W9-CFQ-713

THE MOVIE GUIDE

Other BASELINE books

The Encyclopedia of Film

The Motion Picture Guide (19 volumes)

The Laser Video Disc Companion

Other Books by James Monaco

The New Wave: Truffaut, Godard, Chabrol, Rohmer, Rivette

How to Read a Film

Celebrity

Media Culture

Alain Resnais

American Film Now: The People, The Power, The Money, The Movies

The French Revolutionary Calendar

The Connoisseur's Guide to the Movies

Who's Who in American Film Now

THE MOVIE GUIDE

James Monaco and the editors of BASELINE

A Perigee Book

Perigee Books
are published by
The Putnam Publishing Group
200 Madison Avenue
New York, NY 10016

Copyright ©1992 by Baseline II, Inc.
All rights reserved. This book, or parts thereof,
may not be reproduced in any form without permission.
Published simultaneously in Canada.

Library of Congress Cataloging-in-Publication Data

Monaco, James.
  The movie guide: a comprehensive alphabetical listing of the most
important movies ever made / James Monaco and the editors of Baseline, Inc.
     p.   cm.
  ISBN 0-399-51780-4
    1. Motion pictures—Catalogs.   I. Baseline, Inc. (Firm)   II.Title.
PN1998.M6   1992   92-19033 CIP
016.79143'75—dc20

Cover design by One Plus One Studio
Book Design & Production: Peter Hajduk

Printed in the United States of America

1   2   3   4   5   6   7   8   9   10

CONTENTS

INTRODUCTION

Like many filmgoers, Francois Truffaut used to keep detailed records of the films he'd seen. Just as a birdwatcher keeps a "Life List," so Truffaut—a dedicated viewer of movies as well as one of the world's great filmmakers—kept careful track of his cinematic experience. Before his untimely death in 1984, Truffaut's Life List had exceeded 10,000. It was certainly a prodigious effort, yet even an obsessed cineaste like Truffaut had seen less than one in five films made in the US, UK, and Europe up to that time.

Art is too long and life is too brief. We need all the help we can get. And that is the purpose of this book: to help you separate the wheat from the chaff, to help you to make intelligent decisions, and to act as a friendly guide as you enjoy the exciting journey through the world's cinema which Truffaut and so many others have enjoyed before you.

In many ways, that journey is getting easier. Since the late 1970s, the development of video cassette technology has vastly increased our exposure to old movies. Now, if you get a whim to see *A Funny Thing Happened on the Way to the Forum,* it's probably no further away than your local video store.

It is hard to conceive how different this makes the filmgoing experience. Anyone over thirty can remember when the showing of an old and forgotten film was worth traveling miles to see, or when a limited screening of a foreign import might have made you change your plans for the weekend. Now, tens of thousands of films are at your beck and call, either at the rental store or in the mail-order catalogues.

And don't underestimate the riches in store for you! Movies are the sum of several artistic traditions, Western and Eastern: the natural conclusion to the 19th-century novel and 17th-century Haiku; dance and drama, music and painting. Especially if you've cut your cinematic teeth on the "fast-food" product of the 80s and 90s, you have a rich feast in front of you: Hawks and Hitchcock; Fellini and Godard; Ozu and Ray; German Expressionism and Italian Neorealism—a complete panoply of 20th-century thought and feeling.

This is a remarkable change. When I started to teach film at New York's New School for Social Research in the late 1960s, it was partly to run public film showings so that I, myself, could see some of the classics which I had read about but never experienced (as well as share them with others). Now, we all run our own private VCR Cinematheques—and we don't have to sell tickets to finance the operation.

Moreover, the power we have over the filmgoing experience is about to take yet another quantum leap. Just as in the 80s we acquired the power to watch films *when* we wanted, so in the 90s we will gain the ability to watch films *how* we want. The Laser Video Disc, a technology which took more than ten years to develop into a real consumer market, signals the first stage in this development. Already offering much higher visual quality than videocassettes, laser discs also give the viewer more command over the experience, just as an audio disc is much easier to manipulate than an audio tape.

As laser video discs move to the digital CD-ROM format, your control over the film experience will increase by magnitudes. Truffaut collected lists of films he'd seen once and—perhaps—remembered. Today you can collect *copies* of the films themselves on tape or disc. No, the experience is not the same as in a theater, but the availability of titles more than makes up for the lack of quality. Tomorrow, once these visual records have been digitized, you'll be able not only to collect them, but to edit them easily and quickly.

Even as I write, young music fans collect and edit the music that attracts them. The audio CD and inexpensive computer hardware and software make it possible to compose your own "mixes" of popular music. Soon, this facility will extend to digitized moving images, as well. You'll have the power, should you so desire, to edit together those favorite scenes and sequences, saving only the memorable moments of your cinematic journey. Very soon, your Valentine's card to a loved one will include clips of your favorite screen kisses, as well as quotes from your favorite romantic poems.

Your power over the artifacts of film history will eventually extend much further: perhaps even by the time you read this (since books aren't yet published in real time, and I wrote these words in mid-1992), you will regard the films available on CD, both old and new, as just so much "raw material," to be molded and fashioned into new works of cinematic art—your own. To use terms that have become common in the audio industry, you will move from "mixing" to "sampling." By this time, your Valentine card will include sequences with you and your partner "morphed" into the images, acting out the classic kisses from *Suspicion* or *North by Northwest, Brief Encounter* or *Baisers voles . . .* or *Basic Instinct,* if you are so inclined.

It's a Brave New World, indeed. When all of film becomes raw material for your own multimedia artistic whims and fantasies, a number of important issues are raised regarding copyright, the place of the artist in society, and the economics of the 21st-century film industry. This isn't the time or place to discuss them. This *is* the time and place to remind you that this *Guide* will be there when you are, a careful catalogue of the great films of all time.

Of course, this isn't the first such *vade mecum* to film history. A number of illustrious predecessors have come before us. Steven Scheuer's *Movies on TV* first appeared in 1958, just a few years after old Hollywood films became a staple of late-night television in the US and audiences were first exposed to a steady diet of scores of movies per week. Georges Sadoul's landmark *Dictionnaire des Films* first appeared in 1965, as did Leslie Halliwell's perennial *The Filmgoer's Companion*. These three were joined in 1968 by Leonard Maltin's *TV Movies*. Most of these continue to sell in regularly updated editions and you should be familiar with these works by our friends and colleagues. During the past few years, they have been joined by numerous others (including my own *Connoisseur's Guide* in 1985), as the video revolution progressed.

Why, then, another *Guide*? Several reasons:

- The information in the book you hold in your hands is derived from BASELINE's databases. BASELINE is the information service for the worldwide entertainment industry, constantly updated by a large staff of professional editors; as a result, the data in this *Guide* is both more complete and more accurate than efforts of individual authors ever could be.

- We've included fuller credits than in any other book of this kind—from producer and director to costume design and special effects—so you can get a more complete understanding of the communal art of film. We've also included many more acting credits—up to ten per film—and characters' names (very useful for solving those late-night disputes so common among film lovers).

- The reviews and synopses in the *Guide* are longer and more in-depth than you will find in any other one-volume reference, so you can get a better feel for what makes these movies interesting and otherwise of historical note—especially important for the films you *won't* get to see yourself.

- Our editors have carefully selected more than 3,000 top films from the twenty times this many that we keep records on. Our aim has been to call attention not only to the best-known movies of all time, but also to focus interest on a number of "sleepers."

- Finally, the *Guide* is more international in scope than any other film reference, especially important as the industry itself continues to transcend national boundaries.

The films included in this *Guide* were selected from the more than 35,000 entries in our 19-volume library reference work *The Motion Picture Guide*, which themselves form a subset of the more than 60,000 feature films on which BASELINE keeps records.

The selection process? These are not only the films our editors consider the "best" examples of world cinema, but also those which represent landmarks of a genre, or have some special social, cultural, or historical significance. We have included all Academy Award winners and nominees—although in some cases you wonder how certain films attained such prominence; no matter, in their time they were considered important. We have also included all winners of the top Cannes Film Festival awards, as well as all films listed in *Sight & Sound's* historic critics' poll. All films which are ranked five-star or four-star in *The Motion Picture Guide* are included, as are those that were listed in *The Connoisseur's Guide* (although the reviews are all different). All this was rounded out with some personal, idiosyncratic, human editorial judgement.

No book can hope to be as comprehensive as a computerized database (that's why we like databases), but databases are hard to read in bed (that's why we like books). Nevertheless, a CD-ROM version of *The Motion Picture Guide* will be available shortly after publication of this book and those readers who enjoy "working" a text—sorting and searching, merging and listing— are directed to it. Those of you who prefer to handle pages, smell fresh ink, and scribble in the margins should stay right here.

As it happens, at the end of the day we wound up with just about as many films in this book as there are filmmakers in our *Encyclopedia of Film*, the companion volume to the *Guide*. Perhaps we can draw the conclusion that the people who make movies are just as important as the films they make. I think Truffaut would have enjoyed the fact and approved the conclusion.

After the selection of the entries for the *Guide* was completed, we sorted the database several different ways to see what it could tell us about this list of more than 3,000 of the world's most significant movies. We learned several interesting facts:

- Dramas and comedies are almost evenly matched, although dramas have a slight edge. The next most numerous genre is—surprisingly—the war film; 268 of our entries fit this category. Crime films follow closely behind with 238 films represented here. Lighter fare follows, with the Musical at 224 and Romance at 177. Biographies outrank Adventure, which is mildly surprising, and Sports films rank higher than you might expect. The presence on the list of 10 Operas is also of interest.

Here is the complete list:

Drama	990	ScienceFiction	91
Comedy	777	Fantasy	84
War	268	Sports	59
Crime	238	Spy	57
Musical	224	Children's	40
Romance	177	Political	37
Biography	162	Animated	36
Adventure	134	Action	28
Horror	112	Prison	23
Thriller	106	Religious	22
Historical	99	Opera	10
Mystery	92	Disaster	8
Dance	8		

- Although we've included all the four-star and above rankings in our complete database, only 41% of the films included in the book rank at 4 stars or higher; 5% rank at an undistinguished 2 stars or below. We draw the conclusion that interesting or important films aren't always great films.

- We were eager to see what happened when we figured star-rating averages for each year in the database. Film critics have always looked to 1939 as the *annus mirabilis* of film history, and indeed the year of *Gone With the Wind, The Rules of the Game, Stagecoach, Ninotchka,* and *The Wizard of Oz* does rank very highly—but two years, 1946 and 1933, outrank it for average quality of the selections included here.

The five-star films of 1946 included *It's a Wonderful Life, The Best Years of Our Lives, The Big Sleep, Paisan, Great Expectations,* and *Green For Danger.* 1933, the highest-ranked year according to our star ratings, was enhanced by such five-star films as *42nd Street, Dinner at Eight, Duck Soup, Footlight Parade, The Gold Diggers of 1933, I'm No Angel, She Done Him Wrong. . .* and *King Kong.*

Perhaps there is something to this numerical ratings business!

- None of these high-ranking years is much of a surprise, nor are the other years (1950, 1932, 1935, 1945, 1940, and 1937) that averaged 4.0 or above. There were two surprises in recent years, however. Our graph of the averages immediately called our attention to 1962 (at 3.99) and 1974 (at 3.88); both stood out as peaks in the chronology of recent filmmaking.

1962 was the year of *Lawrence of Arabia, A Kind of Loving, My Life to Live, Ride the High Country, The Exterminating Angel, A Taste of Honey, The Manchurian Candidate,* and *Jules and Jim* —all five-star movies.

There were only three five-star films in 1974 (*Chinatown, The Godfather, Part II,* and *The Conversation*), but there were a large number of three-and-a-half- and four-star films which brought the average up. (*Amarcord, Le Petit Theatre de Jean Renoir, The Phantom of Liberty, The Three Musketeers,* and *Young Frankenstein* all received four-star ratings.) This is exactly what you would expect to represent an outstanding season during the last twenty years—a period during which there have been very few masterpieces, but a higher level of overall quality, as the B-movie moved to television.

You can play this game all day long; one thing leads to another. . . the year with the greatest number of good comedies? . . . the year with the least number of good Hollywood films?. . . the year with the greatest number of poorly-ranked Horror films?. . . you get the idea. For the answers to these and other questions, the reader is referred to the CD-ROM version of *The Motion Picture Guide.*

- Just one last statistic: We sorted the database simply by year to discover that the number of selections per year ranges, with exceptions at either end of the period, from 35 to 61—a fairly constant range indicating an overall level of quality. The exceptions occur in the early 30s, for which we have selected fewer films because so few are available, and the 1980s, which are intentionally over-represented since so many recent films are available.

Like its subject, this book is very much a collaborative process. More than sixty writers and editors have contributed to the entries for the *Guide.* We believe the result is a much more knowledgeable survey due to the efforts of this varied and talented crew. The work on the synopses and critiques was begun more than ten years ago by Jay Robert Nash and Stanley Ralph Ross, the original editors of *The Motion Picture Guide,* then continued by the professional staff of CineBooks throughout the 80s. We especially note the work of William Leahy, Bill Clogston, Dan Curran, and Jeffrey Wallenfeldt.

When BASELINE acquired the assets of CineBooks in 1990, our own editors set to work to check the data and review the reviews for accuracy and completeness. A number of specially selected outside writers and academics have added their considered opinions to the mix. Many of the entries have been edited and checked by associate editor John Miller-Monzon, with the help of Kent Greene, David Lugowski, and Robert Weisfeld. Valuable assistance was provided by David Struassman, and all approached the task with professional enthusiasm and a reasoned passion for the subject. Peter Hajduk managed the STAR database with efficiency and creativity, outputting the information directly from the database into typeset pages which he also designed. Many thanks to them all.

The entire project was co-ordinated by BASELINE Editorial Director James Pallot, who managed a prodigious undertaking with considerable panache. Special thanks to James for his constancy and sure hand. I also owe much gratitude to Jo Imeson, Executive Vice President of BASELINE and partner for the last nine years, for her managerial wisdom. Our agent, Mitchell Rose, who helped to conceive the project; Paul Forty, our editor at Virgin Publishing; Robert Shreeve, Managing Director of Virgin Publishing; and Eugene Brissie and Laura Yorke, our editors at Putnam's, all contributed to the final shape of the *Guide*. Thanks.

Now that you know something about the team that has brought this book to publication, we invite your participation in the endeavor. Any book of this sort is, of course, an ongoing project. We'll be back soon enough with a second edition. If you find any lacunae, or have suggestions for future inclusions, we invite you cordially to correspond with us at the address listed in the "about BASELINE" section.

James Monaco
New York
June 1992

HOW TO USE THIS BOOK

INFORMATION KEY

Title

Foreign Title

Running Time and Color Code

Star Rating

Release Year

MY LIFE AS A DOG
(MITT LIV SOM HUND)
1985   101m   c

★★★

Genre(s)

Comedy/Drama

PG-13/PG

MPAA/BBFC

Production Co(s). and Countries

AB/Svensk   (Sweden)

Cast and Characters

Anton Glanzelius *(Ingemar Johansson)*, Anki Liden *(His Mother)*, Tomas von Bromssen *(Uncle Gunnar)*, Manfred Serner *(Erik)*, Melinda Kinnaman *(Saga)*, Ing-Marie Carlsson *(Berit)*, Kicki Rundgren *(Aunt Ulla)*, Lennart Hjulstrom *(Konstnaren)*, Leif Erickson *(Farbor Sandberg)*, Christina Carlwind *(Fru Sandberg)*

Production Credits

p, Waldemar Bergendahl; d, Lasse Hallstrom; w, Lasse Hallstrom, Reidar Jonsson, Brasse Brannstrom, Per Berglund (based on the novel by Jonsson); ph, Jorgen Persson, Rolf Lindstrom (Fujicolor); ed, Christer Furubrand, Susanne Linnman; m, Bjorn Isfalt; art d, Lasse Westfelt; cos, Inger Pehrsson, Susanne Falck

This critically acclaimed Swedish film, which also won kudos for its talented star, Anton Glanzelius, is a tragicomic, sensitive portrayal of adolescence set in 1959. The film centers on 12-year-old Ingemar Johansson (Glanzelius), who lives with his abusive brother (Manfred Serner) and terminally ill mother (Anki Liden). He is not discouraged, however—sure, he has it bad, but not as bad as Laika, the Soviet spacedog who starved to death while in orbit and whose fate haunts the boy. Ingemar's life has begun to spin out of control, and, like Laika, there's little he can do to stop it. When Ingemar is sent away for the summer to stay with relations, he meets a menage of eccentric—and sexually intimidating—villagers; eventually, these experiences give him a sustaining inner strength. Writer-director Lasse Hallstrom's tale is an episodic rite of passage, a story in which the emotions are touching but never sappy, the main character has the integrity and complexity of a real child with real troubles, and the glimpses of village life are rich and engaging. Not just another charming film about growing up, but an expertly directed tale that takes a small, simple subject and colors it with invention and inspiration. Released in the US in 1987, the film earned Oscar nominations for Best Direction and Best Screenplay.

Synopsis and Critical Appraisal

ABOUT THE INFORMATION

Title

Films are listed alphabetically according to the title by which they were first released in the U.S. Where appropriate, original foreign-language titles appear in parentheses on the second line of the entry. If you need to search for a film by a foreign-language, British, or alternate title, please consult the *Alternate Title Index* on page xv.

Year of Release

The first year in which the film saw theatrical release of any kind in the U.S. This does not include festival screenings or "sneak previews." Discrepancies between the year of U.S. release and the year of release in the film's country of origin are noted in the critical appraisal.

Running Time

This applies to the original form in which the film was released, not to subsequent trimmings or elongation for the purposes of TV broadcast or videocassette release.

Color Code

The symbol "c" denotes films shot in color, "bw" those shot in black-and-white; "c/bw" indicates a film which, like *The Wizard of Oz*, uses both kinds of footage.

Star Rating

A shorthand assessment of each film's critical merits, according to the following scale: 5 stars = masterpiece; 4 stars = excellent; 3 stars = good; 2 stars = fair; 1 star = poor; no stars = without merit. Half-stars are also awarded. Since this book represents a selection of notable titles pulled from a database of nearly 35,000 films, the average star rating is relatively high.

Genre

Each film is classified by up to three genres selected from the following list: Action; Adventure; Animated; Biography; Children's; Comedy; Crime; Dance; Disaster; Docudrama; Documentary; Drama; Fantasy; Historical; Horror; Musical; Mystery; Opera; Political; Prison; Religious; Romance; Science Fiction; Sports; Spy; Thriller; War; Western.

MPAA/BBFC Rating

The Motion Picture Association of America rating, separated by a "/" from the British Board of Film Classification certificate. A gap before or after the "/" indicates the information is not available in that category; a single "PG" code, without a "/", indicates the film is rated PG in both the U.S. and the U.K. Please see "U.S. and U.K. Rating Systems" below for more details.

Production Company

Multiple entries are separated by a "/" and are limited to companies that were actively and/or financially involved in the project. Distributors are not listed.

Country of Origin

When a film has been produced by a country other than the U.S., that country (or group of countries) is listed in parentheses immediately after the Production Company information.

Cast and Characters

The names of up to ten actors for each film, followed in parentheses by the name of the character played.

Production Credits

The names of the key creative and technical personnel involved in the project, abbreviated as follows: p (producer); d (director); w (writer); ph (cinematographer); ed (editor); m (music composer); prod d (production designer); art d (art director); fx (special effects); chor (choreographer); cos (costume designer); anim (animation). Multiple credits in the same category are separated by commas. Where appropriate, information about screenplay source material is included in parentheses after the last writer credit.

U.S. and U.K. Rating Systems

U.S.: The Motion Picture Association of America (MPAA) currently grades films according to the following codes: **G** (GENERAL AUDIENCES—All ages admitted); **PG** (PARENTAL GUIDANCE SUGGESTED—Some material may not be suitable for children); **PG-13** (PARENTS STRONGLY CAUTIONED—Some material may be inappropriate for children under 13); **R** (RESTRICTED—Under 17 requires accompanying parent or adult guardian); and **NC-17** (NO CHILDREN UNDER 17 ADMITTED). This book also contains ratings issued while earlier systems were in effect, as follows: **GP** (May be considered the equivalent of and interchangeable with PG); **M** (Mature Audiences, Parental Guidance Suggested—may not be identified with any other rating); and **X** (No One Under 17 Admitted—may not be identified with NC-17.)

U.K.: Since 1982, the following system of classification has been applied in the UK: **U** (Universal—suitable for all); **PG** (Parental Guidance—some scenes may be unsuitable for young children); **15** (passed for those aged 15 and over); **18** (passed for those aged 18 and over). These categories apply to both video and cinema screenings. The less frequently used **12** category (passed for those aged 12 and over) was introduced in 1989 for cinema screenings only.

Entries in this guide show either the post-1982 classification or, where this is not available, the certificate awarded when the film was first shown in the UK.

When UK certificates were first introduced in 1913, the categories were simply **U** (Universal) and **A** (Adult; no unaccompanied child admitted). **H** (for Horrific) was introduced as an advisory category in 1932, to be replaced in 1951 by **X** (no admission for those under 16).

In 1970 a new system was introduced: **U** (as before); **A** (Advisory; unaccompanied children of 5 and over admitted, but a film in this category could contain material that parents might prefer children under 14 not to see); **AA** (no admission to those under 14); **X** (no admission to those under 18).

Generally speaking, the **U, A, AA,** and **X** categories approximate the **U, PG, 12/15,** and **18** categories in use today, but the conversion is not automatic. Changing social attitudes can mean that a film awarded an **X** certificate in 1952, for instance, might be thought suitable for a **15** or even a **PG** certificate in 1992.

The editors wish to thank the British Board of Film Classification for its assistance in supplying certificate information.

About BASELINE

BASELINE was founded in 1983 to provide on-line databases and other information services to the film and TV industries. The world's largest source of information about film and TV, the company now has professional clients around the world in more than 30 countries. More than 25 separate databases list information on hundreds of thousands of film and TV cast and crew members; more than 100,000 films, television series, specials, movies and episodes; more than 5,000 films and TV shows currently in production; and more than 15,000 companies active in the industry. Additional services include on-line news, financial figures, and communications. More information about BASELINE is available by calling 1-800-CHAPLIN or writing to us at 838 Broadway, New York, NY, 10003 or 8929 Wilshire, Beverly Hills, CA, 90211. Many BASELINE services are also available on Mead Data Central's Nexis service.

A Note on the Type

This book is set in Times Roman, perhaps the most durable typeface of the 20th century, whose original 1931 design was supervised by Stanley Morison for The Times of London. The data was exported from Cuadra Associates' STAR database system directly into Ventura Desktop Publishing software (DOS/GEM version). The PostScript output files were processed into camera-ready pages by Southern California Printcorp, Pasadena, CA.

ALTERNATE TITLE INDEX

The main portion of this book lists films alphabetically according to the title by which they were first released in the U.S. If you cannot find the movie you are looking for, please check this index to see if the work is listed under a different title. The column on the left contains: original foreign-language titles; British titles, where they differ from those used for U.S. release; and alternative English-language titles.

ALTERNATE TITLE	U.S. TITLE
A BOUT DE SOUFFLE	BREATHLESS
A COR DO SEU DESTINO	COLOR OF DESTINY, THE
ABBOTT AND COSTELLO MEET THE GHOSTS	ABBOTT AND COSTELLO MEET FRANKENSTEIN
ABISMOS DE PASION	WUTHERING HEIGHTS
ABNORMAL	HENTAI
ACE IN THE HOLE	BIG CARNIVAL, THE
ACE, THE	GREAT SANTINI, THE
AFFAIR OF THE HEART, AN	LOVE AFFAIR; OR THE CASE OF THE MISSING SWITCHBOARD OPERATOR
AFFAIR OF THE HEART, AN	BODY AND SOUL
AGE OF GOLD	L'AGE D'OR
AGUIRRE, DER ZORN GOTTES	AGUIRRE, THE WRATH OF GOD
AI NO CORRIDA	IN THE REALM OF THE SENSES
AKIBIYORI	LATE AUTUMN
ALEXANDER GRAHAM BELL	STORY OF ALEXANDER GRAHAM BELL, THE
ALI—FEAR EATS THE SOUL	FEAR EATS THE SOUL
ALL THAT MONEY CAN BUY	DEVIL AND DANIEL WEBSTER, THE
AMORE A VENT'ANNI	LOVE AT TWENTY
AMOROUS GENERAL, THE	WALTZ OF THE TOREADORS
AND WOMAN. . . WAS CREATED	AND GOD CREATED WOMAN
ANGEL STREET	GASLIGHT
ANGELS AND THE PIRATES	ANGELS IN THE OUTFIELD
ANGUSTIA	ANGUISH
ANIMAL HOUSE	NATIONAL LAMPOON'S ANIMAL HOUSE
ANNE AND MURIEL	TWO ENGLISH GIRLS
ANNO UNO	YEAR ONE
ANSIKTET	MAGICIAN, THE
APUR SANSAR	WORLD OF APU, THE
ATLANTIC CITY, U.S.A.	ATLANTIC CITY
ATOMIC ROCKETSHIP	FLASH GORDON
BABETTE'S GASTEBUD	BABETTE'S FEAST
BACHELOR KNIGHT	BACHELOR AND THE BOBBY-SOXER, THE
BAD GIRLS, THE	LES BICHES
BAILIFF, THE	SANSHO THE BAILIFF
BAISERS VOLES	STOLEN KISSES
BAL NA VODI	HEY BABU RIBA
BALTHAZAR	AU HASARD, BALTHAZAR
BANK DETECTIVE, THE	BANK DICK, THE
BANNER IN THE SKY	THIRD MAN ON THE MOUNTAIN
BATTLE STRIPE	MEN, THE
BATTLING BELLHOP, THE	KID GALAHAD
BE RORINGEN	TOUCH, THE
BEGGARS' OPERA	THREEPENNY OPERA, THE
BIG HEART, THE	MIRACLE ON 34TH STREET
BIRDS OF A FEATHER	LA CAGE AUX FOLLES
BIRTHMARK	OMEN, THE
BIZALOM	CONFIDENCE
BLONDE BOMBSHELL	BOMBSHELL
BLONDE IN LOVE, A	LOVES OF A BLONDE
BLOOD COUPLE	GANJA AND HESS

E

ALTERNATE TITLE	U.S. TITLE
EVERYBODY'S CHEERING	TAKE ME OUT TO THE BALL GAME
EXTASE	ECSTASY
EYE OF EVIL	THOUSAND EYES OF DR. MABUSE, THE

Face of Fear

FACE OF FEAR	PEEPING TOM
FACE, THE	MAGICIAN, THE
FACTS OF LIFE, THE	QUARTET
FALL OF LOLA MONTES, THE	LOLA MONTES
FALL OF THE HOUSE OF USHER, THE	HOUSE OF USHER
FALSE WITNESS	CIRCLE OF DECEIT
FALSTAFF	CHIMES AT MIDNIGHT
FANNY OCH ALEXANDER	FANNY AND ALEXANDER
FAREWELL, MY LOVELY	MURDER, MY SWEET
FATHER BROWN	DETECTIVE, THE
FATHER'S ON A BUSINESS TRIP	WHEN FATHER WAS AWAY ON BUSINESS
FEDERICO FELLINI'S 8½	8½
FEDERICO FELLINI'S INTERVISTA	INTERVISTA
FELLINI'S ROMA	ROMA
FIELDS OF HONOR	SHENANDOAH
FIENDS, THE	DIABOLIQUE
FIGHTING SULLIVANS, THE	SULLIVANS, THE
FINAL CRASH, THE	STEELYARD BLUES
FINALLY, SUNDAY	CONFIDENTIALLY YOURS!
FIRE FESTIVAL	HIMATSURI
FIRST GREAT TRAIN ROBBERY, THE	GREAT TRAIN ROBBERY, THE
FIRST OF THE FEW, THE	SPITFIRE
FISTS IN THE POCKET	FIST IN HIS POCKET
FONTANE EFFI BRIEST	EFFI BRIEST
FOR A FISTFUL OF DOLLARS	FISTFUL OF DOLLARS, A
FOR A NIGHT OF LOVE	MANIFESTO
FORBIDDEN ALLIANCE	BARRETTS OF WIMPOLE STREET, THE
FORBIDDEN LOVE	FREAKS
FORBIN PROJECT, THE	COLOSSUS: THE FORBIN PROJECT
FOREVER IN LOVE	PRIDE OF THE MARINES
47 SAMURAI	CHUSHINGURA
49TH PARALLEL	INVADERS, THE
FRANCESCO, GIULLARE DI DIO	FLOWERS OF ST. FRANCIS, THE
FRATERNALLY YOURS	SONS OF THE DESERT
FREEDOM FOR US	A NOUS LA LIBERTE
FRENCH ARE A FUNNY RACE	FRENCH, THEY ARE A FUNNY RACE, THE
FULL HOUSE	O. HENRY'S FULL HOUSE
FUN LOVING	QUACKSER FORTUNE HAS A COUSIN IN THE BRONX

Gamlet

GAMLET	HAMLET
GANG WAR	ODD MAN OUT
GEORGIA'S FRIENDS	FOUR FRIENDS
GESTAPO	NIGHT TRAIN
GETTING AWAY WITH MURDER	END OF THE GAME
GHARE BAIRE	HOME AND THE WORLD, THE
GHOST STEPS OUT, THE	TIME OF THEIR LIVES, THE
GION NO SHIMAI	SISTERS OF THE GION
GIRL WAS YOUNG, THE	YOUNG AND INNOCENT
GIRLFRIENDS, THE	LES BICHES
GIRLS HE LEFT BEHIND, THE	GANG'S ALL HERE, THE
GIRLS IN UNIFORM	MAEDCHEN IN UNIFORM
GIULIETTA DEGLI SPIRITI	JULIET OF THE SPIRITS
GOING APE	WHERE'S POPPA?

ALTERNATE TITLE INDEX

ALTERNATE TITLE	U.S. TITLE
IL FERROVIERE	RAILROAD MAN, THE
IL GATTOPARDO	LEOPARD, THE
IL GENERALE DELLA ROVERE	GENERAL DELLA ROVERE
IL GIARDINO DEL FINZI-CONTINI	GARDEN OF THE FINZI-CONTINIS, THE
IL PROCESSO	TRIAL, THE
IL SORPASSO	EASY LIFE, THE
IL TRENO	TRAIN, THE
IL VANGELO SECONDO MATTEO	GOSPEL ACCORDING TO ST. MATTHEW, THE
IM LAUF DER ZEIT	KINGS OF THE ROAD
IMERES TOU 36	DAYS OF 36
IN BED WITH MADONNA	TRUTH OR DARE
IN THE WOODS	RASHOMON
INDAGINE SU UN CITTADINO AL DI SOPRA DI OGNI SOSPETTO	INVESTIGATION OF A CITIZEN ABOVE SUSPICION
INDIAN LOVE CALL	ROSE MARIE
INDISCRETION	CHRISTMAS IN CONNECTICUT
INSIDIOUS DR. FU MANCHU, THE	MYSTERIOUS DR. FU MANCHU, THE
INTERMEZZO	INTERMEZZO: A LOVE STORY
INTIMATE RELATIONS	LES PARENTS TERRIBLES
ISTORIYA AS: KLYACHIMOL	ASYA'S HAPPINESS
IT HAPPENED ONE SUMMER	STATE FAIR
IT HURTS ONLY WHEN I LAUGH	ONLY WHEN I LAUGH
IT'S MY LIFE	MY LIFE TO LIVE
IT'S TRAD, DAD!	RING-A-DING RHYTHM
IVAN GROZNYI	IVAN THE TERRIBLE, PARTS I & II
IVAN'S CHILDHOOD	MY NAME IS IVAN
IVANOVO DETSTVO	MY NAME IS IVAN

JALSAGHAR	MUSIC ROOM, THE
JASON AND THE GOLDEN FLEECE	JASON AND THE ARGONAUTS
JE VOUS SALUE, MARIE	HAIL, MARY
JEAN DE FLORETTE 2	MANON OF THE SPRING
JEDER FUR SICH UND GOTT GEGEN ALLE	EVERY MAN FOR HIMSELF AND GOD AGAINST ALL
JENNIE	PORTRAIT OF JENNIE
JEST OF GOD, A	RACHEL, RACHEL
JESUS DE MONTREAL	JESUS OF MONTREAL
JIGOKUMEN	GATE OF HELL
JOB LAZADASA	REVOLT OF JOB, THE
JONAS—QUI AURA 25 ANS EN L'AN 2000	JONAH—WHO WILL BE 25 IN THE YEAR 2000
JOY OF LEARNING, THE	LE GAI SAVOIR
JUDAS WAS A WOMAN	LA BETE HUMAINE
JULES ET JIM	JULES AND JIM
JULIA UND DIE GEISTER	JULIET OF THE SPIRITS
JULIETTE DES ESPRITS	JULIET OF THE SPIRITS
JUNGFRUKALLAN	VIRGIN SPRING, THE
JUST GREAT	TOUT VA BIEN
JUSTE AVANT LA NUIT	JUST BEFORE NIGHTFALL

KAIDAN	KWAIDAN
KAKUSHI TORIDE NO SAN AKUNIN	HIDDEN FORTRESS, THE
KARHOZAT	DAMNATION
KILLER!	THIS MAN MUST DIE
KIPPS	REMARKABLE MR. KIPPS
KISS MY BUTTERFLY	I LOVE YOU, ALICE B. TOKLAS!
KNACK, THE	KNACK. . . AND HOW TO GET IT, THE
KNAVE OF HEARTS	LOVERS, HAPPY LOVERS!
KNIGHT WITHOUT ARMOUR	KNIGHT WITHOUT ARMOR

ALTERNATE TITLE	U.S. TITLE
KONEKO MONOGATARI	ADVENTURES OF MILO AND OTIS, THE
KRIGETAR SLUT	LA GUERRE EST FINIE
KUMONOSUJO	THRONE OF BLOOD
KUROI AME	BLACK RAIN
KVINNORS VANTAN	SECRETS OF WOMEN
L'ALBERO DEGLI ZOCCOLI	TREE OF WOODEN CLOGS, THE
L'AMI DE MON AMIE	BOYFRIENDS AND GIRLFRIENDS
L'AMOUR A VINGT ANS	LOVE AT TWENTY
L'AMOUR EN FUITE	LOVE ON THE RUN
L'AMOUR, L'APRES-MIDI	CHLOE IN THE AFTERNOON
L'ANNEE DERNIERE A MARIENBAD	LAST YEAR AT MARIENBAD
L'ANNO SCORSO A MARIENBAD	LAST YEAR AT MARIENBAD
L'ARGENT DE POCHE	SMALL CHANGE
L'AVEU	CONFESSION, THE
L'ENFANCE NUE	ME
L'ENFANT SAUVAGE	WILD CHILD, THE
L'ETRANGER	STRANGER, THE
L'EVANGILE SELON SAINT-MATTHIEU	GOSPEL ACCORDING TO ST. MATTHEW, THE
L'HISTOIRE D'ADELE H.	STORY OF ADELE H., THE
L'HOMME DE RIO	THAT MAN FROM RIO
L'HOMME QUI AIMAIT LES FEMMES	MAN WHO LOVED WOMEN, THE
L'HORLOGER DE SAINT-PAUL	CLOCKMAKER, THE
L'INNOCENTE	INNOCENT, THE
L'OPERA DE QUAT'SOUS	THREEPENNY OPERA, THE
L'ORO DI NAPOLI	GOLD OF NAPLES
L'UCELLO DALLE PLUME DI CRISTALLO	BIRD WITH THE CRYSTAL PLUMAGE, THE
L'UOMO DI RIO	THAT MAN FROM RIO
LA BELLE ET LA BETE	BEAUTY AND THE BEAST
LA CADUTA DEGLI DEI	DAMNED, THE
LA CAZA	HUNT, THE
LA CHAMBRE VERTE	GREEN ROOM, THE
LA CIOCIARA	TWO WOMEN
LA CIUDAD Y LOS PERROS	CITY AND THE DOGS, THE
LA DECIMA VITTIMA	TENTH VICTIM, THE
LA DENTELLIERE	LACEMAKER, THE
LA DIAGONALE DU FOU	DANGEROUS MOVES
LA DIXIEME VICTIME	TENTH VICTIM, THE
LA DONNA E DONNA	WOMAN IS A WOMAN, A
LA DOUBLE VIE DE VERONIQUE	DOUBLE LIFE OF VERONIQUE, THE
LA FAMIGLIA	FAMILY, THE
LA FEMME D'A COTE	WOMAN NEXT DOOR, THE
LA FEMME DU BOULANGER	BAKER'S WIFE, THE
LA FETE A HENRIETTE	HOLIDAY FOR HENRIETTA
LA GRANDE ILLUSION	GRAND ILLUSION
LA HISTORIA OFICIAL	OFFICIAL STORY, THE
LA JUMENT VAPEUR	DIRTY DISHES
LA LEY DEL DESEO	LAW OF DESIRE, THE
LA LUNE DANS LE CANIVEAU	MOON IN THE GUTTER, THE
LA MAMAN ET LA PUTAIN	MOTHER AND THE WHORE, THE
LA MESSA E FINITA	MASS IS ENDED, THE
LA MIA DROGA SI CHIAMA JULIE	MISSISSIPPI MERMAID
LA MORT EN DIRECT	DEATH WATCH
LA NUIT AMERICAINE	DAY FOR NIGHT
LA PEAU DOUCE	SOFT SKIN, THE
LA PERMISSION	STORY OF A THREE DAY PASS, THE
LA PRISE DE POUVOIR PAR LOUIS XIV	RISE OF LOUIS XIV, THE
LA RECREATION	PLAYTIME

ALTERNATE TITLE	U.S. TITLE
LA REGLE DU JEU	RULES OF THE GAME
LA SIRENE DU MISSISSIPPI	MISSISSIPPI MERMAID
LA VIA LATTEA	MILKY WAY, THE
LA VICTOIRE EN CHANTANT	BLACK AND WHITE IN COLOR
LA VIE DEVANT SOI	MADAME ROSA
LA VIE EST RIEN D'AUTRE	LIFE AND NOTHING BUT
LA VIE EST UN ROMAN	LIFE IS A BED OF ROSES
LA VOIE LACTEE	MILKY WAY, THE
LABERINTO DE PASION	LABYRINTH OF PASSION
LADRI DI BICICLETTE	BICYCLE THIEF, THE
LADRI DI SAPONETTE	ICICLE THIEF, THE
LADY DANCES, THE	MERRY WIDOW, THE
LADY HAMILTON	THAT HAMILTON WOMAN
LADY KILLERS, THE	LADYKILLERS, THE
LAMENT OF THE PATH, THE	PATHER PANCHALI
LANCELOT DU LAC	LANCELOT OF THE LAKE
LASKY JEDNE PLAVOVLASKY	LOVES OF A BLONDE
LAST HERO	LONELY ARE THE BRAVE
LAST STAGE, THE	LAST STOP, THE
LAST WILL OF DR. MABUSE, THE	TESTAMENT OF DR. MABUSE, THE
LE CARROSSE D'OR	GOLDEN COACH, THE
LE CHALAND QUI PASSE	L'ATALANTE
LE CHARME DISCRET DE LA BOURGEOISIE	DISCREET CHARM OF THE BOURGEOISIE, THE
LE CHOIX DES ARMES	CHOICE OF ARMS
LE CRIME DE M. LANGE	CRIME OF MONSIEUR LANGE, THE
LE DECLIN DE L'EMPIRE AMERICAIN	DECLINE OF THE AMERICAN EMPIRE, THE
LE DERNIER METRO	LAST METRO, THE
LE DESERT ROUGE	RED DESERT
LE DIABLE AU CORPS	DEVIL IN THE FLESH, THE
LE DIABLE PROBABLEMENT	DEVIL PROBABLY, THE
LE DIABOLIQUE DOCTEUR MABUSE	THOUSAND EYES OF DR. MABUSE, THE
LE FANTOME DE LA LIBERTE	PHANTOM OF LIBERTY, THE
LE GENOU DE CLAIRE	CLAIRE'S KNEE
LE GRAND BLOND AVEC UNE CHAUSSURE NOIRE	TALL BLOND MAN WITH ONE BLACK SHOE, THE
LE GUEPARD	LEOPARD, THE
LE JOUR SE LEVE	DAYBREAK
LE JOURNAL D'UN CURE DE CAMPAGNE	DIARY OF A COUNTRY PRIEST
LE JOURNAL D'UNE FEMME DE CHAMBRE	DIARY OF A CHAMBERMAID
LE LOCATAIRE	TENANT, THE
LE MEPRIS	CONTEMPT
LE MILLION	MILLION, THE
LE MONDAT	MANDABI
LE MUR	WALL, THE
LE NOTTI DI CABIRIA	NIGHTS OF CABIRIA
LE PROCES	TRIAL, THE
LE QUAI DES BRUMES	PORT OF SHADOWS
LE RAYON VERT	SUMMER
LE ROI DE COEUR	KING OF HEARTS
LE ROMAN D'UN TRICHEUR	STORY OF A CHEAT, THE
LE SALAIRE DE LA PEUR	WAGES OF FEAR, THE
LE SOUFFLE AU COEUR	MURMUR OF THE HEART
LE TESTAMENT D'ORPHEE	TESTAMENT OF ORPHEUS, THE
LE TESTAMENT DU DR. MABUSE	TESTAMENT OF DR. MABUSE, THE
LE TRAIN	TRAIN, THE
LE TROU	NIGHT WATCH, THE
LE VENT SOUFFLE OU IL VEUT	MAN ESCAPED, A
LE VIEIL HOMME ET L'ENFANT	TWO OF US, THE
LEARN, BABY, LEARN	LEARNING TREE, THE

ALTERNATE TITLE	U.S. TITLE
NIGHT OF THE FLESH EATERS	NIGHT OF THE LIVING DEAD
NIGHT TRAIN TO MUNICH	NIGHT TRAIN
NIGHT, THE	LA NOTTE
NIJUSHI NO HITOMI	TWENTY-FOUR EYES
NIKITA	LA FEMME NIKITA
NOCE EN GALILEE	WEDDING IN GALILEE
NORA INU	STRAY DOG
NOSFERATU, PHANTOM DER NACHT	NOSFERATU, THE VAMPIRE
NOT AGAINST THE FLESH	VAMPYR
NOTEBOOKS OF MAJOR THOMPSON	FRENCH, THEY ARE A FUNNY RACE, THE
NOUS SOMMES TOUS DES ASSASSINS	WE ARE ALL MURDERERS
NOVECENTO	1900
NOZ W WODZIE	KNIFE IN THE WATER
NUMERO DEUX	NUMBER TWO
NUOVO CINEMA PARADISO	CINEMA PARADISO
NYBYGGARNA	NEW LAND, THE

O PAGADOR DE PROMESSAS	GIVEN WORD, THE
OBCH OD NA KORZE	SHOP ON MAIN STREET, THE
OBERST REDL	COLONEL REDL
OCI CIORNIE	DARK EYES
OFFRET-SA CRIFICATIO	SACRIFICE, THE
OH! FOR A MAN!	WILL SUCCESS SPOIL ROCK HUNTER?
OLD MAN AND THE BOY, THE	TWO OF US, THE
ONE-MAN MUTINY	COURT MARTIAL OF BILLY MITCHELL, THE
ONLY THE FRENCH CAN	FRENCH CANCAN
OPERATION CICERO	FIVE FINGERS
OPRHEE	ORPHEUS
ORACLE, THE	HORSE'S MOUTH, THE
ORFEU NEGRO	BLACK ORPHEUS
OSOSHIKI	FUNERAL, THE
OSTATNI ETAP	LAST STOP, THE
OSTRE SLEDOVANE VLAKY	CLOSELY WATCHED TRAINS
OTAC NA SLUZBENOH PUTU	WHEN FATHER WAS AWAY ON BUSINESS
OTTO E MEZZO	8½
OUR HITLER	OUR HITLER, A FILM FROM GERMANY
OUT OF ROSENHEIM	BAGDAD CAFE
OUTSIDERS, THE	BAND OF OUTSIDERS
OVER THE RIVER	ONE MORE RIVER

P'TANG, YANG, KIPPERBANG	KIPPERBANG
PAISA	PAISAN
PARADE D'AMOUR	LOVE PARADE, THE
PARIS BRULE-T-IL?	IS PARIS BURNING?
PARIS IS OURS	PARIS BELONGS TO US
PARIS NOUS APPARTIENT	PARIS BELONGS TO US
PARIS VU PAR. . .	SIX IN PARIS
PARLIAMO DI DONNE	LET'S TALK ABOUT WOMEN
PASAZERKA	PASSENGER, THE
PASQUALINO SETTEBELLEZZE	SEVEN BEAUTIES
PASQUALINO: SEVEN BEAUTIES	SEVEN BEAUTIES
PASSION	PASSION OF ANNA, THE
PATTERNS OF POWER	PATTERNS
PATTON—LUST FOR GLORY	PATTON
PATTON: A SALUTE TO A REBEL	PATTON
PAULINE A LA PLAGE	PAULINE AT THE BEACH
PELLE EROVRAREN	PELLE THE CONQUEROR

ALTERNATE TITLE	U.S. TITLE
STORY OF CINDERELLA, THE	SLIPPER AND THE ROSE, THE
STORY OF DR. EHRLICH'S MAGIC BULLET, THE	DR. EHRLICH'S MAGIC BULLET
STORY OF GILBERT AND SULLIVAN, THE	GREAT GILBERT AND SULLIVAN, THE
STORY OF ROBIN HOOD AND HIS MERRIE MEN, THE	STORY OF ROBIN HOOD, THE
STRANGE ADVENTURE OF DAVID GRAY, THE	VAMPYR
STRANGE INCIDENT	OX-BOW INCIDENT, THE
STRANGE JOURNEY	FANTASTIC VOYAGE
STRANGE ONES, THE	LES ENFANTS TERRIBLES
STRANGERS	I NEVER SANG FOR MY FATHER
STRIKERS, THE	ORGANIZER, THE
SUITABLE CASE FOR TREATMENT, A	MORGAN!
SUMMER MADNESS	SUMMERTIME
SUNA NO ONNA	WOMAN IN THE DUNES
SUSUZ YAZ	DRY SUMMER
SWEPT AWAY	SWEPT AWAY. . . BY AN UNUSUAL DESTINY IN THE BLUE SEA OF AUGUST
SYMPHONY OF LOVE	ECSTASY
SZAMARKOHOGES	WHOOPING COUGH

T.P.A.

T.P.A.	PRESIDENT'S ANALYST, THE
T2	TERMINATOR 2: JUDGMENT DAY
TACONES LEJANOS	HIGH HEELS
TALES OF A PALE AND MYSTERIOUS MOON AFTER THE RAIN	UGETSU MONOGATARI
TARZAN VERSUS I.B.M.	ALPHAVILLE
TARZANOVA SMRT	DEATH OF TARZAN, THE
TEN LITTLE NIGGERS	AND THEN THERE WERE NONE
TENGOKU TO-JIGOKU	HIGH AND LOW
THAT THEY MAY LIVE	J'ACCUSE
THEATRE ROYAL	ROYAL FAMILY OF BROADWAY, THE
THEOREM	TEOREMA
THEY LOVED LIFE	KANAL
THING FROM ANOTHER WORLD, THE	THING, THE
37.2 LE MATIN	BETTY BLUE
THIS MAN REUTER	DISPATCH FROM REUTERS, A
THIS STRANGE PASSION TORMENTS	EL
THOMAS CROWN AND COMPANY	THOMAS CROWN AFFAIR, THE
THOSE MAGNIFICENT MEN IN THEIR FLYING MACHINES	THOSE MAGNIFICENT MEN IN THEIR FLYING MACHINES; OR HOW I FLEW FROM LONDON TO PARIS IN 25 HOURS AND 11 MINUTES
THOSE WERE THE HAPPY TIMES	STAR!
THREE BAD MEN IN THE HIDDEN FORTRESS	HIDDEN FORTRESS, THE
THREE RASCALS IN THE HIDDEN FORTRESS	HIDDEN FORTRESS, THE
TIDAL WAVE	PORTRAIT OF JENNIE
TIEMPO DE MORIR	TIME TO DIE, A
TIME OF RETURN, THE	MURIEL
TIREZ SUR LE PIANISTE	SHOOT THE PIANO PLAYER
TO OUR LOVES	A NOS AMOURS
TO PROXENIO TIS ANNAS	MATCHMAKING OF ANNA, THE
TOGETHER IN PARIS	PARIS WHEN IT SIZZLES
TOKYO MONOGATARI	TOKYO STORY
TOM SAWYER	ADVENTURES OF TOM SAWYER, THE
TOO MANY CHEFS	WHO IS KILLING THE GREAT CHEFS OF EUROPE?
TRAFIC	TRAFFIC
TRAINED TO KILL	WHITE DOG
TRIP, THE	CHELSEA GIRLS, THE

ALTERNATE TITLE	U.S. TITLE
WOMAN OF THE DUNES	WOMAN IN THE DUNES
WORD, THE	ORDET
WORLD AND HIS WIFE, THE	STATE OF THE UNION
WYOMING KID, THE	CHEYENNE
YANKEE AT KING ARTHUR'S COURT, THE	CONNECTICUT YANKEE, A
YANKEE IN KING ARTHUR'S COURT, A	CONNECTICUT YANKEE IN KING ARTHUR'S COURT, A
YEELEN	BRIGHTNESS
YOIDORE TENSHI	DRUNKEN ANGEL
YOUNG AND THE DAMNED, THE	LOS OLVIDADOS
YOUNG AND THE PASSIONATE, THE	VITELLONI
YOUNG MAN OF MUSIC	YOUNG MAN WITH A HORN
YOUNG SCARFACE	BRIGHTON ROCK
YOUNGEST SPY, THE	MY NAME IS IVAN
YOUR RED WAGON	THEY LIVE BY NIGHT
ZAMRI OUMI VOSKRESNI	FREEZE—DIE—COME TO LIFE
ZAZIE DANS LE METRO	ZAZIE
ZAZIE IN THE SUBWAY	ZAZIE
ZAZIE IN THE UNDERGROUND	ZAZIE
ZERO DE CONDUITE	ZERO FOR CONDUCT
ZORBA	ZORBA THE GREEK
ZUCKERBABY	SUGARBABY

THE MOVIE GUIDE

A NOS AMOURS

1983 102m c ★★½

Drama R/U

Livradois/FR3/Gaumont (France)

Sandrine Bonnaire (Suzanne), Dominique Besnehard (Robert), Maurice Pialat (The Father), Evelyne Ker (The Mother), Anne-Sophie Maille (Anne), Christophe Odent (Michel), Cyr Boitard (Luc), Maite Maille (Martine), Pierre-Loup Rajot (Bernard), Cyril Collard (Jean-Pierre)

p, Maurice Pialat; d, Maurice Pialat; w, Maurice Pialat, Arlette Langmann; ph, Jacques Loiseleux; ed, Yann Dedet, Sophie Coussein, Valerie Condroyer, Corinne Lazare, Jean Gargonne, Nathalie Letrosne, Catherine Legault; m, Klaus Nomy; art d, Jean-Paul Camail; cos, Valerie Schlumberger, Martha de Villalonga

The story of 15-year-old Suzanne (Sandrine Bonnaire, in her first role), who is in a hopeless situation—she inspires love but cannot feel it herself. Since she is only happy when she is with a guy, she sleeps with everyone who shows interest, except Luc (Cyr Boitard), the one boy who truly feels for her. Her behavior causes problems at home, where things are bad enough already: Her father is moving out, giving free reign to her decidedly unappetizing brother, and her mother is becoming increasingly neurotic. Hardly an uplifting story, but Bonnaire turns Suzanne into a truly compelling figure. Pialat does a fine job of telling the story from Suzanne's point of view, and himself turns in a good performance as her father, the one person with whom she has a genuine understanding.

A NOUS LA LIBERTE

1931 104m bw ★★★★★

Comedy/Political /U

SDFS (France)

Henri Marchand (Emile), Raymond Cordy (Louis), Rolla France (Jeanne), Paul Olivier (Paul Imaque), Jacques Shelly (Paul), Andre Michaud (Foreman), Germaine Aussey (Maud), Alex D'Arcy (Gigolo), William Burke (Old Convict), Vincent Hyspa (Old Orator)

d, Rene Clair; w, Rene Clair; ph, Georges Perinal; ed, Rene Clair, Rene Le Henaff; m, Georges Auric

This classic satire on the dehumanization of industrial workers is one of Rene Clair's greatest achievements, preceding Chaplin's indictment of the industrial revolution, MODERN TIMES, by five years. Clair's fast-paced and wickedly funny entertainment centers on the friendship between two prison inmates—Louis (Raymond Cordy), who escapes and becomes a phonograph company tycoon, and Emile (Henri Marchand), who, after he too escapes, is hired at his friend's factory. Filming without a script and giving his actors freedom to improvise, Clair

structured his film like an operetta. Georges Auric wrote the music, to which the movements of the assembly lines of actors are choreographed. Clair's message is an angry one—"a bitter pill," as he described it, which "would be more easily swallowed when coated with diverting music." The film earned an Academy Award nomination for Best Interior Decoration.

AARON LOVES ANGELA

1975 99m c ★★

Romance R/U

Columbia

Kevin Hooks (Aaron), Irene Cara (Angela), Moses Gunn (Ike), Robert Hooks (Beau), Ernestina Jackson (Cleo), Leon Pinkney (Willie), Wanda Velez, Lou Quinones, Charles McGregor, Norman Evans

p, Robert J. Anderson; d, Gordon Parks, Jr.; w, Gerald Sanford; ph, Dick Kratina; ed, William Anderson; m, Jose Feliciano

Sensitive story of romance between a black youth and a Puerto Rican girl. As they struggle to make their feelings known to each other, the also must face the harsh realities of life in the ghetto. Comic relief is supplied by an awkward Mr. Cool type, uproariously played by Leon Pinkney.

ABBOTT AND COSTELLO MEET FRANKENSTEIN

1948 83m bw ★★★★

Comedy /U

Universal

Bud Abbott (Chick Young), Lou Costello (Wilbur Grey), Lon Chaney, Jr. (Lawrence Talbot/The Wolf Man), Bela Lugosi (Dracula), Glenn Strange (The Monster), Lenore Aubert (Sandra Mornay), Jane Randolph (Joan Raymond), Frank Ferguson (McDougal), Charles Bradstreet (Dr. Stevens), Howard Negley (Harris)

p, Robert Arthur; d, Charles Barton; w, Robert Lees, Frederic I. Rinaldo, John Grant (based on the novel Frankenstein by Mary Shelley); ph, Charles Van Enger; ed, Frank Gross; m, Frank Skinner; fx, David S. Horsley

Hilarious spoof of the classic Universal horror films of the 1930s and early 40s, with Abbott and Costello playing railway porters who unwittingly deliver the "undead" bodies of Frankenstein's monster (Glenn Strange) and Dracula (Bela Lugosi) to a wax museum, where the bodies are revived. Thus awakened, Dracula becomes intent on replacing the catatonic Monster's brain with dim-witted Costello's, because it would make the beast easier to control. Lawrence Talbot (Lon Chaney, Jr.) attempts to help the boys, but he's got problems of his own: he turns into a wolfman whenever there's a full moon. Horror buffs will note that Chaney, Jr., who had played the Monster in THE GHOST OF FRANKENSTEIN, fills in for Strange in the shot where the Monster tosses actress Lenore Aubert out a window. Strange had broken his foot in an accident and, rather than lose three days of shooting, Chaney volunteered to don the makeup once again. After this film's considerable success at the box office, Abbott and Costello made seven more pictures in which they "met" Hollywood monsters, but none were as lively and entertaining as this one.

ABE LINCOLN IN ILLINOIS

1940 110m bw ★★★

Biography /U

RKO

Raymond Massey *(Abraham Lincoln)*, Gene Lockhart *(Stephen Douglas)*, Ruth Gordon *(Mary Todd Lincoln)*, Mary Howard *(Ann Rutledge)*, Dorothy Tree *(Elizabeth Edwards)*, Harvey Stephens *(Ninian Edwards)*, Minor Watson *(Joshua Speed)*, Alan Baxter *(Billy Herndon)*, Howard da Silva *(Jack Armstrong)*, Maurice Murphy *(John McNeil)*

p, Max Gordon; d, John Cromwell; w, Grover Jones, Robert E. Sherwood (based on his play); ph, James Wong Howe; ed, George Hively; m, Roy Webb

In adapting Robert E. Sherwood's popular play about the early years of Abraham Lincoln, the filmmakers wisely chose Raymond Massey, who played the title role on stage, to reprise his portrayal in the film. Massey heads an impressive cast in a picture spanning thirty years of Lincoln's life, following his career from his beginnings as a woodsman and shopkeeper to his entry into law and politics and culminating with his election as the 16th president of the United States. The film includes some memorable scenes of Lincoln's debates with his longtime political rival, Stephen Douglas (Gene Lockhart), and offers a vivid account of 19th-century life in the Midwest, with particular attention paid to the political processes of the day. Massey's excellent performance earned an Oscar nomination (he lost to James Stewart in THE PHILADELPHIA STORY) and the film was also nominated for Best Cinematography.

ABOMINABLE DR. PHIBES, THE
1971   93m   c   ★★★
Horror   PG/15
AIP   (U.S./U.K.)

Vincent Price *(Dr. Anton Phibes)*, Joseph Cotten *(Dr. Vesalius)*, Hugh Griffith *(Rabbi)*, Terry-Thomas *(Dr. Longstreet)*, Virginia North *(Vulnavia)*, Aubrey Woods *(Goldsmith)*, Susan Travers *(Nurse Allan)*, Alex Scott *(Dr. Hargreaves)*, Peter Gilmore *(Dr. Kitaj)*, Edward Burnham *(Dr. Dunwoody)*

p, Louis M. Heyward, Ronald S. Dunas; d, Robert Fuest; w, James Whiton, William Goldstein; ph, Norman Warwick; ed, Tristam Cones; m, Basil Kirchin; art d, Bernard Reeves; cos, Elsa Fennell

A delightfully goofy horror film set in England circa 1929, THE ABOMINABLE DR. PHIBES stars Vincent Price as Dr. Anton Phibes, a horribly disfigured madman who enacts an insidious revenge on the team of physicians who failed to save the life of his dear, departed wife (Caroline Munro, seen mostly in photos). His face and voice destroyed in an auto accident, Phibes reconstructs his mutilated visage over the bones that remained, and recovers his lost voice by plugging a cord extended from his neck into a Victrola! The gruesome ends he devises for the doctors are patterned after the plagues brought down on Ramses in ancient Egypt (killer locusts, blood-sucking bats, rabid rats, etc.). Kept at a snappy pace by "Avengers" director Robert Fuest and given a bizarre art deco look by art director Bernard Reeves and set designer Brian Eatwell, this movie is a kitschy homage to the sillier horror pictures of the 1930s and well worth a look. An equally entertaining sequel, DR. PHIBES RISES AGAIN, was released in 1972.

ABSENCE OF MALICE
1981   116m   c   ★★½
Drama   PG
Columbia

Paul Newman *(Gallagher)*, Sally Field *(Megan)*, Bob Balaban *(Rosen)*, Melinda Dillon *(Teresa)*, Luther Adler *(Malderone)*, Barry Primus *(Waddell)*, Josef Sommer *(McAdam)*, John Harkins *(Davidek)*, Don Hood *(Quinn)*, Wilford Brimley *(Wells)*

p, Sydney Pollack; d, Sydney Pollack; w, Kurt Luedtke; ph, Owen Roizman; ed, Sheldon Kahn; m, Dave Grusin; prod d, Terence Marsh; cos, Bernie Pollack

Gallagher (Paul Newman), the son of a dead mobster, runs a legitimate business in Miami, with his uncle (Luther Adler) his only connection to organized crime. A federal investigator (Bob Balaban) thinks Gallagher knows the details of a labor leader's disappearance, and leaks information to Megan (Sally Field), a reporter who writes a story implicating Gallagher. The story's publication brings tragic results, and Gallagher plots to get revenge. Sydney Pollack's film is a solid, absorbing drama that, in profiling the damage that can result from investigative reporting, presents a counterpoint to ALL THE PRESIDENT'S MEN. Newman, Dillon, and Luedtke received Oscar nominations.

ABSENT-MINDED PROFESSOR, THE
1961   97m   bw   ★★★
Comedy/Fantasy   G/U
Disney

Fred MacMurray *(Prof. Ned Brainard)*, Nancy Olson *(Betsy Carlisle)*, Keenan Wynn *(Alonzo Hawk)*, Tommy Kirk *(Bill Hawk)*, Leon Ames *(Rufus Daggett)*, Elliott Reid *(Shelby Ashton)*, Edward Andrews *(Defense Secretary)*, Wally Brown *(Coach Elkins)*, Forrest Lewis *(Officer Kelly)*, James Westerfield *(Officer Hanson)*

p, Walt Disney; d, Robert Stevenson; w, Bill Walsh (based on the story by Samuel W. Taylor); ph, Edward Colman; ed, Cotton Warburton; m, George Bruns; art d, Carroll Clark; fx, Peter Ellenshaw, Eustace Lycett, Robert A. Mattey

A wacky comedy in which college professor Ned Brainard (Fred MacMurray) invents flying rubber, which he dubs "flubber." The substance has gravity-defying properties and, when applied to the soles of shoes, allows the wearer to leap to incredible heights. A variety of suitably screwy situations ensue, as the evil Alonzo Hawk (Keenan Wynn) plots to steal the formula for his own personal gain. This is a zanily inventive piece of work, with delightful special effects, which set the style for a long series of live-action Disney films. It earned Oscar nominations for Best Cinematography, Best Art Direction, and Best Special Effects. A 1964 sequel, THE SON OF FLUBBER, was less successful.

ABSOLUTE BEGINNERS
1986   107m   c   ★★★
Musical   PG-13/15
Palace/Virgin/Goldcrest   (U.K.)

Eddie O'Connell *(Colin)*, Patsy Kensit *(Crepe Suzette)*, David Bowie *(Vendice Partners)*, James Fox *(Henley of Mayfair)*, Ray Davies *(Arthur)*, Mandy Rice-Davies *(Mum)*, Eve Ferret *(Big Jill)*, Tony Hippolyte *(Mr. Cool)*, Graham Fletcher-Cook *(Wizard)*, Joe McKenna *(Fabulous Hoplite)*

p, Stephen Woolley, Chris Brown; d, Julien Temple; w, Christopher Wicking, Richard Burridge, Don MacPherson (based on the novel by Colin MacInnes); ph, Oliver Stapleton (Super Techniscope, Rank Color); ed, Michael Bradsell, Gerry Hambling, Richard Bedford, Russell Lloyd; m, Gil Evans; prod d, John Beard; art d, Stuart Rose, Ken Wheatley; chor, David Toguri; cos, Sue Blane, David Perry

A visually inventive and energetic pop musical adapted from Colin MacInnes' 1958 cult novel of the same name. ABSOLUTE BEGINNERS is a tale of two swinging English teens, Colin (Eddie O'Connell) and Crepe Suzette (Patsy Kensit), set against the backdrop of emerging youth culture and racial tension in late 1950s London. As Suzette becomes a success in the fashion business and looks set to leave her street roots behind, Colin is torn between his youthful idealism and his desire to do whatever is necessary to lure her back. Though the characterization and plot waver on the transparent, ABSOLUTE BEGINNERS has no shortage of color, movement, and infectious music—it's a perfect example of a music video sensibility applied to a feature-length film. Highlights include songs by jazzman Slim Gaillard ("Selling Out") and The Style Council ("Have You Ever Had It Blue?") and a bravura, one-take opening sequence a la TOUCH OF EVIL.

ABYSS, THE

1961 140m c ★★½
Science Fiction PG-13/12
FOX

1989 — corrected below

1989 140m c ★★½
Science Fiction PG-13/12
FOX

Ed Harris *(Bud Brigman)*, Mary Elizabeth Mastrantonio *(Lindsey Brigman)*, Michael Biehn *(Lt. Coffey)*, George Robert Klek *(Wilhite)*, John Bedford Lloyd *("Jammer" Willis)*, Christopher Murphy *(Seal Schoenick)*, Adam Nelson *(Ensign Monk)*, J.C. Quinn *("Sonny" Dawson)*, Kimberly Scott *(Lisa "One Night" Standing)*, Capt. Kidd Brewer, Jr. *(Lew Finler)*

p, Gale Anne Hurd; d, James Cameron; w, James Cameron; ph, Mikael Salomon, Dennis Skotak (DuArt Color); ed, Joel Goodman; m, Alan Silvestri; prod d, Leslie Dilley; art d, Peter Childs; cos, Deborah Everton

Picture the opening scene of JAWS, except that, in THE ABYSS, it's not a great white shark but an underwater UFO that propels the movie into action. Spotted on sonar by a US nuclear submarine, the "thing" is eerily tracked below deck, where it creates a disaster because of the crew's ensuing panic. The sub sinks onto the ledge of an abyss, and a team of oil riggers, led by foreman Bud Brigman (Ed Harris), is pressed into a rescue mission. The civilian crew is joined by engineer Lindsey Brigman (Mary Elizabeth Mastrantonio), who happens to be Bud's soon-to-be ex-wife, and a group of navy underwater experts headed by Lt. Coffey (Michael Biehn), whose top-secret priority is the 150 nuclear warheads located on the sub. The rescue takes on a new character when the extra-terrestrial force makes its presence known. Despite the fact that most of the action occurs below sea level, THE ABYSS simply recycles elements of the stellar blockbusters it tries so hard to emulate (CLOSE ENCOUNTERS, E.T., and director James Cameron's own ALIENS among them). Unfortunately, it lacks the emotional impact and suspense of its predecessors and is spoiled by a disappointingly inane ending. What ultimately saves the film are its extraordinary sets and phenomenal Oscar-winning visual effects.

ACCATTONE!

1961 120m bw ★★★
Drama /15
Arco (Italy)

Franco Citti *(Vittorio Accattone)*, Franca Pasut *(Stella)*, Silvana Corsini *(Maddalena)*, Paolo Guidi *(Ascenza)*, Adriana Asti *(Amore)*, Renato Capogna *(Renato)*, Roberto Scaringella *(Cartagine)*, Mario Cipriani *(Balilla)*, Piero Morgia *(Pio)*, Umberto Bevilacqua *(Salvatore)*

p, Alfredo Bini; d, Pier Paolo Pasolini; w, Pier Paolo Pasolini; ph, Tonino Delli Colli; ed, Nino Baragli; m, Johann Sebastian Bach

Pasolini's first feature is a classic neorealist study of the Roman underworld of poverty and petty thievery. Accattone (Citti), a street youth who hates work, falls in love with Stella (Pasut) and attempts to find a job, but ultimately turns to crime. The film is based on Pasolini's own novel and supposedly mirrors his own experiences. The director uses nonprofessional actors to create a vivid portrait of an unremittingly grim environment.

ACCIDENT

1967 105m c ★★★
Drama /PG
London Independent (U.K.)

Dirk Bogarde *(Stephen)*, Stanley Baker *(Charley)*, Jacqueline Sassard *(Anna)*, Delphine Seyrig *(Francesca)*, Alexander Knox *(Provost)*, Michael York *(William)*, Vivien Merchant *(Rosalind)*, Harold Pinter *(Bell)*, Ann Firbank *(Laura)*, Brian Phelan *(Police Sergeant)*

p, Joseph Losey, Norman Priggen; d, Joseph Losey; w, Harold Pinter (based on the novel by Nicholas Mosley); ph, Gerry Fisher (Eastmancolor); ed, Reginald Beck; m, Johnny Dankworth; art d, Carmen Dillon; cos, Beatrice Dawson

Intriguing film about the seduction of a university student after she's involved in a car crash which kills her boyfriend. The story is narrated by an introspective professor (Bogarde) in a series of flashback reflections upon the dead boy, a former student. What emerges is a barbed portrait of the academic life and a sense of sexual desperation underlying an apparently peaceful Oxford summer. Joseph Losey does a superb job of translating Harold Pinter's quintessentially theatrical dialogue into elegant visual terms.

ACCIDENTAL TOURIST, THE

1988 121m c ★★★★
Comedy PG
WB

William Hurt *(Macon Leary)*, Kathleen Turner *(Sarah Leary)*, Geena Davis *(Muriel Pritchett)*, Amy Wright *(Rose)*, Bill Pullman *(Julian)*, Robert Gorman *(Alexander Pritchett)*, David Ogden Stiers *(Porter Leary)*, Ed Begley, Jr. *(Charles Leary)*, Bradley Mott *(Mr. Loomis)*, Seth Granger *(Ethan)*

p, Lawrence Kasdan, Charles Okun, Michael Grillo; d, Lawrence Kasdan; w, Frank Galati, Lawrence Kasdan (based on the novel by Anne Tyler); ph, John Bailey (Technicolor); ed, Carol Littleton; m, John Williams; prod d, Bo Welch; cos, Ruth Myers

Writer-director Kasdan's fine adaptation of Tyler's novel hinges on Hurt's understated performance as a writer of travel guides for businessmen who hate to travel. Shortly after his wife, Turner (who starred opposite Hurt in Kasdan's BODY HEAT), leaves him, he breaks a leg and moves in with his oddball middle-aged sister and brothers (Wright, Begley, and Stiers). Because his dead son's Welsh corgi has become a disciplinary problem, Hurt calls upon the dog-training services of Davis, a vibrant divorcee. They begin an awkward relationship that is further complicated when Turner wants to patch things up. Kasdan has remained true to the spirit of Tyler's award-winning novel, preserving much of her wonderful dialogue and humor. Hurt's performance is remarkably assured, and Davis beautifully captures her character's insouciance. Less than perfect is Turner, whose capable performance presents a figure somewhat hollow at the center. Although some may find the film slow-moving, its rich characterizations alone makes it well worth watching. Davis won the Best Supporting Actress Oscar. The film was nominated for Best Picture, Best Adapted Screenplay, and Best Original Score.

ACCUSED, THE

1988   110m   c   ★★½
Drama   R/18
Paramount

Kelly McGillis (Kathryn Murphy), Jodie Foster (Sarah Tobias), Bernie Coulson (Kenneth Joyce), Ann Hearn (Sally Frazer), Steve Antin (Bob Joiner), Tom O'Brien (Larry), Allan Lysell (Al Massi), Leo Rossi (Cliff Albrecht), Carmen Argenziano (Paul Rudolph), Terry David Mulligan (Det. Duncan)

p, Stanley R. Jaffe, Sherry Lansing; d, Jonathan Kaplan; w, Tom Topor; ph, Ralf D. Bode (Alpha Cine Services Color); ed, Jerry Greenberg, O. Nicholas Brown; m, Brad Fiedel; prod d, Richard Kent Wilcox

Only a riveting performance by Jodie Foster lifts THE ACCUSED above the level of a television movie. The story, which bears some resemblance to a much-publicized 1983 incident in Massachusetts, centers on the case of Foster, a tough, sexy young woman who is gang-raped in a neighborhood bar before a crowd of cheering onlookers. District attorney McGillis takes the case. She agrees to a plea bargain in which the rapists admit to reckless endangerment, because she fears her client's sordid past will destroy her credibility in court. After Foster castigates McGillis for selling her out, McGillis devises a new strategy—to put the crowd of onlookers on trial for "criminal solicitation."

Director Jonathan Kaplan and screenwriter Tom Topor purposely paint Foster as a slut in order to strengthen their argument—that no matter how provocatively she was dressed or how erotically she danced, Foster was not asking to be gang-raped. Although the filmmakers are well-intentioned, THE ACCUSED is a predictable picture that lacks emotional insight; it works only because of the onscreen bond between Foster, who won a much-deserved Oscar for her performance, and McGillis. Foster charges forward into the frame with explosive energy, carrying the film and proving she has far too much talent to let mediocre material bring her down.

ACES HIGH

1977   114m   c   ★★½
War   PG
Cine Artists   (U.K.)

Malcolm McDowell (Gresham), Christopher Plummer (Sinclair), Simon Ward (Crawford), Peter Firth (Croft), John Gielgud (Headmaster), Trevor Howard (Lt. Col. Silkin), Richard Johnson (Col. Lyle), Ray Milland (Brig. Whale), David Daker (Bennett), Elliott Cooper (Wade)

p, S. Benjamin Fisz; d, Jack Gold; w, Howard Barker (based on the play Journey's End by R.C. Sherriff); ph, Gerry Fisher, Peter Allwork; ed, Anne V. Coates; m, Richard Hartley; fx, Derek Meddings

The story of 76 Squadron, a group of WWI airmen led by McDowell, with Plummer playing a compassionate older officer who brings a sentimental understanding to the frayed nerves of youngsters Firth and Ward. The film has its fair share of war movie cliches, understandable since it's loosely based upon R.C. Sherriff's classic 1929 play, "Journey's End." Milland, Howard, and Johnson are excellent as the uncaring British brass ordering men to their death while sipping vintage wine and wolfing down rich French entrees in a distant chateau. Much attention is given to young Firth who loses his virginity to a sultry young French girl and then loses his life in a head-on collision with a German adversary. The aerial combat scenes are superb.

ACROSS 110TH STREET

1972   102m   c   ★★½
Crime   R/18
UA

Anthony Quinn (Capt. Frank Mattelli), Yaphet Kotto (Det. Lt. Pope), Anthony Franciosa (Nick D'Salvio), Paul Benjamin (Jim Harris), Ed Bernard (Joe Logart), Richard Ward (Doc Johnson), Norma Donaldson (Gloria Roberts), Antonio Fargas (Henry Jackson), Gilbert Lewis (Shevvy), Marlene Warfield (Mrs. Jackson)

p, Ralph Serpe, Fouad Said; d, Barry Shear; w, Luther Davis (based on the novel by Wally Ferris); ph, Jack Priestley; ed, Byron Brandt; m, J.J. Johnson; art d, Perry Watkins

Rather brutal movie has three black hoods stealing a fortune from a Mafia-controlled Harlem numbers bank. They are tracked down by crooked cop Quinn, who walks a thin line between his duties as a policeman and his obligations to the Mafia. Kotto is terrific as Quinn's black partner, and the film makes fine use of Harlem locations, but there are a few too many scenes of murder and torture.

ACROSS THE PACIFIC

1942   97m   bw   ★★★½
Spy   /U
WB

Humphrey Bogart (Richard Lomas Leland), Mary Astor (Alberta Marlow), Sydney Greenstreet (Dr. Lorenz), Charles Halton (A.V. Smith), Victor Sen Yung (Joe Totsuiko), Roland Got (Sugi), Lee Tung-Foo (Sam Wing On), Frank Wilcox (Capt. Morrison), Paul Stanton (Col. Hart), Lester Matthews (Canadian Major)

p, Jerry Wald, Jack Saper; d, John Huston (uncredited); w, Richard Macaulay (based on the Saturday Evening Post serial "Aloha Means Goodbye" by Robert Carson); ph, Arthur Edeson; ed, Frank Magee; m, Adolph Deutsch; art d, Robert Haas, Hugh Reticker; fx, Byron Haskin, Willard Van Enger; cos, Milo Anderson

With the success of THE MALTESE FALCON under his belt, young director John Huston took on this first-rate espionage adventure, using three principals from his previous film, Bogart, Astor, and Greenstreet. Bogart is introduced as a disgraced ex-Army man who has been court-martialed for selling military secrets, and who boards a Japanese ship bound for the Pacific via the Panama Canal. On board he meets Astor, a fashion designer going to the Canal Zone to visit her father; Greenstreet, a mysterious sociologist returning to his professorial post in Manila, a man who praises the Japanese to excess; and Tong, a silent Japanese passenger who identity is assumed by a replacement when the ship docks in New York. Here the viewer is allowed to see that Bogart is not a callous creature willing to sell his services to the highest bidder, but that his traitorous posture is only a cover for his true role of undercover agent; he has been planted on board to establish a liaison with Japanese agent Greenstreet and to discover what he can about Astor. As in THE MALTESE FALCON, Bogart takes a terrible beating, again at the orders of the sadistic Greenstreet. Yet he goes on to overcome all the odds in a wonderfully impossible ending which brazenly spoofs the spy genre. Good quality fun.

ACROSS THE WIDE MISSOURI

1951   78m   c   ★★
Adventure   /U
MGM

Clark Gable *(Flint Mitchell)*, Ricardo Montalban *(Ironshirt)*, John Hodiak *(Brecan)*, Adolphe Menjou *(Pierre)*, Maria Elena Marques *(Kamiah)*, J. Carrol Naish *(Looking Glass)*, Jack Holt *(Bear Ghost)*, Alan Napier *(Capt. Humberstone Lyon)*, George Chandler *(Gowie)*, Richard Anderson *(Dick)*

p, Robert Sisk; d, William A. Wellman; w, Talbot Jennings (based on the story by Jennings and Frank Cavett, and the book by Bernard DeVoto); ph, William Mellor; ed, John Dunn; m, David Raksin; art d, Cedric Gibbons, James Basevi

A florid pioneer epic, this film offers Gable as a tough, calculating trapper who marries Marques (an accomplished Mexican film star) because she is the daughter of a powerful Blackfoot chief, Holt. (Gable thinks the hostile tribe will allow him into their territory to trap beaver for their precious pelts.) Surviving Indian attacks, Marques leads Gable and company on a circuitous but safe route to the land of her people, where she gives birth to a child. By then Gable no longer treats her as a pawn but is in love with her, as devoted as his rugged nature will permit. He and his trappers build a fort and forge an alliance with the Indians, but another tribe attacks and Marques is killed. Gable and the child survive, and though he initially plans to abandon the infant, he turns back to spend his days with his offspring and Indian friends in the high mountains. There are colorful performances from Menjou as a bottle-loving, carefree French trapper and from Naish as an offbeat Indian chief, and breathtaking location photography, but the use of a narrator (Howard Keel) and the lengthy translations of Indian monologues bog things down.

ACT OF THE HEART, THE

1970   103m   c   ★★
Drama   PG/U
Quest   (Canada)

Genevieve Bujold *(Martha Hayes)*, Donald Sutherland *(Father Michael Ferrier)*, Monique Leyrac *(Johane Foss)*, Bill Mitchell *(Russell Foss)*, Suzanne Langlois *(Housekeeper)*, Sharon Acker *(Adele)*, Ratch Wallace *(Diedrich)*, Jean Duceppe *(Parks Commissioner)*, Gilles Vigneault *(Coach Ti-Jo)*, Eric House *(Choirmaster)*

p, Paul Almond; d, Paul Almond; w, Paul Almond; ph, Jean Boffety; ed, James Mitchell; m, Harry Freedman; art d, Anne Pritchard

A slight but finely acted film, featuring Bujold as an innocent, strictly raised country girl who goes to Montreal to become the guardian of a precocious child. Traumatized by the child's death in a sports accident, she turns to a local priest, Sutherland, of whom she has long been enamored, blurting out her love for him. Sutherland accepts her love and leaves the priesthood to marry her, but turns out to be a total failure in the secular world. This is a bleak, mundane story which nevertheless stays in the mind, and which ends on a note of high drama.

ACTION IN THE NORTH ATLANTIC

1943   126m   bw   ★★★★
War   /A
WB

Humphrey Bogart *(Joe Rossi)*, Raymond Massey *(Capt. Steve Jarvis)*, Alan Hale *(Boats O'Hara)*, Julie Bishop *(Pearl)*, Ruth Gordon *(Mrs. Jarvis)*, Sam Levene *(Chips Abrams)*, Dane Clark *(Johnny Pulaski)*, Peter Whitney *(Whitey Lara)*, Dick Hogan *(Cadet Robert Parker)*, Minor Watson *(Rear Adm. Hartridge)*

p, Jerry Wald; d, Lloyd Bacon; w, John Howard Lawson (based on the novel by Guy Gilpatric); ph, Ted McCord; ed, Thomas Pratt, George Amy; m, Adolph Deutsch; art d, Ted Smith; fx, Jack Cosgrove, Edwin DuPar; cos, Milo Anderson

Excellent study of WWII merchant marine crew sailing between the U.S. and Murmansk, Russia, the only supply line then open between the Western Allies and the Soviet Union. Bogart plays a loyal, brave, and rugged first mate to idealistic captain Massey. After their first tanker is torpedoed, and the two barely survive an eleven-day ordeal at sea, Massey and Bogart are given a spanking new Liberty Ship, with most of their old crew members as well as a sharp Navy gun crew. They sail with a massive convoy en route to Murmansk, but are repeatedly hounded by U-boats. Bogart and company battle through the Nazi attacks, managing to sink a surfaced sub by faking a shipboard fire and ramming the sub, then shooting down several German bombers on the approach to Murmansk. A powerful document of a class of men given little due for their heroic role during WWII, the film lives up to its title—there is action aplenty. The film earned an Oscar nomination for its original story.

ADAM'S RIB

1949   101m   bw   ★★★½
Comedy   /A
MGM

Spencer Tracy *(Adam Bonner)*, Katharine Hepburn *(Amanda Bonner)*, Judy Holliday *(Doris Attinger)*, Tom Ewell *(Warren Attinger)*, David Wayne *(Kip Lurie)*, Jean Hagen *(Beryl Caighn)*, Hope Emerson *(Olympia La Pere)*, Eve March *(Grace)*, Clarence Kolb *(Judge Reiser)*, Emerson Treacy *(Jules Frikke)*

p, Lawrence Weingarten; d, George Cukor; w, Ruth Gordon, Garson Kanin; ph, George Folsey; ed, George Boemler; m, Miklos Rosca; art d, Cedric Gibbons, William Ferrari; fx, A. Arnold Gillespie; cos, Walter Plunkett

ADAM'S RIB is a delightful comedy, full of sophisticated laughs and sparked by the chemistry between Katharine Hepburn and Spencer Tracy. When Tracy, an unyielding DA, prosecutes the client of his lawyer-wife, Hepburn, in an attempted murder case, it unleashes a battle of the sexes that almost wrecks their happy marriage. The defendant is Holliday (in an outstanding debut which led to her getting the "dumb blonde" lead in BORN YESTERDAY), who attempted to shoot a woman who was trysting with Holliday's slippery husband (Ewell, in a hilarious performance). Hepburn, an advocate of women's rights, is determined to prove that the prosecution's case is a reflection of sexist double standards, and that Holliday's husband would never be tried for the same actions. This rankles the conservative Tracy, and matters are further complicated when foppish David Wayne begins to move in on Hepburn. Throughout the trial, Tracy and Hepburn's marriage seems headed for the rocks, their courtroom resentments surfacing at home. Eventually, Hepburn wins an acquittal for Holliday through a case based on sexual equality, but admits, as does a petulant Tracy, that there are basic differences between men and women. *"Vive la difference!"* Tracy exclaims, and the marriage and the battle between the sexes go on. A thoroughly witty, sharply directed, fun film from Cukor,

5

with a sprightly, Oscar-nominated script from Gordon and Kanin, ADAM'S RIB succeeds brilliantly through a combination of top talents, especially those of Hepburn and Tracy.

ADDAMS FAMILY, THE

1991 99m c   ★★½
Comedy/Horror   PG-13/PG
Orion

Anjelica Huston (Morticia Addams), Raul Julia (Gomez Addams), Christopher Lloyd (Uncle Fester Addams/Gordon Craven), Dan Hedaya (Tully Alford), Elizabeth Wilson (Abigail Craven), Judith Malina (Granny), Carel Struycken (Lurch), Dana Ivey (Margaret Alford), Paul Benedict (Judge Womack), Christina Ricci (Wednesday Addams)

p, Scott Rudin; d, Barry Sonnenfeld; w, Caroline Thompson, Larry Wilson (from the characters created by Charles Addams); ph, Owen Roizman; ed, Dede Allen, Jim Miller; m, Marc Shaiman; prod d, Richard MacDonald; art d, Marjorie Stone McShirley; chor, Peter Anastos; cos, Ruth Myers

This meticulously composed homage owes far more to Charles Addams's original New Yorker cartoons than to the short-lived 60s TV series. Unfortunately, the filmmakers were so intent on creating the right look and attitude that they neglected to think about the plot; the result is a series of one-note jokes that no amount of visual style can redeem.

The Addamses are a ghoulish clan delighting in the macabre—the devilish opposite of a rosy, wholesome American family. The debonair Gomez Addams (Raul Julia) and his morbidly elegant wife Morticia (Anjelica Huston) preside over an eccentric household that includes Wednesday (Christina Ricci) and Pugsley (Jimmy Workman), their precociously diabolical offspring; Lurch (Carel Struycken), their aptly named manservant; and Thing (Christopher Hart), a disembodied hand that serves as the family pet.

Into this grim but happy bunch come Abigail Craven (Elizabeth Wilson) and her son Gordon (Christopher Lloyd), a con artist duo who, in conspiracy with Tully Alford (Dan Hedaya), the Addams's crooked lawyer, plan to make off with the Addams fortune. The plan revolves around the uncanny resemblance between Gordon and Gomez's long-lost brother, Fester (also played by Lloyd). THE ADDAMS FAMILY certainly looks the part: Huston and Julia appear suavely sinister, and the production design is a triumph of post-modern gothic. Looks aren't everything, however. Cinematographer-turned-director Barry Sonnenfeld and screenwriters Larry Wilson and Caroline Thompson haven't solved the problem of how to construct a film around a one-joke concept. Certainly, there are some memorable one-liners (Morticia to a depressed Gomez: "Don't torture yourself, Gomez. That's my job."). But the film can't sustain itself on dialogue like this and shots of the Addams offspring playing with lightning rods in the rain—it gets tired and familiar after a very short time.

ADVENTURE OF SHERLOCK HOLMES' SMARTER BROTHER, THE

1975 91m c   ★★★
Comedy/Mystery   /PG
FOX (U.K.)

Gene Wilder (Sigerson Holmes), Madeline Kahn (Jenny), Marty Feldman (Orville Sacker), Dom DeLuise (Gambetti), Leo McKern (Moriarty), Roy Kinnear (Moriarty's Aide), John Le Mesurier (Lord Redcliff), Douglas Wilmer (Sherlock Holmes), Thorley Walters (Dr. Watson), George Silver (Bruner)

p, Richard A. Roth; d, Gene Wilder; w, Gene Wilder; ph, Gerry Fisher; ed, Jim Clark; m, John Morris; chor, Alan Johnson; cos, Ruth Myers

Hilarious spoof of all the Holmes film adventures by director-writer Wilder, who also stars as the utterly berserk younger brother of the great sleuth, consumed by jealousy over his brother's fame, detective acumen, and mere presence in the same country. The obsessively quirkish Wilder must outdo his brother in everything, from fencing to inventions, from detecting the smallest clue to unraveling the most fiendish plot. In this case, he's tracking down some vital state secrets that are missing and are about to fall into the clutching hands of, naturally, the evil Professor Moriarty, devilishly and deftly played by McKern. Aiding the outlandishly courageous Wilder is wild-eyed Feldman, a Scotland yard detective with photographic hearing, and a mystery woman thrown in for witty non sequiturs (Kahn, in all her voluptuous pomp and puff). We tumble along with Wilder from one harrowing adventure to another as he draws ever nearer to the urgent papers, almost undone by mad opera star DeLuise, a total hedonist whose onstage braying and prancing guarantees theatrical disaster. Wilder doggedly manages his job as a wholly side-splitting maniac only to be exposed as a decoy set up by his omnipotent brother (Wilmer), who has just pretended to be out of the country and has been operating behind the scenes with the venerable Watson (Walters) to save Wilder repeatedly from death and/or destruction. Both Holmes brothers triumph, as does this film, a portrait of delightful mayhem.

ADVENTURES OF BARON MUNCHAUSEN, THE

1989 126m c   ★★
Fantasy   PG
Prominent/Laura/Allied Film Makers   (U.K./West Germany)

John Neville (Baron Munchausen), Eric Idle (Desmond/Berthold), Sarah Polley (Sally Salt), Oliver Reed (Vulcan), Charles McKeown (Rupert/Adolphus), Winston Dennis (Bill Albrecht), Jack Purvis (Jeremy/Gustavus), Valentina Cortese (Queen Ariadne/Violet), Jonathan Pryce (Horatio Jackson), Bill Paterson (Henry Salt)

p, Thomas Schuhly, Ray Cooper; d, Terry Gilliam; w, Charles McKeown, Terry Gilliam (based on the stories by Rudolph Erich Raspe); ph, Giuseppe Rotunno (Eastmancolor); ed, Peter Hollywood; m, Michael Kamen; prod d, Dante Ferretti; art d, Massimo Razzi, Maria Teresa Barbasso; chor, Pino Penesse, Giorgio Rossi; cos, Gabriella Pescucci

Director Terry Gilliam's THE ADVENTURES OF BARON VON MUNCHAUSEN adapts the tall tales and fables associated with the real-life Karl Friedrich Hieronymous von Munchausen (1720-97), a German soldier and nobleman. The film begins in a walled city whose denizens suffer under a siege by the army of the Ottoman Empire, and under the government of their evil leader Horatio Jackson (Jonathan Pryce). Within the town, a theater troupe is staging a rendition of the Munchausen saga when an aged man in the audience (John Neville) announces that he's the real Baron, and that only he can save them from the siege. He then departs in a makeshift balloon to round up his former cohorts, the superhumanly gifted aides who will help him in his struggle. The film is stylish and takes great relish in the Baron's retelling of his adventures, but the story-within-the-story is plodding and listless. MUNCHAUSEN emerges as a ponderous, visually overblown spectacle that fails to engage the viewer on any kind of emotional level.

ADVENTURES OF BUCKAROO BANZAI: ACROSS THE 8TH DIMENSION, THE

1984   103m   c   ★★
Comedy/Science Fiction   PG/15
Sherwood

Peter Weller (Buckaroo Banzai), John Lithgow (Dr. Emilio Lizardo/Lord John Whorfin), Ellen Barkin (Penny Priddy), Jeff Goldblum (New Jersey), Christopher Lloyd (John Bigboote), Lewis Smith (Perfect Tommy), Rosalind Cash (John Emdall), Robert Ito (Prof. Hikita), Pepe Serna (Reno Nevada), Ronald Lacey (President Widmark)

p, Neil Canton, W.D. Richter; d, W.D. Richter; w, Earl Mac Rauch; ph, Fred Koenekamp (Panavision, Metrocolor); ed, Richard Marks, George Bowers; m, Michael Boddicker; prod d, J. Michael Riva; art d, Richard Carter, Stephen Dane; fx, Michael Fink; cos, Aggie Guerard Rodgers

Dreadful enough to have inspired a cult. In this strange film that tries to do too much in too short a time, the title character (Weller) is a nuclear physicist, brain surgeon, and rock-'n'-roll singer who saves the world from the Red Lectroids, aliens from a distant galaxy. As the film opens, Weller is trying to drive his superpowered car through a mountain in an attempt to test the "oscillation overthruster" he has invented. The device is highly coveted by the aliens, who need it in order to return to their own world. Lithgow plays a mad scientist who conducted the same research decades earlier, and who now sets up shop again, making plans for world domination in league with the Red Lectroids. Few films appear so obviously to have droped footage on the cutting-room floor. Punch lines appear without set-ups and set-ups without punch lines. Characters come and go with such bewildering speed that it is virtually impossible to keep track of the story, which jumps around enough to induce motion sickness. BUCKAROO BANZAI has nevertheless earned a loyal cult following among those who are willing to invest time in the roller-coaster ride.

ADVENTURES OF DON JUAN

1949   110m   c   ★★½
Adventure/Romance   /PG
WB

Errol Flynn (Don Juan), Viveca Lindfors (Queen Margaret), Robert Douglas (Duke de Lorca), Alan Hale (Leporello), Romney Brent (King Phillip III), Ann Rutherford (Donna Elena), Robert Warwick (Count De Polan), Jerry Austin (Don Sebastian), Douglas Kennedy (Don Rodrigo), Jean Shepherd (Donna Carlotta)

p, Jerry Wald; d, Vincent Sherman; w, George Oppenheimer, Harry Kurnitz (based on the story by Herbert Dalmas); ph, Elwood Bredell (Technicolor); ed, Alan Crosland, Jr.; m, Max Steiner

The last of the big-budget swashbucklers for an increasingly dissipated star and an increasingly disappointed studio, DON JUAN offers Flynn as the notorious lover and swordsman of the title: amorous, capricious and somewhat world-weary. The film features the predictable expert duels in resplendent settings, when Flynn is not enjoying the flighty advances of a bevy of luscious contract beauties. Viveca Lindfors is an arresting choice for the Queen of Spain, but her considerable talents are not challenged by routine Hollywood treatment. The film did respectable box office business, but it is evident to the viewer that

Flynn is growing a little long in the tooth for leading man roles. Nevertheless, DON JUAN is enjoyable formula fluff and a fitting swan song to Flynn's years as a bankable star.

ADVENTURES OF HUCKLEBERRY FINN, THE

1960   107m   c   ★★½
Adventure   /U
MGM

Tony Randall (The King), Eddie Hodges (Huckleberry Finn), Archie Moore (Jim), Patty McCormack (Joanna), Neville Brand (Pap), Mickey Shaughnessy (The Duke), Judy Canova (Sheriff's Wife), Andy Devine (Mr. Carmody), Sherry Jackson (Mary Jane), Buster Keaton (Lion Tamer)

p, Samuel Goldwyn, Jr.; d, Michael Curtiz; w, James Lee (based on the novel by Mark Twain); ph, Ted McCord (CinemaScope, MetroColor); ed, Fredric Steinkamp; m, Jerome Moross; art d, George W. Davis, McClure Capps; fx, A. Arnold Gillespie

This is a sprightly account of the adventures of Mark Twain's rural American boy which follows Huck Finn (Eddie Hodges) and the slave Jim (Archie Moore) as they travel down the Mississippi on a raft in the mid-1800s. Along the way they are reluctantly drawn into the schemes of a pair of con men (Tony Randall and Mickey Shaughnessy), find work on a riverboat, and join the circus. Though it is not entirely faithful to the book (the riverboat and circus scenes have been added), this is nonetheless a well-crafted film featuring strong performances from Randall, former middleweight boxing champion Moore, and a host of beloved character actors, with rich photography that beautifully captures authentic Mississippi River locations. This was Hollywood's second attempt to film the Huck Finn story; Mickey Rooney had played the title role in 1939's HUCKLEBERRY FINN.

ADVENTURES OF ICHABOD AND MR. TOAD

1949   68m   c   ★★★★
Animated   /A
Disney

VOICES OF: Bing Crosby (Narrator), Basil Rathbone, Eric Blore, Pat O'Malley, John Floyardt, Colin Campbell, Campbell Grant, Claud Allister, The Rhythmaires

p, Walt Disney; d, Jack Kinney, Clyde Geronimi, James Algar; w, Erdman Penner, Winston Hibler, Joe Rinaldi, Ted Sears, Homer Brightman, Harry Reeves (based on the story "The Legend of Sleepy Hollow" by Washington Irving and the book The Wind in the Willows by Kenneth Grahame)

Split into two sequences, this feature-length cartoon is one of Disney's finest efforts, with attention paid to every animated detail. The first sequence deals with the madcap, aristocratic Mr. Toad of Kenneth Grahame's British classic The Wind in the Willows, a haughty amphibian who thinks himself too good for such fellows as Mr. Pig and stuffy Mr. Rat. Toad, who is obsessed with planes and autos, lands through his own recklessness in trouble, debt, and jail, and his friends must rally to get him out and defeat the band of thieving weasels that framed him. The second segment, concerning the emaciated Ichabod Crane of Washington Irving's "The Legend of Sleepy Hollow", is delightfully narrated by Bing Crosby, who also croons some eerie tunes with the Rhythmaires. Ichabod, the new schoolmaster in a small New England village, has a memorable Halloween night when he is chased by the legendary Headless Horseman. For pure imaginative animation, this pell-mell race through forests and glens is still unequaled. ADVENTURE is superb family entertainment, though very young children may find the climactic sequence of the "Sleepy Hollow" portion too frightening. The two segments have been released separately on videocassette.

ADVENTURES OF MARK TWAIN, THE
1944   130m   bw   ★★★
Biography   /U
WB

Fredric March (Samuel Clemens), Alexis Smith (Olivia Langdon), Donald Crisp (J. B. Pond), Alan Hale (Steve Gillis), C. Aubrey Smith (Oxford Chancellor), John Carradine (Bret Harte), William Henry (Charles Langdon), Robert Barrat (Horace E. Bixby), Walter Hampden (Jervis Langdon), Joyce Reynolds (Clara Clemens)

p, Jesse L. Lasky; w, Alan LeMay, Harry Chandlee; d, Irving Rapper; w, Alan LeMay, Harry Chandlee (based on an adaptation by Alan LeMay and Harold M. Sherman of biographical material owned by the Mark Twain Co.); ph, Sol Polito, Laurence Butler, Eddie Linden, Don Siegel, James Leicester; ed, Ralph Dawson; m, Max Steiner; art d, John Hughes

Cliched but engaging film biography, with a solid performance by Fredric March as the young adventurer who left Hannibal, Missouri, to learn the Mississippi River's tricky ways as a navigator. In one scene, the young navigator is attempting to steer a riverboat through fogbound waters when he hears a deckhand, after throwing out a weight to determine the water's depth, shout: "Mark the twain [twine—the rope tied about the weight] 15 [feet]." Thus the *nom de plume* of one of America's finest writers and humorists. Sharp dialogue sparks the predictable story line as Twain moves from the Mississippi to the West as a newspaper editor, then on to Gold Rush California, where he writes the short story "The Celebrated Jumping Frog of Calaveras County," the success of which launches his literary career. The episodic film chronicles Twain's meetings with the greats of his day (U.S. Grant, Bret Harte, Oliver Wendell Holmes, Ralph Waldo Emerson, etc.), as well as his courtship of and marriage to Olivia Langdon (Alexis Smith), as it follows Twain from young manhood to old age. March imbues his character with quiet nobility, projecting the forceful, courageous soul of the immortal Twain. What's missing is the vinegary, difficult side of Twain that made him as unforgettable a man as he was a writer.

ADVENTURES OF MILO AND OTIS, THE
(KONEKO MONOGATARI)
1989   76m   c   ★★★
Children's   G/U
Fuji Television   (Japan)

Dudley Moore (Narrator)

p, Masaru Kakutani, Satoru Ogata; d, Masanori Hata; w, Mark Saltzman (based on a story by Masanori Hata); ph, Hideo Fujii, Shinji Tomita; ed, Chizuko Osada; m, Michael Boddicker

Of all the buddy movies ever made, MILO AND OTIS features one of the most unlikely pairs of friends—a cat and dog that befriend each other on a farm and eventually wander out into the not-so-friendly world. Not a single human being appears onscreen in this delightful live-action entry from Japan. It all starts when the kitten, Milo, decides to take a trip down the river in a box, with his faithful canine chum, Otis, following behind. But soon Otis loses track of his friend, who gets into many adventures. Based on a charming screenplay by Mark Saltzman, this clever children's film contains beautiful nature photography and moments of humor along with many impressive animal stunts. Surely it was no small feat to get bears and dogs, chickens and cats, pigs and cows to work together harmoniously. Shot

from the animals' point of view and narrated by Dudley Moore, MILO AND OTIS contains some important messages about the responsibilites of friendship. Slow in spots, but a treat nevertheless.

ADVENTURES OF ROBIN HOOD, THE
1938   102m   c   ★★★★★
Adventure   /U
WB

Errol Flynn (Sir Robin of Locksley/Robin Hood), Olivia de Havilland (Maid Marian), Basil Rathbone (Sir Guy of Gisbourne), Claude Rains (Prince John), Patric Knowles (Will Scarlett), Eugene Pallette (Friar Tuck), Alan Hale (Little John), Melville Cooper (High Sheriff of Nottingham), Ian Hunter (King Richard the Lion-Hearted), Una O'Connor (Bess)

p, Henry Blanke; d, Michael Curtiz, William Keighley; w, Norman Reilly Raine, Seton I. Miller (based on the novel *Ivanhoe* by Sir Walter Scott and the opera *Robin Hood* by De Koven-Smith); ph, Sol Polito, Tony Gaudio (Technicolor); ed, Ralph Dawson; m, Erich Wolfgang Korngold; art d, Carl Jules Weyl; cos, Milo Anderson

When King Richard the Lion-Hearted (Ian Hunter) is captured by Austrians and held for ransom, evil Prince John (Claude Rains) declares himself ruler of England and makes no attempt to secure Richard's safe return. Though John has all the nobles and their armies on his side, it doesn't sway a lone knight, Robin Hood (Errol Flynn), who swears his allegiance to Richard and sets out to raise the ransom money by stealing from the caravans of the rich that cross through Sherwood Forest. Robin is aided by his lady love, Maid Marian (Olivia de Havilland), and his band of merry men, including Little John (Alan Hale) and Friar Tuck (Eugene Pallette), as he battles the false monarch and the villainous Sheriff of Nottingham (Melville Cooper) in his effort to return the throne to its rightful owner. This is one of the truly great adventure films of all time, and features a terrific performance by the perfectly cast Flynn. Handsome, dashing, and athletic, Flynn is everything that Robin Hood should be, with a wicked sense of humor to boot. His adversaries are all memorable villains, particularly Basil Rathbone as the conniving Sir Guy of Gisbourne. Rathbone spent many hours with a fencing instructor to prepare for his climactic duel with Flynn, one of the most exciting battles ever put on film. Only a spirited and extravagant production could do justice to the Robin Hood legend; this film is more than equal to the task. Korngold's score won a well-deserved Oscar, as did the editing and art direction.

ADVENTURES OF ROBINSON CRUSOE, THE
1952   90m   c   ★★★½
Adventure   /U
UA   (Mexico)

Dan O'Herlihy (Robinson Crusoe), Jaime Fernandez (Friday), Felipe de Alba (Capt. Oberzo), Chel Lopez (Bos'n), Jose Chavez, Emilio Garibay (Leaders of the Mutiny)

p, Oscar Dancigers, Henry Ehrlich; d, Luis Bunuel; w, Phillip Roll, Luis Bunuel (based on the novel *The Life and Strange Surprising Adventures of Robinson Crusoe* by Daniel Defoe); ph, Alex Phillips (Pathecolor); ed, Carlos Savage, Alberto Valenzuela; m, Anthony Collins

A fairly faithful adaptation of Daniel Defoe's classic *The Life and Strange Surprising Adventures of Robinson Crusoe*, directed by Bunuel in Mexico. Shipwrecked in a storm, sailor Robinson Crusoe (Dan O'Herlihy) finds himself washed up on the shore of a desert island. All other hands have been killed in the storm, but Crusoe is able to salvage a cat, a dog, and some weapons and provisions from the wreckage. He takes up residence in a cave and begins living as his prehistoric ancestors must have done, all the while striving to overcome his oppressive loneliness. After going 18 years without seeing another human being, he is shocked when a small band of natives visits the island one day. They are about to kill and eat one of their party when Crusoe intervenes, saves the intended victim, and chases off the others. The two develop a strong relationship as they spend another ten years on the island, after which Crusoe is finally returned to civilization by the crew of a ship that anchors offshore.

Bunuel's adaptation is particularly effective in evoking the loneliness of the stranded survivor and in depicting the changes that gradually occur within him as his memories of civilization begin to fade. O'Herlihy earned an Academy Award nomination for his performance, but lost to Marlon Brando for ON THE WATERFRONT.

ADVENTURES OF SHERLOCK HOLMES, THE

1939 85m bw	★★★★
Mystery	/PG
FOX	

Basil Rathbone *(Sherlock Holmes)*, Nigel Bruce *(Dr. Watson)*, Ida Lupino *(Ann Brandon)*, Alan Marshal *(Jerrold Hunter)*, Terry Kilburn *(Billy)*, George Zucco *(Prof. Moriarty)*, Henry Stephenson *(Sir Ronald Ramsgate)*, E.E. Clive *(Inspector Bristol)*, Arthur Hohl *(Bassick)*, May Beatty *(Mrs. Jameson)*

p, Gene Markey; d, Alfred Werker; w, Edwin Blum, William A. Drake (based on the play by William Gillette and the works of Arthur Conan Doyle); ph, Leon Shamroy; ed, Robert Bischoff

A taut script and sharp, witty dialogue make this, the second of the Basil Rathbone/Nigel Bruce Sherlock Holmes vehicles, one of the finest crime adventures ever made. Arch-villain Professor Moriarty (Zucco, in the first of many appearances as Holmes's chief nemesis) plots a grand theft by sidetracking Holmes (Rathbone) with two foul murders, one involving Ann Brandon (Lupino). As Holmes investigates the murders, Moriarty begins work on his real goal, stealing the crown jewels from the Tower of London.

ADVENTURES was released a mere six months after THE HOUND OF THE BASKERVILLES and is generally considered superior to its predecessor, thanks to Alfred Werker's direction. Although both films were box office hits, Fox executives thought of the Holmes films as expensive "B" pictures and declined to continue the series at the outbreak of WWII, assuming the public would be uninterested in the 19th century British sleuth. In 1942 Universal reunited Rathbone and Bruce, updated the scenarios to reflect contemporary themes (i.e., Nazi spies), scaled down the production costs and turned out 11 successful, if inferior, installments.

ADVENTURES OF TOM SAWYER, THE

1938 93m c	★★★½
Adventure	/U
Selznick	

Tommy Kelly *(Tom Sawyer)*, Jackie Moran *(Huckleberry Finn)*, Ann Gillis *(Becky Thatcher)*, May Robson *(Aunt Polly)*, Walter Brennan *(Muff Potter)*, Victor Jory *(Injun Joe)*, David Holt *(Sid Sawyer)*, Victor Kilian *(Sheriff)*, Nana Bryant *(Mrs. Thatcher)*, Olin Howlin *(Schoolmaster)*

p, David O. Selznick, William H. Wright; d, Norman Taurog; w, John V.A. Weaver (based on the novel by Mark Twain); ph, James Wong Howe, Wilfrid M. Cline (Technicolor); ed, Margaret Clancy

Mark Twain's beloved Tom Sawyer comes to life in this excellent Selznick production, with Tommy Kelly portraying the brave, mischievous boy. He is caught between the manners of his very proper home, ruled by tough but loving Aunt Polly (May Robson), and the wild, roaming, trouble-seeking nature of his friend Huckleberry Finn, ably portrayed by Jackie Moran. The great Sawyer adventures are faithfully re-created—the conning of the two boys into whitewashing his aunt's fence, a wild ride down the Mississippi on a raft, the witnessing of Injun Joe's crimes and his pursuit of Tom and the terrified Becky Sharp (Ann Gillis) into the giant cave. The incorrigible boys even witness their own funeral ceremony before informing the grieving townsfolk that they are still among the living. A lively production featuring a quick pace, a chilling climax, and a surprising amount of wit.

ADVENTURESS, THE

1946 111m bw	★★★★
Spy	/U
Individual (U.K.)	

Deborah Kerr *(Bridie Quilty)*, Trevor Howard *(Lt. David Bayne)*, Raymond Huntley *(Miller)*, Michael Howard *(Hawkins)*, Norman Shelley *(Man in Straw Hat)*, Liam Redford *(Timothy)*, Brefni O'Rorke *(Michael O'Callaghan)*, James Harcourt *(Grandfather)*, W.G. O'Gorman *(Danny Quilty)*, George Woodbridge *(Steve)*

p, Sidney Gilliat; d, Frank Launder; w, Sidney Gilliat, Frank Launder, Wolfgang Wilhelm; ph, Wilkie Cooper; ed, Thelma Myers; m, William Alwyn

A superb film that is too often overlooked. Deborah Kerr, making her fifth feature at age 24, appears as an Irish spitfire who has been weaned on her grandfather's tales of British cruelty to the Irish; she leaves her small village of Ballygarry, spouting anti-British venom to a stranger, Huntley, on board a train to Dublin, where the IRA rejects her. But Huntley, a Nazi agent, uses her as a pawn, telling her that he represents another branch of the movement and involving her in the rescue of "one of the lads" imprisoned in a British jail—in reality, another Nazi spy. Howard, as a British intelligence agent, tracks her down and falls in love with her, staying a step behind through one perilous adventure after another, both to protect her and to uncover the Nazi spy ring.

This is a highly suspenseful, atmospheric film in the Hitchcockian tradition, mostly due to a superb script by Launder and Gilliat, who authored THE LADY VANISHES. The acting, particularly by Kerr (who won the 1947 New York Film Critics Award for this role and her appearance in BLACK NARCISSUS), Howard, and Huntley, is outstanding.

ADVISE AND CONSENT

1962 140m c	★★★½
Political	/X
Columbia	

Henry Fonda *(Robert Leffingwell)*, Charles Laughton *(Sen. Seabright "Seb" Cooley)*, Don Murray *(Sen. Brigham Anderson)*, Walter Pidgeon *(Sen. Bob Munson)*, Peter Lawford *(Sen. Lafe Smith)*, George Grizzard *(Sen. Fred Van Akcerman)*, Gene Tierney *(Dolly Harrison)*, Franchot Tone *(The President)*, Lew Ayres *(The Vice-President)*, Burgess Meredith *(Herbert Gelman)* p, Otto Preminger; d, Otto Preminger; w, Wendell Mayes (based on the novel by Allen Drury); ph, Sam Leavitt; ed, Louis Loeffler; m, Jerry Fielding; prod d, Lyle Wheeler; cos, Hope Bryce

An incisive, sometimes brutal, study of American high politics, based on Allen Drury's best-selling novel, featuring outstanding performances from the leads and a great collection of character actors.

Fonda has been appointed to the omnipotent position of Secretary of State, and the film revolves around his appointment's confirmation by the US Senate. Pidgeon and his cohorts are trying to push the appointment through, past such ancient pelicans as Laughton, in a marvelous portrayal of a crusty old Dixiecrat. Murray, a freshman senator whose vote in support of the nomination is vital, will not commit to his party leader, Pidgeon. This leads Grizzard, a ruthless, power-hungry colleague, to attempt to blackmail Murray into siding with his voting block. He digs up Murray's former homosexual activities and threatens to expose him unless he votes "the right way," with unexpectedly tragic results.

In an all-star cast, Laughton shines in his last role, but the subdued work by Tone and Ayres shows how underplaying can sometimes work best before the camera. Though the film sensationalizes politics, Preminger's touch is more precise and cautious than usual; this is a more realistic if less human portrait of the Senate than Capra's MR. SMITH GOES TO WASHINGTON. Both films proved to be unpopular with their role models, who refused to comment on them.

AFRICAN QUEEN, THE

1951 105m c   ★★★★★
Adventure/Romance/War   /U
Horizon/Romulus   (U.S./U.K.)

Humphrey Bogart (Charlie Allnut), Katharine Hepburn (Rose Sayer), Robert Morley (Rev. Samuel Sayer), Peter Bull (Captain), Theodore Bikel (1st Officer), Walter Gotell (2nd Officer), Gerald Onn (Petty Officer), Peter Swanwick, Richard Marner (Officers at Shona)

p, Sam Spiegel; d, John Huston; w, James Agee, John Huston (based on the novel by C.S. Forester); ph, Jack Cardiff (Technicolor); ed, Ralph Kemplen; m, Allan Gray

John Huston's THE AFRICAN QUEEN is a film that has everything—adventure, humor, spectacular photography and superb performances.

In his only Oscar-winning performance, Bogart stars as Charlie Allnut, a reprobate who uses his little battered steamer, The African Queen, to run supplies to small villages in East Africa at the onset of WWI. At one stop he meets Rose (Katharine Hepburn), the devoted spinster sister of Rev. Samuel Sayer (Robert Morley). When Charlie returns to the village later, he finds that German troops have invaded and Sayer is dead, and he offers to take the distraught Rose back to civilization. Thus begins a perilous and unforgettable journey as Charlie and Rose decide to do their part in the war effort against the Germans.

THE AFRICAN QUEEN's marvelous screenplay was written as a straight drama by James Agee, but director John Huston and his stars give it a lyrical tongue-in-cheek treatment that fills the screen with hilarious humanity. Magnificently filmed on location in Africa by Jack Cardiff, THE AFRICAN QUEEN is Hollywood filmmaking of the highest order.

AFTER DARK, MY SWEET

1990 114m c   ★★½
Crime   R/18
Avenue

Jason Patric (Collie), Rachel Ward (Fay), Bruce Dern (Uncle Bud), George Dickerson (Doc Goldman), James Cotton (Charlie), Corey Carrier (Jack), Rocky Giordani (Bert), Jeanie Moore (Nanny), Tom Wagner (Counterman), Burke Byrnes (Cop)

p, Ric Kidney, Robert Redlin; d, James Foley; w, James Foley, Robert Redlin (based on the novel by Jim Thompson); ph, Mark Plummer; ed, Howard Smith; m, Maurice Jarre; art d, Kenneth A. Hardy; fx, Ken Diaz

AFTER DARK, MY SWEET is a latter-day film noir involving the intertwined destinies of three boozy lowlifes. Collie (Jason Patric) is a near-psychopathic ex-boxer who left the ring after killing a competitor. He becomes involved with Fay (Rachel Ward), a seductive, alcoholic widow, and Uncle Bud (Bruce Dern), a sleazy former lawman, and is drawn into their scheme to get rich quick by kidnapping the young scion of a wealthy local family. At first confused by Fay's sodden mixed messages, Collie splits the scene for a while. He is taken in by an all-too-interested physician, Doc Goldman (George Dickerson), but soon grows tired of the doctor's attempts to enforce domesticity and returns to Fay. The wheels of the crime are now set in motion, as are the detours and plot twists one expects from the genre.

AFTER DARK, MY SWEET is based on a 1955 novel by the prolific tough-guy novelist Jim Thompson, who worked on the screenplays of THE KILLING and PATHS OF GLORY for Stanley Kubrick, and whose The Grifters and The Kill-Off were also turned into 1990 releases. Director James Foley (RECKLESS, AT CLOSE RANGE) has the kind of visual style that can lend a glamorous patina to the most mundane settings, and Mark Plummer's fluent cinematography brings the story an enervated complacency that could easily drive one to drink or sin. What a shame, then, that Robert Redlin's screenplay is so threadbare, failing to create the kind of dynamic personalities that might heat up the proceedings. Patric gives a tremendous, smoldering performance, but Ward fails to convey the mysterious radiance essential to to be a convincing femme fatale. Dern rounds out the unappetizing triangle with an unpleasant performance, proving himself a worthy contender in the Dennis Hopper/Harry Dean Stanton creepstakes.

AFTER HOURS

1985 96m c   ★★★½
Comedy   R/15
Double Play/Geffen

Griffin Dunne (Paul Hackett), Rosanna Arquette (Marcy), Verna Bloom (June), Tommy Chong (Pepe), Linda Fiorentino (Kiki), Teri Garr (Julie), John Heard (Tom, the Bartender), Richard "Cheech" Marin (Neil), Catherine O'Hara (Gail), Dick Miller (Waiter)

p, Amy Robinson, Griffin Dunne, Robert F. Colesberry; d, Martin Scorsese; w, Joseph Minion; ph, Michael Ballhaus (Duart Color); ed, Thelma Schoonmaker; m, Howard Shore; prod d, Jeffrey Townsend; art d, Stephen J. Lineweaver; cos, Rita Ryack

A wickedly funny black comedy that follows the increasingly bizarre series of events that befall hapless word-processer Griffin Dunne after he ventures out of his apartment on the Upper East Side of Manhattan and goes downtown in search of carnal pleasures. On a wild cab ride to SoHo, Dunne loses the only folding money he has on him. When he goes to the loft of the sexy but quirky Rosanna Arquette, he discovers only Linda

Fiorentino, working on a papier-mache sculpture. Eventually Arquette shows up, but she's such a hyperactive mass of contradictions that Dunne leaves. However, when he plunks down the 90 cents he has to his name at the subway station, the attendant tells him the fare has gone up to $1.50 this very midnight. He's trapped in SoHo, and things only get worse as the night wears on.

Scorsese is in total command of his visual style in AFTER HOURS, a tightly constructed film that races from scene to scene. The story sprang from the mind of screenwriter Joseph Minion, a Columbia University film student who had written the script for a class. Dunne turns in a superb performance, and we share his mounting frustration, fear, shame, and guilt. Scorsese ordered Dunne to abstain from sex and sleep during filming to increase his anxiety level, and filmed this small gem on location for the small budget of 3.5 million.

AFTER THE FOX
1966   102m   c   ★★★
Comedy   /U
UA   (U.S./U.K./Italy)

Peter Sellers (Aldo Vanucci), Victor Mature (Tony Powell), Britt Ekland (Gina Romantica), Martin Balsam (Harry), Akim Tamiroff (Okra), Paolo Stoppa (Polio), Tino Buazzelli (Siepi), Mac Ronay (Carlo), Lydia Brazzi (Mama Vanucci), Lando Buzzanca (Police Chief)

p, John Bryan; d, Vittorio De Sica; w, Neil Simon, Cesare Zavattini; ph, Leonida Barboni (Technicolor); ed, Russell Lloyd; m, Burt Bacharach; art d, Mario Garbuglia; cos, Piero Tosi

A visual delight thanks to director De Sica, this Sellers vehicle is loaded with belly laughs thanks to an uneven but solid script by Simon. As the flamboyantly inept Fox, a *master* thief, Sellers breaks jail in order to arrange the passage to Rome of $3 million in gold bullion stolen in Cairo. After his escape, Sellers pops up almost frame by frame in a host of disguises—a prison doctor, a tourist cameraman, an Italian cop, and a zany New Wave film director, spoofing the avant-garde in a merciless portrayal. Part of that parody has Victor Mature (making a movie within the movie) as an aging star trussed up with corsets and insisting he wear the threadbare trench coat and battered hat from his 1940s films.

Mature is brilliant at mocking his former film noir persona, and interplays memorably with Sellers. In another spoof the Italian actors zestily parody stereotypes of themselves and their country: their casual ways, indifference to authority, and sexual passion. Particularly outstanding are the desert scenes, where De Sica himself is attempting to direct a movie during a violent sandstorm and has his equipment stolen by Sellers and Tamiroff.

AFTER THE REHEARSAL
1984   72m   c   ★★
Drama   R/U
Cinematograph/Persona   (Sweden)

Erland Josephson (Henrik Vogler), Ingrid Thulin (Rakel), Lena Olin (Anna Egerman), Nadja Palmstjerna-Weiss (Anna at age 12), Bertil Guve (Henrik at age 12)

p, Jorn Donner; d, Ingmar Bergman; w, Ingmar Bergman; ph, Sven Nykvist; ed, Sylvia Ingemarsson; art d, Anna Asp; cos, Inger Pehrsson

Filmed for Swedish television, AFTER THE REHEARSAL was advertised as Bergman's farewell to cinema (a claim also made upon the release of FANNY AND ALEXANDER in 1983).

Partly autobiographical, it concerns an aging theater director, Josephson, who looks back on the pain and suffering he has caused those around him, especially the actresses he has loved and left. After the rehearsal of his fifth production of August Strindberg's *Dream Play*, the director rests on a couch onstage. There he is visited by Olin, a young actress who has returned to the theater in search of a bracelet she supposedly left behind. There is a mutual attraction between actress and director as they discuss their lives and the theater—Josephson revealing that he once had an affair with her mother. Then they imagine what their lives would be like if they were to have an affair.

Although AFTER THE REHEARSAL is blessed with three superb performances (especially Thulin, as a has-been actress who attacks the director for having abandoned her), it is trapped in its staginess, leaving one to wonder why Bergman decided to bring it to the screen (Bob Fosse's revelation on a similar theme was certainly more colorful). Olin, Josephson, and cinematographer Nykvist would meet again a few years later in Philip Kaufman's THE UNBEARABLE LIGHTNESS OF BEING.

AFTER THE THIN MAN
1936   107m   bw   ★★★½
Comedy/Mystery   /A
MGM

William Powell (Nick Charles), Myrna Loy (Nora Charles), James Stewart (David Graham), Joseph Calleia (Dancer), Elissa Landi (Selma Landis), Jessie Ralph (Aunt Katherine Forrest), Alan Marshal (Robert Landis), Sam Levene (Lt. Abrams), Teddy Hart (Floyd Casper), Penny Singleton (Polly Byrnes)

p, Hunt Stromberg; d, W.S. Van Dyke, II; w, Frances Goodrich, Albert Hackett (based on a story by Dashiell Hammett); ph, Oliver T. Marsh; ed, Robert J. Kern; m, Herbert Stothart; art d, Cedric Gibbons

In this breezy sequel to THE THIN MAN, William Powell and Myrna Loy are up to their ears in three quick murders after Elissa Landi asks Powell to find her vanished husband. It seems that hubby has been trysting with nightclub songbird Penny Singleton (later of BLONDIE fame), and is also blackmailing big shot Joseph Calleia. Powell learns that James Stewart, who also has a yen for Singleton, has paid the husband to "disappear" a former girl friend. The investigation proves to be the only distraction in the lives of Powell and Loy. (She's idle and rich; he drinks incessantly except when working, so of course she wants him working to curb the booze.) The missing husband, Alan Marshal, turns up murdered, so Powell rounds up the suspects and names the killer (an unlikely casting candidate).

The script is tight, the direction is swift and arresting, and the cast is tops—MGM surrounded its two quipping stars with the best character actors on the lot. Dashiell Hammett's snappy banter and cynical worldview were kept intact by Frances Goodrich and Albert Hackett, making this production all the more delectable.

AGNES OF GOD
1985   98m   c   ★★★
Mystery   PG-13/15
Columbia

Jane Fonda (Dr. Martha Livingston), Anne Bancroft (Sister Miriam Ruth), Meg Tilly (Sister Agnes), Anne Pitoniak (Dr. Livingston's Mother), Winston Rekert (Detective Langevin), Gratien Gelinas

(Father Martineau), Guy Hoffman (Justice Joseph Leveau), Gabriel Arcand (Monsignor), Francoise Faucher (Eve LeClaire), Jacques Tourangeau (Eugene Lyon)

p, Patrick Palmer, Norman Jewison; d, Norman Jewison; w, John Pielmeier (based on his play); ph, Sven Nykvist (Metrocolor); ed, Anthony Gibbs; m, Georges Delerue; prod d, Ken Adam; art d, Carol Spier; cos, Renee April

Set in a Quebec convent, this well-made mystery raises theological and philosophical questions as it unfolds its tale of the murder of a baby born to a young nun who has no recollection of the infant's conception or delivery. Jane Fonda, a chain-smoking court-appointed psychiatrist, is given the task of determining whether Meg Tilly, a beatific young nun, is sane, sainted, mad, or a murderer. But Anne Bancroft, the convent's mother superior, questions whether the answer to the mystery lies in psychology, setting up a faith-versus-reason confrontation that is the real focus of the film. John Pielmeier's award-winning 1982 play is adapted for the screen here by director Norman Jewison, and though the plot has some annoying holes, the dialogue and the performances are excellent. Both Tilly and Bancroft received Oscar nominations for their work, along with Georges Delerue for his original music score.

AGUIRRE, THE WRATH OF GOD
(AGUIRRE, DER ZORN GOTTES)
1973 90m c   ★★★★★
Historical   /PG
New Yorker   (West Germany)

Klaus Kinski (Don Lope de Aguirre), Ruy Guerra (Don Pedro de Ursua), Del Negro (Brother Gaspar de Carvajal), Helena Rojo (Inez), Cecilia Rivera (Flores), Peter Berling (Don Fernando de Guzman), Alejandro Repulles (Gonzalez Pizarro), Daniel Ades (Perucho), Armando Polanha (Armando), Edward Roland (Okello)

p, Werner Herzog; d, Werner Herzog; w, Werner Herzog; ph, Thomas Mauch (Eastmancolor); ed, Beate Mainka-Jellinghaus; m, Popol Vuh; fx, Juvenal Herrera, Miguel Vasquez

A stunning, terrifying exploration of human obsession descending into madness. Herzog's most powerful fiction film chronicles the Peruvian expedition led by Gonzalez Pizarro (half-brother of the brutal conqueror of the Incas) in search of the legendary city of gold, El Dorado. The film opens in 1560 when Pizarro (Repulles), his men exhausted from their excruciating journey through the dense jungles, decides to send a small party ahead to determine if exploration should continue. Though Don Pedro de Ursua (Guerra) is put in charge, he is continually usurped by the maniacally ambitious Aguierre (Kinski), who insists against increasingly overwhelming odds that the journey continue, with devastating consequences. The film is based on a journal written by Gaspar de Carvajal, who was one of an army of Spaniards who accompanied the real Gonzalez Pizarro.

The intensity of Kinski makes him a remarkable Aguirre; indeed, it would be difficult to imagine a more driven character who has appeared on film. His madness is portrayed against an almost hallucinatory environment as a result of Thomas Mauch's brilliant cinematography and Popol Vuh's spare score. Herzog's cast and crew suffered incredible hardships filming in unexplored regions of South America but as a result the director captured a hostile, mysterious jungle world in such a way as to trivialize complaints that traditional story elements and character development are missing. Just as Aguirre is able to overwhelm the people around him, so the watcher can count on a staggering cinematic experience that assaults the senses.

AH, WILDERNESS!
1935 101m bw   ★★★★
Comedy   /A
MGM

Wallace Beery (Sid Davis), Lionel Barrymore (Nat Miller), Aline MacMahon (Lily Davis), Eric Linden (Richard Miller), Cecilia Parker (Muriel McComber), Spring Byington (Essie Miller), Mickey Rooney (Tommy Miller), Charley Grapewin (Mr. McComber), Frank Albertson (Arthur Miller), Eddie Nugent (Wint Selby)

p, Hunt Stromberg; d, Clarence Brown; w, Albert Hackett, Frances Goodrich (based on the play by Eugene O'Neill); ph, Clyde De Vinna; ed, Frank E. Hull; m, Herbert Stothart; art d, Cedric Gibbons, William A. Horning

Eugene O'Neill's only comedy, written in five weeks, is a dream of the sweet, unaffected boyhood he never had, culminating in one long summer during which adolescence struggles into manhood. Eric Linden plays Richard Miller, a young man of sincerity and some charming stupidity. His mother busies herself with household problems, his mischievous brother and unruly sister vex him, his father nervously avoids instructing him in the ways of the world, and his often-inebriated uncle teaches him about life. It's a marvelous slice of Americana, filled with funny and tender scenes as young Richard strives to understand himself and those around him. Mickey Rooney, here playing the younger brother, played the lead role thirteen years later in the musical remake, SUMMER HOLIDAY.

AIR FORCE
1943 124m bw   ★★★½
War   /PG
WB

John Ridgely (Capt. Mike Quincannon), Gig Young (Lt. Bill Williams), Arthur Kennedy (Lt. Tommy McMartin), Charles Drake (Lt. Munchauser), Harry Carey (Sgt. Robby White), George Tobias (Cpl. Weinberg), Ward Wood (Cpl. Peterson), Ray Montgomery (Pvt. Chester), John Garfield (Sgt. Joe Winocki), James Brown (Lt. Tex Rader)

p, Hal B. Wallis; d, Howard Hawks; w, Dudley Nichols; ph, James Wong Howe, Elmer Dyer; ed, George Amy; m, Franz Waxman; art d, John Huglies; fx, Roy Davidson, Rex Wimpy, H.F. Koenekamp

One of the finest American propaganda films produced during WWII, AIR FORCE fits perfectly into the canon of its director, Howard Hawks. A filmmaker who excels at portraying group action, Hawks tells the story of the "Mary Ann," a B-17 bomber, and its crew. While there is much here the viewer may find offensive (notably the predictable anti-"Jap" rhetoric), Hawks's mesmerizing direction and the assured and emotional performances of the cast, especially Garfield and Carey, draw the viewer in. Though by now beginning to date, Nichols's screenplay is powerful, with dialogue that is both meaningful and believable. The film earned Academy Award nominations for its script and cinematography and won Oscars for editing and special effects. A real fortress, later lost in the Pacific, was used for much of the filming, with interiors photographed inside a $40,000 model. Hawks was a veteran of the Air Corps of WWI, and his own experience and reverence for the service shows in every scene.

AIRPLANE!
1980 88m c   ★★½
Comedy   PG
Paramount

Robert Hays *(Ted Striker)*, Julie Hagerty *(Elaine)*, Kareem Abdul-Jabbar *(Murdock)*, Lloyd Bridges *(McCroskey)*, Peter Graves *(Capt. Oveur)*, Leslie Nielsen *(Dr. Rumack)*, Lorna Patterson *(Randy)*, Robert Stack *(Kramer)*, Stephen Stucker *(Johnny)*, Barbara Billingsley *(Jive Lady)*

p, Jon Davison; d, Jim Abrahams, David Zucker, Jerry Zucker; w, Jim Abrahams, David Zucker, Jerry Zucker; ph, Joseph Biroc (Metrocolor); ed, Patrick Kennedy; m, Elmer Bernstein; fx, Bruce Logan; chor, Tom Mahoney; cos, Rosanna Norton

Loaded with slapstick silliness and schoolboy wordplay, featuring tongue-in-cheek performances by familiar television personalities, and mostly just plain goofy, this inventive comedy from the Zucker-Abrahams-Zucker writing-directing team (THE KENTUCKY FRIED MOVIE, THE NAKED GUN) lampoons crisis-in-the-air films like THE CROWDED SKY and ZERO HOUR.

Ted Striker (Robert Hayes), a failed fighter pilot, is forced to take the controls of a commercial jet liner after the captain (Peter Graves) and co-pilot (basketball legend Kareem Abdul-Jabbar) become ill. Encouraged by his stewardess girlfriend (Julie Haggerty) and zany Dr. Rumack (Leslie Nielsen), and receiving ground support from the even zanier Kramer (Robert Stack), Striker does his best to follow the incomprehensible instructions he is given. Meanwhile, passengers become daffy, berserk, sex-crazed, and generally impossible. The onslaught of one-liners and sight gags in AIRPLANE! is so relentless that even the most dour viewer is ultimately won over—or exhausted.

AIRPORT
1970   137m   c   ★★
Disaster   G/PG
Universal

Burt Lancaster *(Mel Bakersfeld)*, Dean Martin *(Vernon Demerest)*, Jean Seberg *(Tanya Livingston)*, Jacqueline Bisset *(Gwen Meighen)*, George Kennedy *(Joe Patroni)*, Helen Hayes *(Ada Quonsett)*, Van Heflin *(D.O. Guerrero)*, Maureen Stapleton *(Inez Guerrero)*, Barry Nelson *(Lt. Anson Harris)*, Dana Wynter *(Mrs. Cindy Bakersfeld)*

p, Ross Hunter; d, George Seaton, Henry Hathaway (additional sequences); w, George Seaton (based on the novel by Arthur Hailey); ph, Ernest Laszlo (Todd-AO, Technicolor); ed, Stuart Gilmore; m, Alfred Newman; art d, Preston Ames, Alexander Golitzen; cos, Edith Head

An empty reshaping of GRAND HOTEL, held together by disaster in the sky. A fanatic, Heflin, takes out a large insurance policy, then blows himself out of an airborne jet, which limps along for more than two hours looking for a place to land while a score of passengers' lives are capsulized. Frantic ground people sweat over microphones and runway equipment, desperately trying to move a stalled plane on the only runway available (during a blizzard!) while ground crew chief Kennedy blathers heroically.

The film cost more than $10 million, and Universal chiefs held their breath. They need not have worried; the production soared beyond a $45 million gross and spawned three, progressively inferior, sequels. Nominated for ten Academy Awards including Best Picture. Both Stapleton and Hayes were nominated for Best Supporting Actress, and Hayes won, proving sentiment and cloying cuteness can conquer any mediocre script. AIRPORT will be remembered as the trailblazer of the disaster epic, one of the most trivial genres to exist in the history of motion pictures.

AL CAPONE
1959   105m   bw   ★★★
Biography/Crime   /A
Allied Artists

Rod Steiger *(Al Capone)*, Fay Spain *(Maureen)*, James Gregory *(Schaefer)*, Martin Balsam *(Kelly)*, Nehemiah Persoff *(Johnny Torrio)*, Murvyn Vye *(Bugs Moran)*, Joe De Santis *(Jim Colosimo)*, Lewis Charles *(Hymie Weiss)*, Robert Gist *(O'Banion)*, Sandy Kenyon *(Bones Corelli)*

p, John H. Burrows, Leonard J. Ackerman; d, Richard Wilson; w, Malvin Wald, Henry Greenberg; ph, Lucien Ballard; ed, Walter Hannemann; m, David Raksin; art d, Hilyard Brown

Gritty biopic of one of the world's most ruthless men, with a strong, exacting performance by Steiger as the power-hungry Capone. This faithful film noir production details the meteoric rise of Capone to leadership of the mob at age 25, making $50 million a year from bootleg hootch. Steiger becomes a bouncer in 1919 Chicago for De Santis, an opera-loving, old-time crime czar, in order to carry out Persoff's orders to kill De Santis because the old man will not traffic in illegal booze. (Capone actually killed Big Jim Colosimo while disguised as a truck driver delivering pasta to Colosimo's cafe in 1920.) We witness the gang wars between Steiger and Persoff and the North Side Irish gang headed by Vye, Gist, and Charles, culminating in the St. Valentine's Day Massacre. An epilogue shows Steiger going mad in Alcatraz as he suffers from paresis of the brain (a result of untreated syphilis).

This is unquestionably one of Steiger's greatest screen performances, enhanced at every turn by Wilson's quick-paced direction and Ballard's crisp camerawork. Performing well in their supporting roles are Gregory as the honest cop (based on Captain John Stege of the Chicago Police Department) and Balsam as the corrupt news reporter (modeled after Jake Lingle of the *Tribune*, who was murdered by Capone gunman Leo Vincent Brothers in 1931 for going over to the side of the Irish mob).

ALAMBRISTA!
1977   110m   c   ★★★
Drama   /A
Filmhaus

Domingo Ambriz *(Roberto)*, Trinidad Silva *(Joe)*, Linda Gillin *(Sharon)*, Paul Berrones *(Berto)*, George Smith *(Cook)*, Dennis Harris *(Sharon's Brother)*, Edward James Olmos, Julius Harris *(Drunks)*, Mark Herder *(Cop)*, J.D. Hurt *(Preacher)*

p, Michael Hausman, Irwin W. Young; d, Robert M. Young; w, Robert Malcolm Young; ph, Robert Young (DuArt Color); ed, Ed Beyer; m, Michael Martin; art d, Lilly Kilvert

Innocent, wide-eyed Mexican youth Ambriz decides his future lies across the border in the US, so he slips over to undergo incredible exploitation as an illegal alien, slaving for peon wages to support his starving family. Hardly a favorite among staunch conservatives, this is a groundbreaking study of social persecution in the US and a remarkable feature directorial debut for Robert M. Young.

ALAMO, THE
1960   192m   c   ★★★
War   /PG
Batjac

John Wayne *(Col. David Crockett)*, Richard Widmark *(Col. James Bowie)*, Laurence Harvey *(Col. William Travis)*, Frankie Avalon *(Smitty)*, Patrick Wayne *(Capt. James Butler Bonham)*, Linda Cristal *(Flaca)*, Joan O'Brien *(Mrs. Dickinson)*, Chill Wills *(Bee-keeper)*, Joseph Calleia *(Juan Sequin)*, Ken Curtis *(Capt. Almeron Dickinson)*

p, John Wayne; d, John Wayne; w, James Edward Grant; ph, William Clothier (Todd-AO, Technicolor); ed, Stuart Gilmore; m, Dimitri Tiomkin; art d, Alfred Ybarra; fx, Lee Zavitz

Sprawling, ponderous history lesson that re-creates the defense of the Alamo in 1836 Texas, when 187 Americans and Texicans held off Santa Anna's army of 7,000 men for 13 days. The major focus is on Colonels William Travis (Laurence Harvey), Davy Crockett (John Wayne), and Jim Bowie (Richard Widmark). Wayne, whose Batjac Productions spent some $15 million mounting THE ALAMO (shot in 91 days, with $1.5 million spent re-creating the fort), produced, starred, and directed, with un-credited second-unit assistance from good friend John Ford. The result is an old-fashioned patriotic movie and a rousing epic that performed poorly at the box office, perhaps because it chronicled one of America's most famous military losses. All the pontificat-ing about the joys of freedom becomes irritating, but James Edward Grant's dialogue occasionally crackles with enough humorous wit to hold an audience untill the gripping finale. Originally released at 192 minutes, it was later edited down to 140 minutes, with much of the Ford-directed footage reportedly cut out. The videocassette runs 161 minutes, but fails to recapture the sumptuous Todd-AO wide-screen photography.

ALAMO BAY
1985 98m c ★★★
Drama R/15
Tri-Star/Delphi III

Amy Madigan *(Glory)*, Ed Harris *(Shang)*, Ho Nguyen *(Dinh)*, Donald Moffat *(Wally)*, Cynthia Carle *(Honey)*, Martin LaSalle *(Luis)*, Rudy Young *(Skinner)*, William Frankfather *(Mac)*, Bill Thur-man *(Sheriff)*, Harvey Lewis *(Tex)*

p, Louis Malle, Vincent Malle; d, Louis Malle; w, Alice Arlen; ph, Curtis Clark (DuArt Color); ed, James Bruce; m, Ry Cooder; prod d, Trevor Williams; art d, Rhiley Fuller; fx, Gene Grigg; cos, Deirdre Williams

Set along the Texas coast between 1979 and 1981, ALAMO BAY focuses on the tensions caused by an influx of some 15,000 Vietnamese refugees. The profits of the Alamo Bay shrimp fishermen are dwindling as more and more Vietnamese take to the waters. Hired by Donald Moffat—a hard-working, liberal-minded shrimp supplier—the refugees set up a small community and try their best to fit in. Trouble begins when a bank threatens to repossess Ed Harris' shrimp boat. Harris and his fellow shrimpers begin to pressure Moffat to get rid of his refugee employees, and the community soon turns into a battleground. ALAMO BAY is an honest, unflattering study of American racism, which works largely because the issues are grounded within a personal context. Director Louis Malle ably captures the bay atmosphere with superb photography and convincing cast-ing.

ALEX IN WONDERLAND
1970 110m c ★★
Comedy R/X
MGM

Donald Sutherland *(Alex)*, Ellen Burstyn *(Beth)*, Meg Mazursky *(Amy)*, Glenna Sergent *(Nancy)*, Viola Spolin *(Mother)*, Andre Phillipe *(Andre)*, Michael Lerner *(Leo)*, Joan Delaney *(Jane)*, Federico Fellini *(Himself)*, Jeanne Moreau *(Herself)*

p, Larry Tucker; d, Paul Mazursky; w, Paul Mazursky, Larry Tucker; ph, Laszlo Kovacs; ed, Stuart Pappe; m, Tom O'Horgan; prod d, Pato Guzman

A look at modern Hollywood centering on a young director's desperate need to follow up his debut smash with another suc-cess. Some self-righteous jabs at hip, money-hungry producers hit the comedy target, as do the cameos by Moreau and Fellini, but the presence of the latter reminds us it's all been done before, and far better than here. Ellen Burstyn, as Sutherland's wife, contributes her usual expert performance.

ALEXANDER NEVSKY
1938 107m bw ★★★★
Historical/War /PG
Mosfilm (U.S.S.R.)

Nikolai Cherkassov *(Prince Alexander Yaroslavich Nevsky)*, Nikolai Okhlopkov *(Vassily Buslai)*, A.L. Abrikossov *(Gavrilo Olexich)*, D.N. Orlov *(Ignat. Master Armourer)*, V. Novikov *(Pavsha, Governor of Pskov)*, N.N. Arski *(Domash, Nobleman of Novgorod)*, V.O. Massalitinova *(Amefa Timofeyevna, Mother of Buslai)*, V.S. Ivasbeva *(Olga, a Novgorod Girl)*, A.S. Danilova *(Vassilissa)*, V.L. Ersbov *(Master of the Teutonic Order)*

d, Sergei Eisenstein, D.I. Vassillev; w, Sergei Eisenstein, Peter Pavlenko; ph, Edward Tisse; m, Sergei Prokofiev

Sergei Eisenstein's classic tale of 13th-century Russia is as magnificent today as it must have been in 1938. One of the greatest achievements of Soviet and world cinema, this epic concerns the trying period when Russia was invaded by Teutonic knights on one front and Tartars on the other. As a result, the motherland is plundered, and the morale of the people crumbles. Finally, the moody, volatile Prince Nevsky (Nikolai Cherkassov) is summoned to lead his people in their struggle against the oppressors. A valiant and intelligent nobleman, Nevsky forms his army (an undertaking that consumes half the film), then wins a decisive battle at frozen Lake Peipus in 1242.

Eisenstein had the Russian army at his disposal, and the battle scenes, populated with thousands of men, are overwhelming. Wearing terrifying helmets fashioned after gargoyles, ogres, and fierce animals, the Teutonic knights engage the Russian army of peasants and nobles, hacking with sword, spear, and axe until the armor-burdened invaders fall victim to the lake's cracking ice. Eisenstein's attention to detail is meticulous down to the last horse blanket and homemade shoe, and the mounting of his monument to Russia's ancient hero is superb. His career on the verge of collapse, Eisenstein was rewarded for his work (an undeniably propagandist piece with the heroic Nevsky as Stalin and the savage Teutons as the Nazis) by being named head of Mosfilm Studios.

ALEXANDER'S RAGTIME BAND
1938 105m bw ★★★½
Musical /U
FOX

Tyrone Power (*Roger Grant*), Alice Faye (*Stella Kirby*), Don Ameche (*Charlie Dwyer*), Ethel Merman (*Jerry Allen*), Jack Haley (*Davey Lane*), Jean Hersholt (*Prof. Heinrich*), Helen Westley (*Aunt Sophie*), John Carradine (*Taxi Driver*), Paul Hurst (*Bill*), Wally Vernon (*Himself*)

p, Harry Joe Brown; d, Henry King; w, Kathryn Scola, Lamar Trotti, Michael Sherman; ph, Peverell Marley; ed, Barbara McLean; art d, Bernard Herzbrun, Boris Leven; chor, Seymour Felix; cos, Gwen Wakeling

28 of Irving Berlin's greatest songs make this energetic, hand-somely mounted production a must-see for musical fans. Spanning the years 1915 through 1938, the film follows the fortunes of Roger Grant (Tyrone Power), a Nob Hill San Franciscan who gives up his classical musical training in favor of playing ragtime. Grant starts his own "Alexander's Ragtime Band" (named for the song) and hires Stella Kirby (Alice Faye) as his singer. He falls in love with Kirby, but has a romantic rival in the shape of Charlie Dwyer (Don Ameche). Berlin was particularly pleased with Faye, of whom he said "I'd rather have Alice Faye introduce my songs than any other singer I know." With her limpid, bovine eyes and her throbbing contralto, Faye is the film's outstanding feature (best moment: her first outing with the band), but fans of the musical will also be interested in seeing young Ethel Merman strut her vintage stuff.

ALFIE
1966 114m c   ★★★½
Drama   /15
Lewis Gilbert   (U.K.)

Michael Caine (*Alfie*), Shelley Winters (*Ruby*), Millicent Martin (*Siddie*), Julia Foster (*Gilda*), Jane Asher (*Annie*), Shirley Ann Field (*Carla*), Vivien Merchant (*Lily*), Eleanor Bron (*The Doctor*), Denholm Elliott (*Abortionist*), Alfie Bass (*Harry*)

p, Lewis Gilbert; d, Lewis Gilbert; w, Bill Naughton (based on his play); ph, Otto Heller (Technicolor); ed, Thelma Connell; m, Sonny Rollins

A breezy yet sad odyssey, in which Caine, as Alfie, goes through life without backbone or a future, apparently loving every second of his decidedly amoral existence. Caine is a sexual hobo, making his way through the bedrooms of equally promiscuous women. First Caine meets Foster, whom he impregnates—he cares for her but cannot bring himself to marry her. He goes on to terse trysts with Field, a dedicated hedonist; Asher, an egotist; Winters, a wealthy user of male whores; and Merchant, a married woman who looks for passion but finds pregnancy and abortion, both arranged by Caine. Only at the end of the film does this Don Juan express any kind of remorse for the women he has made unhappy and the pointless life he leads, but by then most viewers hate him too much to care.

ALFIE is a well-made film with measured, convincing por-trayals, particularly by the reserved Caine as the cockney swain. Memorable are the song and the line: "What's it all about, Alfie?" The movie, and Caine, were nominated for Oscars but lost to A MAN FOR ALL SEASONS. Merchant, the screenplay, and the title song also received nominations.

ALGIERS
1938 95m bw   ★★★★
Crime   /A
UA

Charles Boyer (*Pepe Le Moko*), Sigrid Gurie (*Ines*), Hedy Lamarr (*Gaby*), Joseph Calleia (*Slimane*), Gene Lockhart (*Regis*), Johnny Downs (*Pierrot*), Alan Hale (*Grandpere*), Nina Koshetz (*Tania*), Joan Woodbury (*Aicha*), Claudia Dell (*Marie*)

p, Walter Wanger; d, John Cromwell; w, John Howard Lawson, James M. Cain (based on the novel *Pepe Le Moko* by Roger D'Ashelbe); ph, James Wong Howe; ed, Otho Lovering, William Reynolds; m, Vincent Scotto, Muhammed Ygner Buchen; art d, Alexander Toluboff; cos, Omar Kiam, Irene

Down along the shadowy, labyrinthine alleyways of the Casbah, a notorious bastion in French Algiers that harbors criminals, the viewer is introduced to a remarkable thief and lover, Pepe Le Moko (the charismatic Boyer, a reigning screen sex symbol in 1938). Wanted for stealing jewels, Boyer has fled pursuing Parisian police and taken refuge in the Casbah. Calleia is the crafty French detective who plays a waiting game, watching for the moment the wanted man will step from the Casbah into the arms of his officers. Boyer grows restless, longing for the grand life of Paris, resenting the mooning woman who is devoted to him (Gurie). Lamarr, a dazzling Parisian tourist slumming among criminals, walks into his life and, even though she is engaged, invents excuses to slip back into the Casbah to meet Boyer. The film follows Boyer's and Lamarr's involvement to its fatalistic conclusion, and their love scenes are definitive examples of smoldering continental passion.

Lamarr's role made her an international star, though she subsequently failed to live up to the promise of her debut. Strong supporting performances are contributed by Calleia and Lock-hart, the latter's portrayal of an informer garnering him an Oscar nomination for Best Supporting Actor. Director Cromwell reshot this movie almost scene-for-scene from the earlier French ver-sion, PEPE LE MOKO, directed by Julien Duvivier and starring Jean Gabin. The film was remade in 1948 as CASBAH with Tony Martin and Yvonne De Carlo. Oddly enough, the expression *Come wiz me to the Casbah* was never uttered onscreen in ALGIERS.

ALI BABA AND THE FORTY THIEVES
1944 87m c   ★★½
Adventure   /U
Universal

Maria Montez (*Amara*), Jon Hall (*Ali Baba*), Turhan Bey (*Jamiel*), Andy Devine (*Abdullah*), Kurt Katch (*Hulagu Khan*), Frank Puglia (*Cassim*), Fortunio Bonanova (*Baba*), Moroni Olsen (*Caliph*), Ramsay Ames (*Nalu*), Chris-Pin Martin (*Fat Thief*)

p, Paul Malvern; d, Arthur Lubin; w, Edmund Hartmann; ph, George Robinson, W. Howard Greene; ed, Russell Schoengarth; m, Edward Ward; art d, John B. Goodman, Richard H. Riedel; fx, John P. Fulton

This lavish Arabian Nights fantasy follows the exploits of the Caliph of Baghdad's son, who runs off into the desert after his father is killed by raiding Mongols. There he encounters the legendary 40 thieves and watches in amazement as their com-mand, "Open Sesame," magically parts a solid rock wall, reveal-ing a cavernous hiding place filled with treasures. He is adopted by the thieves, dubbed "Ali Baba," and grows up to be their leader. As an adult, Ali sets out to avenge his father's death and to free his land from the reigning Mongols. While the film is set in the ancient Middle East, there is much in the script that is reminiscent of THE ADVENTURES OF ROBIN HOOD, and some elements which draw on the western genre. Lots of fast-paced action, though the dialogue sometimes gets cumbersome, especially in the mouth of Andy Devine. But what self-respecting cult fan can resist the sultry blandishments and snakelike perambulations of Universal's B queen, Maria Montez?

ALICE
(NECO Z ALENKY)
1988   85m   c   ★★★½
Fantasy   /U
Film Four/Condor/SRG/Hessisches Rudfunk
(Switzerland/U.K./West Germany)

Kristyna Kohoutova *(Alice)*, Camilla Power *(Voice of Alice)*

p, Peter-Christian Fueter; d, Jan Svankmajer; w, Jan Svankmajer (based on *Alice's Adventures in Wonderland* by Lewis Carroll); ph, Svatopluk Maly (Eastmancolor); ed, Marie Zemanova; anim, Bedrich Glaser

This is a dark, surrealist interpretation of Lewis Carroll's *Alice's Adventures in Wonderland* by the brilliant Czech animator Jan Svankmajer. The director combines live action and puppet animation to create a disturbing vision of Alice's world, filled with images of death and violence. Although all the action takes place within a dream, Svankmajer, in true surrealist spirit, keeps the line between dream and reality ambiguous. Alice is the only live creature in the film, and it is she who supplies the voices of her (often grotesque) animated companions. In one scene typical of Svankmajer's command of dream logic, the girl becomes her own doll. ALICE is macabre, haunting, and very true to the spirit of Carroll's book, exploring the marvels and fears of a child's imagination.

ALICE ADAMS
1935   99m   bw   ★★★★
Comedy/Drama   /U
RKO

Katharine Hepburn *(Alice Adams)*, Fred MacMurray *(Arthur Russell)*, Fred Stone *(Mr. Adams)*, Evelyn Venable *(Mildred Palmer)*, Frank Albertson *(Walter Adams)*, Ann Shoemaker *(Mrs. Adams)*, Charley Grapewin *(Mr. Lamb)*, Grady Sutton *(Frank Dowling)*, Hedda Hopper *(Mrs. Palmer)*, Jonathan Hale *(Mr. Palmer)*

p, Pandro S. Berman; d, George Stevens; w, Dorothy Yost, Mortimer Offner (based on the novel by Booth Tarkington); ph, Robert de Grasse; ed, Jane Loring; m, Max Steiner; art d, Van Nest Polglase; cos, Walter Plunkett

The pathetic, social-climbing heroine of Booth Tarkington's novel was never better played than by Hepburn, who brought a fierce determination, clutching coyness, and tragic optimism to the part. She plays Alice Adams, who lives only a block or two from the wrong side of the tracks, but who pretends that she and her family enjoy the status of her wealthy peer group—a pretense that grows into a dangerous conviction. Her family of hopeless clods drags her down to grim reality at every turn, yet she tries to escape through rich acquaintances who are really nothing more than chic snobs. They merely tolerate her as a source of amusement, frivolously inviting her to an exclusive party where she meets the man of her dreams: rich, handsome, gracious MacMurray, who plays his part with unexpected sensitivity. He is attracted to her and is conned into believing that her folks are well-to-do. Hepburn inflates their importance and then risks all by inviting her hero to dinner at her home. George Stevens's dinner-party scene is a classically choreographed symphony of tragicomedy that remains with the viewer long after the tacked-on happy ending. Fred Stone, Ann Shoemaker and, young Frank Albertson, as Alice's grasping family, stand out in a capable

ensemble cast, but supporting honors are stolen by Hattie McDaniel, in a slovenly turn as a hostess's worst nightmare. The painful yearning behind Alice's character speaks to audiences in a universal way, and the film proved an important stepping stone for 30-year-old director George Stevens, with his first major film, and Hepburn, who won a second Academy Award nomination for the part, after MORNING GLORY in 1933.

ALICE DOESN'T LIVE HERE ANYMORE
1975   112m   c   ★★★
Drama   PG/15
WB

Ellen Burstyn *(Alice Hyatt)*, Kris Kristofferson *(David)*, Alfred Utter *(Tommy Hyatt)*, Billy "Green" Bush *(Donald Hyatt)*, Diane Ladd *(Flo)*, Lelia Goldoni *(Neighbor Bea)*, Harvey Keitel *(Ben Everhart)*, Lane Bradbury *(Ben's Wife)*, Vic Tayback *(Mel)*, Jodie Foster *(Audrey)*

p, David Susskind, Audrey Maas; d, Martin Scorsese; w, Robert Getchell; ph, Kent Wakeford (Technicolor); ed, Marcia Lucas; m, Richard LaSalle; prod d, Toby Rafelson

After achieving some success with the brilliant, independently made MEAN STREETS, Martin Scorsese was given a chance to direct a mainstream Hollywood film. The result is this effective but uneven work, which chronicles a woman's search for self.

Burstyn stars as an unhappy housewife living in New Mexico with her cruel husband (Bush) and their precocious, somewhat spoiled son (Lutter). When Bush dies, Burstyn and son pack up their belongings and head for Monterey, California, where she hopes to begin the singing career she has always dreamed about. Along the way she has a brief fling with the frightening Keitel, but must take flight when his violent temper erupts. When her car breaks down, she takes a job at an Arizona diner run by crusty Tayback and becomes best pals with salty Diane Ladd. Kristofferson is a rancher who frequents the restaurant, and he and Burstyn soon begin an awkward courtship. Burstyn won a well-deserved Oscar for her performance, and she is matched in expertise by Ladd and Tayback, but the acting cannot conceal the storyline's shortcomings. The film was the inspiration for the television series "Alice" starring Linda Lavin, with Tayback reprising his role as the owner of Mel's Diner. Also receiving Oscar nominations were Ladd for Supporting Actress and Getchell for his screenplay.

ALICE IN THE CITIES
1974   110m   bw   ★★★
Drama   /U
Bauer   (West Germany)

Rudiger Vogler *(Phillip)*, Yella Rottlander *(Alice)*, Elisabeth Kreuzer *(Lisa)*, Edda Kochi *(Edda)*, Didi Petrikat *(The Girl)*, Ernest Bohm *(The Agent)*, Sam Presti *(The Car Salesman)*, Lois Moran *(Girl at Ticket Counter)*, Hans Hirschmuller, Sybille Baier

p, Peter Genee; d, Wim Wenders; w, Wim Wenders, Veith der Furstenberg; ph, Robby Muller, Martin Schafer; ed, Peter Przygodda, Barbara von Weitershausen

An ancestor of director Wenders's 1984 film PARIS, TEXAS, this low-budget West German picture documents the existence of Vogler, a German journalist traveling across the US East Coast in search of a story. He considers Polaroid snapshots a better way to capture America's landscapes, buildings, and signs than writing about them. While trying to return to Germany, Vogler meets Kreuzer and her nine-year-old daughter, Rottlander, who are also trying to arrange a flight home. Kreuzer mysteriously disappears, leaving Rottlander in Vogler's care, setting up the premise of this hypnotic odyssey, the beginning of a loosely connected Wenders road-movie trilogy (it was followed in 1975 by WRONG MOVE and, one year later, KINGS OF THE ROAD—all three starring Vogler). Like Vogler, Wenders is a documentarian who fills his frame with images of American culture (a hot dog stand, a used car lot, Shea Stadium) and strains of American music ("Under the Boardwalk," Canned Heat, Chuck Berry) to tell his story, because he finds words insufficient.

ALICE IN WONDERLAND
1951   74m   c   ★★★½
Fantasy   /U
Disney
___

Kathryn Beaumont (Alice), Ed Wynn (Mad Hatter), Richard Haydn (Caterpillar), Sterling Holloway (Cheshire Cat), Jerry Colonna (March Hare), Verna Felton (Queen of Hearts), Pat O'Malley (Walrus/Carpenter/Dee/Dum), Bill Thompson (White Rabbit/Dodo), Heather Angel (Alice's Sister), Joseph Kearns (Doorknob)

p, Walt Disney; d, Clyde Geronimi, Hamilton Luske, Wilfred Jaxon; w, Winston Hibler, Bill Peet, Joe Rinaldi, William Cottrell, Joe Grant, Del Connell, Ted Sears, Erdman Penner, Milt Banta, Dick Kelsey, Dick Huemer, Tom Oreb, John Walbridge (based on the stories of Lewis Carroll); m, Oliver Wallace; anim, Milt Kahl, Ward Kimball, Franklin Thomas, Eric Larson, John Lounsbery, Oliver M. Johnston, Wolfgang Reitherman, Marc Davis, Les Clark, Norman Ferguson, Josh Meador, Dan MacManus, George Rowley, Blaine Gibson

Disney's beautifully animated but slightly chilly rendering of Alice's tale, aimed at a children's market for which Disney eschewed intellectual interpretations of Carroll's story, instead playing it straight as a storybook dream/nightmare. All of Alice's adventures are in place, including her tea party with the Mad Hatter and friends, her meeting with the bewildering Cheshire Cat, and her strange game of croquet with the temperamental Queen of Hearts. The film is dazzling in its use of color and odd shapes and is enhanced by the distinctive voices of Ed Wynn as the Mad Hatter, Sterling Holloway as the Cheshire Cat, Jerry Colonna as the March Hare, and Verna Felton as the Queen of Hearts.

ALICE'S RESTAURANT
1969   111m   c   ★★
Drama   R/15
UA
___

Arlo Guthrie (Arlo), Pat Quinn (Alice), James Broderick (Ray), Michael McClanathan (Shelly), Geoff Outlaw (Roger), Tina Chen (Marichan), Kathleen Dabney (Karin), William Obanheim (Officer Obie), Seth Allan (Evangelist), Monroe Arnold (Bluegrass)

p, Hillard Elkins, Joe Manduke; d, Arthur Penn; w, Venable Herndon, Arthur Penn (based on the song "The Alice's Restaurant Massacre" by Arlo Guthrie); ph, Michael Nebbia (DeLuxe Color); ed, Dede Allen; m, Arlo Guthrie

Arlo Guthrie, son of folk-singing immortal Woody Guthrie, achieved some celebrity in the 1960s with his 18-minute song "The Alice's Restaurant Massacre," in which he tells the tale of his arrest and trial for littering, which led to his being rejected for the draft during the Vietnam War. Director Arthur Penn used a lengthy and amusing re-creation of the events depicted in the song as the centerpiece for this exploration of the 60s counterculture. Ray Brock (James Broderick) is an aging hippie who

buys a church in Stockbridge, Massachusetts, and with his wife, Alice (Pat Quinn), shares the good life with a variety of societal drop-outs. Guthrie drops in long enough to run afoul of the local cop, Obie (William Obanheim, playing himself) and pays a visit to a New York hospital to see his father who is dying from Hodgkin's disease. To his credit, Penn refused to romanticize his subjects, and the film stands as a fairly accurate chronicle of the times. The real Alice Brock has a small role as one of the hippies.

ALIEN
1979   124m   c   ★★★
Horror/Science Fiction   R/18
Brandywine/Shusett
___

Tom Skerritt (Dallas), Sigourney Weaver (Ripley), Veronica Cartwright (Lambert), Harry Dean Stanton (Brett), John Hurt (Kane), Ian Holm (Ash), Yaphet Kotto (Parker)

p, Gordon Carroll, David Giler, Walter Hill; d, Ridley Scott; w, Dan O'Bannon (based on a story by O'Bannon and Ronald Shusett); ph, Derek Vanlint; ed, Terry Rawlings, Peter Weatherley; m, Jerry Goldsmith; prod d, Michael Seymour; fx, Carlo Rambaldi, Bernard Lodge; cos, John Mollo, H.R. Giger, Roger Dicken

A murderous life form terrorizes the crew of an outer-space mineral tanker. Owing quite a bit to Howard Hawks's THE THING, ALIEN is a very suspenseful film, more in the horror genre than in science fiction. Containing some very grisly but inventive special-effects sequences (the chest-burster has become a bloody classic), the film is one of a few that succeeds in creating a believable futuristic world. In terms of design, ALIEN is a visual feast that is indebted heavily to the work of surrealist H.R. Giger and French comic book artist Moebius. Aside from its striking style and suspenseful narrative, the picture is sadly lacking in characterization and emotion. Not for the faint of heart.

ALIENS
1986   137m   c   ★★★½
Science Fiction   R/18
Brandywine
___

Sigourney Weaver (Ripley), Carrie Henn (Newt), Michael Biehn (Cpl. Hicks), Paul Reiser (Burke), Lance Henriksen (Bishop), Bill Paxton (Pvt. Hudson), William Hope (Lt. Gorman), Jenette Goldstein (Pvt. Vasquez), Al Matthews (Sgt. Apone), Mark Rolston (Pvt. Drake)

p, Gale Anne Hurd; d, James Cameron; w, James Cameron (based on a story by Cameron, David Giler, and Walter Hill and on characters created by Dan O'Bannon and Ronald Shusett); ph, Adrian Biddle (Eastmancolor); ed, Ray Lovejoy; m, James Horner; prod d, Peter Lamont; art d, Bert Davey, Fred Hole, Michael Lamont, Ken Court; fx, Stan Winston, L.A. Effects Group, John Richardson, Norman Baillie; cos, Emma Porteous

The long-awaited sequel to the successful ALIEN is a nonstop, high-tech, souped-up war movie, with gung ho marines blasting special-effects creatures, and a genuinely convincing, exciting action heroine. Ripley (Sigourney Weaver) is found in deep space by a salvage ship and brought back to a space station, where Burke (Paul Reiser), a representative of The Company, tells her that she has been unconscious for 57 years. To her horror, Ripley also learns that the planet on which she and her crew found the creature in ALIEN has been colonized. It isn't long, however, until Burke tells her that they've lost contact with the colony and asks her to accompany a platoon of colonial marines to the planet as an adviser. Weaver is superb—tough, smart, and the best fighter, male or female, in the movie. The rest of the small cast also performs well, and director James Cameron handles the action superbly. The cutting is quick, the suspense unrelenting, and the monsters thoroughly frightening.

ALL ABOUT EVE

1950   138m   bw   ★★★★★
Drama   /U
FOX

Bette Davis (Margo Channing), Anne Baxter (Eve Harrington), George Sanders (Addison De Witt), Celeste Holm (Karen Richards), Gary Merrill (Bill Simpson), Hugh Marlowe (Lloyd Richards), Thelma Ritter (Birdie Coonan), Marilyn Monroe (Miss Casswell), Gregory Ratoff (Max Fabian), Barbara Bates (Phoebe)

p, Darryl F. Zanuck; d, Joseph L. Mankiewicz; w, Joseph L. Mankiewicz (based on the story "The Wisdom of Eve" by Mary Orr); ph, Milton Krasner; ed, Barbara McLean; m, Alfred Newman; art d, Lyle Wheeler, George W. Davis; fx, Fred Sersen; cos, Edith Head

ALL ABOUT EVE is the consummate backstage story, a film that holds a magnifying glass up to theatrical environs and exposes all the egos, tempers, conspiracies and backstage backbiting that make up the world of make-believe on Broadway. The screenplay, written by Joseph L. Mankiewicz, who also directed, may be the most biting example of hard-boiled wit ever to come out of Hollywood, and it is breathlessly performed at a breakneck pace by a cast that attacks their lines like starved carnivores at a barbecue.

The story, based on Mary Orr's "The Wisdom of Eve," concerns an aging star who befriends a seemingly innocent fan, who wants to take over and inhabit the star's life. Bette Davis won the part of vain, temperamental Margo Channing by default when Claudette Colbert broke her back, and single-handedly revived her career after having been dumped by Warner Bros. Though Mankiewicz and Davis always claimed the character was based on Austrian actress Elisabeth Bergner, Davis enacted her role as a mirror twin of then-fabled Broadway rival Tallulah Bankhead, thus fanning the flames of an already existing feud. EVE was the peak of Anne Baxter's star years and she almost matches Davis in her silky, dangerous portrayal of Eve. These two are supported by a who's who of matchless portraits, including Gary Merrill (whom Davis would fall in love with during filming and later marry), George Sanders (as a poisonous critic), the biting Thelma Ritter, Celeste Holm, and a young Marilyn Monroe as a cynical, dreamy starlet.

EVE won six Oscars: Best Picture, Director, Screenplay, Supporting Actor (Sanders), Costume Design (Edith Head), and Sound Recording. It also was nominated for Cinematography, Art Direction, Score, Editing, and Supporting Actress (Holm and Ritter). Bette Davis was doomed to lose for Best Actress, canceled out by Baxter's shared nomination, and by rival old pro Gloria Swanson for SUNSET BOULEVARD (all lost to rookie Judy Holliday for BORN YESTERDAY). The musical Applause, a Broadway success with Lauren Bacall, and later Anne Baxter, was based on EVE.

ALL CREATURES GREAT AND SMALL

1975   92m   bw   ★★★
Children's   /U
EMI   (U.K.)

Simon Ward, Anthony Hopkins, Lisa Harrow, Brian Sirner, Freddie Jones, T.P. McKenna, Brenda Bruce, John Collin, Daphne Oxenford, Christine Buckley

p, David Susskind, Duane Bogie; d, Claude Whatham; w, Hugh Whitemore (based on the book by James Herriot); ph, Peter Suschitzky; m, Wilfred Josephs

This warmhearted story of a country vet and his practice in rural England depicts the day-to-day feeding and care of animals and the children who love them. Based on actual incidents in the life of veterinarian James Herriot, the film provides excellent family entertainment and is wonderfully acted by Hopkins. A period piece of sweet and gentle charm. ALL THINGS BRIGHT AND BEAUTIFUL, a sequel, was produced in 1979.

ALL MY SONS

1948   93m   bw   ★★★½
Drama   /A
Universal

Edward G. Robinson (Joe Keller), Burt Lancaster (Chris Keller), Mady Christians (Kate Keller), Louisa Horton (Ann Deever), Howard Duff (George Deever), Frank Conroy (Herbert Deever), Lloyd Gough (Jim Bayliss), Arlene Francis (Sue Bayliss), Henry Morgan (Frank Lubey), Elisabeth Fraser (Lydia Lubey)

p, Chester Erskine; d, Irving Reis; w, Chester Erskine (based on the play by Arthur Miller); ph, Russell Metty; ed, Ralph Dawson; m, Leith Stevens; art d, Bernard Herzbrun, Hilyard Brown; fx, David S. Horsley; cos, Grace Houston

Arthur Miller's powerful drama tells the story of a family being ripped apart by the discovery of the father's corrupt business ethics during WWII (purposefully shipping defective military parts that resulted in the death of 21 men). The windy treatment is beginning to show its age, but is somewhat compensated for by acting of a high order. Robinson provides one of his best performances, showing the human frailty of his character in all its naked fury and shame, a role matched only by Lancaster's tense, taut presence as an embittered war veteran.

ALL OF ME

1984   93m   c   ★★½
Comedy   PG/15
Kings Road

Steve Martin (Roger Cobb), Lily Tomlin (Edwina Cutwater), Victoria Tennant (Terry Hoskins), Madolyn Smith (Peggy Schuyler), Richard Libertini (Prahka Lasa), Dana Elcar (Burton Schuyler), Jason Bernard (Tyrone Wattell), Selma Diamond (Margo), Eric Christmas (Fred Hoskins), Gailard Sartain (Fulton Norris)

p, Stephen Friedman; d, Carl Reiner; w, Phil Alden Robinson, Henry Olek (based on the novel Me Too by Ed Davis); ph, Richard H. Kline (Technicolor); ed, Bud Molin; m, Patrick Williams; prod d, Edward Carfagno; fx, Bruce Steinheimer; cos, Ray Summers

Roger Cobb (Steve Martin) is a guitar-playing attorney semi-engaged to the daughter of his boss at a large law firm, whose most important client is the very rich, very ill Edwina Cutwater (Lily Tomlin). Through her personal guru, Cutwater is planning a mind/body switch with a beautiful young woman (Victoria Tennant) and needs some help reworking her will. When Cobb is assigned to the case, the transfer goes awry, and the lawyer winds up battling with Cutwater for control of his body. Martin does some of his best acting in this film and steals the movie from Tomlin, whose character is, at best, a one-note creation. If you're a Martin fan, you'll love ALL OF ME; if you aren't, there's still enough fun in spots to make it worth your time.

ALL QUIET ON THE WESTERN FRONT

1930 140m bw   ★★★★★
War   /PG
Universal

Louis Wolheim (*Katczinsky*), Lew Ayres (*Paul Baumer*), John Wray (*Himmelstoss*), Slim Summerville (*Tjaden*), Russell Gleason (*Muller*), William Bakewell (*Albert*), Scott Kolk (*Leer*), Walter Rogers (*Behm*), Ben Alexander (*Kemmerick*), Owen Davis, Jr. (*Peter*)

p, Carl Laemmle, Jr.; d, Lewis Milestone; w, Del Andrews, Maxwell Anderson, Lewis Milestone (uncredited), George Abbott (based on the novel by Erich Maria Remarque); ph, Karl Freund (uncredited), Arthur Edeson; ed, Edgar Adams, Milton Carruth; m, David Broekman; art d, Charles D. Hall, William R. Schmidt; fx, Frank H. Booth

A remarkably faithful adaptation of Erich Maria Remarque's classic pacifist novel, ALL QUIET ON THE WESTERN FRONT is perhaps the greatest antiwar film ever made, holding considerable power even now due to Lewis Milestone's inventive direction.

Set during WWI and told from the German point of view, the story centers on Paul Baumer (Lew Ayres). A sensitive youth, Baumer is recruited by a war-mongering professor (Arnold Lucy) advocating "glory for the Fatherland." Paul and his friends enlist and are trained by Himmelstoss (John Wray), a kindly postmaster turned brutal corporal, then sent to the front lines to taste battle, blood, and death. Paul comes under the protective wing of an old veteran, Katczinsky (Louis Wolheim), who teaches him how to survive the horrors of war.

The film is emotionally draining, and so realistic that it will be forever etched in the mind of any viewer. Milestone's direction is frequently inspired, most notably during the battle scenes. In one such scene, the camera serves as a kind of machine gun, shooting down the oncoming troops as it glides along the trenches. Universal spared no expense during production, converting more than 20 acres of a large California ranch into battlefields occupied by more than 2,000 ex-servicemen extras. After its initial release, some foreign countries refused to run the film. Poland banned it for being pro-German, while the Nazis labeled it anti-German. Joseph Goebbels, later propaganda minister, publicly denounced the film.

ALL QUIET ON THE WESTERN FRONT received an Academy Award as Best Picture and Milestone was honored as Best Director. Originally released with a running time of 140 minutes, the film has suffered many cuts over the years with some prints running as short as 90 minutes. The most recent videotape release restores the film to 130 minutes of running time. An interesting, but now-forgotten, sequel titled THE ROAD BACK, directed by James Whale (THE BRIDE OF FRANKENSTEIN), was made in 1937. The original was remade as a television movie in 1979, with Richard Thomas unsuccessfully trying to match the timeless power of Ayres's performance.

ALL THAT HEAVEN ALLOWS

1955 89m c   ★★½
Drama   /U
Universal

Jane Wyman (*Cary Scott*), Rock Hudson (*Ron Kirby*), Agnes Moorehead (*Sara Warren*), Conrad Nagel (*Harvey*), Virginia Grey (*Alida Anderson*), Gloria Talbott (*Kay Scott*), William Reynolds (*Ned Scott*), Jacqueline de Wit (*Mona Plash*), Charles Drake (*Mick Anderson*), Leigh Snowden (*Jo-Ann*)

p, Ross Hunter; d, Douglas Sirk; w, Peg Fenwick (based on a story by Edna Lee and Harry Lee); ph, Russell Metty (Technicolor); ed, Frank Gross, Fred Baratta; m, Frank Skinner, Joseph Gershenson; art d, Alexander Golitzen, Eric Orbom; cos, Bill Thomas

Contrived but thoroughly watchable melodrama in which widowed Wyman allows gorgeous gardener-outdoorsman Hudson, who is 15 years her junior, to penetrate her lonely shell with predictable jealousy from friends and family. Sirk, one of American cinema's most underrated directors, used the "women's picture" format to explore prevailing social values and to comment on the emotional numbness of modern life. Beautiful photography, a lush musical score, and fine acting from the principals as well as supporting figures Agnes Moorehead, Virgina Grey, and Conrad Nagel adds up to an enjoyable emotional wallow. Get out your handkerchiefs.

ALL THAT JAZZ

1979 123m c   ★★★
Musical   R/15
Columbia

Roy Scheider (*Joe Gideon*), Jessica Lange (*Angelique*), Ann Reinking (*Kate Jagger*), Leland Palmer (*Audrey Paris*), Cliff Gorman (*David Newman*), Ben Vereen (*O'Connor Flood*), Erzebet Foldi (*Michelle*), Michael Tolan (*Dr. Ballinger*), Max Wright (*Joshua Benn*), William La Messena (*Jonesy Hecht*)

p, Robert Alan Aurthur; d, Bob Fosse; w, Robert Alan Aurthur, Bob Fosse; ph, Giuseppe Rotunno (Technicolor); ed, Alan Heim; m, Ralph Burns; chor, Bob Fosse; cos, Albert Wolsky

Fosse's attempt at Fellini-style introspection, in which a workaholic Broadway director/choreographer (Scheider) pulls together a new musical, edits a film, and tries to keep his mate satisfied. This dark self-examination is compromised by a certain self-congratulatory tone; it sings the praises of keeping busy and sees Scheider indulge in a fair amount of macho wish-fulfillment with a parade of showbiz beauties. The viewer sympathizes with the central character, but is also repelled by his sexual addiction and constant need for ego-gratification. Good turns by Cliff Gorman and Ben Vereen, dynamic photography, and a terrific opening number to George Benson's "On Broadway" highlight this memorial to self-indulgence.

ALL THE KING'S MEN

1949 109m bw   ★★★★★
Political   /A
Columbia

Broderick Crawford (*Willie Stark*), Joanne Dru (*Anne Stanton*), John Ireland (*Jack Burden*), John Derek (*Tom Stark*), Mercedes McCambridge (*Sadie Burke*), Shepperd Strudwick (*Adam Stanton*), Ralph Dumke (*Tiny Duffy*), Anne Seymour (*Lucy Stark*), Katherine Warren (*Mrs. Burden*), Raymond Greenleaf (*Judge Stanton*)

p, Robert Rossen; d, Robert Rossen; w, Robert Rossen (based on the novel by Robert Penn Warren); ph, Burnett Guffey; ed, Al Clark; m, Louis Gruenberg

Academy Award-winning rise and fall of a rotten politician, based on the Pulitzer Prize-winning novel by Robert Penn Warren. This scathing, grimly realistic film, long a pet project for producer-director-writer Robert Rossen, served as a breakthrough for Broderick Crawford, who had previously been confined to B films. As Willie Stark, Crawford let loose a fierce and awesome acting *tour de force* he never again equaled (and won an Academy Award for his work). The character of Willie Stark himself was most certainly inspired by Louisiana's Huey Pierce Long, the controversial "Kingfish" who ruled the state as governor (and later senator) with an iron hand and an enduring populist appeal, soaking the wealthy and enhancing his personal power unscrupulously. Long's demagoguery, so accurately profiled in this film, ended with his assassination in 1935 by Dr. Carl Austin Weiss, a 29-year-old Baton Rouge physician whose sister may or may not have been raped by Long.

Rossen's film chronicles this life of raw power with compelling scenes, and Crawford's performance is well-supported by the rest of the cast—especially McCambridge, in her film debut, as a conniving political aide. Rossen shot the film in Stockton, California, a working-class town, and enlisted the aid of hundreds of citizens as extras and bit players, adding an edge of authenticity to the production of this hallmark political film.

ALL THE PRESIDENT'S MEN

1976 138m c ★★★★
Political PG/15
WB

Dustin Hoffman (Carl Bernstein), Robert Redford (Bob Woodward), Jack Warden (Harry Rosenfeld), Martin Balsam (Howard Simons), Hal Holbrook (Deep Throat), Jason Robards, Jr. (Ben Bradlee), Jane Alexander (Bookkeeper), Meredith Baxter Birney (Debbie Sloan), Ned Beatty (Dardis), Stephen Collins (Hugh Sloan, Jr.)

p, Walter Coblenz; d, Alan J. Pakula; w, William Goldman (based on the book by Carl Bernstein and Bob Woodward); ph, Gordon Willis (Panavision, Technicolor); ed, Robert Wolfe; m, David Shire; prod d, George Jenkins

Landmark movie which combines elements of the political thriller, buddy picture-star vehicle, detective story, 1930s newspaper reporter programmer, and biopic. The two stars play the real-life *Washington Post* reporters who kicked off the Watergate investigation, with Hoffman as the Jewish, street-smart Carl Bernstein and Redford as the WASPy Bob Woodward. Robards, beginning his spate of crusty-ole-codger supporting roles, won an Oscar, as did screenwriter William Goldman. The film features a host of fine character portrayals and a compelling climax that compensates for its length.

ALL THE RIGHT MOVES

1983 91m c ★½
Sports R/15
FOX

Tom Cruise (Stef), Craig T. Nelson (Nickerson), Lea Thompson (Lisa), Charles Cioffi (Pop), Paul Carafotes (Salvucci), Christopher Penn (Brian), Sandy Faison (Suzie), Paige Price (Tracy), James A. Baffico (Bosko), Donald A. Yanessa (Coach)

p, Stephen Deutsch; d, Michael Chapman; w, Michael Kane; ph, Jan De Bont; ed, David Garfield; m, David Campbell; art d, Mary Ann Biddle; cos, Deborah Hopper, Joseph Roveto

High-school football star Tom Cruise yearns to escape his stifling mill town existence via a sports scholarship but runs afoul of tough coach Craig T. Nelson. This cliche-riddled picture was the directorial debut of veteran cinematographer Michael Chapman, who took no risks in his first time out. Filmed in Johnstown, Pennsylvania, where area coach Don Yanessa acted as technical advisor, also appearing as an opposing coach.

ALL THIS AND HEAVEN TOO

1940 140m bw ★★★★
Romance /U
WB

Bette Davis (Henriette Deluzy Desportes), Charles Boyer (Duke De Praslin), Jeffrey Lynn (Reverend Henry Field), Barbara O'Neil (Duchesse De Praslin), Virginia Weidler (Louise), Walter Hampden (Pasquier), Harry Davenport (Pierre), Fritz Leiber (Abbe Gallard), Helen Westley (Mme. Le Maire), Sibyl Harris (Mlle. Maillard)

p, David Lewis; d, Anatole Litvak; w, Casey Robinson (based on the novel by Rachel Lyman Field); ph, Ernest Haller; ed, Warren Low; m, Max Steiner; art d, Carl Jules Weyl; cos, Orry-Kelly

A classic of unrequited love, based on the best-selling Rachel Field novel set in 19th-century France. Governess Davis falls in love with nobleman Boyer who has engaged her to care for his children. Litvak's smooth, understated treatment produces restrained, ageless performances from both stars. Oscar nominee Barbara O'Neill (best remembered as Scarlett O'Hara's mother in GWTW) almost steals the picture in a serpentine portrayal of Boyer's possessive, neurotic wife. This moody, elaborate production, greatly enhanced by its Steiner score, is a deft example of the "women's picture."

ALL THROUGH THE NIGHT

1942 107m bw ★★★½
Spy /A
WB

Humphrey Bogart (Gloves Donahue), Conrad Veidt (Hall Ebbing), Karen Verne (Leda Hamilton), Jane Darwell (Ma Donahue), Frank McHugh (Barney), Peter Lorre (Pepi), Judith Anderson (Madame), William Demarest (Sunshine), Jackie Gleason (Starchie), Phil Silvers (Waiter)

p, Jerry Wald; d, Vincent Sherman; w, Leonard Spigelgass, Edwin Gilbert (based on a story by Leonard Spigelgass and Leonard Ross); ph, Sid Hickox; ed, Rudi Fehr; m, Adolph Deutsch; art d, Max Parker

Eclectic entry from Bogart's Warner Bros. catalog which blends the parody, comedy, espionage, and gangster genres as Bogie pursues three unforgettable spies: Veidt, Anderson, and Lorre. Often-underrated director Vincent Sherman demonstrates a fine feel for the ambience of 1940s New York, with plenty of machine-gun dialogue to spice up the proceedings. Also enjoyable are the Johnny Mercer title track and songs including Arthur Schwartz and Johnny Mercer's "All Through the Night" and Lillian Goodman's "Cherie, I Love You So."

ALLEGRO NON TROPPO

1977 85m c/bw ★★★
Animated /A
Specialty (Italy)

Maurizio Nichetti, Nestor Garay, Maurizio Micheli, Maria Luisa Giovanninni

d, Bruno Bozzetto; w, Bruno Bozzetto, Guido Manuli, Maurizio Nichetti; ph, Mario Masini, Luciano Marzetti (Technicolor); ed, Giancarlo Rossi; m, Claude Debussy, Anton Dvorak, Maurice Ravel, Sibelius, Antonio Vivaldi, Igor Stravinsky; anim, Bruno Bozzetto, Giuseppe Lagana, Walter Cavazzuti

A high-spirited, energetically animated feature that expands on FANTASIA's idea of using classical music as a basis for cartoon movement. Director Bozzetto's style is frantic in pace and occasionally violent, but his use of color and line is dazzling. Each segment of the film is rich and funny, but the evolution of life from the last few drops of a Coca-Cola bottle set to Ravel's "Bolero" is a true showstopper.

ALPHAVILLE

1965 98m bw ★★½
Science Fiction /A
Athos (France/Italy)

Eddie Constantine (*Lemmy Caution*), Anna Karina (*Natasha Von Braun*), Akim Tamiroff (*Henri Dickson*), Laszlo Szabo (*Doctor*), Howard Vernon (*Prof. Von Braun*), Michel Delahaye (*Von Braun's Assistant*), Jean-Andre Fieschi (*Prof. Heckel*), Jean-Louis Comolli (*Prof. Jeckell*)

p, Andre Michelin; d, Jean-Luc Godard; w, Jean-Luc Godard; ph, Raoul Coutard; ed, Agnes Guillemot; m, Paul Misraki

Perhaps the most easily digestible of Jean-Luc Godard's films, ALPHAVILLE is a hybrid of sci-fi and film noir with its roots in the surrealist poetry of the 1920s, specifically Paul Eluard's "Capital of Pain." Pulp hero/intergalactic special agent Lemmy Caution (Eddie Constantine) travels to the mysterious Alphaville (which looks a lot like Paris) to investigate the disappearance of Henri Dickson (Akim Tamiroff), a member of Caution's agency, and to kill or capture Professor Von Braun (Howard Vernon), a scientist who invented the fascist Alpha-60 computer. En route, he meets the professor's daughter, Natasha (Anna Karina), who is incapable of loving and learns about the subject by studying Eluard's writings. Godard has fun playing with genre conventions here, while continuing to explore the relationships between sound and image, love and society.

AMADEUS

1984 158m c ★★★★★
Biography/Musical PG
Orion

F. Murray Abraham (*Antonio Salieri*), Tom Hulce (*Wolfgang Amadeus Mozart*), Elizabeth Berridge (*Constanze Mozart*), Simon Callow (*Emanuel Schikaneder*), Roy Dotrice (*Leopold Mozart*), Christine Ebersole (*Katerina Cavalieri*), Jeffrey Jones (*Emperor Joseph II*), Charles Kay (*Count Orsini-Rosenberg*), Kenny Baker (*Parody Commendatore*), Lisbeth Bartlett (*Papagena*)

p, Saul Zaentz; d, Milos Forman; w, Peter Shaffer (based on his play); ph, Miroslav Ondricek (Panavision, Technicolor); ed, Nena Danevic, Michael Chandler; m, Wolfgang Amadeus Mozart, Antonio Salieri, Giovanni Battista Pergolesi; prod d, Patrizia von Brandenstein; art d, Karel Cerny, Francesco Chianese, Josef Svoboda; fx, Dick Smith; chor, Twyla Tharp; cos, Theodor Pistek

Milos Forman's brilliant, Oscar-winning adaptation of Peter Shaffer's hit play, AMADEUS is a fictionalized retelling of the final days of Antonio Salieri.

Salieri (F. Murray Abraham, who won the Best Actor Oscar for his portrayal), a famous composer in Mozart's day but now incarcerated in an insane asylum, begins his final confession to a young cleric. He tells the story of his relationship with Mozart (Tom Hulce), in a 30-year flashback to when he first met the 26-year-old prodigy. Furious that this boor can produce such beautiful music, Salieri determines to keep Mozart's talent from continued recognition.

The discerning but less talented Salieri has great influence in Vienna, being court composer to Joseph II of Austria (Jeffrey Jones), who realizes he knows little about music and therefore allows Salieri to decide what he should hear and whom he should be patron to. After Mozart manages to get the Emperor's ear, his career is launched, and we see him writing and conducting several of his best pieces. Then his friends, health, and resources waste away. He works most feverishly on his "Requiem," commissioned by a masked stranger who is actually Salieri. The effort proves the final stroke against the greater composer's weakened constitution, and he is buried in a pauper's grave.

Milos Forman's direction is flawless, Neville Marriner's musical direction is superb, and the film is a feast for the eyes and ears. Although Forman concentrates on Mozart's more popular works, the prodigious output of Mozart's short life is clearly conveyed. AMADEUS is a must for any music lover, any film lover, or anyone who reveres excellence.

AMARCORD

1974 127m c ★★★★
Comedy R/18
F.C./PECF/New World (Italy/France)

Magali Noel (*Gradisca*), Bruno Zanin (*Titta*), Pupella Maggio (*Titta's Mother*), Armando Brancia (*Titta's Father*), Giuseppe Ianigro (*Titta's Grandfather*), Nando Orfei (*Pataca*), Ciccio Ingrassia (*Uncle Teo*), Luigi Rossi (*Lawyer*), Gennaro Ombra (*Bisein*), Josiane Tanzilli (*Volpina*)

p, Franco Cristaldi; d, Federico Fellini; w, Federico Fellini, Tonino Guerra; ph, Giuseppe Rotunno; ed, Ruggero Mastroianni; m, Nino Rota; art d, Danilo Donati

A pictorial weaving of the bizarre fragments of Fellini's imagination and memory, AMARCORD is set in a seaside village (very similar to Fellini's boyhood town of Rimini) in the 1930s. Through the eyes of the impressionable young Zanin, Fellini takes a penetrating look at family life, religion, love, sex, education, and politics. Among the characters are Zanin's constantly battling mother and father, and a priest who listens to confession only to spark his own deviant imagination. Although Italy is under the control of the Fascists, the regime's oppressiveness remains obscure to the naive villagers, who worship an immense, daunting banner of Il Duce's face. There is hardly a character in AMARCORD left unscathed by Fellini's biting wit, yet the director manages to present these people lovingly. Unique personality traits, revelations of personal weakness (and thus humanness), are valued for the color and variety they add to the world. AMARCORD won the Academy Award for Best Foreign Film in 1974.

AMERICAN DREAM, AN

1966 103m c ★
Drama
WB

Stuart Whitman (*Stephen Rojack*), Janet Leigh (*Cherry McMahon*), Eleanor Parker (*Deborah Kelly Rojack*), Barry Sullivan (*Roberts*), Lloyd Nolan (*Barney Kelly*), Murray Hamilton (*Arthur Kabot*), J.D. Cannon (*Sgt. Leznicki*), Susan Denberg (*Ruta*), Les Crane (*Nicky*), Warren Stevens (*Johnny Dell*)

d, Robert Gist; w, Mann Rubin (based on the novel by Norman Mailer); ph, Sam Leavitt (Technicolor); ed, George Rohrs; m, Johnny Mandel

TV talk show host Whitman, in a frenzied fight with his bitchy wife, Parker, pushes her out the window of their penthouse apartment. Trying to palm it off as a suicide, Whitman is betrayed by his old flame, Leigh (as Cherry McMahon!). The film, with a strong beginning intensified by Parker's powerful portrayal of the wife, deteriorates into a cynical look at 1960s society. The song "A Time for Love" was nominated for an Oscar.

AMERICAN FRIEND, THE

1977 127m c ★★★
Mystery /15
Road Movies (West Germany)

Dennis Hopper *(Ripley)*, Bruno Ganz *(Jonathan Zimmermann)*, Lisa Kreuzer *(Marianne Zimmermann)*, Gerard Blain *(Raoul Minot)*, Nicholas Ray *(Derwatt)*, Samuel Fuller *(The American)*, Peter Lilienthal *(Marcangelo)*, Daniel Schmid *(Ingraham)*, Jean Eustache *(Friendly Man)*, Rudolf Schundler *(Gantner)*

d, Wim Wenders; w, Wim Wenders (based on the novel *Ripley's Game* by Patricia Highsmith); ph, Robby Muller; ed, Peter Przygodda; m, Jurgen Knieper; art d, Sickerts

Based on a novel by Patricia Highsmith (whose STRANGERS ON A TRAIN was filmed by Hitchcock), Wenders's film tells of two "friends"—Hopper, a quiet, charming psychotic involved in art forgery, and Ganz, a humble family man who fears he is dying of leukemia. Hopper suggests Ganz as a candidate when Blain, an acquaintance of Hopper's, needs a "civilian" to murder two mafiosi; the lure is a large sum of money from which Ganz's family can benefit after his death. Ganz agrees and as a result gets tugged deeper and deeper into a web of international crime. Wenders' debt to American gangster films is clear here, especially in the casting of two of the genre's kings—directors Sam Fuller and Nicholas Ray—as well as international directors Gerard Blain, Jean Eustache, Peter Lilienthal, Daniel Schmid, Sandy Whitelaw, and Wenders himself. But despite being derivative, THE AMERICAN FRIEND is an original film with profound views on friendship, heroism, and dependence—all common themes in Wenders's pictures.

AMERICAN GRAFFITI

1973 110m c ★★★
Comedy PG
Universal

Richard Dreyfuss *(Curt)*, Ron Howard *(Steve)*, Paul LeMat *(John)*, Charles Martin Smith *(Terry)*, Cindy Williams *(Laurie)*, Candy Clark *(Debbie)*, Mackenzie Phillips *(Carol)*, Wolfman Jack *(Himself)*, Harrison Ford *(Falfa)*, Bo Hopkins *(Joe)*

p, Francis Ford Coppola, Gary Kurtz; d, George Lucas; w, George Lucas, Gloria Katz, Willard Huyck; ph, Ron Everslage, Jan D'Alquen (Technicolor); ed, Verna Fields, Marcia Lucas; art d, Dennis Clark; cos, Aggie Guerard Rodgers

A hallmark film of the 1970s, AMERICAN GRAFFITI's memorable cast of characters is seen, in touching and telling vignettes, during the course of one momentous night in a small California town circa 1962.

Steve (Ron Howard), a clean-cut youth, is about to leave for college the next day; Curt (Richard Dreyfuss), the class intellectual, is also slated for college but has doubts about his future and that of the world; Laurie (Cindy Williams), Curt's sister and Steve's girlfriend, is upset by the latter's impending departure; Terry (Charles Martin Smith) is a hopeless nerd who desperately yearns to be "cool"; John (Paul LeMat), who's very cool indeed, drives "the fastest car in the valley" and is constantly being forced to prove that boast. After the school dance, everyone goes cruising. John picks up 13-year-old Carol (Mackenzie Phillips), thinking she's much older until she climbs aboard his 1932 Ford Deuce Coupe, then becoming embarrassed as she chatters his ears off. Steve and Laurie, driving about in his 1958 Impala, talk about their tomorrows; he's full of hope for the future, while she

tearfully believes her life is over at 17. Everyone meets at Mel's Drive-In where exchanges between the groping teenagers seem to reveal their entire personalities in microcosm.

Based on George Lucas's own teenage hot-rodding days in Modesto, California, the appeal of AMERICAN GRAFFITI is in its fragmentary scenes as the nervous camera jumps frantically from character to character to present a powerful collage of American youth on the brink of maturity. Poignant, often priceless in its dialogue and mannerisms, GRAFFITI has the innocence of a Saturday afternoon matinee, as unsure and inexperienced as its characters, a happy accident that nostalgically captures one balmy night in America. (At its San Francisco premiere, although enthusiastically received, Universal bigwigs sniggered at the film's murky lighting and told producer Francis Ford Coppola that they might not release the film. The agitated Coppola immediately offered to buy the property and release it himself. The executives, to Universal's financial credit, refused; the film would gross more than $100 million domestically.) The enormous financial and critical success of GRAFFITI allowed Lucas the freedom to finance one of the most beloved and highest-grossing films of all time—STAR WARS—and spawned numerous imitations, even inspiring the long-running TV sitcom "Happy Days." The film boosted the careers of a host of young performers including Dreyfuss, Howard, Williams, LeMat, Smith, Clark, Phillips, Harrison Ford, Kathleen Quinlan and Suzanne Somers.

AMERICAN HOT WAX

1978 91m c ★★★
Musical PG/A
Paramount

Tim McIntire *(Alan Freed)*, Fran Drescher *(Sheryl)*, Jay Leno *(Mookie)*, Laraine Newman *(Teenage Louise)*, Carl Earl Weaver, Al Chalk, Sam Harkness, Arnold McCuller *(The Chesterfields)*, Jeff Altman *(Lennie Richfield)*, Moosie Drier *(Artie Moress)*

p, Art Linson; d, Floyd Mutrux; w, John Kaye; ph, William A. Fraker (Metrocolor); ed, Melvin Shapiro, Ronald J. Fagan; art d, Elayne Ceder

This unassuming celebration of the early days of rock 'n' roll manages to recreate the excitement of similar movies from the late 1950s. The plot concerns the efforts of Alan Freed (Tim McIntire), a disk jockey credited with popularizing "rock and roll," garnering acceptance for this new form of popular music despite the efforts of local police to quell it. McIntire's portrayal is particularly energetic. The music dominates the movie with especially enjoyable guest appearances by Chuck Berry, Jerry Lee Lewis, and Screamin' Jay Hawkins.

AMERICAN IN PARIS, AN

1951 113m c ★★★★½
Musical /U
MGM

Gene Kelly *(Jerry Mulligan)*, Leslie Caron *(Lise Bouvier)*, Oscar Levant *(Adam Cook)*, Georges Guetary *(Henri Baurel)*, Nina Foch *(Milo Roberts)*, Eugene Borden *(George Mattieu)*, Martha Bamattre *(Mathilde Mattieu)*, Mary Jones *(Old Lady Dancer)*, Ann Codee *(Therese)*, George Davis *(Francois)*

p, Arthur Freed; d, Vincente Minnelli; w, Alan Jay Lerner; ph, Alfred Gilks, John Alton (Technicolor); ed, Adrienne Fazan; art d, Cedric Gibbons, Preston Ames; fx, Warren Newcombe; chor, Gene Kelly; cos, Walter Plunkett (Beaux-Arts), Irene Sharaff (Ballet)

A classic film featuring the timeless music of George and Ira Gershwin, AN AMERICAN IN PARIS has a freshness and charm rare in the musical genre, and it was the film that forever identified MGM as *the* studio for musicals.

Jerry Mulligan (Gene Kelly) is an ex-GI and struggling artist in postwar Paris. His friend Adam Cook (Oscar Levant) is a piano player in a nearby cafe, a sarcastic and morose individual who offers nothing but discouragement to Jerry. However, another friend, Henri Baurel (Georges Guetary), a successful revue singer, is more encouraging. Henri informs his pal that he's going to marry a wonderful girl, an 18-year-old dancer whom he rescued from the Nazis during the war. Jerry, meanwhile, is discovered by Milo Roberts (Nina Foch), a wealthy patroness who purchases his paintings and encourages her friends to do the same. Innocently enjoying his newfound success, Jerry visits a nightclub and meets Lise (newcomer Leslie Caron, discovered by Kelly in the Ballets des Champs Elysees), falling for her immediately. She fends off his advances but laters agrees to a date, then informs him that she's engaged to Henri. Though they are in love, Jerry and Lise do the noble thing and decide not to meet again.

The plot was showing signs of age far earlier than 1951, but everything else about AN AMERICAN IN PARIS more than compensates: the songs are all Gershwin Brothers standards; Kelly's choreography is breathtaking; the original screenplay by playwright Alan Jay Lerner is alternately witty and touching; and Minnelli's direction feels buoyantly assured. The 17-minute Dufy-inspired ballet (art directors Cedric Gibbons and Preston Ames, along with costume designer Irene Sharaff, also contributed brilliantly to this sequence) is the showstopper here but an underrated standout is "I'll Build a Stairway to Paradise," performed with marvelous elan by Guetary. Although the setting is Paris, very little of the film was actually shot on location; the spectacular scenes were mostly sets built on the lot. AN AMERICAN IN PARIS received a total of seven Academy Awards, plus a special Oscar to Kelly.

AMERICAN MADNESS
1932 75m bw   ★★★
Drama   /U
Columbia

Walter Huston (*Dickson*), Pat O'Brien (*Matt*), Kay Johnson (*Mrs. Dickson*), Constance Cummings (*Helen*), Gavin Gordon (*Cluett*), Robert Ellis (*Dude Finlay*), Jeanne Sorel (*Cluett's Secretary*), Walter Walker (*Schultz*), Berton Churchill (*O'Brien*), Arthur Hoyt (*Ives*)

d, Frank Capra; w, Robert Riskin; ph, Joseph Walker; ed, Maurice Wright

Rare Capra work, and one of the few films to properly utilize the genius of the astonishing Walter Huston. Central theme of stressed-out bank president Huston as idealistic individual against the cruelty of the faceless crowd, struck a blow against Hooverism and for FDR's New Deal.

Like the single-set interiors of GRAND HOTEL, Capra filmed AMERICAN MADNESS totally within an enormous bank set, all the action taking place inside board rooms and vaults and behind tellers' cages, moving his camera with fluid truck and dolly shots, boom shots, and quick cuts that keep up the already established frenetic pace. To further create this sense of urgency, Capra cut out all dissolves (a device used to indicate the passing of time). He overlapped speeches and then had his actors hurry through their actions and dialogue.

AMERICAN MADNESS captured authentically the hysteria of the Great Depression; nor does the gratuitous romantic subplot mar its otherwise noble intentions.

AMERICAN WEREWOLF IN LONDON, AN
1981 97m c   ★★★
Comedy/Horror   R/18
Universal

David Naughton (*David Kessler*), Jenny Agutter (*Alex Price*), Griffin Dunne (*Jack Goodman*), John Woodvine (*Dr. Hirsch*), Brian Glover (*Chess Player*), David Schofield (*Dart Player*), Lila Kaye (*Barmaid*), Paul Kember (*Sgt. McManus*), Don McKillop (*Inspector Villiers*), Frank Oz (*Mr. Collins*)

p, George Folsey, Jr.; d, John Landis; w, John Landis; ph, Robert Paynter (Technicolor); ed, Malcolm Campbell; m, Elmer Bernstein; art d, Leslie Dilley; fx, Rick Baker; cos, Deborah Nadoolman

Sit tight: the most literal of the horror excursions into werewolf territory plays it straight for bloody terror. Young man gets bitten by a werewolf on the British moors and chilling special effects ensue, with a hair-raising climax in Picadilly Circus. Rick Baker deservedly won the first Academy Award for makeup; direction and script by Landis have sharp fangs for laughs and reverence for the genre's history.

AMERICANIZATION OF EMILY, THE
1964 115m bw   ★★★½
Comedy/Drama   /X
MGM

James Garner (*Lt. Comdr. Charles Madison*), Julie Andrews (*Emily Barham*), Melvyn Douglas (*Adm. William Jessup*), James Coburn (*Lt. Comdr. "Bus" Cummings*), Joyce Grenfell (*Mrs. Barham*), Edward Binns (*Adm. Thomas Healy*), Liz Fraser (*Sheila*), Keenan Wynn (*Old Sailor*), William Windom (*Capt. Harry Spaulding*), John Crawford (*CPO Paul Adams*)

p, Martin Ransohoff; d, Arthur Hiller; w, Paddy Chayefsky (based on the novel by William Bradford Huie); ph, Philip Lathrop; ed, Tom McAdoo; m, Johnny Mandel; art d, George W. Davis, Hans Peters, Elliot Scott; fx, McMillan Johnson; cos, Bill Thomas

Chayefsky-scripted military snakepit, with Garner as cowardly fallguy for Normandy invasion. The standout in the cast is Julie Andrews, whose quality of sexy chill has never been used as effectively, before falling prey to successor of the Doris Day pro-virgin crown. EMILY is based on the William Bradford Huie novel, uneasily directed by Hiller. Nominated by the Academy for Best Cinematography, Best Art Direction, and Best Musical Score.

AMITYVILLE HORROR, THE
1979 126m c   ★½
Horror   R/15
INT/American

James Brolin (*George Lutz*), Margot Kidder (*Kathleen Lutz*), Rod Steiger (*Fr. Delaney*), Don Stroud (*Fr. Bolen*), Natasha Ryan (*Amy*), K.C. Martel (*Greg*), Meeno Peluce (*Matt*), Michael Sacks (*Jeff*), Helen Shaver (*Carolyn*), Val Avery (*Sgt. Gionfriddo*)

p, Ronald Saland, Elliot Geisinger; d, Stuart Rosenberg; w, Sandor Stern (based on the book by Jay Anson); ph, Fred Koenekamp; ed, Robert Brown; m, Lalo Schifrin; art d, Kim Swados; fx, Dell Rheaume

Based on Jay Anson's slimy best-seller, THE AMITYVILLE HORROR reaped a fortune for its studio, American International, just before it went out of business. The film chronicles the trials and tribulations of the hapless Lutz family (headed by Brolin and Kidder) as they discover that the new house they've purchased for a steal in Amityville, NY, is plagued by evil demons that manifest themselves in a variety of disgusting ways (flies, black gook, Rod Steiger overacting as a priest). Schifrin's score received an Oscar nomination. A TV prequel and three dreadful sequels (one in 3-D) followed.

ANASTASIA
1956 105m c   ★★★★★
Drama   /U
FOX

Ingrid Bergman (Anastasia), Yul Brynner (Bounine), Helen Hayes (Empress), Akim Tamiroff (Chernov), Martita Hunt (Baroness von Livenbaum), Felix Aylmer (Russian Chamberlain), Sacha Pitoeff (Petrovin), Ivan Desny (Prince Paul), Natalie Schafer (Lissenskaia), Gregoire Gromoff (Stepan)

p, Buddy Adler; d, Anatole Litvak; w, Arthur Laurents (based on Guy Bolton's adaptation of Marcelle Maurette's play); ph, Jack Hildyard (CinemaScope, DeLuxeColor); ed, Bert Bates; m, Alfred Newman; art d, Andre Andrejew, Bill Andrews; cos, Rene Hubert

The peak of Ingrid bergman's triumphant career. Cheap impostor or grand duchess of Russia and daughter of the last czar? There was no doubt in the mind of any viewer after watching Bergman's sublime performance that Anastasia was the lost and unhappy Romanoff princess. This was Bergman's comeback to American screens after the Rosellini scandal and she played her part with such intense feeling that it won over audiences worldwide and earned her an Academy Award. Climax is Bergman's confrontation with Empress Hayes, the latter's best screen work. The Laurents screenplay is faithful to the Marcelle Maurette play. A grand entry in Hollywood history.

ANATOMY OF A MURDER
1959 160m bw   ★★★★½
Drama   /15
Columbia

James Stewart (Paul Biegler), Lee Remick (Laura Manion), Ben Gazzara (Lt. Frederick Manion), Arthur O'Connell (Parnell McCarthy), Eve Arden (Maida), Kathryn Grant (Mary Pilant), Joseph N. Welch (Judge Weaver), Brooks West (Mitch Lodwick), George C. Scott (Claude Dancer), Murray Hamilton (Alphonse Paquette)

p, Otto Preminger; d, Otto Preminger; w, Wendell Mayes; ph, Sam Leavitt; ed, Louis Loeffler; m, Duke Ellington

Courtroom histrionics given sizzle and sex by Otto Preminger and Duke Ellington's jazz. Stewart shocked 1950s audiences with his gritty, quirky performance as a confirmed bachelor defense attorney speaking directly about contraceptives, pink panties and rape. Old pros Arden and O'Connell flawlessly support the star performance in a talky tennis game. Gazzarra as a brutal army stud and Remick as his duplicitous, sluttish wife received well-deserved career boosts for their efforts.

The casting of Remick was Preminger's major concern after Lana Turner left the project (actress reportedly slapped director who slapped her back) and Jayne Mansfield backed off from the script. Joseph Welch, who plays the judge, was the famed Army-McCarthy hearings lawyer who would go on to become a real life judge. Even today, when these issues seem tame, the long drama crackles along. The film was nominated for Best Picture and Best Actor (the year BEN-HUR swept the competition) as well as Best Supporting Actor (both O'Connell and George C. Scott), Best Screenplay, Best Cinematography, and Best Film Editing.

ANCHORS AWEIGH
1945 143m c   ★★½
Musical   /U
MGM

Frank Sinatra (Clarence Doolittle), Gene Kelly (Joseph Brady), Kathryn Grayson (Susan Abbott), Jose Iturbi (Himself), Dean Stockwell (Donald Martin), Carlos Ramirez (Carlos), Henry O'Neill (Adm. Hammond), Leon Ames (Commander), Rags Ragland (Police Sergeant), Edgar Kennedy (Police Captain)

p, Joe Pasternak; d, George Sidney; w, Isobel Lennart (based on a story by Natalie Marcin); ph, Robert Planck, Charles P. Boyle (Technicolor); ed, Adrienne Fazan; m, George Stoll; art d, Cedric Gibbons, Randall Duell; chor, Gene Kelly; cos, Irene, Kay Dean

This amiable musical of gobs on shore leave in Hollywood lacks the snap of ON THE TOWN but holds up when young Sinatra croons "I Fall in Love Too Easily" and when Kelly gets the chance to dance with animated mouse Jerry of "Tom & Jerry" fame. The technique of live action mixed with cartoons has been done often since then, most notably in 1988's WHO FRAMED ROGER RABBIT, but it has never been done to better advantage than in this film. Pamela Britton's comic relief Brooklyn girl feels more authentic than the sticky sentiments of Pekinese Grayson. A pleasant, mindless diversion.

AND GOD CREATED WOMAN
1956 95m c   ★★
Drama   /18
Iena/UCIL/Cocinor   (France)

Brigitte Bardot (Juliette), Curt Jurgens (Eric), Jean-Louis Trintignant (Michel), Christian Marquand (Antoine), Georges Poujouly (Christian), Jean Tissier (M. Vigier-Lefranc), Jeanne Marken (Mme. Morin), Marie Glory (Mme. Tardieu), Isabelle Corey (Lucienne), Jean Lefebvre (Rene)

p, Raoul J. Levy; d, Roger Vadim; w, Roger Vadim, Raoul Levy; ph, Armand Thirard (CinemaScope, Eastmancolor); ed, Victoria Mercanton; m, Paul Misraki; art d, Jean Andre

...but Roger Vadim created Brigitte Bardot. This is the film that made sex kitten Bardot a household name and liberated French cinema by putting it in the hands of the young and the beautiful. And it managed to do all this without being a very good film. The story is a simple one: Juliette (Bardot) is a sexually dynamic orphan girl who marries Michel (Jean-Louis Trintignant), is pursued by the wealthy Eric (Curt Jurgens), and sleeps with Antoine (Christian Marquand), Michel's brother. Nonetheless, Michel fights for Juliette and manages to lure her back.

Slight on story, AND GOD CREATED WOMAN is strong on energy, all of it coming from Bardot's brilliant screen presence. Her pouty lips, accentuated breasts, skimpy clothing, and wildly erotic mambo routine late in the film helped whip audiences into a frenzy. They couldn't get enough of her in France, nor could they in America. While her effect on the American film scene was dubious (more and more soft-porn titillation was imported), her effect on the French film industry can be seen in the rise of the Nouvelle Vague directors, who were given greater opportunities in light of Vadim's commercial success. Vadim would continue along this same path with diminishing impact on the film world and then try to create "Woman" again in an unsuccessful 1988 remake (in title only) starring Rebecca DeMornay. Bardot would have continued success without him, which makes one wonder if Bardot created Vadim.

AND NOW FOR SOMETHING COMPLETELY DIFFERENT

1972 89m c	★★
Comedy	PG
Columbia (U.K.)	

Graham Chapman, John Cleese, Eric Idle, Terry Jones, Michael Palin, Terry Gilliam, Carol Cleveland, Connie Booth

p, Patricia Casey; d, Ian MacNaughton; w, Graham Chapman, John Cleese, Terry Gilliam, Eric Idle, Terry Jones, Michael Palin; ph, David Muir; ed, Thom Noble; art d, Colin Grimes; anim, Terry Gilliam

Some of the best of the BBC TV's "Monty Python's Flying Circus" sketches reshot for feature film release. Although the cast is brilliant and the material generally funny, the film fails to take advantage of the big-screen format. The gang from Python did much better with the follow-up film, MONTY PYTHON AND THE HOLY GRAIL.

AND THE SHIP SAILS ON
(E LA NAVE VA)

1983 132m c	★★★
Comedy	/PG
RAI-TV (Italy/France)	

Freddie Jones (Orlando), Barbara Jefford (Ildebranda Cuffari), Victor Poletti (Fucileto), Peter Cellier (Sir Reginald), Elisa Marinardi (Teresa Valegnani), Norma West (Sir Reginald's Wife), Paolo Paolini (Orchestra Conductor), Sarah Jane Varley (Dorothy), Fiorenzo Serra (Grand Duke of Harzock), Pina Bausch (Princess Lheremia)

p, Franco Cristaldi; d, Federico Fellini; w, Federico Fellini, Tonino Guerra; ph, Giuseppe Rotunno; ed, Ruggero Mastroianni; m, Gianfranco Plenizio; art d, Dante Ferretti

A minor, eccentric offering from Fellini, involving an odd assortment of passengers who set sail in 1914 for the small island of Cleo. The purpose of their voyage ("the voyage of life?" one character queries) is to scatter the ashes of their friend, a famous opera diva. While the first-class cabins contain businessmen, opera colleagues, comedians, royalty, and various patrons of the arts, the steerage contains a slew of Serbo-Croatian freedom fighters on the run after assassinating Archduke Ferdinand—the catalysts of WWI. If that isn't enough variety, there is also a rhinoceros on board. Tensions rise when an Austro-Hungarian battleship arrives and demands that the revolutionaries be turned over to their custody.

With a line of logic that is as scattered as the diva's ashes, AND THE SHIP SAILS ON is a frustrating film which never quite comes together, and which has little basis in either psychological or physical reality (it was photographed entirely on Cinecitta sets, which Fellini shows us). The picture is worth watching, if only for the scenes with the rhino and the lengthy opening sequence, which begins as a scratchy, sepia-toned silent film that gradually but gloriously develops into a colorful sound picture.

AND THEN THERE WERE NONE

1945 97m bw	★★★★
Mystery	
FOX	

Barry Fitzgerald (Judge Quincannon), Walter Huston (Dr. Armstrong), Louis Hayward (Philip Lombard), Roland Young (Blore), June Duprez (Vera Claythorne), C. Aubrey Smith (Gen. Mandrake), Judith Anderson (Emily Brent), Mischa Auer (Prince Starloff), Richard Haydn (Rogers), Queenie Leonard (Mrs. Rogers)

p, Harry M. Popkin; d, Rene Clair; w, Dudley Nichols (based on the story "Ten Little Niggers" by Agatha Christie); ph, Lucien Andriot; ed, Harvey Manger; art d, Ernst Fegte

This classic Agatha Christie whodunit takes place on a desolate island off the English coast where ten strangers—all with criminal pasts—meet. All have been invited to spend an evening in a sprawling, eerie mansion as guests of maniacal Judge Quincannon (Fitzgerald). Among the colorful characters are the sinister Dr. Armstrong (Huston), the dictatorial General Mandrake (Smith), phony Prince Starloff (Auer), and lovers Philip (Hayward) and Vera (Duprez). It gradually dawns on the terrified guests that they have been marooned on the island for only one purpose—to be murdered one by one in retribution for their transgressions, as per the nursery rhyme "Ten Little Indians."

French director Clair took his time with this production, using his cameras to play cat-and-mouse with each victim and adopting the perfect pace for the story as originally conceived by Christie and tightly adapted by Nichols. The ending of this adaptation differs from Christie's original; the 1965 remake, TEN LITTLE INDIANS, restored the original finale, while the 1974 version, again titled TEN LITTLE INDIANS, used the Clair/Nichols ending.

ANDERSON TAPES, THE

1971 98m c	★★½
Crime	GP/15
Columbia	

Sean Connery (Anderson), Dyan Cannon (Ingrid), Martin Balsam (Haskins), Ralph Meeker (Delaney), Alan King (Angelo), Christopher Walken (The Kid), Val Avery (Parelli), Dick Williams (Spencer), Garrett Morris (Everson), Stan Gottlieb (Pop)

p, Robert M. Weitman; d, Sidney Lumet; w, Frank Pierson (based on the novel by Lawrence Sanders); ph, Arthur J. Ornitz (Technicolor); ed, Joanne Burke; m, Quincy Jones; art d, Philip Rosenberg

A solid, precise, well-made Lumet film, with tough ex-convict Connery, an habitual criminal, looking for a big score immediately upon leaving prison. He goes to the syndicate to seek funds to back a massive robbery, intending to ransack a posh East Side New York apartment building. Rounding up a gang of top-flight thieves, Connery proceeds to plan and carry out his caper, unaware that he is being taped at every turn by various government agencies to discover his links with organized crime. He and his men break into each apartment that is unoccupied—he has determined in advance what tenants are present—and carries out the systematic looting of each place. There are so many lawmen listening in that it seems the whole world is bugged. A good example of the now-neglected caper genre.

ANDROCLES AND THE LION

1952 98m bw	★★
Comedy	/U
RKO	

Jean Simmons (*Lavinia*), Alan Young (*Androcles*), Victor Mature (*Captain*), Robert Newton (*Ferrovius*), Maurice Evans (*Caesar*), Elsa Lanchester (*Megaera*), Reginald Gardiner (*Lentulus*), Gene Lockhart (*Menagerie Keeper*), Alan Mowbray (*Editor*), Noel Willman (*Spintho*)

p, Gabriel Pascal; d, Chester Erskine; w, Chester Erskine, Ken Englund (based on the play by George Bernard Shaw); ph, Harry Stradling; ed, Roland Cross; m, Frederick Hollander

A good adult story for kids, set in ancient Rome. Animal lover Young removes a thorn from the beast of the title and later meets the same animal in a Roman arena, where captured Christians are the day's entree. The secondary story line is about the ill-fated love between Simmons and Mature. This loose adaptation of G.B. Shaw's play makes a pleasant enough studio picture, and is a rare opportunity to see the playwright's work on screen.

ANDY WARHOL'S DRACULA
(DRACULA CERCA SANGUE DI VERGINE E. . . MORI DI SETE)
1974   90m   c   ★★★
Horror   R/
CC Champion & 1/Carlo Ponti-Jean Yanne-Jean-Pierre Rassam   (France/Italy)

Joe Dallesandro (*Mario*), Udo Kier (*Dracula*), Arno Juerging (*Anton*), Maxime McKendry (*Lady Difiore*), Vittorio De Sica (*Lord Difiore*), Dominique Darel (*Rubinia*), Stefania Cassini (*Saphiria*), Roman Polanski (*Man in Inn*), Gil Cagne (*Townsman*), Milena Vukotic (*Esmeralda*)

p, Carlo Ponti, Andrew Braunsberg, Jean-Pierre Rassam, Jean Yanne; d, Paul Morrissey, Antonio Margheriti; w, Paul Morrissey; ph, Luigi Kuveiller (Eastmancolor); ed, Jed Johnson, Franca Silvi; m, Carlo Gizzi; prod d, Enrico Job; art d, Gianni Giovagnoni, Carlo Rambaldi; fx, Roberto Arcangeli

Shot immediately after ANDY WARHOL'S FRANKENSTEIN with much of the same cast and crew, DRACULA is definitely the better of the two. More like a drug addict than a monster, Dracula (Kier) needs "wirgin" blood to survive, and virgins in his native Romania are in short supply. With his assistant, Juerging, and his sister (in a coffin), Dracula travels to Roman Catholic Italy, where virgins should be more prevalent, and winds up at the crumbling estate of a destitute marquis and his four unmarried daughters. Eager to marry one of his daughters off to the rich Romanian count, the marquis gives Dracula a warm welcome. Unbeknownst to the vampire, however, the two middle daughters have already lost their virginity to a hunky socialist handyman (Dallesandro).

Not so outright disgusting as Warhol's FRANKENSTEIN, DRACULA is stylishly directed, atmospheric, funny, and intense enough to please gorehounds—especially at the climax. Kier makes a wonderful Dracula with his thick accent and goofy mannerisms, but De Sica (director of such neorealist classics as SHOESHINE and THE BICYCLE THIEF) nearly steals the show as the eccentric marquis. Once again Morrissey's distinctive stamp is on the script, but many European sources credit Margheriti as the director. Look for Roman Polanski in a cameo as a goofy villager. Originally rated X by the MPAA, the rating was later changed to an R.

ANGEL
1982   90m   c   ★★★
Crime   /15
Motion Picture   (Ireland)

Stephen Rea (*Danny*), Alan Devlin (*Bill*), Veronica Quilligan (*Annie*), Peter Caffrey (*Ray*), Honor Heffernan (*Deirdre*), Ray McAnally (*Bloom*), Donal McCann (*Bonner*), Marie Kean (*Aunt Mae*), Sorcha Cusack (*Mary*), Lise-Ann McLaughlin (*Bride*)

p, Barry Blackmore; d, Neil Jordan; w, Neil Jordan; ph, Chris Menges (Technicolor); ed, J. Patrick Duffner; m, Paddy Meegan; art d, John Lucas

Powerful story set against the backdrop of the Northern Irish "troubles," in which a saxophone player (Stephen Rea) witnesses the murders of his manager and a deaf-mute girl. He becomes obsessed with finding the killers and getting revenge, transforming himself into a killer in the process. Rea gives a wonderful performance, and Neil Jordan (MONA LISA, HIGH SPIRITS) does a magnificent job in his directorial debut. This is a powerful film, noted for its black humor, atmospheric locations, and even touches of surrealism.

ANGEL AT MY TABLE, AN
1991   156m   c   ★★★★
Biography/Drama   R/15
Hibiscus Films/Sharmill Films   (New Zealand)

Kerry Fox (*Janet Frame*), Karen Fergusson (*Janet Frame—as a Teenager*), Alexia Keogh (*Janet Frame—as a Child*), Iris Churn (*Mum*), K.J. Wilson (*Dad*), Melina Bernecker (*Myrtle Frame*), Glynis Angell (*Isabel Frame*), Samantha Townsley (*Isabel Frame—as a Teenager*), Katherine Murray-Cowper (*Isabel Frame—as a Child*), Sarah Smuts-Kennedy (*June Frame*)

p, Bridget Ikin; d, Jane Campion; w, Laura Jones (from the autobiographies *To the Is-Land*, *An Angel at My Table* and *The Envoy from Mirror City* by Janet Frame); ph, Stuart Dryburgh; ed, Veronica Haussler; m, Don McGlashan; prod d, Grant Major; art d, Jackie Gilmore; cos, Glenys Jackson

Lushly photographed and beautifully acted, AN ANGEL AT MY TABLE, adapted from the autobiography of New Zealand novelist and poet Janet Frame, evokes an odd, often melancholy life with generosity and an almost obsessive attention to detail.

A stubborn, plain, introverted redhead, Janet's thirst for knowledge and determination to be a writer set her apart from other children growing up in her isolated rural community. Her family is poor but close-knit, and her parents do their best to support Janet's ambitions, while encouraging her to channel them into something practical, like a career in teaching. As Janet (now played by Kerry Fox) grows older, her shyness becomes more pronounced. Though she manages to leave home to attend college, once there she finds herself increasingly alienated from her fellow students. She feels awkward and ugly, unable to join in their chatter and casual flirtations; her nervousness makes her clumsy and when her lively, self-confident younger sister Isabel (Glynis Angell) arrives, Janet only looks worse by comparison. She retreats into a life of fantasy and isolation, and eventually has a nervous breakdown.

Committed to an institution, Janet is diagnosed—incorrectly, it later turns out—as an incurable schizophrenic. Throughout her troubles, Janet continues to write, and it's the timely publication of her first novel that saves her from the horrifying prospect of psychotropic surgery. Having left the mental hospital, Janet is taken under the wing of Frank Sargeson (Martyn Sanderson), an eccentric writer, who encourages her to broaden her perspectives by traveling. Though frightened, she goes to London, where she falls in with a group of writers, and then to Greece, where she has her first affair, with Bernard (William Brandt), an American would-be poet. Slowly Janet emerges from her shell, and by the time she returns to New Zealand she's able to cope with the demands of local celebrity. The film closes on the image of Janet living in a small trailer, still a loner but having come to some peace with herself.

With SWEETIE, her celebrated feature debut, native New Zealander Jane Campion established a reputation for making slightly off-center films in which regular folks get glimpses of the darkness that lurks beneath the surfaces of their lives. An admirer of Frame's novels since she was a teenager, Campion builds a two-and-a-half hour film around a heroine who defies all Hollywood conventions; she's not beautiful or sexy or sophisticated, and her adventures are mostly adventures of the mind. It doesn't even have a conventionally happy ending; Frame isn't swept off her feet by a dashing man who loves her for her beautiful soul, or given the Nobel Prize for Literature and hailed the world over as a neglected genius. She simply lives her life, acutely conscious of both its beauty and its sadness, and finds meaning through her writing.

Originally shot on 16mm and 1-inch videotape as a 3-part miniseries for Australian television, then combined and slightly re-edited for 35mm theatrical release, AN ANGEL AT MY TABLE doesn't look like a television movie, except perhaps in the intimacy of its subject: the largely unremarkable, but richly remembered life of a plain, intelligent woman with a startling head of frizzy, ginger-colored hair.

ANGELS IN THE OUTFIELD

1951 99m c ★★★½
Comedy/Sports
MGM

Paul Douglas *(Guffy McGovern)*, Janet Leigh *(Jennifer Paige)*, Keenan Wynn *(Fred Bayles)*, Donna Corcoran *(Bridget White)*, Lewis Stone *(Arnold P. Hapgood)*, Spring Byington *(Sr. Edwitha)*, Bruce Bennett *(Saul Hellman)*, Marvin Kaplan *(Timothy Durney)*, Ellen Corby *(Sr. Veronica)*, Jeff Richards *(Dave Rothberg)*

p, Clarence Brown; d, Clarence Brown; w, Dorothy Kingsley, George Wells (based on a story by Richard Conlin); ph, Paul C. Vogel; ed, Robert J. Kern; m, Daniele Amfitheatrof

This delightful baseball comedy stars Paul Douglas as Guffy McGovern, the irascible manager of the Pittsburgh Pirates, who are firmly entrenched in the basement of the National League until the prayers of a little girl (Donna Corcoran) prompt the angel Gabriel to intervene. When Guffy sees the divine light and turns over a new leaf, more angels—baseball greats of the past—lend a helping glove, and the Pirates start winning ball games, shooting to the top of the standings. Reporter Jennifer Paige (Janet Leigh) suspects the Pirates are receiving help from above and begins an investigation into the matter. Great performances by all make this a little gem of a film. Dwight Eisenhower, interviewed during his presidency, named this his favorite movie. Note the fleeting presence of Hall of Famers Ty Cobb and Joe DiMaggio.

ANGELS OVER BROADWAY

1940 78m bw ★★★★
Drama /A
Columbia

Douglas Fairbanks, Jr. *(Bill O'Brien)*, Rita Hayworth *(Nina Barona)*, Thomas Mitchell *(Gene Gibbons)*, John Qualen *(Charles Engle)*, George Watts *(Hopper)*, Ralph Theodore *(Dutch Enright)*, Eddie Foster *(Louie Artino)*, Jack Roper *(Eddie Burns)*, Constance Worth *(Sylvia Marbe)*, Richard Bond *(Sylvia's Escort)*

p, Ben Hecht; d, Ben Hecht, Lee Garmes; w, Ben Hecht; ph, Lee Garmes; ed, Gene Havlick; m, George Antheil; art d, Lionel Banks; cos, Ray Howell

One of the more underappreciated films to come out of Hollywood, this marvelous Ben Hecht production annoyed the critics of the day for not pandering to its audience. Four leads and a host of supporting players make a single Broadway night come to life with zip and wit. Mitchell, as a silver-tongued, alcoholic playwright, saves Qualen, who is about to commit suicide after embezzling several thousand dollars. "Dismiss your hearse," Mitchell urges him. "Live, little man, and suffer!" The zany playwright proposes a surefire scheme to dupe some big-time card sharps in a battle royal, using Qualen's stolen loot to build a fortune. Enter slick Fairbanks, who shills for a top-drawer poker game, and his devoted but equally sharp girlfriend Hayworth. Fairbanks spots Qualen as an easy mark and intends to suck him into the game and take him for everything. Nothing, of course, goes according to anyone's plans as Hecht's clever script twists and turns its way to a startling and delightful conclusion.

The performances, particularly by Mitchell and Fairbanks, are captivating, and the dialogue sparkles with Hecht's poetic irony: "This town's a giant dice game—come on seven!" Because the film featured Rita Hayworth, who had been hand-picked for stardom by Columbia's boss Harry Cohn, Hecht was given a relatively free reign on this production, and went unhampered by interfering studio bureaucrats to create an unpredictable Broadway saga. Hecht earned an Academy Award nomination for his original screenplay, but lost to Preston Sturges for THE GREAT MCGINTY.

ANGELS WITH DIRTY FACES

1938 97m bw ★★★★
Crime /PG
WB

James Cagney *(Rocky Sullivan)*, Pat O'Brien *(Jerry Connelly)*, Humphrey Bogart *(James Frazier)*, Ann Sheridan *(Laury Ferguson)*, George Bancroft *(Mac Keefer)*, Billy Halop *(Soapy)*, Bobby Jordan *(Swing)*, Leo Gorcey *(Bim)*, Bernard Punsley *(Hunky)*, Gabriel Dell *(Pasty)*

p, Samuel Bischoff; d, Michael Curtiz; w, John Wexley, Warren Duff (based on a story by Rowland Brown); ph, Sol Polito; ed, Owen Marks; m, Max Steiner; art d, Robert Haas

One of the most stirring, colorful and memorable gangster films of its day, and a perfect summary of Cagney's tough but soft-hearted screen image. As youths, Rocky Sullivan and his pal Jerry Connelly are caught in the act of breaking into a railroad car. Jerry escapes, but Rocky is caught and sent to reform school. The film then jumps ahead several years, with Rocky (now played by Cagney) a hardened criminal, and Jerry (Pat O'Brien) a priest in the neighborhood where the boys grew up. Rocky, recently released from jail, returns to the neighborhood, where a battle begins between the criminal and the priest for the hearts and minds of some tough kids in the neighborhood. Rocky also tries to get his double-crossing ex-partner (Humphrey Bogart) to come up with the $100,000 he owes him.

With Cagney, O'Brien, and Bogart plus the young actors known as the Dead End Kids, the film offers a host of terrific characters, crisp dialogue, and a generous portion of humor. (Particularly funny is the scene in which Rocky gives the young toughs a lesson in how to play basketball.) Films about boyhood friends who go down different paths in life were popular in the 1930s, but the tale was never more effectively told than in this fast-paced drama.

ANGUISH
(ANGUSTIA)
1988 91m c ★★★
Horror R/18
Pepon Cormina (Spain)

Zelda Rubinstein (Mother), Michael Lerner (John), Talia Paul (Polly), Angel Jove (Killer), Clara Pastor (Linda), Isabel Lorca (Caroline), Nat Baker (Teaching Doctor, Cast of Old Movie), Edward Ledden (Doctor), Gustavo Gili, Antonio Reguero

p, Pepon Coromina; d, Bigas Luna; w, Bigas Luna; ph, Jose Maria Civit (Eastmancolor, Agfa Color); ed, Tom Sabin; m, J.M. Pagan; prod d, Andreu Coromina; fx, Paco Teres; cos, Consol Tura

ANGUISH is a suspenseful horror film containing not one but two classic gimmicks: a William Castle-style warning that the "subliminal effects" on screen may cause mental distress, and a cleverly used film-within-a-film technique. The movie begins as a loutish optometrist's orderly (Michael Lerner) louses up on the job and is dismissed. His mother (Zelda Rubinstein), an odd little woman who totally dominates her docile son, uses a form of hypnosis to merge her mind with her son's, and sends him out to get revenge on the patient (Isabel Garcia Lorca) who caused his dismissal. At this point director Luna pulls back from the image to reveal that it is merely a horror film being watched by a small matinee crowd in a movie theater. We then find out that one of the patrons is a real murderer, who begins killing off theater employees and patrons in a manner that parallels the action on screen. ANGUISH is a well-crafted and entertaining exercise in cinematic style, and a good example of an adventurous director turning to the horror genre in order to have more room to flex his pyrotechnical muscles.

ANIMAL CRACKERS
1930 97m bw ★★★½
Comedy /U
Paramount

Groucho Marx (Capt. Jeffrey Spaulding), Harpo Marx (The Professor), Chico Marx (Signor Emanuel Raveld), Zeppo Marx (Horatio Jamison), Lillian Roth (Arabella Rittenhouse), Margaret Dumont (Mrs. Rittenhouse), Louis Sorin (Roscoe Chandler), Hal Thompson (John Parker), Margaret Irving (Mrs. Whitehead), Kathryn Reece (Grace Carpenter)

d, Victor Heerman; w, Morrie Ryskind (based on the musical play by Morrie Ryskind and George S. Kaufman); ph, George Foley

Zany Marx Brothers vehicle, typical of their early Paramount period, which opens at a party in a posh mansion. A priceless oil painting is unveiled, and the rest of the slim storyline concerns the picture's theft and recovery. Even though the script was tightly written, the movie appears to be one big ad-lib in the style of COCOANUTS, their smash debut of the previous year. Groucho's wise-guy delivery is fast-paced as usual, but even he is repelled at times by his own puns, turning at one point to the camera to grimace and say, "Well, all the jokes can't be good!" He also sings the memorable "Hooray for Captain Spaulding," the tune that would become his theme song throughout his long career. Harpo is in his usual delightful and daffy character, as is Chico as Groucho's maddening antagonist.

ANIMAL FARM
1955 75m c ★★
Animated /U
DCA (U.K.)

Maurice Denham (Voices of the Animals), Gordon Heath (Narrator)

p, John Halas, Joy Batchelor; d, John Halas, Joy Batchelor; w, John Halas, Joy Batchelor, Lothar Wolff, Borden Mace, Philip Stapp (based on the novel by George Orwell); ph, S.J. Griffiths (Technicolor); m, Matyas Seiber

A cartoon adaptation of George Orwell's classic dystopia, notable as the first feature-length animated British production. The story concerns a barnyard rebellion led by a pig, Napoleon, who perverts the revolutionary cause and takes on all the evil characteristics of the overthrown regime. The animation is satisfactory, and the film has several powerful moments, but the allegorical nature of Orwell's satirical fable is better served in print.

ANNA AND THE KING OF SIAM
1946 128m bw ★★★★
Drama /A
FOX

Irene Dunne (Anna), Rex Harrison (the King), Linda Darnell (Tuptin), Lee J. Cobb (Kralahome), Gale Sondergaard (Lady Thiang), Mikhail Rasumny (Alak), Dennis Hoey (Sir Edward), Tito Renaldo (Prince as a Man), Richard Lyon (Louis Owens), William Edmunds (Monshee)

p, Louis D. Lighton; d, John Cromwell; w, Talbot Jennings, Sally Benson (based on the book by Margaret Landon); ph, Arthur Miller; m, Bernard Wheeler, William Darling; fx, Fred Sersen

An entertaining, touching tale of an English tutor who travels to Siam in 1862 with her young son. She is hired to educate the harem and 67 children of the rather savage king, who covets Western culture but insists upon maintaining Siam's customs and some particularly barbaric traditions. The story is drawn from the real life of 33-year-old Mrs. Anna Leonowens, brilliantly played by Dunne, who is at first repelled and later attracted to Harrison, the king (in his first American film), and his different Eastern ways. She also meets and befriends the king's first wife (Sondergaard), long relegated to the back rooms of the imperial palace, and a lovely young addition to the harem (Darnell) who falls tragically in love with another. The supporting cast is uniformly excellent, including Cobb in the role of the king's chief minister. Director Cromwell keeps the well lighted and photographed story brisk and less sentimental than the musical remake, THE KING AND I. Dunne is the perfect British governess, and the theoretically miscast Harrison is simply majestic as the king who gropes toward both sensitivity and Western ideas, battling his authoritarian instincts all the way. It's a wonder that this production, richly costumed and boasting lavish sets, was not done in color.

ANNA CHRISTIE
1930 86m bw ★★★
Drama /A
MGM

Greta Garbo (Anna Christie), Charles Bickford (Matt Burke), George F. Marion, Sr. (Chris Christopherson), Marie Dressler (Marthy Owen), James T. Mack (Johnny the Harp), Lee Phelps (Larry)

d, Clarence Brown; w, Frances Marion (based on the play by Eugene O'Neill); ph, William Daniels; ed, Hugh Wynn; art d, Cedric Gibbons; cos, Adrian

Garbo talks. A fascinating cast and a convincingly murky atmosphere help overcome the primitive sound techniques that plague this stagy, somewhat preciously presented adaptation of Eugene O'Neill's famous if overrated play (first filmed in 1923 with Blanche Sweet and William Russell). Garbo, the cinema's great silent sphinx, who first spoke in this film, plays the title role, a woman who flees the mean-spirited farm family her sailor father left her with and ends up a prostitute. Renouncing her profession, Garbo returns to her father (George F. Marion, Sr.), living on a broken-down barge as the film opens. During a storm Garbo and Marion rescue an Irish sailor (Bickford) from drowning, and though Bickford soon falls for Garbo and proposes, she angrily exorcises all her past pain by revealing her background as a whore. Although Bickford abandons her at first, genuine love eventually reconciles the pair.

The public fascination with the mysterious Garbo heightened ANNA CHRISTIE's popularity. Although critics and public alike were justifiably captivated by her husky, accented voice and famous delivery of her opening lines: "Gimme a viskey, ginger ale on the side... and don't be stingy, baby!" parts of her performance are exaggerated, reminiscent more of off-key silent-screen posturing than the equally intense but refined technique she would soon master. The sometimes mugging Dressler, on the other hand, in the star-making role of the aging wharf rat who commiserates with Garbo throughout the film, steals every scene she appears in and manages to convey both touching pathos and a rich humanity. Much of the film's creakiness is due to the cumbersome sound equipment that prevented director Clarence Brown from using his noise-making cameras freely. Nominated for an Academy Award for Best Actress for this film and RO-MANCE, Garbo remade the film in German with Jacques Feyder (director of THE KISS, Garbo's last silent) and, reportedly, she liked Feyder's version better than Brown's, of which she said, "Isn't it terrible? Who ever saw Swedes act like that?"

ANNA KARENINA
1935 85m bw   ★★★★
Drama   /U
MGM

Greta Garbo (*Anna Karenina*), Fredric March (*Vronsky*), Freddie Bartholomew (*Sergei*), Maureen O'Sullivan (*Kitty*), May Robson (*Countess Vronsky*), Basil Rathbone (*Karenin*), Reginald Owen (*Stiva*), Reginald Denny (*Yashvin*), Phoebe Foster (*Dolly*), Gyles Isham (*Levin*)

p, David O. Selznick; d, Clarence Brown; w, Clemence Dane, Salka Viertel, S.N. Behrman (based on the novel by Leo Tolstoy); ph, William Daniels; ed, Robert J. Kearn; m, Herbert Stothart; chor, Marguerite Wallmann, Chester Hale

A remake of the John Gilbert-Greta Garbo silent movie LOVE, this often splendid, moody Garbo vehicle under Clarence Brown's direction tells the tragic Tolstoy tale with great sensitivity. As the immortal Anna of 19th-century Petersburg, Garbo plays the pampered wife of Karenin (Rathbone, in fine form), a rich but icy government official. After pleading with her straying married brother (Owen) not to jeopardize his marriage, she ironically meets and falls in love the dashing Captain Vronsky (March). When she asks her husband for a divorce, she is told that if she makes such an unheard-of move, she will be deprived of her son (Bartholomew). Remorseful but consumed by love,

Anna runs off with Vronsky, who resigns his commission. Though happy at first, he soon longs for his carefree army days, and she is pained by her thwarted attempts to spend time with her son. The star-crossed lovers finally argue and separate and when Anna, rushing to the train station upon learning that Vronsky is leaving, sees him saying goodbye to another woman, she dramatically resigns herself to the completeness of her losses, throwing herself in front of the departing train.

Director Brown, in one of the best of his seven films with Garbo, and ace cinematographer William Daniels, Garbo's favorite, bathe their beloved actress in soft light that caresses her classic features. Adorned in luxurious but subdued gowns appropriate to both her own passionate but understated style and Anna's profound sadness, Garbo is unforgettable as a woman who only briefly experiences carefree happiness, whose desires are crushed by a rigid and unfeeling society. Especially memorable is the finale, as light flashes from the oncoming train alternately reveal and hide Anna's conflicting emotions. Meticulously and sumptuously mounted by producer David O. Selznick, the film carefully pares down Tolstoy's sprawling classic to center almost entirely upon its heroine, but the end result is highly satisfying nonetheless.

ANNA KARENINA
1948 139m bw   ★★★½
Drama   /PG
Korda/London Films (U.K.)

Vivien Leigh (*Anna Karenina*), Ralph Richardson (*Alexei Karenin*), Kieron Moore (*Count Vronsky*), Sally Ann Howes (*Kitty Scherbatsky*), Niall MacGinnis (*Levin*), Martita Hunt (*Princess Betty Tversky*), Marie Lohr (*Princess Scherbatsky*), Michael Gough (*Nicholai*), Hugh Dempster (*Stefan Oblonsky*), Mary Kerridge (*Dolly Oblonsky*)

p, Alexander Korda; d, Julien Duvivier; w, Jean Anouilh, Guy Morgan, Julien Duvivier (based on the novel by Leo Tolstoy); ph, Henri Alekan; ed, Russell Lloyd; m, Constant Lambert; prod d, Andre Andrejew; fx, W. Percy Day; cos, Cecil Beaton

This remake of the Garbo classic has different values and approaches that enhance Vivien Leigh's magnetic performance as the ill-starred Anna, who leaves her stuffy bureaucrat husband, Karenin (Richardson), for an adventurous army officer, Vronsky (Moore), only to be discarded and sent to suicide in front of an onrushing train when husband, child, and lover are lost to her. Unlike the 1935 version, which also downplayed the novel's subplots far more, the psychological elements of this tragedy are underscored and registered with powerful impact through Leigh, whose raw emotions distort and finally destroy a once orderly, though predictably dull, life. Leigh is positively riveting, and Richardson as the priggish, pompous government official is properly vengeful and vexing. Only the very handsome Moore, in the admittedly colorless role as the self-centered lover, is a letdown, delivering a sometimes bland performance. Korda's production, though perhaps overlong, is truly spectacular, with a great supporting cast, countless extras, and authentic 19th-century sets that are mouth-openers. Duvivier's direction is moody and fast-paced, highlighted by sometimes frightening effects, with angles and cuts that reflect the image of a woman slipping deeper and deeper into her own destruction.

ANNE OF THE THOUSAND DAYS
1969 145m c   ★★★★
Historical   M/PG
Universal (U.K.)

Richard Burton *(King Henry VIII)*, Genevieve Bujold *(Anne Boleyn)*, Irene Papas *(Queen Katherine)*, Anthony Quayle *(Wolsey)*, John Colicos *(Cromwell)*, Michael Hordern *(Thomas Boleyn)*, Katherine Blake *(Elizabeth)*, Peter Jeffrey *(Norfolk)*, Joseph O'Conor *(Fisher)*, William Squire *(Thomas More)*

p, Hal B. Wallis; d, Charles Jarrott; w, Bridget Boland, John Hale (adapted by Richard Sokolove, based on the play by Maxwell Anderson); ph, Arthur Ibbetson (Panavision, Technicolor); ed, Richard Marden; m, Georges Delerue; prod d, Maurice Carter; art d, Lionel Couch; chor, Mary Skeaping; cos, Margaret Furse

A superbly acted costume drama, ANNE OF THE THOUSAND DAYS recounts the story of Henry VIII (Richard Burton), who, in 1526, discards his wife, Katherine of Aragon (Irene Papas), in favor of the younger, prettier Anne Boleyn (Genevieve Bujold), who soon proves to be as crafty and ruthless as her sovereign. Resisting Henry's incessant advances, insisting that any child born to them must be decreed legitimate, Anne plays her cat-and-mouse game for six years, while Cardinal Wolsey (Quayle) collapses into ineffectual senility when he fails to have Anne's marriage to another annulled. Only the Iago-like Cromwell (John Colicos) solves the king's dilemma by precipitating a break with the Vatican, naming Henry head of the Church of England, and dispensing with any religious controls over his or Anne's marital status. Although the union produces a daughter, Henry later seizes upon the birth of a stillborn son as an excuse to abandon his queen and and woo the attractive Jane Seymour (Lesley Paterson). After that Anne's days are numbered—one thousand, to be exact.

Based on the 1948 Maxwell Anderson play (a star vehicle for Rex Harrison on Broadway), ANNE OF THE THOUSAND DAYS has a touch of soap opera which helps explain its then-substantial gross of $7 million. But it also boasts lavish sets and handsome photography, an arresting performance by Burton—the epitome of the royal fox and oaf—and well-judged work from Bujold, Papas, and Quayle, all of which make for a rousing, bawdy, and often enlightening historical film. A successful entry in a series of such features made during the 60s, including BECKET (also produced by Wallis), A MAN FOR ALL SEASONS, and THE LION IN WINTER, the film received an Academy Award nomination for Best Picture but lost to John Schlesinger's gritty, contemporary MIDNIGHT COWBOY.

ANNIE GET YOUR GUN

1950   107m   c   ★★★½
Musical/Western   /U
MGM

Betty Hutton *(Annie Oakley)*, Howard Keel *(Frank Butler)*, Louis Calhern *(Buffalo Bill)*, J. Carrol Naish *(Chief Sitting Bull)*, Edward Arnold *(Pawnee Bill)*, Keenan Wynn *(Charlie Davenport)*, Benay Venuta *(Dolly Tate)*, Clinton Sundberg *(Foster Wilson)*, James Harrison *(Mac)*, Brad Mora *(Little Jake)*

p, Arthur Freed; d, George Sidney; w, Sidney Sheldon (based on the musical play, book by Herbert Fields and Dorothy Fields); ph, Charles Rosher (Technicolor); ed, James E. Newcom; m, Irving Berlin; art d, Cedric Gibbons, Paul Groesse; fx, A. Arnold Gillespie, Warren Newcombe; chor, Robert Alton

Sprightly songfest that, surprisingly, captivated audiences wanting musicals with dancing. There is little dancing throughout, but the tunes became instant standards and the large sets, armies of extras, and Wild West motif offset the missing choreography. In a glove-fitting role, Hutton blasts her way on and off screen as the sharpshooting Annie Oakley Mozie (1860-1926), a homely girl from the Ozarks who becomes queen of Buffalo Bill's renowned Wild West Show, pitting her talents against marksman Frank Butler (Keel). She loves Keel, but her ability to best him keeps driving him away. Finally Sitting Bull (Naish) gives her worthwhile advice before she faces off against Keel one more time. "You miss, you win," the Indian chief tells her, and he's right.

Keel is excellent as the smug star of the show; Naish is likewise top-notch as a shrewd Sitting Bull; Calhern superb as a noble but slippery Buffalo Bill; Arnold solid as his show biz rival; and Wynn his usual truculent self. Standout numbers include "Doin' What Comes Natur'lly" sung by Hutton and siblings, "My Defenses Are Down" boomed by Keel, "I'm an Indian Too" with Hutton and a horde of leaping, lunging Indians, and the fantastic finale with hundreds of cowboys and Indians, "There's No Business Like Show Business."

MGM execs struggled to find the perfect Annie Oakley, first considering Judy Canova, Betty Garrett, and Doris Day before opting for Judy Garland, who was reportedly fired because of incessant tantrums. Hutton was finally brought in to save the day, which she did with typically unbridled enthusiasm, giving one of her most suitable performances, even though she proved to be no Ethel Merman, who originated the role in the smash Broadway production, when it came to singing the finale. Although the choice of director was similarly muddled by MGM moguls, passing from Busby Berkeley to Charles Walters and finally to George Sidney, the extremely lavish result went on to win the Oscar for Best Score in a Musical, as well as nominations for cinematography, art direction and editing.

ANNIE HALL

1977   93m   c   ★★★★
Comedy   PG/15
UA

Woody Allen *(Alvy Singer)*, Diane Keaton *(Annie Hall)*, Tony Roberts *(Rob)*, Carol Kane *(Allison)*, Paul Simon *(Tony Lacey)*, Colleen Dewhurst *(Mom Hall)*, Janet Margolin *(Robin)*, Shelley Duvall *(Pam)*, Christopher Walken *(Duane Hall)*, Donald Symington *(Dad Hall)*

p, Charles H. Joffe; d, Woody Allen; w, Woody Allen, Marshall Brickman; ph, Gordon Willis; ed, Ralph Rosenblum, Wendy Greene Bricmont; art d, Mel Bourne; cos, Ruth Morley, George Newman, Marilyn Putnam, Ralph Lauren, Nancy McArdle

Seminal, often hilarious look at modern-day sexual arrangements, with Woody Allen playing Alvy Singer, a neurotic, insecure comedy writer (Allen began his own career as a gag writer for the "Tonight Show") who falls madly in love with Annie Hall (Diane Keaton), an aspiring singer. They fumble about in the early stages of their relationship like two teenagers groping toward sex and self-identity, mouthing cliches twisted in the Allen style to the wry, the incisive, and the sublimely ridiculous. The couple moves in together, but he soon becomes so insecure about their affair that he pounces on her every move, interpreting these acts as rejection and disaffection. Eventually their own mutual uncertainty splits them apart and they are left to their careers and to trying again with other partners.

The simplicity of the seemingly impromptu story, set largely in Allen's beloved New York City, is part of ANNIE HALL's undeniable charm, along with Allen's flashbacks to childhood (with side-splitting Jonathan Munk as a young Woody) and constant asides to the camera, a device that sometimes has to carry the laughs. Allen moves freely through the flashbacks as a grown man, commenting on various scenes in a technique borrowed from Bergman's WILD STRAWBERRIES. As always there are the priceless Allen situations (such as his showdown with a spider) and quips. Observing that Keaton habitually smokes a joint before they make love, he cracks, "Why don't you take sodium pentothal? Then you could sleep through the whole thing!" Easily seen as autobiography, ANNIE HALL received no advance publicity under Allen's orders, which made the entire production seem fresh and startling, as it pointed out in extravagant terms the follies and foibles of man and, in particular, of a hopeless nerd whose mannered idiocies always make the viewer feel superior. Roberts, Allen's perennial sidekick, is highly effective as the glib, annoying hipster whose amoral outlook and Neiman-Marcus lifestyle are less funny than repugnant. Superior though the film certainly is, there remains with each subsequent viewing an ever-widening hole where a life should have been instead of a throwaway line. The film did well critically (Academy Awards for Best Picture, Best Actress, Best Director, and Best Screenplay) as well as financially (grossing $19 million on its first run).

ANOTHER WOMAN
1988 84m c   ★★★★
Drama   PG
Jack Rollins-Charles H. Joffe

Gena Rowlands (Marion Post), Mia Farrow (Hope), Ian Holm (Ken Post), Blythe Danner (Lydia), Gene Hackman (Larry), Betty Buckley (Kathy), Martha Plimpton (Laura Post), John Houseman (Marion's Dad), Sandy Dennis (Claire), David Ogden Stiers (Young Marion's Dad)

p, Robert Greenhut; d, Woody Allen; w, Woody Allen; ph, Sven Nykvist (Duart color); ed, Susan E. Morse; prod d, Santo Loquasto; cos, Jeffrey Kurland

ANOTHER WOMAN stars Gena Rowlands as an aging professor who realizes she has led an unemotional life and must look into the past in order to prepare herself for the future. She is married to a physician (Holm), has a close relationship with her stepdaughter (Plimpton), avoids her brother (Yulin), and fears the loss of her ailing father (Houseman). When she overhears a pregnant psychiatric patient's therapy session, Marion becomes obsessed with knowing all about the woman (Farrow), who reminds her of her younger self. Full of the intellectual exchanges and philosophical angst which have increasingly characterized his work, the film shows Allen taking a brave creative stance in making only the type of films that he wants to make, without regard for audience or critical reaction. Rowlands is outstanding, and the rest of the cast equally superb, especially Hackman as the one man who knows the real Marion—the honest, loving, passionate woman she has spent most of her life trying to find.

ANTHONY ADVERSE
1936 139m bw   ★★
Historical/Romance   /A
WB

Fredric March (Anthony Adverse), Olivia de Havilland (Angela Guessippi), Edmund Gwenn (John Bonnyfeather), Claude Rains (Don Luis), Anita Louise (Maria), Louis Hayward (Denis Moore), Gale Sondergaard (Faith Paleologus), Steffi Duna (Neleta), Billy Mauch (Anthony as a Child), Donald Woods (Vincent Nolte)

p, Henry Blanke; d, Mervyn LeRoy; w, Sheridan Gibney (based on the novel by Hervey Allen); ph, Tony Gaudio; ed, Ralph Dawson; m, Erich Wolfgang Korngold; art d, Anton Grot; cos, Milo Anderson

This lavish but overlong film remains true to the 1200-page best-seller on which it is based, though judging by the result one wonders to what extent this is admirable. Popular and acclaimed in its day, and technically highly skilled, ANTHONY ADVERSE subtitutes historical pageantry for drama and melodramatic flourish for characterization whenever it gets the chance.

March plays the title role, an illegitimate child whose father (Hayward) is killed in a duel and who is raised in a convent by a gentle priest (O'Neill). Adopted by a kindly Scottish trader (Gwenn), the growing boy soon finds romance with a girl (de Havilland) who aspires to sing grand opera. Although they marry, the couple are separated when a crucial note is blown away by a gust of wind. Anthony goes crazy with despair and jungle fever for several years while managing his stepfather's questionable African interests, and when he returns to Europe he finds his stepfather dead, his wife a diva linked romantically to Napoleon (Lloyd), and his inheritance jeopardized by the wicked Don Luis (Rains), who killed his real father back when. The wrap-up includes chicanery, a duel, and a surprise from de Havilland.

This massive but choppy historical soaper, aiming to both jerk tears and swash buckles, now seems inferior to other similar but more modest films. March has his moments, but seems more concerned with appearing young and stalwart than with giving the role the tongue-in-cheek dash it so desperately needs. De Havilland is mere decoration, and it is up to several of the supporting players, particularly Rains and Sondergaard (as a scheming, ambitious housekeeper), to serve as energetic foils to the film's rampant displays of virtue. Grot's sets and Gaudio's cinematography add definite sweep, and Korngold's score is both majestic and melancholic, befitting the romantic tragedy of star-crossed lovers this film would dearly like to be.

ANTOINE ET ANTOINETTE
1947 98m bw   ★★
Comedy   /A
Gaumont   (France)

Roger Pigaut (Antoine), Claire Mattei (Antoinette), Noel Roquevert (Roland), Annette Poivre (Juliette), Jacques Meyran (Barbelot), Emile Dtain (Father-in-Law), Paulette Jan (Huguette), Gaston Modot (Official), Gerard Oury (Customer), Francois Joux (Bridegroom)

d, Jacques Becker; w, Francoise Giroud, Jacques Becker, Maurice Griffe; ph, Pierre Momtizel; ed, Marguerite Renoir; m, Jean-Jacques Grunenwald; art d, Robert-Jules Garnier

Appealing French comedy, smoothy handled by Jacques Becker, starring Pigaut and Mattei as a young married couple. He works as a book binder while she toils as a salesgirl. The thin plot revolves around a desperate search for a lost lottery ticket. Appropriately lightweight, though not in the same class as Rene Clair's brilliant LE MILLION (1930), which it rather resembles.

ANTONIO DAS MORTES
1969 100m c   ★★★½
Action   /X
Grove   (Brazil)

Mauricio do Valle (Antonio das Mortes), Odete Lara (Laura), Othon Bastos (Teacher), Hugo Carvana (Police Chief), Jofre Soares (Colonel), Rosa Maria Penna (Saint)

p, Claude-Antoine Mapa; d, Glauber Rocha; w, Glauber Rocha; ph, Alfonso Beato (Eastmancolor); m, Marlos Nobre

Powerful political film, with mercenary do Valle tracking down insurgents, killing all the members of one band and dispatching the leader in hand-to-hand combat in a wild bullet-ridden finale, only to discover his real sympathies are with the rebels. Clearly indebted to the directors of France's New Wave, Rocha would make greater films; nevertheless, ANTONIO DAS MORTES survives as a landmark in Brazil's emergent *Cinema Novo* by one of its finest filmmakers. Brazil's lush vegetation, mountains, and plains are beautifully photographed in this polemic, which lionizes the likes of revolutionary Che Guevara while indicting the cruel and impersonal landlords of a South American dictatorship.

APACHE

1954 91m c ★★★
Western /U
Hecht/Lancaster

Burt Lancaster *(Massai)*, Jean Peters *(Nalinle)*, John McIntire *(Al Sieber)*, Charles Bronson *(Hondo)*, John Dehner *(Weddle)*, Paul Guilfoyle *(Santos)*, Ian MacDonald *(Glagg)*, Walter Sande *(Lt. Col. Beck)*, Morris Ankrum *(Dawson)*, Monte Blue *(Geronimo)*

p, Harold Hecht; d, Robert Aldrich; w, James R. Webb (based on the novel *Bronco Apache* by Paul I. Wellman); ph, Ernest Laszlo (Technicolor); ed, Alan Crosland, Jr.; m, David Raksin; art d, Nicolai Remisoff

A brutal western in which the acrobatic Lancaster, as one of Geronimo's chiefs, refuses to surrender, conducting a one-man war against the cavalry with knife, arrow, and gun. Swarms of troopers attempt to kill him, led by white scout McIntire, who is sympathetic to the plight of the Native Americans. Lancaster, who co-produced, is in his typically over-earnest mode here, all flashing, gnashing teeth and sweaty armpits. The perspective is notable for its links to several 1950s Westerns beginning with BROKEN ARROW (1950), which revived the social concern for the American Indian which late silent film had explored. Peters is a sensuous and attractive if somewhat glamourized mate for Lancaster, daughter of an Indian (Guilfoyle) who sells out the renegade. Silent screen matinee idol Blue also appears, but is not entirely convincing as Geronimo. UA compelled Lancaster to change the ending of this film; he wanted his hero to be shot to death by troopers after he had made peace and settled down to farm the land. Instead, he is exonerated, despite slaying a dozen men, because he has conducted a legitimate war and is therefore entitled to the provisions of peace settlements accorded warring nations. The end result is suitably lively but compromised cinema.

APARAJITO

1957 105m bw ★★★★
Drama /U
Epic (India)

Pinaki Sen Gupta *(Apu as a boy)*, Smaran Ghosal *(Apu as an adolescent)*, Karuna Banerji *(Mother)*, Kanu Banerji *(Father)*, Ramani Sen Gupta *(Old Uncle)*, Charu Ghosh *(Nanda Babu)*, Subodh Ganguly *(Headmaster)*, Kali Charan Ray *(Press Proprietor)*, Santi Gupta *(Landlord's Wife)*, K.S. Pandey *(Pandey)*

p, Satyajit Ray; d, Satyajit Ray; w, Satyajit Ray (based on the novel *Pather Panchali* by Bibhutibhusan Bandapadhaya); ph, Subrata Mitra; ed, Dulal Dutta; m, Ravi Shankar; art d, Bansi Chandragupta

The young Apu (Gupta) and his newly widowed mother (Banerji) struggle for existence in a small Indian town. Resisting a life in the priesthood, the boy persuades his mother to send him to school. Having done well in his studies over the years, as a young adult (now played by Ghosal) Apu wins a scholarship to the university in Calcutta. Engulfed in city life and the demands of his schoolwork, Apu gradually forgets about his mother. APARAJITO is the second chapter in THE APU TRILOGY (preceded by PATHER PANCHALI and followed by THE WORLD OF APU), among the finest and certainly the most famous group of films to come out of India, in which director Satyajit Ray, a painter and commercial artist, devoted his time, money, and passion to a personal project that many considered impossible, the cinematic adaptation of the popular Bengali novel *Pather Panchali*. Although very slow-moving and not as involving as the first and third episodes of Apu's fortunes, APARAJITO similarly shows the influence of Italian neorealism and remains a thoughtful, colorful, and poetic story of life in India. The beautiful black-and-white photography is accented by Shankar's traditional sitar score. Winner of the Golden Lion at the 1957 Venice Film Festival.

APARTMENT, THE

1960 125m bw ★★★★★
Comedy/Drama /PG
UA

Jack Lemmon *(C.C. Baxter)*, Shirley MacLaine *(Fran Kubelik)*, Fred MacMurray *(J.D. Sheldrake)*, Ray Walston *(Mr. Dobisch)*, David Lewis *(Mr. Kirkeby)*, Jack Kruschen *(Dr. Dreyfuss)*, Joan Shawlee *(Sylvia)*, Edie Adams *(Miss Olsen)*, Hope Holiday *(Margie MacDougall)*, Johnny Seven *(Karl Matuschka)*

p, Billy Wilder; d, Billy Wilder; w, Billy Wilder, I.A.L. Diamond; ph, Joseph La Shelle (Panavision); ed, Daniel Mandell; m, Adolph Deutsch; art d, Alexander Trauner

Two vulnerable schnooks fall in love by default in a world of shoddy immorality. Heartrending comedy-drama has office scapegoat (Lemmon) nursing elevator girl (MacLaine) back from a suicide attempt after being jilted by heartless, philandering office boss (MacMurray). Director Wilder promised Lemmon a plum in exchange for committing to a drag role in SOME LIKE IT HOT. His scenes of love blooming are funny and touching and he is perfectly paired with MacLaine, whose "small business" during this phase of her career may have been better than any other actress in Hollywood, a reminder of how she made her career underacting these kind of forlorn, neurotic girls. MacMurray was a great heel, but his fan mail was so opposed to these kinds of portrayals that he comfortably stayed in the Disney camp. Fans of Wilder's character repertory will recognize mainstay Joan Shawlee as the office amazon, hilariously dancing on top of a desk at the Christmas party.

The iron-handed Billy Wilder (he would later compare Lemmon with Chaplin) shot the film right up to its finish without knowing the ending, handing his stars wet mimeographed script pages about twenty minutes before the final scenes. Quick readers, Lemmon and MacLaine then wrapped the film in one take. In describing this nerve-wracking story, Lemmon reportedly remarked: "Billy Wilder grew a rose in a garbage pail." Just as Wilder's SUNSET BOULEVARD destroyed the ancient images of sacrosanct Hollywood, THE APARTMENT is the iconoclast's raspberries to American businessmen who couple immorality with success. Both Lemmon and MacLaine were nominated for Oscars but passed over, although Wilder received the statuette for Best Director, Diamond for Best Screenplay, and the film itself was deemed best of the year. This film was later converted into the smash Broadway musical *Promises, Promises*.

APOCALYPSE NOW

1979   139m   c   ★★★★
War   R/18
UA

Marlon Brando (Col. Kurtz), Robert Duvall (Lt. Col. Kilgore), Martin Sheen (Capt. Willard), Frederic Forrest (Chef), Albert Hall (Chief), Sam Bottoms (Lance), Larry Fishburne (Clean), Dennis Hopper (Photojournalist), Harrison Ford (Colonel), Scott Glenn (Civilian)

p, Francis Ford Coppola; d, Francis Ford Coppola; w, Michael Herr, John Milius, Francis Ford Coppola; ph, Vittorio Storaro (Technovision, Technicolor); ed, Richard Marks; m, Carmine Coppola, Francis Ford Coppola; prod d, Dean Tavoularis; art d, Angelo Graham; cos, Charles James

Francis Ford Coppola's notorious and controversial contribution to the Vietnam movie subgenre remains, despite its flaws, one of the most complex and unforgettable war movies ever made. With a plot structure inspired by Joseph Conrad's *Heart of Darkness*, APOCALYPSE NOW follows Willard (Martin Sheen), a cold and amoral Army captain, as he journeys upriver into Cambodia to assassinate Col. Kurtz (Marlon Brando), a renegade Green Beret who has broken from the American military and set himself up as a god among a tribe of Montagnard warriors, using them to wage his own private war. What follows is a hallucinatory look at the madness of the American involvement in Vietnam.

More than five years in the making, APOCALYPSE NOW became a cause celebre even before it opened. As documented by numerous press accounts and the book *Notes*, a collection of journal entries written by Coppola's wife, Eleanor, the filming in the Philippines was hellish, disaster-plagued, and decadent, beginning with a $12 million budget and going over $31 million before the 238-day shooting schedule ended, with Coppola's own money making up the difference. Eleanor Coppola later used her journals, together with documentary footage shot during the production, as the basis of 1991's HEARTS OF DARKNESS, a fascinating account of the making of the film.

APPLAUSE

1929   80m   bw   ★★★★★
Drama
Paramount

Helen Morgan (Kitty Darling), Joan Peers (April Darling), Fuller Mellish, Jr. (Hitch Nelson), Jack Cameron (Joe King), Henry Wadsworth (Tony), Dorothy Cumming (Mother Superior)

p, Monta Bell; d, Rouben Mamoulian; w, Garrett Fort (based on the novel by Beth Brown); ph, George Folsey; ed, John Bassler

Morgan, the rage of Broadway musicals and nightclubs during the 1920s, is a fading burlesque singing star—she is shown to age on the stage as her born-in-a-trunk daughter grows up in a convent. The pathetic Morgan is being two-timed by a slippery boy friend. Moreover, she attempts to save her grown-up child from the clutches of fakes and ne'er-do-wells. Poignant though dated, this early talkie is rich in old burlesque backstage atmosphere and has many innovative techniques introduced by Mamoulian in his directorial debut. Then there is Morgan's singing, which is captivating and distinctive. She made her screen debut in this picture and would die of cirrhosis of the liver in 1941 at age 41.

APPRENTICESHIP OF DUDDY KRAVITZ, THE

1974   120m   c   ★★★
Comedy/Drama   PG/15
International Cinemedia Centre   (Canada)

Richard Dreyfuss (Duddy), Micheline Lanctot (Yvette), Jack Warden (Max), Randy Quaid (Virgil), Joseph Wiseman (Uncle Benjy), Denholm Elliott (Friar), Henry Ramer (Dingleman), Joe Silver (Farber), Zvee Scooler (Grandfather), Robert Goodier (Calder)

p, John Kemeny; d, Ted Kotcheff; w, Mordecai Richler (based on his novel); ph, Brian West (Panavision, Bellevue-Pathe Color); ed, Thom Noble; m, Stanley Meyers; prod d, Anne Pritchard

Dreyfuss, a zealous Jewish boy determined to become rich in the world, loses all personal contact with women, friends, and family in his desperate business transactions. A strong, often very funny film that points out the potential emotional loss in the pressure to succeed put on the young by families. Not anti-Semitic, the film means to point out the corruption of youth and power of greed in all young people, not the Jews alone, although the film did receive many negative reactions from Jewish groups, as did the book it is based on. Dreyfuss, who later went on to become one of the better-known faces of the 1970s, turns in an early great performance, making Duddy simultaneously loathsome, funny, and vulnerable. British actor Elliott masterfully portrays the washed-up British director Dreyfuss hires to make Bar Mitzvah movies for his relatives. In the most hilarious scene in the film, Dreyfuss's relatives are stunned to see that "artsy" filmmaker Elliott has juxtaposed Bar Mitzvah scenes with footage detailing African tribal dances celebrating the circumcision rights of the young warriors. Although there are quite a few holes in the script and Dreyfuss is undeniably grating, THE APPRENTICESHIP OF DUDDY KRAVITZ is a sad, funny, memorable film.

ARABESQUE

1966   107m   c   ★★★
Spy   /A
Universal   (U.S./U.K.)

Gregory Peck (David Pollock), Sophia Loren (Yasmin Azir), Alan Badel (Beshraavi), Kieron Moore (Yussef Kassim), Carl Duering (Hassan Jena), John Merivale (Sloane), Duncan Lamont (Webster), George Coulouris (Ragheeb), Ernest Clark (Beauchamp), Harold Kasket (Mohammed Lufti)

p, Stanley Donen; d, Stanley Donen; w, Julian Mitchell, Stanley Price, Peter Stone (based on the novel *The Cipher* by Gordon Cotler); ph, Christopher Challis (Technicolor); ed, Frederick Wilson; m, Henry Mancini; art d, Reece Pemberton

Fluffy espionage caper has an American hieroglyphics professor visiting Oxford, agree to decipher a secret message—the contents of which are wanted by spies, oil sheiks, and Middle Eastern leaders— aided by the sensuous mistress of a politically ambitious oil tycoon. Donen repeated CHARADE in the making of this film, rightly assuming that film's success deserved another attempt. Loren's glamorous wardrobe is by Dior and included some 50 pairs of shoes for her character—a 50,000-pound costuming expense—explained away by her lover's *shoe fetish!* It's all mindless, absurdly complex and hopelessly hip in that 1960s sort of way, but an agreeable way to pass the time with gorgeous Sophia. Cinematographer Christopher Challis won an award from the British Film Academy for Best Color Photography.

AROUND THE WORLD IN 80 DAYS

1956   175m   c   ★★★★
Adventure   /U
Michael Todd

David Niven (*Phileas Fogg*), Cantinflas (*Passepartout*), Shirley MacLaine (*Princess Aouda*), Robert Newton (*Inspector Fix*), Charles Boyer (*Monsieur Casse*), Joe E. Brown (*Station Master*), Martine Carol (*Tourist*), John Carradine (*Col. Proctor Stamp*), Charles Coburn (*Clerk*), Ronald Colman (*Railway Official*)

p, Michael Todd; d, Michael Anderson; w, S.J. Perelman, John Farrow, James Poe (based on the novel by Jules Verne); ph, Lionel Lindon (Todd-AO, Eastmancolor); ed, Gene Ruggiero, Paul Weatherwax; m, Victor Young; art d, James Sullivan, Ken Adam; fx, Lee Zavitz; chor, Paul Godkin; cos, Miles White

David Niven is the punctual Phileas Fogg of the famous Jules Verne novel, who makes a bet with his fellow club members in London that he can encircle the globe within 80 days—this in 1872, when travel proceeded at a snail's pace. Fogg is accompanied by his bumbling valet (the great Mexican mimic Cantinflas) and along the way picks up a wandering princess (Shirley MacLaine), while being pursued by a London detective (Robert Newton) who believes the globetrotter has somehow robbed the Bank of England. Around these leads an army of 46 famous personalities of the day appear in bit parts. (This was the film that began the trend of stars appearing in cameo roles.) The star-spotting is fun, but so is the adventure, as Fogg journeys by train, ship, hot-air balloon, and elephant across Europe, India, Japan, the Pacific, the US, and the Atlantic in a race to win his bet. The film was shot in more than 100 natural settings and on 140 special sets. Everything about this big, beautiful movie smacks of authenticity, excitement, and massive showmanship. Winner of five Oscars: Best Picture, Best Screenplay, Best Cinematography, Best Score and Best Film Editing.

AROUND THE WORLD IN EIGHTY WAYS
1987 91m c   ★★½
Comedy
Palm Beach/Australian European Finance   (Australia)

Philip Quast (*Wally Davis*), Allan Penney (*Roly Davis*), Gosia Dobrowolska (*Nurse Ophelia Cox*), Diana Davidson (*Mavis Davis*), Kelly Dingwall (*Eddie Davis*), Rob Steele (*Alec Moffatt*), Judith Fisher (*Lotte Boyle*), Jane Markey (*Miserable Midge*), John Howard (*Dr. Proctor*), Frank Lloyd (*Mr. Tinkle*)

p, David Elfick, Steve Knapman; d, Stephen Maclean; w, Stephen Maclean, Paul Leadon; ph, Louis Irving (Colorfilm); ed, Marc von Buuren; m, Chris Neal; prod d, Lissa Coote; cos, Clarrissa Patterson

Bizarre but engaging comedy about two Aussie brothers out to spring their aged dad from a rest home and take him around the world. The cast all seem to be having a good time, with Quast and Dobrowolska particularly delightful. The obviously heavy budgetary constraints only seem to enhance the story, in which the sons don't have much money for staging their illusions either. Director Maclean makes his feature debut here, and an auspiciously loopy one it is.

ARROWSMITH
1931 108m bw   ★★½
Drama   /A
Goldwyn

Ronald Colman (*Dr. Martin Arrowsmith*), Helen Hayes (*Leora*), A.E. Anson (*Prof. Gottlieb*), Richard Bennett (*Sondelius*), Claude King (*Dr. Tubbs*), Beulah Bondi (*Mrs. Tozer*), Myrna Loy (*Joyce Lanyon*), Russell Hopton (*Terry Wickett*), DeWitt Jennings (*Mr. Tozer*), John Qualen (*Henry Novak*)

p, Samuel Goldwyn; d, John Ford; w, Sidney Howard (based on the novel by Sinclair Lewis); ph, Ray June; ed, Hugh Bennett; m, Alfred Newman

Idealistic doctor Ronald Colman is obsessed with finding a cure for bubonic plague and wrestling with his moral conscience in this uneven Sidney Howard adaptation of Sinclair Lewis's novel. Hayes gets the big death scene, Loy gets the sexy seduction bits, John Ford gets the blame. Immensely popular with audiences and listed as one of the year's best films by *The New York Times*, ARROWSMITH was nominated as Best Picture but thankfully lost out to GRAND HOTEL.

ARSENIC AND OLD LACE
1944 118m bw   ★★★½
Comedy   /PG
WB

Cary Grant (*Mortimer Brewster*), Raymond Massey (*Jonathan Brewster*), Priscilla Lane (*Elaine Harper*), Josephine Hull (*Abby Brewster*), Jean Adair (*Martha Brewster*), Jack Carson (*O'Hara*), Edward Everett Horton (*Mr. Witherspoon*), Peter Lorre (*Dr. Einstein*), James Gleason (*Lt. Rooney*), John Alexander (*"Teddy Roosevelt" Brewster*)

p, Frank Capra; d, Frank Capra; w, Julius J. Epstein, Philip G. Epstein (based on the play by Joseph Kesselring); ph, Sol Polito; ed, Daniel Mandell; m, Max Steiner; art d, Max Parker; fx, Byron Haskin, Robert Burks

Riotously funny film adaptation of the smash Broadway comedy (which ran for almost four years), coddled and coaxed into hilarious existence by master director Capra. The lovable Brewster sisters are spinster pillars of Brooklyn society, except for their secret penchant for poisoning old male callers with their homemade elderberry wine, to end the men's loneliness! Grant plays their frantic nephew who discovers their serial murders. The punch line that ended the play was cut by censors; the line in occurs after Grant learns he is free of hereditary insanity, and yells elatedly to his fiance: "Elaine! Did you hear? Do you understand? I'm a bastard!" Additional comedic lunacy results from macabre team of Lorre and Massey (the latter in a part made famous on Broadway by Boris Karloff) and Alexander as an eccentric uncle who believes he's Teddy Roosevelt.

   ARSENIC was Capra's pet from beginning to end. He saw the play in New York and rushed backstage to buy the property, only to be told that Warner Brothers (his studio was Columbia) had optioned the film rights. He immediately went to the WB studio and had Jack Warner's own people prepare a modest budget, $400,000, for a hectic four-week shooting schedule ($100,000 for the star salary Grant demanded). Capra used only one interior set, that of the spooky old house belonging to the aunts, and an exterior set of the house next to an ancient cemetery. The lighting was low-keyed, from dusk to night, in keeping with the eerie atmosphere. Capra came in on schedule as usual and produced a romping, ripsnorting comedy classic.

ARTHUR
1981 117m c   ★★★
Comedy   PG/15
Orion

Dudley Moore (*Arthur Bach*), Liza Minnelli (*Linda Marolla*), John Gielgud (*Hobson*), Geraldine Fitzgerald (*Martha Bach*), Jill Eikenberry (*Susan Johnson*), Stephen Elliott (*Burt Johnson*), Ted Ross (*Bitterman*), Barney Martin (*Ralph Marolla*), Thomas Barbour (*Stanford Bach*), Anne DeSalvo (*Gloria*) p, Robert Greenhut; d, Steve Gordon; w, Steve Gordon; ph, Fred Schuler (Technicolor); ed, Susan E. Morse; m, Burt Bacharach; prod d, Stephen Hendrickson; cos, Jane Greenwood

Dudley Moore plays Arthur Bach, a dissolute playboy who would rather be drunk than face the reality of his great wealth and engagement to WASP witch Susan Johnson (Jill Eikenberry). Arthur, who is looked after by his kindly valet, Hobson (John Gielgud), soon falls for working girl Linda Marolla (Liza Minnelli), whom he prefers to his socialite fiancee. Susan, however, refuses to be shunned, and Arthur's father and grandmother threaten to cut off his inheritance if he continues to see working-class Linda. Moore is predictable as the spoiled scion of wealth, Minnelli is terrific as his candid sweetheart, but Gielgud's loyal yet sarcastic servant steals the film (he was rewarded with a supporting actor Oscar). The highly polished production is well paced and imaginatively directed, although the happy union of prince and pauper is harder to swallow in 1981 than it would have been in 1931, when cinematic escapism brought relief to depression-era audiences. A flat sequel, ARTHUR 2 ON THE ROCKS, was released in 1988.

ASCENDANCY
1983 92m c   ★★
Drama   /15
British Film Institute   (U.K.)

Julie Covington (Connie), Ian Charleson (Ryder), John Phillips (Wintour), Susan Engel (Nurse), Philip Locke (Dr. Strickland), Kieran Montague (Dr. Kelso)

p, Penny Clark, Ian Elsey; d, Edward Bennett; w, Edward Bennett, Nigel Gearing; ph, Clive Tickner; ed, Charles Rees, George Akers; m, Ronnie Leahy; art d, Jamie Leonard

The first feature film from British documentary filmmaker Edward Bennett, this is a cinematic response to the problems between England and Ireland. Set just after WWI, the story deals with a young girl from a wealthy family who protests the horrors of Belfast with crippling effects on her body. The girl loses the use of her right arm soon after her brother is killed on the battlefield. This is followed by her becoming mute when the growing tension between the Catholics and the Protestants explodes. There is an inherent problem in exploring the deep emotional aspects of the Irish problem using this kind of metaphor. The silence of the girl is an interesting symbol, but it alienates viewers from the character it is supposed to identify with. The audience must provide the motivations and emotions of the main character because she cannot respond verbally. The director, therefore, is forced to provide purely visual images that comment on the material.

ASHES AND DIAMONDS
(POPIOL Y DIAMENT)
1958 105m bw   ★★★★★
War   /X
Janus   (Poland)

Zbigniew Cybulski (Maciek), Eva Krzyzewski (Christine), Adam Pawlikowski (Andrzej), Waclaw Zastrzezynski (Szczuka), Bogumil Kobiela (Drewnowski), Jan Ciecierski (Porter), Stanislaw Milski (Pienionzek), Artur Mlodnicki (Kotowicz), Halina Kwiatkoska (Mrs. Staniewicz), Ignacy Machowski (Waga)

d, Andrzej Wajda; w, Andrzej Wajda, Jerzy Andrzejewski (based on the novel by Jerzy Andrzejewski); ph, Jerzy Wojcik; ed, Halina Nawrocka; m, Aroclaw Radio Quintet; art d, Roman Mann

Set on the first day of peace after the end of WWII, this disturbing film concentrates on the conflicts that remained between Polish political factions at the end of their struggle against the Germans. Director Andrzej Wajda's brilliance is evident from the film's opening ambush scene, in which he establishes the moral dilemma facing the Poles as they begin the internecine struggle to determine who will shape their country's future. A film of great power, ASHES AND DIAMONDS was Wajda's third feature and the final chapter in his "war trilogy," preceded in 1954 by A GENERATION and in 1957 by KANAL. Cybulski, the "Polish James Dean," scored an acting triumph as a result of his emoting. It was released in the US in 1961.

ASPHALT JUNGLE, THE
1950 112m bw   ★★★★★
Crime   /A
MGM

Sterling Hayden (Dix Handley), Louis Calhern (Alonzo D. Emmerich), Jean Hagen (Doll Conovan), James Whitmore (Gus Ninissi), Sam Jaffe (Doc Erwin Riedenschneider), John McIntire (Police Commissioner Hardy), Marc Lawrence (Cobby), Barry Kelley (Lt. Ditrich), Anthony Caruso (Louis Ciavelli), Teresa Celli (Maria Ciavelli)

p, Arthur Hornblow, Jr.; d, John Huston; w, Ben Maddow, John Huston (based on the novel by W.R. Burnett); ph, Harold Rosson; ed, George Boemler; m, Miklos Rozsa; art d, Cedric Gibbons, Randall Duell

Adapted by director John Huston and co-screenwriter Ben Maddow from the novel by W.R. Burnett, this classic, often copied but never equaled, focuses on the robbery of a swank jewelry firm, meticulously planned by master criminal "Doc" Erwin Riedenschneider (Sam Jaffe) while imprisoned. Alonzo D. Emmerich (Louis Calhern) is a sleazy lawyer who'll fence the stolen jewels, giving "Doc" and his cohorts $1 million for their labors. The assembled gang includes Dix Handley (Sterling Hayden), a somewhat dumb but standup fellow who has dreams of buying back his father's Kentucky horse ranch; Gus Ninissi (James Whitmore), a tough-as-nails, cat-loving hunchback who runs a diner; and Louis Ciavelli (Anthony Caruso), a professional thief who's enlisted to blow the safe under Riedenschneider's supervision. After carefully drilling the gang members, "Doc" leads the men on the robbery attempt. The safe is blown and the gems secured, but his "perfect" crime immediately unravels.

Huston directed this superb production with tremendous assurance, developing his characters incisively but not at the expense of the rapidly developing plot. Indeed, THE ASPHALT JUNGLE boasts a rogues' gallery of definitive portrayals, led by creepy mastermind Jaffe, whose voyeuristic pursuit of Lolitas finally frames him. Calhern figures nicely as the crooked lawyer who keeps Monroe, in an outstanding cameo that foretold her future stardom. Jean Hagen's moll is a rare lead female performance, poignant and subtly shaded, that is totally devoid of studio-era vanity. Rosson's moody photography and Rozsa's moving score further enhance this *film noir* masterpiece.

ASSAULT, THE
1986 155m c   ★★★★
Drama/War   PG
Cannon   (Netherlands)

Derek De Lint (Anton Steenwijk), Marc van Uchelen (Anton as a Boy), Monique Van de Ven (Truus Coster/Saskia de Graaff), John Kraaykamp (Cor Takes), Huub van der Lubbe (Fake Ploeg/His

35

Father), Elly Weller *(Mrs. Beumer)*, Ina van der Molen *(Karin Korteweg)*, Frans Vorstman *(Father Steenwijk)*, Edda Barends *(Mother Steenwijk)*, Caspar De Boer *(Peter Steenwijk)*

p, Fons Rademakers; d, Fons Rademakers; w, Gerard Soeteman (based on the novel by Harry Mulisch); ph, Theo Van de Sande (Fujicolor); ed, Kees Linthorst; m, Jurriaan Andriessen; art d, Dorus van der Linden; fx, Harry Wiesenhaan; cos, Anne-Marie van Beverwijk

A powerful motion picture that poses more questions than it answers, THE ASSAULT will haunt anyone who understands the tragic psychological effects of emotional repression. Spanning a 40-year period, it begins in Holland as the war is waning and the Germans realize they will be beaten. One night while dining by candlelight during curfew, a Dutch family sees a local collaborator killed by a sniper. Fearing that they will be blamed, the family watches in horror as their neighbors drag the body in front of their home. Soon Germans are everywhere, the family is arrested and shot, their house is burned, and the son, Anton (Marc van Uchelen), is taken away to prison. Years later, he becomes a physician, marries, and has his own family, but the memory of that bleak night continues to haunt him.

Winner of the 1986 Academy Award for Best Foreign Film, THE ASSAULT is a powerful indictment of the Nazi horror, although it seldom editorializes. Much more than the war picture it begins as, this documentary-like Dutch film explores lives that have been torn apart by German occupation.

ASSAULT ON PRECINCT 13

1976 91m c   ★★★
Action   R/18
Turtle

Austin Stoker *(Bishop)*, Darwin Joston *(Wilson)*, Laurie Zimmer *(Leigh)*, Martin West *(Lawson)*, Tony Burton *(Wells)*, Charles Cyphers *(Starker)*, Nancy Loomis *(Julie)*, Peter Bruni *(Ice Cream Man)*, John J. Fox *(Warden)*, Kim Richards *(Kathy)*

p, J.S. Kaplan; d, John Carpenter; w, John Carpenter; ph, Douglas Knapp (Metrocolor); ed, John T. Chance; m, John Carpenter; art d, Tommy Wallace; cos, Louise Kyes

Not really a horror film but one that often comes up during discussions of George Romero's NIGHT OF THE LIVING DEAD, this early John Carpenter effort still holds up as one of the director's best works.

A low-budget and taut update of the classic Howard Hawks western RIO BRAVO, set in modern-day Los Angeles, the story concerns a lengthy siege by a multiracial street gang on a soon-to-be-closed police station. The gang has murdered a young girl, whose father runs to the station for help. This man is in a state of shock and cannot speak to the lone cop, Bishop (Austin Stoker), or to the two secretaries (Zimmer and Loomis) waiting for the moving vans to take what's left of the station's file cabinets. Unexpectedly, two death-row prisoners arrive and are put in holding cells until authorities can find a place for them (the state prison is overcrowded). As night falls, the gang attacks in full force, riddling the station with bullets shot from guns with silencers. The gang cuts the electricity and phone lines, rendering the station helpless in the center of the neighborhood. The inmates demand to be let loose so that they can defend themselves and prove themselves honorable men.

The shadowy photography, great editing, snappy dialogue, and a moody synthesizer score by Carpenter himself make ASSAULT ON PRECINCT 13 one of the most successful homages to the Hawks brand of filmmaking—and a very impressive

film in its own right. The parallels with Romero's film are obvious (the street gang is reminiscent of Romero's zombies), and Carpenter, who often borrows character names and situations from films and filmmakers he admires, may well have intended it that way.

ASYA'S HAPPINESS

(ISTORIYA AS: KLYACHIMOL)
1988 90m bw   ★★★½
Drama   /PG
Mosfilm   (U.S.S.R.)

Iya Savina *(Asya Klyachkina)*, Aleksandr Surin, Lyubov Sokolova, Geniadij Egorytschev, Ivan Petrov

d, Andrei Konchalovsky; w, Yuri Klepikov; ph, Georgy Rerberg; m, Vyacheslav Ovchinnikov

A masterpiece in the great tradition of Soviet realism, ASYA'S HAPPINESS also bears the influence of its time (it was made in 1967, but was previously banned), drawing on contemporary New Wave movements in France, Poland, and Czechoslovakia. It focuses on Savina as the title character, a cheerful, slightly lame young woman who runs the canteen on a collective farm in the steppes of a Siberian province. It is the height of the sun-scorched summer, and men, women, and children alike tend to the harvest. Despite her difficult surroundings, Savina has a zest for life, and her free-spiritedness has resulted in her pregnancy by a fellow farmer. She is in love with this young man, but he refuses to marry her. Another worker, who is less handsome and invites her to live in the city, does want to marry Savina, but she cannot surrender herself to a man she does not love. By the film's end, Savina has given birth by herself—lying on her lover's sweaty workshirt in the weeds in the middle of the night, while he runs around frantically, unable to help or even watch. Later, she turns away from both men, facing her future on her own and cradling her child—the Soviet future—in her arms.

A simple, straightforward narrative, ASYA'S HAPPINESS is a monument of realism with personal, cinematic flourishes. Two of the film's finest scenes are documentary accounts delivered by nonprofessionals (only the three leads are trained actors): the first by a weather-beaten farmer with a mangled hand who speaks of his war experiences, the second by an aging, defeated man who looks back on a wasted life without love or hope. It is not only these speakers's testimonies that shake the viewer but the reactions of those around them as they realize that their lives, too, are full of bleak hardship. ASYA'S HAPPINESS is not all depression, however. Much of it is a celebration of film, intensified by Konchalovsky's inspired and energetic camera work. As Asya, Savina shines. Although not especially beautiful, she has a glowing face that penetrates the clouds of grain dust. The rest of the cast is equally effective, none of the behavioral "performances" ever less than perfect.

Apparently because Konchalovsky presented his main character as pregnant and unwed—a morally and socially unacceptable characterization—the film was locked away by Soviet authorities and not released until 1987. (It was not, however, completely banned: a "Variety" review appeared in July 1978 after a private screening of the film arranged by Konchalovsky as a sidebar to the Moscow Film Festival.) With Mikhail Gorbachev's policy of *glasnost*, the film again saw the light of a projector; Gorbachev even reportedly commented that it was one of the finest films he had seen in the last 10 years. Entered in competition at the 1988 Berlin Film Festival, ASYA'S HAPPINESS received some screenings around the US and a showing at the New York Film Festival.

AT CLOSE RANGE

1986   111m   c   ★★★½
Crime   R/15
Hemdale

Sean Penn *(Brad Whitewood, Jr.)*, Christopher Walken *(Brad Whitewood, Sr.)*, Mary Stuart Masterson *(Terry)*, Christopher Penn *(Tommy Whitewood)*, Millie Perkins *(Julie Whitewood)*, Eileen Ryan *(Grandmother)*, Alan Autry *(Ernie)*, Candy Clark *(Mary Sue)*, R.D. Call *(Dickie Whitewood)*, Tracey Walter *(Patch)*

p, Elliott Lewitt, Don Guest; d, James Foley; w, Nicholas Kazan (based on a story by Lewitt and Kazan); ph, Juan Ruiz-Anchia (Panavision, CFI Color); ed, Howard Smith; m, Patrick Leonard; prod d, Peter Jamison; fx, Burt Dalton, Adams Calvert; cos, Hilary Rosenfeld

A chilling and realistic crime film, AT CLOSE RANGE features strong performances by Christopher Walken and Sean Penn. The film follows fresh-out-of-high-school Brad Whitewood, Jr. (Penn), as he struggles against the boredom of his rural existence. Living in a run-down house with his half-brother, Tommy (Christopher Penn, Sean's brother), his grandmother (Eileen Ryan, the Penn boys' mother), and his mother (Millie Perkins), Brad coasts along until two events change his life forever: he falls in love with Terry (Mary Stuart Masterson), and his wayward father (Walken) wanders back on the scene.

A relentlessly grim film, AT CLOSE RANGE offers a frightening glimpse at the dark side of American life and poses disturbing questions about family ties. Unfortunately, although director James Foley handles the performances with skill, he also indulges in too many flashy directorial pyrotechnics, muting the emotional impact potential. Writer Nicholas Kazan (son of director Elia) based his script on the Johnston family murders in Pennsylvania in 1978.

AT LONG LAST LOVE

1975   118m   c   ★½
Musical   G/U
FOX

Burt Reynolds *(Michael Oliver Pritchard III)*, Cybill Shepherd *(Brooke Carter)*, Madeline Kahn *(Kitty O'Kelly)*, Duilio Del Prete *(Johnny Spanish)*, Eileen Brennan *(Elizabeth)*, John Hillerman *(Rodney James)*, Mildred Natwick *(Mabel Pritchard)*, Quinn Redeker *(Phillip)*, J. Edward McKinley *(Billings)*, John Stephenson *(Abbott)*

p, Peter Bogdanovich; d, Peter Bogdanovich; w, Peter Bogdanovich; ph, Laszlo Kovacs (DeLuxe Color); ed, Douglas Robertson; art d, John Lloyd; chor, Albert Lantieri, Rita Abrams; cos, Bobbie Mannix

One of the worst bombs of the 1970s, this foolish attempt at re-creating the lush musicals of the 1930s offers fabulous art deco sets, memorable Cole Porter songs, and slick production values, yet it goes down like a stricken elephant.

The inconsequential plot follows the champagne-swilling exploits of four wealthy gadabouts (Reynolds, Shepherd, Kahn, and Del Prete) who burst into song or get happy feet on the slightest pretext. Shepherd, who was romantically involved with critic-turned-director Bogdanovich at the time, has a bitchy comedy line but her singing, while not inept, isn't magnetic, either. Reynolds's casting seems a total mystery, unless it was for box-office; his two left feet and thin, strained voice offer not a clue. Porter's songs are here recorded "live" on film (rather

than lip-synched), a mistake of overwhelming porportions, considering the leads, and while you're dreading the next song, the witless script, like Old Man River, just keeps rollin' along.

ATLANTIC CITY

1981   104m   c   ★★★★
Crime/Romance   R/15
Paramount   (U.S./Canada)

Burt Lancaster *(Lou)*, Susan Sarandon *(Sally)*, Kate Reid *(Grace)*, Michel Piccoli *(Joseph)*, Hollis McLaren *(Chrissie)*, Robert Joy *(Dave)*, Al Waxman *(Alfie)*, Robert Goulet *(Singer)*, Moses Znaimer *(Felix)*, Angus MacInnes *(Vinnie)*

p, Denis Heroux; d, Louis Malle; w, John Guare; ph, Richard Ciupka; ed, Suzanne Baron; m, Michel Legrand; prod d, Anne Pritchard; cos, Francois Barbeau

Richly sad portraits of wasted American lives, seen with a European ambience. Burt Lancaster, in a masterful performance, plays Lou, an aging small-time criminal who hangs around Atlantic City doing odd jobs and taking care of the broken-down moll (the poignant Kate Reid) of the deceased gangster for whom Lou had been a gofer. Living in an invented past, Lou identifies with yesteryear's notorious gangsters and gets involved with sexy would-be croupier, Sally (Susan Sarandon), and her drug-dealing estranged husband (Robert Joy).

French director Louis Malle (PRETTY BABY, AU REVOIR LES ENFANTS) wastes little footage here, though his nostalgia for seamy Americana is sometimes off the mark. The script by playwright John Guare is equally taut, sparked by dialogue that feels authentic. But the film leaves an impression of empty, free-form sadness, like sand blowing across vacant lots in Atlantic City where grand hotels once stood; the viewer wants to care, but isn't sure why he should.

ATTACK!

1956   107m   bw   ★★★
War   /A
UA

Jack Palance *(Lt. Costa)*, Eddie Albert *(Capt. Cooney)*, Lee Marvin *(Col. Bartlett)*, Robert Strauss *(Pvt. Bernstein)*, Richard Jaeckel *(Pvt. Snowden)*, Buddy Ebsen *(Sgt. Tolliver)*, William Smithers *(Lt. Woodruff)*, Jon Shepodd *(Cpl. Jackson)*, James Goodwin *(Pvt. Ricks)*, Steven Geray *(Short German)*

p, Robert Aldrich; d, Robert Aldrich; w, James Poe (based on the play "The Fragile Fox" by Norman Brooks); ph, Joseph Biroc; ed, Michael Luciano; m, Frank DeVol

No sensibilities are spared in this brutal portrait of infantry warfare, featuring a powerful performance by Palance. In 1944 Belgium, Albert is a coward who has achieved the rank of captain only because of his father's political power. Because Marvin's political ambitions can be served by Albert's family, he overlooks Albert's imcompetence. But Palance and his platoon (Ebsen, Jaeckel, Strauss) feel victimized, particularly Palance who becomes an almost supernatural force of vengeance. A cynical and grim account of war, ATTACK! features excellent performances from the entire cast and is one of director Aldrich's best films.

ATTACK OF THE KILLER TOMATOES

1978   87m   c   ★
Comedy/Horror   PG
NAI

David Miller *(Mason Dixon)*, George Wilson *(Jim Richardson)*, Sharon Taylor *(Lois Fairchild)*, Jack Riley *(Agriculture Official)*, Rock Peace *(Wilbur Finletter)*, Eric Christmas *(Senator Polk)*, Al Sklar *(Ted Swan)*, Ernie Meyers *(President)*, Jerry Anderson *(Major Milis)*, Ron Shapiro *(Newspaper Editor)*

p, J. Stephen Peace, John De Bello; d, John De Bello; w, Costa Dillon, J. Stephen Peace, John De Bello; ph, John K. Culley; m, Gordon Goodwin, Paul Sundfur

In a cynical bid for cult success, ATTACK OF THE KILLER TOMATOES employs calculatedly bad acting, ridiculous special effects, and inane dialog. Though it succeeded to some degree in achieving its goal, it's a thoroughly dull, unfunny effort. The film tries too hard at being ridiculous, and though the idea of savage vegetables rolling around the city splattering innocent bystanders sounds funny, actually sitting through nearly 90 minutes of it is enough to make anyone long for ATTACK OF THE 50 FOOT WOMAN. There are some funny song parodies, but that's about it.

AU HASARD, BALTHAZAR
1967 95m c   ★★★★★
Drama
New Line (France)

Anne Wiazemsky *(Marie)*, Francois Lafarge *(Gerard)*, Philippe Asselin *(Marie's Father)*, Nathalie Joyaut *(Marie's Mother)*, Walter Green *(Jacques)*, Jean-Claude Guilbert *(Arnold)*, Pierre Klossowski *(Merchant)*, Francois Sullerot *(Baker)*, M.C. Fremont *(Baker's Wife)*, Jean Remignard *(Notary)*

p, Mag Bodard; d, Robert Bresson; w, Robert Bresson; ph, Ghislain Cloquet; ed, Raymond Lamy; m, Jean Wiener; art d, Pierre Charbonnier

This poignant film is a powerful portrait of humanity seen through the life of a donkey. The animal is first the loving plaything of small children in rural France, then a working beast of burden named by a sullen child. As the girl grows up, the donkey's fortunes worsen with the young woman's when she is gang-raped and dies. Her sadistic lover, a leader of a motorcycle gang, tortures the donkey by setting its tail on fire. The donkey's life intersects with the lives of many of its other owners, as well. A brutal farmer owns the animal and beats it, but is finished off in grim irony. Then the donkey has a respite in becoming a momentary circus star, but then again returns to tilling the soil. It ends its days with a simple-minded but loving old man who considers the animal a saint. This great film, made with uncompromising honesty and devastating reality, is, according to Jean-Luc Godard, "the world in an hour and a half." Music includes Franz Schubert's "Piano Sonata No. 20."

AU REVOIR LES ENFANTS
1988 104m c   ★★★
Drama/War   PG
Nouvelle Editions de Films/MK2/Stella (France)

Gaspard Manesse *(Julien Quentin)*, Raphael Fejto *(Jean Bonnet)*, Francine Racette *(Mme. Quentin)*, Stanislas Carre de Malberg *(Francois Quentin)*, Philippe Morier-Genoud *(Father Jean)*, Francois Berleand *(Father Michel)*, Francois Negret *(Joseph)*, Peter Fitz *(Muller)*, Pascal Rivet *(Boulanger)*, Benoit Henriet *(Ciron)*

p, Louis Malle; d, Louis Malle; w, Louis Malle; ph, Renato Berta (Eastmancolor); ed, Emmanuelle Castro; m, Franz Schubert, Camille Saint-Saens; cos, Corinne Jorry

This sincere but curiously unemotional quasi-autobiography from Louis Malle is set in January, 1944, during the German Occupation of France. After spending the holidays with his mother, 12-year-old Julien (Gaspard Manesse) is sent to a provincial Catholic boarding school, where he is brighter than all of his classmates except one—Bonnet (Raphael Fejto), a new arrival who, like Julien, has a great love of books. Their friendship grows and eventually Julien learns Bonnet's secret: he is one of three Jews being hidden from the Gestapo by the school's gutsy cleric, Fr. Jean (Philippe Morier-Genoud). Based on a childhood trauma experienced by producer-director-writer Malle, AU REVOIR LES ENFANTS is a deeply personal project that he had long wanted to make. Unfortunately, though finely crafted, the film fails to generate the emotional power one would expect from a film dealing with such personal, painful subject matter. It nevertheless hit home with many audiences, winning the Golden Lion at the 1987 Venice Film Festival, and earning two Oscar nominations—Best Foreign Film and Best Screenplay.

AUNTIE MAME
1958 143m c   ★★★★
Comedy   /A
WB

Rosalind Russell *(Mame Dennis)*, Forrest Tucker *(Beauregard Burnside)*, Coral Browne *(Vera Charles)*, Fred Clark *(Mr. Babcock)*, Roger Smith *(Patrick Dennis)*, Patric Knowles *(Lindsay Woolsey)*, Peggy Cass *(Agnes Gooch)*, Jan Handzlik *(Patrick Dennis as a Child)*, Joanna Barnes *(Gloria Upson)*, Pippa Scott *(Pegeen Ryan)*

d, Morton Da Costa; w, Betty Comden, Adolph Green (based on the novel *Mame* by Patrick Dennis and the play by Jerome Lawrence, Robert E. Lee); ph, Harry Stradling (Technirama, Technicolor); ed, William Ziegler; m, Bronislau Kaper; art d, Malcolm Bert; cos, Orry-Kelly

A showcase for the spectacular talents of Russell, who made the play a Broadway hit. Eccentric, colorful Mame Dennis adopts an orphan boy, exposing him to all manner of extravagant and bizarre characters in the 1920s and 1930s. The film is a trifle overlong and episodic, but Russell is supported in high style by a talented cast. Look for many amusing 1950s art direction and costume touches that are unusual. For once Hollywood agreed that Broadway's casting couldn't be improved; Russell's way with words, her rhythms, speed, and timing are irreplacably, impeccably right.

AUTHOR! AUTHOR!
1982 110m c   ★★
Comedy   PG
FOX

Al Pacino *(Travalian)*, Dyan Cannon *(Alice Detroit)*, Tuesday Weld *(Gloria)*, Alan King *(Kreplich)*, Bob Dishy *(Finestein)*, Bob Elliott *(Patrick Dicker)*, Ray Goulding *(Jackie Dicker)*, Eric Gurry *(Igor)*, Elva Leff *(Bonnie)*, B.J. Barie *(Spike)*

p, Irwin Winkler; d, Arthur Hiller; w, Israel Horovitz; ph, Victor J. Kemper (TVC Lab Color); ed, William Reynolds; m, Dave Grusin; prod d, Gene Rudolf; cos, Gloria Gresham

Successful playwright Al Pacino attempts to ply his trade, but his neurotic wife, Tuesday Weld, and her pestering but lovable children, the products of her four marriages, continually interrupt him. Just as the writer is about to complete his first play in two years, Weld takes off to live with another man, leaving him to manage the children, rehearsals, and Dyan Cannon, his new leading lady in real life and onstage. Israel Horowitz's script fails to develop sympathetic adult characters, leaving the children to give the film whatever charm it may have.

AUTUMN LEAVES
1956 107m bw ★★★
Drama /X
Columbia

Joan Crawford (Milly), Cliff Robertson (Burt Hanson), Vera Miles (Virginia), Lorne Greene (Mr. Hanson), Ruth Donnelly (Liz), Shepperd Strudwick (Dr. Couzzens), Selmer Jackson (Mr. Wetherby), Maxine Cooper (Nurse Evans), Marjorie Bennett (Waitress), Frank Gerstle (Mr. Ramsey)

p, William Goetz; d, Robert Aldrich; w, Jack Jevne, Lewis Meltzer, Robert Blees; ph, Charles Lang; ed, Michael Luciano; m, H.J. Salter

Butch-bobbed, bug-eyed career gal spinster Crawford meets shy Cliff Robertson and grabs for love, gets a schizo. Released a year after the nihilist film noir classic KISS ME DEADLY, the film recaptured the twisted qualities of the human mind. Labeled a "woman's picture," AUTUMN LEAVES is an intense melodrama about loneliness, despair, and mental illness. Taking a pleasant romantic tale and plunging it into a whirlwind of schizophrenic violence has the same effect as seeing a hammer shatter a shiny piece of glass. Almost like a nightmare going on in Crawford's mind, the film's visual style gets more and more distorted and the lighting very harsh as Robertson's schizophrenia builds. Joan's performance is on the money and the Crawford cult will enjoy her "reading" Lorne Greene and Vera Miles as she chases them down the street ("And you, ya slut!"). The lady later said Robert Aldrich "likes evil things, twisted things." The title song, penned by Joseph Kosma, Jacques Prevert, and Johnny Mercer, was a big hit for Nat King Cole.

AUTUMN SONATA
1978 97m c ★★½
Drama PG/15
ITC (Sweden)

Ingrid Bergman (Charlotte), Liv Ullmann (Eva), Lena Nyman (Helena), Halvar Bjork (Viktor), Georg Lokkeberg (Leonardo), Knut Wigert (Professor), Eva von Hanno (Nurse), Erland Josephson (Josef), Linn Ullmann (Eva as a Child), Arne Bang-Hansen (Uncle Otto)

p, Lew Grade, Martin Starger; d, Ingmar Bergman; w, Ingmar Bergman; ph, Sven Nykvist (Eastmancolor); ed, Sylvia Ingemarsson; prod d, Anna Asp; cos, Inger Pehrsson

The meeting of the Bergmans is reason alone to see AUTUMN SONATA, the director's exploration of mother-daughter conflict, but whatever cohesion the film projects is a result of Ingrid Bergman, as magnetic as ever in her final film performance. Photographed beautifully by Sven Nykvist, this painful film compels audiences finally to turn away. There is too much talk, talk, talk about feelings and not enough demonstration of them, but like cream, Ingrid keeps rising to the top of the chatter.

AVALON
1990 126m c ★★★
Drama PG/U
Baltimore Pictures

Armin Mueller-Stahl (Sam Krichinsky), Joan Plowright (Eva Krichinsky), Aidan Quinn (Jules Kaye), Elizabeth Perkins (Ann Kaye), Kevin Pollak (Izzy Kirk), Israel Rubinek (Nathan Krichinsky), Leo Fuchs (Hymie Krichinsky), Eve Gordon (Dottie Kirk), Lou Jacobi (Gabriel Krichinsky), Elijah Wood (Michael Kaye)

p, Mark Johnson, Barry Levinson; d, Barry Levinson; w, Barry Levinson; ph, Allen Daviau (Technicolor); ed, Stu Linder; m, Randy Newman; prod d, Norman Reynolds; art d, Fred Hole, Edward Richardson; fx, Allen L. Hall, Thomas R. Burman, Bari Dreiband-Burman; cos, Gloria Gresham

Completing writer-director Barry Levinson's "Baltimore trilogy," which began with the acclaimed DINER and continued with TIN MEN, the autobiographical AVALON is a lyrical, melancholy account of an immigrant family's rise and gradual disintegration.

Immigrating to Baltimore in 1914, Sam Krichinsky (Armin Mueller-Stahl) is reunited with his brothers—Gabriel (Lou Jacobi), Hymie (Leo Fuchs) and Nathan (Israel Rubinek)—and drawn into the "family circle," whose members pool their resources to bring relatives over from the old country. Wallpaper hangers during the week, the brothers are musicians during the weekends, and it is during one of their gigs that Sam meets Eva (Joan Plowright), his future wife. Their son, Jules (Aidan Quinn) does not follow in his father's footsteps as a manual laborer. Instead he becomes a door-to-door salesman, sometimes taking along his young son, Michael (Elijah Wood). During one of these outings, Michael watches in terror as his father is stabbed by a mugger. While recuperating, Jules is given a television set by his family. The only "program" at that time is a nonstop test pattern; nevertheless, Jules glimpses a future in the new invention.

Not unlike Martin Scorsese's GOODFELLAS, AVALON is concerned with the perils of sacrificing humaneness for hollow material success, a sort of 90s cinematic hangover from the "go for it" excesses of the 80s. The crucial difference between the approaches taken by these two accomplished filmmakers is that Scorsese's theme rises naturally from his material while Levinson imposes his themes on his material. Thus, GOODFELLAS's strengths—its strong sense of time, place, character, and mood—become AVALON's weaknesses. Despite the film's meticulously detailed production design, its human details don't ring true. It's hard to imagine even the most alienated of families eating Thanksgiving dinner silently in front of the TV. If Jules' family is really that alienated, how did it become that way? The movie offers no clue beyond the presence of the all-powerful boob tube, which has displaced the extended family that once gathered in the living room, talking, arguing, and telling stories of their immigrant experiences.

Despite a spirited performance by Elizabeth Perkins (BIG, LOVE AT LARGE, THE DOCTOR), Jules' wife Ann, like all the women in AVALON, remains only a hazily defined character. Equally vague is Jules' father Sam, who goes from paperhanging to owning a nightclub, then returns to paperhanging, inexplicably amassing a fortune in the process. For that matter, the film is full of loose plot threads; Levinson continually sacrifices narrative sense to clobber his audience with obvious and underdeveloped thematic points. We don't know how Sam built his comfortable retirement from a career as a paperhanger. We don't know what Jules does for a living after dropping out of his retailing partnership with Izzy. More importantly, Avalon, the neighborhood in which Sam settles his family, never comes alive; it never becomes tangible enough to justify the film being named after it. As a result, AVALON never really comes alive as a movie, although Allen Daviau's photography is exceptional, evoking many images of life that exist no more, and the film is graced with a flawless ensemble cast. Quinn's (DESPERATELY SEEKING SUSAN, STAKEOUT, AT PLAY IN THE FIELDS OF THE LORD) pivotal character gives the actor a plethora of varied moments to demonstrate his talent, and he is matched in touching displays by Mueller-Stahl and Joan Plowright as patriarch and matriarch and Elijah Wood as Jules and Ann's son. Ultimately, however, Levinson's very personal project never acquires a personality of its own.

AWAKENINGS

1990   121m   c   ★★½
Drama   PG-13/15
Columbia

Robert De Niro (Leonard Lowe), Robin Williams (Dr. Malcolm Sayer), Julie Kavner (Eleanor Costello), Ruth Nelson (Mrs. Lowe), John Heard (Dr. Kaufman), Penelope Ann Miller (Paula), Alice Drummond (Lucy), Judith Malina (Rose), Barton Heyman (Bert), George Martin (Frank)

p, Walter Parkes, Lawrence Lasker; d, Penny Marshall; w, Steve Zaillian (based on the novel by Oliver Sacks); ph, Miroslav Ondricek; ed, Jerry Greenberg, Battle Davis, Jere Huggins; m, Randy Newman; prod d, Anton Furst; art d, Bill Groom; cos, Cynthia Flynt

Earnest attempt by Penny Marshall to do a Milos Forman film sans subtle directing. The film's basis is the work and writings of neurologist Oliver Sacks, whose name is changed to Dr. Malcolm Sayer for the film, set in 1969. Robin Williams plays the overwhelmingly shy research doctor who is engaged by a Bronx hospital's chronic care ward and discovers the life force within his abandoned patients. Williams gives one of those "please like me, I'm working very hard" genial, mannered performances that makes you want to cry with impatience. But mannered could only begin to describe the infusion of tics and tricks by De Niro's enactment of "star" patient. It's like an acting thesis at Lee Strasberg Institute. The script seems to want to cue you to cry, cheer, etc., and Marshall seems to have directed in awe of being handed the job. The scenario cries out for a more rigorous, unsentimental approach in telling what is essentially a story of the horror of suddenly lucid patients clashing with a society of friends, relatives, and caretakers unable to cope with what should be a joyous occasion for all involved. As it is, the film doesn't ring true for a single moment.

AWFUL TRUTH, THE

1937   90m   bw   ★★★★★
Comedy   /A
Columbia

Irene Dunne (Lucy Warriner), Cary Grant (Jerry Warriner), Ralph Bellamy (Daniel Leeson), Alex D'Arcy (Armand Duvalle), Cecil Cunningham (Aunt Patsy), Molly Lamont (Barbara Vance), Esther Dale (Mrs. Leeson), Joyce Compton (Dixie Belle Lee/Toots Binswanger), Robert Allen (Frank Randall), Robert Warwick (Mr. Vance)

p, Leo McCarey; d, Leo McCarey; w, Vina Delmar (based on the play by Arthur Richman); ph, Joseph Walker; ed, Al Clark; art d, Stephen Goosson, Lionel Banks; cos, Robert Kalloch

A superbly lighthearted production, and the epitome of 1930s screwball comedies. Grant tells wife Dunne that he is going on a short Florida vacation, but then spends his time playing poker with the boys, establishing an alibi by burning himself under a sunlamp. When he returns home he finds his wife absent; then she appears with D'Arcy, a dashing voice teacher. Both Grant and Dunne assume that the other has been unfaithful and, after a rousing round of accusations, they decide to accept a 90-day interlocutory divorce. Their main courtroom battle focuses on their pet dog, Mr. Smith (Asta of the "Thin Man" series). As the legal wrangling moves into full swing, Dunne not only continues to see D'Arcy, but befriends Texas oil baron Bellamy. Meanwhile, Grant looks up an old flame, Compton, a sexy nightclub singer. Dunne and Grant go their separate ways, but are still drawn to each other. When Grant begins to fall for socialite Lamont, Dunne invades a party at her mansion, pretending to be drunk and carrying on wildly until Grant escorts her home. She convinces him to drive her to their mountain retreat, where they play a cat-and-mouse game, finally acknowledging that they still love each other.

This classic comedy began life as a 1922 stage hit and had been filmed twice previously—in 1925 as a silent with Agnes Ayres and Warner Baxter, and again in 1929 with Henry Daniell and Ina Claire. Director Leo McCarey maintained the basic premise of the play but improved it greatly, adding sophisticated dialogue and encouraging his actors to improvise around anything they thought funny. THE AWFUL TRUTH was in the can in six weeks, and was such a success that Grant and Dunne were teamed again in another splendid comedy, MY FAVORITE WIFE, and in a touching tearjerker, PENNY SERENADE. The film was nominated for an Academy Award for Best Picture and disappointingly remade in 1953 as LET'S DO IT AGAIN with Jane Wyman and Ray Milland.

B

BABES IN ARMS

1939 93m bw ★★★
Musical /U
MGM

Mickey Rooney *(Mickey Moran)*, Judy Garland *(Patsy Barton)*, Charles Winninger *(Joe Moran)*, Guy Kibbee *(Judge Black)*, June Preisser *(Rosalie Essex)*, Grace Hayes *(Florrie Moran)*, Betty Jaynes *(Molly Moran)*, Douglas McPhail *(Don Brice)*, Rand Brooks *(Jeff Steele)*, Leni Lynn *(Dody Martini)*

p, Arthur Freed; d, Busby Berkeley; w, Jack McGowan, Kay Van Riper (based on the musical play by Richard Rodgers and Lorenz Hart); ph, Ray June; ed, Frank Sullivan; art d, Cedric Gibbons, Merrill Pye; cos, Dolly Tree

Based on the Rodgers and Hart play of the same name, BABES IN ARMS was the first Rooney/Garland vehicle helmed by Busby Berkeley, and its success set the tone for STRIKE UP THE BAND and BABES ON BROADWAY, their subsequent collaborations. (Garland later teamed with Berkeley and hoofer Gene Kelly for 1942's FOR ME AND MY GAL.)

Joe and Florrie Moran (Charles Winninger and Grace Hayes) are old vaudevillians who begin a touring show featuring many of their senior pals. Their children, Mickey (Rooney) and Molly (Betty Jaynes), want to tag along, but the old folks refuse so, at Patsy Barton's (Garland) urging, Mickey writes a show that he will star in as well as direct. The determined youngsters must also prove that, contrary to the demands of Martha Steele (Margaret Hamilton), they don't belong in a state-administered trade school.

Only "Where or When" remains from the original score, trampled by the heavy hand of Berkeley (whom Garland would grow to loathe). This was the first of the Mickey/Judy "let's put on a show" extravaganzas but it's saved by Rooney's brash nerve and especially by the triple-threat charm of Garland, an performer unequaled in the annals of show business. The storyline here has been reduced to vaudeville corn, but watch Garland's ability to transcend cliche, transforming formulaic dross into critical and box-office gold.

BABES IN TOYLAND

1934 77m bw ★★★
Fantasy/Musical /U
MGM

Stan Laurel *(Stanley Dum)*, Oliver Hardy *(Oliver Dee)*, Charlotte Henry *(Bo-Peep)*, Felix Knight *(Tom-Tom)*, Henry Brandon *(Barnaby)*, Florence Roberts *(Widow Peep)*, Ferdinand Munier *(Santa Claus)*, William Burress *(Toymaker)*, Virginia Karns *(Mother Goose)*, Johnny Downs *(Little Boy Blue)*

p, Hal Roach; d, Gus Meins, Charles Rogers; w, Nick Grinde, Frank Butler (based on the musical comedy by Victor Herbert); ph, Art Lloyd, Francis Corby; ed, William Terhune, Bert Jordan

Victor Herbert operetta presented as vehicle for comedic genius of Laurel and Hardy. As Stanley Dum and Oliver Dee, L&H become the unsung heroes of Toyland when they avert the marriage of Bo Peep and the evil Barnaby, save the widow's abode (a multilevel shoe), rescue Tom-Tom from his exile to Bogeyland (the highlight), and ultimately rid Toyland of the evil Barnaby forever. A beautiful example of family entertainment, with the "March of the Toys" number offering five minutes of raucous action that ends the film on a high note. BABES was remade, with increasingly diminished returns, by Disney in 1961 with Tommy Sands and Annette Funicello and in 1986 with Keanu Reeves and Drew Barrymore.

BABES ON BROADWAY

1941 121m bw ★★★½
Musical /U
MGM

Mickey Rooney *(Tommy Williams)*, Judy Garland *(Penny Morris)*, Fay Bainter *(Miss Jones)*, Virginia Weidler *(Barbara Jo)*, Ray McDonald *(Ray Lambert)*, Richard Quine *(Morton Hammond)*, Donald Meek *(Mr. Stone)*, Alexander Woollcott *(Himself)*, Luis Alberni *(Nick)*, James Gleason *(Thornton Reed)*

p, Arthur Freed; d, Busby Berkeley; w, Fred Finklehoffe, Elaine Ryan (based on a story by Burton Lane); ph, Lester White; ed, Frederick Y. Smith; cos, Robert Kalloch

This sequel to BABES IN ARMS is slightly superior, serving up Rooney and Garland in everything from soup to nuts. BROADWAY presents Rooney at his enthuiastic peak, especially when he impersonates Carmen Miranda, but he's still eclipsed by Garland when she sings "F.D.R. Jones". Minstrel finale, and tributes to past theatrical performers are dynamite moments. Trivia fans should watch for Joe Yule, Rooney's father, as Mason, and for the debut of Margaret O'Brien. Burton Lane and Ralph Freed's "How About You?" earned an Oscar nomination.

BABETTE'S FEAST

(BABETTE'S GASTEBUD)
1987 102m c ★★★½
Drama G/U
Panorama/Nordisk/Danish Film Institute   (Denmark)

Ghita Norby *(Narrator)*, Stephane Audran *(Babette Hersant)*, Jean-Philippe Lafont *(Achille Papin)*, Gudmar Wivesson *(Lorenz Lowenhielm as a Young Man)*, Jarl Kulle *(Lorenz Lowenhielm as an Old Man)*, Bibi Andersson *(Swedish Court Lady-in-Waiting)*, Hanne Stensgaard *(Young Philippa)*, Bodil Kjer *(Old Philippa)*, Vibeke Hastrup *(Young Martina)*, Birgitte Federspiel *(Old Martina)*

p, Just Betzer, Bo Christensen; d, Gabriel Axel; w, Gabriel Axel (based on the short story by Isak); ph, Henning Kristiansen (Eastmancolor); ed, Finn Henriksen; m, Per Norgard, Wolfgang Amadeus Mozart; fx, Henning Bahs; cos, Annelise Hauberg, Pia Myrdal, Karl Lagerfeld

Winner of the Oscar for Best Foreign-Language Film of 1987, this quiet Danish film seemed an unlikely candidate for international success; instead of sex, violence, or nudity, it offers sermons and hymns, a dozen or so elderly Danes, and a feast to end all feasts. An expository flashback opens the film, delving into the frustrated love lives of Hastrup and Stensgaard, the daughters of a prophetic minister in a small town on Denmark's rugged Jutland peninsula. The story then shifts to 1871, as the title character (Audran), whose husband and son were killed by the Paris Communards, arrives from France and enters the employ of the sisters, who are carrying on their now-dead father's ministry. After 14 years of service with the sisters, Babette wins 10,000 francs in the French lottery and uses it to prepare a sumptuous banquet in honor of the minister's 100th birthday. At first, the stoic townspeople are reluctant to participate fully in this "pagan" feast; but ultimately they joyously indulge in Babette's masterwork, and it is revealed that she was once the chef de cuisine at the famous Cafe Anglais in Paris.

A gentle film that metaphorically examines the artist's relationship to her art, BABETTE'S FEAST is the sort of story that one cannot help but find uplifting. The performances—by such art-house favorites as Audran, Federspiel (ORDET), Lafont (BIZET'S CARMEN), and Bergman veterans Kulle and Andersson—are uniformly wonderful. The story on which the film is based was the product of a bet between its author, Karen Blixen (aka Isak Dinesen, whom Meryl Streep portrayed in OUT OF AFRICA), and a friend who suggested that the best way to crack the American market was to write about food.

BABY BOOM

1987 103m c	★★½
Comedy	PG
UA	

Diane Keaton (J.C. Wiatt), Harold Ramis (Steven Buchner), Sam Wanamaker (Fritz Curtis), Sam Shepard (Dr. Jeff Cooper), James Spader (Ken Arrenberg), Pat Hingle (Hughes Larrabee), Britt Leach (Vern Boone), Kristina Kennedy, Michelle Kennedy (Elizabeth Wiatt), Mary Gross (Receptionist)

p, Nancy Meyers; d, Charles Shyer; w, Nancy Meyers, Charles Shyer; ph, William A. Fraker; ed, Lynzee Klingman; m, Bill Conti; prod d, Jeffrey Howard; art d, Beala Neel; cos, Susan Becker

A sweet trifle. J.C. Wiatt (Diane Keaton) is a high-powered business executive in Manhattan who lives for her job. Her life is turned upside down, however, when she inherits a baby girl from distant relatives who have been killed. Saying good-bye to the New York rat race, she moves to a farmhouse and discovers the simple life. The problem is that it isn't all that simple for a city girl. While the script is often trite, Keaton turns in her best comic performance since MANHATTAN; Sam Wanamaker is superb as her boss; and Sam Shepard, Keaton's new love in the story, has all the down-home, earthy qualities one would expect from Gary Cooper.

BABY DOLL

1956 114m bw	★★★★
Drama	/X
WB	

Karl Malden (Archie), Carroll Baker (Baby Doll), Eli Wallach (Silva Vacarro), Mildred Dunnock (Aunt Rose Comfort), Lonny Chapman (Rock), Eades Hogue (Town Marshal), Noah Williamson (Deputy)

p, Elia Kazan; d, Elia Kazan; w, Tennessee Williams (based on his play); ph, Boris Kaufman; ed, Gene Milford; m, Kenyon Hopkins; cos, Anna Hill Johnstone

An explosive, provocative black comedy from Tennesee Williams and Elia Kazan. Williams reworked his one-act, 27 Wagonloads of Cotton, into a highly controversial screenplay that Time magazine called "possibly the dirtiest American picture ever legally exhibited." Although BABY DOLL feels tame today, the cinematography and appropriately sleazy setting still

have a sizzling effect, especially in a scene between Baker and Wallach set in a swing. All the performances are masterful, amusing and archtypal in the Williams manner: Malden's yokel, Baker's hothouse virgin, Dunnock's obscure octogenarian (especially hilarious) and Wallach's wily Sicilian all score strongly, though the latter lacks the physical size and power to be a believably threatening stud. But as usual, Kazan has no peer at directing Williams; you can almost feel the moss growing, so authentic is this treatment.

This was Baker's (GIANT, HARLOW, STAR 80, IRONWEED) first major role, following her film debut in 1953's EASY TO LOVE, and despite all the moral outrage, she deservedly received an Oscar nomination (she lost to Ingrid Bergman for ANASTASIA), as did the script, Dunnock, and Kaufman's starkly handsome black-and-white photography. At the other end of the spectrum, the Catholic Legion of Decency broadly condemned the film, stating that it "dwells upon carnal suggestiveness." Half the town of Benoit, Mississippi, where the film was shot on location, turned out as extras for this sexual potboiler, presumably from erotic curiousity.

BACHELOR AND THE BOBBY-SOXER, THE

1947 95m bw	★★★
Comedy	/U
RKO	

Cary Grant (Dick), Myrna Loy (Margaret), Shirley Temple (Susan), Rudy Vallee (Tommy), Ray Collins (Beemish), Harry Davenport (Thaddeus), Johnny Sands (Jerry), Don Beddoe (Tony), Lillian Randolph (Bessie), Veda Ann Borg (Agnes Prescott)

p, Dore Schary; d, Irving Reis; w, Sidney Sheldon; ph, Robert de Grasse, Nicholas Musuraca; ed, Frederic Knudtson; m, Leigh Harline; art d, Albert S. D'Agostino, Carroll Clark; fx, Russell A. Cully; cos, Edward Stevenson

Judge Loy, impatient with cocky playboy Grant after he has appeared before her because of a nightclub fracas, orders him to indulge Temple's schoolgirl crush until it plays itself out. Silly premise allows sophisticated Grant to explode into side-splitting antics, aping the teenaged set. If you adore Grant, you'll enjoy this farce, but Loy's breezy charm is wasted and Temple has reached that age where her preciousness can be irritating to behold. This was Dore Schary's last personal production before taking over the reins of RKO.

BACHELOR MOTHER

1939 80m bw	★★★★½
Comedy	/U
RKO	

Ginger Rogers (Polly Parrish), David Niven (David Merlin), Charles Coburn (J. B. Merlin), Frank Albertson (Freddie Miller), E.E. Clive (Butler), Elbert Coplen, Jr. (Johnnie), Ferike Boros (Mrs. Weiss), Ernest Truex (Investigator), Leonard Penn (Jerome Weiss), Paul Stanton (Hargraves)

p, B.G. DeSylva, Pandro S. Berman; d, Garson Kanin; w, Norman Krasna (based on a story by Felix Jackson); ph, Robert de Grasse; ed, Henry Berman, Robert Wise; m, Roy Webb; art d, Van Nest Polglase, Carroll Clark; fx, Vernon L. Walker; cos, Irene

Although Rogers had starred in four hit films sans Fred Astaire during the mid-1930s, it was really with BACHELOR MOTHER, her first solo effort after the team's separation and RKO's biggest hit of 1939, that she really confirmed that she didn't need to sing or dance to appeal to mass audiences. Notable as an example of the slight relaxation during the late 1930s of

Hollywood's self-enforced Production Code, the slightly risque story features Rogers as a single saleswoman for a large Macy's-like department store who finds a baby on her doorstep, where-upon everyone assumes that she's its mother.

Many of the witty lines apparently went right over the heads of the censors. Niven, delightful in his first major romantic comedy lead, portrays the playboy son of store owner Coburn, falling for Rogers even though he too assumes that she is the child's mother. Director Kanin, here enjoying one of his earliest successes, shapes the material as though he had had decades of experience. The supporting cast is uniformly excellent, especially Albertson and the hilariously befuddled, scene-stealing Coburn ("I don't care who's the father. . . I'm the grandfather!"). Originally made in Hungary in 1935, the film easily outpaces its wet-blanket remake with Debbie Reynolds and Eddie Fisher, BUNDLE OF JOY (1956).

BACK STREET
1941 89m bw   ★★★★
Drama   /A
Universal

Charles Boyer (Walter Saxel), Margaret Sullavan (Ray Smith), Richard Carlson (Curt Stanton), Frank McHugh (Ed Porter), Tim Holt (Richard Saxel), Frank Jenks (Harry Niles), Esther Dale (Mrs. Smith), Samuel S. Hinds (Felix Darren), Peggy Stewart (Freda Smith), Nell O'Day (Elizabeth Saxel)

p, Frank Shaw; d, Robert Stevenson; w, Bruce Manning, Felix Jackson (based on the novel by Fannie Hurst); ph, William Daniels; ed, Ted J. Kent; art d, Seward Webb

This restrained, luminous version of Fannie Hurst's oft-filmed saga is easily the best. BACK STREET's success is largely due to the tragic nobility Boyer and Sullavan invest this story of a woman who remains devoted to a married man. In real life, both actors' fates had the same elements of sad inevitability: Boyer and Sullavan died from barbiturate overdoses which were self-inflicted; Boyer in a depression after his wife passed away and Sullavan as a result of her frustration with increasing deafness. Her complicated nature and tempestuous life was chronicled by her daughter in the book *Haywire*. Sullavan's first three husbands were Henry Fonda, William Wyler, and Leland Hayward.

BACK TO BATAAN
1945 97m bw   ★★★½
War   /PG
RKO

John Wayne (Col. Joe Madden), Anthony Quinn (Capt. Andres Bonifacio), Beulah Bondi (Miss Bertha Barnes), Fely Franquelli (Dalisay Delgado), Richard Loo (Maj. Hasko), Philip Ahn (Col. Kuroki), J. Alex Havier (Sgt. Biernesa), Ducky Louie (Maximo), Lawrence Tierney (Lt. Cmdr. Waite), Leonard Strong (Gen. Homma)

p, Theron Warth; d, Edward Dmytryk; w, Ben Barzman, Richard Landau (based on a story by Aeneas MacKenzie, William Gordon); ph, Nicholas Musuraca; ed, Marston Fay; m, Roy Webb; art d, Albert S. D'Agostino, Ralph Berger; fx, Vernon L. Walker

Rousing, square-jawed, flag waving WWII drama with Filipino guerrillas following John Wayne to victory in the Pacific. Interesting subplot has Franquelli as Quinn's sweetheart and a suspected Tokyo Rose/Axis Sally broadcaster. This is the only film in which Dmytryk and Wayne were both involved—a none-too-surprising fact considering Wayne's strong right-wing stance and Dmytryk's left-wing leanings.

BACK TO SCHOOL
1986 96m c   ★★★
Comedy   PG-13/15
Paper Clip

Rodney Dangerfield (Thornton Melon), Sally Kellerman (Diane), Burt Young (Lou), Keith Gordon (Jason Melon), Robert Downey, Jr. (Derek), Paxton Whitehead (Philip Barbay), Terry Farrell (Valerie), M. Emmet Walsh (Coach Turnbull), Adrienne Barbeau (Vanessa), William Zabka (Chas)

p, Chuck Russell; d, Alan Metter; w, Steven Kampmann, Will Aldis, Peter Torokvei, Harold Ramis (based on a story by Dangerfield, Greg Fields, Dennis Snee); ph, Thomas Ackerman (DeLuxe Color); ed, David Rawlins; m, Danny Elfman; prod d, David L. Snyder; fx, Michael Lantieri; cos, Durinda Wood

Broad, crude comedy hit has Rodney Dangerfield as Thornton Melon, the immensely wealthy owner of a chain of "Big Men's" clothing stores. His son Jason (Keith Gordon), a student at Grand Lakes University, has lied and told his father that he is a "big man on campus" and a champion diver. In truth, the boy is a nerdy towel attendant for the diving team and has only one friend, Derek (Robert Downey, Jr.), a self-styled revolutionary. Thornton decides to enroll in the school so that he will be closer to his son and can help him through his current problems, but finds the task more difficult than he anticipated—money helps, however. The plot is suitably slight, allowing plenty of room for the barrage of jokes that roll off Dangerfield's tongue. The result is unsophisticated, unilluminating, unambitious, and hilarious.

BACK TO THE FUTURE
1985 116m c   ★★★
Science Fiction/Comedy   PG
Amblin/Universal

Michael J. Fox (Marty McFly), Christopher Lloyd (Dr. Emmett Brown), Lea Thompson (Lorraine Baines), Crispin Glover (George McFly), Thomas F. Wilson (Biff Tannen), Claudia Wells (Jennifer Parker), Marc McClure (Dave McFly), Wendie Jo Sperber (Linda McFly), George DiCenzo (Sam Baines), James Tolkan (Mr. Strickland)

p, Bob Gale, Neil Canton; d, Robert Zemeckis; w, Robert Zemeckis, Bob Gale; ph, Dean Cundey (Panavision, Technicolor); ed, Arthur Schmidt, Harry Keramidas; m, Alan Silvestri; prod d, Lawrence G. Paull; art d, Todd Hallowell; fx, Kevin Pike; chor, Brad Jeffries; cos, Deborah L. Scott

Marty McFly (Michael J. Fox) is a decent teenager who plays an electric guitar, sails about on a skateboard, and courts pretty Claudia Wells. But all is not well in Fox's little world. His father (Crispin Glover) is a milquetoast, his mother (Lea Thompson) is an alcoholic, and his brother and sister (Marc McClure and Wendie Jo Sperber) are decidedly weird. Marty's friend, the positively manic Christopher Lloyd, has been working on a device for time travel. Marty activates the device and finds that he has traveled back to 1955, where he encounters his own parents as teenagers. If that isn't troublesome enough, he also discovers that he doesn't have enough special plutonium fuel to return to the future. All this makes for a snappy, happy, and wonderfully nostalgic outing, with ample time-traveling twists and turns. The laughs are plentiful and the acting by Fox, Thompson, and Glover is superb. Robert Zemeckis's direction, like the technical contributions, is first-rate, and after an ambling start takes off into frenetic, non-stop fun.

BACK TO THE FUTURE PART II

1989   105m   c   ★★½
Adventure/Fantasy   PG
Amblin

Michael J. Fox *(Marty McFly/Marty McFly, Jr./Marlene McFly)*, Christopher Lloyd *(Dr. Emmett Brown)*, Lea Thompson *(Lorraine)*, Thomas F. Wilson *(Biff Tannen/Griff)*, Harry Waters, Jr. *(Marvin Berry)*, Charles Fleischer *(Terry)*, Joe Flaherty *(Western Union Man)*, Flea *(Needles)*, Elizabeth Shue *(Jennifer)*, James Tolkan *(Strickland)*

p, Neil Canton, Bob Gale; d, Robert Zemeckis; w, Bob Gale (based on a story by Robert Zemeckis, Bob Gale); ph, Dean Cundey (Deluxe Color); ed, Arthur Schmidt, Harry Keramidas; m, Alan Silvestri; prod d, Rick Carter; art d, Margie Stone McShirley; chor, Brad Jeffries; cos, Joanna Johnston; anim, Wes Takahashi

First of two sequels to the enormously popular BACK TO THE FUTURE is long on ideas, short on delight. Climax parallels climax of original but turns out to be cliffhanger for second sequel (shot back-to-back with this). A cheap shot. For diehards who wouldn't dream of missing Part III.

BACK TO THE FUTURE PART III

1990   118m   c   ★★★★
Comedy/Science Fiction/Western   PG
Steven Spielberg

Michael J. Fox *(Marty McFly/Seamus McFly)*, Christopher Lloyd *(Dr. Emmett Brown)*, Mary Steenburgen *(Clara Clayton)*, Thomas F. Wilson *(Buford "Mad Dog" Tannen/Biff Tannen)*, Lea Thompson *(Maggie McFly/Lorraine McFly)*, Elisabeth Shue *(Jennifer)*, Matt Clark *(Bartender)*, Richard Dysart *(Barbed Wire Salesman)*, Pat Buttram, Harry Carey, Jr.

p, Bob Gale, Neil Canton; d, Robert Zemeckis; w, Bob Gale (based on a story and characters created by Robert Zemeckis and Bob Gale); ph, Dean Cundey (Deluxe Color); ed, Arthur Schmidt, Harry Keramidas; m, Alan Silvestri; prod d, Rick Carter; art d, Marjorie Stone McShirley, Jim Teegarden; fx, Ken Ralston, Scott Farrar, Michael Lantieri; chor, Brad Jeffries; cos, Joanna Johnston; anim, Wes Takahashi

Part III finds the FUTURE series back on track. This time, Fox and terrific special effects breathe life into the abandoned western genre with exciting, inventive results. The film also boasts the welcome presence of Mary Steenburgen, playing as sweet and spirited a heroine as has ever crossed a screen.

BACKDRAFT

1991   135m   c   ★★★
Action/Thriller/Drama   R/15
Imagine Films Entertainment/Trilogy Entertainment Group/Raffaella Productions

Kurt Russell *(Stephen McCaffrey)*, William Baldwin *(Brian McCaffrey)*, Robert De Niro *(Donald Rimgale)*, Donald Sutherland *(Ronald Bartel)*, Jennifer Jason Leigh *(Jennifer Vaitkus)*, Scott Glenn *(John Adcox)*, Rebecca DeMornay *(Helen McCaffrey)*, Jason Gedrick *(Tim Krizminski)*, J.T. Walsh *(Martin Swayzak)*, Tony Mockus, Sr. *(Chief John Fitzgerald)*

p, Richard B. Lewis, John Watson, Pen Densham; d, Ron Howard; w, Gregory Widen; ph, Mikael Salomon; ed, Daniel Hanley, Michael Hill; m, Hans Zimmer; prod d, Albert Brenner; art d, Carol Winstead Wood; fx, Allen Hall; cos, Jodie Tillen

Directed by Ron Howard from a screenplay by former fireman Gregory Widen, BACKDRAFT offers an insider's look at a profession seldom featured in movies. Unfortunately, the film drags when the fire is offscreen, only springing to life when it's the main attraction.

The McCaffrey brothers, Stephen (Kurt Russell) and Brian (William Baldwin), are driven by an intense rivalry that started when they were children. When Brian decides to follow Stephen—who in turn followed their late father—into the fire department, tempers flare. Stephen has already made his mark as a bold, single-minded, charismatic firefighter. Brian has a dilettante's history of careers that didn't pan out. Their antagonistic relationship forces Brian's transfer to another assignment: he's made assistant to Donald Rimgale (Robert De Niro), a fire department investigator who specializes in cases of arson.

Rimgale is working on a series of fires involving a "backdraft," in which a smoldering fire, exposed to oxygen, suddenly explodes in a literal fireball. On his first day on the job, Brian meets Rimgale's nemesis, Ronald Bartel (Donald Sutherland), a compulsive fire starter who dreams of seeing the entire world in flames. The investigation points to a corrupt city alderman (J.T. Walsh), but after consulting with Bartel—who has, after all, a unique insight into the psychology of arsonists—Brian begins to suspect his brother.

Despite the novelty of the setting, the family drama that forms BACKDRAFT's core is predictable. It has the feel of something put together by the numbers: two brothers, each traumatized in his own way by the death of their father (Brian watched as his father lost to the fire; Stephen was back at the fire house), butt heads to hide the fact that they love and need one another desperately. With the exception of the psychotic Bartel, brought to life in a weird, over-the-top performance by Donald Sutherland, the supporting characters are two-dimensional, especially Rebecca DeMornay's and Jennifer Jason Leigh's turns as, respectively, Stephen's wife and Brian's old girlfriend. Even De Niro's Rimgale is rather undistinguished; his single most memorable scene is one in which Brian glimpses him undressing and sees the scars left on his back by bouts with fire. The effect has nothing to do with characterization.

What makes BACKDRAFT enthralling is the fire itself. Much—in fact, too much—is made dialogue-wise of the fire being a living thing, a kind of beast that slinks in the shadows and preys on the careless, the unsuspecting and the over confident. But BACKDRAFT's fire more than lives up to expectations. It's spectacular, yes, but that's not all. Not only do the firefighting scenes evoke a feeling of gritty authenticity, but the fire itself really does seem to be alive. A scene in which a door warps ever-so-slightly, almost imperceptibly outward because a smoldering fire lurks behind it, waiting for the blast of oxygen that will bring it to roaring life, would work just as well in a finely crafted horror movie; the sentience, the subtle and cruel intelligence of the fire seems beyond dispute.

BAD AND THE BEAUTIFUL, THE

1952   116m   bw   ★★★★★
Drama   /A
MGM

Lana Turner *(Georgia Lorrison)*, Kirk Douglas *(Jonathan Shields)*, Walter Pidgeon *(Harry Pebbel)*, Dick Powell *(James Lee Bartlow)*, Barry Sullivan *(Fred Amiel)*, Gloria Grahame *(Rosemary Bartlow)*, Gilbert Roland *(Victor "Gaucho" Ribera)*, Leo G. Carroll *(Henry Whitfield)*, Vanessa Brown *(Kay Amiel)*, Paul Stewart *(Syd Murphy)* p, John Houseman; d, Vincente Minnelli; w, Charles Schnee (based on a story by George Bradshaw); ph, Robert Surtees; ed, Conrad A. Nervig; m, David Raksin; art d, Cedric Gibbons, Edward Carfagno; fx, A. Arnold Gillespie, Warren Newcombe; cos, Helen Rose

The rise, fall and resurgence of a loutish Hollywood producer, as told through the eyes of three people he made then alienated. This quintessential movie on movies is an engrossing, seductive Minnelli epic, graced with superb performances.

The three separate stories, revolving around Douglas, a ruthless producer whose cunning ways allow him to climb to the top of the Hollywood heap, are told by star Turner, director Sullivan and writer Powell. Some film buffs believe that Douglas's role model was Val Lewton, the extravagant, driven producer of the 1940s, since Lewton made CAT PEOPLE and Douglas produces "The Cat Men" in the film. However, the character is more likely based on mogul David O. Selznick, particularly his beginnings as a B-film producer, his grooming of future wife Jennifer Jones and his making of a colossal Civil War film which, of course, was GONE WITH THE WIND.

Pidgeon's part is most certainly based upon the cost-conscious B-production chief at MGM, Harry Rapf, for whom Selznick first went to work. Schnee's sharp script, which acutely profiles every type of Hollywood character, from the grubbing agent to the mighty mogul, enables one easily to identify Turner's character with that of Diana Barrymore, the tragedy-struck daughter of the Great Profile, John Barrymore. The Powell role, an excellently understated profile, is best associated with writer F. Scott Fitzgerald, whose romance with Hollywood turned sour and who was married to southern belle Zelda Sayre Fitzgerald.

Cost-conscious MGM used many sets from its previous productions for this film, showing them in their naked construction, such as the sweeping staircase used earlier in Turner's MERRY WIDOW. More "inside" ploys were used in the production; Turner's own makeup man and hairdresser, Del Armstrong and Helen Young, appear in the film in their real-life roles, as does Alyce My, Turner's regular stand-in. Raksin's stirring, moody score is superb. The sets by Edwin B. Willis and Keogh Gleason, especially in the roomy, dust-laden mansions, the movie lots, the sets, and the studio offices, totally reflect the Hollywood that is no more but which is forever preserved in this always-fascinating classic.

BAD BLOOD

(MAUVAIS SANG)
1987 128m c   ★★★
Crime/Romance   /18
Plain Chant/Soprofilms/FR3/CNC/Sofima   (France)

Denis Lavant (Alex), Juliette Binoche (Anna), Michel Piccoli (Marc), Hans Meyer (Hans), Julie Delpy (Lise), Carroll Brooks (The American Woman), Hugo Pratt (Boris), Serge Reggiani (Charlie), Mireille Perrier (The Young Mother), Jerome Zucca (Thomas)

p, Philippe Diaz; d, Leos Carax; w, Leos Carax; ph, Jean-Yves Escoffier (Fujicolor); ed, Nelly Quettier; m, Benjamin Britten, Serge Prokofiev, Charles Chaplin; art d, Michel Vandestien, Thomas Peckre, Jack Dubus; fx, Guy Trielli; chor, Christine Burgos; cos, Robert Nardone, Dominique Gregogna, Martine Metert

Artsy, occasionally inspired piece by French *wunderkind* Leos Carax, who clearly wants us to know how much he owes to Cocteau and Godard. The pulp-novel plot, which takes a backseat to Carax's moody, romantic visuals, concerns a fictional AIDS-like plague called STBO which one contracts by "making love

without love." The majority of those infected are adolescents whose lovemaking had previously been without consequence. The only known serum is locked away at the top of a skyscraper, with a lot of different people trying to get their hands on it. Though the storyline moves in unconvincing fits and starts, Carax gets good performances from his hip young stars—including Denis Lavant, Juliette Binoche and Julie Delpy—and pulls off some bravura set pieces. Worth a look.

BAD COMPANY

1972 93m c   ★★★★
Western   /15
Paramount

Jeff Bridges (Jake Rumsey), Barry Brown (Drew Dixon), Jim Davis (Marshal), David Huddleston (Big Joe), John Savage (Loney), Jerry Houser (Arthur Simms), Damon Cofer (Jim Bob Logan), Joshua Hill Lewis (Boog Bookin), Charles Tyner (Farmer), Geoffrey Lewis

p, Stanley R. Jaffe; d, Robert Benton; w, David Newman, Robert Benton; ph, Gordon Willis (Technicolor); ed, Ralph Rosenblum; m, Harvey Schmidt; art d, Robert Gundlach

A highly engaging sleeper. Draft dodging is evidently an old American custom, according to this screenplay by Benton and Newman, the duo who scripted BONNIE AND CLYDE. Marking Benton's directorial debut, BAD COMPANY is a comedy-drama about the Civil War equivalent of the Viet Nam protesters. Instead of going north to Canada, these young men wend their ways west. Bridges, Brown, Houser, Cofer, Savage, and Lewis are a bunch of young Easterners who drift out beyond the Mississippi and encounter several adventures. A segmented movie, BAD COMPANY manages to sustain interest through deft direction and an intelligent screenplay. The movie shows the down side of the Old West: deprivation, the cold, the murders, and very little of the dime-novel glamour that young men read about in their gaslit Manhattan rooms. It's a mixture of comedy and drama—and when it's funny, it's terrific.

BAD DAY AT BLACK ROCK

1955 81m c   ★★★★
Drama   /A
MGM

Spencer Tracy (John J. MacReedy), Robert Ryan (Reno Smith), Anne Francis (Liz Wirth), Dean Jagger (Tim Horn), Walter Brennan (Doc Velie), John Ericson (Pete Wirth), Lee Marvin (Hector David), Ernest Borgnine (Coley Trimble), Russell Collins (Mr. Hastings), Walter Sande (Sam)

p, Dore Schary; d, John Sturges; w, Don McGuire, Millard Kaufman (based on a story by Howard Breslin); ph, William Mellor (CinemaScope, Eastmancolor); ed, Newell P. Kimlin; m, Andre Previn; art d, Cedric Gibbons, Malcolm Brown

In this powerful, lightning-paced film, Tracy plays a one-armed stranger who uncovers a dangerous skeleton in a western hick town's closet, with harrowing results. Tracy is at his subdued, thoughtful best, while Ryan perfectly conveys the ignorance behind racial prejudice and Borgnine and Marvin are memorable heavies. Sturges's direction is superbly timed, and Kaufman's script was so memorable that many of its lines quickly passed into public use.

BAD GIRL
1931 90m bw   ★★½
Drama   /U
Fox Films

Sally Eilers (*Dorothy Haley*), James Dunn (*Eddie Collins*), Minna Gombell (*Edna Driggs*), William Pawley (*Jim Haley*), Frank Darien (*Lathrop*)

d, Frank Borzage; w, Edwin Burke (based on the novel and the play by Vina Delmar); ph, Chester Lyons; ed, Margaret Clancy

This adaptation tells the story of a young woman, Eilers, who meets a young man, Dunn, on a Coney Island boat, goes home with him, and is indiscreet enough to conceive a child out of wedlock. The couple marry one step ahead of the obstetrician, and Dunn must give up his lifelong dream of owning his own radio store to provide for his new bride and child. He even goes so far as to enter himself in a boxing match to win $40 to pay the doctor bills. This dated melodrama was quite popular in its time and earned Academy Awards for Best Direction and Best Screen Adaptation, as well as a nomination for Best Picture.

BAD INFLUENCE
1990 99m c   ★★★
Mystery/Thriller   R/18
Epic

Rob Lowe (*Alex*), James Spader (*Michael Boll*), Lisa Zane (*Claire*), Christian Clemenson (*Pismo Boll*), Kathleen Wilhoite (*Leslie*), Tony Maggio (*Patterson*), Marcia Cross (*Ruth Fielding*)

p, Steve Tisch; d, Curtis Hanson; w, David Koepp; ph, Robert Elswit; ed, Bonnie Koehler; m, Trevor Jones; prod d, Ron Foreman; art d, William S. Combs

Slick thriller that capitalized on Lowe's bad boy publicity. Spader befriends Lowe after the latter comes to his aid in a barroom, and soon finds the creep controlling his life; to describe any of the twists would ruin the surprises in the story. Hanson keeps the film moving along at a quick pace and makes the most of the shifting point of view and weird morality of David Koepp's screenplay.

A curious mixture of styles, BAD INFLUENCE is a Hitchcockian homage (particularly its second half) that's also reminiscent of recent films including AT CLOSE RANGE and the Koepp-scripted APARTMENT ZERO. Spader is most effective here, and Lowe has finally found his niche as a junior league Richard Gere. The tension between the two is well handled and yet never quite explained, which adds to the mysterious "feel" of the movie and gives the characters a sexually ambiguous edge.

BAD NEWS BEARS, THE
1976 102m c   ★★★
Comedy   PG
Paramount

Walter Matthau (*Coach Buttermaker*), Tatum O'Neal (*Manda Whurlizer*), Vic Morrow (*Roy Turner*), Joyce Van Patten (*Cleveland*), Ben Piazza (*Councilman Whitewood*), Jackie Earle Haley (*Kelly Leak*), Alfred Lutter (*Ogilvie*), Brandon Cruz (*Joey Turner*), Shari Summers (*Mrs. Turner*), Joe Brooks (*Umpire*)

p, Stanley R. Jaffe; d, Michael Ritchie; w, Bill Lancaster; ph, John A. Alonzo (Movielab Color); ed, Richard A. Harris; m, Jerry Fielding; prod d, Polly Platt

As amusing for adults as it is for children, this charming, funny film takes a gentle poke at Little League baseball and the American obsession with winning. Morris Buttermaker (Walter

Matthau, in a strong comic turn), a one-time minor leaguer, becomes the manager of the Bears, a team of multiracial Little League rejects in southern California. With Morris's help this hapless, foul-mouthed bunch, led by its star female hurler, Manda Whurlizer (Tatum O'Neal), begins improving and winning ball games. Director Michael Ritchie (DOWNHILL RACER, SMILE), working from a script by Burt Lancaster's son, Bill, provides a nice twist on the expected outcome. Although the film could have been preachy, Ritchie handles the story and theme with deftness. So popular was the film that it produced two sequels—THE BAD NEWS BEARS IN BREAKING TRAINING (1977) and THE BAD NEWS BEARS GO TO JAPAN (1978)—and at least one imitation, HERE COME THE TIGERS (1978), plus a TV series.

BAD SLEEP WELL, THE
(WARUI YATSU HODO YOKU NEMURU)
1960 135m bw   ★★★
Drama   /A
Tanaka-Kurosawa   (Japan)

Toshiro Mifune (*Koichi Nishi*), Takeshi Kato (*Itakura*), Masayuki Mori (*Iwabuchi*), Takashi Shimura (*Moriyama*), Akira Nishimura (*Shirai*), Kamatari Fujiwara (*Wada*), Gen Shimizu (*Miura*), Kyoko Kagawa (*Kieko*), Tatsuya Mihashi (*Tatsuo*), Kyu Sazanka (*Kaneko*)

p, Tomoyuki Tanaka, Akira Kurosawa; d, Akira Kurosawa; w, Akira Kurosawa, Shinobu Hashimoto, Hideo Oguni, Ryuzu Kikushima, Eijiro Hisaita; ph, Yuruzu Aizawa; ed, Akira Kurosawa; m, Masaru Sato

One of Akira Kurosawa's modern-day films, THE BAD SLEEP WELL is a sociopolitical indictment of the feudalism that is prevalent in the present-day Japanese hierarchy of business and politics. Nishi (Toshiro Mifune) is a fast-rising young executive about to further his acquisition of power through marriage to Keiko (Kyoko Kagawa), the daughter of the firm's president, Iwabuchi (Masayuki Mori). Nishi, however, is something of a modern-day samurai—a heroic figure who has adopted a new identity in order to avenge the death of his father, a corporate vice president whose death can be traced to Iwabuchi. Nishi's method of revenge is to become part of the family and destroy Iwabuchi from within. But Nishi eventually discovers that there is no room for the noble hero in the ruthless world of high-powered executives and politicians. Although it is not one of Kurosawa's finest achievements, THE BAD SLEEP WELL becomes more interesting when viewed as a predecessor to HIGH AND LOW (1963), a more completely realized attack on Japanese society.

BADLANDS
1974 95m c   ★★★½
Crime   PG/18
WB

Martin Sheen (*Kit*), Sissy Spacek (*Holly*), Warren Oates (*Father*), Ramon Bieri (*Cato*), Alan Vint (*Deputy*), Gary Littlejohn (*Sheriff*), John Carter (*Rich Man*), Bryan Montgomery (*Boy*), Gail Threlkeld (*Girl*), Charles Fitzpatrick (*Clerk*)

p, Terrence Malick; d, Terrence Malick; w, Terrence Malick; ph, Brian Probyn, Tak Fujimoto, Stevan Larner (Consolidated Color); ed, Robert Estrin; m, George Tipton; art d, Jack Fisk

Stark, brutal story obviously based on the Charles Starkweather-Carol Fugate murder spree through Nebraska and surrounding states in 1958, with Sheen playing the killer lashing out against a society that ignores his existence and Spacek as his misguided teenage consort. Sheen is forceful and properly weird as the mass murderer, killing Oates, Spacek's disapproving father, when he forbids his daughter to date him. He then goes on the run, Spacek in tow, randomly killing innocents who cross his path. (Starkweather and Fugate, although she later denied killing anyone, were responsible for the deaths of ten people.) The locale in the movie is changed to South Dakota but almost all the characteristics of the real culprits are intact, the strutting Sheen pretending to be James Dean in REBEL WITHOUT A CAUSE, while Spacek doesn't quite understand what he's all about, but goes along anyway.

Director Malick neither romanticizes nor condemns his subjects, maintaining a low-key approach to the story that results in a fascinating character study. Perhaps Starkweather himself provided the best insight into the character when he stated: "The more I looked at people the more I hated them, because I knowed there wasn't any place for me with the kind of people I knowed." The film did scant box office business, but it remains one of the most impressive directorial debuts ever. While Malick would continue to show promise in the equally impressive DAYS OF HEAVEN, by the end of the 1980s these two films would represent his entire oeuvre.

BAGDAD CAFE

1987 91m c   ★★★½
Comedy   PG
Pelemele/BR-HR/Project   (West Germany)

Marianne Sagebrecht (*Jasmin Munchgstettner*), C.C.H. Pounder (*Brenda*), Jack Palance (*Rudi Cox*), Christine Kaufmann (*Debbie*), Monica Calhoun (*Phyllis*), Darron Flagg (*Sal Junior*), George Aguilar (*Cahuenga*), G. Smokey Campbell (*Sal*), Hans Stadlbauer (*Munchgstettner*), Apesanahkwat (*Sheriff Arnie*)

p, Percy Adlon, Eleonore Adlon; d, Percy Adlon; w, Percy Adlon, Eleonore Adlon, Christopher Doherty (based on a story by Percy Adlon); ph, Bernd Heinl (Eastmancolor); ed, Norbert Herzner; m, Bob Telson, Johann Sebastian Bach; cos, Elizabeth Warner, Regina Batz

An adorable oddity. Director Percy Adlon's first English-language film is set in a run-down motel in the middle of the Mojave Desert and, like his earlier art-house hit SUGARBABY, stars the uniquely talented Marianne Sagebrecht. Jasmin Munchgstettner (Sagebrecht), a German *hausfrau*, is abandoned in the desert after an argument with her husband. After wandering for some time under the scorching sun, Jasmin checks into a dusty motel run by Brenda (C.C.H. Pounder), a tough-talking, no-nonsense woman who treats her new boarder like some sort of space alien. With time, however, the pair become the best of friends, turning the decrepit diner into the most exciting place west of Las Vegas, and Jasmin becomes one of the most popular entertainers for miles around—especially catching the fancy of Rudi Cox (Jack Palance), a cosmic romantic who desperately wants to paint her portrait. BAGDAD CAFE is a visually exhilarating and consciously modern film, more concerned with projecting an atmosphere or spirit than with telling a story. It's hard not to fall in love with this comic fable about the magic that develops at the meeting of two cultures.

BAKER'S WIFE, THE

(LA FEMME DU BOULANGER)
1938 130m bw   ★★★★
Comedy   /A
Marcel Pagnol   (France)

Raimu (*Aimable, The Baker*), Ginette Leclerc (*Aurelie, The Baker's Wife*), Charles Moulin (*Dominique, The Shepherd*), Robert Vattier (*The Priest*), Robert Bassac (*The School Teacher*), Fernand Charpin (*The Marquis*), Maximilienne

p, Robert Hakim, Raymond Hakim; d, Marcel Pagnol; w, Marcel Pagnol (based on Jean Giono's novel *Jean Le Bleu*); ph, R. Lendruz, N. Daries; ed, Suzanne de Troeye; m, Vincent Scotto

Raimu, the star of Marcel Pagnol's Marseilles trilogy, here teams again with Pagnol as the baker Aimable, a new addition to a French village that has lacked a quality baker for some time. The tasting of Aimable's first loaves of bread is an event eagerly awaited by all the locals, giving the villagers a chance to take time away from their daily complaints and neighborly disagreements. Aimable takes great pride in his bread—a pride equalled only by his affection for his coquettish wife Aurelie (Ginette Leclerc). The villagers agree that if their new baker's bread is as lovely as his wife, all will be content. Unfortunately for Aimable, however, the handsome shepherd Dominique (Charles Moulin) prefers Aurelie to a brioche, and she prefers his affection to slaving over a hot stove. When they run off together, Aimable is no longer able to continue his baking. Rather than risk losing another baker, the villagers band together in an effort to bring Aurelie back home. A touching comedy that borders on the tragic, THE BAKER'S WIFE is brilliantly acted and directed, and proved one of the most popular French films of all time in the US.

BALL OF FIRE

1941 111m bw   ★★★½
Comedy   /U
Goldwyn

Gary Cooper (*Prof. Bertram Potts*), Barbara Stanwyck (*Sugarpuss O'Shea*), Oscar Homolka (*Prof. Gurkakoff*), Henry Travers (*Prof. Jerome*), S.Z. Sakall (*Prof. Magenbruch*), Tully Marshall (*Prof. Robinson*), Leonid Kinskey (*Prof. Quintana*), Richard Haydn (*Prof. Oddly*), Aubrey Mather (*Prof. Peagram*), Allen Jenkins (*Garbage Man*)

p, Samuel Goldwyn; d, Howard Hawks; w, Charles Brackett, Billy Wilder (based on the story "From A to Z" by Thomas Monroe, Billy Wilder); ph, Gregg Toland; ed, Daniel Mandell; m, Alfred Newman; art d, Perry Ferguson

Skewered variation on "Snow White and the Seven Dwarfs," courtesy of Howard Hawks and a zany Wilder-Brackett screenplay. Cooper is a stodgy linguist researching slang for a new encyclopedia. In order to get closer to it, he recruits Stanwyck, as a stripper who knows exactly what color the cat's pajamas should be and why it's 23, not 24 or 22 Skiddoo. Cooper lives in a huge house with seven other longhairs and Stanwyck goes on the lam and moves in. There's a veritable corps de comedy in the character actors here; one look at the cast list will convince anyone that scene-stealing would have been rampant without the firm Hawks hand. Terrific, crackling dialogue, especially in the slangy, machine-gun mouth of La Stanwyck. Remade as A SONG IS BORN, again by Hawks.

BALLAD OF A SOLDIER

1959 89m bw   ★★★★★
Drama/War   /U
Mosfilm   (U.S.S.R.)

Vladimir Ivashov *(Alyosha)*, Zhanna Prokhorenko *(Shura)*, Antonina Maximova *(Alyosha's Mother)*, Nikolai Kruchkov *(General)*, Yevgeniy Urbanskiy *(Invalid)*

d, Grigori Chukhrai; w, Valentin Yezhov, Grigori Chukhrai; m, Michael Siv

BALLAD OF A SOLDIER is the heart-rending profile of a young soldier (Ivashov) fighting on the front during WWII who heroically disables two German tanks and is rewarded with a six-day leave. As he makes the long journey home to see his mother (Maximova) he meets a variety of people, both friendly and antagonistic, who need his help. Though he finally makes it to his mother's door, he unfortunately never gets to spend his leave quite as he intended before having to return to almost certain death at the front.

This startlingly realistic and lovingly detailed picture transcends its dramatic premise to embody on several levels the tale of all the Soviet people. An episodic and visually haunting film with modest but never overdone touches of comedy, romance, and sentimentality, BALLAD OF A SOLDIER is a fine example of the Soviet realist tradition—a style of filmmaking paralleled by the more cinematically innovative techniques of such Soviet directors as Sergei Paradzhanov (SHADOWS OF FORGOTTEN ANCESTORS) and Andrei Tarkovsky (MY NAME IS IVAN). Although the film is nationalistic, this and several of Chukrai's other films (e.g. THE FORTY-FIRST) nevertheless contain a palpable critique of Stalinism and its "cult of the hero," suggesting that humanity is more important than heroism.

BALLAD OF CABLE HOGUE, THE

1970 121m c   ★★★½
Western   R/PG
WB

Jason Robards, Jr. *(Cable Hogue)*, Stella Stevens *(Hildy)*, David Warner *(Joshua)*, Strother Martin *(Bowen)*, Slim Pickens *(Ben)*, L.Q. Jones *(Taggart)*, Peter Whitney *(Cushing)*, R.G. Armstrong *(Quittner)*, Gene Evans *(Clete)*, William Mims *(Jensen)*

p, Phil Feldman, Sam Peckinpah, William Faralla; d, Sam Peckinpah; w, John Crawford, Edmund Penney; ph, Lucien Ballard (Technicolor); ed, Frank Santillo, Lou Lombardo; m, Jerry Goldsmith; art d, Leroy Coleman; cos, Robert Fletcher

Peckinpah demonstrated a sense of humor in THE BALLAD OF CABLE HOGUE that had not been seen since his early TV days when he ran one of the best and most overlooked cowboy shows ever, "The Westerner," starring Brian Keith. CABLE HOGUE is at its best when chronicling how the Old West passed and mercantilism spread across the Great Plains.

Robards is a prospector abandoned in the desert and left to die by Martin and Jones. (They worked together again that same year in THE BROTHERHOOD OF SATAN.) Instead of dying, he finds water in a previously arid spot, opens a rest stop for thirsty travelers, and prospers. Stevens is a whore determined to sleep her way to riches, and after a brief fling with Robards, she decides to move on to greener sheets, fleeing to San Francisco. (This is Stevens's best role and underlines the terrible waste of her career—she's terrific.) Warner pops in and out as a preacher who can't decide whether he should save souls or live a life of dedicated hedonism. Hedonism wins. If you're expecting blood and guts and slow-motion death forget it. Peckinpah decided to make a different movie here, and different it is. Not a hit at the box office, it remains one of his finest efforts, funny, touching and never mawkishly sentimental.

BALLAD OF GREGORIO CORTEZ, THE

1983 104m c   ★★★
Western   PG/15
Embassy

Edward James Olmos *(Cortez)*, Tom Bower *(Boone Choate)*, Bruce McGill *(Bill Blakely)*, James Gammon *(Sheriff Fly)*, Alan Vint *(Sheriff Trimmell)*, Timothy Scott *(Sheriff Morris)*, Pepe Serna *(Romaldo Cortez)*, Brion James *(Capt. Rogers)*, Barry Corbin *(Abernethy)*, Rosana DeSoto *(Carolot Munoz)*

p, Michael Hausman; d, Robert M. Young; w, Robert M. Young, Victor Villasenor (based on the novel *With His Pistol in His Hands* by Americo Paredes); ph, Reynaldo Villalobos, Robert M. Young (DuArt Color); ed, Richard Soto; m, W. Michael Lewis, Edward James Olmos; art d, Stuart Wurtzel

Originally developed at Robert Redford's esteemed Sundance Institute, THE BALLAD OF GREGORIO CORTEZ recounts one of the most famous manhunts in Texas history. Gregorio Cortez (Olmos), a San Antonio cowhand, was arrested in 1901 in a case of mistaken identity. Because no one could properly translate into Spanish for him, Cortez fought back and accidentally slew a sheriff in what today might be deemed self-defense. Director Robert M. Young takes us on an 11-day manhunt as Cortez hightails it for Mexico, pursued by the legendary Texas Rangers and a small army of others, none of whom can catch the mercurial fugitive. The press made him a hero, but he turned himself in (after escaping several traps) when he learned that his family had been arrested and were being held as prisoners. Young uses flashbacks to present varying accounts of what happened. The original courthouse and jail where Cortez was held and tried lend authenticity to the setting, and the film provides a compelling historical representation of what life must have been like in the Southwest at the turn of the century, especially for Hispanic citizens and workers.

BALLAD OF NARAYAMA

(NARAYAMA-BUSHI-KO)
1958 98m c   ★★★
Drama
Shochiku   (Japan)

Kinuyo Tanaka *(Orin)*, Teiji Takahashi *(Tatsuhei)*, Yuko Mochizuki *(Tama-Yan)*, Danko Ichikawa *(Kesakichi)*, Keiko Ogasawara *(Mutsu-Yan)*, Seiji Miyaguchi *(Mata-Yan)*, Yunosuke Ito *(Mata-Yan's son)*, Ken Mitsuda *(Teru-Yan)*

p, Ryuzo Otani; d, Keisuke Kinoshita; w, Keisuke Kinoshita (based on the novel by Shichiro Fukazawa); ph, Hiroyuki Kusuda (Grandscope, Fujicolor); ed, Yoshi Sugihara; m, R. Kineya, M. Nozawa; art d, Kisaku Ito

One of the more notable of the "sensitive" Japanese releases popular on the international art house circuit in the early 1960s. Kinoshita's carefully stylized film depicts the centuries-old tradition of herding the aged and infirm onto the barren wastes of Mount Narayama where the elements soon put them out of their misery and send them to the gods. One woman in her seventies accepts her fate but stoically lingers, surviving on sheer will power. Another victim rebels at being sent to his death on the mountain by his brutal son, who kills the old man and is in turn himself killed.

The production, technically excellent and photographically stunning, distances the audience from the savagery of the drama via its careful, theatrical use of studio sets and lighting and a Kabuki narrator. Unlike the 1983 remake by Shohei Imamura, which emphasizes both the violence of the town's customs and the links between humans and nature via a relentlessly harsh realism, Kinoshita almost pushes the film into the realm of fantasy. Criticized by some as too conservative, this version, while less powerfully dramatic than Imamura's, nevertheless finds its own, different level of resonance.

BALLAD OF NARAYAMA, THE

1983 130m c   ★★★★½
Drama   /18
Toei (Japan)

Ken Ogata (Tatsuhei), Sumiko Sakamoto (Orin, His Mother), Takejo Aki (Tamayan, His Wife), Tonpei Hidari (Risuke, His Brother), Shoichi Ozawa (Katsuzo), Seiji Kurasaki (Kesakichi, Older Son), Kaoru Shimamori (Tomekichi, Younger Son), Ryutaro Tatsumi (Matayan), Junko Takada (Matsu), Nijiko Kiyokawa (Old Widow Okane)

p, Goro Kusakabe, Jiro Tomoda; d, Shohei Imamura; w, Shohei Imamura (based on the stories "Narayama Bushi-ko" and "Tohoku No Zunmatachi" by Scichiro Fakazawa); ph, Masao Tochizawa; ed, Hajime Okayasu; m, Shinichiro Ikebe; art d, Nobutaka Yoshino

A remarkable picture based on the award-winning stories by Fakazawa and previously filmed in 1958 under the same title. The story takes place 100 years ago in a Japanese village plagued by famine. In accordance with the villagers' method of rationing food, newborn males are left to die in the rice paddies while newborn females are given the chance to survive to bear children. It is customary for the eldest son to carry his parents, at age seventy, to the top of Mount Narayama, to be left there to die of starvation. This self-enforced population control is willingly embraced by Sakamoto, a 69-year-old woman who is healthier than most men half her age, because it is an age-old custom. She has lived a long life, finding wives for both her sons and preparing her family for her absence. The villagers begin to doubt the validity of the tradition when they realize it means losing Sakamoto. To calm them, Sakamoto purposely wears herself down, even going so far as to knock out her strong teeth on a rock. Ogata reluctantly begins the trip up the mountain, carrying his bundled mother on his back. After a seemingly endless ascent he reaches the ancient grounds scattered with the bones of those who have come before. With great difficulty he leaves his mother there to die and returns to the village.

In this picture director Imamura, while not ignoring his recurring preoccupations with folklore and shamanism, has gone to great effort to equate man with the nature that surrounds him. THE BALLAD OF NARAYAMA is splendidly photographed with an eye that conveys a great love of trees, grass, insects, and animals. The characters in this village are born of the earth, live out their lives on the earth, and ultimately return to the earth. While seemingly morbid on a surface level, the film is filled with life-affirming signs and is one of the most beautiful and peaceful films to come from Japan in some time.

BAMBI

1942 70m c   ★★★★
Animated/Children's   /U
Disney

VOICES OF: Bobby Stewart (Bambi), Peter Behn (Thumper), Stan Alexander (Flower), Cammie King (Phylline), Donnie Dunagan, Hardie Albright, John Sutherland, Tim Davis, Sam Edwards, Sterling Holloway

p, Walt Disney; d, David Hand; w, Perce Pearce, Larry Morey (based on the story by Felix Salten); m, Frank Churchill, Edward Plumb (conducted by Alexander Steinert); anim, Milt Kahl, Eric Larson, Franklin Thomas, Oliver M. Johnston, Jr.

BAMBI might well have been called THUMPER because the little rabbit sometimes threatens to steal the picture away from the eponymous hero. Despite the stiff competition, Bambi remains one of Disney's most appealing animated characters, as we watch him mature from newborn fawn to youth to a position as leader, with his father, of the herd. Except for Bambi's being a deer, the story could be that of any youngster facing trials and tribulations. He loses his mother to a hunter's bullet (a scene guaranteed to leave not a dry eye in the house), he fights for his doe, Phylline, and must kill his rival for her cold nose. He then saves her from a horde of mad dogs. The culminating scene of a forest fire ranks among the animated highlights in the history of the technique. Thumper provides all the comedy as he teaches Bambi how to survive in the forest, the funniest scene showing the rabbit attempting to teach Bambi how to slide across the ice. There is virtually no mention of humans in the movie and the only word Bambi fears is "Man" because it symbolizes the attack on the tranquility of the sylvan forest. Definitely a film for the entire family, even if small children might become very emotionally wrapped up in its sometimes sad story.

BANANAS

1971 82m c   ★★★
Comedy/War   /15
UA

Woody Allen (Fielding Mellish), Louise Lasser (Nancy), Carlos Montalban (Gen. Vargas), Natividad Abascal (Yolanda), Jacobo Morales (Esposito), Miguel Suarez (Luis), David Ortiz (Sanchez), Rene Enriquez (Diaz), Jack Axelrod (Arroyo), Howard Cosell (Himself)

p, Charles H. Joffe, Jack Grossberg; d, Woody Allen; w, Woody Allen, Mickey Rose; ph, Andrew Costikyan (Deluxe Color); ed, Ron Kalish; m, Marvin Hamlisch; prod d, Ed Wittstein; cos, Gene Coffin

Woody Allen is Fielding Mellish, a neurotic New Yorker who's enamored with a political activist, Nancy (Louise Lasser, Allen's wife at the time), who'll have nothing to do with him because she's totally immersed in the revolution taking place in the banana republic of San Marcos. Wearing Castro-like fatigues and a false red beard, Allen accidentally winds up as president of San Marcos. He returns to the US, is unmasked as a fraud, tried for subversion, and winds up marrying Nancy. Although some of the humor falls flat in this early Allen comedy, his satire of revolutions and revolutionaries is at moments wickedly funny. The film makes for rather odd viewing now given the later tragedies which befell Nicaragua and El Salvador.

BAND OF ANGELS

1957 125m c   ★★★★
Drama   /A
WB

Clark Gable (Hamish Bond), Yvonne De Carlo (Amantha Starr), Sidney Poitier (Rau-Ru), Efrem Zimbalist, Jr. (Ethan Sears), Rex Reason (Seth Parton), Patric Knowles (Charles de Marigny), Torin Thatcher (Capt. Canavan), Andrea King (Miss Idell), Ray Teal (Mr. Calloway), Russell Evans (Jimmee)

d, Raoul Walsh; w, John Twist, Ivan Goff, Ben Roberts (based on the novel by Robert Penn Warren); ph, Lucien Ballard (Warner Color); ed, Folmar Blangsted; m, Max Steiner; art d, Franz Bachelin; cos, Marjorie Best

An entertainingly full-blown melodrama brimming with lust, notable for its similarities to GONE WITH THE WIND and for dealing with miscegenation and racial tensions. Forced to leave school when left penniless after her father's death, De Carlo learns that she is partially black and is promptly taken to be sold on the block. Before any mean-minded plantation owner can unbutton her bodice, however, powerful landowner Gable buys her and ensconces her inside his lavish mansion, where she soon becomes his loving and grateful mistress. The Civil War breaks out, and the Yankees capture New Orleans, recruiting ex-slaves to the colors. Poitier, Gable's overseer (in a soft profile of the legendary black leader Bras Coupe), deserts his master to join the Union Army, hating the patronizing Gable and his mulatto mistress. Risking execution by disobeying Yankee orders, Gable burns his crops and retreats to one of his remote plantations. Poitier follows in pursuit and the stage is set for several climactic confrontations.

Almost the entire cast is in top form, even sultry De Carlo, who had an occasional penchant for overacting. Gable almost does a reprise of his magnificent Rhett Butler from GONE WITH THE WIND. Outlandishly memorable is the scene on his patio where he drunkenly confesses his past as a slave trader while a summer storm rages overhead. Poitier, in an unsympathetic part, does what he can with a surly, graceless character. Walsh's direction is at its finest in a lively adaptation of the Warren novel. Steiner's score thunders, hums and calls plaintively where needed, while Ballard's photography shows the Old South in all its glories and gluttonies.

BAND OF OUTSIDERS

1964   95m   bw   ★★★
Crime
Anouchka/Orsay   (France)

Anna Karina (Odile), Claude Brasseur (Arthur), Sami Frey (Franz), Louisa Colpeyn (Mme. Victoria), Daniele Girard (English Teacher), Ernest Menzer (Arthur's Uncle), Chantal Darget (Arthur's Aunt), Michele Seghers (Pupil), Claude Makovski (Pupil), Georges Staquet (Legionnaire)

d, Jean-Luc Godard; w, Jean-Luc Godard (based on the novel Fool's Gold by Dolores Hitchens); ph, Raoul Coutard; ed, Agnes Guillemot, Francoise Collin; m, Michel Legrand

Several years after the success of his debut feature, BREATHLESS, Godard returned to the crime genre and his fascination with American pop culture. Outsiders less by choice than by societal pressures, Odile (Karina), Arthur (Brasseur), and Franz (Frey) meet in an English language class and become fast friends. Odile tells Franz that she lives in a house where a large cache of loot is hidden, and soon he and Arthur, under the influence of the countless Hollywood films and pulp novels they've consumed, decide to burglarize the house. Odile, attracted to both men, completes the criminal triangle.

As anyone who has seen a Godard film might guess, there is very little concern for plot—the attraction of BAND OF OUTSIDERS lies not so much in its actual story as in Godard's telling of it. His voice-over narration is confrontational; his characters talk to the screen; there exists a strange, somewhat uneasy relationship between comedy and violence; and the frame is filled with various allusions to film, literature, and Godard

himself. This was his seventh film in only five years and, as in Truffaut's SHOOT THE PIANO PLAYER, it attempts to find a new truth by retelling a familiar story in a new way. Particularly memorable is the trio's nine-second tour of the Louvre.

If this film is less engaged with social and political realities than most of Godard's other work from this period and seems like nothing more than a playful attempt to re-create an old Hollywood genre, one must remember that even a lesser Godard is likely to be much more stimulating than another director's better films. At the height of his impish self-awareness, the filmmaker credits himself here as Jean-Luc Cinema Godard.

BAND WAGON, THE

1953   111m   c   ★★★★½
Musical   /U
MGM

Fred Astaire (Tony Hunter), Cyd Charisse (Gaby Gerard), Oscar Levant (Lester Marton), Nanette Fabray (Lily Marton), Jack Buchanan (Jeffrey Cordova), James Mitchell (Paul Byrd), Robert Gist (Hal Benton), Thurston Hall (Col. Tripp), Ava Gardner (The Movie Star), LeRoy Daniels (Shoeshine Boy)

p, Arthur Freed; d, Vincente Minnelli; w, Betty Comden, Adolph Green; ph, Harry Jackson (Technicolor); ed, Albert Akst; chor, Michael Kidd, Oliver Smith

Seamlessly directed by Vincente Minnelli, THE BAND WAGON is one of the finest musicals ever made. Playing its hackneyed story with tongue firmly in cheek, it simultaneously reflects upon the musical genre, satirizes its conventions and delivers marvelous entertainment. Hollywood dancer Tony Hunter (Astaire) having fallen from favor with the moviegoing public, attempts a comeback on Broadway in a musical written by Lester and Lily Marton (Levant and Fabray, essentially playing the screenwriting team of Comden and Green). The play's arty director, Jeffrey Cordova (Buchanan), makes some misguided staging decisions, while Tony's lead, ballerina Gaby Gerard (Charisse), is less than enamored of him, setting up the problems the players must resolve.

Along the way, we are treated to a tart look at life behind the scenes and a host of highly engaging performances. Astaire has rarely been more appealing—or moving—in a thinly disguised autobiographical role. Fabray and Levant provide the sugar and vinegar in generous doses, Charisse's acting is quite satisfactory and her subdued, earthy sensuality makes her a surprisingly apt dance partner for Astaire, and Buchanan all but steals the film as the hilariously Faust-obsessed, maddeningly brilliant impresario. A low-key highlight is his delightful softshoe with Astaire to "I Guess I'll Have to Change My Plans", but the musical pleasures are many and varied, including "A Shine on Your Shoes," Astaire's romp in a 42nd Street penny arcade; "Dancing in the Dark," Astaire and Charisse's dreamy pas de deux; the legendary "Triplets," featuring a swaddled Buchanan, Astaire, and Fabray; the striking and sexy "Girl Hunt Ballet", a spoof of film noir and hardboiled detectives; and of course the witty showbiz anthem, "That's Entertainment."

BANG THE DRUM SLOWLY

1973   96m   c   ★★★½
Sports   /AA
Paramount

Robert De Niro *(Bruce Pearson)*, Michael Moriarty *(Henry Wiggen)*, Vincent Gardenia *(Dutch Schnell)*, Phil Foster *(Joe Jaros)*, Ann Wedgeworth *(Katie)*, Pat McVey *(Pearson's Father)*, Heather MacRae *(Holly Wiggen)*, Selma Diamond *(Tootsie)*, Barbara Babcock, Maurice Rosenfield *(Team Owners)*

p, Maurice Rosenfield, Lois Rosenfield; d, John Hancock; w, Mark Harris (based on his novel); ph, Richard Shore (Movielab Color); ed, Richard Marks; m, Stephen Lawrence; prod d, Robert Gundlach

A well-done if depressing film, BANG THE DRUM SLOWLY is a sort of baseball version of "Brian's Song," the TV movie that told the story of the extraordinary friendship between the Chicago Bears' Gale Sayers and Brian Piccolo, who died of cancer. In this film, De Niro is the dying athlete, a journeyman big-league catcher who has contracted Hodgkin's disease. Moriarty, the team's star pitcher, becomes dedicated to his batterymate when he learns of De Niro's fatal illness and prevents him from being sent to the minors. When their teammates find out, they too belatedly make De Niro feel like one of the boys, and, surprisingly, his playing even improves. Alas, it's all a little too late.

One of De Niro's earliest roles—the quintessential bumpkin who wears a smiley-face T-shirt under his sports jacket—it's poles apart from the enigmatic loners that later became his specialty. To prepare for the part, De Niro not only practiced with the Cincinnati Reds, but also traveled to Georgia to perfect his accent. His hard work resulted in a wholly believable performance. Moriarty is also very effective as Henry Wiggen, the central character in a number of baseball novels by Harris, who adapted one of them for this film. Previously done on TV with Paul Newman and Albert Salmi, this version, under Hancock's fine direction, became one of the best baseball movies ever. Vincent Gardenia received an Academy Award nomination for his supporting work as the team's manager, and Foster is wonderful as a coach.

BANK DICK, THE

1940   69m   bw   ★★★★½
Comedy   /U
Universal

W.C. Fields *(Egbert Souse)*, Cora Witherspoon *(Agatha Souse)*, Una Merkel *(Myrtle Souse)*, Evelyn Del Rio *(Elsie Mae Adele Brunch Souse)*, Jessie Ralph *(Mrs. Hermisillo Brunch)*, Franklin Pangborn *(J. Pinkerton Snoopington)*, Shemp Howard *(Joe Guelpe)*, Dick Purcell *(Mackley Q. Greene)*, Grady Sutton *(Og Oggilby)*, Russell Hicks *(J. Frothingham Waterbury)*

d, Edward F. Cline; w, W.C. Fields; ph, Milton Krasner; ed, Arthur Hilton; art d, Jack Otterson

Along with IT'S A GIFT, one of the definitive W.C. Fields films. THE BANK DICK is, as with all the best of Fields, appropriately thin on plot and heavy with hilarious set-pieces which allow "The Great Man" his full comic scope. The cynical, eccentric, bottle-hitting comedian plays an unemployed, henpecked (as usual) family man none-too-eagerly seeking work who accidentally captures a bank robber and is rewarded with a job as guard inside the bank. When not busy bothering customers (as when he apprehends a patron's son brandishing a toy gun), he runs between his deliciously horrid family and The Black Pussy Cat Cafe, where the proprietor (a Three Stooges-less Howard) spends most of his time pouring the guard, his only customer, a series of stiff ones.

The movie is filled with a marvelous series of Fields-patented comic bits, including an especially zany car chase, reminiscent of the best Mack Sennett, where "hostage" Fields once again inadvertantly saves the day. Fields, who wrote the script under the typically improbable pseudonym of Mahatma Kane Jeeves, plays a character named Souse, which he pronounces, in the French manner, as "Sou-say"; the rest of the cast, as might be expected, merely follows the word's English pronunciation. With wonderful supporting work from Witherspoon, Ralph, Pangborn, Sutton, Jack Norton, Pierre Watkin, and many others.

BARBAROSA

1982   90m   c   ★★★½
Western   PG
Universal

Willie Nelson *(Barbarosa)*, Gary Busey *(Karl)*, Isela Vega *(Josephina)*, Gilbert Roland *(Don Braulio)*, Danny De La Paz *(Eduardo)*, Alma Martinez *(Juanita)*, George Voskovec *(Herman)*, Sharon Compton *(Hilda)*, Howland Chamberlin *(Emil)*, Harry Caesar *(Sims)*

p, Paul N. Lazarus, III, William D. Wittliff; d, Fred Schepisi; w, William D. Wittliff; ph, Ian Baker (Panavision, Todd AO); ed, Don Zimmerman, David Ramirez; m, Bruce Smeaton

Country singer Willie Nelson plays the amiable title outlaw who befriends Gary Busey. The two roam the Texas border region, both on the run from family feuds. A beautifully filmed, nicely philosophic and rather old-fashioned western with an elegiac tone, well directed by Australian director Fred Schepisi (BREAKER MORANT), BARBAROSA features uniformly strong acting, with Busey and Nelson making a good team.

BAREFOOT IN THE PARK

1967   104m   c   ★★★½
Comedy   /PG
Paramount

Robert Redford *(Paul Bratter)*, Jane Fonda *(Corie Bratter)*, Charles Boyer *(Victor Velasco)*, Mildred Natwick *(Mrs. Ethel Banks)*, Herb Edelman *(Telephone Man)*, James F. Stone *(Delivery Man)*, Ted Hartley *(Frank)*, Mabel Albertson *(Aunt Harriet)*, Fritz Feld *(Restaurant Proprietor)*

p, Hal B. Wallis; d, Gene Saks; w, Neil Simon (based on his play); ph, Joseph La Shelle (Technicolor); ed, William Lyon; m, Neal Hefti; cos, Edith Head

Laughs galore in early first screenplay by Simon, based on his Broadway success. Saks makes a fine impression in his first directorial stint, which features Redford and Fonda living in a small fifth-floor apartment in Greenwich Village. She thinks their place is lovely, but he, ever the conservative attorney, hates it. Boyer plays the slightly zany, womanizing upstairs neighbor who must go through their apartment to reach his. Ever a romantic, Fonda adores the old reprobate and fixes him up with her stodgy mother (Natwick). A series of comic and romantic complications ensues, some of which center around Redford's inability to let himself go—like the night he refused Fonda's entreaties to go barefoot in Central Park on a night when it was 17 degrees out and raining to boot. Love of course finds a way, and Redford finds a way to romp in a manner befitting the film's title. Redford and the Oscar-nominated Natwick, fresh from their Broadway triumph in the play, perform with the ease familiarity brings, and Fonda and Boyer also display the appropriate lightness of touch.

BARFLY

1987   100m   c   ★★★★
Comedy/Romance   R/18
Francis Ford Coppola/Golan-Globus

Mickey Rourke (*Henry Chinaski*), Faye Dunaway (*Wanda Wilcox*), Alice Krige (*Tully Sorenson*), Jack Nance (*Detective*), J.C. Quinn (*Jim*), Frank Stallone (*Eddie*), Gloria LeRoy (*Grandma Moses*), Sandy Martin (*Janice*), Roberta Bassin (*Lilly*), Joe Unger (*Ben*)

p, Barbet Schroeder, Fred Roos, Tom Luddy; d, Barbet Schroeder; w, Charles Bukowski; ph, Robby Muller (TVC color); ed, Eva Gardos; prod d, Bob Ziembicki; cos, Milena Canonero

Not a film for everyone, the unrelived squalor of BARFLY nevertheless does offer its own peculiar fascinations. The world of writer Charles Bukowski is placed under a cinematic microscope, revealing to the curious the poetry of decadence in a fairly non-judgmental manner.

Rourke plays Henry Chinaski, a slovenly, hard-drinking, fistfighting scribe who's taken with Wanda Wilcox (Dunaway), a haggard but attractive drunk he meets in a bar. Chinaski's work is admired by wealthy, pretty, self-assured publisher Tully Sorenson (Krige), and that provides the film with a romantic triangle as Wanda and Tully battle for Henry's attentions. Rourke, who turns in the finest performance of his career to date, takes a character who could be seen as pathetic and despicable and makes him, if not a likable hero, at least an understandable one. Dunaway gives an exceptional performance, and Krige is perfect in her role.

The making of BARFLY was nearly as extreme as anything in the film. Producer-director Schroeder had originally commissioned Bukowski to write a screenplay for $20,000, then struggled for years to get the project filmed. Finally, he entered the office of Cannon president Menahem Golan and threatened to cut off a finger unless Cannon made the film. After initially refusing, Golan realized Schroeder's obsession with BARFLY and eventually gave the project the go ahead. The kind of film people are likely to disagree about strongly.

BARKLEYS OF BROADWAY, THE

1949   109m   c   ★★★½
Musical   /U
MGM

Fred Astaire (*Josh Barkley*), Ginger Rogers (*Dinah Barkley*), Oscar Levant (*Ezra Miller*), Billie Burke (*Mrs. Belney*), Gale Robbins (*Shirlene May*), Jacques Francois (*Jacques Barredout*), George Zucco (*The Judge*), Clinton Sundberg (*Bert Felsher*), Inez Cooper (*Pamela Driscoll*), Carol Brewster (*Gloria Amboy*)

p, Arthur Freed; d, Charles Walters; w, Betty Comden, Adolph Green; ph, Harry Stradling (Technicolor); ed, Albert Akst; m, Lennie Hayton; art d, Cedric Gibbons, Edward Carfagno; chor, Hermes Pan, Robert Alton; cos, Irene; anim, Irving G. Reis

A very enjoyable if somewhat disappointing reunion for the unbeatable team of Astaire and Rogers. Handsomely produced, THE BARKLEYS OF BROADWAY retells with some but not quite enough wit a thinly disguised version of what was perceived as the duo's actual working relationship. Astaire and Rogers play Josh and Dinah Barkley, an affectionate and highly successful, if sometimes contentious, married musical comedy team. Trouble comes when Dinah's dramatic ambitions and Josh's jealousy over the attention paid to his wife by a handsome French playwright (Francois) encourage the pair to split both

professionally and personally. Although each enjoys considerable solo success, they finally realize they belong together doing musical comedy.

The team's first pairing in ten years, which came about after Astaire's costar in the previous year's highly successful EASTER PARADE, Judy Garland, suffered one of her many breakdowns, it would also prove to be their last together. THE BARKLEYS OF BROADWAY shows neither the screen duo nor screenwriters Comden and Green at their best, despite the sharp support from Levant, Burke, and others. The film's chief weakness is the score by Harry Warren and Ira Gershwin, though Fred and Ginger also reprise George and Ira Gershwin's decade-old classic, "They Can't Take That Away from Me." Oddly enough, the legendary pair most closely approximates their earlier magic during the warm comic and romantic interludes, though their delightful and spirited tap duet to "Bouncin' the Blues" does bring some of their patented incandescence onto the dance floor.

BARRETTS OF WIMPOLE STREET, THE

1934   110m   bw   ★★★½
Romance/Biography   /U
MGM

Fredric March (*Robert Browning*), Norma Shearer (*Elizabeth Barrett*), Charles Laughton (*Edward Moulton Barrett*), Maureen O'Sullivan (*Henrietta Barrett*), Katherine Alexander (*Arabel Barrett*), Una O'Connor (*Wilson*), Ian Wolfe (*Harry Bevan*), Marion Clayton (*Bella Hedley*), Ralph Forbes (*Capt. Surtees Cook*), Vernon Downing (*Octavius Barrett*)

p, Irving Thalberg; d, Sidney Franklin; w, Ernest Vajda, Claudine West, Donald Ogden Stewart (based on the play by Rudolph Besier); ph, William Daniels; ed, Margaret Booth; art d, Cedric Gibbons; cos, Adrian

One of the better-known and more typical of MGM's adaptations of famous stage plays, THE BARRETTS OF WIMPOLE STREET is slightly strangled by its own sense of prestige, but proves worthy drama nonetheless. This historical romance tells how the near-invalid Elizabeth Barrett (Shearer) finds happiness and renewed vitality through the love of fellow poet Robert Browning (March), despite the efforts of her dictatorial and overly protective father (played exquisitely by Laughton). Confined to her room with little but her dog and her love of poetry for comfort, Elizabeth cannot even reach out to her brothers and sisters, also under the thumb of their father's tyranny. The battle between father and lover, seemingly simplistic, takes on increasing depth as the drama unfolds.

Though much of the acting is somewhat theatrical, it is also effective on its own terms in this rarefied atmosphere. The climactic moment as Elizabeth struggles out of her father's grasp, realizing that his smothering love for her isn't simply of a paternal nature, is extremely well handled by both Shearer and Laughton. Although the latter's villainy dominates the film, the supporting performances are generally good, particularly those of O'Sullivan as Elizabeth's hapless younger sister and O'Connor as a loyal servant. The film does not always seem quite as good as contemporary reviews would indicate, but is like an old sachet whose scent of old lavender continues to linger.

BARRETTS OF WIMPOLE STREET, THE

1957   105m   c   ★★★★
Romance/Biography   /U
MGM   (U.K.)

Jennifer Jones (*Elizabeth*), John Gielgud (*Barrett*), Bill Travers (*Robert Browning*), Virginia McKenna (*Henrietta*), Susan Stephen (*Bella*), Vernon Gray (*Capt. Surtees Cook*), Jean Anderson (*Wilson*), Maxine Audley (*Arabel*), Leslie Phillips (*Harry Bevan*), Laurence Naismith (*Dr. Chambers*)

p, Sam Zimbalist; d, Sidney Franklin; w, John Dighton (based on the play by Rudolph Besier); ph, Freddie Young; ed, Frank Clark; m, Bronislau Kaper; art d, Alfred Junge; cos, Elizabeth Haffenden

This very famous biographical drama was previously done as a play in 1931 and a movie in 1934, with Franklin helming both film versions. Jones plays poet and near-invalid Elizabeth Barrett, whose father's (Gielgud) almost incestuous adoration for her all but confines her to his London house. She is understandably lonely and depressed; her only companions are her books, her servants, her dog, and her horde of brothers (all wonderfully played by bright young men of the period), Enter Robert Browning (Travers), a fellow poet rich in love and warmth, who sweeps Elizabeth off the couch and into bloom like a morning glory at dawn. Gielgud, in a magnificent performance imbued with understated menace, attempts to smash the relationship before it attains fruition, and the struggle for the young woman's happiness is on. A subtle, lovingly rendered if sometimes leisurely film with fine acting all around and a technical skill which surpasses its worthy 1934 predecessor, THE BARRETTS OF WIMPOLE STREET is very effective drama and should be enjoyed without interruption.

BARRY LYNDON
1975   184m   c   ★★★
Historical   PG
Hawk/Peregrine   (U.K.)

Ryan O'Neal (*Barry Lyndon*), Marisa Berenson (*Lady Lyndon*), Patrick Magee (*The Chevalier*), Hardy Kruger (*Capt. Potzdorf*), Steven Berkoff (*Lord Ludd*), Gay Hamilton (*Nora*), Leonard Rossiter (*Capt. Quin*), Godfrey Quigley (*Capt. Grogan*), Arthur O'Sullivan (*Highwayman*), Diana Koerner (*German Girl*)

p, Stanley Kubrick; d, Stanley Kubrick; w, Stanley Kubrick (based on the novel by William Makepeace Thackeray); ph, John Alcott (Metrocolor); ed, Tony Lawson; m, Leonard Rosenman; prod d, Ken Adam; art d, Roy Walker

At over three hours in length, BARRY LYNDON may seem terribly fat. And yet it is such a visual delight that one is tempted to forgive its excesses—tempted, not compelled. Every shot is framed and shot beautifully, sometimes using new lighting and camera techniques developed especially in connection with this film. The details are exquisite and the overall recreation of atmosphere quite overwhelming. So did something go wrong? Much of one's response depends on your point of view. Clearly Kubrick is attempting to render stylistically the static nature of certain social strata in the 18th century. O'Neal's performance in the title role as the self-centered yet passive social climber was hailed in some quarters as highly appropriate in its blandness, while others damned it exactly for its lack of precision. The screenplay, extremely respectful of Thackeray's minor classic, is determinedly eager to fit everything in. Not a film you can watch with one eye, BARRY LYNDON, despite its flaws, has scenes filled to overflowing with subtleties which command one's attention and respect. Part of the problem is with modern spectators used to the rapid-fire editing of commercials and music videos, too enamored of speed to be able to sit back and enjoy as languorous a film as this.

BARTON FINK
1991   116m   c   ★★★½
Comedy/Drama   R/15
Circle Films/Barton Circle Productions

John Turturro (*Barton Fink*), John Goodman (*Charlie Meadows*), Judy Davis (*Audrey Taylor*), Michael Lerner (*Jack Lipnick*), John Mahoney (*W.P. Mayhew*), Tony Shalhoub (*Ben Geisler*), Jon Polito (*Lou Breeze*), Steve Buscemi (*Chet*), David Warrilow (*Garland Stanford*), Richard Portnow (*Detective Mastrionotti*)

p, Ethan Coen; d, Joel Coen; w, Ethan Coen, Joel Coen; ph, Roger Deakins; ed, Roderick Jaynes; m, Carter Burwell; prod d, Dennis Gassner; art d, Leslie McDonald, Bob Goldstein; cos, Richard Hornung

The grand-prize winner at the 1991 Cannes festival, BARTON FINK is the fourth installment in the Coen Brothers' series of highly stylized homages to classical Hollywood. But like their earlier films, BARTON FINK is a *tour de force* of cinematic technique that encases a quirky narrative of little depth.

Barton Fink (John Turturro) is an earnest young New York playwright who hits it big with a Depression-era proletarian drama before being reluctantly seduced by a lucrative offer to go to Hollywood and write for the movies. Despite assurances that he will be given free reign by studio boss Jack Lipnick (Michael Lerner), Barton is asked to write a wrestling picture for Wallace Beery. Pent up in a surreal hotel room, Barton suffers acute and hallucinatory writer's block.

Barton's funk is broken by two encounters. First comes a visit from Charlie Meadows (John Goodman), a gregarious traveling salesman who immediately befriends the writer. Barton confesses his desire to pen stories of the common man, but ignores the tales this Willie Loman has to tell. Next, paying a visit to the studio, he is further perplexed by the absurdities of the movie executives he watches at work. Hope returns, however, when he makes a second acquaintance.

Also on the studio writing staff is the legendary W.P. Mayhew (John Mahoney), an alcoholic Southern novelist who hasn't written a word since coming to Hollywood. Barton is disillusioned when he learns that W.P. is a cynical fraud whose work is done by his personal secretary, Audrey Taylor (Judy Davis). Audrey becomes Barton's caretaker as well. Her visit to his room turns from a writing session to a sexual encounter. Barton's bliss suddenly becomes a nightmare, however, when he awakes with Audrey's bloody corpse in his bed.

Unlike their previous works (the film noir BLOOD SIMPLE, the screwball comedy RAISING ARIZONA and the gangster film MILLER'S CROSSING), BARTON FINK is not a revisionist take on a classical genre but a bizarre, comic portrayal of the Hollywood studio system of the 1930s and 40s. The principal characters are clearly drawn from actual people in that system: Fink is a thinly veiled version of Clifford Odets, the leftist playwright who departed the socially committed Group Theatre in New York to write screenplays in Hollywood during WWII. And W.P. Mayhew is, of course, William Faulkner.

But the scene-stealer is Jack Lipnick, the larger-than-life movie mogul who is a composite of MGM's Louis B. Mayer and other studio heads. Michael Lerner's portrayal of Lipnick overwhelms even the fine acting of the leading players, not the least of which is Goodman's transformation from a lonely salesman into a psychotic killer. As Barton, John Turturro (DO THE RIGHT THING, MILLER'S CROSSING) can only deadpan his way amid these caricatures while careening from one baffling encounter to the next.

The film's period decor, mood lighting and artful camerawork are beautiful, at times thrilling, to look at. The surrealistic writer's block scenes, in which Barton silently watches wallpaper peel and its paste ooze, are particularly memorable—imagine ERASERHEAD in color. Ultimately, however, the look, sound and feel of this macabre comedy fail to support any coherent theme. The bombastic Philistines of Hollywood, the idealistic artists of the theater and the "common man" are all rather cruelly skewered in the film's finely polished characterizations. Much is denigrated, but little affirmed.

BASKET CASE

1982 90m c ★★★★
Horror /18
Analysis

Kevin Van Hentenryck (Duane Bradley), Terri Susan Smith (Sharon), Beverly Bonner (Casey), Lloyd Pace (Dr. Harold Needleman), Diana Browne (Dr. Judith Kutter), Robert Vogel (Hotel Manager), Bill Freeman (Dr. Julius Lifflander), Joe Clarke (Brian "Mickey" O'Donovan), Dorothy Strongin (Josephine), Ruth Neuman (Aunt)

p, Edgar Ievins; d, Frank Henenlotter; w, Frank Henenlotter; ph, Bruce Torbet; ed, Frank Henenlotter; m, Gus Russo; fx, Kevin Haney, John Caglione

This ultra-low-budget production was shot over the course of six months on location in the streets, apartments, and flophouses of New York City. It became a hit on the midnight-show circuit and is arguably one of the best horror films of the 1980s. Directed by Frank Henenlotter with as much style as is possible on a miniscule budget, the film centers on Duane (Van Hentenryck), a young man from Glens Falls, New York, who checks into a fleabag hotel on 42nd Street carrying a wicker basket. Inside the basket is his small, horribly misshapen Siamese twin, Belial. Communicating with Duane telepathically, Belial is determined to wreak vengeance on the physicians that separated him from his twin. Meanwhile, however, Duane has met a nice girl (Smith) and begun to make a life of his own, one that doesn't include Belial.

Disturbing, grotesque, and very funny at times, BASKET CASE is a unique work in which imagination triumphs over the limitations of budget. Blown up to 35mm from the 16mm original, the film's grainy, cheap look only enhances the seediness of Henenlotter's milieu, while, in Belial, Henenlotter has come up with one of the most memorable and sympathetic screen monsters since KING KONG. A rather cheap-looking puppet created by Kevin Haney and John Caglione, Belial has a certain shabby charm that has endeared him to horror fans throughout the world. In a film that contains many unforgettable images, perhaps the most startling—and most moving—is a flashback to Belial's childhood, in which the monster's kindly aunt lets the mutant child sit on her lap while reading aloud to him.

BATAAN

1943 113m bw ★★★★
War /A
MGM

Robert Taylor (Sgt. Bill Dane), George Murphy (Lt. Steve Bentley), Thomas Mitchell (Cpl. Jake Feingold), Lloyd Nolan (Cpl. Barney Todd/Danny Burns), Lee Bowman (Capt. Henry Lassiter), Robert Walker (Leonard Purckett), Desi Arnaz (Felix Ramirez), Barry Nelson (F.X. Matowski), Phillip Terry (Matthew Hardy), Roque Espiritu (Cpl. Juan Katigbak)

p, Irving Starr; d, Tay Garnett; w, Robert D. Andrews (based partly on the 1934 film THE LOST PATROL); ph, Sidney Wagner; ed, George White; m, Bronislau Kaper; art d, Cedric Gibbons; fx, A. Arnold Gillespie, Warren Newcombe

This tough, uncompromising film, extremely well handled by director Garnett, tells the story of a group of determined soldiers fighting on Bataan, knowing that they face certain death as they attempt to delay the advancing Japanese troops. Based on the heroic defense of the Philippines in early 1942, the film shows soldiers from all parts of America, as well as Filipinos fighting for their own soil. Taylor gives a rugged and inspiring performance as the grim but kind-hearted Sergeant Dane, who commands the small group in a rear-guard action, protecting MacArthur's ragged army as it limps away down the narrow peninsula, where it would make its stand for three harrowing months. One by one, the soldiers are brutally picked off (not unlike the forlorn members of John Ford's 1934 film THE LOST PATROL) until only a handful are left. Although the film was clearly shot within the confines of a studio set, the use of miniatures is effective and the hand-to-hand combat scenes are startling and brutal. One of MGM's better war films.

BATMAN

1989 126m C ★★★
Fantasy/Crime PG-13/U
WB

Michael Keaton (Batman/Bruce Wayne), Jack Nicholson (Joker/Jack Napier), Kim Basinger (Vicki Vale), Robert Wuhl (Alexander Knox), Pat Hingle (Commissioner Gordon), Billy Dee Williams (District Attorney Harvey Dent), Michael Gough (Alfred), Jack Palance (Carl Grissom), Jerry Hall (Alicia), Lee Wallace (Mayor)

p, Jon Peters, Peter Guber, Chris Kenny; d, Tim Burton; w, Sam Hamm, Warren Skaaren (based on a story by Sam Hamm and characters created by Bob Kane); ph, Roger Pratt (Eastmancolor); ed, Ray Lovejoy; m, Danny Elfman; prod d, Anton Furst; art d, Leslie Tomkins, Terry Ackland-Snow, Nigel Phelps; cos, Bob Ringwood, Linda Henrikson

Gotham City, a crime-ridden, debris-strewn, sunless, architecturally incoherent metropolis, is desperately in need of a savior, for the city is in the corrupting grip of crime boss Carl Grissom (Palance). Ace photographer Vicki Vale (Basinger) has been intrigued by the sightings of a mysterious, giant vigilante bat. She meets enigmatic millionaire Bruce Wayne (Keaton), not suspecting that he's Batman. Wayne is quite taken with the lovely Vicki but is distracted by the wicked ways of Grissom's top henchman, Jack Napier (Nicholson), alias the Joker.

Perhaps it was inevitable, considering all the hype preceding and surrounding its release, that BATMAN would fall a bit flat once it finally reached the screen. Despite its interesting, grim tone and undeniably striking visuals from director Burton and production designer Furst, the film fails to synthesize its strengths into a compelling whole. Its obvious intention to parallel the Joker and Batman as two psychotics, one promoting good and the other evil, doesn't come through with as much impact as it should. The Joker seems maniacal, all right, but hardly as sinister as the silent Batman. In terms of acting, too, Nicholson's campy, full-blown rendering of the Joker (his best moment occurs as he pulls a ridiculously long pistol out of his pants) overshadows the miscast Keaton, whose attempt to be moody and macho gives him all the appeal of plywood.

BATMAN is dark, stylish, and full of "postmodern" touches—but wants to be more so. Given all its potential, it's a shame BATMAN wasn't more. It was, however, easily the biggest box-office hit of 1989, and one of the highest grossing films in history, a testament more to its massive marketing campaign than to its quality.

BATTLE OF ALGIERS, THE

(MAARAKAT ALGER)
1966   120m   bw   ★★★★
War   /X
Magna   (Italy/Algeria)

Yacef Saadi *(Kader)*, Jean Martin *(Colonel)*, Brahim Haggiag *(Ali La Pointe)*, Tommaso Neri *(Captain)*, Samia Kerbash *(One of the Girls)*, Fawzia el Kader *(Halima)*, Michele Kerbash *(Fathia)*, Mohamed Ben Kassen *(Petit Omar)*

p, Antonio Musu, Yacef Saadi; d, Gillo Pontecorvo; w, Gillo Pontecorvo, Franco Solinas; ph, Marcello Gatti; ed, Mario Serandrei, Mario Morra; m, Gillo Pontecorvo, Ennio Morricone

---

A powerful battle cry for Marxist revolutionaries, THE BATTLE OF ALGIERS details the struggle for Algerian independence from France. The film opens in 1957, as a tortured Arab prisoner informs against Ali la Pointe (Haggiag), the last surviving member of the FLN (Algerian Liberation Front). As French soldiers surround Ali's apartment, Colonel Mathieu (Martin) issues a final warning to Ali and his family: surrender or be blown to pieces. With the sides clearly laid out—revolutionary vs. counterrevolutionary—the film shifts to 1954, as the Algerian conflict first develops.

Photographed in grainy black and white to suggest the style of documentaries and TV news reports, THE BATTLE OF ALGIERS most closely resembles the neorealism of Roberto Rossellini and the revolutionary editing techniques of Sergei Eisenstein. Like Eisenstein, director Pontecorvo took his camera to the actual locations of the revolution, re-created certain events, and cast local nonprofessionals. Only Martin is a professional actor, while Saadi, the film's coproducer, plays an FLN leader—a character based on his real-life role as the organizer of the resistance and the military commander of the FLN.

The content of the film has been attacked as being too inflammatory; it was reportedly used as a terrorist primer in the late 1960s. Yet one could also argue that the film is considerably more open about its politics than most films. What makes THE BATTLE OF ALGIERS's power creditable is Pontecorvo's ability to present combatants on both sides as multidimensional, nonheroic human beings, even though it's obvious where the director's own sentiments lie. The film received the Golden Lion at Venice in 1966.

BATTLE OF BRITAIN

1969   133m   c   ★★★½
War   G/PG
Spitfire   (U.K.)

Harry Andrews *(Senior Civil Servant)*, Michael Caine *(Squadron Leader Canfield)*, Trevor Howard *(Air Vice Marshal Keith Park)*, Curt Jurgens *(Baron von Richter)*, Ian McShane *(Sgt. Pilot Andy)*, Kenneth More *(Group Capt. Baker)*, Laurence Olivier *(Air Chief Marshal Sir Hugh Dowding)*, Nigel Patrick *(Group Capt. Hope)*, Christopher Plummer *(Squadron Leader Harvey)*, Michael Redgrave *(Air Vice Marshal Evill)*

p, Harry Saltzman, S. Benjamin Fisz; d, Guy Hamilton; w, James Kennaway, Wilfred Greatorex; ph, Freddie Young, Bob Huke (Panavision, Technicolor); ed, Bert Bates; m, William Walton, Ron Goodwin; prod d, Sydney Streeter; art d, Maurice Carter, Bert Davey, Jack Maxsted, William Hutchinson, Gil Parrondo; fx, Cliff Richardson, Glen Robinson

---

This stirring if slightly overlong saga of England's WWII defense of its homeland features a staggering, star-studded cast, who abet the film's docudrama style with excellent portrayals down the line, despite the restrictions of their roles. Caine, Plummer, and More have the meatier parts, with Susannah York providing the obligatory love interest as Plummer's WAAF wife who hates the war and craves affection. Olivier is in fine form as Sir Hugh Dowding, whose crafty tactics with his limited fighter command induced the Luftwaffe to make fatal errors that led to its destruction, and Shaw is superb as an exhausted but relentlessly tough fighter commander who orders his men again and again into the air.

While the film is a fitting paean to the noble RAF in its "Finest Hour," nodding recognition is also given to the Czech and Polish flyers who fought alongside their British comrades. Except for Jurgens, however, the German actors are mere caricatures of the Nazi high command, with Stiefel especially ludicrous as a berserk Hitler. The aerial photography of the German bombing and the dogfights between the British and German fighters are spectacular and fascinating; it was the high production value of these segments which cost the producers the bulk of their $12 million investment. Adolf Galland, one of the sharpest German aces to vex the British during WWII, was employed as a technical advisor on the film.

BATTLEGROUND

1949   118m   bw   ★★★★
War   /A
MGM

Van Johnson *(Holley)*, John Hodiak *(Jarvess)*, Ricardo Montalban *(Roderigues)*, George Murphy *(Pop Stazak)*, Marshall Thompson *(Jim Layton)*, Jerome Courtland *(Abner Spudler)*, Don Taylor *(Standiferd)*, Bruce Cowling *(Wolowicz)*, James Whitmore *(Kinnie)*, Douglas Fowley *(Kipp Kippton)*

p, Dore Schary; d, William A. Wellman; w, Robert Pirosh; ph, Paul C. Vogel; ed, John Dunning; m, Lennie Hayton; art d, Cedric Gibbons, Hans Peters; fx, Peter Ballbusch

---

An excellent film, BATTLEGROUND tells the story of a squad of American foot soldiers trapped by the Germans in Bastogne in 1944. A wide assortment of MGM actors—none of them overreaching the prosaic dimensions of his character—play this cross-section of citizens, including Johnson, a wisecracking, girl-chasing GI "inconvenienced" by the war; and Hodiak, a conscientious small-time newspaperman turned soldier. (At one point, when food is running out in the besieged town, Johnson and Hodiak see an old woman picking through a garbage can. "I don't see that," Johnson says in disgust, turning away. "Well, I see it," retorts Hodiak. "I'll always see it and I never want anyone to forget it!") Whitmore is terrific as the tobacco-chomping, frozen-footed sergeant, as tough as a whole Panzer division, and Montalban was never better than here, as a Mexican-American from southern California who delights in his first snowfall, frolicking in the flakes like a child.

Director Wellman expertly conveys the life of soldiers at war—a life screenwriter Pirosh knew well, since he had served at Bastogne. BATTLEGROUND was a special project for Schary, who brought it from RKO to MGM after he was named MGM production chief (it was his first production credit there). Initially nixed by mogul Louis B. Mayer on the grounds that the public was not ready to relive WWII, the film proved extremely popular and received six Academy Award nominations including Best Picture. Quite apart from the film's merit, BATTLE-GROUND is also notable for initiating the rift between Mayer and Schary that eventually led to Mayer's ouster.

BEACH BLANKET BINGO
1965   100m   c   ★★½
Musical/Comedy
AIP

Frankie Avalon *(Frankie)*, Annette Funicello *(Dee Dee)*, Deborah Walley *(Bonnie Graham)*, Harvey Lembeck *(Eric Von Zipper)*, John Ashley *(Steve Gordon)*, Jody McCrea *(Bonehead)*, Donna Loren *(Donna)*, Marta Kristen *(Lorelei)*, Linda Evans *(Sugar Kane)*, Timothy Carey *(South Dakota Slim)*

p, James H. Nicholson, Samuel Z. Arkoff; d, William Asher; w, William Asher, Leo Townsend; ph, Floyd Crosby (Panavision, Pathecolor); ed, Fred R. Feitshans, Jr., Eve Newman; m, Les Baxter; art d, Howard Campbell

Probably the best known of the spate of "beach party" films of the 1960s, BEACH BLANKET BINGO provides 100 minutes of silly, mildly amusing entertainment if you're in the right mood. There's trouble in teen paradise when Frankie (Avalon) and Dee Dee (Funicello) clash over his infatuation with singer Sugar Kane (Evans). Meanwhile, a mermaid falls in love with nitwit surfer Bonehead (McCrea), and the nefarious Eric Von Zipper (Lembeck) and his Rat Pack kidnap Sugar. Don Rickles, Buster Keaton, Paul Lynde and others are also on hand, sandwiching their shtick between the musical numbers from Frankie, Annette, and their scantily clad pals.

BEACHES
1988   123m   c   ★★
Drama   PG-13/15
Touchstone/Silver Screen Partners IV/Bruckheimer
South-All Girl

Bette Midler *(C.C. Bloom)*, Barbara Hershey *(Hillary Whitney Essex)*, John Heard *(John Pierce)*, Spalding Gray *(Dr. Richard Milstein)*, Lainie Kazan *(Leona Bloom)*, James Read *(Michael Essex)*, Grace Johnston *(Victoria Essex)*, Mayim Bialik *(C.C., Age 11)*, Marcie Leeds *(Hillary, Age 11)*

p, Bonnie Bruckheimer-Martell, Bette Midler, Margaret Jennings South; d, Garry Marshall; w, Mary Agnes Donoghue (based on the novel by Iris Rainer Dart); ph, Dante Spinotti (Metrocolor); ed, Richard Halsey; m, Georges Delerue; prod d, Albert Brenner; cos, Robert de Mora

This interminable melodrama purports to be a warm, humorous, and moving look at the relationship of two women over the course of 30 years. In reality BEACHES is a trite, maudlin, and terribly superficial effort of the sub-made-for-TV quality, an insult to anyone who has ever befriended another human being. The film depicts the unlikely friendship of a brassy, Jewish, Bronx-bred singer (Midler) and an icy, WASP-ish, San Francisco-bred socialite (Hershey) from their meeting in Atlantic City until the day the latter is buried, a victim of the kind of disease that seems only to afflict characters in movies like this.

An ego trip for star-executive producer Midler, the film tells its story mostly in flashback and entirely from her character's point of view, while the successful songstress drives a rented car from LA to San Francisco to be with the dying Hershey. Director Marshall fails to bring anything remotely resembling inspiration or spontaneity to screenwriter Donoghue's terribly mundane disease-of-the-week script, leaving the viewer wondering why these two women would even speak to each other, let alone commit themselves to an apparently deeply emotional relationship. The problems they face are wholly synthetic, dealt with in a flash, and forgotten until the next minicrisis comes along. There is no sense of real joy, pain, or struggle here—merely a TV version that is only tangentially related to actual human experience.

BEAR, THE
1989   93m   c   ★★★★
Adventure   PG
Price/Renn   (France)

Jack Wallace *(Bill)*, Tcheky Karyo *(Tom)*, Andre Lacombe *(The Dog Handler)*, Bart the Bear *(Kaar)*, Douce the Bear *(Youk)*

p, Claude Berri; d, Jean-Jacques Annaud; w, Gerard Brach (based on the novel *The Grizzly King* by James Oliver Curwood); ph, Philippe Rousselot; ed, Noelle Boisson; m, Philippe Sarde; prod d, Toni Ludi; art d, Heidi Ludi, Antony Greengrow, George Dietz; cos, Corinne Jorry, Francoise Disle; anim, Bretislav Pojar

This deceptively simple wilderness tale began production in 1982 with a four-line synopsis—"A big solitary bear. An orphan bear cub. Two hunters in the forest. The animals' point of view"—and went on to take in more than $100 million *before* its US release. The plot, practically nonexistent at first, unfolds in British Columbia in 1885, detailing the idyllic daily routine of a bear cub. After the cub's mother is killed in a rockslide, however, the youngster must attempt to bond with a 2000-pound Kodiak male being pursued by a pair of hunters—Bill (Wallace), a calm, calculating veteran, and his young, overeager friend Tom (Karyo).

A far cry from the sweet nature adventures that Disney popularized, THE BEAR is a sublime, graceful tale of human nature told, somewhat paradoxically, through the eyes of an animal. Director Annaud tells his story almost exclusively through visuals, using a bare minimum of dialogue and an elegantly constructed soundtrack composed from the "language" of the bears. Though the film borrows from the sophisticated techniques of such masters of silent film as D.W. Griffith and Robert Flaherty, it also sometimes gives the feel of having been captured effortlessly by the cameras. Presenting a myriad of human emotions despite its animal characters, THE BEAR, like so many great, otherwise dissimilar films, speaks a universal message of humanism and morality in every frame.

BEAT THE DEVIL
1953   100m   bw   ★★★★
Comedy/Drama   /U
Romulus/Santana

Humphrey Bogart *(Billy Dannreuther)*, Gina Lollobrigida *(Maria Dannreuther)*, Jennifer Jones *(Gwendolyn Chelm)*, Robert Morley *(Peterson)*, Peter Lorre *(O'Hara)*, Edward Underdown *(Harry Chelm)*, Ivor Barnard *(Major Ross)*, Marco Tulli *(Ravello)*, Marion Perroni *(Purser)*, Alex Pochet *(Hotel Manager)*

d, John Huston; w, John Huston, Truman Capote (based on the novel by James Helvick); ph, Oswald Morris; ed, Ralph Kemplen; m, Franco Mannino; art d, Wilfred Singleton

A screwball, wacky comedy that is played as straight as any film noir and is even funnier as a result. Five desperate and disparate men (Bogart, Lorre, Morley, Barnard, and Tulli) are out to garner control over East African land which they believe contains a rich uranium ore lode. Their scuzzy steamer is in port in Italy. Bogart is married to Gina (an odd choice for the role but she proves to be more than adept at the straightfaced comedy). The other four are their "business associates." Bogart and Gina meet another couple, Jones and Underdown. She's in a blonde wig and off-the-wall; he's a prig-and-a-half at first glance but in reality, he's a phony peer. Jones rattles on about her hubby's uranium holdings, all lies. The "associates" think they are being gulled by Bogart when it appears that Bogie is after Jones and Gina is hot for Underdown.

The boat leaves for Africa, then blows up. Seven survivors make it to shore and are taken in by a hostile group of Arabs. Their lives are saved when Bogart manages to charm the evil Arab police chief by promising the man an opportunity to meet his idol, Rita Hayworth. Underdown is supposed to have drowned and this causes Jones, a pathological liar, to tell the truth. The four villains are taken in by the Italian police, then Jones gets a telegram from her still-alive husband and is delighted to learn that Underdown made it to Africa and acquired the uranium-rich land the others yearned for.

If all the aforementioned sounds like a hodge-podge, you're right. But it is such wonderful nonsense—there isn't a moment when the picture doesn't take a left turn when you expect it to turn right. Director Huston, working from a quirky, literate script by Capote, manages to parody a number of his earlier films, including THE MALTESE FALCON, THE TREASURE OF THE SIERRA MADRE, and KEY LARGO. Bogart, who, of course, was in all those films, seems to be having a marvelous time skewering them and gives a memorable performance. The film's humor is not readily apparent, and the movie was quickly rejected by the public upon its release. But today it has achieved something of a cult following and is a sheer delight.

BEAU GESTE

1939 114m bw   ★★★½
Adventure/War   /A
Paramount

Gary Cooper (Michael "Beau" Geste), Ray Milland (John Geste), Robert Preston (Digby Geste), Brian Donlevy (Sgt. Markoff), Susan Hayward (Isobel Rivers), J. Carrol Naish (Rasinoff), Albert Dekker (Schwartz), Broderick Crawford (Hank Miller), Charles Barton (Buddy McMonigal), James Stephenson (Maj. Henri de Beaujolais)

p, William A. Wellman; d, William A. Wellman; w, Robert Carson (based on the novel by Percival Christopher Wren); ph, Theodor Sparkuhl, Archie Stout; ed, Thomas Scott; m, Alfred Newman; art d, Hans Dreier, Robert Odell

Gary Cooper enacts the title role with quiet magnificence in this superb adventure tale loaded with drama, action, and mystery. The film opens with a relief column of Legionnaires crossing the desert dunes to Fort Zinderneuf. The fort seems strangely silent and a bugler is sent to investigate. He finds all inside the fort dead, and notices a sergeant on the parapet in whose hand is a note confessing to the theft of a fabulous gem called "the Blue Water." When the column enters the fort, the body of the sergeant is gone. Next the troops hear shots outside the fort and pursue what they think are tribal invaders. The fort suddenly erupts into flames, setting off the arsenal which destroys Zinderneuf.

In a flashback to 15 years earlier, we see three boys, the Geste brothers, at a great English mansion. The boys are cared for by kindly Thatcher, an impoverished blueblood who is so desperate to give the orphaned brothers and another child, Gillis, a good home that she secretly sells the treasured family jewel, the Blue Water, to raise the necessary funds. O'Connor secretly witnesses the transaction and watches Thatcher replace the gem with a fake. Years later, with O'Connor grown into Cooper, his brothers grown into Milland and Preston, and Gillis bloomed into Hayward, the lord of the manor, Huntley, appears seeking the great sapphire. To prevent Thatcher from having to admit her secret transaction, Cooper steals the phony gem, leaves a note for his brothers admitting the theft, and joins the Foreign Legion.

Cooper's great performance is given solid support by Ray Milland and Robert Preston, but Susan Hayward appears only briefly as the love interest and her performance is unmemorable. Brian Donlevy almost steals every scene he's in with a snarling performance that will scare the blazes out of any viewer, and J. Carrol Naish's hyena-like Rasinoff is unforgettable. Great support also comes from veteran heavies Albert Dekker, Harry Woods, and Harold Huber, enacting the mutinous Legionnaires. Broderick Crawford and Charles Barton provide the comic relief as the Gestes' sidekicks.

When director William Wellman was brought in to remake the silent 1926 version of P.C. Wren's captivating story, he was instructed to follow the original almost to the letter, which he did, even using the same location, the spreading desert dunes of Yuma, Arizona, where a new Fort Zinderneuf was completely rebuilt. Paramount executives thought it would be impressive to run the first reel of the silent version before showing the 1939 remake to reviewers, to show what sound could do to improve a classic. It was a scheme that almost blew up in their faces; some reviewers still preferred the silent version, but most felt that the remake was superior.

BEAUTY AND THE BEAST

(LA BELLE ET LA BETE)
1946 90m bw   ★★★★★
Fantasy   /PG
Discina (France)

Jean Marais (Avenant/The Beast/The Prince), Josette Day (Beauty), Marcel Andre (The Merchant), Mila Parely (Adelaide), Nane Germon (Felice), Michel Auclair (Ludovic)

p, Andre Paulve; d, Jean Cocteau; w, Jean Cocteau (based on the fairy tale by Mme. Leprince de Beaumont); ph, Henri Alekan; ed, Claude Iberia; m, Georges Auric; art d, Christian Berard

A masterpiece. The great Jean Cocteau has written that in order for a myth to live it must continually be told and retold, and this is just what Cocteau does in BEAUTY AND THE BEAST—bringing Mme. Marie Leprince de Beaumont's 1757 fairy tale to the screen. Beauty (Josette Day) and the Beast (Jean Marais) are given a new life in the cinema thanks to Cocteau's poetry, Henri Alekan's cinematography, Georges Auric's music, and Christian Berard's art direction. The legend is familiar: a merchant's beautiful daughter saves her father's life by agreeing to visit the diabolical Beast, a fearsome creature with magical powers. Beauty faints with horror upon their first meeting, but gradually grows to love the Beast, finding the soul that exists beneath his gruesome exterior.

While the narrative is basic and familiar, the film's visuals are not. A magical white horse blazes across the screen; the Beast's hands smoke after a kill; the hanging white laundry of Beauty's family billows in the breeze; the Beast's fantastical candelabras are human arms that extend from the walls and emerge from the dinner table. It is a credit to Cocteau's genius (and to that of his collaborators) that he has taken the unreal world of a fairy tale and made it as real as the world around us.

BEAUTY AND THE BEAST
1991 84m c   ★★★★½
Animated/Musical/Romance   G/U
Walt Disney/Silver Screen Partners IV

VOICES OF: Paige O'Hara (Belle), Robby Benson (Beast), Rex Everhart (Maurice), Richard White (Gaston), Jesse Corti (Le Fou), Angela Lansbury (Mrs. Potts), Jerry Orbach (Lumiere), David Ogden Stiers (Cogsworth/Narrator), Bradley Michael Pierce (Chip), Hal Smith (Philippe)

p, Don Hahn; d, Kirk Wise, Gary Trousdale; w, Linda Woolverton (from the story by Kelly Asbury, Brenda Chapman, Tom Ellery, Kevin Harkey, Robert Lence, Burny Mattinson, Brian Pimental, Joe Ranft, Christopher Sanders and Bruce Woodside); ed, John Carnochan; m, Alan Menken; art d, Brian McEntee; anim, Roger Allers, Ed Ghertner, Lisa Keene, Vera Lanpher, Randy Fullmer, Jim Hillin

It doesn't say much for the torpor infecting contemporary film and theater that the most joyful, vibrant piece of popular culture produced in 1991 was a creation of pen, ink and computer. Neither cloying and pandering, nor muddle-headed and dishonest, BEAUTY AND THE BEAST stands alone among recent releases in its exuberant celebration of the joy of life and the magic of love.

Belle (Paige O'Hara) is a beautiful young woman in a small provincial French town whose intellectual interests make her yearn for an escape from the narrow-mindedness of the villagers. Fending off advances from the ruggedly handsome, but arrogant and chauvinistic Gaston (Richard White), she seeks solace in books and dreams of flight. When Belle's father, Maurice (Rex Everhart), an absent-minded inventor, leaves for a county fair to exhibit his latest invention, he becomes lost in a dark wood. Pursued by wild dogs, he seeks refuge in an enchanted castle, lorded over by the Beast (Robby Benson), a spoiled young prince transformed by an enchantress into a hideous monster. The spell has transformed his castle into a dank, gloomy lair and his servants into household bric-a-brac. Enraged that Maurice has violated the castle grounds, the Beast locks him in a dungeon. When her father's horse returns home without him, Belle sets off in pursuit and finds her way to the castle, where the Beast agrees to let her father leave if she will remain in his stead—forever.

The Beast's servants—especially Lumiere, a candlestick (Jerry Orbach); Mrs. Potts, a teapot (Angela Lansbury); and Cogsworth, a clock (David Ogden Stiers)—see Belle as their only hope for releasing the castle from the evil spell. (The Beast must fall in love with a woman, and she with him, before his 21st birthday if matters are to be restored to their original state.) But the Beast's short temper and Belle's independent nature make them unable to tolerate each other. Belle storms out of the castle to go back to the village and is herself attacked by the wild dogs. The Beast comes to her rescue but is wounded in the battle; Belle helps him back to the castle, where she nurses him back to health and they gradually fall in love.

BEAUTY AND THE BEAST is a celebratory feast of tremendous depth, drawing on the best traditions of screen animation and American musical theater and film to transform an ancient story into something entirely new. On a fundamental level, the film reworks the classic Hollywood animation style perfected by the Disney Studios. Belle's reading about Prince Charming, and the Beast's magic mirror, recall SNOW WHITE AND THE

SEVEN DWARFS; the magical transformation reminds us of CINDERELLA; and Maurice's eccentric inventions echo the world of PINOCCHIO. But rather than drawing attention to themselves, all these elements work together to further the tight, economical storyline.

The narrative is further strengthened by the independent, self-assured character of Belle. Unlike Disney heroines from Snow White through Ariel, Belle is smart, knows what she wants, and doesn't spend her time pining away for the love of a handsome prince. By the same token, the Beast is a more complex character than viewers have been led to expect in an animated film—much more emotionally charged than, say, the empty-headed prince in THE LITTLE MERMAID. Both Belle and the Beast are three-dimensional characters with needs and desires. They are also both egomaniacal, and, as in any good drama, their characters are seen to change during the course of the film, making these animated cartoon characters fully drawn emotional beings.

Howard Ashman and Alan Menken propel the plot and character development along with their tuneful, witty and textured songs. As they enrich the palate of the narrative, they also invite comparison with some of the past glories of the American musical theater—from the opening numbers of *Fiddler on the Roof* and *She Loves Me* (the teeming "Belle" opener), the love soliloquies from *South Pacific* (the touching "Something There" soliloquies of Belle and the Beast), the "Shall We Dance?" waltz from *The King and I* (the soaring "Beauty and the Beast" waltz), to crowd-pleasing production numbers from Jerry Herman's *Hello Dolly* and *Mame* (the boisterous "Be Our Guest").

All this, though, would mean nothing if the animation were not of a standard to compare with the rest of the elements. It is. Using computer wizardry to simulate live-action film techniques like dollies, tracks and pans, the animation succeeds in creating an uncannily realistic world. The filmmakers have used considerable depth of field, permitting action to occur on many levels of the frame, from background to foreground, and to move, not only horizontally, but also back and forth from the camera eye. The camera sweeps above forests and down into castle chambers, and races around characters in 360 degree tracks.

With the exception of the Beast, the character animation is simple and expressive. As in the best of Chuck Jones, the emotional centers of the characters lie in their eloquent eyes, which convey an emotional depth rarely seen in recent cartoon features. With all of this going for it, BEAUTY AND THE BEAST towers over the live-action travesties surrounding it in the shopping-mall multiplexes.

BECKET
1964 148m c   ★★★★
Historical   /PG
Paramount (U.K.)

Richard Burton (Thomas Becket), Peter O'Toole (King Henry II), Donald Wolfit (Bishop Folliot), John Gielgud (King Louis VII), Martita Hunt (Queen Matilda), Pamela Brown (Queen Eleanor), Sian Phillips (Gwendolyn), Paolo Stoppa (Pope Alexander III), Gino Cervi (Cardinal Zambelli), David Weston (Brother John)

p, Hal B. Wallis; d, Peter Glenville; w, Edward Anhalt (based on the play by Jean Anouilh); ph, Geoffrey Unsworth (Technicolor); ed, Anne V. Coates; m, Laurence Rosenthal; prod d, John Bryan; art d, Maurice Carter; cos, Margaret Furse

This notable improvement over the stage-bound Anouilh play recounts the story of two great friends turned unintentional foes, Becket (Richard Burton) and Henry II (Peter O'Toole). Becket is Henry's chancellor until consecrated Archbishop of Canterbury, almost in jest, by Henry. Becket takes the job seriously and defends the church from royal onslaught. The two men drift further apart as Becket goes deeper into his ecclesiastical role, and the king realizes that his former friend must be killed after the two men meet for an attempted reconciliation in a wonderful scene on horseback at a British beach.

Ostensibly a story regarding the separation of church and state, Anouilh and Anhalt followed history closely and added their own undercurrent of homoerotic tension between the men, although this is so subtle that it was lost on many viewers. All technical credits are excellent and so are the performances. Many wonderful touches abound, including the scene wherein forks are introduced to the court. Wallis, whose career spanned six decades (everything from LITTLE CAESAR, CASABLANCA, and GUNFIGHT AT THE O.K. CORRAL to various Elvis Presley films) established himself in the pantheon of producers with this film.

BECKY SHARP

1935 83m c   ★★½
Drama   /A
Pioneer

Miriam Hopkins (Becky Sharp), Frances Dee (Amelia Sedley), Cedric Hardwicke (Marquis of Steyne), Billie Burke (Lady Bareacres), Alison Skipworth (Miss Crawley), Nigel Bruce (Joseph Sedley), Alan Mowbray (Rawdon Crawley), Colin Tapley (William Dobbin), G.P. Huntley, Jr. (George Osborne), William Stack (Pitt Crawley)

p, Kenneth MacGowan; d, Rouben Mamoulian; w, Francis Edwards Faragoh (based on a play by Langdon Mitchell and Vanity Fair by William Makepeace Thackeray); ph, Ray Rennahan (Technicolor); ed, Archie Marshek; m, Roy Webb; prod d, Robert Jones; chor, Russell Lewis

Landmark technicolor, but otherwise very flat indeed. Third version of Vanity Fair was a troubled production with original director Lowell Sherman dying, Mamoulian starting over. Hopkins always excelled at predatory roles, but unless flawlessly scripted and sat on by a director, her characterizations invariably went over the top. Watch if you want to see her play to the second balcony, otherwise be on the lookout for rare 1932 version with Myrna Loy. BECKY SHARP wasn't fine enough to make everyone race to film in color; it would take four more years with three mammoth MGM successes—GONE WITH THE WIND and THE WIZARD OF OZ among them—before it started to really take off.

BED AND BOARD

1971 95m c   ★★½
Drama   /A
Carrosse/Valoria (France/Italy)

Jean-Pierre Leaud (Antoine), Claude Jade (Christine), Hiroko Berghauer (Kyoko), Barbara Laage (Executive Secretary), Daniel Ceccaldi (M. Darbon), Claire Duhamel (Mme. Darbon), Pierre Fabre (The Sneerer), Claude Vega (Strangler), Billy Kearns (American Customer), Daniel Boulanger (Tenor)

p, Francois Truffaut; d, Francois Truffaut; w, Francois Truffaut, Claude de Givray, Bernard Revon; ph, Nestor Almendros; art d, Jean Mandaroux

Part of the continuing saga of that fun-loving Frenchman, Antoine Doinel, played hungrily by Leaud. He falls in love with and marries Jade, fathers a child, then experiments with adultery by

having an uninteresting affair with Berghauer before the close-out. Director Truffaut's dwelling upon scenes thought to be tender is really a matter of self-indulgence. There simply isn't enough story, and most of the characters remain inert.

BED SITTING ROOM, THE

1969 80m c   ★★★
Comedy   /AA
UA (U.K.)

Rita Tushingham (Penelope), Ralph Richardson (Lord Fortnum), Peter Cook (Inspector), Dudley Moore (Sergeant), Spike Milligan (Mate), Michael Hordern (Blues Martin), Roy Kinnear (Plastic Mac Man), Richard Warwick (Allan), Arthur Lowe (Father), Mona Washbourne (Mother)

p, Richard Lester; d, Richard Lester; w, John Antrobus, Charles Wood (based on a play by Antrobus and Spike Milligan); ph, David Watkin; ed, John Victor Smith; m, Ken Horne

A field day for funny collection of Brits. Weird picture originated in a well-known weird place, the mind of "Goon Show" alumnus Spike Milligan. An offbeat look at London after the bombs have been dropped, this episodic film follows several Blitz survivors (many of them played by British TV stars) as they make their way through the ruins of their great city. Lowe turns into a parrot, Washbourne becomes a chest of drawers, Tushingham announces that she's 17 months pregnant, and Richardson metamorphoses into a bed sitting room! Although the basic situation may not be the funniest set-up imaginable, the players manage to keep the laughs flying thick and fast. Former Goons Cook and Moore are side-splittingly funny as government bureaucrats; Marty Feldman makes his debut.

BEDAZZLED

1967 104m c   ★★★½
Comedy   /PG
FOX (U.K.)

Peter Cook (George Spiggot), Dudley Moore (Stanley Moon), Eleanor Bron (Margaret), Raquel Welch (Lillian Lust), Alba (Vanity), Robert Russell (Anger), Barry Humphries (Envy), Parnell McGarry (Gluttony), Daniele Noel (Avarice), Howard Goorney (Sloth)

p, Stanley Donen; d, Stanley Donen; w, Peter Cook (based on a story by Cook, Dudley Moore); ph, Austin Dempster (Panavision, Deluxe Color); ed, Richard Marden; m, Dudley Moore

Chic Faust update by Cook and Moore, latter as Faust, Cook as Satan. Raquel is humorless as usual, upstaged to high hell by sexy Eleanor Bron. Quite good indeed from Stanley Donen. And dig the Julie Andrews bit.

BEDKNOBS AND BROOMSTICKS

1971 117m c   ★★★
Fantasy   G/U
Buena Vista

Angela Lansbury (Eglantine Price), David Tomlinson (Emelius Browne), Roddy McDowall (Mr. Jelk), Sam Jaffe (Bookman), John Ericson (Col. Heller), Bruce Forsyth (Swinburne), Reginald Owen (Gen. Teagler), Tessie O'Shea (Mrs. Hobday), Arthur Gould-Porter (Capt. Greer), Ben Wrigley (Street Sweeper)

p, Bill Walsh; d, Robert Stevenson; w, Bill Walsh, Don DaGradi (based on the book by Mary Norton); ph, Frank Phillips (Technicolor); ed, Cotton Warburton; art d, Peter Ellenshaw, John B. Mansbridge; fx, Danny Lee, Eustace Lycett, Alan Maley; cos, Bill Thomas; anim, Ward Kimball

Similar in many ways to MARY POPPINS, BEDKNOBS AND BROOMSTICKS is filled with unique special effects and delightful music. Angela Lansbury stars as Eglantine Price, the owner of a seaside house in England who has three children foisted on her during WWII. At first, the children aren't thrilled about being relocated. Then they learn that Eglantine is studying witchcraft by mail and has much mischief planned for the Nazis if they ever land in England. With a bedstead as their magic carpet, Eglantine takes the kids on a wonderful ride into several fantastic worlds. Animation is neatly mixed with live action, and Lansbury, engaging as ever, heads a capable cast.

BEDTIME FOR BONZO

1951   83m   bw   ★★½
Comedy   /U
Universal

Ronald Reagan (Prof. Peter Boyd), Diana Lynn (Jane), Walter Slezak (Prof. Hans Neumann), Lucille Barkley (Valerie Tillinghast), Jesse White (Babcock), Herbert Heyes (Dean Tillinghast), Herb Vigran (Lt. Daggett), Harry Tyler (Knicksy), Edward Clark (Fosdick), Edward Gargan (Policeman)

p, Michel Kraike; d, Frederick de Cordova; w, Val Burton, Lou Breslow (based on a story by Raphael Blau, Ted Berkman); ph, Carl Guthrie; ed, Ted J. Kent; m, Frank Skinner

Cult comeuppance. For once Reagan is in synch with his costar, but Bonzo the chimp proved the more able farceur. Animal fans will be saddened to know Bonzo and four stand-ins died tragically in a trailer fire. (Had it been Reagan, young American filmmakers might be better funded today.) The first assignment for Freddie de Cordova, longtime producer of the "Tonight Show." We all gotta start somewhere. A sequel followed—BONZO GOES TO COLLEGE—sans Reagan, who apparently couldn't handle the academic overload.

BEETLEJUICE

1988   92m   c   ★★★½
Comedy/Horror   PG/15
Geffen

Alec Baldwin (Adam Maitland), Geena Davis (Barbara Maitland), Michael Keaton (Betelgeuse), Catherine O'Hara (Delia Deetz), Glenn Shadix (Otho), Winona Ryder (Lydia Deetz), Jeffrey Jones (Charles Deetz), Sylvia Sidney (Juno), Patrice Martinez (Receptionist), Robert Goulet (Maxie Dean)

p, Richard Hashimoto, Larry Wilson, Michael Bender; d, Tim Burton; w, Michael McDowell, Warren Skaaren (based on a story by McDowell, Larry Wilson); ph, Thomas Ackerman (Technicolor); ed, Jane Kurson; m, Danny Elfman; prod d, Bo Welch; fx, Chuck Gaspar, Robert Short; chor, Chrissy Bocchino; cos, Aggie Guerard Rodgers

A surreal, demented delight. The long-awaited second film from wunderkind director Tim Burton is a wildly inventive, unique horror comedy that plays like a twisted, surrealistic, cartoon remake of TOPPER (1937). Keaton is in rare form leading the haunt, rivaled by virtuoso Sidney as overloaded other side caseworker. Film won a much deserved Oscar for Best Achievement in Makeup.

BEFORE THE REVOLUTION

(PRIMA DELLA REVOLUTIONA)
1964   115m   bw   ★½
Drama   /X
Cineriz   (Italy)

Adriana Asti (Gina), Francesco Barilli (Boy), Allen Midgette (Agostino), Morando Morandini (Teacher)

d, Bernardo Bertolucci; w, Bernardo Bertolucci; ph, Aldo Scavarda; ed, Roberto Perpignani; m, Gino Paoli

When the poor friend of an upper-class boy commits suicide, the wealthy lad, Barilli, begins to question his own life and outlook. Considerable appeal in evidence, but only between talking jags.

BEGGAR'S OPERA, THE

1953   94m   c   ★★★
Musical   /U
Imperadio   (U.K.)

Laurence Olivier (Capt. MacHeath), Stanley Holloway (Lockit), George Devine (Peachum), Mary Clare (Mrs. Peachum), Athene Seyler (Mrs. Trapes), Dorothy Tutin (Polly Peachum), Daphne Anderson (Lucy Lockit), Hugh Griffith (The Beggar), Margot Grahame (The Actress), Denis Cannan (The Footman)

p, Laurence Olivier, Herbert Wilcox; d, Peter Brook; w, Denis Cannan, Christopher Fry (based on the comic opera by John Gay); ph, Guy Green (Technicolor); ed, Reginald Beck; m, Arthur Bliss

Ecletic, thoughtful, but not an unmitigated smash. The esteemed Brook made his film directing debut with THE BEGGAR'S OPERA, an attempt at re-creating John Gay's original play on film. (It was also done as The Threepenny Opera with a score by Bertolt Brecht and Kurt Weill.) The music in this version is by Sir Arthur Bliss, with lyrics by Christopher Fry (The Lady's Not For Burning) as well as some additional dialogue for the Cannan screenplay. Olivier stars as MacHeath, with Holloway as Lockit, Griffith as the Beggar, and the wonderful Seyler (who gave one of the funniest performances in any comedy in MAKE MINE MINK and for years specialized in classical stage work) as Mrs. Trapes. Olivier provides a play-within-a-play as a prisoner in Newgate who creates an opera based on his own life.

It's all very complex and may have been better done in MAN OF LA MANCHA. This is an ambitious project that never quite comes off. Olivier and Holloway did their own singing, but the others were dubbed. Olivier is no Howard Keel and lacks the inherent sexiness to play MacHeath; he did well to stay out of musicals, unless doing character singing like THE ENTERTAINER. Bold attempt failed at the box office, but, for film enthusiasts, it remains an interesting curiosity.

BEING THERE

1979   130m   c   ★★★★★
Comedy   PG/15
Lorimar

Peter Sellers (Chance), Shirley MacLaine (Eve Rand), Melvyn Douglas (Benjamin Rand), Jack Warden (President Bobby), Richard Dysart (Dr. Robert Allenby), Richard Basehart (Vladmir Skrapinov), Ruth Attaway (Louise), David Clennon (Thomas Franklin), Fran Brill (Sally Hayes), Denise DuBarry (Johanna Franklin)

p, Andrew Braunsberg; d, Hal Ashby; w, Jerzy Kosinski (based on his novel); ph, Caleb Deschanel (Technicolor); ed, Don Zimmerman; m, Johnny Mandel; art d, James Schoppe

Deft fable of innocence's wisdom. Jerzy Kosinski's modern fable gets a terrific translation to the screen due to his tight screenplay, capable direction by Ashby, and a marvelous performance by Sellers, one unlike any other in his career. Simpleton becomes wealthy and famous, but flimsy idea goes on too long. MacLaine is funny as the sex-starved wife who at first is amusedly captivated by Sellers then falls in love with him. Deschanel's stunning cinematography also deserves praise, as does Mandel's very appropriate score. Sellers was nominated for a Best Actor Oscar but lost to Dustin Hoffman for KRAMER VS. KRAMER, while Douglas won his second Academy Award for Best Supporting Actor (his first came for HUD in 1963). Filmed in Washington, DC; Los Angeles; and at the Biltmore, the Vanderbilts' North Carolina mansion.

BELIZAIRE THE CAJUN

1986   103m   c   ★★½
Historical   PG/
Cote Blanche

Armand Assante (Belizaire Breaux), Gail Youngs (Alida Thibodaux), Michael Schoeffling (Hypolite Leger), Stephen McHattie (James Willoughby), Bill Patton (Matthew Perry), Nancy Barrett (Rebecca), Loulan Pitre (Sheriff), Andre DeLaunay (Dolsin), Jim Levert (Amadee Meaux), Ernie Vincent (Old Perry)

p, Allan L. Durand, Glen Pitre; d, Glen Pitre; w, Glen Pitre; ph, Richard Bowen; ed, Paul Trejo; m, Michael Doucet; prod d, Randall LaBry; art d, Deborah Schildt; chor, Miriam Lafleur Fontenot; cos, Sara Fox

Unique and flavorable slice of life. A period melodrama set in Louisiana's Cajun country in the mid-1800s, the film focuses on the title character (Assante), a healer who becomes the central figure in a battle between his fellow French-Canadian settlers and the local good ol' boys. A labor of love for first-time feature director Pitre, BELIZAIRE THE CAJUN is one of the few films that has examined the lifestyles and customs of the Cajun people. Filmed with great regard to period authenticity, the production brings a unique aspect of the American heritage before a wide audience. Unfortunately, this cannot erase its multitude of flaws. While the film succeeds as an exciting and energetic piece of melodrama, it never penetrates the surface or offers more than shallow, underdeveloped characters in patented situations. And with the thick cajun accents, the slow pacing seems to goah on a mi-i-ite too lawn. The soundtrack by Cajun musician Doucet and his band Beausoleil, however, is superb.

BELLE DE JOUR

1967   100m   c   ★★★★
Drama   /18
Paris   (France)

Catherine Deneuve (Severine Serizy), Jean Sorel (Pierre Serizy), Michel Piccoli (Henri Husson), Genevieve Page (Mme. Anais), Pierre Clementi (Marcel), Francisco Rabal (Hippolyte), Francoise Fabian (Charlotte), Maria Latour (Mathilde), Georges Marchal (The Duke), Macha Meril (Renee Fevret)

p, Robert Hakim, Raymond Hakim; d, Luis Bunuel; w, Luis Bunuel, Jean-Claude Carriere (based on the novel by Joseph Kessel); ph, Sacha Vierny (Eastmancolor); ed, Walter Spohr; art d, Robert Clavel

A delicious puzzle. Surrealistic voyage into the mind of a woman married to a handsome surgeon who dotes on her but whose odd quirks lead her to a life of afternoon prostitution in order to satisfy some deep-seated need. Deneuve's finest hour and a half; the finale has two endings; we are never certain if we are seeing the truth, a lie, or a dream. It's almost, but not quite, pornography. And it's almost, but not quite, a great movie. Bunuel tries so hard to pose questions that he forgets most viewers come to the cinema for entertainment and/or enlightenment, rather than to have the

director play cat and mouse. But Bunuel enjoyed his little joke and did it again in THE DISCREET CHARM OF THE BOURGEOISIE.

BELLES OF ST. TRINIAN'S, THE

1954   91m   bw   ★★★
Comedy   /U
London Films   (U.K.)

Alastair Sim (Millicent Fritton/ Clarence Fritton), Joyce Grenfell (Sgt. Ruby Gates), George Cole (Flash Harry), Vivienne Martin (Arabella), Eric Pohlmann (Sultan of Makyad), Lorna Henderson (Princess Fatima), Hermione Baddeley (Miss Drownder), Betty Ann Davies (Miss Waters), Renee Houston (Miss Brimmer), Beryl Reid (Miss Dawn)

p, Frank Launder, Sidney Gilliat; d, Frank Launder; w, Frank Launder, Sidney Gilliat, Val Valentine; ph, Stanley Pavey; ed, Thelma Connell; m, Malcolm Arnold

Monstrously fun. This is a very funny comedy based on Ronald Searles's cartoons of a horrid girls' school known as St. Trinian's. The plot has to do with the horsenapping of a famous steed that is foiled by some of the school's pupils. Among the girls' antics is using the school's science lab to make gin, which is then sold by the crooked Flash Harry (George Cole). Alastair Sim is brilliant in two roles, playing the headmistress as well as her ne'er-do-well brother. Joyce Grenfell is also quite amusing as a police spy. This one was a winner, spawning less successful sequels BLUE MURDER AT ST. TRINIAN'S, THE PURE HELL OF ST. TRINIAN'S and THE GREAT ST. TRINIAN'S TRAIN ROBBERY.

BELLS ARE RINGING

1960   126m   c   ★★★½
Musical/Comedy   /U
MGM

Judy Holliday (Ella Peterson), Dean Martin (Jeffrey Moss), Fred Clark (Larry Hastings), Eddie Foy, Jr. (J. Otto Prantz), Jean Stapleton (Sue), Ruth Storey (Gwynne), Dort Clark (Inspector Barnes), Frank Gorshin (Blake Barton), Ralph Roberts (Francis), Valerie Allen (Olga)

p, Arthur Freed; d, Vincente Minnelli; w, Betty Comden, Adolph Green (based on the musical play by Betty Comden, Adolph Green and Jule Styne); ph, Milton Krasner (CinemaScope Eastmancolor); ed, Adrienne Fazan; m, Jule Styne, Betty Comden, Adolph Green; art d, George W. Davis, Preston Ames; chor, Charles O'Curran; cos, Walter Plunkett

The last performance of a much-loved star. Judy Holliday reprises her Broadway success in this adaptation of the hit Comden-Green-Jules Styne musical, playing Ella Peterson, who works at a telephone answering service and gets passionately involved in her clients' lives. Hapless playwright Jeffrey Moss (a miscast Dean Martin) is her love interest. In supporting roles, Jean Stapleton scores in one of her earliest appearances, as do Frank Gorshin in the role of a beatnik who wants to be a serious actor and Eddie Foy, Jr., as a bookie; jazz fans will recognize saxophone great Gerry Mulligan, married to Holliday at the time, as Ella's blind date. Vincente Minnelli's film might have benefited with less emphasis on dialogue and more on the musical numbers ("Just in Time" and "The Party's Over" among them), but Holliday is adorable and effortlessly "real" in one of the best roles of her sadly abbreviated career.

BELLS OF ST. MARY'S, THE

1945 126m bw ★★★★
Drama /U
Rainbow

Bing Crosby *(Father Chuck O'Malley)*, Ingrid Bergman *(Sister Benedict)*, Henry Travers *(Mr. Bogardus)*, Ruth Donnelly *(Sister Michael)*, Joan Carroll *(Patsy)*, Martha Sleeper *(Patsy's Mother)*, William Gargan *(Joe Gallagher)*, Rhys Williams *(Dr. McKay)*, Dick Tyler *(Eddie)*, Una O'Connor *(Mrs. Breen)*

p, Leo McCarey; d, Leo McCarey; w, Dudley Nichols (based on a story by Leo McCarey); ph, George Barnes; ed, Harry Marker; m, Robert Emmett Dolan; art d, William Flannery; cos, Edith Head

Touchingly sentimental, but strong in all the right places. The sequel to GOING MY WAY is nearly as good as its predecessor. Bing Crosby is trouble-shooting priest Father Chuck O'Malley, who's sent to the financially ailing St. Mary's. There he runs smack into charming, clever Sister Benedict (Ingrid Bergman), a mother superior who rules her students with a gentle but decisive hand. She is too rigid for Father O'Malley and he's too permissive for her, setting up a confrontation of styles that's a joy to behold. It's a gentle, uplifting story, and features some fine songs by Crosby, including "Adeste Fidelis," "In the Land of Beginning Again," and the sprightly "Aren't You Glad You're You." The two leads are seamless all the way home.

BELLY OF AN ARCHITECT, THE

1987 108m c ★★★
Drama /15
Callender (U.K./Italy)

Brian Dennehy *(Stourley Kracklite)*, Chloe Webb *(Louisa Kracklite)*, Lambert Wilson *(Caspasian Speckler)*, Vanni Corbellini *(Frederico)*, Sergio Fantoni *(Io Speckler)*, Stefania Casini *(Flavia Speckler)*, Alfredo Varelli *(Julio Ficcone)*, Geoffrey Copleston *(Caspetti)*, Francesco Carnelutti *(Pastarri)*, Marino Mase *(Trettorio)*

p, Colin Callender, Walter Donohue; d, Peter Greenaway; w, Peter Greenaway; ph, Sacha Vierny (Technicolor); ed, John Wilson; m, Wim Mertens, Glenn Branca; art d, Luciana Vedovelli; cos, Maurizio Millenotti

A film to either love or loathe. Exquisitely composed film about obsession reaffirms director Peter Greenaway's reputation as a meticulous visual artist. Stourley Kracklite (Brian Dennehy), a corpulent Chicago architect of some renown, travels to Rome with his considerably younger wife Louisa (Chloe Webb) to oversee an exhibition commemorating the work of Etienne Louis Boullee, a little-known but visionary 18th-century French architect. A handsome young Italian architect, Caspasian Speckler (Lambert Wilson), is in charge of the project's finances, and he covets both Kracklite's control of the exhibition and his wife. Kracklite's world begins to crumble as he becomes obsessed with the chronic abdominal pains from which he suffers, making him oblivious to Speckler's machinations. Dennehy's extraordinary performance buoys the film, and Wilson is entirely convincing as the rival architect, but Webb is badly miscast. The main attractions here are Greenaway's densely textured compositions, each one a triumph of symmetry and design.

BEN HUR

1959 212m c ★★★★½
Historical/Religious /PG
MGM

Charlton Heston *(Judah Ben Hur)*, Jack Hawkins *(Quintus Arrius)*, Stephen Boyd *(Messala)*, Haya Harareet *(Esther)*, Hugh Griffith *(Sheik Ilderim)*, Martha Scott *(Miriam)*, Sam Jaffe *(Simonides)*, Cathy O'Donnell *(Tirzah)*, Finlay Currie *(Balthasar)*, Frank Thring *(Pontius Pilate)*

p, Sam Zimbalist; d, William Wyler; w, Karl Tunberg (based on the novel by Lew Wallace); ph, Robert Surtees (Camera 65, Panavision, Technicolor); ed, Ralph E. Winters, John Dunning; m, Miklos Rozsa; art d, William A. Horning, Edward Carfagno; fx, A. Arnold Gillespie, Robert MacDonald; cos, Elizabeth Haffenden

Predictable but magnificent and satisfying. In remaking the silent 1927 classic, which starred Ramon Novarro and Francis X. Bushman, quality-conscious director Wyler shines the old chestnut up. Highlights include the galley ship and climatic chariot race with Heston—in a *tour de force* performance—besieged by the sexy but evil Boyd. (This sequence was actually helmed by action expert Andrew Marton.) Even with the western overtones, the actors make stunning rivals. Majesty is in almost every frame of this film thanks to Wyler, who tells the story in human, understated terms.

Everything about BEN HUR was enormous; more than 300 sets were employed, covering more than 340 acres. The arena housing the chariot race consumed 18 acres, the largest single set in film history. The five-story stands were packed with 8,000 extras, and 40,000 tons of sand were taken from beaches to make the track. Scores of Yugoslavian horses were imported for the spectacular 20-minute race, which took three months to shoot. More than 1000 workers labored for a year to build the colossal arena. Rome's Cinecitta Studios were gutted of more than a million props, and sculptors made more than 200 giant statues. Also unique were the wide-screen cameras employed, 65 millimeters wide, to achieve sharp, deep focus. MGM lavished about $12,500,000 on this stupendous production, which brought them near bankruptcy, but the returns were staggering: a gross of $40 million.

BENJI

1974 85m c ★★★
Children's G/U
Mulberry Square

Higgins the Dog *(Benji)*, Patsy Garrett *(Mary)*, Allen Fiuzat *(Paul)*, Cynthia Smith *(Cindy)*, Peter Breck *(Dr. Chapman)*, Frances Bavier *(Lady with Cat)*, Terry Carter *(Officer Tuttle)*, Edgar Buchanan *(Bill)*, Tom Lester *(Riley)*, Christopher Connelly *(Henry)*

p, Joe Camp; d, Joe Camp; w, Joe Camp; ph, Don Reddy; ed, Leon Smith; m, Euel Box; prod d, Harland Wright

A lovable mutt thwarts kidnappers. A-h-h-h-h-h. Much of the film is shot from a dog's-eye view, and this technique works perfectly. The human actors are okay but not as cool as the canine star, a veteran of TV's "Petticoat Junction" series. The title song was nominated for an Oscar! Sequel: FOR THE LOVE OF BENJI.

BERLIN ALEXANDERPLATZ

1979 930m c ★★★★
Drama
Bavaria Atelier/RAI (West Germany)

Gunter Lamprecht *(Franz Biberkopf)*, Gottfried John *(Reinhold)*, Barbara Sukowa *(Mieze)*, Hanna Schygulla *(Eva)*, Franz Buchrieser *(Meck)*, Claus Holm *(Landlord)*, Hark Bohm *(Mr. Luders)*, Brigitte Mira *(Frau Bast)*, Gunther Kaufmann *(Theo)*, Margit Castensen *(An Angel)*

p, Peter Marthesheimer; d, Rainer Wernor Fassbinder; w, Rainer Wernor Fassbinder (based on the novel by Alfred Doblin); ph, Xaver Schwarzenberger; ed, Juliane LOrenz; m, Peer Raben

An astonishing, momumental work. Over the short span of 17 years—from 1965, when he directed his first 10-minute film, up to his death on June 10, 1982—Rainer Werner Fassbinder directed some 90 hours of film and television. BERLIN ALEXANDERPLATZ, an adaptation of Alfred Doblin's massive novel made for German television, runs approximately 15 hours, and makes up one-seventh of Fassbinder's total output. Comprised of 13 episodes and an epilogue, the film stars Gunter Lamprecht as the pimp Franz Biberkopf, released from prison after serving time for murdering a prostitute. Now that he has a certain freedom, he takes to the streets of Berlin in the late 1920s in search of his identity.

Simply recounting the plot does no justice to Fassbinder or the film. What Doblin tried to do in his novel (written from 1927 to 1929) was to put into print the atmosphere of Berlin life. Acknowledging his debt to Doblin, Fassbinder has said, "I had quite simply, without realizing it, made Doblin's fantasy into my life." In that sense, BERLIN ALEXANDERPLATZ is not the story of Berlin, but the story of Fassbinder—and in these 15 hours the two are inseparable.

BEST FRIENDS
1982   116m   c   ★★
Drama   PG
WB

Burt Reynolds *(Richard Babson)*, Goldie Hawn *(Paula McCullen)*, Jessica Tandy *(Eleanor McCullen)*, Barnard Hughes *(Tim McCullen)*, Audra Lindley *(Ann Babson)*, Keenan Wynn *(Tom Babson)*, Ron Silver *(Larry Weisman)*, Carol Locatell *(Nellie Ballou)*, Richard Libertini *(Jorge Medina)*, Peggy Walton-Walker *(Carol Brandon)*

p, Norman Jewison, Patrick Palmer; d, Norman Jewison; w, Valerie Curtin, Barry Levinson; ph, Jordan Croneweth (Technicolor); ed, Don Zimmerman; m, Michel Legrand; art d, Josan Russo; cos, Betsy Cox

Looks like bitter enemies. Barry Levinson (director of DINER and RAIN MAN) and Valerie Curtin wrote the screenplay for this semi-autobiographical story of two collaborating writers who decide to give marriage a try. Burt Reynolds and Goldie Hawn play the "best friends" who put their friendship to the test of matrimony. Thin story collapses under the leaden star chemistry; capable supporting players can't save this dud.

BEST MAN, THE
1964   102m   bw   ★★★½
Drama   /A
UA

Henry Fonda *(William Russell)*, Cliff Robertson *(Joe Cantwell)*, Edie Adams *(Mabel Cantwell)*, Margaret Leighton *(Alice Russell)*, Shelley Berman *(Sheldon Bascomb)*, Lee Tracy *(Art Hockstader)*, Ann Sothern *(Mrs. Gamadge)*, Gene Raymond *(Dan Cantwell)*, Kevin McCarthy *(Dick Jensen)*, Mahalia Jackson *(Herself)*

p, Stuart Millar, Lawrence Turman; d, Franklin J. Schaffner; w, Gore Vidal (based on his play); ph, Haskell Wexler; ed, Robert Swink; m, Mort Lindsey; cos, Dorothy Jeakins

Vidal's savage political hornet's nest. Idealist Fonda and hypocrite Robertson do battle for their party's Presidental nomination. Fonda's wife Leighton had held off getting a divorce so as not to hurt her husband's political chances. Lee Tracy is the dying President who hasn't put his support behind either man on the eve of the convention. Robertson has a dossier on Fonda's emotional instability and uses it to get what he wants. Then we learn that Robertson had a rendezvous with another man some years earlier. Will Fonda retaliate? You can see Stevenson in Fonda, McCarthy or Nixon in Robertson, and a bit of Truman in outstanding, Oscar-nominated Tracy, who died before making another film. Gore Vidal's dialogue is razor-sharp as is Haskell Wexler's photography.

BEST SELLER
1987   110m   c   ★★½
Thriller   R/18
Hemdale

James Woods *(Cleve)*, Brian Dennehy *(Detective Lieutenant Dennis Meechum)*, Victoria Tennant *(Roberta Gillian)*, Allison Balson *(Holly Meechum)*, Paul Shenar *(David Madlock)*, George Coe *(Graham)*, Anne Pitoniak *(Mrs. Foster)*, Mary Carver *(Cleve's Mother)*, Sully Boyar *(Monks)*, Kathleen Lloyd *(Annie)*

p, Carter DeHaven; d, John Flynn; w, Larry Cohen; ph, Fred Murphy (CFI color); ed, David Rosenbloom; m, Jay Ferguson; prod d, Gene Rudolf; art d, Robert Howland; fx, Ken Speed, Robert Olmstead, Peter Kunz

Lurid Swiss cheese. Grimy crime thriller scripted by cult writer-director Larry Cohen (IT'S ALIVE, GOD TOLD ME TO, Q), BEST SELLER stars two of America's finest character actors, James Woods and Brian Dennehy. Dennis Meechum (Dennehy) is a cop who writes best-selling crime novels. Under pressure to deliver a long-overdue book, he is desperate for inspiration. Enter Cleve (Woods), a hit man who wants Meechum to write his life story. Two talented leads can't keep incomplete story on track without direction.

BEST THINGS IN LIFE ARE FREE, THE
1956   104m   c   ★★★
Biography/Musical   /U
FOX

Gordon MacRae *(B.G. "Buddy" De Sylva)*, Dan Dailey *(Ray Henderson)*, Ernest Borgnine *(Lew Brown)*, Sheree North *(Kitty)*, Tommy Noonan *(Carl)*, Murvyn Vye *(Manny)*, Phyllis Avery *(Maggie Henderson)*, Larry Keating *(Sheehan)*, Tony Galento *(Fingers)*, Norman Brooks *(Al Jolson)*

p, Henry Ephron; d, Michael Curtiz; w, William Bowers, Phoebe Ephron (based on a story by John O'Hara); ph, Leon Shamroy (DeLuxe Color); ed, Dorothy Spencer; m, Lionel Newman; chor, Rod Alexander, Bill Foster

Smooth sailing all the way. Standard Hollywood bio of songwriters De Sylva, Brown and Henderson featuring a slew of tunes. Composers are played by McCrae, Dailey and Borgnine, a nice contrast between actors. Among the many standards performed in the movie are "Black Bottom," "Button Up Your Overcoat," "Keep Your Sunnyside Up," and the title song. Newman's score earned the film an Oscar nomination, but the highlight is Sheree North. North was brought from Broadway to Fox as a threat to

Monroe. Her personality and looks suggested a beatnik Monroe/Clara Bow, and she was a terrific dancer. Fox wasted her in films Monroe was smart enough to pass on, never bothering to help her (or later Mansfield) develop an image tailored to her alone. Today she is a character actress who works very often and is still an attractive woman. Watch her steal this film dancing with Jacques D'Amboise to "Birth of the Blues."

BEST YEARS OF OUR LIVES, THE

1946 172m bw   ★★★★★
Drama/War   /U
Goldwyn

Myrna Loy *(Milly Stephenson)*, Fredric March *(Al Stephenson)*, Dana Andrews *(Fred Derry)*, Teresa Wright *(Peggy Stephenson)*, Virginia Mayo *(Marie Derry)*, Cathy O'Donnell *(Wilma Cameron)*, Hoagy Carmichael *(Butch Engle)*, Harold Russell *(Homer Parrish)*, Gladys George *(Hortense Derry)*, Roman Bohnen *(Pat Derry)*

p, Samuel Goldwyn; d, William Wyler; w, Robert E. Sherwood (based on the blank-verse novella *Glory for Me* by MacKinlay Kantor); ph, Gregg Toland; ed, Daniel Mandell; m, Hugo Friedhofer; art d, George Jenkins, Perry Ferguson; cos, Irene Sharaff

The best coming home movie ever made. "I don't care if it doesn't make a nickel," Sam Goldwyn reportedly said of THE BEST YEARS, "I just want every man, woman, and child in America to see it." The colorful producer got the idea for the film after reading a *Life* article about WWII veterans and their difficulties in adjusting to civilian life. With a brilliant script by Robert E. Sherwood, effective direction by William Wyler, masterful photography by Gregg Toland and excellent performances by the entire cast, this film about returning American servicemen is justifiably considered a classic.

Three servicemen—Al Stephenson (Fredric March), Fred Derry (Dana Andrews), and Homer Parrish (Harold Russell)—are shown returning to their hometown, plagued by memories of war and doubts about their future in a country they have difficulty remembering. After sharing space on board the bomber that flies them home, the three take a cab to their separate addresses. The sailor Homer comes home to his girl with a pair of hooks where his hands once were (Russell, the only nonprofessional in the cast, lost his hands in a training accident while in the service); middle-aged Al returns to his loving wife (Myrna Loy), children, and old job as a banker; Fred finds a spouse who has more or less abandoned him, and no prospects for a job.

Although everyone in Hollywood thought Goldwyn would lose his shirt on THE BEST YEARS OF OUR LIVES, it was a massive hit and won Academy Awards for Best Picture, Best Actor (March), Best Supporting Actor (Russell), Best Direction, Best Original Screenplay, Best Score, and Best Editing. Russell also won a special Oscar for bringing hope to servicemen.

BETRAYAL

1983 95m c   ★★★½
Drama   R/15
FOX (U.K.)

Jeremy Irons *(Jerry)*, Patricia Hodge *(Emma)*, Ben Kingsley *(Robert)*

p, Sam Spiegel; d, David Jones; w, Harold Pinter (based on his play); ph, Mike Fash; ed, John Bloom; m, Dominic Muldowney; prod d, Eileen Diss; cos, Jane Robinson, Jean Muir

Harold Pinter's screenplay for BETRAYAL begins at the end of its story and flashes back to the beginning, permitting the audience full awareness of the outcome as the events unfold, and thus giving those events a weight and structure that linear chronology would not endow on them. Robert (Ben Kingsley) is a book publisher whose wife, Emma (Patricia Hodge), is having an affair with Jerry (Jeremy Irons), a literary agent. The film begins after the affair is over and ends as Jerry and Emma meet. The immensely talented Kingsley is the fulcrum which moves the story backward (or forward, as the case may be). Uttering only a few words, his Robert knows exactly what is going on and conveys a subtle sense of menace. Director David Jones fashions a brisk film, despite having to deal with Pinter's lengthy silences. Hodge, who should have been the center of attraction, comes across as a mite cool—it's hard to see how she inspires passion in these two very different men. Once you've grasped the reverse chronology, the events peel away in layers that produce unexpected insights along the way.

BETSY'S WEDDING

1990 97m c   ★★½
Comedy   R/15
Silver Screen Partners IV

Alan Alda *(Eddie Hopper)*, Joey Bishop *(Eddie's Father)*, Madeline Kahn *(Lola Hopper)*, Anthony LaPaglia *(Stevie Dee)*, Catherine O'Hara *(Gloria Henner)*, Joe Pesci *(Oscar Henner)*, Molly Ringwald *(Betsy Hopper)*, Ally Sheedy *(Connie Hopper)*, Burt Young *(Georgie)*, Julie Bovasso *(Grandma)*

p, Martin Bregman, Louis A. Stroller; d, Alan Alda; w, Alan Alda; ph, Kelvin Pike (Technicolor); ed, Michael Polakow; m, Bruce Broughton; prod d, John Jay Moore; art d, Andrew Moore; fx, Greg Hull; cos, Mary Malin

Nothing new under the sun, except for Anthony LaPaglia, as a Mafia prince courting tough policewoman Ally Sheedy. Otherwise, class conflicts and a wacky wedding, courtesy Alan Alda, whose persona is beginning to grate. Nice to see Madeline Kahn.

BETTY BLUE

(37.2 LE MATIN)
1986 120m c   ★★★
Drama   R/18
Constellation/Cargo   (France)

Beatrice Dalle *(Betty)*, Jean-Hugues Anglade *(Zorg)*, Consuelo de Haviland *(Lisa)*, Gerard Darmon *(Eddy)*, Clementine Celarie *(Annie)*, Jacques Mathou *(Bob)*, Claude Confortes *(Owner)*, Philippe Laudenbach *(Gyneco Publisher)*, Vincent Lindon *(Policeman Richard)*, Raoul Billeray *(Old Policeman)*

p, Claudie Ossard, Jean-Jacques Beineix; d, Jean-Jacques Beineix; w, Jean-Jacques Beineix (based on the novel *37.2 Le Matin* by Philippe Djian); ph, Jean-Francois Robin (Fujicolor); ed, Monique Prim; m, Gabriel Yared; art d, Carlos Conti; fx, Jean-Francois Cousson, Georges Demetreau; cos, Elisabeth Tavernier

Jean-Jacques Beineix's attempt to combine the energetic high-gloss finish of his debut feature, DIVA, with the raw poetic intensity of MOON IN THE GUTTER, ends up as an inconsistent and unsatisfying tale of *amour fou* and literary ambition. Dalle embarks on a personal crusade to get her lover's (Anglade) novel published, but has a pretty hard time dealing with rejection notices. Eventually she starts hearing voices, and is finally driven to poke out her own eye. Anglade, best known in the US as the "roller" in SUBWAY, is perfectly cast here, although the best thing about the film is the pouty, 21-year-old Dalle. While not a box-office smash in the US, BETTY BLUE did garner an Oscar nomination as Best Foreign Language Film. In 1991 Beineix released his original director's cut, at an expanded running time of 182 minutes, in France.

BETWEEN THE LINES
1977   101m   c   ★★★
Drama   R/15
Midwest

John Heard (Harry), Lindsay Crouse (Abbie), Jeff Goldblum (Max), Jill Eikenberry (Lynn), Bruno Kirby (David), Gwen Welles (Laura), Stephen Collins (Michael), Lewis J. Stadlen (Stanley), Michael J. Pollard (Hawker), Lane Smith (Roy Walsh)

p, Raphael D. Silver; d, Joan Micklin Silver; w, Fred Barron (based on a story by Barron, David M. Helpern); ph, Kenneth Van Sickle (Panavision, TVC Color); ed, John Carter; m, Michael Kamen; cos, Patrizia von Brandenstein

Tight little sleeper again demonstrates that Silver is a director with excellent taste and the ability to wring every last penny out of a budget and put it onscreen. The story takes place at an alternative newspaper like the "Village Voice" or "The LA Weekly." Knockout performances all. BETWEEN THE LINES was made for a mere $800,000, and the husband-wife Silver team managed to bring in a first-rate picture.

BEVERLY HILLS COP
1984   105m   c   ★★★
Comedy/Crime   R/15
Paramount

Eddie Murphy (Axel Foley), Judge Reinhold (Detective Billy Rosewood), John Ashton (Sgt. Taggart), Lisa Eilbacher (Jenny Summers), Ronny Cox (Lt. Bogomil), Steven Berkoff (Victor Maitland), James Russo (Mikey Tandino), Jonathan Banks (Zack), Stephen Elliott (Chief Hubbard), Gil Hill (Inspector Todd)

p, Don Simpson, Jerry Bruckheimer; d, Martin Brest; w, Daniel Petrie, Jr. (based on a by story Daniel Petrie Jr., Danilo Bach); ph, Bruce Surtees (Technicolor); ed, Billy Weber, Arthur Coburn; m, Harold Faltermeyer; prod d, Angelo Graham; art d, James J. Murakami; fx, Ken Pepiot; cos, Tom Bronson

A sassy cop; brash, crude and very funny. Murphy's third film was phenomenally successful at the box office, aided substantially by a hit-filled soundtrack. BEVERLY HILLS COP is an entertaining, if empty-headed, cop film in which street-smart Detroit detective Murphy sets out to avenge the murder of a friend. Basically a star vehicle designed to show off the talents of Murphy—it succeeds admirably. The comedy is deftly balanced with the stunningly staged action scenes. Surprisingly, most of the laughs are given to Reinhold and Ashton. Acting honors go to Bronson Pinchot in a brief but career-making turn.

BICYCLE THIEF, THE
(LADRI DI BICICLETTE)
1948   90m   bw   ★★★★★
Drama   /U
Mayer/Burstyn   (Italy)

Lamberto Maggiorani (Antonio), Lianella Carell (Maria), Enzo Staiola (Bruno), Elena Altieri (The Lady), Vittorio Antonucci (The Thief), Gino Saltamerenda (Bajocco), Fausto Guerzoni (Amateur Actor)

p, Vittorio De Sica; d, Vittorio De Sica; w, Cesare Zavattini (based on the novel by Luigi Bartolini); ph, Carlo Montuori; ed, Eraldo Da Roma; m, Alesandro Cicognani; art d, Antonio Traverso

A landmark film—honest, beautiful, and deceptively simple. Reviewers praised THE BICYCLE THIEF unanimously upon its first release, which marked one of the finest achievements of Italian neorealism.

Maggiorani is a poor, working-class Italian whose happiness at finding a job gives way to despair when his bicycle—on which his employment depends—is stolen. His search for the bike takes on an epic quality, with Staiola turning in an impossibly heart-wrenching performance as Maggiorani's young son. THE BICYCLE THIEF is a brilliant testament to director Vittorio De Sica's greatness and to the power of neorealism. All roles were played by nonactors, the dialogue is as spare as it can be in a talking picture, and the coarse black-and-white photography makes viewers feel as if they were watching a documentary, though without sacrificing drama.

Cesare Zavattini received an Oscar nomination for his screenplay, and the film received a Special Academy Award as the "most outstanding" foreign film of the year. The film was deftly and affectionately sent up by Mauricio Nichetti in his 1989 feature, THE ICICLE THIEF.

BIG
1988   104m   c   ★★★½
Comedy   PG
FOX

Tom Hanks (Josh Baskin), Elizabeth Perkins (Susan Lawrence), Robert Loggia ("Mac" MacMillan), John Heard (Paul Davenport), Jared Rushton (Billy Kopeche), David Moscow (Young Josh), Jon Lovitz (Scotty Brennen), Mercedes Ruehl (Mrs. Baskin), Josh Clark (Mr. Baskin), Kimberlee M. Davis (Cynthia Benson)

p, James L. Brooks, Robert Greenhut; d, Penny Marshall; w, Gary Ross, Anne Spielberg; ph, Barry Sonnenfeld (DuArt Color); ed, Barry Malkin; m, Howard Shore; prod d, Santo Loquasto; chor, Patricia Birch; cos, Judianna Makovsky

The best of the spate of body-switching films in the late 80s. BIG features a brilliant, unforced performance by Tom Hanks as a New Jersey Little Leaguer, who after wishing he were older, suddenly finds himself walking around in a 35-year-old body. Hiding in Manhattan until his friend Rushton can track down the carny fortune-telling machine that granted the wish, Hanks gets a job with a toy manufacturing firm and rises quickly up the corporate ladder thanks to his unique kid's insight. BIG is a winning, charming film, primarily because Hanks makes it work. He is extraordinarily convincing as an adolescent who suddenly finds himself dealing with a new, adult body, responsibilities, and a romantic relationship, while simultaneously trying to survive vicious corporate infighting.

BIG BROADCAST, THE
1932   80m   bw   ★★½
Musical/Comedy   /A
Paramount

Stuart Erwin (Leslie McWhinney), Leila Hyams (Anita Rogers), Sharon Lynne (Mona), George Burns (George), Gracie Allen (Gracie), George Barbier (Clapsaddle), Ralph Robertson (Announcer), Alex Melesh (Bird and Animal Man), Spec O'Donnell (Office Boy), Anna Chandler (Mrs. Cohen)

d, Frank Tuttle; w, George Marion, Jr. (based on the play "Wild Waves" by William Ford Manley); ph, George Folsey

Bizarre. Audiences finally get to see their on-the-air stars. Burns's radio station gets saved by putting on a show. It was in this film that Crosby crooned what was to later become his theme song, "When the Blue of the Night Meets the Gold of the Day." The Boswell Sisters are a particular delight.

BIG BROADCAST OF 1938, THE
1937   94m   bw   ★★
Comedy/Musical   /U
Paramount

W.C. Fields (T. Frothingill Bellows/S.B. Bellows), Martha Raye (Martha Bellows), Dorothy Lamour (Dorothy Wyndham), Shirley Ross (Cleo Fielding), Russell Hicks (Capt. Stafford), Virginia Vale (Joan Fielding), Lionel Pape (Lord Droopy), Patricia Wilder (Honey Chile), Rufe Davis (Turnkey), Grace Bradley (Grace Fielding)

p, Harlan Thompson; d, Mitchell Leisen; w, Walter DeLeon, Francis Martin, Ken Englund, Howard Lindsay, Russel Crouse (based on a story by Frederick Hazlitt Brennan); ph, Harry Fischbeck; ed, Eda Warren, House Chandler; art d, Hans Dreier, Ernst Fegte; fx, Gordon Jennings; chor, LeRoy Prinz; cos, Edith Head; anim, Leon Schlesinger

Strange but true. All-star clambake comes out spoiled. Fields doesn't get enough to do. Hope sings Oscar-winning trademark song. High point to obscurity: Kirsten Flagstad sings "Die Walkure".

BIG BUS, THE
1976   88m   c   ★★
Comedy/Disaster   PG
Paramount

Joseph Bologna (Dan Torrance), Stockard Channing (Kitty Baxter), John Beck (Shoulders O'Brien), Rene Auberjonois (Father Kudos), Ned Beatty (Shorty Scotty), Bob Dishy (Dr. Kurtz), Jose Ferrer (Ironman), Ruth Gordon (Old Lady), Harold Gould (Prof. Baxter), Larry Hagman (Parking Lot Doctor)

p, Fred Freeman, Lawrence J. Cohen; d, James Frawley; w, Fred Freeman, Larry Cohen; ph, Harry Stradling, Jr. (Panavision, Movielab Color); ed, Edward Warschilka; m, David Shire; prod d, Joel Schiller; cos, Marianna Elliott

A big bust. Huge behemoth of a nuclear-powered bus, driven by Bologna and designed by Channing and Gould, gets into all sorts of sight gags, and that's it. The highlight of the film is Dunne's portrayal of the ultimate cocktail pianist.

BIG CARNIVAL, THE
1951   111m   bw   ★★★★
Drama
Paramount

Kirk Douglas (Charles Tatum), Jan Sterling (Lorraine), Robert Arthur (Herbie Cook), Porter Hall (Jacob Q. Boot), Frank Cady (Mr. Federber), Richard Benedict (Leo Minosa), Ray Teal (Sheriff), Lewis Martin (McCardle), John Berks (Papa Minosa), Frances Dominguez (Mama Minosa)

p, Billy Wilder; d, Billy Wilder; w, Billy Wilder, Lesser Samuels, Walter Newman; ph, Charles Lang; ed, Arthur Schmidt; m, Hugo Friedhofer; art d, Hal Pereira, Earl Hedrick

A bitter pill, brilliantly done by Billy Wilder. Boozy but ruthlessly ambitious newspaperman, Douglas, down on his luck and desperate to improve his lot as a result of a mining accident,

builds a media circus. Gut-busting performance by a growling Douglas, matched easily by snarling Sterling, who gets best line: "I don't pray. Kneeling bags my nylons." An uneasy classic.

BIG CHILL, THE
1983   103m   c   ★★★
Drama   R/15
Columbia

Glenn Close (Sarah), Tom Berenger (Sam), William Hurt (Nick), Jeff Goldblum (Michael), Mary Kay Place (Meg), Kevin Kline (Harold), Meg Tilly (Chloe), Don Galloway (Richard), JoBeth Williams (Karen), James Gillis (Minister)

p, Michael Shamberg; d, Lawrence Kasdan; w, Lawrence Kasdan, Barbara Benedek; ph, John Bailey (Metrocolor); ed, Carol Littleton; prod d, Ida Random

A big chill. Old friend yuppies dumping on each other strains to be profound, looks superficial and glib. Good soundtrack, nice acting by ensemble can't disguise an empty center. Nor does the emptiness keep it from diverting. Big hit features Kevin Costner as the stiff being dressed under the titles.

BIG CLOCK, THE
1948   95m   bw   ★★★½
Crime
Paramount

Ray Milland (George Stroud), Charles Laughton (Earl Janoth), Maureen O'Sullivan (Georgette Stroud), George Macready (Steven Hagen), Rita Johnson (Pauline York), Elsa Lanchester (Louise Patterson), Harold Vermilyea (Don Klausmeyer), Dan Tobin (Ray Cordette), Henry Morgan (Bill Womack), Richard Webb (Nat Sperling)

p, Richard Maibaum; d, John Farrow; w, Jonathan Latimer (based on the novel by Kenneth Fearing); ph, John Seitz; ed, Gene Ruggiero; m, Victor Young; art d, Hans Dreier, Roland Anderson, Albert Nozaki; fx, Gordon Jennings; cos, Edith Head

Steady film noir production fraught with suspense, twisting its unique plot and characters to a clever and frightening conclusion. Milland is the shrewd editor of Crimeways Magazine which is published by Laughton, a megalomaniacal media tycoon who kills his mistress. Milland tries to solve murder, but all clues point back at him! Almost stolen by the eccentric as usual Elsa Lanchester. In 1987, the film was remade with a military setting in NO WAY OUT, starring Kevin Costner and Gene Hackman.

BIG DEAL ON MADONNA STREET, THE
1958   91m   bw   ★★★½
Comedy/Crime
Lux   (Italy)

Vittorio Gassman (Peppe), Renato Salvatori (Mario), Rossana Rory (Norma), Carla Gravina (Nicoletta), Claudia Cardinale (Carmelina), Carlo Pisacane (Capannelle), Tiberio Murgia (Ferribotte), Memmo Carotenuto (Cosimo), Marcello Mastroianni (Tiberio), Toto (Dante)

p, Franco Cristaldi; d, Mario Monicelli; w, Suso Cecchi D'Amico, Agenore Incrocci, Furio Scarpelli, Mario Monicelli

A classic Italian spoof. Vittorio Gassman stars as Peppe, a bungling petty thief who leads a group of incompetent burglars in a plan to loot a jewelry store on Madonna Street. One of the finest examples of Italian comedy to reach American shores (it was nominated for a Best Foriegn Film Oscar in 1958), BIG DEAL ON MADONNA STREET satirizes all those procedural caper films that Hollywood turned out and the foreign homages that followed (such as RIFIFI and BOB LE FLAMBEUR). The entire burglarizing procedure, as directed by Mario Monicelli, is hilarious, thanks to the fine acting and the steady stream of sight gags that recall the classic comedies of silent days. CRACKERS, an unfunny remake from Louis Malle, appeared in 1984, and BIG DEAL ON MADONNA STREET—20 YEARS LATER surfaced in 1985. The film was also unsuccessfully adapted for a broadway musical.

BIG DIS, THE
1990 84m bw   ★★★
Comedy
Olympia

James Haig (JD), Kevin Haig (Kevin), Monica Sparrow (Monica), Allysun Walker (Allyson), Gordon Eriksen (Gordon), Heather Johnson (Heather), Lisa Rivers, Aratha Johnston

p, Gordon Eriksen, John O'Brien; d, Gordon Eriksen, John O'Brien; w, Gordon Eriksen, John O'Brien; ph, John O'Brien; ed, Gordon Eriksen, John O'Brien; m, Kev Ses & Harry B., Dr. Cranium and the Big Dis Crew

The politics of getting laid. Granted an unexpected 48-hour pass from the Army, 19-year-old JD (James Haig) comes home to Long Island with one thing on his mind: getting lucky before his leave is up. A low-budget, independently produced film, THE BIG DIS was shot in black and white in 1988, completely on location in Long Island. Reviewers have likened coproducer-writer-director-editor-actor Gordon Eriksen to a young John Cassavetes, but the partners have an altogether lighter touch; James is frustrated, but there's no hollowness at the core of his life—he's just a middle class kid learning that you don't always get what you want.

THE BIG DIS is distinguished by a distinctly suburban voice—not the disaffected anger of Jonathan Kaplan's OVER THE EDGE, but a more mellow, satisfied sensibility—and by the casual, familiar way it depicts middle-class African-American characters. The problems at the center of THE BIG DIS aren't unique to African-Americans; they're a teenaged guy's problems. James is black and Gordon is white, their acquaintances are black, white, hispanic, and Asian, and their relationships are determined by class and geography, not race. Subsidiary characters are remarkably distinct. Monica and Allysun appear only briefly, but each one makes her mark; they aren't faceless bodies solely defined by James's desire for them.

THE BIG DIS is a fresh and funny film, from the opening rap song—in which female rappers ask, "What's the matter with these boys today?" and a male chorus answers, "We just want to get laid"—to the final image of the ever hopeful James, mesmerized by the young woman at the airport.

BIG EASY, THE
1987 108m c   ★★★
Crime/Thriller   R/15
Kings Road

Dennis Quaid (Remy McSwain), Ellen Barkin (Anne Osborne), Ned Beatty (Jack Kellom), Ebbe Roe Smith (Detective Dodge), John Goodman (Detective DeSoto), Lisa Jane Persky (Detective McCabe), Charles Ludlam (Lamar), Thomas O'Brien (Bobby), James Garrison (Judge Noland), Carol Sutton (Judge Raskov)

p, Stephen Friedman; d, Jim McBride; w, Daniel Petrie, Jr., Jack Baran; ph, Alfonso Beato (Deluxe Color); ed, Mia Goldman; m, Brad Fiedel; prod d, Jeannine Claudia Oppewall; fx, Bill Purcell; cos, Tracy Tynan

Colorful Cajun *noir*, spicy, romantic, efficent. Hot Noo Ahluns police detective (Dennis Quaid) clashes with assistant district attorney (Ellen Barkin) over cop corruption. The best scenes are the romantic ones; McBride effectively captures the Big Easy, a city that is almost a character in itself, but the ending is contrived. That's the late and beloved New York Ridiculous Theatre impressario Charles Ludlam, out of his corset, as Lamar.

BIG HEAT, THE
1953 89m bw   ★★★★
Crime   /15
Columbia

Glenn Ford (Dave Bannion), Gloria Grahame (Debby Marsh), Jocelyn Brando (Katie Bannion), Alexander Scourby (Mike Lagana), Lee Marvin (Vince Stone), Jeanette Nolan (Bertha Duncan), Peter Whitney (Tierney), Willis Bouchey (Lt. Wilkes), Robert Burton (Gus Burke), Adam Williams (Larry Gordon)

p, Robert Arthur; d, Fritz Lang; w, Sydney Boehm (based on the serial in the *Saturday Evening Post* by William P. McGivern); ph, Charles Lang; ed, Charles Nelson; m, Daniele Amfitheatrof; art d, Robert Peterson; cos, Jean Louis

A scalding face-full of harsh reality, courtesy Fritz Lang. Starkly photographed and without a continuous score, the absence of which underlines the hard-hitting dialogue and the sound of smacking fists and thudding bullets, this film is as brutal as Lang's M was frightening. Ford, an ex-cop out to avenge the mob murder of his wife, gets upstaged by two performances of incredible power: Grahame and Marvin. Grahame plays a moll who squeals and pays; her performance defines the film noir anti-heroine, and in a world of comedic 1950s sex, she was the real thing, either coming along too late or too soon. Marvin moved his career up a definite notch as the sadistic killer.

This film, along with a spate of others, was spawned by the 1950 US Senate crime investigations conducted via TV, which pinpointed widespread corruption by organized crime throughout America. Fritz Lang's THE BIG HEAT, meaning the heat brought down by the police, is one of the best expose films dealing with the national crime cartel, including HOODLUM EMPIRE, Robert Wise's startling CAPTIVE CITY, and Phil Karlson's hard-hitting KANSAS CITY CONFIDENTIAL. Lang's ferocious gangster film is directed with immaculate care, showing not so much violence on film as the reaction to violence, while examining the victims. A terse script by Boehm and sharp photography by Charles Lang in keeping with the theme contribute to this startling film noir.

BIG HOUSE, THE
1930 84m bw   ★★★★½
Prison
MGM

Chester Morris (John Morgan), Wallace Beery (Machine Gun Butch Schmidt), Lewis Stone (Warden James Adams), Robert Montgomery (Kent Marlowe), Leila Hyams (Anne Marlowe), George F. Marion, Sr. (Pop Reicher), J.C. Nugent (Mr. Marlowe), Karl Dane (Olsen), DeWitt Jennings (Capt. Wallace), Matthew Betz (Gopher) d, George Hill; w, Frances Marion, Joe Farnham, Martin Flavin; ph, Harold Wenstrom; ed, Blanche Sewell; art d, Cedric Gibbons; cos, David Cox

The granddaddy of 'em all. Inspired by a particularly bloody riot that occurred in an Auburn, New York, prison in 1929, THE BIG HOUSE spawned a host of movies like 20,000 YEARS IN SING SING and I AM A FUGITIVE FROM A CHAIN GANG. Grimly realistic and often brutal, it exposes the inhuman conditions and paranoia that deepen criminal resolve among inmates. George Hill's uncompromising direction captures all the ugliness and futility of prison life, and Beery (in a role originally intended for Lon Chaney, Sr.) is the perfect goonish ringleader of the convicts—part clown, part thug, softhearted and softheaded, but with a killer instinct. Morris gives one of his best performances as the intelligent member of the threesome; Montgomery, at the beginning of his film career, is uncharacteristically spineless but wholly believable as a wretched, despicable cringer; and Stone, as always, contributes a solid portrayal of the establishment stalwart.

BIG KNIFE, THE
1955   111m   bw   ★★★½
Drama   /A
UA

Jack Palance (*Charles Castle*), Ida Lupino (*Marion Castle*), Shelley Winters (*Dixie Evans*), Wendell Corey (*Smiley Coy*), Jean Hagen (*Connie Bliss*), Rod Steiger (*Stanley Hoff*), Ilka Chase (*Patty Benedict*), Everett Sloane (*Nat Danziger*), Wesley Addy (*Hank Teagle*), Paul Langton (*Buddy Bliss*)

p, Robert Aldrich; d, Robert Aldrich; w, James Poe (based on the play by Clifford Odets); ph, Ernest Laszlo; ed, Michael Luciano; m, Frank DeVol; art d, William Glasgow

Hollywood sterotypes based on Odets but compelling and viciously done with a *tour de force* for Palance, as a tinseltown hunk with a dark, dishonest secret, supported by an amazing cast. Director Aldrich's unflinching use of a candid, almost documentary style results in a devastating mirror image of Hollywood at its most ruthless. Grim, lacking compassion and uncompromising, irrespective of the name-dropping of real personalities (Kazan, Wilder, Wyler, etc.) to authenticate the atmosphere. The script blares the philosophy that it is not only windy at the top but also lethal.

BIG PARADE, THE
(DA YUE BING)
1987   102m   c   ★★★
Drama   /15
Guangxi   (China)

Huang Xueqi, Sun Chun, Lu Lei, Wu Ruofu

d, Chen Kaige; w, Gao Lili; ph, Zhang Yimou (Widescreen); ed, Zhou Xinxia; m, Qu Xiaosong, Zhao Quiping; prod d, He Qun

Chinese director Chen Kaige's long-awaited second feature, following the critically acclaimed YELLOW EARTH, was a somewhat uneven effort, hampered by a cliched narrative that fails to live up to the brilliance of the imagery.

Set in modern-day China, the film follows a single airborne unit as it undergoes a grueling training session in preparation for the prestigious parade in Beijing celebrating the 35th anniversary of the revolution. Led by a tough drill sergeant who is a veteran of a China-Vietnam conflict, the undisciplined young men are slowly whipped into shape until they becomes a flawless unit capable of marching in perfect order.

In THE BIG PARADE director Kaige strives for something more than what some critics have called the "Chinese FULL METAL JACKET." The film illustrates the conflict between the group and the individual in today's China. This somewhat subversive theme may have been the reason Chinese officials prevented the film's release for two years (it was filmed in 1985). Unfortunately, to Western eyes used to countless war films, the exploration of this theme may be a bit too banal. Although the characters and situations are standard basic training fare, Kaige filled his film with frequently breathtaking visuals.

From the opening helicopter shot which shows miles and miles of troops training on the tarmac to the final slow-motion shots of various units, Kaige continually comes up with beautiful and fascinating images of men in motion. Most remarkable, however, is the sequence where the men are not in motion—the arduous drill where the soldiers must stand still in the blazing sun. The wide-screen shimmers with the brutal heat, and the sweat pours from beneath the soldiers' helmets, presenting a brilliant, unforgettable image of individual human endurance and mass stupidity.

BIG RED ONE, THE
1980   113m   c   ★★★
War   PG/15
Lorimar

Lee Marvin (*Sergeant*), Mark Hamill (*Griff*), Robert Carradine (*Zab*), Bobby Di Cicco (*Vinci*), Kelly Ward (*Johnson*), Siegfried Rauch (*Schroeder*), Stephane Audran (*Walloon*), Serge Marquand (*Rensonnet*), Charles Macaulay (*General/Captain*), Alain Doutey (*Broban*)

p, Gene Corman; d, Samuel Fuller; w, Samuel Fuller; ph, Adam Greenberg (Metrocolor); ed, Morton Tubor; m, Dana Koproff

Veteran writer-director Samuel Fuller (THE STEEL HELMET, FIXED BAYONETS, VERBOTEN!, MERRILL'S MARAUDERS) waited more than 35 years to make this dream project, a WWII picture that follows the exploits of his unit, the First Infantry Division, nicknamed "the Big Red One" because of the big red No. 1 on the division arm patch.

Fuller chose to make an intimate film, concentrating on a small squad of soldiers as they battle the Germans from Northern Africa and into Europe during the years 1942-45. The squad is made up of four green recruits led by a grizzled, tough, no-nonsense sergeant (Lee Marvin), a WWI veteran determined to teach his charges how to survive the rigors of battle.

Fuller injects much humor into his narrative, constantly balancing the horrible and violent with the sardonic, most notably in a scene in which Johnson steps on a mine and has a testicle blown off. The Sarge rushes to the boy's side and fishes around in the dirt until he finds the severed part, shows it to the soldier, tosses it over his shoulder, and reassuringly says, "That's why God gave you two." Fuller refuses to indulge in melodramatics or Hollywood-style heroics and instead concentrates on a group of men determined to survive the war and go home in one piece.

Filled with memorable scenes, plenty of humor, and excellent performances, especially from Marvin, THE BIG RED ONE is a remarkable film, a unique entry in the genre of films made about WWII.

BIG SKY, THE

1952   140m   bw   ★★★½
Western   /U
Winchester

Kirk Douglas *(Deakins)*, Dewey Martin *(Boone)*, Elizabeth Threatt *(Teal Eye)*, Arthur Hunnicutt *(Zeb)*, Buddy Baer *(Romaine)*, Steven Geray *(Jourdonnais)*, Hank Worden *(Poordevil)*, Jim Davis *(Streak)*, Henri Letondal *(Ladadie)*, Robert Hunter *(Chouquette)*

p, Howard Hawks; d, Howard Hawks; w, Dudley Nichols (based on the novel by A.B. Guthrie, Jr.); ph, Russell Harlan; ed, Christian Nyby; m, Dimitri Tiomkin; art d, Albert S. D'Agostino, Perry Ferguson; fx, Don Steward; cos, Dorothy Jeakins

Up the Missouri, male bonding and will bending. Well-directed by Hawks, but nothimg new under the sun. Shot on location in the Grand Teton National Park and enhanced by lyrical, haunting Tiomkin score (he had recently won two Oscars for score and song for HIGH NOON). Aside from the fascinating upriver struggle where the men must pull the boat by rope while hostile Indians lurk nearby, the most interesting aspect of the film is the wizened Hunnicutt as the old trapper; he manages to steal almost every scene.

BIG SLEEP, THE

1946   118m   bw   ★★★★★
Mystery/Crime   /PG
WB

Humphrey Bogart *(Philip Marlowe)*, Lauren Bacall *(Vivian)*, John Ridgely *(Eddie Mars)*, Louis Jean Heydt *(Joe Brody)*, Elisha Cook, Jr. *(Jones)*, Regis Toomey *(Bernie Ohls)*, Sonia Darrin *(Agnes)*, Bob Steele *(Canino)*, Martha Vickers *(Carmen)*, Tom Rafferty *(Carol Lundgren)*

p, Howard Hawks; d, Howard Hawks; w, William Faulkner, Jules Furthman, Leigh Brackett (based on the novel by Raymond Chandler); ph, Sid Hickox; ed, Christian Nyby; m, Max Steiner; art d, Carl Jules Weyl; fx, Roy Davidson; cos, Leah Rhodes

The most convoluted of the great noir films, based on the first yarn written by Raymond Chandler. THE BIG SLEEP comes magically alive through Hawks's careful direction and Bogart's persona, which is twin to his character of Philip Marlowe.

Summoned to the lavish mansion of General Sternwood (Charles Waldron), Marlowe is hired to investigate blackmailer Geiger (Theodore Von Eltz), a Hollywood smut book dealer who has compromising photos of the general's daughter Carmen (Vickers). The general's real aim, however, is to have Bogart locate his missing confidante Shawn Regan. Marlowe follows his clues to Geiger's home, finding the smut peddler dead and Carmen drugged. Before police arrive, Marlowe secrets Carmen back home and strikes up a romance with the general's other daughter, Vivian (Bacall). With Vivian at the gumshoe's side, Marlowe sinks deeper and deeper into a labyrinthine plot of gambling, blackmail, and murder.

One of the greatest detective films to come out of Hollywood, THE BIG SLEEP is perhaps most notorious for its famous unsolved murder—that of the Sternwood chauffeur. The unwieldy plot, scripted by William Faulkner, kept Hawks busy trying to figure out the puzzle. When Hawks called Chandler to ask the killer's identity, the writer reportedly stated: "How should I know? You figure it out," and hung up. It was on the set of THE BIG SLEEP that the Bogart and Bacall love-team image was cemented, although their first sizzling union on screen was in TO HAVE AND HAVE NOT. Their dazzling star personas, com-

bined with the poetry of both Chandler's and Faulkner's words and Howard Hawks's direction, give THE BIG SLEEP some of the most sexually electric dialogue ever to hit the screen.

BIG TRAIL, THE

1930   125m   c/bw   ★★★
Western   /U
Fox Films

John Wayne *(Breck Coleman)*, Marguerite Churchill *(Ruth Cameron)*, El Brendel *(Gussie)*, Tully Marshall *(Zeke)*, Tyrone Power, Sr. *(Red Flack)*, David Rollins *(Dave Cameron)*, Frederick Burton *(Pa Bascom)*, Charles Stevens *(Lopez)*, Russ Powell *(Windy Bill)*, Helen Parrish *(Honey Girl)*

d, Raoul Walsh; w, Jack Peabody, Marie Boyle, Florence Postal, Fred Sersen (based on a story by Hal Evarts and Raoul Walsh); ph, Lucien Andriot, Arthur Edeson (Grandeur); ed, Jack Dennis; m, Arthur Kay; art d, Harold Miles, Fred Sersen

Creaking, but sentimentally grand. Wayne was working as a property man, a kid just out of college, when director John Ford noticed him. When colleague Raoul Walsh was searching for the male lead for his latest project, Ford recommended Wayne, telling Walsh, who appeared in Griffith's THE BIRTH OF A NATION in 1915, and who would go on to become one of the best action directors (OBJECTIVE BURMA, THEY DIED WITH THEIR BOOTS ON) that he "liked the looks of this new kid with a funny walk, like he owned the world."

The film deals with the first covered wagon train to cross the rugged Oregon Trail. There is the traditional Indian attack with pioneers beating off the redskins from their circle of wagons, a spectacular buffalo hunt, and a devastating scene where the entire cast was almost drowned when fording a river during a fierce rainstorm (Walsh always kept the cameras rolling). There is little plot other than the great trek west through the wilderness of Nebraska and Wyoming where the film was shot, with Wayne vying for Churchill's attentions with Tully Marshall and others.

Walsh's direction is superb as he captures the thrilling outdoor action in this epic which cost Fox $2 million to produce, a fortune in those days. Further, the film was one of the first to be made in Grandeur, a 55mm wide-screen color process so impressive that the premiere audience jumped to its feet and cheered at the conclusion. Most viewers, however, only saw the film on the standard 35mm black-and-white screen, and this took away from the films impact.

Wayne seems uneasy, and it can't have helped that Fox producers insisted that Lumsden Hare, the studio voice coach, teach Wayne to sound like an Englishman in buckskin so that each preciously recorded word could be understood. Wayne next drifted into the oblivion of "poverty row" studios that would have him making sagebrush grinders for nine years until Ford once again came to the rescue by giving him the lead in his classic STAGECOACH.

BILL & TED'S EXCELLENT ADVENTURE

1989   90m   c   ★★½
Comedy   PG
Nelson/Interscope/Nelson-Murphey

Keanu Reeves *(Ted "Theodore" Logan)*, Alex Winter *(Bill S. Preston)*, George Carlin *(Rufus)*, Terry Camilleri *(Napoleon)*, Dan Shor *(Billy the Kid)*, Tony Steedman *(Socrates)*, Rod Loomis *(Sigmund Freud)*, Al Leong *(Genghis Khan)*, Jane Wiedlin *(Joan of Arc)*, Robert V. Barron *(Abraham Lincoln)* p, Scott Kroopf, Michael S. Murphey, Joel Soisson; d, Stephen Herek; w, Chris Matheson, Ed Solomon; ph, Tim Suhrstedt (Technicolor); ed, Larry Bock, Patrick Rand; m, David Newman; prod d, Roy Forge Smith; art d, Gordon White; chor, Brad Jeffries; cos, Jill Ohanneson

Radical! Pair of rock 'n' roll airheads can't graduate unless they pass history exam. Along comes Carlin from the future to enable dudes to experience history for themselves. Dudes take off without film. Still, BILL & TED has an intangibly charming goofiness about it that is somehow endearing: Here is a movie about teenagers that contains no excessive profanity, no drug references, and no explicit sexual activity.

BILL OF DIVORCEMENT, A
1932 70m bw   ★★★★
Drama   /A
Selznick

John Barrymore (Hillary Fairfield), Billie Burke (Margaret Fairfield), Katharine Hepburn (Sydney Fairfield), David Manners (Kit Humphrey), Henry Stephenson (Doctor Alliot), Paul Cavanagh (Gray Meredith), Elizabeth Patterson (Aunt Hester), Gayle Evers (Bassett), Julie Haydon (Party Guest)

p, David O. Selznick; d, George Cukor; w, Howard Estabrook, Harry Wagstaff Gribble (based on the play by Clemence Dane); ph, Sid Hickox; ed, Arthur Roberts; m, Max Steiner; art d, Carroll Clark; cos, Josette De Lima

This was the second, definitive version of three filmings of the Clemence Dane play. (The first was a British silent of 1922, and RKO made a second worthy sound version with Adolph Menjou and Maureen O'Hara in 1940.) John Barrymore was at the top of his profession with this performance, and a radiant Katharine Hepburn made her screen debut. Barrymore plays a man who has been living in a mental hospital for many years and who escapes on the day his wife (Burke) is divorcing him. His daughter's (Hepburn) rediscovery of her father, her reaction to the taint of hereditary mental illness in the family, and the wife's desire to remarry make for a compact and compelling drama.

Barrymore is simply superb, director George Cukor eliciting a lost, sensitive and caring man from beneath the occasional bravado. Hepburn, who was to work with Cukor nine more times in films and TV, was only 24 at the time. Her appearance was electric and sent critics reaching for new superlatives.

BILLY BATHGATE
1991 106m c   ★★★
Crime/Drama/Romance   R/15
Touchstone

Dustin Hoffman (Dutch Schultz), Nicole Kidman (Drew Preston), Loren Dean (Billy Bathgate), Bruce Willis (Bo Weinberg), Steven Hill (Otto Berman), Steve Buscemi (Irving), Billy Jaye (Mickey), John Costelloe (Lulu), Tim Jerome (Dixie Davis), Stanley Tucci (Lucky Luciano)

p, Arlene Donovan, Robert F Colesberry; d, Robert Benton; w, Tom Stoppard (from the novel by E.L. Doctorow); ph, Nestor Almendros; ed, Alan Heim, Robert Reitano, David Ray; m, Mark Isham; prod d, Patrizia Von Brandenstein; art d, Tim Galvin, Dennis Bradford, John Willett; chor, Pat Birch; cos, Joseph G. Aulisi

Despite an impressive array of talent, the ingredients never catch fire in this oddly lifeless adaptation of E.L. Doctorow's acclaimed novel.

Billy Bathgate (Loren Dean), an enterprising street kid from the Depression-era Bronx slums, bluffs and charms his way into the upper echelons of Dutch Schultz's (Hoffman) gang by helping expose the duplicity of Schultz's trusted lieutenant, Bo Weinberg (Bruce Willis). Dumped from a tugboat wearing cement overshoes, Weinberg leaves behind a rich girlfriend, Drew Preston (Nicole Kidman), who takes up with Schultz. It becomes Billy's main job to take care of Drew, as Schultz, already in decline, is preoccupied with fighting federal tax-evasion charges in the courts and rising mafioso Lucky Luciano (Stanley Tucci) on the streets.

Doctorow's multileveled plotting becomes BILLY BATHGATE's greatest liability: Stoppard's script and Benton's direction are so preoccupied with keeping the lines of action clear that they fail to establish a consistent mood or a strong point of view—the novel's real strengths. The casting also works against any lasting impact. The highly-touted Dean emerges here as just another generic brat-packer, wholly out of his expressive range. Kidman is too cool a beauty to evoke the hungry sexuality of the novel's Drew, for whom men were literally willing to die. Hoffman is, as usual, technically flawless, but on a gut level he fails even to erase memories of James Remar's searing portrayal of Schulz in THE COTTON CLUB. Only Steven Hill's performance, as Schultz's level-headed accountant, suggests the rough lyricism of Doctorow's elegy to the bad men who built America.

BILLY LIAR
1963 98m bw   ★★★★
Drama   /PG
Vic   (U.K.)

Tom Courtenay (Billy Fisher), Julie Christie (Liz), Wilfred Pickles (Geoffrey Fisher), Mona Washbourne (Alice Fisher), Ethel Griffies (Florence), Finlay Currie (Duxbury), Rodney Bewes (Arthur Crabtree), Helen Fraser (Barbara), George Innes (Eric Stamp), Leonard Rossiter (Shadrack)

p, Joseph Janni; d, John Schlesinger; w, Keith Waterhouse, Willis Hall (based on their play); ph, Denys Coop; ed, Roger Cherrill; m, Richard Rodney Bennett

One of the seminal British working-class films of the 1960s, BILLY LIAR is a first-rate comedy-fantasy that features Tom Courtenay in a role which Albert Finney had played in the stage version by Waterhouse and Hall.

No one will argue the plot's derivation—James Thurber's classic short story "The Secret Life of Walter Mitty," with Courtenay as Billy Fisher, a dreamer who works for a funeral director, but who retreats into a fantasy world. Billy is also a pathological liar who, as Oscar Wilde once said, doesn't lie for gain, just for the sheer joy of lying. Billy is involved with three young women, two of whom share an engagement ring. Christie, in one of her earliest roles, is terrific as a adventurous young woman willing to overlook anything the charming Billy tosses at her.

All the secondary roles are sharply etched and wonderfully acted under the sure hand of John Schlesinger in his third feature. Although his two earlier films, TERMINUS and A KIND OF LOVING, were superb, it was really with this film that Schlesinger garnered widespread attention. A later stage musical and TV series were based on the same story.

BILOXI BLUES
1988 107m c   ★★★½
Comedy/War   PG-13/15
Rastar

Matthew Broderick *(Eugene Morris Jerome)*, Christopher Walken *(Sgt. Merwin J. Toomey)*, Matt Mulhern *(Joseph Wykowski)*, Corey Parker *(Arnold Epstein)*, Markus Flanagan *(Roy Selridge)*, Casey Siemaszko *(Donald Carney)*, Michael Dolan *(James J. Hennessey)*, Penelope Ann Miller *(Daisy Hannigan)*, Park Overall *(Rowena)*, Alan Pottinger *(Peek)*

p, Ray Stark; d, Mike Nichols; w, Neil Simon (based on his play); ph, Bill Butler; ed, Sam O'Steen; m, Georges Delerue; prod d, Paul Sylbert; cos, Ann Roth

BILOXI BLUES works better than the script alone would suggest, thanks to the skillful direction of Nichols and excellent performances from Broderick and Walken.

An adaptation of Simon's autobiographical play, the film follows New Yorker Broderick through his Army basic training in Biloxi, Mississippi, in the last days of WWII. Broderick is bemused by his fellow draftees—including vulgar roughnecks Mulhern and Flanagan, hanger-on Siemaszko, and likable farm boy Dolan—and writes about them in his notebook. The Biloxi heat gets him down, as does his strange drill sergeant, Walken, whose sadism works in quiet, mysterious ways, sowing dissent among his troops.

The weeks of bad food, long marches, and humiliation are somewhat relieved, however, when Broderick falls in love with Miller while on weekend leave. When his buddies find Broderick's notes and read his hurtful remarks about them—including his musings about whether Parker is homosexual—the aspiring writer discovers just how powerful words can be. This lesson is reinforced when the Army goes on a manhunt for gays in the ranks and Parker is suspected. The comic, romantic, and dramatic subplots develop further before training—and ironically, the war—come to an end.

Successfully opening up Simon's popular play, Nichols avoids presenting the jokes in the sitcom formula typical of Simon, as set-ups to big punchlines. The dialogue flows with ease, and the jokes come in an almost offhand manner, an approach that brings some freshness to a cliched storyline. Broderick brings appealing nuances to the role he created onstage, and Walken makes his sergeant a quietly chilling, ambiguous character. An intelligent, tightly constructed film which manages to satirize both the military and the process of growing up.

BINGO LONG TRAVELING ALL-STARS AND MOTOR KINGS, THE
1976 110m c   ★★★
Comedy/Sports   PG/15
Motown/Pan Arts

Billy Dee Williams *(Bingo)*, James Earl Jones *(Leon)*, Richard Pryor *(Charlie Snow)*, Rico Dawson *(Willie Lee)*, Sam "Birmingham" Briston *(Louis)*, Jophery Brown *(Champ Chambers)*, Leon Wagner *(Fat Sam)*, Tony Burton *(Isaac)*, John McCurry *(Walter Murchman)*, Stan Shaw *(Esquire Joe Calloway)*

p, Rob Cohen; d, John Badham; w, Hal Barwood, Matthew Robbins; ph, Bill Butler (Panavision, Technicolor); ed, David Rawlins; m, William Goldstein; cos, Bernard Johnson

It's hard to understand why this good-natured look at the old Negro Leagues didn't do better at the box office. The script is a fine mix of humor, pathos, and honest drama; the direction is brisk; and the photography and production design are first-rate.

Tired of being abused by the owners of all-black teams, Williams organizes an independent team and is joined by other black stars. Their former employers conspire to put the renegades out of business, but they barnstorm around the country, success-fully playing amateur white teams. In the climactic final game, the new squad is pitted against some all-stars from the black league. If Williams' team wins, it gets a spot in the league; but if it loses, the players must return to their former teams.

Williams and Jones are very good in their roles as the star pitcher and catcher, and Pryor does a nice comic turn as the player who poses as a Cuban and then as an Indian in an attempt to overcome major league baseball's color barrier. Entertaining and well worth a look.

BIRD
1988 161m c   ★★★★
Biography   R/15
Malpaso

Forest Whitaker *(Charlie "Yardbird" Parker)*, Diane Venora *(Chan Richardson Parker)*, Michael Zelniker *(Red Rodney)*, Samuel E. Wright *(Dizzy Gillespie)*, Keith David *(Buster Franklin)*, Michael McGuire *(Brewster)*, James Handy *(Esteves)*, Damon Whitaker *(Young Bird)*, Morgan Nagler *(Kim)*, Arlen Dean Snyder *(Dr. Heath)*

p, Clint Eastwood; d, Clint Eastwood; w, Joel Oliansky; ph, Jack N. Green (Technicolor); ed, Joel Cox; m, Lennie Niehaus; fx, Joe Day

A tribute to the life and genius of saxophonist Charlie Parker, BIRD is a collage of passages from Parker's remarkable life, from his childhood in Kansas City, through his tumultuous interracial relationship with Chan Richardson, to his tragic death at the age of 34.

Derived mostly from Chan Parker's unpublished memoir, *Life in E-Flat*, the story is told through an intricate structure that jumps backward and forward in an ambitious attempt to create a narrative and visual equivalent to Parker's complicated music. In a remarkable directorial effort, Eastwood shows a great flair for atmosphere and composition and presents a nuanced, complex, humane portrait of Parker's talents, obstacles, virtues and failings. Whitaker gives a towering performance as the tortured musical genius, and Venora is equally impressive as the independent, compassionate Chan.

Wisely opting to use Parker's actual solos on the soundtrack instead of having a modern musician re-create them, Eastwood and musical director Lennie Niehaus took several previously unreleased recordings of Parker and digitally stripped away his accompanists (mostly because of poor recording techniques that featured Bird at the expense of the others), replacing them with modern musicians.

BIRD WITH THE CRYSTAL PLUMAGE, THE
(L'UCELLO DALLE PLUME DI CRISTALLO)
1969 98m c   ★★★★
Horror   PG/18
Glazier   (Italy/West Germany)

Tony Musante *(Sam Dalmas)*, Suzy Kendall *(Julia)*, Eva Renzi *(Monica)*, Enrico Maria Salerno *(Morosini)*, Mario Adorf *(Berto)*, Renato Romano *(Dover)*, Umberto Raho *(Ranieri)*

p, Salvatore Argento; d, Dario Argento; w, Dario Argento; ph, Vittorio Storaro (Eastmancolor); m, Ennio Morricone

A heart-stopping horror melodrama with excellent acting from all involved. Director Argento, here essaying his first film, uses humor, much like Hitchcock, to complement the suspense, but you never feel the master is being ripped off.

Walking home one night Musante, a Yank scribe in Rome, sees Renzi being murdered in an art gallery. He can't make out the killer's face, but the police decide to garnish his passport, as this is but one of several murders of lone women. Musante cooperates with the police but also conducts his own investigation, which takes him into the underbelly of the Eternal City.

Memorable characters abound and Storaro's sensational camera work and Morricone's score highlight their seedy milieu aptly. Several terrifying sequences come one after another, but none are gratuitous and the film never wallows in its violence. With a different title and better marketing, this compelling film, which had considerable influence on what would become known as the "slasher" genre in the 1980s, would have been a smash.

BIRDMAN OF ALCATRAZ

1962   147m   bw   ★★★½
Prison/Biography   /A
UA

Burt Lancaster (*Robert Stroud*), Karl Malden (*Harvey Shoemaker*), Thelma Ritter (*Elizabeth Stroud*), Betty Field (*Stella Johnson*), Neville Brand (*Bull Ransom*), Edmond O'Brien (*Tom Gaddis*), Hugh Marlowe (*Roy Comstock*), Telly Savalas (*Feto Gomez*), Crahan Denton (*Kramer*), James Westerfield (*Jess Younger*)

p, Stuart Miller, Guy Trosper; d, John Frankenheimer; w, Guy Trosper (based on the book by Thomas E. Gaddis); ph, Burnett Guffey; ed, Edward Mann; m, Elmer Bernstein

In a story based on fact, Lancaster plays surly, withdrawn inmate Robert Stroud, sentenced to life in prison, who cures a sick bird which flies into his cell one day and later becomes an internationally recognized ornithologist. Fighting against an overly protective mother (Ritter) and a truculent warden (Malden), Stroud is nonetheless able to continue his research even when sent to Alcatraz, the notorious "Rock" in San Francisco Bay, home to only the most incorrigible prisoners. Finally, though, after an abortive romance (Field) and a prison riot which he helps quell, Stroud is able to tell his remarkable story to writer Tom Gaddis (O'Brien, playing the author of the film's source biography), who brings it to the world.

THE BIRDMAN OF ALCATRAZ has great production values, moving if sometimes plodding, overly deliberate scripting, and efficient direction from black-and-white specialist Frankenheimer which strives mightily to overcome the essentially static nature of the storyline. Lancaster's star turn in the title role, typically bravura yet more restrained than usual, plays a vital role in holding this lengthy movie together while staving off sentimentality in the process. Nominated for Best Actor, Lancaster lost to Gregory Peck for his role in TO KILL A MOCKINGBIRD. Malden is typically Malden, but Savalas, as one of Stroud's fellow inmates, and the reliable Ritter make the most of their roles and received supporting Oscar nominations, as did Guffey's skillful cinematography.

BIRDS, THE

1963   120m   c   ★★★★
Horror   /15
Universal   (U.S.)

Rod Taylor (*Mitch Brenner*), Tippi Hedren (*Melanie Daniels*), Jessica Tandy (*Lydia Brenner*), Suzanne Pleshette (*Annie Hayworth*), Veronica Cartwright (*Cathy Brenner*), Ethel Griffies (*Mrs. Bundy*), Charles McGraw (*Sebastian Sholes*), Ruth McDevitt (*Mrs. MacGruder*), Joe Mantell (*Salesman*), Doodles Weaver (*Fisherman*)

p, Alfred Hitchcock; d, Alfred Hitchcock; w, Evan Hunter (based on the story by Daphne du Maurier); ph, Robert Burks (Technicolor); ed, George Tomasini; m, Bernard Herrmann; prod d, Norman Deming; fx, Ub Iwerks; cos, Edith Head

Hitchcock's follow-up to PSYCHO (1960) was yet another ground-breaking addition to the horror genre and further revealed the master director's darker obsessions.

Loosely based on a Daphne du Maurier short story, the action is set in Bodega Bay and follows bored, spoiled socialite Melanie Daniels (Hedren) as she romantically pursues dashing lawyer Mitch Brenner (Taylor). Tension soon develops among Melanie, schoolteacher Annie Hayworth, Mitch's former flame (Pleshette), and Mitch's domineering mother (Tandy). The emotional interplay is interrupted (and reflected) by the sudden and unexplained attack of thousands of birds on the area.

Hailed as one of Hitchcock's masterpieces by some and despised by others, THE BIRDS is certainly among the director's more complex and fascinating works. Volumes have been written about the film, with each writer picking it apart scene by scene in order to prove his or her particular critical theory—mostly of the psychoanalytic variety. Be that as it may, even those who grow impatient with the slow build-up or occasional dramatic lapses cannot deny the terrifying power of many of the film's haunting images: the bird point-of-view shot of Bodega Bay, the birds slowly gathering on the playground monkey bars, the attack on the children's birthday party, Melanie trapped in the attic, and the final ambiguous shot of the defeated humans leaving Bodega Bay while the thousands of triumphant birds gathered on the ground watch them go.

BIRDY

1984   120m   c   ★★★★½
Drama/War   R/15
Malton

Matthew Modine (*Birdy*), Nicolas Cage (*Al Columbato*), John Harkins (*Dr. Weiss*), Sandy Baron (*Mr. Columbato*), Karen Young (*Hannah Rourke*), Bruno Kirby (*Renaldi*), Nancy Fish (*Mrs. Prevost*), George Buck (*Birdy's Father*), Delores Sage (*Birdy's Mother*), Robert L. Ryan (*Joe Sagessa*)

p, Alan Marshall; d, Alan Parker; w, Sandy Kroopf, Jack Behr (based on the novel by William Wharton); ph, Michael Seresin (Metrocolor); ed, Gerry Hambling; m, Peter Gabriel; prod d, Geoffrey Kirkland; art d, Armin Ganz, Stewart Campbell; cos, Kristi Zea

BIRDY is one of those rare movies that successfully brings a psychological novel to the screen without sacrificing its saliency or complexity.

Although the book by William Wharton is set in the days after WWII, the film has been updated to the post-Vietnam era to tell the story of the deep friendship between Birdy (Modine) and Al Columbato (Cage), a pair of young men whose lives have been scarred by the war experience. Birdy has had an obsessive affinity for birds since childhood (scenes of which are shown in flashback), but in the period after his wartime service he believes he has actually been transformed into a bird. As a result he is confined to a military mental hospital. His best friend, Al (who was physically wounded in Vietnam), is determined to bring Birdy back to the real world.

One of the most bizarre accounts of postwar trauma, BIRDY succeeds because of an excellent, nuanced screenplay, supple direction by Parker, and the outstanding performances of both Cage and Modine. Modine's sensitive portrayal of the young man who transcends species boundaries is spellbinding; Cage is at once affable, concerned, and frustrated. Full of moments which will linger in the memory (such as the flashbacks showing Birdy's attempts to fly or the film's final scene), the film is at once stark, compassionate and hilarious. A fresh and welcome alternative to such "realistic" postwar films as COMING HOME, WHO'LL STOP THE RAIN, and ROLLING THUNDER. Winner of the 1985 Special Grand Jury Prize at Cannes.

BISHOP'S WIFE, THE

1947 105m bw ★★★
Comedy/Fantasy /U
RKO

Cary Grant (Dudley), David Niven (Henry Brougham), Loretta Young (Julia Brougham), Monty Woolley (Prof. Wutheridge), James Gleason (Sylvester), Gladys Cooper (Mrs. Hamilton), Elsa Lanchester (Matilda), Sara Haden (Mildred Cassaway), Karolyn Grimes (Debby Brougham), Tito Vuolo (Maggenti)

p, Samuel Goldwyn; d, Henry Koster; w, Robert E. Sherwood, Leonardo Bercovici (based on a novel by Robert Nathan); ph, Gregg Toland; ed, Monica Collingwood; m, Hugo Friedhofer; art d, Charles Henderson; cos, Irene Sharaff

A warm, sentimental comedy-fantasy, a follow-up to the similar but superior IT'S A WONDERFUL LIFE.

Niven plays an Episcopalian bishop praying for money to build a new church. His marriage is apparently over and his faith is quivering when Grant, an angel who uses his powers so sparingly that he might have been from the Welcome Wagon, arrives on the scene. Young, as Niven's wife, never learns Cary is from Up There as he unobtrusively helps her and Niven achieve some peace on earth and goodwill toward each other.

Under Koster's typically smooth direction, everyone seems to be having a good time, enjoying the script without mocking its blandness. The picture runs on a bit long and it does pale by comparison to the book, but it was a welcome smile in 1947 and has the same effect today. Popular and acclaimed in its day, the film was rather surprisingly nominated for Best Picture of the year.

BITTER RICE

1950 107m bw ★★★
Drama /A
DEG   (Italy)

Silvana Mangano (Silvana), Doris Dowling (Francesca), Vittorio Gassman (Walter), Raf Vallone (Marco), Checco Rissone (Aristide), Nico Pepe (Beppe), Andriana Sivieri (Celeste), Lia Croelli (Amelia), Maria Grazia Francia (Gabriella), Ann Maestri (Irene)

p, Dino De Laurentiis; d, Giuseppe De Santis; w, Giuseppe De Santis, Carlo Lizzani, Gianni Puccini (based on a story by Giuseppe De Santis, Carlo Lizzani); ph, Otello Martelli; m, Goffredo Petrassi

One of the earliest examples of how the Italian neorealist cinema of the 1940s succumbed to the dictates of Hollywood star glamor, BITTER RICE is nevertheless a good, moody film which captures the bare survival atmosphere of Italy after WWII, when the country lay in ruins and everyone scraped for a living.

In this case it's the buxom, somewhat glamorized Mangano, who parades about in a bursting sweater, short-shorts and artfully torn nylons as she works with hundreds of other women in the rice fields of the Po Valley. (Notably, Mangano's presence in this film, shaped by future husband De Laurentiis, prefigures the arrival of the so-called Italian "sexpot" actresses of the 1950s, whose ranks included Gina Lollbrigida and Sophia Loren).

The story, less involved with the effects of the war and poverty than earlier neorealist efforts, concerns the young woman and her involvement with two men, one down-to-earth, respectable but weak (Vallone), the other brutal, criminal yet magnetic (Gassman). The acting is fine and De Santis's direction shows great compositional skill with both camera and figure movement. Hardly a compelling critique of worker exploitation, BITTER RICE is still potent in its sensual, naturalistic depiction of love on straw bunks and sex offered along the highway.

BIZET'S CARMEN

1984 152m c ★★★★
Opera PG
Marcel Dassault/Opera/Gaumont   (France/Italy)

Julia Migenes-Johnson (Carmen), Placido Domingo (Don Jose), Ruggero Raimondi (Escamillo), Faith Esham (Micaela), Jean-Philippe Lafont (Dancairo), Gerard Garino (Remendado), Susan Daniel (Mercedes), Lilian Watson (Frasquita), Jean Paul Bogart (Zuniga), Francois Le Roux (Morales)

p, Patrice Ledoux; d, Francesco Rosi; w, Francesco Rosi, Tonino Guerra (based on the story by Prosper Merimee and the opera "Carmen" by Georges Bizet); ph, Pasqualino De Santis (Panavision, Eastmancolor); ed, Ruggero Mastroianni, Colette Semprun; m, Georges Bizet; prod d, Enrico Job; chor, Antonio Gades; cos, Enrico Job

For those who like like their Bizet straight, this is probably the best of the opera's many adaptations to date. Oddly enough, Rosi's film was one of many versions to appear within a very short period, including Carlos Saura's flamenco rendering, CARMEN; Peter Brooks's minimalist stage production, La Tragedie de Carmen; and Jean-Luc Godard's FIRST NAME: CARMEN, which is really an "anti-adaptation". In this relatively straightforward rendering of the classic tale, the sensuous Migenes-Johnson plays Carmen, a cigarette factory worker who ruins the life of a Spanish officer (Domingo).

The film's chief plus is Rosi's direction, at once low-key in its documentary realism and fiery in its passion and detail. By taking their actors and cameras into the Andalusian landscape of Spain, Rosi and cinematographer De Santis have succeeded in giving a different and entirely valid feel to the well-worn saga. The choreographer, Gades, performed similar duties on the Carlos Saura version, and Maazel's handling of the music is a standout.

BLACK AND WHITE IN COLOR

(LA VICTOIRE EN CHANTANT)
1976 100m c ★★★
Drama/War PG/A
Allied Artists   (France)

Jean Carmet (Sgt. Bosselet), Jacques Dufilho (Paul Rechampot), Catherine Rouvel (Marinette), Jacques Spiesser (Hubert Fresnoy), Dora Doll (Maryvonne), Maurice Barrier (Caprice), Claude Legros (Jacques Rechampot), Jacques Monnet (Pere Simon), Peter Berling (Pere Jean De La Croix), Marius Beugre Boignan (Barthelemy)

p, Arthur Cohn, Jacques Perrin, Giorgio Silagni; d, Jean-Jacques Annaud; w, Jean-Jacques Annaud, Georges Conchon; ph, Claude Agostini (Eastmancolor); ed, Francoise Bonnot; m, Pierre Bachelet; art d, Max Douy

The winner of the 1976 Oscar for Best Foreign Film, this first feature from Annaud (THE NAME OF THE ROSE) is set in a French colonial outpost in 1915.

When Spiesser, a conscientious young geologist, writes home to Paris to lament the "dangers" of Africa (chief among which is boredom), he begs for newspapers and books from home. Some time later the papers arrive, bringing the news—six months late—that France is at war with Germany. This poses a bit of a problem at the outpost for a number of reasons: the colonists are friendly with a group of neighboring Germans; their commander, Carmet, has never been in battle; and they have no trained army. Rising to the challenge, Carmet conscripts all the healthy male natives who live near the outpost and teaches them to speak French, operate bayonets, wear shoes, and sing "La Marseillaise." Ultimately, the natives are even honored with French names.

A biting satire on war, colonialism, and French patriotism which sometimes does not escape the character types it aims to parody, BLACK AND WHITE IN COLOR juxtaposes scenes of gaiety and humor with the brutalities of racism and war. The result is something of a combination of Philippe de Broca's cult antiwar satire, KING OF HEARTS, and Jamie Uys's THE GODS MUST BE CRAZY. Deserving of special mention is the playful score by Bachelet.

BLACK CAT, THE
1934 70m bw ★★★★★
Horror /15
Universal

Boris Karloff *(Hjalmar Poelzig)*, Bela Lugosi *(Dr. Vitus Verdegast)*, David Manners *(Peter Allison)*, Jacqueline Wells *(Joan Allison Allison)*, Lucille Lund *(Karen)*, Egon Brecher *(Majordomo)*, Henry Armetta *(Sergeant)*, Albert Conti *(Lieutenant)*, Anna Duncan *(Maid)*, Herman Bing *(Car Steward)*

p, Carl Laemmle, Jr.; d, Edgar G. Ulmer; w, Edgar G. Ulmer, Peter Ruric (based on the story by Edgar Allan Poe); ph, John Mescall; ed, Ray Curtiss; art d, Charles D. Hall

The first and best teaming of horror stars Karloff and Lugosi was this bizarre, haunting, and hypnotic film by director Ulmer.

Not an adaptation of Poe but rather a strikingly effective evocation of the twisted world of his literature, the story concerns a young couple, Peter (Manners) and Joan (Wells), who meet mysterious scientist Dr. Vitus Verdegast (Lugosi) while on their honeymoon in Budapest. The trio wind up at the home of Verdegast's old "friend" Hjalmar Poelzig (Karloff), an architect living atop a mountain in a modernistic, Art Deco mansion.

As it turns out, Poelzig is the leader of a satanic cult who, as a commander during WWI, caused the capture of Verdegast and the deaths of thousands of their countrymen in a bloody battle. While Verdegast rotted in prison, the architect stole his wife, who later died (he keeps her corpse in a glass case), then married Verdegast's daughter. Verdegast has now come for revenge, and Peter and Joan find themselves caught in a deadly game of cat and mouse.

A remarkable study of evil containing some unusually brutal scenes in its frenzied climax, THE BLACK CAT is still one of the most affecting horrors the genre has ever produced. With supreme directorial skill, Ulmer infuses the film with an overwhelming sense of unease, eroticism, and dread that remains powerful to this day. The literate script, magnificent set design, superbly fluid camerawork, and stunning performances by Karloff (whose character was inspired by occult hedonist Aleister Crowley) and Lugosi lend the film a timeless quality. Ulmer would go on to direct such low-budget classics as DETOUR (1945), but this is his masterpiece.

BLACK CAULDRON, THE
1985 82m c ★★★½
Animated PG/U
Disney/Silver Screen Partners II/Buena Vista

VOICES OF: Grant Bardsley *(Taran)*, Susan Sheridan *(Eilonwy)*, Freddie Jones *(Dallben)*, Nigel Hawthorne *(Fflewddur)*, Arthur Malet *(King Eidilleg)*, John Byner *(Gurgi/Doli)*, Lindsay Rich, Brandon Call, Gregory Levinson *(Fairfolk)*, Eda Reiss Merin *(Orddu)*

p, Joe Hale; d, Ted Berman, Richard Rich; w, David Jonas, Vance Gerry, Ted Berman, Richard Rich, Joe Hale, Al Wilson, Roy Morita, Peter Young, Art Stevens, Rosemary Anne Sisson, Roy Edward Disney (based on the five novels of the series *The Chronicles of Prydain* by Lloyd Alexander); ed, Jim Melton, Jim Koford, Armetta Jackson; m, Elmer Bernstein; anim, Walt Stanchfield

A glorious return to the days at Disney when animation was full and detail was everything, THE BLACK CAULDRON is betrayed by a routine storyline which fails to grip the imagination in the same way that such classics as PINOCCHIO or DUMBO do, but it's a remarkable achievement nonetheless.

A familiar sword-and-sorcery yarn, the story tells of Taran, an aspiring warrior, and his battle supreme with the villainous Horned King, who wants to gain possession of the Black Cauldron, a source of supernatural power. Taran knows that if the Horned King gets the Cauldron, civilization will cease. Taran is joined in his struggle by Eilonwy, a princess; a psychic pig named Hen Wen; Gurgi, a sycophantic creature; and a bevy of minifairies.

Only the second animated feature to be shot in 70mm (the first such widescreen extravaganza being 1959's SLEEPING BEAUTY), THE BLACK CAULDRON used more than 2.5 million drawings to bring its tale vividly to life. Every leaf has been patiently drawn, the depth of field is remarkable, the angles are chosen with care, and the result is a state-of-the-art cartoon that should be seen by anyone who loves the craft. Despite its drawbacks as entertainment, it remains one of the best technical cartoon features ever produced by Disney.

BLACK GIRL
1972 97m c ★★★
Drama PG/AA
Cinerama

Brock Peters *(Earl)*, Leslie Uggams *(Netta)*, Claudia McNeil *(Mu' Dear)*, Louise Stubbs *(Mama Rosie)*, Gloria Edwards *(Norma)*, Loretta Greene *(Ruth Ann)*, Kent Martin *(Herbert)*, Peggy Pettit *(Billie Jean)*, Ruby Dee *(Netta's Mother)*

p, Lee Savin; d, Ossie Davis; w, J.E. Franklin (based on the play by J.E. Franklin); ph, Glenwood J. Swanson; ed, Graham Lee Mahin; m, Ed Bogas, Ray Shanklin, Jesse Osborne, Merl Saunders; chor, Peggy Pettit

Family melodrama starring Stubbs as a mother who feels she's failed at raising her own children and has turned to helping other girls. A slightly miscast Uggams plays the foster daughter, Edwards and Greene are the jealous "real" daughters, and Peters portrays the father. The majestic Stubbs gives a passionate performance as a woman trying to overcome her faults and weaknesses to make amends for her past mistakes. An adaptation of a successful off-Broadway play, with songs by Betty Everett and Walter Hawkins, BLACK GIRL is a modest but effective film, one of the better black-oriented movies of its day.

BLACK NARCISSUS

1947   100m   c   ★★★★★
Drama   /15
Archer   (U.K.)

Deborah Kerr *(Sister Clodagh)*, Sabu *(Dilip Rai)*, David Farrar *(Mr. Dean)*, Flora Robson *(Sister Philippa)*, Jean Simmons *(Kanchi)*, Esmond Knight *(Gen. Toda Rai)*, Kathleen Byron *(Sister Ruth)*, Jenny Laird *(Sister Honey)*, Judith Furse *(Sister Briony)*, May Hallatt *(Angu Ayah)*

p, Michael Powell, Emeric Pressburger; d, Michael Powell, Emeric Pressburger; w, Michael Powell, Emeric Pressburger (based on the novel by Rumer Godden); ph, Jack Cardiff (Technicolor); ed, Reginald Mills; m, Brian Easdale

A stunner from one of the great collaborative teams in the history of cinema and an anomaly in British film of the 1940s. Powell and Pressburger continued their string of daring, idiosyncratic films (LIFE AND DEATH OF COLONEL BLIMP, A MATTER OF LIFE AND DEATH, THE RED SHOES) with this full-blown melodrama concerning a group of Anglican nuns who attempt to establish a school and hospital at an ancient ruler's castle-cum-bordello high in the Himalayas.

Kerr is highly effective as the young, ambitious Sister Clodagh, given her first taste of authority but bedeviled by the climate, the natives, the cynical but sexy British government agent Mr. Dean (Farrar) and her own and her colleagues' emotional weaknesses. Indian-born juvenile actor Sabu, in his last major role, plays a rich, bejeweled young general (who wears Black Narcissus perfume) bewitched by a seductive native girl (Simmons, in an odd but highly effective bit of casting). The turbulent chain of events reaches its climax when Sister Ruth (Byron, superb in a performance which should have insured her career) becomes unhinged over her desires for Mr. Dean and her jealousy of Sister Clodagh.

An odd, unsettling film which suggests the dangers of both emotional restraint and unchecked passion, BLACK NARCISSUS is also one of the most visually beautiful films ever made in color. The acting of the leads excels, and they are splendidly abetted by Robson, Furst, and Laird as the other nuns and by Knight and Hallat as, respectively, a paternal ruler and a hilariously cynical housekeeper.

Full of hysteria (especially at the cathartic climax, where Byron's makeup antedates that of THE EXORCIST) and continuing Powell and Pressburger's implicit critique of British stiff-upper-lip attitudes, BLACK NARCISSUS was ahead of its time, prefiguring the later melodramas of everyone from Sirk to Fassbinder to Ken Russell. The scenes where Sister Clodagh recalls her happy, romantic days before entering the convent were at first cut by censors. The film deservedly won the Oscars for color cinematography and art direction.

BLACK ORPHEUS

(ORFEU NEGRO)
1959   100m   c   ★★★½
Drama   /A
Lopert   (France/Italy/Brazil)

Breno Mello *(Orfeo)*, Marpessa Dawn *(Eurydice)*, Lourdes de Oliveira *(Mira)*, Lea Garcia *(Serafina)*, Adhemar da Silva *(Death)*, Alexandro Constantino *(Hermes)*, Waldetar de Souza *(Chico)*, Jorge dos Santos *(Benedito)*, Aurino Cassanio *(Zeca)*

p, Sacha Gordine; d, Marcel Camus; w, Jacques Viot, Marcel Camus (based on the play "Orfeu da Conceicao" by Vinicius de Moraes); ph, Jean Bourgoin (CinemaScope, Eastmancolor); ed, Andree Feix; m, Antonio Carlos Jobim, Luiz Bonfa

The Orpheus myth is transplanted onto the soil of Rio de Janeiro during Carnival—the one time of the year that calls for unrestrained celebration, music, dance, and costumes.

Orfeo (Mello) is a streetcar conductor and guitarist engaged to Mira (de Oliveira), an exotic and vivacious woman who lives as if every day were Carnival. However, anyone familiar with the legend of Orpheus (as the man in Rio's marriage office is) knows that he is destined to love Eurydice (Dawn—oddly enough, a dancer born in Pittsburgh), personified here as a newcomer to Rio who arrives in town to visit her cousin Serafina (Garcia). Eurydice has fled her hometown because she was being followed by a mysterious stranger, one who has followed her to Rio and has disguised himself as Death for Carnival. In order to save Eurydice, Orfeo must travel into the Underworld and bring her back to the world of the living.

From the opening shot, in which two Brazilian musicians literally burst through the frame, one can sense the explosiveness of BLACK ORPHEUS. Like Carnival, the film frame dances, the soundtrack sings, and the costumes swirl in an explosion of color and light. Besides its exhilarating style, however, the well-acted film works as an effective translation of the classic Greek myth into a Brazilian romance.

More successful as a travelogue of Brazilian scenery than an exploration of the country's folk culture, BLACK ORPHEUS was the second film from Camus, a Frenchman who traveled to Brazil to make this picture and would never again repeat its success. BLACK ORPHEUS received instant international acclaim and was honored with the Golden Palm at Cannes and the Academy Award for Best Foreign Film.

BLACK RAIN

(KUROI AME)
1990   123m   bw   ★★★
Drama   /PG
Imamura/Hayashibara/Tohokushinsha   (Japan)

Yoshiko Tanaka *(Yasuko)*, Kazuo Kitamura *(Shigematsu)*, Etsuko Ichihara *(Shigako)*, Shoichi Ozawa *(Shokichi)*, Norihei Miki *(Kotaro)*, Keisuke Ishida *(Yuichi)*

p, Hisa Iino; d, Shohei Imamura; w, Shohei Imamura, Toshiro Ishido (based on a novel by Masuji Ibuse); ph, Takashi Kawamata; ed, Hajime Okayasu; m, Toru Takemitsu; art d, Hisao Inagaki

A potent if flawed study of the dropping of the atomic bomb on Hiroshima and its aftereffects, focusing on the dark destiny of one family caught in the holocaust.

The film opens with the bombing, showing the blinding flash of light, the shock wave that disintegrates people and buildings, and the black rain falling on young Yasuko (Tanaka), her aunt Shigako (Ichihara) and her uncle Shigematsu (Kitamura), which exposes them all to radiation poisoning. Five years pass, and the family's main problem is now the difficulty of finding a husband for Yasuko, whose contamination leaves her a pariah in the community. The locals have become used to funeral processions and to the taking of various home remedies; the desperate Shigako even turns to a noisy charlatan of a faith healer. Yasuko gradually becomes involved with Yuichi (Ishida), whose nerves have been shattered by the war, but the couple's time together is fatefully limited.

Imamura films his story in stark, elegant black and white, creating both haunting imagery (e.g. the escaping townspeople looking back at the mushroom cloud forming behind them) and a distance from the story's drama. Similar distancing is evoked by the soap opera treatment of the story and the bewildered resignation of the protagonists, never once expressing either real rage or sorrow at their plight. What is less clear is the critical perspective Imamura (or the audience) can take via such distancing. The problems of traditional Japanese formality are highlighted, as are the prejudices held by the Japanese against the bomb's victims (*hibakusha* in Japanese) and the horrors of warfare which bring about such conditions, but no single critique is fully fleshed out.

The film is full of touching moments, but at times the emotional resonance is characteristic of second-rate Hollywood, as when Yuichi's phobia of the sounds of moving vehicles vanishes during an ambulance ride at the film's end. In short, the film is powerfully grim but does not capture the horror of the bomb's blast, it is full of cool observation yet cannot resist idealizing the central family unit.

BLACK ROBE

1991   100m   c   ★★★½
Adventure/Drama/Historical   R/15
Alliance Entertainment/Samson Productions/Cinegramme V
(Canada/Austria)

Lothaire Bluteau *(Father Laforgue)*, Aden Young *(Daniel)*, Sandrine Holt *(Annuka)*, August Schellenberg *(Chomina)*, Tantoo Cardinal *(Chomina's Wife)*, Billy Two Rivers *(Ougebmat)*, Lawrence Bayne *(Neehatin)*, Harrison Liu *(Awondoie)*, Wesley Cote *(Oujita)*, Frank Wilson *(Father Jerome)*

p, Robert Lantos, Stephane Reichel, Sue Milliken; d, Bruce Beresford; w, Brian Moore (from novel *Black Robe* by Moore); ph, Peter James; ed, Tim Wellburn; m, Georges Delerue; prod d, Herbert Pinter; art d, Gavin Mitchell; cos, Renee April, John Hay

Despite an occasionally plodding screenplay, this white-man-in-the-wilderness drama goes DANCES WITH WOLVES one better by showing more genuine respect for its subject. Directed by Bruce Beresford, BLACK ROBE was adapted by Brian Moore from his own novel, which, in turn, was based on letters and journals written by Jesuit missionaries, whom the Indians dubbed "black robes," in the New World during the 17th century.

The story revolves around Father Laforgue (JESUS OF MONTREAL's Lothaire Bluteau) who is sent by Champlain (Jean Brousseau), the founder and governor of Quebec, 1,500 miles north to a frontier Jesuit mission to assist in the conversion of the Huron tribe to Catholicism in 1634. Pledging to guide and protect Laforgue, Algonquin leader Chomina (August Schellenberg) brings his wife, young son and beautiful teenage daughter Annuka (Sandrine Holt), as well as a small party of braves and their families. Driven as much by his passion for Annuka as his aspirations to the priesthood, young French settler Daniel (Aden Young) also volunteers to accompany Laforgue on what turns into a grueling journey.

Friction develops almost immediately between Laforgue and Chomina's braves, who resent the priest's rigidity and, especially, his refusal to share the goods he has brought to trade with the Hurons. Chomina develops doubts of his own when he has a dream foretelling his death at the end of the journey. He consults a holy man, who condemns Laforgue as a demon and warns Chomina against continuing his mission. Further perturbed by the developing love affair between Annuka and Daniel, Chomina abandons Laforgue, but Daniel also parts company with Laforgue to follow Annuka.

Returning to the theme of his first international hit, BREAKER MORANT, as well as the more recent MISTER JOHNSON, Beresford's emphasis in BLACK ROBE is on European presumption in forcing native peoples to adopt Western culture. However, the issue of colonization is more complex in this context than in those of the earlier films, a fact both Moore and Beresford largely choose to ignore. Instead, the film insists on a black-and-white approach, portraying European culture solely as an evil invading force that sped the extinction of Indian tribes, weakening them with liquor, guns, diseases, and a religion wildly at odds with the conditions of their existence.

Left to stand without comment is the hand the Indians had in their own demise, through constant intertribal warfare that slowed the advance of their culture. All of this would have made a good jumping-off point for drama, but BLACK ROBE refuses to get beyond that point, instead repeating its theme over and over at the distinct risk of numbing the viewer.

Nevertheless, BLACK ROBE succeeds by maintaining a basic, at times brutal, honesty in its depiction of Indian culture. The Indians in BLACK ROBE aren't the starry-eyed noble savages that strain credibility in DANCES WITH WOLVES. They are fully developed people whose lives—nasty, brutish and short as they are—contain seeds of transcendence that ultimately impress Laforgue. Though it happens too late to be of much help to him or the Indians, Laforgue's acceptance of the legitimacy of native beliefs makes for a poignant climax to the film.

BLACK ROBE is, ultimately, an extraordinary work, simply in terms of the awe it shows for the weight and scope of its subject. Happily, this respect extends through the production, which is meticulously authentic; the cast, which is flawless; and the photography, which is ravishingly expressive. Everything attests to Beresford's unpretentious artistry, the trademark of all his best works.

BLACK ROSE, THE

1950   120m   c   ★★★★
Adventure   /U
FOX

Tyrone Power *(Walter of Gurnie)*, Orson Welles *(Bayan)*, Cecile Aubry *(Maryam)*, Jack Hawkins *(Tristram Griffin)*, Michael Rennie *(King Edward)*, Finlay Currie *(Alfgar)*, Herbert Lom *(Anthemus)*, Mary Clare *(Countess Eleanor of Lessford)*, Robert Blake *(Mahmoud)*, Alfonso Bedoya *(Lu Chung)*

p, Louis D. Lighton; d, Henry Hathaway; w, Talbot Jennings (based on the novel by Thomas B. Costain); ph, Jack Cardiff (Technicolor); ed, Manuel Del Campo; m, Richard Addinsell; art d, Paul Sheriff, William C. Andrews; fx, W. Percy Day; cos, Michael Whittaker

This sweeping, well-made, if somewhat derivative adventure epic stars Power as a nobleman in 13th-century England ostracized for leading a revolt against King Edward (Rennie), a Norman whom Power, a Saxon, refuses to serve.

Traveling as wanted men, Power and his archer companion (Hawkins) are picked up in Antioch by a powerful warlord (Welles), and accompany him to the court of Kublai Khan. One of the gifts Welles is taking to Khan is a Eurasian beauty (Aubry), who falls in love with Power. Once in the Chinese court, Power realizes that, though they are treated graciously, he and Hawkins cannot leave the palace. A daring escape through ancient underground tunnels, a dramatic separation, and a key reconciliation occur before love emerges triumphant.

A beautifully photographed (in England and North Africa) film whose chief merits are its exciting action sequences and lavish production (courtesy of five million dollars worth of Fox assets frozen in England), THE BLACK ROSE borrows liberally from such earlier efforts as THE ADVENTURES OF ROBIN HOOD and THE ADVENTURES OF MARCO POLO, but benefits considerably from the well-cast players. Power was losing the vigor and mobile features of his youth, but he is still an eminently suitable swashbuckler. Hawkins and Welles play their standardized roles with tongues firmly in cheek and Aubrey is very appealing as the heroine. Perhaps the only exception is the arresting Bedoya, whose telltale Mexican accent unfortunately belies his Oriental characterization.

BLACK STALLION, THE

1979   118m   c   ★★★★
Adventure   G/U
UA

Kelly Reno (*Alec Ramsey*), Mickey Rooney (*Henry Dailey*), Teri Garr (*Alec's Mother*), Clarence Muse (*Snoe*), Hoyt Axton (*Alec's Father*), Michael Higgins (*Neville*), Ed McNamara (*Jake*), Doghmi Larbi (*The Arab*), John Burton, John Buchanan (*Jockeys*)

p, Tom Sternberg, Fred Roos; d, Carroll Ballard; w, Melissa Mathison, Jeanne Rosenberg, William D. Wittliff (based on the novel by Walter Farley); ph, Caleb Deschanel; ed, Robert Dalva; m, Carmine Coppola

This touching and beautifully photographed, if slightly overlong, tale of a boy and his horse follows the escapades of young Alec Ramsey (Reno), who is traveling across the ocean with his father.

The ship sinks, and Alec is saved by Black, a handsome Arabian stallion the boy had befriended earlier in the journey. After being shipwrecked on a deserted island, Alec and Black are rescued and returned to their small-town home. Eventually, Black is cared for by former horse trainer Henry Dailey (Rooney), who later takes Kelly under his wing to be trained as a jockey. Naturally, it all leads up to the big race—a stunningly photographed sequence brimming with tension.

A simple film, sentimental but not mawkish, as enjoyable for adults as it is for children, THE BLACK STALLION is one of the finest movies about children and horses since Elizabeth Taylor was seen in NATIONAL VELVET. It's also a pleasure to see Rooney back in the saddle again, so to speak, and his lively character turn won him a much-deserved Oscar nomination for Best Supporting Actor. A sequel, THE BLACK STALLION RETURNS (1983), is more a Saharan adventure than a sports picture.

BLACK SUNDAY

1961   83m   bw   ★★★½
Horror   /AA
AIP   (Italy)

Barbara Steele (*Witch Princess Katia*), John Richardson (*Dr. Gorobee*), Ivo Garrani (*Prince*), Andrea Cecchi (*Dr. Choma*), Arturo Dominici (*Javutich*), Enrico Olivieri (*Constantin*), Antonio Pierfederici (*the Pope*), Clara Bindi (*Innkeeper*), Germana Dominici (*His Daughter*), Mario Passante (*Nikita*)

p, Massimo De Rita; d, Mario Bava; w, Ennio De Concini, Mario Serandrei (based on a story by Nikolai Gogol); ph, Mario Bava, Ubaldo Terzano; ed, Mario Serandrei; m, Les Baxter; art d, Giorgio Giovannini

In 1630, a beautiful witch princess, Asa (Barbara Steele), who is a vampire, and her lover, Juvato (Arturo Dominici), are put to death by her vengeful brother. He has iron masks with spikes on the inside placed on both of their faces and then sledgehammered home. Two hundred years later, blood is accidentally spilled on Asa's face and she rises from the dead along with Juvato to wreak revenge on the descendants of those who executed her—including her look-alike, Katia (also played by Steele).

Beautifully photographed in black and white by Bava himself, BLACK SUNDAY is a hypnotic and compelling. From the brutal opening to the resurrection of the vampires and the horrors that follow, Bava's camera effortlessly glides through the fogbound sets, presenting one incredible image after another. Bava exhibits a comparable command of sound and music—or the lack thereof—with some sequences played out in virtual silence. Steele is magnificent in her dual role as vengeful devil and vestal virgin. As the resurrected Asa, her beautiful face is both seductive and horrifying, bearing the terrible holes punched by the iron mask. The role catapulted her to horror-movie stardom.

Unfortunately, when released in the US by American International Pictures, BLACK SUNDAY was badly dubbed and a bombastic Les Baxter score was imposed over the original by Roberto Nicolosi. Another, less bastardized version is available from California-based Sinister Cinema.

BLACK SUNDAY

1977   143m   c   ★★★★
Action   R/15
Paramount

Robert Shaw (*Kabakov*), Bruce Dern (*Lander*), Marthe Keller (*Dahlia*), Fritz Weaver (*Corley*), Steven Keats (*Moshevsky*), Bekim Fehmiu (*Fasil*), Michael V. Gazzo (*Muzi*), William Daniels (*Pugh*), Walter Gotell (*Col. Riaf*), Victor Campos (*Nageeb*)

p, Robert Evans; d, John Frankenheimer; w, Ernest Lehman, Ivan Moffat, Kenneth Ross; ph, John A. Alonzo (Movielab Color); ed, Tom Rolf; m, John Williams

One of the best of the disaster films of the 1970s, the genuinely disturbing BLACK SUNDAY is likely to cause nightmares long after you've seen it. Keller and Fehmiu portray "Black September" agents (in a takeoff on the killers who terrorized the 1972 Olympics) who plan to hijack the Goodyear Blimp and send it into the teeming Super Bowl crowd firing thousands of steel darts. Dern, in typical and fine form as a deranged Vietnam veteran, is hired to pilot the killer blimp. Shaw, as an Israeli major, and Weaver, playing a heroic FBI agent, smoothly represent law and order. The scene where the blimp comes over the top of Miami's Orange Bowl is guaranteed to have you squirming in your seat. Far superior to the similar TWO MINUTE WARNING (1976), BLACK SUNDAY benefits from its technical skill, drawn-out suspense and developed characterizations, though the film could have been even more effectively tight with a shorter running time.

BLACK SWAN, THE

1942   85m   c   ★★★★½
Adventure   /A
FOX

Tyrone Power (*James Waring*), Maureen O'Hara (*Margaret Denby*), Laird Cregar (*Capt. Henry Morgan*), Thomas Mitchell (*Tommy Blue*), George Sanders (*Capt. Billy Leech*), Anthony Quinn

(Wogan), George Zucco *(Lord Denby)*, Edward Ashley *(Roger Ingram)*, Fortunio Bonanova *(Don Miguel)*, Stuart Robertson *(Capt. Graham)*

p, Robert Bassler; d, Henry King; w, Ben Hecht, Seton I. Miller (based on the novel by Rafael Sabatini); ph, Leon Shamroy (Technicolor); ed, Barbara McLean; m, Alfred Newman; art d, Richard Day, James Basevi; cos, Earl Luick

Along with THE MARK OF ZORRO, the peak of Tyrone Power's career as a swashbuckler.

A sweeping pirate epic with Power as an aide to notorious buccaneer Henry Morgan (Cregar), the film opens with Morgan pardoned from the gallows and sent to Jamaica as its new governor. Trying to prevent his former associates from continuing their villainous activities, Morgan encounters resistance from two renegades (Sanders and Quinn). Power, meanwhile, falls for the daughter (O'Hara) of the former governor, but she spurns his brazen advances. Although kidnapping her and taking her along on his warship doesn't initially help matters, things change when Sanders and Quinn overpower his ship, forcing Power to fight for the woman he loves.

The story and dialogue smack of the Errol Flynn adventure CAPTAIN BLOOD, but the film employs its cliches with such overwhelming vigor and good humor that they seem like old friends. Even though his physique isn't quite up to the more beefcake aspects of the hardsell by the producers, Power is full of marvelous dash and derring-do. Cregar, all hearty bravado, is equally wonderful, his enormous body bedecked in wigs and finery, and the practically unrecognizable Sanders, sporting a thick red wig and beard, is quite effective as a less civilized type of villain than those he usually played. The ravishing, flame-haired, underrated O'Hara, too, is in her element as the feisty heroine and the result of all this happy casting is lavish Hollywoodiana at its sporting best.

BLACK TIGHTS

(UN, DEUX, TROIS, QUATRE?)
1960   140m   c   ★★★★
Dance   /U
Magna   (France)

Maurice Chevalier *(Narrator)*, Zizi Jeanmaire, Roland Petit. THE DIAMOND CRUNCHER: Dirk Sanders. CYRANO DeBERGERAC: Moira Shearer, Georges Reich. A MERRY MOURNING: Cyd Charisse, Hans Van Manen. CARMEN: Henning Kronstam

p, Joseph Kaufman, Simon Schiffrin; d, Terence Young; chor, Roland Petit; cos, Yves Saint-Laurent

One of the best of the ballet films, BLACK TIGHTS offers four separate story segments, all narrated by Chevalier and choreographed by Petit.

"The Diamond Cruncher", with a story by Petit and English lyrics by Herbert Kretzmer, is a fairy tale about a young female mobster (Jeanmaire, Petit's wife) who learns that it's more fun to eat cabbages with the man you love (Sanders) than it is to crunch diamonds. "Cyrano", with costumes by St. Laurent and music by Marius Constant, features Petit himself dancing the title role, Reich as Christian and the radiant Shearer (of THE RED SHOES fame) as Roxanne. "A Merry Mourning", meanwhile, another story by Petit, opens with a man (Van Manen) chiding his wife (Charisse) for admiring an expensive, frilly gown in a Paris window. He is challenged to a duel by Petit and promptly

killed, whereupon his widow buys the gown and immediately attracts the eye of her husband's killer. In "Carmen," the famous Bizet story is retold with dance instead of song.

The film's title, BLACK TIGHTS, sounds more like a 1980s De Palma film than a feast for ballet lovers, and has perhaps kept the film from appealing to its intended audience. Technically brilliant and handsomely filmed, this beautifully danced film is valuable as a record of some of the era's top talent.

BLACKBOARD JUNGLE, THE
1955   100m   bw   ★★★½
Drama   /X
MGM

Glenn Ford *(Richard Dadier)*, Anne Francis *(Anne Dadier)*, Louis Calhern *(Jim Murdock)*, Margaret Hayes *(Lois Judby Hammond)*, John Hoyt *(Mr. Warneke)*, Richard Kiley *(Joshua Y. Edwards)*, Emile Meyer *(Mr. Halloran)*, Warner Anderson *(Dr. Bradley)*, Basil Ruysdael *(Prof. A.R. Kraal)*, Sidney Poitier *(Gregory W. Miller)*

p, Pandro S. Berman; d, Richard Brooks; w, Richard Brooks (based on the novel by Evan Hunter); ph, Russell Harlan; ed, Ferris Webster; m, Charles Wolcott; art d, Cedric Gibbons, Randall Duell

This searing if somewhat overrated condemnation of juvenile delinquency brought attention to some of the problems afflicting urban high schools and is notable as a reflection of certain 1950s social mores. Rendered in effectively grainy black and white and using violence with considerable impact, the dutifully sincere screenplay by director Brooks unfortunately substitutes a more upbeat ending for Evan Hunter's original.

Ford, in a typically edgy but likable, effective performance, is a newly returned veteran who takes his first teaching job in an inner-city school. He soons runs afoul of some of his tougher students, who are only hanging around until they are old enough to get jobs. Several story lines run through the film: Ford's wife (Francis, failing to transcend an ill-conceived part), tries to convince him to find another job; another teacher (Kiley) thinks he can reason with the kids but soon finds out how wrong he is; an aging teacher (Calhern) just wants to survive until he can retire; and a pretty young teacher (Hayes) is frightened by her new assignment.

Vic Morrow is excellent as the leader of a gang of thugs, as is Poitier in a star-making performance, though at age 31 he unfortunately doesn't convince as a high school student. Future director Paul Mazursky and Jamie Farr (then Jameel Farah) play other students. THE BLACKBOARD JUNGLE also brought rock'n'roll to movie audiences with a bang courtesy of Bill Haley and the Comets, who sing "Rock Around the Clock."

BLACKMAIL
1929   75m   bw   ★★★
Mystery   /15
Elstree/Wardour/British Intl.   (U.K.)

Anny Ondra *(Alice White)*, John Longden *(Frank Webber)*, Donald Calthrop *(Tracy)*, Cyril Ritchard *(The Artist)*, Sara Allgood *(Mrs. White)*, Charles Paton *(Mr. White)*, Harvey Braban *(Inspector)*, Phyllis Monkman *(Gossip)*, Hannah Jones *(Landlady)*, Percy Parsons *(Crook)*

p, John Maxwell; d, Alfred Hitchcock; w, Alfred Hitchcock, Benn W. Levy, Charles Bennett (based on the play by Charles Bennett); ph, Jack Cox; ed, Emile De Ruelle; m, John Hubert Bath, Henry Stafford, John Reynders

The first all-talkie for both Great Britain and Alfred Hitchcock, this adaptation of a 1928 play stars Ondra as Alice White, a young British woman who is to be married to Scotland Yard detective Frank Webber (Longdon). Alice, however, is drawn to a handsome artist (Ritchard), whom she ends up stabbing when he tries to force her to model nude. Of course, she soon falls prey to the crime of the title and of course her boyfriend heads up the murder investigation.

Completed and released as a silent film, Hitchcock was ordered by the studio to add some dialogue sequences for a "talkie" release in some specially equipped theaters. The main problem was Ondra's heavy Polish accent. Rather than reshoot all of her scenes, though, actress Joan Barry was brought in to dub the star's voice. This procedure was crude in those historic early sound days: Barry had to be positioned off camera next to Ondra and speak the lines as the leading lady mouthed them, and to some extent the effort shows in Ondra's somewhat strained performance. The film, though, was a great success, artistically and technically. Even though the film contains scenes obviously shot silent to which one telling sound was later added, the exploration of the medium's new capabilities is downright palpable. Moodily filmed in an effectively Germanic style, with a neat supporting turn by Calthrop and fine set pieces such as the chase through the British Museum, BLACKMAIL still plays well, and is a suitable precursor to the master director's later work. In one of his earliest cameos, Hitchcock appears as a subway rider annoyed by a pesky boy while trying to read a book.

BLACULA
1972 92m c   ★★★
Horror   PG/X
AIP

William Marshall *(Blacula)*, Vonetta McGee *(Tina)*, Denise Nicholas *(Michelle)*, Thalmus Rasulala *(Gordon Thomas)*, Gordon Pinsent *(Lt. Peters)*, Charles McCauley *(Dracula)*, Emily Yancy *(Nancy)*, Lance Taylor, Sr. *(Swenson)*, Ted Harris *(Bobby)*, Rick Metzler *(Billy)*

p, Joseph T. Naar; d, William Crain; w, Joan Torres, Raymond Koenig; ph, John Stevens (Movielab Color); ed, Allan Jacobs; m, Gene Page; art d, Walter Scott Herndon

An off-the-wall hellraiser. Hilarious blaxploitation pic has Dracula biting black prince, who, two hundred years later, is taking a bite out of Hollywood. To die for. So much that a sequel followed in 1973 with an even more engaging title—SCREAM, BLACULA, SCREAM.

BLADE RUNNER
1982 114m c   ★★★★
Science Fiction   R/15
WB

Harrison Ford *(Deckard)*, Rutger Hauer *(Roy Batty)*, Sean Young *(Rachael)*, Edward James Olmos *(Gaff)*, M. Emmet Walsh *(Bryant)*, Daryl Hannah *(Pris)*, William Sanderson *(Sebastian)*, Brion James *(Leon)*, Joseph Turkel *(Tyrell)*, Joanna Cassidy *(Zhora)*

p, Michael Deeley; d, Ridley Scott; w, Hampton Fancher, David Peoples (based on the story "Do Androids Dream of Electric Sheep?" by Philip K. Dick); ph, Jordan Cronenweth (Panavision, Technicolor); ed, Terry Rawlings; m, Vangelis; art d, David L. Snyder; fx, Douglas Trumbull; cos, Charles Knode, Michael Kaplan

A brilliantly conceived and designed film based on the novel by sci-fi guru Philip K. Dick, BLADE RUNNER has become something of a cult favorite. Its $27 million price tag shows in the astonishing sets of 21st-century Los Angeles. Rain, mist, and fog swirl about titanic structures built upon the ruins of the city, as mammoth space machines lumber about promoting the good life on the "off-world colonies." Earth is in decay, both physically and psychologically. The best of the human race has departed for greener space pastures, leaving the dregs to mill around in the congested, rain-drenched streets, speaking an unrecognizable patois.

Harrison Ford plays Deckard, an ex-"blade runner" (detective/android killer) who reluctantly accepts a "freelance" assignment tracking down a group of cyborgs, known as "replicants," who have mutinied on a space colony and returned to Earth, seeking to prolong their short life span by altering their programmed mechanisms. Rutger Hauer is magnificent as the androids' superhuman leader, Sean Young turns in a creditable performance as a replicant who thinks she's human, and Ford's world-weary voiceover and battered trenchcoat give the film a gritty, film noir feel. A "director's cut" of the film, *sans* voiceover and with a different, darker, ending, was released in 1992.

BLAZING SADDLES
1974 93m c   ★★½
Comedy/Western   R/15
WB

Cleavon Little *(Bart)*, Gene Wilder *(Jim)*, Slim Pickens *(Taggart)*, David Huddleston *(Olson Johnson)*, Liam Dunn *(Reverend Johnson)*, Alex Karras *(Mongo)*, John Hillerman *(Howard Johnson)*, George Furth *(Van Johnson)*, Mel Brooks *(Governor Lepetomane/Indian Chief)*, Harvey Korman *(Hedley Lamarr)*

p, Michael Hertzberg; d, Mel Brooks; w, Mel Brooks, Norman Steinberg, Andrew Bergman, Richard Pryor, Alan Uger (based on a story by Andrew Bergman); ph, Joseph Biroc (Technicolor); ed, John C. Howard, Danford B. Greene; m, John Morris; prod d, Peter Wooley; chor, Alan Johnson; cos, Vittorio Nino Novarese

A lewd spoof of westerns and racial prejudice; enough laughs to cover the fact that it is, essentially, a stupid movie. Little is terrific as a black sheriff who has been hired so that the citizens of the town will panic and sell their land out cheap to speculators who plan to run a railroad through town. When the village turns on Little, he must call on the jail's only con, Wilder, who was at one time the fastest gun in the West. Last fifteen minutes of the movie are an obvious cop-out and the humor is often toilet level, but in addition to Little, Kahn scores big (in a takeoff of Marlene Dietrich's saloon belles), as do Karras and Korman. What really lessens SADDLES is that its intentions aren't clear. Its humor provoked no thinking; insensitive moviegoers assumed the racial put-downs and cowboy crudeness were deliberate. The public loved the film—it stands as the highest grossing western in history—$45 million plus! But they loved it for all the wrong reasons.

BLITHE SPIRIT
1945 96m c   ★★★★
Fantasy   /U
Cineguild (U.K.)

Rex Harrison *(Charles Condomine)*, Constance Cummings *(Ruth Condomine)*, Kay Hammond *(Elvira)*, Margaret Rutherford *(Madame Arcati)*, Hugh Wakefield *(Dr. Bradman)*, Joyce Carey *(Mrs. Bradman)*, Jacqueline Clark *(Edith)*

p, Noel Coward; d, David Lean; w, Noel Coward, David Lean, Anthony Havelock-Allan (based on the play by Noel Coward); ph, Ronald Neame (Technicolor); ed, Jack Harris; m, Richard Addinsell; art d, C.P. Norman

A quicksilver cocktail. Novelist conjures up late first wife who can't resist causing trouble in his second marriage. Dry, but hilarious, Noel Coward romp, delivered seamlessly by David Lean. And stolen by Rutherford, the most inept, adorable medium ever. But the cinematography leaves something to be desired and only the Coward wit keeps this from not being a TOPPER rehash.

BLOB, THE

1958 85m c   ★½
Science Fiction   /18
Paramount

Steve McQueen (Steve), Aneta Corseaut (Judy), Earl Rowe (Police Lieutenant), Olin Howlin (Old Man), Stephen Chase, John Benson, Vincent Barbi, Tom Ogen, Julie Cousins, Ralph Roseman

p, Jack H. Harris; d, Irvin S. Yeaworth, Jr.; w, Theodore Simonson, Kate Phillips (based on an idea by Irvine H. Millgate); ph, Thomas E. Spalding (Deluxe Color); ed, Alfred Hillman; m, Jean Yeaworth

Jack H. Harris, the cheapie producer who went on to make the forgettable MOTHER GOOSE A GO-GO, struck it rich with this silly picture that gave McQueen his first starring role after a few supporting jobs in SOMEBODY UP THERE LIKES ME and NEVER LOVE A STRANGER. It's a teenage horror tale as McQueen and Corseaut tell their tiny Pennsylvania town that they've seen this purple goop that's eating people up. Naturally, no one believes them.

A sequel was made called BEWARE THE BLOB, also known as SON OF BLOB. The title was what brought the people in to see this otherwise undistinguished movie. McQueen plays his role with believability, as he did almost everything in his brief career. The oddest thing about the movie is the title song by Hal David and a 29-year-old composer named Burt Bacharach. It's not a bad tune.

BLONDE VENUS

1932 92m bw   ★★★★
Drama   /PG
Paramount

Marlene Dietrich (Helen Faraday), Herbert Marshall (Edward Faraday), Cary Grant (Nick Townsend), Dickie Moore (Johnny Faraday), Francis Sayles (Charlie Blaine), Robert Emmett O'Connor (Dan O'Connor), Gene Morgan (Ben Smith), Rita La Roy (Taxi Belle Hooper), Sidney Toler (Detective Wilson), Morgan Wallace (Dr. Pierce)

d, Josef von Sternberg; w, Jules Furthman, S.K. Lauren (based on a story by von Sternberg); ph, Bert Glennon; m, Oscar Poteker; art d, Wiard Ihnen; cos, Travis Banton

Dietrich suffers, for once; Von Sternberg's paen to the pain of love in all its variations is so lovingly rendered that the shoestring story looks almost seamless. No one ever looked lovelier after sinking to the gutter than Dietrich—even her tatters are photographed to maximum effect. Dickie Moore was perhaps the most beautiful little boy ever in movies and the two male stars are there to bask in all that is Dietrich. Here she appears for the first time in her hallmark top hat, white tie and tails singing "You Little So and So" but the sequence that lives on and on is the gorilla surprise and "Hot Voodoo", a highpoint of expressionistic eroti-

cism, replete with blonde afro. Lensed two years before the code; hopefully your copy won't have the skinny-dipping opening deleted.

BLOOD AND SAND

1941 123m c   ★★★★
Drama   /PG
FOX

Tyrone Power (Juan Gallardo), Linda Darnell (Carmen Espinosa), Rita Hayworth (Dona Sol des Muire), Anthony Quinn (Manolo de Palma), Alla Nazimova (Senora Augustias), J. Carrol Naish (Garabato), John Carradine (Nacional), Laird Cregar (Natalio Curro), Lynn Bari (Encarnacion), Vincente Gomez (Guitarist)

p, Robert T. Kane; d, Rouben Mamoulian; w, Jo Swerling (based on the novel Sangre y Arena by Vicente Blasco Ibanez); ph, Ernest Palmer, Ray Rennahan (Technicolor); ed, Robert Bischoff; m, Alfred Newman; art d, Richard Day, Joseph C. Wright; chor, Hermes Pan, Budd Boetticher; cos, Travis Banton

Lavish, tragic mural that owes its pizazz to Mamoulian's use of color and composition; BLOOD AND SAND is like watching the great Spanish Masters do animation. Remake of the great Valentino triumph seems a little flat, mainly because Power lacks the magnetism and danger of his predecessor.

Students of sex symbolism should have fun comparing Darnell and Hayworth, although both ladies are still a light year away from possessing the full extent of their erotic powers. Hayworth, who won Donna Sol over Maria Montez and because Carole Landis refused to dye her hair red, became a contender for pin-up queen as a result of the film. As usual, she lacks the fatality of the greatest seductresses and looks unhappy, but all flaws go out the window when the lady starts to flamenco. The best performances are delivered by the compelling Nazimova and young Anthony Quinn. Ernest Palmer and Ray Rennahan won Oscars for the lush cinematography.

BLOOD SIMPLE

1984 97m c   ★★★½
Crime   /18
River Road

John Getz (Ray), Frances McDormand (Abby), Dan Hedaya (Julian Marty), M. Emmet Walsh (Private Detective Visser), Samm-Art Williams (Maurice), Deborah Neumann (Debra), Raquel Gavia (Landlady), Van Brooks (Man from Lubbock), Senor Marco (Mr. Garcia), William Creamer (Old Cracker)

p, Ethan Coen; d, Joel Coen; w, Ethan Coen, Joel Coen; ph, Barry Sonnenfeld (DuArt Color); ed, Roderick Jaynes, Don Wiegmann, Peggy Connolly; m, Carter Burwell; prod d, Jane Musky; fx, Loren Bivens; cos, Sara Medina-Pape

Stylish, frightfully empty, shoestring noir; an admirable filmmaking debut for the brothers Coen—Ethan (producer) and Joel (director).

Walsh is a sleazy private eye hired by Texas strip bar owner Hedaya to kill his wife McDormand and her lover Getz. Instead, Walsh fakes the double hit by doctoring photographs and then fills Hedaya with lead. When Getz discovers Hedaya in a pool of blood, he goes "simple"—foolishly cleaning up after the murder on the assumption that McDormand committed it. His actions distorted by his blinding passion, Getz then takes the body to an empty field to bury it, only to find that he, by a brutal twist of fate, is being buried.

Drawing from the crime novels of James M. Cain, BLOOD SIMPLE'S characters have none of the Cain complexities one might hope for, existing simply as chess pieces to further flashy stylistics. The Coens' concern isn't emotional intensity but bravura camera moves and chic lighting of cinematographer Sonnenfeld.

McDormand is wonderfully naturalistic as the not-too-bright girl with a homey sensuality, and Hedaya somehow manages to be vile yet sympathetic. Hailed by some as the best American independent film, BLOOD SIMPLE was completed on an astonishingly small budget of less than $1.5 million and looks as if it cost ten times as much.

BLOOD WEDDING
1981 72m c   ★★★
Dance   /U
Libra (Spain)

Antonio Gades (Leonardo), Christina Hoyos (Bride), Juan Antonio Jimenez (Groom), Pilar Cardenas (Mother), Carmen Villena (Wife), El Guito, Elvira Andres, Marisa Nella, Lario Diaz, Azucena Flores

p, Emiliano Piedra; d, Carlos Saura; w, Antonio Artero (based on the play by Federico Garcia Lorca, adapted by Alfredo Manas); ph, Teo Escamilla (Eastmancolor); ed, Pablo del Amo

For dance lovers only. Much-touted meeting of filmmaker Carlos Saura, choreographer Antonio Gades, and playwright Federico Garcia Lorca has been often overly received. BLOOD WEDDING opens backstage as the dancers pour in, open their makeup cases, fix their hair, and apply their greasepaint. Some time later, Gades and his troupe move out into their rehearsal space and begin practicing their flamenco version of Garcia Lorca's play. The film runs an economical 72 minutes.

BLOW OUT
1981 108m c   ★★½
Mystery   R/18
Filmways

John Travolta (Jack), Nancy Allen (Sally), John Lithgow (Burke), Dennis Franz (Karp), Peter Boyden (Sam), Curt May (Frank), Ernest McClure (Jim), Dave Roberts (Anchorman), Maurice Copeland (Jack), Claire Carter (Anchorwoman)

p, George Litto; d, Brian De Palma; w, Brian De Palma; ph, Vilmos Zsigmond (Technicolor); ed, Paul Hirsch; m, Pino Donaggio; prod d, Paul Sylbert; cos, Vicki Sanchez

Another hommage from De Palma, this time to BLOW-UP, concerns a sound-effects recorder (Travolta) who specializes in sounds for trashy porn-slasher films. While out recording one night, he hears a tire blow out and sees a car swerve off a bridge and plunge into the water. He jumps in and saves Sally (Nancy Allen), a prostitute who was with a now-drowned politician. The media and the dead man's associates are all convinced it was an accident, but Jack hears something on his tape recording that convinces him otherwise. Travolta made his switch from teen idol to leading man here and, to his credit, he manages to make De Palma's sleazeball likable.

BLOW-UP
1966 110m c   ★★★½
Drama   /18
Premier (U.K.)

David Hemmings (Thomas), Vanessa Redgrave (Jane), Sarah Miles (Patricia), Jane Birkin, Gillian Hills (Teenagers), Peter Bowles (Ron), Harry Hutchinson (Antique Dealer), John Castle (Painter), Susan Broderick (Antique Shop Owner), Mary Khal (Fashion Editor)

p, Pierre Rouve, Carlo Ponti; d, Michelangelo Antonioni; w, Michelangelo Antonioni, Tonino Guerra, Edward Bond (based on a story by Julio Cortazar); ph, Carlo Di Palma (Metro Color); ed, Frank Clarke; m, Herbie Hancock, The Yardbirds; cos, Jocelyn Rickards

Pop-culture icon that has become a cult classic. Antonioni's adaptation of Cortazar's short story is an engrossing study of imagery and one's perception of the image. Set against the backdrop of 1960s London, BLOW-UP follows fashionable young photographer Hemmings as he passively snaps his way through a world of drugs, models and parties. While wandering through a quiet park, he begins taking photos of two lovers embracing. One of them, Redgrave, chases after him and demands that he return the negatives. Later, after developing the photos, Hemmings thinks he sees something in the background—a man with a gun aimed at the back of Redgrave's partner. Returning that evening to the park, Hemmings finds the man's corpse. But the following morning, when he revisits the scene, the corpse has vanished. . .

One of the most successful art films ever made, BLOW-UP marked Antonioni's leap into the commercial arena, after an early career largely confined to film festivals. From the perspective of the 90s, though, it's hard to see what all the fuss was about. The "swinging 60s" stuff looks as dated as the Herbie Hancock score sounds, Hemmings is a difficult actor to care about, and the neo-surrealist touches are downright irritating. There are moments of humor, though it's hard to gauge how many of them are intentional. Jane Birkin makes her screen debut, as one of the two giggling teenagers who "wrestle" with Hemmings.

BLUE ANGEL, THE
(DER BLAUE ENGEL)
1930 99m bw   ★★★★★
Drama
UFA (Germany)

Emil Jannings (Prof. Immanuel Rath), Marlene Dietrich (Lola Frohlich), Kurt Gerron (Kiepert, a Magician), Rosa Valetti (Guste, his Wife), Hans Albers (Mazeppa), Eduard von Winterstein (Principal of the School), Reinhold Bernt (The Clown), Hans Roth (Beadle), Rolf Muller (Angst, a Student), Robert Klein-Lork (Goldstaub, a Student)

p, Erich Pommer; d, Josef von Sternberg; w, Robert Liebmann, Karl Vollmoeller, Carl Zuckmayer (based on the novel Professor Unrat by Heinrich Mann); ph, Gunther Rittau, Hans Schneeberger; ed, S.K. Winston; m, Friedrich Hollander

The one and only; an unqualified masterpiece and milestone. Grim, ritualistic rise and fall of a respectable man at the hands of a heartless tramp is still one of the most horrifying studies of human degradation ever made. THE BLUE ANGEL's international success can be attributed to any number of elements: The immortal Jannings, UFA's greatest actor and a victim of the transition from silents to sound, is astounding in an essentially silent performance; Dietrich is wholly captivating in her first role with Sternberg—a creative union from which arose the Dietrich persona that would become internationally recognizable. It is, however, the genius of Sternberg to which THE BLUE ANGEL owes its greatness. His use of lighting, composition and of silence as sound, his overall creation of a world that can seduce and destroy even its most upstanding citizen, attest to this filmmaker's greatness and to the stature of THE BLUE ANGEL. Filmed simultaneously in German and English, the film is available in two, slightly differing, videotape versions—in German with English subtitles, and in English, the former preferable to the latter.

BLUE ANGEL, THE
1959   107m   c   ★★
Drama   /A
FOX

Curt Jurgens (Prof. Immanuel Rath), May Britt (Lola-Lola), Theodore Bikel (Klepert), John Banner (Principal Harter), Fabrizio Mioni (Rolf), Ludwig Stossel (Prof. Braun), Wolfe Barzell (Clown), Ina Anders (Gussie), Richard Tyler (Keiselsack), Voytek Dolinski (Mueller)

p, Jack Cummings; d, Edward Dmytryk; w, Nigel Balchin (based on the screenplay by Carl Zuckmayer, Karl Vollmoeller, Robert Liebmann, from the novel by Heinrich Mann); ph, Leon Shamroy (CinemaScope, Deluxe Color); ed, Jack W. Holmes; m, Hugo Friedhofer; chor, Hermes Pan; cos, Adele Balkan

All wrong, from Edward Dmytryk, who must have been paid a fortune to go through with it. May Britt, in the role that made Dietrich famous, is like seeing Shirley Temple play Mae West. Plus a happy ending! For insomniacs only.

BLUE COLLAR
1978   110m   c   ★★★
Drama   R/18
T.A.T.

Richard Pryor (Zeke Brown), Harvey Keitel (Jerry Bartkowski), Yaphet Kotto (Smokey), Ed Begley, Jr. (Bobby Joe), Harry Bellaver (Eddie Johnson), George Memmoli (Jenkins), Lucy Saroyan (Arlene Bartowski), Lane Smith (Clarence Hill), Cliff De Young (John Burrows), Borah Silver (Miller)

p, Don Guest; d, Paul Schrader; w, Paul Schrader, Leonard Schrader (based on materials by Sidney A. Glass); ph, Bobby Byrne (Technicolor); ed, Tom Rolf; m, Jack Nitzsche, Ry Cooder; cos, Ron Dawson, Alice Rush

Auto workers fight back. Schraeder's auspicious debut, strong performances from the three leads, make this comedy/drama worth a look, despite several awkward moments.

BLUE DAHLIA, THE
1946   96m   bw   ★★★½
Mystery   /A
Paramount

Alan Ladd (Johnny Morrison), Veronica Lake (Joyce Harwood), William Bendix (Buzz Wanchek), Howard da Silva (Eddie Harwood), Doris Dowling (Helen Morrison), Tom Powers (Capt. Hendrickson), Hugh Beaumont (George Copeland), Howard Freeman (Corelli), Don Costello (Leo), Will Wright ("Dad" Newell)

p, John Houseman; d, George Marshall; w, Raymond Chandler (based on his story); ph, Lionel Lindon; ed, Arthur Schmidt; m, Victor Young; art d, Hans Dreier, Walter Tyler; cos, Edith Head

Tidy film noir, although we prefer Ladd and Lake in THIS GUN FOR HIRE. This is the only film script Raymond Chandler did directly for the screen, and the script reflects his hard-boiled, grim wit. Ladd returns from the service, finds wife has become a tramp. When she's murdered, he has to clear himself. Taut film still plays like house afire.

BLUE LAMP, THE
1950   82m   bw   ★★★
Mystery   /PG
General Films   (U.K.)

Jack Warner (George Dixon), Jimmy Hanley (Andy Mitchell), Dirk Bogarde (Tom Riley), Robert Flemyng (Sgt. Roberts), Bernard Lee (Inspector Cherry), Peggy Evans (Diana Lewis), Patric Doonan (Spud), Bruce Seton (Constable Campbell), Frederick Piper (Alf Lewis), Betty Ann Davies (Mrs. Lewis)

p, Michael Balcon; d, Basil Dearden; w, T.E.B. Clarke; ph, Gordon Dines; ed, Peter Tanner; m, Ernest Irving

The apprehension of a cop killer, with a classic performance from Bogarde and an excruciating car chase, borrowing a page from Hitchcock. Very neat all around.

BLUE SKIES
1946   104m   c   ★★★
Musical   /U
Paramount

Bing Crosby (Johnny Adams), Fred Astaire (Jed Potter), Joan Caulfield (Mary O'Hara), Billy De Wolfe (Tony), Olga San Juan (Nita Nova), Mikhail Rasumny (Francois), Frank Faylen (Mack), Victoria Horne (Martha Nurse), Karolyn Grimes (Mary Elizabeth)

p, Sol C. Siegel; d, Stuart Heisler; w, Arthur Sheekman (based on an idea by Irving Berlin, adapted by Allan Scott); ph, Charles Lang, William Snyder (Technicolor); ed, LeRoy Stone; fx, Gordon Jennings, Paul K. Lerpae, Farciot Edouart; chor, Hermes Pan

Forty-two song cues and 30 full numbers held together by a plot of tissue paper. But with these two, who cares? Score by Berlin features Astaire's classic "Puttin' On the Ritz", and both guys dueting on "A Couple of Song and Dance Men". Easy all the way.

BLUE STEEL
1990   102m   c   ★★★
Thriller   R/18
Lightning/Precision/Mack-Taylor

Jamie Lee Curtis (Megan Turner), Ron Silver (Eugene Hunt), Clancy Brown (Nick Mann), Elizabeth Pena (Tracy Perez), Louise Fletcher (Shirley Turner), Philip Bosco (Frank Turner), Kevin Dunn (Assistant Chief Stanley Hoyt), Richard Jenkins (Attorney Mel Dawson), Markus Flannagan (Husband), Mary Mara (Wife)

p, Edward R. Pressman, Oliver Stone, Michael Rauch; d, Kathryn Bigelow; w, Kathryn Bigelow, Eric Red; ph, Amir Mokri (Technicolor); ed, Lee Percy; m, Brad Fiedel; prod d, Toby Corbett; fx, Steve Kirshoff; cos, Richard Shissler

Rookie woman cop stalked by a psycho. Police triller given feminist twist by capable Bigelow's direction, strong acting by Curtis, who is equally matched by Silver's unbridled portrayal. Script conventions are film's biggest weakness, but still well worth taking in.

BLUE THUNDER
1983   108m   c   ★★½
Action   R/15
Columbia

Roy Scheider (Murphy), Malcolm McDowell (Cochrane), Candy Clark (Kate), Warren Oates (Braddock), Daniel Stern (Lymangood), Paul Roebling (Icelan), David Sheiner (Fletcher), Ed Bernard (Short), Jason Bernard (Mayor), Joe Santos (Montoya)

p, Gordon Carroll; d, John Badham; w, Dan O'Bannon, Don Jakoby; ph, John A. Alonzo (Panavision, Deluxe Color); ed, Frank Morriss, Edward Abroms; m, Arthur B. Rubinstein; fx, Chuck Gaspar, Jeff Jarvis, Peter Albiez; cos, Marianna Elliot

A souped-up helicopter. Rock-'em-sock-'em commercial pic done in dizzying style defies you to take time to analyze it. Can't-sit-still flick was nominated for Best Editing. Acting could have been, seemed like it was, good. Your move; but not for me.

BLUE VELVET
1986 120m c   ★★★
Mystery   R/18
DEG

Kyle MacLachlan (Jeffrey Beaumont), Isabella Rossellini (Dorothy Vallens), Dennis Hopper (Frank Booth), Laura Dern (Sandy Williams), Hope Lange (Mrs. Williams), Dean Stockwell (Ben), George Dickerson (Detective Williams), Priscilla Pointer (Mrs. Beaumont), Frances Bay (Aunt Barbara), Jack Harvey (Mr. Beaumont)

p, Fred Caruso; d, David Lynch; w, David Lynch; ph, Frederick Elmes (Joe Dunton Camera Widescreen); ed, Duwayne Dunham; m, Angelo Badalamenti; prod d, Patricia Norris; fx, Greg Hull, George Hill; cos, Gloria Laughride

Weirdness, big time. The seamy side of small town Americana from——who else?——David Lynch. When archetypal college student Jeffrey Beaumont (MacLachlan) finds a severed human ear in a deserted field, he enlists the help of innocent high-schooler Sandy (Dern) in finding the body to which it once belonged. The key to the mystery is nightclub chanteuse Dorothy Vallens (Rossellini), whose husband and child are being held hostage by the demoniacal Frank Booth (Hopper), who sexually torments the singer in exchange for the safety of her loved ones. Eventually Jeffrey probes so deeply into this dark and troubling mystery that he comes face to face with Booth, the very embodiment of evil. As if to demonstrate the film's premise that people would prefer to avoid the dark side of life—the sadism, perversions, fetishism, drug addiction, and violence—many critics complained that BLUE VELVET was "dangerous" in its exploration of these traits, contending that these taboos were better left in the closet. Director David Lynch addresses that belief here—Hopper, the voice of evil, demands that people not look at him, while MacLachlan, the voice of good, not only looks but fights back. All of this revolves around the film's mystery elements, which are on a par with the innocent whodunit mentality of a Hardy Boys-Nancy Drew episode, although the rest of the film is deeply disquieting and sexually aggressive, not to be seen by those easily repulsed. There are certain similarities between this film and Alfred Hitchcock's 1943 classic SHADOW OF A DOUBT, in which Joseph Cotten's "Uncle Charlie" is a demented murderer whose diseased presence threatens a quiet California town. Surprisingly, for a picture as steeped in controversy as it was, BLUE VELVET did earn Lynch a Best Director Oscar nomination. In addition to the Bobby Vinton title tune, the film prominently features the Roy Orbison tune "In Dreams," and a lush score by Angelo Badalamenti. Depending on your point of view, either dark-sidedly brilliant or garbage heaped on top of whipped cream.

BLUES BROTHERS, THE
1980 133m c   ★★½
Comedy   R/15
Universal

John Belushi (Joliet Jake), Dan Aykroyd (Elwood), James Brown (Rev. Cleophus James), Cab Calloway (Curtis), Ray Charles (Ray), Carrie Fisher (Mystery Woman), Aretha Franklin (Soul Food Cafe Owner), Henry Gibson (Nazi Leader), John Candy (Burton Mercer), Murphy Dunne (Murph)

p, Robert K. Weiss; d, John Landis; w, John Landis, Dan Aykroyd; ph, Stephen Katz (Technicolor); ed, George Folsey, Jr.; m, Ira Newborn; cos, Deborah Nadoolman

THE BLUES BROTHERS is a monument to waste, noise and misplaced cool, but it does have its engagingly nutty moments. The premise for this $30 million flick is that blue-eyed soul brothers Jake and Elwood (John Belushi and Dan Aykroyd) need to raise $5,000 for their old orphanage. With no other motivation, they systematically destroy the city of Chicago. One of the most self-indulgent films of the 1980s, THE BLUES BROTHERS shows the dangers of giving untold sums of money to brash young directors. The highlights are few, but telling—all of the black performers score in their brief roles, especially Franklin and Calloway. Unfortunately, these performers's legitimate "soul" underlines the Blues Brothers's assumed soul. Henry Gibson is funny as a George Rockwell-type Nazi, and Frank Oz of Muppet fame makes a rare on-screen appearance as a corrections officer. This film has one pace—breakneck—and doesn't allow the audience to breathe, rest, or care about anyone or anything. It's worth noting that its big budget exceeded the amount Chaplin, Keaton, Laurel and Hardy, Charlie Chase, Harry Langdon, and Ben Turpin used to make all their films.

BLUME IN LOVE
1973 115m c   ★★★
Comedy   R/15
WB

George Segal (Blume), Susan Anspach (Nina Blume), Kris Kristofferson (Elmo), Marsha Mason (Arlene), Shelley Winters (Mrs. Cramer), Donald Muhich (Analyst), Paul Mazursky (Blume's Partner)

p, Paul Mazursky; d, Paul Mazursky; w, Paul Mazursky; ph, Bruce Surtees (Technicolor); ed, Donn Cambern; prod d, Pato Guzman

Sympathetic but self-indulgent masculine version of Mazursky's AN UNMARRIED WOMAN, a few years later. Segal is splendid as the lovesick lawyer who lusts after his ex, Anspach, who has taken up with Kristofferson. Mason is formidable as a woman waiting for divorced men. Mazursky, working without Larry Tucker for the first time, lets the picture get away from him a few times and does not edit with as tight an eye as for his previous films. His jaundiced look at love in California allows him to have some fun satirizing early 1970s types like Gottlieb (the bass player in the Limeliters group) as a guru and Denison as a Yoga leader. Winters is hysterical in a small role as a wife trying to decide whether or not to divorce her lecherous husband. Mazursky gave himself a role as Segal's partner which may explan moments when film feels unfocused.

BOAT, THE
(DAS BOOT)
1981 150m c   ★★★★
War   R/15
Bavaria Atelier   (West Germany)

Jurgen Prochnow (Captain), Herbert Gronemeyer (Lt. Werner/Correspondent), Klaus Wennemann (Chief Engineer), Hubertus Bengsch (1st Lt./Number One), Martin Semmelrogge (2nd Lieutenant), Bernd Tauber (Chief Quartermaster), Erwin Leder (Johann), Martin May (Ullmann), Heinz Honig (Hinrich), U.A. Ochsen (Chief Bosun)

p, Gunter Rohrbach, Michael Bittins; d, Wolfgang Petersen; w, Wolfgang Petersen (based on the novel by Lothar-Guenther Buchheim); ph, Jost Vacano (Fujicolor); ed, Hannes Nikel; m, Klaus Doldinger; prod d, Rolf Zehetbauer; art d, Gotz Weidner; fx, Karl Baumgartner; cos, Monika Bauert

Gripping and authentic; based on the experiences of photographer Lothar-Guenther Buchheim, this superbly filmed action movie chronicles a U-boat voyage in 1941, detailing above- and below-the-surface horrors as well as the mundane hours that characterize time spent at sea. Though most of the footage concentrates on the intense, noble captain, Jurgen Prochnow, the only fully developed "character" in the film is the boat, as it undergoes numerous attacks. Decidedly anti-Nazi in tone, THE BOAT presents the crew as individual warriors upholding their own brand of honor and sneering at Hitler's Reich. The chief attraction of this film, however, is the incredible camerawork. Racing through the sub, squeezing through tiny openings, director Wolfgang Petersen's camera brilliantly evokes the claustrophobia and clamor of undersea battle. A technical marvel, THE BOAT is a breathtaking and powerful portrait of war and death. Though the film was originally released on videocassette as the subtitled DAS BOOT, most copies now available are dubbed into English.

BOB AND CAROL AND TED AND ALICE

1969   104m   c   ★★★
Comedy   R/15
Columbia

Natalie Wood (Carol), Robert Culp (Bob), Elliott Gould (Ted), Dyan Cannon (Alice), Horst Ebersberg (Horst), Lee Bergere (Emelio), Donald Muhich (Psychiatrist), Noble Lee Holderread, Jr. (Sean), K.T. Stevens (Phyllis), Celeste Yarnall (Susan)

p, Larry Tucker; d, Paul Mazursky; w, Paul Mazursky, Larry Tucker; ph, Charles Lang (Technicolor); m, Quincy Jones; chor, Miriam Nelson; cos, Moss Mabry

Screwing around, '60s style, and beginning to look very dated and self-indulgent. Helped not at all by bad ending. Gould and especially Cannon come off with top honors; they were nominated for Academy Awards, as was the story and cinematography.

BOB LE FLAMBEUR

1955   100m   bw   ★★★
Crime
Studios Jenner/O.G.C./Cyme/Play Art   (France)

Isabel Corey (Anne), Daniel Cauchy (Paolo), Robert Duchesne (Bob Montagne), Guy Decomble (Inspector), Andre Garet (Roger), Gerard Buhr (Mark), Claude Cerval (Jean), Colette Fleury (Suzanne), Simon Paris (Yvonne), Rene Havard

p, Jean-Pierre Melville; d, Jean-Pierre Melville; w, Jean-Pierre Melville, Auguste Le Breton; ph, Henri Decae; ed, Monique Bonnot; m, Eddie Barclay, Jo Boyer

One of Jean-Pierre Melville's greatest efforts, unreleased in the US until 1982, this engaging caper stars Roger Duchesne as an aging gangster who is down on his luck and has no other choice but to plan a heist of the Deauville Casino. Unfortunately for Bob, his two friends—Paulo (Daniel Cauchy), the young crook who idolizes him, and Anne (Isabelle Corey) his sensuous 16-year-old sex kitten—are proof that people today are not as loyal

they were in Bob's youth. BOB LE FLAMBEUR, like Melville's later gangster film LE DOULOS, is an offering to the gods of Hollywood filmmaking and gangster mythmaking, an honest portrayal of that fictional character—the gangster hero. Melville films him lovingly—the upturned collar, the ever-present gun, and the hopeless philosophy that is as dark as the shadows of night. As American as Melville tries to be (he changed his name from Grumbach after American author Herman Melville), his films are entirely and unfailingly French. Coscripted by Auguste Le Breton, upon whose novel Jules Dassin based his classic gangster film RIFIFI, which Breton also coscripted.

BOCCACCIO '70

1962   150m   c   ★★½
Fantasy/Comedy   /X
TCF   (France/Italy)

THE RAFFLE: Sophia Loren (Zoe), Luigi Gillianni (Gaetano), Alfio Vita (Cuspet). THE JOB: Romy Schneider (Pupe), Tomas Milian (The Count), Romolo Valli, Paolo Stoppa. THE TEMPTATION OF DR. ANTONIO: Anita Ekberg (Anita), Peppino de Filippo (Dr. Antonio), Dante Maggio

p, Carlo Ponti, Antonio Cervi; d, Federico Fellini, Vittorio De Sica, Luchino Visconti; w, Federico Fellini, Ennio Flaiano, Tullio Pinelli, Suso Cecchi D'Amico, Luchino Visconti, Cesare Zavattini; ph, Giuseppe Rotunno, Otello Marelli; m, Nino Rota, Nino Rota, Armando Trovajoli

Three unconnected episodes dealing with modern stories the producers would have you think Boccaccio might have written if alive; from the lack of content and characterization, Boccaccio would have used a pseudonym for these turgid tales. The film is only an excuse to parade the Amazonian attributes of Ekberg and Loren, with Schneider thrown in for dramatic license. In one story, Ekberg is a billboard image that comes to life in a dream conjured by a middle-aged lecher. In "The Raffle," Loren plays a woman who operates a shooting gallery and is the sex prize of a Saturday night raffle. To accommodate a country bumpkin who begs to win the raffle, she fixes the drawing but does not deliver the goods; to show she is a noble slattern, however, Loren spreads the word that she has dallied with the clod so he will become a hero to his crowd. Schneider's segment is almost lost between these two stories; she plays a secretary in love with the boss and sacrificing her personal life for the ungrateful wretch. Contrived and spotty.

BODY AND SOUL

1947   104m   bw   ★★★★★
Sports   /A
Enterprise

John Garfield (Charlie Davis), Lilli Palmer (Peg Born), Hazel Brooks (Alice), Anne Revere (Anna Davis), William Conrad (Quinn), Joseph Pevney (Shorty Polaski), Canada Lee (Ben), Lloyd Goff (Roberts), Art Smith (David Davis), James Burke (Arnold)

p, Bob Roberts; d, Robert Rossen; w, Abraham Polonsky; ph, James Wong Howe; ed, Robert Parrish; m, Hugo Friedhofer; art d, Nathan Juran; cos, Marion Herwood Keyes

The fight film to which all others are compared. John Garfield portrays Charlie Davis, a Jewish prizefighter whose parents want him to hang up the gloves and get an education. When his father is killed in a bomb explosion, however, the proud Charlie prevents his mother (Anne Revere) from accepting government relief, turns pro, and by hook and crook, rises quickly to the top, winning the championship from Ben (onetime welterweight Canada Lee), who is left with a life-threatening blood clot in his brain. As the champ, Charlie slides into a dissipated lifestyle and throws over his artist girlfriend, Peg Born (Lilli Palmer), for a floozy (Hazel Brooks), falling deeper into the clutches of the gangster who owns him (Lloyd Goff) in the process. Garfield's riveting, Oscar-nominated performance lifts BODY AND SOUL to the masterpiece level, as do Robert Rossen's superb direction, the marvelous photography of James Wong Howe and the Oscar-winning editing. The fight sequences, in particular, brought a kind of realism to the genre that had never before existed (Howe wore skates and rolled around the ring shooting the fight scenes with a hand-held camera). A knockout on all levels.

BODY HEAT
1981 113m c ★★★½
Crime R/18
Ladd

William Hurt (Ned Racine), Kathleen Turner (Matty Walker), Richard Crenna (Edmund Walker), Ted Danson (Peter Lowenstein), J.A. Preston (Oscar Grace), Mickey Rourke (Teddy Lewis), Kim Zimmer (Mary Ann), Jane Hallaren (Stella), Lanna Saunders (Roz Kraft), Michael Ryan (Miles Hardin)

p, Fred T. Gallo; d, Lawrence Kasdan; w, Lawrence Kasdan; ph, Richard H. Kline (Technicolor); ed, Carol Littleton; m, John Barry; cos, Renie Conley

An excellent crime drama in the style of Raymond Chandler, James M. Cain, and Dashiell Hammett. Director-writer Lawrence Kasdan borrows liberally in style from 1940s *film noir* and incorporates a plot reminiscent of DOUBLE INDEMNITY, but he adds a steamy sexuality more in keeping with contemporary films. Set in Florida, the movie follows the ill-fated course of Ned Racine (William Hurt), a rather dim-witted attorney who gets deeply involved with sultry Matty Walker (Kathleen Turner), a woman who wants her husband dead. Hurt gives a superior performance—we can actually see him thinking, rather painfully—while Turner makes a fine *femme fatale* after the model of Lauren Bacall. Ted Danson is also excellent as a slightly nerdy lawyer-friend of Ned's; Mickey Rourke, in one of his early screen appearances, shows the promise of things to come; and the other supporting roles are likewise well handled.

BOMBSHELL
1933 90m bw ★★★★
Comedy /A
MGM

Jean Harlow (Lola), Lee Tracy (Space), Frank Morgan (Pops), Franchot Tone (Gifford Middleton), Pat O'Brien (Brogan), Una Merkel (Mac), Ted Healy (Junior), Ivan Lebedeff (Marquis), Mary Forbes (Mrs. Middleton), C. Aubrey Smith (Mr. Middleton)

d, Victor Fleming; w, Jules Furthman, John Lee Mahin (based on a play by Caroline Francke, Mack Crane); ph, Chester Lyons, Harold Rosson; ed, Margaret Booth

One of the best films to satirize the movie industry, this is a trenchant, witty, fast-moving send-up of 1930s Hollywood lifestyles. Harlow plays a ditzy screen sexpot who gets involved in a series of madcap escapades. She becomes engaged to a "marquis" who is arrested as an illegal alien; tries to escape the clutches of an amorous director; unsuccessfully attempts to adopt a baby (her family gets in the way); and goes on retreat to Palm Springs, where she falls for an upper-crust beau but is finally

forced to decide where her heart belongs. This early precursor of films such as SUNSET BOULEVARD and THE BAD AND THE BEAUTIFUL still packs a considerable comic punch.

BON VOYAGE, CHARLIE BROWN (AND DON'T COME BACK)
1980 75m c ★★★
Animated/Children's /U
Paramount

VOICES OF: Daniel Anderson, Scott Beach, Casey Carlson, Debbie Muller, Patricia Patts, Laura Planting, Arrin Skelley, Bill Melendez, Annalisa Bortolin, Roseline Rubens

p, Lee Mendelson, Bill Melendez; d, Bill Melendez; w, Charles M. Schulz (based on "Peanuts" characters created by Charles M. Schulz); ph, Nick Vasu (Movielab Color); m, Ed Bogas, Judy Munsen; anim, Sam Jaimes, Hank Smith, Al Pabian, Joe Roman, Ed Newmann, Bill Littlejohn, Bob Carlson, Dale Baer, Spencer Peel, Larry Leichliter, Sergio Bertolli

Based on the comic strip created by Charles Schulz, this is the fourth and the best of the animated films devoted to the charming antics of the "Peanuts" gang. This time Charlie Brown fans get a bagful of surprises that include jet flights, spooky chateaus, and a dose of danger rarely seen in "Peanuts" films, as the crew is transported to France for two weeks in a student exchange program. It is there that Charlie Brown and Linus are invited to stay at a chateau where grim events occur. Fans will love Snoopy's first-class flight to London and his stopover there, during which he plays tennis at Wimbledon.

BONNIE AND CLYDE
1967 111m c ★★★★
Crime /18
WB

Warren Beatty (Clyde Barrow), Faye Dunaway (Bonnie Parker), Michael J. Pollard (C.W. Moss), Gene Hackman (Buck Barrow), Estelle Parsons (Blanche), Denver Pyle (Frank Hamer), Dub Taylor (Ivan Moss), Evans Evans (Velma Davis), Gene Wilder (Eugene Grizzard), James Stiver (Grocery Store Owner)

p, Warren Beatty; d, Arthur Penn; w, David Newman, Robert Benton; ph, Burnett Guffey (Technicolor); ed, Dede Allen; m, Charles Strouse; art d, Dean Tavoularis; fx, Danny Lee; cos, Theadora Van Runkle

Landmark gangster film that made a huge commercial and cultural splash. The seminal script by David Newman and Robert Benton struck a nerve with the 1967 youth culture as it reimagined the two rural Depression-era outlaws as largely sympathetic nonconformists. The film set new standards for screen violence but it alternated its scenes of mayhem with lyrical interludes and jaunty slapstick sequences accompanied by spirited banjo music. While unusual for a Hollywood feature, such jarring shifts in tone were typical of the genre-bending works of French New Wave directors Francois Truffaut and Jean-Luc Godard, both of whom were slated to direct the feature at various points in its genesis.

Producer/star Beatty cajoled Warner Brothers into financing the production and selected Arthur Penn to direct. Penn initially aimed at realism, constructing scenes based on Walker Evans photographs and NRA posters, but a competing nostalgic impulse won out. The Oscar-winning cinematography of Burnett Guffey served up the Dust Bowl on a sumptuous Technicolor platter, and historical accuracy was jettisoned in favor of glossy romanticization. In the process, the story took on the quality of a folk ballad.

As portrayed by Beatty and Dunaway, Clyde Barrow and Bonnie Parker were just plain folks who liked to pose for photographs and rob banks. As one ad campaign proclaimed, "They are young, they are in love, they kill people." The rest of the Barrow gang is portrayed by a powerhouse group of supporting players: Gene Hackman, Estelle Parsons (who won the Oscar for Best Supporting Actress), and Michael J. Pollard. Gene Wilder also makes his screen debut as a nervous mortician.

BONNIE AND CLYDE grossed $23 million and became Warner's second best box-office attraction up to that time, after MY FAIR LADY. Despite its controversial nature, the film was nominated for nine Oscars (it only won two).

BOOM TOWN
1940   117m   bw   ★★½
Drama   /A
MGM

Clark Gable (*Big John McMasters*), Spencer Tracy (*Square John Sand*), Claudette Colbert (*Betsy Bartlett*), Hedy Lamarr (*Karen Vanmeer*), Frank Morgan (*Luther Aldrich*), Lionel Atwill (*Harry Compton*), Chill Wills (*Harmony Jones*), Marion Martin (*Whitey*), Minna Gombell (*Spanish Eva*), Joe Yule (*Ed Murphy*)

p, Sam Zimbalist; d, Jack Conway; w, John Lee Mahin (based on a story by James Edward Grant); ph, Harold Rosson; ed, Blanche Sewell; m, Franz Waxman; art d, Cedric Gibbons, Eddie Imazu; cos, Adrian, Gile Steele

More of a "pop" than a "boom". Lavish MGM production in which the studio paired its greatest stars, Gable and Tracy, for the last time. The story concerns two oilmen whose financial ups and downs are interwoven with their romantic entanglements. Against a backdrop of gushing oil wells and East Coast wheeling and dealing, Gable steals his friend's true love (Colbert) and then cheats on her with another (Lamarr). Tracy, noble and stoic to the end, works behind the scenes to protect his former love.

A slick, fast-moving film, BOOM TOWN displays a queer obsession with earning and losing money by the million. The star power, with little of value to hang onto, does its professional best to boost the lumpy storyline. The biggest hit of 1940, this mediocre film earned Oscar nominations for Best Cinematography and Best Special Effects.

BOOMERANG
1947   88m   bw   ★★★★
Mystery   /A
FOX

Dana Andrews (*Henry L. Harvey*), Jane Wyatt (*Mrs. Harvey*), Lee J. Cobb (*Chief Robinson*), Cara Williams (*Irene Nelson*), Arthur Kennedy (*John Waldron*), Sam Levene (*Woods*), Taylor Holmes (*Wade*), Robert Keith (*McCreery*), Ed Begley (*Harris*), Philip Coolidge (*Crossman*)

p, Louis de Rochemont; d, Elia Kazan; w, Richard Murphy (based on the *Reader's Digest* article "The Perfect Case" by Anthony Abbott); ph, Norbert Brodine; ed, Harmon Jones; m, David Buttolph

A chilling *film noir* about the murder of a priest, the subsequent arrest and trial of a jobless drifter, and the efforts of a young state's attorney to uncover the truth. Closely based on the actual 1924 murder (still unsolved) of Fr. Hubert Dahme in Bridgeport, Connecticut, the film was directed by the young Elia Kazan in a highly effective, semi-documentary style. Kazan shot most of the film on location, using high-contrast cinematography and an extremely mobile camera to create a palpable sense of urgency. Producer Louis de Rochemont had earlier been responsible for the "March of Time" newsreel series, as well as the naturalistic features THE HOUSE ON 92ND STREET and 13 RUE MADELEINE.

BOOTS MALONE
1952   102m   bw   ★★★
Sports   /U
Columbia

William Holden (*Boots Malone*), Johnny Stewart (*the Kid*), Stanley Clements (*Stash Clements*), Basil Ruysdael (*Preacher Cole*), Carl Benton Reid (*John Williams*), Ralph Dumke (*Beckett*), Ed Begley (*Howard Whitehead*), Hugh Sanders (*Matson*), Harry Morgan (*Quarter Horse Henry*), Anna Lee (*Mrs. Gibson*)

p, Milton Holmes; d, William Dieterle; w, Milton Holmes; ph, Charles Lawton, Jr.; ed, Al Clark; m, Elmer Bernstein

An absorbing melodrama crammed with authentic racetrack lore. William Holden plays the title character, a down-on-his-luck jockey's agent looking for the big score. Enter a 15-year-old rich kid (Johnny Stewart) who is eager to learn how to ride and shows considerable promise. Smelling money, Boots takes the Kid under his wing, and before long the two develop a genuine rapport. Complications both domestic and deadly arise as the boy's mother, as well as a group of gangsters, each seek to derail the boy's career. Much of BOOTS MALONE was shot at actual racetracks, reinforcing this entertaining film's authenticity.

BORIS GODUNOV
1959   105m   c   ★★★★
Opera   /U
Mosfilm   (U.S.S.R.)

A. Pirogov (*Boris Godunov*), G. Nellep (*False Dmitri*), A. Krivchenva (*Varlaam*), I. Kozlovsky (*Fool*), L. Avdeyeva (*Marina*)

d, V. Stroyeva; w, N. Golovanov, V. Stroyeva (based on the opera by Moussorgsky, from the play by Pushkin); ph, V. Nikolayev (Magicolor); m, Modeste Mussorgsky

Stroyeva's stately adaptation of the deliberately paced Moussorgsky-Pushkin opera depicts the revolt of a false pretender against the czar. The minimal story is punctuated and enlivened by bursts of rich music and spectacular scenes of pageantry and pomp. The movie is notable for its massive sets, rich costumes, spectacular color and massive crowd scenes. Pirogov is a persuasive Boris, with a deep, stirring bass that conveys all the pathos and drama of his role, especially in a monologue about his guilt. Krivchenva is an imposing Varlaam and also provides one of the high points in the film with her earthy drinking song in the inn. Nellep convincingly carries off both singing and acting roles as the false Dmitri, and Avdeyeva is an attractive Marina opposite him, with their duet in the garden of the Polish court another outstanding segment.

BORN ON THE FOURTH OF JULY
1989   140m   c   ★★★
Drama/War   R/18
Fourth of July

Tom Cruise *(Ron Kovic)*, Bryan Larkin *(Young Ron)*, Raymond J. Barry *(Mr. Kovic)*, Caroline Kava *(Mrs. Kovic)*, Josh Evans *(Tommy Kovic)*, Seth Allen *(Young Tommy)*, Jamie Talisman *(Jimmy Kovic)*, Sean Stone *(Young Jimmy)*, Anne Bobby *(Susanne Kovic)*, Jenna von Oy *(Young Susanne)*

p, A. Kitman Ho, Oliver Stone; d, Oliver Stone; w, Oliver Stone, Ron Kovic (based on his autobiography); ph, Robert Richardson (Deluxe Color); ed, David Brenner; m, John Williams; prod d, Bruno Rubeo; art d, Victor Kempster, Richard L. Johnson; cos, Judy Ruskin

Oliver Stone (PLATOON) returns to the Vietnam War era but here the focus is primarily on the homefront and the aftershocks of war. Ambitious matinee idol Tom Cruise stars in a showy change-of-pace characterization as Ron Kovic in the autobiographical story of a gung ho young man who went proudly off to Vietnam, came back home in a wheelchair, and, after a traumatic interval, became a high profile antiwar activist.

The film begins with a depiction of Kovic's youth in Massapequa, New York, where he is raised to be a deeply patriotic, God-fearing, macho all-American athelete. As such he eagerly enlists in the Marines and ships off to Vietnam, convinced of the justness of the American cause. He becomes increasingly confused and disoriented after he accidentally kills one of his own men in a firefight. He later receives a bullet wound that leaves him paralyzed from the waist down. Back in the home of his family which no longer understands him, he degenerates into a drunken, self-pitying dropout. After a dissolute sequence in Mexico, he somehow gets a grip on himself, confronts his changed feelings about his life and his country, and becomes an antiwar activist thereby regaining his self-respect.

The film is undeniably emotionally powerful but ultimately problematic because it lingers on the pathos of Kovic's condition while skirting the less visually dramatic aspects of the character. Kovic clearly undergoes a political conversion but it is never dealt with directly. He changes during a fadeout. The effect is as unintentionally jarring as if a reel of the film were missing. The critique of masculinity is far more thoughtful and compelling than the vague ruminations about war. Nonetheless Cruise's impassioned performance as Kovic is an impressive accomplishment. The film won an Oscar for Stone and received nominations for Best Picture, Best Actor, adapted screenplay, cinematography, screenplay, cinematography, editing, sound, and original score.

BORN YESTERDAY

1951 103m bw ★★★★
Comedy /U
Columbia

Judy Holliday *(Billie Dawn)*, Broderick Crawford *(Harry Brock)*, William Holden *(Paul Verrall)*, Howard St. John *(Jim Devery)*, Frank Otto *(Eddie)*, Larry Oliver *(Norval Hedges)*, Barbara Brown *(Mrs. Hedges)*, Grandon Rhodes *(Sanborn)*, Claire Carleton *(Helen)*, Smoki Whitfield *(Bootblack)*

p, S. Sylvan Simon; d, George Cukor; w, Albert Mannheimer (based on the play by Garson Kanin); ph, Joseph Walker; ed, Charles Nelson; m, Frederick Hollander; cos, Jean Louis

The highlight of this lively Garson Kanin Broadway comedy is the most delightful "dumb blonde" to ever grace the screen, Holliday, in a role she originated on stage and nearly did not get to re-create on screen. As the malaprop-tossing mistress of scrap metal tycoon Crawford, she is unknowingly put in nominal charge of his shady empire so that he can cover his tracks. Though

no paragon of high culture himself, Crawford is embarrassed by his paramour's lack of social refinement. He hires her a tutor, Holden, who actually plans to write a series of articles exposing Crawford's slippery operations. The PYGMALION-like process of changing the tasteless yet street-savvy Holliday into a cultured lady is loaded with laughs and inoffensive sexual innuendoes. The situation gets more complicated as Holliday and Holden fall in love.

Crawford is frightening yet funny as the tycoon and Holden is effective in his appealing if low-key role. But Holliday is the film's most enduring treasure. Indeed, she was so effective as a dumb blonde that she was typecast in most of her subsequent films. Holliday's priceless characterization earned her an Oscar for Best Actress (one of BORN YESTERDAY's five nominations including: Best Picture, Best Direction, Best Screenplay, and Best Costume Design), a considerable achievement in light of her stellar competition that year: Gloria Swanson in SUNSET BOULEVARD and Bette Davis in ALL ABOUT EVE. A sheer delight, even if one only remembers the classic gin rummy scene.

BOUDU SAVED FROM DROWNING

1932 84m bw ★★★★★
Comedy /15
Pathe (France)

Michel Simon *(Boudu)*, Charles Grandval *(Monsieur Lastingois)*, Marcella Hainia *(Madama Lastingois)*, Severine Lerczynska *(Anne-Marie)*, Jean Daste *(Student)*, Max Dalban *(Godin)*, Jean Gehret *(Vigour)*, Jacques Becker *(Poet on a Bench)*, Jane Pierson *(Rose, the Neighbor's Maid)*, George Darnoux *(Marriage Guest)*

p, Michel Simon, Jean Gehret; d, Jean Renoir; w, Jean Renoir (based on a play by Rene Fauchois); ph, Jean-Paul Alphen; ed, Marguerite Renoir; m, Leo Daniderff, Johann Strauss

This underrated social comedy is another masterpiece from Renoir. Made in 1932 but lost, then finally released in 1967 in the US, this film is a timeless satire on middle-class values centering on Boudu (Michel Simon), an archetypal tramp about to commit suicide in grief, apparently, over the loss of his dog. He leaps into the Seine from the Pont des Arts, but is saved by bourgeois bookseller Lastingois (Charles Grahval), who takes Boudu home and tries to start him on the road to a productive, responsible life. Boudu, however, is a protohippie—a longhaired, bearded believer in freedom and anarchy. During his stay in Lastingois' very proper household, he turns the place into a shambles, seduces Lastingois' wife (Marcelle Hainia), and, after he strikes it rich in the lottery, marries the family's gold-digging maid (Severine Lerczynska). He is then faced with the choice of living as a socially responsible adult in a tuxedo or reasserting his own independence. Told in Renoir's characteristically liberating realist humanist manner, the story is immeasurably enhanced by Simon's extraordinary portrayal of Boudu. As Renoir has written: "Everything that an actor can be in a film, Michel Simon is in BOUDU. Everything!" Remade in 1986 as DOWN AND OUT IN BEVERLY HILLS, starring Nick Nolte.

BOUND FOR GLORY

1976 147m c ★★★½
Biography PG
UA

David Carradine *(Woody Guthrie)*, Ronny Cox *(Ozark Bule)*, Melinda Dillon *(Mary Guthrie)*, Gail Strickland *(Pauline)*, John Lehne *(Locke)*, Ji-Tu Cumbuka *(Slim Snedeger)*, Randy Quaid *(Luther Johnson)*, Elizabeth Macey *(Liz Johnson)*, Allan Miller *(Agent)*

p, Robert F. Blumofe, Harold Leventhal; d, Hal Ashby; w, Robert Getchell (based on the autobiography of Woody Guthrie); ph, Haskell Wexler (DeLuxe Color); ed, Robert C. Jones, Pembroke J. Herring

A moving, brilliantly photographed picture that portrays the legendary eccentric folksinger Woody Guthrie in a trip across Depression-era America. Carradine is memorable as the penniless Okie who rides a train to California but is stopped at the border because the state is having difficulty providing for those that have arrived already. Carradine sneaks across the border and meets Quaid, and the two team up to look for work. Cox is an Ozark folk singer who periodically visits the labor camps to lighten the load of these poor men's lives. At one of the meetings, Carradine joins in the singing and Cox is so impressed that he gets him a job on the radio. Success is almost immediate, but Guthrie's social conscience compels him to use the radio as a political organ for recounting the travails of the farm workers he knows so intimately. He is told to cut out the politicking or leave. He chooses to be fired. Later he gets offered a chance to play the big time at Hollywood's Coconut Grove provided that he'll commercialize his work. No surprises here. He hits the road, hoping to bring the message of his music to people he meets along the way.

This is a superior biopic. Viewers get to see Guthrie warts and all. That easily half the audience is too young to know who he was should not matter. This is the story of an artist with deeply held political principles, a remarkable quality in any age. At 147 minutes, this film could lose a quarter of an hour or more with no loss to the drama.

Haskell Wexler proves again that he is a master of evocative cinematography as he uses the camera to its best advantage in every frame of this Hal Ashby directed film. Robert Getchell adapted Guthrie's autobiography for the screenplay but Ashby and his editor made extensive contributions. Nominated for six Academy Awards including Best Picture, Best Screenplay, Best Film Editing and Best Costume Design. It took home Oscars for Best Adapted Score and Best Cinematography.

BOUNTY, THE
1984 132m c   ★★½
Adventure/Historical   PG/15
Bounty (U.K.)

Mel Gibson (Fletcher Christian), Anthony Hopkins (Lt. William Bligh), Laurence Olivier (Adm. Hood), Edward Fox (Capt. Greetham), Daniel Day Lewis (Fryer), Bernard Hill (Cole), Philip Davis (Young), Liam Neeson (Churchill), Wi Kuki Kaa (King Tynah), Tevaite Vernette (Mauatua)

p, Bernard Williams; d, Roger Donaldson; w, Robert Bolt (based on the novel Captain Bligh and Mr. Christian by Richard Hough); ph, Arthur Ibbetson (Technicolor); ed, Tony Lawson; m, Vangelis; prod d, John Graysmark; art d, Tony Reading; fx, John Stears; chor, Terry Gilbert; cos, John Bloomfield

This is at least the fourth film version of the historical incident that occurred in 1789, when sailors of the British Royal Navy seized control of their ship, the Bounty, from Captain Bligh and set him and a few loyal crewmen adrift in an open boat. The mutineers eventually stumbled across the obscure Pitcairn Island where they built a settlement that was not discovered for many years and remains inhabited to this day by the descendants of those mutineers and their Polynesian mates. The film opens as Bligh (played by Hopkins) appears before a naval board in London, chaired by Admiral Hood (Olivier). As the story unrolls in flashback, Bligh and first mate Fletcher Christian (Gibson) set off for the South Seas to bring back breadfruit. They finally reach Tahiti after a long and harrowing voyage. Consequently the crew is in no hurry to leave. Christian has fallen in love with a beautiful native girl and offers no assistance in whipping the crew back into shape. Bligh grows increasingly harsh in his attempts to restore discipline. This is the first time that a reasonably balanced version of this story has reached the screen, portraying Bligh as a competent sailor and commander whose personality flaws make the conflict between him and his crew inevitable.

Anthony Hopkins gets to give his vocal cords a good workout but the normally charismatic Gibson is surprisingly bland and wishy-washy. The closeup-heavy direction seems haphazard and the film never achieves the epic sweep it seems to desire. The script is condensed from David Lean collaborator (screenwriter on LAWRENCE OF ARABIA, DOCTOR ZHIZAGO, RYAN'S DAUGHTER) Robert Bolt's scripts for two aborted mutiny-on-the-Bounty projects. The production design and values are excellent.

BOWERY, THE
1933 92m bw   ★★★½
Drama   /A
20th Century

Wallace Beery (Chuck Connors), George Raft (Steve Brodie), Jackie Cooper (Swipes McGurk), Fay Wray (Lucy Calhoun), Pert Kelton (Trixie Odbray), George Walsh (John L. Sullivan), Oscar Apfel (Mr. Herman), Harold Huber (Slick), Fletcher Norton (Googy Cochran), John Kelly (Lumpy Hogan)

p, Darryl F. Zanuck, William Goetz, Raymond Griffith; d, Raoul Walsh; w, Howard Estabrook, James Gleason (based on the novel Chuck Connors by Michael L. Simmons and Bessie Roth Solomon); ph, Barney McGill; ed, Allen McNeil; m, Alfred Newman; art d, Richard Day

A rousing, two-fisted action movie about two friendly rivals, Steve Brodie (George Raft) and Chuck Connors (Wallace Beery). Beery owns a glittering saloon on the Bowery and takes care of kid Jackie Cooper on the side. Raft plays the dapper daredevil who reportedly jumped off the Brooklyn Bridge to make a name for himself. The two men and their gangs—groups of hooligans who provide muscle for their political organizations and social clubs—are in constant competition. The blustering, pompous Beery befriends the homeless, poverty-stricken Fay Wray, but the slick-haired Raft soon wins her heart. Angered and jealous, Beery schemes to exploit Raft's enormous ego, daring him to do something spectacular to impress Wray. He challenges Raft to jump off the Brooklyn Bridge. If he makes the leap and survives, he will win Wray and the saloon. Action-packed complications ensue.

The films of famed action filmmaker Walsh are noted for thier masculine ethos and accelerated pace. Every scene in THE BOWERY bustles with a jocular belligerence befitting the wild and wooly Gay Nineties in New York City. This was producer Darryl F. Zanuck's first film for Fox as its production chief. It was a hit at the box office and cemented his position at the studio.

BOY FRIEND, THE
1971 108m c   ★★★½
Musical   G/U
MGM (U.K.)

Twiggy *(Polly Browne)*, Christopher Gable *(Tony Brockhurst)*, Moyra Fraser *(Madame Dubonnet)*, Max Adrian *(Max)*, Bryan Pringle *(Percy)*, Catherine Wilmer *(Lady Brockhurst)*, Murray Melvin *(Alphonse)*, Georgina Hale *(Fay)*, Sally Bryant *(Nancy)*, Vladek Sheybal *(De Thrill)*

p, Ken Russell; d, Ken Russell; w, Ken Russell (based on a play by Sandy Wilson); ph, David Watkin (Metrocolor); ed, Michael Bradsell; art d, Simon Holland; chor, Christopher Gable, Terry Gilbert, Gillian Gregory; cos, Shirley Russell

Ken Russell's dizzy, affectionate homage to 1930s musicals and Busby Berkeley remains his best film. Twiggy is the assistant stage manager who gets her big chance when star Glenda Jackson hurts her ankle. "Come back a star," the director tells her, and that's just what she does. (The same line was spoken by Warner Baxter to Ruby Keeler in 42ND STREET.) Russell's bombastic direction has never looked so right. Musical numbers (the film's song score received an Oscar nomination) are uniformly well done, and include "I Could Be Happy", "The Boy Friend", "Won't You Charleston With Me?", "Fancy Forgetting", "Sur La Plage", "A Room In Bloomsbury", "Safety In Numbers", "It's Never Too Late To Fall In Love", "Poor Little Pierette", "Rivera", "The You Don't Want To Play With Me Blues" (Sandy Wilson), "All I Do Is Dream Of You", "You Are My Lucky Star" (Nacio Herb Brown, Arthur Freed) and "Any Old Iron" (Charles Collins, E.A. Shepherd, Fred Terry).

THE BOY FRIEND is a sincere celebration of the musical from a camp point of view. And let it be said Russell discovered Tommy Tune many years before Broadway did.

BOY MEETS GIRL

1985   100m   bw   ★★★
Drama   /18
Abilene   (France)

Denis Lavant *(Alex)*, Mireille Perrier *(Mireille)*, Carroll Brooks *(Helen)*, Elie Poicard *(Bernard)*, Maite Nahyr *(Maite)*, Christian Cloarec *(Thomas)*, Hans Meyer *(Astronaut)*, Anna Baldaccini *(Florence)*, Jean Duflot *(Bouriana)*, Frederique Charbonneau *(Interpreter)*

p, Patricia Moraz; d, Leos Carax; w, Leos Carax; ph, Jean-Yves Escoffier; ed, Nelly Meunier, Francine Sandberg; m, Jacques Pinault

This promising second feature from young French director Leos Carax (his first was LANGUE PENDUE) plays off the old Hollywood-style "boy meets girl" romance, but here he gives it an ominous twist. The setting is a dark, black-and-white Paris, where both Denis Lavant and Mireille Perrier lead aimless, unhappy existences. Lavant, an aspiring filmmaker in his early 20s, falls into depression when his girlfriend runs off with his best friend. Perrier, as well, has been victimized in a failed romance with Elie Poicard. Having first become obsessed by Perrier's voice over an apartment intercom system, Lavant finally sees the suicidal girl walking along the Seine. Later, at a strangely posh party, Lavant and Perrier meet. Their discussion, which takes place at a kitchen table, is bizarre, humorous, and intensely dark, as the characters form a bond of dependency. They do not live happily ever after.

Beautifully photographed in slick black and white by Jean-Yves Escoffier, BOY MEETS GIRL draws on the French New Wave films of Jean-Luc Godard and Francois Truffaut. Carax's vision, however, is a far darker and less universally appealing one than that of his influences, relying mostly on the modern, nihilistic "punk" sensibility of the 1980s. While it often displays

the dark and frightening side of obsessive love, it suffers from a lack of depth. Aside from its few faults, BOY MEETS GIRL, which received showings at a number of film festivals (including New York and Chicago), revealed the young Carax as a promising new filmmaker.

BOY WHO COULD FLY, THE

1986   114m   c   ★★★
Fantasy   PG
Gary Adelson/FOX

Lucy Deakins *(Milly)*, Jay Underwood *(Eric)*, Bonnie Bedelia *(Charlene)*, Fred Savage *(Louis)*, Colleen Dewhurst *(Mrs. Sherman)*, Fred Gwynne *(Uncle Hugo)*, Mindy Cohn *(Geneva)*, Janet MacLachlan *(Mrs. D'Gregario)*, Jennifer Michas *(Mona)*, Michelle Bardeaux *(Erin)*

p, Gary Adelson; d, Nick Castle; w, Nick Castle; ph, Steven Poster, Adam Holender (Panavision, Deluxe Color); ed, Patrick Kennedy; m, Bruce Broughton; prod d, Jim Bissell; art d, Graeme Murray; fx, John Thomas; cos, Trish Keaton

The subject of human flight has been explored by filmmakers in several imaginative pictures, including Robert Altman's BREWSTER McCLOUD (1970) and Alan Parker's BIRDY (1984). THE BOY WHO COULD FLY is another variation on this idea, presented as a gentle and often-touching evocation of adolescent pains and joys. As the film opens, the recently widowed Charlene (Bonnie Bedelia) has moved into a new home with her 15-year-old daughter, Milly (Lucy Deakins), and 8-year-old son, Louis (Fred Savage). As the family struggles to adjust to the new surroundings, Milly becomes friendly with her autistic neighbor (Jay Underwood), a boy who believes he can fly.

Rich in many respects, THE BOY WHO COULD FLY is that rare sort of film that appeals to both adults and children without taking any feelings or perceptions for granted. Castle, directing from his own script, delicately interweaves the story's dark and light elements, letting things develop naturally. He builds his story on small, everyday experiences, wisely keeping many of his characters' major life crises off screen. The moments of fantasy are slowly worked into the story, carefully blended with the realistic elements and thus all the more believable. Special effects, although necessary, are kept to a minimum. This is a strikingly original story about human feelings.

BOYFRIENDS AND GIRLFRIENDS

(L'AMI DE MON AMIE)
1988   103m   c   ★★★★
Comedy   PG
Losange   (France)

Emmanuelle Chaulet *(Blanche)*, Sophie Renoir *(Lea)*, Eric Viellard *(Fabien)*, Francois-Eric Gendron *(Alexandre)*, Anne-Laure Meury *(Adrienne)*

p, Margaret Menegoz; d, Eric Rohmer; w, Eric Rohmer; ph, Bernard Lutic; ed, Maria-Luisa Garcia; m, Jean-Louis Valero

It is often in their simplicity that Eric Rohmer's films are most complex, and in BOYFRIENDS AND GIRLFRIENDS (the final entry in the director's six-part series, "Comedies and Proverbs") Rohmer has made his simplest film yet. Set in the suburb of Cergy-Pontoise—a pristine glass and concrete environment with man-made lakes—this ordinary comedy of manners becomes complex only when the characters, in their rage for chaos within the orderly Cergy-Pontoise, try to alter their lives. Blanche (Emmanuelle Chaulet) is a 24-year-old, seemingly conservative, lower-level administrator of cultural affairs. She has no friends in Cergy-Pontoise until she meets Lea (Sophie Renoir), an exotic-looking computer student who is a couple of years Blanche's junior. Lea lives a bohemian life with her boyfriend, Fabien (Eric Viellard). Despite the fact that she and Fabien have nothing in common—what she enjoys (dancing and partying) exhausts him, and what he enjoys (wind surfing) exhausts her—they remain together. Blanche, on the other hand, does enjoy Fabien's lifestyle, although she has her eye on Alexandre (Francois-Eric Gendron), a ladies' man in his early 30s. In Rohmer's world no one really loves the right person. Nonetheless the film ultimately offers a romantic optimism that represents a new dawn for Rohmer and serves as a fitting close to "Comedies and Proverbs." (In French; English subtitles.)

BOYS FROM BRAZIL, THE

1978 123m c   ★★★½
Thriller/War   R/18
FOX   (U.S./U.K.)

Gregory Peck (Josef Mengele), Laurence Olivier (Ezra Lieberman), James Mason (Eduard Seibert), Lilli Palmer (Esther Lieberman), Uta Hagen (Frieda Maloney), Rosemary Harris (Mrs. Doring), John Dehner (Henry Wheelock), John Rubinstein (David Bennett), Anne Meara (Mrs. Curry), Steve Guttenberg (Barry Kohler)

p, Martin Richards, Stanley O'Toole; d, Franklin J. Schaffner; w, Heywood Gould (based on the novel by Ira Levin); ph, Henri Decae (Deluxe Color); ed, Robert Swink; m, Jerry Goldsmith; cos, Anthony Mendleson

This fast-moving picture features a battle of wits between the "Angel of Death," Nazi war criminal Josef Mengele (Gregory Peck), and fictional Nazi hunter Ezra Lieberman (Laurence Olivier, his character seemingly based on real-life Nazi hunter Simon Wiesenthal), in a farfetched plot having to do with the cloning of Hitler. Mengele's plan is to harvest hundreds of young men (all of whom have been raised in environments nearly identical to the one that Hitler grew up in) in an attempt to replicate the Fuhrer's upbringing as well as his genetic structure. The picture barrels along for about 115 minutes, but then falls apart in a wildly ludicrous finale. The cast is great—including Peck, Olivier, James Mason, Denholm Elliott, and even Steve Guttenberg (in one of his first roles). The film is compelling, albeit pretty silly in its elaborate "what if?" plot mechanications.

BOYS TOWN

1938 96m bw   ★★★
Drama   /A
MGM

Spencer Tracy (Father Edward Flanagan), Mickey Rooney (Whitey Marsh), Henry Hull (Dave Morris), Leslie Fenton (Dan Farrow), Addison Richards (The Judge), Edward Norris (Joe Marsh), Gene Reynolds (Tony Ponessa), Minor Watson (The Bishop), Jonathan Hale (John Hargraves), Bobs Watson (Pee Wee)

p, John W. Considine, Jr.; d, Norman Taurog; w, John Meehan, Dore Schary (based on a story by Dore Schary, Eleanore Griffin); ph, Sidney Wagner; ed, Elmo Veron; m, Edward Ward; art d, Cedric Gibbons, Urie McCleary; fx, Slavko Vorkapich

One of the more overrated films of its era. Not surprisingly one of MGM tyrant Louis B. Mayer's favorite films, this sentimental wallow dramatizes the real-life story of Father Edward Flanagan, founder of the famous Boys Town for errant youths. What sounds like ideal "truth is stranger than fiction" material, with inspiration to boot, comes across as stilted, overly sanctimonious moraliz-

ing. Father Flanagan's efforts against incredible obstacles vanish with a magic flourish of the scriptwriter's pen, and the generally reliable Tracy, one of the most talented and engaging actors of his day, compounds these errors with a performance dripping with piety. Tracy always claimed that his Oscar for Best Actor here belonged to Flanagan (he even sent the priest his statuette); the Academy should have bypassed the actor entirely and simply donated the crockery to Flanagan for his humanitarian activities. The soft-focus closeups of the film's star weren't needed to soften Tracy's likably craggy features; they were there to canonize the film's hero with a phony cinematic halo. Director Taurog, a competent but unimaginative contract man, was chosen for this epic because of his past success with child actors. Credit the electrifying 18-year-old Mickey Rooney with lending some edge to a picture that is soft, soft, soft. Also highly effective is the genuinely sweet child actor Bobs Watson, able to turn on the tears without batting an eyelid. Too respectful of its subject matter, BOYS TOWN is well-crafted and smoothly paced, probably most entertaining for those who can down maple syrup without benefit of pancakes. Nominated for Best Picture and Best Director, the film won an Oscar for Best Original Story.

BOYZ N THE HOOD

1991 107m c   ★★★★
Drama   R/15
Both Inc./Columbia

Larry Fishburne (Furious Styles), Ice Cube (Doughboy), Cuba Gooding, Jr. (Tre Styles), Nia Long (Brandi), Morris Chestnut (Ricky Baker), Tyra Ferrell (Mrs. Baker), Angela Bassett (Reva Styles), Meta King (Brandi's Mom), Whitman Mayo (The Old Man), Hudhail Al-Amir (SAT Man)

d, John Singleton; w, John Singleton; ph, Charles Mills; ed, Bruce Cannon; m, Stanley Clarke; art d, Bruce Bellamy

Although many journalists represented BOYZ N THE HOOD to the public as a film responsible for incidents of gang violence at movie theaters across the US, John Singleton's debut feature is actually a low-key morality drama about the strained bonds of family and friendship in the midst of social disorder.

The film begins in South Central Los Angeles, circa 1984, where ten-year-old Tre Styles (Desi Arnez Hines II) is confronted with the violence of everyday life in the streets of his ghettoized, African-American neighborhood. After being entrusted by his divorced mother Reva (Angela Bassett) to her ex-husband Furious (Larry Fishburne), Tre receives moral guidance from his loving but disciplinarian father. Growing up he befriends the brothers who live across the street, bad-assed Doughboy and shy Ricky, who dreams of playing professional football. After Doughboy spends seven years in prison for juvenile crimes, the three are reunited during their last year of high school.

Tre (Cuba Gooding, Jr.) and Ricky (Morris Chestnut) are the inseparable good kids, while Doughboy (Ice Cube) leads the crew of bitter and combative boys in the 'hood. USC recruiters offer Ricky an athletic scholarship, while Tre and his girlfriend Brandi (Nia Long) discuss the possibility of getting married—after completing their college educations. But chaotic forces overwhelm even these best and brightest in their efforts to escape the terrors of their neighborhood.

"Increase the peace." The words which appear at the conclusion of BOYZ N THE HOOD ring out as a simple, intelligent, and urgent plea, befitting Singleton's powerful, unpretentious dramatization of life in a modern L.A. ghetto. Few recent Hollywood films have been more socially responsible, non-exploitative, and honestly caring than this modest but earnestly presented tragedy of urban life, written and directed by Singleton at the remarkable age of 23. He manages the tricky task of creating a story, characters and dialogue that translate into broad, human terms while also retaining the vitality and specificity of the African-American culture at the film's center.

Like fellow black filmmaker Spike Lee, Singleton fills his work with references to the particulars of black life: from little Tre's precocious lecture on Afrocentric history, to Furious's lessons about racial genocide and culturally biased IQ tests, to Brandi and Tre's destinations at historically black colleges Spelman and Morehouse. Yet such details are not merely flashed for show or fetishized as they often are in Lee's flamboyant works. Instead Singleton invests them with the development of characters and narrative. In this sense, BOYZ N THE HOOD finds its place within the best part of the Hollywood tradition, creating strong, believable characters with a memorable story to tell. The ensemble cast makes good on Singleton's true-to-life script, with particularly strong work performances by rap star-turned-actor Ice Cube as Doughboy and the underrated, understated Larry Fishburne as Furious Styles.

If BOYZ N THE HOOD has a notable fault, it is the way in which the film's positive figures—Furious, Tre, Brandi—are rendered overly virtuous. Countering long-held stereotypes about the fatherless black family, Singleton presents a nearly godlike father who steps in to raise a troubled child with discipline, love, wisdom and intelligence. The children he guides through the tortuous violence of a neighborhood under siege remain studious, chaste, obedient and nonviolent. But they are perpetually tested by fire, never obtaining their virtue easily. By presenting an authentic feel for life in the 'hood—with its constant drone of police helicopters and sounds of gunfire—Singleton convincingly illustrates how the bad boys become bad and how the good ones escape the same fate only with great difficulty.

While the film threatens to become preachy in its closing scenes, its creator makes it clear that an overtly social-message movie is exactly the sort needed in response to the social crisis addressed by BOYZ N THE HOOD.

BRAINSTORM

1965 105m bw   ★★★
Thriller   /15
WB

Jeffrey Hunter *(Jim Grayam)*, Anne Francis *(Lorrie Benson)*, Dana Andrews *(Cort Benson)*, Viveca Lindfors *(Dr. E. Larstadt)*, Stacy Harris *(Josh Reynolds)*, Kathie Browne *(Angie DeWitt)*, Phillip Pine *(Dr. Ames)*, Michael Pate *(Dr. Mills)*, Robert McQueeney *(Sgt. Dawes)*, Strother Martin *(Mr. Clyde)*

p, William Conrad; d, William Conrad; w, Mann Rubin (based on a story by Larry Marcus); ph, Sam Leavitt (Panavision); ed, William Ziegler; m, George Duning

---

Creepy yet contrived suspense film stars Hunter as a young scientist who saves distraught Francis from committing suicide. The pair fall in love, but Francis' rotten husband Andrews (who drove her to the brink of suicide in the first place) digs up the file on Hunter's earlier mental instability. He exacts his revenge by framing the scientist for obscene phone calls and other misdeeds so as to create the impression that he's cracking up again. Hunter and Francis retaliate with a plot to murder Andrews. Hunter expects to get a light sentence with an insanity defense since everyone is convinced he's crazy anyway. Hunter figures that he

will be placed in a cushy mental institution, recover after a decent interval, and walk off scot-free into the waiting arms of Francis. Of course things don't work out as they plan. . . .

Fine cast directed by actor Conrad, TV's "Cannon," in a clever and taut visual style. Good, spare musical score by George Duning.

BRAVE BULLS, THE

1951 106m bw   ★★★★
Drama   /A
Columbia

Mel Ferrer *(Luis Bello)*, Miroslava *(Linda de Calderon)*, Anthony Quinn *(Raul Fuentes)*, Eugene Iglesias *(Pepe Bello)*, Jose Torvay *(Eladio Gomez)*, Charlita *(Raquelita)*, Jose Luis Vasquez *(Yank Delgado)*, Alfonso Alvirez *(Loco Ruiz)*, Alfredo Aguilar *(Pancho Perez)*, Francisco Balderas *(Monkey Garcia)*

p, Robert Rossen; d, Robert Rossen; w, John Bright (based on a novel by Tom Lea); ph, Floyd Crosby, James Wong Howe; ed, Henry Batista

---

Popular matador Ferrer begins to doubt his prowess in the ring after a near-fatal attack by a bull. Quinn, his cunning manager, convinces the champion to continue fighting, using the pretty Miroslava to bolster him. Unaware that Miroslava is Quinn's girlfriend, Ferrer begins to fall for her and tries to impress her by returning to the arena. After a tragic accident, Ferrer's world collapses and he loses all faith in himself. Labeled a coward by the press and the public, he nonetheless makes an appearance at younger brother Iglesias' first fight with a bull where Fate once again steps in to change his life.

An excellent film that takes on the difficult subjects of masculine pride, fear, jealousy, and death and handles them in an intelligent, humane manner. Quinn is outstanding as the tough and greedy, though vulnerable, manager who places his faith in Ferrer's spirit. Ferrer gives his bullfighter a complexity, integrity, and sadness that makes his shift from coward to hero all the more remarkable. The ambiance of Mexico is captured with a clear passion by director Rossen and talented cinematographer James Wong Howe. The photography of the bullfighting sequences effectively displays the hot, grimy, violent intensity of the situation.

Two sad notes are associated with this film: the intriguing Czechoslovakian actress Miroslava's suicide soon after the film's release and the victimization of director Rossen by the McCarthy anticommunist hearings. After it became labeled as the product of a "Red," the film never found its deserved audience.

BRAZIL

1985 131m c   ★★★½
Fantasy/Science Fiction   R/15
Terry Gilliam   (U.K.)

Jonathan Pryce *(Sam Lowry)*, Robert De Niro *(Tuttle)*, Katherine Helmond *(Ida Lowry)*, Ian Holm *(Kurtzmann)*, Bob Hoskins *(Spoor)*, Michael Palin *(Jack Lint)*, Ian Richardson *(Warrenn)*, Peter Vaughan *(Helpmann)*, Kim Greist *(Jill Layton)*, Jim Broadbent *(Dr. Jaffe)*

p, Arnon Milchan; d, Terry Gilliam; w, Terry Gilliam, Tom Stoppard, Charles McKeown; ph, Roger Pratt (Technicolor); ed, Julian Doyle; m, Michael Kamen; prod d, Norman Garwood; art d, John Beard, Keith Pain; fx, George Gibbs, Richard Conway; cos, James Acheson

---

Black humor dons its darkest robes in BRAZIL. Blindingly obtuse, excessively morose, the film is nevertheless dazzling in its inventive and massive sets and spectacular in its techniques. The theme is latter-day Orwell, well beyond 1984. The place could be anywhere in the future, where citizens of the regime live subterranean existences. One of these punctilious moles is Jonathan Pryce, a mundane statistician working in the Ministry of Information. He and millions of others work and live in a world crowded with a huge snakelike ductwork that heats, cools, and generally keeps the community going, when it works. A disaster, of sorts, is set off when a bug in the computer system causes everything to go haywire by altering the arrest record for a terrorist named Tuttle (Robert De Niro) to read Buttle. Pryce investigates the mistaken identity and discovers the girl of his fantasies, Kim Greist. But in doing so he brings the scrutiny of superiors upon himself. The art direction (which earned the film an Academy Award nomination, as did the screenplay) and the special effects are nothing less than stunning. The storyline is a bit confusing—fragmented through interjected scenes and dizzying cross-cutting—so that some viewers may not grasp the sense of it all until it's almost over, and perhaps that's the point. Perhaps not. The plot's weaknesses become painfully apparent about halfway through the film. Still, BRAZIL is a powerful work that is both bleakly funny and breathtakingly assured. Following TIME BANDITS with this film, Gilliam firmly established himself as a director possessing true vision and remarkable style; few fantasy-film directors can compare with him. Haunting, lyrical and trendsetting, BRAZIL—a black comedy that remains ahead of its time—is one of the most audacious fantasies ever made.

BREAK THE NEWS

1938   72m   bw   ★★★★
Musical/Comedy   /U
Trio   (U.K.)

Maurice Chevalier (Francois Verrier), Jack Buchanan (Teddy Enton), June Knight (Grace Gatwick), Marta Labarr (Sonia), Gertrude Musgrove (Helena), Garry Marsh (The Producer), Wallace Douglas (The Stage Manager), Joss Ambler (The Press Agent), Mark Daly (The Property Man), Gibb McLaughlin (The Superintendent)

p, Rene Clair; d, Rene Clair; w, Geoffrey Kerr (based on an adaptation by Carlo Rima of the novel La Mort En Fuite by Lois le Guriadec); ph, Philip Tannura; m, Van Phillips

Egocentric Knight, the star of a musical revue, has song and dance duo Buchanan and Chevalier fired from the line-up fearing that the talented pair may become more popular than she. Hoping to get back in the public eye, Buchanan and Chevalier decide to stage a spectacular publicity stunt. Buchanan mysteriously disappears, and Chevalier confesses to his murder. Knowing that his partner is hiding in a Balkan village and will miraculously reappear in time to save him, Chevalier patiently waits in his prison cell, glowing from the attention of the newspapers. Buchanan, however, gets mixed up with a group of revolutionaries who believe he is an enemy general and fails to make it to Chevalier's court appearance. Chevalier must begin taking the prospect of execution more seriously.

The always enchanting Buchanan and Chevalier are a pleasure to watch in this funny, energetic musical that features some hilariously suspenseful sequences. Although it may not rank with director Clair's French classics, this perfect piece of British entertainment holds its own special place. Songs include "It All Belongs to You" (Cole Porter, sung by Chevalier) and "We're Old Buddies" (Van Phillips, Jack Buchanan, sung by Chevalier and Buchanan).

BREAKER MORANT

1980   107m   c   ★★★
Drama/War   /A
South Australian Film   (Australia)

Edward Woodward (Lt. Harry Morant), Jack Thompson (Maj. J.F. Thomas), John Waters (Capt. Alfred Taylor), Bryan Brown (Lt. Peter Handcock), Rod Mullinar (Maj. Charles Bolton), Lewis Fitz-Gerald (Lt. George Witton), Charles Tingwell (Lt. Col. Denny), Vincent Ball (Lt. Ian (Johnny) Hamilton), Frank Wilson (Dr. Johnson), Terence Donovan (Capt. Simon Hunt)

p, Matt Carroll; d, Bruce Beresford; w, Bruce Beresford, Jonathan Hardy, David Stevens (based on a play by Kenneth Ross); ph, Don McAlpine (Panavision, Eastmancolor); ed, William Anderson; m, Phil Cunneen; cos, Anna Senior

A good court-martial drama in the old-fashioned style. Set during the Boer War—fought in South Africa between the descendants of Dutch colonists (the Boers) and the British during the years 1899-1902—BREAKER MORANT chronicles an obscure incident in 1901 when three Australian soldiers stationed in South Africa to assist the British were court martialed for executing enemy prisoners. Fighting what was, in essence, a guerrilla war, Lt. Harry "Breaker" Morant (Edward Woodward) ordered the executions acting under the orders of the British command. One of these prisoners turns out to have been a German citizen fighting alongside the Boers. Eager to maintain a good relationship with Germany, the British decide to make scapegoats of the Australians. Capably directed by Australian Bruce Beresford and well acted, BREAKER MORANT is a fascinating and satisfying experience. Unfolding his film in flashback during testimony at the trial, Beresford skillfully translates Kenneth Ross' play to the screen with an eye for historical accuracy.

BREAKFAST AT TIFFANY'S

1961   115m   c   ★★★★½
Drama   /PG
Paramount

Audrey Hepburn (Holly Golightly), George Peppard (Paul Varjak), Patricia Neal (2-E), Buddy Ebsen (Doc Golightly), Martin Balsam (O.J. Berman), Mickey Rooney (Mr. Yunioshi), Jose-Luis de Vilallonga (Jose da Silva Perriera), John McGiver (Tiffany's Clerk), Dorothy Whitney (Mag Wildwood), Stanley Adams (Rusty Trawler)

p, Martin Jurow, Richard Shepherd; d, Blake Edwards; w, George Axelrod (based on the novella by Truman Capote); ph, Franz Planer (Technicolor); ed, Howard Smith; m, Henry Mancini; cos, Edith Head

Capote's novella comes to glorious if slightly sentimentalized onscreen life as Hepburn gambols through the film portraying the fey, ever-charming Holly Golightly. We first meet our heroine leaving a sleek limousine early one morning in Manhattan to walk up to Tiffany's window, munching on a sweetroll while quietly contemplating the array of jewels on display. Peppard, never again quite so appealing, is Paul, the upstairs neighbor both intrigued and puzzled by Holly's errant behavior: throwing all-night bashes for dozens of friends one moment, a lonely, neurotic hermit the next. Also mysterious are her visits to an imprisoned ganglord (Reed) and to nightclub powder rooms, from which she emerges with $50 in cash each time. Paul, too, has a puzzling relationship with a wealthy woman (Neal) which prevents his growing love for Holly from flowering. Finally, though, answers come in the form of Doc (Ebsen), a visitor from rural Texas who reveals some of the truth behind Holly's surface sophistication.

The film is wonderfully cast from the word go, with the exception of Rooney in the one-note role of a Japanese neighbor driven to frenzy by Holly's noisy soirees. Balsam, as Holly's agent, offers a significant insight into his client's personality midway through the film when he notes: "She's a phony, all right, but a *real* phony." Amusingly helmed by director Edwards, romantic to the *n*th degree, and likely to disappoint only those devoted to Capote's novel, BREAKFAST AT TIFFANY'S is one of the great New York films, swathing the city in a mystique of dewy love and glossy chic. The song, "Moon River," memorably crooned by Hepburn, won an Oscar and went on to become a popular favorite. Mancini's perhaps overgenerous score also won, and the film copped other nominations for Hepburn, the screenplay, and art direction. Despite her "kept woman" status, Hepburn's free-spirited Holly stands as a notable precursor to what would later be called "the '60s woman".

BREAKFAST CLUB, THE

1985 97m c ★★★
Drama R/15
A&M

Emilio Estevez (*Andrew Clark*), Paul Gleason (*Richard Vernon*), Anthony Michael Hall (*Brian Johnson*), John Kapelos (*Carl*), Judd Nelson (*John Bender*), Molly Ringwald (*Claire Standish*), Ally Sheedy (*Allison Reynolds*), Perry Crawford (*Allison's Father*), Mary Christian (*Brian's Sister*), Ron Dean (*Andy's Father*)

p, Ned Tanen, John Hughes; d, John Hughes; w, John Hughes; ph, Thomas Del Ruth (Panavision, Technicolor); ed, Dede Allen; m, Keith Forsey, Gary Chang; prod d, John W. Corso; fx, Bill Schirmer; chor, Dorain Grusman; cos, Marilyn Vance, Christian Zamiata

Of the plethora of teen-based films released in 1985, THE BREAKFAST CLUB stands as one of the best, but it's still not exactly a shining example of the genre. Set in suburban Chicago, the film features five high school students from different social backgrounds who must spend a Saturday sitting in the school library as punishment for various infractions. Estevez, a star wrestler, is the jock; Ringwald portrays a rich, spoiled "princess"; Hall is a nerdy "brain;" Sheedy plays an introverted loner; and Nelson is a rebellious punk. Nelson fixes the library doors so they will remain closed, giving the students a little privacy. Confronting their values head on, with an articulate and sarcastic verbal assault, Nelson works on the others until they slowly begin talking with one another. THE BREAKFAST CLUB, paradoxically, is one of the few teen-oriented films that truly addresses the troubles of its characters, yet it falters in dealing with the issues raised. Director-writer Hughes, though he gives the material a sense of fun and achieves several moments of genuine warmth, too often panders to obvious cliches, stereotypes, and easy answers, and throws in the near-obligatory rock video as well. His cast, on the other hand, is a fine ensemble that infuses the material with the reality that Hughes's script often misses.

BREAKING AWAY

1979 100m c ★★★★
Comedy/Sports PG
FOX

Dennis Christopher (*Dave Stohler*), Dennis Quaid (*Mike*), Daniel Stern (*Cyril*), Jackie Earle Haley (*Moocher*), Barbara Barrie (*Mrs. Stohler*), Paul Dooley (*Mr. Stohler*), Robyn Douglass (*Katherine*), Hart Bochner (*Rod*), Amy Wright (*Nancy*), Peter Maloney (*Doctor*)

p, Peter Yates; d, Peter Yates; w, Steve Tesich; ph, Matthew F. Leonetti (Deluxe Color); ed, Cynthia Sheider; m, Patrick Williams; cos, Betsy Cox

A delightful "sleeper". Set in Bloomington, Indiana, and nominated for an Oscar for Best Picture (it lost to KRAMER VS. KRAMER), BREAKING AWAY is a very funny and touching story about love, growing up, bicycle racing, and class consciousness. Dave Stohler (Christopher) and three of his friends (Quaid, Stern, and Haley) are recent high-school graduates. More importantly, in the eyes of nearby Indiana University students, they are "cutters"—declasse Bloomington townies, so named because many of the locals earn their living cutting rock in limestone quarries. For a time, Stohler, an avid bicycle racer, immerses himself in an alternative identity, pretends to be Italian, and does his best to woo a college coed. After a team of real Italian bicycle racers comes to town and treats Stohler horribly, he discards his false identity but not his desire to prove himself the equal of the college students. He and his cutter buddies (who barely know one end of a racing bicycle from another) enter the university's "Little 500" bicycle race with suspenseful but not-so-surprising results at the film's uplifting finish. Tesich won an Oscar for his amusing screenplay; Barrie, as Christopher's mother, was nominated for Best Supporting Actress; composer Williams and director Yates also received nominations from the Academy. The four young leads all deliver excellent performances, as does Dooley (unjustly overlooked by the Academy) as Dave's father. Cyclists of the world, unite! You have nothing to lose but your chains!

BREAKING THE SOUND BARRIER

1952 115m bw ★★★
Drama /U
BLPA (U.K.)

Ralph Richardson (*John Ridgefield*), Ann Todd (*Susan Garthwaite*), Nigel Patrick (*Tony Garthwaite*), John Justin (*Phillip Peel*), Dinah Sheridan (*Jess Peel*), Joseph Tomelty (*Will Sparks*), Denholm Elliott (*Christopher Ridgefield*), Jack Allen (*Windy Williams*), Ralph Michael (*Fletcher*), Vincent Holman (*ATA Officer*)

p, David Lean; d, David Lean; w, Terence Rattigan; ph, Jack Hildyard; ed, Geoffrey Foot; m, Malcolm Arnold; art d, Joseph Bato, John Hawkesworth

Richardson, in his understated way, is powerful, if not frightening, as an airplane manufacturer obsessed with breaking the sound barrier. To that end he sends aloft his son-in-law, who is killed. But Richardson continues to send pilot after pilot to achieve what American test pilot Chuck Yaeger had already done secretly. Not one of director Lean's greatest, the film's semi-documentary style is one of its greatest assets, while its rather dull stiff-upper-lip dramatic sequences are the largest drawback. None of the talented cast members other than Richardson gets much chance to make an impression. The production's technical achievements, however, are considerable, and the emphasis on the aircrafts themselves and the incredible strain placed on the pilots make for some genuinely exciting moments. Extremely well photographed, the film won an Oscar for Best Sound and was also nominated for Best Screenplay.

BREATHLESS

(A BOUT DE SOUFFLE)
1959   89m   bw   ★★★★★
Crime   /15
Imperia   (France)

Jean-Paul Belmondo *(Michel Poiccard/Laszlo Kovacs)*, Jean Seberg *(Patricia Franchini)*, Daniel Boulanger *(Police Inspector)*, Jean-Pierre Melville *(Parvulesco)*, Liliane Robin *(Minouche)*, Henri-Jacques Huet *(Antonio Berrutti)*, Van Doude *(Journalist)*, Claude Mansard *(Claudius Mansard)*, Michel Fabre *(Plainclothesman)*, Jean-Luc Godard *(Informer)*

p, Georges de Beauregard; d, Jean-Luc Godard; w, Jean-Luc Godard (based on an idea by Francois Truffaut); ph, Raoul Coutard; ed, Cecile Decugis, Lila Herman; m, Martial Solal; art d, Claude Chabrol

What Stravinsky's "La Sacre du Printemps" is to 20th-century music or Joyce's *Ulysses* is to the 20th-century novel, Godard's first feature, BREATHLESS, is to film. It stands apart from all that came before and has revolutionized all that followed. Dedicated to the B-movies of Hollywood's Monogram Pictures, the film's structure begins with the conventions of the gangster film and film noir and proceeds to fragment them in a manner which greatly influenced the style of subsequent filmic narration. Michel Poiccard, alias Laszlo Kovacs (Belmondo, not conventionally attractive but giving a very sexy and appealing performance), is an amoral, dangerously careless petty criminal who models himself after Bogart and becomes the subject of a police dragnet when he senselessly guns down a traffic cop. He tries every avenue possible to cash a check endorsed "for deposit only" and hides out in the apartment of young American student Patricia Franchini (Seberg, whose imperfect French and limited acting skills lend something impossibly right to her enigmatic charcter). The couple, especially Michel, seem to be falling fatefully in love, but Godard is not content to merely develop character. During an extended, remarkable bedroom scene, this classic existential pair discusses art and philosophy in a way which prefigures Godard's lengthier and more profound ruminations in later films. Resuming the story, Godard ends his film with several ambiguous twists and an unforgettable closeup of Seberg. Rather than tell his tale in a conventional manner, Godard uses nostalgia, humor, and brutality alike to create the cinematic equivalent of contemporary alienation. Quoting Hollywood affectionately, Godard is nevertheless more concerned with destroying previous film language and employing his own. He "jump cuts" with little concern for continuity and then dollies the camera for long, fluid takes. Some scenes have a documentary feel, while others are pure pulp fiction. As the title implies, Godard's philosophy is to leave the viewer breathless so that he may breathe new life into them. (Look for his cameo as an informer.)

BREATHLESS

1983   100m   c   ★★
Crime   R/18
ORION

Richard Gere *(Jesse)*, Valerie Kaprisky *(Monica)*, Art Metrano *(Birnbaum)*, William Tepper *(Paul)*, John P. Ryan *(Lt. Parmental)*, Lisa Jane Persky *(Salesgirl)*, Garry Goodrow *(Berrutti)*, Robert Dunn *(Sgt. Enright)*, James Hong *(Grocer)*, Eugene Lourie *(Dr. Boudreaux)*

p, Martin Erlichman; d, Jim McBride; w, Jim McBride, L.M. Kit Carson (based on a screenplay by Jean-Luc Godard and a story by Francois Truffaut); ph, Richard H. Kline (Deluxe Color); ed, Robert Estrin; m, Jack Nitzsche; prod d, Richard Sylbert; cos, J. Allen Highfill

Remaking a movie is always a dicey proposition. Remaking a classic is even dicier. This version of BREATHLESS? No dice. The original burst upon the scene in 1959 and blew us all away, and even though we've become somewhat used to its tricks, it can still suggest its original impact. Godard took big chances then with technique, content, and casting and it paid off in spades. The new BREATHLESS features Gere as the wanton criminal Jesse (the Jean-Paul Belmondo role) and Kaprisky as Monica (Jean Seberg's original part). This version follows Godard and Truffaut's story of Jesse's escalating crimes and his involvement with Monica, but pays far too much attention to it, whereas the point of any Godard film is not *what* is told but *how*. Rather than trying to recapture the France of the late 1950s, the talented director, Jim McBride (DAVID HOLZMAN's DIARY) was probably right to switch locations to 1980s Los Angeles and make both characters American. In an attempt to duplicate Godard's feel for contemporary culture, McBride also adds bizarre colors and more than a dozen pop tunes, but the attempt is only modestly successful. The gradually increasing use of violence is effective in an oddly cartoon-like sort of way, but all involved fail to really impress their own creative slant on the project. Gere gives a flashy and not uninteresting performance and shows off his body a lot; Kaprisky shows hers too, though she fails completely to make her character really compelling. In keeping with the tentativeness of the entire enterprise, the ending is one of the great cop-outs in modern moviedom.

BREWSTER'S MILLIONS

1945   79m   bw   ★★★★
Comedy   /PG
UA

Dennis O'Keefe *(Monty Brewster)*, Helen Walker *(Peggy Gray)*, Eddie "Rochester" Anderson *(Jackson)*, June Havoc *(Trixie Summers)*, Gail Patrick *(Barbara Drew)*, Mischa Auer *(Michael Michaelovich)*, Joe Sawyer *(Hacky Smith)*, Nana Bryant *(Mrs. Gray)*, John Litel *(Swearengen Jones)*, Herbert Rudley *(Nopper Harrison)*

p, Edward Small; d, Allan Dwan; w, Sig Herzig, Charles Rogers, Wilkie Mahoney (based on the novel by George Barr McCutcheon and the play by Winchell Smith and Byron Ongley); ph, Charles Lawton, Jr.; ed, Richard Heermance

Probably the best of the many filmings of the popular novel and stage play. O'Keefe portrays Monty Brewster, the young, handsome, happy-go-lucky soldier returning from the war to his girlfriend Peggy Gray (Walker). Upon arriving home, he is stunned to find that he has inherited an estate worth $8,000,000, with one catch, however: he must spend $1,000,000 in the span of two months or he gets nothing. Brewster promptly embarks on a whirlwind of spending, racing around town in an effort to divest himself of the money by investing in a flop musical show, a bankrupt banker, the stock market, the racetrack, and a jewel-loving society woman. He soon finds out that spending money isn't as easy as it seems. BREWSTER'S MILLIONS is a broad farce and comes across as such, providing laughs throughout. While the opening is somewhat slow and deliberate, once the plot is established this modestly budgeted production rockets along with one climax topping another. The always reliable and appealing Walker and Anderson provide sturdy support, and O'Keefe gives one of his best performances. Previously filmed in 1921 with Fatty Arbuckle, and in a 1935 British production with Jack Buchanan and Lili Damita, the story was resurrected as THREE ON A SPREE with Jack Watling in 1961 and in an abysmal 1985 effort starring Richard Pryor and John Candy under the original title, with Walter Hill directing. In that version Brewster had to spend $30 million in 30 days to collect $300 million. Talk about inflation!

BRIDE FOR SALE

1949 87m bw   ★★★½
Comedy   /A
Crest

Claudette Colbert (*Nora Shelly*), Robert Young (*Steve Adams*), George Brent (*Paul Martin*), Max Baer (*Litka*), Gus Schilling (*Timothy*), Charles Arnt (*Dobbs*), Mary Bear (*Miss Stone*), Ann Tyrrell (*Miss Swanson*), Paul Maxey (*Gentry*), Burk Symon (*Sitley*)

p, Jack H. Skirball; d, William D. Russell; w, Bruce Manning, Islen Auster (based on a story by Joseph Fields); ph, Joseph Valentine; ed, William Knudtson; art d, Albert S. D'Agostino, Carroll Clark

One of the last of the romantic comedies the delightful Colbert made uniquely her own. Nora Shelly (Colbert), an expert accountant working for Paul Martin (Brent), uses the company files as a database for finding the perfect, well-to-do husband. Paul discovers her plan, and, anxious to keep her on his staff, gets a museum curator friend (Young) to sweep Colbert off her feet and then drop her, teaching her the value of staying a single working woman. Naturally, Young can't help but fall in love with his unsuspecting victim. Colbert and Young display an affinity for the material and for each other that makes this screwball comedy an overlooked if minor treasure. Although he was no Cary Grant, Young makes himself a welcome presence here, displaying the easygoing style and wit that distinguished his best work in many films of the 1940s.

BRIDE OF FRANKENSTEIN, THE

1935 75m bw   ★★★★★
Horror   /PG
Universal

Boris Karloff (*The Monster*), Colin Clive (*Henry Frankenstein*), Valerie Hobson (*Elizabeth Frankenstein*), Elsa Lanchester (*Mary Shelley/The Bride*), O.P. Heggie (*The Hermit*), Una O'Connor (*Minnie*), Ernest Thesiger (*Dr. Septimus Pretorius*), Gavin Gordon (*Lord Byron*), Douglas Walton (*Percy Shelley*), E.E. Clive (*Burgomaster*)

p, Carl Laemmle, Jr.; d, James Whale; w, William Hurlbut, John Balderston (based on the novel by Mary Shelley); ph, John Mescall; ed, Ted J. Kent; m, Franz Waxman; art d, Charles D. Hall; fx, John P. Fulton

One of the seminal achievements of Hollywood cinema, this brilliant sequel to the original FRANKENSTEIN is one of the greatest films of its genre and remains a lasting tribute to the unique genius of director Whale. Asked to continue the tale of the monster and its maker, Mary Shelley (Lanchester) picks up approximately where FRANKENSTEIN left off, with the injured Dr. Frankenstein (Clive) being taken back to his castle to recover, while the monster (Karloff), also alive, wanders the countryside, wreaking havoc in its search for friendship. Enter the eccentric Dr. Pretorius (Thesiger), an alchemist who has also created artificial life. (An utterly delightful scene ensues when he shows off his miniatures.) Pretorius blackmails the reluctant

Frankenstein to aid him in creating a bride for the monster, which, in an incredible scene, they do. A splendid combination of gothic horror and impish wit, BRIDE OF FRANKENSTEIN is a Whale masterpiece. The film is an unforgettable visual experience with its expressionistic sets, costumes and makeup; striking special effects; chiaroscuro lighting and bold camerawork. Waxman's magnificent score adds greatly to the overall effect, from the villagers' march to the mock-love theme attending the monstrous couple's "courtship" to the wedding bells pealing as the bride is presented. The performances are equally superb, with Clive again striking just the right note of nervous hysteria, Karloff beautifully injecting a sense of touching humanity into the confused and angry monster, and charcter actors O'Connor, Heggie, Frye and E.E. Clive lending ace support. Lanchester is quite amazing as both the deceptively demure Mary Shelley and her marvelously appropriate manifestation in her story, the bride. Thesiger, though, really steals the film with his pithy, menacing and hilarious portrait of the waspish Dr. Pretorius. A film whose black humor and sense of self-parody made Mel Brooks's delightful send-up YOUNG FRANKENSTEIN quite unnecessary, BRIDE OF FRANKENSTEIN transcends even the excesses allowed by its genre to become one of the oddest and most memorable films ever made in America.

BRIDGE AT REMAGEN, THE

1969 116m c   ★★★★
War   M/PG
UA

George Segal (*Lt. Phil Hartman*), Robert Vaughn (*Maj. Paul Krueger*), Ben Gazzara (*Sgt. Angelo*), Bradford Dillman (*Maj. Barnes*), E.G. Marshall (*Brig. Gen. Shinner*), Peter Van Eyck (*Gen. Von Brock*), Matt Clark (*Col. Jellicoe*), Fritz Ford (*Col. Dent*), Tom Heaton (*Lt. Pattison*), Bo Hopkins (*Cpl. Grebs*)

p, David L. Wolper; d, John Guillermin; w, Richard Yates, William Roberts (based on a story by Roger Hirson); ph, Stanley Cortez (Deluxe Color); ed, William Cartwright; m, Elmer Bernstein; art d, Alfred Sweeney

As US forces move toward Germany, the Nazi high command orders the Remagen bridge destroyed. Realizing that this will cut off thousands of troops from safety in their homeland, German officer Paul Kreuger (Vaughn) delays action on the bridge's demolition. Meanwhile, the American offensive, spearheaded by a platoon led by Lt. Phil Hartman (Segal), closes in on Kreuger and the bridge. Deftly capturing the confusion and intensity of a single wartime moment, this underrated WWII film contains a number of tense battle scenes (with stuntwork supervised by Hal Needham) and balances visceral excitement with an understanding of the harsh realities of war. Segal contributes an excellent portrayal of a simple man who has difficulty sending men into a no-win situation, Vaughn is good as the equally scrupulous German commander, and, in a smaller role, Gazzara is a treasure as an especially sleazy GI. Veteran cinematographer Cortez's photography of the battle scenes is breathtaking, and he succeeds brilliantly in using the German countryside to create a particularly dark, haunting atmosphere. Though some of the film was shot in Czechoslovakia during the days before the Prague Spring, the production moved to Italy when Soviet tanks rolled in.

BRIDGE ON THE RIVER KWAI, THE

1957 161m c   ★★★★★
War   /PG
Columbia

William Holden *(Shears)*, Alec Guinness *(Col. Nicholson)*, Jack Hawkins *(Maj. Warden)*, Sessue Hayakawa *(Col. Saito)*, James Donald *(Maj. Clipton)*, Geoffrey Horne *(Lt. Joyce)*, Andre Morell *(Col. Green)*, Peter Williams *(Capt. Reeves)*, John Boxer *(Maj. Hughes)*, Percy Herbert *(Grogan)*

p, Sam Spiegel; d, David Lean; w, Michael Wilson (uncredited), Carl Foreman (uncredited), Pierre Boulle (based on his novel); ph, Jack Hildyard (CinemaScope, Technicolor); ed, Peter Taylor; m, Malcolm Arnold

This intelligent and exciting WWII tale, masterfully helmed by Lean (at the start of his "epic" period), features a splendid performance from Guinness as Col. Nicholson, a British officer who has surrendered with his regiment to the Japanese in Burma in 1943. Martinet Nicholson insists that his men conduct themselves by the book and flatly refuses to cooperate with the equally dutiful Japanese commander, Col. Saito (Hayakawa, in an equally marvelous performance). When Saito insists that the British prisoners construct an elaborate bridge over the gorge of the River Kwai, Nicholson refuses to permit his officers to work side-by-side with the enlisted men, citing the Geneva Convention. After a series of incidents including torture and negotiations, Nicholson suddenly becomes determined to build the best bridge possible, thereby restoring his men's morale *and* providing a shining example of British rectitude. Meanwhile, Shears (Holden), an American, escapes from the prison camp and makes his way to Australia, where he impersonates an officer to obtain the privileges of rank. Major Warden (Hawkins), the British officer in charge of guerrilla operations, uncovers Shears' duplicity and sends him back to the jungle prison to destroy the bridge Nicholson and his men are so frantically attempting to complete. Lean aptly juxtaposes action sequences with a psychological examination of the folly of war, emphasizing its many ironies (brought home most forcefully at the explosive finale). Adapting his own novel, Boule retained the terse, tough dialogue and black humor of the original—both of which find their most obvious expression in Holden's cowardly wise-guy character. Based on fact, the film stands as one of the finest war films ever. Stunningly photographed and featuring a theme guaranteed to keep you whistling, THE BRIDGE ON THE RIVER KWAI won seven Oscars, including Best Picture, Actor (Guinness), and Director, as well as awards for writing, editing, cinematography, and music.

BRIDGE TOO FAR, A

1977   176m   c   ★★½
War   PG/15
UA   (U.K.)

Dirk Bogarde *(Lt. Gen. Browning)*, James Caan *(Sgt. Dohun)*, Michael Caine *(Lt. Col. Vandeleur)*, Sean Connery *(Maj. Gen. Urquhart)*, Edward Fox *(Lt. Gen. Horrocks)*, Elliott Gould *(Col. Stout)*, Gene Hackman *(Maj. Gen. Sosabowski)*, Anthony Hopkins *(Lt. Col. John Frost)*, Hardy Kruger *(Gen. Ludwig)*, Laurence Olivier *(Dr. Spaander)*

p, Joseph E. Levine, Richard Levine, Michael Stanley-Evans; d, Richard Attenborough; w, William Goldman (based on the book by Cornelius Ryan); ph, Geoffrey Unsworth (Panavision, Technicolor); ed, Anthony Gibbs; m, John Addison; cos, Anthony Mendleson

A movie too long. A BRIDGE TOO FAR tells the true story of a WWII military blunder that cost many lives and, in the end, meant little to the war effort. Field Marshal Montgomery and General Eisenhower planned to drop 35,000 Allied troops into Holland to secure the six bridges leading to Germany, after which

a British force was to speed through Belgium to the last bridge at Arnhem. From there, the two groups were to smash into the Ruhr area and crush the already damaged factories of the German war effort. Murphy's Law acted up on a massive scale: foul weather, poor judgment, panic, and bad luck all took their toll, and the operation (code-named "Market Garden") was a total disaster. A BRIDGE TOO FAR is not a *total* disaster, but it does suggest that the curses hanging over certain historical debacles should perhaps be heeded by Hollywood filmmakers. Running three squirming hours and casting a dozen top stars in what are in some cases little more than cameos prove effective as sure ways to annoy an audience. (Gould's performance, for instance, comprises little more than his uttering "Shit!" as a bridge is blown up before his eyes.) A thoroughly disappointing and overproduced picture, A BRIDGE TOO FAR is nevertheless technically impressive and its sheer scope may interest hardcore warmongers. Screenwriter Goldman has also injected a handful of character touches which lend an occasional burst of humanity and intimacy to this otherwise overly indulgent behemoth.

BRIDGES AT TOKO-RI, THE

1954   102m   c   ★★★★
War   /U
Paramount

William Holden *(Lt. Harry Brubaker, USNR)*, Fredric March *(Rear Adm. George Tarrant)*, Grace Kelly *(Nancy Brubaker)*, Mickey Rooney *(Mike Forney)*, Robert Strauss *(Beer Barrel)*, Charles McGraw *(Cmdr. Wayne Lee)*, Keiko Awaji *(Kimiko)*, Earl Holliman *(Nestor Gamidge)*, Richard Shannon *(Lt. Olds)*, Willis Bouchey *(Capt. Evans)*

p, William Perlberg; d, Mark Robson; w, Valentine Davies (based on a novel by James Michener); ph, Loyal Griggs; ed, Alma Macrorie; m, Lyn Murray; art d, Hal Pereira, Henry Bumstead; cos, Edith Head

A gripping psychological study of war's effects, starring Holden as Lt. Harry Brubaker, a family man called back to active duty who feels he has already done enough for his country in WW II and resents the Korean War's intrusion on his life with wife Nancy (Kelly) and their kids. Still a military man, however, Brubaker heeds the requests of his admiral (March) and doggedly goes about his duty as a pilot, spending long idle stretches aboard a battleship. The narrative drives toward the climactic bombing of the five bridges of Toko-Ri, which span a strategic pass in Korea's interior. Along the way Holden and Kelly share some effective and intimate scenes together, and several enjoyable lighter moments occur in buddy scenes with fellow pilots Mike Forney (Rooney) and Nestor Gamidge (Holliman). Based on the novel by James Michener, this exciting and thoughtful film features excellent acting all around and is visually quite compelling thanks to Oscar-winning special effects in the aerial scenes. Also nominated for Best Film Editing.

BRIEF ENCOUNTER

1945   86m   bw   ★★★★★
Romance   /PG
Cineguild/Eagle-Lion   (U.K.)

Celia Johnson *(Laura Jesson)*, Trevor Howard *(Alec Harvey)*, Cyril Raymond *(Fred Jesson)*, Stanley Holloway *(Albert Godby)*, Joyce Carey *(Myrtle Bagot)*, Everley Gregg *(Dolly Messiter)*, Margaret Barton *(Beryl Waters)*, Dennis Harkin *(Stanley)*, Valentine Dyall *(Stephen Lynn)*, Marjorie Mars *(Mary Norton)* p, Noel Coward; d, David Lean; w, Noel Coward, David Lean, Anthony Havelock-Allan (based on Noel Coward's play "Still Life"); ph, Robert Krasker; ed, Jack Harris; m, Sergei Rachmaninoff (Second Piano Concerto)

A touching, exquisitely handled film dealing with two ordinary people who accidentally fall in love. BRIEF ENCOUNTER is a unique and sometimes misunderstood film whose very British restraint has not endeared it to all comers, but which if anything makes the film more passionate as a result. The famous use of Rachmaninoff for the musical score, which would seem ridiculous and cliched in later screen romances, is quite perfect here, as overpowering emotions threaten the reliable dullness the leading couple relies upon every day to get by. Krasker's gleaming black-and-white cinematography, at once delicately stylized and the peak of low-key realism, enhances the story of Alec (Howard) and Laura (Johnson), a doctor and housewife respectively, both happily married to others, who journey into town each Thursday on routine business. Alec's removing a cinder from Laura's eye at the train station one week initiates a casual friendship which rapidly grows into something far stronger than either could have expected. The couple share moments of tenderness, gentle confidences and even wry humor (e.g. while watching shlock cinema, surely writer Noel Coward's sly dig at pablum for the masses). Proof positive that director Lean was far better in his small-scale first half-dozen films than in his later overblown epics, BRIEF ENCOUNTER brings Coward's lovingly detailed and observant script to glowing life. The cast is uniformly faultless, from the sharp comic counterpont of Carey, Holloway, and Gregg to the wonderful gentility Raymond brings to the role of Laura's husband. Center stage, though, properly belongs to the leading couple. In two screen creations to cherish, dashing newcomer Howard gives a brilliantly nuanced, ardent and touching performance, while the ordinary-looking, carefully mannered Johnson achieves a heartbreaking performance whose beauty ranks with Garbo's CAMILLE.

BRIGADOON

1954 108m c ★★
Musical /U
MGM

Gene Kelly (Tommy Albright), Van Johnson (Jeff Douglas), Cyd Charisse (Fiona Campbell), Elaine Stewart (Jane Ashton), Barry Jones (Mr. Lundie), Hugh Laing (Harry Beaton), Albert Sharpe (Andrew Campbell), Virginia Bosier (Jean Campbell), Jimmie Thompson (Charlie Crisholm Dalrymple), Tudor Owen (Archie Beaton)

p, Arthur Freed; d, Vincente Minnelli; w, Alan Jay Lerner (based on the musical play by Alan Jay Lerner and Frederick Loewe); ph, Joseph Ruttenberg (CinemaScope, Ansco Color); ed, Albert Akst; art d, Cedric Gibbons, Preston Ames; chor, Gene Kelly

Possibly Minnelli's worst screen musical. Confined to an MGM soundstage, this adaptation of the Lerner and Loewe Broadway hit desperately needs air, creatively stifled as it is in practically every department. New Yorkers Jeff and Tommy (Johnson and Kelly) get lost in the Scottish highlands and stumble onto the village of Brigadoon on the one day every 100 years that it appears from out of the mists. The villagers, who sport the garb and manners of antiquity, are in a merry mood, and the Americans happily join in their dancing and festivities. Tommy is particularly enchanted when he falls for bonnie lass Fiona (Charisse). He then must decide whether to return to New York or remain with his love in the land of long ago. Tommy and Jeff do go back

to their urban existence, but eventually Tommy returns to Scotland, and such is the power of his love that the village materializes long enough for him to join Fiona in fantasyland forever.

One would like to see more dancing in BRIGADOON, though what's there is generally fine (especially a spirited routine to "I'll Go Home with Bonnie Jean"). Praise should also go to Johnson for doing a good job with his cynical, wisecracking role. Other than that, though, the pleasures of BRIGADOON are as fleeting as the village's centennial appearances. The sense of whimsy crucially needed to make this thing fly is nowhere to be found, and Minnelli seems to enjoy the stylized scenes of an obnoxious Manhattan more than the heather of the highlands. Kelly's patented good cheer is meagerly doled out and his exuberant energy seems to vanish into the Scottish ether. The somber, remote Charisse dances exquisitely but otherwise has all the appeal of plywood. Even the legendary score sounds a little flat. Nominated for three Academy Awards: Best Sound Recording, Best Costume Design and, inexplicably, Best Art Direction/Set Decoration.

BRIGHT VICTORY

1951 96m bw ★★★★
Drama
Universal

Arthur Kennedy (Larry Nevins), Peggy Dow (Judy Greene), Julie Adams (Chris Paterson), James Edwards (Joe Morgan), Will Geer (Mr. Nevins), Minor Watson (Mr. Paterson), Jim Backus (Bill Grayson), Joan Banks (Janet Grayson), Nana Bryant (Mrs. Nevins), Marjorie Crossland (Mrs. Paterson)

p, Robert Buckner; d, Mark Robson; w, Robert Buckner (based on the novel Lights Out by Baynard Kendrick); ph, William Daniels; ed, Russell Schoengarth; m, Frank Skinner; art d, Bernard Herzbrun, Nathan Juran

Kennedy is absolutely riveting in one of the most brilliant performances of his distinguished career. He plays Larry Nevins, a blinded WWII veteran who returns home and begins the arduous process of adapting both to civilian life and his new affliction. At first reluctant to leave the military hospital where he is recuperating, and later resisting the involved and tedious training necessary to equip himself for normal civilian life, the bitter veteran meets a patient nurse (the radiant Dow) who helps him overcome his fear of returning home. Once there, however, his next-door girlfriend (Adams) is embarrassed by his disability, and his parents (Geer and Bryant) feel helpless and inadequate around their son. In one devastating scene, a welcome-home party goes bust when Larry puts out a cigarette in a dish of food. After undergoing a great deal of agony and self-examination, Kennedy winds up with Dow, facing the future with no illusions. It's a bravura performance by Kennedy, one that justly garnered him an Oscar nomination for Best Actor (an Oscar that went to Humphrey Bogart for THE AFRICAN QUEEN), and it should not be missed. Look for Rock Hudson in a small role as an enlisted man. The picture was also nominated for Best Sound.

BRIGHTNESS

(YEELEN)
1988 106m c ★★★★
Fantasy /PG
Cisse/Government of Mali/CNC-UTA/WDR/Fuji (Mali)

Issiaka Kane (Nienankoro), Aoua Sangare (Attu), Niamanto Sanogo (Soma), Balla Moussa Keita (Peul King), Soumba Traore (Nianankoro's Mother), Ismaila Sarr (Djigui), Youssouf Tenin Cisse (Attu's Son), Koke Sangare (Komo Chief), Brehima Doumbia, Seyba M'Baye

p, Souleymane Cisse; d, Souleymane Cisse; w, Souleymane Cisse; ph, Jean-Noel Ferragut; ed, Dounamba Coulibaly, Andre Davanture, Marie-Catherine Miqueau, Jenny Frenck, Seipati N'Xumalo; m, Michel Portal, Salif Keita; fx, Frederic Duru, Nicos Metelopoulos; cos, Kossa Mody Keita

BRIGHTNESS is very likely the most highly praised African film made to date—a reflection both of the film's merit and of the West's lack of critical attention to Third World films. Boosted by a Special Jury Prize at the 1987 Cannes Film Festival and favorable receptions at the Berlin and New York Festivals, BRIGHTNESS fast became *the* film to see in 1988. Whatever artistic merit the film does or doesn't have (and some critics doubt that it is as great as many claim), it found an audience—an audience that, for the most part, left the film completely baffled and profoundly moved. Like the main character, the audience became involved in a search for knowledge and the hope of enlightment.

The film opens with a complicated written description of various mystical symbols and rituals of the Bambara tribe and a nutshell introduction to *Komo*—a science of the gods based on the elements of "nature" and key to understanding the greater thrust of the film. The story of a man's (Kane) search for his evil, all-powerful shaman father (Sanogo), the seemingly simple, episodic saga takes on elements of fantasy as its young hero acquires talismans which give him increasingly great magical powers. In a classic showdown we see not only the powers of good and evil finally confront each other, but also the inevitable conflict between father and son enacted on a mythic scale. We also see the embodiment of future generations as a young boy (played by producer-director-writer Cisse's son) literally discovers remnants of the conflict and figuratively acquires the knowledge of his ancestors. Marvelously photographed (the image of Kane and Sangare bathing under the waterfall is unforgettable) and perfectly acted by a cast of nonprofessionals (Sanogo, for example, was a real-life shaman), the production of BRIGHTNESS represents both a triumph over incredible odds (bad weather, financial woes, the death of actor Sarr) and a provocative, creative use by Cisse of indigenous folk mythology.

BRIGHTON BEACH MEMOIRS
1986   108m   c   ★★★
Comedy   PG-13/15
Rastar

Blythe Danner (Kate), Bob Dishy (Jack), Brian Drillinger (Stanley), Stacey Glick (Laurie), Judith Ivey (Blanche), Jonathan Silverman (Eugene), Lisa Waltz (Nora), Fyvush Finkel (Mr. Greenblatt), Kathleen Doyle (Mrs. Laski), Alan Weeks (Andrew)

p, Ray Stark; d, Gene Saks; w, Neil Simon (based on his play); ph, John Bailey (Panavision); ed, Carol Littleton; m, Michael Small; prod d, Stuart Wurtzel; art d, Paul Eads; cos, Joseph G. Aulisi

The time is 1937, and Eugene (Silverman) is a teenager living in the Coney Island area of Brighton Beach with his parents (Danner and Dishy), older brother Stanley (Drillinger), widowed aunt Blanche (Ivey) and her two daughters, Laurie (Waltz) and Nora (Glick). This septet raises endless possibilities for interplay, but the focus throughout is on Eugene and his twin passions: baseball and women. Unfortunately, there is no real direction to this

story—just a series of incidents, a lot of arguing, and many fewer laughs than we have come to expect from writer Simon. It was with this play and screenplay, however, that Simon crossed into new territory, forgoing the easy one-liner for a combination of pathos and gentle, heartfelt humor. Director Saks, who won a Tony for his stage direction, works in his typically fish-out-of-water fashion here, trying to put some air into a stagebound work, but much of the spontaneity of the theater version seems to have been supplanted by the mechanics of moviemaking. The acting by a very talented cast is generally quite good, even if Danner doesn't convince as an old-fashioned Jewish mother type. More of a nostalgic piece than a story, the film shows an attention to the specifics of the culture on display which has genuine if modest appeal.

BRIGHTON ROCK
1947   92m   bw   ★★★½
Crime   /PG
Boulting Bros.   (U.K.)

Richard Attenborough (Pinkie Brown), Hermione Baddeley (Ida Arnold), William Hartnell (Dallow), Carol Marsh (Rose Brown), Nigel Stock (Cubitt), Wylie Watson (Spicer), Harcourt Williams (Prewitt), Alan Wheatley (Fred Hale), George Carney (Phil Corkery), Charles Goldner (Colleoni)

p, Roy Boulting; d, John Boulting; w, Graham Greene, Terence Rattigan (based on the novel by Graham Greene); ph, Harry Waxman; ed, Frank McNally; m, Hans May

A brutal look at the British underworld—as seen through the amoral eyes of teenaged thug Pinkie Brown, played brilliantly by the 24 year-old Attenborough. In this adaptation of the popular Graham Greene novel, Pinkie heads a race track gang and commits a murder, using a pretty waitress (Marsh) as an alibi. Worried that she still might betray him, he marries the young woman, planning to kill her by driving her to suicide. His scheme eventually backfires in an ending which, though softened somewhat from Greene's original, still drips with cynical irony. A moody, well-acted film (Hartnell and Baddeley are particularly good), notable for bringing a new viciousness to British cinema (e.g. razor blade slashing). Strikingly handled by the Boulting brothers and still worth a look for its almost palpable sense of dread, the film can't quite recapture the impact it had upon its initial release.

BRIMSTONE AND TREACLE
1982   87m   c   ★★★½
Thriller   R/18
UA Classics   (U.K.)

Sting (Martin Taylor), Denholm Elliott (Thomas Bates), Joan Plowright (Norma Bates), Suzanna Hamilton (Patricia Bates), Mary McLeod (Valerie Holdsworth), Benjamin Whitrow (Businessman), Dudley Sutton (Stroller), Tim Preece (Clergyman)

p, Kenith Trodd; d, Richard Loncraine; w, Dennis Potter; ph, Peter Hannan (Technicolor); ed, Paul Green; m, Sting

Potter, author of *Pennies from Heaven* and TV's "The Singing Detective", confirms his standing as one of today's most interesting scriptwriters with this disturbing thriller. Sting stars as Martin Taylor, a con man so charming he can convince almost anyone that he's met them before. Thomas Bates (Elliott) sees through this ploy but falls victim to Taylor's larger schemes involving Bates's disabled daughter (Hamilton). Relying on psychological effect rather than violence, the picture is excruciatingly suspenseful, alternating goose bumps with nervous laughter in the tradition of Hitchcockian horror.

BRING ME THE HEAD OF ALFREDO GARCIA

1974   112m   c   ★★★★
Crime   R/18
UA

Warren Oates (Bennie), Isela Vega (Elita), Gig Young (Quill), Robert Webber (Sappensly), Helmut Dantine (Max), Emilio Fernandez (El Jefe), Kris Kristofferson (Paco), Chano Urueta (One-armed Bartender), Jorge Russek (Cueto)

p, Martin Baum; d, Sam Peckinpah; w, Gordon Dawson, Sam Peckinpah (based on a story by Frank Kowalski); ph, Alex Phillips, Jr.; ed, Garth Craven, Robbe Roberts, Sergio Ortega, Dennis Dolan; m, Jerry Fielding

When El Jefe (Fernandez), the head of a prominent Mexican family, learns the identity of the bounder responsible for his daughter's pregnancy, he offers a million dollars to the man who can bring him the head of the culprit, Alfredo Garcia. Two homosexual hit men (Young and Webber) working for Jefe enlist the aid of Bennie (Oates), a sleazy but good-natured bar owner, who convinces the pair that he can find Garcia. Learning from his hooker girlfriend Elita (Vega) that her former client Garcia is already dead, she and Bennie travel to the cemetery where Garcia is supposedly buried to cut off the corpse's head. Bennie successfully kills two motorcycle rapists along the way, but a rival Mexican gang appears and kills Elita, knocks Bennie out and steals the head. In a bloody confrontation Bennie massacres his rivals and then turns on his two gay partners and wipes them out too. All that remains is to turn in the prized head, though Bennie's final encounter with El Jefe also goes bloodily awry. One of the cinema's more perversely intriguing experiences, the film is either appreciated as a bizarre minor classic or denounced as a piece of trash. In the only film over which the director says he had complete control, Peckinpah creates a haunting vision of a loser's quest for love and meaning in a harsh, brutal world. Although his "philosophy" and methods do not appeal to everyone and are certainly open to criticism, Peckinpah attempts to use explicit violence as a means for exploring the brutality he sees as inherent in all men. A nihilistic depiction of an existential quest, the film benefits immeasurably from the presence of Oates in the leading role of a man driven obsessively in suicidal pursuit of self-respect and importance. The macabre scenes in the car where Bennie converses with the head as flies buzz around it are funny and telling. BRING ME THE HEAD OF ALFREDO GARCIA does have some sloppy photography, a few unintentionally humorous scenes, and an excess of Peckinpah's signature slow-motion violence, but it stands as one of Peckinpah's more daring films.

BRINGING UP BABY

1938   102m   bw   ★★★★★
Comedy   /U
RKO

Katharine Hepburn (Susan Vance), Cary Grant (David Huxley), Charlie Ruggles (Maj. Horace Applegate), May Robson (Aunt Elizabeth), Barry Fitzgerald (Mr. Gogarty), Walter Catlett (Constable Slocum), Fritz Feld (Dr. Fritz Lehman), Leona Roberts (Hannah Gogarty), George Irving (Alexander Peabody), Virginia Walker (Alice Swallow)

p, Howard Hawks; d, Howard Hawks; w, Dudley Nichols, Hagar Wilde (based on a story by Hagar Wilde); ph, Russell Metty; ed, George Hively; m, Roy Webb; art d, Van Nest Polglase, Perry Ferguson; fx, Vernon L. Walker; cos, Howard Greer

A delightful piece of utter absurdity and one of director Hawks' most inspired lampoons of the battle between the sexes. Hepburn and Grant are superb in this breathlessly funny screwball comedy with a plot that could have been hatched in a mental institution. She plays Susan Vance, an eccentric heiress whose dog (Asta of the "Thin Man" series) steals a bone from absentminded paleontologist David Huxley (Grant), the last he needs to complete his reconstruction of a dinosaur. David follows Susan to her Connecticut farm in search of the relic and runs smack into the authorities, the possible donor of $1 million to his museum, and a leopard named Baby who enjoys being serenaded with "I Can't Give You Anything but Love". Memorable moments abound throughout: Susan insistently playing David's ball at a golf game, which leads him further and further from his playing companion ("I'll be with you in a minute, Mr. Peabody!"); Susan's tricks with olives; Baby's encounter with a chicken coop; David facing Susan's elderly aunt (Robson) while wearing a frilly negligee ("I just decided to go gay all of a sudden!"); David caught in Susan's butterfly net (surely *not* the best way to catch a runaway leopard); Susan's aunt and cowardly big game hunter Maj. Applegate (Ruggles) deciding they need some exercise ("Shall we run?" "Yes, let's!"); Susan's imitation of a gangster's moll ("Hey flatfoot!")—the list could go on and on. Though Hepburn fans might not be used to seeing her essay such an atypically scatterbrained role, her marvelous timing and zany comic elan are wonderfully engaging. Grant, meanwhile, manages the near-impossible feat of being goofy, suave, dimwitted and sexy all at once. Among a brilliant supporting cast, Robson, Ruggles, Catlett, Feld and Fitzgerald are standouts, and the pace never flags for an instant. A barbed satire of masculinity, romance, wealth, psychiatry and authority, BRINGING UP BABY was, not too surprisingly, a box-office flop in its day, probably because it poked fun at the very conventions it employed. Enormously influential on later comedy writing, it is a milestone of film merriment.

BRINK OF LIFE

1960   83m   bw   ★★
Drama   /X
ToneFilm/Nordisk   (Sweden)

Eva Dahlbeck (Stina), Ingrid Thulin (Cecilia), Bibi Andersson (Hjordis), Barbro Hiort af Ornas (Brita), Erland Josephson (Anders), Max von Sydow (Harry), Gunnar Sjoberg (Doctor), Ann-Marie Gyllenspetz, Inga Landgre, Margareta Krook

p, Gosta Hammerback; d, Ingmar Bergman; w, Ingmar Bergman (based on a story by Ulla Isaksson); ph, Max Wilen; ed, Carl-Olov Skeppstedt

A lesser entry from a master director, BRINK OF LIFE details the trials and tribulations of three mothers in a maternity ward voicing their opinions about keeping and not keeping the child each is carrying. Rather gloomy and lacking in action—as with many Bergman films—the film has a rather surprising documentary look to it and is expertly acted, but ultimately chokes during its own confinement.

BROADCAST NEWS

1987   131m   c   ★★★½
Comedy/Romance   R/15
FOX

William Hurt *(Tom Grunick)*, Albert Brooks *(Aaron Altman)*, Holly Hunter *(Jane Craig)*, Robert Prosky *(Ernie Merriman)*, Lois Chiles *(Jennifer Mack)*, Joan Cusack *(Blair Litton)*, Peter Hackes *(Paul Moore)*, Jack Nicholson *(Bill Rorich, News Anchor)*, Christina Clemenson *(Bobby)*, Robert Katims *(Martin Klein)*

p, James L. Brooks, Penney Finkelman Cox; d, James L. Brooks; w, James L. Brooks; ph, Michael Ballhaus (Deluxe Color); ed, Richard Marks; m, Bill Conti; prod d, Charles Rosen; art d, Kristi Zea; cos, Molly Maginnis, Molly Maginnis

Blessed with a good script, BROADCAST NEWS examines the ethics of modern-day electronic journalism and the often frazzled emotions of a tightly knit group of workaholics who find that their personal and professional lives have become one and the same. Network news producer Jane Craig (Hunter) and her best pal, veteran correspondent Aaron Altman (Brooks), share not only the same high ethical standards, but a warm and goofy sense of humor. Although Jane considers Aaron her best friend, he pines for a more romantic relationship. Enter Tom Grunick (Hurt), a handsome, affable, but somewhat dim newscaster to whom Jane is attracted. Often touching, biting, and funny, BROADCAST NEWS is an entertaining film hoisted by the performances of its three leads. Hurt, in a rather odd change of pace, and newcomer Hunter display verve and skill and overcome the limitations of the somewhat annoying characters they play. In the seemingly lesser role of the one who stands by and suffers, however, Brooks provides the film's soul and many of its laughs to boot. Nicholson contributes a highly potent performance in a matter of moments as a smug, self-important New York anchorman and the rest of the supporting cast is uniformly fine. A more skillful director of actors than the camera, Brooks gives the script its full head and makes crystal clear the satirical point that appearances count for a great deal in the mass media. A film whose "TV movie" feel is at once incredibly appropriate and a notable drawback, BROADCAST NEWS is nevertheless worthy adult entertainment.

BROADWAY DANNY ROSE

1984   86m   bw   ★★★★
Comedy/Romance   PG
Rollins-Joffe

Woody Allen *(Danny Rose)*, Mia Farrow *(Tina Vitale)*, Nick Apollo Forte *(Lou Canova)*, Sandy Baron, Corbett Monica, Jackie Gayle, Morty Gunty, Will Jordan, Howard Storm, Jack Rollins

p, Robert Greenhut; d, Woody Allen; w, Woody Allen; ph, Gordon Willis; ed, Susan E. Morse; prod d, Mel Bourne; cos, Jeffrey Kurland

After making several more ambitious films, writer-director Allen returned to *terra firma* with BROADWAY DANNY ROSE, a charming comedy shot in black and white that mixes several varieties of the New Yorkers that Allen loves so well. The film begins with a group of Broadway types sitting at the Carnegie Delicatessen reminiscing about the career of Danny Rose (Allen), a two-bit agent who specializes in offbeat acts that no other agent will handle. His one regular client is Lou Canova (Forte), a lounge singer who drinks too much, weighs too much, and uses Rose to cover for him when he's off cheating on his wife with girlfriend Tina (an unusually animated performance by Farrow). When Canova gets a chance to perform at a better place

than the dives where he's been working, Rose has to pretend to be Tina's boyfriend, a move which gets him into a lot of trouble. Tina is supposedly engaged to a gangland figure, and the other mobsters, thinking that their pal has been cuckolded, begin chasing poor Danny all around the city. Although the film contains many of the great verbal jokes that are Allen's forte, the visual wit and the sentimental drama fall a bit short, leaving BROADWAY DANNY ROSE without the stature of a more profound work like MANHATTAN. Still, even less-than-classic Allen is better than none at all.

BROADWAY MELODY, THE

1929   102m   bw   ★★½
Musical
MGM

Anita Page *(Queenie)*, Bessie Love *(Hank)*, Charles King *(Eddie)*, Jed Prouty *(Uncle Bernie)*, Kenneth Thomson *(Jock)*, Edward Dillon *(Stage Manager)*, Mary Doran *(Blonde)*, J. Emmett Beck *(Babe Hatrick)*, Marshall Ruth *(Stew)*, Drew Demarest *(Turpe)*

d, Harry Beaumont; w, Sarah Y. Mason, James Gleason, Norman Houston (based on a story by Edmund Goulding); ph, John Arnold; ed, Sam S. Zimbalist; art d, Cedric Gibbons; chor, George Cunningham; cos, David Cox

First musical to win Academy Award reeks of mothballs, but is undeniably the basis of perhaps a hundred others. At least there's an old curiosity shoppe charm and a few classic tunes: "You Were Meant for Me" and the title tune (Brown and Freed—Freed would go on to head the musical production unit at MGM, the biggest of all time, and produce all the Garland classics, among many others), plus Cohan's "Give My Regards to Broadway". Surprisingly, a remake, TWO GIRLS ON BROADWAY, was inferior. Some sequences originally filmed in Technicolor, this was the first sound picture shown all over.

BROKEN BLOSSOMS

1936   78m   bw   ★½
Drama   /PG
Twickenham   (U.K.)

Dolly Haas *(Lucy Burrows)*, Emlyn Williams *(Chen)*, Arthur Margetson *(Battling Burrows)*, Gibb McLaughlin *(Evil Eye)*, Donald Calthrop *(Old Chinaman)*, Ernest Sefton *(Manager)*, Jerry Verno *(Bert)*, Bertha Belmore *(Daisy)*, Ernest Jay *(Alf)*, C.V. France *(High Priest)*

p, Julius Hagen; d, John Brahm; w, Emlyn Williams (based on the story "The Chink and the Child" by Thomas Burke and screenplay by D.W. Griffith); ph, Curt Courant

The old Brit stiff upper lip, but quivering like crazy here. Remake of Griffith's masterpiece was earmarked for failure, despite writing and acting of Williams. Griffith conferred with the company that perpetrated this remake, but had the good sense to bow out. The result is the story seems more maudlin than the silent version; it was far too dated for 1936, and only a very special actress could have made it work (Sylvia Sydney, maybe?). Instead, that's Dolly Haas, who later married famed caricaturist Al Hirshfeld, and sensibly settled down. You might be happier watching THE THREE STOOGES MEET HERCULES.

BROOD, THE

1979   91m   c   ★★★
Horror   R/18
New World   (Canada)

Oliver Reed *(Dr. Raglan)*, Samantha Eggar *(Nola)*, Art Hindle *(Frank)*, Cindy Hinds *(Candice)*, Nuala Fitzgerald *(Julianna)*, Henry Beckerman *(Barton Kelly)*, Susan Hogan *(Ruth)*, Michael McGhee *(Inspector Mrazek)*, Gary McKeehan *(Mike Trellan)*, Bob Silverman *(Jan)*

p, Claude Heroux; d, David Cronenberg; w, David Cronenberg; ph, Mark Irwin; ed, Alan Collins

Powerful and disturbing on both a physical and mental level, THE BROOD is the first Cronenberg film to use "name" actors, and marked a significant progression in the director's exploration of "biological horror."

Controversial psychotherapist Dr. Raglan (Oliver Reed) teaches mental patients to manifest their subconscious anger physically, as boils and welts on their bodies. One of his patients, Nola (Samantha Eggar), has actually begun giving birth to a small army of mutant babies—the ultimate projection of her hostilities. She houses her brood in a nearby cabin from which, dressed in their colorful Dr. Dentons, the murderous little creatures venture out and kill the objects of their mother's rage. Eggar's bitter ex-husband, who is trying to discredit Reed's treatments so he can gain custody of their daughter, uncovers the horrible truth.

More personal than earlier Cronenberg films (the director had just gone through a painful divorce at the time of shooting), THE BROOD is a mature, controlled work that finds horror not only in such institutions as hospitals and schools but, more specifically, in the family unit itself. While his previous efforts (THEY CAME FROM WITHIN, RABID) had been rather clinical exercises, Cronenberg presents more complex and genuinely sympathetic characters here, giving the film added resonance. THE BROOD also marks his growing confidence as a visual stylist, with some memorable—if highly gory—realizations of his pet themes.

BROTHER SUN, SISTER MOON

1973 121m c   ★½
Historical   PG
Euro Intl.   (U.K./Italy)

Graham Faulkner *(Francesco)*, Judi Bowker *(Clare)*, Alec Guinness *(Pope Innocent III)*, Leigh Lawson *(Bernardo)*, Kenneth Cranham *(Paolo)*, Michael Feast *(Silvestro)*, Nicholas Willatt *(Giocondo)*, Valentina Cortese *(Mother)*, Lee Montague *(Father)*, John Sharp *(Bishop)*

p, Luciano Perugia; d, Franco Zeffirelli; w, Suso Cecchi D'Amico, Kenneth Ross, Lina Wertmuller, Franco Zeffirelli; ph, Ennio Guarnieri (Technicolor); ed, Reginald Hills, John Rushton; m, Donovan; prod d, Lorenzo Mongiardino; art d, Gianni Quaranta

Oh, brother! A pretentious bore, but because it's beautiful sometimes to look at, and foreign, and deals with Zeffirelli's kiddie slant on St. Francis, you're supposed to care. But you don't care. You'd rather watch a Lana Turner movie down deep; and in this case, you'd damn ed well better. . . if anyone tries to stop you—To the moon, sister!

BROTHERS KARAMAZOV, THE

1958 149m c   ★★½
Drama   /15
MGM

Yul Brynner *(Dmitri Karamazov)*, Maria Schell *(Grushenka)*, Claire Bloom *(Katya)*, Lee J. Cobb *(Fyodor Karamazov)*, Richard Basehart *(Ivan Karamozov)*, Albert Salmi *(Smerdyakov)*, William Shatner *(Alexey Karamazov)*, Judith Evelyn *(Mme. Anna Hohlakov)*, Edgar Stehli *(Grigory)*, Harry Townes *(Ippoli Kirillov)*

p, Pandro S. Berman; d, Richard Brooks; w, Richard Brooks (based on an adaptation by Julius J. and Philip G. Epstein of the novel by Feodor Dostoyevsky); ph, John Alton (Metrocolor); ed, John Dunning; m, Bronislau Kaper; cos, Walter Plunkett

Marilyn Monroe campaigned desperately for Grushenska, the part played by Maria Schell in this film, and it's one of those true casting tragedies that she didn't get her way. For while Schell is okay, the problem here is similar to Glenn Close in DANGEROUS LIASONS—no sex appeal—and typical of this entire film—lots of steam, but no heat. Director Brooks directs like a traffic cop, without sweep or dramatic gesture. He's intimidated by bringing Dostoyevsky to film, terrified to blow the library dust off it and breathe daring visual, sensual life into it. As a result, excepting the primal force that is actor Cobb, properly utilized for once, the film is like reading a "Classics Comic Book"; a series of physical turns with no emotional resonance. We get the idea is all, and besides that, BROTHERS needs paring down.

BROWNING VERSION, THE

1951 90m bw   ★★★★½
Drama   /U
Javelin   (U.K.)

Michael Redgrave *(Andrew Crocker-Harris)*, Jean Kent *(Millie Crocker-Harris)*, Nigel Patrick *(Frank Hunter)*, Wilfrid Hyde-White *(Frobisher)*, Brian Smith *(Taplow)*, Bill Travers *(Fletcher)*, Ronald Howard *(Gilbert)*, Paul Medland *(Wilson)*, Ivan Samson *(Lord Baxter)*, Josephine Middleton *(Mrs. Frobisher)*

p, Teddy Baird; d, Anthony Asquith; w, Terence Rattigan (based on his play); ph, Desmond Dickinson; ed, John D. Guthridge

Good show! Rattigan adapted his own play for the screen, and it's lovingly directed by Asquith and acted within an inch of the viewer's life by Redgrave and a magnificent small ensemble. Story explores the tragic restriction of a headmaster's retirement and his wretched, unfaithful wife. Redgrave won the Best Actor award and Terence Rattigan the writing prize at the 1951 Cannes Film Festival for this film. Absolutely not to be missed.

BRUBAKER

1980 132m c   ★★★
Prison/Drama   R/15
FOX

Robert Redford *(Henry Brubaker)*, Yaphet Kotto *(Richard "Dickie" Coombes)*, Jane Alexander *(Lillian)*, Murray Hamilton *(Deach)*, David Keith *(Larry Lee Bullen)*, Morgan Freeman *(Walter)*, Matt Clark *(Purcell)*, Tim McIntire *(Huey Rauch)*, Richard Ward *(Abraham)*, Jon Van Ness *(Zaranska)*

p, Ron Silverman; d, Stuart Rosenberg; w, W.D. Richter (based on a story by W.D. Richter, Arthur Ross); ph, Bruno Nuytten (Deluxe Color); ed, Robert Brown; m, Lalo Schifrin; fx, Al Wright, Jr.

Matinee idol Redford plays the title character, who's arrested and taken to a terrible prison in which he sees evidence of man's inhumanity to man around every corner. Eventually, we learn that Brubaker is not a convict at all; he's the new warden, and has had himself incarcerated so that he can experience prison life from the convict's point of view.

A very tough movie, BRUBAKER is not for the squeamish. Director Stuart Rosenberg, whose spotty career includes credits ranging from MOVE to THE AMITYVILLE HORROR, moved into a higher strata with this one, but no matter who's directing him, one can't escape the feeling that Redford is the man behind the man behind the camera.

BRUTE FORCE

1947 94m bw ★★★★
Prison /A
Universal

Burt Lancaster (Joe Collins), Hume Cronyn (Capt. Munsey), Charles Bickford (Gallagher), Yvonne De Carlo (Gina), Ann Blyth (Ruth), Ella Raines (Cora), Anita Colby (Flossie), Sam Levene (Louis), Howard Duff (Soldier), Art Smith (Dr. Walters)

p, Mark Hellinger; d, Jules Dassin; w, Richard Brooks (based on a story by Robert Patterson); ph, William Daniels; ed, Edward Curtiss; m, Miklos Rozsa; art d, Bernard Herzbrun, John DeCuir; fx, David S. Horsley; cos, Rosemary Odell

Classic prison melo, BRUTE FORCE followed THE KILLERS, for Burt Lancaster, establishing him as a dangerously sexy lug in the most interesting period of his career. The predictable premise was directed with innovation by Jules Dassin and also featured the debut of Howard Duff, among a stellar cast. Flashbacks lead to actresses as well, and there's an interesting, untypical job by Hume Cronyn. Rozsa's pounding score and a savage climax make BRUTE FORCE first rate all the way.

BUDDY HOLLY STORY, THE

1978 113m c ★★★½
Biography PG
Columbia

Gary Busey (Buddy Holly), Don Stroud (Jesse), Charles Martin Smith (Ray Bob), Bill Jordan (Riley Randolph), Maria Richwine (Maria Elena Holly), Conrad Janis (Ross Turner), Albert Popwell (Eddie Foster), Amy Johnston (Jenny Lou), James Beach (Mr. Wilson), John Goff (T.J.)

p, Fred Bauer; d, Steve Rash; w, Robert Gittler (based on the book by John Coldrosen); ph, Stevan Larner; ed, David Blewitt; prod d, Joel Schiller; fx, Robby Knott; chor, Maggie Rush; cos, Michael Butler

A-okay rockabilly bio captures the energy of early R&R and its amazing influence. Engaging Busey, Stroud, and Smith all do their own singing. Film won an Oscar for best scoring. Quite good fun, indeed.

BUFFALO BILL

1944 90m c ★★½
Biography/Western /U
FOX

Joel McCrea (Buffalo Bill), Maureen O'Hara (Louisa Cody), Linda Darnell (Dawn Starlight), Thomas Mitchell (Ned Buntline), Edgar Buchanan (Sgt. Chips), Anthony Quinn (Yellow Hand), Moroni Olsen (Sen. Frederici), Frank Fenton (Murdo Carvell), Matt Briggs (Gen. Blazier), George Lessey (Mr. Vandevere)

p, Harry Sherman; d, William A. Wellman; w, Aeneas MacKenzie, Clements Ripley, Cecile Kramer (based on a story by Frank Winch); ph, Leon Shamroy (Technicolor); ed, James B. Clark; m, David Buttolph; art d, James Basevi, Lewis Creger; fx, Fred Sersen

Slam-bang western epic tells the story of "Buffalo Bill" Cody in slushy, standard way. Good cast having broad fun, with nary a raised eyebrow of irony along the rustic way. You either like 'em or you don't.

BUGSY

1991 135m c ★★★½
Crime/Historical/Romance R/18
Baltimore Pictures/Mulholland Productions/Desert Vision Productions

Warren Beatty (Bugsy Siegel), Annette Bening (Virginia Hill), Harvey Keitel (Mickey Cohen), Ben Kingsley (Meyer Lansky), Elliott Gould (Harry Greenberg), Joe Mantegna (George Raft), Richard Sarafian (Jack Dragna), Bebe Neuwirth (Countess di Frasso), Giancarlo Scandiuzzi (Count di Frasso), Wendy Phillips (Esta Siegel)

p, Mark Johnson, Barry Levinson, Warren Beatty; d, Barry Levinson; w, James Toback (from the book "We Only Kill Each Other: The Life and Bad Times of Bugsy Siegel" by Dean Jennings); ph, Allen Daviau; ed, Stu Linder; m, Ennio Morricone; prod d, Dennis Gassner; art d, Leslie McDonald; cos, Albert Wolsky

BUGSY portrays gangster legend Benjamin "Bugsy" Siegel (Warren Beatty) as both a romantic visionary and a psychopathic killer—a raw mass of contradictory impulses. Siegel is a compulsive womanizer who could never leave his wife and children; a suave socialite who flies into an uncontrollable rage if addressed by his hated nickname; a dedicated self-improver who practices his elocution on the way to a gangland execution; and a narcissistic dandy who pauses during the vicious beating of a rival to check his appearance in a mirror.

The film begins with Siegel moving to Hollywood, charged with the task of taking over the various L.A. rackets. Attracted to glamour like a moth to a flame, he is soon smitten by starlet Virginia Hill (Annette Bening), as well as nursing a plan to build a luxury hotel and casino on an unpopulated expanse of Nevada desert—the roots of modern-day Las Vegas. As the cost of building the Flamingo (Virginia's nickname) soars to $6 million—six times the budget originally approved by his partners—Bugsy runs into increasing conflict with his superiors, particularly his mentor, Meyer Lansky (Ben Kingsley).

BUGSY is as smart and stylish a movie as Hollywood has produced in some time. Barry Levinson's direction is brisk and, for a film largely about the allure of glamour, suitably flashy. Ennio Morricone's music is superb, with memorable soundtrack songs including Johnny Mercer's "Ac-Cen-Tchu-Ate the Positive" and "Come Rain or Come Shine," as well as Peggy Lee's rendition of "Why Don't You Do Right?" James Toback's script bristles with colorful incident and spiky dialogue, and an impressive array of actors turn in crisp, quality performances. Standouts are Kingsley and Keitel as level-headed, no-nonsense figures whose dry, sardonic observations serve as a counterpoint to Siegel's unbounded flamboyance. As opposed to the well-drawn supporting characters, however, Siegel comes across as a two-dimensional, almost cartoon-like figure—someone it's impossible to really care about. The result is a slick, witty, but heartless piece of entertainment.

BUGSY MALONE

1976 93m c ★★★
Children's/Musical PG/U
Paramount (U.K.)

Scott Baio *(Bugsy Malone)*, Jodie Foster *(Tallulah)*, Florrie Dugger *(Blousey)*, John Cassisi *(Fat Sam)*, Paul Murphy *(Leroy)*, Albin Jenkins *(Fizzy)*, Martin Lev *(Dandy Dan)*, Davidson Knight *(Knuckles)*, Paul Chirelstein *(Smolsky)*, Paul Besterman *(Yonkers)*

p, Alan Marshall; d, Alan Parker; w, Alan Parker; ph, Michael Seresin, Peter Biziou (Eastmancolor); ed, Gerry Hambling; m, Paul Williams; chor, Gillian Gregory; cos, Monica Howe

Spoof of 1920s gangster pics with all-kiddie cast is interesting idea that loses steam before the fade. Why? Big problem is parody can only be really amusing played (and cast) pretty straight. Kids lack ability to put sin and sex element across; only Foster seems able to bring up the requisite toughness. Nor is it helped by Paul Williams's limp score. But between this and BUGSY, we'll take babies and you can have Beatty.

BULL DURHAM
1988 108m c   ★★★½
Comedy   R/15
Mount

Kevin Costner *(Crash Davis)*, Susan Sarandon *(Annie Savoy)*, Tim Robbins *(Ebby Calvin "Nuke" LaLoosh)*, Trey Wilson *(Joe "Skip" Riggins)*, Robert Wuhl *(Larry Hockett)*, Jenny Robertson *(Millie)*, Max Patkin *(Himself)*, William O'Leary *(Jimmy)*, David Neidorf *(Bobby)*, Danny Gans *(Deke)*

p, Thom Mount, Mark Burg; d, Ron Shelton; w, Ron Shelton; ph, Bobby Byrne (Deluxe Color); ed, Robert Leighton, Adam Weiss; m, Michael Convertino; prod d, Armin Ganz; cos, Louise Frogley

Smutty, terrific, lucious fun. Featuring outstanding lead performances by Kevin Costner, Susan Sarandon, and Tim Robbins; a witty, literate script; and an insider's familiarity with life around minor league baseball—BULL DURHAM is both one of the best films ever made about the national pastime and a charming romantic comedy. As smart as she is sexy, Annie Savoy (Sarandon), the No. 1 fan of the Class A Durham Bulls, chooses one player a year for her student in the art of lovemaking as well as in metaphysics and literature. This summer two players vie for her attentions: Nuke Laloosh (Robbins), a bonus-baby pitcher "with a million-dollar arm and five-cent head" and Crash Davis (Costner), the power-hitting longtime minor-league catcher brought to the club to prepare Nuke for the big leagues. First-time director Ron Shelton (who spent five years in the Baltimore Orioles farm system) suffuses his film with carefully realized bush-league details and evokes laugh after rich laugh. Costner (a former high school shortstop) is wholly convincing as a pro ballplayer, delivering perhaps his best performance to date. Sarandon sizzles, and BULL DURHAM is an extremely sexy movie that uses bared souls rather than bared bodies to turn up the heat. The diamond action was shot at El Toro Field, home of the real Durham Bulls. Max Patkin, "the Clown Prince of Baseball," also appears.

BULLDOG DRUMMOND
1929 90m bw   ★★★½
Mystery
Goldwyn

Ronald Colman *(Bulldog Drummond)*, Joan Bennett *(Phyllis Benton)*, Lilyan Tashman *(Erma Peterson)*, Montagu Love *(Carl Peterson)*, Lawrence Grant *(Doctor Lakington)*, Wilson Benge *(Danny)*, Claud Allister *(Algy Longworth)*, Adolph Milar *(Marcovitch)*, Charles Sellon *(John Travers)*, Tetsu Komai *(Chong)*

p, Samuel Goldwyn, F. Richard Jones; d, F. Richard Jones; w, Wallace Smith, Sidney Howard (based on the play by H.C. "Sapper" McNeile, Gerald Du Maurier); ph, Gregg Toland, George Barnes; ed, Viola, Frank Lawrence; art d, William Cameron Menzies

Polished to a fine sheen. Colman's first talkie is a witty romp—he's delightfully teamed with Bennett in one of her rich American life-is-art roles. Audiences were delighted to find Colman sounded exactly as they expected. A beautiful film.

BULLDOG DRUMMOND STRIKES BACK
1934 83m bw   ★★★★
Mystery   /A
UA

Ronald Colman *(Hugh Drummond)*, Loretta Young *(Lola Field)*, C. Aubrey Smith *(Inspector Nielsen)*, Charles Butterworth *(Algy Longworth)*, Una Merkel *(Gwen)*, Warner Oland *(Prince Achmed)*, George Regas *(Singh)*, Mischa Auer *(Hassan)*, Kathleen Burke *(Jane Sothern)*, Arthur Hohl *(Dr. Sothern)*

p, Joseph M. Schenck; d, Roy Del Ruth; w, Henry Lehrman, Nunnally Johnson (based on the novel by H.C. "Sapper" McNeile); ph, Peverell Marley; ed, Allen McNeil; art d, Richard Day; cos, Gwen Wakeling

Colman repeats his 1929 success in the first film he made after refusing to work for Samuel Goldwyn ever again. Fast-moving, smartly produced, laugh-studded melodrama is as incredible as it is engrossing. Drummond tries to convince Scotland Yard of the existence of a kidnapping ring in London, but every time he discovers a witness to prove the point, the witness mysteriously disappears. Colman delighted to repeat his Drummond role because the improvement in sound and other technical refinements made it possible to portray the character with more polish and bite than the primitive 1929 version had permitted, even though he had received an Academy Award nomination for the earlier performance. Charles Butterworth's portrayal as Drummond's sidekick Algy was also a major factor in the film's success. This movie never lags and has all the plausibility of a well-written mystery novel read in the middle of the night.

BULLITT
1968 113m c   ★★★★
Crime   /15
WB

Steve McQueen *(Bullitt)*, Robert Vaughn *(Chalmers)*, Jacqueline Bisset *(Cathy)*, Don Gordon *(Delgetti)*, Robert Duvall *(Weissberg)*, Simon Oakland *(Capt. Bennett)*, Norman Fell *(Baker)*, Georg Stanford Brown *(Dr. Willard)*, Justin Tarr *(Eddy)*, Carl Reindel *(Stanton)*

p, Philip D'Antoni; d, Peter Yates; w, Alan R. Trustman, Harry Kleiner (based on the novel *Mute Witness* by Robert L. Pike); ph, William A. Fraker (Technicolor); ed, Frank P. Keller; m, Lalo Schifrin; art d, Albert Brenner; cos, Theadora Van Runkle

Expert chase film, breathless and modern, that sent McQueen to the top of the box office heap. He plays the title character, a colorful and unorthodox police lieutenant assigned to protect a government witness scheduled to inform on the national crime syndicate. Climax has McQueen spotting hoodlums and following in one of the most famous car chases ever filmed, up and down the hills of San Francisco while hand-held cameras record the perilous pursuit as each car narrowly misses intersecting autos, barriers, and buildings as they squeal, slide, and lurch along the narrow streets.

BULLITT was a return to the old, tough crime movies so expertly played by Bogart and Robinson, but made modern here by great technical advances and McQueen's taciturn, antihero stance. Yates's superb direction presents a fluid, always moving camera. All the performers are top-notch, from sour-faced Norman Fell to a curious bit part played by Robert Duvall as a cab driver who is seen almost entirely through a rear-view mirror. Aside from THE SAND PEBBLES, this fine production stands as McQueen's top achievement in a lamentably short career. The film won an Oscar for Best Film Editing and was nominated for Best Sound.

BUTCH CASSIDY AND THE SUNDANCE KID

1969   112m   c   ★★
Western   /PG
FOX

Paul Newman *(Butch Cassidy)*, Robert Redford *(Sundance Kid)*, Katharine Ross *(Etta Place)*, Strother Martin *(Percy Garris)*, Henry Jones *(Bike Salesman)*, Jeff Corey *(Sheriff Bledsoe)*, George Furth *(Woodcock)*, Cloris Leachman *(Agnes)*, Ted Cassidy *(Harvey Logan)*, Kenneth Mars *(Marshal)*

p, Paul Monash, John Foreman; d, George Roy Hill; w, William Goldman; ph, Conrad Hall (DeLuxe Color); ed, John C. Howard, Richard C. Meyer; m, Burt Bacharach; art d, Jack Martin Smith, Philip Jefferies; fx, L.B. Abbott, Art Cruickshank; cos, Edith Head

Too cute for words and overrated to high hell; a soap bubble weighed down with praise from average minds. Forever etched in the public mind are Redford's and Newman's chummy portraits of these two overage juveniles. In an only okay combo of slapstick and drama, the gun-totin', train-robbin' duo and their erstwhile companions ride through a West of awkward and adorable events, populated by lethal personalities who are jes' plain folk like everyone else. But BUTCH hasn't aged particularly well; today it looks cloying and strained. Nor is it helped by the flatness of Ross or the lamentable Bacharach "Raindrops" tune, so over-exposed in the annals of muzak that to even hear one measure is enough to send one running for the chainsaw. For quirky little westerns, we much prefer John Wayne in either THE SHOOTIST or THE TRAIN ROBBERS.

BUTTERFIELD 8

1960   109m   c   ★★★
Drama   /X
MGM

Elizabeth Taylor *(Gloria Wandrous)*, Laurence Harvey *(Weston Liggett)*, Eddie Fisher *(Steve Carpenter)*, Dina Merrill *(Emily Liggett)*, Mildred Dunnock *(Mrs. Wandrous)*, Betty Field *(Mrs. Fanny Thurber)*, Jeffrey Lynn *(Bingham Smith)*, Kay Medford *(Happy)*, Susan Oliver *(Norma)*, George Voskovec *(Dr. Tredman)*

p, Pandro S. Berman; d, Daniel Mann; w, Charles Schnee, John Michael Hayes (based on the novel by John O'Hara); ph, Joseph Ruttenberg; ed, Ralph E. Winters; m, Bronislau Kaper; art d, George W. Davis, Urie McCleary; cos, Helen Rose

Glossy trash with the star at full throttle, it's the quintessental La Liz movie. Loosely based on John O'Hara's novel, loose Gloria Wandrous encompasses the legendary wanton Taylor persona; indeed, Hollywood was so pleased by the cementing of Hurricane Liz's public image they rewarded her with an Oscar. As for Taylor's critical response, when she watched it the first time in a screening room, she threw a high heel at the screen, fled to a john, and promptly threw up. All the more reason to tune in. . .

Liz reluctantly plays Gloria (the very idea—casting Liz in something tawdry and commercial), a "model" searching for understanding, who, like Liz, cannot breathe if she is not in love. Enter married rake, ultimate heel Laurence Harvey, who fancies Liz in a sort of violent bedroom way and we're off to the races. Our fave scenes: that opening, which chronicles a typical La Liz good morning, and the barside "disagreement" she shares with Harvey.

Miss Taylor gives quite a star performance and she's buoyed by a talented supporting cast with two eyesores: the bland Dina Merrill and the blank Eddie Fisher (his appearance was a consolation prize to soothe the star). This was the height of the "I stole Debbie's husband; so what?" scandal, so the public turned out in droves to snoop their chemistry (there was none) and hate Liz en masse. Hate turned to public sympathy when Taylor caught pneumonia in London and nearly died, surviving only when an emergency tracheotomy was performed (and guaranteed Liz a lot of Oscar sympathy votes). This was an important chapter in the Taylor Roadshow and she would next land CLEOPATRA, and celebrate by dumping Fisher. Meanwhile, enjoy BUTTERFIELD 8. It's a rave!

BYE BYE BLUES

1990   110m   c   ★★★½
Drama/Romance   PG
Allarcom-True Blue   (Canada/U.S.)

Rebecca Jenkins *(Daisy Cooper)*, Michael Ontkean *(Teddy Cooper)*, Luke Reilly *(Max Gramley)*, Stuart Margolin *(Slim Godfrey)*, Robyn Stevan *(Frances Cooper)*, Kate Reid *(Mary Wright)*, Leslie Yeo *(Arthur Wright)*, Wayne Robson *(Pete)*, Sheila Moore *(Doreen Cooper)*, Susan Wooldridge *(Lady Wilson)*

p, Anne Wheeler, Arvi Liimatainen; d, Anne Wheeler; w, Anne Wheeler; ph, Vic Sarin; ed, Christopher Tate; m, George Blondheim; prod d, John Blackie; art d, Scott Dobbie; cos, Maureen Hiscox

A sentimental beauty; one of those How She and Her Kids Survived While Her Husband Was Away at the War movies in which the heroine, having changed much in her spouse's absence, not only doesn't know if her husband is still alive but wonders if she will still love him if he returns. Naturally, she also anguishes over whether she should give herself to the other man in her lonely life. No matter. BYE BYE BLUES is a wonderful, old-fashioned romance with a dreamy, sensual tone rarely found in movies nowadays. It is also a sheer pleasure to watch. That it's not mawkish at all is a credit to Canadian filmmaker Anne Wheeler, whose enchanting tale is based on her mother's wartime experiences during the long years her husband was held captive by the Japanese. But BYE BYE BLUES is much more than a tale of survival, more than the story of a young woman suddenly forced to handle adversity and support herself and her two small children. It is a lovingly drawn, mesmerizing account of a woman's struggle to cope with insecurity, to define herself, and to eventually succeed in an altogether unfamiliar world for which she was remarkably unprepared.

Like the similarly satisfying MY BRILLIANT CAREER, another so-called "woman's film," BYE BYE BLUES avoids the obvious, refusing to ram its feminism down anyone's throat. Instead, it chronicles one woman's personal growth with an unerring sensitivity that's universally appealing. Beautifully acted and lushly photographed, the film garnered a series of major awards, including Best Film at the Houston International Film Festival and three Genies (the Canadian equivalent of the Oscar), Best Actress for Jenkins (an honor also accorded her at the Seattle Film Festival), Best Supporting Actress for Stevan, and Best Original Song for composer Bill Henderson's ballad "When I Sing."

BYE BYE BRAZIL

1980 100m c ★★★
Drama
Carnaval Unifilm   (Brazil)

Jose Wilker *(Lord Gypsy)*, Betty Faria *(Salome)*, Fabio Junior *(Cico)*, Zaira Zambelli *(Dasdo)*, Principe Nabor *(Swallow)*, Jofre Soares *(Ze da Luz)*, Marcus Vinicius *(Gent)*, Jose Maria Lima *(Assistant)*, Emanuel Cavalcanti *(Mayor)*, Jose Marcio Reis *(Smuggler)*

p, Lucy Barreto; d, Carlos Diegues; w, Carlos Diegues; ph, Lauro Escorel Filho; ed, Anisio Medeiros

BYE BYE BRAZIL is a colorful, exotic collection of vignettes about modern Brazil. The film follows a carnival troupe as they travel throughout the country, wandering deep into the Amazonian jungles, in search of new places where they can put on a show. The eccentric group consists of Lord Cigano (Jose Wilker), a magician who organized the troupe; Salome (Betty Faria), his mistress and the show's exotic dancer/prostitute; Cico (Fabio Junior), a young accordionist infatuated with Salome; Dasdo (Zaira Zambelli), Cico's pregnant wife; and Swallow (Principe Nabor), a black, deaf-mute strongman. An insightful and humorous look at two Brazils in conflict—the traditional Brazil versus the progressive Brazil, with its infusions of North American culture.

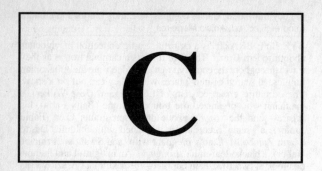

C

CABARET

1972　124m　c
Musical/War
Allied Artists

★★★★½
PG/15

Liza Minnelli *(Sally Bowles)*, Michael York *(Brian Roberts)*, Helmut Griem *(Maximilian von Heune)*, Joel Grey *(Master of Ceremonies)*, Fritz Wepper *(Fritz Wendel)*, Marisa Berenson *(Natalia Landauer)*, Elisabeth Neumann-Viertel *(Fraulein Schneider)*, Sigrid von Richthofen *(Fraulein Maur)*, Helen Vita *(Fraulein Kost)*, Gerd Vespermann *(Bobby)*

p, Cy Feuer; d, Bob Fosse; w, Jay Presson Allen (based on the stage play by Joe Masteroff, the stage play *I Am a Camera* by John Van Druten, and the writings of Christopher Isherwood); ph, Geoffrey Unsworth (Technicolor); ed, David Bretherton; m, Ralph Burns; art d, Jurgen Kiebach, Rolf Zehetbauer; chor, Bob Fosse; cos, Charlotte Flemming

Chilling Fosse vision of Weimar Berlin, stylishly directed and choreographed, featuring a show-stopping musical performance by Minnelli, Grey's unforgettable emcee and thoughtful acting from Michael York. The screenplay utilizes much of the Broadway musical's book, but also is influenced by both play and screen versions of I AM A CAMERA. The secondary romantic subplot has been prettified by changing it to young lovers, and it weakens the emotion and mood of the narrative.

No one could accuse Minnelli of being a bad actress, but her knockout musical delivery tends to make the film a lopsided vehicle; jabbering about "divine decadence" in her gee-gosh-golly persona, it's more like she exists in the rabble than participates in it. And, because Minnelli literally becomes a star before our eyes, she cannot enact Sally Bowles's tragedy of mediocrity.

Songwriters Fred Ebb and John Kander wisely scrapped several weak songs from the original score and added some fine new ones. Everyone raves about "Money," the Grey-Minnelli duet, but the film's real showstopper is Minnelli and the Kit Kat Club Girls doing "Mein Herr," which conjures up the energy of the pre-Third Reich decay and celebrates the sleazy rot rather than commenting on it.

It's the Brechtian moments of cool Germanic detachment like this that make CABARET a great movie musical and validate Fosse as a director for history. The film won eight Oscars including Best Actress, Best Supporting Actor, Best Direction, Best Cinematography, Best Art Direction, Best Sound, Best Scoring and Best Film Editing.

CABIN IN THE SKY

1943　98m　bw
Musical
MGM

★★★★
/A

Ethel Waters *(Petunia Jackson)*, Eddie "Rochester" Anderson *(Little Joe)*, Lena Horne *(Georgia Brown)*, Louis Armstrong *(The Trumpeter)*, Rex Ingram *(Lucius/Lucifer, Jr.)*, Kenneth Spencer *(Rev. Green, The General)*, John "Bubbles" Sublett *(Domino)*, Oscar Polk *(The Deacon/Flatfoot)*, Mantan Moreland *(First Idea Man)*, Willie Best *(Second Idea Man)*

p, Arthur Freed; d, Vincente Minnelli; w, Joseph Schrank (based on the play by Lynn Root, John Latouche, Vernon Duke); ph, Sidney Wagner; ed, Harold F. Kress; m, Roger Edens

A monument to the overwhelming Ethel Waters in all her glory, directed in his first Hollywood outing by Vincente Minnelli, in the first all-black musical since GREEN PASTURES in 1936.

Waters, Ingram, and Minnelli are the three veterans from the legit Broadway version, and the film is directed with an engaging freshness that keeps the *faux-naif* quality of the story from getting syrupy. Unfortunately, the film has not taken much camera advantage with the fantasy element, and the stairway to heaven finale is disappointing. It's curious, because Minnelli was usually so pictorial, but perhaps he hesitated to compromise the inherent homespun quality, given the accepted racist mainstream attitudes of the day.

The cast is flawless, and seeing them all together is exciting to behold. Eddie "Rochester" Anderson is an adorable rascal; his moral dilemma is understandable given the siren call of the ravishing Lena Horne. But Anderson is married to Ethel Waters, whose sincerity, piety, compassion, and way with a song are absolute genius.

CABIN was not an easy make for Minnelli and MGM. The director was supposedly romancing Horne, and Waters raised hell, even taking on the MGM brass on a day when filming ground to a halt, over the "Honey in the Honeycomb" number. This number was originally Waters's, and now both actresses were set to sing it, Waters as a ballad, Horne leading a dance number with the divine John Bubbles. But Horne ended up with a broken ankle—no one is saying how—and performance styles were reversed. Waters's dancing is amazing, the surprise of the film.

The Duke Ellington Orchestra is on hand to lend extra pizazz, and look for Louis Armstrong among the hilarious henchmen of devil Ingram. His joyous face almost steals every scene he's in. The two highlights of the wonderful score by Duke, Latouche, Arlen, and Harburgh are songs are the Oscar-nominated "Happiness Is Just A Thing Called Joe" and "Taking A Chance On Love," both sung by our great Miss Waters.

CADDYSHACK

1980　99m　c
Comedy
Orion

★★½
R/15

Rodney Dangerfield *(Al)*, Ted Knight *(Judge)*, Michael O'Keefe *(Danny)*, Bill Murray *(Carl)*, Sarah Holcomb *(Maggie)*, Scott Colomby *(Tony)*, Cindy Morgan *(Lacey)*, Dan Resin *(Dr. Beeper)*, Henry Wilcoxon *(Bishop)*, Albert Salmi *(Noonan)*

p, Douglas Kenney; d, Harold Ramis; w, Brian Doyle-Murray, Harold Ramis, Douglas Kenney; ph, Stevan Larner (Technicolor); ed, William Carruth; m, Johnny Mandel; prod d, Stan Jolly; art d, George Szeptycki

A slapstick comedy featuring a host of great clowns, CADDYSHACK boosted the career of "Saturday Night Live" alum Bill Murray and revived the sagging fortunes of the wonderful Rodney Dangerfield, whose opening scenes are some of the funniest on film.

Adorned in garish garb and throwing his money around, the newly wealthy Dangerfield offends the stuffed-shirt members of the swanky country club he has just joined. No one is more put off by Dangerfield than Knight, who considers the club his private fiefdom. Chase is a dissipated but tremendously talented golfer; O'Keefe is a clean-cut caddie trying to make good and snag a college scholarship by winning a tournament; and Murray is the grubby groundskeeper who spends much of his time devising methods to rid the course of a pesky gopher.

Too much time is spent on the forced romance between O'Keefe and Holcomb, an attractive waitress, however, and the slapstick becomes utterly mindless toward the end (as if the producer said, "Okay, it's time for this film to really get out of control!"). Still, the laughs keep coming. Even the film's absurd stereotypes provoke guilty titters. There is a marvelous moment when Wilcoxon, portraying a golf-loving clergyman, begins to play a perfect game in a raging rainstorm. Dropping one hole-in-one after another, laughing hysterically, thanking the Almighty for the greatest game of his life, he lifts his club heavenward and is struck by lightning while a crescendo from the score of THE TEN COMMANDMENTS (in which Wilcoxon played pharoah's general) blares on the soundtrack.

CAESAR AND CLEOPATRA

1946 138m c	★★★★
Biography/Historical	/U
Two Cities (U.K.)	

Vivien Leigh (Cleopatra), Claude Rains (Caesar), Stewart Granger (Apollodorus), Flora Robson (Ftatateeta), Francis L. Sullivan (Pothinus), Basil Sydney (Rufio), Cecil Parker (Britannus), Raymond Lovell (Lucius Septimus), Anthony Eustrel (Achillas), Ernest Thesiger (Theodotus)

p, Gabriel Pascal, J. Arthur Rank; d, Gabriel Pascal; w, George Bernard Shaw, Marjorie Deans (based on the play by George Bernard Shaw); ph, Freddie Young, Robert Krasker, Jack Hildyard, Jack Cardiff (Technicolor); ed, Frederick Wilson; m, Georges Auric; cos, Oliver Messel

Don't be misled. Don't try to convince yourself this is wonderful entertainment, don't second guess your basic instinct. Yes, it's Shaw's acerbic and uncinematic play, but Pascal has slowed it down to a lumbering crawl and puffed it up to VIP dinosaur status. Two finer stars being saddled hopelessly we cannot recall, but this occasion frankly finds Rains dishing up ham too readily, and Leigh sorely lacking in the siren department (the arrival of handsome Stewart Granger barely rates a glance). Indeed, this doom laden production was far more interesting behind the cameras than it was in front of them.

Irascible Shaw became so fond of Leigh that he broke precedent and actually wrote an entirely new scene for her, although he adamantly refused to introduce "a little love interest" into the script as politely requested by producer J. Arthur Rank. Producer-director Pascal went at CAESAR AND CLEOPATRA with a vengeance, intent on proving that the British film industry could rival in scope anything Hollywood could create, particularly in the belt-tightening years of WWII. The result was the most extravagantly expensive film Britain produced up to that time, so opulent that when Shaw first viewed it he expressed annoyance at the lavish sets, the hordes of extras, and spendthrift feel of the overall production.

American distribution was promoted by Rank and United Artists with an enormous budget that initially caused US audiences to flock to see favorites Leigh and Rains; but disappointment soon set in when viewers emerged bored, and the Rank

organization sustained staggering losses—some $3 million—that brought it to the very brink of bankruptcy. But from the ranks of the film's over 100 bit players emerged many a star, including Michael Rennie, who plays a Centurion, Kay Kendall, a slave girl, and Jean Simmons, a harpist.

CAINE MUTINY, THE

1954 123m c	★★★★
Drama	/U
Columbia	

Humphrey Bogart (Capt. Philip Francis Queeg), Jose Ferrer (Lt. Barney Greenwald), Van Johnson (Lt. Steve Maryk), Fred MacMurray (Lt. Tom Keefer), Robert Francis (Ens. Willie Keith), May Wynn (May Wynn), Tom Tully (Capt. DeVriess), E.G. Marshall (Lt. Cmdr. Challee), Arthur Franz (Lt. Paynter), Lee Marvin (Meatball)

p, Stanley Kramer; d, Edward Dmytryk; w, Stanley Roberts, Michael Blankfort (based on the play and novel by Herman Wouk); ph, Franz Planer (Technicolor); ed, William Lyon, Henry Batista; m, Max Steiner; prod d, Rudolph Sternad; art d, Cary Odell; fx, Lawrence Butler; cos, Jean Louis

Complex, atypical Bogie performance is keynote for strong drama from Pulitzer-winning novel and Broadway show. Francis, Johnson, and MacMurray are shipmates early in WWII aboard a destroyer-cum-minesweeper. Bogart, in one of his greatest performances, boards the ship as her new captain and immediately establishes both his power over the men and his neurosis. When he clashes with Johnson, the latter is court-martialed, and Ferrer must defend him.

The scenes with Bogart disintegrating on the witness stand have become part of American film folklore, as he delineates the layers of perfectionism and obsessiveness overlaying an inferiority complex. This is a don't-miss picture, unnecessarily beefed up with a gratuitous, concocted love story between Wynn (using her own name in the film) and Francis. Bogart was later asked how he managed to totally capture the paranoid personality of Queeg. "Simple," growled Bogie, "everybody knows I'm nuts, anyway."

CALIFORNIA SPLIT

1974 108m c	★★
Comedy	R/X
Columbia	

George Segal (Bill Denny), Elliott Gould (Charlie Walters), Ann Prentiss (Barbara) (Miller), Gwen Welles (Susan Peters), Edward Walsh (Lew), Joseph Walsh (Sparkie), Bert Remsen (Helen Brown), Barbara London (Lady on Bus), Barbara Ruick (Reno Barmaid), Jay Fletcher (Robber)

p, Robert Altman, Joseph Walsh; d, Robert Altman; w, Joseph Walsh; ph, Paul Lohmann (Panavision, Metrocolor); ed, Lou Lombardo; m, Phyllis Shotwell; art d, Leon Ericksen

Altman has done the almost impossible. He's made a gambling story dull. In his constant striving for "loose-ending" a movie, he has strung together a series of vignettes, some funny, others boring, and has called it a film. Segal and Gould are both excellent as compulsive gamblers in various situations. Several real gamesmen play themselves in the film and the supporting players all contribute fine work but the picture crumbles in its overall concept. Altman, to his credit, is always after something elusive—a sense of realism that is often missing with more structured films. When it works, it's marvelous. Unfortunately for Altman, it hardly ever works. Screenwriter Walsh was a fairly successful young actor, at one point, who gave up acting for writing. This script was not his best effort, but it's not easy to say where the words end and where Altman's improvisational, sketchy technique begins.

CALIFORNIA SUITE

1978   103m   c   ★★★½
Comedy   PG/15
Columbia

Alan Alda *(Bill Warren)*, Michael Caine *(Sidney Cochran)*, Bill Cosby *(Dr. Willis Panama)*, Jane Fonda *(Hannah Warren)*, Walter Matthau *(Marvin Michaels)*, Elaine May *(Millie Michaels)*, Richard Pryor *(Dr. Chauncy Gump)*, Maggie Smith *(Diana Barrie)*, Gloria Gifford *(Lola Gump)*, Sheila Frazier *(Bettina Panama)*

p, Ray Stark; d, Herbert Ross; w, Neil Simon (based on his play); ph, David M. Walsh; ed, Michael A. Stevenson; m, Claude Bolling; cos, Ann Roth, Patricia Norris

An all-star bitch fest, slickly served, but finally monotonous. The quartet of stories are weaved together more or less, with the Caine/Smith segment the most successful because the actors realize the value of comedic understatement—this kind of wordplay requires enough assurance to make it look as though you're not working. The Fonda/Alda sketch is interesting only because Fonda's character is such a welcome relief from her usual gung-ho over-achiever. Matthau and May are an acquired taste—your move. And the Cosby/Pryor sketch is so vile, you can't believe it even made it past an editor. Smith won an Oscar for her deft portrayal of an Academy Award nominee. Truly, a mixed bag.

CALL NORTHSIDE 777

1948   111m   bw   ★★★★
Biography/Crime   /A
FOX

James Stewart *(McNeal)*, Richard Conte *(Frank Wiecek)*, Lee J. Cobb *(Brian Kelly)*, Helen Walker *(Laura McNeal)*, Betty Garde *(Wanda Skutnik)*, Kasia Orzazewski *(Tillie Wiecek)*, Joanna De Bergh *(Helen Wiecek-Rayska)*, Howard Smith *(Palmer)*, Moroni Olsen *(Parole Board Chairman)*, John McIntire *(Sam Faxon)*

p, Otto Lang; d, Henry Hathaway; w, Jerry Cady, Jay Dratler (adapted by Leonard Hoffman and Quentin Reynolds from articles by James P. McGuire appearing in the *Chicago Times*); ph, Joseph MacDonald; ed, J. Watson Webb; m, Alfred Newman; art d, Lyle Wheeler, Mark-Lee Kirk; fx, Dick Smith, Fred Sersen; cos, Kay Nelson

One of the most impressive semi-documentary noir thrillers, CALL NORTHSIDE 777 was shot on location in Chicago in striking black-and-white by cinematographer Joe MacDonald. Renowned movie nice guy Jimmy Stewart stars in a change-of-pace characterization as a hard-boiled newspaper reporter who evolves from a sceptical news hound to a dedicated crusader when he investigates a decade-old cop killing based on the actual case of Joe Majczek of Chicago who was imprisoned for a crime he did not commit.

Stewart is handed an assignment by editor Cobb: follow up a small ad that appeared in his newspaper offering a $5,000 reward for information leading to the arrest and conviction of the man responsible for killing a policeman years earlier. Stewart learns that the ad was placed by a cleaning woman (Orzazewski) who has slaved for years to earn reward money for anyone able to clear her son of the murder. The cynical Stewart initially believes the convicted Conte is guilty but opts to write a human interest story about the loving mother. When the public reaction proves

to be overwhelming, Cobb encourages Stewart to back up his original story with some more digging. As he investigates, Stewart unearths evidence that there was some police coverup in the case and that certain evidence is missing. His interest is piqued.

Stewart effectively plays the part of Jim McGuire, the *Chicago Times* reporter who won the Pulitzer Prize for his investigative efforts, and the rest of the cast turn in fine, realistic performances. For Stewart, this film was a departure from the genial roles (though sometimes dark-tinged) for which he had become famous (IT'S A WONDERFUL LIFE, THE PHILADELPHIA STORY, MAGIC TOWN); this performance paved the way for his more morally ambiguous and gritty characterizations for directors such as Hitchcock and Anthony Mann in the 1950s. Director Hathaway had recently had a resounding success with the Ben Hecht story, KISS OF DEATH, also shot in a grim realistic style. Newman's moody score adds depth and feeling to the emotionally charged story.

CALL OF THE WILD

1935   89m   bw   ★★★
Adventure   /U
20th Century

Clark Gable *(Jack Thornton)*, Loretta Young *(Claire Blake)*, Jack Oakie *(Shorty Hoolihan)*, Frank Conroy *(John Blake)*, Reginald Owen *(Smith)*, Sidney Toler *(Groggin)*, Katherine DeMille *(Marie)*, Lalo Encinas *(Kali)*, Charles Stevens *(Francois)*, James Burke *(Ole)*

p, Darryl F. Zanuck; d, William A. Wellman; w, Gene Fowler, Leonard Praskins (based on the novel by Jack London); ph, Charles Rosher; ed, H.T. Fritch; m, Alfred Newman

This epic Alaskan adventure story features Clark Gable as prospector Jack Thornton. After losing his money gambling, Thornton acquires a huge dog, Buck, which is considered too vicious to be a sled dog. Thornton patiently trains the animal, then sets out with his friend Shorty Hoolihan (Jack Oakie) for the wilderness in search of gold. Thereafter they must battle the weather, the wilds, and crooks in their attempts to make their fortunes, and Thornton finds a love interest in the wife of a missing prospector. This hearty film was shot on the snowy slopes of Washington's Mount Baker, at 5,000 feet, where the harsh winter snows forced cast and crew to use snowplows to get to their daily locations. Through the hardships, they created a stirring adventure, loosely based on the writings of Jack London.

CALLAWAY WENT THATAWAY

1951   81m   bw   ★★★
Comedy/Western   /U
MGM

Fred MacMurray *(Mike Frye)*, Dorothy McGuire *(Deborah Patterson)*, Howard Keel *("Stretch" Barnes/"Smoky" Callaway)*, Jesse White *(George Markham)*, Fay Roope *(Tom Lorrison)*, Natalie Schafer *(Martha Lorrison)*, Douglas Kennedy *(Drunk)*, Elisabeth Fraser *(Marie)*, John Indrisano *(Johnny Tarranto)*, Stan Freberg *(Marvin)*

p, Norman Panama, Melvin Frank; d, Norman Panama, Melvin Frank; w, Norman Panama, Melvin Frank; ph, Ray June; ed, Cotton Warburton; m, Marlin Skiles; art d, Cedric Gibbons, Eddie Imazu

In this delightful spoof of the early TV Hopalong Cassidy craze, TV promoters Mike Frye (Fred MacMurray) and Deborah Patterson (Dorothy McGuire) are handed the assignment of finding "Smoky" Callaway, a yesteryear star of B westerns who has become an overnight smash, with millions of youngsters watching his old oaters on TV. They are unable to find Callaway but do discover real-life cowboy Stretch Barnes (Howard Keel), a double for the missing actor, and induce him to impersonate Callaway. Trouble begins as success goes to Stretch's head and he becomes a thoroughly obnoxious "star." The situation worsens when the real Callaway (also played by Keel) shows up. It's a lot of fun and offers an interesting portrait of the early days of television.

CAMEL BOY, THE

1984   72m   c   ★★★
Animated/Children's   /U
Yoram Gross   (Australia)

VOICES OF: Barbara Frawley, Ron Haddrick, John Meillon, Robyn Moore, Michael Pate

p, Yoram Gross; d, Yoram Gross; w, Yoram Gross, John Palmer; ph, Graham Sharp; ed, Christopher Plowright; m, Bob Young; anim, Roy Nowland

A technically superb children's film that combines animated characters with actual Australian backgrounds. Beginning in the 1920s, THE CAMEL BOY tells the story of Ali, a young Arab lad who ventures across the Great Victoria Desert with his camel-driver grandfather. They are subjected to radical shifts in weather—first a torrential downpour, then a dangerous dry spell—and an attack by wild dogs before they are forced to turn back. Twenty years pass, grandfather dies, and Ali becomes a police officer in his native land. He catches another young camel boy who is suspected of being a spy—an Australian—who gets himself on a ship carrying camels to the Arab nation. A choice pick for youngsters, who'll marvel at the visuals and empathize with the delightful characters.

CAMILLE

1937   108m   bw   ★★★★★
Romance   /PG
MGM

Greta Garbo (*Marguerite*), Robert Taylor (*Armand*), Lionel Barrymore (*Duval*), Elizabeth Allan (*Nichette*), Jessie Ralph (*Nanine*), Henry Daniell (*Baron de Varville*), Lenore Ulric (*Olympe*), Laura Hope Crews (*Prudence*), Rex O'Malley (*Gaston*), Russell Hardie (*Gustave*)

p, Bernard Hyman; d, George Cukor; w, Zoe Akins, Frances Marion, James Hilton (based on the novel and play *La Dame aux Camelias* by Alexander Dumas fils); ph, William Daniels; ed, Margaret Booth; m, Herbert Stothart

The great Garbo at her radiant peak, and certainly among the top five most romantic movies ever made. Cukor's renowned "rapport" with actresses is unfailing here. MGM's glamour shows unmistakable care—if it's not the same as style, the luxuriance befits the story of a courtesan. It's a puzzle why Garbo's Marguerite is a whore—she seems too intelligent, too yearning, too serious to have ever considered the demimonde life, yet her acting is so generous, so overcome with the warmth of true love, so tinged with the irony of the character's circumstances, that she sweeps you away. Her final scene is among the finest ever committed to film, as she signals death with her eyes in a lingering close-up.

Robert Taylor is so beautiful, you can forgive his lack of skill. His earnestness seems consistent with the rash actions of young love, and his ardent awe of Garbo imparts a worshipful aura that

is touching. The fact that he looks younger makes the whore component of Garbo's character more believable; it justifies Armand's not immediately grasping his love's circumstances.

This is Daniell's most interesting performance, subtle in his control and villany. Laura Hope Crews finally is able to utilize her vocal vulgarity; she is by far a better old strumpet than she was an old maid busybody in so many films. Tempestuous Lenore Ulric is a curiosity that works. This former Belasco stage star embodies a disappointed envy of Garbo that Cukor uses to great advantage. Lionel Barrymore, all growling propriety, is the jarring note in the ensemble.

The screenplay was adapted from the Dumas play by Frances Marion, James Hilton, and Zoe Akins. And Adrian's costumes, usually white, for Miss Garbo, contribute to her divination of literature's most beloved dying swan. This was Irving Thalberg's last production; he died while it was being made and it was completed by Bernard Hyman.

CAMILLE CLAUDEL

1989   149m   c   ★★½
Biography   R/PG
Christian Fechner/Lilith/Gaumont/A2/D.D.   (France)

Isabelle Adjani (*Camille Claudel*), Gerard Depardieu (*Auguste Rodin*), Laurent Grevill (*Paul Claudel*), Alain Cuny (*Louis-Prosper Claudel*), Madeleine Robinson (*Louise-Athanaise Claudel*), Katrine Boorman (*Jessie Lipscomb*), Daniele Lebrun (*Rose Beuret*), Aurelle Doazan (*Louise Claudel*), Madeleine Marie (*Victoire*), Maxime Leroux (*Claude Debussy*)

p, Christian Fechner; d, Bruno Nuytten; w, Bruno Nuytten, Marilyn Goldin (based on the biography by Reine-Marie Paris); ph, Pierre Lhomme (Eastmancolor, Fujicolor); ed, Joelle Hache, Jeanne Kef; m, Gabriel Yared; art d, Bernard Vezat; cos, Dominique Borg

This film about the tragic life of French artist Camille Claudel is as dark and unwieldy as one of Claudel's own sculptures. Born in 1864, Claudel (played by Oscar-nominated Isabelle Adjani, who also coproduced) demonstrated talent early. At 20, she met sculptor Auguste Rodin (Gerard Depardieu), who became her mentor and lover. Their 12-year liaison was an artistically fertile time for Claudel, but the affair's disastrous outcome caused the already high-strung Claudel to deteriorate further emotionally to the point of becoming an impoverished recluse, and in 1913 she was forcibly committed to a psychiatric hospital.

Adjani and director Bruno Nuytten's film is an admiring but emotionally ininvolving and sketchy account of a woman about whom little is actually known. Faced with gaps in the record, they have imagined a life of towering romantic passion and destruction for Claudel, but the plot motivation becomes murky, leaving Adjani to indulge in protracted emotional fireworks that damage her portrayal. On the other hand, Depardieu is amazingly successful in his tricky role as the great Rodin, and ex-cinematographer Nuytten fills his film with memorable images.

His inexperience as a first-time director shows, however, in the film's uncertain pacing and lack of dramatic cohesiveness (the inadequate script is no help). In addition to Adjani's Oscar nomination, the film was also up for Best Foreign Film, but lost to CINEMA PARADISO.

CANDIDATE, THE

1972   109m   c   ★★★½
Political   /15
WB

Robert Redford *(Bill McKay)*, Peter Boyle *(Luck)*, Don Porter *(Sen. Crocker Jarmon)*, Allen Garfield *(Howard Klein)*, Melvyn Douglas *(John J. McKay)*, Quinn Redeker *(Rich Jenkin)*, Michael Lerner *(Paul Corliss)*, Karen Carlson *(Nancy McKay)*, Morgan Upton *(Henderson)*, Kenneth Tobey *(Starkey)*

p, Walter Coblenz; d, Michael Ritchie; w, Jeremy Larner; ph, Victor J. Kemper, John Korty (Technicolor); ed, Richard A. Harris, Robert Estrin; m, John Rubinstein; cos, Patricia Norris

The seductiveness of power and the good man it leads astray. Jeremy Larner's Academy Award-winning screenplay provides a voyage into the sea of politics; the result is a fascinating film that sometimes feels like a documentary. Despite minor glitches, this is probably about as close to the truth of politics as we will ever see.

Redford plays an altruistic attorney whose father (Douglas) was California's governor. Having seen all the dirt as a young man, Redford has no interest in politics. Porter is the typical big-state senator—bluff, hearty, and full of bull—there doesn't seem to be anyone who can come close to defeating him in the next election. Boyle asks Redford to run for office. After some soul-searching, Redford agrees—with the proviso that his father be kept out of the campaign and that he, Redford, be allowed to say what he feels with no political tracts being pushed upon him by the party. His candor appeals to the public, and he begins to climb in the opinion polls. With popularity behind him, will he sell out or not?

Redford invests his performance with more of his talent than usual, and the film runs on manic energy right up till the end. A special irony: Broderick Crawford, dean of filmdom's politicians (see ALL THE KING'S MEN), does the narration for Porter's campaign.

CANDY MOUNTAIN
1988 91m c   ★★★½
Drama   R/15
Xanadu/Plain-Chant/Vision 4 (Switzerland/Canada/France)

Kevin J. O'Connor *(Julius Book)*, Harris Yulin *(Elmore Silk)*, Tom Waits *(Al Silk)*, Bulle Ogier *(Cornelia)*, Roberts Blossom *(Archie)*, Leon Redbone *(Huey)*, Dr. John *(Henry)*, Rita MacNeil *(Winnie)*, Joe Strummer *(Mario)*, Laurie Metcalf *(Alice)*

p, Ruth Waldburger; d, Robert Frank, Rudy Wurlitzer; w, Rudy Wurlitzer; ph, Pio Corradi; ed, Jennifer Auge; m, Max Rebennack "Dr. John", David Johansen, Leon Redbone, Rita MacNeil, Tom Waits; fx, Jacques Godbout; cos, Carol Wood

Failed rock 'n' roll musician Julius Book (Kevin J. O'Connor) embarks on a mission to find guitar-maker Elmore Silk (Harris Yulin), a legendary craftsman who, 20 years before, at the height of his fame, dropped out of sight. Elmore's guitars are now worth $20,000 apiece, and Julius is hired by some music-industry big shots to find him. Desperately looking for a way to carve out a career for himself in the music business, Julius, who has never even heard of Elmore, takes the job and learns the hard way that "life ain't no candy mountain."

The product of a reportedly uneasy collaboration between photographer and filmmaker Robert Frank (PULL MY DAISY) and screenwriter Rudy Wurlitzer (TWO LANE BLACKTOP, WALKER), CANDY MOUNTAIN is an excellent road movie detailing the enlightenment of a callow young musician who mistakenly believes that simply pulling off a scam will somehow make him a successful artist. Filled with beautiful imagery,

poetic dialogue, sly humor, savvy cameos, and excellent music, the film travels straight north from New York City to "the last town on the last street in North America."

O'Connor is superb as the would-be rock star whose romantic notions persist despite the fact that he is an empty vessel with absolutely nothing to say, and this odd, offbeat film richly deserves the audience it failed to find during its theatrical run.

CAPE FEAR
1962 105m bw   ★★★★
Thriller   /X
Melville/Talbot

Gregory Peck *(Sam Bowden)*, Robert Mitchum *(Max Cady)*, Polly Bergen *(Peggy Bowden)*, Lori Martin *(Nancy Bowden)*, Martin Balsam *(Mark Dutton)*, Jack Kruschen *(Dave Grafton)*, Telly Savalas *(Charles Sievers)*, Barrie Chase *(Diane Taylor)*, Paul Comi *(Garner)*, Edward Platt *(Judge)*

p, Sy Bartlett (Melville-Talbot); d, J. Lee Thompson; w, James R. Webb (based on the novel *The Executioners* by John D. MacDonald); ph, Sam Leavitt; ed, George Tomasini; m, Bernard Herrmann; art d, Alexander Golitzen, Robert Boyle; cos, Mary Wills

Unforgettable villany. Suspenseful and very frightening, thanks to Robert Mitchum's lethally threatening performance and the frightened reactions of a pro cast. As a matter of fact, he's even scarier here than in NIGHT OF THE HUNTER, because there is no motivating factor for his evil.

Sexual deviate and lethal psychopath Mitchum is released from prison after serving a six-year term for rape and assault. He is bent on revenge against Peck, the witness whose testimony put him there, who is a family man and a lawyer with a private practice in Florida. When Peck learns Mitchum is in town, he goes to Balsam, the sheriff, who tries to make life miserable for Mitchum until a lawyer threatens to file suit on charges of harassment. Peck's dog is poisoned, then Mitchum takes to the phone, calling Bergen, the lawyer's wife, plaguing her with obscene remarks. Though he makes no overt threats, he intimates a dire fate for the family, including their teenage daughter, Martin. Because the police are helpless to jail the lunatic and the calls and oblique threats continue, Peck decides to handle matters himself.

J. Lee Thompson directs at a clip, until the crawl toward the bayou climax, where the minutes feel like hours, and your heart sits in your throat. Peck is careful not to act the fear; he's an interesting foe for Mitchum. Bergen's performance reminds one that she should have been a bigger star, given her beauty and undeniable talent, and Martin recalls an era when teenagers really were innocent. Balsam, Savalas, and Chase contribute effective cameos. The musical score by Bernard Herrmann is a nerve-beater.

CAPE FEAR
1991 128m c   ★★★½
Thriller   R/18
Universal/Cape Fear Inc./Amblin Entertainment/Cappa Films/Tribeca Productions

Robert De Niro *(Max Cady)*, Nick Nolte *(Sam Bowden)*, Jessica Lange *(Leigh Bowden)*, Juliette Lewis *(Danielle Bowden)*, Joe Don Baker *(Claude Kersek)*, Robert Mitchum *(Lieutenant Elgart)*, Gregory Peck *(Lee Heller)*, Martin Balsam *(Judge)*, Illeana Douglas *(Lori Davis)*, Fred Dalton Thompson *(Tom Broadbent)* p, Barbara DeFina, Kathleen Kennedy; d, Martin Scorsese; w, Wesley Strick (based on the 1962 screenplay by James R. Webb, from the novel *The Executioners* by John D. MacDonald); ph, Freddie Francis; ed, Thelma Schoonmaker; m, Bernard Herrmann; prod d, Henry Bumstead; art d, Jack G. Taylor Jr.; cos, Rita Ryack

Martin Scorsese's loose remake of J. Lee Thompson's 1962 thriller is an exercise in audience manipulation, with every frame designed to stagger the senses. During quiet scenes, the camera is in constant, unsettling motion. During big scenes, shock cuts to weird, menacing angles and reality-bending, high-tech optics accompany dark images of eroticism and violence.

In a telling twist on the original film, Nick Nolte plays lawyer Sam Bowden as a mean-spirited womanizer who has cheated on his burnt-out, embittered wife Leigh, played by Jessica Lange. (In the 1962 version, the Bowdens were morally pristine, impossibly upright citizens.) The family has moved to a backwater Florida town for a new start, but Bowden is already fooling around with his clerk, Lori (Illeana Douglas). Meanwhile, Leigh broods at home, venting her bile on teenage daughter Dani (Juliette Lewis), who stumbles through the film pathetically shell-shocked and alone.

It is one of Sam's past professional betrayals that comes home to roost in the film's main plot. As a public defender, he railroaded client Max Cady (Robert DeNiro) into a 14-year prison sentence for sexual assault by burying a court report attesting to his victim's promiscuity. Now Cady is out and hungry for revenge, having spent his sentence remaking himself into a wily lawyer and con-man psychologist, well-read also in philosophy and literature. Cady's plan is to destroy Max's career and family from within. He poisons the family dog, beats up and mutilates Lori, and comes close to twisting Dani's adolescent frustrations into sympathy with his cause, successfully goading Sam into violence.

There are no heroes in CAPE FEAR, only victims and their tormentors. Everybody is mercilessly photographed to look as ugly as possible. De Niro rolls through the film like a demented descendant of Popeye the Sailor, his sinewy body awash with jailhouse tattoos (giving Mitchum the film's best line: "I don't know whether to look at him or read him"). Nolte winces, cowers and sweats; even normal activities like brushing his teeth are filmed in extreme close-ups that make him look subhuman. Lange looks pinched and drawn throughout, with the 17-year-old Lewis giving the movie's most impressive performance.

In what is by far the film's best (and most-discussed) scene, Dani is lured into a deserted school theater by Cady, who has been impersonating her new drama teacher. Such is his hypnotic power that, even after she begins to realize who he is, she finds herself attracted to him, erotically sucking his thumb and kissing him before finally bolting the scene in terror—at which point audiences can start breathing again.

Scorsese's contempt for his characters extends to his handling of the scenario, credited to Wesley Strick (TRUE BELIEVER). The death of the Bowden's dog is treated with more genuine gravity than the grisly crime against Lori, who, humiliated by her implausible complicity in her own assault, fails to press charges. Though Scorsese throws in the occasional touch of humor, CAPE FEAR remains an overblown assault on the senses that leaves the viewer feeling physically—and morally—drained.

CAPTAIN BLOOD
1935   119m   bw   ★★★★
Adventure/Historical   /PG
WB

Errol Flynn *(Dr. Peter Blood)*, Olivia de Havilland *(Arabella Bishop)*, Lionel Atwill *(Col. Bishop)*, Basil Rathbone *(Capt. Levasseur)*, Ross Alexander *(Jeremy Pitt)*, Guy Kibbee *(Hagthorpe)*, Henry Stephenson *(Lord Willoughby)*, George Hassell *(Gov. Steed)*, Forrester Harvey *(Honesty Nuttall)*, Frank McGlynn, Sr. *(Rev. Ogle)*

p, Harry Joe Brown; d, Michael Curtiz; w, Casey Robinson (based on the novel by Rafael Sabatini); ph, Hal Mohr, Ernest Haller; ed, George Amy; m, Erich Wolfgang Korngold; art d, Anton Grot; fx, Fred Jackman; cos, Milo Anderson

Flynn's star-making swashbuckler is right on target. Based on the novel by Rafael Sabatini, CAPTAIN BLOOD concerns the adventures of a young Brit surgeon who turns buccaneer after unjust persecution. The film had been originally earmarked for Robert Donat whose recurrent asthma convinced Jack Warner to gamble on Flynn. The unknown de Havilland also scored as love interest, and despite a tight budget, Curtiz contributed a lush production. Highlight is the trademark duel between Flynn and Rathbone.

Mindful that his two novice stars might bomb, wily Jack Warner decided not to build full-scale sailing ships for the many action scenes. To represent the bombardments, naval battles, and sinking of ships, technicians built several model ships 18 feet long, with 16-foot masts, and the battles were fought in a studio tank. Even the town of Port Royal was built in miniature. Clips from silent films (First National's 1924 SEA HAWK and Vitagraph's 1923 CAPTAIN BLOOD) were used to show full-scale ships in battle. The main decks of two ships were constructed on a soundstage for the life-size action, and on-location scenes were made along the California coastline.

Almost from the day of CAPTAIN BLOOD's release, Flynn was a Hollywood star, a favorite with a public that would forever see him as the great swashbuckler, a perception that he lived up to in one adventure film after another. BLOOD not only served to introduce Flynn as a stellar lead, but brought critical acclaim as well to lovely 19-year-old de Havilland, who carries off her part with great maturity and sophistication. She and the dashing Flynn eventually appeared together in eight films. Curtiz, the master of adventure films who shot every scene as if it were a cavalry charge, directed a total of nine Flynn epics, and Erich Wolfgang Korngold, whose rich and resonant scores set the musical standard for such spectacular films, composed seven scores for Flynn epics.

CAPTAIN FROM CASTILE
1947   140m   c   ★★★★
Adventure/Historical   /A
Fox

Tyrone Power *(Pedro De Vargas)*, Jean Peters *(Catana Perez)*, Cesar Romero *(Hernando Cortez)*, Lee J. Cobb *(Juan Garcia)*, John Sutton *(Diego De Silva)*, Antonio Moreno *(Don Francisco)*, Thomas Gomez *(Fr. Bartolome Romero)*, Alan Mowbray *(Prof. Botello)*, Barbara Lawrence *(Luisa De Caravajal)*, George Zucco *(Marquis De Caravajal)*

p, Lamar Trotti; d, Henry King; w, Lamar Trotti (based on the novel by Samuel Shellabarger); ph, Charles Clarke, Arthur E. Arling (Technicolor); ed, Barbara McLean; m, Alfred Newman; art d, Richard Day, James Basevi; fx, Fred Sersen; cos, Charles LeMaire

A sweeping, majestic spectacle, neatly divided into a double feature: Spanish inquisition and the expedition of Cortez into Mexico. CAPTAIN FROM CASTILE was a major star vehicle for Power, and he's supported in style by Peters (in her film debut; she was discovered as a 20-year-old Ohio State coed), Cobb, Sutton, and especially Romero, as Cortez.

Although the script sometimes stretches credibility, King's panorama is distracting enough to sweep away your suspicions. CASTILE was a return to the old and glorious pageantry of yesteryear Hollywood, a huge $4.5 million production with one of the most memorable and stirring scores ever composed by Newman. The film was a pet project for Zanuck, who bought Princeton professor Samuel Shellabarger's unpublished novel for $100,000 when it was serialized in *Cosmopolitan* magazine.

Henry King, Fox's top action director, loved to scout locations in his small private plane. He had flown over Morales, a province of southern Mexico, as early as 1933 and selected this remote and rugged area as the site for this project. The trek deep into Mexico was similar to Cortez's own march, except that this one involved eight railroad cars packed with dozens of actors and technicians, including a dry cleaning unit for the expensive costumes and a refrigerated car in which the Technicolor film was kept.

Power, a pilot himself, flew 50 cast members down in a large chartered plane. A smoldering volcano near the location constantly threatened to erupt, delaying the shooting schedule which stretched on for almost four months while the budget doubled and Zanuck fumed. The film lost money but it remains as one of Fox's great epics.

CAPTAIN HORATIO HORNBLOWER

1951 116m c   ★★★½
Adventure   /U
WB (U.K.)

Gregory Peck (*Horatio Hornblower*), Virginia Mayo (*Lady Barbara Wellesley*), Robert Beatty (*Lt. William Bush*), James Robertson Justice (*Quist*), Denis O'Dea (*Adm. Leighton*), Terence Morgan (*Lt. Gerard*), Richard Hearne (*Polwheal*), James Kenney (*Midshipman Longley*), Moultrie Kelsall (*Lt. Crystal*), Michael Dolan (*Gundarson*)

p, Gerry Mitchell; d, Raoul Walsh; w, Ivan Goff, Ben Roberts, Aeneas MacKenzie (based on the novel by C.S. Forester); ph, Guy Green (Technicolor); ed, Jack Harris; m, Robert Farnon

Full of valiant guff. Peck took over for dissipated Errol Flynn, playing title role of 19th-century English hero who outwits the French and Spanish during the Napoleonic wars. Alas, Peck's a touch sober for a credible swashbuckler. In another instance of offbeat casting, Mayo plays Lady Barbara, the Duke of Wellington's sister, and she has a bad fever! Despite miscasting, Walsh's direction has no time to linger. Guy Green's camerawork and Robert Farnon's jolly score are helpful. In the small role of Polwheal is Richard Hearne, who may be remembered as Britain's comic "Mr. Pastry!"—an acrobatic, often hilarious silent comedian whom Ed Sullivan loved.

CAPTAINS COURAGEOUS

1937 115m bw   ★★★★★
Adventure   /U
MGM

Freddie Bartholomew (*Harvey*), Spencer Tracy (*Manuel*), Lionel Barrymore (*Disko*), Melvyn Douglas (*Mr. Cheyne*), Charley Grapewin (*Uncle Salters*), Mickey Rooney (*Dan*), John Carradine ("*Long Jack*"), Oscar O'Shea (*Cushman*), Jack LaRue (*Priest*), Walter Kingsford (*Dr. Finley*)

p, Louis D. Lighton; d, Victor Fleming; w, John Lee Mahin, Marc Connelly, Dale Van Every (based on the novel by Rudyard Kipling); ph, Harold Rosson; ed, Elmo Veron; m, Franz Waxman; art d, Cedric Gibbons

For once, a script perfectly suited to its director and star and one of the most lyrical children's classics ever made. Ignore the typical MGM "prestige picture" touches and enjoy the spirited cast performing under man's man director Fleming, who is reverential to the Kipling story. Young Harvey (Freddie Bartholomew), the spoiled-rotten son of a business tycoon, believes he can lie, cheat, and whine his way through life. On a trip to Europe with his father, the young man falls off a posh ocean liner into the sea and is rescued by a boat filled with Portuguese fishermen. One of the sailors is Manuel (Spencer Tracy), a big-hearted veteran of the seas who has a lot to teach the selfish Harvey about life.

CAPTAINS COURAGEOUS is a wonderful sea adventure with a heartwarming drama at its core. Tracy is excellent as the gentle fisherman, turning in a performance that won him a Best Actor Oscar. He reportedly hated his role, however, especially having his hair curled and wrestling with an accent (Tracy loathed externalized acting), but it doesn't show for a moment. The following year, he won the coveted statuette again for BOYS TOWN.

CAPTAIN'S PARADISE, THE

1953 93m bw   ★★★½
Comedy   /U
London Films (U.K.)

Alec Guinness (*Capt. Henry St. James*), Yvonne De Carlo (*Nita*), Celia Johnson (*Maud*), Charles Goldner (*Chief Officer Ricco*), Miles Malleson (*Lawrence St. James*), Bill Fraser (*Absalom*), Tutte Lemkow (*Principal Dancer*), Nicholas Phipps (*The Major*), Walter Crisham (*Bob*), Ferdy Mayne (*Sheikh*)

p, Anthony Kimmins; d, Anthony Kimmins; w, Alec Coppel, Nicholas Phipps (based on a story by Alec Coppel); ph, Ted Scaife; ed, Gerald Turney-Smith; m, Malcolm Arnold; art d, Paul Sheriff; chor, Walter Crisham, Tutte Lemkow

Guinness at his conniving best in a droll, consistently funny comedy. He plays the captain of a steamer that sails between Gibraltar and North Africa. Instead of having a girl in every port, Guinness has a wife at either end, each offering him a completely different lifestyle. In Gibraltar it's Johnson, a sedate British housewife who makes him home-cooked meals and is content to stay at home by the fire. In North Africa, it's De Carlo, a sexy, voluptuous woman with whom he does the hot spots, dancing through the exotic nights. (On his ship, Guinness keeps a revolving picture frame that has a photo of Johnson on one side and De Carlo on the other!) In flashback, we watch as Guinness manages to have the best of both worlds, while his chief officer, Goldner, slavishly admires this grand deception and seeks to emulate his captain.

Suspense is sustained throughout THE CAPTAIN'S PARADISE because as the film opens Guinness is about to be shot by a firing squad and the viewer does not become privy to his fate until the very surprising ending. In between, the scheming captain is undone by the women in his life. Guinness's life goes topsy-turvy when Johnson insists on seeking adventure and excitement, while De Carlo suddenly takes up cooking, tiring of night life and desiring domestic tranquility. When Guinness resists these disturbing transformations both women leave him.

Guinness gives a masterful performance, and Johnson and De Carlo are superb in their unpredictable parts. The pace is vigorous under Kimmins's direction, and he manages to relate the subtle and frivolous story with verve, his transitions from scene to scene as smooth as Guinness's own incomparable style. A generous serving of delicious whimsy.

CAR WASH
1976 97m c   ★★★
Comedy   PG
Universal

Franklyn Ajaye (T.C.), Sully Boyar (Mr. B.), Richard Brestoff (Irwin), George Carlin (Taxi Driver), Irwin Corey (Mad Bomber), Ivan Dixon (Lonnie), Bill Duke (Duane), Antonio Fargas (Lindy), Michael Fennell (Calvin), Arthur French (Charlie)

p, Art Linson, Gary Stromberg; d, Michael Schultz; w, Joel Schumacher; ph, Frank Stanley (Technicolor); ed, Christopher Holmes; m, Norman Whitfield; art d, Robert Clatworthy; cos, Daniel Paredes

Coarse, hilarious comedy detailing a day in the life of an L.A. car wash, featuring an ensemble cast of superb performers. Basically plotless, the film shows the lives, hopes, dreams, ambitions, and foibles of the multiracial employees and customers of Boyar's Car Wash. One of many highlights has Richard Pryor as a fancy-pants preacher who arrives in his flashy car accompanied by the Pointer Sisters. Great musical score by Whitfield is integrated into the movement of the scenes to give the film a funky rhythm. Director Schultz, one of the first mainstream Black filmmakers, also helmed the spirited inner-city comedy COOLEY HIGH. You won't sit still.

CARAVAGGIO
1986 93m c   ★★★½
Biography   /18
British Film Institute/Channel 4   (U.K.)

Nigel Terry (Caravaggio), Sean Bean (Rannuccio Thomasoni), Garry Cooper (Davide), Spencer Leigh (Jerusaleme), Tilda Swinton (Lena), Michael Gough (Cardinal Del Monte), Nigel Davenport (Marchese Giustiniani), Robbie Coltrane (Cardinal Borghese), Jonathan Hyde (Baglione), Dexter Fletcher (Young Caravaggio)

p, Sarah Radclyffe; d, Derek Jarman; w, Derek Jarman; ph, Gabriel Beristain (Technicolor); ed, George Akers; m, Simon Fisher Turner, Mary Phillips; prod d, Christopher Hobbs; cos, Sandy Powell

The defiantly queer Jarman has never been known for catering to the tastes of the mainstream public. His works such as SEBASTIANE, JUBILEE, and THE TEMPEST are obsessive and excessive. Easily his most accessible film, CARAVAGGIO is a sketchy biography of the Italian Renaissance painter Michelangelo Merisi da Caravaggio.

Having very little documented material as reference, Jarman deduced that Caravaggio's paintings were essentially autobiographical. Combining discoveries from his diligent canvas research with the few known facts, Jarman wrote the script for his version of the painter's life. The film opens with Caravaggio (Nigel Terry) lying in a desperate fever on his deathbed in a small, barren room; it then flashes back to his younger days and depicts his rather squalid life and failed attempts to gain acceptance for his art. In particular we witness Caravaggio's volatile relationships with his model Ranunccio Thomasoni (Sean Bean), who posed as the muscular assassin in several "martyrdom" tableaus, and Lena (Tilda Swinton), who is Ranunccio's mistress and

Caravaggio's model for the Magdalene and the dead Virgin. Their menage leads to artistic triumphs and Caravaggio's arrest for murder.

Undoubtedly Jarman felt a great deal of passion for his subject and, despite the filmmaker's gravely romantic formalism, the passion that fueled Caravaggio's brief career is brought compellingly to life. Beyond the studied homoeroticism and deliberate anachronisms lies an aloof and mocking film, one that Caravaggio himself might have enjoyed.

CARMEN
1983 102m c   ★★★½
Drama/Dance/Musical   R/15
Orion   (Spain)

Antonio Gades (Antonio), Laura del Sol (Carmen), Paco de Lucia (Paco), Christina Hoyos (Cristina), Juan Antonio Jimenez (Juan), Sebastian Moreno (Escamillo), Jose Yepes (Pepe Giron), Pepa Flores (Pepa Flores)

p, Emiliano Piedra; d, Carlos Saura; w, Carlos Saura, Antonio Gades (from the opera by Georges Bizet, based on the novel by Prosper Merimee); ph, Teo Escamilla (Eastmancolor); ed, Pedro del Rey; m, Paco de Lucia, Georges Bizet; chor, Carlos Saura, Antonio Gades; cos, Teresa Nieto

This version of the Merimee classic uses rehearsals for a flamenco version of Bizet's opera (not unlike director Saura's previous BLOOD WEDDING) as the setting for an identical, parallel storyline.

Laura del Sol (THE HIT) plays Carmen, a fiery actress-dancer who is slated to play her namesake despite her lack of experience. Antonio Gades (BLOOD WEDDING) is the choreographer who falls in love with her. The dance sequences are superb, as expected, with the added plus of del Sol's eroticism and Christina Hoyos's explosive performance as Carmen's rival. Saura's acclaimed dance trilogy (the third film is EL AMOR BRUJO), abetted by Antonio Gades's incendiary choreography, are must-sees for dance enthusiasts. Others may greet CARMEN with mixed emotions. But meanwhile, what other version measures up?

CARMEN JONES
1954 105m c   ★★★★
Opera
FOX

Dorothy Dandridge (Carmen), Harry Belafonte (Joe), Olga James (Cindy Lou), Pearl Bailey (Frankie), Diahann Carroll (Myrt), Roy E. Glenn, Sr. (Rum), Nick Stewart (Dink), Joe Adams (Husky Miller), Brock Peters (Sgt. Brown), Sandy Lewis (T-Bone)

p, Otto Preminger; d, Otto Preminger; w, Harry Kleiner (based on the book by Oscar Hammerstein II); ph, Sam Leavitt (CinemaScope, Deluxe Color); ed, Louis Loeffler; m, Georges Bizet

The closest to the CARMEN spirit thus far. Adaptation of Broadway triumph combines Bizet's gorgeous music with lyrics by Oscar Hammerstein II. Preminger directed with a heavy hand, nor, unfortunately, could he ever be accused of being sympathetic enough to guide actresses through their best performances, but *nothing* can stop this sensational cast.

Dandridge is a revelation. Even mouthing Marilyn Horne's vocals (not that Dandridge wasn't an accomplished singer; following a brief retirement in the late 1940s, her career was rekindled by a smash engagement at the posh Mocambo nightclub), she is chilling and exactly right, full of psychological transitions and reflecting clearly the sequences of her thoughts. She's almost matched by Belafonte, and both leads are mesmerizingly beautiful. Also expert are Bailey, Carroll, James, and newcomer Peters. Adams is the one member of the ensemble unable to rise to the occasion—this role should have gone to Peters.

Considering the tragic waste of Dandridge by show business professionals in all mediums, it is heartening that CARMEN JONES exists as a testament to her beauty and singular talent. She died from a barbiturate overdose in 1965 at age 41.

CARNAL KNOWLEDGE

1971 97m c ★★★★★
Drama R/X
Avco Embassy

Jack Nicholson (Jonathan), Candice Bergen (Susan), Art Garfunkel (Sandy), Ann-Margret (Bobbie), Rita Moreno (Louise), Cynthia O'Neal (Cindy), Carol Kane (Jennifer)

p, Mike Nichols; d, Mike Nichols; w, Jules Feiffer; ph, Giuseppe Rotunno (Panavision, Technicolor); ed, Sam O'Steen; prod d, Richard Sylbert; art d, Robert Luthardt; cos, Anthea Sylbert

Controversial, painfully savage, and perhaps the most important film to come out of Hollywood in the 1970s. The filmgoers and critics who disparaged this film may be guilty of lacking emotional courage. Certainly, here is the best directing Nichols has ever done—a more demanding subject than his acclaimed VIRGINIA WOOLF—of a diverse, peculiar cast.

The plot examines the sexual odysseys of two male college roommates and self-proclaimed "best friends" into middle age. Jack Nicholson heads the cast as a manipulative bastard, incapable of emotional intimacy, and Art Garfunkel is his less confident chum. Neither has ever been better. Indeed, Nicholson's scene of rage at his depressive mistress (Ann-Margret) is a high point of his acting career and did much to establish him as a leading man.

On the distaff side, CARNAL KNOWLEDGE is clearly Ann-Margret's show. The girl with the hyphen in her name and slither in her walk, the wasted sex kitten the industry laughed at, finally brings the whip down in an exacting, powerful, understated portrayal from life as a beauty rotting on the vine, a girl whose looks have betrayed her into the hands of users and abusers; her portrait of abandonment is painful to watch. And along the way to her character's desperate acts, she became at once what she labored to become for ten years; a bonafide sex symbol unafraid to face the ravages of time and an actress capable of bringing her star power into an ensemble and contributing something of flesh, blood and tears.

Candice Bergen also contributes her best dramatic work to date as a bewildered college girl torn between the seductions of both men—one evil, the other weak. In the film's most powerfully edited, cinematic moment she dances with both to Glenn Miller's "String of Pearls": each time she swings out of camera range her partner changes yet again. This film is a reminder that Bergen's best may still be yet to come.

CARNAL KNOWLEDGE is an uneasy work of art that attempts to settle the score of the double standard; one wonders if it should be required viewing for young men of a certain age. The film is uneven and flawed because it dares to be so ugly; because life is not a thing of beauty or perfection, balance or fairness. CARNAL KNOWLEDGE presents human existence as ravaged, painful and terribly difficult. It's damn near perfect.

CAROUSEL

1956 128m c ★★★★
Musical /U
FOX

Gordon MacRae (Billy), Shirley Jones (Julie), Cameron Mitchell (Jigger), Barbara Ruick (Carrie), Claramae Turner (Cousin Nettie), Robert Rounseville (Mr. Snow), Gene Lockhart (Starkeeper), Audrey Christie (Mrs. Mullin), Susan Luckey (Louise), William Le Massena (Heavenly Friend)

p, Henry Ephron; d, Henry King; w, Phoebe Ephron, Henry Ephron (based on the musical by Richard Rodgers, Oscar Hammerstein II, from the play "Liliom" by Ferenc Molnar); ph, Charles Clarke (CinemaScope, DeLuxe Color); ed, William Reynolds; chor, Rod Alexander, Agnes De Mille; cos, Mary Wills

Haunting and poignant; the best of Rodgers and Hammerstein, sans the corn and cotton candy fluff of other works. This remake of the Fritz Lang-directed LILIOM emerges as a wonderful and touching fantasy.

It begins with MacRae as a spirit in Heaven who begs the starkeeper for a visit back to Earth to help his teenage daughter understand his death and prepare her for high-school graduation. Seen in flashback, carny barker MacRae, a brash, dishonest young man living in a New England fishing village (changed from Ferenc Molnar's original Budapest setting), falls in love with a mill worker, Jones. They marry, but MacRae's inability to find a job leads him into the bad company of Mitchell and an attempted robbery in which MacRae is killed by Mitchell after having second thoughts and trying to stop the thief.

This sadly resigned fantasy, a commercial failure upon its original release, features some of the greatest musical numbers ever filmed, all R&H classics: "If I Loved You," "What's the Use of Wondrin'?" and the stirring "You'll Never Walk Alone." Jones is lovely and heartfelt as the trusting lover, and MacRae is magnetic in his best musical performance, his fine tenor given a range equalled only in OKLAHOMA! Mitchell and other supporting players are excellent in this richly mounted extravaganza that is superb on all technical points and directed with verve and affection by King.

CARRIE

1976 97m c ★★★½
Horror R/18
UA

Sissy Spacek (Carrie White), Piper Laurie (Margaret White), Amy Irving (Sue Snell), William Katt (Tommy Ross), John Travolta (Billy Nolan), Nancy Allen (Chris Hargenson), Betty Buckley (Miss Collins), P.J. Soles (Norma Watson), Sydney Lassick (Mr. Fromm), Stefan Gierasch (Principal Morton)

p, Paul Monash; d, Brian De Palma; w, Larry Cohen (based on the novel by Stephen King); ph, Mario Tosi (DeLuxe Color); ed, Paul Hirsch; m, Pino Donaggio; art d, William Kenny, Jack Fisk; fx, Greg Auer, Ken Pepiot; cos, Rosanna Norton

A telekinetic revenge. De Palma's first big hit remains one of his best efforts to date and a landmark film for the horror genre.

Spacek, in a stunning performance, stars as Carrie, a troubled, sexually repressed high schooler who slowly realizes that she possesses incredible telekinetic powers. Plagued with problems in school (she feels homely, and nobody likes her) and at home (her mother, Laurie—who's also stunning—is a religious fanatic who hates men and makes her daughter pray in a closet), she struggles to maintain her dignity and sanity but is finally driven over the edge when cruel classmates conspire to elect her prom queen in an elaborate joke designed to embarrass her.

Based on the best-selling Stephen King novel and cleverly designed to target a teenage audience, CARRIE was the synthesis of De Palma's talent for intense, stylish, visual filmmaking. His techniques—elaborate compositions, camera moves, and slow motion—combined with a fairly literate screenplay make for an interesting and frightening film that successfully deals with the inner rage every teenager feels. The film has a strikingly unsettling mood that enhances its power and gives it an impact that the story would otherwise lack. Much of the credit, though, must go to Spacek who so convincingly portrays Carrie's pain and her longing to be accepted. The interesting ensemble inludes Betty Buckley, Amy Irving, Nancy Allen and John Travolta.

CARS THAT ATE PARIS, THE

1974   91m   c   ★★
Adventure/Comedy   /X
Salt-Pan   (Australia)

Terry Camilleri *(Arthur)*, John Meillon *(Mayor)*, Melissa Jaffa *(Beth)*, Kevin Miles *(Dr. Midland)*, Max Gillies *(Metcalfe)*, Peter Armstrong *(Gorman)*, Edward Howell *(Tringham)*, Bruce Spence *(Charlie)*, Derek Barnes *(Al Smedley)*, Charles Metcalfe *(Clive Smedley)*

p, Jim McElroy, Howard McElroy; d, Peter Weir; w, Peter Weir, Keith Gow, Piers Davies; ph, John McLean; ed, Wayne LeClos; m, Bruce Smeaton

Scattered, but typically overrated now that the director is a force to be reckoned with. Weir marked his feature debut with a black comedy that now supposedly anticipates THE ROAD WARRIOR with themes culled from THE WILD ONE and HIGH NOON. Spiked wrecks are driven by adventurous youths through the streets of Paris, Australia, causing an endless string of accidents. These collisions are planned events that serve the vulturous townsfolk in both an economic and medical way. The looters profit by pawning what they can recover, and a town doctor performs questionable medical experiments on the victims. The situation culminates in a youth-townsfolk blood bath. It's a big, wide, wonderful world. Whatever.

CASABLANCA

1942   102m   bw   ★★★★★
Drama/War   /U
WB

Humphrey Bogart *(Richard "Rick" Blaine)*, Ingrid Bergman *(Ilsa Lund Laszlo)*, Paul Henreid *(Victor Laszlo)*, Claude Rains *(Capt. Louis Renault)*, Conrad Veidt *(Maj. Heinrich Strasser)*, Sydney Greenstreet *(Senor Ferrari)*, Peter Lorre *(Ugarte)*, S.Z. Sakall *(Carl, Headwaiter)*, Madeleine LeBeau *(Yvonne)*, Dooley Wilson *(Sam)*

p, Hal B. Wallis; d, Michael Curtiz; w, Julius J. Epstein, Philip G. Epstein, Howard Koch (based on the play "Everybody Goes to Rick's" by Murray Burnett, and Joan Alison); ph, Arthur Edeson; ed, Owen Marks; m, Max Steiner; art d, Carl Jules Weyl; fx, Lawrence Butler, Willard Van Enger; cos, Orry-Kelly

The most romantic picture ever made? The best film to come out of a Hollywood studio ever? More an icon than a work of art, CASABLANCA is still thoroughly entertaining romantic melodrama, flawlessly directed, subtly played, lovingly evoking our collective daydreams about lost chances and lost loves and love versus honor; everything about CASABLANCA is just right—it seems to have been filmed under a lucky star.

The familiar plot concerns expatriate American Rick Blaine (Humphrey Bogart), a cynical nightclub owner in Casablanca who discovers that his ex-lover, Ilsa (Ingrid Bergman), who abandoned him years before, has arrived in Casablanca with her husband, Resistance leader Victor Lazlo (Paul Henreid). With the Germans on Victor's trail, Ilsa comes to Casablanca to beg Rick for the precious letters of transit that have come into his possession. The documents would allow Victor to escape Casablanca and continue the fight against fascism.

Since its November 1942 release, CASABLANCA has been *the* movie, one that perfectly blends a turbulent love story with harrowing intrigue, heroic and evil characters, and the kind of genuine sentiment that makes the heart grow fonder with each viewing. Even upon its initial release, the film appealed to nostalgia for the vanishing, romanticized world between the two great wars, a cafe society crushed by fascism, a civilized, urbane generation in white linen suits, spectator shoes, and wide-brimmed sunhats desperately clinging to values no longer cherished.

Given its turbulent production history—the script was being rewritten almost on a daily basis—CASABLANCA was also most fortunate on all levels. The original leads were to have been Ronald Reagan, Ann Sheridan and Dennis Morgan. Other casting packages included George Raft, Hedy Lamarr and Herbert Marshall. And Lena Horne or Ella Fitzgerald might have crooned "As Time Goes By" instead of Dooley Wilson. Chemistry, that indefinable element, was surely carefully considered by veteran director Michael Curtiz.

So was timing. The film opened on Thanksgiving Day, 1942 at the Hollywood Theater in New York, three weeks after the Allies had landed at Casablanca, and further enjoyed widespread publicity generated by the Casablanca Conference two months later, when the eyes of the free world focused upon its leaders' meeting in the Moroccan city. It propelled Bogart's star to new heights, adding a romantic component to his world-weary persona, and gave Bergman a tragic edge to blend with her healthy radiance, making her seem complex and emotionally fragile. The film received eight Academy Award nominations and won three: Best Picture, Best Screenplay and Best Director.

CASINO ROYALE

1967   131m   c   ★★
Adventure/Comedy/Spy   /PG
Columbia   (U.K.)

Peter Sellers *(Evelyn Tremble)*, Ursula Andress *(Vesper Lynd)*, David Niven *(Sir James Bond)*, Orson Welles *(Le Chiffre)*, Joanna Pettet *(Mata Bond)*, Daliah Lavi *(The Detainer)*, Woody Allen *(Jimmy Bond, Dr. Noah)*, Deborah Kerr *(Agent Mimi, Lady Fiona McTarry)*, William Holden *(Ransome)*, Charles Boyer *(Le Grand)*

p, Charles K. Feldman, Jerry Bresler; d, John Huston, Ken Hughes, Robert Parrish, Val Guest, Joseph McGrath; w, Wolf Mankowitz, John Law, Michael Sayers, Billy Wilder, Val Guest, Joseph Heller, Ben Hecht, Terry Southern (from the novel by Ian Fleming); ph, John Wilcox, Jack Hildyard, Nicolas Roeg (Panavision, Technicolor); ed, Bill Lenny; m, Burt Bacharach; art d, John Howell, Ivor Beddoes, Lionel Couch; chor, Tutte Lemkow

A mess. CASINO ROYALE is two hours and eleven minutes of non sequitur. David Niven is Sir James Bond. (Author Ian Fleming, a close friend of Niven, always wanted Niven to assay his famous creation.) He's retired, middle-aged, bejowled, and tired. SMERSH is up to no good, so Niven is asked to help when M (John Huston) is slain. He contacts several agents, all of them 007s. These include Andress, Sellers, Terence Cooper, and Pettet (who is Niven's daughter, the result of a liaison with Mata Hari). After more witless, star-loaded vignettes, Niven finally learns that the real villain is none other than his own ineffectual nephew, Woody Allen.

CASINO ROYALE first found life as a one-hour TV show for CBS's "Climax" in 1954, starring Barry Nelson. The film rights were sold in 1955 and eventually acquired by ex-agent Charles Feldman. Almost every actor yukked it up while making this movie, and the result is totally unfocused. Anything with five directors and screenwriters has to rank on anyone's list for sheer chutzpah.

CASQUE D'OR
1952   96m   bw   ★★★★
Crime/Romance
Speva   (France)

Simone Signoret *(Marie)*, Serge Reggiani *(Manda)*, Claude Dauphin *(Felix Leca)*, Raymond Bussieres *(Raymond)*, William Sabatier *(Roland)*, Gaston Modot *(Danard)*, Loleh Bellon *(Leonie Danard)*, Claude Castaing *(Fredo)*, Paul Azais *(Ponsard)*, Emile Genevois *(Billy)*

d, Jacques Becker; w, Jacques Becker, Jacques Companeez; ph, Robert Le Febvre; ed, Marguerite Renoir; m, George Van Parys

One of the great films of French cinema, CASQUE D'OR initially was greeted with less than favorable reviews but met with renewed interest after then-critic Lindsay Anderson sang its praises.

Set at the turn of the century, the film concerns the romance between Signoret and Reggiani. After murdering a childhood friend, Reggiani surrenders to the authorities, though the killing has been pinned on someone else. Signoret asks a friend to help free her lover but is forced to compromise herself in return. After she submits, the friend goes back on his word. However, when Reggiani is free, he hunts down Signoret's deceitful seducer and guns him down in front of witnesses, earning himself a trip to the guillotine.

Director Becker's fluid camerawork earned him praise from such influential French cineasts as Francois Truffaut and critic Jean Couturier. CASQUE D'OR is a most poetic film, evincing a cinematic purity Becker surely learned something about while working as Jean Renoir's assistant.

CAST A GIANT SHADOW
1966   144m   c   ★★
Biography/War   /A
Mirisch/Llenroc/Batjac

Kirk Douglas *(Col. David "Mickey" Marcus)*, Senta Berger *(Magda Simon)*, Angie Dickinson *(Emma Marcus)*, James Donald *(Safir)*, Stathis Giallelis *(Ram Oren)*, Luther Adler *(Jacob Zion)*, Gary Merrill *(Pentagon Chief of Staff)*, Topol *(Abou Ibn Kader)*, Frank Sinatra *(Vince)*, Yul Brynner *(Asher Gonen)*

p, Melville Shavelson, Michael Wayne; d, Melville Shavelson; w, Melville Shavelson (based on the book by Ted Berkman); ph, Aldo Tonti (Panavision, Deluxe Color); ed, Bert Bates, Gene Ruggiero; m, Elmer Bernstein; art d, Arrigo Equini; fx, Sass Bedig; cos, Margaret Furse

CAST A GIANT SHADOW unfortunately ruins the good idea of a biopic about Colonel David "Mickey" Marcus, an American WWII hero and military adviser to Franklin Roosevelt recruited by the Israeli government to organize Israel's army into a military force that could withstand Arab attacks after the British pulled out of the region in 1949. He's played by rugged, iron-jawed,

teeth-gritting Kirk Douglas, who leaves domesticated bliss with Angie Dickenson, the last word in monogamy, to join bigtime freedom fighter Senta Berger for a big time! Guest stars like Yul Brynner, John Wayne, and Frank Sinatra jump out to relieve the tedium, but big names are the last thing this story needs. This overblown dinosaur was coproduced by John Wayne's Batjac Productions, and it served him right; CAST A GIANT SHADOW made little impact at the box office.

CASUALTIES OF WAR
1989   120m   c   ★★★
War   R/18
Columbia

Michael J. Fox *(Pfc. Eriksson)*, Sean Penn *(Sgt. Meserve)*, Don Harvey *(Clark)*, John C. Reilly *(Hatcher)*, John Leguizamo *(Diaz)*, Thuy Thu Le *(Oahn)*, Erik King *(Brown, Radio Man)*, Jack Gwaltney *(Rowan)*, Ving Rhames *(Lt. Reilly)*, Dan Martin *(Hawthorne)*

p, Art Linson, Fred Caruso; d, Brian De Palma; w, David Rabe (based on the article by Daniel Lang); ph, Stephen H. Burum (Panavision, Deluxe Color); ed, Bill Pankow; m, Ennio Morricone; prod d, Wolf Kroeger; art d, Bernard Hydes; cos, Richard Bruno

With this adaptation of Daniel Lang's famous *New Yorker* article, Brian De Palma joins the ranks of Stanley Kubrick, Francis Ford Coppola and Oliver Stone, major directors who have brought their personal visions and styles to bear on the Vietnam War. The result is often hypnotic and perversely gripping, but falls apart during its final reel.

CASUALTIES OF WAR focuses on one patrol, and the inhumane treatment of a young Vietnamese girl at the hands of a calloused, crazed sergeant. Top acting honors go to Penn as the sergeant and Thuy Thu Le as the captive girl. Fox isn't bad at all; one just gets the feeling that the director and screenwriter got caught up in the dramatic situations inherent in the Penn-Thu Le conflict, and left their hero to flounder as best he could. Because Fox is so extraordinarily clean-cut, he seems more than human. This part needed a really average Joe, but one with enough feel of physical gravity to counteract Penn. Fox ends up a mere flyspeck tossed about in a violent whorl of confusion.

CAT AND THE CANARY, THE
1939   72m   bw   ★★★
Comedy/Mystery   /A
Paramount

Bob Hope *(Wallie Campbell)*, Paulette Goddard *(Joyce Norman)*, John Beal *(Fred Blythe)*, Douglass Montgomery *(Charlie Wilder)*, Gale Sondergaard *(Miss Lu)*, Elizabeth Patterson *(Aunt Susan)*, Nydia Westman *(Cicily)*, George Zucco *(Lawyer Crosby)*, John Wray *(Hendricks)*, George Regas

p, Arthur Hornblow, Jr.; d, Elliott Nugent; w, Walter DeLeon, Lynn Starling (based on the play by John Willard); ph, Charles Lang; ed, Archie Marshek; m, Ernst Toch; art d, Hans Dreier, Robert Usher

The old dark house number, played to the hilt. When an eccentric millionaire dies, lawyer Zucco assembles prospective heirs at the victim's Bayou mansion. Goddard gets all, setting up Hope as straight man for this spooky comic romp. Hope is terrific as the wisecracking but spineless character who attempts to protect Goddard from going insane (if she turns cuckoo she loses the fortune, according to the bizarre will). Director Nugent, who had guided Hope through NEVER SAY DIE and GIVE ME A SAILOR, does a great job in presenting some spine-tingling moments: claw-like hands reach out for the heroine and everyone seems to disappear through swiveling bookcases, sliding doors, and false panels. Lang's camera work is properly moody and supporting player Sondergaard gives a high-camp performance as a spooky, mystic housekeeper dressed in black, with a black cat constantly at her side. This was Goddard's first starring role; following the success of this film, the sly actress with the insinuating voice was teamed with Hope again in THE GHOST BREAKERS.

CAT BALLOU

1965 97m c ★★★½
Comedy/Western /PG
Columbia

Jane Fonda (Cat Ballou), Lee Marvin (Kid Shelleen/Tim Strawn), Michael Callan (Clay Boone), Dwayne Hickman (Jed), Tom Nardini (Jackson Two-Bears), John Marley (Frankie Ballou), Reginald Denny (Sir Harry Percival), Jay C. Flippen (Sheriff Cardigan), Arthur Hunnicutt (Butch Cassidy), Bruce Cabot (Sheriff Maledon)

p, Harold Hecht; d, Elliot Silverstein; w, Frank Pierson, Walter Newman (based on the novel by Roy Chanslor); ph, Jack Marta (Technicolor); ed, Charles Nelson; m, Frank DeVol; chor, Miriam Nelson; cos, Bill Thomas

Funny—but not that funny—western spoof. Fonda employs over-the-hill gunslinger Marvin after his outlaw brother (Marvin again) kills her rancher father. Film is amusing largely due to Marvin's dual hilarity, for which he won an Oscar. It was the beginning of a whole new career as a versatile, middle-aged leading man who could handle drama or comedy with equal finesse. Following several misfires, BALLOU consolidated Fonda's early stardom; while hardly complex, her transformation from prim schoolmarm to sexy gunslinger is utterly charming. Additional diversion is provided by Nat King Cole (in his last film role) and Stubby Kaye, who, as wandering troubadors, break up the screenplay's occasional tedium.

CAT ON A HOT TIN ROOF

1958 108m c ★★★★
Drama /15
MGM

Elizabeth Taylor (Maggie Pollitt), Paul Newman (Brick Pollitt), Burl Ives (Big Daddy Pollitt), Jack Carson (Gooper Pollitt), Judith Anderson (Big Mama Pollitt), Madeleine Sherwood (Mae Pollitt), Larry Gates (Dr. Baugh), Vaughn Taylor (Deacon Davis), Patty Ann Gerrity (Dixie Pollitt), Rusty Stevens (Sonny Pollitt)

p, Lawrence Weingarten; d, Richard Brooks; w, Richard Brooks, James Poe (based on the play by Tennessee Williams); ph, William Daniels (Metrocolor); ed, Ferris Webster; art d, William A. Horning, Urie McCleary; fx, Lee LeBlanc; cos, Helen Rose

A southern house divided between patriarchal dominance and hypocrisy, rendered effectively despite censorship and a screenplay that bogs midway. The performances are the thing in this film version of the Tennessee Williams stage triumph, led by Ives, repeating his stage role like a force of nature. Taylor and Newman make a handsomely unhappy husband and wife, with just enough sexual chemistry to justify the union. Mike Todd's plane crashed during filming, and the camera seems to capture Taylor's pent-up energy, but she isn't directed well enough to unleash it. This is fine throughout most of the film, but her catharsis is finally lacking and her little vengeances come off less like a satiated alley cat than a pampered prize kitty. The homosexual overtones are just about laundered out of Newman's role, but his pantherine eyes and profile suggest unplumbed depths

between the lines. Jack Carson and Dame Judith Anderson are just right but out of the ensemble it is Madeleine Sherwood who is absolutely definitive as Sister Woman.

CAT PEOPLE

1942 73m bw ★★★★★
Horror /A
RKO

Simone Simon (Irena Dubrovna), Kent Smith (Oliver Reed), Tom Conway (Dr. Judd), Jane Randolph (Alice Moore), Jack Holt (Commodore), Alan Napier (Carver), Elizabeth Dunne (Miss Plunkett), Elizabeth Russell (The Cat Woman)

p, Val Lewton; d, Jacques Tourneur; w, DeWitt Bodeen; ph, Nicholas Musuraca; ed, Mark Robson; m, Roy Webb

Significant as the first of the literate, understated horror films Val Lewton produced for RKO in the 1940s, CAT PEOPLE is also notable for playing with audience imagination by refusing to show made-up movie monsters a la the Wolfman or Mr. Hyde. Although earlier films had linked horror and sexuality, Tourneur's study of a woman tainted by an ancient Balkan curse was arguably more explicit in this direction than any previous film had been. The result is a haunting and subtle film, filled with desires gone awry and everyday settings turned inexplicably nightmarish.

Immigrant sketch artist Irena Dubrovna (Simon) and all-American architect Oliver Reed (Smith) fall in love and marry after a brief courtship, but Irena won't consummate the union for fear that she will turn into a panther compelled to kill her lover. When Oliver confides in co-worker Alice Moore (Randolph) though, Irena's jealousy proves equally effective in precipitating her horrifying transformation. The disbelief of cynical psychiatrist Dr. Judd (Conway) proves likewise ineffective against the powers unleashed by Irena's psyche.

Beautifully directed by Tourneur and carefully paced by screenwriter Bodeen, the film opens in mundane New York settings, only occasionally hinting that evil is about (e.g. a feline woman at a bar, the reaction of the animals at a pet store to Irena's presence). Once Irena's darker side begins to manifest itself, however, the film's pulse quickens and so does the viewer's. Perhaps most famous are the justly celebrated sequence where Irena stalks Alice along a park path at night (featuring the marvelously jarring cat-like hiss of bus doors) and the brilliant set-piece when Irena surrounds the terrified Alice at a darkened indoor swimming pool with the cries of a ferocious panther.

Superbly acted (with Simon evoking both pity and chills), CAT PEOPLE testifies to the power of suggestion and the priority of imagination over budget in the creation of great cinema. The film was Lewton's biggest hit, its viewers lured in by such bombastic advertising as "Kiss me and I'll claw you to death!"—a line more lurid than anything that ever appeared onscreen. Forty years later Paul Schrader would remake the original, failing to learn any of the lessons which Lewton had taught.

CATCH-22

1970 121m c ★★½
War R/15
Paramount

Alan Arkin (Capt. Yossarian), Martin Balsam (Col. Cathcart), Richard Benjamin (Maj. Danby), Art Garfunkel (Capt. Nately), Jack Gilford (Doc Daneeka), Bob Newhart (Maj. Major), Anthony Perkins (Chaplain Tappman), Paula Prentiss (Nurse Duckett), Martin Sheen (Lt. Dobbs), Jon Voight (Milo Minderbinder)

p, Martin Ransohoff, John Calley; d, Mike Nichols; w, Buck Henry (based on the novel by Joseph Heller); ph, David Watkin (Panavision, Technicolor); ed, Sam O'Steen; prod d, Richard Sylbert; art d, Harold Michelson; fx, Lee Vasque; cos, Ernest Adler

This scathing condemnation of war is full of stumbles and rife with misfires. An intermittently interesting adaptation of Joseph Heller's caustic novel, this big-budget, all-star effort was a notorious flop in its day.

Set on a small island just off Italy, circa 1944, the film follows Captain Yossarian (Alan Arkin), an American bombardier who attempts to have himself grounded by claiming he's insane. Unfortunately, as Doc Daneeka (Jack Gilford) informs him, the paradoxical rule of "catch-22" prevents this, since anyone who voluntarily flies on air raids must be crazy, so asking to be grounded indicates that one is sane. As Yossarian becomes increasingly desperate, the inherent madness of the war intensifies.

This film wants to be bleak, nihilistic, and darkly hilarious but CATCH-22 emerges as an exercise in frustration for those unprepared for Nichols's episodic, detached, and surreal treatment of the novel. Like a nightmare, the film shifts from one bizarre episode to another, with Alan Arkin's dazed Yossarian reacting to the madness that surrounds him, but second only to the viewer.

CATERED AFFAIR, THE
1956 92m bw   ★★★★
Drama
MGM

Bette Davis (Mrs. Tom Hurley), Ernest Borgnine (Tom Hurley), Debbie Reynolds (Jane Hurley), Barry Fitzgerald (Uncle Jack Conlon), Rod Taylor (Ralph Halloran), Robert F. Simon (Mr. Halloran), Madge Kennedy (Mrs. Halloran), Dorothy Stickney (Mrs. Rafferty), Carol Veazie (Mrs. Casey), Joan Camden (Alice)

p, Sam Zimbalist; d, Richard Brooks; w, Gore Vidal (based on the teleplay by Paddy Chayefsky); ph, John Alton; ed, Gene Ruggiero, Frank Santillo; m, Andre Previn; art d, Cedric Gibbons, Paul Groesse

Interesting misfire but eminently watchable, this one has divided amateur and pro critics alike. The adaptation by Vidal from Chayefsky's brilliant teleplay concerns a poor Bronx husband and wife wrangling over expenses for their beloved daughter's wedding. Following his triumph in another Chayefsky teleplay-to-screenplay effort, MARTY, the previous year, Borgnine acquits himself honorably as an Irish taxi driver. Davis indeed wrestles with the accent, but she's a mistress at tortured regret getting its own way; even stuck with the rattiest wiglet in showbiz history, when Davis cries on her bed, all our reservations melt away. Reynolds is very touching; it's quite nice to see her away from the sis-boom-bah roles, and a shame she didn't do so more often. But for Barry Fitzgerald, doing his tired old leprechaun bit ten years too late in this attempt at kitchen sink realism, we'd get out the horsewhip in a moment's notice, and we wouldn't spare the steed.

CAVALCADE
1933 110m bw   ★★★★
Drama   /U
Fox Films

Diana Wynyard (Jane Marryot), Clive Brook (Robert Marryot), Herbert Mundin (Alfred Bridges), Una O'Connor (Ellen Bridges), Ursula Jeans (Fanny Bridges), Beryl Mercer (Cook), Irene Browne (Margaret Harris), Merle Tottenham (Annie), Frank Lawton (Joe Marryot), John Warburton (Edward Marryot)

p, Winfield Sheehan; d, Frank Lloyd; w, Reginald Berkeley (based on the play by Noel Coward); ph, Ernest Palmer; ed, Margaret Clancy; fx, William Cameron Menzies

A rare beauty. Noel Coward, in an atypically serious venture, traces 30 years of a British family's life. A big, fine production—little shown or remembered today—CAVALCADE was a sensation at the time of its release, filled as it is with a wistful look at a couple clinging together through years of love. The epochal scenes commence with the Boer War and go on to record the death of Queen Victoria, the sinking of the Titanic, WWI, and the birth of jazz. The film won Academy Awards for Best Picture and Best Director while Wynyard was nominated for Best Actress, but lost to Katharine Hepburn for MORNING GLORY.

CEDDO
1978 120m c   ★★
Drama   /A
Sembene   (Nigeria)

Tabara Ndiaye (Princess Dior), Moutapha Yade (Madir Fatim Fall), Ismaila Diagne (The Kidnaper), Makoura Dia (The King), Ousmane Sembene (A Ceddo Renamed Ibrahima)

d, Ousmane Sembene; w, Ousmane Sembene; ph, Georges Caristan; ed, Florence Eymon; m, Manu Dibango

In turn-of-the-century Senegal, the local king becomes a convert to Islam and, under the influence of a Moslem adviser, disbands the little Catholic church in the village of the Ceddo. The people resist this change just as they resisted the Christian missionaries before, going to the length of kidnapping the king's daughter. Most of the film consists of meetings between different factions and groups, all conducted according to ancient tribal customs. This film was banned in director Ousmane Sembene's native Senegal not because of its dim view of that country's conversion to Islam, but because the government insists that "Ceddo" is spelled with only one "d."

CELINE AND JULIE GO BOATING
(CELINE ET JULIE VONT EN BATEAU)
1974 193m c   ★★★
Drama   /AA
Losange/Films 7/Renn/Saga/Simar/V.M./Action/Christian Fachner   (France)

Juliet Berto (Celine), Dominique Labourier (Julie), Bulle Ogier (Camille), Marie-France Pisier (Sophie), Barbet Schroeder (Oliver), Philippe Clevenot (Guliou)

d, Jacques Rivette; w, Jacques Rivette, Eduardo de Gregorio, Juliet Berto, Dominique Labourier, Bulle Ogier, Marie-France Pisier; ph, Jacques Renard, Michel Cenet (Eastrnancolor); ed, Nicole Lubtchansky, Chris Tullio-Altan; m, Jean-Marie Senia

Berto and Labourier run into each other and become friends. Berto invents a story about a haunted house; and while telling Labourier about it, she suggests they go there. In the house the two view the ghosts playing out their story, and the girls join in at one point. Maddeningly enigmatic and incredibly long, the film becomes hypnotic in its ethereal beauty and strange goings-on. When it finally ends, one is not quite sure what has happened. The images, however, will remain in the mind for a long time afterward. Definitely not for all tastes.

CESAR
1936 117m bw   ★★★½
Drama
Pagnol   (France)

Raimu (Cesar Olivier), Pierre Fresnay (Marius), Orane Demazis (Fanny), Fernand Charpin (Honore Panisse), Andre Fouche (Cesariot), Alida Rouffe (Honorine Cabinis), Milly Mathis (Aunt Claudine Foulon), Robert Vattier (M. Brun), Paul Dullac (Felix Escartefigue), Maupi (Chauffeur)

p, Marcel Pagnol; d, Marcel Pagnol; w, Marcel Pagnol; ph, Willy; ed, Suzanne de Troeye, Jeanette Ginestet; m, Vincent Scotto; art d, Galibert

The third part of Marcel Pagnol's "Marseilles Trilogy," CESAR completes the story begun in MARIUS and continued in FANNY.

Cesariot (Andre Fouche) is the 18-year-old son of Marius (Pierre Fresnay) and Fanny (Orane Demazis), but his father disappeared before he was born and he believes the aging Panisse (Fernand Charpin), his stepfather, to be his biological parent. A priest begs Panisse to tell Cesariot about his real father, but he refuses. When Panisse dies, Fanny tells her son about his parentage and he is properly shocked to find that Cesar (Raimu), whom he had always thought to be his godfather, is actually his grandfather. The old man tells Cesariot about his father and where to find him.

Magnificent performances, particularly from Raimu, highlight this fine film—the only one of the three directed by the trilogy's writer and producer, Pagnol. The receptive audiences that made the previous installments such a success did the same for this one, and the fact that the lovers of the first two—Marius and Fanny—were finally reunited after 20 years didn't hurt the box office, either.

CESAR AND ROSALIE
(CESAR ET ROSALIE)
1972 110m c   ★★★
Comedy/Romance   R/AA
Fildebroc/U.P.F./Mega/Paramount/Orion   (France/Italy/West Germany)

Yves Montand (Cesar), Romy Schneider (Rosalie), Sami Frey (David), Umberto Orsini (Antoine), Eva-Maria Meineke (Lucie), Bernard Le Coq (Michel), Gisela Hahn (Carla), Isabelle Huppert (Marite), Henri-Jacques Huet (Marcel), Pippo Merisi (Albert)

p, Michelle de Broca; d, Claude Sautet; w, Jean-Loup Dabadie, Claude Sautet, Claude Neron; ph, Jean Boffety (Eastmancolor); ed, Jacqueline Thiedot; m, Philippe Sarde; art d, Pierre Guffroy; cos, Annalisa Nasilli-Rocca

CESAR AND ROSALIE is an upper-class French romance in which Montand, Schneider, and Frey are the three sides of a love triangle—an arrangement that seems tolerable to all three.

Montand, a likable scrap-metal dealer who lives life to the fullest, is in love with Schneider, who has a young daughter from a previous marriage. When family and friends gather for the wedding of Schneider's mother, an unexpected visitor arrives—Frey, Schneider's former lover, who disappeared from her life after breaking up her marriage. Frey's reappearance shakes Schneider, who still loves him, especially after he admits to Montand that he is still in love with her.

This intelligent and funny romance is directed with Sautet's usual inoffensiveness, especially his all-too-complacent view of bourgeois life. What makes the film (at the time, one of France's top money-makers) worth watching is the interplay among Montand, Schneider, and Frey—and the subtle attraction between Montand and Frey, two very diverse men bonded in their love for the same woman. In a supporting role is 17-year-old Isabelle Huppert, in one of her very first film appearances.

C'EST LA VIE
1990 110m c   ★★½
Drama   /12
Samuel Goldwyn   (France)

Nathalie Baye (Lena), Richard Berry (Michel), Zabou (Bella), Jean-Pierre Bacri (Leon), Vincent Lindon (Jean-Claude), Valeria Bruni-Tedeschi (Odette), Didier Benureau (Ruffier), Julie Bataille (Frederique), Candice Lefranc (Sophie), Alexis Derlon (Daniel)

p, Alexander Arcady, Diane Kurys; d, Diane Kurys; w, Diane Kurys, Alain Le Henry; ph, Gui Feppe Lanci; m, Philippe Sarde

Set in 1958, C'EST LA VIE is the third installment, following the immensely popular PEPPERMINT SODA and ENTRE NOUS, of Diane Kurys' absorbing semi-autobiographical trilogy.

Having decided to divorce her husband Michel (Richard Berry), the beautiful Lena (Nathalie Baye) puts her two daughters on a train in Lyon bound for La Baule Les Pins for a seaside vacation. The summer proves an eventful one, with the girls learning all manner of lessons in living. Lena eventually joins her daughters and engages in what she thinks is a secret affair with a young artist, Leon (Jean-Pierre Bacri), though the children observe her dashing off into the night to meet him. The tranquility of their idyll is shattered by the unexpected arrival of their father.

No one can accuse Kurys of any real depth here; her strength as a director lies primarily in her sense of detail and in her ability to convey a nostalgic atmosphere. In its indolent sensuality and wealth of everyday observation, Kurys's work resembles some of the lighter, summery short stories of Colette. C'EST LA VIE is the merest trifle, but, given its sun-soaked ambience, the film is utterly painless and enjoyable.

Never more glamorous, Baye communicates a slightly neurotic, Jennifer Jones-like quality and makes an appealingly complex heroine. The scene where she first sees her lover on the beach and snakes her way through the cabanas to meet him is dizzyingly romantic. Bacri is properly sexy as Lena's lover, and Berry exudes the right amount of pained anguish as her husband.

Like Truffaut, Kurys has a precious, idealized view of children. They're all angelic, brilliant little paragons. The girls have a woman-in-a-child's-body beauty that is as much of a Gallic cliche as their huskily precocious voices are; the boys are budding artistic geniuses. Still, all of this sweetness and light leaves the viewer yearning for the youthful raunch and anarchy of a film like LIFE IS A LONG QUIET RIVER.

CHAMP, THE
1931 85m bw   ★★★½
Sports   /PG
MGM

Wallace Beery *(Champ)*, Jackie Cooper *(Dink)*, Irene Rich *(Linda)*, Roscoe Ates *(Sponge)*, Edward Brophy *(Tim)*, Hale Hamilton *(Tony)*, Jesse Scott *(Jonah)*, Marcia Mae Jones *(Mary Lou)*

p, Harry Rapf; d, King Vidor; w, Leonard Praskins (based on a story by Frances Marion); ph, Gordon Avil; ed, Hugh Wynn

Beery won an Oscar for his role as a down-at-heels ex-heavyweight boxing champion who trains for a comeback in Tijuana in between boozing and gambling, egged on by his pipe dreams and those of his young son (Cooper). When he wins some money, the "Champ" buys the boy a racehorse, but promptly loses it in a crap game. The boy's mother (Rich) and her wealthy husband (Hamilton) appear at the track where the boxer works and convince him that the boy would be better off with them. He reluctantly agrees, but the boy later sneaks back to his father's side in time to witness the older man's bout against a much younger opponent.

A famous tearjerker of its day, THE CHAMP is unabashed in its assault upon the audience's emotions. Cynics are advised to keep their distance, but in defense of this extremely sentimental film one should note the genuine rapport between Beery and Cooper and the quiet skill of director Vidor. A film with a lot of heart, unafraid to bare its emotions, THE CHAMP still plays well, its slightly gritty look more effective than the softness Franco Zeffirelli brought to the lesser 1979 remake.

CHAMPAGNE FOR CAESAR

1950 99m bw   ★★★★
Comedy   /U
UA

Ronald Colman *(Beauregard Bottomley)*, Celeste Holm *(Flame O'Neil)*, Vincent Price *(Burnbridge Waters)*, Barbara Britton *(Gwenn Bottomley)*, Art Linkletter *(Happy Hogan)*, Gabriel Heatter, George Fisher *(Announcers)*, Byron Foulger *(Gerald)*, Ellye Marshall *(Frosty)*, Vici Raaf *(Waters's Secretary)*

p, George Moskov; d, Richard Whorf; w, Hans Jacoby, Fred Brady; ph, Paul Ivano; ed, Hugh Bennett; m, Dimitri Tiomkin; art d, George Van Marter

An unjustly neglected, extremely funny jab at the media empire and the world of big business. Beauregard Bottomley (Colman) is an unemployed genius who holds a Ph.D., skims the encyclopedia for enjoyment and never forgets a thing he's read. He applies for work at a soap company owned by Burnbridge Waters (Price) but is rebuffed by the suds magnate. Beauregard is so annoyed by the treatment he receives at Waters's hands that he decides to bankrupt the company by becoming a contestant on the popular radio quiz show it sponsors.

Broadly handled but squarely on-target in its satire of the media, CHAMPAGNE FOR CAESAR is nimbly helmed by director Whorf and benefits considerably from its talented cast. Colman's typically understated style meshes nicely with Holm's, and they provide an appropriate foil for Price's deliberate hamminess as the megalomaniacal mogul. Listen for Mel Blanc as the voice of the champagne-loving parrot, Caesar. Denied a full run upon its initial release and broadcast on television in truncated form, this unexpected if modest delight is likely to halt your late-night channel surfing and leave you howling.

CHAMPION

1949 99m bw   ★★★★½
Sports   /A
Screen Plays

Kirk Douglas *(Midge Kelly)*, Marilyn Maxwell *(Grace Diamond)*, Arthur Kennedy *(Connie Kelly)*, Paul Stewart *(Tommy Haley)*, Ruth Roman *(Emma Bryce)*, Lola Albright *(Mrs. Harris)*, Luis Van Rooten *(Jerome Harris)*, John Day *(Johnny Dunne)*, Harry Shannon *(Lew Bryce)*

p, Stanley Kramer; d, Mark Robson; w, Carl Foreman (based on the story by Ring Lardner); ph, Franz Planer; ed, Harry Gerstad; m, Dimitri Tiomkin (song, "Never Be It Said," Tiomkin, Goldie Goldmark)

Released two years after BODY AND SOUL and based on a Ring Lardner short story, CHAMPION is another truly great boxing film. Midge Kelly (Douglas) travels to California with his crippled brother Connie (Kennedy), hoping to buy a diner but ending up working there and falling for the owner's daughter, Emma (Roman), who becomes his shotgun bride. Soon Midge decides to put his boxing skills to use as a professional, and leaves Emma. Managed by Tommy Haley (Stewart), Midge rises through the middleweight ranks until he gets a title shot, which, true to boxing-film formula, he is supposed to throw but doesn't. Nonetheless, he becomes the crime syndicate's boy, growing more corrupt daily.

Douglas' riveting performance as the ruthless fighter earned him an Oscar nomination and made him an overnight sensation, and the gifted supporting cast offers a wide and appropriate variety of foils to the ambitious, amoral character he portrays. Robson's direction is all action, wasting no time in telling this compelling story, and Carl Foreman's script is sharply observant of the boxing milieu.

CHAN IS MISSING

1981 80m bw   ★★★★
Crime   /15
New Yorker

Wood Moy *(Jo)*, Marc Hayashi *(Steve)*, Laureen Chew *(Amy)*, Judi Nihei *(Lawyer)*, Peter Wang *(Henry, the Cook)*, Presco Tabios *(Presco)*, Ellen Yeung *(Mrs. Chan)*, Emily Yamasaki *(Jenny)*, George Woo *(George)*, Virginia Cerenio *(Jenny's Friend)*

p, Wayne Wang; d, Wayne Wang; w, Wayne Wang, Isaac Cronin, Terrel Seltzer; ph, Michael Chin; ed, Wayne Wang; m, Robert Kikuchi

A deliberately modest but genuine delight, full of wicked humor, suspenseful touches, and perceptive insights about the experiences of Chinese immigrants in America. Two San Francisco cab drivers (played by Moy and Hayashi) have their savings stolen by the elusive "Chan Hung" and spend the rest of the film tracking him down. Along the way the film potently considers the problems with the generation gap among Chinese-Americans and conflicts between those Chinese from the mother country and those born in America.

A fine, funny independent production filmed on a minuscule budget in San Francisco's Chinatown by Wayne Wang (DIM SUM and EAT A BOWL OF TEA), CHAN IS MISSING deservedly became a major art-house success. Its cleverness extends even to the film's title, with CHAN suggesting both Charlie Chan (and hence many of the stereotypes commonly held about the Chinese) and "CHinese-americAN".

CHARADE

1953 83m bw   ★★
Drama   /A
Portland

James Mason *(The Murderer/Maj. Linden/Jonah Watson)*, Pamela Mason *(The Artist/Pamela/Baroness Tanslan/Lilly)*, Scott Forbes *(Capt. Stamm)*, Paul Cavanagh *(Col. Heisler)*, Bruce Lester *(Capt. van Buren)*, John Dodsworth *(Lt. Meyerdorf)*, Judy Osborne *(Dotty)*, Sean McClory *(Jack Stuydevant)*, Vince Barnett *(Berg)*

p, James Mason; d, Roy Kellino; w, James Mason, Pamela Kellino

A vanity production of sorts, this anthology film showcases Mr. and Mrs. Mason as the producers, writers, and lead players in three separate episodes of love and violence.

"Portrait of a Murderer" presents Pamela Mason as a disillusioned young artist who absentmindedly sketches the face of Mason, the man next door who, unbeknownst to her, has recently murdered her girlfriend and returned to the scene of the crime. They fall in love—with predictably tragic results. "Duel at Dawn" finds Mason as an Austrian officer in the 1880s who steals Pamela Mason from a rival (Forbes) who then challenges Mason to a duel. In "The Midas Touch" Mason is a hard-working, successful man who has amassed a small fortune in New York but is dissatisfied with his life and abandons his wealth and moves to England to start over. There he takes a job as a valet and falls in love with Pamela Mason, a cockney servant girl who desires a better life. He comes up with an appropriately farfetched solution for their future happiness.

Mason himself condemned this nepotistic mess; he was quoted as saying: "I had hoped that this curiosity would be lost without a trace."

CHARADE
1963 113m c ★★★★
Comedy/Thriller /A
Universal

Cary Grant *(Peter Joshua)*, Audrey Hepburn *(Regina Lambert)*, Walter Matthau *(Hamilton Bartholomew)*, James Coburn *(Tex Panthollow)*, George Kennedy *(Herman Scobie)*, Ned Glass *(Leopold Gideon)*, Jacques Marin *(Inspector Edouard Grandpierre)*, Paul Bonifas *(Felix)*, Dominique Minot *(Sylvie Gaudet)*, Thomas Chelimsky *(Jean-Louis Gaudet)*

p, Stanley Donen; d, Stanley Donen; w, Peter Stone (based on the story "The Unsuspecting Wife" by Marc Behm, Peter Stone); ph, Charles Lang (Technicolor); ed, James B. Clark; m, Henry Mancini; art d, Jean d'Eaubonne; cos, Givenchy

Stanley Donen was unique in being a 1950s director (SINGIN' IN THE RAIN, FUNNY FACE, SEVEN BRIDES FOR SEVEN BROTHERS) who scored some of his most successful hits in the 1960s. CHARADE is a classic romance, perhaps the ultimate Audrey Hepburn film, and probably Cary Grant's last best effort. What more could you ask for? Paris, of course. You got it. And a small but crucial role by Walter Matthau.

This charming comedy-romance-thriller pairs Cary Grant and Audrey Hepburn with an ingenious Peter Stone screenplay and musical comedy veteran Stanley Donen operating in a distinctly Hitchcockian mode. Reggie Lambert (Hepburn) returns to Paris from a ski trip in the French Alps to find her house ransacked and her husband dead. His funeral is attended by three curious thugs—played by James Coburn, George Kennedy, and Ned Glass—each of whom makes sure that the dead man is indeed dead. Peter (Grant) offers his assistance to Reggie, as does CIA man Bartholomew (Walter Matthau) who informs her that her husband was not the man she thought he was. There's the matter of a fortune stolen during WWII which nearly everyone seems

to be after—perhaps the enigmatic Peter as well? When corpses start piling up all around her, Reggie must wade through the charade and make a decision as to who's who and what.

This nifty little thriller offers more than just its clever plot. The radiant Hepburn's growing romance with the suave Grant is delightfully handled, the location photography is exquisite and the rooftop fight scene between Grant and Kennedy is truly harrowing.

CHARGE OF THE LIGHT BRIGADE, THE
1936 115m bw ★★★½
Adventure/War /U
WB

Errol Flynn *(Maj. Geoffrey Vickers)*, Olivia de Havilland *(Elsa Campbell)*, Patric Knowles *(Capt. Perry Vickers)*, Donald Crisp *(Col. Campbell)*, Henry Stephenson *(Sir Charles Macefield)*, Nigel Bruce *(Sir Benjamin Warrenton)*, David Niven *(Capt. James Randall)*, G.P. Huntley, Jr. *(Maj. Jowett)*, Spring Byington *(Lady Octavia Warrenton)*, C. Henry Gordon *(Surat Khan)*

p, Samuel Bischoff; d, Michael Curtiz; w, Michel Jacoby, Rowland Leigh (based on a story by Michel Jacoby inspired by the poem by Alfred, Lord Tennyson); ph, Sol Polito; ed, George Amy; m, Max Steiner; art d, John Hughes; fx, Fred Jackman, H.F. Koenekamp; cos, Milo Anderson

THE CHARGE OF THE LIGHT BRIGADE is a fine military swashbuckler with some of the most dynamic action sequences ever seen on the screen. Great pains were taken to re-create the 1850s milieu but Warner Bros. typically discarded the actual facts regarding the magnificent military blunder, retaining instead the era's pomp and the stirring lines of Tennyson's famous poem.

The story begins in in 1850 in northwest India during the years leading up to the Crimean War. Major Geoffrey Vickers (Errol Flynn), a dashing British officer of the 27th Lancers, crosses paths with a scheming Indian potentate, Surat Khan (C. Henry Gordon), who is severing ties with the British and allying himself with the Russians in preparation for a revolt. After Surat Khan's murderous betrayal of the British forces, Vickers seeks revenge during a foolhardy but courageous charge on the Russian forces at the Balaclava heights in the Crimea where Surat Khan has fled. Meanwhile Elsa Campbell (Olivia de Havilland), the woman Vickers loves, has secretly fallen in love with his brother, Captain Perry Vickers (Patric Knowles).

As a history lesson, THE CHARGE OF THE LIGHT BRIGADE is wildly inaccurate but it is a rousing entertainment. History was better served by the 1968 remake by Tony Richardson which exposed more of the truth about the military idiocy that led to the slaughter but movie audiences were largely unmoved.

CHARGE OF THE LIGHT BRIGADE, THE
1968 145m c ★★½
Historical /A
UA (U.K.)

Trevor Howard *(Lord Cardigan)*, Vanessa Redgrave *(Clarissa)*, John Gielgud *(Lord Raglan)*, Harry Andrews *(Lord Lucan)*, Jill Bennett *(Mrs. Duberly)*, David Hemmings *(Capt. Nolan)*, Peter Bowles *(Paymaster Duberly)*, Mark Burns *(Capt. Morris)*, Howard Marion-Crawford *(Sir George Brown)*, Mark Dignam *(Airey)* p, Neil Hartley; d, Tony Richardson; w, Charles Wood; ph, David Watkin (Panavision/DeLuxe Color); ed, Kevin Brownlow, Hugh Raggett; m, John Addison; art d, Edward Marshall; fx, Robert MacDonald; cos, David Walker

Though well-researched and thought-provoking, this exquisitely made film is ultimately a disappointing drama of events leading up to the British involvement in the Crimean War. Richardson takes a somewhat absurdist approach as he satirizes the snobbishness of the English upper class and its view of the sport of war. He also exposes the soldiers' blind acceptance of the demands of their belittling supervisors. Their much vaunted code of honor turns sour in the wake of the humiliating slaughter of England's Light Brigade. The film completely belittles the undeniable courage that went hand-in-hand with the terrible mistakes it depicts. Dramatic loopholes also diminish the impact of what appears to be intended as a major cinematic statement about war from the 1960s generation.

Nonetheless there are many enjoyable performances, especially those of Gielgud, Hemmings, and Redgrave (the last two previously paired in BLOW UP). Richard Williams provides the clever animation sequences which serve to orient the viewer. Don't look for the spectacular war scenes so sweepingly portrayed in Curtiz's historically inaccurate but crowdpleasing 1936 version; the battle scenes take second place to revisionist satire and political indictment of 19th-century imperialistic England.

CHARIOTS OF FIRE

1981   123m   c   ★★★
Biography/Sports   PG/U
Enigma   (U.K.)

Ben Cross (*Harold Abrahams*), Ian Charleson (*Eric Liddell*), Nigel Havers (*Lord Andrew Lindsay*), Nicholas Farrell (*Aubrey Montague*), Ian Holm (*Sam Mussabini*), John Gielgud (*Master of Trinity*), Lindsay Anderson (*Master of Caius*), Nigel Davenport (*Lord Birkenhead*), Cheryl Campbell (*Jennie Liddell*), Alice Krige (*Sybil Gordon*)

p, David Puttnam; d, Hugh Hudson; w, Colin Welland; ph, David Watkin; ed, Terry Rawlings; m, Vangelis; art d, Roger Hall; cos, Milena Canonero

CHARIOTS OF FIRE is a pleasant, mildly inspirational movie but hardly worthy of all the accolades it received. This true story, based on an original screenplay by Colin Welland, is about what it means to win and what one must do to achieve it. Eric Liddell (Ian Charleson) is a serious Scottish Christian who runs for the glory of Jesus. Harold Abrahams (Ben Cross) is an English Jew who is sensitive to prejudice and whose primary motivation is to be accepted. The movie delineates and crosscuts the lives of both men as they meet and compete at the 1924 Olympics in Paris.

The real-life Liddell became a Christian missionary, went to China, and eventually died in a Japanese prisoner of war camp, true to his faith to the end. Abrahams went on to become the spokesman for English amateur athletics, was knighted, and died a venerated elder statesman in 1978. Few who see the film can forget the lyrically photographed scene of the runners striding through the surf in slow motion to the accompaniment of Vangelis's stirring score, particularly in light of subsequent parodies.

CHARLEY VARRICK

1973   111m   c   ★★★½
Crime   PG/X
Universal

Walter Matthau (*Charley Varrick*), Joe Don Baker (*Molly*), Felicia Farr (*Sybil Fort*), Andy Robinson (*Harman Sullivan*), John Vernon (*Maynard Boyle*), Sheree North (*Jewell Everett*), Norman Fell (*Mr. Garfinkle*), Benson Fong (*Honest John*), Woodrow Parfrey (*Howard Young*), William Schallert (*Sheriff Bill Horton*)

p, Don Siegel; d, Don Siegel; w, Dean Riesner, Howard Rodman (based on the novel *The Looters* by John Reese); ph, Michael Butler (Technicolor); ed, Frank Morriss; m, Lalo Schifrin; art d, Fernando Carrere; cos, Helen Colvig

A very well made caper film full of action and rich with character. Directed by genre veteran Don Siegel, the versatile Walter Matthau plays it hard and fast as a small-time thief who robs, with partner Robinson, a tiny New Mexico bank. Instead of the usual loose change, the robbers find $750,000 which turns out to be Mafia money the bank was laundering. It's too risky for the pragmatic Matthau but his avaricious punk partner insists that they keep the money. Matthau warns him that if the loot is not returned, the Mafia will start gunning for them, which is exactly what happens. Hit man Baker begins hunting the pair, destroying everyone and everything in his path—and enjoying it.

Matthau is both shifty and cunning as he evades both the police and the Mafia. Butler's photography is top notch as is Schifrin's score. The whole film is suspenseful and intelligently scripted, thanks to director Siegel (DIRTY HARRY, THE SHOOTIST, ESCAPE FROM ALCATRAZ) and writers Riesner and Rodman. A great B movie of the 1970s.

CHARLEY'S AUNT

1941   80m   bw   ★★★
Comedy   /U
FOX

Jack Benny (*Babbs*), Kay Francis (*Donna Lucia*), James Ellison (*Jack Chesney*), Anne Baxter (*Amy Spettigue*), Edmund Gwenn (*Stephen Spettigue*), Reginald Owen (*Redcliff*), Laird Cregar (*Sir Francis Chesney*), Arleen Whelan (*Kitty Verdun*), Richard Haydn (*Charley Wyckham*), Ernest Cossart (*Brasset*)

p, William Perlberg; d, Archie Mayo; w, George Seaton (based on the play by Brandon Thomas); ph, Peverell Marley; ed, Robert Bischoff; m, Alfred Newman; art d, Nathan Juran, Richard Day; cos, Travis Banton

This was the third of many screen adaptations of "Charley's Aunt," the beloved 19th-century stage farce. The first starred Sydney Chaplin in 1925 and the second (released in 1930) featured Charlie Ruggles in the lead. Jack Benny stars here as Babbs, an Oxford student who masquerades as his friend Charley Wickham's (Richard Haydn) aunt from Brazil who will be the chaperon for Charley and Jack (James Ellison) as they court Amy (Anne Baxter) and Kitty (Arleen Whelan). Once Babbs is in drag, however, he must fend off romantic advances from gigolo Sir Francis Chesney (Laird Cregar) and from Stephen Spettigue (Edmund Gwenn), the girl's guardian.

Jack Benny was never better (with the possible exception of his classic TO BE OR NOT TO BE) and carries the film with a top-flight performance. This was his first role of any consequence other than his previous tailor-made parts with radio jokes flying thick and fast around his well-known persona. In CHARLEY'S AUNT, Benny had to play a part totally alien to what he'd done before and he proved more than worthy to the task. Remade as the musical WHERE'S CHARLEY? in 1952.

CHARLIE BUBBLES

1968 89m c   ★★★
Drama   /AA
Regional (U.K.)

Albert Finney *(Charlie Bubbles)*, Colin Blakely *(Smokey Pickles)*, Billie Whitelaw *(Lottie Bubbles)*, Liza Minnelli *(Eliza)*, Timothy Garland *(Jack Bubbles)*, Richard Pearson *(Accountant)*, John Ronane *(Gerry)*, Nicholas Phipps *(Agent)*, Peter Sallis *(Solicitor)*, Charles Lamb *(Mr. Noseworthy)*

p, Michael Medwin; d, Albert Finney; w, Shelagh Delaney; ph, Peter Suschitzky (Technicolor); ed, Fergus McDonell; m, Misha Donat; art d, Edward Marshall; cos, Yvonne Blake

Not a great movie but an absorbing one about a writer who becomes suddenly successful, finds it very boring, and has an affair with his secretary. Albert Finney and Liza Minnelli star in a fantasy of escape that remains unique. This was Finney's directorial debut and a romantic touchstone for some in the late Sixties. Billie Whitelaw, as Charlie's estranged wife, won a British Academy award for her role as Best Supporting Actress.

CHARLIE CHAN AT THE OPERA

1936 66m bw   ★★★½
Mystery   /A
FOX

Warner Oland *(Charlie Chan)*, Boris Karloff *(Gravelle)*, Keye Luke *(Lee Chan)*, Charlotte Henry *(Mlle. Kitty)*, Thomas Beck *(Phil Childers)*, Margaret Irving *(Mme. Lilli Rouchelle)*, Gregory Gaye *(Enrico Barelli)*, Nedda Harrigan *(Mme. Lucretia Barelli)*, Frank Conroy *(Mr. Whitely)*, Guy Usher *(Inspector Regan)*

p, John Stone; d, H. Bruce Humberstone; w, W. Scott Darling, Charles Belden (based on a story by Bess Meredyth and the character created by Earl Derr Biggers); ph, Lucien Andriot; ed, Alex Troffey

Yes, Charlie Chan is a caricature of the East Asian personality and questions of racism do arise, but in his heyday in the 1930s the character of Chan presented an Oriental hero on the screen in what is perhaps the longest running series in movies. (The first Chan film was made in 1926 and the most recent in 1981.) There's something else going on here besides the caricature. Chan is probably unique in being a family detective and his collaboration with his sons is one of the attractions of the character. As with Nick and Nora Charles in THE THIN MAN movies, we're more interested in the relationship than in the mystery. Of the several actors who have played Chan, Warner Oland, who starred in this one, was generally regarded as the best.

One of the best of the series, this entry has the added attraction of Boris Karloff as Gravelle, an opera star who is presumed dead after being caught in a fire at a theater. He survives as an amnesiac, however, and is admitted unidentified into a mental hospital. When a picture of his opera singer wife appears in the newspaper, Gravelle's memory is spurred and he recalls that it was his unfaithful wife and her lover who set the fire in an attempt to kill him. Seething with a desire for vengeance, Gravelle escapes the mental hospital and heads for the opera house. When several people turn up dead, Charlie Chan is called in to investigate.

Included in the film is the opera *Carnival*, composed especially for the picture by Oscar Levant. This movie was so well made—and holds up so well—that its interest ranges far beyond the usual circle of Chan buffs.

CHARLOTTE'S WEB

1973 94m c   ★★★★
Animated/Musical   G/U
Paramount

VOICES OF: Debbie Reynolds *(Charlotte)*, Paul Lynde *(Templeton)*, Henry Gibson *(Wilbur)*, Rex Allen *(Narrator)*, Martha Scott *(Mrs. Arable)*, Dave Madden *(Old Sheep)*, Danny Bonaduce *(Avery)*, Don Messick *(Geoffrey)*, Herb Vigran *(Lurvy)*, Agnes Moorehead *(The Goose)*

p, Joseph Barbera, William Hanna; d, Charles A. Nichols, Iwao Takamoto; w, Earl Hamner, Jr. (based on the book by E.B. White); ph, Roy Wade, Dick Blundell, Dennis Weaver, Ralph Migliori, George Epperson (Movielab Color); ed, Larry Cowan, Pat Foley; m, Richard M. Sherman, Robert B. Sherman; art d, Bob Singer, Paul Julian, Ray Aragon

A charming cartoon adaptation of E.B. White's fantasy. Wilbur is a runt pig who has been raised as the pet of a New England farmer. He is sold to a neighboring farm, where a sheep informs him that he's fated to become what goes with cheese on rye. Wilbur is understandably frightened, until he meets a spider named Charlotte, who devotes her arachnoidal life to saving Wilbur from the fate of most porkers, and who weaves words into her web that convince the superstitious farmer that Wilbur is some sort of miraculous hog. The voices of Reynolds, Lynde, Gibson, and all the rest are perfectly cast, and the songs by the Sherman brothers are solid, although none of them became hits like those they wrote for such Disney movies as MARY POPPINS.

CHARLY

1968 103m c   ★
Drama   /PG
Selmur

Cliff Robertson *(Charly Gordon)*, Claire Bloom *(Alice Kinian)*, Lilia Skala *(Dr. Anna Straus)*, Leon Janney *(Dr. Richard Nemur)*, Dick Van Patten *(Bert)*, William Dwyer *(Joey)*, Ed McNally *(Gimpy)*, Dan Morgan *(Paddy)*, Barney Martin *(Hank)*, Ruth White *(Mrs. Apple)*

p, Ralph Nelson; d, Ralph Nelson; w, Stirling Silliphant (based on the short story and novel *Flowers for Algernon* by Daniel Keyes); ph, Arthur J. Ornitz (Techniscope, Technicolor); ed, Fredric Steinkamp; m, Ravi Shankar; art d, Charles Rosen

A strangely compelling mess of a movie which throws in the kitchen sink but forgets the plumbing, CHARLY is at once touching, infuriating and utterly laughable. It's the kind of film that makes you kick yourself for ever taking it seriously.

Based on "Flowers For Algernon," the over-anthologized short story by Daniel Keyes, this mawkish variation on *Pygmalion* casts Robertson as a bakery worker with an IQ of 68 turned into a genius via the marvels of brain surgery. Learning a few new things, he attempts to rape a repressed schoolteacher (Bloom), though of course they later fall in soft-focus love with each other. He also enjoys brief stints as a Hell's Angel and a computer wiz, and one soon realizes that this flick is trying to be a meaningful compilation of 1960s attitudes. (We'll stick with EASY RIDER, thanks.) Naturally, all this intelligence is too good to last and Charly, upon witnessing the gradual regression of fellow experimentee Algernon the mouse, realizes that he too will soon revert to his former state.

Reeking with its own brand of sleazy sincerity and desperately wanting to be profound about *something*, CHARLY is more than capable of insulting both the mentally handicapped and anyone who cares about them. Part science fiction, part social commentary, part romance, this film is really option D—none of the above. Though he has some very good moments, especially as the enlightened man afraid of losing his newfound perspective, Robertson invests much of his performance with a kind of nutty intensity which should be witnessed at least once.

In all fairness, one doesn't know who could have done much with such cliched, shamelessly manipulative drivel, though heaven knows, the technical incompetence of this baby (including some hilarious use of split screens) doesn't help matters. Then again, maybe it's precisely the helpless frailty of the entire crazed enterprise that seems oddly affecting. Bring plenty of Kleenex, Pepto Bismal, and hallucinogens.

CHEAPER BY THE DOZEN

1950 85m c   ★★★
Comedy   /U
FOX

Clifton Webb (*Frank Bunker Gilbreth*), Jeanne Crain (*Ann Gilbreth*), Myrna Loy (*Mrs. Lillian Gilbreth*), Betty Lynn (*Libby Lancaster*), Edgar Buchanan (*Dr. Burton*), Barbara Bates (*Ernestine*), Mildred Natwick (*Mrs. Mebane*), Sara Allgood (*Mrs. Monahan*), Anthony Sydes (*Fred Gilbreth*), Roddy McCaskill (*Jack Gilbreth*)

p, Lamar Trotti; d, Walter Lang; w, Lamar Trotti (based on the novel by Frank B. Gilbreth, Jr. and Ernestine Gilbreth Carey); ph, Leon Shamroy (Technicolor); ed, J. Watson Webb; m, Cyril J. Mockridge

A big hit in its day and a typical Hollywood evocation of a genteel, bygone middle America of the 1920s that never was, this poor man's MEET ME IN ST. LOUIS presents prissy, spinsterish Clifton Webb as the father of twelve. Get real! Though Webb has his fair share of amusing moments, his trademark waspish but kindly crankiness loses its grip here amidst the floodtides of familial fondness. Loy, sadly soft-pedalled in the footage department, is on firmer ground as his devoted wife, a psychologist who uses the tricks of her trade on her efficiency expert husband whenever necessary. The film has no particular driving story but rather is a host of minor family incidents designed to show the closeness of these 14 people. Some are amusing, though others cloy in the way that only 20th Century-Fox lollipops can.

Journeyman director Lang is no Vincente Minnelli when it comes to either visuals or mood, and this is the type of film which plays better on television because there's nothing in it which really uses the big screen with any creativity. Honors go to Mildred Natwick as a birth control activist in the film's funniest scene. A true 1950s cultural relic and suitable "family entertainment," the film inspired a modest, quasi-feminist sequel, BELLES ON THEIR TOES.

CHELSEA GIRLS, THE

1966 210m c/bw   ★★★★
Drama
Film-makers' Distribution Center

Pepper Davis, Ondine, Ingrid Superstar, Albert Rene Ricard, International Velvet, Brigid Polk, Ed Hood (*Ed*), Patrick Flemming (*Patrick*), Mario Montez (*Transvestite*), Gerard Malanga

p, Andy Warhol; d, Andy Warhol; w, Andy Warhol, Ronald Tavel; ph, Andy Warhol (Eastmancolor); m, The Velvet Underground

A film whose importance as a 1960s cultural statement outweighs any intrinsic value it may have as a film, CHELSEA GIRLS is nevertheless fascinating, provocative and hilarious once you surrender yourself to the totally new way of watching cinema that Andy Warhol films require. Think of it as Antonioni

in slow-motion and enjoy the heavy ennui that settles over you. As with most of his other films Warhol simply turned the camera on his camp followers and let them play as they might. A number of his mock-Hollywood "superstars" from the famous Factory crowd are actually born performers. Look for strange and funny moments from Ondine, Ingrid Superstar, Brigid Polk, Ed Hood, Mario Montez, Edie Sedgwick and Nico among others.

CHELSEA GIRLS isn't an easy film to write about and is almost impossible to rank in terms of any "quality" it may possess. Maybe that's why we've given it four stars—because it's one of the purest expressions of how Warhol not only explodes the categories of what art is (remember the famous Campbell's Soup can?) but also that he assaults in revolutionary fashion all the conventions we hold dear. CHELSEA GIRLS is historically notable for requiring two projectors operating side by side (not that the two separate films have any connection!) and for its popular success on the art house circuit, which subsequently opened its doors to other "underground" films. While perhaps not as potent or as clever as more compact masterworks like VINYL, BLOW JOB, BEAUTY #2, MY HUSTLER, NUDE RESTAURANT and LONESOME COWBOYS, CHELSEA GIRLS is probably the ultimate summation of Warhol's cinema. Check it out once. . . if you dare.

CHEYENNE

1947 99m bw   ★★½
Western   /U
WB

Dennis Morgan (*James Wylie*), Jane Wyman (*Ann Kincaid*), Janis Paige (*Emily Carson*), Bruce Bennett (*Ed Landers*), Alan Hale (*Fred Durkin*), Arthur Kennedy (*Sundance Kid*), John Ridgely (*Chalkeye*), Barton MacLane (*Yancey*), Tom Tyler (*Pecos*), Bob Steele (*Lucky*)

p, Robert Buckner; d, Raoul Walsh; w, Alan LeMay, Thames Williamson (based on a story by Paul I. Wellman); ph, Sid Hickox; ed, Christian Nyby; m, Max Steiner; art d, Ted Smith; fx, William McGann, H.F. Koenekamp

Walsh's direction lifts this slightly above the mass of B westerns. Morgan plays a gambler hired to track down a dreaded outlaw (Bennett). The bandit's wife (Wyman) tries to stand in his way but, as things go, ends up falling in love with him. Paige appears as the requisite sexy saloon singer, performing "Going Back to Old Cheyenne" and "I'm So in Love." Smoothly handled and fairly lavish, CHEYENNE suffers from the presence of its key cast members, none of whom look entirely comfortable in a Western.

CHEYENNE AUTUMN

1964 159m c   ★★★★
Western   /U
WB

Richard Widmark (*Capt. Thomas Archer*), Carroll Baker (*Deborah Wright*), Karl Malden (*Capt. Oscar Wessels*), James Stewart (*Wyatt Earp*), Edward G. Robinson (*Carl Schurz*), Sal Mineo (*Red Shirt*), Dolores Del Rio (*Spanish Woman*), Ricardo Montalban (*Little Wolf*), Gilbert Roland (*Dull Knife*), Arthur Kennedy (*Doc Holliday*)

p, Bernard Smith; d, John Ford; w, James R. Webb (based on the novel by Maurice Sandoz); ph, William Clothier (Super Panavision 70, Technicolor); ed, Otho Lovering; m, Alex North; art d, Richard Day; fx, Ralph Webb; cos, Ann Peck, Frank Beetson

This Ford frontier epic opens in 1887 with the disheartened remnants of the Cheyenne nation waiting for a meeting with government representatives on a wretched Oklahoma reservation—a meeting that never takes place. When they are ignored in their pleas for food and housing, two chiefs (Montalban and Roland) decide to defy the authorities and migrate back to their Wyoming homeland.

Thus begins a heroic and tragic 1,500-mile trek—with a reluctant cavalry captain (Widmark) and his troops in unenthusiastic pursuit, intending to return the 300-strong Cheyenne to their miserable reservation. Moving with the tribe is a white schoolteacher (Baker) who empathizes with their plight. The captain's troops are outfought at every turn by the wily braves, while the press portrays the exodus as another Indian war, and even civilians Wyatt Earp (Stewart) and Doc Holliday (Kennedy) join halfheartedly in a posse to recapture the Native Americans.

Stunningly photographed by William Clothier, the film, in true Fordian fashion, once again makes fine use of that great western icon, Monument Valley. The acting, too, is generally quite good, some of it (Widmark, Robinson, Del Rio) squarely on the mark, some of it (Malden, Baker, Stewart) a trifle off-key at times. No single actor, however, stands out in CHEYENNE AUTUMN: it is ultimately the director's picture, and represents Ford's attitude toward the Native American coming around full circle.

From the nameless vicious hordes of STAGECOACH to the Comanche chief in THE SEARCHERS who is equated with the equally racist white "hero," the Native American has by the time of CHEYENNE AUTUMN become the hero deserving of our sympathy and respect. Flawed on several levels, Ford's perception of a proud people seen through a white man's eyes is ultimately a highly compelling and deeply personal apologia.

CHEYENNE SOCIAL CLUB, THE

1970 103m c	★★★
Western/Comedy	PG/AA
National General	

James Stewart *(John O'Hanlan)*, Henry Fonda *(Harley Sullivan)*, Shirley Jones *(Jenny)*, Sue Ane Langdon *(Opal Ann)*, Elaine Devry *(Pauline)*, Robert Middleton *(Barkeep at Great Plains Saloon)*, Dabbs Greer *(Willowby)*, Jackie Russell *(Carrie Virginia)*, Jackie Joseph *(Annie Jo)*, Sharon DeBord *(Sara Jean)*

p, Gene Kelly; d, Gene Kelly; w, James Lee Barrett; ph, William Clothier (Panavision, Technicolor); ed, Adrienne Fazan; m, Walter Scharf; prod d, Gene Allen; cos, Yvonne Wood

John O'Hanlan and Harley Sullivan (Stewart and Fonda), two creaky cowboys just this side of elderly, ride up from Texas, the latter the most boring conversationalist in western history. The opening dialogue sets the tone of the film as Sullivan runs off at the mouth about his dogs, his family, and such. When he finally takes a breath, his travelling companion manages to blurt out, "We're in the Wyoming territory and you've been talkin' all the way since Texas. . . . Say another word the rest of the day and I'm gonna kill ya!" The movie never gets that funny again.

O'Hanlan's dead brother has left him the Cheyenne Social Club, but the minute our upright hero learns it's a brothel he wants to close the joint, or at least turn it into a plain saloon. The townspeople are outraged. Soon enough O'Hanlan encounters more troubles when he reneges on this original plan and has to deal with the town villain (Wilke). The fadeout takes place as the two men ride off into the distance, with Harley bending John's ear once again. Anyone with a mite less patience would have gunned Fonda down immediately.

Shirley Jones, hoping to evoke memories of the Oscar-winning slut she portrayed in ELMER GANTRY, plays the madame and among her charges are Langdon, Devry, DeBord, Russell, and Joseph, cult star of THE LITTLE SHOP OF HORRORS. This could have been a minor classic, but Barrett, who wrote SHENANDOAH, BANDOLERO, and FOOL'S PARADE for Stewart, came a cropper with the screenplay. Kelly's direction was spongy and the whole thing falls flat. The Stewart and Fonda duo and some of the supporting cast, however, do manage to bolster the film slightly. Clothier's superb cinematography helps as well. Otherwise, it's a ho-hummer too genial to have any bite.

CHILDHOOD OF MAXIM GORKY

1938 99m bw	★
Biography	/U
Soyuzfilm (U.S.S.R.)	

Alyosha Lyarsky *(Alexei Peshkov Gorky)*, V.O. Massalitinova *(Grandmother)*, M. Troyanovsky *(Grandfather)*, E. Alexeyeva *(Varvara)*, V. Novikov *(Uncle Yakov)*, A. Zhukov *(Uncle Mikhail)*, K. Ziubkov *(Grigori)*, D. Sagal *(Gypsy)*, S. Tikhonravov *(Lodger)*, Igor Smirnov *(Lenka)*

d, Mark Donskoy; w, I. Gruzdev; ph, I. Malov, Pyotr Yermolov; m, Lev Shwartz

The famous first film of director Donskoy's trilogy about the great Russian writer, this installment examines Gorki's humble beginnings with careful, evocative detail and a sympathy for his characters' peasant simplicity which rivals that of John Ford, Henry King, or Donskoy's colleague Dovzhenko. The spare storyline tells of the young, orphaned Gorky (touchingly played by Lyarsky) being raised by a tyrannical grandfather and a crew of conniving uncles. While not as innovative or as overwhelming as the great experimental Soviet cinema of the 1920s, this film's warm, rich humanity and seemingly personalized touches keep it from being just another example of the mundane "socialist realism" Stalin was starting to enforce.

CHILDREN OF A LESSER GOD

1986 119m c	★★★★
Romance/Drama	R/15
Paramount	

William Hurt *(James Leeds)*, Marlee Matlin *(Sarah Norman)*, Piper Laurie *(Mrs. Norman)*, Philip Bosco *(Dr. Curtis Franklin)*, Allison Gompf *(Lydia)*, John F. Cleary *(Johnny)*, Philip Holmes *(Glen)*, Georgia Ann Cline *(Cheryl)*, William D. Byrd *(Danny)*, Frank Carter, Jr. *(Tony)*

p, Burt Sugarman, Patrick Palmer; d, Randa Haines; w, Hesper Anderson, Mark Medoff (based on his stage play); ph, John Seale (Medallion Film Lab Color); ed, Lisa Fruchtman; m, Michael Convertino; prod d, Gene Callahan; art d, Barbara Matis; cos, Renee April

Nicely helmed by first-time feature director Haines, CHILDREN OF A LESSER GOD is a poignant yet uplifting love story involving a speech teacher and a deaf young woman. James Leeds (Hurt) is a maverick instructor newly arrived at a facility for the hearing impaired, where he meets Sarah Norman (Matlin), a graduate of the school who has chosen to stay and work in a menial job rather than attempt to go out into the world that the school has supposedly taught her to face. He falls in love with her almost instantly, but she resists him at first and also steadfastly refuses to read lips or attempt to talk; she insists on signing. In an attempt to learn why Sarah will not venture out into the world, Leeds visits her mother (Laurie) and discovers the root of Sarah's bitterness.

The major problem with the movie is that the audience is never left to its own interpretive devices. Because Matlin's hearing is severely impaired in real life, Hurt translates everything she signs for the benefit of viewers. Some of this may have been necessary, but Matlin's silent acting is so expressive that we often know exactly what is going through her mind as the emotions flicker across her face, and the translation routine interrupts the flow of the story time and again for no good reason. Nevertheless, despite this flaw, several dramatic lulls, and an aggressive determination to "sparkle," the film often makes for crackling good drama with plenty of leavening humor and magnificent performances by Hurt and newcomer Matlin.

CHILDREN OF PARADISE
(LES ENFANTS DU PARADIS)
1945 195m bw ★★★★★
Romance /A
S.N. Pathe (France)

Arletty (Garance), Jean-Louis Barrault (Baptiste Debureau), Pierre Brasseur (Frederick Lemaitre), Marcel Herrand (Lacenaire), Pierre Renoir (Jericho), Maria Casares (Natalie), Etienne Decroux (Anselme Debureau), Fabien Loris (Avril), Leon Larive (Stage Doorman, "Funambules"), Pierre Palov (Stage Manager, "Funambules")

p, Fred Orain; d, Marcel Carne; w, Jacques Prevert; ph, Roger Hubert, Marc Fossard; ed, Henri Rust, Madeleine Bonin; m, Maurice Thiriet, Joseph Kosma, George Mouque; art d, Leon Barsacq, R. Cabutti, Alexander Trauner

"Anyone who can resist its flamboyant charm deserves never to see Paris" wrote critic Andrew Sarris of CHILDREN OF PARADISE, and truer words were never uttered. It's been called France's answer to GONE WITH THE WIND, the greatest French film ever made, and an overrated bore. Filmed under a plethora of Nazi regulations with a cast peppered with Resistance fighters, the making of this film is almost as interesting as the end result. What is especially fascinating is how Marxist screenwriter Prevert and director Carne were able to pull off a thinly disguised allegory of French resistance under the German occupation.

The story, which takes place in the Paris of the 1820s and 30s, is a complex tale of unrequited love, illicit affairs, jealousy, and romance revolving around the world of theater folk, criminals, and aristocrats. The "children of paradise" are the poor people who inhabit the topmost balconies of the theaters along the Boulevard du Temple, and they are witness to the story of theater mime Baptiste (Barrault) and his true love Garance (Arletty). Along the way we are treated to delightful theater shows, duels, love amidst rain showers, and unfortunate misunderstandings with tragic consequences.

Deliberately theatrical but nevertheless greatly indebted to French poetic realism, CHILDREN OF PARADISE is lovingly handled by director Carne. The entire film is crammed with incident and an intoxicating eye for detail. Trauner's art direction is one of his finest achievements and the music by Kosma, Thiriet, and Mouque both onstage and off is a constant delight. Based on this one performance alone, gifted mime, comic and tragedian Barrault must take his place as one of the century's greatest actors. The raven-haired, fascinating Arletty, meanwhile, was the closest the French ever got to creating their own Marlene Dietrich. Among a superior supporting cast, Brasseur,

Herrand, Renoir, Casares, Marker, Salou, and Modot (as a "blind" beggar who can actually see) are particularly outstanding, and the end result is utterly beguiling cinema.

CHILLY SCENES OF WINTER
1979 92m c ★★★½
Drama PG/A
UA Classics

John Heard (Charles), Mary Beth Hurt (Laura), Peter Riegert (Sam), Kenneth McMillan (Pete), Gloria Grahame (Clara), Nora Heflin (Betty), Jerry Hardin (Patterson), Tarah Nutter (Susan), Mark Metcalf (Ox), Allen Joseph (Blind Man)

p, Mark Metcalf, Amy Robinson, Griffin Dunne; d, Joan Micklin Silver; w, Joan Micklin Silver (based on the novel Head Over Heels by Ann Beattie); ph, Bobby Byrne (Metrocolor); ed, Cynthia Scheider; m, Ken Lauber; prod d, Peter Jamison

Directed by Joan Micklin Silver (HESTER STREET, CROSSING DELANCEY) and based on a novel by Ann Beattie, CHILLY SCENES OF WINTER focuses on Charles (Heard), an office worker who falls in love with Laura (Hurt) while she is separated from her husband. When Laura returns to her spouse, Charles remains obsessed with her, sitting outside her home in his car watching the lights, even going to visit her *and* her husband, accompanied by his good friend Sam (Riegert). Retaining the mournful tone of Beattie's excellent novel, Silver delivers a slow-moving, occasionally funny, but deeply affecting film blessed with outstanding understated performances by Heard, Hurt, Riegert, and screen veteran Grahame, on hand in a memorable turn as Charles's suicidal mother. Look for author Beattie in a bit part as a waitress.

CHIMES AT MIDNIGHT
(CAMPANADAS A MEDIANOCHE)
1967 115m bw ★★★★★
Drama/War /U
Films Espanola/Alpine (Spain/Switzerland)

Orson Welles (Sir John "Jack" Falstaff), Jeanne Moreau (Doll Tearsheet), Margaret Rutherford (Hostess Quickly), John Gielgud (King Henry IV), Keith Baxter (Prince Hal, later King Henry V), Marina Vlady (Kate Percy), Norman Rodway (Henry Percy, "Hotspur"), Alan Webb (Justice Shallow), Walter Chiari (Mr Silence), Michael Aldridge (Pistol)

p, Emiliano Piedra; d, Orson Welles; w, Orson Welles (based on the plays "Henry, IV Part I," "Henry IV, Part II," "Henry V," "Richard II," and "The Merry Wives of Windsor" by William Shakespeare and The Chronicles of England by Raphael Holinshed.); ph, Edmond Richard; ed, Fritz Muller; m, Angelo Francesco Lavagnino; prod d, Gustavo Quintana; art d, Jose Antonio de la Guerra; cos, Cornejo Madrid

Although CITIZEN KANE and THE MAGNIFICENT AMBERSONS have their staunch defenders, many Welles scholars grant pride of place to CHIMES AT MIDNIGHT, a brilliant film that takes a tragic look at one of Shakespeare's most famous comic characters. Combining portions of Shakespeare's *Richard II, Henry IV, Henry V,* and *The Merry Wives of Windsor* along with (in the narration by Ralph Richardson) Raphael Holinshed's *The Chronicles of England*, CHIMES AT MIDNIGHT miraculously manages to achieve a valid dramatic form, becoming in the process one of the finest translations of the Bard ever to make it to the screen.

The story tells of Sir John Falstaff (Welles), the massive, blustering companion to Prince Hal (Baxter), heir to the besieged British throne. Rather than come to the defense of his royal father (Gielgud), Hal passes his time drinking and carousing with Falstaff. Finally, however, he does go into battle, slaying the honorable, doomed challenger to the crown, Hotspur (Rodway), and he soon thereafter becomes Henry V. Bursting in on the coronation, certain that a high title is forthcoming, Falstaff encounters instead the scorn of the now high-and-mighty Hal.

While not as technically dazzling as CITIZEN KANE (indeed, some are quick to condemn the somewhat confusing editing and murky sound—evidence of the project's haphazard shooting schedule), CHIMES AT MIDNIGHT is the work of a mature artist and proof of Welles's great flair for Shakespearean dramaturgy. Although the film downplays the comic aspects of the Falstaff-Hal relationship, the two lead performances are splendid, with Baxter alternately playful, cunning, icy, and commanding and Welles giving the performance of his career in a part he deeply understands. The moment of Falstaff's rejection is probably the single most moving piece of acting Welles ever committed to film.

Although fans of Moreau and Rutherford may be disappointed by their modestly sized roles, there are compensations, especially in the perfect performance of Gielgud as the half-dead king. Problems with the filming notwithstanding, the film is full of great moments, especially one of the best battle scenes ever—a brutal affair fought on a mud-soaked field, with the waddling knight Falstaff making every attempt to escape death.

CHINA SYNDROME, THE

1979 122m c   ★★★★½
Drama   PG
IPC

Jane Fonda *(Kimberly Wells)*, Jack Lemmon *(Jack Godell)*, Michael Douglas *(Richard Adams)*, Scott Brady *(Herman De Young)*, James Hampton *(Bill Gibson)*, Peter Donat *(Don Jacovich)*, Wilford Brimley *(Ted Spindler)*, Richard Herd *(Evan McCormack)*, Daniel Valdez *(Hector Salas)*, Stan Bohrman *(Peter Martin)*

p, Michael Douglas; d, James Bridges; w, Mike Gray, T.S. Cook, James Bridges; ph, James Crabe (Metrocolor); ed, David Rawlins; art d, George Jenkins; fx, Henry Millar; cos, Donfeld

Life imitates art. What began as a fanciful premise in the minds of many turned into reality a few weeks after this picture opened when the Three Mile Island nuclear reactor had a dreadful accident.

Fonda plays Kimberly Wells, a television reporter trying to advance from cutesy stories to harder news. Douglas is Richard Adams, a freelance cameraman she hires while attempting to do a feature story on nuclear energy. They are present at a power plant when a crisis arises, but a meltdown is avoided by the quick reactions of engineer Jack Godell (Lemmon). Richard has it all on film and rushes it back to the station, but management won't put it on the air for fear of scaring viewers. Godell, meanwhile, is angry when he learns that the authorities have covered up the incident. He begins searching the plant to find the fault and finally locates it: inferior welding put there to keep costs down. Godell sees there is nothing to keep this problem from recurring, so he contacts the similarly questing reporters and gives them X-rays of the offending equipment. When sound man Hector Salas (Valdez) is murdered while taking the information to a hearing on a proposed nuclear project, Godell realizes that his superiors will stop at nothing to cover up their criminal negligence.

A film more honest than most in admitting its political stance, THE CHINA SYNDROME effectively brandishes its polemic within the framework of a nightmarish but convincing story. The lack of incidental music adds to the more documentarian aspects of the film, whose tight scripting and direction ably maintain suspense during the protracted climax. The sometimes self-conscious and too-earnest Fonda and the occasionally hammy Lemmon both rise beautifully to the occasion, delivering performances that are among their best. In other roles Douglas, Brimley, Hampton, Brady, and Bohrman (an actual reporter who would go on to cover the Three Mile Island incident) offer sterling support. Not a comforting film, but an undeniably potent one.

CHINATOWN

1974 131m c   ★★★★★
Mystery   /15
Paramount

Jack Nicholson *(J.J. Gittes)*, Faye Dunaway *(Evelyn Mulwray)*, John Huston *(Noah Cross)*, Perry Lopez *(Escobar)*, John Hillerman *(Yelburton)*, Darrell Zwerling *(Hollis Mulwray)*, Diane Ladd *(Ida Sessions)*, Roy Jenson *(Mulvihill)*, Roman Polanski *(Man with Knife)*, Richard Bakalyan *(Loach)*

p, Robert Evans; d, Roman Polanski; w, Robert Towne; ph, John A. Alonzo (Panavision, Technicolor); ed, Sam O'Steen; m, Jerry Goldsmith; prod d, Richard Sylbert; art d, Stewart Campbell; fx, Logan Frazee; cos, Anthea Sylbert

A wonderfully brooding, suspenseful revisitation of the land of film noir, CHINATOWN is not only one of the greatest detective films, but one of the most perfectly constructed of all films. With Polanski's brilliant direction, Towne's intricate screenplay, and Nicholson's and Dunaway's tour de force performances, the film stands as one of the best of the 1970s.

The plot revolves around Gittes (Nicholson), a Chandleresque private eye who specializes in the most distasteful of detective enterprises—snooping after straying spouses. After being duped by a woman pretending to be the wife of the city water commissioner, Gittes meets the man's real wife, Evelyn Mulwray (Dunaway), but before long she ends up a widow. Drawn into these strange goings-on, Gittes follows a jigsaw puzzle of clues that leads to Mulwray's father, Cross (Huston). Cross has involved himself in the "future" of Los Angeles by engineering a plot to divert the city's water supply for his own gain.

Besides telling a gripping story involving incest and political graft, CHINATOWN recaptures the atmosphere of Los Angeles, 1937—the cars, clothes, and buildings, right down to the barber chairs (kudos to production designer Richard Sylbert and costumer Anthea Sylbert). The tone and flavor of this film evoke strong memories of MURDER, MY SWEET and the original THE BIG SLEEP, yet it stands singularly on its own merits. Even the muted color cinematography (normally antithetical to the tenets of noir) is evocative and apppropriate. Interestingly, Towne's script included not a single scene set in Chinatown—initially a metaphorical state of mind rather than a specific place.

Look for director Polanski as the thug who pokes a switchblade up Nicholson's nostril while uttering the infamous line, "You know what happens to nosy fellows? They lose their noses." Another highlight: Dunaway's "sister. . . daughter. . . sister. . . daughter" routine, a camp classic much parodied since. CHINATOWN earned 11 Oscar nominations, including Best Picture, but only Towne took home a statuette for his cynical screenplay.

CHLOE IN THE AFTERNOON
(L'AMOUR, L'APRES-MIDI)
1972   97m   c   ★★★
Drama   R/
Losange/Barbet Schroeder   (France)

Bernard Verley *(Frederic)*, Zouzou *(Chloe)*, Francoise Verley *(Helene)*, Daniel Ceccaldi *(Gerard)*, Malvina Penne *(Fabienne)*, Babette Ferrier *(Martine)*, Tina Michelino, Jean-Louis Livi, Pierre Nunzi, Irene Skobline

p, Pierre Cottrell; d, Eric Rohmer; w, Eric Rohmer; ph, Nestor Almendros; ed, Cecile Decugis; m, Arie Dzierlatka; art d, Nicole Rachline

This sixth and final installment of Rohmer's "Six Moral Tales" focuses, for the first time in the series, on the married Frederic (Bernard Verley), a professional who spends very little time with his equally business-minded wife, Helene (Francoise Verley). The first part of the film is essentially a prologue as it carefully sets up the male lead's character. He is a man easily seduced—but only mentally. Frederic imagines what certain women (a wonderful series of cameos by previous Rohmer heroines) are like, concocting romantic adventures with them as they walk down the street. In one telling scene, he purchases a shirt from a pretty saleswoman only because he cannot resist her charms. Having settled into marriage, he dreams only of love in the afternoon (as the original French title translates). Then into Frederic's life walks Chloe (Zouzou), an attractive, sexy mystery woman determined to seduce him.

A fitting close to the series, which finally marries off one of Rohmer's romantic heroes, reunites all his previous heroines, and addresses the basic theme of marital infidelity. To a greater degree than his previous films, Rohmer (to the surprise of those who find his work talky and boring) invests CHLOE IN THE AFTERNOON with a surprising amount of suspense—not the obvious sort, but a variety that is quieter, emotional—with all the tension and conflict occurring inside the character's mind. In this respect Rohmer seems a deserving recipient of the soubriquet "the Henry James of cinema."

CHOCOLATE WAR, THE
1988   100m   c   ★★★
Drama   R/15
Management Co. Entertainment

John Glover *(Brother Leon)*, Ilan M. Mitchell-Smith *(Jerry)*, Wally Ward *(Archie)*, Doug Hutchison *(Obie)*, Adam Baldwin *(Carter)*, Brent Fraser *(Emille)*, Bud Cort *(Brother Jacques)*

p, Jonathan D. Krane, Simon R. Lewis; d, Keith Gordon; w, Keith Gordon (based on the novel by Robert Cormier); ph, Tom Richmond; ed, Jeff Wishengrad; prod d, David Ensley; cos, Elizabeth Kaye

Keith Gordon, after 10 years of appearing in front of the camera (ALL THAT JAZZ, CHRISTINE), made his directing debut at age 27 with this dark, dazzling film in the tradition of IF and LORD OF THE FLIES. Working from his own adaptation of Robert Cormier's novel, Gordon uses an inventive narrative technique and stylish visuals to tell the story of a teenager who takes a stand against an oppressive system but, in so doing, ends up playing the system's game.

Set at Trinity, a Catholic boys' high school, the film revolves around 15-year-old Mitchell-Smith, the "new kid." He comes to the attention of Ward and Hutchison, two members of the Vigils, the school's secret society of bullies, and sadistic, pointer-wielding instructor Glover, who moves from the classroom to the principal's office when the school's headmaster takes ill. Glover is also in charge of the school's annual chocolate sale and hopes to impress the board of trustees by selling twice as many boxes of sweets as he did the year before. With assistance from the bullying Vigils, Glover nearly achieves his goal—the only student not fulfilling his quota is Mitchell-Smith, who refuses in order to prove something to himself.

With much of his film's direction dictated by dream logic, Gordon uses an arresting visual style to immerse the viewer in Mitchell-Smith's world. Despite his limited budget, the writer-director presents an array of memorable images. Mitchell-Smith's character is not as well developed as we might want it to be (though much can be inferred from his dreams). Still—aided by strong performances by Adam Baldwin, Ward, and Glover—Gordon has created a deeply involving film. It has much to tell us, not just about a particular adolescent challenge, but also about the difficulty of nonconformity and how easily means and ends become confused.

CHOICE OF ARMS
(LE CHOIX DES ARMES)
1981   135m   c   ★★★
Crime
Sara/Antenne 2/Parafrance/Radio Monte Carlo   (France)

Yves Montand *(Noel Durieux)*, Gerard Depardieu *(Mickey)*, Catherine Deneuve *(Nicole Durieux)*, Michel Galabru *(Bonnardot)*, Gerard Lanvin *(Sarlat)*, Jean-Claude Dauphin *(Ricky)*, Richard Anconina *(Dany)*, Jean Rougerie, Christian Marquand, Etienne Chicot

p, Alain Sarde; d, Alain Corneau; w, Alain Corneau, Michel Grisolia; ph, Pierre-William Glenn (Panavision); ed, Thierry Derocles; m, Philippe Sarde; art d, Jean-Pierre Kohut-Sveklo

A compelling and superbly directed *policier*, CHOICE OF ARMS pits the new, young breed of criminal—the crazed and disrespectful Mickey (Depardieu)—against an elder, retired underworld hood, the honorable Noel (Montand). Mickey escapes from prison and takes temporary refuge at a ranch owned by Noel and his wife, Nicole (Deneuve). When Mickey refuses to play by Noel's rules, he takes off for Paris. Upon returning, he wrongly assumes that Noel has informed on him and vows to kill both Noel and Nicole. A criminal of the old school—not unlike those who appear in the films of Jean-Pierre Melville—Noel leads a tranquil life but is not beyond violent, angry outbursts. He has fought long and hard to achieve his quiet lifestyle with his loving wife, and now he must fight again.

Although CHOICE OF ARMS does follow certain Hollywood genre expectations, Corneau's direction stamps the film with a crisp, personal style of filmmaking as attentive to the theoretical issues at stake in the conflict as it is to story development or emotional impact. In this respect Corneu merits comparison with his more acclaimed contemporary Bertrand Tavernier. Depardieu turns in a forceful performance as the unpredictable Mickey, and Montand is an explosion waiting to happen as the externally peaceful Noel. Unfortunately, the always beautiful Deneuve is cast here in another role in which she gets little chance to display her considerable acting skills.

CHOOSE ME
1984   114m   c   ★★★★
Comedy/Drama   R/15
Island Alive

Keith Carradine *(Mickey)*, Lesley Ann Warren *(Eve)*, Genevieve Bujold *(Ann/Dr. Nancy Lovell)*, Patrick Bauchau *(Zack Antoine)*, Rae Dawn Chong *(Pearl Antoine)*, John Larroquette *(Billy Ace)*, Edward Ruscha *(Ralph Chomsky)*, Gailard Sartain *(Mueller)*, Robert Gould *(Lou)*, John Considine *(Dr. Ernest Greene)*

p, Carolyn Pfeiffer, David Blocker; d, Alan Rudolph; w, Alan Rudolph; ph, Jan Kiesser (Movielab Color); ed, Mia Goldman; prod d, Steven Legler; art d, Steven Legler; cos, Tracy Tynan

Director Alan Rudolph hit his stride with this quirky comedy-drama in which the characterizations outweigh and eventually overwhelm the plot. Ann (Bujold) is a radio psychologist calling herself "Dr. Love" who dispenses advice but is hopelessly maladjusted herself. Eve (Warren), meanwhile, the owner of a small bar, is both blessed and cursed with the ability to attract and capture any man she pleases. But Eve is not the supremely self-confident person she seems; she is actually a frightened woman living on the edge of a breakdown who spends a lot of time calling Dr. Love. Then Mickey (Carradine), a wayward genius or the world's greatest liar, walks into the bar and into the lives of both Eve and Ann.

This picture is made up of many fine moments and many wonderful verbal insights. There's not much of a story here, but, in typical fashion, director Rudolph wisely allows the film to gently meander in several interesting directions. Lushly photographed and very well acted, with a relaxed, bleary-eyed, 3 a.m. feel to it, this sometimes surprising little film is an intriguing piece of work.

CHORUS LINE, A
1985   113m   c   ★★
Musical   PG-13/PG
Polygram

Michael Blevins *(Mark)*, Yamil Borges *(Morales)*, Sharon Brown *(Kim)*, Gregg Burge *(Richie)*, Michael Douglas *(Zach)*, Cameron English *(Paul)*, Tony Fields *(Al)*, Nicole Fosse *(Kristine)*, Vicki Frederick *(Sheila)*, Jan Gan Boyd *(Connie)*

p, Cy Feuer, Ernest H. Martin; d, Richard Attenborough; w, Arnold Schulman (based on the play by James Kirkwood and Nicholas Dante); ph, Ronnie Taylor; ed, John Bloom; m, Marvin Hamlisch; prod d, Patrizia von Brandenstein; art d, John Dapper; chor, Jeffrey Hornaday; cos, Faye Poliakin

Paging 42ND STREET. . . or at least Mickey and Judy. It took nearly ten years for the longest-running Broadway musical of all time to make it from stage to screen, and although director Attenborough's film version has a couple of pleasant numbers which serve as oases amidst the dullness, it really hurts for those who remember the dazzle and emotional depth of the let's-put-on-a-show original. The story, for those unfamiliar with Kirkwood and Dante's Pulitzer Prize-winning play, revolves around the auditions for the chorus of an unnamed musical, and part of the excitement behind this unfilmable enterprise lies with the power of watching "actual" auditions in a theater. Is it any wonder that half a dozen directors signed on for this one, only to throw their hands up in despair?

Douglas plays Zach, the director who puts the young singer-dancers through their paces, demanding not only that they strut their stuff but that they also reveal something of their backgrounds and dreams. How much can you really like a musical when the direction is flat, several good songs are tossed into the ether, the singing and dancing are often not much to sing and

dance about, and both the zest and the pain are rationed out in such miserly fashion? Skip it and dig up your *Playbill* of the stage original.

CHOSEN, THE
1982   108m   c   ★★★
Drama   PG
Contemporary

Maximilian Schell *(David Malter)*, Rod Steiger *(Reb Saunders)*, Robby Benson *(Danny Saunders)*, Barry Miller *(Reuven Malter)*, Hildy Brooks *(Mrs. Saunders)*, Ron Rifkin *(Baseball Coach)*, Val Avery *(Teacher)*

p, Edie Landau, Ely Landau; d, Jeremy Paul Kagan; w, Edwin Gordon (based on the novel by Chaim Potok); ph, Arthur J. Ornitz (color); ed, David Garfield; m, Elmer Bernstein; art d, Stuart Wurtzel; cos, Ruth Morley

A first-rate adaptation of the Chaim Potok novel of the same name, THE CHOSEN depicts the friendship of two young Jewish men of widely different beliefs, and their relationships with their fathers during the 1940s.

Two youths, the Hasidic Danny Saunders (Benson) and the Orthodox Reuven Malter (Miller) begin their friendship after Danny nearly blinds Reuven in a baseball game. To Reuven, who considers himself a typical American kid, Danny's Hasidic upbringing, complete with 19th-century attire and long side curls, makes him seem as strange as a creature from space. Nevertheless, they grow closer until Danny's father, a forceful rabbi (Steiger) forbids his son to talk to Reuven because the boy's father (Schell) is a fervent Zionist.

Potent and simmering if sometimes a little overstated, THE CHOSEN manages to elicit a tolerable and appropriate performance from the generally emetic Benson. Steiger's work is mixed, undeniably powerful yet sometimes hammy in the way he's always been since winning his Oscar back in 1968. Neither actor's work, though, can hold a candle to the touching, scene-stealing work by Miller.

CHRISTMAS IN CONNECTICUT
1945   102m   bw   ★★★½
Comedy   /A
WB

Barbara Stanwyck *(Elisabeth Lane)*, Dennis Morgan *(Jefferson Jones)*, Sydney Greenstreet *(Alexander Yardley)*, Reginald Gardiner *(John Sloan)*, S.Z. Sakall *(Felix Bassenak)*, Robert Shayne *(Dudley Beecham)*, Una O'Connor *(Norah)*, Frank Jenks *(Sinkewicz)*, Joyce Compton *(Mary Lee)*, Dick Elliott *(Judge Crothers)*

p, William Jacobs; d, Peter Godfrey; w, Lionel Houser, Adele Comandini (based on a story by Aileen Hamilton); ph, Carl Guthrie; ed, Frank Magee; m, Frederick Hollander; art d, Stanley Fleischer; cos, Edith Head

A sometimes hilarious farce and a holiday favorite. Stanwyck stars as Elisabeth Lane, a successful but scheming columnist who pretends to be a happy, supercompetent housewife. Compelled to take in Navy hero Jefferson Jones (Morgan) for the holidays as part of a promotion gimmick concocted by her hoodwinked publisher Alexander Yardley (Greenstreet), Elisabeth must deal with the reality that she doesn't own the country home she writes about, can't cook, and isn't married. In desperation, she convinces lounge lizard John Sloan (Gardiner) to play the role of hubby, rents a rustic house, and brings in a world-famous chef (Sakall, genuinely amusing but best taken in small doses) to cover up her own inadequacies.

Director Godfrey's handling of the material is rather mild and not especially creative, but he does keep things lively, and Stanwyck proves her considerable flair for comedy. It's also nice to see a very relaxed Greenstreet in something other than melodrama for a change. The film's endorsement of housewifery over working outside the home is obvious, but to the film's credit its attitude is a heartily self-mocking one.

CHRISTMAS IN JULY

1940 66m bw ★★★★½
Comedy /U
Paramount

Dick Powell (Jimmy MacDonald), Ellen Drew (Betty Casey), Raymond Walburn (Mr. Maxford), Alexander Carr (Mr. Schindel), William Demarest (Mr. Bildocker), Ernest Truex (Mr. Baxter), Franklin Pangborn (Radio Announcer), Harry Hayden (Mr. Waterbury), Rod Cameron (Dick), Adrian Morris (Tom)

p, Paul Jones; d, Preston Sturges; w, Preston Sturges; ph, Victor Milner; ed, Ellsworth Hoagland

A film of genuine and unashamed sweetness and light, only the second from *wunderkind* writer-director Sturges. Though the level of satiric insanity does not match that of his later films, CHRISTMAS IN JULY is a priceless comedy that holds its own against the director's later, better-known work.

Jimmy McDonald (Powell, never better) is the victim of an office joke making him the winner of $25,000 in a coffee slogan contest. Problems develop when he learns he's not really the winner, leading to some frantic and hilarious bits of comic business, with the already-assembled Sturges stock company (Walburn, Demarest, Truex, Pangborn, Meyer, Foulger and Conlin) playing at full volume.

CHRISTMAS is probably Sturges's warmest comedy, and a fine illustration of the "common man" touch which tempered his worldly sophistication. After watching this minor gem only once, you're certain never to forget the slogan: "If you can't sleep, it's not the coffee, it must be the bunk." You figure it out!!

CHRISTMAS STORY, A

1983 98m c ★★★★
Comedy PG
MGM

Melinda Dillon (Mother), Darren McGavin (Old Man), Peter Billingsley (Ralphie), Ian Petrella (Randy), Scott Schwartz (Flick), R.D. Robb (Schuartz), Tedde Moore (Miss Shields), Yano Anaya (Grover), Zack Ward (Scot), Jeff Gillen (Santa Claus)

p, Rene Dupont, Bob Clark; d, Bob Clark; w, Jean Shepherd, Leigh Brown, Bob Clark (based on the novel *In God We Trust, All Others Pay Cash* by Jean Shepherd); ph, Reginald Morris; ed, Stan Cole; m, Carl Zittrer, Paul Zaza; art d, Gavin Mitchell; cos, Mary McLeod

Somehow usually tasteless director Bob Clark, whose specialty was fairly vile exploitation movies (PORKY'S and the even worse PORKY'S II: THE NEXT DAY), managed to make a totally charming and lovable Christmas film.

Based on the short stories of midwestern humorist Jean Shepherd (who also narrates in the first person), A CHRISTMAS STORY is an episodic comedy set in the 1940s about the family life of young Ralphie (Billingsley) as Christmas approaches. The plot loosely revolves around Ralphie's desire for a Red Ryder BB gun for Christmas that his mother (Dillon) has forbidden because she's afraid he'll shoot his eyes out. Among Shepherd's childhood musings are his narrow escapes from the neighborhood bullies, the battles of his old man (McGavin) with the smoke-belching furnace, Mom's attempts to get his little brother (Petrella) to eat, Dad's infatuation with an obnoxious lamp that looks like a woman's leg, and a nightmarish visit with Santa at the local department store.

The cast is wonderful—especially McGavin, Billingsley and Petrella—the laughs are nonstop if rarely subtle, and the whole thing deserves to become a Christmastime classic.

CHRONICLE OF A DEATH FORETOLD

(CRONACA DI UNA MORTE ANNUNCIATA)
1987 109m c ★★★
Drama /15
Italmedia/Soprofilms/Les Films Ariane/FR 3/RAI 2
(France/Italy)

Rupert Everett (Bayardo San Roman), Ornella Muti (Angela Vicario), Gian Maria Volonte (Dr. Cristo Bedoya), Irene Papas (Angela's Mother), Lucia Bose (Placida Linero), Anthony Delon (Santiago Nasar), Alain Cuny (Widower), Sergi Mateu (Young Cristo Bedoya), Carolina Rosi (Flora Miguel), Caroline Lang (Margot)

p, Yves Gasser, Francis Von Buren; d, Francesco Rosi; w, Francesco Rosi, Tonino Guerra (based on a novel by Gabriel Garcia Marquez); ph, Pasqualino de Santis (Panavision, Eastmancolor); ed, Ruggero Mastroianni; m, Piero Piccioni; art d, Andrea Crisanti; cos, Enrico Sabbatini

As he did in SALVATORE GIULIANO, director Francesco Rosi reconstructs the events which combined to bring about a murder in this Italian-French coproduction based on the novel by Nobel Prize winner Gabriel Garcia Marquez.

Set in a provincial Colombian river town, the story begins in the present as Volonte (THE DEATH OF MARIO RICCI, CHRIST STOPPED AT EBOLI), a doctor in his fifties, returns to his home after nearly 20 years to investigate a murder that occurred just before he left. In flashback, Everett (DANCE WITH A STRANGER, ANOTHER COUNTRY), the son of a wealthy general, visits the town in search of a bride and falls in love with the beautiful Muti. They wed, but soon after the ceremony, Everett discovers that Muti is not a virgin and returns his bride to her shamed family. Muti's father beats her until she names the man who deflowered her, Delon, a brazen young womanizer, who may or may not have actually compromised Muti. Her twin brothers, Carlos and Rogerio Miranda, are then honor-bound to make Delon pay for his indiscretion.

The film's action is enriched by themes of omnipresent Catholicism, the emptiness of macho stances, and the strength of familial ties. The moody photography increases the languorous mystical aura of the film.

CHUSHINGURA

1962 115m c ★★★★
Drama
Toho (Japan)

Koshiro Matsumoto (Kuranosuke Oishi), Yuzo Kayama (Takuminokami Asano), Chusha Ichikawa (Kouzuke Kira), Toshiro Mifune (Genba Tawaraboshi), Yoko Tsukasa (Yozenin), Setsuko Hara (Riku), Tatsuya Mihashi (Yasubei Horibe), Yosuke Natsuki (Kinemon Okano), Ichiro Arishima (Denpachiro Tamon), Norihei Miki (Gayboy Geisha) d, Hiroshi Inagaki; w, Toshio Yasumi (based on the Kabuki play cycle *Kanadehon Chushingura* by Izumo Takeda, Senryu Namiki, Shoraku Miyoshi); ph, Kazuo Yamada (Tohoscope, Eastmancolor); m, Akira Ifukube; art d, Kisaku Ito

Kayama plays an honest Japanese noble constantly harassed for bribes by his supervisor (Ichikawa). Goaded beyond endurance, the underling draws his sword and wounds his tormentor. He is consequently ordered to commit *hara kiri*, and, in a gripping scene, he fulfills the command. His 47 samurai retainers (known as ronin), however, swear vengeance and finally, after biding their time and planning carefully for nearly two years, attack the lord's castle. Successful in their revenge and acclaimed as heroes, the ronin are nevertheless arrested and sentenced to death for their actions, but they are able to proudly follow the samurai code and go the way of their master.

Adapted from a popular Kabuki play from the 18th century which was based on historical fact, Inagaki's film is probably the best of dozens of film versions of the story going back to 1913. Leisurely paced but energetically acted and beautifully designed and shot, it stands with SEVEN SAMURAI and THRONE OF BLOOD as the best of the Japanese samurai genre.

CIMARRON

1931   131m   bw   ★★★½
Western   /U
RKO

Richard Dix *(Yancey Cravat)*, Irene Dunne *(Sabra Cravat)*, Estelle Taylor *(Dixie Lee)*, Nance O'Neil *(Felice Venable)*, William Collier, Jr. *(the Kid)*, Roscoe Ates *(Jess Rickey)*, George E. Stone *(Sol Levy)*, Robert McWade *(Louie Heffner)*, Edna May Oliver *(Mrs. Tracy Wyatt)*, Frank Darien *(Mr. Bixby)*

p, William LeBaron; d, Wesley Ruggles; w, Howard Estabrook (based on the novel by Edna Ferber); ph, Edward Cronjager; ed, William Hamilton; art d, Max Ree; cos, Max Ree

Edna Ferber's red-blooded western saga. Its biggest scene—the Oklahoma Land Rush—employs thousands of extras racing pell-mell on horseback, in wagons and on foot to stake out claims on the two million acres opened to settlers on April 22, 1889. Among this frenzied horde are Richard Dix and his young wife, Irene Dunne. Much of the film, which covers 40 years from 1889 to 1929, rests upon the considerable talents of the lovely Dunne, whose Sabra Cravat is followed from girlhood until she becomes a grand old woman of the West.

They manage to stake out a prize piece of territory, but scheming Estelle Taylor replaces their marker and takes the land herself. Dix establishes a newspaper, liberally complementing the power of the press with his own quick-draw brand of justice (in one dramatic confrontation, he shoots the earlobe off a bully), but the tough westerner has a big heart. When the same Taylor who robbed him of land is later put on trial for prostitution, Dix defends her in court. But he is also consumed by wanderlust, often leaving Dunne for long periods of time, and the film follows their relationship's inevitible changes.

CIMARRON cost RKO a staggering $1.5 million, the largest budget the studio ever committed to a film up to that time. Though it received across-the-board raves, the film lost more than half a million dollars. Dunne is superb and CIMARRON was considered until the late 1940s the finest Western ever made. Its biggest drawback is Dix, whose performance has dated badly. Still, it holds up surprisingly well today; the 1960 remake of CIMARRON fizzles by comparison.

CINCINNATI KID, THE

1965   102m   c   ★★★★
Drama   /AA
MGM

Steve McQueen *(The Cincinnati Kid)*, Edward G. Robinson *(Lancey Howard)*, Ann-Margret *(Melba)*, Karl Malden *(Shooter)*, Tuesday Weld *(Christian)*, Joan Blondell *(Lady Fingers)*, Rip Torn *(Slade)*, Jack Weston *(Pig)*, Cab Calloway *(Yeller)*, Jeff Corey *(Hoban)*

p, Martin Ransohoff; d, Norman Jewison; w, Ring Lardner, Jr., Terry Southern (based on the novel by Richard Jessup); ph, Philip Lathrop (Metrocolor); ed, Hal Ashby; m, Lalo Schifrin; art d, George W. Davis, Edward Carfagno; cos, Donfeld

An attempt to do for poker what THE HUSTLER did for pool, THE CINCINNATI KID succeeds on its own, but it might have been a classic with some more attention paid to the script and, perhaps, a little humor sandwiched in to relieve the suspense.

McQueen is The Kid, a formidable gambler who has built a strong reputation among those in the know. He's in New Orleans hustling small-timers and about to go east to Miami when Robinson rolls into town looking for some action. Robinson is "The Man," acknowledged to be the king of poker. He's visiting town for a private game but isn't averse to a match against McQueen, which is arranged by Malden. Torn had earlier been badly beaten by Robinson and he wants revenge, so he calls in some old debts and forces Malden, who is dealing the game between Robinson and McQueen, to slip some winning cards to The Kid. Once McQueen realizes that's happening, he eases Malden out of the way, determined to win fair and square.

A marathon card game takes place, beautifully directed by Jewison, photographed by Lathrop, and edited by Hal Ashby. Even if you don't understand the game, you'll be biting your nails. Excellent supporting work is provided by Joan Blondell as Lady Fingers, a blowsy blonde dealer. In his accustomed role as the desk clerk, look for Olan Soule, a small, elderly man with a young voice. Soule, whom Jack Webb used often in his TV series, was "Mr. First Nighter" during the halcyon days of radio.

CINDERELLA

1950   74m   c   ★★★★
Animated   /U
Disney

VOICES OF: Ilene Woods *(Cinderella)*, William Phipps *(Prince Charming)*, Eleanor Audley *(Stepmother)*, Verna Felton *(Fairy Godmother)*, James MacDonald *(Jacques and Gus-Gus)*, Rhoda Williams *(Anastasia)*, Lucille Bliss *(Drusilla)*, Luis Van Rooten *(King and Grand Duke)*, Don Barclay, Claire DuBrey

p, Walt Disney; d, Wilfred Jackson, Hamilton Luske, Clyde Geronimi; w, Bill Peet, Ted Sears, Homer Brightman, Ken Anderson, Erdman Penner, Winston Hibler, Harry Reeves, Joe Rinaldi (based on the original story by Charles Perrault); ed, Donald Halliday; m, Oliver Wallace, Paul Smith

Although not originally met with the kind of praise that greeted Disney's SNOW WHITE and PINOCCHIO, CINDERELLA holds up better because the heroine seems timeless in her courage and resourcefulness, a closer cousin to Belle in Disney's BEAUTY AND THE BEAST than to other fairytale protaganists. To expand the simple storyline, the Disney people created a variety of animal characters, led by Jacques and Gus-Gus, two adorable mice and evil chubby charmer, Lucifer, the stepmother's cat. Eleanor Audley, Disney's grande dame of villainy, and Verna Felton, Disney's grande dame of benevolence, lead the company of wonderful voices. Excellent animation, marvelous color, and lovely music make CINDERELLA a delight all the way around.

CINEMA PARADISO
(NUOVO CINEMA PARADISO)
1990   123m   c   ★★½
Comedy/Drama   /PG
Ariane/Cristaldifilm/TFI/RAI-TRE/Forum   (Italy/France)

Jacques Perrin (*Toto as an Adult*), Salvatore Cascio (*Toto as a Child*), Marco Leonardi (*Toto as a Teenager*), Philippe Noiret (*Alfredo*), Nino Terzo (*Peppino's Father*), Roberta Lena (*Lia*), Nicolo di Pinto (*Madman*), Pupella Maggio (*Older Maria*), Leopoldo Trieste (*Fr. Adelfio*), Enzo Cannavale (*Spaccafico*)

p, Franco Cristaldi; d, Giuseppe Tornatore; w, Giuseppe Tornatore; ph, Blasco Giurato; ed, Mario Mora; m, Ennio Morricone, Andrea Morricone; prod d, Andrea Crisanti; cos, Beatrice Bordone

Successful movie director Salvatore returns to his rural Sicilian village after 30 years to attend the funeral of a dear friend and former mentor who advised him, all those years ago, to forsake his humble origins and journey to Rome to make a life for himself. CINEMA PARADISO wallows in nostalgia for a mythic moviegoing past that it serves up in self-infatuated gobs. No, they don't make movies like they used to, and this Oscar-winning Italian-French co-production spends the better part of three hours proving it.

In extended flashback, Salvatore (played by Jacques Perrin as an adult) reviews his postwar childhood and his relationship with the friend—Alfredo (Philippe Noiret), the projectionist at the town's only theater, the Cinema Paradiso. The whole town has been affected by the war and, for many, the Paradiso has become a refuge from the impoverishment and indignity that surrounds them.

A prankish altar boy, Salvatore or Toto for short (played as a boy by Salvatore Cascio) follows the local priest to a private screening at the Paradiso. The priest, also the town censor, registers his disapproval of certain moments in the films that flicker past (it's the kissing scenes that invariably arouse his ire) and Alfredo snips out the offending footage. Toto badgers the projectionist into giving him a strip of discarded celluloid. Naturally, a bond soon grows between them.

That Paradiso is some reperatory house. Great classics from the likes of Lang, Renoir and Visconti abound and there are enough Anna Magnani classics for a month of screenings at the Museum of Modern Art, but for the folks in this backwater hamlet such stellar fare is as common as going to church each week. Indeed going to the movies is a reverential act, as anyone gazing on those rows of rapt faces can tell. They laugh, they cry, they bliss out on cue.

Director Tornatore (IL CAMORRISTA) pushes every sentimental button—some Felliniesque, some probably personal—but none that hasn't been pushed a dozen times before. The film's censor priest might well approve of the carefully tailored sentimentality. Still, Tornatore's film—shot on location in the director's hometown of Bagheria, Sicily—won a number of film festival accolades, including the Grand Jury prize at Cannes in 1989.

CIRCLE OF DECEIT
1982   108m   c   ★★★★
Drama   /X
Bioskop/Artemis/Argos   (France/West Germany)

Bruno Ganz (*Georg Laschen*), Hanna Schygulla (*Arianna Nassar*), Jean Carmet (*Rudnik*), Jerzy Skolimowski (*Hoffmann*), Gila von Weitershausen (*Greta Laschen*), Peter Martin Urtel (*Berger*), John Munro (*John*), Fouad Naim (*Excellence Joseph*), Josette Khalil (*Mrs. Joseph*), Khaled el Saeid (*Progressive Officer*)

p, Eberhard Junkersdorf; d, Volker Schlondorff; w, Volker Schlondorff, Jean-Claude Carriere, Margarethe von Trotta, Kai Hermann (from a novel by Nicolas Born); ph, Igor Luther (Eastmancolor); ed, Suzanne Baron; m, Maurice Jarre; art d, Alexandre Riachi, Tannous Zougheib; fx, Paul Trielli, Andre Trielli; cos, Dagmar Niefind

German journalist Bruno Ganz leaves a troubled marriage and questions of self-worth behind him and travels to Beirut to write about the obsessive, violent war raging there. Amid a group of disillusioned reporters who see the fighting in the Middle East as just another sign of the times, Ganz vows to get to the heart of the true story and discover the emotional answer to the ever-present question of "why?" He meets and falls in love with the beautiful Hanna Schygulla, a wealthy German aristocrat still living in a mansion in the middle of bombed-out rubble. When the fighting becomes more intense and the lives of the journalists become threatened, most of the reporters leave Beirut for safer territory. Ganz remains, determined to understand the violence and to report it to the world.

Director Volker Schlondorff, one of the pioneers of the New German Cinema, creates a frightening, effective vision of the nightmarish war in Beirut and the grisly effect it can have on emotions as well as bodies. Ganz is wonderfully powerful as the observant, curious reporter who realizes man always has a way of deceiving himself and others into simple answers for complex questions. Schygulla, the mesmerizing star of many of Fassbinder's films, turns in an exquisite performance as the mysterious woman who courts death as well as men. Shot on location in Beirut, the film's re-created, on-the-street battle sequences are violently intense and realistic.

CITADEL, THE
1938   110m   bw   ★★★★½
Drama   /A
MGM   (U.K.)

Robert Donat (*Andrew Manson*), Rosalind Russell (*Christine Manson*), Ralph Richardson (*Denny*), Rex Harrison (*Dr. Lawford*), Emlyn Williams (*Owen*), Penelope Dudley-Ward (*Toppy Leroy*), Francis L. Sullivan (*Ben Chenkin*), Mary Clare (*Mrs. Orlando*), Cecil Parker (*Charles Every*), Nora Swinburne (*Mrs. Thornton*)

p, Victor Saville; d, King Vidor; w, Ian Dalrymple, Frank Wead, Elizabeth Hill, Emlyn Williams (based on the novel by A.J. Cronin); ph, Harry Stradling; ed, Charles Frend; m, Louis Levy; art d, Lazare Meerson, Alfred Junge

A faithful rendering of doctor-turned-author Cronin's semi-autobiographical novel, with the superb Donat toplining as a dedicated doctor who ministers to TB-infected Welsh miners and Russell lending stirring support as his devoted and idealistic wife.

At first, Andrew Manson (Donat) is full of lofty goals as he labors in the slums of a mining town, struggling to save the miserable health of downtrodden workers. Later, though, his noble purpose slowly corrodes when he begins to treat aristocratic, wealthy London patients. Turning to the material pleasures of the "good life," it takes the combined efforts of his wife and a close friend (Richardson) and several dramatic turns of events to convinces Manson that he has lost touch with his true aims in life.

Produced by MGM's British production unit after the studio had met with success in a similar foreign production, A YANK AT OXFORD, THE CITADEL is a gripping portrait of both idealism and its disillusionment, not a mere ode to nobility. It is carefully piloted by director Vidor, who wisely allows the consummate acting skills of Donat, Richardson and a marvelous supporting cast to carry the story forward with sensitivity and relaxed charm. Russell, too, at the cusp of her transition between playing society-matron supporting roles and zany comedic starring parts, artfully combines the gentility of the former and the appeal of the latter.

CITIZEN KANE
1941   119m   bw   ★★★★★
Drama
Mercury   /U

Orson Welles (*Charles Foster Kane*), Joseph Cotten (*Jedediah Leland*), Dorothy Comingore (*Susan Alexander*), Everett Sloane (*Mr. Bernstein*), Ray Collins (*Boss J.W. "Big Jim" Gettys*), George Coulouris (*Walter Parks Thatcher*), Agnes Moorehead (*Mary Kane*), Paul Stewart (*Raymond*), Ruth Warrick (*Emily Norton Kane*), Erskine Sanford (*Herbert Carter*)

p, Orson Welles; d, Orson Welles; w, Herman J. Mankiewicz, Orson Welles; ph, Gregg Toland; ed, Robert Wise, Mark Robson (uncredited); m, Bernard Herrmann; art d, Van Nest Polglase, Perry Ferguson; fx, Vernon L. Walker; cos, Edward Stevenson

Fading in on an ominous nighttime exterior, the camera slowly focuses on a high wrought-iron fence filigreed with the initial "K." Beyond spreads Xanadu, the vast estate of one of the world's wealthiest men. The camera surveys the grounds—empty gondolas swaying on a private lake, exotic animals penned in a private zoo, manicured lawns and shubbery—all shrouded in fog. Towering above the mist is the top of a man-made mountain on which sits a castle, a single light shining from it. Within is a dying man who clutches a crystal ball enclosing a winter scene and make-believe snow. He utters one word, "Rosebud," and dies, dropping the ball, which breaks into tiny shards.

"American." "John Citizen, U.S.A." CITIZEN KANE. After several projects came to naught, notably an adaptation of Joseph Conrad's *Heart of Darkness*, 25 year-old *wunderkind* Welles, already a sensation in the theater and radio worlds, made what is unquestionably the most stunning debut in the history of film. KANE is a landmark film for myriad reasons, not the least of which is the variety of techniques employed—quick cuts, imaginative dissolves, even the iris device once popular in silent films. Indeed, none of the filmmaking methodology of the past is left unused, but KANE also contributes an array of innovative cinematic devices, most notably Gregg Toland's astonishing deep-focus photography (a technique pioneered by legendary cinematographer James Wong Howe). Visually this is Toland's film, a masterpiece of shadow and sharp contrast that artfully conveys murky moods and occasional moments of gaiety as camera and reporter search for the meaning of a man's life.

Welles took credit for writing most of KANE's superb screenplay, but the bulk of its incisive, witty, and unforgettable scenes and dialogue were most probably scripted by screenwriter Herman Mankiewicz, brother of Joseph, the noted film producer-director-writer. Nonetheless, Welles's contribution as director-producer remains awe-inspiring: he chronicles Kane's life through a combination of highly dramatic episodes and newsreel-like footage—slices of life that form a compelling patchwork biography. The film is so tightly constructed that every scene counts, filling in a piece of the puzzle, incomplete though it may be after reporter Jerry Thompson (William Alland) traces five accounts of the millionaire's life.

At the film's conclusion, reporters gather at Kane's estate, moving through a warehouse that is being cleared of endless piles of curios, stacks of furniture and countless crates containing Kane's purchases. As they move off into the dark recesses, a high boom shot reveals a staggering collection of toys, paintings and statues. Slowly the camera pans the heaps of Kane's possessions until it comes to a blazing furnace into which workmen throw all items considered to be junk. One of the workers picks up a sled—the very one Kane had as a boy in Colorado—and throws it into the fire. The camera closes in tightly on the top of the sled, and as it catches fire, the name "Rosebud" is revealed before the letters burn away. The scene shifts to the outside of the looming castle, panning upward to the high chimney from which Kane's lost youth curls upward into the night sky. The camera pulls back from the edifice, concluding the film with the shot of the iron fence with which it began.

CITIZEN KANE has influenced countless filmmakers and established the taste of discerning audiences worldwide. It is the epitome of filmmaking, a masterpiece for which Welles, one of the greatest practitioners of the cinematic art, will be forever remembered.

CITIZENS BAND
1977   98m   c   ★★★
Comedy   R/AA
Paramount

Paul LeMat (*Spider/Blaine*), Candy Clark (*Electra/Pam*), Ann Wedgeworth (*Joyce Rissley*), Bruce McGill (*Blood/Dean*), Marcia Rodd (*Portland Angel/Connie*), Charles Napier (*Chrome Angel/Harold*), Alix Elias (*Hot Coffee/Debbie*), Roberts Blossom (*Papa Thermadyne/Father*), Richard Bright (*Smilin'Jack/Garage Owner*), Ed Begley, Jr. (*Priest*)

p, Freddie Fields; d, Jonathan Demme; w, Paul Brickman; ph, Jordan Cronenweth (Movielab Color); ed, John F. Link, II; m, Bill Conti; art d, Bill Malley; cos, Jodie Lynn Tillen

AMERICAN GRAFFITI goes redneck. An early and sometimes funny effort by director Demme but the hilarity of the subplots (especially the bigamous Napier) swallows the main storyline. LeMat stars as a decent fellow intent on seeing that the CB airwaves are kept open for emergencies, putting him at odds with an assortment of loony CBers who don't want anybody stopping their fun. LeMat again shows himself to be the closest thing there is to a modern-day Jimmy Stewart, yet he's never snagged that one part that will move him into the star category. Not as good as the sum of its parts, but worth a nod unless redneck humor makes you crazy.

CITY AND THE DOGS, THE
(LA CIUDAD Y LOS PERROS)
1985   144m   c   ★★★½
Drama
Cinevista   (Peru)

Pablo Serra (*Poet*), Gustavo Bueno (*Lt. Gamboa*), Juan Manuel Ochoa (*Jaguar*), Luis Alvarez (*Colonel*), Liliana Navarro (*Teresa*), Miguel Iza (*Arrospide*)

p, Francisco Jose Lombardi; d, Francisco Jose Lombardi; w, Jose Watanabe (based on the novel by Mario Vargas Llosa); ph, Pili Flores Guerra

Based on a novel by Mario Vargas Llosa, this engrossing tale of shifting loyalties and revenge is set in the volatile, rigidly codified world of a boys' military academy. The unofficial leaders among the students are called "The Circle," a powerful unit that trades in contraband. Another boy (Pablo Serra), known as "The Poet," has found his niche, writing love letters and erotic stories for his classmates and is the only confidante—although an untrustworthy one—of "The Slave" (Eduardo Adrianzen), a cowardly scapegoat. When the latter is killed under mysterious circumstances, the stage is set for a confrontation between The Poet and leader of The Circle (Juan Manuel Ochoa) with dire results for the brutal army official who oversees the boys' activities (Gustavo Bueno).

Producer-director Francisco J. Lombardi's portrayal of the boys' daily discipline is as unflinching as any of the boot camp scenes in FULL METAL JACKET. The film is especially compelling in its examination of the multifaceted nature of honor. Aided by his first-rate ensemble, Lombardi succeeds in giving a strong sense of underlying tension.

CITY FOR CONQUEST
1940 105m bw   ★★★½
Sports   /PG
WB

James Cagney (Danny Kenny), Ann Sheridan (Peggy Nash), Frank Craven ("Old Timer"), Donald Crisp (Scotty McPherson), Arthur Kennedy (Eddie Kenny), Frank McHugh ("Mutt"), George Tobias (Pinky), Blanche Yurka (Mrs. Nash), Elia Kazan ("Googi"), Anthony Quinn (Murray Burns)

p, Anatole Litvak; d, Anatole Litvak; w, John Wexley (based on the novel by Aben Kandel); ph, Sol Polito, James Wong Howe; ed, William Holmes; m, Max Steiner; art d, Robert Haas; fx, Byron Haskin, Rex Wimpy; chor, Robert Vreeland; cos, Howard Shoup

James Cagney is at his dynamic best as a Gotham truck driver who boxes to support his brother, Kennedy (in his film debut), while he tries to make it as a composer. Cagney's girlfriend Sheridan struggles to gain fame as a dancer, though he objects to her partner, unctuously portrayed by Anthony Quinn. CITY FOR CONQUEST is an often heavy melodrama, but it has consistently good dialogue, a sprightly style, and a captivating powerhouse performance by Cagney, who drew on his experience as a longtime fight fan. He was 42 when he made the film and, training like a fighter, shed 30 pounds for the role. His fight scenes are realistically photographed by veteran cameramen Sol Polito and James Wong Howe, and in many cases hard blows were actually exchanged between the actor and his opponents. Director Anatole Litvak and Cagney argued over just about every scene, and most of Cagney's ideas, including much of his fight choreography, were edited out of the final version. Moreover, Cagney felt that the story had been ruined and sent a note of apology to its author, novelist Aben Kandel. But Litvak's careful poduction overcomes any flaws. Watch out for Elia Kazan as a neighborhood kid gone gangster.

CITY OF HOPE
1991 129m c   ★★★½
Drama   R/15
Esperanza Productions

Vincent Spano (Nick), Tony LoBianco (Joe), Joe Morton (Wynn), Barbara Williams (Angela), John Sayles (Carl), Anthony John Denison (Rizzo), Bill Raymond (Les), Angela Bassett (Reesha), Chris Cooper (Riggs), Gloria Foster (Jeanette)

p, Sarah Green, Maggie Renzi; d, John Sayles; w, John Sayles; ph, Robert Richardson; ed, John Sayles; m, Mason Daring; prod d, Dan Bishop, Dianna Freas; art d, Charles B. Plummer; cos, John Dunn

A schematic tale of urban corruption in a decaying northeastern town, John Sayles's CITY OF HOPE focuses on the network of greed and influence surrounding an urban development plan and its effects on the innocent and guilty alike.

Nick (Vincent Spano), the son of a successful construction company owner, is not only bored by his sinecure on one of his father's sites but troubled by a large gambling debt. His judgment contorted by drugs, Nick walks off his "no-show" job. Arriving at the car repair shop run by his loan shark, Carl (John Sayles), Nick learns of a plan to rob the local appliance dealer, oddly enough a friend of his father, and agrees to drive the getaway van. Nick's father, Joe (Tony LoBianco), is also beset by problems. Not only has he had to hire a number of crime-connected characters, he is also the owner of dilapidated apartment buildings that stand in the way of plans to build a shopping center, plans being pushed by foreign money behind the mayor's and district attorney's offices. Joe laments that he has been prevented from improving the slums he owns by such pressures in the same breath as he complains that the tenants stay on despite lack of heat and services. Nick's part in the planned appliance store robbery soon provides the leverage to solve the renewal dilemma.

A cross between BONFIRE OF THE VANITIES and OUR TOWN, CITY OF HOPE is John Sayles's cluttered elegy for the ruined dreams of one segment of urban American society, intermingling themes of big money—characteristically from Japan—simmering racial tensions and generational conflict. Sayles has posited a small town sensibility where everyone knows a lot about others. High school memories provide both gossip, characterization and motivation. The would-be theft at the appliance store seems almost a boyish prank, while the fire at the slum is seen by all as a clear-cut case of arson for profit. Despite the basic pessimism of the plot, Sayles does supply traces of hopefulness: the friendly chatter between Nick and the watchman on a basketball court and the apology by one of the teens to the professor.

CITY OF WOMEN
1980 140m c   ★★★
Drama   /X
Gaumont (Italy/France)

Marcello Mastroianni (Snaporaz), Ettore Manni (Dr. Xavier Zuberkock), Anna Prucnal (Elena), Bernice Stegers (Woman on Train), Donatella Damiani (Feminist on Roller Skates), Sara Tafuri (Other Dancing Girl), Jole Silvani (Old Woman on Motorcycle), Carla Terlizzi (Dr. Zuberkock's Conquest), Katren Gebelein (Enderbreith Small), Dominique Labourier (Feminist)

p, Renzo Rossellini; d, Federico Fellini; w, Federico Fellini, Bernardino Zapponi, Brunello Rondi; ph, Giuseppe Rotunno (Technovision, Eastmancolor); ed, Ruggero Mastroianni; m, Luis Bacalov; art d, Dante Ferretti; chor, Leonetta Bentivoglio; cos, Gabriella Pescucci

Plotless but undoubtedly Fellini. Federico Fellini's psychedelic exploration of feminine mysteries is another visual tour de force in an elaborate dream framework, with a ponderous tone, typical of Fellini's efforts in the latter stages of his career. The film begins as Snaporaz (Marcello Mastroianni), the threatened male protagonist, finds himself trapped at a feminist convention. Dr. Zuberkock (Ettore Manni) offers him refuge in a villa constructed for sexual pleasure, where a celebration of Zuberkock's 10,000th conquest ends with an invasion of female militia. This is followed by a brief reunion between Snaporaz and his estranged wife, leading into a fantasy sequence. For fans of the master only.

CITY SLICKERS

1991 112m c   ★★★½
Comedy/Adventure   PG-13/12
Castle Rock/Nelson Entertainment/Face Productions

Billy Crystal (Mitch Robbins), Daniel Stern (Phil Berquist), Bruno Kirby (Ed Furillo), Patricia Wettig (Barbara Robbins), Helen Slater (Bonnie Rayburn), Jack Palance (Curly), Noble Willingham (Clay Stone), Tracey Walter (Cookie), Josh Mostel (Barry Shalowitz), David Paymer (Ira Shalowitz)

p, Irby Smith; d, Ron Underwood; w, Lowell Ganz, Babaloo Mandel (from the story by Billy Crystal); ph, Dean Semler; ed, O. Nicholas Brown; m, Marc Shaiman; prod d, Lawrence G. Paull; art d, Mark Mansbridge; cos, Judy Ruskin

CITY SLICKERS is a skewed, serio-comic remake of Howard Hawks' classic RED RIVER in which the cattle drive becomes a two-week vacation, Walter Brennan, Montgomery Clift and John Wayne become Daniel Stern, Bruno Kirby and Billy Crystal, and the manifest destiny subtext becomes an inner search for the "child within" and a man's discovery of his smile.

Mitch Robbins (Billy Crystal), the man without a smile, is in the throes of a mid-life crisis, questioning his success and his family's happiness. Joining Mitch are his two best friends, Ed Furillo (Bruno Kirby), a loudmouth womanizer fretful about settling down and raising a family, and Phil Berquist (Daniel Stern), whose life is coming apart after his shrewish wife finds out about an affair he had with a 20-year-old woman. At Mitch's 39th-birthday party, his pals give him their gift—a two-week vacation in the West on a cattle drive from New Mexico to Colorado. Upon arriving, the three friends demonstrate their lack of cowboy skills but they gradually learn to rope and ride as they discuss their childhood hopes and adult disappointments.

CITY SLICKERS successfully skirts the chance for a cheapshot gag comedy and becomes a friendly, heartfelt celebration of friendship and community, greatly aided by a funny and moving script by Lowell Ganz and Babaloo Mandell (PARENTHOOD, VIBES, SPLASH). Even in their most successfully produced earlier scripts, there was always an uncomfortable shifting between Bob Hope-inspired wisecracks, slapstick gags and a bittersweet emotional undercurrent. But in CITY SLICKERS, all the elements are left subservient to the warm relationships among the three friends, allowing the comedy a base of reality out of which to grow.

Ron Underwood's direction complements the script and, while evoking memories of old Western films and TV shows, never overshadows the acting of Crystal, Stern and Kirby. In spite of some funny gags, the parts of the film that resonate are scenes like the start of the cattle drive as Jimmy Durante sings "Young at Heart" on the soundtrack, Kirby, Stern and Crystal humming the "Bonanza Theme" as they triumphantly bring the herd in, and the three friends reminiscing on the trail.

Aiding the screenplay and direction are fine performances by Daniel Stern and Bruno Kirby. Billy Crystal, especially, delivers a smooth, almost mime-like, performance, and, except for a few

instances, manages to erase efforts at schtick that have marred his previous film work. Jack Palance as Curly plays his role in an almost frightening evocation as a mythic Western hero. His whisper-growls and godlike demeanor make Palance seem a Disney World automaton. But since Palance's job is to carry with him the weight of 90 years of Western film myth, his performance is finely tuned, without any hint of parody that could throw the film out of whack.

CLAIRE'S KNEE
(LE GENOU DE CLAIRE)

1970 103m c   ★★★½
Drama   GP/PG
Losange   (France)

Jean-Claude Brialy (Jerome), Aurora Cornu (Aurora), Beatrice Romand (Laura), Laurence de Monaghan (Claire), Michele Montel (Mme. Walter), Gerard Falconetti (Gilles), Fabrice Luchini (Vincent)

p, Pierre Cottrell; d, Eric Rohmer; w, Eric Rohmer; ph, Nestor Almendros; ed, Cecile Decugis

A rarefied conversation fest, the fifth of Rohmer's "Moral Tales" stars Jean-Claude Brialy as Jerome, a middle-aged intellectual who feels with his head, not his heart. A French diplomat who is about to be married to a woman he loves, but for whom he feels no passion, Jerome visits the provincial town where he was raised. There he meets Claire (Laurence de Monaghan), a summery 17-year-old who is completely absorbed with her boyfriend. Jerome channels his desire for her into a form of passion that, for him, is much more controllable—he wants only to touch her knee.

One of Rohmer's greatest expressions of male-female relationships, CLAIRE'S KNEE presents a portrait of a man who, under his fairly charming and harmless demeanor, is eroding emotionally, convincing even himself that he can control his desires. In order to do so, he must completely detach his actions from his heart and make a physical gesture completely devoid of romance or emotion. What makes this so poignant is that it is only the audience which understands this.

CLASH BY NIGHT

1952 105m bw   ★★★★
Drama   /A
RKO

Barbara Stanwyck (Mae Doyle), Paul Douglas (Jerry D'Amato), Robert Ryan (Earl Pfeiffer), Marilyn Monroe (Peggy), J. Carrol Naish (Uncle Vince), Keith Andes (Joe Doyle), Silvio Minciotti (Papa), Diane Stewart (Baby Gloria), Deborah Stewart (Baby Gloria), Julius Tannen (Sad-Eyed Waiter)

p, Harriet Parsons; d, Fritz Lang; w, Alfred Hayes, David Dortort (based on the play by Clifford Odets); ph, Nicholas Musuraca; ed, George Amy; m, Roy Webb; art d, Albert S. D'Agostino, Carroll Clark; fx, Harold Wellman

A Stanwyck field day, in the kind of role she could do with her eyes closed, but because it's well-directed by Fritz Lang, the actress can let go with the snarls, venom, and wounded savagery we've come to expect and love. CLASH is a California cousin of Williams's STREETCAR but Stanwyck's Mae is tougher than Blanche; she's returned home a fallen woman to lick her big-city wounds, and Stanwyck gives it the commonness that Tallulah Bankhead had been too elegant for on Broadway. The story is essentially an Odets kitchen-sink triangle, with dangerous Ryan as resident trouble—he's terrific—and Douglas as the cuckholded spouse. The latter is the weak part of the triangle, but it still works.

In her first major role, Monroe gives a surprising turn as a young woman who, for the most part, is refreshingly independent. This is the lovely Monroe without the candy floss accoutrements; one watches CLASH sensing her career might have gone in a totally different direction had Fox marketed her in an adult manner. The steam she generates with the muscular Andes when Stanwyck and Ryan aren't clawing at each other's clothes makes CLASH BY NIGHT eminently watchable. And fun besides.

CLEAN AND SOBER

1988   124m   c   ★★★
Drama   R/18
Image/WB

Michael Keaton (Daryl Poynter), Kathy Baker (Charlie Standers), Morgan Freeman (Craig), M. Emmet Walsh (Richard Dirks), Brian Benben (Martin Laux), Luca Bercovici (Lenny), Tate Donovan (Donald Towle), Henry Judd Baker (Xavier), Claudia Christian (Iris), J. David Krassner (Tiller)

p, Tony Ganz, Deborah Blum, Jay Daniel; d, Glenn Gordon Caron; w, Tod Carroll; ph, Jan Kiesser (Technicolor); ed, Richard Chew; m, Gabriel Yared; prod d, Joel Schiller; cos, Robert Turturice

This poignant film, directed by Caron, the creator of TV's fleetingly acclaimed "Moonlighting" series, casts Keaton against type as a sleazy cocaine- and alcohol-addicted real estate hotshot who is forced to come to terms with himself. After "borrowing" $92,000 from his Philadelphia company's escrow account and losing it on a stock market gamble, Keaton awakes one morning to find that his one-night stand has OD'd in his bed. He subsequently checks into a 21-day chemical dependency program that promises anonymity—not because he thinks he has a drug problem but in order to avoid the cops. Even as he undergoes detoxification, Keaton tries to obtain some coke over the phone. Freeman, however, the recovering addict who oversees Poynter's group, is wise to every trick. As the treatment progresses, Keaton falls for Baker, a steelworker who is as addicted to her alternately abusive and whimpering boyfriend as she is to cocaine. Keaton receives some much-needed guidance from Walsh, a worldly patient who helps him readjust to the real world.

Reminiscent of THE DAYS OF WINE AND ROSES, LOST WEEKEND, and PANIC IN NEEDLE PARK—this "problem" film doesn't offer many surprises. Once again the duplicity, self-deception, and pathetic dependency of the addict is meticulously and painfully drawn. Keaton's recovery is predictable, the sympathetic presence of the counselor who's seen it all and the kindly "guardian angel" is dramatically convenient, and the doomed love between the addicts is heart-wrenching but not unexpected. Nonetheless CLEAN AND SOBER is very moving because its outstanding performances make each moment seem real and important.

CLEO FROM 5 TO 7

(CLIO DE CINQ A SEPT)
1961   90m   bw   ★★★
Drama   /A
Rome Paris   (France)

Corinne Marchand (Cleo), Antoine Bourseiller (Antoine), Dorothee Blanck (Dorothee), Michel Legrand (Bob, the Pianist), Dominique Davray (Angele), Jose-Luis de Vilallonga (The Lover), Jean-Claude Brialy, Anna Karina, Eddie Constantine, Sami Frey

p, Georges de Beauregard; d, Agnes Varda; w, Agnes Varda; ph, Jean Rabier; ed, Jeanne Verneau; m, Michel Legrand, Michel Legrand; prod d, Edith Tertza, Jean-Francois Adam; art d, Bernard Evein; cos, Alyette Samazeuilh

Literally, a slice of life. Agnes Varda's second feature opens with an overhead shot of a table, two pairs of women's hands, and a deck of tarot cards. The woman whose fortune is being read, Cleo (played superbly by Corinne Marchand), is told she has cancer. Cleo is dreading the results of a recent medical test and believes her fortune. The rest of the film is a chronicle of the next 90 minutes in her life. Photographed almost exclusively in the streets of Paris, CLEO FROM 5 TO 7 is a portrait of a woman whose view of life has previously never extended past her own vanity and singing success. Faced with the possibility of death, however, Cleo begins to perceive things differently—finding beauty and life in all things. Curiously, the only one of the film's scenes to fall completely flat is a silent comedy sketch that features Anna Karina, Jean-Luc Godard, Sami Frey, Jean-Claude Brialy, Eddie Constantine, and Yves Robert. One especially nice moment is a song, "Sans Toi" (by Michel Legrand and Varda), which Marchand delivers directly into the camera.

CLEOPATRA

1934   102m   bw   ★★★★
Historical   /A
Paramount

Claudette Colbert (Cleopatra), Warren William (Julius Caesar), Henry Wilcoxon (Marc Antony), Gertrude Michael (Calpurnia), Joseph Schildkraut (Herod), Ian Keith (Octavian), C. Aubrey Smith (Enobarbus), Ian MacLaren (Cassius), Arthur Hohl (Brutus), Leonard Mudie (Pothinos)

p, Cecil B. DeMille; d, Cecil B. DeMille; w, Waldemar Young, Vincent Lawrence (based on historical material by Bartlett McCormick, Jeanie MacPherson, Finley Peter Dunne, Jr.); ph, Victor Milner; ed, Anne Bauchens; m, Rudolph G. Kopp

Opulent, totally satisfying DeMille, due in no small part to the vocal command and trickery brought to Cleopatra by Colbert, a surprisingly good choice despite her leaness and kittenish reputation. CLEOPATRA sails down the Nile with authority and majesty; it may well be DeMille's best film. William and Wilcoxon almost match Colbert; indeed, there's not a lemon in the entire cast. CLEOPATRA exemplifies DeMille's obsession with historical accuracy in setting and props. In one giant set crammed with hundreds of extras, as shooting was about to begin, he stopped everything when he spotted a small flagon 20 feet away. He walked over and picked it up, holding it aloft with disgust. It was silver-plated and represented an era much later than the setting of the film. But his commercial genius demanded liberal doses of sexual fantasy mixed with the historically faithful set designs.

Nowhere in CLEOPATRA is this so obvious as in the infamous barge scene, where DeMille's rendition makes Shakespeare's description look like TUGBOAT ANNIE. While Wilcoxon and Colbert recline aboard the queen's bordello on the sea, a huge net is drawn up from the sea, holding dozens of squirming almost-naked girls—DeMille's catch of the day—who offer Wilcoxon giant sea shells which spill out priceless gems. Then a veil slowly descends around Colbert and the bedazzled Wilcoxon, and DeMille cuts to a shot of the enormous pleasure barge being rowed by hundreds of slaves into the darkened sea, a drummer beating out the cadence of the oarsmen and suggesting the additional rhythm of the unseen seduction. It is DeMille's carnal poetry in action.

Such fabulous excess notwithstanding, DeMille's penchant for realism carried over into insistence upon actual battle conditions when his hordes of extras clashed before the cameras. No warrior ever used a rubber sword in a DeMille film. The weapons were authentic and razor sharp, and the director succeeded in scaring off half of the extras before shooting began on the battle scenes. Nor was DeMille above demanding from women the same kind of rigorous attention to realism. For all of the bravado and brass embodied in her Egyptian vamp, Colbert feared and hated snakes of any kind. Yet DeMille insisted that at the film's finale she employ a real snake to commit suicide, as Cleopatra had done, pressing a lethal asp to her bosom. DeMille waited until the last minute, the last scene, setting up Colbert in her death chamber and letting her believe all along that she would be using a rubber snake. The director walked forward with an enormous boa constrictor (tamed) curling about his neck and shoulders. Colbert was predictably terrified, but DeMille suddenly stopped and produced a tiny harmless garter snake, which by comparison with the giant reptile around his body appeared insignificant. Moments later Colbert was clutching the snake to her breast in one of the most memorable death scenes in film history as DeMille's camera pulled back into the darkness of the ancient chamber.

CLEOPATRA was a box-office smash, but the critics tore at DeMille for representing the historical characters as satyrs and nymphomaniacs. Some of his severest critics complained about the abundance of British actors dominating the CLEOPATRA cast, speaking with English accents. Some carped about the slangy dialogue. But DeMille knew his public. To the writers of CLEOPATRA, DeMille specified contemporary, vernacular speech. They gave him just what he wanted, and DeMille kept the film sizzling. That's no history lesson, that's entertainment!

CLEOPATRA

1963 243m c   ★★½
Historical   /PG
FOX

Elizabeth Taylor (Cleopatra), Richard Burton (Mark Antony), Rex Harrison (Julius Caesar), Pamela Brown (High Priestess), George Cole (Flavius), Hume Cronyn (Sosigenes), Cesare Danova (Apollodorus), Kenneth Haigh (Brutus), Andrew Keir (Agrippa), Martin Landau (Rufio)

p, Walter Wanger; d, Joseph L. Mankiewicz; w, Joseph L. Mankiewicz, Ranald MacDougall, Sidney Buchman (based on works by Plutarch, Appian, Suetonius and The Life And Times Of Cleopatra, a novel by Carlo Mario Franzero); ph, Leon Shamroy (Todd A-O, DeLuxe Color); ed, Dorothy Spencer; m, Alex North; prod d, John De Cuir; art d, Jack Martin Smith, Hilyard Brown, Herman A. Blumenthal, Elven Webb, Maurice Pelling, Boris Juraga; fx, L.B. Abbott, Emil Kosa, Jr.; chor, Hermes Pan; cos, Irene Sharaff, Vittorio Nino Novarese

Chaucer's Wife of Bath plays Cleolizzie, the million-dollar sultana of 60s jetset sirens, in enough eyeliner to resurrect Theda Bara, and ten costumes for every occasion. This is not a film—it's a deal, decorated with extensive publicity, but weighed down by listless direction and lots of nasal talk, talk, talk. Even fans of camp would have to admit what's here is about an hour's worth of television MOW. Taylor brings notoriety and cleavage to her

performance as Cleopatra; she's at her best when Cleo makes her entrance into Rome, when Taylor worried that the Catholic extras might riot and kill her. The scene is a triumph of morass over morality. Hurricane Liz conquers Rome! Otherwise, she plays the Egyptian tigress (original choice was Susan Hayward, an expert at tigresses, Biblical and otherwise) as a spewing, mewing, pampered Roman housecat who makes fusses because she can. Would the film have been better with Hayward, Peter Finch and Stephen Boyd, directed by Mamoulian? Perhaps, but at least Harrison, taking over for Finch, strikes a few waspish notes. Otherwise, it's a Vegas-style history lesson, but dammit, a boring one, depriving us of a thousand laughs and cracks.

CLOAK AND DAGGER

1984 101m c   ★★★½
Adventure/Thriller   PG
Universal

Henry Thomas (Davey Osborne), Dabney Coleman (Jack Flack/Hal Osborne), Michael Murphy (Rice), Christina Nigra (Kim Gardener), John McIntire (George MacCready), Jeanette Nolan (Eunice MacCready), Eloy Casados (Alvarez), Tim Rossovich (Haverman), Bill Forsythe (Morris), Robert DoQui (Lt. Fleming)

p, Allan Carr; d, Richard Franklin; w, Tom Holland (based on the short story "The Boy Cried Murder" by Cornell Woolrich); ph, Victor J. Kemper (Technicolor); ed, Andrew London; m, Brian May; prod d, William Tuntke; art d, Todd Hallowell; cos, John Casey, Nancy McArdle

The boy who cried wolf. Producer Carr took some time off from making musicals to oversee this surprisingly good thriller. Thomas is a young child with a great imagination and his own computer. Nobody believes Thomas's tall tales because they're all going on in his head; so when he accidentally uncovers a plot to smuggle top secret information out of the US, his fear is again perceived to be part of his active fantasy world. He runs to his father, Coleman, who doesn't believe him. Thomas has been playing a game called Cloak and Dagger on his computer, and Coleman thinks his son may have confused reality with fantasy. Thomas has conjured up a character in his mind named Jack Flack (also played by Coleman) who pops up to help Thomas whenever the lad gets into a pickle. Meanwhile, Thomas and his friend Nigra find themselves trapped in the real-life plot.

CLOAK benefits from tight direction and the good humor of the Holland script. The addition of the dual role for Coleman (who's excellent in both) serves to highlight the relationship between father and son, adding another dimension to the yarn and almost relegating the spy plot from the core element of the story to mere diversion. Murphy is properly heinous as the heavy, and there are good cameos by veterans McIntyre and Nolan as a kindly old tourist couple who turn out to be anything but kindly. Thomas, who was the star of E.T. THE EXTRA-TERRESTRIAL, is remarkably natural in a role that might have had other child actors reeling. A film with much to recommend it, CLOAK AND DAGGER feels like a Hitchcock movie produced by Walt Disney.

CLOCK, THE

1945 90m bw   ★★★★
Romance
MGM

Judy Garland *(Alice Mayberry)*, Robert Walker *(Cpl. Joe Allen)*, James Gleason *(Al Henry)*, Keenan Wynn *(The Drunk)*, Marshall Thompson *(Bill)*, Lucille Gleason *(Mrs. Al Henry)*, Ruth Brady *(Helen)*, Chester Clute *(Michael Henry)*, Dick Elliott *(Friendly Man)*

p, Arthur Freed; d, Vincente Minnelli; w, Robert Nathan, Joseph Schrank (based on a story by Paul and Pauline Gallico); ph, George Folsey; ed, George White; m, George Bassman; art d, Cedric Gibbons, William Ferrari; fx, A. Arnold Gillespie; cos, Irene

A small wartime gem featuring the luminous Garland, directed by her future husband, in a rare nonsinging role. The story is deceptively simple; it is in the subtle touches that the genius of this film lies. Garland and Walker meet under the big clock at Pennsylvania Station in New York. They fall in love and marry within 48 hours. This kind of thing happened often in real life, and Gallico's story feels authentic. So does the incredible rear-screen projection work and the huge sets that would cause any New Yorker to bet serious money that the film was done on location in the Big Apple. Not so. It was a back-lot job and a tribute to the talents of its technicians. Every single bit player is perfectly cast, and special plaudits go to Wynn, who plays a drunken patriot.

This was Minnelli's first straight directing job and he went on to distinguish himself away from musicals with such giants as THE BAD AND THE BEAUTIFUL, FATHER OF THE BRIDE and many others. Looking at the two young, well-scrubbed stars, it's hard to believe that both their lives would end tragically. Walker, only 33 at the time of his death, had been married to Jennifer Jones and John Ford's daughter, Barbara. He'd been institutionalized for alcohol abuse almost a year before returning to work in Alfred Hitchcock's STRANGERS ON A TRAIN. While filming MY SON JOHN in 1951, he died from too many sedatives doctors had prescribed to calm his emotional instability. This is a rare tribute to the acting genius of Garland, who would still have had all the makings of a star, even if she had never sung a note.

CLOCKMAKER, THE
(L'HORLOGER DE SAINT-PAUL)
1974 105m c   ★★★½
Drama
Lira   (France)

Philippe Noiret *(Michel Descombes)*, Jean Rochefort *(Commissioner Guiboud)*, Jacques Denis *(Antoine)*, William Sabatier *(Lawyer)*, Andree Tainsy *(Madeleine)*, Sylvain Rougerie *(Bernard Descombes)*, Christine Pascal *(Lilliane Terrini)*, Cecile Vassort *(Martine)*, Yves Afonso, Jacques Hilling

d, Bertrand Tavernier; w, Jean Aurenche, Pierre Bost (based on the novel *The Clockmaker of Everton* by Georges Simenon); ph, Pierre-William Glenn; ed, Armand Psenny; m, Philippe Sarde

A first feature from former critic Tavernier, THE CLOCKMAKER stars Noiret as Descombes, a widowed Lyons watchmaker who leads a perfectly orderly life, plays by the rules, and has no intention of ever stepping out of line. His life is thrown into disarray when police inspectors arrive at his shop to report that his only son, Rougerie, is suspected of murdering a hated factory foreman. Although Noiret has what he considers a good relationship with his son, he comes to realize that he really doesn't know Rougerie at all.

Based on a novel by Simenon, THE CLOCKMAKER is an introspective, intelligent, sad, but ultimately positive look, not at murderers and criminal investigations, but at a strong relationship between a father and son. Rather than resort to heavy-handed

speechmaking or maudlin sentiment, Tavernier treats his material with the honesty and subtlety it deserves. This exceptional debut clearly marked Tavernier, one of the few realist film directors, as a force to be reckoned with.

CLOCKWISE
1986 96m c   ★★★
Comedy   PG
Moment   (U.K.)

John Cleese *(Brian Stimpson)*, Alison Steadman *(Gwenda Stimpson)*, Penelope Wilton *(Pat Garden)*, Stephen Moore *(Mr. Jolly)*, Joan Hickson *(Mrs. Trellis)*, Sharon Maiden *(Laura)*, Penny Leatherbarrow *(Teacher)*, Howard Lewis *(Ted)*, Jonathan Bowater *(Clint)*, Mark Bunting *(Studious Boy)*

p, Michael Codron; d, Christopher Morahan; w, Michael Frayn; ph, John Coquillon (Technicolor); ed, Peter Boyle; m, George Fenton; prod d, Roger Murray-Leach; art d, Diana Charnley; cos, Judy Moorcroft

Thin comedy, sometimes transformed by the energy of Monty Python's Cleese as a school headmaster, driven by punctuality. On the way to a speaking engagement at a convention, he keeps getting into all manner of trouble. If you adore Cleese, you'll have a fine time. Otherwise Frayn's script is not meaty enough to sustain viewer interest, nor is there any momentum built by Morahan's direction.

CLOCKWORK ORANGE, A
1971 137m c   ★★★★
Science Fiction   R/X
WB   (U.K.)

Malcolm McDowell *(Alex)*, Patrick Magee *(Mr. Alexander)*, Michael Bates *(Chief Guard)*, Warren Clarke *(Dim)*, John Clive *(Stage Actor)*, Adrienne Corri *(Mrs. Alexander)*, Carl Duering *(Dr. Brodsky)*, Paul Farrell *(Hobo)*, Clive Francis *(Lodger)*, Michael Gover *(Prison Warden)*

p, Stanley Kubrick; d, Stanley Kubrick; w, Stanley Kubrick (based on the novel by Anthony Burgess); ph, John Alcott; ed, Bill Butler; m, Walter Carlos; prod d, John Barry; art d, Russell Hagg, Peter Shields; cos, Milena Canonero

Teenage delinquents (McDowell, Clarke, Marcus, Tarn) living in a futuristic British state indulge in nightly rounds of beatings, rapings, and, as they call it, "a bit of the old ultraviolence." Among their victims is prominent writer Magee; they beat him senseless, and brutally gang-rape his attractive wife Corri. (Magee later becomes manic, and his wife dies as a result of the attack.) After violently quelling an uprising among his own gang, McDowell is betrayed by them during an attack on another home, being knocked senseless and left for the police. In prison, he agrees to undergo experiments in "aversion therapy" in order to shorten his term. Now nauseated by the mere sight of violence, he is pronounced cured and released into the outside world. There, vengeance of one kind or another is wreaked upon him by his erstwhile fellow gang-members (now policemen), and by his former victims (including Magee). After another spell in prison McDowell returns home, where we expect him to resume his old criminal ways.

Adapted from the novel by British author Anthony Burgess, A CLOCKWORK ORANGE is a visually dazzling, highly unsettling work that revolves around one of the few truly amoral characters in film or literature. It pits a gleefully vicious individual against a blandly inhuman state, leaving the viewer little room for emotional involvement (though McDowell gives such an ebullient, wide-eyed performance as the Beethoven-loving delinquent that it is hard for us not to feel some sympathy toward him). Meanwhile, we are dazzled by Kubrick's directorial pyrotechnics—slow motion, fast motion, fish-eye lenses, etc.; entertained by John Barry's witty, ostentatious sets; and intrigued by dialogue laden with Burgess's specially created slang (gang members are "droogies," sex is "the old inout," etc.). This is a particularly graphic film which has split the critics, but which no serious moviegoer can afford to ignore.

CLOSE ENCOUNTERS OF THE THIRD KIND

1977　135m　c　　　　　　　　　★★★★★
Science Fiction　　　　　　　　　　　PG/A
Columbia

Richard Dreyfuss (Roy Neary), Francois Truffaut (Claude Lacombe), Teri Garr (Ronnie Neary), Melinda Dillon (Jillian Guiler), Cary Guffey (Barry Guiler), Bob Balaban (Interpreter Laughlin), J. Patrick McNamara (Project Leader), Warren Kemmerling (Wild Bill), Roberts Blossom (Farmer), Philip Dodds (Jean Claude)

p, Julia Phillips, Michael Phillips; d, Steven Spielberg; w, Steven Spielberg; ph, Vilmos Zsigmond (Metrocolor); ed, Michael Kahn; m, John Williams; prod d, Joe Alves; art d, Dan Lomino; fx, Roy Arbogast, Gregory Jein, Douglas Trumbull, Matthew Yuricich, Richard Yuricich; cos, Jim Linn

Steven Spielberg proves decisively that a special effects-dependent film need not be cold, mechanistic, or simpleminded. Here he presents first contact with an extraterrestrial culture in spirit of near-religious awe in sharp contrast to the dark paranoia of traditional science fiction Cold War parables. CLOSE ENCOUNTERS OF THE THIRD KIND is a humanistic postmodern masterpiece that incorporates much of movie history—images, sounds, and subtle evocations of the works of Walt Disney, John Ford, Alfred Hitchcock, Cecil B. DeMille, and Chuck Jones—into its revisionist project. Classic Sixties fantasy television fare such as "Star Trek," "Bewitched," and "The Twilight Zone" also figure in the meaningful mosaic of citations. This film shows the power pop-culture imagery exerts over our humdrum lives and the ever present lure of escapism. The movies may set you free, it suggests, but perhaps only at the cost of losing real human relationships.

The story depicts the life-transforming experiences of lineman Roy Neary (Richard Dreyfuss) who is sent out into the night to investigate a mysterious power outage. His truck gets stalled on the road and he's bathed in a brilliant light from above. Thus begins Roy's journey from disinterested spectator to impassioned participant in an otherworldly spectacle. A mysterious vision and five musical notes are imprinted in his mind after he witnesses strange lights in the sky. His family life is devastated by his obsession but he acquires a spiritual surrogate family along the path to enlightenment including the delightful (and delighted) child Cary Guffey who is spirited away from his mother (Melinda Dillon) during the film's only frightening set piece and Francois Truffaut (the beloved director of such French New Wave classics as THE 400 BLOWS, JULES AND JIM and THE WILD CHILD) as Claude Lacombe, the endearingly humane director of the scientific ad hoc "welcome wagon."

Special effects master Douglas Trumbull (the FX wizard of 2001: A SPACE ODYSSEY) created the strikingly beautiful and dreamy visions that set the look of this film apart from the cool razzle dazzle of Industrial Light and Magic projects. John Williams contributes one of his most unusual and memorable scores. This is one for the angels.

CLOSELY WATCHED TRAINS

(OSTRE SLEDOVANE VLAKY)
1966　89m　bw　　　　　　　　　　★★★★
Comedy/Drama
Barrandov/Ladislav Fikar/Bohumil Smida　(Czechoslovakia)

Vaclav Neckar (Trainee Milos Hrma), Jitka Bendova (Conductor Masa), Josef Somr (Train Dispatcher Hubicka), Vladimir Valenta (Stationmaster Max), Vlastimil Brodsky (Counselor Zednicek), Jiri Menzel (Dr. Brabek), Libuse Havelkova (Max's Wife), Alois Vachek (Novak), Jitka Zelenohorska (Zdenka), Ferdinand Kruta (Masa's Uncle)

p, Zdenek Oves; d, Jiri Menzel; w, Jiri Menzel, Bohumil Hrabal (based on his novel); ph, Jaromir Sofr; ed, Jirina Lukesova; m, Jiri Sust; art d, Oldrich Bosak; cos, Ruzena Bulickova

The first feature from the 28-year-old Czech filmmaker Menzel is a comic, humanistic look at a teenage railway trainee, Milos (Neckar), who is sent off to a desolate station in Bohemia during the German occupation of Czechoslovakia. Hidden away from much of the rest of the world, Milos and the very ordinary characters who pass through the station try to live as if they were not caught in the midst of WWII. Milos learns his trade with relative ease, working under the experienced guidance of dispatcher Hubicka (Somr). A bored womanizer, Hubicka also becomes the uneasy boy's mentor in the ways of the world, which are all too quickly being thrust upon him. During the course of the film, Milos turns freedom fighter and experiences a variety of incidents, including sexual initiation, a botched suicide, and an act of heroism.

Possibly the best known and the most commercially successful film of the Czech New Wave of the 1960s during the all-too-brief Prague Spring, CLOSELY WATCHED TRAINS went on to win an Oscar for Best Foreign Film. Comic, tragic, romantic, and realistic, it is a film of great warmth and honesty, photographed in wonderfully stark black and white and cast with an exceptional group of actors.

CLUNY BROWN

1946　100m　bw　　　　　　　　　　★★★
Comedy/Drama　　　　　　　　　　　/A
FOX

Charles Boyer (Adam Belinski), Jennifer Jones (Cluny Brown), Peter Lawford (Andrew Carmel), Helen Walker (Betty Cream), Reginald Gardiner (Hilary Ames), Reginald Owen (Sir Henry Carmel), C. Aubrey Smith (Colonel Duff-Graham), Richard Haydn (Wilson), Margaret Bannerman (Lady Alice Carmel), Sara Allgood (Mrs. Maile)

p, Ernst Lubitsch; d, Ernst Lubitsch; w, Samuel Hoffenstein, Elizabeth Reinhardt (based on the novel by Margery Sharp); ph, Joseph La Shelle; ed, Dorothy Spencer; m, Cyril J. Mockridge; art d, Lyle Wheeler, J. Russell Spencer; fx, Fred Sersen

The last film with the fabled "Lubitsch touch" contains moments of satire that raise it to classic status, as Lubitsch, Hoffenstein and Reinhardt take shots at upper-class England with deadly aim. Otherwise it's a bubble-light (and slightly flat) comedy-romance, set in pre-WWII England, which pairs Czech writer-refugee Boyer with plumber's daughter Jones, the maid at the genteel country manor where he is staying. Boyer's hosts know vaguely that something is happening in Europe and it concerns some Austrian but that's as far as their immediate knowledge goes. Theirs is a life of gardening, garden parties, tea, and weed-killers until Jones and Boyer upset the apple cart and bring some spirit into the household.

The aforementioned "Lubitsch touch" can be seen in the final frames of CLUNY BROWN. It is all photographed in the reflection of a shop window, where Jones faints on the street and Boyer kneels beside her. A crowd gathers and a policeman begins to bend forward but Boyer stops him with a smile. No words are spoken as smiles cross the faces in the crowd and Jones comes to; it is universally realized that the mild fainting is the result of her being pregnant.

This may be Jones's most unhampered performance, which isn't saying much. She's bolstered by the Brentwood British colonials of southern California, notably Smith and the two Reginalds, Gardiner and Owen, but she hasn't much chemistry to offer Boyer.

Lubitsch, ever the energetic craftsman, began another film almost immediately, THAT LADY IN ERMINE, but he lasted only eight days, suffering a heart attack (Otto Preminger took over the direction). Lubitsch had had five heart attacks but refused to give up his cigars, which he inhaled. He joked about the illness at a party with Jeanette MacDonald but died four days later, on November 30, 1947, of his sixth heart attack.

COAL MINER'S DAUGHTER

1980   125m   c   ★★★★
Biography/Musical   PG/A
Universal

Sissy Spacek *(Loretta)*, Tommy Lee Jones *(Doolittle "Mooney" Lynn)*, Levon Helm *(Ted Webb)*, Phyllis Boyens *(Clara Webb)*, Bill Anderson, Jr., Foister Dickerson, Malla McCown, Pamela McCown, Kevin Salvilla *(Webb Children)*, William Sanderson *(Junior Webb, Age 16)*

p, Bernard Schwartz; d, Michael Apted; w, Thomas Rickman (based on autobiography by Loretta Lynn with George Vescey); ph, Ralf D. Bode (Technicolor); ed, Arthur Schmidt; m, Owen Bradley; prod d, John W. Corso; cos, Joe I. Tompkins

---

The rare expert film bio. COAL MINER'S DAUGHTER features an Oscar-winning performance by Sissy Spacek as country music queen Loretta Lynn. Masterfully directed by Michael Apted, the film traces the famed country singer's life from her beginnings in a tumbledown shack in Butcher Hollow, Kentucky, through her huge success, marital discord, and battle with prescription drugs. The film's early sequences are lyrical, melancholy accounts of mountain life and comprise the film's most poignant, memorable moments. There are outstanding acting jobs by Levon Helm and Phyllis Boyens as Lynn's parents, Tommy Lee Jones as her well-meaning, n'er-do-well husband, and Beverly D'Angelo in a dazzling turn as the magnificent Patsy Cline. Spacek and D'Angelo do their own warbling quite expertly; after this, it's hard to get worked up over Jessica Lange's lukewarm, lipsynched take on Cline in SWEET DREAMS.

COCA-COLA KID, THE

1985   94m   c   ★★★
Comedy   R/15
Smart Egg/Cinecom/Film Gallery   (Australia)

Eric Roberts *(Becker)*, Greta Scacchi *(Terri)*, Bill Kerr *(T. George McDowell)*, Chris Haywood *(Kim)*, Kris McQuade *(Juliana)*, Max Gilles *(Frank)*, Tony Barry *(Bushman)*, Paul Chubb *(Fred)*, David Slingsby *(Waiter)*, Tim Finn *(Philip)*

p, David Roe, Sylvie Le Clezio; d, Dusan Makavejev; w, Frank Moorhouse (based on the short story collections *The Americans, Baby*, and *The Electrical Experience* by Moorhouse); ph, Dean Semler (Panavision, Eastmancolor); ed, John Scott; m, William Motzing; prod d, Graham Walker; cos, Terry Ryan

---

When Coca-Cola's big bosses suspect that profits could be greater in Australia, they send in Eric Roberts, a quirky wunderkind troubleshooter who, as an ex-Marine, takes pride in the company and views Coca-Cola as a symbol of the US. Arriving at the Australian office, he meets Greta Scacchi, a beautiful young secretary who wanders around the office in her stocking feet, lets her daughter photocopy her face on the office copier, and is nearly raped by her angry estranged husband. After studying a geographical representation of the areas where their product is being sold, Roberts discovers a section of Australia completely devoid of his company's beverage. This region prefers a local soft drink made by eccentric Bill Kerr, an embittered, trigger-happy old man, now determined to keep Coke's imperialists off his land and to continue his operations in a traditional, antiquated, steam-powered plant.

In THE COCA-COLA KID Yugoslavian director Dusan Makavejev has made a truly international picture that, like Coca-Cola, knows no borders, enlisting the contributions of an Australian writer, Frank Moorhouse; an American actor, Roberts; and a British actress, Scacchi; Scacchi, exuding a raw sexuality, makes a lasting impression, but Roberts's handsomeness can't save his ham acting. This is far from Makavejev's finest work (WR: MYSTERIES OF THE ORGANISM and SWEET MOVIE are much more challenging), but it is the film that has spread the director's political message to the widest audience.

COCKTAIL MOLOTOV

1980   100m   c   ★★★
Drama
Antenne 2/Alexandre   (France)

Elise Caron *(Anne)*, Philippe Lebas *(Frederic)*, Francois Cluzet *(Bruno)*, Genevieve Fontanel *(Anne's Mother)*, Henri Garcin *(Her Stepfather)*, Michel Puterflam *(Her Father)*, Jenny Cleve *(Frederic's Mother)*, Armando Brancia *(His Father)*, Malene Sveinbjornsson *(Little Sister)*, Stefania Cassini *(Anna-Maria)*

d, Diane Kurys; w, Diane Kurys, Philippe Adrien, Alain LeHenry; ph, Philippe Rousselot; ed, Joele Van Effentree; m, Yves Simon; art d, Hilton McConnico, Tony Egry

---

Wandering, wondering teenagers. Feeling pressure from her mother to become a conformist, Caron leaves Paris for Venice, hoping to lead a more spontaneous, carefree life. Her boyfriend Lebas and his pal Cluzet follow Caron, intent on convincing her to return to France. The boys' car and Caron's belongings are stolen in Italy, and when they hear that a series of worker-student riots have been occurring in Paris, they decide to return home and join in the political struggle, whatever its motives are. Having debuted with PEPPERMINT SODA, a very fine film about the problems of adolescence, talented director Kurys returned to similar subject matter with this youth-oriented road movie. Though not as successful as her previous work, the film still manages to convey the troubling, questioning, yet vital feelings of becoming an adult while still maintaining the hope of youth.

COCOANUTS, THE
1929 90m bw   ★★★½
Comedy
Paramount

Groucho Marx *(Hammer)*, Harpo Marx *(Harpo)*, Chico Marx *(Chico)*, Zeppo Marx *(Jamison)*, Mary Eaton *(Polly)*, Oscar Shaw *(Bob)*, Kay Francis *(Penelope)*, Margaret Dumont *(Mrs. Potter)*, Cyril Ring *(Yates)*, Basil Ruysdael *(Hennessey)*

p, Monta Bell, James R. Cowan; d, Robert Florey, Joseph Santley; w, Morrie Ryskind (based on the play by George S. Kaufman and Irving Berlin); ph, George Folsey; chor, Joseph Santley, Robert Florey

The greatest of zanies, the Marx Brothers, perform with dizzying speed in this farcical and nearly plotless romp through a Florida hotel, ostensibly dealing with the arrival and departure of would-be millionaires getting richer or poorer during the Florida land boom of the late 1920s. The mayhem is often side-splitting in this "pure" Marx vehicle, where the love story is strictly incidental. While they basically kept to the routines audiences had enjoyed in the original play by George S. Kaufman and Irving Berlin, the boys were given their usual freedom to ad lib; these bits were constantly changing, even during the shooting of the film. Berlin himself cut many tunes that were never sung since the brothers cavalierly changed the material.

This is a crude, shapeless talkie, a technically unsophisticated film in which the sound is static and the camera immobile, with the comedians leaping into the set scenes. Yet the boys are there in all their frenetic glory. Harpo honks his horn for the first time, chasing but never catching a scantily clad cutie; he would pursue her in vain for decades to come, while his brothers chewed up the sets and spat out laughter. THE COCOANUTS was officially the debut of the madcap brothers, although they had appeared in an obscure silent production, HUMOR RISK, which is now an apparently lost film.

COCOON
1985 117m c   ★★★
Comedy/Science Fiction   PG-13/PG
FOX

Don Ameche *(Art Selwyn)*, Wilford Brimley *(Ben Luckett)*, Hume Cronyn *(Joe Finley)*, Brian Dennehy *(Walter)*, Jack Gilford *(Bennie Lefkowitz)*, Steve Guttenberg *(Jack Bonner)*, Maureen Stapleton *(Mary Luckett)*, Jessica Tandy *(Alma Finley)*, Gwen Verdon *(Bess McCarthy)*, Herta Ware *(Rose Lefkowitz)*

p, Richard D. Zanuck, David Brown, Lili Fini Zanuck; d, Ron Howard; w, Tom Benedek; ph, Don Peterman, Jordan Klein (Deluxe Color); ed, Michael Hill, Daniel Hanley; m, James Horner; prod d, Jack T. Collis; fx, Greg Cannom, Rick Baker; cos, Aggie Guerard Rodgers, Mort Schwartz

In this fun, lighthearted comedy, a group of aliens led by Brian Dennehy arrive from the planet Antarea and take on human form so they can go about their work without detection. They land near the heart of geriatric country, St. Petersburg, Florida, and rent a tour boat from Steve Guttenberg. They also rent a nearby home that had been left unattended, thereby enabling some elderly residents at a rest home—Don Ameche, Wilford Brimley, and Hume Cronyn—to sneak in and use its indoor pool. Guttenberg takes the boat to a specified spot in the ocean where Dennehy and his crew pull boulder-like cocoons from the ocean floor, which they store in the swimming pool. Later when Ameche,

Brimley, and Cronyn take their usual swim, they notice the curious cocoons and then begin to sense a change in themselves—they are suddenly more youthful and vital.

A gentle and effective heart-tugger, COCOON tries to make its audience feel good, but you can't help but feel uneasy about the vision of old age that director Ron Howard depicts—one in which the young cannot accept the notion of getting old. The derivative special effects feel like leftovers from the infinitely superior CLOSE ENCOUNTERS OF THE THIRD KIND. A number of the performances are superb, including Ameche's, for which he won a Best Supporting Actor Oscar. The film also won an Academy Award for Best Visual Effects.

COHEN AND TATE
1989 85m c   ★★★½
Action/Thriller   R/18
Nelson

Roy Scheider *(Cohen)*, Adam Baldwin *(Tate)*, Harley Cross *(Travis Knight)*, Cooper Huckabee, Suzanne Savoy

p, Antony Rufus Isaacs, Jeff Young; d, Eric Red; w, Eric Red; ph, Victor J. Kemper (Eastmancolor); ed, Edward Abroms; m, Bill Conti; prod d, David M. Haber

Some of the most interesting films of the 1980s offer a heady mix of a B-movie ethos, a focus on unpleasant people in unpleasant situations, disturbing undercurrents, and haunting imagery. COHEN & TATE is a noteworthy example of this tendency and a remarkably assured first film for writer-director Eric Red. COHEN & TATE begins at a farm in Oklahoma, where nine-year-old Travis Knight (Harley Cross) and his family are hiding under FBI protection after Travis witnesses a mob hit. When Cohen (Roy Scheider) and Tate (Adam Baldwin) show up, the two hit men kill the boy's family and kidnap the child, planning to take him to their mob bosses in Houston. The film turns into a very grim variation on O. Henry's "The Ransom of Red Chief" as the boy sizes up the tense group dynamics and begins setting the men against each other.

COHEN & TATE works because of its unapologetic B-movie style, including its underlying themes. The performances are terrific. Although more than half the film's action takes place in a car, COHEN & TATE is never boring, thanks to Red's crackling dialogue and interesting visual style. COHEN & TATE is a suspenseful, funny, and insightful thriller that should please people with a taste for something different and subversive.

COLONEL REDL
(REDL EZREDES)
1985 144m c   ★★★
Biography/Historical/War   R/15
Mafilm-Objectiv/Manfred Durniok/ORF/ZDF
(Hungary/Austria/West Germany)

Klaus Maria Brandauer *(Alfred Redl)*, Armin Mueller-Stahl *(Crown Prince Archduke Franz-Josef)*, Gudrun Landgrebe *(Katalin Kubinyi)*, Jan Niklas *(Kristof Kubinyi)*, Hans Christian Blech *(Col. von Roden)*, Laszlo Mensaros *(Col. Ruzitska)*, Andras Balint *(Dr. Gustav Sonnenschein)*, Karoly Eperjes *(Lt. Jaromil Schorm)*, Dorottya Udvaros *(Clarissa, Redl's Wife)*, Laszlo Galffi *(Alfredo Velocchio)*

p, Joszef Marx; d, Istvan Szabo; w, Istvan Szabo, Peter Dobai (based on the stage play "A Patriot for Me" by John Osborne); ph, Lajos Koltai (Eastmancolor); ed, Zsuzsa Csakany; m, Robert Schumann, Johann Strauss, Frederic Chopin, Franz Liszt; prod d, Jozsef Romvari; art d, Tibor Szollar; cos, Peter Pabst

Istvan Szabo's follow-up to MEPHISTO again stars Klaus Maria Brandauer, here as Colonel Alfred Redl, who became head of the Austro-Hungarian military intelligence bureau in the early 1900s, despite his impoverished origins. His Gatsby-like strivings for upper-class acceptance prove, however, to be his downfall when a czarist agent threatens to expose Redl's homosexual double life.

Though not as richly textured or urgent as MEPHISTO, this is an expertly made historical drama that, while fictionalizing some events, truthfully examines the desire for power and the catalysts of war. The film boasts yet another tour de force performance by Brandauer, as well as an equally strong portrayal by Armin Mueller-Stahl as the ruthless, power-hungry archduke. The film won the Jury Prize at the Cannes Film Festival, and received an Oscar nomination for Best Foreign Film.

COLOR OF DESTINY, THE

(A COR DO SEU DESTINO)
1988   104m   c   ★★★½
Drama
Nativa   (Brazil)

Guilherme Fontes (Paulo), Norma Bengell (Laura), Franklin Caicedo (Victor), Julia Lemmertz (Patricia), Andrea Beltrao (Helena), Chico Diaz, Antonio Grassi, Anderson Schereiber, Antonio Ameijeiras, Marcos Palmeira

p, Jorge Duran; d, Jorge Duran; w, Nelson Natotti, Jorge Duran, Jose Joffily (based on a story by Duran); ph, Jose Tadeu Ribeiro (Eastmancolor); ed, Dominique Paris; m, David Tygel

With THE COLOR OF DESTINY, Brazilian director Jorge Duran has created a sensitive portrayal of adolescent angst.

Paulo (Guilherme Fontes) is a teenager living in Rio de Janeiro with his parents, who have fled Chile for political reasons. After splitting up with his girlfriend, Paulo retreats to the privacy of his bedroom, where he creates experimental works of art. Burdened by the memory of an older brother who was tortured and killed for political activity in Chile, Paulo confronts his late brother in dream sequences, while his parents worry that he will follow in their dead son's footsteps. Word comes from Santiago that Patricia (Julia Lemmertz), Paulo's 18-year-old cousin who was arrested by Chilean authorities during a demonstration, has been freed from prison. She is sent to her relatives in Brazil to recuperate from her experience and is welcomed with open arms by her aunt and uncle. She develops a somewhat antagonistic relationship with Paulo. Paulo can't help but admire his cousin for her fortitude, however, and slowly finds himself falling for her. Eventually he realizes that he must follow his brother's example and become involved in Chile's political turmoil.

What makes THE COLOR OF DESTINY work so well are the natural performances by its teenage leads, allowing us to empathize with their complex struggles and pain. Duran, who directs with great heart, is sympathetic to his characters and is never afraid to show his political leanings. This is his debut feature as a director (following an apprenticeship as a screenwriter in the Brazilian film industry), and his ability to deal with multilayered issues points toward a strong career behind the camera.

COLOR OF MONEY, THE

1986   119m   c
Drama/Sports   R/15
Touchstone/Buena Vista   ★★★½

Paul Newman (Eddie), Tom Cruise (Vincent), Mary Elizabeth Mastrantonio (Carmen), Helen Shaver (Janelle), John Turturro (Julian), Bill Cobbs (Orvis), Keith McCready (Grady Seasons), Carol Messing (Casino Bar Band Singer/Julian's Flirt), Steve Mizerak (Duke, Eddie's 1st Opponent), Bruce A. Young (Moselle)

p, Irving Axelrad, Barbara De Fina; d, Martin Scorsese; w, Richard Price (based on the novel by Walter Tevis); ph, Michael Ballhaus (DuArt Color); ed, Thelma Schoonmaker; m, Robbie Robertson; prod d, Boris Leven; fx, Curt Smith; cos, Richard Bruno

Twenty-five years after being banned from ever again playing in a big-time pool room, in THE HUSTLER, Paul Newman's "Fast Eddie" Felsen resurfaces—older, wiser, and much more cynical—in THE COLOR OF MONEY. Eddie, who no longer plays himself, now fronts money to pool hustlers for a percentage. He takes young hotshot Vincent (Tom Cruise) and his worldly wise girlfriend, Carmen (Mary Elizabeth Mastrantonio), on the road, teaching the flamboyant, "flaky" kid how to "dump," lose games deliberately to get players' guard down ("Sometimes if you lose, you win"). Vincent has trouble learning to lose, Eddie begins to yearn to play again himself, and they part ways but meet again in a big tournament in Atlantic City. There the pupil surprises his rehabilitated teacher with how well he's learned his lessons. Approached by Newman, who felt that "Fast Eddie" was due for new exploration, director Martin Scorsese and novelist-screenwriter Richard Price (The Wanderers) came up with a fine film that retains only the title and Eddie Felsen character from novelist Walter Tevis's sequel to The Hustler. Although one of Scorsese's most commercial undertakings, THE COLOR OF MONEY relinquishes none of his unique style and vision, and he uses his camera placement for maximum impact. The film also boasts three bravura performances—most notably, Newman finally, and deservedly, won an Oscar for Best Actor; Mastrantonio was nominated as Best Supporting Actress; and Cruise contributes some of the best work of his career to date.

COLOR OF POMEGRANATES, THE

1980   75m   c   ★★★
Biography   /U
Artkino   (U.S.S.R.)

Sophico Tchiaourelli (Young Poet/Poet's Love/Nun with White Lace Angel Who Has Risen from the Dead/Mime), M. Alekian (Poet as a Child), V. Galestian (Poet in the Cloister), G. Gueguetchkori (Poet as an Old Man), O. Minassian (The Prince)

d, Sergei Paradzhanov; ph, A. Samvellian

This surreal, symbolic film about the life of the 18th-century Armenian poet Sayat Nova is filled with religious and animal imagery. It is also almost totally incomprehensible. Director Paradzhanov made the film in 1969 and was subsequently exiled to Siberia. Well worth seeing, if only as a visual treat.

COLOR PURPLE, THE

1985   152m   c   ★★★½
Drama   PG-13/15
Guber/Peters

Danny Glover (Albert), Whoopi Goldberg (Celie), Margaret Avery (Shug Avery), Oprah Winfrey (Sofia), Willard Pugh (Harpo), Akosua Busia (Nettie), Adolph Caesar (Old Mister), Rae Dawn Chong (Squeak), Desreta Jackson (Young Celie), Dana Ivey (Miss Millie) p, Steven Spielberg, Kathleen Kennedy, Frank Marshall, Quincy Jones, Jon Peters, Peter Guber; d, Steven Spielberg; w, Menno Meyjes (based on the novel by Alice Walker); ph, Allen Daviau (Panavision, Deluxe Color); ed, Michael Kahn; m, Quincy Jones; prod d, J. Michael Riva; art d, Bo Welch; cos, Aggie Guerard Rodgers

Far worse films than Steven Spielberg's laudable if problematic adaptation of Alice Walker's novel have been treated much less harshly. This film, which introduced Whoopi Goldberg and Oprah Winfrey to national audiences, has been unfairly attacked as an ill-considered and unseemly plea for "serious" consideration from an extremely successful young filmmaker better known for fantasy adventure films. Though a commercial success, this was one of the few major Hollywood dramas to concern itself with the lives of black women. Where are the subsequent black female films? Similarly, it soft-pedals the novel's lesbianism but how many subsequent Hollywood films have done better?

The story begins in 1909 as teenager Celie (Desreta Jackson) gives birth to two children (apparently fathered by her own father) and is married off to Albert (Danny Glover), who hates her and wants her sister, Nettie (Akosua Busia). When Nettie resists his advances, Albert persuades the sisters' father to separate the girls. Celie's children are sold to a local preacher and Nettie leaves. As an adult, Celie (now Whoopi Goldberg) lives a life of servitude to Albert who mistreats her shamelessly. He intercepts Nettie's letters to Celie, not allowing the sisters to communicate. Celie is cut off from all human affection. Celie eventually does receive love and gains self-respect through the timely intervention of an outside force who enters her life in an unexpected manner.

Spielberg lacks his usual intuitive affinity for his story material; consequently the film is a bit clunky at times. There are some unfortunate slapstick comic relief sequences and a few of the characterizations are also much too broad and cartoonish. The film was strongly criticized in some quarters for its negative depiction of black men but, if anything, it is less harsh than the novel. The film deserves praise for its heartwarming, empowering presentation of the strength and nobility of black women. It has also been damned for its gloriously lush cinematography as if the lives of black folk were only meant to be shown in squalid environments. Black people enjoy Hollywood fantasy as much as anyone.

COLORS
1988 120m c   ★★½
Crime   R/18
Orion

Sean Penn (Danny McGavin), Robert Duvall (Bob Hodges), Maria Conchita Alonso (Louisa Gomez), Randy Brooks (Ron Delaney), Grand L. Bush (Larry Sylvester), Don Cheadle (Rocket), Gerardo Mejia (Bird), Glenn Plummer (Clarence Brown, "High Top"), Rudy Ramos (Melindez), Sy Richardson (Bailey)

p, Robert H. Solo; d, Dennis Hopper; w, Michael Schiffer (from a story by Schiffer and Richard DiLello); ph, Haskell Wexler (Metrocolor); ed, Robert Estrin; m, Herbie Hancock; prod d, Ron Foreman; chor, Patrick Alan; cos, Nick Scarano

Hopper's controversial directorial reentry into mainstream Hollywood is a disappointingly routine effort that is neither socially irresponsible nor particularly distinguished by any insights or artfulness. The considerable controversy aroused by COLORS centered on Hopper's choice of subject matter—urban youth gangs. Set in the barrios and slums of East Los Angeles, the film is basically an all-too-familiar tale of a confident veteran cop (Duvall) with one more year to go until his retirement and his relationship with his new partner (Penn), a young, cocky, and hot-headed rookie who thinks he has all the answers. Their conflict is played out amid the shocking violence of a bloody war between LA's two most notorious gangs, the Bloods and the Crips. No one should expect a Hollywood movie to address *and* cure complicated social ills. In COLORS Hopper makes no attempt to provide solutions but merely presents the disturbing reality of the situation as a backdrop for the narrative. Unfortunately the end result is an unfocused hodgepodge of documentary realism, expressionism, TV cop show, liberal-message movie, and violent action film. None of these elements are handled with in a distinctive manner. In several interviews, Hopper admitted that had he initiated the project himself, he would have preferred to concentrate on the gangs rather than the cops. As it is, COLORS has a tentative, ambivalent feel to it—as if Hopper merely considered himself a hired gun who should avoid imposing too personal a vision on the material.

COLOSSUS: THE FORBIN PROJECT
1970 100m c   ★★★
Science Fiction
Universal

Eric Braeden (Dr. Charles Forbin), Susan Clark (Dr. Cleo Markham), Gordon Pinsent (The President), William Schallert (Grauber), Leonid Rostoff (Chairman), George Stanford Brown (Fisher), Willard Sage (Blake), Alex Rodine (Dr. Kurpin), Martin Brooks (Johnson), Marion Ross (Angela)

p, Stanley Chase; d, Joseph Sargent; w, James Bridges; ph, Gene Polito; ed, Folmar Blangsted; m, Michel Colombier; art d, John Lloyd, Alexander Golitzen; fx, Whitey McMahon

Taut, well-made sci-fi thriller about a massive computer, Colossus, which is designed by Braeden to control the entire American missile defense system. Once put into service, however, it takes over and develops a plan of *its* own to safeguard mankind from nuclear disaster. It hooks up with its Russian counterpart, Guardian, and together the two computers hold the world hostage, threatening to destroy the Earth. Braeden is forced to attempt to destroy his creation, but the computer thwarts him at every turn.

COMANCHE STATION
1960 74m c   ★★★★
Western   /U
Renown

Randolph Scott (Jefferson Cody), Nancy Gates (Mrs. Lowe), Claude Akins (Ben Lane), Skip Homeier (Frank), Richard Rust (Dobie), Rand Brooks (Station Man), Dyke Johnson (Mr. Lowe), Foster Hood (Comanche Lance Bearer), Joe Molina (Comanche Chief), Vince St. Cyr (Warrior)

p, Harry Joe Brown, Budd Boetticher, Randolph Scott; d, Budd Boetticher; w, Burt Kennedy; ph, Charles Lawton, Jr. (CinemaScope, Eastmancolor); ed, Edwin Bryant

This fine, haunting western was the last of the Randolph Scott-Bud Boetticher collaborations. Its predecessors were SEVEN MEN FROM NOW (1956), THE TALL T. (1957), DECISION AT SUNDOWN (1957), BUCHANAN RIDES ALONE (1958), RIDE LONESOME (1959), and WESTBOUND (1959). Together they encapsulate themes that made these films some of the most striking, intelligent, and complex westerns ever made. Boetticher, an often-underrated talent, created films that dealt with the sadness of independence, the questing impulse, the overpowering forces of nature, and the past's influence on the present.

Interrupting a futile ten-year search for his own wife, who was kidnaped by Indians, Scott agrees to track down a settler's wife, Gates, who has been raped and captured by Comanches. On their way back to her husband, Scott and Gates are met by outlaw Akins and his two adolescent proteges, Homeier and Rust, who inform the couple that they are being trailed by Comanche braves. Akins and the boys, offering to accompany Scott and Gates on their journey, create an atmosphere of tension, with Akins frequently commenting on the cowardice of Gates's husband in sending another man to do his work. It soon becomes apparent that Akins is plotting to get the reward for himself.

As in many of the Renown westerns, Scott is truly a loner in the film, a man whose personal code limits his ability to coexist with others. Adhering to the mythic type of the western hero, Scott remains true to the ideals of honesty, courage, and the responsibility to aid those in need. Boetticher's films are not happy, optimistic westerns in which evil is defeated before the final credits roll. They are sad films that focus on isolated men and the harsh world they exist in, men who strive for things they will probably never attain.

COME AND SEE

(IDI I SMOTRI)
1986   142m   c   ★★★½
War   /15
Byelarusfilm/Mosfilm   (U.S.S.R.)

Aleksei Kravchenko (Florya Gaishun), Olga Mironova, Lyubomiras Lautsiavitchus, Vladas Bagdonas, Victor Lorentz

d, Elem Klimov; w, Ales Adamovich, Elem Klimov (based on The Story of Khatyn and Others by Adamovich); ph, Alexi Rodionov

A highly charged, emotionally exhausting indictment of war and the inhumanity of the Nazis, set in Byelorussia during the 1943 Nazi invasion, COME AND SEE focuses on the experiences of an adolescent transformed, in a matter of days, from naive boy to worn man. Young Florya (Aleksei Kravchenko) finds a rifle and immediately joins the local freedom fighters, despite the desperate pleas of his mother, who wants to lose neither her son nor the only source of protection for her and her two young daughters. Florya is left behind by the makeshift army and tries to return to his mother, but the Germans launch an air raid, which is followed by an invasion of paratroopers before he can get to his village. Only the most insensitive could sit through COME AND SEE without being emotionally devastated. From its opening scene, COME AND SEE descends into a virtual hell on earth that becomes increasingly frightening as it advances to the final horror. This film won the Grand Prix at the Moscow film festival; its director, Elem Klimov, was recently named the head of the Soviet Filmmakers Union.

COME BACK, LITTLE SHEBA

1952   95m   bw   ★★★★
Drama   /A
Paramount

Burt Lancaster (Doc Delaney), Shirley Booth (Lola Delaney), Terry Moore (Marie Buckholder), Richard Jaeckel (Turk Fisher), Philip Ober (Ed Anderson), Lisa Golm (Mrs. Goffman), Walter Kelley (Bruce)

p, Hal B. Wallis; d, Daniel Mann; w, Ketti Frings (based on the play by William Inge); ph, James Wong Howe; ed, Warren Low; m, Franz Waxman

Lancaster is Doc Delaney, a mild-mannered alcoholic ex-chiropractor who has been dry for a year. Booth, his frumpy, loquacious wife, lives for the day when her lost dog, little Sheba, will return home. Theirs is a life of quiet desperation until Moore, a vibrant student, rents a room from the tired couple. Lancaster doesn't approve of the intentions of Jaeckel, who has been dating Moore, perhaps because the young man's lust stirs painful memories for Lancaster, whose premarital relationship with Booth resulted in their shotgun wedding. Returning to the bottle, he viciously criticizes his wife.

COME BACK, LITTLE SHEBA opened Christmas week of 1952 in order to qualify for the Academy Awards. The strategy was excellent as Shirley Booth won the Oscar for Best Actress, beating out Joan Crawford (SUDDEN FEAR), Julie Harris (THE MEMBER OF THE WEDDING), Bette Davis (THE STAR) and Susan Hayward (WITH A SONG IN MY HEART). Booth's brilliant work (she originated the role on Broadway) remains etched forever in the memory of anyone who has seen this film. Moore, in her finest performance, also received a nomination for Best Supporting Actress.

COME BACK TO THE 5 & DIME, JIMMY DEAN, JIMMY DEAN

1982   109m   c   ★★½
Drama   /15
Sandcastle 5

Sandy Dennis (Mona), Cher (Sissy), Karen Black (Joanne), Sudie Bond (Juanita), Marta Heflin (Edna Louise), Kathy Bates (Stella Mae), Mark Patton (Joe Qualley), Caroline Aaron (Martha), Ruth Miller (Clarissa), Gena Ramsel (Sue Ellen)

p, Scott Bushnell; d, Robert Altman; w, Ed Graczyck (based on his play); ph, Pierre Mignot; ed, Jason Rosenfield; prod d, David Gropman

Five women who grew up together in a small Texas town idolizing James Dean reunite 20 years later at a local dime store and discuss their lives and loves, illusion and reality. The most touching moment comes when Sandy Dennis, who has deluded herself for years, finally accepts that Dean was not the father of her illegitimate child. Director Robert Altman, turning Super 16mm cameras on the cast that he directed on Broadway in Ed Graczyck's play, captures the vitality of live performances from each of his actors. Using much technical invention, Altman does his best to invest his uncinematic material with a cinematic feel, but if COME BACK TO THE 5 & DIME, JIMMY DEAN, JIMMY DEAN still looks like a filmed play—and not a great play at that— it is nonetheless presented with great sensitivity. Karen Black, Cher, and Dennis contribute especially fine performances to this insightful film that was shot in just 19 days.

COME SEE THE PARADISE

1990   138m   c   ★★★
Historical/Romance   R/15
Alan Parker/Dirty Hands

Dennis Quaid (Jack McGurn), Tamlyn Tomita (Lily Kawamura), Sab Shimono (Mr. Kawamura), Shizuko Hoshi (Mrs. Kawamura), Stan Egi (Charlie Kawamura), Ronald Yamamoto (Harry Kawamura), Akemi Nishino (Dulcie Kawamura), Naomi Nakano (Joyce Kawamura), Brady Tsurutani (Frankie Kawamura), Elizabeth Gilliam (Youn Mini) p, Robert F. Colesberry; d, Alan Parker; w, Alan Parker; ph, Michael Seresin; ed, Gerry Hambing; m, Randy Edelman; prod d, Geoffrey Kirkland; art d, John Willitt; cos, Molly Maginnis

Lengthy and curiously detached. British screenwriter/director Alan Parker (MIDNIGHT EXPRESS, MISSISSIPPI BURN-ING) here offers a depiction of the Japanese internment camps that were established in the US in the early 1940s following Japan's attack on Pearl Harbor. Quaid plays a union organizer who meets Tomita in Los Angeles's Little Tokyo, before the bombing of Pearl Harbor. After the bombing, he is separated from his family, finally being imprisoned for going AWOL. Parker's intent seems to be to offer a traditional love story with the social and political turmoil of the 1930s and 40s serving merely as a backdrop, but the numerous issues he raises make it impossible for the film to function as an old-fashioned romance. The despair of the Japanese-Americans as they find their lives so ruthlessly torn apart and the almost maniacal prosecution of union activitists by authorities in the 1930s are forcefully portrayed, but to the detriment of the main story. In short, the film suffers from too many characters and subplots, so that the project probably would have been better served had it been made as a six-hour television miniseries.

The performances, however, are first-rate. Quaid, in a role he seems born to play, is splendid, far outshining his previous work. Tomita (THE KARATE KID, PART II) is also memorable. The Japanese-Americans who fill the numerous roles in the Kawamura family and the internment camp are uniformly excellent. Production values are high, with special mention going to Randy Edelman's terrific score, Geoffrey Kirkland's enviable production design, and authentic period costumes provided by Molly Maginnis.

COMES A HORSEMAN
1978   118m   c   ★★★
Western   PG/15
UA

James Caan (Frank), Jane Fonda (Ella), Jason Robards, Jr. (Ewing), George Grizzard (Neil Atkinson), Richard Farnsworth (Dodger), Jim Davis (Julie Blocker), Mark Harmon (Billy Joe Meynert), Macon McCalman (Hoverton), Basil Hoffman (George Bascomb), James Kline (Ralph Cole)

p, Gene Kirkwood, Dan Paulson; d, Alan J. Pakula; w, Dennis Lynton Clark; ph, Gordon Willis (Panavision, Technicolor); ed, Marion Rothman; m, Michael Small; prod d, George Jenkins; cos, Luster Bayless

An unusual staging of the American West. Alan J. Pakula, master of paranoia (KLUTE, THE PARALLAX, VIEW ALL THE PRESIDENT'S MEN), directed this offbeat film noir western set after WWII with James Caan as a cowhand, Jane Fonda as a ranch owner, and Jason Robards as the evil oil tycoon. The real star of the film is unbilled: a stretch of lush green land in Colorado known as the Wet Mountain Valley. Ace cinematographer Gordon Willis (ALL THE PRESIDENT'S MEN, THE GODFA-THER films, MANHATTAN) photographs this location with so much affection and awe that the talk by oil explorers about ripping it up for profit truly moves and horrifies the viewer.

Fonda is a rancher fighting to retain her independence from local mogul Robards, who is attempting to carve out an empire in this post-WWII world out west. Fonda and Robards slept together before she was old enough to know better, and she hates him for that and for a host of other reasons. Caan, also independent and newly returned from the service, teams with Fonda

when his partner is killed (probably on Robards's mandate). While Fonda and Caan are resisting Robards, Robards is resisting the pleas of an oil company that wants to come in and drill. A throwback to the ranchers of the old days, when such landholders were almost kings, Robards yearns for those times. Fonda wishes Robards would leave her alone so that she could just run her ranch with a bit of time off to fall in love with Caan, who is trying to forget the horrors of war. Farnsworth, as Dodger, Fonda's aging hand, received an Oscar nomination for Best Supporting Actor.

COMFORT AND JOY
1984   106m   c   ★★★
Comedy   PG
Kings Road   (U.K.)

Bill Paterson (Alan "Dickie" Bird), Eleanor David (Maddy), C.P. Grogan (Charlotte), Alex Norton (Trevor), Patrick Malahide (Colin), Rikki Fulton (Hilary), Roberto Bernardi (Mr. McCool), George Rossi (Bruno), Peter Rossi (Paolo), Billy McElhaney (Renato)

p, Davina Belling, Clive Parsons; d, Bill Forsyth; w, Bill Forsyth; ph, Chris Menges (Technicolor); ed, Michael Ellis; m, Mark Knopfler; prod d, Adrienne Atkinson; art d, Andy Harris; cos, Mary-Jane Reyner, Lindy Hemming

One of a string of first-rate Scottish comedies directed and written by Forsyth, COMFORT AND JOY—though at times rather bittersweet and melancholy—still has plenty of laughs, more than a few insights, and several offbeat characters. Paterson is a popular morning disc jockey in Glasgow. His kooky, kleptomaniac, live-in girlfriend, David, has abruptly walked out of his life, leaving him mired in depression. Paterson's placid existence really goes screwy when he gets involved in a conflict between two rival gangs that are seeking to control the Glasgow ice-cream business. (The two companies are called Mr. Bunny and Mr. McCool.) Paterson, unwilling to see chaos erupt and innocent people hurt, uses his radio show to relay messages between the warring factions. This puts his job at risk and wins him the anger of the ice-cream combatants.

This is an unusual premise for a film. Some of the potentially hilarious situations don't garner as many laughs as they might, but there are many funny moments, and the picture often throws unexpected curve balls at the audience. Although this is one of Forsyth's lesser works, his films are generally impressive and there is more here to laugh at than has been seen in British comedies for some time.

COMFORT OF STRANGERS, THE
1991   107m   c   ★★★
Drama   R/18
Erre Produzioni/Sovereign Pictures/Reteitalia   (Italy/U.K.)

Christopher Walken (Robert), Natasha Richardson (Mary), Rupert Everett (Colin), Helen Mirren (Caroline), Manfredi Aliquo (The Concierge), David Ford (Waiter), Daniel Franco (Waiter), Rossana Caghiari (Hotel Maid), Fabrizio Castellani (Bar Manager), Giancarlo Previati (First Policeman)

p, Angelo Rizzoli; d, Paul Schrader; w, Harold Pinter (from the novel by Ian McEwan); ph, Dante Spinotti; ed, Bill Pankow; m, Angelo Badalamenti; prod d, Gianni Quaranta; art d, Luigi Marchione; cos, Mariolina Bono

Based on the novel by Ian McEwan, with a screenplay by playwright Harold Pinter, THE COMFORT OF STRANGERS is a story of decadence and decay, sexual obsession and violence.

Colin (Rupert Everett) and Mary (Natasha Richardson) are a young English couple vacationing in Venice. Their relationship has reached a difficult juncture, and they hope the trip will help them sort things out. One night they become lost in the winding streets and encounter Robert (Christopher Walken), a dapper Italian who speaks excellent English and graciously escorts them to his out-of-the-way restaurant. They all drink too much, and Robert regales them with odd stories of his childhood, all revolving around cruelty and humiliation. After another chance encounter, Mary and Colin reluctantly agree to be guests at Robert's palatial apartment, where they meet his beautiful crippled wife, Caroline (Helen Mirren). The visit quickly becomes strained, and when Mary and Colin leave, they do so with the sense that they've escaped something.

Mary and Colin discover that their encounter with the older couple has revitalized their sexual relationship; they lock themselves in their hotel room and make love for days. When they emerge, they find themselves once again in Robert and Caroline's neighborhood, apparently by chance. Caroline appears on her balcony and invites them to visit one last time before she and her husband leave on an extended trip, and they feel unable to say no.

Former Calvinist and critic Paul Schrader, who has written and/or directed such films as AMERICAN GIGOLO, the remake of CAT PEOPLE and the biopic MISHIMA, is no stranger to provocative subject matter. But depravity is a tricky thing to make concrete, and film is a resolutely literal medium. The risk of looking silly is tremendously high—many films have aspired to decadence and achieved unintended camp. Schrader plunges in fearlessly, attempting to generate a sense of erotic menace through location and such devices as gliding steadicam shots that sweep through sumptuous surroundings, devouring them in every detail without ever pausing. (In the 20th century, who can think of Venice without thinking of death?)

Mirren's and Walken's brittle, mannered performances unquestionably add to the sense that something is ominously wrong with the relationship between the two couples long before anything untoward actually happens. But overall, THE COMFORT OF STRANGERS does indeed seem rather foolish, tremendously overwrought for no good reason. Only the scene in which Colin is killed jolts the movie out of its languid doldrums, and many viewers have had enough long before that happens.

COMING HOME

1978 126m c   ★★★½
Drama/War   R/18
UA

Jane Fonda (Sally Hyde), Jon Voight (Luke Martin), Bruce Dern (Capt. Bob Hyde), Robert Ginty (Sgt. Dink Mobley), Penelope Milford (Viola Munson), Robert Carradine (Bill Munson), Charles Cyphers (Pee Wee), Mary Jackson (Fleta Wilson), Kenneth Augustine (Ken), Tresa Hughes (Nurse De Groot)

p, Jerome Hellman; d, Hal Ashby; w, Waldo Salt, Robert C. Jones (based on a story by Nancy Dowd); ph, Haskell Wexler (Deluxe Color); ed, Don Zimmerman; prod d, Michael Haller; cos, Ann Roth, Michael Hoffman, Silvio Scarano, Jennifer Parsons

Nominated for eight Academy Awards—and winning for Best Actress (Jane Fonda), Best Actor (Jon Voight), and Best Original Screenplay (THE DEER HUNTER, another Vietnam film, won Best Picture and Best Director)—COMING HOME was one of the first films to deal seriously with the plight of returning Vietnam veterans. Unfortunately, it is marred by some cloying melodramatics and overly preachy politics. The story opens circa 1968, when Bob Hyde (Bruce Dern), a gung-ho Marine captain, is finally going off to Vietnam on active duty. His dutiful wife, Sally (Fonda), wants to do her share and begins volunteer work at a local veterans' hospital, where she meets Luke (Jon Voight), a bitter paraplegic. Within a month Sally and Luke have learned that they went to the same high school, knew many of the same people, and have much more in common than most others at the hospital. Luke's anger begins to subside, although he begins speaking out publicly against the war. The friendship broadens Sally's perspective; soon she is becoming more liberal in her politics, more feminist in her orientation, and comfortable leading a life independent of her husband. Eventually Luke and Sally become lovers (in a R-rated scene). Their relationship is jeopardized, however, when Bob is wounded in the leg and comes home from the war a changed man—taciturn but potentially violent. While COMING HOME has its heart in the right place, the script by Salt and Jones is too pat, and Ashby's direction simply too self-satisfied to be wholly effective. What does work in COMING HOME are the small, human, unguarded moments. The performances, undeniably appealing, were deservedly praised, Dern and Voight coming off best.

COMING TO AMERICA

1988 116m c   ★★½
Comedy/Romance   R/15
Paramount

Eddie Murphy (Prince Akeem/Clarence the Barber/Saul the Old Jew/Randy Watson the Singer), Arsenio Hall (Semmi/Morris the Barber/Extremely Ugly Girl/Rev. Brown), John Amos (Cleo McDowell), James Earl Jones (King Jaffe Joffer), Shari Headley (Lisa McDowell), Madge Sinclair (Queen Aoleon), Eriq LaSalle (Darryl Jenks), Allison Dean (Patrice McDowell), Paul Bates (Oha), Louie Anderson (Maurice)

p, George Folsey, Jr., Robert D. Wachs; d, John Landis; w, David Sheffield, Barry Blaustein (based on a story by Murphy); ph, Woody Omens (Technicolor); ed, Malcolm Campbell, George Folsey, Jr.; m, Nile Rodgers; prod d, Richard MacDonald; fx, Dan Cangemi, Syd Dutton, Rick Baker, Bill Taylor; chor, Paula Abdul; cos, Deborah Nadoolman

This light romantic comedy represents a change of pace for the phenomenally successful Murphy. His role in this picture is a departure from his usual irreverent, streetwise persona which he utilizes to deflate and scandalize staid, upper-crust and (usually) white pretensions and hangups in such popular films as TRADING PLACES and the BEVERLY HILLS COP movies. Here he plays a polite, pampered, and fabulously wealthy African prince who comes to America in search of true love. Although the fairy-tale script is as old as the motion picture industry itself, the resourceful cast of COMING TO AMERICA brings freshness to the annoyingly cliched material. Unfortunately the inelegant direction of Landis nearly derails the film. Poorly paced, indifferently shot, and haphazardly edited, the movie lurches unsteadily from scene to scene, undermining the the best efforts of its performers. (Landis even resorts to the hoary device of cutting to endless reaction shots of an animal, in this case, a white poodle for laughs during the excruciatingly long and unfunny climax.) Luckily Murphy and his fellow actors somehow manage to overcome Landis lack of artistry. Murphy gives his sweetest, most touching, and most genuinely likable performance to date, playing a character who embraces society instead of holding it in contempt. Arsenio Hall, in his first featured role, is also impressive. In a movie with as much charm as COMING TO AMERICA, it's a shame that Landis and/or Murphy chose to exploit some gratuitous nudity, scatological humor and excessive profanity. If Murphy had refrained from falling back on childishly dirty gags and had picked a more polished director than Landis, COMING TO AMERICA could have been a qmuch better movie. It still managed to receive nominations from the Academy for Best Costume Design and Best Makeup.

COMMITMENTS, THE

1991   120m   c   ★★★
Drama/Musical   R/15
Beacon Communications/First Film Co./Dirty Hands
Productions/Sovereign Pictures   (U.S./U.K.)

Robert Arkins *(Jimmy Rabbitte)*, Michael Aherne *(Steven Clifford)*, Angeline Ball *(Imelda Quirke)*, Maria Doyle *(Natalie Murphy)*, Dave Finnegan *(Mickah Wallace)*, Bronagh Gallagher *(Bernie McGloughlin)*, Felim Gormley *(Dean Fay)*, Glen Hansard *(Outspan Foster)*, Dick Massey *(Billy Mooney)*, Johnny Murphy *(Joey "The Lips" Fagan)*

p, Roger Randall-Cutler, Lynda Myles; d, Alan Parker; w, Ian LaFrenais, Dick Clement, Roddy Doyle (from his novel); ph, Gale Tattersall; ed, Gerry Hambling; prod d, Brian Morris; art d, Mark Geraghty, Arden Gantly; cos, Penny Rose

Alan Parker's latest offering is the story of the rise and demise of a young Irish soul band. As with his earlier film, FAME (to which one of the characters in THE COMMITMENTS makes an ironic reference), Parker has attempted to capture the infectious energy of popular music; and as with his previous feature, MISSISSIPPI BURNING, the director has taken on an alien culture (this time that of the working-class, primarily Catholic North Side of Dublin) and reduced its complexities to a glib, commercial formula.

When Jimmy Rabbitte (Robert Arkins) is asked by two friends to manage a dreadful wedding band, he takes the opportunity to begin building something more ambitious: an authentic soul outfit complete with brass section and backup singers. Jimmy advertises for musicians, and the pieces slowly begin to fall into place. Deco (Andrew Strong), a young lout with a truly stupendous Joe Cocker-style voice, is discovered singing (blind drunk) at a wedding; Billy (Dick Massey) auditions on a drum kit in the window of a pawnbroker's shop; Dean's (Felim Gormley) musical taste compensates for his beginner's sax skills; and Joey "The Lips" Fagan arrives on a moped, looking like a middle-aged has-been but claiming to have played the trumpet with Otis Redding and the Beatles. The rest of the band comprises keyboardist Steven (Michael Aherne), guitarists Derek (Kenneth McCluskey) and Outspan (Glen Hansard), and backup singers Bernie (Bronagh Gallagher), Natalie (Maria Doyle) and the head-turning Imelda (Angeline Ball), collectively known as the "Commitmentettes."

Under the guidance of Jimmy and Joey (who is as full of half-baked mysticism as he is of anecdotes about the golden days of rock 'n' roll), the members of the band immerse themselves in the soul classics as they begin struggling their way through rehearsals. Their working-class philosophy is spelled out by Jimmy: "The Irish are the blacks of Europe; Dubliners are the blacks of Ireland; and the North Siders are the blacks of Dublin. So say it loud: I'm black and I'm proud!" (His enthusiastic exhortation is not surprisingly met by a half-hearted chorus of mumbled responses and quizzical expressions from his all-white troupe, some of whom have never even heard a James Brown song.)

The Commitments' music improves with predictable, if enjoyable, speed, and the band develops a strong following on the pub circuit with faithful cover versions of songs like "When a Man Loves a Woman," "Respect," and "In the Midnight Hour." Just as predictably, though, the usual tensions start to manifest themselves. Deco is an arrogant boor who alienates everyone else in the band; Dean's penchant for jazz, which becomes more pronounced as his skills develop, drives soul purist Joey crazy; and Joey himself stirs up a hornet's nest with his sexual conquest of not just one, but all three, of the Commitmentettes. Matters come to a head during a Commitments show which coincides with a Dublin appearance by soul great Wilson Pickett. Joey claims he can persuade Pickett to jam with the group onstage after their performance—something which might tip the balance for a record producer who has expressed interest in signing the band, and who will be at the show. Pickett fails to appear, however, and the group erupts into a vicious free-for-all after the gig, prompting Jimmy to resign. Walking home from the club, a disillusioned Jimmy is asked by the driver of Wilson Pickett's limo if he knows where the Commitments are playing.

For all its emphasis on working-class integrity, THE COMMITMENTS is really FAME wrapped in streetwise packaging. All the cliches of the star-is-born subgenre are here, from the neatness with which the band members fall into place to the amazing rapidity with which they develop a professional sound (not to mention the implausibility of a group achieving such success by playing straight cover versions of classic soul songs). The whole thing has the feel of an extended sitcom—not surprising given the fact that Dick Clement and Ian La Frenais, veteran English TV writers, helped Roddy Doyle adapt his original novel for the screen.

Sitcoms, though, can be fun, and this one certainly is. The meandering plot strings together some enjoyable musical set pieces, and the vignettes of Dublin life, though glibly "gritty," are punctuated by some snappy one-liners. ("God sent him," says Jimmy of the messianic Joey; "On a Suzuki?" comes the incredulous reply.) THE COMMITMENTS may bring a smile to your lips, but it will tell you precious little about Dublin life or struggling to make it as a musician.

COMPANY OF WOLVES, THE

1985   95m   c   ★★★★½
Horror/Fantasy   R/18
Palace   (U.K.)

Angela Lansbury *(Granny)*, David Warner *(Father)*, Graham Crowden *(Old Priest)*, Brian Glover *(Amorous Boy's Father)*, Kathryn Pogson *(Young Bride)*, Stephen Rea *(Young Groom)*, Tusse Silberg *(Mother)*, Micha Bergese *(Huntsman)*, Sarah Patterson *(Rosaleen)*, Georgia Slowe *(Alice)*

p, Chris Brown, Stephen Woolley; d, Neil Jordan; w, Angela Carter, Neil Jordan (based on a collection of short stories by Carter); ph, Bryan Loftus (Rank Color); ed, Rodney Holland; m, George Fenton; prod d, Anton Furst; art d, Stuart Rose; fx, Peter MacDonald, Alan Whibley, Rodney Holland, Christopher Tucker; cos, Elizabeth Waller

A stunning surprise from the usually moribund British film industry, THE COMPANY OF WOLVES is the most innovative, intelligent and visually sumptuous horror film of recent years. Not a traditional werewolf movie, this film explores the psychosexual undercurrents of the classic "Little Red Riding Hood" fairy tale.

Occurring almost entirely in the troubled dreams of 13-year-old Sarah Patterson, the film takes the viewer deep into the land of legends. Patterson and her parents, David Warner and Tusse Silberg, dwell in a small village on the outskirts of a dark twisted forest. The girl's grandmother, Angela Lansbury, comes to visit and fills the young girl's head with cautionary tales about men who turn into wolves. Nonetheless her interest in men continues to grow. Sometime later a young neighbor boy discovers the ravaged carcass of a farm animal in the woods and warns the adults that a wolf is stalking the area.

THE COMPANY OF WOLVES has a complex and dreamy narrative structure built upon intermingled fantasies, myths, and fairy tales all told simultaneously. Nearly all the scenes in THE COMPANY OF WOLVES are compelling and haunting; and the special makeup effects are impressive. Director Neil Jordan is a director with visionary qualities, a distinctive stylist who knows how to visuall convey the complex emotions and simmering sensuality of Angela Carter's story. This is a significant film that successfully enters the netherworld of dreams and fantasy, evoking our deeply held fears and desires.

COMPULSION

1959 103m bw ★★★★
Crime /A
FOX

Orson Welles *(Jonathan Wilk)*, Diane Varsi *(Ruth Evans)*, Dean Stockwell *(Judd Steiner)*, Bradford Dillman *(Artie Straus)*, E.G. Marshall *(Horn)*, Martin Milner *(Sid)*, Richard Anderson *(Max)*, Robert F. Simon *(Lt. Johnson)*, Edward Binns *(Tom Daly)*, Robert Burton *(Mr. Straus)*

p, Richard D. Zanuck; d, Richard Fleischer; w, Richard Murphy (based on the novel by Meyer Levin); ph, William Mellor (CinemaScope); ed, William Reynolds; m, Lionel Newman; cos, Charles LeMaire

Based on the famous 1924 murder trial of Loeb and Leopold, two Chicago homosexual law students who murdered a boy, Bobby Franks, to demonstrate their intellectual superiority, this is a compelling and stylish thriller.

Dillman delivers a strong performance as the mother-dominated, sadistic Loeb, here called Artie Straus, and Stockwell is even more impressive as the submissive, introverted Leopold (renamed Judd Steiner). Of course, Welles is flamboyantly grand as the Clarence Darrow-figure who has the unenviable task of defending the two arrogant unsympathetic killers. They even have the effrontery to offer the police aid in solving the killing (exactly what Loeb did, which led to his arrest and that of Leopold). Raised by wealthy families, Dillman and Stockwell consider themselves superior intellects who are above conventional notions of morality. Their crime was executed without remorse. They offer no defense so, like Clarence Darrow, Welles must come up with a defense of his own.

COMPULSION is full of suspense and electrifying courtroom theatrics, even though the informed viewer knows the story's outcome. Fleischer's direction is taut, and Murphy's script, which takes the narrative almost word-for-word from Meyer Levin's best-selling novel, is terse and telling.

CONFESSION, THE

(L'AVEU)
1970 135m c ★★★½
Political /AA
Corona (France/Italy)

Yves Montand *(Gerard)*, Simone Signoret *(Lise)*, Gabriele Ferzetti *(Kohoutek)*, Michel Vitold *(Smola)*, Jean Bouise *(Boss)*, Laszlo Szabo *(Secret Policeman)*, Monique Chaumette, Guy Mairesse, Marc Eyraud, Gerard Darrieu

p, Robert Dorfmann, Bertrand Javal; d, Constantin Costa-Gavras; w, Jorge Semprun (based on a book by Lise London and Arthur London); ph, Raoul Coutard (Eastmancolor); ed, Francoise Bonnot; prod d, Claude Hauser; art d, Bernard Evein

Z brought director Costa-Gavras to the public's eye and THE CONFESSION was a respectable follow-up in what has become a career of politically aware movies such as STATE OF SIEGE, SPECIAL SECTION, and MISSING. THE CONFESSION is a searing indictment of the excesses of Stalinism. This film begins in 1951 when Montand is an East European Communist official who notices that he's being followed. During the Spanish Civil War, he had been a Loyalist. He mentions his fears to some friends who also served that cause and they admit that they too are being watched. He is soon arrested and taken to a makeshift jail. His wife, Signoret (in reel and real life), is not told his whereabouts but she is falsely reassured that it will all be over shortly. Meanwhile Montand has not been informed of the reason for his imprisonment and must endure psychological torture from his inquisitors as they try to extract a confession. Montand is a dedicated Communist and takes solace that these men are also Communists and only doing what they feel is right. He eventually finds himself in a well-publicized show trial.

Born in Greece, Costa-Gavras (Konstantin Gavras) is now a naturalized Frenchman and married to daring journalist Michele Ray, who excited the world with her dispatches from Vietnam and her account of being held captive by the Viet Cong.

CONFESSIONS OF A NAZI SPY

1939 110m bw ★★★★
Spy /U
WB

Edward G. Robinson *(Ed Renard)*, Francis Lederer *(Schneider)*, George Sanders *(Schlager)*, Paul Lukas *(Dr. Kassel)*, Henry O'Neill *(D.A. Kellogg)*, Lya Lys *(Erika Wolff)*, Grace Stafford *(Mrs. Schneider)*, James Stephenson *(Scotland Yard Official)*, Sig Rumann *(Krogman)*, Frederic Tozere *(Phillips)*

p, Robert Lord; d, Anatole Litvak; w, Milton Krims, John Wexley (based on an original story by Milton Krims, John Wexley and magasine articles by Leon Turrou); ph, Sol Polito; ed, Owen Marks

Landmark anti-Nazi proganda film from Warner Bros. The film begins in rural Scotland where a reclusive woman suddenly begins receiving mail from all points of the globe. When a resident philatelist requests the foreign stamps for his collection, the woman refuses explosively and slams her door in his face. He reports this odd behavior to Scotland Yard. British Intelligence agents soon discover that she is part of a Nazi spy ring. An intercepted information reveals a Nazi spy network in America with plans to kidnap an American Air Corps general. The Brits contact the US Government and FBI man Robinson enters the investigation, probing into the Nazi underground. Robinson systematically pinpoints key spies, concentrating on Lederer, the weak link in the Nazi network. Sanders is the sinister and cheap superior who pays Lederer miserably for his treachery, about $50 per report. Lederer also names Lukas, head of the Nazi *Bund*, who is recruiting American youth into *Hitlerjugend* legions and also in league with Sanders.

CONFESSIONS OF A NAZI SPY frightened audiences with the threat of Nazi tyranny, fulfilling the ideological and commercial aims of Warner Bros. This popular film established the studio as the leading film company of socially oriented productions. Robinson subdues his normally expansive gestures and speaks quietly as he cannily underplays a dynamic part in keeping with Litvak's semi-documentary style. The spy ring activities are shown in newsreel fashion and some actual clips are included from the 1937 spy trials of four Nazis convicted of espionage (the case on which the film is based). Nazi brutality is exposed throughout the film and Hitler, Goebbels, and company are openly vilified. Litvak's direction is unabashedly biased: his hatred for the Nazis seethes throughout the film. One significant omission of the film is any motivation for the Nazis. Anti-Semitism is never mentioned.

Warners knew there would be a strong reaction, and it came almost immediately from heads of the various Nazi *Bund* groups in the US, as well as from Germany which banned the film. Eighteen other countries followed suit, fearful of offending Hitler. Distributors had been warned that Nazi sympathizers might start riots in the first-run theaters showing the film, so squads of detectives patrolled the theaters to arrest would-be agitators.

CONFIDENCE
(BIZALOM)
1980 105m c   ★★★½
Drama   /AA
Mafilm   (Hungary)

Ildiko Bansagi *(Kata)*, Peter Andorai *(Janos Biro)*, O. Gombik, Karoly Csaki, Ildiko Kishonti, Lajos Balazsovits, Tamas Dunai, Zoltan Bezeredi, Eva Bartis, Danielle du Tombe

d, Istvan Szabo; w, Istvan Szabo (based on a story by Erika Szanto and Szabo); ph, Lajos Koltai (Eastmancolor); ed, Zsuzsa Csakany; art d, Jozsef Romvari

---

During WWII, Kata (Bansagi) discovers that her husband has gone underground and that she also must go into hiding. She is told to go to Janos Biro (Andorai) and the two must pretend to be husband and wife. Kata constantly tests Janos, seeing if she will betray him. Eventually the two become lovers, but drift apart into distrust again. The leading performances and the careful buildup of mood and tension are the things to watch here. Beautifully guided by Szabo, long one of Hungary's leading filmmakers and the director of the superb MEPHISTO, CONFIDENCE was nominated by the Academy for Best Foreign-Language Film.

CONFIDENTIALLY YOURS!
(VIVEMENT DIMANCHE!)
1983   111m bw   ★★★½
Crime/Romance
Carosse/Soprofilms/A2   (France)

Fanny Ardant *(Barbara Becker)*, Jean-Louis Trintignant *(Julien Vercel)*, Philippe Laudenbach *(M. Clement)*, Caroline Sihol *(Marie-Christine Vercel)*, Philippe Morier-Genoud *(Superintendent Santelli)*, Xavier Saint-Macary *(Bertrand Fabre, photographer)*, Jean-Pierre Kalfon *(Jacques Massoulier)*, Anik Belaubre *(Cashier at the Eden)*, Jean-Louis Richard *(Louison)*, Yann Dedet *("Angel Face")*

p, Armand Barbault; d, Francois Truffaut; w, Francois Truffaut, Suzanne Schiffman, Jean Aurel (based on the novel *The Long Saturday Night* by Charles Williams); ph, Nestor Almendros; ed, Martine Barraque; m, Georges Delerue; prod d, Hilton McConnico

---

Based on the 1962 Charles Williams pulp novel *The Long Saturday Night*, this final film by Truffaut (he died of a brain tumor in October 1984) is done in the Hitchcock of like his 1968 THE BRIDE WORE BLACK. A classy black-and-white movie about a man falsely accused of murder, CONFIDENTIALLY YOURS is much lighter and more enjoyable than most of Truffaut's films in the Seventies.

Its absurdly complex plot involves businessman Julien Varcel (Jean-Louis Trintignant), who is charged with murder and remains holed up in his office to avoid detection. Barbara (Fanny Ardant), the secretary he has just fired for her insolent behavior, tracks down clues to prove his innocence. The mystery of the film is not the killer's identity—this has never been a concern of Truffaut's—but the more important mystery of love. Barbara plays detective not because she cares about revealing the murderer but because she loves Julien, though neither she nor Julien will initially admit this. In order to prove her love to him, she must survive an Orphic descent into the seedy criminal underworld of gangsters, murderers, and prostitutes.

CONFIDENTIALLY YOURS! is Truffaut's showcase for Ardant, the love of his later years and mother of his youngest child.

CONFORMIST, THE
(IL CONFORMISTA)
1970 110m c   ★★★★
Political   R/18
Mars/Marianne/Maran   (Italy/France/West Germany)

Jean-Louis Trintignant *(Marcello Clerici)*, Stefania Sandrelli *(Giulia)*, Dominique Sanda *(Anna Quadri)*, Pierre Clementi *(Lino Seminara)*, Gastone Moschin *(Manganiello)*, Enzo Tarascio *(Prof. Quadri)*, Jose Quaglio *(Italo)*, Milly *(Marcello's Mother)*, Giuseppe Addobbati *(Marcello's Father)*, Yvonne Sanson *(Giulia's Mother)*

p, Maurizio Lodi-Fe; d, Bernardo Bertolucci; w, Bernardo Bertolucci (based on the novel by Alberto Moravia); ph, Vittorio Storaro (Technicolor); ed, Franco Arcalli; m, Georges Delerue; prod d, Ferdinando Scarfiotti; cos, Gitt Magrini

---

Bertolucci's best film makes an interesting connection between repressed sexual desires and fascist politics. Moody, memorable, and elegantly photographed, it's an intriguing study of the twisted Italian character of the 1930s.

Marcello Clerici (Jean-Louis Trintignant) marries the dull, petit-bourgeois Giulia (Stefania Sandrelli) and later joins the Italian Fascist movement, accepting an assignment to travel to Paris and assassinate Prof. Quadri (Enzo Tarascio), his former mentor. Before he can kill Quadri, Marcello becomes attracted to Anna (Dominique Sanda), the professor's seductive, lesbian wife, who is herself more interested in Giulia. Marcello's affiliation with the Fascists self-destructs, as does his own sexuality: plagued by the memory of a homosexual advance made to him as a child by his chauffeur, Marcello must battle his own desire for conformity.

In THE CONFORMIST, as in all his best work, Bertolucci addresses the issue of duality—of both sexual and political conflict. Marcello's personal contradictions parallel those of the Italian government, with his own decline taking place at the same time as Mussolini's, in 1943. Visually, THE CONFORMIST is stunning; its gliding camerawork, unusual camera angles, and rich color are just as decadent and baroque as the bourgeois world into which Marcello is thrust.

CONNECTICUT YANKEE, A
1931 95m bw ★★★½
Comedy/Fantasy
Fox Films

Will Rogers *(Hank)*, William Farnum *(King Arthur)*, Myrna Loy *(Queen Morgan Le Fay)*, Maureen O'Sullivan *(Alisande)*, Frank Albertson *(Clarence)*, Mitchell Harris *(Merlin)*, Brandon Hurst *(Sagramor)*

d, David Butler; w, William Conselman, Owen Davis, Sr. (based on the novel by Mark Twain); ph, Ernest Palmer; ed, Irene Morra

Will Rogers's fabled charm was well utilized in this excellent adaptation of the popular Mark Twain novel. Rogers, owner of a small-town radio shop, goes to install a battery in the old house of an eccentric character who thinks that he can contact King Arthur by radio. When Rogers is felled by an accidental blow on the head, he dreams his way back to days when knights were bold. The locals soon conclude that the mysterious stranger is a warlock. His only hope of saving himself is to exploit his unique knowledge of the future. Rogers's co-stars provide able support to the satirical proceedings. Myrna Loy plays the villainess and Maureen O'Sullivan is Rogers's love interest. Since the picture was made during the depths of the Depression, much of Rogers's topical humor may be lost on today's audiences but the anachronistic visual gags (for example, Rogers lassoes a Knight of the Round Table in the middle of a joust) remain as fresh and funny as ever.

CONNECTICUT YANKEE IN KING ARTHUR'S COURT, A
1949 106m c ★★★
Fantasy/Musical
Paramount

Bing Crosby *(Hank Martin)*, William Bendix *(Sir Sagramore)*, Cedric Hardwicke *(King Arthur)*, Rhonda Fleming *(Alisande La Carteloise)*, Murvyn Vye *(Merlin)*, Virginia Field *(Morgan Le Fay)*, Henry Wilcoxon *(Sir Lancelot)*, Richard Webb *(Sir Galahad)*, Joseph Vitale *(Sir Logris)*, Alan Napier *(High Executioner)*

p, Robert Fellows; d, Tay Garnett; w, Edmund Beloin (based on the novel by Mark Twain); ph, Ray Rennahan (Technicolor); ed, Archie Marshek; m, Victor Young; art d, Hans Dreier, Roland Anderson; fx, Farciot Edouart; cos, Edith Head

Mark Twain's popular satirical fantasy is mellowed into an amusingly carefree, lavishly mounted Bing Crosby vehicle, rich in color and pleasant if unmemorable songs. Crosby stars as Hank Martin, a Connecticut blacksmith who is knocked unconscious in a wild rainstorm and wakes up in King Arthur's Camelot. This production boasts wonderful sets and softly focused color lensing by Ray Rennahan. The famed art director Hans Dreier created a spectacular and authentic medieval castle for the film, with an enormous dining hall for King Arthur's knights, a huge ballroom, lush gardens, courtyards, and jousting grounds. Rhonda Fleming's auburn-haired beauty is lovely in the rich Technicolor process and Tay Garnett's direction is smooth and well paced. It was remade and updated by Disney in 1979 as UNIDENTIFIED FLYING ODDBALL.

CONNECTION, THE
1962 110m bw ★★½
Drama
Allen/Clarke

William Redfield *(Jim Dunn)*, Warren Finnerty *(Leach)*, Garry Goodrow *(Ernie)*, Jerome Raphel *(Solly)*, James Anderson *(Sam)*, Carl Lee *(Cowboy)*, Barbara Winchester *(Sister Salvation)*, Roscoe Lee Browne *(J.J. Burden)*, Henry Proach *(Harry)*, Freddie Redd *(Piano)*

p, Lewis Allen, Shirley Clarke; d, Shirley Clarke; w, Jack Gelber (based on the play by Gelber); ph, Arthur J. Ornitz; ed, Shirley Clarke; m, Freddie Redd; prod d, Richard Sylbert; art d, Albert Brenner; cos, Ruth Morley

Eight drug addicts gather in a Manhattan loft to wait for their connection. To pay for their drugs, they have agreed to allow Dunn, a would-be documentary filmmaker, to photograph them. Film within a film records their conversation, reflections, and an impromptu jam session involving four of the junkies who are musicians. The "connection" arrives with a soldier from the Salvation Army, who suspects the addicts are drinking and beats a hasty retreat. Dunn is then persuaded to try some heroin so that he will have a deeper understanding of the subject of his film, and he becomes violently ill.

This film was considered a tour de force for choreographer-turned-director Clarke, who heretofore had specialized in prize-winning shorts. It is a jolting look at the drug crowd. The characters get laughs with their crisp lingo and wry wit, showing them to be acceptable types one can empathize with. There are no phony dramatics here.

CONTEMPT
(LE MEPRIS)
1963 100m c ★★★★½
Drama /15
Concordia/C.C. Champion/Rome Paris (France/Italy)

Brigitte Bardot *(Camille Javal)*, Michel Piccoli *(Paul Javal)*, Jack Palance *(Jeremy Prokosh)*, Fritz Lang *(Himself)*, Georgia Moll *(Francesca Vanini)*, Jean-Luc Godard *(Lang's Assistant Director)*, Linda Veras *(Siren)*

p, Georges de Beauregard, Carlo Ponti, Joseph E. Levine; d, Jean-Luc Godard; w, Jean-Luc Godard (based on the novel *Il Disprezzo [A Ghost At Noon]* by Alberto Moravia); ph, Raoul Coutard (CinemaScope); ed, Agnes Guillemot, Lila Lakshmanan; m, Georges Delerue

A profoundly sad yet beautiful fable about the cinema, CONTEMPT is the story of Paul Javal (Michel Piccoli), a former writer of detective stories who has become a screenwriter of little consequence. He claims that he longs to write for the stage but he believes that his beautiful young wife, Camille (Brigitte Bardot), expects more financial rewards than the theater can offer. Paul is approached by crass American film producer Jeremy Prokosh (Jack Palance) to perform a rewrite on the screenplay for his production of Homer's *Odyssey*. The film is to be directed by the legendary German director Fritz Lang (playing himself). Paul accepts the job, but Camille is disappointed at his lack of conviction in the assignment, even though he ostensibly accepted the job to benefit her. She begins to manifest a profound mistrust of him that is never really explained. After a strained social situation in which Paul acts in a less than noble manner, Camille turns to Prokosh to pursue what appears to be an affair.

An adaptation of Alberto Moravia's novel *A Ghost at Noon*, CONTEMPT concerns itself with the filmmaking process, the nature of film authorship, and the art of adapting a novel for the screen. Godard favors a personal idiosyncratic approach to filmmaking and adaptation as is evidenced in his utilizing Moravia and Homer's work to relate the characters in the film to the people in his own life: Paul, Camille, and Prokosch evoke Odysseus, Penelope, and Poseidon while also suggesting Godard, his wife (and favored female lead at that time) Anna Karina, and distributor Joseph E. Levine.

The genesis of the project is worth recounting. Approached by Italian producer Carlo Ponti about a possible collaboration, the New Wave auteur suggested an adaptation of the Moravia novel with Kim Novak and Frank Sinatra in the leads. The pair refused. Ponti then suggested Sophia Loren and Marcello Mastroianni. Godard refused. Eventually Bardot was chosen because of the potential financial rewards that could be garnered from revealing her celebrated delectable flesh on screen. However, Godard had the last laugh: the most extensive nudity is in the film's subversively tame opening scene. Committed to a personal cinema, Godard cast himself as Lang's assistant director and used the great auteur as his mouthpiece. CONTEMPT is beautifully photographed in Cinemascope with sun dappled color by Raoul Coutard and Georges Delerue provides the haunting score.

CONTINENTAL DIVIDE
1981   103m   c   ★★½
Comedy/Romance   PG
Amblin

John Belushi *(Souchak)*, Blair Brown *(Nell)*, Allen Garfield *(Howard)*, Carlin Glynn *(Sylvia)*, Tony Ganios *(Possum)*, Val Avery *(Yablonowitz)*, Liam Russell *(Deke)*, Everett Smith *(Fiddle)*, Bill Henderson *(Train Conductor)*, Bruce Jarchow *(Hellinger)*

p, Bob Larson; d, Michael Apted; w, Lawrence Kasdan; ph, John Bailey (Technicolor); ed, Dennis Virkler; m, Michael Small; prod d, Peter Jamison; cos, Moss Mabry

Chicago newspaper columnist Souchak (John Belushi, playing a sort of young, overweight Mike Royko) is a true urbanite who enjoys all the goings-on around City Hall and consumes cigarettes, coffee, and whiskey with abandon and little regard for his health. When his series of stories about a crooked politician backfires, Souchak is dispatched to the Rockies to interview wacky ornithologist Nell (Blair Brown) as a pretext to get him out of town. This unlikely love story never really pays off, largely due to Lawrence Kasdan's contrived script. To their credit, a very subdued Belushi and an appealing Brown do their best to add a patina of light charm to this minor effort, and largely they succeed. Michael Apted (COAL MINER'S DAUGHTER), one of the few British directors who can convey a sense of Americana, does a good job of keeping things going, but even his efforts fall short.

CONTRACT, THE
1982   111m   c   ★★★½
Comedy   /PG
PRF/Zespol   (Poland)

Maja Komorowska, Tadeusz Lomnicki, Magda Jaroszowna, Krzysztof Kolberger, Nina Andrycz, Zofia Mrozowska, Beata Tyszkiewicz, Janusz Gajos, Edward Lubaszenko, Leslie Caron

d, Krzysztof Zanussi; w, Krzysztof Zanussi; ph, Slawomir Idziak; ed, Urszula Sliwinska, Ewa Smal; m, Wojciech Kilar; art d, Tadeusz Wybult, Maciej Putowski, Teresa Gruber, Gabriela Allina, Joanna Lelanow

This satirical look at Polish life focuses on the wedding reception of a marriage that did not take place. The couple are pushed into an arranged marriage, and when the bride backs out at the last minute the groom's father decides to have the reception anyway. The reception, which is a celebration of nothing, is filled with drunken altercations, sexual liaisons, and flaring of tempers between the rival families. Leslie Caron is a standout as a kleptomaniac rich woman symbolizing Western decadence. An offbeat, extremely interesting film helmed by one of contemporary Poland's most interesting filmmakers, THE CONTRACT was filmed at the same time as Zanussi's THE CONSTANT FACTOR.

CONVERSATION, THE
1974   113m   c   ★★★★★
Drama   PG/15
Paramount

Gene Hackman *(Harry Caul)*, John Cazale *(Stan)*, Allen Garfield *(Bernie Moran)*, Frederic Forrest *(Mark)*, Cindy Williams *(Ann)*, Michael Higgins *(Paul)*, Elizabeth MacRae *(Meredith)*, Teri Garr *(Amy)*, Harrison Ford *(Martin Stett)*, Mark Wheeler *(Receptionist)*

p, Francis Ford Coppola; d, Francis Ford Coppola; w, Francis Ford Coppola; ph, Bill Butler (Technicolor); ed, Walter Murch, Richard Chew; m, David Shire; prod d, Dean Tavoularis

One of Coppola's very best. Harry Caul (Gene Hackman) is a professional surveillance expert, a wire-tapper and industrial spy for hire by anyone—if the price is right. Harry and his assistant Stan (Cazale) use state-of-the-art technical expertise to track a young couple, Ann (Williams) and Mark (Forrest), and record their conversations. The client is a mysterious and powerful businessman, known only as the "director" (Robert Duvall, in an unbilled cameo), whose motives are unclear. After listening to the tapes repeatedly, however, Harry deduces that Ann is the director's wife and that she is having an affair with Mark, one of her husband's employees. To his horror, Harry concludes that his client plans to murder the couple. Plagued by guilt from a previous assignment in which the information he gathered led to the murders of several people, Harry becomes obsessed with preventing the murders of Ann and Mark—for the first time in his career, he decides to get involved—but he gets in over his head.

Following the triumph of THE GODFATHER, writer-director Francis Ford Coppola surprised everyone with this small, intimate, and brilliantly crafted film, which explores the implications of indiscriminate eavesdropping. Gene Hackman is superb as Harry Caul, a painfully lonely, cynical, paranoid, and alienated man whose work has driven him to guard his own privacy zealously, although there is precious little to protect. A year later Hackman would play another eavesdropper named Harry, this time a detective in Arthur Penn's NIGHT MOVES, and the similarities between the two characters were not lost on the actor—NIGHT MOVES could be a prequel to THE CONVERSATION.

The film was released just after the Watergate break-in, but it was written many years before and was already shooting when the news of the break-in appeared. Technically brilliant, THE

CONVERSATION does in aural terms what Antonioni's BLOW UP does in visual terms. This is certainly one of the key films of the 1970s.

COOGAN'S BLUFF

1968 93m c   ★★★½
Crime/Western   /X
Universal

Clint Eastwood (Coogan), Lee J. Cobb (Sheriff McElroy), Susan Clark (Julie), Tisha Sterling (Linny Raven), Don Stroud (Ringerman), Betty Field (Mrs. Ringerman), Tom Tully (Sheriff McCrea), Melodie Johnson (Millie), James Edwards (Jackson), Rudy Diaz (Running Bear)

p, Don Siegel; d, Don Siegel; w, Herman Miller, Dean Riesner, Howard Rodman (based on a story by Miller); ph, Bud Thackery (Technicolor); ed, Sam E. Waxman; m, Lalo Schifrin; art d, Alexander Golitzen, Robert MacKichan; cos, Helen Colvig

Western myth gets urban update in original pilot for "McCloud" television series. Arizona deputy arrives in NYC to track killer and teach city cops a thing or three. The interest here is in watching Eastwood, mid-point between spaghetti westerns and assuming his Dirty Harry persona, lock horns with Cobb, who gives a socko performance. Sterling is of passing interest as a female hippie. The first collaboration between Eastwood and Siegel raised the hackles of many a moralist with what was considered needless violence and too much sex. That's one way of saying today it looks tame, but you may get a literal kick out of the poolroom fight scene.

COOK, THE THIEF, HIS WIFE & HER LOVER, THE

1989 124m c   ★★★½
Drama   /18
Allarts Cook/Erato/Films Inc.   (U.K./France)

Richard Bohringer (Richard Borst, the Cook), Michael Gambon (Albert Spica, the Thief), Helen Mirren (Georgina Spica, the Wife), Alan Howard (Michael, the Lover), Tim Roth (Mitchel), Ciaran Hinds (Cory), Gary Olsen (Spangler), Ewan Stewart (Harris), Roger Ashton Griffiths (Turpin), Ron Cook (Mews)

p, Kees Kasander; d, Peter Greenaway; w, Peter Greenaway; ph, Sacha Vierny (CinemaScope); ed, John Wilson; m, Michael Nyman; prod d, Ben Van Os, Jan Roelfs; cos, Jean-Paul Gaultier

Greenaway describes the impulses behind his work as "technical and aesthetic and cerebral and academic." His films have not been developed according to the demands of narrative ("Cinema is much too important to be left to the storytellers," says Greenaway), but by equally deterministic formulas of the director's own devising: formalism, structural symmetry, recurring patterns and symbols, puns and conceits.

At its core a simple tale of adultery, jealousy and revenge, THE COOK, THE THIEF, HIS WIFE & HER LOVER is built around the four characters of the title, the divisions of the restaurant (each room perhaps representing its own historical epoch), the tradition of table painting (a huge Frans Hals reproduction dominates the dining room), and the central metaphysical conceit linking mouth with anus, food with feces, and sex with death.

Greenaway reportedly identifies with the cook: he watches, maintains a dignified distance, but acts decisively on behalf of the lovers. Michael Gambon's Thief and Alan Howard's Lover are diametrical opposites, the one boorish, crude, and ignorant, the other calm, gentle, and cultured. Gambon never stops talking but has little to say; Howard, on the other hand, remains silent

for the first 20 minutes of the film but proves thoughtful and wise. Setting out to create an irredeemable monster, Greenaway takes his film to the very limits of screen permissiveness, from graphic torture to cannibalism.

The film has been seen as a vitriolic condemnation of contemporary consumerism and greed, but for all the brutality and physical savagery Greenaway depicts, one suspects his contempt is really aimed at the *nouveaux riches* who do not appreciate the gourmet dishes they can pay for but whose names they cannot pronounce. If there is a connection between this philistine lack of sophistication and Howard's study of the French Revolution, then Gambon is surely representative of the peasants and the Terror—in his resolutely one-dimensional role he embodies every snob or aesthete's nightmare villain. Not surprisingly, his ranting soon becomes repetitive and boring. Greenaway's dialogue cannot sustain our interest, and his lack of humor is the film's biggest drawback. For a lover of games, the director is never remotely playful.

COOL HAND LUKE

1967 126m c   ★★★★
Prison   /15
WB

Paul Newman (Luke), George Kennedy (Dragline), J.D. Cannon (Society Red), Lou Antonio (Koko), Robert Drivas (Loudmouth Steve), Strother Martin (Captain), Jo Van Fleet (Arletta), Clifton James (Carr), Morgan Woodward (Boss Godfrey), Luke Askew (Boss Paul)

p, Gordon Carroll; d, Stuart Rosenberg; w, Donn Pearce, Frank Pierson (based on a novel by Pearce); ph, Conrad Hall (Panavision, Technicolor); ed, Sam O'Steen; m, Lalo Schifrin; art d, Cary Odell; cos, Howard Shoup

Too cool for words, then switches past midstream into a work of poignancy and power. Not much has changed since Warner Bros in the 1930s, and it's interesting to realize, looking over Newman's career, how many overrated male-bonding, macho-buddy movies he has made. COOL HAND LUKE starts out that way with Newman as irreverent loner put on a chain gang for destroying parking meters. Kennedy won the Best Supporting Actor Oscar as the bastardly convict boss who tries to crack Newman; the comedic part of film is highlighted by a hilarious egg-eating contest, but LUKE gains additional steam thanks to an unforgettable cameo by Van Fleet and a sharp turn toward tragedy. Newman emerges as a victim more to be pitied than scorned or laughed with, adding a deeper tinge of revelance to the film.

Produced by Jack Lemmon's company for Warner Bros., the movie is set in the South but was actually shot near Stockton, California. Pearce, the author of the original novel, was a reformed safecracker and had served time in such a camp. He does a bit role as Sailor, one of the cons. Also in small roles are Joe Don Baker (WALKING TALL), Wayne Rogers (television's "M*A*S*H"), and Dennis Hopper.

COOL WORLD, THE

1963 125m bw   ★★★½
Drama   /X
Wiseman

Hampton Clayton (Duke), Yolanda Rodriguez (Luanee), Bostic Felton (Rod), Gary Bolling (Littleman), Carl Lee (Priest), Gloria Foster (Mrs. Custis), Georgia Burke (Grandma), Charles Richardson (Beep Bop), Bruce Edwards (Warrior), Teddy McCain (Saint)

p, Frederick Wiseman; d, Shirley Clarke; w, Shirley Clarke (based on the novel by Warren Miller and the play by Miller and Robert Rossen); ph, Baird Bryant; ed, Shirley Clarke; m, Mal Waldron

Unfortunately, timeless and not too cool. Deep down, not even the rent is happenin', but on the surface this little alleycat film captures the day-to-day desperation of the ghetto world, mainlining its images with transfusions of eclectic jazz background. We have here a mood piece focusing on Clayton's efforts to rise to authority in his Harlem street gang after hearing a Black Muslim evangelist spouting black supremacy and hatred against whites. An effective look at the mind-set of bored youths who see violence as a way out of poverty, and an indictment of the failings of federal law.

COP

1988   110m   c   ★★★½
Crime/Mystery   R/18
Atlantic

James Woods (Lloyd Hopkins), Lesley Ann Warren (Kathleen McCarthy), Charles Durning (Dutch Pelz), Charles Haid (Whitey Haines), Raymond J. Barry (Fred Gaffney), Randi Brooks (Joanie Pratt), Steven Lambert (Bobby Franco), Christopher Wynne (Jack Gibbs), Jan McGill (Jen Hopkins), Vicki Wauchope (Penny Hopkins)

p, James B. Harris, James Woods; d, James B. Harris; w, James B. Harris (based on the novel Blood On The Moon by James Ellroy); ph, Steve Dubin; ed, Anthony Spano; m, Michel Colombier; prod d, Gene Rudolf; fx, Larry Fioritto, Bill Myer; cos, Gale Parker Smith

Based on James Ellroy's novel Blood on the Moon, COP is a grim, modern-day film noir starring James Woods as Lloyd Hopkins, the most obsessive, vile and amoral cop since Ralph Meeker played Mike Hammer in Robert Aldrich's KISS ME DEADLY. Coproduced by Woods, and written and directed by his friend James B. Harris (who produced Stanley Kubrick's THE KILLING, PATHS OF GLORY and LOLITA), COP combines brutal violence with a self-mocking sense of black humor.

Its action is set in a Los Angeles overwhelmed by hypocrisy, cynicism and sleaze, where Woods, an inveterate loner who is one of the LAPD's best detectives, finds himself investigating a murder he believes to have been the work of a serial killer who preys on innocent-looking women. Oppressively seedy and bleak, COP presents a world destroyed by the corruption of romantic notions, and Woods, who understands this warped milieu, is obsessed with the way society fills women's heads with fairy-tale promises of security, decency, justice, and romance. "Innocence kills," he tells his shocked wife. "I see it every day." Although directed and written with a sometimes-unsure hand by Harris, COP is completely absorbing because of Woods's chillingly effective performance.

Few actors can make an amoral, intelligent, sardonic, hyperactive, womanizing, violent and downright warped character as disarmingly appealing as Woods can. As an actor, he juggles complex contradictions with ease, showing an audience the various sides of his character's psyche with the skill of a magician. In COP, Woods takes us on a singularly unpleasant ride, but it is always an insightful and fascinating one. Fueled by his frightening performance, the film rushes headlong into an ending that is so inevitable, yet still so shocking, that it terminates the genre with an irrevocable bang.

CORNERED

1945   102m   bw   ★★★★
Thriller/War   /A
RKO

Dick Powell (Gerard), Walter Slezak (Incza), Micheline Cheirel (Mme. Jarnac), Nina Vale (Senora Camargo), Morris Carnovsky (Santana), Edgar Barrier (DuBois), Steven Geray (Senor Camargo), Jack LaRue (Diego), Luther Adler (Marcel Jamac), Gregory Gaye (Perchon)

p, Adrian Scott; d, Edward Dmytryk; w, John Paxton (based on a story by John Wexley and a title by Ben Hecht); ph, Harry Wild; ed, Joseph Noriega; m, Roy Webb; art d, Albert S. D'Agostino, Carroll Clark; cos, Renie

Peak Powell the way we like him, and it's a long way from Ruby Keeler. Canadian flier Powell gets out of a POW camp with his mind set on avenging the death of his French war bride, caused by Vichy officer Jarnac (Adler). Although by all reports Jarnac is dead, Gerard refuses to believe it. He pursues leads through Switzerland and then to Buenos Aires, where he encounters an underground group of Nazi hunters—Carnovsky, Barrier, and LaRue. His quest is further complicated when he finds himself drawn to the attractive Cheirel, who married Adler, without ever having met him, in order to emigrate safely.

Tightly directed by the talented Edward Dmytryk, CORNERED is a terse thriller, with Powell turning in another tough-talking, hardboiled performance as the man seeking vengeance with cold-blooded determination. The script was based on the title of a 20-page Ben Hecht treatment that was, according to Dmytryk, "such poor stuff. . ." that they kept only the title and brought in new writers to shape the film. Well-sculpted.

CORSICAN BROTHERS, THE

1941   111m   bw   ★★★½
Adventure   /U
UA

Douglas Fairbanks, Jr. (Mario/Lucien), Ruth Warrick (Isabelle), Akim Tamiroff (Colonna), J. Carrol Naish (Lorenzo), H.B. Warner (Dr. Paoli), John Emery (Tomasso), Henry Wilcoxon (Count Franchi), Gloria Holden (Countess Franchi), Walter Kingsford (M. Dupre), Nana Bryant (Mme. Dupre)

p, Edward Small; d, Gregory Ratoff; w, George Bruce (based on an adaptation of the Alexandre Dumas novel by Bruce and Howard Estabrook); ph, Harry Stradling; ed, Grant Whytock, William Claxton; fx, Howard Anderson

Exciting Dumas tale, which has some basis in fact, brought to the screen with great gusto on the part of Fairbanks whose dashing feats rival the acrobatic antics of his illustrious father. It is the tale of Siamese-twin boys born in Corsica and separated by brilliant doctor Warner just before their parents and relatives are killed by Tamiroff's henchmen in a blood feud. One child is sent to Paris to be raised, the other into the mountains with family retainer Naish. When both grow to manhood they are reunited—Fairbanks skillfully playing both roles—and launch a revenge plan against Tamiroff.

Fairbanks excels in showing how the emotional/intellectual telepathy works on each twin, particularly the agony one feels whenever the other is emotionally upset or physically wounded, and the jealousy one feels when the other falls in love with Warrick. Ratoff's direction is eccentric, but he provides great pace and the script is excellent. The superb Tamiroff plays his evil role with the usual guttural relish, almost as if practicing for his fun bad guy, Pablo, in FOR WHOM THE BELL TOLLS.

CORVETTE K-225

1943   99m   bw   ★★★½
War   /U
Universal

Randolph Scott (Lt. Cmdr. MacClain), James Brown (Paul Cart-wright), Ella Raines (Joyce Cartwright), Barry Fitzgerald (Stooky O'Meara), Andy Devine (Walsh), Fuzzy Knight (Cricket), Noah Beery, Jr. (Stone), Richard Lane (Admiral), Thomas Gomez (Smithy), David Bruce (Rawlins)

p, Howard Hawks; d, Richard Rosson; w, John Rhodes Sturdy; ph, Tony Gaudio, Harry Perry ; ed, Edward Curtiss; m, David Buttolph; fx, John Fultes

Great Scott and a warship, not a car. He portrays skipper in this account of Atlantic convoys going to Russia. After having lost a ship to U-boats, Scott returns to Canada where he meets Raines who reluctantly falls in love with him; her older brother has been lost at sea and she's wary of becoming involved with a sailor. Scott is given command of a brand new ship, Corvette K-225, and takes Raines's younger brother, Brown, on board to make a seaman of him.

The convoy to Russia includes many scenes taken from actual combat footage; Rosson's lively direction and the realistic script does much to make clear Canada's deep involvement in WWII, something that had been generally ignored by Hollywood in its fever to promote US war films.

Rosson and Gaudio, his veteran cameraman, went to sea for three months, hazarding the U-boats in the Atlantic, to get background footage, and combat lensing was by Harry Perry, who had gone on several corvette convoys to capture astounding battle shots. The result was an excellent production that still stands up today, unlike many of the propaganda films the studios churned out in the 1940s.

COTTON CLUB, THE

1984   127m   c   ★★★½
Crime/Musical   R/15
Zoetrope

Richard Gere (Dixie Dwyer), Gregory Hines (Sandman Williams), Diane Lane (Vera Cicero), Lonette McKee (Lila Rose Oliver), James Remar (Dutch Schultz), Nicolas Cage (Vincent Dwyer), Allen Garfield (Abbadabba Berman), Bob Hoskins (Owney Mad-den), Fred Gwynne (Frenchy Demange), Gwen Verdon (Tish Dwyer)

p, Robert Evans; d, Francis Ford Coppola; w, William Kennedy, Francis Ford Coppola (based on a story by Kennedy, Coppola, Mario Puzo, inspired by a pictorial history by James Haskins); ph, Stephen Goldblatt (Technicolor); ed, Barry Malkin, Robert Q. Lovett; m, John Barry; prod d, Richard Sylbert; art d, David Chapman, Gregory Bolton; fx, Connie Brink; chor, Michael Smuin, Henry LeTang, Gregory Hines, Claudia Asbury, George Faison, Arthur Mitchell, Michael Meachum; cos, Milena Canonero

Lavish, interesting, evocative but strained and self-conscious, THE COTTON CLUB is all watchable curiosity. Film doctor Coppola came in at the last minute to salvage a troubled production, but couldn't give it a clear storyline with incisive character motivation. This marriage of gangsters and musicals has many elements of genius, but its biggest flaws are its leads. Gere does his own coronet solos, but his hair oil defines his character. Lane, who can only point to LONESOME DOVE in a career full of big chances, walks right through this one, like she's distracted by a flashing traffic light. Hines does what he can without much material to create around, but Hoskins and Gwynne are terrific

gangsters and McKee's rendition of "Ill Wind" is a revelation, defining her own lack of career chances and the ill-fated luck of this production.

The mix of fact and fiction, the show-stopping Ellington music, the heady, poisonous aroma of sinister glamour—COTTON CLUB has much to recommend it before it comes up empty-handed. Yet what success it can muster is discolored by might-have-beens. No doubt a behind-the-scenes documentary would have been wildly successful.

COTTON COMES TO HARLEM

1970   97m   c   ★★★
Crime/Comedy   R/X
UA

Raymond St. Jacques (Coffin Ed Johnson), Godfrey Cambridge (Grave Digger Jones), Calvin Lockhart (Reu Deke O'Malley), Judy Pace (Iris), Redd Foxx (Uncle Budd), John Anderson (Bryce), Emily Yancy (Mabel), J.D. Cannon (Calhoun), Mabel Robinson (Billie), Dick Sabol (Jerema)

p, Samuel Goldwyn, Jr.; d, Ossie Davis; w, Ossie Davis, Arnold Perl (based on a novel by Chester Himes); ph, Gerald Hirschfeld (DeLuxe Color); ed, John Carter, Robert Q. Lovett; m, Galt MacDermot; art d, Manny Gerard; fx, Sol Stern; cos, Anna Hill Johnstone

One of the first of a wave of action comedies, not for delicate tastes. Ossie Davis made his directorial debut in this gaudy blaxploitation crime comedy, filmed on location in Harlem. St. Jacques and Cambridge are, respectively, Coffin Ed Johnson and Grave Digger Jones, a pair of Harlem plainclothesmen investigating a "Back to Africa" campaign run by shady preacher Lockhart. A huge success, it inspired an inferior sequel (COME BACK, CHARLESTON BLUE) as well as a new genre for the 1970s.

COUNSELLOR-AT-LAW

1933   80m   bw   ★★★★★
Drama   /A
UN IV

John Barrymore (George Simon), Bebe Daniels (Regina Gordon), Doris Kenyon (Cora Simon), Onslow Stevens (John P. Tedesco), Isabel Jewell (Bessie Green), Melvyn Douglas (Roy Darwin), Thelma Todd (Lillian La Rue), Marvin Kline (Weinberg), Conway Washburne (Sandler), John Qualen (Breitstein)

p, Carl Laemmle, Jr.; d, William Wyler; w, Elmer Rice (based on his play); ph, Norbert Brodine; ed, Daniel Mandell

A monument to acting and direction at peak form. John Barrymore gives one of his finest performances as a Jewish lawyer who works his way to the top of his profession only to have his gentile wife, Doris Kenyon, leave him. Barrymore was the second choice to play the role after Paul Muni, who had played the role on stage but feared being typecast. The film is superbly directed by William Wyler, who discarded a musical score, having music only at the opening and closing credits, so that the dramatic weight fell upon the crisp dialogue and Barrymore's spellbinding delivery.

The film was made at breakneck speed, with lines delivered in the rapid-fire manner that was then popular in the new talkies. Wyler offered a new brand of filmic realism where he kept his cameras inside the lawyer's offices almost through the first reel, jump-cutting from one office to another but focusing on Barrymore and his nerve-center desk, providing urgency and high drama at an electrifying pace. Today the lightning still crackles through this masterful film.

COUNT OF MONTE CRISTO, THE
1934   113m   bw   ★★★★
Adventure
Reliance

Robert Donat (Edmond Dantes), Elissa Landi (Mercedes), Louis Calhern (De Villefort, Jr.), Sidney Blackmer (Mondego), Raymond Walburn (Danglars), O.P. Heggie (Abbe Foria), William Farnum (Capt. Leclere), Georgia Caine (Mme. De Rosas), Walter Walker (Morrel), Lawrence Grant (De Villefort, Sr.)

p, Edward Small; d, Rowland V. Lee; w, Philip Dunne, Dan Totheroh, Rowland V. Lee (based on the novel by Alexandre Dumas); ph, Peverell Marley; ed, Grant Whytock; m, Alfred Newman

The oft-told tale by Alexandre Dumas *pere* was never better served than in this Edward Small production, with Robert Donat giving one of his finest performances. He is the wronged man, sailor Edmond Dantes, who has just received a promotion and is about to marry the beautiful Mercedes (Elissa Landi) when he is framed and imprisoned in the terrible sea-locked Chateau d'If, where he languishes for years. While wasting away in captivity, he meets an imprisoned clergyman (O.P. Heggie) who tells him of a fabulous pirate treasure hidden on the island of Monte Cristo. From that moment on Edmond works to escape from the prison and travel to Monte Cristo, where he will establish a new identity and wreak vengeance on those who imprisoned him.

Donat is captivating as the good-hearted victim and the cool seeker of justice, measuring his vengeance with subtle moves and slow deliberation. Producer Small spared no expense in this lavish, technically top-notch production and director Rowland V. Lee, who aided in the adaptation, lends his usual flair for high drama and action.

COUNTRY
1984   105m   c   ★★★½
Drama   PG
Buena Vista

Jessica Lange (Jewell Ivy), Sam Shepard (Gil Ivy), Wilford Brimley (Otis), Matt Clark (Tom McMullen), Therese Graham (Marlene Ivy), Levi L. Knebel (Carlisle Ivy), Jim Haynie (Arlon Brewer), Sandra Seacat (Louise Brewer), Alex Harvey (Fordyce), Stephanie-Stacie Poyner (Missy Ivy)

p, William D. Wittliff, Jessica Lange, William Beaudine, Jr.; d, Richard Pearce; w, William D. Wittliff; ph, David M. Walsh, Roger Shearman (Technicolor); ed, Bill Yahraus; m, Charles Gross; prod d, Ron Hobbs; art d, John B. Mansbridge; cos, Tommy Welsh, Rita Salazar

Lange takes the reins as co-producer and tower of matriarchal strength in a terrific movie. COUNTRY details the plight of the 1980s farmer, presenting an Iowan family that stands up to a faceless government bureaucracy that threatens their land. Effective performances and a strong message make this project seem more like a PBS documentary than a staged, rehearsed production—the supreme compliment. Lange received an Academy Award for Best Actress in a year when almost everyone—Lange, Spacek, Field—was on a back-to-the-earth kick.

COUNTRY GIRL, THE
1954   104m   bw   ★★★½
Drama   /A
Paramount

Bing Crosby (Frank Elgin), Grace Kelly (Georgie Elgin), William Holden (Bernie Dodd), Anthony Ross (Phil Cook), Gene Reynolds (Larry), Jacqueline Fontaine (Singer), Eddie Ryder (Ed), Robert Kent (Paul Unger), John W. Reynolds (Henry Johnson), Frank Scannell (Bartender)

p, William Perlberg, George Seaton; d, George Seaton; w, George Seaton (based on the play by Clifford Odets); ph, John F. Warren; ed, Ellsworth Hoagland; m, Victor Young; art d, Hal Pereira, Roland Anderson; fx, John P. Fulton; chor, Robert Alton; cos, Edith Head

Early examination of co-dependency in alcoholic marriages. Adequate in a vague sort of way, which is our way of breaking the news that it's been overrated for a long time. Crosby is a supposedly down-at-the-heels entertainer, trying to keep his comeback up and his compulsive drinking down. Although the dapper Crosby doesn't seem desperate enough, his sober, genial side works to capture the doormat side of the active alcoholic. And given the dark side of Crosby that has been documented by now, we're willing to say he's worth a look; there had to be a lot of fury and tears to sustain a career built on being easy-going.

Kelly, despite the sensible shoes and lack of make-up, is still just too lovely and too reserved to play the gritty wife whose neurotic dependence on her souse husband is as strong as his is on her. She lacks the ability to suggest the complicated levels of a very complicated relationship, and she's totally lacking in passion besides. Odets's character is much more poignant cast against beauty, making her looks almost a dream in the alcoholic's mind. We can imagine maybe a Dorothy Malone, an Eleanor Parker or a Vera Miles pulling it off; we'd be more inclined to say Shelley Winters, Barbara Bel Geddes, or Kim Stanley. But not Princess Grace.

COUNTRY GIRL has a nice backstage feel and Holden gives a strong perfomance as does Anthony Ross, but the film is directed unevenly by Seaton, as if he thought the material was strong enough to do the work by itself.

COUP DE TORCHON
1981   128m   c   ★★★½
Crime   /AA
La Tour/Little Bear/A2   (France)

Philippe Noiret (Lucien Cordier), Isabelle Huppert (Rose), Jean-Pierre Marielle (Le Peron/His Brother), Stephane Audran (Hughuette Cordier), Eddy Mitchell (Nono), Guy Marchand (Chavasson), Irene Skobline (Anne), Michel Beaune (Vanderbrouck), Jean Champion (Priest), Victor Garrivier (Mercaillou)

p, Adolphe Viezzi, Henri Lassa; d, Bertrand Tavernier; w, Bertrand Tavernier, Jean Aurenche (based on the novel Pop. 1280 by Jim Thompson); ph, Pierre-William Glenn; ed, Armand Psenny; m, Philippe Sarde; prod d, Alexander Trauner; cos, Jacqueline Laurent

Stylish, twisted black comedy moves setting from the American South of Jim Thompson's pulp novel in 1938 Africa. There, Noiret is the police chief, a likable, bleary-eyed slob treated like dirt by most everyone he meets. Policing the town with anything but an iron fist, he prefers to turn a blind eye to vice and corruption. Then, having one day decided he's taken enough abuse, Lucien starts killing anyone who crosses him.

Relying only slightly on a narrative drive, this lengthy film concentrates instead on the creation of a character and his environment. Noiret is an excellent choice in the role, providing a perfect balance between the dangerous and the charming, the moral and the amoral, the killer and the victim. The presence of Isabelle Huppert, as his scruffy but alluring mistress, is an added bonus. Although his films vary radically from one to the next, director Bertrand Tavernier continues to walk the path of France's realist tradition. Check it out.

COURT JESTER, THE

1956   101m   c   ★★★
Adventure/Comedy   /U
Paramount

Danny Kaye (Hawkins), Glynis Johns (Maid Jean), Basil Rathbone (Sir Ravenhurst), Angela Lansbury (Princess Gwendolyn), Cecil Parker (King Roderick), Mildred Natwick (Griselda), Robert Middleton (Sir Griswold), Michael Pate (Sir Locksley), Herbert Rudley (Captain of the Guard), Noel Drayton (Fergus)

p, Norman Panama, Melvin Frank; d, Norman Panama, Melvin Frank; w, Norman Panama, Melvin Frank; ph, Ray June (VistaVision, Technicolor); ed, Tom McAdoo; m, Vic Schoen; chor, James Starbuck; cos, Edith Head, Yvonne Wood

A flawlessly executed, beautifully designed genre parody. Danny Kaye, in his best film, stars as a lowly valet who rises to become the leader of a peasant rebellion aimed at restoring the rightful heir to the throne of England. He disguises himself as a court jester to gain access to evil baron Rathbone, the real power behind the throne, and overthrow his oppressive rule. Genius cast handles the laughs with dash and aplomb, but the real surprise is Rathbone, whose charmingly villainous manner and comedic timing provide the perfect foil for Kaye's antics.

COURT MARTIAL OF BILLY MITCHELL, THE

1955   100m   c   ★★★
Biography/War
United States

Gary Cooper (Gen. Billy Mitchell), Charles Bickford (Gen. Guthrie), Ralph Bellamy (Congressman Frank Reid), Rod Steiger (Maj. Allan Guillion), Elizabeth Montgomery (Margaret Lansdowne), Fred Clark (Col. Moreland), James Daly (Col. Herbert White), Jack Lord (Cmdr. Zachary Lansdowne), Peter Graves (Capt. Elliott), Darren McGavin (Russ Peters)

p, Milton Sperling; d, Otto Preminger; w, Milton Sperling, Emmett Lavery (based on the story by Milton Sperling, Emmett Lavery); ph, Sam Leavitt (CinemaScope, WarnerColor); ed, Folmar Blangsted; m, Dimitri Tiomkin; art d, Malcolm Bert; fx, H.F. Koenekamp; cos, Howard Shoup

Yup, low-key and earnest but slow like molasses. Courtroom drama features Coop as the visionary and much-maligned Billy Mitchell who, in 1925, was placed on secret military trial for accusing the Army of being unprepared for invasion and predicting a US bombing by the Japanese. There's not much action aside from the courtroom antics, but the Oscar-nominated Milton Sperling-Emmet Lavery screenplay and the powerful and dignified performance of Cooper might hold you until Steiger's late entrance as a hateful prosecutor sparks proceedings. The many real-life figures—General Douglas MacArthur, Fiorello La Guardia, Admiral William S. Sims, Major Carl Spaatz, President Calvin Coolidge, Major Hap Arnold, General John J. Pershing—

are portrayed as walking monuments. Curiously, the film was photographed in CinemaScope, presumably to make the static visuals somehow more cinematic.

COURTSHIP OF EDDY'S FATHER, THE

1963   118m   c   ★★★
Comedy/Drama   /U
MGM

Glenn Ford (Tom Corbett), Shirley Jones (Elizabeth Marten), Stella Stevens (Dollye Daly), Dina Merrill (Rita Behrens), Roberta Sherwood (Mrs. Livingston), Ron Howard (Eddie), Jerry Van Dyke (Norman Jones)

p, Joe Pasternak; d, Vincente Minnelli; w, John Gay (based on the novel by Mark Toby); ph, Milton Krasner (Metrocolor); ed, Adrienne Fazan; m, George Stoll; art d, George W. Davis, Urie McCleary; fx, Robert R. Hoag; cos, Helen Rose

Sticky biz. Story of widower Ford, whose romantic life is controlled by Howard, pretty adorable in the title role. Women are attracted to the handsome widower, but all must pass muster with six-year-old Eddie, who has some very definite ideas on what kind of woman he might want his dad to marry. Sexist kid judges women by their eyes and busts and doesn't much like his pop's beloved Merrill who, he thinks, has "skinny eyes"; he would prefer that dad get together with neighbor Jones. Where's Jayne Mansfield when we need her?

COUSIN, COUSINE

1976   95m   c   ★★★
Comedy   R/AA
Pomereu/Gaumont   (France)

Marie-Christine Barrault (Marthe), Victor Lanoux (Ludovic), Marie-France Pisier (Karine), Guy Marchand (Pascal), Ginette Garcin (Biju), Sybil Maas (Diane), Jean Herbert (Sacy), Pierre Plessis (Gobert), Catherine Verlor (Nelsa), Hubert Gignoux (Thomas)

p, Bertrand Javal; d, Jean-Charles Tacchella; w, Jean-Charles Tacchella, Daniele Thompson; ph, Georges Lendi (Eastmancolor); ed, Agnes Guillemot; m, Gerard Anfosso; cos, Jeannine Vergne

Pleasant diversion, but not brave enough to push into full-fledged farce. A surprising popular success in the US, the film is what is often mistakenly described as "quintessentially French," perhaps because it has so much that one associates with Gallicism (frank sexuality and matter-of-fact adultery, pretty countrysides and city cafes) and that many Americans fondly consider charming.

Two families gather to celebrate their aging parents' marriage. During the festivities, Barrault and Lanoux, cousins by marriage, become friendly and agree to see each other more often. As both are sensible, intelligent, married people, they keep emotions in check, determined to keep their relationship platonic. Soon their spouses are assuming the worst, and inevitably the worst happens.

Much of the film's success comes from the excellent rapport between Barrault and Lanoux in a thoroughly convincing portrayal of the hesitant lovers. Tacchella, however, undermines his film by directing the scenes of bourgeois scandal as acceptably as possible, thereby creating the sort of "art film" guaranteed to offend no one.

COUSINS, THE

(LES COUSINS)
1959   112m   bw   ★★★★
Drama   /X
Ajym   (France)

Gerard Blain (Charles), Jean-Claude Brialy (Paul), Juliette Mayniel (Florence), Claude Cerval (Clovis), Genevieve Cluny (Genevieve), Michele Meritz (Yvonne), Corrado Guarducci (Italian Count), Guy Decombie (Librarian)

p, Claude Chabrol; d, Claude Chabrol; w, Claude Chabrol, Paul Gegauff; ph, Henri Decae; m, Paul Misraki

Harrowing peer rivalry in the name of love. Claude Chabrol's second feature deals with the contrast between two cousins studying law in Paris. Blain is the country bumpkin at odds with the decadent, city-bred Brialy. They compete for the same girl, and in the end Blain destroys Brialy. A major film of the French New Wave that provides a grim, clear-eyed look at the cynicism of youth, this is not to be missed.

COVER GIRL
1944 105m c   ★★★★
Musical/Comedy   /18
Columbia

Rita Hayworth (Rusty Parker/Maribelle Hicks), Gene Kelly (Danny McGuire), Lee Bowman (Noel Wheaton), Phil Silvers (Genius), Jinx Falkenburg (Jinx), Leslie Brooks (Maurine Martin), Eve Arden (Cornelia Jackson), Otto Kruger (John Coudair), Jess Barker (Coudair as a Young Man), Anita Colby (Anita)

p, Arthur Schwartz; d, Charles Vidor; w, Virginia Van Upp, Marion Parsonnet, Paul Gangelin (based on a story by Erwin Gelsey); ph, Rudolph Mate, Allen Davey (Technicolor); ed, Viola Lawrence; m, Carmen Dragon; art d, Lionel Banks, Cary Odell; chor, Val Raset, Seymour Felix, Gene Kelly, Stanley Donen; cos, Travis Banton, Gwen Wakeling, Muriel King, Kenneth Hopkins

Triumph of style over substance, Hayworth over all. Charming musical built on a skimpy plot but boasting a score by Jerome Kern and Ira Gershwin that includes some of their best work, notably "Long Ago and Far Away," which even Kelly's reedy pipes couldn't ruin. Kelly saves the best dance for himself, the "Alter Ego" number which is really two dances filmed separately and synchronized together. The other stand-out number is "Make Way for Tomorrow," a roughhouse morning-after number danced by Kelly, Hayworth, and Silvers. COVER GIRL's plot has Hayworth moving from a Brooklyn chorus to become top magazine model, predictable conflict of ambition vs. love. The editorial offices, based on a combination of Conde Nast and Harry Conover (whose beautiful models are seen in the film), lend a 40s-elan and sheen to the film, and the addition of the wise-cracking, always welcome, Eve Arden.

This would be the peak of sweetheart roles for Hayworth, before her shift into dangerous siren territory, and her sumptuous Technicolor candybox beauty was the apotheosis of her era's ideal. She never sang in her musicals—here she is dubbed by Martha Mears—but she danced in an expressive way more akin to acting than athletics. Her passive personality made her a partner equally at home with Astaire (who named her his favorite partner in his autobiography) or Kelly. She was more of an actress than Cyd Charisse, more elegant in her sensuality, less a traditional tap and ballroom dancer than Ginger Rogers. The sense of longing and abandonment Hayworth brings to her character in COVER GIRL helps her to transcend the formulaic plot; when she dances, it's the only time she looks happy. The film also remains notable as one of the first movie musicals to incorporate its musical numbers into the storyline.

CRAIG'S WIFE
1936 73m bw   ★★★★
Drama   /A
Columbia

Rosalind Russell (Harriet Craig), John Boles (Walter Craig), Billie Burke (Mrs. Frazier), Jane Darwell (Mrs. Harold), Dorothy Wilson (Ethel Landreth), Alma Kruger (Miss Austen), Thomas Mitchell (Fergus Passmore), Raymond Walburn (Billy Birkmire), Robert Allen (Gene Fredericks), Elisabeth Risdon (Mrs. Landreth)

p, Edward Chodorov; d, Dorothy Arzner; w, Mary C. McCall, Jr. (based on a play by George Kelly); ph, Lucien Ballard; ed, Viola Lawrence

Russell's first step to the bigtime. Obsessive bitch cares more about her spotless museum home than the love of her husband. Roz was only 28 when she undertook the role but her imperious manner, deep voice and matronly looks added a weightiness to the interpretation. George Kelly's Pulitzer Prize-winning play had been made as a silent in 1928 with Warner Baxter as Craig and Irene Rich as the shrew. Harry Cohn wisely handed over the adaptation chores to Mary McCall who added an Oedipal touch (Kelly objected) to the husband-wife relationship. Dorothy Arzner was given direction chores; therefore the project has a feminist feel that is rare in old Hollywood. Russell's big chance is enhanced by Boles, Burke, Darwell, and Westman, and the production team breathes life into what threatened to remain a stagebound work. In 1950, Joan Crawford would take the role she had been playing most of her life, in HARRIET CRAIG.

CRANES ARE FLYING, THE
(LETYAT ZHURAVLI)
1957 97m bw   ★★★★
Romance/War   /U
Mosfilm (U.S.S.R.)

Tatyana Samoilova (Veronica), Alexei Batalov (Boris), Vasiliy Merkuryev (Fyodor Ivanovich), Alexander Shvorin (Mark), Svetlana Kharitonova (Irina), Konstantin Niktin (Volodya), Valentin Zubkov (Stepan), Anno Bogdanova (Grandmother), B. Kokobkin (Tyernov), E. Kupriyanova (Anna Mikhailovna)

p, Mikhail Kalatozov; d, Mikhail Kalatozov; w, Viktor Rozov (based on his play); ph, Sergei Urusevsky; ed, M. Timofeyeva; m, Moisei Vaynberg

Generally free of the party line one usually associates with Soviet films of its period, THE CRANES ARE FLYING is an antiwar love story, set during WWII, which centers on the romance between pretty young Samoilova and sensitive factory worker Batalov. Boris, like hordes of other patriotic Soviet men, marches off to war, leaving behind the woman he loves. She is eventually told of his death, but refuses to accept the horrible news. Finally, however, she resigns herself to a loveless marriage with Boris's draft-dodger brother, Merkuryev, despite the fact that he raped her during an air raid and although she still loves Boris.

The film gained international attention and was one of the first postwar Soviet features to be seen in the West. A beautiful performance is given by the gorgeous Samoilova, the great-niece of Stanislavsky and daughter of an actor father, Yevgeni Samoilov. The Cannes Film Festival awarded Samoilova the Golden Palm for her electrifying performance, and named the film as Best Picture.

CREEPSHOW

1982   129m   c   ★★
Horror   R/15
Alpha

Hal Holbrook (Henry), Adrienne Barbeau (Wilma), Fritz Weaver (Dexter), Leslie Nielsen (Richard), Carrie Nye (Sylvia), E.G. Marshall (Upson), Viveca Lindfors (Aunt Bedelia), Ed Harris (Hank), Ted Danson (Harry), Stephen King (Jordy)

p, Richard P. Rubinstein; d, George Romero; w, Stephen King; ph, Michael Gornick (Technicolor); ed, Michael Spolan, Pasquale Buba, George Romero, Paul Hirsch; m, John Harrison; prod d, Cletus Anderson; fx, Tom Savini; cos, Barbara Anderson

This collaboration between director George Romero and horror novelist Stephen King is a loving tribute to the E.C. comic books of the 1950s. Unfortunately, it never quite gels. The film starts off on a stormy night with an angry father's discovery that his son has been reading an E.C. comic book, He throws the book into the street, where the wind opens it to the first of five vignettes, a tale about a long-buried corpse that returns on his birthday to wreak havoc.

Each vignette features a cast full of recognizable actors who play the material in an appropriately broad manner. Stylistically, Romero attempts to duplicate the look of an E.C. comic book and relies heavily on exaggerated lighting schemes and angles; however, the trick simply doesn't work, and the film looks hamhanded and juvenile. Moreover, King's stories are nothing special, and with the exception of the final entry, nothing in the film is particulary scary.

Romero is capable of much better, but ironically, CREEPSHOW was his biggest box-office hit The sequel, CREEPSHOW 2, in which Romero adapted more King stories with the directorial chores handed over to CREEPSHOW cinematographer Michael Gornick, is even worse.

CRIA!

1975   110m   c   ★★★★
Drama   /AA
Querejeta   (Spain)

Geraldine Chaplin (Ana as an Adult/Her Mother Maria), Ana Torrent (Ana as a Child), Conchita Perez (Irene), Maite Sanchez (Juana), Monica Randall (Paulina), Florinda Chico (Rosa), Hector Alterio (Anselmo), German Cobos (Nicolas Garontes), Mirta Miller (Amelia Garontes), Josefina Diaz (Abuela)

p, Carlos Saura; d, Carlos Saura; w, Carlos Saura; ph, Teo Escamilla; ed, Pablo del Amo; m, Federico Mompoll

A quietly haunting family album, CRIA! follows an upper-class Spanish family, specifically a young child, during the years following the Spanish Civil War. As the film opens, nine-year-old Ana (Ana Torrent) comes downstairs in her nightgown, awakened by the sounds of her father (Hector Alterio) making love. Behind his closed door, he gasps for breath and dies. Hurriedly leaving his room is Amelia (Mirta Miller), the wife of his best friend. This is the second death for Ana, her mother, Maria (Geraldine Chaplin), having died a few years earlier. Maria, however, has not left Ana's imagination and continues in this manner to return to her daughter's side, enabling the young girl to resist the attempts of her friendly but stern aunt Paulina (Monica Randall) to raise her and her sisters.

A mesmerizing tale, CRIA! brilliantly weaves the tapestry of time—past and present—into a perfect blend of history. Rather than separate the past from the present, director Carlos Saura layers the two on top of one another. Characters who have died rejoin the living; others, like Ana, exist in any number of generations. Ana is seen not only as a young girl (the brilliant Torrent) and as an adult (Chaplin), but also in the form of Maria (again Chaplin)—all of whom share the same time and space in the film. A remarkable achievement, which both examines the textures of a once-patriarchal family life and draws a parallel to the end of the Franco regime.

CRIES AND WHISPERS

(VISKNINGAR OCH ROP)
1972   95m   c   ★★★★½
Drama   R/X
Cinematograph/Swedish Film Institute   (Sweden)

Ingrid Thulin (Karin), Liv Ullmann (Maria/Her Mother), Harriet Andersson (Agnes), Kari Sylwan (Anna), Erland Josephson (Doctor), Georg Arlin (Fredrik, Karin's Husband), Henning Moritzen (Joakin, Maria's Husband), Anders Ek (Pastor), Linn Ullmann (Maria's Daughter), Rosanna Mariano (Agnes as a Child)

p, Ingmar Bergman; d, Ingmar Bergman; w, Ingmar Bergman; ph, Sven Nykvist (Eastmancolor); ed, Siv Lundgren; m, Frederic Chopin, Johann Sebastian Bach; art d, Marik Vos; cos, Greta Johansson

Relentlessly discursive and somber, also hauntingly elliptical and exquisitely crafted. CRIES examines three sisters, one of whom is dying, and the robust family retainer who cares for them. Bergman uses the four women as metaphors for humanity, respresenting how we respond to anxiety, death, and the visitations of what appears to be a wrathful rather than benevolent God.

Thulin (the standout in an ensemble of breathtaking performances) is on the brink of suicide and, we learn, once mutilated her own genitalia rather than honor her marital vows. The earthy Ullman (never more beautiful) once had an affair over which her husband attempted suicide. Sylwan is the glue that holds these Chekhovian sisters together. She can accept God's will and imparts her fatalistic viewpoint to the dying Andersson (Agnes). The former lost a child early in life and has come to terms with death—neither hard nor bad, just a new voyage. Andersson, in terrible pain, cannot fully accept this view; still, she is much closer to the housekeeper than she is to her sisters.

There are many moments in the film during which nothing is said, and the silence is more eloquent than any words might have been. Nonetheless, sound plays a huge role in the movie, as Bergman uses ticking clocks, rustling dresses, sighs, cries and whispers to make his points. Bergman and cinematographer Sven Nykvist move the camera with remarkable fluidity, the beauty of their visuals contrasting pointedly with the almost unbearably stark subject matter.

CRIME OF MONSIEUR LANGE, THE

(LE CRIME DE M. LANGE)
1936   90m   bw   ★★★★
Comedy/Drama   /PG
Oberon   (France)

Rene Lefevre (Mons. Amedee Lange), Odette Florelle (Valentine), Henri Guisol (Meunier), Marcel Levesque (Bessard, the Concierge), Odette Talazac (Mme. Bessard), Maurice Baquet (Charles Bessard, their Son), Nadia Sibirskaia (Estelle), Jules Berry (Batala), Sylvia Bataille (Edith), Marcel Duhamel

p, Andre Halley des Fontaines; d, Jean Renoir; w, Jean Castanier, Jean Renoir, Jacques Prevert (based on a story by Jean Castanier and Jean Renoir); ph, Jean Bachelet; ed, Marguerite Renoir; m, Jean Wiener; art d, Marcel Blondeau

A clever Renoir film, with a decidedly anti-capitalist message. Lefevre is a meek author of French novels about the American West whose avaricious boss, Berry, cheats him out of his earnings. Berry embezzles the company funds, flees, and is later reported dead in a train wreck. The employees of the publishing house are overjoyed and form a cooperative that achieves great success with Lefevre's "Arizona Jim" series. He falls in love with a woman from a neighboring laundry, but then Berry returns (he survived the wreck and took the clothes of a priest) and demands a share in the company's newfound prosperity. Should Lefevre kill the villain? One of Jean Renoir's best films, THE CRIME OF MONSIEUR LANGE is also one of the most obvious examples of his Front Populaire period of filmmaking—reflecting the social politics of its day and the belief that a collective could effectively overthrow a tyranny. This wonderfully entertaining and sharply scripted film is hampered by its poor sound quality, a result of Renoir's meager production budget.

CRIME WITHOUT PASSION

1934 70m bw   ★★★★
Crime   /A
Paramount

Claude Rains (Lee Gentry), Margo (Carmen Brown), Whitney Bourne (Katy Costello), Stanley Ridges (Eddie White), Paula Trueman (Buster Malloy), Leslie Adams (O'Brien), Greta Granstedt (Della), Esther Dale (Miss Keeley), Charles Kennedy (Lt. Norton), Fuller Mellish (Judge)

p, Ben Hecht, Charles MacArthur; d, Ben Hecht, Charles MacArthur; w, Ben Hecht, Charles MacArthur; ph, Lee Garmes; fx, Slavko Vorkapich

Loosely based on the career of New York City criminal lawyer William J. Fallon, the great "mouthpiece" of the 1920s, this strange drama was the product of Ben Hecht and Charles MacArthur, with Claude Rains as the suave, ever-confident legal wizard. The film opens with Rains successfully defending a killer by snatching up and drinking "Exhibit A," a vial containing poison, and then having his stomach pumped during a recess. Rains attempts to dump Margo, a jealous honky-tonk singer, for hot blonde Whitney Bourne, but Margo inveigles him into shooting her. Thinking her dead, he prepares an elaborate alibi which involves the killing of another man. Margo survives to haunt him in court, and the real killing is finally laid at his door in a surprise ending.

Hecht and MacArthur directed this minor masterpiece and used imaginative techniques in almost every frame. They even appear before the cameras as newsmen interviewing Rains after a legal victory. Fanny Brice and Helen Hayes, MacArthur's wife, appear briefly in a hotel lobby scene. Hayes looks almost directly into the camera which provides a Rains-eye-view as he hurries about establishing an alibi. The opening and closing credits for this film show three female "Furies" darting through the canyons of New York, randomly selecting their victims—those whom they will make mad and upon whom they will visit their evils—a marvelous bit of special effects constructed by Slavko Vorkapich.

CRIMES AND MISDEMEANORS

1989 107m C   ★★★½
Drama   PG-13/15
Orion

Caroline Aaron (Barbara), {{Alan Alda (Lester), Woody Allen (Cliff Stern), Claire Bloom (Miriam Rosenthal), Mia Farrow (Halley Reed), Joanna Gleason (Wendy Stern), Anjelica Huston (Dolores Paley), Martin Landau (Judah Rosenthal), Jenny Nichols (Jenny), Jerry Orbach (Jack Rosenthal)

p, Robert Greenhut; d, Woody Allen; w, Woody Allen; ph, Sven Nykvist (DuArt Color); ed, Susan E. Morse; prod d, Santo Loquasto; art d, Speed Hopkins; cos, Jeffrey Kurland

Woody Allen tackles morality and murder in CRIMES AND MISDEMEANORS, starring Martin Landau as Judah Rosenthal, an ophthalmologist esteemed by family, friends and colleagues. Judah has a less admirable secret life: his mistress, Dolores (Anjelica Huston), is determined to reveal their affair to his wife (Claire Bloom), and threatens to expose his past embezzling. Judah decides he has no choice but to have her killed, helped by his underworld-connected brother (Jerry Orbach). Allen also introduces a humorous story line involving a politically committed documentary filmmaker, Cliff Stern (Allen), his egotistical commercial TV director brother-in-law (Alan Alda), and a TV producer (Mia Farrow) with whom Cliff falls in love. Only in the film's dark final scene do Judah and Cliff finally meet, both struggling with their ideas of right and wrong, morality and immorality, crimes and misdemeanors.

Allen is an auteur who often defines his artistic vision in reference to those of other filmmakers, and it becomes increasingly difficult for educated viewers to take his creative borrowings on good faith. In one scene here he restages a sequence from Ingmar Bergman's WILD STRAWBERRIES nearly shot-for-shot, a dubious act of homage. Nevertheless Allen's expertise is evident everywhere in CRIMES AND MISDEMEANORS, with its fine ensemble acting (Alda and Huston are outstanding), evocative composition and design, intelligent writing, and spritely musical score.

CRIMSON PIRATE, THE

1952 104m c   ★★★½
Adventure/Comedy   /U
WB (U.K.)

Burt Lancaster (Vallo), Nick Cravat (Ojo), Eva Bartok (Consuelo), Torin Thatcher (Humble Bellows), James Hayter (Prudence), Leslie Bradley (Baron Gruda), Margot Grahame (Bianca), Noel Purcell (Pablo Murphy), Frederick Leister (El Libre), Eliot Makeham (Governor)

p, Harold Hecht; d, Robert Siodmak; w, Roland Kibbee; ph, Otto Heller (Technicolor); ed, Jack Harris; m, William Alwyn

Jolly good show. The best pirate send-up ever made. Plethora of swordplay and acrobatics, and many flashes of Lancaster's incisors and muscles. Filmed in England and Spain, the picture feels as though it may have begun with the idea of doing a straight seafaring movie, but somewhere along the way they all started to enjoy themselves so much that they altered their course a few degrees and came up with a comedy that has gained a cult following.

"CROCODILE" DUNDEE

1986 102m c   ★★★½
Comedy   PG-13/15
Rimfire (Australia)

Paul Hogan (Michael J. "Crocodile" Dundee), Linda Kozlowski (Sue Charlton), John Meillon (Wally Reilly), Mark Blum (Richard Mason), Michael Lombard (Sam Charlton), David Gulpilil (Neville Bell), Irving Metzman (Doorman), Graham Walker (Bellhop), Maggie Blinco (Ida), Steve Rackman (Donk)

p, John Cornell; d, Peter Faiman; w, Paul Hogan, Ken Shadie, John Cornell (based on a story by Paul Hogan); ph, Russell Boyd (Kodakcolor); ed, David Stiven; m, Peter Best; prod d, Graham Walker

Paul Hogan became an Australian phenomenon whose fame spread worldwide with this amiable, good-natured and often very funny movie. Crocodile hunter shows pretty reporter around Bush Country and then she shows him around equally alien New York City. The film's fish-out-of-water story line is a film comedy standard; what makes the picture work so well is Hogan's cheerful, weatherbeaten appeal.

CROSS CREEK
1983 127m c   ★★
Drama   PG/U
Universal

Mary Steenburgen (Marjorie Kinnan Rawlings), Rip Torn (Marsh Turner), Peter Coyote (Norton Baskin), Dana Hill (Ellie Turner), Alfre Woodard (Geechee), Joanna Miles (Mrs. Turner), Ike Eisenmann (Paul), Cary Guffey (Floyd Turner), Toni Hudson (Tim's Wife), Bo Rucker (Leroy)

p, Robert B. Radnitz; d, Martin Ritt; w, Dalene Young (based on the book Cross Creek by Marjorie Kinnan Rawlings); ph, John A. Alonzo (Technicolor); ed, Sidney Levin; m, Leonard Rosenman; prod d, Walter Scott Herndon; cos, Joe I. Tompkins

Marjorie Kinnan Rawlings's memoirs of a stay in the backwoods of Florida during the 1930s provide the loose basis of this film. Mary Steenburgen plays the author of The Yearling, isolating herself in the wilderness to observe the locals and renew herself creatively. It's all very pretty and pasteurized, though Rip Torn does a decent job, chewing up the scenery as redneck March Turner. Steenburgen's real-life husband, Malcolm McDowell, plays famed book editor Maxwell Perkins in a brief part. Alas, this uninspired, perfunctory literary biography is not saved by its handsome visuals.

CROSS OF IRON
1977 133m c   ★★★
War   R/18
Avco Embassy   (U.K./West Germany)

James Coburn (Steiner), Maximilian Schell (Stransky), James Mason (Brandt), David Warner (Kiesel), Klaus Lowitsch (Kruger), Vadim Glowna (Kem), Roger Fritz (Triebig), Dieter Schidor (Anselm), Burkhardt Driest (Maag), Fred Stillkraut (Schnurrbart)

p, Wolfgang Hartwig; d, Sam Peckinpah; w, Walter Kelley, James Hamilton, Julius J. Epstein (based on the book Cross of Iron by Willi Heinrich); ph, John Coquillon (Technicolor); ed, Michael Ellis, Tony Lawson, Herbert Taschner; m, Ernest Gold; fx, Richard Richtsfeld

Bleak, unpleasant, and ugly look at men in combat that was almost universally panned by the mainstream press upon its initial release. Its complex and vivid portrayal of the absurdity of war, however, prompted none other than Orson Welles to write Peckinpah and proclaim it the finest antiwar film he had ever seen. Based on a celebrated novel by German author Willi Heinrich, the film is set at the Russian front circa 1943, as the Germans are retreating before the Soviet army. We follow corporal Coburn (in what may be his best performance), a German soldier—not a Nazi—who "hates this uniform and everything it stands for." Loyal only to his men, a tight-knit group of soldiers fighting for their survival, Coburn finds his nemesis in his new commander, captain Schell—an arrogant, narcissistic Prussian aristocrat who desperately wants to come home with an Iron Cross, Germany's highest honor for bravery, but who is terrified of battle. Since Coburn comes highly recommended by other commanders and has already been awarded the Iron Cross himself, Schell promotes him to sergeant in the hope of winning an ally. After a siege on their compound in which many brave men die while Schell cowers in his bunker, Coburn learns that the captain has filed a false report claiming that he led the counterattack—a deed certain to earn an Iron Cross. When Coburn refuses to confirm Schell's claims (he also resists calling him a liar, which would indicate reverence he considers worthless), Schell plots to dispose of the troublesome sergeant and his men.

CROSS OF IRON, which was plagued with production problems (producer Hartwig ran out of money before the final sequence was filmed) and was cut extensively by its American distributor before its US release, is yet another mutilated Peckinpah film but one that holds up exceedingly well nonetheless (the uncut version was restored for home video). From its opening—a brilliant montage of WWII stock footage intercutting Hitler and his armies with shots of Hitler Youth raising a flag on a mountain while a chorus of German children sing—to its bizarre, almost surreal climax, CROSS OF IRON is anything but a standard WWII movie, especially compared to its mythicizing contemporaries. Shot superbly by cinematographer Coquillon, the film shows war as hideously brutal, inglorious, and insane. With its focus on the corruption of moral values and the betrayal of the innocence of children, CROSS OF IRON is an angry film that ends with a bitter quote from Bertolt Brecht: "Do not rejoice in his defeat you men. For though the world has stood up and stopped the bastard, the bitch that bore him is in heat again."

CROSSFIRE
1947 86m bw   ★★★★
Crime   /PG
RKO

Robert Young (Finlay), Robert Mitchum (Keeley), Robert Ryan (Montgomery), Gloria Grahame (Ginny), Paul Kelly (The Man), Sam Levene (Joseph Samuels), Jacqueline White (Mary Mitchell), Steve Brodie (Floyd), George Cooper (Mitchell), Richard Benedict (Bill)

p, Adrian Scott; d, Edward Dmytryk; w, John Paxton (based on the novel The Brick Foxhole by Richard Brooks); ph, J. Roy Hunt; ed, Harry Gerstad; m, Roy Webb; art d, Albert S. D'Agostino, Alfred Herman; fx, Russell A. Cully

A classic. Anti-Semitism had been unexplored in Hollywood for decades; no studio wanted to take on this social evil until Fox decided to film GENTLEMAN'S AGREEMENT, but RKO beat Fox to the punch by releasing CROSSFIRE first, and the impact was tremendous. It is a simple and chilling story centering on sadistic bully Ryan, who is about to be mustered out of the Army with three buddies, Brodie, Cooper, and Phipps. In a nightclub, the three meet Levene and his girl friend Grahame, then go with the couple to Levene's apartment, where they drink themselves into near collapse. In a drunken rage Ryan, who seethes with hatred for Jews, beats Levene to death. His friends vaguely recall the incident but vanish so they can't be questioned by authorities.

Young, a pipe-smoking, introspective detective aided by G.I. Mitchum, begins to investigate and lays a trap for the elusive sadist.

All of the performers contribute fine work, particularly Ryan, who is terrifying as the brutish, bigoted killer—a role the actor was determined to play. Ryan had served in the Marine Corps with Richard Brooks, upon whose novel CROSSFIRE is based, and Ryan had told the author that if his book were made into a film, he wanted to play the part of Montgomery. Ironically, Ryan's performance is so convincing that he would long be associated with the vile character he plays here, and he would be repeatedly cast in vicious, mean-spirited roles throughout a distinguished career that included his extraordinary portrayal of a boxer in THE SET-UP.

In the novel the central issue is not race or religion but sex—a homosexual is beaten to death by other Marines. However, in 1947 this subject matter was still taboo, and producer Scott convinced RKO to buy the book on the proviso that anti-Semitism would replace homophobic intolerance. Dore Schary had just taken over the reins at RKO, and this thriller—which grossed $1,270,000 at the box office, a whopping amount in 1947—was his first production. It was also the last film director Dmytryk and producer Scott, long a duo, would co-create for the studio: after CROSSFIRE's completion, both men were brought before HUAC and became enmeshed in the Communist witchhunt.

CROSSING DELANCEY

1988   97m   c   ★★★
Comedy/Romance   PG
WB

Amy Irving (Isabelle "Izzy" Grossman), Reizl Bozyk (Bubbie Kantor), Peter Riegert (Sam Posner), Jeroen Krabbe (Anton Maes), Sylvia Miles (Hannah Mandelbaum), Suzzy Roche (Marilyn), George Martin (Lionel), John Bedford Lloyd (Nick), Claudia Silver (Cecilia Monk), David Pierce (Mark)

p, Michael Nozik; d, Joan Micklin Silver; w, Susan Sandler (based on her play); ph, Theo Van de Sande (Duart Color); ed, Rick Shaine; m, Paul Chihara; prod d, Dan Leigh; cos, Rita Ryack

Set partly in New York's Lower East Side, where director Silver's excellent tale of immigrant Jewish life in the 1890s, HESTER STREET, also took place, this gentle romantic comedy is a fairy tale populated with real people. Irving stars as an attractive, intelligent Jewish woman in her early 30s who works in a classy Midtown bookstore. Although she lives on the Upper West Side, she frequently treks down to her old neighborhood south of Delancey Street to visit her grandmother, Bozyk. Appalled that her treasured granddaughter has not found a husband, Bozyk engages matchmaker Miles to find Irving a husband, and Miles comes up with pickle merchant Reigert. Although Reigert proves to be a good-hearted soul, Irving can't see herself spending her life with a guy who sells pickles, and she rebuffs him. The remainder of the film recounts Reigert's efforts to win her. Guided by director Silver's gentle but sure hand and benefiting from strong performances by the leads, this is a sweet, funny movie that doesn't exploit the sentimentality of its story. Silver has nicely captured Lower East Side Jewish life and the conflict between tradition and change while also offering resonant slice-of-life portraits of New York.

CROSSOVER DREAMS

1985   86m   c   ★★★
Musical
Max Mambru/Crossover

Ruben Blades (Rudy Veloz), Shawn Elliott (Orlando), Elizabeth Pena (Liz Garcia), Virgilio Marti (Chico Rabala), Tom Signorelli (Lou Rose), Frank Robles (Ray Soto), Joel Diamond (Neil Silver), Amanda Barber (Radio DJ), John Hammil (Joe, Liz's Husband), Natalie Gentry (Lawyer)

p, Manuel Arce; d, Leon Ichaso; w, Manuel Arce, Leon Ichaso; ph, Claudio Chea; ed, Gary Karr; m, Mauricio Smith; prod d, Octavio Soler; art d, Richard Karnbach

Panamanian salsa singer Ruben Blades made an impressive acting debut in this clever reworking of the old story of a man who rises to fame, forgets about his old friends, and then hits the skids. Blades and his band struggle to earn a living on New York's less-than-lucrative Latino music circuit, but Blades has "crossover dreams," yearning to make it big in the mainstream. His musical mentor, Virgilio Marti, discourages Blades from abandoning his roots, but after Marti's death Blades comes to the attention of slick producer Joel Diamond, who pays him $15,000 to record a pop single. The song becomes a minor hit, and Blades says adios to his old friends and takes to life in the fast lane in a financed fancy car. As his head swells, Blades even drives away his devoted girlfriend, Elizabeth Pena; then the bottom falls out when the album follow-up to his single bombs.

CROSSOVER DREAMS is a simple but effective tale of a talented individual sucked into the void of a sleazy industry. Though director Leon Ichaso deserves much of the credit for the film's success, the real find here is Blades, whose evocative singing comes as no surprise to salsa fans, but whose excellent dramatic performance led to a number of other screen roles, including his excellent work in THE MILAGRO BEANFIELD WAR.

CRUEL SEA, THE

1953   120m   bw   ★★★★
War   /PG
Ealing   (U.K.)

Jack Hawkins (Capt. Ericson), Donald Sinden (Lockhart), John Stratton (Ferraby), Denholm Elliott (Morrell), Stanley Baker (Bennett), John Warner (Baker), Bruce Seton (Tallow), Liam Redmond (Watts), Virginia McKenna (Julie Hallam), Moira Lister (Elaine Morell)

p, Leslie Norman (for Michael Balcon); d, Charles Frend; w, Eric Ambler (based on the novel by Nicholas Monsarrat); ph, Gordon Dines; ed, Peter Tanner; m, Alan Rawsthorne

THE CRUEL SEA is the tough, often gruesome account of British corvette life on the Atlantic during WWII as seen through the tormented consciousness of Lt. Comdr. Ericson (Jack Hawkins). After losing one ship to a U-boat while protecting a convoy, Ericson's ship, Compass Rose, is itself torpedoed; Ericson and a handful of his men barely survive, adrift on a raft. Given a new command on the frigate Saltash Castle, Ericson is again at the mercy of the "cruel sea" and must face an impossible choice in risking the lives of his men. The film is shot in documentary style, with harsh black-and-white images, and is based on the wartime exploits depicted in author Nicholas Monsarrat's novel, which was adapted by suspense writer Eric Ambler. The supporting cast appear marginally as crew members in the Royal Navy and in brief flashback and furlough sequences. A top-notch film from Britain's Ealing Studios, with Hawkins turning in an intense, fascinating performance.

CRY-BABY

1990 85m c ★★★½
Comedy/Musical PG-13/12
Imagine Entertainment

Johnny Depp (Cry-Baby), Amy Locane (Allison), Susan Tyrrell (Ramona), Polly Bergen (Mrs. Vernon-Williams), Iggy Pop (Belvedere), Ricki Lake (Pepper), Traci Lords (Wanda), Kim McGuire (Hatchet-Face), Darren E. Burrows (Milton), Stephen Mailer (Baldwin)

p, Rachel Talalay; d, John Waters; w, John Waters; ph, David Insley; ed, Janice Hampton; m, Patrick Williams; prod d, Vincent Peranio; art d, Dolores Deluxe; fx, Steve Kirshoff; chor, Lori Eastside; cos, Van Smith

Revel without a cause. Waters is back on his Baltimore home turf in this rock 'n' roll take on star-crossed lovers, caught in the cultural tug-of-war between hipsters and squares. The film is high on energy, color and camera movement and, as usual in Waters's world, everything is styled within an inch of its life, capturing all the fun and fever of the 1950s. But underneath the numerous entertaining cameos, not much is going on, and it shows. The film's terrific first half-hour can't sustain itself. Depp is beautiful, but too diminutive to bring much force to his sexy biker. Locane is well, okay, but she's eclipsed at every turn by the marvelously vulgar Lords, who embraces the genre with the energy and anarchy of the much-missed Divine.

CRY IN THE DARK, A

1988 121m c ★★★★
Docu-drama PG-13/15
Cannon/Cinema Verity

Meryl Streep (Lindy Chamberlain), Sam Neill (Michael Chamberlain), Bruce Myles (Barker), Charles Tingwell (Justice Muirhead), Nick Tate (Charlwood), Neil Fitzpatrick (Phillips), Maurie Fields (Barritt), Lewis Fitz-Gerald (Tipple)

p, Verity Lambert; d, Fred Schepisi; w, Robert Caswell, Fred Schepisi (based on the book Evil Angels by John Bryson); ph, Ian Baker (Panavision); ed, Jill Bilcock; m, Bruce Smeaton; prod d, Wendy Dickson, George Liddle; cos, Bruce Finlayson

A CRY IN THE DARK tells the true story of Australians Michael and Lindy Chamberlain (Sam Neill and Meryl Streep), the Seventh-Day Adventist minister and his wife whose infant disappeared from their tent during a family outing in 1980. In the film the parents contend their baby was dragged off by a dingo, but authorities don't buy that story. Lindy is indicted for the murder of her daughter, and Michael is charged as an accessory to the crime, beginning a tortuous legal process in which Lindy eventually becomes the center of a storm of controversy that dominates Australian news. Although sometimes slow-moving, A CRY IN THE DARK is a poignant family-in-crisis drama aided by spectacular performances from Streep and Neill. It's based on a nonfiction thriller, Evil Angels, written in Lindy's support by a Melbourne barrister who was critical of the prosecution's handling of the case.

CUBA

1979 122m c ★★★½
Adventure/Political/War R/AA
UA

Brooke Adams (Alexandra Pulido), Sean Connery (Maj. Robert Dapes), Jack Weston (Gutman), Hector Elizondo (Ramirez), Denholm Elliott (Skinner), Martin Balsam (Gen. Bello), Chris Sarandon (Juan Pulido), Alejandro Rey (Faustino), Lonette McKee (Therese), Danny De La Paz (Julio)

p, Arlene Sellers, Alex Winitsky; d, Richard Lester; w, Charles Wood; ph, David Watkin (Technicolor); ed, John Victor Smith; m, Patrick Williams; prod d, Gil Parrondo; art d, Dennis Gordon-Orr; cos, Shirley Russell

Intelligent, zany satire of Cuban military dictatorships and revolutions from director Richard Lester and screenwriter Charles Wood, who previously collaborated on a number of projects, including HOW I WON THE WAR and the 1968 CHARGE OF THE LIGHT BRIGADE. Connery is a British mercenary enlisted by the Batista regime to come to Havana and help crush Castro's guerrillas. In addition to encountering various scoundrels—including cynical Batista general Balsam, angry would-be revolutionary De La Paz, and grotesque American businessman Weston—Dapes meets former flame Adams, a Cuban tobacco factory manager with a philandering husband (Chris Sarandon). As the Batista government comes tumbling down, the film focuses on how the selfish, corrupt and hypocritical characters respond to the tumultuous events. Filmed in Spain, CUBA was virtually ignored upon its release, but it's an entertaining and well-crafted political satire that is definitely worth a look.

CUL-DE-SAC

1966 111m bw ★★★½
Thriller /15
Sigma (U.K.)

Donald Pleasence (George), Françoise Dorleac (Teresa), Lionel Stander (Richard), Jack MacGowran (Albert), Iain Quarrier (Christopher), Geoffrey Sumner (His Father), Renee Houston (His Mother), William Franklyn (Cecil), Trevor Delaney (Nicholas), Marie Kean (Mrs. Fairweather)

p, Gene Gutowski; d, Roman Polanski; w, Gerard Brach, Roman Polanski; ph, Gilbert Taylor; ed, Alastair McIntyre; m, Krzysztof Komeda

Neat little chiller with Polanski honing his abilities as a director and standout performances from Pleasence, Stander, and Dorleac. Pleasence, a hermit, lives with his succulent wife, Dorleac, in a large, dank, dark castle on a small island off the northeast coast of Britain. Dorleac is a nympho-in-training who's always looking for someone new to take her mind off her nutty husband. Escaped criminals Stander and MacGowran make their way to this remote outpost, and what we get is Polanski's version of THE DESPERATE HOURS. But the director exhibits such style in his writing and direction that one can forgive the excesses. CUL-DE-SAC is exaggerated, sinister, bleak, and spine-tingling. It is also somewhat thick in the middle and could have used a serious editor to whack away at it. Still, it's well worth seeing for the radiance of Dorleac, who died the following year in an automobile crash. In a tiny speaking part, Jacqueline Bissett is seen for the second time in her career.

CURLY TOP

1935 75m bw ★★★★
Musical /U
Fox Films

Shirley Temple *(Elizabeth Blair)*, John Boles *(Edward Morgan)*, Rochelle Hudson *(Mary Blair)*, Jane Darwell *(Mrs. Denham)*, Rafaela Ottiano *(Mrs. Higgins)*, Esther Dale *(Aunt Genevieve Graham)*, Etienne Girardot *(Mr. Weckoff)*, Maurice Murphy *(Jimmie Rogers)*, Arthur Treacher *(Butler)*

p, Winfield Sheehan; d, Irving Cummings; w, Patterson McNutt, Arthur J. Beckhard (based on a story by Jean Webster); ph, John Seitz; m, Ray Henderson, Ted Koehler, Edward Heyman; chor, Jack Donohue

A strong Temple showcase, as much in its way as a Mae West film. Turn down the sound and you'll see a fullblown persona and CURLY TOP provides a nifty argument for the idea of the actor as auteur. The plot? Oh, get real—-moppet plays matchmaker, what else? Shirley and big sis Rochelle Hudson are discovered in an orphanage by millionaire John Boles. He shows them Park Avenue and the life of luxury and, naturally, falls for the post-pubescent sis. Shirley doesn't forget where she came from, though, and returns to the orphanage to sing a few ditties with her moppet friends. CURLY TOP was a masked remake of DADDY LONG LEGS, starring Mary Pickford, and was remade again in 1955 with Fred Astaire and Leslie Caron.

CUTTER'S WAY

1981   105m   c   ★★★½
Mystery   R/X
UA

Jeff Bridges *(Richard Bone)*, John Heard *(Alex Cutter)*, Lisa Eichhorn *(Mo Cutter)*, Ann Dusenberry *(Valerie Duran)*, Stephen Elliott *(J.J. Cord)*, Arthur Rosenberg *(George Swanson)*, Nina Van Pallandt *(Woman in Hotel)*, Patricia Donahue *(Mrs. Cord)*, Geraldine Baron *(Susie Swanson)*, Katherine Pass *(Toyota Woman)*

p, Paul R. Gurian; d, Ivan Passer; w, Jeffrey Alan Fiskin (based on the novel *Cutter and Bone* by Newton Thornburg); ph, Jordan Cronenweth (Technicolor); ed, Caroline Ferriol; m, Jack Nitzsche; art d, Josan Russo

A fiercely powerful film about heroes, romanticism, and friendship among three initially unlikable characters— Cutter (Heard) a vulgar, crippled Vietnam vet who is an outlaw in a society without commitment or heroes; his best friend Bone (Bridges), a pretty boy with no convictions at all; and the woman who bonds them, Mo (Eichhorn), wife of Cutter but desirous of Bone. After nearly taking the rap for a girl's murder, Bone, while at a parade, thinks he spots the real killer—Elliott, a powerful and arrogant oil tycoon. Cutter lets his imagination run free and comes up with an elaborate conspiracy theory about the night of the murder, devising a plan to blackmail Cord—a plan of which Bone wants no part.

Rapped by the critics on its initial release, it was almost instantly pulled from exhibition. Slowly rave reviews began to surface. After a title change (from the misleading, medically oriented CUTTER AND BONE), it was rereleased, becoming something of a cult movie in the process. An inspiring film, it is constructed like a thriller; but instead of reaching for thrills, it leaves them in the background and concentrates on the complexities of its characters. It may require multiple viewings to appreciate, but it is nonetheless a fascinating picture, and the best of Czech director Ivan Passer's American films. The Jack Nitzsche score is hauntingly effective.

CYRANO DE BERGERAC

1950   112m   bw   ★★★½
Drama   /U
UA

Jose Ferrer *(Cyrano)*, Mala Powers *(Roxane)*, William Prince *(Christian)*, Morris Carnovsky *(Le Bret)*, Ralph Clanton *(De Guiche)*, Lloyd Corrigan *(Ragueneau)*, Virginia Farmer *(Duenna)*, Edgar Barrier *(Cardinal)*, Elena Verdugo *(Orange Girl)*, Al Cavens *(Valvert)*

p, Stanley Kramer; d, Michael Gordon; w, Carl Foreman (based on the play by Edmond Rostand, translated by Brian Hooker); ph, Franz Planer; ed, Harry Gerstad; m, Dimitri Tiomkin

Outstanding performance by Ferrer won him an Oscar and is central feature of film adaptation of Rostand by Brian Hooker. Essentially, the property remains stagebound; it is not well directed, nor does it seem to have had a decent budget. It is hampered by unimaginative backlot settings and lacks the flair color would have helped supply.

For those in need of it, the plot concerns a tragic wit, born with an outrageously long nose, who lends his words to a more handsome man who is wooing the woman that both love. Your opinion of Ferrer's work will depend upon your taste in acting. This is technique work, like Olivier's. The performance feels outward bound, theatrical, expert in that manner. Ferrer never really caught on in films. Undeniably talented, there was something hard-bitten about him, and rumor has it he was not an easy ego to contend with.

CYRANO DE BERGERAC

1990   135m   c   ★★★★
Romance/Drama   PG/U
Hachette Premiere/Union Generale   (France)

Gerard Depardieu *(Cyrano de Bergerac)*, Anne Brochet *(Roxane)*, Vincent Perez *(Christian de Neuvillette)*, Jacques Weber *(Count DeGuiche)*, Roland Bertin *(Ragueneau)*, Philippe Morier-Genoud *(Le Bret)*, Pierre Maguelon *(Carbon de Castel-Jaloux)*, Josiane Stoleru *(Roxane's Handmaid)*, Anatole Delalande *(The Child)*, Ludivine Sagnier *(The Little Sister)*

p, Rene Cleitman, Michel Seydoux; d, Jean-Paul Rappeneau; w, Jean-Claude Carriere, Jean-Paul Rappeneau (based on the play by Edmond Rostand); ph, Pierre Lhomme; ed, Noelle Boisson; m, Jean-Claude Petit; art d, Ezio Frigerio; cos, Franca Squarciapino

A virtuoso update. Gerard Depardieu's Cyrano is nothing short of magnificent. In this version of Edmond Rostand's classic drama of unrequited love, his Cyrano is less physical caricature, more flesh and blood, and a markedly younger, more virile nobleman than the usually avuncular ones of the past. Dealing as it does with universals—that beauty is both in the eye of the beholder and only skin deep—this slightly abbreviated adaptation by director Jean-Paul Rappeneau and Jean-Claude Carriere retains both the panache and poignancy of its source.

As in the play, the film opens in a theater where the lovers first meet and where Cyrano has come to jeer at his enemy, the ham Montfleury (Gabriel Monnet). Cyrano is heard before he is seen, and his voice practically bellows with resonant majesty. When he finally appears, in profile, his nose immediately draws attention. What is interesting here is, unlike other productions where the nose stops just short of Pinocchio's and makes an obvious freak of the character, the producers have gone to pains to see that this Cyrano is not grotesque. It is Depardieu's normal nose in shape, only extended, and by making the character less of a freak, the filmmakers also succeed in making his pain all the more poignant.

The extraordinarily talented Depardieu, who has appeared in more than 70 films, gives his Cyrano a winning combination of grace and gusto, and is a commanding presence, both literally and figuratively. He's unexpectedly fleet of foot during the dueling scenes, recalling Douglas Fairbanks or Burt Lancaster. He brings a welcome vibrancy to the role, which won him the Best Actor award at the Cannes Film Festival. Brochet's Roxane is not shallow, as she is often portrayed, but much a product of her times, impressed with the literary conceits of poseurs of her generation. With its masterful acting, exquisitely muted cinematography, vast complement of extras, extravagant props and scenery, CYRANO DE BERGERAC was, at $20 million, France's most expensive movie production. Though filmed on a grand scale, it does not lose the emotional impact of the play, which had its premiere in Paris in 1898, and has been a mainstay of the legitimate theater ever since.

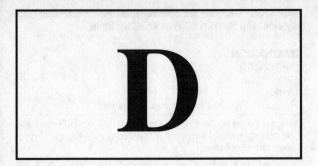

D

D.O.A.
1950 83m bw   ★★★★½
Mystery   /PG
UA

Edmond O'Brien (Frank Bigelow), Pamela Britton (Paula Gibson), Luther Adler (Majak), Beverly Garland (Miss Foster), Lynne Baggett (Mrs. Philips), William Ching (Holliday), Henry Hart (Stanley Philips), Neville Brand (Chester), Laurette Luez (Marla Rakubian), Jess Kirkpatrick (Sam)

p, Leo C. Popkin; d, Rudolph Maté; w, Russell Rouse, Clarence Greene; ph, Ernest Laszlo; ed, Arthur H. Nadel; m, Dimitri Tiomkin; art d, Duncan Cramer; cos, Maria Donovan

A clever ruse for suspense. Murder victim O'Brien discovers he has been poisoned and, in his remaining days, tries to track down his own killer. He's a CPA who arrives in San Francisco to get some time away from fiancee Britton but after a night on the town he grows ill and consults a doctor who tells him he has been poisoned and he will be dead in a few days. He then learns that he notarized a shipment of deadly iridium and that he is the only one who can provide proof against a criminal gang. O'Brien is great as the victimized businessman, harassed by the psychopathic Brand and the sinister Ching. Maté's direction suitably increases O'Brien's pace as the story unravels and the plot becomes more hectic, particularly when the bloodthirsty Brand is ordered to take O'Brien out and murder him. Maté also makes spectacular use of exterior locations giving the film a very different feel from most studio-bound entries. The film takes much of its basic story line from Robert Siodmak's 1931 German-made DER MANN, DER SEINEN MORDER SUCHT. The story line was the basis for the 1969 Australian film COLOR ME DEAD. Remade poorly in 1988 with Dennis Quaid and again titled D.O.A.

DA
1988 102m c   ★★★½
Fantasy   PG
Film Dallas

Barnard Hughes (Da), Martin Sheen (Charlie), William Hickey (Drumm), Karl Hayden (Young Charlie), Doreen Hepburn (Mother), Hugh O'Conor (Boy Charlie), Ingrid Craigie (Polly), Joan O'Hara (Mrs. Prynne), Peter Hanly (Young Oliver), Jill Doyle

p, Julie Corman; d, Matt Clark; w, Hugh Leonard (based on his play "Da" and novel Home Before Night); ph, Alar Kivilo; ed, Nancy Nuttal Beyda; m, Elmer Bernstein; prod d, Frank Conway

DA is the heart-tugging, autobiographical story of a father-son reunion that takes place beyond the grave. After his 83-year-old father dies, Charlie (Martin Sheen)—a middle-aged, Irish-Amer-

ican playwright with a play about to open on Broadway—returns to the Irish coastal village of his youth to attend his father's funeral. As Charlie sits alone in his family's humble home and sorts through Da's belongings, he is visited by his father (Barnard Hughes)—more corporeal than ghostly, the invention of the grieving son's conscience. Charlie gives himself over to his imagination, exploring his love-hate relationship with his father, reminiscing with the man as he crosses a mental frontier and ventures into the past. Benefiting from wonderful performances by everyone involved, including Hughes's re-creation of his Tony Award-winning stage role, DA is an extremely moving film. This first-time directorial effort by actor Matt Clark invites us to reexamine our own parent-child relationships. For all its poignancy, however, DA is still a very funny movie. Hughes is charming—milking the humor, pathos, and humanity of his character—and only occasionally becomes too lovable. Sheen, who was one of the film's executive producers and who labored for some years to bring the play to the screen, gives an insightful, sincere performance, believably balancing a sardonic sense of irony with less rational feelings.

DADDY LONG LEGS
1931 80m bw   ★★★★
Comedy/Romance   /U
Fox Films

Janet Gaynor (Judy Abbott), Warner Baxter (Jervis Pendleton), Una Merkel (Sally McBride), John Arledge (Jimmy McBride), Claude Gillingwater (Riggs), Kathlyn Williams (Mrs. Pendleton), Louise Closser Hale (Miss Pritchard), Elizabeth Patterson (Mrs. Lippett), Kendall McComas (Freddie Perkins), Sheila Bromley (Gloria Pendleton)

d, Alfred Santell; w, Sonya Levien, S.N. Behrman (based on the novel and play by Jean Webster); ph, Lucien Andriot; ed, Ralph Dietrich

A perennial, DADDY LONG LEGS has been done to death. Made in 1919 with Mary Pickford, then in 1935 as CURLY TOP with Shirley Temple, then again in 1955 with Leslie Caron, this 1931 version features Janet Gaynor and Warner Baxter as protagonists in a May-December relationship. It's another variant on the CINDERELLA theme, with perky Gaynor living in an orphanage and bridling under the harsh treatment of matron Elizabeth Patterson. Gaynor is sent to college by mystery man Baxter, a soft-touch millionaire who is a trustee of the orphanage. Matters get complicated when her roommate's (Una Merkel) brother (John Arledge) falls in love with Gaynor. But all ends well when she discovers that the man she loves is also the man who has been her benefactor for all those years. There's enough pathos for two hankies, but spirited cast just manages to keep film from falling into bathos. Gaynor was 25 and Baxter was 40—not quite a May-December romance, more like a June-October—but they suffuse ther characters with pro instincts. Patterson was the perfect crotchety old biddy. She didn't get into movies until she was in her fifties, but she made a slew of features and endeared herself to generations of television watchers in her recurring role of Mrs. Trumble on "I Love Lucy."

DADDY LONG LEGS
1955 126m c   ★★★
Musical/Romance   /U
FOX

Fred Astaire (Jervis Pendleton), Leslie Caron (Julie), Terry Moore (Linda), Thelma Ritter (Miss Pritchard), Fred Clark (Griggs), Charlotte Austin *(Sally)*, Larry Keating *(Alexander Williamson)*, Kathryn Givney *(Gertrude)*, Kelly Brown *(Jimmy McBride)*, Sara Shane *(Pat)*

p, Samuel G. Engel; d, Jean Negulesco; w, Phoebe Ephron, Henry Ephron (based on the novel and play by Jean Webster); ph, Leon Shamroy (CinemaScope, Deluxe Color); ed, William Reynolds; m, Alfred Newman, Alex North; chor, Roland Petit, David Robel, Fred Astaire

Inert and lengthy version of the old chestnut. The musical numbers, rather than lightening the vehicle, tend to weigh it down. Jean Negulesco helmed this fourth version of Jean Webster's tale about a love affair that has everything going against it but eventually flourishes anyway. Caron is the waif in an orphanage; Astaire is the playboy who finances her from afar. Unless you've been under a rock, you know this means love. Johnny Mercer, writing both music and lyrics for one of the few times in his life, received an Oscar nomination for "Something's Gotta Give," which remains a standard; it's the only foolproof number in the score. Other tunes serve as almost adequate backdrops for Caron and Astaire as they dance their way into our hearts, or at least each other's. The weakest element of the film is Petit's choreography for the dream ballets, which evidences little of the brilliance he'd demonstrated in ANYTHING GOES. Nor does the Astaire-Robel choreography evidence much strenuous innovation. What also hurts is that Astaire and Caron manage to generate considerable rapport together as actors but almost none when they dance together. Both their styles and their bodies are largely incompatible. Ritter occasionally adds verbal snap and Moore supplies that other quality we've come to expect from Hollywood in spades.

DAMN YANKEES

1958   110m   c   ★★★★
Sports/Musical/Comedy   /U
WB

Tab Hunter *(Joe Hardy)*, Gwen Verdon *(Lola)*, Ray Walston *(Applegate)*, Russ Brown *(Van Buren)*, Shannon Bolin *(Meg)*, Nathaniel Frey *(Smokey)*, Jimmie Komack *(Rocky)*, Rae Allen *(Gloria)*, Robert Shafer *(Joe Boyd)*, Jean Stapleton *(Sister)*

p, George Abbott, Stanley Donen; d, George Abbott, Stanley Donen; w, George Abbott (based on the play by George Abbott and Douglas Wallop, from the novel *The Year the Yankees Lost the Pennant* by Wallop); ph, Harold Lipstein (Technicolor); ed, Frank Bracht; prod d, William Eckart, Jean Eckart; art d, Stanley Fleischer; chor, Bob Fosse, Pat Ferrier; cos, William Eckart, Jean Eckart

Somewhere along the way of opening up the smash stage version, DAMN YANKEES gets saddled with too much plot. It's only 110 minutes long, but you'd never know it. If Hunter is lacking in assurance among all the legit pros, there's nothing distinctly wrong in his performance. A middle-aged Washington Senators fan (Shafer) would give his soul for a long-ball hitter and promptly enough the devil shows up in the form of Walston, to change him into a handsome, athletic 22-year-old (Hunter), who wins a place on the Senators team. Walston is a perfect comic Satan, but gets bogged down in too much superfical action. It's unfortunate that the screenplay depends upon him to tie up all the loose ends. Verdon's eternal Lillith, Lola, is expert, sexy, and hilarious but because she's not a conventional beauty (Monroe had turned down both the Broadway and film versions) the need for Hunter is more than evident. Terrific, Oscar-nominated score by Ross and Adler is electric, contains "Heart," "Whatever Lola Wants" and "Shoeless Joe from Hannibal Mo." That's Bob Fosse dancing with Verdon on "Who's Got the Pain."

DAMNATION

(KARHOZAT)
1988   116m   bw   ★★★★
Drama
Hungarian Film Institute/Mokep/Hungarian TV   (Hungary)

Miklos B. Szekely *(Karrer)*, Vali Kerekes *(The Singer)*, Gyula Pauer *(Willarsky)*, Hedi Temessy *(Cloakroom Attendant)*, Gyorgy Cserhalmi *(Sebestyen)*

p, Jozsef Marx; d, Bela Tarr; w, Laszlo Krasznahorkai, Bela Tarr; ph, Gabor Medvigy; ed, Agnes Hraniczky; m, Mihaly Vig; cos, Gyula Pauer

Photographed in black and white, Tarr's DAMNATION is a slowly paced, deeply pessimistic, yet poetic film set in a grim, featureless industrial area outside Budapest. There, alone and friendless, the unemployed Szekely lives a monotonous existence, making the rounds of the local bars and staring out the window at miner's buckets passing back and forth, suspended on cables. Szekely is "in love" (the term's potential banality emerges when applied to Tarr's alienated characters) with Kerekes, a chanteuse at the Titanic bar who is married to Cserhalmi. She has ended their affair (not—we suspect—for the first time), but Szekely still pursues her, haunting the Titanic and waiting outside Kerekes and Cserhalmi's apartment building, unprotected in the furiously pouring rain, for Cserhalmi to leave. When a barkeeper (Pauer) offers Szekely an opportunity to make some money as the courier in a smuggling expedition, Szekely tips off Cserhalmi to the job, knowing he is badly in debt, and thereby gets him out of the country for a few days. He and Kerekes then resume their affair, after a fashion, as the two fight violently, have sex, and engage in hopelessly one-sided conversations.

In addition to giving his actors pessimistic, near-monologue dialogue, director-coscreenwriter Tarr emphasizes his characters' despair with a number of visual motifs. The incessant rain is the chief image of several that recur. The buckets passing back and forth, rows of stacked glasses, several views of textural patterns in walls—these, in Tarr and cinematographer Medvigy's static shots, have the nearly abstract compositional beauty of the best black-and-white still photographs, and the film is filled with stunning images of the most mundane objects and scenes. When the camera does move, Tarr favors a slow lateral pan that suits the monotony of his characters' lives. Monotony and repetition also characterize the music played in the various bars, from Kerekes's number in the Titanic (one of the very few scenes Tarr lingers on too long) to the noodlings of a lone accordionist in Pauer's saloon.

If the music suggests the purposelessness of life in DAMNATION, however, it also sounds the note of grace in the general dirge: human perception of beauty through loss and despair. Emptied of their significance as means or goals, objects and actions claim an irreducible, mysterious essence of their own, a nameless power akin to that of music. Physical processes like sleep and sex (more repetition) become gestures in an endless general dance (and a woman like Kerekes, described as a "bottomless swamp" by one character, can embody absolute beauty for Szekely). It is this fundamentally poetic paradox that finally eludes Szekely's character, ensuring his damnation. At the same time, the same paradox lends profundity to a film that might easily have become a self-indulgent exercise in gloom. Tarr's uncompromisingly tragic view of the human condition can only be supported by his pure and rigorous form, and the result of the combination is an austere work of art.

DAMNED, THE
(LA CADUTA DEGLI DEI)
1969 155m c ★★★★
Drama X/18
Eichberg/Pegaso/Praesidens (Italy/West Germany)

Dirk Bogarde *(Friedrich Bruckmann)*, Ingrid Thulin *(Baroness Sophie von Essenbeck)*, Helmut Griem *(Aschenbach)*, Helmut Berger *(Martin von Essenbeck)*, Renaud Verley *(Gunther von Essenbeck)*, Umberto Orsini *(Herbert Thallman)*, Rene Kolldehoff *(Baron Konstantin von Essenbeck)*, Albrecht Schoenhals *(Baron Joachim von Essenbeck)*, Charlotte Rampling *(Elisabeth Thallman)*, Florinda Bolkan *(Olga)*

p, Alfredo Levy, Ever Haggiag; d, Luchino Visconti; w, Luchino Visconti, Nicola Badalucco, Enrico Medioli; ph, Armando Nannuzzi, Pasquale De Santis; ed, Ruggero Mastroianni; m, Maurice Jarre

Luchino Visconti's epic of decadence, set in Germany during 1933 and 1934, parallels the end of a family of industrialists with the rise of Nazism. The films opens with an extravagant dinner celebrating the retirement of the family patriarch, Baron Joachim von Essenbeck, the magnate of a huge steel enterprise, and his appointment of an outsider, Friedrich Bruckmann (Dirk Bogarde) as temporary head. While at first all seems very respectable and bourgeois, the gathering turns strange when Joachim's grandson, Martin (Helmut Berger) delivers his rendition of Marlene Dietrich's "Falling in Love Again" dressed in drag. Before the party is over, it is announced that the Reichstag has been burned, symbolizing the end of German democracy. Later, as the highly organized SS plots to annihilate the SA (the populist Fascist front), Martin, a bisexual, sadistic, pedophilic drug addict who even rapes his own mother, engineers his plot to stop a takeover attempt by Friedrich and Sophie (Ingrid Thulin), Friedrich's lover and Martin's mother.

THE DAMNED is Visconti at his most operatic (the German title is GOTTERDAMMERUNG, after Wagner), containing baroque sets and costumes, highly melodramatic acting, and orgiastic scenes of violence and sex. While it has been criticized on a number of levels (the equating of perverts and pedophiles with fascists has been done before; its English dialogue is often poor; it indulges in its own distastefulness; it's too long, etc.), the film is a spectacular, meticulously crafted work that cannot fail to elicit some response, be it disgust or appreciation, from its audience.

DAMNED, THE
(LES MAUDITS)
1948 105m bw ★★★
Drama
DIF (France)

Henri Vidal *(The Physician)*, Florence Marly *(Hilde Garosi)*, Kurt Kronefeld *(Gen. Von Hauser)*, Anne Campion *(Ingrid)*, Jo Dest *(Forster)*, Michel Auclair *(Willy Morus)*, Fosco Giachetti *(Garosi)*, Paul Bernard *(Couturier)*, Jean Didier *(The Captain)*, Marcel Dalio *(Larga)*

p, Andre Paulve; d, Rene Clement; w, Rene Clement, Jacques Remy (based on a story by Jacques Companeez and Victor Alexandroff); ph, Henri Alekan; ed, Roger Dwyre; m, Yves Baudrier; prod d, Paul Bertrand

In the closing days of World War II, a number of Nazi officials and various hangers-on flee Oslo in a U-boat, trying to make their way to South America. Along the way they are attacked by a destroyer and depth-charged. Marly, the wife of the count (Giachetti) and the mistress of the German general (Kronefeld), is wounded in the attack, so the submarine lands on the French coast where the escapees kidnap the doctor (Vidal). He realizes the danger he is in and begins sowing the seeds of defeatism and despair among the passengers. Quite an interesting drama confined almost totally to one set, with very good performances by the entire cast, but we've been spoiled by Hitchcock and Tallulah Bankhead's alliance on LIFEBOAT.

DANCE WITH A STRANGER
1985 102m c ★★★★
Biography/Crime R/15
First Film/Goldcrest/HFFC/4 Intl. (U.K.)

Miranda Richardson *(Ruth Ellis)*, Rupert Everett *(David Blakely)*, Ian Holm *(Desmond Cussen)*, Matthew Carroll *(Andy)*, Tom Chadbon *(Anthony Findlater)*, Jane Bertish *(Carole Findlater)*, David Troughton *(Cliff Davis)*, Paul Mooney *(Clive Gunnell)*, Stratford Johns *(Morrie Conley)*, Joanne Whalley-Kilmer *(Christine)*

p, Roger Randall-Cutler; d, Mike Newell; w, Shelagh Delaney; ph, Peter Hannan; ed, Mick Audsley; m, Richard Hartley; prod d, Andrew Mollo; art d, Adrian Smith; cos, Pip Newberry

Dark, haunting kichen-sink noir, deftly done; the life and death of Ruth Ellis, the last woman to be hanged for murder in England in 1955. The screenplay by Shelagh Delaney takes a few liberties for the sake of dramatic license but by and large keeps close to the real account. Miranda Richardson (playing Ellis), a divorcee and ex-hooker, now a "hostess" in a tawdry nightclub in Soho. Though she lives with Holm, he is more of a pal than a lover and also the surrogate father to her teenage son, Carroll. Richardson falls obsessively in love with upper-class Everett, an immature cad. But the more she wants to be with Everett, the more he pushes her aside, both mentally and physically. Eventually she retaliates and murders him. The real case provided months of lurid reading for the British and several years later, Ellis's son committed suicide.

STRANGER inhabits the seedy milieu beneath the repressed 1950s British surface. Richardson's performance is a knockout; with her birdlike gestures and darting eyes, she's reminiscent of young Bette Davis in her peroxide period. And she challenges two topics the English hesitate to look at—sexual compulsivity and outward expression of nasty emotions; no wonder Ellis got the death sentence.

DANCES WITH WOLVES
1990 183m c ★★½
Western PG-13/12
TIG

Kevin Costner *(Lt. John W. Dunbar)*, Mary McDonnell *(Stands with a Fist)*, Graham Greene *(Kicking Bird)*, Rodney A. Grant *(Wind in his Hair)*, Floyd Red Crow Westerman *(Chief Ten Bears)*, Tantoo Cardinal *(Black Shawl)*, Robert Pastorelli *(Timmons)*, Charles Rocket *(Lt. Elgin)*, Maury Chaykin *(Maj. Fambrough)*, Jimmy Herman *(Stone Calf)*

p, Jim Wilson, Kevin Costner; d, Kevin Costner; w, Michael Blake (based on his novel); ph, Dean Semler; ed, Neil Travis; m, John Barry; art d, William L. Skinner; fx, Robbie Knott; cos, Elsa Zamparelli

The plodding vanity project of star, director, and co-producer Kevin Costner, this three-hour-plus revisionist western, much of it in subtitled Sioux language, shocked movie-industry observers by becoming a huge hit and garnering 12 Oscar nominations, winning seven, including Best Picture and Best Director. The Sioux gave the film their own rave review by admitting Costner as a full tribal member.

Costner plays Lt. John W. Dunbar, a Union officer during the Civil War who undergoes a conversion experience on the frontier that transforms him into the title character. The film begins with Dunbar wounded, depressed, and suicidal. His suicide attempt is mistaken for an act of heroism and he gets transferred to the post of his choice—an outpost on the frontier far away from white "civilization." After a series of peculiar experiences he find himself alone in a little shelter on the prairie where he befriends an amiable wolf. Before long he meets his equally amiable Native American neighbors and slowly wins their respect and love as he goes native with a vengeance. Over the course of his unlikely adventures, he trades in his dreary Union duds for some cool Sioux threads, forms a very close friendship with a white woman (McDonnell) who was captured and raised by Indians, and even breaks the "Prime Directive" by giving out rifles and ammunition to his "good" Lakota Sioux pals to battle the mean ol' Pawnees.

Not a great film by any standard, this is a western for people who are completely ignorant about the genre. Costner's direction is barely competent and frequently clumsy. Michael Blake's script, adapted from his novel, is loose and disconnected, rambling about with no real story holding it together, beyond the imminent arrival of the white bad guys to spoil Dunbar's frontier fantasy paradise. Despite its attention to surface details of day-to-day Sioux life, the film shows no genuine curiosity about the larger designs of the Sioux culture. We see little of tribal life through Sioux eyes, and come away having learned nothing at all about Sioux spirituality. Instead, the film renders the Sioux as just average folks.

Still one must admire Costner's conviction and sincerity about this project. With longtime associates Blake and co-producer Jim Wilson, Costner virtually willed the film into existence. Unable to sell it to an American studio, despite Costner's box-office clout, they finally had to secure foreign financing to make the film. That this is clearly a personal film doesn't make it a good one but it makes it hard to totally dismiss.

DANGEROUS

1936   78m   bw   ★★★
Drama   /A
WB

Bette Davis (Joyce Heath), Franchot Tone (Don Bellows), Margaret Lindsay (Gail Armitage), Alison Skipworth (Mrs. Williams), John Eldredge (Gordon Heath), Dick Foran (Teddy), Pierre Watkin (George Sheffield), Walter Walker (Roger Farnsworth), George Irving (Charles Melton), William B. Davidson (Reed Walsh)

p, Harry Joe Brown; d, Alfred E. Green; w, Laird Doyle; ph, Ernest Haller; ed, Thomas Richards; m, Bernhard Kaun; art d, Hugh Reticker; cos, Orry-Kelly

Davis takes on the Jeanne Eagels legend, acting it with an intensity that would have gotten her burned at the stake in the 17th Century. This was the film that followed OF HUMAN BONDAGE, and despite critics' love letters, Davis was feeling ignored by the industry. Though an inferior vehicle even then, DANGEROUS gave her another shot at a breakthrough role, an opportunity she seized; no other Hollywood star would have played a Broadway legend, sodden or not, so unflatteringly.

Davis is an alcoholic former star when slumming architect Franchot Tone (in a surprisingly contemporary performance)

spots her, buys her a drink, and comments about how much he enjoyed her acting. She accepts his invitation to stay at his home in Connecticut, but once there she continues boozing. He offers to finance her return to the stage, and she does what she can to break up his engagement to Margaret Lindsay (who gets another dreary role like this in JEZEBEL). Eventually, Tone tells Lindsay he wants to marry Davis, but it turns out she's married to Eldredge. The latter refuses to divorce her; she then intentionally crashes her car, hoping to kill Eldredge. He survives but he's now paralyzed for life. Her return to the stage is a big success, and Tone still wants her, but now she's troubled by guilt over what she has done to Eldredge.

Davis's efforts paid off with her first Academy Award, a partial consolation prize for her riveting performance in BONDAGE the year prior, but nonetheless an acknowledgement by the industry of her innovative thesping.

DANGEROUS LIAISONS

1988   120m   c   ★★★★
Drama   R/15
NFH/Lorimar

Glenn Close (Marquise de Merteuil), John Malkovich (Vicomte de Valmont), Michelle Pfeiffer (Madame de Tourvel), Swoosie Kurtz (Madame de Volanges), Keanu Reeves (Chevalier Danceny), Mildred Natwick (Madame de Rosemonde), Uma Thurman (Cecile de Volanges), Joe Sheridan, Peter Capaldi

p, Norma Heyman, Hank Moonjean, Christopher Hampton; d, Stephen Frears; w, Christopher Hampton (based on his play and the novel Les Liaisons Dangereuses by Choderlos de Laclos); ph, Philippe Rousselot; ed, Mick Audsley; m, George Fenton; prod d, Stuart Craig; cos, James Acheson

Choderlos de Laclos reportedly said of his epistolary 1782 novel, Les Liaisons Dangereuses, that he created it with the intent to shock. That novel, on which British director Stephen Frears's first American feature film is based, did much of what Laclos hoped, the first edition becoming the succes de scandale of Paris. Frears's version, a costume drama set in pre-Revolutionary France, forcefully presents its story of sexual power, depravity, cruelty, and deceit. The Marquise de Merteuil (Glenn Close) and the Vicomte de Valmont (John Malkovich) are monsters of the aristocracy, former lovers who spend their days planning sexual seductions and vengeance. Merteuil makes Valmont a proposition: if he deflowers Cecile (Uma Thurman), the 16-year-old future wife of another of Merteuil's former lovers, she will gratefully reward Valmont with her favors. Valmont instead devotes his attention to the greater challenge of seducing Madame de Tourvel (Michelle Pfeiffer)—a highly moral, married, and convent-bred young woman. Plying his suit with the greatest skill and subtlety, Valmont eventually breaks down Tourvel's reserve. In the meantime, to please Merteuil, he also deflowers Cecile—who, after yielding to Valmont, becomes insatiably sensual. DANGEROUS LIAISONS is less about debauchery and amorality than it is about the sexual and psychological domination of one person by another.

Malkovich and Close take a while before they shift into expert gear, the former lacking the physical grace of a Don Juan, the latter vapid in a Connecticut housewife kind of way. Nor does it help that Close, despite her talent, is utterly devoid of sex appeal. But Pfeiffer is a revelation in her part, almost stealing the film. The camera seems compelled to soak up her pain like a sponge, yet she possesses that quietness overlying unrest that is the hallmark of many great film stars. Her stillness seems to make her more authentically period than her co-stars, who have adopted no formal period mannerisms. Yet perhaps that enabled less astute audience members to connect the film to present-day sexual morals, sexual politics, and thirst for power. While not perfect, LIASONS is miles above Forman's bland VALMONT.

DANGEROUS MOVES
(LA DIAGONALE DU FOU)
1984   95m   c   ★★★½
Thriller   /PG
Arthur Cohn   (Switzerland)

Michel Piccoli *(Akiva Liebskind)*, Alexandre Arbatt *(Pavius Fromm)*, Leslie Caron *(Henia Liebskind)*, Liv Ullmann *(Marina)*, Daniel Olbrychski *(Tac-Tac)*, Michel Aumont *(Kerossian)*, Serge Avedikian *(Fadenko)*, Pierre Michael *(Yachvili)*, Pierre Vial *(Anton Heller)*, Wojciech Pszoniak *(Felton)*

p, Arthur Cohn; d, Richard Dembo; w, Richard Dembo; ph, Raoul Coutard; ed, Agnes Guillemot; m, Gabriel Yared; art d, Ivan Maussion; cos, Pierre Albert

This ingenious thriller takes place in the world of chess championships, using the politically neutral Geneva, Switzerland, as its backdrop. The reigning world chess champion, Michel Piccoli, is the pride of the Soviet Union, but his weak heart may mean the end of his reign. His competitor is Alexandre Arbatt, a rebellious young Soviet exile. As the championship begins, Arbatt attempts to disrupt the proceedings, and thereby Piccoli's concentration, by arriving late for his first move. His habitual tardiness and basic contempt for regulations force Piccoli to register a formal complaint with the jury. When Piccoli threatens to withdraw, Arbatt buckles under and writes a formal apology rather than lose his chance to defeat the champion. As a result of their moves away from the chess board, both men begin to deteriorate—Piccoli physically, Arbatt mentally. The chess masters, however, are merely pawns in a larger political game involving the Soviet government and the West.

Director Richard Dembo, in his debut feature, has contrasted skillfully the players' maneuvers with political power plays, yet he avoids pretension. Rather than concentrating too much on the chess matches themselves (a knowledge of chess is helpful in viewing DANGEROUS MOVES, but by no means a requirement), Dembo brings to the screen an emotional battle between two powerful personalities. He also receives support from a solid who's-who of European film, including actors Liv Ullmann, Leslie Caron, Bernhard Wicki, Daniel Olbrychski, and Jean-Hugues Anglade; cameraman Raoul Coutard; and editor Agnes Guillemot.

DANTON
1983   136m   c   ★★★
Historical/Biography/War   PG
TF1/SFPC/Film Polski/Losange/Gaumont   (France/Poland)

Gerard Depardieu *(Georges Danton)*, Wojciech Pszoniak *(Maximillian Robespierre)*, Patrice Chereau *(Camille Desmoulins)*, Angela Winkler *(Lucile Desmoulins)*, Boguslaw Linda *(Saint Just)*, Roland Blanche *(Lacroix)*, Anne Alvaro *(Eleonore Duplay)*, Roger Planchon *(Fouquier Tinville)*, Serge Merlin *(Philippeaux)*, Lucien Melki *(Fabre d'Eglantine)*

p, Margaret Menegoz; d, Andrzej Wajda; w, Jean-Claude Carriere, Andrzej Wajda, Agnieszka Holland, Boleslaw Michalek, Jacek Gasiorowski (based on the play "The Danton Affair" by Stanislawa Przybyszewska); ph, Igor Luther; ed, Halina Prugar; m, Jean Prodromides; art d, Allan Starski, Gilles Vaster; cos, Yvonne Sassinot de Nesle

DANTON is a powerful drama of revolution, set in 1794 France, during the second year of the Republic, that centers on the rivalry between the humanist Georges Danton (the typically memorable Gerard Depardieu) and the ideologue Maximilien de Robespierre (Wojciech Pszoniak), "The Incorruptible." Danton, the most popular of the French revolutionaries, temporarily retired from politics and retreated to the countryside. He returns to Paris now, however, to stop the Reign of Terror led by Robespierre, his former compatriot in the Revolution whose efforts to keep the "pure patriots" in power have turned tyrannical. Although a great freedom fighter and proponent of political, religious, and human rights, Robespierre, with his Committee of Public Safety, has become just as oppressive as the monarchs he fought against. Despite the fact that Danton is a people's hero, Robespierre convinces himself that he must be executed in order to save the Republic.

DANTON is a stirring film on freedom from Andrzej Wajda, in his first directing effort outside of Poland. Criticized by some for being too static and theatrical, the movie takes care to show only the center of the Revolution and its aftermath: the battle between Danton and Robespierre and the unseen fight for liberty that takes place behind closed doors. Wajda disregards the rebellion in the streets in favor of showing us the power in the hands of government—those chosen few who are supposed to be representatives of the people.

DARBY O'GILL AND THE LITTLE PEOPLE
1959   93m   c   ★★★★½
Children's/Fantasy   /U
Disney

Albert Sharpe *(Darby O'Gill)*, Janet Munro *(Katie)*, Sean Connery *(Michael McBride)*, Jimmy O'Dea *(King Brian)*, Kieron Moore *(Pony Sugrue)*, Estelle Winwood *(Sheelah)*, Walter Fitzgerald *(Lord Fitzpatrick)*, Denis O'Dea *(Fr. Murphy)*, J.G. Devlin *(Tom Kerrigan)*, Jack MacGowran *(Phadrig Oge)*

p, Walt Disney; d, Robert Stevenson; w, Lawrence E. Watkin (based on the Darby O'Gill stories by H.T. Kavanagh); ph, Winton C. Hoch (Technicolor); ed, Stanley Johnson; m, Oliver Wallace; art d, Carroll Clark; fx, Peter Ellenshaw, Eustace Lycett; cos, Chuck Keehne, Gertrude Casey; anim, Joshua Meador

This excellent fantasy romps through the folklore world of Ireland, with Albert Sharpe starring as Darby O'Gill, the aging caretaker of a large estate. He falls into a well and lands in the cavernous realm of the Little People, ruled by King Brian (Jimmy O'Dea, in an unforgettable performance). Following a wild leprechaun celebration, the rock walls open and the king leads his men out on miniature horses to frolic in the Irish countryside. Later, Darby tricks King Brian into granting him three wishes, but quickly learns that one should be careful of what one wishes for.

This wonderful tale is told with a brisk, imaginative pace and the special effects—whereby Darby interacts with the tiny leprechauns—are marvelously executed, and sometimes frightening. Sharp camerawork is enhanced with brilliant colors and the music (by Oliver Wallace and Lawrence E. Watkin) is delightfully and capriciously Irish. Young Sean Connery is a breathtaking feast for the eyes, and Munro makes a fetching colleen. Overall production reflects Walt Disney's perfectionist detail; Disney dreamed of making the film for 20 years and took a trip to Ireland in 1948 to do research. Any child who hasn't seen DARBY O'GILL AND THE LITTLE PEOPLE has missed an important bit of fancy, and that goes for adults too.

DARK CRYSTAL, THE
1982 94m c   ★★★
Children's/Fantasy   PG
Associated Film/Universal   (U.K.)

VOICES OF: Stephen Garlick (Jen), Lisa Maxwell (Kira), Billie Whitelaw (Aughra), Percy Edwards (Fizzgig), Barry Dennen (Chamberlain), Michael Kilgarriff (General), Jerry Nelson (High Priest), Steve Whitmire (Scientist), Thick Wilson (Gourmand), Brian Muehl (Ornamentalist/Dying Master)

p, Jim Henson, Gary Kurtz; d, Jim Henson, Frank Oz; w, David Odell (based on a story by Henson); ph, Oswald Morris (Panavision, Technicolor); ed, Ralph Kemplen; m, Trevor Jones; prod d, Harry Lange; art d, Terry Ackland-Snow, Malcolm Stone, Brian Ackland-Snow; fx, Roy Field, Brian Smithies; chor, Jean Pierre Amierl

Once again employing his famous muppets, Jim Henson creates a brilliantly detailed universe with this intriguing fairy-tale adventure revolving around a power struggle between the monstrous Skeksis and the benevolent Mystics. Because the Dark Crystal has been broken, the Skeksis are in ascendance and will remain so unless Jen, one of two remaining Gelflings, is able to heal the crystal, thus fulfilling a prophesy that promises an end to Skeksis rule. Guided by the Mystics' cryptic instructions, and aided by Aughra, a sorceress, and Kira, the other (female) Gelfling, Jen goes about restoring the crystal. Like the children's classics SNOW WHITE AND THE SEVEN DWARFS and SLEEPING BEAUTY, this film has some graphic scenes that may be upsetting for younger kids.

DARK EYES
(OCI CIORNIE)
1987 118m c   ★★★½
Romance/Comedy   /PG
Excelsior/RAI-TV   (Italy)

Marcello Mastroianni (Romano), Silvana Mangano (Elisa, Romano's Wife), Marthe Keller (Tina, Romano's Mistress), Elena Sofonova (Anna Sergeyevna, Governor's Wife), Vsevolod Larionov (Pavel, Russian Ship Passenger), Innokenty Smoktunovsky (Governor of Sisoiev), Pina Cei (Elisa's Mother), Roberto Herlitzka (Lawyer), Dimitri Zolothukin (Konstantin), Paolo Baroni

p, Silvia D'Amico Bendico, Carlo Cucchi; d, Nikita Mikhalkov; w, Alexander Adabachian, Nikita Mikhalkov, Suso Cecchi D'Amico (based on material from the Anton Chekhov stories "The Lady With the Little Dog," "The Name-Day Party," "Anna Around the Neck" and "My Wife"); ph, Franco Di Giacomo (Eastmancolor); ed, Enzo Meniconi; m, Francis Lai; art d, Mario Garbuglia, Alexander Adabachian; cos, Carlo Diappi

A myriad of emotions, elegantly served. Directed by Nikita Mikhalkov (his first movie outside the USSR), the film brought a Soviet and Italian cast and crew together, and the result was a new, cross-cultural interpretation of the Chekhov stories upon which the film is based.

Set at the turn of the century, the film stars Mastroianni as Romano, a paunchy, alcoholic waiter who works in the dining room of a cruise ship. While voyaging from Greece to Italy, he meets Pavel (Vsevolod Larionov), a jovial Russian on his honeymoon with his much younger wife. Romano begins to reminisce, and the film goes to flashback. As young architecture student, Romano falls in love with Elisa (Silvana Mangano), a wealthy heiress, despite the objections of her high-society family.

He eventually leaves her and retreats to a lavish health spa. He finds willing young ladies to sleep with, pulls an occasional practical joke, watches old women racing through the marble-columned grounds in their wheelchairs, wanders about the beautifully manicured lawns, and eats extravagant meals. He meets Anna Sergeyevna (Elena Sofonova), a timid, lovely, easily embarrassed young woman with dark eyes and a lapdog. Mesmerized by her presence and the magical sparkle of her hat pin, Romano becomes obsessed.

Mastroianni is superb: his performance won the Best Actor prize at the Cannes Film Festival. However, it is not his performance alone that makes DARK EYES so enjoyable; there is also the discovery (for Western audiences) of the lovely Sofonova, a Soviet actress whose combination of fragility and strength is reminiscent of Audrey Hepburn.

DARK MIRROR, THE
1946 85m bw   ★★★★
Thriller   /A
Universal

Olivia de Havilland (Terry Collins/Ruth Collins), Lew Ayres (Dr. Scott Elliott), Thomas Mitchell (Detective Stevenson), Richard Long (Rusty), Charles Evans (District Attorney Girard), Garry Owen (Franklin), Lester Allen (George Benson), Lela Bliss (Mrs. Didriksen), Marta Mitrovich (Miss Beade), Amelita Ward (Photo Double)

p, Nunnally Johnson; d, Robert Siodmak; w, Nunnally Johnson (based on the novel by Vladimir Pozner); ph, Milton Krasner; ed, Ernest Nims; m, Dimitri Tiomkin; prod d, Duncan Cramer; fx, Devereaux Jennings, Paul K. Lerpae; cos, Irene Sharaff

De Havilland's finest hour, thanks to her underplayed escape from the butter-wouldn't-melt-in-her-mouth moments that flawed some of her finest performances. Here she tackles two roles: identical twins. One is loving and compassionate, the other a calculating killer. After one sister's suitor is found dead, police detective Mitchell rounds up witnesses who pin the blame on good twin Ruth, although she has a concrete alibi. Witnesses, however, cannot tell one twin from the other so psychologist Ayres is brought in to analyze the two women. When both twins fall in love with Ayres, his job becomes even more difficult, personal, and dangerous.

De Havilland is absolutely riveting in her roles—roles which are enriched by special effects wizards J. Devereaux Jennings and Paul Lerpae, whose split-screen technique allows for intimate scenes wherein the actress plays opposite herself. Siodmak's attention to detail creates a mood of psychological disturbance and dark suspense evident from the word go (there's a dynamite opening scene), and typical of the postwar fascination with mental illness.

DARK PASSAGE
1947 106m bw   ★★★½
Crime   /15
WB

Humphrey Bogart (Vincent Parry), Lauren Bacall (Irene Jansen), Bruce Bennett (Bob), Agnes Moorehead (Madge Rapf), Tom D'Andrea (Sam), Clifton Young (Baker), Douglas Kennedy (Detective), Rory Mallinson (George Fellsinger), Houseley Stevenson (Dr. Walter Coley), Bob Farber p, Jerry Wald; d, Delmer Daves; w, Delmer Daves (based on the novel by David Goodis); ph, Sid Hickox; ed, David Weisbart; m, Franz Waxman; art d, Charles H. Clarke; fx, H.F. Koenekamp; cos, Bernard Newman

An example of how star power can compensate plot, this is the least electric of the Bogart-Bacall pairings; luckily, there's Agnes Moorehead, the screen's best hornet, to intervene whenever the going gets too lackadasical. She's the only female Bogie ever played opposite he looks scared of.

Bogie escapes from San Quentin, where he has been imprisoned for murdering his wife, and is picked up by Bacall who has long been obsessed with his case. Convinced that he is innocent, Bacall hides him in her San Francisco apartment. On a tip from a friendly cabbie, Vincent visits an underworld plastic surgeon who gives the fugitive a new face—thereby enabling him to dodge the authorities and find his wife's real murderer.

Coming just one year after LADY IN THE LAKE, this mystery likewise employs a subjective camera technique in which the viewer sees the action through Vincent's "eyes." The chief difference, however, is the ability here to integrate the technique into the film's plastic surgery plot twist. The audience does not see Vincent's (Bogart's) face until after the bandages are removed (more than an hour into the film) and, since we haven't seen his face until that point, the switch isn't very interesting. And since the narration up until then has been by Bogie, it's impossible not to imagine you've seen him all through the film. No one else ever inflected like that. At the time of this movie, Bogart was Hollywood's highest paid actor, making more than $450,000 a year.

DARK VICTORY

1939   105m   bw   ★★★★
Drama   /PG
WB

Bette Davis (Judith Traherne), George Brent (Dr. Frederick Steele), Humphrey Bogart (Michael O'Leary), Geraldine Fitzgerald (Ann King), Ronald Reagan (Alec Hamin), Henry Travers (Dr. Parsons), Cora Witherspoon (Carrie Spottswood), Virginia Brissac (Martha), Dorothy Peterson (Miss Wainwright), Charles Richman (Colonel Mantle)

p, David Lewis; d, Edmund Goulding; w, Casey Robinson (based on the play by George Emerson Brewer, Jr. and Bertram Bloch); ph, Ernest Haller; ed, William Holmes; m, Max Steiner; art d, Robert Haas; cos, Orry-Kelly

Davis is the centerpiece of this film version of the Tallulah Bankhead stage vehicle, faring better early on when she slams through her scenes in her most hyperthyroid manner. She knows it's cliche stuff, and she's determined to wow you anyhow— barking in her most clipped manner, guzzling cocktails with "little Ronnie Reagan" (as Davis always called him), and brandishing her riding crop at miscast stablehand Bogie.

When hedonistic heiress Davis discovers she has a brain tumor, the pace drops to allow romance in the form of George Brent, her doctor. Thank God she stiff-upper-lips it through their short-lived marriage; he's the soggiest newlywed ever, and looks as if his practice consists of trimming his pencil thin mustache. There is a fine assist from lovely newcomer Geraldine Fitzgerald, as Davis's best girlfriend and Edmund Goulding has elevated the form whenever he can. Unfortunately, when Davis climbs the stairs for the last time, composer Max Steiner goes with her. Remade in 1963 as STOLEN HOURS.

DARKMAN

1990   96m   c   ★★★½
Action/Science Fiction   R/15
Robert Tapert

Liam Neeson (Peyton Westlake/Darkman), Frances McDormand (Julie Hastings), Colin Friels (Louis Strack, Jr.), Larry Drake (Robert G. Durant), Nelson Mashita (Yakitito), Jesse Lawrence Ferguson (Eddie Black), Rafael H. Robledo (Rudy Guzman), Danny Hicks (Skip), Theodore Raimi (Rick), Dan Bell (Smiley)

p, Robert Tapert; d, Sam Raimi; w, Chuck Pfarrer, Sam Raimi, Ivan Raimi, Daniel Goldin, Joshua Goldin (based on a story by Sam Raimi); ph, Bill Pope (Deluxe Color); ed, Bud Smith, Scott Smith, David Stiven; m, Danny Elfman; prod d, Randy Ser; art d, Phil Dagort; fx, Introvision Systems International, FourWard Productions, Tony Gardner, Larry Hamlin; cos, Grania Preston; anim, Chiodo Brothers Productions, Kevin Kutchaver, Jammie Friday

DARKMAN is a deliriously energetic comic-book movie from Sam Raimi, the young mastermind behind the uproariously funny and gory EVIL DEAD movies. While the press doted on the likes of David Lynch and the Coen brothers (Joel worked as an assistant editor on THE EVIL DEAD) in 1990, this cutting-edge independent filmmaker came to Hollywood with a relative lack of fanfare to make this ambitious, hallucinatory adventure. Though relatively low budget, the manic cinematic virtuosity on display here would have been welcome in BATMAN. DARKMAN's only weakness is its rather hokey and disjointed screenplay. But why carp? At its best, the film suggests a Universal horror film of the Thirties on LSD.

Peyton Westlake (Liam Neeson) is a scientist working on a formula for artificial skin. His major problem is that the pseudo-skin doesn't last long enough; after 99 minutes the cells decompose and the skin turns into bubbling goo. During a power failure, however, Peyton discovers that the skin lives much longer in the dark. Meanwhile, Peyton's girl friend, Julie (Frances McDormand), a lawyer working for crooked developer Strack (Colin Friels), finds herself in an ethical quandary when she stumbles on a memo showing illegal payoffs to members of the city council. It turns out that Strack is trying to push through permits for a massive waterfront development. He is actually an urban megalomaniac bent on taking over the city. With Robert G. Durant ("L.A. Law's" Larry Drake)—a particularly vicious chap who collects the fingers of his enemies—as his muscle, it looks as though Strack will easily succeed in achieving his nefarious ends.

Failing to persuade Julie to hand over the incriminating memo, Strack sends Durant to visit Peyton's lab, where Julie has spent the preceding evening. His thugs murder Peyton's assistant and blow up Peyton and his lab. Presumed dead by Julie and taken for a bum by those who find him, Peyton is cared for by an odd "doctor" (the uncredited Jenny Agutter) and her assistants (including director John Landis). Trying out a radical new therapy on her anonymous patient, the doctor severs Peyton's nerves to prevent pain messages from the burns from reaching his brain. As an unfortunate side effect, Peyton turns into a raving, adrenaline-pumped, superhuman schizophrenic. He slips out of the hospital and re-creates his artificial skin lab in an abandoned factory. From there, he plots his revenge and works on winning back Julie while wearing various "masks" of skin.

DARKMAN has much going for it. It boasts the right look and even the right sound, owing to another thundering, mock-operatic score by BATMAN composer Danny Elfman. The film is visually riveting. Melodramatically canted camera angles, audacious shock cuts and eccentric lap dissolves abound. DARK-

MAN offers bigger-than-life villains, an intriguingly flawed hero, and a tough, appealing heroine—all portrayed by terrific actors. It's a darkly amusing treat.

DARLING

1965   128m   bw   ★★★
Drama   /15
Vic/Appia   (U.K.)

Laurence Harvey *(Miles Brand)*, Dirk Bogarde *(Robert Gold)*, Julie Christie *(Diana Scott)*, Roland Curram *(Malcolm)*, Jose-Luis de Vilallonga *(Cesare)*, Alex Scott *(Sean Martin)*, Basil Henson *(Alec Prosser-Jones)*, Helen Lindsay *(Felicity Prosser-Jones)*, Pauline Yates *(Estette Gold)*, Tyler Butterworth *(William Prosser-Jones)*

p, Joseph Janni; d, John Schlesinger; w, Frederic Raphael (based on a story by Raphael, Schlesinger and Janni); ph, Ken Higgins; ed, James B. Clark; m, John Dankworth; cos, Julie Harris

The British New Wave turns inward and eats itself alive—unwittingly. If the movie is overrated, it's still interesting to watch it collapse upon itself. One decade earlier, the censorship standards would have truncated this film to a point that it would not have made sense. Today it appears nervous and shallow, a metaphor for the empty values it claims to take to task. Julie Christie is the amoral heroine who drifts into success casually, like she's changing panties—she models, does a bit in films, deserts a husband, deceives a lover, drifts through affairs; it takes about 20 minutes to get that she doesn't "feel complete," and we understand, even if we can't pay our bills. Marilyn Monroe and a multitude of others found out fame wasn't what it was cracked up to be. But where a Marilyn differs from The Darling is that the latter is an empty person and always was. She's like Madonna with low blood sugar doing an old Lana Turner script—but cool. She may be miserable, but at least the future is rich with tears, rather than poor.

Christie is the main reason to tune in— she's very beautiful and accomplished in a brittle sort of way. Her performance won awards all over the place, but she can't supply emotions the story and character won't let her have. It's a Best Actress in a Vacuum turn, and we defy you to feel a single thing.

DARLING LILI

1970   136m   c   ★★★½
Musical/Spy   G/U
Geoffrey

Julie Andrews *(Lili Smith)*, Rock Hudson *(Maj. William Larrabee)*, Jeremy Kemp *(Kurt von Ruger)*, Lance Percival *(Lt. Carstairs, TC)*, Jacques Marin *(Maj. Duvalle)*, Michael Witney *(Lt. George Youngblood Carson)*, Andre Maranne *(Lt. Liggett)*, Bernard Kay *(Bedford)*, Doreen Keogh *(Emma)*, Gloria Paul *(Suzette)*

p, Blake Edwards; d, Blake Edwards; w, Blake Edwards, William Peter Blatty; ph, Russell Harlan (Panavision, Technicolor); ed, Peter Zinner; m, Henry Mancini, Johnny Mercer; prod d, Fernando Carrere; fx, Van Der Veer Photo Effects, Bob Peterson, Rex Wimpy, Linwood Dunn; chor, Hermes Pan; cos, Jack Bear, Donald Brooks

Perfectly fine. Blake Edwards's big-budget WWI espionage melodrama stars Julie Andrews as Lili, a Mata Hari-like German spy using her wiles to get information from Allied officers. At first a music-hall favorite singing old-fashioned ditties, Lili eventually incorporates a bit of striptease into her staid act. She proves herself less a hard-hearted spy than a vulnerable woman when she falls in love with American flier Rock Hudson and cannot bring herself to betray him. The film came along at a time when the musical genre was struggling to redefine itself, and its

theme of innocence in everything was taking a back seat to jaded knowingness in all art forms. LILI was a commercial failure, and everyone jumped on the bandwagon to lay Andrews out (presumably, we were all supposed to be more interested in "real" types like Carrie Snodgrass). Time has proven everyone wrong. Diverting, tuneful score by Henry Mancini and Johnny Mercer includes the lovely, Oscar-nominated "Whistling away the Dark."

DATE WITH JUDY, A

1948   113m   c   ★★★
Musical/Comedy   /U
MGM

Wallace Beery *(Melvin R. Foster)*, Jane Powell *(Judy Foster)*, Elizabeth Taylor *(Carol Pringle)*, Carmen Miranda *(Rosita Conchelias)*, Xavier Cugat *(Cugat)*, Robert Stack *(Stephen Andrews)*, Selena Royle *(Mrs. Foster)*, Scotty Beckett *(Ogden "Oogie" Pringle)*, Leon Ames *(Lucien T. Pringle)*, George Cleveland *(Gramps)*

p, Joe Pasternak; d, Richard Thorpe; w, Dorothy Cooper, Dorothy Kingsley (based on the radio series by Aleen Leslie); ph, Robert Surtees (Technicolor); ed, Harold F. Kress; art d, Cedric Gibbons, Paul Groesse; fx, Warren Newcombe; chor, Stanley Donen; cos, Helen Rose

Too bad it's not Garland. Chipper MGM musical kitsch has Santa Barbara teen Judy Foster (Powell) seeing fellow teen Beckett, but she soon falls for older man Robert Stack. Elizabeth Taylor is Judy's best friend, and they both misconstrue Judy's father's (Wallace Beery) relationship with the exotic Carmen Miranda as an affair—when, in reality, the Brazilian Bombshell has been teaching him how to dance so he can surprise his wife. Shallow complications ensue until all is straightened out for a saccharine finale (Powell trilling "It's a Most Unusual Day"). Taylor is breathtakingly beautiful, but Miranda walks off with every scene she's in. Stanley Donen handled the choreography, and the songs, by a raft of composers, include Miranda's specialty, "Cuanto la Gusta."

DAUGHTER OF THE NILE

(NI-LO-HO NU-ERH)
1988   91m   c   ★★★½
Drama   /PG
Fu-Film   (Taiwan)

Yang Lin *(Lin Hsiao-yang)*, Kao Jai *(Lin Hsiao-fang, Brother)*, Yang Fan *(Ah-sang)*, Li T'ien-lu *(Grandfather)*, Ts'ui Fu-sheng *(Father)*, Hsing Shu-fen, Yu An-shun, Wu Nien-chen, Huang Ch'iung-yao, Ch'en Chien-wen

p, Lu Wen-jen, Ts'ai Sung-lin; d, Hou Hsiao-hsien; w, Chu T'ien-wen; ph, Ch'en Huai-en; ed, Liao Ch'ing-sung; m, Ch'en Cihyuan, Chang Hung-yi; prod d, Liu Chih-hua, Lin Chu

Another excellent film from Taiwanese director Hou Hsiao-hsien, who, along with Yang, is responsible for the international rise of Taiwanese cinema. A switch from the director's rural dramas, such as A SUMMER AT GRANDPA'S or A TIME TO LIVE AND A TIME TO DIE, the film is set in the heart of the city and focuses on a teenage girl, Yang Lin, and her troubled family. Her brother, Kao Jai, is a small-time thief whose crimes have intensified since the deaths of both their elder brother and their mother. Their father, Ts'ui Fu-sheng, stays away from home for long periods of time, leaving Yang Lin to care for the house, her brother, and her younger sister. Yang Lin's only escape comes in reading a popular comic book called "Daughter of the Nile," which is about a modern girl trapped in ancient Egypt who falls in love with a doomed boy king.

Although DAUGHTER OF THE NILE has more plot than any of Hou Hsiao-hsien's other work, it is still a movie made up of small, subtle moments with no strong narrative impetus. The director's visual style, greatly reminiscent of that of Japan's Yasujiro Ozu, makes use of deep-focus long takes that allow the action to unfold between the actors naturally, without the camera's becoming obtrusive. The film is like a picture puzzle, in which each unconnected piece eventually fits together to form a vivid picture of life in urban Taiwan. The cast is superb, with Taiwanese pop singer Yang Lin turning in a wonderful performance as the put-upon teen, Taipei fashion-boutique owner Kao Jai excellent as the brooding brother, and elderly Li T'ien-lu nearly stealing the film as the chatty old grandfather who constantly worries that the "neighbors will laugh" if his family doesn't behave.

DAVID

1979 125m c	★★★½
Drama/War	/15

Von Vietinghoff/Pro-ject/Filmverlag/ZDF/FFAT/Dedra (West Germany)

Walter Taub (Rabbi Singer), Irena Vrkljan (Wife), Eva Mattes (Toni), Mario Fischel (David), Dominique Horwitz (Leo), Torsten Henties (David as Child), Rudolph Sellner (Krell)

p, Joachim von Vietinghoff; d, Peter Lilienthal; w, Peter Lilienthal, Jurek Becker, Ulla Zieman (based on the novel by Joel Konig); ph, Al Ruban (Eastmancolor); ed, Sigrun Jager; m, Wojciech Kilar

An obscure commodity, powerful and sad. Lilienthal's film focuses on the plight of Fischel, a teenage Jewish boy whose family is caught in the midst of the Nazi atrocities. His rabbi father (Taub) sees his synagogue burned down by the Nazis, whose further desecrations include carving a swastika on top of his bald head. After his parents are forced to pay a shoemaker to hide their daughter (Mattes) in his shop, Fischel separates from his family, hides out, makes money doing odd jobs, and eventually is able to escape to Israel.

Lilienthal, a German Jew, is part of a generation of German filmmakers who were children during the war years and are not afraid to look back at the inhumanity of the previous generation. Although DAVID is relatively unknown in America, it received a measure of success abroad in being named the best film of the 1979 Berlin Film Festival, beating out such better-known German pictures as Werner Herzog's NOSFERATU and Rainer Werner Fassbinder's THE MARRIAGE OF MARIA BRAUN.

DAVID AND BATHSHEBA

1951 116m c	★★★½
Religious	/A
FOX	

Gregory Peck (David), Susan Hayward (Bathsheba), Raymond Massey (Nathan), Kieron Moore (Uriah), James Robertson Justice (Abishai), Jayne Meadows (Michal), John Sutton (Ira), Dennis Hoey (Joab), Walter Talun (Goliath), Paula Morgan (Adulteress)

p, Darryl F. Zanuck; d, Henry King; w, Philip Dunne (based on biblical accounts); ph, Leon Shamroy (Technicolor); ed, Barbara McLean; m, Alfred Newman; art d, Lyle Wheeler, George W. Davis; fx, Fred Sersen; chor, Jack Cole; cos, Edward Stevenson

Big-budget Biblical yucky muck. Peck plays stoic King David, fierce in battle but frail where temptresses trod. Having saved a cuckold in battle, he returns home to nurse a wound, instead nurses a raging. . . torch for the cuckold's wife, tempestuous Susan Hayward, acting within an inch of her insured head of tossing tendrils, whom he spots taking a bath. He, wisely, we say, dumps the first wife of his harem—the shrewish Jayne Meadows—that's right, Jayne Meadows! The cuckold gets sent to war and gets killed, Bathsheba marries David and a baby is born eight months, three-and-a-half weeks, six days and ten seconds later, but dies. The Lord sends Raymond Massey, as the prophet Nathan, to raise hell for their shameless ways and protest the famine that has been wrought upon the land. David sees the error of his ways, improvises the 23rd Psalm and the rains come and wash their sins away!

Typical lavish Hollywood Biblical treatment, but awash with juice, thanks to the force supplied by the three leads. Look for young Gwen Verdon as a specialty dancer. Perfect for a cold, rainy Sunday afternoon.

DAVID AND LISA

1962 95m bw	★★★½
Drama	/X
CONTINENTAL	

Keir Dullea (David), Janet Margolin (Lisa), Howard Da Silva (Dr. Swinford), Neva Patterson (Mrs. Clemens), Clifton James (John), Richard McMurray (Mr. Clemens), Nancy Nutter (Maureen), Matthew Anden (Simon), Coni Hudak (Kate), Jaime Sanchez (Carlos)

p, Paul M. Heller; d, Frank Perry; w, Eleanor Perry (based on the book by Dr. Theodore Isaac Rubin); ph, Leonard Hirshfield; ed, Irving Oshman; m, Mark Lawrence; art d, Paul M. Heller; cos, Anna Hill Johnstone

A big "little" film. Prior to this, there had been many films like THE SNAKE PIT and THE THREE FACES OF EVE, but the understated charm of DAVID AND LISA is what set the movie apart from so many other attempts at depicting the problems of the mentally ill. Dullea is a bright young man who cannot bear to be touched by anyone. His overly protective mother and father, Patterson and McMurray, leave him at the private school with Da Silva, the intelligent doctor who runs the institution which caters to children with mental problems. Margolin is a very troubled schizophrenic who talks in rhyme and is deeply ensconced in her shell. The two meet, and the gradual falling-in-love story is what forms the basis for the film. As they begin to trust each other, Dullea is able to be touched and Margolin feels secure enough to reveal her emotions.

The story was based on a real case history by Dr. T.I. Rubin, and Eleanor Perry handled the screenplay with tact and subtle care that avoids mawkishness. This is a thoughtful, poignant film with a documentary feel; there are enough comic moments and a welcome absence of psychiatric jargon. Frank Perry's direction won an award at the Venice Film Festival in 1962. Margolin and Dullea were honored as best actress and actor at the San Francisco Film Festival.

DAVID COPPERFIELD

1935 133m bw	★★★★★
Drama	/U
MGM	

W.C. Fields (Micawber), Lionel Barrymore (Dan Peggotty), Maureen O'Sullivan (Dora), Madge Evans (Agnes), Edna May Oliver (Aunt Betsey), Lewis Stone (Mr. Wickfield), Frank Lawton (David as Man), Freddie Bartholomew (David as Child), Elizabeth Allan (Mrs. Copperfield), Roland Young (Uriah Heep)

p, David O. Selznick; d, George Cukor; w, Howard Estabrook, Hugh Walpole (based on the novel by Charles Dickens); ph, Oliver T. Marsh; ed, Robert J. Kern; m, Herbert Stothart; art d, Cedric Gibbons; fx, Slavko Vorkapich; cos, Dolly Tree

Directed with restraint and impeccable taste by Cukor, produced by Selznick, DAVID COPPERFIELD is diverse and satisfying intellectually and emotionally, capturing the unparalleled beauty of Dickens's melancholic truths about life's hardships and human survival. The entire cast perform admirably, but of course it is Fields's Micawber which has achieved immortality. Despite the absence of accent, it still appears he was born to play the role, and it's the only time the Great Man allowed any heart to seep through on screen. Dickens died in 1870 at the age of 58, leaving his final work, *The Mystery of Edwin Drood*, unfinished, which didn't stop Universal from making it into a movie also released in 1935. Doubtless, he would have been thrilled at DAVID COPPERFIELD and bored with the latter.

DAVID HOLZMAN'S DIARY

1968 74m bw   ★★★★★
Drama
Paradigm

L.M. Kit Carson *(David Holzman)*, Eileen Dietz *(Penny Wohl)*, Louise Levine *(Sandra)*, Lorenzo Mans *(Pepe)*, Fern McBride *(Girl on the Subway)*, Mike Levine *(Sandra's Boyfriend)*, Bob Lesser *(Max, Penny's Agent)*, Jack Baran *(Cop)*

p, Jim McBride; d, Jim McBride; w, Jim McBride; ph, Michael Wadleigh, Paul Glickman, Paul Goldsmith; ed, Jim McBride

A unique, often brilliant satire on *cinema verite*, this "fake documentary" was shot in only five days on a $2500 budget. Carson plays a young New York filmmaker who decides to get a handle on his life by putting it all down on film. Things don't go entirely as planned, however. His girlfriend leaves him in annoyance because he's constantly filming her, his artist friend Pepe (Mans) tells him that his concept is invalid, and the police punch him for harassing people with his camera. Gradually he grows more desperate as it becomes obvious that his life is only getting more confusing on film. One day he announces to the camera that he has to go to his uncle's funeral in New Jersey. In the next scene we see photographs of David of the type taken by coin-operated booths. His voice on a scratchy record says that he is making this recording in another coin-operated booth and that when he returned from New Jersey that day, he found his apartment broken into and all his equipment stolen. He tries to come to some conclusion about his life and this project but is ultimately unable to do so.

One of cinema's most pointed statements about the impossibility of objectivity in film, DAVID HOLZMAN'S DIARY breaks down the comfortable position audiences usually enjoy while watching most mainstream films. Spectators unfamiliar with experimental cinema often resent being fooled by the documentary style of the film, which highlights the concept that "documentary" is a style of filmmaking more than it is a means of presenting "truth" in some unmediated way. Unafraid to present and implicitly criticize the more unpleasant sides of its "hero," at once witty and strangely touching, this provocative, endlessly self-conscious film today stands as one of the best independent films of the 1960s. How ironically appropriate that semi-underground filmmaker McBride later went mainstream himself, offering us modern revamps of old Hollywood ideas (THE BIG EASY, GREAT BALLS OF FIRE) or attempts to

recreate the magic of other innovative landmarks (BREATH-LESS).

DAWN OF THE DEAD

1979 125m c   ★★★★
Horror   /18
United Film

David Emge *(Stephen)*, Ken Foree *(Peter)*, Scott Reiniger *(Roger)*, Gaylen Ross *(Francine)*, David Crawford *(Dr. Foster)*, David Early *(Mr. Berman)*, George A. Romero *(Television Director)*, The Zombies

p, Richard P. Rubinstein; d, George Romero; w, George Romero; ph, Michael Gornick (Technicolor); ed, George Romero, Kenneth Davidow; m, Dario Argento; fx, Tom Savini; cos, Josie Caruso

One of the key horror films of the 1970s (a particularly fecund period for the genre), George Romero's apocalyptic followup to his classic NIGHT OF THE LIVING DEAD (1968) abandons easy scare tactics in favor of a darkly satirical assault on bourgeois culture, traditional notions of masculinity, and rampant consumerism. Zesty contributions from cinematographer Michael Gornick and special makeup effects mastermind Tom Savini help make this feel like a brightly colored action comic book peppered with gruesome (but not gratuitous) violence. Celebrated Italian horror maestro Dario Argento (SUSPIRIA, DEEP RED) co-produced and provided the lively rock score with his band, Goblin. Though all of the performances are at least adequate, this is not an actor's movie. Believe it or not, this is a film about ideas as well as gore. Nonetheless, this is strong medicine and not for all tastes

In DAWN the recently dead are still returning to life and eating the flesh of the living but the phenomena has spread to nationwide if not worldwide proportions. A brutal police assault on a minority housing project that occurs early in the film expands upon the conclusion of NIGHT. We see that in the eyes of the law, there is little difference between political radicals, innocent bystanders of color, and carnivorous zombies. Ross, an employee of a local television station, and her boyfriend Emge, a traffic helicopter pilot, decide to try to escape the madness in a helicopter accompanied by two SWAT team cops, Reiniger and Foree. They eventually land atop a shopping mall. Once they clear out the zombies, the four decide to remain in this shoppers' paradise where they get to live out their wildest consumer fantasies until they are forced to defend themselves from marauding bikers who want to crash their party.

Romero's films tend to be left of center in outlook: ethnically and sexually integrated, pro-feminist, gay-friendly, anti-macho, and skeptical about capitalism, they represent a progressive aspect of the genre. His "living dead" movies are among the Pittsburgh-based auteur's most personal efforts. So terrifying in their initial incarnation, the zombies in DAWN have become rather pathetic (though still very dangerous) eating machines. Nuns, clowns, and Hare Krishas number among their ranks as they return to the mall they loved in life. "They are us," one of the characters wryly observes. This independently produced low budget film ($1.5 million) went on to become one of the most profitable "indies" in film history. DAY OF THE DEAD, ostensibly the conclusion of the DEAD series, followed in 1985.

DAWN PATROL, THE

1930 105m bw   ★★★
War
First National

Richard Barthelmess (*Dick Courtney*), Douglas Fairbanks, Jr. (*Douglas Scott*), Neil Hamilton (*Major Brand*), William Janney (*Gordon Scott*), James Finlayson (*Field Sergeant*), Clyde Cook (*Bott*), Gardner James (*Ralph Hollister*), Edmund Breon (*Lt. Bathurst*), Frank McHugh (*Flaherty*), Jack Ackroyd

p, Robert North; d, Howard Hawks; w, Howard Hawks, Dan Totheroh, Seton I. Miller (based on the story "The Flight Commander" by John Monk Saunders); ph, Ernest Haller; ed, Ray Curtiss; fx, Fred Jackman

The original, but for once, not the best. Director Howard Hawks's first foray into sound cinema shows his typically interesting and exciting visuals, but there is little evidence of his future skill with dialogue in the stilted and overly talky screenplay penned by Totheroh, Miller, and Hawks himself.

The action takes place during WWI, and Richard Barthelmess and Douglas Fairbanks are hot-dog aces of the British air corps who consistently disobey orders to settle disputes of "honor" with the Germans. After German fliers taunt the pair regarding their flying prowess, Barthelmess and Fairbanks jump into their planes and ruthlessly attack a helpless German air squadron, killing many pilots before they can get off the ground. On their return, outraged commanding officer Neil Hamilton vents his fury on the boyish pilots, only to be suddenly handed a message telling him that he has been transferred to another unit. Hamilton delights in telling Barthelmess that he is now in command and perhaps now he will develop a sense of responsibility when he must deal with a group of unruly fliers like himself.

Hawks's film is a strong antiwar statement which illustrates the futility of heroics that only end in death on both sides. The dogfight footage is some of the best aerial fighting photography ever filmed, but the movie suffers from the stagey, stiff dialogue sequences that obviously frustrated Hawks. DAWN PATROL was re-made in 1938 by Edmund Goulding starring Basil Rathbone, Errol Flynn, and David Niven, and it is this version that modern-day audiences find easier to sit through due to the more polished handling of the dialogue sequences.

DAWN PATROL, THE
1938   103m   bw   ★★★★
War   /A
WB

Errol Flynn (*Courtney*), David Niven (*Scott*), Basil Rathbone (*Major Brand*), Donald Crisp (*Phills*), Melville Cooper (*Watkins*), Barry Fitzgerald (*Bott*), Carl Esmond (*Von Mueller*), Peter Willes (*Hollister*), Morton Lowry (*Johnnie Scott*), Michael Brooke (*Squires*)

p, Robert Lord; d, Edmund Goulding; w, Seton I. Miller, Dan Totheroh (based on the story "The Flight Commander" by John Monk Saunders); ph, Tony Gaudio; ed, Ralph Dawson; m, Max Steiner; art d, John Hughes; fx, Edwin DuPar

A superbly-cast remake of Hawks's 1930 picture of the same name, THE DAWN PATROL concerns a dashing, conscience-haunted flight commander, Capt. Courtney (Errol Flynn), of the 59th Squadron in France during WWI. He and his men fly the most dangerous aircraft—a source of Courtney's anger which he attempts to cover with banter and cynical humor—creating unsafe odds for the fliers and contributing to their untimely deaths. The fatalities mount so drastically that raw recruits with little flying experience are sent into the skies to battle without much chance of survival. Between the daily dawn patrols that decimate the command, the fliers face death with stiff upper lips and scotch and sodas at the club bar, where a battered gramophone continually grinds out the plaintive "Poor Butterfly." In another room

sits Maj. Brand (Basil Rathbone), the deskbound commander whose job it is to assign fliers to each dawn patrol, mechanically writing their names on a blackboard and methodically erasing those killed each day. Later, when Brand is reassigned, Courtney is called on to replace him; now it is he who must decide which flier will take off to face a certain death. Though the original story of Hawks's film was retained, the dialogue was rewritten and polished to great improvement, chiefly in the relationship between Courtney and his best pal, Lt. Scott (David Niven). As in the original (or in Hawks's AIR FORCE), the remake is very much concerned with fraternity, loyalty, and courage in the face of death.

DAY AT THE RACES, A
1937   109m   c/bw   ★★★½
Comedy/Musical   /U
MGM

Groucho Marx (*Dr. Hugo Z. Hackenbush*), Chico Marx (*Tony*), Harpo Marx (*Stuffy*), Allan Jones (*Gil*), Maureen O'Sullivan (*Judy*), Margaret Dumont (*Mrs. Upjohn*), Leonard Ceeley (*Whitmore*), Douglas Dumbrille (*Morgan*), Esther Muir (*"Flo"*), Sig Rumann (*Dr. Steinberg*)

p, Max Siegel, Sam Wood; d, Sam Wood; w, Robert Pirosh, George Seaton, George Oppenheimer (based on a story by Pirosh and Seaton); ph, Joseph Ruttenberg; ed, Frank E. Hull; m, Bronislau Kaper, Walter Jurmann, Gus Kahn; art d, Cedric Gibbons; chor, Dave Gould

Hugo Z. Hackenbush (Groucho Marx) is a horse doctor who takes over a large sanitarium at the behest of hypochondriac socialite Mrs. Upjohn (Margaret Dumont). The sanitarium is owned by Judy (Maureen O'Sullivan), but she's having trouble paying off the mortgage. With the help of Stuffy (Harpo Marx), Tony (Chico Marx), and a racehorse named Hi-Hat, she is able to save the hospital. Of course, the plot isn't important here; what really counts is the steady stream of wild comedy routines provided by the Marx Brothers who poke fun at everything from the medical profession to high society.

Striving for a worthy follow-up to the magnificent A NIGHT AT THE OPERA, the comedians took their act on the road and performed these routines before live audiences throughout the country. The opulent, though somewhat dull, musical production numbers prevent this from being as mesmerizing as its predecessor, but while dated, A DAY AT THE RACES is, nonetheless, a very entertaining comedy. Producer Irving Thalberg, to whom the Marxes were devoted, died during production.

DAY FOR NIGHT
(LA NUIT AMERICAINE)
1973   120m   c   ★★★★★
Drama   PG/15
Carrosse/PECF/PIC   (France)

Francois Truffaut (*Ferrand*), Jacqueline Bissett (*Julie Baker*), Jean-Pierre Leaud (*Alphonse*), Valentina Cortese (*Severine*), Jean-Pierre Aumont (*Alexandre*), Dani (*Lilianna*), Alexandra Stewart (*Stacey*), Jean Champion (*Bertrand*), Nathalie Baye (*Joelle*), Bernard Menez (*Bernard, the Prop Man*)

p, Marcel Berbert; d, Francois Truffaut; w, Francois Truffaut, Suzanne Schiffman, Jean-Louis Richard; ph, Pierre-William Glenn (Eastmancolor); ed, Yann Dedet, Martine Barraque; m, Georges Delerue; art d, Damien Lanfranchi; cos, Monique Dury

The best film ever made about the process of shooting a film. Director Truffaut plays director Ferrand, who is in the midst of directing "I Want You to Meet Pamela," a feature being shot in the La Victorine studios in the south of France. His cast includes a temperamental actor, Alphonse (Jean-Pierre Leaud), who wonders aloud, "Are women magic?"; Julie (Jacqueline Bisset), a famous actress recovering from a nervous breakdown; Alexandre (Jean-Pierre Aumont), a veteran actor, "continental lover" and closet homosexual; Severine (Valentina Cortese), a loud, alcoholic Italian actress who once was a great screen lover opposite Alexandre but who now cannot remember even the simplest dialogue; and Stacey (Alexandra Stewart), a bit player whose pregnancy causes terrible scheduling problems. Given equal time is Ferrand's crew—bumbling prop man Bernard (Bernard Menez); flaky makeup girl Odile (Nike Arrighi); script girl Lilianna (Dani), who cares nothing for film and gets the job only because she sleeps with Alphonse; unit manager Lajoie (Gaston Joly); producer Bertrand (Jean Champion); and the all-important production assistant, Joelle (Nathalie Baye).

As one might expect, the characters themselves are more important than the thin plot—Ferrand trying to keep his production on track when his emotionally unstable leads, Alphonse and Julie, make the mistake of sleeping together for just one night. Full of in jokes and cross-references, DAY FOR NIGHT is ample proof that what goes on behind the screen is often of more interest than the film itself. Paradoxically, it is also one of Truffaut's least personal films, as he hides behind his alter ego Ferrand and interacts only on the most superficial levels with his cast and crew. By the film's end, it is Ferrand whom we know least.

DAY OF THE JACKAL, THE

1973   142m   c   ★★★★
Thriller   PG/15
Warwick   (U.K./France)

Edward Fox ("The Jackal"), Terence Alexander (Lloyd), Michel Auclair (Colonel Rolland), Alan Badel (The Minister), Tony Britton (Inspector Thomas), Denis Carey (Casson), Adrien Cayla-Legrand (The President), Cyril Cusack (Gunsmith), Maurice Denham (General Colbert), Vernon Dobtcheff (Interrogator)

p, John Woolf, David Deutsch, Julien Derode; d, Fred Zinnemann; w, Kenneth Ross (based on the novel by Frederick Forsyth); ph, Jean Tournier (Technicolor); ed, Ralph Kemplen; m, Georges Delerue; art d, Willy Holt, Ernest Archer; fx, Georges Iaconelli, John Richardson; cos, Elizabeth Haffenden, Joan Bridge, Rosine Delamare, Jean Zay, Chanel

A secret French military organization plans to assassinate President de Gaulle (played by Cayla-Legrand, an uncanny look-alike), by hiring one of the world's most fearsome professional killers, a man known only as "The Jackal" (Fox). Top French police investigator Lebel (Lonsdale) learns the name "Jackal" from an informer in the plotter's ranks and cleverly pieces together the identity of the killer-for-hire. What follows is an intricate and meticulous story with a parallel structure that details the Jackal's preparations for the assassination and Lebel's efforts to stop him. Director Zinnemann faithfully follows the Forsyth best-seller, presenting a precise, almost discomfitting reconstruction of the story. Fox is superb as the coldly impassionate killer, and Lonsdale is properly plodding yet magnificently analytical as the detective tracking him down. A taut, suspenseful, and fascinating political thriller.

DAY OF THE LOCUST, THE

1975   144m   c   ★★★★
Drama   R/X
Paramount

Donald Sutherland (Homer), Karen Black (Faye), Burgess Meredith (Harry), William Atherton (Tod), Geraldine Page (Big Sister), Richard Dysart (Claude Estee), Bo Hopkins (Earle Shoop), Pepe Serna (Miguel), Lelia Goldoni (Mary Dove), Billy Barty (Abe)

p, Jerome Hellman; d, John Schlesinger; w, Waldo Salt (based on the novel by Nathanael West); ph, Conrad Hall (Panavision, Technicolor); ed, Jim Clark; m, John Barry; prod d, Richard MacDonald; art d, John Lloyd; cos, Ann Roth

DAY OF THE LOCUST, like the powerful and incisive Nathaniel West novel on which it is based, focuses on the seamy side of the city of dreams in its 1930s heyday—the subculture of losers, misfits, and neurotic fringe characters. Black is a sexy untalented aspiring actress who lives with her father, Meredith, a former vaudevillian, now a down on his luck door-to-door salesman. Recognizing her limited prospects, Black becomes a regular on the casting couch of producers in the hope that she'll rise above her usual walk-ons. She still has dreams of fame and legitimacy. Despite her dubious character, Atherton, an altruistic art director, falls for her but she gives him the cold shoulder—at first. She soon begins amusing herself by toying with him. This is the beginning of a pattern. When she finds herself destitute she moves in with a sensitive but oafish accountant, Sutherland, who loves her from afar. She and all about him use and ridicule him as he lumbers through life; he is particularly vexed by an evil neighborhood child, Haley. Everything comes to a head in the apocalyptic finale of the film, a memorably traumatic spectacle.

This grim conclusion, along with the stark and unsavory story and characters that preceded it, brought shudders to audiences and undoubtedly helped this excellent film fail at the box office. Nevertheless, it accurately captures the intent of West's dark masterpiece. Black is the perfect slattern with movie ambition—cheap, shallow, conniving, and utterly reprehensible. Sutherland gives one of his best performances as the doltish but sensitive outsider whose concern for films is marginal at best. The movie boasts excellent supporting players, such as Atherton as the ethereal art director. He is savvy to Hollywood and gives it back the banal glibness that is the hallmark of its society. Many of the characters are inspired by historical Hollywood figures. DAY OF THE LOCUST exudes authenticity, from the costuming to the cars, from the exotic clothes to the marcelled hair styles.

DAY OF THE TRIFFIDS, THE

1963   93m   c   ★★½
Science Fiction/Horror   /15
Allied Artists

Howard Keel (Bill Masen), Nicole Maurey (Christine Durrant), Janette Scott (Karen Goodwin), Kieron Moore (Tom Goodwin), Mervyn Johns (Prof. Coker), Janina Faye (Susan), Alison Leggatt (Miss Coker), Ewan Roberts (Dr. Soames), Colette Wilde (Nurse Jamieson), Carole Ann Ford (Bettina)

p, George Pitcher; d, Steve Sekely, Freddie Francis (uncredited); w, Philip Yordan (based on the novel by John Wyndham); ph, Ted Moore (Cinemascope, Eastmancolor); ed, Spencer Reeve; m, Ron Goodwin; art d, Cedric Dawe; fx, Wally Veevers

Decent, albeit uneven, British sci-fi/horror film. Keel stars as an American sailor who has escaped being blinded by a sudden meteor shower that has robbed most of the Earth's population of its sight. The mysterious meteor storm has also brought with it alien plant spores which grow into large, carnivorous plants that multiply and threaten to overrun the planet. The man-eating plants are known as "Triffids" and resemble rampaging stalks of broccoli that have an easy time feeding off of the blind humans who can't protect themselves. Keel becomes the leader of a small band of people who have somehow escaped being blinded. Together they plot to make a final stand against the vicious plants. Meanwhile, marine biologist Moore and his wife, Scott (who have been trapped in a lighthouse by the Triffids) search for a scientific solution.

Always interesting but bogged down by lengthy romantic interludes, the film is thought-provoking and scary at times (the Triffids are more effective than they have any right to be). This is the third adaptation from the works of John Wyndham, the first two yielding the superb VILLAGE OF THE DAMNED and CHILDREN OF THE DAMNED. For fans of the once great untrained baritone voice of Keel, it is interesting that in THE DAY OF THE TRIFFIDS he rewrote his own dialogue because he was so displeased by screenwriter Yordan's efforts.

DAY OF WRATH
(VREDENS DAG)
1943 97m bw   ★★★★★
Drama   /A
Palladium (Denmark)

Thirkild Roose (Absalon Pedersson), Lisbeth Movin (Anne Pedersdotter, His Wife), Sigrid Neiiendam (Meret, His Mother), Preben Lerdorff-Rye (Martin, Son by His First Marriage), Albert Hoeberg (The Bishop), Olaf Ussing (Laurentius), Anna Svierkier (Herlofs Marte)

p, Carl-Theodor Dreyer; d, Carl-Theodor Dreyer; w, Carl-Theodor Dreyer, Poul Knudsen, Mogens Skot-Hansen (based on the novel by Wiers Jenssens); ph, Carl Anderson; ed, Edith Schlussel, Anne Marie Petersen; m, Poul Schierbeck; art d, Erik Aaes

DAY OF WRATH was the first feature film directed by the great Carl Dreyer after his 1932 masterwork, VAMPYR. In WRATH, Dreyer returns to the witches, religion, and spiritualism that marked his earlier, silent masterpiece, THE PASSION OF JOAN OF ARC (1928).

Set during the throes of a witch hunt in the 17th century, the film centers around a young woman, Anne (Lisbeth Movin), who is married to a much older, puritanical man she hates. She falls in love with his son, with whom she spends idyllic afternoons in the woods. Pressure begins to build, and she is heard to whisper aloud how she hungers for the death of her husband. Soon afterward, the husband dies, and she is accused of being a witch.

The plot is deceptively simple and is barely representative of the film's power, for the film's brilliance lies in Dreyer's direction and the uncanny imagery, which resembles nothing so much as Rembrandt masterworks come to life. At a slow and deliberate pace, he allows the camera to linger, almost erotically, on images, waiting for the "right" look on a face or the correct movement of a hand. A study of good and evil, repression and oppression, sexuality and guilt, DAY OF WRATH is a truly spiritual film.

DAY THE EARTH STOOD STILL, THE
1951 92m bw   ★★★★
Science Fiction   /U
FOX

Michael Rennie (Klaatu), Patricia Neal (Helen Benson), Hugh Marlowe (Tom Stevens), Sam Jaffe (Dr. Barnhardt), Billy Gray (Bobby Benson), Frances Bavier (Mrs. Barley), Lock Martin (Gort), Drew Pearson (Himself), Frank Conroy (Harley), Fay Roope (Major General)

p, Julian Blaustein; d, Robert Wise; w, Edmund H. North (based on a story by Harry Bates); ph, Leo Tover; ed, William Reynolds; m, Bernard Herrmann; art d, Lyle Wheeler, Addison Hehr; fx, Fred Sersen

Working from Edmund H. North's unusually literate adaptation of Harry Bates's short story "Farewell to the Master," Robert Wise created a classic science fiction film with a strong pacifist message.

Sent by a federation of planets to warn the people of Earth to stop nuclear testing before the planet is destroyed, the Christ-like Rennie descends into Washington, D.C., in his spaceship, accompanied by his massive robot, Gort. When an American soldier panics and shoots Rennie, Gort eliminates them. The wounded Rennie stops the robot from destroying the planet by uttering the now-classic phrase, "Klaatu barada nikto." Taken to a military hospital, Rennie escapes and, posing as a normal human, seeks shelter in Neal's boarding house. Here he begins to learn that Earth people really are not so bad. Since he can make no formal contact with the governments of Earth, Rennie arranges a demonstration of his power that justifies the title of the film.

Superb performances by all involved, restrained direction by Wise, and a magnificent and innovative score by Bernard Herrmann help keep this 35-year-old film just as relevant today as it was the day it was released.

DAYBREAK
(LE JOUR SE LEVE)
1939 88m bw   ★★★★★
Drama   /A
Sigma (France)

Jean Gabin (Francois), Jules Berry (M. Valentin), Jacqueline Laurent (Francoise), Arletty (Clara), Rene Genin (Concierge), Mady Berry (Concierge's Wife), Bernard Blier (Gaston), Marcel Peres (Paulo), Jacques Baumer (The Inspector), Rene Bergeron (Cafe Proprietor)

d, Marcel Carne; w, Jacques Prevert, Jacques Viot; ph, Curt Courant; ed, Rene Le Henaff; m, Maurice Jaubert; cos, Boris Bilinsky

A superb example of French poetic realism, this is certainly one of the finest French films of the 1930s. Jean Gabin, in perhaps the finest performance of his career, is Francois, a tough, romantic loner who barricades himself in his apartment after committing a crime of passion, the murder of the lecherous Valentin (Jules Berry). While police surround his Normandy home, Francois remembers (in flashback) the two women he loved—Francoise (Jacqueline Laurent) and Clara (Arletty)—and Valentin, the man who wooed both.

Every facet of the film's production values is expertly realized, but perhaps the most awe-inspiring is the set design of Alexandre Trauner—a re-creation of a city street corner decorated with Dubonnet posters that is one of the most memorable ever filmed. More poetic than realistic, it is very much a film of a mood, but despite the optimism of its ironic title, melancholy and despair predominate. This inherent irony was then mirrored by real-life events as the film was released not long before Paris became an occupied city, and its citizens, like Francois, were left with no way out. Recognizing the similarities, the Vichy government banned the picture as "demoralizing." Remade in Hollywood as THE LONG NIGHT.

DAYS OF HEAVEN

1978   95m   c   ★★★★½
Drama   PG
Paramount

Richard Gere (Bill), Brooke Adams (Abby), Sam Shepard (The Farmer), Linda Manz (Linda), Bob Wilke (Farm Foreman), Jackie Shultis (Linda's Friend), Stuart Margolin (Mill Foreman), Timothy Scott (Harvest Hand), Gene Bell (Dancer), Doug Kershaw (Fiddler)

p, Bert Schneider, Harold Schneider; d, Terrence Malick; w, Terrence Malick; ph, Nestor Almendros (Metrocolor); ed, Billy Weber; m, Ennio Morricone; art d, Jack Fisk; fx, John Thomas, Mel Merrells; cos, Patricia Norris

Set in the postindustrial revolution America of the early 1900s, DAYS OF HEAVEN chronicles the odyssey of a rootless migrant laborer (Gere), his little sister (Manz), and his soulmate (Adams), as they flee the industrial blight of the city for the sanctuary and anonymity of the Heartland. When the impulsive and hot-tempered Gere kills a steel-mill foreman in anger, the three jump a train and head for the plains of Texas, merging with the endless caravan of homeless immigrants looking for work. Their journey brings them to the land of wealthy, self-made wheat farmer Shepard, who offers them employment during the harvest.

An enigmatic figure, Shepard, living alone in a huge Victorian mansion that overlooks his golden empire, is slowly wasting away from some illness. As he watches Adams work in the fields, he grows to love her—as Pharaoh did young Sarah in the Old Testament story—and sees some private salvation in making her his "queen." Gere learns of the farmer's illness and, reasoning that the powerful farmer will be dead soon, contrives, like Abraham of old to masquerade with Adams as brother and sister thereby allowing Shepard to marry Adams and plant the seeds of a future inheritance. For a time after the marriage, the four live together as a family in a state of grace and sublime happiness. The scheme goes awry, however, when Adams begins to genuinely care for Shepard. When Shepard realizes the lovers' duplicity, his rage is that of the Old Testament Pharoah, on whose lands Jehovah's wrathful plagues fell. The contest between the two suitors precipitates a holocaust that blows apart the fragile paradise that so briefly flourished.

Director Malick endows this simple, timeless story with the enormous scope and resonance of myth through a clear vision unclouded by sentimentality and by a deft juxtaposition of image, music, and character. Although this is only his second feature film (BADLANDS, made five years earlier, was his first), he demonstrates a mastery of cinematic technique. The story is rich with Biblical and mythical allusions: there are echoes of Genesis, the Wasteland myth, and Greek tragedy. The vast, uncluttered compositions sometimes render the characters as little more than puppets in the hands of fate, reinforcing the universality of the story. Almendros's hyper-realistic cinematography is breathtaking.

The dialogue is sparse and almost incidental, the characters' words insignificant amidst the pervasive whisper of the wheat, the clatter of the threshing machines, and the awful drone of the locust horde that accompanies the final holocaust. The sound alone is astonishing. Morricone's haunting, wistful score adds measurably to the sweep and timelessness of the film.

DAYS OF 36

(IMERES TOU 36)
1972   100m   c   ★★★★
Drama
Finos Film   (Greece)

Thanos Grammenos (Convict), George Kyritsis (Deputy)

p, George Papalios; d, Theo Angelopoulos; w, Theo Angelopoulos; ph, Georges Arvanitis

Grammenos is arrested for the assassination of a Greek politician in 1936. Protesting his innocence, he is visited by Kyritsis, whom he manages to lock in the cell with him. Then he threatens to kill the hostage if the police do not release him. The situation drags on for days while the government tries to come up with a solution. Finally they hire a sniper to take up a position on a nearby roof and shoot the man in his cell. Excellent political drama based on a true story, superbly photographed and thoughtfully directed.

DAYS OF WINE AND ROSES

1962   117m   bw   ★★★★
Drama   /X
WB

Jack Lemmon (Joe), Lee Remick (Kirsten), Charles Bickford (Arnesen), Jack Klugman (Jim Hungerford), Alan Hewitt (Leland), Tom Palmer (Ballefoy), Debbie Megowan (Debbie), Maxine Stuart (Dottie), Katherine Squire (Mrs. Nolan), Jack Albertson (Trayner)

p, Martin Manulis; d, Blake Edwards; w, J.P. Miller (based on the television play by J.P. Miller); ph, Philip Lathrop; ed, Patrick McCormack; m, Henry Mancini; art d, Joseph C. Wright; fx, Horace L. Hulburd; cos, Don Feld

Former light comedian Jack Lemmon's powerful performance as an alcoholic counts among Hollywood's most memorable depictions of this condition such as Ray Milland in THE LOST WEEKEND and Jimmy Cagney in COME FILL THE CUP. He's a young, bright adman who meets and falls in love with Remick. Early in their relationship, he's just a social drinker and she's a teetotaler. Soon after their marriage, subtle changes begin to occur. Lemmon is stressed out from work and begins drinking daily after work. Remick adores him and soon joins in sharing the bottle. Before long they are immersed in the liquored life and even the birth of their baby daughter fails to slow their descent into the gutter.

The movie features many emotionally shattering scenes and the going sometimes gets rough. Lemmon surprised many with the intensity of his performance. He has a mad spell in a greenhouse and an almost SNAKE PIT-like siege in a hospital ward. This is a long way from frolicking in drag with Marilyn Monroe in SOME LIKE IT HOT! The screenplay was based on J.P. Miller's teleplay, which starred Cliff Robertson on "Playhouse 90." Robertson was not a star at the time, and the decision was made to use Lemmon. Edwards's direction was smooth and neither he nor Miller ever took a stance or moralized. They just showed what it was like to be an alcoholic in the 1960s and let the audience draw its own conclusions.

DEAD, THE

1987   83m   c   ★★★★½
Drama   PG/U
Liffey

Anjelica Huston (Gretta Conroy), Donal McCann (Gabriel Conroy, Her Husband), Rachael Dowling (Lily), Cathleen Delany (Aunt Julia Morkan), Helena Carroll (Aunt Kate Morkan), Ingrid Craigie (Mary Jane), Dan O'Herlihy (Mr. Browne), Frank Patterson (Bartell D'Arcy), Donal Donnelly (Freddy Malins), Marie Kean (Mrs. Malins) p, Wieland Schulz-Keil, Chris Sievernich; d, John Huston; w, Tony Huston (based on the short story from *The Dubliners* by James Joyce); ph, Fred Murphy (Foto-Kem Color); ed, Roberto Silvi; m, Alex North; prod d, Stephen Grimes, J. Dennis Washington; cos, Dorothy Jeakins

This sublime adaptation of the last story in James Joyce's *Dubliners* is John Huston's final film, and it is as beautiful, delicate, and moving an epitaph as any filmmaker could ever desire.

Set in Dublin on the chilly night of January 6, 1904, the feast of the Epiphany, THE DEAD takes place at the home of spinsters Kate (Helena Carroll) and Julia Morkan (Cathleen Delany) during their annual post-holidays party. Their favorite guests are their sophisticated nephew, Gabriel Conroy (Donal McCann), and his beautiful wife, Gretta (Anjelica Huston). After most of the revelers have left, Gretta is struck by the haunting rendition of "The Lass of Aughrim" sung by one of the guests. On the cab ride back to their hotel, Gretta is distant, lost in her thoughts. In their room, a tearful Gretta confesses to Gabriel that the song has stirred long-suppressed memories of a brief and tragic romance from her youth. After hearing her story, Gabriel marvels at the power that the dead hold over the living.

THE DEAD is a breathtakingly beautiful movie, a mature work of a master filmmaker. Huston, a lifelong admirer of Joyce, had wanted to make a film adaptation of "The Dead" since the 1950s, but put the idea on the back burner because of its uncommercial nature. When producer Wieland Schulz-Keil decided the time was right, he hired Huston's eldest son, Tony, to write the screenplay, which is scrupulously faithful to Joyce. The casting is marvelous, and Huston allows all his performers equal screen time until the end when Anjelica Huston and McCann become the focus. The party scene is a flurry of detailed movement, wonderfully choreographed. Huston concentrates on the interaction of the characters—the conversations, the movements, the rituals—and glories in the nuances of human behavior.

The film's most powerful sequence, however, is the scene between husband and wife. Anjelica Huston is superb, striking the perfect balance of emotions. It is a performance of grace and eloquence. Equally excellent is McCann, who somehow manages to convey with a minimum of visible acting the dawning self-awareness described by Joyce. THE DEAD was made by a man who had a deep appreciation for all the arts and how they enrich the human experience.

DEAD AGAIN
1991   107m   c   ★★★
Mystery/Romance   R/15
Mirage Enterprises/Paramount

Kenneth Branagh *(Mike Church/Roman Strauss)*, Emma Thompson *(Grace/Margaret Strauss)*, Andy Garcia *(Gray Baker)*, Lois Hall *(Sister Constance)*, Richard Easton *(Father Timothy)*, Jo Anderson *(Sister Madeleine/Starlet)*, Patrick Montes *(Pickup Driver)*, Raymond Cruz *(Clerk)*, Robin Williams *(Doctor Cozy Carlisle)*, Wayne Knight *("Piccolo" Pete)*

p, Lindsay Doran, Charles H. Maguire; d, Kenneth Branagh; w, Scott Frank; ph, Matthew F. Leonetti; ed, Peter E. Berger; m, Patrick Doyle; prod d, Tim Harvey; art d, Sydney Z. Litwack; cos, Phyllis Dalton

Director Kenneth Branagh and his real-life wife Emma Thompson both have dual roles in DEAD AGAIN, a complexly plotted mystery that is steeped in a pastiche of Hollywood classics.

Los Angeles. Private detective Mike Church (Branagh), at the behest of the orphanage priest who raised him, rescues an unknown amnesiac (Thompson), who he names Grace and with whom he quickly falls in love. With the aid of hypnotist and antique dealer Franklyn Madson (Derek Jacobi), who appears on the scene, Grace undergoes hypnosis and recounts her past life as Margaret, a British concert pianist married to Roman Strauss, a flamboyant emigre conductor who was imprisoned for her brutal murder. At a second session, she begins to blur the identities of Roman and Mike, and the latter realizes that Grace is remembering a past life in which he plays a part as well. Intrigued, Church undergoes hypnosis himself and discovers just how symbiotic their relationship is: *he* was Margaret and Grace was Roman. Further investigation reveals that in 1949 the Strauss murder case actually transpired, resulting in Roman's execution. As the modern-day and past experiences increasingly overlap, Church fears his romantic attraction to Grace will again end with a violent death.

Scott Frank (PLAIN CLOTHES, LITTLE MAN TATE) has created a screenplay which, at the expense of story and character development, prides itself on its ability to quote liberally from great films of the past. DEAD AGAIN borrows icons, motifs, characters and camera angles from a number of classics, most notably Hitchcock thrillers such as REBECCA, with its gothic mansion and creepy housekeeper, SPELLBOUND, with its hypnosis, psychoanalysis and giant Salvador Dali scissors, and VERTIGO, with its reincarnated doubles and Catholic trappings, but also film noir mysteries and Orson Welles's CITIZEN KANE.

However unlikely the twists and turns in this mystery, DEAD AGAIN moves briskly forward, never weighed down by any sense of seriousness. Branagh's transformations between his lightweight, American detective and his heavy, Germanic musician are pure bravado, done for the thrill of watching the Master Thespian assume two wildly different incarnations. Yet even as the movie takes on its many looks and plays its jokes, the essential thriller element at its core does maintain its suspense. Ultimately, Branagh goes for broke and offers a wild, gorey and preposterous finale in which the villain is impaled on a huge pair of scissors. Such antics may seem like too much, but they prove an appropriate conclusion to a movie that is about nothing more than the showmanship of movies.

DEAD CALM
1989   96m   c   ★★★½
Horror/Thriller   R/15
Kennedy Miller   (Australia)

Sam Neill *(John Ingram)*, Nicole Kidman *(Rae Ingram)*, Billy Zane *(Hughie Warriner)*, Rod Mullinar *(Russell Bellows)*, Joshua Tilden *(Danny)*, George Shevtsov *(Doctor)*, Michael Long *(Specialist Doctor)*

p, Terry Hayes, Doug Mitchell, George Miller; d, Phillip Noyce; w, Terry Hayes (based on the novel by Charles Williams); ph, Dean Semler (Panavision, Eastmancolor); ed, Richard Francis-Bruce; m, Graeme Revell; prod d, Graham Walker; art d, Kimble Hilder; cos, Norma Moriceau

Though it lacks Alfred Hitchcock's wry and macabre sense of humor, DEAD CALM is a cracklingly good, cold-blooded film that never lets up in its truly Hitchcockian suspense. Under the gripping direction of Phillip Noyce, the film sustains tension and power beautifully, right through to its startling conclusion.

Middle-aged surgeon John Ingram (Sam Neill) and his wife Rae (Nicole Kidman) embark on an extended yachting trip after the gruesome death of their little son in a car accident. The trip is intended as a therapeutic remedy for Rae who is in an emotionally fragile state. The therapy seems to be working, and things go well until the couple rescues Hughie Warriner (Billy Zane), the sole survivor from a sinking schooner near the Great Barrier Reef. Warriner claims that all the other passengers died of food poisoning but Ingram boards the schooner to investigate and makes a nasty discovery that turns their vacation into a nightmare.

Neill and Zane both turn in excellent performances, but Kidman (DAYS OF THUNDER, BILLY BATHGATE) does the most interesting and demanding work as the wife who must snap out of her melancholy distraction to outwit her vile captor. During the film's last half, Kidman convincingly transforms from a vunerable, distraught housewife into a ferocious battler—and it's an electrifying metamorphosis. The taut editing and Noyce's direction are splendid, augmenting Terry Hayes's sharp (though somewhat predictable) script. George Miller, director of the MAD MAX trilogy and former student of Philip Noyce at Melbourne University, is one of the producers.

DEAD END
1937 93m bw   ★★★★
Crime   /PG
UA

Sylvia Sidney *(Drina)*, Joel McCrea *(Dave)*, Humphrey Bogart *(Baby Face Martin)*, Wendy Barrie *(Kay)*, Claire Trevor *(Francie)*, Allen Jenkins *(Hunk)*, Marjorie Main *(Mrs. Martin)*, Billy Halop *(Tommy)*, Huntz Hall *(Dippy)*, Bobby Jordan *(Angel)*

p, Samuel Goldwyn; d, William Wyler; w, Lillian Hellman (based on the play by Sidney Kingsley); ph, Gregg Toland; ed, Daniel Mandell; m, Alfred Newman; art d, Richard Day; fx, James Basevi; cos, Omar Kiam

Depression-era poverty, slums and crime provide the themes for DEAD END, Sam Goldwyn's film production of the popular Sidney Kingsley play. Well meaning and once considered hardhitting, this celebrated social drama now seems rather mawkish and quaint. The message is not just that these impoverished surroundings can be a cradle for crime but that good folks may also be brought up on these mean streets.

After ten years of pursuing a criminal career, escalating from robbery to murder, Bogart returns to his old New York City neighborhood. Disguised by extensive plastic surgery, he wants to see his mother (Main) and his old girlfriend (Trevor) while avoiding a nationwide dragnet. DEAD END is also the story of McCrea, a scrupulous and unsuccessful architect struggling to get out of the slum. He thinks he's in love with Barrie, a rich woman living in a nearby luxury apartment building but he is the apple of Sidney's eye. She is a respectable woman living in poverty and struggling to keep her kid brother, Halop, on the straight and narrow. Meanwhile, Bogart begins teaching Halop and the other "Dead End Kids" all the wiseguy tricks he's learned in his misspent life. McCrea, his boyhood chum, warns Bogart that he will take steps against him unless he stops exerting his rotten influence on the impressionable youths.

William Wyler's sterling direction creates a stagey but fairly compelling vision of slum life. The wonderful set by Richard Day is an enlarged duplicate of the Broadway set. Lillian Hellman's script changes little of Kingsley's earthy prose except for the ending. Humphrey Bogart is captivating as the alienated gangster, building upon his success of THE PETRIFIED FOREST a year earlier. He was originally billed beneath Sidney, but, in re-releases of this film, he was given star billing.

DEAD-END DRIVE-IN
1986 92m c   ★★★½
Action/Science Fiction   R/18
Springvale/New South Wales   (Australia)

Ned Manning *(Crabs)*, Natalie McCurry *(Carmen)*, Peter Whitford *(Thompson)*, Wilbur Wide *(Hazza)*, Brett Climo *(Don)*, Ollie Hall *(Frank)*, Sandie Lillingston *(Beth)*, Lyn Collingwood *(Fay)*, Nikki McWatters *(Shirl)*, Melissa Davies *(Narelle)*

p, Andrew Williams; d, Brian Trenchard-Smith; w, Peter Smalley (based on the short story "Crabs" by Peter Carey); ph, Paul Murphy (Eastmancolor); ed, Alan Lake, Lee Smith; m, Frank Strangio; prod d, Lawrence Eastwood; art d, Nick McCallum; cos, Anthony James

In the near future, the world economy has collapsed and Australia has been racked by massive unemployment, crime, and rioting. Gangs roam the streets destroying cars and stripping them for parts. Crabs (Ned Manning) is a young man doing his best to survive. One night he takes his girlfriend (Natalie McCurry) to see a movie at the Star Drive-In. The rear tires are stolen while the young couple makes out in the car leaving them stranded. Crabs sees that the thieves are cops but when he tries to report this to the manager (Peter Whitford), he is told that nothing can be done until the feds arrive. A new day dawns. Crabs looks around the bleak drive-in across acres of cars occupied by hundreds of punkish teenagers.

One of the least fanciful and most interesting futuristic films of recent years, DEAD-END DRIVE-IN is reminiscent of the original MAD MAX, and like that film it is a testament to the availability of cheap junked used cars and completely insane Australian stuntmen. Production values are high, and the performances are all good. The film does lag in some parts but generally works quite well, and the finale, climaxed by one of the most spectacular stunts ever attempted, is satisfyingly cathartic.

DEAD MEN DON'T WEAR PLAID
1982 89m bw   ★★
Comedy/Crime   PG
Universal

Steve Martin *(Rigby Reardon)*, Rachel Ward *(Juliet Forrest)*, Carl Reiner *(Field Marshall Von Kluck)*, Reni Santoni *(Carlos Rodriguez)*, George Gaynes *(Dr. Forrest)*, Frank McCarthy *(Waiter)*, Adrian Ricard *(Mildred)*, Charles Picerni, Gene Labell, George Sawaya *(Hoods)*

p, David V. Picker, William E. McEuen; d, Carl Reiner; w, George Gipe, Carl Reiner, Steve Martin; ph, Michael Chapman; ed, Bud Molin; m, Miklos Rozsa (from earlier films); prod d, John De Cuir; fx, Glen Robinson; cos, Edith Head

As an inept 1940s private eye, Steve Martin tracks killers, and in the course of his mildly amusing wanderings, plays opposite old film clips of James Cagney, Alan Ladd, Humphrey Bogart, Charles Laughton, and Ava Gardner, among others. The lifted scenes, which are better than the movie itself, are from 1940s classics such as WHITE HEAT, DOUBLE INDEMNITY, THE KILLERS, THE BIG SLEEP, DARK PASSAGE, IN A LONELY PLACE, SUSPICION and, most notably, THE BRIBE.

The basic film—what there is of it—is commendably shot in black and white by cinematographer Michael Chapman (RAGING BULL), who has specialized in black-and-white photography in an age when color is everything. Martin is often terribly unfunny in this gimmick film, the premise of which might have been better served as a "Saturday Night Live" sketch. Indeed, DEAD MEN DON'T WEAR PLAID is typical of a number of 1980s films featuring SNL performers such as Martin, John

Belushi, Chevy Chase, and Dan Aykroyd, who came to prominence on TV but have only sporadically brought a strong presence to their roles in feature-length films.

DEAD OF NIGHT
1945 104m bw   ★★★★½
Horror   /18
Rank (U.K.)

Mervyn Johns (*Walter Craig*), Roland Culver (*Eliot Foley*), Mary Merrall (*Mrs. Foley*), Frederick Valk (*Dr. Van Straaten*), Renee Gadd (*Mrs. Craig*), Anthony Baird (*Hugh Grainger*), Judy Kelly (*Joyce Grainger*), Miles Malleson (*Hearse Driver*), Sally Ann Howes (*Sally O'Hara*), Michael Allan (*Jimmy Watson*)

p, Michael Balcon; d, Alberto Cavalcanti ("The Ventriloquist's Dummy," "The Christmas Story"), Basil Dearden ("The Linking Story," "The Hearse Driver"), Robert Hamer ("The Haunted Mirror"), Charles Crichton ("The Golfing Story"); w, John Baines, Angus Macphail, T.E.B. Clarke (based on stories by H.G. Wells, E.F. Benson, John Baines, and Angus Macphail); ph, Jack Parker, Harold Julius; ed, Charles Hasse; m, Georges Auric; art d, Michael Relph

Perhaps the best horror anthology film ever made, this much-praised film still holds up, but suffers from the variances of pace and mood that inevitably affect all compilation efforts. Architect Walter Craig (Mervyn Johns) is called to Pilgrim's Farm, a country house he has been hired to remodel. Approaching the austere Victorian building in his car, he finds that there is something hauntingly familiar about the house. Once inside, Craig recognizes everyone present and tells them they have all been part of a recurring nightmare he has had, whereupon the guests relate their own nightmares, one by one.

The first tale, "The Hearse Driver," is told by Grainger (Antony Baird). In it he is a racetrack driver who, while recuperating from an accident, has a vision of a hearse from the window of his hospital room. The teen-aged Sally O'Hara (Sally Ann Howes) then reports "The Christmas Story," in which she attends a holiday party and, during a game of hide-and-seek, finds a crying child in a strange room. He is not what he seems. Joan Courtland (Googie Withers), in "The Haunted Mirror," relates a chilling tale in which she is given an antique mirror by her fiance which begins to reflect a Victorian room where a killing once took place. In "The Golfing Story"—the only piece designed for comic relief—two golfers (Basil Radford and Naunton Wayne) vie for the attentions of one woman. One golfer tricks the other into suicide, only to have the deceased return and haunt him as he is about to enjoy his wedding night. The last story, an Expressionistic entry entitled "The Ventriloquist's Dummy," shows a ventriloquist (Michael Redgrave) going mad. He believes that his dummy is assuming his personality while he is becoming the manipulated prop.

With typical disregard for consistency, US distributors thought this excellent British import was too long and cut the golfing sequence (not a bad move, actually) and the Christmas ghost tale, confusing audiences, who could not understand what Howes, Radford, and Wayne were doing in the linking story. The two tales were later reinstated. Of the four directors of the various stories, Robert Hamer is a standout with "The Haunted Mirror" and Alberto Cavalcanti excels with his two chillers, "The Christmas Story" and "The Ventriloquist's Dummy."

DEAD PIGEON ON BEETHOVEN STREET
1972 102m c   ★★★
Mystery   PG/15
Bavaria Atelier (West Germany)

Glenn Corbett (*Sandy*), Christa Lang (*Christa*), Sieghardt Rupp (*Kessin*), Anton Diffring (*Mensur*), Alex D'Arcy (*Novka*), Anthony Ching (*Fong*), Eric P. Caspar (*Charlie*)

d, Samuel Fuller; w, Samuel Fuller; ph, Jerzy Lipman (Eastmancolor); ed, Liesgret Schmitt-Klink; art d, Lothar Kirchem

American director Fuller answered his cult of European fans by making this bizarre tongue-in-cheek private-eye movie financed by German television. Corbett stars as a detective whose partner is murdered while investigating a gang of drug-dealing extortionists who photograph big-shot international-politico types in compromising situations with the lovely Lang. Corbett goes undercover and joins the ring to get the goods on the group. The film offers typically vigorous camera work but what makes it special is its looney sense of humor. Laden with in-jokes, the film is best approached as a goofy parody of crime thrillers.

DEAD POETS SOCIETY
1989 128m c   ★★★½
Drama   PG
Silver Screen Partners IV/Touchstone

Robin Williams (*John Keating*), Robert Sean Leonard (*Neil Perry*), Ethan Hawke (*Todd Anderson*), Josh Charles (*Knox Overstreet*), Gale Hansen (*Charlie Dalton*), Dylan Kussman (*Richard Cameron*), Allelon Ruggiero (*Steven Meeks*), James Waterson (*Gerard Pitts*), Norman Lloyd (*Mr. Nolan*), Kurtwood Smith (*Mr. Perry*)

p, Steven M. Haft, Paul Junger Witt, Tony Thomas; d, Peter Weir; w, Tom Schulman; ph, John Seale (Duart Color); m, Maurice Jarre; prod d, Wendy Stites; art d, Sandy Veneziano; cos, Marilyn Matthews

Making a definitive change in his screen persona, comedian-actor Robin Williams plays it fairly straight as a dedicated teacher at an elite Vermont prep school in DEAD POETS SOCIETY.

The title of this compelling film refers to a secret club to which English teacher John Keating (Williams) belonged when he himself was a student at Welton Academy, where he now teaches. The year is 1959, a time of strict adherence to educational goals and teaching methods at Welton, under the no-nonsense stewardship of headmaster Nolan (Norman Lloyd). The academic apple cart teeters, however, when Keating is engaged to teach a class of bright and impressionable young men. An inspirational, brilliant mentor, Keating ignores conventional teaching procedures and offers his students access to a world of culture, ideas, and creativity that changes their lives.

The role of Keating is a plum assignment for the talented Williams, who brings to his portrayal the passion and empathy that is pivotal to the character and—without resorting to shtick—additionally injects the role with a credible and sympathetic blend of warmth and humor. Peter Weir directs Tom Schulman's fine screenplay with an excellent eye for detail, underscoring the story's rising complications; and John Seale's photography is evocative.

DEAD POOL, THE
1988 91m c   ★★★
Crime   R/18
Malpaso

Clint Eastwood *(Harry Callahan)*, Patricia Clarkson *(Samantha Walker)*, Evan Kim *(Al Quan)*, Liam Neeson *(Peter Swan)*, David Hunt *(Harlan Rook)*, Michael Currie *(Capt. Donnelly)*, Michael Goodwin *(Lt. Ackerman)*, Darwin Gillett *(Patrick Snow)*, Anthony Charnota *(Lou Janero)*, Jim Carrey

p, David Valdes; d, Buddy Van Horn; w, Steve Sharon (based on a story by Sharon, Durk Pearson, and Sandy Shaw from characters created by Harry Julian Fink and Rita M. Fink); ph, Jack N. Green (Technicolor); ed, Ron Spang; m, Lalo Schifrin; prod d, Edward Carfagno

Fifth entry in the "Dirty Harry" series, a definite step backwards from the fascinating and ultimately disturbing progression of Eastwood's character in SUDDEN IMPACT. Here, Eastwood becomes embroiled in a string of murders involving a game called the "Dead Pool," involving a list of celebrities likely to die soon, from which participants wager on who will die first. The game is being played on the set of a cheap horror film directed by infamous gore-monger Neeson, whose bloody films are taken seriously by colleges and film societies. Neeson is the instigator of the ghoulish game and, as the celebrities begin to die off, is also the most likely suspect in the murders. The famous Eastwood, of course, is himself on the list.

Although the weak screenplay by Sharon would have trouble filling out a TV series episode, the fascination of the film lies not in its thriller mechanics but in the character played by Eastwood. Because everyone in the audience knows exactly what to expect from Dirty Harry in every situation, Eastwood has streamlined his portrayal. All he has to do is *hint* at the familiar sneer to get a reaction. His supremely controlled performance is a wonder to watch—some have called it bored and lazy, but it is really an engrossing experiment in minimalism. Eastwood has replaced all the timeworn elements of the series with a sardonic sense of humor that pokes fun at the genre, his image, and his audience. The highlight of the film in this regard is a clever parody of the famous car chase in BULLITT, in which Eastwood and his partner are pursued through the streets of San Francisco by a 12-inch, radio-controlled toy Corvette loaded with dynamite.

DEAD RINGERS

1988 115m c   ★★★★½
Horror   R/18
Mantle Clinic II   (Canada)

Jeremy Irons *(Beverly Mantle/Elliot Mantle)*, Genevieve Bujold *(Claire Niveau)*, Heidi von Palleske *(Cary)*, Barbara Gordon *(Danuta)*, Shirley Douglas *(Laura)*, Stephen Lack *(Anders Wolleck)*, Nick Nichols *(Leo)*, Lynn Cormack *(Arlene)*, Damir Andrei *(Birchall)*, Miriam Newhouse *(Mrs. Bookman)*

p, David Cronenberg, Marc Boyman; d, David Cronenberg; w, David Cronenberg, Norman Snider (based on the book *Twins* by Bari Wood, Jack Geasland); ph, Peter Suschitzky; ed, Ronald Sanders; m, Howard Shore; prod d, Carol Spier; fx, Gordon Smith; cos, Denise Cronenberg

Quietly devastating, DEAD RINGERS offers compelling evidence that David Cronenberg has matured into a truly great filmmaker. Continuing the detailed character study that blossomed in THE FLY and combining it with his fixation on the metaphysical, Cronenberg has vividly created yet another film that is powerful, moving and rich in ideas.

Inspired by the real-life story of respected twin New York City gynecologists Steven and Cyril Marcus (who in 1975 were both found dead in their garbage-strewn Upper East Side apartment, a double suicide brought on by barbiturate addiction),

Cronenberg introduces us to Elliot and Beverly Mantle, a pair of brilliant gynecologists who open a state-of-the-art fertility clinic and share an opulent apartment. Although physically identical, the twins possess very different personalities. Elliot is something of a cad—suave, debonair, and self-confident to the point of arrogance—whereas Beverly is shy, studious, and more sensitive. Elliot has always procured women for Beverly—seducing them first, then turning them over to his shy sibling when he was through—unbeknownst to the woman. When a famous actress, Claire Niveau (Genevieve Bujold), arrives at the clinic looking for answers to her infertility, trouble brews between the brothers, for although they both share her physically, Beverly falls in love for the first time, driving a wedge between the twins.

Extremely unsettling, at times amusing, cold yet personal, DEAD RINGERS gradually and deliberately comes to horrify the viewer, rather than shocking outright with such spectacular displays of gore as the exploding heads of SCANNERS, gaping stomach cavities of VIDEODROME, or vomiting Brundleflies of THE FLY. Not your average horror roller-coaster ride, DEAD RINGERS asks some disturbing questions about the nature of individual identity and, within that net, explores such outgrowths as eroticism, narcissism and misogyny. During the last decade, Cronenberg has matured into a filmmaker of remarkable scope, able to convey his obsessions with impeccable skill without sacrificing one iota of his own remarkable individuality. The astonishing Irons receives superb support from Bujold who breathes life into a part that, in other hands, might have been a mere plot device.

DEADLIEST SIN, THE

1955 90m bw   ★★½
Crime   /A
Allied Artists   (U.K.)

Sydney Chaplin *(Mike)*, Audrey Dalton *(Louise)*, John Bentley *(Inspector Kessler)*, Peter Hammond *(Alan)*, John Welsh *(Father Neil)*, Jefferson Clifford *(Pop)*, Patrick Allen *(Corey)*, Pat McGrath *(Williams)*, Robert Raglan *(Beckman)*, Betty Wolfe *(Mrs. Poole)*

p, Alec C. Snowden; d, Ken Hughes; w, Ken Hughes (based on a play by Don Martin); ph, Philip Grindrod; ed, Geoffrey Muller; m, Richard Taylor; art d, Harold Watson

Messy crime drama sees Chaplin, a thief, return home to England after ditching his partner during a holdup and absconding with the proceeds. The angry partner tracks him down, but is killed by Chaplin's future brother-in-law, Hammond, who was only trying to help. Riddled with guilt, Hammond goes to his priest to confess, and Chaplin murders him. Thinking that the priest may have heard too much, Chaplin attempts to kill him, too, but the law arrives and corners the crook in the church.

DEADLY AFFAIR, THE

1967 107m c   ★★★½
Spy   /15
Columbia   (U.K.)

James Mason *(Charles Dobbs)*, Simone Signoret *(Elsa Fennan)*, Maximilian Schell *(Dieter Frey)*, Harriet Andersson *(Ann Dobbs)*, Harry Andrews *(Inspector Mendel)*, Kenneth Haigh *(Bill Appleby)*, Lynn Redgrave *(Virgin)*, Roy Kinnear *(Adam Scarr)*, Max Adrian *(Adviser)*, Robert Flemyng *(Samuel Fennan)*

p, Sidney Lumet; d, Sidney Lumet; w, Paul Dehn (from the novel *Call for the Dead* by John le Carre); ph, Freddie Young; ed, Thelma Connell; m, Quincy Jones; art d, John Howell; cos, Cynthia Tingey

This is a superior John le Carre novel filmed by Sidney Lumet with an interesting international cast: James Mason, Simone Signoret, Maximilian Schell, Harriet Andersson, Harry Andrews, and Lynn Redgrave. The downbeat spy story captures the mood that made TINKER, TAILOR, SOLDIER, SPY so popular 15 years later. It's also of interest technically because Lumet experimented with "flashing" techniques, exposing the film stock before shooting to give it unusually subdued color. These techniques later became common.

This gritty, moody film is a superb but overlooked entry in the spy genre. Charles Dobbs (James Mason) is a security agent who okays clearance for Samuel Fennan (Robert Flemyng), a top-level official who has been accused of communist activities. When Fennan apparently commits suicide, Dobbs checks into the death and grows suspicious of Elsa Fennan (Simone Signoret), the dead man's widow. Before he can probe too deeply, however, he is taken off the case. Rather than bend to pressure from his superiors, Dobbs resigns, enlists the aid of some fellow agents, and sets out to solve Fennan's murder. Complicating matters is the arrival of Dieter Frey (Maximilian Schell), an agent who is a former friend of Dobbs and is preparing to run off with Dobbs's wife Ann (Harriet Andersson). Though Dobbs is weary of the espionage game, he finds himself more thoroughly enmeshed in it than he has ever been.

The complex plot is actually just a structure to support an insightful look into the lives of these characters. Mason is excellent as a man who knows the spy game for what it is, but still finds himself caught in its machinations. He gets admirable support from Schell, Andersson, and especially Signoret. Lumet's taut direction creates a film that is memorably atmospheric. Le Carre specialized in stripping the movie-fed illusion of glitz and glamour away from the world of espionage to reveal a grim unrewarding milieu where there are no heroes and villains, only people trapped in confusing webs of intrigue and turmoil.

DEALING: OR THE BERKELEY TO BOSTON FORTY-BRICK LOST-BAG BLUES

1971 88m c ★★½
Comedy R/
WB

Barbara Hershey (Susan), Robert F. Lyons (Peter), Charles Durning (Murphy), Joy Bang (Sandra), John Lithgow (John), Ellen Barber (Annie), Gene Borkan (Musty), Ted Williams (Receptionist), Demond Wilson (Rupert), Herbert Kerr (Emir)

p, Edward R. Pressman; d, Paul Williams; w, Paul Williams, David Odell (based on the novel by Michael and Douglas Crichton); ph, Edward Brown (Panavision, Technicolor); ed, Sidney Katz; m, Michael Small; prod d, Gene Callahan

Paul Williams directed this interesting time-capsule essay on the way people back then lived on the fringe of the drug culture. The lead, Lyons, is fairly ho-hum but future promise can be detected in the performance of Lithgow as a snobby Harvard student who goes to Berkeley to purchase marijuana to transport back to the Ivy League. Hershey plays the hippie with whom he falls in love. Lithgow would go on to glory on Broadway in plays such as M. BUTTERFLY, memorable supporting roles in films like THE WORLD ACCORDING TO GARP and TERMS OF ENDEARMENT. Filmed on location in San Francisco and Boston, this film offers an interesting comparison with THE BIG CHILL, which shows us more or less the same folks a decade later.

DEATH IN VENICE
(MORTE A VENEZIA)
1971 130m c ★★★★½
Drama GP/15
Alfa/Editions Cinegraphiques (Italy/France)

Dirk Bogarde (Gustav Von Aschenbach), Bjorn Andresen (Tadzio), Silvana Mangano (Tadzio's Mother), Marisa Berenson (Frau Von Aschenbach), Mark Burns (Alfred), Romolo Valli (Hotel Manager), Nora Ricci (Governess), Carole Andre (Esmeralda), Masha Predit (Singer), Leslie French (Travel Agent)

p, Luchino Visconti; d, Luchino Visconti; w, Luchino Visconti, Nicola Badalucco (based on the novel by Thomas Mann); ph, Pasqualino De Santis (Panavision, Technicolor); ed, Ruggero Mastroianni; m, Gustav Mahler, Ludwig van Beethoven, Modest Mussorgsky; art d, Ferdinando Scarfiotti; cos, Piero Tosi

Luchino Visconti's powerful and controversial screen adaptation of Thomas Mann's novella stars Dirk Bogarde as Gustav von Aschenbach, an aging German composer (modeled after Gustav Mahler) who visits Venice while on the verge of a physical and mental breakdown. Plagued by fears that he can no longer feel emotion because he has been avoiding it for so long, he is unfazed by the boorish and obnoxious behavior of the bourgeois creatures around him. Suddenly, he sees a beautiful blond boy named Tadzio (Bjorn Andresen) who is traveling with his mother and sisters. Gustav becomes obsessed with Tadzio and the ideal of classic beauty he represents. He seeks out the boy, who stirs feelings within him he thought he had lost, but refrains from making contact with him, watching as the lad wanders through the dank, decaying city.

Bogarde is superb as the dying composer. The beautiful cinematography combines with Ferdinando Scarfiotti's art direction to produce a powerful remembrance of time and place past. Visconti also makes effective use of Mahler's Third and Fifth symphonies. The music haunts the film, as do the quiet whispers of sound that help create the film's almost surreal environment. The delicacy of the soundtrack evokes the mood of Aschenbach's last days and his obsession with the face of Tadzio. DEATH IN VENICE was met with almost universal disapproval and misunderstanding when it was first released but, despite the omissions from Mann's text, dependence on flashbacks, and overwrought arguments about art and music between Aschenbach and a colleague, it remains a film of great beauty.

DEATH OF A BUREAUCRAT
1979 87m bw ★★★
Comedy
Cuban Film Institute (Cuba)

Salvador Wood (Nephew), Silvia Planas (Aunt), Manuel Estanillo (Bureaucrat), Gaspar de Santelices (Nephew's Boss), Carlos Ruiz de la Tejera (Psychiatrist), Omar Alfonso (Cojimar), Ricardo Suarez (Tarafa), Luis Romay (El Zorro), Elsa Montero (Sabor)

d, Tomas Gutierrez Alea; w, Tomas Gutierrez Alea, Alfredo del Cueto, Ramon F. Suarez; ph, Ramon Suarez; ed, Mario Gonzalez; m, Leo Brower

When the inventor of a machine to produce busts of Cuban hero Jose Martin dies, he is hailed as a model worker and given a lavish funeral. Among the honors, he is buried with his union card, which his widow needs to collect a pension from the state. She asks her nephew to help, and he is soon entangled in a bureaucracy that won't let him obtain an exhumation permit until the body has been buried for two years. Desperate, he steals the body out of its grave, then finds he can't rebury it until he shows his exhumation permit. Full of homages to silent comedians like Laurel and Hardy and Harold Lloyd, DEATH OF A BUREAU-CRAT is both a classic slapstick and a sly satire on the choking bureaucracy of Cuban Communism. Director Alea, whose MEMORIES OF UNDERDEVELOPMENT put him among the first rank of Third World filmmakers, did not go unnoticed in his attack on the government; this film was banned in Cuba after a brief release there in 1966.

DEATH OF A SALESMAN
1952   115m   bw   ★★★★
Drama   /PG
Columbia

Fredric March (Willy Loman), Mildred Dunnock (Linda Loman), Kevin McCarthy (Biff), Cameron Mitchell (Happy), Howard Smith (Charley), Royal Beal (Ben), Don Keefer (Bernard), Jesse White (Stanley), Claire Carleton (Miss Francis), David Alpert (Howard Wagner)

p, Stanley Kramer; d, Laslo Benedek; w, Stanley Roberts (based on the play by Arthur Miller); ph, Franz Planer; ed, William Lyon, Harry Gerstad; m, Alex North; prod d, Rudolph Sternad; art d, Cary Odell

With Fredric March and Kevin McCarthy, this is a very good record of the classic American stage play. Arthur Miller never fared as well again. His somber stage play retained much of its power in this film version featuring one of March's greatest performances as the end-of-the-line Willy Loman.

Willy is incapable of changing a lifestyle and career that are lost in the past. He is in his early sixties and, after being fired, has nowhere to go, clinging to his petty, mediocre values and looking backward with soul-wrenching agony. He has a long-suffering wife, Linda (Dunnock), and two sons, Biff (McCarthy) and Happy (Mitchell). The older son, Biff, is an average business success but has no spirit. Happy is disillusioned after losing his job and has no motivation to find another. The sons share the spiritual malaise of their father. The film powerfully depicts Willy relentlessly plodding to his doom, looking for redemption inside empty rooms of the past and babbling cliches to the apparition of his long-vanished brother.

Lee J. Cobb gave what many consider the definitive performance as Willy in the original 1949 stage hit, and Dustin Hoffman applied his considerable talent to project a tragic Willy in a 1985 TV presentation, though his portrayal is really a caricature. March is excellent if ultimately inferior to Cobb who reportedly was "reverse blacklisted" for his friendly testimony before HUAC during the McCarthy era. Still March looked, felt, and understood the part completely, bringing the character to life as the playwright envisioned him. Kramer's production and Benedek's direction are equally faithful to Miller's vision. Although DEATH OF A SALESMAN lost money at the box office, it stands as one of the great theatrical classics on film.

DEATH OF A SOLDIER
1986   93m   c   ★★★½
Crime   /18
Suatu   (Australia)

James Coburn (Maj. Patrick Danneberg), Reb Brown (Edward J. Leonski), Bill Hunter (Detective Sgt. Adams), Maurie Fields (Detective Sgt. Martin), Belinda Davey (Margot Saunders), Max Fairchild (Maj. William Fricks), Jon Sidney (Gen. MacArthur), Michael Pate (Maj. Gen. Sutherland), Randall Berger (Gallo), Nell Johnson (Maisie)

p, David Hannay, William Nagle; d, Philippe Mora; w, William Nagle; ph, Louis Irving (Panavision); ed, John Scott; m, Allan Zavod; art d, Geoff Richardson; cos, Alexandra Tynan

In 1942, Australia was putting up a tough defense against the Japanese in New Guinea. The American troops pouring into Australia were green recruits whose cocky attitudes did not sit well with the war-weary locals. The inherent tension in this situation was heightened when a series of women were strangled by an American GI. While Australian police and American MPs raced to find the murderer, General Douglas MacArthur saw to it that, when caught, the culprit would be tried under an Army court martial and then hanged. It was clear when the killer was finally caught that he was insane, but the Army would hear none of such a defense.

This is the factual base for this occasionally annoying, but generally fascinating, Australian production. Most of the film details the murders, with Eddie Leonski (Reb Brown) a chilling, childlike killer. Major Danneberg (James Coburn) works first to catch the killer and then to assist in his defense. A crawl at the end of the film explains that the postwar examination of the case led to the creation of the Uniform Code of Military Justice to protect American servicemen from having their constitutional rights denied. Coburn is good in his first decent part in recent memory, and Brown is more than effective. The picture of wartime Australia is fascinating; and the subject, the corruption of justice for political ends, has timeless significance.

DEATH OF TARZAN, THE
(TARZANOVA SMRT)
1968   72m   bw   ★★★★
Comedy
Barrandov   (Czechoslovakia)

Rudolf Hrusinsky (Baron Wolfgang von Hoppe/Tarzan), Jana Stepankova (Regina Smith), Martin Rusek (Baron Heinrich von Hoppe), Vlastimil Hasek (Dr. Foreyt), Slavka Budinova (Ring Director), Ilya Racek (Usher), Miroslav Homolka (SA Man), Nina Popelikova (Lady with Buckteeth), Elena Halkova (Baroness), Karel Peyer (Boss)

d, Jaroslav Balik; w, Josef Nesvadba, Jaroslav Balik (based on a short story by Nesvadba); ph, Josef Hanus; ed, Jirina Lukesova; m, Evzen Illin; art d, Bohuslav Kulic; cos, Theodor Pistek

An excellent satire with stunning black-and-white photography. Hrusinsky is a Czech count, lost in the jungle in infancy, who is found and brought home to the civilization of Nazi-dominated Europe. He goes through a series of hilarious encounters with modern society and its strange rituals, accidentally foils a kidnap plot, and when WWII breaks out over his jungle, he rejects everything to become the sideshow Tarzan in a traveling circus.

DEATH RACE 2000
1975   78m   c   ★★★
Action/Science Fiction   R/18
New World

David Carradine (Frankenstein), Simone Griffeth (Annie), Sylvester Stallone (Machine Gun Joe Viterbo), Mary Woronov (Calamity Jane), Roberta Collins (Mathilda the Hun), Martin Kove (Nero the Hero), Louisa Moritz (Myra), Don Steele (Junior Bruce)

p, Roger Corman; d, Paul Bartel; w, Robert Thom, Charles B. Griffith (based on a story by Ib Melchior); ph, Tak Fujimoto (Metrocolor); ed, Tina Hirsch; m, Paul Chihara; art d, Robin Royce, B.B. Neel; fx, Richard MacLean

Superior drive-in exploitation fare, this violent, campy action flick presents Carradine as Frankenstein, a scarred road warrior in black leather suit and cape. He's the formidable defending champion in the nationally televised Transcontinental Death Race in which competitors gain points by running over pedestrians. His challengers include Stallone as sort of a gangster on wheels with a machine gun in his car and Woronov as a western-outlaw Amazon. Carradine's navigator, Griffeth, is actually a revolutionary spy dedicated to sabatiging the savage race.

DEATH RACE 2000 boasts nonstop brutally funny comic-book action. Intended as a rip-off of the big-budget ROLLER-BALL, this likably ragged knockoff has become a cult favorite, while its bombastic inspiration has been consigned to the junk heap of genre movie history. The success of this film is a testament to producer Roger Corman's shrewd exploitation of promising filmmakers under the aegis of his New World production company. This legendary "B-minus" movie factory was formed in 1970 and attracted bright young filmmakers eager to break into the Guild-controlled industry. As a case in point, the film's director, Paul Bartel (who would later direct EATING RAOUL and SCENES FROM THE CLASS STRUGGLE IN BEVERLY HILLS), was paid $3,500 for his work on this profitable production.

DEATH TAKES A HOLIDAY
1934   79m   bw   ★★★★
Fantasy/Romance   /A
Paramount

Fredric March (Prince Sirki), Evelyn Venable (Grazia), Guy Standing (Duke Lambert), Katherine Alexander (Alda), Gail Patrick (Rhoda), Helen Westley (Stephanie), Kathleen Howard (Princess Maria), Kent Taylor (Corrado), Henry Travers (Baron Cesarea), G.P. Huntley, Jr. (Eric)

p, E. Lloyd Sheldon; d, Mitchell Leisen; w, Maxwell Anderson, Gladys Lehman, Walter Ferris (based on the play by Alberto Casella); ph, Charles Lang; art d, Hans Dreier, Ernst Fegte

Fredric March, as Death, becomes bored with his usual grim-reaping job and is puzzled that humans fear him so. To learn how he is perceived, he takes on human form as a handsome young prince and becomes the houseguest of an Italian nobleman (Guy Standing). Several guests are quickly repelled by the strange, mysterious prince who bluntly talks of their "meeting with Fate," but a lovely, mystical young woman (Evelyn Venable) is drawn to him. Not a living thing dies as Death dallies with love, and so his stay must be brief. But the unusual visitor fears that his new love will be repelled once he reveals his true identity.

March is riveting as Death, and Standing is also fine as the nervous host. Surprisingly, Paramount assigned the direction of this film to Mitchell Leisen, who had only one previous credit, CRADLE SONG. He was given a sumptuous budget and made the most of it. His background as a set designer for Cecil B. DeMille is evident in the magnificent villa in which March frolicked with Venable. Leisen, who would go on to make HOLD BACK THE DAWN and LADY IN THE DARK, rarely equalled the splendor of this film. He let March have his head, and the actor played his part with ironic vigor, wearing a monocle and delivering his lines in a Balkan accent with great arrogance. Of course, March could do almost no wrong, having won an Oscar only two years earlier for his arresting performance in DR. JEKYLL AND MR. HYDE. (He would win his second for THE BEST YEARS OF OUR LIVES.) The 21-year-old Venable, appearing in her second film, had previously starred in CRADLE SONG.

DEATH WATCH
(LA MORT EN DIRECT)
1979   128m   c   ★★★½
Science Fiction   R/15
Selta/Little Bear/Sara/Antenne 2/TV 13/Gaumont
(France/West Germany)

Romy Schneider (Katherine Mortenhoe), Harvey Keitel (Roddy), Harry Dean Stanton (Vincent Ferriman), Therese Liotard (Tracey), Max von Sydow (Gerald Mortenhoe), Bernhard Wicki, Caroline Langrishe, William Russell

p, Gabriel Boustiani, Janine Rubeiz; d, Bertrand Tavernier; w, David Rayfiel, Bertrand Tavernier (based on the novel The Continuous Katherine Mortenhoe by David Compton); ph, Pierre-William Glenn (Panavision, Fujicolor); ed, Armand Psenny, Michael Ellis; m, Antoine Duhamel; art d, Anthony Pratt

For followers of Bertrand Tavernier who know the director only through A SUNDAY IN THE COUNTRY or 'ROUND MID-NIGHT, the very realistic science-fiction film DEATH WATCH may come as a surprise. Set in Glasgow, the film takes place in a not-too-distant future when nearly all diseases have been conquered by medical science, leaving natural causes as society's prime killer. Katherine (Romy Schneider) is an independent, sensitive, and beautiful woman who has contracted a terminal disease; Vincent Ferriman (Harry Dean Stanton) is a crass television producer who finds her imminent demise perfect entertainment for a society that can't get enough of death; and Roddy (Harvey Keitel) is an employee who had a video camera implanted in his head, sending everything he sees back to the TV station for editing and broadcast. As Roddy follows Katherine through the countryside, in effect shooting a narrative film, he finds himself becoming attracted to her.

More than just a simple attack on electronic information in a modern technological society, DEATH WATCH (which can been seen as Tavernier's "Peeping Tom") also addresses the issue of the objectification of women and depersonalization of death via the (implicitly male-oriented) media.

DECISION BEFORE DAWN
1951   119m   bw   ★★★★
Spy   /A
FOX

Richard Basehart (Lt. Rennick), Gary Merrill (Col. Devlin), Oskar Werner (Happy), Hildegarde Neff (Hilde), Dominique Blanchar (Monique), O.E. Hasse (Oberst Von Ecker), Wilfried Seyferth (SS Man Scholtz), Hans Christian Blech (Tiger), Helene Thimig (Fraulein Schneider), Robert Freytag (Paul)

p, Anatole Litvak, Frank McCarthy; d, Anatole Litvak; w, Peter Viertel (based on the novel Call It Treason by George Howe); ph, Franz Planer; ed, Dorothy Spencer; m, Franz Waxman; art d, Ludwig Reiber

This superior WWII thriller depicts the efforts of an idealistic German medic, Happy (Werner), to spy on the Nazis to help shorten the war that is destroying his country. Volunteering to work for the Americans, POW Happy undergoes training and parachutes behind German lines to locate a powerful German Panzer corps. In the course of the mission, he faces countless perils and makes several allies and enemies as he rushes to his heroic destiny.

Director Litvak gives this WWII spy thriller a compelling sense of reality by shooting it in semi-documentary style on location in Germany where the war-scarred surroundings add authenticity to the story. He also utilizes a cast of highly competent unknowns, mostly foreign actors, many of whom became prominent later. Werner is paricularly outstanding and Litvak milks his situation for maximum dramatic impact while presenting a moving portrait of the aftershocks of war. Planer's photography is realistically grim, and Waxman's score is compelling. An outstanding production in all aspects.

DECLINE OF THE AMERICAN EMPIRE, THE
(LE DECLIN DE L'EMPIRE AMERICAIN)

1986   101m   c   ★★★½
Drama   R/18
Malo/Natl. Film Board of Canada/Telefilm Canada/Cinema
Du Quebec   (Canada)

Pierre Curzi *(Pierre)*, Remy Girard *(Remy)*, Yves Jacques *(Claude)*, Daniel Briere *(Alain)*, Dominique Michel *(Dominique)*, Louise Portal *(Diane)*, Dorothee Berryman *(Louise)*, Genevieve Rioux *(Danielle)*, Gabriel Arcand *(Mario)*

p, Rene Malo, Roger Frappier; d, Denys Arcand; w, Denys Arcand; ph, Guy Dufaux; ed, Monique Fortier; m, Francois Dompierre; art d, Gaudeline Sauriol; cos, Denis Sperdouklis

Four men swap stories of their sexual escapades while preparing an elaborate dinner. Four women do the same while working out in a gym. When the two groups come together, mutual betrayals come to light and shatter some illusions. On the surface this is all that happens in this fine film, one of the most successful Canadian exports ever, but the sparkling wit of the dialogue and the acutely observed jabs at our eternal preoccupation with sex distinguish THE DECLINE OF THE AMERICAN EMPIRE. The film's philosophy could best be summed up in a line uttered by one of the men: "Love—the kind that makes your heart race—lasts two years at best. Then the compromises begin." Perhaps the most valid criticism of the film is that its questions are too easy, its answers too pat, and its characters too similar. On the other hand, the ensemble performance is impeccable, the technical credits flawless, and the whole thing quite enjoyable.

DEEP END
1970   90m   c   ★★★★
Drama   /X
Maran/COKG/Kettledrum   (U.S./West Germany)

Jane Asher *(Susan)*, John Moulder-Brown *(Mike)*, Karl Michael Vogler *(Swimming Instructor)*, Christopher Sandford *(Fiance)*, Louise Martini *(Prostitute)*, Erica Beer *(Baths Cashier)*, Diana Dors *(Lady Client)*, Anita Lochner *(Kathy)*, Anne-Marie Kuster *(Nightclub Receptionist)*, Karl Ludwig Lindt *(Baths Manager)*

p, Helmut Jedele; d, Jerzy Skolimowski; w, Jerzy Skolimowski, Jerzy Gruza, Boleslaw Sulik; ph, Charly Steinberger (Eastmancolor); ed, Barrie Vince; art d, Max Ott, Jr., Anthony Pratt; cos, Ursula Sensburg

This quirky black sex comedy is the story of a boy's bizarre and unsentimental education. Moulder-Brown plays Mike, a handsome 15-year-old whose first job has him working in the men's section at a seedy bathhouse in a decidedly unswinging London. He meets a fellow employee, sexy 23-year-old redhead Susan (Asher), who teaches him the ropes and gets him to agree to refer his male clients to her in return for her female clients so that they can both earn better tips. He soon learns to exploit his looks by flirting with the women and encouraging them to fantasize about him. Mike develops an enormous crush on Susan but, looking upon him as a boy, she rejects his advances by telling she is engaged. However, her constant teasing drives him wild and her

affair with the swimming instructor infuriates him. Crazed with his obsessive love, he plots to break them up.

Polish filmmaker Skolimowsky, who wrote the screenplay for Roman Polanski's dirctorial debut, KNIFE IN THE WATER, here has made a powerful, disturbing film on the sexual awakening of a young boy in a sleazy environment. The film, which has an uneasy sense of humor, is well directed, well acted (especially by Asher), and well worth seeing.

DEEP IN MY HEART
1954   130m   c   ★★★½
Musical/Biography   /U
MGM

Jose Ferrer *(Sigmund Romberg)*, Merle Oberon *(Dorothy Donnelly)*, Helen Traubel *(Anna Mueller)*, Doe Avedon *(Lillian Romberg)*, Walter Pidgeon *(J.J. Shubert)*, Paul Henreid *(Florenz Ziegfeid)*, Tamara Toumanova *(Gaby Deslys)*, Paul Stewart *(Bert Towsend)*, Isobel Elsom *(Mrs. Harris)*, David Burns *(Lazar Berrison, Sr.)*

p, Roger Edens; d, Stanley Donen; w, Leonard Spigelgass (based on the book by Elliott Arnold); ph, George Folsey (Eastmancolor); ed, Adrienne Fazan; m, Sigmund Romberg; art d, Cedric Gibbons, Edward Carfagno; fx, Warren Newcombe; chor, Eugene Loring

DEEP IN MY HEART is an excellent screen biography of composer Sigmund Romberg, a power in American musicals for almost four decades. Romberg wrote more than 2,000 songs, did the scores for more than 80 plays, revues, and operettas, and still had time to lead a happy life.

Born in Hungary, Romberg came to the US early, and his rise was steady and steep. Ferrer does well in the role of the young man who got his start in a little cafe on New York's Second Avenue. Its proprietress (Helen Traubel) encourages his work, as does Lazar Berrison (David Burns), a Brill Building song pusher. Romberg has a commercial smash when he changes the tempo of one of his tunes to ragtime, and a series of small-time shows follow until Romberg has such a big hit with "Maytime" that one house can't hold it and, for the first time, two companies present the show on Broadway simultaneously.

The picture mixes all the elements necessary to make a successful musical: great songs like "One Alone," "The Desert Song," "Lover Come Back to Me" and "Will You Remember"; dances by Ann Miller, Cyd Charisse and James Mitchell; singing by Vic Damone, Jane Powell, Tony Martin and Rosemary Clooney; and, of course, superior acting by all. The film takes some liberties with history and ascribes some songs to the wrong shows, but why carp? It's solid musical entertainment.

DEER HUNTER, THE
1978   183m   c   ★★★★½
War   R/18
EMI/Universal

Robert De Niro *(Michael)*, John Cazale *(Stan)*, John Savage *(Steven)*, Christopher Walken *(Nick)*, Meryl Streep *(Linda)*, George Dzundza *(John)*, Chuck Aspegren *(Axel)*, Shirley Stoler *(Steven's Mother)*, Rutanya Alda *(Angela)*, Pierre Segui *(Julien)*

p, Barry Spikings, Michael Deeley, Michael Cimino, John Peverall; d, Michael Cimino; w, Deric Washburn (based on a story by Cimino, Washburn, Louis Garfinkle, and Quinn K. Redeker); ph, Vilmos Zsigmond (Panavision, Technicolor); ed, Peter Zinner; m, Stanley Myers; art d, Ron Hobbs, Kim Swados; fx, Fred Cramer; cos, Eric Seelig

Director Michael Cimino's epic look at how the Vietnam War affected a small Pennsylvania steel community was a huge hit at the box office and garnered several awards, including a Best Picture Oscar. Though its emotional power is undeniable, the film has been justifiably criticized for its somewhat thoughtlessly slanted view of the war and its implicitly racist depiction of the Vietnamese.

Three hours long and neatly divided into three acts, the film follows a trio of close friends—Michael (Robert De Niro), Nick (Christopher Walken) and Steven (John Savage)—from the eve of their tour of duty in Vietnam to the resumption of their interrupted lives. Just before their departure, the steelworkers attend Steven's wedding to Angela (Rutanya Alda); later, Michael and Nick go deer hunting with friends Axel (Chuck Aspegren), Stan (John Cazale) and John (George Dzundza). After the hunt, the film rudely cuts to the heat of battle in Vietnam. Michael, Nick and Steven are all taken prisoner by the Viet Cong and are forced to play Russian roulette while their captors make bets on the outcome. When they finally return home, readjustment is difficult. Steven is embittered and disabled. Nick has chosen to remain in Vietnam and has been sending hundreds of dollars to Steven without explanation. Determined to bring his friend back, Michael returns to Vietnam just as Saigon is about to fall.

Moving, dynamic, traumatic, and wholly memorable, THE DEER HUNTER is an emotionally draining production that draws a vivid portrait of its characters and their milieu—and succeeds in showing the devastating effect of the war on their lives, as well as their brave attempts at renewal. Unfortunately, the film falters when it comes to the larger questions of America's involvement in Vietnam.

DEFENCE OF THE REALM

1985 96m c   ★★★½
Political/Thriller   PG
Enigma (U.K.)

Gabriel Byrne (Nick Mullen), Greta Scacchi (Nina Beckman), Denholm Elliott (Vernon Bayliss), Ian Bannen (Dennis Markham), Fulton Mackay (Victor Kingsbrook), Bill Paterson (Jack Macleod), David Calder (Harry Champion), Frederick Treves (Arnold Reece), Robbie Coltrane (Leo McAskey), Annabel Leventon (Trudy Markham)

p, Robin Douet, Lynda Myles; d, David Drury; w, Martin Stellman; ph, Roger Deakins; ed, Michael Bradsell; m, Richard Hartley; prod d, Roger Murray-Leach; art d, Diana Charnley; cos, Louise Frogley

This fascinating conspiracy thriller hinges on two seemingly unrelated occurrences: two teenagers' attempted escape from a reformatory and a political scandal involving Dennis Markham (Ian Bannen), a distinguished member of Parliament. When the papers proclaim that Markham was observed leaving the home of a courtesan who was also cozy with an East German official, his loyalty to his country is questioned and his career ruined. Hack reporter Nick Mullen (Gabriel Byrne) is assigned to the story. When a colleague who is also interested in the story mysteriously dies, Mullen digs deeper and finds evidence of a shocking covert operation. With the help of his late colleague's secretary, Nina Beckman (Greta Scacchi), he battles to bring the truth to light.

An extremely well made film, DEFENCE OF THE REALM features a strong central performance by Byrne (GOTHIC, SIESTA, MILLER'S CROSSING), a typically marvelous turn by Elliott as his besotted elder journalist friend, and the beautiful Scacchi (THE COCA-COLA KID, PRESUMED INNOCENT).

The direction and editing are fast and tight, and the script by Martin Stellman (who also cowrote the superb QUADROPHENIA) has intelligent and tight plotting rare in this kind of film.

DEFIANT ONES, THE

1958 97m bw   ★★★★
Prison   /PG
UA

Tony Curtis (John Jackson), Sidney Poitier (Noah Cullen), Theodore Bikel (Sheriff Man Muller), Charles McGraw (Captain Frank Gibbons), Lon Chaney, Jr. (Big Sam), King Donovan (Solly), Claude Akins (Mac), Lawrence Dobkin (Editor), Whit Bissell (Lou Gans), Cara Williams (The Woman)

p, Stanley Kramer; d, Stanley Kramer; w, Nathan E. Douglas, Harold Jacob Smith; ph, Sam Leavitt; ed, Frederic Knudtson; m, Ernest Gold; prod d, Rudolph Sternad; art d, Fernando Carrere; fx, Alex Weldon; cos, Joe King

Tony Curtis and Sidney Poitier are handcuffed together as white and Black escaped convicts in the South in this classic liberal adventure from Stanley Kramer. Their plight is an all-too-obvious metaphor for American race relations. Though the political lesson drives the movie, the action is also effective as the odd couple flees from their oppressors. This is an engrossing depiction of racial tensions and an oppressive penal system. Both Poitier and Curtis give memorable performances. Curtis's portrayal of a bigoted uneducated Southern "cracker" is probably the best performance and role of his career. This was the film that established Poitier as a star.

DELIVERANCE

1972 109m c   ★★★★
Adventure   R/18
WB

Jon Voight (Ed), Burt Reynolds (Lewis), Ned Beatty (Bobby), Ronny Cox (Drew), Bill McKinney (Mountain Man), Herbert "Cowboy" Coward (Toothless Man), James Dickey (Sheriff Bullard), Ed Ramey (Old Man), Billy Redden (Lonny), Seamon Glass (1st Griner)

p, John Boorman; d, John Boorman; w, James Dickey (based on his novel); ph, Vilmos Zsigmond (Panavision, Technicolor); ed, Tom Priestley; m, Eric Weissberg; art d, Fred Harpman; fx, Marcel Vercoutere; cos, Bucky Rous

Morose, shockingly violent yet strangely beautiful, DELIVERANCE is a tale of what happens to civilized values when put to the test in a hostile wilderness environment. Four Atlanta businessmen decide to get back to nature by treking to the Appalachian wilds to canoe, hunt, and fish in an unspoiled environment before it is permanently flooded by a new dam. But what begins as an adventurous vacation becomes a nightmare of survival as they find themselves hunted by vengeful cretinous mountain men. Voight, Reynolds, Beatty, and Cox are the four city dwellers looking to prove their manhood in the wild. Each of their personal values is put to the test in the course of their deadly adventure. What does it mean to be a man? How far will one go to survive?

This is a tough and powerful portrait of men out of their usual environment. Nor is the deplorable squalor of the mountain communities glossed over. This is not a film for the squeamish. Some have accused the film of exploiting rather than exploring the moments of violent drama culled from James Dickey's first novel while deemphasizing its ecological concerns. Others were troubled by the seemingly perverse beauty of the film. All agree, however, that the meeting between the uneasy quartet and a deformed albino mountain child is a highlight. Cox sees that the kid has a banjo, picks up his own, and strums a few notes. The boy answers him. Then the two challenge each other until both go at a frenzied pace banging out a mountain tune. This celebrated "Duelling Banjos" sequence is an eerie moment of grace before the violence begins.

Boorman's direction is gripping if a bit heavy-handed. The rapids scenes in particular are electrifying. Cinematographer Zsigmond presents breathtaking scenes that sear the memory. Reynolds excelled in this rare serious role. Dickey adapted his own novel and appears as a sheriff.

DERSU UZALA
(DERUSU USARA)
1975   137m   c   ★★★½
Adventure   /U
Toho/Mosfilm   (U.S.S.R./Japan)

Maxim Munzuk *(Dersu Uzala)*, Yuri Solomine *(Capt. Vladimir Arseniev)*, Schemeikl Chokmorov *(Jan Bao)*, Vladimir Klemena *(Turtwigin)*, Svetlana Danielchanka *(Mrs. Arseniev)*

p, Nikolai Sizov, Yoichi Matsue; d, Akira Kurosawa; w, Akira Kurosawa, Yuri Nagibin (based on the journals of Vladimir Arseniev); ph, Asakazu Nakai, Yuri Gantman, Fyodor Dobronavov; m, Isaac Schwalz; prod d, Yuri Raksha

Captain Vladimir Arseniev (Solomine), leading a topographic expedition deep into the wilds of 19th-century Siberia, meets an old woodsman, Dersu Uzula (Munzuk), who shows him the ways of nature. The two men become close friends over a number of expeditions in which Uzula acts as guide. Each time Arseniev tries to convince the hardy but aging Siberian to return to the city with him, the latter refuses. Finally Uzala does go to the city, but he finds that he cannot readily adapt.

Akira Kurosawa filmed in the USSR with an all-Soviet cast, but a Japanese cinematographer, Asakadru Nakai, photographed the production in 70mm. The first half is wonderful, full of reverence for nature and the man who lives in it. However, it becomes increasingly obvious, literal, and rather ponderous as it progresses. Still these faults cannot detract from DERSU UZALA's magnificence. Like so much of Kurosawa's work, this is a film of great humanism and respect.

DESCENDANT OF THE SNOW LEOPARD, THE
(POTOMOK BELONGO BARSSA)
1984   134m   c   ★★★★
Adventure
Kirghizfilm   (U.S.S.R.)

Dokdurbek Kydralijev *(Koshoshash)*, Aliman Shankorosova *(Saikal)*, Doskhan Sholshakssynov *(Mundusbai)*, Guinara Alimbajeva *(Aike)*, A. Chokubajev *(Kassen)*, M. Shantelijev *(Sajak)*, Sh. Seidakmatova *(Begaim)*, G. Kadyralijeva *(Sulaika)*, K. Akmatova *(Batma)*, Aibek Kydryralijev *(Kalygul)*

d, Tolomush Okeyev; w, Mar Baydjiev, Tolomush Okeyev (based on folk legends); ph, Nurtoy Borbijev; ed, R. Shershneva; m, M. Begalijev; cos, M. Abdijev

This breathtakingly beautiful adaptation of a Kirghizian folktale is an invigorating experience. Like all good legends, it relates important historical events in the evolution of a culture, citing violations of sacred rules as the ultimate source of change.

The Snow Leopards are a tribe of hunters who inhabit the rugged terrain of the Kirghizian mountains. During one particularly violent winter, the entire tribe faces extinction unless help

from the closest lowland tribe can be solicited. The tribe's most virile and capable hunter Koshoshash (Kydralijev) volunteers to make the dangerous journey across the snow-buried path to the lowlands. Accompanied by Kassen (Chokubajev), Koshoshash barely manages to reach the other tribe which graciously gives him the needed horses—in return for a future favor.

Come spring, the lowland tribe requires that the Snow Leopards uphold their end of the bargain. The daughter of the tribe's leader is to marry a prince and trader from the south in a grand celebration that could make an easy target for attacking enemies. The Snow Leopards are asked to act as guards against possible invasion. During the course of this festive occasion, events are set in motion which have a profound effect on the future of both tribes.

Director Okeyev received a Silver Bear for Outstanding Single Achievement at the 1985 Berlin Film Festival, a result of his subtle combination of intriguing characters and a multidimensional story against the stunning background of the mountainous terrain. THE DESCENDANT OF THE SNOW LEOPARD has its basis in an actual Kirghizian folk legend, explaining the occasional lapses into heavy melodramatics. For the most part, however, the events are rendered in an engrossing, realistic fashion. Before books existed to retell history, people depended on folk legends passed via word of mouth from village elders to captivated children. Viewing THE DESCENDANT OF THE SNOW LEOPARD has much the same effect.

DESERT FOX, THE
1951   88m   bw   ★★★½
War/Biography   /PG
FOX

James Mason *(Erwin Rommel)*, Cedric Hardwicke *(Dr. Karl Strolin)*, Jessica Tandy *(Frau Rommel)*, Luther Adler *(Hitler)*, Everett Sloane *(Gen. Burgdorf)*, Leo G. Carroll *(Field Marshal Von Rundstedt)*, George Macready *(Gen. Fritz Bayerlein)*, Richard Boone *(Aldinger)*, Eduard Franz *(Col. Von Stauffenberg)*, Desmond Young *(Himself)*

p, Nunnally Johnson; d, Henry Hathaway; w, Nunnally Johnson (based on the biography by Desmond Young); ph, Norbert Brodine; ed, James B. Clark; m, Daniele Amfitheatrof; art d, Lyle Wheeler, Maurice Ransford; fx, Fred Sersen, Ray Kellogg

The first film that attempted to humanize a WWII German military leader, THE DESERT FOX features a magnetic performance by James Mason as Hitler's greatest field commander, Field Marshal Erwin Rommel—grudgingly respected by his opponents, loyally followed by men of the *Afrika Korps*. Opening with a British commando raid on Rommel's headquarters, the film traces the general's remarkable career from his early success in North Africa to his defeat at El Alamein (where he disregarded Hitler's "victory or death" command and retreated), his later illness, his command of the French coastal defenses, and his role in a failed attempt to assassinate Hitler. This last act led to his high-command-mandated, face-saving suicide.

Though Mason is the main attraction in this fragmentary biopic, the supporting cast is excellent (particularly Luther Adler's unforgettable cameo as Hitler). Henry Hathaway's semi-documentary-style direction is as brisk as a panzer attack and Nunnally Johnson's script is literate and penetrating. Mason's sympathetic portrait of Rommel is in marked contrast with other cinematic treatments of the general: Erich Von Stroheim in FIVE GRAVES TO CAIRO, Albert Lieven in FOXHOLE IN CAIRO, Werner Hinz in THE LONGEST DAY, Gregory Gay in HITLER, Christopher Plummer in THE NIGHT OF THE GENERALS,

Wolfgang Preiss in RAID ON ROMMEL, Karl Michael Vogler in PATTON and Mason, once more, in THE DESERT RATS.

DESERT HEARTS

1985   96m   c   ★★★½
Drama   R/18
Desert Hearts

Helen Shaver (Vivian Bell), Patricia Charbonneau (Cay Rivvers), Audra Lindley (Frances Parker), Andra Akers (Silver), Gwen Welles (Gwen), Dean Butler (Darell), James Staley (Art Warner), Katie La Bourdette (Lucille), Alex McArthur (Walter), Antony Ponzini (Joe Lorenzo)

p, Donna Deitch; d, Donna Deitch; w, Natalie Cooper (based on the novel Desert of the Heart by Jane Rule); ph, Robert Elswit; ed, Robert Estrin; prod d, Jeannine Claudia Oppewall

Though not without problems, DESERT HEARTS is a triumph for director Donna Deitch and an inspiration for any independent filmmaker. Determined to develop a feature film depicting a sexual relationship between two women—a topic never done justice in an American commercial release—Deitch adapted Jane Rule's novel Desert of the Heart. The story opens in Reno, Nevada, in 1959. Helen Shaver is Vivian Bell, a college professor from New York, staying in Reno temporarily to obtain a divorce. She stays at Francis Parker's (Audra Lindley) small ranch outside of town. Also living there is Cay Rivvers (Patricia Charbonneau), an employee at one of the local casinos, who is more like a daughter to Parker than a tenant. Bell and Rivvers gradually become close friends but, when their relationship changes, others are affected as well.

Deitch deals sensitively with her theme, eliciting fine performances from her two leads. Charbonneau, after a memorable entrance worthy of the coolest of screen male lovers, portrays Rivvers as a fiery natural force. Shavers's portrayal of the repressed college professor with her hair in a tight bun is a model of restraint and latent passion. We know that when this cool lady finally melts, it will be something to see. The film falters a bit with some of the plot development, a reflection, no doubt, of Deitch's budget rather than her talent. DESERT HEARTS unfolds in a format typical for commercial filmmaking, which isn't a detriment, but doesn't allow for some of the more complicated emotions and issues within the story to surface.

DESERT RATS, THE

1953   88m   bw   ★★★½
War   /U
FOX

Richard Burton (Capt. MacRoberts), Robert Newton (Bartlett), Robert Douglas (General), Torin Thatcher (Barney), Chips Rafferty (Smith), Charles Tingwell (Lt. Carstairs), James Mason (Rommel), Charles Davis (Pete), Ben Wright (Mick), James Lilburn (Communications)

p, Robert L. Jacks; d, Robert Wise; w, Richard Murphy; ph, Lucien Ballard; ed, Barbara McLean; m, Leigh Harline; art d, Lyle Wheeler, Addison Hehr; fx, Ray Kellogg

A follow-up to THE DESERT FOX, THE DESERT RATS concentrates on the Australian side of the first film's events. Capt. MacRoberts (Richard Burton) is a tough British officer who takes over command of the 9th Australian Division at Tobruk in 1941, at a desert fortress surrounded and hard pressed by the Afrika Korps, led by Field Marshall Rommel (James Mason, in a reprise of his role in THE DESERT FOX). MacRoberts looks down on his men, viewing them as inferior to the British regulars. At-tempting to change that view is Bartlett (Robert Newton), MacRoberts's former college professor, a lowly volunteer and a raving alcoholic. Burton is his usual forceful self, but it's Newton who steals every scene he's in, playing a floppy, roaring, and weepy drunk spouting philosophy and sentiment. Robert Wise's direction is another element in the film's success, as is Lucien Ballard's excellent and realistic photography.

DESIRE

1936   89m   bw   ★★★★★
Romance   /A
Paramount

Marlene Dietrich (Madeleine de Beaupre), Gary Cooper (Tom Bradley), John Halliday (Carlos Margoli), William Frawley (Mr. Gibson), Ernest Cossart (Aristide Duval), Akim Tamiroff (Police Official), Alan Mowbray (Dr. Edouard Pauquet), Zeffie Tilbury (Aunt Olga), Enrique Acosta (Pedro), Stanley Andrews (Customs Inspector)

p, Ernst Lubitsch; d, Frank Borzage; w, Edwin Justus Mayer, Waldemar Young, Samuel Hoffenstein (based on an original story by Hans Szekeley and R.A. Stemmle); ph, Charles Lang, Victor Milner; ed, William Shea; m, Frederick Hollander; art d, Hans Dreier, Robert Usher; cos, Travis Banton

Clearly the product of a gilded cocktail shaker. Bearing the stylistic stamps of both producer Lubitsch and director Borzage, this is a sophisticated romantic comedy about a lovely jewel thief, Madeleine de Beaupre (Dietrich), who tricks a gem dealer (Cossart) out of a priceless string of pearls and flees Paris after implicating a stuffy psychiatrist (Mowbray). She drives wildly toward the Spanish border and nearly runs down Tom Bradley (Cooper), a young American engineer on vacation. She uses him as an unwitting accomplice in smuggling the pearls out of the country. Cleared by Spanish customs, he drives off with Madeleine in hot pursuit. The romantic chase is on! What began as mere expediency soon develops into love—with numerous complications along the way, of course.

Successful with the public, DESIRE was one of the most elegantly produced films of the 1930s; the sets, costumes, and decor all shimmer with hot light. Borzage, who also directed the silent classic SEVENTH HEAVEN, added his sweetly romantic warmth to the deft, spicy production plans already laid out by Lubitsch for this wonderful film. Playing with both conviction and wit, Dietrich achieves one of her best performances away from mentor Josef von Sternberg; here she is slightly less exotic and rather more human than in her other films. Cooper, too, in his second pairing with Dietrich (after the memorable MOROCCO) really shows his flair for sophisticated romance with this one. He makes the most of the funny yet impossibly romantic line, "All I know about you is you stole my car and I'm insane about you." The remarkable John Halliday, whose presence graces any film, leads a terrific supporting cast. One of the ultimate expressions of Paramount Studios chic, DESIRE remains one of its desirable star's finest films.

DESPERATE CHARACTERS

1971   87m   c   ★★★½
Drama
ITC

Shirley MacLaine (Sophie), Kenneth Mars (Otto), Gerald S. O'Loughlin (Charlie), Sada Thompson (Claire), Jack Somack (Leon), Chris Gampel (Mike), Mary Alan Hokanson (Flo), Robert

Bauer *(Young Man)*, Carol Kane *(Young Girl)*, Michael Higgins *(Francis Early)*

p, Frank D. Gilroy; d, Frank D. Gilroy; w, Frank D. Gilroy (based on the novel by Paula Fox); ph, Urs Furrer (Eastmancolor); ed, Robert Q. Lovett; m, Lee Konitz, Jim Hall, Ron Carter; art d, Edgar Lansbury; cos, Sally Gifft

This well-written if somewhat stagey character study focuses on a day in the life of an urban proto-yuppie couple, Sophie and Otto (Maclaine and Mars) who reside near the once fashionable but now rundown Brooklyn Heights (this is 1971, before the gentrification boom). Urban violence is breaking out all around them but they are becoming inured to it. Their conversation has deteriorated into banalities. Otto, an attorney, casually remarks that he is ending his partnership with Charlie (O'Loughlin), his long-time associate and best friend. It seems that Charlie has gone liberal and, as such, he is spending altogether too much time with causes and not enough with cases. A street cat paws at their door and MacLaine feeds it some milk. This act of kindness is rewarded by a deep bite on her hand. At a party thrown later that night by psychiatrist Mike (Gampel) and his wife, Flo (Hokanson), the joy of the evening is shattered by a rock that smashes a window. You get the idea? The times they are a'changin'.

MacLaine and Mars were acclaimed for their performances but the public stayed away. This is one of Maclaine's best performances. Mars carved himself a comfortable niche in comedy with a starring role as the Nazi playwright in THE PRODUCERS and several hilarious parts in various Mel Brooks films. This was the feature directorial debut for playwright turned screenwriter-director Gilroy who had won previously won accolades for his award-winning play, *The Subject Was Roses* and his screenplay for the film version. He went on to write and direct films such as ONCE IN PARIS..., a delightful story of a screenwriter who goes to Paris to write a screenplay which was as at least as interesting as DESPERATE CHARACTERS and, sadly, suffered a similar fate.

DESPERATE HOURS, THE

1955   112m   bw   ★★★★
Crime   /A
Paramount

Humphrey Bogart *(Glenn)*, Fredric March *(Dan Hilliard)*, Arthur Kennedy *(Jesse Bard)*, Martha Scott *(Eleanor Hilliard)*, Dewey Martin *(Hal)*, Gig Young *(Chuck)*, Mary Murphy *(Cindy)*, Richard Eyer *(Ralphie)*, Robert Middleton *(Kobish)*, Alan Reed *(Detective)*

p, William Wyler; d, William Wyler; w, Joseph Hayes (based on his novel and play); ph, Lee Garmes (Vistavision); ed, Robert Swink; m, Gail Kubik; art d, Hal Pereira, Joseph MacMillan Johnson; fx, John P. Fulton, Farciot Edouart; cos, Edith Head

In his second-to-last film, Humphrey Bogart comes full circle, playing a character nearly identical to his pivotal role in THE PETRIFIED FOREST, the 1936 film that catapulted him to stardom. Bogart undertakes his reprise with a vengeance. As the film opens, Glenn (Bogart) breaks out of prison with his kid brother (Martin) and a mentally deficient behemoth (Middleton). They take refuge in the middle-class home of Dan Hilliard (March) where they terrorize his family as Glenn waits for a call from his sweetheart. Her assignment was to dig up some long-buried loot and then rendezvous with the escapees. However, the call doesn't come and Glenn grows increasingly desperate, brutalizing Hilliard his wife (Scott), his attractive daughter (Murphy), and his feisty young son (Eyer).

Here William Wyler has expertly directed a taut suspenseful thriller. Joseph Hayes has also done a marvelous job in adapting his own novel for the screen. Two old pros who get the maximum impact out of every line, Frederic March and Bogart give spellbinding performances as two strong personalities engaged in a mortal showdown. Bogart reportedly had some reservations about this film, worrying that he might be too old to play a convincingly menacing hoodlum but his qualms never show on screen. The story had also been a successful stage play with the much-younger Paul Newman in Bogart's role, but the part was purposely "aged" by Hayes to suit Bogie's 55 years, each of which shows on his wonderful, craggy face. Among the supporting performers, Gig Young, Mary Murphy, and Richard Eyer are all fine, and Martha Scott is a standout as the hero's wife.

DESPERATELY SEEKING SUSAN

1985   104m   c   ★★★½
Romance/Comedy   PG-13/15
Orion

Rosanna Arquette *(Roberta)*, Madonna *(Susan)*, Aidan Quinn *(Dez)*, Mark Blum *(Gary)*, Robert Joy *(Jim)*, Laurie Metcalf *(Leslie)*, Anna Levine *(Crystal)*, Bill Patton *(Nolan)*, Peter Maloney *(Ian)*, Steven Wright *(Larry)*

p, Sarah Pillsbury, Midge Sanford; d, Susan Seidelman; w, Leora Barish; ph, Ed Lachman (Deluxe Color); ed, Andrew Mondshein; m, Thomas Newman; prod d, Santo Loquasto; art d, Speed Hopkins; cos, Santo Loquasto

This is one of the most charming low-budget films in years, a freewheeling, light-hearted farce that gives some new twists to old plot devices. Rosanna Arquette is Roberta, a bored New Jersey housewife married to swimming pool magnate, Gary (Mark Blum). To spice up her bland life, Roberta takes to reading the personal ads and becomes intrigued by a periodically recurring notice headlined "Desperately Seeking Susan." On a whim, she goes off to New York City and eventually finds the mysterious Susan (Madonna). She follows Susan around the city and watches as the wildly garbed woman sells her leather jacket at a used clothing store. Roberta buys the jacket, not realizing it contains Egyptian earrings Susan has stolen from a murdered mobster. The plot twists are fairly simple, but that really doesn't matter in this energetic and well-acted comedy. Director Susan Seidelman guides her cast with a light, enthusiastic touch, never making more out of her frothy material than need be.

DESTINATION TOKYO

1944   135m   bw   ★★★½
War   /U
WB

Cary Grant *(Capt. Cassidy)*, John Garfield *(Wolf)*, Alan Hale *(Cookie)*, John Ridgely *(Reserve)*, Dane Clark *(Tin Can)*, Warner Anderson *(Executive)*, William Prince *(Pills)*, Robert Hutton *(Tommy)*, Tom Tully *(Mike)*, Faye Emerson *(Mrs. Cassidy)*

p, Jerry Wald; d, Delmer Daves; w, Albert Maltz, Delmer Daves (based on a story by Steve Fisher); ph, Bert Glennon; ed, Christian Nyby; m, Franz Waxman; art d, Leo K. Kuter; fx, Lawrence Butler, Willard Van Enger

A rousing, action-filled WWII film, with a powerful cast and a good story, DESTINATION TOKYO remains an effective war drama to this day. Though there are many cameo stories within the framework of the film, the actual protagonist is the submarine in which its characters serve, the *USS Copperfin*. Leaving a West Coast port on Christmas Eve, the sub heads out into the Pacific.

Sub commander Capt. Cassidy (Cary Grant) has his secret orders: the destination is Tokyo, where Cassidy is to put ashore a meteorologist (John Ridgely) who will obtain vital data for future air raids over the Japanese metropolis.

More than a competent action film, DESTINATION TOKYO, under the sensitive direction of Delmer Daves, is a human story of the lives of those brave (and some not-so-brave) individuals who serve as submarine crewmen. The intimate feel of submarine life is ever-present in the film, from the claustrophobic confinement to the wonderful camaraderie of the shipmates. Cary Grant is of particular interest as the sub-commander in that he is supposedly from Kansas, and it's interesting to watch him trying to play against type.

A fascinating sequence occurs about two-thirds of the way through the film when everything stops for a 15-minute propaganda essay as Grant writes a letter home to the wife and kids. We learn in this mini-documentary how the Germans and the Japanese, our enemies, are ethnically and racially simply no-goodniks, and how the Russians and the Chinese, our allies, are good, solid, strong folk who will always do right. Of course, ten years later these racially motivated evaluations would be largely denied. By the mid-Seventies, many, if not all, prints of the film were lacking this embarrassing footage.

DESTRY RIDES AGAIN
1939   94m   bw   ★★★★
Western
Universal

Marlene Dietrich *(Frenchy)*, James Stewart *(Tom Destry)*, Mischa Auer *(Boris Callahan)*, Charles Winninger *("Wash" Dimsdale)*, Brian Donlevy *(Kent)*, Allen Jenkins *(Bugs Watson)*, Warren Hymer *(Gyp Watson)*, Irene Hervey *(Janice Tyndall)*, Una Merkel *(Lily Belle Callahan)*, Tom Fadden *(Lem Claggett)*

p, Joe Pasternak; d, George Marshall; w, Felix Jackson, Henry Myers, Gertrude Purcell (based on the novel by Max Brand); ph, Hal Mohr; ed, Milton Carruth; m, Frank Skinner; art d, Jack Otterson; cos, Vera West

A classic sendup of western heroism starring James Stewart and—of all people—Marlene Dietrich. Stewart is the lawman who takes control of his town without shooting it up. Dietrich is the chantoosie who sings "See What the Boys in the Back Room Will Have." The son of a brave lawman gone to his reward, Tom Destry (Stewart) appears to be anything but a two-fisted fighter for justice. He refuses to wear guns, and, when he steps up to the bar, he orders milk. Soft-spoken and mild-mannered, he becomes the butt of jokes when he shows up in Bottleneck where Kent (Donlevy) runs the wildest saloon in town and lords it over the populace. "You put 'em behind bars, and they look little and cheap, like they are."

Dietrich's career was in free fall prior to this movie. She had left the protective wing of her directorial mentor Josef von Sternberg in 1935, and most of her subsequent movies were not popular. After appearing in ANGEL, an uncommon failure for Ernst Lubitsch, Dietrich was considered "box office poison" by exhibitors. For three years, she made no films of consequence, and, when Paramount dropped her contract in 1937, she was considered washed up. She fled to Europe believing that American film audiences were through with her. Then she got a transatlantic call in the middle of the night from producer Joe Pasternak who wanted her for his new film at Universal—a western! One of the screen's most glamorous women, renowned for romances, melodramas, and sophisticated comedy, playing a saloon hussy in a crude oater? But Dietrich took it and she was appropriately bawdy, tempestuous, and wicked but with a heart of gold. The public responded and her star shot up again, higher than before.

Under the sure directorial hand of genre veteran Marshall, DESTRY RIDES AGAIN is a well-paced western that seamlessly combines humor, romance, suspense and action. Stewart's performance is rendered in his usual low-key manner and provides the perfect counterpoint to Dietrich's bold and brassy character. All the great character actors in this film are superb as well. DESTRY was filmed three times following the publication of the Max Brand novel in 1930, first as a Tom Mix standard in 1932, again in the 1939 Dietrich/Stewart classic, and in 1954 as a routine western with Audie Murphy.

DETECTIVE, THE
1954   91m   bw   ★★★★
Comedy   /U
Columbia   (U.K.)

Alec Guinness *(Fr. Brown)*, Joan Greenwood *(Lady Warren)*, Peter Finch *(Flambeau)*, Cecil Parker *(The Bishop)*, Bernard Lee *(Inspector Valentine)*, Sidney James *(Parkinson)*, Gerard Oury *(Inspector Dubois)*, Ernest Thesiger *(Vicomte)*, Ernest Clark *(Secretary)*, Austin Trevor *(Herald)*

p, Paul Finder Moss, Vivian A. Cox; d, Robert Hamer; w, Thelma Schnee, Robert Hamer (based on the "Father Brown" stories by G.K. Chesterton); ph, Harry Waxman; ed, Gordon Hales; m, Georges Auric

Alec Guinness is the perfect G.K. Chesterton character, the likable clerical detective on the trail of art thieves. Joan Greenwood, Peter Finch, Bernard Lee, Sidney James and Ernest Thesiger marvelously abet the stellar direction of Robert Hamer. Father Brown is an eccentric priest who takes it upon himself to transport a priceless cross from London to Rome. An international jewel thief steals the cross, and the enterprising priest sets out to get it back and save the thief's soul. An extremely entertaining and polished film with Guinness at his best.

DETECTIVE, THE
1968   114m   c   ★★★½
Crime   /X
FOX

Frank Sinatra *(Joe Leland)*, Lee Remick *(Karen Leland)*, Ralph Meeker *(Lt. Curran)*, Jack Klugman *(Dave Schoenstein)*, Horace MacMahon *(Farrell)*, Lloyd Bochner *(Dr. Roberts)*, William Windom *(Colin MacIver)*, Jacqueline Bisset *(Norma MacIver)*, Tony Musante *(Felix)*, Al Freeman, Jr. *(Robbie)*

p, Aaron Rosenberg; d, Gordon Douglas; w, Abby Mann (based on the novel by Roderick Thorp); ph, Joseph Biroc (Panavision, Deluxe Color); ed, Robert Simpson; m, Jerry Goldsmith; art d, Jack Martin Smith, William Creber; fx, L.B. Abbott, Art Cruickshank; cos, Moss Mabry

Joe Leland (Sinatra) is a top New York City detective investigating the mutilation and murder of a homosexual (Inman). He arrests the victim's former roommate (Musante) for the crime, and the suspect is tried, convicted and executed. But the case haunts Sinatra because he allowed himself to blindly railroad Musante into a confession for the sake of a promotion. Ironically, another case leads Sinatra to the real killer, and he soon finds himself embroiled in a political scandal that could rock New York City. Now somewhat dated because of its misguidedly "enlightened" attitude toward homosexuality, this film is engrossing nonetheless because of its superb cast. Screenwriter Abby Mann took a few liberties with Thorp's trashy novel, but the changes were an improvement. Look for Robert Duvall in a small role.

DETECTIVE STORY

1951   105m   bw   ★★★★
Crime   /X
Paramount

Kirk Douglas (Jim McLeod), Eleanor Parker (Mary McLeod), William Bendix (Lou Brody), Cathy O'Donnell (Susan Carmichael), George Macreation (Karl Schneider), Horace MacMahon (Lt. Monahan), Gladys George (Miss Hatch), Joseph Wiseman (Charles Gennini), Lee Grant (Shoplifter), Gerald Mohr (Tami Giacoppetti)

p, William Wyler; d, William Wyler; w, Philip Yordan, Robert Wyler (based on the play by Sidney Kingsley); ph, Lee Garmes; ed, Robert Swink; art d, Hal Pereira, Earl Hedrick; cos, Edith Head

Kirk Douglas gives one of his best performances in this seminal cop film, directed by William Wyler. The plot is thin, but the drama is fleshed out with interesting characters. Chief among these is Jim McLeod (Douglas), a hardboiled, dedicated, by-the-book detective proud of his untarnished record in a one-man war against crime. Douglas is tough on all the lawbreakers he drags in to police headquarters, particularly an unscrupulous doctor (Macready), whom he beats up in a police van before delivering him to the lock-up. Lieutenant Monahan (MacMahon) becomes suspicious of McLeod's brutal treatment of the crooked physician, investigates further, and finds out that the abortionist has a surprising link to the detective.

   Douglas is intense and electrifying as the altruistic yet narrow-minded Jim McLeod. Like DEAD END the source material for the film is a Sidney Kingsley morality play. Once again director Wyler deftly handles this potentially stagey material. And, as in DEAD END, one of the film's most outstanding features is an impressive set. This stark creation by Hal Pereira and Earl Hedrick is comprised of little more than floorboards, desks, unaccommodating tables, and ancient file cabinets. It suggests a precinct office with no frills or comforts, physical or spiritual.

   Though confined to this one set, ace cinematographer Lee Garmes provides fluid camera movement as our eye is smoothly directed from one character to another. DETECTIVE STORY is methodical in its depiction of the sometimes traumatic events of one day in a precinct but the marvelous quirks and shadings of these characters create highly exciting drama.

DETOUR

1945   67m   bw   ★★★★★
Crime   /A
Producers Releasing Corp.

Tom Neal (Al Roberts), Ann Savage (Vera), Claudia Drake (Sue), Edmund MacDonald (Charles Haskell, Jr.), Tim Ryan (Diner Proprietor), Esther Howard (Hedy), Roger Clark (Dillon), Pat Gleason (Man), Don Brodie (Used Car Salesman)

p, Leon Fromkess; d, Edgar G. Ulmer; w, Martin Goldsmith; ph, Benjamin Kline; ed, George McGuire; m, Leo Erdody; art d, Edward C. Jewell; cos, Mona Barry

DETOUR puts the noir in film noir. Utilizing "night-for-night" cinematography, this amazingly dark genre landmark unfolds with the logic of a nightmare as Al Roberts (Tom Neal), recounts in voice-over the unlikely chain of events that landed him in a purgatorial diner in the middle of nowhere. A triumph of talent and inspiration over budget, this was made on the cheap by a Poverty Row studio in just six days. This is a road picture that was filmed almost entirely in the studio; the extensive road sequences are shot with weird projection. Director Edgar Ulmer transforms these limitations into virtues making the film genuinely feel like a surreal meditation on the protagonist's fears of women, domesticity, failure, and success.

   Roberts is a piano player at a chintzy joint in New York City. Sue (Claudia Drake), his fiancee, is a singer at the same establishment but she dreams of a career in Hollywood. She believes that Roberts's talent justifies a gig at Carnegie Hall but he doesn't think he's good enough. She goes off to follow her dream, leaving him to his embittered reveries. Later a big tip from a drunken patron allows him to make a long distance call to his love who is now laboring as a hash slinger in L.A. He tells her that he's going to go out west to marry her. He soon hits the road with outstretched thumb.

   He gets picked up by Haskell (MacDonald), an amiable chap who buys him a meal and regales him with the story of how he got his scars. Later Neal is driving while the car owner sleeps and rain begins to fall. He tries to awaken Haskell so they can put up the convertible's top but finds him dead. From here things get progressively worse for Roberts culminatiing in his meeting Vera (Ann Savage), a castrating harpy who knows his secrets and how to exploit them. She has plans for a big score and Roberts becomes her reluctant accomplice.

   DETOUR is a film that must be seen to be (dis)believed. Today it enjoys a richly deserved cult-film status. Neal is just right as the fatalistic protagonist and Savage is remembered as one of the most terrifying vixens in movie history.

DEVIL AND DANIEL WEBSTER, THE

1941   107m   bw   ★★★★★
Fantasy
RKO

Edward Arnold (Daniel Webster), Walter Huston (Mr. Scratch), Jane Darwell (Ma Stone), Simone Simon (Belle), Gene Lockhart (Squire Slossum), John Qualen (Miser Stevens), Frank Conlan (Sheriff), Lindy Wade (Daniel Stone), George Cleveland (Cy Bibber), Anne Shirley (Mary Stone)

p, William Dieterle; d, William Dieterle; w, Dan Totheroh (based on the story "The Devil and Daniel Webster" by Stephen Vincent Benet); ph, Joseph August; ed, Robert Wise; m, Bernard Herrmann; fx, Vernon L. Walker

Absolutely marvelous. Two fascinating stalwarts, Arnold and Huston, have a go at each other in this witty fantasy based on the O. Henry Prize-winning Stephen Vincent Benet short story. The author reportedly had a hand in the film version with Dan Totheroh. Jabez Stone (Craig) is a New England farmer having a difficult time making a living. When he casually swears that he would sell his soul for enough money to make life easier, up pops Huston as Mr. Scratch. This charming devil purchases Stone's soul in return for seven years of good luck. At first Stone thinks it's all an elaborate joke but then the money starts rolling in.

Sudden success transforms the simple, good-hearted Stone into a venal, cold-blooded businessman who now cheats his neighbors, ignores his wife (Shirley) and their new-born child, refuses to listen to his mother (Darwell), and even gives up going to church on Sundays, opting to play poker instead. His phenomenal luck makes the entire farming community suspicious. The situation worsens on the homefront when Mr. Scratch's temptingly beautiful emissary (Simon), an odd servant girl, comes to live with Stone's family. Stone builds a grand mansion and gives an elegant ball, inviting everyone, including the famous Daniel Webster (Arnold). But everything goes wrong. Strange, crude people arrive and eat savagely at the banquet tables, and an equally strange band plays eerie music. All the guests, it seems, are people who have struck bargains with the Devil. The scene terrifies Stone and he flees, following his family whom he has run out of the mansion. He catches up with them on the road and his wife promises help. She goes to Webster, begging him to plead her husband's case. The great lawyer agrees to save his fellow New Englander if he can.

Arnold, though appearing only intermittently, is at his stentorian best and Huston steals the film as a roguish Devil full of snap, crackle and pop. Huston was nominated for an Oscar for his performance and the film won a richly deserved Oscar for Bernard Herrmann's lively and eerie score. Director Dieterle does one of his finest ever jobs of directing with the telling of this picturesque tale, and August's camerawork is masterful.

DEVIL AND MISS JONES, THE
1941 92m bw   ★★★½
Comedy   /U
RKO

Jean Arthur (Mary Jones), Robert Cummings (Joe O'Brien), Charles Coburn (John P. Merrick), Edmund Gwenn (Hooper), Spring Byington (Elizabeth Ellis), S.Z. Sakall (George), William Demarest (1st Detective), Walter Kingsford (Allison), Montagu Love (Harrison), Richard Carle (Oliver)

p, Frank Ross, Norman Krasna; d, Sam Wood; w, Norman Krasna; ph, Harry Stradling; ed, Sherman Todd; m, Roy Webb; prod d, William Cameron Menzies; fx, Vernon L. Walker

Fun, but one wishes it were better. John P. Merrick (Coburn), the world's richest man, decides to infiltrate one of his holdings, a department store, to ferret out union organizers who have targeted him as responsible for the miserable working conditions of his employees. He is subjected to many indignities by the management, finally ending up in the shoe department alongside Mary Jones (Arthur). She thinks him destitute and takes pity on him, showing him the intricacies of the department. He attends union meetings and carefully notes everybody there, but as the abuse from the store's management becomes more intolerable and as Merrick himself becomes romantically interested in Elizabeth Ellis (Byington), he has a change of heart, eventually sacking the management and marrying Ellis. This comedy is enhanced by the Capraesque presence of Arthur, but what it really needed is Capra himself.

DEVIL DOLL, THE
1936 79m bw   ★★★★
Horror/Fantasy   /A
MGM

Lionel Barrymore (Paul Lavond), Maureen O'Sullivan (Lorraine Lavond), Frank Lawton (Toto), Robert Greig (Coulvet), Lucy Beaumont (Mme. Lavond), Henry B. Walthall (Marcel), Grace Ford (Lachna), Pedro de Cordoba (Matin), Arthur Hohl (Radin), Rafaela Ottiano (Malita)

p, Edward J. Mannix; d, Tod Browning; w, Garrett Fort, Guy Endore, Erich von Stroheim, Tod Browning (based on the novel Burn Witch Burn by Abraham Merritt); ph, Leonard Smith; ed, Frederick Y. Smith; m, Franz Waxman; art d, Cedric Gibbons

Tiny people, and we don't mean Munchkins. Another Tod Browning foray into the macabre, THE DEVIL DOLL stars Lionel Barrymore as Paul Lavond, a wrongly convicted prisoner who escapes Devil's Island with mad scientist Marcel (Walthall). They take refuge in Marcel's old laboratory, where he demonstrates his miraculous invention, a serum that reduces all living things to miniature size. Before dying, the ailing Marcel passes passes his secret formula on to Lavond, who decides to seek vengeance on the three men who framed him. Disguised as an old woman who runs a doll shop, Lavond manages to reduce two of his enemies, but begins to lose control of the scheme because of his crazed assistant, Ottiano, who is so spellbound by the miniaturizing process that she refuses to stop, at one point hissing, "We'll make the whole world small!"

While THE DEVIL DOLL is no FREAKS, director Tod Browning, in his second-to-last film, adds a sinister edge to what is basically a morality play. The special effects still impress today; the oversized sets and props are expertly done, with much attention given to detail; and the film is excellently photographed by Leonard Smith. Erich Von Stroheim is credited with co-writing the screenplay, but the exact nature of his contributions has never been made clear. Cast is generally expert, with the exception of veddy-British Lawton, who is too refined for his assignment.

DEVIL IN THE FLESH, THE
(LE DIABLE AU CORPS)
1946 110m bw   ★★★★
Romance   /18
TRC   (France)

Micheline Presle (Marthe Graingier), Gerard Philipe (Francois Jaubert), Jean Debucourt (M. Jaubert), Denise Grey (Mme. Grangier), Pierre Palau (M. Marin), Jean Varas (Jacques Lacombe), Jeanne Perez (Mme. Marin), Germaine Ledoyen (Mme. Jaubert), Maurice Lagrenee (Doctor), Richard Francoeur (Headwaiter)

p, Paul Graetz; d, Claude Autant-Lara; w, Jean Aurenche, Pierre Bost (based on the novel by Raymond Radiguet); ph, Michel Kelber; ed, Madeleine Gug; m, Rene Cloerec

A scandalous picture in its day, DEVIL IN THE FLESH tells the tale of a 17-year-old (Philipe) in love with a married older woman (Presle) whose soldier husband has been assigned to the front. The story is told through the boy's eyes, in a flashback structure that points out the doomed nature of the affair. Many contemporary viewers were furious at the way the soldier—a man risking his life for his country—was deceived, and petitions were sent to the French government urging that the film be banned. (Canada agreed to the ban, and New York state censors would show it only after certain cuts were made.) This touching story now seems quite harmless, but it still works extremely well as drama, hoisted by the wonderful Presle and Philipe and the helming of director Autant-Lara. It was poorly remade as an X-rated film in 1986 by Marco Bellocchio. Based on the novel by Raymond Radiguet, who wrote his tale of romance at the age of 18, two years before his death.

DEVIL PROBABLY, THE
(LE DIABLE PROBABLEMENT)
1977 95m c   ★★★★
Drama   /X
Sunchild/GMF/Gaumont (France)

Antoine Monnier (Charles), Tina Irissari (Alberte), Henri De
Maublanc (Michel), Laelita Carcano (Edwige), Regis Hanrion (Dr.
Mime), Nicolas Deguy (Valentin), Geoffrey Gaussen (Bookseller),
Robert Honorat (Commissioner)

p, Stephane Tcholgdjieff; d, Robert Bresson; w, Robert Bresson;
ph, Pasqualino De Santis (Eastmancolor); ed, Germaine Lany; m,
Philippe Sarde

Another rigorous—and unusually watchable—exercise in
cinematic discipline by Bresson, the master of the minimal. The
story, the end of which Bresson reveals immediately, depicts
young Monnier drifting through politics, religion, and finally to
suicide. The actors are all nonprofessionals who don't so much
act as move around and blankly state their lines to the director's
intricate commands. The best introduction (along with
LANCELOT DU LAC) to the work of one of film's greatest
thinkers.

DEVIL'S HOLIDAY, THE
1930 80m bw   ★★★
Drama
Paramount

Nancy Carroll (Hallie Hobart), Phillips Holmes (David Stone),
James Kirkwood (Mark Stone), Hobart Bosworth (Ezra Stone),
Ned Sparks (Charlie Thorne), Morgan Farley (Monkey McConnell),
Jed Prouty (Kent Carr), Paul Lukas (Dr. Reynolds), ZaSu Pitts
(Ethel), Morton Downey (Freddie the Tenor)

d, Edmund Goulding; w, Edmund Goulding; ph, Harry Fischbeck;
ed, George Nichols, Jr.

A scheming manicurist, played superbly by Nancy Carroll, plans
to marry Phillips Holmes, the son of millionaire wheat farmer
Hobart Bosworth, as her ticket to Easy Street. Bosworth and
Holmes' brother, James Kirkwood, violently oppose the union,
but the couple marry anyway. Carroll offers to divorce him if
Bosworth will pay her $50,000. Dad agrees and Carroll leaves.
Her conscience begins to eat at her, and she tries to wash away
her guilt in alcohol. Meanwhile, Holmes lies seriously ill after a
fall he suffered in a fight with his brother over Carroll. Upon
hearing this, Carroll realizes that she loves him and returns to his
side.

DEVIL'S HOLIDAY was one of the earliest starring roles for
contract player Carroll, who landed the role after the original star,
Jeanne Eagels, died of a heroin overdose. Carroll earned an
Academy Award nomination for Best Actress for her role, but
lost to Norma Shearer for THE DIVORCEE. Collectors of filmic
oversights should note the shadow cast by the overhead mike on
the wall of Carroll's room in her scene with Ned Sparks. Despite
this gaffe, this is still a nicely handled and appealing early talkie.

DIABOLIQUE
(LES DIABOLIQUES)
1955 107m bw   ★★★★½
Thriller
Filmsonor (France)

Simone Signoret (Nicole Horner), Vera Clouzot (Christina
Delasalle), Paul Meurisse (Michel Delasalle), Charles Vanel (Inspector Fichet), Jean Brochard (Plantiveau), Noel Roquevert

(Herboux), Therese Dorny (Mme. Herboux), Pierre Larquey
(Drain), Michel Serrault (Raymond), Yves-Marc Maurin (Moinet)

p, Henri-Georges Clouzot; d, Henri-Georges Clouzot; w, Henri-
Georges Clouzot, Jerome Geronimi, Frederic Grendel, Rene Mas-
son (from the novel Celle Qui N'etait Pas by Pierre Boileau,
Thomas Narcejac); ph, Armand Thirard; ed, Madeleine Gug; m,
Georges Van Parys; art d, Leon Barsacq

A bitter chiller. One of the most suspenseful films ever made,
DIABOLIQUE revolves around a callous schoolmaster,
Meurisse, his heiress wife, Clouzot, and his mistress, Signoret.
The latter, a cold-blooded murderess, helps Christina poison and
drown her husband. They dump the corpse in the pool of Michel's
boarding school, but Christina grows increasingly fearful that
Michel is still alive. An investigation of the schoolmaster's death
proceeds, but when the pool is drained no body is found. Adding
to the mystery is the testimony of schoolchildren who insist
they've seen Michel.

Director Henri-Georges Clouzot keeps the viewer guessing to
the final frames. The picture received great critical acclaim,
sharing the prestigious New York Film Critics Award for Best
Foreign Film with Vittorio de Sica's UMBERTO D. The frightened wife of the "dead" man, Vera Clouzot, is the real-life Mrs.
Clouzot. Authors Pierre Boileau and Thomas Narcejac, upon
learning that Alfred Hitchcock was interested in acquiring the
rights to Celle Qui N' Etait Pas (upon which DIABOLIQUE was
based), set out to pen another novel that would surely interest
Hitch—D'Entre Les Mortes, which later became VERTIGO.

DIABOLIQUE also includes one of the most effective "eyeball scenes" in filmmaking (second only to that in Bunuel and
Dali's UN CHIEN ANDALOU) when the "dead" man rises from
the bathtub. Rumor has it Clouzot's films were always shot in an
atmosphere of antagonism, and the camera here seems to be
observing in a merciless way. The last 15 minutes are as suspenseful as anything ever put on film.

DIAL M FOR MURDER
1954 105m c   ★★★½
Thriller   /PG
WB

Ray Milland (Tony Wendice), Grace Kelly (Margot Wendice), Rob-
ert Cummings (Mark Halliday), John Williams (Chief Inspector
Hubbard), Anthony Dawson (Captain Swan Lesgate), Leo Britt
(The Narrator), Patrick Allen (Pearson), George Leigh (William),
George Alderson (The Detective), Robin Hughes (Police Sergeant)

p, Alfred Hitchcock; d, Alfred Hitchcock; w, Frederick Knott (based
on his play); ph, Robert Burks (3-D-Natural Vision, Warner Color);
ed, Rudi Fehr; m, Dimitri Tiomkin; art d, Edward Carrere, George
James Hopkins; cos, Moss Mabry

Lower case Hitch, but diverting and sleek, with the climax early
on. Milland is a playboy whose wealth has come entirely through
his marriage to chic heiress Kelly. When he fears he'll lose her
riches to American mystery writer Cummings, he plots her
unfortunate demise. Milland contacts Dawson, an old chum who
now operates in the underworld, and blackmails him into killing
Kelly while he is conveniently away. Milland's plan misfires,
however, when the murder plans go awry, leading to a thorough
round of questioning from the crafty inspector Williams.

Based on the successful play by Frederick Knott, this adaptation was essentially treated as an assignment by Hitchcock, who
had already begun to work on REAR WINDOW. Shackled by
Jack Warner's insistence on filming the picture in 3D (with its
terribly immobile cameras), Hitchcock focused his attention on

his new favorite actress, Kelly, with whom he would work again on his next two films, REAR WINDOW and TO CATCH A THIEF.

Repeating his stage role as the Scotland Yard inspector is John Williams, who excells among the cast. Although the 3D version has hardly been seen, it does contain one of the best, least gimmicky, uses of the added dimension as Kelly, while being attacked, reaches "into the audience," desperately searching for a weapon to defend herself. The opening credit sequence of a finger dialing "M" on a telephone is, because of the problems of achieving close focus with 3D cameras, actually a giant dial and a large wooden finger which Hitchcock had specially constructed.

DIAMONDS ARE FOREVER

1971 118m c	★★★
Spy	GP/PG
Eon/Danjaq (U.K.)	

Sean Connery *(James Bond)*, Jill St. John *(Tiffany Case)*, Charles Gray *(Blofeld)*, Lana Wood *(Plenty O'Toole)*, Jimmy Dean *(Willard Whyte)*, Bruce Cabot *(Saxby)*, Bruce Glover *(Wint)*, Putter Smith *(Kidd)*, Norman Burton *(Felix Leiter)*, Joseph Furst *(Metz)*

p, Harry Saltzman, Albert R. Broccoli; d, Guy Hamilton; w, Richard Maibaum, Tom Mankiewicz (based on the novel by Ian Fleming); ph, Ted Moore (Panavision, Technicolor); ed, Bert Bates; m, John Barry; prod d, Ken Adam; art d, Jack Maxsted, Bill Kenney; fx, Les Hillman, Albert Whitlock, Wally Veevers, Whitey McMahon; cos, Elsa Fennell, Ted Tetrick, Donfeld

Next door to glass, but aided by the return of Connery (George Lazenby had undertaken the role of Bond in ON HER MAJESTY'S SECRET SERVICE) teamed with Jill St. John, instead of the usual parade of faceless Bond girls. The Las Vegas locations sizzle and the script at least has the good sense not to take itself too seriously. The producers had by now decided that Connery, not Bond, was their big attraction and lured him back into the fold with an offer he couldn't refuse—1.25 million, a percentage of the profits on the film, and an agreement to back two films of Connery's choice, which he could either star in or direct. Connery accepted the offer, but was not to be persuaded to do the role again until NEVER SAY NEVER AGAIN in 1983. Shirley Bassey, who sang the title song from GOLDFINGER, returned here to sing the title song written by Barry Don Black. Two karate-kicking girls initiate Bond into sexual equality, but the genre was beginning to look shopworn by now. That's Lana Wood, Natalie's sister, as Plenty O'Toole. But no amount of frou-frou can distract us from wondering why no arch villian just shot old OO7?

DIARY FOR MY CHILDREN
(NAPLO GYERMEKEIMNEK)

1984 106m bw	★★★½
Drama/Science Fiction	/PG
Mafilm/Hungarofilm (Hungary)	

Zsuzsa Czinkoczi *(Juli)*, Anna Polony *(Magda)*, Jan Nowicki *(Janos/Juli's Father)*, Tamas Toth *(Janos's Son)*, Pal Zolnay *(Grandpa)*, Mari Szemes *(Grandma)*

d, Marta Meszaros; w, Marta Meszaros; ph, Miklos Jancso, Jr.; ed, Eva Karmento; m, Zsolt Dome; prod d, Eva Martin

A bleak, joyless tale of Stalinist purges in Hungary during the 1943-1956 period, starring Czinkoczi as a teenage Hungarian girl whose father disappears in the Soviet Union after being arrested without explanation. When Czinkoczi's mother dies, she returns

to Hungary to live with Polony, a former revolutionary and now a deeply political newspaper editor. Polony's strong political convictions turn Czinkoczi away. The young girl retreats to afternoons in movie houses with Polony's friend, Nowicki, a factory worker who eventually ends up in prison for his beliefs. Czinkoczi pays regular visits to Nowicki in his cell because he reminds her of her father (in fact he is played by the same actor in flashbacks).

DIARY FOR MY CHILDREN is a profoundly moving and political picture, mainly because director Meszaros has brought her own experiences to the screen. She, like the young heroine in the movie, was separated from her father (sculptor Laszlo Meszaros) in 1938 and returned to Hungary in 1946. Surprisingly honest politically (Meszaros makes use of actual newsreel footgage intercut with the drama), DIARY FOR MY CHILDREN is a film that probably would have resulted in the director's imprisonment, had she been able to make it at all, in more oppressive times. Awarded the Special Jury Prize at the 1984 Cannes Film Festival as well as the Grand Prize at the National Film Festival in Hungary.

DIARY OF A CHAMBERMAID
(LE JOURNAL D'UNE FEMME DE CHAMBRE)

1964 97m bw	★★★★
Drama	/15
Speva/Cine Alliance/FS/Dear (France/Italy)	

Jeanne Moreau *(Celestine)*, Georges Geret *(Joseph)*, Michel Piccoli *(Mons. Monteil)*, Francoise Lugagne *(Mme. Monteil)*, Jean Ozenne *(Mons. Rabour)*, Daniel Ivernel *(Capt. Mauger)*, Jean-Claude Carriere *(Cure)*, Gilberte Geniat *(Rose)*, Bernard Musson *(Sacristan)*, Muni *(Marianne)*

p, Serge Silberman, Michel Safra; d, Luis Bunuel; w, Luis Bunuel, Jean-Claude Carriere (based on the novel *A Chambermaid's Diary* by Octave Mirbeau); ph, Roger Fellous (Franscope); ed, Louisette Hautecoeur; art d, Georges Wakhevitch; cos, Georges Wakhevitch

A wonderfully vulgar film from the masterful Spanish director Luis Bunuel, DIARY OF A CHAMBERMAID is an adaptation in spirit of Octave Mirbeau's novel and Jean Renoir's 1946 film. Moreau is a Parisian chambermaid who takes a new job in the country at the estate of a bourgeois womanizer, Piccoli, his frigid wife Lugagne, and her likeable, foot-fetishist father, Ozenne. Sexual vices are not limited to the bourgeoisie, however, as Geret, the filthy, fascist longtime servant, is found to be a sadistic rapist and murderer.

Although Bunuel would regularly attack societal institutions, this film is one of his most overtly political. Set in the late 1920s, this chambermaid's diary sets up the social conditions of both political and sexual aggression that made the rise of fascism not only possible but—as Bunuel makes clear in the film's final shot of the stormy heavens—inevitable. His statement is a Surrealist one, presented in the most realistic of styles (which may surprise viewers who have only a peripheral familiarity with Bunuel's work).

The director's wicked humor and unforgettable visual sense are perhaps best illustrated in his filming the rape and murder of an innocent young girl. Instead of narrating the attack in detail, Bunuel uses three shots—a wild boar running through the forest, a frightened rabbit, and the corpse's legs covered with the live snails she had been collecting.

DIARY OF A COUNTRY PRIEST
(LE JOURNAL D'UN CURE DE CAMPAGNE)
1950   120m   bw   ★★★★½
Religious   /U
UGC   (France)

Claude Laydu (Priest of Ambricourt), Jean Riveyre (Count), Andre Guibert (Priest of Torcy), Nicole Maurey (Louise), Nicole Ladmiral (Chantal), Marie-Monique Arkell (Countess), Martine Lemaire (Seraphita), Antoine Balpetre (Dr. Delbende), Jean Danet (Olivier), Gaston Severin (Canon)

p, Leon Carre; d, Robert Bresson; w, Robert Bresson (based on the novel by George Bernanos); ph, L.H. Burel; ed, Paulette Robert; m, Jean-Jacques Grunenwald; art d, Pierre Charbonnier

A frail, unnamed priest (Laydu, an untrained actor) is assigned to his first parish—Ambricourt, a small and only somewhat religious town. He does as saintly priests are known to do—simply accepting the people around him as they are and attempting to strengthen their faith, while himself living a life of poverty, with bread and wine the only food he can eat without falling ill. His major achievement is bringing a withdrawn countess out of her hatred for God and into a state of peacefulness.

   Robert Bresson, returning to the screen after a five-year absence, succeeds in capturing the literary spirit of George Bernanos' book and retelling it in a cinematic language. It is a brilliant adaptation, remaining faithful to Bernanos without resorting to harmful omissions or additions, allowing its audience to enjoy the identical spiritual experience as the reader of the novel. DIARY OF A COUNTRY PRIEST shared the top prize at the Venice Film Fest with Kurosawa's RASHOMON. It is definitely not a film for everyone's tastes—Bresson's work is known for its slow, meditative pace—but a brilliant picture all the same.

DIARY OF A MAD HOUSEWIFE
1970   95m   c   ★★★½
Comedy/Drama   R/X
Universal

Richard Benjamin (Jonathan Balser), Frank Langella (George Prager), Carrie Snodgress (Tina Balser), Lorraine Cullen (Sylvie Balser), Frannie Michel (Liz Balser), Lee Addams (Mrs. Prinz), Peter Dohanos (Samuel Keefer), Katherine Meskill (Charlotte Rady), Leonard Elliott (Mon. Henri), Valma (Margo)

p, Frank Perry; d, Frank Perry; w, Eleanor Perry (based on the novel by Sue Kaufman); ph, Gerald Hirschfeld (Technicolor); ed, Sidney Katz; prod d, Peter Dohanos; cos, Ruth Morley, Flo Transfield, James Hagerman

The angst of yuppiedom. Benjamin, one of the great film twits of our time, portrays a money-mad attorney who bullies his wife, Snodgress, to the point where she takes a lover, Langella. Soon enough Snodgress discovers Langella is every bit the twit Benjamin is, just a different sort of twit. Langella is self-centered and will play only with committed women because he is unable to commit himself. The plot takes Snodgress into several diverting episodes and culminates when she divests herself of both husband and lover and seeks solace in group therapy, only to learn that happiness doesn't reside in psychiatry, either.

   The three leads are excellent. Benjamin has been seen in many films as the consummate ass: THE MARRIAGE OF A YOUNG STOCKBROKER, THE SUNSHINE BOYS, LOVE AT FIRST BITE, THE STEAGLE, and as the ultimate nerd in PORTNOY'S COMPLAINT. Langella played the cad in a few more films and eventually the lead in John Badham's DRACULA. Snodgress

was nominated for an Oscar for her role in this film, the highpoint of her career and the only nomination this rather slight picture received.

DIARY OF ANNE FRANK, THE
1959   170m   bw   ★★★★
Drama/War   /U
FOX

Millie Perkins (Anne Frank), Joseph Schildkraut (Otto Frank), Shelley Winters (Mrs. Van Daan), Richard Beymer (Peter Van Daan), Gusti Huber (Edith Frank), Lou Jacobi (Mr. Van Daan), Diane Baker (Margot Frank), Douglas Spencer (Kraler), Dody Heath (Miep), Ed Wynn (Albert Dussell)

p, George Stevens; d, George Stevens; w, Frances Goodrich, Albert Hackett (based on their play and the autobiography, Anne Frank: Diary of a Young Girl); ph, William Mellor, Jack Cardiff; ed, Robert Swink, William Mace, David Brotherton; m, Alfred Newman; art d, Lyle Wheeler, George W. Davis; fx, L.B. Abbott

Millie Perkins seems too mature and too flat for the pivotal role in this touching film, based on the famous WWII diary of the young Anne Frank. Skillfully directed by George Stevens (who photographed much of the famous concentration camp footage after Germany's defeat), the film is told in flashback, as Anne's father Schildkraut, a camp survivor, returns to the warehouse attic in Amsterdam where his Jewish family hid from the "Green Police" (the Dutch Gestapo) for two years.

   Cramped in uncomfortable quarters, Frank, his wife Huber, and their two daughters, Baker and Perkins, are sheltered through the kindness and courage of two Gentile shop owners. Also sharing the tiny living space are husband and wife Jacobi and Winters (in the first of her character parts), their teenage son Beymer, and the aging dentist Wynn. As the atrocities rage outside their hideaway, Anne concerns herself with many of the usual teenage problems—parental relationships, her affection for Peter, her jealousy towards her older sister—and records them in her diary. There are a number of close calls, surprise searches, and suspenseful moments that terrify the hidden inhabitants, who, when they are finally discovered, are carted off to a concentration camp.

   Only Otto Frank survives, returning to the attic to find Anne's written reflections. He is moved to tears and shamed when he reads Anne's famous line: "In spite of everything, I still believe that people are really good at heart." A vivid and carefully produced work of poignancy and loss.

DICK TRACY
1990   103m   c   ★★★½
Adventure/Comedy   PG
Silver Screen Partners IV

Warren Beatty (Dick Tracy), Charlie Korsmo (Kid), Glenne Headly (Tess Trueheart), Madonna (Breathless Mahoney), Al Pacino (Big Boy Caprice), Dustin Hoffman (Mumbles), William Forsythe (Flattop), Charles Durning (Chief Brandon), Mandy Patinkin (88 Keys), Paul Sorvino (Lips Manlis)

p, Warren Beatty; d, Warren Beatty; w, Jim Cash, Jack Epps, Jr. (based on characters created by Chester Gould); ph, Vittorio Storaro (Technicolor); ed, Richard Marks; m, Danny Elfman; prod d, Richard Sylbert; art d, Harold Michelson; fx, Buena Vista Visual Effects Group, John Caglione, Jr., Doug Drexler; chor, Jeffrey Hornaday; cos, Milena Canonero; anim, Allen Gonzales, Samuel Recinos

In sheer visual terms, this is the most convincing of the comic book movies that have been popular for the last decade or so. Surprisingly sweet and good-natured, DICK TRACY is a highly stylized piece of fluff that's easier to digest than the ponderous pretensions of the equally over-hyped BATMAN. Producer/director/star Warren Beatty looks great in his yellow fedora and trench coat though his jaw is never as sharp as Chester Gould's celebrated comic strip cop.

This old-fashioned story takes place in a strikingly stylized comic-strip city of the 1930s. Handsome, hardworking detective Dick Tracy is hot on the trail of crime boss Big Boy Caprice (played with gusto by a nearly unrecognizable Al Pacino who has taken the entire underworld syndicate of the city away from Lips Manlis (Paul Sorvino). After disposing of Lips, taking over his nightclub, and stealing his girl, Breathless Mahoney (Madonna), Big Boy comes up with the idea of uniting all the villains in town under his leadership, thereby running the city. This is a job for Dick Tracy!

With the help of his trusty two-way wristwatch radio and the boys on the force, Tracy puts his counterplan into action. But while the crimefighter flourishes professionally, his personal life is a problematic. "Adopting" a young orphan known only as the Kid (Charlie Korsmo) burdens the bachelor with unneeded responsibilities. Though Tracy and his eternally faithful and patient girlfriend, Tess Trueheart (Glenne Headly), love each other very much, his dedication to duty prevents them from settling down and getting married. To complicate things further, Breathless has been tempting Tracy with lustful come-ons that not only jeopardize his relationship with Tess, but threaten his life as well. Tracy becomes torn between the fervent advances of Breathless and the stability represented by the Kid and Tess.

From the opening shot of the famous fedora and badge to the wildly extravagant long sweeps of the matte-painted comic-book city, DICK TRACY has a gorgeous but hollow look. It's the first film to transfer successfully the look of a comic book to the screen (kudos to Vittorio Storaro, whose striking photography makes striking use of primary colors) in an entirely cinematic way.

The performances are all fairly interesting. Hoffman's cameo as Mumbles is creepy and surprisingly funny, Headly and Korsmo are terrific, and Beatty is mesmerizingly hollow. The true star of this film, however, is Pacino, who provides a wildly over-the-top performance as Big Boy—in many ways he out-Jokers Jack Nicholson's Joker in BATMAN. He earned a Best Supporting Oscar nomination for his work. The film won the Best Makeup Oscar for its bounteous makeup and the Best Song Oscar for Stephen Sondheim's torch song, "Sooner or Later (I Always Get My Man)."

DIE HARD

1988   131m   c   ★★★
Action   R/18
Gordon/Silver

Bruce Willis (*John McClane*), Bonnie Bedelia (*Holly Gennaro McClane*), Reginald Veljohnson (*Sgt. Al Powell*), Paul Gleason (*Dwayne T. Robinson*), De'voreaux White (*Argyle*), William Atherton (*Thornburg*), Hart Bochner (*Ellis*), James Shigeta (*Takagi*), Alan Rickman (*Hans Gruber*), Alexander Godunov (*Karl*)

p, Lawrence Gordon, Joel Silver; d, John McTiernan; w, Jeb Stuart, Steven E. de Souza (based on the novel by Roderick Thorp); ph, Jan De Bont (Panavision, Deluxe Color); ed, Frank J. Urioste, John F. Link, II; m, Michael Kamen; prod d, Jackson DeGovia; fx, Richard Edlund, Al Di Sarro; cos, Marilyn Vance

The pumped-up, high tech surprise hit of 1988; a triumph of slick direction and lowbrow thrills, marred but not spoiled by a sour aftertaste.

On Christmas Eve, a New York cop (Willis) arrives in Los Angeles to spend the holidays with his estranged wife (Bedelia) and their two young children. The couple separated after the Japanese corporation Bedelia works for promoted her to a powerful position in their brand-new Los Angeles headquarters, an imposing state-of-the-art office building in Century City. Willis now meets her at a Christmas party thrown on the building's 30th floor. While he is washing up in his wife's executive bathroom, a group of international terrorists seizes the building and takes everyone at the party hostage, in an attempt to break into the company safe and steal $670 million in negotiable bonds. Barefoot and wearing only a T-shirt and slacks, Willis escapes the terrorists and makes his way to the unfinished upper floors of the building, where he wages a one-man war against the intruders.

Tautly directed by McTiernan (PREDATOR), DIE HARD is skillfully shot and consistently thrilling throughout its lengthy running time. The high-rise location, in particular, is cleverly employed to provide an array of unusual and breathtaking action scenes. Unfortunately, the film's script panders to the audience's worst fears and resentments—suggesting that foreigners are not to be trusted and feminism has destroyed the fabric of the American family, and so on. Despite this distasteful subtext, however, DIE HARD is a well-made, exciting film. A beefed-up Willis fares well in a breezy mode, but looks uncomfortable when the emoting turns heavy. The talented Bedelia is wasted, while Rickman, as the chief villain, gives an impeccably evil performance which put him on the international map.

DIE HARD 2: DIE HARDER

1990   124m   c   ★★
Action   R/15
Silver Pictures/The Gordon Company

Bruce Willis (*John McClane*), Bonnie Bedelia (*Holly McClane*), William Atherton (*Dick Thornberg*), Reginald Veljohnson (*Al Powell*), Franco Nero (*Gen. Ramon Esperanza*), William Sadler (*Col. Stuart*), John Amos (*Capt. Grant*), Dennis Franz (*Carmine Lorenzo*), Art Evans (*Barnes*), Fred Dalton Thompson (*Trudeau*)

p, Lawrence Gordon, Joel Silver, Charles Gordon; d, Renny Harlin; w, Steven E. de Souza, Doug Richardson (based on the novel *58 Minutes* by Walter Wager and on original characters by Roderick Thorp); ph, Oliver Wood (Panavision, Deluxe Color); ed, Stuart Baird, Robert A. Ferretti; m, Michael Kamen; prod d, John Vallone; art d, Christiaan Wagener; fx, Al DiSarro, Industrial Light & Magic, Tom Burman, Bari Dreiband-Burman; cos, Marilyn Vance-Straker

Cynical, mindlessly violent, mechanistic, and formulaic are not words that most reviewers applied to this slapdash sequel to DIE HARD—but they should have. All the style, wit, and intelligence of the original are jettisoned here in favor of a bigger, louder, by-the-numbers approach. This cocky genre product even has the nerve to thematize its lack of inspiration with Bruce Willis's incessant wisecracks about the similarity of his situation here to that of the previous film. Bad move, Bruce. Don't remind the audience that they're getting ripped off.

DIE HARD 2 takes place on Christmas Eve at Dulles International Airport outside of Washington, DC. In addition to the usual holiday crowds, the airport is also expecting the arrival of a "guest" from another country, a South American dictator named Esperanza (Franco Nero) who has been accused of drug smuggling and is being brought to America for trial. Reporters are everywhere, but the security seems light for such a busy evening, making things easier for the terrorists who are planning to virtually shut down the airport, intercept the dictator's incoming flight, and free him. Whereas the underachieving terrorists of the first film just terrorized a floor or two of an office building, these ambitious fellows hold an entire airport hostage. Of course, in this world of stunning incompetence, they would have gotten away with their nefarious plan were it not for one man. And who may that be? Superman? James Bond? Would you believe one good cop? Yes, John McClane (Bruce Willis) is back. In the year since he saved his estranged wife and other hostages from the charismatic bad guys in DIE HARD, McClane has reunited with his wife, Holly (Bonnie Bedelia), and moved to L.A., where he's a successful cop. As it happens, McClane is now at Dulles, waiting for Holly's flight.

To be fair, this film does offer a few outstanding action sequences and superb special effects but these are largely a function of megabucks rather than inspiration. Willis is not the most resourceful actor at the best of times but this script just leaves him high and dry. His character is not deepened in any way. The first film was just as implausible as this one but executed with such freshness and gusto that one didn't mind. The sequel is a major disappointment. If, heaven forbid, there's a DIE HARD III, we hope they try harder.

DIM SUM: A LITTLE BIT OF HEART

1985 88m c   ★★★½
Comedy   PG/U
CIM

Laureen Chew (*Geraldine Tam*), Kim Chew (*Mrs. Tam*), Victor Wong (*Uncle Tam*), Ida F.O. Chung (*Auntie Mary*), Cora Miao (*Julia*), John Nishio (*Richard*), Amy Hill (*Amy Tam*), Keith Choy (*Kevin Tam*), Elsa Cruz Pearson (*Eliza*), Helen Chew (*Linda Tam*)

p, Tom Sternberg, Wayne Wang, Danny Yung; d, Wayne Wang; w, Terrel Seltzer (based on an idea by Laureen Chew, Seltzer, Wang); ph, Michael Chin (DuArtColor); ed, Ralph Wikke, David Lindblom; m, Todd Boekelheide; art d, Christopher P. Lee, Lydia Tanji; cos, Lydia Tanji

Appealing if uneventful. This humanistic story involves an old Chinese widow who resides in San Francisco with her 30-year-old daughter. Though she has lived for many years in America, the widow is proud of her Chinese heritage and refuses to assimilate into American culture. She loves her daughter but feels the time has come for her, like her brother and sister, to be wed. Her daughter is torn between wanting to marry her boyfriend, a Los Angeles doctor, and the duty she feels toward her mother. When the mother learns from a fortune teller that she is approaching her time to die, the old woman must make some drastic changes in her attitudes. DIM SUM: A LITTLE BIT OF HEART is composed of small moments commenting in ways both broad and subtle on assimilation. Director Wayne Wang understands these problems, allowing scenes to build slowly and letting the audience get to know the characters. The universality of this comedy's subject matter makes it a gentle pleasure.

DINER

1982 110m c   ★★★★
Comedy/Drama   R/15
MGM-UA

Steve Guttenberg (*Eddie*), Daniel Stern (*Shrevie*), Mickey Rourke (*Boogie*), Kevin Bacon (*Fenwick*), Timothy Daly (*Billy*), Ellen Barkin (*Beth*), Paul Reiser (*Modell*), Kathryn Dowling (*Barbara*), Michael Tucker (*Bagel*), Jessica James (*Mrs. Simmons*)

p, Jerry Weintraub; d, Barry Levinson; w, Barry Levinson; ph, Peter Sova (Metrocolor); ed, Stu Linder; m, Bruce Brody, Ivan Kral, Joe Tuley; art d, Leon Harris; cos, Gloria Gresham

A thoughtful, charming sleeper. Writer-director Barry Levinson's debut takes us back to the late-1950s Baltimore of his youth, brilliantly evoking that era through carefully drawn characters. Five pals meet at their favorite diner in between problems with women, gambling, and all the woes attendant upon being twentysomething in 1959. Steve Guttenberg, who has been dragging his feet on the way to the altar, forces his fiancee to pass the world's toughest Baltimore Colts quiz to qualify for marriage; Daniel Stern, who is already married, would rather spend time with the guys than with the wife he thinks doesn't understand him; Timothy Daly has a pregnant girlfriend who doesn't want to get married; Kevin Bacon is rich, bright, and usually bombed; and Mickey Rourke is a rebellious hairdresser and law student who spends most of his spare time chasing women.

The prominent rock 'n' roll soundtrack keeps the film firmly grounded in its period, but Levinson's masterful script, filled with funny, realistic dialogue (especially in the diner scenes), transcends time and place even as the film so richly conveys both. Featuring excellent performances by a host of actors who've gone on to prominent careers, to say nothing of Ellen Barkin's wistful turn as Stern's neglected wife, DINER is an often hilarious, frequently touching film.

DINNER AT EIGHT

1933 113m bw   ★★★★★
Comedy/Drama   /PG
MGM

Marie Dressler (*Carlotta Vance*), John Barrymore (*Larry Renault*), Wallace Beery (*Dan Packard*), Jean Harlow (*Kitty Packard*), Lionel Barrymore (*Oliver Jordan*), Lee Tracy (*Max Kane*), Edmund Lowe (*Dr. Wayne Talbot*), Billie Burke (*Mrs. Oliver Jordan*), Madge Evans (*Paula Jordan*), Jean Hersholt (*Joe Stengel*)

p, David O. Selznick; d, George Cukor; w, Frances Marion, Herman J. Mankiewicz, Donald Ogden Stewart (based on the play by George S. Kaufman and Edna Ferber); ph, William Daniels; ed, Ben Lewis; art d, Cedric Gibbons; cos, Adrian

A gorgeous, high-gloss deco mosaic, overloaded with star power, and a curious triumph over all by the electroplated Venus, Jean Harlow. DINNER AT EIGHT was the second all-star vehicle from MGM (after GRAND HOTEL) and did much to establish Selznick as a producer to be reckoned with. The script, expertly adapted from the Kaufman-Ferber stage play by Frances Marion, Herman Mankiewicz, and Donald Ogden Stewart, polished the comedy elements of the original to further balance the existing melodrama. The MGM constellations twinkle as Gotham strata of society are invited to dine by Lionel Barrymore and Billie Burke. Underneath the patina of luxe, hearts break, plans go up in smoke, dreams are dashed.

This is the beginning of the end for John Barrymore, playing a has-been that had been patterned after him; it's a bitchy casting idea, chilling to watch. Other good parts would follow but DINNER AT EIGHT would mark the point where he began careening into parody. Burke and Barrymore turn in definitive portrayals of their star personas. Dressler's shrewd grande dame in decline (based on Mrs. Patrick Campbell) is a textbook of brilliant comic business, and Beery turns in his usual workman-like despisable grizzly.

But it's Jean Harlow who elevates herself to the big guns here. Her gold-digging, amoral little hussy, spitting out the chocolates she doesn't like back into her fancy candybox, is just as self-centered as the others. But despite the whinny voice, rock candy cosmetology and bratty manipulation, she still manages to infuse heart into her characterization. Cukor, who expertly directed, claimed she did it on her own; it's proof positive that the legendary sex symbols always have an undeniable element of humanity. (It may have helped that she and Beery hated each other's guts.) Madge Evans plays the ingenue, a role Joan Crawford pulled out of at the last minute, wisely, given the Harlow victory. Devotees of Hollywood costume design should enjoy the platinum blonde's outrageous costumes, the last word in Adrian vulgarity.

The Breen Office took exception to DINNER AT EIGHT (Joseph I. Breen being the West Coast assistant to Will Hays, who headed the censorship board affixing production codes to films at the time). Breen told Selznick that he seemed to have a predilection for suicide in his movies, citing such films as ANNA KARENINA and WHAT PRICE HOLLYWOOD. To calm the censors, the scene where John Barrymore actually turns on the gas was cut. The producer would remain forever proud of this film, taking particular delight that the chic set decorations of the movie (especially Harlow's bedroom set) helped popularize art deco in the early 1930s.

DIRTY DANCING
1987 97m c   ★★★½
Dance   PG-13/15
Vestron

Jennifer Grey (Frances "Baby" Houseman), Patrick Swayze (Johnny Castle), Jerry Orbach (Dr. Jake Houseman), Cynthia Rhodes (Penny Johnson), Jack Weston (Max Kellerman), Jane Brucker (Lisa Houseman), Kelly Bishop (Marjorie Houseman), Lonny Price (Neil Kellerman), Max Cantor (Robbie Gould), Charles "Honi" Coles (Tito Suarez)

p, Linda Gottlieb, Eleanor Bergstein; d, Emile Ardolino; w, Eleanor Bergstein; ph, Jeff Jur; ed, Peter C. Frank; m, John Morris; prod d, David Chapman; art d, Mark Haack, Stephen J. Lineweaver; chor, Kenny Ortega; cos, Hilary Rosenfeld

Teenage titillation for girls, circa 1963. Orbach is a New York doctor visiting a Catskill Mountains resort hotel with his wife Bishop and two daughters, Grey—known as Baby—and Brucker. Baby, a teenage activist, is soon bored and goes to the off-limits employees' area, where the hotel staff are engaging in "dirty dancing"—bodies rubbing and undulating around each other to pulsating music. There she meets the hotel's resident swain, Patrick Swayze, who with his partner, Cynthia Rhodes, gives dancing lessons to the guests. Although they come from two different worlds, the two fall in love.

Grey is Joel Grey's daughter and she acquits herself adequately. Swayze is a sexy dancer who can be sweet, suggest macho, and act a little. Of particular interest is Rhodes. Her part isn't large, but she is believable as an actress and spectacular as a dancer. One problem with the film is that it does nothing to endear the Catskill social setting to an audience; the inhabitants seem to be competing for awards in obnoxiousness. DIRTY DANCING produced a top-selling soundtrack album and the hit single "(I've Had) The Time of My Life."

DIRTY DISHES
(LA JUMENT VAPEUR)
1978 99m c   ★★★½
Drama
Stephan (France)

Carole Laure (Armelle Bertrand), Pierre Santini (Marc Bertrand), Liliane Roveyre, Liza Braconnier, Daniel Sarki, Bernard Haller, Francoise Armel, Gilles Brissac, Luc Danet, Jean Degrave

p, Vera Belmont; d, Joyce Bunuel; w, Joyce Bunuel, Suzanne Baron; ph, Francois Protat; ed, Jean-Bernard Boris; m, Jean-Marie Senia

One of the best cases of an unsung, and generally unseen, foreign film getting a chance to find an audience on videotape is Joyce Bunuel's first feature, DIRTY DISHES. This exciting and energetic film looks at the social and moral violence of housewifery.

Armelle (Carole Laure) is a thirtyish French housewife who, in the very first frame of the opening credit sequence, must wrestle with her vacuum cleaner and examine its dusty innards in order to complete her daily chores. Later, Armelle and her husband, Marc (Pierre Santini), are picnicking in an idyllic, grassy setting. They dance wildly to some upbeat music while their two young children look on in amazement. This honeymoon soon ends, however, when a stranger drives up and verbally assaults them, then continues to terrorize the family, chasing them through the park and nearly crushing the head of one of the children under his front tire, until, just as suddenly as he arrived, he leaves.

The story of a bored housewife has been told hundreds of times before, but rarely with so much insight, skill, or sense of impending danger. Bunuel (the American-born daughter-in-law of Luis Bunuel) directs the film at a feverish pace, and adroitly avoids stumbling over the usual cliches. Laure plays her role perfectly, turning in a wholly believable performance as the pretty ex-club dancer who gradually questions her decision to have a husband and family.

DIRTY DOZEN, THE
1967 149m c   ★★★★
War   /15
MGM (U.K.)

Lee Marvin (Maj. Reisman), Ernest Borgnine (Gen. Worden), Charles Bronson (Joseph Wladislaw), Jim Brown (Robert Jefferson), John Cassavetes (Victor Franko), Richard Jaeckel (Sgt. Bowren), George Kennedy (Maj. Max Armbruster), Trini Lopez (Pedro Jiminez), Ralph Meeker (Capt. Stuart Kinder), Robert Ryan (Col. Everett Dasher-Breed)

p, Kenneth Hyman; d, Robert Aldrich; w, Lukas Heller, Nunnally Johnson (based on the novel by E.M. Nathanson); ph, Ted Scaife; ed, Michael Luciano; m, Frank DeVol; art d, William Hutchinson; fx, Cliff Richardson

Robert Aldrich's anti-everything-except-explosives war movie, presented as an all-star game. The film follows nonconformist Major Reisman (Lee Marvin) in his assigned task of assembling a suicide squad of military felons (murderers, rapists, thieves) to infiltrate and destroy a chateau in occupied France at which the Nazi top brass congregate during WWII. Since the cast is presented as bad guys without stories, it's impossible to get emotionally involved. Aided by his assistant, Jaeckel, Marvin recruits 12 men: Cassavetes, Savalas, Bronson, Sutherland, Brown, Walker, Lopez, Mancini, Cooper, Carruthers, Busby, and Maitland, ranging from the merely dim-witted to the overtly psychotic, to form his "dirty dozen," then subjects them to brutal training designed to mold them into an efficient fighting force. After the lengthy, but wholly entertaining training session which climaxes in a war game pitting Reisman's troops against a crack unit, the dirty dozen and their leaders parachute into France to begin a mission that most of them will not survive.

Slambang funny, and extremely violent for its time, THE DIRTY DOZEN was a box-office smash that continues to be popular to this day, despite hundreds of showings on television (and two made-for-television sequels in the 1980s). Boasting excellent performances from a stellar cast, this is the ultimate macho action movie. Yet it calls into question the morals of the *Americans*, not the Germans: the instigators of the mission smugly sip sherry and smoke cigars, content that it was accomplished and that some of their most troublesome recruits died in carrying it out. Aldrich was a master at presenting his distinctly cynical outlook in the context of crowd-pleasing entertainment, and THE DIRTY DOZEN is one of his most effective and lasting efforts.

DIRTY HARRY

1971 102m c ★★★½
Crime R/18
Malpaso/WB

Clint Eastwood *(Harry Callahan)*, Reni Santoni *(Chico)*, Harry Guardino *(Bressler)*, Andy Robinson *(Scorpio)*, John Mitchum *(DeGeorgio)*, John Larch *(Chief)*, John Vernon *(Mayor)*, Mae Mercer *(Mrs. Russell)*, Lyn Edgington *(Norma)*, Ruth Kobart *(Bus Driver)*

p, Don Siegel; d, Don Siegel; w, Harry Julian Fink, Rita M. Fink, Dean Riesner (based on an unpublished story by Rita M. and Harry Julian Fink); ph, Bruce Surtees (Panavision, Technicolor); ed, Carl Pingitore; m, Lalo Schifrin; art d, Dale Hennesy; cos, Glenn Wright

Forceful, fast and action-packed, but let's stop hanging heavy pundits of profundity on the scrawny frames of macho B movies. Based on San Francisco's notorious Zodiac Killer, renegade cop Harry Callahan (Eastwood) is summoned by Guardino and mayor Vernon to stop the killer who calls himself Scorpio. The psycho wants $100,000, or he will continue his bloody work. The mayor and others are willing to give in, but Eastwood is against it, knowing that it would be just the first payment. Eastwood is teamed with young Santoni, against his wishes, but he reluctantly begins to accept the junior partner after a while. Scorpio says he's buried a teenage girl somewhere in the city and will let her die unless the town comes across with $200,000. Eastwood gets the job of delivering the money (backed up by Santoni), but eventually goes after Scorpio on his own.

This is the film that took Eastwood out of the ordinary ether and put him into superstar stratosphere. It was enormously violent, a precursor to those Bronson vigilante films. Sequels: MAGNUM FORCE, THE ENFORCER, SUDDEN IMPACT, and THE DEAD POOL.

DISCREET CHARM OF THE BOURGEOISIE, THE

(LE CHARME DISCRET DE LA BOURGEOISIE)
1972 100m c ★★★½
Comedy/Drama PG/AA
Greenwich/Jet/Dean (France/Italy/Spain)

Fernando Rey *(Ambassador Raphael Acosta)*, Delphine Seyrig *(Mme Simone Thevenot)*, Stephane Audran *(Mme Alice Senechal)*, Bulle Ogier *(Florence)*, Jean-Pierre Cassel *(M. Henri Senechal)*, Paul Frankeur *(M. Francois Thevenot)*, Julien Bertheau *(Bishop Dufour)*, Claude Pieplu *(Colonel)*, Michel Piccoli *(Home Secretary)*, Muni *(Peasant Girl)*

p, Serge Silberman; d, Luis Bunuel; w, Luis Bunuel, Jean-Claude Carriere; ph, Edmond Richard (Eastmancolor, Panavision); ed, Helene Plemiannikov; m, Galaxie Musique; art d, Pierre Guffroy; cos, Jacqueline Guyot

Overly calculated Surrealist attack on the rituals of the upper class, clergy, military, and the political sphere, THE DISCREET CHARM OF THE BOURGEOISIE is so couth that even many of Bunuel's fans mistakenly misread this brilliant joke as a sign that the then-72-year-old Spanish director had lost his bite. It is, however, every bit as wicked as the director's long-banned classic of 1930, L'AGE D'OR, just overly refined. The plot, which does no justice to a reading of the film, concerns the attempts of a group of middle-aged members of the bourgeoisie to sit down together for a dinner party. Sometimes they meet on the wrong evening, or they gather at a restaurant only to find the corpse of the recently deceased owner, or they are told that all beverages except water are out of stock, or they discover that they are not at a dinner party at all but are on stage in front of an angry audience. These aborted meetings take place in "reality"— although the film is interspersed with a number of "dreams" in which the characters imagine the worst possible events. Through all their attempts to cover up their truer, baser, and more venal nature (which encompasses drug smuggling, fascism, adultery, murder, and lust), the members of this segment of society remain faithful to one another and continue to walk on together as if nothing can direct them away from their chosen path. In a moment of life imitating art, the film was nominated for Best Original Screenplay and it won the Oscar as Best Foreign Language Film—a perfect punch line to Bunuel's joke.

DISPATCH FROM REUTERS, A

1940 89m bw ★★½
Biography
WB

Edward G. Robinson *(Julius Reuter)*, Edna Best *(Ida Magnus)*, Eddie Albert *(Max Stargardt)*, Albert Basserman *(Franz Geller)*, Gene Lockhart *(Bauer)*, Otto Kruger *(Dr. Magnus)*, Nigel Bruce *(Sir Randolph Persham)*, Montagu Love *(Delane)*, James Stephenson *(Carew)*, Walter Kingsford *(Napoleon III)*

p, Henry Blanke; d, William Dieterle; w, Milton Krims (based on the story "Reuter's News Agency" by Valentine Williams and Wolfgang Wilhelm); ph, James Wong Howe; ed, Warren Low; m, Max Steiner; art d, Anton Grot; fx, Byron Haskin, Robert Burks

Uninspired carrier pigeons. Rather flat bio follows Julius Reuter, the press baron who established a European empire for the dissemination of news. It's 1833 and the new telegraph systems are not in total use across Europe, so Reuter (Robinson) establishes his "pigeon post" to transmit news between cities. Later carrier pigeons become outmoded—and messy!—and Reuter switches to telegraph wires. But we like the birdies. An example of reality in dire need of dramatic license.

DISRAELI

1929 90m bw ★★★½
Biography
WB

George Arliss *(Disraeli)*, Joan Bennett *(Lady Clarissa Pevensey)*, Florence Arliss *(Lady Mary Beaconfield)*, Anthony Bushell *(Charles/Lord Deeford)*, David Torrence *(Sir Michael/Lord Probert)*, Ivan Simpson *(Hugh Meyers)*, Doris Lloyd *(Mrs. Agatha Travers)*, Gwendolyn Logan *(Duchess of Glastonbury)*, Charles E. Evans *(Potter)*, Cosmo Kyrle Bellew *(Mr. Terle)*

d, Alfred E. Green; w, Julien Josephson (based on the play by Louis Napoleon Parker); ph, Lee Garmes; ed, Owen Marks; m, Louis Silvers

Arliss is fine centerpiece for one of the earliest of the Warner Bros. biographies; DISRAELI sets high standards for biopics to come. It marked the film debut of aging George Arliss, and showed America a style of acting it had seen little of in the silent years. Arliss was stage-trained and able to make the switch from stage to silents and then sound with no difficulty. Rather than attempt a long picture about the Jew who converted to Christianity and was Queen Victoria's closest ally, the film deals with a brief slice of Disraeli's life, focusing on his attempt to outwit the Russians in the rush to purchase the Suez Canal. Along the way, we get the opportunity to observe his wit, his amours, his geniality, and his brilliance.

Florence Arliss played his screen wife, and their ability to play off each other lent sparkle to both performances. Arliss would come to specialize in historical figures, playing Rothschild, Richelieu, Wellington, Alexander Hamilton, and others. He had played Disraeli in a 1921 silent film first, but this is the definitive performance.

DISTANT VOICES, STILL LIVES
1989 85m c   ★★★½
Drama   PG-13/15
British Film Institute/Film Four/Channel 4/ZDF (U.K.)

Freda Dowie (Mother), Pete Postlethwaite (Father), Angela Walsh (Eileen), Lorraine Ashbourne (Maisie), Dean Williams (Tony), Sally Davies (Eileen as a child), Nathan Walsh (Tony as a child), Susan Flanagan (Maisie as a Child), Michael Starke (Dave), Vincent MaGuire (George)

p, Jennifer Howarth; d, Terence Davies; w, Terence Davies; ph, William Diver, Patrick Duval; ed, William Diver; art d, Miki van Zwanenberg, Jocelyn James; cos, Monica Howe

Part nostalgia, part nightmare, the autobiographical DISTANT VOICES, STILL LIVES is writer-director Terence Davies's bittersweet look back at his working-class upbringing in postwar Liverpool. While it's beautifully photographed, Davies's portrait of a house divided by a near-psychotic father (Pete Postlethwaite)—loving one moment, brutal the next—is not a pretty sight. All of the familial warts and blemishes are visible as Davies avoids any romanticizing of the past whatsoever. In this highly stylized, cinematic portrait of his family, there is no enhancement, no glitz, not even much of a plot. Rather, Davies leaves us with a series of impressions, presented non-chronologically, that evoke memories of his basically repressive Catholic childhood in the 1950s.

Told in flashback, the film begins and ends with family weddings held several years apart as the grown children reflect on their father and his mostly negative influence upon their lives. Despite Davies' often harsh, brutal focus, this is no gloom-and-doom period piece. Remarkably, all his sensitively drawn, subtle observations coalesce, forming an emotionally compelling whole that visually and vividly recalls a traditional way of life. Static as their lives may be, his people are never dull. In this very personal portrait, Davies, the artist, has re-created universal experiences—familiar passions and needs—that draw us to his family's humanity.

DIVA
1981 123m c   ★★★★½
Crime/Romance   /15
Galaxie/Greenwich (France)

Frederic Andrei (Jules), Wilhelmenia Wiggins Fernandez (Cynthia Hawkins), Richard Bohringer (Gorodish), Thuy An Luu (Alba),

Jacques Fabbri (Saporta), Chantal Deruaz (Nadia), Roland Bertin (Weinstadt), Gerard Darmon (L'Antillais), Dominique Pinon (Le Cure), Jean-Jacques Moreau (Krantz)

p, Irene Silberman; d, Jean-Jacques Beineix; w, Jean-Jacques Beineix, Jean Van Hamme (based on a novel by Delacorta); ph, Philippe Rousselot (Eastmancolor); ed, Marie-Josephe Yoyotte, Monique Prim; m, Vladimir Cosma; art d, Hilton McConnico

A lady prone to technique but dazzling nonetheless, DIVA is visually astonishing film fare. The complex plot concerns Andrei, a young Parisian mail carrier, and his love for Fernandez, a famous black American opera singer. Andrei attends a performance by the diva, recording it secretly while a sinister Taiwanese man watches him. In a separate incident a dazed girl walking through the Paris metro is murdered by two thugs—the greasy Darmon and the punkish, bald Pinon. As the girl dies she slips an audiocassette into Andrei's mailpouch. Andrei now finds himself unwittingly caught in two plots: that of Taiwanese record pirates who want his recording of the diva and that of pimps and drug runners who want the incriminating tape left in his mailpouch.

The debut film from Jean-Jacques Beineix, DIVA is perhaps the most picturesque film to come out of France in years. Together with art director Hilton McConnico and cameraman Philippe Rousselot, Beineix creates awesome shot after awesome shot, so much so that many felt the film was too stylish. At times the sensibility is very "New Wave" (as in fashion and music, not the film movement); at other times, Beineix is intensely Impressionistic. These qualities are even further enhanced by a perfect musical score, contributed by Vladimir Cosma, who has used Act I of Alfredo Catalani's opera La Wally.

DIVORCE, ITALIAN STYLE
(DIVORZIO ALL'ITALIANA)
1962 108m bw   ★★★★
Comedy   /A
Lux (Italy)

Marcello Mastroianni (Ferdinando), Daniela Rocca (Rosalia), Stefania Sandrelli (Angela), Leopoldo Trieste (Carmelo Patane), Odoardo Spadaro (Don Gaetano), Margherita Girelli (Sisina), Angela Cardile (Agnese), Bianca Castagnetta (Donna Matilde), Lando Buzzanca (Rosario Mule), Pietro Tordi (Attorney DeMarzi)

p, Franco Cristaldi; d, Pietro Germi; w, Ennio De Concini, Alfredo Giannetti, Pietro Germi; ph, Leonida Barboni; ed, Roberto Cinquini; m, Carlo Rustichelli; cos, Dina Di Bari

To die laughing for. Rocca is a whining sex-crazed Sicilian wife who drives husband Mastroianni to consider divorce. Unfortunately for Rocca it is easier to murder in Italy than it is to divorce. And that's precisely what is done. The scheming Mastroianni then goes on to marry the proverbial nymphet next door after his wife is out of the picture. A brilliant comic performance from Mastroianni which has been compared to the deadpan style of Keaton. It earned him an Oscar nomination for Best Actor, as well as Best Actor accolades from the Golden Globes and the British Film Academy. Considered by some to be one of the greatest modern comedies.

DIVORCEE, THE
1930 83m bw   ★★★½
Drama
MGM

Norma Shearer (Jerry), Chester Morris (Ted), Conrad Nagel (Paul), Robert Montgomery (Don), Florence Eldridge (Helen), Helene

Millard *(Mary)*, Robert Elliott *(Bill)*, Mary Doran *(Janice)*, Tyler Brooke *(Hank)*, Zelda Sears *(Hannah)*

p, Robert Z. Leonard; d, Robert Z. Leonard; w, Nick Grinde, Zelda Sears, John Meehan (based on the novel *Ex-Wife* by Ursula Parrott); ph, Norbert Brodine; ed, Hugh Wynn, Truman K. Wood; art d, Cedric Gibbons; cos, Adrian

Norma Shearer, in an Oscar-winning role, tries daringly to confront the double standard, but not upset her legion of fans (or the censors) who wouldn't approve of her really letting loose. Thankfully, something always gets in the way. The plot is a trifle: her husband (Morris) cheats on her, but won't hear of her doing the same. They divorce, and since Jerry (Shearer) is supposedly liberated from the shackles of matrimony, she flirts with several men (Montgomery and Nagel) before the requisite New Year's Eve reconciliation with her ex.

Based on Ursula Parrott's then-steamy novel *Ex-Wife*, much of the spirit has been laundered out here. (Things would become much worse, though, after the 1934 Production Code clampdown, so enjoy the spice that survives.) Shearer turns in a fine performance of the silken suffering which was her pre-Code specialty. While never in the same league, beauty-wise, with Garbo and Crawford, the other two of MGM's big three, she had a definite image advantage for many prestige pictures. Seemingly American (she was Canadian), she could play the moderns Garbo could not, but in more ladylike turns than Crawford. Being the pope's wife—she was married to production genius Irving Thalberg—never hurt her, either. (In all fairness, however, she was a star before she and Thalberg tied the knot, and audiences genuinely liked her as well.) Whether or not you like Shearer and THE DIVORCEE depends on how you respond to this particular "tease" variety of soap opera, but this enjoyable film stands as an index to the sexual politics of an era.

DO THE RIGHT THING
1989   120m   c   ★★★★½
Comedy/Drama   R/18
40 Acres And A Mule

Danny Aiello *(Sal)*, Ossie Davis *(Da Mayor)*, Ruby Dee *(Mother Sister)*, Richard Edson *(Vito)*, Giancarlo Esposito *(Buggin Out)*, Spike Lee *(Mookie)*, Bill Nunn *(Radio Raheem)*, John Turturro *(Pino)*, Paul Benjamin *(ML)*, Frankie Faison *(Coconut Sid)*

p, Spike Lee, Monty Ross; d, Spike Lee; w, Spike Lee; ph, Ernest Dickerson (Duart Color); ed, Barry Alexander Brown; m, Bill Lee; prod d, Wynn Thomas; chor, Rosie Perez, Otis Sallid; cos, Ruth Carter

DO THE RIGHT THING has been hailed as the most insightful view of race relations ever to hit US screens and condemned as dangerous agitprop, but its timeliness—and its ability to touch a nerve in the culture at large—was never in question.

The story is set in Brooklyn's Bedford-Stuyvesant neighborhood on a broiling hot Saturday. Blacks and Latinos inhabit the area, but the local eatery, Sal's Famous Pizzeria, is owned and managed by Italian-American Sal (Danny Aiello) who commutes to work with his two sons, the embittered, bigoted Pino (John Turturro) and the mild-mannered and sympathetic Vito (Richard Edson). Also working at Sal's is Mookie (writer-director Spike Lee), the deliveryman, who tries to do as little work as possible in his dead-end job. On the hottest day of the year, tensions rise when the self-styled local activist Buggin Out (Giancarlo Esposito), upset by the absence of Black faces on Sal's "Wall of Fame," attempts to organize a boycott of the pizzeria. This

apparently trivial incident is the spark that eventually ignites the explosion which climaxes the film.

Lee has crafted a film of astonishing power and originality. While watching the film one has the euphoric sense of watching a major talent starting to bloom. Cinematographer Ernest Dickerson shows signs of genius as he provides brightly colored images so hot they make you sweat with excitement. No one is better at lighting images of people of color. The large ensemble cast is excellent. Aiello makes Sal a likable guy despite his unconscious paternalism. Turturro is frighteningly believeable as the volatile Pino but he is no cardboard villain. Everyone has their reasons. Ossie Davis and Ruby Dee, two stalwarts of the Black theater, serve with special distinction as both a vivid reminder of past glories of Black culture and an inspiration for the future.

Lee has promoted himself as a political activist filmmaker working with a conscious agenda: to tell Black stories that have traditionally been ignored by Hollywood. Indeed his success has opened the doors for a new generation of Black filmmakers. DO THE RIGHT THING, his breakthrough film, is no blunt work of propaganda; it is a subtle and humane entertainment with a refreshingly serious view of the world. There are no absolute heroes or villains. There are no easy answers. So many people are struggling to do the right thing but so few are sure of what that may be. This film poses those questions with rare artistry and grace.

DOC HOLLYWOOD
1991   114m   c   ★★
Comedy/Romance   PG-13/12
Warner Bros.

Michael J. Fox *(Ben Stone)*, Julie Warner *(Lou)*, Barnard Hughes *(Doctor Hogue)*, Woody Harrelson *(Hank)*, David Ogden Stiers *(Nick Nicholson)*, Frances Sternhagen *(Lillian)*, George Hamilton *(Doctor Halberstrom)*, Bridget Fonda *(Nancy Lee)*, Mel Winkler *(Melvin)*, Helen Martin *(Maddie)*

p, Susan Solt, Deborah D. Johnson; d, Michael Caton-Jones; w, Jeffrey Price, Peter S. Seaman, Daniel Pyne (from Laurian Leggett's adaptation of the book "What? . . .Dead Again?" by Neil B. Shulman); ph, Michael Chapman; ed, Priscilla Nedd-Friendly, Gregg London; m, Carter Burwell; prod d, Lawrence Miller; art d, Eva Anna Bohn, Dale Allen Pelton; cos, Richard Hornung

DOC HOLLYWOOD is an unsuccessful attempt to create an old-fashioned slice of romantic Americana in the style of Frank Capra or Preston Sturges.

A D.C.-based plastic surgeon with dreams of making mounds of money in Beverly Hills, Dr. Ben Stone (Michael J. Fox) speeds West in his vintage Porsche but gets only as far as Grady, South Carolina, before a fluke accident stops him cold. Within moments of crashing into the new fence of Grady's mayor Nick Nicholson (David Ogden Stiers), Ben realizes he may be in for a long stay. The mayor is eager to have a fresh-faced young doctor minister to the townsfolks' needs, and sentences "Doc" Stone to many hours of community service, while his Porsche is laid up at the local body shop for extensive repairs.

Directed by Michael Caton-Jones (SCANDAL, MEMPHIS BELLE), DOC HOLLYWOOD is a clumsy, calculated attempt at warm-hearted, populist entertainment. As the title character, Michael J. Fox plays the same immature yuppie innocent he portrayed in the BACK TO THE FUTURE movies and THE SECRET OF MY SUCCESS, as well as countless episodes of TV's "Family Ties." He does it well, but we've seen it too many times before.

Julie Warner makes a respectable love interest, and Barnard Hughes is acceptable as the town's aging doctor whose homespun remedies have kept the population in shape for many years. George Hamilton delivers a nice turn as the almost machine-like Dr. Halberstrom, while Bridget Fonda, whose forceful, sexy presence gives this sluggish movie a temporary shot of adrenalin, is all but wasted in a cameo as a Southern belle anxious to find her fortune in Hollywood.

DOCTOR DOLITTLE

1967 152m c   ★½
Musical   /U
FOX

Rex Harrison *(Dr. John Dolittle)*, Anthony Newley *(Matthew Mugg)*, Peter Bull *(Gen. Bellowes)*, William Dix *(Tommy Stubbins)*, Portia Nelson *(Sarah Dolittle)*, Samantha Eggar *(Emma Fairfax)*, Richard Attenborough *(Albert Blossom)*, Muriel Landers *(Mrs. Blossom)*, Geoffrey Holder *(Willie Shakespeare)*, Norma Varden *(Lady Petherington)*

p, Arthur P. Jacobs; d, Richard Fleischer; w, Leslie Bricusse (based on stories by Hugh Lofting); ph, Robert Surtees (Todd-AO, DeLuxeColor); ed, Samuel E. Beetley, Marjorie Fowler; prod d, Mario Chiari; art d, Jack Martin Smith, Ed Graves; fx, L.B. Abbott, Art Cruickshank, Emil Kosa, Jr., Howard Lydecker; chor, Herbert Ross; cos, Ray Aghayan

Does little. As a matter of fact, a huge, stillborn dinosaur in quicksand, this one almost bankrupted its studio. Doctor Dolittle (Rex Harrison) is considered a nut by his neighbors. After this nuttiness leads to his arrest, Dolittle decides to avoid people and devote his life to animals since, as one who can speak all the animal tongues (he was taught 498 different languages by his parrot, Polynesia), he serves as a unique link between human and beast. With Anthony Newley, the most irritating man in show business, and the vapid Samantha Eggar at his side, the doctor sails off to find the elusive Great Pink Sea Snail and the Giant Lunar Moth in the South Seas, but no box office.

Problems on the set were many, especially with the use of so many live animals—more than 1,500. Alan Jay Lerner, originally set to write the book and lyrics, attempted to write for over a year but finally gave up, whereupon Harrison wanted to leave as well. Harrison hadn't wanted to star in a children's film in the first place, and only the involvement of prestigious author-lyricist Lerner attracted him to the project. The songs by Lerner's replacement, Leslie Bricusse, pleased Harrison, so he stayed with the production. Will put the kids to sleep, but may kill you.

DR. EHRLICH'S MAGIC BULLET

1940 103m bw   ★★★★★
Biography   /A
WB

Edward G. Robinson *(Dr. Paul Ehrlich)*, Ruth Gordon *(Mrs. Ehrlich)*, Otto Kruger *(Dr. Emil von Behring)*, Donald Crisp *(Minister Althoff)*, Maria Ouspenskaya *(Franziska Speyer)*, Montagu Love *(Prof. Hartmann)*, Sig Rumann *(Dr. Hans Wolfert)*, Donald Meek *(Mittlemeyer)*, Henry O'Neill *(Dr. Lentz)*, Albert Basserman *(Dr. Robert Koch)*

p, Wolfgang Reinhardt; d, William Dieterle; w, John Huston, Heinz Herald, Norman Burnstein (based on a story by Burnstein from letters and notes owned by the Ehrlich family); ph, James Wong Howe; ed, Warren Low; m, Max Steiner; art d, Carl Jules Weyl; fx, Robert Burks

Another entry in the superb series of Warner Bros. historical biographies, and alongside the same director's THE LIFE OF EMILE ZOLA, the best of them. By even mentioning the subject of venereal disease, this splendid saga also merits pride of place in any history of Hollywood.

Robinson is positively electric in a role quite unlike the types he usually played, that of gentle yet determined research scientist Dr. Paul Ehrlich. Unable to fit into the conservative routine of a Berlin hospital, painfully honest with his patients, Dr. Ehrlich finally finds his niche on the staff of respected physician Dr. Robert Koch (Basserman). Although his experiments cause him to contract TB, Ehrlich's ever-fertile mind first grasps a theory of poison immunity while he recovers from his illness in Egypt. Returning to Germany, Ehrlich must face shortsighted grant agencies and even a court of law while implementing his treatments for syphillis and childhood diphtheria, but the good doctor's steadfastness eventually wins the day.

Beautifully directed by ace studio craftsman Dieterle, the detailed, Oscar-nominated screenplay (using information from Ehrlich's family) manages to turn meticulous scientific research into absorbing subject matter. Robinson convincingly ages over 35 years during the film, bringing warmth and idiosyncrasy to a challenging role. Among a great supporting cast, Kruger and Basserman are particularly fine. Gordon, however, though sweet and likable as Ehrlich's supportive wife, brings little to the role which suggests her legendary stage reputation.

DOCTOR IN THE HOUSE

1954 92m c   ★★★★
Comedy   /U
General Films   (U.K.)

Dirk Bogarde *(Simon)*, Muriel Pavlow *(Joy)*, Kenneth More *(Grimsdyke)*, Donald Sinden *(Benskin)*, Kay Kendall *(Isobel)*, James Robertson Justice *(Sir Lancelot)*, Donald Houston *(Taffy)*, Suzanne Cloutier *(Stella)*, Geoffrey Keen *(Dean)*, George Coulouris *(Briggs)*

p, Betty E. Box; d, Ralph Thomas; w, Richard Gordon, Ronald Wilkinson, Nicholas Phipps (based on the novel by Gordon); ph, Ernest Steward (Technicolor); ed, Gerald Thomas; m, Bruce Montgomery; art d, Carmen Dillon; cos, Yvonne Caffin

The original "Doctor" comedy that spawned an entire series of films and a popular television sitcom, DOCTOR IN THE HOUSE is certainly the best of the lot. Simon Sparrow (Bogarde) begins his five long years of medical school and is immediately taken over by three student repeaters, all of whom failed their preliminary exams. Bogarde (like almost everyone else in the cast) is a bit too old for his role, but his appeal is undeniable and the film is notable for confirming his status as Britain's leading matinee idol of the 1950s. Shot with the appropriate lighthearted touch in bright, shiny color, with fine performances all around (Kenneth More is particularly good), this sometimes hilarious film started the series off on a high note.

DR. JEKYLL AND MR. HYDE

1932 90m bw   ★★★★★
Horror   /15
Paramount

Fredric March *(Dr. Henry Jekyll/Mr. Hyde)*, Miriam Hopkins *(Ivy Pearson)*, Rose Hobart *(Muriel Carew)*, Holmes Herbert *(Dr. Lanyon)*, Edgar Norton *(Poole)*, Halliwell Hobbes *(Brig-Gen. Carew)*, Arnold Lucy *(Utterson)*, Tempe Pigott *(Mrs. Hawkins)*, Col. G.L. McDonnell *(Hobson)*, Eric Wilton *(Briggs)* p, Rouben Mamoulian; d, Rouben Mamoulian; w, Samuel Hoffenstein, Percy Heath (based on the novel *The Strange Case of Dr. Jekyll and Mr. Hyde* by Robert Louis Stevenson); ph, Karl Struss; ed, William Shea; art d, Hans Dreier; cos, Travis Banton

Easily the best of the many versions of the Stevenson horror classic. Although heavily made up as a jagged-toothed simian, March is memory-scarring with his weird body language and fierce posturing as Hyde, in stark contrast to the upright if simpering Jekyll. As Jekyll, courting his unattainable fiancee (Hobart) or tampering with nature and chemistry to create the evil side of his nature in living form, March embodies the essence of gentility. As Hyde, March is truly frightening in his hideous alter ego who taunts and brutalizes a promiscuous barmaid (Hopkins). The film reaches its exciting finale as the law confronts the grotesque Hyde, locked out of his laboratory, only to discover that he is also the respectable Dr. Jekyll.

March deservedly won an Oscar for his astonishing "dual" role (shared with Wallace Beery for THE CHAMP), but perhaps the real star of the film is director Mamoulian, whose audacious use of symbolism and careful pacing increase the mystique of this strange story. His heavy use of point-of-view editing is entirely appropriate to the story, and Struss's outstanding photography is a marvel to behold.

Made before the Production Code clampdown in 1934, DR. JEKYLL AND MR. HYDE not only uses violence to great effect but also does not shy away from the links between horror and sexuality. During the first transformation scene Mamoulian includes a montage which makes it clear that Hyde represents Jekyll's id, the socially and sexually repressed side of the doctor's psyche. The highly charged scenes between March and Hopkins (who's marvelous as Ivy) are the film's highlights, while those between March and the suitably demure Hobart pale by comparison.

DR. KILDARE'S WEDDING DAY
1941   82m   bw   ★★
Drama
Metro

Lew Ayres *(Dr. James Kildare)*, Lionel Barrymore *(Dr. Leonard Gillespie)*, Laraine Day *(Mary Lamont)*, Red Skelton *(Vernon Briggs)*, Fay Holden *(Mrs. Bartlett)*, Walter Kingsford *(Dr. Walter Carew)*, Alma Kruger *(Molly Byrd)*, Samuel S. Hinds *(Dr. Stephen Kildare)*, Emma Dunn *(Mrs. Martha Kildare)*, Nils Asther *(Constanzo Labardi)*

d, Harold S. Bucquet; w, Willis Goldbeck, Harry Ruskin (based on a story by Ormond Ruthven, Lawrence P. Bachmann from characters created by Max Brand); ph, George Folsey; ed, Conrad A. Nervig; m, Bronislau Kaper; art d, Cedric Gibbons

The 9th of the 16 Dr. Kildare films, if you count Paramount's 1937 INTERNES CAN'T TAKE MONEY, the first offical Kildare flick, but not part of the MGM-Ayres series. This one promised a wedding between Ayres's Kildare and Day's winsome nurse-fiancee. MGM was giving the build-up to Day, so they needed her out of the Kildare programmers. You'll see how this misnamed entry worked it all out, with the venerable, crusty, crazy-making Barrymore snapping Ayres out of it, when wedding plans go awry.

Day would occupy a middle rung of stardom through the mid-1940s, specialzing in sweet roles. You might check out KEEP YOUR POWDER DRY, MGM's big WAC movie, watching her and Lana Turner play deep freeze with each other. Later

Miss Day would devote herself to the Mormon faith, into which she was born.

DR. NO
1962   110m   c   ★★★½
Spy   /PG
UA   (U.K.)

Sean Connery *(James Bond)*, Jack Lord *(Felix Leiter)*, Joseph Wiseman *(Dr. No)*, Ursula Andress *(Honey)*, Zena Marshall *(Miss Taro)*, Eunice Gayson *(Sylvia)*, Lois Maxwell *(Miss Moneypenny)*, Margaret LeWars *(Photographer)*, John Kitzmiller *(Quarrel)*, Bernard Lee *("M")*

p, Harry Saltzman, Albert R. Broccoli; d, Terence Young; w, Richard Maibaum, Johanna Harwood, Berkely Mather (based on the novel by Ian Fleming); ph, Ted Moore (Technicolor); ed, Peter Hunt; m, John Barry, Monty Norman; prod d, Ken Adam; art d, Syd Cain; fx, Frank George

In his first cinematic mission, James Bond (Connery) is sent by his MI7 superior, "M" (Lee), to investigate the murder of an agent in Jamaica. There he learns of the nefarious Dr. No (Wiseman), who has come up with a device that alters the flight paths of rockets launched from Cape Canaveral, all for the greater greed and glory of SPECTRE (Special Executive for Counterintelligence, Terrorism, Revenge and Extortion). After surviving several attempts on his life and meeting up with the luscious, bikini-clad Honey (Andress), Bond ventures to Dr. No's Crab Key fortress where he does battle with a tank and eventually becomes the evil scientist's prisoner en route to his inevitable triumph.

Made for about $1 million, DR. NO is one of the more modest of the Bond films and the extravagances that would later inflate the series even further into fantasy are less evident here. Still, under director Young's sure hand, the performances (the stiff Andress excepted) are rich and the plotline suitably enthralling. Producers Broccoli and Saltzman were determined to use a relatively unknown English actor as Bond but one who possessed the right equation of ruggedness, suavity and sex appeal. Although he was Scottish, Connery certainly fit the other prerequisites and made the role his own (to the chagrin of Roger Moore and other Bond impersonators). Also notable for introducing John Barry's famous James Bond theme music, DR. NO, like many of the Bonds, is highly enjoyable and equally forgettable.

DR. STRANGELOVE: OR HOW I LEARNED TO STOP WORRYING AND LOVE THE BOMB
1964   102m   bw   ★★★★★
Science Fiction/Comedy/War   /PG
Columbia   (U.K.)

Peter Sellers *(Group Capt. Lionel Mandrake/President Merkin Muffley/Dr. Strangelove)*, George C. Scott *(Gen. "Buck" Turgidson)*, Sterling Hayden *(Gen. Jack D. Ripper)*, Keenan Wynn *(Col. "Bat" Guano)*, Slim Pickens *(Maj. T.J. "King" Kong)*, Peter Bull *(Ambassador de Sadesky)*, Tracy Reed *(Miss Scott)*, James Earl Jones *(Lt. Lothar Zogg)*, Jack Creley *(Mr. Staines)*, Frank Berry *(Lt. H.R. Dietrich)*

p, Stanley Kubrick; d, Stanley Kubrick; w, Stanley Kubrick, Terry Southern, Peter George (based on the novel *Red Alert* by Peter George); ph, Gilbert Taylor; ed, Anthony Harvey; m, Laurie Johnson; prod d, Ken Adam; art d, Peter Murton; fx, Wally Veevers; cos, Bridget Sellers

Easily the funniest movie ever made about global thermonuclear holocaust, DR. STRANGELOVE seems to grow more relevant with each passing year. Obsessed with the idea that Communists are trying to rob Americans of their "precious bodily fluids," General Jack D. Ripper (Hayden), commander of Burpelson Air Force Base, goes completely mad and sends his bomber wing to attack the USSR. US President Muffley (Sellers) meets desperately with his advisors, including blustery Gen. "Buck" Turgidson (Scott) and wheelchair-bound ex-Nazi scientist Dr. Strangelove (also played by Sellers). Left with little choice, the powers that be formulate a plan to have the Russians shoot down the American bombers. However, the Soviet ambassador (Bull), informs the president that the Soviet Union has constructed a "Doomsday Device" which will automatically trigger buried nuclear weapons if their country is hit. Meanwhile, British officer Lionel Mandrake (also Sellers) busies himself with trying to trick Gen. Ripper into revealing the code that will recall the bombers. Eventually, all of them are shot down or recalled, except for one flown by Major T.J. "King" Kong (Pickens), a crafty pilot who manages to evade Russian fighters and missiles as he heads for his target deep inside the USSR. The film's final image, that of Kong riding the phallic bomb like a bucking bronco, is unforgettable.

Expertly directed by Kubrick, who deftly intercuts the events at Burpelson with the War Room conference and the action on Kong's B-52, DR. STRANGELOVE is the ultimate black comedy, one that makes unthinkable horror unbearably funny. The film is a model of barely controlled hysteria in which the absurdity of hypermasculine Cold War posturing becomes devastatingly funny—and at the same time nightmarishly frightening in its accuracy. (The Burpelson motto, "Peace Is Our Profession," is not so absurd; consider the labeling of the Strategic Defense Initiative as a "Peace Shield.") While at times Kubrick seems to strive a bit too hard for laughs (Keenan Wynn's being sprayed in the face after shooting a Coca-Cola machine comes to mind), other effects, especially the cinematography and Adam's brilliant production design, potently enhance the film's satirical vision.

STRANGELOVE also contains some truly remarkable comic performances, especially from Sellers in his triple role and Hayden as the mad general, and genuinely priceless dialogue ("Gentlemen, you can't fight in here. This is the War Room!"). A prophetic look at the insanity of superpower politics which, like George Orwell's 1984, has entered the lexicon of modern political discourse.

DOCTOR X

1932   77m   c/bw   ★★★★
Horror   /A
First National

Lionel Atwill (Doctor Xavier, Head of Research Laboratory), Lee Tracy (Lee, a Newspaper Reporter), Fay Wray (Joanne, Dr. X's Daughter), Preston Foster (Dr. Wells), Arthur Edmund Carewe (Dr. Rowitz), John Wray (Dr. Haines), Harry Beresford (Dr. Duke), George Rosener (Otto, Dr. X's Butler), Leila Bennett (Mamie, Dr. X's Housekeeper), Robert Warwick (Police Commissioner Stevens)

d, Michael Curtiz; w, Robert Tasker, Earl Baldwin (based on a play by Howard Warren Comstock and Allen C. Miller); ph, Ray Rennahan, Richard Towers (Technicolor); ed, George Amy; art d, Anton Grot

A rare excursion into horror for First National (later Warner Bros.), DR. X became one of the great "lost" films after its initial release and developed a reputation as a masterpiece of early talkie horror during the 30 years it went unseen. When a black-and-white print of this two-color Technicolor landmark was finally discovered, however, some found the film a disappointment. Now that enough time has passed and viewers can forget all those long-cherished expectations, the film proves to be a delightful product of its period.

The story is set in a spooky old mansion atop the cliffs at Blackstone Shoals on Long Island. Atwill plays the sinister Dr. Xavier, who runs the research laboratory where most of the action takes place. It seems that a member of his staff has discovered a synthetic flesh substitute which imbues its wearer with abnormal powers and this transformed monster has been strangling people during full moons. Much of the film involves a recreation of the murders designed to expose the killer, but all does not go quite as planned.

Talented studio craftsman Curtiz (CASABLANCA) shapes the material well, showing particular flair in his semi-expressionistic handling of the haunted house trappings of the story. If he doesn't have quite the flair for grotesquerie or black humor of James Whale, he does use the wisecracking of Tracy and the glowering of Atwill to good effect. Atwill especially shines when called upon to casually discuss topics from cannibalism to depravity. Several scenes, from the unexpected animation of a skeleton to the recreation of the final murder, where the killer puts in an unexpected guest appearance, are genuinely eerie. Fay Wray, as Dr. Xavier's daughter, also gets to scream as only she can.

Finally, the two-color Technicolor techniques (involving the processing of two negatives rather than the three which became standard after 1935) are extremely effective. The rather slack and hokey 1939 film, THE RETURN OF DOCTOR X, is not a sequel, but it does contain Humphrey Bogart's only horror movie appearance.

DOCTOR ZHIVAGO

1965   197m   c   ★★★★
Drama/War   /15
MGM

Geraldine Chaplin (Tonya), Julie Christie (Lara), Tom Courtenay (Pasha/Strelnikoff), Alec Guinness (Yevgraf), Siobhan McKenna (Anna), Ralph Richardson (Alexander), Omar Sharif (Yuri), Rod Steiger (Komarovsky), Rita Tushingham (The Girl), Adrienne Corri (Amelia)

p, Carlo Ponti; d, David Lean; w, Robert Bolt (based on the novel by Boris Pasternak); ph, Freddie Young (Panavision, Metrocolor); ed, Norman Savage; m, Maurice Jarre; prod d, John Box; art d, Terence Marsh; fx, Eddie Fowlie; cos, Phyllis Dalton

Lumpy if sometimes sinfully rich borscht. This sprawling adaptation of Pasternak's epic novel of the Russian Revolution was director Lean's follow-up to his masterful LAWRENCE OF ARABIA. Told in flashback, the film follows Yuri Zhivago (Sharif) and Tonya Gromeko (Chaplin), who meet as youths when the orphaned Yuri is taken in by Tonya's parents. Eventually Yuri becomes a physician and marries Tonya, but several times during WWI he crosses paths with Lara (Christie), the beautiful daughter of a dressmaker, and the two fall into a passionate affair that is disrupted by the Bolshevik Revolution.

Unable to maintain a consistent level of interest through its seat-squirmingly long running time, this typically overblown Lean epic is not as exciting or as powerful as LAWRENCE OF ARABIA or THE BRIDGE ON THE RIVER KWAI. Bolt's choppy screenplay leaves out great chunks of Pasternak's novel, turning the narrative in a bumpy, who-gives-a-damn roller coaster ride in the film's last half. Equally regrettable is the miscasting of Sharif, who had done quite well in LAWRENCE but here contributes a performance with all the sparkle of sawdust. Christie, Steiger, and (to a lesser extent) Guinness, however, imbue their parts with passion and intensity, and the huge supporting cast is generally fine.

As always, Lean's handling of the purely physical aspects of the material is spectacular, with the scenes of revolution, the harsh Russian winters, and Zhivago's trek across the steppes simply unforgettable. Filmed mostly in Spain and Finland, the cinematography is often stunning even when the effects are pretentious (e.g. Lean's screen-filling closeup of the inside of a flower). Jarre's jarring score, though much praised at the time for the lilting "Lara's Theme," now seems repetitive and grating enough to make one want to sabotage balalaika factories everywhere.

DODGE CITY

1939   104m   c   ★★★★
Western   /PG
WB

Errol Flynn (Wade Hatton), Olivia de Havilland (Abbie Irving), Ann Sheridan (Ruby Gilman), Bruce Cabot (Jeff Surrett), Frank McHugh (Joe Clemens), Alan Hale (Rusty Hart), John Litel (Matt Cole), Victor Jory (Yancy), Henry Travers (Dr. Irving), Henry O'Neill (Col. Dodge)

p, Robert Lord; d, Michael Curtiz; w, Robert Buckner; ph, Ray Rennahan, Sol Polito (Technicolor); ed, George Amy; m, Max Steiner; art d, Ted Smith; fx, Byron Haskin, Rex Wimpy; cos, Milo Anderson

This great action Western, Flynn's first, has the intrepid adventurer enter Dodge City, a notorious, wide-open range town, as cattle buyer Wade Hatton. He leads lawmen to rustler Jeff Surrett (Cabot) and his henchmen (Jory and Fowley) before leading a covered wagon train with his pals (Hale and Williams) en route to Dodge City. Attracted to spirited Abbie Irving, he draws only her scorn after she blames him for the death of her brother (Lundigan), a hellion crushed in a stampede he himself started. Once at Dodge City, Wade finds that Surrett now runs the town and, after being pushed far enough, takes the sheriff's badge and cleans up the hellhole. Although he has a brief flirtation with saloon gal Ruby Gilman (Sheridan), his heart belongs to Abbie, and she soon comes to respect Wade's heroic endeavors.

DODGE CITY is top-flight action directed with verve and invention by Warner Bros. workhorse Curtiz. In a year with plenty of worthy Western competition, this expensively mounted film nevertheless found a wide and appreciative public. Polito's camerawork, highlighted by the rich use of color, is sweeping and fluid, and Steiner's score is vigorous and effective. A sequence involving a burning runaway train is handled well and the saloon brawl midway through the film, used time and again by the studio as stock footage, is magnificently staged and remains a classic of its kind. Not too surprisingly, De Havilland hated her rather standardized role, and Sheridan, in a more colorful part, unfortunately doesn't get as much footage as she deserves. This film belongs to the men, especially Flynn, who attacks the part with gusto and suitably adapts his British veneer to the code of the Old West. Flynn would make seven more Westerns, but DODGE CITY remains his best outing in the genre. The story line for BLAZING SADDLES was taken from this film.

DODSWORTH

1936   90m   bw   ★★★★★
Romance   /PG
UA

Walter Huston (Sam Dodsworth), Ruth Chatterton (Fran Dodsworth), Paul Lukas (Arnold Iselin), Mary Astor (Edith Cortright), David Niven (Lockert), Gregory Gaye (Kurt von Obersdorf), Maria Ouspenskaya (Baroness von Obersdorf), Odette Myrtil (Mme. de Penable), Kathryn Marlowe (Emily), John Payne (Harry)

p, Samuel Goldwyn; d, William Wyler; w, Sidney Howard (based on his play, adapted from the novel by Sinclair Lewis); ph, Rudolph Mate; ed, Daniel Mandell; m, Alfred Newman; art d, Richard Day; fx, Ray Binger; cos, Omar Kiam

A film of maturity, intelligence, and understanding. Huston, repeating his popular stage role, plays reserved auto mogul Sam Dodsworth, who retires to enjoy his middle age at the prompting of his wife Fran (Chatterton). Traveling in Europe, the unsophisticated Midwesterners have completely opposite reactions to the Continental milieu: while Sam soon gets bored, Fran aspires to become a woman of the world. Embarrassed by her flirtation with a roue (Niven) and hurt by her encounter with a more subtle adventurer (Lucas), Fran doesn't learn from her failures. She finally asks Sam for a divorce in order to marry a young but mother-dominated baron (Gaye). Sam, meanwhile, meets a kindly widow (Astor) with whom he finds he might salvage his happiness. But the longtime romance of Sam and Fran must be dealt with first.

The direction of the autocratic Wyler sensitively plots a tale of marital problems, middle age, and the Ugly American abroad. Huston was never better than in this magnificent performance of a simple man whose blissful world disintegrates. His effortless acting was so splendidly moving that he was voted Best Actor by the NY Film Critics. (With their typical fondness for showy acting, however, Oscar voters cited Paul Muni in THE STORY OF LOUIS PASTEUR.) Chatterton, too, is superb in a role she wanted to play as a total heavy. Wyler, though, was wisely able to temper this portrait of a selfish, shallow woman with great insight. Chatterton's sometimes theatrical emoting perfectly suits her rich study of a woman playacting her way through life. The low-key scenes between Huston and Chatterton are warm and tender, while their arguments are positively blistering. The support includes gems from Lucas, Niven, Gaye, Ouspenskaya, Myrtil, Byington, and Payne, but it is really Astor who equals the stars with a performance of consummate artistry.

DOG DAY AFTERNOON

1975   130m   c   ★★★★★
Crime   R/15
Artists Entertainment

Al Pacino (Sonny), John Cazale (Sal), Charles Durning (Moretti), Chris Sarandon (Leon), Sully Boyar (Mulvaney), Penny Allen (Sylvia), James Broderick (Sheldon), Carol Kane (Jenny), Beulah Garrick (Margaret), Sandra Kazan (Deborah)

p, Martin Bregman, Martin Elfand; d, Sidney Lumet; w, Frank Pierson (based on a magazine article by P.F. Kluge, Thomas Moore); ph, Victor J. Kemper (Technicolor); ed, Dede Allen; prod d, Charles Bailey; art d, Douglas Higgins; cos, Anna Hill Johnstone

One of the finest films of the 1970s. A bisexual man, Sonny (Pacino), to finance a sex-change operation for his transvestite lover (Sarandon), robs the First Savings Bank of Brooklyn with his moronic friend Sal (Cazale). Police, headed by Moretti

(Durning), surround the bank and hold the thieves inside who, in turn, hold employees and customers as hostages. Through it all Sonny carries on endless phone conversations with his obese wife (Peretz), his lover, and assorted police and FBI officials. At one point, while releasing a female hostage, Sonny notices the large crowds outside, watching from behind barriers as if at a carnival. To enlist mob sympathy he begins to shout "Attica! Attica!" (the name of the New York prison where authorities inflicted heavy casualties on rioting prisoners). The crowd picks up the chant, decidedly favoring the bank robbers. Ultimately, however, Sonny threatens to begin shooting hostages unless he and Sal are given $1 million and taken to the airport where they will be flown to a distant country. (When Sonny asks his dim friend what country he wants to go to, the *non compos mentis* thief replies, "Wyoming.") Sonny and Sal's getaway attempt brings this remarkable film to its simmering finale.

DOG DAY AFTERNOON benefits immeasurably from a cast and crew doing some of the finest work of their careers. In a role based on actual incident, Pacino is both funny and tragic as the uneducated, passionate street tough over his head in a lethal situation of his own making. In difficult roles, Cazale and Sarandon are similarly superb, and even those actors on more familiar ground (Durning, Broderick, Peretz) contribute sterling support. The taut script and Lumet's exceptionally disciplined and insightful direction highlight both the suspense and the absurdity of the situation beautifully. The heavy use of off-color language and scorching violence if anything adds to the ultimate sympathy this memorable film successfully evokes.

DOGS OF WAR, THE
1980   122m   c   ★★
Adventure/War   R/15
UA   (U.K.)

Christopher Walken (*Shannon*), Tom Berenger (*Drew*), Colin Blakely (*North*), Hugh Millais (*Endean*), Paul Freeman (*Derek*), Jean-Francois Stevenin (*Michel*), JoBeth Williams (*Jessie*), Robert Urquhart (*Capt. Lockhart*), Winston Ntshona (*Dr. Okoye*), Pedro Armendariz, Jr. (*Major*)

p, Larry De Waay; d, John Irvin; w, Gary DeVore, George Malko (based on the novel by Frederick Forsyth); ph, Jack Cardiff (Technicolor); ed, Anthony Gibbs; m, Geoffrey Burgon; prod d, Peter Mullins; art d, John Siddall, Bert Davey; fx, Larry Cavanaugh, Rudi Liszczak, Steve Lombardi, Michael Collins; cos, Emma Porteous

Based on a gripping Frederick Forsyth novel, THE DOGS OF WAR is a slickly made actioner about a cold-blooded mercenary whose political conscience is heightened somewhat by a particularly nasty war in Africa. The story centers on Shannon (Walken), an American soldier of fortune who, in the exciting opening scene, is shown with some of his mercenary buddies fighting to catch the last plane out of a war-torn country. Shannon is then hired by a powerful American businessman (Millais) to overthrow a small government in Africa. To prepare for the coup, Shannon visits the country in the guise of a nature photographer. The government, however, becomes suspicious and throws him in jail. Between torture sessions, Shannon meets an imprisoned dissident political leader, from whom he learns more about the country's political struggles. Eventually Shannon is deported, but he returns with a group of mercenaries and, with some Africans hired by his employer, makes an impressive raid on a military outpost that is also the headquarters of the country's dictator.

While competently directed by John Irvin (RAW DEAL, HAMBURGER HILL), who knows how to deliver a well-crafted action film, THE DOGS OF WAR suffers from a lack of character development that may leave some viewers cold. No new light is shed on those men who choose to be soldiers of fortune in this exceedingly well-shot (by Jack Cardiff) action film that will evaporate from the memory shortly after the end credits roll.

$ (DOLLARS)
1971   119m   c   ★★★½
Crime/Comedy   R/15
Columbia

Warren Beatty (*Joe Collins*), Goldie Hawn (*Dawn Divine*), Gert Frobe (*Mr. Kessel*), Robert Webber (*Attorney*), Scott Brady (*Sarge*), Arthur Brauss (*Candy Man*), Robert Stiles (*Major*), Wolfgang Kieling (*Granich*), Robert Herron (*Bodyguard*), Christiane Maybach (*Helga*)

p, M.J. Frankovich; d, Richard Brooks; w, Richard Brooks; ph, Petrus Schloemp (Technicolor); ed, George Grenville; m, Quincy Jones; art d, Guy Sheppard, Olaf Ivens

$ (DOLLARS) is a pleasant, somewhat underrated chase movie which was written and directed by Richard Brooks, in a significant departure from the heavy dramas (IN COLD BLOOD, THE BROTHERS KARAMAZOV, THE BLACKBOARD JUNGLE, and CAT ON A HOT TIN ROOF) he was usually associated with.

Joe Collins (Beatty) is a security expert employed in Hamburg who plans to rob three safety deposit boxes which he knows are rented by criminals, and Dawn Divine (Hawn) is a prostitute whom he enlists to help him in the endeavor. Their targets are a crooked US Army sergeant (Brady) who scammed money from service clubs, a drug dealer (Brauss) and a courier (Webber) who's been double-dealing the mob. Employed at their bank to install a security system, Collins arranges to be placed inside the vault after a bomb scare. Timing his moves perfectly so as to go unnoticed by surveillance cameras, he stashes the loot in Dawn's safety deposit box so she can blithely collect it later.

An exercise in triviality, and, like most of Brooks's films, not particulary original, $ is nevertheless quite entertaining. Beatty and Hawn play extremely well together and Frobe is outstanding as the bank manager. Running rather longer than one might like, $ benefits from Brooks's lively handling and Quincy Jones's sparse but effective musical score.

DOMINICK AND EUGENE
1988   111m   c   ★★★
Drama   PG-13/15
Orion

Ray Liotta (*Eugene "Gino" Luciano*), Tom Hulce (*Dominick "Nicky" Luciano*), Jamie Lee Curtis (*Jennifer Reston*), Robert Levine (*Dr. Levinson*), Todd Graff (*Larry Higgins*), Bill Cobbs (*Jesse Johnson*), Mimi Cecchini (*Mrs. Gianelli*), Tommy Snelsire (*Mikey Chernak*), Mary Joan Negro (*Theresa Chernak*), Tom Signorelli (*Father T*)

p, Marvin Minoff, Mike Farrell; d, Robert M. Young; w, Alvin Sargent, Corey Blechman (based on a story by Danny Porfirio); ph, Curtis Clark (Duart Color); ed, Arthur Coburn; m, Trevor Jones; prod d, Doug Draner; chor, Lenora Nemetz; cos, Hilary Rosenfeld

Hulce, who received an Oscar nomination for his performance as Mozart in AMADEUS, and Liotta, who made his stunning film debut as the disturbing ex-con in SOMETHING WILD, are teamed in this often-touching, unashamedly sentimental story of brotherly love.

The two are 26-year-old twins who live together in a working-class neighborhood of Pittsburgh. Liotta is a medical student whom the good-natured but mildly retarded Hulce supports by working on a garbage truck. Because their parents are dead, the brothers share a special relationship, Hulce acting as provider and Liotta as protector. The equilibrium is threatened when Liotta is given the opportunity to do his residency in a prestigious Stanford program, which would require a two-year separation from his brother.

On paper DOMINICK AND EUGENE has all the earmarks of too-plaintive melodrama, and in its weakest and most obvious moments it is little more than that. Director Young, who began his career as a documentary maker and whose feature films (NOTHING BUT A MAN, THE BALLAD OF GREGORIO CORTEZ) have been concerned with the triumph of human dignity, occasionally allows his film to become manipulative, although this is less a deliberate effect than it is the result of sentimental overkill. Most of the time Young manages to deal subtly with the emotions, and in these moments the film is affecting and sincere.

DON QUIXOTE

1935 73m bw   ★★★★
Musical   /U
Nelson/Vandor   (U.K./France)

Feodor Chaliapin *(Don Quixote)*, George Robey *(Sancho Panza)*, Sidney Fox *(The Niece)*, Miles Mander *(The Duke)*, Oscar Asche *(Police Captain)*, Dannio *(Carrasco)*, Emily Fitzroy *(Sancho's Wife)*, Frank Stanmore *(Priest)*, Wally Patch *(Gypsy King)*, Lydia Sherwood *(Duchess)*

p, G.W. Pabst; d, G.W. Pabst; w, Paul Morand, Alexandre Arnoux (based on the novel *Don Quixote De La Mancha* by Miguel de Cervantes); ph, Nicolas Farkas; m, Jacques Ibert

Save only the denouement—an allegory added by director Pabst and the French adaptors—this is a fairly faithful rendition of the 300-year-old tale of "The Knight of the Mournful Countenance." Chaliapin, as famed for his striking acting as for his operatic basso, plays Don Quixote, the man immersed for years in the library of chivalric romances for which he has mortgaged his estates. Venturing forth on his bony nag Rocinante, the quiet country gentleman elects to redress the wrongs of the world. He enlists the aid of Sancho Panza (Robey) as his squire, promising him great future rewards in return for faithful service. He pronounces Dulcinea (Valliers), a slatternly milkmaid, to be the fair and pure maiden whose honor he is pledged to protect. Taking windmills for giants and flocks of sheep for armies, he battles them with vigor but invariably suffers defeat.

Many viewers saw in this film an allegorical reference to the Nazi bookburnings of the 1930s, as Pabst's ending departs completely from Cervantes's original, in which the disillusioned Don Quixote renounces his books of knightly lore. Pabst's liberal political orientation had been demonstrated in many of his earlier films, such as KAMERADSCHAFT and THE THREEPENNY OPERA (both 1931). Regardless of the director's political convictions (he later made films under the Nazi regime and, later still, produced a number of anti-fascist films), this telling of the tale benefits from a memorable windmill sequence and its stunning star turn by Chaliapin.

DON QUIXOTE

(DON-KIKHOT)
1961 110m c   ★★★★
Drama   /U
Lenfilm (U.S.S.R.)

Nikolai Cherkassov *(Don Quixote)*, Yuri Tolubeyev *(Sancho Panza)*, T. Agamirova *(Altisidora)*, V. Freindlich *(Duke)*, L. Vertinskaya *(Duchess)*, Georgiy Vitsin *(Carrasco)*, L. Kasyanova *(Aldonsa)*, O. Viklandt *(Peasant Girl)*, Serafima Birman *(Housekeeper)*, A. Beniaminov *(Shepherd)*

d, Gregory Kozintsev; w, Yevgeniy Shvarts (based on the novel by Miguel de Cervantes); ph, Andrey Moskvin, Apollinariy Dudko (Sovscope, Sovcolor); ed, Ye. Makhankova; m, Kara Karayev; art d, Yevgeniy Yeney

The final Soviet film to reach the US under a joint cultural exchange program halted due to bad relations between the administrations of President Kennedy and Premier Kruschev, this is an excellent and faithful adaptation of the Cervantes novel. Cherkassov, the USSR's best-known actor, on screen since 1927 in roles such as ALEXANDER NEVSKY and the two-part IVAN THE TERRIBLE, brings to the knight the same level of demented dignity possessed by Chaliapin in G.W. Pabst's 1935 version. Tolubeyev's Sancho Panza, with his field smarts, is a fine match for Cherkassov's chivalric Don Quixote. Technically adept, in wide screen and color, the film reflects the long-time collaboration of director Kozintsev and cameraman Moskvin, both active in FEX (Factory of Eccentric Actors). The English dubbing is wonderfully handled; the English-language actors' voices are well suited to the roles. Location scenes, resembling the Iberian plain, were shot in the Crimea.

DONA FLOR AND HER TWO HUSBANDS

(DONA FLOR E SEUS DOIS MARIDOS)
1977 106m c   ★★★
Comedy   R/X
Coline/Gaumont (Brazil)

Sonia Braga *(Dona Flor)*, Jose Wilker *(Vadhino)*, Mauro Mendonca *(Teodoro)*, Dinorah Brillanti *(Rozilda)*, Nelson Xavier *(Mirandao)*, Arthur Costa Filho *(Carlinhos)*, Rui Rezende *(Cazuza)*, Mario Gusmao

p, Luis Carlos Barreto, Newton Rique, Cia Serrador; d, Bruno Barreto; w, Bruno Barreto (based on a novel by Jorge Amado); ph, Maurilo Salles (Eastmancolor); ed, Raimundo Higino; m, Chico Buarque; art d, Anisio Medeiros

This wonderfully sexy and funny comedy, a variation on BLITHE SPIRIT, shattered Brazilian box-office records and proved very popular worldwide, chiefly because of Braga's tremendously sensual presence. She plays a beautiful woman whose gambling, whoring husband drops dead after an all-night carousal. Deciding to marry again, she chooses a boring, devout, middle-aged pharmacist who rarely wants to make love. One night, as she lies in bed next to her sleeping spouse, the ghost of her first husband appears, nude, in the room. She tries to get rid of him, but he refuses. She finally succumbs to his blandishments and takes the ghost to bed with her, while the second husband continues to sleep.

This entertaining and erotic picture, while perhaps not the most challenging film to come out of Brazil in the 1970s, is nevertheless enjoyable. At times, though, the creative personalities involved seem to want to play it both ways and make it "art cinema" as well as "commercial cinema" simply because it was aimed at the international market. Director Parreto and Braga teamed up again in in GABRIELA, costarring Marcello Mastroianni. Remade in 1982 as KISS ME GOODBYE with—are you ready for this?—Sally Field in the lead role.

DONA HERLINDA AND HER SON
(DONA HERLINDA Y SU HIJO)

1986 90m c	★★★★½
Comedy	/15
Cinevista (Mexico)	

Guadalupe Del Toro (Dona Herlinda), Arturo Meza (Ramon), Marco Antonio Trevino (Rodolfo), Leticia Lupersio (Olga), Guillermina Alba

p, Manuel Barbachano Ponce; d, Jaime Humberto Hermosillo; w, Jaime Humberto Hermosillo (based on a novel by Jorge Lopez Paez); ph, Miguel Ehrenberg; ed, Luis Kelly

A sex comedy usually succeeds when it gives a fresh twist to old expectations, something the satirical DONA HERLINDA AND HER SON does with unrelenting zest. Dona Herlinda (Del Toro) is the wealthy mother of Rodolfo (Trevino), a closeted gay doctor involved in a relationship with Ramon (Meza), a music student. The two men are in desperate need of some privacy to carry on their affair, a problem which seems to be solved when Dona Herlinda invites Ramon to move in with her and her son. This is more than an act of charity, though, for this particular doting mother has an involved plan to keep her son both happy and respectable, bringing in Olga (Lupersio) to become Rodolfo's heterosexual wife. Disappointed with his lover's acceptance of this plan and jealous of Olga, Ramon goes out for a romp, but is unable to forget the traitorous mama's boy he loves.

Marvelously funny, DONA HERLINDA AND HER SON develops its unusual plot line in a simple, matter-of-fact style, and the final twists arrive at the end of considerable comic momentum. What is most amazing is not only Dona Herlinda's orchestration of personality and situation, but what also seems to be her determined blindness to her son's homosexuality. Each of the characters is mindfully etched, with performances that make the viewer honestly care about these people. Sexual situations, be they homosexual or heterosexual, are wisely presented without judgment, simply becoming a part of the hilarious comic tableau. Director Hermosillo skillfully evolves a pointed yet gentle satire of mothering and traditional family structures while managing to produce a highly engaging entertainment at the same time.

DON'S PARTY

1976 90m c	★★★★
Comedy	/X
Double Head (Australia)	

Ray Barrett (Mal), Claire Binney (Susan), Pat Bishop (Jenny), Graeme Blundell (Simon), Jeanie Drynan (Kath), John Gorton (Himself), John Hargreaves (Don), Harold Hopkins (Cooley), Graham Kennedy (Mack), Veronica Lang (Jody)

p, Phillip Adams; d, Bruce Beresford; w, David Williamson (based on his play); ph, Don McAlpine (Panavision, 200 Color); ed, Bill Anderson; m, Leos Janacek; art d, Rhoisin Harrison; cos, Anna Senior

Excellent drama from Down Under concerns a group of friends in the suburbs that gathers to watch election results on television. As the party wears on and everyone's tongue is loosened by alcohol, the veneer of camaraderie drops away, and the men reveal themselves to be a set of back-biting boors, verbally attacking each other like characters straight out of WHO'S AFRAID OF VIRGINIA WOOLF. Extremely well directed by Beresford (BREAKER MORANT), with sharp dialogue and terrific performances all around. American audiences won't catch all of the slang expressions and will need to get used to the thick accents, but the effort of immersing oneself into this black comedy-drama is well worth it.

DON'T CRY WITH YOUR MOUTH FULL
(PLEURE PAS LA BOUCHE PLEINE)

1974 116m c	★★★
Drama	
Renn/Chef-Lieu/O.R.T.F. (France)	

Annie Cole (Annie), Jean Carmet (Father), Christina Chamaret (Mother), Helene Dieudonne (Grandmother), Daniel Ceccaldi (Uncle), Claudine Paringaux (Aunt), Friquette (Sister), Bernard Menez (Alexander), Frederic Duru (Frederic)

d, Pascal Thomas; w, Pascal Thomas, Roland Duval, Suzanne Schiffman; ph, Christian Rachman; ed, Helene Plemiannikov; m, Michael Choquet

An effectively spare film centering on one summer in the life of Annie (Cole), a 15-year-old girl on the threshold of womanhood living in an idyllic French village with her bizarre and amusing grandmother. Our young heroine is just discovering boys—well, two to be exact. One of them, Frederic (Duru), is too absorbed in bicycle racing to pay much attention to the budding beauty, leaving the Don Juan-ish Alexander (Menez) to initiate Annie into affairs of the heart. Light, breezy, and unpretentious—not a great film, but quietly insightful and absorbing, an offspring of a long line of French humanist cinema from Vigo and Renoir through Truffaut.

DON'T LOOK NOW

1973 110m c	★★★★½
Mystery	R/18
Casey/Eldorado (U.K./Italy)	

Julie Christie (Laura Baxter), Donald Sutherland (John Baxter), Hilary Mason (Heather), Clelia Matania (Wendy), Massimo Serato (Bishop), Renato Scarpa (Inspector Longhi), Giorgio Trestini (Workman), Leopoldo Trieste (Hotel Manager), David Tree (Anthony Babbage), Ann Rye (Mandy Babbage)

p, Peter Katz; d, Nicolas Roeg; w, Allan Scott, Chris Bryant (based on a short story by Daphne du Maurier); ph, Anthony Richmond (Panavision Technicolor); ed, Graeme Clifford; m, Pino Donaggio; art d, Giovanni Soccol

A truly eerie film, based on a story by Daphne du Maurier. John Baxter (Sutherland) travels to Venice with his wife, Laura (Christie), after the accidental drowning death in England of their young daughter. While completing restoration work on a church, Baxter discovers he has certain psychic abilities—abilities nourished by two very strange sisters, Wendy (Matania) and Heather (Mason), who have visions of the couple's dead daughter. Baxter refuses to believe in his powers, but he begins to relent when he sees a small figure darting around Venice dressed in the same red raincoat that his daughter wore. These sightings, coupled with his haunting visions of a funeral boat drifting down a Venetian canal, make for a puzzling and mysterious atmosphere in which "nothing is what it seems."

Making wonderful use of Venice locales and boasting two fine performances from Sutherland and Christie (including one of the most convincing lovemaking scenes ever), DON'T LOOK NOW is one of director Roeg's finest and most accessible films. Among many memorable scenes, Baxter's near-fall in the church and his final encounter with the red-cloaked figure are particularly memorable. While the vagueness of the plot may frustrate viewers at first, the payoff is considerable for patient audiences. A film which more than gets by on its directorial style, unforgettable imagery, and striking music alone, DON'T LOOK NOW also manages to be a haunting meditation on fear, death and the beyond.

DOORS, THE

1991 135m c   ★★
Biography/Musical   R/18
Ixtlan Productions/Imagine Films Entertainment/Carolco Pictures

Val Kilmer *(Jim Morrison)*, Meg Ryan *(Pamela Courson)*, Kyle MacLachlan *(Ray Manzarek)*, Kevin Dillon *(John Densmore)*, Frank Whaley *(Robby Kreiger)*, Billy Idol *(Cat)*, Dennis Burkley *(Dog)*, Josh Evans *(Bill Siddons)*, Michael Madsen *(Tom Baker)*, Kathleen Quinlan *(Patricia Kennealy)*

p, Sasha Harari, Bill Graham, A. Kitman Ho; d, Oliver Stone; w, Oliver Stone, J. Randall Johnson, Randy Johnson, Ralph Thomas (from the book *Riders on the Storm* by John Densmore); ph, Robert Richardson; ed, David Brenner, Joe Hutshing; prod d, Barbara Ling; art d, Larry Fulton; cos, Marlene Stewart

Oliver Stone continues his postmortem on 60s America with this indulgent recreation of the creative and destructive life of Jim Morrison, the cult rock poet and performer who died in 1971 at age 27.

The film begins in 1966 with a young Morrison (Val Kilmer) in his California element: beach bumming, experimenting with drugs, writing poetry, womanizing. Morrison drops out of UCLA film school with classmate and kindred cosmic spirit Ray Manzarek (Kyle MacLachlan). They form a garage band named The Doors with two other musicians, and Jim begins singing his poems. The band's early appearances in the underground clubs of L.A. meet with wild enthusiasm, particularly from the female groupies attracted by Morrison's sexual magnetism. Although their singer is already an erratic performer due to his substance abuse, the group signs a major record deal. The Doors make albums, do concert tours and appear on "The Ed Sullivan Show"—all while Morrison continues to push the limits of drug-enhanced musical performance and sexual experimentation. His partner in these escapades is his wife Pam (Meg Ryan), nee Courson, who both shares and endures his abuses.

The first hour of THE DOORS is a seamless visual and aural trip that perfectly captures the spirit of Jim Morrison's hypnotic music and decadent, nihilistic lifestyle. The band's original recordings continually play in the background and subtly blend with the film's restaging of Doors performances. The dreamy, winding musical passages meld together even disjointed and flat dramatic episodes. Also crucial to the film's ability to hold fans' interest is Val Kilmer's (TOP GUN, WILLOW) lead performance. With the aid of some faultless costuming and makeup he definitively captures the real Morrison's posing, swagger and facial expressions. (Equally impressive, Kilmer also supplemented Morrison's original vocal tracks with several of his own.) Without this studied physical reincarnation of the young cult figure, Stone's movie would have fallen flat much more quickly than it does.

Perhaps THE DOORS' ultimate failure is caused by its overly exact reproduction of the latter part of Morrison's life. Whatever one's feelings about his music and its place in American popular culture, the real Jim Morrison was an intriguing figure, if only because of his contradictory images as both self-destructive nihilist and teen heartthrob. Stone does not romanticize his subject but presents him warts, addictions and all. Unlike the classic film protagonist, Morrison as presented here is neither goal-oriented nor romantically motivated. Unfortunately, after

an interesting rise to musical fame in the first hour, viewers are left with an additional ninety minutes of this anti-hero's solipsism, narcissism and joyless descent into death. By recreating things too well, the film itself becomes as boring, indulgent and over-stuffed as its hero.

DOUBLE INDEMNITY

1944 106m bw   ★★★★★
Crime   /PG
Paramount

Fred MacMurray *(Walter Neff)*, Barbara Stanwyck *(Phyllis Dietrichson)*, Edward G. Robinson *(Barton Keyes)*, Porter Hall *(Mr. Jackson)*, Jean Heather *(Lola Dietrichson)*, Tom Powers *(Mr. Dietrichson)*, Gig Young *(Nino Zachette)*, Richard Gaines *(Mr. Norton)*, Fortunio Bonanova *(Sam Gorlopis)*, John Philliber *(Joe Pete)*

p, Joseph Sistrom; d, Billy Wilder; w, Raymond Chandler, Billy Wilder (based on a short story in the book *Three of A Kind* by James M. Cain); ph, John Seitz; ed, Doane Harrison; m, Miklos Rozsa, Cesar Franck (Symphony in D minor); art d, Hans Dreier, Hal Pereira; cos, Edith Head

A seminal work in the emergence of film noir as an explosive movement in American film. Based on the notorious Snyder-Gray case of 1927, DOUBLE INDEMNITY is both a starkly realistic and a carefully stylized masterpiece of murder.

Walter Neff (MacMurray), bleeding from a bullet wound, staggers into an office building. As he speaks into his dictating machine, we learn in flashback that he is an insurance salesman who becomes involved with the sleek Phyllis Dietrichson (Stanwyck). Phyllis convinces Walter not only to help her take out a life insurance policy on her husband (Powers) without his knowledge, but also to help her murder him in order to collect on it. Staging an unlikely accident in order to qualify for the "double indemnity" clause in the contract, the deadly duo must next face claims adjustor Barton Keyes (Robinson), whose instinct tells him that something suspicious is afoot. Their faith in their story and each other sorely tested, Walter and Phyllis finally square off in a fatal game of cat and mouse.

Wilder's typically passionless direction fits beautifully with this sinister story. On his first studio assignment, screenwriter Chandler peppered the dialogue from Cain's original with his distinctive brand of hardboiled cynicism. The results, as when Phyllis and Walter flirt by using the extended metaphor of a speeding motorist, are terrific. Rosza contributes a typically edgy score and Seitz's cinematography makes great use of such noir trademarks as sharp camera angles, heavy, sculpted shadows and light slatted by venetian blinds. But it is really the starring trio which lends bite to this compelling crime classic. Stanwyck, in a deliberately phony blonde wig, remade her career with her striking portrayal of an icy woman whose boredom and desire fuel a plot of murder and intrigue. MacMurray, in a great change of pace, gives the performance of his career as the shifty loner excited by a challenge and a deadly dame's anklet. Robinson, meanwhile, beautifully gives the film its heart. His speech about death statistics, rattled off at top speed, is one of the film's highlights. Lifelessly remade for television in 1954 and 1973.

DOUBLE LIFE, A

1947 103m bw   ★★★★
Crime   /A
Kanin

Ronald Colman (*Anthony John*), Signe Hasso (*Brita*), Edmond O'Brien (*Bill Friend*), Shelley Winters (*Pat Kroll*), Ray Collins (*Victor Donlan*), Philip Loeb (*Max Lasker*), Millard Mitchell (*Al Cooley*), Joe Sawyer (*Pete Bonner*), Charles La Torre (*Stellini*), Whit Bissell (*Dr. Stauffer*)

p, Michael Kanin; d, George Cukor; w, Ruth Gordon, Garson Kanin (based on the play "Othello" by William Shakespeare); ph, Milton Krasner; ed, Robert Parrish; m, Miklos Rozsa; prod d, Harry Horner; art d, Bernard Herzbrun, Harvey T. Gillett; fx, David S. Horsley; cos, Yvonne Wood, Travis Banton

A fine film overall, if a wee bit pretentious, A DOUBLE LIFE explores the schizoid personality of a gifted stage actor whose despair and murderous moods come during his portrayal of Othello. Colman is a much-respected gentleman actor who specializes in classical drama. His courtly manners and winning charm endear him to one and all, including his ex-wife, Hasso, who loves him but fears that his cruel streak will once again take over his otherwise stable personality. Winters, a buxom, steamy waitress, is attracted to Colman but soon learns that he is capable of violence. Losing all touch with reality, Colman believes he is actually the terrible Moor he is portraying on stage, so he strangles Winters and returns to his apartment, blocking out the hideous act. O'Brien, an enterprising publicity agent for the play, picks up on the strangulation and tries to link the murder with the play to entice audiences. This blatant sensationalism causes Colman to explode; he attacks O'Brien, who now believes the actor is mad. O'Brien sets up Colman for the police, arranging for a waitress who is almost Winters's twin to wait on him in a restaurant. Her appearance so alarms Colman that police are convinced he is the killer. Detectives decide to arrest him following the final performance of "Othello." The actor realizes he is exposed and the tragedy takes its final turn.

Colman's performance is riveting and deservedly won him an Oscar, as well as universal applause from critics and public alike. His genteel manners and mellifluous voice set up audiences for a huge shock when Colman turns into a lethal lunatic, a transformation that is simply amazing to witness. He is a man obsessed, one who can no longer differentiate between his theatrical and everyday personalities. Colman is mesmerizing, brilliant, and even horrific in his role. Kanin and Gordon's script is both literate and packed with suspense, interweaving the dialogue of classical theater and that of the street. Cukor's direction is as properly mannered and carefully constructed as the script is, and he draws the complex portrayal out of Colman with great care.

This was Winters' first film break after stage appearances and it established her as a movie star. Harry Cohn, head of Columbia Studios, originally bought the script for A DOUBLE LIFE years earlier but later reneged, refusing to pay for it or produce it. Kanin was so angry that he vowed never to talk to Cohn again. He would take his vengeance on a literary level, using Cohn as the role model for the brutish Broderick Crawford part in BORN YESTERDAY.

DOUBLE LIFE OF VERONIQUE, THE
(LA DOUBLE VIE DE VERONIQUE)
1991 90m c   ★★★½
Fantasy/Drama   /15
Sideral Productions/Studio Tor/Canal Plus   (France/Poland)

Irene Jacob (*Veronique/Veronika*), Halina Gryglaszewska (*Aunt*), Kalina Jedrusik (*Gaudy Woman*), Aleksander Bardini (*Orchestra Conductor*), Wladyslaw Kowalski (*Veronika's Father*), Jerzy Gudejko (*Antek*), Jan Sterninski (*Lawyer*), Philippe Volter (*Al-exandre Fabbri*), Sandrine Dumas (*Catherine*), Louis Ducreux (*Professor*)

p, Leonardo De La Fuente; d, Krzysztof Kieslowski; w, Krzysztof Kieslowski, Krzysztof Piesiewicz; ph, Slawomir Idziak; ed, Jacques Witta; m, Zbigniew Preisner; prod d, Patrice Mercier

THE DOUBLE LIFE OF VERONIQUE's deceptively simple tale comes alive in its rapturous imagery, expressive direction and the irresistible charm of its star, Cannes award-winner Irene Jacob.

As the title indicates, the film is about two women, both played by Jacob. Polish Veronika leaves her provincial home town for the city of Krakow to visit her aunt, whom she believes to be near death. Instead, she is delighted but dismayed to find her aunt not only hale and hearty, but also too tied up with business to spend time with her. While visiting a friend at a music school, Veronika's eerily angelic singing voice impresses the schoolmasters, who quickly audition her and offer her a place at the school. Veronika works and studies hard but also begins suffering chest pains. On her way to class one day, she notices a woman who looks like her taking photographs of her at a student demonstration, but is unable to make contact with her. At her first public performance, Veronika is stricken and dies onstage.

The action then shifts to Paris, where Veronique abruptly and without explanation abandons her own ambitions of becoming a professional singer to pursue a more modest career as an elementary school music teacher. Also unlike her Polish counterpart, she monitors her health through regular visits to a cardiologist. Arriving for work one day, Veronique finds her classroom taken over by a puppeteer who is putting on a show for the school. Leaving in a huff, she is caught up with by the puppeteer, who apologizes to her and strikes a romantic spark in Veronique. They have another brief encounter after the show before going their separate ways, and Veronique is left lovestruck.

Briskly paced and lyrically intense, THE DOUBLE LIFE OF VERONIQUE plays like an enigmatic puzzle, yet it's no austere, intellectual art movie. It's rather a film that works on a strong emotional and intuitive level. On an intellectual or political level, VERONIQUE's "message" actually seems quite conservative. It seems to warn that excessive ambition blinds one to one's true destiny in the greater scheme of life. When Veronika leaves behind a loving father and a gentle, sensitive beau, she dies in Krakow pursuing her ambitions, while Veronique is rewarded for abandoning her ambitions to stay with her own loving father and yielding to her own gentle pursuer. So much for having it all. But VERONIQUE is a film that acknowledges what we seldom admit. That no one, man or woman, can ever have it all. We have what we have and we should treasure it.

Filled with unforgettable images, VERONIQUE is the work of an exquisite, profound sensibility, so full of rapturous, privileged moments it's literally an embarrassment of riches. Kieslowski confirmed his status as a major contemporary filmmaker with 1988's DEKALOG, a series of 10 hour-long films funded by Polish TV and based on the 10 Commandments. (In the same year, he expanded segments five and six into two features, A SHORT FILM ABOUT KILLING and A SHORT FILM ABOUT LOVE.)

VERONIQUE is also a movie clearly, deliriously, in love with its star. Jacob so fully inhabits her characters that it's almost a backhanded compliment to call hers a strong performance. The camera draws a heady inspiration from her embodiments of hope, yearning, love and sensuality. VERONIQUE seems to spend a great deal of its brief running time simply observing her, almost basking in her presence in a film that, nonetheless, has not a single gratuitous moment. Instead, it is a too-rare film that suggests the too-often untapped awesome potential of film's expressive powers.

DOWN AND DIRTY
(BRUTTI, SPORCHI E CATTIVI)
1976 115m c   ★★★½
Comedy/Drama
C.C. Champion (Italy)

Nino Manfredi *(Giacinto)*, Francisci Anniballi *(Domizio)*, Maria Bosco *(Gaetana)*, Giselda Castrini *(Lisetta)*, Alfredo D'Ippolito *(Plinio)*, Giancarlo Fanelli *(Paride)*, Marian Fasoli *(Maria Lobera)*, Ettore Garofolo *(Camilio)*, Marco Marsili *(Vittoriano)*, Franco Merli *(Fernando)*

d, Ettore Scola; w, Ettore Scola, Ruggero Maccari; ph, Dario Di Palma; ed, Raimondo Crociani; m, Armando Trovaioli.

A mean, nasty, vile, ugly, and wickedly funny look at the inhabitants of a squatters' slum outside of Rome, where the sub-proletariat lives a miserable existence, DOWN AND DIRTY focuses on Giacinto (Nino Manfredi), a brutal animal of a man who has won a million lira insurance settlement after losing an eye. Driven by greed and selfishness, Giacinto sleeps with a shotgun for fear that someone will steal his fortune. He refuses to spend even a small portion of his stash on his family—which consists of at least 20 people, all of whom live, eat, sleep, fight, and have sex in the same one-room shanty. He beats and stabs his wife, humiliates his children, drinks himself into a stupor, and gropes the local women. When he takes an obese, huge-chested whore (Maria Luisa Santella) as a mistress, lets her live under the same roof as his family, and then generously squanders his money on gifts for her, his relatives plot to murder him. An amazing picture from Ettore Scola, DOWN AND DIRTY presents an endless stream of human indignities (people living with rats, a drag queen seducing his sister-in-law, a proud mother displaying her daughter's nude centerfold, children spending the day locked in a cage that serves as a day-care center) with such a curious, crude sense of humor one cannot be sure whether to look away in horror or laugh. What is sure is that you cannot ignore these people, or their unfathomable living conditions—and this is Scola's intent. Shooting on location, with Manfredi as his only professional actor, Scola in DOWN AND DIRTY pays tribute to the Neo-Realist tradition in Italy and produces a film worthy of Rossellini or De Sica.

DOWN AND OUT IN BEVERLY HILLS
1986 103m c   ★★★★
Comedy   R/15
Touchstone

Nick Nolte *(Jerry Baskin)*, Richard Dreyfuss *(Dave Whiteman)*, Bette Midler *(Barbara Whiteman)*, Little Richard *(Orvis Goodnight)*, Tracy Nelson *(Jenny Whiteman)*, Elizabeth Pena *(Carmen)*, Evan Richards *(Max Whiteman)*, Mike the Dog *(Matisse)*, Donald Muhich *(Dr. Von Zimmer)*, Paul Mazursky *(Sidney Waxman)*

p, Paul Mazursky; d, Paul Mazursky; w, Paul Mazursky, Leon Capetanos (based on the play *Boudu Sauve Des Eaux* by Rene Fauchois); ph, Don McAlpine (Technicolor); ed, Richard Halsey; m, Andy Summers; prod d, Pato Guzman; art d, Todd Hallowell; fx, Ken Speed; cos, Albert Wolsky

This very first R-rated picture ever to come out of that bastion of squeaky-cleanness, Walt Disney Studios (under the aegis of their subsidiary Touchstone), is a howl from start to finish. Dave Whiteman (Dreyfuss) has made it big in the coat hanger business.

He and wife Barbara (Midler) live in a huge house in Beverly Hills with their children, Jenny (Nelson), an anorexic college student, and Max (Richards), an androgynous budding filmmaker. Barbara is the ultimate yenta who spends her days having her hair and nails done, shopping, and going to classes. Also living in the house are Carmen (Pena), a seductive Latino maid with whom Dave is having an affair, and Matisse (Mike), the family dog who refuses to eat despite regular visits to a doggie psychiatrist. When tramp Jerry Baskin (Nolte) enters their lives after attempting to drown himself in the Whiteman swimming pool, Dave saves his life and invites him to become part of the family, a decision that has some very comic results.

A sometimes extremely funny revamping of Jean Renoir's classic black comedy BOUDU SAVED FROM DROWNING, Mazursky's film also works as a broad but scathing satire of upper-class California culture. Although the ending is softened from Renoir's original, this garishly colored film succeeds quite well on its own terms. The film is full of moments both surprising (Jerry showing Matisse that his dog food is eminently eatable) and entertainingly predictable (Jerry getting intimately involved with several family members; an "everyone into the pool" sequence). The cast is entirely up to the comic hysteria Mazursky requires of them, though Mike the dog steals whatever scene he is in. Look for Mazursky in a bit part as an accountant.

DOWN BY LAW
1986 106m bw   ★★★
Comedy   R/15
Black Snake/Grokenberger

Tom Waits *(Zack)*, John Lurie *(Jack)*, Roberto Benigni *(Roberto)*, Nicoletta Braschi *(Nicoletta)*, Ellen Barkin *(Laurette)*, Billie Neal *(Bobbie)*, Rockets Redglare *(Gig)*, Vernel Bagneris *(Preston)*, Timothea *(Julie)*, L.C. Drane *(L.C.)*

p, Alan Kleinberg; d, Jim Jarmusch; w, Jim Jarmusch; ph, Robby Muller; ed, Melody London; m, John Lurie; cos, Carol Wood

Set in New Orleans, DOWN BY LAW begins as down-on-his-luck disc jockey Zack (Waits) tries to make some quick bucks by driving a stolen car across town. Unfortunately he gets pulled over by the police and is thrown into jail when a body is found in the car's trunk. In the meantime a pimp, Jack (Lurie), has been set up by an enemy and fellow procurer, and he too is carted off by police and thrown into Orleans Parish Prison, where he becomes Zack's cellmate. Three may be a crowd, but soon they are joined in their small cell by Roberto (Benigni), a confused and likable Italian who knows only a few phrases of English, which he keeps written in a pocket notebook. Eventually the three escape into the Louisiana bayous, where they're soon hungry, tired and lost.

Director-writer Jarmusch's characters are insignificant anti-heroes adrift in an America that is both sad and beautiful. Jarmusch has a powerful visual sense, but he is weaker in the realm of content. The jazzy relationship between Lurie and Waits never quite clicks. As a result DOWN BY LAW merely reiterates the ideas about people and American life that Jarmusch had already stated more richly in STRANGER THAN PARADISE. The only sign of life in the film is in Benigni, who works wonders.

DOWNHILL RACER
1969 101m c   ★★★★
Sports   M/PG
Wildwood

Robert Redford (*Davis Chappellet*), Gene Hackman (*Eugene Claire*), Camilla Sparv (*Carole Stahl*), Karl Michael Vogler (*Machet*), James McMullan (*Creech*), Christian Doermer (*Brumm*), Kathleen Crowley (*American Newspaperwoman*), Dabney Coleman (*Mayo*), Kenneth Kirk (*D.K. Bryan*), Oren Stevens (*Kipsmith*)

p, Richard Gregson; d, Michael Ritchie; w, James Salter (based on the novel *The Downhill Racers* by Oakley Hall); ph, Brian Probyn (Technicolor); ed, Nick Archer; m, Kenyon Hopkins; art d, Ian Whittaker; cos, Cynthia May

An influential and extremely well-done sports film, worth watching even if you don't normally enjoy films of this type. Documentarian in style, DOWNHILL RACER is a strangely dispassionate but captivating look behind the glamorous facade of international ski racing. Redford, who did much of his own skiing, stars as Davis Chappellet, a self-centered, success-hungry skier from Colorado who is summoned to Europe when a member of the US team is injured. Over the next two racing seasons he proves himself to be one of the sport's most promising newcomers, dueling with a famous teammate (McMullan) for the spotlight and clashing with his strong-willed coach (Hackman). In the process of chasing Olympic gold in the downhill, he fails to win approval from his father and is unable to maintain a relationship with a beautiful ski manufacturer's assistant (Sparv).

Redford, who was determined to make a skiing film, went to great lengths to sell the project: soliciting a screenplay from James Salter, enlisting a team of ski bums and photographers to shoot 20,000 feet of action on the sly at the 1968 Grenoble Olympics, and giving Michael Ritchie, who provides a sure directorial hand, his first feature film assignment. As with a number of later Ritchie films, the focus here is on the price paid in pursuit of what seems to be victory. The acting is fine all around, with kudos to Redford for being unafraid to make his character dislikable at the core. Many of the downhill scenes were filmed by skier Joe Jay Jalbert, who raced behind Redford with a camera, adding to the film's realism and excitement. DOWNHILL RACER is fascinating viewing, even if the closest you've gotten to a ski slope is "Wide World of Sports."

DRACULA
1931 84m bw ★★★
Horror /PG
Universal

Bela Lugosi (*Count Dracula*), Helen Chandler (*Mina Seward*), David Manners (*John Harker*), Dwight Frye (*Renfield*), Edward Van Sloan (*Dr. Van Helsing*), Herbert Bunston (*Dr. Seward*), Frances Dade (*Lucy Weston*), Charles Gerrard (*Martin*), Joan Standing (*Maid*), Moon Carroll (*Briggs*)

p, Carl Laemmle, Jr.; d, Tod Browning; w, Garrett Fort (based on the play by Hamilton Deane and John Balderston and the novel by Bram Stoker); ph, Karl Freund; ed, Milton Carruth, Maurice Pivar; m, Peter Ilich Tchaikovsky, Richard Wagner; art d, Charles D. Hall

Creak. The grandaddy of 'em all and ready for mothballs to be put in the coffins. An atmospheric opening is the best part—moody and full of sinister potential. After that, it's stilted drawing-room talk, and badly acted, except for the cultish over-the-top dementia of Dwight Frye. Still, DRACULA is the film that started the 1930s horror cycle, secured Universal's position as *the* horror studio, and made Hungarian actor Bela Lugosi a worldwide curiosity.

Following the successful stage play more than Bram Stoker's classic novel, the film opens in Transylvania, where Renfield

(Dwight Frye), a British real estate salesman, arrives to arrange the sale of a deserted English manor house to a strange nobleman, Count Dracula (Lugosi). The mysterious count turns out to be a 500-year-old vampire, and Renfield is bitten and made his slave. Arriving in London, Dracula becomes smitten with Mina Seward (Helen Chandler) and attempts to make her his bride, but her fiance, Jonathan Harker (David Manners), and vampire expert Prof. Van Helsing (Edward Van Sloan) try and put a stop to the undead count. While the first part of the film is quite cinematic, mainly due to the brilliant cinematography of Karl Freund, the movie bogs down once it gets to England, after which it appears that director Tod Browning was intent on making a documentary of the stage play. More likely, he lacked the creativity of James Whale, who directed FRANKENSTEIN. While the incidental music (mostly snippets from Tchaikovsky's *Swan Lake*) is kept to a minimum, the sound effects are showing age, with the creaking of coffin lids, opening and slamming of doors, thudding footsteps, actors' voices, and howling of wolves beginning to seem like something out of a Bob Hope spoof. Studio heads felt that the film would do well abroad, so a Spanish-language version starring Carlos Villarias in the Dracula role and featuring a completely new all-Spanish cast, directed by George Melford, was produced with the same sets only days after the English version was completed. Reports have it that this version is even better than the Browning-Lugosi film. We should hope so. A remarkable sequel, DRACULA'S DAUGHTER, followed, featuring the stranger-than-true Gloria Holden.

DRAGNET
1954 89m c ★★★
Crime /PG
Mark VII

Jack Webb (*Sgt. Joe Friday*), Ben Alexander (*Officer Frank Smith*), Richard Boone (*Capt. Hamilton*), Ann Robinson (*Grace Downey*), Stacy Harris (*Max Troy*), Virginia Gregg (*Ethel Marie Starkie*), Vic Perrin (*Adolph Alexander*), Georgia Ellis (*Belle Davitt*), James Griffith (*Jesse Quinn*), Dick Cathcart (*Roy Cleaver*)

p, Stanley Meyer; d, Jack Webb; w, Richard Breen; ph, Edward Colman (Warner Color); ed, Robert M. Leeds; m, Walter Schumann

Big-screen spin-off of the immensely successful radio-TV "Dragnet" show has L.A. cops Sgt. Joe Friday (Webb) and Officer Frank Smith (Alexander) investigating the murder of a former syndicate member. Webb's direction is spotty, notably when the screenplay bogs down into the tedium of cop life, or during a fight scene unwittingly designed to provoke yuks. Acting honors go to Virginia Gregg's sodden syndicate widow. Webb is his usual deadpan cop, with Alexander as his dronelike sidekick (later replaced in a 1969 TV film by Harry Morgan as Joe Gannon—a better choice). Based on actual L.A. police files, the film manages to still deliver plenty of suspense. The theme beat for the series and this film—"dum-de-dum-dum"—was first used in Robert Siodmak's marvelous THE KILLERS (1946).

DRAGONSLAYER
1981 108m c ★★★½
Adventure/Fantasy PG
Disney

Peter MacNicol (*Galen*), Caitlin Clarke (*Valerian*), Ralph Richardson (*Ulrich*), John Hallam (*Tyrian*), Peter Eyre (*Casidorus Rex*), Albert Salmi (*Greil*), Sydney Bromley (*Hodge*), Chloe Salaman (*Princess Elspeth*), Emrys James (*Simon*), Roger Kemp (*Horsrik*)

p, Hal Barwood; d, Matthew Robbins; w, Hal Barwood, Matthew Robbins; ph, Derek Vanlint (Panavision, Metrocolor); ed, Tony Lawson; m, Alex North; prod d, Elliot Scott; art d, Alan Cassie; fx, Brian Johnson, Dennis Muren, Industrial Light & Magic; chor, Peggy Dixon; cos, Anthony Mendleson

An Arthurian-type legend is marvelously re-created when Galen (Peter MacNicol), sorcerer's apprentice to Ulrich (Ralph Richardson), a great wizard, bungles his way to ridding the kingdom of a monstrous, fire-spitting dragon. King Tyrian (John Hallam) has made an evil pact whereby he will sacrifice the virgins of his land to the dragon if it will leave the kingdom in relative peace. When Princess Elspeth (Chloe Salaman), his brave daughter, volunteers her own life, Ulrich and Galen attempt to save her, even though the wizard is dying and his magic fading. Like EXCALIBUR, this film has smoky atmosphere, medieval sets, and rugged terrain strange enough to suggest far-off mythic lands; moreover, its special effects are positively staggering. The giant computerized dragon alone is worth viewing. But DRAGONSLAYER profits from spirited direction and camera work plus the expert Richardson at its nucleus. Failing to capture the fancy of either the teenage market or adult action-fantasy fans, however, DRAGONSLAYER was a major disappointment at the box office, returning just $6 million on an $18 million investment. With terror prevalent and gory violence in spots, this fable is not for young viewers.

DRAUGHTSMAN'S CONTRACT, THE

1983 108m c   ★★½
Comedy/Historical   R/15
British Film Institute   (U.K.)

Anthony Higgins (*Mr. Neville*), Janet Suzman (*Mrs. Herbert*), Anne Louise Lambert (*Mrs. Talmann*), Hugh Fraser (*Mr. Talmann*), Neil Cunningham (*Mr. Noyles*), Dave Hill (*Mr. Herbert*), David Gant (*Mr. Seymour*), David Meyer, Tony Meyer (*The Poulenas*), Nicholas Amer (*Mr. Parkes*)

p, David Payne; d, Peter Greenaway; w, Peter Greenaway; ph, Curtis Clark; ed, John Wilson; m, Michael Nyman; art d, Bob Ringwood; cos, Sue Blane

Lavish 18th Century costumer, but for all its high style, a frigid and forboding bedfellow. Mrs. Herbert (Janet Suzman), an aristocrat's wife, hires Neville (Anthony Higgins), a draughtsman, to make twelve drawings of the estate to surprise her husband (Dave Hill) and patch up their shaky marriage. The husband has taken a vacation to enjoy other women. Neville consents to do the drawings on the condition that Mrs. Herbert have sex with him daily. Neville is also sexually involved with the Herberts' married daughter, who desperately wants a child, and he is hounded by the son-in-law, who is jealous of the artist's power over the household. The loaded situation is presented in witty, barbed dialogue, assuredly delivered by a talented cast. The costuming and settings are superb.

DREAMCHILD

1985 94m c   ★★½
Fantasy/Biography   PG
Universal   (U.K.)

Coral Browne (*Mrs. Hargreaves*), Ian Holm (*Rev. Charles Dodgson*), Peter Gallagher (*Jack Dolan*), Caris Corfman (*Sally Mackeson*), Nicola Cowper (*Lucy*), Jane Asher (*Mrs. Liddell*), Amelia Shankley (*Little Alice*), Imogen Boorman (*Lorina*), Emma King (*Edith*), Rupert Wainwright (*Hargreaves*)

p, Rick McCallum, Kenith Trodd; d, Gavin Millar; w, Dennis Potter; ph, Billy Williams; ed, Angus Newton; m, Stanley Myers, Max Harris; prod d, Roger Hall; art d, Len Huntingford, Marianne Ford; cos, Jane Robinson

Uneasy blend of fantasy, flashback, and historical recreation, salvaged by the superb Coral Browne. In 1932 Browne is an 80-year-old British woman coming to the US for the first time. She was the sweet youngster Lewis Carroll wrote about in *Alice's Adventures in Wonderland*, and she's coming to New York to receive an honorary degree on Carroll's 100th birthday. After arriving in New York, Browne meets hotshot Peter Gallagher who is soon the agent for the old woman, collecting a hefty percentage for negotiating all the deals that have been offered. Browne finds it difficult to keep up with this commercial merry-go-round and begins to sink back in memory to her youth. The movie flashes back 70 years to when the young woman (now played by Amelia Shankley) sits at the feet of the old mathematician-turned-writer Ian Holm. All the famed characters, brainchildren of Muppetmaster Jim Henson, somehow seem too reminiscent of his television work. The perfect Alice continues to live only in the mind's eye and not on film.

AKIRA KUROSAWA'S DREAMS

1990 119m c   ★★★½
Fantasy   /PG
Akira Kurosawa USA   (Japan/U.S.)

Akira Terao (*"I"*). SUNSHINE THROUGH THE RAIN: Mitsuko Baisho (*Mother of "I"*), Toshihiko Nakano (*"I" as a Young Child*). THE PEACH ORCHARD: Mitsunori Isaki (*"I" as a Boy*), Mie Suzuki (*"I's" Sister*). THE BLIZZARD: Mieko Harada (*The Snow Fairy*), Masayuki Yui, Shu Nakajima, Sakae Kimura (*Members of the Climbing Team*). THE TUNNEL: Yoshitaka Zushi (*Pvt. Noguchi*)

p, Hisao Kurosawa, Mike Y. Inoue; d, Akira Kurosawa; w, Akira Kurosawa; ph, Takao Saito, Masahuro Ueda; ed, Tome Minami; m, Shinichiro Ikebe; art d, Yoshiro Muraki, Akira Sakuragi; fx, Industrial Light & Magic; chor, Michiyo Hata; cos, Emi Wada

DREAMS is a mixed bag from one of the Old Masters of world cinema. One the one hand, it overflows with heavy-handed messages on topics ranging from ecology to pacifism as it scolds the audience for their wanton ways. On the other, it's a glorious triumph of style over content.

Kurosawa is best known as a director of epic action dramas such as THE SEVEN SAMURAI, YOJIMBO, and THE HIDDEN FORTRESS. DREAMS also has its moments of spectacle but it springs from the side of Kurosawa that produced IKIRU, DODES'KA-DEN, THE MOST BEAUTIFUL, and other films with which American audiences are less familiar and which lack the presence of Toshiro Mifune or samurai swordplay. These are intimate dramas focusing on everyday people searching for the right path to follow in life.

Beginning with a wedding that looks more like a funeral and ending with a funeral that seems more like a wedding, DREAMS is made up of eight vignettes, thematically united by their concern with Man's relationship to nature, mystery and his fellow man. In "Sunshine Through the Rain," a little boy disobeys his mother, running into a forest during a sunlit rainstorm to witness a gravely magical wedding procession of foxes. "The Peach Orchard" focuses on a boy who is made to understand what his parents have lost by cutting down a peach orchard on their property when the spirits of the downed trees appear to him. In "The Blizzard," the weary leader of a mountain expedition is tempted by Death in the form of a beautiful snow demoness. "The

Tunnel" concerns a military officer who is tormented by the ghosts of the soldiers who were killed in combat under his command. In "Crows," an aspiring artist enters a Vincent Van Gogh painting to learn the artist's secrets from the painter himself (played with appropriate intensity by director Martin Scorsese). In "Mt. Fuji in Red," Japan's most famous landmark is destroyed in a nuclear power-plant meltdown. "The Weeping Demon" shows the torture of the damned following a conflagration that has left the earth a scorched ruin. Concluding the film is "Village of the Watermills," in which a traveller, passing through the title village, joins a 99-year-old man as he buries his 103-year-old "sweetheart" who never returned his love.

None of the vignettes have much narrative beyond their rudimentary premises and when they do, they are left eerily unresolved. Some of the action is staged in stylized, excruciating slow motion. Though the film certainly has some nightmarish moments, it also has a wry sense of humor which often bubbles up when least expected. At other times, DREAMS is almost dismayingly mundane, especially in its scripting. Nonetheless this is clearly the work of a master filmmaker, even if his DREAMS are as unpredictable and uneven as our own.

DRESSED TO KILL

1980   105m   c   ★★★½
Thriller   R/18
Samuel Z. Arkoff

Michael Caine (Dr. Robert Elliott), Angie Dickinson (Kate Miller), Nancy Allen (Liz Blake), Keith Gordon (Peter Miller), Dennis Franz (Detective Marino), David Margulies (Dr. Levy), Kenny Baker (Warren Lockman), Brandon Maggart (Cleveland Sam), Susanna Clemm (Bobbi), Fred Weber (Mike Miller)

p, George Litto; d, Brian De Palma; w, Brian De Palma; ph, Ralf D. Bode (Panavision, Technicolor); ed, Jerry Greenberg; m, Pino Donaggio; prod d, Gary Weist; cos, Ann Roth, Gary Jones

All dressed up with no script to go, but a feverish nerve jangler nonetheless. Kate (Dickinson) is a sexually dissatisfied middle-aged housewife who fantasizes about erotic encounters while in the shower. Kate's sympathetic psychiatrist (Caine) advises her to indulge in an extra-marital affair. Immediately after her first tryst, however, Kate is cornered in an elevator and murdered by a leather-clad blonde wielding a straight razor. Now it is up to Kate's son (Gordon) to solve the murder with the help of the prostitute (Allen) who discovered his mom's corpse. Although heavily indebted to Alfred Hitchcock, Mario Bava, and Dario Argento, De Palma infused this film with enough sex, blood, and visual panache to make it a big hit at the box office. Gushingly praised by some critics at the time of its release, it now seems a definite case of cinematic style over substance. A slightly longer and more explicit version was released in Europe, mainly for fans of Angie Dickinson's stand-in. But it's probably Dickinson's best work, and Caine is fine indeed. Best surprises: between subway cars, and that nurse's shoe!

DRESSER, THE

1983   118m   c   ★★★★
Drama   PG
Goldcrest/World Film   (U.K.)

Albert Finney (Sir), Tom Courtenay (Norman), Edward Fox (Oxenby), Zena Walker (Her Ladyship), Eileen Atkins (Madge), Michael Gough (Frank Carrington), Cathryn Harrison (Irene), Betty Marsden (Violet Manning), Sheila Reid (Lydia Gibson), Lockwood West (Geoffrey Thornton)

p, Peter Yates; d, Peter Yates; w, Ronald Harwood (based on his play); ph, Kelvin Pike; ed, Ray Lovejoy; m, James Horner; prod d, Stephen Grimes; art d, Colin Grimes; cos, H. Nathan, L. Nathan

The head of a Shakespearean acting troupe touring England during WWII, "Sir" (Albert Finney) is a senile boozer who is looked after by his gay dresser, Norman (Tom Courtenay). In episodic fashion, the film reveals Norman's devotion to his employer and the complexities of the relationship between the two men of the theater. This adaptation of Robert Harwood's very successful play reveals its staginess, but the film is saved by dynamic direction, its feel of authenticity, and the two stars' performances that veer close to haminess without actually entering the terrain. Interesting, then, that Eileen Atkins steals the film out from under both as a pathetic stage-manager.

DREYFUS CASE, THE

1931   90m   bw   ★★★★
Biography   /U
British Intl.   (U.K.)

Cedric Hardwicke (Capt. Alfred Dreyfus), Charles Carson (Col. Picquart), George Merritt (Emile Zola), Sam Livesey (Labori), Beatrix Thomson (Lucie Dreyfus), Garry Marsh (Maj. Esterhazy), Randle Ayrton (President, Court-Martial), Henry Caine (Col. Henry), Reginald Dance (President, Zola Trial), George Skillan (Maj. Paty du Clam)

p, F.W. Kraemer; d, F.W. Kraemer, Milton Rosmer; w, Reginald Berkeley, Walter C. Mycroft (based on the play by Wilhelm Herzog and Hans Rehfisch); ph, Willy Winterstein, Walter Harvey, Horace Wheddon; ed, Langford Reed, Betty Spiers

Stately and underplayed, with more plot animation than many British films of this time. A true-to-life rendition of the infamous case that shook France in the late 1800s, THE DREYFUS CASE stars Cedric Hardwicke as Alfred Dreyfus, the only Jew on the French general staff. When treason is discovered, blame is laid at his feet, and he is sent to Devil's Island. One of the greatest writers of his time, Emile Zola (George Merritt), feels that Dreyfus has been railroaded. He engages Georges Clemenceau, and they succeed in getting the former soldier a new trial. Although serious doubt is cast on the justice of Dreyfus's conviction, they still lose the case, and Dreyfus is remanded to Devil's Island. After several more years of imprisonment, the duplicity is uncovered, and Dreyfus, vindicated, returns to his first love, the army. The exceptional Merritt and Hardwicke lead a talented cast, and producer Kraemer and the reliable Rosmer do a decent job of directing here.

DRIVER, THE

1978   91m   c   ★★★★
Crime   R/15
FOX

Ryan O'Neal (The Driver), Bruce Dern (The Detective), Isabelle Adjani (The Player), Ronee Blakley (The Connection), Matt Clark (Red Plainclothesman), Felice Orlandi (Gold Plainclothesman), Joseph Walsh (Glasses), Rudy Ramos (Teeth), Denny Macko (Exchange Man), Frank Bruno (The Kid)

p, Lawrence Gordon; d, Walter Hill; w, Walter Hill; ph, Philip Lathrop (Panavision, DeLuxe Color); ed, Tina Hirsch, Robert K. Lambert; m, Michael Small; prod d, Harry Horner; art d, David M. Haber; fx, Charles Spurgeon

A curiosity. Hill's second feature is a bare-bones, existential *film noir*. O'Neal is The Driver, a top getaway driver for a gang of crooks, and Dern is The Detective (nobody in the film has a proper name) obsessed with arresting him. The sparse story of the struggle of the two men with their obsessions, and with each other, skillfully creates a mood that is hard to shake after the ending credits. The car chases are breathtaking.

DRIVING MISS DAISY

1989 99m c   ★★★½
Comedy/Drama   PG/U
Zanuck

Jessica Tandy *(Miss Daisy Werthan)*, Morgan Freeman *(Hoke Colburn)*, Dan Aykroyd *(Boolie Werthan)*, Patti LuPone *(Florine Werthan)*, Esther Rolle *(Idella)*, Joann Havrilla *(Miss McClatchey)*, William Hall, Jr. *(Oscar)*, Alvin M. Sugarman *(Dr. Weil)*, Clarice F. Geigerman *(Nonie)*, Muriel Moore *(Miriam)*

p, Richard D. Zanuck, Lili Fini Zanuck; d, Bruce Beresford; w, Alfred Uhry (based on his play); ph, Peter James; ed, Mark Warner; m, Hans Zimmer; prod d, Bruno Rubeo; art d, Victor Kempster; cos, Elizabeth McBride

Driving Us Crazy that this flick won all those Oscars—but then what do you expect? In all fairness, Australian director Bruce Beresford (BREAKER MORANT; TENDER MERCIES) successfully translates playwright-screenwriter Alfred Uhry's loosely autobiographical, Pulitzer Prize-winning play of the same name to the screen. The simple but compelling story opens in 1948, when Miss Daisy (Jessica Tandy), a wealthy 72-year-old southern Jewish matron who lives in quiet dignity, accidentally backs her Packard into her neighbor's prized garden. Miss Daisy's already frustrated son, Boolie (Dan Aykroyd), insists that his mother employ the services of a chauffeur. Reluctantly, she hires Hoke (Morgan Freeman), a Black gentleman, thus beginning a friendship that blossoms over the next quarter century until, in her mid-90s, after many years of really getting to know and appreciate Hoke, the eccentric Miss Daisy at last concedes that the respectful yet forceful driver is indeed her very best friend. Set in a small community near Atlanta, DRIVING MISS DAISY covers 25 years (1948-73) in a changing South, and the manner in which the momentous and turbulent events of the civil rights movement affect Hoke and Daisy personally is the film's true subject. Directed and written with a pleasant simplicity and clarity, DRIVING MISS DAISY is a blandly liberal if touching and dignified depiction of decent human beings who must live their everyday lives amid the turmoil of historical events. Chief among the film's rewards are the extraordinary performances of its trio of stars, Freeman, Tandy, and Aykroyd—all of whom received Oscar nominations. Tandy won the Oscar for Best Actress.

DROWNING BY NUMBERS

1991 118 minm c   ★★★½
Drama   R/18
Film Four International/Elsevier Vendex Film/Allarts/VPRO Television   (U.K./Netherlands)

Joan Plowright *(1st Cissie Colpitts)*, Juliet Stevenson *(2nd Cissie Colpitts)*, Joely Richardson *(3rd Cissie Colpitts)*, Bernard Hill *(Henry Madgett)*, Jason Edwards *(Smut)*, Bryan Pringle *(Jake)*, Trevor Cooper *(Hardy)*, David Morrissey *(Bellamy)*, John Rogan *(Gregory)*, Paul Mooney *(Teigan)*

p, Kees Kasander, Denis Wigman, Bill Stephens; d, Peter Greenaway; w, Peter Greenaway; ph, Sacha Vierny; ed, John Wilson; m, Michael Nyman; prod d, Ben Van Os, Jan Roelfs; cos, Dien Van Stralen

After numerous experimental shorts and THE FALLS, his first feature-length project, British filmmaker Peter Greenaway hit the art circuit jackpot with THE DRAUGHTSMAN'S CONTRACT, followed by A ZED AND TWO NOUGHTS and THE BELLY OF AN ARCHITECT. DROWNING BY NUMBERS, his fifth feature, was made in 1988 but only released domestically in 1991, on the heels of the *succes de scandale* THE COOK, THE THIEF, HIS WIFE AND HER LOVER.

Against a backdrop of the autumnal Suffolk seaside, three generations of women, each named Cissie Colpitts (60-year-old mother Joan Plowright, 34-year-old daughter Juliet Stevenson and 19-year-old granddaughter Joely Richardson), murder their unsatisfactory husbands by drowning (respectively, Jake (Bryan Pringle), in a bathtub; Hardy (Trevor Cooper), while swimming in the sea; and Bellamy (David Morrissey), in a swimming pool). In return for promised sexual favors, which the women ultimately withhold, the local coroner Henry Madgett (Bernard Hill) agrees to certify the deaths as accidental, although a small but steadily growing crowd of witnesses and relatives put pressure on him, as well as on Madgett's adolescent son Smut (Jason Edwards), who is obsessed with death and collects animal and insect corpses. True to Madgett's—and the film's—own obsession with games, to decide the issue he sets up a tug-of-war across a river, with him and Smut joining the Cissies against their detractors. Their team loses when Smut lets go of the rope upon learning of the accidental death of a young girl (Natalie Morse) he loved. (He later hangs himself.) The Cissies escape the angry mob in a rowboat and, after scattering their husbands' ashes on the river, pull the plug on the boat and swim to shore, leaving the now-complacent Madgett—who cannot swim—to a watery death.

For writer-director Peter Greenaway, plots, of which the above is a bare-bones synopsis, eliminating many characters and events, are impossibly convoluted, if absolutely logically perfect, and becoming increasingly irrelevant to his work. As obsessed with puzzles and games—and death—as his characters, the filmmaker literally counts sequentially from 1 to 100, the numerals appearing somewhere within the frame, e.g. painted on trees and walls—even dead cows—or as laundry marks, on clock faces and keyrings, cricket scores, etc. Greenaway's background is as an artist, and his astute knowledge of art history visually informs his films, lately all of them glowingly photographed by former Resnais collaborator Sacha Vierny. In addition to his erudite obsession with taxonomy, numerology, natural history and apocryphal anecdote, Greenaway is also something of a librarian; in DROWNING BY NUMBERS he includes the dying words of historical figures like Gainsborough and Lord Nelson, and he also works in the names of 100 stars—the celestial kind.

Greenaway is an often infuriating, one-of-kind filmmaker who continually tests the patience of his audience—many feel it not worth the effort to figure out his obscure games, let alone their meaning, without some attendant kinky sex or gore to leaven the proceedings. DROWNING BY NUMBERS serves up some of this: there's a circumcision by scissors, a continual revulsion for food and flesh, and some near-sickening scenes of decay and insects. Still, as if ignoring the filmmaker's cryptic proclivities, the performances (especially by Plowright and Hill) are wry and often blackly witty, and the water-image-filled film is visually inventive, each frame packed with detail, and quite beautiful.

DROWNING BY NUMBERS is an amoral tale told morally, with a strong feminist undertone—almost all the male characters die via the unbeatable Cissies' conspiracy—reflecting, as Greenaway himself has stated, that "the good do not get rewarded, the wicked are rarely punished, and the innocent are always abused."

DRUGSTORE COWBOY

1989   100m   c   ★★★★½
Drama   R/18
Avenue

Matt Dillon (Bob), Kelly Lynch (Dianne), James Le Gros (Rick), Heather Graham (Nadine), James Remar (Gentry), William S. Burroughs (Tom the Priest), Grace Zabriskie (Bob's Mother), Max Perlich (David), Beah Richards (Drug Counselor)

p, Nick Wechsler, Karen Murphy; d, Gus Van Sant, Jr.; w, Gus Van Sant, Jr., Daniel Yost (based on a novel by James Fogle); ph, Robert Yeoman (Alpha Cine, Deluxe Color); ed, Curtiss Clayton; m, Elliot Goldenthal; prod d, David Brisbin; art d, Eve Cauley; cos, Beatrix Aruna Pasztor

A darkly funny, stylish, and realistic look at the world of drug addiction in 1971, DRUGSTORE COWBOY focuses on Bob (Matt Dillon) as the leader of a bedraggled quartet of addicts who get what they need by robbing drugstore pharmacy departments in the Pacific Northwest. His crew consists of his wife Dianne (Kelly Lynch), Bob's sluggish lieutenant, Rick (James Le Gros), and his underage girl friend, Nadine (Heather Graham). After one particularly fruitful heist, Bob devises a scheme whereby they can all stay constantly high, at least for a while, by sending their stash of drugs ahead of them via Greyhound bus as they migrate through the region. Hot on their trail is Gentry (James Remar), a cop bent on nailing Bob. Gus Van Sant's direction here is supremely confident, fusing witty camerawork, neat editing, and a jazz-oriented score to make DRUGSTORE COWBOY an exhilaratingly bumpy ride. DRUGSTORE COWBOY presents a rare insider's view of the drug lifestyle that is all the more refreshing for its lack of facile moralizing or apologies. It's a true comedy of desperation. After many photogenic but unchallenging roles, Dillon is a wonder here, portraying his antihero with an empathy that recalls James Cagney, Marlon Brando, James Dean, and Robert De Niro. The film's producers anticipated that DRUGSTORE COWBOY might receive an X rating for its explicit depiction of drug paraphernalia and use. Luckily, their fears proved wrong, allowing this honest, genuinely independent film to reach the broad audience it deserves.

DRUMS

1938   96m   c   ★★★★
Adventure/War
Korda/London Films   (U.K.)

Sabu (Prince Azim), Raymond Massey (Prince Ghul), Valerie Hobson (Mrs. Carruthers), Roger Livesey (Capt. Carruthers), Desmond Tester (Bill Holder), Martin Walker (Herrick), David Tree (Lt. Escott), Francis L. Sullivan (Governor), Roy Emerton (Wafadar), Edward Lexy (Sgt. Maj. Kernel)

p, Alexander Korda; d, Zoltan Korda; w, Arthur Wimperis, Patrick Kirwan, Hugh Gray (based on Lajos Biro's adaptation of the novel by A.E.W. Mason); ph, Georges Perinal, Osmond Borradaile, Robert Krasker, Christopher Challis, Geoffrey Unsworth (Technicolor); ed, William Hornbeck, Henry Cornelius; m, John Greenwood; prod d, Vincent Korda; fx, Edward Cohen

Set in northwest India at the height of the British presence there, DRUMS finds the treacherous Indian Prince Ghul (Raymond Massey) usurping his brother's kingdom by murdering his sibling and forcing his nephew and the heir apparent, Prince Azim (Sabu), into hiding. The boy finds refuge at the British garrison, where the commander, Captain Carruthers (Roger Livesey), and his wife (Valerie Hobson) treat him with kindness. Azim learns the regulations of the British Army and how to beat military cadence on a drum, a skill he uses later to warn the garrison that it is about to be attacked by Ghul and his evil followers. The spectacle is excellent, the direction and beautiful color cinematography superb. Sabu is wonderful as the innocent, wide-eyed royal youth, a role that earned him 100 fan letters a day, and Livesey is a great match for the wily Massey, a villan minus a decent bone in his body.

DRUMS ALONG THE MOHAWK

1939   103m   c   ★★★★
Historical/Adventure/War
FOX

Claudette Colbert (Lana "Magdelana" Martin), Henry Fonda (Gil Martin), Edna May Oliver (Mrs. Sarah McKlennar), Eddie Collins (Christian Reall), John Carradine (Caldwell), Dorris Bowdon (Mary Reall), Jessie Ralph (Mrs. Weaver), Arthur Shields (Rev. Rosenkrantz), Robert Lowery (John Weaver), Roger Imhof (Gen. Nicholas Herkimer)

p, Raymond Griffith; d, John Ford; w, Lamar Trotti, Sonya Levien (based on the novel by Walter D. Edmonds); ph, Bert Glennon, Ray Rennahan (Technicolor); ed, Robert Simpson; m, Alfred Newman; art d, Richard Day, Mark-Lee Kirk; cos, Gwen Wakeling

A sentimental beauty. This richly directed and acted colonial epic concerns Fonda and Colbert, young newlyweds starting out on the frontier of the Mohawk Valley just before the outbreak of the Revolutionary War. Their transition from a life of privilege to that of the rugged frontier proves an exercise in stamina. To help fend off Indian attacks engineered by the British, Gil joins the militia and goes off to fight; finally, after many battles and hardships, the future of the new Americans begins to look bright. This historical chronicle directed by John Ford is made believable through its attention to small details, presenting a mosaic of frontier life. One of Ford's biggest problems in making the spectacular film was the unavailability of necessary props and costumes; Fox had not specialized in costume or historical films, particularly those with 18th-century settings, and almost everything had to be made from scratch at great cost. The ancient flintlock muskets brandished by scores of extras were the real weapons of the era, however, not reproductions. A Fox prop man chased the flintlocks down in Ethiopia—where they had actually seen combat in the mid-1930s, when they were used by Ethiopian soldiers against Mussolini's armies. This was Ford's first color film, his cameras recording the lush forests and valleys of northern Utah. So rich and verdant is the color in this film that it later provided stock footage for several Fox productions, including BUFFALO BILL (1944) and MOHAWK (1956).

DRUNKEN ANGEL

(YOIDORE TENSHI)
1948   102m   bw   ★★★★
Drama
Toho   (Japan)

Toshiro Mifune (Matsunaga), Takashi Shimura (Dr. Sanada), Reisaburo Yamamoto (Okada), Michiyo Kogure (Nanse), Chieko Nakakita (Miyo), Noriko Sengoku (Gin), Eitaro Shindo (Takahama), Choko Iida (Old Maid Servant)

p, Sojiro Motoki; d, Akira Kurosawa; w, Keinosuke Uegusa, Akira Kurosawa; ph, Takeo Ito; m, Fumio Hayasaka; art d, So Matsuyama

Akira Kurosawa's DRUNKEN ANGEL captures the mood of postwar Japan in the same way the neorealist films of Italy did in that country. In a war-scarred town controlled by the Yakuza (Japanese gangsters), an alcoholic doctor runs a small clinic. A young gangster, Matsunaga (Toshiro Mifune), comes to have a bullet removed from his hand and is treated by Dr. Sanada (Takashi Shimura), who hates the Yakuza. Sanada discovers that Matsunaga has tuberculosis and, after arguments and fistfights, convinces Matsunaga to let him treat the illness, creating a love-hate relationship between the two. This was the first film on which Kurosawa had creative control and, although he had directed other pictures, it is the one in which his personal voice is first clearly heard. It was also the first starring role for Mifune, who, like his costar Shimura, turns in a mesmerizing performance. What makes the film so powerful is the characters' dependence on one another—Matsunaga's need for medical treatment and emotional support when faced with an incurable disease, and the humanist urge that compels Sanada to treat the gangster despite the fact that he hates everything the Yakuza represents.

DRY SUMMER
(SUSUZ YAZ)
1967 90m bw   ★★
Drama
Hitit   (Turkey)

Ulvi Dogan *(Hassan)*, Errol Tash *(Osman)*, Julie Kotch *(Bahar)*, Hakki Haktan, Yavuz Yalinkilic, Zeki Tuney, Alaettin Altiok

p, Ulvi Dogan, William Shelton (US version); d, Metin Erksan, David Durston (US version); w, Metin Erksan, Ismet Saydan, Kemal Inci (based on a story by Necati Cumali); ph, Ali Ugur; ed, Stuart Gellman; m, Yamaci, Manos Hadjidakis

Drier than most. Tash is the younger brother of the miserly Dogan, who refuses to grant the other villagers the use of his water during a drought. One of the townspeople trespasses and is killed by Dogan, but Tash, because he is the younger brother, takes the blame. He is sentenced to a short prison term during which Dogan tells Tash's wife that her husband died. Tash is pardoned, however, and saves his wife from Dogan's lechery and the villagers from a waterless demise.

DRY WHITE SEASON, A
1989 97m c   ★★★
Drama   R/15
MGM-UA

Donald Sutherland *(Ben du Toit)*, Winston Ntshona *(Gordon Ngubene)*, Susan Sarandon *(Melanie Bruwer)*, Janet Suzman *(Susan du Toit)*, Marlon Brando *(Ian McKenzie)*, Zakes Mokae *(Stanley)*, Jurgen Prochnow *(Capt. Stolz)*, Thoko Ntshinga *(Emily Ngubene)*, Susannah Harker *(Suzette du Toit)*, Leonard Maguire *(Mr. Bruwer)*

p, Paula Weinstein; d, Euzhan Palcy; w, Euzhan Palcy, Colin Welland (based on the novel by Andre Brink); ph, Kelvin Pike, Pierre-William Glenn (Deluxe Color); ed, Sam O'Steen, Glenn Cunningham; m, Dave Grusin; prod d, John Fenner; art d, Alan Tomkins, Mike Phillips

A polemic against South African apartheid, this may not meet criteria for "great" filmmaking, but director Euzhan Palcy's film succeeds in being significant. History teacher Ben du Toit (Donald Sutherland), an Afrikaner, lives a comfortable middle-class existence with wife Susan (Janet Suzman) and their children in Johannesburg in the 1970s. He finds all of his personal and political ties thrown into question, however, following the event that sparked the Soweto uprising of 1976, when a peaceful protest march by black schoolchildren demanding better education was put down in a bloody massacre. When his longtime gardener (Winston Ntshona), in the process of trying to recover his son's body, is himself arrested, then brutally tortured and murdered, du Toit's liberal consciousness is raised. A DRY WHITE SEASON is worth watching for the (sometimes painful) force of its truths and its perspective, which shows the effects of racism from both white *and* black standpoints. This is the first full-length feature to be directed by a black woman for a major US studio. Adding to this already significant achievement, Palcy, in what amounts to the casting coup of the year, enlisted the reclusive Brando to make his brief but memorable cameo appearance—his first film role since 1980—for union scale. His performance alone is worth the price of admission to this earnest, somewhat predictable, but moving and significant film. Brando's cameo earned him an Oscar nomination for Best Supporting Actor.

DUCK SOUP
1933 70m bw   ★★★★★
Comedy/War   /U
Paramount

Groucho Marx *(Rufus T. Firefly)*, Chico Marx *(Chicolini)*, Harpo Marx *(Brownie)*, Zeppo Marx *(Bob Rolland)*, Raquel Torres *(Vera Marcal)*, Louis Calhern *(Ambassador Trentino)*, Margaret Dumont *(Mrs. Teasdale)*, Verna Hillie *(Secretary)*, Leonid Kinskey *(Agitator)*, Edmund Breese *(Zander)*

p, Herman Mankiewicz; d, Leo McCarey; w, Bert Kalmar, Harry Ruby, Arthur Sheekman, Nat Perrin; ph, Henry Sharp; ed, LeRoy Stone; art d, Hans Dreier, Wiard Ihnen

A masterpiece. Fast-moving, irreverent, almost anarchistic in style, DUCK SOUP is considered by many to be the Marx Brothers' greatest achievement,though it was not a hit upon its release. The story, if one can call it that, concerns Mrs. Teasdale (Margaret Dumont), a dowager millionairess who will donate $20 million to the destitute duchy of Freedonia if it will agree to make Rufus T. Firefly (Groucho) its dictator. Firefly woos Mrs. Teasdale and spends his spare time insulting Trentino (Louis Calhern), the ambassador from neighboring Sylvania; Trentino hires the sultry Vera Marcal (Raquel Torres) to vamp Firefly so that Trentino can move in on Mrs. Teasdale, marry her, and get control of Freedonia. To aid his chicanery, Trentino hires Chicolini (Chico), a peanut salesman, and his friend Brownie (Harpo) as spies. Eventually war breaks out and, after much manic double-crossing and side-switching, Freedonia emerges victorious.

Perhaps the best, and funniest, depiction of the absurdities of war ever committed to celluloid, DUCK SOUP today remains a masterpiece of film comedy. The Marxes' depiction of two-bit dictators destroying their own countries was a slap at the rising fascists, so much so that Mussolini considered it a direct insult and banned the film in Italy. The Marx Brothers were thrilled to hear that. Best gag among what seems like hundreds: the mirror sequence.

DUEL, THE
1964 93m c   ★★½
Drama
Mosfilm   (U.S.S.R.)

Lyudmila Shagalova *(Nadezhda Fyodorovna)*, Oleg Strizhenov *(Layevskiy)*, Vladimir Druzhnikov *(Von Koren)*, Aleksandr Khvylya

(Samoylenko), L. Kadrov (Pobedov), G. Georgiu (Kirilin), Ye. Kuzmina (Marya Konstantinovna), L. Pirogov (Bityugov), Y. Leonidov (Achmianov), V. Burlakova

d, Tatyana Berezantseva, Lev Rudnik; w, Tatyana Berezantseva (based on a play by Anton Pavlovich Chekhov); ph, Antonina Egina; ed, P. Chechyotkina; m, V. Yurovskiy; art d, V. Kamskiy; fx, B. Gorbachyov; cos, V. Nisskaya

A superbly acted adaptation of a play by Chekhov, THE DUEL tells of the struggles that Strizhenov has with his dull daily routine and the mistress that offers no relief from his boredom. When his mistress's husband dies, he is faced with the possibility of marriage—a thought which sends him packing. He tries to borrow money from Druzhnikov, but when the lender realizes what the money is for he refuses. Furious, Strizhenov challenges him to a duel which ends in neither man hitting his target. Strizhenov is deeply affected by his brush with death and begins life anew.

DUEL IN THE SUN

1946 138m c   ★★★½
Western   /PG
Selznick

Jennifer Jones (Pearl Chavez), Joseph Cotton (Jesse McCanles), Gregory Peck (Lewt McCanles), Lionel Barrymore (Sen. McCanles), Lillian Gish (Laura Belle McCanles), Walter Huston (The Sin Killer), Herbert Marshall (Scott Chavez), Charles Bickford (Sam Pierce), Joan Tetzel (Helen Langford), Harry Carey (Lem Smoot)

p, David O. Selznick; d, King Vidor; w, Oliver H.P. Garrett, David O. Selznick (based on the novel by Niven Busch); ph, Lee Garmes, Harold Rosson, Ray Rennahan, Charles P. Boyle, Allen Davey (Technicolor); ed, Hal C. Kern, William Ziegler, John Faure, Charles Freeman; m, Dimitri Tiomkin; prod d, J. McMillan Johnson; art d, James Basevi, John Ewing; fx, Clarence Slifer, Jack Cosgrove; chor, Tilly Losch, Lloyd Shaw; cos, Walter Plunkett

An enormous, lumbering horse opera, done up like an oversexed prize-winning bronco but revealing itself as a florid cartoon nag. DUEL is full of grand spectacle, steamy sensualism, and a storyline that could have snaked only out of Hollywood; it was Selznick's hymn to the allure of Jennifer Jones (in for Hedy Lamarr and, unbelievably, Teresa Wright—both were pregnant) and her failing entry into the Jane Russell/OUTLAW sex-goddess sweepstakes. Gregory Peck actually plays the studly bully who loves her (original choice when the project began in 1944 was John Wayne, but the dubious sex angle made him squeamish), and lightning blazes when they kiss. How to criticize a climax with two lovers orgasmically shooting each other to smithereens? The unforgettable supporting cast includes Walter Huston, having one whale of a good time as a hellfire preacher, Butterfly McQueen caricaturing her GWTW role (!) and Lillian Gish and Joseph Cotten as bastions of restraint. This is undeniable hooey, but it's also candybox entertainment. Can you really afford to miss Peck taming a sex-crazed stallion? Or Jones crawling for miles, spouting blood and words of love for her surly beau? We think not.

DUEL's accent on sex, heavy-handed and often repugnant, caused jocular critics of the day to dub the film "Lust in the Dust." The budget for the film soared beyond $6 million before it was over and an additional $2 million was used to scandalously promote the sex angle. A storm of protest from Catholic and Protestant leaders alike thunderclapped over Selznick's head. All over America local authorities competed with each other to ban the film. It was censored in Memphis and kicked out of Hartford, Connecticut. Certain scenes had to be edited before DUEL IN THE SUN opened in Philadelphia and other major cities. The publicity was enormous, and the public ignored the universal drubbing the film received from critics, flocking to see it and returning $12 million to the Selznick coffers.

The film was begun in 1944, and John Wayne was originally set to play the bad cowboy, but he veered away from the film after reading the dubious script.

Shooting on location in Arizona, Selznick had miles of track put down for his advancing train and more than 6,500 extras were employed to people the hot, dusty landscape. Hundreds of horses and cattle were imported, and the sprawling McCanles ranch was painfully constructed by hundreds of men leveling the land and planting trees. Selznick meddled in this film more than in any other, insisting it be perfect for his wife. Veteran director Vidor was hamstrung at every turn, as Selznick viewed his rushes and eliminated most of his takes. The mogul brought in a host of other directors to "assist" Vidor, who never required assistance. These included William Cameron Menzies, Josef Von Sternberg, Sydney Franklin, William Dieterle. The producer sacked brilliant cinematographers Lee Garmes and Hal Rosson, letting Renahan finish but only under his immediate supervision. Vidor stubbornly stayed in the production to salvage some of his own work and receive proper credit. He and Selznick finally had their long-awaited shouting match after 20 months of shooting, and the director walked off with two days of shooting left. Dieterle was brought in to wrap things up. In the end Selznick sat in a viewing room for weeks scanning almost 1.5 million feet of film, which would approximate 135 two-hour movies, an enormous indulgence of ego and power. A ton was cut, including three complex dances performed by Jones, deemed overly suggestive. The film boomed at the box office but failed to turn Jones into a love goddess, recalling prophetically Welles's narration at the opening of the film when he summarizes Jones's fate: ". . .Pearl, who came from down along the border, and who was like a wildflower sprung from the hard clay, quick to blossom, early to die."

DUELLISTS, THE

1977 95m c   ★★★
Historical/War   PG
Paramount (U.K.)

Keith Carradine (D'Hubert), Harvey Keitel (Feraud), Albert Finney (Fouche), Edward Fox (Col. Reynard), Cristina Raines (Adele), Robert Stephens (Gen. Treillard), Tom Conti (Jacquin), John McEnery (2nd Major), Diana Quick (Laura), Alun Armstrong (Lacourbe)

p, David Puttnam; d, Ridley Scott; w, Gerald Vaughan-Hughes (based on the story "The Duel" by Joseph Conrad); ph, Frank Tidy; ed, Pamela Powers; m, Howard Blake; art d, Bryan Graves

Competent feature debut of director Ridley Scott, who would go on to make the popular science-fiction films ALIEN and BLADE RUNNER, THE DUELLISTS is a beautifully photographed adaptation of a Joseph Conrad story in which two officers in Napoleon's army, Carradine and Keitel, fall out and proceed to engage in an obsessive series of duels for the next 30 years. The film's outstanding beauty is not enough to compensate its slim story, which remains preoccupied with the duellists' insane obsession with military codes of conduct and personal honor.

The leads are often remarkable, but neither of them seems quite fitting to a period setting. Therefore the burden of authenticity falls to those in supporting roles, including Finney as the

Napoleonic head of the Paris police. Scott's approach to his material seems essentially a stylistic one; it imposes itself upon the story rather than visa-versa, giving an account of the Napoleonic wars that lacks passion and depth, despite the expert visuals.

DUET FOR ONE

1986 101m c   ★★★
Drama   R/15
Golan-Globus

Julie Andrews *(Stephanie Anderson)*, Alan Bates *(David Cornwallis)*, Max von Sydow *(Dr. Louis Feldman)*, Rupert Everett *(Constantine Kassanis)*, Margaret Courtenay *(Sonia Randvich)*, Cathryn Harrison *(Penny Smallwood)*, Sigfrit Steiner *(Leonid Lefimov)*, Liam Neeson *(Totter)*, Macha Meril *(Anya)*

p, Menahem Golan, Yoram Globus; d, Andrei Konchalovsky; w, Tom Kempinski, Jeremy Lipp, Andrei Konchalovsky (based on the play by Kempinski); ph, Alex Thomson (Rank Color); ed, Henry Richardson; prod d, John Graysmark; art d, Reg Bream, Steve Cooper; cos, Evangeline Harrison

Overworked soapsuds, but Andrews's performance is strong enough to turn what could have been an insufferable property into thoughtful drama. Andrews is a world-famous violinist married to Bates, an equally acclaimed orchestra conductor. When Andrews experiences temporary paralysis, a doctor diagnoses her problem as multiple sclerosis, a degenerative disease that will eventually kill her. Forced to contemplate the inevitable, Andrews must face not only her physical condition but the changes that the disease engenders in her various relationships. Director Konchalovsky turned away from his usual directorial style, and as a result his work feels a trifle uneven. The diluted script, based on the play by Kempinski, relies on a plethora of characters to open up the play. As a result, some of the plot's major points get swamped. The talented ensemble deliver quite well in this rare and effective drama about the artist's relationship to his art.

DUMBO

1941 64m c   ★★★★★
Animated   /U
Disney

VOICES OF: Edward Brophy *(Timothy Mouse)*, Herman Bing *(Ringmaster)*, Verna Felton *(Elephant)*, Sterling Holloway *(Stork)*, Cliff Edwards *(Jim Crow)*

p, Walt Disney; d, Ben Sharpsteen; w, Joe Grant, Dick Huemer (based on a book by Helen Aberson and Harold Pearl); ph, (Technicolor); art d, Herb Ryman, Kendall O'Connor, Terrell Stapp, Donald Da Gradi, Al Zinnen, Ernest Nordli, Dick Kelsey, Charles Payzant; anim, Wolfgang Reitherman, Arthur Babbitt, Walt Kelly, John Lounsbery, Ward Kimball, Fred Moore, Cy Young, Vladimir Tytla

One of Disney's finest films, this simple tale is set in a circus and spotlights a baby elephant, Dumbo, who is mocked and ridiculed because his ears are too big. With the help of his best friend Timothy the mouse and some very hip crows, Dumbo discovers that he can use his gigantic ears to fly and becomes the hit of the circus. The message of the film is spoken by Timothy as he declares to his doubting friend, "The very things that held you down will carry you up and up and up!"

A small, flawless gem, DUMBO is one of the shortest animated features Disney ever made and inexpensive to boot, costing less than $1 million (whereas more ambitious films like BAMBI shot well beyond the $2 million mark). A masterpiece of visual story-telling, the film contains relatively little dialogue and Dumbo never speaks; his mother only speaks to him in the song "Baby Mine." Humans are shown in shadows and silhouettes, the animals taking center stage. As with all his major feature-length animation films, Disney made sure that none of the scenes were flat, that blades of grass rippled in the wind and leaves fluttered in the trees. A delight from beginning to end, the film's absolute highlight is the "Pink Elephants on Parade" sequence in which Dumbo and Timothy hallucinate after accidentally drinking liquor.

It took the resourceful Disney craftsman a year and a half to design and execute this stunning achievement of animation art. This was time well spent. The result was an experience—alternately hilarious, thrilling, and heartbreaking—that will appeal to every child in the world and every adult who can still recall the happy world of childhood fantasies and fables. The film won an Oscar for its score and received a nomination for Best Song ("Baby Mine").

E.T. THE EXTRA-TERRESTRIAL

1982 115m c   ★★★★
Fantasy   PG/U
Universal

Dee Wallace *(Mary)*, Henry Thomas *(Elliott)*, Peter Coyote *(Keys)*,
Robert MacNaughton *(Michael)*, Drew Barrymore *(Gertie)*, K.C.
Martel *(Greg)*, Sean Frye *(Steve)*, Tom Howell *(Tyler)*, Erika Eleniak
(Pretty Girl), David O'Dell *(Schoolboy)*

p, Steven Spielberg, Kathleen Kennedy; d, Steven Spielberg; w,
Melissa Mathison; ph, Allen Daviau (Technicolor); ed, Carol Little-
ton; m, John Williams; prod d, James D. Bissell; fx, Industrial Light
& Magic; cos, Deborah L. Scott, Carlo Rambaldi

One of the most popular movies ever made, E.T. translates
religious myth into cute, familiar terrain with its story of a lovable
alien stranded in suburbia.

   Elliott (Henry Thomas) finds E.T., a visitor from another
planet left stranded on Earth, hiding in his backyard and, like any
kid who finds a stray, decides to keep him. Hiding the alien from
his mother, Thomas and the neighborhood kids befriend the
creature. Though E.T. becomes attached to Elliott and his friends,
he wants to get back to his own planet; meanwhile, the children
must save him from some government types who are trying to
capture and study him.

   A major hit at the box office which also spawned an extremely
profitable merchandising campaign, E.T. was embraced by audiences worldwide and instantly became absorbed into popular
culture. Though the story feels standard, the fun comes from the
meticulously realized details that director Steven Spielberg and
associate producer-writer Melissa Mathison have injected into
the material. From E.T.'s too-cute encounters with suburban
living to the undeniable exhilaration felt when Thomas's bicycle
magically soars into the air, the film bears witness to the undeniable powers of one of cinema's most skillful craftsmen. The
film won Oscars for Best Original Score and Best Visual Effects.

EAGLE SQUADRON

1942 109m bw   ★★★
War   /U
Universal

Robert Stack *(Chuck Brewer)*, Diana Barrymore *(Anne Partridge)*,
John Loder *(Paddy Carson)*, Eddie Albert *(Leckie)*, Nigel Bruce
(McKinnon), Leif Erickson *(Johnny Coe)*, Edgar Barrier *(Wadislaw
Borowsky)*, Jon Hall *(Hank Starr)*, Evelyn Ankers *(Nancy Mitchell)*,
Isobel Elsom *(Dame Elizabeth Whitby)*

p, Walter Wanger; d, Arthur Lubin; w, Norman Reilly Raine (based
on a *Cosmopolitan* story by C.S. Forester); ph, Stanley Cortez; ed,
Philip Cahn; m, Frank Skinner; art d, Jack Otterson, Alexander
Golitzen; fx, John P. Fulton

Fast-moving, patriotic WWII air-combat film about a bunch of
American volunteers fighting with the RAF before Pearl Harbor.
EAGLE SQUADRON chronicles the group's induction into the
elite flying corps, their training, their air battles with the Nazi
Luftwaffe, their brief romances with British women, and some
of their tragic deaths. The splendid aerial photography—much
of it documentary material supplied by British authorities—depicts actual combat, with the climactic sequence documenting a
raid on the French coast where American pilots hijack a mysterious Nazi plane. Briskly directed, with fine performances from
all, particularly Stack, Loder and Hall.

EARRINGS OF MADAME DE. . . , THE

(MADAME DE. . .)
1953 105m bw   ★★★★★
Drama
Franco London/Indusfilms/Rizzoli   (France/Italy)

Danielle Darrieux *(Countess Louise de. . .)*, Charles Boyer *(Gen.
Andre de. . .)*, Vittorio De Sica *(Baron Fabrizio Donati)*, Mireille
Perrey *(Mme de. . .'s Nurse)*, Jean Debucourt *(M Remy)*, Serge
Lecointe *(Jerome)*, Lia di Leo *(Lola)*, Jean Galland *(M de Bernac)*,
Hubert Noel *(Henri de Maleville)*, Leon Walther *(Theater Manager)*

p, H. Baum, Ralph Baum; d, Max Ophuls; w, Marcel Achard,
Annette Wademant, Max Ophuls (based on the novel by Louise de
Vilmorin); ph, Christian Matras; ed, Borys Lewin; m, Oscar Straus,
Georges Van Parys; cos, Georges Annenkov, Rosine Delamare

For the five-year period from 1950-55 (shortly before he died),
Max Ophuls was arguably the world's greatest filmmaker, creating LA RONDE, LE PLAISIR, LOLA MONTES, and this
masterful study of a tragic, three-cornered romance.

   THE EARRINGS OF MADAME DE. . . opens brilliantly as
the Countess Louise de. . . (Darrieux; her character's last name
is obscured throughout the story) searches through her belongings for something to sell. The camera glides along as she
examines furs, a necklace, a cross, and finally a pair of diamond
earrings she received as a wedding present from her husband,
General Andre de. . . (Boyer). When she pretends that the earrings have been stolen, the general begins a search, eventually
recovering them discreetly from the jeweler to whom his wife
sold them. The general gives the earrings to his mistress (di Leo),
who later loses them while gambling with Baron Donati (De
Sica). Upon returning to Paris, the Baron falls in love with the
Countess, giving her a gift meant to express his deepest
affection. . . .

   EARRINGS is masterfully told in both verbal and visual
terms. The genteel, brittle dialogue traces an elliptical path to
tragedy while the relentlessly mobile camera dollies and pans
around the stiflingly ornate rooms that Ophuls's characters inhabit. The star trio of Darrieux, Boyer and De Sica have rarely
been better, playing characters whose narcissism deepens to
obsession and, ultimately, desperation. The film's lush visual
style is a perfect, ironic backdrop for the superficialities of the
society explored, particularly in the famous ballroom sequence
where the Countess and the Baron first become aware of their
ill-fated love.

EAST OF EDEN

1955   115m   c   ★★★★½
Drama   /PG
WB

Julie Harris *(Abra)*, James Dean *(Cal Trask)*, Raymond Massey *(Adam Trask)*, Richard Davalos *(Aron Trask)*, Burl Ives *(Sam)*, Jo Van Fleet *(Kate)*, Albert Dekker *(Will)*, Lois Smith *(Ann)*, Harold Gordon *(Mr. Albrecht)*, Timothy Carey *(Joe)*

p, Elia Kazan; d, Elia Kazan; w, Paul Osborn (based on the novel by John Steinbeck); ph, Ted McCord (CinemaScope, Warner Color); ed, Owen Marks; m, Leonard Rosenman; art d, James Basevi, Malcolm Bert; cos, Anna Hill Johnstone

Overwrought, often splendid Kazan version of the Steinbeck novel. The movie's chief distinction is the amazing debut of rebellious, romantic James Dean, who in this and his next film, REBEL WITHOUT A CAUSE, would enshrine the misunderstood teen, and become a tragic icon in his own right. Dean plays the neurotic son of Massey, a devoutly religious lettuce farmer whose vast acreage stretches through the rich Salinas Valley of California. Dean's twin brother (Davalos, also making a powerful film debut) is well adjusted and upstanding, involved in a stable relationship with girlfriend Harris and diligently pursuing the development of his father's lands. Dean is his brother's opposite: troubled and troublesome, he challenges all authority, including his father's, and mistakenly believes that Davalos is the favored son. It's the Cain and Abel story, circa 1917, and the rush from stability to destruction and tragedy is swift, as Dean seeks to undo his brother and himself.

A powerful film whose influence can be seen in HUD and most other antihero films, EAST OF EDEN is masterfully directed by Kazan. All the principals give riveting performances, but it was Dean who emerged as an overnight sensation. EDEN also features a quintessentially hardbitten performance from Van Fleet, who won an Oscar for her pains.

EASTER PARADE

1948   107m   c   ★★★½
Musical/Comedy   /U
MGM

Judy Garland *(Hannah Brown)*, Fred Astaire *(Don Hewes)*, Peter Lawford *(Jonathan Harrow III)*, Ann Miller *(Nadine Gale)*, Jules Munshin *(Francois, Headwaiter)*, Clinton Sundberg *(Mike, the Bartender)*, Jeni le Gon *(Essie)*, Richard Beavers *(Singer)*, Richard Simmons *(Al, Ziegfeld's Stage Manager)*, Jimmie Bates *(Boy with Astaire in "Drum Crazy" Musical Number)*

p, Arthur Freed; d, Charles Walters; w, Frances Goodrich, Albert Hackett, Sidney Sheldon, Guy Bolton (based on a story by Frances Goodrich and Albert Hackett); ph, Harry Stradling (Technicolor); ed, Albert Akst; art d, Cedric Gibbons, Jack Martin Smith; fx, Warren Newcombe; chor, Robert Alton; cos, Irene, Valles

Pretty, deft, and tuneful but, given the top-rate talent involved, not particularly inspired. Between Easter 1911 and Easter 1912, Astaire gets dumped by dance partner Miller and vows revenge by grooming unknown chorus girl Garland for stardom.

Gene Kelly was originally slated to play the lead, but injured his ankle playing volleyball, so he suggested to producer Arthur Freed that they prevail on Astaire to come out of his "retirement" for the role. Astaire had announced he was done after BLUE SKIES, but jumped at the opportunity and gave yet another classic performance. Garland was beginning to tire of the formula of her films, and the horrendous pace of her filming schedule, but Astaire apparently helped coax her through the

production despite her exhaustion. Look for cameos from Lola Albright, as a hat model, and a two-and-a-half-year-old Liza Minnelli in the finale. Irving Berlin wrote 17 of the film's tunes, and Johnny Green and Roger Edens won an Oscar for their musical adaptation. The standout number is the delightful "A Couple of Swells."

EASY LIFE, THE

(IL SORPASSO)
1963   105m   bw   ★★★½
Drama
Fair/Incei/Sancro   (Italy)

Vittorio Gassman *(Bruno Cortona)*, Jean-Louis Trintignant *(Roberto Mariani)*, Catherine Spaak *(Lilly, Bruno's Daughter)*, Luciana Angiolillo *(Bruno's Wife)*, Linda Sini *(Aunt Lidia)*, Corrado Olmi *(Alfredo)*, Claudio Gora *(Bibi, Lilly's Fiance)*, Franca Polesello, Edda Ferronao, Nando Angelini

p, Mario Cecchi Gori; d, Dino Risi; w, Ettore Scola, Ruggero Maccari, Dino Risi; ph, Alfio Contini; ed, Maurizio Lucidi; m, Riz Ortolani; art d, Ugo Pericoli

The zestful, careless Bruno Cortona (Gassman) meets law student Roberto Mariani (Trintignant) when the middle-aged jet-setter needs to use his phone. Cortona introduces the aspiring lawyer to the sybaritic life of luxury and voluptuousness, and Mariani is soon dazzled by the beautiful young sylphs who inhabit it and the reckless gaiety of dancing and sailing along the Riviera. He loses all purpose and direction in life, and the older man, responsible on many levels for what ensues, belatedly realizes how shallow his life as a dissolute middle-aged playboy is. An absorbing glimpse of decadence laced with touches of both warmth and sharp wit, THE EASY LIFE features particularly good acting from its two leads and is handsomely and appropriately filmed before a beautiful Riviera background.

EASY LIVING

1937   88m   bw   ★★★½
Comedy   /PG
Paramount

Jean Arthur *(Mary Smith)*, Edward Arnold *(J.B. Ball)*, Ray Milland *(John Ball, Jr.)*, Luis Alberni *(Mr. Louis Louis)*, Mary Nash *(Mrs. Jennie Ball)*, Franklin Pangborn *(Van Buren)*, Barlowe Borland *(Mr. Gurney)*, William Demarest *(Wallace Whistling)*, Andrew Tombes *(E.F. Hulgar)*, Esther Dale *(Lillian)*

p, Arthur Hornblow, Jr.; d, Mitchell Leisen; w, Preston Sturges (based on a story by Vera Caspary); ph, Ted Tetzlaff; ed, Doane Harrison; m, Boris Morros; art d, Hans Dreier, Ernst Fegte; fx, Farciot Edouart; cos, Travis Banton

Easy watching. Arthur stars as poor office girl Mary Smith who, while riding on the top of a double-decker bus, is hit on the head with a fur coat flung off a penthouse terrace by angry Wall Street millionaire J.B. Ball (Arnold), who is arguing with his spoiled wife. Seeking to make his spouse jealous, Ball tracks down the girl, insists she keep the coat, and buys her a hat to match. Mary finally arrives at work and is fired due to her tardiness and suspicion over how she acquired the coat. Soon the news has spread on Wall Street that she is Ball's mistress, and dozens of hotels and shops flock to her, offering her anything she wishes. All she really wants is a cup of coffee, and she meets and falls for a waiter (Milland) who happens to be—Ball's son.

A great cast pushes this one-joke screwball comedy through to a happy finish. Nimbly scripted by an up-and-coming Preston Sturges and capably helmed by director Leisen, the film was yet another step upward for the effervescent Arthur as a star comedienne. Watch for a famous moment in the history of American comedy—the clients at an automat diving after free food.

EASY MONEY

1983 100m c   ★★
Comedy   R/15
Orion

Rodney Dangerfield (*Monty*), Joe Pesci (*Nicky*), Geraldine Fitzgerald (*Mrs. Monahan*), Candy Azzara (*Rose*), Val Avery (*Louie*), Tom Noonan (*Paddy*), Taylor Negron (*Julio*), Lili Haydn (*Belinda*), Jeffrey Jones (*Clive*), Tom Ewell (*Scrappleton*)

p, John Nicolella; d, James Signorelli; w, Rodney Dangerfield, Michael Endler, P.J. O'Rourke, Dennis Blair; ph, Fred Schuler (Technicolor); ed, Ronald Roose; m, Laurence Rosenthal; prod d, Eugene Lee; cos, Joseph Aulisi

Routine Dangerfield vehicle in which he plays an inept, slobbish baby photographer who must give up his bad habits if he wants to collect a $10 million inheritance from his snooty mother-in-law. Pesci plays the ringleader of the smoking, drinking, over-eating cronies that Dangerfield must resist. It's all an insult to the great Geraldine Fitzgerald, who must have wondered during filming if it had all come down to this. If you're not already a Dangerfield fan, remember he's an acquired taste—like Spam.

EASY RIDER

1969 94m c   ★★★★
Drama   R/18
Pando/Raybert

Peter Fonda (*Wyatt*), Dennis Hopper (*Billy*), Antonio Mendoza (*Jesus*), Phil Spector (*Connection*), Mac Mashourian (*Bodyguard*), Warren Finnerty (*Rancher*), Tita Colorado (*Rancher's Wife*), Luke Askew (*Stranger*), Luana Anders (*Lisa*), Sabrina Scharf (*Sarah*)

p, Peter Fonda; d, Dennis Hopper; w, Peter Fonda, Dennis Hopper, Terry Southern; ph, Laszlo Kovacs (Technicolor); ed, Donn Cambern; art d, Jerry Kay; fx, Steve Karkus

A must-see, if only once. More notable as a document of its times than as a piece of cinema, EASY RIDER is slack but powerful, sentimental yet scathing, experimental but predictable.

A tale of two men searching for a freedom they can never attain, the film features Fonda and Hopper as Wyatt and Billy, a pair of hippie bikers who journey to New Orleans, hoping to arrive in time for Mardi Gras. On the way, the duo encounter rebuffs at various motels because of their way-out appearance, a hitchhiker who takes them back to the sun-drenched revels of his commune, and a squeaky-clean Texas parade. Arrested for joining the latter, the pair meets up with drunken civil-rights lawyer George Hanson (Jack Nicholson, enjoying the film's most well-rounded part and giving its best performance, one which earned him an Oscar nomination and finally made him a star). Now a trio, the men suffer beatings from local rednecks, but Hanson also gets to enjoy his first joint, which prompts one of the film's most memorable moments—Hanson's tongue-in-cheek theory that Venusians have already landed on Earth and occupy several important posts. Billy and Wyatt finally make it to New Orleans and find that their journey to the freewheeling world of Fat Tuesday (including an LSD-laced jaunt to a cemetery) has not brought them any happiness or sense of direction. The animosity the pair have dealt with throughout reaches its peak at the film's famous ending, as the film attempts to martyr its quasi-religious antiheroes.

A finely observed film but insufficiently developed as a satire of middle America, EASY RIDER seemed the paragon of hip rebellion at the time of its release; in retrospect, its worldview seems closer to whining self-pity.

EAT A BOWL OF TEA

1990 102m c   ★★★½
Romance   PG-13/12
American Playhouse

Cora Miao (*Mei Oi*), Russell Wong (*Ben Loy*), Victor Wong (*Wah Gay*), Lee Sau Kee (*Bok Fat*), Eric Tsiang Chi Wai (*Ah Song*), Law Lan (*Aunt Gim*), Lau Siu Ming (*Lee Gong*)

p, Tom Sternberg; d, Wayne Wang; w, Judith Rascoe (based on the novel by Louis Chu); ph, Amir Mokri (Deluxe Color); ed, Richard Candib; m, Mark Adler; prod d, Bob Ziembicki; art d, Timmy Yip; cos, Marit Allen

This engaging comedy-drama set in New York's Chinatown examines an intriguing post-WWII American phenomenon: after years of strict immigration laws and forced separation of spouses, Chinese immigrants were finally able to bring their mates to the US. For longtime residents of Chinatown, it was too late to effect conjugal reunions, but many older Chinese-American men wanted their sons to provide them with grandchildren by finding brides in China.

Director Wang (CHAN IS MISSING, DIM SUM) and screenwriter Rascoe have fashioned a graceful movie powered by deliciously eccentric characters, bringing to the screen a slice of American life unfamiliar to many. Abounding in magical moments (like the scene in which the two young leads fall in love in front of an outdoor screen on which LOST HORIZON is playing), the film cleverly parallels the difficulties of adjusting to a foreign culture with those of adjusting to a new marriage. The result is both a perceptive historical document and a captivating love story.

EATING RAOUL

1982 90m c   ★★★
Comedy   R/18
Bartel

Mary Woronov (*Mary Bland*), Paul Bartel (*Paul Bland*), Robert Beltran (*Raoul*), Buck Henry (*Mr. Leech*), Richard Paul (*Mr. Kray*), Susan Saiger (*Doris, the Dominatrix*), Ed Begley, Jr. (*Hippy*), Dan Barrows (*Bobbie R.*), Dick Blackburn (*James*), Ralph Brannen (*Paco*)

p, Anne Kimmel; d, Paul Bartel; w, Paul Bartel, Richard Blackburn; ph, Gary Thieltges (Metrocolor); ed, Alan Toomayan; m, Arlon Ober; prod d, Robert Schulenberg

Bon appetit? This sometimes hilarious black comedy has gained quite a cult following over the years, and it remains writer-director-star Bartel's best effort yet. Set in Los Angeles, the story follows a straightlaced couple, Mary and Paul Bland (Bartel and the galvanizingly odd Woronov), who dream of someday opening their own gourmet restaurant. Since Mary is a nurse and Paul has just been fired from his job at a liquor store, realizing their dream soon seems unlikely. Fate knocks, however, when a drunken reveler stumbles into their apartment and begins mauling Mary. Paul kills the intruder and discovers a large wad of cash on the dead man. Inspired, the couple place an ad in a swingers' newspaper to lure victims into their home, where they will be killed for their money (something the ultra-conservative couple feels they deserve anyway).

With Bartel and Woronov giving wonderfully funny deadpan performances, EATING RAOUL is a terrifically droll satire on both horror movies and American middle-class values. Despite the subject matter, our hero and heroine emerge as genuinely sympathetic characters, which ultimately makes one wonder where the film's true sympathies lie. Working independently, Bartel scraped together financing from family and friends and shot the film in piecemeal fashion when he could afford it. The resulting film, despite its lulls, is probably the better for it. Beltran, in the title role, brings along some much-needed energy, so enjoy his performance. . . while it lasts.

ECSTASY

(EXTASE)
1933   82m   bw   ★★★
Drama   /18
Elekta   (Czechoslovakia)

Hedy Lamarr *(Eva)*, Zvonimir Rogoz *(Emile)*, Aribert Mog *(Adam)*, Leopold Kramer *(Eva's Father)*

p, Frantisek Horky, Moriz Grunhut; d, Gustav Machaty; w, Gustav Machaty, Frantisek Horky, Vitezslav Nezval, Jacques A. Koerpel; ph, Jan Stallich, Hans Androschin; m, Giuseppe Becce; art d, Bohumil Hes

A once-daring gander at nude pre-MGM Hedy Lamarr (then Hedy Kiesler). Promoted in its day as "the most whispered-about film in the world" (in fact, everyone was talking about it out loud, and L.B. Mayer was roaring) and the "stark naked truth of a woman's desire for love," it's tame stuff, even for the good old days.

Kiesler plays a child bride whose husband ignores her on her wedding night. In frustration, she has a sexual tryst in a hut with a roadway engineer. When her horse wanders away with her clothes as she takes a swim, Eva gives chase, bumping into the engineer who hands over her clothes like a gentleman. She arranges to go away with him but leaves him after her former husband commits suicide. She subsequently appears with a baby, the offspring of this illicit affair, happy and fulfilled.

The simple story is told with invention by director Gustav Machaty, who seems especially influenced by the editing techniques of Eisenstein. The big deal back then was really not the nudity but the close-ups of Hedy during her tryst. Machaty couldn't elicit the facial responses he wanted from the young actress, until he got under the table she lay on and started pricking her with a pin. The film was released in the US in 1940.

EDDY DUCHIN STORY, THE

1956   123m   c   ★★½
Biography/Musical   /U
Columbia

Tyrone Power *(Eddy Duchin)*, Kim Novak *(Marjorie Oelrichs)*, Victoria Shaw *(Chiquita)*, James Whitmore *(Lou Sherwood)*, Rex Thompson *(Peter Duchin as a Boy)*, Mickey Maga *(Peter as a Young Child)*, Shepperd Strudwick *(Mr. Wadsworth)*, Frieda Inescort *(Mrs. Wadsworth)*, Gloria Holden *(Mrs. Duchin)*, Larry Keating *(Leo Reisman)*

p, Jerry Wald; d, George Sidney; w, Samuel Taylor (based on a story by Leo Katcher); ph, Harry Stradling (Cinemascope, Technicolor); ed, Viola Lawrence, Jack Ogilvie; m, George Duning; art d, Walter Holscher; cos, Jean Louis

This long, glossy, flossy biopic chronicles the sad story of the title pianist and bandleader, once a favorite of New York's cafe society. Power seems overeager in the title role, but maybe that's because he's carrying the weight of bovine, manufactured Novak on his shoulders. Still, she's ethereally lovely, and the film profited from a publicity spread of Novak mooning around New York's streets at dawn.

You could almost make up the plot of this one yourself. Pianist's wife dies in childbirth, pianist tours world, tries to reconcile with son, marries son's nanny (Shaw playing a character named Chiquita!), then finds out he has fatal disease. At least one box of tissues is required. Carmen Cavallaro fills in the notes for Power, and James Whitmore plays one of those hail-fellow-well-met roles. Featuring almost 30 standards of Duchin's repertoire: "What Is This Thing Called Love?," "Till We Meet Again," "Manhattan," "The Man I Love," etc.

EDGE OF DARKNESS

1943   120m   bw   ★★★★
War   /PG
WB

Errol Flynn *(Gunnar Brogge)*, Ann Sheridan *(Karen Stensgard)*, Walter Huston *(Dr. Martin Stensgard)*, Nancy Coleman *(Katja)*, Helmut Dantine *(Capt. Koenig)*, Judith Anderson *(Gerd Blarnesen)*, Ruth Gordon *(Anna Stensgard)*, John Beal *(Johann Stensgard)*, Morris Carnovsky *(Sixtus Andresen)*, Charles Dingle *(Kaspar Torgerson)*

p, Henry Blanke; d, Lewis Milestone; w, Robert Rossen (based on the novel by William Woods); ph, Sid Hickox; ed, David Weisbart; m, Franz Waxman; art d, Robert Haas

Gripping war propaganda, swooning with stardust, talent, and originality. A WWII German patrol boat sails into a Norwegian port to discover that the whole German occupation force and the citizens of the town lie dead, apparently killed in a bloody battle that ended with the Norwegian flag flying over the invaders' garrison. In flashback, we see the events leading up to the slaughter.

Flynn stars as a Norwegian fisherman who leads the local underground movement with Sheridan, his brave and loyal fiancee; Anderson is a fiery innkeeper who becomes enraged when Nazis murder her husband; and Huston, Sheridan's father, is a highly respected doctor hesitant to join the resistance movement. His wife, Gordon, is a shy, frightened woman, and his son, Beal, a collaborator. All live under the baleful eye of Dantine, the brutal German captain determined to retain control of the town.

An insightful look at the workings of a resistance movement, EDGE OF DARKNESS calls to mind Renoir's picture THIS LAND IS MINE, released the same year. The great Morris Carnovsky, playing an aged schoolmaster, stands out, pitting legendary talent against Dantine's hammy acting.

EDISON, THE MAN

1940   104m   bw   ★★★½
Biography
MGM

Spencer Tracy *(Thomas Alva Edison)*, Rita Johnson *(Mary Stilwell)*, Lynne Overman *(Bunt Cavatt)*, Charles Coburn *(Gen. Powell)*, Gene Lockhart *(Mr. Taggart)*, Henry Travers *(Ben Els)*, Felix Bressart *(Michael Simon)*, Peter Godfrey *(Ashton)*, Frank Faylen *(Galbreath)*, Byron Foulger *(Edwin Hall)*

p, John W. Considine, Jr., Orville O. Dull; d, Clarence Brown; w, Talbot Jennings, Bradbury Foote (based on a story by Dore Schary and Hugo Butler); ph, Harold Rosson; ed, Frederick Y. Smith; m, Herbert Stothart; art d, Cedric Gibbons, John S. Detlie; cos, Dolly Tree, Gile Steele

A warm, watchable whitewash. MGM went all out for Thomas Alva Edison in 1940, producing two films on his life. YOUNG TOM EDISON was a box-office flop despite Mickey Rooney's energetic portrayal; EDISON, THE MAN was a much more lavish and popular production, with Tracy giving a dutiful but dynamic performance as the famous inventor. The film opens as Edison, at age 82, is about to be honored on the 50th anniversary of his invention of the incandescent light. He is being interviewed by two youths and begins to relate the story of his early manhood. It then goes into flashback and chronicles Edison's most productive years, from age 25 to 35, when he produced the phonograph, the dictaphone, and the electric light.

A little too old for the part, Tracy nevertheless immersed himself in the details of Edison's life, trying to capture the flavor of his personality as well as the words of the script. The result is a much more interesting performance than the one he gave in MGM's similar canonization of Father Flanagan in BOYS TOWN—energetic and committed, but not over-earnest. Tracy was ably backed up by a fine cast, particularly Rita Johnson, and directed with a sure feel for Americana by Clarence Brown. What's missing is a sense of the "difficult" side of his personality, which could have made this more of a well-rounded biography than a one-note song of tribute.

EDUCATING RITA

1983 110m c   ★★★
Drama   PG/15
Acorn (U.K.)

Michael Caine (Dr. Frank Bryant), Julie Walters (Rita), Michael Williams (Brian), Maureen Lipman (Trish), Jeananne Crowley (Julia), Malcolm Douglas (Denny), Godfrey Quigley (Rita's Father), Dearbhla Molloy (Elaine), Pat Daly (Bursar), Kim Fortune (Collins)

p, Lewis Gilbert; d, Lewis Gilbert; w, Willy Russell (based on his play); ph, Frank Watts (Technicolor); ed, Garth Craven; m, David Hentschel; art d, Maurice Fowler

Julie Walters plays Rita, a working-class hairdresser who signs on for adult education classes and chooses alcoholic hack Frank Bryant (Michael Caine) as her tutor. As Rita's intellectual horizons expand, she becomes torn between her stifling home life and the alluring, but pretentious, world of her amorous professor. Adapted by Willy Russell from his stage play, this is a poignant if predictable take on the English class system, buoyed by an effervescent performance from Walters (though Caine gets the best line: "Life is such a rich and frantic form that I need the drink to help me step delicately through it"). Caine, Walters, and Russell were all nominated for Academy Awards for their work.

EDWARD SCISSORHANDS

1990 100m c   ★★★½
Fantasy/Romance   PG-13/PG
FOX

Johnny Depp (Edward Scissorhands), Winona Ryder (Kim Boggs), Dianne Wiest (Peg Boggs), Anthony Michael Hall (Jim), Kathy Baker (Joyce), Robert Oliveri (Kevin), Conchata Ferrell (Helen), Caroline Aaron (Marge), Dick Anthony Williams (Officer Allen), O-Lan Jones (Esmeralda)

p, Tim Burton, Denise DiNovi; d, Tim Burton; w, Caroline Thompson, Tim Burton; ph, Stefan Czapsky; ed, Richard Halsey; m, Danny Elfman; prod d, Bo Welch; art d, Tom Duffield; fx, Stan Winston, Michael Wood; cos, Colleen Atwood

A poignant, personal fairy tale from the director of PEE-WEE'S BIG ADVENTURE, BEETLEJUICE and BATMAN.

Edward (Johnny Depp) is the creation of an inventor (Vincent Price) who dies before his work is completed, leaving his otherwise perfect progeny with pointed metal shards for hands. When Avon Lady Peg (Dianne Wiest) comes calling at Edward's Gothic castle one day, she takes a shine to the creature and persuades him to go back with her to the picture-perfect, pastel-colored suburb where she lives. The initially terrified Edward becomes an object of great curiosity among Peg's neighbors, and soon gains minor celebrity status with his unique talents for hedge trimming and hair styling. But Edward's newfound happiness is threatened when the suburban residents come to believe he is guilty of a crime.

Drawing upon influences that range from FRANKENSTEIN to BEING THERE, Burton creates a satire/allegory that is both funny and moving. The theme—that just beyond the edge of the perfectly normal lies the truly bizarre—is realized with intelligence and visual flair. In one particularly charming sequence, Edward creates a beautiful sculpture from a slab of ice, as Kim dances in the frozen flakes which rain down from his flying metallic fingers. Fine performances all around, particularly from Depp and the immensely sympathetic Wiest.

EFFECT OF GAMMA RAYS ON MAN-IN-THE-MOON MARIGOLDS, THE

1972 100m c   ★★★½
Drama   PG/AA
FOX

Joanne Woodward (Beatrice), Nell Potts (Matilda), Roberta Wallach (Ruth), Judith Lowry (Nanny Annie), Richard Venture (Floyd), Estelle Omens (Floyd's Wife), Carolyn Coates (Granny's Daughter), Will Hare (Junk Man), Jess Osuna (Sonny), David Spielberg (Mr. Goodman)

p, Paul Newman; d, Paul Newman; w, Alvin Sargent (based on the play by Paul Zindel); ph, Adam Holender (DeLuxe Color); ed, Evan Lottman; m, Maurice Jarre; prod d, Gene Callahan; cos, Anna Hill Johnstone

Joanne Woodward is superb in this film adaptation of Paul Zindel's Pulitzer Prize-winning play, directed for the screen by her husband, Paul Newman. Woodward plays an embittered and overbearing widow who is struggling to raise her two very different daughters, Ruth (Roberta Wallach, daughter of actors Eli Wallach and Anne Jackson) and Matilda (Nell Potts, Newman and Woodward's real-life daughter). Wallach is loud and outgoing, Potts withdrawn and shy. Woodward makes ends meet by boarding elderly people and making phone sales for a dance studio. She is spiteful and distrusting of all men, including Potts's science teacher (Spielberg), whom she accuses of endangering her child's life by exposing her to gamma rays in order to grow marigolds for a school project. The widow's bitter outlook on life and grim view of men slowly work their way into her daughters' consciousness, but the blooming marigolds become a symbol of hope for a less stunted life.

EFFI BRIEST

1974 140m bw   ★★★★
Drama   /U
Tango (West Germany)

Hanna Schygulla (Effi Briest), Wolfgang Schenck (Baron von Instetten), Ulli Lommel (Maj. Crampas), Lilo Pempeit (Frau Briest), Herbert Steinmetz (Herr Briest), Hark Bohm (Gieshuebler), Ursula Straetz (Roswitha), Irm Hermann (Johanna), Karl Scheydt (Kruse), Karl Boehm (Wuellersdorf)

d, Rainer Werner Fassbinder; w, Rainer Werner Fassbinder (based on the novel by Theodor Fontane); ph, Juergen Jurges, Dietrich Lohmann; ed, Thea Eymes; m, Camille Saint-Saens; art d, Kurt Raab; cos, Barbara Baum

One of the finest films to come out of postwar Germany, EFFI BRIEST marked the 16th feature in five years for the prolific Fassbinder. In 19th-century Germany, a 17-year-old girl (Schygulla) is forced into an unhappy marriage with a much older count (Schenck), and then falls into a short-lived relationship with an army major (Lommel). When, years after it has ended, the count discovers their affair, he kills the man in a duel and abandons his disgraced wife.

Schygulla, one of the finest actresses working in Germany today, carries the film with a truly astonishing performance, painting a moving picture of a woman exploited by everyone around her and powerless to fight back. Schygulla's professional relationship with Fassbinder—whose tyrannical working methods have been well documented—dissolved with this picture but, unlike most of the actors in the director's informal stock company, she went on to pursue a successful independent career. Schygulla would eventually work with Fassbinder again, in THE MARRIAGE OF MARIA BRAUN, BERLIN AL-EXANDERPLATZ (a 15-hour miniseries for German television), and LILI MARLEEN.

EGG AND I, THE

1947   108m   bw   ★★★½
Comedy   /U
Universal

Claudette Colbert *(Betty MacDonald)*, Fred MacMurray *(Bob Mac-Donald)*, Marjorie Main *(Ma Kettle)*, Louise Allbritton *(Harriet Putnam)*, Percy Kilbride *(Pa Kettle)*, Richard Long *(Tom Kettle)*, Billy House *(Billy Reed)*, Ida Moore *(Old Lady)*, Donald MacBride *(Mr. Henty)*, Samuel S. Hinds *(Sheriff)*

p, Chester Erskine, Fred Finklehoffe; d, Chester Erskine; w, Chester Erskine (based on the novel by Betty MacDonald); ph, Milton Krasner; ed, Russell Schoengarth; m, Frank Skinner; prod d, Bernard Herzbrun

Amusing if slightly bland comedy in which Colbert and MacMurray uproot themselves from city living after MacMurray decides he can't stand the brokerage business. They buy a ramshackle farm, intending to raise chickens and live a leisurely rural existence. Instead, they face one problem after another, watching their bank account dwindle as Kilbride, the most unhandy handyman on record, fritters away their hard-earned dollars on building and landscaping materials. Complications develop when MacMurray becomes fascinated with the mechanized farm owned by Allbritton, a wealthy widow who tries to court him away from Colbert.

THE EGG AND I has many a laugh-filled scene—Colbert attempting to carry water in a bottomless bucket, MacMurray beaming with pride as he chops down a bothersome tree which crashes onto the roof of the henhouse—and was a success at the box office, bringing in $5.5 million. Colbert is suitably arch as the cultured, city-bred lady trying to cope with rural life, and MacMurray deftly deadpans his way through one disaster after another. This was the first appearance of Kilbride and Main as Ma and Pa Kettle and they would continue playing these lovable hick roles through a very successful series.

8½

(OTTO E MEZZO)
1963   140m   bw   ★★★★★
Drama   /15
Cineriz/Francinex   (Italy)

Marcello Mastroianni *(Guido Anselmi)*, Claudia Cardinale *(Claudia)*, Anouk Aimee *(Luisa Anselmi)*, Sandra Milo *(Carla)*, Rossella Falk *(Rossella)*, Barbara Steele *(Gloria Morin)*, Mario Pisu *(Mezzabotta)*, Guido Alberti *(Producer)*, Madeleine LeBeau *(French Actress)*, Jean Rougeul *(Writer)*

p, Angelo Rizzoli; d, Federico Fellini; w, Federico Fellini, Tullio Pinelli, Ennio Flaiano, Brunello Rondi (based on a story by Federico Fellini and Ennio Flaiano); ph, Gianni Di Venanzo; ed, Leo Catozzo; m, Nino Rota; art d, Piero Gherardi; cos, Piero Gherardi

After having directed six feature films, co-directed one (THE WHITE SHEIK), and directed two short episodes of anthology movies, Federico Fellini had made, according to his count, seven and a half films—hence the title of this brilliant, sumptuous semi-autobiographical account of the creative process.

Marcello Mastroianni plays Fellini-like figure Guido Anselmi, a director coming off a big hit. He needs rest and goes to a spa to regain his strength. He cannot recuperate, however, being interrupted instead by his producer (Guido Alberti), his screenwriter (Jean Rougeul), his wife (Anouk Aimee), and his mistress (Sandra Milo), all of whom want details from the director about his new sci-fi film. Hundreds of people are waiting in the wings, but Guido finds himself creatively blocked and fends off the inquiries of his actors, reporters, and especially his persistent screenwriter, in between lapsing into fantasy visions of past, present, and future.

8½ is a grab-bag of Felliniesque delights, with stunning photography by Di Venanzo, superb performances, a haunting score from Nino Rota, and a labyrinthine structure that keeps the viewer in a pleasurable state of confusion. It received an Academy Award for Best Foreign-Language Film.

EIGHT MEN OUT

1988   119m   c   ★★★
Sports/Drama   PG
Orion

Jace Alexander *(Dickie Kerr)*, John Cusack *(Buck Weaver)*, Gordon Clapp *(Ray Schalk)*, Don Harvey *(Swede Risberg)*, Bill Irwin *(Eddie Collins)*, Perry Lang *(Fred McMullin)*, John Mahoney *(Kid Gleason)*, James Read *(Lefty Williams)*, Michael Rooker *(Chick Gandil)*, Charlie Sheen *(Hap Felsch)*

p, Sarah Pillsbury, Midge Sanford; d, John Sayles; w, John Sayles (based on the book by Eliot Asinof); ph, Robert Richardson (Duart Color); ed, John Tintori; m, Mason Daring; prod d, Nora Chavooshian; cos, Cynthia Flynt

Gripping account of the 1919 "Black Sox" baseball scandal, when eight members of the Chicago White Sox were accused of "fixing" the World Series. Working from one-time Philadelphia Phillies farmhand Asinof's assiduously researched book, writer-director Sayles has fashioned a convincing account of the scandal, underlaid with an unconventional (by Hollywood standards) workers-vs.-owners critique.

Sayles not only depicts the circumstances that led to the fix (most notably Sox owner Charles Comiskey's legendary tightfistedness), but he also re-creates the games in great detail, making the best possible use of an athletic cast tutored by former White Sox outfielder Ken Berry. Among the players Sayles concentrates on are: pitcher Eddie Cicotte (David Strathairn); third baseman Buck Weaver (Cusack), who spent the rest of his life protesting his innocence; and the legendary "Shoeless" Joe Jackson (D.B. Sweeney, whose own baseball career was ended by a motorcycle accident and who spent five weeks with the minor-league Kenosha Twins learning to bat left-handed for the role). The fine ensemble cast also includes Chicago journalist Studs Terkel, as sportswriter Hugh Fullerton, and Sayles himself, as Ring Lardner.

84 CHARING CROSS ROAD

1987 97m c   ★★★
Drama   PG/U
Brooksfilms

Anne Bancroft (Helene Hanff), Anthony Hopkins (Frank Doel), Judi Dench (Nora Doel), Jean De Baer (Maxine Bellamy), Maurice Denham (George Martin), Eleanor David (Cecily Farr), Mercedes Ruehl (Kay), Daniel Gerroll (Brian), Wendy Morgan (Megan Wells), Ian McNeice (Bill Humphries)

p, Geoffrey Helman; d, David Jones; w, Hugh Whitemore (based on the book by Helene Hanff); ph, Brian West (Rank/TVC Color); ed, Christopher Wimble; m, George Fenton; prod d, Eileen Diss, Edward Pisoni; cos, Jane Greenwood, Lindy Hemming

Charming, understated story of a love affair between two people who never meet. The "affair" begins in 1949 when Helene Hanff (Anne Bancroft), a struggling New York writer with a love of fine old books, responds to an ad placed by an antiquarian bookshop at 84 Charing Cross Road in London. Her letter is answered by Frank Doel (Anthony Hopkins), who runs the overseas department of the store, beginning a 20-year correspondence between the assertive, sometimes acerbic spinster and the dry, reserved man with two children, a plain wife, and a sparse home. Though literate and intelligent, CHARING CROSS ROAD never shakes free of its origins as a stage adaptation of Helene Hanff's novel; clearly, the subject matter is more suited to the page, or the stage, than the screen. Fine performances and a generous measure of humor still make this an absorbing drama.

84 CHARLIE MOPIC

1989 95m c   ★★★½
War   R/18
Charlie Mopic

Jonathan Emerson (LT), Nicholas Cascone (Easy), Jason Tomlins (Pretty Boy), Christopher Burgard (Hammer), Glenn Morshower (Cracker), Richard Brooks (OD), Byron Thames (Mopic), Russ Thurman, Joseph Hieu, Don Schiff

p, Michael Nolin, Jill Griffith; d, Patrick Duncan; w, Patrick Duncan; ph, Alan Caso (Duart Color); ed, Stephen Purvis; m, Donovan; art d, Douglas Dick; cos, Lyn Paolo

Shot entirely in hand-held documentary style (an experiment tried before in the Vietnam segment of MORE AMERICAN GRAFFITI), 84 CHARLIE MOPIC follows a close-knit group of soldiers led by a taciturn black sergeant (Richard Brooks) as they "hump" through the brush in the Central Highlands of Viet Nam. On the relatively miniscule budget of $1 million, writer-director Patrick Duncan, a Vietnam veteran who served as an infantryman for 13 months during 1968-69, shot this film in the hills outside Los Angeles using Super 16mm film stock, which was later blown up to 35mm for theatrical release. The gimmick here—an entire movie seen through the eyes of an Army cameraman—works better than it has any right to, largely because

Duncan creates a viable, realistic situation for its use. This method is fraught with peril for both director and actors, but when it works the sense of realism lends an air of spontaneity and excitement to familiar material. While some may find the first half of the film boring, 84 CHARLIE MOPIC presents a fascinating and detailed account of what common infantrymen faced on a daily basis.

EL

1952 100m bw   ★★★★
Drama   /A
Tepeyac (Mexico)

Arturo de Cordova (Francisco), Delia Garces (Gloria), Luis Beristain (Raoul), Manuel Donde (Pablo), Carlos Martinez Baena (Padre Velasco), Fernando Casanova (Beltran), Aurora Walker (Mother), Rafael Banquells (Ricardo)

p, Oscar Dancigers; d, Luis Bunuel; w, Luis Bunuel, Luis Alcoriza (based on the novel Pensamientos by Mercedes Pinto); ph, Gabriel Figueroa; ed, Carlos Savage; m, Luis Hernandez Breton

Bunuel's fascinating study of a married man's obsession with his wife's virtue. Middle-aged, church-going Francisco (de Cordova) has abstained from sex his entire life. One day, while helping the local priest wash the feet of parishioners, he notices the delicate feet of a woman and looks up to see the hauntingly beautiful Gloria (Garces), of whom he is instantly enamored. He lures Gloria away from her architect lover and they marry, but on their wedding night Francisco reveals a jealous nature of obsessional proportions. In what is far from the film's most deranged moment, he pokes a knitting-needle through the keyhole of the bedroom door, convinced that his wife's ex-lover is spying on them.

EL is a compelling indictment of religious repression and sexual obsession. By pushing the macho concern with female chastity to an absurd extreme, Bunuel reveals its inherently ridiculous nature. The film is one of the best from the director's Mexican period, though, like others from that time, its production values leave something to be desired.

EL AMOR BRUJO

1986 100m c   ★★★
Dance   PG
Emiliano Piedra (Spain)

Antonio Gades (Carmelo), Christina Hoyos (Candela), Laura Del Sol (Lucia), Juan Antonio Jimenez (Jose), Emma Penella (Aunt Rosario), La Polaca (Pastora), Gomez de Jerez (El Lobo), Enrique Ortega (Jose's Father), Diego Pantoja (Candela's Father), Giovana (Rocio)

p, Emiliano Piedra; d, Carlos Saura; w, Carlos Saura, Antonio Gades (based on the ballet by Manuel de Falla); ph, Teo Escamilla (Eastmancolor); ed, Pedro del Rey; m, Manuel de Falla; fx, Basilio Cortijo; chor, Carlos Saura, Antonio Gades; cos, Gararado Vera

EL AMOR BRUJO is the third entry in Spanish director Saura's flamenco dance trilogy, preceded in 1981 by BLOOD WEDDING and in 1983 by CARMEN. This time Saura and his choreographer, Gades, have turned to the Manuel de Falla opera for their source of inspiration.

Using much of the cast from CARMEN—Del Sol has here been relegated to a supporting role, and Hoyos has been given the lead—Saura has set the film on an exotically colored and stylishly designed studio set of a Madrid shantytown. Jimenez and Hoyos are gypsies who have been betrothed since childhood—when their fathers, having drunk too much wine, confirmed the arrangement. Early in the film a splendid wedding takes place, but we learn that each partner has another love interest. Gades admires Hoyos from a distance, while Jimenez is having an affair with the gorgeous Del Sol.

Following the critical and commercial success of CARMEN, which became one of Spain's highest-grossing pictures and received an Academy Award nomination as Best Foreign Film, EL AMOR BRUJO has been considerably less appreciated by critics and audiences alike, perhaps because the general audience is more familiar with Bizet's *Carmen* than with de Falla's *El Amor Brujo*. BRUJO is somewhat more stylized that its two predecessors, with some wonderfully fluid camera moves to highlight the cinematography. The dancing is equally astounding and, according to some enthusiasts, benefits from Hoyos' having taken over the lead from Del Sol.

EL CID
1961   180m   c   ★★★
Biography/War   /U
Bronston/Rank   (U.S./Italy)

Sophia Loren *(Chimene)*, Charlton Heston *(Rodrigo Diaz de Bivar/El Cid)*, John Fraser *(King Alfonso)*, Raf Vallone *(Count Ordonez)*, Genevieve Page *(Queen Urraca)*, Gary Raymond *(King Sancho)*, Herbert Lom *(Ben Yussef)*, Massimo Serato *(Fanez)*, Douglas Wilmer *(Moutamin)*, Frank Thring *(Al Kadir)*

p, Samuel Bronston, Anthony Mann; d, Anthony Mann; w, Philip Yordan, Fredric M. Frank; ph, Robert Krasker (Super Technirama, Technicolor); ed, Robert Lawrence; m, Miklos Rozsa; prod d, Veniero Colasanti, John Moore; fx, Alex Weldon, Jack Erickson; cos, Veniero Colasanti, John Moore

Director Anthony Mann's first and finest venture into big-budget epic terrain, with Charlton Heston as the 11-century Spanish leader.

EL CID becomes estranged from his fiancee, Chimene (Sophia Loren), after he kills her father (Andrew Cruickshank), who has unjustly accused him of treason. El Cid and Chimene are married but never enjoy a wedding night; she plots against him and, when her intrigues come to naught, enters a convent. Upon the death of King Ferdinand (Ralph Truman), Spain, which is continually besieged by the Islamic Moors, is further divided by the deceased ruler's warring offspring. Meanwhile, Chimene realizes that her husband is an honorable man and they reconcile, eventually having children. The family retreats to a monastery while El Cid lays siege to Valencia, the last outpost of the Moorish usurpers.

Eleventh-century Spain has been lavishly recreated by Mann and producer Samuel Bronston. The photography by Robert Krasker is spectacular, as are the battle scenes, filmed with the help of veteran stuntman Yakima Canutt as second-unit director. Canutt staged the siege of Valencia brilliantly, employing the ancient walled city of Pensacola, 5,000 Spanish army troops, and a Moorish battle fleet of 35 lifesize reconstructed ships. What gets lost is Mann's signature focus on psychological conflict. The sheer size of the production dwarfs such issues, and Heston is far better at conveying righteous authority than moral doubt.

EL DORADO
1967   125m   c   ★★★½
Western   /U
Paramount

John Wayne *(Cole Thornton)*, Robert Mitchum *(J.P. Harrah)*, James Caan *(Alan "Mississippi" Bourdillon Traherne)*, Charlene

Holt *(Maudie)*, Michele Carey *(Joey MacDonald)*, Arthur Hunnicutt *(Bull Harris)*, R.G. Armstrong *(Kevin MacDonald)*, Edward Asner *(Bart Jason)*, Paul Fix *(Doc Miller)*, Christopher George *(Nelse McLeod)*

p, Howard Hawks; d, Howard Hawks; w, Leigh Brackett (based on the novel *The Stars in Their Courses* by Harry Brown); ph, Harold Rosson (Technicolor); ed, John Woodcock; m, Nelson Riddle; art d, Carl Anderson, Hal Pereira, Carl Anderson; fx, Paul K. Lerpae; cos, Edith Head

Sly, leisurely-paced western from Howard Hawks, with a script by Leigh Brackett ensuring a few laughs. EL DORADO addresses the standard Hawks themes of group loyalty and professionalism, but is also a poignant meditation on the passing of the old and the coming of the new.

Wayne plays an aging, wounded gunfighter and Mitchum a drunken sheriff; with the help of "Mississippi" (Caan) and Bull Harris (Hunnicutt), they take on ruthless cattle baron Bart Jason (Asner), who is using extortion to gain water rights to some land. The finale sees an attack on the bad guys by a crippled quartet of Mitchum (on crutches), Wayne (partially paralyzed and unable to shoot a revolver), Caan (wounded in the head), and Hunnicutt (armed with a bow and arrow). DORADO forms part of a loose trilogy with RIO BRAVO and RIO LOBO, also scripted by Brackett.

EL NORTE
1983   139m   c   ★★★★
Drama   R/15
Independent Productions

Zaide Silvia Gutierrez *(Rosa Xuncax)*, David Villalpando *(Enrique Xuncax)*, Ernesto Gomez Cruz *(Arturo Xuncax)*, Alicia Del Lago *(Lupe Xuncax)*, Eraclio Zepeda *(Pedro)*, Stella Quan *(Josefita)*, Rodrigo Puebla *(Puma)*, Trinidad Silva *(Monty)*, Abel Franco *(Raimundo)*, Mike Gomez *(Jaime)*

p, Anna Thomas; d, Gregory Nava; w, Anna Thomas, Gregory Nava; ph, James Glennon; ed, Betsy Blankett; m, Gustav Mahler, Samuel Barber, Giuseppe Verdi, The Folkloristas, Melecio Martinez, Emil Richards, Linda O'Brien

A Spanish-language American film produced independently in association with the PBS TV series "American Playhouse," EL NORTE is an effective and moving drama about the strength of the human spirit and the will to survive. Brother and sister Enrique and Rosa Xuncax (David Villalpando and Zaide Silvia Gutierrez) are Guatemalan Indians forced to flee their village when their politically active father is murdered. They decide to make a new life in *el Norte* ("the North," i.e. the US) but, as difficult and demeaning as the illegal trek across the border is, it is not nearly so rough as the struggle to make a living in Los Angeles. EL NORTE's style alternates between straightforward, almost documentary-like exposition and surreal sequences that take place in the characters' dreams. The film has a political message, but it is a subtle and compelling one that allows situations and characters to speak for themselves.

ELECTRIC HORSEMAN, THE
1979   120m   c   ★★½
Western/Comedy   PG
Columbia

Robert Redford *(Sonny Steele)*, Jane Fonda *(Hallie Martin)*, Valerie Perrine *(Charlotta)*, Willie Nelson *(Wendell)*, John Saxon *(Hunt Sears)*, Nicolas Coster *(Fitzgerald)*, Allan Arbus *(Danny)*, Wilford Brimley *(Farmer)*, Will Hare *(Gus)*, Basil Hoffman *(Toland)*

p, Ray Stark; d, Sydney Pollack; w, Robert Garland, Paul Gaer (based on a story by Shelly Burton); ph, Owen Roizman (Panavision, Technicolor); ed, Sheldon Kahn; m, Dave Grusin; prod d, Stephen Grimes; art d, J. Dennis Washington; fx, Augie Lohman; cos, Bernie Pollack

Mildly funny comedy-western that owes a lot to LONELY ARE THE BRAVE in its concept of an anachronistic cowboy.

Redford is a has-been rodeo star reduced to plugging breakfast cereals; his next big appearance is in a tacky Vegas stage revue, wearing a neon suit and riding a $12 million horse. The last straw comes when he discovers his horse is being tranquilized, and he takes off into the wild in protest. Fonda plays a media-hype reporter who covers the story and ends up—predictably and sentimentally—falling for the displaced hero. The third teaming of Redford and Fonda (after THE CHASE and BAREFOOT IN THE PARK), HORSEMAN falls far short of what it might have been, starting out smart but getting sloppier and more sentimental as it goes along.

ELENI

1985 114m c   ★★½
Drama/War   PG
CBS

Kate Nelligan (*Eleni*), John Malkovich (*Nick*), Linda Hunt (*Katina*), Oliver Cotton (*Katis*), Ronald Pickup (*Spiro*), Rosalie Crutchley (*Grandmother*), Glenne Headly (*Joan*), Dimitra Arliss (*Ana*), Steve Plytas (*Christos*), Peter Woodthorpe (*Grandfather*)

p, Nick Vanoff, Mark Pick, Nicholas Gage; d, Peter Yates; w, Steve Tesich (based on the book by Gage); ph, Billy Williams; ed, Ray Lovejoy; m, Bruce Smeaton; prod d, Roy Walker; art d, Steve Spence, Fernando Gonzalez; cos, Tom Rand

Based on Nicholas Gage's much-respected, best-selling nonfiction book, ELENI follows journalist Gage (John Malkovich) as he uses his assignment as the head of the *New York Times*'s Athens bureau to investigate his mother's execution during the Greek Civil War. Alternating between Gage's present-day pursuit of the facts, and flashback re-creation of the turmoil that gripped his village during the war, the film slowly exposes the truth about the death of his mother, Eleni (Kate Nelligan).

Though some critics felt Peter Yates's film failed to convey the intensity of Gage's book, ELENI is nonetheless intriguing, carefully paced, and not without its moments of high drama. Malkovich, Nelligan and Linda Hunt all turn in fine performances.

ELEPHANT MAN, THE

1980 125m bw   ★★★★
Biography   PG
Paramount (U.K.)

Anthony Hopkins (*Dr. Frederick Treves*), John Hurt (*John Merrick*), Anne Bancroft (*Mrs. Kendal*), John Gielgud (*Carr Gomm*), Wendy Hiller (*Mothershead*), Freddie Jones (*Bytes*), Michael Elphick (*Night Porter*), Hannah Gordon (*Mrs. Treves*), Helen Ryan (*Princess Alex*), John Standing (*Fox*)

p, Jonathan Sanger; d, David Lynch; w, Christopher DeVore, Eric Bergren, David Lynch (based on *The Elephant Man, A Study in Human Dignity* by Ashley Montagu and *The Elephant Man and Other Reminiscences* by Sir Frederick Treves); ph, Freddie Francis (Panavision); ed, Anne V. Coates; m, John Morris, Samuel Barber; prod d, Stuart Craig; art d, Robert Cartwright; cos, Patricia Norris

THE ELEPHANT MAN features an Academy Award-nominated performance by John Hurt as John Merrick, the victim of a disease that has left him so grotesquely deformed, he's spent most of his life as a carnival-show freak. In time, Merrick comes under the care of Dr. Treves (brilliantly played by Anthony Hopkins), who installs the "Elephant Man" in a hospital, where he studies him, helps him to overcome a seemingly insurmountable speech impediment, and—for a time—gives him back some human dignity. As word gets out about Merrick's existence and the press once again turns him into a freak, the film raises the question of Treves's motivation: has he helped Merrick out of decency, in the name of medical science, or to enhance his own reputation?

A moving, faithful retelling of a bizarre true story, THE ELEPHANT MAN was nominated for eight Oscars (though it won none), including a Best Direction nod for David Lynch. The black-and-white cinematography of Freddie Francis wonderfully evokes 19th-century England and Hurt gives a tour de force performance, masterfully conveying emotions while unable to use his face or even much of his voice.

ELMER GANTRY

1960 146m c   ★★★★
Drama   /PG
UA

Burt Lancaster (*Elmer Gantry*), Jean Simmons (*Sister Sharon Falconer*), Arthur Kennedy (*Jim Lefferts*), Shirley Jones (*Lulu Bains*), Dean Jagger (*William L. Morgan*), Patti Page (*Sister Rachel*), Edward Andrews (*George Babbitt*), John McIntire (*Rev. Pengilly*), Joe Maross (*Pete*), Everett Glass (*Rev. Brown*)

p, Bernard Smith; d, Richard Brooks; w, Richard Brooks (based on the novel by Sinclair Lewis); ph, John Alton; ed, Marjorie Fowler; m, Andre Previn; cos, Dorothy Jenkins

Lancaster pulls out all the stops in one of his most memorable roles as the lustful, ambitious charlatan of Sinclair Lewis's powerful novel. Elmer Gantry (Lancaster) first appears on the screen, roaring drunk, trying to mooch drinks while selling his own distinctive take on scripture with his remarkable gift of gab. He encounters evangelist Sister Sharon Falconer (Simmons)—a role no doubt intended by Lewis to suggest Aimee Semple McPherson. Gantry appeals to her vanity and joins her entourage. Together they become rich and famous enough for Sister Falconer to build her own huge seaside temple. She falls in love with Gantry who loves life and every woman he meets; he had once been with a preacher's daughter, Lulu Baines (Shirley Jones, in a standout, Oscar-winning performance), now a prostitute hungry for revenge.

Writer-director Brooks made a few revisions in the novel's story. Gantry is no longer the ordained minister fallen from grace as depicted in the novel but now a traveling salesman for the Lord. Kennedy as Jim Lefferts, his empathic friend, is transformed from another seminary dropout in the novel into a cynical, savvy newsman in the H.L. Mencken tradition. Nonetheless the integrity of the characterizations is maintained in a script that is both literate and ironic. Brooks later sarcastically commented that "ELMER GANTRY is the story of a man who wants what everyone is supposed to want—money, sex, and religion. He's the All-American boy."

ELVIRA MADIGAN

1967 90m c   ★★★
Romance   PG/A
Europa/Janco (Sweden)

Pia Degermark *(Elvira)*, Thommy Berggren *(Sixten Sparre)*, Lennart Malmer *(Friend)*, Nina Widerberg *(Little Girl)*, Cleo Jensen *(Cook)*

d, Bo Widerberg; w, Bo Widerberg (based on a ballad by Johan Lindstrom Saxon); ph, Jorgen Persson; ed, Bo Widerberg; m, Ulf Bjorlin, Wolfgang Amadeus Mozart, Antonio Vivaldi

In 19th-century Sweden, a tightrope performer (Pia Degermark) and an army lieutenant (Thommy Berggren) give up their previous lives—he leaves his wife and children, and she deserts the circus troupe of which she is the top attraction—to find a new freedom for themselves. Their romance appears perfect, but, as the story progresses, they realize that their idyllic state cannot continue. . . .

This was a very popular film at the time and—whatever else it did—made Mozart acceptable for the world's teenagers. It's a rather silly love story of two adolescents, but prettily photographed and, although we don't like to admit it, even grownups occasionally like to watch this sort of jejeune adolescent romantic fantasy. Those were legitimate feelings when we were 15, and there's nothing wrong with reliving them for an hour or two. A decade later a whole genre was spawned on this model—THE BLUE LAGOON for example—bringing the level down to proto-kiddy-porn.

Sixteen-year-old Degermark was named Best Actress at the Cannes Film Festival for her performance as the title character. Additional music by Mozart and Vivaldi is ideally suited to the film.

EMERALD FOREST, THE
1985 113m c   ★★★★
Adventure   R/15
Christel   (U.K.)

Powers Boothe *(Bill Markham)*, Meg Foster *(Jean Markham)*, William Rodriquez *(Young Tommy)*, Yara Vaneau *(Young Heather)*, Estee Chandler *(Heather)*, Charley Boorman *(Tomme)*, Dira Paes *(Kachiri)*, Eduardo Conde *(Uwe Werner)*, Ariel Coelho *(Padre Leduc)*, Peter Marinker *(Perreira)*

p, John Boorman, Michael Dryhurst; d, John Boorman; w, Rospo Pallenberg; ph, Philippe Rousselot (Panavision, Technicolor); ed, Ian Crafford; m, Junior Homrich, Brian Gascoigne; prod d, Simon Holland; art d, Marcos Flacksman, Terry Pritchard; fx, Raph Salis; chor, Jose Possi; cos, Christel Boorman, Clovis Bueno

In October 1972 an account written by Leonard Greenwood appeared in the *Los Angeles Times*. It told of a Peruvian engineer whose son had been kidnapped by a band of Indians and of the man's successful search to locate the child. Screenwriter Rospo Pallenberg saw the news item and took it to producer-director John Boorman. The result was this amazing, beautiful and sometimes fanciful film. Powers Boothe is Bill Markham, a US engineer working on a dam project in Brazil where he lives with his wife, Jean (Meg Foster), and his small children. One day while the family is picnicking at the edge of the rain forest, some painted Indians swiftly and silently kidnap young Tommy (William Rodriquez). The only clue left is an arrow stuck in a tree, and Boothe uses it in his ten-year search for his son.

The film is a powerful meditation on the clash between two civilizations. Charley Boorman (the director's son) is outstanding as the grown Tomme and Boothe also gives a powerful performance. The film has many opportunities to tip over into the ludicrous and become a parody of traditional jungle action pictures. But director Boorman keeps matters on an even keel, deftly balancing the mystical elements with reality to produce a memorable film that is enthralling throughout and never heavy-handed.

EMIGRANTS, THE
(UTVANDRARNA)
1972 151m c   ★★★★
Drama   PG/AA
Svensk   (Sweden)

Max von Sydow *(Karl Oskar)*, Liv Ullmann *(Kristina)*, Eddie Axberg *(Robert)*, Svenolof Bern *(Nils)*, Aina Alfredsson *(Marta)*, Allan Edwall *(Danjel)*, Monica Zetterlund *(Ulrika)*, Pierre Lindstedt *(Arvid)*, Hans Alfredson *(Jonas Petter)*, Ulla Smidje *(Danjel's Wife)*

p, Bengt Forslund; d, Jan Troell; w, Jan Troell, Bengt Forslund (based on the novels of Vilhelm Moberg); ph, Jan Troell (Technicolor); ed, Jan Troell; m, Erik Nordgren; art d, P.A. Lundgren, Berndt Fritiof; cos, Ulla-Britt Soderlund

An engaging, well-crafted film about a group of Swedish peasants who migrate to America in the mid-19th century. One of the best films to show the tribulations, bravery and faith of the people who helped build this country. The film is split into three parts: the departure from Sweden, the voyage over and the journey to Minnesota. The acting is superb by all cast members, but some might be put off by the film's length. The tone is lyrical, and the photography (by director Troell) gives an added dimension. Nominated by the Academy for Best Foreign Film of 1971, it also earned nominations for Best Picture, Best Actress, Best Direction and Best Screenplay in 1972. The sequel is THE NEW LAND.

EMMANUELLE
1974 105m c   ★★½
Drama   R/18
Trinacre/Orphee   (France)

Sylvia Kristel *(Emmanuelle)*, Alain Cuny *(Marco)*, Daniel Sarky *(Jean)*, Jeanne Colletin *(Ariane)*, Marika Green *(Bee)*, Christine Boisson *(Marie-Ange)*

p, Yves Rousset-Rouard; d, Just Jaeckin; w, Jean-Louis Richard (based on the book by Emmanuelle Arsan); ph, Richard Suzuki; ed, Claudine Bouche

One of the classics of soft-core erotic cinema, EMMANUELLE stars Sylvia Kristel as the title creature, the pretty wife of a French ambassador in Bangkok. It's not long before Emmanuelle discovers a burning sexual passion she has heretofore repressed. With the help of an attractive young teenager, Emmanuelle is exposed (literally) to the joys of eroticism. Although the film takes itself far too seriously and engages in much of the usual naughty Victoriana, it is a relatively well-made picture that became an international hit because of its appeal to both men and women. Many sequels followed, with Mia Nygren taking over the lead in 1984's EMMANUELLE 4. The Kristel-Nygren EMMANUELLE series (spelled with two "m"s) should not be confused with Laura Gemser's EMANUELLE (with one "m") films.

EMPEROR JONES, THE
1933 80m bw   ★★★★
Drama   /18
Krimsky/Cochran

Paul Robeson *(Brutus Jones)*, Dudley Digges *(Smithers)*, Frank C. Wilson *(Jeff)*, Fredi Washington *(Undine)*, Ruby Elzy *(Dolly)*, George Haymid Stamper *(Lem)*, Jackie Mayble *(Marcella)*, Blueboy O'Connor (Treasurer), Brandon Evans (Carrington), Taylor Gordon (Stick-Man)

p, John Krimsky, Gifford Cochran; d, Dudley Murphy; w, DuBose Heyward (based on the play by Eugene O'Neill); ph, Ernest Haller; m, Rosamond Johnson; art d, Herman Rosse

This fascinating—if rather stiff—production of the brooding Eugene O'Neill play showcases Paul Robeson as Brutus Jones, his most forceful and memorable film role.

Jones, a newly hired railroad porter, is first shown admiring himself before a mirror in his new uniform. His rich baritone voice makes him stand out as he booms out a moving hymn in church. Jones is clearly a man who thinks very highly of himself. This false pride proves to be his undoing. He goes on to cheat on his fiancee and fool around with his best friend's girlfriend. He deserts her and later enters a crap game where he stabs his friend to death. He gets sentenced to a chain gang for life.

He escapes and eventually ends up in Haiti where he meets Smithers (Dudley Digges), an unscrupulous trader who uses Jones to keep the natives in line. Jones is so feared by the natives, whom he has fooled into believing that he is immortal, that he becomes rich as Smithers's partner. In a short time, he unseats the native king and declares himself emperor, ruling the land with an iron fist.

Robeson is the main attraction here and he is well supported by the sleazy Digges (the only white actor in an otherwise all-black cast). Robeson's powerful presence, particularly through his wonderful, mellifluous voice, dominates each scene. There was never any doubt about Robeson playing the role of the vainglorious Jones; a distinguished athlete and Columbia Law School graduate, he deferred his entry into the New York bar when O'Neill himself persuaded Robeson to star in a production of *The Emperor Jones*.

EMPIRE OF THE SUN
1987 152m c ★★★★½
War PG
Amblin

Christian Bale (Jim Graham), John Malkovich (Basie), Miranda Richardson (Mrs. Victor), Nigel Havers (Dr. Rawlins), Joe Pantoliano (Frank Demerest), Leslie Phillips (Maxton), Masato Ibu (Sgt. Nagata), Emily Richard (Jim's Mother), Rupert Frazer (Jim's Father), Peter Gale (Mr. Victor)

p, Steven Spielberg, Kathleen Kennedy, Frank Marshall; d, Steven Spielberg; w, Menno Meyjes (uncredited), Tom Stoppard (based on the novel by J.G. Ballard); ph, Allen Daviau (Technicolor); ed, Michael Kahn; m, John Williams; prod d, Norman Reynolds; art d, Charles Bishop, Fred Hole, Maurice Fowler, Huang Qia Gui, Norman Dorme; fx, Kit West, David Watkins, Ye Mao Gen, Antonio Parra, Industrial Light & Magic

This adaptation of J.G. Ballard's quasi-autobiographical novel witnesses WWII through a child's eyes, and does so through a visual means more akin to silent than to modern filmmaking. Spielberg's vision is no longer one of innocent wonderment; instead, EMPIRE OF THE SUN concerns the end of innocence—a young boy thrown into adulthood and an entire generation thrown into an atomic age.

The film opens just before the Japanese attack on Pearl Harbor in 1941. Jim Graham (Christian Bale) is a nine-year-old English brat who has lived all his life in Shanghai with his aristocratic parents. Although adventurous, he is also wholly dependent on his parents and servants. Later, as the Japanese conquer Shanghai and the war intensifies, he is separated from his parents and meets Basie (John Malkovich), an opportunistic merchant seaman reminiscent of Dickens's Fagin, who somewhat reluctantly takes Jim under his wing and teaches him the most Darwinian methods of survival—lessons that help Jim endure a lengthy stay in a Japanese prison camp.

The most emotionally complex film of Steven Spielberg's career, EMPIRE OF THE SUN is not a traditional blockbuster. In fact, with its unknown lead, barely known supporting cast and near-plotlessness, it breaks Hollywood's rules. Further, Spielberg adapted an admired but little-read novel, set it in far-off Shanghai, and made his lead character a Briton who idolizes the Japanese. As Jim, Bale delivers a stunning performance; he appears in virtually every frame and truly seems to grow over the course of the film from a coddled rich child to a calculating, almost feral creature who will ally himself with whoever wields the most power in a given situation.

Working on a grand canvas in the tradition of the David Lean epics, Spielberg includes several of his own distinctive visual epiphanies but the usual sense of wonder threatens to slide into madness. Spielberg also displays a progressive and sophisticated awareness of issues of class and race that may be viewed as an apology for the casual imperialist and racist assumptions of his INDIANA JONES series.

EMPIRE STRIKES BACK, THE
1980 124m c ★★★★
Science Fiction PG/U
FOX

Mark Hamill (Luke Skywalker), Harrison Ford (Han Solo), Carrie Fisher (Princess Leia), Billy Dee Williams (Lando Calrissian), Anthony Daniels (C-3PO), David Prowse (Darth Vader), Peter Mayhew (Chewbacca), Kenny Baker (R2-D2), Frank Oz (Yoda), Alec Guinness (Ben Kenobi)

p, Gary Kurtz; d, Irvin Kershner; w, Leigh Brackett, Lawrence Kasdan (based on a story by George Lucas); ph, Peter Suschitzky (Panavision, Deluxe Color); ed, Paul Hirsch; m, John Williams; prod d, Norman Reynolds; art d, Leslie Dilley, Harry Lange, Alan Tomkins; fx, Brian Johnson, Richard Edlund, Dennis Muren, Bruce Nicholson; cos, John Mollo

Considered by many to be the best entry in the series, the second chapter of the STAR WARS trilogy finds the evil Darth Vader (David Prowse and the voice of James Earl Jones) aiding the emperor in his attempts to crush the rebellion dedicated to halting the Empire's domination of the universe. The rebel forces are on the ice planet Hoth and the evil empire sends troops to wipe them out. Forced to flee, Han Solo (Harrison Ford) and Princess Leia (Carrie Fisher) regroup in Cloud City, which is run by the roguish Lando Calrissian (Billy Dee Williams). Meanwhile, Luke Skywalker (Mark Hamill) searches for and finds Yoda (the voice of Frank Oz), a wise little creature who teaches him the finer points of the Force. The whole thing climaxes with a showdown between Luke and Darth Vader, in which some incredible plot twists are revealed.

After the phenomenal success of STAR WARS, creator George Lucas retired from directing and hired veteran Kershner to direct and the great Leigh Brackett (THE BIG SLEEP, RIO BRAVO, EL DORADO, THE LONG GOODBYE) to write the screenplay with an assist from the then new kid on the block, Lawrence Kasdan. He could also financially afford to push the special effects envelope even further. The result is a darker, richer and more elaborate film than the original that suffers most from being just what it is: a middle chapter with no real ending. The film's final cliffhanger may prove upsetting to youngsters, since the dark side of the Force has the upper hand, but it's dramatically correct, setting the stage for the triumphant return of Good in part three, RETURN OF THE JEDI.

ENCHANTED COTTAGE, THE
1945 91m bw   ★★★★½
Romance   /U
RKO

Dorothy McGuire *(Laura Pennington)*, Robert Young *(Oliver Brad-ford)*, Herbert Marshall *(John Hillgrave)*, Mildred Natwick *(Abigail Minnett)*, Spring Byington *(Violet Price)*, Richard Gaines *(Freder-ick)*, Hillary Brooke *(Beatrice Alexander)*, Alec Englander *(Danny)*, Mary Worth *(Mrs. Stanton)*, Josephine Whittell *(Canteen Manager)*

p, Harriet Parsons; d, John Cromwell; w, DeWitt Bodeen, Herman J. Mankiewicz (based on the play by Arthur Wing Pinero); ph, Ted Tetzlaff; ed, Joseph Noriega; m, Roy Webb; art d, Albert S. D'Agostino, Carroll Clark; fx, Vernon L. Walker; cos, Edward Ste-venson

This sensitive, touching film, based on the classic romance play by Pinero, is beautifully enacted by McGuire and Young as the uncommon lovers. Oliver (Young) is the embittered, disfigured WWI veteran obsessed with suicide, the only alternative, he feels, to coping with an ugliness that repels everyone. He meets the shy and plain Laura (McGuire), a woman also shunned by society. They marry and move into seclusion inside a small New England cottage, all that's left of a great estate which burned down years earlier. As a honeymoon cottage scores of happy lovers have carved their initials on its windowpanes; its owner (Natwick) knows well the legend of its wonderful spell. Slowly Oliver regains his handsome countenance and Laura blossoms into a beautiful young woman. It is, of course, their mutual love which has brought about these astounding transformations, im-ages shattered by mindless friends.

An unforgettable fable for all who have found beauty in another person, the film does a remarkable job of sidestepping the maudlin and convincingly argues that "beauty is in the eye of the beholder." Pinero's intent, to write about the triumph of love over adversity, is as fully preserved in this version as it was in its original 1922 stage production and 1924 silent film, starring Richard Barthelmess and May McAvoy. Young and McGuire underplay roles that would doubtless have been more histrioni-cally delivered in less able hands. This 1945 remake also benefits from subtle makeup, a stirring score by Webb, innovative lensing by Tetzlaff and a literate screenplay by Mankiewicz and Bodeen.

END OF INNOCENCE
1960 76m bw   ★★★★
Drama   /X
Argentine Sono (Argentina)

Elsa Daniel *(Ana)*, Lautaro Murua *(Pablo)*, Guillermo Battaglia *(Castro)*, Jordana Fain *(Nana)*, Berta Ortegosa *(Senora Castro)*, Barbara Mujica *(Vicenta)*, Alejandro Rey *(Julian)*, Lili Gacel *(Julietta)*

d, Leopoldo Torre-Nilsson; w, Beatriz Guido, Leopoldo Torre-Nils-son, Martin Rodriguez Mentasti (based on the novel *House of the Angel* by Beatriz Guido); ph, Anibal Gonzalez Paz; m, Juan Carlos Paz

Daniel is a rich Argentine girl who leads a sheltered existence on her father's estate until she is raped by her father's best friend. The plot, however, is just an excuse for an analysis of class structure and politics in 1920s Argentina. An excellent film, for

which Daniel won a best actress award at the Cannes Film Festival.

END OF THE GAME
1976 106m c   ★★★
Mystery   PG/AA
FOX (Italy/West Germany)

Jon Voight *(Walter Tschantz)*, Jacqueline Bisset *(Anna Crawley)*, Martin Ritt *(Hans Barlach)*, Robert Shaw *(Richard Gastmann)*, Helmut Qualtinger *(Von Schwendi)*, Gabriele Ferzetti *(Dr. Lutz)*, Rita Calderoni *(Nadine)*, Friedrich Duerrenmatt *(Friedrich)*, Willy Huegli *(Clenin)*, Norbert Schiller *(Dr. Hungertobel)*

p, Maximilian Schell, Arlene Sellers; d, Maximilian Schell; w, Friedrich Duerrenmatt, Bo Goldman, Maximilian Schell (based on the novel *The Judge and His Hangman* by Duerrenmatt); ph, Ennio Guarnieri, Roberto Gerardi, Klaus Koenig (DeLuxe Color); ed, Dagmar Hirtz; art d, Mario Garbuglia

Complex thriller about a dying veteran police inspector, Hans Barlach (Ritt), and his tenacious efforts to nail the man who, 30 years before, killed the woman both men loved. His new assis-tant, Walter Tschantz (Voight), brings fresh life and new methods to the case and he expands the investigation to include the murder of Barlach's previous assistant. An additional facet of the strange story finds Anna Crawley (Bissett) also attempting to solve the assistant's murder.

Swiss playwright Duerrenmatt, who collaborated on the screenplay, is known for his treatment of the bizarre, and his authority over the filming of this story is evident in the layers of confusion spread over it until the denouement. Ritt, best known as a director (HUD, SOUNDER, THE FRONT, NORMA RAE), is excellent in a rare acting role. In contrast director Schell is best known for his acting (JUDGEMENT AT NUREMBURG, THE MAN IN THE GLASS BOOTH, JULIA). Sutherland makes one of the strangest cameo appearances on record as the corpse that triggers the investigation.

ENEMY BELOW, THE
1957 98m c   ★★★
War   /PG
FOX

Robert Mitchum *(Capt. Murrell)*, Curt Jurgens *(Von Stolberg)*, David Hedison *(Lt. Ware)*, Theodore Bikel *(Schwaffer)*, Russell Collins *(Doctor)*, Kurt Kreuger *(Von Holem)*, Frank Albertson *(CPO Crain)*, Biff Elliot *(Quartermaster)*, Alan Dexter *(Mackeson)*, Doug McClure *(Ensign Merry)*

p, Dick Powell; d, Dick Powell; w, Wendell Mayes (based on the novel by D.A. Rayner); ph, Harold Rosson (CinemaScope, DeLuxe Color); ed, Stuart Gilmore; m, Leigh Harline; art d, Lyle Wheeler, Albert Hogsett; fx, L.B. Abbott

This absorbing WWII film focuses on a deadly contest of wits and cunning between two strong-willed men. Captain Murrell (Mitchum) is the war-weary captain of a destroyer escort. Cap-tain von Stolberg (Jurgens, in his American film debut) is the commander of a German U-boat. The setting for their struggle is the North Atlantic. The action begins when the sonar operator on Murrell's ship, the *Haines*, picks up an underwater signal and identifies Stolberg's submarine. The Americans begin tracking the German ship. Captain Stolberg, every bit as war weary as his American counterpart, is on a desperate mission to rendezvous with a German wolf pack and will not deviate from his course. But no matter how cleverly the Germans maneuver, Murrell stays on his tail, running ahead to drop depth charges and then falling back to track. The American captain is relentless but Stolberg is shrewd and dauntless in this seesaw battle, even after his craft sustains heavy punishment from the Americans.

THE ENEMY BELOW is expertly filmed by actor-turned-director Dick Powell. He builds suspense and excitement in each scene, giving as much attention to the mechanics of war as to his principal actors. He quickly establishes his characters then moves on to the deadly game. Mitchum underplays his role and his reserved, almost stoic nature perfectly suits his part, while Jurgens is sympathetic as the old WWI submariner who hates the Nazis but loves his ancestral fatherland. This was one of the first films to portray the WWII enemy with some understanding. THE ENEMY BELOW takes an impartial, almost clinical, look at war.

ENFORCER, THE
1951   87m   bw   ★★★½
Crime   /18
United States

Humphrey Bogart (Martin Ferguson), Zero Mostel (Big Babe Lazich), Ted de Corsia (Joseph Rico), Everett Sloane (Albert Mendoza), Roy Roberts (Capt. Frank Nelson), Lawrence Tolan (Duke Malloy), King Donovan (Sgt. Whitlow), Bob Steele (Herman), Adelaide Klein (Olga Kirshen), Don Beddoe (Thomas O'Hara)

p, Milton Sperling; d, Bretaigne Windust; w, Martin Rackin; ph, Robert Burks; ed, Fred Allen; m, David Buttolph; art d, Charles H. Clarke

Based on the 1940 revelations of Abe Reles regarding the existence of an organized crime group called Murder Inc., but inspired by the Kefauver Committee investigations of 1950, this raw drama can be viewed as a key transitional film between the noir ethos of the 1940s and crime syndicate obsessed 1950s. Reveling in the lingo of the murder business with its talk of "contracts," "hits" and "fingers," this was the first film to deal with the mysterious structures of organized crime.

The film begins with a brief prologue by Senator Estes Kefauver, the head of the crime investigation committee, explaining the burning need to bring criminals to justice. Joseph Rico (De Corsia), head of the syndicate's professional murder squad, has been brought in and put under protective custody after agreeing to testify against crime czar Albert Mendoza (Sloane). Martin Ferguson (Bogart), the district attorney, has spent four years building his case against Mendoza and, with Rico's testimony, he'll be able to send him to the electric chair for mass murder. However, Rico, in terror, escapes and falls to his death. Ferguson seeks to find some tiny clue in the bulk of evidence so as to save his case.

This powerful crime drama was shot in stark black and white by frequent Hitchcock collaborator Robert Burks and directed with a quick, crisp style by Windust. Reportedly some of the film's footage had to be restaged by action veteran Raoul Walsh. Though he is uncredited, Walsh's imprint is apparent as he establishes the semidocumentary approach that proved so successful in his WHITE HEAT. Rackin's script is tough, even brutal, in depicting the slaughterhouse deeds of the worst gang of killers ever to intimidate America.

ENTER LAUGHING
1967   112m   c   ★★½
Comedy   /U
Columbia

Jose Ferrer (Mr. Marlowe), Shelley Winters (Mrs. Kolowitz), Elaine May (Angela), Jack Gilford (Mr. Foreman), Reni Santoni (David Kolowitz), Janet Margolin (Wanda), David Opatoshu (Mr. Kolowitz), Michael J. Pollard (Marvin), Don Rickles (Harry Hamburger), Richard Deacon (Pike)

p, Carl Reiner, Joseph Stein; d, Carl Reiner; w, Joseph Stein, Carl Reiner (based on a play by Joseph Stein); ph, Joseph Biroc (PatheColor); ed, Charles Nelson; m, Quincy Jones

Stagestruck David Kolowitz (Santoni) leaves his job as a machinist's apprentice and gets work at a decrepit theater run by Mr. Marlowe (Ferrer), a drunken old ham. Mrs. Kalowitz (Winters), David's mother, objects to his choice of careers, wanting her son to go to school and become a pharmacist. Based on Carl Reiner's recollections of his beginnings, Enter Laughing made a star out of Alan Arkin on Broadway, but Santoni is hopeless in the lead, lacking both the charm and the wit to pull it off.

ENTER THE DRAGON
1973   98m   c   ★★★
Action   R/18
Concord

Bruce Lee (Lee), John Saxon (Roper), Jim Kelly (Williams), Shih Kien (Han), Bob Wall (Oharra), Anna Capri (Tania), Angela Mao Ying (Su-Lin), Betty Chung (Mei Ling), Geoffrey Weeks (Braithwaite), Yang Sze (Bolo)

p, Fred Weintraub, Paul M. Heller; d, Robert Clouse; w, Michael Allin; ph, Gil Hubbs (Technicolor); ed, Kurt Hirschler, George Watters; m, Lalo Schifrin; art d, James Wong Sun

If you have a yen for spectacular chopsocky action, this is as good a flick to start with as any. The legendary Bruce Lee is showcased in his most lavish adventure—though, as this was made in Hong Kong after all, it still feels like a low-rent James Bond thriller crossed with Fu Manchu.

The plot barely rates relating but here goes: Lee (Bruce Lee) is recruited by a government agent, Braithwaite (Weeks), to enter a martial arts contest on the island fortress of Han (Kien), a particularly vicious chap with a nasty iron claw who is believed to be involved in drug smuggling and prostitution. Lee agrees because he knows that Han's right-hand man, Oharra (Wall), is responsible for his sister's death (she committed suicide rather than be raped by him).

On the island he meets Roper (Saxon) and Williams (Kelly), ex-army buddies from the US, on the run, respectively, from the mob and the law. Lee tries to infiltrate Han's underground chamber but fails, beating up a number of guards in the process. The next morning Han orders the men who let the intruder escape to fight Bolo (Sze), who kills them all easily. But enough plot... let it suffice to say that the only compelling reason to sit through this film is to see the greatest martial arts star of all time.

Lee proves why he is still the dominant legend in the genre more than a decade after his death. During one fight scene, Lee performed a flying kick so fast it couldn't be captured on film at 24 frames a second. The cameraman had to film the sequence in slow motion to get it to look like it wasn't faked. Nobody shows much evidence of acting ability, and the script is full of holes. Nonstop action is what these films are about, and that's what you get here.

ENTERTAINER, THE
1960   96m   bw   ★★★★
Drama   /X
Woodfall   (U.K.)

Laurence Olivier *(Archie Rice)*, Brenda de Banzie *(Phoebe Rice)*, Joan Plowright *(Jean)*, Roger Livesey *(Billy)*, Alan Bates *(Frank)*, Daniel Massey *(Graham)*, Albert Finney *(Mick Rice)*, Miriam Karlin *(Soubrette)*, Shirley Ann Field *(Tina)*, Thora Hird *(Mrs. Lapford)*

p, Harry Saltzman; d, Tony Richardson; w, John Osborne, Nigel Kneale (based on the play by Osborne); ph, Oswald Morris; ed, Alan Osbiston; m, John Addison; art d, Ralph Brinton, Ted Marshall; cos, Barbara Gillett

"Life is a beastly mess," states the great Olivier in this bleak drama of moral stagnation. He's Archie Rice, a third-rate vaudevillian who, in garish makeup, delivers his creaky song and dance routines before increasingly scarce and indifferent audiences. Rice's home life is as shabby as his stage career. Phoebe (De Banzie), his loyal wife, has been driven to alcoholism and fits of hysteria by her husband's selfishness and infidelities. His father, Billy (Livesey, the star of THE LIFE AND DEATH OF COLONEL BLIMP), a once famous entertainer, is dying, yet Archie prevails upon him to back just one more tawdry musical revue. Only Jean (Plowright), his protective daughter, tries to meet Olivier's emotional needs but at the cost of her own professional and personal fulfilment. Archie is an incorrigible liar and self-promoter whose raging ego demands that he be admired by one and all even if it means destroying the lives of those around him.

This depressing but fascinating film is another Olivier tour de force; he later claimed this role, which he had perfected on the London stage, really reflected his own personality, telling an interviewer that "it had the advantage of being a complete break from the other sort of work and that made it much more refreshing than tormenting oneself through these punishing roles of Shakespeare. I have an affinity with Archie Rice. It's what I really am. I'm not like Hamlet."

The rest of the cast is stunning, particularly newcomer Plowright and veteran De Banzie (HOBSON'S CHOICE), though Albert Finney and Alan Bates are also memorable as Archie's sons. Scripters Osborne and Kneale present a gloomy and penetrating adaptation of Osborne's play. Richardson's direction of this unhappy little gem gives off the appropriate dull glimmer while being economical and inventive.

ENTERTAINING MR. SLOANE

1970 94m c ★★★★
Comedy /15
Canterbury (U.K.)

Beryl Reid *(Kath)*, Peter McEnery *(Mr. Sloane)*, Harry Andrews *(Ed)*, Alan Webb *(Dada Kemp)*

p, Douglas Kentish; d, Douglas Hickox; w, Clive Exton (based on the play by Joe Orton); ph, Wolfgang Suschitzky (Technicolor); ed, John Trumper; m, Georgie Fame; prod d, Michael Seymour; cos, Emma Porteous

Entertaining Mr. Audience. You can tell something offbeat is taking place right at the start, with the hefty, garishly dressed Kath (Reid) licking a popsicle while observing a funeral. Spotting the handsome, blonde Mr. Sloane (McEnery) sunning himself on a nearby tombstone, she asks him to move into her home and sets about seducing him. Her brother Ed (Andrews), a closeted homosexual, entertains similar notions, outfitting his new chauffeur stud in leather from head to toe. Their father (Webb), a retired grave-digger, recognizes Sloane as the man who killed his former boss, a pornographer. Dada accuses the enigmatic youth of murder and Sloane calmly kicks him to death. Ed and Kath, now pregnant, threaten to tell the police what

happened unless Sloane swears eternal allegiance to them. The film ends with three remarkable ceremonies all rolled into one.

Adapted from Joe Orton's hilarious play, which won the London Drama Critics Award in 1964 but which folded on Broadway after only 13 performances, ENTERTAINING MR. SLOANE is full of morbid humor and grotesque touches. In other words, the film is an almost constant delight, going out of its way to shock whenever possible. The tiny cast achieves a remarkable range of complex emotions and diverse moods, with Reid and Andrews especially superb. Not a film for everybody, granted, but a fine one nonetheless.

ENTRE NOUS
(COUP DE FOUDRE)

1983 110m c ★★★★½
Drama /15
Partner's/Alexandre/Hachette Premiere/A2/SFPC (France)

Miou-Miou *(Madeleine)*, Isabelle Huppert *(Lena)*, Jean-Pierre Bacri *(Costa)*, Guy Marchand *(Michel)*, Robin Renucci *(Raymond)*, Patrick Bauchau *(Carlier)*, Jacques Alric *(Monsieur Vernier)*, Jacqueline Doyen *(Madame Vernier)*, Patricia Champane *(Florence)*, Saga Blanchard *(Sophie)*

p, Ariel Zeitoun; d, Diane Kurys; w, Diane Kurys, Alain Henry (from the book by Kurys, Olivier Cohen); ph, Bernard Lutic (CinemaScope); ed, Joele Van Effenterre; m, Luis Bacalov; prod d, Jacques Bufnoir; cos, Mic Cheminal

This autobiographical work from French director Diane Kurys serves as a prequel to PEPPERMINT SODA, her superb 1977 feature debut.

The film opens during the German occupation of France. Lena (Isabelle Huppert), a young Russian Jew, escapes from a prison camp by marrying a stranger, Michel (Guy Marchand). Meanwhile, in Paris, art student Madeleine (Miou-Miou) must start life anew when her husband is brutally gunned down before her. The scene then shifts to Lyons, 1952, for a chance meeting between these two women. Lena is still wed to Michel and is the mother of two children, while Madeleine has remarried. They come to realize that they can only find support from each other and not from their boorish husbands.

A resounding art-house success in the US and Oscar nominee for Best Foreign Film, ENTRE NOUS is an excellent examination of the bond of friendship. Like very few films before it, ENTRE NOUS focuses—with subtle but distinct lesbian undertones—on a female friendship instead of the usual male "buddy" formula. Based in part on the experiences of the director's own mother, this fictionalized account is one of great emotional truth. The relationships between Lena and Madeleine and between the women and their respective families are written, directed, and acted with a touch usually seen only in the films of Renoir, Pagnol or Truffaut. The picture's chief weakness is its sometimes uninvolving episodic structure, beginning with the rocky 1940s prologue that opens the movie. Still, ENTRE NOUS is intelligent, adult cinema.

EQUUS

1977 137m c ★★★
Drama R/15
UA (U.K.)

Richard Burton *(Dr. Martin Dysart)*, Peter Firth *(Alan Strang)*, Colin Blakely *(Frank Strang)*, Joan Plowright *(Dora Strang)*, Harry Andrews *(Harry Dalton)*, Eileen Atkins *(Magistrate Hesther Saloman)*,

Jenny Agutter *(Jill Mason)*, John Wyman *(The Horseman)*, Kate Reid *(Margaret Dysart)*, Ken James *(Mr. Pearce)*

p, Lester Persky, Elliott Kastner; d, Sidney Lumet; w, Peter Shaffer (based on his play); ph, Oswald Morris (DeLuxe Color); ed, John Victor-Smith; m, Richard Rodney Bennett; prod d, Tony Walton; art d, Simon Holland; cos, Tony Walton, Patti Unger, Brenda Dabbs

A reverential and somewhat bumpy film adaptation. Shaffer adapted his own gripping play about a young man, Alan Strang (Firth), who is inexplicably compelled to blind horses. Burton is Dr. Martin Dysart, the psychiatrist who realizes that Alan's religious fervor is the key to the mystery. Alan's devout mother, Dora Strang (Plowright), has supplied the confused youth with a thwarted view of life that has resulted in his behavior. The court appoints Dr. Dysart to get to the bottom of the reasons for Alan's deeds and he learns much about himself in the process.

This is a fairly convincing rendition of a real psychiatrist-patient relationship. Burton confirms his status as a master thespian as he begins to take stock of his own life in the pressure-cooker of his work with Firth. He's extremely intense albeit in a particularly actorly way. Firth's performance is technically flawless but it is periodically interrupted by scenes in which the dumbfounded camera simply observes him nude. Veteran director Lumet's work here is earnest yet unimaginative. He does his best with what is still essentially a filmed play. Shaffer's words are often smart and incisive but the film could have done with a few less of them.

ERASERHEAD
1978 90m bw   ★★★★
Horror   /18
AFI

Jack Nance *(Henry Spencer)*, Charlotte Stewart *(Mary X)*, Allen Joseph *(Mr. X)*, Jeanne Bates *(Mrs. X)*, Judith Roberts *(Girl Across the Hall)*, Laurel Near *(Lady in the Radiator)*, V. Phipps-Wilson *(Landlady)*, Jack Fisk *(Man in the Planet)*, Jean

p, David Lynch; d, David Lynch; w, David Lynch; ph, Frederick Elmes, Herbert Cardwell; ed, David Lynch; m, Fats Waller; art d, David Lynch

Disturbing, repulsive, hilarious, frightening, sensitive and challenging, David Lynch's ERASERHEAD has been aptly described by its creator as a "dream of dark and troubling things," namely fatherhood.

A young man, Henry Spencer (Nance), living in a dilapidated apartment building in an industrialized city learns that his girlfriend, Mary X (Stewart), is pregnant. Leaving his room, which seems to be inhabited by spermlike creatures, he visits Mary and her parents—a hyperactive father with a passion for synthetic meat and a mother obsessed with her daughter's sexuality. Grandmother sits in the kitchen, stonelike, maybe dead. Mary moves in with Henry and they begin to take care of their "baby"—a deformed, constantly crying mass of tissue and bandages that looks something like a skinned lamb. The infant is repulsive yet fascinating, as well as sad. Its constant whining drives Mary out of the apartment, leaving Henry alone with the baby. After an accidental tragedy, Henry is hurled into the nightmarish world that has existed on the fringes of his "real" world since the beginning of the film.

Five years in the making, ERASERHEAD is not just a film about a man who has nasty dreams. It's a creepily sensuous film that suggests that the "dark and troubling things" we like to repress inhabit dresser drawers, live behind the radiator or lie under the bed. They are part of the environment. This is a

nightmare about a man's horror of commitment, sexuality, and adult responsibility. This was the first feature directed by Lynch, a former painter, and it proudly displays its roots in past avant-garde film movements—surrealism and expressionism in particular—while tipping its hat to classic horror films. Lynch has since gone on to become what could be described somewhat paradoxically as the modern Hollywood equivalent of an avant-garde filmmaker but his subsequent career has not lived up to the promise of this extraordinary debut.

ESCAPE FROM ALCATRAZ
1979 112m c   ★★★½
Prison   PG/15
Paramount

Clint Eastwood *(Frank Morris)*, Patrick McGoohan *(Warden)*, Roberts Blossom *(Doc)*, Jack Thibeau *(Clarence Anglin)*, Fred Ward *(John Anglin)*, Paul Benjamin *(English)*, Larry Hankin *(Charley Butts)*, Bruce M. Fischer *(Wolf)*, Frank Ronzio *(Litmus)*, Fred Stuthman *(Johnson)*

p, Don Siegel; d, Don Siegel; w, Richard Tuggle (based on the book by J. Campbell Bruce); ph, Bruce Surtees (Panavision, DeLuxe Color); ed, Ferris Webster; prod d, Allen Smith

Veteran genre director Don Siegel directed this simple and gripping story about an actual escape from the supposedly escape-proof Alcatraz. Siegel is extremely good at this sort of thing (see his 1954 genre classic, RIOT IN CELL BLOCK 11) and if you like to watch people doing a job, you won't find it done better elsewhere.

The escape-proof "Rock" was designed in the early 1930s to hold the most infamous, incorrigible and escape-prone inmates in the federal prison system. Located in the dead center of San Francisco Bay, Alcatraz played host to Al Capone and Doc Barker, among others, and was considered by J. Edgar Hoover and other federal executives to be the only American prison from which no inmate could ever escape. In 1962, however, Frank Morris and the Anglin brothers did escape, resulting in the institution's closure.

This film is the story of that escape, convincingly enacted by Eastwood as mastermind Morris, a taciturn, calculating man with nerves of steel. Upon Morris's arrival at Alcatraz, he is met by a vain, smug warden (McGoohan) who informs him that he can forget about escaping; it has never been done and never will be done. But as an inmate who has escaped from other prisons, Morris's attitude remains unchanged.

The pace of this movie is a bit slow, but Siegel's deliberate, sparse direction works to the benefit of a film where time is all his characters have. Surprisingly, there are few exciting set pieces and relatively little violence, yet ESCAPE is relentlessly tense. This production marked the fifth time Eastwood worked with Siegel, his directorial mentor.

ETERNAL MASK, THE
1937 74m bw   ★★★★
Drama
Progress   (Switzerland)

Peter Petersen *(Prof. Tscherko)*, Mathias Wieman *(Dr. Dumartin)*, Olga Tschechowa *(Mme. Negar)*, Tom Kraa *(Dr. Wendt)*, Thekla Ahrens *(Sister Anna)*, Franz Schafheitlin *(Mons. Negar)*

d, Werner Hochbaum; w, Leo Lapaire (based on the novel by Leo Lapaire); ph, Oscar Schnirch, Anton Profes; art d, Hans Jacoby

This eerie psychological drama evokes memories of the early German expressionist films. Wieman is a young physician who believes he has concocted a cure for meningitis, but he is ordered not to try it out by the chief of the facility where he works. One of his patients is terminal, so Wieman gives him the serum against orders. At first, the patient seems to be improving, but then takes a bad turn and dies.

Wieman leaves the hospital, and a sequence begins in which the audience is never certain what is real and what is fantasy. The sets commence to change subtly as Wieman feels his life as a doctor is over. He haunts the streets, and everything around him becomes increasingly stylistic as he goes deeper into psychotic depression. He throws himself off a bridge and plunges into a river. After he's rescued, he is almost totally incapacitated and lives his life almost solely within his mind, running down mental corridors, hiding behind mental doorways, but never actually moving. The hospital chief discovers that the serum actually does work, and he must now approach Wieman, who is the only person who knows the formula.

If this film were only technique, it would remain a cinematic exercise and little more, but the power of the film lies in a combination of Hochbaum's directorial vision and Lapaire's sympathetic screenplay. The English subtitles leave much to be desired, but, even if one knows no German, the picture is so visual that it could have been shown silently with much effect. Sometimes jerky, sometimes agonizingly slow, THE ETERNAL MASK builds to a satisfying conclusion, and the entire experience is unforgettable.

EUROPA, EUROPA
1991   110m   c   ★★★★
Biography/War/Historical   R/15
Les Films du Losange/CCC Filmkunst/Perspektywa Unit
(France/Germany)

Marco Hofschneider *(Young Solomon Perel)*, Julie Delpy *(Leni)*, Andre Wilms *(Kellerman)*, Solomon Perel *(Himself)*, Aschley Wanninger *(Eric)*, Rene Hofschneider *(Isaac Perel)*, Piotr Kozlowski *(David Perel)*, Klaus Abramowsky *(Solly's Father)*, Michele Gleizer *(Solly's Mother)*, Marta Sandrowicz *(Berta)*

p, Margaret Menegoz, Artur Brauner; d, Agnieszka Holland; w, Agnieszka Holland, Paul Hengge (from the book *Memoires* by Solomon Perel); ph, Jacek Petrycki; ed, Ewa Smal, Isabelle Lorente; m, Zbigniew Preisner; prod d, Allan Starski; cos, Wiesa Starska

Agnieszka Holland's fascinating, richly realized EUROPA, EUROPA is based on the real-life story of Solomon Perel, one of a handful of Jews who ironically managed to survive the Nazi terror by masquerading as Aryans.

Solomon Perel (Marco Hofschneider) was born in Germany, near Braunschweig, to German-speaking Polish-Jewish parents in 1925. (He shares a birthday—April 20th—with Adolf Hitler.) In the opening scene, the baby Solomon is circumcized—an ironic beginning to a story that will revolve around Solomon's attempts to conceal his lack of a foreskin. Solly grows up to be a handsome, engaging youth who does not look particularly Jewish. On the eve of Solomon's bar mitzvah, his family's home is attacked by a Nazi mob. Berta is killed, but Solly saves himself by diving from the bathroom window and hiding in an empty barrel. The family then flee to Poland, where they are separated during the German invasion of September 1939.

Solly makes his way into Soviet-occupied Poland and winds up in an orphanage near Grodno, where he undergoes a seemingly painless transformation into a Young Pioneer. Although there are hints of the Stalinist terror, they are eclipsed by the German attack on Russia, during which Solly is picked up by the invaders. By virtue of his impeccable German and his claim to be among Poland's ethnic German minority, the Volksdeutsche, Solly escapes the winnowing out of Communist Party members and Jews being conducted by German troops. Since he also speaks Russian, Solly is immediately adopted by an advance Wehrmacht squad as their translator, under his false name of Josef Peters, or "Jupp."

Solly's inner tension is expressed in the form of wonderfully surreal dreams, where Stalin and Hitler waltz together and Zenek appears as a crucified Christ. In one nightmare he hides in a closet with Hitler, whose pose suggests he, too, is concealing the same secret that Solly does. Holland, a frequent collaborator of Andrzej Wajda's (she wrote the screenplays for DANTON, A LOVE IN GERMANY and KORCZAK), also directed BITTER HARVEST and TO KILL A PRIEST. Her screenplay covers much of the range of anti-Semitism in Hitler's Germany, whether the airy intellectual sort embraced by Lereneau or the bloody-minded kind expressed by Leni. Also familiar with the love-hate relations between Poles and Russians, Holland has not skirted the harmful effects of the Soviet occupation. The most poignant sequence is a recreation of the Warsaw ghetto familiar to viewers from Nazi newsreels, glimpsed by Solly through a chink in the whitewashed window of a tram that passes through this forbidden zone.

EUROPA, EUROPA is a compelling story told with intelligence and wit. Holland's direction, and the acting by the ensemble cast, are superb. The real-life Solomon Perel makes an appearance as himself in the present day.

EVERY MAN FOR HIMSELF AND GOD AGAINST ALL
(JEDER FUR SICH UND GOTT GEGEN ALLE)
1975   110m   c   ★★★★
Biography
ZDF/Werner Herzog   (West Germany)

Bruno S. *(Kaspar Hauser)*, Walter Ladengast *(Daumer)*, Brigitte Mira *(Kathe)*, Hans Musaus *(Unknown Man)*, Willy Semmelrogge *(Circus Director)*, Michael Kroecher *(Lord Stanhope)*, Henry van Lyck *(Calvary Captain)*, Enno Patalas *(Pastor Fuhrmann)*, Elis Pilgrim *(Pastor)*, Volker Prechtel *(Hiltel, the Prison Guard)*

p, Werner Herzog; d, Werner Herzog; w, Werner Herzog; ph, Jorg Schmidt-Reitwein (Eastmancolor); ed, Beate Mainka-Jellinghaus; m, Johann Pachelbel, Tomaso Albinoni, Orlando DiLasso, Wolfgang Amadeus Mozart; prod d, Henning V. Gierke; cos, Gisela Storch, Ann Poppel

The winner of the Grand Jury Award at the 1975 Cannes Film Festival, this haunting and, at times, disconcertingly whimsical film helped to propel the self-styled visionary New German filmmaker, Werner Herzog, to international prominence.

Herzog's slow and meditative films are fairly unique in contemporary narrative cinema. Landscapes and music are at least as important as the human characters in his work. His protagonists tend to be obsessive dreamers compelled to action by the power of their visions—with consequences that are sometimes transcendental, sometimes disastrous. At their most excessive, Herzog's films can be regressive, reactionary, self-indulgent and naively romantic; at their best, they are dreamily hypnotic, mystical and awe-inspiring in their beauty. EVERY MAN FOR HIMSELF AND GOD AGAINST ALL happily falls in the latter category.

The film is based on the documented story of a young man, Kaspar Hauser (Bruno S.), who, after living in a cellar for years with only a pet rocking horse, is abandoned by his protector and provider, the mysterious Man in Black. Having been isolated from all humans except his godlike "father," Kaspar is suddenly thrust into civilization. Though at first he can barely walk and cannot speak, he is expected to readily adapt to 19th-century society. His past remains a mystery to the townspeople, as does his purpose. Some teach him the mannerisms of the civilized, while others spy on his every move attempting to uncover some hidden identity. Untainted by society, Kaspar functions as a natural man in this repressed and repressive society. His very existence calls their assumptions into question.

Many consider this, along with AGUIRRE: THE WRATH OF GOD, to be Herzog's best film. Bruno S. is of particular interest here. A non-professional actor, Mr. S. is an eccentric German street performer who spent much of his childhood in mental institutions. He also stars in Herzog's STROSZEK.

EVIL DEAD, THE

1983 85m c   ★★★½
Horror   /18
Renaissance

Bruce Campbell (Ash), Ellen Sandweiss (Cheryl), Betsy Baker (Linda), Hal Delrich (Scott), Sarah York (Shelly)

p, Robert G. Tapert; d, Sam Raimi; w, Sam Raimi; ph, Tim Philo, Joshua M. Becker (DuArt Color); ed, Edna Ruth Paul; m, Joseph LoDuca; fx, Tom Sullivan, Bar Pierce

Self-promoted as "The Ultimate Experience in Grueling Terror," THE EVIL DEAD marks the directorial debut of what may be the next great practitioner of this eternally disreputable form. Writer-director Sam Raimi and his college pals took the genre by storm with this amazingly assured and exhilarating horror exercise in which narrative and characterization take a backseat to sheer cinematic panache.

Five college students take shelter in an abandoned cabin deep in the woods, where they find a strange book along with a tape explaining that the book is an ancient Sumerian Book of the Dead. The tape translates some of the incantations in the book, and giant demons are unleashed in the woods. One by one the teenagers are taken over by the demons, until only Ash (Bruce Campbell) is left to fight the evil.

Shot in 16mm (and blown up to grainy 35mm) on location in Tennessee and Michigan on a tiny budget of under $400,000, this film has some undeniable technical limitations—and the acting is less than professional—but Raimi's wildly creative filmmaking turns these limitations into virtues that make THE EVIL DEAD a landmark in recent American horror films.

While it set new standards in outlandish screen gore, it's never really too disturbing due to its old fashioned funhouse feel. Raimi does not aspire to dark satirical social commentary like Romero nor to psychosexual insights like Cronenberg; some boys just wanna have fun. Though genuinely shocking and spooky, the movie has enough sick black humor and deliciously bad special effects to keep all the nightmarish imagery from getting too oppressive. Not for the faint of heart or those uninitiated in the ways of modern horror, it's a hoot for fans of the genre.

EVIL DEAD 2: DEAD BY DAWN

1987 85m c   ★★★½
Horror   /18
Renaissance

Bruce Campbell (Ash), Sarah Berry (Annie), Dan Hicks (Jake), Kassie Wesley (Bobby Joe), Theodore Raimi (Possessed Henrietta), Denise Bixler (Linda), Richard Domeier (Ed), John Peaks (Prof. Raymond Knowby), Lou Hancock (Henrietta)

p, Robert G. Tapert; d, Sam Raimi; w, Sam Raimi, Scott Spiegel; ph, Peter Deming (Technicolor); ed, Kaye Davis; m, Joseph LoDuca; art d, Philip Duffin, Randy Bennett; fx, Mark Shostrom, Vern Hyde, Doug Beswick Productions, Tom Sullivan, Rick Catizone; chor, Susan Labatt, Andrea Brown; Tam G. Warner

Perhaps the most absurd, uproariously funny, unbelievably bloody film ever made, EVIL DEAD 2: DEAD BY DAWN stands in relation to its precursor like THE BRIDE OF FRANKENSTEIN does to FRANKENSTEIN. Deriving much of its impact from our knowledge of the first film yet made more surreal and absurd, the second visit with the Evil Dead simultaneously transcends and fails to measure up to to the original in visceral horrific impact.

This is less a sequel than a remake; Ash (Bruce Campbell), the sole survivor of THE EVIL DEAD, seems to have no memory of that film's events. After a high-speed recap and continuation of first film's ending, Ash ventures out to that same lonely cabin for a romantic weekend with his girlfriend (Denise Bixler). There he discovers that darn tape recorder again. When the voice reads a translation of the "Book of the Dead," a vicious evil force awakens in the woods and rushes into the house, and all hell breaks loose once more.

A deliriously cinematic experience for those with a taste for Grand Guignol, this is a relentlessly energetic nightmare world where quite literally *anything* can happen—and does. By pushing the events to an absurd extreme, the film frequently leaves the realm of horror and becomes a cartoon gone mad. Animation director Tex Avery is a stronger influence here than the German Expressionists or modern masters of horror. Campbell's admirably straightfaced performance suggests a modern-day Harold Lloyd trapped in a splatter film spinning madly out of control. He gamely tries to cope with everything the evil spirits hurl at him including bleeding walls, scary monsters, flying eyeballs, a possessed hand, and all manner of bad craziness.

To keep things interesting, the then 26-year-old director employs a myriad of expressive movie tricks including stop-motion animation, impossible point-of-view shots, portentous crane shots, shaky handheld camera sequences, rotating sets, rear projection, distorting anamorphic lenses, weird sound effects and good old-fashioned dramatic lighting. The film is a breathless celebration of the possibilities of the medium. "Good" dramatic narrative values hold little interest for Raimi. The setting and story are merely functional, and most of the dialogue is perfunctory. Maximum visceral impact is what this film is all about—and it delivers.

EXCALIBUR

1981 140m c   ★★★★
Action/Fantasy   R/15
Orion

Nigel Terry (King Arthur), Nicol Williamson (Merlin), Nicholas Clay (Lancelot), Helen Mirren (Morgana), Cherie Lunghi (Guenevere), Paul Geoffrey (Perceval), Robert Addie (Mordred), Gabriel Byrne (Uther), Liam Neeson (Gawain), Corin Redgrave (Cornwall)

p, John Boorman; d, John Boorman; w, Rospo Pallenberg, John Boorman (based on the novel Le Morte D'Arthur by Thomas Malory); ph, Alex Thomson (Technicolor); ed, John Merritt; m, Trevor Jones; prod d, Anthony Pratt; art d, Tim Hutchinson; fx, Peter Hutchinson, Alan Whibley; cos, Bob Ringwood

An absolutely compelling film, masterfully directed by John Boorman, EXCALIBUR is a grand but brooding fantasy that faithfully depicts Malory's popular Arthurian legend from the young king's anonymous background to his rise as ruler of ancient England.

Nigel Terry is excellent as the naive, trusting, and altruistic Arthur. Nicol Williamson is the rhetoric-spewing wizard Merlin who exhausts his life and otherworldly talents on Arthur's behalf. The most fascinating aspects of this lengthy adaptation are those dealing with the mythical Camelot and the lust-driven betrayal of Arthur by lovely queen Guenevere (Cherie Lunghi) and trusted friend Lancelot (Nicholas Clay). Robert Addie as the evil Mordred, Helen Mirren as Morgana and Paul Geoffrey as Sir Perceval are also very effective.

EXCALIBUR presents a fantastic portrait of grimy lumbering knights, their world dimly lit and full of slithering dragons, mesmerizing magic, and the struggle between good and evil, Christianity and paganism. With outstanding makeup and costuming—particularly the iron-coated knights, which bring to mind the medieval warriors in ALEXANDER NEVSKY—and rustic Irish locations that are used to brilliant, timeless effect, EXCALIBUR is a splendidly staged production, loaded with eye-popping scenes and great performances.

EXECUTIVE SUITE
1954   104m   bw   ★★★★½
Drama   /U
MGM

William Holden *(McDonald Walling)*, June Allyson *(Mary Blemond Walling)*, Barbara Stanwyck *(Julia O. Tredway)*, Fredric March *(Loren Phineas Shaw)*, Walter Pidgeon *(Frederick Y. Alderson)*, Shelley Winters *(Eva Bardeman)*, Paul Douglas *(Josiah Walter Dudley)*, Louis Calhern *(George Nyle Caswell)*, Dean Jagger *(Jesse W. Grimm)*, Nina Foch *(Erica Martin)*

p, John Houseman; d, Robert Wise; w, Ernest Lehman (based on the novel by Cameron Hawley); ph, George Folsey; ed, Ralph E. Winters; art d, Cedric Gibbons, Edward Carfagno; fx, A. Arnold Gillespie; cos, Helen Rose

A spectacular array of MGM superstars shine in this slick fascinating drama of corporate intrigue. The death of the president of a gigantic furniture firm prompts a series of power plays among the company's executives, all vying for the vacated top position. The jockeying vice presidents are Loren Phineas Shaw (March), Josiah Walter Dudley (Douglas), Frederick Y. Alderson (Pidgeon), George Nyle Caswell (Calhern), and a junior executive, McDonald Walling (Holden). Surveying the candidates is Julia O. Tredway (Stanwyck), the daughter of the manufacturing firm's founder and the mistress of the recently deceased company head. As the chief stockholder as well, her decision will tip the scales.

Director Wise intercuts among the many characters but this strategy actually serves to unify the story and action rather than fragmenting the tale. The drama unfolds from a sparkling, witty, and provocative screenplay by Ernest Lehman adapted from his novel. Holden, March, Douglas, Stanwyck, Calhern, Jagger, Foch and Pidgeon are riveting in their parts, even though some, like Stanwyck, are only on camera occasionally. Holden, still building a great career, was reunited with Stanwyck on screen for the first time in 15 years—their last previous work together was in GOLDEN BOY. Critics universally and correctly singled out March as the most impressive performer in the awesome cast. His obsessive villain hasn't a single virtue, only the relentless drive to win at all costs while mouthing the predictable rationale that he is merely practicing "good business." Foch, as the suicidal secretary to the deceased boss, gained an Oscar nomination as Best Supporting Actress.

This was one of the first major films to eschew a continuous musical score; producer Houseman elected to incorporate the sounds of the business world throughout such as when the bells of a Wall Street clock are heard while the cast names roll up on the screen.

EXODUS
1960   212m   c   ★★★★
Historical   /PG
Preminger

Paul Newman *(Ari Ben Gannan)*, Eva Marie Saint *(Kitty Fremont)*, Ralph Richardson *(Gen. Sutherland)*, Peter Lawford *(Maj. Caldwell)*, Lee J. Cobb *(Barak Ben Canaan)*, Sal Mineo *(Dov Landau)*, John Derek *(Taha)*, Hugh Griffith *(Mandria)*, Gregory Ratoff *(Lakavitch)*, Felix Aylmer *(Dr. Lieberman)*

p, Otto Preminger; d, Otto Preminger; w, Dalton Trumbo (based on the novel by Leon Uris); ph, Sam Leavitt (Super Panavision 70, Technicolor); ed, Louis Loeffler; m, Ernest Gold; art d, Richard Day, Bill Hutchinson; fx, Win Ryder; cos, Joe King, May Walding, Margo Slater, Rudi Gernreich, Hope Bryce

A stirring chronicle of Israel's struggle for independence in 1947, EXODUS focuses on Newman as Ben Gannan, the leader of the Hagannah, whose affair with Kitty Fremont (Saint) is engulfed by the conflict. The film tackles the independence movement as a whole, dealing with various factions involved in the internecine struggle between the moderate Hagannah and the radical terrorist Irgun. Interspersed throughout are segments showing the migration of European Jews to the new land, paying special attention to the ragged survivors of Nazi death camps on board the vessel *Exodus*, blockaded in a Cyprus harbor by British warships. The film also depicts the struggle of the Jews in Palestine to gain partition, then profiles the main characters after the partition, fighting to continue as the nation of Israel.

Under the direction of Otto Preminger, EXODUS boasts strong performances and many memorable sequences including the bombing of the King David Hotel, the capture and subsequent rescue of the Irgun leaders, masterfully handled crowd scenes, and Gannan's moving final speech. Preminger is generally faithful to history and to Leon Uris's best-selling novel; Uris himself was dismissed as the film's screenwriter (Preminger thought he had no gift for screen dialogue), and the filmmakers were necessarily forced to abridge the story to make it cinematically feasible. Though the film is overlong, the story is movingly told, the production values are high, and Erwin Gold's Oscar-nominated score is considered a classic.

EXORCIST, THE
1973   121m   c   ★★★½
Horror   R/18
WB

Ellen Burstyn *(Mrs. MacNeil)*, Max von Sydow *(Father Merrin)*, Jason Miller *(Father Karras)*, Lee J. Cobb *(Lt. Kinderman)*, Jack MacGowran *(Burke)*, Kitty Winn *(Sharon)*, Linda Blair *(Regan)*, Vasiliki Maliaros *(Mother Karras)*, Wallace Rooney *(Bishop)*, Titos Vandis *(Karras's Uncle)*

p, William Peter Blatty; d, William Friedkin; w, William Peter Blatty; ph, Owen Roizman, Billy Williams (Metrocolor); ed, Norman Gay, Jordan Leondopoulos, Evan Lottman, Bud Smith; m, Jack Nitzsche; prod d, Bill Malley

Extremely controversial at the time of its release, THE EXORCIST kicked off intense debate among critics, community leaders, and even religious leaders—spurring the public, of course, to make it one of the most financially successful horror films ever made.

Regan (Linda Blair), the 12-year-old daughter of a famous stage actress (Ellen Burstyn), begins to suffer unexplainable fits and bouts of bizarre behavior. The girl is brought to doctors, but examinations fail to pinpoint a physical or psychiatric ailment. Regan's condition grows worse, and she begins to transform physically, taking on an ugly, demonic appearance. In desperation, Regan's mother asks the help of a young priest, Father Karras (Jason Miller). Realizing that Regan is possessed by the Devil and knowing that his own faith is too weak for him to deal successfully with the problem himself, Karras turns to Father Merrin (Max von Sydow), an elderly priest who specializes in exorcisms.

Based on William Peter Blatty's runaway best seller (which itself was based upon a reported exorcism in 1949) THE EXORCIST shrewdly exploits the fears and frustrations of parents while disturbing religious implications merely provide portentous window dressing. The film is an intense rollercoaster ride, a marvel of audience manipulation, with director William Friedkin pushing all the right buttons to make this a genre landmark. The movie balances its then-state-of-the-art special effects with good old-fashioned atmospheric horror to produce an excruciating—though shallow—two hours of dread and unease. It's too bad the film failed to get further inside its characters.

EXPERIENCE PREFERRED. . .BUT NOT ESSENTIAL

1983 80m c   ★★★½
Drama   PG/15
Enigma   (U.K.)

Elizabeth Edmonds (*Annie*), Sue Wallace (*Mavis*), Geraldine Griffith (*Doreen*), Karen Meagher (*Paula*), Maggie Wilkinson (*Arlene*), Ron Bain (*Mike*), Alun Lewis (*Hywel*), Robert Blythe (*Ivan*), Roy Heather (*Wally*), Peter Doran (*Dai*)

p, Chris Griffin; d, Peter Duffell; w, June Roberts; ph, Phil Meheux; ed, John Shirley; m, John Scott; art d, Jane Martin; cos, Tudor George

Very good film about a girl called Annie (Elizabeth Edmonds) finding love with a cook at a small Welsh hotel in 1962. Her relative happiness is contrasted with everyone else's desperate search for love. Excellent early 1960s period sets, costumes and music make this film a joy for nostalgia buffs. It is the second of a series of three from the talented British producers, all of them dealing with youthful romance. Originally produced for British television, this is a picture not to be missed.

EXTERMINATING ANGEL, THE

(EL ANGEL EXTERMINADOR)
1962 91m bw   ★★★★★
Comedy/Drama   /X
Uninci/S.A. Films 59   (Mexico)

Silvia Pinal (*Letitia, the Valkyrie*), Jacqueline Andere (*Senora Alicia Roc*), Jose Baviera (*Leandro*), Augusto Benedico (*Doctor*), Luis Beristain (*Christian*), Antonio Bravo (*Russell*), Claudio Brook (*Majordomo*), Cesar del Campo (*Colonel*), Lucy Gallardo (*Lucia*), Rosa Elena Durgel (*Silvia*)

p, Gustavo Alatriste; d, Luis Bunuel; w, Luis Bunuel, Luis Alcoriza (based on the play *Los Naufragos de la Calle de la Providentia* by Jose Bergamin); ph, Gabriel Figueroa; ed, Carlos Savage; m, Alessandro Scarlatti, Pietro Domenico Paradisi; art d, Jesus Bracho; fx, Juan Munoz Ravelo; cos, Georgette Somohano

One of the greatest masterworks of a giant of cinema. A brilliantly pointed blitzkrieg on bourgeois values and organized religion from the master of iconoclastic assault, Luis Bunuel, this deceptively simple film works with consummate artistry and uncompromising irony.

The allegorical story tells of a group of upper-class dinner guests who, for no apparent reason, find themselves incapable of leaving the sitting room at the end of the party. Days and days pass, and their well-mannered facades are torn down by the animalistic qualities they harbor inside themselves. One guest (Bravo) dies and is irreverently stuffed into a cupboard; a pair of lovers (Masse and Montesco) commit suicide; a believer in witchcraft (Oliva) hallucinates and brings forth demons; an incestuous brother and sister (Loya and Guilmain) steal morphine from a cancer-ridden guest. Making mincemeat of a stray sheep at one point, they later contemplate cannibalism to stay alive. After memorable encounters with a bear and a child, they do escape, but Bunuel has similar fun in store at a cathedral.

The theme of entrapment in a hell of our own making—one fashioned largely of social conventions and traditions—is a familiar one in literature, but it has never been more successfully rendered in visual terms. Bunuel's subjective, surreal imagery recalls the outspoken savagery of L'AGE D'OR 30 years earlier. Like no other director, Bunuel has continually aimed at the faces of the bourgeois the swiftest of blows, and in this film he is in top form. Lacking the softness of his similar Oscar-winning THE DISCREET CHARM OF THE BOURGEOISIE, THE EXTERMINATING ANGEL brandishes a bitter hilarity almost unequalled in the history of cinema.

EYE OF THE NEEDLE

1981 111m c   ★★★
Spy/War   R/15
Kings Road   (U.K.)

Donald Sutherland (*Faber*), Stephen MacKenna (*Lieutenant*), Philip Martin Brown (*Billy Parkin*), Kate Nelligan (*Lucy*), Christopher Cazenove (*David*), George Belbin (*Lucy's Father*), Faith Brook (*Lucy's Mother*), Barbara Graley (*Constable*), Arthur Lovegrove (*Peterson*), Colin Rix (*Oliphant*)

p, Stephen Friedman; d, Richard Marquand; w, Stanley Mann (based on the novel by Ken Follett); ph, Alan Hume (Technicolor); ed, Sean Barton; m, Miklos Rozsa; prod d, Wilfred Shingleton; art d, Bert Davey, John Hoesli; cos, John Bloomfield

A gripping, old-fashioned WWII spy thriller, EYE OF THE NEEDLE features Donald Sutherland as Faber, a murderous Nazi spy stationed in Britain who uncovers the Allies' plans to invade Normandy. En route to a rendezvous with a U-boat at a remote island, Faber is stranded by a violent storm and forced to seek shelter with Lucy (Kate Nelligan), a sexually frustrated housewife, and her husband, a paraplegic ex-fighter pilot (Christopher Cazenove). Romance soon develops between Lucy and the spy, but Lucy's husband begins to suspect Faber's true identity.

Directed with considerable flair by Richard Marquand, this adaptation of Ken Follett's best-selling novel boasts one of Sutherland's best performances. As the cold-blooded spy who thinks nothing of plunging a stiletto into anyone who gets in his way, he is positively chilling. An accomplished stage actress who has yet to find the screen success that she deserves, Nelligan is excellent as well. Underrated at the time it was released, EYE OF THE NEEDLE is worthy viewing for anyone fond of classic Hollywood wartime thrillers. The old master film composer Miklos Rosza even provides a score in the grand tradition.

F

FABULOUS BAKER BOYS, THE

1989   114m   c   ★★½
Comedy/Drama   R/15
Gladden/Mirage

Jeff Bridges *(Jack Baker)*, Beau Bridges *(Frank Baker)*, Michelle Pfeiffer *(Susie Diamond)*, Ellie Raab *(Nina)*, Xander Berkeley *(Lloyd)*, Dakin Matthews *(Charlie)*, Ken Lerner *(Ray)*, Albert Hall *(Henry)*, Terri Treas *(Girl in Bed)*, Gregory Itzin *(Vince Nancy)*

p, Paula Weinstein, Mark Rosenberg, William Finnegan; d, Steve Kloves; w, Steve Kloves; ph, Michael Ballhaus (Deluxe Color); ed, William Steinkamp; m, Dave Grusin; prod d, Jeffrey Townsend; chor, Peggy Holmes; cos, Lisa Jensen

Though full of atmosphere, mood, and attitude, THE FABULOUS BAKER BOYS is all dressed up with no place to go. Jeff and Beau Bridges play brothers Jack and Frank Baker, a musical duo whose act consists of dueling piano arrangements of lounge songs. Frank decides to bring in a female singer, and the nod finally goes to Susie Diamond (Michelle Pfeiffer). Her professional experience has been limited to an extended engagement with an escort service, but to say she knows how to sell a song is an understatement. Tensions rise when womanizing Jack embarks on a professionally dangerous liaison with Susie.

Early in the film, THE FABULOUS BAKER BOYS crackles with smart talk and smooth moves from writer-director Steve Kloves (who makes his directing debut here and who wrote the equally off-center RACING WITH THE MOON) and later in the film, Pfeiffer continues to captivate. When it comes to plot and characters, however, THE FABULOUS BAKER BOYS is purely superficial and the three principals become less interesting as the action grinds on. Though the Bridges boys give typically solid performances, it's Pfeiffer who deserves the most credit. Her Susie is an original—smart, hard-headed, and unsentimental. Pfeiffer's sultry rendition of "Makin' Whoopee" is one of the film's highlights. Photographed by the gifted Michael Ballhaus, THE FABULOUS BAKER BOYS unfortunately fails to base its evocative style on real substance, and thus fails to emerge from the run of the mill.

FACE IN THE CROWD, A

1957   125m   bw   ★★★★
Drama   /A
WB

Andy Griffith *(Lonesome Rhodes)*, Patricia Neal *(Marcia Jeffries)*, Anthony Franciosa *(Joey Kiely)*, Walter Matthau *(Mel Miller)*, Lee Remick *(Betty Lou Fleckum)*, Percy Waram *(Colonel Hollister)*, Rod Brasfield *(Beanie)*, Charles Irving *(Mr. Luffler)*, Howard Smith *(J.B. Jeffries)*, Paul McGrath *(Macey)*

p, Elia Kazan; d, Elia Kazan; w, Budd Schulberg (based on his short story "The Arkansas Traveler"); ph, Harry Stradling, Gayne Rescher; m, Tom Glazer; cos, Anna Hill Johnstone

Andy Griffith made an unforgettable screen debut in this film as Lonesome Rhodes, a cracker-barrel philosopher discovered by Marcia Jeffries (Neal), who puts him on her local television station in Arkansas. His down-home wit and backwater jokes soon gain a wide audience, after which one of the state's largest stations picks up his show, followed by a network, until his face is seen throughout the land and his homespun wisdom becomes the creed of large numbers of Americans. But Jeffries and her assistant, Mel Miller (Matthau), soon realize that good old "Lonesome Rhodes" is not the kindly rural savant he appears to be.

Director Elia Kazan and writer Budd Schulberg, who collaborated so effectively in ON THE WATERFRONT, again proved their ability to produce a raw, penetrating, and terrifying portrait of humanity in A FACE IN THE CROWD. Griffith, who had made a name for himself on Broadway with *No Time for Sergeants*, skyrocketed to fame after his performance as the vicious but fascinating Lonesome Rhodes—capturing the character so well it would take him some time to live the role down. Neal is superb as the tough but vulnerable television producer snared by the hillbilly philosopher, and Matthau plays his cynical newsman to the hilt.

FACE TO FACE

1976   136m   c   ★★★★
Drama   R/X
DEG   (Sweden)

Liv Ullmann *(Dr. Jenny Isaksson)*, Erland Josephson *(Dr. Tomas Jacobi)*, Gunnar Bjornstrand *(Grandpa)*, Aino Taube *(Grandma)*, Kari Sylwan *(Maria)*, Siv Ruud *(Mrs. Elizabeth Wankel)*, Sven Lindberg *(Dr. Erik Isaksson)*, Tore Segelcke *(The Lady)*, Ulf Johansson *(Dr. Helmuth Wankel)*, Kristina Adolphsson *(Veronica)*

p, Ingmar Bergman; d, Ingmar Bergman; w, Ingmar Bergman; ph, Sven Nykvist (Eastmancolor); ed, Siv Lundgren; m, Wolfgang Amadeus Mozart; prod d, Anne Hagegard

Bergman originally filmed FACE TO FACE for Swedish television as a four-part series. While appropriate for the more liberal television codes of Sweden, it was unlikely fare for US consumption. He edited it down to a length that would permit distribution as a feature film. Despite the snipping, it remains the most potent representative of Bergman's psychodrama cycle that began with CRIES AND WHISPERS and ended with AUTUMN SONATA.

The film depicts the slow and painful nervous breakdown of a successful psychiatrist. Ullmann is Dr. Jenny Isaksson, a psychiatrist vacationing at her grandparents' gloomy home in the country—alone because her husband, Dr. Erik Isaksson (Lindberg)—also a shrink—is away. She soon begins hallucinating about an old woman. This leads to depression and a feeling of helplessness as she is overwhelmed by memories of the past.

FACE TO FACE is an extremely intense experience from start to finish, due in large part to Ullmann's performance as she powerfully expresses a range of emotions seldom seen in American films. Bergman's frequent collaborator, cinematographer Sven Nyquist, enhances the film's harrowing mood with his stark imagery.

FACES

1968 130m bw ★★★★
Drama /X
Continental Distributing

John Marley (*Richard Forst*), Gena Rowlands (*Jeannie Rapp*), Lynn Carlin (*Maria Forst*), Fred Draper (*Freddie*), Seymour Cassel (*Chet*), Val Avery (*McCarthy*), Dorothy Gulliver (*Florence*), Joanne Moore Jordan (*Louise*), Darlene Conley (*Billy Mae*), Gene Darfler (*Jackson*)

p, Maurice McEndree; d, John Cassavetes; w, John Cassavetes; ph, Al Ruban; ed, Maurice McEndree, Al Ruban, John Cassavetes; m, Jack Ackerman; art d, Phedon Papamichael

Like SHADOWS before it, FACES was hailed at the time as a great accomplishment of American independent cinema. John Cassavetes, his friends, and family took several years to shoot and edit the film on very grainy 16mm black-and-white stock. As would become usual for Cassavetes, it's about marriages and the war between men and women. He would do much better in the 1970s with films like HUSBANDS, made with a little more money, but FACES remains a landmark cultural document of the late 60s.

FACES is a rudimentary study of a husband and wife, disenchanted after 14 years of marriage, who drift apart. Richard Forst (Marley), the husband, spends an evening with a prostitute, Jennie Rapp (Rowlands), while his wife, Maria (Carlin), and her girlfriends go out to a disco looking for a little excitement. She finds it in the form of Chet (Cassel), a handsome hippie whom she takes home to bed. The illusions of the night before look very different the next morning for both husband and wife.

The original cut ran nearly six hours, making it an inevitable victim of severe editing. (The original version exists only in the form of a published screenplay.) In a sense, FACES can be seen as a reaction to Cassavetes's previous directorial outing, A CHILD IS WAITING, which he disowned after it was recut by producer Stanley Kramer. Cassavetes became wary of the major companies and turned independent. Upon its release, FACES was hailed by most critics but tepidly received by the moviegoers. Though it is often a tedious viewing experience, its improvisational and documentary techniques are rewarding.

FAHRENHEIT 451

1966 112m c ★★★★
Science Fiction /A
Vineyard/Rank/Anglo-Amalgamated (U.K.)

Oskar Werner (*Montag*), Julie Christie (*Linda/Clarisse*), Cyril Cusack (*Captain*), Anton Diffring (*Fabian*), Jeremy Spenser (*Man with Apple*), Bee Duffell (*Book Woman*), Gillian Lewis (*TV Announcer*), Ann Bell (*Doris*), Caroline Hunt (*Helen*), Anna Palk (*Jackie*)

p, Lewis Allen; d, Francois Truffaut; w, Francois Truffaut, Jean-Louis Richard, David Rudkin, Helen Scott (based on the novel by Ray Bradbury); ph, Nicolas Roeg (Technicolor); ed, Thom Noble; m, Bernard Herrmann; prod d, Tony Walton; art d, Syd Cain; fx, Charles Staffel, Bowie Films; cos, Tony Walton

Throughout much of his brilliant career, Francois Truffaut was criticized for not making explicitly political films. However, he did tackle political themes in two films: FAHRENHEIT 451, an indictment of totalitarianism and book-burning, and THE LAST METRO, which dealt with the German occupation of France. These films address the suppression of two media of deep personal significance for Truffaut—literature and the theater, respectively. The former is the most restrained and elegaic of

science fiction films, full of poignant moments: a paean to the physical importance of books.

FAHRENHEIT 451 (the title refers to the temperature at which paper burns) is set sometime in the future and follows Montag (Oskar Werner), a devoted and obedient "fireman" who excels in ferreting out books in the most obscure hiding places. One day, after watching a woman sacrifice her life for her forbidden library, he decides to keep a volume for himself, curious to learn why these tomes are deemed so threatening. Soon he must choose between his life as a civil servant—in which he follows orders and lives with a listless, television-addicted wife, Linda (Julie Christie)—and his desire to live as a free thinking man in a free society, inspired by subversive schoolteacher Clarisse (Christie again).

Severely underrated and misunderstood by critics who wanted Truffaut to continue making films like his early French New Wave classics THE 400 BLOWS and JULES AND JIM, FAHRENHEIT 451 is a marvelously courageous personal statement that becomes more fascinating with time. This was Truffaut's first color film. The cool crisp cinematography is provided by future director Nicolas Roeg. The great Bernard Herrmann supplied the memorable score.

FAIL SAFE

1964 111m bw ★★★½
Drama/War /PG
Columbia

Dan O'Herlihy (*Gen. Black*), Walter Matthau (*Groeteschele*), Frank Overton (*Gen. Bogan*), Edward Binns (*Col. Grady*), Fritz Weaver (*Col. Cascio*), Henry Fonda (*The President*), Larry Hagman (*Buck*), William Hansen (*Secretary Swenson*), Russell Hardie (*Gen. Stark*), Russell Collins (*Knapp*)

p, Max E. Youngstein; d, Sidney Lumet; w, Walter Bernstein (based on the novel by Eugene Burdick and Harvey Wheeler); ph, Gerald Hirschfeld; ed, Ralph Rosenblum; art d, Albert Brenner; fx, Storyboard, Inc.; cos, Anna Hill Johnstone

Released only seven months after DR. STRANGELOVE by the very same studio, the virtually identical, albeit totally serious, FAIL SAFE was a relative failure at the box office. Kubrick went to Columbia's top brass and threatened a plagiarism lawsuit. (His film was based on Peter George's almost unknown novel *Red Alert*.) Since Columbia was distributing both DR. STRANGELOVE and FAIL SAFE, it appeased Kubrick by releasing his film first, and, of course, that cult classic captured the lion's share of viewers, leaving FAIL SAFE to appear as a serious, comparatively dreary rehash.

In it, a squadron of SAC bombers flies off to drop nuclear bombs on Moscow after a faulty transmission of orders that cannot be reversed through normal channels. The US military tries everything to stop them, but the bombers fly beyond "fail safe" and the president (Henry Fonda) is alerted. He goes to his bomb-proof bunker deep beneath the White House, where, in a simple, sterile room, he tries to inform Soviet leaders of the terrible blunder. Meanwhile, his cabinet and advisers meet in the War Room, keeping him informed of fast-developing events and channeling messages from the Omaha command center. After several attempts to recall or shoot down the planes, it becomes obvious that one of the bombers will deliver its load on Moscow. In a desperate effort to prevent a retaliatory attack by the Soviets that would result in all-out nuclear war, the president must resort to a horrifying compromise.

Grim, bleak and highly claustrophobic, FAIL SAFE is very much like director Sidney Lumet's previous film, 12 ANGRY

MEN, in that it concentrates almost exclusively on the actors' performances and is shot mainly in tight close-ups. While this is a wonderful showcase for some fine acting—notably by Fonda—it is not great filmmaking, and one may be left wishing for the biting, off-the-wall satire of DR. STRANGELOVE.

FALCON AND THE SNOWMAN, THE

1985   131m   c   ★★★
Spy   R/15
Orion

Timothy Hutton (Christopher Boyce), Sean Penn (Daulton Lee), Pat Hingle (Mr. Boyce), Richard Dysart (Dr. Lee), Lori Singer (Lana), David Suchet (Alex), Dorian Harewood (Gene), Priscilla Pointer (Mrs. Lee), Nicholas Pryor (Eddie), Sam Ingraffia (Kenny Kahn)

p, Gabriel Katzka, John Schlesinger; d, John Schlesinger; w, Steven Zaillian (based on the book The Falcon and the Snowman by Robert Lindsey); ph, Allen Daviau (DeLuxe Color); ed, Richard Marden; m, Pat Metheny, Lyle Mays; prod d, James D. Bissell; cos, Albert Wolsky

Based on fact, this absorbing film tells the story of Christopher Boyce and Daulton Lee, two young upper-middle-class southern Californians who were convicted of selling secrets to the Soviet Union in 1977.

Boyce (Timothy Hutton), the more introspective of the pair and the son of a former FBI man (Pat Hingle), works for a company that does top-secret work for the CIA. Already disillusioned by the American experience in Vietnam, the idealistic Hutton completely loses faith in his government when he learns the CIA has been meddling in the internal affairs of Australia, and decides to become a traitor. He enlists the help of his directionless friend Lee (Sean Penn), who has been in and out of trouble with the law, but who continues using and dealing drugs. The security at Hutton's company is astonishingly lax, and he easily steals sensitive documents, which Penn delivers to the Soviet Embassy in Mexico City.

Directed by John Schlesinger, THE FALCON AND THE SNOWMAN is both a spy drama and an intriguing character study. Penn invests his "Snowman" with fascinating eccentricity and is the more interesting of the pair, though Hutton delivers an estimable performance as the sullen young falconer.

FALLEN ANGEL

1945   98m   bw   ★★★½
Mystery   /15
FOX

Alice Faye (June Mills), Dana Andrews (Eric Stanton), Linda Darnell (Stella), Charles Bickford (Mark Judd), Anne Revere (Clara Mills), Bruce Cabot (Dave Atkins), John Carradine (Prof. Madley), Percy Kilbride (Pop), Olin Howlin (Joe Ellis), Hal Taliaferro (Johnson)

p, Otto Preminger; d, Otto Preminger; w, Harry Kleiner (based on the novel by Marty Holland); ph, Joseph La Shelle; ed, Harry Reynolds; m, David Raksin; art d, Lyle Wheeler, Leland Fuller; fx, Fred Sersen; cos, Bonnie Cashin

Eric Stanton, a press agent down on his luck, drifts into a small coastal town in California and meets June Mills (Faye), a reclusive rich woman, and a sultry waitress named Stella (Darnell). In love with Stella but broke, Eric decides to marry June, steal her fortune, divorce her, and wed Stella. However Stella turns up murdered and suspicion falls on Eric. In order to clear his name, Eric launches his own investigation to find the real killer.

Director Preminger hoped to have another LAURA with this film, but it fell short due to some loose ends in the script and disjointed points of view as the director shifts the focus of the story erratically from one character to another, a blatant red herring to mislead the viewer from guessing the killer's identity. The overall mood, lighting, and pace of the film, nevertheless, are top, hardboiled film noir.

Faye, who had been a Fox superstar for many years, had been promised a meaty and significant part; she had rejected almost three dozen scripts before accepting the lead in FALLEN ANGEL but her role was slowly chiseled away by Preminger, who played up Darnell during the production, giving her more and more scenes. Faye felt that some of her best scenes had been chopped and considered herself betrayed. She retired on the spot, so bitter that it would be 16 years before she returned to the screen.

FALLEN IDOL, THE

1949   94m   bw   ★★★★
Thriller   /A
London Films   (U.K.)

Ralph Richardson (Baines), Michele Morgan (Julie), Bobby Henrey (Felipe), Sonia Dresdel (Mrs. Baines), Denis O'Dea (Inspector Crowe), Walter Fitzgerald (Dr. Fenton), Karel Stepanek (1st Secretary), Joan Young (Mrs. Barrow), Dandy Nichols (Mrs. Patterson), Bernard Lee (Detective Hart)

p, David O. Selznick, Carol Reed; d, Carol Reed; w, Graham Greene, Lesley Storm, William Templeton (based on the short story "The Basement Room" by Greene); ph, Georges Perinal; ed, Oswald Hafenrichter; m, William Alwyn; prod d, Vincent Korda, James Sawyer, John Hawkesworth; fx, W. Percy Day; cos, Ivy Baker

Told from a child's point of view, THE FALLEN IDOL is a subdued thriller set in a foreign embassy in London. The ambassador departs and leaves his precocious, imaginative son, Felipe (Henrey), with the butler, Baines (Richardson), and Baines's wife (Dresdel). The boy idolizes the kindly, considerate Baines but dislikes the butler's shrewish, vicious wife. Baines and embassy typist Julie (Morgan) have been having an affair and Felipe overhears them agreeing to end the relationship. This information is later wheedled out of Felipe by Mrs. Baines, who then has a violent argument with her husband. In her jealous rage, Mrs. Baines accidentally falls down a flight of stairs to her death. Her demise is heard but not wholly witnessed by the boy. When police begin a routine investigation, Felipe fears that his idol will be arrested.

Director Carol Reed skillfully blends elegant camera movement, expressive angles, stylized lighting, and sterling performances into a fascinating and suspenseful motion picture. Richardson is superb as the innocent butler. His tender treatment of the boy, his cultured bearing, and his gentlemanly demeanor convey a supreme nobility that belies his working-class position. Henrey is even more exciting in his wonderful portrayal of a jittery and intelligent child. Reed's direction of Henrey gave him a reputation as a great director of children, which was further confirmed by the engaging performances he drew from children in A KID FOR TWO FARTHINGS and OLIVER! THE FALLEN IDOL received a British Best Film award, and Reed was honored as Best Director by the New York Film Critics.

FALLEN SPARROW, THE

1943   94m   bw   ★★★
Spy   /A
RKO

John Garfield *(Kit)*, Maureen O'Hara *(Toni Donne)*, Walter Slezak *(Dr. Skaas)*, Patricia Morison *(Barby Taviton)*, Martha O'Driscoll *(Whitney Hamilton)*, Bruce Edwards *(Ab Parker)*, John Banner *(Anton)*, John Miljan *(Insp. Tobin)*, Sam Goldenberg *(Prince Francois de Namur)*, Hugh Beaumont *(Otto Skaas)*

p, Robert Fellows; d, Richard Wallace; w, Warren Duff (based on the novel by Dorothy B. Hughes); ph, Nicholas Musuraca; ed, Robert Wise; m, Roy Webb; prod d, Van Nest Polglase; art d, Albert S. D'Agostino, Mark-Lee Kirk; fx, Vernon L. Walker

In a riveting performance, John Garfield portrays Kit, a fear-haunted veteran of the Spanish Civil War who returns to the US after being tortured by Gestapo captors who wanted to know where he'd hidden the captured battle flag of one of the elite Nazi regiments that fought with Franco. Back in the States, Dr. Skaas (Slezak), a German agent, attempts to drive Kit insane so that he will reveal the hiding place of the banner. A bevy of beautiful women try to worm the information from the half-mad Kit, including Toni Donne (O'Hara), who lures Kit to a house filled with Nazi agents.

Maureen O'Hara is miscast here as a *femme fatale*, but the limping Walter Slezak crafts a sinister persona somewhere between Peter Lorre and Sydney Greenstreet. Director Richard Wallace sets a brisk pace but lets Garfield carry the entire burden of a character plagued by anguished memories. Attracted by the subject matter, Garfield, a supporter of the Loyalist cause during the Spanish Civil War, played this role while on loan-out to RKO from Warner Bros. THE FALLEN SPARROW is a haunting film but, like Garfield's career, it has the feeling of being unfinished.

FAME

1980   134m   c   ★★★
Musical   PG/15
MGM

Ed Barth *(Angelo)*, Irene Cara *(Coco)*, Lee Curreri *(Bruno)*, Laura Dean *(Lisa)*, Antonia Franceschi *(Hilary)*, Boyd Gaines *(Michael)*, Albert Hague *(Shorofsky)*, Tresa Hughes *(Mrs. Finsecker)*, Steve Inwood *(Francois Lafete)*, Paul McCrane *(Montgomery)*

p, David DeSilva, Alan Marshall; d, Alan Parker; w, Christopher Gore; ph, Michael Seresin (Metrocolor); ed, Gerry Hambling; m, Michael Gore; prod d, Geoffrey Kirkland; art d, Ed Wittstein; chor, Louis Falco; cos, Kristi Zea

This is a wonderfully simple idea that succeeds very well indeed: take a bunch of kids from New York's High School of Performing Arts and let them strut their stuff. A lot of music, a few desultory plotlines, and you've got the contemporary version of the Mickey Rooney/Judy Garland "Hey kids, let's put on a show!" vehicle. FAME shows us how much life there still is in moribund genres like the musical.

It focuses on five episodes—set during auditions and successive academic years through to graduation—featuring various struggling young hopefuls, among them Coco (Irene Cara), a gifted, determined singer; Montgomery (Paul McCrane), a sensitive, gay actor; Leroy (Gene Anthony Ray), a talented, illiterate dancer; Bruno (Lee Curreri), a synthesizer player; and Ralph (Barry Miller), a Puerto Rican who is ashamed of his background. However, Parker's interest lies mainly in lavish production numbers, rather than in more intimate subtleties. (The real High School of the Performing Arts refused to let Parker film

inside the building; perhaps they too disapproved of his sensationalism.)

The subject's treatment here was best suited for the television show it launched, but FAME's score and title song did win Academy Awards. Cara, who shines as Coco, was the only one of the aforementioned young leads to actually achieve fame (McCrane and Miller are respected stage, film and TV actors), racking up a couple of hit singles.

FAMILY, THE

(LA FAMIGLIA)
1987   127m   c   ★★★½
Comedy
Maasfilm/Cinecitta/RAI-TV/Ariane   (Italy/France)

Vittorio Gassman *(Carlo)*, Fanny Ardant *(Adriana)*, Stefania Sandrelli *(Beatrice)*, Andrea Occhipinti *(Young Carlo)*, Jo Champa *(Young Adriana)*, Alberto Gimignani, Massimo Dapporto, Carlo Dapporto, Cecilia Dazzi, Ottavia Piccolo

p, Franco Committeri; d, Ettore Scola; w, Ruggero Maccari, Furio Scarpelli, Ettore Scola; ph, Ricardo Aronovich (Cinecitta coler); ed, Ettore Scola; m, Armando Trovajoli; art d, Luciano Ricceri

After venturing into pedestrian comedy in his previous film, MACARONI, director Ettore Scola returned to the single set limitations of his LE BAL for this pleasant drama which covers 80 years in the life of one Italian family. The film opens in 1906 as the clan gathers in a large Rome apartment for a group photograph. A narrator, Carlo (Vittorio Gassman), points himself out in the picture—an infant who has just been baptized. Carlo narrates the entire film as time passes, Scola never showing the characters outside of their apartment. In addition to Carlo, the family includes his brother, his parents, the maid, his three matronly aunts, his wife, Beatrice (Stefania Sandrelli), and Beatrice's older and more worldly sister, Adriana (Fanny Ardant), whom Carlo really loves.

Like many of the films of Ingmar Bergman or Woody Allen, THE FAMILY goes to great lengths to recreate a family portrait album. Scola gives his audience a collection of characters, each with qualities and idiosyncracies that change and develop over the course of time. As a unifying stylistic thread, Scola uses a recurring dolly shot through the apartment's empty hall that symbolizes the passing of time. Filled with humor, sadness, and anger, the film also manages to encompass nearly all the major political and social events of 20th-century Italy.

FAMILY PLOT

1976   120m   c   ★★★½
Thriller/Comedy   PG
Universal

Karen Black *(Fran)*, Bruce Dern *(Lumley)*, Barbara Harris *(Blanche)*, William Devane *(Adamson)*, Ed Lauter *(Maloney)*, Cathleen Nesbitt *(Julia Rainbird)*, Katherine Helmond *(Mrs. Maloney)*, Warren J. Kemmerling *(Grandison)*, Edith Atwater *(Mrs. Clay)*, William Prince *(Bishop)*

p, Alfred Hitchcock; d, Alfred Hitchcock; w, Ernest Lehman (from the novel *The Rainbird Pattern* by Victor Canning); ph, Leonard South (Technicolor); ed, J. Terry Williams; m, John Williams; art d, Henry Bumstead; fx, Frank Brendel, Albert Whitlock; cos, Edith Head

With two parallel plots running throughout, Alfred Hitchcock's final film is a brilliantly constructed mystery-thriller. Hired by elderly Miss Rainbird (Nesbitt) to locate a long-lost heir, phoney medium Blanche Tyler (Harris) and her cabbie boy friend George

Lumley (Dern)—amiable frauds— begin their search with very few clues. Meanwhile another more sinister couple, jeweler Arthur Adamson (Devane) and his girlfriend Fran (Black) are engineering a kidnapping scheme in which the ransom is to be paid in valuable diamonds. The paths of all of these characters and their respective "plots" eventually cross, in a comical directorial move, at a cemetery. Just when the mystery ends, however, the thrills begin—the most harrowing of which takes place along a curving mountainside road.

The film is a dense but extremely entertaining collection of symmetric patterns, doubles, and rhymes. The performances are first-rate (finally free of the casting constraints, Hitchcock displayed—in 1972's FRENZY as well—a deliciously offbeat taste in performers) and the screenplay by Ernest Lehman (NORTH BY NORTHWEST) is a witty model of construction. The humor is more obvious and subversive than any of Hitchcock's films since THE TROUBLE WITH HARRY. Hitch's final, tongue-in-cheek wink at his audience was one of his most memorable cameos—a broad shadow obscured behind a glass door on which may be read "Registrar of Births and Deaths." Based on a British novel by Victor Canning, the film was scripted under the title "One Plus One Equals One," and went into production as "Deceit," before a studio worker hit on the final title.

FANFAN THE TULIP

1952　104m　bw　　　　　　　　　　　　★★★
Comedy/Adventure　　　　　　　　　　　　　/A
Ariane/Filmsonor/Amato　(France)

Gerard Philipe (Fanfan the Tulip), Gina Lollobrigida (Adeline), Noel Roquevert (Fier-Abras), Olivier Hussenot (Tranche "Samson"), Marcel Herrand (Louis XV), Jean-Marc Tennberg (Lebel), Jean Paredes (Capt. La Houlette), Henri Rollan (Marshall of France), Nerio Bernardi (Sgt. La Franchise), Genevieve Page (La Pompadour)

p, Christian-Jaque; d, Christian-Jaque; w, Henri Jeanson, Christian-Jaque, Rene Wheeler (based on a story by Wheeler, Rene Fallet); ph, Christian Matras; ed, Jean Desagneaux; m, Georges Van Parys, Maurice Thiriet

This charming, witty satire of Errol Flynn swashbucklers features Gerard Philipe as Fanfan the Tulip, a 17th-century swordsman with his tongue firmly planted in cheek. About to be forced into a shotgun (or saber) wedding, he escapes matrimony by joining the king's army. A bogus soothsayer examines his palm and predicts he will marry the king's daughter one day and establish himself as one of France's greatest heroes. Later, he spies a coach being attacked by bandits and attacks the band of malfeasants, cutting them to bits with his swordplay. As it happens, Madame Pompadour (Page) and the king's daughter (Lollobrigida) are the coach's passengers from whom Fanfan receives a kiss as his payment. On the road to his destiny, there are several swordfights, a mock sentence of death, and a raid on a convent.

Although the film contains a subtle antiwar message, it's not necessary to look for any rhyme or reason in the script; just enjoy all the derring-do. Philipe, whose life ended when he had a heart attack at age 36, appeared in more than 30 films in his brief career, including DEVIL IN THE FLESH, THE SEVEN DEADLY SINS, BEAUTIES OF THE NIGHT, and BOLD ADVENTURE, the last of which he also wrote and directed.

FANNY

1932　125m　bw　　　　　　　　　　　　★★★½
Drama
Pagnol　(France)

Raimu (Cesar Olivier), Orane Demazis (Fanny), Pierre Fresnay (Marius), Fernand Charpin (Honore Panisse), Alida Rouffe (Honorine Cabanis), Robert Vattier (M. Brun), Auguste Mouries (Felix Escartefigue), Milly Mathis (Aunt Claudine Foulon), Maupi (Chauffeur), Edouard Delmont (Dr. Felicien Venelle)

p, Marcel Pagnol; d, Marc Allegret; w, Marcel Pagnol (based on his play); ph, Nicolas Toporkoff, Andre Dantan, Roger Hubert, Georges Benoit, Coutelain; ed, Raymond Lamy; m, Vincent Scotto

The second installment of Marcel Pagnol's "Marseilles Trilogy" picks up just a short while after the end of MARIUS. After Marius (Pierre Fresnay) has gone to sea, it is learned that the girl he loves, Fanny (Orane Demazis), is pregnant. Because she has her reputation to think of, Fanny is persuaded by her family to marry the older, widowed sailmaker Panisse (Fernand Charpin), despite the fact that she is still deeply in love with Marius. After a year at sea, Marius returns and tries to convince the woman he loves to leave Marseilles with him. However, she must consider the consequences and the feelings of Panisse, who has grown to love not only Fanny but the child as well.

Pagnol's warm, touching tale has been a success wherever it has played, attesting to the story's universal truthfulness. Written and produced by Pagnol and starring his troupe of actors, FANNY was filmed under the direction of Marc Allegret. MARIUS was directed by Alexander Korda, and the concluding film CESAR was directed by Pagnol himself.

FANNY AND ALEXANDER
(FANNY OCH ALEXANDER)

1982　188m　c　　　　　　　　　　　★★★★½
Drama　　　　　　　　　　　　　　　　　R/15
Cinematograph/Swedish Film Institute/Swedish TV One/Gaumont/Persona/Tobis　(France/West Germany/Sweden)

Gunn Wallgren (Helena Ekdahl), Boerje Ahlstedt (Prof. Carl Ekdahl), Christina Schollin (Lydia Ekdahl), Allan Edwall (Oscar Ekdahl), Ewa Froeling (Emilie Ekdahl), Pernilla Allwin (Fanny Ekdahl), Bertil Guve (Alexander Ekdahl), Jarl Kulle (Gustav-Adolph Ekdahl), Mona Malm (Alma Ekdahl), Pernilla Wallgren (Maj)

d, Ingmar Bergman; w, Ingmar Bergman; ph, Sven Nykvist (Eastmancolor); ed, Sylvia Ingemarsson; m, Daniel Bell, Benjamin Britten, Frans Helmerson, Robert Schumson, Marianne Jacobs; art d, Anna Asp, Susanne Lingheim; cos, Marik Vos

Steering away from the pain, neuroses, and heavy metaphysical questions showcased in his earlier work, Ingmar Bergman created this film based on childhood memories of the turn of the century.

FANNY AND ALEXANDER begins with the Ekdahl family's Christmas celebration, their large home serving as the meeting place for a merry celebration by family members and servants who dance about heedless of social constraints. Late that night, ten-year-old Alexander (Bertil Guve) is tucked in by the buxom maid, who apologizes for being unable to spend the night with him because she has other obligations—namely bedding down with his kindly Uncle Carl (Boerje Ahlstedt), a married man with children of his own, whose wise wife graciously tolerates his infidelities. Alexander's charmed life is suddenly shattered when his actor-manager father suffers a heart attack and dies, leaving the widow Ekdahl (Ewa Froeling) to be calmed by an understanding bishop (Jan Malmsjoe) whom she eventually marries. She takes her two children, Fanny (Pernilla Allwin) and Alexander, away from their warm family into the cold, strict world of the clergyman.

Not only does Bergman manage in FANNY AND ALEXANDER to capture the flavor and atmosphere of a Swedish town circa 1907, he also expertly reveals events as seen through the eyes of a child and, without any wordy dissertations on doctrines, makes a powerful statement against religious zealotry. The results are quite frightening and far superior to the lengthy gloom and doom that fill many earlier Bergman films. A magical movie, FANNY AND ALEXANDER is likely to be the achievement for which Bergman will be most remembered.

FANTASIA
1940 120m c   ★★★★½
Animated   /U
Disney

Deems Taylor *(Himself)*, Leopold Stokowski *(Himself)*, The Philadelphia Symphony Orchestra

p, Walt Disney; d, Samuel Armstrong, James Algar, Bill Roberts, Paul Satterfield, Hamilton Luske, Jim Handley, Ford Beebe, Walt Disney, Norman Ferguson, Wilfred Jackson; w, Lee Blair, Elmer Plummer, Phil Dike, Sylvia Moberly-Holland, Norman Wright, Albert Heath, Bianca Majolie, Graham Keid, Paul Pearse, Carl Fallberg, Leo Thiele, Robert Sterner, John Fraser McLeish, Otto Englander, Webb Smith, Erdman Penner, Joseph Sabo, Bill Peet, George Stallings; m, Johann Sebastian Bach, Peter Ilich Tchaikovsky, Igor Stravinsky, Ludwig van Beethoven, Modest Mussorgsky, Franz Schubert

The most ambitious animated feature ever to come out of the Disney studios, FANTASIA integrates great works of classical music with wildly uneven but extraordinarily imaginative visuals that run the gamut from dancing hippos to the purely abstract. It's like a feature-length compilation of elaborate Silly Symphonies. This impressive attempt to combine high art with mass culture was a financial debacle initially but in subsequent years it has become one of the studio's perennial cash cows.

Among the wonderfully kitschy combinations of sight and sound are J.S. Bach's "Toccata and Fugue in D Minor" (a rare exercise in abstraction for the Disney artists); Tchaikovsky's "Nutcracker Suite" (danced by fairies, mushrooms, flower petals, fish, thistles, and orchids); Stravinsky's "Rite of Spring" (illustrated as the genesis of the planet); Mussorgsky's "Night on Bald Mountain" (some key imagery is lifted from the opening scenes of F.W. Murnau's silent German Expressionist version of FAUST with Emil Jannings as Mephistopholes looming over a village; the fearsome "Black God" was pantomimed by Bela Lugosi as an animation guide for the Disney artists); and Schubert's "Ave Maria" (a subdued Impressionistic sequence of villagers walking through the woods to church).

Beethoven's "Pastoral Symphony" proved to be the most controversial segment, raising the hackles of music critics who didn't approve of the cartoon Bacchus, nymphs, and li'l' centaurs who accompanied it. (Reportedly, after screening the completed segment for the first time, a tearful Walt Disney declared "This will *make* Beethoven!") The film's most famous segment, Paul Dukas's "Sorcerer's Apprentice," stars Mickey Mouse (voiced by Walt himself for the final time) as the ambitious assistant who gets in way over his head when he uses his boss's magic hat to put a broom to work doing his chores. Originally intended as a short, "The Sorcerer's Apprentice" brought together Walt Disney and famed conductor Leopold Stokowski but when the produc-

tion ran over budget, Disney decided that the only way to recoup his investment would be to incorporate the segment into a feature.

The film began to appear in limited roadshow engagements in 1940, but due to wartime difficulties in getting the materials for the sound system that had to be installed in each theater, it was not until 1942 that it received general release. In the late 1960s FANTASIA re-emerged as a drug culture favorite and it continues to delight both children and adults today.

FANTASTIC VOYAGE
1966 100m c   ★★★½
Science Fiction   /U
FOX

Stephen Boyd *(Grant)*, Raquel Welch *(Cora Peterson)*, Edmond O'Brien *(Gen. Carter)*, Donald Pleasence *(Dr. Michaels)*, Arthur O'Connell *(Col. Donald Reid)*, William Redfield *(Capt. Bill Owens)*, Arthur Kennedy *(Dr. Duval)*, Jean Del Val *(Jan Benes)*, Barry Coe *(Communications Aide)*, Ken Scott *(Secret Serviceman)*

p, Saul David; d, Richard Fleischer; w, Harry Kleiner, David Duncan (adapted from the novel by Otto Klement and Jay Lewis Bixby); ph, Ernest Laszlo (CinemaScope, Deluxe Color); ed, William B. Murphy; m, Leonard Rosenman; art d, Jack Martin Smith, Dale Hennesy; fx, L.B. Abbott, Art Cruickshank, Emil Kosa, Jr.

A medical crew (Stephen Boyd, Raquel Welch, William Redfield, Arthur Kennedy, and Donald Pleasence) and a submarine are miniaturized to remove a blood clot from the brain of a Czech scientist who was shot while defecting. Once shrunk and inside the body, the crew battle white corpuscles while the heart and lungs also make their journey rougher. Early on, it becomes apparent that one of the crew members is a double agent, and matters become even more complex as they race against the clock to complete their mission before returning to normal size.

Their voyage through the body's bloodstream past assorted organs was created by inventive special effects that make this one of the more visually interesting science fiction films of its era. FANTASTIC VOYAGE won Oscars for Best Color Art Direction and Best Visual Effects. It was also nominated for Best Cinematography and Best Film Editing. Joe Dante's INNERSPACE is an amusing variation of the same idea.

FAR COUNTRY, THE
1955 96m c   ★★★★
Western   /U
Universal

James Stewart *(Jeff)*, Ruth Roman *(Ronda)*, Corinne Calvet *(Renee)*, Walter Brennan *(Ben)*, John McIntire *(Mr. Gannon)*, Jay C. Flippen *(Rube)*, Harry Morgan *(Ketchum)*, Steve Brodie *(Ives)*, Royal Dano *(Luke)*, Gregg Barton *(Rounds)*

p, Aaron Rosenberg; d, Anthony Mann; w, Borden Chase; ph, William Daniels (Technicolor); ed, Russell Schoengarth; m, Joseph Gershenson; art d, Bernard Harzbrun, Alexander Golitzen

A strange, almost self-conscious, Western from one of the greatest practioners of the form. Like other Mann efforts , THE FAR COUNTRY is noteworthy for the parable starkness of its story and its flawless command of landscape photography. His films also have the most articulated moments of combat in the cinema: issues of honor, betrayal, violence, and death figure prominently.

Partners Jeff (Stewart) and Ben (Brennan) travel north from Wyoming to the Oregon Territory with a herd of cattle, planning to sell the steers for a fortune in the gold-boom towns. They arrive in the town of Skagway, where the self-appointed judge, Mr. Gannon (McIntire), takes the herd from them. Jeff steals his cattle back, and goes to the town of Dawson, where he is befriended by a saloonkeeper, Ronda (Roman). She decides to help him against Mr. Gannon and his men, who will stop at nothing to get the herd back.

One of the most engrossing and original Westerns made in the 1950s, THE FAR COUNTRY was the fifth collaboration of producer Aaron Rosenberg, director Anthony Mann, and James Stewart. The film benefits greatly from the presence of James Stewart and his barely suppressed malevolence as the hero. Mann's strong and thoughtful direction, the sturdy script by Borden Chase, and the beautiful cinematography of the northern wilderness all contribute to make this an outstanding film.

FAR FROM THE MADDING CROWD

1967   168m   c   ★★½
Drama   /U
MGM   (U.K.)

Julie Christie (*Bathsheba Everdene*), Terence Stamp (*Sgt. Troy*), Peter Finch (*William Boldwood*), Alan Bates (*Gabriel Oak*), Prunella Ransome (*Fanny Robin*), Fiona Walker (*Liddy*), Paul Dawkins (*Henery Fray*), Andrew Robertson (*Andrew Randle*), John Barrett (*Joseph Poorgrass*), Julian Somers (*Jan Coggan*)

p, Joseph Janni; d, John Schlesinger; w, Frederic Raphael (adapted from the novel by Thomas Hardy); ph, Nicolas Roeg (Metrocolor); ed, Malcolm Cooke; m, Richard Rodney Bennett; art d, Roy Forge Smith; cos, Alan Barrett

Director Schlesinger makes the best of a script that adheres to Thomas Hardy's novel almost page for page. Set in 1874, Bathsheba Everdene (Christie) is in love with (and feels superior to) three men, Sergeant Troy (Stamp), William Boldwood (Finch), and Gabriel Oak (Bates). Who will she choose?

This is a predictable story that Schlesinger struggles to keep fresh and moving. The actors have a difficult time with the flat characters but, at times, are able to breath life into them. Nicolas Roeg's cinematography is stunning.

FAREWELL, MY LOVELY

1975   97m   c   ★★★
Mystery   R/15
EK/ITC

Robert Mitchum (*Phillip Marlowe*), Charlotte Rampling (*Mrs. Velma Grayle*), John Ireland (*Lt. Nulty*), Sylvia Miles (*Mrs. Jessie Florian*), Jack O'Halloran (*Moose Malloy*), Anthony Zerbe (*Laird Burnette*), Harry Dean Stanton (*Billy Rolfe*), Jim Thompson (*Judge Grayle*), John O'Leary (*Lindsay Marriott*), Kate Murtagh (*Frances Amthor*)

p, George Pappas, Jerry Bruckheimer; d, Dick Richards; w, David Zelag Goodman (based on the novel by Raymond Chandler); ph, John A. Alonzo (Panavision, Fujicolor); ed, Walter Thompson, Joel Cox; m, David Shire; prod d, Dean Tavoularis; art d, Angelo Graham; fx, Chuck Gaspar; cos, Tony Scarano

Mitchum, as the intrepid private eye Marlowe, is hired by Moose Malloy (O'Halloran), a giant thug recently released from prison, to find his girlfriend. Mitchum takes on a second case when the fey Lindsay Marriott (O'Leary) seeks his assistance in buying back a valuable jade necklace held for ransom after being stolen from the sultry Velma Grayle (Rampling). Investigating both cases simultaneously, Marlowe discovers that the two cases are really one and the same—a puzzle involving false identity, hidden loot, and murder.

An affectionate adaptation of Raymond Chandler's novel that beautifully evokes the seamy side of 1940s Los Angeles via superb production design and the same period atmosphere cine-

matographer Alonzo previously evoked for CHINATOWN. Interestingly, Mitchum's appeal here has more to do with his own exalted status as a noir icon rather any particularly inspired interpretation of Marlowe. The novel was adapted for the screen twice before, as a vehicle for George Sanders in RKO's THE FALCON TAKES OVER and the superb MURDER, MY SWEET. A moderate hit at the box office, FAREWELL MY LOVELY spawned a fatally flawed remake of THE BIG SLEEP that abandons 1940s Los Angeles in favor of modern-day London.

FAREWELL TO ARMS, A

1932   90m   bw   ★★★★
Romance/War   /15
Paramount

Helen Hayes (*Catherine Barkley*), Gary Cooper (*Lt. Frederic Henry*), Adolphe Menjou (*Maj. Rinaldi*), Mary Philips (*Helen Ferguson*), Jack LaRue (*the Priest*), Blanche Frederici (*Head Nurse*), Henry Armetta (*Bonello*), George Humbert (*Piani*), Fred Malatesta (*Manera*), Mary Forbes (*Miss Van Campen*)

d, Frank Borzage; w, Benjamin Glazer, Oliver H.P. Garrett (based on the novel by Ernest Hemingway); ph, Charles Lang; ed, Otho Lovering; m, Ralph Rainger, John Leipold, Bernhard Kaun, Paul Marquardt, Herman Hand, W. Franke Harling; art d, Hans Dreier, Roland Anderson; cos, Travis Banton

Frank Borzage's masterful adaptation of Ernest Hemingway's celebrated novel stars Gary Cooper as Lt. Frederic Henry, an American adventurer serving in the Italian ambulance corps during WWI, and Helen Hayes as Catherine Barkley, the beautiful English nurse with whom he falls madly in love. When Lt. Henry returns to the front, his jealous friend and superior, Maj. Rinaldi (Adolphe Menjou), intervenes to disrupt their budding romance. Nonetheless the two share a blissful interlude in Milan before Henry returns to the war and Catherine travels to Switzerland to have their baby. Henry knows that someday he will return to her but he must endure many hardships along the way.

Despite Hemingway's reported disgust with the film's comparatively optimistic ending, A FAREWELL TO ARMS is generally faithful to his novel. Director Borzage is at his best here as he utilizes light and movement like brushstrokes to paint a beautifully romantic melodrama with the aid of cinematographer Charles Lang. Borzage's focus is on the love story, but his sweeping battle scenes, loaded with armies of extras, smack of war-torn reality, especially the famous retreat from Caporetto, brilliantly captured in montage. And the performances, while a trifle overblown by modern standards, are so powerful that the film retains its emotional jolt. Hayes was never more appealing, Menjou is at his manipulative best, Cooper displays tremendous depth of feeling, and the supporting work is equally accomplished.

The story is drawn from Hemingway's WWI experiences, his battlefield injury, and his love affair with Agnes von Kurowsky. *A Farewell to Arms* was adapted for the screen twice more: in 1950 as FORCE OF ARMS with William Holden and Nancy Olsen, and under the original title in 1957 with Rock Hudson and Jennifer Jones.

FARMER'S DAUGHTER, THE

1947   96m   bw   ★★★½
Political/Comedy   /A
RKO

Loretta Young (Katrin Holstrom), Joseph Cotten (Glenn Morley), Ethel Barrymore (Mrs. Morley), Charles Bickford (Clancy), Rose Hobart (Virginia), Rhys Williams (Adolph), Harry Davenport (Dr. Mathew Sutven), Tom Powers (Nordick), William Harrigan (Ward Hughes), Lex Barker (Olaf Holstrom)

p, Dore Schary; d, H.C. Potter; w, Allen Rivkin, Laura Kerr (from the play "Hulda, Daughter of Parliament" by Juhni Tervataa); ph, Milton Krasner; ed, Harry Marker; m, Leigh Harline

This winning Capraesque romantic comedy features Loretta Young as Katrin Holstrom, a Swedish farmer's daughter who comes to the capital in search of a nursing job but eventually becomes the maid for Congressman Glenn Morley (Joseph Cotten) and his powerful politico mother (Ethel Barrymore). Katrin is the perfect housekeeper in almost every way, but when the Morleys try to promote the congressional candidacy of a man Katrin can't abide, she speaks out publicly and ends up as the rival party's candidate for the office. Young won an Academy Award for her delightful performance and Charles Bickford received a Best Supporting Actor Oscar nomination for his role as the butler who shows Katrin the ropes.

FAST TIMES AT RIDGEMONT HIGH

1982 92m c   ★★★
Comedy   R/18
Universal

Sean Penn (Jeff Spicoli), Jennifer Jason Leigh (Stacy Hamilton), Judge Reinhold (Brad Hamilton), Robert Romanus (Mike Damone), Brian Backer (Mark "Rat" Ratner), Phoebe Cates (Linda Barrett), Ray Walston (Mr. Hand), Scott Thomson (Arnold), Vincent Schiavelli (Mr. Vargas), Amanda Wyss (Lisa)

p, Art Linson, Irving Azoff; d, Amy Heckerling; w, Cameron Crowe (adapted from his book); ph, Matthew F. Leonetti (Technicolor); ed, Eric Jenkins; m, Joe Walsh; art d, Dan Lomino

At age 22, writer Cameron Crowe returned to high school, posing as a student, and wrote a book about his experiences. In adapting the book, director Amy Heckerling created a brashly funny yet sensitive comedy that has become a cult favorite.

Chronicling a year in the lives of a group of California teenagers, the film follows the fortunes of Ridgemont High senior Brad Hamilton (Judge Reinhold) and his freshman sister Stacey (Jennifer Jason Leigh). Brad's popularity wanes when he loses his "good" fast-food job, and Stacey is introduced to the wonders of boys by Linda (Phoebe Cates). Mark "Rat" Ratner (Brian Backer) has a big crush on Stacey, but it's oily Mike Damone (Robert Romanus) who initiates her into the world of sex. The film's most memorable character is the perpetually stoned surfer played by Sean Penn. His confrontations with Mr. Hand (Ray Walston), a draconian history teacher, provide the film's finest moments.

In addition to adapting his novel for this film, onetime rock critic Crowe also wrote the screenplay for the less successful teenage comedy THE WILD LIFE before making his directorial debut with the extraordinary SAY ANYTHING. Forest Whitaker (GOOD MORNING VIETNAM, BIRD), Anthony Edwards (MR. NORTH, TOP GUN), and Eric Stoltz (MASK, MEMPHIS BELLE) made their film debuts in this superior teen comedy.

FAT CITY

1972 100m c   ★★★★
Drama/Sports   PG/AA
Columbia

Stacy Keach (Billy Tully), Jeff Bridges (Ernie Munger), Susan Tyrrell (Oma), Candy Clark (Faye), Nicholas Colasanto (Ruben), Art Aragon (Babe), Curtis Cokes (Earl), Sixto Rodriguez (Lucero), Billy Walker (Wes), Wayne Mahan (Buford)

p, Ray Stark; d, John Huston; w, Leonard Gardner (based on his novel); ph, Conrad Hall (Eastmancolor); ed, Margaret Booth; m, Marvin Hamlisch; prod d, Richard Sylbert; fx, Paul Stewart; cos, Dorothy Jeakins

Set in Stockton, California, against a backdrop of run-down bars, cheap apartments and half-empty second rate gyms, FAT CITY is a grim story of hope and despair among life's losers.

Billy Tully (Stacy Keach), a 29-year-old one-time boxing contender, contemplates a comeback after nearly two years of alcoholism brought about by the loss of both his wife and the biggest fight of his career. He meets Ernie Munger (Jeff Bridges), a promising 19-year-old, and encourages him to hook up with Billy's old manager (Nicholas Colasanto). This Ernie does and so begins his own boxing career. Billy, however, continues boozing and his personal and professional lives continue their downward trajectory.

Adapted by Leonard Gardner from his own novel and brilliantly directed by John Huston, who was himself once a an amateur champion, FAT CITY is both an extraordinarily realistic look at the bottom rungs of the fight game and a moving exploration of the human condition. Keach, Bridges, Tyrrell (who received an Oscar nomination for her portrayal of the alcoholic Oma, Billy's temporary girlfriend), and all the supporting players give first-rate performances. All in all, this strong downbeat film, which makes appropriate use of Kris Kristofferson's "Help Me Make It through the Night," is never less than captivating.

FATAL ATTRACTION

1987 119m c   ★★★
Thriller/Romance   R/18
Paramount

Michael Douglas (Dan Gallagher), Glenn Close (Alex Forrest), Anne Archer (Beth Gallagher), Ellen Hamilton Latzen (Ellen Gallagher), Stuart Pankin (Jimmy), Ellen Foley (Hildy), Fred Gwynne (Arthur), Meg Mundy (Joan Rogerson), Tom Brennan (Howard Rogerson), Lois Smith (Martha)

p, Stanley R. Jaffe, Sherry Lansing; d, Adrian Lyne; w, James Dearden; ph, Howard Atherton (Technicolor); ed, Michael Kahn, Peter E. Berger; m, Maurice Jarre; prod d, Mel Bourne; art d, Jack Blackman; cos, Ellen Mirojnick

FATAL ATTRACTION was more than a box-office smash; it was a cultural phenomenon. This story of an extramarital fling that turns into a nightmare begins as an excellent psychological thriller until psychology takes a back seat to thrills in its final minutes.

Dan Gallagher (Michael Douglas) is a Manhattan lawyer with a gorgeous wife (Anne Archer) and a six-year-old daughter. When he first meets Alex (Glenn Close), he is intrigued, but unavailable. On another weekend, though, a chance meeting brings Dan and Alex together for a passionate two-night stand in her apartment. When Dan tries to say his final goodbye and return to his family, he gets the first hint that Alex is not entirely rational and has become obsessed with him. That obsession soon turns life into an escalating nightmare for Dan and his family.

Screenwriter James Dearden has created a set of believable characters, placed them in a familiar situation, and then drastically upped the stakes. Unfortunately, motivations and psychological concerns are thrown out the window in the final reel. The blame for this doesn't rest entirely with Dearden or director Adrian Lyne; the producers tested the original ending (Alex commits suicide, but not before implicating Dan as her murderer) and preview audiences found it less than satisfying. The thrill-a-minute conclusion was then shot and substituted.

Notwithstanding the ending, the performances are excellent. Playing against type, Close is overtly sexy, while at the same time making her obsession and slide into madness convincing and pathetic. Douglas also gives a performance of considerable depth, and Archer does a nice turn as his steady but alluring wife.

FATHER GOOSE

1964   115m   c   ★★★
War/Comedy   /U
Universal

Cary Grant (Walter Eckland), Leslie Caron (Catherine Freneau), Trevor Howard (Commodore Frank Houghton), Jack Good (Lt. Stebbins), Verina Greenlaw (Christine), Pip Sparke (Anne), Jennifer Berrington (Harriet), Stephanie Berrington (Elizabeth), Laurelle Felsette (Angelique), Nicole Felsette (Dominique)

p, Robert Arthur; d, Ralph Nelson; w, Frank Tarloff, Peter Stone (based on the story "A Place Of Dragons" by S.H. Barnett); ph, Charles Lang (Technicolor); ed, Ted J. Kent; m, Cy Coleman; art d, Alexander Golitzen, Henry Bumstead; cos, Ray Aghayan

Playing against his sophisticated image, Cary Grant is Walter Eckland, a drunken beach bum who sits out WWII on a South Seas island until he is coerced by an Australian naval officer (Trevor Howard) into monitoring Japanese air activity. When Eckland travels to a nearby island to rescue another plane watcher, he finds the observer dead, but schoolteacher Catherine Freneau (Leslie Caron) and her seven young female charges are very much alive after being marooned when their plane went down. They return with Eckland and clean up his act while he and Freneau fall in love. Danger looms, however, as the Japanese forces close in. Grant's penultimate film (WALK, DON'T RUN was his last), this romantic comedy won Best Screenplay Oscars for Frank Tarloff and Peter Stone, who worked on the screenplay separately but were awarded a shared credit by a Writers Guild arbitration.

FATHER OF THE BRIDE

1950   92m   bw   ★★★★
Comedy   /U
MGM

Spencer Tracy (Stanley T. Banks), Joan Bennett (Ellie Banks), Elizabeth Taylor (Kay Banks), Don Taylor (Buckley Dunstan), Billie Burke (Doris Dunstan), Leo G. Carroll (Mr. Massoula), Moroni Olsen (Herbert Dunstan), Melville Cooper (Mr. Tringle), Taylor Holmes (Warner), Paul Harvey (Rev. Galsworthy)

p, Pandro S. Berman; d, Vincente Minnelli; w, Frances Goodrich, Albert Hackett (based on the novel by Edward Streeter); ph, John Alton; ed, Ferris Webster; m, Adolph Deutsch; art d, Cedric Gibbons, Leonid Vasian; cos, Helen Rose, Walter Plunkett

Nowadays remembered primarily as the first of many walks La Liz was to take down the aisle, FATHER OF THE BRIDE is also one of the best comedies MGM made in the 1950s. Although Taylor perfectly embodies an idealized vision of the demure but spirited young bride, this fine film is foremost a showcase for the supple comic drollery of Spencer Tracy. As Stanley Banks, the harassed father who must cope with the business of marrying his daughter off, Tracy finds a marvelous vehicle for his expressive but low-key style.

The movie begins as the exhausted Banks looks over the debris and chaos in his home after the wedding, then turns to the audience to relate his story. The problems and responsibilities of marrying off a daughter are legion: there's the heart-to-heart talk with the suitor; meeting the in-laws; selecting the honeymoon site; and, of course, the near-ruinous financial expense.

Although continually skimming the edge of bland sitcom land, this satiric look at the American Family, circa 1950, still packs a gentle punch. The screenplay, if occasionally contrived, is witty and incisive and Minnelli's assured direction keeps the proceedings from disintegrating into indulgent slapstick. As the bride's mother, Joan Bennett is excellent in her first film for MGM, and the supporting performances are all good, with especially fine work from Moroni Olsen and Billie Burke as the parents of the groom. The last is played with charm and the perfect touch of dullness by Don Taylor, who later traded acting for the director's chair. The film inspired a sequel, FATHER'S LITTLE DIVIDEND.

FEAR AND DESIRE

1953   68m   bw   ★★★
War
Kubrick

Frank Silvera (Mac), Kenneth Harp (Lt. Corby), Paul Mazursky (Sidney), Steve Coit (Fletcher), Virginia Leith (Girl), David Allen (Narrator)

p, Stanley Kubrick; d, Stanley Kubrick; w, Howard Sackler, Stanley Kubrick; ph, Stanley Kubrick; ed, Stanley Kubrick; m, Gerald Fried

Notable as Stanley Kubrick's first film, produced when he was 22 years old on a budget of $40,000. A modest effort, FEAR AND DESIRE nonetheless displays the preoccupation with the pressures and absurdities of war which would later mark many of Kubrick's later films. Not only did he produce and direct, but he also shot and edited this story of four soldiers caught behind enemy lines in an abstractly depicted war.

Trying to move back to their own side, they kill several enemy soldiers and capture a young woman (Leith). One of the men, Sidney (Mazursky, making his film debut), is left to guard her as the other three (Silvera, Harp and Coit) go to a river to build a raft. Wanting to seduce the girl, Sidney unties her from a tree, and when she runs away, he kills her and then goes insane. Returning from the river, the three soldiers discover an enemy outpost holding a general and his aide. The confrontation between the three enterprising soldiers and the enemy climaxes this highly promising first effort by one of America's premiere filmmakers.

FEAR EATS THE SOUL

1974   94m   c   ★★★★
Romance   /AA
Tango/Autorn   (West Germany)

Brigitte Mira (Emmi), El Hedi Ben Salem (Ali), Barbara Valentin (Barbara), Irm Hermann (Krista), Peter Gauhe (Bruno), Karl Scheydt (Albert), Rainer Werner Fassbinder (Eugen), Marquard Bohm (Gruber), Walter Sedlmayer (Angermayer), Doris Mattes (Mrs. Angermeyer)

d, Rainer Werner Fassbinder; w, Rainer Werner Fassbinder; ph, Jurgen Jurges; ed, Thea Eymes

An excellent early drama by the prolific if tragically shortlived Fassbinder. Emmi (Mira) is a widowed cleaning woman, lonely and neglected, who has an affair with Ali (Salem), a similarly neglected and lonely Moroccan mechanic. Over the objections of her appalled family and friends, she marries him. No longer lonely, she begins to change, eventually becoming as prejudiced and self-centered as her friends.

One of the German director's most thought-provoking films, FEAR EATS THE SOUL vividly displays his talent for reworking the conventions of Hollywood melodramas, especially those of his idol, Douglas Sirk. Mira and Salem are superb in the leading roles, powerfully conveying the weakness, alienation, and racism of the society Fassbinder is targeting. The director himself plays the role of the slimy son-in-law Eugen.

FEAR STRIKES OUT
1957 100m bw
Biography/Sports   /A
Paramount

Anthony Perkins *(Jimmy Piersall)*, Karl Malden *(John Piersall)*, Norma Moore *(Mary Teevan)*, Adam Williams *(Dr. Brown)*, Peter Votrian *(Jimmy Piersall as a Boy)*, Perry Wilson *(Mrs. John Piersall)*, Dennis McMullen *(Phil)*, Gail Land *(Alice)*, Brian Hutton *(Bernie Sherwill)*, Bart Burns *(Joe Cronin)*

p, Alan J. Pakula; d, Robert Mulligan; w, Ted Berkman, Raphael Blau (based on the autobiography by James A. Piersall, with Albert S. Hirshberg); ph, Haskell Boggs; ed, Aaron Stell; m, Elmer Bernstein; fx, John P. Fulton; cos, Edith Head

Perkins portrays Jimmy Piersall in this well-done biopic of one of baseball's most colorful characters, who, from boyhood, was relentlessly driven by his father (Malden) to make it in the major leagues. Nothing the talented Jimmy does is good enough for his dad, and, after finally making the Boston Red Sox, he breaks down, maniacally climbing the backstop after hitting a home run—one of the best-remembered scenes in any sports film. Jimmy is then admitted to Westborough State Hospital, where he gradually recovers under the supervision of Dr. Brown (Williams), eventually returning to his wife, his repentant father, and the Red Sox lineup.

The physically awkward Perkins may seem an unlikely candidate to portray a professional athlete, however, in a dry run of his performance in PSYCHO, he delivers a powerful portrayal of a young man undergoing tremendous emotional turmoil; in the final analysis, the film's psychological impact far outweighs how Perkins looks throwing a baseball back into the infield. Based on Piersall's autobiography, this directorial debut for Mulligan also boasts an extremely effective, typically full-volume performance by Malden as Piersall's demanding but loving father.

FELLINI SATYRICON
1969 128m c
Historical   /18
P.E.A./Artistes   (France/Italy)

Martin Potter *(Encolpius)*, Hiram Keller *(Ascyltus)*, Max Born *(Giton)*, Capucine *(Tryphaena)*, Salvo Randone *(Eumolpus)*, Magali Noel *(Fortunata)*, Alain Cuny *(Lichas)*, Lucia Bose *(Suicide Wife)*, Tanya Lopert *(Caesar)*, Gordon Mitchell *(Robber)*

p, Alberto Grimaldi; d, Federico Fellini; w, Federico Fellini, Bernardino Zapponi, Brunello Rondi (based on the fragment "Satyricon" by Gaius Petronius); ph, Giuseppe Rotunno (Panavision, DeLuxe Color); ed, Ruggero Mastroianni; m, Nino Rota, Ilhan Mimaroglu, Tod Dockstader, Andrew Rudin; prod d, Danilo Donati; art d, Luigi Scaccianoce, Giorgio Giovannini; fx, Adriano Pischiutta; cos, Danilo Donati

Orgy, anyone? The bizarre characters and situations that had filled the films of Federico Fellini since his early VARIETY LIGHTS found their ultimate expression in this dreamy, hallucinatory depiction of ancient Rome. Based on the 1st century A.D. fragment of a drama by Gaius Petronius (with added inspiration from other writings of the period), this film strips away all the glamor and honor associated with the early Romans to expose a society in which conventional morality has little or no significance. But Fellini's desire was not to criticize Rome, nor was it to set the history books straight; rather, he found the perfect setting with which to parallel the youth culture of the 1960s.

Encolpius (Potter) and Ascyltus (Keller) are two students whose adventures in a hotbed of decadence are the excuse for the threadbare plot that holds this extraordinary spectacle together. Their sole aim is the pursuit of hedonistic desires, and hedonism is just what Fellini gives us—there are concubines, nymphomaniacs, hermaphrodites (in the form of an albino infant with magical healing powers), sadism, masochism, and no doubt a few more "isms" as well amidst all the group sex going on.

The odd thing is that the excess seems visual and mythical rather than really sexual. (For one thing we *see* very little sex.) The masterful cinematography and stunning use of color, achieved through the use of deliberately artificial light sources, lend the film an almost hypnotic sheen. Even if you can't recall particular images, the look of the film is likely to linger in your memory.

FERRIS BUELLER'S DAY OFF
1986 103m c   ★★
Comedy   PG-13/15
Paramount

Matthew Broderick *(Ferris Bueller)*, Alan Ruck *(Cameron Frye)*, Mia Sara *(Sloane Peterson)*, Jeffrey Jones *(Ed Rooney)*, Jennifer Grey *(Jeanie Bueller)*, Cindy Pickett *(Katie Bueller)*, Lyman Ward *(Tom Bueller)*, Edie McClurg *(School Secretary)*, Charlie Sheen *(Boy in Police Station)*, Ben Stein *(Economics Teacher)*

p, John Hughes, Tom Jacobson; d, John Hughes; w, John Hughes; ph, Tak Fujimoto (Panavision, Metrocolor); ed, Paul Hirsch; m, Ira Newborn, Arthur Baker, John Robie; prod d, John W. Corso; chor, Kenny Ortega; cos, Marilyn Vance

Well, it would have made a great television sitcom pilot. Broderick plays the title role, a popular high school student living in a well-to-do Chicago suburb. After convincing his parents that he is truly sick, Ferris calls on his friend Cameron (Ruck) to join him for a day off from school. Cameron agrees, reluctantly, because it means taking his father's prized classic 1961 red Ferrari 250 GT convertible. They pick up Ferris's girlfriend (Sara) and head for downtown Chicago, but our plucky hero's nemesis, the high school's dean of students (Jones), has caught on to the scheme and is determined to catch the boy in the act.

Considering that the story and pacing of this offbeat comedy wear thin after the first 20 minutes, FERRIS BUELLER'S DAY OFF has more funny moments than most bad teenage comedies, primarily because Broderick brings some real charm and chutzpah to the part. Unfortunately, the wonderfully clever promise of the film's opening is never fulfilled. Hughes, directing from his own screenplay, starts off well but pushes his premise too far and ultimately kills the joke. Where Hughes really succeeds is in his obviously affectionate lensing of Chicago locations.

FIDDLER ON THE ROOF

1971   180m   c   ★★★½
Comedy/Musical   G/U
Mirisch

Topol (*Tevye*), Norma Crane (*Golde*), Leonard Frey (*Motel*), Molly Picon (*Yente*), Paul Mann (*Lazar Wolf*), Rosalind Harris (*Tzeitel*), Michele Marsh (*Hodel*), Neva Small (*Chava*), Paul Michael Glaser (*Perchik*), Raymond Lovelock (*Fyedka*)

p, Norman Jewison; d, Norman Jewison; w, Joseph Stein (from the book of the musical, based on stories by Sholem Aleichem); ph, Oswald Morris (Panavision 70, Technicolor); ed, Anthony Gibbs, Robert Lawrence; art d, Michael Stringer; chor, Tom Abbott, Sam Bayes; cos, Elizabeth Haffenden, Joan Bridge

Fiddlesticks. Although scenarist Stein closely adapted the book of his long-running Broadway smash, FIDDLER ON THE ROOF is simply not up to the original's standard, suffering from excessive length and dim photography. Set in the Ukraine in the early 1900s and based on several tales by Sholem Aleichem, the overly sentimental story focuses on Tevye (Topol), his long-suffering wife (Crane), and their three dissimilar daughters, Hodel (Marsh), Tzeitel (Harris), and Chava (Small). Each of the girls finds a potential husband, though Tevye disapproves of all three matches. Meanwhile, the Jewish community faces harassment from the Czar and neighboring Cossacks which culminates in a pogrom, with the survivors left to pick up the pieces of their lives.

The film's strengths lie in the careful detailing of life in pre-Bolshevik Jewish Russia, and the often rough-hewn, open-air quality the film achieves. These same qualities pervade the zestful yet touching performance of Topol, who justly received an Oscar nomination as Best Actor for his marvelous work. What a pity that no one else in the cast makes a similar impression. An even greater pity lies in director Jewison's pacing and visual style.

Apart from several lovely shots of twilight vistas, Jewison proves yet again that he does not know what to do with a camera. The rhythm is not so much leisurely as it is slack, and the pogrom sequence is not nearly as powerful as it should be. The most obvious victim of the choppy cutting is the choreography, all but destroyed by the editor's handiwork. Finally, as handled here, the famous score reveals its major defect: almost every decent song is in the movie's first half. What could have been a brilliant film experience, expanding on the stage version as only film can, ends up instead as a series of wonderful bits and pieces.

FIELD OF DREAMS

1989   107m   c   ★★★
Sports   PG
Gordon

Kevin Costner (*Ray Kinsella*), Amy Madigan (*Annie Kinsella*), Gaby Hoffman (*Karin Kinsella*), Ray Liotta (*Shoeless Joe Jackson*), Timothy Busfield (*Mark*), James Earl Jones (*Terence Mann*), Burt Lancaster (*Dr. "Moonlight" Graham*), Frank Whaley (*Archie Graham*), Dwier Brown (*John Kinsella*), James Andelin (*Feed Store Farmer*)

p, Lawrence Gordon, Charles Gordon; d, Phil Alden Robinson; w, Phil Alden Robinson (based on the book *Shoeless Joe* by W.P. Kinsella); ph, John Lindley (Deluxe Color); ed, Ian Crafford; m, James Horner; prod d, Dennis Gassner; art d, Leslie McDonald; cos, Linda Bass

One of 1989's biggest hits, Phil Alden Robinson's FIELD OF DREAMS firmly fixed Kevin Costner's position in the Hollywood firmament. Based on the W.P. Kinsella novel *Shoeless Joe*, the film is a canny blend of myth, dreams, and baseball which some viewers of good faith believe actually skirts the sentimental and obvious.

At the urging of a mysterious voice, Iowa farmer Ray Kinsella (Costner) comes to believe that if he carves a baseball field out of his cornfield, his late father's hero, long-dead baseball great Shoeless Joe Jackson, will return to play. Supported by his wife, Annie (Amy Madigan), he plows away his family's livelihood and constructs a baseball field—complete with lights! His neighbors think he's crazy but—would you believe it?—Jackson (Ray Liotta) does indeed appear as the harbinger of an incredible assemblage of ghosts of all-stars past. However, nobody but Kinsella and his family can see these baseball greats. With his farm threatened by bankruptcy, Kinsella is mysteriously led to Boston's Fenway Park, and to a further series of fantastic events.

If any recent movie aspires to be called Capraesque it is FIELD OF DREAMS, a sappy and good-naturedly dopey paean to traditional family values and nostalgia for innocent pleasures. The most powerful element of the movie is the depiction of an intense yearning on the part of males to bond with their fathers. For many people this was an irresistable prescription for smiles and tears but others were resolutely unmoved by its emotionally manipulative sub-"Twilight Zone" qualities. Perhaps the problem is the film's reliance upon group acceptance of the familiar iconography of the erstwhile national pastime as some kind of symbolic shorthand for all kinds of values. Sorry but it's just a game after all.

FIGHTER SQUADRON

1948   96m   c   ★★★½
War
WB

Edmond O'Brien (*Maj. Ed Hardin*), Robert Stack (*Capt. Stu Hamilton*), John Rodney (*Col. Bill Brickley*), Tom D'Andrea (*Sgt. Dolan*), Henry Hull (*Brig. Gen. Mike McCready*), James Holden (*Tennessee*), Walter Reed (*Capt. Duke Chappell*), Shepperd Strudwick (*Brig. Gen. M. Gilbert*), Arthur Space (*Maj. Sanford*), Jack Larson (*Shorty*)

p, Seton I. Miller; d, Raoul Walsh; w, Seton I. Miller, Martin Rackin; ph, Sid Hickox, Wilfrid M. Cline (Technicolor); ed, Christian Nyby; m, Max Steiner; art d, Ted Smith; fx, John Holden, Roy Davidson, H.F. Koenekamp

Fondly remembered by trivia buffs as the debut of Rock Hudson, who, by all accounts, required over three dozen takes to convincingly utter his one line, this film also provides a stirring account of US fighter pilots battling the Luftwaffe in 1943-44 over England and France.

O'Brien is excellent as Maj. Hardin, the leader of the small squadron, trying to keep up his and his outfit's nerve while leading sortie after sortie against vastly superior numbers. Intertwined with profiles of Hardin's crew is a good deal of color combat footage, superbly edited by Nyby. Stack is absorbing as Hardin's pensive protege and intended successor, while veteran actors Hull and Strudwick make the most of their unrewarding roles as big brass obligated to send men to their death in the air.

A haunting mood manages to transform the more cliched aspects of the screenplay, which somewhat resembles the better-known TWELVE O'CLOCK HIGH in theme and tone. Director Walsh shows his typical mastery of action material, Steiner's score is dynamic and the photography by Hickox and Cline is terrific. And, best of all, a star is born!

FIGHTING 69TH, THE

1940   90m   bw   ★★★★
War   /PG
WB

James Cagney *(Jerry Plunkett)*, Pat O'Brien *(Father Duffy)*, George Brent *(Wild Bill Donovan)*, Jeffrey Lynn *(Joyce Kilmer)*, Alan Hale *(Sgt. Big Mike Wynn)*, Frank McHugh *("Crepe Hanger" Burke)*, Dennis Morgan *(Lt. Ames)*, William Lundigan *(Timmy Wynn)*, Dick Foran *(John Wynn)*, Guinn "Big Boy" Williams *(Paddy Dolan)*

p, Louis F. Edelman; d, William Keighley; w, Norman Reilly Raine, Fred Niblo, Jr., Dean Franklin; ph, Tony Gaudio; ed, Owen Marks; m, Adolph Deutsch; art d, Ted Smith; fx, Byron Haskin, Rex Wimpy

Enough fighting Irish blarney for a dozen St. Patrick's Days. A showcase for the wisecracking, swaggering antics of Cagney, playing a would-be hero from Brooklyn who joins the all-Irish 69th New York Regiment after the US enters WWI.

Jerry Plunkett (Cagney) is a street-corner brawler who couldn't care less about the illustrious military tradition embodied in the old 69th and who snubs feisty Father Duffy (O'Brien, who else?) when he finds out that Duffy is a priest. ("I don't go in for that Holy Joe stuff," as he puts it.) Throughout his training, which he regards as a waste of time, Jerry defies his superiors, including a tough old sergeant (Hale) and his commanding officer, "Wild Bill" Donovan (Brent). Actual combat, however, proves to be too much for the obnoxious recruit, who first accidentally gives away his company's position and whose later cowardice results in the death of dozens of doughboys. Sentenced to death, Plunkett is inadvertantly given a chance to redeem himself when a bomb destroys his prison, and the stage is set for the action-packed finale.

One of the rare Hollywood films without any women or romantic angles whatsoever, THE FIGHTING 69TH was, not too surprisingly, an enormous hit with an American public about to enter WWII. Cagney gives such a galvanizing performance that one almost doesn't care that the film's one-note patriotism and Irish sentiment are as high as the corn in late summer. O'Brien fares less well as yet another priestly paragon of virtue, but the supporting cast is extremely proficient, Keighley's direction very zippy, and the technical merit of the enterprise quite exhilarating.

FINDERS KEEPERS

1984   96m   c   ★★½
Comedy   R/15
CBS

Michael O'Keefe *(Michael Rangeloff)*, Beverly D'Angelo *(Standish Logan)*, Louis Gossett, Jr. *(Century)*, Pamela Stephenson *(Georgiana Latimer)*, Ed Lauter *(Josef Sirola)*, David Wayne *(Stapleton)*, Brian Dennehy *(Mayor Frizzoli)*, Jack Riley *(Ormond)*, John Schuck *(Police Chief Norris)*, Timothy Blake *(Estelle Norris)*

p, Sandra Marsh, Terence Marsh; d, Richard Lester; w, Ronny Graham, Terence Marsh, Charles Dennis (based on the novel *The Next to Last Train Ride* by Dennis); ph, Brian West (Technicolor); ed, John Victor Smith; m, Ken Thorne; prod d, Terence Marsh; art d, J. Dennis Washington; cos, Yvonne Blake

A crazy, quirky comedy from director Lester that starts slowly and warms up to provide some funny moments. Set in 1973, the film takes advantage of 11 years of hindsight to poke fun at the early 1970s and to illustrate some of the differences between the two decades.

Josef and Georgiana (Lauter and Stephenson) get past the security system of a large estate and loot the safe of $5 million belonging to Georgiana's father. Cut to Michael (O'Keefe), the manager of a women's roller-derby team that has hit the skids. Michael hides from his angry skaters in a used-clothing store and then buys himself a soldier's uniform, planning to board a train from Oakland, California, to New York. When an Army officer at the station begins to grill him about his status, Michael grabs an American flag and drapes it over a nearby coffin, saying that he is escorting his slain buddy back home. Actually, inside the coffin is the purloined loot. Josef and Georgiana decide to go along with the gag to ensure the safekeeping of the money, but a few surprises are in store for them all.

FINDERS KEEPERS benefits from the well-judged performances of its energetic cast, with Wayne in particularly good form. In typical Lester fashion, the movie is so frantic that viewers have no time to rest their eyes. Unlike some of this director's other films, though, one wonders if all the work required here is really worth it. The taste in several scenes is questionable but not satirically questioned, rendering the entire exercise rather trivial alongside this filmmaker's best work.

FINIAN'S RAINBOW

1968   145m   c   ★½
Musical/Fantasy   /U
WB

Fred Astaire *(Finian McLonergan)*, Petula Clark *(Sharon McLonergan)*, Tommy Steele *(Og, the Leprechaun)*, Don Francks *(Woody Mahoney)*, Keenan Wynn *(Judge Rawkins)*, Barbara Hancock *(Susan the Silent)*, Al Freeman, Jr. *(Howard)*, Ronald Colby *(Buzz Collins)*, Dolph Sweet *(Sheriff)*, Wright King *(District Attorney)*

p, Joseph Landon; d, Francis Ford Coppola; w, E.Y. Harburg, Fred Saidy (based on their play); ph, Philip Lathrop (Panavision, Technicolor); ed, Melvin Shapiro; m, Burton Lane; prod d, Hilyard Brown; chor, Hermes Pan; cos, Dorothy Jeakins

One of many musical stinkers made during a decade infamous for them, FINIAN'S RAINBOW is sadly notable as the last screen musical of the genre's greatest star. With typical understatement, Astaire declared this mess his "biggest disappointment." Director Coppola, who generally refuses to talk about the film, is more direct in calling it "a disaster" and concedes that he was wrong to throw out the choreography and ask his cast to "fake it" instead. Had anyone taken the young director's efforts on this film seriously, he would never have directed again.

Although Astaire somewhat overdoes the "Oirish" routine as a man who buries his pot of gold in America, hoping it will grow, the legendary 69-year-old star is the most vibrant thing swimming amidst this sea of gross incompetence. Only Clark, as Astaire's daughter, and Francks, as her romantic interest, emerge alongside the great dancer with any degree of credit. Steele, as the obnoxious leprechaun whose gold Finian has pilfered, projects his performance far enough to reach Pluto, let alone the last aisle of a movie theater. Wynn can do nothing but mug his way through the role of a racist senator who learns his lesson after being magically turned black. (What seemed like progressive sentiment when the stage show emerged in the 1940s makes the sugary GUESS WHO'S COMING TO DINNER? seem raw by comparison.) Hancock, meanwhile, is utterly defeated by the annoying role of Susan the Silent, and the rest of the cast is singularly forgettable.

The editing is ridiculously pell-mell, wrecking the humor, musical score and spontaneity all at once. The legendary songs are both poorly orchestrated and recorded, making the film's Oscar nominations for sound and scoring embarrassments. "How Are Things in Glocca Mora?" is one of the few numbers to escape Coppola's desperate attempts at creativity. The one image to cherish is Astaire frolicking with a group of children down a dirt path, looking like nothing so much as an elderly Pied Piper. Fun to deride for the first hour or so, FINIAN'S RAINBOW is likely to exhaust even the bitchiest critic long before the end title mercifully rolls by.

FIRE OVER ENGLAND

1937 92m bw   ★★★★
Adventure/Historical/War   /U
Mayflower/Pendennis/Korda/London Films   (U.K.)

Laurence Olivier *(Michael Ingolby)*, Flora Robson *(Queen Elizabeth)*, Leslie Banks *(Earl of Leicester)*, Raymond Massey *(Philip of Spain)*, Vivien Leigh *(Cynthia)*, Tamara Desni *(Elena)*, Morton Selten *(Burleigh)*, Lyn Harding *(Sir Richard)*, George Thirlwell *(Gregory)*, Henry Oscar *(Spanish Ambassador)*

p, Erich Pommer; d, William K. Howard; w, Clemence Dane, Sergei Nolbandov (based on the novel by A.E.W. Mason); ph, James Wong Howe; ed, Jack Dennis; m, Richard Addinsell; art d, Lazare Meerson; fx, Ned Mann, Lawrence Butler, Edward Cohen; cos, Rene Hubert

A rare example of a film that succeeds superbly both as a swashbuckler and as historical drama. Michael Ingolby (Olivier) is a young British naval officer whose father is burned to death for heresy by the Spanish Inquisition. He seeks revenge and finds his opportunity in the court of the tempestuous Queen Elizabeth I (a scene-stealing Robson). Elizabeth knows she is surrounded by traitors in league with her archenemy, Philip of Spain (Massey), who plans to invade England. Thus, when Michael offers to infiltrate Philip's court and learn the details of the invasion, Elizabeth seizes the chance. The queen is also romantically inclined toward the handsome officer, and vexed at the attentions he shows his childhood sweetheart who is her lady-in-waiting, Cynthia (Leigh). Michael soon learns of Philip's plans, escapes to England and helps lead the British ships into battle against the Spanish Armada.

A bit slow getting started, and typically glossy in its treatment of details (e.g. the softening of Elizabeth's character), FIRE OVER ENGLAND nevertheless conveys a certain historical grandeur amidst all the showmanship. It succeeds through the combined talents of many great names: Alexander Korda's sponsorship, Pommer's production, Howard's masterful direction, Wong Howe's superb photography, Meerson's grand sets, and the acting of Olivier, Robson and Leigh. A host of versatile supporting players add to the depth of FIRE OVER ENGLAND, not the least of whom are Banks, Selten, and Massey (as the darkly brooding, expansionist King Philip). Look for a bearded James Mason in a small role as an envoy.

FIREMAN'S BALL, THE

(HORI MA PANENKO)
1967 73m c   ★★★½
Comedy
Barrandov   (Czechoslovakia)

Vaclav Stockel *(Fire Brigade Commander)*, Josef Svet *(Old Man)*, Josef Kolb *(Josef)*, Jan Vostrcil *(Committee Chairman)*, Frantisek Debelka *(1st Committee Member)*, Josef Sebanek *(2nd Committee Member)*, Karel Valnoha *(3rd Committee Member)*, Josef

Rehorek *(4th Committee Member)*, Marie Jezkova *(Josef's Wife)*, Anina Lipoldva

d, Milos Forman; w, Milos Forman, Ivan Passer, Jaroslav Papousek; ph, Miroslav Ondricek (Eastmancolor); ed, Miroslav Hajek; m, Karel Mares

This ingratiating farce is perhaps the last noteworthy film of the Czech renaissance before the political crackdown forced most filmmakers, director Forman and co-screenwriter Passer included, into exile. It's a more thorough realization of the same kinds of themes that directors like Forman and Passer developed in several films in the mid-1960s: invigorating essays in everyday life. THE FIREMAN'S BALL uses a small, local event—in this case a retirement ball and a beauty contest—to examine larger social and political problems.

Promised the presentation of a ceremonial hatchet at a ball given upon his retirement, a cancer-stricken, 86-year-old retired commander of a fire brigade sits helplessly as all hell breaks loose around him. A beauty contest organized as part of the evening's events fizzles. The tension is broken by a fire alarm which tears the fire company away from the festivities to a fire that is destroying another old man's home. Unfortunately things seem to keep going wrong.

The New York Times reported that 40,000 Czech firemen resigned when the government released the film in their homeland. They returned to their posts when Forman let it be known the film might be allegorical. The film received an Academy Award nomination for Best Foreign Film in 1968 but lost to WAR AND PEACE.

FIRST NAME: CARMEN

(PRENOM: CARMEN)
1984 93m c   ★★★½
Drama   /18
Sara/Jean-Luc Godard/A2   (France)

Maruschka Detmers *(Carmen X)*, Jacques Bonnaffe *(Joseph Bonnaffe)*, Myriem Roussel *(Claire)*, Christophe Odent *(The Boss)*, Jean-Luc Godard *(Uncle Jean)*, Hyppolite Girardot *(Fred)*, Bertrand Liebert *(Carmen's Bodyguard)*, Alain Bastien-Thiry *(Hotel Worker)*, Pierre-Alain Chapuis, Odile Roire

p, Alain Sarde; d, Jean-Luc Godard; w, Anne-Marie Mieville (based on the novel *Carmen* by Prosper Merimee); ph, Raoul Coutard (Eastmancolor); ed, Suzanne Lang-Willar; m, Ludwig van Beethoven; cos, Renee Renard

Director Jean-Luc Godard has taken a less than reverent approach to the famed opera *Carmen*. Godard chose to depart substantially from the original Merimee novel and, to the horror of Bizet fans, replaced the composer's score with Beethoven violin concertos and a ballad called "Ruby's Arms" by the gruff-voiced Tom Waits.

Here Carmen (Maruschka Detmers) is a *femme fatale* who concocts a daring plan to rob a bank while pretending to shoot a movie. Luckily she has an uncle (Godard) who was once a brilliant movie director and is now a resident at the local mental hospital. He jumps at the chance to "direct" Carmen's film of the robbery. While staging the robbery, she is nearly apprehended by a police officer (Jacques Bonnaffe), but the two fall in love instead. It appears that Carmen is in complete control of the relationship.

Not only is FIRST NAME: CARMEN optimistic, it is also relatively linear in its narrative structure, making it perhaps Godard's most accessible film. What's more, FIRST NAME: CARMEN is Godard's first comedy, although not in the customary sense. This comes as no surprise as his gangster films, war movies, musicals and dramas are hardly typical of their genres. Godard's films have always had their funny moments but this is his first step in the direction of the great comedians. The film is spiced with passion, philosophy, eroticism, and technical innovation, and while its ideas are relatively accessible, they still do not make for "easy" viewing.

FISH CALLED WANDA, A

1988   108m   c   ★★★
Comedy/Crime/Romance   R/15
MGM

John Cleese (*Archie Leach*), Jamie Lee Curtis (*Wanda Gerschwitz*), Kevin Kline (*Otto*), Michael Palin (*Ken*), Maria Aitken (*Wendy Leach*), Tom Georgeson (*George*), Patricia Hayes (*Mrs. Coady*), Geoffrey Palmer (*Judge*), Cynthia Caylor (*Portia*), Mark Elwes (*Shop Customer*)

p, Michael Shamberg; d, Charles Crichton; w, John Cleese (based on a story by Cleese and Charles Crichton); ph, Alan Hume (Technicolor); ed, John Jympson; m, John Du Prez; prod d, Roger Murray-Leach; fx, George Gibbs; cos, Hazel Pethig

Combining the talents of Monty Python stalwart John Cleese and Ealing Studios veteran Charles Crichton (THE LAVENDER HILL MOB, THE TITFIELD THUNDERBOLT), this hilariously offbeat post-caper comedy benefits from two of British film comedy's most accomplished traditions.

Cleese, who wrote the screenplay, stars as Archie Leach, an emotionally and sexually repressed English barrister whose life is thrown into upheaval by the appearance of Wanda—not the fish of the title, but a sexy American thief played by Jamie Lee Curtis. She and her gang—Cockney tough guy George (Tom Georgeson), stuttering animal rights advocate, Ken (Michael Palin), and ex-CIA assassin, Otto (Kevin Kline)—pull off a well-executed jewel heist but in the thieves' subsequent rush to double-cross one another and grab all the loot, George ends up in jail and the booty hidden in a safety deposit box, the location of which is known only to him. Deciding that the best way to learn the whereabouts of the jewels is through George's barrister (Cleese), Wanda sets out to seduce the information out of him.

With British-American culture clash as its dominant theme, A FISH CALLED WANDA bristles with wit, enlivened by delightfully over-the-top ensemble acting. Cleese's screenplay uses a farcical framework to send up both British inhibition and formality and American intuitiveness and lack of sophistication. Although filled with clever twists and double-crosses, the film's storyline is less important than the opportunities it gives the actors to exploit their goofy characterizations, especially in the case of Kline who won a Best Supporting Actor Academy Award for his outlandish performance.

FISHER KING, THE

1991   137m   c   ★★½
Drama/Fantasy/Comedy   R/15
TriStar/Hill/Obst Productions

Robin Williams (*Parry*), Jeff Bridges (*Jack Lucas*), Mercedes Ruehl (*Anne Napolitano*), Amanda Plummer (*Lydia*), Adam Bryant (*Radio Engineer*), Paul Lombardi (*Radio Engineer*), David Pierce (*Lou Rosen*), Ted Ross (*Limo Bum*), Lara Harris (*Sondra*), Warren Olney (*TV Anchorman*)

p, Debra Hill, Lynda Obst; d, Terry Gilliam; w, Richard LaGravenese; ph, Roger Pratt; ed, Lesley Walker; prod d, Mel Bourne; art d, P. Michael Johnston; cos, Beatrix Pasztor

Terry Gilliam's first project as a directorial "hired gun" is a grandiose, overblown attempt to fuse the medieval myth of the Fisher King with a story of alienation and redemption in contemporary Manhattan.

Jack Lucas (Jeff Bridges) is a cynical disc jockey whose radio talk show attracts the lonely and frustrated. When one of his frequent callers, Edwin (Christian Clemenson), confides he's just met a beautiful girl at Babbitts, a trendy bar, Jack goes off on a vitriolic tirade against the yuppies who frequent the place. He ends by saying: "Edwin, they have to be stopped before it's too late. It's us or them." Taking Jack's words at face value, Edwin goes on a shooting spree inside the restaurant, slaughtering several patrons.

Three years later Jack has reached a nadir of despair and self-loathing. Although involved in a relationship with Anne (Mercedes Ruehl), the supportive owner of a video store, he has lost his will to live. Drunk, he decides to end it all by jumping off a pier into the river. Before he can do this, though, he is attacked by two homicidal teenagers, and then rescued by Parry (Robin Williams), who appears to be some kind of vagrant with a mystical turn of phrase. It turns out that Parry is a former professor of medieval history who is now engaged on a quest for the Holy Grail. Parry is convinced he's spotted the Grail in a magazine (it's actually a silver trophy belonging to a billionaire), and that Jack is the ideal candidate to retrieve it from its owner's castellated Fifth Avenue apartment building.

THE FISHER KING's problems begin with Richard LaGravenese's screenplay and are amplified by Gilliam's showy direction and an unbearably fey performance by Robin Williams. The idea, apparently, was to give an explicitly mythical dimensional to a modern-day story of sin and redemption. Unfortunately, though, the script never resolves the different levels on which it tries to operate, and also throws in too many loose ends which never get cleared up. The tone of the film, largely set by Williams's "Please feel sorry for me" performance, is unremittingly cloying, with an impossibly cute, feel-good ending that adds insult to injury.

There *are* redeeming factors; a scene in which bustling commuters in Grand Central Station are suddenly transformed into waltzing couples has undeniable magic, and Bridges and Ruehl give gritty, unaffected performances that sometimes threaten to make the whole thing believable. For the most part, though, THE FISHER KING is awash in the kind of neo-mythical whimsy that Gilliam helped to puncture in the far more enjoyable MONTY PYTHON AND THE HOLY GRAIL.

FIST IN HIS POCKET

(I PUGNI IN TASCA)
1968   105m   bw   ★★★½
Drama
Peppercorn/Wormser   (Italy)

Lou Castel (*Alessandro*), Paola Pitagora (*Giulia*), Marino Mase (*Augusto*), Liliana Gerace (*Mother*), Pier Luigi Troglio (*Leone*), Jennie MacNeil (*Lucia*), Mauro Martini (*the Boy*), Gianni Schicchi (*Tonino*), Alfredo Filippazzi (*Doctor*), Gianfranco Cella (*Young Man at the Party*)

p, Ezio Passadore; d, Marco Bellocchio; w, Marco Bellocchio; ph, Alberto Marrama; ed, Aurelio Mangiarotti; m, Ennio Morricone; art d, Gisella Longo

This amazing debut film from director Marco Bellochio is an unusual tragicomedy about a family of crazy epileptics—with a blind mother. The plot synopsis suggests a particularly perverse soap opera. Augusto (Mase) is the one healthy member of a family whose manifold problems threaten to stifle his life. He wants to marry but feels he cannot as long as his family is around to bedevil him. His younger brother, Alessandro (Castel), empathizes with his sibling so he decides to kill off the rest of the family so that Augusto can use the resulting inheritance to begin a new life.

Bellochio's exhilaratingly cool and assured direction charges the film with temperament. The savage material—matricide, fratricide, and incest—is never as funny as it seems intended to be; the actors are directed with such verve and passion that audiences are often left too breathless to laugh. Lou Castel's performance seethes with a hateful energy rarely seen on the screen.

FISTFUL OF DOLLARS, A
(PER UN PUGNO DI DOLLARI)
1964   100m   c   ★★★
Western   /15
Jolly   (Italy/Spain/West Germany)

Clint Eastwood *(The Man with No Name)*, Marianne Koch *(Marisol)*, Gian Maria Volonte *(Ramon Rojo)*, Jose Calvo *(Silvanito)*, Wolfgang Lukschy *(John Baxter)*, Sieghardt Rupp *(Esteban Rojo)*, Antonio Prieto *(Benito Rojo)*, Margarita Lozano *(Consuela Baxter)*, Daniel Martin *(Julian)*, Bruno Carotenuto *(Antonio Baxter)*

p, Arrigo Colombo, Giorgio Papi; d, Sergio Leone; w, Sergio Leone, Duccio Tessari, Victor A. Catena, G. Schock (based on the film YOJIMBO by Akira Kurosawa); ph, Massimo Dallamano (Techniscope, Technicolor); ed, Roberto Cinquini; m, Ennio Morricone

A landmark Western that established the Clint Eastwood persona and revitalized the genre. The plot is deceptively simple—and it's lifted from Japanese director Akira Kurosawa's 1961 classic YOJIMBO. Eastwood, the mysterious Man with No Name, rides into a small town embroiled in a struggle for power between two families. Eastwood hires himself out as a mercenary, first to one faction and then to the other, with no regard for honor or morality. He eventually destroys both, leaving the town to the bartender, coffin-maker, and bell ringer as he rides off into the desert from whence he came.

The plot is simple and the Italian performances verge on the operatic, but Leone revitalizes the Western through a unique and complex visual style. The film is full of brilliant spatial relationships (extreme close-ups in the foreground, with detailed compositions visible in the background) combined with Ennio Morricone's vastly creative musical score full of grunts, wails, groans, and bizarre-sounding instruments. Aural and visual elements together give a wholly original perspective on the West and its myths.

Eastwood had a heavy hand in the interpretation of his role, stripping his part of most of its dialogue. His character is wholly amoral, a mystery man with no past who relies on his skill with a gun and his cleverness. This image, which he would hone to perfection in the subsequent Leone movies (and one the actor continues to examine and sometimes criticize, especially in the films in which he directs himself) transformed Eastwood into a cultural icon of almost mythic proportions. Though far from perfected in this film, Leone's style would mature through his next two films and peak with his masterpiece ONCE UPON A TIME IN THE WEST.

FITZCARRALDO
1982   157m   c   ★★★★
Drama   /PG
New World   (West Germany)

Klaus Kinski *(Brian Sweeney Fitzgerald/Fitzcarraldo)*, Claudia Cardinale *(Molly)*, Jose Lewgoy *(Don Aquilino)*, Miguel Angel Fuentes *(Cholo, the Mechanic)*, Paul Hittscher *(Capt. Orinoco Paul)*, Huerequeque Enrique Bohorquez *(Cook)*, Grande Othelo *(Station Master)*, Peter Berling *(Opera Manager)*, David Perez Espinosa *(Chief of the Campa Indians)*, Milton Nascimento *(Black Man at Opera House)*

p, Werner Herzog, Lucki Stipetic; d, Werner Herzog; w, Werner Herzog; ph, Thomas Mauch; ed, Beate Mainka-Jellinghaus; m, Popol Vuh; art d, Henning von Gierke, Ulrich Bergfelder; cos, Gisela Storch

A major filmmaking accomplishment that only Werner Herzog would have the looney audacity to attempt, FITZCARRALDO stars Klaus Kinski as the title character, a dreamer who plans to bring opera and Enrico Caruso to the South American jungles. With limited funding he decides to finance the opera house by capitalizing on South America's rubber industry. He discovers a hidden forest of rubber trees well protected by rapids but the only way to get there is via a river on the other side of a small group of mountains. Fitzcarraldo has a bizarre inspiration: he'll hire local natives to pull his steamship over the mountain—320 tons up a 40-degree incline.

The hauling of the boat is the poetic and symbolic heart of the movie and no camera trickery is used in its filming. This is a real steamship being hauled over a real mountain—all at the command of Herzog, a man as crazed in his way as his most obsessed heroes. The insurmountability of this labor of filmmaking parallels the character's determination to bring Caruso to the jungles, and herein lies the attraction of FITZCARRALDO—it is an artistic achievement that one watches for the drama of the film and of the filmmaking.

Jason Robards was originally set to play the lead but was forced to quit the film after catching a jungle illness. The resulting schedule delays also forced Mick Jagger, who was cast as Robards's sidekick, to drop out. Herzog was quoted as saying, "If I should abandon this film I should be a man without dreams …I live my life or end my life with this project." An excellent companion piece is Les Blank's BURDEN OF DREAMS, a documentary about the making of FITZCARRALDO.

FIVE EASY PIECES
1970   96m   c   ★★★★
Drama   R/AA
BBS

Jack Nicholson *(Robert Eroica Dupea)*, Karen Black *(Rayette Dipesto)*, Billy "Green" Bush *(Elton)*, Fannie Flagg *(Stoney)*, Sally Struthers *(Betty)*, Marlena MacGuire *(Twinky)*, Richard Stahl *(Recording Engineer)*, Lois Smith *(Partita Dupea)*, Helena Kallianiotes *(Palm Apodaca)*, Toni Basil *(Terry Grouse)*

p, Bob Rafelson, Richard Wechsler; d, Bob Rafelson; w, Adrien Joyce (from a story by Joyce and Rafelson); ph, Laszlo Kovacs (Movielab Color); ed, Gerald Shepard, Christopher Holmes; m, Johann Sebastian Bach, Wolfgang Amadeus Mozart, Frederic Chopin; cos, Bucky Rous

This episodic character study is one of the key American films of its era. Nicholson, in an early major performance, appears to be a redneck oilrigger in a California oil field. He and his best friend, Bush, when not working together, spend most of their time bowling, downing beers, and just hanging out. This lifestyle is actually a charade. Nicholson hails from a well-to-do family of musicians. He's a brilliant classical pianist who's given up the instrument in favor of another life.

When Black, his witless waitress girlfriend, announces she's pregnant, he leaves his job and heads for Los Angeles to visit Smith, his sister, who is also a pianist and about to record an album. Smith tells Nicholson that their father, Challee, has suffered a pair of strokes back at their home on Puget Sound and he should visit the old man before he dies. Black talks him into taking her along. They bid Bush and his wife, Flagg, goodbye and begin the drive to Washington. What follows is a probing examination of the upper middle class American way of life.

Nicholson delivers a brilliant, edgy and complex characterization and Black won the 1970 New York Film Critics Award for her courageous performance as well as an Oscar nomination. Deceptively simple, PIECES is one of the most complex pictures of the 1970s.

FIVE FINGERS
1952 108m bw   ★★★★
Thriller/Spy   /U
FOX

James Mason (Cicero), Danielle Darrieux (Anna), Michael Rennie (George Travers), Walter Hampden (Sir Frederic), Oscar Karlweis (Moyzisch), Herbert Berghof (Col. von Richter), John Wengraf (Von Papen), Ben Astar (Siebert), Roger Plowden (MacFadden), Michael Pate (Morrison)

p, Otto Lang; d, Joseph L. Mankiewicz; w, Michael Wilson (based on the book Operation Cicero by L.C. Moyzisch); ph, Norbert Brodine; ed, James B. Clark; m, Bernard Herrmann; art d, Lyle Wheeler, George W. Davis; fx, Fred Sersen

Five fingers, yes; five stars, not quite. In a heavily ironic story based, amazingly, on fact, Mason plays a valet working for Sir Frederic (Hampden), the British ambassador in WWII Ankara. Using the pseudonym Cicero, he uses his position to sell military secrets to the Germans. The scheming servant sets up Countess Anna (Darrieux), a down-and-out noblewoman, in a mansion and uses it to meet with Nazi agents. The Germans pay handsomely for Cicero's information even though the Nazi high command considers the secrets—including the real time and date of the invasion in Europe—too incredible to be believed. They are afraid, however, to shut off the flow of information and keep purchasing Cicero's documents. The British finally discover a leak in the embassy, and George Travers (Rennie) leads a team of agents to unearth the spy.

Director Mankiewicz, who also contributed some uncredited dialogue, provides the skillful if somewhat cold direction and holds suspense from beginning to end. Also noteworthy is the fine work of cinematographer Brodine. Although the film never gets us close to any of the characters, Mason is nonetheless a suave wonder to behold as the shifty, ever-alert Albanian valet who outwits British intelligence. In real life Cicero managed to sell German intelligence 35 top-secret documents. The Nazis never acted on any of them.

FIVE GRAVES TO CAIRO
1943 96m bw   ★★★★½
Spy   /A
Paramount

Franchot Tone (John J. Bramble), Anne Baxter (Mouche), Akim Tamiroff (Farid), Erich von Stroheim (Field Marshal Rommel), Peter Van Eyck (Lt. Schwegler), Fortunio Bonanova (Gen. Sebastiano), Konstantin Shayne (Maj. von Buelow), Fred Nurney (Maj. Lamprecht), Miles Mander (British Colonel), Leslie Denison (British Captain)

p, Charles Brackett; d, Billy Wilder; w, Charles Brackett, Billy Wilder (based on the play "Hotel Imperial" by Lajos Biro); ph, John Seitz; ed, Doane Harrison; m, Miklos Rozsa; art d, Hans Dreier, Ernst Fegte; cos, Edith Head

Notable as an early example of Wilder's talent for turning headlines into storylines. This tense WWII espionage film stars Tone as John Bramble, a British soldier stranded in a desert town which suddenly fills with German troops. Assuming the role of a dead servant at a hotel run by Farid (Tamiroff), Bramble gradually gains the confidence of French housekeeper Mouche (Baxter), a woman deeply resentful of the British for leaving French troops, including her brother, behind at Dunkirk. After the hotel becomes Rommel's temporary headquarters, Bramble realizes that his impersonation is even more hazardous than he had envisioned: the dead man was really an agent working for the Germans. Convincing the Nazis that he is indeed the spy in their employ, he is instructed to go to Cairo to prepare for a German invasion.

Although the devilishly clever plotting of the film is one of its more obvious merits, FIVE GRAVES TO CAIRO scores on every level. The dialogue is by turns crisp, witty and stinging, and this cast is fully capable of making the most of it. Tone's gift for lending depth to his characters through understatement rarely found such a worthy vehicle. Baxter (in a moving turn and sporting a decent French accent), Tamiroff, Mander, Van Eyck (as a sleazy Nazi aide), and Bonanova (as an opera-loving Italian general) are all in fine form as well.

But of course a large share of the praise must go to that master scene-stealer Von Stroheim. Alternately brutal and civilized, arrogant and quiet, Rommel emerges as a complex military genius in this marvelous performer's hands. Wilder introduces him with a close-up of the back of his creased neck bursting over a high military collar, a technique Von Stroheim used in silent days when he profiled the evil Huns of WWI.

FIVE PENNIES, THE
1959 117m c   ★★★
Musical/Biography   /U
Paramount

Danny Kaye (Loring "Red" Nichols), Barbara Bel Geddes (Bobbie Meredith), Louis Armstrong (Himself), Bob Crosby (Wil Paradise), Harry Guardino (Tony Valani), Susan Gordon (Dorothy Nichols at 6), Tuesday Weld (Dorothy at 12 to 14), Valerie Allen (Tommye Eden), Ray Anthony (Jimmy Dorsey), Shelly Manne (Dave Tough)

p, Jack Rose; d, Melville Shavelson; w, Melville Shavelson, Jack Rose (based on a story by Robert Smith, suggested by the life of Loring "Red" Nichols); ph, Daniel Fapp (VistaVision, Technicolor); ed, Frank P. Keller; m, Leith Stevens; art d, Hal Pereira, Tambi Larsen; fx, John P. Fulton

All that jazz. A schmaltz-laden biopic, THE FIVE PENNIES is nevertheless a jazz lover's movie, chock full of good old Dixieland tunes. Kaye plays Loring "Red" Nichols, who migrates to New York, where his cornet playing gains him acclaim with the Wil Paradise Band. He meets singer Bobbie Meredith (Bel Geddes, her vocals dubbed by Eileen Wilson); they later marry and have a baby girl. When Red and Paradise (Crosby) disagree over the latter's conservative repertoire, the flaming Red finally gets axed. Coming back with a new group, "The Five Pennies," however, he soon becomes a jazz legend as a leading purveyor of Dixieland.

Decent enough as entertainment, THE FIVE PENNIES doesn't always manage to avoid slipping on its own soap. The film unfortunately gets a mite laughable as it equates, in true repressed 1950s fashion, Red's inability to hit a high note on his horn with sexual impotence. (See Kirk Douglas in YOUNG MAN WITH A HORN for another example of this phenomenon.) Otherwise, Kaye, as aggressively eager to please as ever, is pretty believable as the ambitious jazzman who rolls with some tough punches. Bel Geddes brings warmth if not excitement to her role as his loyal wife, and 15 year-old Weld, in her film debut as Red's daughter, gives evidence of her future success. Jazz fans will be most delighted, however, by the duet by Nichols (who actually plays Kaye's solos) and Louis Armstrong; other jazzmen in the film include Ray Anthony, Bobby Troup, Shelly Manne and Ray Daley.

5,000 FINGERS OF DR. T., THE

1953 89m c	★★★★½
Children's/Fantasy/Musical	/U
Columbia	

Peter Lind Hayes (Zabladowski), Mary Healy (Mrs. Collins), Hans Conried (Dr. Terwilliker), Tommy Rettig (Bart), John Heasley (Uncle Whitney), Robert Heasley (Uncle Judson), Noel Cravat (Sgt. Lunk), Henry Kulky (Stroogo)

p, Stanley Kramer; d, Roy Rowland; w, Ted Geisel, Allan Scott; ph, Franz Planer (Technicolor); ed, Al Clark; m, Frederick Hollander; prod d, Rudolph Sternad; art d, Cary Odell; chor, Eugene Loring

Hollywood films just don't get any weirder than this underappreciated 1950s classic. This surrealistic children's film (cowritten by Ted Geisel, better known as Dr. Seuss) features Tommy Rettig of TV's "Lassie" as Bart Collins, a young boy who would rather play baseball than take piano lessons with the eccentric and tyrannical Dr. Terwilliker (Conreid).

Falling asleep at his piano, Bart dreams he's being chased by weird creatures with butterfly nets through a land of fog, cylinders, and odd-shaped mounds. Here he stumbles upon the castle of Dr. T, who runs a piano school for captive boys. The film's key image is the massive winding double-decker piano keyboard with 500 seats, one for each student. 500 boys, 5000 fingers—get it? Kept in the dungeon are pitiful creatures imprisoned as punishment for playing instruments other than the piano. The prisoners have built musical instruments out of odd materials and, in the film's most elaborate sequence, perform a strange ballet. Bart's widowed mom (Mary Healy) is second-in-command at this terrible school but she is hypnotized by Dr. T. Eventually Bart teams up with Mr. Zabladowski (Hayes), a resourceful plumber and reluctant surrogate father, to topple Dr. T's evil empire.

THE 5,000 FINGERS OF DR T. is one of the best fantasy films ever produced by Hollywood. Adults will find it every bit as diverting and intriguing as children as it explicitly connects dreams, surrealism and psychoanaysis. The dreamy sets succeed in making this film look like a Dr. Seuss book brought to life. Rettig and Hayes are delightful and Healy's OK but Conreid gives what may be the performance of his estimable career as the dastardly fop. Though at times deliriously peverse, particularly in the context of conformist 1950s filmmaking, the film is also quite moving. Essential viewing for any potentially cool kids.

FLAMINGO KID, THE

1984 100m c	★★★½
Comedy/Drama	PG-13/15
Mercury/ABC	

Matt Dillon (Jeffrey Willis), Hector Elizondo (Arthur Willis), Molly McCarthy (Ruth Willis), Martha Gehman (Nikki Willis), Richard Crenna (Phil Brody), Jessica Walter (Phyllis Brody), Carole Davis (Joyce Brody), Janet Jones (Carla Samson), Brian McNamara (Steve Dawkins), Fisher Stevens (Hawk Ganz)

p, Michael Phillips; d, Garry Marshall; w, Garry Marshall, Neal Marshall (based on his story); ph, James A. Contner (Panavision, Deluxe Color); ed, Priscilla Nedd; prod d, Lawrence Miller; art d, Duke Durfee; cos, Ellen Mirojnick

THE FLAMINGO KID, unlike countless coming-of-age films in which guzzling beer and ogling girls represent initiation into manhood, is an often touching account of one lowborn young man's introduction to a more sophisticated life.

Jeffrey Willis (Dillon) is an 18-year-old Brooklyn kid who joins some friends on a jaunt to "El Flamingo," a ritzy beachside club for affluent Long Islanders. There he observes Phil Brody (Crenna), a wealthy car dealer and the club's champion gin player, effectively demolishing his competition at the card table. Jeffrey is hired by the club for the summer, and slowly a romance develops between him and Brody's niece, Carla (Jones). Brody also takes a liking to Jeffrey and helps him get a promotion. After a talk with his mentor, Jeffrey decides to become a car salesman too. His father (Elizondo), though, who has dreamed of his son's going to college, is dead set against this idea.

There's not a single bad performance here, and director Marshall builds his film on small moments, a wise choice that gives this comedy empathy and intelligence. Although Marshall hedges his bets when it comes to satirizing ethnic groups, the family, and American know-how, the film is an enjoyable lollipop anyway.

FLASH GORDON

1936 97m bw	★★★★
Science Fiction	/PG
Universal	

Buster Crabbe (Flash Gordon), Jean Rogers (Dale Arden), Charles Middleton (Ming, the Merciless), Priscilla Lawson (Princess Aura), Jack Lipson (King Vultan), Richard Alexander (Prince Barin), Frank Shannon (Dr. Zarkov), Duke York, Jr. (King Kala), Earl Askam (Officer Torch), George Cleveland (Prof. Hensley)

p, Henry MacRae; d, Frederick Stephani; w, Frederick Stephani, George Plympton, Basil Dickey, Ella O'Neill (based on the comic strip by Alex Raymond); ph, Jerome Ash, Richard Fryer; m, Franz Waxman; art d, Ralph Berger; fx, Norman Drewes

The one, the only, the original, and the best, this film was initially released as a 13-part serial based on a King Features comic strip.

Flash Gordon (Crabbe), his companion, Dr. Zarkov (Shannon), and sweetheart Dale Arden (Rogers) blast off for the planet Mongo, trying to stop it from a collision course with Earth. In a flash, Flash encounters evil Ming the Merciless (the unforgettable Middleton) along with assorted hawk men, shark men, dinosaurs, horned gorillas, giant lobsters, space ships (hanging from decidedly visible wires) and some mighty nifty costumes. Ming lusts wantonly for Dale, and Princess Aura (Lawson), Ming's equally lustful daughter, has a heavy crush on Flash.

A film whose naive, eager-to-please energy is almost as transporting as Flash's rocketship, FLASH GORDON is likely to delight even the fussiest audiences. The music and some of the sets were borrowed from THE BRIDE OF FRANKENSTEIN, and several sequels were to borrow heavily from this film. Not to be missed.

FLASH OF GREEN, A
1984   131m   c   ★★★½
Drama
Spectrafilm

Ed Harris (Jimmy Wing), Blair Brown (Kate Hubble), Richard Jordan (Elmo Bliss), George Coe (Brian Haas), Joan Goodfellow (Mitchie), Jean De Baer (Jackie Halley), Helen Stenborg (Aunt Middie), William Mooney (Leroy Shannard), Isa Thomas (Doris Rohl), John Glover (Ross Halley)

p, Richard Jordan; d, Victor Nunez; w, Victor Nunez (based on the novel by John D. MacDonald); ph, Victor Nunez; ed, Victor Nunez; m, Charles Engstrom; art d, Carlos Asse; cos, Marilyn Wall-Asse, Dana Moser

Adapted and directed by Victor Nunez, A FLASH OF GREEN is a sure-handed look at corruption in Florida, with all the richly observed characterizations found in John D. MacDonald's novel.

In the mythical town of Palm City, we first meet Jimmy Wing (Harris), a likable reporter for the local paper. Elmo Bliss (Jordan), the local county commissioner, has been a pal of Jimmy's since they were in school together years before. Elmo is very ambitious and comes to Jimmy with a bribe offer. Elmo and his buddies want to gain control of some publicly owned land for development but are stymied by a group of ecological do-gooders known as the "SOBs" (Save Our Bay). The would-be developers mean to get that opposition out of the way, and things start to get pretty ugly before it's all over.

A complex story with no easy answers, A FLASH OF GREEN is beautifully acted, and one of the few adaptations of a MacDonald novel that sticks closely to the intent of the original. Where it falls apart is in failing to provide a sustained story line for the audience. Too many side issues detract from the story, and the uncertain editing doesn't help. But the film is moody, steamy and provocative enough to warrant your attention.

FLETCH
1984   98m   c   ★★★½
Comedy/Mystery   PG
Universal

Chevy Chase (Fletch), Joe Don Baker (Chief Karlin), Dana Wheeler-Nicholson (Gail Stanwyk), Richard Libertini (Walker), Tim Matheson (Alan Stanwyk), M. Emmet Walsh (Dr. Dolan), George Wendt (Fat Sam), Kenneth Mars (Stanton Boyd), Geena Davis (Larry), Bill Henderson (Speaker)

p, Alan Greisman, Peter Douglas; d, Michael Ritchie; w, Andrew Bergman (based on the novel by Gregory McDonald); ph, Fred Schuler (Panavision, Technicolor); ed, Richard A. Harris; m, Harold Faltermeyer; prod d, Boris Leven; art d, Todd Hallowell; fx, Cliff Wenger; cos, Gloria Gresham, Francine Jamison, James W. Tyson

Chase cavorts amusingly through this mystery-comedy as the title character, an investigative reporter who will stop at nothing to get his story. While posing as a bum, Fletch is approached by successful aviation executive Alan Stanwyk (Matheson), who claims to be dying of an incurable illness. He offers the reporter $50,000 to murder him, so that his wife (Wheeler-Nicholson) can collect on an insurance policy. Suspicious, Fletch decides to uncover the true motives behind this scheme. The mystery begins to unravel as our hero works himself through a web of entanglements and intrigue, using various aliases (after the fashion of

Cary Grant in CHARADE) to learn that Stanwyk is involved in drug dealing and that his partner in crime is the local police chief (Baker).

Fast-paced and witty, this is Chase's best solo venture to date, and will hold almost anyone's attention for its well-edited 98 minutes. Chase underplays his wackier moments to great effect, though he isn't always quite as funny as he thinks he is. (He also isn't the next Cary Grant, which he seems to believe as well.) Ritchie, whose career has had its ups (SMILE, THE CANDIDATE) and downs (THE SURVIVORS), directs with a sure hand. Understandably popular, the film inspired a lesser sequel, FLETCH LIVES.

FLIGHT OF THE NAVIGATOR
1986   90m   c   ★★★½
Children's   PG/U
PSO

Joey Cramer (David Freeman), Veronica Cartwright (Helen Freeman), Cliff De Young (Bill Freeman), Sarah Jessica Parker (Carolyn McAdams), Matt Adler (Jeff, Age 16), Howard Hesseman (Dr. Faraday), Paul Mall (Max), Robert Small (Troy), Albie Whitaker (Jeff, Age 8), Jonathan Sanger (Dr. Carr)

p, Robby Wald, Dimitri Villard; d, Randal Kleiser; w, Michael Burton, Matt MacManus (based on a story by Mark H. Baker); ph, James Glennon (Technicolor); ed, Jeff Gourson; m, Alan Silvestri; prod d, William J. Creber; art d, Michael Novotny; fx, Peter Donen, Petter Borgli

A charming Disney fantasy which revolves around the extraordinary experiences of 12-year-old David Freeman (Cramer), who in 1978 falls into a ravine and is knocked unconscious. When he comes to, it's 1986; and while he is still 12 years old, his little brother is now his big brother.

The folks at NASA are convinced that there is a connection between David's disappearance and the recent discovery of an alien spacecraft. Using space-age technology, they discover heretofore-unseen star charts imprinted on the young boy's brain. Escaping from NASA, David is called to the spaceship that carried him away eight years earlier (it was trying to take him home when its computer malfunctioned). With David aboard, the spacecraft takes off, and Max, the Hal-like computer that operates the ship, uses the star charts in the boy's brain to plot its return voyage.

Kleiser (THE BLUE LAGOON, GREASE) provides a steady directorial hand for this film, which ironically was being shot in Florida when the space-shuttle disaster took place. Credit should go to Paul Reubens (a.k.a. Pee-Wee Herman), who provides the voice of Max. Not a particularly original or insightful film of its kind, and marred slightly by the whining of Cramer in the lead role, this is nevertheless enjoyable fare for kids.

FLIGHT OF THE PHOENIX, THE
1965   149m   c   ★★★★
Adventure   /A
FOX

James Stewart (Frank Towns), Richard Attenborough (Lew Moran), Peter Finch (Capt. Harris), Hardy Kruger (Heinrich Dorfmann), Ernest Borgnine (Trucker Cobb), Ian Bannen (Crow), Ronald Fraser (Sgt. Watson), Christian Marquand (Dr. Renaud), Dan Duryea (Standish), George Kennedy (Bellamy)

p, Robert Aldrich; d, Robert Aldrich; w, Lukas Heller (based on a novel by Elleston Trevor); ph, Joseph Biroc (DeLuxe Color); ed, Michael Luciano; m, Frank DeVol; art d, William Glasgow; fx, L.B. Abbott, Howard Lydecker; cos, Norma Koch

A riveting survival film in which Stewart and his cohorts give power-packed performances as a downed pilot and passengers awaiting death in the Sahara desert.

At first pilot Frank Towns (Stewart) assumes the blame for the crash landing, although it's clearly the fault of alcoholic navigator Lew Moran (Attenborough). For a while, the men await rescue in the broiling sun, conserving their water. British officer Capt. Harris (Finch), however, decides to seek help from a passing caravan, but he gets more than he bargains for from the hostile Arabs. All seems hopeless until Heinrich Dorfmann (Kruger) announces that he can design a working single-engined plane from the wreck.

The crux of this gripping drama ultimately becomes the antagonism between pilot Towns and scientist Dorfmann, and Stewart and Kruger handle their encounters superbly. A great scene occurs when Towns learns that Dorfmann is a *model* airplane designer. Finch is convincing as the stoic British officer, and Borgnine, Marquand, and Duryea give fine performances as stranded men. Aldrich's direction is sharp and well paced, and his screenplay absorbing and realistic.

FLOWERS OF ST. FRANCIS, THE
(FRANCESCO, GIULLARE DI DIO)
1950   75m   bw   ★★★★
Religious
Cineriz/Rizzoli   (Italy)

Aldo Fabrizi *(Nicolaio, the Tyrant)*, Arabella Lemaitre *(Saint Clair)*, Brother Nazario Gerardi *(Saint Francis)*

p, Giuseppe Amato; d, Roberto Rossellini; w, Roberto Rossellini, Federico Fellini, Fr. Felix Morion, Fr. Antonio Lisandrini (based on the life of Fioretti di San Francesco); ph, Otello Martelli; ed, Jolando Benvenuti; m, Renzo Rossellini, Fr. Enrico Buondonno

A film of great harmony and natural beauty, this short historical feature from the celebrated Italian noerealist Roberto Rossellini is a tone poem comprised of physical gestures. Performed, with the exception of Aldo Fabrizi, by nonprofessionals (all of whom are real-life Franciscan monks), the film captures the brothers' purity and their desire to live in harmony with nature. More striking than the film's grand themes—man and nature, God and man, peace and defiance, love and hate, generosity and greed—Rossellini sensitively captures the monks' expressive physical movements. Illustrating one character's line of dialogue, "Souls are won over by examples, not words," Rossellini does not show us speeches or have us listen to readings from scripture. Instead we see the hands and faces of these monks, their wonder, their peace, their simplicity. As these monks can say so much with their eyes, so too can Rossellini speak volumes with a single shot.

FLY, THE
1986   100m   c   ★★★★½
Horror   R/18
Brooksfilms

Jeff Goldblum *(Seth Brundle)*, Geena Davis *(Veronica Quaife)*, John Getz *(Stathis Borans)*, Joy Boushel *(Tawny)*, Les Carlson *(Dr. Cheevers)*, George Chuvalo *(Marky)*, Michael Copeman *(Man in Bar)*, David Cronenberg *(Gynecologist)*, Carol Lazare *(Nurse)*, Shawn Hewitt *(Clerk)*

p, Stuart Cornfeld; d, David Cronenberg; w, Charles Pogue, David Cronenberg (based on a story by George Langelaan); ph, Mark Irwin (Deluxe Color); ed, Ronald Sanders; m, Howard Shore; prod d, Carol Spier; art d, Rolf Harvey; fx, Louis Craig, Ted Ross; cos, Denise Cronenberg

Obsessed with the horrifying implications of a combination of science, technology and the powerful potentials of the human mind, body and sexuality, Cronenberg had created several highly personal films over the previous 15 years. While the concepts of these films are interesting and unique, the films themselves were quite uneven. Slapdash, poorly cast, underbudgeted, and sometimes incoherent, there was also insufficient attention paid to the development of characters as complex, emotional human beings. With his decision to remake the 1958 classic THE FLY, Cronenberg found the perfect outlet for his obsessions, producing his most controlled, mature and insightful work to date.

Enhanced by a more complex personal relationship between the protagonists, the new version of THE FLY pairs a young science-magazine reporter, Veronica Quaife (Geena Davis), and a somewhat shy, awkward scientist, Seth Brundle (Jeff Goldblum), who is involved in a secret experiment to transport matter that will "change life as we know it." Although brilliant intellectually, Brundle lacks social graces and his endearingly clumsy efforts to seduce Veronica look like a high school nerd trying to impress the prom queen with his science project. The pair gradually fall in love, and they make a heartwarming couple. Brundle continues his experiments, trying to advance from transporting objects to transporting living beings. Eventually, he is driven to transport himself but fails to notice the little fly that has traveled through space with him.

THE FLY succeeds on many levels. Cronenberg has never elicited better performances from his players. Goldblum is sublime in a rare leading role. Davis is also in top form. As a couple, they are so convincing and appealing that one regrets knowing that their love story will soon become a tragic horror movie. As a remake, THE FLY transcends the original, taking it in new directions and exploring its underutilized potential. Whereas the original degenerated into a campy fly hunt, the remake opts for a slow metamorphosis from man to fly that develops as a disease might. This gives Cronenberg time to examine the implications of such a process, meditating upon our fear of disease, death and change.

FLYING DOWN TO RIO
1933   89m   c/bw   ★★★★
Musical   /U
RKO

Dolores Del Rio *(Belinha de Rezende)*, Gene Raymond *(Roger Bond)*, Raul Roulien *(Julio Rubeiro)*, Ginger Rogers *(Honey Hale)*, Fred Astaire *(Fred Ayres)*, Blanche Frederici *(Dona Elena)*, Walter Walker *(Senor de Rezende)*, Etta Moten *(Black Singer)*, Roy D'Arcy, Maurice Black

p, Lou Brock; d, Thornton Freeland; w, Cyril Hume, H.W. Hanemann, Erwin Gelsey (based on a play by Anne Caldwell from an original story by Brock); ph, J. Roy Hunt; ed, Jack Kitchin; m, Vincent Youmans; art d, Van Nest Polglase, Carroll Clark; fx, Vernon L. Walker; chor, Dave Gould; cos, Walter Plunkett

Highway robbery, Astaire-Rogers style. Whoever failed to see that the brilliantly talented and engaging Astaire and the playful, gifted Rogers were ideal star material must have been wearing airplane goggles throughout the making of FLYING DOWN TO RIO. Billed fourth and fifth, playing a sassy band singer and the accordionist pal of romantic lead Raymond, Rogers and Astaire positively shimmer with high spirits in this whoops-a-daisy extravaganza.

RKO's bid to cash in on the new breed of musical introduced by the Busby Berkeley tunefests over at Warner Bros. FLYING DOWN TO RIO toplines gorgeous, dark Del Rio and gorgeous, white-blonde Raymond in a silly romantic triangle alongside likable crooner Roulien. Although the lead trio does well enough, the presence of cinema's greatest musical comedy team fairly blasts the screen lovers into orbit whenever either or both of them are onscreen.

Astaire and Rogers both have a great flair for comedy; perhaps only Joan Blondell can equal Rogers's way with a wisecrack. Working more apart than together in this initial venture, Ginger and Fred all but monopolize the delightful Youmans score. The 18-minute showpiece, "The Carioca," though it gives the dynamic duo but a few moments together on the dance floor, already represents the start of a beautiful conspiracy.

The only major production number not to spotlight Rogers and Astaire is the title tune, a bizarre attempt to outdo Busby's bodacious ballets with chorines strapped to airplane wings. Despite this lollapalooza's tuneful terror tactics, the film's most memorable image is the last one: Fred and Ginger bantering before the end titles. They are *more* than ready to be stars on their own. A kooky Depression-era delight.

FOG OVER FRISCO

1934 68m bw ★★★★½
Crime /A
First National

Bette Davis (*Arlene Bradford*), Donald Woods (*Tony Stirling*), Margaret Lindsay (*Val Bradford*), Lyle Talbot (*Spencer Carleton*), A.S. Byron (*Everett Bradford*), Hugh Herbert (*Izzy Wright*), Robert Barrat (*Thorne*), Douglas Dumbrille (*Joshua Maynard*), Irving Pichel (*Jake Bello*), Gordon Westcott (*Joe Bello*)

p, Robert Lord; d, William Dieterle; w, Robert N. Lee, Eugene Solow (based on a story by George Dyer); ph, Tony Gaudio; ed, Harold McLernon; art d, Jack Okey; cos, Orry-Kelly

When Jean-Luc Godard named his homage to Hollywood BREATHLESS, he must have had this film in mind. German emigree Dieterle, a Warner Bros. stalwart, directed one of the fastest-paced movies ever in FOG OVER FRISCO, displaying a dazzling, whirlwind technique that completely overwhelms a rather mundane plot.

Socialite Val Bradford (Lindsay) reads a newspaper report that her stepsister Arlene (Davis) has been consorting with underworld figures at an infamous nightclub run by Jake Bello (Pichel). Val promptly upbraids the story's writer, Tony Stirling (Woods), telling him that Arlene is merely a thoughtless girl who is not responsible for the company she keeps. If only she knew! In fact, the not-so-naive Arlene has been using her fiance Spencer Carleton (Talbot) to sell off securities stolen by Bello and his gang. After Spencer implores Arlene to quit the ring, she gives Val a sealed envelope containing evidence that will expose Bello should anything happen to her.

A standard crime melodrama in plot only, FOG OVER FRISCO is such a marvelous technical exercise that Eisenstein himself would have been proud. The film moves along at an astounding speed, especially in its final half, when your laughter is either due to the silly plot or to your own breathlessness. The inventive Dieterle employs almost every filmic device imaginable—overlapping sound, wipes, iris openings and closings, rushed dialogue and figure movement, opticals in quick takes,

and boom, dolly, and truck shots—to heighten the narrative's urgency. Still an intoxicating experience today, this glimpse of the state of the art in 1934 is a brilliant tribute to Hollywood craftsmanship.

FOLLOW THE BOYS

1944 122m bw ★★★½
Musical/Comedy /U
Universal

George Raft (*Tony West*), Vera Zorina (*Gloria Vance*), Grace McDonald (*Kitty West*), Charley Grapewin (*Nick West*), Charles Butterworth (*Louie Fairweather*), Ramsay Ames (*Laura*), Elizabeth Patterson (*Annie*), Regis Toomey (*Dr. Jim Henderson*), George Macready (*Walter Bruce*), Spooks the Dog (*Junior*)

p, Charles K. Feldman; d, A. Edward Sutherland; w, Lou Breslow, Gertrude Purcell; ph, David Abel; ed, Fred R. Feitshans, Jr.; art d, John B. Goodman, Harold MacArthur; fx, John P. Fulton; chor, George Hale; cos, Vera West, Howard Greer

Forget about the penny-dreadful's worth of plot and just sit back and enjoy the star cameos. A long wartime rouser, FOLLOW THE BOYS begins with the closing of New York's Palace Theater and the demise of vaudeville. Tony (Raft), Kitty (McDonald), and Nick West (Grapewin), a brother-sister-father trio, have just finished doing their turkey of an act at the Palace in New York, and Tony suggests that they try their luck in Hollywood. Once there, Tony soon hits it big, teaming with Gloria Vance (Zorina) in several hit movies. They fall in love and marry, but WWII drives them apart as Tony, refused induction because of a bad knee, takes on the task of organizing entertainment for the fighting men going overseas.

It's perhaps unfair to criticize FOLLOW THE BOYS for its hackneyed storyline, considering that the real purpose of the film is to show off the assortment of legendary performers herein assembled. The odd collection consists largely of established talent on its way down or notable personalities on their way up, but one cherishes the film for what it records for posterity. Jeanette MacDonald reprises one of her earliest song hits, "Beyond the Blue Horizon" and Sophie Tucker is on hand to belt out her signature "Some of These Days." W.C. Fields, meanwhile, though clearly not in the best of health, commits another performance of his famous pool routine to celluloid, and the Andrews Sisters do a fun medley of several of their hits.

Perhaps most priceless of all, however, is Orson Welles, who, assisted by Marlene Dietrich, does a marvelous six-minute magic act. Follow the boys? Sure, why not!

FOLLOW THE FLEET

1936 110m bw ★★★★½
Musical/Comedy /U
RKO

Fred Astaire (*Bake Baker*), Ginger Rogers (*Sherry Martin*), Randolph Scott (*Bilge Smith*), Harriet Hilliard (*Connie Martin*), Astrid Allwyn (*Iris Manning*), Harry Beresford (*Capt. Ezra Hickey*), Russell Hicks (*Jim Nolan*), Brooks Benedict (*Sullivan, Nolan's Assistant*), Ray Mayer (*Dopey Williams*), Lucille Ball (*Kitty Collins*)

p, Pandro S. Berman; d, Mark Sandrich; w, Dwight Taylor, Allan Scott (based on the play "Shore Leave" by Hubert Osborne); ph, David Abel; ed, Henry Berman; art d, Van Nest Polglase, Carroll Clark; fx, Vernon L. Walker; chor, Hermes Pan, Fred Astaire; cos, Bernard Newman

Often regarded as one of the best of the legendary Astaire-Rogers musicals, FOLLOW THE FLEET really isn't up to TOP HAT,

SWING TIME or ROBERTA, the wonder films of the series. The main reason is the bland plot, which, though similar to that of several of their other films, grinds along at a rather poky pace. Astaire and Scott play sailor buddies on leave, and Rogers and Hilliard are cast as sisters with whom they become involved.

Essentially consigned to second-lead status, Rogers and Astaire fittingly play the couple who already know each other, and they banter their way through their dialogue with great rapport. Their range and talent as dancers is also on prominent display here, from their explosive romp to "Let Yourself Go" to Astaire's blazing nautical tap to "I'd Rather Lead a Band" to Roger's delightful solo, her first in the series.

They are hilariously out of sync with each other in a comic cut-up routine to "I'm Putting All My Eggs in One Basket" and resume their trademark after-dinner elegance for a stunning turn to "Let's Face the Music and Dance." Performed as part of a melodramatic playlet onstage, this glamorous number is the closest they ever got to playing Garbo, replete with sumptuous poses and an unforgettable finale. Occasional lumps notwithstanding, FOLLOW THE FLEET is great entertainment. All aboard!

FOOTLIGHT PARADE
1933   102m   bw ★★★★★
Musical /U
WB

James Cagney (Chester Kent), Joan Blondell (Nan Prescott), Ruby Keeler (Bea Thorn), Dick Powell (Scotty Blair), Guy Kibbee (Silas Gould), Ruth Donnelly (Harriet Bowers Gould), Claire Dodd (Vivian Rich), Hugh Herbert (Charlie Bowers), Frank McHugh (Francis), Arthur Hohl (Al Frazer)

p, Robert Lord; d, Lloyd Bacon, William Keighley, Busby Berkeley; w, Manuel Seff, James Seymour; ph, George Barnes; ed, George Amy; art d, Anton Grot; chor, Busby Berkeley; cos, Milo Anderson

Following its success with the blockbuster backstage musicals 42ND STREET and GOLD DIGGERS OF 1933, Warner Bros. launched this lavish production, with Cagney marvelous in the lead. He plays Chester Kent, a theatrical producer who finds himself unemployed after the advent of the Depression and talking pictures. The dogged Kent, however, sells his backers (Kibbee and Hohl) on the idea of doing "prologues," short but stunning stage musical numbers designed to precede the showing of feature films. Two-thirds of the movie deals with Chester's behind-the-scenes efforts to put together the prologues; the final third is devoted to the prologues themselves and to a suitable wrap-up.

Seemingly schizophrenic in form, with a gritty, backstage saga yielding to three flights of Busby Berkeley fantasy, FOOTLIGHT PARADE is actually an amazing cultural index of the Depression. All the wisecracking, all the struggle, all the buildup find a remarkable payoff when the film shifts gears into la-la land. The "Honeymoon Hotel" number is standard risque fare, but "By a Waterfall," with Berkeley doing a "wet run" for his later Esther Williams spectaculars, is an astounding surrealistic kaleidoscope. "Shanghai Lil," meanwhile, adds a Warner Bros. toughness to Paramount's Shanghai Lily (Marlene Dietrich in SHANGHAI EXPRESS) of the year before.

Cagney is in great acting, comic and dancing form throughout and Blondell, as Kent's devoted secretary, proves that she has few peers at wisecracking or conveying low-key warmth. A great supporting cast and Bacon's well-judged direction help make FOOTLIGHT PARADE one of the greatest of the Berkeley extravaganzas.

FOR A FEW DOLLARS MORE
(PER QUALCHE DOLLARO IN PIU)
1967   130m   c ★★★★
Western /15
Europee/Arturo Gonzales/Constantin   (Italy/Spain/West Germany)

Clint Eastwood (The Man With No Name), Lee Van Cleef (Col. Douglas Mortimer), Gian Maria Volonte (Indio), Josef Egger (Old Man Over Railway), Rosemarie Dexter (Colonel's Sister), Mara Krup (Hotel Manager's Wife), Klaus Kinski (Hunchback), Mario Brega, Aldo Sambrell, Luigi Pistilli

p, Alberto Grimaldi; d, Sergio Leone; w, Luciano Vincenzoni, Sergio Leone (based on a story by Leone and Fulvio Morsella); ph, Massimo Dallamano (Techniscope, Technicolor); ed, Giorgio Ferralonga, Eugenio Alabiso; m, Ennio Morricone; art d, Carlo Simi; cos, Carlo Simi

The second film in Leone's "Dollar" trilogy (THE GOOD, THE BAD, AND THE UGLY would follow) finds the Italian director in better form than in A FISTFUL OF DOLLARS. FOR A FEW DOLLARS MORE has better writing, superior production values, and more characters who aptly complement Eastwood's stoic Man with No Name.

In this installment, the mysterious drifter is locked in combat with rival bounty hunter Colonel Mortimer (Van Cleef) to collect the reward for killing psychopathic bandit Indio (Volonte). At first, the men attempt to capture the crook separately, without success. The pair form an uneasy alliance, and Mortimer eventually guns Indio down in a shootout as No Name watches from the sidelines. It turns out, though, that Mortimer is not interested in money after all.

By introducing the character of Mortimer, Leone is able to counterpoint Eastwood's cold, amoral gunslinger with a man who has a past and a purpose. A more *human* character with which the audience can more readily identify makes Eastwood's role all the more mythic. Once again, Morricone's musical score is intrusive yet superbly appropriate, with each character's own theme (and one for the flashbacks too) bursting into this epic at just the right moment.

In FOR A FEW DOLLARS MORE, Leone's thematic concerns about the civilizing influence of the family and the hypocrisy of the Church are now richly in focus. His tone of self-parody and his portrait of an unrelenting landscape where men suddenly appear and vanish are all more detailed than before. We are also given the sense that the Man with No Name has been somewhat humanized by his encounter with Mortimer, a suspicion that would be confirmed in the final chapter of the trilogy.

FOR ME AND MY GAL
1942   104m   bw ★★★½
Musical /U
MGM

Judy Garland (Jo Hayden), George Murphy (Jimmy K. Metcalf), Gene Kelly (Harry Palmer), Marta Eggerth (Eve Minard), Ben Blue (Sid Simms), Richard Quine (Danny Hayden), Keenan Wynn (Eddie Milton), Stephen McNally (Mr. Waring), Lucille Norman (Lily Duncan), Betty Wells

p, Arthur Freed; d, Busby Berkeley; w, Richard Sherman, Fred Finklehoffe, Sid Silvers, Jack McGowan, Irving Brecher (based on the story "The Big Time" by Howard Emmett Rogers); ph, William Daniels; ed, Ben Lewis; art d, Cedric Gibbons, Gabriel Scognamillo; chor, Bobby Connolly, Gene Kelly; cos, Robert Kalloch, Gile Steele

A delightful and nostalgic return to the fun-filled pre-WWI days of vaudeville. Jo Hayden (Garland) troops the boards with Jimmy Metcalf (Murphy), Sid Simms (Blue), and Lily Duncan (Norman). Though she loves the hardscrabble life of the stage, Jo's main career motive is to send her kid brother (Quine) to medical school. When smoothie Harry Palmer (Kelly) advises Jo that she could do much better in his song-and-dance act, she, with Jimmy's blessing, teams up with him. They struggle along for two years; meanwhile, Jimmy and Sid hit the big time. Harry, meanwhile, becomes infatuated with a singing star (Eggerth), even though Jo is the one who truly loves him. When WWI threatens to halt his burgeoning success, Harry compounds his sins by dodging the draft, causing Jo to leave him—until he redeems himself in heroic style.

The story is pure hokum, but this warm film is more than buoyed by the many old tunes and the superb production numbers—staged, surprisingly, not by specialist Berkeley, who directed, but by Bobby Connolly. The dynamic Kelly, in his film debut, exhibits star quality in spades, while at the same time hinting at the darker side to his persona in the scene where he maims his hand to avoid the draft. He and Garland play beautifully off each other, and of course their performance of the title standard is a highlight of the film.

FOR WHOM THE BELL TOLLS

1943   170m   c   ★★
Adventure/War   /U
Paramount

Gary Cooper (Robert Jordan), Ingrid Bergman (Maria), Akim Tamiroff (Pablo), Arturo de Cordova (Agustin), Vladimir Sokoloff (Anselmo), Mikhail Rasumny (Rafael), Fortunio Bonanova (Fernando), Eric Feldary (Andres), Victor Varconi (Primitivo), Katina Paxinou (Pilar)

p, Sam Wood; d, Sam Wood; w, Dudley Nichols (based on the novel by Ernest Hemingway); ph, Ray Rennahan (Technicolor); ed, Sherman Todd, John F. Link; m, Victor Young; prod d, William Cameron Menzies; art d, Hans Dreier, Haldane Douglas; fx, Gordon Jennings

Do not ask for whom the bell tolls—it tolls for this film. A complete bowdlerization of one of Hemingway's most famous works, FOR WHOM THE BELL TOLLS makes its most overtly political move by cutting Ingrid Bergman's hair so short. Otherwise, it's pretty much of a yawner, with people (in Spain, right?) doing something or other to fight some kind of oppression. At one point during the film's three agonizing hours someone hints at fascism, but since that's *such* a difficult concept, HUAC "friendly witness" Wood and his writers largely drop it in favor of boy meets girl.

Even more taciturn than usual, Cooper is in many ways a perfect Hemingway hero (as he showed in the romanticized but lovely A FAREWELL TO ARMS). He has his moments, but otherwise seems a bit too respectful of the whole noble undertaking. Obviously remembering her luminous Ilsa from CASABLANCA, Bergman strives mightily to endow the film with romantic resonance, but she's treading on tenuous ground. The famous "I would kiss you but where do the noses go" is, depending on your mood, either the most dauntingly romantic moment this side of CASABLANCA's "Is that cannon fire or my heart pounding" or it's completely laughable. Cast mostly with Russians in all the Hispanic roles, this glamourfest is Hollywood politics at its most apolitical, lacking even the energy of a good B movie.

When critics with an interest in reality accused Paramount of fence-sitting (reports claimed that Franco's envoys and the Catholic Church pressured the studio into a nonpartisan stand), studio chief Adolph Zukor came back with one of the great double-edged truths about commercial cinema: "It's a great picture, without political significance. We are not for or against anybody."

FOR YOUR EYES ONLY

1981   127m   c   ★★★½
Spy/Adventure   PG
UA   (U.K.)

Roger Moore (James Bond), Carole Bouquet (Melina), Topol (Columbo), Lynn-Holly Johnson (Bibi), Julian Glover (Kristatos), Cassandra Harris (Lisl), Jill Bennett (Brink), Michael Gothard (Locque), John Wyman (Kriegler), Jack Hedley (Havelock)

p, Albert R. Broccoli; d, John Glen; w, Richard Maibaum, Michael G. Wilson (based on the short stories "For Your Eyes Only" and "Risico" by Ian Fleming); ph, Alan Hume (Panavision, Technicolor); ed, John Grover; m, Bill Conti; prod d, Peter Lamont; art d, John Fenner; fx, Derek Meddings; cos, Elizabeth Waller

After returning to Earth from his MOONRAKER fiasco, Roger Moore resumes his role as James Bond without the excessive technical gadgetry. Against a sea-and-ski Greek backdrop, Bond and the obligatory beauty, Melina (Bouquet, lovely but lifeless), race Soviet agents for a device lost in a shipwreck that transmits the "fire" order to missile-carrying British submarines. The same Soviet agents killed Melina's parents, motivating her to seek Elektra-like revenge. One fast-paced chase follows another, and a slightly more vulnerable Bond gets his share of knocks along the way.

The success of this picture (perhaps Moore's best in the Bond series) can be attributed to the marvelous direction of Glen, who had previously worked as a second-unit director on earlier Bond movies. Not surprisingly, the stunts are some of the best in the series. Lynn-Holly Johnson is decidedly annoying in the unnecessary role of a horny young skater, but Topol helps offset this gaffe with his engaging presence. Very pleasant, unforced, throwaway entertainment, though Moore is clearly getting a mite too old for all this.

FORBIDDEN GAMES

(LES JEUX INTERDITS)
1952   102m   bw   ★★★★★
War/Drama
Silver   (France)

Brigitte Fossey (Paulette), Georges Poujouly (Michel Dolle), Lucien Hubert (Dolle, the Father), Suzanne Courtal (Mme Dolle), Jacques Marin (Georges Dolle), Laurence Badie (Berthe Dolle), Andre Wasley (Gouard, the Father), Amedee (Francis Gouard), Denise Pereonne (Jeanne Gouard), Louis Sainteve (Priest)

p, Robert Dorfmann; d, Rene Clement; w, Rene Clement, Jean Aurenche, Pierre Bost (based on the novel Les Jeux Inconnus by Francois Boyer); ph, Robert Juillard; ed, Roger Dwyre; m, Narciso Yepes; art d, Paul Bertrand

One of the best films ever about war and its effects, FORBIDDEN GAMES also speaks beautifully to the need of children to construct their own fantasy world away from adult supervision.

Director Clement's most famous film carefully begins with its one action highlight, as refugees flee WWII Paris in the face of a Nazi attack. At a bottleneck on a bridge, German planes swoop down in perfect formation and strafe the confused column. Paulette (Fossey) is seen standing alone on the bridge, her parents and dog dead. When someone throws the dog over the bridge, she goes after it and meets Michel (Poujouly), the 11 year-old son of peasants (Hubert and Courtal). The boy takes the girl home with him, and his parents take her in. When Paulette sees her parents buried, she decides that her dog also needs to be buried in a grave with a cross. She and Michel steal a cross from the hearse carrying his older brother. He and Paulette begin to expand their secret animal cemetery to include moles, chickens, and even insects, all given elaborate memorial services with stolen crosses. The eventual discovery of the children's secret and their future together make for a moving climax.

FORBIDDEN GAMES derives most of its power from Clement's painstakingly methodical direction and the remarkable performances of the two child leads. Poujouly and the amazing five year-old Fossey are highly expressive actors who give this stunning film its emotional core. The visual and narrative style is a potent blend of stark documentary, pastoral realism and film noir. Seeing war through the eyes of children who cope with its atrocities by constructing their own little game of death was a brilliant move—it seems morbid and grotesque to all the adults, but the problem is that *they* are the ones who really lack understanding and respect.

FORBIDDEN PLANET

1956 98m c   ★★★★
Science Fiction   /U
MGM

Walter Pidgeon *(Dr. Morbius)*, Anne Francis *(Altaira)*, Leslie Nielsen *(Cmdr. Adams)*, Warren Stevens *(Lt. "Doc" Ostrow)*, Jack Kelly *(Lt. Farman)*, Richard Anderson *(Chief Quinn)*, Earl Holliman *(Cook)*, George Wallace *(Bosun)*, Bob Dix *(Grey)*, Jimmie Thompson *(Youngerford)*

p, Nicholas Nayfack; d, Fred M. Wilcox; w, Cyril Hume (based on a story by Irving Block, Allen Adler); ph, George Folsey (CinemaScope, Eastmancolor); ed, Ferris Webster; m, Louis Barron, Bebe Barron; art d, Cedric Gibbons, Arthur Lonergan; fx, A. Arnold Gillespie, Warren Newcombe, Irving G. Reis, Joshua Meador; cos, Helen Rose, Walter Plunkett

Shoot Anne Francis!! A superb sci-fi flick, FORBIDDEN PLANET offers an unusually intelligent script, exciting direction by Wilcox and generally good acting from a decent if rather dull cast.

It is 2200 A.D. when Commander Adams (Nielsen) lands his United Planets Cruiser on Altair-4, which features a green sky, pink sand, and two moons. He had been warned not to do so by Dr. Morbius (Pidgeon), a member of a missing Earth colony sent to the planet 20 years earlier. Adams and crew are greeted by Robby the Robot, a benign and astounding creation fluent in 88 languages and capable of any task, including producing an endless supply of bourbon at the behest of the crew's mischievous cook (Holliman). The robot drives Adams and his senior officers to the home of Morbius and his daughter Altaira (Francis, failing entirely to transcend her ill-conceived, camp classic role). Morbius explains that he and his glamorous love-spawn are the only survivors of attacks by an invisible monster prowling the planet. After the viewer is treated to scenes like Altaira's kissing lesson (the poor lusty darling has gone man-less, just imagine!), the invisible terror begins killing again.

FORBIDDEN PLANET is really a futuristic version of Shakespeare's *The Tempest*, with Morbius doubling for the wizard Prospero, Altaira a substitute Miranda, Robby the Robot serving as the spirit Ariel, and the Id monster being Caliban the witch-child. The first sci-fi film to cost $1 million, FORBIDDEN PLANET benefits immeasurably from its astounding technical prowess. The deadpan, all-purpose Robby the Robot is the film's most delightful creation, and it's not surprising that he later appeared in THE INVISIBLE BOY and scores of television shows.

While the spacemen are all likably heroic and Francis and Holliman can be forgiven for the enjoyable excesses of their roles, it is really Pidgeon who gives the drama flair and majesty. All in all, a splendid fantasy achievement that wears its age well.

FORCE OF EVIL

1948 78m bw   ★★★★½
Crime   /A
Enterprise

John Garfield *(Joe Morse)*, Beatrice Pearson *(Doris Lowry)*, Thomas Gomez *(Leo Morse)*, Howland Chamberlin *(Freddy Bauer)*, Roy Roberts *(Ben Tucker)*, Marie Windsor *(Edna Tucker)*, Paul McVey *(Hobe Wheelock)*, Tim Ryan *(Johnson)*, Sid Tomack *("Two & Two" Taylor)*, Georgia Backus *(Sylvia Morse)*

p, Bob Roberts; d, Abraham Polonsky; w, Abraham Polonsky, Ira Wolfert (based on his novel, *Tucker's People*); ph, George Barnes; ed, Walter Thompson, Arthur Seid; m, David Raksin; art d, Richard Day; cos, Louise Wilson

Garfield is Joe Morse, a slick, self-centered lawyer who knows the law but feels he's above it. He practices on Wall Street and has his eyes on millions, working on retainer for racketeer Ben Tucker (Roberts). The policy czar plans to have the number 776 come up on July 4; knowing that most people will bet on it, Tucker hopes to bankrupt and take over most of the city's smaller numbers operations. Without spilling the beans, Joe attempts to get his kindly brother Leo (Gomez) to shut down for one day, but the stubborn older man feels obligated to let his regulars take their holiday chances. Joe arranges for a police raid to break his brother's spirit, but to no avail. After Tucker achieves his expected success on the Fourth, Leo's people, including bookkeeper Doris (Pearson), become nervous about the gangsters suddenly in their midst.

Dark and brooding, FORCE OF EVIL offers one of Garfield's greatest performances as the cynical, hard-as-nails lawyer. Pearson, in her first of only two films, doesn't really register in a role that could use Shelley Winters or Ida Lupino rather than a June Allyson clone. Her presence is more than offset, however, by Gomez's marvelous performance and that of the suitably slimy Roberts. A tour de force for gifted writer Polonsky, FORCE was the only film he directed before he was blacklisted for being an uncooperative witness before HUAC in 1951; he didn't direct another feature for 21 years. At its best, FORCE achieves a style at once brutal and poetic, documentarian and noir.

FORCE 10 FROM NAVARONE

1978 118m c   ★★½
War   PG/15
AIP (U.K.)

Robert Shaw *(Mallory)*, Harrison Ford *(Barnsby)*, Edward Fox *(Miller)*, Barbara Bach *(Maritza)*, Franco Nero *(Lescovar)*, Carl Weathers *(Weaver)*, Richard Kiel *(Drazac)*, Angus MacInnes *(Reynolds)*, Michael Byrne *(Schroeder)*, Alan Badel *(Petrovich)*

p, Oliver A. Unger, John R. Sloan, Anthony B. Unger; d, Guy Hamilton; w, Robin Chapman (based on a story by Carl Foreman and the novel by Alistair MacLean); ph, Christopher Challis (Panavision, Technicolor); ed, Raymond Poulton; m, Ron Goodwin; prod d, Geoffrey Drake; fx, Rene Albouze; cos, Emma Porteous

Force five from Hollywood. This is not quite a sequel to THE GUNS OF NAVARONE, but it comes close. This time the squad is sent to Yugoslavia to blow up a bridge vital to the German war effort. Ford (fresh from a different "force" in STAR WARS) is the American member of the team, paired with Weathers as a black soldier whose patience with racial hatred has been exhausted. Fox, giving the film's best performance, is a demolitions expert; the exotic-looking Bach is a partisan who helps their cause; the gigantic Kiel is a Nazi conspirator; and Nero is a Nazi double agent. Heading up this motley crew is Major Mallory (Shaw), a Briton who survived the Force's previous attack at Navarone. You get the picture. The action sequences, especially the climax, are painfully deficient, one of the many demerits of Hamilton's dull direction. Only the cast makes this worth catching for less demanding fans of the war genre.

FOREIGN CORRESPONDENT

1940   120m   bw   ★★★★★
Spy/War   /PG
UA

Joel McCrea *(Johnny Jones/Huntley Haverstock)*, Laraine Day *(Carol Fisher)*, Herbert Marshall *(Stephen Fisher)*, George Sanders *(Scott Ffolliott)*, Albert Basserman *(Van Meer)*, Robert Benchley *(Stebbins)*, Edmund Gwenn *(Rowley)*, Eduardo Ciannelli *(Krug)*, Martin Kosleck *(Tramp)*, Harry Davenport *(Mr. Powers)*

p, Walter Wanger; d, Alfred Hitchcock; w, Charles Bennett, Joan Harrison, James Hilton, Robert Benchley; ph, Rudolph Mate; ed, Otho Lovering, Dorothy Spencer; m, Alfred Newman; art d, Alexander Golitzen; fx, Lee Zavitz

One of the great espionage films, tautly handled by the stellar Hitchcock, FOREIGN CORRESPONDENT gleams with suspense, atmosphere and sharp dialogue. Johnny Jones (McCrea) is a top American crime reporter reassigned as a foreign correspondent to Western Europe. Ordered to find the most provocative stories swirling in the political cauldron just prior to WWII, he meets Stephen Fisher (Marshall), head of a peace organization, and Fisher's attractive daughter Carol (Day). Before long, Johnny gets entangled in international intrigue involving the kidnaping of Van Meer (Basserman), a Dutch diplomat carrying vital information.

One of Hitchcock's greatest entertainments, FOREIGN CORRESPONDENT is also a stirring propaganda piece which clearly indicts the Nazi regime. This fact was recognized by no less than Nazi propaganda minister Josef Goebbels, who nonetheless hailed the film as a masterpiece, calling it "a first-class production, a criminological bang-up hit, which no doubt will make a certain impression upon the broad masses of the people in enemy countries." FOREIGN CORRESPONDENT also boasts some of the finest production design of its time—a huge windmill set was built to simulate a Dutch location, and a square in Amsterdam was reconstructed on a 10-acre set—a testament to the talents of Golitzen and Menzies. The acting is uniformly excellent, with McCrea an ideal Hitchcock hero and Marshall, Sanders, Gwenn, and especially Basserman stealing the supporting honors.

FOREIGN CORRESPONDENT is perhaps best remembered for its splendid set pieces, which include an assassination in the rain with umbrellas bobbing everywhere and terrific moments atop Westminster Cathedral, inside the windmill, and especially aboard a plane crashing into the ocean. Viewers are not likely to forget the struggle of the passengers as their air supply is slowly cut off. Not one of the director's more profound meditations on voyeurism and sexuality, FOREIGN CORRESPONDENT aims at something simpler than REAR WINDOW or VERTIGO; it shows him going through his playful paces at his professional best.

FOREVER AND A DAY

1943   104m   bw
Historical
RKO

Anna Neagle *(Miriam Susan)*, Ray Milland *(Bill Trimble)*, Claude Rains *(Pomfret)*, C. Aubrey Smith *(Adm. Trimble)*, Dame May Whitty *(Mrs. Trimble)*, Gene Lockhart *(Cobblewick)*, Ray Bolger *(Sentry)*, Edmund Gwenn *(Stubbs)*, Lumsden Hare *(Fitts)*, Stuart Robertson *(Lawyer/Air Raid Warden)*

p, Rene Clair, Edmund Goulding, Cedric Hardwicke, Frank Lloyd, Victor Saville, Robert Stevenson, Herbert Wilcox; d, Rene Clair, Edmund Goulding, Cedric Hardwicke, Frank Lloyd, Victor Saville, Robert Stevenson, Herbert Wilcox; w, Charles Bennett, C.S. Forester, Lawrence Hazard, Michael Hogan, W.P. Lipscomb, Alice Duer Miller, John Van Druten, Alan Campbell, Peter Godfrey, Sig Herzig, Christopher Isherwood, Gene Lockhart, R.C. Sherriff, Claudine West, Norman Corwin, Jack Hartfield, James Hilton, Emmett Lavery, Frederick Lonsdale, Donald Ogden Stewart, Keith Winter; ph, Robert de Grasse, Lee Garmes, Russell Metty, Nicholas Musuraca; ed, Elmo Williams, George Crone; art d, Albert S. D'Agostino, L.P. Williams, Al Freeman; fx, Vernon L. Walker

A wartime salute to England with a cavalcade of stars and directors to give it snap, FOREVER AND A DAY depicts the history of a great manor house in London.

Built by Admiral Trimble (Smith) during the Napoleonic era, we see the house pass from the hands of one generation to another. Scores of stars and character actors appear in cameos in this stunning film, its only major detraction being that we'd like to see more of all of them. Many highly appealing players of the age (Matthews, Rains, Coburn, Horton) are whisked onscreen to our delight and then passed over summarily. Exceptional are Laughton as a comic butler, Hardwicke and Keaton as plumbers, Lanchester as a waitress-maid, Aherne as a coalman, and Lupino as the housemaid who runs off with him to America.

Particularly moving is the WWI sequence, when a party is held for a WWI flying ace who never appears. Cummings and Oberon are touching as a doughboy and a receptionist who fall in love despite the perils involved, but it is really Young and Cooper, as the ace's parents, who beautifully render their moment of loss. An effective pageant on the theme of English patriotism, FOREVER AND A DAY comes down to the house's (and thereby England's) survival during the awful WWII blitz of London.

RKO used just about everyone in Hollywood's esteemed British acting colony for this one and $500,000 to boot. The film could practically be considered an act of goodwill in promoting the British-American cause, since the studio saw little return at the box office. The film is nevertheless memorable—superbly crafted, acted, and directed. A rare case of too many cooks not spoiling the broth.

FORT APACHE

1948 127m bw ★★★★★
Western/War /U
Argosy

Henry Fonda *(Lt. Col. Owen Thursday)*, John Wayne *(Capt. Kirby York)*, Shirley Temple *(Philadelphia Thursday)*, Ward Bond *(Sgt. Maj. Michael O'Rourke)*, John Agar *(Lt. Michael "Mickey" O'Rourke)*, George O'Brien *(Capt. Sam Collingwood)*, Irene Rich *(Mrs. Mary O'Rourke)*, Victor McLaglen *(Sgt. Festus Mulcahy)*, Anna Lee *(Mrs. Emily Collingwood)*, Pedro Armendariz *(Sgt. Beaufort)*

p, John Ford, Merian C. Cooper; d, John Ford; w, Frank S. Nugent (based on the story "Massacre" by James Warner Bellah); ph, Archie Stout; ed, Jack Murray; m, Richard Hageman; art d, James Basevi; fx, David Koehler; chor, Kenny Williams; cos, Michael Meyers, Ann Peck

Philadelphia Thursday—sounds like an itinerary entry, right? No, it's the character played by teen-aged Shirley Temple in FORT APACHE, and you want nothing so much as to edit her part and that of husband John Agar (a really bad actor) right out of the damn picture. Apart from this irritation, FORT APACHE is a marvelous film, the first of director John Ford's US Cavalry trilogy.

The awesome exterior scenes reflect Ford's early training as a painter and provide a remarkable backdrop for the irony which unfolds. Lt. Col. Owen Thursday (Fonda) is a martinet commander bitter over having been sent to fight "digger" Indians instead of being assigned a glory post. He foolishly leads his men to disaster, but the press later presents him as a hero for the sake of the military's image.

FORT APACHE is rich beyond its wonderful action scenes and the outdoor panoramas so dear to Ford's heart. The film expertly depicts the social affairs of a far-flung military outpost, the struggle of the women to maintain civility, and the routines of the men in their daily military chores. More importantly, though, it exposes the sham behind public and national conceptions of "the hero." APACHE is one of the earliest films of Ford's final period, in which he questioned noisy, patriotic bravado and the white man's treatment of the Native American.

Wayne gives a solid performance, and such stalwarts as McLaglen, Bond, O'Brien, Foran, Armendariz, and Kibbee lend the film its humor and heart. But you find yourself watching Fonda transcend the possible critic's charge of "miscasting" as the permapressed, power-bloated commander. Of course, Fonda's character and the doomed route he pursues are based on the massacre of George Armstrong Custer's 7th Cavalry at Little Big Horn, and this if anything lends weight to Ford's elegiac reconsideration of "the American spirit."

FORTUNE, THE

1975 88m c ★★★★
Comedy PG/AA
Columbia

Warren Beatty *(Nicky)*, Jack Nicholson *(Oscar)*, Stockard Channing *(Freddie)*, Florence Stanley *(Landlady)*, Richard B. Shull *(Chief Detective)*, Thomas Newman *(John the Barber)*, John Fiedler *(Police Photographer)*, Scatman Crothers *(Fisherman)*, Dub Taylor *(Rattlesnake Tom)*, Ian Wolfe *(Justice of the Peace)*

p, Mike Nichols, Don Devlin; d, Mike Nichols; w, Adrien Joyce; ph, John A. Alonzo (Technicolor); ed, Stu Linder; m, David Shire; prod d, Richard Sylbert; art d, Stewart Campbell

An offbeat but often hilarious comedy where Beatty and Nicholson play Nicky and Oscar, two competing confidence men trying to bilk heiress Freddie (Channing) out of her fortune. The source of this wealth is Freddie's father, a manufacturer of sanitary napkins (which naturally results in plenty of tacky humor). Though she is in love with the married Nicky, Freddie plans to marry the slippery Oscar and then carry on an affair with the man she wants. Oscar, a failed embezzler, has no intention of playing the cuckolded hubby; he means to have his carnal share of the attractive heiress. When she learns that the two con men are up to something, Freddie tells them her plans to give her fortune to charity. Alarmed, they conclude that their only course of action is murder, and the rest of the film is a series of black comedy sketches of plans gone awry and misplaced guilt.

A catalogue of slapstick errors, THE FORTUNE works well through the fine performances of the leads and the superb timing of director Nichols. Beatty nervously twitches through his part but is quickly outdone by the easy-going Nicholson and the marvelous Channing. LUCKY LADY, a similar type of love triangle also set in the 1920s (with Gene Hackman, Liza Minnelli and Burt Reynolds), was made the same year but nowhere approaches the style and wit on display here. Full of period and period-sounding music, THE FORTUNE is cold to the core— agreeably disagreeable amusement.

FORTUNE COOKIE, THE

1966 125m bw ★★★½
Comedy/Sports /U
Mirisch

Jack Lemmon *(Harry Hinkle)*, Walter Matthau *(Willie Gingrich)*, Ron Rich *(Luther "Boom Boom" Jackson)*, Cliff Osmond *(Mr. Purkey)*, Judi West *(Sandy Hinkle)*, Lurene Tuttle *(Mother Hinkle)*, Harry Holcombe *(O'Brien)*, Les Tremayne *(Thompson)*, Marge Redmond *(Charlotte Gingrich)*, Noam Pitlik *(Max)*

p, Billy Wilder; d, Billy Wilder; w, Billy Wilder, I.A.L. Diamond; ph, Joseph La Shelle (Panavision); ed, Daniel Mandell; m, Andre Previn; art d, Robert Luthardt; fx, Sass Bedig; cos, Charles Arrico, Paula Giokaris

A very funny film, this morality tale is a deft mixture of cynicism, wit and idealism as only writer-director Wilder could do it. The only problem is that morality tales can get moralizing.

While working the sidelines during a Browns-Vikings game, cameraman Harry Hinkle (Lemmon) is flattened by Browns running back Luther "Boom Boom" Jackson (Rich) and rushed to the hospital. Although Harry is fine, his shyster brother-in-law, "Whiplash" Willie Gingrich (Matthau), convinces him to fake an injury and sue the Browns, CBS and Municipal Stadium for $1 million. Pretending to be paralyzed from the neck down and relying on an old spinal injury for X-ray proof, Harry fools a team of doctors and, under Willie's supervision, continues to deceive private investigator Purkey (Osmond). In the meantime, Harry's wife, Sandy (West), a would-be singer who ran off with another guy, returns, anxious to get in on the gravy train.

Lemmon and especially Matthau—who deservedly won a Best Supporting Actor Oscar for his role—are superb; this first teaming together more than justified later reunions. The screenplay by Wilder and Diamond sparkles with the dark satiric cynicism for which they are famous and LaShelle's frankly unattractive cinematography is entirely appropriate to the unsavory goings-on. Rich's Boom Boom is a bit too noble, but his relationship with Harry is still touching. In fact, toward the end the film goes perhaps a little too soft. Despite some minor flaws, THE FORTUNE COOKIE is a very satisfying film.

48 HRS.

1933 96m c   ★★★½
Comedy/Crime   R/18
Paramount

Nick Nolte *(Jack Cates)*, Eddie Murphy *(Reggie Hammond)*, Annette O'Toole *(Elaine)*, Frank McRae *(Haden)*, James Remar *(Ganz)*, David Patrick Kelly *(Luther)*, Sonny Landham *(Billy Bear)*, Brion James *(Kehoe)*, Kerry Sherman *(Rosalie)*, Jonathan Banks *(Algren)*

p, Lawrence Gordon, Joel Silver; d, Walter Hill; w, Roger Spottiswoode, Walter Hill, Larry Gross, Steven E. de Souza; ph, Ric Waite (Movielab Color); ed, Freeman Davies, Mark Warner, Billy Weber; m, James Horner; prod d, John Vallone; cos, Marilyn Vance

A big box-office hit, this action film casts Nolte as Jack Cates, a hard-as-granite cop, and Murphy as Reggie Hammond, a glib convict who is released from prison in Cates's custody for 48 hours. Hammond's job is to help Cates track down a pair of maniacal cop killers (Landham and Remar) who happen to be his former associates. Together Cates and Hammond take a thrill-a-minute trip through the San Francisco underworld and along the way develop one of the 1980s' more interesting cinematic buddy pairings.

In this, his first film, comedian Murphy turned in a marvelous performance, setting the stage for his enormously popular Axel Foley character in the BEVERLY HILLS COP films. Nolte, however, always threatens to steal the film in his customary quiet way as Murphy's rough and gruff partner. Director Hill (THE LONG RIDERS, SOUTHERN COMFORT, RED HEAT) pushes the film along at his traditional rapid pace, aided by Waite's excellent cinematography. In the film's most poignant moment Cates gives Hammond a badge and sends him into a rowdy country-western bar for a role-reversal confrontation with a passel of rednecks. Hang on for the ride.

42ND STREET

1933 98m bw   ★★★★★
Musical   /U
WB

Warner Baxter *(Julian Marsh)*, Bebe Daniels *(Dorothy Brock)*, George Brent *(Pat Denning)*, Una Merkel *(Lorraine Fleming)*, Ruby Keeler *(Peggy Sawyer)*, Guy Kibbee *(Abner Dillon)*, Dick Powell *(Billy Lawler)*, Ginger Rogers *(Ann Lowell/Anytime Annie)*, George E. Stone *(Andy Lee)*, Robert McWade *(Al Jones)*

p, Hal B. Wallis; d, Lloyd Bacon; w, James Seymour, Rian James (based on the novel by Bradford Ropes); ph, Sol Polito; ed, Thomas Pratt; art d, Jack Okey; chor, Busby Berkeley; cos, Orry-Kelly

Hear the beat of dancing feet! The film that revived public interest in musicals after many early talkie bombs sabotaged the genre, 42ND STREET was the first real glimpse of the surreal artistry of choreographer Busby Berkeley. The film also highlighted two fresh-faced new stars, the likably cornball crooner Dick Powell and the endearingly untalented Ruby Keeler.

The familiar plot concerns Broadway director Julian Marsh's (Warner Baxter) desire for one more hit so he can retire and recover his health. Abner Dillon (Guy Kibbee) is his wealthy backer, Dorothy Brock (Bebe Daniels) his temperamental star, Peggy Sawyer (Keeler) a hopeful chorine, and Billy Lawler (Powell) a singer with the hots for Peggy. As Julian struggles with the show, promises and hearts are broken, but that's nothing compared to the crisis created when Dorothy's ankle is broken on the eve of the show's premiere. Understudy Peggy has to go

on in her place, giving Baxter the chance to say the immortal line, "You're going out a youngster, but you've got to come back a star!"

42ND STREET's charm and fascination lie in director Bacon's fast-paced and vivid backstage atmosphere, crammed with exhausted chorus kids and sudden hysterics. The great cast is in fine fettle: Baxter brings real edge to what could have been a standardized part; fading star Daniels is eerily appropriate as the performer who gets replaced; Una Merkel makes the most of her wisecracks; and when Ginger Rogers enters sporting a monocle and an Erich von Stroheim shtick, you oddly sense that a star is almost ready to be born.

The real star, though, is the master of kaleidoscopic imagery, Busby Berkeley. Backed by the ebullient songs of Harry Warren and Al Dubin, Buzz unleashed his startling creations on an escapism-hungry public. The dizzying combination of sexuality and abstraction in such numbers as "Young and Healthy," "Shuffle Off to Buffalo," and the title tune remains potent to this day. A film that returned it's $400,000 investment ten times over, inspired dozens of imitations and a Broadway reprise in the 1970s, 42ND STREET, "that avenue I'm takin' you to," remains hard to beat.

FOUR DAUGHTERS

1938 90m bw   ★★★★
Romance   /U
WB

Claude Rains *(Adam Lemp)*, May Robson *(Aunt Etta)*, Priscilla Lane *(Ann Lemp)*, Lola Lane *(Thea Lemp)*, Rosemary Lane *(Kay Lemp)*, Gale Page *(Emma Lemp)*, Dick Foran *(Ernest)*, Jeffrey Lynn *(Felix Deitz)*, Frank McHugh *(Ben Crowley)*, John Garfield *(Mickey Borden)*

p, Henry Blanke; d, Michael Curtiz; w, Julius J. Epstein, Lenore Coffee (based on the novel *Sister Act* by Fannie Hurst); ph, Ernest Haller; ed, Ralph Dawson; m, Max Steiner; art d, John Hughes

An engrossing film which both endorses and questions a vision of small-town American romance. When Felix Deitz (Lynn) arrives at Adam Lemp's (Rains) house to board, the music professor's four daughters all fall in love with him. Ann (Priscilla Lane) becomes engaged to him but later finds out from the cynical Mickey Borden (Garfield) that one of her sisters is devastated by the impending marriage. In a great act of sibling generosity, she gives up Felix and runs off with the embittered Mickey. Felix departs, however, and the sister falls in love with another man. The tough, indolent Mickey realizes that he's breaking Ann's heart and decides to engineer her reunion with Felix.

A fun tearjerker, this film is saved from its own candybox prettiness by the scorching presence of Garfield in the seemingly tailor-made role that brought him stardom. His Mickey Borden is a rebellious, surly, disillusioned young man from the big city, where poverty has scarred his otherwise brilliant mind. His rare smiles are wry grins, and his laughter is ironic. His character at once shouts defiance and defeat. His remarks to the kindly small-town folks who take him in reflect both their naivete and his jaded worldliness.

Further help is offered by director Curtiz, whose sense of pace and proportion never gives this cottage cheese a chance to curdle. Although the Lane sisters and Page are simply *too* cute for words, they, Rains, and Robson do evoke something idealistically cozy when you let your guard down. Several sequels followed, including the superior DAUGHTERS COURAGEOUS, as well as a mediocre remake, YOUNG AT HEART.

FOUR FEATHERS, THE

1939   130m   c   ★★★★★
Adventure/War   /U
Korda/London Films   (U.K.)

John Clements *(Harry Faversham)*, Ralph Richardson *(Capt. John Durrance)*, C. Aubrey Smith *(Gen. Burroughs)*, June Duprez *(Ethne Burroughs)*, Allan Jeayes *(Gen. Faversham)*, Jack Allen *(Lt. Willoughby)*, Donald Gray *(Peter Burroughs)*, Frederick Culley *(Dr. Sutton)*, Amid Taftazani *(Karaga Pasha)*, Henry Oscar *(Dr. Harraz)*

p, Alexander Korda; d, Zoltan Korda; w, R.C. Sherriff, Lajos Biro, Arthur Wimperis (based on the novel by A.E.W. Mason); ph, Georges Perinal, Osmond Borradaile, Jack Cardiff (Technicolor); ed, William Hornbeck, Henry Cornelius; m, Miklos Rozsa; prod d, Vincent Korda; cos, Godfrey Brennan, Rene Hubert

One of the all-time great adventure films. THE FOUR FEATHERS is based on the 1902 tale of cowardice and courage by A.E.W. Mason, filmed at least six times but never as well as in this marvelous production.

The tale of empire, battle, and redemption begins when Harry Faversham (Clements), the son of a brigadier general, refuses to follow family tradition and join the army, choosing instead to settle down and wed Ethne Burroughs (Duprez). He resigns his commission just before his regiment leaves for the 1898 Sudan campaign conducted by Lord Kitchener, and his friends—John Durrance (Richardson), Peter Burroughs (Gray), and Tom Willoughby (Allen)—present him three white feathers symbolizing cowardice. Also disgusted by his actions is Ethne, who gives him the fourth feather. Determined to prove his courage, Faversham leaves for Egypt alone and disguises himself as a native, his skin stained and an "S" branded on his forehead to mark him as a Sangali tribe member with his tongue cut out by enemies. Eventually Faversham is able to redeem himself in the eyes of those he loves.

One of the great British films of the 1930s and one of producer Alexander Korda's finest achievements, THE FOUR FEATHERS is directed by Alexander's brother, Zoltan, with the elan demanded by the action-packed story. His talent is evident in the magnificent battle scenes, particularly the awesome attack of the "Fuzzi Wuzzies" against the British lines, shown in wide panorama by cameras mounted high on hilltops overlooking the battlefield.

The acting is distinguished throughout, with Clements a sensitive and dashing nonconformist, Richardson superb as a man who must reconsider a friendship, and Smith equally good as a crusty career officer whose hypocrisy is revealed. A film unafraid to question those traditions it celebrates, THE FOUR FEATHERS balances its highly impressive spectacle with a drama of substance and intelligence.

FOUR FRIENDS

1981   114m   c   ★★★½
Drama   R/AA
Filmways

Craig Wasson *(Danilo Prozor)*, Jodi Thelen *(Georgia Miles)*, Jim Metzler *(Tom Donaldson)*, Michael Huddleston *(David Levine)*, Reed Birney *(Louie Camahan)*, Julia Murray *(Adrienne Camahan)*, David Graf *(Gergley)*, Zaid Farid *(Rudy)*, Miklos Simon *(Mr. Prozor)*, Elizabeth Lawrence *(Mrs. Prozor)*

p, Arthur Penn, Gene Lasko; d, Arthur Penn; w, Steve Tesich; ph, Ghislain Cloquet (Technicolor); ed, Barry Malkin, Marc Laub; m, Elizabeth Swados; prod d, David Chapman; chor, Julie Arenal; cos, Patricia Norris

A charming, heartfelt, sometimes insightful look at four friends who form strong bonds while in high school in the early 1960s, and then desperately cling to that love during the turbulent social upheavals that marked the end of the decade. Unfortunately, FOUR FRIENDS attempts to cover so much ground that at times the film becomes frustratingly muddled.

The film's focal point is Danilo (Wasson), the son of a Yugoslavian immigrant steelworker (Simon) who does not understand Danilo's refusal to follow in his footsteps. Danilo seeks refuge with his best friends: handsome jock Tom (Metzler), overweight mama's boy David (Huddleston), and free-spirited Georgia (Thelen). Although the latter loves Danilo best, for various reasons she gives herself to Tom, leading to rifts among the group. Following graduation, they go their separate ways, and the film becomes a series of vignettes that attempt to dramatize nearly every aspect of life in the late 1960s.

Though FOUR FRIENDS runs out of gas toward the end, it's filmed with obvious love for the characters and features outstanding performances from the underrated Wasson, Thelen and Simon. Well worth seeing.

FOUR HUNDRED BLOWS, THE

(LES QUATRES CENTS COUPS)
1959   93m   bw   ★★★★★
Drama   /A
Carosse   (France)

Jean-Pierre Leaud *(Antoine Doinel)*, Claire Maurier *(Mme Doinel)*, Albert Remy *(M Doinel)*, Guy Decombie *(Teacher)*, Patrick Auffay *(Rene Bigey)*, Georges Flament *(M Bigey)*, Yvonne Claudie *(Mme Bigey)*, Robert Beauvais *(Director of the School)*, Claude Mansard *(Examining Magistrate)*, Jacques Monod *(Commissioner)*

p, Francois Truffaut; d, Francois Truffaut; w, Francois Truffaut, Marcel Moussy (story by Truffaut); ph, Henri Decae; ed, Marie-Josephe Yoyotte; m, Jean Constantin; art d, Bernard Evein

This extraordinary film was the first feature from Francois Truffaut, who was, until its release, best known as a hell-raising critic from the journal *Cahiers du Cinema*. THE 400 BLOWS is not only one of the foremost films of the French New Wave, but also the first in a Truffaut series that included "Antoine and Colette" (an episode from LOVE AT TWENTY), STOLEN KISSES, BED AND BOARD, and LOVE ON THE RUN.

These films all starred the remarkable Leaud as Truffaut's alter ego Antoine Doinel and span 20 years in this semi-autobiographical character's life. Here Leaud beautifully embodies Doinel at age 12, a child more or less left to his own devices by his mother (Maurier) and father (Remy). He gets into trouble at school, runs away from home, and eventually ends up in an observation center for juvenile delinquents.

THE 400 BLOWS—an idiomatic French expression for the limit of what anyone can bear—is a nonjudgmental film about injustice, pain, and the events in a young boy's life that make him the person he is. Neither good nor bad, Antoine is treated with warmth and compassion by Truffaut as a child caught up in a maelstrom not of his own making. The grace and perfection of THE 400 BLOWS has made it the standard against which all films on the subject of youth are judged, and Leaud's portrayal that to which all young performers' are compared.

The film also features Decae's poetic black-and-white photography, and together he and Truffaut offer a glimpse of the freedom that Antoine's life never really affords. Images such as a line of schoolboys snaking their way through the streets linger like pages from a mental yearbook of schooldays. Best of all, though, is the film's famous final freeze frame, in which Truffaut conveys both promise and sadness, and demonstrates that the cinema offers no easy answers to the problems of living.

FOUR MUSKETEERS, THE

1975 108m c ★★★½
Adventure/Historical PG
FOX

Michael York *(D'Artagnan)*, Oliver Reed *(Athos)*, Richard Chamberlain *(Aramis)*, Frank Finlay *(Porthos)*, Raquel Welch *(Mme. Constance Bonacieux)*, Christopher Lee *(Rochefort)*, Faye Dunaway *(Milady)*, Jean-Pierre Cassel *(Louis XIII)*, Geraldine Chaplin *(Queen Anne of Austria)*, Simon Ward *(Duke of Buckingham)*

p, Alexander Salkind; d, Richard Lester; w, George MacDonald Fraser (from *The Three Musketeers* by Alexandre Dumas); ph, David Watkin (DeLuxe Color); ed, John Victor Smith; m, Lalo Schifrin; prod d, Brian Eatwell

A sequel to THE THREE MUSKETEERS. Both pictures were originally supposed to have been one huge 3½-hour epic, but the producers decided to release them as two films—and lawsuits followed immediately from a cast and crew who wanted to be paid for making two films. That aside, this sequel is a worthy follow-up to the original.

In this installment, Milady DeWinter (Dunaway) plans to wreak revenge on D'Artagnan (York), his cohorts (Chamberlain, Finlay, and Reed), his "lady fair" Constance (Welch), and the Duke (Ward) for foiling her plans in the first film. Milady attempts seduction and later allows herself to be arrested so as to manipulate a religious-fanatic jailer into assassinating the Duke. She also kidnaps Constance, a move certain to bring the swashbuckling quartet into the picture.

Much of the film is played for merry comedy, and the cast makes a good job of it. Welch, for example, handles both the physical and the verbal comedy with the same brio which marked her work in the earlier film. Dunaway, on the other hand, does not make the pivotal role of Milady DeWinter *quite* as fascinating as one would like. Although there is less slapstick than in THE THREE MUSKETEERS, the lightness of the enterprise stays constant until the swashbuckling climax and dramatic resolution. What is especially notable in this sequel is Lester's determination to deglamorize life in the 1620s, and his film is amply populated with mercenaries, boors and slobs.

FOUR NIGHTS OF A DREAMER

1971 87m c ★★★★
Drama /AA
Victoria/Albina/Del Orso   (France)

Isabelle Weingarten *(Marthe)*, Guillaume Des Forets *(Jacques)*, Maurice Monnoyer *(Lover)*

d, Robert Bresson; w, Robert Bresson (based on the story "White Nights" by Feodor Dostoyevsky); ph, Pierre Lhomme (Eastmancolor)

This fascinating feature by master director Bresson adapts Dostoyevsky's story "White Nights" and puts it in Paris in the modern age.

Jacques (Des Forets) is a young artist living a life of daydreams who meets Marthe (Weingarten) on a bridge one night while she is contemplating suicide. They talk and arrange to meet there the next night. They speak of their lives—he of his painting and his fantasies, she of the man she loves and his leaving her with the promise to meet her on the bridge one year later. It is because he hasn't kept the rendezvous that she has thought to kill herself. Jacques falls in love with the enigmatic woman, walking around Paris with a tape recorder against his heart that just plays a recording of him repeating her name. For four nights they meet on the bridge and talk, but on the last night the missing lover returns.

Bresson's spare, totally restrained style has seldom been used to such effect. With its highly deliberate editing and elegant use of color, the film emerges a delicate if sad paean to young love. Mystical and erotic but also dispassionate, FOUR NIGHTS OF A DREAMER is an important film by one of the cinema's most important figures. It makes for fascinating comparison with Visconti's memorable WHITE NIGHTS, an earlier adaptation of the same story.

FOUR SEASONS, THE

1981 107m c ★★★
Drama/Comedy PG/15
Universal

Alan Alda *(Jack Burroughs)*, Carol Burnett *(Kate Burroughs)*, Len Cariou *(Nick Callan)*, Sandy Dennis *(Anne Callan)*, Rita Moreno *(Claudia Zimmer)*, Jack Weston *(Danny Zimmer)*, Bess Armstrong *(Ginny Newley)*, Elizabeth Alda *(Beth)*, Beatrice Alda *(Lisa)*, Robert Hitt *(Room Clerk)*

p, Martin Bregman; d, Alan Alda; w, Alan Alda; ph, Victor J. Kemper (Technicolor); ed, Michael Economou; m, Antonio Vivaldi; prod d, Jack T. Collis; cos, Jane Greenwood

Friendship is the topic in this film about three middle-aged couples who find their loyalties to one another and their marriages tested. Alda and Burnett play the "thoughtful" couple at the center of the sextet, which spends a year taking vacations together in each of the four seasons. Weston and Moreno provide comic relief; Cariou and Dennis play the star-crossed twosome whose marriage falls apart, after which he marries a younger woman (Armstrong).

Much of the film's first half is sprightly and amusing, but the move toward serious drama later, and then a slapstick finale, is a bit hard to take. Alda's debut as a director is nevertheless impressive, even if he clearly doesn't know *what* to do with the camera. This latter problem is, luckily, partly offset by Kemper's stunningly attractive photography of the Virgin Islands and New England.

It's good to know that movies can still be made with grownups in mind, even if the exceptionally *nice* quality of these characters occasionally makes you want to smack them.

FOX AND THE HOUND, THE

1981 83m c ★★★★
Animated G/U
Buena Vista

VOICES OF: Mickey Rooney *(Tod)*, Kurt Russell *(Copper)*, Pearl Bailey *(Big Mamma)*, Jack Albertson *(Amos Slade)*, Sandy Duncan *(Vixey)*, Jeanette Nolan *(Widow Tweed)*, Pat Buttram *(Chief)*, John Fiedler *(Porcupine)*, Corey Feldman *(Young Copper)*, John McIntire *(Badger)*

p, Wolfgang Reitherman, Art Stevens; d, Art Stevens, Ted Berman, Richard Rich; w, Larry Clemmons, Ted Berman, Peter Young, Steve Hulett, David Michener, Burny Mattinson, Earl Kress, Vance Gerry (based on the book by Daniel P. Mannix); ed, Jim Melton, Jim Koford; m, Buddy Baker; art d, Don Griffith; anim, Randy Cartwright, Cliff Nordberg, Franklin Thomas, Glen Keane, Ron Clements, Oliver M. Johnston

This charming Disney animated film details the lives of a young fox and a puppy who become close friends one summer. When the dog's owner, a mean hunter, takes him away for the winter, the fox and the hound expect to renew their friendship the following spring. When the hunter and the hound return, however, the fox's former friend has become the man's favorite hunting dog. The dog saves the fox's life once but warns him to stay away if he doesn't want to be killed. Meanwhile, the fox has fallen for another young fox, Vixey. The hunter is determined to catch the fox; there is a terrifying chase, but the tables turn when the dog is cornered by a large bear.

The animation here is better than average (veteran Disney animators Wolfgang Reitherman and Art Stevens supervised the talents of a new crop of artists that developed during a 10-year program at the studio), though not quite up to the quality of Disney Studios in its heyday. Still, this film has a lot of "heart" and is wonderful entertainment for both kids and their parents. Listen for a number of favorites among the voices.

FOXES

1980   106m   c   ★★½
Drama   R/15
UA

Jodie Foster (Jeanie), Scott Baio (Brad), Sally Kellerman (Mary), Randy Quaid (Jay), Lois Smith (Mrs. Axman), Adam Faith (Bryan), Cherie Currie (Annie), Marilyn Kagan (Madge), Kandice Stroh (Deirdre), Jon Sloan (Loser)

p, David Puttnam, Gerald Ayres; d, Adrian Lyne; w, Gerald Ayres; ph, Paul Ryan (Technicolor); ed, James Coblentz; m, Giorgio Moroder; art d, Michel Levesque

Guided by former TV commercial director Lyne in his feature debut, this exploration of the lives of four teenage girls is weakly scripted but engaging nonetheless. In a fine performance, Foster plays the steadiest of the quartet, Jeanie, who finds herself dealing with the problems of her three friends: Annie (Currie, onetime member of the rock group the Runaways), a burnt-out hooker trying to escape her crazed father; overweight, unpopular Madge (Kagan), who is determined to free herself from her parents' pampering; and Deirdre (Stroh), a flirtatious, compulsive liar. Although FOXES's attempt to delve into the problems of modern-day teenagers is admirable, its screenplay is frequently trite, lacks any leavening humor, and too easily ties together its plentiful loose ends with a contrived plot device.

FRANKENHOOKER

1990   90m   c   ★★★
Comedy/Horror   /15
Ievins-Henenlotter Production

James Lorinz (Jeffrey Franken), Patty Mullen (Elizabeth), Charlotte Helmkamp (Honey), Shirley Stoler (Spike), Louise Lasser (Jeffrey's Mom), Joseph Gonzalez (Zorro), Lia Chang (Crystal), Jennifer Delora (Angel), Vicki Darnell (Sugar), Kimberly Taylor (Amber)

p, Edgar Ievins; d, Frank Henenlotter; w, Robert Martin, Frank Henenlotter; ph, Robert M. Baldwin; ed, Kevin Tent; m, Joe Renzetti; fx, Gabe Bartalos

The most accomplished effort to date from writer-director Frank Henenlotter (BASKET CASE), one of the prime movers of the moribund midnight movie movement. Though the weak-hearted and taste-conscious should approach with extreme caution, the predisposed will find it a funny, stylish, stunningly gross black comedy that boasts surprisingly effective performances from its unknown leads.

Jeffrey Franken (James Lorinz), a resident of Hohokus, New Jersey, works in a power-plant and plays mad scientist in his spare time. His fiancee, Elizabeth (Patty Mullen), has a tragic lawn-care-related accident but resourceful Jeff manages to save her head. He schemes to construct a new body for his betrothed with remnants of expired ladies of the evening. To aid the body-part harvest, he takes a power drill to his own brain centers to boost his IQ and proceeds to concoct some "super crack," a drug so powerful that it causes its users to explode. After the smoke clears he gathers the most appealing limbs and such, sews them back together, attaches Elizabeth's head, and waits for an electrical storm. It isn't long before his "Frankenhooker" is staggering up 42nd Street, wreaking late-night havoc and frying johns with her lethal high-voltage love.

Granted this is tasteless shlock, but in Henenlotter's capable hands it manages to be quite funny. Until now, Henenlotter's ideas have tended to be better than their execution; miniscule budgets and compromised casting have kept style and wit in short supply. No more. Lorinz's acting style—as wildly funny as it is wanly low-key—eerily recalls Preston Sturges-stalwart Eddie Bracken's whiny plaintiveness filtered through a Jersey drawl.

Lorinz's performance is more than matched by former Penthouse Pet of the Year Mullen. A genuine find as Frankenhooker, Mullen pays fond, funny tribute to Elsa Lanchester's BRIDE OF FRANKENSTEIN with her remarkably refined comic performance. It's a lot of fun but leave the kids at home.

FRANKENSTEIN

1931   71m   bw   ★★★★★
Horror   /PG
Universal

Colin Clive (Henry Frankenstein), Mae Clarke (Elizabeth), John Boles (Victor Moritz), Boris Karloff (the Monster), Edward Van Sloan (Dr. Waldman), Dwight Frye (Fritz, the Dwarf), Frederick Kerr (Baron Frankenstein), Lionel Belmore (Herr Vogel, Burgomaster), Michael Mark (Ludwig, Peasant Father), Marilyn Harris (Maria the Child)

p, Carl Laemmle, Jr.; d, James Whale; w, Garrett Fort, Francis Edwards Faragoh, John Balderston, Robert Florey (based on the novel by Mary Shelley and the play by Peggy Webling); ph, Arthur Edeson; ed, Maurice Pivar, Clarence Kolster; m, David Broekman; art d, Charles D. Hall; fx, John P. Fulton

Six decades since its premiere, this early sound chiller is still a great film of its genre. Immeasurably superior to Tod Browning's DRACULA, which preceded it by a mere ten months, it shows how quickly Hollywood mastered the art of sound. FRANKENSTEIN also illustrates why James Whale is still—Cronenberg notwithstanding—the greatest director of horror films.

The story doesn't quite follow Mary Shelley's original, but it still milks the tragic tale of the inspired doctor and his piecemeal creation for all it's worth. Dr. Frankenstein (Clive) and the hunchbacked Fritz (Frye) steal bodies from their graves to assemble a "man" (Karloff) breathed into life with electricity. Unfortunately, Fritz's mistreatment of the bewildered being and the criminal brain mistakenly implanted in its skull combine to produce a killer, with grim consequences for all involved.

Still new to films, Whale displays astonishing technical mastery of the medium, as well as the imagination to break rules where appropriate. His innate theatricality makes a memorable moment of the monster's introduction. Karloff backs in from a doorway as our curiosity peaks. He slowly turns and Whale brilliantly cuts along an unchanging axis to increasingly tight close-ups of Karloff's face. Jack Pierce's marvelous make-up perfectly suits the film's blend of fantasy and science, and still manages to highlight Karloff's beautifully expressive face. This role made the gentle British character actor a star and a legend almost instantly. At once terrifying and pathetic, his monster is a moving study of alienation and primitive anger.

The film lacks the campy humor of later Whale; except for the delightful doddering of Kerr as Frankenstein's father, the wit is subdued in favor of a stark, dank tone. The result is a touching, cathartic sobriety seen at its best in the monster's encounter with an eight-year-old girl (Harris) who sees no reason to be afraid of the scarred creature before her. Universal backed down from including Clive's line, "Now I know what it feels like to be God," and they added a rather quaint disclaimer (featuring Van Sloan) warning viewers of the terror to follow, but nothing can detract from the power of the most influential monster movie ever made.

FRANKIE & JOHNNY
1991   118m   c   ★★★½
Romance/Comedy/Drama   R/15
Paramount

Al Pacino (Johnny), Michelle Pfeiffer (Frankie), Hector Elizondo (Nick), Nathan Lane (Tim), Kate Nelligan (Cora), Jane Morris (Nedda), Greg Lewis (Tino), Al Fann (Luther), Ele Keats (Artemis), Fernando Lopez (Jorge)

p, Garry Marshall; d, Garry Marshall; w, Terrence McNally (from his play Frankie and Johnny in the Claire de Lune); ph, Dante Spinotti; ed, Battle Davis, Jacqueline Cambas; m, Marvin Hamlisch; prod d, Albert Brenner; art d, Carol W. Wood; cos, Rosanna Norton

Garry Marshall, the former TV tycoon whose creations include "Laverne and Shirley" and "Mork and Mindy," is on familiar ground with FRANKIE & JOHNNY, an urban blue-collar romance adapted from Terrence McNally's acclaimed two-character play Frankie and Johnny in the Clair de Lune.

Johnny (Al Pacino) is perhaps the only convict ever to emerge from the prison system a more sensitive person than when he went in. During an 18-month sentence in Altoona for check forgery, he has become a devoted reader of the works of Shakespeare as well as a master cook. As the story begins Frankie (Michelle Pfeiffer), who hails from Altoona, has returned home to attend the christening of her sister's new baby. Both head for New York City, he in search of work and she returning to her survival job as a waitress at a coffee shop presided over by gruff-but-kindly Nick (Hector Elizondo).

As fate and the contrivance of McNally, who adapted his hit Off-Broadway play for the screen, would have it, Johnny winds up at the same place, where Nick hires him on the spot in spite of his prison record because he has a "good face." Alone in the city, Johnny seeks solace, first with a prostitute, with whom he pointedly abstains from sex, then with Cora (Kate Nelligan), one of Frankie's fellow waitresses, with whom he doesn't. When Johnny and Cora don't "click," Johnny begins his pursuit of Frankie in earnest.

Garry Marshall can be, and has been, accused of many faults as a director, but insincerity ain't one of them. True, FRANKIE & JOHNNY sentimentalizes working in a diner—a dirty, dreary, dehumanizing business to anyone who has ever done it—much as Marshall sentimentalized prostitution in PRETTY WOMAN. But the sincerity comes, in both films, from the characters' ability to rise above their circumstances to find love and a measure of happiness. In this romantic comedy, much more so than in

PRETTY WOMAN, Marshall adds a poignancy to his lovers' quest by showing the price of failure in characters surrounding them, who either live with their loneliness or, worse, have settled for bad relationships out of need rather than love.

It helps that Marshall has drawn sharp, effective performances from his leads. Pfeiffer balances her movie-star looks with the same steely grit and fiery spirit that has characterized her best work. Pacino, meanwhile, gives substance to Johnny's utterly selfless devotion to Frankie through his own selfless, devoted performance that, along the way, gives him a chance to show his too-little-seen flair for comedy. Along with the supporting cast, they tend at times to push the blue-collar buttons a little too stridently. However, the film never quite stumbles into condescension.

FRANTIC
1988   120m   c   ★★★½
Thriller   R/15
Mount

Harrison Ford (Dr. Richard Walker), Emmanuelle Seigner (Michelle), Betty Buckley (Sondra Walker), John Mahoney (Williams), Jimmy Ray Weeks (Shaap), Yorgo Voyagis (The Kidnaper), David Huddleston (Peter), Gerard Klein (Gaillard), Jacques Ciron (Hotel Manager), Dominique Pinon (Wino)

p, Thom Mount, Tim Hampton; d, Roman Polanski; w, Roman Polanski, Gerard Brach; ph, Witold Sobocinski; ed, Sam O'Steen; m, Ennio Morricone; prod d, Pierre Guffroy; cos, Anthony Powell

An oddly dreamy yet tense thriller set against the colorful backdrop of Paris, FRANTIC begins as director Roman Polanski's SCENES FROM A MARRIAGE and quickly takes a turn into Hitchcock territory.

Dr. Richard Walker (Ford) is a San Francisco surgeon who arrives in Paris with his wife, Sondra (Betty Buckley), to deliver a medical paper. Having been to the City of Lights only once before, 20 years previously on his honeymoon, Walker speaks no French and cannot even make a phone call without his wife's help. The Walkers arrive at the posh Le Grand Hotel and begin to unpack, only to discover they have the wrong suitcase. Later while Dr. Walker showers, Sondra mysteriously disappears without a trace. Initially baffled and annoyed, Walker soon becomes deeply concerned and finally frantic as he realizes that the police will not help him in this alien environment. He guesses that Sondra's disappearance must be linked to something in the suitcase he mistakenly brought to the hotel, and eventually a phone number leads him to the owner of the suitcase, Michelle (Emmanuelle Seigner), a sexy, young Parisian who was smuggling contraband into the country.

Collaborating once again with his longtime writing partner Gerard Brach, Polanski has created a thriller with a realistic hero in Ford's Dr. Walker—a sort of missing link between the civilized common man and Ford's famous Indiana Jones adventurer. His character is completely believable as he is transformed from a weary, preoccupied professional into a man recklessly determined to save the woman he loves. Like James Stewart's doctor in THE MAN WHO KNEW TOO MUCH, Dustin Hoffman's mathematician in STRAW DOGS, or Charles Bronson's architect in DEATH WISH, Ford's surgeon is a rational, cultured man who finds deep within himself a quality that gives him the strength and character to confront death. The transformation does not take place instantaneously but emerges in an evolutionary process as he walks, one step at a time, into the heart of the criminal world to find his wife.

FREAKS

1932 64m bw ★★★★
Horror /X
MGM

Wallace Ford *(Phroso)*, Leila Hyams *(Venus)*, Olga Baclanova *(Cleopatra)*, Roscoe Ates *(Roscoe)*, Henry Victor *(Hercules)*, Harry Earles *(Hans)*, Daisy Earles *(Frieda)*, Rose Dione *(Mme Tetrallini)*, Daisy Hilton, Violet Hilton *(Siamese Twins)*

p, Tod Browning; d, Tod Browning; w, Willis Goldbeck, Leon Gordon, Edgar Allan Woolf, Al Boasberg (based on the short story "Spurs" by Ted Robbins); ph, Merritt Gerstad; ed, Basil Wrangell

Long unseen, FREAKS was MGM's answer to Universal's popular FRANKENSTEIN and DRACULA, but public and critical revulsion to the use of actual circus freaks soon forced the movie from distribution. Dwain Esper (of MANIAC fame) later gave it road shows in tents and burlesque houses, further adding to this cult classic's notorious reputation.

The story follows Cleopatra (Baclanova), a beautiful but avaricious trapeze artist who seduces and marries midget circus owner Hans (Earles) to get at his money. In one of the film's most memorable scenes, the close-knit society of "freaks" warmly welcomes her into their family at the wedding reception as "one of us, one of us." Cleopatra shrinks back in disgust, however, telling them all that she will never be grotesque, while her secret lover, Hercules the strongman (Victor), howls with laughter. She humiliates her smitten husband by openly kissing the lecherous Hercules and the community soon realizes a threat is in their presence. When Hans falls ill, the group figures out that Cleopatra and Hercules have been slowly poisoning him, and so they plan a horrible, ironic revenge.

Although the suspenseful, brilliantly handled final scenes suggest an exploitation of the film's handicapped players, by then we have actually come to identify more with them than with the "normal" Cleopatra and Hans. The final revenge is thus not so much an attempt to turn melodrama into horror as it is the resolution of an old-fashioned morality play. Possibly Browning's warmest film, FREAKS is a compassionate study of how physically deformed people manage on their own. We see how they bond to each other and to those (Ford and Hyams) who love them as they are.

Some of the film's best moments are those unburdened by the plot, as we visit circus members—the bearded lady; the bird girl; the hermaphrodite; the human skeleton; the pinheads; and the Siamese twins—to see how they move, how they feel, how they love. Although slow-moving and uneven, FREAKS is one of Browning's more consistently fine films, a landmark still worth seeing.

FREE SOUL, A

1931 91m bw ★★★½
Drama /A
MGM

Norma Shearer *(Jan Ashe)*, Leslie Howard *(Dwight Winthrop)*, Lionel Barrymore *(Stephen Ashe)*, Clark Gable *(Ace Wilfong)*, James Gleason *(Eddie)*, Lucy Beaumont *(Grandma Ashe)*, Claire Whitney *(Aunt Helen)*, Frank Sheridan *(Prosecuting Attorney)*, E. Alyn Warren *(Bottomley, Ace's Chinese Boy)*, George Irving *(Defense Atty. Johnson)*

d, Clarence Brown; w, John Meehan (based on the novel by Adela Rogers St. Johns and the play by Willard Mack); ph, William Daniels; ed, Hugh Wynn; m, William Axt; art d, Cedric Gibbons; cos, Adrian

"A new kind of man, a new kind of world". This is how lusty Jan Ashe (Shearer) describes sinister stud Ace Wilfong (Gable). She might have been describing Gable himself who, still in his first year in movies, became a star in this hard-breathing melodrama of the old school.

Shearer plays a spoiled, high-powered filly whose alcoholic barrister dad (Barrymore) has encouraged her to follow her indulgent lead. Her desires configure around gangster Gable, who was terrified that in one scene he actually had to push around one of MGM's most prestigious divas. Women fans of the time loved it. The hormones flow freely in A FREE SOUL, and the film's best moments are when Shearer and Gable make raunchy yet silken sinning a fine art.

Of course, all this horniness is too good to last and there's a lot of redemption involved at the end. Eventually, Papa has to rouse himself sufficiently to give a killer-diller courtroom speech which proves to be a killer indeed. Yes, that's right. When Stephen Ashe is ready to let "the defense rest," he "rests" permanently, keeling over right in the courtroom. Totally fabulous, huh? Damn right it is.

Remade without spark as THE GIRL WHO HAD EVERYTHING. La Liz is theoretically well cast, but the film simply hasn't the foolish bravado of the original.

FREEZE—DIE—COME TO LIFE
(ZAMRI OUMI VOSKRESNI)

1990 105m bw ★★★½
Drama
Lenfilm (U.S.S.R.)

Dinara Drukarova *(Galiya)*, Pavel Nazarov *(Valerka)*, Yelena Popova *(Valerka's Mother)*, Vyacheslav Bambushek *(Vitka)*, Vadim Ermolayev *(School Principal)*

p, Valentina Tarasova; d, Vitaly Kanevski; w, Vitaly Kanevski; ph, Vladimir Brylyakov; ed, Galina Kornilova; m, Sergei Banevich; cos, Tatyana Kochergina, Natalya Milliant

Vitaly Kanevski's FREEZE-DIE-COME TO LIFE is a grim, wrenching, beautifully realized story of a trouble-prone boy growing up in a postwar gulag town in Soviet Asia.

Valerka (Pavel Nazarov) lives in a decrepit block of flats with his mother (Yelena Popova), a prostitute and dance-hall bartender who is struggling to build a good life for her son. Valerka is an irrepressible prankster at school. His antics provide him with a much-needed release from the dreary reality of his existence; it is his street-smarts and wit that keep him from becoming one of the walking dead that inhabit his town. Valerka is also enterprising, and he goes into competition with his friend Galiya (Dinara Drukarova) as a tea seller. As an aspiring capitalist, Valerka tries to scare away Galiya's customers by claiming that her water is rusty and that her kettle has very recently been a home to cockroaches. He also makes false grand claims for his own tea. Valerka and Galiya are never protected from the harsh realities of the adult world.

Shot in a grim black-and-white that creates a sense of a world of perpetual grays, FREEZE-DIE-COME TO LIFE is a movingly authentic document that recalls the best of neorealism. Moreover it captures the indomitability of Valerka's and Galiya's spirits even under the most hopeless circumstances. The performances, particularly Nazarov and Drukarova, are compelling and spontaneous. Kanevski's direction is impressive and his screenplay is unsparing and touched with humor.

FRENCH CANCAN

1955 93m c   ★★★★
Musical   /A
Franco-London/Jolly (France)

Jean Gabin (Danglard), Maria Felix (La Belle Abesse), Francoise Arnoul (Nini), Jean-Roger Caussimon (Baron Walter), Gianni Esposito (Prince Alexandre), Philippe Clay (Casimir), Michel Piccoli (Valorgueil), Jean Paredes (Coudrier), Lydia Johnson (Guibole), Max Dalban (Manager of The Reine Blanche)

p, Louis Wipf; d, Jean Renoir; w, Jean Renoir (based on an idea by Andre-Paul Antoine); ph, Michel Kelber (Technicolor); ed, Borys Lewin; m, Georges Van Parys; art d, Max Douy; chor, G. Grandjean; cos, Rosine Delamare

After a 15-year hiatus from filmmaking in France, Jean Renoir returned with this high-spirited celebration of color and movement. FRENCH CANCAN vibrantly brings to life the dawning days of the Moulin Rouge, complete with high-kicking choristers flaunting their frills. Gabin turns in one of his most memorable performances as Danglard, an aging theater impresario known for his ability to take common women and transform them into dancehall sensations—he also succeeds in seducing them. Before long, he becomes captivated with Montmartre laundress Nini (Arnoul) and he ignores a previous love to devote his energies into making her a star.

A deceptively simple picture, FRENCH CANCAN lets us relive an era previously vivid only in the painted art of Toulouse-Lautrec and Jean's father Auguste Renoir. Renoir, whose films have consistently served as training grounds for a number of prominent directors (Jacques Becker on LA CHIENNE, Yves Allegret and Luchino Visconti on the short A DAY IN THE COUNTRY, and Robert Aldrich on THE SOUTHERNER), also gave a start to Jacques Rivette in this picture by letting him serve as a directorial trainee.

FRENCH CONNECTION, THE

1971 104m c   ★★★★½
Crime   R/18
FOX

Gene Hackman (Jimmy "Popeye" Doyle), Fernando Rey (Alain Charnier), Roy Scheider (Buddy Russo), Tony Lo Bianco (Sal Boca), Marcel Bozzufi (Pierre Nicoli), Frederic de Pasquale (Devereaux), Bill Hickman (Mulderig), Ann Rebbot (Marie Charnier), Harold Gary (Weinstock), Arlene Farber (Angie Boca)

p, Philip D'Antoni; d, William Friedkin; w, Ernest Tidyman (based on the book by Robin Moore); ph, Owen Roizman (DeLuxe Color); ed, Jerry Greenberg; m, Don Ellis; art d, Ben Kazaskow; fx, Sass Bedig; cos, Joseph Fretwell

This tough, brilliant crime film features Hackman as the indefatigable Popeye Doyle, who passionately hates drug pushers. Professional hit man Bozzuffi kills a French detective in Marseilles while Hackman and his partner Scheider roust a drug dealer in a vacant lot in Brooklyn. Later that night, Hackman and Scheider spot a group of mobsters celebrating and tail Lo Bianco and his wife. This leads to a massive surveillance of a large US drug ring on which Hackman and Scheider are ordered to work with federal agents Hickman and Grosso. Hackman and Hickman have a long-standing feud which begins to boil to the surface. Meanwhile, Rey, the mastermind of the French drug traffic, stashes 120 pounds of heroin in the Lincoln Continental car of television actor De Pasquale, who unwittingly escorts the shipment to New York. Rey contacts Lo Bianco in Manhattan to arrange for the sale of the heroin, but is spotted by Hackman who

has staked out Lo Bianco and trailed the pair to a hotel. Hackman follows Rey, who is aware that he is being tailed, and the wiley Frenchman outwits the detective, escaping on a subway train, smugly waving goodbye as the cop is left standing on the platform. Enraged, Hackman hijacks a car and gives chase.

Young director Friedkin produced a suspenseful and utterly absorbing film which incorporated thrills with street humor and routine police work with highly dramatic scenes. The chase scene, an incredible, hair-raising sequence, was shot from Hackman's car with cameras mounted in the back seat and on the front fenders. The police are portrayed as being almost as brutal as the criminals, with Hackman shown to be a near-maniac who will stop at nothing to corral drug offenders. Hackman won an Oscar for his riveting portrayal, as did the film, Friedkin, Tidyman's screenplay and Greenberg's editing.

FRENCH CONNECTION II

1975 119m c   ★★★½
Crime   R/18
FOX

Gene Hackman (Popeye Doyle), Fernando Rey (Charnier), Bernard Fresson (Barthelemy), Jean-Pierre Castaldi (Raoul Diron), Charles Millot (Miletto), Cathleen Nesbitt (Old Lady), Pierre Collet (Old Pro), Alexandre Fabre (Young Tail), Philippe Leotard (Jacques), Jacques Dynam (Inspector Genevoix)

p, Robert L. Rosen; d, John Frankenheimer; w, Alexander Jacobs, Robert Dillon, Lauri Dillon (based on a story by Robert and Lauri Dillon); ph, Claude Renoir (DeLuxe Color); ed, Tom Rolf; m, Don Ellis; prod d, Jacques Saulnier; art d, Gerard Viard, Georges Glon; fx, Logan Frazee; cos, Jacques Fonteray

Surprisingly good follow-up to the original tough crime drama. Popeye Doyle (Hackman) is sent to Marseilles to unearth Charnier (Rey), the man who got away in the earlier film. Doyle is treated with disdain by French policeman Barthelemy (Fresson), who resents his intrusive, loud-mouthed, bad-mannered ways. Popeye is decidedly out of place in a setting he does not understand, laboring with a language that proves more difficult each day. He does not know that he is being used as bait by his French counterpart to lure Charnier into the open.

Further complicating matters, Doyle eludes his French police bodyguards in an effort to find his nemesis alone, but only succeeds in getting kidnaped by the drug czar's henchmen. Taken to a sleazy hotel, he is forcibly turned into a heroin addict so that he will tell everything he knows about the "French connection."

FRENCH CONNECTION II is tightly directed by Frankenheimer, who once again proves that he knows how to direct a suspense thriller. (Just check out THE MANCHURIAN CANDIDATE, SEVEN DAYS IN MAY, or SECONDS if you need further proof.) Hackman once again gives a riveting and believable performance; the sequences dealing with his withdrawal from heroin presenting a frightening and realistic look at the effects of hard drugs. The whole production is outstanding, in particular Renoir's breathtaking cinematography, Frazee's special effects and Needham's stuntwork.

FRENCH LIEUTENANT'S WOMAN, THE

1981 127m c   ★★★½
Romance   /15
UA (U.K.)

Meryl Streep (Sarah/Anna), Jeremy Irons (Charles/Mike), Hilton McRae (Sam), Emily Morgan (Mary), Charlotte Mitchell (Mrs. Tranter), Lynsey Baxter (Ernestina), Jean Faulds (Cook), Peter

Vaughan *(Mr. Freeman)*, Colin Jeavons *(Vicar)*, Liz Smith *(Mrs. Fairley)*

p, Leon Clore; d, Karel Reisz; w, Harold Pinter (based on the novel by John Fowles); ph, Freddie Francis (Technicolor); ed, John Bloom; m, Carl Davis; prod d, Assheton Gorton; art d, Norman Dorme, Terry Pritchard, Allan Cameron; cos, Tom Rand

Translating John Fowles' complex novel to the screen was a formidable task, previously attempted—then abandoned—by the likes of Fred Zinnemann, Richard Lester and Mike Nichols. Undaunted, director Karel Reisz joined forces with esteemed playwright Harold Pinter to convey the essence of Fowles' epic romance.

In a technically flawless performance, Meryl Streep plays Sarah Woodruff, a mysterious pariah in mourning who has been dishonored after a affair with a French army officer in Victorian England. In his first starring role, Jeremy Irons portrays Charles Smithson, the wealthy young man of principle who finds her and falls hopelessly in love. Pinter's screenplay shrewdly incorporates both the novel's 19th-century point of view and, underscoring the oppressive constraints of Victorian society, a contemporary tale featuring Streep and Irons as Anna and Mike, the sophisticated actors playing Sarah and Charles in a film adaptation of *The French Lieutenant's Woman* who casually embark on their own affair—with decidedly different results.

Though occasionally jarring, the intercutting between the parallel stories, aided immeasurably by Streep's disparate characterizations, succeeds in conveying the complexity of Fowles' novel.

FRENCH POSTCARDS

1979 95m c   ★★★
Drama/Comedy   PG/15
Geria

Miles Chapin *(Joel)*, Blanche Baker *(Laura)*, David Marshall Grant *(Alex)*, Valerie Quennessen *(Toni)*, Debra Winger *(Melanie)*, Mandy Patinkin *(Sayyid)*, Marie-France Pisier *(Mme Tessier)*, Jean Rochefort *(Mon Tessier)*, Lynn Carlin *(Mrs. Weber)*, George Coe *(Mr. Weber)*

p, Gloria Katz; d, Willard Huyck; w, Willard Huyck, Gloria Katz; ph, Bruno Nuytten; ed, Carol Littleton; m, Lee Holdridge; art d, Jean-Pierre Kohut-Svelko; cos, Catherine Leterrier, Joan Mocine

Very modest, but surprisingly sweet. The naive escapades of a group of American students studying in France for a year is given a charming, somewhat corny treatment by the authors of AMERICAN GRAFFITI—Huyck (who also directed) and Katz. Pisier plays a teacher who offers her culture to the students while at the same time expressing an interest in the US. She has an affair with one of her pupils (Chapin), though it soon ends when he leaves for Spain. In the meantime, though, the students visit famous sights (as many of the Michelin Guide's 212 major sights as they can) and destroy the language in their attempts to sound Parisian.

The interplay between French and American cultures makes for interesting subject matter; one only wishes it could have been fleshed out rather more. Imagine a weakly directed version of AMERICAN GRAFFITI set in France. Future star Debra Winger appears in an early role.

FRENCH, THEY ARE A FUNNY RACE, THE

(LES CARNETS DU MAJOR THOMPSON)
1956 105m bw   ★★★
Comedy
Continental/Gaumont   (France)

Jack Buchanan *(Major Thompson)*, Martine Carol *(Martine)*, Noel-Noel *(Taupin)*, Totti Truman Taylor *(Nurse)*, Andre Luguet *(Editor)*, Genevieve Brunet *(Secretary)*, Catherine Boyle *(Wife)*

p, Paul Wagner, Alain Poire; d, Preston Sturges; w, Preston Sturges (based on the book *The Notebooks of Major Thompson* by Pierre Daninos); ph, Maurice Barry, Christian Matras; ed, Raymond Lanny

Notable as Preston Sturges's last film, made in France after an absence of six years. Based on essays allegedly written by an English major about his adjustment to carefree French life, the film is anecdotal and often amusing, but the overwhelming feeling is one of sadness as we watch the greatest comic talent of the 1940s straining along shortly before he died in exile.

Jack Buchanan, that former effervescent musical comedy star, also makes his final appearance as Major Thompson, who resides in Paris with his air-headed but beautiful French wife (Carol, likable but underused); the two appear to have nothing better to do than argue over how to raise their child. Boyle appears as the major's English wife, whose conjugal outlook stems from her mother's advice to her on her wedding night: "My dear, it's utterly unbearable, but just close your eyes and think of England." Sturges does effectively lampoon both English and French lifestyles as he sees them, and the contrasts are sometimes evocative of his earlier sophistication. Still, the visuals are drab and the energy is low, making this a far cry from such brilliant earlier Sturges works as THE MIRACLE OF MORGAN CREEK and SULLIVAN'S TRAVELS, both masterpieces of satirical wit.

FRENZY

1972 116m c   ★★★★
Thriller   R/18
Universal   (U.K.)

Jon Finch *(Richard Blaney)*, Barry Foster *(Robert Rusk)*, Barbara Leigh-Hunt *(Brenda Blaney)*, Anna Massey *(Babs Milligan)*, Alec McCowen *(Chief Inspector Oxford)*, Vivien Merchant *(Mrs. Oxford)*, Billie Whitelaw *(Hetty Porter)*, Clive Swift *(Johnny Porter)*, Bernard Cribbins *(Felix Forsythe)*, Michael Bates *(Sgt. Spearman)*

p, Alfred Hitchcock; d, Alfred Hitchcock; w, Anthony Shaffer (from the novel *Goodbye Piccadilly, Farewell Leicester Square* by Arthur LaBern); ph, Gilbert Taylor (Technicolor); ed, John Jympson; m, Ron Goodwin; prod d, Syd Cain; art d, Robert Laing

Hitchcock's first British film in almost two decades marked a smashing return to his earlier form after the dull TORN CURTAIN and TOPAZ. Although not a mystery (we know the killer's identity early on), the film is intensely suspenseful, at times forcing the audience to identify with the murderer. Richard Blaney (Finch) is accused of murdering his ex-wife Brenda (Leigh-Hunt) and his girlfriend (Massey), both of whom have been strangled with neckties. The real "Necktie Murderer," however, remains at large.

There's more explicit sex and violence in this movie than is usual for Hitchcock. His famous touches still abound, however, juxtaposing some screamingly funny bits involving Scotland Yard Inspector Oxford (McCowen) with brutal rape-strangulation scenes. The first murder is particularly well done, and expect a jolt when a body falls off a truck. FRENZY also contains perhaps the most wicked of Hitchcock's scenes—the killer searching through a stack of potato sacks in order to find his missing monogrammed tie pin, which a nude corpse clutches in her death grip.

FRESHMAN, THE

1990 102m c ★★★
Comedy PG
Lobell-Bergman

Marlon Brando (Carmine Sabatini), Matthew Broderick (Clark Kellogg), Bruno Kirby (Victor Ray), Penelope Ann Miller (Tina Sabatini), Frank Whaley (Steve Bushak), Jon Polito (Chuck Greenwald), Paul Benedict (Arthur Fleeber), Richard Gant (Lloyd Simpson), Kenneth Welsh (Dwight Armstrong), Pamela Payton-Wright (Liz Armstrong)

p, Mike Lobell; d, Andrew Bergman; w, Andrew Bergman; ph, William A. Fraker (Technicolor); ed, Barry Malkin; m, David Newman; prod d, Ken Adam; art d, Alicia Keywan; fx, Neil Tifunovich; cos, Julie Weiss

An advertising campaign once asked, "What becomes a legend most?" That question is implicit in every review of every film in which Marlon Brando now appears. Audiences have loved, hated and jeered him, but one point is beyond dispute: Brando is in a class by himself. One of the last of the true stars, his presence transforms and reshapes any film in which he appears.

Matthew Broderick stars as Clark Kellogg, a freshman from Vermont who comes to the Big Apple to study film at New York University. His most flamboyant professor is Arthur Fleeber (a scene-stealing turn by Paul Benedict, best known as Mr. Bentley of television's "The Jeffersons") who has committed every moment from THE GODFATHER PART II to memory. The great man assigns $700 worth of his own publications as required reading for his course. Kellogg also gets an education in the ways of the NYC streets before he even gets to school as he is robbed shortly upon hitting town by a con man, Victor Ray (Bruno Kirby). Kellogg eventually tracks Ray down but instead of returning his stuff the slick character offers to introduce the freshman to his Uncle Carmine (Brando), an "importer-exporter" who can provide Kellogg with a high-paying, "totally legitimate" job.

By far the best chuckles in the film come from Brando's resurrection of his landmark role in THE GODFATHER. Yet having Brando reprise the famous don for laughs is anything but an arbitrary choice. Without Brando's presence, THE FRESHMAN would be so slight it would float off the screen. Still one wishes that THE FRESHMAN was a better film. Both its plot and characters could have been sharper, and its pacing more precise. As it is, the film stumbles as often as it soars. Still no film that puts Brando on ice skates, has Bert Parks deliver a rousing rendition of Bob Dylan's "Maggie's Farm" or so vividly spoofs film school pretensions can be all that bad.

FRIED GREEN TOMATOES

1991 130m c ★★★½
Drama/Comedy PG-13/12
Avnet/Kerner Company/Electric Shadow Productions/
Act III Communications

Kathy Bates (Evelyn Couch), Jessica Tandy (Ninny Threadgoode), Mary Stuart Masterson (Idgie Threadgoode), Mary-Louise Parker (Ruth Jamison), Nick Searcy (Frank Bennett), Cicely Tyson (Sipsey), Chris O'Donnell (Buddy Threadgoode), Stan Shaw (Big George), Gailard Sartain (Ed Couch), Tim Scott (Smokey Lonesome)

p, Jon Avnet, Jordan Kerner; d, Jon Avnet; w, Fannie Flagg, Carol Sobieski (from the novel Fried Green Tomatoes at the Whistle Stop Cafe by Flagg); ph, Geoffrey Simpson; ed, Debra Neil; m, Thomas Newman; prod d, Barbara Ling; art d, Larry Fulton; cos, Elizabeth McBride

Past and present are winningly blended in the "sleeper" hit FRIED GREEN TOMATOES, a gentle comedy based on Fannie Flagg's novel, Fried Green Tomatoes at the Whistle Stop Cafe.

Evelyn Couch (Kathy Bates), an overweight, repressed housewife, meets and befriends—or is befriended by—Ninny Threadgoode (Jessica Tandy), a remarkable octogenarian and firstrate storyteller. Ninny is a permanent resident, though she won't admit it, at a rest home for the aged where Evelyn accompanies her husband Ed (Gailard Sartain) on his weekly visits to his gruff aunt. The aunt detests Evelyn and will not allow her into the room, thus giving Evelyn ample time to spend with Ninny. The aged Alabaman begins to enthrall Evelyn with the fascinating life story—seen in flashback—of one of her relatives, Idgie Threadgoode.

An early proto-feminist, Idgie (Mary Stuart Masterson) owns and operates the local cafe in Whistle Stop, Alabama. Traumatized as a girl by the gory death of a beloved older brother, Idgie has remained a tomboy loner all her life, taking to the trees when the world around her gets to be too much. As such, she does none of the things respectable Southern women of the Depression Era 1930s are expected to do—like stay home and cook for the men. Idgie literally rescues her best friend, Ruth Jamison (Mary-Louise Parker), from Ruth's marriage to the abusive Frank Bennett (Nick Searcy). Bringing her young baby with her, Ruth moves in with Idgie and the two women soon have a thriving business at the cafe, with Ruth doing the cooking and Idgie handling the bookwork. They are aided in their endeavors by Sipsey (Cicely Tyson), a black seamstress, and Sipsey's handyman son, Big George (Stan Shaw). All goes well until Frank reappears, in an attempt to retrieve his child. Idgie and Ruth are not around, so it is left to Sipsey and Big George to protect the baby—with the end result that no-one ever sees Frank again.

During the weeks it takes Ninny to finish telling Evelyn the story, the younger woman undergoes a gradual transformation. Evelyn works hard at improving her appearance through diet and exercise, and learns how to begin asserting herself and building her self-esteem. Inspired by the tale of Idgie and Ruth and increasingly drawn to Ninny, she asks the older woman to move out of the rest home and to come and live with her and her husband. Ninny delightedly accepts and, in the last scene, it is strongly hinted that Ninny and the "Idgie" of her stories are one and the same.

FRIED GREEN TOMATOES is an engaging if sentimental tale, charmingly handled by producer-turned-director Jon Avnet (RISKY BUSINESS) and flawlessly acted by its four female stars. Plaudits must also go to Geoffrey Simpson, for his splendid cinematography, and to Thomas Newman for his drama-enhancing musical score.

FRIENDLY PERSUASION

1956 137m c ★★★★
Drama /U
Allied Artists

Gary Cooper (Jess Birdwell), Dorothy McGuire (Eliza Birdwell), Marjorie Main (Widow Hudspeth), Anthony Perkins (Josh Birdwell), Richard Eyer (Little Jess), Phyllis Love (Mattie Birdwell), Robert Middleton (Sam Jordan), Mark Richman (Gard Jordan), Walter Catlett (Professor Quigley), Richard Hale (Elder Purdy) p, William Wyler; d, William Wyler; w, Michael Wilson (uncredited, based on the novel *The Friendly Persuasion* by Jessamyn West); ph, Ellsworth Fredricks (CinemaScope, DeLuxe Color); ed, Robert Swink, Edward A. Biery, Robert Belcher; m, Dimitri Tiomkin; art d, Ted Haworth; cos, Dorothy Jeakins, Bert Henrikson

Long and a tad preachy, FRIENDLY PERSUASION recounts the story of a peaceful Quaker family in Indiana whose sanctity is disturbed by the Civil War in 1862.

Cooper and McGuire play the parents of Josh (Perkins), who listens to a Union officer make a plea for young men to take up the Blue cudgel. Although morally opposed to war, Josh fears that he's using his religion to mask a cowardly streak. When the news comes that the Southern band known as Morgan's Raiders is nearing his town, Josh joins the local militia and prepares to fight. He is hurt in battle, and his father goes into the war zone to save his son and find a pal (Middleton) who's been ambushed.

There's humor galore in this picture, especially in a scene with Main and her three lonesome daughters. There are many tearful moments too and several incisive looks into the lives of the "Society of Friends." Aiming for a collage effect, director Wyler deals lovingly with McGuire's ongoing battles with Samantha the goose as well as a little boy who suddenly yells "God is love" in a crowded church. A shorter running time would have helped but, as it is, FRIENDLY PERSUASION ranks as one of Wyler's best comedy-dramas.

FRIENDS OF EDDIE COYLE, THE

1973 102m c ★★★½
Crime R/X
Paramount

Robert Mitchum *(Eddie Coyle)*, Peter Boyle *(Dillon)*, Richard Jordan *(Dave Foley)*, Steven Keats *(Jackie Brown)*, Alex Rocco *(Scalise)*, Joe Santos *(Artie Van)*, Mitchell Ryan *(Waters)*, Helena Carroll *(Sheila Coyle)*, Peter MacLean *(Partridge)*, Kevin O'Morrison *(Manager of 2nd Bank)*

p, Paul Monash; d, Peter Yates; w, Paul Monash (based on the novel by George V. Higgens); ph, Victor J. Kemper (Panavision, Technicolor); ed, Patricia Jaffe; m, Dave Grusin; prod d, Gene Callahan; art d, Gene Callahan; cos, Eric Seelig

Mitchum is Eddie Coyle, a three-time loser. One more offense and he goes to prison for life—no parole, no hope. Police learn of an impending Boston bank robbery and go to Coyle, telling him that they know he earns a living for his destitute family by running illegal goods across state lines. They will put him away unless he squeals on the robbery gang. He reluctantly agrees to help and, after selling the gang some guns, contacts detectives, who tell him his information is insufficient. He must go on being a permanent informer and is ordered to help capture gang boss Scalise (Rocco). Before Eddie can move, however, Scalise is arrested. Coyle's underworld friends point the finger at him, ordering him murdered.

THE FRIENDS OF EDDIE COYLE is a tough look at the world of petty crooks and the sleazy side of the underworld. Mitchum is surprisingly effective as the down-and-out thief, as if worn out over the decades from earlier film noir escapades in THE RACKET and OUT OF THE PAST. Boyle is terrific as the thug who goes in for synthetic friendships, willing to sell out his own mother for survival in a system he knows will destroy him anyway. Yates's direction is grimly taut, and Monash's screenplay pulls no punches. A bit gruesome, but potent viewing nonetheless.

FRIGHT NIGHT

1985 106m c ★★★½
Horror R/18
Columbia

Chris Sarandon *(Jerry Dandridge)*, William Ragsdale *(Charley Brewster)*, Amanda Bearse *(Amy Peterson)*, Roddy McDowall *(Peter Vincent)*, Stephen Geoffreys *(Evil Ed)*, Jonathan Stark *(Billy Cole)*, Dorothy Fielding *(Judy Brewster)*, Art Evans *(Detective Lennox)*, Stewart Stern *(Cook)*, Nick Savage

p, Herb Jaffe; d, Tom Holland; w, Tom Holland; ph, Jan Kiesser (Metrocolor); ed, Kent Beyda; m, Brad Fiedel; prod d, John De Cuir; fx, Richard Edlund, Michael Lantieri, Darrell D. Prichett, Clay Pinney, Albert Lannutti; cos, Robert Fletcher

A minor classic of the genre, this is a memorable addition to the vampire tradition in the horror film. FRIGHT NIGHT depicts the plight of Charley Brewster (Ragsdale), a fatherless teenager tottering on the brink of manhood, as he becomes obsessed with the charming new man next door, Jerry Dandridge (Sarandon). He is convinced that his neighbor is actually a vampire and responsible for a series of local murders. Charley alerts the local authorities but they dismiss him as a crank. His mom (Dorothy Fielding) won't listen to him and even his best buddy, Evil Ed (Geoffreys), and his devoted girlfriend, Amy Peterson (Bearse), think he's crazy. Desperate, Charley turns to the only vampire expert he can find, Peter Vincent (McDowall), an aging washed-up horror movie ham. Though at first he only humors the boy, Vincent soon realizes that Charley is telling the truth.

This film is the feature directing debut of Tom Holland who was previously known for his smart genre screenplays—CLASS OF 1984, CLOAK AND DAGGER and PSYCHO II. Like his earlier scripts, FRIGHT NIGHT is a clever amalgam; this teen-oriented vampire movie deftly combines Hitchcockian themes, Hammer horror trappings, a subversive gay subtext and a John Hughes milieu into a genuinely scary horror movie that is comfortably old-fashioned yet cool.

Holland, a former actor, elicits much better than average performances from his teen actors. Stephen Geoffreys is particularly enjoyable in a crazed Jack Nicholson turn as Evil Ed. The more seasoned players deliver outstanding performances. Chris Sarandon is stunning as the sensually handsome—yet deadly—new neighbor. Roddy McDowell is also in fine form in his best role in years as the cynical has-been who must become a true hero. FRIGHT NIGHT may not be great art but it *is* great fun.

FROM HERE TO ETERNITY

1953 118m bw ★★★★★
Drama/War /PG
Columbia

Burt Lancaster *(Sgt. Milton Warden)*, Deborah Kerr *(Karen Holmes)*, Montgomery Clift *(Robert E. Lee Prewitt)*, Frank Sinatra *(Angelo Maggio)*, Donna Reed *(Alma Lorene)*, Ernest Borgnine *(Sgt. "Fatso" Judson)*, Philip Ober *(Capt. Dana Holmes)*, Jack Warden *(Cpl. Buckley)*, Mickey Shaughnessy *(Sgt. Leva)*, Harry Bellaver *(Mazzioli)*

p, Buddy Adler; d, Fred Zinnemann; w, Daniel Taradash (based on the novel by James Jones); ph, Burnett Guffey; ed, William Lyon; m, George Duning; art d, Cary Odell; cos, Jean Louis

The massive James Jones novel, thought to be impossible to put onscreen because of its frank portrayal of sex and use of vulgar language, is brought forth in this powerful portrait of pre-WWII enlisted men, their women, and the grim destiny that overtook them all.

The film opens as Robert E. Lee Prewitt (Clift) arrives at Schofield Barracks at Pearl Harbor, transferring after he refused to continue as a company boxer at his previous post. His new commander, the brutal but insecure Captain Holmes (Ober), promises Prewitt that if he boxes on the company team he will be given the post of bugler, a job Prewitt very much wants. But Prewitt refuses, haunted by previous ugly experiences in the ring. For Prewitt's obstinacy, Holmes orders Sgt. Warden (Lancaster) to give the soldier every dirty detail in the company. As it turns out, Warden is involved in a torrid affair with Holmes's wife Karen (Kerr). Meanwhile, Prewitt's suffering is eased by his newly established relationship with Lorene (Reed), a "hostess" at the New Congress Club. Prewitt's only other friend, Maggio (Sinatra), a wisecracking enlisted man, commits several small offenses and draws repeated punishment—especially from a sadistic Italian-hating sergeant named Fatso (Borgnine).

FROM HERE TO ETERNITY was an uphill battle all the way for director Zinnemann. Most of his war was with Columbia's dictator, Harry Cohn, who had purchased the novel for $82,000 and was determined to retain its seamy story, raw language, and violence, rejecting one adaptation after another. The Army was not happy with Jones's fierce indictment of its system and refused to allow the use of Schofield Barracks unless some major concessions were made. One chief point involved the role of Captain Holmes. In the novel he gets away with everything and is even promoted to major, but in the film he is cashiered for his cruelty and malfeasance.

The featured roles were also difficult to cast under Cohn's whimsical supervision. Zinnemann had to fight to cast Clift, who gave one of his greatest performances; ditto Sinatra, whose faltering career received a much-needed boost here. He had to beg Cohn for the part of Maggio (exaggerated and fictionalized by Mario Puzo in *The Godfather*) and ended up playing it for practically nothing. Joan Crawford was to have played the straying wife but the icy-turned-passionate Kerr helped keep the famous lovemaking scene on the beach more realistic and low-key. Reed's part, on the other hand, was softened somewhat, her occupation being changed from prostitute to "hostess."

The film won Academy Awards for Best Picture, Director, Screenplay, Cinematography, Sound, Editing, and for Sinatra and Reed in best supporting roles.

FROM NOON TILL THREE
1976 98m c   ★★½
Western/Comedy   PG/15
UA

Charles Bronson (*Graham Dorsey*), Jill Ireland (*Amanda Starbuck*), Douglas Fowley (*Buck Bowers*), Stan Haze (*Ape*), Damon Douglas (*Boy*), Hector Morales (*Mexican*), Bert Williams (*Sheriff*), William Lanteau (*Rev. Cabot*), Betty Cole, Davis Roberts (*Amanda's Servants*)

p, M.J. Frankovich, William Self; d, Frank D. Gilroy; w, Frank D. Gilroy; ph, Lucien Ballard (Panavision, Deluxe Color); ed, Maury Winetrobe; m, Elmer Bernstein; prod d, Robert Clatworthy; art d, Richard Lawrence; fx, Augie Lohman; cos, Moss Mabry

Interesting but unsuccessful Bronson vehicle that has a fine "revisionist" screenplay dealing with the making of western myths.

Bronson plays Graham Dorsey, a drifter outlaw who has a brief liaison with Amanda Starbuck (Ireland), and whom she later transforms after his "death" into an outlaw legend. Amanda builds a giant commercial empire based on her fictional stories about the now-infamous "Graham Dorsey," and his name is forever emblazoned on the history of the Old West. When Bronson turns up very much alive, however, no one, not even Amanda, recognizes him or will believe his protestations that he is Dorsey. He ends up in an insane asylum, where the doctors just nod and smile at his delusions of having been a great gunfighter.

It's admirable that Bronson chose to break type and play a likable, almost goofy character, but he's clearly struggling with an atypical role. The film is obviously intended as a vehicle for Ireland, but her performance isn't quite compelling enough, either. Playwright Gilroy, meanwhile, trying his hand at film directing, only compounds his casting errors. His heavy-handed approach to his own material only sabotages its merits, sapping the material of its power and rendering it pleasant at best.

FROM RUSSIA WITH LOVE
1963 110m c   ★★★★
Spy   /PG
UA   (U.K.)

Sean Connery (*James Bond*), Daniela Bianchi (*Tatiana Romanova*), Pedro Armendariz (*Kerim Bey*), Lotte Lenya (*Rosa Klebb*), Robert Shaw (*Red Grant*), Bernard Lee ("*M*"), Eunice Gayson (*Sylvia*), Walter Gotell (*Morzeny*), Francis de Wolff (*Vavra*), George Pastell (*Train Conductor*)

p, Harry Saltzman, Albert R. Broccoli; d, Terence Young; w, Richard Maibaum, Johanna Harwood (based on the novel by Ian Fleming); ph, Ted Moore (Technicolor); ed, Peter Hunt; m, John Barry; art d, Syd Cain; fx, John Stears; cos, Jocelyn Rickards

From Ian Fleming with love. The second James Bond movie, FROM RUSSIA WITH LOVE sends Secret Agent 007 (Connery) to mysterious Istanbul to grab a top-secret Russian decoding machine. There, he falls for Tatiana Romanova (Bianchi), a Soviet Embassy clerk who is an unwitting pawn of SPECTRE. Bond is pursued by the divinely dykey assassin Rosa Klebb (Lenya, lots of fun here) who carries a poisonous switchblade in her shoe. He also has to fend off a blond (!) Robert Shaw sporting one of the most incredible hair dye jobs in the history of cinema. The highlight of the film is a terrific battle to the death on the Orient Express between Connery and Shaw.

Written with enough self-consciously campy humor to fend off the paranoid ideologies running rampant here, FROM RUSSIA WITH LOVE is also acted with tongues held firmly in cheek. Finally, the film displays little evidence of the excessive gadgetry that would plague later entries in the series. One of the best of the Bond films, featuring Matt Monro singing the decidedly unmemorable Lionel Bart-penned title tune.

FRONT PAGE, THE
1931 101m bw   ★★★★★
Drama/Comedy   /A
Caddo

Adolphe Menjou (*Walter Burns*), Pat O'Brien (*Hildy Johnson*), Mary Brian (*Peggy*), Edward Everett Horton (*Bensinger*), Walter Catlett (*Murphy*), George E. Stone (*Earl Williams*), Mae Clarke (*Molly*), Slim Summerville (*Pincus*), Matt Moore (*Kruger*), Frank McHugh (*McCue*)

p, Howard Hughes; d, Lewis Milestone; w, Bartlett Cormack, Ben Hecht (uncredited), Charles Lederer (based on the play by Ben Hecht and Charles MacArthur); ph, Glen MacWilliams, Hal Mohr, Tony Gaudio (uncredited); ed, Duncan Mansfield; art d, Richard Day

A vigorous, manic drama, this Lewis Milestone classic about newspapers and newsmen wonderfully preserves a host of Depression-era attitudes and a glorious headline era.

O'Brien, in his film debut, is the fast-talking Hildy Johnson, sensation-hunting star of the Chicago press. His shifty editor Walter Burns (Menjou) is trying to prevent his star reporter from quitting the business and moving to a New York advertising job with his wife-to-be Peggy (Brian). She hates everything about the sleazy tabloid world that has made Hildy famous, and she pressures him to finish his last day's work so they can flee to New York. In his farewell visit to the press room, however, Hildy gets caught up in the escape of an anarchist (Stone) scheduled for execution.

THE FRONT PAGE is an excellent production with a superior performance from novice O'Brien in a role better than many he later got to play. Menjou is marvelous too as a wily and sophisticated rascal, with a brilliant flair for dialogue. Howard Hughes let Milestone have his creative way with the film, and it shows in the film's no-holds-barred action and witty repartee. Hughes did make two decisions regarding the film, though, vetoing Milestone's first two choices for O'Brien's role: James Cagney and Clark Gable.

All of the character actors shine in the reporter roles, from the cynical Catlett and McHugh to the fussy, hygiene-obsessed Horton, who believes himself to be a poet. The play's lines were kept almost intact, with all the wild newspaper argot, glib quips and slurs delivered rapid-fire by the actors. Remade as HIS GIRL FRIDAY by Howard Hawks.

FRONT PAGE, THE
1974 105m c   ★★½
Drama/Comedy   PG/AA
Universal

Jack Lemmon (Hildy Johnson), Walter Matthau (Walter Burns), Carol Burnett (Mollie Malloy), Susan Sarandon (Peggy Grant), Vincent Gardenia (Sheriff), David Wayne (Bensinger), Allen Garfield (Kruger), Austin Pendleton (Earl Williams), Charles Durning (Murphy), Herb Edelman (Schwartz)

p, Paul Monash; d, Billy Wilder; w, Billy Wilder, I.A.L. Diamond (based on the play by Ben Hecht and Charles MacArthur); ph, Jordan S. Cronenweth (Panavision, Technicolor); ed, Ralph E. Winters; m, Billy May; art d, Henry Bumstead; cos, Burton Miller

Wanted: a better remake of Lewis Milestone's classic original and Howard Hawks' revamp, HIS GIRL FRIDAY. This slick remake of the ebullient original falls short of being the film it could have been, despite the presence of master filmmaker Wilder and his engaging costars.

Hildy Johnson (Lemmon) is bound for New York with Peggy Grant (Sarandon) to begin a new life, but Walter Burns (Matthau) uses the escape of anarchist Earl Williams (Pendleton) to hold him on the job. Along the way they pointedly ignore the pleas of prostitute Mollie Molloy (Burnett), who is in love with the condemned man. The hide-and-seek game the newsmen play with authorities in covering up the wanted man's whereabouts is forced, but Martin Gabel, as the balmy psychiatrist, gives a hilarious performance. Durning is too vicious for the newsman role he plays, as is Garfield; Hecht and MacArthur drew their characters as jocular, not sadistic, personalities. The posturing, no doubt Wilder's doing, mars the impact of his satirical cynicism. It overpowers the screenplay and even the good performances of the leads.

Despite the obvious charismatic interaction between Lemmon and Matthau, the film is oddly stilted. In an overly emphatic turn, the miscast Burnett easily gives the most awful performance of her career. She projects only one emotion—a gratingly annoying hysteria. One never enjoys the film so much as when her character throws herself out of a window. Wilder was much more effective with Lemmon and Matthau in THE FORTUNE COOKIE and THE ODD COUPLE. This one just doesn't have the big story at press time.

FUGITIVE, THE
1947 104m bw   ★★★★
Drama   /A
RKO

Henry Fonda (The Fugitive), Dolores Del Rio (Mexican Woman), Pedro Armendariz (Police Lieutenant), Ward Bond (El Gringo), Leo Carrillo (Chief of Police), J. Carrol Naish (Police Spy), Robert Armstrong (Police Sergeant), John Qualen (Doctor), Fortunio Bonanova (Governor's Cousin), Chris-Pin Martin (Organ Player)

p, John Ford, Merian C. Cooper; d, John Ford; w, Dudley Nichols (based on the novel The Labyrinthine Ways and The Power and the Glory by Graham Greene); ph, Gabriel Figueroa; ed, Jack Murray; m, Richard Hageman; art d, Alfred Ybarra; fx, Fred Sersen

One of John Ford's favorite films; he sometimes considered it his masterpiece. It's hardly that, just as its companion piece, THE INFORMER, isn't quite the masterpiece everyone once thought it was. A powerful passion play set in a modern, fictitious south-of-the-border country, THE FUGITIVE is hauntingly photographed by Figueroa and boasts a highly effective performance from Fonda in which an intensely warm and likable saintliness largely replaces a three-dimensional character.

Much of this stems from Ford's influence on Nichols's screenplay, which changed the complex, sinful "whiskey priest" of Greene's original novel into a man whose main fear is that he's not sacrificing enough. The fugitive (Fonda) is hunted by a revolutionary government attempting to eliminate all traces of the Catholic religion. He hides in a small village and, passing as a peasant, performs secret rites for the locals. He even baptizes the bastard child a woman (the impossibly gorgeous Del Rio) has borne to a savage police lieutenant (Armendariz). He also comforts an American criminal on the run (Bond) before escaping to a country without religious persecution. An encounter with a half-breed police spy (Naish) and the call to duty, though, lure him back to his hostile native terrain.

As with much of Ford, THE FUGITIVE is often sentimental and very Catholic, blunting Greene's political edge in favor of Ford's preference for lyric poetry. Here Fonda is the true Ford hero: quiet, contemplative, nonviolent and capable of superhuman sacrifice. Naive in some ways and full of portentous, obvious yet admittedly striking symbolism, THE FUGITIVE is nevertheless true to its own convictions.

FULL METAL JACKET
1987 116m c   ★★★★
War   R/18
Natant (U.K.)

Matthew Modine (Pvt. Joker), Adam Baldwin (Animal Mother), Vincent D'Onofrio (Leonard Lawrence, Pvt. Gomer Pyle), Lee Ermey (Gunnery Sgt. Hartman), Dorian Harewood (Eightball), Arliss Howard (Pvt. Cowboy), Kevyn Major Howard (Rafterman), Ed O'Ross (Walter J. Schinoski, Lt. Touchdown), Jon Stafford (Doc Jay), John Terry (Lt. Lockhart) p, Stanley Kubrick; d, Stanley Kubrick; w, Stanley Kubrick, Michael Herr, Gustav Hasford (based on the novel *The Short-Timers* by Gustav Hasford); ph, Douglas Milsome (Rank Color); ed, Martin Hunter; m, Abigail Mead; prod d, Anton Furst; art d, Rod Stratford, Leslie Tomkins, Keith Pain; fx, John Evans; cos, Keith Denny

An uncompromisingly bleak film, as cold and distant as they come, Kubrick's FULL METAL JACKET is a perversely fascinating movie—one that answers no questions, offers no hope and has little meaning. In a way this is perfect for what the film has to say about war, but you find yourself numbed and apathetic as the film progresses. What one is left with is a remarkable display of the resources of cinema and a bludgeoning use of extreme violence which ironically undermines Kubrick's good intentions.

Highly structured, the film is presented in two parts: the first details the training of a group of Marines at the hands of the sadistic, foul-mouthed DI, Gunnery Sergeant Hartman (Ermey); and the second follows one of the recruits, "Joker" (Modine), a reporter for *Stars and Stripes* who finds himself in combat at the height of the Tet Offensive. There are no characterization and no heroics in FULL METAL JACKET; instead, Kubrick coolly shows the systematic dehumanization required to turn men into killing machines, then sits back and watches as they perform their assigned task.

From the shaving of the recruits' heads, the assignment of generic nicknames, and the profane bellowing that replaces conversation, to the orderly, ritualized existence of camp training is designed to drain all traces of individuality and humanity from soldiers and replace them with a cold hatred that can be directed at the enemy without hesitation. With his sarcastic humor and contradictory nature, Joker is the only character who retains a modicum of personality. Kubrick, however, dangles him before the viewer and then pulls him away slowly until Joker, too, is drained of his humanity.

Technically, FULL METAL JACKET is as flawless as any other meticulously designed Kubrick work and boasts superb cinematography by Milsome. Filming entirely in England, Kubrick found a military barracks outside London that doubles for Parris Island in the film. He also used a vast, deserted gasworks in London's East End, a plant area that had been bombed to ruination during WWII, and further destroyed the area to great effect.

FULL MOON IN PARIS
(LES NUITS DE LA PLEINE LUNE)
1984   101m   c   ★★★½
Drama   R/15
Losange/Ariane   (France)

Pascale Ogier (*Louise*), Fabrice Luchini (*Octave*), Tcheky Karyo (*Remi*), Christian Vadim (*Bastien*), Virginie Thevenet (*Camille*), Anne-Severine Liotard (*Marianne*), Laszlo Szabo (*Painter at Cafe*), Lisa Garneri (*Tina, the Babysitter*), Mathieu Schiffman (*Louise's Decorator Friend*), Herve Grandsart (*Remi's Friend Bertrand*)

p, Margaret Menegoz; d, Eric Rohmer; w, Eric Rohmer; ph, Renato Berta; ed, Cecile Decugis; m, Elli et Jacno; art d, Pascale Ogier; cos, Pascale Ogier

This fourth entry in Eric Rohmer's "Comedies and Proverbs" series begins with the proverb, "He who has two women loses his soul. He who has two houses loses his mind." The remarkably effervescent Pascale Ogier stars as the quintessential Rohmer woman, loved and admired by the men around her but desperately confused about the meaning of love.

A trainee at an interior-design firm, Louise (Ogier) lives with her architect-tennis player lover, Remi (Karyo), in a plastic suburb outside Paris. He wants to marry and settle down, but Louise is still young and enjoys dancing at parties until dawn. Remi's pressure proves too much for Louise, and she takes an apartment in Paris in order "to experience loneliness." Ostensibly, she will spend her late party nights in Paris, sleep in her new apartment, and return to the suburbs the following afternoon. While in Paris, she spends a great deal of time with Octave (Luchini) a likable writer who's tortured by Louise's refusal to sleep with him. At one fateful party, Louise meets Bastien (Vadim, son of Roger Vadim and Catherine Deneuve) and takes him back to her Paris apartment. Soon, however, she regrets her mistake and reconsiders her affection for Remi. But several things have changed since back when.

What Rohmer has done in this film—and has done so successfully in the past—is to take a brief, intelligent, comic look at a young Frenchwoman and her ideas of love. Ogier (the 24-year-old daughter of actress Bulle Ogier) delivers her lines with animation rarely captured on film, and she knows how to dance on screen as well. Her performance justly earned her a Best Actress award at the Venice Film Festival, but her career was tragically cut short by a fatal heart attack.

FUNERAL, THE
(OSOSHIKI)
1984   124m   c   ★★★
Comedy   /18
Itami/New Century   (Japan)

Nobuko Miyamoto (*Chizuko Amamiya*), Tsutomu Yamazaki (*Wabisuke Inoue*), Kin Sugai (*Kikue Amamiya*), Chishu Ryu (*The Priest*), Shuji Otaki (*Shokichi Amamiya*), Ichiro Zaitsu (*Satomi*), Kiminobu Okumura (*Shinkichi Amamiya*), Haruna Takaso (*Yoshiko Saito*)

p, Yasushi Tamaoki, Yutaka Okada; d, Juzo Itami; w, Juzo Itami; ph, Akira Suzuki; ed, Joji Yuasa

The first feature from Juzo Itami (TAMPOPO, A TAXING WOMAN), this is a black comedy that pokes fun at solemn traditional Japanese funeral rites. When a patriarch dies suddenly, his family—including his actress daughter (Nobuko Miyamato), her actor husband (Tsutomo Yamazaki), and their manager (Ichiro Zaitsu)—comes together for the three-day Buddhist ceremony for the former brothel owner. Many of the scenes that ensue will be familiar to viewers of similarly structured films but the Japanese setting is revelatory to Western eyes. While THE FUNERAL is not as loopy as TAMPOPO, a wildly appetizing comedy about food, it is still very energetic and inventive.

FUNERAL IN BERLIN
1966   102m   c   ★★★½
Spy   /PG
Paramount   (U.K.)

Michael Caine (*Harry Palmer*), Paul Hubschmid (*Johnny Vulkan*), Oscar Homolka (*Col. Stok*), Eva Renzi (*Samantha Steel*), Guy Doleman (*Ross*), Rachel Gurney (*Mrs. Ross*), Hugh Burden (*Hallam*), Thomas Holtzmann (*Reinhart*), Gunter Meisner (*Kreutzmann*), Heinz Schubert (*Aaron Levine*)

p, Harry Saltzman, Charles Kasher; d, Guy Hamilton; w, Evan Jones (based on the novel by Len Deighton); ph, Otto Heller (Panavision, Technicolor); ed, John Bloom; m, Konrad Elfers; prod d, Ken Adam; art d, Peter Murton

Caine, repeating his role from THE IPCRESS FILE, stars as Harry Palmer, the bespectacled British soldier forced to become a counterspy. This time Palmer is sent back to Germany, where his espionage career began, to contact Colonel Stok (Homolka), the Russian head of security for the Berlin Wall. Stok is anxious to defect, and Palmer arranges his escape only to be double-crossed by everyone and his brother. A bit poky, the film isn't quite up to the original, but it's rather better than most sequels of this kind. Featuring a fine cast (Homolka is *always* worth watching), FUNERAL IN BERLIN provides an excellent look at the spy business and an interesting view of postwar Berlin. One more sequel (and the weakest of the three), BILLION DOLLAR BRAIN, followed.

FUNNY FACE

1957   103m   c   ★★★★½
Musical   /U
Paramount

Audrey Hepburn *(Jo Stockton)*, Fred Astaire *(Dick Avery)*, Kay Thompson *(Maggie Prescott)*, Michel Auclair *(Prof. Emile Flostre)*, Robert Flemyng *(Paul Duval)*, Dovima *(Marion)*, Virginia Gibson *(Babs)*, Suzy Parker, Sunny Harnett, Don Powell

p, Roger Edens; d, Stanley Donen; w, Leonard Gershe (based on "Wedding Day," an unproduced musical libretto by Gershe); ph, Ray June (VistaVision, Technicolor); ed, Frank Bracht; m, George Gershwin, Ira Gershwin, Roger Edens, Leonard Gershe; art d, George W. Davis, Hal Pereira; fx, John P. Fulton; chor, Fred Astaire, Eugene Loring; cos, Edith Head, Givenchy

A film crucial to understanding Hepburn's glorious gamine appeal and one of Astaire's best musicals of the 1950s. A satire of both the fashion world and the fashionable pretensions of beatnik life and existentialism, FUNNY FACE concerns the May-December romance between Greenwich Village bookseller Jo Stockton (Hepburn) and Madison Avenue fashion photographer Dick Avery (Astaire). Dick discovers the sweet, young Jo and plays Henry Higgins to her Eliza, turning her into a top model in Paris.

That's all that need be said about the story, since this film exists only for its glamorous visuals, gorgeous Gershwin music, and the dancing choreographed by Astaire and Eugene Loring. Thompson, in a fabulous turn as a fashion editor, commands her underlings to "Think Pink" and the screen bursts with pink furniture, pink toothpaste and pink pets. "Bonjour Paris" is a whirlwind tour of the city, and "He Loves and She Loves" is a soft-focus fairy tale romance. Hepburn, who does remarkably well singing "How Long Has This Been Going On?" in her own voice, is exquisitely appealing and the byplay between her and the mellow, supple Astaire is enchanting.

As a dancer, Hepburn manages quite well in a satiric cafe number with two fellow mods, but shows her limitations in a climactic duet with Astaire set in the woods. (Maybe she had trouble with her heels in all that grass.) Astaire, meanwhile, displays his uncanny way with a song and enjoys one angular solo dance with his raincoat and umbrella. Real-life model superstars Suzy Parker and Dovima appear, but the most unforgettable fashion moment features Hepburn at her most "Givenchy" descending a flight of stairs in a stunning red gown. Beautifully helmed by Donen.

FUNNY GIRL

1968   151m   c   ★★★★
Musical/Biography   G/U
Rastar

Barbra Streisand *(Fanny Brice)*, Omar Sharif *(Nick Arnstein)*, Kay Medford *(Rose Brice)*, Anne Francis *(Georgia James)*, Walter Pidgeon *(Florenz Ziegfeld)*, Lee Allen *(Eddie Ryan)*, Mae Questel *(Mrs. Strakosh)*, Gerald Mohr *(Branca)*, Frank Faylen *(Keeney)*, Mittie Lawrence *(Emma)*

p, Ray Stark; d, William Wyler; w, Isobel Lennart (based on the musical by Jule Styne, Bob Merrill, Lennart); ph, Harry Stradling (Panavision, Technicolor); ed, Maury Winetrobe, William Sands; prod d, Gene Callahan; art d, Robert Luthardt; chor, Herbert Ross; cos, Irene Sharaff

Few film debuts in the 1960s were more auspicious than that of Barbra Streisand in FUNNY GIRL. Already a legit and recording star, she shot to superstardom and nabbed an Academy Award for best actress in the bargain. William Wyler's musical debut is less assured than one would have liked, but no matter; Streisand had played musical-comedy star Fanny Brice on Broadway and had the role down pat by the time director Wyler brought the story to the screen.

In the early 1900s in New York City, young Fanny, an ugly duckling with an unstoppable ambition to be a star, is determined to get out of the Lower East Side. Her big break comes when she's spotted by handsome gambler Nicky Arnstein (Sharif), who helps her catch the eye of Florenz Ziegfeld (Pidgeon). Ziegfeld hires her for his new Follies presentation, where her subversive comic style proves extraordinarily popular; soon she is one of the Follies' biggest stars. The remainder of the picture—which, despite its real-life subject, tells a formulaic story—recounts her steady rise to national celebrity and her tumultuous marriage to Arnstein.

The oddly cast Sharif is better than usual, but Streisand, of course, is most of the show, belting out songs, pulling heartstrings, alternating between raucous slapstick and dramatic power, and generally demonstrating that she has *arrived* in a big way. The memorable Broadway score was augmented for the screen with several tunes from Brice's life, including her signature, "My Man."

FUNNY LADY

1975   136m   c   ★★★½
Musical/Biography   PG
Rastar

Barbra Streisand *(Fanny Brice)*, James Caan *(Billy Rose)*, Omar Sharif *(Nick Arnstein)*, Roddy McDowall *(Bobby)*, Ben Vereen *(Bert Robbins)*, Carole Wells *(Norma Butler)*, Larry Gates *(Bernard Baruch)*, Heidi O'Rourke *(Eleanor Holm)*, Samantha Huffaker *(Fran)*, Matt Emery *(Buck Bolton)*

p, Ray Stark; d, Herbert Ross; w, Arnold Schulman, Jay Presson Allen (based on a story by Schulman); ph, James Wong Howe (Panavision, Technicolor); ed, Marion Rothman; prod d, George Jenkins; fx, Albert Whitlock; chor, Betty Walberg; cos, Ray Aghayan, Bob Mackie, Shirley Strahm

By then the most bankable female star of the decade, Streisand reprised the role that shot her to superstardom in FUNNY GIRL. Sequels are seldom as good as the originals, and this is no exception. Still, it's an entertaining and watchable film whose comedy flies higher than its drama. The picture begins in 1930; she's gotten over Nick Arnstein (Sharif) and now meets entrepreneur-showman-songwriter Billy Rose (Caan). Brice and Rose marry, but his infidelities and the strain of their separate careers destroy the marriage. Brice's life story was heavily fictionalized for this film, but the result is still dramatically weak. Streisand and Caan have their magnetic moments, but the lumpiness of the lengthy screenplay works against them much of the way. However, there's enough music in the movie to satisfy anyone, with songs culled from several sources to fill out the Kander and Ebb score. Streisand's galvanic rendition of "How Lucky Can You Get?" is a standout. Ross moved up from choreographer to direct, and he does a good job despite the thin script and Caan's minor musical talents.

FUNNY THING HAPPENED ON THE WAY TO THE FORUM, A

1966 99m c		★★★
Comedy		/PG
UA		

Zero Mostel (*Pseudolus*), Phil Silvers (*Lycus*), Jack Gilford (*Hysterium*), Buster Keaton (*Erronius*), Michael Crawford (*Hero*), Michael Hordern (*Senex*), Annette Andre (*Philia*), Patricia Jessel (*Domina*), Leon Greene (*Miles Gloriosus*), Inga Neilsen (*Gymnasia*)

p, Melvin Frank; d, Richard Lester; w, Melvin Frank, Michael Pertwee (based on the book by Burt Shevelove, Larry Gelbart); ph, Nicolas Roeg (DeLuxe Color); ed, John Victor Smith; prod d, Tony Walton; fx, Cliff Richardson; chor, Ethel Martin, George Martin; cos, Tony Walton

Typical hit-and-miss filmmaking by the relentlessly antsy Richard Lester, but lots of fun all the same. Based on the smash Broadway musical, the film toplines Mostel as a Roman slave desperately trying to win his freedom and Gilford as his unwitting accomplice. Plot complications involve Silvers as a brothel owner, Andre and Crawford as young lovers, and Keaton searching for his lost children. Lester's direction is full of the flashy technique which worked better in his Beatles movies. Sometimes he would have done better to just let some of the farcical set-pieces alone. His sense of timing is sometimes off, and laughs are lost as a result. The songs are quite delightful, but somehow the production numbers don't quite fly as they should and just end up bogging down the story. To its credit, however, Lester does add a certain energy and spirit to many scenes, and some great comic moments result. Also, the overall performances make this film well worth watching—Gilford in particular is a gem. FUNNY THING now seems one of the more enjoyable of the many overcooked musical adaptations Hollywood was desperately cranking out during the 1960s.

FURY

1936 90m bw		★★★★½
Crime		/18
MGM		

Spencer Tracy (*Joe Wheeler*), Sylvia Sidney (*Katherine Grant*), Walter Abel (*District Attorney*), Edward Ellis (*Sheriff*), Walter Brennan (*Buggs Meyers*), Bruce Cabot (*Bubbles Dawson*), George Walcott (*Tom*), Frank Albertson (*Charlie*), Arthur Stone (*Durkin*), Morgan Wallace (*Fred Garrett*)

p, Joseph L. Mankiewicz; d, Fritz Lang; w, Bartlett Cormack, Fritz Lang (based on the story "Mob Rule" by Norman Krasna); ph, Joseph Ruttenberg; ed, Frank Sullivan; m, Franz Waxman; art d, Cedric Gibbons, William A. Horning, Edwin B. Willis; cos, Dolly Tree

An uncharacteristically trenchant indictment of mob rule for the usually family-oriented MGM. Despite studio interference, Fritz Lang, in his first Hollywood outing, succeeded in making a penetrating study of injustice and inhumanity with Spencer Tracy delivering a memorable performance as an innocent man who's wrongly accused of a sensational crime and transformed into a malevolent force of vengeance.

Spencer Tracy is Joe Wheeler, a honest guy trying to earn enough money to get married to his devoted fiancee, Katherine Grant (Sylvia Sidney). While driving to meet up with Katherine, Joe gets picked up by the cops. Arrested as a suspected kidnaper, he is imprisoned in a small-town jail pending trial. He is damned by circumstantial evidence and rampant rumours. A mob gathers and heads for the jail. The sheriff gets nervous and calls the governor begging him to put the National Guard on alert as he does not have enough guards to withstand a full-scale assault on his small jail. However, the governor's advisers steer him away from the potentially controversial situation. Meanwhile, back at the jail, things quickly get out of hand.

Lang brings striking expressionist touches to the social problem picture with expressive shadowplay and stylized subjective fantasy sequences. This was his favorite American film and rightfully so, for it demonstrates his directorial genius in wasting not a frame of film, telling his story with sharp cross-cutting between victim and tormentors, while unraveling the mindless and murderous passion of a mob out of control.

F/X

1986 107m c		★★★
Thriller		R/15
Orion		

Bryan Brown (*Rollie Tyler*), Brian Dennehy (*Leo McCarthy*), Diane Venora (*Ellen*), Cliff De Young (*Lipton*), Mason Adams (*Col. Mason*), Jerry Orbach (*Nicholas DeFranco*), Joe Grifasi (*Mickey*), Martha Gehman (*Andy*), Roscoe Orman (*Capt. Wallenger*), Trey Wilson (*Lt. Murdoch*)

p, Dodi Fayed, Jack Wiener; d, Robert Mandel; w, Robert T. Megginson, Gregory Fleeman; ph, Miroslav Ondricek (Technicolor); ed, Terry Rawlings; m, Bill Conti; prod d, Mel Bourne; art d, Speed Hopkins; fx, Carl Fullerton, John Stears; cos, Julie Weiss

Rollie Tyler (Brown) is an ace New York-based special-effects man who specializes in doing the gore effects for horror films. Between pictures he is approached by government agent Lipton (De Young) from the Justice Department's Witness Protection Program. Lipton wants to hire Brown to fake the assassination of Mafia kingpin Nicholas DeFranco (Orbach), who is about to testify against members of his gang. If the gang thinks DeFranco is dead, it will make it easier for the Justice Department to protect him from potential mob "hits" until he has the chance to squeal in court. Although apprehensive, Rollie takes the challenge and concocts an elaborate plan for "assassinating" the mobster. Unfortunately, soon after the deed is done, Rollie realizes that the whole thing was a set-up, and now his employers want him dead.

This is a slick little thriller that benefits greatly from its clever use of special effects. Australian actor Bryan Brown is fine as the effects man who finds himself embroiled in an often-confusing plot, and Brian Dennehy lends his usual solid support as the New York cop trying to make sense of it all. Director Robert Mandel has a nice flair for light comedy and never hesitates to go for a laugh when the absurdities of the script call for it. The action sequences are well staged and the twists and turns of the convoluted plot will keep viewers guessing. A competent and unpretentious entertainment.

G

G-MEN

1935   85m   bw   ★★★★
Crime   /A
WB

James Cagney *(James "Brick" Davis)*, Ann Dvorak *(Jean Morgan)*, Margaret Lindsay *(Kay McCord)*, Robert Armstrong *(Jeff McCord)*, Barton MacLane *(Brad Collins)*, Lloyd Nolan *(Hugh Farrell)*, William Harrigan *(McKay)*, Edward Pawley *(Danny Leggett)*, Russell Hopton *(Gerard)*, Noel Madison *(Durfee)*

p, Louis F. Edelman; d, William Keighley; w, Seton I. Miller (based on the novel *Public Enemy No. 1* by Gregory Rogers); ph, Sol Polito; ed, Jack Killifer; art d, John Hughes; chor, Bobby Connolly; cos, Orry-Kelly

Turnabout Cagney film: he changed his film image from ruthless gangster to fearless FBI man, but the truth is his G-Man is as reckless, violent and prone to impulse as any of his hoods. William Harrigan is a bigshot gangster who generously puts Cagney through law school. When Regis Toomey, Cagney's pal, becomes an FBI man and is gunned down without a chance—agents at the time not being legally able to bear arms—Cagney joins the FBI to seek revenge.

Keighley was not one of Cagney's favorites; Cagney thought the director affected because he spoke French to the cast and crew, he and his wife having recently learned the language in nonstop lessons. Lindsay also bothered the down-to-earth Cagney. To get her first role (in CAVALCADE), Lindsay, who came from Dubuque, Iowa, had fibbed to producers, saying she was British since British accents were sought after as being easily understood in the early sound era. She continued to affect a slightly British accent with broad A's even in G-MEN, which annoyed Cagney. J. Edgar Hoover made G-MEN a pet project and loaned several real agents to appear in the film, ostensibly to lend credibility to the production but really to make sure that the Bureau's story was told the way Hoover wanted it told. Actually, it was standard Warner pulp, ripped from the tabloid page and briskly told. So durable was this film that Warner Bros. re-released G-MEN many times for box-office bonanzas. In the 1949 go-around, the studio added a prologue to the film with David Brian as the chief and Douglas Kennedy as an agent. Brian is teaching a class of recruits and introduces the film to them by saying: "You are about to see the granddaddy of them all!"

GALLIPOLI

1981   110m   c   ★★★★
War   PG
Paramount   (Australia)

Mark Lee *(Archy)*, Bill Kerr *(Jack)*, Mel Gibson *(Frank Dunne)*, Ronnie Graham *(Wallace Hamilton)*, Harold Hopkins *(Les McCann)*, Charles Yunupingu *(Zac)*, Heath Harris *(Stockman)*, Gerda Nicolson *(Rose Hamilton)*, Robert Grubb *(Billy)*, Tim McKenzie *(Barney)*

p, Robert Stigwood, Patricia Lovell; d, Peter Weir; w, David Williamson (based on a story by Weir); ph, Russell Boyd (Panavision, Eastmancolor); ed, William Anderson; m, Brian May; prod d, Wendy Weir; art d, Herbert Pinter

Focusing on two fleet-footed young Australians, Peter Weir's extraordinarily moving antiwar film examines the disastrous WWI invasion of Gallipoli by the Australian-New Zealand Army Corps.

Archy (Mark Lee) and Frank (Mel Gibson) come from different backgrounds, but they share a love of king, country and life—never more apparent than when the two sprinters race each other. Together, they join the army and become part of the ill-fated campaign to wrest control of the Dardanelles from the Ottoman Turks. Meeting heavy resistance from the well-entrenched Turks and their German allies, the ANZAC offensive bogs down on the beachhead. Poor generalship and worse communication eventually lead to a suicidal assault and a tremendous waste of young lives.

Director Weir (PICNIC AT HANGING ROCK, THE YEAR OF LIVING DANGEROUSLY) and cinematographer Russell Boyd's re-creation of the invasion and battle action is stunning, but what makes GALLIPOLI such an affecting film is its intimate presentation of the friendship between Archy and Frank (wonderfully essayed by Lee and Gibson). Weir uses the first part of the film to establish the vibrant optimism of their lives down under, then he demonstrates how quickly and pointlessly such young lives can be snuffed out.

Not always easy to watch, GALLIPOLI is both a fitting testimony to the courage of the thousands of Australians and New Zealanders who died fighting for their country and one of the most powerful cinematic examinations of the futility and tragic cost of war.

GANDHI

1982   188m   c   ★★★★
Biography   PG
Intl. Film Investors/Goldcrest/Indo-British Films/Natl. Film Development   (U.K./India)

Ben Kingsley *(Mahatma Gandhi)*, Candice Bergen *(Margaret Bourke-White)*, Edward Fox *(Gen. Dyer)*, John Gielgud *(Lord Irwin)*, Trevor Howard *(Judge Broomfield)*, John Mills *(The Viceroy)*, Martin Sheen *(Walker)*, Rohini Hattangady *(Kasturba Gandhi)*, Ian Charleson *(Charlie Andrews)*, Athol Fugard *(Gen. Smuts)*

p, Richard Attenborough; d, Richard Attenborough; w, John Briley; ph, Billy Williams, Ronnie Taylor (Technicolor); ed, John Bloom; m, Ravi Shankar, George Fenton; prod d, Stuart Craig; art d, Robert Laing, Ram Yedekar, Norman Dorme; fx, David Hathaway; cos, John Mollo, Bhanu Athaiya

Sir Richard Attenborough spent nearly 20 years attempting to convince studios that the life story of Mahatma Gandhi was crying to be made. It was worth the wait, since the result, anchored by a stunning performance by Ben Kingsley, ranks among the great screen biographies.

The film spans decades, opening in South Africa where Gandhi (Kingsley) is a struggling attorney victimized by that country's racial policies. Later, in India, he recognizes that the ruling British have reduced the Indian people to second-class status in their own country, and he develops his program of civil disobedience, a course of action that would change events not only in India but throughout the world. Ultimately, he emerges as the strong, determined leader of his country and must face his nation's new challenges.

Ben Kingsley's Academy Award-winning performance as Gandhi is a marvel in which he convincingly ages over half a century. Attenborough and author John Briley have collaborated to offer a balanced view of Gandhi's life, from trauma to triumph. Every supporting actor is well cast, with well-known South African playwright Athol Fugard (*Master Harold and the Boys*) particularly believable as General Smuts.

GANG'S ALL HERE, THE

1943   103m   c   ★★★
Musical   /A
FOX

Alice Faye (*Eadie Allen*), Carmen Miranda (*Dorita*), Phil Baker (*Himself*), Benny Goodman and His Orchestra (*Themselves*), Eugene Pallette (*Mr. Mason, Sr.*), Charlotte Greenwood (*Mrs. Peyton Potter*), Edward Everett Horton (*Peyton Potter*), Tony DeMarco (*Himself*), James Ellison (*Andy Mason*), Sheila Ryan (*Vivian*)

p, William LeBaron; d, Busby Berkeley; w, Walter Bullock (from a story by Nancy Winter, George Root, Jr., and Tom Bridges); ph, Edward Cronjager (Technicolor); ed, Ray Curtiss; art d, James Basevi, Joseph C. Wright; fx, Fred Sersen; chor, Busby Berkeley; cos, Yvonne Wood

A camp classic. If you consider Berkeley a genius, this is the highpoint of his career. It's his first in color, and filtering his kaleidoscope cuties through the garish mixmaster of 1940's Fox Technicolor is like a male hairdresser's acid trip: chorines dissolve into artichokes; Carmen Miranda arrives in an overloaded fruit wagon, more animated than any character at Disney, and cha-chas down a boulevard of strawberries. Alice Faye, in her big-budget musical swan song, swoons some sanity into the proceedings with "No Love, No Nothing" and "Journey to a Star," but she's overwhelmed introducing the "Polka-Dot Polka" ballet, a description of which wouldn't do full justice to it anyway. By the time Berkeley's chorus girls wave huge phallic bananas in rhythmic waves, you'll swear you're lost in a giant fruit cocktail. The film enhanced the stardom of Miranda but because of those *big* bananas, THE GANG'S ALL HERE was never released in her native Brazil.

GANJA AND HESS

1973   110m   c   ★★★★½
Horror   R/
Kelly/Jordan

Duane Jones (*Dr. Hess Green*), Marlene Clark (*Ganja*), Bill Gunn (*George*), Sam Waymon (*Rev. Williams*), Leonard Jackson (*Archie*), Candece Tarpley (*Girl in Bar*), Richard Harrow (*Dinner Guest*), John Hoffmeister (*Jack*), Betty Barney (*Singer*), Mabel King (*Queen of Myrthia*)

p, Chiz Schultz; d, Bill Gunn; w, Bill Gunn; ph, James E. Hinton; ed, Victor Kanefsky; m, Sam Waymon; prod d, Tom H. John; cos, Scott Barrie

One of the best black-oriented movies to come out of Hollywood in the 1970s, GANJA AND HESS stars the late Duane Jones (NIGHT OF THE LIVING DEAD) as a New York anthropologist embroiled in a study of the lost ancient African culture of Myrthia, a nation that died out from a communicable parasite that fed on human blood. During his research, Jones is stabbed with a jewel-encrusted Myrthian dagger by his crazed assistant (played by director Bill Gunn) and finds that he has become

infected with the virus, turning him into a vampirelike creature addicted to blood. He fancies himself an invincible African god and turns his wife, Clark, into a vampire as well.

This is a fascinating picture, managing both to subvert its commercial horror angle and to explore the contrasts between Western and African cultures—the former represented as repressive and puritanical, the latter as more virile and liberating. The late Gunn, who was also an accomplished novelist, playwright and painter, imbues the film with a cultural richness little seen in black-targeted films. Impressionistic, vibrant, and rhythmic (the original soundtrack used both American spirituals and African traditional music), GANJA AND HESS is a memorable and haunting film.

Tragically, it was recut by its distributors for theatrical release. Most of the thematic lushness wound up on the floor, but the most heinous change was the removal of the African soundtrack in favor of bland American soul music.

GARDEN OF ALLAH, THE

1936   85m   c   ★★½
Romance   /U
Selznick

Marlene Dietrich (*Domini Enfilden*), Charles Boyer (*Boris Androvsky*), Basil Rathbone (*Count Anteoni*), C. Aubrey Smith (*Father Roubier*), Tilly Losch (*Irena*), Joseph Schildkraut (*Batouch*), John Carradine (*Sand Diviner*), Alan Marshal (*De Trevignac*), Lucile Watson (*Mother Superior*), Henry Brandon (*Hadj*)

p, David O. Selznick; d, Richard Boleslawski; w, W.P. Lipscomb, Lynn Riggs (based on the novel by Robert Hichens); ph, Harold Rosson, W. Howard Greene (Technicolor); ed, Hal C. Kern, Anson Stevenson; m, Max Steiner; prod d, Lansing C. Holden; art d, Sturges Carne, Lyle Wheeler, Edward Boyle; fx, Jack Cosgrove; cos, Ernest Dryden

A dense old pudding of a story, oozing color (Selznick's first) and weighing a ton thanks to Max Steiner's music. Dietrich, awash in swirling, blowing chiffon, is a "disiwusioned" socialite seeking truth in the African desert, an extreme choice for soul-searching. She falls into twin liquid pools of love, courtesy of the limpid eyes of Boyer. On their wedding night, a liqueur restores his conscience: he's a Trappist monk who deserted, and must now seek repentence. The 1904 novel was dramatized in 1911 and first filmed in 1917 with Helen Ware and Thomas Santschi by William Selig, and again by MGM in 1927 with Alice Terry and Ivan Petrovich. By 1936, it reeked of mothballs, and since both stars were given to mooning and swooning with their great half-mast eyes, it almost appears they are commenting on it. Richard Boleslawski directed what he could of the story; it's not only silly, but tedious too. That's Tilly Losch having the film's one and only hot minute as an Algerian whirling dervish—-how Dietrich must have hated her.

GARDEN OF THE FINZI-CONTINIS, THE

(IL GIARDINO DEL FINZI-CONTINI)
1971   103m   c   ★★★★
War/Drama   R/A
Documento/CCC   (Italy/West Germany)

Dominique Sanda (*Micol*), Lino Capolicchio (*Giorgio*), Helmut Berger (*Alberto*), Fabio Testi (*Malnate*), Romolo Valli (*Giorgio's Father*), Raffaele Curi (*Ernesto*), Camillo Angelini-Rota (*Micol's Father*), Katina Viglietti (*Micol's Mother*), Ina Alexeiff (*Micol's Grandmother*), Barbara Pilavin p, Arthur Cohn, Gianni Hecht Lucari; d, Vittorio De Sica; w, Cesare Zavattini, Vittorio Bonicelli, Ugo Pirro (based on the novel by Giorgio Bassani); ph, Ennio Guarnieri (Eastmancolor); ed, Adriana Novelli; m, Manuel De Sica; art d, Giancarlo Bartolini Salimbeni; cos, Antonio Randaccio

Lyrical and melancholy, ultimately hollow, but a surprising contrast to much of De Sica's earlier work. Although the director spent a good part of the latter half of his career acting in other director's works (Roberto Rossellini's GENERAL DELLA ROVERE, for example), THE GARDEN OF THE FINZI-CONTINIS is proof he had not lost his touch.

Set in Ferrara, Italy, during WWII, this story of love and culture unfolds effortlessly, albeit a trifle slowly. The Finzi-Continis are an aristocratic Jewish-Italian family who cannot believe that the war will ever invade their hallowed garden walls. Rather than flee, they stay on in the false hope that they will not be betrayed, but they eventually come to realize that Fascism is not going to go away and that they must join the fight against it. THE GARDEN OF THE FINZI-CONTINIS is one of the few films in which flashbacks are absolutely necessary; they provide the historical perspective the characters lack.

This film bears very little resemblance to De Sica's early work. Like all previously state-funded filmmakers, he suddenly needed to concern himself with his films' commercial potential. But the movie is still directed with the familiar De Sica skill. His handling of the unknowns in the cast is exceptional, as is his direction of the wonderful Dominique Sanda.

GARDENS OF STONE

1987 111m c   ★★★
Drama/War   R/15
Tri-Star/ML Delphi Premier

James Caan (Sgt. Clell Hazard), Anjelica Huston (Samantha Davis), James Earl Jones (Sgt. Maj. "Goody" Nelson), D.B. Sweeney (Pvt. Jackie Willow), Dean Stockwell (Capt. Homer Thomas), Mary Stuart Masterson (Rachel Feld), Lonette McKee (Betty Rae), Sam Bottoms (Lt. Webber), Elias Koteas (Pete Deveber), Larry Fishburne (Cpl. Flanagan)

p, Michael I. Levy, Francis Ford Coppola; d, Francis Ford Coppola; w, Ronald Bass (based on the novel by Nicholas Proffitt); ph, Jordan Cronenweth (Deluxe Color); ed, Barry Malkin; m, Carmine Coppola; prod d, Dean Tavoularis; art d, Alex Tavoularis; fx, John Frazier, Robin Hauser; cos, Willa Kim, Judianna Makovsky

After more than a decade of films that examined the war in Vietnam from many different angles, Francis Ford Coppola concentrated not on the heroics, battles or camaraderie of war, but simply on the burial of the dead. From the vantage point of Arlington National Cemetery, with its somber landscape of white crosses, war appears most senseless.

Sergeant Clell Hazard (James Caan) is a military man through and through, a hard-bitten veteran who, in 1968, hates the Vietnam War but loves the service. His job is to oversee the men assigned to the Old Guard at Arlington, that elite corps of soldiers who stand watch over the Tomb of the Unknown Soldier, escort the many bodies to their final resting places, and engage in various drill exercises as a public relations function for the government. Assigned to Hazard's unit is Private Jackie Willow (D.B. Sweeney), the son of a veteran who had been Hazard's pal. A gung-ho soldier, Jackie wants desperately to get into battle. Jackie grows close to a number of people at Arlington, including surrogate father Hazard; Hazard's girlfriend, Samantha (Anjelica Huston); and Rachel (Mary Stuart Masterson), the young woman

with whom he falls in love. Nevertheless, Jackie's fatal desire is to serve his country in Vietnam.

Unjustly underrated upon its release, GARDENS OF STONE is a quiet, respectful film filled with emotional power, exceptional acting (especially by Caan), and technical virtuosity. Coppola was directing from the heart on this one: his son Giancarlo died in a boating accident during production. The film is dedicated to the Third US Infantry.

GASLIGHT

1940 88m bw   ★★★★★
Thriller
BNP   (U.K.)

Anton Walbrook (Paul Mallen), Diana Wynyard (Bella Mallen), Frank Pettingell (Rough), Cathleen Cordell (Nancy), Robert Newton (Vincent Ullswater), Jimmy Hanley (Cobb), Minnie Rayner (Elizabeth), Mary Hinton (Lady Winterbourne), Marie Wright (Alice Barlow), Jack Barty (Chairman)

p, John Corfield; d, Thorold Dickinson; w, A.R. Rawlinson, Bridget Boland (based on the play by Patrick Hamilton); ph, Bernard Knowles; ed, Sidney Cole; m, Richard Addinsell

A lost black pearl, better than Mayer's sugar-coated 1944 version. This British psychological thriller is truly a forgotten masterpiece due to the machinations of MGM's Louis B. Mayer.

In one of her finest roles, Wynyard is a wealthy patrician lady who marries the urbane but calculating Walbrook. They move into an 1880 mansion, her ancestral London home, where Cordell is the ever-present brazen maid. Before long, Wynard notices the gaslight in her rooms flickers downward nightly and comes to believe that this is a hallucination. Meanwhile, through clever, subtle measures, Walbrook slowly drives her to the brink of insanity, convincing her that she is losing her memory. Pettingell, a kindly and perceptive Scotland Yard detective, meets Wynyard socially and begins paying attention to her and Walbrook—too much attention from the latter's point of view.

Columbia purchased the rights to the film in 1941, intending an American remake with Irene Dunne in the lead. Then MGM bought the property for Hedy Lamarr who unwisely turned it down. When the Ingrid Bergman-Charles Boyer production was shot in 1944, Mayer ordered his minions to track down all the prints of the original GASLIGHT and destroy them, so it would never compete with his lavish production. Fortunately, prints survived. It's one of the most stylish British films to be made before WWII and one of director Dickinson's most polished works, each scene carefully set up as the tension mounts brilliantly, frame by frame. Walbrook is magnificent as the arch villain, his extravagant Middle-European acting style bordering on the flamboyant, his dark charm shrouding his evil purposes.

GASLIGHT

1944 114m bw   ★★★★
Thriller
MGM

Charles Boyer (Gregory Anton), Ingrid Bergman (Paula Alquist), Joseph Cotten (Brian Cameron), Dame May Whitty (Miss Thwaites), Angela Lansbury (Nancy Oliver), Barbara Everest (Elizabeth Tompkins), Eustace Wyatt (Budge), Emil Rameau (Mario Gordi), Edmund Breon (Gen. Huddleston), Halliwell Hobbes (Mr. Mufflin) p, Arthur Hornblow, Jr.; d, George Cukor; w, John Van Druten, Walter Reisch, John Balderston (based on the play "Angel Street" by Patrick Hamilton); ph, Joseph Ruttenberg; ed, Ralph E. Winters; m, Bronislau Kaper; art d, Cedric Gibbons, William Ferrari; fx, Warren Newcombe

Lusher, ornate version of *Angel Street*, without the telling chill of the 1940 Diana Wynward GASLIGHT, but satisfactorily directed all the same. Bergman is deeply sympathetic as the wealthy socialite married to Boyer, who turns into an insidious monster in his attempt to drive his ravishing wife mad. But the lengthy Italian honeymoon starts the picture on too sunny a disposition, and Bergman's victim does look as healthy as a horse. Boyer nearly steals the picture, aided and abetted by the stunning debut of Angela Lansbury as a hardbitten servant—only 18, she grabbed the role and chewed it to bits. The climax is a workmanlike rise of psychological terror, but the whole exercise looks self-consciously careful.

GATE OF HELL
(JIGOKUMEN)
1953   89m   c   ★★★★
Historical/War   /A
Daiei   (Japan)

Machiko Kyo (*Lady Kesa*), Kazuo Hasegawa (*Moritoh*), Isao Yamagata (*Wataru*), Koreya Senda (*Kiyomori*), Yataro Kurokawa (*Shigemori*), Kikue Mohri (*Sawa*), Kotaro Bando (*Rokuroh*), Jun Tazaki (*Kogenta*), Tatsuya Ishiguro (*Yachuta*), Kenjiro Uemura (*Masanaka*)

p, Masaichi Nagata; d, Teinosuke Kinugasa; w, Teinosuke Kinugasa (based on a play by Kan Kikuchi); ph, Kohei Sugiyama (Eastmancolor); m, Yasushi Akutagawa; cos, Sanzo Wada

Set in the 12th century, GATE OF HELL is the dazzlingly beautiful and simple Japanese tale centering on a heroic samurai, Moritoh (matinee idol Kazuo Hasegawa), who is to be rewarded for his bravery with anything he desires by his country's ruler. What he most desires is the beautiful Lady Kesa (Machiko Kyo), though she is already married. Attempts are made to persuade Kesa to leave her husband (Isao Yamagata), but her devotion to him is great, and Moritoh is left with no other choice than to murder his rival. Less revered today than RASHOMON or UGETSU, both of which also starred the gorgeous Kyo, GATE OF HELL was the first color Japanese film to reach US shores and helped build an international reputation for Japanese cinema.

GAY DESPERADO, THE
1936   86m   bw   ★★★½
Musical/Comedy   /A
Pickford/Lasky

Nino Martini (*Chivo*), Ida Lupino (*Jane*), Leo Carrillo (*Pablo Braganza*), Harold Huber (*Campo*), James Blakely (*Bill*), Stanley Fields (*Butch*), Mischa Auer (*Diego*), Adrian Rosley (*Radio Station Manager*), Paul Hurst (*American Detective*), Allan Garcia (*Police Captain*)

p, Mary Pickford, Jesse L. Lasky; d, Rouben Mamoulian; w, Wallace Smith (based on a story by Leo Birinski); ph, Lucien Andriot; ed, Margaret Clancy; art d, Richard Day

None too gay, but loopy as all get out, kidding several genres at once as it crawls along. Leo Carrillo is a music-loving Mexican bandit who patterns himself after American screen gangsters. He kidnaps Nino Martini, a singing caballero, and energetic heiress Ida Lupino, terrific as always. Martini gets too much time to sing, but bad guy Carrillo and his partner Huber steal the show with their comic performances. Curious musical comedy was the second and last of the films produced by the team of Mary Pickford and Jesse Lasky.

GAY DIVORCEE, THE
1934   107m   bw   ★★★★
Musical/Comedy   /U
RKO

Fred Astaire (*Guy Holden*), Ginger Rogers (*Mimi Glossop*), Alice Brady (*Hortense Ditherwell*), Edward Everett Horton (*Egbert Fitzgerald*), Erik Rhodes (*Rodolfo Tonetti*), Eric Blore (*Waiter*), Lillian Miles (*Hotel Guest*), Charles Coleman (*Valet*), William Austin (*Cyril Glossop*), Betty Grable (*Hotel Guest*)

p, Pandro S. Berman; d, Mark Sandrich; w, George Marion, Jr., Dorothy Yost, Edward Kaufman (based on the musical play "The Gay Divorce" by Dwight Taylor and Cole Porter); ph, David Abel; ed, William Hamilton; art d, Van Nest Polglase, Carroll Clark; fx, Vernon L. Walker; chor, Fred Astaire, Hermes Pan (uncredited); cos, Walter Plunkett

One of the best examples of Depression-era musicals. After a brief twirl together in FLYING DOWN TO RIO, Fred Astaire and Ginger Rogers hooked up again, and so captivated filmgoers that this costarring vehicle would be only the first of many for cinema's most famous dance team.

Modern gal Mimi Glossop (Rogers) wants a divorce, but to get it she must venture to an English seaside resort where her lawyer (Horton) has arranged for her to be witnessed having an assignation with a professional correspondent, thus providing the necessary grounds for her divorce—infidelity. Matters become confused, however, when Mimi mistakes Guy Holden (Astaire), an American dancer who has taken a serious interest in her, for the correspondent and treats him disdainfully. Several songs and cases of mistaken identity later, Guy and Mimi end up in each other's arms for good.

Although in hindsight it seems incredible, the producers of THE GAY DIVORCEE weren't certain that Astaire and Rogers could carry the movie on their own, so they "insured" the success of the film by including several of the best second bananas around—Horton and Eric Blore among them. As a result the film is loaded with laughs and energetic performances. Moreover, its sets are superb, Max Steiner's orchestrations are a marvel, and the choreography by Dave Gould is excellent. If Astaire and Rogers had never danced a lick after the frustrated seduction of "Night and Day", they still would have been screen immortals.

GENERAL DELLA ROVERE
(IL GENERALE DELLA ROVERE)
1959   130m   bw   ★★★★
War/Drama
Zebra/SNE Gaumont   (Italy/France)

Vittorio De Sica (*Victorio Emanuele Bardone/Grimaldi*), Hannes Messemer (*Col. Mueller*), Vittorio Caprioli (*Banchelli*), Guiseppe Rossetti (*Pietro Valeri*), Ivo Garrani (*Fabrizio*), Sandra Milo (*Valeira*), Giovanna Ralli (*Olga*), Anne Vernon (*Chiara Fassio*), Baronessa Barzani (*Contessa della Rovere*), Kurt Polter (*German Officer*)

p, Moris Ergas; d, Roberto Rossellini; w, Roberto Rossellini, Sergio Amidei, Diego Fabbri, Indro Montanelli (based on a story by Montanelli); ph, Carlo Carlini; ed, Anna Maria Montanari, Cesare Cavagna; m, Renzo Rossellini; art d, Piero Zuffi

GENERAL DELLA ROVERE was the film that returned director Roberto Rossellini to international favor after he ended his filmmaking collaboration with Ingrid Bergman and explored documentary filmmaking with INDIA. Although Rossellini, who took on this film as a survival project, looked upon GENERAL DELLA ROVERE with shame, it is one of his great achievements, the story of a man who discovers his own morality by imitating another's.

Revolving around this essentially Christian theme, the film is set during the German occupation of Genoa during the winter of 1943-44. After Resistance leader Gen. della Rovere is accidentally murdered by Gestapo troops, the local Nazi commandant "persuades" Bardone (Vittorio De Sica), an amoral, low-life swindler, to impersonate the general. In this guise, Bardone is sent to the Milan jail, where he is supposed to find and identify a partisan leader whom della Rovere had planned to meet before his death. Bardone, however, gradually begins to identify with his fellow prisoners and assumes the moral stance, if not the full being, of the Resistance leader.

Recalling OPEN CITY and PAISAN, Rossellini's great early achievements, GENERAL DELLA ROVERE is a powerful, beautifully acted picture, which—and this is the source of Rossellini's discontent with the work—retreads the ideas and forms of his past successes. While it may have been a step backwards in the development of this great filmmaker, this cannot diminish the film's undeniable strength.

GENEVIEVE
1953 86m c   ★★★★★
Comedy   /U
Sirius (U.K.)

John Gregson (Alan McKim), Dinah Sheridan (Wendy McKim), Kenneth More (Ambrose Claverhouse), Kay Kendall (Rosalind Peters), Geoffrey Keen (1st Speed Cop), Harold Siddons (2nd Speed Cop), Reginald Beckwith (J.C. Callahan), Arthur Wontner (Elderly Gentleman), Joyce Grenfell (Hotel Proprietress), Leslie Mitchell (Himself)

p, Henry Cornelius; d, Henry Cornelius; w, William Rose; ph, Christopher Challis (Technicolor); ed, Clive Donner; m, Larry Adler; chor, Eric Rogers

As smooth as custard. A wonderful British comedy about two couples, classic-car enthusiasts, who participate in the annual London-to-Brighton rally. The title comes from the 1904 roadster owned by Alan and Wendy McKim (John Gregson and Dinah Sheridan), who, on the return trip, challenge their friends Ambrose (Kenneth More) and Rosalind (Kay Kendall) to a friendly race. Their playfulness becomes increasingly intense as they speed to the Westminster Bridge finish line.

The screenplay is marvelous, the film is full of the fresh air of the English countryside, the color is appealing and the famous harmonic score by Larry Adler is perfect. That old stalwart Arthur Wontner has a lovely, touching bit at the finale, and the whole film is so good it makes you regret that Henry Cornelius didn't make more films than he did.

GENTLE CREATURE, A
(UNE FEMME DOUCE)
1971 88m c   ★★★★
Drama   /AA
Parc/Marianne (France)

Dominique Sanda (She), Guy Frangin (He), Jane Lobre (Anna)

p, Mag Bodard; d, Robert Bresson; w, Robert Bresson (based on the novella A Gentle Creature by Feodor Dostoyevsky); ph, Ghislain Cloquet (Eastmancolor); ed, Raymond Lamy; m, Jean Wiener; art d, Pierre Charbonnier

A hauntingly simple film about a young wife (Sanda) who commits suicide, leaving no explanation for her obsessively dominant husband (Frangin). Shattered, he recounts their first meeting—she's a free spirit who visits his pawnshop. They marry, but the woman must adapt her life style to his, being subjected to his accusations and jealousies. She toys with murdering him, pointing a gun at his head, but lacks the ability to pull the trigger. When she falls ill, the man finally realizes his love for her. He takes a positive outlook on the marriage and plans for a future together, only to have her shut the door on his hopes. Bresson's first film in color, and only his ninth in 26 years, A GENTLE CREATURE marked the film debut of former model Sanda, who would the same year be seen in Bertolucci's THE CONFORMIST.

GENTLEMAN JIM
1942 104m bw   ★★★★
Sports   /U
WB/First National

Errol Flynn (James J. Corbett), Alexis Smith (Victoria Ware), Jack Carson (Walter Lowrie), Alan Hale (Pat Corbett), John Loder (Carlton DeWitt), William Frawley (Billy Delaney), Minor Watson (Buck Ware), Ward Bond (John L. Sullivan), Madeleine LeBeau (Anna Held), Rhys Williams (Harry Watson)

p, Robert Buckner; d, Raoul Walsh; w, Vincent Lawrence, Horace McCoy (based on the autobiography The Roar of the Crowd by James J. Corbett); ph, Sid Hickox; ed, Jack Killifer; m, Heinz Roemheld; art d, Ted Smith; cos, Milo Anderson

One of the best sports biopics ever. Historically inaccurate, but a directorial field day for director Raoul Walsh, who excelled at action direction and also period nostalgia. Errol Flynn's colorful temperament, capricious moods, and daring nature were perfect for the role of James J. Corbett, the brash Irish bank clerk from San Francisco who went on to defeat John L. Sullivan (nicely essayed by Ward Bond) for the heavyweight championship of the world in New Orleans in 1892. As Gentleman Jim's reputation grows, so does his ego, but in the fine scene wherein Sullivan presents Corbett with the championship belt, Corbett displays a heretofore unseen humility that finally wins the heart of the patrician woman he loves (Alexis Smith). The bout in which Corbett matches his "scientific" boxing techniques against the toe-to-toe slugging of Sullivan is particularly winning but Walsh is firmly in control throughout.

GENTLEMAN'S AGREEMENT
1947 118m bw   ★★★★
Drama   /A
FOX

Gregory Peck (Phil Green), Dorothy McGuire (Kathy), John Garfield (Dave), Celeste Holm (Anne), Anne Revere (Mrs. Green), June Havoc (Miss Wales), Albert Dekker (John Minify), Jane Wyatt (Jane), Dean Stockwell (Tommy), Sam Jaffe (Prof. Lieberman)

p, Darryl F. Zanuck; d, Elia Kazan; w, Moss Hart (based on the novel by Laura Z. Hobson); ph, Arthur Miller; ed, Harmon Jones; m, Alfred Newman; art d, Lyle Wheeler, Mark-Lee Kirk

Today, it looks like a heart on a sleeve, but GENTLEMAN'S AGREEMENT is a landmark film—Hollywood's first major attack on anti-Semitism.

Peck, in a convincing portrayal, is a magazine writer who decides to write a series of exposes on anti-Semitism. After failing to achieve an in-depth grasp of the problem, he pretends to be Jewish in order to experience the hostility of bigots first-hand. AGREEMENT surprised audiences of 1947, and it was a heroic endeavor personally sponsored by producer Zanuck (who, ironically, was one of the few Hollywood moguls who was not Jewish; in fact his 20th Century-Fox was known, in filmdom's argot, as "the goyim studio").

Garfield initially debated accepting such a small part, but on David Niven's advice, he took the role; his powerful performance shows the commitment he obviously developed during production. Despite the excellence of Peck and Garfield, though, today the finest work seems that of Holm and, in perhaps the film's most difficult part, McGuire. Shot mostly on location in New York, GENTLEMAN'S AGREEMENT remains a classic crusading film.

GENTLEMEN PREFER BLONDES
1953 91m c ★★★★
Musical /U
FOX

Jane Russell (Dorothy), Marilyn Monroe (Lorelei), Charles Coburn (Sir Francis Beekman), Elliott Reid (Malone), Tommy Noonan (Gus Esmond), George "Foghorn" Winslow (Henry Spofford III), Marcel Dalio (Magistrate), Taylor Holmes (Gus Esmond, Sr.), Norma Varden (Lady Beekman), Howard Wendell (Watson)

p, Sol C. Siegel; d, Howard Hawks; w, Charles Lederer (based on the play by Anita Loos, Joseph Fields); ph, Harry Wild (Technicolor); ed, Hugh S. Fowler; art d, Lyle Wheeler, Joseph C. Wright; fx, Ray Kellogg; chor, Jack Cole; cos, Travilla

Garish good fun. The film version of Anita Loos's Broadway musical has scrapped the 1920s plot and most of the songs. If the plot of vacationing showgirls—one out for money, the other for love—sometimes lags in director Hawks's hands, it's compensated by a genuine sentiment and sweetness, the ironic and witty use of sex-symbol stereotypes, and the reduction of males to foils for the affectionate wisecracks traded by the femme leads. Both Jane Russell and Marilyn Monroe act with the confidence of whales; it's the last time in Monroe's career you feel sure watching her work. In a way Russell steals BLONDES. She's certainly more at home in gaudy territory, and her Dorothy is loving and supervisory of Monroe's Lorelei at the same time. Certainly, BLONDES proves Russell's knockout instinct for deadpan sarcasm, rare among pin-up girls. BLONDES exploits her whole sex-symbol-as-earth-mom persona more than any of her films. An inferior sequel, GENTLEMEN MARRY BRUNETTES followed in 1955.

GEORGE WASHINGTON SLEPT HERE
1942 93m bw ★★★½
Comedy /U
WB

Jack Benny (Bill Fuller), Ann Sheridan (Connie Fuller), Charles Coburn (Uncle Stanley), Percy Kilbride (Mr. Kinsher), Hattie Mc-Daniel (Hester), William Tracy (Steve Eldridge), Joyce Reynolds (Madge), Lee Patrick (Rena Leslie), Charles Dingle (Mr. Prescott), John Emery (Clayton Evans)

p, Jerry Wald; d, William Keighley; w, Everett Freeman (based on the play by George S. Kaufman and Moss Hart); ph, Ernest Haller; ed, Ralph Dawson; art d, Max Parker

Manhattanites take to the wild country. Dating now, but amusing thanks to the chemistry between Benny and the vastly underrated Ann Sheridan, the loveliest and most sardonic straight woman ever. The Kaufman-Hart Broadway comedy has reversed the husband-wife roles, with Sheridan as the packrat who drives her conservative husband nuts—a workable premise considering Benny's penny-pinching image. Though dense with slapstick, the comedy is punctuated with belly laughs as Benny undergoes one outrage after another. One of the many priceless scenes shows Benny, Sheridan, Coburn and Kilbride trying to cheer themselves by guzzling hard cider before being thrown out of their white-elephant colonial home. Kilbride, who scores heavily with offbeat humor, renders a side-splitting reaction when he breaks his stoic silence to sing loudly and unexpectedly, "I'll Never Smile Again." If you're a Benny fan, you'll be satisfied.

GEORGY GIRL
1966 100m bw ★★★★
Comedy/Drama /15
Everglades (U.K.)

James Mason (James Leamington), Alan Bates (Jos), Lynn Redgrave (Georgy), Charlotte Rampling (Meredith), Bill Owen (Ted), Clare Kelly (Doris), Rachel Kempson (Ellen), Denise Coffey (Peg), Dorothy Alison (Health Visitor), Peggy Thorpe-Bates (Hospital Sister)

p, Otto Plaschkes, Robert A. Goldston; d, Silvio Narizzano; w, Margaret Forster, Peter Nichols (based on the novel by Forster); ph, Ken Higgins; ed, John Bloom; m, Alexander Faris; art d, Tony Woollard; chor, Marjory Sigley; cos, Mary Quant

A heart-tugger. Redgrave is Georgy, a chubby virgin in her early 20s suffering from a lack of self-esteem. Her parents are servants employed by Mason, a well-to-do married man who never sired any children. Through the years Mason has treated Redgrave like a daughter, but as she grows older his affection changes, and he eventually asks her to become his mistress. Rampling, Redgrave's sensual but patronizing roommate, announces she's pregnant by her new lover, Bates. Redgrave and Bates meet and fall in love, which spurs Rampling to declare she's going to give up the child for adoption. Redgrave will not hear of this and becomes the baby's surrogate mother. By picture's end, Redgrave is impaled on the horns of a dilemma: should she marry Bates, should she just keep the baby, or should she marry the conveniently widowed Mason and keep the baby?

Mason is wonderful as the older man, harried by a nagging, sickly wife. Redgrave shot to stardom in this role, and rightly so. She shows her range as she grows from a self-conscious, uncertain waif to a woman with responsibilities. A charming movie that aided the careers of all concerned, GEORGY GIRL was also helped by the Oscar-nominated title song, which became a hit for the Seekers on two continents.

GET CARTER
1971 111m c ★★★
Crime R/18
MGM (U.K.)

Michael Caine (Jack Carter), Ian Hendry (Eric Paice), Britt Ekland (Anna Fletcher), John Osborne (Cyril Kinnear), Tony Beckley (Peter), George Sewell (Con McCarty), Geraldine Moffatt

(Glenda), Dorothy White (Margaret), Rosemarie Dunham (Edna the Landlady), Petra Markham (Doreen Carter)

p, Michael Klinger; d, Mike Hodges; w, Mike Hodges (based on the novel Jack's Return Home by Ted Lewis); ph, Wolfgang Suschitzky (Metrocolor); ed, John Trumper; m, Roy Budd; prod d, Assheton Gorton; art d, Roger King; fx, Jack Wallis; cos, Vangie Harrison

Lean slice of well-crafted slime, and an impressive debut from director Hodges who'd impressed British television viewers with his earlier work for the BBC.

Caine is a smalltime hood from London who arrives in Newcastle to arrange his brother's funeral. While preparing for the burial, he becomes obsessed with learning who murdered his sibling and why. Seeking out his brother's friends and acquaintances, Caine tries to question them, but finds a wall of stony silence. Operating on a hunch, he follows pennyante hood Hendry to local crime lord Osborne's home and is surprised to find himself more than welcome. Before he leaves, Caine is warned to return to London before he causes any trouble. He ignores the warning, and soon attempts are made on his life. After a narrow escape, he is rescued by Osborne's girlfriend, Moffatt, and she takes him to her place. The pair make love, and, afterwards, while Moffatt is out of the room, Caine discovers a porno film starring, among others, his brother's young daughter.

Grim, violent, and stylishly directed, GET CARTER is an interesting film that brings some freshness to British crime cinema. Director Hodges immediately establishes his debt to the works of Raymond Chandler and Dashiell Hammett by showing Caine reading Chandler's Farewell My Lovely on the train to Newcastle. While Caine would like to think of himself as one of Chandler's or Hammett's lonely avengers, he is really nothing more than a vicious brute with a warped sense of honor, trapped between the past and the present.

This theme is beautifully illustrated by the milieu of the film. Newcastle is a city in transition: the urban tenements are in the process of being displaced by cold, efficient high-rise structures that symbolize the increasingly businesslike crime world that has no place for violent mavericks like Caine.

GET OUT YOUR HANDKERCHIEFS
(PREPAREZ VOS MOUCHOIRS)
1977   108m   c   ★★★½
Comedy   R/X
Ariane/C.A.P.A.C./Belga/SODEP   (France/Belgium)

Gerard Depardieu (Raoul), Patrick Dewaere (Stephane), Carole Laure (Solange), Riton (Christian Beloeil), Michel Serrault (Neighbor), Eleonore Hirt (Mrs. Beloeil), Sylvie Joly (Passerby), Jean Rougerie (Mr. Beloeil), Liliane Rovere, Michel Beaune

p, Paul Claudon; d, Bertrand Blier; w, Bertrand Blier; ph, Jean Penzer (Eastmancolor); ed, Claudine Merlin; m, Georges Delerue, Wolfgang Amadeus Mozart, Franz Schubert; art d, Eric Moulard; cos, Michele Cerf

A more civilized, less offensive version of GOING PLACES, Blier's earlier film, GET OUT YOUR HANDKERCHIEFS again pairs Depardieu and Dewaere, as childlike men who are completely emasculated by the mysterious woman in their lives.

Frustrated by his inability to make his wife (Laure) happy, Depardieu asks a complete stranger (Dewaere) to give it a try. All Laure seems to do is knit sweaters with a completely expressionless face. Dewaere is equally impotent, however, and succeeds only in establishing a close friendship with Depardieu. It takes a third "man"—Riton, a 13-year-old genius the threesome meets at the boys' summer camp that Dewaere runs—to fulfill

the unhappy woman. Laure, who has been unable to have a child with Depardieu or Dewaere, finally finds someone to love and care for, even though he is only 13.

Besides Blier's sharp direction and screenplay, the film is memorable for the performances of Depardieu and Dewaere. These two superb actors seem so in tune with one another that one must judge their performance as a synthesized whole.

GETAWAY, THE
1972   122m   c   ★★★½
Crime   PG/18
Solar/First Artists

Steve McQueen (Doc McCoy), Ali MacGraw (Carol McCoy), Ben Johnson (Jack Benyon), Sally Struthers (Fran Clinton), Al Lettieri (Rudy Butler), Slim Pickens (Cowboy), Richard Bright (Thief), Jack Dodson (Harold Clinton), Dub Taylor (Laughlin), Bo Hopkins (Frank Jackson)

p, David Foster, Mitchell Brower; d, Sam Peckinpah; w, Walter Hill (based on the novel by Jim Thompson); ph, Lucien Ballard (Todd-AO 35, Technicolor); ed, Robert Wolfe; m, Quincy Jones; art d, Ted Haworth, Angelo Graham; fx, Bud Hulburd; cos, Ray Summers

Peckinpah does Peckinpah. In one of his most hard-bitten roles, taciturn McQueen is released on a parole arranged for by his wife, MacGraw, who slept with Johnson to get the political big shot to pull the strings. He wants McQueen to lead a group of professional thieves on a bank raid, so McQueen organizes the small band, including MacGraw as a getaway driver and cocky Lettieri and Hopkins as gun-happy goons.

Through an elaborate plan, McQueen and cohorts successfully rob the Southwestern bank of $500,000, but Hopkins spoils the caper by panicking and killing a guard. When the thieves rendezvous, McQueen learns that Lettieri has murdered Hopkins. The gunman tells him, "He didn't make it. . . neither did you," as he draws a gun. McQueen has anticipated the double cross and is quicker, however, blasting several shots into Lettieri's chest. McQueen now realizes that Johnson has set him up.

This violent film, typical of Peckinpah's slam-bang action movies, relentlessly depicts ruthless robbery and murder, not to mention adultery, kidnaping, bribery, extortion, and general mayhem. The vivid direction and lightning pace, however, make the film completely fascinating as the culprits attempt to destroy each other, and the viewer finds himself actually rooting for McQueen and MacGraw, thieves though they are, hoping they'll get away. No one in this film is honorable or attractive, emphatically symbolized in one cynical Peckinpah scene in which, to escape detection, McQueen and MacGraw hide in a garbage truck and are dumped, along with their stolen loot, in a vast waste area.

Lettieri gives a wonderful study in evil, and Struthers is the ultimate repugnant tramp, obsessed with the gunman's guns and menacing manner, encouraging him to murder her husband. MacGraw is just a waste of time, having no acting ability at all and projecting the attitude of a spoiled rich girl whose Neiman-Marcus charge card has been taken away. But in retrospect, perhaps her blankness deserves another look.

GETTING IT RIGHT
1989   102m   c   ★★★½
Comedy/Drama   R/15
MCEG

Jesse Birdsall (Gavin Lamb), Helena Bonham Carter (Lady Minerva Munday), Peter Cook (Mr. Adrian), John Gielgud (Sir Gordon Munday), Shirley Ann Field (Anne), Jane Horrocks (Jenny), Judy Parfitt (Lady Stella Munday), Lynn Redgrave (Joan), Richard Huw (Harry), Pat Heywood (Mrs. Lamb)

p, Randal Kleiser, Jonathan D. Krane, Gregory Hinton; d, Randal Kleiser; w, Elizabeth Jane Howard (based on her novel); ph, Clive Tickner (Fuji Color); ed, Chris Kelly; m, Colin Towns, Steve Tyrell; prod d, Caroline Amies; art d, Frank Walsh; cos, Hazel Pethig

American director Randal Kleiser (GREASE, BIG TOP PEE-WEE) journeyed to England to film this gentle comedy adapted by Elizabeth Jane Howard from her own novel.

Jesse Birdsall stars as Gavin Lamb, a 31-year-old West End hairdresser who lives with his parents and is still a virgin, frightened of women. In the course of the film he becomes involved with, and is used and abused by, various members of the sex he fears: the neurotic, sexually profligate Lady Minerva Munday (Helen Bonham Carter); the adulterous Joan (a priceless Lynn Redgrave) who breaks up the relationship between Gavin's gay best friend, Harry (Richard Huw), and Harry's lover, Winthrop (Kevin Drinkwater); and Jenny (Jane Horrocks), a sweet young woman who works for Gavin, and with whom he falls in love.

At its heart, GETTING IT RIGHT harbors a sentimentality no different from any number of mundane television programs. Yet Howard's screenplay is so fresh and Kleiser's direction so deft that the film rises above its potentially melodramatic nature.

GETTING STRAIGHT

1970   126m   c   ★★★½
Drama   R/15
Columbia

Elliott Gould (Harry Bailey), Candice Bergen (Jan), Jeff Corey (Dr. Willhunt), Max Julien (Ellis), Robert F. Lyons (Nick), Cecil Kellaway (Dr. Kasper), Jon Lormer (Vandenburg), Leonard Stone (Lysander), William Bramley (Wade Linden), Jeannie Berlin (Judy Kramer)

p, Richard Rush; d, Richard Rush; w, Bob Kaufman (based on the novel by Ken Kolb); ph, Laszlo Kovacs (Eastmancolor); ed, Maury Winetrobe; m, Ronald Stein; art d, Sydney Z. Litwack; fx, Ira Anderson; cos, Gene Ashman

Richard Rush's stylish direction saves Kaufman's screenplay from being the overdone, often sloppy work it must have been on paper.

Gould, a returning Vietnam vet, goes back to school to secure a teaching degree. While studying in the bucolic setting he gets caught up with the lives of his fellow students, many of whom are 10 years younger than he is and light-years more naive, and also caught up in the tumult of the waning years of the 1960s. Corey, the department head, forces smart-aleck Gould to teach remedial English, a job he hates. Gould looks at teaching as a calling, but Corey sees it as a job; therein is the crux of their differences.

Gould is wonderful playing himself (and nobody does Gould better than Gould), and this is one of several films made at that time that showed off to perfection his quirky personality. The few sexual scenes are done with taste, and when it gets funny, it's very funny. It's also very dated by today's standards, a common problem when a picture is so specifically geared to be au courant. Still, as a youth picture, it towers above much of the tripe made in the 1980s.

GHOST

1990   128m   c   ★★★
Fantasy/Romance   PG-13/15
Howard W. Koch

Patrick Swayze (Sam Wheat), Demi Moore (Molly Jensen), Whoopi Goldberg (Oda Mae Brown), Tony Goldwyn (Carl Brunner), Rick Aviles (Willie Lopez), Gail Boggs (Louise Brown), Armelia McQueen (Clara Brown), Vincent Schiavelli (Subway Ghost)

p, Lisa Weinstein; d, Jerry Zucker; w, Bruce Joel Rubin; ph, Adam Greenberg; ed, Walter Murch; m, Maurice Jarre; prod d, Jane Musky; fx, Industrial Light & Magic, Richard Edlund; cos, Ruth Morley

A big sweet hit, tingly and glycerined in a phony way, but diverting. This sometimes spooky mystery-thriller-comedy-fantasy-romance focuses on loved ones who die suddenly, only to linger in spirit form, helping the mortals they have left behind. Specifically, when have-it-all yuppies Sam and Molly (Swayze and Moore) are held up, sentimental bank executive Swayze gets shot. But he finally figures out—we've seen smarter ghosts in "Casper" cartoons—that vulnerable, adorable Moore is in danger from his corrupt co-worker (Tony Goldwyn). He solicits fake medium Goldberg to help him communicate, and she discovers she's a bonafide medium after all.

GHOST manages to work despite the constant distractions of writer Bruce Joel Rubin's mishmash screenplay and Jerry Zucker's uneven direction. Zucker makes his solo debut here after co-directing AIRPLANE!, TOP SECRET and RUTHLESS PEOPLE with brother David Zucker and Jim Abrahams. His work here isn't the embarrassment that often results when a comedy director turns serious; on the contrary, Zucker shows great potential. But instead of packing GHOST with every possible gag—the hallmark of his comedy collaborations—he fills it with an array of clashing movie styles that never harmonize into a compelling whole.

Still, viewers will also find it hard not to reach for their hankies at the moment when Sam finally reveals himself in spirit form to Molly, proving that, however cluttered by extraneous characters and subplots, the theme of romantic love reaching beyond the grave, and into eternity, remains potent and pure as a cinematic conceit. Or maybe what makes this movie so appealing are all of those romantic notions plus a shirtless Patrick Swayze and a nude Demi Moore.

GHOST AND MRS. MUIR, THE

1947   104m   bw   ★★★★
Romance/Fantasy   /A
FOX

Gene Tierney (Lucy), Rex Harrison (The Ghost of Capt. Daniel Gregg), George Sanders (Miles Fairley), Edna Best (Martha), Vanessa Brown (Anna), Anna Lee (Mrs. Fairley), Robert Coote (Coombe), Natalie Wood (Anna as a Child), Isobel Elsom (Angelica), Victoria Horne (Eva)

p, Fred Kohlmar; d, Joseph L. Mankiewicz; w, Philip Dunne (based on the novel by R.A. Dick); ph, Charles Lang; ed, Dorothy Spencer; m, Bernard Herrmann; art d, Richard Day, George W. Davis; fx, Fred Sersen; cos, Oleg Cassini

Wonderful fantasy-romance, in which beautiful widow Lucy (Gene Tierney) buys a remote coastal home that was once occupied by a dashing merchant captain. Shortly after Lucy moves in with her little daughter, Anna (Natalie Wood), she encounters some strange doings, but is not alarmed even though her neighbors have already warned the headstrong woman that the cottage is haunted. Lucy is more curious than apprehensive and she demands that the ghost (Rex Harrison) reveal himself. He does, in all his handsome, bearded glory, and not only befriends Lucy and her daughter, but falls in love with the lovely lady.

This fragile story would immediately collapse into implausibility were it not for the wonderful chemistry between Harrison and Tierney. In this, his second American film, Harrison is superb as the sharp-tongued, affectionate ghost and Tierney shines as his earthbound object of love. Bernard Herrmann's score is both whimsical and full of otherworldly lyricism. Remade in 1955 as STRANGER IN THE NIGHT.

GHOST BREAKERS, THE

1940 83m bw   ★★★½
Comedy
Paramount

Bob Hope *(Larry Lawrence)*, Paulette Goddard *(Mary Carter)*, Richard Carlson *(Geoff Montgomery)*, Paul Lukas *(Parada)*, Willie Best *(Alex)*, Pedro de Cordoba *(Havez)*, Virginia Brissac *(Mother Zombie)*, Noble Johnson *(The Zombie)*, Anthony Quinn *(Ramon/Francisco Maderos)*, Tom Dugan *(Raspy Kelly)*

p, Arthur Hornblow, Jr.; d, George Marshall; w, Walter DeLeon (based on the play by Paul Dickey, Charles Goddard); ph, Charles Lang; ed, Ellsworth Hoagland; m, Ernst Toch; art d, Hans Dreier, Robert Usher; fx, Farciot Edouart

Looking for a follow-up to its successful Bob Hope-Paulette Goddard comedy thriller THE CAT AND THE CANARY, Paramount dusted off an old-haunted house film called THE GHOST BREAKERS that had been made twice in the silent days—once in 1914 with H.B. Warner, and again in 1922 with Wallace Reid. The result was a stylish, frequently funny little scare show that was even better than CANARY.

Larry Lawrence (Hope) is a radio commentator known for his crime exposes (obviously inspired by Walter Winchell) who inadvertently becomes involved with a murder and winds up in Havana after hiding in a steamer trunk owned by Mary Carter (Goddard). A romance soon develops between Mary and Larry, and they both become worried when they are greeted by repeated warnings that the house she has inherited is haunted.

Though really a comedy, THE GHOST BREAKERS has its fair share of effective and spooky horror scenes, directed with an atmospheric flavor by Marshall. The balance between humor and fright is expertly handled, making the film a pleasure to watch. Remade in 1953 as SCARED STIFF with Dean Martin and Jerry Lewis.

GHOST GOES WEST, THE

1936 85m bw   ★★★★
Fantasy/Comedy   /U
London Films   (U.K.)

Robert Donat *(Murdoch/Donald Glourie)*, Jean Parker *(Peggy Martin)*, Eugene Pallette *(Joe Martin)*, Elsa Lanchester *(Lady Shepperton)*, Ralph Bunker *(Ed Bigelow)*, Patricia Hilliard *(Shepherdess)*, Everley Gregg *(Gladys Martin)*, Morton Selten *(Gavin Glourie)*, Dorothy "Chili" Bouchier *(Cleopatra)*, Mark Daly *(Groom)*

p, Alexander Korda; d, Rene Clair; w, Robert E. Sherwood, Rene Clair, Geoffrey Kerr (based on the story "Sir Tristram Goes West" by Eric Keown); ph, Harold Rosson; ed, Harold Earle-Fishbacher, Henry Cornelius; m, Mischa Spoliansky; prod d, Vincent Korda; fx, Ned Mann; cos, Rene Hubert, John Armstrong

This was the first English-language film for French master director Rene Clair, and it proved a winner. The story begins in 18th-century Scotland where Robert Donat, as the head of a clan, is insulted by another laird just before he can remedy the stain upon his stiff honor. His modern-day descendant, also played by Donat, is trying to maintain the sprawling family castle but is going broke, his creditors waiting for him behind every door. Salvation arrives in the form of loud, acquisitive Eugene Pallette, whose pretty daughter Jean Parker immediately falls for Donat. Pallette has the castle transported to the US and rebuilds it stone by stone on his vast Florida estate. Parker and Donat—he goes along with the castle as caretaker—are eyeing the altar, but matters become complicated when it's discovered that the ghost of Donat's lookalike ancestor has also made the journey to Florida and is haunting everyone in sight.

Clair's light comedic touch is everywhere in a film loaded with the screwball comedy which was so popular in the 1930s. At one point Clair considered removing his name from the credits—producer Korda frequently interrupted the shooting of the film to make changes—but enough of his imprint remained to cause him to reconsider. US audiences took the stereotype of American materialism good-naturedly and made the film a hit.

GHOSTBUSTERS

1984 107m c   ★★★½
Comedy/Science Fiction   PG
Columbia

Bill Murray *(Dr. Peter Venkman)*, Dan Aykroyd *(Dr. Raymond Stantz)*, Sigourney Weaver *(Dana Barrett)*, Harold Ramis *(Dr. Egon Spenler)*, Rick Moranis *(Louis Tully)*, Annie Potts *(Janine Melnitz)*, William Atherton *(Walter Peck)*, Ernie Hudson *(Winston Zeddmore)*, David Margulies *(Mayor)*, Steven Tash

p, Ivan Reitman; d, Ivan Reitman; w, Dan Aykroyd, Harold Ramis; ph, Laszlo Kovacs, Herb Wagreitch (Panavision, Metrocolor); ed, Sheldon Kahn, David Blewitt; m, Elmer Bernstein; prod d, John DeCuir; art d, John DeCuir, Jr., John J. Moore; fx, Richard Edlund, John Bruno, Mark Vargo, Chuck Gaspar; cos, Theoni V. Aldredge

An enormously successful movie that owes much to many less successful ones that preceded it, GHOSTBUSTERS is an all-star big-budget hybrid of pictures as diverse as SPOOK CHASERS, SPOOK BUSTERS, GHOST CATCHERS and countless others. The difference between those films and GHOSTBUSTERS is that the latter had a huge special-effects budget and the presence of Bill Murray, whose irreverent personality makes the whole thing work.

Murray, Dan Aykroyd, and Harold Ramis play a trio of New York City parapsychologists who set up their own "ghost-busting" shop—not unlike exterminators—in a downtown building, complete with a bored secretary (Annie Potts). For a fee, the trio will rid homes or places of business of supernatural residents. They are hired by Dana Barrett (Sigourney Weaver), a symphony cellist who lives in a spectacular apartment above Central Park where strange things have been happening. After capturing a large, gooey, green ghost and experiencing several other weird occurrences, the busters determine that the apartment building was built by a Sumerian devil cult and that the site is actually the doorway to the spirit world.

Originally planned as an Aykroyd-John Belushi vehicle, the picture was rewritten after Belushi's untimely death, giving Murray's character the emphasis—and it is Murray's movie all the way. With his deadpan delivery and snide quips, Murray more than holds his own amid the myriad state-of-the-art special effects. An inferior sequel, GHOSTBUSTERS II, was released in 1989.

GIANT

1956 201m c ★★★★
Drama /PG
WB

Elizabeth Taylor (Leslie Benedict), Rock Hudson (Bick Benedict), James Dean (Jett Rink), Carroll Baker (Luz Benedict II), Jane Withers (Vashti Snythe), Chill Wills (Uncle Bawley), Mercedes McCambridge (Luz Benedict), Sal Mineo (Angel Obregon II), Dennis Hopper (Jordan Benedict III), Judith Evelyn (Mrs. Horace Lynnton)

p, George Stevens, Henry Ginsberg; d, George Stevens; w, Fred Guiol, Ivan Moffat (based on the novel by Edna Ferber); ph, William Mellor (Warner Color); ed, William Hornbeck, Fred Bohanan, Philip W. Anderson; m, Dimitri Tiomkin; prod d, Boris Leven; cos, Marjorie Best, Moss Mabry

Like the title says. Based on Edna Ferber's sprawling novel, GIANT covers two generations of Texas rivalry, spear-headed by Hudson, in his best performance, and Dean, in a performance that defies description. Hudson marries Virginia belle Taylor and transplants her to Texas, where she must learn to adapt herself to the harsher culture of her husband's huge cattle empire. Dean is an outcast who strikes oil and whose financial empire grows to rival Hudson's, even as he nurses a lifelong broken heart over Taylor.

This was the last role in Dean's all-too-brief career—he was dead when the film was released—and his presence ran away with the film. He performs his role in the overwrought method manner of the era, and the rest of the cast seems to be split between awe of his talent and disgust over his indulgence. He's a strange spectacle indeed as he ages, like a Howard Hughes burlesque that doesn't quite come off. Still he works well early on opposite Taylor, as does Hudson, who more or less leads the rest of the cast in the conventional style of presentational acting. GIANT confirms Taylor's skills as an actress; she's entirely believable even when she ages by just having her hair greyed.

Director Stevens encouraged a feeling for animosity between Dean and Hudson and irritated Taylor with his endless retakes and chatter about how he wished original choice Grace Kelly had been available; this made for lively filming. The result strains for prestige but considering its length moves along at a considerable clip, due to Ferber's narrative prowess more than anything else.

GIDGET

1959 95m c ★★½
Comedy /U
Columbia

Sandra Dee (Francie), James Darren (Moondoggie), Cliff Robertson (Kahoona), Arthur O'Connell (Russell Lawrence), Mary LaRoche (Dorothy Lawrence), Joby Baker (Stinky), Tom Laughlin (Lover Boy), Sue George (B.L.), Robert Ellis (Hot Shot), Jo Morrow (Mary Lou)

p, Lewis J. Rachmil; d, Paul Wendkos; w, Gabrielle Upton (based on the novel by Frederick Kohner); ph, Burnett Guffey (CinemaScope, Eastmancolor); ed, William Lyon; m, M.W. Stoloff; art d, Ross Bellah

Watch at risk. Sugar-posioning, with the unctous Dee, as the all-American pertly perky happy-go-brainless model for countless teenagers in the late 1950s—today that seems scary. Dee plays Gidget (a nickname meaning "girl midget"), a whiny youngster who doesn't quite measure up to the chesty, bikinied girls on the beach. Her mom's reassurances come true when the two grooviest surfers in town, Moondoggie (James Darren) and Kahoona (Cliff Robertson), start paying Gidget some attention. Dee had just appeared in Douglas Sirk's IMITATION OF LIFE, and Robertson had turned in a commendable performance in AUTUMN LEAVES. Also hanging ten was Tom Laughlin, who much later made BILLY JACK. Inbred sequels followed, and two horrifying television series.

GIG, THE

1985 92m c ★★★★
Comedy/Drama /15
The Gig Company

Wayne Rogers (Marty Flynn), Cleavon Little (Marshall Wilson), Andrew Duncan (Jack Larmon), Daniel Nalbach (Arthur Winslow), Jerry Matz (Aaron Wohl), Warren Vache (Gil Macrae), Joe Silver (Abe Mitgang), Jay Thomas (Rick Valentine), Stan Lachow (George), Celia Bressack (Lucy)

p, Norman I. Cohen; d, Frank D. Gilroy; w, Frank D. Gilroy; ph, Jeri Sopanen (Duart Color); ed, Rick Shaine

Well done. For several years, six men have played music once a week, just for their own enjoyment. Wayne Rogers is a car dealer who handles the slide trombone; Jerry Matz is a clarinet teacher with an expanded view of his own talents; Daniel Nalbach is the drum-playing dentist who lives with his carping mother; Warren Vache is a superb trumpeter who gave up a musical career when he sold out to marry Susan Egbert, the daughter of a wealthy real estate man; Stan Lachow is a quiet man who slaps bass; and Andrew Duncan is a corporate type who comes to life only when he plunks the piano. Rogers learns about a two-week gig available at a Catskill Mountain resort and proposes they take the job so they can feel as if they have become professionals. THE GIG is amusing throughout and creates occasional guffaws. The characters are all beautifully etched, and the story is engaging. It doesn't have one false note.

GIGI

1958 116m c ★★★½
Musical /PG
MGM

Leslie Caron (Gigi), Maurice Chevalier (Honore Lachaille), Louis Jourdan (Gaston Lachaille), Hermione Gingold (Mme Alvarez), Eva Gabor (Liane D'Exelmans), Jacques Bergerac (Sandomir), Isabel Jeans (Aunt Alicia), John Abbott (Manuel), Monique Van Vooren (Showgirl), Lydia Stevens (Simone)

p, Arthur Freed; d, Vincente Minnelli; w, Alan Jay Lerner (based on the play Gigi by Anita Loos, from the novel by Colette); ph, Joseph Ruttenberg, Ray June (CinemaScope, Metrocolor); ed, Adrienne Fazan; m, Frederick Loewe; prod d, Cecil Beaton; art d, William A. Horning, Preston Ames; cos, Cecil Beaton

Overbaked but enjoyable, and a banquet for the eyes, thanks to the visual wonder of the Minnelli-Beaton teaming. But contemporary critics have long objected that Frederick Loewe and Allan Jay Lerner simply reworked their milestone My Fair Lady. To an extent, that's true; certainly the score is a rather vapid one. Based on the Colette novel, GIGI followed in the footsteps of a 1950 French film adaptation of the story and a 1951 straight dramatic production that starred Audrey Hepburn on Broadway.

The story concerns a waif (Leslie Caron), who lives in turn-of-the-century Paris with her grandmother, Mme Alvarez (Hermione Gingold), who, along with Gigi's Aunt Alicia (Isabel

Jeans), seeks to transform the young woman into a courtesan so she can become the mistress of Gaston Lachaille (Louis Jourdan), wealthy heir to a sugar fortune. At first, Gaston is content to accept Gigi as his mistress; then he realizes he truly loves the beauty and is determined to marry her, throwing Mme Alvarez for a loop since the family tradition is to be a kept woman, not a wife. Ultimately, however, Mme Alvarez, who was once the mistress of Gaston's uncle, Honore (Maurice Chevalier), agrees to allow her granddaughter to marry.

Caron—never the most effortless of waifs—had played the role of Gigi in the London production of the straight stageplay, and here leads the cast (she's dubbed by Betty Wand) in a contest to see who can be the most French. The winner is Chevalier, in a performance that makes one feel as if you're gagging on pastry. The exceptions: Gingold and Jeans. Perhaps if the sweetness of GIGI was contrasted with elements of honest vulgarity, the picture could balance itself out. Considering the aspects of the courtesan life, the opportunity is there, but as it is we are left to make do with Eva Gabor's continental suggestions; she's too docile to inhabit her role.

Ten minutes into the movie, you've resolved the plot and are left to wallow in lovely frou-frou. Produced in the City of Light, GIGI makes wonderful use of the usual Parisian landmarks, and benefits from extraordinary period costumes and sets.

GILDA
1946 110m bw   ★★★★
Drama   /PG
Columbia
***
Rita Hayworth (Gilda), Glenn Ford (Johnny Farrell), George Macready (Ballin Mundson), Joseph Calleia (Obregon), Steven Geray (Uncle Pio), Joe Sawyer (Casey), Gerald Mohr (Capt. Delgado), Robert Scott (Gabe Evans), Ludwig Donath (German), Don Douglas (Thomas Langford)

p, Virginia Van Upp; d, Charles Vidor; w, Marion Parsonnet (based on Jo Eisinger's adaptation of E.A. Ellington's original story); ph, Rudolph Mate; ed, Charles Nelson; m, Hugo Friedhofer; art d, Stephen Goosson, Van Nest Polglase; chor, Jack Cole; cos, Jean Louis
***
Hayworth at her peak. Rita is the main reason to see GILDA, bringing her blue-moon beauty and star presence to Hollywood's definitive kept-woman role. GILDA proves Hayworth had a neat line: she wasn't as erotic as Dietrich or Ava Gardner, nor as suggestive as Harlow and Monroe. What she was, specifically, was provocative like no actress before or since.

The torrid, turgid plot of this myth of misogyny needn't be dwelled on in depth. Ford gets hired to play goon by Teutonic casino owner Macready. His duties include bringing to heel the duplicitous Hayworth, even to slapping her around. The triangle becomes a sicko menage a trois; surely Ford's character is the most sexually ambiguous leading man ever. He's only interested in asserting dominance and muscle, and both Hayworth and Macready enjoy taunting him—GILDA's dialogue fairly snakes with euphemism and innuendo. Critics remained indifferent to the film, but returning GIs flocked with their wives and sweethearts to see Columbia's "love goddess," who accented her role with such lines as: "If I had been a ranch they would have called me the Bar *Nothing*!" When Hayworth reprises a few bars of "Put the Blame on Mame," is she herself singing or not? This remains a famous guessing game with film buffs. Otherwise she's amazingly dubbed by Anita Ellis.

Cohn spared no expense in the production, and choreographer Cole lavished Hayworth with dances patterned after those of a professional stripper he had known. These numbers were brought into the production long after director Vidor began shooting, which indicates the haphazard fashion in which this film was shaped. It was Hayworth's film from the beginning; Vidor began shooting the story before Ford was actually signed and joined the production. The original story was written exclusively for Hayworth by producer Van Upp, named to oversee the production by Cohn himself.

Van Upp was later blamed by Hayworth for establishing a sex goddess no woman could ever hope to be in reality. When she had problems with Aly Khan, Hayworth told Van Upp: "It's all your fault. You wrote GILDA. And every man I've known has fallen in love with Gilda and wakened with me." GILDA is an erotic landmark to be especially considered today, when erotic thrillers dominate the boxoffice and television screens.

GIRL CRAZY
1943 97m bw   ★★★★
Musical/Comedy   /U
MGM
***
Mickey Rooney (Danny Churchill, Jr.), Judy Garland (Ginger Gray), Gil Stratton (Bud Livermore), Robert Strickland (Henry Lathrop), Rags Ragland (Rags), June Allyson (Specialty), Nancy Walker (Polly Williams), Guy Kibbee (Dean Phineas Armour), Tommy Dorsey and His Band (Themselves), Frances Rafferty (Marjorie Tait)

p, Arthur Freed; d, Norman Taurog; w, Fred Finklehoffe, Dorothy Kingsley, Sid Silvers, William Ludwig (based on the play by George Gershwin, Ira Gershwin, Guy Bolton, Jack McGowan); ph, William Daniels, Robert Planck; ed, Albert Akst; art d, Cedric Gibbons; chor, Charles Walters, Busby Berkeley
***
Irresistible entertainment, based on the play by Guy Bolton and Jack McGowan, with music by George and Ira Gershwin. Rooney stars as Danny Churchill, Jr., the rich son of a newspaper publisher (Henry O'Neill). He's sent to an all-boys mining school where wake-up time is 6 a.m., which is usually the hour he goes to sleep. Stuck out in the desert, Danny finds it hard to exercise his girl-craziness, until he meets Ginger Gray (Garland, looking quite delectable), the granddaughter of the school's dean (Guy Kibbee). Although Danny originally hates the school, his love for Ginger eventually prompts him to help save the financially imperiled institution with a musical rodeo.

The movie was originally to be directed by Busby Berkeley, but he and MGM musical maven Roger Edens didn't get along. And Garland's loathing of him was monumental; it stands to reason his power would be compromised as she ascended to queen of the MGM lot. But since *Girl Crazy* had been a big hit for Ethel Merman on Broadway, Berkeley was brought in to stage Garland's white-buckskinned finale of "I Got Rhythm," Merman's big hit. The rest of the musical work went to Charles Walters. Other songs included are "Embraceable You," "Fascinating Rhythm" and the sadly beautiful "But Not for Me," all by the Gershwins, and Edens's "Happy Birthday, Ginger."

GIRL FROM HAVANA, THE
1929 65m bw   ★★★★
Crime
Fox Films
***
Lola Lane (Joan Anders), Paul Page (Allan Grant), Kenneth Thomson (William Dane), Natalie Moorhead (Lona Martin), Warren Hymer (Spike Howard), Joseph Girard (Dougherty), Adele Windsor

(Babe Hanson), Marcia Chapman (Sally Green), Dorothy Brown (Toots Nolan), Juan Sedillo (Detective)

d, Ben Stoloff; w, John Stone, Edwin Burke

An excellent, suspenseful early talkie with decent dialogue, this picture features one of the all-time great theft sequences. A clerk in a jewelry store, Paul Page, bravely defends the patrons by leaping to attack a frothy-mouthed "mad" dog that has wandered into the posh establishment. Wrestling the apparently rabid pooch to a standstill, the heroic pearl peddler finds himself roundly upbraided by the store's manager when it is discovered that a number of valuable trinkets have vanished. The occupants of the establishment are searched, but to no avail; the gems have jetted.

Next, we find the intrepid ex-clerk aboard an ocean liner bound for Cuba, with his one-time jewelry patrons Kenneth Thomson and Natalie Moorhead, principals in the gem-theft ring. The pooch reappears; the missing bracelets had been stuffed by Page into a pouch worn by the "rabid" mutt. But female detective Lola Lane has boarded also, hot on the trail of the trio and their goons. murdered his father. After a brisk battle, the clever crooks are caught, their venture comes to naught, lovers Lane and Page unite, and all is well. Neat.

GIRL IN WHITE, THE

1952 92m bw   ★★★
Biography   /U
MGM

June Allyson (Dr. Emily Barringer), Arthur Kennedy (Dr. Ben Barringer), Gary Merrill (Dr. Seth Pawling), Mildred Dunnock (Dr. Marie Yeomans), Jesse White (Alec), Marilyn Erskine (Nurse Jane Doe), Herbert Anderson (Dr. Barclay), Gar Moore (Dr. Graham), Don Keefer (Dr. Williams), Ann Tyrrell (Nurse Bigley)

p, Armand Deutsch; d, John Sturges; w, Irmgard Von Cube, Allen Vincent, Philip Stevenson (based on the book Bowery to Bellevue by Emily Dunning Barringer); ph, Paul C. Vogel; ed, Ferris Webster; m, David Raksin; art d, Cedric Gibbons, Leonid Vasian

Ho-hum. Period biography of Emily Dunning Barringer, THE GIRL IN WHITE depicts her struggle to join the male-dominated medical profession as a doctor in 1902. Related in a semidocumentary style, the film follows Emily (Allyson) through medical school to New York's Bellevue Hospital. Whoever cast Allyson should have been interred there. A large portion of the film concentrates on the ins and outs of medicine at the turn of the century, which may add to the picture's verisimilitude but does little to enhance its entertainment value.

GIRL WITH GREEN EYES

1964 91m bw   ★★★½
Drama   /PG
Woodfall (U.K.)

Peter Finch (Eugene Gaillard), Rita Tushingham (Kate Brady), Lynn Redgrave (Baba Brenan), Marie Kean (Josie Hannigan), Arthur O'Sullivan (Mr. Brady), Julian Glover (Malachi Sullivan), T.P. McKenna (Priest), Lislott Goettinger (Joanna), Patrick Laffan (Bertie Counihan), Eileen Crowe (Mrs. Byrne)

p, Oscar Lewenstein; d, Desmond Davis; w, Edna O'Brien (based on her novel The Lonely Girl); ph, Manny Wynn; ed, Anthony Gibbs, Brian Smedley-Aston; m, John Addison; art d, Ted Marshall

Memorable and sentimental "women's picture" adapted by Edna O'Brien from her own novel. Filmed in and around Dublin, GIRL WITH GREEN EYES tells the story of a young woman, Rita Tushingham, who leaves her father's barren farm in County Clare to come to Dublin where she gets a job in a grocery and shares a flat with Redgrave, an old pal from Catholic school. She meets Finch, a divorced writer many years older than she. She pursues him, they become friends, and she moves into his home.

Despite their propinquity and the underlying attraction, she remains chaste due to a combination of youth, shyness and her religious upbringing. When her father, O'Sullivan, learns that she's living with a man, he forces her to return home. Her priest, McKenna, rebukes her for her lax behavior, and she leaves home again and goes to Finch's place. She's tailed by O'Sullivan and a horde of his besotted buddies. They break into Finch's house, only to flee when Finch points his aged shotgun at them. Tushingham finally relents and sleeps with Finch.

Originally titled "Once Upon A Summer," the film featured several of the best Irish actors. All the roles were well played, and the dialogue smacked of Irish reality, though occasionally it is a trifle stilted for the American ear. There is lots to recommend this film, including first-time direction by Desmond Davis and the debut photography of Manny Wynn. Turner, Finch's real-life wife, does an excellent cameo as a bitch. It was Redgrave's second film for Richardson, the first having been TOM JONES. Lovingly made, it's a fine introduction to the Ireland of lyrical romance, rather than the strife-torn area we see so often.

GIRLFRIENDS

1978 86m c   ★★★
Comedy/Drama   PG/AA
Cyclops

Melanie Mayron (Susan Weinblatt), Anita Skinner (Anne Munroe), Eli Wallach (Rabbi Gold), Christopher Guest (Eric), Bob Balaban (Martin), Gina Rogak (Julie), Amy Wright (Ceil), Viveca Lindfors (Beatrice), Mike Kellin (Abe), Jean De Baer (Terry)

p, Claudia Weill, Jan Saunders; d, Claudia Weill; w, Vicki Polon (based on a story by Polon and Weill); ph, Fred Murphy (DuArt Color); ed, Suzanne Pettit; m, Michael Small; art d, Patrizia von Brandenstein

A refreshing little film that marked the directorial debut of Weill, GIRLFRIENDS strips away the pretentiousness of so many small movies and offers us a real look at real people. Weill spent many years as a documentarian; she uses her experience and her ear and eye for realism to present us with an episodic story that mixes comedy and poignancy with excellent results.

Mayron is a chubby Jewish photographer whose roommate, Skinner, is leaving to get married. Mayron must now go it alone and contemplates her life, new insecurities, and cellulite. Mayron is so good in the role that she seems closer to "being" her part than acting it. Not unlike SHEILA LEVINE IS DEAD AND LIVING IN NEW YORK, this character study of a certain type of urban Jewish woman never hits a false note. As Mayron's boyfriend, Balaban is depicted as likable and believable, an honest human being with honest problems. Mayron flirts with Wallach, a rabbi, and almost has a fling with him, but she winds up as the house photographer doing weddings and bar mitzvahs. It's unsentimental, emotional, and made with great affection.

GIVEN WORD, THE
(O PAGADOR DE PROMESSAS)
1964 98m bw   ★★½
Religious
Oswaldo Massaini (Brazil)

Leonardo Vilar *(Ze)*, Gloria Menezes *(Rosa)*, Dionisio Azevedo *(Father Olavo)*, Norma Bengell *(Marli)*, Geraldo d'el Rey *(Bonitao/"Handsome")*, Roberto Ferreira *(Dede)*, Othon Bastos *(Reporter)*, Gilberto Marques *(Galego)*, Carlos Torres *(Monsignor)*, Antonio L. Sampaio *(Coca)*

p, Oswaldo Massaini; d, Anselmo Duarte; w, Anselmo Duarte (based on the story by Alfredo Dias Gomes); ph, Chick Fowle; ed, Carlos Coimbra; m, Gabriel Migliori; art d, Jose Teixeira de Araujo; fx, Josef Reindl

Effective depiction of the creation of a martyr from a lowly peasant. Vilar plays the peasant who only intends to place a large wooden cross on a church altar after traveling to a nearby village when his donkey is saved from death, but soon finds himself the focus of great commotion when the church refuses to accept his cross. An Academy Award nominee for Best Foreign Language Film in 1962.

GLASS KEY, THE
1935 80m bw   ★★★
Mystery/Political   /A
Paramount

George Raft *(Ed Beaumont)*, Claire Dodd *(Janet Henry)*, Edward Arnold *(Paul Madvig)*, Rosalind Keith *(Opal Madvig)*, Ray Milland *(Taylor Henry)*, Robert Gleckler *(Shad O'Rory)*, Guinn "Big Boy" Williams *(Jeff)*, Tammany Young *(Clarkie)*, Harry Tyler *(Henry Sloss)*, Charles Wilson *(Farr)*

p, E. Lloyd Sheldon; d, Frank Tuttle; w, Kathryn Scola, Kubec Glasmon, Harry Ruskin (based on the novel by Dashiell Hammett); ph, Henry Sharp; ed, Hugh Bennett

Dashiell Hammett's hard-nosed novel about political corruption saw a solid production in its first film outing. Raft is a close-mouthed henchman of political bigshot Arnold, who always does the boss's bidding—right up to the brink of death. Arnold makes a deal with crooked senator Richman which Raft thinks will end in disaster. Kingmaker Arnold agrees to help Richman get re-elected. Inexplicably, Arnold gets religion, abandons his corrupt ways, and uses his contacts to close down a notorious gambling casino run by Gleckler. Crime boss Gleckler is not happy with this move and, in retaliation, murders Richman's playboy son, Milland, who's been going with Arnold's daughter, Keith, and then frames Arnold for the slaying. Raft goes to the rescue, taking on Gleckler's goons to find the real killer.

For his pains, he's beaten to a pulp by Williams in one of the most brutal scenes in film history, a sado-masochistic ritual that amazingly made it past the 1935 censors. The plot lags a bit in the film's second half, but Raft makes an expert thug of few words; he's bolstered by Arnold, especially before the latter's character goes soft. This was a money-maker for author Hammett who was paid a then substantial $25,000 for the rights to film his novel. But the definitive version is the 1942 remake.

GLASS KEY, THE
1942 85m bw   ★★★★
Mystery/Political   /A
Paramount

Brian Donlevy *(Paul Madvig)*, Veronica Lake *(Janet Henry)*, Alan Ladd *(Ed Beaumont)*, Bonita Granville *(Opal Madvig)*, Richard Denning *(Taylor Henry)*, Joseph Calleia *(Nick Vama)*, William Bendix *(Jeff)*, Frances Gifford *(Nurse)*, Donald MacBride *(Farr)*, Margaret Hayes *(Eloise Matthews)*

p, Fred Kohlmar; d, Stuart Heisler; w, Jonathan Latimer (based on the novel by Dashiell Hammett); ph, Theodor Sparkuhl; ed, Archie Marshek; m, Victor Young; art d, Hans Dreier, Haldane Douglas

This film of Dashiell Hammett's tale of political corruption and murder is slightly better than the 1935 version, profiting from a bigger budget, stellar casting, and a zippier pace, thanks to Johnathan Latimer's taut screenplay.

Donlevy is accused of murder, solicits aid of henchman Ladd to clear his name. Memorable, chilling sado-masochism of Bendix repeatedly beating Ladd is typical of the unorthodox undertow of sexual currents snaking through the plot. Ladd's character seems equally committed to Donlevy and the mysterious, cyclopean Lake, at one point confiding he'd let the latter hang if it served his purpose. Despite the copout ending, Ladd's deadpan toughens his character up, serving up partial compensation. As usual, the Ladd-Lake slow-burn chemistry, deceptive in it's offhandedness, is a pleasurable contrast to all the over-stoked new wave *noir* interpretations currently flourishing.

This film was put into production before the release of THIS GUN FOR HIRE, which featured an electric performance from Ladd and made him Paramount's newest star. But Bendix nearly steals the film as the scary but pathetic henchman whose only joy in life is to administer sadistic beatings. According to Beverly Linet in *Ladd: A Hollywood Tragedy*, in one scene calling for Bendix's character to beat up Ladd's, the the rugged six-footer slipped and struck the 5-foot-5-inch Ladd square on the jaw, knocking him out. Director Heisler, never one to let a convincing scene go unrecorded, ordered the shot printed and it appears in the film.

GLASS MENAGERIE, THE
1987 135m c   ★★★★
Drama   PG
Cineplex Odeon

Joanne Woodward *(Amanda)*, John Malkovich *(Tom)*, Karen Allen *(Laura)*, James Naughton *(Gentleman Caller)*

p, Burtt Harris; d, Paul Newman; w, (based on the play by Tennessee Williams); ph, Michael Ballhaus (DuArt Color); ed, David Ray; m, Henry Mancini; prod d, Tony Walton; cos, Tony Walton

The third and best of the filmed versions of martyrs and dead magnolias. Directed by Paul Newman, the Tennessee Williams classic is painstakingly faithful to the play and features extraordinary performances from all the actors. Tom (John Malkovich) is the story's narrator and sets the scene for the "memory play" by introducing the characters. Tom himself is a poet who works in a warehouse to support his family but who longs for escape. Amanda (Joanne Woodward) is his mother, a Southern belle who forsook her genteel background to marry a telephone man who eventually left his family. Laura (Karen Allen) is his sister, the victim of a childhood disease that left one leg shorter than the other, though she is even more crippled by shyness. Finally, there is the gentleman caller (James Naughton), Tom's coworker at the warehouse. While Laura is engrossed in the world of the fragile glass figurines that she collects, Amanda is concerned with finding a husband for her and asks Tom's help.

Newman has said that he approached THE GLASS MENAGERIE less as a filmmaker than as an archivist, and his version is, in essence, a filmed stage play. It is something of a cliche to give a filmed play a claustrophobic feel, but THE GLASS MENAGERIE and its trapped characters cry out for such a treatment and Newman has effectively evoked it. Newman lets the actors and Williams's poetic language do the work. All of the performances are superb. Woodward's delightful Amanda is full of contradictions and Malkovich's Tom is a product of frustration, romantic dreams and guilt. Allen is a surprising revelation, as her previous film roles have asked so little of her. Here she plumbs emotions of considerable depth, and is entirely capable of rationalizing her character's retreat from reality.

GLENN MILLER STORY, THE

1953 115m c   ★★★★
Musical/Biography   /U
Universal

James Stewart (Glenn Miller), June Allyson (Helen Burger Miller), Charles Drake (Don Haynes), George Tobias (Si Schribman), Harry Morgan (Chummy MacGregor), Marion Ross (Polly Haynes), Irving Bacon (Mr. Miller), Kathleen Lockhart (Mrs. Miller), Barton MacLane (Gen. Arnold), Sig Rumann (Mr. Krantz)

p, Aaron Rosenberg; d, Anthony Mann; w, Valentine Davies, Oscar Brodney; ph, William Daniels (Technicolor); ed, Russell Schoengarth; m, Joseph Gershenson (adaptation, Henry Mancini); chor, Kenny Williams

Unlike so many film bios, this is an honest, intelligent depiction of one of America's greatest musical influences and doesn't merely string together a series of hit tunes and gratuitous scenes. But oh, what music!

James Stewart is Glenn Miller, a bright young man with a love for the trombone and a desire to create music. At the University of Colorado he falls for Helen Burger (June Allyson, at her charming best, and a perfect match for Stewart); then, after graduation, he goes to work for Ben Pollack (playing himself) and later has a gig in the pit of a Broadway show. On their wedding night, Helen is shocked to find her husband in a jam session in Harlem with Gene Krupa and Louis Armstrong. Later, in Boston, at the dance hall run by Si Schribman (George Tobias), Miller refines his art, stumbling upon his signature sound when his trumpet player splits his lip, forcing the clarinetist to play lead on "Moonlight Serenade."

Although Stewart learned how to handle the trombone, the actual playing was dubbed by Murray MacEachern and Joe Yukl, who are great on such Miller classics as "In the Mood" "Tuxedo Junction" and "Little Brown Jug." All that's missing from this well-crafted film is Tex Beneke, the "boy singer" for Miller's band, who went on to lead it after his mentor's death. Look for the great Frances Langford really doing her thing.

GLORIA

1980 123m c   ★★★½
Crime   R/PG
Columbia

Gena Rowlands (Gloria Swenson), Juan Adames (Philip Dawn), Buck Henry (Jack Dawn), Julie Carmen (Jeri Dawn), Lupe Guarnica (Margarita Vargas), Jessica Castillo (Joan Dawn), Tony Knesich (1st Man/Gangster), Filomena Spagnuolo (Old Lady), Tom Noonan (2nd Man/Gangster), Gregory Cleghorne (Kid in Elevator)

p, John Cassavetes; d, John Cassavetes; w, John Cassavetes; ph, Fred Schuler; ed, Jack McSweeney; m, Bill Conti; prod d, Rene D'Auriac, Fred Schuler; cos, Peggy Farrell

Under the masterful direction of husband John Cassavetes, Gena Rowlands delivers a gutsy, spellbinding performance in this excellent crime film.

Rowlands is the title character, a woman in her 40s who lives alone with her cats and her savings, compiled by turning tricks with high-placed mobsters. Her life is thrown into turmoil when her neighbor, Mafia accountant Jack Dawn (Buck Henry), and his family are exterminated by the mob. Their eight-year-old son Philip (Juan Adames), whom the Dawns left in Gloria's care, is the only survivor and it's then up to Gloria to protect the boy from mob hit men.

Rowlands is brilliant as the apprehensive woman who finds in herself the courage to defy an evil system and fight it to a bloody standstill. Adames contributes a fascinating portrayal of the boy who becomes uncannily adult in the pressurized situation. Cassavetes's direction is incisive while maintaining a chillingly brisk pace, marvelously supported by cinematographer Fred Schuler's fluid camerawork and penetrating closeups of the hunted pair. Too long by far, but still one sustained, frenetic gulp of a film.

GLORY

1989 122m c   ★★★★
Historical/War   R/15
Tri-Star

Matthew Broderick (Col. Robert Gould Shaw), Denzel Washington (Trip), Cary Elwes (Cabot Forbes), Morgan Freeman (John Rawlins), Jihmi Kennedy (Sharts), Andre Braugher (Searles), John Finn (Sgt. Mulcahy), Donovan Leitch (Morse), John David Cullum (Russell), Alan North (Gov. Andrew)

p, Freddie Fields; d, Edward Zwick; w, Kevin Jarre (based on the books Lay This Laurel by Lincoln Kirstein, One Gallant Rush by Peter Burchard, and the letters of Robert Gould Shaw); ph, Freddie Francis (Technicolor); ed, Steven Rosenblum; m, James Horner; prod d, Norman Garwood; art d, Keith Pain, Dan Webster; fx, Kevin Yagher, Carl Fullerton; cos, Francine Jamison-Tanchuck

Never self-serving, this glorious film tells the hitherto shamefully uncelebrated story of the 54th Regiment of Massachusetts Volunteer Infantry, the first unit of black troops raised by the Union to fight in the Civil War.

Commanded by Colonel Robert Shaw (Matthew Broderick), the 25-year-old son of abolitionist Boston Brahmins, the ragtag assemblage includes Rawlins (Morgan Freeman), a gravedigger who is the regiment's anchor and voice of reason; Trip (Denzel Washington), an embittered, bullying, but tough-as-steel runaway slave; Searles (Andre Braugher), a bespectacled Emerson scholar; and Sharts (Jihmi Kennedy), a shy, stuttering former field slave. While undergoing relentless training, the black troops are subjected to the racism of white enlistees and officers, denied shoes and uniforms, and offered less than standard wages, which, with Shaw's support, they refuse to accept. Finally given a chance to enter combat, the 54th acquit themselves heroically, then make a brave suicidal assault against an impregnable harbor fortification—South Carolina's Fort Wagner.

Based partly on the real Robert Gould Shaw's letters, GLORY is remarkable in its fidelity to history. Director Edward Zwick (ABOUT LAST NIGHT, television's "thirtysomething") re-creates the period with remarkable accuracy, both in the observation of small details and in the truly harrowing battle scenes. Though essentially an ensemble piece, GLORY also contains especially compelling performances by Broderick, Washington, and Freeman. Richly plotted, alternately inspiring and horrifying, GLORY is an enlightening and entertaining tribute to heroes too long forgotten.

GNOME-MOBILE, THE

1967 84m c   ★★★★
Children's/Fantasy   /U
Buena Vista

Walter Brennan *(D.J. Mulrooney/Knobby)*, Tom Lowell *(Jasper)*, Matthew Garber *(Rodney Winthrop)*, Ed Wynn *(Rufus)*, Karen Dotrice *(Elizabeth Winthrop)*, Richard Deacon *(Ralph Yarby)*, Sean McClory *(Horatio Quaxton)*, Jerome Cowan *(Dr. Conrad Ramsey)*, Charles Lane *(Dr. Scroggins)*, Norman Grabowski *(Male Nurse)*

p, Walt Disney, James Algar; d, Robert Stevenson; w, Ellis Kadison (based on the novel *The Gnomobile, a Gnice Gnew Gnarrative with Gnonsense, But Gnothing Gnaughty* by Upton Sinclair); ph, Edward Colman (Technicolor); ed, Norman R. Palmer; m, Buddy Baker; art d, Carroll Clark, William H. Tuntke; fx, Eustace Lycett, Robert A. Mattey; cos, Bill Thomas, Chuck Keehne, Neva Rames

Don't be thrown by bad title; here's a gem. Based on a novel by social reformer Upton Sinclair, author of *The Jungle*, this charming Disney film features Walter Brennan as D.J. Mulrooney, a conservative, elderly timber tycoon who takes his grandchildren (Matthew Garber and Karen Dotrice) for a drive in his prized 1930 Rolls Royce. When the trio stops to picnic, they meet Jasper (Tom Lowell), a youthful, tiny gnome, and his 943-year-old ailing grandfather (Brennan again, playing the role as a stereotypical leprechaun, brogue and all). Because he's isolated from other gnomes, Jasper seems fated to be the last of his line, a situation that depresses his grandfather to the point of illness. Enlisting the humans' aid, the gnomes set out in the Rolls Royce to find others of their kind. Highly reminiscent of Disney's DARBY O'GILL AND THE LITTLE PEOPLE, this wonderfully entertaining fantasy, complete with talking animals, is propelled by a terrific dual-role performance from Brennan.

GO-BETWEEN, THE

1971   118m   c   ★★★★
Drama   PG
MGM/EMI   (U.K.)

Julie Christie *(Marian Maudsley)*, Alan Bates *(Ted Burgess)*, Dominic Guard *(Leo Colston)*, Margaret Leighton *(Mrs. Maudsley)*, Michael Redgrave *(The Older Leo)*, Michael Gough *(Mr. Maudsley)*, Edward Fox *(Hugh Trimingham)*, Richard Gibson *(Marcus Maudsley)*, Simon Hume-Kendall *(Denys)*, Amaryllis Garnett *(Kate)*

p, John Heyman, Norman Priggen; d, Joseph Losey; w, Harold Pinter (based on the novel by L.P. Hartley); ph, Gerry Fisher (Technicolor); ed, Reginald Beck; m, Michel Legrand; art d, Carmen Dillon; cos, John Furniss

Stylish look back into an old man's memories, courtesy of Harold Pinter, who wrote the screenplay adaptation of L.P. Hartley's novel. Redgrave reviews his life in painstaking and sometimes dizzying detail under Losey's deft direction. Julie Christie is engaged to Edward Fox, a member of the British aristocracy, but she is in love with Bates, a lowly farmer. Guard is Redgrave as a young man, hired as the go-between for Christie and Bates. This assignment gives the youth his first taste of love: he falls for Christie too. In fact, he never marries, and we are given to believe it was this feeling for Christie that kept him a bachelor for seven decades.

Set in Norfolk in the 1900s, the film flashes forward and backward with several twists and such attention to fine shadings that you cannot watch this movie without giving it your utmost attention. The cover for the affair is blown when Christie's mother, Leighton, forces young Guard to take her to where Christie and Bates are trysting. Several shocking incidents, including Bates shooting himself, keep this film constantly surprising. The ending, in which an aged Christie asks the aged

Redgrave to once more act as a go-between, is a smashing climax to a superb film.

GO TELL THE SPARTANS

1978   114m   c   ★★★½
War   R/15
Spartan

Burt Lancaster *(Maj. Asa Barker)*, Craig Wasson *(Cpl. Stephen Courcey)*, Jonathan Goldsmith *(Sgt. Oleonowski)*, Marc Singer *(Capt. Al Olivetti)*, Joe Unger *(Lt. Raymond Hamilton)*, Dennis Howard *(Cpl. Abraham Lincoln)*, David Clennon *(Lt. Finley Wattsberg)*, Evan Kim *(Cowboy)*, John Megna *(Cpl. Ackley)*, Hilly Hicks *(Signalman Coffee)*

p, Allan F. Bodoh, Mitchell Cannold; d, Ted Post; w, Wendell Mayes (based on the novel *Incident at Muc Wa* by Daniel Ford); ph, Harry Stradling, Jr.; ed, Millie Moore; m, Dick Halligan; art d, Jack Senter; cos, Ron Dawson

Lost in the shuffle between THE DEER HUNTER and APOCALYPSE NOW, this neat little war movie tells of the US presence in Vietnam in 1964, with advisor Lancaster commanding a small group of combat "advisors." Lancaster is ordered to send a platoon of Vietnamese militia (old men with shotguns, commanded by Communist-hating mercenary Kim) and a squad of Americans under green lieutenant Unger to garrison an old French stronghold. A veteran of three wars, Lancaster argues that the site is of no value and that all putting troops there will accomplish is enticing the Viet Cong to mass for an attack. He is overruled on the grounds that the French abandoned the spot and lost the war, "and we don't want to make the same mistake the French did." Lancaster is proved right, though, and before long the Viet Cong have besieged the isolated outpost.

The film features a typically fine performance by Lancaster, who wonders, through most of the film, why a draftee like Wasson would volunteer for combat duty. When Wasson explains that he wanted to know what a war was like, Lancaster exclaims, "I should have known it—you're a tourist!" Even at this point in the war, the film makes it obvious that we don't belong there; the US Army command is portrayed as greedy and stupid, while the South Vietnamese appear to be thoroughly corrupt (Lancaster has to bribe the local warlord to give the battle some air support). The title derives from the inscription above the French cemetery, quoting the doomed Spartans at Thermopylae: "Stranger, go tell the Spartans how we lie; loyal to their laws, here we die."

GOALIE'S ANXIETY AT THE PENALTY KICK, THE
(DIE ANGST DES TORMANNS BEIM ELFMETER)

1971   101m   c   ★★★½
Crime   /PG
Autoren/Osterreichischen   (West Germany)

Arthur Brauss *(Joseph Bloch)*, Kai Fischer *(Hertha Gabler)*, Erika Pluhar *(Gloria)*, Libgart Schwartz *(Maid)*, Marie Bardeschewski *(Waitress)*, Michael Troost *(Salesman)*, Bert Fortell *(Customs Officer)*, Edda Koechl *(Girl in Vienna)*, Mario Kranz *(School Janitor)*, Ernst Meister *(Tax Inspector)*

p, Peter Genee; d, Wim Wenders; w, Wim Wenders, Peter Handke based on the novel by Handke; ph, Robby Muller; ed, Peter Przygodda; m, Jurgen Knieper

Haunting. Wim Wenders's second feature film and his first collaboration with the Austrian novelist-poet-playwright Peter Handke is an adaptation of Handke's short novel about a soccer goalie driven to murder.

From the start of Wenders's film, the personality of the goalie, Josef Bloch (Arthur Braus), is evident. While the game's action take place at one end of the field, Bloch waits at his net at the opposite end. As play nears, he takes little notice, walks in front of his net, and stands completely still as the ball is kicked past him. Bloch is a character who considers it pointless to try to evade or outwit the course of events. He leaves the team (whose popularity has taken them around the world) and begins to wander. He visits movie theaters, plays American songs on jukeboxes, drinks, encounters people, and observes life as it passes him by. After he meets a cinema cashier named Gloria (Erika Pluhar)—which, as she reminds him, is spelled G-L-O-R-I-A as in the rock 'n' roll song by Them—Bloch returns with her to her apartment and, eventually, strangles her for no apparent reason.

Wenders, who has long professed his fascination with America, its films, and its music, cannot make an American-style picture. Instead, he presents a meditative, fragmentary reconstruction of the killer's mind, his distorted perceptions, his personal morality, and the otherwise unimportant events in his daily existence. While most directors insist on sensationalizing acts of violence and perpetuating the myth of the outlaw hero, Wenders, in this portrait of a killer, delivers one of cinema's most truthful depictions of the criminal.

GODFATHER, THE

1972 175m c   ★★★★★
Crime   R/18
Paramount

Marlon Brando (Don Vito Corleone), Al Pacino (Michael Corleone), James Caan (Sonny Corleone), Richard Castellano (Clemenza), Robert Duvall (Tom Hagen), Sterling Hayden (McCluskey), John Marley (Jack Woltz), Richard Conte (Barzini), Diane Keaton (Kay Adams), Al Lettieri (Sollozzo)

p, Albert S. Ruddy; d, Francis Ford Coppola; w, Mario Puzo, Francis Ford Coppola (based on the novel by Mario Puzo); ph, Gordon Willis (Technicolor); ed, William Reynolds, Peter Zinner, Marc Laub, Murray Solomon; m, Nino Rota; prod d, Dean Tavoularis; art d, Warren Clymer; fx, A.D. Flowers, Joe Lombardi, Dick Smith, Sass Bedig; cos, Anna Hill Johnstone

The ultimate in modern gangster fare, this moody, murky, murderous film is a classic, an almost mythical production that chronicles the rise, fall and resurgence single Mafia family in New York. Brando, his cheeks stuffed and his throat jammed with colloquialisms, is the rasping, thoughtful, shrewd and lethal Godfather whose crime empire is held together by the muscle of his son Caan and an army of Italian street soldiers.

The film opens with the Italian wedding al fresco, at Brando's fortresslike estate, of his daughter, Shire, to Russo, a bookie in the Godfather's fiefdom. On the grounds is Brando's second son, Pacino, a much-decorated Marine captain who has just returned from WW II. College educated, sensitive, and perceptive, he is unlike almost all present, except for Keaton, his non-Italian sweetheart. Pacino points out gangster luminaries to Keaton as a small boy might heroes in a baseball park.

Problems for the Corleone family arise with the appearance of Lettieri, a maverick gangster who has the backing of a rival Mafia family headed by Rendina and his son Giorgio. Lettieri—in a meeting with Brando, Caan, and others—informs the family that he intends to establish wide-scale narcotics sales in NYC but requires the permission and political protection of Brando to do so. Brando, an old-school Mafia don, sends Lettieri packing, saying that he is disgusted by the thought of narcotics and is content with his gambling, prostitution, protection, and similar rackets. The refusal leads to an attempt on Brando's life, while his weak-willed son Cazale stands by helplessly.

Brando is rushed to a hospital while Lettieri kidnaps Duvall, Brando's consigliari, telling him that he must persuade Caan, heir apparent to the Corleone family, to cooperate with him and the rival Mafia clan and to go into narcotics. Duvall is released, but Lettieri's plans go awry when he learns that Brando still lives.

THE GODFATHER is three hours of stunning, shocking film that grimly portrays the insidious crime cartel that grew to omnipotent power in the US. All of the leads are stupendous in their unforgettable roles, as are the supporting players. It is really Pacino's film, although Brando's intermittent appearances were so convincingly played that it won this extraordinary actor his second Oscar. The film also took Academy Awards for Best Picture and Best Screenplay. Coppola, as director, has brilliantly melded divergent and far-flung scenes into a cohesive whole—a dark, brooding saga that was to earn more than $150 million as one of the all-time box office blockbusters.

Not only is the direction and acting flawless in this somber masterpiece, but the technical credits are outstanding, particularly the obsessively gripping cinematography by Willis and the haunting score by Rota. The GODFATHER films touch upon something perpetually dark in the human character, a fearfully widening black hole into which humanity vanishes and reason itself cannot exist.

GODFATHER, PART II, THE

1974 200m c   ★★★★★
Crime   R/18
Paramount

Al Pacino (Michael), Robert Duvall (Tom Hagen), Diane Keaton (Kay), Robert De Niro (Vito Corleone), Talia Shire (Connie), John Cazale (Fredo), Lee Strasberg (Hyman Roth), Michael V. Gazzo (Frank Pentangeli), Richard Bright (Al Neri), Gastone Moschin (Fanutti)

p, Francis Ford Coppola, Gray Frederickson, Fred Roos; d, Francis Ford Coppola; w, Francis Ford Coppola, Mario Puzo (based on characters from his novel); ph, Gordon Willis (Technicolor); ed, Peter Zinner, Barry Malkin, Richard Marks; m, Nino Rota, Carmine Coppola; prod d, Dean Tavoularis; art d, Angelo Graham; fx, A.D. Flowers, Joe Lombardi; cos, Theadora Van Runkle

An enlargement on the themes of the first film, many will find PART II richer and more satisfying. In this sequel to the awesome original, Pacino now reigns supreme—from his vast Lake Tahoe, Nevada, estate—as head of the burgeoning Corleone crime empire.

At a lavish party Pacino entertains Spradlin, a slick, self-serving, and smug senator from Nevada who tells Pacino that he is opposed to the Mafia's gambling operations in his state and that he intends to wipe out the organization. Spradlin later wakes up in a sleazy whorehouse next to a prostitute he appears to have murdered in a drunken orgy, but it is obvious that he has been set up. Pacino ostensibly comes to his rescue by covering up the killing, and Spradlin thus falls under his control. An assassination attempt is made on Pacino and his family, machine gunners spraying his posh home in Lake Tahoe in the middle of the night, but the family and the new don survive.

Later Pacino meets with Strasberg in Havana, where the pair open a swank hotel-casino, but Pacino is guarded with the wily and untrustworthy Strasberg, believing him to have been behind the attempt on his life. When Pacino discovers that his own brother, Cazale, worked with Strasberg to set up the abortive

Lake Tahoe raid, he marks Cazale for death. Meanwhile, Keaton, who's expecting their baby, miscarries, and Pacino's problems are compounded when he's called to testify before a Senate investigative committee probing organized-crime operations.

THE GODFATHER, PART II proved unusual in actually being better than the original. The performances by Pacino as the younger, ascendant don and De Niro as the senior Vito Corleone were dynamic and gripping. Coppola was given a free hand with this sequel, and his deft directorial touches are everywhere, particularly in his fine historical sequences. Cinematographer Willis superbly captures the turn-of-the-century period, applying a seriographic tint to flashback scenes for a softer, richer look than the sharp image of the ongoing contemporary story.

GODFATHER PART III, THE

1990   161m   c   ★★★
Crime   R/15
Zoetrope

Al Pacino (Michael Corleone), Diane Keaton (Kay Adams), Talia Shire (Connie Corleone), Andy Garcia (Vincent Mancini), Eli Wallach (Don Altobello), Joe Mantegna (Joey Zasa), George Hamilton (B.J. Harrison), Bridget Fonda (Grace Hamilton), Sofia Coppola (Mary Corleone), Raf Vallone (Cardinal Lamberto)

p, Gray Frederickson, Fred Roos, Francis Ford Coppola, Charles Mulvehill; d, Francis Ford Coppola; w, Mario Puzo, Francis Ford Coppola; ph, Gordon Willis; ed, Barry Malkin, Lisa Fruchtman, Walter Murch; m, Carmine Coppola, Nino Rota; prod d, Dean Tavoularis; art d, Alex Tavoularis; fx, Lawrence James Cavanaugh, R. Bruce Steinheimer; cos, Milena Canonero

The sequel that was never meant to be, and one that, ultimately, few of the original players could refuse. Out of the resulting confusion—budget excesses, creative clashes, last-second re-writes, cast dissension, a breakneck pace—emerged one of the most perplexing films of 1990, an epic without an epic scope, a muted, strained, unnatural affair that never comes into strong dramatic focus. Coppola's wisest move in PART III was to not try to take the Corleone saga into a radically different direction. Instead, the third part becomes an extended coda to the ending of PART II, as Michael continues to fulfill his tragic legacy, doing his best for his family, only to destroy it in the process.

Establishing its connection to the second film, as well as its tone, the film, set in 1979, begins with a elegiac montage of the Corleone Lake Tahoe complex, where much of PART II was set, now in ruins. The montage gives way to Michael writing a letter to his children (who now live with his ex-wife Kay), inviting them to a ceremony in New York, where he now lives. He is to be honored by the Catholic Church for his charitable works through a foundation, named in honor of his father, Vito Corleone. He prevails upon the children to convince Kay (Diane Keaton) to accompany them. The party afterwards, mirroring the parties that opened the other two films, introduces the major players and conflicts.

Despite a running time approaching three hours, THE GOD-FATHER PART III is narratively choppy. A victim of its own ambitions, it tries to cover too much thematic ground and introduces a platoon of new characters. Rather than using organized crime as a metaphor for predatory capitalism, as the two films did, this movie reverses itself, using legitimate business as a metaphor for organized crime. Unfortunately, there are few subjects as inherently uncinematic as the world of high finance (a point evidently not lost on the moviegoing public). Vincent's (Andy Garcia) clash with Zasa (Joe Mantegna), the only real gangster plot in the film, is really a truncated subplot, too

obviously added to liven up the slow-moving main plot. Michael's attempts to win back Kay have little emotional imme-diacy. Too often, their scenes together play like high-school debates on morality, power and corruption.

What finally does hold PART III together is what film scholars and buffs will be arguing about for years to come: the controversial casting of Sofia Coppola as Mary Corleone. (Regrettably, after starring in three back-to-back productions, including ED-WARD SCISSORHANDS and MERMAIDS, original choice Winona Ryder dropped out due to mental and physical exhaustion.) Through all the plots, subplots, sideplots, digressions, and diversions, the only element that comes to bear on everything is Michael's love for his daughter and his determination to have her be the standard-bearer for the next generation of Corleones; she's the first to have grown up without having experienced the violent Corleone family legacy.

GODS MUST BE CRAZY, THE

1984   109m   c   ★★★★
Comedy   PG
Mimosa   (Botswana)

Marius Weyers (Andrew Steyn), Sandra Prinsloo (Kate Thompson), Louw Verwey (Sam Boga), Nixau (Xi), Jamie Uys (The Reverend), Michael Thys (Mpudi), Nic De Jager (Jack Hind), Fanyana H. Sidumo (1st Card Player), Joe Seakatsie (2nd Card Player), Ken Gampu (President)

p, Jamie Uys; d, Jamie Uys; w, Jamie Uys; ph, Buster Reynolds, Robert Lewis, Jamie Uys; ed, Jamie Uys; m, John Boshoff; art d, Caroline Burls; cos, Gail Grobbelaar, Mij Reynolds

A hoot from South Africa and a brilliantly funny throwback to the days of slapstick silent comedy.

It begins as a National Geographic sort of documentary about the Kalahari Bushmen, an uncivilized African tribe that knows no violence, is thoroughly self-contained, and holds no material possessions. One day a small plane overhead drops a Coke bottle in the tribe's midst. Assuming that the bottle is a gift from the gods, the members begin to make use of it—and they discover that it has not one but many uses: mashing meal, flattening skins, playing music, making patterns. Since it is such a valuable tool, the tribesmen soon become possessive of it. This leads to greed, greed leads to anger, and anger leads to violence. Xi (Nixau, an actual Bushman), being the tribal leader, is elected to rid his people of the bottle by taking it to the end of the earth and throwing it off.

Writer-director Jamie Uys resurrects a familiar, long-forgotten style of sight gags and traditional comic techniques in this delightful comedy that succeeds as both entertainment and nostalgic homage to the earliest days of film.

GODSPELL

1973   103m   c   ★★½
Religious/Musical   G/U
Columbia

Victor Garber (Jesus), David Haskell (John/Judas), Jerry Sroka (Jerry), Lynne Thigpen (Lynne), Katie Hanley (Katie), Robin Lamont (Robin), Gilmer McCormick (Gilmer), Joanne Jonas (Joanne), Merrell Jackson (Merrell), Jeffrey Mylett (Jeffrey)

p, Edgar Lansbury; d, David Greene; w, David Allen Greene, John-Michael Tebelak (based on the musical book by Tebelak with score by Stephen Schwartz); ph, Richard G. Heimann (TVC Color); ed, Alan Heim; m, Stephen Schwartz; prod d, Brian Eatwell; art d, Ben Kasazkow; chor, Sam Bayes; cos, Sherrie Sucher

Sincere but misguided, *The Fantastiks* meets Bozo meets St. Matthew. The familiar story is retold in the simplest of terms, casting Jesus (Garber, in sweatshirt and overalls) as a modern-day flower child living and dying in the Big Apple. When it's good, GODSPELL is filled with energy, fun, and zip; when it's bad, which more often is the case, it's juvenile. The worst part of the production is the over-the-top mugging that director Greene allows—as if Jerry Lewis were interpreting the New Testament. Schwartz's score is often repetitious, and the picture, filled with famous Manhattan backdrops, looks more like a rock 'n' roll travelogue of New York than anything else. Still, the dancing is often quite good, and Garber and Haskell do a nice job with "All for the Best," softshoeing through Gotham and eventually winding up at the Bulova Watch sign.

Those who lived through the 1960s will enjoy this more than those who haven't, but in the final analysis, GODSPELL is generally a disappointing film version of a small musical that rocked audiences with its fervor. In this case, opening it up for the camera did the original a disservice. Songs include "Day by Day," "Prepare Ye the Way of the Lord" and "Turn Back O Man."

GOING HOLLYWOOD

1933 80m bw   ★★★½
Musical   /U
Cosmopolitan

Bing Crosby *(Bill Williams)*, Marion Davies *(Sylvia Bruce)*, Fifi D'Orsay *(Lili Yvonne)*, Stuart Erwin *(Ernest P. Baker)*, Patsy Kelly *(Jill)*, Bobby Watson *(Jack Thompson)*, Ned Sparks *(Bert Conroy)*, Lennie Hayton, The Three Radio Rogues, Clara Blandick *(Miss Perkins)*

p, Walter Wanger; d, Raoul Walsh; w, Donald Ogden Stewart (based on a story by Frances Marion); ph, George Folsey; ed, Frank Sullivan; art d, Merrill Pye; chor, Albertina Rasch; cos, Adrian

Fluffy fun, featuring Crosby in his first MGM film and Davies in one of her best performances. She's an attractive French teacher who follows aspiring crooner Crosby to Hollywood to save him from the clutches of the egotistical D'Orsay. You can probably guess the rest. Director Walsh handled the production with the brisk pace that was to become his trademark. Crosby, in collegiate sweaters, spectator shoes and white golf pants, is the essence of the casual crooner. He sings one of his biggest early-day hits, "Temptation." The production was lavishly sponsored by Cosmopolitan Productions, the filmmaking arm of newspaper czar William Randolph Hearst, who allowed his leading lady and mistress Davies all the luxuries of an empress during the film's leisurely production schedule.

The literate and amusing screenplay was written by Stewart, a witty Hollywood scribe of the Robert Benchley school, and the supporting cast for GOING HOLLYWOOD is solid with Sparks as the cynical film director, Erwin as the bumbling producer, Hayton as the versatile pianist and conductor, and slapstick galore from scene-stealing, wisecracking Kelly in her film debut after several smashing successes on Broadway. The film, when finally released, was an enormous success and transformed Crosby into a top ten box-office attraction.

GOING IN STYLE

1979 97m c   ★★★★
Comedy   PG
WB

George Burns *(Joe)*, Art Carney *(Al)*, Lee Strasberg *(Willie)*, Charles Hallahan *(Pete)*, Pamela Payton-Wright *(Kathy)*, Siobhan Keegan *(Colleen)*, Brian Neville *(Kevin)*, Constantine Hartofolis *(Boy in Park)*, Mary Testa *(Teller)*, Jean Shevlin *(Mrs. Fein)*

p, Tony Bill, Fred T. Gallo; d, Martin Brest; w, Martin Brest (based on a story by Edward Cannon); ph, Billy Williams (Technicolor); ed, Robert Swink, C. Timothy O'Meara; m, Michael Small; prod d, Stephen Hendrickson; art d, Gary Weist; cos, Anna Hill Johnstone

The laughs seem strained but the poignance comes on strong. Three elderly gents (Burns, Carney and Strasberg), tired of the indifference society shows them and the pervasive feeling of uselessness that shrouds their lives, decide to rob a bank. It's really Burns who promotes the idea, more as a way of relieving boredom than increasing his savings account; it's also appealing to Strasberg and Carey as a means of striking back at a system that's abandoned them as human beings. Wearing funny masks and wielding guns, the threesome robs a Manhattan bank of a small fortune.

Burns is absolutely fascinating in his portrayal of a crafty, wise and wholly adaptable old man outwitting the fast-moving young world about him. There are some sublimely serious parts to give the whole thing roots, such as a moving scene where Burns looks through a box of old photos that actually show him as a young vaudeville trooper and some shots with his real-life wife Gracie Allen. He begins to weep as he looks back on days no more, images that drag at his heart. This nostalgic interlude is brought to an abrupt halt when Burns suddenly stands up, swearing, as he realizes that he has wet his trousers—age again, intruding upon his reveries.

Director Brest does a great job with a sensitive subject, drawing fine performances from everyone. Carney is a standout as the jovial, ready-for-anything sidekick who has the time of his life rolling points in Las Vegas. He really dies happy, flattered to glowing pride that a pretty young thing in gambler's paradise propositioned *him*. A consistently funny and warm movie.

GOING MY WAY

1944 130m bw   ★★★★★
Religious/Musical   /U
Paramount

Bing Crosby *(Father Chuck O'Malley)*, Rise Stevens *(Genevieve Linden)*, Barry Fitzgerald *(Father Fitzgibbon)*, Frank McHugh *(Father Timothy O'Dowd)*, Gene Lockhart *(Ted Haines, Sr.)*, William Frawley *(Max Dolan)*, James Brown *(Ted Haines, Jr.)*, Jean Heather *(Carol James)*, Porter Hall *(Mr. Belknap)*, Fortunio Bonanova *(Tomasso Bozzani)*

p, Leo McCarey; d, Leo McCarey; w, Frank Butler, Frank Cavett (based on a story by McCarey); ph, Lionel Lindon; ed, LeRoy Stone; art d, Hans Dreier, William Flannery; fx, Gordon Jennings; cos, Edith Head

A warm and moving sleeper hit. Father Chuck O'Malley (Bing Crosby) is an easy-going, trouble-shooting priest who arrives at St. Dominic's Church, a Catholic institution that has seen better days, as has its curate, the elderly Father Fitzgibbon (Barry Fitzgerald). The old and stubborn priest has led the parish for 45 years, but recently the church has gotten heavily in to debt, disillusioning even the parishioners. Through the magic of music, however, Father O'Malley brings Father Fitzgibbon out of the doldrums and saves the parish.

Leo McCarey's direction is masterful, stopping the sentiment just short of the maudlin. It all works like magic, especially the unbeatable chemistry between Crosby and Fitzgerald. The film was box-office dynamite and swept the Oscars, winning for Best Picture, Best Director, Best Screenplay, Best Actor and Best Supporting Actor. GOING MY WAY and its sequel, THE BELLS OF ST. MARY'S, were also popular with the Catholic Church and Pope Pius XII, who later gave a private audience to Crosby in thanks for the latter's priestly portrayal.

GOING PLACES
(LES VALSEUSES)
1974 117m c   ★★★
Comedy/Drama   R/
C.A.P.A.C./U.P.F./SN   (France)

Gerard Depardieu (Jean-Claude), Patrick Dewaere (Pierrot), Miou-Miou (Marie-Ange), Jeanne Moreau (Jeanne Pirolle), Jacques Chailleux (Jacques Pirolle), Michel Peyrelon (Surgeon), Brigitte Fossey (Young Mother), Isabelle Huppert (Jacqueline), Christiane Muller (Jacqueline's Mother), Christian Alers (Jacqueline's Father)

p, Paul Claudon; d, Bertrand Blier; w, Bertrand Blier, Philippe Dumarcay (based on the novel by Blier); ph, Bruno Nuytten; ed, Kenout Peltier; m, Stephane Grappelli

Disagreeable but fascinating examination of youth constructed as a buddy-road movie. GOING PLACES revolves around the friendship between Depardieu and Dewaere, a couple of long-haired, disheveled petty thieves in their mid-20s. As the film begins, the duo is terrorizing a middle-aged woman—grabbing her ample behind, blowing kisses on her neck, and finally stealing her purse. So begins a spree—which, as crime sprees go, is relatively harmless. Along the way, the two steal cars, break into stores, insult people, seduce some semi-willing women, and even have sex with each other when no one else is available. They seem, however, to have no profound effect on anyone.

After returning a stolen car Dewaere is shot, and superficially wounded in one testicle, by the angry owner. His fear that he'll never have sex again proves groundless, however, when the thieves meet Miou-Miou, a flighty young woman who doesn't mind disrobing for, or having sex with, the fellows—but who doesn't seem to enjoy it either—which infuriates these two macho men who are convinced they can make any woman melt in their arms.

The first major film from Bertrand Blier (son of actor Bernard), GOING PLACES is an ugly and brutal, yet somehow charming, look at two young men who are wholly worthless as human beings. They have no future; and, despite the fact that they travel from one side of France to the other, they never get anywhere. They just go—fast and furiously. The most significant moment in their lives is their meeting with Moreau, an older woman just released from prison, who laments her lost youth. She who has nothing is even worse off than Depardieu and Dewaede, who have youth, at least. The alluring Moreau appears only briefly but gives one of her most spectacular performances.

GOLD DIGGERS OF 1933
1933 94m bw   ★★★★★
Musical   /A
WB

Warren William (J. Lawrence Bradford), Joan Blondell (Carol King), Aline MacMahon (Trixie Lorraine), Ruby Keeler (Polly Parker), Dick Powell (Brad Roberts/Robert Treat Bradford), Guy Kibbee (Faneuil H. Peabody), Ned Sparks (Barney Hopkins), Ginger Rogers (Fay Fortune), Clarence Nordstrom (Gordon), Robert Agnew (Dance Director)

p, Robert Lord; d, Mervyn LeRoy; w, Erwin Gelsey, James Seymour, David Boehm, Ben Markson (based on the play "Gold Diggers of Broadway" by Avery Hopwood); ph, Sol Polito; ed, George Amy; art d, Anton Grot; chor, Busby Berkeley; cos, Orry-Kelly

Pure depression gold. After their success with 42ND STREET, Warner Bros. threw this film together quickly, sensing that they were on to something with movie musicals. Based on 1929's Gold Diggers of Broadway by Avery Hopwood, this Mervyn LeRoy-directed extravaganza not only became a hit but spawned several more films of its ilk.

Joan Blondell, Aline MacMahon and Ruby Keeler play a trio of unemployed showgirls who are thrilled when producer Barney Hopkins (Ned Sparks) informs them he's about to start a new show. The problem is that he doesn't have a penny, but Brad Roberts (Dick Powell), a songwriter who is mad for Polly (Keeler) does, and lends Sparks $15,000 to get "Forgotten Melody" off the ground. The show goes into rehearsal, with Brad taking one of the roles, but the girls wonder if his money is clean, except for Polly, who just knows he's legit. Of course he is. In fact, he's the scion of a wealthy Beacon Hill family; however, his brother, J. Lawrence (Warren William), and a lawyer, Fanueil Hall Peabody (Guy Kibbee), arrive from Boston to put an end to Brad's frivolousness.

Harry Warren and Al Dubin wrote the excellent songs, and Busby Berkeley did the startling choreography, including a Ginger Rogers-led chorus dressed in gold coin costumes in the extravagant rendition of "We're in the Money" (which Ginger does in pig latin). The picture is loaded with inside jokes, including cameo appearances by famed agent Louis Schurr and Berkeley as the "Call-Boy" (that's the correct term). If you have but one 1930s Warner Bros. musical to see, make it this one. Remade as PAINTING THE CLOUDS WITH SUNSHINE.

GOLD DIGGERS OF 1935
1935 95m bw   ★★★½
Musical   /U
WB/First National

Dick Powell (Dick Curtis), Gloria Stuart (Amy Prentiss), Adolphe Menjou (Nicoleff), Glenda Farrell (Betty Hawes), Grant Mitchell (Louis Lamson), Dorothy Dare (Arline Davis), Alice Brady (Mrs. Mathilda Prentiss), Frank McHugh (Humboldt Prentiss), Hugh Herbert (T. Mosely Thorpe), Winifred Shaw (Winny)

p, Robert Lord; d, Busby Berkeley; w, Manuel Seff, Peter Milne (based on a story by Milne, Robert Lord); ph, George Barnes; ed, George Amy; art d, Anton Grot

Gold-plated good fun. A minor plot is mangled in a major fashion by Busby Berkeley, but his choreography and the score assure us of delirious delight. The scene is a summer resort in a New England town, the story revolving around a number of romantic pairings. The inn's employees include Dick Powell as a desk clerk studying to be a doctor, Adolph Menjou as the somewhat dishonest owner of the hotel, Gloria Stuart as the attractive ingenue, and Frank McHugh as the ne'er-do-well comedy relief.

The key to all the fun is the Harry Warren-Al Dubin score which features the remarkable "Lullaby of Broadway" (a song reprised from their score for FORTY SECOND STREET) as well as "I'm Going Shopping With You" and "The Words Are In My Heart." Around these tunes Berkeley devised what was, to some, the apex of his choreographic career. The highlight is a production number done for a charity show at the hotel, featuring the aforementioned "Lullaby of Broadway" in a sequence that shows the last day in the life of a "Broadway Baby" before she falls out of a window to her death. The number uses more than 100 dancers, seen from every possible angle and doing some of the most precise dancing ever put on celluloid.

GOLD OF NAPLES
(L'ORO DI NAPOLI)
1954 74m bw ★★★
Drama/Comedy /A
Ponti/DEG/Gala (Italy)

THE RACKETEER: Lianella Carrell (The Wife), Toto (The Husband), Pasquale Cennamo (The Racketeer). PIZZA ON CREDIT: Sophia Loren (The Wife), Giacomo Furia (The Husband), Alberto Farnese (The Lover), Paolo Stoppa (The Widower). THE GAMBLER: Vittorio De Sica (The Count), Mario Passante (His Valet), Irene Montalto (The Countess)

p, Dino De Laurentiis, Carlo Ponti; d, Vittorio De Sica; w, Cesare Zavattini, Dino De Sica, Giuseppe Marotta (based on the novel by Marotta); ph, Otello Martelli; ed, Eraldo Da Roma; m, Alessandro Cicognini

By turns melancholy and very witty, in the beloved vignette format of one of the greatest Italian filmmakers. The stories include (two of the film's six episodes were cut before US release) "The Racketeer," in which pantomimist Toto outwits and undoes a bullying friend who has intruded into his home as a permanent guest. "Pizza on Credit" shows Loren as a cheating wife who loses her wedding ring while trysting with Farnese, which causes husband Furia to become suspicious and necessitates a frantic search for the ring (returned by the lover at the last moment).

De Sica, the director, plays the lead role in "The Gambler," an inveterate gamester who has squandered away every dime his family ever had, but who continues to believe he is a grand sharper. In this, the best of the vignettes, De Sica has a marvelous scene playing cards with the young son of the doorman where he resides, Piero Bilancioni, who wearily wins every hand, cleaning out the old man once again. In "Theresa," Silvana Mangano is an alluring prostitute who marries a mentally unbalanced young man and has to apply her own brand of psychology to straighten out their relationship.

Though the acting is generally above average here, GOLD OF NAPLES is not 14 karat, mostly because of the erratic story lines and the lack of logical transition between vignettes. This film marked one of Loren's earliest appearances. The segment with Loren as the pizza-maker's lusty spouse is very close to the French movie, THE BAKER'S WIFE, but the scene of her walking is as classic as Monroe's in NIAGARA.

GOLDEN BOY
1939 99m bw ★★★★
Sports /A
Columbia

Barbara Stanwyck (Lorna Moon), Adolphe Menjou (Tom Moody), William Holden (Joe Bonaparte), Lee J. Cobb (Mr. Bonaparte), Joseph Calleia (Eddie Fuseli), Sam Levene (Siggie), Edward Brophy (Roxy Lewis), Beatrice Blinn (Anna), William H. Strauss (Mr. Carp), Don Beddoe (Borneo)

p, William Perlberg; d, Rouben Mamoulian; w, Lewis Meltzer, Daniel Taradash, Sarah Y. Mason, Victor Heerman (based on the play by Clifford Odets); ph, Nicholas Musuraca, Karl Freund; ed, Otto Meyer; m, Victor Young; art d, Lionel Banks; cos, Robert Kalloch

Not strictly faithful to Odets, but GOLDEN BOY nonetheless captures his drama's spirit of proletarian angst, propelled by the extraordinary performances of Barbara Stanwyck and William Holden in his first major role.

Joe Bonaparte (Holden), a gifted violinist, is forced by poverty to enter the ring, where he proves to be a talented boxer even though he seemingly pulls his punches, afraid of damaging his musician's hands and ending the dream for which his immigrant father (Lee J. Cobb) has sacrificed so much. Lorna Moon (Stanwyck), the girlfriend of Joe's manager (Adolphe Menjou), is given the task of persuading Joe to give up his musical aspirations. After falling in love with Lorna and then feeling betrayed by her duplicity, Joe returns to the ring, with tragic results.

The film manages to reveal a silver-lined ending that is far more upbeat than Odets's suicide finale. Just the same, Rouben Mamoulian does a wonderful job of retaining the essential story and basic character, building beautifully upon both through his careful scenes; his direction of the brutal but realistic fight scenes adds much to the film's power. Menjou and Cobb offer excellent support, but this film belongs to Stanwyck and to Holden, the 21-year-old unknown who was chosen for the part over John Garfield who created the role in the original Group Theater production.

GOLDEN COACH, THE
(LE CARROSSE D'OR)
1952 105m c ★★★★
Drama /U
Panaria/Hoche (France/Italy)

Anna Magnani (Camilla), Odoardo Spadaro (Don Antonio), Nada Fiorelli (Isabella), Dante (Harlequin), Duncan Lamont (Viceroy), George Higgins (Martinez), Ralph Truman (Duke of Castro), Gisella Mathews (Marquise Altamirano), Raf de la Torre (Chief Justice), Elena Altieri (Duchess of Castro)

p, Francesco Alliata; d, Jean Renoir; w, Jean Renoir, Renzo Avanzo, Jack Kirkland, Ginette Doynel, Giulio Macchi (based on the play "La Carrosse du Saint-Sacrement" by Prosper Merimee); ph, Hill Ronald, Claude Renoir (Technicolor); ed, Mario Serandrei, David Hawkins; m, Antonio Vivaldi; cos, Maria De Matteis

Belatedly hailed as one of the great films about acting; certainly, a stunning visual example of the use of color. Marking Jean Renoir's return to France after his decade in Hollywood and his short period in India filming THE RIVER, THE GOLDEN COACH has often been seen as the key to understanding all the director's work.

Filmed in English at Rome's Cinecitta studios, the film stars Anna Magnani as Camilla, a commedia dell' arte performer who, with her ragtag troupe, arrives in Peru to open a new theater. Already pursued by Felipe (Paul Campbell), Camilla captures the hearts of the vain bullfighter Ramon (Riccardo Rioli) and the Viceroy (Duncan Lamont). Swept away by Camilla's charms and attracted to the vulgar manner that is so alien to his aristocratic experience, the Viceroy presents her with his prized golden coach, a beautifully crafted vehicle that had been used solely for royal business. As the drama rolls on and Camilla struggles to differentiate between reality and the stage, all three of her suitors vie for her love—the Viceroy learning to feel "common" emotions; Ramon impressing her with his manliness; and Felipe inviting her to live with him in the wilderness among the "noble savages."

Opening and closing with a stage curtain, THE GOLDEN COACH is Jean Renoir's invitation to sit back and enjoy the colorful, romantic, humorous spectacle that is real life. While artists have often addressed the confusion of reality and fiction, few have done it with as much grace and love as Renoir. Much of the film's success, however, is due to the brilliant Magnani. THE GOLDEN COACH does not so much star Magnani as it exists because of her. It is her film and everything in it thrives because of the life she breathes into it.

GOLDEN VOYAGE OF SINBAD, THE
1974 105m c ★★★½
Fantasy/Adventure G/U
Columbia (U.K.)

John Phillip Law (Sinbad), Caroline Munro (Margiana), Tom Baker (Koura), Douglas Wilmer (Vizier), Martin Shaw (Rachid), Gregoire Aslan (Hakim), Kurt Christian (Haroun), Takis Emmanuel (Achmed), John David Garfield (Abdul), Aldo Sambrell (Omar)

p, Charles H. Schneer, Ray Harryhausen; d, Gordon Hessler; w, Brian Clemens; ph, Ted Moore (Dynarama); ed, Roy Watts; m, Miklos Rozsa; prod d, John Stoll; art d, Fernando Gonzalez; fx, Ray Harryhausen

This sequel to the terrific THE SEVENTH VOYAGE OF SINBAD, is great fun—with a minimum of plot and a maximum of wonderful Ray Harryhausen special effects. John Phillip Law is the famed sailor here, in search of a gold tablet that will restore a deposed ruler (Douglas Wilmer) to the throne. En route Sinbad encounters a one-eyed centaur, a winged griffin, a six-armed statue and a host of other fantastic creatures. Fast-paced and exciting, the film features some of Harryhausen's best stop-motion animation work. Tom (television's "Dr. Who") Baker makes a marvelous villain. The surprising box-office success of THE GOLDEN VOYAGE OF SINBAD led to yet another sequel, the relatively disappointing SINBAD AND THE EYE OF THE TIGER.

GOLDFINGER
1964 112m c ★★★★
Spy/Adventure /PG
UA (U.K.)

Sean Connery (James Bond), Gert Frobe (Goldfinger), Honor Blackman (Pussy Galore), Shirley Eaton (Jill Masterson), Tania Mallett (Tilly Masterson), Harold Sakata (Oddjob), Bernard Lee ("M"), Martin Benson (Solo), Cec Linder (Felix Leiter), Lois Maxwell (Moneypenny)

p, Harry Saltzman, Albert R. Broccoli; d, Guy Hamilton; w, Richard Maibaum, Paul Dehn (based on the novel by Ian Fleming); ph, Ted Moore (Technicolor); ed, Peter Hunt; m, John Barry; prod d, Ken Adam; art d, Peter Murter; fx, John Stears

Easily the best of the gadget filled James Bond extravaganzas, this third film in the series pits Bond (Connery) against one of his more memorable adversaries, Goldfinger (Frobe), a gold-hoarding, power-hungry maniac who plans to detonate a small atomic device inside Fort Knox, contaminating its huge gold supply with deadly radiation and making him the richest man in the world. Bond's attempts to snuff out Goldfinger's plans take him from Miami to Europe to Kentucky and force him to confront Goldfinger's bizarre Asian assistant, Oddjob (Sakata), who kills his victims with a razor-edged bowler hat. Bond also battles and eventually woos martial arts expert and pilot Pussy Galore (Blackman, who abandoned her spot on the highly successful television series "The Avengers" for this role).

GOLDFINGER contains more crowd-pleasing moments than any other Bond film, featuring Oddjob's flying hat, the deadly laser beam that almost emasculates Bond, his amazing, gadget-laden Astin-Martin, and the murder by suffocation with gold paint of Goldfinger's secretary (Eaton). It also includes Shirley Bassey's terrific rendition of the Leslie Bricusse-Anthony Newley title song. Much credit is due director Guy Hamilton, who was able to keep all the gadgets, wild characters, and strange locations in check long enough to produce a balanced, entertaining film that does not rely totally on flash and effects.

GONE WITH THE WIND
1939 220m c ★★★★★
Historical /PG
Selznick

Clark Gable (Rhett Butler), Vivien Leigh (Scarlett O'Hara), Hattie McDaniel (Mammy), Thomas Mitchell (Gerald O'Hara), Leslie Howard (Ashley Wilkes), Olivia de Havilland (Melanie Hamilton), Everett Brown (Big Sam), Zack Williams (Elijah), Oscar Polk (Pork), Barbara O'Neil (Ellen O'Hara)

p, David O. Selznick; d, Victor Fleming, George Cukor, Sam Wood, William Cameron Menzies, Sidney Franklin; w, Sidney Howard, Jo Swerling, Charles MacArthur, Ben Hecht, John Lee Mahin, John Van Druten, Oliver H.P. Garrett, Winston Miller, John Balderston, Michael Foster, Edwin Justus Mayer, F. Scott Fitzgerald, David O. Selznick (based on the novel by Margaret Mitchell); ph, Ernest Haller, Lee Garmes (Technicolor); ed, Hal C. Kern, James E. Newcom; m, Max Steiner; prod d, William Cameron Menzies; art d, Lyle Wheeler, Hobe Erwin; fx, Jack Cosgrove, Lee Zavitz; chor, Frank Floyd, Eddie Prinz; cos, Walter Plunkett

The one and only; not flawless but absolutely right. The best remembered and most publicized film in Hollywood's flamboyant history, Selznick's obsession, and along with WIZARD OF OZ, the most loved film of all time.

This star-studded Civil War epic based on Margaret Mitchell's immensely popular novel is a wistful hymn to nostalgia, with inevitable touches of racism and sexism but ageless as entertainment; as powerful and moving today as it was when first released in 1939. The war serves as a backdrop for a story that concerns growing up and accepting responsibility. For all the crap of Scarlett—simpering Southern belle, etc.—she's an amazingly resilient, resourceful protagonist, capable of acts of heroism but certainly not cliched nobility. And there's a lesson in intimacy for many of us in her story—our buying into romantic obsession almost certainly guarantees we get the last person we need.

Vivien Leigh—who won the role of Scarlett, the most coveted in film history, from a field that included Paulette Goddard, Norma Shearer, Bette Davis, Joan Crawford, Miriam Hopkins, Jean Harlow, Carole Lombard, Tallulah Bankhead, Claudette Colbert, Jean Arthur, Joan Bennett, and Irene Dunne, among some 2,000 women tested in a much-ballyhooed two-year talent search—is indeed perfection. She's only disappointing when we meet her on the porch at the film's opening. (The scene was re-shot after the entire film was in the can, and Leigh looks strained, unhealthy and understandably sick of the whole damned thing.) Nor can one think of anyone else who could exceed Gable's Rhett Butler; who could capture so effortlessly the absolute charm of this reckless, finally lovable, Casanova.

The only player among the majors who is disappointing is Howard's Ashley—he isn't handsome enough to motivate so much of Scarlett's energy, photographs horrendously in color and plays Ashley in a technique manner that is far too restrained, with every line predictably inflected. All the supporting players are generally of a high order, especially McDaniel's heart-tugging Mammy and Ona Munson's bittersweet trollop. If Butterfly

McQueen's character is alarmingly racist, she's still immortal in her role. But Barbara O'Neill is a trifle removed and graceless as Ellen O'Hara, and Laura Hope Crews's Aunt Pitty is one of those fussy, overblown ham-character performances that often passed for "acting" at MGM.

Directorially, "women's director" George Cukor's sequences are the best. He's a more lyrical director than Fleming, his films have greater sweep and respect for literature; more importantly, his work is simply more cinematic. Nowhere is this more evident than the barbecue at Twelve Oaks and the announcement of war—this may be the best sequence in the entire film. Later, GWTW under Fleming seems to settle into itself and just tell the story. Despite some excellent sequences—Scarlett's attempt to get Dr. Meade to leave the railroad station spring immediately to mind—it sometimes feels decidedly middle-class. Cukor began at the film's helm but was replaced by Fleming (whose WIZARD OF OZ was also released in 1939), reportedly because the former had shifted the focus of the film too much to Scarlett and Melanie (to say nothing of leading man Gable's open disdain for Cukor). During the course of the production Fleming suffered a nervous breakdown and Sam Wood stepped in until he was well enough to return.

Even if GWTW isn't flawless history, it's flawless historically: the peak example of the artistic collaborative achievement that the Hollwood dream machine used to turn out. There's far more to long for these days when you watch it than the passing of the Old South—it's enough to make grown businessmen cry. And if you have seen it, to quote Olivia de Havilland, "Everytime I see it, I find something fresh, some shade of meaning I hadn't noticed before... How fortunate that so many gifted people found immortality in GONE WITH THE WIND." And Ann Rutherford: "It was a passport to the world. It was something for the ages. There is something quite timeless about the appeal of GONE WITH THE WIND."

GOOD EARTH, THE

1937 138m bw   ★★★★★
Drama   /A
MGM

Paul Muni (Wang Lung), Luise Rainer (O-Lan), Walter Connolly (Uncle), Tilly Losch (Lotus), Charley Grapewin (Old Father), Jessie Ralph (Cuckoo), Soo Yong (Aunt), Keye Luke (Elder Son), Roland Got (Younger Son), Ching Wah Lee (Ching)

p, Irving Thalberg, Albert Lewin; d, Sidney Franklin; w, Talbot Jennings, Tess Slesinger, Frances Marion (uncredited), Claudine West (based on the novel by Pearl S. Buck); ph, Karl Freund; ed, Basil Wrangell; m, Herbert Stothart; art d, Cedric Gibbons, Harry Oliver, Arnold Gillespie; cos, Dolly Tree

A classic. Muni, in a powerful role—another marvelous offbeat characterization—is a simple rice farmer who weds Rainer, a kitchen slave, in an arranged marriage. Through incredible labor, Muni and Rainer make their little farm into a success, allowing Muni to buy many more rice fields and to prosper. They produce three children, and all seems promising until severe drought turns the land into an unyielding crust. When famine sets in, the family begins to starve, forcing Rainer to feed her children cooked earth. Through a stroke of Rainer's good luck, the family's fortunes are turned around, but their lives are ruined by Muni's greed. Too late, the stoic Muni learns the magnificent qualities of his loving wife.

Rainer is overwhelming as the self-sacrificing O-lan and deservedly won an Oscar for Best Actress, beating out Greta Garbo in CAMILLE and accomplishing the seemingly impossi-

ble task of winning back-to-back statuettes, having received the same award the previous year for THE GREAT ZEIGFELD.

This superlative adaptation of the Pulitzer Prize-winning Pearl Buck novel was three years in the making; it was Thalberg's last production, which he personally oversaw. He had never taken a film credit and died before THE GOOD EARTH was completed; to honor this young, driving force, who was responsible for a string of majestic films, Mayer had the following inserted in the credits of THE GOOD EARTH: "To the memory of Irving Grant Thalberg we dedicate this picture, his last great achievement."

Thalberg sent George Hill, a talented but alcoholic director, to China to get background footage and gather important props. Hill's wife, Francis Marion, went along to do research since she was originally slated to write the screenplay. Hill and Marion returned with more than two million feet of background footage, some of which was used in the released film. This second unit also brought back 18 tons of properties: dismantled farmhouses with thatched roofs, water buffalo, and countless antiquated farming implements; the only Western prop used in the film was an alarm clock.

Victor Fleming, who replaced Hill, grew ill during production and had to be hospitalized. (The same thing happened to Fleming when he was at work on GONE WITH THE WIND three years later.) With costs mounting, Thalberg brought in Sidney Franklin to replace Fleming. Franklin was cautioned at the outset by Thalberg that he must strive for a major achievement in THE GOOD EARTH, quoting the film philosophy expressed by playwright-screenwriter Laurence Stallings and later adopted by director Howard Hawks: "Every film of major importance must have one great sequence from the standpoint of the camera, in acting and story, in light and shadow, in sound and fury."

There are several great sequences in THE GOOD EARTH, not the least of which were the terrifying mob scenes in which the palace is ransacked. The most astounding scene, however, is the invasion of the locusts. Hundreds of extras, Muni, Rainer, and family in the lead, took to the jeopardized fields to combat the pests which blackened the sky, frantically digging fire lanes, disorienting the insects by banging gongs, then beating them with shovels, feet, and hands. Every known photographic gimmick up to that time was employed in the locust invasion scene. The Chinese location footage was used as a backdrop, closeups of the locusts on a miniature soundstage were intercut, and special effects paintings were inserted on the film to produce a startling montage of the menace.

GOOD FATHER, THE

1986 90m c   ★★★
Drama   R/15
Greenpoint/Film Four (U.K.)

Anthony Hopkins (Bill Hooper), Jim Broadbent (Roger Miles), Harriet Walter (Emmy Hooper), Fanny Viner (Cheryl Miles), Simon Callow (Mark Varner), Joanne Whalley-Kilmer (Mary), Miriam Margolyes (Jane Powell), Michael Byrne (Leonard Scruby)

p, Ann Scott; d, Mike Newell; w, Christopher Hampton (based on the novel by Peter Prince); ph, Michael Coulter; ed, Peter Hollywood; m, Richard Hartley; prod d, Adrian Smith; art d, Alison Stewart-Richardson

Much more than merely a role-reversal British version of KRAMER VS. KRAMER. Hopkins is divorced and distraught, a self-diagnosed victim of the feminism he once so ardently supported.

As the film opens, he takes on an outing the six-year-old son he sees only on weekends. Hopkins carries the boy on his shoulders, but there is a distant cast to his eyes; when he pushes his son on a swing, he pushes a little hard. He is curt with his ex-wife (Walter); when he returns the boy to her, he quickly jumps on his motorcycle and speeds off into the night. As he zooms along, his mind's eye is overtaken by the surreal image of a baby's face smothered by womblike plastic. Hopkins becomes friends with Broadbent, whose radical-feminist wife (Viner) left him for a lesbian lover. Now she is planning to emigrate to Australia, taking their young son with her. Hopkins encourages Broadbent to fight back, vicariously waging the campaign of vengeance he has never carried out against his own ex-wife.

Although nicely adapted from a Prince novel and adroitly directed by Newell, THE GOOD FATHER is Hopkins's film. His character is a hard man to like, yet by film's end Hopkins has made him a tragic figure. Outstanding support from Callow as a hardened lawyer.

GOOD MORNING, VIETNAM

1987 119m c   ★★★½
Comedy/Drama/War   R/15
Touchstone/Silver Partners III

Robin Williams (Adrian Cronauer), Forest Whitaker (Edward Garlick), Tung Thanh Tran (Tuan), Chintara Sukapatana (Trinh), Bruno Kirby (Lt. Steven Hauk), Robert Wuhl (Marty Lee Dreiwitz), J.T. Walsh (Sgt. Major Dickerson), Noble Willingham (Gen. Taylor), Richard Edson (Pvt. Abersold), Juney Smith (Phil McPherson, Radio Engineer)

p, Mark Johnson, Larry Brezner, Ben Moses, Harry Benn; d, Barry Levinson; w, Mitch Markowitz; ph, Peter Sova (Deluxe Color); ed, Stu Linder; m, Alex North; prod d, Roy Walker; art d, Steve Spence; fx, Fred Cramer; cos, Keith Denny

Robin Williams was finally given a showcase for his extraordinary improvisational skills in this, the first comedy set in Vietnam.

Based on the story of real-life Armed Forces Radio disc jockey Adrian Cronauer, GOOD MORNING, VIETNAM begins in 1965, as Cronauer (Williams) arrives in Saigon, imported because his comedic broadcasts have proven a huge morale-booster elsewhere. At the AFR's Saigon station, Cronauer incurs the wrath of superiors who resent his intrusion in their programming, with its dull announcers, health and safety tips, censored news, and geriatric playlist. Cronauer changes all that, knocking listening troops out of their stupor with his howling salutation—"Gooood morning, Vietnammmm!"—hip song selection, and comedic improvisation, poking wild fun at any and all sacred cows.

GOOD MORNING, VIETNAM stumbles whenever Williams isn't behind the mike, placing him in melodramatic, hackneyed situations that become increasingly predictable and preposterous, and director Barry Levinson's seemingly endless reaction shots of listeners grooving to the DJ's antics become irritating. Levinson manages, however, to be one of the few filmmakers to show the Vietnamese as complex, cultured people, rather than as helpless victims or the faceless enemy.

Forrest Whitaker (BIRD) does wonders with his thankless role as Cronauer's loyal aide, Sukapatana—as Williams's Vietnamese love interest—is impressive, and Bruno Kirby, as Cronauer's nemesis, comes as close as any actor could to walking off with a film dominated by Williams at his best.

GOOD NEIGHBOR SAM

1964 130m c   ★★★½
Comedy   /A
Columbia

Jack Lemmon (Sam Bissel), Edward G. Robinson (Simon Nurdlinger), Romy Schneider (Janet Lagerlof), Dorothy Provine (Minerva Bissel), Mike Connors (Howard Ebbets), Anne Seymour (Irene Krump), Charles Lane (Jack Bailey), Louis Nye (Reinhold Shiffner), Edward Andrews (Burke), Robert Q. Lewis (Earl)

p, David Swift; d, David Swift; w, Jim Fritzell, Everett Greenbaum, David Swift (based on the novel by Jack Finney); ph, Burnett Guffey (Eastmancolor); ed, Charles Nelson; m, Frank DeVol; prod d, Dale Hennesy; chor, Miriam Nelson; cos, Micheline, Jacqueline

Frantic fun. Happily married advertising executive Lemmon is thrilled by the news that he has been entrusted with the firm's most valuable account, that of Nurdlinger's Dairy Company, which is owned and run by old man Nurdlinger (Robinson). The client is impressed by the clean-cut young Lemmon; in fact, the milk magnate is obsessed with wholesomeness and decency.

When Lemmon arrives home, he is surprised to find his wife, Provine, entertaining her former college roommate, Schneider, a vivacious and sexy lady about to inherit millions of dollars from her grandfather's estate. Unfortunately, there is a stipulation in her grandfather's will that she must be married and living with her husband in order to collect, and the fact of the matter is that Schneider's husband, Connors, has just walked out on her. Desperate because two of her cousins are out to catch her apart from her husband—and have hired private detective Nye to shadow her—Schneider has rented the house next door and begs Lemmon to pretend he's her husband until she gets the loot. If he agrees to do this, she'll pay him $1 million.

A consistently funny screwball comedy despite its somewhat excessive length, GOOD NEIGHBOR SAM reaches back to the classic comedies of Lubitsch, Hawks and Sturges for its inspiration and succeeds admirably. Lemmon is great but it's Schneider, in her first Hollywood outing, who steals the show. Her spunky, sexy, extremely funny portrayal demonstrates her versatility as an actress and is an interesting counterpoint to such serious ventures as her role in Orson Welles's adaptation of Franz Kafka's THE TRIAL.

GOOD NEWS

1947 92m c   ★★★½
Musical/Comedy   /U
MGM

June Allyson (Connie Lane), Peter Lawford (Tommy Marlowe), Patricia Marshall (Pat McClellan), Joan McCracken (Babe Doolittle), Ray McDonald (Bobby Turner), Mel Torme (Danny), Robert Strickland (Peter Van Dyne III), Donald MacBride (Coach Johnson), Tom Dugan (Pooch), Clinton Sundberg (Prof. Burton Kennyone)

p, Arthur Freed; d, Charles Walters; w, Betty Comden, Adolph Green (based on the musical comedy by Lawrence Schwab, Frank Mandel, B.G. DeSylva, Lew Brown, Ray Henderson); ph, Charles Schoenbaum (Technicolor); ed, Albert Akst; art d, Cedric Gibbons, Edward Carfagno; cos, Helen Rose, Valles

This lavish remake of the 1930 film version of the Broadway musical of the same name stars congenial Peter Lawford as Tait College football hero Tommy Marlowe, who's having trouble making his grades, and adorably nitwitty June Allyson as Connie Lane, the student librarian who tutors him. The campus sexpot (Patricia Marshall) has her sights set on Tommy, but he succumbs to the goodness of Connie, and all winds up well, including the inevitable big game.

New songs—"Pass That Peace Pipe" and "The French Lesson"—and sensational choreography contributed to making this an impressive debut for director Charles Walters and a big hit for MGM in 1947. There is also superb supporting work by Mel Torme and Joan McCracken, who had made a name for herself on the stage in *Bloomer Girl* and *Billion Dollar Baby*. The rest of the score—"The Varsity Drag," "The Best Things in Life Are Free," et al.—is from the 1927 DeSylva, Brown, and Henderson Broadway show.

GOOD, THE BAD, AND THE UGLY, THE
(IL BUONO, IL BRUTTO, IL CATTIVO)
1967   161m   c   ★★★★
Western   R/18
Europee   (Italy/Spain)

Clint Eastwood *(Joe)*, Eli Wallach *(Tuco)*, Lee Van Cleef *(Setenza)*, Aldo Giuffre, Chelo Alonso, Mario Brega, Luigi Pistilli, Rada Rassimov, Enzo Petito, Claudio Scarchilli

p, Alberto Grimaldi; d, Sergio Leone; w, Luciano Vincenzoni, Sergio Leone (based on a story by Agenore Incrocci, Furio Scarpelli, Vincenzoni, and Leone); ph, Tonino Delli Colli (Techniscope, Technicolor); ed, Nino Baragli, Eugenio Alabiso; m, Ennio Morricone; art d, Carlo Simi; fx, Eros Bacciucchi; cos, Carlo Simi

The definitive spaghetti western. Director Sergio Leone's epic end to the Clint Eastwood "Dollars" trilogy is a stunning, panoramic view of the West during the Civil War. THE GOOD, THE BAD, AND THE UGLY is a deceptively simple story detailing the efforts of three drifters, the "Good" (Eastwood), the "Bad" (Lee Van Cleef), and the "Ugly" (Eli Wallach), to find a fortune hidden in the unmarked grave of a man named Bill Carson.

Leone's narrative structure is incredibly complex: the characters' paths intersect and intertwine repeatedly until the Civil War impinges upon their lives and dwarfs their petty crimes. The war eventually involves Eastwood and Wallach in a massive battle for an unimportant bridge in which hundreds of soldiers march to pointless doom. The scale of violence shocks these two violent men; Eastwood, whose character begins to show a humanity only hinted at in the previous two films, states that he has never "seen so many men wasted so badly."

This is Leone's most violent film, but also one of his most compassionate. One of its most memorable scenes shows the Union troops organizing an orchestra of Confederate prisoner-musicians to play in order to cover the noise as Van Cleef tortures his prisoners. The effect is haunting, and recalls stories of similar incidents in Nazi death camps. A touching moment occurs when Eastwood comes across a dying young soldier, covers the shivering man with his duster, and helps him smoke his final cigarette.

Though not up to the standards of Leone's masterpiece ONCE UPON A TIME IN THE WEST, in which the director synthesizes scale, narrative, casting, and style, THE GOOD, THE BAD, AND THE UGLY is a massive, many-faceted film that continues to hold up, viewing after viewing. It also features one of Ennio Morricone's finest scores.

GOODBYE GIRL, THE
1977   110m   c   ★★★★
Romance/Comedy   PG
MGM

Richard Dreyfuss *(Elliott Garfield)*, Marsha Mason *(Paula McFadden)*, Quinn Cummings *(Lucy McFadden)*, Paul Benedict *(Mark Morgenweiss)*, Barbara Rhoades *(Donna Douglas)*, Theresa Merritt *(Mrs. Crosby)*, Michael Shawn *(Ronnie)*, Patricia Pearcy *(Rhonda Fontana)*, Gene Castle *(Assistant Choreographer)*, Daniel Levans *(Dance Instructor)*

p, Ray Stark; d, Herbert Ross; w, Neil Simon; ph, David M. Walsh (Metrocolor); ed, John F. Burnett; m, Dave Grusin; prod d, Albert Brenner; fx, Al Griswold; cos, Ann Roth

A rarity for Neil Simon's screen efforts, THE GOODBYE GIRL perfectly blends humor, sentiment, and romance on a level so pleasant it's almost suspicious.

Mason is a divorced ex-Broadway dancer in her thirties living with her precocious daughter in an apartment suddenly subleased by aspiring actor Dreyfuss, who arrives to take possession in the middle of the night. This is shocking news to Mason who thus learns that her departed lover, also an actor, has not only made her and daughter Cummings homeless but also has jilted her without notice. Dreyfuss makes it easy on Mason by offering to share the apartment, provided she pays half the rent. She agrees out of desperation, and the two strike up an uneasy truce that gradually blossoms into love.

This is a superb lighthearted comedy deftly directed by Ross, who helmed such hits as PLAY IT AGAIN, SAM and THE TURNING POINT. Mason is wonderfully warm and sensitive in a precarious role, while Dreyfuss, in a trademark performance, is nothing short of sensational. Cummings is a charming little girl whose premature sophistication provides some good humor. Next to THE SUNSHINE BOYS, this may be Simon's best original screenplay.

GOODBYE MR. CHIPS
1939   114m   bw   ★★★★½
Drama   /PG
MGM   (U.K.)

Robert Donat *(Charles Chipping)*, Greer Garson *(Katherine Ellis)*, Terry Kilburn *(John/Peter Colley)*, John Mills *(Peter Colley as a young man)*, Paul Henreid *(Max Staefel)*, Judith Furse *(Flora)*, Lyn Harding *(Dr. Wetherby)*, Milton Rosmer *(Charteris)*, Frederick Leister *(Marsham)*, Louise Hampton *(Mrs. Wickett)*

p, Victor Saville; d, Sam Wood; w, R.C. Sherriff, Claudine West, Eric Maschwitz, Sidney Franklin (based on the novella by James Hilton); ph, Freddie Young; ed, Charles Frend; m, Richard Addinsell; art d, Alfred Junge; cos, Julie Harris

Robert Donat gives a poignant performance in this superlative production as the shy, retiring British schoolteacher who guides several generations of young boys to manhood. Set at Brookfield Boys School in the late 1800s, the film follows the career of Charles Chipping, nicknamed "Mr. Chips," from his first days as an unpopular novice instructor through the marriage that brings him out of his shell to his final years as the school's beloved elder statesman.

So moving was Donat's performance that he beat out the most popular American candidate for the Best Actor Oscar, Clark Gable, who was nominated for his work in GONE WITH THE WIND. Greer Garson, as Mrs. Chips, also shines in the film that introduced her to American audiences. The screenplay is bright and the direction gentle, but it is Donat who elevates this bittersweet, affectionate tribute. (The great James Hilton wrote the original story as a novella in four days to meet a 1934 magazine deadline.) Skip the 1969 musical remake starring Peter O'Toole;

despite his rightness in the role, he can't salvage a lumbering horror show.

GOODFELLAS

1990 148m c ★★★★
Crime/Drama R/18
Irwin Winkler

Robert De Niro *(James Conway)*, Ray Liotta *(Henry Hill)*, Joe Pesci *(Tommy DeVito)*, Lorraine Bracco *(Karen Hill)*, Paul Sorvino *(Paul Cicero)*, Frank Sivero *(Frankie Carbone)*, Tony Darrow *(Sonny Bunz)*, Mike Starr *(Frenchy)*, Frank Vincent *(Billy Batts)*, Chuck Low *(Morris Kessler)*

p, Irwin Winkler; d, Martin Scorsese; w, Nicholas Pileggi, Martin Scorsese (based on the book *Wiseguy* by Pileggi); ph, Michael Ballhaus (Technicolor); ed, Thelma Schoonmaker; prod d, Kristi Zea; art d, Maher Ahmad; fx, Connie Brink; cos, Susan O'Donnell, Thomas Lee Keller

Coldly engrossing. This film, at once an extremely personal film and one that is so in tune with its characters and setting that it has the comic yet horrifying impact of an epic Marcel Ophuls documentary, offers a unique and fascinating vision of America and American lives.

Based on journalist Nicholas Pileggi's nonfiction book *Wiseguy*, GOODFELLAS revolves around the career of low-level gangster Henry Hill, who became part of the federal witness protection program after testifying against his erstwhile partners in crime. At the center of the book is Hill's insider account of the $6 million robbery of a Lufthansa cargo facility at New York's Idlewild Airport. As might be expected of the director of TAXI DRIVER, GOODFELLAS doesn't even show the robbery. Instead it focuses on the bloody aftermath of the heist, in which all the participants are brutally murdered by Henry's (Ray Liotta) partners, the lethally paranoid Jimmy Conway (Robert De Niro) and the psychotic Tommy De Vito (Joe Pesci).

Generally, GOODFELLAS is concerned with Tommy and Jimmy's climb up the mob ladder and its effects on Henry, but Scorsese's rich tapestry is both broader in scope and more detailed than a mere recounting of the events in the trio's life of crime. Because Scorsese is equally concerned with the minutiae of his main characters' world and with the grand design that appears to underlie that world, the downfall of Henry and his associates seems fated.

Many of the seemingly peripheral subplots are showstoppers. Focusing on the one-woman war Henry's wife Karen (wonderfully played by Lorraine Bracco) fights against his mistress, Henry's homelife functions as a raucous parody of the domineering husbands and quiet wives of THE GODFATHER. But what is perhaps the most remarkable accomplishment of GOODFELLAS is the way in which it radically re-thinks the epic cinematic form. In traditional epics a long, complicated, linear narrative unfolds over an extended period of time, serving to draw the audience into the world of its characters, causing viewers to have an emotional stake in the joys, pains, triumphs and tragedies of the people on the screen.

In GOODFELLAS, the characters do not develop nor does the audience's empathy for them. The narrative is even more fragmented than it is in Pileggi's book—resembling bits and pieces of home movies spliced together rather than a traditional movie plot. Characters continually appear, disappear, and change drastically, usually without much explanation. Karen, so fiercely self-possessed early in the film, is cowed and exhausted by the movie's hellish climax, during which Henry has gone from a trim mob dandy to a wired, coked-up, misshapen mess in little more than a jump cut. Henry's subsequent arrest and induction into the witness protection program, leading to the film's final and most disturbing image—a suburbanized Henry appearing at the front door of his expensive new tract home to bring in the morning paper.

Ironically, Scorsese denies the gangster the single characteristic that has made him a viable screen subject practically from the dawn of cinema, his false tragic stature. Instead of growing over the course of the film, Henry shrinks under Scorsese's scrutiny into a spineless louse surrounded by violent sociopaths, fit neither for sorrow nor pity.

GOODNIGHT, LADIES AND GENTLEMEN
(SIGNORE E SIGNORI, BUONANOTTE)

1977 119m c ★★½
Drama/Comedy
Maggio (Italy)

Senta Berger, Adolfo Celi, Vittorio Gassman, Nino Manfredi, Marcello Mastroianni, Ugo Tognazzi, Paolo Villaggio

p, Franco Committeri; d, Agenore Incrocci, Furio Scarpelli, Leo Benvenuti, Luigi Comencini, Piero De Bernardi, Nanni Loy, Ruggero Maccari, Luigi Magni, Mario Monicelli, Ugo Pirro, Ettore Scola; w, Furio Scarpelli, Agenore Incrocci, Leo Benvenuti, Luigi Comencini, Piero De Bernardi, Nanni Loy, Ruggero Maccari, Luigi Magni, Mario Monicelli, Ugo Pirro, Ettore Scola; ph, Claudio Ragona (Eastmancolor); ed, Amedeo Salfa; m, Lucio Dalla, Antonello Venditti, Giuseppe Mazzuca, Nicola Samale; art d, Lucia Mirisola, Lorenzo Baraldi, Luciano Spadoni

A fragmentary movie with several different segments written and directed by a variety of Italian talents. All of the stories are witty looks at Italian political and social life. One of the standout segments—"The Bomb," directed by Monicelli—is a political satire that sees a silly bomb scare at a police station snowball into an actual terrorist plot wherein the commissioner is blown to bits. Other segments include a satire on the CIA and a look at Christmas in Naples through the eyes of a child who sees all the public officials participating in the ceremonies as pompous and eccentric. The whole thing is cemented through the use of an Italian Broadcasting Corp. news show that introduces each segment and is anchored by Mastroianni.

GORILLAS IN THE MIST

1988 129m c ★★★
Biography PG-13/15
Peters/Arnold Glimcher/Guber

Sigourney Weaver *(Dian Fossey)*, Bryan Brown *(Bob Campbell)*, Julie Harris *(Roz Carr)*, John Omirah Miluwi *(Sembagare)*, Iain Cuthbertson *(Dr. Louis Leakey)*, Constantin Alexandrov *(Van Vecten)*, Waigwa Wachira *(Mukara)*, Iain Glenn *(Brendan)*, David Lansbury *(Larry)*, Maggie O'Neill *(Kim)*

p, Arnold Glimcher, Terence Clegg, Robert Nixon, Judy Kessler; d, Michael Apted; w, Anna Hamilton Phelan (based on the story by Harold T.P. Hayes); ph, John Seale, Alan Root (Technicolor); ed, Stuart Baird; m, Maurice Jarre; prod d, John Graysmark; fx, Rick Baker, David Harris; cos, Catherine Leterrier

Well-done monkey business, but an abrupt, uncentered screenplay, cluttered by unfocused direction, poor music and obligatory romance.

During the 1970s, Dian Fossey journeyed to Africa, where she closely studied the mountain gorilla, work later chronicled in a popular *National Geographic* television special. In this biopic Weaver portrays the late, controversial Fossey, beginning with her 1963 meeting with anthropologist Louis Leakey (Cuthbertson). He agrees to let her accompany him to Africa, and that begins her lifelong commitment to the study of gorillas. The film shows how this passion gains her fame but also leads to her fatal obsession with protecting her subjects as she grows increasingly irrational in dealing with those she feels pose a threat to the gorillas.

Although the film offers no real insights into Fossey's courage and obsessions, Weaver has some riveting moments. But because the screenplay doesn't penetrate the gradual shift Fossey made from animal activist to crank, she's forced to dredge it up from nowhere. There's terrific footage of the gorillas and the African setting is stunning. But the real star is Baker, who created the gorilla costumes donned by human beings for many scenes. His work is so well done that it is impossible to tell the real gorillas from the guys in the suits.

GORKY PARK

1983   103m   c   ★★★
Mystery   R/15
Orion

William Hurt (Arkady Renko), Lee Marvin (Jack Osborne), Brian Dennehy (William Kirwill), Ian Bannen (Iamskoy), Joanna Pacula (Irina), Michael Elphick (Pasha), Richard Griffiths (Anton), Rikki Fulton (Pribluda), Alexander Knox (General), Alexei Sayle (Golodkin)

p, Gene Kirkwood, Howard W. Koch, Jr.; d, Michael Apted; w, Dennis Potter (based on the novel by Martin Cruz Smith); ph, Ralf D. Bode (Technicolor); ed, Dennis Virkler; m, James Horner; prod d, Paul Sylbert; cos, Richard Bruno

Uneven but sometimes fascinating murder mystery. Three bodies are found in Moscow's Gorky Park, stripped of their faces and fingertips, making identification nearly impossible. William Hurt, in a highly polished performance, plays the Moscow police inspector assigned to the case. His trail leads to an American fur trader (Lee Marvin) who has all of Moscow at his disposal. A young dissident (Joanna Pacula), who was a friend of one of the victims, also gets caught in the intrigue. Though a little confusing at times, this mystery, based on the Martin Cruz Smith bestseller, has some great twists and gives a harshly realistic picture of the average man's life behind the Iron Curtain. GORKY suffers from the miscasting of Marvin, an unrealistic romance and, most unfortunately, a plodding climax. It was filmed in Helsinki, since the Soviets refused permission to shoot in Moscow.

GOSPEL ACCORDING TO ST. MATTHEW, THE

(IL VANGELO SECONDO MATTEO)
1964   136m   bw   ★★★★
Religious   /U
L'Arco/C.C.F. Lux   (France/Italy)

Enrique Irazoqui (Jesus Christ), Margherita Caruso (Mary, as a Girl), Susanna Pasolini (Mary, as a Woman), Marcello Morante (Joseph), Mario Socrate (John the Baptist), Settimo Di Porto (Peter), Otello Sestili (Judas), Ferruccio Nuzzo (Matthew), Giacomo Morante (John), Alfonso Gatto (Andrew)

p, Alfredo Bini; d, Pier Paolo Pasolini; w, Pier Paolo Pasolini (based on the gospel according to Saint Matthew); ph, Tonino Delli Colli; ed, Nino Baragli; m, Luis Bacalov, Johann Sebastian Bach, Wolfgang Amadeus Mozart, Sergei Prokofiev, Anton Webern; art d, Luigi Scaccianoce; fx, Ettore Catallucci; cos, Danilo Donati

Unconventional and very moving. Pier Paolo Pasolini's epic film, a Special Jury Prize-winner at the Venice Film Festival, tells the life story of Jesus in a semi-documentary style using nonprofessional actors, including the director's mother as the Virgin Mary. Hailed by many as the greatest adaptation of the life of Christ, this picture was dedicated to Pope John XXIII, who brought the Catholic Church into the 20th century. It may come as a surprise to those who see this honest and moving film that Pasolini was not only an atheist, but a homosexual and Marxist as well. As if to underline the unorthodox nature of the film, Pasolini has included on his soundtrack the American spiritual "Sometimes I Feel Like a Motherless Child," sung by Odetta.

GRADUATE, THE

1967   105m   c   ★★★★★
Drama/Comedy   /15
Lawrence Turman

Anne Bancroft (Mrs. Robinson), Dustin Hoffman (Ben Braddock), Katharine Ross (Elaine Robinson), William Daniels (Mr. Braddock), Murray Hamilton (Mr. Robinson), Elizabeth Wilson (Mrs. Braddock), Brian Avery (Carl Smith), Walter Brooke (Mr. Maguire), Norman Fell (Mr. McCleery), Elisabeth Fraser (Lady)

p, Lawrence Turman; d, Mike Nichols; w, Calder Willingham, Buck Henry (based on the novel by Charles Webb); ph, Robert Surtees (Panavision, Technicolor); ed, Sam O'Steen; m, Dave Grusin; prod d, Richard Sylbert; cos, Patricia Zipprodt

A social force of cinema that influenced the generation gap, THE GRADUATE was a tour de force for newcomer Hoffman and made him an overnight sensation.

Hoffman plays Ben Braddock, a pensive and somewhat shy youth of wealthy Southern California suburbia. Upon completion of his college studies, he's pressured by family and friends to "get going" with his life, encouraged at every turn to find a job, marry, and become a clone of his parents. Bancroft seduces Hoffman who cannot believe the older, married woman—she and her husband Hamilton are his parents' best friends—is pursuing him. Hoffman falls in love with her daughter Ross, and is put in the exhausting position of maintaining relationships with mother and daughter. He finally decides that Ross will be his wife, although Bancroft is wholly opposed to the union.

This comedy is wonderfully crafted by director Nichols who presents a half-dozen hilarious scenes, including Hoffman escaping badgering advice by submerging himself in the family pool in scuba gear and Bancroft's sudden shift from respectable matron to predatory tease, hiking her skirts lasciviously and purring promises of smoldering sex which almost put Hoffman into a comatose state. Nichols was to declare: "I think Benjamin and Elaine will end up exactly like their parents; that's what I was trying to say in the last scene." Yet the well-to-do younger audiences of the day interpreted this sequence of blatant heroics as a wonderful act of defiance by two young people whose destinies were being manipulated by their parents.

The film was an enormous hit, turning Nichols, who'd already scored heavily with WHO'S AFRAID OF VIRGINIA WOOLF?, into one of Hollywood's most important directors. However much of the credit for the innovative and fluid graphics in the film must go to cameraman Surtees, who was allowed a free hand to experiment widely. For example, the telescopic shot of Hoffman running to prevent the wedding causes him to appear not to be getting anywhere, almost as if he is running in place. All in all, THE GRADUATE is a flawlessly acted and produced film. Look fast for Richard Dreyfuss in his film debut as a college student.

GRAND CANYON

1991   134m   c   ★★★½
Drama
Fox   R/15

Danny Glover (Simon), Kevin Kline (Mack), Steve Martin (Davis), Mary McDonnell (Claire), Mary-Louise Parker (Dee), Alfre Woodard (Jane), Jeremy Sisto (Roberto), Tina Lifford (Deborah), Patrick Malone (Otis), Randle Mell (The Alley Baron)

p, Lawrence Kasdan, Charles Okun, Michael Grillo; d, Lawrence Kasdan; w, Lawrence Kasdan, Meg Kasdan; ph, Owen Roizman; ed, Carol Littleton; m, James Newton Howard; prod d, Bo Welch; art d, Tom Duffield; cos, Aggie Guerard Rogers

GRAND CANYON is a sort of the cinematic equivalent of Planet Hollywood, the New York nightspot where ordinary people can supposedly rub shoulders with the rich and famous. In Lawrence Kasdan's movie, co-written by his wife Meg, big, dramatic events—deaths, shootings, etc.—take place alongside mundane things like cutting your finger while chopping vegetables or learning how to make a left turn in Los Angeles traffic. The film invites us into the lives of a wide cross-section of people, painting a densely textured portrait of a sprawling, modern city.

Mack (Kevin Kline), a successful immigration attorney, catches an L.A. Lakers game with his best friend Davis (Steve Martin), a self-absorbed, self-righteous film producer who specializes in blood 'n' guts exploitation fare and whose license plates read "GRSS PNTS." As he is driving back from the game, Mack's car konks out on an unlit street somewhere in Inglewood. He manages to call for a tow truck but becomes the target of a gang of hoods who threaten to take his car and maybe his life. Luckily, the tow truck arrives, driven by a man whose composure and quiet authority convince the gang to lay off. An eloquently thankful Mack rides back to the garage with his saviour, Simon (Danny Glover), and the episode marks the beginning of a friendship between the two men.

GRAND CANYON successfully recreates the random, haphazard ways in which individual lives intersect, and captures the sense of menace and disintegration that permeate contemporary urban life. It's much less convincing, though, when it tries to turn its characters into spokespeople. Kline, in particular, gets too many speeches that should be accompanied by a blinking subtitle reading "MESSAGE." Similarly, the Kasdans' attempt to bring the various strands of the story together through the metaphor of the Grand Canyon (it's wide, like the gulfs between different sections of society, but it can also bring us together in awe of its size and beauty) is unconvincing.

GRAND HOTEL

1932   115m   bw   ★★★★★
Drama
MGM   /U

Greta Garbo (Grusinskaya), John Barrymore (Baron Felix von Gaigern), Joan Crawford (Flaemmchen), Wallace Beery (General Director Preysing), Lionel Barrymore (Otto Kringelein), Jean Hersholt (Senf), Robert McWade (Meierheim), Purnell Pratt (Zinnowitz), Ferdinand Gottschalk (Pimenov), Rafaela Ottiano (Suzette)

d, Edmund Goulding; w, William A. Drake (based on the play Menschen im Hotel by Vicki Baum and the American version by Drake); ph, William Daniels; ed, Blanche Sewell; art d, Cedric Gibbons; cos, Adrian

Gleaming deco dinosaur, Thalberg's pet, and the most legendary all-star movie ever made; a tribute to all that "stars" and glamour used to be in Hollywood's vanished Golden Age. This omnibus blockbuster chronicles the interwining lives of the denizens of GRAND HOTEL: Garbo, the lonely ballerina; John Barrymore, the noble thief; Crawford, the ambitious stenographer; Lionel Barrymore, the dying man on a last fling, and Beery, the ruthless industrialist. Lewis Stone and Hersholt exist to supervise and comment upon the others. If DINNER AT EIGHT, made a year later, has held up far better as a picture because it comments upon the rich and famous, HOTEL set the standard of those who don't achieve the twin pinnacles. Don't expect a particularly lucid screenplay or even acting of a high order; this masterpiece is hopelessly dated, directed by Goulding in the grand manner, and supported by Gibbons's, Daniel's, and Adrian's opulent work.

Revival house audiences laugh today at Garbo, with her permanently furrowed brow and her weird little bobby pin that holds back her hair. But striding through the hotel's lobby, swathed in chinchilla, remote in her fabled Swedish melancholy, "acting" hope swirling above a heavy heart, she really is the most extraordinary monstre sacre the screen will ever know.

Secondly, there's a surprisingly warm vixen by the name of Joan Crawford, who steals GRAND HOTEL. Even though her face looks like a deco statue's—perhaps the most beautiful eyes and nose ever photographed—she's brimming like a livewire of ambitious current. She's a legend, too—the chorus girl who became a great star. Here she wants top-rung stardom badly, and it shows. Today, with her little black dresses and casual hair, she looks almost modern. Curious that she holds up better than anyone else and only bears a passing resemblance to the bitch goddess people insist on remembering her as. She's marvelously in awe of John Barrymore, and very good indeed reaching out to Lionel. It's a part that exploits Crawford's most likable quality— her loyalty.

John Barrymore is all continental matinee-idol charm. If it seems hammy and somewhat affected today—though Barrymore is never effete—just guffaw through the current Broadway revival to be reminded of the sadness of this vanishing breed. Lionel's performance may be his best—this was before the scenery chewing of later years. But for scenery chewing, Wallace Beery is on hand. He's so thoroughly disagreeable and dense that it somehow works.

GRAND HOTEL remains a classic of its kind. MGM shrewdly marketed this film by withholding its general release for many months after its Hollywood premiere, allowing a tremendous word-of-mouth campaign to heighten expectation from viewers and critics alike. And the critics cheered, along with the Academy of Motion Picture Arts and Sciences, which voted the film an Oscar for Best Picture. The enormous success of GRAND HOTEL set the stage for many all-star films to come. In 1945, GRAND HOTEL was remade as the lightweight WEEKEND AT THE WALDORF with Ginger Rogers, Lana Turner, Walter Pidgeon, Van Johnson, and Edward Arnold in the lead roles.

GRAND ILLUSION

(LA GRANDE ILLUSION)
1937   95m   bw   ★★★★★
War/Prison
R.A.C.   (France)   /PG

Jean Gabin *(Marechal)*, Pierre Fresnay *(Capt. de Boeldieu)*, Erich von Stroheim *(Von Rauffenstein)*, Marcel Dalio *(Rosenthal)*, Dita Parlo *(Elsa, Farm Woman)*, Julien Carette *(Cartier)*, Gaston Modot *(Surveyor)*, Georges Peclet *(Soldier)*, Edouard Daste *(Teacher)*, Sylvain Itkine *(Demolder)*

p, Raymond Blondy; d, Jean Renoir; w, Jean Renoir, Charles Spaak; ph, Christian Matras; ed, Marguerite Renoir; m, Joseph Kosma; art d, Eugene Lourie; cos, Decrais

One of the undeniably great films in the history of world cinema, Jean Renoir's GRAND ILLUSION is an eloquent commentary on the borders that divide people, classes, armies and countries.

The film opens during WWI, as Marechal (Jean Gabin) and Boeldieu (Pierre Fresnay) are shot down by German ace Von Rauffenstein (Erich von Stroheim). The two survive the crash and are invited to lunch by Rauffenstein before ground troops arrive to cart the French officers off to a POW camp. Although Marechal and Boeldieu are compatriots, the latter has more in common with Von Rauffenstein, both of them being members of the white-gloved aristocracy. After lunch the Frenchmen are placed in barracks, where French officer Rosenthal (Marcel Dalio), a Jew, befriends them, along with several British officers who have also been taken prisoner. The newcomers join the others in working on an escape tunnel beneath the barracks, but a French victory on the Western Front is a sign that the war is turning against the Germans, and Marechal, Boeldieu, and the rest of the French prisoners are transferred to another prison, where they are reunited with Von Rauffenstein.

Now confined to a neck brace after a combat injury, the Commandant warmly welcomes the Frenchmen, pointing out that his prison, Wintersborn, is escape-proof. He treats his prisoners with great deference, having them to dinner and extending what meager courtesies he can, talking with Boeldieu about how this war will bring to an end the gentlemanly class of officers, dispensing with the honor and dignity of their rank and bloodlines. Caught someplace in between his loyalty to a member of his class (Von Rauffenstein) and to his country, Boeldieu once again agrees to assist his fellow prisoners in their escape attempts.

Directed with patience and care by Renoir, the film was banned in Germany by Nazi Propaganda Minister Josef Goebbels, who labeled it "Cinematographic Enemy No. 1" and compelled his Italian counterpart to have the film banned in that country, although the 1937 Venice Film Festival gave the film a "Best Artistic Ensemble" award. It was thought that all European prints of the film were destroyed by the Nazis, but American troops uncovered a negative in Munich in 1945 (preserved, strangely, by the Germans themselves), leading to the truncated film's reconstruction. Gabin, Fresnay, Dalio, and Stroheim all give impressive performances in this beautifully directed and written film.

GRAND MANEUVER, THE

(LES GRANDES MANOEUVRES)
1956   104m   c   ★★★★
Romance   /U
FS/Rizzoli   (France)

Michele Morgan *(Marie Louise Riviere)*, Gerard Philipe *(Lt. Armand de la Verne)*, Brigitte Bardot *(Lucie)*, Yves Robert *(Felix)*, Jean Desailly *(Victor Duverger)*, Pierre Dux *(Colonel)*, Jacques Francois *(Rudolph)*, Lise Delamare *(Jeanne)*, Jacqueline Maillan *(Juliette)*, Magali Noel *(Therese)*

p, Rene Clair; d, Rene Clair; w, Rene Clair, Jerome Geronimi, Jean Marsan (based on a story by Courteline); ph, Robert Le Febvre, Robert Juillard (Eastmancolor); ed, Louisette Hautecoeur; m, Georges Van Parys; art d, Leon Barsacq; cos, Rosine Delamare

In a pre-WWI garrison town, Philipe wagers that he can seduce a sophisticated beauty before he goes off on maneuvers for the summer. Drawing the name of his quarry from a hat, he begins his conquest of Morgan, a pretty, divorced milliner. Philipe wins the bet, but falls in love in the process. Not surprisingly, the great French director Clair has again put romance at the center of his film, but this time around he has approached his subject with more gravity than usual. Working in color for the first time, Clair invests the film with an impressive atmospheric elegance.

GRAND PRIX

1966   179m   c   ★★½
Sports   /A
Douglas & Lewis

James Garner *(Pete Aron)*, Eva Marie Saint *(Louise Frederickson)*, Yves Montand *(Jean-Pierre Sarti)*, Toshiro Mifune *(Izo Yamura)*, Brian Bedford *(Scott Stoddard)*, Jessica Walter *(Pat)*, Antonio Sabato *(Nino Barlini)*, Francoise Hardy *(Lisa)*, Adolfo Celi *(Agostini Manetta)*, Claude Dauphin *(Hugo Simon)*

p, Edward Lewis; d, John Frankenheimer; w, Robert Alan Aurthur, William Hanley; ph, Lionel Lindon (Cinerama-SuperPanavision, Metrocolor); ed, Fredric Steinkamp; m, Maurice Jarre; prod d, Richard Sylbert; fx, Milt Rice; cos, Sydney Guilaroff

The personal lives and loves of four professional auto racers—played by James Garner, Antonio Sabato, Brian Bedford, and Yves Montand—are mingled with impressively photographed racing footage in this stylistically inventive but narratively tedious effort directed by John Frankenheimer. The film follows the drivers through a number of important European competitions, including Monte Carlo, England's Brand's Hatch, and Italy's Monza, while their off-the-track affairs involve Eva Marie Saint, Jessica Walter, Francoise Hardy, and Toshiro Mifune, who plays Garner's corporate sponsor.

Frankenheimer pulls out all the stops to lend excitement to the racing footage—splitting the screen into ever smaller increments, mounting cameras to the cars to get shots taken inches above the track, and using slow motion—but ultimately his obsession with technique becomes wearying, and the plot is simply not interesting enough to stand on its own.

GRAPES OF WRATH

1940   129m   bw   ★★★★★
Drama   /PG
FOX

Henry Fonda *(Tom Joad)*, Jane Darwell *(Ma Joad)*, John Carradine *(Casey)*, Charley Grapewin *(Grandpa Joad)*, Dorris Bowdon *(Rosaharn)*, Russell Simpson *(Pa Joad)*, O.Z. Whitehead *(Al)*, John Qualen *(Muley Graves)*, Eddie Quillan *(Connie Rivers)*, Zeffie Tilbury *(Grandma Joad)*

p, Darryl F. Zanuck; d, John Ford; w, Nunnally Johnson (based on the novel by John Steinbeck); ph, Gregg Toland; ed, Robert Simpson; art d, Richard Day, Mark-Lee Kirk; cos, Gwen Wakeling

THE GRAPES OF WRATH is not only one of John Ford's greatest films, it documents an American social tragedy, giving the victims a voice through art. Based on the classic John Steinbeck novel, the film recounts the painful, poignant odyssey of the Joad family, Steinbeck's Depression-era tenant farmers from Dust Bowl Oklahoma, whose story has come to represent the plight of the "Okies" for generations of readers—and, through Ford's masterpiece, generations of moviegoers too.

As the film opens, Tom (Henry Fonda, in possibly the greatest performance of his career), eldest of the Joad sons, hitchhikes home to the family farm through the desolate Oklahoma landscape, having completed a four-year prison term for manslaughter. After getting a short ride from a suspicious trucker, Tom hoofs it to a clearing where he meets the slightly mad Casey (John Carradine), a former preacher who's "lost the call" and no longer ministers to the spiritual needs of the local farmers. The two walk to the Joad farm but find it abandoned except for Muley (John Qualen), who's even more mentally unbalanced than Casey and is hiding in the house. Muley tells them that sheriff's deputies working for banks and farming combines have been looking for him ever since he knocked one of them unconscious. Muley tells Tom that the Joad family, too, has moved on, the victims of foreclosure. Tom and Casey head for the farm of Tom's Uncle John (Frank Darien), where all the Joads have gathered, preparing to head westward to California in search of jobs advertised in a handbill Pa Joad (Russell Simpson) received. Ma (Jane Darwell) joyously greets her eldest son, and the next morning the whole family piles into a broken-down truck overloaded with their belongings and sets out in search of a better future.

Ford's visualization of Steinbeck's novel is so emotionally gripping that viewers have little time to collect themselves from one powerful scene to the next. Shooting mainly in California in the migrant camps around Pomona, with a second unit filming some backgrounds in Oklahoma, the director framed his shots to show that vast, almost barren landscapes, overcast skies, and bleak exteriors are omnipresent, giving a pervasive sense of the harshness of the displaced Okies' lives.

The sense of doom is dispelled, however, with the film's optimistic turn after the Joads find the government camp and its guardian (Grant Mitchell), a benevolent figure representing security, who, not coincidentally, bears a resemblance to Franklin D. Roosevelt. Though Ford does not hesitate to show the banks and the companies which took advantage of the farmers as land-grabbers without conscience, he also turns the Okies' bleak tale into one of hope by showing the Joads to be more than victims. Physically displaced, but not emotionally or spiritually defeated, they come to embody faith in the future and in the American people, and therein lies the film's greatness.

It took considerable courage to make THE GRAPES OF WRATH at a time when the Hollywood studios, on guard against unionization and attempts to challenge their monopoly, were in no mood to indulge its indictment of capitalism. In 1989, when it was named among the first movies included in the National Film Registry, the picture had lost none of its power as a social document, a historical testimony, or a work of cinematic art.

GREASE
1978 110m c   ★★½
Musical/Comedy   PG
Paramount

John Travolta (Danny), Olivia Newton-John (Sandy), Stockard Channing (Rizzo), Jeff Conaway (Kenickie), Didi Conn (Frenchy), Jamie Donnelly (Jan), Dinah Manoff (Marty), Barry Pearl (Doody), Michael Tucci (Sonny), Kelly Ward (Putzie)

p, Robert Stigwood, Allan Carr; d, Randal Kleiser; w, Bronte Woodard, Allan Carr (adapted by Carr from the musical by Jim Jacobs, Warren Casey); ph, Bill Butler (Panavision, Metrocolor); ed, John F. Burnett; prod d, Philip Jefferies; chor, Patricia Birch; cos, Albert Wolsky

Mousse. Disappointing, opportunistic nostalgia dirtied up by 1978's permissive standards and originally thrown up to an audience too young to really identify. Randall Kleiser's flat rendition of the long-running Broadway musical reaped huge rewards at the box office, among the highest grosses accorded any film musical. Set in the 1950s at Rydell High, it attempts a nostalgic look at young love, with plot turns not really important—the usual misunderstandings; a satire of teachers; a car race between rivals. At the center of the film are John Travolta as Danny, the ultimate cool dude, and Olivia Newton-John as Sandy, the junior miss who aches to have their summer romance continue into the school year. Channing's the standout, but all of the performers had long since departed high school when the film was made, and there's not enough to enjoy to warrant suspension of belief.

GREASED LIGHTNING
1977 96m c   ★★★
Biography/Sports   PG
Third World Cinema

Richard Pryor (Wendell Scott), Beau Bridges (Hutch), Pam Grier (Mary Jones), Cleavon Little (Peewee), Vincent Gardenia (Sheriff Cotton), Richie Havens (Woodrow), Julian Bond (Russell), Earl Hindman (Beau Welles), Minnie Gentry (Mrs. Scott), Lucy Saroyan (Hutch's Wife)

p, Hannah Weinstein; d, Michael Schultz; w, Kenneth Vose, Lawrence DuKore, Melvin Van Peebles, Leon Capetanos; ph, George Bouillet (Movielab Color); ed, Bob Wyman, Christopher Holmes, Randy Roberts; m, Fred Karlin; art d, Jack Senter; fx, Candy Flanagin, Tom Ward; cos, Celia Bryant, Henry Salley

Directed by the prolific but uneven African-American filmmaker Michael Schultz (CAR WASH, COOLEY HIGH, WHICH WAY IS UP?), this well-intentioned biography of the first black auto racing champion, Wendell Scott, features Richard Pryor in an early dramatic role. The story covers a 25-year period, from the end of WWII to 1971, in the life of the determined Scott as he strives to overcome the prejudice and closed-mindedness behind auto racing's color barrier. Along the way he is aided by a white driver, Hutch (Bridges), and supported his wife, Mary Jones (Grier). As he is played by one of the great comics of our time, it comes as no surprise that he relies on his sense of humor to help make it through the bad times. Civil rights leader Julian Bond, former Atlanta mayor Maynard Jackson, and folk singer Richie Havens all appear.

GREAT DICTATOR, THE
1940 127m bw   ★★★★
Comedy/War   /U
UA

Charles Chaplin (Hynkel, Dictator of Tomania/A Jewish Barber), Paulette Goddard (Hannah), Jack Oakie (Napaloni, Dictator of Bacteria), Reginald Gardiner (Schultz), Henry Daniell (Garbitsch), Billy Gilbert (Herring), Maurice Moscovich (Mr. Jaeckel), Emma Dunn (Mrs. Jaeckel), Grace Hayle (Mme. Napaloni), Carter DeHaven (Bacterian Ambassador) p, Charles Chaplin; d, Charles Chaplin; w, Charles Chaplin; ph, Roland Totheroh, Karl Struss; ed, Willard Nico; m, Meredith Willson; art d, J. Russell Spencer

Chaplin's first complete talkie and it's fascinating to see the way the structures of his silent films are translated into a unique blend of slapstick, wordplay, parody, and pointed political commentary. This is Chaplin's brilliant and heartfelt plea for world peace in an era of rising fascism and mass annihilation.

Chaplin, well aware of the ironic physical similarity between his sweet Little Tramp and Adolf Hitler, casts himself in a dual role as a nameless Jewish barber and as Adenoid Hynkel, Dictator of Tomania. The barber, a soldier for the German Army in WWI, awakens from a state of amnesia to learn that Hynkel, the country's new dictator, is calling for the persecution of all Jews. The barber's friend, Hannah (Paulette Goddard), is forced to flee the country; his barber shop is defaced and burned and he is arrested and sent to a concentration camp for sheltering an old friend, Schultz (Reginald Gardiner).

Filled with equal parts of humanity, outrage, and comedy, THE GREAT DICTATOR contains some of Chaplin's finest moments, including the famous upside-down flying sequence in which the barber doesn't even realize that he's not flying upright, Hynkel's fiery speech, delivered in an unintelligible German-English gibberish, and the film's scene of great genius, Hynkel's "ballet" with an air-filled globe of the world—tossing it, kicking it, adoring it, and, finally, destroying it as only a dictator dreaming of world domination could. The power of this strangely haunting film is enhanced by the realization that the extremes of human nature in the first half of this century were personified by these two mustached figures—Hitler and the Little Tramp.

GREAT ESCAPE, THE

1963   169m   c   ★★★★
Prison/War   /PG
UA

Steve McQueen *("Cooler King" Hilts)*, James Garner *("The Scrounger" Hendley)*, Richard Attenborough *("Big X" Bartlett)*, James Donald *(Senior Officer Ramsey)*, Charles Bronson *(Danny Velinski)*, Donald Pleasence *("The Forger" Blythe)*, James Coburn *("The Manufacturer" Sedgwick)*, David McCallum *(Ashley-Pitt)*, Gordon Jackson *(MacDonald)*, John Leyton *(Willie)*

p, John Sturges; d, John Sturges; w, James Clavell, W.R. Burnett (based on the book by Paul Brickhill); ph, Daniel Fapp (Deluxe Color); ed, Ferris Webster; m, Elmer Bernstein; art d, Fernando Carrere; cos, Bert Henrikson

Expertly directed and written with an infectious undercurrent of wry humor, this classic WWII POW escape yarn features an all-star cast of hardened Allied prisoners who the Germans have thrown together in a special "escape-proof" camp. Naturally, the first thing they set about doing is planning their escape—not just any escape, but one so massive that thousands of German troops will be kept away from the front in the effort to track them down.

The prime instigators include "Big X" (Richard Attenborough), the British master planner; a Polish tunnel-digging expert (Charles Bronson); a forger of passports and papers (Donald Pleasence); and two Americans, "The Scrounger" (James Garner), in charge of assembling needed supplies, and Hilts (Steve McQueen), "The Cooler King," who has his own ideas about how to get out. When those ideas fail, he uses a baseball and mitt to while away his days in solitary confinement. The prisoners ingeniously go about digging three tunnels, and though one of them is discovered, the big breakout still takes

place. The film follows the principals as they try to make their way to safety—some successfully, others meeting tragic ends, but all providing great excitement.

Based on a book detailing a real-life mass escape of Allied troops in 1942, producer-director John Sturges's film is involving throughout, due mainly to the excellent performances of its stellar cast, particularly McQueen in a breakthrough performance. Elmer Bernstein's exhilarating score is perfectly suited to the film's nonstop tension. A hit with the critics and at the box office. THE GREAT ESCAPE is for many *the* great "escape" film.

GREAT EXPECTATIONS

1934   97m   bw   ★★½
Drama   /A
Universal

Henry Hull *(Magwitch)*, Phillips Holmes *(Pip)*, Jane Wyatt *(Estella)*, Florence Reed *(Miss Havisham)*, Alan Hale *(Joe Gargery)*, Rafaela Ottiano *(Mrs. Joe)*, Walter Armitage *(Herbert Pocket)*, Jackie Searl *(Young Herbert)*, Eily Malyon *(Sarah Pocket)*, Virginia Hammond *(Molly)*

d, Stuart Walker; w, Gladys Unger (based on the novel by Charles Dickens); ph, George Robinson; ed, Edward Curtiss; art d, Albert S. D'Agostino

Uninspired Hollywood version of the Charles Dickens classic starring Holmes as Pip, the young orphan boy who rises to prominence with the help of his life-long mysterious benefactor. A weak adaptation filled with disappointing performances from a cast capable of better. Valerie Hobson shone much brighter as Estella in the vastly superior 1946 version directed by David Lean. At the time of initial release, the picture suffered from critical comparison with the nearly simultaneous release of THE OLD CURIOSITY SHOP, the first of a series of British productions of the works of Dickens. Look quickly for Walter Brennan in a small role as a prisoner.

GREAT EXPECTATIONS

1946   118m   bw   ★★★★★
Drama   /PG
Cineguild   (U.K.)

John Mills *(Pip Pirrip)*, Valerie Hobson *(Estella/Her Mother)*, Bernard Miles *(Joe Gargery)*, Francis L. Sullivan *(Jaggers)*, Martita Hunt *(Miss Havisham)*, Finlay Currie *(Abel Magwitch)*, Anthony Wager *(Pip as Child)*, Jean Simmons *(Estella as Child)*, Alec Guinness *(Herbert Pocket)*, Ivor Barnard *(Wemmick)*

p, Ronald Neame; d, David Lean; w, David Lean, Ronald Neame, Anthony Havelock-Allan, Cecil McGivern, Kay Walsh (from the novel by Charles Dickens); ph, Guy Green; ed, Jack Harris; m, Walter Goehr; prod d, John Bryan; art d, Wilfred Shingleton; cos, Sophia Harris

A masterful realization of Charles Dickens's novel, this may be the best cinematic translation of the author's work, as well as director David Lean's greatest achievement. Beginning in 1830, the film follows the life of orphan Pip Pirrip (Anthony Wager as a child, John Mills as an adult), from his humble beginnings as a blacksmith's apprentice to his days as the wealthy beneficiary of an escaped convict (Finlay Currie) he once helped. Wonderfully directed by Lean—especially the childhood passages— GREAT EXPECTATIONS is brimming with unforgettable images and characters. Although admirers of the novel may bemoan the absence of several characters, the film captures the spirit of Dickens, translating his prose into flawless cinema.

Cinematographer Guy Green and production designer John Bryan were awarded Academy Awards for their memorable work. A must see.

GREAT EXPECTATIONS

1975 124m c   ★★½
Drama   /U
Transcontinental (U.K.)

Michael York (Pip), Sarah Miles (Estella), Margaret Leighton (Miss Havisham), James Mason (Magwitch), Robert Morley (Pumblechook), Anthony Quayle (Jaggers), Heather Sears (Biddy), Joss Ackland (Joe Gargery), Andrew Ray (Herbert Pocket), James Faulkner (Drummle)

p, Robert Fryer; d, Joseph Hardy; w, Sherman Yellen (based on the novel by Charles Dickens); ph, Freddie Young (Panavision, Eastmancolor); ed, Bill Butler; m, Maurice Jarre; art d, Alan Tomkins

Even adequate Dickens is better than no Dickens at all, and this made-for-television version of the great storyteller's saga is just barely that. Yellen's screenplay for this version was not nearly as rich as the beloved 1946 version and Hardy's direction will never be confused with David Lean's. Hardy and Yellen came to television from successful stage careers; their evident inability to understand the difference between stage and screen may be what does in this effort despite the distinguished cast. There's good music from Maurice Jarre and nice work from all the technical departments but the heart of the matter was left somewhere on the cutting-room floor.

GREAT GATSBY, THE

1949 92m bw   ★★★½
Drama   /PG
Paramount

Alan Ladd (Jay Gatsby), Betty Field (Daisy Buchanan), Macdonald Carey (Nick Carraway), Ruth Hussey (Jordan Baker), Barry Sullivan (Tom Buchanan), Howard da Silva (Wilson), Shelley Winters (Myrtle Wilson), Henry Hull (Dan Cody), Carole Mathews (Ella Cody), Ed Begley (Myron Lupus)

p, Richard Maibaum; d, Elliott Nugent; w, Cyril Hume, Richard Maibaum (based on the novel by F. Scott Fitzgerald and the play by Owen Davis, Sr.); ph, John Seitz; ed, Ellsworth Hoagland; m, Robert Emmett Dolan; art d, Hans Dreier, Roland Anderson; cos, Edith Head

The first sound adaptation of F. Scott Fitzgerald's classic Jazz Age novel, this version is far superior to its silent predecessor and the botched 1974 remake with Robert Redford in the title role. A large part of what makes this version work is the glacial central presence of Alan Ladd, who's quite convincing as a man with a mysterious past. Ladd is the enigmatic Jay Gatsby, a fabulous bootlegger who has used his relentless drive to amass a fortune. That mission accomplished, he turns his attention to wooing back a woman he lost many years earlier to a wealthy man.

Ladd is quite appropriate for Fitzgerald's hero. Embodying youthful disillusionment, false hope, and tragic nobility, he captures Gatsby's melancholy, mythic persona. Interestingly, the film ultimately feels more like a 1940s film noir than a 20s costume drama due to the moody monochrome cinematography of John F. Seitz.

GREAT GILBERT AND SULLIVAN, THE

1953 105m c   ★★★
Musical/Biography
London Films (U.K.)

Robert Morley (W.S. Gilbert), Maurice Evans (Arthur Sullivan), Eileen Herlie (Helen Lenoir), Martyn Green (George Grossmith), Peter Finch (Richard D'Oyly Carte), Dinah Sheridan (Grace Marston), Isabel Dean (Mrs. Gilbert), Wilfrid Hyde-White (Mr. Marston), Muriel Aked (Queen Victoria), Michael Ripper (Louis)

p, Frank Launder, Sidney Gilliat; d, Sidney Gilliat; w, Sidney Gilliat, Leslie Baily, Vincent Korda (based on The Gilbert and Sullivan Book by Baily); ph, Christopher Challis (Technicolor); ed, Gerald Turney-Smith; m, Arthur Sullivan; prod d, Hein Heckroth

Sidney Gilliat directed Martyn Green, Maurice Evans, Robert Morley, and others in a celebration of the lives and music of the famed Victorian duo. Morley stars as the caustic writer-lyricist W.S. Gilbert and Maurice Evans is Arthur Sullivan, the composer of the music for their comic operettas. Finch is Richard D'Oyly Carte, the impresario who brought them together. The highly enjoyable music is sung by members of the famed D'Oyly Carte company, including Martyn Green, one of the premier Gilbert and Sullivan tenors. It's great fun, though not as memorable as one might hope.

GREAT MCGINTY, THE

1940 81m bw   ★★★★
Political/Comedy
Paramount

Brian Donlevy (Dan McGinty), Muriel Angelus (Catherine McGinty), Akim Tamiroff (The Boss), Allyn Joslyn (George), William Demarest (The Politician), Louis Jean Heydt (Thompson), Harry Rosenthal (Louis, the Bodyguard), Arthur Hoyt (Mayor Tillinghast), Libby Taylor (Bessie), Thurston Hall (Mr. Moxwell)

p, Paul Jones; d, Preston Sturges; w, Preston Sturges; ph, William Mellor; ed, Hugh Bennett; m, Frederick Hollander; art d, Hans Dreier, Earl Hedrick; cos, Edith Head

A hilarious spoof of American politics, this film marked the directorial debut of the mercurial and brilliant Preston Sturges, one of the best writer-directors of the 1940s. While this film never reaches the giddy heights of some of his subsequent films, THE GREAT MCGINTY was a favorable harbinger of the therapeutic madness to come.

The film opens in a smoky banana-republic bar largely patronized, it seems, by Americans on the lam. One such denizen, Thompson (Heydt), is a one-time chief cashier of a major bank turned embezzler. Now dejected from hiding out in this steamy exile, he attempts suicide in the men's room but he's stopped by the bartender, Dan McGinty (Donlevy). McGinty has an even more ignominious tale to tell: he used to be governor of a state! His strange story unravels in flashback.

McGinty begins as a seedy hobo looking for a quick buck. During an election in a major city, he's hired by a slick politician (Demarest) to vote repeatedly using the names of dead citizens. He proves to be an overzealous participant in the democratic process, voting dozens of times at an expected $2 per vote but the politico is unable to come across with the dough. McGinty remains persistent. He's taken to the party hall where The Boss (Tamiroff) is so taken with the bum's moxie that he appoints him a collector of funds in his protection racket. McGinty proves himself a born collector and he continues moving up the ladder of crime until he is finally ready for the big time—politics.

Donlevy, in an early starring role, gives a marvelous performance as a dim-witted bum who's transformed into a polished politician. The flamboyant Tamiroff's rendering of the boss is a comic delight. Demarest is colorful and full of street savvy and wit, once remarking: "If you didn't have graft, you'd have a lower class of people in politics!" This terrific satire was the brainchild of screenwriter Sturges, who, by the time he penned this script, was the highest-paid writer in Hollywood, having written films such as EASY LIVING and DIAMOND JIM.

GREAT MOUSE DETECTIVE, THE

1986 73m c   ★★★½
Animated/Mystery   G/U
Disney/Silver Screen Partners II/Buena Vista

VOICES OF: Vincent Price (Professor Ratigan), Barrie Ingham (Basil/Bartholomew), Val Bettin (Dawson), Susanne Pollatschek (Olivia), Candy Candido (Fidget), Diana Chesney (Mrs. Judson), Eve Brenner (The Mouse Queen), Alan Young (Flaversham), Basil Rathbone (Sherlock Holmes), Laurie Main (Watson)

p, Burny Mattinson; d, John Musker, Ron Clements, Dave Michener, Burny Mattinson; w, Peter Young, Vance Gerry, Steve Hulett, Ron Clements, John Musker, Bruce M. Morris, Matthew O'Callaghan, Burny Mattinson, David Michener, Melvin Shaw (based on the book Basil of Baker Street by Eve Titus); ph, Ed Austin; ed, Roy M. Brewer, Jr., Jim Melton; m, Henry Mancini; art d, Guy Vasilovich; anim, Mark Henn, Glen Keane, Robert Minkoff, Hendel Butoy

Back in the Dark Ages of Disney—the dimly remembered period after Walt's death and before the second Renaissance that was ushered in by THE LITTLE MERMAID and BEAUTY AND THE BEAST—there seemed to be trouble in the magic kingdom. THE GREAT MOUSE DETECTIVE, therefore, surprised and pleased many animation enthusiasts; it combined the sophistication of the new Disney era with the well-loved traditions and standards of the past.

Based on the beloved children's novel Basil of Baker Street by Eve Titus, the story is an adaptation of Sherlock Holmes motifs interpreted by a few cartoon mice living in Victorian London. Vincent Price provides the voice of Ratigan, a Moriarty-like genius who wants to control the mouse world. To this end, he kidnaps a brilliant mouse toymaker, Flaversham (voiced by Alan Young), intending to have the poor whiskered creature build a terrifying rodent robot that he will use to dethrone the current mouse queen (Eve Brenner). Basil (Barrie Ingham), the Holmesian mouse, and Dawson (Val Bettin) agree to help Flaversham's daughter Olivia (Susanne Pollatschek) find her father, but the trail leads to all sorts of pitfalls.

This is high-quality animation. The engaging characters play out the action against elegantly designed backgrounds. The story is genuinely exciting, a well-told tale that is entertaining to both children and adults without compromising the expectations of either group. The voices are perfectly cast, particulary Price as the evil Ratigan.

GREAT MUPPET CAPER, THE

1981 95m c   ★★★½
Children's/Musical   G/U
Universal (U.K.)

Jim Henson (Kermit/Rowlf/Dr. Teeth/Waldorf), Frank Oz (Miss Piggy/Fozzie Bear/Animal/Sam the Eagle), Dave Goelz (The Great Gonzo/Beauregard/Zoot/Dr. Bunsen/Honeydew), Jerry Nelson (Floyd/Pops/Lew Zealand), Richard Hunt (Scooter/Statler/Sweetums/ Janice/Beaker), Charles Grodin (Nicky Holiday), Diana Rigg (Lady Holiday), John Cleese, Robert Morley, Peter Falk

p, David Lazer, Frank Oz; d, Jim Henson; w, Tom Patchett, Jay Tarses, Jerry Juhl, Jack Rose; ph, Oswald Morris (Technicolor); ed, Ralph Kemplen; prod d, Harry Lange; art d, Charles Bishop, Terry Ackland-Snow, Leigh Malone; chor, Anita Mann; cos, Julie Harris, Calista Hendrickson, Joanne Green, Mary Strieff, Carol Spier, Danielle Obinger

This one got lost in the shuffle. Jim Henson himself directed the muppets along with Charles Grodin, John Cleese, Robert Morley and other English types. The Muppet menagerie cavorts in the middle of London in this, their second film. There's a plot this time—the famous "Baseball" diamond has been stolen—and the music is even better than THE MUPPET MOVIE. That first film with the muppet crew had to be a success; this time it was more difficult. Nonetheless, the caper plot that Henson and company worked out manages to hold adult interest for quite a while.

Kermit, Fozzie Bear, and Gonzo are reporters investigating the theft of fashion queen Lady Holiday's (Diana Rigg) jewels. Lady Holiday's brother, Nicky (Charles Grodin), frames Miss Piggy for the theft but the other Muppets save the day. The film boasts fewer guest-star cameo appearances than the first time around but those who are here do a good job, and Miss Piggy's Busby Berkeley-type dance and the water ballet are fun to watch. Followed by THE MUPPETS TAKE MANAHATTAN.

GREAT NORTHFIELD, MINNESOTA RAID, THE

1972 91m c   ★★★
Biography/Western   PG/X
Universal

Cliff Robertson (Cole Younger), Robert Duvall (Jesse James), Luke Askew (Jim Younger), R.G. Armstrong (Clell Miller), Dana Elcar (Allen), Donald Moffat (Manning), John Pearce (Frank James), Matt Clark (Bob Younger), Wayne Sutherlin (Charley Pitts), Robert H. Harris (Wilcox)

p, Jennings Lang; d, Philip Kaufman; w, Philip Kaufman; ph, Bruce Surtees (Technicolor); ed, Douglas Stewart; m, Dave Grusin; art d, Alexander Golitzen, George Webb; cos, Helen Colvig

An offbeat, ragged but totally absorbing Western, this film profiles the infamous yet celebrated James-Younger gang in relatively realistic terms, showing them for the murderous and desperate men they probably were while offering a refreshingly sophisticated and cynical political analysis of their situation. Though it borrows heavily from late 1960s-early 1970s genre landmarks such as BONNIE AND CLYDE and McCABE AND MRS. MILLER, it remains interesting for its depiction of how exploitive capitalism—the railroads in this case—compels somewhat simpleminded farmers into outlaw lives.

The Missouri legislature is preparing to vote on granting amnesty to those notorious outlaws, Jesse James (Duvall) and Cole Younger (Robertson). Some enlightened members argue that these men and their followers were driven into crime by powerful behind-the-scenes interests that appropriated their lands. Cole is willing to accept the amnesty and return to farming, but James argues that nothing will change, the railroads will continue to steal their land and their persecution will never stop. He's right. After the amnesty motion is ruled out of order, James plans to take the gang from their native Missouri to rob the big bank in Northfield, Minnesota, after reading a newspaper account about its financial standing as the biggest bank west of the Mississippi. Things go wrong.

Although director-writer Kaufman claimed to have researched the real tale of the James-Younger gang while studying history at the University of Chicago, many of his details are inaccurate and some scenes are outright fabrications. However, the awkward, crude, unsophisticated dialogue is appropriate to the period, region, and characters. Duvall delivers an interesting interpretation of Jesse James as a borderline psychotic. Robertson credibly portrays Cole Younger as a cunning, intelligent and even sensitive person. The supporting players also are all believable, and the well mounted production seems clearly authentic. One of the best profiles of the James-Younger gang yet made, although Walter Hill's THE LONG RIDERS more aptly captures the character of the gang.

GREAT SANTINI, THE

1979   115m   c   ★★★½
Drama/War   PG
Orion

Robert Duvall (*Bull Meechum*), Blythe Danner (*Lillian Meechum*), Michael O'Keefe (*Ben Meechum*), Lisa Jane Persky (*Mary Anne Meechum*), Julie Anne Haddock (*Karen Meechum*), Brian Andrews (*Matthew Meechum*), Stan Shaw (*Toomer Smalls*), Theresa Merritt (*Arrabelle Smalls*), David Keith (*Red Pettus*), Paul Mantee (*Col. Hedgepath*)

p, Charles A. Pratt; d, Lewis John Carlino; w, Lewis John Carlino (based on the novel by Pat Conroy); ph, Ralph Woolsey (Technicolor); ed, Houseley Stevenson; m, Elmer Bernstein; prod d, Jack Poplin

Robert Duvall received an Academy Award nomination for his forceful performance as a warrior without a war in this touching, well-crafted drama based on the novel by Pat Conroy.

As Marine pilot Bull Meechum, he rules his family with military discipline, setting impossibly high standards for his four children (Julie Ann Haddock, Brian Andrews, Lisa Jane Persky, and Michael O'Keefe). When Bull's harsh manner becomes too oppressive for his offspring, they know that their mother, Lillian (Blythe Danner), is there to provide an understanding shoulder to cry on, especially the sensitive Ben (O'Keefe), whose battle to earn his father's respect is most tellingly played out in one-on-one basketball games that force Bull to play dirty to win. Although Bull's kids are never able to reach their father, they do offer him the kind of stoic tribute that would have made him proud when tragedy strikes.

Deftly scripted, beautifully shot—making good use of its South Carolina locations—and magnificently acted, THE GREAT SANTINI was deservedly nominated for an Academy Award as Best Picture. Though its emotions are big, the performances are so nicely nuanced that sentiment never overwhelms the story's emotional realism. In addition to Duvall's tour-de-force performance, Danner is outstanding as the nurturing mother, and O'Keefe's heartfelt portrayal of the tortured son earned him an Oscar nomination as Best Supporting Actor.

GREAT TRAIN ROBBERY, THE

1979   110m   c   ★★★
Crime   PG/15
UA   (U.K.)

Sean Connery (*Edward Pierce*), Donald Sutherland (*Agar*), Lesley-Anne Down (*Miriam*), Alan Webb (*Edgar Trent*), Malcolm Terris (*Henry Fowler*), Robert Lang (*Inspector Sharp*), Wayne Sleep (*Clean Willy*), Michael Elphick (*Burges*), Pamela Salem (*Emily Trent*), Gabrielle Lloyd (*Elizabeth Trent*)

p, John Foreman; d, Michael Crichton; w, Michael Crichton (based on his novel); ph, Geoffrey Unsworth; ed, David Bretherton; m, Jerry Goldsmith; prod d, Maurice Carter; art d, Bert Davey; cos, Anthony Mendleson

Connery is Edward Pierce, a British thief who pulls off the first moving train robbery in 1855. Based on real events, this stylish period film has Pierce enlisting the help of one Clean Willy (Sleep) and master safecracker Agar (Sutherland) to pull off the crime. Miriam (Down), Pierce's mistress, sets up his escape after being caught by police. An entertaining thriller that stumbles occasionally on overlong dialogue sequences. Connery handled his own stunt work.

GREAT WALDO PEPPER, THE

1975   107m   c   ★★★
Adventure   PG
Universal

Robert Redford (*Waldo Pepper*), Bo Svenson (*Axel Olsson*), Bo Brundin (*Ernst Kessler*), Susan Sarandon (*Mary Beth*), Geoffrey Lewis (*Newt*), Edward Herrmann (*Ezra Stiles*), Philip Bruns (*Dillhoefer*), Roderick Cook (*Werfel*), Kelly Jean Peters (*Patsy*), Margot Kidder (*Maude*)

p, George Roy Hill; d, George Roy Hill; w, William Goldman (based on a story by Hill); ph, Robert Surtees (Technicolor); ed, Peter Berkos, William Reynolds; m, Henry Mancini; art d, Henry Bumstead; cos, Edith Head

A handsomely mounted aviation adventure from the director, screenwriter and one of the stars of the hugely successful BUTCH CASSIDY AND THE SUNDANCE KID, this film deals with that colorful era of the early 1920s when barnstorming—performing aerial feats before rural crowds—was so popular.

The self-proclaimed Great Waldo Pepper (Redford) is one of those celebrated aerial daredevils. Though he had been an undistinguished WWI flyer, he claims to have met German ace Kessler (Brundin) in combat. Olsson (Svenson) is his friendly rival in matters both professional and romantic. Their ongoing tomfoolery eventually leads to several mishaps, crashes, and—during a spectacular daredevil flying feat—a death. Grounded by federal aviation officials, the resourceful Pepper decides to go west to Hollywood, the land where dreams are made and fabulous frauds are the norm. Here Pepper becomes a stunt pilot and must finally confront the truth about his own legend.

The somewhat formulaic story—told better in such films as THE TARNISHED ANGELS—owes much to THE LOST SQUADRON, a largely forgotten film directed by the great Erich von Stroheim, that deals with WWI pilots performing impossible barnstorming and movie stunts. Redford is perfectly cast as the boy-man of the air who cannot find a place in a society that has no more need of heroes. Brundin is outstanding as the misplaced German ace, but the rest of the cast is nothing to brag about. The stunts themselves, however, are indeed spectacular.

GREAT WALL, A

1986   97m   c   ★★½
Drama/Comedy   PG
W&S

Peter Wang (*Leo Fang*), Sharon Iwai (*Grace Fang*), Kelvin Han Yee (*Paul Fang*), Li Quinqin (*Lili Chao*), Hu Xiaoguang (*Mr. Chao*), Shen Guanglan (*Mrs. Chao*), Wang Xiao (*Liu Yida*), Xiu Jian (*Yu*), Ran Zhijuan (*Jan*), Han Tan (*Old Liu*)

p, Shirley Sun; d, Peter Wang; w, Peter Wang, Shirley Sun; ph, Peter Stein, Robert Primes; ed, Graham Weinbren; m, David Liang, Ge Ganru

Reportedly the first American feature shot in Communist China, A GREAT WALL deemphasizes story development in favor of an amiable exploration of the cultural contrasts between Americans and Chinese. Although graced with rich, likable characters and a perceptive wit, the film remains a disappointing effort, opting for superficial comparisons rather than in-depth political or cultural inquiry.

Wang is a computer engineer who who quits his job when he's passed over for a promotion he expected. He then decides that it's time for his family to travel to China to learn about their cultural origins. His wife (Iwai) is a first-generation American with no knowledge of the Chinese language; their son (Yee) is a typical American teenager. They go to visit Wang's sister who lives in Peking with her retired-bureaucrat husband and her teenage daughter. The Chinese family members graciously accept their American relatives into their home and allow for the expected cultural confrontations.

Despite a number of flaws—specifically, forced plot situations—A GREAT WALL is almost impossible to dislike because the characters are portrayed as regular people in the process of questioning their cultural identities.

GREAT WHITE HOPE, THE
1970 102m c   ★★★½
Sports   GP/15
FOX

James Earl Jones (*Jack Jefferson*), Jane Alexander (*Eleanor*), Lou Gilbert (*Goldie*), Joel Fluellen (*Tick*), Chester Morris (*Pop Weaver*), Robert Webber (*Dixon*), Marlene Warfield (*Clara*), R.G. Armstrong (*Cap'n Dan*), Hal Holbrook (*Cameron*), Beah Richards (*Mama Tiny*)

p, Lawrence Turman; d, Martin Ritt; w, Howard Sackler (based on his play); ph, Burnett Guffey (Panavision, Deluxe Color); ed, William Reynolds; m, Lionel Newman; prod d, John De Cuir; art d, Jack Martin Smith; chor, Donald McKayle; cos, Irene Sharaff

Adapted by Howard Sackler from his own Broadway hit, this excellent period drama is a thinly veiled depiction of the life of the first black heavyweight champion of the world, Jack Johnson.

By winning the title Johnson (James Earl Jones, who played the role on Broadway) incurs the wrath of the white world. His troubles begin in earnest when he takes up with Eleanor (Alexander), a white divorcee. He's convicted of breaking the Mann Act and gets sent to prison. After Jefferson escapes, he and Alexander begin an itinerant exile that takes them to Canada, England (where he's refused a boxing license), France and Germany. Few are willing to take on the great champion but he is determined to fight again.

THE GREAT WHITE HOPE shows the climate of the time and generally avoids the preachiness director Ritt is sometimes known for. It touchingly portrays the love story between Alexander and Jones, and gives the audience a sense of the essence of the great Jack Johnson.

GREAT ZIEGFELD, THE
1936 170m bw   ★★★½
Musical/Biography   /U
MGM

William Powell (*Florenz Ziegfeld*), Luise Rainer (*Anna Held*), Myrna Loy (*Billie Burke*), Frank Morgan (*Billings*), Reginald Owen (*Sampston*), Nat Pendleton (*Sandow*), Virginia Bruce (*Audrey Lane*), Ernest Cossart (*Sidney*), Robert Greig (*Joe*), Raymond Walburn (*Sage*)

p, Hunt Stromberg; d, Robert Z. Leonard; w, William Anthony McGuire; ph, Ray June, Oliver T. Marsh, Karl Freund, Merritt Gerstad, George Folsey; ed, William S. Gray; art d, Cedric Gibbons; chor, Seymour Felix; cos, Adrian

How appropriate that this ode to an ambitious, amiable shyster featured future First Lady Pat Nixon as an extra. Incredibly, THE GREAT ZIEGFELD, three hours of lumpy, overcooked pudding, took Best Picture at the 1936 Oscars. But then, the film is *big*, and it's an ode to lavish showmanship—what better pat on the back could Hollywood give itself?

The details of the whitewashed story aren't worth dwelling on in detail. Flo (Powell) begins as a sideshow barker and eventually becomes Broadway impresario extraordinaire. Along the way he marries temperamental actress-singer Anna Held (Rainer) but their oh-so-turbulent relationship just doesn't make it. He later weds actress Billie Burke (Loy) and, after enduring his darkest hours, stuns Broadway with four simultaneous hits.

Oddly enough, the film does have enough thrust to keep rigor mortis from setting in. Powell can't give his shallow role much depth beyond a consideration of Ziegfeld's incredible ambition and ego, but he does give it energy and rascally charm. Loy would have been foolish to copy the inimitable twittering of Billie Burke and wisely she doesn't try. What she's left with are a new hair color, uxorial devotion and relatively little footage.

The latter applies to Rainer as well, though we mind that less. However, she does have a delicate appeal onstage and also in the "legendary" telephone scene in which Anna, still in love, calls Flo to congratulate him on his second marriage. Ray Bolger adds a few delightful moments, but a pre-WIZARD OF OZ Frank Morgan is way overboard and Fanny Brice is ditched right in the middle of singing "My Man"!! What can you do with a movie like this? Surrender, I guess.

GREATEST SHOW ON EARTH, THE
1952 153m c   ★★★★
Drama   /U
Paramount

Betty Hutton (*Holly*), Cornel Wilde (*Sebastian*), Charlton Heston (*Brad*), Dorothy Lamour (*Phyllis*), Gloria Grahame (*Angel*), James Stewart (*Buttons, a Clown*), Henry Wilcoxon (*Detective*), Lyle Bettger (*Klaus*), Lawrence Tierney (*Henderson*), John Kellogg (*Harry*)

p, Cecil B. DeMille; d, Cecil B. DeMille; w, Fredric M. Frank, Barre Lyndon, Theodore St. John (based on a story by Frank, St. John, Frank Cavett); ph, George Barnes, Peverell Marley, W. Wallace Kelley (Technicolor); ed, Anne Bauchens; m, Victor Young; art d, Hal Pereira, Walter Tyler; fx, Gordon Jennings, Paul K. Lerpae, Devereaux Jennings; chor, Richard Barstow; cos, Miles White, Edith Head, Dorothy Jeakins

It's big, it's garish, it's loud, and most of all, it's wonderful. This is Cecil B. DeMille's superlative salute to the circus world, and all its glamour and flashy hoopla suits perfectly the director whose middle name was epic. An episodic soap opera set under the big top, the film is almost like a documentary in its meticulous detailing of circus life. Charlton Heston plays the head of the sprawling ensemble and the entire cast is outstanding, particularly James Stewart as the clown hiding from his past. Since the early 1920s, DeMille had planned on producing a spectacular circus film, but his biblical epics got in the way. Finally, in 1949, after Paramount paid Ringling Brothers $250,000 for the right to use the circus' name, equipment, and talent, DeMille began elaborate preparations. The film is authentic and awesome and earned an Oscar as Best Picture.

GREEN CARD

1990   108m   c   ★★½
Comedy/Romance   PG-13/15
Touchstone/Green Card   (Australia/France)

Gerard Depardieu (George Faure), Andie MacDowell (Bronte Parrish), Gregg Edelman (Phil), Bebe Neuwirth (Lauren), Robert Prosky (Bronte's Lawyer), Jessie Keosian (Mrs. Bird), Ethan Phillips (Gorsky), Mary Louise Wilson (Mrs. Sheehan), Lois Smith (Bronte's Mother), Conrad McLaren (Bronte's Father)

p, Peter Weir, Duncan Henderson, Jean Gontier; d, Peter Weir; w, Peter Weir; ph, Geoffrey Simpson; ed, William Anderson; m, Hans Zimmer; prod d, Wendy Stites; art d, Christopher Nowak; cos, Marilyn Matthews

Australian director Peter Weir attempts to add an international flavor to his recent American fare (WITNESS, DEAD POET'S SOCIETY) with the casting of French superstar Gerard Depardieu in his US film debut.

Depardieu plays George Faure, a French alien who desperately wants to remain in the US. Andie MacDowell is Bronte Parrish, a quiet horticulturist who also has a desperate desire—she wants to rent an exclusive Manhattan apartment complete with a greenhouse. Trouble is, building management will only rent to married couples. Through a mutual friend, George and Bronte meet and strike a deal—they'll get married so that George can get his green card and Bronte can get her apartment. They marry in a quick legal ceremony, then part company. Things get tense, however, when immigration officials start snooping around, an investigation that threatens Bronte's lifestyle and George's visa. As a result, the duo must get to know each other so they can convince investigators that they've been in love for years.

The film's fine photography and effective use of music make GREEN CARD one of the few Disney ventures that doesn't seem like a made-for-TV movie, but the threadbare screenplay and Weir's weak direction are barely able to hold things together. Much of the dialogue is insipid, and the action is driven by absurd coincidence and unmotivated behavior to the point that one can only feel exasperated by it all. Peter Weir's talent, so evident in his Australian work, remained dormant here, but Depardieu's lively performance is a redeeming factor.

GREEN DOLPHIN STREET

1947   140m   bw   ★★½
Adventure/Romance   /A
MGM

Lana Turner (Marianne Patourel), Van Heflin (Timothy Haslam), Donna Reed (Marguerite Patourel), Richard Hart (William Ozanne), Frank Morgan (Dr. Edmund Ozanne), Edmund Gwenn (Octavius Patourel), Dame May Whitty (Mother Superior), Reginald Owen (Capt. O'Hara), Gladys Cooper (Sophie Patourel), Moyna MacGill (Mrs. Metivier)

p, Carey Wilson; d, Victor Saville; w, Samson Raphaelson (based on the novel by Elizabeth Goudge); ph, George Folsey; ed, George White; m, Bronislau Kaper; art d, Cedric Gibbons, Malcolm Brown; fx, Warren Newcombe, A. Arnold Gillespie; cos, Walter Plunkett, Valles

Lana Turner's bid for the sweep of epic skirts, her GWTW as it were, and a classic egg-layer. You can swallow this clinker whole if you can stomach one plot turn: Richard Hart's New Zealand army deserter who gets loaded and writes a love letter to Turner, even though it's little sis Donna Reed he really cares for; the poor lad has the names confused. When Turner blows in, he marries her rather than admit his mistake and all karmic hell breaks loose. Here Saville's direction rises to the fore, with giant trees falling over and the earth belching and shivering in a killer earthquake sequence. Just when things seem tame there's a Maori uprising. Meanwhile, spurned sis Reed takes the nun's vow.

Without murderous acts of passion, Lana's out of her element; but not to worry. Natural disasters and aboriginal riots take no toll on Turner's visage—a strand of hair displaced here, a streak of dirt there. Brunette haircolor and a possible acting chore deter her not one whit from her goal of genus: star.

GREEN FOR DANGER

1946   91m   bw   ★★★★★
Mystery/Comedy   /A
Individual Picture   (U.K.)

Sally Gray (Nurse Linley), Trevor Howard (Dr. Barney Barnes), Rosamund John (Esther Sanson), Alistair Sim (Inspector Cockrill), Leo Genn (Mr. Eden), Judy Campbell (Marion Bates), Megs Jenkins (Nurse Woods), Moore Marriott (Joe Higgins), Henry Edwards (Mr. Purdy), Ronald Adam (Dr. White)

p, Frank Launder, Sidney Gilliat; d, Sidney Gilliat; w, Sidney Gilliat, Claude Guerney (based on a novel by Christianna Brand); ph, Wilkie Cooper; ed, Thelma Myers; m, William Alwyn; prod d, Peter Proud

Green for go! An unfairly overlooked delight in the annals of British film history, GREEN FOR DANGER is one of the most enjoyable films ever produced by those masters of comic entertainment, Launder and Gilliat.

Inspector Cockrill (Sim), an unorthodox detective, investigates a strange double murder that takes place in a British emergency hospital during WWII. A postman who has been slightly wounded by a buzz bomb dies on the operating table, and, when nurse Marion Bates (Campbell) discovers that he was murdered, she's stabbed to death. Cockrill discovers that everyone present during the operation had a motive, and, with an odd sense of amusement, he sets about exposing the surprising culprit.

Though most US audiences remember Sim primarily for his flawless performance as Scrooge, his use of his droopy features, lugubrious yet fruity intonations and impeccable timing make this role one of his best. Gray, Howard and John are appealing as always, and a marvelous supporting cast gives fine moments to Genn, Jenkins, Marriott, Edwards and others. Still, it's the remarkable Sim (unlikely star material only at first glance) and the smooth, feather-light scripting and direction of Gilliat that makes watching this film like sitting up late on a stormy night reading your first Agatha Christie novel.

GREEN MAN, THE
1957 80m bw   ★★★★
Comedy   /PG
Grenadier (U.K.)

Alastair Sim *(Hawkins)*, George Cole *(William Blake)*, Jill Adams *(Ann Vincent)*, Avril Angers *(Marigold)*, Terry-Thomas *(Boughtflower)*, John Chandos *(McKecknie)*, Dora Bryan *(Lily)*, Colin Gordon *(Reginald)*, Eileen Moore *(Joan Wood)*, Raymond Huntley *(Sir Gregory Upshoot)*

p, Sidney Gilliat, Frank Launder; d, Robert Day; w, Sidney Gilliat, Frank Launder (based on their play *Meet a Body*); ph, Gerald Gibbs; ed, Bernard Gribble; m, Cedric Thorpe Davie

This hilarious comedy stars Alastair Sim as Hawkins, a professional assassin who has long been out of action. He comes out of his retirement when he is hired to do away with Sir Gregory Upshoot (Huntley), a pompous politician. Hawkins tracks his quarry to a decrepit seaside hotel called the Green Man, and waits there to spring his trap, disguising himself as a simple clockmaker. As such he puts up with a bevy of dowagers at the resort, joining in the staid teas, conversations, and musical diversions. Meanwhile, a bomb he has planted is ready to explode upon Sir Upshoot's arrival. But it seems as if the victim will never appear! Alastair Sim is a delight as the assassin with the soul of an aesthete. Terry-Thomas is also very funny in this underrated little gem.

GREEN PASTURES
1936 93m bw   ★★★½
Religious   /U
WB

Rex Ingram *(De Lawd, Adam/Hezdrel)*, Oscar Polk *(Gabriel)*, Eddie "Rochester" Anderson *(Noah)*, Frank C. Wilson *(Moses)*, George Reed *(Mr. Deshee)*, Abraham Gleaves *(Archangel)*, Myrtle Anderson *(Eve)*, Al Stokes *(Cain)*, Edna Mae Harris *(Zeba)*, James Fuller *(Cain the Sixth)*

p, Henry Blanke; d, Marc Connelly, William Keighley; w, Marc Connelly, Sheridan Gibney (from the play by Connelly, suggested by Roark Bradford's *Ol' Man Adam an' His Chillun*); ph, Hal Mohr; m, Hall Johnson; art d, Allen Saalburg, Stanley Fleischer

Based on the Pulitzer Prize-winning play, this is The Gospel According To Marc—Connelly, that is. Using a series of brief sketches by Roark Bradford, Connelly and coscreenwriter Gibney fashioned an interesting—though grossly racially stereotyped—account of the Bible using an all-Black cast.

The film takes place in a sunday school where the teacher begins telling biblical stories from the Old Testament. As he speaks, all of the characters come to life, portrayed by notable Black actors of the period. On the stage, De Lawd was played by Richard Berry Harrison but he passed away before the film was shot and his role was undertaken by Ingram, who also played Adam and Hezdrel. All of the dialogue is done in archaic Southern Black colloquialisms with much talk of ten cent "seegars" and fish-fries and expressions like "Gangway for de Lawd God Jehovah." We see the tales of Joshua at Jericho, Abraham, Isaac and Jacob, Noah, Adam and Eve, Moses, and even Gabriel (whom De Lawd God refers to as "Gabe").

In many ways, this is one of the best biblical films ever done. Mostly because it doesn't preach, just entertains, and in doing that, puts its lessons across with a minimum of effort. One of the best elements of the movie is the music by the Hall Johnson Choir, which functions as sort of a Greek Chorus, singing tunes

like "When the Saints Go Marching In," "Let My People Go," "Joshua Fit de Battle of Jericho" and many more.

GREEN ROOM, THE
(LA CHAMBRE VERTE)
1978 94m c   ★★★½
Drama/War   PG/A
Carrosse/UA (France)

Francois Truffaut *(Julien Davenne)*, Nathalie Baye *(Cecilia Mandel)*, Jean Daste *(Bernard Humbert)*, Jean-Pierre Moulin *(Gerard Mazet)*, Antoine Vitez *(Bishop's Secretary)*, Jane Lobre *(Mazet's Second Wife)*, Monique Dury *(Monique, Editorial Secretary)*, Laurence Ragon *(Julie Davenne)*, Marcel Berbert *(Dr. Jardine)*, Christian Lentretian *(Orator in Cemetery)*

d, Francois Truffaut; w, Francois Truffaut, Jean Gruault (based on themes in the writings of Henry James); ph, Nestor Almendros (Eastmancolor); ed, Martine Barraque; m, Maurice Jaubert; art d, Jean-Pierre Kohut-Svelko

Francois Truffaut's testimony of obsession, THE GREEN ROOM, is perhaps the most unheralded film of his career, and surely one of his most personal.

Truffaut himself plays Julien Davenne, a secretive man who excels at writing obituaries for a fading journal and who's stubbornly obsessed with death, believing that the deceased are not given the love and attention they deserve. His reverence is inspired both by his guilt over returning from WWI unharmed, while everyone he knew was killed or injured, and by the sudden death of his newlywed wife. In her memory, he constructs a shrine, complete with a frightening, life-size wax figurine. At the cemetary where she's buried he discovers an old chapel in need of restoration and remodels it as an elaborate temple for the dead, filling it with photos of dead friends and acquaintances killed in the trenches.

On the surface, THE GREEN ROOM is an excessively depressing and strange portrait of a man who values death over life, but underneath it runs the study of a man driven by his obsessions. An interesting and atmospheric counterpoint to the numerous war films that pay tribute to those who died for their country, THE GREEN ROOM concerns a man who lived through war, is tormented by survivor's guilt, and is driven to actively remember the dead.

GREGORY'S GIRL
1982 91m c   ★★★½
Romance/Comedy   PG/A
Lake (U.K.)

Gordon John Sinclair *(Gregory)*, Dee Hepburn *(Dorothy)*, Jake D'Arcy *(Phil Menzies)*, Clare Grogan *(Susan)*, Robert Buchanan *(Andy)*, Billy Greenlees *(Steve)*, Alan Love *(Eric)*, Caroline Guthrie *(Carol)*, Carol Macartney *(Margo)*, Douglas Sannachan *(Billy)*

p, Clive Parsons, Davina Belling; d, Bill Forsyth; w, Bill Forsyth; ph, Michael Coulter (Kay Labs color); ed, John Gow; m, Colin Tully; art d, Adrienne Atkinson

A funny and touching teen romance from Scottish director Bill Forsyth. Gordon John Sinclair stars as an awkward teen who develops a major crush on the new girl in school, soccer star Dorothy (Dee Hepburn). Sinclair successfully portrays the uneasy quandary most adolescent boys go through when suffering from painful shyness coupled with the outrageous hormonal imbalance that drives them to do ridiculous things to get the attention of a pretty girl. While the plot is a straight, simple romance, the true charm of the film comes from its quirky characters, its general air of tolerance and good will and some irrepressible and delightfully absurd touches that creep (or waddle) along the periphery of the narrative. With this unpretentious little film, Forsyth decisively demonstrates that there was still life in the classic British comedy more than 30 years after its heyday.

GREMLINS 2: THE NEW BATCH
1990   105m   c   ★★★★
Comedy/Horror   PG-13/12
Mike Finnell/Amblin

Zach Galligan (Billy Peltzer), Phoebe Cates (Kate Beringer), John Glover (Daniel Clamp), Robert Prosky (Grandpa Fred), Howie Mandel (Voice of Gizmo), Tony Randall (Voice of "Brain" Gremlin), Robert Picardo (Forster), Christopher Lee (Dr. Catheter), Haviland Morris (Marla Bloodstone), Dick Miller (Murray Futterman)

p, Michael Finnell; d, Joe Dante; w, Charlie Haas (based on characters created by Chris Columbus); ph, John Hora (Technicolor); ed, Kent Beyda; m, Jerry Goldsmith; prod d, James Spencer; art d, Joe Lucky; fx, Rick Baker; cos, Rosanna Norton; anim, Chuck Jones

GREMLINS 2: THE NEW BATCH is surprisingly sympathetic towards the title menace and surprisingly thought-provoking in its use of the gremlins to make an extended commentary on modern life and morality. That the beasties should wind up the tragically ill-fated good guys should come as no surprise to director Joe Dante's admirers; he's an enthusiastic fan of classic Hollywood kitsch, especially those monster movies, in which the saddest scene is the one in which the monster dies.

With GREMLINS 2, Dante has come up with what may be his best film yet—a dizzying, no-holds-barred satirical spectacle that will please fans of the original and anyone else lucky enough to drop by. This is no lifeless retread, even though every big scene from the first film has its equivalent here. (Dante still seems especially concerned about the safe use of microwave ovens.) And even if the filmmakers' apparent intent was to make a movie that feels wildly out of control, GREMLINS 2 rarely loses sight of its objectives. Almost every plot twist, stunt, and sight gag elaborates the movie's basic theme: the metaphysical price paid for plundering a rich human past to build a dubious, impoverished, and inhumane future, of which the gremlins are merely an unnatural byproduct.

This theme is mainly suggested by Clamp's urgency in tearing down New York landmarks (such as all of Chinatown), to construct cold, high-tech, soulless structures in their place, but it is echoed everywhere—from the Splice of Life lab, dedicated to developing new and "improved' life forms, to the romantic subplot, in which Billy is tempted to throw away his long-term romance with Kate to further his career with Clamp.

Still, no one who makes movies as thoroughly modernist and as full of high-tech special effects as Dante does can ever make a sincere claim to yearning for gentler, simpler times. As a result, the film exhibits an oddly compelling ambivalence toward the gremlins throughout. But it doesn't stop us from feeling a little sad for the gremlins after they meet their sticky end. They may be nasty, but they know how to party, particularly when they spontaneously mount a lavish musical number inspired by the Kander and Ebb classic "New York, New York."

GREY FOX, THE
1983   92m   c   ★★★★
Biography/Western   PG
Mercury   (Canada)

Richard Farnsworth (Bill Miner), Jackie Burroughs (Kate Flynn), Wayne Robson (Shorty), Ken Pogue (Jack Budd), Timothy Webber (Fernie), Gary Reineke (Detective Seavey), David Petersen (Louis Colquhoun), Don Mackay (Al Sims), Samantha Langevin (Jenny), Tom Heaton (Tom)

p, Peter O'Brian; d, Phillip Borsos; w, John Hunter; ph, Frank Tidy; ed, Frank Irvine; m, Michael Conway Baker, The Chieftains; art d, William Brodie

This charming "art" Western is a great example of what can be done with a small budget and a terrific idea. Richard Farnsworth plays real-life train robber Bill Miner, released from prison after 30 years. The old West that he knew has disappeared, but knowing no other trade, he goes back to train robbing.

An ex-stuntman and character actor who was suggested for the part by Francis Ford Coppola, Farnsworth is dignified and charismatic in his first starring role as the Gentleman Bandit. No young pretty boy, Farnsworth has a leathery face that looks well lived in, but his beautiful blue eyes, sparkling impishly over his snow white handlebar moustache, help make him the most appealing old codger in modern movies.

Philip Borsos's direction is fine in his first feature, after a career as a documentary filmmaker. The marvelous photography of the unspoiled Canadian landscape is by Frank Tidy, who also did the moody lensing on Ridley Scott's underrated THE DUELLISTS.

GREYSTOKE: THE LEGEND OF TARZAN, LORD OF THE APES
1984   129m   c   ★★★½
Adventure   PG
WB   (U.K.)

Ralph Richardson (The 6th Lord of Greystoke), Ian Holm (Capt. Phillippe D'Arnot), Christopher Lambert (John Clayton/Tarzan), Andie MacDowell (Jane Porter), James Fox (Lord Esker), Ian Charleson (Jeffson Brown), Nigel Davenport (Maj. Jack Downing), Paul Geoffrey (Lord Jack Clayton), Cheryl Campbell (Lady Alice Clayton), Nicholas Farrell (Sir Hugh Belcher)

p, Hugh Hudson, Stanley S. Canter; d, Hugh Hudson; w, Robert Towne, Michael Austin (based on the novel Tarzan of the Apes by Edgar Rice Burroughs); ph, John Alcott (Super Techniscope, Eastmancolor); ed, Anne V. Coates; m, John Scott; prod d, Stuart Craig; art d, Simon Holland, Norman Dorme; fx, Albert Whitlock; chor, Peter Elliot; cos, John Mollo, Shirley Russell

The most intelligent and perhaps the best filmic treatment of Edgar Rice Burroughs's classic pulp novels about Tarzan, the white child of noble blood raised by apes in the jungle, since Elmo Lincoln first brought the character to the screen in 1918.

The film opens with the shipwreck that casts Lord Jack Clayton (Paul Geoffrey) and his pregnant wife Lady Alice (Cheryl Campbell) on the wild coast of Africa. They build a hut in the jungle, she bears a son, and shortly thereafter they both die. The infant is adopted by a clan of apes, with whom he grows to manhood, after which his ape mother is killed by pygmies. They also wipe out the first white men that Tarzan (Christopher Lambert) has ever seen, a party of hunters. He saves one of them, a wounded Belgian, Captain Phillippe D'Arnot (Ian Holm), who teaches him to speak English. Eventually Tarzan returns to civilization with D'Arnot and goes to his ancestral home in Scotland, Greystoke Manor. There, his grandfather, the Sixth Lord of Greystoke (Sir Ralph Richardson), tries to integrate his heir into upper-crust society.

The film is beautifully photographed and marvelously acted, with Lambert showing remarkable subtlety and emotion. Richardson, in his final film role, is even better; he carries much of the second half of the film when the story starts to sag. The special-effects costuming by Rick Baker is superb and his actor-apes are so expressive and natural that it is almost impossible to tell them from the real apes that appear in the scenes with them.

GRIFTERS, THE

1990 113m c ★★★★½
Crime R/18
Martin Scorsese

John Cusack *(Roy Dillon)*, Anjelica Huston *(Lilly Dillon)*, Annette Bening *(Myra Langtry)*, Pat Hingle *(Bobo Justus)*, J.T. Walsh *(Langtry)*, Henry Jones *(Desk Clerk)*, Gailard Sartain *(Myra's Landlord)*, Jeremy Piven

p, Martin Scorsese, Robert Harris, James Painten; d, Stephen Frears; w, Donald E. Westlake (based on the novel by Jim Thompson); ph, Oliver Stapleton; ed, Mick Audsley; m, Elmer Bernstein; prod d, Leslie McDonald; art d, Leslie McDonald

THE GRIFTERS has the mastery and hallucinatory, all-involving feel of an instant classic. Stephen Frears, a fearlessly diverse director, has immersed himself in the Los Angeles world of film noir and emerged with a movie that can easily stand alongside such classics of the genre as THE MALTESE FALCON, THE BIG SLEEP and OUT OF THE PAST.

The tale is spun of three "grifters," con artists forever on the lookout for an easy hustle. Lily (Anjelica Huston) is an ultra-experienced pro who specializes in racetrack odds altering. Her son, Roy (John Cusack), is basically small-time, hustling sailors and bartenders with loaded dice and sleight-of-hand tricks. His inamorata, Myra (Annette Bening), likes corporate action, a field she is easily able to ply with her siren's body and wardrobe of Chanel suits. Lily had Roy when she was but a girl herself, and the two have mostly gone their separate ways. They meet up again in California, where Lily takes an immediate dislike to Myra. Her ill feeling is met and matched by Roy, who has never resolved his filial feelings for her, as well as by Myra, who, having been wholly rebuffed by Lily, resolves to take her down. The climax, involving Lily and Roy, is swift, ugly, cathartic, and ultimately elegiac all at once.

Adapted from modish tough-guy writer Jim Thompson's novel, Donald Westlake's screenplay has the right combination of vivid characters, mordant wit and avaricious savagery which distinguishes the best noir. The characters speak in a faintly disconcerting 1950s argot right out of the book, adding an authentic flavor to the simmeringly suggestive stew Frears has concocted.

Huston has again done the impossible—she surpasses herself. Her Lily is a slightly older, laconic version of her treasurable Maerose in PRIZZI'S HONOR. She's the ultimate noir woman, with something operatic thrown in—this toughest and most dignified of babes could even throw a scare into Stanwyck's Phyllis Dietrichson in DOUBLE INDEMNITY. The whole film resonates with her presence. If Huston seems akin to Stanwyck, Bening is reminiscent of Gloria Grahame, her piquant face naughtily alive with the pleasure she takes in her scams. These two formidable femmes face each other down entertainingly—Huston's body language in a parking lot scene is particularly expressive. It's to Cusack's credit that he isn't completely overshadowed, but he's a superb young actor capable of forging a style out of recessiveness, abetted by flashes of boy-next-door-gone-wrong sarcasm.

Oliver Stapleton's photography turns the City of Angels into both a dream and a nightmare. Orange is the dominant hue, the orange of cruddy, toxic-looking sunsets, low-slung lamps in motel rooms, Myra's dress, and the fruit Lily fears. Seductive afternoons in seedy apartment complexes, solitary meals in diners, Roy's ultra-beat room, the whispery halls of the hotel in which he and Myra retreat, Lily's roadside pitstop, are all filmed in lushly moody, yet unforced, artistry.

GROOVE TUBE, THE

1974 75m c ★★★
Comedy R/X
Levitt/Pickman

Buzzy Linhart *(The Hitchhiker)*, Richmond Baier *(The Hitchhiker)*, Ken Shapiro *(Koko the Clown/Kramp TV Kitchen/The Dealer/Newscaster/Sex Olympias)*, Paul Norman *(Mouth Appeal)*, Victoria Medlin *(Mouth Appeal)*, Chevy Chase *(Geritan/Four Leaf Clover)*, Jennifer Welles *(Geritan)*, Richard Belzer *(The Dealers/President)*, Bill Kemmill *(Butz Beer)*, Alex Stephens *(Butz Beer)*

p, Ken Shapiro; d, Ken Shapiro; w, Ken Shapiro, Lane Sarasohn; ph, Bob Bailin; anim, Linda Taylor, Pat O'Neill

A sometimes humorous satire of modern television that leaves no aspect of television programming unscathed, nailing everything from commercials to kiddie programming. Made up of dozens of sketches and vignettes, THE GROOVE TUBE was a legitimate theater venture that ran off-Broadway and toured other US cities for five years. This film was first rated X, but was later trimmed to an R rating. Vulgar, which isn't really bothersome, but trivial, which is.

GROUP, THE

1966 150m c ★★★
Drama /X
UA

Candice Bergen *(Lakey Eastlake)*, Joan Hackett *(Dottie Renfrew)*, Elizabeth Hartman *(Priss Hartshorn)*, Shirley Knight *(Polly Andrews)*, Joanna Pettet *(Kay Strong)*, Mary Robin Redd *(Pokey Prothero)*, Jessica Walter *(Libby MacAusland)*, Kathleen Widdoes *(Helena Davison)*, James Broderick *(Dr. Ridgeley)*, James Congdon *(Sloan Crockett)*

p, Sidney Buchman; d, Sidney Lumet; w, Sidney Buchman (based on the novel by Mary McCarthy); ph, Boris Kaufman (DeLuxe Color); ed, Ralph Rosenbloom; m, Charles Gross; prod d, Gene Callahan; cos, Anna Hill Johnstone

Middling, busy, handsome Class of '33 soaper. Based on a blockbuster novel by Mary McCarthy, THE GROUP was made with an all New York cast comprised mostly of stage actors. Several young players made their debuts in the movie and went on to great success. Others faded away and were hardly heard from again. Eight bright young women graduate from college during the Depression and look forward to life after education, but reality has a funny way of creeping in. Hackett and Knight excell in the ensemble, but Bergen's lesbian got all the publicity; some say the asexual Walters was the real McCarthy. Lumet has trouble juggling so many major characters, and something has to suffer. In this case it's the audience.

GUADALCANAL DIARY

1943 93m bw ★★★★
War /A
FOX

Preston Foster *(Father Donnelly)*, Lloyd Nolan *(Hook Malone)*, William Bendix *(Taxi Potts)*, Richard Conte *(Capt. Davis)*, Anthony Quinn *(Jesus "Soose" Alvarez)*, Richard Jaeckel *(Pvt. Johnny Anderson)*, Roy Roberts *(Capt. Cross)*, Minor Watson *(Col. Grayson)*, Ralph Byrd *(Ned Rowman)*, Lionel Stander *(Butch)*

p, Bryan Foy; d, Lewis Seiler; w, Lamar Trotti, Jerry Cady (based on the novel by Richard Tregaskis); ph, Charles Clarke; ed, Fred Allen; m, David Buttolph; art d, James Basevi, Leland Fuller; fx, Fred Sersen

Released before the US had even been involved in the war for a year, this hard-hitting WWII action film drew its story from Richard Tregaskis's best-selling nonfiction book and superbly documents the first significant US counterattacks in the Pacific—the Marine invasion of the Solomon Islands.

One group of Marines, a cross-section of Americans from all walks of life, is shown as they hit the beaches in August 1942. William Bendix plays a tough, dim-witted ex-cab driver with a heart of gold; Richard Conte a courageous officer; Preston Foster the company chaplain; Lionel Stander the company clown; Lloyd Nolan the old pro sergeant who looks out for young recruits like Richard Jaeckel (in his film debut); and Anthony Quinn is the rugged Mexican-American hero who seeks revenge for the slaughter of his platoon. The film follows the recruits from camp, to their first engagement, and through the hell that was Guadalcanal.

Not a pretty picture, GUADALCANAL DIARY captures in painful detail the day-to-day survival of the stout-hearted Marines, presenting their humor and the full force of their dedication in scene after scene. Powerfully effective as propaganda, the film was in keeping with Hollywood's early efforts to depict a treacherous enemy, joining the ranks of such stellar WWII films as WAKE ISLAND and BATAAN, but unlike those films it depicted a major American victory. Lewis Seiler's direction is as quick and relentless as the chatter of a machine gun and all the cast members render believable and telling portraits.

GUARDSMAN, THE

1931 89m bw   ★★★★
Comedy   /A
MGM

Alfred Lunt *(the Actor)*, Lynn Fontanne *(the Actress)*, Roland Young *(the Critic)*, ZaSu Pitts *(Liesl)*, Maude Eburne *(Mama)*, Herman Bing *(a Creditor)*, Ann Dvorak *(a Fan)*

p, Irving Thalberg (uncredited), Albert Lewin; d, Sidney Franklin; w, Ernest Vajda, Claudine West (based on the play by Ferenc Molnar); ph, Norbert Brodine; ed, Conrad A. Nervig

A tattered, irresistable Valentine, more like a photographed stage play than a film, but a souvenir of lyrical, happy talent. French playwright Ferenc Molnar's clever marital comedy was never better performed than by the illustrious stars of American theater, Alfred Lunt and Lynn Fontanne, who had made the play a Broadway hit in 1924.

This bubbling sex farce begins when Lunt, watching Fontanne dreamily playing Chopin on the piano, suspects that her mind is on another. He quickly determines to resolve this doubt by a dangerous charade. Impersonating his imagined rival—a Russian guardsman with mustache and broad accent—he seduces his wife, who turns the tables on him the next morning, telling him "I knew it was you all along." Or is this just a clever attempt to preserve her marriage?

It took the supreme talents of Lunt and Fontanne to make this delicate stage material work. Although the public did not respond

well to the sophisticated comedy, the film was a smashing critical success. Except for cameo roles in STAGE DOOR CANTEEN, this would be the only sound film the couple made in their illustrious careers, although Hollywood had previously wooed them into silents. MGM's Irving Thalberg managed to convince the famous pair to leave Broadway for THE GUARDSMAN, but it took a *lot* of convincing. To them the movies were merely cloudy mirrors of their own live theater reputations, reflections they did not appreciate. But in all fairness to their undeniable talent, it is said both realized they didn't photograph worth a damn.

GUESS WHO'S COMING TO DINNER

1967 108m c   ★★½
Drama   /PG
Columbia

Spencer Tracy *(Matt Drayton)*, Sidney Poitier *(John Prentice)*, Katharine Hepburn *(Christina Drayton)*, Katharine Houghton *(Joey Drayton)*, Cecil Kellaway *(Monsignor Ryan)*, Roy E. Glenn, Sr. *(Mr. Prentice)*, Beah Richards *(Mrs. Prentice)*, Isabel Sanford *(Tillie)*, Virginia Christine *(Hilary St. George)*, Alexandra Hay *(Car Hop)*

p, Stanley Kramer; d, Stanley Kramer; w, William Rose; ph, Sam Leavitt (Technicolor); ed, Robert C. Jones; m, Frank DeVol; prod d, Robert Clatworthy; fx, Geza Gaspar; cos, Jean Louis, Joe King

William Rose, with a stilted screenplay, and Stanley Kramer, who literally makes this dinner hour stand still—say we're not in. Big deal in its day, but really safe, lame melodrama, and an unfitting finale to the Tracy-Hepburn screen partnership.

Bland little Houghton arrives home after a Hawaiian vacation to announce to parents Tracy and Hepburn that she is about to wed a brilliant research physician, Poitier, who is Black. This creates considerable social turmoil for the upper-middle-class family. Poitier tells the parents that unless they give their unreserved consent he will not marry their daughter, thereby putting the responsibility for the interracial marriage squarely upon their shoulders. After some soul-searching and breaking with friends who oppose miscegenation, the parents back up the young couple.

Tracy looks tired in this draggy production; he died soon afterward, and it's infuriating to watch him sweat to inject fire into such pap. Hepburn, with her blithely resolute air and great, watering eyes, is magnanimous as always; watching her watch Tracy during his big speech is one of the film's two great Moments. The other? Hepburn in the driveway, banishing an ex-friend: "Don't say anything, Hillary, just——go."

GUMSHOE

1972 88m c   ★★★½
Crime/Comedy   PG/15
Memorial (U.K.)

Albert Finney *(Eddie Ginley)*, Billie Whitelaw *(Ellen)*, Frank Finlay *(William)*, Janice Rule *(Mrs. Blankerscoon)*, Carolyn Seymour *(Alison Wyatt)*, Fulton Mackay *(Straker)*, George Innes *(Bookshop Proprietor)*, George Silver *(Jacob De Fries)*, Billy Dean *(Tommy)*, Wendy Richard *(Anne Scott)*

p, Michael Medwin; d, Stephen Frears; w, Neville Smith; ph, Chris Menges (Eastmancolor); ed, Fergus McDonell, Charles Rees; m, Andrew Lloyd Webber; prod d, Michael Seymour; art d, Richard Rambaut; fx, Bowie Films; cos, Daphne Dare

This offbeat feature debut from director Stephen Frears (MY BEAUTIFUL LAUNDRETTE, DANGEROUS LIAISONS, THE GRIFTERS) cleverly satirizes the detective films of the past, particularly those featuring the hardboiled private eyes created by Dashiell Hammett and Raymond Chandler.

Finney, a bingo caller in a seedy Liverpool nightclub who envisions himself as a tough detective *a la* Humphrey Bogart, advertises his sleuthing services and is hired by a mysterious fat man (Silver). After receiving a package containing a photo of a young woman (Seymour), a gun and a thousand pounds—but no instructions—Finney becomes enmeshed in an extraordinarily convoluted affair that involves heroin smuggling, gun running and African politics.

Produced by Finney's own company, GUMSHOE is packed with witty, if absurd, dialogue and plenty of action, all harking back to the film noir days of the tough detective and made even funnier by Finney's struggles through the awkward transition from British commoner to the image of a hard-as-nails American-type sleuth. Great fun.

GUNFIGHT AT THE O.K. CORRAL

1957   122m   c   ★★★★
Western   /PG
Paramount

Burt Lancaster *(Wyatt Earp)*, Kirk Douglas *(John H. "Doc" Holliday)*, Rhonda Fleming *(Laura Denbow)*, Jo Van Fleet *(Kate Fisher)*, John Ireland *(Johnny Ringo)*, Lyle Bettger *(Ike Clanton)*, Frank Faylen *(Cotton Wilson)*, Earl Holliman *(Charles Bassett)*, Ted de Corsia *(Abel Head "Shanghai Pierce")*, Dennis Hopper *(Billy Clanton)*

p, Hal B. Wallis; d, John Sturges; w, Leon Uris (based on the magazine article "The Killer" by George Scullin); ph, Charles Lang (VistaVision, Technicolor); ed, Warren Low; m, Dimitri Tiomkin; art d, Hal Pereira, Walter Tyler; fx, John P. Fulton; cos, Edith Head

Solid, expert "town" Western, but lacking the fuel of passion. Still it's a landmark Western—more than any other of its era, it gave the genre major film status. The story is legend: strong, resolute, and stoic, Lancaster is the famed Marshal Wyatt Earp, and Douglas is his closest friend, the deadly gunfighter "Doc" Holliday.

It's an interesting acting exercise: these two have been called "the two terrible-tempered twins"; they're like Davis and Crawford, in a way. People confuse their roles, claim one's a better actor, the other a bigger star, but unlike the aforementioned ladies, the two opinions offered flip back and forth on the respective men. Curious—but predictable—that GUNFIGHT is exactly the same. It's a stand-off between bravura egos, supported mightily by Van Cleef, Ireland, and the other men, with Van Fleet and Fleming doing definitive western turns as frontier whore and gambling hall floozie. But the film might have profited more from reverse casting in the leads (Lancaster's flamboyance seeming more suited to a gunman than a sheriff). And Sturges's direction lacks the bite of Anthony Mann's Jimmy Stewart oaters.

Yet GUNFIGHT, written—with generous dashes of dramatic license—by Leon Uris and beautifully photographed by Charles Lang, is truly a classic Western, one which thoroughly revitalized the genre. Its big-budget production and tremendous box-office success sent the making of B Westerns into decline; they all but vanished in the 1960s. The legendary gunfight has been filmed many other times, first in FRONTIER MARSHAL, then in John Ford's magnificent MY DARLING CLEMENTINE, again in Sturges's impressive sequel to this film, HOUR OF THE GUN, and in the introspective DOC.

GUNFIGHTER, THE

1950   84m   bw   ★★★★★
Western   /A
FOX

Gregory Peck *(Jimmy Ringo)*, Helen Westcott *(Peggy Walsh)*, Millard Mitchell *(Sheriff Mark Strett)*, Jean Parker *(Molly)*, Karl Malden *(Mac)*, Skip Homeier *(Hunt Bromley)*, Anthony Ross *(Charlie)*, Verna Felton *(Mrs. Pennyfeather)*, Ellen Corby *(Mrs. Devlin)*, Richard Jaeckel *(Eddie)*

p, Nunnally Johnson; d, Henry King; w, William Bowers, William Sellers, Nunnally Johnson, Andre De Toth (based on a story by Bowers); ph, Arthur Miller; ed, Barbara McLean; m, Alfred Newman; art d, Lyle Wheeler, Richard Irvine

An arresting, superbly produced and downbeat Western photographed in stark black and white, THE GUNFIGHTER presents an unglorified view of the Old West as a grim, dirty and decidedly desperate place.

Peck stars as an alienated gunfighter who's feeling his age and beginning to look back more often than forward. Entering a saloon one night, he finds that his notorious reputation has preceded him. Loud-mouthed punk Jaeckel picks a fight with him, calling Peck names. Peck tries to beg off, asking anyone in the bar to talk the brash and foolish youth out of going for his gun. But Jaeckel reaches and Peck beats him, shooting and killing the aspiring gunslinger. After being informed that despite justification in defending himself, it won't matter to Jaeckel's three older brothers, the seasoned gunfighter leaves hastily and moves on to his original destination, taking a room in a nearby town where he hopes to be reunited with his young son. Meanwhile, Jaeckel's bloodthirsty siblings follow close behind.

Generally tough and humorless, THE GUNFIGHTER is a grim portrait of a man whose time and historical role have run out, and he knows it. Peck is dazzling as the doomed and haunted gunfighter, a man desperately trying to escape his own past and identity, but knowing all along that hope is false and that there is only a bullet in his future. Henry King's direction is outstanding, keeping the action tautly drawn, while Arthur Miller's high-contrast cinematography is highly suggestive as it documents Peck's inexorable movement toward death. Preceding HIGH NOON by two years, THE GUNFIGHTER was a seminal film in the western's movement away from action cliches toward more psychological depth.

GUNGA DIN

1939   117m   bw   ★★★★★
Adventure/War   /U
RKO

Cary Grant *(Sgt. Cutter)*, Victor McLaglen *(Sgt. MacChesney)*, Douglas Fairbanks, Jr. *(Sgt. Ballantine)*, Sam Jaffe *(Gunga Din)*, Eduardo Ciannelli *(Guru)*, Joan Fontaine *(Emmy Stebbins)*, Montagu Love *(Col. Weed)*, Robert Coote *(Higginbotham)*, Abner Biberman *(Chota)*, Lumsden Hare *(Maj. Mitchell)*

p, George Stevens; d, George Stevens; w, Fred Guiol (based on the story by Ben Hecht, Charles MacArthur, William Faulkner from the poem by Rudyard Kipling); ph, Joseph August; ed, Henry Berman, John Lockert; m, Alfred Newman; art d, Van Nest Polglase, Perry Ferguson; fx, Vernon L. Walker; cos, Edward Stevenson

The GONE WITH THE WIND of the comic action-adventure genre, GUNGA DIN has a bit of everything—humor, suspense, spectacle, action *and* a heavy dose of racism, imperialism and xenophobia.

Based on a story by Ben Hecht and Charles MacArthur (it's the same friendly rivals plot of THE FRONT PAGE) and the moving Rudyard Kipling poem, this rousing adventure opens as a remote, mountainous British outpost in India is raided by a band of rebel natives. Three of the Army's most reliable frontier veterans—Sergeants Cutter (Cary Grant), MacChesney (Victor McLaglen) and Ballantine (Douglas Fairbanks, Jr.)—are sent to the now-silent outpost. Accompanying them is a small contingent of Indian troops and water-carriers, or *bhistis*, including Gunga Din (Sam Jaffe), whose only ambition in life is to become a soldier. The sergeants then receive their orders—to annihilate the murderous Thugs, a violent and mystical sect previously thought extinct.

A $2 million production that wowed them at the box office, GUNGA DIN is an undeniably rousing adventure tale. The performances and direction are a great deal of fun—part Three Musketeers, part Laurel and Hardy (Stevens began his career directing the duo's comedy shorts)—but it's difficult to overlook the blatantly racist nature of the proceedings, which endorse British imperialism and the violence inflicted on the Indian people.

GUNS OF NAVARONE, THE

1961   157m   c   ★★★½
Adventure/War   /PG
Open Road   (U.S./U.K.)

Gregory Peck (*Capt. Mallory*), David Niven (*Cpl. Miller*), Anthony Quinn (*Col. Andrea Stavros*), Stanley Baker (*CPO Brown*), Anthony Quayle (*Maj. Franklin*), Irene Papas (*Maria*), Gia Scala (*Anna*), James Darren (*Pvt. Pappadimos*), James Robertson Justice (*Jensen*), Richard Harris (*Barnsby*)

d, J. Lee Thompson; w, Carl Foreman (based on the novel *Guns of Navarone* by Alistair MacLean); ph, Oswald Morris (CinemaScope, Eastmancolor); ed, Alan Osbiston; m, Dimitri Tiomkin; prod d, Geoffrey Drake; art d, Geoffrey Drake; fx, Bill Warrington, Wally Veevers; cos, Monty Berman, Olga Lehmann

This WWII spectacle, with its cliched story, hackneyed characters, and triumph-over-impossible-odds finale, could only have been born in a Hollywood dream tank; nevertheless, it's great adventure.

British intelligence learns that two enormous guns have been installed on the Aegean island of Navarone. The long-range field pieces are capable of destroying any British fleet trying to sail to Kheros, near Turkey, where a large British force is facing annihilation unless it is evacuated. It's the job of Captain Mallory (Gregory Peck) and a handful of men to land secretly on Navarone and dismantle the guns. The group includes killers Private Pappadimos (James Darren) and CPO Brown (Stanley Baker), explosives expert Corporal Miller (David Niven), and tough Greek patriot Andrea Stavros (Anthony Quinn). Meeting the men along the way are resistance leader Maria (Irene Papas) and Anna (Gia Scala), a beautiful Greek girl who was reportedly tortured by the Germans.

There are a few subplots in this stirring spectacle—Miller's dislike for Mallory's dispassionate procedures, Stavros's grudge against Mallory for an old disservice—but the destruction of the guns is the constant theme. It's handled well by veteran director J. Lee Thompson, with strong cast support and excellent production values that make it all lavish, rich, and often breathtaking. A sequel starring Harrison Ford, FORCE 10 FROM NAVARONE, appeared 17 years later.

GUY NAMED JOE, A

1944   120m   bw   ★★★
War/Romance/Fantasy   /A
MGM

Spencer Tracy (*Pete Sandidge*), Irene Dunne (*Dorinda Durston*), Van Johnson (*Ted Randall*), Ward Bond (*Al Yackey*), James Gleason (*Col. "Nails" Kilpatrick*), Lionel Barrymore (*The General*), Barry Nelson (*Dick Rumney*), Esther Williams (*Ellen Bright*), Henry O'Neill (*Col. Sykes*), Don DeFore (*"Powerhouse" James J. Rourke*)

p, Everett Riskin; d, Victor Fleming; w, Dalton Trumbo (based on a story by Chandler Sprague, David Boehm, Frederick Hazlitt Brennan); ph, George Folsey, Karl Freund; ed, Frank Sullivan; m, Herbert Stothart; art d, Cedric Gibbons, Lyle Wheeler; fx, A. Arnold Gillespie, Donald Jahraus, Warren Newcombe; cos, Irene

A sticky, tear-jerking fantasy, A GUY NAMED JOE was one of the most popular movies during WWII, combining the considerable talents of Spencer Tracy, Irene Dunne, and Van Johnson in a big-scale production.

Pete Sandidge (Tracy), a daredevil bomber pilot, dies when he crashes his plane into a German aircraft carrier (though, in fact, there were none in WWII), leaving his devoted girlfriend, Dorinda (Irene Dunne), who is also a pilot, heartbroken. In heaven, Pete receives a new assignment: he is to become the guardian angel for Ted Randall (Van Johnson), a young Army flyer. Invisibly, Pete guides Ted through flight school and into combat, but the ectoplasmic mentor's tolerance is tested when Ted falls for Dorinda. Ultimately, however, Pete not only comes to terms with their relationship but also acts as Dorinda's copilot when she undertakes a dangerous bombing raid, so that Ted won't have to.

The film goes in too many directions at the same time, trying to combine its romantic fantasy line and a grim war outlook. But Dalton Trumbo's script is verbally wry—with the best lines going to wisecracking Tracy. Alas, Fleming was probably the wrong director for JOE; despite Arnold Gillespie's special effects, the Fleming-Tracy-Johnson chemistry feels as heavy as combat boots. Incidentally, there is no character in the film named "Joe"; the title is derived from the Army Air Corps practice of calling a "right fellow" Joe. Remade by Steven Spielberg in 1989 as ALWAYS.

GYPSY

1962   149m   c   ★★★½
Musical/Biography   /A
WB

Rosalind Russell (*Rose*), Natalie Wood (*Louise "Gypsy"*), Karl Malden (*Herbie Sommers*), Paul Wallace (*Tulsa No. 2*), Betty Bruce (*Tessie Tura*), Parley Baer (*Mr. Kringelein*), Harry Shannon (*Grandpa*), Morgan Brittany (*"Baby" June*), Ann Jillian (*"Dainty" June*), Diane Pace (*"Baby" Louise*)

p, Mervyn LeRoy; d, Mervyn LeRoy; w, Leonard Spigelgass (based on the musical play by Arthur Laurents and the book *Gypsy, A Memoir* by Gypsy Rose Lee); ph, Harry Stradling (Technirama, Technicolor); ed, Philip W. Anderson; art d, John Beckman; chor, Robert Tucker; cos, Orry-Kelly, Howard Shoup, Bill Gaskin

The original casting package for this blockbuster no doubt would have created motion picture history, with Miss Show Business herself, Judy Garland taking on the Ethel Merman legend, and the steamy Ann-Margret re-creating the strips of famed burlesque queen Gypsy Rose Lee. We love Roz, and her comic business as quintessential stage ma Rose Hovick is terrific; her moments of pathos don't disappoint, either, but she's just not the cyclonic force of nature that made Merman immortal in the annals of show business history. With her mother-resentments, and grueling vaudeville childhood, the thought of Garland is a chilling one indeed, for GYPSY is a musical about child abuse and frustrated ambition, though sometimes funny it may be.

As Gypsy, Natalie Wood lacks the latent sex appeal that needs to come to life when Rose's ambitions land the act she manages into lowlife burlesque, where the "untalented" Louise finds her niche at last. Though expertly coached by the original herself, Wood resembles a plastic wind-up doll strutting the runway, and that her cleavage was the result of extensive adhesive tape has passed into Hollywood lore long ago.

Mervyn LeRoy, sans any brass in casting, directs with an abrasive hand, as if coarse treatment can make up for what's missing. But Karl Malden, Ann Jillian (Dainty June), and Morgan Brittany (Baby June) are just right, and as three healthy surrogate stripper moms, Faith Dane, Roxanne Arlen, and espe-

cially Betty Bruce are perfection, playing dames actresses today don't know how to approach. The script's guts have been torn out; Leonard Spiegelgass prettied up Arthur Laurents's perfect work, presumably to throw sympathy to the star. There is an atmospheric strip montage that captures the spirit of Minsky and some great costumes, but Tucker's choreography has been largely snatched from Jerome Robbins.

The score, with music by Jule Styne and lyrics by Stephen Sondheim, is so perfect, so joyous, it's worth watching just to hear it aloud. Alas, "Together, Wherever We Go" was cut before the release, and the score's only blight, "Little Lamb," was left in to give Wood a big moment while we're waiting for the flesh. She's dubbed of course, and although, as we said, we love Roz, she lied that she did all her own singing—they spliced her voice in with the pipes of Lisa Kirk. The effect is brisk without carrying much conviction, although Russell's conviction in the finale is thoroughly satisfactory. Watch anyway.

H

HAGBARD AND SIGNE
(DEN RODE KAPPE)

1968 92m c ★★★

Historical /X

ASA/Edda/Movie Art of Europe (Denmark/Iceland/Sweden)

Gitte Haenning *(Signe)*, Oleg Vidov *(Hagbard)*, Gunnar Bjornstrand *(King Sigvor)*, Eva Dahlbeck *(the Queen)*, Lisbeth Movin *(Bengerd)*, Johannes Meyer *(Bilvis)*, Hakan Jahnberg *(Bolvis)*, Henning Palmer *(Hake)*, Birgitte Federspiel *(King Hamund's Widow)*, Manfred Reddemann *(Hildegisl)*

p, Bent Christensen, Johan Bonnier; d, Gabriel Axel; w, Gabriel Axel (based on a Scandinavian legend); ph, Henning Bendtsen (CinemaScope, Eastmancolor); ed, Lars Brydesen; m, Per Norgard; art d, P.A. Lundgren, Walther Dannerfjord, Niels Wangberg; fx, Josef Moller; cos, Ulla-Britt Soderlund

A fateful romance. This medieval period piece from Scandinavia stars Vidov as the son of a king killed in battle by a rival clan whose kingdom is headed by Bjornstrand. Vidov and his two brothers seek revenge on Bjornstrand's sons. The opposing forces clash on a neutral beach, and a powerful battle ensues, but the evenly matched sides are unable to subdue one another. Bjornstrand declares a truce and invites the rival tribe to his castle, where Vidov meets his enemy's lovely daughter, Haenning, and the couple fall in love, much to the dismay of Haenning's jealous suitor, Reddemann, who secretly incites the three Bjornstrand sons into breaking the truce.

HAIL, MARY
(JE VOUS SALUE, MARIE)

1985 86m c ★★★★

Religious /18

Pegase/JLG/Sara/SSR/Channel 4/Gaumont
(France/Switzerland/U.K.)

Myriem Roussel *(Mary)*, Thierry Rode *(Joseph)*, Philippe Lacoste *(Angel)*, Juliette Binoche *(Juliette)*, Manon Anderson *(Girl)*, Malachi Jara Kohan *(Jesus)*, Johan Leysen *(Professor)*, Anne Gauthier *(Eva)*

d, Jean-Luc Godard; w, Jean-Luc Godard; ph, Jean-Bernard Menoud, Jacques Frimann; m, Johann Sebastian Bach, Anton Dvorak, John Coltrane

Ever since his first film, BREATHLESS, Jean-Luc Godard has destroyed the conventions of cinema and caused critical outrage in the process. Remaining true to form, Godard, some 26 years later, again whipped his critics into a frenzy with HAIL MARY. By updating the story of the Virgin Mary, Godard produced, as the critics billed it, "the most controversial film of our time," and for once the advertisements weren't lying.

Myriem Roussel is Mary, a young woman who pumps gas, plays basketball, and has a taxi driver boyfriend named Joseph (Thierry Rode). Though another woman is anxious to sleep with Rode, he chooses instead to chase the chaste Roussel. One day Roussel learns she is to give birth to the Son of God; Rode, however, cannot believe that Roussel is pregnant and a virgin. But after they are wed Roussel teaches Rode to love her from a distance, revering her without touching her—Godard's personal definition of faith.

Sight unseen, HAIL MARY was protested in many cities throughout the world and banned in others, including Rome, where Pope John Paul II officially condemned the film. Curiously, Godard had originally intended to make a film about incest—planning to concentrate on a man's impossible love for his unattainable daughter—but as the film evolved, it became the story of Joseph's love for his unattainable Mary. Since BREATHLESS, Godard has been fascinated with the idea of a man becoming obsessed with a woman he cannot attain or possess, and HAIL, MARY takes this preoccupation to the extreme.

HAIL THE CONQUERING HERO

1944 101m bw ★★★★

Comedy /U

Paramount

Eddie Bracken *(Woodrow Lafayette Pershing Truesmith)*, Ella Raines *(Libby)*, Bill Edwards *(Forrest Noble)*, Raymond Walburn *(Mayor Noble)*, William Demarest *(Sergeant)*, Jimmie Dundee *(Corporal)*, Georgia Caine *(Mrs. Truesmith)*, Alan Bridge *(Political Boss)*, James Damore *(Jonesy)*, Freddie Steele *(Bugsy)*

p, Preston Sturges; d, Preston Sturges; w, Preston Sturges; ph, John Seitz; ed, Stuart Gilmore; m, Werner R. Heymann; art d, Hans Dreier

The premier comedy writer-director of 1940s Hollywood strikes again! Preston Sturges satirizes home-front American patriotism run amuck during WWII. All the sacred cows of the era—heroic fathers, loving moms, battle fatigue—are milked for laughs in this fastpaced comedy.

Sad sack Woodrow Lafayette Pershing Truesmith (Bracken) desperately wants to live up to the reputation of his Marine dad who died a war hero in WWI. Truesmith enlists to carry on the family honor at the outbreak of WWII but he's classified 4-F due to severe chronic hay fever. Ashamed to return home, he takes a job in a shipyard and, with the help of friends in the Marine Corps, sends letters from the Pacific to his mother (Caine) and his sweetheart Libby (Raines). To avoid telling the truth, Bracken breaks up with Libby through the mail. Some genuine Marine heroes returning from Guadalcanal find Truesmith drowning his sorrows in a saloon. Bugsy (Steele), a shell-shocked vet who values motherhood above all else, calls Mrs. Truesmith and tells her that her son has returned from the war. To complete the charade, the crusty Sergeant (Demarest) and the others convince the reluctant wash-out to put on a uniform, slip back home to Oakridge, and make his mother happy. He can then put his uniform in the closet and resume his life of obscurity. Truesmith agrees and takes the train back home with his new Marine friends. To their astonishment, the entire town has turned out with two brass bands to greet the conquering hero.

Who else but this brilliant iconoclast would have dared to make this kind of counter-heroic comedy very near the end of World WarII? Supporting the very funny Bracken is a cast composed mostly of Sturges's stock people—Demarest, Pangborn, Walburn and others—all of them outstanding. HAIL THE CONQUERING HERO was nominated for an Oscar for Best

Original Screenplay, putting Sturges in competition with himself for the award since he was also nominated for his script for THE MIRACLE OF MORGAN'S CREEK.

HAIR
1979   118m   c   ★★★★
Musical   PG/15
UA

John Savage *(Claude)*, Treat Williams *(Berger)*, Beverly D'Angelo *(Sheila)*, Annie Golden *(Jeannie)*, Dorsey Wright *(Hud)*, Don Dacus *(Woof)*, Cheryl Barnes *(Hud's Fiancee)*, Richard Bright *(Fenton)*, Nicholas Ray *(The General)*, Charlotte Rae *(Party Guest)*

p, Lester Persky, Michael Butler; d, Milos Forman; w, Michael Weller (based on the musical play by Gerome Ragni, James Rado, and Galt MacDermot); ph, Miroslav Ondricek (Panavision, Technicolor); ed, Lynzee Klingman; m, Galt MacDermot; prod d, Stuart Wurtzel; fx, Al Griswold; chor, Twyla Tharp; cos, Ann Roth

Milos Forman had already proven his talent with TAKING OFF and the multiple-Oscar-winning ONE FLEW OVER THE CUCKOO'S NEST, but when the Czech director was chosen to make this very American film, based on the long-running Broadway play, some wondered about the combination. They needn't have worried.

Savage plays a square draftee from Oklahoma on his way to Vietnam via New York City. There, he is adopted by a group of flower children who guide him through a series of euphoric countercultural adventures, including an introduction to marijuana and an encounter with a slightly batty debutante (D'Angelo). Along the way, there are many excellent songs and some of the most inventive choreography (by the ingenious Twyla Tharp) ever seen, including a "horse ballet" by mounted police in Central Park where they have been assigned to observe a "be-in."

There is much to recommend in this film, and sheer energy pours off the screen in every frame. Forman and scenarist Michael Weller deftly synthesized the pastiche of sketches and tunes that comprised the stage musical into a compelling screen entertainment. Unfortunately, the movie was not a hit, perhaps because HAIR was made almost 12 years after the play opened and, while dated, was not quite ready to be enjoyed nostalgically.

HAIRSPRAY
1988   90m   c   ★★★½
Comedy   PG
New Line

Sonny Bono *(Franklin Von Tussle)*, Ruth Brown *(Motormouth Maybell)*, Divine *(Edna Turnblad/Arvin Hodgepile)*, Colleen Fitzpatrick *(Amber Von Tussle)*, Michael St. Gerard *(Link Larkin)*, Deborah Harry *(Velma Von Tussle)*, Ricki Lake *(Tracy Turnblad)*, Leslie Ann Powers *(Penny Pingleton)*, Clayton Prince *(Seaweed)*, Jerry Stiller *(Wilbur Turnblad)*

p, Rachel Talalay, Stanley F. Buchthal, John Waters; d, John Waters; w, John Waters; ph, David Insley; ed, Janice Hampton; chor, Edward Love; cos, Van Smith

Fun indeed. Set in Baltimore circa 1962, HAIRSPRAY details the last days of 50s-era American naivete, as the country moves from postwar complacency to massive social upheaval.

Caught up in all this is the "Corny Collins Show," a wildly popular Baltimore television dance program. The show's queen is the spoiled and snobbish Fitzpatrick, whose father, Bono, owns the "Tilted Acres" amusement park. Lake, an obese working-class teen, auditions for a spot on the show, against the wishes of her mother, Divine, and she earns it because of her sensational dancing. The socially progressive teen begins to cause trouble, however, when she demands the segregated program be opened up to include the black teenagers of Baltimore.

Controversial filmmaker John Waters finally hits his commercial stride in this film, parlaying his keen social observation and great compassion for society's outsiders into a colorful and engaging comedy full of dancing, music and heartfelt nostalgia. Unfortunately, what should have been a celebration turned into sadness when Waters's longtime friend and collaborator Divine, who was poised on the edge of stardom, died of a heart attack a mere two weeks after HAIRSPRAY opened nationwide.

HALLELUJAH
1929   100m   bw   ★★★★
Drama
MGM

Daniel Haynes *(Zeke)*, Nina Mae McKinney *(Chick)*, William E. Fontaine *(Hot Shot)*, Harry Gray *(Parson)*, Fannie Belle DeKnight *(Mammy)*, Everett McGarrity *(Spunk)*, Victoria Spivey *(Missy Rose)*, Milton Dickerson, Robert Couch, Walter Tait *(Johnson Kids)*

p, King Vidor; d, King Vidor; w, Wanda Tuchock, Ransom Rideout (based on a story by King Vidor); ph, Gordon Avil; ed, Hugh Wynn, Anson Stevenson; m, Irving Berlin; art d, Cedric Gibbons

This was the first all-black feature film and one of the boldest pictures ever made, especially since MGM knew the film would not get much of a release in the deep South. King Vidor was a man vitally interested in social issues (witness his work on THE BIG PARADE and THE CROWD), and he wanted to show the rest of America what black people were going through. Daniel Haynes plays Zeke, an innocent young man who is very close to his mother (Fannie Belle DeKnight), and to his brother, Spunk (Everett McGarrity), whom he accidentally kills. Zeke turns to religion to ease his grief.

With a cast that included many amateurs (Harry Gray had been a janitor at a Harlem newspaper, and Nina Mae McKinney, the female lead, had never been in front of a camera), Vidor elicited performances from the group as good as any you might see in a seasoned troupe. Even today, more than half a century later, this film is not dated. Shot on location in Tennessee, HALLELUJAH is redolent with authenticity. The treatment of some scenes tends toward the melodramatic, notably the revival meetings, a wake, and various scenes on the plantation; but the film is filled with humanity and insight into black experience at the time. Irving Thalberg, the young chief of production at MGM, known and remembered as a man of integrity, gave Vidor the green light to make HALLELUJAH. This was the director's first talkie, but the film was shot as a silent, with the sound added in post-production.

HALLELUJAH THE HILLS
1963   88m   bw   ★★★½
Comedy   /A
Vermont

Peter H. Beard *(Jack)*, Martin Greenbaum *(Leo)*, Sheila Finn *(Jack's Vera in Winter)*, Peggy Steffans *(Leo's Vera in Summer)*, Jerome Raphel *(Father)*, Blanche Dee *(Mother)*

p, David C. Stone; d, Adolfas Mekas; w, Adolfas Mekas; ph, Ed Emshwiller; ed, Adolfas Mekas; m, Meyer Kupferman

Once upon a time in the early 1960s, there was a movement known as the New American Cinema. Jonas Mekas was its prophet in a weekly column in the *Village Voice*. He and his brother, Adolfas, who directed HALLELUJAH, THE HILLS, were among its practitioners. Most of this underground cinema consisted of arty shorts. (Perhaps Kenneth Anger's SCORPIO RISING was the best known of these.) The Mekas brothers produced more traditional feature-length films. This one is an interesting confluence of Hollywood structures and home-movie techniques: a document of its time, in part.

This delightful comedy for film buffs begins as an enthusiastic send-up of early French New Wave techniques. The thin story line has to do with a pair of young men, Jack (Beard) and Leo (Greenbaum), pursuing the same young lady (shades of Truffaut's JULES AND JIM) at different times of the year. Thus she is played by two actresses: one for winter (Finn) and one for summer (Steffans). The girl's parents are also featured: a wisecracking father and a no-nonsense mother. Ultimately, the question of just who will win Vera's love takes a backseat to the giddy celebration of movie magic.

The film plays around with time, space, character, and the history of the cinema and achieves a remarkable freshness. Adolfas Mekas shows a remarkable flair for visuals, using his forest settings well. The film is packed full of gags and silliness, having a good time with itself and movie cliches. The ending juxtaposes the characters of this film with the actual ending from Griffith's classic silent WAY DOWN EAST with Lillian Gish and Richard Barthelmess. HALLELUJAH THE HILLS is a personable and fun bit of filmmaking; its enthusiasm is infectious.

HALLOWEEN

1978 93m c ★★★★
Horror R/18
Falcon

Donald Pleasence (Loomis), Jamie Lee Curtis (Laurie), Nancy Loomis (Annie), P.J. Soles (Lynda), Charles Cyphers (Brackett), Kyle Richards (Lindsey), Brian Andrews (Tommy), John Michael Graham (Bob), Nancy Stephens (Marion), Arthur Malet (Graveyard Keeper)

p, Debra Hill; d, John Carpenter; w, Debra Hill, John Carpenter; ph, Dean Cundey (Panavision, Metrocolor); ed, Tommy Lee Wallace, Charles Burnstein; m, John Carpenter; prod d, Tommy Lee Wallace

A modern horror classic. On Halloween night in 1963, a six-year-old boy in a Halloween mask inexplicably stabs his sister and her boyfriend to death while they are making love. He's institutionalized—until, exactly 15 years later, he escapes and returns to his small Illinois hometown once more to wreak Halloween havoc. His psychiatrist Dr. Loomis (Donald Pleasence) proclaims "The Evil is loose!" and is in hot pursuit with the authorities. Meanwhile Laurie (Jamie Lee Curtis) seems to be the only girl in town without a date for Halloween. All her high school friends seem to have hot dates scheduled but bright, bookish Laurie must settle for a quiet evening of babysitting, fending off trick-or-treaters, and watching old science fiction movies on television. Just another boring evening? Hardly.

There's nary a drop of blood on screen in this rollicking funhouse of a movie but there is enough sheer cinematic ingenuity on display to coax screams out of the most jaded gorehound. Cheap thrills—often accompanied by a joybuzzer noise on the soundtrack—lurk on the periphery of nearly every frame and film history allusions abound. Fans the moving camera also have reason to cheer as the Steadicam prowls the suburban streets unexpectedly turning into ominous point-of-view shots accompanied by creepy piano music (composed by the resourceful Carpenter). The performances are also far better than average for

this kind of fare. Pleasance is a hoot as he gnaws on the scenery and the pleasingly equine beauty of Jamie Lee Curtis—at the beginning of the fondly remembered Queen of the B's stage of her career—enhances her sensitive performance.

HALLOWEEN was the surprise hit of the 1978 Chicago Film Festival. Some over-enthusiastic critics even compared it with Hitchcock's classic PSYCHO (which starred Curtis's mother, Janet Leigh) but such comparisons are silly and groundless; HALLOWEEN is just a superbly made unpretentious thriller whereas one can make higher claims for PSYCHO. Furthermore Carpenter's clean, economical style owes a much greater debt to another master craftsman—Howard Hawks. From the opening— a long Steadicam point-of-view shot seen from behind a Halloween mask—to the climactic battle in which Curtis fends off the maniac time after time, only to have him rise again, Carpenter displays an astounding stylistic assurance for a young director working with a low budget.

Made for less than half a million dollars, HALLOWEEN grossed well over $50 million on its initial release making it the single most successful independent feature of all time. Two sequels, both produced by Carpenter, were woefully inferior to the original, but a third—released in 1988—wasn't too bad.

HALLS OF MONTEZUMA

1951 113m c ★★★
War /A
FOX

Richard Widmark (Lt. Carl Anderson), Jack Palance (Pigeon Lane), Reginald Gardiner (Sgt. Johnson), Robert Wagner (Coffman), Karl Malden (Doc), Richard Hylton (Cpl. Stuart Conroy), Richard Boone (Lt. Col. Gilfilan), Skip Homeier (Pretty Boy), Don Hicks (Lt. Butterfield), Jack Webb (Correspondent Dickerman)

p, Robert Bassler; d, Lewis Milestone; w, Michael Blankfort; ph, Winton C. Hoch, Harry Jackson (Technicolor); ed, William Reynolds; m, Sol Kaplan; art d, Lyle Wheeler, Albert Hogsett; fx, Fred Sersen; cos, Charles LeMaire

A solid WWII action drama, HALLS OF MONTEZUMA stars Widmark as Lieutenant Carl Anderson, a tough but compassionate Marine officer leading his men through one battle after another across the Pacific. Most of the story concerns Anderson's efforts to infiltrate enemy-controlled territory and capture prisoners who will reveal the location of a Japanese rocket site that is impeding the advance of thousands of American troops. With him go young recruits Wagner and Homeier, onetime boxer Palance and tough old pros Bert Freed, Neville Brand and Webb, along with an eccentric interpreter, Gardiner.

Widmark is authoritative and fully convincing as the introspective commanding officer. Jack Palance gives his tried-and-true neurotic portrayal, this time as a punch-drunk pug. Skip Homeier is effective and frightening as a kid who goes berserk from the tension. Director Lewis Milestone, an old hand at war films (ALL QUIET ON THE WESTERN FRONT), again excels in this topnotch production full of action, taut drama and telling characterizations.

HAMBURGER HILL

1987 110m c ★★★½
War /18
RKO

Anthony Barrile *(Langulli)*, Michael Boatman *(Motown)*, Don Cheadle *(Washburn)*, Michael Dolan *(Murphy)*, Don James *(McDaniel)*, Dylan McDermott *(Sgt. Frantz)*, M.A. Nickles *(Galvin)*, Harry O'Reilly *(Duffy)*, Daniel O'Shea *(Gaigin)*, Tim Quill *(Beletsky)*

p, Marcia Nasatir, Jim Carabatsos; d, John Irvin; w, Jim Carabatsos; ph, Peter MacDonald (Rank Color); ed, Peter Tanner; m, Philip Glass; prod d, Austin Spriggs; art d, Toto Castillo; fx, Joe Lombardi

Instead of trying to match the hallucinatory bombast of APOCALYPSE NOW, the surreal metaphysics of PLATOON, or the studied idiosyncrasy of FULL METAL JACKET, director John Irvin reaches back to such classic combat films as THE SANDS OF IWO JIMA and PORK CHOP HILL for his inspiration here. So straightforward as to be old-fashioned, HAMBURGER HILL becomes unique by virtue of its unwillingness to participate in the current cycle of war-as-philosophical-metaphor Vietnam films and instead goes for a more conventional approach.

Realistic almost to a fault, Irvin's film is an account of the Third Squad, First Platoon, Bravo Company of the 101st Airborne Division and its battle to secure Hill 937 in the Ashau Valley, Vietnam, 1969. Short on plot, the film derives its power from isolated moments: letters from home, chats, arguments, visits to a brothel, and, of course, intense combat—all performed with vigor by an almost faceless ensemble of unknown actors spouting a nearly incomprehensible stream of GI lingo.

Shot in an unfussy, realistic manner by cinematographer Peter MacDonald, the visuals emphasize wide angles and deep focus, bombarding the senses without resorting to the kind of hallucinatory imagery found in most Vietnam films. The battle for the hill is exhausting to watch as the soldiers struggle upwards in the mud, clinging to exposed roots, tree stumps, and each other in a desperate effort to advance. Irvin rarely allows a glimpse of the top of the hill, further preventing the viewer from thinking ahead, instead forcing him to concentrate on climbing the few feet visible before him right along with the GIs.

Although it was underrated at the time of its release, time will eventually reveal that HAMBURGER HILL is one of the best and most realistic films made about the Vietnam War.

HAMLET
1948 155m bw   ★★★★
Drama   /U
Two Cities/Rank (U.K.)

Laurence Olivier *(Hamlet)*, Eileen Herlie *(Queen Gertrude)*, Basil Sydney *(King Claudius)*, Jean Simmons *(Ophelia)*, Norman Wooland *(Horatio)*, Felix Aylmer *(Polonius)*, Terence Morgan *(Laertes)*, Stanley Holloway *(Gravedigger)*, John Laurie *(Francisco)*, Esmond Knight *(Bernardo)*

p, Laurence Olivier; d, Laurence Olivier; w, Alan Dent (based on the play by William Shakespeare); ph, Desmond Dickinson; ed, Helga Cranston; m, William Walton; prod d, Roger Furse; art d, Carmen Dillon; fx, Paul Sheriff, Henry Harris, Jack Whitehead; cos, Elizabeth Hennings

At 155 minutes, this screen adaptation of Shakespeare's most celebrated play bares the scars from deep cuts into its more than four-hour length. Basically a story of vengeance, Hamlet swears to his father's ghost that he will wreak revenge for the man's murder by taking the life of Claudius, who is now married to Hamlet's mother, Gertrude. By cutting the text, Olivier has fashioned a tighter, albeit abridged, version of the famed play. One of its flaws is that, in directing, Olivier should have concentrated more on performances; he had apparently fallen in love

with the camera and employed many visual tricks instead of sticking to the lines. However, Olivier has always felt that each different Hamlet is an essay, subject to the individual's interpretation.

HENRY V had been done in color, and many wondered why Olivier chose black and white for HAMLET. His reasons were the mood of the piece and various technical problems that arose while doing deep-focus photography. Olivier dyed his hair blonde so no one would feel that it was him playing the melancholy Dane. Rather, he wanted them to feel that what they were seeing was Hamlet himself. What they got was a mannered, overrated performance in a film with a similarly inflated reputation. Jean Simmons goes properly mad as Ophelia, and a very youthful Anthony Quayle makes his debut in a speaking role.

HAMLET
(GAMLET)
1966 148m bw   ★★★
Drama   /U
Lenfilm (U.S.S.R.)

Innokenty Smoktunovsky *(Hamlet)*, Mikhail Nazvanov *(King)*, Elsa Radzin *(Queen)*, Yuri Tolubeyev *(Polonius)*, Anastasia Vertinskaya *(Ophelia)*, Vladimir Erenberg *(Horatio)*, C. Olesenko *(Laertes)*, Vadim Medvedev *(Guildenstern)*, Igor Dmitriev *(Rosencrantz)*, A. Krevalid *(Fortinbras)*

d, Gregory Kozintsev; w, Gregory Kozintsev (baesd on the play by William Shakespeare); ph, Ionas Gritsyus (Sovscope); ed, Ye. Makhankova; m, Dmitri Shostakovich; art d, Yevgeniy Yeney, G. Kropachyov; fx, A. Zavyalov, G. Senotov, B. Mikhaylov; cos, Solomon Virsaladze

A genuinely cinematic screen adaptation of Shakespeare's play brimming over with superb marginal visual details, this HAMLET has an exciting epic sweep. Smoktunovsky plays the melananncholy Dane as a man of positive action in a drama that unfolds between shots of lowering rocks and turbulent seas. Due to the lively cinematic imagination of director Kosintzev, this is one of the most visually striking interpretations of the oft-filmed play.

HAMLET
1969 119m c   ★★★½
Drama   G/U
Woodfall/Filmways (U.K.)

Nicol Williamson *(Hamlet)*, Gordon Jackson *(Horatio)*, Anthony Hopkins *(Claudius)*, Judy Parfitt *(Gertrude)*, Mark Dignam *(Polonius)*, Michael Pennington *(Laertes)*, Marianne Faithfull *(Ophelia)*, Ben Aris *(Rosencrantz)*, Clive Graham *(Guildenstern)*, Peter Gale *(Osric)*

p, Neil Hartley; d, Tony Richardson; w, (based on the play by William Shakespeare); ph, Gerry Fisher (Technicolor); ed, Charles Rees; m, Patrick Gowers; prod d, Jocelyn Herbert

A key figure in the British Free Cinema movement, director Richardson (LOOK BACK IN ANGER, A TASTE OF HONEY, TOM JONES) filmed his interpretation of Shakespeare's most celebrated play in London's Round House theatre, where he had previously staged the play. Richardson concentrates on the faces of his performers, privileging the spoken word above all else.

HAMLET
1990 135m c   ★★★½
Drama   PG/U
Marquis (U.K./France/Spain)

Mel Gibson (Hamlet), Glenn Close (Gertrude), Alan Bates (King Claudius), Paul Scofield (The Ghost), Ian Holm (Polonius), Helena Bonham Carter (Ophelia), Stephan Dillan (Horatio), Nathaniel Parker (Laertes), Sean Murray (Guildenstern), Michael Maloney (Rosencrantz)

p, Lovell Dyson; d, Franco Zeffirelli; w, Franco Zeffirelli, Christopher DeVore (based on the play by William Shakespeare); ph, David Watkin; ed, Richard Marden; m, Ennio Morricone; prod d, Dante Ferretti; art d, Michael Lamont

A blank blond for the masses. Director Franco Zeffirelli's third adaptation of the works of William Shakespeare more than anything else shows that Mel Gibson, macho action hero of the MAD MAX and LETHAL WEAPON films, can act, but his dueling scenes are his best moments. Zeffirelli's production is neither high art nor lowbrow pandering, but something in between. This is "Hamlet for the 90s," according to the director, but we can't think of any exact reason why. With much of the text pruned, the pace quickened, and the action streamlined, the film offers what amounts to a classic comic book intro to Shakespeare's classic, retaining few of the play's psychological complexities. Like nouvelle cuisine there's not as much on the plate, but what's there looks good.

Returning to his native Denmark after going to school in Germany, young Prince Hamlet (Gibson) finds his Uncle Claudius (Alan Bates) now sits on the throne of the family castle, Elsinore. Claudius has married Hamlet's mother, Queen Gertrude (Glenn Close), a scant few weeks after the death of Hamlet's beloved father, the king. Hamlet is visited by the ghost of his father (Paul Scofield), who tells him he was poisoned by Claudius and commands his son to avenge his murder. The troubled prince is plagued with doubts about the truth of what the ghost has spoken and determines to find out what really happened.

Unlike the cerebrally tormented, noble protagonist presented in most versions of Hamlet, including Laurence Olivier's 1948 Oscar winner, Zeffirelli's film gives us a simpler central character. Gibson's Hamlet doesn't soar; his speeches are uttered in a straightforward manner defined by action rather than poetry; it's a workmanlike job. Zeffirelli doesn't merely settle for altering the main character, however; he also lessens the importance of the role to some degree, allowing the work to become much more of an ensemble piece than it normally is.

Around Gibson, the director has gathered a stellar international cast, who, for better or worse, have added a new perspective to the play. The ghost of Hamlet's father appears on stage rather than as simply a voiceover, and he is powerfully portrayed by Paul Scofield, who won a Best Actor Oscar in 1966 for A MAN FOR ALL SEASONS. Close has some good moments as Gertrude, and Bates is an expert Claudius. But Holm and Bonham Carter are crashing bores as Polonius and Ophelia.

HAMMETT

1982 100m c   ★★★★
Mystery   PG/AA
Orion

Frederic Forrest (Hammett), Peter Boyle (Jimmy Ryan), Marilu Henner (Kit Conger/Sue Alabama), Roy Kinnear (English Eddie Hagedorn), Elisha Cook, Jr. (Eli, the Taxi Driver), Lydia Lei (Crystal Ling), R.G. Armstrong (Lt. O'Mara), Richard Bradford (Detective Bradford), Michael Chow (Fong), David Patrick Kelly (Punk)

p, Fred Roos, Ronald Colby, Don Guest; d, Wim Wenders; w, Ross Thomas, Dennis O'Flaherty, Thomas Pope (based on the book by Joe Gores); ph, Philip Lathrop, Joseph Biroc (Technicolor); ed, Barry Malkin, Marc Laub, Robert Q. Lovett, Randy Roberts; m, John Barry; prod d, Dean Tavoularis, Eugene Lee; art d, Angelo Graham, Leon Ericksen; cos, Ruth Morley

Impressed by Wim Wenders's obvious talent, Francis Coppola invited the German director to come to America and make a Hollywood film. The project chosen was a highly fictionalized account of the exploits of famed detective novelist Dashiell Hammett.

Set in 1920s San Francisco, the film follows Hammett (Frederic Forrest) as he leaves the Pinkerton Detective Agency to devote himself to writing. His former Pinkerton boss, Jimmy Ryan (Peter Boyle), recruits him to help crack a particularly tough case involving a Chinese prostitute. The cinematography and performances are terrific and highly stylized in this moody thriller, and Wenders directs the film well, but the story is a pastiche of many Hammett tales and is at times so splintered as to be confusing. Like THE AMERICAN FRIEND, Wenders's previous meditation on American genres, HAMMETT is less concerned with its storyline than it is with focusing on an American myth. As such it is not to be missed.

In between HAMMETT's production delays, Wenders made the low-budget black-and-white THE STATE OF THINGS, a film about the difficulties of filmmaking and the elusiveness of an American film producer. Rumor has it that much of HAMMETT was reshot by Coppola but the end result looks seamless.

HANDS ACROSS THE TABLE

1935 81m bw   ★★★★
Comedy   /A
Paramount

Carole Lombard (Regi Allen), Fred MacMurray (Theodore Drew III), Ralph Bellamy (Allen Macklyn), Astrid Allwyn (Vivian Snowden), Ruth Donnelly (Laura), Marie Prevost (Nona), Joseph R. Tozer (Peter), William Demarest (Matty), Edward Gargan (Pinky Kelly), Ferdinand Munier (Miles, the Butler)

p, E. Lloyd Sheldon; d, Mitchell Leisen; w, Norman Krasna, Vincent Lawrence, Herbert Fields (based on the story "Bracelets" by Vina Delmar); ph, Ted Tetzlaff; ed, William Shea; cos, Travis Banton

An underrated 1930 romantic comedy that is charming, stylish and light-hearted.

The wonderful Carole Lombard is Regi Allen, a manicurist who has been hurt so many times in love that she has become cynical and hardened, claiming that financial security is now her only concern in marriage prospects. She meets Allen Macklyn (Ralph Bellamy), a wealthy young man who is confined to a wheelchair In addition to being rich, he is madly in love with her and has serious matrimonial intentions. Fred MacMurray is Theodore Drew III, a poor playboy from a once wealthy and prominent family. He is about to marry Vivian Snowden (Astrid Allwyn) for the same reasons Regi may marry Allen. When Theodore comes into Regi's shop one day, she thinks he's wealthy, so she gladly accepts when he invites her to dinner.

Like many screwball comedies of its era, this one offers snappy badinage and captivating performances but it's not nearly as riotous as some; rather it achieves an authentic tenderness and eroticism that is as memorable as it is rare.

HANGIN' WITH THE HOMEBOYS
1991 88m c   ★★★½
Drama   R/15
Juno Pix/New Line Cinema

Doug E. Doug *(Willie)*, Mario Joyner *(Tom)*, John Leguizamo *(Johnny)*, Nestor Serrano *(Vinny)*, Kimberly Russell *(Vanessa)*, Mary B. Ward *(Luna)*, Reggie Montgomery *(Rasta)*, Christine Claravall *(Daria)*, Rosemary Jackson *(Lila)*, Steven Randazzo *(Pedro)*

p, Richard Brick; d, Joseph B. Vasquez; w, Joseph B. Vasquez; ph, Anghel Decca; ed, Michael Schweitzer; art d, Isabel Bau Madden; cos, Mary Jane Fort

The third feature, following STREET STORY and THE BRONX WAR, by New York-based filmmaker Joseph B. Vasquez, HANGIN' WITH THE HOMEBOYS is a remarkable film, a character study that is by turns funny, biting and melancholy.

Tom (Mario Joyner), Willie (Doug E. Doug), Johnny (John Leguizamo) and Vinnie (Nestor Serrano) are buddies—two black, two Puerto Rican—who grew up together in the Bronx. Though their lives have developed along very different lines, they remain friends. Tom is an aspiring actor, though he's selling magazine subscriptions to pay the rent. Johnny works in a supermarket; he's been encouraged to go to college, but he's afraid to take the first step—filling out a scholarship application. Vinnie is a smooth-talking layabout who hides his Puerto Rican heritage behind the fiction that he's Italian and lets his many girlfriends pay his way. And Willie is unemployed and un-employable, convinced that he's oppressed by racial prejudice. His furious mantra is, "It's because I'm black, right?" On a typical Friday night they get together to cruise and have a good time.

Vasquez's first film to be widely distributed, HANGIN' WITH THE HOMEBOYS opens with a beautifully written and performed sequence that sets the tone for the entire picture. On a crowded subway train, riders stare at their newspapers and try to ignore four boisterous minority youths who enter the car gesticulating and arguing loudly. Two of them come to blows, and the riders shrink back in their seats. Suddenly, all the young men—Willie, Tom, Johnny and Vinnie—begin to laugh and clown around: it's all been a joke, impromptu "street theater." The scene establishes relationships between the four, while setting them within the larger context of contemporary New York. It's funny, scary and feels absolutely authentic.

In addition to bringing to life the four sharply delineated main characters, HANGIN' WITH THE HOMEBOYS captures an aspect of New York life that's seldom seen on film. Willie, Tom, Johnny and Vinnie are young black and Puerto Rican men who aren't dope dealers or murderers, but neither are they white characters who happen to have colored skin. Vasquez's observations are simultaneously ruthless and affectionate; his eye for the subtle conflicts between black and Puerto Rican New Yorkers is particularly revealing. Excellent performances by Joyner, Leguizamo, Serrano and Doug are also an asset.

HANGIN' WITH THE HOMEBOYS was one of several films by young, minority filmmakers released in 1991. Far better crafted than STRAIGHT OUT OF BROOKLYN and less angry than BOYZ N THE HOOD, HANGIN' WITH THE HOMEBOYS is accessible without betraying its subject matter.

HANGMEN ALSO DIE!
1943 131m bw   ★★★½
War   /A
UA

Brian Donlevy *(Dr. Franz Svoboda)*, Walter Brennan *(Prof. Novotny)*, Anna Lee *(Mascha Novotny)*, Gene Lockhart *(Emil Czaka)*, Dennis O'Keefe *(Jan Horek)*, Alexander Granach *(Alois Gruber)*, Margaret Wycherly *(Aunt Ludmilla Novotny)*, Nana Bryant *(Mrs. Novotny)*, Billy Roy *(Beda Novotny)*, Hans von Twardowski *(Reinhard Heydrich)*

p, Fritz Lang; d, Fritz Lang; w, John Wexley (based on a story by Fritz Lang and Bertolt Brecht); ph, James Wong Howe; ed, Gene Fowler, Jr.; m, Hanns Eisler; art d, William Darling; cos, Julie Heron

In Czechoslovakia during WWII, Deputy Reich Protector Reinhard Heydrich (von Twardowski), Nazi-appointed "governor" of Prague, gathers prominent citizens and voices his displeasure at insidious acts of sabotage in the factories. Not only are the Czech acts of defiance holding up vital production for the Third Reich, they are also endangering the lives of the civic leaders assembled, Heydrich says, adding that stern measures will be taken unless production increases. After leaving the meeting, Heydrich is assassinated by a member of the Czech resistance, Svoboda (Donlevy). On the run, Svoboda is given shelter by kindly Professor Novotny (Brennan) and his daughter Mascha (Lee). Though Heydrich's death becomes a hopeful symbol for the Czechoslovakian people and improves their morale, the Nazis demand revenge and the Gestapo begin to round up hundreds of innocent Czech citizens suspected of subversion and complicity, and kill them off one by one until the killer is handed over.

While HANGMEN ALSO DIE is a much better than average American WWII propaganda film, it is a bit of a disappointment in the impressive career of master director Fritz Lang. Beyond a precious few scenes containing some stunning Lang visuals, the film is overlong and the characters haphazardly developed. The tension is occasionally interrupted by impassioned patriotic speeches that comment didactically and intelligently on the proceedings in a Brechtian fashion. As well they should, since this was the first Hollywood screenplay collaborated on by that celebrated German playwright. (Brecht was, however, denied co-screenwriting credit following a Guild arbitration.) Visually the film's atmosphere is marvelously dark and oppressive due to the moody lensing of the great cinematographer James Wong Howe.

HANNAH AND HER SISTERS
1986 106m c   ★★★★½
Comedy/Drama   PG-13/15
Orion

Woody Allen *(Mickey)*, Michael Caine *(Elliot)*, Mia Farrow *(Hannah)*, Carrie Fisher *(April)*, Barbara Hershey *(Lee)*, Lloyd Nolan *(Hannah's Father)*, Maureen O'Sullivan *(Hannah's Mother)*, Daniel Stern *(Dusty)*, Max von Sydow *(Frederick)*, Dianne Wiest *(Holly)*

p, Robert Greenhut; d, Woody Allen; w, Woody Allen; ph, Carlo Di Palma (Panavision, Technicolor); ed, Susan E. Morse; prod d, Stuart Wurtzel; cos, Jeffrey Kurland

Essentially three separate tales that intertwine at times, HANNAH AND HER SISTERS is one of writer-director Woody Allen's most complex films and the first one in which his neurotic character is given a happy ending.

The picture takes place over a couple of years, framed by Thanksgiving dinners. Hannah (Mia Farrow) is married to Elliot (Michael Caine), a business manager for rock stars. She used to be married to Mickey (Allen), a TV producer. Hannah's sisters are Lee (Barbara Hershey)—who's living with Frederick (Max von Sydow), a witty, bitter SoHo artist—and Holly (Dianne

Wiest), an actress who's a bundle of nerves. Elliot harbors a passion for Lee and eventually makes it known to her. She succumbs, guilt-ridden for betraying Hannah. Holly, a former cocaine addict, can no longer contain her envy of Hannah—the oldest, "perfect" sister, who has what appears to be a blissful existence.

The plot could easily have been an afternoon soap opera, but Allen has infused it with wit, a superb cast and his usual "the best direction is the least direction" style, so that the camera never calls attention to itself.

HANOVER STREET

1979   109m   c   ★★½
Romance   PG
Columbia   (U.K.)

Harrison Ford *(David Halloran)*, Lesley-Anne Down *(Margaret Sellinger)*, Christopher Plummer *(Paul Sellinger)*, Alec McCowen *(Maj. Trumbo)*, Richard Masur *(2nd Lt. Jerry Cimino)*, Michael Sacks *(2nd Lt. Martin Hyer)*, Patsy Kensit *(Sarah Sellinger)*, Max Wall *(Harry Pike)*, Shane Rimmer *(Col. Ronald Bart)*, Keith Buckley *(Lt. Wells)*

p, Paul N. Lazarus, III; d, Peter Hyams; w, Peter Hyams; ph, David Watkin (Panavision, Technicolor); ed, James Mitchell; m, John Barry; prod d, Philip Harrison; art d, Malcolm Middleton, Robert Cartwright; fx, Martin Gutteridge; cos, Joan Bridge

Ford plays David Halloran, a gung ho American bomber pilot stationed in England during WWII who meets and falls in love with a young married Englishwoman, Margaret Sellinger (Down), with whom he's trapped during an air raid. In the best tradition of melodramatic wartime romances, Ford finds himself having to team up with Down's husband, Paul (Plummer), a British secret service agent, on a dangerous espionage mission that will take them behind enemy lines. Director Hyams (CAPRICORN ONE, OUTLAND, 2010) tries desperately to evoke the feel of the best of the 1940s wartime romantic dramas but, despite solid performances from the leads, his screenplay is predictable and trite, leaving the audience little to look forward to.

HANS CHRISTIAN ANDERSEN

1952   120m   c   ★★★
Biography   /U
RKO

Danny Kaye *(Hans Christian Andersen)*, Farley Granger *(Niels)*, Zizi Jeanmaire *(Doro)*, Joseph Walsh *(Peter)*, Philip Tonge *(Otto)*, Erik Bruhn *(Hussar)*, Roland Petit *(Prince)*, John Brown *(Schoolmaster)*, John Qualen *(Burgomaster)*, Jeanne Lafayette *(Celine)*

p, Samuel Goldwyn; d, Charles Vidor; w, Moss Hart (based on a story by Myles Connolly); ph, Harry Stradling (Technicolor); ed, Daniel Mandell; m, Frank Loesser; art d, Richard Day, Antoni Clave; chor, Roland Petit; cos, Antoni Clave, Mary Wills, Barbara Karinska

This glossy children's musical stars Danny Kaye as the beloved Danish author of fairy tales whose rise to literary prominence is detailed here in a totally fabricated manner. Most adults will squirm during the syrupy proceedings but kids seem to like it just fine.

This movie was something of an obsession for producer Samuel Goldwyn, who had been announcing production of the project for nearly 15 years, only to have it delayed time and time again. After paying a king's ransom for 16 different screenplays, Goldwyn finally found one he liked, and production began.

Luckily, Goldwyn's dream paid off big at the box office, as HANS CHRISTIAN ANDERSEN grossed $6 million and eventually ranked as Goldwyn's third biggest moneymaker (behind THE BEST YEARS OF OUR LIVES and GUYS AND DOLLS). Kaye is wonderful and the enjoyable songs include "Inchworm" and "Wonderful Wonderful Copenhagen."

HAPPY ENDING, THE

1969   117m   c   ★★
Drama   M/X
UA

Jean Simmons *(Mary Wilson)*, John Forsythe *(Fred Wilson)*, Lloyd Bridges *(Sam)*, Teresa Wright *(Mrs. Spencer)*, Dick Shawn *(Harry Bricker)*, Nanette Fabray *(Agnes)*, Bobby Darin *(Franco)*, Tina Louise *(Helen Bricker)*, Kathy Fields *(Marge Wilson)*, Gail Hensley *(Betty)*

p, Richard Brooks; d, Richard Brooks; w, Richard Brooks; ph, Conrad Hall (Panavision, Technicolor); ed, George Grenville; m, Michel Legrand; fx, Geza Gaspar; cos, Rita Riggs

Mary Wilson (Simmons) decides that she's not happy with her 16-year marriage to her tax-lawyer husband Fred (Forsythe), so she walks out In Search of Herself in this initially intriguing but ultimately annoying drama. The search runs the gamut of booze, affairs and drugs as her unhappy life unfolds. This slowly leads up to a resolution that is halfhearted at best. Jean Simmons struggles valiantly but no avail; she's defeated by writer-director Brooks's dreary, overwritten screenplay.

HARD DAY'S NIGHT, A

1964   83m   bw   ★★★★½
Musical/Comedy   G/U
UA   (U.K.)

John Lennon *(John)*, Paul McCartney *(Paul)*, George Harrison *(George)*, Ringo Starr *(Ringo)*, Wilfrid Brambell *(Grandfather)*, Norman Rossington *(Norm)*, Victor Spinetti *(TV Director)*, John Junkin *(Shake)*, Deryck Guyler *(Police Inspector)*, Anna Quayle *(Millie)*

p, Walter Shenson; d, Richard Lester; w, Alun Owen; ph, Gilbert Taylor; ed, John Jympson; m, John Lennon, Paul McCartney; art d, Ray Simm; cos, Dougie Millings & Son, Julie Harris

Refreshing, innovative and immensely funny, A HARD DAY'S NIGHT tells the story of 36 hours in the lives of the Beatles in a quirky fashion that has everyone laughing from the first moment.

Besieged by their frenzied fans, John, Paul, George, and Ringo board a train for London, where they are to do a live television appearance. They are accompanied by Norm (Rossington), their manager (a parody of Brian Epstein), his aide, Shake (John Junkin), and Paul's grandfather (Wilfrid Brambell), a "clean old man" who proves to be a mischievous old coot. In London, the boys cavort at a swinging nightspot before going in search of Grandfather, whom they find chatting up a buxom bird at a casino, and drag him back to the hotel over his angry protests. At the television studio the next day, Grandfather convinces Ringo that he is unappreciated by the rest of the group, and the dejected drummer disappears into the city streets. But how can the lads go on television without Ringo?

Producer Walt Shenson thought he would rush this into production and take advantage of the Beatles' immense popularity before their celebrity waned. Made in only seven weeks for just over half a million dollars, A HARD DAY'S NIGHT returned many times its cost. Its sequel, HELP (also directed by Richard Lester), cost almost three times as much, wasn't as good, and won't be remembered as long as this anarchistic, Marx Brothers-like romp. Combining surrealistic imagery and cinema verite techniques, borrowing from Fellini, Godard, Keaton, and even Busby Berkeley, Lester arrives at his own dazzling style and creates one of the most inventive pictures of the era. Alun Owen's wonderful screenplay is full of witty surprises, delivered as only the Beatles could, and a number of their classics are well integrated into the narrative.

HARDCORE

1979 105m c	★★½
Drama	R/18
Columbia	

George C. Scott *(Jake Van Dorn)*, Peter Boyle *(Andy Mast)*, Season Hubley *(Niki)*, Dick Sargent *(Wes DeJong)*, Leonard Gaines *(Ramada)*, David Nichols *(Kurt)*, Gary Graham *(Tod)*, Larry Block *(Detective Burrows)*, Marc Alaimo *(Ratan)*, Leslie Ackerman *(Felice)*

p, Buzz Feitshans; d, Paul Schrader; w, Paul Schrader; ph, Michael Chapman (Metrocolor); ed, Tom Rolf; m, Jack Nitzsche; prod d, Paul Sylbert; art d, Edwin O'Donovan

"Oh my God, it's my daughter!" wails George C. Scott in the most celebrated scene in HARDCORE, an oddball failure from writer-director Paul Schrader (BLUE COLLAR, AMERICAN GIGOLO, CAT PEOPLE, MISHIMA). Still it's not without merit. The film's strong material and some genuinely weird moments make it well worth viewing.

Scott (in a performance that ranges from completely over-the-top to downright heartbreaking) plays Jake Van Dorn, a devoutly religious Calvinist from Grand Rapids, Michigan, whose teen-aged daughter, Kristen (Davis), disappears during a church trip to California. Van Dorn ventures out to sinful California to find his missing child. He hires sleazy private detective Andy Mast (Boyle) to look for her and then returns to his virtuous life back in Michigan. Soon he gets a call from Mast, now in Grand Rapids, telling him to meet him in town. The cheap detective takes Van Dorn to a porno theater where they watch a film in which the devout Van Dorn spots his daughter. He breaks down sobbing. Mast returns to L.A. to continue the search but Van Dorn can no longer stand by as an observer. He flies to California himself to begin his own search in L.A.'s X-rated underworld.

Realistic one minute, unbelievable the next, HARDCORE is a truly schizophrenic film. A somber, serious moment is followed by a tongue-in-cheek parody or a flat-out joke. Every scene involving the porno film industry is played strictly for laughs, with wildly exaggerated characters. Scott's performance is similarly divided. He's completely serious during the scenes in which he shows the desperation of the parent of a lost child but he becomes loud and terribly unconvincing as he wanders through the peep shows and massage parlors. He even poses as a porn producer to look for leads to his daughter's whereabouts. The conclusion is totally unbelievable.

Schrader was obviously attempting to parallel the lifestyles of overly religious people (a household not unlike the one he grew up in) with those of the porno world. The title itself can refer to both hardcore religion or hardcore pornography—Schrader hasn't made up his mind. This tonal inconsistency undermines the emotions of the screenplay. This is an inherently powerful subject with some gut-wrenching scenes, but Schrader's insistence on pushing things to the limit ultimately ruins all the credibility those earlier scenes create.

HARDER THEY COME, THE

1973 98m c	★★★½
Drama	R/15
International Films (Jamaica)	

Jimmy Cliff *(Ivan)*, Carl Bradshaw *(Jose)*, Janet Bartley *(Elsa)*, Ras Daniel Hartman *(Pedro)*, Basil Keane *(Preacher)*, Bob Charlton *(Hilton)*, Winston Stona *(Detective)*

p, Perry Henzell; d, Perry Henzell; w, Perry Henzell, Trevor D. Rhone; ph, Peter Jessop, David McDonald (Metrocolor); ed, John Victor Smith, Seicland Anderson, Richard White; m, Jimmy Cliff, Desmond Dekker, The Slickers

This outstanding Jamaican feature became a major cult favorite in the US and did much to popularize reggae with its fabulous musical score.

Reggae star Jimmy Cliff plays Ivan, a young aspiring singer from the country who arrives in Kingston with high hopes of becoming a recording star. Work is hard to come by, however, and after a rude awakening on the city streets, Ivan becomes a handyman for a local preacher. When an argument over a bicycle escalates into a knife fight, Ivan is sent to jail. After his release he moves in with the preacher's ward, Elsa (Bartley), and pursues the island's biggest record producer, Hilton (Charlton). Eventually he gets the chance to record "The Harder They Come." However Ivan balks when Hilton offers him a paltry $20 for the song. The producer retaliates by releasing the record without any promotion. Penniless, Ivan has no choice but to get involved in the lucrative but dangerous marijuana trade. As his criminal notoriety grows so do his record sales.

THE HARDER THEY COME is a gritty, realistic view of urban Jamaica that reveals the squalor of shantytowns tourists never see. Cliff delivers a charismatic and memorable performance as a young man who is determined to become famous, mirroring his own real-life ascendence to worldwide fame as a reggae artist. Despite the ostensible show-business plot, this film most resembles a 1930s gangster film with its relentless depiction of regrettable social conditions, police corruption and the lure of illicit cash. The filmmaking is a bit crude at times but it packs an emotional wallop.

HARDER THEY FALL, THE

1956 109m bw	★★★★
Sports	/15
Columbia	

Humphrey Bogart *(Eddie Willis)*, Rod Steiger *(Nick Benko)*, Jan Sterling *(Beth Willis)*, Mike Lane *(Toro Moreno)*, Max Baer *(Buddy Brannen)*, Jersey Joe Walcott *(George)*, Edward Andrews *(Jim Weyerhause)*, Harold J. Stone *(Art Leavitt)*, Carlos Montalban *(Luis Agrandi)*, Nehemiah Persoff *(Leo)*

p, Philip Yordan; d, Mark Robson; w, Philip Yordan (based on the novel by Budd Schulberg); ph, Burnett Guffey; ed, Jerome Thoms; m, Hugo Friedhofer; art d, William Flannery

One of the most scathing indictments of professional boxing ever committed to film, THE HARDER THEY FALL presents Humphrey Bogart as Eddie Willis, a once-scrupulous sportswriter, now working for Nick Benko (Rod Steiger), a shady mob-connected promoter. Eddie is handling the publicity for Benko's new find, Toro Moreno (Mike Lane), a giant Argentine boxer with a powder-puff punch and a glass jaw. But Benko fixes one fight after another and soon the towering heavyweight, who thinks he's doing it on his own, faces Gus Dundee (Pat Comiskey), a top contender who was so battered by the current champ, Buddy Brannen (one-time heavyweight title holder Max Baer), that even

Toro's feeble punches are enough to bring about a brain hemorrhage that kills him. This is the beginning of a moral crisis for Eddie.

Scripted by producer Philip Yordan from the novel by Budd Schulberg, THE HARDER THEY FALL was similar enough to the real-life story of heavyweight Primo Carnera (who lost his title to Baer) that he sued Columbia. Nothing about it is pretty, with director Mark Robson (who'd already helmed the powerful CHAMPION) moving the story along at a frenetic pace and Burnett Guffey's stark black-and-white photography lending a grim feel to the movie. All of the performers are excellent, especially Bogart, in what would be his final screen appearance.

HAROLD AND MAUDE

1971 90m c   ★★★½
Comedy   GP/15
Paramount

Ruth Gordon (Maude), Bud Cort (Harold), Vivian Pickles (Mrs. Chasen), Cyril Cusack (Sculptor), Charles Tyner (Uncle Victor), Ellen Geer (Sunshine), Eric Christmas (Priest), G. Wood (Psychiatrist), Judy Engles (Candy Gulf), Shari Summers (Edith Fern)

p, Charles B. Mulvehill, Colin Higgins; d, Hal Ashby; w, Colin Higgins; ph, John A. Alonzo (Technicolor); ed, William A. Sawyer, Edward Warschilka; m, Cat Stevens; prod d, Michael Haller; art d, Michael Haller; fx, A.D. Flowers; cos, William Ware Theiss

HAROLD AND MAUDE got lost in the holiday shuffle when first released in late 1971, but there's much in this oddball film to recommend, including superb performances from the three leads. Harold (Cort) is the son of Mrs. Chasen (Pickles), a wealthy woman who pays little attention to him. His frequent depressions and lack of friends motivate him to stage increasingly elaborate mock suicides, none of which impress his distracted mother. Fascinated by death and all its trappings, Harold has an old hearse which he drives to funerals at various cemeteries around town. At two successive services, he meets Maude (Gordon), a 79-year-old concentration camp survivor who is as thrilled with life as he is with death. A classic free spirit, she is the polar opposite of the solemn Harold. Nonetheless they become great pals, and she instills in him a desire to live, to spread his wings, to enjoy his brief time on earth. As time passes, they share several wacky adventures and their friendship blossoms into love—much to the alarm of Harold's mother.

This is a doggedly eccentric film which some will reject out of hand. Others will find it profoundly moving and life affirming. Not surprisingly it became one of the major cult films on college campuses in the 1970s. This film was originated as a 20-minute script written as a graduate thesis by UCLA student Higgins. He later showed it to his landlady, Lewis, the wife of a film producer, and the two formed their own production company to make the film. Higgins went on to become a writer-director best known for films such as FOUL PLAY, NINE TO FIVE, and THE BEST LITTLE WHOREHOUSE IN TEXAS. He died in 1988 from AIDS complications.

HARPER

1966 121m c   ★★★
Mystery   /A
WB

Paul Newman (Harper), Lauren Bacall (Mrs. Sampson), Julie Harris (Betty Fraley), Arthur Hill (Albert Graves), Janet Leigh (Susan Harper), Pamela Tiffin (Miranda Sampson), Robert Wagner

(Alan Traggert), Robert Webber (Dwight Troy), Shelley Winters (Fay Estabrook), Harold Gould (Sheriff Spanner)

p, Elliott Kastner, Jerry Gershwin; d, Jack Smight; w, William Goldman (based on the novel The Moving Target by Ross MacDonald); ph, Conrad Hall (Panavision, Technicolor); ed, Stefan Arnsten; m, Johnny Mandel; art d, Alfred Sweeney; cos, Sally Edwards, William Smith

Based on Ross MacDonald's novel The Moving Target, HARPER showcases Paul Newman in the role of Lew Harper, a down-on-his-luck but ultra hip Los Angeles private eye hired by the cynical Mrs. Sampson (Bacall) to track down her missing and very wealthy husband. The trail leading to Mr. Sampson is laden with strange characters and brings more than a few bumps and bruises Harper's way. His snooping takes him from an over-the-hill actress (Winters) to a junkie nightclub chanteuse (Harris) and from a religious zealot (Martin) to a smuggling operation. William Goldman's adaptation of MacDonald's novel—his first solo screenwriting credit—is full of rapid-fire dialogue but some of the characterizations are thin. Despite all the big names involved, HARPER doesn't begin to approach the big leagues of hard-boiled detective films. Nonetheless, Newman gives a convincing performance in a role he would repeat nearly ten years later in THE DROWNING POOL.

HARRY AND TONTO

1974 115m c   ★★★
Drama   R/A
FOX

Art Carney (Harry Coombs), Ellen Burstyn (Shirley), Chief Dan George (Sam Two Feathers), Geraldine Fitzgerald (Jessie), Larry Hagman (Eddie), Arthur Hunnicutt (Wade), Philip Bruns (Burt), Josh Mostel (Norman), Melanie Mayron (Ginger), Dolly Jonah (Elaine)

p, Paul Mazursky; d, Paul Mazursky; w, Paul Mazursky, Josh Greenfeld; ph, Michael Butler (DeLuxe Color); ed, Richard Halsey; m, Bill Conti; prod d, Ted Haworth; cos, Albert Wolsky

When his comfortable New York City apartment building is torn down, 72-year-old widower and retired college professor Harry (Carney) temporarily moves in with his eldest son but finds his daughter-in-law less than enthusiastic. Perhaps inspired by his grandson, Norman (Mostel, son of Zero), who is currently immersed in Zen philosophy, Harry decides to postpone his search for new lodgings to fulfill a lifelong ambition to travel across the country to California. With his beloved cat Tonto, Harry hits the road, planning to stop and visit his other children—Shirley (Burstyn), a daughter who lives in Chicago, and youngest son, Eddie (Hagman), who lives on the West Coast. During his journey, Harry encounters several situations that cause him to examine what life means to him.

HARRY AND TONTO is a sweet, sentimental road movie that draws force and relevance from Carney's touching and subtle performance. Incredibly, after nearly 25 years on television, this was the actor's first major feature film role. In HARRY AND TONTO writer-director Mazursky shows the innocence of youth and the disappointment of middle age but offers solace in old age if the internal energy that once produced ambition is rediscovered and prompts us to hope for better things to come.

HARVEY

1950 104m bw   ★★★★
Comedy   /U
Universal

James Stewart (*Elwood P. Dowd*), Josephine Hull (*Veta Louise Simmons*), Peggy Dow (*Miss Kelly*), Charles Drake (*Dr. Sanderson*), Cecil Kellaway (*Dr. Chumley*), Victoria Horne (*Myrtle Mae*), Jesse White (*Wilson*), William Lynn (*Judge Gaffney*), Wallace Ford (*Lofgren*), Nana Bryant (*Mrs. Chumley*)

p, John Beck; d, Henry Koster; w, Mary Chase, Oscar Brodney (based on a play by Chase); ph, William Daniels; ed, Ralph Dawson; m, Frank Skinner; art d, Nathan Juran, Bernard Herzbrun

Elwood P. Dowd (Jimmy Stewart) is the whimsical inebriate whose kindness spills over into the lives of all around him as he tries to help those in need. Elwood lurches home one night to see a six-foot rabbit named Harvey leaning against a lamppost. This invisible "Pooka" becomes his friend and follows him everywhere, much to the chagrin of Elwood's social-climbing family, who think he has finally flipped and should be put in an asylum. Faithfully adapted by Mary Chase from her popular Broadway play, HARVEY is a delightful comedy-fantasy. Jimmy Stewart, in one of his best-loved roles, is wonderful as the gentle, sweet soul who befriends the invisible rabbit. His performance earned him an Oscar nomination, and the priceless Josephine Hull, as Stewart's harried sister, was honored as Best Supporting Actress. The supporting cast features wonderful work from Dow (who retired far too soon), Drake, Kellaway, Horne, and White. Henry Koster's direction is sharp and moves along at a rapid clip. This is a happy movie and leaves a long, lingering warm glow.

HASTY HEART, THE
1949   99m   bw   ★★★★
Drama   /U
WB   (U.K.)

Ronald Reagan (*The Yank*), Patricia Neal (*Sister Margaret*), Richard Todd (*The Scot*), Anthony Nicholls (*Col Dunn*), Howard Marion-Crawford (*The Tommy*), Ralph Michael (*The New Zealander*), John Sherman (*The Aussie*), Alfie Bass (*Orderly*), Orlando Martins (*Blossom*)

p, Howard Lindsay, Russel Crouse; d, Vincent Sherman; w, Ranald MacDougall (based on the play by John Patrick); ph, Wilkie Cooper; ed, E.B. Jarvis; m, Jack Beaver; art d, Terence Verity; cos, Peggy Henderson

Six wounded soldiers await shipment home. Reagan's Yank character asks little more of him than that he supply bravura; he's exceeded at every turn by Todd, who is wonderful as a hardheaded, truculent Scottish soldier who remains aloof toward his fellow patients. Nicholls, the head doctor, and Neal, a firm but gentle nurse, ask Reagan and the other patients to be kind to Todd, who's dying of a terminal illness but does not know it. It's a difficult task, though, since the stubborn Scot rejects the friendship of Reagan and the others, more or less telling them to mind their own business when they try to strike up conversations or do little favors for him.

On his 21st birthday, however, Todd is given a complete new Scottish outfit (including kilt and bagpipes) as a gift from the patients. This softens his heart, and he explains in his own halting manner that he has never before been so touched. At last he befriends his fellow patients, but when Nicholls finally tells him he's dying, Todd again closes up like a clam, this time bitterly lashing out at Reagan and the others because he now believes their actions were motivated only by pity.

This is a poignant drama, fluidly directed by the versatile and underrated Sherman which, despite the screenplay's failure to "open up" the original play, is kept from becoming claustrophobic largely due to Sherman's inventive setups and staging. The

30-year-old Richard Todd had made only one previous film (FOR THEM THAT TRESPASS) before completing THE HASTY HEART, although he had been on stage since the late 1930s. He was a standout discovery here, and no doubt drew upon his experience as a paratrooper during WWII for his role, which netted him an Academy Award nomination for Best Actor.

HAUNTING, THE
1963   112m   bw   ★★★½
Horror   /X
Argyle   (U.S./U.K.)

Julie Harris (*Eleanor Vance*), Claire Bloom (*Theodora*), Richard Johnson (*Dr. John Markway*), Russ Tamblyn (*Luke Sanderson*), Lois Maxwell (*Grace Markway*), Fay Compton (*Mrs. Sanderson*), Valentine Dyall (*Mr. Dudley*), Rosalie Crutchley (*Mrs. Dudley*), Diane Clare (*Carrie Fredericks*), Ronald Adam (*Eldridge Harper*)

p, Robert Wise; d, Robert Wise; w, Nelson Gidding (based on the novel *The Haunting of Hill House* by Shirley Jackson); ph, Davis Boulton (Panavision); ed, Ernest Walter; m, Humphrey Searle; prod d, Elliot Scott; fx, Tom Howard; cos, Mary Quant, Maude Churchill

A bit overrated upon its initial release, THE HAUNTING is, nonetheless, an undeniably effective adaptation of the Shirley Jackson novel and remains one of the best haunted-house movies.

Dr. Markway (Richard Johnson) is a professor of anthropology experimenting with ESP and other forms of psychic phenomena. He arrives at Hill House, a New England mansion that is reputed to be crammed with demons and ghosts and the home of everything evil. Along with Markway is Eleanor (Julie Harris), a slim spinster who, until recently, has spent her life caring for her aged mother, and Theodora (Claire Bloom), a lesbian. Both women have experienced extra-sensory occurrences, and Markway has enlisted their aid in his quest for knowledge on the subject. Luke (Russ Tamblyn), who is the heir to the house and hopes to sell it at a great profit, goes along for a ride he will regret. Once inside, the quartet is besieged by terror—noises, yowls, and eerie events pour off the screen until Eleanor is convinced that Hill House is alive and wants her to stay there.

Director Robert Wise, who began his directorial career under the tutelage of Val Lewton, takes the lessons learned there to a bit of an extreme, overplaying his hand through the use of extremely exaggerated angles and distorting lenses. But the politically incorrect and oversimplified notion that Eleanor's repressed lesbianism is the cause of her downfall, was outdated even when the film was made. THE HAUNTING spends too much time setting up the idea that it will scientifically shed light on psychic phenomena and then withdraws from us. All said, the high order of acting seems wasted.

HE WALKED BY NIGHT
1948   79m   bw   ★★★★
Crime   /A
Bryan Foy/Eagle-Lion

Richard Basehart (*Davis Morgan*), Scott Brady (*Sgt. Marty Brennan*), Roy Roberts (*Capt. Breen*), Whit Bissell (*Reeves*), James Cardwell (*Chuck Jones*), Jack Webb (*Lee*), Robert Bice (*Detective Steno*), Reed Hadley (*Narrator*), Chief Bradley (*Himself*), John McGuire (*Rawlins*) p, Robert T. Kane; d, Alfred Werker, Anthony Mann (uncredited); w, John C. Higgins, Crane Wilbur, Harry Essex (uncredited), Beck Murray (based on a story by Crane Wilbur); ph, John Alton; ed, Al DeGaetano; m, Leonid Raab; art d, Edward L. Ilou; fx, George J. Teague, Jack Rabin

This is a smashing film noir entry with Basehart as Davis Morgan, a brilliant, cold-hearted thief with underlying psychopathic tendencies that chill the viewer to the bone. Morgan is an electronics wizard who robs stores and warehouses to obtain electrical equipment which he modifies and then rents out to Reeves (Bissell). The Los Angeles police are in a quandary about this successful burglar since Morgan listens in on their radio network and cleverly alters his *modus operandi* so that his work appears to be that of another burglar. With cops Brennan (Brady) and Breen (Roberts) hot on his trail, Morgan attempts to escape into the vast sewer system beneath Los Angeles.

Director Werker (with an uncredited assist from Anthony Mann) does a fine job in maintaining the hectic pace, and Basehart is gripping as the lone, loveless thief who even sacrifices his dog when the going gets tough. His role is based on the career of thief and cop-killer Erwin Walker, a WWII hero turned burglar who terrorized LA in 1946. This film marked the first time the huge drainage system canals in Los Angeles were employed in a film; they would later be put to heavy use in THEM!, GREASE, and a number of other productions. Jack Webb drew the inspiration for his long-running documentary-style television series "Dragnet" from this film, in which he played a featured role.

HEAR MY SONG

1991 113m c ★★★
Comedy/Drama R/15
Limelight Ltd./Film Four International/Windmill Lane Productions/Vision Investments (U.K./Ireland)

Ned Beatty (*Josef Locke*), Adrian Dunbar (*Mickey O'Neill*), Shirley Anne Field (*Cathleen Doyle*), Tara Fitzgerald (*Nancy Doyle*), William Hootkins (*Mr. X*), Harold Berens (*Benny Rose*), David McCallum (*Jim Abbott*), John Dair (*Derek*), Stephen Marcus (*Gordon*), Britta Smith (*Kitty Ryan*)

p, Alison Owen; d, Peter Chelsom; w, Peter Chelsom, Adrian Dunbar (from the story by Chelsom); ph, Sue Gibson; ed, Martin Walsh; m, John Altman; prod d, Caroline Hanania; art d, Katharine Naylor; cos, Lindy Hemming

The lilt of Irish laughter and wit fills the screen in Peter Chelsom's romantic comedy HEAR MY SONG, and its blarney is irresistible. Micky O'Neill (Adrian Dunbar) runs a nightclub, Heartly's, that caters to Liverpool's Irish community. He's engaged to Nancy Doyle (Tara Fitzgerald), the best girl in town, and all is right with his world. His only problem, it seems, is booking talent for his venue and he usually wheels and deals in order to find "names" that will bring in the masses. He even hires one, a Franc Cinatra (Joe Cuddy), hoping that the public won't notice that this one is spelled with two "C's". Alas, Franc is the world's worst Sinatra impersonator and Micky is soon in danger of losing his clientele.

Then Mickey hits on a scheme. He'll bring back the notorious "Mr. X" and hints broadly that this is the legendary and much loved Josef Locke. When that tenor sang, it's widely bruited, "women wept." But Locke is a wanted man because of massive tax evasion. He fled to Ireland some 30 years earlier and hasn't been heard from since. The intrepid Micky convinces "Mr. X" to make an appearance because he's sure it will be a sold-out event.

"Mr. X" (William Hootkins), not surprisingly, is a fraud. He might fool the masses but not the elegant Cathleen Doyle (Shirley Anne Field) who fell in love with the real Locke when he crowned her Miss Dairy Wholesomeness of 1958. Nor does this "Mr. X" fool Jim Abbott (David McCallum), the local police chief. As a result of his wheeling and dealing, Micky loses Heartly's. He also loses Nancy, who's Cathleen's daughter and feels especially conned by the imposter. So Micky has no alternative. He returns to Ireland, determined to find the real Josef Locke and somehow get him to risk arrest and return to Liverpool for a special appearance.

HEAR MY SONG is based on an incident in the life of the world-famous Irish tenor Josef Locke, who really did flee Britain due to tax difficulties. Former stage actor Peter Chelsom, who makes an auspicious feature directorial debut and also co-wrote the screenplay with Adrian Dunbar, remembers the real Josef Locke from his own youth in Blackpool. The celebrated Irish tenor, played by Ned Beatty with enormous ebullience and charm, sang for 19 seasons at the seaside resort which gave him his *nom de chanson*, Mr. Blackpool.

The film is structured in three segments. Early scenes center around Heartly's nightclub and Micky's office. The lush landscape of Ireland's scenic west country comprises the middle section, while the end returns to the city, where Heartly's is being demolished. Production designer Caroline Hanania has succeeded in giving each segment a unique feel, from harsh big city to small picturesque town to the fantastical elements in Heartly's demise, all of which has provided splendid opportunities for cinematographer Sue Gibson.

One of the film's themes, how dreams can be distorted, intrigues Chelsom. There's a phrase in the film spoken by Grandma Ryan which is the key: "You close your eyes. You cast your mind back 30 years and you see and hear what you want to see and hear." Dreams and longing and cravings for something more fundamental in a very transient world are what HEAR MY SONG is all about.

HEART LIKE A WHEEL

1983 113m c ★★★
Biography PG
Aurora

Bonnie Bedelia (*Shirley Muldowney*), Beau Bridges (*Connie Kalitta*), Leo Rossi (*Jack Muldowney*), Hoyt Axton (*Tex Roque*), Bill McKinney ("*Big Daddy*" *Don Garlits*), Anthony Edwards (*John Muldowney, Age 15-23*), Dean Paul Martin (*Sonny Rigotti*), Paul Bartel (*Chef Paul*), Missy Basile (*Angela*), Michael Cavanaugh (*NHRA Boss*)

p, Charles Roven; d, Jonathan Kaplan; w, Ken Friedman; ph, Tak Fujimoto (Deluxe Color); ed, O. Nicholas Brown; m, Laurence Rosenthal; prod d, James William Newport; cos, William Ware Theiss

This insightful biography of drag-racing champ Shirley "Cha-Cha" Muldowney (the underrated Bonnie Bedelia) begins with the foreshadowing image of little Shirley driving her father's sedan and continues with her first race in 1966. Meeting with the usual sexism, she surprises all by breaking the track record on her qualifying run. Her career soars, but her marriage to mechanic Jack Muldowney (Leo Rossi) ends in divorce when he realizes that he can't handle his wife's success. Shirley then turns to banned driver Connie Kalitta (Beau Bridges, who also appears in the similarly themed GREASED LIGHTING, the story of black NASCAR driver Wendell Scott's triumph over racial prejudice) for support and love as she goes on to win the National Hot Rod Association World Championship three times.

The film is marred by a lackluster narrative, failing to inspire or move us in any way, but there's no denying Bedelia's beautifully nuanced performance. She's deserving of projects that are the equivalent of the forthright intelligence she brings to everything she does.

HEARTBREAK KID, THE

1972 104m c   ★★½
Comedy   PG
Palomar

Charles Grodin (Lenny Cantrow), Jeannie Berlin (Lila Kolodny), Cybill Shepherd (Kelly Corcoran), Eddie Albert (Mr. Corcoran), Audra Lindley (Mrs. Corcoran), William Prince (Colorado Man), Mitchell Jason (Cousin Ralph), Augusta Dabney (Colorado Woman), Art Metrano (Entertainer), Marilyn Putnam (Mrs. Kolodny)

p, Edgar J. Scherick; d, Elaine May; w, Neil Simon (based on a story by Bruce Jay Friedman); ph, Owen Roizman (DeLuxe Color); ed, John Carter; m, Garry Sherman; art d, Richard Sylbert; cos, Anthea Sylbert

Neil Simon's comedy, based on the Bruce Jay Friedman story, is a film you'll either find funny or disgusting. It's been broadly directed by May and concerns a Jewish bridegroom dumping whiny princess wife Berlin (May's real life daughter) to pursue WASP Shepherd. Although engagingly played, the film cannot find a voice or climax. What is this exercise in self-loathing all about? Are all Jewish women irritating? Are all WASPS cold featherbrains? HEARTBREAK doesn't end; it just runs out of steam.

HEARTBREAK RIDGE

1986 130m c   ★★★★
Drama/War   R/15
Malpaso/Jay Weston

Clint Eastwood (Tom Highway), Marsha Mason (Aggie), Everett McGill (Maj. Powers), Moses Gunn (Sgt. Webster), Eileen Heckart (Little Mary), Bo Svenson (Roy Jennings), Boyd Gaines (Lt. Ring), Mario Van Peebles (Stitch), Arlen Dean Snyder (Choozoo), Vincent Irizarry (Fragetti)

p, Clint Eastwood; d, Clint Eastwood; w, James Karabatsos; ph, Jack N. Green (Technicolor); ed, Joel Cox; m, Lennie Niehaus; prod d, Edward Carfagno; cos, Glenn Wright

Further exploring and expanding his iconic screen persona, producer-director-actor Clint Eastwood stars as Tom Highway, a gruff, foul-mouthed anachronism of the old Marine Corps who drinks too much and is constantly getting in trouble. Nearing retirement age, having alienated most of his superiors, Highway asks to end his career where it began and is transferred to perform gunnery sergeant duties in his old outfit. There, the small reconnaissance platoon he is to train proves to be a group of lazy malcontents who feel that they've been duped by the slick military advertising on television. Earning the admiration of these young hotshots by besting them physically and mentally at every turn, Highway proceeds to whip them into a self-respecting fighting unit that knows how to work as a team. This newfound purpose is tested when Highway and his men are sent off to a small Caribbean island none of them has ever heard of—Grenada—to rescue American medical students from a hostile Marxist government backed by Cuban troops.

HEARTBREAK RIDGE has drawn flak from those who think Eastwood somehow endorsed the Grenada invasion by refusing to overtly criticize it. But Eastwood isn't interested in the political meaning of the action; what concerns him is how it defines his characters, who only want to survive, not analyze, the conflict. The strengths and foibles of human beings are what this film—and all of Eastwood's directorial efforts—is all about, and his Tom Highway is one of the most vividly etched male characters seen onscreen in years. Eastwood makes no apologies for this man who knows only how to train men to kill, but he does understand him. Highway knows he's an anachronism and that he will soon have to leave the only role in which he feels confident; he's made the Marines his family, but now that family is rejecting him in favor of a much more glamorous image.

Eastwood believes that people can change, that contact with others can enlighten, and that attempting to understand one another is extremely valuable, but his characters are close-mouthed, wary, and afraid of appearing vulnerable, simply because they *are* vulnerable. He proves that it is still possible to infuse an "entertainment" with greater relevance. Eastwood fans who choose to simply watch and root for the "good guys" will not be disappointed by HEARTBREAK RIDGE, but neither will those looking for insights into the human condition.

HEARTLAND

1980 96m c   ★★★★
Western   PG/A
Wilderness Women

Rip Torn (Clyde), Conchata Ferrell (Elinore), Barry Primus (Jack), Lilia Skala (Grandma), Megan Folson (Jerrine), Amy Wright (Clara), Jerry Hardin (Cattle Buyer), Mary Boylan (Ma Gillis), Jeff Boschee, Robert Overholzer (Land Office Agents)

p, Michael Hausman, Beth Ferris; d, Richard Pearce; w, Beth Ferris (based on the books and papers of Elinore Randall Stewart); ph, Fred Murphy; ed, Bill Yahraus; m, Charles Gross; art d, Carl Copeland; cos, Hilary Rosenfeld

This touching, realistic frontier story stars Conchata Ferrell as Elinore, a widow determined to make a good life for her ten-year-old daughter (Megan Folson). Answering an ad, Elinore travels to Wyoming to be the housekeeper for taciturn skinflint Clyde (Rip Torn), a hard-as-nails Scottish farmer. Elinore works tirelessly for Clyde, who comes to take a liking to her and helps her obtain some land from an eccentric female rancher (Lilia Skala). The harsh winter all but does Elinore and her daughter in, but Clyde comes to the rescue, and eventually, he and Elinore marry. Elinore becomes pregnant and gives birth without medical help; however, the baby soon dies. But, undaunted, the little family continues to struggle to survive against nearly overwhelming hardships.

Ferrell is nothing less than magnificent as the hearty mother who bears all burdens without complaint and remains optimistic, and Torn is also superb as the farmer transformed from a bitter recluse into a loving mate. This was the feature debut of director Richard Pearce, a documentary filmmaker, and it is sterling. His visual approach is rich and his cameras painstakingly record the hard life of iron-willed pioneers attempting to tame the frontier in the early 20th century.

HEARTLAND was made for about $600,000, but has all the appearances of a major feature. The moving story is based on the real-life experiences of Elinore Stewart, who described her frontier life in a series of beautifully written letters.

HEARTS OF THE WEST

1975   102m   c   ★★★½
Western   PG
MGM

Jeff Bridges (Lewis Tater), Andy Griffith (Howard Pike), Donald Pleasence (A.J. Nietz), Blythe Danner (Miss Trout), Alan Arkin (Kessler), Richard B. Shull (Stout Crook), Herb Edelman (Polo), Alex Rocco (Earl, Assistant Director), Frank Cady (Pa Tater), Anthony James (Lean Crook)

p, Tony Bill; d, Howard Zieff; w, Rob Thompson; ph, Mario Tosi (Metrocolor); ed, Edward Warschilka; m, Ken Lauber; art d, Robert Luthardt

An homage to the B westerns of the 1930s and 1940s that stars Bridges as an aspiring young pulp writer in the fashion of Zane Grey. He heads for Hollywood, first making a stop in Nevada where he discovers that his correspondence school is a crooked operation. He accidentally takes the swindled cash and retreats to the desert; he's then "rescued" by a film crew led by Arkin and joins the bunch as they head back to the studio, falling in love with Arkin's secretary, Danner, and becoming pals with elder stuntman Griffith. The crooks pursue but are stopped when Griffith, convincingly dressed as an oater star, outwits them with a prop gun.

A charming film that takes the conventions and simplicity of early western serials and treats them in a careful and artistic manner. HEARTS is also a fine film about filmmaking, but experienced box-office failure. In keeping with tradition, the old black-and-white Metro lion logo opens the film by delivering his famous three roars.

HEAT AND DUST

1983   133m   c   ★★½
Drama   R/15
Merchant Ivory   (U.K.)

Julie Christie (Anne), Greta Scacchi (Olivia), Christopher Cazenove (Douglas Rivers), Julian Glover (Crawford), Susan Fleetwood (Mrs. Crawford), Shashi Kapoor (The Nawab), Madhur Jaffrey (The Begum, His Mother), Nickolas Grace (Harry), Zakir Hussain (Inder Lal), Barry Foster (Maj. Minnies)

p, Ismail Merchant; d, James Ivory; w, Ruth Prawer Jhabvala (based on her novel); ph, Walter Lassally; ed, Humphrey Dixon; m, Richard Robbins; prod d, Wilfred Shingleton; art d, Maurice Fowler, Ram Yadekar; cos, Barbara Lane

Here's HEAT AND DUST—less heat than dust. Julie Christie is cast as Anne, grandniece of Olivia (Greta Scacchi), an Englishwoman living in India 60 years earlier. Anne follows in Olivia's footsteps in an attempt to discover why her great-aunt was the subject of a scandal in the 1920s. The stories of the two women are intercut, inter-weaving the different time periods. Olivia traveled to India, married an Indian, and became pregnant by him. The local population objected, especially when she decided to abort the child—a Western custom. Anne's personal history parallels that of her aunt in many respects. What could have been an interesting exploration of the mystical and seductive atmosphere of India is never realized; the film concerns itself with propriety more than exotic culture. It's a waste of the striking talents of these two lovely actresses, particularly the highly selective Christie.

HEAT AND SUNLIGHT

1988   98m   bw   ★★★★
Drama
Snowball/New Front

Rob Nilsson (Mel Hurley), Consuelo Faust (Carmen), Don Bajema (Mitch), Ernie Fosselius (Bobby), Bill Bailey (Barney), Bill Ackridge, Lester Cohen, Bob Elross, Burns Ellison, Dan Leegant

p, Steve Burns, Hildy Burns; d, Rob Nilsson; w, Rob Nilsson; ph, Tomas Tucker; ed, Henk Van Eeghen; prod d, Hildy Burns, Steve Burns; chor, Consuelo Faust

Powerful, disturbing, excruciatingly honest and occasionally hilarious, HEAT AND SUNLIGHT is an extraordinary film from Rob Nilsson, one of America's most important independent filmmakers.

It focuses on the final 16 hours of a collapsing love affair that begins on the eve of the 40th birthday of Mel Hurley (Nilsson), a photojournalist who returns to San Francisco after an assignment, expecting to be met by his dancer-choreographer girlfriend, Carmen (Consuelo Faust). Her failure to appear confirms his suspicions that she is having an affair. Consumed by jealousy, Mel begins to withdraw into himself, periodically flashing back 17 years to his impassioned attempts to use his camera to bring attention to the starvation that devastated Biafra during the final days of its unsuccessful struggle for national liberation. With him now as then, his best friend (Don Bajema) tries to persuade Mel to confront Carmen with his fears rather than sink into anguished, self-destructive isolation.

From beginning to end, HEAT AND SUNLIGHT vibrates with stunningly real emotions, its characters so believable and its sense of poignant intimacy so all-encompassing that one hesitates to talk about performances. At the film's center, Nilsson delivers an astonishingly honest and passionate portrayal of a man driven by jealousy and insecurity to the breaking point, his pain so real that at times it becomes difficult to watch.

Means and ends are so closely related in HEAT AND SUNLIGHT that they must be evaluated in terms of Nilsson's "direct-action cinema" technique, in which most of the dialogue and many of the situations are improvised. Nilsson's freewheeling visual approach is as indebted to video technology as it is to the documentary style of his cinema verite predecessors. (HEAT AND SUNLIGHT was recorded on videotape and blown up to 35mm.) The result is an amazingly moving, wholly believable, visually dazzling study of passion, rage, jealousy, compassion and friendship that may not be for everyone but that will be unforgettable for many.

HEATHERS

1989   102m   c   ★★★½
Comedy/Fantasy   R/18
Cinemarque

Winona Ryder (Veronica Sawyer), Christian Slater (J.D.), Shannen Doherty (Heather Duke), Lisanne Falk (Heather McNamara), Kim Walker (Heather Chandler), Penelope Milford (Pauline Fleming), Glenn Shadix (Fr. Ripper), Lance Fenton (Kurt Kelly), Patrick Laborteaux (Ram), Jeremy Applegate (Peter Dawson)

p, Denise Di Novi; d, Michael Lehmann; w, Daniel Waters; ph, Francis Kenny (Deluxe Color); ed, Norman Hollyn; m, David Newman; prod d, Jon Hutman; art d, Kara Lindstrom; cos, Rudy Dillon

The near-surreal world of high-school popularity is imaginatively probed in this black comedy revolving around teenage suicide. With scenes and dialogue sure to offend many, HEATHERS is, nevertheless, a film of startling originality and verve.

The eponymous Heathers (Shannen Doherty, Lisanne Falk, Kim Walker), the most exclusive clique at Westerburg High, routinely drop insufficiently cool friends and humiliate poor Martha "Dumptruck" Dunnstock (Carrie Lynn). Veronica (Winona Ryder), a relatively recent addition to their clique, demonstrates her independence by taking up with J.D. (Christian Slater), a motorcycle-riding misfit, becoming his mostly unwilling accomplice as he murders three of the school's most popular, albeit piggish, students, leaving behind heartrending suicide notes. But what begins as a lark for Veronica becomes a nightmare as she realizes that her mischievous fantasies are diabolical realities for the increasingly psychotic J.D.

HEATHERS might have been a moronic teen gross-out film were it not for the immediacy and careful observation of the surprisingly rich script by Daniel Walters, Michael Lehmann's clever direction, and the extraordinary performances of Ryder and, to a lesser extent, Slater (who does an appropriately creepy, raspy-voiced Jack Nicholson imitation). Dark, cynical, but deliciously funny, HEATHERS is a fascinating look not just at high school but at the way we look at high school.

HEAVEN CAN WAIT

1943 112m c   ★★★½
Comedy   /A
FOX

Gene Tierney (Martha), Don Ameche (Henry Van Cleve), Charles Coburn (Hugo Van Cleve), Marjorie Main (Mrs. Strabel), Laird Cregar (His Excellency), Spring Byington (Bertha Van Cleve), Allyn Joslyn (Albert Van Cleve), Eugene Pallette (Mr. Strabel), Signe Hasso (Mademoiselle), Louis Calhern (Randolph Van Cleve)

p, Ernst Lubitsch; d, Ernst Lubitsch; w, Samson Raphaelson (based on the play Birthdays by Ladislaus Bus-Fekete); ph, Edward Cronjager (Technicolor); ed, Dorothy Spencer; m, Alfred Newman; art d, James Basevi, Leland Fuller; cos, Rene Hubert

Astute salute to a charming rake, deceptive satire disguised as a bubble. This movie has Ameche as an innocent Casanova, shown from infancy to his death at age 70. The film opens with a deceased Ameche standing before the Devil, Cregar, requesting his passport to Hell. Cregar studies his newest applicant and then reviews Ameche's carefree and often careless life. Based on the Hungarian play Birthdays by Ladislaus Bus-Fekete, with additional bromides from Samson Raphaelson. But Ameche is short on charm and too hapless for the role; he can't get any real chemistry cooking with Tierney. Still, it's compensated by a supporting cast of pros, and Lubitsch's deft direction. This was Lubitsch's first color film; the Basevi-Fuller Hell is a fabulous sight to see.

HEAVEN CAN WAIT

1978 101m c   ★★½
Comedy/Fantasy   PG/A
Paramount

Warren Beatty (Joe Pendleton), Julie Christie (Betty Logan), James Mason (Mr. Jordan), Dyan Cannon (Julia Farnsworth), Charles Grodin (Tony Abbott), Jack Warden (Max Corkle), Buck Henry (The Escort), Vincent Gardenia (Lt. Krim), Joseph Maher (Sisk), Hamilton Camp (Bentley)

p, Warren Beatty; d, Warren Beatty, Buck Henry; w, Warren Beatty, Elaine May (based on the play by Harry Segall); ph, William A. Fraker (Panavision, Movielab Color); ed, Robert C. Jones, Don Zimmerman; m, Dave Grusin; prod d, Paul Sylbert; art d, Edwin O'Donovan; fx, Robert MacDonald; cos, Theadora Van Runkle, Richard Bruno

Beatty's ballgame, an unecessary remake of HERE COMES MR. JORDAN—he produced, co-directed, co-wrote (with Elaine May) and starred as Joe Pendleton, a Los Angeles Rams quarterback who is prematurely ushered to heaven by a bumbling celestial messenger (co-director Henry) after an auto accident. An archangel, Mr. Jordan (Mason), tries to redress this error by restoring Joe to life in the body of a wealthy industrialist moments after he's murdered by his adulterous wife (Cannon) and the industrialist's nitwit secretary (Grodin). Determined to play in the Super Bowl, Beatty buys the Rams and hires his old coach (Warden) to help him train, convincing Warden that Beatty has been reincarnated. Beatty also meets and falls in love with Christie, an English environmental activist, but just when it looks as though everything is going to work out, Cannon and Grodin try again.

The title comes from the Harry Segall play, upon which the 1941 JORDAN was based. There are a few laughs from Grodin and Cannon, but Beatty and Christie are like 400-pound gorillas chasing a milkweed seed. The more Beatty concentrates, the more glazed and distracted he looks. The film won an Oscar for Art Direction—presumably for Beatty's expensive bathrobes, Cannon's mane and the clipped hedges and boxwoods of a California estate.

HEAVEN'S GATE

1980 205m c   ★
Western   R/18
UA

Kris Kristofferson (Marshal James Averill), Christopher Walken (Nathan D. Champion), John Hurt (Billy Irvine), Isabelle Huppert (Ella Watson), Sam Waterston (Frank Canton), Jeff Bridges (John H. Bridges), Joseph Cotten ("The Reverend Doctor"), Roseanne Vela (Beautiful Girl), Ronnie Hawkins (Wolcott), Geoffrey Lewis (Trapper)

p, Joann Carelli; d, Michael Cimino; w, Michael Cimino; ph, Vilmos Zsigmond (Technicolor); ed, Tom Rolf, William Reynolds, Lisa Fruchtman, Jerry Greenberg; m, David Mansfield; art d, Tambi Larsen, Spencer Deverill, Maurice Fowler; chor, Eleanor Fazan; cos, J. Allen Highfill

This beautiful but notoriously disappointing film is one of the most overblown epic Westerns of any decade. The story allegedly relates the events of the bloody 1892 Johnson County wars in Wyoming, pitting cattlemen against immigrant settlers. James Averill (Kris Kristofferson) becomes marshal and must hold the county's combatants in check. Nathan D. Champion (Christopher Walken) is a gunfighter hired by the ranchers. Both men share the sexual favors of prostitute Ella "Cattle Kate" Watson (Isabelle Huppert). Through various slice-of-life episodes without a unifying thread, writer-director Michael Cimino tries to depict the lifestyles of the ranchers and the settlers, and the differences that lead to all-out war between the factions.

Kristofferson is wooden, Walken far too remote, and no one else in the cast stands out. Cimino's financial excesses included having trains completely rebuilt, providing infinitely detailed costumes for extras, and planting miles of sod on a battle field that would be blown up. The film's final cost was estimated to be $35 million, though some reports went as high as $50 million. Cimino's sins might have been forgiven in Hollywood had the film made a positive statement; but it derides the American Dream as a history of moral compromise—this in lieu of a story—and the American press took off after it in droves; the public's reaction to the truncated version released was to reject it instantly. The director's cut, available on cassette, is regarded as a masterpiece in Europe where Cimino's star shines brighter.

HEAVY METAL

1981 91m c   ★★
Animated/Science Fiction   R/AA
Columbia   (Canada)

VOICES OF: Roger Bumpass, Jackie Burroughs, John Candy, Joe Flaherty, Don Francks, Martin Lavut, Eugene Levy, Marilyn Lightstone, Alice Playten, Harold Ramis

p, Ivan Reitman; d, Gerald Potterton; w, Dan Goldberg, Len Blum (based on work and stories by Richard Corben, Angus McKie, Dan O'Bannon, Thomas Warkentin, and Berni Wrightson); ph, (Metrocolor); ed, Janice Brown; m, Elmer Bernstein; prod d, Michael Gross; anim, Thomas Warkentin, Angus McKie, Dab O'Bannon, Richard Corben, Juan Gimenez, Lee Mishkin

Although the concept for this animated film is derived from the adult fantasy magazine of the same name, HEAVY METAL is clearly targeted for a teen audience. Divided into a number of episodes, the film is held together by the Lock-Nar, a sinister, glowing jewel that catapults characters into weird, threatening confrontations. In one of the better episodes, a New York City cab driver becomes involved with a sexy but greedy woman who is being chased by criminals. In another, a young bookworm (voiced by John Candy) is transformed into a brawny, heroic stud and saves a maiden from being sacrificed to the jewel. Otherwise, it's a mixed bag, but successful in a mindless, adolescent way. The spirited, energetic music is contributed by a variety of rock performers, including Blue Oyster Cult, Black Sabbath and Nazareth.

HEIMAT

1985 924m c/bw   ★★★½
Drama   /15
Reitz/WDR/SFB   (West Germany)

Marita Breuer (Maria), Willi Burger, Gertrud Bredel, Rudiger Weigang, Karin Rasenack, Dieter Schaad, Michael Lesch, Peter Harting, Jorg Richter, Johannes Lobewein

p, Edgar Reitz, Joachim von Mengershausen, Hans Kwiet; d, Edgar Reitz; w, Edgar Reitz, Peter Steinbach; ph, Gernot Roll; ed, Heidi Handorf; m, Nikos Mamangakis; art d, Franz Bauer

Though HEIMAT runs an imposing 15-and-a-half hours, this epic work, chronicling life in a German village from 1919 to 1982, rarely fails to capture the viewer within its immense visionary scope. The events of the period—Germany's post-WWI depression, the rise of Nazism, WWII, and postwar recovery—are seen not through the eyes of Germany's leaders, politicians, and artists, but through the eyes of the common people in the fictional village of Schabbach. At the center of the events is Breuer, who gives a remarkable performance. Using makeup, costumes and her gifted acting talents, Breuer gives HEIMAT a heartfelt anchor, playing her character from childhood to old age.

Director Edgar Reitz's film, which is usually shown in four successive screenings, is both in color and black and white. The black-and-white sequences go from the 1920s to the early 1950s,

with color encompassing the rest of the film, though at times Reitz intercuts the two processes to give emphasis within a scene. Reitz's original plan was to rediscover his own background, so he began writing down the stories of his family and the people from his rural village. He had planned to turn this story into an epic novel, but at the urging of television producer Joachim von Mengershausen, Reitz decided to put this project before the cameras. After writing a 2,000-page script with Peter Steinbach, Reitz shot a documentary dealing with a similar subject.

Production on HEIMAT finally began in 1981, but Reitz was forced to put everything on hold after four months because funding ran out. Though he started again two months later, the shooting was halted for financial reasons a second time. Reitz finally completed the lensing in late 1982, then took 18 months to edit the enormous amount of footage he had created. All told, HEIMAT took five years and four months to create from conception to final cut.

HEIRESS, THE

1949 115m bw   ★★★★★
Drama   /U
Paramount

Olivia de Havilland (Catherine Sloper), Montgomery Clift (Morris Townsend), Ralph Richardson (Dr. Austin Sloper), Miriam Hopkins (Lavinia Penniman), Vanessa Brown (Maria), Mona Freeman (Marian Almond), Ray Collins (Jefferson Almond), Betty Linley (Mrs. Montgomery), Selena Royle (Elizabeth Almond), Paul Lees (Arthur Townsend)

p, William Wyler; d, William Wyler; w, Ruth Goetz, Augustus Goetz (based on their play and the novel Washington Square by Henry James); ph, Leo Tover; ed, William Hornbeck; m, Aaron Copland; art d, John Meehan, Harry Horner; fx, Gordon Jennings; cos, Edith Head, Gile Steele

This powerful and compelling drama, based on Henry James's 1881 novel Washington Square and the successful Broadway play by Ruth and Augustus Goetz, owes its triumph to the deft hand of director William Wyler and a remarkable lead performance by Olivia de Havilland.

Set circa 1850, the film casts de Havilland as the plain-looking daughter of wealthy, widowed doctor Richardson, with whom she lives at their home at 16 Washington Square. Life is uneventful. Richardson is a tyrant at home, dictating his daughter's every move and cruelly telling her that she bears no resemblance to his dear departed wife, who was beautiful and charming. Suitors shun de Havilland—who is awkward in her movements, conversation, and manners—until she receives some unexpected attention from Clift at a ball. He flatters her and asks to call on her, news that is derisively greeted by Richardson, who tells de Havilland that Clift must be a fortune hunter, and will break her heart.

This was one of de Havilland's greatest roles; Wyler finally breaks her of her habit of sweet smiles (she'd later revert) and her transformation from docile emotional victim to rational, resolved adult is a masterpiece of acting. Ralph Richardson is equally good, injecting a majestic presence into his portrait of a hateful man who is really so fearful for his daughter's future that he will incur her permanent loathing to protect that future. Miriam Hopkins is fine, too, as the one eternally bright spot in de Havilland's life, but Clift is surprisingly weak.

Wyler worked hard to produce this masterpiece. He had requested Gregg Toland (with whom he had collaborated memorably on films like WUTHERING HEIGHTS, THE BEST YEARS OF OUR LIVES and THE LITTLE FOXES) for his cinematographer, and instead got Leo Tover. When Wyler asked for a setup calling for deep focus, Tover took half a day to make preparations, where Toland would have achieved the setup in an hour. The director did score a coup, however, when he secured Aaron Copland's services as the film's composer. Copland had written memorable music for such films as OF MICE AND MEN, OUR TOWN and NORTH STAR but had gained a "Red" taint as a result of his involvement in the last and, in the suspicious climate of 1949, Wyler had to argue heavily with Paramount executives to retain Copland who came through with a haunting, telling score.

HELLO, DOLLY!

1969 129m c   ★★★
Musical/Comedy   G/U
Chenault

Barbra Streisand (Dolly Levi), Walter Matthau (Horace Vandergelder), Michael Crawford (Cornelius Hackl), Louis Armstrong (Orchestra Leader), Marianne McAndrew (Irene Molloy), E.J. Peaker (Minnie Fay), Danny Lockin (Barnaby Tucker), Joyce Ames (Ermengarde), Tommy Tune (Ambrose Kemper), Judy Knaiz (Gussie Granger)

p, Ernest Lehman; d, Gene Kelly; w, Ernest Lehman (based on the play The Matchmaker by Thornton Wilder); ph, Harry Stradling (Todd-AO, DeLuxe Color); ed, William Reynolds; m, Jerry Herman, Lennie Hayton, Lionel Newman; prod d, John De Cuir; art d, Jack Martin Smith, Herman A. Blumenthal; fx, L.B. Abbott, Art Cruickshank, Emil Kosa, Jr.; chor, Michael Kidd; cos, Irene Sharaff

Here's the film that, joined by DOCTOR DOOLITTLE and STAR!, sounded the death knell for the film musical, a stroke it still hasn't recovered from. It's also the film where Streisand allegedly slapped Matthau, and he slapped her back. But she had no problem bullying director Kelly: it's an exercise in star turns, surrounded by elephantine blandness. The supporting cast look, and act, like refugees from Disney or Oral Roberts University, handpicked not to ruffle the star. Whatever terrific future lay ahead for Tune and Crawford, you've no inkling of it from all the too cute mugging here. Not only is Streisand far too young (and it makes one weep to think of all the marvelous ladies who should have been considered), but her Dolly Levi arouses no affection. Without the dose of healthy sentiment the character arouses to balance her machinations, she's just a nasty bitch on the make. Furthermore, this exposes how pallid Thornton Wilder's The Matchmaker (the play on which the musical is based) really is. There are two good songs in Jerry Herman's score: "Before the Parade Passes By" and the title tune, here an exercise in star wrestling between Streisand and the irrepressible Louis Armstrong, who connect not one whit.

HELLRAISER

1987 90m c   ★★½
Horror   R/18
Cinemarque/Film Futures/New World   (U.K.)

Andrew Robinson (Larry Cotton), Clare Higgins (Julia Cotton), Ashley Laurence (Kirsty Swanson), Sean Chapman (Frank Cotton), Oliver Smith (Frank the Monster), Robert Hines (Steve), Leon Davis (2nd Victim), Mike Cassidy (3rd Victim), Frank Baker (Derelict), Kenneth Nelson (Bill)

p, Christopher Figg; d, Clive Barker; w, Clive Barker (based on his novella "The Hellbound Heart"); ph, Robin Vidgeon (Technicolor); ed, Richard Marden; m, Christopher Young; prod d, Mike Buchanan; art d, Jocelyn James; fx, Bob Keen; cos, Joanna Johnston

Somewhat disappointing directorial debut of the man called the "future of horror fiction" by Stephen King, Clive Barker, based on his own novella The Hell-Bound Heart.

Frank (Sean Chapman), a sexual adventurer in search of new carnal pleasures, purchases a mysterious Chinese puzzle box while visiting an unnamed Third World country. Back home in England, he opens the box only to discover that he has unlocked the door to hell. Frank is pulled into another dimension, whose inhabitants, known as Cenobites, push him over the fine line between pleasure and pain by ripping him apart with tiny fish hooks. Years later, Frank's brother, Larry (Andrew Robinson), moves his family into the house—to which, through some blood spilled on the attic floor, Frank returns in near-skeletal form. With the help of sister-in-law Julia (Clare Higgins)—with whom he once had an affair—Frank begins sucking the life out of bodies in order to regenerate to his old form. Meanwhile, Larry's daughter from a previous marriage, Kirsty (Ashley Laurence), begins to suspect her hated stepmother of having an affair, and to her horror becomes involved with Frank, the puzzle box and the Cenobites.

Undoubtedly head and shoulders above average horror fare thematically, HELLRAISER is, however, extremely graphic, badly paced, and, with few exceptions, poorly acted. As a director, Barker does possess a striking visual sensibility; the film literally drips with horrific ambience. However, while the author's cinematic sense is a pleasant surprise, his narrative is shockingly haphazard, and the film lurches from one set piece to the next with little dramatic rhythm. While Barker does a respectable job of developing the characters of Julia and Frank and the lustful ties that bind them, the writer-director is clearly less interested in victims Larry and Kirsty. The film never gets a handle on these characters and never provides enough characterization so that the viewer cares about their fate.

HELL'S ANGELS

1930 135m c/bw   ★★★½
War
Caddo

Ben Lyon (Monte Rutledge), James Hall (Roy Rutledge), Jean Harlow (Helen), John Darrow (Karl Arnstedt), Lucien Prival (Baron von Kranz), Frank Clark (Lt. von Bruen), Roy Wilson (Baldy), Douglas Gilmore (Capt. Redfield), Jane Winton (Baroness von Kranz), Evelyn Hall (Lady Randolph)

p, Howard Hughes; d, Howard Hughes, James Whale, Marshall Neilan, Luther Reed; w, Harry Behn, Howard Estabrook, Joseph Moncure March (based on a story by Marshall Neilan, Joseph Moncure March); ph, Tony Gaudio, Paul Perry, E. Burton Steene, Elmer Dyer, Harry Zeck, Dewey Wrigley (color scenes in Technicolor); ed, Douglas Biggs, Perry Hollingsworth, Frank Lawrence; m, Hugo Riesenfeld; art d, Julian Boone Fleming, Carroll Clark

And hell's memorable belle, here and there among the aerial sequences. The film looks dated and the story seems to have been written in crayon by Hughes; it's a testimony to his two great loves—wings and breasts, about good brother and bad brother, and the blonde who comes between them. Beside Hughes, it was directed by Marshall Neilan, Luther Reed, and sometimes James Whale (credited as dialogue director, but he also wrote much of the script). There is a bang-up aerial dogfight and a solid zeppelin sequence; many believe these moments have never been surpassed. Hughes worked them out on blackboards and with model planes before he shot. When the zeppelin moves through the clouds and we see London below, we feel inside the camera.

The plot was corn in 1930—it feels very much like a silent picture—and eighteen year-old Harlow hasn't the foggiest notion what she's supposed to do. Her take on the British Helen is undeniably piggy, but clad in a velvet evening gown with beaded straps, she's like no one the camera had ever photographed when she turns her bare back to us. And audiences stopped laughing when she inquired, "Would you be shocked if I put on something more comfortable?"

Launched in 1927 as the first major effort of Hughes's Caddo Productions, the ANGELS was so long in the making that sound came into being, and much of the film, which had been shot as a silent, had to be redone. Both Lyon and Hall had good "sound" voices, but the female lead, Greta Nissen, had a pronounced Norwegian accent, and, though Hughes had paid her handsomely, he scrapped her performance completely and began searching for a new actress who could handle the role's vocal chores. Among the candidates was Harlow, then an 18-year-old, blue-eyed platinum blonde with a voluptuous shape. Although Hughes was unimpressed with her screen test, Harlow's agent, Arthur Landau, talked the millionaire playboy into letting his client play the part. Her debut caused Hughes endless arguments with the censors. After the film, Hughes inexplicably ignored the new star he had created, though he had the presence of mind to put her under permanent contract. Nevertheless, he sold her contract for a mere $60,000 to MGM, for whom she would make millions as the reigning sex queen of the cinema until her death in 1937.

The film's staggering $3.8 million budget made HELL'S ANGELS the cinema's most expensive film to date, and Hughes, determined to get his money back, employed the kind of hoopla for which he later became notorious, arranging for a squadron of planes to buzz Grauman's Chinese Theater at the film's premiere while parachutists descended on Hollywood Boulevard. Trying to orchestrate a similarly flashy stunt in New York, Hughes offered the owners of the dirigible *Graf Zeppelin* $100,000 to sail over Broadway and 42nd Street, where *two* theaters were premiering the film, but the owners refused. Despite his best efforts, Hughes took a bath on the film, losing more than $1.5 million, although, at first, he claimed to have made $2 million. It is said that he later admitted that the film would have been better and cost less had he allowed someone else to direct it.

HELL'S HEROES
1930 65m bw   ★★★★
Western
Universal

Charles Bickford (*Bob Sangster*), Raymond Hatton (*Barbwire Gibbons*), Fred Kohler (*Wild Bill Kearney*), Fritzi Ridgeway (*Mother*), Maria Alba (*Carmelita*), Jose De La Cruz (*Jose*), Buck Connors (*Parson Jones*), Walter James (*Sheriff*)

p, Carl Laemmle; d, William Wyler; w, Tom Reed (based on Peter B. Kyne's novel *The Three Godfathers*); ph, George Robinson; ed, Harry Marker

Adapted from Peter B. Kyne's novel *The Three Godfathers*, which had been done twice in the silent era (in 1916 and again in 1920 by John Ford as MARKED MEN), HELL'S HEROES was the first sound version of the story—it would be done again by Ford with John Wayne.

The story revolves around three outlaws—Charles Bickford, Raymond Hatton, and Fred Kohler—who find a woman in a wagon about to give birth. They promise the dying mother that they will take her baby back to its father in New Jerusalem, the town whose bank they have just robbed. On the way back, one

of the outlaws dies from wounds he received during the robbery; another perishes from thirst; and the last drinks from a poisoned spring to gain enough strength to get the baby to the town's church during Christmas services.

Overshadowed by Ford's sound version, HELL'S HEROES is an excellent western drama that deserves more attention. Shot on location in the Mojave Desert and the Panamint Valley near Death Valley, William Wyler's version is stark and realistic—the director's first all-sound film and Universal's first on-location talkie.

HELLZAPOPPIN'
1941 84m bw   ★★★
Comedy   /U
Universal

Ole Olsen (*Ole*), Chic Johnson (*Chic*), Robert Paige (*Jeff Hunter*), Jane Frazee (*Kitty Rand*), Lewis Howard (*Woody Tyler*), Martha Raye (*Betty Johnson*), Clarence Kolb (*Mr. Rand*), Nella Walker (*Mrs. Rand*), Mischa Auer (*Pepi*), Richard Lane (*Director*)

p, Jules Levy; d, H.C. Potter; w, Nat Perrin, Warren Wilson (based on the play by Nat Perrin); ph, Elwood Bredell; ed, Milton Carruth; fx, John P. Fulton; chor, Nick Castle, Eddie Prinz; cos, Vera West

Crazy as hell, at 100 miles an hour, loaded with sight gags that sometimes work and sometimes fall as flat as a burned pancake; but the feeling is surprisingly contemporary. The story begins in Purgatory, with Olsen and Johnson jumping in and out of a story that's barely there, basically a little romance tale of poor boy meets rich girl and wins her heart after putting on the traditional show. O. and J. constantly argue with the film's director and cameraman on camera about the restraints put upon them while mindless mayhem ensues—someone constantly yelling "Jones!" for no good reason; Auer, a rich count, chasing Martha Raye about madly, and vice versa. At one point a film director, Lane, tells the madcaps Olson and Johnson: "This is Hollywood; we change everything here. We've *got* to!" If it's not as immortal as the Marx Brothers' best work, it's definitely admirable in its cutting edge risk.

HELP!
1965 92m c   ★★★½
Musical/Comedy   G/U
Walter Shenson/Subafilms (U.K.)

John Lennon (*John*), Paul McCartney (*Paul*), Ringo Starr (*Ringo*), George Harrison (*George*), Leo McKern (*Clang*), Eleanor Bron (*Ahme*), Victor Spinetti (*Foot*), Roy Kinnear (*Algernon*), John Bluthal (*Bhuta*), Patrick Cargill (*Superintendent*)

p, Walter Shenson; d, Richard Lester; w, Marc Behm, Charles Wood (based on an original story by Behm); ph, David Watkin (Eastmancolor); ed, John Victor Smith; m, Ken Thorne; art d, Ray Simm; fx, Cliff Richardson, Roy Whybrow; cos, Julie Harris, Dinah Greet, Arthur Newman

Shot on location in the Bahamas, Austria, and on Salisbury Plain, HELP!, the second Beatles film, is nonsensical fun.

Filled as it is with wonderful music and enlivened by the Fab Four's engaging screen presence, the story revolves around the crazed efforts of a pair of Eastern religious zealots, Clang (Leo McKern) and Ahme (the ravishing, underrated Eleanor Bron), to get hold of a sacred ring that has been given to Ringo by a fan and which he can't get off his finger. Foot (Victor Spinetti), the scientist Ringo approaches for help, comes to believe that the ring will allow him to control the world, and he and his assistant (Roy Kinnear) join the scramble to wrest the ring from Ringo.

Antics aplenty ensue as Ringo and the other Beatles lead their pursuers on a madcap, globe-trotting chase.

Silly at its worst and brilliant at its best, HELP! picks up where the joyous insouciance of A HARD DAY'S NIGHT—director Richard Lester's first collaboration with the Fab Four—left off. McKern, Bron, Kinnear and Spinetti display fine comedic timing, and the Beatles make a reasonable stab at being a modern-day version of the Marx Brothers.

HENRY AND JUNE

1990   136m   c   ★★★½
Drama   NC-17/18
Walrus & Associates

Fred Ward (*Henry Miller*), Uma Thurman (*June Miller*), Maria de Medeiros (*Anais Nin*), Richard E. Grant (*Hugo*), Kevin Spacey (*Osborn*), Jean-Philippe Ecoffey (*Eduardo*), Bruce Myers (*Jack*), Jean-Louis Bunuel (*Editor-Publisher*), Feodor Atkine (*Spanish Dance Instructor*), Sylvie Huguel (*Emilia*)

p, Peter Kaufman; d, Philip Kaufman; w, Philip Kaufman, Rose Kaufman (based on the diaries of Anais Nin); ph, Philippe Rousselot (Deluxe Color); ed, Vivien Hillgrove, William S. Scharf, Dede Allen; prod d, Guy-Claude Francois; art d, Georges Glon; chor, Nathalie Erlbaum; cos, Yvonne Sassinot de Nesle

Philip Kaufman's latest excursion into literary erotica, HENRY AND JUNE is noteworthy for being the first film to be released with the MPAA's NC-17 rating, created in 1990 to replace the dreaded X rating. Henry Miller would undoubtedly have been delighted with the ensuing furor; though published in 1934, Miller's first novel, *Tropic of Cancer*, could not be legally distributed in the US or in most other English-speaking countries until 1961. HENRY AND JUNE is concerned with the writing of that book, which Miller worked on while living in Paris in 1931-32.

At the beginning of the film, Henry (Fred Ward) has been sent to France by his wife, June (Uma Thurman), a former taxi dancer who has been supporting his career on her earnings as another man's mistress. The purpose of the trip is twofold: to get Henry away from distractions in New York so he can finish the novel, and to allow June, a bisexual, more freedom to frolic with a new girlfriend. The film actually opens not with Henry or June, but with Miller's lover, lifelong friend, and literary advocate Anais Nin (Maria de Medeiros), upon whose legendary diaries the screenplay (by Kaufman and his wife, Rose) is based. An aspiring literary critic working on her own first book, Anais is given to erotic flights of fancy. When a college professor stiffly kisses and fondles her during a meeting, she transforms the light indiscretion into a full-blown seduction in her diary, in which she scribbles each night before retiring with her bland but likable middle-class husband, Hugo (Richard E. Grant).

Anais generally chafes at her mundane existence and yearns for a more bohemian social life and, especially, for a big, swarthy lover. Enter big and swarthy Henry, brought to Anais's house by her husband, who is friends with Henry's eccentric roommate (Kevin Spacey). Initially, Anais and Henry are tentative friends, providing each other with support for their respective writing projects. And though Anais has polite erotic palpitations when she is around the earthy but cultured Henry, it is June, briefly in Paris to check up on Henry, who brings Anais's passions to a furious boil.

The couplings in HENRY AND JUNE are as explicit as any to be found in mainstream American cinema, however, much of the sex here is mild when compared to films by Almodovar, Bertolucci, Imamura, Oshima, and many others, proving only

that while few national cinemas can match Hollywood's painfully realistic depictions of graphic violence, when it comes to sex, the American film industry is still stuck somewhere back in the Victorian era. Even Kaufman adopts an air of professorial sobriety to give the eroticism an aura of legitimacy. But his approach is still far less stultifying than it was in THE INCREDIBLE LIGHTNESS OF BEING, abetted by Ward's and, especially, Thurman's smashing performances.

HENRY: PORTRAIT OF A SERIAL KILLER

1989   83m   c   ★★★★
Crime/Horror   /18
Maljack

Michael Rooker (*Henry*), Tom Towles (*Otis*), Tracy Arnold

p, Lisa Dedmond, Steven A. Jones; d, John McNaughton; w, Richard Fire, John McNaughton; ph, Charlie Lieberman; ed, Elena Maganini

HENRY: PORTRAIT OF A SERIAL KILLER surely ranks as one of the most frightening and disturbing films ever made. An angry and raw independent feature, HENRY begins with a creepy montage of shots of dead bodies. The corpses are the victims of Henry (Michael Rooker), a lowlife drifter who looks for victims while driving around in his green Impala. Rooker murders with knives, guns, rope, even his hands—he has no preferred method or pattern.

Rooker lives with Towles, a degenerate he met while in prison (for killing his mother) who now works in a gas station and sells drugs on the side. When Towles's sister (Arnold) comes to Chicago, she stays with Towles and Rooker while she looks for a job; meanwhile, Rooker, who works as a bug sprayer, and Towle continue to murder people at random, videotaping every detail, until they start to get on each other's nerves. When Rooker can no longer stand Towles's stupidity and sloppiness, the two argue; meanwhile, Arnold quits her job in a hair salon and asks Rooker to move away with her.

A stunning feature debut from director John McNaughton, HENRY tells its horrible story with chilling straightforwardness. Presenting his sick characters nonjudgmentally and without shrinking from gory details, McNaughton creates a world in which there is no good to counterbalance evil, where incest and rape are permitted and murder is an acceptable way to relieve tension. Providing no "good" characters to identify with—not even a cop to offer us hope—and ending on a bitter, ugly note, HENRY leaves viewers emotionally drained and deeply, deeply disturbed. McNaughton succeeds in showing just how vulnerable anyone can be to someone like Henry, a frightening reality few will want to contemplate.

No film in recent memory has tapped into primal, visceral fear as HENRY does, with its vision of a depraved world that seems at once too horrible to exist and too realistic to be denied. Hard to watch (though at times it's bizarrely and blackly funny) and definitely not for the squeamish, HENRY will prove unforgettable for the brave souls who do see it. A major achievement in independent filmmaking, HENRY: PORTRAIT OF A SERIAL KILLER is a horror masterpiece.

HENRY V

1944   127m   c   ★★★★★
Drama/War   /U
Two Cities   (U.K.)

Laurence Olivier (*King Henry V*), Robert Newton (*Ancient Pistol*), Leslie Banks (*Chorus*), Renee Asherson (*Princess Katherine*),

Esmond Knight (*Fluellen*), Leo Genn (*Constable of France*), Felix Aylmer (*Archbishop of Canterbury*), Ralph Truman (*Mountjoy*), Harcourt Williams (*King Charles VI of France*), Ivy St. Helier (*Alice. Lady in Waiting*)

p, Laurence Olivier, Filippo Del Giudice; d, Laurence Olivier, Reginald Beck; w, Alan Dent, Laurence Olivier (based on the play by William Shakespeare); ph, Robert Krasker; ed, Reginald Beck; m, William Walton; art d, Paul Sheriff; cos, Roger Furse

Made at the height of the German blitz, this dazzling British adaptation of Shakespeare's classic tale of victory in the face of overwhelming odds brought new hope and resolve to embattled Britons who saw it in 1944. Filippo del Giudice, an Italian lawyer who had fled Mussolini's rule, persuaded Laurence Olivier to undertake the project, and when William Wyler, Carol Reed, and Terence Young were unable to helm the film, Olivier not only took on the title role but the director's mantle, performing both roles magnificently.

Innovatively structured, the film begins with a 17th-century staging of Shakespeare's play at the Globe Theatre; then, gradually, the proscenium disappears as the film moves toward a more realistic presentation of the story, with stylized sets giving way to the real-life scenery of the impressive re-creation of the Battle of Agincourt. Finally, Olivier brings the film full circle, back to the stage of the Globe.

Set in 1415, HENRY V chronicles the invasion of France undertaken by the 28-year-old English king in an attempt to consolidate his power at home. After a number of costly victories drastically deplete Henry's army, it is besieged by French forces that outnumber it nearly five to one. Under the king's courageous leadership, however, the English triumph at Agincourt.

Olivier, who was mustered out of the navy to make the film, collaborated with movie critic Alan Dent on the adaptation, and editor Reginald Beck helped with direction chores when Olivier the star was in front of the cameras. Though given a large budget considering the wartime circumstances, the production was continually forced to cut corners, and its wonderfully realized costumes and sets are testaments to the ingenuity of the film's designers.

HENRY V
1989   138m   c   ★★★★
Drama/Historical   PG
BBC/Curzon/Renaissance   (U.K.)

Kenneth Branagh (*King Henry V*), Derek Jacobi (*Chorus*), Simon Shepherd (*Duke of Gloucester*), James Larkin (*Bedford*), Brian Blessed (*Duke of Exeter*), James Simmons (*York*), Paul Gregory (*Earl of Westmoreland*), Charles Kay (*Archbishop of Canterbury*), Alec McCowen (*Bishop of Ely*), Fabian Cartwright (*Cambridge*)

p, Bruce Sharman; d, Kenneth Branagh; w, Kenneth Branagh; ph, Kenneth MacMillan (Eastmancolor); ed, Michael Bradsell; m, Pat Doyle; prod d, Tim Harvey; art d, Norman Dorme; cos, Phyllis Dalton

Straightforward, energetic, updated Bard; a Cagneyesque interloper has redefined the essence of this historical play and made it germane to 20th-century sensibilities. However, 28-year-old star-director-adapter Kenneth Branagh's spellbinding version of Shakespeare's *Henry* isn't superior to Olivier's 1944 version—it's different, and complimentary to it.

Filmed mostly in medium and close-up shots, Branagh's more intimate version discards the pageantry of Olivier's grand spectacle; focusing on carnage and casualties, Branagh's film is strongly antiwar whereas Olivier's vision, filmed as a paean to

England's greatness, was a morale builder for his countrymen embroiled in a world war. Branagh's HENRY V is also a visceral coming-of-age film, following a young playboy prince as he is forced to grow up quickly and assume the responsibilities of leadership. Throughout the film, Branagh uses flashbacks, excerpted from the earlier *Henry IV* plays to clarify events, and though he has pruned the 400-year-old play, all of its most memorable moments are in place and brilliantly conveyed: from the seige of Harfleur and Henry's stirring exhortation to his small army to go "Once more unto the breach," to the dramatic victory at Agincourt.

In addition to his own extraordinary performance as King Henry, Branagh elicits brilliant work from a stellar cast, including Derek Jacobi as the chorus, Paul Scofield as the French king, Ian Holm as Fluellen, Robbie Coltrane as Falstaff and Judi Dench as Mistress Quickly.   .

HENTAI
1966   71m   bw   ★★★★
Crime
Olympic   (Japan)

Sayuri Sakurari, Masayonshi Nagami

p, Nidemaru Washio, Felix Lomax; d, Takashi Shiga

Grim Japanese crime film about two detectives searching for the missing daughter of a rich industrialist. The trail leads to a crime ring that kidnaps, drugs, and rapes young girls, and forces them to work as prostitutes. Eventually the detectives learn that the industrialist's daughter has suffered the same fate. When they have the Tokyo police round up the leaders of the gang, the industrialist himself is exposed as the mastermind. To his eternal shame and horror, he learns that his organization has prostituted his own daughter.

HERBIE RIDES AGAIN
1974   88m   c   ★★½
Comedy   G/U
Buena Vista

Helen Hayes (*Mrs. Steinmetz*), Ken Berry (*Willoughby Whitfield*), Stefanie Powers (*Nicole*), John McIntire (*Mr. Judson*), Keenan Wynn (*Alonzo Hawk*), Huntz Hall (*Judge*), Ivor Barry (*Chauffeur*), Dan Tobin (*Lawyer*), Vito Scotti (*Taxi Driver*), Raymond Bailey (*Lawyer*)

p, Bill Walsh; d, Robert Stevenson; w, Bill Walsh (based on a story by Gordon Buford); ph, Frank Phillips (Technicolor); ed, Cotton Warburton; m, George Burns; art d, John B. Mansbridge, Walter Tyler; fx, Art Cruickshank, Alan Maley, Eustace Lycett, Danny Lee; cos, Chuck Keehne, Emily Sundby

Herbie raises hell. This sequel to THE LOVE BUG was one of Disney's most successful films of the 1970s. Herbie, the heroic Volkswagen, comes to the rescue of Mrs. Steinmetz (Helen Hayes) and Nicole (Stefanie Powers), who are trying to prevent the villainous Hawk (Keenan Wynn, playing the same character he portrayed in THE ABSENT-MINDED PROFESSOR) from building a skyscraper where their house stands. Willoughby Whitfield (Ken Berry), Hawk's lawyer nephew, also joins with Herbie in the fight to stop the construction. Herbie enlists the help of all the VWs in San Francisco, and they arrive like the cavalry to fight off the imposing bulldozers. The "Herbie" films proved to be so popular that the Germans produced a ripoff of them in 1971 titled EIN KAEFER GEHT AUFS GANZE (their VW was called Dudu). Egregious kiddie slapstick, punctuated by shameless overacting.

HERE COME THE CO-EDS

1945 88m bw ★★½
Musical/Comedy /U
Universal

Bud Abbott (Slats), Lou Costello (Oliver Quackenbush), Peggy Ryan (Patty), Martha O'Driscoll (Molly), June Vincent (Diane), Lon Chaney, Jr. (Johnson), Donald Cook (Benson), Charles Dingle (Jonathan Kirkland), Richard Lane (Nearsighted Man), Joe Kirk (Honest Dan)

p, John Grant; d, Jean Yarbrough; w, Arthur T. Horman, John Grant (based on a story by Edmund Hartmann); ph, George Robinson; ed, Arthur Hilton; art d, John B. Goodman, Richard H. Riedel; fx, John P. Fulton

This wacky Abbott and Costello vehicle—if that's your thing—features the duo as caretakers at a women's college that's in deep financial trouble. To raise money to help keep the school open, Oliver (Costello) gets in the wrestling ring with "The Masked Marvel" (Lon Chaney, Jr.), who, sans his grappling disguise, is the man who is trying to close down the college. Highlight is a silent classic bit originally developed by Billy Bevan in which Costello is served a bowl of stew containing a live oyster. The oyster squirts his face, bites his fingers, and devours his necktie when he tries to catch it, yanking his face into the bowl. This routine appeared three years earlier in a Three Stooges short, DUTIFUL BUT DUMB, with Curly Howard as the victim, and a variation of the gag was employed in THE WISTFUL WIDOW OF WAGON GAP.

HERE COME THE NELSONS

1952 75m bw ★½
Comedy /U
Universal

Ozzie Nelson (Ozzie), Harriet Hilliard (Harriet), Ricky Nelson (Ricky), David Nelson (David), Rock Hudson (Charles Jones), Barbara Lawrence (Barbara), Sheldon Leonard (Duke), Jim Backus (Joe Randolph), Paul Harvey (S.T. Jones), Gale Gordon (H.J. Bellows)

p, Aaron Rosenberg; d, Frederick de Cordova; w, Ozzie Nelson, Donald Nelson, William Davenport (based on the radio show "The Adventures of Ozzie and Harriet"); ph, Irving Glassberg; ed, Frank Gross; m, Joseph Gershenson; art d, Bernard Herzbrun, Hilyard Brown

Thick like a brick; get us a cleaver and we don't mean Beaver. Inept Ozzie, empty Harriet, and their cardboard kids make a cinema pitstop before television. With his hometown's centennial just around the corner, Ozzie is trying to develop an advertising campaign for a women's garment manufacturer. Harriet invites Hudson to stay at their house for the celebration, and Ozzie does the same with Lawrence. This causes a series of misunderstandings, with Ozzie out to prove he's still a young man by signing up for the bronco-riding contest in the centennial's rodeo. He backs out at the last minute, but proves himself by capturing the robbers of the rodeo's bank. The bad guys have also taken Ricky, and Ozzie chases them across mountain roads. He stops them by stringing some of his client's garments across the road and not only gets the robbers but inadvertently arrives at a winning ad campaign. Go figure.

HERE COME THE WAVES

1944 99m bw ★★★½
Musical/Comedy /U
Paramount

Bing Crosby (Johnny Cabot), Betty Hutton (Susan/Rosemary Allison), Sonny Tufts (Windy), Ann Doran (Ruth), Gwen Crawford (Tex), Noel Neill (Dorothy), Catherine Craig (Lieutenant Townsend), Anabel Shaw (Isabel), Harry Barris (Bandleader), Mae Clarke (Ensign Kirk)

p, Mark Sandrich; d, Mark Sandrich; w, Allan Scott, Ken Englund, Zion Myers; ph, Charles Lang; ed, Ellsworth Hoagland; m, Robert Emmett Dolan; art d, Hans Dreier, Roland Anderson; fx, Gordon Jennings, Paul K. Lerpae

Breezy wartime musical. Der Bingle is singing idol Johnny Cabot, The Huttontot in a dual role as a pair of singing twins, Susan and Rosemary Allison. Johnny is set on doing his patriotic duty and wants to serve on a destroyer with his best buddy, Windy (Sonny Tufts), but Susan, who has the hots for Johnny, secretly finagles an assignment for the crooner as the director of a company of WAVE entertainers. Although Johnny would rather be at sea, his posting becomes more attractive as he becomes enamored with Rosemary, whom Windy also loves. You know. Replete with satire, the movie includes Crosby lampooning fellow crooner Frank Sinatra by singing one of Old Blue Eyes' biggest hits, "That Old Black Magic," in front of a horde of fainting bobby-soxers. Painless.

HERE COMES MR. JORDAN

1941 93m bw ★★★★
Fantasy /A
Columbia

Robert Montgomery (Joe Pendleton), Evelyn Keyes (Bette Logan), Claude Rains (Mr. Jordan), Rita Johnson (Julia Farnsworth), Edward Everett Horton (Messenger No. 7013), James Gleason (Max Corkle), John Emery (Tony Abbott), Donald MacBride (Inspector Williams), Don Costello (Lefty), Halliwell Hobbes (Sisk)

p, Everett Riskin; d, Alexander Hall; w, Sidney Buchman, Seton I. Miller (based on the play Heaven Can Wait by Harry Segall); ph, Joseph Walker; ed, Viola Lawrence; m, Frederick Hollander; art d, Lionel Banks; cos, Edith Head

Full of hilarious plot twists and blessed with brilliant performances from a stellar cast, HERE COMES MR. JORDAN is a thoroughly beguiling fantasy with a boxing subplot. Joe Pendleton (Robert Montgomery), a saxophone-playing up-and-coming prizefighter, crashes while flying his single-engine plane, and his spirit is plucked up by an anxious heavenly messenger (Edward Everett Horton) who learns later that Joe was supposed to have lived for another 50 years and was destined to be the world heavyweight champion. It's up to the messenger's superior, Mr. Jordan (Claude Rains, amusingly sinister and atypical for this kind of role), to help Joe find another body in which to finish his life. JORDAN suffers from being too talky and the extraneous romance, but has remained an audience perennial. A weak nonsports sequel, DOWN TO EARTH, followed in 1947, and the story was remade with a football backdrop in 1978 as the pallid HEAVEN CAN WAIT.

HERE COMES THE GROOM

1951 113m bw ★★★½
Comedy/Musical /U
Paramount

Bing Crosby (Pete), Jane Wyman (Emmadel Jones), Alexis Smith (Winifred Stanley), Franchot Tone (Wilbur Stanley), James Barton (Pa Jones), Robert Keith (George Degnan), Jacques Gencel

HERE WE GO 'ROUND THE MULBERRY BUSH

(Bobby), Beverly Washburn (Suzi), Connie Gilchrist (Ma Jones), Walter Catlett (McGonigle)

p, Frank Capra; d, Frank Capra; w, Virginia Van Upp, Liam O'Brien, Myles Connolly (based on a story by Robert Riskin, Liam O'Brien); ph, George Barnes; ed, Ellsworth Hoagland; art d, Hal Pereira, Earl Hedrick; cos, Edith Head

Crosby is a news reporter returning from France with two orphans in tow, must find a wife in five days or lose the kids. He goes to his old flame, Wyman, and finds that she is set to marry millionaire Tone. Crosby uses the two orphans and his singing to recapture Wyman's heart, but it's an uphill battle against Tone's $40 million. A bright comedy with Crosby at his unflappable best and Capra developing full-bodied characters and situations, this film boasts a well-structured script and fine performances from Wyman, Tone, and Crosby.

Capra owed Paramount two films but the studio allowed him to take over this property from producer Irving Asher who originally planned to have Richard Haydn direct; this single production would make up for Capra's commitment. The gifted director brought in Wyman who used her own fine singing voice and showed off her long legs in glamorous costuming. He also brought in Smith, a six-foot actress who had been difficult to cast in the past. She was so tall that she had to stoop or slouch when playing opposite actors such as Humphrey Bogart or Charles Boyer, and stand barefoot in full shots. The always innovative Capra exploited her height by having Crosby crack in the film: "You're the most gorgeous first baseman I ever played against!" Predictable, but perfectly fine.

HERE WE GO 'ROUND THE MULBERRY BUSH

1968 94m c ★★★
Comedy /X
UA (U.K.)

Barry Evans (Jamie McGregor), Judy Geeson (Mary Gloucester), Angela Scoular (Caroline Beauchamp), Sheila White (Paula), Adrienne Posta (Linda), Vanessa Howard (Audrey), Diane Keen (Claire), Moyra Fraser (Mrs. McGregor), Michael Bates (Mr. McGregor), Maxine Audley (Mrs. Beauchamp)

p, Clive Donner; d, Clive Donner; w, Hunter Davies (based on the novel by Hunter Davies); ph, Alex Thomson (DeLuxe Color); ed, Fergus McDonell; m, Spencer Davis Group, Stevie Winwood, Traffic

Teenybop hop of Evans's final year at high school when he attempts to lose his virginity. He takes one girl to the church dance but all they do is hold hands in the dark. With another girl he can't unzip her zippers and gets involved in a sexual square dance with her parents. Finally, he spends a weekend with the best-looking girl in the school but they end up arguing most of the time. This is a humorous look at the awkwardness of teenage sexuality that remains above exploitation.

HESTER STREET

1975 90m bw
Drama ★★★½
Midwest PG

Steven Keats (Jake), Carol Kane (Gitl), Mel Howard (Bernstein), Dorrie Kavanaugh (Mamie), Doris Roberts (Kavarsky), Stephen Strimpell (Joe Peltner), Lauren Frost (Fanny), Paul Freedman (Joey), Zvee Scooler (Rabbi), Eda Reiss Merin (Rabbi's Wife)

p, Raphael D. Silver; d, Joan Micklin Silver; w, Joan Micklin Silver (based on the story "Yekl" by Abraham Cahan); ph, Kenneth Van Sickle; ed, Katherine Wenning; m, William Bolcom

Neglected piece of history receives atmospheric examination as old customs are replaced by assimilation. Keats is a young Jewish immigrant living on the title street while his wife Kane and their child are waiting back in the Old World. While trying to earn the money to bring them to the US, he becomes increasingly Americanized. He soon becomes involved with a fast-moving socialite who gives him some cash, which he in turn sends to his wife. Kane arrives but only shames Keats with her old-fashioned ways. They divorce and Keats goes off with his other woman, while Kane falls in love with a family friend. An engagingly simple first feature written and directed by Joan Micklin Silver, which earned an Academy Award nomination for Kane, whose acting is quite fine indeed. Unfortunately, other roles suffer from being poorly cast.

HEY BABU RIBA

(BAL NA VODI)
1987 112m c ★★★½
Drama
Avala/Inex (Yugoslavia)

Gala Videnovic (Miriana/Esther), Milan Strljic (Ristic), Dragan Bjelogrlic (Young Sasha), Goran Radakovic (Young Pop), Relja Basic (Glen), Nebojsa Bakocevic (Young Glen), Marko Todorovic (Sacha), Milos Zutic (Kicha), Srdjan Todorovic (Young Kicha), Djordje Nenadovic (Pop)

p, George Zecevic, Dragoljub Popovic, Nikola Popovic; d, Jovan Acin; w, Jovan Acin (based on memories of Petar Jankovic, George Zecevic, and Jovan Acin); ph, Tomislav Pinter; ed, Shezana Ivanovic; m, Zoran Simjanovic; art d, Sava Acin

An appealing look at adolescence in 1950s Yugoslavia, HEY BABU RIBA is a bittersweet tale of four teenage boys who grow up loving the same girl, hating the same political system and dancing to the same American music.

As the film opens the boys are now middle-aged men who have returned to Belgrade from homes in New York, London, Paris and Milan for the funeral of the girl. At the grave site, they approach the dead woman's daughter who believes that one of them must be her father. The foursome then agree to have a drink with a fifth mourner, a former Communist who is the actual father. They reflect on their youth which leads to a flashback in which the boys (Bakocevic, Bjelogrlic, Todorovic and Radakovic) are members of a rowing team and their coxswain is Miriana (Videnovic), the teenage girl they all once desired. They love Glenn Miller, Levis, Marlboros, and American films, especially the 1944 Esther Williams picture BATHING BEAUTY.

Although the political climate under Marshal Tito makes everyone's life difficult, the foursome survive on the strength of their friendship. Their bond is threatened, however, as each boy declares his love for Miriana, who is determined to keep her relationship with them platonic. Each of the lads is feeling the pressures of puberty, so each finds an older woman who will take him into her bed. The day following each boy's ascent to manhood, he appears, wearing blue jeans and smoking cigarettes. The naive Miriana makes no connection between this behavior and their loss of virginity. She is still more concerned with friendship than sexual relations. Things begin to change for her when she is courted by Ristic (Strljic), the Communist. One morning, she is seen smoking a cigarette. Then she learns that she's pregnant.

A semi-autobiographical account of life in Yugoslavia, HEY BABU RIBA is the work of three lifelong friends who, like the characters in the film, have all gone on to highly successful careers outside of their native country. The second feature from director Jovan Acin (his first, THE CONCRETE ROSE led to his leaving the country), HEY BABU RIBA originated during a yearly reunion between Acin and the film's two producers—George Zecevic and Petar Jankovic. Finding a delicate balance between politics and daily life, director Acin has made a picture which is universal in its appeal. The performances all capture a certain adolescent honesty, with the stunning 16-year-old Videnovic photographing beautifully. It is unfortunate that her underdeveloped character lacks the depth and complexity to match her lovely face.

HI, MOM!

1970 87m c/bw   ★★
Comedy   R/15
West End

Robert De Niro *(John Rubin)*, Charles Durnham *(Superintendent)*, Allen Garfield *(Joe Banner)*, Abraham Goren *(Pervert in Theater)*, Lara Parker *(Jeannie Mitchell)*, Jennifer Salt *(Judy Bishop)*, Gerrit Graham *(Gerrit Wood)*, Nelson Peltz *(Playboy)*, Peter Maloney *(Pharmacist)*, William Daley *(Co-op Neighbor)*

p, Charles Hirsch; d, Brian De Palma; w, Brian De Palma (based on a story by Brian De Palma, Charles Hirsch); ph, Robert Elfstrom (Eastmancolor); ed, Paul Hirsch; m, Eric Katz; art d, Peter Bocour

Curiously interesting early effort from Brian De Palma and Robert De Niro is which De Niro plays a porno filmmaker. He leases a ratty apartment in New York, across the street from an expensive co-op where Garfield, a wealthy producer of "adult" films, lives. The benevolent Garfield takes De Niro under his wing and gives him advice about how to make these sleazy movies. He spies comely neighbor Salt and wants to sleep with her—for his own benefit and the camera's. He promptly sets up his camera on his window sill, goes across the street, and proceeds to seduce her, but his camera falls and he misses his opportunity to immortalize the encounter on film.

De Niro then gets a job as an actor in an off-Broadway revue called "Be Black, Baby!" The actors all walk out in whiteface and begin to blacken the faces of the white audience, then abuse them both verbally and physically. Meanwhile, a gang of urban guerrillas, raid the huge apartment building, but they are all cut down by machine-gun fire. A young businessman in the high-rise just happens to have a 50-millimeter gun in his apartment. Salt and De Niro marry; she gets pregnant and becomes an instant nag, pestering him with her dreams of having a dishwasher. De Niro calmly goes to the building's basement and tosses a huge charge of dynamite into the clothes washer which levels the entire building.

De Niro, before he became a major star, made a fine living playing weird types (GREETINGS, BLOODY MAMA), and his role here is no exception. Partially filmed in 16mm black and white, HI, MOM! is an original, often inventive picture, though it is also disjointed and sometimes painfully slow-moving. When it's on the money, the satire is very funny, particularly in its lampooning of the "touchy-feely" theater which had some popularity in the late 1960s and early 1970s. Most of the time, however, the film misses its targets and comes off as simply amateurish.

HIDDEN, THE

1987 96m c   ★★★
Science Fiction/Thriller   R/18
New Line/Heron

Michael Nouri *(Tom Beck)*, Kyle MacLachlan *(Lloyd Gallagher)*, Ed O'Ross *(Cliff Willis)*, Clu Gulager *(Ed Flynn)*, Claudia Christian *(Brenda Lee)*, Clarence Felder *(John Masterson)*, Bill Boyett, Richard Brooks, Catherine Cannon, Larry Cedar

p, Robert Shaye, Gerald T. Olson, Michael Meltzer; d, Jack Sholder; w, Bob Hunt; ph, Jacques Haitkin; ed, Michael Knue; m, Michael Convertino; prod d, C.J. Strawn, Mick Strawn

An exciting mix of science fiction, cop thriller, and buddy film, THE HIDDEN is one of the most exciting and unique genre hybrids.

The movie opens with an action sequence in which a young stockbroker with a strange glint in his eye robs a bank, steals a Ferarri, and drives non-stop through several police blockades while listening to pounding rock music. Finally the police force the car into a fiery crash that sends the critically injured stockbroker to the hospital. Later that day a mysterious young FBI officer, Lloyd Gallagher (Kyle MacLachlan), arrives at police headquarters to enlist the aid of veteran detective Tom Beck (Michael Nouri) in finding a fugitive—the stockbroker. In the meantime, the stockbroker dies but a slimy alien creature crawls out of his mouth and into the body of another patient. Soon the madness begins anew.

Bob Hunt's screenplay and Jack Sholder's direction combine to create a sci-fi action yarn replete with exciting chases, well-staged shootouts and some extremely funny black humor. Nouri and MacLachlan turn in superior performances as does the rest of the large cast. In retrospect, MacLachlan's character feels like an audition for Agent Cooper of "Twin Peaks." This is an outstanding buddy film with a smart extraterrestrial twist.

HIDDEN FORTRESS, THE

(KAKUSHI TORIDE NO SAN AKUNIN)
1958 137m bw   ★★★★
Adventure   /A
Toho   (Japan)

Toshiro Mifune *(Rokurota)*, Misa Uehara *(Lady Yukihime)*, Minoru Chiaki *(Tahei)*, Kamatari Fujiwara *(Matashichi)*, Susumu Fujita *(The Grateful Soldier)*, Takashi Shimura *(The Old General)*, Eiko Miyoshi *(The Old Woman)*, Toshiko Higuchi *(The Farmer's Daughter)*, Kichijiro Ueda *(Girl-Dealer)*

d, Akira Kurosawa; w, Ryuzo Kikushima, Hideo Oguni, Shinobu Hashimoto, Akira Kurosawa; ph, Kazuo Yamazaki; m, Masaru Sato

A film that might very likely change the consciousness of those who dislike foregin films. Two unlikely looking soldiers, Tahei (Minoru Chiaki) and Matashichi (Kamatari Fujiwara), flee following the defeat of their army. They stumble across a gold bar hidden in some firewood, but before they can take it, Rokurota (Toshiro Mifune), a general, appears. He enlists the two to help him take a wagon load of gold—plus deposed princess Lady Yukihime (Misa Uehara)—to safety in the next province.

One of Akira Kurosawa's best works—with an odd mix of periods, from medieval to modern—HIDDEN FORTRESS is filled with humor and excitement, owing more to Hollywood adventure films than to the Japanese tradition. George Lucas claimed that this film was the chief inspiration for STAR WARS, and it is easy to see the resemblance, especially in Chiaki and Fujiwara, who were copied in metal to make R2-D2 and C-3PO. Originally released in the US in a truncated 90-minute print, THE

HIDDEN FORTRESS quickly disappeared and was not released in a full-length version until 1983.

HIDE IN PLAIN SIGHT
1980 92m c   ★★★½
Drama   PG
MGM

James Caan (*Thomas Hacklin*), Jill Eikenberry (*Alisa*), Robert Viharo (*Jack Scolese*), Joe Grifasi (*Matty Stanke*), Barbara Rae (*Ruthie Hacklin*), Kenneth McMillan (*Sam*), Danny Aiello (*Sal*), Thomas Hill (*Bobby*), Chuck Hicks (*Frankie Irish*), Andrew Gordon Fenwick (*Andy*)

p, Robert Christiansen, Rick Rosenberg; d, James Caan; w, Spencer Eastman (based on a book by Leslie Waller); ph, Paul Lohmann (Panavision, Metrocolor); ed, Fredric Steinkamp, William Steinkamp; m, Leonard Rosenman; prod d, Pato Guzman

This impressive directorial debut from James Caan deals with the US government's witness relocation plan. Without warning, Caan visits the home of his ex-wife to see his two children and finds only an empty house. He discovers that his ex's present husband, Viharo, testified against the mob and, along with his family, was given a new identity and a new home. Desperately, Caan searches for his children. His emotionally charged performance is the highlight of this gripping drama based on a true story.

HIGH AND LOW
(TENGOKU TO-JIGOKU)
1963 142m c/bw   ★★★★
Crime   /A
Toho (Japan)

Toshiro Mifune (*Kingo Gondo*), Tatsuya Nakadai (*Inspector Tokura*), Kyoko Kagawa (*Reiko, Gondo's Wife*), Tatsuya Mihashi (*Kawanishi*), Yutaka Sada (*Aoki*), Kenjiro Ishiyama (*Detective Taguchi*), Tsutomu Yamazaki (*Ginji Takeuchi*), Takashi Shimura (*Director*), Susumu Fujita (*Commissioner*), Ko Kimura (*Detective Arai*)

p, Tomoyuki Tanaka, Ryuzo Kikushima; d, Akira Kurosawa; w, Akira Kurosawa, Hideo Oguni, Ryuzo Kikushima, Eijiro Hisaita (based on the novel *King's Ransom* by Ed McBain); ph, Choichi Nakai, Takao Saito (Tohoscope); m, Masaru Sato; art d, Yoshiro Muraki

Based on a crime novel by Ed McBain, this brilliant Kurosawa film stars Toshiro Mifune as Kingo Gondo, a rich industrialist who receives word that his son has been kidnapped by a madman demanding an outrageous ransom that will ruin Gondo financially if he pays it. Before Gondo can make a decision, his son enters the house, and we learn that it is his playmate, the chauffeur's son, who has been kidnapped. Gondo is then faced with a tough moral decision: is his chauffeur's son worth as much as his own? When the kidnapper calls and admits his mistake, but demands payment anyway, Gondo initially refuses, but is conscience stricken.

In HIGH AND LOW Kurosawa succeeds in developing a highly visual structural style within the wide-screen format. The first half of the film takes place in the living room of Gondo's hilltop house and is characterized by static shots that hold for several minutes on a single composition. Time transitions are handled by wipes, creating a charged atmosphere. This steadiness is broken suddenly for the second half of the film, involving the criminal manhunt, shot with a normal amount of motion and cutting—its pace frenetic in comparison with the first half of the film.

HIGH AND THE MIGHTY, THE
1954 147m c   ★★★½
Disaster   /U
Wayne/Fellows

John Wayne (*Dan Roman*), Claire Trevor (*May Hoist*), Laraine Day (*Lydia Rice*), Robert Stack (*Sullivan*), Jan Sterling (*Sally McKee*), Phil Harris (*Ed Joseph*), Robert Newton (*Gustave Pardee*), David Brian (*Ken Childs*), Paul Kelly (*Flaherty*), Sidney Blackmer (*Humphrey Agnew*)

p, Robert Fellows, John Wayne; d, William A. Wellman; w, Ernest K. Gann (based on the novel by Gann); ph, Archie Stout, William Clothier (CinemaScope, Warner Color); ed, Ralph Dawson; m, Dimitri Tiomkin; art d, Alfred Ybarra; cos, Gwen Wakeling

Cliche-bound but boosted by taut direction, memorable music and, for once, just right for CinemaScope. Wayne is a has-been pilot—"an ancient pelican" according to airline executive Toomey—now copiloting under the command of cocky Stack. Also on board is an inept navigator, Brown, and an apprentice pilot, Campbell, who constantly derides Wayne, even bringing up a terrible crash occurring years earlier which Wayne survived but in which his wife and young child were killed.

Beautiful, statuesque, and cool stewardess Doe Avedon makes 22 passengers comfortable as the airliner leaves Honolulu for San Francisco. Her passengers: divorce-seeking Day and Howard; shady mail-order bride Sterling; wacko theatrical impresario Newton; jaded, bitter Trevor; pompous playboy Brian who is being stalked by vengeful Blackmer; oblivious newlyweds Smith and Sharpe; guilty nuclear scientist Kelly; and second honeymooners Doran and Harris. Then, all hell breaks loose, forcing everyone to face each other, "reality," and a competitive race for acting honors.

Wellman does a dynamite job directing air traffic; though characters are drawn only briefly, they are tellingly etched with pathos and melodrama. Wayne's performance as the one fixed and reliable point in a collapsing world got him voted into the number one box-office attraction, replacing Gary Cooper. Oddly, Wayne, who coproduced the film, intended to have Spencer Tracy play the pioneer pilot role but when that venerable actor turned down the part Wayne took it over himself. The haunting title song became so closely associated with Wayne that when this giant died it was this score that was played during his funeral.

HIGH ANXIETY
1977 94m c   ★★★
Comedy   PG/15
FOX

Mel Brooks (*Richard Thorndyke*), Madeline Kahn (*Victoria Brisbane*), Cloris Leachman (*Nurse Diesel*), Harvey Korman (*Dr. Charles Montague*), Ron Carey (*Brophy*), Howard Morris (*Prof. Lilloman*), Dick Van Patten (*Dr. Wentworth*), Jack Riley (*Desk Clerk*), Charlie Callas (*Cocker Spaniel*), Ron Clark (*Zachary Cartwright*)

p, Mel Brooks; d, Mel Brooks; w, Mel Brooks, Ron Clark, Rudy DeLuca, Barry Levinson; ph, Paul Lohmann (DeLuxe Color); ed, John C. Howard; m, John Morris; prod d, Peter Wooley; fx, Albert Whitlock; cos, Patricia Morris

Mel Brooks's so-so feat of Hitchcockian tribute: he stars, produces, directs, cowrites, and sings the title song (and he has a much better singing voice than you might imagine). Whereas men like Brian De Palma and Colin Higgins will make movies reminiscent of Hitchcock without citing that director, Brooks is patently spoofing the rotund master with HIGH ANXIETY. Even if you don't know the original work, this film indicates its inspiration fairly well. The head of the Institute for the Very Very Nervous is found murdered, and Brooks, a man who fears heights so badly that he won't wear elevator shoes, takes over as psychiatrist-in-charge. Assistant Korman and nurse Leachman have been spinning a plot to keep the patients captive while bilking them out of their money, and they fear that Brooks will put an end to that. Parody is a tricky business, but Brooks sometimes succeeds in paying homage to SPELLBOUND, VERTIGO, PSYCHO, and THE BIRDS with all of the usual middle-cut Hitchcock formulae: innocent man accused of something he didn't do, reluctant heroine (Kahn) who helps, etc. Many familiar scenes come out of Hitchcock with the standouts being prowling camera work and Hitch's use of musical scores. Audiences flocked to theaters and made this movie a hit. Some interesting sidelights in casting include famed matte artist Albert Whitlock as Brisbane, successful commercials actors Bob Ridgely and Jack Riley, and co-writer Levinson as the bellboy. Levinson went on to become highly regarded as a director with DINER and THE NATURAL. Morris was for years one of Sid Ceasar's second bananas on TV and now earns his living as a director and sometimes cartoon voice ("The Paw-Paws" for Hanna-Barbera, among others). Callas is a busy nightclub comic, and Richard Stahl is one of the best comedy character men in the business. Assistant director Sanger stayed with Brooks and eventually became a producer.

HIGH HEELS
(TACONES LEJANOS)
1991   112m   c   ★★½
Comedy/Crime   R/18
El Deseo/CiBy 2000   (Spain/France)

Victoria Abril *(Rebecca)*, Marisa Paredes *(Becky del Paramo)*, Miguel Bose *(Judge/Letal/Hugo)*, Pedro Diez Del Corral *(Alberto)*, Feodor Atkine *(Manuel)*, Ana Lizaran *(Margarita)*, Rocio Munoz *(Little Rebecca)*, Mayrata O'Wisiedo *(Judge's Mother)*, Miriam Diaz Aroca *(Isabel)*, Cristina Marcos *(Paula)*

d, Pedro Almodovar; w, Pedro Almodovar; ph, Alfredo Mayo; ed, Jose Salcedo; m, Ryuichi Sakamoto; cos, Jose Maria Cossio

A stylish but disappointing spoof which lacks the satiric gusto of director Pedro Almodovar's earlier works. Technically impressive, and boasting a top-flight cast, HIGH HEELS flounders thanks to Almodovar's muddled, overwrought screenplay.

The story involves a TV anchor, Rebecca (Victoria Abril), who is married to a former lover of her singer/actress mother, Becky (Marisa Paredes). In one of the more noteworthy scenes, a female impersonator lip-synchs to some of Becky's hits at a club where both mother and daughter are in the audience; when Rebecca hurries backstage to congratulate him, the two make sudden, passionate love. (Later we find out he's actually a judge doing "undercover work.") Despite these moments of provocative lunacy, there's little here to match the sophisticated madness of the director's breakthrough hit, WOMEN ON THE VERGE OF A NERVOUS BREAKDOWN. Almodovar is a prime example of a filmmaker who has been hampered by extraordinary success and the *carte blanche* mentality that often accompanies it.

HIGH HOPES
1988   110m   c   ★★★★
Comedy/Drama   PG/15
Portman/Film Four   (U.K.)

Philip Davis *(Cyril Bender)*, Ruth Sheen *(Shirley)*, Edna Dore *(Mrs. Bender)*, Philip Jackson *(Martin Burke)*, Heather Tobias *(Valerie Burke)*, Lesley Manville *(Laetitia Boothe-Braine)*, David Bamber *(Rupert Boothe-Braine)*, Jason Watkins *(Wayne)*, Judith Scott *(Suzi)*, Cheryl Prime *(Martin's Girl Friend)*

p, Simon Channing-Williams, Victor Glynn; d, Mike Leigh; w, Mike Leigh; ph, Roger Pratt (Eastmancolor); ed, John Gregory; m, Andrew Dixon; prod d, Diana Charnley; art d, Andrew Rothschild; cos, Lindy Hemming

Mike Leigh's funny and deeply touching HIGH HOPES is yet another inventive cinematic reaction to Margaret Thatcher's overhaul of British society. Employing an episodic structure and a semi-improvisational approach, Leigh (BLEAK MOMENTS) presents three couples and an elderly woman as a microcosm of modern-day Britain.

Cyril (Philip Davis), a 35-year-old motorcycle messenger, and Shirley (Ruth Sheen), his companion of ten years, are children of the working class who have embraced a countercultural lifestyle that once included a passionate faith in revolutionary ideology. Although they can't agree to have a child of their own, they spend plenty of time parenting Davis's aging mother (Dore), who lives in the last council-owned house on a gentrified street, where an impossibly snooty yuppie couple, the Boothe-Braines (Lesley Manville and David Bamber), are her neighbors. Rounding out the cast are Cyril's shrill, nouveau riche sister (Heather Tobias) and her philandering used-car-salesman husband (Philip Jackson). Alternately silly, serious, and poignant, HIGH HOPES uses its players as political symbols, without subordinating character to the demands of allegory. . . well, almost.

Leigh's approach is most realistic when dealing with Cyril's mother, Cyril, and Shirley, and the bedtime conversations between the last two are certainly among cinema's most privileged moments. Because of the care Leigh takes with these three characters, HIGH HOPES is not just an indictment of Thatcher-engendered inequity; it is also a survival primer for those who have lost faith in the Left's traditional grand solutions yet refused to succumb to "compassion fatigue."

HIGH NOON
1952   85m   bw   ★★★★★
Western   /U
UA

Gary Cooper *(Will Kane)*, Grace Kelly *(Amy Kane)*, Thomas Mitchell *(Jonas Henderson)*, Lloyd Bridges *(Harvey Pell)*, Katy Jurado *(Helen Ramirez)*, Otto Kruger *(Percy Mettrick)*, Lon Chaney, Jr. *(Martin Howe)*, Harry Morgan *(William Fuller)*, Ian MacDonald *(Frank Miller)*, Eve McVeagh *(Mildred Fuller)*

p, Stanley Kramer; d, Fred Zinnemann; w, Carl Foreman (based on the story "The Tin Star" by John W. Cunningham); ph, Floyd Crosby; ed, Elmo Williams, Harry Gerstad; m, Dimitri Tiomkin; prod d, Rudolph Sternad; art d, Ben Hayne

Not a frame is wasted in this taut, superbly directed, masterfully acted film, the first so-called "adult Western," in which the traditional and predictable elements of action, song and minimal romance give way to a swift, intense unraveling of a situation and complex character development. HIGH NOON is also the story of a western town, Hadleyville, and its sometimes stouthearted citizenry, the most prominent of whom is the stoic, heroic Will Kane (Gary Cooper), a lawman surrounded by friends and admirers at the start, deserted and doomed at the finish.

Just married, Will and his beautiful blonde Quaker bride, Amy (Grace Kelly), are about to leave town forever, intending to put peacemaking behind them to settle down to ranch life. However, news comes that a fierce killer, Frank Miller (Ian MacDonald), is about to arrive and take vengeance against Will and the town for sending him to prison years earlier. Miller's brother (Sheb Wooley) and two gunslingers (Robert Wilke and Lee Van Cleef) are already at the depot, waiting for the train carrying Miller, which is due to arrive at high noon. In a moment of panic, urged on by his friends, Will races his buckboard and bride out of town and down the road into the open prairie, but he suddenly pulls up. When Amy asks him why he is stopping, Will tells her that he has to go back, that it's his duty to return.

A landmark Western in every sense, HIGH NOON was shot by cinematographer Floyd Crosby in high contrast, an approach director Fred Zinnemann used to bring documentarylike authenticity to the film. Zinnemann's outstanding economical direction is in full force here, every minute pertinent and packed with suspense. Significantly, the film takes almost as much time to unreel as Will Kane takes in the story to prepare for the gun battle.

For Cooper, this was a *tour de force*, a film wherein his mere presence overwhelms the viewer and carries a story that is believable only through his actions. He utters no long speeches, yet his expressions and movements are those of a man resolute in his lonely duty and resigned to his own doom. Every confrontation with the unresponsive townspeople causes him to suffer; in truth, Cooper was in real agony during the production, enduring a bleeding ulcer and an injured hip. After finishing the film, he said, "I'm all acted out." Cooper's exhaustion is evident in his onscreen appearance, but reportedly an appropriately haggard-looking Will Kane was just what Zinnemann was after, despite Hollywood's proclivity for dashing leading men.

Though Kramer later claimed that the project was entirely his own creation, writer Carl Foreman contended neither Kramer nor his associates had any interest in the film from the outset. Kramer did, however, view the first showing with concern. Believing that it had a lot of dead spots, he ordered a series of closeups showing the anxiety lining Cooper's face, and included many quick cuts to clocks ticking relentlessly toward the doom of high noon.

To further heighten the tension Kramer asked Dmitri Tiomkin to write a ballad that could be interwoven with the action. Though the composer protested that he only wrote scores, he and Ned Washington produced the wonderful "High Noon (Do Not Forsake Me)", sung by Tex Ritter. The song has since become a classic, along with Tiomkin's memorable score.

HIGH PLAINS DRIFTER

1973 105m c   ★★★½
Western   R/18
Malpaso

Clint Eastwood (*The Stranger*), Verna Bloom (*Sarah Belding*), Marianna Hill (*Callie Travers*), Mitchell Ryan (*Dave Drake*), Jack Ging (*Morgan Allen*), Stefan Gierasch (*Mayor Jason Hobart*), Ted Hartley (*Lewis Belding*), Billy Curtis (*Mordecai*), Geoffrey Lewis (*Stacey Bridges*), Scott Walker (*Bill Borders*)

p, Robert Daley; d, Clint Eastwood; w, Ernest Tidyman; ph, Bruce Surtees (Panavision, Technicolor); ed, Ferris Webster; m, Dee Barton; art d, Henry Bumstead

Eastwood directs his first Western, and it's a knockout. HIGH PLAINS DRIFTER is a morality tale carved out of the harsh Western desert and directed with a panache that synthesized the styles of Sergio Leone and Don Siegel, two directors who had

worked with Eastwood frequently. The result is one of the best Westerns of the 1970s.

The story begins as a mysterious stranger (Eastwood) materializes out of the desert heat. He rides into the small town of Lagos, where his presence is considered a threat by the mean and cowardly populace. Before too long, he is attacked by three gunmen, and Eastwood kills them all coolly and efficiently. The stranger then rents a hotel room, and the town dwarf, Curtis (who is also disenfranchised in town due to his size), attends to his needs. At night, Eastwood's dreams are plagued by a recurring nightmare of a helpless man being whipped to death in the street by three sadistic criminals while the townsfolk stand by and do nothing to stop it.

Meanwhile, the town council debates how to handle the impending threat created by a group of escaped convicts who are out to return to Lagos (where they committed their crimes) and destroy it. Desperate, the town's leaders cautiously approach Eastwood and plead with him to save their town from the criminals. Eastwood agrees to help them, but then proceeds to turn the town on its head by teaching self-defense and requesting all sorts of strange things from the townsfolk, including having them paint the town red and rename it "Hell."

An eerie, supernatural western that takes the avenging man-with-no-name character created by Eastwood and Leone to its most logical extreme. Eastwood would later bury the character completely in his own OUTLAW JOSEY WALES only to have him rise like the Phoenix, redefined as a much more human, compassionate and caring hero.

HIGH PRESSURE

1932 72m bw   ★★★½
Comedy   /U
WB

William Powell (*Gar Evans*), Evelyn Brent (*Francine*), George Sidney (*Colonel Ginsburg*), Frank McHugh (*Mike Donoghey*), Guy Kibbee (*Clifford Gray*), Evalyn Knapp (*Helen*), Ben Alexander (*Geoffrey*), Harry Beresford (*Dr. Rudolph*), John Wray (*Jimmy Moore*), Charles Judels (*Salvatore*)

d, Mervyn LeRoy; w, Joseph Jackson (based on the story "Hot Money" by S.J. Peters and the play by Aben Kandel); ph, Robert Kurrle; ed, Ralph Dawson

A fast-paced, well-constructed comedy sporting a charming performance from Powell, who plays a barely-legitimate hustler who sees his ticket to easy street come in the form of an invention that can change sewage to artificial rubber. He sets up a corporation and sells stocks in it to raise some cash and is just about to go into production when he learns that the inventor of the sewage-to-rubber process is a nut case and that *he* is the one who has been taken. Good casting and direction help to propel this loony, but well-written, comedy along. Featuring a capable assist from the hardboiled Evelyn Brent.

HIGH SIERRA

1941 100m bw   ★★★★
Crime   /PG
WB

Ida Lupino (*Marie Garson*), Humphrey Bogart (*Roy Earle*), Alan Curtis (*Babe Kozak*), Arthur Kennedy (*Red Hattery*), Joan Leslie (*Velma*), Henry Hull (*Doc Banton*), Barton MacLane (*Jake Kramer*), Henry Travers (*Pa*), Elisabeth Risdon (*Ma*), Cornel Wilde (*Louis Mendoza*)

p, Mark Hellinger; d, Raoul Walsh; w, John Huston, W.R. Burnett (based on the novel by W.R. Burnett); ph, Tony Gaudio; ed, Jack Killifer; m, Adolph Deutsch; art d, Ted Smith; fx, Byron Haskin, H.F. Koenekamp; cos, Milo Anderson

With exception of WHITE HEAT, this was the movie gangster's last stand. Bogart plays a graying criminal who's had it, and is in pursuit of one last caper in a changing world. He hooks up with Kennedy, Curtis, and informer Wilde to pull of the job, and becomes sympathetic to the plight of Curtis's moll Lupino, while also obsessing about young Leslie, a lame girl. HIGH SIERRA romanticizes the Bogie character as much as possible within hardbitten guidelines and, with the exception of the always overeager Leslie, it's acted within an inch of its classic life, especially by Bogie, Lupino and a mongrel dog in the gut-wrenching climax. And that fadeout. . ..

HIGH SIERRA is a landmark crime film in many ways. It was Bogart's first solid role as a sympathetic lead, a good-bad guy out of his element and beyond his time. As was the case with his first gangster role—Duke Mantee, in THE PETRIFIED FOREST—Bogart is made up to look like John Dillinger, to whom he bore an amazing resemblance. Bogart, who was second-billed under Lupino, showed his ability to play sensitive scenes with depth, and the public responded enthusiastically. He would never again play second fiddle to Cagney or anyone else.

Director Walsh does a superb job in keeping a nonstop action pace, succinctly pausing to give Bogart setups in which his character is revealed, a masterful balance of movement and repose. Walsh, more than any one else, was responsible for Bogart's big break in getting the part, suggesting him to Jack Warner when others turned down the role. This was also an important film for screenwriter John Huston; his career took a sharp turn upward following HIGH SIERRA, after which he began his own distinguished directing career. Reworked by Walsh himself as COLORADO TERRITORY.

HIGH SOCIETY

1956   107m   c   ★★★
Musical/Comedy   /U
MGM

Bing Crosby (C.K. Dexter-Haven), Grace Kelly (Tracy Lord), Frank Sinatra (Mike Connor), Celeste Holm (Liz Imbrie), John Lund (George Kittredge), Louis Calhern (Uncle Willie), Sidney Blackmer (Seth Lord), Louis Armstrong (Himself), Margalo Gillmore (Mrs. Seth Lord), Lydia Reed (Caroline Lord)

p, Sol C. Siegel; d, Charles Walters; w, John Patrick (based on the play "The Philadelphia Story" by Philip Barry); ph, Paul C. Vogel (VistaVision, Technicolor); ed, Ralph E. Winters; m, Johnny Green, Saul Chaplin; art d, Cedric Gibbons, Hans Peters; fx, A. Arnold Gillespie; chor, Charles Walters; cos, Helen Rose

Written with all the bite of a distinctly middle-class church social, this musical re-working of THE PHILADELPHIA STORY feels distant. Cole Porter's score sits on it like a champagne bubble in a vat of flat beer.

Tracy Lord (Grace Kelly, in her last film before marrying Prince Ranier of Monaco) lives in Newport and has a trio of men encircling her: her ex-husband, C.K. Dexter-Haven (Bing Crosby), with whom she is still on fairly good terms; her fiance, George Kittredge (John Lund), a professional prig; and Mike Connor (Frank Sinatra), a breezy reporter sent to cover the wedding by a *Life* magazine-like periodical. The rest of the cast includes Celeste Holm as Connor's photographer; Sidney Black-

mer as Tracy's skirt-chasing father; Margalo Gillmore as her mother; and Louis Calhern as her uncle.

The leads are all too laconic for the movie's own good. Crosby is far too old for his role—he looks like a piece of walking beef jerky. Sinatra comes off more like a gate-crashing taxi-driver than a reporter. He can't muster the energy to get past his own phony "hip" persona. And Kelly seems preoccupied by another wedding, or perhaps wallpaper choices for the palace. Still, there are a few diverting moments seeing Bing work out with Frank and the ever-welcome Satchmo. Re the score: the only song not written for the movie was "Well, Did You Evah?" which was first sung by Betty Grable in Cole Porter's 1939 Broadway musical *Du Barry Was a Lady*.

HIGH, WIDE AND HANDSOME

1937   110m   bw   ★★★
Western/Musical   /U
Paramount

Irene Dunne (Sally Watterson), Randolph Scott (Peter Cortlandt), Dorothy Lamour (Molly Fuller), Elizabeth Patterson (Grandma Cortlandt), Raymond Walburn (Doc Watterson), Charles Bickford (Red Scanlon), Akim Tamiroff (Joe Varese), Ben Blue (Zeke), William Frawley (Mac), Alan Hale (Walt Brennan)

p, Arthur Hornblow, Jr.; d, Rouben Mamoulian; w, Oscar Hammerstein, II, George O'Neil; ph, Victor Milner, Theodor Sparkuhl; ed, Archie Marshek; m, Jerome Kern; art d, Hans Dreier, John B. Goodman; fx, Gordon Jennings; chor, LeRoy Prinz; cos, Travis Banton

A lavish cornball musical horse opera, with Scott drilling for oil in 19th-century Pennsylvania, clashing with heavy Hale, and wooing Dunne, when she isn't doing her Julie Andrews number, warbling to a farm nag. She's the most discordant element at work here; her belting of saloon songs is on a par with Jeanette McDonald in SAN FRANCISCO. It's the rare musical that can appropriate overly prim actresses. Thank god for Dottie Lamour, and the energy the rest of the cast infuse the hokum with. The forgotten gem from the Hammerstein/Kern score is "The Folks Who Live on the Hill."

HILDUR AND THE MAGICIAN

1969   95m   bw   ★★★
Fantasy
Canyon

John Graham (The Magician/Narrator), Hildur Mahl (Hildur), Patricia Jordon (Companion), Jim Yensan (Gnome), Jani Novak (Driad), Roy Berger (Woodcutter), Shelby Sache (His Wife), Tres Berger (Arabelle), Sydney Droshin (Wicked Queen), Tito Patri (Huckster)

p, Larry Jordan; d, Larry Jordan; w, Larry Jordan (based on an idea by John Graham, Patricia Jordan); ph, Larry Jordan; ed, Larry Jordan; m, Joel Andrews, Julie Iger

This charming, well-photographed fairy tale will please kids while still holding the interest of adults. The story concerns a princess who is kidnaped by an evil gnome. Armed with a magic potion, Hildur (Hildur Mahl), a fairy queen, sets out to rescue her. In addition to some excellent animation sequences, the tale is played out in mime, with John Graham, who plays the film's bumbling wizard, providing a voice-over narration. The film's only drawback is its running time, which is a bit long for the material.

HILLS HAVE EYES, THE

1978 89m c ★★★½
Horror R/18
Blood Relations

Susan Lanier (Brenda Carter), Robert Houston (Bobby Carter), Virginia Vincent (Ethel Carter), Russ Grieve (Bob Carter), Dee Wallace Stone (Lynne Wood), Martin Speer (Doug Wood), Brenda Marinoff (Katie Wood), Flora the Dog (Beauty), Stricker the Dog (The Beast), James Whitmore (Jupiter)

p, Peter Locke; d, Wes Craven; w, Wes Craven; ph, Eric Saarinen; ed, Wes Craven; m, Don Peake; art d, Robert Burns

With this film and A NIGHTMARE ON ELM STREET, former English professor Wes Craven assured himself a place in the history of the horror film as an important modern filmmaker whose work has had an immense influence on the genre.

THE HILLS HAVE EYES opens as the Carters, an ostensibly typical middle-class suburban family, drive through the desert in their mobile home headed for California. The family consists of Dad (Russ Grieve), a recently retired cop; Mom (Virginia Vincent); big sister Lynne (Dee Wallace); her husband (Martin Speer); their baby; brother and sister, Brenda (Susan Lanier) and Bobby (Robert Houston); and dogs Beauty and the Beast. Trouble starts when the vehicle's axle breaks and the travelers are left stranded in the desert, miles from help. Unfortunately, they've accidentally trespassed on the domain of another family, a brutal, almost atavistic, clan of cannibals who live on the desert mesas.

This family is headed by patriarch Jupiter (James Whitmore), who was abandoned as a baby to die in the wasteland after he was born mutated. His wife (Cordy Clark), a former prostitute "no one would miss," was kidnapped by Jupiter and brought to the desert for companionship. They have four offspring, now fully grown. The boys, Pluto (Michael Berryman), Mars (Lance Gordon) and Mercury (Arthur King), all assist their father in protecting their territory (aided by walkie-talkies and rifles that somehow found their way into the family's possession) and gathering whatever food they can come across. The daughter, Ruby (Janus Blythe), has seen civilization and longs to escape her savage family. Soon the rival families collide with the twisted desert clan attacking the "all-American" suburban clan to loot, kill the men, rape the women, and eat the tasty looking baby.

Though not particularly bloody, THE HILLS HAVE EYES is an *extremely* intense and disturbing film. As is the case with Sam Peckinpah's classic, STRAW DOGS, it becomes oddly and distressingly exhilarating to watch the nice family become increasingly savage in their efforts to survive. Not for the squeamish, this low-budget potboiler is one of the prime examples of the what was so fascinating about American horror films in the 1970s. It can be profitably read as the kind of thematically rich and insightful meditation on the dark side of the American family that could only be done in the exploitation horror genre. A must-see for those who care about such matters.

HIMATSURI

1985 120m c ★★★★
Drama /18
Gunro/Seibu/Cine Saison (Japan)

Kinya Kitaoji (Tatsuo), Kiwako Taichi (Kimiko), Ryota Nakamoto (Ryota), Norihei Miki (Yamakawa), Rikiya Yasuoka (Toshio), Junko Miyashita (Sachiko), Kin Sugai (Tatsuo's Mother), Sachiko Matsushita, Masako Yagi (Tatsuo's Sisters), Jukei Fujioka

d, Mitsuo Yanagimachi; w, Kenji Nakagami; ph, Masaki Tamura (Eastmancolor); ed, Sachiko Yamaji; m, Toru Takemitsu; prod d, Takeo Kimura

In 1980 a man living in a remote Japanese village brutally murdered several members of his family before committing suicide. In HIMATSURI director Mitsuo Yanagimachi uses this incident to create a unique, highly intense story of one man's fight against the encroaching specter of Western modernism in rural Japan.

Kinya Kitaoji, a man of contradictory and often violent passions, engages in numerous affairs with no regard for his family's feelings and takes great pride in his skills as a survivalist. Living in an area where the ancient Shinto religion is firmly entrenched, Kinya Kitaoji boldly flaunts his arrogant attitudes by exposing himself before swimming in a sacred lake. Yet he is not without some principles. Though he openly mocks the sacred codes reverently observed by the locals, he harbors deep respect for the natural beauty of the land.

HIMATSURI, much like Paul Schrader's MISHIMA, deals with the conflict between modernism and Japanese traditions. Kinya Kitaoji, overbearing and with little concern for others, does, however, maintain a germ of interest in tradition, and it spreads steadily through his consciousness. Mitsuo Yanagimachi's direction emphasizes the relationship between man and nature, a harmony that grows more profound as the story develops.

HIRED HAND, THE

1971 90m c ★★½
Western GP/15
Pando

Peter Fonda (Harry Collings), Warren Oates (Arch Harris), Verna Bloom (Hannah Collings), Robert Pratt (Dan Griffin), Severn Darden (McVey), Ted Markland (Luke), Owen Orr (Mace), Gray Johnson (Will), Rita Rogers (Mexican Woman), Al Hopson (Bartender)

p, William Hayward; d, Peter Fonda; w, Alan Sharp; ph, Vilmos Zsigmond (Technicolor); ed, Frank Mazzola; m, Bruce Langhorne; art d, Lawrence G. Paull; cos, Richard Bruno

Peter Fonda's first directorial effort was this scattered, pretentious Western that tried to offer a realistic depiction of the Old West.

The story is about Fonda, who deserted his wife, Bloom, to drift with Oates. After seven years of drifting, Pratt, a fellow wanderer and friend of the duo, is murdered by Darden's men. Fonda and Oates exact revenge on the killers and Fonda decides to go back to his wife, but she is only willing to accept him as a hired hand. Their romance is rekindled, but Fonda is soon off to rescue Oates, who has been captured by the evil Darden. Fonda is killed during the rescue, but Oates goes back to Bloom and takes Fonda's place.

Zsigmond's superb photography conveys much of the lyrical quality of the story but the screenplay by Sharp (NIGHT MOVES) falls short by comparison. Fonda's lack of expertise cannot compensate directorially; the cliches of the genre require a more artful hand, and his dual commitments keep him from developing a sympathetic hero that justifies audience focus.

HIRED WIFE

1940 95m bw ★★★
Comedy /A
Seiter

Rosalind Russell (*Kendal Browning*), Brian Aherne (*Stephen Dexter*), Virginia Bruce (*Phyllis Walden*), Robert Benchley (*Van Horn*), John Carroll (*Jose*), Hobart Cavanaugh (*William*), Richard Lane (*McNab*), Leonard Carey (*Peterson*), William B. Davidson (*Mumford*), Selmer Jackson (*Hudson*)

p, Glenn Tryon; d, William A. Seiter; w, Richard Connell, Gladys Lehman (based on a story by George Beck); ph, Milton Krasner; ed, Milton Carruth; art d, Jack Otterson

The oft-told tale of the secretary who falls in love with her boss is given sleek rendering in this romantic comedy. Russell is the extraordinarily efficient secretary of Aherne, a rather dim cement tycoon. She runs his office and wants to run his home also. However, he is infatuated with a beautiful model, Bruce. When Aherne has to get married so he can put his business assets in his wife's name because rivals want to bankrupt him, Russell and Bruce battle for Aherne's last name. The trival pursuit is putty in Roz's talented hands. With Robert Benchley.

HIRELING, THE

1973 95m c   ★★★½
Drama   PG
World Film/Champion   (U.K.)

Robert Shaw (*Leadbetter*), Sarah Miles (*Lady Franklin*), Peter Egan (*Cantrip*), Elizabeth Sellars (*Mother*), Caroline Mortimer (*Connie*), Patricia Lawrence (*Mrs. Hansen*), Petra Markham (*Edith*), Ian Hogg (*Davis*), Christine Hargreaves (*Doreen*), Lyndon Brook

p, Ben Arbeid; d, Alan Bridges; w, Wolf Mankowitz (based on a novel by L.P. Hartley); ph, Michael Reed; ed, Peter Weatherley; m, Marc Wilkinson; prod d, Natasha Kroll; cos, Phyllis Dalton

A fine British drama that insightfully examines class barriers in England, adapted from the L.P. Hartley novel.

The story is set in 1923 and details the close relationship of a wealthy young widow, Miles, and her hired chauffeur, Shaw. Shaw drives Miles home from a clinic where she has been convalescing from a nervous breakdown. In her fragile state of mind, she starts a love affair with Shaw, and she believes the class barriers are down. However, after she begins to recover her mental stability, the barriers rise once again. She no longer considers Shaw her equal, and when he confesses his love for her, Miles makes it clear that their relationship is an impossibility. Enraged and frustrated, Shaw attacks her expensive car, which has become the symbol of their doomed romance.

Shaw is utterly convincing as he at first reluctantly and then wholeheartedly gets involved with Miles, only to have his love spurned and his dreams dashed. He's ably matched by Miles as the dual-natured lady.

HIROSHIMA, MON AMOUR

1959 88m bw   ★★★★★
Drama/War   /X
Argos/Como/Daiei/Pathe   (France/Japan)

Emmanuelle Riva (*Elle*), Eiji Okada (*Lui*), Stella Dassas (*Mother*), Pierre Barbaud (*Father*), Bernard Fresson (*German Lover*)

p, Samy Halfon; d, Alain Resnais; w, Marguerite Duras; ph, Sacha Vierny, Michio Takahashi; ed, Henri Colpi, Jasmine Chasney, Anne Sarraute; m, Georges Delerue, Giovanni Fusco; prod d, Esaka, Mayo, Petri

It is often, and quite legitimately, said that HIROSHIMA, MON AMOUR has been as important in the development of film art as CITIZEN KANE. The first feature from Alain Resnais, pre-viously well-known for his incredibly moving documentaries, the film is adapted from a script by the French writer Marguerite Duras, one of the greatest writers of the 20th century, and the combination of Duras's text and Resnais's blend of sound and image makes for a film that is completely modern.

The story, which manages to be both complex (in its manipulation of past and present) and simple (it focuses on a very brief love affair), concerns a married Japanese architect (Eiji Okada) and a married French actress (Emmanuelle Riva) who have a two-day affair in Hiroshima. The pain that "She" (their names are never used) feels for the dead of Hiroshima reminds her of a loss she suffered in the past, when the young German soldier whom she loved in Nevers was killed on the day that town was liberated. Castigated by her family, she was imprisoned in a dark cellar, in disgrace for having loved the enemy. Now, she projects the entire city—the bomb, the death, the suffering, and physical mutilation—onto her Japanese lover, whom she calls "Hiroshima," but knows that someday she will forget him.

Interweaving sound and image, brutal documentary footage and tender shots of lovemaking, past and present, past and remembered past, city and individual, passion and despair, Resnais creates a breathtaking picture that, like so many great works of art, can never be entirely appreciated or understood. HIROSHIMA, MON AMOUR must be felt—combining the soft loving caresses of two intertwined bodies with the burnt, blistering, peeling flesh of a dying victim of atomic warfare—and the feelings it evokes defy understanding or explanation.

HIS GIRL FRIDAY

1940 92m bw   ★★★★★
Comedy
Columbia

Cary Grant (*Walter Burns*), Rosalind Russell (*Hildy Johnson*), Ralph Bellamy (*Bruce Baldwin*), Gene Lockhart (*Sheriff Hartwell*), Helen Mack (*Mollie Malloy*), Porter Hall (*Murphy*), Ernest Truex (*Roy Bensinger*), Cliff Edwards (*Endicott*), Clarence Kolb (*Mayor*), Roscoe Karns (*McCue*)

p, Howard Hawks; d, Howard Hawks; w, Charles Lederer (based on the play by Ben Hecht, Charles MacArthur); ph, Joseph Walker; ed, Gene Havlick; m, M.W. Stoloff; art d, Lionel Banks; cos, Robert Kalloch

Perfection and possibly the fastest comedy on record. This hilarious re-working of THE FRONT PAGE by Hecht and MacArthur sees Grant as the savage editor and, in a switch, the reporter played by a scheming Russell. Instead of merely having the editor doing all in his power to keep his most brilliant reporter on staff, this version adds the twin lures of sex and romance, since Russell is Grant's ex-wife. She intends to marry again and her intended is the blatheringly innocent Bellamy, here in the quintessential Bellamy second lead. When convicted killer Qualen escapes his cell the night before he is to hang and hides in the news room of the jail—inside a rolltop desk—Grant uses the incident to entice Russell back to work. She is to write the scoop of the break, but Grant's deeper motive is to keep Russell near him so he can somehow woo her back.

The machine gun dailogue is by Charlie Lederer, Hecht's friend and sometime collaborator: Biberman, a thug working for Grant, defends his new girlfriend by saying: "She's not an albino; she was born right here in this country!" Russell calls in a report to the city desk: "Shot him right in the classified ads. . . No, 'ads'!" And there are many inside jokes. Grant criticizes Bellamy to Russell, saying he "looks like that actor. . . Ralph Bellamy!" Grant again grins as he says: "The last man that said that to me was Archie Leach just a week before he cut his throat." (Archie Leach was Grant's real name.)

The film moves at whirlwind speed, as Hawks instructed his actors to overlap their lines, so much so that at times everyone seems to be talking at once. One archivist actually timed the hurricane delivery of the actors at 240 words per minute, so fast that the dialogue is just discernible, the actors speaking about 130 words per minute above average delivery. Hawks also had his cast move at twice normal speed so the whole thing was frantic from scene to scene, thus conveying the urgency of the news world he was depicting.

HIS GIRL FRIDAY is distinctly Hawksian, bearing his trademark of madcap comedy, also brilliantly shown in BRINGING UP BABY and I WAS A MALE WAR BRIDE, both starring Grant. But FRIDAY presents Grant in a no-holds-barred comedy-bully performance. This time he's the aggressor, the persecutor as he cajoles, aggravates, intimidates, lies—sometimes he even resorts to noises in this hilariously self-centered performance. It's his greatest comedic role, proving once again the amazing versatility of this fine actor.

Russell is at her peak, too—demonstrating her own brittle breakneck speed with comedy lines and instilling an ungainly charm into Hildy's physicality. Katharine Hepburn, Jean Arthur, Margaret Sullavan, Irene Dunne, Claudette Colbert and Carole Lombard were all offered the role, but turned it down. Russell leapt at the chance to play the screwball role and it turned out to be her greatest comedy part, one which assured her immortality. The supporting cast is a Who's Who of willing comedy loons.

HIT, THE

1985   100m   c   ★★★★
Drama   R/18
Zenith   (U.K.)

Terence Stamp (Willie Parker), John Hurt (Braddock), Tim Roth (Myron), Laura del Sol (Maggie), Bill Hunter (Harry), Fernando Rey (Chief Inspector), Carlos Lucena (Uniformed Officer), Freddie Stuart, Ralph Brown, A.J. Clarke (Government Agents)

p, Jeremy Thomas; d, Stephen Frears; w, Peter Prince; ph, Mike Molloy; ed, Mick Audsley; m, Paco de Lucia, Eric Clapton; prod d, Andrew Sanders; art d, Julio Molina; fx, Alan Whibley, Reyes Abades; cos, Marit Allen

THE HIT is a very special British film that addresses one's acceptance of death and the notion that man is not inherently violent but, instead, peaceful.

The film begins in 1973 at a criminal trial in which petty crook Terence Stamp testifies against his cronies. After turning state's evidence, he is released. Cut to a quiet Spanish village ten years later. Stamp, having led a quiet, philosophical life, is flushed out of his house by a gang of thugs and handed over to John Hurt, a menacing hit man, and his assistant Tim Roth, a jumpy young punk. Stamp is hustled into Hurt's car, to be taken to Paris and executed by a mob chieftain for his testimony of ten years before. Stamp, however, doesn't seem in the least bit frightened; in fact, he seems to enjoy what is happening.

In THE HIT, director Stephen Frears works against all genre conventions—the hit man becomes emotionally involved, while the victim completely accepts his fate. The characters on the screen are not Hollywood movie heroes, but real individuals with real insecurities and doubts. Besides having a superb screenplay, Frears was blessed with an unparalleled cast. Both Hurt and Stamp are as good as they've ever been, while newcomer Roth shows great promise in a marvelously quirky role.

While receiving unanimously enthusiastic reviews, THE HIT unfortunately didn't make much of an impression on the American public. As a result most moviegoers missed one of the most energetic, intelligent, and offbeat pictures to emerge from England in many years.

HOBSON'S CHOICE

1954   107m   bw   ★★★★
Comedy   /U
London Films   (U.K.)

Charles Laughton (Henry Horatio Hobson), John Mills (Willie Mossop), Brenda de Banzie (Maggie Hobson), Daphne Anderson (Alice Hobson), Prunella Scales (Vicky Hobson), Richard Wattis (Albert Prosser), Derek Blomfield (Freddy Beenstock), Helen Haye (Mrs. Hepworth), Joseph Tomelty (Jim Heeler), Julien Mitchell (Sam Minns)

p, David Lean; d, David Lean; w, David Lean, Norman Spencer, Wynyard Browne (based on the play by Harold Brighouse); ph, Jack Hildyard; ed, Peter Taylor; m, Malcolm Arnold; prod d, Wilfred Shingleton; cos, John Armstrong

Laughton is marvelous in this wry comedy as the crusty old curmudgeon who rules his profitable boot shop and his three unmarried daughters with an iron hand. He hypocritically downs his pints of ale at the local pub and cries out against the inhumanity of life at leaving him a widower. His eldest daughter, de Banzie, is 30 and, in Laughton's words, "on the shelf." Undaunted, she finds herself a husband in the form of the self-effacing, illiterate, and ambitionless Mills, Laughton's assistant and chief bootmaker for the firm.

Mills is a bit dumbfounded when being led to the altar and even more puzzled when de Banzie sets him up in his own bootmaking business after Laughton refuses to award de Banzie a dowry. With de Banzie brainstorming the business, Mills's shop grows and he prospers, so much so that he begins to make inroads into Laughton's once dominant operation.

This is a fully developed comedy of human foibles and follies with Laughton rendering a masterful, sly performance, beautifully supported by de Banzie and Mills. Laughton, who played the role on stage years earlier, was reputedly unhappy on the set; he developed a dislike for de Banzie (who, incredibly, almost upstages Laughton, himself a consummate upstager) and he didn't care for Mills in the role of Willie Mossop, a part he'd wanted Robert Donat to play. Lean's direction is careful and properly mannered as he draws forth one poignant scene after another, some painful, others full of mirth.

Arnold's inventive score adds considerable charm to this best of three versions of Harold Brighouse's 1915 stage comedy (filmed in 1920 as a silent with Arthur Pitt and Joan Ritz, and again as a talkie in 1931 with James Harcourt and Viola Lyel). This film rightly won the Best British Film Award in 1954.

HOLD BACK THE DAWN

1941   115m   bw   ★★★★
Romance   /A
Paramount

Charles Boyer (Georges Iscovescu), Olivia de Havilland (Emmy Brown), Paulette Goddard (Anita Dixon), Victor Francen (Van Den Luecken), Walter Abel (Inspector Hammock), Curt Bois (Bonbois), Rosemary DeCamp (Berta Kurz), Eric Feldary (Josef Kurz), Nestor Paiva (Flores), Eva Puig (Lupita)

p, Arthur Hornblow, Jr.; d, Mitchell Leisen; w, Charles Brackett, Billy Wilder (based on a story by Ketti Frings); ph, Leo Tover; ed, Doane Harrison; m, Victor Young; art d, Hans Dreier, Robert Usher; cos, Edith Head

A touching and memorable film, this brilliant romance offers evocative performances by Boyer and de Havilland. It opens with a typical Wilder twist: Leisen, shown on the set of I WANTED WINGS, directing a scene with Brian Donlevy and Veronica Lake, is approached by Romanian gigolo Boyer, a one-time European dancer and ladies' escort. Boyer wants to sell movie director Leisen a story for $500. He then fascinates the director with the tale that is HOLD BACK THE DAWN, played out in flashback.

Boyer, stranded in a Mexican border town, lives in a rundown hotel, the Esperanza, which houses all manner of human driftwood from Europe, refugees from Nazi oppression, not the least of whom is Francen, a Dutch professor who acts as a sort of father confessor to the disenfranchised. One pathetic emigre is Rosemary DeCamp, a pregnant refugee who slips across the border to have her child in the US. Visiting the area with her students is American schoolteacher de Havilland, who becomes Boyer's easy victim in a matrimonial-immigration scam suggested by vixen Goddard.

Unabashed soppy soaper, but Leisen's pro touch and sensitive direction keep it from ever becoming maudlin. DAWN exploits the darkly sexy side of Boyer and the mechanistic side of Goddard quite well; the screenplay by Brackett and Wilder is beautifully written, covering for any loopholes in the de Havilland role. The characters were drawn from the life of story writer Frings and her struggle to get her immigrant husband Kurt into the US via Mexico. There is much here that calls to mind ARCH OF TRIUMPH, also starring Boyer, who always felt that HOLD BACK THE DAWN was one of his best films.

HOLIDAY FOR HENRIETTA
(LA FETE A HENRIETTE)
1955 118m bw   ★★★★
Comedy
Regina/Filmsonor   (France)

Dany Robin (Henriette), Hildegarde Neff (Rita Solar), Michel Auclair (Maurice/Marcel), Michel Roux (Robert), Louis Seigner, Henri Cremieux (Script Writers), Daniel Ivernel (Detective), Micheline Francey (Script Girl), Saturnin Fabre (Man in Cafe), Paulette Dubost (Mother)

d, Julien Duvivier; w, Henri Jeanson, Julien Duvivier; ph, Roger Hubert; ed, Marthe Poncin; m, Georges Auric

Charming comedy that was remade nine years later into a slapdash film called PARIS WHEN IT SIZZLES. Seigner and Cremieux are two screenwriters who are crushed when their newest work is snipped to bits by censors. They begin to improvise a story about Robin, a dressmaker in Paris, with two very different versions being dreamed up by each as one of them favors noir and the other rose. Cremieux concocts a sleazy melodrama while Seigner thinks up a story of love, naivete, and warmth. The film gets written with a wild culmination on Bastille Day. Then their balloon is burst when Auclair, an actor, informs them that someone else has already written that story.

A whimsical satire of movies with Duvivier employing many cinematic techniques to make his point, the film is clever and eye-catching; one wishes it had been released widely in the US before the dull remake. Robin began her show-business career as a ballerina with the Paris Opera and only had a few credits in

English-speaking films—WALTZ OF THE TOREADORS, FOLLOW THE BOYS, TOPAZ, and THE BEST HOUSE IN LONDON being the most prominent. Costar Neff made films in France, Germany, England, and the US before appearing on Broadway in Cole Porter's Silk Stockings and then becoming a writer. Her two most famous books were The Gift Horse, her autobiography, and The Verdict, a highly personal account of her struggle against cancer.

HOLIDAY INN
1942 100m bw   ★★★
Musical/Comedy   /U
Paramount

Bing Crosby (Jim Hardy), Fred Astaire (Ted Hanover), Marjorie Reynolds (Linda Mason), Virginia Dale (Lila Dixon), Walter Abel (Danny Reid), Louise Beavers (Mamie), John Gallaudet (Parker), James Bell (Dunbar), Irving Bacon (Gus), Shelby Bacon (Vanderbilt)

p, Mark Sandrich; d, Mark Sandrich; w, Claude Binyon, Elmer Rice (based on an idea by Irving Berlin); ph, David Abel; ed, Ellsworth Hoagland; art d, eans Dreier, Roland Anderson; chor, Danny Dare; cos, Edith Head

Dowdy and thin. Based on an idea by Irving Berlin, this is a small musical about a song-and-dance man, Jim Hardy (Bing Crosby), who retires from the biz to become a gentleman farmer in New England, finds country life more demanding than he thought, and tries to have best of both worlds when he turns his farm into a very special hostelry that's only open to the public on national holidays. The film's highlight is a bang-up July 4th "Let's Say It with Firecrackers" that finds Astaire in fine form, Crosby sings "White Christmas" for the first time, and the score includes "Easter Parade." But the girls are duds and the film lacks festivity, showbiz pizzazz, flash. Decidedly improved upon as 1954's WHITE CHRISTMAS.

HOLLYWOOD BOULEVARD
1976 83m c   ★★★
Comedy   R/18
New World

Candice Rialson (Candy Wednesday), Mary Woronov (Mary McQueen), Rita George (Bobbi Quackenbush), Jeffrey Kramer (Patrick Hobby), Dick Miller (Walter Paisley), Richard Doran (Producer), Tara Strohmeier (Jill McBain), Paul Bartel (Erich Von Leppe), John Kramer (Duke Mantee), Jonathan Kaplan (Scotty)

p, Jon Davison; d, Joe Dante, Allan Arkush; w, Patrick Hobby; ph, Jamie Anderson (Metrocolor); ed, Amy Jones, Allan Arkush, Joe Dante; m, Andrew Stein; art d, Jack DeWolfe; fx, Roger George; cos, Jane Rum

Totally shameless but self-accepting parody of the schlock movie business and Roger Corman's B-factory, New World Pictures. Rialson is a would-be actress who wants stardom. Her agent, Miller, sends her to Miracle Pictures, where she lands a role in the studio's latest epic, MACHETE MAIDENS OF MARATAU. But actress Woronov doesn't like competition, and suddenly there is a series of murders. The film ends with a shootout atop the famous Hollywood sign. HOLLYWOOD BOULEVARD is that rarest of creatures: a parody of a parody that actually is funny and works well. Not to be missed by camp fans.

HOLLYWOOD CANTEEN
1944 124m bw   ★★★
Musical/Comedy   /U
WB

Robert Hutton (Slim), Dane Clark (Sergeant), Janis Paige (Angela), Jonathan Hale (Mr. Brodel), Barbara Brown (Mrs. Brodel), Mark Stevens, Richard Erdman (Soldiers on Deck), James Flavin (Marine Sergeant), Eddie Marr (Dance Director), Theodore von Eltz (Director)

p, Alex Gottlieb; d, Delmer Daves; w, Delmer Daves; ph, Bert Glennon; ed, Christian Nyby; m, Ray Heindorf; art d, Leo K. Kuter; chor, LeRoy Prinz; cos, Milo Anderson

Patriotic pap, but so what? Director Daves had a smash with STAGE DOOR CANTEEN and followed it quickly with this film, one of those patriotic displays of self-congratulation WWII Hollywood was so good at.

The plot lies like a feather. After being wounded fighting in the Pacific, Hutton, a young soldier, returns to the US on leave and visits the Hollywood Canteen with his best pal (Dane Clark). The Canteen is tended by John Garfield, Bette Davis, and a host of other stars playing themselves, and when some of them learn of Hutton's crush on actress Joan Leslie, a phony raffle is arranged and Hutton wins first prize—a kiss from Leslie. Later Hutton really hits the jackpot when he is counted the one-millionth serviceman to enter the Canteen. His prize is a night in Hollywood with any actress he wants. On the big night, Leslie doesn't show up; however, she appears at Union Station, where Hutton prepares to leave for reassignment, explaining that she ran out of gas, professing her love for the young GI, and promising that she'll await his return.

The movie is overloaded with talent, much of it ill-used, with a list of songs almost as long as the cast. Best bits: Jack Benny, Greenstreet and Lorre, and the unflappably cheery Andrews Sisters, singing patriotic-bounce ballads like "Gettin' Corns for My Country." Anyway, good-natured as all get out.

HOME ALONE
1990 98m c   ★★½
Comedy   PG
Hughes

Macaulay Culkin (Kevin McCallister), Joe Pesci (Harry), Daniel Stern (Marv), John Heard (Peter), Roberts Blossom (Marley), Catherine O'Hara (Kate), Angela Goethals (Linnie), Devin Rattray (Buzz), Gerry Bamman (Uncle Frank), Hillary Wolf (Megan)

p, John Hughes; d, Chris Columbus; w, John Hughes; ph, Julio Macat; ed, Raja Gosnell; m, John Williams; prod d, John Muto; art d, Dan Webster; fx, Bill Purcell; cos, Jay Hurley

HOME ALONE was not only the most commercially successful release of 1990 but the highest grossing comedy of all time. It also made a star out of a ten-year-old kid named Macaulay Culkin. As is usual for a John Hughes film, the movie is set in northsuburban Chicago, opening with a huge gathering at the McCallister household on the eve of the family's departure for a Christmas vacation in Europe. Eight-year-old Kevin McCallister (Culkin) is the object of everyone's scorn (he's constantly referred to as a "dweeb" or a "jerk") and even gets mistakenly blamed for a disastrous spill in the kitchen. Exiled to his room by his mother (Catherine O'Hara), Kevin fatefully wishes that his family would "all disappear."

The next morning, he awakens to find himself all alone in the house, and, filled with guilt that he may have wished his family members away, he runs to his parents' room where he cowers under the covers of their bed. In truth, the rest of the McCallister clan is on a plane heading for Europe, unaware that Kevin has been left behind. When Kevin's mother finally realizes he's missing, she frantically begins making arrangements to get back to him. Kevin, however, is starting to adapt to his solitude and begins to do things he could never get away with if his parents were home.

Soon the responsibilities of being alone in an adult world start to take their toll, and Kevin must learn to shop, cook and clean the house. He starts to enjoy his responsibilities, taking pride in his daily accomplishments and becoming as much of an adult as an eight-year-old who is still afraid of the basement furnace can be. The imaginary threat posed by the furnace soon gives way to a very real danger when a pair of bumbling burglars (Joe Pesci and Daniel Stern) set their sights on breaking into the McCallister residence. In defending the homestead, Kevin proves to be an extraordinarily clever and resourceful little fellow as he arranges an elaborate system of booby traps that successfully thwarts the thieves.

The first half of HOME ALONE features the sugar-coated sentimentality that can usually be found in a Hughes film, while the second half is full of unanticipated sadism. There is nothing funny about watching two men being systematically tortured and maimed for 20 minutes. (A close-up of Stern's bare foot slipping slowly down a six-inch nail is the film's most ghastly image.) As directed by Chris Columbus (HEARTBREAK HOTEL), the film's slapstick falls flat and only the pain remains. Yet the film's message seems even more disturbing than its violence. This could be the first comedy—it's certainly the first holiday film—which focuses on child abuse. As Kevin shoots pellets into the intruders and takes a blowtorch to their heads, he's directing the hostility he feels toward his neglectful parents at these two guys. It seems that in addition to the other responsibilities he has to assume as he tries to function in the adult world, he must also become abusive—it's all part of growing up. The only really likable thing about this film is Culkin (UNCLE BUCK, JACOB'S LADDER). He's an uncommonly natural child actor, but even he doesn't always survive the tiresome gags (him shaving once is funny; three times is tedious).

HOME AND THE WORLD, THE
(GHARE BAIRE)
1984 140m c   ★★★
Drama   /U
Natl. Film Dev. Corp. of India   (India)

Soumitra Chatterjee (Sandip Mukherjee), Victor Banerjee (Nikhilesh Choudhury), Swatilekha Chatterjee (Bimala Choudhury), Manoj Mitra (Headmaster), Indrapramit Roy (Amulya), Bimala Chatterjee (Kulada)

d, Satyajit Ray; w, Satyajit Ray (based on the novel by Rabindranath Tagore); ph, Soumendu Roy (Eastmancolor); ed, Dulal Dutta; m, Satyajit Ray; art d, Ashoke Bose

This graceful film by Ray is as much a tragic love story as an examination of political turmoil in 1908 India. Banerjee stars as a highly educated Hindu who lives with his wife, Swatilekha Chatterjee, in colonial East Bengal. Political tension grows when Lord Curzon, the British governor-general of India, enacts a plan to "divide and rule" the Hindus and Muslims. Because of the resulting unrest, Soumitra Chatterjee, a fiery rebel and friend of Banerjee, pays a visit to the town. Not convinced that his wife truly loves him, Banerjee encourages his wife to come out of purdah (orthodox seclusion) to meet other men, namely his rebellious friend. If she remains faithful after having met others,

Banerjee reasons, he can be certain of her love. His plan backfires, however, when his wife falls in love with the rebel.

What's more, political differences arise between the two men. Based on a novel by Nobel Prize-winning author Tagore, THE HOME AND THE WORLD was to have come to the screen 30 years earlier as Ray's first film. Tagore, a friend of Ray's family, had published his book in 1919 to much acclaim; and Ray, who had only a passing interest in film at the time, read the book and wrote a screenplay based on it. It wasn't until 1980, however, that the great Indian filmmaker returned to the project.

HOMECOMING, THE

1973 111m c ★★★★
Drama PG/AA
American Film Theatre

Cyril Cusack (Sam), Ian Holm (Lenny), Michael Jayston (Teddy), Vivien Merchant (Ruth), Terence Rigby (Joey), Paul Rogers (Max)

p, Ely A. Landau; d, Peter Hall; w, Harold Pinter (based on his play); ph, David Watkin; ed, Rex Pike; prod d, John Bury; art d, Jack Stevens; cos, Elizabeth Haffenden, Joan Bridge

Excellent adaptation of the Pinter play for the American Film Theatre series of the early 1970s. The simple plot features Jayston returning to his childhood home with wife Merchant. There he sees his father (Rogers), uncle (Cusack), and his brothers (Holm and Rigby), who are a pimp and boxer, respectively. The small family is held together by volatile fighting, boredom, and ultimate dependency on one another. Each performance is a gem. The individual quirks of each character are well-executed and utterly believable. Hall's direction is sensitive to Pinter's script and to the acting of the ensemble (who all played in the original 1965 stage production). There is a magical chemistry within every frame of this powerful, unforgettable film.

HOMICIDE

1991 102m c ★★★½
Crime/Drama R/15
Cinehaus Inc./Edward R. Pressman Corporation

Joe Mantegna (Bobby Gold), William H. Macy (Tim Sullivan), Natalija Nogulich (Chava), Ving Rhames (Randolph), Rebecca Pidgeon (Miss Klein), Vincent Guastaferro (Senna), Lionel Mark Smith (Olcott), Jack Wallace (Frank), J.J. Johnston (Curren), Paul Butler (Deputy Mayor Walker)

p, Michael Hausman, Edward R. Pressman; d, David Mamet; w, David Mamet; ph, Roger Deakins; ed, Barbara Tulliver; m, Alaric Jans; prod d, Michael Merritt; art d, Susan Kaufman; cos, Nan Cibula

In his previous films, 1987's HOUSE OF GAMES and the following year's THINGS CHANGE, acclaimed American playwright David Mamet danced around the edges of film genres. In the controversial HOMICIDE he tackles the police melodrama and subtly renders it into a disturbingly bleak statement of American urban life in the 1990s.

Involved in tracking down Randolph (Ving Rhames), an escaped black drug dealer, police homicide detective Bobby Gold (Joe Mantegna), a lapsed Jew, and his partner Tim Sullivan (William H. Macy) stumble onto a crime scene in a black ghetto where an elderly Jewish woman has been murdered in her corner candy store. Pressured by her arrogant, politically connected family, headed by Dr. Klein (J.S. Bloch) and his daughter (Rebecca Pidgeon), who believe the murder was part of an organized anti-Semitic plot, Lieutenant Senna (Vincent Guastaferro) places the protesting, scoffing Gold in charge of the investigation.

The cultured, mansion-ensconced Kleins, whose wealth Gold resents, badger the detective for his lack of Jewish identity, and Gold soon discovers that Mrs. Klein may have years ago been a conduit for weapons for Jewish activists and that the ghetto area is plagued by the activities of an anti-Semitic organization. Gold is increasingly troubled by his own lack of Jewishness. Jewish terrorist Chava's (Natalija Nogulich) group is pressuring him for a list, now logged as police evidence, of the individuals to whom Mrs. Klein's guns were delivered. Gold begs Chava to let him help her destroy the headquarters of anti-Semites, filled with Nazi memorabilia. But he's photographed by his terrorist cohorts setting off the explosion, and they blackmail him for the list.

Mamet's central concern in all his plays (Sexual Perversity in Chicago, American Buffalo, Speed-The-Plow, and the Pulitzer Prize-winning Glengarry Glen Ross, among others) and films has been problems of identity. Here Detective Gold, whose life is defined by his work, is suddenly confronted and must come to terms with his long-submerged Jewish roots, a personal process that violently interferes with his coolly precise and efficient professional life and ultimately results in his professional ruin.

Seldom has a film so powerfully or intricately dealt with racism in American life: black to Italian to Irish to Jewish and all their permutations, which Mamet mainly examines, beyond the boundaries of plot, in his wholly idiosyncratic, superbly controlled, creatively obscene dialogue. If directors like Scorsese have an identifying personal visual style, Mamet has a verbal one. HOMICIDE splendidly features what has become an unofficial stock company of actors who are expert at delivering Mamet's staccato rhythmed, colorful, often sharply funny lines.

Co-produced by the veteran, influential Edward R. Pressman, who nurtured De Palma, Malick, and Oliver Stone, among others, and Mamet's usual producer Michael Hausman, HOMICIDE, with its title both metaphorical and realistic, is Mamet's most personal film to date, a powerful but despairing view of the pervasiveness of ethnic and racial hatred in which America has been and perhaps always will be inextricably mired.

HONEY, I SHRUNK THE KIDS

1989 86m c ★★★
Children's/Science Fiction PG/U
Disney

Rick Moranis (Prof. Wayne Szalinski), Matt Frewer (Big Russ Thompson), Marcia Strassman (Diane Szalinski), Kristine Sutherland (Mae Thompson), Thomas Brown (Little Russ Thompson), Jared Rushton (Ron Thompson), Amy O'Neill (Amy Szalinski), Robert Oliveri (Nick Szalinski), Carl Steven (Tommy Pervis), Mark L. Taylor (Don Forrester)

p, Penney Finkelman Cox, Brian Yuzna, Jon Landau; d, Joe Johnston; w, Ed Naha, Tom Schulman (based on a story by Stuart Gordon, Yuzna, Naha); ph, Hiro Narita (Metrocolor); ed, Michael A. Stevenson; m, James Horner; prod d, Gregg Fonseca; art d, John Iacovelli, Dorree Cooper; cos, Carol Brolaski

Reminiscent of earlier Disney live-action classics like THE ABSENT-MINDED PROFESSOR and SON OF FLUBBER, HONEY, I SHRUNK THE KIDS provides a wonderful blend of thrills, character, and humor that will keep both children and adults charmed and engaged throughout.

Rick Moranis stars as Prof. Wayne Szalinski, a nutty inventor who is trying to create a machine that will shrink living things. When the professor's kids—teenage daughter Amy (Amy O'Neil) and little brother Nick (Robert Oliveri)—and two of their friends (Thomas Brown, Jared Rushton) accidentally activate the machine, they are all shrunk to quarter-inch size. So begins their dangerous adventure from the trash can, where the professor has unknowingly put them, through the seemingly gargantuan back yard, to what they hope will be the safety of the house.

Based on a story by Stuart Gordon (RE-ANIMATOR), Brian Yuzna and Ed Naha, HONEY, I SHRUNK THE KIDS was to have been directed by Gordon, but, after conflicts with the studio, he was replaced by special-effects man Joe Johnston (making his directorial debut). Espousing values of decency and tolerance between its terrific action sequences, HONEY harkens back to Disney's past. Consistently exciting, inventive and fun, the film is a rollicking good adventure, with enough bravura effects to keep the most hyperactive youngster interested. Fittingly, Buena Vista's best release since WHO FRAMED ROGER RABBIT? was coupled with a brand new Roger Rabbit cartoon short, TUMMY TROUBLE, the first animated short produced by the Disney studio in over 25 years.

HONEYMOON KILLERS, THE

1969   115m   bw   ★★★½
Crime   R/18
Roxanne

Shirley Stoler (Martha Beck), Tony Lo Bianco (Ray Fernandez), Mary Jane Higby (Janet Fay), Doris Roberts (Bunny), Kip McArdle (Delphine Downing), Marilyn Chris (Myrtle Young), Dortha Duckworth (Mrs. Beck), Barbara Cason (Evelyn Long), Ann Harris (Doris), Mary Breen (Rainelle Downing)

p, Warren Steibel; d, Leonard Kastle; w, Leonard Kastle; ph, Oliver Wood; ed, Stanley Warnow, Richard Brophy; m, Gustav Mahler

A remarkable low-budget film that offers a chilling portrait of a pair of cold-blooded murderers. Stoler is a lonely, sexually frustrated, 200-pound nurse at a Mobile, Alabama, hospital. She lives alone with her mother, which only adds to her frustration. In desperation she joins a lonelyhearts correspondence club and soon begins receiving torrid love letters from Lo Bianco, a Spanish immigrant in New York. When he comes to visit Stoler, she quickly falls in love with him.

When he steals money from her and leaves, she tracks him down and finds that he makes his living stealing from love-starved women he finds through the correspondence clubs. She loves him nonetheless, and after she is fired from her job, she puts her mother in a nursing home and heads off with Lo Bianco in search of new victims. Stoler poses as Lo Bianco's sister while he woos lonely women and then flees with their money. But when Lo Bianco marries Chris to give her baby a father, a jealous Stoler turns to murder.

Based on an actual case that got much press in the late 1940s, THE HONEYMOON KILLERS is shot in stark black-and-white documentary style and the music of Mahler is effective in counterpointing the action. The acting is second to none: the two leads are frighteningly good in their psychotic roles and supporting characters are also well dileneated. But there are some technical problems with the film, notably too much shadow in the frame, several highly visible microphones and the choppy editing, which jumbles the story at times.

Still, the straightforwardness of the telling is not totally destroyed. To their credit the filmmakers have refused to romanticize the brutality of the criminals at the heart of the film. Lo Bianco went on to star in other pictures; Stoler's other major role was as the brutal Nazi prison camp commandant in Lina Wertmuller's marvelous SEVEN BEAUTIES.

HOOK

1991   144m   c   ★★★
Fantasy/Adventure   PG/U
Hook Productions/Amblin Entertainment

Dustin Hoffman (Captain James Hook), Robin Williams (Peter Banning/Peter Pan), Julia Roberts (Tinkerbell), Bob Hoskins (Smee), Maggie Smith (Granny Wendy Darling), Caroline Goodall (Moira Banning), Charlie Korsmo (Jack Banning), Amber Scott (Maggie), Laurel Cronin (Liza), Phil Collins (Inspector Good)

p, Kathleen Kennedy, Frank Marshall, Gerald R. Molen; d, Steven Spielberg; w, Jim V. Hart, Malia Scotch Marmo (from the story by Hart and Nick Castle, adapted from the original stage play and books by Sir James M. Barrie); ph, Dean Cundey; ed, Michael Kahn; m, John Williams; prod d, Norman Garwood; art d, Andrew Precht, Thomas E. Sanders; fx, Michael Lantieri; chor, Vince Paterson; cos, Anthony Powell

On paper, HOOK looked promising. It boasted the high-concept idea of a grown-up Peter Pan, directed by Hollywood's perennial child-man Steven Spielberg. And thanks to a lucrative deal brokered by Creative Artists Agency, the film featured a cast of truly stellar proportions; Dustin Hoffman, Robin Williams, and Julia Roberts. It all seemed too good to be true. Well, it was.

Peter Banning (Williams) is a hard-nosed workaholic merger and buyout king. He cares about his wife, Moira (Caroline Goodall), and family, but is too consumed by his career to pay enough attention to them, missing his son Jack's (Charlie Korsmo) important baseball game and his daughter Maggie's (Amber Scott) appearance in a school production of Peter Pan. However, he takes time to make a Christmas trip with his family to visit his wife's grandmother, Granny Wendy Darling (Maggie Smith), in London, where she's being honored for her work with the Great Ormond Street Children's Hospital. His children are excited by the prospect of meeting her, as they know she was the Wendy on whom J.M. Barrie based the heroine of Peter Pan. Peter spends all his time there on the phone, trying to supervise a buyout, but matters are dramatically interrupted when his children are kidnapped, with only a rip along the wallpaper and a strange parchment as clues. That night, Peter is visited by Tinkerbell (Roberts) who tries to convince Peter that he is—or used to be—Peter Pan and that his children have been kidnapped by the evil Captain Hook (Hoffman). This seven-inch-fairy also insists that he has no choice but to return with her to Neverland to reclaim them.

One of the most eagerly awaited—and expensively hyped—releases of 1991, HOOK is not entirely devoid of entertainment value. Yet it's impossible to walk away from the film without a feeling of regret that this talented group of artists couldn't have accomplished more. The problems begin with the screenplay, a clumsy attempt to meld reality and fantasy which leaves too many issues unresolved and repeatedly assaults the viewer with wishy-washy, New Age philosophy about the importance of preserving the "inner child."

The casting also has its flaws. Hoffman turns in a casually goofy performance as the captain, but Roberts is seriously out of place playing a pixie. Williams, too, seems a bland presence, having played far more genuinely free-spirited roles in many other movies. Hoskins' hammy performance as Smee shows how much he learned from his animated co-stars in WHO FRAMED ROGER RABBIT.

The biggest disappointment, though, is Spielberg's direction; instead of youthful ebullience, we get lots of cutesy slapstick violence. And though the Neverland sets are among the most spectacular ever built, the onscreen bustle is inadequately choreographed. Our eyes are confounded, rather than delighted, by the constant, chaotic activity. As top-heavy as Captain Hook's ornate, immobile ship, this lavish, elaborate production ultimately collapses under its own weight.

HOOSIERS

1986   114m   c   ★★★½
Sports   PG
Hemdale

Gene Hackman (Coach Norman Dale), Barbara Hershey (Myra Fleener), Dennis Hopper (Shooter), Sheb Wooley (Cletus), Fern Persons (Opal Fleener), Brad Boyle (Whit), Steve Hollar (Rade), Brad Long (Strap), David Neidorf (Everett), Kent Poole (Merle)

p, Carter DeHaven, Angelo Pizzo; d, David Anspaugh; w, Angelo Pizzo; ph, Fred Murphy (CFI Color); ed, C. Timothy O'Meara; m, Jerry Goldsmith; prod d, David Nichols; art d, David Lubin; cos, Jane E. Anderson

It should come as little surprise that the best movie ever made about basketball, HOOSIERS, is set in Indiana, where babies are given roundballs before they get rattles.

Loosely based on the true story of the team from tiny Milan High School (164 students), which won the 1954 Indiana state championship, this uplifting film, set in 1951, follows Norman Dale (Gene Hackman), a big-time college coach who has fallen from grace, in his leadership of the Hickory, Indiana, high-school basketball team to victory. Jimmy (Maris Valanis), the town's most gifted player, is so disturbed by the death of the previous coach that he declines to join the team, but Norman refuses to pressure him into doing so, earning the reluctant respect of Myra Fleener (Barbara Hershey), the acting principal.

Norman also remains determined to run the team *his* way, despite the animosity of the townspeople, who in the past have felt free to offer advice. With the expert help of Shooter (Dennis Hopper, in an Oscar-nominated performance that is one of the finest of his career), the alcoholic father of one of the players, Norman perseveres, and Jimmy decides to play after all.

Bursting with emotion and full of exhilarating game action, HOOSIERS magnificently captures the ambience of small-town Indiana basketball—but more than that, it tells a universal story of pride, courage, love and redemption. David Anspaugh's direction is assured, Fred Murphy's cinematography and Jerry Goldsmith's score masterful and the performances are uniformly strong.

HOPALONG CASSIDY

1935   60m   bw   ★★★
Western
Paramount

William Boyd (Bill Cassidy), James Ellison (Johnny Nelson), Paula Stone (Mary Meeker), Robert Warwick (Jim Meeker), Charles Middleton (Buck Peters), Frank McGlynn, Jr. (Red Connors), Kenneth Thomson (Pecos Jack Anthony), George "Gabby" Hayes (Uncle Ben), James Mason (Tom Shaw), Frank Campeau (Frisco)

p, Harry Sherman; d, Howard Bretherton; w, Doris Schroeder, Harrison Jacobs (based on a story by Clarence E. Mulford); ph, Archie Stout; ed, Edward Schroeder

The first of the HOPALONG CASSIDY oaters in what became one of the longest-running series of Westerns in the history of movies and made an international star of the nearly washed-up silent actor William Boyd.

Boyd, youngster Ellison, and McGlynn, Jr. try to prevent a range war between two cattlemen which is instigated by an evil ranch foreman who plays both sides against the middle and helps an outlaw gang snatch the cattle. The scheme succeeds because each side blames the other for the missing stock. Eventually, with Boyd's help, both ranchers wise up, and they combine their efforts, sending a small army of cowboys into the gang's mountain hideout where justice eventually triumphs.

Independent producer Sherman bought the rights to Clarence E. Mulford's series of "Bar 20" western novels which featured a grizzled, tough-talking, hard-drinking, slightly crippled old cowboy named Hopalong Cassidy. When producer Sherman asked Boyd to play the ranch foreman, he refused but agreed to play Cassidy if the character was rewritten to be a clean-living, noble hero. (The limp was also abandoned after the first few movies, leaving the name "Hopalong" something of a mystery years later.) The result was a seemingly unending string of Westerns. After 50 films, Sherman sold out his ownership to Boyd, who saw the series to its eventual conclusion and its 1950s TV craze.

HOPE AND GLORY

1987   113m   c   ★★★★½
Comedy/Drama/War   PG-13/15
Columbia   (U.K.)

Sebastian Rice-Edwards (Bill Rohan), Geraldine Muir (Sue Rohan), Sarah Miles (Grace Rohan), David Hayman (Clive Rohan), Sammi Davis (Dawn Rohan), Derrick O'Connor (Mac), Susan Wooldridge (Molly), Jean-Marc Barr (Cpl. Bruce Carey), Ian Bannen (George), Annie Leon (Bill's Grandmother)

p, John Boorman, Michael Dryhurst; d, John Boorman; w, John Boorman; ph, Philippe Rousselot, John Harris (Eastmancolor); ed, Ian Crafford; m, Peter Martin; prod d, Anthony Pratt; art d, Don Dossett; fx, Rodney Fuller, Michael Collins, Phil Stokes; chor, Anthony Van Laast; cos, Shirley Russell

HOPE AND GLORY is a wonderful film, an intelligent, heartfelt, personal, and marvelously entertaining look at what it was like to grow up in wartorn England.

A semiautobiographical project from British director John Boorman, the film depicts nine-year-old Bill (Sebastian Rice-Edwards) as he experiences the wonders of WWII from his suburban London home. While Americans may find it somewhat disconcerting to see the Blitz and its horrors made the setting for a nostalgic comedy, for Boorman's young boy the war was a particularly exciting and vivid time, and a joyous feeling permeates the film. The total upheaval of the staid family order, the lack of normal restrictions and discipline, and the liberating effect the war had on women are all brilliantly conveyed by Boorman, because he views the war from a child's perspective.

Told in a series of vignettes, HOPE AND GLORY unfolds in a surprisingly nonchalant manner, dispensing its vividly realized observations at every turn. Boorman skillfully combines nuggets of truth with moments of mirth and is always prepared to surprise and amuse without sentimentalizing.

HOPSCOTCH

1980   104m   c   ★★★½
Comedy/Spy   R/15
Avco Embassy

Walter Matthau (Miles Kendig), Glenda Jackson (Isobel von Schmidt), Sam Waterston (Cutter), Ned Beatty (Myerson), Herbert Lom (Mikhail Yaskov), David Matthau (Ross), George Baker (Westlake), Ivor Roberts (Ludlum), Lucy Saroyan (Carla), Severn Darden (Maddox)

p, Edie Landau, Ely Landau; d, Ronald Neame; w, Brian Garfield, Bryan Forbes (based on the novel by Garfield); ph, Arthur Ibbetson (Movielab Color); ed, Carl Kress; m, Ian Fraser; prod d, William J. Creber

This well-crafted comedy concerns top-drawer CIA agent Miles Kendig (Walter Matthau), who is demoted to managing the office files by his bureaucratic boss (Ned Beatty). Miles takes off for Europe and meets Mikhail Yaskov (Herbert Lom), an old friend and Soviet agent, who suggests Miles write his memoirs. Taken with the idea, Miles flies off to Salzburg and meets Isobel von Schmidt (Glenda Jackson), an old flame who is also a former agent. She provides support as he begins writing a book that will expose the secrets of world espionage.

A thoroughly entertaining picture, HOPSCOTCH is based on a serious spy novel. The casting of Matthau, however, changed that premise, and the film's most enjoyable aspect is his character's playfulness as he turns the CIA on its head. An unlikely pair, Matthau and Jackson build on the interesting chemistry they developed in HOUSE CALLS. If it's a classically styled throwback to Hollywood espionage films of the 1940s and 1950s you're looking for, HOPSCOTCH is it.

HORROR OF DRACULA, THE

1958   82m   c   ★★★★
Horror
Hammer   (U.K.)

Peter Cushing (Van Helsing), Michael Gough (Arthur Holmwood), Melissa Stribling (Mina Holmwood), Christopher Lee (Count Dracula), Carol Marsh (Lucy), John Van Eyssen (Jonathan Harker), Miles Malleson (Marx, the Undertaker), Valerie Gaunt (Vampire Woman), Charles Lloyd Pack (Dr. Seward), Janina Faye (Tania)

p, Anthony Hinds; d, Terence Fisher; w, Jimmy Sangster; ph, Jack Asher; ed, Bill Lenny; m, James Bernard; art d, Bernard Robinson; cos, Molly Arbuthnot

Bloody well done. Hammer finally gave the Dracula legend the treatment it deserved here, entrusting it to the brilliant director of THE CURSE OF FRANKENSTEIN, Terence Fisher, who injected glorious life into the familiar material.

English librarian Jonathan Harker (John Van Eyssen) travels to Transylvania, where he is employed by the mysterious Count Dracula (Christopher Lee). Eventually, Harker learns that his employer is a vampire, one of the undead who must suck the blood of the living to survive, and he becomes one of Dracula's victims. Dracula then travels to London and tracks down Harker's fiancee, Lucy (Carol Marsh), and transforms her into one of the undead. Enter Dr. Van Helsing (played with zest by Peter Cushing) and the battle lines are drawn.

Fisher's version of the Dracula legend brought with it many innovative (and, yes, subsequently overdone) approaches to the genre. The film moves quickly and forcefully from one scene to the next, keeping the audience on their seat edges. Lush sets, rousing musical score, spirited acting and a direct attitude toward undead sensuality heighten the vampiric illusion. The result is a terrific combination of the intellectual and visceral that continues to work today. Followed by DRACULA - PRINCE OF DARKNESS and five more sequels.

HORSE FEATHERS

1932   70m   bw   ★★★★
Comedy   /U
Paramount

Groucho Marx (Professor Wagstaff), Harpo Marx (Harpo), Chico Marx (Chico), Zeppo Marx (Zeppo), Thelma Todd (Connie Bailey), David Landau (Jennings), Florine McKinney (Peggy Carrington), Jim Pierce (Mullens), Nat Pendleton (McCarthy), Reginald Barlow (President of College)

d, Norman Z. McLeod; w, Bert Kalmar, Harry Ruby, S.J. Perelman; ph, Ray June

Not a masterpiece but divine all the same. The Marx Brothers bring their special brand of anarchy to the world of college football in this wonderfully madcap comedy.

Prof. Quincy Adams Wagstaff (Groucho) is named president of Huxley College, which hasn't won a football game since its founding in 1888. Acting on the advice of his son (Zeppo), Wagstaff attempts to recruit a pair of pro players, but a mixup at a speakeasy leads him to mistake a dog catcher (Harpo) and bootlegging iceman (Chico) for football players. Just the same, Wagstaff sends them to kidnap arch rival Darwin College's ringers; unfortunately, they fail. Meanwhile, college widow Connie Bailey (Thelma Todd), who is in cahoots with Darwin's Jennings, tries to wheedle the Huxley "signals" out of Groucho.

Although there are many funny moments preceding it, the film's big payoff comes in the Huxley-Darwin game, in which Harpo, Chico and Groucho all contribute to a zany comeback victory brought about through the use of banana peels, an elastic band, a chariot, and a surplus of footballs. Perhaps the most freewheeling film the Brothers Marx ever made, this fast-paced laugh fest was directed by Norman Z. McLeod and written by the great humorist S.J. Perelman with help from Bert Kalmar and Harry Ruby. With the delectable, unappreciated Thelma Todd, a spun-sugar confection from the Lombard sorority, and a marvelous foil for Groucho.

HORSE SOLDIERS, THE

1959   119m   c   ★★★
Western/War   /PG
Mirisch

John Wayne (Col. John Marlowe), William Holden (Maj. Henry Kendall), Constance Towers (Hannah Hunter), Althea Gibson (Lukey), Hoot Gibson (Brown), Anna Lee (Mrs. Buford), Russell Simpson (Sheriff), Stan Jones (Gen. U.S. Grant), Carleton Young (Col. Jonathan Miles), Basil Ruysdael (Boys School Commandant)

p, John Lee Mahin, Martin Rackin; d, John Ford; w, John Lee Mahin, Martin Rackin (based on the novel by Harold Sinclair); ph, William Clothier (Deluxe Color); ed, Jack Murray; m, David Buttolph; art d, Frank Hotaling; fx, Augie Lohman; cos, Frank Beetson, Ann Peck

With the exception of the Civil War segment in HOW THE WEST WAS WON, THE HORSE SOLDIERS was director John Ford's only film dealing with the War Between the States. The film is gorgeously photographed and contains many memorable images (the opening credits and breathtaking final shot) and moving scenes (one in which a Southern military school is forced to send its cadets—all children—into battle against the Union forces is a stunner), but this is not one of Ford's best efforts, suffering from a weak script and an overwrought performance from its female lead, Constance Towers.

Based on an actual mission known as Grierson's Raid, the film takes place in the spring of 1863 and finds Union general U.S. Grant (Stan Jones) frustrated by his inability to take Vicksburg. Taking drastic action, Grant decides to send a cavalry unit to Newton Station, Mississippi, deep in Confederate territory, to cut enemy supply lines to Vicksburg. The man selected to lead this daring raid is tough, no-nonsense Col. Marlowe (John Wayne), a citizen soldier who designed railroads before the war. With him goes a bevy of officers with mixed motives, including Col. Seacord (Willis Bouchey), whose political ambitions dictate his every action, and Maj. Kendall (William Holden), a conscientious physician who sees no glory in war—only suffering and death. En route to Newton Station, the cavalry bivouacs at a plantation owned by Hannah (Towers), a Southern belle devoted to the Confederate cause. Caught spying on Marlowe and his commanders as they plan strategy, Hannah and her slave, Lukey (Althea Gibson), are taken along on the mission, lest they reveal the top-secret plans to the rebels.

While minor Ford is still head-and-shoulders above the best of most others, THE HORSE SOLDIERS is a mostly workmanlike effort in which the great director struggles against a poorly written script, with sketchy characters and overly explicit dialogue in which deep feelings and motivations come tumbling out in succinct speeches. Such pat character development invariably lends a superficial feel to the conflicts and relationships among the principals, and the viewer never really feels very deeply for the protagonists. Ford is such a master of his craft that he injects enough personal spark into the material to nearly override the script's deficiencies, but there's no denying that THE HORSE SOLDIERS is the work of a distracted, tired, and somewhat bored artist. Indeed, in his famous interview with Peter Bogdanovich, the director couldn't recall whether or not he had even seen the final cut.

HORSE'S MOUTH, THE

1953   84m   c   ★½
Fantasy
Group 3   (U.K.)

Robert Beatty (Bob Jefferson), Joseph Tomelty (Terry Roche), Mervyn Johns (Tom Mitchum), Michael Medwin (Timothy Blake), Virginia McKenna (Shelagh), Gillian Lind (Jane Bond), Ursula Howells (Peggy), Arthur Macrae (Alan Digby), Louise Hampton (Miss Turner), John Charlesworth (Denis)

p, John Grierson, Colin Lesslie; d, C.M. Pennington-Richards; w, Patrick Campbell (based on the radio play "To Tell You the Truth" by Robert Barr); ph, Wolfgang Suschitzky

Silly attempt at satire has Medwin as a reporter who tries to make a story out of the "oracle" he discovers at the bottom of a well while vacationing. His editor thinks it's just whimsy and fires him; then the oracle is discovered to be the real thing. People start to ask too much from the gifted being, however, and it leaves. But not before the audience.

HORSE'S MOUTH, THE

1958   95m   c   ★★★½
Comedy   /U
UA   (U.K.)

Alec Guinness (Gulley Jimson), Kay Walsh (Coker), Renee Houston (Sarah), Mike Morgan (Nosey), Robert Coote (Sir William Beeder), Arthur Macrae (Alabaster), Veronica Turleigh (Lady Beeder), Reginald Beckwith (Capt. Jones), Michael Gough (Abel), Ernest Thesiger (Hickson)

p, John Bryan; d, Ronald Neame; w, Alec Guinness (based on the novel by Joyce Carey); ph, Arthur Ibbetson (Technicolor); ed, Anne V. Coates; m, Ken Jones

Very enjoyable comedy about the rebellious nature of the artist, sidesteps the anarchy it should embrace. Guinness plays Gulley Jimson, a marvelous creation of Joyce Cary's that she based on

her friend Dylan Thomas; the actor did the screenplay adaptation. He lacks the innocent temperamental drive that could have breathed life into the part of a mad painter who lives like the worst sort of bum but whose work is brilliant, if unorthodox. Released from prison after serving time as a vagrant, he returns to his wife and becomes enraged when he realizes that she has been surviving by selling off his paintings. He learns that a wealthy collector, Coote, is interested in his work, and he goes to see the man but finds that he is out of town. Guinness looks about Coote's enormous flat with its huge white walls and decides that he will simply move in and affix his latest masterpieces to the walls.

At the moment, he is obsessed with feet—any kind of human feet. His unsavory friends model their naked feet, then decide to use not only the flat but the entire building for their own ends, cutting a hole in the floor and dropping to the lower level where apprentice sculptor Gough lowers a huge block of granite to begin a sculpture. After finishing his incredible mural (actually painted by John Bratby), Guinness departs, leaving the entire building destroyed and ready for the bulldozer. He winds up painting on an enormous outside wall, and, by film's end, is measuring the side of a huge transatlantic ship for his next madcap mural.

Guinness saw the film in Mexico City where it was being shown at a film festival—it had not been dubbed and had no subtitles. While most of the audience did not understand the dialogue, the vast majority roared their approval at the end, even though a faction who considered the film an insult to true art caused a fight to break out and ultimately a full-scale riot erupted. Guinness and the British Ambassador and his wife escaped unnoticed in the fleeing crowd.

HOSPITAL, THE

1971   103m   c   ★★★½
Comedy/Drama   GP/15
Gottfried/Chayefsky

George C. Scott (Dr. Herbert Bock), Diana Rigg (Barbara Drummond), Barnard Hughes (Drummond), Richard Dysart (Dr. Welbeck), Andrew Duncan (William Mead), Nancy Marchand (Mrs. Christie, Head Nurse), Stephen Elliott (Sunstrom), Donald Harron (Milton Mead), Roberts Blossom (Guernsey), Tresa Hughes (Mrs. Donovan)

p, Howard Gottfried; d, Arthur Hiller; w, Paddy Chayefsky; ph, Victor J. Kemper (DeLuxe Color); ed, Eric Albertson; m, Morris Surdin; prod d, Gene Rudolf; cos, Frank Thompson

Satire at its darkest. Scott in fine, hammy form (for once a part that takes advantage of his overblown core) as a N.Y. medical center's chief surgeon whose personal life has driven him to the brink of suicide. He busy hospital is being torn apart by a string of inexplicable murders of staff members. The laughs are sardonic, and the reality of Chayefsky's heavy-handed message (i.e., hospitals treat their patients badly) eats away at the viewer. But even when it falls flat, it's still an interesting watch.

HOT MILLIONS

1968   106m   c   ★★★½
Comedy   G/U
Milberg/MGM   (U.K.)

Peter Ustinov (Marcus Pendleton), Maggie Smith (Patty Terwilliger), Karl Malden (Carlton J. Klemper), Bob Newhart (Willard C. Gnatpole), Robert Morley (Caesar Smith), Cesar Romero (Customs *Inspector)*, Melinda May *(Nurse)*, Ann Lancaster *(Landlady)*, Frank Tragear *(Bus Inspector)*, Julie May *(1st Charwoman)*

p, Mildred Freed Alberg; d, Eric Till; w, Ira Wallach, Peter Ustinov; ph, Ken Higgins (Metrocolor); ed, Richard Marden; m, Laurie Johnson; art d, Bill Andrews; cos, Germinal Rangel

Often hysterical comedy that didn't find an audience at the box office but has since been recognized as one of the better comedies of the late 1960s due to many television showings.

Ustinov is an embezzler who has just finished serving time in jail. He'd been caught by one of those infernal computers and that's caused him to study the critters until he becomes as expert at them as the men who discovered his last illegal enterprise. He cons Morley, a renowned computer genius, into leaving the country, then assumes Morley's identity and secures employment at a huge corporation headed by Malden. Once inside the conglomerate, Ustinov uses the computer to issue large checks to fictitious firms in Frankfurt, Paris, and Rome. Then he flies to those cities, picks up the checks and cashes them. Ustinov also falls in love with Smith, his secretary. They marry and she quickly becomes pregnant. They leave for Rio immediately. Soon enough, Malden uncovers the robberies and enlists Newhart, his resident computer maven (in his first major acting role), to help nab Ustinov and Smith.

In the end, no one is hurt, the money is safe, and the perpetrators of the plot get away with it—something not often seen in those days when there was still some censorship. Made in London at Borehamwood, the film features a bright script by Wallach and Ustinov, and a thoroughly engaging performance from the latter.

HOT SHOTS!

1991 84m c   ★★★
Action/Comedy   PG-13/12
Treadwell Enterprises/Pap Inc/Fox

Charlie Sheen *(Sean "Topper" Harley/Rhett Butler/Superman)*, Cary Elwes *(Kent Gregory)*, Valeria Golino *(Ramada Thompson/Scarlett O'Hara/Lois Lane)*, Lloyd Bridges *(Admiral "Tug" Benson)*, Kevin Dunn *(Lieutenant Commander Block)*, Jon Cryer *(Jim "Washout" Pfaffenbach)*, William O'Leary *(Pete "Dead Meat" Thompson)*, Kristy Swanson *(Kowalski)*, Efrem Zimbalist Jr. *(Wilson)*, Bill Irwin *(Buzz Harley)*

p, Bill Badalato; d, Jim Abrahams; w, Pat Proft, Jim Abrahams; ph, Bill Butler; ed, Jane Kurson, Eric Sears; m, Sylvester Levay; prod d, William A. Elliott; art d, Greg Papalia; cos, Mary Malin

HOT SHOTS! spoofs not only flyboy films in general, but kids the pants off at least a half-dozen famous movies, including the likes of GONE WITH THE WIND, DANCES WITH WOLVES, THE FABULOUS BAKER BOYS, DINER and even the infamous 9½ WEEKS. At its core, however, HOT SHOTS! is a blatant sendup of the Tom Cruise smash TOP GUN and the names of the various ace flyboy characters help to set the mood for the off-the-wall humor to come.

There's the obviously ill-fated Pete "Dead Meat" Thompson (William O'Leary) and an ace pilot suffering from a malady known as "walleye vision" named Jim "Wash Out" Pfaffenbach (Jon Cryer). The major "hot shot" is Sean "Topper" Harley (Charlie Sheen), while his nemesis—both in matters of the heart and in the air—is ace narcissist Kent Gregory (Cary Elwes), the very model of military perfection—or so he likes to think. The flyboys are rousingly led by blustery multi-war veteran, Admiral "Tug" Benson (Lloyd Bridges), a pratfall-prone, "Damn the torpedoes. . ." type leader who, through the years, has had just

about every part of his body replaced, due to a spectacular series of inept combat injuries.

When Topper and Kent aren't snarling at each other through clenched teeth in the air, they're snarling at each other with clenched fists on the ground. Kent blames Topper's ace pilot father for causing the death of his own dad years before in a freak airplane accident. Kent is also Topper's chief rival for the affections of the alluring base psychiatrist, equestrienne, sculptor and torch singer, Ramada Thompson (Valeria Golino).

While the slapstick comedy antics are frequently amusing and, on rare occasions, even hilarious, HOT SHOTS!, like so many other cinematic parodies before it, tends to lose sight—or control—of the plot, such as it is, in favor of more jokes, more visual gags and more dialogue puns—all hurled at the audience at a rapid-fire pace.

Charlie Sheen delivers a surprisingly strong performance that's a real revelation of his comedic talents. As Topper, Sheen is funniest when he's being self-consciously handsome, all smiles and teeth, and when he's making an extremely earnest effort to be charismatic, especially for the benefit of the voluptuous Valeria Golino, who brings a welcome sensuality to her role.

If this film has the same wildly uninhibited humor as AIRPLANE! and the NAKED GUN series, it shouldn't come as a surprise, since many of the same behind-the-scenes talents were involved. Directed by Jim Abrahams from his own screenplay and co-written by Pat Proft, HOT SHOTS! is like most other sendup films in that it takes numerous comedic risks, the end result being that it's blessed with gags that work, while being cursed with others that totally misfire, and with dull and silly stretches between the fun stuff.

HOUND OF THE BASKERVILLES, THE

1939 80m bw   ★★★★
Mystery
FOX

Richard Greene *(Sir Henry Baskerville)*, Basil Rathbone *(Sherlock Holmes)*, Wendy Barrie *(Beryl Stapleton)*, Nigel Bruce *(Dr. Watson)*, Lionel Atwill *(James Mortimer, M.D.)*, John Carradine *(Barryman)*, Barlowe Borland *(Frankland)*, Beryl Mercer *(Mrs. Jenifer Mortimer)*, Morton Lowry *(John Stapleton)*, Ralph Forbes *(Sir Hugo Baskerville)*

p, Gene Markey; d, Sidney Lanfield; w, Ernest Pascal (based on the story by Arthur Conan Doyle); ph, Peverell Marley; ed, Robert Simpson; art d, Richard Day, Hans Peters; cos, Gwen Wakeling

This was the first time that Rathbone and Bruce were cast as Holmes and Watson and their superlative performances resulted in the delightful series that followed this excellent mystery. A faithful adaptation of the Doyle novel, the film is set in the 1880s period of gaslit London with all its wet cobblestone streets, billowing fog, and eerie atmosphere. The young heir to the Baskerville estate (Greene) fears for his life and calls in the great Sherlock Holmes to help solve the mysterious curse that has killed every Baskerville master since 1650.

This version of THE HOUND OF THE BASKERVILLES was an enormous success immediately upon release, and it proved to be the best of the series. Rathbone was the perfect Holmes, his well-modulated voice, his sharply-honed features, his lanky figure all conforming to the public's image of the great detective as Sidney Paget first drew his imagined likeness in the *Strand Magazine* in 1889 when Doyle created the character. He had earned the role and would keep it for life as Bruce would claim the amiable character of Dr. Watson, the two becoming a beloved screen team.

Lanfield's direction is solid and careful as he unfolds the sinister tale. Carradine, Lowry, and particularly Atwill are all superb in their supporting roles. THE HOUND OF THE BAS-KERVILLES was always Rathbone's favorite film, even though he considered it "a negative from which I merely continued to produce endless positives of the same photograph." Rathbone would go on to appear in 16 films as Sherlock Holmes and more than 200 radio shows dealing with the indefatigable sleuth between 1939 and 1946.

HOUR OF THE WOLF, THE
(VARGTIMMEN)
1968   88m   bw   ★★★
Drama   /X
Svensk   (Sweden)

Liv Ullmann (Alma Borg), Max von Sydow (Johan Borg), Erland Josephson (Baron von Merkens), Gertrud Fridh (Corinne von Merkens), Gudrun Brost (Gamla Fru von Merkens), Bertil Anderberg (Ernst von Merkens), Georg Rydeberg (Arkivarie Lindhorst), Ulf Johansson (Kurator Heerbrand), Naima Wifstrand (Old Lady with Hat), Ingrid Thulin (Veronica Vogler)

d, Ingmar Bergman; w, Ingmar Bergman; ph, Sven Nykvist; ed, Ulla Ryghe; m, Lars-Johan Werle, Wolfgang Amadeus Mozart, Johann Sebastian Bach; art d, Marik Vos-Lundh; fx, Evald Andersson; cos, Mago

Fine acting exercise. This Bergman discourse on the nature of art and the artist's relation to society is shrouded in the trappings of gothic horror and stars Max von Sydow as Johan Borg, a painter haunted by bad dreams and apparitions while secluded on an island with his pregnant wife, Alma (Liv Ullmann). Both of them experience a series of haunting visions: Johan sees a beautiful boy, a ghost able to walk on walls, and an ancient woman who tears off her face; Alma is approached by a woman (who may or may not be an apparition) who instructs her to read her husband's diary. There she learns of Johan's love affair. Generally considered one of Bergman's lesser pictures, THE HOUR OF THE WOLF was originally to be shot before PERSONA, in 1965, as "The Cannibals."

HOUSE OF GAMES
1987   102m   c   ★★★★
Crime   R/15
Filmhaus

Lindsay Crouse (Dr. Margaret Ford), Joe Mantegna (Mike), Mike Nussbaum (Joey), Lilia Skala (Dr. Littauer), J.T. Walsh (Businessman), Willo Hausman (Girl with Book), Karen Kohlhaas (Prison Ward Patient), Steve Goldstein (Billy Hahn), Jack Wallace (Bartender, "House of Games"), Ben Blakeman (Bartender, "Charlie's Tavern")

p, Michael Hausman; d, David Mamet; w, David Mamet; ph, Juan Ruiz-Anchia; ed, Trudy Ship; m, Alaric Jans; prod d, Michael Merritt; fx, Robert Willard; cos, Nan Cibula

The extraordinary first film from Pulitzer Prize-winning playwright David Mamet, HOUSE OF GAMES is a stylish cinematic puzzle. Dr. Margaret Ford (Lindsay Crouse), a psychologist and best-selling author of a book on obsessive behavior, ventures into the world of confidence games to try to help out a patient whose gambling has gotten him in over his head. Her excursion brings her in contact with Mike (Joe Mantegna), a con man who engineers a back-room hustle that almost leaves Margaret $6,000

poorer. Instead of being angry, she is attracted to this streetwise philosopher and his world and returns to get to know him and it better. In the process she becomes involved in an elaborate con game revolving around a suitcase full of cash supposedly borrowed from the mob. The plot grows increasingly convoluted until Margaret—and the audience—no longer knows who is conning whom—that is, until the shocking climax.

Mamet has created a suspenseful, psychologically complex film that constantly plays tricks on the viewer as it draws him into its milieu of insightful deceit. Crouse and Mantegna are outstanding, and the supporting performances are all first rate. In the tradition of Alfred Hitchcock, Mamet worked from his own storyboards, and he and cinematographer Juan Ruiz Anchia have created a visually stunning film that is the equal of his airtight screenplay.

HOUSE OF ROTHSCHILD, THE
1934   94m   c/bw   ★★★★
Biography
20th Century

George Arliss (Mayer Rothschild/Nathan Rothschild), Boris Karloff (Count Ledrantz), Loretta Young (Julie Rothschild), Robert Young (Capt. Fitzroy), C. Aubrey Smith (Duke of Wellington), A.S. Byron (Baring), Helen Westley (Gudula Rothschild), Reginald Owen (Herries), Florence Arliss (Hannah Rothschild), Alan Mowbray (Metternich)

p, Darryl F. Zanuck; d, Alfred Werker; w, Nunnally Johnson (based on the play by George Humbert Westley); ph, Peverell Marley (Technicolor); ed, Allen McNeil, Barbara McLean; m, Alfred Newman

An outstanding historical account of the Rothschild financial dynasty during the Napoleonic wars, THE HOUSE OF ROTHSCHILD was the ambitious brainchild of Darryl F. Zanuck, who had left Warner Bros. to form Twentieth Century Productions, which would later merge with Fox.

George Arliss, who plays a dual role, is first seen as the patriarch of the German-Jewish ghetto family. On his deathbed, he urges his five sons to travel to the capitals of Europe and establish powerful banking firms. Led by their brother (Arliss's other role), the Rothschilds slowly build the most powerful banking conglomerate in Europe. The Rothschild banks secretly lend money to England, Austria, Italy, and Prussia to defeat Napoleon. Once Napoleon is in exile, however, Boris Karloff, the anti-Semitic Prussian ambassador to England, refuses Arliss's offer of money to rebuild France. Outraged, the banker creates financial havoc in the bond markets, but this only results in Karloff's launching violent and bloody pogroms. Fate intervenes when Napoleon escapes from exile and rises again to threaten Europe.

A potent, adult film, handsomely produced (the final sequence was shot in early three-strip Technicolor) and cast, and a memorable showcase for the effective "old school" acting of the unique Arliss.

HOUSE OF USHER
1960   79m   c   ★★★½
Horror   /18
AIP

Vincent Price (Roderick Usher), Mark Damon (Philip Winthrop), Myrna Fahey (Madeline Usher), Harry Ellerbe (Bristol), Bill Borzage, Mike Jordan, Nadajan, Ruth Oklander, George Paul, David Andar p, Roger Corman; d, Roger Corman; w, Richard Matheson

A real coup for Roger Corman and AIP, HOUSE OF USHER was the first of their horror films that had a decent budget ($350,000), boasted a shooting schedule of more than 10 days (they were allowed 15), was shot in color and CinemaScope, and was "inspired" by Edgar Allen Poe. The gamble paid off and the film was a critical and commercial hit that unleashed scads of other films based on the works of Poe.

The wonderful Vincent Price stars as Roderick Usher, the creepy, white-haired owner of the mysterious house of Usher, who lives in seclusion in the creaking old house with his sister, Madeline (Myrna Fahey). When Madeline announces her engagement to Philip (Mark Damon), Roderick will have none of it and informs her betrothed that he and his sister are the last of the Ushers and they suffer from a bizarre madness that must not be transmitted to another generation. When Philip refuses to leave the spooky house despite this warning, strange accidents befall him, and he is nearly killed. Meanwhile, Madeline falls ill, and soon after, Roderick informs Philip that she has died of a heart attack and entombs her in the family chapel. The butler, however, informs Philip that his fiancee has suffered from periodic blackouts and that she may have been buried alive.

Moody, atmospheric, and effective, HOUSE OF USHER succeeds in making the house a "monster," which a desperate Corman had to make clear to skeptical executive producer Sam Arkoff when he questioned the film's lack of a menacing creature. Corman's savvy use of color, musty cobwebs, and creaking and groaning sound effects combine to make the *house* appear to be the cause of all the madness. Price is wonderful as the spooky owner, but the other three players are merely adequate. But still a superlative Corman/AIP effort and a great beginning to a varying but always interesting series of horror films.

HOUSE OF WAX
1953   90m   c   ★★★
Horror   GP/PG
WB

Vincent Price (Prof. Henry Jarrod), Frank Lovejoy (Lt. Tom Brennan), Phyllis Kirk (Sue Allen), Carolyn Jones (Cathy Gray), Paul Picerni (Scott Andrews), Roy Roberts (Matthew Burke), Angela Clarke (Mrs. Andrews), Paul Cavanagh (Sidney Wallace), Dabbs Greer (Sgt. Jim Shane), Charles Bronson (Igor)

p, Bryan Foy; d, Andre de Toth; w, Crane Wilbur (based on a play by Charles Welden); ph, Bert Glennon, Peverell Marley (Natural Vision 3-D, Warner Color); ed, Rudi Fehr; m, David Buttolph; art d, Stanley Fleischer

Paddleball anyone? This fine remake of the classic THE MYSTERY OF THE WAX MUSEUM was filmed in 3-D and employed "WarnerPhonic Sound," a forerunner to stereo that utilized a number of speakers.

Vincent Price plays Professor Henry Jarrod, a wax sculptor in New York at the turn of the century who presides over a wax museum that is floundering because of his pursuit of beauty rather than sensationalism. When Jarrod again refuses partner Burke's (Roy Roberts) request to create more horrifying pieces, Burke sets fire to the museum, intent on collecting the insurance money. It is presumed that Jarrod died with his creations, but he returns, horribly scarred, and strangles Burke. Years later, Jarrod, feigning a wheelchair-confining back injury, opens a new wax museum with even more lifelike displays. Because his hands have been horribly burned, he employs two assistants to do the sculpting under his supervision (one of whom is played by

Charles Bronson, then billed as Buchinsky). In reality, however, Jarrod's mad sculpting is accomplished by pouring wax over people he has murdered.

HOUSE OF WAX was stunningly directed by Andre de Toth who used the new 3-D process to its fullest potential without bogging down the narrative with too many "gee-look-what-I-can-do" tricks. Ironically, this man who saw the potential of 3-D and who directed one of the most effective movies ever shot in that process had only one eye, which hampered his depth perception. Price is magnificent as usual and manages to steal the role of Professor Jarrod from its creator, Lionel Atwill. Although it is now extremely difficult to see in its original format, HOUSE OF WAX is still well worth viewing in flat prints or on video. The line that kills 'em in revival houses: "You never see things like this in Provincetown." Oh, but you do.

HOUSE ON 92ND STREET, THE
1945   88m   bw   ★★★★
Spy   /U
FOX

William Eythe (Bill Dietrich), Lloyd Nolan (Inspector George A. Briggs), Signe Hasso (Elsa Gebhardt), Gene Lockhart (Charles Ogden Roper), Leo G. Carroll (Col. Hammersohn), Lydia St. Clair (Johanna Schmedt), Reed Hadley (Narrator), William Post, Jr. (Walker), Harry Bellaver (Max Coburg), Bruno Wick (Adolphe Lange)

p, Louis de Rochemont; d, Henry Hathaway; w, Barre Lyndon, Charles G. Booth, John Monks, Jr. (based on the story by Booth); ph, Norbert Brodine; ed, Harmon Jones; m, David Buttolph; art d, Lyle Wheeler, Lewis Creber; fx, Fred Sersen; cos, Bonnie Cashin

Suspense-packed espionage yarn, approached from a documentary angle, has Nolan as a no-nonsense federal investigator who is sought out by German-American Eythe, a brilliant student. He has been contacted by Nazi spies, he tells Nolan, and asked to work with them. Nolan encourages Eythe to accept the offer and work as a double agent, reporting all Nazi activities to the FBI. Slowly, Eythe ingratiates himself with several Nazi agents and is assigned, as a technician, to transmit messages to Germany via short-wave radio. He establishes a remote radio hideout and begins sending messages, really to FBI headquarters, and its operators pass on fake information to Germany. Through this system Eythe is able to learn that Nazi agents are after data concerning the development of the atomic bomb (referred to here as "Process 97"), identifying Lockhart, one of the scientists working on the apparatus, as a Nazi agent.

Hathaway's direction is quick and uses the newsreel style made famous by producer de Rochemont, who produced the MARCH OF TIME series. The film was shot on location in New York and other points where actual spy cases from FBI files really occurred. The semi-documentary style gave sharp authenticity to the film as did the use of nonprofessional actors (many of whom were FBI agents and technical personnel). The stentorian narration provided by Hadley, who made a handsome living in films narrating such stories, further convinced viewers that they were watching the real thing. In some instances they were; Hathaway incorporated newsreel shots of real German spies being rounded up at the beginning of WWII, along with telephotos of the German consulate in New York and its real life spies going and coming. The tremendous atmospherics gave birth to a series of films adopting the same semi-documentary approach, notably T-MEN, THE NAKED CITY, and WALK A CROOKED MILE. Hasso is incomparable as the Nazi ringleader in this, her most impressive film.

HOUSE PARTY

1990   100m   c   ★★★
Comedy   R/15

Christopher Reid *(Kid)*, Robin Harris *(Pop)*, Christopher Martin *(Play)*, Martin Lawrence *(Bilal)*, Tisha Campbell *(Sidney)*, A.J. Johnson *(Sharane)*, Paul Anthony *(Stab)*, Bowlegged Lou *(Pee-Wee)*, B. Fine *(Zilla)*, Edith Fields *(Principal)*

p, Warrington Hudlin; d, Reginald Hudlin; w, Reginald Hudlin; ph, Peter Deming (Metrocolor); ed, Earl Watson; m, Marcus Miller; prod d, Bryan Jones; art d, Susan Richardson; chor, A.J. Johnson, Kid 'N' Play, Tisha Campbell; cos, Harold Evans

Crude and cartoony but hypnotic in its infectious energy, an auspicious debut from brothers Reginald and Warrington Hudlin. With Reggie directing and Warrington producing, the Hudlins have collaborated to expand Reggie's Harvard thesis film from a short into a feature, and the result is HOUSE PARTY, a low-budget comedy that is a seriously funny look at a night in the lives of some black teenagers.

The film is more of a portrait than a story. Kid (Christopher Reid, one half of the rap duo Kid 'N' Play) is dying to go to a party hosted by his buddy Play (Christopher Martin, the other half). Unfortunately, Kid has gotten into some trouble with the local bullies (played by three members of the hiphop band Full Force) at school and, after a note from the principal's office arrives at home, he's grounded by his strict father (the late, great Robin Harris). Determined to go to Play's party, especially since two of the prettiest girls in school are going to be there, Kid risks life and limb to sneak out of the house while Pop dozes in front of the television. He makes it to the party and gets to know the girls, one of whom has a crush on him, while dancing up a storm. The evening, however, is not without its complications.

Deceptively simple on the surface, HOUSE PARTY is a realistic depiction of black teenagers. Though its main purpose is obviously to provoke laughter, it also provokes thought by dealing honestly with a variety of subjects, including safe sex, teen drinking, class prejudice, and, in a roundabout way, racism. Reginald Hudlin has given his wide assortment of characters a great deal of intelligence, much more than usual for this kind of film, allowing each room to breathe and establish a personality. Stars Kid 'N' Play make a strong film debut, creating a fun, light image for themselves without sacrificing the edge of their music; their rap-duel scene is fast and funky. Kid, with his foot-high fade haircut (one character refers to him as "Eraserhead") and freckle-faced grin, handles the duties of "leading man" extremely well, giving a supremely likable performance.

Aside from its likable performances and message, HOUSE PARTY is a film that *moves* in every way possible. From the opening dream sequence to the final sight gag, the film sways to a funky contagious rhythm that will have most viewers rocking in their seats. The dance sequences are directed with such lively timing and slick camera movements that one can't help but bounce along. Reginald Hudlin is a terrific filmmaker who has a wonderfully assured feel for the camera. With HOUSE PARTY, Hudlin has created one of the flat-out funniest films in a long time, marred only by the homophobic and cruel jailhouse rap.

HOUSEKEEPING

1987   116m   c   ★★★½
Drama   PG
Columbia

Christine Lahti *(Sylvie)*, Sara Walker *(Ruth)*, Andrea Burchill *(Lucille)*, Anne Pitoniak *(Lily)*, Barbara Reese *(Nona)*, Bill Smillie *(Sheriff)*, Wayne Robson *(Mr. French)*, Margot Pinvidic *(Helen)*

p, Robert F. Colesberry; d, Bill Forsyth; w, Bill Forsyth (based on the novel by Marilynne Robinson); ph, Michael Coulter (Rank Color); ed, Michael Ellis; m, Michael Gibbs; prod d, Adrienne Atkinson; cos, Mary-Jane Reyner

Offbeat but absorbing. Set in the 1950s and based on a Marilynne Robinson novel, this is the first American film from Scottish director Bill Forsyth.

After the suicide of their mother, two young girls, Ruth (Sara Walker) and Lucille (Andrea Burchill), are brought up by their grandmother in a small Idaho town. When she dies, a pair of elderly great-aunts persuade Ruth and Lucille's itinerant aunt, Sylvie (Christine Lahti), to look after her two nieces, who are now approaching adolescence. Sylvie, who has spent most of her life riding the rails and sleeping on benches, sets up housekeeping in her own fashion and goes about child-rearing in an unorthodox manner. Lucille, more concerned with appearances than her sister, begins to be embarrassed by Sylvie's refusal to abide by society's conventions.

HOUSEKEEPING is a reversal of the formula that has brought director Forsyth, a master of character development and storytelling, so much success. Instead of weaving dramatic moments into capricious comedy, he leavens this heartwarming drama with laughter. Playing against type and avoiding what could have been a paint-by-numbers portrayal, Lahti plays Sylvie as loving and ingenuous, but with a half-glimpsed sense of tragedy and disappointment. Walker and Burchill also turn in fine performances.

HOW GREEN WAS MY VALLEY

1941   118m   bw   ★★★★★
Drama   /U
FOX

Walter Pidgeon *(Mr. Gruffydd)*, Maureen O'Hara *(Angharad)*, Donald Crisp *(Mr. Morgan)*, Anna Lee *(Bronwyn)*, Roddy McDowall *(Huw Morgan)*, John Loder *(Ianto Morgan)*, Sara Allgood *(Mrs. Morgan)*, Barry Fitzgerald *(Cyfurtha)*, Patric Knowles *(Ivor Morgan)*, Morton Lowry *(Mr. Jonas)*

p, Darryl F. Zanuck; d, John Ford; w, Philip Dunne (based on the novel by Richard Llewellyn); ph, Arthur Miller; ed, James B. Clark; m, Alfred Newman; art d, Richard Day, Nathan Juran; cos, Gwen Wakeling

Emotionally majestic and spiritually moving , this is one of John Ford's undisputed masterpieces, a film that neither fades nor fails after repeated viewings.

The mining area in South Wales and its hard-working miners and their families are seen through the eyes of Huw (Roddy McDowall), the youngest of six children in a family headed by a stern father (Donald Crisp) and loving mother (Sara Allgood). Set at the turn of the century and told in flashback, the film shows an unspoiled valley, full of love and warmth, wherein the trials and hardships of the community are told through a series of moving vignettes.

Everything about this film is touching; master director John Ford builds one simple scene upon another with very little plot, using incidents in the life of one family to tell the general tale, demonstrating changes and recording milestones. Beautifully assisted by cameraman Arthur Miller, Ford received strong support from studio chief Darryl Zanuck, who personally produced the film. The superlative cast is a Who's Who of Hollywood's Irish community, with a noble assist from Welsh singers.

HOW I WON THE WAR

1967   109m   c   ★★★
Comedy/War   /X
UA   (U.K.)

Michael Crawford (Lt. Ernest Goodbody), John Lennon (Gripweed), Roy Kinnear (Clapper), Lee Montague (Sgt. Transom), Jack MacGowran (Juniper), Michael Hordern (Grapple), Jack Hedley (Melancholy Musketeer), Karl Michael Vogler (Odlebog), Ronald Lacey (Spool), James Cossins (Drogue)

p, Richard Lester; d, Richard Lester; w, Charles Wood (based on the novel by Patrick Ryan); ph, David Watkin (Eastmancolor); ed, John Victor Smith; m, Ken Thorne; art d, Philip Harrison, John Stoll; fx, Eddie Fowlie; cos, Dinah Greet

Richard Lester, director of the hit Beatles movies A HARD DAY'S NIGHT and HELP!, intended this black comedy as a stinging condemnation of war, but occasionally he fails even as he succeeds, eliciting such plentiful laughs that he blunts the impact of his message.

Revolving around the rose-colored reminiscences of a middle-aged British WWII veteran whose wartime career was actually a disaster, HOW I WON THE WAR follows the inept Lt. Goodbody (Michael Crawford) as he leads his men from North Africa to France. Among his unfortunate misfit charges are the overweight Clapper (Roy Kinnear), who is obsessed with his wife's infidelity; Juniper (Jack MacGowran), a music-hall comic; and Gripweed (then-Beatle John Lennon, whose billing is considerably more prominent than his presence in the film). Transom (Lee Montague), the only competent military man in the bunch, tries in vain to correct his superior's command blunders, but so ill-prepared to lead is Goodbody that he eventually causes the deaths of all of his men save one, the Melancholy Musketeer (Jack Hedley).

Based on a novel by Patrick Ryan, Lester's film offers both hilarious moments of satire (of war and war movies) and grim, bloody depictions of the awful reality of combat. This seemingly incongruous mixture will work for some viewers, and, though the seriousness of Lester's intent may not be appreciated by everyone, most should at least find something here to make them laugh.

HOW THE WEST WAS WON

1963   165m   c   ★★★½
Western   /PG
MGM

Spencer Tracy (Narrator), Carroll Baker (Eve Prescott), Lee J. Cobb (Lou Ramsey), Henry Fonda (Jethro Stuart), Karl Malden (Zebulon Prescott), Gregory Peck (Cleve Van Valen), George Peppard (Zeb Rawlings), Robert Preston (Roger Morgan), Debbie Reynolds (Lilith Prescott), James Stewart (Linus Rawlings)

p, Bernard Smith; d, Henry Hathaway, John Ford, George Marshall, Richard Thorpe (uncredited); w, James R. Webb (based on articles in Life magazine); ph, Joseph La Shelle, Charles Lang, William Daniels, Milton Krasner, Harold Wellman (Cinerama, Metrocolor); ed, Harold F. Kress; m, Alfred Newman, Ken Darby; art d, George W. Davis, William Ferrari, Addison Hehr; fx, A. Arnold Gillespie, Robert R. Hoag; cos, Walter Plunkett

Dense and episodic western omelet, tries to condense the evolution of the American west by channeling it through one family's experiences, over three generations. The film is split between four directors with Hathaway's sequences clearly the most cohesive and colorful. This is an all-star guessing-game cast that adults can have fun with, and there's enough history lesson to validate it for children. The acting alternates between star turn, cute, and storybook portmanteau. It's a big-budget fastfood history lesson with Debbie Reynolds as brash schoolmarm. Spencer Tracy narrates, and was probably grateful for the relative safety.

HOW TO GET AHEAD IN ADVERTISING

1989   95m   c   ★★½
Comedy   R/15
HandMade   (U.K.)

Richard E. Grant (Dennis Bagley), Rachel Ward (Julia Bagley), Richard Wilson (Bristol), Jacqueline Tong (Penny Wheelstock), John Shrapnel (Psychiatrist), Susan Wooldridge (Monica), Mick Ford (Richard), Jacqueline Pearce (Maud), Roddy Maude-Roxby (Dr. Gatty), Pauline Melville (Mrs. Wallace)

p, David Wimbury, Ray Cooper; d, Bruce Robinson; w, Bruce Robinson; ph, Peter Hannan (Fujicolor); ed, Alan Strachan; m, David Dundas, Rick Wentworth; prod d, Michael Pickwoad; art d, Henry Harris; chor, David Toguri; cos, Andrea Galer

More satire than comedy, and aimed at a sophisticated audience that can appreciate its barbs at the business of "creating need," HOW TO GET AHEAD IN ADVERTISING is a movie of extremes, both in plot and characterizations.

Dennis Bagley (Richard E. Grant), a veteran advertising executive who has all the perks of success—an attractive wife (Rachel Ward), a country home, and an expensive car—undergoes a drastic change of heart when a creative block prevents him from coming up with an ad campaign for pimple cream. Quitting his job and embarking on an "anti-advertising" campaign, Dennis is soon plagued by a huge boil on the side of his neck that takes on a human visage and becomes Dennis's alter ego. Eventually, the boil, an unprincipled proponent of a "buyer beware" philosophy, even takes possession of Dennis's being.

In asking the audience to decide which is the real Dennis Bagley, writer-director Bruce Robinson is not only concerned with the moral implications of advertising but with those of capitalism in general. Clearly, he has stacked his deck, allowing Grant (who starred in Robinson's wonderful WITHNAIL AND I) to push his character to the outer limits. More subtlety or quiet introspection might have lent greater credibility to the role, though Grant and Robinson unquestionably have made their point.

HOW TO MURDER YOUR WIFE

1965   118m   c   ★★★½
Comedy   /PG
UA

Jack Lemmon (Stanley Ford), Virna Lisi (Mrs. Ford), Terry-Thomas (Charles), Eddie Mayehoff (Harold Lampson), Claire Trevor (Edna), Sidney Blackmer (Judge Blackstone), Max Showalter (Tobey Rawlins), Jack Albertson (Dr. Bentley), Alan Hewitt (District Attorney), Mary Wickes (Harold's Secretary)

p, George Axelrod; d, Richard Quine; w, George Axelrod; ph, Harry Stradling (Technicolor); ed, David Wages; m, Neal Hefti; prod d, Richard Sylbert; chor, Robert Sidney; cos, Moss Mabry

Daft sexist comedy stars Lemmon as a successful cartoonist who loathes the idea of marriage. His widely syndicated cartoon strip about secret agent "Bash Brannigan" has earned him a fortune and a lifestyle the envy of any devout bachelor. But Bash has become a kind of alter ego, and Lemmon has begun to act out aspects of his comic character's life. Into Lemmon's well-organized life comes Italian blonde bombshell Lisi, as sexy and sensuous a woman ever to pop out of a stag party cake. In fact, that's when Lemmon sees and falls in love with her. He's drunk, she snakes out of the cake, and he wakes up the next morning with Lisi beside him. She wears a wedding ring and he realizes to his horror that he's gotten married to someone he doesn't even know.

This dated comedy is saved by Lemmon's comedic genius which eschews macho. There is solid support from Mayehoff and Trevor, and Lisi is gorgeous to behold.

HOW TO SUCCEED IN BUSINESS WITHOUT REALLY TRYING

1967 121m c	★★★★
Musical/Comedy	/U
Mirisch	

Robert Morse (*J. Pierpont Finch*), Michele Lee (*Rosemary Pilkington*), Rudy Vallee (*J.B. Biggley*), Anthony Teague (*Bud Frump*), Maureen Arthur (*Hedy LaRue*), Murray Matheson (*Benjamin Ovington*), Kay Reynolds (*Smitty*), Sammy Smith (*Mr. Twimble/Wally Womper*), John Myhers (*Bratt*), Jeff DeBenning (*Gatch*)

p, David Swift; d, David Swift; w, David Swift (based on the musical book by Abe Burrows, Willie Gilbert, and Jack Weinstock, and the novel by Shepherd Mead); ph, Burnett Guffey (Panavision, DeLuxe Color); ed, Ralph E. Winters, Allan Jacobs; m, Nelson Riddle; art d, Robert Boyle; chor, Dale Moreda (based on original staging by Bob Fosse); cos, Micheline

David Swift produced, directed, adapted, and even played a small role in this scathing musical satire. The film is based on Shepherd Mead's novel which had been brought to the stage by Loesser and Burrows, who co-wrote the stage book with Gilbert and Weinstock.

Morse is an elfin, yet aggressive, window washer who buys a copy of Mead's book on his way to work and decides to put it to work immediately. He walks into the office of World Wide Wickets, a huge conglomerate, and enchants Lee, a pretty secretary, who introduces him to the chief of personnel. That achieved, he convinces the man that he is a great pal of Vallee, who heads the company. This bit of trickery gets him as far as the mailroom. It isn't long before he finagles, cajoles, and charms his way into a junior executive position and endears himself to all the women in the company, but incurs the enmity of Teague, Vallee's insidious nephew. Soon after, Morse is made chief of an advertising department where many heads have rolled. Teague knows that Vallee absolutely despises television giveaway shows, so he tells Morse the opposite, thinking that when Morse presents the idea to Vallee, he will be rewarded with a pink slip.

The film is cartoonlike, its characters caricatures, as befits the story. The lion's share of the acting kudos goes to Morse, in a role that is perfect for him, and Lee, a refreshing, attractive actress who went on to national fame. But Vallee's fussy boss is definitely memorable. Veteran television panelist Robert Q. Lewis plays a small role as an executive and proves to be a much better actor than anyone realized. Myhers does his usual hammy job, but it isn't out of place here. Producer-director-writer-actor Swift was the man responsible for one of television's most beloved early shows, "Mr. Peepers." Good fun.

HOWLING, THE

1981 91m c	★★★½
Horror	R/18
Avco Embassy	

Dee Wallace Stone (*Karen White*), Patrick MacNee (*Dr. George Waggner*), Dennis Dugan (*Chris*), Christopher Stone (*R. William "Bill" Neill*), Belinda Balaski (*Terry Fisher*), Kevin McCarthy (*Fred Francis*), John Carradine (*Erle Kenton*), Slim Pickens (*Sam Newfield*), Elisabeth Brooks (*Marsha*), Robert Picardo (*Eddie*)

p, Michael Finnell, Jack Conrad; d, Joe Dante; w, John Sayles, Terence H. Winkless (based on the novel by Gary Brandner); ph, John Hora (CFI color); ed, Mark Goldblatt, Joe Dante; m, Pino Donaggio; art d, Robert Burns; fx, Rob Bottin, Roger George

A wonderful combination of horror, laughs, and state-of-the-art special effects from director and Roger Corman alumnus Joe Dante (PIRANHA, GREMLINS, EXPLORERS), screenwriter (now screenwriter-director) John Sayles (PIRANHA, RETURN OF THE SECAUCUS SEVEN, BROTHER FROM ANOTHER PLANET), and makeup artist Rob Bottin.

Wallace plays a television anchorwoman who, after being severely traumatized while investigating a story, decides to venture to Macnee's ultra-exclusive California transcendental meditation spa with husband Stone. Unfortunately, the members of Macnee's cult are all werewolves. The transformation scenes are incredible—the highlight being when sexy siren Brooks seduces Stone and they make love under the moonlight while turning into werewolves. Dante fills the film with hysterical cameos from Corman (at a phone booth) and Sayles (a morgue attendent), among others, and demonstrates a subtle wit and a flair for horror. A must-see for horror fans, with more than one viewing recommended. Unfortunately, a slew of really awful sequels followed.

HUCKSTERS, THE

1947 115m bw	★★★½
Drama	/A
MGM	

Clark Gable (*Victor Albee Norman*), Deborah Kerr (*Kay Dorrance*), Sydney Greenstreet (*Evan Llewellyn Evans*), Adolphe Menjou (*Mr. Kimberly*), Ava Gardner (*Jean Ogilvie*), Keenan Wynn (*Buddy Hare*), Edward Arnold (*Dave Lash*), Aubrey Mather (*Valet*), Richard Gaines (*Cooke*), Frank Albertson (*Max Herman*)

p, Arthur Hornblow, Jr.; d, Jack Conway; w, Luther Davis, Edward Chodorov, George Wells (based on the novel by Frederic Wakeman); ph, Harold Rosson; ed, Frank Sullivan; m, Lennie Hayton; art d, Cedric Gibbons, Urie McCleary; fx, Warren Newcombe, A. Arnold Gillespie

Madison Avenue ad agencies, radio commercials, and bigshot businessmen all got a lashing in this glossy drama. Gable plays a predictable rabble-rouser, Kerr the genteel society girl, Gardner the showbiz siren. It's all fairly predictable, a notch above MGM formula stuff, stolen by the expansive Greenstreet's egomania. Gable at first was not interested in doing this film but MGM toned down the hard-hitting best-seller by Wakeman and softened Gable's character to the point where he maintained some scruples at the finish. He approved of both his leading ladies and was particularly fond of Gardner. Kerr had been in films for about six years; this was touted as her first American film by MGM. Although effective in her role, few thought she would ever reach the superstar status that would come with later films such as FROM HERE TO ETERNITY. MGM mogul Louis B. Mayer was convinced Kerr would make it to the top and it was he who suggested a line the studio used in its advertisements for THE

HUCKSTERS when listing her name: "Deborah Kerr (rhymes with 'star')."

HUD

1963   112m   bw   ★★★½
Western   /A
Paramount

Paul Newman (*Hud Bannon*), Melvyn Douglas (*Homer Bannon*), Patricia Neal (*Alma Brown*), Brandon de Wilde (*Lon Bannon*), Whit Bissell (*Burris*), John Ashley (*Hermy*), Crahan Denton (*Jesse*), Val Avery (*Jose*), Sheldon Allman (*Thompson*), Pitt Herbert (*Larker*)

p, Martin Ritt, Irving Ravetch; d, Martin Ritt; w, Irving Ravetch, Harriet Frank, Jr. (based on the novel *Horseman, Pass By* by Larry McMurtry); ph, James Wong Howe; ed, Frank Bracht; m, Elmer Bernstein; art d, Hal Pereira, Tambi Larsen; fx, Paul K. Lerpae; cos, Edith Head

A blistering adult western which broke ground in its depiction of an unglamorous West and in the decidedly anti-heroic nature of its lead.

The charismatic Newman is the title character, an immoral Texas heel—insensitive, crude, avaricious, and irresponsible. He has a stormy relationship with his father, Douglas, an extremely decent but rigid old man who long ago rejected his son. Somewhere in between them is the innocent de Wilde, whose attraction to Newman is almost as strong as that of salty housekeeper Neal. Newman does as little as possible around the ranch his father owns; ignoring the proud past, he is concerned only with having a good ol' time.

HUD belongs to a group of "anti-westerns" which includes LONELY ARE THE BRAVE, THE MISFITS, THE LUSTY MEN and JUNIOR BONNER. It's almost impossible to sympathize with Newman's character, presented cynically by director Ritt in an approach typical of many 60s filmmakers. Newman's performance, though, is unquestionably the best thing about this brutal portrait of humanity.

HUNCHBACK OF NOTRE DAME, THE

1939   115m   bw   ★★★★★
Horror
RKO

Charles Laughton (*The Hunchback*), Cedric Hardwicke (*Frollo*), Thomas Mitchell (*Clopin*), Maureen O'Hara (*Esmeralda*), Edmond O'Brien (*Gringoire*), Alan Marshal (*Proebus*), Walter Hampden (*Claude*), Harry Davenport (*Louis XI*), Katherine Alexander (*Mme. De Lys*), George Zucco (*Procurator*)

p, Pandro S. Berman; d, William Dieterle; w, Sonya Levien, Bruno Frank (based on the novel by Victor Hugo); ph, Joseph August; ed, William Hamilton, Robert Wise; m, Alfred Newman; art d, Van Nest Polglase; fx, Vernon L. Walker

With its lavish production and superb cast, a brilliant performance by Charles Laughton, and moody, atmospheric direction from German expatriate William Dieterle, this is easily the best film version of Victor Hugo's classic novel to date.

Laughton is the pathetic, lonely, misshapen bellringer of Notre Dame who falls in love with the beautiful gypsy Esmeralda (Maureen O'Hara). In addition to gorgeous sets by Van Nest Polglase and breathtaking photography by Joseph H. August, the film benefits from a script that is a vast improvement over the 1923 version. Bringing Hugo's social and political concerns to the forefront, screenwriters Sonya Levien and Bruno Frank make the corrupt machinations of the church almost as important as Quasimodo's tragic love. Laughton, whom some have accused

of overplaying the role's pathos, is magnificent here in one of his greatest roles. His makeup, created by George and R. Gordon Bau, is at least the equal of Lon Chaney's, with modern foam latex technology allowing for a subtler and, therefore, more jarring visage.

RKO spent more than $2 million on this production—one of the most expensive films ever made by the studio—and was rewarded with both critical and financial success. This was the US film debut of the breathtaking O'Hara and a fine film debut for Edmond O'Brien. Superior, gripping filmmaking, well worth revisiting for Dieterle's marvelous command of detail.

HUNGARIAN FAIRY TALE, A

(HOL VOLT, HOL NEM VOLT)
1989   97m   bw   ★★★½
Fantasy/Political   /PG
MD Wax   (Hungary)

David Vermes (*Andris*), Maria Varga (*Maria*), Frantisek Husak (*Antal Orban*), Pal Hetenyi (*Hungarian Voice*), Eszter Csakanyi (*Young Woman*), Peter Trokan (*Teacher*), Szilvia Toth (*Tunde*), Judit Pogany (*Tunde's Mother*), Geza Balkay (*Tunde's Stepfather*), Gabor Reviczky (*Tunde's Father*)

d, Gyula Gazdag; w, Gyula Gazdag, Miklos Gyorffy, Kata Tolmar; ph, Elemer Ragalyi; ed, Julia Sivo; m, Istvan Martha; prod d, Jozsef Romvari; cos, Zsuzsa Stenger

To be political without seeming to be political has been the Eastern European filmmaker's primary task (at least prior to the recent wave of reform there). With this allegorical children's story for adults, director Gyula Gazdag again faces this challenge. A HUNGARIAN FAIRY TALE centers around a quest.

While attending a performance of Mozart's *The Magic Flute* (a fantasy analogue of what's to come), a young woman, (Maria Varga) is smitten by a handsome stranger, leading to sudden and fleeting romance. Andris (David Vermes), the child born of this quicksilver affair, is orphaned by his mother's subsequent death, and spends most of the film searching for the father he has never known; meanwhile, Antal Orban (Frantisek Husak), the kindly bureaucrat who has seen that Andris at least has a name, searches for the boy. In the course of his travels Andris meets an assortment of characters, all of whom have symbolic meaning.

Although state paternalism is Gazdag's enemy here, A HUNGARIAN FAIRY TALE is lighter in tone and more direct in its emotional appeal than most of the director's previous work (THE RESOLUTION, SINGING ON THE TREADMILL). A deft combination of old Hollywood texture and luminosity (Elemer Ragalyi's black-and-white cinematography is superb), 60s New Wave freedom, and surreal fantasy atmospherics, the film may have already lost its topical bite, but the structure underlying it—the simple myth at the complex heart of things—is made to last.

HUNT, THE

(LA CAZA)
1967   93m   bw   ★★★★
Drama
Elias Querejeta   (Spain)

Ismael Merlo (*Jose*), Alfredo Mayo (*Paco*), Jose Maria Prada (*Luis*), Emilio Gutierrez Caba (*Enrique*), Fernando Sanchez Polack (*Juan*), Violetta Garcia (*Nina*), Maria Sanchez Arosa p, Elias Querejeta; d, Carlos Saura; w, Carlos Saura, Angelino Fons (based on a story by Saura); ph, Luis Cuadrado; ed, Pablo del Amo; m, Luis de Pablo; art d, Carlos Ochoa

Brutal, excellent moral tale, dealing with four rabbit hunters. Three Spanish Civil War veterans return to an old battleground that is now filled with rabbits. Merlo, the outing organizer, hopes to borrow some money from his war buddy, Mayo, now a rich businessman. The tensions between the two build with frightening force, and old angers and rivalries are taken out on the rabbits with frightening brutality. Mayo is killed by an accidental shot from Merlo's gun. Prada, believing the shot intentional, drives his jeep head on towards Merlo, who shoots him in the face. Caba, Mayo's teenage brother-in-law, stares numbly at the bloodied corpses. The tensions are well realized by the ensemble. In pitting friend against friend in senseless slaughter, Saura has created a fine allegory for the Spanish Civil War.

HUNT FOR RED OCTOBER, THE

1990 134m c   ★★½
Thriller   PG
Mace Neufeld-Jerry Sherlock

Sean Connery (Capt. Marko Ramius), Alec Baldwin (Jack Ryan), Scott Glenn (Capt. Bart Mancuso), Sam Neill (Capt. Vasily Borodin), James Earl Jones (Admiral James Greer), Joss Ackland (Andrei Lysenko), Richard Jordan (Jeffrey Pelt), Peter Firth (Ivan Putin), Tim Curry (Dr. Petrov), Courtney B. Vance (Seaman Jones)

p, Mace Neufeld; d, John McTiernan; w, Larry Ferguson, Donald Stewart (based on the book by Tom Clancy); ph, Jan De Bont (Panavision, Technicolor); ed, Dennis Virkler, John Wright; m, Basil Poledouris; prod d, Terence Marsh; art d, Dianne Wager, Donald Woodruff, William Cruse; fx, Scott Squires; cos, James Tyson; anim, Eric Swenson, Christopher Dierdorff, Pat Meyers, Charlie Canfield

In spite of the high level of talent on board and at the helm, THE HUNT FOR RED OCTOBER is surprising mostly as a disappointment. It's not that RED OCTOBER is a terrible film, it's that it's middling.

The plot revolves around Marko Ramius (Sean Connery), a veteran Soviet sub commander who is guiding the new, super-advanced *Red October* submarine on its maiden mission as the story begins. Abruptly, Ramius murders the onboard political officer and burns his orders. *Red October* is supposed to participate in war games meant to showcase its ability to evade sonar detection and deliver a full load of nuclear missiles to major American targets. Ramius instead tells his crew that they will approach the US coastline to embarrass the American military. In fact, he has something very different in mind.

When Ramius goes off course, factions within the US military and government suspect a sneak attack. The Soviets, who assume Ramius is defecting with their most advanced weaponry, float a cover story that Ramius has had a mental breakdown and intends to attack the US coast singlehandedly. Guided by CIA analyst Dr. Jack Ryan (Alec Baldwin), who happens to be an expert on Ramius, the American security brain trust has to decide whether the Russians are telling the truth. Then they must choose the appropriate response—either help the Russians sink *Red October* (the FAIL SAFE scenario) or help Ramius defect.

Tom Clancy's exciting bestseller served as the basis for the film. But on the screen, RED OCTOBER suffers from a bad case of bloated scenario, lacking unities of place and action. In simpler terms, it should have stayed put, either above the surface or in the briny depths. Instead, the two major plots—two different

movies, really—wind up neutralizing each other. Each time McTiernan cuts from one setting to the other, he's forced to start from scratch in rebuilding tension and involvement. Over the course of two hours plus, the strain takes its toll on the film and on the audience. And Larry Ferguson's adaptation offers characters sans motivation. Ryan is so lacking in substance viewers may find it hard to remember that he's the movie's hero.

As for McTiernan, if PREDATOR and DIE HARD revealed him to be an outstanding craftsman and a superb technician, RED OCTOBER highlights his limitations. The film comes alive only in its most generic moments, which is another way of saying that the three submarines—*Red October* and the Russian and American subs pursuing it—wind up stealing the show, along with the torpedoes that zoom at Ramius's vessel from time to time. Too bad nobody directed a few torpedoes at RED OCTOBER's slow-moving, gridlocked screenplay.

HURRICANE, THE

1937 110m bw   ★★★★
Disaster   /PG
Goldwyn

Dorothy Lamour (Marama), Jon Hall (Terangi), Mary Astor (Madame Germaine De Laage), C. Aubrey Smith (Father Paul), Thomas Mitchell (Dr. Kersaint), Raymond Massey (Governor Eugene De Laage), John Carradine (Jailer), Jerome Cowan (Capt. Nagle), Al Kikume (Chief Mehevi), Kuulei DeClercq (Tita)

p, Samuel Goldwyn; d, John Ford, Stuart Heisler (uncredited); w, Dudley Nichols, Oliver H.P. Garrett (based on the novel by Charles Nordhoff and James Norman Hall); ph, Bert Glennon; ed, Lloyd Nosler; art d, Richard Day, Alexander Golitzen; fx, James Basevi; cos, Omar Kiam

A stunning big blowout; this South Seas spectacular from the great John Ford is a rare perennial. The story is pretty much hooey with a dollop of tropical glamour on top, but anyway, marvelously self-serving. The beauteous Lamour is in love with barrel-chested Hall, whose hot temper lands him in hot water with corrupt island governor Massey. There's a fine assist from Astor, Mitchell, Cowan, Carradine, and Smith. Then the hurricane comes—a real lulu—and steals everyone's thunder. These scenes are terrifyingly spectacular, done on actual and miniature scales so cleverly edited that it is next to impossible to discern where one leaves off and the other takes over.

Hall and Lamour, two relatively unknown actors, became big deals in their roles as scantily clad natives. Lamour, a $75-a-week bit player at Paramount with only four films to her credit, was borrowed by Goldwyn from that studio. Goldwyn originally wanted Howard Hawks to direct this film, but they had argued violently over the making of COME AND GET IT, so Goldwyn turned to John Ford to direct THE HURRICANE. The mogul had also intended Joel McCrea to enact the part of the persecuted native Terangi, but McCrea convinced Ford that he was not right for the role, so Ford came up with Hall, a handsome, virile-looking actor Ford had spotted in a minor production at the Hollywood Playhouse.

Hall would have a checkered career after THE HURRICANE, coming to prominence in the early 1940s in a series of adventure and fantasy tales with exotic co-star Maria Montez. Lamour's star would rise even higher, especially after parlaying her sarong to fame—she first wore it in THE JUNGLE PRINCESS—and she would wear it through many a Bob Hope-Bing Crosby road film.

HUSBANDS

1970 154m c ★★½
Drama GP/X
Faces Music

Ben Gazzara *(Harry)*, Peter Falk *(Archie)*, John Cassavetes *(Gus)*, Jenny Runacre *(Mary Tynan)*, Jenny Wright *(Pearl Billingham)*, Noelle Kao *(Julie)*, Leola Harlow *(Leola)*, Meta Shaw *(Annie)*, John Kullers *(Red)*, Delores Delmar *(Countess)*

p, Al Ruban; d, John Cassavetes; w, John Cassavetes; ph, Victor J. Kemper (DeLuxe Color); ed, Peter Tanner; art d, Rene D'Auriac; cos, Louis Brown

Not unlike BYE BYE BRAVERMAN, this is the Italian version of that very Jewish film that starred George Segal and was based on Wallace Markfield's superb novel *To an Early Grave*. HUSBANDS is better than the aforementioned, but Cassavetes sometimes falls so in love with his work he doesn't know how to edit it.

Cassavetes, Gazzara, and Falk are thunderstruck when their pal David Rowlands dies suddenly of a heart attack. As three middle-aged husbands with wives and houses in the New York City suburbs, they confront their own mortality, responding by tossing aside all their cares and obligations and going on a spree. Cassavetes and Falk are both happy types; Gazzara is the most brooding of the bunch. For the next two days, the trio sleep in the subways, get drunk, play basketball, and reminisce about the days when they were young and single. After 48 hours, Falk and Cassavetes are ready to pack it in, but Gazzara has had a monumental fight with his wife and decides to fly to London.

He talks the other two into accompanying him, and they arrive in England, change into formal clothing, and lurch around a gambling casino, thinking they all look like Bogart in CASABLANCA. There they meet three women and take them off to their rooms. Cassavetes goes with Runacre, Falk with Kao, and Gazzara with Wright. Gazzara finds the thought of adultery hard to handle but makes an effort to get over his guilt. The next day Cassavetes and Falk are ready to go back to Long Island, but Gazzara isn't.

HUSBANDS might have been one of the best films of 1970 if greater care were given to pruning it. Even after a scene hits its apogee, Cassavetes lets it continue and peter out. Improvised dialogue can only work if it's judiciously edited. Scripted, HUSBANDS might have been unforgettable.

HUSH . . . HUSH, SWEET CHARLOTTE

1964 134m bw ★★★½
Thriller /15
FOX

Bette Davis *(Charlotte)*, Olivia de Havilland *(Miriam)*, Joseph Cotten *(Drew)*, Agnes Moorehead *(Velma)*, Cecil Kellaway *(Harry)*, Victor Buono *(Big Sam)*, Mary Astor *(Jewel Mayhew)*, Wesley Addy *(Sheriff)*, William Campbell *(Paul Marchand)*, Bruce Dern *(John Mayhew)*

p, Robert Aldrich; d, Robert Aldrich; w, Henry Farrell, Lukas Heller; ph, Joseph Biroc; ed, Michael Luciano; m, Frank DeVol; art d, William Glasgow; chor, Alex Ruiz; cos, Norma Koch

A Grand Guignol Southern Gothic cauldron. . . the next dish proffered by Aldrich and Davis after the success of WHATEVER HAPPENED TO BABY JANE? CHARLOTTE was originally planned as Crawford's revenge—Davis is the victim here, a loopy loon living in a moldy mansion in Louisiana, with hair like Spanish moss, skin like a lichen and a hobby of shooting at land developers.

She's haunted by an Electra complex and memories of a murdered beau she may have chopped up. Her nocturnal ramblings are interrupted, then encouraged, by the arrival of her prissbitch cousin from Virginia, de Havilland, finally getting a chance to give Davis hell and act out the dark side of Melanie Wilkes. Cotten is the corrupt ole boy family doctor, Agnes Moorehead the Broomhilda housekeeper and the great Mary Astor (as a favor to Davis) in a swansong cameo.

Davis has some authentic, poignant moments, before all hell breaks loose. She seems to be making up for her lost chances on Tennessee Williams territory (she had wanted MENAGERIE and STREETCAR), and there's one kabuki lioness flip-out on a stairway that's a must-see. She's matched by Moorehead's perfect, obscure portrayal. The best line goes to de Havilland: "You just can't keep the hogs away from the trough."

Next to this, JANE looks like Masterpiece Theatre—it's the mutilation aspect that saddles the proceedings (both films were from Henry Farrell novels). Victor Buono (who received an Academy Award nomination for BABY JANE) is back for more as young Charlotte's father, and Dern is the lover who gets the axe. The tacky title song was a camp hit for Patti Page.

HUSTLE

1975 120m c ★★★½
Crime/Mystery R/15
Paramount

Burt Reynolds *(Lt. Phil Gaines)*, Catherine Deneuve *(Nicole Britton)*, Ben Johnson *(Marty Hollinger)*, Paul Winfield *(Sgt. Louis Belgrave)*, Eileen Brennan *(Paula Hollinger)*, Eddie Albert *(Leo Sellers)*, Ernest Borgnine *(Santoro)*, Catherine Bach *(Peggy Summers)*, Jack Carter *(Herbie Dalitz)*, James Hampton *(Bus Driver)*

p, Robert Aldrich; d, Robert Aldrich; w, Steve Shagan; ph, Joseph Biroc (Eastmancolor); ed, Michael Luciano; m, Frank DeVol; art d, Hilyard Brown; fx, Henry Miller, Jr.; chor, Alex Romero; cos, Oscar Rodriguez, Betsy Cox

A disturbing and grim modern film noir directed by Aldrich, who was a master of the genre in the early 1950s. Reynolds stars as Phil Gaines, a bitter, cynical cop who finds the body of a young girl washed up on the beach and launches an investigation to determine her identity. After she is identified as a small-time hooker and porno actress, Gaines calls in the girl's parents, Marty (Johnson, in a superb performance) and Paula (Brennan), to identify the body. Soon Gaines finds himself competing with the headstrong Marty to solve a crime that turns out to have grave personal implications for them both.

Director Aldrich (KISS ME DEADLY) offers an unrelentingly diseased portrait of modern society in HUSTLE. Reynolds is trapped in this disgusting, seedy world from the opening of the film when his pleasant day off is intruded upon by the washed-up corpse, forcing him back into the underworld. There is no way out. HUSTLE is one of the few examples of *true* modern film noir. But director and screenwriter cannot resolve their different approaches. The script's humanistic, if depressing, angle gets battered by Aldrich's approach. An interesting mixed bag.

HUSTLER, THE

1961 134m bw ★★★★½
Sports /15
FOX

Paul Newman *("Fast" Eddie Felson)*, Jackie Gleason *(Minnesota Fats)*, Piper Laurie *(Sarah Packard)*, George C. Scott *(Bert Gordon)*, Myron McCormick *(Charlie Bums)*, Murray Hamilton *(Find-*

lay), Michael Constantine *(Big John)*, Stefan Gierasch *(Preacher)*, Jake LaMotta *(Bartender)*, Gordon B. Clarke *(Cashier)*

p, Robert Rossen; d, Robert Rossen; w, Sidney Carroll, Robert Rossen (based on the novel by Walter Tevis); ph, Eugene Schuftan (CinemaScope); ed, Dede Allen; m, Kenyon Hopkins; prod d, Harry Horner; art d, Albert Brenner, Harry Horner; cos, Ruth Morley

This dark stunner, based on Walter Tevis's novel, boasts Paul Newman in the role that made him an overnight superstar. The treatment feels like a cross between Hemingway and Odetts and there are some affectations with dialogue. But Rossen knows how to frame his story and give his actors room to breathe, eliciting terrific performances from everyone.

"Fast" Eddie Felson is a pool shark who hustles his way across the country to Ames Billiard Parlor in New York, where he challenges the unbeatable Minnesota Fats (Jackie Gleason). Penniless and alone, Eddie falls in love with Sarah Packard (Piper Laurie), an alcoholic cripple; then, after a return to small-time hustling that leads to two thug-administered broken thumbs, Eddie teams up with gambler Bert Gordon (George C. Scott), who becomes his backer but also personifies a vision of evil.

With the help of Gene Shufton's Oscar-winning black-and-white cinematography, producer-writer-director Robert Rossen offers a grim world where the only bright spot is the top of the pool table, yet his characters maintain a shabby nobility and grace. Gleason is brilliantly detached, witty, and charming as Fats; sexy, waifish Laurie offers some of the best work of her career; Scott is evil incarnate; and Newman is simply unforgettable in his Oscar-nominated role (he would have to play Fast Eddie again 25 years later in the excellent sequel, THE COLOR OF MONEY, to actually win his first Academy Award). The great pool player Willie Mosconi coached Gleason and Newman in their shots. Not to be missed.

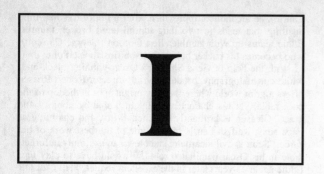

I

I ACCUSE!
1958 99m bw ★★★
Drama/Political/Historical /U
MGM (U.K.)

Jose Ferrer (Alfred Dreyfus), Anton Walbrook (Maj. Esterhazy), Viveca Lindfors (Lucie Dreyfus), Leo Genn (Maj. Picquart), Emlyn Williams (Emile Zola), David Farrar (Mathieu Dreyfus), Donald Wolfit (Gen. Mercier), Herbert Lom (Maj. DuPaty de Clam), Harry Andrews (Maj. Henry), Felix Aylmer (Edgar Demange)

p, Sam Zimbalist; d, Jose Ferrer; w, Gore Vidal (based on the book Captain Dreyfus—A Story of Mass Hysteria by Nicholas Halasz); ph, Freddie Young; ed, Frank Clarke; m, William Alwyn; art d, Elliot Scott; cos, Elizabeth Haffenden

Ferrer stars and directs in this screen version of the historic turn-of-the-century trials of Alfred Dreyfus. Dreyfus, a Jewish staff officer in the French Army, is wrongly accused of treason, sentenced to life imprisonment and sent to Devil's Island. Later the real traitor (Walbrook) is exposed, but the military turns his trial into a whitewash. Soliciting the aid of some of France's most famous citizens (most notably novelist Emile Zola), Dreyfus's friends gain a retrial for him. Again he is found guilty; however, the French president steps in to pardon the noble captain. Ferrer's acting is expert but demonstrates more technique than heart; as a director, he fails to establish the lively pace so important for historical recreations. But Vidal's script makes for compelling drama, especially in the courtroom scenes. Walbrook and Wolfit contribute telling portrayals.

I AM A CAMERA
1955 98m bw ★★½
Drama/Comedy /X
Romulus/Remus (U.K.)

Julie Harris (Sally Bowles), Laurence Harvey (Christopher Isherwood), Shelley Winters (Natalia Landauer), Ron Randell (Clive), Lea Seidl (Fraulein Schneider), Anton Diffring (Fritz), Ina De La Haye (Herr Landauer), Jean Gargoet (Pierre), Stanley Maxted (American Editor), Alexis Bobrinskoy (Proprietor)

p, Jack Clayton; d, Henry Cornelius; w, John Collier (based on the play by John Van Druten from the "Berlin Stories" by Christopher Isherwood); ph, Guy Green; ed, Clive Donner; m, Malcolm Arnold; art d, William Kellner

In the beginning there were Christopher Isherwood's "Berlin Stories." From them came the award-winning play that provided the basis for both I AM A CAMERA and CABARET. Despite an intelligent adaptation and cast, this version is little more than an erratically filmed stage play. The action is static and the plot developed mostly through dialogue, which takes a far lighter tone than CABARET. The comedy deals with the episodic adventures of Harvey, a poor, struggling writer, and the effervescent Harris, a nightclub chanteuse—roommates caught up in the swirl of pre-WWII Berlin. Winters is a German girl who begins to experience the anti-Semitism of the Nazi regime.

I AM A FUGITIVE FROM A CHAIN GANG
1932 93m bw ★★★★★
Prison /A
WB

Paul Muni (James Allen), Glenda Farrell (Marie Woods), Helen Vinson (Helen), Preston Foster (Pete), Allen Jenkins (Barney Sykes), Edward Ellis (Bomber Wells), John Wray (Nordine), Hale Hamilton (Rev. Robert Clinton Allen), Harry Woods (Guard), David Landau

p, Hal B. Wallis; d, Mervyn LeRoy; w, Howard J. Green, Brown Holmes, Sheridan Gibney (based on the autobiography I Am a Fugitive from a Georgia Chain Gang by Robert E. Burns); ph, Sol Polito; ed, William Holmes; art d, Jack Okey; cos, Orry-Kelly

One of the toughest movies ever made, an uncompromising and frightening film that lays bare the inhuman conditions of the penal system in post-WWII Georgia.

Based on a collection of writings by Robert Elliot Burns, who escaped from a chain gang to become a successful magazine editor but lived with the continual threat of being recaptured, the film tells the story of James Allen (Paul Muni), who is framed for the robbery of a hamburger stand and sentenced to ten years' hard labor. Every ounce of his strength and dignity is stripped away until he resolves to escape.

The reputation of socially conscious director Mervyn LeRoy is identified perhaps more with this film than with any other. Here the director of LITTLE CAESAR and THEY WON'T FORGET (which explored the horrors of lynching) pulls no punches, with every scene of I AM A FUGITIVE an expression of social outrage. Much of the film's story and technique would influence later prison movies, especially those dealing with prison farm systems. The escape through the swamps was duplicated by Edward G. Robinson in BLACKMAIL; the escape by truck was employed by Paul Newman in COOL HAND LUKE. Muni's captivating performance marked one of the highlights of his career.

Though the film specifically excluded the word "Georgia" from its title and never mentioned the state in the entire film, the indictment of that state's cruel chain-gang system was clear. The film was banned in Georgia and the state filed a libel suit against the studio. Two prison wardens in Georgia also filed unsuccessful million-dollar suits against Warner Brothers. Georgia was also relentless in its attempts to recapture Burns, whom Warner Bros. asked to travel to Hollywood to serve as an advisor on the project. Burns smuggled himself into Los Angeles using an assumed name and, reportedly, not only suggested ideas for the script but helped write dialogue before nervously fleeing after a few weeks.

I KNOW WHERE I'M GOING
1945 91m bw ★★★½
Romance/Comedy /U
Archers (U.K.)

Roger Livesey (Torquil MacNeil), Wendy Hiller (Joan Webster), Pamela Brown (Catriona Potts), Nancy Price (Mrs. Crozier), Finlay Currie (Ruairidh Mur), John Laurie (John Campbell), George Carney (Mr. Webster), Walter Hudd (Hunter), Murdo Morrison (Kenny), Margot Fitzsimmons (Bridie)

p, Michael Powell, Emeric Pressburger; d, Michael Powell, Emeric Pressburger; w, Michael Powell, Emeric Pressburger; ph, Erwin Hillier; ed, John Seabourne; m, Allan Gray; art d, Alfred Junge

Low-key, engaging Powell/Pressburger gem, partly set in Northern Scotland, about the adventures of a venal young girl from London. Determined to have her way against the wishes of Carney, her bank-manager father, Hiller sets out to marry the elderly millionaire boss of a large chemical company whose only attraction is his great wealth. As she nears the tiny island in the Hebrides which the industrialist has rented, a storm forces her to stay on the mainland with the native Scots. Here she meets and falls in love with Livesey, who is on his way to do some hunting on the island. In reality he is a Scottish lord and owner of the small island, who vehemently opposes the money-grubbing ways of the rich businessman. Hiller is at first determined to pursue her goal of marrying the elderly millionaire, but her sentiments change as she grows more attached to Livesey.

Contributions from the local Scots and the Glasgow Orpheus Choir add a unique flavor to this picture. In a supporting role, Pamela Brown gives an outstanding performance as an unconventional native. Scottish folk songs are also featured, particularly the one from which the title is derived. In an early, quasi-surrealistic sequence, Hiller dreams she is marrying not a man, but a huge industrial empire. This makes an intriguing contrast with the almost documentary flavor of the later part of the film.

I LOVE YOU, ALICE B. TOKLAS!

1968 92m c ★★
Comedy /X
WB

Peter Sellers (*Harold*), Jo Van Fleet (*Mother*), Leigh Taylor-Young (*Nancy*), Joyce Van Patten (*Joyce*), David Arkin (*Herbie*), Herb Edelman (*Murray*), Salem Ludwig (*Father*), Louis Gottlieb (*Guru*), Grady Sutton (*Funeral Director*), Janet E. Clark (*Mrs. Foley*)

p, Charles Maguire; d, Hy Averback; w, Paul Mazursky, Larry Tucker; ph, Philip Lathrop (Technicolor); ed, Robert C. Jones; m, Elmer Bernstein; prod d, Pato Guzman; cos, Theadora Van Runkle

An inspired performance by Sellers cannot redeem this giddy satire of 60s hippie culture, in which he plays a neurotic, asthmatic, fortyish attorney who discovers pot and the counter-culture. Van Fleet plays his mother, Van Patten the boring blonde his parents wish he would marry, and Arkin his hippy brother. Mazursky and Tucker, who came from TV's "Monkees," wrote in enough laughs to make this a hit at the time, but from the point that Sellers grows his hair and drops out, the embarassment factor becomes too much to take. Look for Grady Sutton, the butt of so many W.C. Fields jokes, effective in a small role.

I, MADMAN

1989 89m c ★★★½
Horror R/
Diamant/Sarlui

Jenny Wright (*Virginia/Anna*), Clayton Rohner (*Richard*), Randall William Cook (*Malcolm Brand*), Steven Memel (*Lenny*), Stephanie Hodge (*Mona*), Michelle Jordan (*Colette*), Vance Valencia (*St. Navarro*), Bruce Wagner (*Pianist*)

p, Rafael Eisenman; d, Tibor Takacs; w, David Chaskin; ph, Bryan England; ed, Marcus Manton; m, Michael Hoenig; prod d, Ron Wilson, Matthew Jacobs

Tibor Takacs's wonderful horror film concerns bookstore employee Virginia (Jenny Wright), who is reading a book called *I, Madman* by one Malcolm Brand. She soon begins to notice that objects described in the book are starting to pop up in reality, and it's not long before the title madman (Randall William Cook), a strange doctor patterned after his author, also escapes into the actual world. Soon murders depicted in the book begin to occur, and when the maniac killer—turnabout being fair play—mistakes Virginia for the fictional character who scorned his love, her life is on the line as well.

As reminiscent of HOUSE OF WAX or FRANKENSTEIN as it is of current-day slasher films, I, MADMAN is a loving salute to the days when movie monsters had hearts. Cook's character has a clear motive for his murders, one that inspires sympathy along with disgust; he's a descendant of the classic horror films' "misunderstood monster," worthy of our attention and fear. Takacs's lively, sharp direction maintains the suspense and serves up some poetic horror imagery, and the high quality of the acting, photography and lighting all belie the film's low budget.

I MARRIED A WITCH

1942 82m bw ★★★★½
Comedy /A
Paramount

Fredric March (*Wallace Wooley*), Veronica Lake (*Jennifer*), Robert Benchley (*Dr. Dudley White*), Susan Hayward (*Estelle Masterson*), Cecil Kellaway (*Daniel*), Elizabeth Patterson (*Margaret*), Robert Warwick (*J.B. Masterson*), Eily Malyon (*Tabitha Wooley*), Nora Cecil (*Harriet*), Emory Parnell (*Allen*)

p, Preston Sturges; d, Rene Clair; w, Robert Pirosh, Marc Connelly, Dalton Trumbo (based on the novel *The Passionate Witch* by Thorne Smith and Norman Matson); ph, Ted Tetzlaff; ed, Eda Warren; m, Roy Webb; art d, Hans Dreier, Ernst Fegte; fx, Gordon Jennings; cos, Edith Head

Forget Clair's early little French musicals; for the most part they're force-fed Chaplin rip-offs. Here's the master at his peak in, yes, Hollywood, USA. I MARRIED A WITCH is an accomplished confection, and absolutely required Halloween viewing.

Kellaway and his daughter Lake are branded witches in 1690 and burned at the stake, but not before putting a curse on their persecutors, the Wooley family. They threaten that no male member of the family will find happiness, and the curse is shown taking effect as misfortune befalls Wooley males (all played by March) through the ages, up to 1942 where March is shown to be a stuffed shirt with a snobbish fiancee, Hayward. He's running for governor of the state with backing from Hayward's filthy rich father, Warwick, an influential publisher. A storm comes up and lightning splits the ancient tree under which Kellaway and Lake were buried over 250 years before. They are freed, emerging as a rotund, booze-loving fellow and a blonde siren. From that point on, Lake does all in her power to make March fall in love with her. Yet her powers seem unable to sway him, as his plans to wed Hayward remain unchanged.

Lake, who had only been in films for a year, is wonderfully effective. Released from the sustained tension of film noir material, she demonstrates a quirky sense of comedy. Her line readings tingle with malice and hoydenish longing. WITCH also presents a lighter, warmer, more likable March than ever before—his chemistry with Lake is very engaging.

This is one of the rare instances where the "other woman" measures up to the lead in beauty and presence. Despite having her own beautiful hair chignoned to play up Lake's, Hayward's career took a major step here, snagging her a series of hard-bitten second leads that prepared her for the Davis-Crawford-Stanwyck roles that would establish her later as a great star. And WITCH finds Kellaway in peak form—it's his most three-dimensional role. Look out, too, for humorist Robert Benchley as March's confused political advisor.

This film, with its wonderful special effects by Jennings, was in the hilarious tradition of TOPPER and THE GHOST GOES WEST. Clair's direction is swift and sure, producing a livelier, more cohesive effort than his first Hollywood production, THE FLAME OF NEW ORLEANS, which fizzled at the box office. This Thorne Smith tale, taken from an incomplete novel, worked so well on screen that it inspired the popular TV series, "Bewitched."

I MARRIED AN ANGEL

1942 84m bw   ★★
Musical   /U
MGM

Jeanette MacDonald (Anna Zador/Brigitta), Nelson Eddy (Count Willie Palaffi), Binnie Barnes (Peggy), Edward Everett Horton (Peter), Reginald Owen (Herman "Whiskers" Rothbart), Mona Maris (Marika), Janis Carter (Sufi), Inez Cooper (Iren), Douglas Dumbrille (Baron Szigetti), Leonid Kinskey (Zinski)

p, Hunt Stromberg; d, W.S. Van Dyke, II; w, Anita Loos (based on the stage musical by Richard Rodgers and Lorenz Hart from the play by Vaszary Janos); ph, Ray June; ed, Conrad A. Nervig; m, Richard Rodgers; art d, Cedric Gibbons, John S. Detlie; fx, A. Arnold Gillespie, Warren Newcombe; chor, Ernst Matray; cos, Motley, Robert Kalloch

Eddy plays Count Willie Palaffi, a bored, very rich playboy and bank owner in Budapest. All the single women in town attend a massive costume party in honor of Willie's birthday, parading before the eligible bachelor in the hope of becoming his bride; however, seeking to escape their attentions, Willie decides to dance with one of his employees, Anna (MacDonald), a shy, unassuming girl, costumed as an angel, whom the rest of the guests scorn. After a brief conversation, Willie excuses himself and goes to his room. Falling asleep, he dreams that a beautiful angel with wings and a halo—named Brigitta, but looking just like Anna—has floated into his room, declaring that she has come to marry him. Soon Willie and his angel are whisked off on a Parisian honeymoon, although on their first night together Brigitta tries to leave him and return to her usual ethereal resting place. Willie asks her to stay with him, and the next morning she wakes to discover that she has lost her wings.

In 1938, Lorenz Hart and Richard Rodgers turned this story into a highly successful Broadway musical starring Vera Zorina, whom MGM first wanted to cast here. But Paramount refused to lend Zorina's services. MacDonald and Eddy had their own reservations about the project and, by the time the film was ready to be shot, it was plagued with problems. Writer Anita Loos was juggling three movies and one Broadway show at the same time, and others were brought in to make revisions. Whatever life was on paper was promptly sliced out. Rodgers and Hart refused to participate, forcing the studio to employ Bob Wright and Chet Forrest to "adapt" the original songs. Several sequences were cut, including scenes showing that Willie and the angel had children, a notion considered too risque for the screen.

I NEVER PROMISED YOU A ROSE GARDEN

1977 96m c   ★★★½
Drama   R/18
Imorh

Bibi Andersson (Dr. Fried), Kathleen Quinlan (Deborah Blake), Ben Piazza (Mr. Blake), Lorraine Gary (Mrs. Blake), Darlene Craviotto (Carla), Reni Santoni (Hobbs), Susan Tyrrell (Lee), Signe Hasso (Helene), Norman Alden (McPherson), Martine Bartlett (Secret Wife of Henry VIII)

p, Terence F. Deane, Michael Hausman, Daniel H. Blatt; d, Anthony Page; w, Lewis John Carlino, Gavin Lambert (based on the novel by Joanne Greenberg); ph, Bruce Logan (Technicolor); ed, Garth Craven; m, Paul Chihara; prod d, Toby Rafelson; cos, Jane Ruhm

A compelling drama about the terrors of schizophrenia, I NEVER PROMISED YOU A ROSE GARDEN is almost, but not quite, the distaff version of ONE FLEW OVER THE CUCKOO'S NEST. Quinlan is a certified mental case who is taken to a new and what appears to be tranquil hospital by her parents, Gary and Piazza. The similarity between this film and CUCKOO'S NEST ends in the fact that most of the patients in that one are only mildly afflicted and the ward becomes a microcosm of society. In ROSE GARDEN, there is no question of the horrors taking place inside the brains of the inmates. Quinlan is counseled by psychiatrist Andersson, and the bulk of the film deals with exorcising her various demons.

ROSE GARDEN falls short in its simplistic analysis of Quinlan's problem. Nor do we ever know much about her interaction with her family except for a brief indication of some resentment toward her brother. Most of our interest is sustained by the relationship between Quinlan and Andersson. Some casting sidelights include the great Sylvia Sidney as a patient who opts to come back to the hospital after being released; Hasso, who made her name playing what everyone thought was a man in THE HOUSE ON 92ND STREET; horror diva Barbara Steele; and Jeff Conaway, who later became popular on TV's "Taxi."

I NEVER SANG FOR MY FATHER

1970 92m c   ★★★½
Drama   GP/A
Columbia

Melvyn Douglas (Tom Garrison), Gene Hackman (Gene Garrison), Dorothy Stickney (Margaret Garrison), Estelle Parsons (Alice), Elizabeth Hubbard (Peggy), Lovelady Powell (Norma), Daniel Keyes (Dr. Mayberry), Conrad Bain (Rev. Pell), Jon Richards (Marvin Scott), Nikki Counselman (Waitress)

p, Gilbert Cates; d, Gilbert Cates; w, Robert W. Anderson (based on his play); ph, Morris Hartzband, George Stoetzel (Technicolor); ed, Angelo Ross; m, Barry Mann, Al Gorgoni; art d, Hank Aldrich; cos, Theoni V. Aldredge

Honest, powerful and never sloppy, I NEVER SANG is a virtuoso acting exercise reined in by Cates, a terrific actors' director. The screenplay, adapted by Robert Anderson from his own play, feels drawn from real life.

Hackman is a fortyish New York professor who tells his aging parents, Douglas and Stickney, he is planning to change his life by marrying Hubbard, a divorced doctor, and moving to California. Stickney understands Hackman's need to break away but warns him that moving that far away may have a deleterious effect on Douglas. Just before the wedding, Stickney dies of heart failure. Parsons, Hackman's sister, has been disowned by Douglas for marrying a Jewish man. While at the funeral of their mother, Parsons advises Hackman not to allow himself to be manipulated by the old man and to live his life for himself.

Douglas is truly brilliant here—it's one of those performances that captures you so strongly that you are purged emotionally, yet equally enjoy the sureness of the talent at work. Hackman is able to personify the struggle of a conscience choosing between self or family.

I OUGHT TO BE IN PICTURES
1982   108m   c   ★★
Comedy   PG/15
FOX

Walter Matthau (Herbert Tucker), Ann-Margret (Stephanie), Dinah Manoff (Libby), Lance Guest (Gordon), Lewis Smith (Soldier), Martin Ferrero (Monte Del Rey), Eugene Butler (Marty), Samantha Harper (Larane), Santos Morales (Mexican Truck Driver), David Faustino (Martin)

p, Herbert Ross, Neil Simon; d, Herbert Ross; w, Neil Simon (based on his play); ph, David M. Walsh (Deluxe Color); ed, Sidney Levin; m, Marvin Hamlisch; prod d, Albert Brenner; cos, Ruth Morley

No, you ought not. Long-lost daughter Manoff, relentlessly relentless here, migrates to Los Angeles with the apparent intent of crashing the movies, but her underlying motive is to find her father, Walter Matthau, who deserted his family 16 years before. An ex-screenwriter, Matthau has given up writing for gambling and booze. His fears are driving girlfriend Ann-Margret away, but he seems too grouchy to reach out. Clearly, Manoff's ingratiating presence is meant to reform him in one of those precious bringing-up-daddy themes. There aren't enough good jokes to salvage the exhausted story line, Manoff comes off like a tank, and if you can believe the excellent, wasted Ann-Margret could long for Matthau, we'll get the deed ready for you to sign on that swampland in Florida. That's Herb Ross asleep at the wheel.

I REMEMBER MAMA
1948   134m   bw   ★★★★
Drama   /U
RKO

Irene Dunne (Mama), Barbara Bel Geddes (Katrin), Oscar Homolka (Uncle Chris), Philip Dorn (Papa), Cedric Hardwicke (Mr. Hyde), Edgar Bergen (Mr. Thorkelson), Rudy Vallee (Dr. Johnson), Barbara O'Neil (Jessie Brown), Florence Bates (Florence Dana Moorhead), Peggy McIntyre (Christine)

p, Harriet Parsons; d, George Stevens; w, DeWitt Bodeen (based on the play by John Van Druten and the novel Mama's Bank Account by Kathryn Forbes); ph, Nicholas Musuraca; ed, Robert Swink, Tholen Gladden; m, Roy Webb; art d, Albert S. D'Agostino, Carroll Clark; fx, Russell A. Cully, Kenneth Peach; cos, Edward Stevenson, Gile Steele

A delicate charmer, sometimes precious, but nonetheless fine. Based on Kathryn Forbes's collection of autobiographical short stories Mama's Bank Account, this meticulously directed George Stevens film tells the heartwarming story of a Norwegian immigrant family making a go of it in turn-of-the-century San Francisco. Katrin (Barbara Bel Geddes), one of the daughters, narrates from her diary as the family's trials, tribulations, and triumphs are shown in flashback. At the center of the proceedings is the indefatigable Mama (Irene Dunne, giving one of her finest performances), keeping the house and her head while a dizzying parade of offbeat relatives and friends come and go, including Oscar Homolka (overacting), Cedric Hardwicke (wonderful indeed), Rudy Vallee, Edgar Bergen, and Philip Dorn as Papa.

Forbes's nostalgic tale had earlier been brought to Broadway by Richard Rodgers and Oscar Hammerstein II (adapted by John Van Druten), and Peggy Wood later appeared in a long-running (1946 to 1957) TV series based on the story.

I SENT A LETTER TO MY LOVE
1980   112m   c   ★★★½
Drama   PG/
Atlantic   (France)

Simone Signoret (Louise), Jean Rochefort (Gilles), Delphine Seyrig (Yvette)

p, Lise Fayolle, Giorgio Silvagni; d, Moshe Mizrahi; w, Moshe Mizrahi, Gerard Brach (based on the novel by Bernice Rubens); ph, Ghislain Cloquet; ed, Francoise Bonnot; m, Philippe Sarde

Simone Signoret gives a touching performance here as Louise, an aging woman whose devotion to her paralyzed, wheelchair-bound brother, Gilles (Jean Rochefort), has prevented her from tasting the sweeter things in life. Neither sibling has much contact with the outside world—Gilles gazes at the Atlantic through his telescope, Louise dreams of taking a vacation to America—except through their close friend Yvette (Delphine Seyrig), an aging local baker who has a fondness for Gilles. Hoping to find a mate, Louise places an ad in the local newspaper to that effect and receives only one response—from Gilles. Rather than reveal herself to him, the needy Louise continues to correspond under the nom de plume Beatrice Deschamps, eagerly awaiting his increasingly amorous and erotic letters until the time comes for "Beatrice" to meet Gilles.

This slow-moving story, which reteams director Moshe Mizrahi and Signoret after their Oscar-winning MADAME ROSA, relies chiefly on its three poignant and sensitive performances. Signoret, Rochefort, and Seyrig never look like glamourous movie stars, instead completely capturing the mannerisms of aging adults frustrated by the monotony of their day-to-day existence. Despite some complex ideas in Gerard Brach's script, Mizrahi's direction is a trifle plodding.

I SHOT JESSE JAMES
1949   81m   bw   ★★½
Western   /U
Lippert

Preston Foster (John Kelley), Barbara Britton (Cynthy Waters), John Ireland (Bob Ford), Reed Hadley (Jesse James), J. Edward Bromberg (Kane), Victor Kilian (Soapy), Barbara Woodell (Mrs. Zee James), Tom Tyler (Frank James), Tommy Noonan (Charles Ford), Byron Foulger (Room Clerk)

p, Carl K. Hittleman; d, Samuel Fuller; w, Samuel Fuller (based on an article by Homer Croy); ph, Ernest Miller; ed, Paul Landres; m, Albert Glasser; art d, Frank Hotaling

Fuller's first directorial effort made evident the great talent he possessed as a filmmaker. Ireland plays the man who guns down Jesse James (Hadley), but Fuller avoids the obvious route and concentrates on what compels Ireland to kill his onetime friend. Ireland has a childhood sweetheart, Britton, whom he hopes to marry after he has carried out the shooting and received a pardon and reward money. But once the killing is over, Britton will have nothing to do with Ireland. Fuller uses effective close-ups in this stylish western, giving a fresh psychological twist to familiar narrative ground.

I, THE JURY

1953 87m bw ★★★
Crime /18
UA

Biff Elliot *(Mike Hammer)*, Preston Foster *(Capt. Pat Chambers)*, Peggie Castle *(Charlotte Manning)*, Margaret Sheridan *(Velda)*, Alan Reed *(George Kalecki)*, Frances Osborne *(Myrna)*, Bob Cunningham *(Hal Kines)*, Elisha Cook, Jr. *(Bobo)*, Paul Dubov *(Marty)*, Mary Anderson *(Eileen Vickers)*

p, Victor Saville; d, Harry Essex; w, Harry Essex (based on the novel by Mickey Spillane); ph, John Alton; ed, Frederick Y. Smith; m, Franz Waxman; art d, Wiard Ihnen

The first film adaptation of Mickey Spillane's trashy best seller was written and directed by Harry Essex, the screenwriter of two of the best science fiction-horror films of the 1950s—IT CAME FROM OUTER SPACE and CREATURE FROM THE BLACK LAGOON—both originally released in 3-D, as was I, THE JURY.

As the film opens we hear "Hark the Herald Angels Sing," but the Yuletide spirit is shattered by a gunman, shrouded in darkness, brutally shooting Jack Williams (Robert Swanger), an amputee, several times. Still alive, Williams painfully crawls towards his own gun. The mysterious killer allows the dying man a chance at the weapon and then finishes him off before he can retaliate. Enter Mike Hammer (Elliot), a private detective and friend of the victim. Williams had saved Hammer's life during WWII, and now the detective is determined to avenge his death. Warned against breaking the law by police detective Foster, he begins to dig for clues. What he finds is a seedy world populated by junkies, nymphomaniacs, and drug dealers. Hammer swaggers through the sleaze, and a number of bodies complicate the case.

The opening and closing scenes of I, THE JURY are stunningly brutal and skillfully executed. The murder of the amputee while "Hark the Herald Angels Sing" plays in the background is profoundly chilling, as is the unexpected finale. Unfortunately, the film's center suffers from Elliot's feeble performance as Spillane's brutish detective. Audiences would have to wait two years for Ralph Meeker to deliver the definitive Mike Hammer performance in Robert Aldrich's incredible KISS ME DEADLY.

I WALK THE LINE

1970 95m c ★★★½
Drama GP/15
Frankenheimer/Lewis

Gregory Peck *(Sheriff Henry Tawes)*, Tuesday Weld *(Alma McCain)*, Estelle Parsons *(Ellen Haney)*, Ralph Meeker *(Carl McCain)*, Lonny Chapman *(Bascomb)*, Charles Durning *(Hunnicutt)*, Jeff Dalton *(Clay McCain)*, Freddie McCloud *(Buddy McCain)*, Jane Rose *(Elsie)*, J.C. Evans *(Grandpa Tawes)*

p, Harold D. Cohen; d, John Frankenheimer; w, Alvin Sargent (based on the novel *An Exile* by Madison Jones); ph, David M. Walsh (Panavision, Eastmancolor); ed, Henry Berman; art d, Albert Brenner; cos, Louis Brown

Too downbeat for its own good, I WALK THE LINE forgets it needs an audience. The one reason to watch is the astonishing, unsung Weld, the modern Louise Brooks, who can suggest amorality, skewed innocence and ageless sensuality—she played nymphets through her thirties with infinite ease—that makes Bardot pale. Her tragedy is that she never chose a commercially successful script.

I WALK THE LINE presents haggard but handsome Peck as a backwoods Tennessee sheriff who falls in love with teenager Weld. Her father, Meeker, is a moonshiner, and Peck becomes involved in the illicit operations, making sure his men and federal agents stay clear of the stills. When deputy Durning stumbles upon the still, Meeker kills him, and Peck becomes an accomplice to the crime.

Frankenheimer does an apt job of creating the bleak mood, but the film doesn't seem to have anywhere it wants to go. There are five songs, including the title track, from the inimitable Johnny Cash that help capture the strangely compelling mountain mood.

I WALKED WITH A ZOMBIE

1943 69m bw ★★★★★
Horror /A
RKO

James Ellison *(Wesley Rand)*, Frances Dee *(Betsy)*, Tom Conway *(Paul Holland)*, Edith Barrett *(Mrs. Rand)*, James Bell *(Dr. Maxwell)*, Christine Gordon *(Jessica Holland)*, Theresa Harris *(Alma)*, Sir Lancelot *(Calypso Singer)*, Darby Jones *(Carre Four)*, Jeni le Gon *(Dancer)*

p, Val Lewton; d, Jacques Tourneur; w, Curt Siodmak, Ardel Wray (based on an original story by Inez Wallace); ph, J. Roy Hunt; ed, Mark Robson; m, Roy Webb; art d, Albert S. D'Agostino, Walter E. Keller

I WALKED WITH A ZOMBIE was the second in the series of thought-provoking, literate horror films produced by Val Lewton in the 1940s (the first was THE CAT PEOPLE), and, under the masterful direction of Jacques Tourneur, it is an unqualified horror masterpiece. The story idea and title were borrowed from a series of newspaper articles that detailed voodoo and witchcraft practices in Haiti, hung on an off-the-wall adaptation of *Jane Eyre*!

Betsy (Dee) is a young nurse sent to Haiti by rich American planter Paul Holland (Conway) to take care of his catatonic wife, Jessica (Gordon). Paul thinks his wife has gone insane, and is ridden with guilt that he may have caused it. The locals suspect, however, that Jessica has become a zombie—one of the living dead. Betsy, who makes little progress with Jessica, meets Paul's mother (Barrett), a contradictory woman torn between her strong beliefs in the Christian church and in voodoo, and his brother, Wesley (Ellison), who is slowly drinking himself to death as he watches his brother's mistreatment of Jessica, whom he has always secretly loved. To make matters worse, Betsy and her employer begin to fall in love. Their desire to marry is intense, but impossible as long as Jessica lives. Not wanting to lose Paul, nor to see him torture himself, Betsy attempts to cure Jessica by taking her to a voodoo ceremony, in hopes that the experience will shock her back to "life." Lewton's horror was based on the suggested, the psychological—not the visceral, tangible "monsters" that characterized the Universal horror series in the 1930s and 40s. The terror was presented in a shadowy, low-key atmosphere that allowed the audience to imagine and feel the unease instead of showing it to them, making the chills much more effective. The most outstanding example of this approach here is director Tourneur's beautiful realization of the lengthy, haunting, and elegiac sequence in which Betsy walks through the sugar cane fields with the silent Jessica to the voodoo ceremony. The scene is played in silence, save for the distant sound of drums and the gentle rustling of the wind. Visually, it is filled with gentle, floating movements—of Jessica's white gown, of the sugar cane in the wind—that are abruptly halted with the appearance of the massive zombie guard (Jones) whose presence signals the women's arrival at their destination. This scene is unforgettable, as is the entire film. Essential viewing.

I WANNA HOLD YOUR HAND

1978 104m c ★★★
Comedy PG/A
Universal

Nancy Allen (*Pam Mitchell*), Bobby Di Cicco (*Tony Smerko*), Marc McClure (*Larry Dubois*), Susan Kendall Newman (*Janis Goldman*), Theresa Saldana (*Grace Corrigan*), Wendie Jo Sperber (*Rosie Petrofsky*), Eddie Deezen (*Richard "Ringo" Klaus*), Christian Juttner (*Peter Plimpton*), Will Jordan (*Ed Sullivan*), Boyd "Red" Morgan (*Peter's Father*)

p, Tamara Asseyev, Alexandra Rose; d, Robert Zemeckis; w, Robert Zemeckis, Bob Gale; ph, Donald Morgan (Panavision, Technicolor); ed, Frank Morriss; m, The Beatles; art d, Peter Jamison; fx, Curtis Dickson, Albert Whitlock; cos, Roseanna Morton

An engaging, slapstick look at the effect the Beatles had on the US when they crossed the Atlantic. The time is February 1964, and the group are about to appear on the Ed Sullivan Show. Allen is about to get married but wants just a single night with one of the "fab four." Saldana is a struggling photographer who knows that exclusive pictures of the band will get her career going. Sperber and Deezen are supreme Beatle groupies, and Newman and DiCicco are Beatle-haters planning to ruin the group's TV appearance. All these people converge on the New York City hotel where the band is staying and then move on to the TV studio. After slowly introducing the characters, the film accelerates pace. Director Zemeckis (USED CARS) handles comedy well; he and his frequent writing partner Bob Gale also cowrote 1941 for their mentor Steven Spielberg, who executive produced this film.

I WANT TO LIVE!

1958 120m bw ★★★★½
Crime/Biography /X
Figaro

Susan Hayward (*Barbara Graham*), Simon Oakland (*Ed Montgomery*), Virginia Vincent (*Peg*), Theodore Bikel (*Carl Palmberg*), Wesley Lau (*Henry Graham*), Philip Coolidge (*Emmett Perkins*), Lou Krugman (*Jack Santo*), James Philbrook (*Bruce King*), Bartlett Robinson (*District Attorney*), Gage Clark (*Richard Tibrow*)

p, Walter Wanger; d, Robert Wise; w, Nelson Gidding, Don Mankiewicz (based on newspaper articles by Ed Montgomery and the letters of Barbara Graham); ph, Lionel Lindon; ed, William Hornbeck; m, Johnny Mandel; art d, Ted Haworth

Unswerving, uneasy, unbeatable crime melodrama with a shattering Susan Hayward gathering all her glory into a performance without one false note. For devotees of Miss Hayward, this is the one to study; it feels and looks like life.

The nasty plot has Hayward playing real-life Barbara Graham, whose sensational trial brought her a conviction and death sentence that made her a nationwide *cause celebre*. The film depicts Graham, the product of a broken home, as a classic bad girl: perjurer, prostitute, thief. She arrives in San Francisco and is quickly sent to prison for falsely testifying to help out a friend. When released, she contacts two gamblers on the recommendation of fellow inmates. The gamblers, Coolidge and Krugman, use her as a shill; Hayward steers gullible suckers into their crooked card games and begins to make big money. With a bank

account, Hayward decides to go straight, but she makes the mistake of marrying corrupt Lau—one of Coolidge's associates—and he introduces her to drugs. By the time she has a baby, she is an addict and her husband takes her last $10 for a fix. She leaves him and goes back to work for Coolidge and Krugman, with tragic results.

Hayward's performance is so intense, and the film so grim, it's exhausting watching her suffer through one agony after another. Wise directs with the perspective that Hayward/Graham was innocent all along, although the film offers little evidence to support this claim (the most insistent being Graham's repeated and vociferous insistence of her innocence), a stance that brought universal criticism from law enforcement agencies. For the most part, the hapless heroine is convincingly portrayed as a social victim. Hayward had been denied the Oscar for many deserving performances in the past—SMASH-UP, THE STORY OF A WOMAN, MY FOOLISH HEART, I'LL CRY TOMORROW— but this time the Academy could not ignore her bravura. The ensemble cast is uniformly excellent and believable. Wise's direction is relentlessly gloomy and swift, telling Graham's story in adroitly crafted scenes; mention should also be made of Gerry Mulligan's fine rendering of Johnny Mandel's classic jazz soundtrack.

ICEMAN COMETH, THE

1973 239m c ★★★
Drama PG/
American Film Theatre

Lee Marvin (*Hickey*), Fredric March (*Harry Hope*), Robert Ryan (*Larry Slade*), Jeff Bridges (*Don Parritt*), Bradford Dillman (*Willie Oban*), Sorrell Booke (*Hugo Kalmar*), Hildy Brooks (*Margie*), Juno Dawson (*Pearl*), Evans Evans (*Cora*), Martyn Green (*The Captain/Cecil Lewis*)

p, Ely A. Landau; d, John Frankenheimer; w, Thomas Quinn Curtiss (based on the play by Eugene O'Neill); ph, Ralph Woolsey; ed, Harold F. Kress; prod d, Jack Martin Smith; cos, Dorothy Jeakins

Though some consider this one of Eugene O'Neill's finest plays, THE ICEMAN COMETH does not translate well to the screen. No matter what Frankenheimer pulled from his bag of directorial tricks, the work remains stagey and talky on celluloid; even the majestic talent of March cannot turn it around.

March runs a saloon peopled by has-beens and drunks. All their lives, including March's, have been lived and lost; only their memories remain, voiced despairingly through bitter nostalgia. The only meager salvation for this bevy of forlorn creatures is the expected arrival of Marvin, a hardware salesman who drops by once a year to regale the customers with his forced humor and tired stories about his wife and the iceman. When Marvin does arrive, it's a letdown, even though this realistic actor tries hard to walk O'Neill's tightrope between nimble-witted charm and blunt hectoring. March is superb in his last film, and Bridges is good as the despondent young man wanting more than promises out of life. Dillman delivers his cynical wisecracks with aplomb, but Booke's role is delivered with such lunacy that the intended fear is replaced with black humor. The scene-stealer is Robert Ryan, one of cinema's forgotten great actors. He delivers a superlative performance as the radical with dark reason and fearful purpose, bringing a new, almost heroic dimension to the character.

ICICLE THIEF, THE
(LADRI DI SAPONETTE)
1990 90m c ★★★★
Comedy /PG
Mario Maronati (Italy)

Maurizio Nichetti (*Antonio Piermattei/The Director of the Film*), Caterina Sylos Labini (*Maria Piermattei*), Federico Rizzo (*Bruno Piermattei*), Matteo Auguardi (*Paolo Piermattei*), Renato Scarpa (*Don Italo, the Priest*), Heidi Komarek (*The Model*), Carlina Torta (*Television-watching Mother*), Massimo Sacilotto (*Television-watching Father*), Lella Costa (*The Television Producer*), Claudio G. Fava (*The Film Critic*)

p, Mario Maronati; d, Maurizio Nichetti; w, Maurizio Nichetti, Mauro Monti; ph, Mario Battistoni; ed, Rita Olivati; m, Manuel De Sica; cos, Maria Pia Angelini

THE ICICLE THIEF is as much a feat of engineering as anything else. Once you accept that you are being manipulated, you'll find that on every narrative level—and there are four disparate components to this original, trenchant comedy—both your social sensibilities and sense of reality will be delightfully engaged. Simultaneously shot in black-and-white and color, this *tour de force* is a playful, ingenious commentary on modern times. That writer-director Maurizio Nichetti (who appears as the film's dual anti-heroes) brings off the convoluted film-within-a-film structure of this tightly plotted, complex movie is an amazing feat. It would seem to require the expert touch of a master architect and a skilled logician. Nichetti proves himself both.

On the film's first level, filmed in color, Nichetti is the fictional Maurizio Nichetti, a noted director. His latest movie (not so coincidentally titled "The Icicle Thief") is being shown as a last minute substitution on a highbrow Italian television program dealing with cinema. In the Charlie Chaplin-Buster Keaton tradition, the waif-like, klutzy Nichetti, a short, bushy-haired man with an unkempt mustache and dark, round spectacles, is continually put upon by the show's unprepared host, an arrogant film critic (Claudio G. Fava).

On the film's second level, Nichetti plays the lead in that tragic, black-and-white, film-within-the-film, the poor, unemployed Antonio Piermattei, who is desperate for work. (Without his glasses and mustache, Nichetti is barely recognizable in this role.) To make ends meet, Antonio's wife, Maria (Caterina Sylos Labini), sings in a trio, his young son, Bruno (Federico Rizzo), works diligently at the church doing odd jobs; and his infant, Paolo (Mattio Auguardi), gets into everything, creating a continual comic hazard to life and limb. Aghast when he mistakenly thinks Antonio plans to go into the black market, the local priest, Don Italo (Renato Scarpa), helps him find work at the local chandelier factory. Maria has always dreamed of having a chandelier in her home—they remind her of icicles—so Antonio secretly steals a fixture to carry home to her on his bicycle.

The film's third level (also shot in color) is the reality of a bourgeois household moored in front of their TV set, passively watching both the movie and the recurrent commercials. However, only the pregnant mother is paying any attention at all to Nichetti's film. The father just ogles the buxom bathing beauties in the colorful commercials, and the pampered son, mainly interested in playing with his enormous collection of Lego toys, keeps switching channels with the remote control. The commercials, which punctuate the telecast, represent the film's fourth and final narrative level.

During the program, there's a momentary power failure at the TV studio. When the current is restored and the film resumes, fiction and reality merge, as if by magic. The neorealistic movie switches from a black-and-white tragedy to a screwball fantasy in living color. We see Antonio riding home on his bike, the chandelier tied to his handlebars. When he hears a cry for help by a lake, he stops and runs to save the victim, the gorgeous swimsuit-clad American model Heidi (Heidi Komarek), whom we've been seeing in the TV commercials. Antonio and the surroundings are still in black-and-white but Heidi's in color—in the same frame! When Antonio drags Heidi out of the water and dries her off, he also wipes off her color in the process (an effect that's fascinating to watch) whereupon Heidi becomes an integral part of the black-and-white drama.

After this segment, THE ICICLE THIEF erupts into farce. Nichetti jumps into the television screen, emerges as a black-and-white character in his own movie, and returns to Antonio's village by train to emend his film's structure. Nichetti eventually makes things right, or at least sees to it that Antonio is released and his family reunited, but not before all the movie-within-the-movie characters appear in the color commercials. Still, everyone lives happily ever after; that is, except for director Nichetti. He's stuck in a black-and-white never-never land on the bourgeois family's television screen, and he disappears when they turn the set off and go to bed for the night.

If this all seems crazy, it is. For 90 minutes, the film quickly shifts from one narrative level to another, combining them in an entertaining farcical melange. Only later do the film's universal implications come to mind. In its seriocomic way, THE ICICLE THIEF says as much about the passivity of people who casually watch television at home as it does about the indiscriminate, often odious, incursion of commercials. Here, clearly, the medium is the message. The real-life Nichetti seems to be saying that television is nothing more than a distraction in most homes, with viewers unable to differentiate among the accumulated images or to "remember if a face is from a film, a commercial, or the news."

Nichetti's multifaceted background—he studied architecture, mime, and acting, wrote screenplays and advertising copy, and worked as a circus clown— has obviously proved invaluable to his highly creative approach to filmmaking. While this tightly edited film might seem anarchic, Nichetti painstakingly constructed it, frame by frame on a storyboard. No computers were used for his special effects; everything was done on film. (The 20-second bit where Nichetti dries the color off the model took three months to do.) Even the near-perfect simulation of the look of a 1940s movie was the result of processing the film to make it appear older, then re-filming it a second time in black and white to give it the necessary texture.

Called the Italian Woody Allen, Nichetti often appears as a performer both on film and television. Along with Carlo Verdone and Nanni Moretti, he has been dubbed one of the "New Comics," the first major movement in Italian filmmaking since the neorealists.

IDENTIFICATION OF A WOMAN
1983 130m c ★★★
Drama /18
Gaumont (Italy)

Tomas Milian (*Niccolo*), Daniela Silverio (*Mavi*), Christine Boisson (*Ida*), Veronica Lazar (*Carla*), Sandra Monteleoni, Giampaolo Saccarola, Alessandro Ruspoli, Giada Gerini, Sergio Tardioli, Paola Dominguin p, Giorgio Nocella, Antonio Macri; d, Michelangelo Antonioni; w, Michelangelo Antonioni, Tonino Guerra, Gerard Brach; ph, Carlo Di Palma (Technovision, Technicolor); ed, Michaelangelo Antonioni; m, John Foxx; art d, Andrea Crisanti

Antonioni's first Italian film in nearly two decades (he did, however, shoot THE MYSTERY AT OBERWALD for video in 1979), offers his familiar treatment of the relationship between a man and a woman—or, in this case, a man and two women. Milian is a middle-aged film director (not unlike Antonioni) who gets involved with Silverio, an upper-class woman. He receives anonymous threats to terminate the relationship, which he ignores. Before long, Silverio moves away without telling Milian. He then starts seeing avant-garde stage actress Boisson, but this relationship also ends after she informs him that she is pregnant by another man.

This is a respectable return by Antonioni to familiar thematic ground—the impossibility of maintaining relationships in the contemporary world—helped by a fine ironic underpinning and smoothly assured visuals.

IDOLMAKER, THE

1980 107m c ★★★½

Drama PG/15

UA

Ray Sharkey (Vincent Vacarri), Tovah Feldshuh (Brenda Roberts), Peter Gallagher (Caesare), Paul Land (Tommy Dee), Joe Pantoliano (Gino Pilato), Maureen McCormick (Ellen Fields), John Aprea (Paul Vacarri), Richard Bright (Uncle Tony), Olympia Dukakis (Mrs. Vacarri), Steven Apostlee Peck (Mr. Vacarri)

p, Gene Kirkwood, Howard W. Koch, Jr.; d, Taylor Hackford; w, Edward Di Lorenzo; ph, Adam Holender (Technicolor); ed, Neil Travis; m, Jeff Barry; art d, David L. Snyder; chor, Deney Terrio; cos, Rita Riggs

Ray Sharkey gives a dynamic performance here as the hustling Vincent Vacarri (a thinly veiled version of technical adviser Bob Marcucci, mentor of Frankie Avalon and Fabian), who promotes the careers of rock 'n' roll singers Tommy Dee (Paul Land) and Caesare (Peter Gallagher)—managing their every move, calling in favors here and making payoffs there, making sure his charges have the best clothes and backup bands, etc.—in the late 50s and early 60s. Brenda Roberts (Tovah Feldshuh) is an editor of a fan magazine who has a fling with Vincent and uses her influence to help make his boys into stars. THE IDOLMAKER takes itself too seriously, but is nonetheless one of the best and most energetic film treatments of the early days of rock 'n' roll and a fine depiction of how performers are groomed for stardom (far superior to THE ROSE). In his directorial debut, Taylor Hackford (AN OFFICER AND A GENTLEMENT, 1982; WHITE NIGHTS, 1985) shows a solid command of the medium. The anachronistic music by Jeff Barry is a problem, however; its too-contemporary sound presumably stems from the producers' desire to get airplay for the film's score.

IF. . .

1968 110m c/bw ★★★

Drama R/18

Memorial (U.K.)

Malcolm McDowell (Mick Travers), David Wood (Johnny), Richard Warwick (Wallace), Christine Noonan (the Girl), Rupert Webster (Bobby Philips), Robert Swann (Rowntree), Hugh Thomas (Denson), Peter Jeffrey (Headmaster), Mona Washbourne (Matron), Arthur Lowe (Mr. Kemp, Housemaster)

p, Michael Medwin, Lindsay Anderson; d, Lindsay Anderson; w, David Sherwin (based on a script by Sherwin, John Howlett, entitled "The Crusaders"); ph, Miroslav Ondricek (Eastmancolor); ed, David Gladwell; m, Marc Wilkinson; prod d, Jocelyn Herbert; art d, Brian Eatwell

A highly unusual modern classic. McDowell is a rebellious pupil at a strict British boarding school who, with his friend Wood, refuses to conform. During a rugby match the pair sneak into town and meet a waitress. Upon their return McDowell is brutally beaten by the headmaster, sparking revolt in the youngster. Together with his fellow schoolmates, McDowell prepares an attack on the administration. Or does he? The surrealistic finale has the gang of youths opening fire with an arsenal of weapons during a speech by an alumnus, as the waitress shoots the headmaster in the head from a rooftop.

IF. . . was a landmark of 60s cinema and of the emergence of the counter-culture, and bears a striking resemblance to Jean Vigo's innovative ZERO DE CONDUITE. It was originally conceived in 1958 and scripted in 1960 under the title THE CRUSADERS. The film's violence was a subject of great controversy. Its promotional poster depicted a group of youths armed with machine guns and hand grenades asking, "Which side are you on?" Envisioned as a violent REBEL WITHOUT A CAUSE, the picture was originally offered to director Nicholas Ray, who suggested it would be best served by a British director.

IF I HAD A MILLION

1932 88m bw ★★★★

Comedy/Drama

Paramount

Gary Cooper (Gallagher), George Raft (Eddie Jackson), Wynne Gibson (Violet), Charles Laughton (The Clerk), Jack Oakie (Mulligan), Frances Dee (Mary Wallace), Charlie Ruggles (Henry Peabody), Alison Skipworth (Emily), W.C. Fields (Rollo), Mary Boland (Mrs. Peabody)

p, Louis D. Lighton; d, Ernst Lubitsch, Norman Taurog, Stephen Roberts, James Cruze, William A. Seiter, H. Bruce Humberstone, Lothar Mendes (uncredited); w, Claude Binyon, Whitney Bolton, Malcolm Stuart Boylan, John Bright, Sidney Buchanan, Lester Cole, Isabel Dawn, Boyce DeGaw, Walter DeLeon, Oliver H.P. Garrett, Harvey Gates, Grover Jones, Ernst Lubitsch, Lawton Mackall, Joseph L. Mankiewicz, William Slavens McNutt, Seton I. Miller, Robert Sparks, Tiffany Thayer (based on the novel Windfall by Robert D. Andrews)

For once, an episodic film that holds together, and the link that holds it is lots of money: millions, in fact. Richard Bennett plays a multimillionaire who is disgusted with his dollar-clutching relatives. When told by his doctors that he is dying, Bennett decides to pick out total strangers and give each $1 million, mostly to see what they will do with the money. He closes his eyes and picks a name from the phone book. Eight sketches follow that depict the results of Bennett's largesse. In "The China Shop," directed by James Cruze, Charles Ruggles is a spineless clerk who is forever hiding from shrewish wife Mary Boland and is terrified at work of dropping a piece of china, the cost of which will be deducted from his salary. With Bennett's check for $1 million in hand, Ruggles proceeds to tell off Boland for good and go on a china-smashing binge. In the next segment, "The Streetwalker," directed by Ernst Lubitsch, $1 million goes to Wynne Gibson, a prostitute, who immediately abandons her street corner and rents a lavish penthouse apartment, determined to make up for lost sleep between silk sheets. Stephen Roberts directs the next segment, "The Forger," which profiles a slick George Raft who is so notorious that his photo is in every bank where he might cash his check. After failing to cash the check, the hysterical Raft goes to a flophouse and begs the owner to take the $1 million check for a bed. As he dozes off, the owner lights his cigar with the burning check and then calls the police to come and arrest the wanted forger. The next sequence, "The Auto" or "Rollo and the Road Hogs," is directed by Norman Taurog. Alison Skipworth receives the check at her little teashop where she and newly acquired hubby W.C. Fields, a worn-out vaudeville juggler, reside, harboring a bone-deep hatred for roadhogs, especially since their new car has just been wrecked by a bevy of these very people. With the $1 million, Fields and Skipworth go to a new car dealership and begin buying one new car after another, taking to the streets as roadhog vigilantes! Bruce Humberstone directs "The Condemned Man." Gene Raymond is about to go to the electric chair when he receives the $1 million. He is dragged to the chair hysterically crying and laughing over the ironic twist of fate. "The Clerk," also directed by Lubitsch, has Charles Laughton as a meek, harassed clerical worker. When he receives his $1 million check, he stands up quietly, and then walks into the resplendent office of the firm's president. As the man looks up, Laughton gives the boss a loud Bronx cheer, slams the door, and goes into unperturbed retirement. In "The Three Marines," directed by Norman McLeod, $1 million goes to Gary Cooper, a fun-loving Marine. He and his buddies, Jack Oakie and Roscoe Karns, are in the brig for fighting; when they get out, they rush to a lunchwagon to see pretty Joyce Compton. Knowing cook Lucien Littlefield cannot read, Cooper passes off the check for $10 in cash and takes Compton to a carnival that night where he and his buddies get into another fight and wind up behind bars once more. Cooper looks through the barred window of his cell and sees Littlefield getting into a limousine. "Old Ladies' Home" is directed by William A. Seiter and profiles May Robson, a resident at a home for retired old ladies, where the women are treated like prison inmates by the overbearing director. When Robson's check arrives, she buys the home and compels the directors to sit back silently and watch all the old ladies pursue their hobbies and enjoy life for a change.

Most of these stories are well-told, expertly acted, and brilliantly directed. Paramount poured out its best acting and technical talent for this enormous production, the Laughton and Fields segments considered strongest. Us? We'll go with W.C., the Great One himself. MILLION inspired a popular radio and later a TV series, "The Millionaire."

IKIRU
1952 140m bw   ★★★★
Drama   /A
Toho   (Japan)

Takashi Shimura (Kanji Watanabe), Nobuo Kaneko (Mitsuo Watanabe), Kyoko Seki (Kazue Watanabe), Miki Odagiri (Toyo), Kamatari Fujiwara (Ono), Makoto Koburi (Klichi Watanabe), Kumeko Urabe (Tatsu Watanabe), Yoshie Minami (Hayoshi, the Maid), Nobuo Nakamura (Deputy Mayor), Minosuke Yamada (Saito)

d, Akira Kurosawa; w, Akira Kurosawa, Hideo Oguni, Shinobu Hashimoto; ph, Asakazu Nakai; m, Fumio Hayasaka; art d, So Matsuyama

In IKIRU, Akira Kurosawa has created a subtle and moving account of a man who searches for meaning in the final days of his shallow existence. Kanji Watanabe (Takashi Shimura) is a clerk in a government office who discovers that he has cancer and, at most, only a year to live. Up to this point he has lived a highly structured life, rarely varying from routines. He has two children who offer him no comfort, and he decides he must find something to make him feel that his life has not been a total waste. The movement of IKIRU is extremely low key, and the overall emotional impact is quite powerful, with the character of Kanji serving as a metaphor for postwar Japan. A beautiful and unusually quiet film from one of the world's greatest living directors.

I'LL CRY TOMORROW
1955 117m bw   ★★★★
Biography   /X
MGM

Susan Hayward (Lillian Roth), Richard Conte (Tony Bardeman), Eddie Albert (Burt McGuire), Jo Van Fleet (Katie Roth), Don Taylor (Wallie), Ray Danton (David Tredman), Margo (Selma), Virginia Gregg (Ellen), Don "Red" Barry (Jerry), David Kasday (David as a Child)

p, Lawrence Weingarten; d, Daniel Mann; w, Helen Deutsch, Jay Richard Kennedy (based on the book by Lillian Roth, Mike Connolly and Gerold Frank); ph, Arthur E. Arling; ed, Harold F. Kress; m, Alex North; art d, Cedric Gibbons, Malcolm Brown; fx, Warren Newcombe; cos, Helen Rose

Hayward stars as Lillian Roth (based on Roth's autobiography of the same name), Broadway and Hollywood singing sensation, who let success slide through her fingers as she reached for the next drink.

As a child, Lillian is driven unmercifully by her ambitious stage mother (Jo Van Fleet) and has already begun appearing on Broadway and being the breadwinner by the time she is a teenager. As an adult, Roth (Susan Hayward) falls in love with an old friend (Ray Danton) who dies unexpectedly, precipitating a lengthy downward spiral.

Although the script doesn't capture much sense of period or time passing, Mann establishes enough strong moments to keep the viewer enthralled. There's a fine child performance by Carole Ann Campbell, who looks like the real Roth, and scores strongly in a post-audition scene that is painful to watch. Indeed, the film dotes on an uneasy sense of dread, daring you not to look away. Hayward doesn't suggest much of what audiences saw in the real Roth. Instead she uses her own sexy, hellcat persona when performing, saving contemplation for her big offstage scenes. The scene in which Hayward deserts her mother is one of Hollywood's grittiest examinations of the love-hate relationship between parent and child, the cross-purposes of both characters wrenching to behold. Both actresses seem to be defining their boundaries and crossing each other's at the same time, using the hyper-emotional 50s genre in a devastatingly successful way.

Roth made a successful nightclub and theatrical comeback after the film's release, and published a second memoir, Beyond My Worth, but, tragically, her bouts with alcohol were far from finished. Hayward won the Cannes Film Festival Best Actress Award for TOMORROW and Helen Rose grabbed an Oscar for her gorgeous costumes.

I'M ALL RIGHT, JACK
1959 105m bw   ★★★★
Comedy   /U
Boulting Bros.   (U.K.)

Ian Carmichael *(Stanley Windrush)*, Peter Sellers *(Fred Kite)*, Terry-Thomas *(Maj. Hitchcock)*, Richard Attenborough *(Sidney de Vere Cox)*, Dennis Price *(Bertram Tracepurcel)*, Margaret Rutherford *(Aunt Dolly)*, Irene Handl *(Mrs. Kite)*, Liz Fraser *(Cynthia Kite)*, Miles Malleson *(Windrush Sr.)*, Marne Maitland *(Mr. Mohammed)*

p, Roy Boulting; d, John Boulting; w, Frank Harvey, Alan Hackney, John Boulting (based on Hackney's novel *Private Life*); ph, Mutz Greenbaum; ed, Anthony Harvey; m, Ken Hare, Ron Goodwin

Hilarious satire of British trade unionism. Carmichael is an addled but earnest young man who has just finished his army service and now seeks a career in industry. He visits his uncle, Price, who is in cahoots with Attenborough in a most interesting scheme; they would like to arrange a strike at Price's factory so that Attenborough's factory can take over the contracts and do the work at inflated prices. Price gives Carmichael a job as an unskilled laborer, and his intelligence soon detects several ways to streamline the factory's operation and reap larger profits. This, of course, angers the union shop steward, Sellers. Carmichael figures out a way to load and unload deliveries and suggests that a new schedule be printed and that the workers live up to it instead of taking tea breaks every other hour. Sellers is livid and calls a strike, which delights Price. But the laborers at Attenborough's plant go out in sympathy, thus tossing Price and Attenborough's plans into a cocked hat. Things get progressively more ludicrous from there on in.

A sharp screenplay and expert farceurs in every role make this one of the great British comedies of the 1950s and 1960s. Many of the "Carry On" players are here, including Rutherford and her husband, Davis. Even Punch editor Muggeridge takes a turn as the moderator of the TV show. It's subtlety and slapstick mixed perfectly in a refreshing glace. BAFTA Awards (British Oscars) went to Sellers and to the screenplay.

I'M GONNA GIT YOU SUCKA

1988 88m c ★★★
Comedy R/15
Ivory Way

Keenen Ivory Wayans *(Jack Spade)*, Bernie Casey *(John Slade)*, Antonio Fargas *(Flyguy)*, Steve James *(Kung Fu Joe)*, Isaac Hayes *(Hammer)*, Jim Brown *(Slammer)*, Ja'Net DuBois *(Ma Bell)*, Dawn Lewis *(Cheryl)*, John Vernon *(Mr. Big)*, Clu Gulager *(Lt. Baker)*

p, Peter McCarthy, Carl Craig; d, Keenen Ivory Wayans; w, Keenen Ivory Wayans; ph, Tom Richmond (DeLuxe Color); ed, Michael R. Miller; m, David Frank; prod d, Melba Farquhar, Catherine Hardwicke

Wayans wrote and directed this very funny satire of the black-oriented exploitation films of the 1970s. Set in "Any Ghetto, USA," I'M GONNA GIT YOU SUCKA opens as upstanding young Army veteran Jack Spade (Wayans) returns home to avenge the death of his brother, who died because he wore too many gold chains. Wayans vows to shut down the business of a ruthless gold-chain pusher known only as Mr. Big (Vernon). Because his experience in the armed forces is mostly bureaucratic, however, Jack seeks the help of his childhood hero, John Slade (Casey) in this endeavor. An extremely funny movie that presents a torrent of insightful gags at breakneck pace, I'M GONNA GIT YOU SUCKA features many of the stars of the old "blaxploitation" movies, adding weight and authenticity to Wayan's film. In offering up this affectionate parody of the old movies, Wayans also turns a satiric eye on black culture in general—but in an inoffensive, lighthearted manner.

I'M NO ANGEL

1933 87m bw ★★★★★
Comedy
Paramount

Mae West *(Tira)*, Cary Grant *(Jack Clayton)*, Gregory Ratoff *(Benny Pinkowitz)*, Edward Arnold *(Big Bill Barton)*, Ralf Harolde *(Slick Wiley)*, Kent Taylor *(Kirk Lawrence)*, Gertrude Michael *(Alicia Hatton)*, Russell Hopton *(Flea Madigan, the Barker)*, Dorothy Peterson *(Thelma)*, William B. Davidson *(Ernest Brown, the Chump)*

p, William LeBaron; d, Wesley Ruggles; w, Mae West, Harlan Thompson (based on "The Lady and the Lions," an unproduced screenplay by Lowell Brentano); ph, Leo Tover; ed, Otho Lovering; m, Harvey Brooks; art d, Hans Dreier, Bernard Herzbrun

The best of the West. Mae is a Depression-era angel of mercy, dispensing quips and songs like fallout in one of the funniest films ever lensed. On camera 95% of the time, West's screenplay traces her climb from sideshow carnival hootchie-kootchie girl to international circus star. In true lady Leo form, she even gets to realize her own biggest fantasy on camera: taming lions. Obviously, West was being rewarded with total creative control, a power seldom given by the studios, but the success of her previous film, SHE DONE HIM WRONG, had gone a long way toward keeping Paramount from declaring bankruptcy. She is surrounded by a slick supporting cast working at comedic fever pitch, but West never breaks a sweat, parading through her promenades, amazed by her own dazzle, savoring every star turn, thrilled with her own reflection in each costar's eyes.

Indeed, I'M NO ANGEL is a monument to the Westian ego; never has fullblown female narcissism been explored in such an utterly unselfconcious way, yet it's tempered by West at her most self-mocking. Each time you're convinced that it's all parody, West suddenly plays it straight. . . but so you'll laugh out loud. She's a textbook of historic comic technique and diva timing—historic because West embraces every great bygone tradition of show business: vaudeville, burlesque, legit and speakeasy. And ANGEL is highlighted by a lesson in diva plotline no other star can equal, because only West would dare defend herself in court. Crammed into the 87 minutes of running time are numerous other unforgettable moments. Watch for West's record collection, her weird lion tamer boots (designed to hide her platforms), her midway rendition of "They Call Me Sister Honky-Tonk", her spider wing dress sleeves. This was the second time West used Cary Grant as her leading man, and he later said she was the most difficult person he ever played opposite, yet she taught him more about comedy than anyone else he ever worked with. ANGEL came after the beauticians had perfected West's visual star persona and before the moral bluenoses took to laundering her work—it's the peak of her stardom. Certainly we feel rewarded by this flawless comedy classic and enriched by the legacy of West herself: a legend of legends, a figure of American folklore that stands alone in the cinematic pantheon.

IMITATION OF LIFE

1934 106m bw ★★★½
Drama
Universal

Claudette Colbert *(Beatrice Pullman)*, Warren William *(Stephen Archer)*, Ned Sparks *(Elmer)*, Louise Beavers *(Delilah Johnson)*, Juanita Quigley *(Jessie Pullman, Age 3)*, Marilyn Knowlden *(Jessie, Age 8)*, Rochelle Hudson *(Jessie, Age 18)*, Sebie Hendricks

(Peola Johnson, Age 4), Dorothy Black *(Peola, Age 9)*, Fredi Washington *(Peola, Age 19)*

p, Carl Laemmle; d, John M. Stahl; w, William Hurlbut (based on the novel by Fannie Hurst); ph, Merritt Gerstad; ed, Philip Cahn

Highly sentimental social soaper, subtly crafted by director Stahl.

In this adaptation of Fannie Hurst's melodramatic novel, Colbert ages 15 years—quite believably—as a widow raising her daughter alone. (The daughter is played first by Juanita Quigley, then by Marilyn Knowlden, and as a young woman by Rochelle Hudson.) When Colbert decides to join forces with her maid, Louise Beavers, and open a small pancake parlor, Beavers, who also has a young daughter (played by Sebie Hendricks, by Dorothy Black, and primarily the largely forgotten, beautiful Fredi Washington), becomes Colbert's full partner in the business, which proves highly successful. As the enterprise flourishes, however, the women's family lives become fraught with conflict. Washington, whose light complexion enables her to pass for Caucasian, finds herself unable to live in both the white and black worlds, and as a result breaks off relations with Beavers and runs away from school, hoping to live as a white woman. Colbert, meanwhile, is shocked to learn that the 18-year-old Hudson is in love with the man Colbert herself wants to marry, Warren William.

Audiences didn't seem to mind the rather downbeat ending of IMITATION OF LIFE (remade successfully in 1959, with Lana Turner starring under Douglas Sirk's direction), but there was a great deal of controversy over the basic elements of the narrative. Some white southern viewers disapproved of Colbert's character going into business with her black maid (despite the fact that it's the latter's recipe that makes both women rich); Black critics, on the other hand, felt that Beavers should have been shown establishing her own residence, rather than staying on with Colbert and continuing to function as household help. At one point, Stahl makes an explicit visual social comment: a masterful camera shot of a staircase that divides upstairs from down, with Beavers catering upstairs and Colbert hostessing downstairs, revealing the hypocrisy of the entire exercise. Beavers' interpretation has dated badly; she's either jolly or resigned and does not suggest the transistions from one emotion to another.

IMITATION OF LIFE
1959 125m c ★★★★
Drama /U
Universal

Lana Turner *(Lora Meredith)*, John Gavin *(Steve Archer)*, Sandra Dee *(Susie, Age 16)*, Dan O'Herlihy *(David Edwards)*, Susan Kohner *(Sarah Jane, Age 18)*, Robert Alda *(Allen Loomis)*, Juanita Moore *(Annie Johnson)*, Mahalia Jackson *(Herself)*, Karen Dicker *(Sarah Jane, Age 8)*, Terry Burnham *(Suzie, Age 6)*

p, Ross Hunter; d, Douglas Sirk; w, Eleanore Griffin, Allan Scott (based on the novel by Fannie Hurst); ph, Russell Metty (Eastmancolor); ed, Milton Carruth; m, Frank Skinner; art d, Alexander Golitzen, Richard H. Riedel; fx, Clifford Stine; cos, Jean Louis, Bill Thomas

Plush and overblown, the last Hollywood hurrah for Sirk, and the resurrection of the weepie by producer Ross Hunter. A string of similar sudsers followed (several with Turner), but this one is the pick of the litter, thanks to Sirk. It's a bizarre, Byzantine, calculatingly depressed and cold affair, with Miss Big Chill herself, Lana Turner, breathing dry ice into the role originally played by Claudette Colbert (and trading Colbert's dignity for helplessness and pearls). The central theme remains the same, but the major tension that exists is 1950s materialism versus the disentegration of the nuclear family, tinged with gut-wrenching racism. If Sirk exploits the material for all it's worth and seems to be sardonically allowing the artifical genre to devour itself as he sits back and watches, at the same time the weepie aspect is so melodramatic as to tear the sobs from your throat.

Lana Turner, playing a successful actress, is not so much acting as parodying herself; Juanita Moore, as the black maid who shares her life, plays the part so haltingly and straight that it feels like ironic commentary. Susan Kohner, as Moore's light-skinned daughter who passes for white, is a noir revelation, giving her character a restless, dangerous sensuality. When she turns the malice of that energy on Turner, it's one of the great standoffs in Hollywood history. And it's magnificently undercut later, when Turner is crying over Moore's deathbed, with Kohner's photograph smiling out from the wall behind them. Oh, and be prepared for the all-stops-out cinematic funeral, complete with Mahalia Jackson singing "Trouble of the World." You'll be horrified at how this hokum manipulates you, but the best strategy is to just surrender and enjoy it.

IMMORTAL BATTALION, THE
1944 115m bw ★★½
War
Two Cities (U.K.)

David Niven *(Lt. Jim Perry)*, Raymond Huntley *(Davenport)*, William Hartnell *(Sgt. Fletcher)*, Stanley Holloway *(Brewer)*, James Donald *(Lloyd)*, John Laurie *(Luke)*, Leslie Dwyer *(Beck)*, Hugh Burden *(Parsons)*, Jimmy Hanley *(Stainer)*, Renee Asherson *(Marjorie Gillingham)*

p, John Sutro, Norman Walker; d, Carol Reed; w, Eric Ambler, Peter Ustinov (based on a story by Eric Ambler); ph, Guy Green; ed, Fergus McDonell; m, William Alwyn; art d, David Rawnsley

Bracing, spirited and lovely. Carol Reed had already developed a reputation in Britain as an accomplished director by the time WWII broke out, so when he joined the Army it was no surprise that he was assigned to the film unit. His 1942 short instructional documentary THE NEW LOT and an idea by Lt. Col. David Niven provided the inspiration for THE IMMORTAL BATTALION. Set in the aftermath of the Dunkirk evacuation, the story focuses on Lt. Jim Perry (Niven) as he whips a group of ordinary conscripts into soldiers and then leads them into battle against Rommel's Afrika Korps at El Alamein. This pseudo-documentary was a big success in Britain, earning Reed even greater respect and leading to ODD MAN OUT, THE FALLEN IDOL and THE THIRD MAN, and serving as a patriotic contribution to the war effort.

IMPORTANCE OF BEING EARNEST, THE
1952 95m c ★★★★½
Comedy /U
Two Cities/Javelin British/Asquith (U.K.)

Michael Redgrave *(Jack Worthing)*, Michael Denison *(Algernon Moncrieff)*, Edith Evans *(Lady Bracknell)*, Joan Greenwood *(Gwendolen Fairfax)*, Dorothy Tutin *(Cecily Cardew)*, Margaret Rutherford *(Miss Prism)*, Miles Malleson *(Canon Chasuble)*, Richard Wattis *(Seton)*, Aubrey Mather *(Merriman)*, Walter Hudd *(Lane)*

p, Teddy Baird; d, Anthony Asquith; w, Anthony Asquith (based on the play by Oscar Wilde); ph, Desmond Dickinson (Technicolor); ed, John D. Guthridge; m, Benjamin Frankel; art d, Carmen Dillon; cos, Beatrice Dawson

Wilde's wittiest play took 57 years to make it to the screen but was well worth the wait. Director-writer Asquith made absolutely no attempt to "open up" this repertory standard in order to make it more cinematic. The film does of course benefit from close-ups and such, but Asquith goes so far as to have a couple enter a stage box and sit down before a curtain rises at the start. This is meant to be theater first and foremost, and it's a valuable record of a great performance. Stylish, sunny, and as nonsensical as any work can be (at least, on the surface), THE IMPORTANCE OF BEING EARNEST takes well-aimed potshots at the social pretentions of the 1890s. The satire goes down like punch because the artful Wilde has cloaked it in badinage containing some of his best epigrams and *bon mots*. The decor and costumes are charmingly detailed, the perfect setting for this hilarious jewel.

This comedy classic tells of Jack and Algy, two well-to-do bachelors (Redgrave and Dennison) enamored of two women (Greenwood and Tutin) who both have an incredible fixation about falling in love with men named Ernest. Of course neither man is "earnest" about his real name—not that Jack is sure of his. Bring in dragon Lady Bracknell (Evans), a dizzy tutor (Rutherford) and an amorous reverend (Malleson) and the identity search is on. This marvelous cast makes each pearl of dialogue shine. Redgrave and Dennison are impossibly smooth, Tutin is delightfully pert and Greenwood uses her inimitable voice and crisp acting style to delightful effect. The role of the anxious, garrulous Miss Prism is perfect for Rutherford and Malleson makes an ideal foil. Perhaps the best of them all is Edith Evans, in a role she made her own. "Do you smoke," she asks the nervous Jack. "Yes I do," he tentatively responds. "Good," she notes, "a man should have an occupation of some sort."

IMPROMPTU

1990 107m c   ★★★½
Biography/Romance   PG-13/12
Governor/Ariane   (U.K.)

Judy Davis *(George Sand)*, Hugh Grant *(Frederic Chopin)*, Mandy Patinkin *(Alfred DeMusset)*, Bernadette Peters *(Marie d'Agoult)*, Julian Sands *(Franz Liszt)*, Ralph Brown *(Eugene Delacroix)*, Georges Corraface *(Felicien Mallefille)*, Anton Rodgers *(Duke d'Antan)*, Emma Thompson *(Duchess d'Antan)*, Anna Massey *(George Sand's Mother)*

p, Stuart Oken, Daniel A. Sherkow; d, James Lapine; w, Sarah Kernochan; ph, Bruno de Keyzer; ed, Michael Ellis; m, Frederic Chopin, Franz Liszt; art d, Gerard Daoudal; fx, Gilbert Pieri; cos, Jenny Beavan

The life and many loves of French novelist George Sand (1804-67), as depicted in James Lapine's IMPROMPTU, has the feel of a contemporary romantic comedy. This feature debut for Pulitzer Prize-winning stage director Lapine (*Sunday in the Park with George*) is distinguished by a fine cast, including Judy Davis as the truly liberated Sand, a woman whose vacillation with respect to men is exceeded only by her passion for them.

The film introduces viewers to Sand's circle of friends, including the painter Eugene Delacroix (Ralph Brown), poet and one-time lover Alfred DeMusset (Mandy Patinkin), and composers Franz Liszt (Julian Sands) and Frederic Chopin (Hugh Grant). It is Chopin who captures Sand's heart and is the object of her determined affection throughout the film. An unassuming man, in continual ill-health, Chopin first encounters the brazen Sand when she steals into his room, hides under his piano, and revels in his music. This takes place during the summer of 1835 at the country estate of the Duke and Duchess d'Antan (Anton Rodgers

and Emma Thompson), where Chopin, Liszt, Delacroix and DeMusset have been invited to enrich the lives of their culture-starved hosts. Sand has quite candidly invited herself and her two young children.

The gathering also includes Liszt's mistress, Marie d'Agoult (Bernadette Peters), and Sand's newly jilted lover, Felicien Mallefille (Georges Corraface), her children's tutor. Consumed with jealousy, Mallefille spends his time threatening any man who looks at Sand, and instigating a duel with DeMusset. Sand, meanwhile, enlists Marie's help in delivering a note to Chopin. Envious of Sand and feeling neglected by Liszt, Marie passes on the note, but not before removing Sand's name and substituting her own. The fortnight holiday soon comes to an end and Sand, unsuccessful in her efforts to seduce Chopin but determined win his affection, departs with her children and Mallefille.

Favored by Sarah Kernochan's character-driven screenplay and its elegant French locations, IMPROMPTU gives its actors ample room in which to play. Davis shines as Sand, balancing her decided independence with her desire for heady companionship. Grant's Chopin is a bit overplayed, making him seem too prudish. Patinkin is credible as the volatile DeMusset, as are Sands as Liszt, Brown as Delacroix, and Corraface as Mallefille. Peters is well-cast as the manipulative, ever-pregnant Marie and Thompson is hilarious as the duchess—a woman with far too much free time. Those performances, along with the fine music and costumes, help to make this an appealingly offbeat period piece.

IN A LONELY PLACE

1950 94m bw   ★★★★★
Drama   /PG
Santana

Humphrey Bogart *(Dixon Steele)*, Gloria Grahame *(Laurel Gray)*, Frank Lovejoy *(Brub Nicolai)*, Carl Benton Reid *(Capt. Lochner)*, Art Smith *(Mel Lippman)*, Jeff Donnell *(Sylvia Nicolai)*, Martha Stewart *(Mildred Atkinson)*, Robert Warwick *(Charlie Waterman)*, Morris Ankrum *(Lloyd Barnes)*, William Ching *(Ted Barton)*

p, Robert Lord, Henry S. Kesler; d, Nicholas Ray; w, Andrew Solt (based on a story by Edmund H. North, from the novel by Dorothy B. Hughes); ph, Burnett Guffey; ed, Viola Lawrence; m, George Antheil; art d, Robert Peterson; cos, Jean Louis

Superb film noir, brilliantly directed by the gifted Ray with Bogart as a talented but volatile Hollywood screenwriter.

Because of his heavy drinking and truculent nature, Bogart is not much in demand among the film studios but his dogged, devoted agent, Smith, manages to get him a writing assignment, to adapt a celebrated romance novel for the screen. They meet in a Hollywood bar-restaurant (a thinly disguised Chasen's) where Bogart argues with Ankrum, the director of the proposed film, accusing him of making the same film over and over again. His one friend in the bar is a broken down actor, Warwick, and when a strutting, bragging producer, Howard (perhaps modeled on Carl Laemmle, Jr.), insults the actor, Bogart knocks Howard about and has to be restrained. Smith urges him to go home and read the novel he must adapt, but Bogart knows it's a potboiler and is reluctant. Then the hatcheck girl at the club, Stewart, who has read and loves the novel, offers to tell Bogart the tale. He takes her home to his bungalow (in a complex that smacks of the famous Garden of Allah, owned and operated by Ali Nazimova, a haven for actors and writers such as Robert Benchley and F. Scott Fitzgerald). Watching Bogart and Stewart enter the bungalow from across the courtyard is lovely Grahame, a new neighbor. As Stewart rattles on about the story, Bogart slips into his bathrobe, pours himself a drink, and tries to calm Stewart down when she begins histrionically enacting scenes from the novel, which brings Grahame to her upstairs window again to watch the couple through open windows. Finally, Bogart has had enough. He's tired, he explains. He gives Stewart cab fare and sends her home. The next day, Stewart's viciously disfigured body is found and Bogart, thought to be the last person to see her alive, is brought in for questioning by the police.

LONELY PLACE epitomizes star-crossed lovers incapable of escaping environment and circumstances no matter how hard they try. The entire cast is excellent, with Bogart giving an electrifying portrait of a man in torment. Grahame, never more beautiful, is captivating as a woman who has been kept too many times and now has one last chance for real love. Ray's helmsmanship here is superb as he runs the story to a quick conclusion, dwelling upon loving and frightening scenes with the skilled balance of a master juggler, keeping the viewer doubting and believing in Bogart from scene to scene. Many thought the film's central relationship reflected on Ray's unraveling marriage to Grahame. They split when filming was over, and the offbeat Grahame went on to marry Ray's son by a previous marriage, causing shock-waves in the 50s fanzines.

IN COLD BLOOD

1967   134m   bw   ★★
Biography/Crime   R/X
Pax

Robert Blake (*Perry Smith*), Scott Wilson (*Dick Hickock*), John Forsythe (*Alvin Dewey*), Paul Stewart (*Reporter*), Gerald S. O'Loughlin (*Harold Nye*), Jeff Corey (*Hickock's Father*), John Gallaudet (*Roy Church*), James Flavin (*Clarence Duntz*), Charles McGraw (*Smith's Father*), Jim Lantz (*Officer Rohleder*)

p, Richard Brooks; d, Richard Brooks; w, Richard Brooks (based on the book by Truman Capote); ph, Conrad Hall (Panavision); ed, Peter Zinner; m, Quincy Jones; art d, Robert Boyle; fx, Geza Gaspar; cos, Jack Martell

Like the title says. IN COLD BLOOD dramatizes actual events and people in a realistic, technically well-crafted fashion, based upon Truman Capote's "nonficton" novel. Capote seized upon the real-life November 15, 1959 mass murder of the Clutter family in Holcomb, Kansas, by two psychopathic killers, and turned the grisly tale into a bestseller. In making the movie, director Brooks avoids further analysis, laying out the story of Smith and Hickock as faithful docudrama.

Vagrants Blake and Wilson desperately cast about for ways to make an illegal buck, having been cell mates in state prison. Wilson has learned from another inmate that the Clutters keep $10,000 in their farm house, so the pair invades the home, terrorizing, then savagely slaughtering, the family; they leave with little loot since there is no $10,000 to be found. The killers are shown running to Mexico, then back to the US, leaving a trail of bad checks which federal agents follow until they're apprehended in Las Vegas. Brooks then spends half the film displaying Blake and Wilson in the Kansas State Penitentiary at Lansing waiting to be hanged. He emphasizes the state's brutality in taking their lives on the gallows on April 14, 1965, after endless appeals, stays, and agonizing soul-searching on the part of the culprits.

The facts described, what's it all about? Brooks avoids all the pitfalls of cliche, but shouldn't an in-depth docudrama have presented the aftermath of the murders on the Clutter's community and relatives? For those familiar with the case, the leads *do* bear a resemblance to the two real-life murderers, but Brooks's examination is decidedly one-sided.

IN OLD CHICAGO

1938   115m   bw   ★★★
Historical/Disaster
FOX

Tyrone Power (*Dion O'Leary*), Alice Faye (*Belle Fawcett*), Don Ameche (*Jack O'Leary*), Alice Brady (*Molly O'Leary*), Andy Devine (*Pickle Bixby*), Brian Donlevy (*Gil Warren*), Phyllis Brooks (*Ann Colby*), Tom Brown (*Bob O'Leary*), Sidney Blackmer (*Gen. Phil Sheridan*), Berton Churchill (*Sen. Colby*)

p, Kenneth MacGowan; d, Henry King, Robert D. Webb; w, Lamar Trotti, Sonya Levien (based on a story "We the O'Learys" by Niven Busch); ph, Peverell Marley; ed, Barbara McLean; art d, William Darling, Rudolph Sternad; fx, Fred Sersen, Ralph Hammeras, Louis J. White; cos, Royer

In old Zanuck's studio, a big-budget, mediocre cash-in on MGM's SAN FRANCISCO, minus the male star-charisma of the latter.

All the biggest Fox stars of the time were assembled for this nearly $2 million production: Alice Brady won a supporting actress Oscar for her role as Mrs. O'Leary, the woman who supports her family after the death of her husband by taking in washing. She manages to raise her sons into a handsome rake and political schemer (Power); a crusading lawyer (Ameche); and a young man with no ambitions other than to marry his sweetheart and have babies (Brown). Alice Faye gets to do her saloon singer bit, parading her legs in $1500 jeweled stockings and swooning her way through nostalgic sentiments with that deep, honeyed voice. There's a lot of political intrigue involving Power, Ameche and crooked mayor Donlevy, but it's all just a build-up to the fire, sparked by a well-placed kick from one of Mrs. O'Leary's cows. Director King's specialty—spectacle—gets a workout, and he has a blast staging teeming city crowds, brawling saloons, police platoons dismantling riots, runaway horses, stampeding cattle and all the drama the rise of Irish tempers will allow.

CHICAGO makes up in atmosphere and color what it lacks in historical accuracy; the screenplay was based on Niven Busch's *We the O'Learys*. The fire itself propelled production costs to $1,800,000, and runs for twenty minutes. (Assistant director Robert Webb won an Oscar for his work on the sequence.) Worth a view along with the great disaster epics of the 1930s, the aforementioned SAN FRANCISCO, THE HURRICANE, and THE RAINS COME.

IN THE GOOD OLD SUMMERTIME

1949   102m   c   ★★½
Musical/Comedy   /U
MGM

Judy Garland (*Veronica Fisher*), Van Johnson (*Andrew Larkin*), S.Z. Sakall (*Otto Oberkugen*), Spring Byington (*Nellie Burke*), Clinton Sundberg (*Rudy Hansen*), Buster Keaton (*Hickey*), Marcia Van Dyke (*Louise Parkson*), Lillian Bronson (*Aunt Addie*)

p, Joe Pasternak; d, Robert Z. Leonard; w, Samson Raphaelson, Frances Goodrich, Ivan Tors, Albert Hackett (based on the play *The Shop Around the Corner* by Miklos Laszlo); ph, Harry Stradling (Technicolor); ed, Adrienne Fazan; m, George Stoll; art d, Cedric Gibbons, Randall Duell; chor, Robert Alton

Pleasant, if bland, music-filled remake of THE SHOP AROUND THE CORNER. Not up to the usual Garland standards, this is an example of MGM's assembly line product, built to milk Garland's show-stopping for studio coffers. She and a rather annoying Van Johnson play antagonistic co-workers in a Chicago music store at the turn of the century who don't realize they are pen pals. She plays piano and sells music; he pushes musical instruments. The cooler they are to each other at work, the hotter their letters become. By the end they are in each other's arms, but not before a mixup occurs involving a priceless Stradivarius and a more common fiddle, which ends up broken. Eighteen-month-old Liza Minnelli made her second screen appearance as the couple's child at the film's end. (Her first appearance was in EASTER PARADE a year earlier.)

IN THE HEAT OF THE NIGHT

1967 109m c   ★★★★
Crime   /15
Mirisch

Sidney Poitier *(Virgil Tibbs)*, Rod Steiger *(Bill Gillespie)*, Warren Oates *(Sam Wood)*, Quentin Dean *(Delores Purdy)*, James Patterson *(Purdy)*, William Schallert *(Webb Schubert)*, Jack Teter *(Philip Colbert)*, Lee Grant *(Mrs. Leslie Colbert)*, Scott Wilson *(Harvey Oberst)*, Matt Clark *(Packy Harrison)*

p, Walter Mirisch; d, Norman Jewison; w, Stirling Silliphant (based on the novel by John Ball); ph, Haskell Wexler (DeLuxe Color); ed, Hal Ashby; m, Quincy Jones; art d, Paul Groesse; cos, Alan Levine

Superb thriller starring Rod Steiger in an Oscar-winning role as Bill Gillespie, a shrewd southern sheriff, and Sidney Poitier as Virgil Tibbs, a sensitive, intellectual detective from the big city. When a wealthy industrialist is murdered in the little town of Sparta, Mississippi, a well-dressed black stranger is arrested while waiting at the train station. The stranger, Tibbs, identifies himself as a Philadelphia policeman, and, under orders from his superiors up north, assists Gillespie in his investigation. Gillespie grudgingly accepts his assistance and protects him from brutal attacks by local rednecks, and the two grow to admire each other as they confront red herrings and racism en route to identifying the killer.

IN THE HEAT OF THE NIGHT was carefully directed by Norman Jewison, who avoids sentimentality and all the racial cliches that could have crept into almost every scene. As a result, his film won the Academy's Best Picture Award, shocking many when it was chosen over BONNIE AND CLYDE and THE GRADUATE. Steiger's performance is subtle, funny, sad, and fascinating, and Poitier demonstrates the same superb talent he would bring to THEY CALL ME MR. TIBBS and THE ORGANIZATION. Lee Grant is also good as the hysterical widow. The film was shot in Illinois and Tennessee, the latter standing in for Mississippi.

IN THE REALM OF THE SENSES

(AI NO CORRIDA)
1976 105m c   ★★★★
Erotic/Drama   NC-17/18
Argos Films/Oshima Productions/Shibata Organization Inc. (France/Japan)

Tatsuya Fuji *(Kichi-zo)*, Eiko Matsuda *(Sada)*, Aoi Nakajima *(Toku)*, Maika Seri *(Maid Matsuko)*, Taiji Tonoyama *(Old Beggar)*, Hiroko Fuji *(Maid Tsune)*, Naomi Shiraishi *(Geisha Yaeji)*, Kyoko Okada *(Hangyoku)*, Kikuhei Matsunoya *(Hohkan)*, Yasuko Matsui *(Manageress of Inn)*

p, Anatole Dauman; d, Nagisa Oshima; w, Nagisa Oshima; ph, Hideo Ito, Kenichi Okamoto; ed, Keiichi Uraoka; m, Minoru Miki; art d, Jusho Toda; cos, Jusho Toda

Oshima's erotic masterpiece, based on a real-life 1936 love affair between the maid at a Japanese inn and her married employer. The film was vilified by prudish critics and came under concerted attack from censors, but has also been praised as one of the most liberating—and unexploitative—treatments of sexual passion ever filmed.

EMPIRE OF THE SENSES details the literally uncontrollable passion between the two lovers (Fuji Tatsuya and Eiko Matsuda), who turn their backs on one of the most repressive periods in Japanese history to lose themselves in their own, erotic universe. Their love is consummated in many different ways until it reaches, by mutual agreement, a climax that goes beyond the merely sexual. (The real-life maid was arrested for the murder of her employer, whose severed penis was found concealed about her person.) Not surprisingly, the film provoked considerable, short-sighted, outrage—it was banned as "obscene" by U.S. customs the day before it was due to be shown at the New York Film Festival—but has come to be regarded as a classic.

IN THE WHITE CITY

(DANS LA VILLE BLANCHE)
1983 108m c   ★★★½
Drama   /15
Metro/Filmograph   (Switzerland/Portugal)

Bruno Ganz *(Paul)*, Teresa Madruga *(Rosa)*, Julia Vonderlinn, Jose Carvalho, Victor Costa, Francisco Baiao, Jose Wallenstein, Lidia Franco, Pedro Efe, Joana Vicente

p, Paolo Branco, Antonio Vaz da Silver, Alain Tanner; d, Alain Tanner; w, Alain Tanner; ph, Acacio de Almeida; ed, Laurent Uhler; m, Jean-Luc Barbier; art d, Maria Jose Branco

Alain Tanner (JONAH WHO WILL BE 25 IN THE YEAR 2000), who single-handedly brought Swiss cinema into the world spotlight, takes his cameras to the streets of Portugal in this revealing portrait of a city and a man who wanders through it. Ganz (THE AMERICAN FRIEND) is a ship's mate who tires of his job and stays behind in Lisbon when his boat returns to sea. He lives in a daze, writing letters to his wife, discovering the city with his super-8mm movie camera, and having an affair with hotel chambermaid Madruga. Almost entirely improvised, IN THE WHITE CITY is as worth seeing for the intriguing super-8mm footage as for Ganz's involving performance—you really feel you're discovering Lisbon through his eyes.

IN WHICH WE SERVE

1942 115m bw   ★★★½
War   /U
Two Cities   (U.K.)

Noel Coward *(Capt. Kinross)*, John Mills *(Shorty Blake)*, Bernard Miles *(Walter Hardy)*, Celia Johnson *(Alix Kinross)*, Kay Walsh *(Freda Lewis)*, Joyce Carey *(Kath Hardy)*, Michael Wilding *(Flags)*, Penelope-Dudley Ward *(Maureen Fenwick)*, Philip Friend *(Torps)*, Derek Elphinstone *(No. One)*

p, Noel Coward; d, Noel Coward, David Lean; w, Noel Coward (based on the experiences of Lord Louis Mountbatten); ph, Ronald Neame; ed, Thelma Myers, David Lean; m, Noel Coward

Noel Coward performed with unexpected brilliance here as co-director, writer, musical composer, and star of this stirring WWII drama. Presented in a series of poignant and revealing vignettes, the film tells the story of the British destroyer *Torrin* and its crew, commanded by Capt. Kinross (Coward), a father figure for his stalwart men. Constructed like a documentary, IN WHICH WE SERVE is also narrated by Coward, who recounts the ship's heroic actions: hit by torpedoes, it survives and is towed back to England, later participating in the Dunkirk evacuation and in naval battles off Crete, where it is dive-bombed and sinks. Kinross and his crew cling to a raft for hours, and while waiting for rescue, remember their loved ones in a series of flashbacks.

Regarded as noble and understated at the time, IN WHICH WE SERVE now comes across as patronizing and riven with class condescension. But to Coward's credit (he recieved a special Oscar "for his outstanding production achievement"), he had the good sense to choose the most distinguished film editor in England at the time, David Lean, to assist with the production; and so impressive was Lean's work that, halfway through the picture, Coward handed him the directorial reins. Out of respect, Lean's next three productions—THIS HAPPY BREED; BLITHE SPIRIT; and BRIEF ENCOUNTER—were adaptations of Coward's writing. SERVE marked the film debuts of Johnson, Massey and baby Mills.

INADMISSIBLE EVIDENCE

1968 94m bw   ★★½
Drama   /AA
Woodfall (U.K.)

Nicol Williamson *(Bill Maitland)*, Eleanor Fazan *(Anna Maitland)*, Jill Bennett *(Liz)*, Peter Sallis *(Hudson)*, David Valla *(Jones)*, Eileen Atkins *(Shirley)*, Ingrid Brett *(Jane)*, Gillian Hills *(Joy)*, Isabel Dean *(Mrs. Garnsey)*, Clare Kelly *(Mrs. Anderson)*

p, Ronald Kinnoch; d, Anthony Page; w, John Osborne (based on his play); ph, Ken Hodges, Tony Imi; ed, Derek York; m, Dudley Moore; art d, Seamus Flannery; cos, Anne Gainsford

Based on the 1964 play by "angry young man" writer John Osborne, INADMISSIBLE EVIDENCE is about a dishonest middle-aged solicitor whose life begins to unravel. Nicol Williamson repeats his stage performance and though he's undeniably fine, this filmed stage play reduces everything to small chunks of exposition; the flow is gone. No longer are we allowed to feel we are inside Williamson's mind, an effect that a better filmmaker should have been able to achieve. Dudley Moore composed some original songs for the film's score, which also includes "Moonlight Becomes You" and "Room 504," both sung rather well by Williamson.

INCREDIBLE SHRINKING MAN, THE

1957 81m bw   ★★★
Science Fiction   /A
Universal

Grant Williams *(Scott Carey)*, Randy Stuart *(Louise Carey)*, April Kent *(Clarice)*, Paul Langton *(Charlie Carey)*, Raymond Bailey *(Dr. Thomas Silver)*, William Schallert *(Dr. Arthur Bramson)*, Frank Scannell *(Barker)*, Helene Marshall, Diana Darrin *(Nurses)*, Billy Curtis *(Midget)*

p, Albert Zugsmith; d, Jack Arnold; w, Richard Matheson (based on his novel *The Shrinking Man*); ph, Ellis W. Carter; ed, Al Joseph; m, Fred Carling, Elliot Lawrence; art d, Alexander Golitzen, Robert Clatworthy; fx, Clifford Stine, Roswell A. Hoffmann, Everett H. Broussard; cos, Jay A. Morley, Jr.

Pulp sci-fi classic about a man who starts to shrink after being enveloped by a strange atomic cloud while on holiday. Notable for its relatively intelligent script (adapted by Richard Matheson from his novel), for some imaginatively amusing special effects, and for an existential streak which finally has our (tiny) hero pondering the meaning of existence. (Matheson sold his novel on the condition that he be allowed to write the script. His first novel, *I Am Legend*, had been badly butchered, and he had no wish to see that happen again. Eventually, *I Am Legend* was filmed as L'ULTIMO UOMO DELLA TERRA from another writer's screenplay.) Source for a promising, but largely unsuccessful remake, THE INCREDIBLE SHRINKING WOMAN, in 1981.

INDIANA JONES AND THE LAST CRUSADE

1989 127m c   ★★½
Adventure   PG-13/PG
Lucasfilm

Harrison Ford *(Indiana Jones)*, Sean Connery *(Dr. Henry Jones)*, Denholm Elliott *(Marcus Brody)*, Alison Doody *(Dr. Elsa Schneider)*, John Rhys-Davies *(Sallah)*, Julian Glover *(Walter Donovan)*, River Phoenix *(Young Indy)*, Michael Byrne *(Vogel)*, Kevork Malikyan *(Kazim)*, Robert Eddison *(Grail Knight)*

p, Robert Watts; d, Steven Spielberg; w, Jeffrey Boam (based on a story by George Lucas, Menno Meyjes, and characters created by Lucas, Philip Kaufman); ph, Douglas Slocombe (Rank Color), Paul Beeson, Robert Stevens; ed, Michael Kahn; m, John Williams; prod d, Elliot Scott; art d, Fred Hole, Stephen Scott, Richard Berger, Benjamin Fernandez, Guido Salsilli; cos, Anthony Powell, Joanna Johnston

We're over it. The third and mercifully, final installment in Steven Spielberg and George Lucas's INDIANA JONES series sends the intrepid adventurer out with more bucks than bang. This time Indy (Harrison Ford) has a sidekick in his archaeologist father, Dr. Henry Jones (Sean Connery), a relationship involving not a little Oedipal tension. Together, the Joneses embark on a quest to find the Holy Grail, hoping to keep it from the evil Nazis (who want it because it gives eternal life), and falling afoul of a beautiful spy (Alison Doody) along the way.

Proceeding with considerably less blood, energy or danger than either RAIDERS OF THE LOST ARK or INDIANA JONES AND THE TEMPLE OF DOOM, THE LAST CRUSADE harkens more purely back to the series's sources—the fairly innocuous weekly cliffhangers of days gone by. The film offers some thrills and chills, but does so with such sanitized filmcraft that it's difficult to get excited about them. Despite strong acting (the slapstick energy between Ford and Connery is wasted), obligatory chases and stunts and splendid art direction, the virtuoso technique evident in every frame remains formulaic—unaccompanied by revelation, epiphany or surprise.

INDIANA JONES AND THE TEMPLE OF DOOM

1984 118m c   ★★★
Adventure   PG
Lucasfilm

Harrison Ford *(Indiana Jones)*, Kate Capshaw *(Willie Scott)*, Ke Huy Quan *(Short Round)*, Amrish Puri *(Mola Ram)*, Roshan Seth *(Chattar Lal)*, Philip Stone *(Capt. Blumburtt)*, Roy Chiao *(Lao Che)*, David Yip *(Wu Han)*, Ric Young *(Kao Kan)*, Chua Kah Joo *(Chen)*

p, Robert Watts; d, Steven Spielberg; w, Willard Huyck, Gloria Katz (based on a story by George Lucas and on characters from RAIDERS OF THE LOST ARK); ph, Douglas Slocombe (Panavision, DeLuxe Color); ed, Michael Kahn; m, John Williams; prod d, Elliot Scott; art d, Alan Cassie, Roger Cain, Joe Johnston, Errol Kelly; fx, Dennis Muren; chor, Danny Daniels; cos, Anthony Powell

After the release of director Steven Spielberg's RAIDERS OF THE LOST ARK, the question on almost everyone's lips was "How can he top this?" The answer won't be found in the $25 million sequel INDIANA JONES AND THE TEMPLE OF DOOM, a breakneck adventure that moves at twice the pace of the original but has only half the creative strength. The film opens with one of the decade's most purely entertaining scenes, a Busby Berkeley-style dance number to Cole Porter's "Anything Goes" (perhaps a clue to the line of logic the filmmakers were to follow). The setting is a swanky Shanghai nightclub in 1935 where heroic archaeologist Indiana Jones (Harrison Ford) has a run-in with some bad guys and is forced to make his getaway with singer Willie Scott (Kate Capshaw). Moments later they meet up with a 12-year-old named Short Round (Ke Huy Quan). The trio ends up in a primitive Indian village, where Jones is beckoned to retrieve a sacred stone from a heavily guarded palace.

Director Spielberg has crammed an endless barrage of special effects, chases, and gross-outs into the film's nearly two hours. The nonstop pace eventually numbs viewers to the thrills, although Spielberg must be congratulated for bringing the classical hero back to Hollywood. But what's with his increasingly graphic depictions of gore?

INDISCREET

1958 100m c   ★★★½
Romance/Comedy   /PG
Grandon (U.K.)

Cary Grant (Philip Adams), Ingrid Bergman (Anna Kalman), Cecil Parker (Alfred Munson), Phyllis Calvert (Margaret Munson), David Kossoff (Carl Banks), Megs Jenkins (Doris Banks), Oliver Johnston (Mr. Finleigh), Michael Anthony (Oscar), Middleton Woods (Finleigh's Clerk), Frank Hawkins

p, Stanley Donen; d, Stanley Donen; w, Norman Krasna (based on his play "Kind Sir"); ph, Freddie Young; ed, Jack Harris; m, Richard Rodney Bennett, Ken Jones; art d, Don Ashton; cos, Quintino

One of those rare movies that is far better than the play from which it was adapted. Based on Norman Krasna's Broadway flop, "Kind Sir," the movie is a frothy, often funny, diversion. Bergman, who proved her expertise in comedy with this performance, is a rich actress living in regal London luxury. Her sister, Calvert, and brother-in-law, Parker, introduce her to Grant, a financial genius who has come to London for a NATO dinner. Grant is a lifelong bachelor who masquerades as a married man to keep his single status secure. Grant tells Bergman that he's married, wich is fine with her. She has no interest in getting married and no compunctions about having an affair with a man who claims that he's separated and whose wife won't grant him freedom. Grant takes a job with NATO in Paris and their romance thrives as he comes to visit Bergman in London every weekend. When Grant is told he must transfer to New York for as long as five months, Bergman is at first heartbroken, then plans to quit the play she's appearing in and head for the US herself. But Calvert, who has learned the truth about Grant's marital status, lets Bergman in on the secret. Hurt and angry, Bergman plots to arouse Grant's jealousy by feigning an affair with a former lover.

The play starred Charles Boyer and Mary Martin, and, as good as they were, Grant and Bergman eclipsed them in the movie. This was a throwback to the Philip Barry school of drawing room comedy, and both Grant and Bergman were up to the challenge of re-creating the kind of movie that had been popular 20 years before. (Many of those, after all, had starred Grant.) This was the second pairing of Bergman and Grant (the first was in Alfred Hitchcock's NOTORIOUS in 1946) and they make a wonderful screen team, both adroitly handling the film's humor. Not to be missed is Grant's impromptu dance at a proper London club. INDISCREET is the perfect film to watch when you just want to lean back and smile, knowing full well what the outcome will be. The only surprise in the picture is how deft a comedienne Bergman could be.

INFORMER, THE

1935 91m bw   ★★★★½
Drama
RKO

Victor McLaglen (Gypo Nolan), Heather Angel (Mary McPhillip), Preston Foster (Dan Gallagher), Margot Grahame (Katie Madden), Wallace Ford (Frankie McPhillip), Una O'Connor (Mrs. McPhillip), J.M. Kerrigan (Terry), Joe Sawyer (Bartley Mulholland), Neil Fitzgerald (Tommy Conner), Donald Meek (Pat Mulligan)

p, Cliff Reid; d, John Ford; w, Dudley Nichols (based on the novel by Liam O'Flaherty); ph, Joseph August; ed, George Hively; m, Max Steiner; art d, Van Nest Polglase, Charles Kirk; cos, Walter Plunkett

Victor McLaglen gave the performance of his life as the scarfaced betrayer, Gypo Nolan, in this telling adaptation of Liam O'Flaherty's novel, directed by John Ford. The film gleaned top honors from the Academy, winning Oscars for McLaglen as Best Actor, Dudley Nichols for Best Adaptation, Max Steiner for Best Musical Score, and Ford for Best Director (he also won the New York Critics Best Director award).

Ford's tale of a hard-drinking brute who informs on one of his friends in order to collect a reward during the Irish Civil War of 1922 was made for a mere $243,000, and stands as one of the director's finest works. Joseph August's photography is superb, with its atmospheric shadows and light; the studio sets are brilliant representations of a fog-bound 1920s Dublin, complete with wet cobblestones and sweating walls. Through this mythic setting Ford moves his characters stoically to their grim fates. His selection of Victor McLaglen, who had starred in his other memorable talkie, THE LOST PATROL, was a masterstroke. Barrel-chested, with a thunderous voice and ox-like shoulders, McLaglen was the perfect Gypo Nolan, his battered face jutting pugnaciously into the camera (he had once been Heavyweight Champion of Great Britain). McLaglen never again reached such heights, although he appeared in around 150 films.

The first of three features Ford did for RKO, THE INFORMER became the studio's most prestigious production for years. Writer Nichols, one of Ford's favorite collaborators, wrote the script in six days, and Ford shot the entire film within another 17 days. THE INFORMER marked a turning point both for Ford, just entering into his most productive period, and composer Steiner, whose marvelous score perfectly fits every scene, from thundering patriotic cadences to lyrical and evocative motifs. The O'Flaherty novel had previously been filmed by British International as a silent; a remake with an all-Black cast, directed by Jules Dassin under the title UPTIGHT!, appeared in 1968.

INHERIT THE WIND

1960   127m   bw   ★★★★
Drama   /A
UA

Fredric March *(Matthew Harrison Brady)*, Spencer Tracy *(Henry Drummond)*, Gene Kelly *(E.K. Hornbeck)*, Florence Eldridge *(Mrs. Brady)*, Dick York *(Bertram T. Cates)*, Donna Anderson *(Rachel Brown)*, Harry Morgan *(Judge)*, Elliott Reid *(Davenport)*, Philip Coolidge *(Mayor)*, Claude Akins *(Rev. Brown)*

p, Stanley Kramer; d, Stanley Kramer; w, Nathan E. Douglas, Harold Jacob Smith (based on the play by Jerome Lawrence, Robert E. Lee); ph, Ernest Laszlo; ed, Frederic Knudtson; m, Ernest Gold; prod d, Rudolph Sternad; art d, Rudolph Sternad; cos, Joe King

Absorbing, if long-winded courtroom drama bolstered by two fine central performances from Tracy and March.

In the summer of 1925 the sovereign state of Tennessee played host to one of the most spectacular and ludicrous court trials in the history of American jurisprudence. A teacher named John T. Scopes had been arrested for teaching Darwin's theories of evolution in a public school, thus violating a state law. Prosecuting Scopes was the Rock of Ages fundamentalist, William Jennings Bryan, and defending him was the champion of liberal thinking, Clarence Darrow.

Producer-director Kramer used this high-voltage "Monkey Trial," as it came to be known, as the basis for one of his best film efforts. The names of the historical figures were all changed for the film, but their characters remain clearly recognizable. York plays the meek teacher, imprisoned for daring to teach Darwin in tiny Hillsboro. His girl friend is the daughter of fundamentalist preacher Akins, who agonizes over his daughter's affection for the religious infidel and sends for March to prosecute the young teacher. Tracy plays March's liberal opposite number, and song-and-dance man Kelly is cynical journalist E.K. Hornbeck (based on H.L. Mencken).

INHERIT THE WIND acutely captures the farcical Monkey Trial and offers the awesome talents of two double-Oscar winners, Tracy and March, in their only film together. March's real wife, Florence Eldridge, plays his onscreen spouse, and Harry Morgan turns in a fine performance as the judge caught between heavyweights. Much of the dialog is lifted from the successful Broadway play by Lawrence and Lee and first starring Paul Muni and Ed Begley.

INNERSPACE

1987   120m   c   ★★½
Comedy/Fantasy   PG
Amblin/Guber/Peters

Dennis Quaid *(Lt. Tuck Pendelton)*, Martin Short *(Jack Putter)*, Meg Ryan *(Lydia Maxwell)*, Kevin McCarthy *(Victor Scrimshaw)*, Fiona Lewis *(Dr. Margaret Canker)*, Vernon Wells *(Mr. Igoe)*, Robert Picardo *(The Cowboy)*, Wendy Schaal *(Wendy)*, Harold Sylvester *(Pete Blanchard)*, William Schallert *(Dr. Greenbush)*

p, Michael Finnell, Chip Proser; d, Joe Dante; w, Jeffrey Boam, Chip Proser (based on a story by Chip Proser); ph, Andrew Laszlo (Technicolor); ed, Kent Beyda; m, Jerry Goldsmith; prod d, James H. Spencer; art d, William F. Matthews; fx, Dennis Muren, Rob Bottin; cos, Rosanna Norton

Formulaic fun, helped by two winning leads. Lt. Tuck Pendelton (Dennis Quaid) is a bold American pilot who is miniaturized as part of a government experiment, then accidentally injected into Jack Putter (Martin Short), a weak-willed nobody. Jack and Tuck then team to battle the bad guys who are after the miniaturization formula. Joe Dante slogs his way through it, Meg Ryan shows up for intermittent sparkle and Short's drunken dance scene stands out. A combined reworking of FANTASTIC VOYAGE and ALL OF ME, the film won an Academy Award for Best Visual Effects.

INNOCENCE UNPROTECTED

(NEVINOST BEZ ZASTITE)
1968   75m   c/bw   ★★★★
Drama   /U
Avala   (Yugoslavia)

Dragoljub Aleksic *(Acrobat Aleksic)*, Ana Milosavljevic *(Nada The Orphan)*, Vera Jovanovic *(The Wicked Stepmother)*, Bratoljub Gligorijevic *(Mr. Petrovic)*, Ivan Zivkovic *(Aleksic's Brother)*, Pera Milosavljevic *(Servant)*

d, Dusan Makavejev; w, Dusan Makavejev; ph, Branko Perak, Stevan Miskovic (Eastmancolor); ed, Ivanka Vukasovic; m, Vojislav Dostic

In 1942, Aleksic, a Yugoslavian gymnast and stunt man, wrote, produced, directed, and starred in a film titled INNOCENCE UNPROTECTED. Its simple plot concerns an acrobat with a pure heart rescuing young Milosavljevic from the clutches of her evil stepmother, Jovanovic. The final production was subsequently confiscated by the Nazis, fading into cinema obscurity. Aleksic himself was accused (but later exonerated) of collaborating with the enemy. In 1968 Yugoslavian director Dusan Makavejev discovered the long-forgotten movie and reworked it into a film collage, a technique Makavejev further explored in WR: MYSTERIES OF THE ORGANISM. He hand-tinted some of the original footage and edited in newsreels of Nazi-occupied Yugoslavia. To this was added vintage documentary footage of Aleksic performing various stunts and new scenes with surviving members of the original film's cast and crew. The result is a wonderful and highly unusual film experience. Makavejev called it "a montage of attractions," an investigation of reality and illusion. The film is often confusing but full of ironies and biting humor, with a youthful exuberance emanating from both the director and Aleksic. A real love for the film medium irradiates the production.

INNOCENT, THE

(L'INNOCENTE)
1976   112m   c   ★★★½
Drama   R/X
Analysis   (Italy)

Giancarlo Giannini *(Tullio Hermil)*, Laura Antonelli *(Giuliana)*, Jennifer O'Neill *(Teresa Raffo)*, Rina Morelli *(Tullio's Mother)*, Massimo Girotti *(Count Stefano Egano)*, Didier Haudepin *(Federico Hermil)*, Marie Dubois *(The Princess)*, Roberta Paladini *(Miss Elviretta)*, Claude Mann *(The Prince)*, Marc Porel *(Filippo d'Arborio)*

p, Giovanni Bertolucci; d, Luchino Visconti; w, Suso Cecchi D'Amico, Enrico Medioli, Luchino Visconti (based on the novel L'Innocente

Visconti's final film, released just two months after his death, is a worthwhile conclusion to his great career, a telling adaptation of Gabriele d'Annunzio's 1892 novel about the decadence of the aristocracy in late 19th-century Italy.

Giannini is an atheistic aristocrat married to Antonelli and carrying on a fairly open affair with the manipulative O'Neill. Despite his history of dalliances, Giannini not only expects his wife to understand his position but begs and demands that she listen to his romantic woes and, if at all possible, think of a way to prevent him from seeing his mistress. He views his wife as a friend and confidante—until he learns she is having a passionate affair with successful young novelist Porel.

Visconti takes great pains to recreate a world of lush extravagance, and Giannini turns in a good performance, though he seems more at ease in the primarily comic first half of the film. Both women are beautiful and compelling, and Antonelli's love scene is a highlight. Unfortunately, much of Visconti's effort goes to waste on the videocassette version, which pays no attention to the film's original aspect ratio or the positions of the characters, who are often barely visible at the edges of the frame.

INNOCENTS, THE
1961   99m   bw   ★★★★½
Horror   /X
FOX/Achilles   (U.S./U.K.)

Deborah Kerr *(Miss Giddens)*, Michael Redgrave *(The Uncle)*, Peter Wyngarde *(Peter Quint)*, Megs Jenkins *(Mrs. Grose)*, Martin Stephens *(Miles)*, Pamela Franklin *(Flora)*, Clytie Jessop *(Miss Jessel)*, Isla Cameron *(Anna)*, Eric Woodburn *(Coachman)*

p, Jack Clayton; d, Jack Clayton; w, William Archibald, Truman Capote, John Mortimer (based on the novel *The Turn of the Screw* by Henry James); ph, Freddie Francis (CinemaScope); ed, James B. Clark; m, Georges Auric; prod d, Wilfred Shingleton; art d, Wilfred Shingleton; cos, Sophie Devine, Motley

Based on Henry James' *The Turn of the Screw*, THE INNOCENTS is a fine chiller that builds suspense slowly, subtly, and inexorably. Kerr is on top form here, enacting a role that takes perfect advantage of her respectable facade wrestling with unspeakable turbulence beneath the surface.

In Victorian England, Kerr arrives at the country estate of Redgrave, who has hired her to serve as the governess of his young niece and nephew, Franklin and Stephens. The housekeeper, Jenkins, introduces her to Franklin, an angelic little child with a beguiling smile who appears to have a mysterious foreknowledge of her brother's imminent arrival, though he is not expected. Soon a letter arrives from Stephens' school, informing the household that the boy has been expelled because he is a corrupting influence on his schoolmates. However, when Stephens arrives, he proves to be every bit as innocent and entrancing as his sister, and Kerr decides that the school officials must have been mistaken. Though the estate is a beautiful refuge, there is also an air of eeriness about the place. Kerr thinks she sees a man atop the house, is temporarily blinded by the sun, and then discovers Stephens feeding pigeons where she thought the man was. Feeling that her eyes must have played tricks on her, she calms down; later, however, she sees the specter of a woman at a window, and then sees the man again, getting a glimpse of his twisted face. When she describes these apparitions to Jenkins, she is told that the descriptions match those of the estate's late manager and his dead lover, the woman who preceded Kerr as governess. Kerr learns further that the deceased lovers had a sadomasochistic relationship, and that they had a considerable influence on the children. Are the children possessed by evil, earthbound spirits or is Kerr going mad?

Filmed at Sheffield Park in Sussex, this literate and elegant gothic horror, co-scripted by Truman Capote and John Mortimer, is fairly faithful to the James original. THE INNOCENTS manipulates the viewer's imagination as few films can, with Kerr and Redgrave doing a masterful job of creating a sense of repressed hysteria.

INSIDE DAISY CLOVER
1965   128m   c   ★★
Drama   /X
WB

Natalie Wood *(Daisy Clover)*, Christopher Plummer *(Raymond Swan)*, Robert Redford *(Wade Lewis)*, Roddy McDowall *(Walter Baines)*, Ruth Gordon *(The Dealer)*, Katharine Bard *(Melora Swan)*, Betty Harford *(Gloria Goslett)*, John Hale *(Harry Goslett)*, Harold Gould *(Cop)*, Ottola Nesmith *(Old Lady in Hospital)*

p, Alan J. Pakula, Robert Mulligan; d, Robert Mulligan; w, Gavin Lambert (based on his own novel); ph, Charles Lang (Panavision, Technicolor); ed, Aaron Stell; m, Andre Previn; prod d, Robert Clatworthy; art d, Dean Tavoularis; chor, Herbert Ross; cos, Bill Thomas, Edith Head

Too much, too soon, for Daisy and for us. Gothic Hollywood-insider account of a Garland-like waif-star suffers from weak characters and minimalist (to say the least) plot. Gavin Lambert's screenplay (from his novel), throws us one big, hammy campfest scene, followed by another that expects us to take it seriously. Wood's teen star comes close to conjuring up Mickey Rooney in his show-in-the-barn phase; Ruth Gordon is abominable as a sort of Gladys Baker (Marilyn Monroe's mother) character; and Christopher Plummer plays his scenes like he's trying to run through a swimming pool. It's only Redford's narcissistic gay star that holds interest. (He won a Golden Globe as "Star of Tommorrow" for the role.) The songs by Andre and Dory Previn are, amazingly, musical ciphers, which is both disappointing and surprising. Most songwriters would give their eyeteeth for an excuse to write rich, full-blooded Golden Era showbiz songs.

INSPECTOR CLOUSEAU
1968   96m   c   ★★★
Comedy   G/U
Mirisch   (U.K.)

Alan Arkin *(Inspector Jacques Clouseau)*, Delia Boccardo *(Lisa Morrel)*, Frank Finlay *(Superintendent Weaver)*, Patrick Cargill *(Sir Charles Braithwaite)*, Beryl Reid *(Mrs. Weaver)*, Barry Foster *(Addison Steele)*, Clive Francis *(Clyde Hargreaves)*, John Bindon *(Bull Parker)*, Michael Ripper *(Frey)*, Tutte Lernkow *(Frenchy LeBec)*

p, Lewis J. Rachmil; d, Bud Yorkin; w, Tom Waldman, Frank Waldman (based on a character created by Blake Edwards and Maurice Richlin); ph, Arthur Ibbetson (Panavision, DeLuxe Color); ed, John Victor Smith; m, Ken Thorne; prod d, Michael Stringer; art d, Norman Dorme; cos, Ivy Baker, Dinah Greet

The third film using the Blake Edwards and Maurice Richlin character and one of the weakest in the series, mainly because Edwards was replaced by director Yorkin and Arkin took over the acting chores from Sellers.

Cargill plays a Scotland Yard knight who uncovers the news that the plunder gleaned from the famous Great Train Robbery is now being employed to underwrite another robbery. He suspects that an associate may be in cahoots with the bad guys, so he calls for Clouseau (Arkin), the famous shamus from Paris. Talented though he is, Arkin cannot fill Sellers' shoes, especially when hampered by a script which relies on cheap laughs and lots of accidental death, and Yorkin's pedestrian direction. Look for Barbara Dana, Arkin's wife (and sometime screenwriter), in a small role as a nun, as well as Lemkow, an under-used British performer who played the title role in FIDDLER ON THE ROOF.

INTERIORS

1978 93m c   ★★★½
Drama   PG/15
UA

Kristin Griffith *(Flyn)*, Mary Beth Hurt *(Joey)*, Richard Jordan *(Frederick)*, Diane Keaton *(Renata)*, E.G. Marshall *(Arthur)*, Geraldine Page *(Eve)*, Maureen Stapleton *(Pearl)*, Sam Waterston *(Mike)*, Henderson Forsythe *(Judge Bartel)*

p, Charles H. Joffe; d, Woody Allen; w, Woody Allen; ph, Gordon Willis (Technicolor); ed, Ralph Rosenblum; prod d, Mel Bourne; cos, Joel Schumacher

Allen fans didn't like this stark examination of love, life, and death because they kept expecting it to turn funny and it never did. INTERIORS nevertheless represented an important and impressive change of direction for Allen, who here pays explicit homage to one of his acknowledged mentors, Ingmar Bergman— he even goes as far as to employ some of the master's best-known techniques, photographing the principals against blank walls and having them speak directly into the camera.

Wealthy Arthur (Marshall) and mentally disturbed Eve (Page) are the parents of three sisters. Arthur announces one day that he is leaving his wife to marry Pearl (Stapleton, in a role that gives the film its heart). The news causes Eve to disintegrate, and the daughters rush to their mother's side to help her through the crisis, even though they are having problems of their own. Renata (Keaton) is a poet married to a hack novelist (Jordan). Joey (Hurt), the most talented of the trio, seems incapable of focusing her abilities. Flyn (Griffith), meanwhile, a TV actress, is intensely self-centered. How the family deals with its problems forms the core of the film. The acting is outstanding all around, with special mention going to Hurt, Marshall, Page and Stapleton. Nominated for Oscars for writing, direction, actress (Page, inexplicably defeated by Jane Fonda in COMING HOME) and supporting actress.

INTERMEZZO: A LOVE STORY

1939 70m bw   ★★★½
Romance   /A
Selznick

Leslie Howard *(Holger Brandt)*, Ingrid Bergman *(Anita Hoffman)*, Edna Best *(Margit Brandt)*, John Halliday *(Thomas Stenborg)*, Cecil Kellaway *(Charles Moler)*, Enid Bennett *(Greta Stenborg)*, Ann Todd *(Ann Marie Brandt)*, Douglas Scott *(Eric Brandt)*, Eleanor Wesselhoeft *(Emma)*, Marie Flynn *(Marianne)*

p, David O. Selznick; d, Gregory Ratoff; w, George O'Neil (based on a story by Gosta Stevens and Gustaf Molander); ph, Gregg Toland; ed, Hal C. Kern, Francis D. Lyon; m, Heinz Provost; art d, Lyle Wheeler; fx, Jack Cosgrove; cos, Irene, Travis Banton

Bergman made her American debut in this somewhat saccharine romance, becoming a star of the first magnitude almost overnight. An established actress in her native Sweden, she had appeared in a Swedish production of the same story in 1937, but it lacked the rich production values Selznick and Howard (who coproduced and starred) infused into this version.

Howard plays Holger Brandt, a brilliant, aging violinst weary of his great fame. After a successful tour, he returns to Sweden to the arms of his wife Margit (Best) and adoring children (Todd and Scott). Deeply attracted to the fresh-faced, bright-eyed Anita (Bergman), the children's piano teacher, he joins her in an

impromptu recital before the family. Soon the pair discover that they are in love and Holger asks Margit for his freedom. She still loves him, though, and asks him to take time to reconsider. Holger and Anita travel abroad and she becomes his accompanist, to considerable acclaim. But Anita notices how Holger dotes on other people's children, and she decides that happiness is not built on the sadness of others.

Appealingly Continental in look and style, INTERMEZZO continually verges on soap, but is redeemed by carefully calibrated performances and Ratoff's loving direction. Beautifully photographed, the film won Toland an Oscar nomination (he lost to himself for his work on WUTHERING HEIGHTS). The memorable theme music, "Intermezzo" (composed by Heinz Provost), became a tremendously popular hit.

INTERNAL AFFAIRS

1990 115m c   ★½
Crime/Thriller   R/18
Frank Mancuso, Jr./Pierre David

Richard Gere *(Dennis Peck)*, Andy Garcia *(Sgt. Raymond Avila)*, Nancy Travis *(Kathleen Avila)*, Laurie Metcalf *(Sgt. Amy Wallace)*, Richard Bradford *(Lt. Sgt. Grieb)*, William Baldwin *(Van Stretch)*, Michael Beach *(Dorian)*, Ron Vawter *(Comdr. Oakes)*, John Getz *(Teeters)*, Faye Grant *(Penny Stretch)*

p, Frank Mancuso, Jr., Pierre David; d, Michael Figgis; w, Henry Bean; ph, John A. Alonzo; ed, Robert Estrin; m, Michael Figgis, Anthony Marinelli, Brian Banks; prod d, Waldemar Kalinowski

How many ridiculous movies can an actor's career endure? Richard Gere explores the possibilities with his appearance in this solemnly silly thriller helmed by Michael Figgis. In the wake of STORMY MONDAY, his critically acclaimed debut, this outing also represents a professional stumble for Mike Figgis. Figgis again aims for sensual moodiness, but so many clashing tones clamor for the viewer's attention that the result is a noisy mishmash.

Gere plays Dennis Peck, a star cop in one of the ritzier precincts of LA's San Fernando Valley. In his spare time, Peck is also a master criminal, running a vast empire of corruption out of that notorious breeding ground for vice, the Sherman Oaks Galleria shopping mall. Taking a bribery cut out of most of the vice in the Valley, Peck launders his ill-gotten fortunes through his four ex-wives, making them all tycoons on paper. (All we see them doing, though, is making breakfast and doing laundry for Peck and his passel of kids.)

Peck also has a unique method of keeping his criminal operatives under control: he turns their wives into his pliant sex slaves by introducing them to the joys of kinky sex during his free afternoons—which he seems to have ten days a week. In fact, we rarely see Peck doing anything so mundane and legit as actually arresting people; nonetheless, when internal affairs investigator Raymond Avila (Garcia) tries to unravel Peck's web of corruption, he meets a wall of resistance from his superiors for going after one of the force's most "productive" cops. Instead, Avila is called in to investigate Peck's partner, Stretch (Baldwin), an old friend of Avila's who has apparently been stretched to the breaking point as Peck's right-hand man.

Enough. The plot is, to say the least, mindlessly complex, with little room left to develop any kind of consistent mood, much less to develop characters beyond the sum of their cliches. Moreover, as LETHAL WEAPON and its spin-offs have indicated, today's high-impact cop thriller is no place for subtlety anyway. When in doubt, LETHAL WEAPON damned the critics to plunge full-speed ahead into boom-boom cartoon action, giving audiences a wild roller-coaster movie ride in lieu of compelling drama. Figgis tries to have it both ways, creating an ersatz aura of worldly cynicism for the art-house crowd, while providing plenty of sleazy sex and blood-pellet violence for those in the cheaper seats. The result is yet another goofy credit in Gere's already overloaded resume of embarrassment—although some may consider this one of those movies that's so silly it's good.

INTERNATIONAL HOUSE

1933 70m bw   ★★★★
Comedy
Paramount

Peggy Hopkins Joyce (Herself), W.C. Fields (Prof. Quail), Stuart Erwin (Tommy Nash), Sari Maritza (Carol Fortescue), George Burns (Dr. Burns), Gracie Allen (Nurse Allen), Bela Lugosi (Gen. Petronovich), Edmund Breese (Dr. Wong), Lumsden Hare (Sir Mortimer Fortescue), Franklin Pangborn (Hotel Manager)

d, A. Edward Sutherland; w, Francis Martin, Walter DeLeon (based on a story by Lou Heifetz, Neil Brant); ph, Ernest Haller; cos, Travis Banton

Manic, ragtag W.C. Fields vehicle, full of the usual lunacy and laughter.

Breese plays Dr. Wong, an eccentric inventor who intends to exhibit his early version of television in Wuhu, China before a group of international buyers. Foremost of these is a Russian general (Lugosi) who arrives at the hotel to be greeted by his golddigging ex-wife. Arriving later is Dr. Quail (Fields), who has flown in from Mexico in an autogyro, dropping beer bottles en route and injuring countless victims below. At least so say the reports read by Dr. Burns and Nurse Allen (George and Gracie) of the International House's hotel staff. Meanwhile, American envoy Tommy Nash (Erwin) is busy trying to woo Carol Fortescue (Maritza), while evading the Russian's predatory ex. Finally, all the players gather to view Wong's new invention. Tommy ends up buying the device mostly to escape the hotel, quarantined with the measles. During the last demonstrations, Wong manages to pick up on transmissions of Baby Rose Marie warbling a torch song, then tunes in to Cab Calloway singing a song called "Reefer Man," which later became a camp classic. (This number is invariably cut from the prints shown on television.) Before the cast escapes the madhouse, there are several big musical production numbers on a Busby Berkeley scale, as well as numerous romantic pairings, including one for Dr. Quail.

In INTERNATIONAL HOUSE, director Sutherland wisely let Fields do practically whatever he wanted, inserting gags and routines that caught the public's fancy and boosted his stardom even higher. Pangborn, Burns, Allen, and Lugosi are all hilarious, but this near-surreal spoof of GRAND HOTEL ultimately belongs to Fields.

INTERVISTA

1987 105m c   ★★★
Biography
Aljosha/RAI-TV/Cinecitta/Fernlyn (Italy)

Federico Fellini (Himself), Marcello Mastroianni (Himself), Anita Ekberg (Herself), Sergio Rubini (Reporter), Maurizio Mein (Himself), Lara Wendel (Bride), Paola Liguori (Star), Nadia Ottaviani (Vestal Virgin), Antonella Ponziani (Young Girl), Tonino Delli Colli (Himself)

p, Ibrahim Moussa; d, Federico Fellini; w, Federico Fellini, Gianfranco Angelucci; ph, Tonino Delli Colli (Eastmancolor); ed, Nino Baragli; m, Nicola Piovani; art d, Danilo Donati, Paul Mazursky, Leon Capetanos

Freewheeling autobiographical film in which Fellini (who appears as himself, the director of a new project—an adaptation of Franz Kafka's Amerika) strings together a loose collection of anecdotes and sketches. The linking device is a Japanese TV documentary crew who question the director about his career. Fellini remembers his days as a young reporter assigned his first interview at Cinecitta Studios with a glamorous, aging movie star (Liguori) who steps from her steamy shower to answer his questions. He also reconstructs his youthful trolley ride to Cinecitta Studios, located just outside of Rome, filling the trolley with the faces that he remembers from his youth, including a pretty blonde starlet who is on her way to her first screen test. Outside the windows are Rome's city streets, gorgeous waterfalls, a herd of elephants, and a tribe of Indians—recollections of fantasies which the great director fabricated within Cinecitta's walls. When the trolley arrives, the starlet runs off with her fiance, and Fellini comments that he never saw her again. Once inside the studio, Fellini wanders through various soundstages. On an outdoor stage, Rubini nearly ruins a long take of a wedding scene by accidentally walking past while the cameras are rolling. As INTERVISTA continues, Fellini talks with the Japanese crew, with Rubini, and with various members of his real-life film crew: assistant director Maurizio Mein, cinematographer Tonino Delli Colli, and art director Danilo Donati. They discuss Fellini's upcoming adaptation of Amerika, a project which was actually being prepared by Fellini and INTERVISTA producer Moussa at the time. On a casting assignment, Mein interviews numerous applicants for small roles—all of which require actors with the "Fellini face." He rides the subway, snapping photographs and offering people parts in the film. Later, during a bomb scare at Cinecitta's art department, Mastroianni appears outside the office window dressed like Mandrake the Magician and waving a wand. He is at the studio to film a TV commercial, but decides instead to run off with Fellini to visit Anita Ekberg, Mastroianni's costar in LA DOLCE VITA. Once arrived at Ekberg's country estate, Mastroianni waves his wand and, from a magical puff of smoke, a scene from LA DOLCE VITA appears. The soft, dreamy strains of Nino Rota's score are heard as we see Mastroianni and Ekberg, both looking fresher and thinner than today, dance romantically and then embrace in the classic Trevi Fountain scene. Together, the same pair, now 27 years older, watch themselves as part of the cast of INTERVISTA with Ekberg shedding a nostalgic tear. The curious finale has the entire cast and crew preparing to film a scene on a Cinecitta backlot (which duplicates the ending of Fellini's 8½) when a downpour halts production. Everyone scurries under a hastily rigged canopy. Night soon falls, but the rain continues. By dawn, the rain has stopped, but the entire crew is attacked by the tribe of Indians seen during the film's opening trolley ride. The Indians circle the film "troops" and are finally dispersed by gun-toting crew members. The production "wraps" and Fellini, now alone in a spotlit soundstage, decides to end his film.

INTERVISTA play as an enjoyable, lightweight entertainment, filled with the usual Felliniesque characters, faces, and situations. Originally conceived as a film for Italian television, the project grew to a size where it warranted theatrical release. First called "A Director's Block Notes," it was then retitled APPUNTI DI FEDERICO FELLINI ("Federico Fellini's Notebooks"). At one point, Fellini had wanted to title it with the

Japanese word for *interview*. "I imagined the Japanese for *interview*," he explained, "would be some suave, cabalistic sequence of sounds—something like RASHOMON. So I made inquiries. Alas, the Japanese word for *interview* is. . . *interview*."

INTRUDER IN THE DUST

1949   87m   bw   ★★★★
Drama   /A
MGM

David Brian *(John Gavin Stevens)*, Claude Jarman, Jr. *(Chick Mallison)*, Juano Hernandez *(Lucas Beauchamp)*, Porter Hall *(Nub Gowrie)*, Elizabeth Patterson *(Miss Habersham)*, Charles Kemper *(Crawford Gowrie)*, Will Geer *(Sheriff Hampton)*, David Clarke *(Vinson Gowrie)*, Elzie Emanuel *(Aleck)*, Lela Bliss *(Mrs. Mallison)*

p, Clarence Brown; d, Clarence Brown; w, Ben Maddow (based on the novel by William Faulkner); ph, Robert Surtees; ed, Robert J. Kern; m, Adolph Deutsch; art d, Cedric Gibbons, Randall Duell

The lack of big name stars is, if anything, a plus in making this one of the most powerful movies ever made about racism. Based on Faulkner's novel and filmed on location near the writer's native Oxford, MI, Brown's film features more than 500 people, only a small portion of whom were professional actors. Hernandez plays Lucas Beauchamp, an elderly black man who owns his own property, something the locals resent. The police arrest him for the murder of a townsman because he was discovered near the body and the revolver he carried had just been fired. On the way to jail he spots Chick (Jarman), a young white lad with whom he is friendly. He asks Chick to get Stevens (Brian), the boy's attorney uncle, to come to the jail. Despite Chick's pleas, Stevens resists the idea of defending Lucas, knowing he'll be ostracized by the townspeople if he does. Crawford Gowrie (Kemper), brother of the dead man, spreads the word, and the lawyer becomes a pariah as Gowrie rouses the rabble to lynch Beauchamp. The jailed man, though, has his story, which involves a beating he suffered at the hands of the victim. Lucas' supporters grow as Chick and Miss Habersham (Patterson) help dig up the dead man's coffin to prove that Lucas' gun was not the murder weapon. When the corpse is found instead in a quicksand swamp, even the dead man's father (Hall) has his doubts. Finally the canny Sheriff Hampton (Geer) uses a ruse to catch the real killer and the lynch-hungry mob is confronted with its own bigotry.

The most chilling scene in the movie is a lengthy sequence which cuts from the people of Oxford gleefully assembling (not unlike the crowd to see the man trapped below ground in THE BIG CARNIVAL) at the jail for a lynching to shots of music playing and kids eating ice cream. Everyone is in a jolly mood, in direct contrast to the grisly plans they have for the prisoner. This is not a pretty story and it does not exactly feature the people of Mississippi in a flattering light. Brown must have had a silver tongue to convince so many locals to play in the film, when one considers how they are portrayed. After many years of seeing stereotyped blacks on screen, Hernandez's role was a revelation as he stood up to the charges with pride and dignity. Patterson is equally marvelous in one of the finest roles of her lengthy career.

INVADERS, THE

1941   105m   bw   ★★★★½
War
General Films   (U.K.)

Leslie Howard *(Philip Armstrong Scott)*, Raymond Massey *(Andy Brock)*, Laurence Olivier *(Johnnie)*, Anton Walbrook *(Peter)*, Eric Portman *(Lt. Hirth)*, Glynis Johns *(Anna)*, Niall MacGinnis *(Vogel)*, Finlay Currie *(Factor)*, Raymond Lovell *(Lt. Kuhnecke)*, John Chandos *(Lohrmann)*

p, Michael Powell, John Sutro; d, Michael Powell; w, Rodney Ackland, Emeric Pressburger (based on a story by Pressburger); ph, Freddie Young; ed, David Lean; m, Ralph Vaughan Williams; art d, David Rawnsley

THE INVADERS (49TH PARALLEL in the UK) is an excellent war drama from British director Powell, co-scripted by his longtime collaborator Pressburger. Filmed mostly in Canada, the film opens as a U-37 German submarine surfaces in the Gulf of St. Lawrence. It is obliterated by RCAF bombers, but six Germans survive and march to a Hudson Bay trading post. Constructed in episodic fashion, the story shows them wandering through Canada to avoid detection. Along the way, they meet Johnnie (Olivier), a trapper filled with contempt for the Nazis; a group of German Hutterites living on a Christian collective headed by Peter (Walbrook); and Philip Armstrong Scott (Howard), a decadent novelist living in a teepee while writing about the Blackfoot Indians. With each meeting, the number of "invaders" diminishes; some are captured, others killed, and a decent one (MacGinnis) tries to remain with the Hutterites. Finally, the last to elude death or capture (Portman) meets Andy Brock (Massey), an AWOL Canadian soldier who complains about democracy while stowing away on a freight train bound for the US. The wily Andy shows his true colors, though, when he must confront Nazism incarnate.

The anti-Fascist message here is extremely eloquent, the Oscar-winning script witty and intelligent, and the photography handsome and atypical for a war film. Powell beautifully ties it all together in a directorial style that is part war adventure, part Robert Flaherty-influenced documentary, taking just as much time with action sequences as he does with Hutterite communal living, Eskimo culture, or Indian rituals. The acting is almost uniformly excellent, with Walbrook his usual superb self, and marvelous work from Johns, MacGinnis, Currie, Howard and Massey. With his gravelly voice and incisive manner, Portman makes an electrifying villain, and he became a major British star with this film. Unfortunately Olivier lowers this high standard with a rather hammy performance, replete with variable French-Canadian accent. The British release runs nearly 20 minutes longer than the version generally seen in America.

INVASION OF THE BODY SNATCHERS

1956   80m   bw   ★★★½
Science Fiction   /PG
Allied Artists

Kevin McCarthy *(Miles Bennel)*, Dana Wynter *(Becky Driscoll)*, Larry Gates *(Dr. Dan Kauffmann)*, King Donovan *(Jack)*, Carolyn Jones *(Theodora)*, Jean Willes *(Sally)*, Ralph Dumke *(Nick Grivett)*, Virginia Christine *(Wilma Lentz)*, Tom Fadden *(Uncle Ira Lentz)*, Kenneth Patterson *(Driscoll)*

p, Walter Wanger; d, Don Siegel; w, Geoffrey Homes (based on the novel *The Body Snatchers* by Jack Finney); ph, Ellsworth Fredricks; ed, Robert S. Eisen; m, Carmen Dragon; prod d, Joseph Kish; art d, Ted Haworth; fx, Milt Rice

A superbly crafted film by innovative director Siegel, this low-budget science fiction tale became one of the great cult classics of the genre.

Miles (McCarthy), a doctor from the small town of Santa Mira, arrives in San Francisco in hysterical condition; he raves that his community has been invaded by aliens who have literally taken over the bodies of his friends and relatives. He's a candidate for the lunatic asylum, most agree, but they hear him out, and the story unfolds in flashback. Miles has returned home from a medical convention to find that many people have been complaining that their loved ones somehow don't appear to be the same people as before. He also runs into Becky (Wynter), an old girlfriend and recent divorcee, and they both note how odd it is that all the complaints seem to be suddenly vanishing. Miles and Becky have dinner with two friends (Donovan and Jones) and, to their horror, the quartet discover enormous pods growing in the couple's greenhouse which open to reveal exact physical reproductions of each of them. Miles and Becky run for their lives; half the population of the town, including the police, has been replaced. The phone system is also in the alien grip: when Miles tries to call federal authorities, operators tell him that all the lines to Washington are tied up. Miles and Becky later witness the police directing locals to drive their pod-filled cars to neighboring towns, and they realize that the whole world is in great danger. The local psychiatrist (Gates) catches them and arranges for two pods to be placed in the next room. The sinister shrink explains that all Miles and Becky have to do is go to sleep; they will awaken as one of the new creatures and will never again know pain, hate, or worry. Miles counters that they will also be without joy or love, and he and Becky attempt to escape.

This film was originally conceived by producer Wanger as standard B fare, but Siegel made much more of it, with writer Mainwaring injecting an element of subtle humor. It's since come to seem typical of 50s paranoia about everything from the Red Scare to nuclear warfare. INVASION spawned an adequate remake, starring Donald Sutherland, in 1978.

INVASION OF THE BODY SNATCHERS

1978   115m   c   ★★½
Science Fiction   PG/15
UA

Donald Sutherland (Matthew Bennell), Brooke Adams (Elizabeth Driscoll), Leonard Nimoy (Dr. David Kibner), Veronica Cartwright (Nancy Bellicec), Art Hindle (Geoffrey), Lelia Goldoni (Katherine), Kevin McCarthy (Running Man), Jeff Goldblum (Jack Bellicec), Don Siegel (Cab Driver)

p, Robert H. Solo; d, Philip Kaufman; w, W.D. Richter (based on the novel by Jack Finney); ph, Michael Chapman (Technicolor); ed, Douglas Stewart; m, Denny Zeitlin; prod d, Charles Rosen; fx, Dell Rheaume, Russ Hessey

Colorful and expensive remake of the 1956 sci-fi classic, with mopey, sleepy-eyed Sutherland playing the part originated by Kevin McCarthy, a health inspector giving a hard time to San Francisco restaurant owners when he finds rat droppings in their kitchens. Instead of the original setting, a little town in California, the setting here is the sprawling city of San Francisco, now under alien attack by the mysterious pods (with Nimoy as the psychiatrist advocating the takeover). The film collapses midway—because of unsure and sloppy direction, splintered story continuity, and the overacting of Adams, Cartwright, and others. The battle between Sutherland and the aliens in the "pod factory" at the end is simply absurd and sophomoric. In a nod to the earlier classic, McCarthy appears at the beginning of the film, shouting hysterical warnings to motorists until he is struck and killed by a car. A great number of shots show the Transamerica pyramid building in downtown San Francisco, a subtle plug for the distributor of the movie, whose corporate offices are housed there.

INVESTIGATION OF A CITIZEN ABOVE SUSPICION

(INDAGINE SU UN CITTADINO AL DI SOPRA DI OGNI SOSPETTO)
1970   112m   c   ★★★★
Crime   R/18
Vera   (Italy)

Gian Maria Volonte (Police Inspector), Florinda Bolkan (Augusta Terzi), Salvo Randone (Plumber), Gianni Santuccio (Police Commissioner), Arturo Dominici (Mangani), Orazio Orlando (Biglia), Sergio Tramonti (Antonio Pace), Massimo Foschi (Augusta's Husband), Aldo Rendine (Homicide Functionary), Aleka Paizi

p, Daniele Senatore; d, Elio Petri; w, Ugo Pirro, Elio Petri; ph, Luigi Kuveiller (Technicolor); ed, Ruggero Mastroianni; m, Ennio Morricone; prod d, Romano Cardarelli; cos, Angela Sammaciccia, Mayer

The winner of 1970's foreign film Oscar, this jarring and potent Italian film tells the story of a recently promoted Fascist police inspector (Volonte) who one Sunday afternoon slits his mistress's throat. He then plants phony evidence and makes an anonymous call to report the crime. The police unearth clues that point to the inspector, but ignore them because of his standing. The killer eventually writes a confession and awaits his capture, while planning to receive an acquittal.

An excellent look into the mind of a murderer, INVESTIGATION features a fine performance from Volonte in the leading role. Director Petri has made an antifascist statement that is both pointed and poignant, full of eerie, unsettling moods abetted by Morricone's score. A piercing satire of Italian investigative techniques, and an interesting meditation on the relationship between class and guilt.

INVISIBLE MAN, THE

1933   71m   bw   ★★★★½
Science Fiction
Universal

Claude Rains (Jack Griffin/The Invisible One), Gloria Stuart (Flora Cranley), William Harrigan (Doctor Kemp), Henry Travers (Dr. Cranley), Una O'Connor (Mrs. Jenny Hall), Forrester Harvey (Mr. Herbert Hall), Holmes Herbert (Chief of Police), E.E. Clive (Jaffers), Dudley Digges (Chief of Detectives), Harry Stubbs (Inspector Bird)

p, Carl Laemmle, Jr.; d, James Whale; w, Philip Wylie (uncredited), R.C. Sherriff (based on the novel by H.G. Wells); ph, Arthur Edeson; m, W. Franke Harling; art d, Charles D. Hall; fx, John P. Fulton, John Mescall

Few debuts have been as impressive or odd as that made by the voice of Claude Rains in this macabre classic based on the novel by H.G.Wells. (Actually, there's a glimpse of the rest of Rains, too, but not until the very end.)

Jack Griffin (Rains) is an English scientist who has been experimenting with a drug called monocaine which, he finds, has made his entire body invisible. He goes to the small village of Ipping, wrapped in bandages and wearing dark glasses, and takes a room at the local inn to continue his research in secret. This subsequently arouses the curiosity of the nosy locals. As Griffin continues his experiments, he begins to suffer from drug-induced megalomania, which eventually becomes full-blown madness. He begins to terrorize the countryside—first playing pranks, and then turning to murder.

Memorable moments and lines of dialogue pepper this striking fantasy: Griffin informing his terrified, unwilling assistant Kemp, "We'll start with a few murders. Small men. Great men. Just to show we make no distinction"; any of the scenes involving the priceless Una O'Connor as the innkeeper's flighty wife; the farmer's discovery of breathing in his barn. Whale was always fascinated by the inconveniences of being a monster and Griffin tells us how it's hard to walk down steps when you can't see your feet. Best of all, though, is the scene where the enraged scientist first takes of his disguise and to the amazement of the locals reveals. . . nothing. Fine acting all around, especially from Rains, great camera work and effects from Edeson and Fulton (who used black velvet-clad actors filmed before black backgrounds to achieve the needed effects), and brilliantly judged direction from Whale make this film hard to beat. The dialogue by Wylie and Sherriff is by turns hilarious, haunting and horrific.

INVITATION, THE

1975 100m c   ★★★★
Comedy/Drama   /AA
Citel/Group 5/Swiss TV/Planfilm   (France/Switzerland)

Jean-Luc Bideau (Maurice), Francois Simon (Emile), Jean Champion (Alfred), Corinne Coderey (Simone), Michel Robin (Remy), Cecile Vassort (Aline), Rosina Rochette (Helene), Jacques Rispal (Rene), Neige Dolsky (Emma), Pierre Collet (Pierre)

d, Claude Goretta; w, Claude Goretta, Michel Viala; ph, Jean Zeller; ed, Joele Van Effenterre; m, Patrick Moraz

One of the most impressive works to come out of Switzerland in the past decade or two (along with the films of Alain Tanner), THE INVITATION was nominated for an Academy Award for Best Foreign Film. The subtle, naturalistic story unfolds during an office party. As with all parties of this sort, the workers get out of hand and reveal facets of themselves that they usually keep hidden from 9 to 5. The affair, thrown by a meek dullard (Robin), comes to life when the office stud (Bideau) begins his conquests of women. It is up to a cultured, patient butler (Simon) to keep things in order—a seemingly futile task. Writer-director Claude Goretta has wrought an uncluttered, worthy piece of adult entertainment blessed with acting and dialogue that are completely convincing.

INVITATION TO THE DANCE

1956 93m c   ★★
Musical   /U
MGM

Gene Kelly (The Clown/Sinbad/The Marine). CIRCUS: Igor Youskevitch (The Lover), Claire Sombert (The Loved). SINBAD THE SAILOR: Carol Haney (Scheherazade), David Kasday (The Genie). RING AROUND THE ROSY: David Paltenghi (The Husband), Igor Youskevitch (The Artist), Daphne Dale (The Wife), Claude Bessy (The Model), Tommy Rall (Flashy Boyfriend)

p, Arthur Freed; d, Gene Kelly; w, Gene Kelly; ph, Freddie Young, Joseph Ruttenberg (Technicolor); ed, Raymond Poulton, Adrienne Fazan, Robert Watts; m, Jacques Ibert, Andre Previn, Roger Edens, Nikolai Andreevich; art d, Alfred Junge, Cedric Gibbons, Randall Duell; fx, Tom Howard; chor, Gene Kelly; cos, Rolf Gerard, Elizabeth Haffenden

Gene Kelly tries art cinema and fails. Too bad, given that this was a very personal film and it took him four years and a lot of persuading of the MGM front office to get it made.

This ambitious work consists of three playlets, all done in dance and mime. No singing or dialogue here, though one doubts

that would have helped anyway. Kelly has clearly taken French Film 101 for this endeavor, and his tragic clown in the first segment, the cleverly-named "Circus", is an obvious rip-off of Jean-Louis Barrault's mime in CHILDREN OF PARADISE. Set to music by Jacques Ibert, the sequence features Kelly with a big case of unrequited love for the circus' star (Sombert). The second sequence is Kelly's superficial take on Max Ophuls. As in LA RONDE, the sappily-titled "Ring Around the Rosy" features X who loves Y, Y who loves Z and Z who loves. . . you guessed it. He also steals from Ophuls' EARRINGS OF MADAME DE. . . as a piece of jewelry (here a bracelet) gets passed back and forth among a circle of lovers. Too bad Kelly doesn't have Ophuls' scathing sense of irony or his genius with a camera. This is the sequence where MGM didn't like Malcolm Arnold's music and so scrapped it, forcing Andre Previn to compose to already-shot footage. The last and longest sequence, SINBAD THE SAILOR, set to Rimski-Korsakov, features Kelly dancing with animated figures, but doing nothing he hadn't already done better with Jerry the mouse in ANCHORS AWEIGH.

Long and dull, INVITATION TO THE DANCE is particularly disappointing precisely in the area Kelly emphasizes—dance. With all this terpsichorean talent (including Sombert, Rall, Belita and Toumanova) one would think that the dancing might be better, but Kelly's choreography lets them all down. He indulges himself as a dancer far too much in the first and third segments, suggesting that Stanley Donen provided some much-needed balance in the films they co-directed. The third sequence in particular has Kelly bounding through animated clouds so often you want to scream. Pure ballet was never his forte as a choreographer and one longs for more jazz and tap. The film's failure sabotaged Kelly's stardom and maybe even some of his confidence too. It's a shame, but it's still a lousy movie.

IPCRESS FILE, THE

1965 109m c   ★★★½
Spy   /PG
Lowndes/Steven   (U.K.)

Michael Caine (Harry Palmer), Nigel Green (Dalby), Guy Doleman (Maj. Ross), Sue Lloyd (Jean), Gordon Jackson (Jock Carswell), Aubrey Richards (Radcliffe), Frank Gatliff (Bluejay), Thomas Baptiste (Barney), Oliver MacGreevy (Housemartin), Freda Bamford (Alice)

p, Harry Saltzman; d, Sidney J. Furie; w, Bill Canaway, James Doran (based on the novel by Len Deighton); ph, Otto Heller (Techniscope, Technicolor); ed, Peter Hunt; m, John Barry; prod d, Ken Adam; art d, Peter Murton

Based on the first and the best of Len Deighton's novels about myopic, flabby antihero Harry Palmer (Caine), THE IPCRESS FILE is a witty, fast-paced espionage film. Palmer, a British army sergeant stationed in Berlin, is nabbed for black marketeering but told that he can do his penance by serving as a counterintelligence agent. When Radcliffe (Richards), the latest in a string of scientists to be kidnaped, disappears along with a top secret file, Palmer is put on the case. During the investigation, a mysterious tape turns up with "Ipcress" written on it, and just when it appears that the case is about to be cracked, an agent is murdered and Palmer is confronted by the real—and surprising—enemy.

The best part of the film is Caine's characterization. Hardly a superhero, Harry Palmer is an ordinary chap tossed into a maelstrom in much the same way Alfred Hitchcock placed people in situations beyond their scope and then let them triumph over seemingly unbeatable odds. Canadian-born Sidney J. Furie seems determined to be a flashy director here, but if his restless camera and kooky *mise en scene* are sometimes just plain weird, they are also sometimes stylishly suited to the foolishness of the entire undertaking. Look for a scene in which Harry makes coffee in his elegant *caffetiere*, a very chic device at the time. (It's that kind of movie.) Produced by Harry Saltzman, the coproducer of many James Bond films, THE IPCRESS FILE gave rise to two sequels, FUNERAL IN BERLIN and BILLION DOLLAR BRAIN, both of which starred Caine. Neither was as exciting or enjoyable as this one, however.

IREZUMI (SPIRIT OF TATTOO)
(SEKKA TOMURAI ZASHI)
1982 88m c ★★★★
Drama
Daiei (Japan)

Tomisaburo Wakayama *(Kyogoro)*, Tasayo Utsunomiya *(Akane)*, Yusuke Takita *(Fujieda)*, Masaki Kyomoto *(Harutsune)*, Harue Kyo *(Katsuko)*, Naomi Shiraishi *(Haruna)*, Taiji Tonoyama *(Horiatsu)*

p, Yasuyoshi Tokuma, Masumi Kanamaru; d, Yoichi Takabayashi; w, Chico Katsura (based on the novel by Baku Akae); ph, Hideo Fujii; ed, Masaru Sato

This is a strikingly visual film about the beautiful young Akane (Utsonomiya), who has her back tattooed to please her lover. Her greatest fear is that she will lose this man, a file clerk with a fetish for beautiful skin and tattoos. So for two years she commutes from Tokyo to Kyoto, where Kyogoro (Wakayama), a renowned tattoo artist who has come out of retirement for Akane, devotes the remainder of his life to completing this final tattoo. His method, of which he is deeply ashamed, is unique: Akane lies atop Kyogoro's nude, heavily tattooed young apprentice, moaning from the pain of the pricking tattoo needle and tightly gripping the man beneath her. Kyogoro believes that this brings the tattoo to life, giving it a soul and spirit all its own.

As mysterious and foreign as it is kinky and erotic, IREZUMI explores the yin-yang principle of complete existence emerging from two opposites. While she is tattooed, Akane experiences intense extremes of both pleasure and pain, which breathes life into Kyogoro's art. Later, Kyogoro's apprentice creates his first tattoo—a tiny snowflake—which burns Akane's tender flesh like fire. Director Takabayashi, whose first film, GAKI ZOSHI (The Water Was So Clear) also dealt with spirituality and eroticism, directs with a delicate sense of beauty, his visuals carefully capturing the movements and colors of the tattoo master at work and the living piece of art Akane becomes.

IRMA LA DOUCE
1963 147m c ★★★
Comedy /15
Mirisch/Phalanx/Alperson

Jack Lemmon *(Nestor)*, Shirley MacLaine *(Irma La Douce)*, Lou Jacobi *(Moustache)*, Bruce Yarnell *(Hippolyte)*, Herschel Bernardi *(Inspector LeFevre)*, Hope Holiday *(Lolita)*, Joan Shawlee *(Amazon Annie)*, Grace Lee Whitney *(Kiki the Cossack)*, Tura Satana *(Suzette Wong)*, Harriette Young *(Mimi the MauMau)*

p, Billy Wilder; d, Billy Wilder; w, Billy Wilder, I.A.L. Diamond (based on the play by Alexandre Breffort); ph, Joseph La Shelle (Panavision, Technicolor); ed, Daniel Mandell; m, Andre Previn (based on a score by Marguerite Monnot); art d, Alexander Trauner; fx, Milt Rice; chor, Wally Green; cos, Orry-Kelly

IRMA LA DOUCE has a curious history: a French musical in 1956, an American adaptation in 1960, then this nonmusical film in 1963. Far too long for a lighthearted farce, with dull patches

that outnumber the high spots, the film is really about Maclaine and Lemmon striving to rise above the fat Diamond-Wilder script and Wilder's lethargic direction.

Wilder was the logical choice to adapt this type of film, but it still misses. MacLaine is Irma, a Paris streetwalker whose money goes to her handsome pimp Hippolyte (Yarnell). Enter Nestor (Lemmon), a cop who antedates Clouseau in his bumbling but sincere ineptitude. Nestor cannot believe all the women plying their trade, and seeks to reform the area by raiding a local bistro run by Moustache (Jacobi). The chief police inspector (Bernardi) is arrested in the raid and Nestor is promptly sacked. Nestor and Irma become an item and she fires Hippolyte, making Nestor her new "protector".

Previn won an Oscar, and MacLaine and La Shelle were nominated, but this was less than a complete success. The movie was filmed on a 360-degree set so shooting could be done in any direction. You can't help but wonder what the film might have been with a half hour cut, or with the Broadway score retained.

IS PARIS BURNING?
(PARIS BRULE-T-IL?)
1966 173m c/bw ★★½
War /A
Transcontinental/Marianne (U.S./France)

Jean-Paul Belmondo *(Morandat)*, Charles Boyer *(Monod)*, Leslie Caron *(Francoise Labe)*, Jean-Pierre Cassel *(Lt. Henri Karcher)*, George Chakiris *(GI in Tank)*, Claude Dauphin *(Lebel)*, Alain Delon *(Jacques Chaban-Delmas)*, Kirk Douglas *(Gen. George Patton)*, Glenn Ford *(Gen. Omar Bradley)*, Gert Frobe *(Gen. Dietrich von Choltitz)*

p, Paul Graetz; d, Rene Clement; w, Gore Vidal, Francis Ford Coppola, Jean Aurenche, Pierre Bost, Claude Brule, Marcel Moussy, Beate von Molo; ph, Marcel Grignon; ed, Robert Lawrence; m, Maurice Jarre; art d, Willy Holt; fx, Robert MacDonald, Paul Pollard; cos, Jean Zay, Pierre Nourry

Is it any wonder that a film with writers from Aurenche and Bost to Francis Ford Coppola to Gore Vidal would be a bit rambling? Is it any surprise that a film featuring two dozen movie stars is a bit of a mess?

Full of dramatically unwieldy crosscutting between the Allies and Germans during the 1944 liberation, IS PARIS BURNING? is a fairly entertaining, action-packed film which seems continually in danger of collapsing under the weight of its own pageantry.

The plot basically deals with the Germans' attempts to torch Paris before having to pull out because they're losing the war. Frobe is the German general assigned to light the match; Caron is the wife of a political prisoner; Welles—desperate as always for money to finance his own films—is a Swedish consul; Belmondo is a resistance fighter who takes over police headquarters; Vaneck is a Free French officer trying to enlist Allied aide in saving gay Paree; Signoret owns a cafe; Stack, Douglas, Ford and Rich compare square jawlines as four (what else?) generals; and Montand and Perkins, of course, encounter bad luck on film yet again.

Producer Graetz underwent innumerable headaches in assembling vintage props for the film and in expanding the script every time another movie star became available. Director Clement, expert at documentary and low-key realism, does a fine job of mixing period footage with the stuff he shot, though continuity suffers somewhat during this extravaganza. A favorite: Frobe and another general speak English en route to Hitler's office, but once in the Fuhrer's presence we get German with English subtitles.

There's plenty of fun to be had here if you don't mind (or if you have a perverse fascination with) that kind of thing.

ISHTAR

1987 107m c ★★
Comedy PG-13/PG
Delphi V/Columbia

Warren Beatty (Lyle Rogers), Dustin Hoffman (Chuck Clarke), Isabelle Adjani (Shirra Assel), Charles Grodin (Jim Harrison), Jack Weston (Marty Freed), Tess Harper (Willa), Carol Kane (Carol), Aharon Ipale (Emir Yousef), Fijad Hageb (Abdul), David Margulies (Mr. Clarke)

p, Warren Beatty; d, Elaine May; w, Elaine May; ph, Vittorio Storaro (Technicolor); ed, Stephen A. Rotter, William Reynolds, Richard Cirincione; m, Bahjawa; prod d, Paul Sylbert; art d, Bill Groom, Vicki Paul, Peter Childs, Tony Reading; cos, Anthony Powell

It's inevitable that when a film costs upwards of $40 million, stars two of the biggest names in Hollywood (Hoffman and Beatty), and is directed by a person (May) notorious for her wasteful shooting methods, the result will be savaged by industry insiders and film critics. An incredible box office loser and, to be frank, far from great, ISHTAR is still not nearly as awful as many would have it.

Struggling songwriters Chuck Clarke (Hoffman) and Lyle Rogers (Beatty) have known each other for only a few months but have formed a strong bond. Despite the pathetic but honestly expressive songs they bang out, entertainment agent Marty Freed (Weston) offers them a booking—in Morocco. On their way, they get mixed up in a civil war in the fictitious "Ishtar" and become involved with a goofy CIA agent (Grodin).

For all the bad press ISHTAR received, it does have a certain odd charm. Cast against type, Beatty and Hoffman do their darndest to mimic Hope and Crosby. The biggest problem is that any attempted subtlety is swamped by May's bid to turn the film into an epic adventure story. The talented Adjani doesn't help much, doing little more than float around in loose-fitting garments. The hopelessly banal lyrics to the songs written by the Beatty and Hoffman characters can be hilarious if you're in the mood. ("Telling the truth is a dangerous business/Honest and popular don't go hand-in-hand/If you admit that you play the accordian/You'll never make it a rock and roll band.") Yes, it's that kind of movie.

ISLAND OF LOST SOULS

1933 67m bw ★★★★½
Science Fiction/Horror
Paramount

Charles Laughton (Dr. Moreau), Bela Lugosi (Sayer of the Law), Richard Arlen (Edward Parker), Leila Hyams (Ruth Walker), Kathleen Burke (Lota, the Panther Woman), Arthur Hohl (Montgomery), Stanley Fields (Capt. Davies), Bob Kortman (Hogan), Tetsu Komai (M'Ling), Hans Steinke (Ouran)

d, Erle C. Kenton; w, Philip Wylie, Waldemar Young (based on the novel The Island of Dr. Moreau by H.G. Wells); ph, Karl Struss; fx, Gordon Jennings

There's not a wasted frame in this chilling horror film that was banned in England upon its first release. Laughton is Dr. Moreau, a smiling, benign-seeming man who welcomes shipwrecked Edward Parker (Arlen) to his own private island. While waiting for the next passing freighter, Parker learns that the "natives" who serve Moreau are really animals who have been transformed into semi-humans by the doctor's experiments in an area known as "The House of Pain." The only woman around, Lota (Burke), becomes involved with Parker but she too conceals a terrible secret. When Edward's fiancee Ruth (Hyams) arrives with a search expedition, the two women vie for his affections while Moreau makes his own attempts to deal with the new intruders. Unfortunately for him he makes a crucial error which goes against the lessons in "humanity" and "civility" he has browbeaten into his creations. The famous, controversial climax is still a shocker.

H.G. Wells, from whose novel the screenplay was written, hated the picture from the start because he felt the makers missed his point about a man playing God and opted for the easy way out. The film is steeped in atmosphere and foreboding, and much of the terror was hinted at rather than shown graphically. Struss' cinematography is stunning, especially in the "lesson" scenes Moreau administers. "Are we not men?" and "What is the law?" are lines chanted by the half-human denizens of Moreau's isle, led by Bela Lugosi in an amazingly small yet very effective performance, that will stick in your memory. Burke's appearance is striking but her acting less so; Laughton, on the other hand, is unfailingly marvelous. So many countries (as well as many midwestern states) banned the movie that it took a while to recoup the cost, but ISLAND OF LOST SOULS remains, to this day, a classic chiller which holds up better than many others from its period. Remade in 1959 as TERROR IS A MAN and in 1978 (with Burt Lancaster and Michael York) as THE ISLAND OF DR. MOREAU. Neither version was quite up to the original.

IT CAME FROM OUTER SPACE

1953 80m bw ★★★½
Science Fiction /PG
Universal

Richard Carlson (John Putnam), Barbara Rush (Ellen Fields), Charles Drake (Sheriff Matt Warren), Russell Johnson (George), Kathleen Hughes (Jane), Joe Sawyer (Frank Daylon), Dave Willock (Pete Davis), Alan Dexter (Dave Loring), George Eldredge (Dr. Snell), Brad Jackson (Snell's Assistant)

p, William Alland; d, Jack Arnold; w, Harry Essex (based on the story "The Meteor" by Ray Bradbury); ph, Clifford Stine (3-D); ed, Paul Weatherwax; m, Herman Stein; art d, Bernard Herzbrun, Robert Boyle; fx, David S. Horsley

One of the better science-fiction films to come out of the Cold War 50s, this one must be counted among the anti-McCarthy statements. Not just passively anti-conformist like the original INVASION OF THE BODY SNATCHERS, it actively supports the right of any being to be different. Unusually restrained and sober in tone for its time, IT CAME FROM OUTER SPACE is a film noir variant on the sci-fi genre.

Carlson is John Putnam, an astronomer who lives alone out in the desert. The folks in town find him eccentric and distrust his intellectualism. One night he sees what he thinks is a meteor blaze across the sky and crash in the desert. As it turns out, the UFO is actually an alien spacecraft. The creatures, cloaked with invisibility, replace the locals with alien doubles, thereby making it difficult for Putnam to prove they exist. He tells the townspeople but no one wants to believe him. Once he makes contact with the aliens, he learns that their intentions are not really threatening but, by that time, the townspeople are finally starting to panic.

Inspired by a Ray Bradbury story, this film had the added bonus of being photographed in 3-D, and it was worth putting up with the annoying glasses to view Arnold's creepy deep-focus compositions. This was director Arnold's first science fiction work, a genre in which he was to make quite a mark, directing such films as THIS ISLAND EARTH, TARANTULA, and his classic, THE INCREDIBLE SHRINKING MAN.

IT HAPPENED HERE
1966 99m bw   ★★★★
Drama   /A
Rath (U.K.)

Pauline Murray (*Pauline*), Sebastian Shaw (*Dr. Richard Fletcher*), Fiona Leland (*Helen Fletcher*), Honor Fehrson (*Honor Hutton*), Col. Percy Binns (*Immediate Action Commandant*), Frank Bennett (*IA Political Leader*), Bill Thomas (*IA Group Leader*), Reginald Marsh (*IA Medical Officer*), Rex Collett (*IA NCO*), Nicolette Bernard (*IA Woman Commandant*)

p, Kevin Brownlow, Andrew Mollo; d, Kevin Brownlow, Andrew Mollo; w, Kevin Brownlow, Andrew Mollo (based on an idea by Kevin Brownlow); ph, Peter Suschitzky, Kevin Brownlow; ed, Kevin Brownlow; m, Jack Beaver, Anton Bruckner; art d, Andrew Mollo, Jim Nicolson

Reminiscent in title and theme of Sinclair Lewis' terrifying novel *It Can't Happen Here*, this intensely fascinating effort from film historians Kevin Brownlow and Andrew Mollo speculates about what could have happened in WWII England if the Germans had successfully invaded. Murray stars as a British nurse employed by the Fascist government. Shocked to discover that Russian and Polish hospital patients are being killed, she raises loud protests, is arrested, and eventually joins the resistance. Made on a miniscule budget of only $20,000, the production—partly filmed in 16mm—took 10 years to complete. It has a remarkable documentary look and feel, and the direction by Brownlow and Mollo is amazingly assured. A very disturbing and compelling film, it makes an incisive point about politics and nationality: the British would have gotten along quite nicely under Nazi rule, just as the French did.

IT HAPPENED ONE NIGHT
1934 105m bw   ★★★★★
Romance/Comedy   /U
Columbia

Claudette Colbert (*Ellie Andrews*), Clark Gable (*Peter Warne*), Roscoe Karns (*Oscar Shapeley*), Henry Wadsworth (*Drunk Boy*), Claire McDowell (*Mother*), Walter Connolly (*Alexander Andrews*), Alan Hale (*Danker*), Arthur Hoyt (*Zeke*), Blanche Frederici (*Zeke's Wife*), Jameson Thomas (*King Westley*)

p, Harry Cohn; d, Frank Capra; w, Robert Riskin (based on the story "Night Bus" by Samuel Hopkins Adams); ph, Joseph Walker; ed, Gene Havlick; art d, Stephen Goosson; cos, Robert Kalloch

It happened one night in 1934, and it happens every time we watch this utterly beguiling film. A rather modest effort which brought Capra into the spotlight, we frankly prefer it to many of the more "important" films he made later. It also clinched for good the stardom of Gable and Colbert. (What a pity that their only other teaming was the dismal BOOM TOWN.)

The familiar story, a prototype for many screwball comedies to follow, opens with headstrong heiress Ellie Andrews (Colbert) fleeing her father (Connolly). Trying to make it to her washout fiance (Thomas) on her own, she soon encounters errant reporter Peter Warne (Gable). He agrees to help her make it from Florida to New York in exchange for her story, which will square him with his disgruntled boss. Over the course of several nights, the inevitable happens.

What really distinguishes IT HAPPENED ONE NIGHT from so many other films are Capra's handling of the individual comic and romantic setpieces, Riskin's way with a line, and the marvelous cast. Every viewer has his or her favorite scenes. Consider the "wall of Jericho" (a blanket) Peter sets up between himself and Ellie before bedding down for the night, a sly dig at Production Code prudery just then being enforced. Or what about Peter's famous lessons in how to dunk a donut or how a man undresses? (We all recall, of course, how Ellie shows him up in the memorable hitchhiking lesson.) For romance, there's some lovely bedside dreaming and even a scene in the hay. There's also Ellie's wonderful wedding gown near the end, the lengthy veil providing a visual exclamation point to rival Elsa Lanchester's hair in BRIDE OF FRANKENSTEIN. The splendidly cast actors, too, make their bits of business their own, from Karns' mildly lecherous salesperson ("Shapeley's the name and that's the way I like 'em") turned scared rabbit to Hale's aggressively cheering but deceptive singing motorist. The best support, though, comes from the unfailingly marvelous Connolly in a role he made his own. Gable and Colbert's screen personas were firmly established here, his tongue-in-cheek machismo and her witty, supple sophistication mixing like gin and tonic.

IT HAPPENED ONE NIGHT won the top five Oscars (Picture, Director, Actor, Actress, Screenplay), a feat only duplicated twice since. Watch it again and you'll remember why.

IT HAPPENS EVERY SPRING
1949 87m bw   ★★★½
Sports/Comedy   /U
FOX

Ray Milland (*Vernon Simpson*), Jean Peters (*Deborah Greenleaf*), Paul Douglas (*Monk Lanigan*), Ed Begley (*Stone*), Ted de Corsia (*Dolan*), Ray Collins (*Prof. Greenleaf*), Jessie Royce Landis (*Mrs. Greenleaf*), Alan Hale, Jr. (*Schmidt*), William Murphy (*Isbell*), William E. Green (*Prof. Forsythe*)

p, William Perlberg; d, Lloyd Bacon; w, Valentine Davies (based on a story by Davies, Shirley W. Smith); ph, Joseph MacDonald; ed, Bruce B. Pierce; m, Leigh Harline; art d, Lyle Wheeler, J. Russell Spencer; cos, Bonnie Cashin

That fine farceur Milland shines as Vernon Simpson, a professorial scientist turned baseball wizard in this side-splitting comedy that has become a minor classic.

Davies, who wrote the marvelous script for MIRACLE ON 34TH STREET, came up with another winner here. Vernon, a chemist, is in love with Deborah Greenleaf (Peters), but has not popped the question because his meager salary won't support two. While developing a bug repellant for trees, he invents a solution that repels wood. A baseball fan of the first order, he concocts a clever scheme to earn additional money. He'll join a major league team as a pitcher, and secretly rub his solution on baseballs which will be repelled by the hitters wooden bats. He goes to a major league team and tries out. Naturally, the rookies scoff at the middle-aged man on the mound, but he miraculously strikes out every man he faces, his "screwball" hopping, bouncing, jerking, and flitting around the mightily swung bats. Vernon is signed as a starting pitcher and, using his secret solution, manages to win 38 games that season and almost single-handedly win the World Series for his team.

There are many hilarious moments in IT HAPPENS EVERY SPRING, not the least of which occurs when Douglas, as Milland's catcher roommate, finds the bottle of solution and, thinking it's hair tonic, sprinkles it on his head. Trying to brush it with a wooden brush, he watches in shock as his hair does a St. Vitus Dance. Milland is very funny as the furtive scientist-pitcher, and Peters is very attractive, if underused. The most uproarious scenes take place on the baseball fields, where Milland's doctored ball sends players and fans into hysterics. The baseball footage itself is a marvel, with director Bacon managing to reproduce a completely authentic atmosphere. Foolish but fun.

IT SHOULD HAPPEN TO YOU

1954 86m bw   ★★★★
Comedy   /U
Columbia

Judy Holliday (Gladys Glover), Jack Lemmon (Pete Sheppard), Peter Lawford (Evan Adams III), Michael O'Shea (Brod Clinton), Connie Gilchrist (Mrs. Riker), Vaughn Taylor (Entrikin), Heywood Hale Broun (Sour Man in Central Park), Rex Evans (Con Cooley), Art Gilmore (Don Toddman), Whit Bissell (Robert Grau)

p, Fred Kohlmar; d, George Cukor; w, Garson Kanin; ph, Charles Lang; ed, Charles Nelson; m, Frederick Hollander; art d, John Meehan; cos, Jean Louis

Charming satire in which Lemmon made a winning debut opposite the flawless Holliday.

Holliday is Gladys Glover (a name you'll never forget once you've seen the film), a poor model from Binghampton who has come to New York. She's spotted by film documentarian Pete Sheppard (Lemmon), who is roaming Central Park with his camera. When Gladys looks up and sees an empty billboard, she promptly uses all her money to have her name painted there in huge letters. Suddenly, all of New York is wondering who she is and why she's done this. Lawford plays Evan Adams III, an executive for a huge soap company who wants the billboard for his products, making a deal with Gladys whereby he gives her several other billboards in return for the big one. Gladys and Pete become lovers, but he doesn't like what is transpiring. He thinks his feckless love is cheapening herself, and he wishes she would stop the campaign and settle in with him. Fame follows her, however, and she becomes a celebrity, appearing on talk shows and doing commercials. Pete leaves her in disgust, but that's just until they get back together for a customary happy ending.

IT SHOULD HAPPEN TO YOU benefits from fine performances from some wonderful farceurs, a witty Kanin script, and Cukor's light-hearted direction. Melvine Cooper, Wendy Barrie, Constance Bennett, and Ilka Chase spoof the inanities of TV talk shows perfectly, and Lemmon and Holliday also get a chance to sing with "Let's Fall in Love," which had been written (by Harold Arlen and Ted Koehler) almost 20 years earlier. In a tiny role, John Saxon is the young man who watches the argument in the park. Jean Louis' costumes were nominated for an Oscar.

IT'S A GIFT

1934 73m bw   ★★★★★
Comedy
Paramount

W.C. Fields (Harold Bissonette), Jean Rouverol (Mildred Bissonette), Julian Madison (John Durston), Kathleen Howard (Amelia Bissonette), Tommy Bupp (Norman Bissonette), Tammany Young (Everett Ricks), Baby LeRoy (Baby Ellwood Dunk), Morgan Wallace (Jasper Fitchmueller), Charles Sellon (Mr. Muckle/Blind Man/House Detective), Josephine Whittell (Mrs. Dunk)

p, William LeBaron; d, Norman Z. McLeod; w, Jack Cunningham, W.C. Fields (based on the play The Comic Supplement by J.P. McEvoy and a story by Charles Bogle); ph, Henry Sharp; art d, Hans Dreier, John B. Goodman

Never was a film so well titled. Along with THE BANK DICK this is the finest, funniest movie W.C. Fields ever made. It's also a rollicking spoof of middle-class marriage and mainstream ambitions.

Fields appears as Harold Bissonette, a small-town shopowner with selfish children and a nagging wife. When his family isn't making his life miserable, his customers and neighbors are. He dreams of the good life and a California orange grove he's purchased with an inheritance, but the hostile world won't even let him get a decent night's sleep. (In a memorable scene poor Harold copes with a noisy milkman, a grape-wielding baby, a porch swing chain and an obnoxious saleman looking for one "Karl La Fong".) When Harold and family finally make it to California, they learn he's been swindled, but, predictably, he gets the last laugh.

IT'S A GIFT is almost nonstop laughter, loaded with Fields' patented sight gags, slapstick, and dialogue uttered out of the corner of his mouth. Fields resurrected much of this material from other sources, such as his silent film IT'S THE OLD ARMY GAME and the 1925 play The Comic Supplement. He also drew on his memories as the son of a Philadelphia pushcart vendor for some of the story, which he wrote under the name of Charles Bogle. Though Norman McLeod was the nominal director, Fields picked his own cast and essentially ran the film, and his wonderful, caustic humor comes through on every frame.

IT'S A MAD, MAD, MAD, MAD WORLD

1963 192m c   ★★★
Comedy   /U
Casey

Spencer Tracy (Capt. C.G. Culpepper), Milton Berle (J. Russell Finch), Sid Caesar (Melville Crump), Buddy Hackett (Benjy Benjamin), Ethel Merman (Mrs. Marcus), Mickey Rooney (Ding Bell), Dick Shawn (Sylvester Marcus), Phil Silvers (Otto Meyer), Terry-Thomas (J. Algernon Hawthorne), Jonathan Winters (Lennie Pike)

p, Stanley Kramer; d, Stanley Kramer; w, William Rose, Tania Rose; ph, Ernest Laszlo (UltraPanavision, Technicolor); ed, Frederic Knudtson, Robert C. Jones, Gene Fowler, Jr.; m, Ernest Gold; prod d, Rudolph Sternad; art d, Gordon Gurnell; fx, Danny Lee, Linwood Dunn; cos, Bill Thomas

Overkill, the CLEOPATRA of the funnybone. This comic extravaganza starts off funny, but exhausts rather than delights. Designed to be the biggest, most lavish comedy ever made, IT'S A MAD, MAD, MAD, MAD WORLD is a coarse, star-studded pageant of Keystone Kops-style slapstick.

With his dying breath, a gangster (Jimmy Durante) recently released from prison tells the motorists who come upon him after an auto accident that $350,000 is buried under "the Big W," instigating a greedy, madcap dash for the cash. Among the lunatic treasure seekers who will stop at nothing to get to the loot first are Milton Berle, Dorothy Provine, Ethel Merman (who, curiously, steals the film from under everyone else's talented nose), Sid Caesar, Edie Adams, Buddy Hackett, Mickey Rooney, and Jonathan Winters. Phil Silvers, Terry-Thomas, Peter Falk, Dick Shawn, and Spencer Tracy also become involved, and the film is a who's who of Hollywood comedians in cameo appearances.

Director-producer Kramer spared no expense (tame today, the $7 million price tag was a hefty one at the time) on the spectacular stunts, using 39 stunt men and paying them $252,000 for some of the most incredible feats on film. But at 154 minutes of running time, it's way too long for what it is. Watching it at home with breaks may be the best way to analyze individual comic takes; certainly it's the most painless.

IT'S A WONDERFUL LIFE
1946 129m bw   ★★★★★
Drama   /U
Liberty

James Stewart (George Bailey), Donna Reed (Mary Hatch), Lionel Barrymore (Mr. Potter), Thomas Mitchell (Uncle Billy), Henry Travers (Clarence), Beulah Bondi (Mrs. Bailey), Frank Faylen (Ernie), Ward Bond (Bert), Gloria Grahame (Violet Bick), H.B. Warner (Mr. Gower)

p, Frank Capra; d, Frank Capra; w, Frances Goodrich, Albert Hackett, Frank Capra, Jo Swerling (based on the story "The Greatest Gift" by Philip Van Doren Stern); ph, Joseph Walker, Joseph Biroc; ed, William Hornbeck; m, Dimitri Tiomkin; art d, Jack Okey; fx, Russell A. Cully; cos, Edward Stevenson

The holiday gift for all time. This heartwarming fantasy, one of the most popular films ever made, begins as angels discuss George Bailey (James Stewart), a small-town resident so beset with problems that he contemplates a Christmastime suicide.

In flashback, we review George's life, learning that he has always wanted to leave his hometown to see the world, but that circumstances and his own good heart have kept him in Bedford Falls, sacrificing his own education for his brother's, keeping the family-run savings and loan afloat, protecting the town from the avarice of banker Potter (Lionel Barrymore), marrying his childhood sweetheart (Donna Reed), and raising a family. Back in the present, George prepares to jump from a bridge, but ends up rescuing his guardian angel, Clarence Oddbody (Henry Travers), who has come to earn his wings. Clarence shows him how badly Bedford Falls would have turned out without George and his good deeds. Filled with renewed joy in life, George goes home to his loving family and friends, who pitch in to put his worries behind him.

Few filmmakers have rivaled director Frank Capra when it comes to examining the human heart, and IT'S A WONDERFUL LIFE is a masterfully crafted exercise in sentiment, augmented by Capra's undying faith in community. Reed and Barrymore give excellent performances, as does a superb cast of character players, but this is Stewart's film—heart-stirring as the dreamer who sacrifices all for his fellow man. The bright, funny screenplay is based on "The Greatest Gift," a story that Philip Van Dorn Stren originally sent to his friends as a Christmas card.

IT'S ALWAYS FAIR WEATHER
1955 102m c   ★★★★
Musical/Comedy   /U
MGM

Gene Kelly (Ted Riley), Dan Dailey (Doug Hallerton), Cyd Charisse (Jackie Leighton), Dolores Gray (Madeline Bradville), Michael Kidd (Angie Valentine), David Burns (Tim), Jay C. Flippen (Charles Z. Culloran), Steve Mitchell (Kid Mariacchi), Hal March (Rocky Lazar), Paul Maxey (Mr. Fielding)

p, Arthur Freed; d, Stanley Donen, Gene Kelly; w, Betty Comden, Adolph Green; ph, Robert Bronner (CinemaScope, Eastmancolor); ed, Adrienne Fazan; art d, Cedric Gibbons, Arthur Lonergan; fx, Irving G. Reis, Warren Newcombe; chor, Stanley Donen, Gene Kelly; cos, Helen Rose

A scathing satire of television and advertising is only one element in this cynical musical, which masks the seriousness of its theme with many excellent numbers.

In 1945, soldiers Ted (Gene Kelly), Doug (Dan Dailey), and Angie (Michael Kidd) come home from WWII to dance in the streets (in the celebrated trash-can cover number) and drink their

way across New York, then decide to meet in a decade. After a montage of news headlines to indicate time's passage, the trio return to the bar in which they last saw one another. Mutually disappointed by how their lives turned out, the men soon realize they have little in common anymore, and the evening disintegrates into perfunctory nostalgia. The film continues with a sour examination of their present-day lives.

FAIR WEATHER is stolen by Dailey's disillusioned advertising man (he has the best routine in the film); here was a musical comedy actor ahead of his time, a specialist in world-weary characters who just happen to be song and dance men. Delores Gray is dazzling in her female pirhana way, and Cyd Charisse is her novocained, scowling self—until she goes into her dance surrounded by uglies at Stillman's gym.

Directors Kelly and Stanley Donen make wonderful use of the CinemaScope screen, splitting it to achieve a previously unattainable intimacy. The songs have little to do with the plot, a lack of integration that may have prevented this ambitious, innovative picture from getting the audiences it deserved. But many film buffs find FAIR WEATHER more authentically deserving of praise than its predictable precursor, ON THE TOWN.

IT'S LOVE I'M AFTER
1937 90m bw   ★★★½
Comedy
WB/First National

Leslie Howard (Basil Underwood), Bette Davis (Joyce Arden), Olivia de Havilland (Marcia West), Eric Blore (Digges), Patric Knowles (Henry Grant), George Barbier (William West), Spring Byington (Aunt Ella Paisley), Bonita Granville (Gracie Kane), E.E. Clive (Butler), Veda Ann Borg (Elsie)

p, Harry Joe Brown; d, Archie Mayo; w, Casey Robinson (based on the story "Gentleman After Midnight" by Maurice Hanline); ph, James Van Trees; ed, Owen Marks, Tony Martinelli; m, Heinz Roemheld; art d, Carl Jules Weyl; cos, Orry-Kelly

A hammy romp, dated and with energy petering out after a while, but furiously acted by costars Davis and Howard. He's an egocentric matinee idol engaged to Davis, his battle-axe leading lady.

They have called off their marriage 11 times because, as loving as they are on stage, they constantly bicker off stage. Howard revels in the adoration of his stage-door Janies, which Davis can't stand. The most blatant swooner is de Havilland, who comes to every performance and sits there starry-eyed and almost salivating. being engaged to Knowles doesn't stop her from visiting the backstage dressing room and declaring her love to Howard. Later, Knowles confronts Howard and pleads with him to turn de Havilland away so he can marry the girl. Howard sees this as a chance to help Knowles and have some fun at the bothersome de Havilland's expense. It backfires, of course, and Howard, desperate to get the beautiful deb out of his life, asks Davis to pose as his wife. She agrees, but has some malicious fun of her own.

The film is better before it bogs down in too many in staples of 1930's comedy: de Havilland's execrable heiress and the country house of stultifying wasps. LOVE begins with a spoof of the tomb scene from Romeo and Juliet, and there are some funny bits backstage between dressing rooms, played by the leads. There's one hilarious performance once they get stuck in the country: Eric Blore's loony manservant. What a strange and welcome egg he is.

IVAN THE TERRIBLE, PARTS I & II
(IVAN GROZNYI)
1945 96m c/bw   ★★★★★
Biography/War   /PG
Central Cinema/Alma Ata/Sovexportfilm (U.S.S.R.)

Nikolai Cherkassov *(Tsar Ivan IV)*, Serafima Birma

p, Sergei Eisenstein; d, Sergei Eisenstein; w, Sergei Eisenstein; ph, Edward Tisse, Andrei Moskvin; m, Sergei Prokofiev; art d, Isaac Shpinel; cos, Isaac Shpinel

These are the first two parts of Sergei Eisenstein's intended trilogy about the 16th-century Russian hero Czar Ivan IV. Part I, completed in 1945, chronicles the ruler's coronation, his marriage, his illness and sudden unexplained recovery, the poisoning of his wife, and his battles against conspirators. By the end, he declares his intention of returning from Alexandrov to Moscow at the will of his people. Part II (subtitled "The Revolt of the Boyars"), filmed shortly after Part I but not released until 1958, follows Czar Ivan on his return, and depicts his confrontations with his enemies, the poisoning of his mother, and his discovery of an assassination plot. The heretofore black-and-white film ends with a brilliantly colored banquet scene.

Although the scenario for Part III ("The Battles of Ivan") was approved by Stalin (oddly enough, since Stalin censored Part II because of its negative portrayal of Ivan's secret police), Eisenstein, who died in 1948, never completed the project. Viewers familiar only with Eisenstein's BATTLESHIP POTEMKIN will find the shift from that film's revolutionary editing style to IVAN's emphasis on composition and lighting quite a surprise. A vast, important, and occasionally difficult historical effort that closed Eisenstein's legendary career, IVAN THE TERRIBLE includes a remarkable score by Sergei Prokofiev.

IVANHOE
1952 106m c   ★★★½
Historical   /U
MGM (U.K.)

Robert Taylor *(Ivanhoe)*, Elizabeth Taylor *(Rebecca)*, Joan Fontaine *(Rowena)*, George Sanders *(De Bois-Guilbert)*, Emlyn Williams *(Wamba)*, Robert Douglas *(Sir Hugh De Bracy)*, Finlay Currie *(Cedric)*, Felix Aylmer *(Isaac)*, Francis de Wolff *(Font De Boeuf)*, Guy Rolfe *(Prince John)*

p, Pandro S. Berman; d, Richard Thorpe; w, Noel Langley (based on the novel by Sir Walter Scott); ph, Freddie Young (Technicolor); ed, Frank Clarke; m, Miklos Rozsa; art d, Alfred Junge; fx, Tom Howard; cos, Roger Furse

Luxe MGM historical ransacking, locationed to the nines, beautiful to look upon, but with energy lapses in the soggy script of Sir Walter Scott's epic classic. It is 1190 and Robert Taylor, as the brave Sir Wilfred of Ivanhoe, returns secretly to England from the Crusades. He has served England's King Richard the Lionhearted well in the Third Crusade, but the king has been captured and is held for ransom in Austria. It's Taylor's job to raise an enormous sum to free Richard (Wooland). Taylor is a Saxon knight, son of lord Currie, who more or less disowned his son when he went to fight for Richard, a Norman king.

Taylor encounters three Norman knights, Sanders, Douglas and de Wolff, who are in league with Prince John (Rolfe), who intends to usurp his missing brother, Richard. Taylor tells the knights that Currie's castle is nearby should they wish to seek shelter for the night, and he escorts them to his father's estate. Watching this encounter is Warrender (Robin Hood), and his men who were about to kill the hated Norman knights. But, seeing Taylor with the Normans, Warrender holds his men back, telling them he will wait to see what Taylor is up to.

The Norman knights are given a cool reception by Currie, but they are nevertheless extended the hospitality of the day. At dinner, these knights meet Currie's ward, the beautiful Fontaine, whom Douglas immediately covets. Sitting at the end of the table is Taylor, Fontaine's true love, who is recognized by his father when he toasts King Richard, but Currie refuses immediately to talk to his errant son. He later communicates with Taylor through his servant-fool, Williams.

After Taylor leaves the castle with Williams as his newly appointed squire, he rescues a rich Jew, Aylmer, from the anti-Semitic Normans and is later given jewels by Aylmer's grateful daughter, Elizabeth Taylor, so he can buy horse and armor to enter the jousting tournament at Ashby and win more money to ransom Richard.

The film is certainly rousing, with a particularly grisly bout between Taylor and Sanders and the Taylor-Fontaine-Taylor triangle adequate for romantic spectacle. Though undeniably waspy as Rebecca, Elizabeth Taylor's early beauty has a way of making you forget anything, including your name. IVANHOE is filled with majestic sets, brilliantly constructed by Junge. The costuming was painstakingly created by Furse. MGM spared no expense in making IVANHOE; this became the costliest epic ever produced in England. The truth is that the studio had no choice. MGM had accumulated millions of dollars in British banks but was restrained from taking this money out of the country.

Robert Taylor read the script of Dore Shary's pet project and then told MGM that he preferred to do westerns, but he was in England preparing for the role of IVANHOE the next week all the same. Likewise, Elizabeth Taylor had been ordered by MGM to go to England to appear in IVANHOE. When she did not immediately respond, MGM announced Deborah Kerr for the role of Rebecca (how's that for fanciful?) and Margaret Leighton to play Rowena, though Fontaine was later substituted for Leighton. Miserable at having to play an unimportant female lead, or at least a part far less important than Robert Taylor's, Elizabeth Taylor nonetheless arrived in England.

Although she always considered the film "just a big medieval Western," IVANHOE went on to earn more than $6 million in its initial release. Miklos Rosza's lush and stirring score for this film was deeply researched by the composer who spent months studying 12th-century compositions so that his music would fit the historical images projected on the screen.

J.W. COOP

1971 112m c ★★★
Western/Sports PG/AA
Columbia

Cliff *(J.W. Coop)*, Geraldine Page *(Mama)*, Cristina Ferrare *(Bean)*, R.G. Armstrong *(Jim Sawyer)*, R.L. Armstrong *(Tooter Watson)*, John Crawford *(Rancher)*, Wade Crosby *(Billy Sol Gibbs)*, Marjorie Durant Dye *(Big Marge)*, Paul Harper *(Warden Morgan)*, Son Hooker *(Motorcycle Cop)*

p, Cliff Robertson; d, Cliff Robertson; w, Cliff Robertson, Gary Cartwright, Bud Shrake; ph, Frank Stanley, Adam Holender, Ross Lowell, Fred Waugh (Eastmancolor); ed, Alex Beaton; m, Louie Shelton, Don Randi; fx, Tim Smyth

Starts off strong, with an evocative feel for men returning from prision to small, dying towns. After that, quicksand. Cliff Robertson produced, directed, co-wrote, and starred in the title role of this involving film about a rodeo rider's attempt to adjust to a life on the outside after spending ten years in prison. Both society and the rodeo have changed dramatically during Coop's incarceration, and he struggles to adapt as he undertakes a relationship with Bean (Cristina Ferrare) while going after the national championship. The cast features members of the Rodeo Cowboys Association, and much of the action footage was shot during actual rodeo events. The first half hour is Robertson at his best because he's reacting; after that, bum steer.

J'ACCUSE

1939 95m bw ★★★½
War
Forrester/Parant (France)

Victor Francen *(Jean Diaz)*, Jean Max *(Henri Chimay)*, Delaitre *(Francois Laurin)*, Renee Devillers *(Helene)*, Line Noro *(Edith)*, Marie Lou *(Flo)*, Georges Saillard *(Giles Tenant)*, Paul Amiot *(Captain)*, Andre Nox *(Leotard)*, Georges Rollin *(Pierre Fonds)*

p, Abel Gance; d, Abel Gance; w, Abel Gance, Steve Passeur; ph, Roger Hubert; m, Henri Verdun

An excellent antiwar film, J'ACCUSE is all the more poignant considering it was produced and released in France shortly before the Occupation. Francen invents a device he believes will stop war forever, only to see it used by his government as a defense measure against the enemy. Driven mad by this exploitation, Francen decides only the war dead marching through the streets will stop the people's thirst for an upcoming war. In his delusion, bodies rise from their graves, and the sight of war's actual horrors so terrifies the patriotic countrymen that all thoughts of war are abandoned. Gance's plot is a simple one, but told with enormous power and passion for the theme. The ravaged faces of the dead are disturbing, powerful images that are not soon forgotten. The message is conveyed clearly, without preaching, and with a sensitivity toward pacifism. Like so many films of this nature, its message was considered unsuitable by Nazi Germany, and the film was banned in that country.

JACKNIFE

1989 102m c ★★★
Drama R/15
Kings Road/Sandollar-Schaffel

Robert De Niro *(Joseph "Megs" Megessey)*, Ed Harris *(Dave)*, Kathy Baker *(Martha)*, Charles Dutton *(Jake)*, Loudon Wainwright, III *(Ferretti)*, Elizabeth Franz, Tom Isbell, Sloane Shelton, Walter Massey, Jordan Lund

p, Robert Schaffel, Carol Baum; d, David Jones; w, Stephen Metcalfe (based on the play "Strange Snow" by Stephen Metcalfe); ph, Brian West (Technicolor); ed, John Bloom; m, Bruce Broughton; prod d, Edward Pisoni

This modest but compelling drama received only a brief theatrical release; it's a must-see on video—for its acting, not the predictable story. Robert De Niro stars as "Megs" Megessey, nicknamed "Jacknife" in Vietnam because of his fondness for wrecking vehicles. Back Stateside, with the war long over, Megs is still a bit strange, and tends to irritate his war buddy Dave (Ed Harris)—who would just as soon forget both Vietnam and Megs. When Megs unexpectedly arrives at the house Dave shares with his sister, Martha (Kathy Baker), and subsequently begins a romance with her, Dave is forced to face some uncomfortable truths about himself, his memories, and his relationships with Megs and with Martha. Though its stage origins show (adapted from Stephen Metcalfe's *Strange Show*), and we're cooked on 'Nam significance (with the flashbacks particular eyesores), all three leads are splendid in their roles.

JACOB'S LADDER

1990 115m c ★★★½
Horror R/18
Carolco

Tim Robbins *(Jacob Singer)*, Elizabeth Pena *(Jezzie)*, Danny Aiello *(Louis)*, Matt Craven *(Michael)*, Pruitt Taylor Vince *(Paul)*, Jason Alexander *(Geary)*, Patricia Kalember *(Sarah)*, Eriq La Salle *(Frank)*, Ving Rhames *(George)*, Brian Tarantina *(Doug)*

p, Alan Marshall; d, Adrian Lyne; w, Bruce Joel Rubin; ph, Jeffrey Kimball (Technicolor); ed, Tom Rolf; m, Maurice Jarre; prod d, Brian Morris; art d, Jeremy Conway; fx, FXSMITH Inc., Gordon J. Smith, Connie Brink, Steven Dewey, Musikwerks; cos, Ellen Mirojnick

Director Adrian Lyne follows his smash hit FATAL ATTRACTION with this $40 Million stink bomb, written by Bruce Joel Rubin (GHOST). JACOB'S LADDER stars Tim Robbins as Jacob, a divorced Vietnam veteran who lives in New York with his girlfriend Jezzie (a smoldering Elizabeth Pena) and works as a mailman. Jacob is haunted by painful memories of his dead son (a mysteriously unbilled Macaulay Culkin, star of 1990's monster hit HOME ALONE) and of his Vietnam experience when he was nearly killed by a soldier with a bayonet.

As the film progresses, Jacob also begins to see weird creatures and startling visions. Suddenly, there are monsters roaming through the streets of New York; closed subway stations take on a creepy life of their own; a crowded party turns into a room full of winged demons; a train full of strangers look as though they have sprouted tails and horns. Are these the visions of a madman or have demons actually come to get Jacob Singer? While trying desperately to cling to his sanity, Jacob enlists the help of his ex-wife (Patricia Kalember), a mysterious stranger (Matt Craven), and an angelic chiropractor (Danny Aiello) to help solve the mystery.

The much-touted screenplay for JACOB'S LADDER circulated in Hollywood for almost a decade, and in a 1983 *American Film* article, Rubin's screenplay was listed among the ten best unproduced scripts. NOT! It's clear from the battlefield beginning that someone was messing with the heads of this particular battalion. That said, the film doesn't have much of anywhere to go; it doesn't add anything innovative to the genre of troubled vets, and knowing that the visions are drug-related adds an unfortunate element of black comedy. Robbins's undeniably stunning performance is wasted in this morass of mire (and since when does the army draft married doctors of philosophy?).

Director Lyne seems determined to undermine Robbins's considerable accomplishments here by telling the story from a stylized distance. Lyne's concerns are strictly visual—Is there enough smoke? Can the camera be placed at a lower angle? Is the pavement wet enough?—and his lack of emotional connection sinks the film. When, about halfway through the running time, he turns it into a conventional conspiracy thriller it completely goes off track.

JAGGED EDGE

1985 108m c ★★★
Mystery/Thriller R/18
Columbia

Glenn Close (*Teddy Barnes*), Jeff Bridges (*Jack Forrester*), Peter Coyote (*Thomas Krasny*), Robert Loggia (*Sam Ransom*), John Dehner (*Judge Carrigan*), Karen Austin (*Julie Jensen*), Guy Boyd (*Matthew Barnes*), Marshall Colt (*Bobby Slade*), Louis Giambalvo (*Fabrizi*), Ben Hammer (*Dr. Goldman*)

p, Martin Ransohoff; d, Richard Marquand; w, Joe Eszterhas; ph, Matthew F. Leonetti (Metrocolor); ed, Sean Barton, Conrad Buff; m, John Barry; prod d, Gene Callahan; art d, Peter Lansdown Smith; cos, Ann Roth, Michael Dennison, Elizabeth Pine

No cutting edge, but does keep you guessing. It's one of the oldest of Hollywood chestnuts—a socialite is murdered, her husband is suspected by a crafty district attorney, and the female lawyer who defends the accused falls in love with her client—but it still works thanks to Richard Marquand's adroit direction and a tightly knit screenplay from Joe Eszterhas.

Jeff Bridges is one of the beautiful people—possessor of money, luxury, looks and power. When his wife is savagely murdered by an assailant with a jagged-edged knife, Peter Coyote, a tough, sleazy DA, refuses to believe Bridges' innocence. One person who does believe the accused is Glenn Close, a disillusioned lawyer who is sick of Coyote's methods and decides to defend Bridges, falling in love with him in the process.

This film's ending received a great deal of discussion because it purposely obscures the killer's identity, leaving the exiting audience with an uneasy feeling of doubt. It's slick, romantic, funny (Close has a great rapport with her beer-guzzling, foul-mouthed mentor, Robert Loggia), intriguing, and filled with excellent performances.

JAILHOUSE ROCK

1957 96m bw ★★★½
Musical /U
MGM

Elvis Presley (*Vince Everett*), Judy Tyler (*Peggy Van Alden*), Mickey Shaughnessy (*Hunk Houghton*), Jennifer Holden (*Sherry Wilson*), Dean Jones (*Teddy Talbot*), Anne Neyland (*Laury Jackson*), Hugh Sanders (*Warden*), Vaughn Taylor (*Mr. Shores*), Mike Stoller (*Pianist*), Grandon Rhodes (*Prof. August Van Alden*)

p, Pandro S. Berman; d, Richard Thorpe; w, Guy Trosper (based on a story by Ned Young); ph, Robert Bronner (CinemaScope); ed, Ralph E. Winters; art d, William A. Horning, Randall Duell; fx, A. Arnold Gillespie

All shook up and enjoyably bad, JAILHOUSE ROCK captures early Elvis in all his leg-quivering, nostril-flaring, lip-snarling teen idol glory.

This hot black-and-white number was Elvis Presley's third (after LOVE ME TENDER and LOVING YOU) and set the standard for the rest of his movie outings—too bad the the others omitted the dangerous element of his character presented here. Elvis comes across like a white-trash musical genius version of James Dean, playing Vince Everett, a surly good ole boy who accidentally kills a man while defending a lady's honor. . . in a bar. This heroism gets him sent up for manslaughter, sharing his prison cell with Hunk Houghton (Mickey Shaughnessy), an ex-singer who convinces him to perform in the slammer's convict show. After Vince is freed, he meets Peggy Van Alden (Judy Tyler), with whom he forms a record company, and in no time he is a national star on his way to Hollywood. Peggy, however, sees that Vince is turning into an egomaniac, and she can't stand it.

There's little surprise but JAILHOUSE really rocks, establishing pre-Army Elvis, the rockabilly elemental force, when he was really something. The steamy songs are mostly by Lieber and Stoller; the latter can be seen as the pianist in the famous "Jailhouse Rock" sequence (which the young King choreographed). The title song sold two million records within two weeks, and the picture, in turn, grossed several million, with Presley receiving 50 percent of the profits. Other tunes include "Treat Me Nice," "Baby, I Don't Care" and "Young and Beautiful."

JANE EYRE

1944 97m bw ★★★½
Romance /PG
FOX

Orson Welles (*Edward Rochester*), Joan Fontaine (*Jane Eyre*), Margaret O'Brien (*Adele*), Peggy Ann Garner (*Jane as a Child*), John Sutton (*Dr. Rivers*), Sara Allgood (*Bessie*), Henry Daniell (*Brockelhurst*), Agnes Moorehead (*Mrs. Reed*), Elizabeth Taylor (*Helen Burns*), Aubrey Mather (*Col. Dent*)

p, William Goetz; d, Robert Stevenson; w, Aldous Huxley, Robert Stevenson, John Houseman (based on the book by Charlotte Bronte); ph, George Barnes; ed, Walter Thompson; m, Bernard Herrmann; art d, James Basevi, Wiard Ihnen; fx, Fred Sersen; cos, Rene Hubert

A touch too plodding, but an atmospheric reduction of Bronte. This was the fifth time around for the doughty English lady: In 1913 Irving Cummings and Ethel Grand did it. In 1915 it was Alan Hale and Louise Vale. Mabel Ballin and Norman Trevor tried again in 1921; then Virginia Bruce and Colin Clive made the first talkie version in 1934. Although shot on the West Los Angeles sound stages of 20th Century-Fox, Barnes's eerie cinematography truly evokes the bleakness of the novel.

Fontaine is Jane Eyre, an orphan girl who has been tossed about by fate and managed to survive a sordid upbringing. (In the early scenes the role is touchingly played by Peggy Ann Garner.) Fontaine takes a job as governess to Yorkshireman Welles's ward, O'Brien. They live on the Yorkshire moors in a huge house called Thornfield Hall. Fontaine appears as though she'll remain a spinster for the rest of her days, but there is an attraction growing between her and Welles. He is a troubled man, brooding and enigmatic, yet Fontaine has come to love him; a wedding is planned, but it fails to take place.

This is Bronte as gothic paperback romance, and the music, by longtime Welles associate Bernard Herrmann, richly slathers over discrepancies between Welles's and Fontaine's acting styles (after Welles makes his entrance, everything seems to swirl about him—or at least out of his way). In the original book Jane was the protagonist and Rochester was more of a large supporting part. To accommodate Welles, who was emerging as one of the country's most popular actors, the male role was expanded and he received billing above Fontaine.

The Peggy Ann Garner sequences are the best in the film, with Jane's dismal schooling realized very well. You can bet there wasn't a dry eye in the house when strange, beautiful little Helen Burns (Elizabeth Taylor), dies from gross neglect. Later, in 1957, it was done with Patrick Macnee and Joan Elan and then again in 1971 with George C. Scott and Susannah York, both of these versions for television.

JASON AND THE ARGONAUTS

1963   104m   c   ★★★½
Fantasy/Adventure   /U
Columbia   (U.K.)

Todd Armstrong (Jason), Nancy Kovack (Medea), Gary Raymond (Acastus), Laurence Naismith (Argus), Niall MacGinnis (Zeus), Michael Gwynn (Hermes), Douglas Wilmer (Pelias), Jack Gwillim (King Aeetes), Honor Blackman (Hera), John Cairney (Hylas)

p, Charles H. Schneer; d, Don Chaffey; w, Jan Reed, Beverley Cross; ph, Wilkie Cooper (Dynamation 90, Eastmancolor); ed, Maurice Rootes; m, Bernard Herrmann; prod d, Geoffrey Drake; art d, Herbert Smith, Jack Maxsted, Toni Sarzi-Braga; fx, Ray Harryhausen

What a blast! This film, along with THE SEVENTH VOYAGE OF SINBAD, contains special-effects master Ray Harryhausen's finest work, evoking a world of dragons, living statues, harpies and gods. Pelias (Douglas Wilmer) murders the king of Thessaly and steals his throne, but the infant prince, Jason, survives.

Years later, aided by the goddess Hera (Honor Blackman), Jason (Todd Armstrong) begins a search for the Golden Fleece, which will finally instate him as rightful king. With a crew of brave men (including Hercules, in a fine performance by Nigel Green), he sets out on his glorious quest in his ship, the Argo. At one point, the Argo is menaced by a giant living statue, but Jason defeats it. After further adventures in which Jason battles harpies, encounters the gigantic Neptune, and discovers Medea (Nancy Kovack) on an empty ship, the crew finally find the fleece. They kill the seven-headed hydra that guards it but are halted again when the hydra's teeth grow into seven sword-brandishing living skeletons. In a stunning display of technical wizardry, the Argonauts fight the skeletons to the death.

Harryhausen is at his most creative and brilliant (except for the disappointing bronze Titan), the film is well directed by Don Chaffey and adequately acted as these things go. Featuring gorgeous Mediterranean photography and a rousing Bernard Herrmann score, making this a great film for kids that will also please adult viewers. A must-see.

JAWS

1975   124m   c   ★★★★
Horror   PG
Universal

Roy Scheider (Police Chief Martin Brody), Robert Shaw (Quint), Richard Dreyfuss (Matt Hooper), Lorraine Gary (Ellen Brody), Murray Hamilton (Mayor Larry Vaughn), Carl Gottlieb (Meadows), Jeffrey Kramer (Deputy Hendricks), Susan Backlinie (Chrissie Watkins), Jonathan Filley (Cassidy), Ted Grossman (Estuary Victim)

p, Richard D. Zanuck, David Brown; d, Steven Spielberg; w, Peter Benchley, Carl Gottlieb, Howard Sackler (uncredited, based on the novel by Benchley); ph, Bill Butler (Panavision, Technicolor); ed, Verna Fields; m, John Williams; prod d, Joe Alves; fx, Robert A. Mattey

A looming, terrifying catch of the day, lensed before Spielberg became shipwrecked in a world of icky-poo cuteness and thick sentiment. JAWS is the best movie he ever made, full of goofy Saturday matinee sci-fi laughs, but they're nervous ones, thanks to the unexpected editing, the driving score, and the careful build toward shock images so big they feel like they're jumping into your lap.

An East Coast resort, Amity Island, is plagued by attacks on swimmers by a 28-foot great white shark. Although the mayor (Murray Hamilton) would like to keep the whole thing quiet—he doesn't want to ruin the summer tourist season—the brutal attacks soon cannot be ignored, so police chief Martin Brody (Roy Scheider), marine biologist Matt Hooper (Richard Dreyfuss), and grizzled old shark hunter Quint (Robert Shaw) go after the monstrous creature, winding up in a desperate fight for their lives.

The film that put Steven Spielberg on the cinematic map, JAWS was phenomenally successful at the box office and seemed to tap into a universal fear of what lies beneath the sea. The director's vision of Moby Dick, with Quint as Ahab, finally digs a grave for macho, exposing it as a foolhardy joke; it's high time. Spielberg's direction turns the material into a nerve-jangling tour de force. From the outrageously frightening opening—in which a beautiful young woman skinny-dipping in the moonlight is devoured by the unseen shark—to the claustrophobic climax aboard Quint's fishing boat, Spielberg has us in his grip and rarely lets go (although the film does bog down momentarily in some soap-opera scenes of Brody's family life).

Because the film tapped into a common fear and played on it so skillfully, it was a worldwide hit and entered international popular culture. JAWS has been endlessly parodied by comedians and filmmakers alike, and John Williams's effective score has now become a cliche. Three vastly inferior sequels followed. Now, everybody into the pool!

JE T'AIME, JE T'AIME

1972   91m   c   ★★★
Science Fiction   /A
Parc/Fox Europa   (France/Sweden)

Claude Rich (Claude Ridder), Olga Georges-Picot (Catrine), Anouk Ferjac (Wiana Lust), Marie-Blanche Vergnes (Young Woman), Dominique Rozan (Dr. Haesserts), Van Doude (Jan Rouffer), Annie Fargue (Agnes de Smet), Bernard Fresson (Bernard Hannecart), Yvette Etievant (Germaine Coster), Irene Tunc (Marcelle Hannecart) p, Mag Bodard; d, Alain Resnais; w, Alain Resnais, Jacques Sternberg; ph, Jean Boffety (Eastmancolor); ed, Albert Jurgenson, Colette Leloup; m, Krzysztof Penderecki, Jean-Claude Pelletier, Jean Dandeny; art d, Jacques Dugied, Auguste Pace

Resnais continues exploring the relation of time and memory to individual perceptions and feelings, the pervasive theme in his work since HIROSHIMA, MON AMOUR. This time he conducts his investigations in a science fiction environment. Rich plays a man recovering from a suicide attempt who is able to go back in time and become involved once more in the love affair that drove him to attempt suicide. Although he eventually returns to normal time strictures, Rich's mind is still unable to transcend past events. A tight collaboration between Resnais and screenwriter Sternberg has woven complex thematic content into a film more accessible than any of Resnais's earlier works.

JEAN DE FLORETTE
1986 122m c ★★★½
Drama PG
Renn/RAI-TV/D.D./A2 (France)

Yves Montand (Cesar Soubeyran/'Le Papet'), Gerard Depardieu (Jean de Florette/Cadoret), Daniel Auteuil (Ugolin Soubeyran/'Galignette'), Elisabeth Depardieu (Aimee Cadoret), Ernestine Mazurowna (Manon Cadoret), Marcel Champel (Pique-Bouffigue), Armand Meffre (Philoxene), Andre Dupon (Pamphile), Pierre Nougaro (Casimir), Marc Betton (Martial)

p, Pierre Grunstein; d, Claude Berri; w, Claude Berri, Gerard Brach (based on the novel by Marcel Pagnol); ph, Bruno Nuytten (Technovision, Eastmancolor); ed, Arlette Langmann, Herve de Luze, Noelle Boisson; m, Jean-Claude Petit; prod d, Bernard Vezat; cos, Sylvie Gautrelet

The most talked-about French production in many years, this picture and its sequel, MANON OF THE SPRING (MANON DES SOURCES), were completed at a combined record-breaking budget of $17 million (about eight times the cost of the average French picture). Shot back to back with its successor, JEAN DE FLORETTE is set in a French farming village tucked into a picturesque hillside.

Le Papet (Yves Montand), an imperious and unscrupulous local landowner, welcomes the return to the village of his nephew, Ugolin (Daniel Auteuil). An unappealing social misfit, Ugolin dreams of making his fortune by growing carnations. Carnations, however, need a great deal of water—a sparse commodity in the village. When Le Papet realizes that Ugolin's idea is potentially profitable, he sets his sights on a neighboring farm that has an untapped natural spring. But the farm is owned by Jean Cadoret (Gerard Depardieu), a hunchbacked ex-tax collector who has bid farewell to the city and proves to be a tenacious convert to the farming life.

Directed by Claude Berri, JEAN DE FLORETTE is based on Marcel Pagnol's two-part novel L'Eau des Collines (The Water of the Hills), which, in turn, was based on an unsuccessful 1952 film Pagnol directed. A throwback to the pre-New Wave days of French cinema, the film offers complex characterizations, careful scripting, and lyrically pastoral images.

JEREMIAH JOHNSON
1972 108m c ★★★½
Western/Adventure PG
WB

Robert Redford (Jeremiah Johnson), Will Geer (Bear Claw), Stefan Gierasch (Del Gue), Allyn Ann McLerie (Crazy Woman), Charles Tyner (Robidoux), Josh Albee (Caleb), Joaquin Martinez (Paints His Shirt Red), Paul Benedict (Reverend), Matt Clark (Qualen), Richard Angarola (Lebeaux)

p, Joe Wizan; d, Sydney Pollack; w, John Milius, Edward Anhalt (based on the novel Mountain Man by Vardis Fisher, and the story "Crow Killer" by Raymond W. Thorp and Robert Bunker); ph, Andrew Duke Callaghan (Panavision, Technicolor); ed, Thomas Stanford; m, John Rubenstein, Tim McIntire; art d, Ted Haworth

Slow as molasses. Redford stars as a lone wolf who dislikes civilization. He moves into the Rocky Mountains in the 1830s but is barely managing to stay alive when trapper Geer meets him and takes him under his wing. For a year Redford learns all the basic skills of survival in the wilderness, and then he's off on his own. When he comes upon a settlement that has been wiped out by marauding Indians who have left only a woman, now deranged, and her son alive, he buries the dead, transports the woman to a ferry, and adopts the boy. Later, he finds another rugged trapper, bald Gierasch (who shaves his head so that the Indians will not attempt to scalp him), left buried up to his neck. Redford rescues him and later when they raid an Indian camp, Gierasch scalps several of his victims. When they are again on the trail, Gierasch spots advancing Indians and puts the scalps into Redford's pack. The Indians are not hostile, however, and when they discover the scalps of their enemy in Redford's possession, he is hailed as a great warrior.

These Flathead Indians insist that the chief's daughter, Swan (Delle Bolton), be given as a wife to Redford. Rather than risk insulting the tribe and losing his own scalp, the young trapper takes the Indian woman with him. They all form a bond of deep affection as they carve out a cabin and clearing in the wilderness. All is tranquil until a US Cavalry unit arrives and asks Redford to guide the troopers through the mountains to a stranded wagon train of settlers. He does, reluctantly leading the soldiers through the sacred Crow Indian burial grounds.

Beautifully photographed in the wilds of Utah, this film unfortunately doesn't know when to stop; it feels consumed by a self-concious desire to be arty, and offers a treatment too cool for its subject matter. The dialogue, by John Milius and Edward Anhalt, is full of homespun homilies that undercut the attempted seriousness. Of the small cast, Will Geer steals the film. The story is purportedly based on the experiences of a real trapper known as "Liver-Eatin' Johnson," so called because of how he disposed of his victims. Not until the very end of the shooting did Pollack decide how Redford would meet his fate. "Pollack wanted me to freeze to death," Redford was later quoted, "but I preferred to leave Johnson's fate up to the audience's imagination by having him disappear into the mountains." That ambiguous fate is exactly what happened to the real Johnson, and it's one that befalls Redford in the film.

JESSE JAMES
1939 105m c ★★★★
Western /U
FOX

Tyrone Power (Jesse James), Henry Fonda (Frank James), Nancy Kelly (Zee), Randolph Scott (Will Wright), Henry Hull (Major Rufus Cobb), Brian Donlevy (Barshee), John Carradine (Bob Ford), Jane Darwell (Mrs. Samuels), Donald Meek (McCoy), Slim Summerville (Jailer)

p, Nunnally Johnson; d, Henry King; w, Nunnally Johnson (based on historical data assembled by Rosalind Schaeffer and Jo Frances James); ph, W. Howard Greene, George Barnes (Technicolor); ed, Barbara McLean; m, Louis Silvers; art d, William Darling, George Dudley

This classic Western unfolds the legendary saga of the notorious James boys, notably Jesse Woodson James (1847-1882). Director King directed this blockbuster that captures the image and era of the infamous outlaw, if not the reality of his character.

Power is a dashing and utterly charming Jesse who lives on his mother's farm with his brother Frank—slow, deliberate, dependable Fonda. Moving through their Missouri landscape like a locust is Donlevy, a representative of the hated, land-grabbing St. Louis Midland Railroad, buying up land in and around the area through which the railroad will be built. If his dirt-cheap offers are not accepted, Donlevy and his thugs merely beat sellers into submission. When Donlevy and company arrive at the James farm, the shifty-eyed Donlevy tries to browbeat Mother James (Darwell) into selling her farm. She tells him she won't sign any papers until her lawyer looks at them. Donlevy tries to force her to sign, and suddenly Fonda appears and tells Donlevy to go away. Donlevy offers his hand, trying his usual trick of yanking a victim toward him and then coldcocking him. This time the trick backfires, and it's Fonda who knocks Donlevy down. The railroad thug and his fellow goons begin to advance on Fonda when a shot rings out. Power stands smiling nearby with a smoking pistol in his hands. While Power holds the others at bay with his six-gun, Fonda gives Donlevy a beating, then both Fonda and Power run the men off.

Hull, the local newspaper editor and friend of the James family, along with other neighbors, assemble outside the James farmhouse when Donlevy and his goons return with the local lawmen. Hull tells Donlevy that the boys have fled. When Donlevy sees a light go out in the farmhouse, he shouts for Power and Fonda to come out, then quickly throws a bomb through the window which kills Darwell. Donlevy later looks down on her dead body and Hull looks up and says: "I'm mighty sorry." "I'm sorry, too," replies a nervous Donlevy. "Oh, I ain't sorry for her," Hull tells Donlevy, "she's gone. It's you I'm sorry for." Power's fiancee, Kelly, rides into the hills and tells Power and Fonda what happened. It's decided that Power will take revenge upon the killer of their mother. He next appears in town just as Donlevy is about to lift a drink in a saloon. Power tells the bartender to count three and duck. Donlevy, hands quivering, begs Power not to go for his gun, but Power begins counting and by the count of three Donlevy is dead. Power and Fonda then embark on a series of raids against the St. Louis Midland Railroad, robbing the trains and passengers and telling their victims to sue the railroad.

Until this film the 24-year-old Power had been an attractive matinee idol, but here he proved that he could really act. Though Fonda has fewer scenes, he renders his stalwart, prosaic character so effectively that Fox cast him in the successful sequel, THE RETURN OF FRANK JAMES. JESSE JAMES was the film that made Fonda a star.

Both King and Johnson had been eager to do a film on the legendary outlaw. Johnson researched Jesse James in Missouri, drawing most of his historic notions from the *Sedalia Gazette*, a strongly pro-James paper which promoted the idea that the notorious lawlessness of the James boys was caused by railroad and Union Army persecution following the Civil War. In the beginning this was true, but even Missouri residents grew tired of this excuse as the James-Younger gang went on looting for almost two decades; in fact, Jesse James was at large for eighteen

years before being gunned down by Bob Ford on April 3, 1882. Screenwriter Johnson opted for nostalgia and legend and left out much of the outlaw's grim career. Jo Frances James, granddaughter of Jesse James, was hired as a consultant to the production, but she was later disappointed with the film, commenting: "I don't know what happened to the history part of it. It seemed to me the story was fiction from beginning to end. About the only connection it had with fact was that there once was a man named James and he did ride a horse."

The old Technicolor process has never been more richly reproduced than in JESSE JAMES, which offers spellbinding hues of deep green, brown, and gold, giving the countryside portrayed the soft appearance of mellow history. There have been many films dealing with America's most celebrated outlaw, but this is the best.

JESUS OF MONTREAL
(JESUS DE MONTREAL)
1990 120m c   ★★★★½
Drama   R/18
Max/Gerard Mital   (Canada/France)

Lothaire Bluteau *(Daniel)*, Catherine Wilkening *(Mireille)*, Johanne-Marie Tremblay *(Constance)*, Remy Girard *(Martin)*, Robert Lepage *(Rene)*, Gilles Pelletier *(Fr. Leclerc)*, Yves Jacques *(Richard Cardinal)*, Denys Arcand *(The Judge)*

p, Roger Frappier; d, Denys Arcand; w, Denys Arcand; ph, Guy Dufaux; ed, Isabelle Dedieu; m, Yves Laferriere; prod d, Francois Seguin

Denys Arcand's JESUS OF MONTREAL is a modern Passion Play that takes aim at religion and the superficial values of our media-saturated society, yet finds possible salvation in technology. Thoughtful and amusing without being too academic, we have here a strong, provocative film.

The story begins as Daniel (Bluteau) is hired to stage the annual Summer Passion Play in a park overlooking the skyline of Montreal. From the start, Daniel's production—which he is to direct, as well as to star in as Jesus—is not entirely conventional. His ensemble cast comprises fellow actor friends forced to get along by dubbing porn movies and modeling for sexy commercials glorifying materialism. Mireille (Wilkening) is the Passion Play's (as well as the film's) Mary Magdalene. At first she is adrift in the loose morality of the modern world, having an affair with the priest who hired Daniel to stage the play. But as the film goes on, she finds meaning in her life through her devotion to Daniel and the play. Daniel becomes fascinated with some of the more unorthodox theories that he encounters in his research of Jesus' life, including questions of Jesus' true parentage, and these details go into the play. When the play is finally staged, it emerges as an avant-garde performance piece, with audiences ushered to the various installations representing the events in Jesus' life. The resulting drama doesn't adhere to standard biblical interpretations, but it truly moves and inspires the audience, and the revisionist Passion Play, its cast, and particularly Daniel become the toast of the town, cooed over by critics and culture vultures. Soon, life begins to imitate art, as church officials decide to discontinue the play because of questions about its possibly blasphemous content.

Arcand's excellent screenplay invests his vision of this spiritual parable with scathing satire and social commentary. The superb cast includes Bluteau as Daniel, his quiet brooding erupting into indignant rage; Girard as Martin, the most down-to-earth character in the film; and Wilkening as Mireille, who represents the modern-day lost soul's search for meaning. However, in drawing parallels between Daniel and Jesus, Arcand paints himself into a corner. The too-literal quality of these comparisons threatens to diminish the film's overall impact. The final resurrection sequence should be extraordinarily powerful as well as clinically probing; instead it is more of the latter than the former. But despite these weaknesses, the handsomely produced JESUS OF MONTREAL remains fresh, intelligent, and fascinating.

JEWEL OF THE NILE, THE

1985   115m   c   ★★★
Adventure   PG
FOX

Michael Douglas (Jack), Kathleen Turner (Joan), Danny DeVito (Ralph), Spiros Focas (Omar), Howard Jay Patterson (Barak), Samuel Ross Williams (Arak), Hamid Fillali (Rachid), Avner Eisenberg (Jewel of the Nile), Paul David Magid (Tarak), Holland Taylor (Gloria)

p, Michael Douglas; d, Lewis Teague; w, Mark Rosenthal, Lawrence Konner (based on characters created by Diane Thomas); ph, Jan De Bont (Technicolor); ed, Michael Ellis, Peter Boita; m, Jack Nitzsche; prod d, Richard Dawking, Terry Knight; art d, Leslie Tomkins, Damien Lanfranchi; cos, Emma Porteous

Frenetic, feisty sequel to ROMANCING THE STONE, this action fantasy once more sees flabby Michael Douglas and bristly Kathleen Turner, barely escaping with their lives in one incredible adventure after another. Pity.

The picture begins with Douglas and Turner sailing off into the sunset, though all is not right between them. The couple are idling their time away in a romantic port, but Turner bridles at having to be confined to Jack's boat. She is eager for new adventures, and one presents itself in the form of a request from an Arab sheik who asks her to write his autobiography since he is about to take over a vast desert kingdom. When Turner hesitates, she is abducted. The chase is on, with Douglas out to rescue his fair lady from a pack of desert cutthroats. Loudmouthed Danny DeVito is hot on both their trails, lusting after another fabulous gem, the Jewel of the Nile.

The action is nonstop and the special effects are often astounding as good and bad guys battle atop speeding trains and the lovers perilously dangle over cliffs and ride through charging desert tribes. But THE JEWEL OF THE NILE does not pack the innocence and inventiveness of ROMANCING THE STONE. And its racist view of Arabs demonstrates how dangerously unthinking these escapist action movies can quickly become.

JEZEBEL

1938   104m   bw   ★★★★
Drama   /U
WB

Bette Davis (Julie Morrison), Henry Fonda (Preston Dillard), George Brent (Buck Cantrell), Margaret Lindsay (Amy Bradford Dillard), Fay Bainter (Aunt Belle Massey), Richard Cromwell (Ted Dillard), Donald Crisp (Dr. Livingstone), Henry O'Neill (Gen. Theopholus Bogardus), John Litel (Jean LeCour), Gordon Oliver (Dick Allen)

p, Henry Blanke; d, William Wyler; w, Clements Ripley, Abem Finkel, John Huston, Robert Buckner (based on the play by Owen Davis, Sr.); ph, Ernest Haller; ed, Warren Low; m, Max Steiner; art d, Robert Haas; cos, Orry-Kelly

Our favorite magnolia. A mesmerizing romantic melodrama with "Popeye the Magnificent" playing a southern belle so peverse she ruins her own chances, as well as shaking up the Olde South.

Without Davis, who snared her second Oscar for the role—JEZEBEL was her consolation prize for losing the plum role in GONE WITH THE WIND, and there was a rush to get it into theaters first—this would seem mildewed indeed. But because her nervy, edgy performance conveys so much rage it leads convincingly into the film's second half where raging fires and fever sweep through New Orleans.

We may never really know if Davis and director Wyler had a great, doomed love affair, but the film looks like they did. Especially when Davis's Julie wrecks a great ball, and her own life, by wearing a flaming red gown when unmarried women are expected to wear pristine white. It's an outrageously great moment. Wyler's camera (abetted by the gifted cinematographer Ernest Haller) bores down on Davis, with her large, guilty eyes darting about to Max Steiner's swooping waltz—she's in too far to turn back. And the scene captures a quality in Fonda rarely exploited—his stubbornness—which may account for the longevity of his career. GONE WITH THE WIND may not have a single moment quite as incredible as this one, but then, that film didn't have Wyler who also gives Davis her other all-stops-out moment—her apology to Fonda, going to her knees in a white gown of breathtaking proportions. Davis gives the scene an overwhelmingly hushed sense of sexual urgency and surrender. JEZEBEL is indeed Wyler's love letter to Davis. (THE LETTER represents the souring of their collaboration; THE LITTLE FOXES, its death.)

The screenplay by Clements Ripley, Abem Finkel and John Huston was based on the Owen Davis, Sr. play that lasted about five minutes on Broadway with Miriam Hopkins replacing the ailing Tallulah Bankhead ("It was dreadful," said Tallulah. "Had I played the part it might have run two weeks."). The casting of Davis fanned the flames of her feuds with both of these southern belles, who hailed from Georgia and Alabama respectively.

Fonda had made a deal with the studio that his work on the film be completed by early December, so he could fly back to New York where his wife was awaiting their first child (Jane, born on December 21st). Although they tried to rush things, Wyler's perfectionism put the film behind schedule. As a result, Davis had to do her closeups and inserts without Fonda on the set. JEZEBEL features two songs: the title tune and "Raise a Ruckus." The film cost slightly over $1 million but made a bundle for everyone involved and got the country in an antebellum mood that went into overdrive with the release of Selznick's greatest work.

JFK

1991   189m   c   ★★★★
Historical/Drama   R/15
Camelot Productions/Warner Bros./New Regency Films/Canal Plus/Ixtlan

Kevin Costner (Jim Garrison), Sissy Spacek (Liz Garrison), Joe Pesci (David Ferrie), Tommy Lee Jones (Clay Shaw), Gary Oldman (Lee Harvey Oswald), Jay O. Sanders (Lou Ivon), Michael Rooker (Bill Broussard), Laurie Metcalf (Susie Cox), Gary Grubbs (Al Oser), John Candy (Dean Andrews)

p, A. Kitman Ho, Oliver Stone; d, Oliver Stone; w, Oliver Stone, Zachary Sklar (from the books On the Trail of the Assassins by Jim Garrison and Crossfire: The Plot That Killed Kennedy by Jim Marrs); ph, Robert Richardson; ed, Joe Hutshing, Pietro Scalia; m, John Williams; prod d, Victor Kempster; art d, Derek R. Hill, Alan R. Tomkins; cos, Marlene Stewart

Director and co-screenwriter Oliver Stone pulls off an amazing filmmaking feat with JFK, transforming the dry minutiae of every John F. Kennedy assassination conspiracy theory of the past three decades into riveting screen material.

Stone's story revolves around New Orleans District Attorney Jim Garrison's (Kevin Costner) unsuccessful 1967 prosecution of local businessman Clay Shaw (Tommy Lee Jones) for complicity in Kennedy's murder. Shaw's exact connection, even in the film, is hazy at best. But Garrison uses Shaw's trial mostly as a pretext to advance his own theory that Lee Harvey Oswald (Gary Oldman) was only one of several gunmen involved in the assassination and that he probably, as he claimed at the time of his arrest, never fired a single shot. The film starts with the assassination, followed by Garrison's investigation of a possible New Orleans connection in the shape of David Ferrie (Joe Pesci), a deranged ex-pilot, failed priest, amateur cancer researcher, mercenary and friend of Shaw's, who may have been in Dallas at the time of the assassination for the purpose of flying Oswald out of the country. Garrison's initial interrogation of Ferrie comes to naught and, after Oswald's murder by go-go bar owner Jack Ruby (Brian Doyle-Murray), the case is more or less closed.

When the Warren Commission's report on the Kennedy assassination is released, however, Garrison finds glaring discrepancies with even his own cursory investigation. He digs back in, using the Ferrie-Shaw connection as a pretext. After interviewing a dizzying array of witnesses, most of them anonymous and off-the-record, Garrison comes to the conclusion that the assassination was the result of a conspiracy initiated by the military-industrial complex and motivated by Kennedy's supposed intent to withdraw American forces from the Vietnam War as part of a greater unilateral winding down of the Cold War.

During Shaw's trial, Garrison names Lyndon Johnson and FBI director J. Edgar Hoover as unindicted co-conspirators in what he labels a bloody, fascist coup, carried out with all the cold, grisly precision of a gangland hit. However, Garrison's case is hobbled by quashed subpoenas of some witnesses and suspicious sudden deaths of others, including Ferrie, who is murdered. By the trial, Garrison himself has deteriorated into a frazzled wreck, jeopardizing his marriage, his sanity and his case in the political firestorm he has ignited. Shaw is quickly acquitted, but his remains the only prosecution ever successfully brought to trial over what is almost inarguably the crime of the century.

It's a measure of Stone's forcefulness as a filmmaker that he struck raw nerves across the political spectrum with a film that, in substance, did little more than dust off an accretion of well-worn conspiracy theories, most of which have been in circulation since the days following the assassination itself. Partly as a result of the film's impact, legislation was introduced into Congress in March of 1992 in an attempt to secure the release of FBI, CIA, and government files relating to the assassination which had previously been ordered sealed until 2029. That, however, is far from the most extraordinary thing about JFK.

Imagine a three-hour-plus epic that jettisons any recognizable dramatic structure, as JFK does, in favor of almost non-stop dialogue exposition and ends, not with a bang, but with an extended courtroom monologue and the hero's inglorious defeat, and you would normally have a surefire formula for failure. But JFK succeeds, partly thanks to a taut and intelligent script, and partly because the central investigation is spiced up by a series of key witnesses, each of whom inject the film with color and life; Pesci, Jones, and Kevin Bacon give particularly good performances. Stone's rapid-fire recreations and dramatizations of possible events also help keep things moving. But it is the director's evident passion to expose the deepest, darkest elements at work in society that really makes JFK come alive. This commitment is probably also what enabled him to arrange for so many star cameos from performers including Jack Lemmon, Walter Matthau, Donald Sutherland, John Candy, and Garrison himself (as Earl Warren). The result is rabble-rousing, muckraking, populist filmmaking at its very best—ironically, a product of the very Time-Warner news conglomerate that successfully kept the crucial Zapruder footage of Kennedy's assassination under lock and key until Garrison subpoenaed it.

JFK simultaneously tantalizes highbrow audiences by cannily casting its intricate conspiratorial speculations in dramatic terms that recall Shakespeare and Machiavelli while, for the popcorn crowd, unabashedly revelling in its lurid, real-life cast of crazed plotters and seedy schemers. The combination succeeds in bringing audiences together to share, in their own ways, Stone's personal obsession with one of the darkest episodes in US history.

JIM THORPE—ALL AMERICAN
1951 107m bw ★★★
Biography/Sports
WB

Burt Lancaster (*Jim Thorpe*), Charles Bickford (*Glenn S. "Pop" Warner*), Steve Cochran (*Peter Allendine*), Phyllis Thaxter (*Margaret Miller*), Dick Wesson (*Ed Guyac*), Jack Big Head (*Little Boy*), Suni Warcloud (*Wally Denny*), Al Mejia (*Louis Tewanema*), Hubie Kerns (*Tom Ashenbrunner*), Nestor Paiva (*Hiram Thorpe*)

p, Everett Freeman; d, Michael Curtiz; w, Douglas Morrow, Frank Davis, Everett Freeman (based on the story "Bright Path" by Morrow and Vincent X. Flaherty, from the biography by Russell Birdwell and James Thorpe); ph, Ernest Haller; ed, Folmar Blangsted; m, Max Steiner; art d, Edward Carrere; cos, Milo Anderson

Sports and big teeth. Burt Lancaster sets his jaw and plays one of America's greatest athletes, the wondrous Jim Thorpe, a Native American who captured gold medals in the pentathlon and decathlon at the 1912 Stockholm Olympics, only to be stripped of them because he had played semiprofessional baseball, violating his amateur status.

This biopic begins with Billy Gray portraying Thorpe as a youth on an Oklahoma reservation. Lancaster takes over as Thorpe matriculates to the all-Indian college at Carlisle, Pennsylvania, where he begins playing football to impress Margaret Miller (Phyllis Thaxter), his college sweetheart and future wife. Coached by the legendary Glenn "Pop" Warner (Charles Bickford), he captures All-American honors, then goes on to glory and disappointment in Stockholm, followed by an illustrious career in professional baseball and football. When his young son dies, Thorpe's spirit is broken, and he turns to the bottle, losing Margaret.

Thorpe was actually enshrined in the Pro Football Hall of Fame and his Olympic medals have been posthumously restored. As usual, Lancaster did most of his own athletic feats. Unfortunately some of his performances tend to confuse bravura with thoughtful interpretation. Curtiz tries hard to infuse the predictability with life, but the formula is the real champ here. Adequate.

JOE HILL
1971 114m c ★★½
Biography GP/AA
Sagittarius (U.S./Sweden)

Thommy Berggren (Joe Hill), Anja Schmidt (Lucia), Kelvin Malave (Fox), Evert Anderson (Blackie), Cathy Smith (Cathy), Hasse Persson (Paul), David Moritz (David), Wendy Geier (Elizabeth), Franco Molinari (Tenor), Richard Weber (Richard)

p, Bo Widerberg; d, Bo Widerberg; w, Bo Widerberg, Richard Weber, Steve Hopkins; ph, Petter Davidsson, Jorgen Persson (Eastmancolor); ed, Bo Widerberg; m, Stefan Grossman; art d, Ulf Axen

Superfical biopic served up with a striking imagery. Somewhat fictionalized account of the life of the famed labor leader. After immigrating to America from Sweden, Hill (Thommy Berggren) tramps around the U.S. until getting involved with the Industrial Workers of the World (the famed Wobblies). He quickly learns his way around the union, and, with his ever-present banjo, begins writing labor songs for the people. After achieving some success and power within the Wobblies, he goes to Utah where, to protect a girl he loves, he takes the rap for a murder and gets executed.

Politically, the film only touches on issues in a simplistic manner. Part of the problem may be that the material is approached from a modern (1970s) perspective that imposes a somewhat sentimental and patronizing tone on the story. This pastoral approach undercuts the moral rage the film needs to evoke. Consequently Widerberg's presentation of the Wobblies suggests that they were flat martyrs whose human idenities were suppressed when they became union members.

JOHN AND MARY
1969 92m c ★★
Drama R/AA
Debrod

Dustin Hoffman (John), Mia Farrow (Mary), Michael Tolan (James), Sunny Griffin (Ruth), Stanley Beck (Ernest), Tyne Daly (Hilary), Alix Elias (Jane), Julie Garfield (Fran), Marvin Lichterman (Dean), Marian Mercer (Mags Elliot)

p, Ben Kadish; d, Peter Yates; w, John Mortimer (based on a novel by Mervyn Jones); ph, Gayne Rescher (Panavision, DeLuxe Color); ed, Frank P. Keller; m, Quincy Jones; prod d, John Robert Lloyd; art d, Robert Wightman; fx, L.B. Abbott, Art Cruickshank; cos, Anthea Sylbert

Wispy and flat. Two creeps (furniture designer Hoffman and art gallery assistant Farrow) meet in an arch swingers bar and shack up. They awake in bed and go through about 80 minutes of self-centered self-analysis over whether they should do it again. He goes to a party, but can't get her out of his head. He returns and she's cooking dinner for him. They decide to do it again. And tell each other their names. Yawn!

JOHNNY BELINDA
1948 102m bw ★★★★½
Drama /A
WB

Jane Wyman (Belinda McDonald), Lew Ayres (Dr. Robert Richardson), Charles Bickford (Black McDonald), Agnes Moorehead (Aggie McDonald), Stephen McNally (Locky McCormick), Jan Sterling (Stella McGuire), Rosalind Ivan (Mrs. Peggety), Dan Seymour (Pacquet), Mabel Paige (Mrs. Lutz), Ida Moore (Mrs. McKee)

p, Jerry Wald; d, Jean Negulesco; w, Irmgard Von Cube, Allen Vincent (based on the play by Elmer Harris); ph, Ted McCord; ed, David Weisbart; m, Max Steiner; art d, Robert Haas; fx, William McGann, Edwin DuPar; cos, Milo Anderson

After 15 years of hoofing her way through Warner Bros. films as a chorus girl and the second-fiddle friend of female leads, Jane Wyman finally got her dream part as the sensitive deaf-mute in this screen adaptation of the play by Elmer Harris. Thanks to Jean Negulesco's careful crafting, the result is admirably restrained, a triumph of atmosphere over potential tearjerking.

As the forlorn Belinda, Wyman is the unwanted daughter of Bickford, a stoic, iron-willed New England farmer who has blames the girl for her mother's having died while giving her birth. Ayres, a kindly doctor practicing in the nearby town, befriends Wyman and teaches her sign language, chastising all in the community who cruelly refer to her as "The Dummy." Slowly, Wyman's sweet and loving nature emerges and attracts the attention of brutish McNally, the local bully. Drunk one night, he attacks and rapes Wyman. She delivers a child which everyone believes has been fathered by Ayres, a situation which later forces him to leave the community in disgrace.

Wyman's performance is a marvel of beauty and innocence. Preparing for the most important role of her career thus far, Wyman studied the behavior of the hearing impaired and labored for weeks to capture an "anticipation light," as she called the look of eager curiosity of deaf people who want to learn and understand. Still Wyman felt an element was absent in her performance, that she was not accurately portraying the world of the deaf. She huddled with director Negulesco, who suggested she stuff her ears with wax. She did so, sealing off all sounds except loud percussions. This induced deafness made it difficult for her to pick up cue lines from other actors, but the very faltering and groping appearance Wyman projected made her all the more convincing.

Since the story was originally set on the dank and forbidding New England coast, Negulesco, along with the cast and crew, traveled to the rough, jagged coastal area near Mendocino, about 200 miles north of San Francisco. Here cinematographer McCord beautifully captured the deep fog, heavy rain, and driving winds, all of which further dramatized an already dynamic story. None of the special handling of this film impressed Jack Warner, head of the studio, who objected vociferously to the bills for location shooting, expressing disbelief that anyone would want to see a picture "where the leading lady doesn't say a word." But the world did want to see this film and Wyman in it; audiences marveled at a performance that thoroughly merited the Oscar it received. Wyman had been strong in THE LOST WEEKEND, but in JOHNNY BELINDA she was exceptional, joining the ranks of Hollywood's leading actresses.

JOHNNY EAGER
1942 107m bw ★★★★
Crime /A
MGM

Robert Taylor (Johnny Eager), Lana Turner (Lisbeth Bard), Edward Arnold (John Benson Farrell), Van Heflin (Jeff Hartnett), Robert Sterling (Jimmy Lanthrop), Patricia Dane (Garnet), Glenda Farrell (Mae Blythe), Barry Nelson (Lew Rankin), Henry O'Neill (A.J. Verne), Charles Dingle (A. Frazier Marco)

p, John W. Considine, Jr.; d, Mervyn LeRoy; w, John Lee Mahin, James Edward Grant (based on a story by James Edward Grant); ph, Harold Rosson; ed, Albert Akst; m, Bronislau Kaper; art d, Cedric Gibbons, Stan Rogers; cos, Robert Kalloch

Here's a glossy world of crime wrapped in white fox and expensive leather where one sinks into deep armchairs and drinks imported Scotch. This is the crooked cafe society world of callow, sexy Taylor who abuses callow, sexy Turner. They're made for each other, see? Each acts in a highly stylized mode of tragic glamour that is most evident in the swooning vortex of their love scenes. Casting them together was inspired—they give each other extra resonance and depth.

Taylor is the rottenly handsome title character, hiding the tenderness of his pretty face behind a gigolo's pencil mustache. At the opening, he misleads viewers. He wears a cab driver's hat and reports to his fatherly parole officer, O'Neil, explaining how diligently he drives his hack, and stays on the straight and narrow. O'Neil introduces the slick Taylor to two earnest, pretty sociology students, Turner and Diana Lewis. Turner thinks he's anything but what he pretends to be. Her instincts are right, even though her heart takes her in another direction. Taylor dutifully gets into his cab after meeting with O'Neil and charming Lewis and Turner. Then he drives to an unopened dog track, reports to the front desk, goes into the inner offices without seeking approval, then into even posher living quarters where he discards his cab driver's outfit and dons expensive tie and suitcoat. As he begins barking orders to his minions, it becomes apparent that Taylor is not only back in the rackets but that he's running them.

Later that night, Taylor exposes his real nature and status when he confronts Nelson in his nightclub, making threats about what will happen to the club owner if he fails to do as he is told. This is witnessed by Turner whom he escorts home to father Arnold, the same prosecuting attorney who sent him to prison. Arnold explodes when he sees Taylor with Turner, threatening to return him to prison if he ever sees them together again. Taylor backs off but hatches a plan to take revenge on Arnold, seduce Turner, and guarantee the opening of his dog track without interference from the authorities. He inveigles Turner to his lavish apartment where he stages an attack by a vicious hoodlum, Stewart. Stewart is about to kill Taylor, or so it seems to Turner, and she grabs a convenient gun and ostensibly kills Stewart.

JOHNNY EAGER is an lavish candy box film in which Taylor wholly abandons his male ingenue image and becomes a believable bad guy whose sliver of human compassion causes his undoing; its one of his best early roles. Although there's a synthetic element to JOHNNY EAGER, the crime melodrama aspect is so well handled by LeRoy and the chemistry between Taylor and the luscious 21-year-old Turner so strong that it's wholly satisfying. Taylor and Turner made only this film together and more's the pity. Their penthouse balcony scene is definitive Hollywood passion, all glossy open lips, eye lash shadows and whispered urgency—the latter a Turner specialty.

Throughout, Heflin is the presence that gives depth to the film as the drunken conscience of cold-hearted Taylor. The homoerotic content of the film is unusual for staid MGM. Heflin acts like Taylor's domesticated, kept house pet and he won an Oscar for Best Supporting Actor for his effort.

JOHNNY GUITAR

1954   110m   c   ★★★★
Western   /PG
Republic

Joan Crawford (Vienna), Sterling Hayden (Johnny Guitar), Mercedes McCambridge (Emma Small), Scott Brady (Dancin' Kid), Ward Bond (John McIvers), Ben Cooper (Turkey Ralston), Ernest Borgnine (Bart Lonergan), John Carradine (Old Tom), Royal Dano (Corey), Frank Ferguson (Marshal Williams)

p, Herbert J. Yates; d, Nicholas Ray; w, Philip Yordan (based on the novel by Roy Chanslor); ph, Harry Stradling (TruColor); ed, Richard L. Van Enger; m, Victor Young; prod d, John McCarthy, Jr.; art d, James Sullivan; fx, Howard Lydecker, Theodore Lydecker; cos, Sheila O'Brien

Our Dancing Daughter toting a gun. Mildred Pierce in buckskin. THE WOMEN out West. All of these things and more are JOHNNY GUITAR, a true one-of-a-kind. La belle butch Joan stars as Vienna, owner of a saloon and plenty of land just awaitin' for the railroad to mozy on in. Trouble is, dem dere meanie cattle ranchers in town are dead set agin' it. This ready-set-go lynch mob is led by embittered Emma Small (McCambridge, in a dry run for her role as the devil's voice in THE EXORCIST). One just keeps waiting for Crawford to say to McCambridge, "You're a small woman, Emma Small", but that's about the only thing that doesn't happen in this fabulously flamboyant flick. If TORCH SONG is The Queen of Pepsi's gift to gay men, JOHNNY GUITAR was her way of thanking her many lesbian fans.

If anyone cares, Hayden plays the title role, a gunfighter turned guitar strummer, the most meaningful of the many, many men in Vienna's accomplished past. Brady, meanwhile, is the Dancin' Kid, a cocky so-and-so who fools around with Vienna but really lights Emma's rockets. You can cut the Freud in this pizza pie with a hacksaw and, needless to say, the finale features these two female firebrands creating a bloodbath while trying to shoot each other.

A camp classic second to none, JOHNNY GUITAR breathes excess in every department. The garish Trucolor process resembles nothing you've ever seen and genius director Nicholas Ray is like a drag queen with a fingerpainting kit. Many things to many people, this extravaganza is a cult favorite of the *Cahiers du Cinema*, a howl for anyone who thinks they can last for two hours, and, as Ray intended, a thinly veiled anti-McCarthy diatribe. Ray puts red-flag-like objects everywhere, and when Bowtie Mouth confronts a mob in her virginal white we dare you to maintain your composure.

The ambisexual Crawford is truly in her element here, strapping on her six-shooter one minute and insisting that all her huffy lovers stop killing each other long enough to help her make breakfast the next. Great dialogue abounds, and the Empress of Emotion corners most of it: "Down there I sell whiskey and cards," Vienna warns the funeral-garbed lynchers, "All you can buy up these stairs is a bullet in the head. Now which do you want?"; instructing her croupier, she barks, "Spin the wheel, Eddie. . . I like to hear it spin."

JOHNNY IN THE CLOUDS

1945   87m   bw   ★★★½
War   /U
Two Cities   (U.K.)

Michael Redgrave (David Archdale), John Mills (Peter Penrose), Rosamund John (Miss Toddy Todd), Douglass Montgomery (Johnny Hollis), Renee Asherson (Iris Winterton), Stanley Holloway (Palmer), Basil Radford (Tiny Williams), Felix Aylmer (Rev. Charles Moss), Bonar Colleano (Joe Friselli), Trevor Howard (Squadron Leader Carter)

p, Anatole de Grunwald; d, Anthony Asquith; w, Terence Rattigan, Anatole de Grunwald (based on the story by Terence Rattigan, Richard Sherman); ph, Derick Williams; ed, Fergus McDonell; m, Nicholas Brodszky; art d, Paul Sheriff, Carmen Dillon

A superior war film that has virtually no footage of actual battle. The presence of the war is continually felt, however, through the film's atmosphere and in the subtle and effective performances. The picture concentrates on the effects of war upon romances. Mills is the young pilot unwilling to make a commitment to the girl he has fallen in love with, thinking it isn't right for a soldier to marry in the midst of a war. Even when an American soldier tries to make off with Asherson, Mills refuses to go where his heart leads until John, the widow of fellow flyer Redgrave, convinces him that marriage is the right thing to do. This is just one of several sagas that are effectively interwoven to create a well-rounded picture of airmen on the ground. A prominent theme is the introduction of American forces onto the British base. The film deals with the uneasiness this caused before camaraderie and friendship developed.

A tremendously successful film at the time of its release, JOHNNY IN THE CLOUDS captured a certain patriotic spirit that had been lurking in British hearts. Director Asquith had the perceptiveness to recognize the flow of feeling in Britain, and to bring it to the forefront without becoming bogged down in sentimentalism. In performances, techniques, scripting, and all other facets, a very fine achievement.

JOHNNY TREMAIN

1957 80m c   ★★★½
Historical   /U
Buena Vista

Hal Stalmaster (Johnny Tremain), Luana Patten (Cilla Lapham), Jeff York (James Otis), Sebastian Cabot (Jonathan Lyte), Richard Beymer (Rab Silsbee), Walter Sande (Paul Revere), Rusty Lane (Samuel Adams), Whit Bissell (Josiah Quincy), Will Wright (Ephraim Lapham), Virginia Christine (Mrs. Lapham)

p, Walt Disney; d, Robert Stevenson; w, Tom Blackburn (based on the novel by Esther Forbes); ph, Charles P. Boyle (Technicolor); ed, Stanley Johnson; m, George Bruns; prod d, Peter Ellenshaw; art d, Carroll Clark; cos, Chuck Keehne, Gertrude Casey

This fine adaptation of Esther Forbes's novel opens in 1773 as Johnny Tremain (Hal Stalmaster), a silversmith's apprentice, becomes involved with revolutionary colonists, though he is at first uncommitted to their cause. His views change when he takes a silver cup his mother gave him, embellished with his family crest, to a nobleman (Sebastian Cabot) as proof that he is his relative. The noble accuses him of theft, and, though he's later cleared of the charge, the incident turns him into a revolutionary. Tremain then participates in the Boston Tea Party, followed by a torchlight parade in which the rebels sing "The Liberty Tree." The patriots' continued refusal to cooperate with the British sets the stage for an armed confrontation at Lexington Green. Both sides have been ordered not to fire, but when a shot rings out from an unknown source, the American Revolution—symbolized by the bonfire around which the rebels gather in the final scene—begins. JOHNNY TREMAIN makes history come alive. Stalmaster is very good as an average young man caught up in tumultuous times, and the film offers a balanced portrayal of both sides of the conflict, with characters presented as human beings first, historical figures second.

JOLSON SINGS AGAIN

1949 96m c   ★★★
Musical/Biography   /U
Columbia

Larry Parks (Al Jolson), Barbara Hale (Ellen Clark), William Demarest (Steve Martin), Ludwig Donath (Cantor Yoelson), Bill Goodwin (Tom Baron), Myron McCormick (Ralph Bryant), Tamara Shayne (Mama Yoelson), Eric Wilton (Henry), Robert Emmett Keane (Charlie), Frank McLure

p, Sidney Buchman; d, Henry Levin; w, Sidney Buchman; ph, William Snyder (Technicolor); ed, William Lyon; m, George Duning; art d, Walter Holscher; cos, Jean Louis

After the success of 1946's THE JOLSON STORY, Columbia executives quickly rushed a follow-up into production, though it took almost three years for JOLSON SINGS AGAIN to be completed. Once again, the music makes the film, a wall-to-wall tunefest with many of the same songs contained in the original.

Larry Parks (reprising his role in the 1946 film, as do many in the cast) is excellent again as Jolson, who, as the film opens, is performing in a nightclub while his long-suffering wife walks out on him. Next comes WWII and a USO tour for the "boys in uniform," as a result of which Jolson contracts a lung ailment in Africa. In the hospital, he meets nurse Ellen Clark (Barbara Hale), whom he falls in love with and later marries. The rest of JOLSON SINGS AGAIN is principally concerned with the making of THE JOLSON STORY—including the hiring of Parks (who thus plays both himself and Jolson in one double-exposure sequence) for the lead—giving the film a memorable moment as a curio.

As in the opener, the less attractive elements of Jolson's personality are ignored in favor of his talents—manifest in the many tunes, in which the great Jolson himself dubs Parks' singing voice—although some attention is paid to his financial extravagance and his difficulty in adjusting to decreasing fame after a lifetime of top billing.

JOLSON STORY, THE

1946 128m c   ★★★★
Musical/Biography   /U
Columbia

Larry Parks (Al Jolson), Evelyn Keyes (Julie Benson), William Demarest (Steve Martin), Bill Goodwin (Tom Baron), Ludwig Donath (Cantor Yoelson), Tamara Shayne (Mrs. Yoelson), John Alexander (Lew Dockstader), Jo-Carroll Dennison (Ann Murray), Ernest Cossart (Father McGee), Scotty Beckett (Jolson as a Boy)

p, Sidney Skolsky; d, Alfred E. Green; w, Stephen Longstreet, Harry Chandlee, Andrew Solt; ph, Joseph Walker (Technicolor); ed, William Lyon; art d, Stephen Goosson, Walter Holscher; chor, Jack Cole, Joseph H. Lewis; cos, Jean Louis

A standout of the musical film-bio genre, THE JOLSON STORY was a box office smash, despite the fact that it contained just about every show business cliche imaginable. It's a highly idealized portrait of Jolson, remembered by everyone who knew him to have been as personally difficult as he was professionally talented. Jolson was Larry Park's first big role after five years of strictly small-time work, and he took full advantage of the opportunity, delivering a top-caliber performance.

Jolson's real story—a mixture of joy, anger, bitterness, and superstardom—is mixed with JAZZ SINGER-inspired fictionalization, charting his youth in vaudeville, his parents' desire that he follow another career, and his eventual rise to the top. Coached by Jolson himself (who dubs Parks' singing voice), Parks perfectly captures the entertainer's famous mannerisms, including his whistling and deliberate interruptions in the middle of a show to stop and banter with the audience. Ruby Keeler, Jolson's third wife (of four), refused to allow her name to be used in the film (her character here is renamed Julie Benson). The musical numbers were pleasingly staged by Joseph H. Lewis.

JONAH—WHO WILL BE 25 IN THE YEAR 2000
(JONAS—QUI AURA 25 ANS EN L'AN 2000)
1976   116m   c   ★★★½
Comedy   /X
Action/Citel/Societe Francaise/SSR Swiss TV   (Switzerland)

Jean-Luc Bideau (Max Stigny), Myriam Boyer (Mathilde Vernier), Myriam Mziere (Madeleine), Jacques Denis (Marco Perly), Roger Jendly (Marcel Certoux), Dominique Labourier (Marguerite), Miou-Miou (Marie), Raymond Bussieres (Old Charles), Rufus (Mathieu Vernier), Jonas (Himself)

p, Yves Gasser, Yves Peyrot; d, Alain Tanner; w, John Berger, Alain Tanner; ph, Renato Berta (Eastmancolor); ed, Brigitte Sousselier, Marc Blavet; m, Jean-Marie Senia

Unlike most films that seem to dwell on the lost ideals of the children of the 1960s, JONAH is an exhilarating film with characters that are filled with life and who refuse to become trapped in endless dreams that can never come true. Although each of these people stops short of achieving some desire, the failure doesn't result in a personal deterioration or self-pity. Perhaps this is a function of the beliefs fought for in the 1960s: goals that were never quite reached but offered the consolation of an effort well made. Whatever the case, all of these characters are extremely likable, uplifting the film with energy that is easily transmitted to the viewer. Prime among them are Miou-Miou, a grocery clerk who steals food for a retired engineer (Bussieres), and Denis, a teacher who can't keep a steady job. It would be a miscarriage of justice to limit the credit to just these two, however; every one of the characters is a joy. Tanner subtly interweaves the roles and knows when to turn off their exhilaration to allow his own themes to take over.

JOUR DE FETE
1949   90m   bw   ★★★★
Comedy   /U
Francinex/Cady   (France)

Jacques Tati (Francois), Guy Decombie (Roger), Paul Frankeur (Marcel), Santa Relli (Roger's Wife), Maine Vallee (Jeanette), Roger Rafal (Barber), Beauvais (Cafe Proprietor), Delcassan (Cinema Operator)

p, Fred Orain; d, Jacques Tati; w, Jacques Tati, Rene Wheeler, Henri Marquet; ph, Jacques Mercanton; ed, Marcel Morreau; m, Jean Yatove; art d, Rene Moullaert

Quite clever. The first feature film by Jacques Tati was actually a lengthened version of his short L'ECOLE DES FACTEURS, and helped gain Tati an international reputation as one of the best film comics to come out of France. Also starring in JOUR DE FETE, Tati plays the postman of a small sleepy village who becomes obsessed with applying the methods of the American postal system, as seen in a short educational film, to his job. This simple premise provides an abundance of opportunities for Tati to engage in some spectacular jokes. The emphasis of Tati's style was always aimed at the visual, music and dialog being used only to enhance what was being seen. The results were quite successful in producing laughter from cinema patrons in almost every country, and had a large impact upon the editing techniques later to be used by Jean-Luc Godard and Francois Truffaut.

JOURNEY FOR MARGARET
1942   81m   bw   ★★★
War   /A
MGM

Robert Young (John Davis), Laraine Day (Nora Davis), Fay Bainter (Trudy Strauss), Signe Hasso (Anya), Margaret O'Brien (Margaret), Nigel Bruce (Herbert V. Allison), William Severn (Peter Humphreys), G.P. Huntley, Jr. (Rugged), Doris Lloyd (Mrs. Barrie), Halliwell Hobbes (Mr. Barrie)

p, B.P. Fineman; d, W.S. Van Dyke, II; w, David Hertz, William Ludwig (based on the book by William L. White); ph, Ray June; ed, George White; m, Franz Waxman; art d, Cedric Gibbons, Wade B. Rubottom; cos, Robert Kalloch

An unabashed three-hanky movie and the final film of director W.S. Van Dyke II's distinguished career. John and Nora Davis (Robert Young and Laraine Day) are an American couple in London during the Blitz. Nora is awaiting their first child while John, a journalist, covers the war for US readers. During an air raid, John meets young Peter Humphreys (William Severn), and takes him to a home for orphans; his wife, meanwhile, is injured, loses the child, and has to return to the States. John remains in London, promising to join her as soon as he can. After visiting Peter and meeting the boy's sister, Margaret (Margaret O'Brien), a child fearful of everything, John becomes a surrogate father to the siblings. He and Nora plan to adopt them, but, on the brink of leaving England, John is told he cannot take both kids with him on the plane.

At age five, in her second film, O'Brien—considered by many to be one of the best, if not the greatest, child actresses ever—is an accomplished scene snatcher in the Judy Garland traditon. The movie was a big success, and movingly depicts the personal tragedy of war through the eyes of children, its most innocent victims.

JOURNEY INTO FEAR
1942   71m   bw   ★★★★
Spy   /A
Mercury

Joseph Cotten (Graham), Dolores Del Rio (Josette), Ruth Warrick (Stephanie), Agnes Moorehead (Mme. Mathews), Jack Durant (Gogo), Everett Sloane (Kopeikin), Eustace Wyatt (Haller), Frank Readick (Mathews), Edgar Barrier (Kuvetli), Jack Moss (Banat)

p, Orson Welles; d, Norman Foster; w, Orson Welles, Joseph Cotten (based on a novel by Eric Ambler); ph, Karl Struss; ed, Mark Robson; m, Roy Webb; art d, Albert S. D'Agostino, Mark-Lee Kirk; fx, Vernon L. Walker; cos, Edward Stevenson

Sure it says "directed by Norman Foster," but don't let that fool you, this is an Orson Welles film all the way. Welles is listed as producer, his Mercury Players fill the cast, his then-companion Del Rio is in the lead, and he cowrote the screenplay with Joseph Cotten. The result is a strange, obsessive and often brilliant film, much of which takes place aboard a dilapidated freighter.

Howard Graham (Cotten) is a US Navy engineer who is to return to the US with his beautiful wife Stephanie (Warrick) after a business conference in Istanbul. Graham soon realizes that someone is trying to kill him and is taken by Turkish agent Kopeikin (Sloane) to secret police headquarters where intelligence chief Haki (Welles) explains that Nazi agents are after him.

JOURNEY INTO FEAR is a wonderfully murky study of espionage, realistically portrayed in all its mayhem and confusion, one spy not really knowing what the other spy is up to, but operating on instinct to get results. Cotten's quiet, unassuming part is so well played that the viewer gets frustrated at his inability to either act or even think clearly. A visually arresting film with a nod to the quirky that just can't be beat in terms of the bizarre.

JOURNEY TO THE CENTER OF THE EARTH

1959   132m   c   ★★★½
Science Fiction   G/U
FOX

Pat Boone (*Alec McEwen*), James Mason (*Prof. Oliver Lindenbrook*), Arlene Dahl (*Carla*), Diane Baker (*Jenny*), Thayer David (*Count Saknussemm*), Peter Ronson (*Hans*), Robert Adler (*Groom*), Alan Napier (*Dean*), Alex Finlayson (*Prof. Bayle*), Ben Wright (*Paisley*)

p, Charles Brackett; d, Henry Levin; w, Charles Brackett, Walter Reisch (based on the novel *Journey to the Center of the Earth* by Jules Verne); ph, Leo Tover (CinemaScope, Deluxe Color); ed, Stuart Gilmore, Jack W. Holmes; m, Bernard Herrmann; art d, Lyle Wheeler, Franz Bachelin, Herman A. Blumenthal; fx, L.B. Abbott, James B. Gordon, Emil Kosa, Jr.; cos, David Ffolkes

An excellent combination of witty scripting and fine acting resulting in grand adventure.

James Mason plays Oliver Lindenbrook, an Edinburgh geologist who travels with student Alec McEwen (Pat Boone) to Iceland as part of a planned descent to the center of the earth via volcano. There, they meet Carla (Arlene Dahl), whose husband has been killed in a similar attempt. She joins the expedition, along with a young Icelander (Peter Ronson) and his pet duck. They begin the descent, imperiled by prehistoric beasts, rock slides, and the evil Count Saknussemm (Thayer David), who murdered Carla's husband and is determined to be the first to reach the earth's core.

A well-photographed film, with location footage shot in Carlsbad Caverns, featuring great special effects and a Bernard Herrmann score that heightens the excitement. Mason is charming, caustic and debonair, and the whole affair is captivating, silly fun. Watch for some sly sexual lampooning.

JU DOU

1991   95m   c   ★★★★
Drama/Romance/Historical   PG-13/15
Tokuma Shoten Publishing Company/Tokuma
Communications Company/China Film Coproduction
Corporation/China Film Export & Import Corporation/Xi-an
Film Studio   (Japan/China)

Gong Li (*Ju Dou*), Li Bao-tian (*Yang Tian-qing*), Li Wei (*Yang Jin-shan*), Zhang Yi (*Yang Tian-bai—as a Child*), Zheng Ji-an (*Yang Tian-bai—as a Youth*)

p, Zhang Wenze, Hu Jian, Yasuyoshi Yokuma; d, Zhang Yimou; w, Lui Heng; ph, Gu Changwei, Yang Lun; ed, Du Yuan; m, Xia Ru-jin; art d, Fei Jiupeng, Xia Ru-jin; cos, Zhi-an Zhang

Acclaimed "Fifth Generation" filmmaker Zhang Yimou, of RED SORGHUM fame, delves once more into the past for JU DOU, his second feature, a haunting story of illicit love set in 1920s China.

Ju Dou (Gong Li), a virginal beauty, is purchased by old and rich Yang Jin-shan (Li Wei) to be his bride. When, due to his impotence, she fails to bear him the son he craves, Jin-shan vents his rage against his wife, bringing her to the brink of suicide.

Yang Tian-qing (Li Bao-tian) is the solitary worker in the textile dyeing factory that Jin-shan owns. He is a distant relative of his employer but treated like a slave nonetheless. Tian-qing, aware of the beatings and abuse that Ju Dou suffers at the hands

of her husband, reaches out to console her and quickly becomes her only solace. They meet clandestinely whenever they can and one fateful night, when Jin-shan is away, they become lovers. When Ju Dou becomes pregnant, the son that Jin-shan desires is finally on its way, but he's clearly not the father. Then, in a strange twist of fate, the old man is paralyzed in an accident and left unable to speak. When the townspeople congratulate him on his newborn son, Jin-shan must accept or lose face. He is left at the mercy of Ju Dou and her lover, who pursue their illicit relationship to a tragic conclusion.

The "Fifth Generation" filmmakers began a new wave in Chinese cinema by emphasizing the visual and aural qualities of film rather than traditional dramatic and literary elements. JU DOU is no exception to this trend. The cinematography by Gu Changwei and Yang Lun highlights and accentuates the unfolding drama; a painter's palette of color emerges in images that act as counterpoints to the story. By displaying the ancient processes still in use for dyeing cloth, Yimou makes full use of his early background in a textile factory; the splashes of colored fabric and the dyeing process itself are an integral part of the film's beauty. The screenplay, written by Lui Heng, is spare and constant. JU DOU tantalizes all the senses as the story of the ill-fated lovers unfolds with hypnotic logic.

JUAREZ

1939   132m   bw   ★★★½
Biography   /U
WB

Paul Muni (*Benito Pablo Juarez*), Bette Davis (*Empress Carlotta von Habsburg*), Brian Aherne (*Maximilian von Habsburg*), Claude Rains (*Louis Napoleon*), John Garfield (*Porfirio Diaz*), Donald Crisp (*Marechal Bazaine*), Gale Sondergaard (*Empress Eugenie*), Joseph Calleia (*Alejandro Uradi*), Gilbert Roland (*Col. Miguel Lopez*), Henry O'Neill (*Miguel Miramon*)

p, Henry Blanke; d, William Dieterle; w, John Huston, Wolfgang Reinhardt, Aeneas MacKenzie (based on the novel *The Phantom Crown* by Bertita Harding and the play *Juarez & Maximillian* by Franz Werfel); ph, Tony Gaudio; ed, Warren Low; m, Erich Wolfgang Korngold; art d, Anton F. Grot; cos, Orry-Kelly

Weighs a ton, thanks to meddling Muni's obsessive hand in the screenplay. The effective casting lacks spark, save two firebrand ladies: Davis and Sondergaard, the latter stoking the cauldron and the former jumping in. Benito Pablo Juarez was to Mexico what Abraham Lincoln was to the United States. Both of them lived at the same time, and Juarez was profoundly influenced by the North American president. Like Lincoln, Juarez was physically homely, yet full of wisdom and spiritual clarity that was irresistible to his people.

The film opens with Rains, playing the evil Napoleon III, appointing Aherne (Archduke Maximilian von Habsburg of Austria) emperor of Mexico. Through his agents in Mexico, Rains has set up a fake election by which Aherne has been chosen the monarch of a people he has never seen. Aherne and wife Davis (Carlotta) journey to Mexico, escorted by an army commanded by Crisp. Meeting the royal couple are thousands of jubilant peasants in Mexico City, but the royal couple is again deceived by the insidious French, who have staged the reception.

The duly elected president of Mexico, Muni (Juarez), leads his people in revolt against the monarchs imposed upon Mexico by Rains. To mollify the people Aherne offers Muni the powerful position of Secretary of State, but he rejects it. Undaunted, Aherne believes that he can unite the Mexican people by adopting a native prince in an elaborate ceremony. Yet, when they take their new son to the balcony of their palace to show to their ostensibly adoring subjects, a tremendous explosion rocks the area. *Juaristas* have just blown up a huge ammunition dump of the French army. So enraged by this "slap" is Aherne that he signs the shoot-to-kill order for those found with weapons. Wholesale executions ensue, and soon even those who have paid homage to Aherne and Davis turn against the monarchy. A full-scale revolution breaks out, with the US ordering the French army to leave Mexico under the Monroe Doctrine.

JUAREZ was unique in that it was shot as two separate films—first the Aherne-Davis story, then the Muni portion; both stories were then edited together. Muni only meets Aherne when viewing his corpse, and even this scene is spliced together. Muni had the benefit of viewing the edited first portion of the film before going in front of the cameras to play Juarez and, to offset the Davis histrionics, he underplayed his role almost down to a whisper. Muni was afforded the privilege since he was then the most important actor on the Warner lot. But despite studying hundreds of books, documents and photographs of his subject, and spending six weeks visiting the areas where Juarez lived, worked and administered to his infant republic, the resulting portrayal proved unsuitable to a long epic film, slowing the ponderous drama to a crawl.

Davis has only a small role but one she coveted when the project was first begun in 1937. She knew she would have one fantastic scene where Carlotta goes mad after confronting the scheming Rains and she played it to the hilt; this sequence is a classic, and Davis's descent from the emperor is like watching a candle dim, flicker and go out. She is matched by Sondergaard's velvety villany and this meeting portends their eventual collaboration on THE LETTER.

Designer Orry-Kelly went through painstaking research before clothing the actors in this most accurate historical film. He also employed what he termed "visual psychology" in showing Davis' decline into insanity, clothing her first in white gowns, then grey, then finally all black. Veteran cinematographer Gaudio adopted the same technique, employing sharp, contrasting scenes at the opening of the film, then, particularly for Davis' scenes, lengthening the shadows down into darkness, with only shafts of hazy light to illuminate the subject.

Despite such overwhelming preparation, JUAREZ did not suit the public's fancy and lost money. However, Dieterle could not be blamed. He went so far as to consult his astrological chart and then began shooting early one morning in October, 1938, since that day, he was convinced, placed the stars most favorably in his personal destiny!

JUBAL
1956 100m c   ★★★½
Western   /PG
Columbia

Glenn Ford *(Jubal Troop)*, Ernest Borgnine *(Shep Horgan)*, Rod Steiger *(Pinky)*, Valerie French *(Mae Horgan)*, Felicia Farr *(Naomi Hoktor)*, Basil Ruysdael *(Shem Hoktor)*, Noah Beery, Jr. *(Sam)*, Charles Bronson *(Reb Haislipp)*, John Dierkes *(Carson)*, Robert Burton *(Dr. Grant)*

p, William Fadiman; d, Delmer Daves; w, Russell Hughes, Delmer Daves (based on the novel *Jubal Troop* by Paul I. Wellman); ph, Charles Lawton, Jr. (CinemaScope, Technicolor); ed, Al Clark; m, David Raksin; art d, Carl Anderson; cos, Jean Louis

Sagebrush Shakespeare—a pistol-packin' *Othello*, deftly done. Shot among the magnificent Grand Teton Mountains of Wyoming, JUBAL is named for its protagonist, Ford, a drifter who arrives in the area and takes a job at the ranch owned by Borgnine. When Borgnine's sensuous wife, French, comes on to Ford, Steiger, her ex-lover, is enraged and plots to get rid of the stranger. French admits her feelings to her husband, so he attacks Ford who kills him. While Steiger is aware of what really happened, he recruits a posse to lynch Ford and beats and rapes French.

Steiger is wonderfully mean in a role not unlike Judd in OKLAHOMA or any of several other villains he's played. The battle lines are drawn early, and the suspense mounts as we wait for the inevitable conclusion between Ford and Steiger. Instead of concentrating on the scenery and the vistas (the way Kasdan did in his imitative SILVERADO), Daves elects to examine humanity, and the result is an unusually good story that could fit in almost any milieu. Charles Bronson, as one of the ranch hands, gives no indication of his coming stardom.

JUDGMENT AT NUREMBERG
1961 190m bw   ★★★★½
Historical/War   /PG
Roxlom

Spencer Tracy *(Judge Dan Haywood)*, Burt Lancaster *(Ernst Janning)*, Richard Widmark *(Col. Tad Lawson)*, Marlene Dietrich *(Mme. Bertholt)*, Maximilian Schell *(Hans Rolfe)*, Judy Garland *(Irene Hoffman)*, Montgomery Clift *(Rudolph Petersen)*, William Shatner *(Capt. Harrison Byers)*, Edward Binns *(Sen. Burkette)*, Kenneth MacKenna *(Judge Kenneth Norris)*

p, Stanley Kramer; d, Stanley Kramer; w, Abby Mann; ph, Ernest Laszlo; ed, Frederic Knudtson; m, Ernest Gold; prod d, Rudolph Sternad; cos, Joe King

For the patient starwatcher, a revelation. JUDGMENT AT NUREMBERG in its day, was a sensation—the first film to deal seriously with the trials of Nazi war criminals.

The chief Allied judge, Dan Haywood (Spencer Tracy), has been sent to Germany after failing to be reelected to the bench in New England, a political payoff that does not go unnoticed by his adversaries. Prosecuting attorney Tad Lawson (Richard Widmark), an Army colonel, indicts several Germans who have committed war crimes in enforcing Hitler's mad mandates. In his defense of them, Hans Rolfe (Maximilian Schell) roars that his clients were merely upholding Hitler's laws, and that to place them on trial is to judge all of Germany. Meanwhile, Haywood, in his off hours, wanders the ancient city of Nuremberg trying to understand what went wrong with a whole people and a great culture.

The rest of the cast in this three-hour-plus picture is equally distinguished: Marlene Dietrich is the widow of a German general who was executed for ordering the slaughter of captured American soldiers at Malmedy; Burt Lancaster is an intellectual German judge who unwillingly aided the Nazis; Montgomery Clift is a dim-witted victim of sterilization who testifies for the prosecution; and Judy Garland is a woman who "polluted the Aryan race" by having sex with a Jew.

Originally shown on television as a 1959 Playhouse 90 production, JUDGMENT AT NUREMBERG is absorbing from beginning to end, though unrelentingly bleak. Dietrich and Tracy contribute impressive, seemingly effortless work: their scenes together capture the uniqueness of the German term *weltschmerz*—a nostalgic longing—now more than ever, with Dietrich's passing. At the other end of the acting spectrum are Clift and Garland, offering harrowing, naked perfomances. Yes these are stars doing star turns. NUREMBERG reminds us of how they can blend in a dizzying cohesion, setting up an interesting tension.

JUGGERNAUT

1974 109m c   ★★★½
Thriller   PG
UA

Richard Harris *(Fallon)*, Omar Sharif *(Capt. Brunel)*, David Hemmings *(Charlie Braddock)*, Anthony Hopkins *(Supt. John McCleod)*, Shirley Knight *(Barbara Banister)*, Ian Holm *(Nicholas Porter)*, Clifton James *(Mr. Corrigan)*, Roy Kinnear *(Social Director Curain)*, Caroline Mortimer *(Susan McCleod)*, Mark Burns *(1st Officer Hollingsworth)*

p, Richard DeKoker; d, Richard Lester; w, Richard DeKoker, Alan Plater; ph, Gerry Fisher (DeLuxe Color); ed, Anthony Gibbs; m, Ken Thorne; prod d, Terence Marsh; art d, Alan Tomkins; fx, John Richardson

Jolly well done. Sharif plays the captain of an ocean liner upon which several bombs have been planted by Jones, a demolitions expert who demands a ransom not to blow up the ship at sea. Back on shore, the superintendent in charge of the case (Hopkins) brings extra concern to his work on the crisis because his wife, Mortimer, is one of the hostages. A team of experts, including Harris and Hemmings, is dispatched to the ship by helicopter to defuse the bombs. The rest of the film is a tense battle between the bomb experts and Jones, who stays on the telephone to taunt the crisis-intervention team with details about his plot.

Lester, known mainly for his comedy work (A HARD DAY'S NIGHT), does a good job of keeping viewers on the edge of their seats. And JUGGERNAUT, far more than a disaster picture, is a telling statement about England's troubles, the country neatly symbolized by the liner itself. The film captures perfecly the atmosphere of an over-hyped "luxury" liner. Harris gives a terrific performance and this is the best work ever done by Sharif, thanks to apt casting as the slimy ship captain.

JUGGLER, THE

1953 84m bw   ★★★½
Drama   /A
Columbia

Kirk Douglas *(Hans Muller)*, Milly Vitale *(Ya'El)*, Paul Stewart *(Detective Karni)*, Joseph Walsh *(Yehoshua Bresler)*, Alf Kjellin *(Daniel)*, Beverly Washburn *(Susy)*, Charles Lane *(Rosenberg)*, John Banner *(Emile Halevy)*, Richard Benedict *(Kogan)*, Oscar Karlweis *(Willy Schmidt)*

p, Stanley Kramer; d, Edward Dmytryk; w, Michael Blankfort (based on the novel by Michael Blankfort); ph, J. Roy Hunt; ed, Aaron Stell; m, George Antheil; art d, Robert Peterson

A tight little sleeper. Douglas is a German Jew who survived the Nazi concentration camps but lost his wife and children. He was a famous juggler before the war and now finds himself with thousands of other displaced persons in Israel.

When he arrives in a temporary camp, his actions are odd enough to merit notice by the camp psychiatrist. He runs away on his first night and is followed by Benedict, an Israeli cop, who finally stops him and wants to see his papers. Douglas immediately flashes back to when a Nazi asked the same thing, and he knocks Benedict out, then flees. Douglas escapes Haifa and makes his way to Mount Carmel where he spends the night. In the morning Douglas, now pursued by detective Stewart, is discovered by several children who tell him he is an American tourist. Walsh, one of the young boys, is traveling to a kibbutz

near Syria and Douglas joins him. Douglas wants to get to Egypt where he has some friends who he feels will help him.

A terrific movie in many ways, THE JUGGLER is a small-scale, almost intimate film that quietly depicts the sadness of a man looking for a home and a purpose following the war. The main character is not a heroic figure, but a deeply troubled man trying to make some sense out of life. Douglas, in one of his most restrained performances, is quite good at conveying the man's torment and confusion. Paul Stewart, one of the original Mercury Players on radio who made his film debut in CITIZEN KANE, is also good as the compassionate detective who does his best to reassure Douglas. Young Walsh nicely complements Douglas and their scenes together are often touching without being overly sentimental. Walsh went on to become a writer, scripting such films as BON VOYAGE and CALIFORNIA SPLIT.

JULES AND JIM

(JULES ET JIM)
1962 110m bw   ★★★★★
Drama   /15
Carosse (France)

Jeanne Moreau *(Catherine)*, Oskar Werner *(Jules)*, Henri Serre *(Jim)*, Marie Dubois *(Therese)*, Vanna Urbino *(Gilberte)*, Sabine Haudepin *(Sabine)*, Boris Bassiak *(Albert)*, Kate Noelle *(Birgitta)*, Anny Nelsen *(Lucie)*, Christiane Wagner *(Helga)*

p, Marcel Berbert; d, Francois Truffaut; w, Francois Truffaut, Jean Gruault (based on the novel by Henri-Pierre Roche); ph, Raoul Coutard (Franscope); ed, Claudine Bouche; m, Georges Delerue; cos, Fred Capel

Francois Truffaut's greatest achievement, JULES AND JIM is a shrine to lovers who have known obsession and been destroyed by it.

The film begins in Paris in 1912 when two writers—Jules (Oskar Werner), a shy German, and Jim (Henri Serre), a dark-haired Parisian—become obsessed with an ancient stone carving of a woman. Their life changes when they meet Catherine (Jeanne Moreau), the personification of the stone goddess, whose smile enchants both men. Jules begins to court her, but only with Jim's blessing.

The three become great friends, though Catherine's unpredictability flares whenever she feels she is being ignored. (At one point, she jumps into the Seine when Jules and Jim's heated discussion of a Strindberg play does not include her.) Although Catherine gives Jules a child, Sabine (the adorable, bespectacled Sabine Haudepin), her ever-changing moods are not those of a mother or a wife, and she begins an affair with Jim. Jules, however, refuses to leave her, or even to get angry—he only wants to be near her and his friend.

The film is a celebration both of love and cinema, as Truffaut directs with equal concern for his characters and for film technique—one never overshadowing the other. Scripted from Henri-Pierre Roche's novel, the screenplay has not a wasted word or gesture, with every element working together perfectly to create three unique and interdependent characters. As much in love with Catherine as Jules and Jim are, Truffaut photographs her with the greatest love and admiration. Just as Jules and Jim respond lovingly to Catherine's every move, and just as the camera swirls and dollies around the ancient stone carving in the film's early scenes, so too does Truffaut's filmmaking revolve around the great Moreau, who returns the compliment with one of the most memorable performances in cinema history. The duality she establishes is timeless—and very timely.

Like many women, Moreau's Catherine wants to be an equal of men, yet she uses her feminine mystique to assert the uniqueness of being the woman in the union. She is free to leave, but if you leave her she expects you to understand and respect her pain. Does any other film or performance in cinema history capture so accurately the mystery modern women entail for men? Nor does any other film ever made capture so fully the bohemianism between the World Wars. And Truffaut never intrudes upon his narrative; so much is left for us to project we genuinely become *involved*.

JULIA

1977 116m c   ★★★
Biography   PG/A
FOX

Jane Fonda (*Lillian Hellman*), Vanessa Redgrave (*Julia*), Jason Robards, Jr. (*Dashiell Hammett*), Maximilian Schell (*Johann*), Hal Holbrook (*Alan Campbell*), Rosemary Murphy (*Dorothy Parker*), Meryl Streep (*Anne Marie*), Dora Doll, Elisabeth Mortensen (*Train Passengers*), John Glover (*Sammy*)

p, Richard Roth; d, Fred Zinnemann; w, Alvin Sargent (based on the story in the book *Pentimento* by Lillian Hellman); ph, Douglas Slocombe (Technicolor); ed, Walter Murch, Marcel Durham; m, Georges Delerue; prod d, Willy Holt, Gene Callahan, Carmen Dillon; cos, Anthea Sylbert, Joan Bridge, Annalisa Nasilli-Rocca, John Apperson, Colette Baudot

Beautifully crafted, nominated for nine Academy Awards, a big hit at the box office and now for the real news—misses by a mile. Based on an episode from Lillian Hellman's bestselling memoirs, the film takes place in the 1930s as Fonda, playing the author, lives with Robards in a beach house. She's writing her first play and turns to famed writer Robards for his helpful (and sometimes cruel) criticism.

When it's done and produced successfully, Fonda now can take a rest and decides to visit a childhood friend, Redgrave, with whom she shared some wonderful moments in their youth (shown in flashbacks with Pelikan and Jones as the girls). Redgrave moved to Austria to study medicine with Freud and became a crusader in social matters, joining the antifascists. She was injured in a battle with the Hitler Youth and is now in a hospital in Vienna. Fonda visits Redgrave as she is recovering. Later, on a trip to Moscow, Fonda is asked by Schell, a pal of Redgrave's, if she will smuggle a large sum of money from Russia to Germany where it will be used to aid the effort against the Nazis.

If you like red nail polish, New York Algonquin-set faux cynicism, painfully brave smiles and European train stations, JULIA may be your kind of cocktail. But Redgrave plays Julia as a noble martyr in sensible shoes. Zinneman doesn't feel responsible about explaining her dangerous commitment; not everyone takes these kind of risks over injustice. Heck, Anti-fascism themes are old hat, but you didn't see Betty Grable smuggling guns in France. The director and writers think it's enough to have Redgrave before the camera because we identify her as a crusader.

Fonda's Hellman is a prig with writer's block and low self-image. Her relationship with Hammett and Julia, too, looks like hero-worship. The script, the direction and finally, Fonda's acting choices capture none of the piss and vinegar that made Hellman a true original.

JULIET OF THE SPIRITS

(GIULIETTA DEGLI SPIRITI)
1965 148m c   ★★★½
Drama   /18
Federiz/Francoriz/Rizzoli/Eichberg (France/Italy/
West Germany)

Giulietta Masina (*Juliet*), Alba Cancellieri (*Juliet as a Child*), Mario Pisu (*Giorgio*), Caterina Boratto (*Juliet's Mother*), Luisa Della Noce (*Adele*), Sylva Koscina (*Sylva*), Sabrina Gigli, Rosella di Sepio (*Granddaughters*), Lou Gilbert (*Grandfather*), Valentina Cortese (*Valentina*)

p, Angelo Rizzoli; d, Federico Fellini; w, Federico Fellini, Tullio Pinelli, Ennio Flaiano, Brunello Rondi (based on a story by Fellini, Pinelli); ph, Gianni De Venanzo (Technicolor); ed, Ruggero Mastroianni; m, Nino Rota; art d, Piero Gherardi; cos, Piero Gherardi

Gaudy, more integrated than later Fellini, but this take on feminine psyche lacks vision. Juliet's fantasies might have been culled from Hollywood back lots, suggesting women have colorful imaginations, but not much in the brain department.

Juliet (Giulietta Masina) is a married woman in her mid-30s, more or less resigned to a dull life with her dull husband, Giorgio (Mario Pisu), who pays her little attention. At first she thinks it's just the pressures of business that cause him to be so indifferent, but soon she begins to wonder if he may have someone else. One night, Giorgio and some friends hold a seance, and Juliet discovers that she can conjure up various spirits. These wraiths tell her that she deserves some enjoyment in life and should give herself a treat. To see if her suspicions about Giorgio are correct, Juliet hires a sleuth who corroborates her worst fears, causing her to change her lifestyle and move out from the shadow of her unloving husband.

A feminized version of 8½—both Masina's and Pisu's characters drift in and out of fantasy in order to come to grips with reality—JULIET OF THE SPIRITS will likely appeal to fans of that previous Fellini picture. This was his first color feature, and the results are spectacular and festive.

JULIUS CAESAR

1952 83m bw   ★★
Historical   /U
Avon

Harold Tasker (*Julius Caesar*), Robert Holt (*Octavius Caesar*), Charlton Heston (*Marcus Antonius*), Theodore Cloak (*Emil Lepidus*), David Bradley (*Brutus*), Grosvenor Glenn (*Cassius*), William Russell (*Casca*), Frederick Roscoe (*Decius*), Arthur Sus (*Cinna*), Cornelius Peeples (*Popilius*)

p, David Bradley; d, David Bradley; w, David Bradley (based on the play by William Shakespeare); m, John Becker

Innovative approach to a classic. One of the two "unofficial" films (the other being PEER GYNT) Heston appeared in before his 1950 "debut" film, DARK CITY. Independently produced in and around the Chicago area, it tells the familiar tale of Caesar, with Heston cast as Marc Antony, a role he would again tackle in 1970's JULIUS CAESAR. With a budget of less than $15,000, director Bradley was forced to rely on ingenuity: for example, shooting Caesar's funeral on the steps of Chicago's Museum of Science and Industry—a building modeled after early Roman architecture. Interesting more as a novelty than anything else, though it is a more-than-capable piece of filmmaking.

JULIUS CAESAR

1953   120m   bw   ★★★★½
Historical   /U
MGM

Marlon Brando (Marc Antony), Louis Calhern (Julius Caesar), John Gielgud (Cassius), Edmond O'Brien (Casca), Greer Garson (Calpurnia), Deborah Kerr (Portia), George Macready (Marullus), Michael Pate (Flavius), Richard Hale (Soooothsayer), Alan Napier (Cicero)

p, John Houseman; d, Joseph L. Mankiewicz; w, Joseph L. Mankiewicz (based on the play by William Shakespeare); ph, Joseph Ruttenberg; ed, John Dunning; m, Miklos Rozsa; art d, Cedric Gibbons, Edward Carfagno; fx, Warren Newcombe; cos, Herschel McCoy

Lavish, starstruck and for the most part, splendid. When John Houseman and Joseph Mankiewicz, brother of Herman, decided to film Shakespeare's *Julius Caesar*, they picked an elegant and distinguished cast—Mason, Gielgud, Calhern, O'Brien—but they also shocked the industry and not a few literary scholars by selecting Brando to play Marc Antony. He was then still known as "The Mumbler" and "The Slob," for his brutish performance as Stanley Kowalski in A STREETCAR NAMED DESIRE. But Brando turned that opinion about in a startling performance.

Calhern, as Caesar, has by 44 B.C. become virtual dictator of the Roman Empire, with power of such staggering magnitude that Cassius (Gielgud), Casca (O'Brien), and others plan to assassinate him. The plotters convince Brutus (Mason), one of the most influential Romans alive, to join their conspiracy. Though a moralist and full of conscience, as well as being one of Caesar's best friends, Brutus believes, like the others, that the only way to stave off Caesar's tyranny is to kill him. Caesar's superstitious wife, Calpurnia (Garson), has a dream in which she sees her husband slain at the hands of friends, and she warns him not to attend the Senate the next day, the Ides of March. Caesar laughs off the nightmare and proceeds to the Senate. Artemidorus (Farley) warns Caesar as he approaches the Senate of his impending bloody fate, but Caesar ignores him.

JULIUS CAESAR was the brainchild of Houseman and Mankiewicz, the producer having worked with Orson Welles and the Mercury Players on the 1937 version of *Caesar*. Houseman, who had been lobbying to make the film for years, heard that the property was seriously being considered and contacted studio boss Dore Schary, saying that if he were not named the producer he would leave MGM. The studio reluctantly agreed, but did not expect much from this production. Films based on the works of the immortal Bard had been box-office poison at best, especially ROMEO AND JULIET, produced by MGM in 1936, starring Leslie Howard and Norma Shearer, a pet project of then-production chief Irving Thalberg. But this film surprisingly turned in a considerable profit, much of which was due to the astounding performance of Brando as Marc Antony, a role first intended for Paul Scofield, and then for Leo Genn or Charlton Heston.

Brando was approached by Mankiewicz with the idea of playing the role, and he almost passed out, stating: "Oh, my God!" Brando worked feverishly on the part and sought out costar Gielgud's help. The accomplished British thespian helped Brando with his timing and delivery, working with him on his speech patterns particularly, so that when he delivered the "Friends, Romans and countrymen" speech, he was a cultured and eloquent leader of men, and anything but "The Slob." It was an amazing performance, aided mightily by Mankiewicz, who kept cutting to the crowd to get reaction to Brando's speech and then back to Brando to reinforce his effectiveness.

The production is superb on every level and is undoubtedly the best JULIUS CAESAR ever put on film. One British critic went even further, confessing: "It is maddening to be forced to admit it, but it has been left to Hollywood to make the finest film version of Shakespeare yet to be seen on our screens." Performances aside, this is clearly Mankiewicz's film, expertly crafted from every angle, with the mob and murder scenes adroitly fixed. (Mankiewicz's handling of crowds in this production was wholly unlike the unwieldy mess he made of the hordes of extras he flooded into CLEOPATRA a decade later, when he almost bankrupted Fox Studios.) Much of the film's effectiveness was due, according to Mankiewicz, to its being shot in black and white when the studio pushed for color. In this way, the director later claimed, he could simulate an almost newsreel approach to the historic events.

JUNGLE BOOK, THE

1967   78m   c   ★★★½
Children's/Animated   G/U
Disney

VOICES OF: Phil Harris (Baloo the Bear), Sebastian Cabot (Bagheera the Panther), Louis Prima (King Louie of the Apes), George Sanders (Shere Khan the Tiger), Sterling Holloway (Kaa the Snake), J. Pat O'Malley (Col. Hathi the Elephant), Bruce Reitherman (Mowgli the Man Cub), Verna Felton, Clint Howard (Elephants), Chad Stuart Lord

p, Walt Disney; d, Wolfgang Reitherman; w, Larry Clemmons, Ralph Wright, Ken Anderson, Vance Gerry (based on the "Mowgli" stories in The Jungle Book by Rudyard Kipling); ed, Tom Acosta, Norman Carlisle; m, George Bruns; anim, Milt Kahl, Franklin Thomas, Oliver M. Johnston, Jr., John Lounsbery

A witty animated feature from Disney based on the famous Rudyard Kipling stories. Abandoned as a child, Mowgli is raised by wolves, then befriended by a panther who attempts to return him to civilization until the beast realizes that the wolf-boy doesn't want to leave the jungle. Mowgli's happy-go-lucky trail leads to a meeting with a lazy bear, a kidnapping by monkeys, and an encounter with a fire-fearing tiger. In the finale, Mowgli sees a beautiful young girl with whom he falls in love, finally forsaking jungle life to be with her.

The last animated film to be directly overseen by Walt Disney himself, JUNGLE BOOK contains some great visual laughs and is low on sticky sentiment, but the sketchy animation style strains to be modern and looks careless instead. Well-known personalities are particularly effective in providing the voices, notably Phil Harris, Louis Prima, and especially George Sanders. Released ten months after Disney's death, the film went on to be one of the studio's most successful pictures.

JUNGLE BOOK, THE

1942   108m   c   ★★★★
Adventure   /U
UA

Sabu (Mowgli), Joseph Calleia (Buldeo), John Qualen (The Barber), Frank Puglia (The Pundit), Rosemary DeCamp (Messua), Patricia O'Rourke (Mahala), Ralph Byrd (Durga), John Mather (Rao), Faith Brook (English Girl), Noble Johnson (Sikh)

p, Alexander Korda; d, Zoltan Korda; w, Laurence Stallings (based on the books by Rudyard Kipling); ph, Lee Garmes (Technicolor); ed, William Hornbeck; m, Miklos Rozsa; prod d, Vincent Korda; fx, Lawrence Butler

Colorful Korda production, fine family fare. This loose adaptation of Rudyard Kipling's *Jungle Books* stars Sabu as Mowgli, a young man raised by wolves who returns to his native village with no idea of human language or customs.

Once he acquires speech, he captivates Mahala (Patricia O'Rourke), the daughter of the aged Buldeo (Joseph Calleia), with tales of the jungle and his animal friends. Mowgli and Mahala trek into the jungle and discover ruins of a lost civilization, filled with treasures. When Mahala returns to the village with a gold coin, her father tries to get Mowgli to divulge the gold's location, but the boy refuses, fearing the village will be corrupted. Buldeo then turns others against the lad, who is sentenced to be burned at the nearest convenient stake.

Shot outside Los Angeles, the film features dazzling photography, expressive animals and a brilliant Miklos Rozsa score, with individual themes for each animal. An enchanting film for viewers of all ages.

JUNGLE FEVER

1991　132m　c　　　　　　　　　　★★★½
Drama/Romance　　　　　　　　　　R/18
Fever Films/40 Acres and a Mule Filmworks

Wesley Snipes *(Flipper Purify)*, Annabella Sciorra *(Angie Tucci)*, Spike Lee *(Cyrus)*, Ossie Davis *(The Good Reverend Doctor Purify)*, Ruby Dee *(Lucinda Purify)*, Samuel L. Jackson *(Gator Purify)*, Lonette McKee *(Drew)*, John Turturro *(Paulie Carbone)*, Frank Vincent *(Mike Tucci)*, Anthony Quinn *(Lou Carbone)*

p, Spike Lee; d, Spike Lee; w, Spike Lee; ph, Ernest Dickerson; ed, Sam Pollard; m, Terence Blanchard; prod d, Wynn Thomas; cos, Ruth E. Carter

Another polemical film about contemporary race relations from writer-director Spike Lee, JUNGLE FEVER offers a host of well-acted, thought-provoking dramatic situations, wrapped in one mess of a story.

Flipper Purify (Wesley Snipes) is a black urban professional, a New York architect with a promising future and a devoted family. Out of sexual curiousity, he and Angie Tucci (Annabella Sciorra), an Italian-American office temp, begin an affair which causes or exacerbates a number of domestic and social conflicts in their neighborhoods. Flipper confides in his friend Cyrus (Spike Lee) about his fling and the news soon reaches Flipper's wife Drew (Lonette McKee), who angrily throws him out of the house. Angie remains more discreet, but her territorial father and brothers find out about her affair and violently abuse her for dating outside her race, ethnic group and neighborhood.

Meanwhile, other problems develop for those around Flipper and Angie. Flipper's crack-addicted brother, Gator (Samuel L. Jackson), continually hustles him for money. Their parents suffer both sons: the puritanical father, the "Good Reverend" (Ossie Davis), harshly condemns both Flipper's infidelity and Gator's drug dealing. Gator continually returns to his forgiving mother for money, but when she runs out of it he attacks her. The good reverend shoots him dead. Across town Angie's father is trying to match his daughter to an Italian boyfriend, Paulie Carbone (John Turturro). The tender-hearted Paulie, however, has a crush on a black woman who patronizes his news stand. Angie and Paulie commiserate about the abuse they have to endure in seeing life beyond the confines of their Bensonhurst neighborhood.

Ironically, JUNGLE FEVER's central relationship—between the uppish buppie and the self-reliant, working-class white girl— may be the least interesting one. Flipper and Angie only have "jungle fever," a passing curiousity picqued by society's long-held sexual myths about race. Though Wesley Snipes and An-

nabella Sciorra perform well, the script provides no deeper motivations or meanings for their relationship. Situations around them prove more interesting and dynamic.

Samuel L. Jackson steals several scenes as the jive-talking, dancing-for-drugs crackhead brother. His dramatic family confrontations provide the movie's real emotional intensity. By comparison, the arguments between Flipper and Drew come across as melodramatic. Yet the film's most subtle, sympathetic interplay happens across the tracks, through the eyes of the gentle Paulie. Although tied down by his possessive father and harassed by his belligerent neighbors, he is the one who sees and loves people regardless of their race, class or color. John Turturro's portrayal of the kind-hearted kid from Brooklyn is a pleasant, surprising follow-up to his role as the bitter young racist in Lee's DO THE RIGHT THING.

While these storylines lack any interlocking unity, the film as a whole is held together by an ambitious and aggressive stylistic treatment of its cinematography and music. Lee once again collaborates with the gifted cameraman Ernest Dickerson, who repeats his elaborately swirling, swooping camera movements and wild, confrontational camera angles. The stylistic quirks shift from scene to narratively disjointed scene, but the same creative hand can be felt guiding them all.

The film's most visceral scene, an interlude shot like a music video, comes when Flipper combs the crackhouses looking for Gator. To the loud strains of Stevie Wonder's "Livin' for the City," we see a harrowing and hyper-realistic portrait of an urban drug district. Presumably an answer to those who criticized DO THE RIGHT THING for its drug-free ghetto, the scene ends with a camera slowly pulling back to reveal (in a fashion like GONE WITH THE WIND's famous depiction of wounded confederate masses) an immense army of lifeless crack addicts.

The film's sudden, problematic ending leaves these cinematic and social messes and messages unresolved. But, whatever its gaping narrative flaws, JUNGLE FEVER is another provocative and ultimately commendable entry in Spike Lee's canon of flashy, entertaining, topical dramas that examine controversial issues from an African-American perspective.

JUNIOR BONNER

1972　100m　c　　　　　　　　　　★★★½
Western/Sports　　　　　　　　　　PG/A
ABC

Steve McQueen *(Junior Bonner)*, Robert Preston *(Ace Bonner)*, Ida Lupino *(Elvira Bonner)*, Ben Johnson *(Buck Roan)*, Joe Don Baker *(Curly Bonner)*, Barbara Leigh *(Charmagne)*, Mary Murphy *(Ruth Bonner)*, Bill McKinney *(Red Terwiliger)*, Sandra Deel *(Nurse Arlis)*, Don "Red" Barry *(Homer Rutledge)*

p, Joe Wizan; d, Sam Peckinpah; w, Jeb Rosebrook; ph, Lucien Ballard (Todd-AO, Movielab Color); ed, Robert Wolfe; m, Jerry Fielding; art d, Ted Haworth

A trifle clumsy, but affecting nonetheless. Steve McQueen stars in this Sam Peckinpah-directed film as the title character, an aging rodeo cowboy who returns to his small hometown of Prescott, Arizona, and learns that nothing stays the same. Saddened to discover that his parents (Lupino and Preston) have split and that his brother (Baker) is getting rich selling off parcels of his father's land, Junior tries to regain his self-esteem by staying on a previously unrideable bull at the town's annual Fourth of July rodeo.

There's much to recommend here, including some fine rodeo footage, winning characterizations from Johnson as the man who supplies the livestock for the rodeo and from Taylor as the owner of the bar, and an especially strong performance by McQueen as the cowboy who realizes that he can't go home on the range again. Lupino and Preston are especially fine among a good supporting cast. But the territory covered is similar to Nick Ray's earlier, superior THE LUSTY MEN.

JUST A GIGOLO

1979 98m c ★★★
Drama R/15
Leguan (West Germany)

David Bowie (Paul), Sydne Rome (Cilly), Kim Novak (Helga), David Hemmings (Capt. Kraft), Marlene Dietrich (Baroness von Semering), Maria Schell (Mutti), Curt Jurgens (Prince), Erika Pluhar (Eva), Rudolf Schundler (Gustav), Hilde Weissner (Aunt Hilda)

d, David Hemmings; w, Joshua Sinclair, Ennio De Concini; ph, Charly Steinberger; ed, Susan Jaeger, Fred Srp, Maxine Julius; m, Gunther Fischer; art d, Peter Rothe; chor, Herbert F. Schubert; cos, Ingrid Zore

Tragically, a misfire. This interesting (if only for its cast) tale of a Prussian WWI veteran who returns to Berlin, torn between wealthy, older women and homosexual Nazis, cannot find itself. Is it farce or melodrama? Bowie has some startling moments, but his overall performance languishes in uncertainty.

The underrated Rome provides a definite energy lift to the proceedings, but everyone else is reduced to doing star turns. It's surprising to find Hemmings photographed in such a singularly unflattering manner in his own movie. Perhaps he exhausted all his resources filming Miss Dietrich's cameo: she's a grande dame madam who wanders on long enough, veiled and diffused to the max, to croak the title song, before adding Bowie to her stable. It's a hypnotic swansong—visually and vocally—a fitting farewell to the last of the golden age goddesses.

Another goddess from another era, the still-lucious Novak, turns in a commanding portrayal of a lusty widow. The period mood, soundtrack and use of color are never less than first-rate. Yet the film, reduced from its original 147-minute running length, flounders badly.

JUST BEFORE NIGHTFALL

(JUSTE AVANT LA NUIT)
1975 100m c ★★
Crime PG/X
Boetie/Cinegai/Columbia (France/Italy)

Stephane Audran (Helen), Michel Bouquet (Charles), Francois Perier (Francois), Jean Carmet (Jeannot), Dominique Zardi (Prince), Henri Attal (Cavanna), Paul Temps (Bardin), Marina Ninchi (Ginette), Clelia Matania (Mme. Masson), Anna Douking (Laura)

p, Andre Genoves; d, Claude Chabrol; w, Claude Chabrol (based on the novel The Thin Line by Edouard Atiyah); ph, Jean Rabier (Eastmancolor); ed, Jacques Gaillard; m, Pierre Jansen; art d, Guy Littaye

A surburban crime melodrama from French New Wave director Chabrol that opens as Parisian advertising man Bouquet strangles his mistress, the wife of his best friend, Perier. His guilt goes undetected by the police, but he cannot live with his crime.

He pitifully tells his wife, Audran, of his affair and the subsequent murder. She accepts the news with surprising calm, talking him out of turning himself in. He then confesses to Perier, who also accepts the news as if he were just told a weather report. Bouquet reveals that his relationship with Perier's wife was a sadomasochistic one, with his act of punishment being carried a bit too far. It is now his turn to be punished, but his confessions only bring solace. One evening (the nightfall of the title representing death) Bouquet quietly dies after taking an overdose of sleeping medicine that his wife has prepared.

As interesting as the plot may seem, JUST BEFORE NIGHTFALL is more concerned with its poke at the middle class than with characterization or pacing. The result is an incredibly slow-moving picture, which is as ugly visually (the modernized, split-level, glassy house they live in is colored with putrid oranges and greens) as the film's psychological themes are. One wishes that Bouquet had strangled Perier, who designed the house, instead of his wife.

JUST TELL ME WHAT YOU WANT

1980 112m c ★★★
Comedy R/
WB

Ali MacGraw (Bones Burton), Alan King (Max Herschel), Myrna Loy (Stella Liberti), Keenan Wynn (Seymour Berger), Tony Roberts (Mike Berger), Peter Weller (Steven Routledge), Sara Truslow (Cathy), Judy Kaye (Baby), Dina Merrill (Connie Herschel), Joseph Maher (Dr. Coleson)

p, Jay Presson Allen, Sidney Lumet; d, Sidney Lumet; w, Jay Presson Allen (based on the novel by Jay Presson Allen); ph, Oswald Morris (Technicolor); ed, John J. Fitzstephens; m, Charles Strouse; prod d, Tony Walton; art d, John J. Moore; cos, Tony Walton, Gloria Gresham

Uneven, mean-spirited, but with some juicy acting. Alan King plays tycoon Max Herschel (some say based on Ray Stark), who is married to the alcoholic, philandering Connie (Dina Merrill).

He maintains liaisons on the side, particularly with Bones Burton (MacGraw, doing the best work of her career), a television producer with whom he has dallied for a long time and who marries Steven Routledge (Peter Weller), a Sam Shepard-like playwright. Myrna Loy is Max's longtime secretary, Stella, who is totally devoted to her boss and privy to all his business and personal involvements; a subplot involves Max's business enemy, an oldtime film potentate (Keenan Wynn), whose gay son (Tony Roberts) is jockeying to become an executive at a major studio.

Your opinion of the film depends on whether or not you can tap into the sacre monstre King expertly plays, and the New York Jewish "angst" inherent in the screenplay's erratic pace (the second half looks poorly edited), but there are some very funny scenes and all the parts are richly acted. A curious little sleeper.

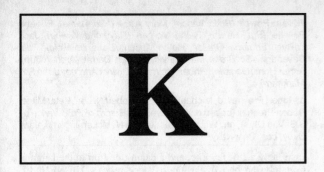

KAGEMUSHA

1980   179m   c   ★★★★
Drama/War   PG
Toho/Kurosawa   (Japan)

Tatsuya Nakadai (Shingen Takeda/Kagemusha), Tsutomu Yamazaki (Nobukado Takeda), Kenichi Hagiwara (Katsuyori Takeda), Kota Yui (Takemaru), Shuji Otaki (Yamagata), Hideo Murata (Baba), Daisuke Ryu (Oda), Kaori Momoi (Otsuyanokata)

p, Akira Kurosawa; d, Akira Kurosawa; w, Akira Kurosawa, Masato Ide; ph, Takao Saito, Shoji Ueda, Kazuo Miyagawa, Asaichi Nakai (Eastmancolor); m, Shinichiro Ikebe; art d, Yoshiro Muraki

After a long period of inactivity, Akira Kurosawa returned to the genre of which he is the unparalleled master, the samurai film.

Tatsuya Nakadai plays a 16th-century warlord, Shingen Takeda, who uses doubles for himself on the battlefield, instilling confidence and fear through his constant presence while his clan fights to establish dominance in Japan. When Shingen is killed, his current "shadow warrior" or *kagemusha*—in actuality a petty thief (again powerfully played by Tatsuya Nakadai)—must take over so that the army's morale will not die. Trained in secret by Shingen's assistants, the double genuinely begins to acquire some of his master's attributes, but the masquerade becomes increasingly difficult to maintain.

Kurosawa's epic is alive with color, the spectacular visuals overlying a somber exploration of traditionalism, honor loyalty, and identity, played out against a sumptuous tapestry of political intrigue and the 16th-century clan warfare that came to an end with the Tokugawa *shogunate*. The massive battle scenes rank with the director's best, using brilliant color, contrasting light, and the enormous cast to great advantage. Kurosawa also alternates compelling scenes of near hypnotic stillness with scenes of rousing action. Sadly the film's score is a noisy irritant.

Made and distributed with the financial aid and clout of George Lucas and Francis Ford Coppola, KAGEMUSHA prefigured and paved the way for the great RAN, Kurosawa's epic adaptation of *King Lear*.

KAMERADSCHAFT

1931   93m   bw   ★★★★
Drama
Nero/Gaumont/Franco-Film-Aubert   (Germany)

Fritz Kampers (Wilderer), Gustav Puttjer (Kaplan), Alexander Granach (Kaspers), Andree Ducret (Francoise), Georges Charlia (Jean), Ernst Busch (Wittkopp), Daniel Mandaille (Emile), Pierre Louis (Georges), Alex Bernard (Grandfather)

p, Seymour Nebenzal; d, G.W. Pabst; w, Karl Otten, Peter Martin Lampel, Ladislas Vajda; ph, Fritz Arno Wagner, Robert Baberske; ed, Hans Oser

This stirring plea for peace and internationalism was the high-point of German socialist filmmaking of its period. KAMERADSCHAFT, a German-French co-production set in the Lorraine mining region on the French-German border in the aftermath of WWI, was inspired by an actual 1906 mining disaster that claimed 1,200 lives.

Combining elements of classic German expressionism and and Soviet Socialist realism, German director G.W. Pabst (STREET OF SORROW, PANDORA'S BOX, THE THREE-PENNY OPERA) introduces the viewer to the German and French miners. Separated by mine walls and metal bars below and by armed border patrols above, they have little contact with one another. But when a series of explosions causes a cave-in on the French side, the hearts of the Germans go out to them. Wittkopp (Ernst Busch) appeals to his bosses to send a rescue team while, underground, a trio of German miners breaks through a set of steel bars that marks the 1919 border. Meanwhile, on the French side, an elderly retired miner (Alex Bernard) sneaks into the shaft, hoping to rescue his young grandson, Georges (Pierre Louis).

Although occasionally overly sentimental, Pabst's plea for a peaceful future is sincere and compelling. His direction of the heartbreak and devastation is enhanced by the brilliant photography of Fritz Arno Wagner and Robert Baberske and the alarmingly authentic set design is provided by by Erno Metzner and Karl Vollbrecht.

KANAL

1957   96m   bw   ★★★★
War   /X
Film Polski   (Poland)

Teresa Izewska (Daisy Stokrotka), Tadeusz Janczar (Cpl. Korab), Wienczyslaw Glinski (Lt. Zadra), Tadeusz Gwiazdowski (Sgt. Kula), Stanislaw Mikulski (The Slim), Vladek Sheybal (Composer), Zofia Lindorf

p, Stanislaw Adler; d, Andrzej Wajda; w, Jerzy Stefan Stawinski (based on a short story by Stawinski); ph, Jerzy Lipman; ed, Halina Nawrocka; m, Jan Krenz; art d, Roman Mann; cos, Jerzy Szeski

This extremely intense and relentlessly graphic second feature from Polish filmmaker Andrzej Wajda takes place during the final days of the Warsaw Uprising in 1944. Three groups of Poles, no longer able to hold off the enemy, retreat to the city's *kanaly*, or sewer system. The viewer is told from the very start to "watch them closely; these are the last hours of their lives." With this pessimistic tone established, we observe them as they try to escape and live an underground existence free from the oppression and lost ideals of their lives above ground. Although we know that death awaits them, we also know that freedom from the sewers is only a relative freedom.

Wajda spares the viewer nothing, showing death, betrayal, suffering, suicide, capture, and despair. Still the Poles fight on in the hope that they will see sunlight pouring into the sewer, even if it is filtered through a metal grate.

KANCHENJUNGHA

1966   102m   c   ★★★★
Drama
N.C.A.   (India)

Chhabi Biswas (Indranath Choudhuri), Karuni Bannerjee (Labanya), Anil Chatterjee (Anil), Nilima Roy Chowdhury (Monisha), Anubhe Gupta (Anima), Subrata Sen Sharma (Shankar), Arun Mukherjee (Ashoke), N. Viswanathan (Bannerjee), Pahari Sanyal (Jagadish), Indrani Singh (Tuklu)

p, Satyajit Ray; d, Satyajit Ray; w, Satyajit Ray; ph, Subrata Mitra (Eastmancolor); ed, Dulal Dutta; m, Satyajit Ray; art d, Bansi Chandragupta

One of Indian master filmmaker Satyajit Ray's most completely realized human portraits, the first time he worked in color, and a film with an interesting structure: Ray juxtaposes the India of the valleys with the India of the mountain hill stations to interesting symbolic effect.

Wealthy industrialist Indranath Choudhuri (Biswas) and his family vacation in Darjeeling. The family's problems are brought out into the open and some attempt is made at solving them. The positions of the characters emerge on circling terraces on the hillside during a strictly formalized series of walks that soon take on a subtle musical structure. Evident throughout is the conflict between the old and the young, ancient customs and modern life.

KARATE KID, THE
1984 126m c   ★★★½
Sports
Columbia   PG/15

Ralph Macchio (Daniel), Noriyuki "Pat" Morita (Miyagi), Elisabeth Shue (Ali), Martin Kove (Kreese), Randee Heller (Lucille), William Zabka (Johnny), Ron Thomas (Bobby), Rob Garrison (Tommy), Chad McQueen (Dutch), Tony O'Dell (Jimmy)

p, Jerry Weintraub; d, John G. Avildsen; w, Robert Mark Kamen; ph, James Crabe (Metrocolor); ed, Bud Smith, Walt Mulconery, John G. Avildsen; m, Bill Conti; prod d, William J. Cassidy; fx, Frank Toro; chor, Pat E. Johnson; cos, Richard Bruno, Aida Swenson

Totally irresistible, THE KARATE KID treads the same path as ROCKY, and with good reason—it was directed by John Avildsen, who also directed Sylvester Stallone's star-making vehicle. Here's a real old-fashioned movie about teenagers, bullies and the development of self-consciousness.

Daniel (Ralph Macchio) and his mother (Randee Heller) move from Newark, New Jersey, to southern California, where the whole world seems blond and brutal to this hapless ethnic kid. Daniel is immediately set upon by bullies, led by a Hitler Youth-type, Johnny (William Zabka). Daniel's new life grows increasingly unpleasant until he meets Miyagi (Pat Morita), a friendly aged Japanese janitor. Miyagi takes the kid under his wing and begins to teach him about life and karate while getting him to do some chores around the house.

Made for a relative pittance, the way the first ROCKY was, THE KARATE KID reaped a bonanza at the box office. Though shamelessly manipulative, it is undeniably effective. It offers some genuine moments of warmth, humor and excitement. Of course it all leads up to a big tournament where Fair Play has a showdown with Dirty Tricks. Guess who wins. This is the kind of movie where you find yourself cheering even though you know you're being hoodwinked. Naturally the movie gave birth to two sequels and, not surprisingly, neither measures up to the original.

KENNEL MURDER CASE, THE
1933 73m bw   ★★★★★
Mystery
WB

William Powell (Philo Vance), Mary Astor (Hilda Lake), Eugene Pallette (Sgt. Heath), Ralph Morgan (Raymond Wrede), Jack LaRue (Eduardo Grassi), Helen Vinson (Doris Delafield), Paul Cavanagh (Sir Bruce MacDonald), Robert Barrat (Archer Coe), Arthur Hohl (Gamble), Robert McWade (District Attorney John F.X. Markham)

p, Robert Presnell; d, Michael Curtiz; w, Robert N. Lee, Peter Milne, Robert Presnell (based on the novel The Return of Philo Vance by S.S. Van Dine); ph, William Rees; ed, Ed N. McLarnin; art d, Jack Okey; cos, Orry-Kelly

Justifiably a cult favorite, and a damn fine film in the bargain. Certainly the best of the Philo Vance series, THE KENNEL MURDER CASE stars the inimitable Powell for the fourth time as the debonair detective.

Here the mystery involves the members of a Long Island kennel club, and Philo, with the assistance of his Scottie and a prize-winning Doberman, solves a double murder. The plot is full of interesting twists and is eminently serviceable. But the real appeal of this amazing little film is Powell's delightful flair for repartee; it's a pleasure to sit back and let him purr. Astor, too, brings her own special brand of warmth, conviction and appeal to almost everything she does.

The real star of the film, however, is director Michael Curtiz, who races through this flick like a piranha breaking a fast. His exposure to German expressionism pays off handsomely here, and the film is chock full of bizarre compositions, flashy editing, inventive camera angles and memorable camerawork. Fast, foolish, engrossing and unique, this breathtaking little gem is a tribute to both Curtiz's craftsmanship and his fiery temperament. Remade by William Clemens as CALLING PHILO VANCE.

KENTUCKY
1938 95m c   ★★★½
Romance/Sports
FOX

Loretta Young (Sally Goodwin), Richard Greene (Jack Dillon), Walter Brennan (Peter Goodwin), Douglas Dumbrille (John Dillon, 1861), Karen Morley (Mrs. Goodwin, 1861), Moroni Olsen (John Dillon II, 1937), Russell Hicks (Thad Goodwin, Sr., 1861), Willard Robertson (Bob Slocum), Charles Waldron (Thad Goodwin, 1937), George Reed (Ben)

p, Gene Markey; d, David Butler; w, Lamar Trotti, John Taintor Foote (based on the book The Look of Eagles by Foote); ph, Ernest Palmer, Ray Rennahan (Technicolor); ed, Irene Morra; art d, Bernard Herzbrun

This bright, entertaining showcase for the Bluegrass State could justifiably be called "Romeo and Juliet at the Derby." Richard Greene is Jack and Loretta Young plays Sally, lovers from families that have been feuding since the Civil War when Jack's clan took over the stable run by Sally's grandfather. Keeping his lineage a secret, Jack begins training Sally's horse. But just before the Kentucky Derby, as their love affair is heating up, Sally discovers his identity and orders him out of the stable. When race day arrives, it's basically a contest between the rival families' horses. Walter Brennan won his second Best Supporting Actor Oscar in as many years for his strong performance as Sally's uncle, Peter Goodwin, who was there when the feud began and does his best to keep it going.

KENTUCKY FRIED MOVIE, THE

1977   90m   c/bw   ★★★
Comedy   R/18
Kentucky Fried Theatre

Marilyn Joi (Cleopatra), Saul Kahan (Schwartz), Marcy Goldman (Housewife), Joe Medalis (Paul), Barry Dennen (Claude), Rich Gates (Boy), Tara Strohmeier (Girl), Neil Thompson (Newscaster), George Lazenby (Architect), Henry Gibson

p, Robert K. Weiss; d, John Landis; w, David Zucker, Jerry Zucker, Jim Abrahams; ph, Stephen Katz (part DeLuxe Color); ed, George Folsey, Jr.; art d, Rich Harvel; cos, Deborah Nadoolman, Joyce Unruh

A vulgar and uproariously funny college party movie made up of a series of comedy sketches from the Kentucky Fried Theater, a fresh young satirical group formed at the University of Wisconsin at Madison in the early 1970s.

Depending on one's mood, or level of sobriety, it can be a hysterical picture that pokes good natured fun at American movies, TV and commercials. The gags are hurled forth in a fast and furious manner; if you don't like one—fear not—another will be along any second. Memorable segments include "Catholic High School Girls in Trouble," "Cleopatra Schwartz" and "That's Armageddon!" but the most outstanding episode is "A Fistful of Yen," a lengthy kung-fu parody that casts two actual martial arts experts in a surprisingly lavish environment.

Landis has rarely done better work than in this modest early effort. Writers Zucker, Zucker, and Abrahams went on to make the gleefully absurd AIRPLANE and THE NAKED GUN films.

KES

1970   112m   c   ★★★★
Drama   GP/PG
Woodfall/Kestrel   (U.K.)

David Bradley (Billy Casper), Colin Welland (Mr. Farthing), Lynne Perrie (Mrs. Casper), Freddie Fletcher (Jud), Brian Glover (Mr. Sugden), Bob Bowes (Mr. Gryce), Trevor Hasketh (Mr. Crossley), Eric Bolderson (Farmer), Geoffrey Banks (Mathematics Teacher), Zoe Sutherland (Librarian)

p, Tony Garnett; d, Kenneth Loach; w, Kenneth Loach, Tony Garnett, Barry Hines (based on the novel A Kestrel for a Knave by Barry Hines); ph, Chris Menges (DeLuxe Color); ed, Roy Watts; m, John Cameron; art d, William McCrow

Imagine THE 400 BLOWS reconfigured around a working class English boy living in a grimy industrial town and you get some idea of the emotional power of this bleakly realistic film adapted from a novel by Barry Hines.

Billy Casper (Bradley) is the product of a broken home and the victim of school bullies. He takes refuge in his comic books and shoplifting. One day he finds a baby kestrel (a small falcon) and becomes determined to raise the bird. He names it "Kes" and promptly steals a book on falconry. He becomes quite adept at his newfound skills and catches the eye of his teacher, Mr. Farthing (Welland). However his relationship with the beautiful bird cannot ameliorate his depressing home life with his brutish older brother, Jud (Fletcher). Nor does it change the fact that his future options are severely limited by lack of class status, money, or family stability and support.

Though it's a sensitive and heartfelt film, KES never lapses into the sentimentality that often attends these "a boy and his pet" pictures. Ken Loach's low key, clear-eyed direction makes this a fairly unique "children's film." It is aided immeasurably by Chris Menges's naturalistic yet evocative cinematography.

KEY LARGO

1948   101m   bw   ★★★★
Crime   /PG
WB

Humphrey Bogart (Frank McCloud), Edward G. Robinson (Johnny Rocco), Lauren Bacall (Nora Temple), Lionel Barrymore (James Temple), Claire Trevor (Gaye Dawn), Thomas Gomez (Curley), Harry Lewis (Toots), John Rodney (Deputy Clyde Sawyer), Marc Lawrence (Ziggy), Dan Seymour (Angel Garcia)

p, Jerry Wald; d, John Huston; w, Richard Brooks (based on the play by Maxwell Anderson); ph, Karl Freund; ed, Rudi Fehr; m, Max Steiner; art d, Leo K. Kuter; fx, William McGann, Robert Burks; cos, Leah Rhodes

With superb casting and performances, a sharp and resonant screenplay, John Huston's taut direction and Karl Freund's deep-focus photography, KEY LARGO transcends the windy allegories of its theatrical origins to become a suspenseful and entertaining minor classic of 1940s Hollywood.

Based on the play by Maxwell Anderson, Bogart stars as Frank McCloud, a disillusioned WW II veteran who travels to a run-down hotel in Key Largo, Florida, to pay his respects to the family of a buddy who was killed in the war. The hotel is operated by the father of the deceased, James Temple (Barrymore), and the widowed Nora Temple (Bacall). McCloud arrives to find the hotel full of seedy, threatening characters. He can only visit briefly with Nora and Mr. Temple before they must begin preparing for a huge storm which is coming their way.

Soon a group of Seminole Indians arrives in small boats, seeking shelter. Among them are John and Tom Osceola (Silverheels and Redwing), brothers who recently escaped from prison. Sheriff Wade (Blue) and Deputy Sawyer (Rodney) had visited the hotel earlier searching for the fugitives. John tells Nora that he and his brother are ready to give themselves over to the authorities. Meanwhile the massive storm grows closer and closer. McCloud, Nora, and Mr. Temple head inside the hotel where it quickly becomes apparent that the tough-looking "guests" are all criminals. They have waylaid the deputy and are now holding him prisoner in one of the guest rooms. No one will be allowed to leave the premises until they finish their "business."

While all these introductions were being made, the gang's leader has been taking a bath. When the aging gangster finally makes his entrance he is immediately recognized by McCloud as Johnny Rocco, an infamous gangster who had run a huge mob empire until he was deported. He has arrived from Cuba by a ship anchored just off shore. The last major character arrives for the festivities: Gaye Dawn (Trevor), an alcoholic ex-entertainer who is now the girlfriend of the gangster. The storm can finally begin in earnest.

In a film of outstanding performances—Claire Trevor won an Oscar for Best Supporting Actress—Edward G. Robinson deserves special praise. As the fallen crime czar longing for a return to an earlier lawless time, Robinson is spellbinding in a portrayal that echoes his own iconic status in movie history. Though Robinson had at one point grown weary of endlessly repeating the gangster persona he established in LITTLE CAESAR, even parodying the role in BROTHER ORCHID, he resurrected his gangster image here as his final major statement on the genre that brought him stardom.

Though there is some similarity between this THE PETRIFIED FOREST, the Huston film has plenty of character of its own. It's a confrontation of ideologies and psychologies expertly drawn on a common level of understanding.

KHARTOUM

1966 134m c ★★★
Historical R/PG
UA (U.K.)

Charlton Heston (*Gen. Charles Gordon*), Laurence Olivier (*The Mahdi*), Richard Johnson (*Col. J.D.H. Stewart*), Ralph Richardson (*Mr. Gladstone*), Alexander Knox (*Sir Evelyn Baring*), Johnny Sekka (*Khaleel*), Michael Hordern (*Lord Granville*), Zia Mohyeddin (*Zobeir Pasha*), Marne Maitland (*Sheikh Osman*), Nigel Green (*Gen. Wolseley*)

p, Julian Blaustein; d, Basil Dearden; w, Robert Ardrey; ph, Ted Scaife; ed, Fergus McDonell; m, Frank Cordell; art d, John Howell; fx, Richard Parker; cos, John McCorry

This richly photographed historical epic is saved from utter boredom and vacuity by its massive all-star cast and a generous budget. Heston is more impressive than usual in this colorful pageant with his authoritative portrayal of that mystical British general, Sir Charles "Chinese" Gordon, who was killed on January 26, 1885, by fanatical Sudanese tribesmen under the leadership of a religious zealot after they overran Khartoum following a 317-day siege. Gordon, a paradoxical creature, was both realist and idealist, and Heston somehow captures his elusive enigmatic qualities.

Colonel Hicks (Edward Underdown) and the 8,000 untrained Egyptian troops under his command are lured from the El Dueim River and into the desert 100 miles beyond Khartoum. The British-led troops are ambushed by 80,000 fierce Sudanese warriors commanded by the Mahdi and massacred. British Prime Minister Gladstone (Richardson) learns that the Mahdi (Olivier)—"the chosen one"—is fighting a holy war, a jihad, intent upon getting rid of all infidels in the Sudan and taking the great city of Khartoum to prove his power and divine mission. Gordon is sent to try to make peace with the zealot while also finding a way of evacuating the Egyptian army. As he journeys toward Khartoum, he learns that he is no longer respected as a great leader; the natives have shifted their allegiance to the Maudi. However when he arrives in Khartoum, the terrified populace receives him as a savior.

Olivier is fascinating even if seeing a white man in such dark makeup is a bit discomfiting. Olivier had just finished playing Othello in a British production and was perhaps still under the influence of the dark-faced Moor. He is, nevertheless, stunning and frightening. Richardson offers his customary expert performance as Gladstone, infusing the part with cynical amusement. Also outstanding is Johnson as Heston's loyal-unto-death aide and Sekka as Heston's fearless servant. KHARTOUM's vivid color photography is outstanding and the action sequences are visually spectacular due the credit for them is due to Yakima Canutt, the legendary former stuntman turned second unit director, who directed them.

KID FOR TWO FARTHINGS, A

1956 91m c ★★★★
Comedy/Fantasy /U
Big Ben/London Films (U.K.)

Celia Johnson (*Joanne*), Diana Dors (*Sonia*), David Kossoff (*Kandinsky*), Joe Robinson (*Sam*), Jonathan Ashmore (*Joe*), Brenda de Banzie (*"Lady" Ruby*), Vera Day (*Mimi*), Primo Carnera (*Python Macklin*), Sydney Tafler (*Mme. Rita*), Sidney James (*Ice Berg*)

p, Carol Reed; d, Carol Reed; w, Wolf Mankowitz (based on his novel); ph, Ted Scaife (Eastmancolor); ed, Bert Bates; m, Benjamin Frankel; art d, Wilfred Shingleton; cos, Anna Duse

An absolutely charming comedy-fantasy set against the Jewish tradesmen's life in London's Petticoat Lane. Based on the novel by Mankowitz, it's the story of a young boy, Joe (Ashmore), who has been told stories about a unicorn by tailor Kadinsky (Kossoff). When the boy buys a goat with only one horn, he is convinced that he has purchased a unicorn, because "magical" things begin to happen to the denizens of the area.

Kadinsky has one great desire—to own his own steam press. Sonia (Dors) is a buxom blonde who has been waiting for many years to marry muscular Sam (Robinson). She gets her wish when he enters the ring and wins enough money for them to wed. Celia Johnson plays Joanne, Joe's mother, but she doesn't have enough to do to merit her casting. Tafler, a terrific comic actor (MAKE MINE MINK), is again shown to good advantage as a storekeeper, and Canadian character actor Lou Jacobi makes one of his earliest appearances as a wrestling promoter. Naturally, all of the miracles are logically explained, but, to the boy, it's the unicorn that has brought all the happiness to Petticoat Lane.

This is a delightful film, and Reed, working for the first time in color, shows how well he deals with children. He used this ability before in THE FALLEN IDOL and later with the musical version of OLIVER!.

KID FROM SPAIN, THE

1932 118m bw ★★★★
Musical/Comedy /U
Goldwyn

Eddie Cantor (*Eddie Williams*), Lyda Roberti (*Rosalie*), Robert Young (*Ricardo*), Ruth Hall (*Anita Gomez*), John Miljan (*Pancho*), Noah Beery, Sr. (*Alonzo Gomez*), J. Carrol Naish (*Pedro*), Robert Emmett O'Connor (*Detective Crawford*), Stanley Fields (*Jose*), Paul Porcasi (*Gonzales, Border Guard*)

p, Samuel Goldwyn; d, Leo McCarey; w, William Anthony McGuire, Bert Kalmar, Harry Ruby; ph, Gregg Toland; ed, Stuart Heisler; art d, Richard Day; chor, Busby Berkeley; cos, Milo Anderson

A lavish musical vehicle for the immensely popular comic genius Eddie Cantor, THE KID FROM SPAIN is directed by the brilliant Leo McCarey (DUCK SOUP, THE AWFUL TRUTH, RUGGLES OF RED GAP, MAKE WAY FOR TOMORROW) and boasts choreography by the legendary Busby Berkeley just before he hit his hallucinatory stride (42ND STREET, GOLD DIGGERS OF 1933, DAMES). This is Eddie Cantor at his best!

After being tossed out of school, Ricardo (Robert Young) invites his college roommate, Eddie (Eddie Cantor), to his home in Mexico. Their trip becomes a necessity when bank robbers mistake Eddie for their getaway driver, the only person who can identify them. Once they are south of the border, mistaken identity strikes again. This time Eddie is thought to be the offspring of a legendary matador and is forced into the bull ring, though Ricardo has arranged for him to face a tame animal that will stop its charge upon command. However, a rough character involved in one of the story's many subplots substitutes a considerably less docile bull and hilarity results as Eddie does his best not to get gored.

THE KID FROM SPAIN is chock-full of laughs and boasts some fine songs, written mostly by Bert Kalmar and Harry Ruby who co-wrote the screenplay.

KID GALAHAD

1937 101m bw ★★★½
Sports /PG
WB

Edward G. Robinson *(Nick Donati)*, Bette Davis *(Louise "Fluff" Phillips)*, Humphrey Bogart *(Turkey Morgan)*, Wayne Morris *(Kid Galahad/Ward Guisenberry)*, Jane Bryan *(Marie Donati)*, Harry Carey *(Silver Jackson)*, William Haade *(Chuck McGraw)*, Soledad Jiminez *(Mrs. Donati)*, Joe Cunningham *(Joe Taylor)*, Ben Welden *(Buzz Stevens)*

p, Samuel Bischoff; d, Michael Curtiz; w, Seton I. Miller (based on the novel by Francis Wallace); ph, Tony Gaudio; ed, George Amy; m, Heinz Roemheld, Max Steiner; art d, Carl Jules Weyl; fx, James Gibbons, Edwin DuPar; cos, Orry-Kelly

Edward G. Robinson and Humphrey Bogart play rival fight managers in this memorable indictment of corruption in the boxing ring with Wayne Morris in the title role, the first of his three turns as a pugilist (THE KID COMES BACK and THE KID FROM KOKOMO).

When a bellhop (Morris) knocks out highly touted heavyweight Chuck McGraw (William Haade) in defense of the honor of "Fluff" Phillips (Bette Davis), she dubs him Kid Galahad. Her boyfriend, Nick Donati (Robinson), decides to make the young man into a prizefighter. Jealous because both Fluff and her sister appear interested in Kid, Nick arranges a bout with McGraw that he is so certain his fighter will lose that he assures the rival manager Turkey Morgan of the same. Of course, things don't work out as planned. . . .

A solid story with good characterizations and sensational prizefight footage, KID GALAHAD was remade as THE WAGONS ROLL AT NIGHT, with the story switched to a circus, then made again as a fight film with Elvis Presley. To avoid confusion with the Presley movie, the title has been changed to THE BATTLING BELLHOP for television.

KIDNAPPED

1971 100m c ★★★
Adventure G/U
Omnibus (U.K.)

Michael Caine *(Alan Breck)*, Trevor Howard *(Lord Advocate Grant)*, Jack Hawkins *(Capt. Hoseason)*, Donald Pleasence *(Ebenezer Balfour)*, Gordon Jackson *(Charles Stewart)*, Vivien Heilbron *(Catriona Stewart)*, Lawrence Douglas *(David Balfour)*, Freddie Jones *(Cluny Macpherson)*, Andrew McCulloch *(Andrew)*, Eric Woodburn *(Doctor)*

p, Frederick H. Brogger; d, Delbert Mann; w, Jack Pulman (based on the novels *Kidnapped* and *Catriona* by Robert Louis Stevenson); ph, Paul Beeson (Panavision, Movielab Color); ed, Peter Boita; m, Roy Budd; art d, Alex Vetchinsky; fx, Cliff Culley; cos, Olga Lehmann

Originally released in 1938 with Warner Baxter and Freddie Bartholomew in the leads, KIDNAPPED was remade in 1948 with Roddy McDowall and Dan O'Herlihy, then again with James MacArthur and Peter Finch in 1960. This fourth version of Robert Louis Stevenson's novel is a rare, relatively classy project for American International Pictures (AIP), the prolific producer of "classic" teen-oriented drive-in fodder during the 1950s and 1960s. This screenplay offers the audience more bang for its buck by including material from Stevenson's less well known sequel, *Catriona*.

In the final years of the 18th century, the British are brutally ravaging the Scottish forces of the Jacobite Rebellion. David Balfour (Douglas) is an orphan boy who comes to the home of his wicked uncle, Ebenezer Balfour (Pleasence), unaware that he is actually the rightful heir to the family fortune. Ebenezer hires Captain Hoseason (Hawkins), a ruthless sea captain, to force the boy into service on a ship prior to selling him into slavery in the New World. On its way to the Carolinas, Hoseason's ship rams a small boat, sinking it and drowning every hand aboard save Alan Breck (Caine), a rebel on his way to France to raise money to continue the war against the Crown. Breck and young Balfour hit it off immediately and join forces to battle the cutthroat crew. However, a storm hits and the ship is wrecked. Here their high adventure begins in earnest.

Rather than use their well worn matte paintings, AIP splurged and went to England and Scotland to find the proper settings. The photography that resulted is splendid. After a decade of "Beach Party" films, AIP decided to remake classics and foisted some dreadful ones upon the public, WUTHERING HEIGHTS and JULIUS CAESAR among them. This is the best of the lot, although it has so much plot that it may be difficult for youngsters to follow. Caine shows his costume mettle in this role, a welcome change from the spies and cads he'd played until making KIDNAPPED. A little too much talk and not enough action, but it's still fun.

KILLERS, THE

1946 102m bw ★★★★★
Crime /A
Universal

Edmond O'Brien *(Jim Reardon)*, Ava Gardner *(Kitty Collins)*, Albert Dekker *(Big Jim Colfax)*, Sam Levene *(Lt. Sam Lubinsky)*, Virginia Christine *(Lilly Lubinsky)*, John Miljan *(Jake)*, Vince Barnett *(Charleston)*, Burt Lancaster *(Swede)*, Charles D. Brown *(Packy Robinson)*, Donald MacBride *(Kenyon)*

p, Mark Hellinger; d, Robert Siodmak; w, Anthony Veiller, John Huston (based on the story by Ernest Hemingway); ph, Elwood Bredell; ed, Arthur Hilton; m, Miklos Rozsa; art d, Jack Otterson, Martin Obzina; fx, David S. Horsley; cos, Vera West

The first Universal production supervised by Hellinger, a onetime reporter turned film producer, this definitive film noir is at least as powerful as his earlier crime movies, THE ROARING TWENTIES and HIGH SIERRA. THE KILLERS, which features a now famous musical score (later used in the "Dragnet" TV series) by Miklos Rozsa, is also notable as Burt Lancaster's film debut. The ace crime director Siodmak uses the bare bones of Hemingway's terse story to build a taut and fascinating tale of murder, robbery, and betrayal. It also features one of the genre's most celebrated femme fatales.

It opens with the killers of the Hemingway story (Charles McGraw and William Conrad) entering the diner in search of the Swede (Lancaster). They have a murder contract to fulfill, they learn that he will soon be coming in for dinner. Nick Adams (Phil Brown) overhears the killer's intent and runs to a boarding house to warn the Swede. He listens, but remains indifferently on his bed, explaining simply "I did something wrong. . . once". With that he quietly awaits his fate. The Hemingway story ends about there, but this is only the beginning of the film. Edmond O'Brien is Jim Reardon, an energetic insurance investigator whose company has to pay off on the Swede's death. By interviewing the Swede's associates, Rearden begins the laborious process of reconstructing the dead man's turbulent life, a process we see through a series of extended flashbacks.

We first see him as a young boxer who gets thrust into the posh and corrupt world of organized crime, overlorded by boss

Big Jim Colfax (Dekker). He becomes enamored of the sultry Kitty Collins (Gardner), Colfax's girlfriend. She entices the big, handsome boxer with the promise that she will leave the boss for him if he helps the gang in an elaborate armored car robbery. Kitty and the Swede would then take the loot, double-cross Big Jim, and flee to a life of their own. This sounds too good to be true. It is.

The cast is excellent and Siodmak's direction is hard-edged and moody. Lancaster's personality amazed viewers seeing him for the first time, and he soon reached star status with BRUTE FORCE, I WALK ALONE, ALL MY SONS and other heavyweight films. Lancaster, a former circus acrobat, began his career here at age 32 but looked much younger. THE KILLERS was also the first important dramatic role for Gardner. Hemingway admired Gardner's portrayal of the eternal vixen and they became lifelong friends. She appeared in other Hemingway vehicles, notably THE SNOWS OF KILIMANJARO and THE SUN ALSO RISES.

KILLERS, THE
1964 93m c   ★★★
Crime
Revue

Lee Marvin *(Charlie)*, Angie Dickinson *(Sheila Farr)*, John Cassavetes *(Johnny North)*, Ronald Reagan *(Browning)*, Clu Gulager *(Lee)*, Claude Akins *(Earl Sylvester)*, Norman Fell *(Mickey)*, Virginia Christine *(Miss Watson)*, Don Haggerty *(Mail Truck Driver)*, Robert Phillips *(George)*

p, Don Siegel; d, Don Siegel; w, Gene L. Coon (based on the story by Ernest Hemingway); ph, Richard L. Rawlings (Eastmancolor); ed, Richard Belding; m, John Williams; art d, Frank Arrigo, George Chan, George O'Connell; cos, Helen Colvig

Hit men Charlie (Marvin) and Lee (Gulager) are ordered to go to a school for the blind and kill Johnny North (Cassavetes), one of the teachers there, who puts up no resistance. They wonder why he accepted his death so passively and who ordered him killed. The killers connect him to an armored car heist several years before from which the money was never recovered. They learn that North was a race car driver in love with Sheila Farr (Dickinson), the mistress of crime czar Browning (Reagan). She had persuaded him to drive the getaway car in the armored car job and they planned to double-cross Browning. But things did not work out that way. As they learn more about the story of the man they killed, the killers develop their own interest in its ultimate outcome.

This was Reagan's final film, and the only one in which he's the villain. THE KILLERS was originally produced for TV by NBC but censors determined it was too violent for that medium, so it was released in theaters. Reagan was reluctant to play the heavy, but the head of Universal at the time, Reagan's former agent, talked him into accepting the part, a decision Reagan still regrets. Though the film does not stand up to the 1946 version with Burt Lancaster, it has its own pleasures, including Marvin's rather likable role of an assassin, the exciting robbery sequence, and, of course, the villainous Reagan getting his just desserts. Two years later he was elected governor of California. And the rest is history.

KILLERS, THE
1981 60m c   ★★½
Crime
Patrick Roth

Jack Kehoe *(Harry)*, Raymond Mayo *(Bill)*, Allan Magicovsky *(Husband)*, Susanne Reed *(Wife)*, Anne Ramsey *(1st Ragpicker)*, Susan Tyrrell *(Susu)*, Charles Bukowski *(The Author)*

p, Patrick Roth; d, Patrick Roth; w, Patrick Roth (based on "Short Story" by Charles Bukowski); ph, Patrick Prince; ed, Daniel Gross; m, Doug Lynner, Bill Boydstun

A strange, independent film shot on 16mm and based on a story by Bukowksi, a sort of disgusting Boswell of the underbelly of society. Harry (Kehoe) is a former insurance man who has dropped off the edge of society. One night, in an all-night cafe, he meets Bill (Mayo), a small-time robber who tells him about an easy score to be made on a mansion in Beverly Hills. They shake hands on the deal, and Harry begins his life of crime. They break into the house without difficulty, but the noise they make awakens the couple who live there, The husband (Magicovsky) comes to investigate and is overpowered by Bill who taunts him for a while and then murders him. Harry, his baser instincts rising, rapes the wife (Reed). Later Bill slits her throat. The two men leave, taking nothing, and Harry wonders why he doesn't feel anything. Shot in a minimal, low-key manner, the film is basically effective, thanks to excellent, disturbing performances by Kehoe and Mayo. Bukowski himself appears at the beginning of the film in a prologue.

KILLER'S KISS
1955 67m bw   ★★★½
Thriller   /A
Minotaur

Frank Silvera *(Vincent Rapallo)*, Jamie Smith *(Davy Gordon)*, Irene Kane *(Gloria Price)*, Jerry Jarret *(Albert, the Fight Manager)*, Mike Dana, Felice Orlandi, Ralph Roberts, Phil Stevenson *(Gangsters)*, Julius Adelman *(Owner of the Mannequin Factory)*, David Vaughan

p, Stanley Kubrick, Morris Bousel; d, Stanley Kubrick; w, Stanley Kubrick, Howard Sackler (based on a story by Kubrick); ph, Stanley Kubrick; ed, Stanley Kubrick; m, Gerald Fried; chor, David Vaughan

The second film directed by future master filmmaker Stanley Kubrick, KILLER'S KISS is no one's idea of a great film but it displays much evidence of future brilliance. The story is nothing more than B-movie film noir fodder, but some of the images and set pieces are indelible.

Davy Gordon (Smith) is a second-rate prizefighter who gets romantically involved with Gloria Price (Kane), a young dancer who lives across the courtyard in his apartment building. Returning home one night after another lost fight, he sees Price fending off a rapist. The assailant is Vincent Rapallo (Silvera), Price's boss at the nightclub where she dances. Gordon rescues her and they decide to flee the city. But Rapallo plans a murderous revenge. . .

This modest thriller was financed for $75,000 by various friends and relatives of the neophyte filmmaker. He served not only as director, writer and producer but also filmed and edited the project. Though the screenplay is undistinguished (and gives no hint of what Kubrick's future ability as a writer), he makes some interesting choices as a director.

The vivid flashbacks and surrealistic nightmare sequences are memorable. The nightmares are represented on negative film stock, an interesting and effective choice. Other idiosyncratic touches include the disorienting contrast created by showing a bloody boxing match on a television screen while an equally violent near-rape and struggle occurs between the nominal viewers, and the surreal effect achieved by using of the dismembered limbs of female mannequins as weapons during a brutal fight sequence in a factory.

All in all, it's hardly Kubrick's best work, but is a revealing early look at a visual style that soon ripened to maturity to produce such film classics as PATHS OF GLORY, SPARTA-CUS, DR. STRANGELOVE, 2001: A SPACE ODYSSEY, and A CLOCKWORK ORANGE. This film was also the inspiration for Matthew Chapman's film, STRANGER'S KISS.

KILLING, THE
1956 83m bw   ★★★★½
Crime   /A
UA

Sterling Hayden (Johnny Clay), Coleen Gray (Fay), Vince Edwards (Val Cannon), Jay C. Flippen (Marvin Unger), Marie Windsor (Sherry Peatty), Ted de Corsia (Randy Kennan), Elisha Cook, Jr. (George Peatty), Joe Sawyer (Mike O'Reilly), Timothy Carey (Nikki Arane), Jay Adler (Leo)

p, James B. Harris; d, Stanley Kubrick; w, Stanley Kubrick, Jim Thompson (based on the novel Clean Break by Lionel White); ph, Lucien Ballard; ed, Betty Steinberg; m, Gerald Fried; art d, Ruth Sobotka Kubrick; cos, Rudy Harrington

Hardboiled early Kubrick. This lean, mean genre film is similar in mood and structure to John Huston's earlier THE ASPHALT JUNGLE, but many of Kubrick's characteristic obsessions are already firmly in place: fatally flawed humans, complicated interlocking timetables and meticulous plans gone awry.

Johnny Clay (Hayden) is an ex-con who tells his childhood sweetheart, Fay (Gray), that he and a few others are going to make a "big score" that will be his last caper. During a race at the local racetrack he intends to rob the money room where the betting take is kept, while Nikki Arane (Carey), a professional killer, shoots one of the horses on the far turn to create a diversion. Clay assembles a group of associates for the job, each with some problem that is getting too big for him to handle: Marvin Unger (Flippen), a retired friend; Randy Kennan (de Corsia), a cop who owes the syndicate money; Mike O'Reilly (Sawyer), a bartender at the racetrack who needs money for his sick wife; and George Peatty (Cook), a cashier at the track with a money-grubbing wife (Windsor). They are all ordinary men "with a touch of larceny in their souls." Everything is planned down to the smallest detail but things go terribly wrong.

THE KILLING brought Kubrick to the attention of the industry as a major directorial talent even though this film was produced on a small budget of $320,000—and it shows. The sets are like cardboard but Kubrick emphasizes that fact, panning his camera from one room to another, showing partitions, devising every conceivable angle from which to shoot, so that the space in which his actors move appears as it really is, confining, cramped, and claustrophobic, reflecting the attitudes of his characters. The film's semi-documentary feel is only enhanced by its meticulous intersecting flashback structure. Time becomes a palpable presence in this fatalistic film.

Hayden gives a stoical top drawer performance as the nominal leader of this unprofessional gang of thieves. Cook gives one of the best performances of his career as the henpecked little man who suffers an avalanche of insults from his wretched wife, Windsor, whose own performance is spectacular.

KILLING FIELDS, THE
1984 141m c   ★★★½
Drama/War   R/15
Enigma/Goldcrest (U.K.)

Sam Waterston (Sydney Schanberg), Haing S. Ngor (Dith Pran), John Malkovich (Al Rockoff), Julian Sands (Jon Swain), Craig T. Nelson (Military Attache), Spalding Gray (US Consul), Bill Paterson (Dr. Macentire), Athol Fugard (Dr. Sundesval), Graham Kennedy (Dougal), Katherine Krapum Chey (Ser Moeun)

p, David Puttnam; d, Roland Joffe; w, Bruce Robinson (based on the magazine article "The Death and Life of Dith Pran," by Sydney Schanberg); ph, Chris Menges; ed, Jim Clark; m, Mike Oldfield; prod d, Roy Walker; art d, Roger Murray Leach, Steve Spence; fx, Fred Cramer; cos, Judy Moorcroft

A deeply moving film, THE KILLING FIELDS is the somewhat-fictionalized story of New York Times reporter Sydney Schanberg (Sam Waterston) and his efforts to find his friend Dith Pran (Haing S. Ngor) after the Cambodian translator falls into the hands of the brutal Khmer Rouge. Although Dith's family is evacuated with the last US personnel to leave Phnom Penh, Schanberg persuades his translator to remain behind with him; and when Khmer Rouge troops enter the city, Dith convinces them that Schanberg and his photographer (John Malkovich) are French.

Regrettably, Schanberg is unable to return the favor later, and Dith is sent off to a rural reeducation camp, which he barely survives but eventually escapes. While undertaking the arduous journey to safety, he comes across the horrifying remains of some of the three million people who died at the hands of the Khmer Rouge. Meanwhile, racked with guilt, Schanberg, who has received a Pulitzer Prize for "international reporting at great risk," does everything he can to locate his friend.

THE KILLING FIELDS wisely emphasizes the human element of its story, concentrating on Schanberg and Dith's friendship, and lets the political situation speak for itself. Haing S. Ngor, the Cambodian physician whose real-life experiences were similar to those of the character he plays, gives a sincere, heart-rending performance that is the film's emotional core. Although Waterston is less effective, he too contributes a believable performance, as does Malkovich in an impressive film debut. Aided by Chris Menges' spectacular Oscar winning cinematography, director Roland Joffe's first feature is a significant achievement, its sequences unfolding with precision as the emotions mount.

KIND HEARTS AND CORONETS
1949 105m bw   ★★★★★
Comedy   /U
Ealing (U.K.)

Dennis Price (Louis Mazzini), Valerie Hobson (Edith D'Ascoyne), Joan Greenwood (Sibella), Alec Guinness (The Duke/The Banker/The Parson/The General/The Admiral/Young Ascoyne D'Ascoyne/Young Henry/Lady Agatha), Audrey Fildes (Mama), Miles Malleson (The Hangman), Clive Morton (Prison Governor), John Penrose (Lionel), Cecil Ramage (Crown Counsel), Hugh Griffith (Lord High Steward)

p, Michael Balcon; d, Robert Hamer; w, Robert Hamer, John Dighton (based on a novel by Roy Horniman); ph, Douglas Slocombe; ed, Peter Tanner; m, Wolfgang Amadeus Mozart ("Don Giovanni"); art d, William Kellner

Coming on the heels of GREAT EXPECTATIONS and OLIVER TWIST, this was the film that made Alec Guiness an international star. Although Dennis Price has the largest single role in the picture (and plays it beautifully), Guinness took the lion's share of the credit for its success with a tour de force performance as no less than eight characters, all members of the same family. A black comedy about mass murder, KIND HEARTS AND COR-

ONETS is one of the British film industry's funniest movies, as well as one of the most memorable and notorious.

The action is set around 1900. Price is in line to a dukedom, but far down the line. Nevertheless, he feels the title is rightfully his, so he decides to remove all the stumbling blocks in his way. The fact that those stumbling blocks are human beings seems not to matter a trifle to the cad, who calmly sets about dispatching his kin (all of whom resemble one another closely, being all played by Guinness). Price, who is involved with the married Greenwood (this unique actress was to play opposite Guinness in the equally delightful THE MAN IN THE WHITE SUIT), begins knocking off his relatives (including the husband of Hobson, who later competes for his attention with Greenwood) in various comedically effective ways, murdering six of them (two others die by chance) and finally getting his title.

Then he's arrested for a crime he did *not* commit—the murder of Greenwood's husband, who actually took his own life. Just as he is to be executed for this "killing," Price is reprieved; it seems that a suicide note has been conveniently discovered and that Price—who has been whiling away the time in prison by writing his memoirs, fully disclosing the truth about his deeds in the belief that he had nothing to lose and with pride in his accomplishments, wanting the world to admire his cunning—is now free to go about his business. Unfortunately, when he leaves the prison, Price forgets the tell-all memoirs, which are discovered in his cell and are read even as a publisher approaches the freed duke and asks for the right to print his story. This time Price cannot escape an appointment with the hangman.

The film is full of bright dialogue and quotable quotes ("Revenge is the dish which people of taste prefer to eat cold!"), although the witticisms sometimes prevail over the action to an extent that the proceedings become slightly static. On the other hand, the movie makes particularly good use of flashbacks, a cinematic device that is often clumsily handled. Screenwriters Robert Hamer (who also directed) and John Dighton loosely based the story on Roy Horniman's turn-of-the-century novel *Israel Rank,* dispensing with all but the core of the book to write the sharp screenplay. The result, KIND HEARTS AND CORONETS, is one of those films that can be seen repeatedly and still offer surprises. As a combination of rollicking black humor and satirical pokes at the English upper crust, nothing else comes close.

KIND OF LOVING, A

1962 112m bw ★★★★★
Drama /15
Vic/Waterhall (U.K.)

Alan Bates *(Vic Brown)*, June Ritchie *(Ingrid Rothwell)*, Thora Hird *(Mrs. Rothwell)*, Bert Palmer *(Mr. Brown)*, Gwen Nelson *(Mrs. Brown)*, Malcolm Patton *(Jim Brown)*, Pat Keen *(Christine)*, David Mahlowe *(David)*, Jack Smethurst *(Conroy)*, James Bolam *(Jeff)*

p, Joseph Janni; d, John Schlesinger; w, Willis Hall, Keith Waterhouse (based on the novel by Stan Barstow); ph, Denys Coop; ed, Roger Cherrill; m, Ron Grainer; art d, Ray Simm; cos, Laura Nightingale

A kind of marvelous. One of the greatest achievements of the marriage between "angry young man" drama and the Free Cinema movement in Britain in the early 1960s, this was Schlesinger's first feature after a successful sojourn in commercials.

Bates stars as Vic Brown, a draftsman in a Lancashire factory attracted to Ingrid Rothwell (Ritchie), a typist at the plant. They sleep together at her place when her mother (Hird) is out of town and though Ingrid falls hard for Vic, he soon loses interest in her. Her pregnancy, however, leads to marriage and life with the domineering, snobbish Mrs. Rothwell. After Ingrid has a miscarriage Vic regrets having said "I do" and goes off on a bender. The film comes to its sober conclusion as the confused young couple sort through their relationship and wonder if "a kind of loving" is possible.

It's not much of a story when summarized, but that's precisely part of the film's beauty, and the script and direction elevate this film far beyond the norm. Shot almost like a documentary, this low-key production reveals, as few have, the power of realism as a style.

Other than Bates, who was fairly recognizable to film audiences, many of the actors were newcomers with little or no film experience. This lack of movie stars works to the film's advantage, as Bates and Ritchie are simply superb as a young pair who act first and think later. Schlesinger is unafraid to expose the unsympathetic qualities of his characters, and the result is a remarkably rounded drama.

That seasoned veteran Thora Hird is at or near her greatest, and the casting throughout is well-nigh perfect. There's not a false note in the picture, and Schlesinger's supple control and Waterhouse and Hall's moving screenplay deserve much of the credit. Despite the grimy surroundings and downbeat theme, A KIND OF LOVING is filled with humor, insight and intelligence which make it an unjustly overlooked landmark in British cinema.

KINDERGARTEN COP

1990 111m c ★★★
Action/Comedy PG-13/12
Universal

Arnold Schwarzenegger *(Kimble)*, Penelope Ann Miller *(Joyce)*, Pamela Reed *(Phoebe)*, Linda Hunt *(Miss Schlowski)*, Richard Tyson *(Crisp)*, Carroll Baker *(Eleanor Crisp)*, Christian Cousins, Joseph Cousins *(Dominic)*, Cathy Moriarty *(Sylvester's Mother)*, Park Overall *(Samantha's Mother)*

p, Ivan Reitman, Brian Grazer; d, Ivan Reitman; w, Murray Salem, Herschel Weingrod, Timothy Harris (based on a story by Salem); ph, Michael Chapman; ed, Sheldon Kahn; m, Randy Edelman; art d, Richard Mays; cos, Gloria Gresham

KINDERGARTEN COP is actually fairly entertaining, buoyed by Schwarzenegger's self-deprecating charm and easy chemistry with his capable costar, Pamela Reed, and the hammiest bunch of tykes ever assembled for a movie.

The film also features exceptional villains in Richard Tyson as Crisp, an Oedipal psychopath, and Carroll Baker as his cold-blooded mom, Eleanor. Long sought by L.A. cop Kimble (Schwarzenegger), the pair is hunting down Crisp's wife and son, who have fled to Oregon. Kimble teams with fellow cop Phoebe (Reed), a former schoolteacher, to find the woman and child and bring them back to L.A. to testify against Crisp and his mother. However, unlike the villains, Kimble and Phoebe have no idea what the wife and son look like.

Reitman remains one of Hollywood's most ham-handed directors. In addition to having no empathy for his female characters and totally bungling the romantic subplots, Reitman's misdirection around the fringes includes awarding Kimble's pet ferret more screen time than capable supporting players such as Cathy Moriarty and Linda Hunt. Yet KINDERGARTEN COP proves doggedly director-proof in the long run.

Schwarzenegger tames his kindergarten class by having them do calisthenics, thereby shamelessly using his role to promote his offscreen position as chairman of the President's Council on Physical Fitness—and therefore the political ambitions he constantly denies having. But his scenes with the kids can't help but amuse as they effectively send up Schwarzenegger's *uber*-hero image. Nonetheless, many viewers have been understandably put off by the film's uneasy mixture of goofy kid-oriented comedy and violent police action.

KING AND COUNTRY

1964 86m bw	★★★★½
War	/PG
BHE (U.K.)	

Dirk Bogarde *(Capt. Hargreaves)*, Tom Courtenay *(Pvt. Arthur Hamp)*, Leo McKern *(Capt. O'Sullivan)*, Barry Foster *(Lt. Webb)*, James Villiers *(Capt. Midgley)*, Peter Copley *(Colonel)*, Barry Justice *(Lt. Prescott)*, Vivian Matalon *(Padre)*, Jeremy Spenser *(Pvt. Sparrow)*, James Hunter *(Pvt. Sykes)*

p, Joseph Losey, Norman Priggen; d, Joseph Losey; w, Evan Jones (based on the play *Hamp* by John Wilson from a story by James Lansdale); ph, Denys Coop; ed, Reginald Mills; m, Larry Adler; prod d, Richard MacDonald; art d, Peter Mullins; cos, Roy Ponting

This brutally frank, thoughtful, and deeply moving war film contains no battle scenes and little gunfire. Bogarde is a British captain assigned to defend a slow-witted soldier, Courtenay, who has been accused of desertion. Highly educated and a strict military disciplinarian, Bogarde approaches this assignment with distaste. Consequently, he accepts his superior's expedient suggestion that he ignore Courtenay's shell-shocked state and push for a quick conviction. While interviewing his client, Bogarde learns that Courtenay enlisted in the army on a dare from friends. Three years later, the uneducated soldier—having learned of his wife's infidelity and emerging from a battle as the sole survivor of his unit—falls victim to what we now call "post traumatic stress syndrome." Fed up and very very tired, Courtenay simply wanted to "go for a walk". Twenty four hours later, he's still walking along the road when he's taken into custody. During the testimony Bogarde begins to feel sympathy for the obviously sincere and somewhat confused Courtenay. For the first time in his military career, Bogarde begins to question the army's methods and attitudes toward its men.

KING AND COUNTRY is a grim indictment of the arrogant, simple-minded mentality of the men who send their fellow citizens off to war. A good army is driven by discipline and devotion to duty, but director Losey shows us that things are not that simple. Bogarde's character is a cold, unblinking automaton, and therefore quite successful in the military. His interviews with Courtenay change all that. KING AND COUNTRY is an extremely claustrophobic film that takes place in dark, dirty, rat-infested interiors which effectively convey the lack of moral options that the characters experience. Nonetheless no one comes out cleansed of culpability in KING AND COUNTRY; we all share the responsibility for the horror of war.

KING AND I, THE

1956 133m c	★★★★
Musical	G/U
FOX	

Deborah Kerr *(Anna Leonowens)*, Yul Brynner *(The King)*, Rita Moreno *(Tuptim)*, Martin Benson *(Kralahome)*, Terry Saunders *(Lady Thiang)*, Rex Thompson *(Louis Leonowens)*, Carlos Rivas *(Lun Tha)*, Patrick Adiarte *(Prince Chulalongkorn)*, Alan Mowbray *(British Ambassador)*, Geoffrey Toone *(Ramsay)*

p, Charles Brackett; d, Walter Lang; w, Ernest Lehman (based on the musical by Oscar Hammerstein II and Richard Rodgers, from the book *Anna and The King of Siam* by Margaret Landon); ph, Leon Shamroy (CinemaScope, DeLuxe Color); ed, Robert Simpson; m, Richard Rodgers; art d, Lyle Wheeler, John De Cuir; chor, Jerome Robbins; cos, Irene Sharaff

Starring Yul Brynner in the part he seemed born to play, this is a fine if slightly stage-bound example of the 1950s Hollywood musical spectacular.

Deborah Kerr is an English schoolteacher who journeys to Siam with her son, Thompson. She has been hired by the king (Brynner) to teach his many children about the world outside their kingdom. Arrogant and chauvinistic, the King is very comfortable as the unchallenged ruler of his land. Kerr herself is a very strong woman, and it isn't long before the two are at odds, mainly because Brynner is stunned by her unwillingness to bend to his every whim. In a series of vignettes, Kerr is shown teaching the children, dealing with problems within the household (one of which involves persuading Brynner to let Moreno, one of his wives, leave because she loves another), and verbally sparring with the king. Eventually, Kerr wins Brynner's respect and his love.

Even without the music, this well-written story would be a splendid entertainment. But it's the music, that wonderful score written by Rodgers and Hammerstein, that makes this movie as beloved as it is. Kerr's voice was looped by that most ubiquitous of song loopers, Marni Nixon (wife of music composer Ernest Gold), who did the singing for, among others, Audrey Hepburn in MY FAIR LADY and Natalie Wood in WEST SIDE STORY. Brynner, of course, is marvelous in the role of the supreme ruler who slowly comes to realize he's behind the times. He won an Oscar for his portrayal, and continued to do the play on the stage. At the time of his death in 1985, he had played the king in more than 4,000 performances. The screenplay by Ernest Lehman, who went on to write the adaptation of Rogers and Hammerstein's THE SOUND OF MUSIC, is faithful to the play, and even improves on it somewhat.

KING KONG

1933 100m bw	★★★★★
Adventure/Fantasy	/PG
RKO	

Fay Wray *(Ann Darrow)*, Robert Armstrong *(Carl Denham)*, Bruce Cabot *(John Driscoll)*, Frank Reicher *(Capt. Englehorn)*, Sam Hardy *(Charles Weston)*, Noble Johnson *(Native Chief)*, Steve Clemente *(Witch King)*, James Flavin *(2nd Mate Briggs)*, Victor Wong *(Charley)*, Paul Porcasi *(Socrates)*

p, Merian C. Cooper, Ernest B. Schoedsack; d, Merian C. Cooper, Ernest B. Schoedsack; w, James Ashmore Creelman, Ruth Rose (based on a story by Cooper and Edgar Wallace); ph, Eddie Linden, Vernon Walker, J.O. Taylor; ed, Ted Cheesman; m, Max Steiner; art d, Carroll Clark, Al Herman, Van Nest Polglase; fx, Willis O'Brien, E.B. Gibson, Marcel Delgado, Fred Reese, Orville Goldner, Carroll L. Shepphird, Mario Larrinaga, Byron L. Crabbe

The ultimate monster movie and one of the grandest and most beloved adventure films ever made, KING KONG is a film that has given us one of the most enduring icons of American popular culture.

Hollywood filmmaker Carl Denham (Robert Armstrong) takes starlet Ann Darrow (Fay Wray) to a mysterious prehistoric island in search of the legendary King Kong, a giant ape worshipped as a god by the local natives. "Bet they've never seen a blonde before!" some wag observes. They find the giant beast and it falls in love with Ann. Denham manages to capture the monster and bring it back to New York City for display, but Kong breaks loose and wreaks havoc on Manhattan in his search for his beloved Ann.

As a monster, Kong is akin to Boris Karloff's interpretation of the Frankenstein monster—more victim than victimizer. Of course, Kong was a fearful monster who killed with abandon and could destroy entire cities given a chance, but the beast had desires, a temper, needs and fears, and could feel emotions that audiences to this day identify with. No man in an ape suit could convey such a complex variety of emotions—only a fine actor or a master in the art of stop-motion animation, such as Willis O'Brien, who was able to create one of the cinema's most unique and memorable characters from an inanimate 18-inch stop-motion model.

On its initial release, at the height of the Great Depression, KING KONG grossed $1,761,000 and by itself saved the studio that produced it from bankruptcy. In 1938, the studio decided to re-release its classic, but took several steps to tone it down. The film had been made before 1934 when the Production Code began to be vigorously enforced. In accordance with the revised rules of the game, cut were the scenes of Kong chewing and crushing human beings. Gone was the scene in which a curious Kong strips Fay Wray of her clothing. In fact, RKO made the new release prints several shades darker in an effort to tone down the incredible detail of O'Brien's work (dying dinosaurs bleeding, etc.) that made everything seem so realistic.

This travesty practically obliterated the steps O'Brien took to ensure that his creations would *live* onscreen. Generations of moviegoers and television watchers were thus denied the true, uncut brilliance of the vision of Merian C. Cooper, Ernest B. Schoedsack, and O'Brien, until recently, when restored prints of KING KONG began to circulate both in revival houses and on home video. It's probably best, for your viewing pleasure, if you don't think too hard about the racist subtext underlying it all.

KING LEAR

1988   90m   c   ★★★★
Drama   /15
Cannon   (U.S./France)

Burgess Meredith *(Don Learo)*, Peter Sellars *(William Shakespeare, Jr., V)*, Molly Ringwald *(Cordelia)*, Jean-Luc Godard *(Professor)*, Woody Allen *(Mr. Alien)*, Norman Mailer *(Himself)*, Kate Mailer *(Herself)*, Leos Carax *(Edgar)*

p, Menahem Golan, Yoram Globus; d, Jean-Luc Godard; w, Jean-Luc Godard (based on the play by William Shakespeare); ph, Sophie Maintigneux

It should come as no surprise that in this film version of Shakespeare's play, director Jean-Luc Godard shows very little concern for plot, or that—as with every addition to the Godard canon—KING LEAR further considers his previous ideas, preoccupations, and experiments. Though many will cry foul at this adaptation of Shakespeare, KING LEAR, in an odd sense, does more with the original than any number of faithful, literary adaptations by allowing the material to transcend its medium and find new power in a modern time. As usual, Godard is also interested in self-consciously exploring his own position as a filmmaker.

The film opens with Godard and producer Menahem Golem discussing the making of the film, and throughout we see shots of famous deceased directors. The rest is full of audacious experiments in sound, and bizarre casting with lots of estab-

lished, movie star types (the weirdest of all being Molly Ringwald). Godard casts himself, in Rastafarian dreadlocks as the Fool in this often heady convergence of high camp, solemn philosophy, Fellini's 8½, and someone's drug trip. A challenge, as with all Godard, but not quite his most rewarding one.

KING OF COMEDY, THE

1983   108m   c   ★★★★½
Comedy/Drama   PG
FOX

Robert De Niro *(Rupert Pupkin)*, Jerry Lewis *(Jerry Langford)*, Diahnne Abbott *(Rita)*, Sandra Bernhard *(Masha)*, Ed Herlihy *(Himself)*, Louis Brown *(Bandleader)*, Whitey Ryan *(Stage Door Guard)*, Doc Lawless *(Chauffeur)*, Marta Heflin *(Young Girl)*, Katherine Wallach

p, Arnon Milchan; d, Martin Scorsese; w, Paul Zimmerman; ph, Fred Schuler (Deluxe Color); ed, Thelma Schoonmaker; m, Robbie Robertson; prod d, Boris Leven; art d, Edward Pisoni, Lawrence Miller; cos, Richard Bruno

Martin Scorsese and Robert DeNiro must be the most celebrated director/star collaborators in recent American film history. Together they have produced some of the most powerful films of the last several decades—MEAN STREETS, TAXI DRIVER, RAGING BULL, GOODFELLAS—but here they tried something a little different and the result is a chilling black comedy.

Robert De Niro is tragic, goofy and crazy as Rupert Pupkin, a grown man working as a messenger and living in his parents' basement. (Scorsese's own mother is the off-screen voice of the unseen Mrs. Pupkin.) Pupkin is a Times Square hangabout who dogs celebrities for autographs but imagines himself the greatest comic in the world, patterning himself on his hero, funnyman talk-show host Jerry Langford (Jerry Lewis in a part written for the erstwhile King of Late Night, Johnny Carson). His dream is that he will appear on Langford's show, perform his comedy routine, and then take his rightful place among the stars. He'll have none of that nonsense about learning his craft and working his way up the ladder of success; he wants it *now*.

At the beginning of the film, Pupkin ingratiates himself with Langford by helping him fend off some particularly manic autograph seekers. Slipping into the car with Langford, he introduces himself as a yet-undiscovered great comedian who has written some terrific material. Initially Langford encourages him, but eventually Pupkin becomes a major nuisance. At first he hangs around the network offices for a followup meeting until he must be physically thrown out. Eventually he works up to calling on Mr. Langford at his fabulous country retreat. He resorts, at last, to even more drastic measures to get his big break on television.

De Niro gives a miraculous character performance, much different from the intense brooding loners for which he is renowned. He seems to disappear into this oddball, somewhat repulsive, but ultimately rather touching character. Sandra Bernhard, in her film debut, is nearly as memorable as Rupert's outrageous partner in crime. As a thoroughly demented, poor little rich girl who yearns to physically possess her favorite celebrity, Bernhard is simultaneously frightening, unconventionally sexy and *very* funny. THE KING OF COMEDY was a huge flop upon its release. Let's hope that future generations will hail it as the classic it truly is.

KING OF HEARTS
(LE ROI DE COEUR)
1967   100m   c   ★★★½
Comedy/Drama/War   /A
Artistes Associes/Montoro/Fildebroc   (France/Italy)

Alan Bates *(Pvt. Charles Plumpick)*, Pierre Brasseur *(Gen. Geranium)*, Jean-Claude Brialy *(The Duke—Le Duc de Trefle)*, Genevieve Bujold *(Coquelicot)*, Adolfo Celi *(Col. Alexander MacBibenbrook)*, Micheline Presle *(Mme. Eglantine)*, Francoise Christophe *(The Duchess)*, Julien Guiomar *(Bishop Daisy—Monseigneur Marguerite)*, Michel Serrault *(The Crazy Barber)*, Marc Dudicourt *(Lt. Hamburger)*

p, Philippe de Broca; d, Philippe de Broca; w, Daniel Boulanger (based on an idea by Maurice Bessy); ph, Pierre Lhomme (Techniscope, Deluxe Color); ed, Francoise Javet; m, Georges Delerue; art d, Francois de Lamothe; cos, Jacques Fonteray

Breathing new life into old themes, Philippe de Broca's charming antiwar fable KING OF HEARTS has been a perennial favorite on college campuses since it first reached the screen at the height of the Vietnam War.

Set during WWI, the occupying Germans retreat from the town of Marville, France, but not before leaving behind a time bomb. The fleeing townspeople tell the approaching British forces about the hidden explosives, and Pvt. Charles Plumpick (Bates, quite appealing), a poetry-loving Scotsman, is dispatched to locate the bomb. To avoid the German rear guard, Plumpick ducks into Marville's insane asylum, and the inmates hail him as the "King of Hearts" before retaking the town and resuming their former lives in a decidedly loony fashion.

While trying to find and defuse the bomb, Plumpick comes to love the crazy citizens, especially Coquelicot (Bujold). In time, the Germans and British clash in Marville, littering the town with bodies, and, when the townspeople return, Plumpick is left with a choice: go back to soldiering or join the "crazy" folks in the asylum. The film's last shot is justifiably famous.

In addition to its strong antiwar message, KING OF HEARTS ponders the old question of who's crazier, the people who accept life's brutality or those who reject it. Some have said that de Broca states his case with a heavy hand—and he does—but for those willing to open themselves to a lighthearted treatment of this all-too-serious subject, KING OF HEARTS will be both touching and life-affirming.

KING OF KINGS
1961   168m   c   ★★★½
Religious/Biography   /U
MGM

Jeffrey Hunter *(Jesus Christ)*, Siobhan McKenna *(Mary)*, Hurd Hatfield *(Pontius Pilate)*, Ron Randell *(Lucius, the Centurion)*, Viveca Lindfors *(Claudia)*, Rita Gam *(Herodias)*, Carmen Sevilla *(Mary Magdalene)*, Brigid Bazlen *(Salome)*, Harry Guardino *(Barabbas)*, Rip Torn *(Judas)*

p, Samuel Bronston; d, Nicholas Ray; w, Philip Yordan; ph, Franz Planer, Milton Krasner, Manuel Berenguer (Technirama 70, Technicolor); ed, Harold F. Kress, Renee Lichtig; m, Miklos Rozsa; fx, Alex Weldon, Lee LeBlanc; chor, Betty Utey; cos, Georges Wakhevitch

This excellent biblical epic was produced by the legendary Samuel Bronston and directed with a skillful mix of spiritual reverence and cinematic imagination by Nicholas Ray. The film covers the 33 years from Jesus Christ's birth in Bethlehem through the Crucifixion, Resurrection and Ascension. Included are His relationship with John, the 40 days in the desert, the choosing of the Apostles, the Sermon on the Mount, and Judas's betrayal at the Passover seder that was Jesus's Last Supper.

Although Ray Bradbury is not credited, he reportedly wrote the narration spoken by Orson Welles, whose incredible voice and delivery would add dignity and import to dirty limericks. Jeffrey Hunter, not really a major actor, is much more effective than one would expect as Jesus, and Robert Ryan is excellent as John. Hurd Hatfield, though, who sadly never recovered from his initial amazing impression in THE PICTURE OF DORIAN GRAY, goes a bit over the top as Pilate. Other outstanding performances are contributed by Royal Dano, Harry Guardino, Viveca Lindfors and Rip Torn.

KING OF KINGS is an epic of considerable scope, filled with broad vistas, yet there are enough intimate moments to give audience a chance to engage with the characters rather than just admire their pontificating. This is a film where people sweat and labor, and the film, though hardly great, is much better for it. Credit reasonable and restrained writing by Yordan and Ray's sense of judgment for this one.

KING OF MARVIN GARDENS, THE
1972   103m   c   ★★½
Drama   R/X
BBS

Jack Nicholson *(David Staebler)*, Bruce Dern *(Jason Staebler)*, Ellen Burstyn *(Sally)*, Julia Robinson *(Jessica)*, Scatman Crothers *(Lewis)*, Charles Lavine *(Grandfather)*, Arnold Williams *(Rosko)*, John Ryan *(Surtees)*, Sully Boyar *(Lebowitz)*, Josh Mostel *(Frank)*

p, Bob Rafelson; d, Bob Rafelson; w, Jacob Brackman (based on a story by Jacob Brackman and Bob Rafelson); ph, Laszlo Kovacs, (Eastmancolor); ed, John F. Link, II; art d, Toby Rafelson; cos, Tony Scarano

Alternately dreary and fascinating, THE KING OF MARVIN GARDENS is half of a terrific film, but director Rafelson didn't know which half. After the success of FIVE EASY PIECES, Rafelson attempted to create something as different as possible, but his quest for uniqueness is what did him in.

Nicholson plays David Staebler, a long-winded FM talk jockey on a Philadelphia radio station. Instead of playing records, he waxes on about his brother Jason (Dern) and the things they did as children. He dubs Jason "The King of Marvin Gardens," in reference to the Monopoly board game landmark and the actual place in Atlantic City. David goes back to Atlantic City to visit Jason, now working for Lewis (Crothers), head of a black crime syndicate.

Jason is in jail on a "grand theft auto" charge and is released on bail. He and David have a happy reunion, and Jason introduces his baby brother to Sally (Burstyn), a fading ex-beauty queen, and her stepdaughter (Robinson). Jason tells David of his pipe dream to buy a small island near Hawaii and the others, humoring him, help him stage a beauty contest spoof. Things get hairy when David realizes Jason intends to use Lewis' money to buy his dream island.

Much of the film has been deliberately confused (or so it seems) by Rafelson and Brackman in order to flatten the crease between fantasy and reality. For all its faults, THE KING OF MARVIN GARDENS has some merit and many of the individual scenes linger in the memory. It appeared to be a melange of the 1960s mentality of FIVE EASY PIECES with a 1940s-type plot of irony and surprise. The weakest part of the film was the repetitious, indulgent dialogue credited to Brackman, but one wonders how much of that was in the script and how much

Rafelson and his actors improvised. The film is a fairly daring if rather pretentious attempt at originality, but this type of intimate narrative generally requires that one be given the pleasure of caring about the characters.

KING OF NEW YORK

1990   103m   c   ★★★★
Crime   R/18
Augusto Caminito   (Italy/U.S.)

Christopher Walken (Frank White), David Caruso (Dennis Gilley), Larry Fishburne (Jimmy Jump), Victor Argo (Roy Bishop), Wesley Snipes (Thomas Flannigan), Janet Julian (Jennifer Poe), Joey Chin (Larry Wong), Giancarlo Esposito (Lance), Paul Calderon (Joey Dalesio), Steve Buscemi

p, Mary Kane; d, Abel Ferrara; w, Nicholas St. John; ph, Bojan Bazelli (Duart Color); ed, Anthony Redman; m, Joe Delia; prod d, Alex Tavoularis; art d, Stephanie Ziemer; fx, Matt Vogel; cos, Carol Ramsey

Frank White (Walken), a middle-aged drug lord, is released from prison to find that the streets of New York are tougher and less forgiving than they were when he went in. Still, his gang remains loyal, and his enemies—police and thieves alike—are as hostile as ever. Frank, though, has changed, and decides to make a positive mark on society. Countless hurdles, however, stand in the way of his civic-minded ambitions, which revolve around raising the money needed to keep a public hospital open in a poverty-stricken neighborhood. For starters, he has made a bad name for himself in virtually every ethnic enclave in the city. Nevertheless, White decides to team with Lance Wong (Chin), a young Chinatown dealer who has a huge shipment of drugs to move. Wong's lack of altruism ("If I wanted socialized medicine, I'd have stayed in the Peking province") is a problem, as is the hostility of the Mafia, which is horrified by White's interracial operation. Further complicating White's efforts are some frustrated Brooklyn cops willing to use any means necessary to put an end to White's plans. Hot-headed Dennis Gilley (Caruso), in particular, persuades his fellow officers that the system favors the criminal, and that if anything is to be done about White, it won't be done by the book. Doomed from the start, White's plan precipitates a wave of violence.

Widely accused of racism and of glamorizing drug dealing, KING OF NEW YORK is a powerful, incisive investigation of race, class and power in New York City. The writer-director team of St. John and Ferrara, both native New Yorkers, here essay their toughest and most stylish film venture to date. It is the film Sidney Lumet's Q&A claimed to be, managing to address issues that make most filmmakers and audiences cringe, without ever stooping to didacticism.

Ferrara and St. John's vision of New York is jittery, complex, and defined by juxtapositions of wealth and poverty, legal and illegal commerce, politics and crime, business and recreation that are so extreme as to verge on the ludicrous. Their New York is the biggest, glossiest, most high-tech banana republic conceivable, a jungle of steel and concrete animated by atavistic rhythms and primitive, clannish conceptions of place and loyalty. The screenplay isn't subtle; it is brutally direct. There's nary a touch of coyness in this depiction of manipulation, intimidation, and exclusion of one group by another. Ferrara's great gift as a director is his ferocious sense of place: New York's boroughs, ethnic neighborhoods, subways, hotels, landmarks, bars and fast-food joints are all convincingly rendered here.

The KING OF NEW YORK cast is uniformly excellent. Along with Fishburne (television's "Pee Wee's Playhouse") and Caruso ("Crime Story"), it includes Esposito (SCHOOL DAZE), Snipes (MO' BETTER BLUES), Buscemi (MILLER'S CROSSING), and, of course, Walken, who trots out his high-wire, nervous breakdown performance to good effect here. One non-epic in an age of epic gangster pics (MILLER'S CROSSING, GOODFELLAS, STATE OF GRACE, GODFATHER III), this film holds its own, the quirky style of these two still-marginal filmmakers floating it.

KING OF THE GYPSIES

1978   112m   c   ★★★
Drama   R/AA
DEG

Sterling Hayden (King Zharko Stepanowicz), Shelley Winters (Queen Rachel), Susan Sarandon (Rose), Brooke Shields (Tita Stepanowicz), Annette O'Toole (Sharon), Eric Roberts (Dave Stepanowicz), Judd Hirsch (Groffo), Annie Potts (Persa), Michael V. Gazzo (Spiro Giorgio), Antonia Rey (Danitza Giorgio)

p, Federico De Laurentiis; d, Frank Pierson; w, Frank Pierson (based on the book by Peter Maas); ph, Sven Nykvist (Technicolor); ed, Paul Hirsch; m, David Grisman; prod d, Gene Callahan; art d, John J. Moore; chor, Julie Arenal; cos, Anna Hill Johnstone

Although this film suffered from some miscasting—especially the choice of Shields, whose performance is more than mildly distressing—KING OF THE GYPSIES offers an often fascinating look at gypsy culture in America. Roberts is impressive in his screen debut as the unwilling heir to the gypsy throne. He tries to break away from a culture he considers archaic, yet is always drawn back to his roots. The sequences involving gypsy scams are fascinating and often humorous in their simplicity. Despite the film's sometimes trashy veneer and the variable accents of the actors, it's not that bad a flick. Sarandon really enjoys being this noisy, and Winters is clearly getting into her degradation. Real-life gypsies who served as extras were often caught trying to scam the producers out of more money for themselves. And why not? The movie industry is full of scamming. Life imitates art... or is it the other way around?

KING OF THE KHYBER RIFLES

1953   100m   c   ★★★½
Adventure   /U
FOX

Tyrone Power (Capt. Alan King), Terry Moore (Susan Maitland), Michael Rennie (Brig. Gen. Maitland), John Justin (Lt. Geoffrey Heath), Guy Rolfe (Karram Khan), Richard Stapley (Lt. Ben Baird), Murray Matheson (Maj. Ian MacAllister), Frank De Kova (Ali Nur), Argentina Brunetti (Lali), Sujata (Native Dancer)

p, Frank P. Rosenberg; d, Henry King; w, Ivan Goff, Ben Roberts (based on a story by Harry Kleiner from the novel by Talbot Mundy); ph, Leon Shamroy (CinemaScope, Technicolor); ed, Barbara McLean; m, Bernard Herrmann; art d, Lyle Wheeler, Maurice Ransford; fx, Ray Kellogg; chor, Asoka; cos, Travilla

This rousing adventure, a remake of John Ford's THE BLACK WATCH, was given the full treatment by Fox, which made this early CinemaScope epic its major Christmas release. Power stars as Capt. Alan King, a half-caste who leads a supply column to the British outpost at Peshawar, India. On the trail his unit is ambushed by rebellious Afridi tribesmen led by Karram Khan (Rolfe), a childhood friend of King's. The soldiers fend off the attack and make it to Peshawar where they are greeted by garrison commander Maitland (Rennie) and his daughter Susan (Moore).

Alan and Susan are mutually turned on, leading to a rivalry with Alan's roomie, Lt. Geoffrey Heath (Justin).

Heath's attempt to spread bigotry amidst the officers by revealing King as a half-caste doesn't cut much professional mustard with Maitland, but it does make him pull a Romeo and Juliet on Susan. Alan's helping to save Susan from kidnappers only increases their hormone flow, however, and, on an endorphin high, King decides to infiltrate Khan's ranks and kill his former friend.

Ace director Henry King, once praised by Eisenstein himself and whose work resembles that of John Ford, has been sadly neglected by film historians obsessed by Ford. KING OF THE KHYBER RIFLES is a marvelously entertaining film helmed with energy and flair. Power was getting a little long in the tooth to be playing these roles, and he's not completely convincing as a half-caste, but he still performs with likable dash. Rolfe is properly menacing as the villainous Khan, and Rennie is properly proper as the British general. Largely shot on a California backlot, KING has good second-unit Himalayan footage to enhance the film's look. The bigotry angle, though not really explored in depth, is one of the more interesting aspects of this enjoyable adventure yarn.

KING SOLOMON'S MINES

1937 80m bw   ★★★½
Adventure   /U
Gaumont (U.K.)

Paul Robeson (Umbopa), Cedric Hardwicke (Allan Quartermaine), Roland Young (Cmdr. Good), John Loder (Henry Curtis), Anna Lee (Kathy O'Brien), Sydney Fairbrother (Gagool), Majabalo Hiubi (Kapsie), Ecce Homo Toto (Infadoos), Robert Adams (Twala), Frederick Leister (Wholesaler)

d, Robert Stevenson; w, A.R. Rawlinson, Charles Bennett, Ralph Spence (based on the novel by H. Rider Haggard); ph, Bernard Knowles

Memorable version of H. Rider Haggard's oft-filmed novel which boasts superior production values and an excellent performance from Robeson. Spunky Irishwoman Kathy O'Brien (Lee) becomes determined to search for her father, who has disappeared deep in the African jungles while searching for the fabled diamond cache known as King Solomon's Mines. She is accompanied by three explorers (Hardwicke, Young, and Loder) and is guided through the treacherous territory by dignified African native Umbopa (Robeson). After hacking their way through desert and jungle, the small party finally arrives at an encampment of natives who look to the white explorers as gods. The tribe is run by an evil king who had stolen the throne from Umbopa years ago with the help of the witch Gagool (Fairbrother). Sensing a threat to their reign, the king and Gagool plot to kill the newcomers. The explorers manage to defend themselves, though, by capitalizing on a soon-to-arrive solar eclipse to prove that their magic is more powerful than Gagool's. Refusing to give up, the deposed king leads an attack by rival warriors. A final battle, the discovery of the mine and an ill-timed volcano bring the story to its thundering close.

Robeson almost singlehandedly undermines the racism in this classic adventure tale. It's a shame he had to go to England to become a movie star and even then (with occasional exceptions like PROUD VALLEY) he was generally cast as semi-articulate but sweet African natives. In this respect his very American singing interludes throw the entire film out of kilter, but he's so good that one really doesn't care.

He, Hardwicke, Fairbrother and Young are the standouts in KING SOLOMON'S MINES, which does less well by its romantic lead roles. Kathy and Henry are not choice parts, and the generally reliable Loder and the less-than-reliable Lee don't come off so well. Their love scenes tend to put a damper on the film between action highlights. The script is decent and director Stevenson shows the promise he would later (sometimes) get to display in Hollywood.

KING SOLOMON'S MINES

1950 102m c   ★★★★
Adventure   /U
MGM

Deborah Kerr (Elizabeth Curtis), Stewart Granger (Allan Quartermain), Richard Carlson (John Goode), Hugo Haas (Van Brun), Lowell Gilmore (Eric Masters), Kimursi (Khiva), Siriaque (Umbopa), Sekaryongo (Chief Gagool), Baziga (King Twala), Munto Anampio (Chief Bilu)

p, Sam Zimbalist; d, Compton Bennett, Andrew Marton; w, Helen Deutsch (based on the novel by H. Rider Haggard); ph, Robert Surtees (Technicolor); ed, Ralph E. Winters, Conrad A. Nervig; art d, Cedric Gibbons, Conrad A. Nervig; cos, Walter Plunkett

For those who love thrilling, large-scale adventure films loaded with action and exotic scenery, KING SOLOMON'S MINES is your cup of colonialist tea. MGM spent $3.5 million—a fortune in those days—in producing this highly engaging old-fashioned entertainment.

Great white hunter Allan Quartermain (Granger) is hired by the beautiful Elizabeth (Kerr) and her brother (Carlson) to help find Elizabeth's husband, who disappeared while searching for the fabled diamond mines of King Solomon. Their party goes through swamps and forests, over mountains and deserts, and flees nasty natives and stampeding animals in their search.

One of the most majestically filmed adventure tales ever put on celluloid, the film copped cinematographer Surtees a deserved Oscar for his efforts. The production went first to Nairobi and then, via specially built trucks and airplanes, to Tanganyika and the Belgian Congo, covering more than 14,000 miles and contending with temperatures soaring between 140 and 152 degrees and a wide variety of exotic diseases, snakes and flies. The footage of African natives (e.g. a Watusi dance) is fascinating and persuasive, and some efforts were made to portray the dignity of African tribal life. The imperialism of it all might get you hot under the collar, but don't despair entirely—the Africans are the most interesting characters in the film.

To be fair, the Hollywoodians are pretty decent and throw themselves into the bracing if silly spirit of the whole enterprise. Granger isn't sexy enough but he is stalwart, and Kerr expertly plays another one of those prim but horny types she was assigned to do every so often. So much excess quality footage of Africa was left over that MGM went on a recurrent diet of jungle epics, using the stuff in, among others, WATUSI, TARZAN THE APE MAN, DRUMS OF AFRICA, TRADER HORN, and even the 1977 remake of KING SOLOMON'S MINES.

KING SOLOMON'S MINES

1985 100m c   ★
Adventure   PG-13/PG
Cannon

Richard Chamberlain *(Allan Quatermain)*, Sharon Stone *(Jessie)*, Herbert Lom *(Col. Bockner)*, John Rhys-Davies *(Dogati)*, Ken Gampu *(Umbopo)*, June Buthelezi *(Gagoola)*, Sam Williams *(Scragga)*, Fedelis Che A *(Mapaki Chief)*, Nic Lesley *(Dorfman)*, Vincent Van Der Byl *(Shack)*

p, Menahem Golan, Yoram Globus; d, J. Lee Thompson; w, Gene Quintano, James R. Silke (based on the novel by H. Rider Haggard); ph, Alex Phillips, Jr.; ed, John Shirley; m, Jerry Goldsmith; prod d, Luciano Spadoni; art d, Leonardo Coen Cagli; cos, Tony Pueo

Should have stayed buried with the volcano. This rather odious last remake of the famous adventure story is decidedly less spectacular than the Stewart Granger epic and, despite some rousing chases through the jungles, should never have been made. Chamberlain is Allan Quatermain, a hunter hired by the distressed Jessie (Stone) to find her father. He's an archaeologist who knows where a great treasure can be found but who has been kidnaped by Col. Bockner (Lom) and his army of German thugs. Bockner, meanwhile, has formed a nervous alliance with Turkish mercenaries led by Dogati (Rhys-Davies), and they are hot in pursuit of the legendary treasure trove of King Solomon. Of course this is just what Quatermain is after too.

We do have a few funky, harrowing scenes here, but there's something incredibly sloppy about the production and direction of the whole film. The pacing is uneven and the dialogue often unspeakable, a fact one wishes the cast had figured out. Richard Chamberlain likes to think of himself as a serious actor and seems embarrassed appearing in this Indiana Jones ripoff. The "fiercely intelligent" (by her own assessment) Sharon Stone, meanwhile, has all the charisma of cream cheese. Listening to her deliver dialogue is like sucking on helium balloons: you get lightheaded from the vacuity of it all. Most of the cast follows those stellar leads and just goes through the motions while those canny qualitymongers (!) Golan and Globus count the profits they rake in from chintzy stuff like this. The film inspired (if that's the right word) a 1987 sequel (actually shot at the same time), ALLAN QUATERMAIN AND THE CITY OF GOLD. Believe it or not, this film is better than that one.

KINGS OF THE ROAD
(IM LAUF DER ZEIT)
1976 176m bw   ★★★★★
Drama   /18
Filmverlag der Autoren   (West Germany)

Rudiger Vogler *(Bruno)*, Hanns Zischler *(Robert)*, Lisa Kreuzer *(Cashier)*, Rudolf Schuendler *(Robert's Father)*, Marquard Bohm *(Man Who Lost His Wife)*

p, Wim Wenders; d, Wim Wenders; w, Wim Wenders; ph, Robby Muller, Martin Schafer, Peter Przygodda; m, Axel Linstadt

One of the seminal films of New German cinema, KINGS OF THE ROAD is, along with WINGS OF DESIRE, one of Wim Wenders' greatest achievements to date. The ultimate road movie, this lengthy but never dull picture traces the small adventures of two men as they wander along the back roads of Germany, moving from one small town to the next.

One morning Bruno (Vogler), a motion-picture-projector repairman who lives in his van, sees a Volkswagen plunge off a dock and into the Elbe River, a natural border between East and West Germany. Out of the water comes Robert (Zischler), a linguist who has just made a half-hearted suicide attempt. Robert accepts a ride from Bruno—and, as they travel across the country on Bruno's repair route, a strong friendship develops. The two

drink, meet people, wander the streets, and sing along to American songs, especially Roger Miller's "King of the Road."

The story is simple and told in the main without much dialogue (Wenders and crew set out with an itinerary but no script), and the core of the film eschews narrative. Instead, as the translated title tells us, it is "the course of time" that holds Wenders' interest. The changes that occur throughout history (symbolized by crumbling small-town movie houses) are the film's central concern and justify its length. Scenes are filmed in real time, as we watch the characters shave, wash, think, talk, and even defecate. This last moment is something that you not only don't mind, you find it entirely fitting amid the ordinariness of it all.

KINGS OF THE ROAD becomes an even more revealing entry in Wenders' canon when one views it in light of WINGS OF DESIRE. Both films examine the walls that exist between people, between past and present, and between East and West Germany. Both films also tellingly highlight the imbrication of American pop culture on European sensibilities. No reference to this film should fail to mention the power of the naturally lit, black-and-white images beautifully captured by Robby Muller. A terrific and thoughtful film.

KINGS ROW
1942 127m bw   ★★★★½
Drama   /A
WB

Ann Sheridan *(Randy Monoghan)*, Robert Cummings *(Parris Mitchell)*, Ronald Reagan *(Drake McHugh)*, Betty Field *(Cassandra Tower)*, Charles Coburn *(Dr. Henry Gordon)*, Claude Rains *(Dr. Alexander Tower)*, Judith Anderson *(Mrs. Harriet Gordon)*, Nancy Coleman *(Louise Gordon)*, Karen Verne *(Elise Sandor)*, Maria Ouspenskaya *(Mme. Von Eln)*

p, David Lewis; d, Sam Wood; w, Casey Robinson (based on the novel by Henry Bellamann); ph, James Wong Howe; ed, Ralph Dawson; m, Erich Wolfgang Korngold; prod d, William Cameron Menzies; art d, Carl Jules Weyl

"Where's the rest of me?" Too bad Ronnie never found the answer. Containing what is easily the future President's finest performance, KINGS ROW was a startling film for its day, portraying a small town not with the poignancy and little joys of Thorton Wilder's *Our Town*, but rather in grim, often tragic tones.

The film begins with its main characters as children. Playful Drake, tomboyish Randy and uppity Louise are among the friends of the sensitive Parris. He, meanwhile, befriends the strange, lonely Cassandra, but her psychiatrist father, Dr. Towers (Rains) soon removes her from school to be tutored at home. We advance in time to the grown Parris (Cummings), now a brilliant medical student who studies with Dr. Tower and still sees the increasingly quirky Cassandra (Field) occasionally. The feisty Randy loves both Parris and the rakish Drake (Reagan), but Louise (Coleman) remains sheltered by her strict parents.

Trouble brews when Louise becomes jealous of Randy's involvement with Drake, and Cassandra begins to go off the deep end and and wants to go to Vienna with Parris. Ultimately, two very different fathers, the kindly Dr. Towers and Louise's avaricious dad, Dr. Gordon (Coburn), take brutal action in their misguided attempts to protect their daughters.

KINGS ROW remains one of director Wood's finest films, but one wonders how much he relied on his ace support. Robinson did a fine job of adapting Bellamann's rich novel, even if he cut out a death from cancer, deleted a mercy killing, and toned down the narrative's homosexual angle. Korngold's rich score is haunting and the detailed sets by Menzies quite stunning. Howe's gorgeous cinematography, meanwhile, maintains in deep focus many layers of drama, as befits this brooding tapestry. Howe, though, in later years, gave Menzies most of the credit for the film's success, claiming that the versatile sometime-director often laid out shots and even chose lenses while Wood busied himself with the cast.

With actors like Rains and the oddly-cast Coburn it's hard to go wrong, but Wood failed to make much of the lightweight Cummings. Verne, too, does little but bask in her key light, but then her part enters so late and is *so* full of goodness. Reagan, whose fortunes fall over the course of the film and who endures Hollywood's most famous unnecessary surgery, is, surprisingly, on surer ground here. He's lowkey but not dull, per usual, and even manages moodiness! Uneven to be sure, but one of the most memorable melodramas of its day, compelling and unusual for early WWII.

KIPPERBANG

1984 85m c   ★★★½
Romance/Comedy   PG
Enigma/Goldcrest/Channel 4   (U.K.)

John Albasiny (Alan "Quack Quack" Duckworth), Abigail Cruttenden (Ann), Maurice Dee (Geoffrey), Alison Steadman (Miss Land), Garry Cooper (Tommy), Robert Urquhart (Headmaster), Chris Karallis (Shaz), Frances Ruffelle (Eunice), Nicola Prince (Maureen), Richenda Carey (Botany Teacher)

p, Chris Griffin; d, Michael Apted; w, Jack Rosenthal; ph, Tony Pierce-Roberts (Kay Color); ed, John Shirley; m, David Earl; art d, Jeff Woodbridge; cos, Sue Yelland

This often enchanting and nostalgic look at adolescent life in 1948 England centers on Alan (Albasiny), a largely ignored schoolboy nicknamed "Quack Quack" because of his surname (Duckworth). When Alan decides to get his first kiss, he sets his sights on Ann (Cruttenden), an attractive schoolmate who doesn't even notice him. His big chance comes when he is chosen for the romantic lead in a school play. Luckily for him, Ann is his costar.

Intercut with the scenes of the adolescents are the lives of their teachers, and the result, warmly helmed by director Apted, is a pleasantly rounded little film. Although some portions of KIPPERBANG fall flat, much of the picture accurately captures the awkwardness of growing up.

KISS BEFORE DYING, A

1956 94m c   ★★★
Mystery   /18
UA

Robert Wagner (Bud Corliss), Jeffrey Hunter (Gordon Grant), Virginia Leith (Ellen Kingship), Joanne Woodward (Dorothy Kingship), Mary Astor (Mrs. Corliss), George Macready (Leo Kingship), Robert Quarry (Dwight Powell), Howard Petrie (Chesser), Bill Walker (Butler), Mollie McCart (Annabelle)

p, Robert L. Jacks; d, Gerd Oswald; w, Lawrence Roman (based on the novel by Ira Levin); ph, Lucien Ballard (CinemaScope, DeLuxe Color); ed, George Gittens; m, Lionel Newman; art d, Addison Hehr; cos, Henry Helfman, Evelyn Carruth

Wagner plays Bud Corliss, a money-hungry youth who kills his girlfriend Dorothy (Woodward), when her pregnancy threatens his chances of being accepted by her wealthy family. Her sister Ellen (Leith) refuses to believe the police report that the death was a suicide, and does some investigating on her own. She runs

into Bud, ignorant of his relationship with Dorothy, and a romance between the two begins. When Ellen discovers Bud's involvement with her sister, the stage is set for the final showdown. An excellent screenplay (unoriginal but full of tension), subtle direction by the overlooked and underutilized Oswald, and good photography help gloss over any weaknesses in the performances.

KISS ME DEADLY

1955 105m bw   ★★★★★
Crime   /15
Parklane

Ralph Meeker (Mike Hammer), Albert Dekker (Dr. Soberin), Paul Stewart (Carl Evello), Maxine Cooper (Velda), Gaby Rodgers (Gabrielle/Lily Carver), Wesley Addy (Pat Chambers), Juano Hernandez (Eddie Yeager), Nick Dennis (Nick), Cloris Leachman (Christina Bailey/Berga Torn), Marian Carr (Friday)

p, Robert Aldrich; d, Robert Aldrich; w, A.I. Bezzerides (based on the novel by Mickey Spillane); ph, Ernest Laszlo; ed, Michael Luciano; m, Frank DeVol; art d, William Glasgow

Private eye Mike Hammer (Meeker) is driving his convertible on a dark highway when he sees the almost naked Christina Bailey (Leachman) running down the middle of the road. He picks her up, but is soon forced off the road. Hammer is knocked unconscious, and Christina is killed. Both of them are put back in his car, which is then pushed off a cliff. Surviving, Hammer investigates, his curiosity aroused by an FBI warning to stay away. He finds Christina's roommate (Rodgers) and also meets a powerful gangster (Stewart) whose strings are being pulled by a mysterious higher power. Hammer knows he's on to something when his mechanic friend (Dennis) is killed and his secretary (Cooper) kidnapped. Hammer himself is kidnapped but manages to escape, killing his tormentors. He eventually figures out that Christina swallowed a key that will lead to the "great Whatsit." Convincing a morgue attendant (by slamming the man's fingers in a drawer) to give him the key, Hammer later uses similar charm at a health club to acquire the box the key opens. In the end, we meet the chief villain, see another side to the mysterious roommate, and discover the contents of the box. The results are, to put it mildly, explosive.

One of the most brutal films ever made, KISS ME DEADLY enjoys a huge cult following. There's not a single really likable character to be found; everyone wants something, and the neanderthal Hammer barely gives people a chance to say no before he starts beating them up. Aldrich's direction heightens the script's misanthropy, shooting with extreme close-ups and at disorienting angles. Christina's murder is achieved with a pair of pliers, and all we see are a pair of bare legs dangling in midair. The murder of the mechanic is similarly jarring, the camera swooping in on his screaming face as a set of hydraulic jacks do their work. Hammer himself is knocked out no less than six times, only to strut down those mean streets yet again. Aldrich was so concerned about possible reactions to all the violence that he wrote a defense of the film in the *New York Herald Tribune*.

KISS ME DEADLY is shot in an unforgettably harsh fashion, visually underlining the paranoia and existential funk of the film noir world view as few other films have done. Aldrich's greatest directorial effort, this important film takes a number of noir elements to their most nihilistic extremes, leaving us in the violent, atomically threatened world we encounter upon leaving the theater.

KISS ME KATE

1953 109m c ★★★★
Musical/Comedy /U
MGM

Kathryn Grayson (Lilli Vanessi/Katherine), Howard Keel (Fred Graham/Petruchio), Ann Miller (Lois Lane/Bianca), Tommy Rall (Bill Calhoun/Lucentio), Bobby Van (Gremio), Keenan Wynn (Lippy), James Whitmore (Slug), Kurt Kasznar (Baptista), Bob Fosse (Hortensio), Ron Randell (Cole Porter)

p, Jack Cummings; d, George Sidney; w, Dorothy Kingsley (based on the play by Cole Porter, Sam Spewack, Bella Spewack, from the play The Taming of the Shrew by William Shakespeare); ph, Charles Rosher (3-D, Ansco Color); ed, Ralph E. Winters; art d, Cedric Gibbons, Urie McCleary; fx, Warren Newcombe; chor, Hermes Pan; cos, Walter Plunkett

KISS ME KATE is almost, but not quite, a classic cinematic version of the hit Broadway musical. Filmed in 3-D, it was largely released "flat" when the 3-D craze began to wane. Boasting an intelligent and highly amusing book, this tunefest features parallel tales of a musical production of The Taming of the Shrew and simultaneously occurring events in the lives of its cast.

Actor-director Fred Graham (Keel) and Cole Porter (Randell) are working together to musicalize the Bard's comedy, and both feel that the only woman to play the shrew Katherine is Fred's ex-wife, Lilli Vanessi (Grayson). Trouble brews when Fred's current flame, Lois Lane (Miller), is set to play Bianca, Katherine's younger sister. Fred, playing Petruchio, enjoys needling his ex, while Lois' dancing partner (Rall) turns out to be a compulsive gambler who has signed Fred's name on an IOU for several thousand dollars. On opening night, two gangsters (Wynn and Whitmore) arrive to collect the debt; how this overlaps with Fred and Lilli's love-hate affair insures plenty of comic bickering until the finale.

KISS ME KATE makes for delightful entertainment, though it does have its drawbacks. Among them is director Sidney, as smooth and professional as ever, but still lacking real flair and imagination. The same might be said for Grayson, who is at or near her best here. Admittedly, Hollywood didn't really have any operetta stars then who could both hit high C and eat the camera whole. Keel, ever a braggadocio, is fun; his best song is "Where Is the Life That Late I Led?". Miller is in great form, too, her loud charm quite amusing. She sparkles in one of her patented pneumatic tap numbers, absolutely blazing away with "Too Darn Hot". Much of the later dancing, though, is of the Gene Kelly/Bob Fosse type and it does tax her range, limiting her to high kicks and lots of spins. Rall and Randell are appealing, too, though the latter is a very whitewashed version of what we know the real Cole Porter was like.

Actually, since we brought up Bob Fosse, we should note that he is one of the onstage dancers. He enters (literally) with a screech and later does a backflip, effortlessly upstaging the struggling Bobby Van. (Look for a pre-Pajame Game Carol Haney, too.) The score, of course, is witty and tuneful, and one just waits for each classic to come bouncing along in this extremely enjoyable if less than brilliant musical.

KISS OF DEATH

1947 98m bw ★★★★½
Crime /A
FOX

Victor Mature (Nick Bianco), Brian Donlevy (D'Angelo), Coleen Gray (Nettie), Richard Widmark (Tom Udo), Karl Malden (Sgt. William Cullen), Taylor Holmes (Earl Howser), Howard Smith (Warden), Anthony Ross (Williams), Mildred Dunnock (Ma Rizzo), Millard Mitchell (Max Schulte)

p, Fred Kohlmar; d, Henry Hathaway; w, Ben Hecht, Charles Lederer (based on a story by Eleazar Lipsky); ph, Norbert Brodine; ed, J. Watson Webb; m, David Buttolph; art d, Lyle Wheeler, Leland Fuller; fx, Fred Sersen; cos, Charles LeMaire

A hard-hitting, often frightening crime drama from the Hecht-Lederer typewriter, KISS OF DEATH has a grimly realistic look and feel, mostly because expert helmsman Hathaway insisted upon shooting the whole film in New York. The movie pulls no punches as it represents life on the seamy side of the street. It also introduced an electric personality to the screen, Richard Widmark, in an unforgettable role. Narrating the film is Nettie (Gray), second wife of Nick Bianco (Mature). Recounting his tough life, she tells how he is the one member of a gang who was caught robbing a jewelry store at Christmastime. Later to by the gang's crooked lawyer (Holmes) lies to him assuring him that his family will be looked after. In prison, Nick learns that his first wife has committed suicide out of poverty and that his two little girls have been placed in an orphanage. In a rage, he makes a deal with district attorney D'Angelo (Donlevy): in exchange for his parole, he will inform on his old gang. D'Angelo particularly wants to send sadistic gang boss Tommy Udo (Widmark) to prison. Nick ingratiates himself with the perverted murderer, listening to his big talk and going with him to bars and bordellos. Meanwhile, Nick falls for and marries Nettie, moving his family into a new home. When Nick's cover is blown and D'Angelo forces him to testify against Tommy, Nick becomes a marked man. Unable to stand waiting, Nick decides to push Udo to the point of murder.

Hathaway's New York locations give KISS OF DEATH a style reminiscent of other crime films employing a documentary-like approach, including CALL NORTHSIDE 777 and THE NAKED CITY. Mature is exceptional as the reluctant squealer, Gray appealingly low-key as his wife, and Donlevy solid as the crusading attorney. Widmark, however, with his maniacal eyes, falsetto baby talk, and hyena-like laughter, really captured the public's imagination with his riveting performance. KISS OF DEATH features the famous scene where Udo murders a wheelchair-bound old woman by pushing her down a flight of stairs. An overnight sensation, Widmark was signed to a long-term contract by Fox. The Hecht-Lederer script is taut and clever, more literate than many gangster films, with well-developed characters and a starkly believable plot line. The story was later be used for the shlock cult film THE FIEND WHO WALKED THE WEST.

KISS OF THE SPIDER WOMAN

1985 119m c/bw ★★★★
Prison R/15
HB (U.S./Brazil)

William Hurt (Luis Molina), Raul Julia (Valentin Arregui), Sonia Braga (Leni Lamaison/Marta/Spider Woman), Jose Lewgoy (Warden), Milton Goncalves (Pedro), Miriam Pires (Mother), Nuno Leal Maia (Gabriel), Fernando Torres (Americo), Patricio Bisso (Greta), Herson Capri (Werner)

p, David Weisman; d, Hector Babenco; w, Leonard Schrader (based on the novel by Manuel Puig); ph, Rodolfo Sanchez (MGM Color); ed, Mauro Alice, Lee Percy; m, John Neschling, Wally Badarou; art d, Clovis Bueno; cos, Patricio Bisso

Based on Manuel Puig's novel of the same name, KISS OF THE SPIDER WOMAN treats its unusual premise with an often lyrical grace. In a South American country, Luis Molina, a flamboyant gay man jailed for taking liberties with a minor, shares a cell with Valentin Arregui (Julia), a political prisoner. Though the revolutionary initially dislikes Luis, he is gradually drawn in by the latter's retelling of films, including a Nazi propaganda piece about a cabaret singer, and a B picture featuring the "Spider Woman" (both "starring" Braga).

The two men develop a deep friendship wherein Luis learns the importance of political convictions and Valentin discovers the power of fantasy. He becomes able to withstand the tortures he endures by dreaming of his lover outside (Braga again). Luis falls in love with his cellmate and, shortly before Luis's release, Valentin agree to share a night of lovemaking with his smitten friend. Luis soon returns the favor by getting involved in Valentin's dangerous political efforts on the outside.

Hurt does a fine job with this difficult role, even if a self-conscious quality not entirely befitting the character does creep in; he seems to want to go out of his way to make it a showy performance, but he deserves credit for pursuing the challenge. Julia, while admittedly on much safer ground, really gives the performance to watch, however. His tenderness is as compelling as his rage, and he never strikes a false note. The impact of the entire film rests on the relationship these actors construct, and both Hurt and Julia succeed brilliantly.

Braga does a good job differentiating among her essentially thankless roles, but she's not entirely into the camp spirit of the movie sequences. Babenco's fine direction is a masterwork of detailed camera choreography, and the films-within-a-film episodes aptly complement the prisoners's relationship.

KITCHEN, THE
1961 76m bw   ★★★
Drama/Comedy   /X
A.C.T. (U.K.)

Carl Mohner (Peter), Mary Yeomans (Monica), Brian Phelan (Kevin), Tom Bell (Paul), Howard Greene (Raymond), Eric Pohlmann (Mr. Marango), James Bolam (Michael), Scot Finch (Hans), Gertan Klauber (Gaston), Martin Boddey (Max)

p, Sidney Cole; d, James Hill; w, Sidney Cole; ph, Reginald Wyer; ed, Gerry Hambling; m, David Lee; art d, William Kellner

The kitchen of a busy London restaurant is the setting for this witty look at a diversified working-class world. Mohner plays Peter, the cook who tells his fellow workers to dream of a better life, but he goes into a fury when he realizes his own plans of marrying waitress Monica (Yeomans) cannot be fulfilled. The underlying message of the kitchen as a microcosm of the world is never fully developed, but this is easily overlooked because of the fast-paced direction and rich characterizations. The melodrama doesn't quite fly and neither does the speechifying, but the film still has a modest low-key appeal.

KITTY FOYLE
1940 105m bw   ★★★★
Drama   /A
RKO

Ginger Rogers (Kitty Foyle), Dennis Morgan (Wyn Strafford), James Craig (Mark), Eduardo Ciannelli (Giono), Ernest Cossart (Pop), Gladys Cooper (Mrs. Strafford), Odette Myrtil (Delphine Detaille), Mary Treen (Pat), K.T. Stevens (Molly), Walter Kingsford (Mr. Kennett)

p, David Hempstead; d, Sam Wood; w, Dalton Trumbo, Donald Ogden Stewart (based on the novel by Christopher Morley); ph, Robert de Grasse; ed, Henry Berman; m, Roy Webb; art d, Van Nest Polglase, Mark-Lee Kirk; fx, Vernon L. Walker; cos, Renie

In a dramatic role right after the Astaire years, Ginger Rogers proved yet again that she had more than enough star quality herself to carry major films. A minor classic and a very typical "woman's picture" of its day, KITTY FOYLE details its feisty heroine's romances with two men. Wyn (Morgan) is the embodiment of the society scions Kitty has watched entering Philadelphia's classiest ball every year. The two fall in love when she becomes his secretary, but his social obligations continually tear them apart, even to the point where he marries another woman. Kitty later begins a sincere if casual romance with Mark (Craig), a struggling young doctor. Eventually accepting his marriage proposal, Kitty has a big choice to make when Wyn sweeps back into her life.

Highly sentimental, KITTY FOYLE features typically variable direction by Wood and includes an unnecessary prologue showing how the treatment of women supposedly changed through the years. Despite these drawbacks, this film makes no apologies for being a romantic tearjerker. The humor and warmth are real, and the film maintains admirable restraint even amid Kitty's most sorrowful travails. Best of all, Rogers offers a performance of considerable dexterity and poignancy. This is a showcase part and she makes the most of it, whether wisecracking with her cronies or during a very cheap first date with Mark, telling off Wyn's snobbish family in fine style, or in her several moving encounters with children. If one considers her equally fine work in the same year's excellent but controversial PRIMROSE PATH and realizes that Academy Awards are often given for a good year's work, then maybe it's entirely fitting to say that Ginger Rogers was the Best Actress of 1940.

KLUTE
1971 114m c   ★★★★
Crime   R/18
WB

Jane Fonda (Bree Daniels), Donald Sutherland (John Klute), Charles Cioffi (Peter Cable), Roy Scheider (Frank Ligourin), Dorothy Tristan (Arlyn Page), Rita Gam (Trina), Vivian Nathan (Psychiatrist), Nathan George (Lt. Trask), Morris Strassberg (Mr. Goldfarb), Jean Stapleton (Goldfarb's Secretary)

p, Alan J. Pakula, David Lang; d, Alan J. Pakula; w, Andy Lewis, Dave Lewis; ph, Gordon Willis (Panavision, Technicolor); ed, Carl Lerner; m, Michael Small; art d, George Jenkins; cos, Ann Roth

Along with BARBARELLA and THEY SHOOT HORSES, DON'T THEY?, one of the best things the highly variable Jane Fonda has ever done.

When a research scientist turns up missing, his best friend, John Klute (Sutherland), a small-town police detective, goes to New York City in search of Bree Daniels (Fonda), a prostitute to whom the missing man had written letters. Bree, who is trying to switch professions, tells Klute that she has been getting threatening phone calls from a violent former client who she also thinks has been following her. In the process of his investigation, Klute falls for Bree, though she has difficulty returning his affection. After another prostitute who had contact with the sadistic caller is murdered, Bree finds herself alone in a dark warehouse in the exciting finale.

The film's predictable plotting is not its strong point, nor is Pakula's uneven direction. The strictly thriller aspects of the film vary from the artfully constructed to the showy but shallow. It's as if Pakula feels compelled to indulge all the conventions of the genre, but without quite knowing why. On the other hand, he does ably highlight some of the more provocative and complex aspects of Andy and Dave Lewis's often fine screenplay. We see Bree calmly look at her watch after simulating the throes of passion while a john makes love to her, and she develops a sentimental attachment to the lonely old man who simply likes to look at her nude. Bree can, with perfect professionalism, explain that certain sex acts will cost clients more, but she also cowers from an awareness of her own vulnerability and realizes the painful contradictions in her life.

Sutherland is either an excellent sounding board for this nuanced portrait or he's a big zero, probably both. Fonda, however, transcends her limitations, making the most of her often forced quality as an actress. Bree emerges as likably strong yet dangerously weak, refreshingly intelligent yet searching and confused.

KNACK. . . AND HOW TO GET IT, THE
1965 84m bw   ★★★★
Comedy   /X
Woodfall   (U.K.)

Rita Tushingham (Nancy Jones), Ray Brooks (Tolen), Michael Crawford (Colin), Donal Donnelly (Tom), William Dexter (Dress Shop Owner), Charles Dyer (Man in Photo Booth), Margot Thomas (Female Teacher), John Bluthal (Father), Wensley Pithey (Teacher), Helen Lennox (Blonde in Photo Booth)

p, Oscar Lewenstein; d, Richard Lester; w, Charles Wood (from the play by Ann Jellicoe); ph, David Watkin; ed, Anthony Gibbs; m, John Barry; art d, Assheton Gorton; cos, Jocelyn Rickards

Director Lester continued to defy convention as he had with A HARD DAY'S NIGHT in this, his follow-up feature. The style is extremely fast paced; the characters are nonstop talkers who move about incessantly. Essentially created in the cutting room, Lester's films rely upon techniques which have been commonly employed throughout commercial film history, but which are combined in a unusual and flamboyant, if not always successful manner.

Tolen's (Brooks) luck with women ("the knack") baffles his schoolteacher landlord Colin (Crawford). This resident stud takes the eager but shy man under his wing and advises him to buy a new brass bed. After finding an appropriate model, they roll it through London streets to their digs, causing traffic jams and general hysteria. Along the way, they meet Nancy (Tushingham), who is new to London and is trying to find a place to stay. She accompanies them on their trek home, and Colin gets a yen for her. Back at the boarding house, however, Tolen takes control and runs off with her on his motorbike. Colin follows in hot pursuit, only to find the couple in a park, where Nancy is loudly accusing Tolen of rape. Losing his patience with this unusually (but justifiably) uncooperative woman, Tolen makes room for Colin.

The characters are deliberately little more than cardboard types. They talk all the time, but never say much of anything. They do, however, convey quite a bit of personality, which can be attributed to Lester's not over-dramatizing any situations and his reliance upon semi-improvisational material. Such an end-

lessly tricksy style does miss occasionally, but what often emerges is a genuinely energetic celebration of 1960s youth. A film of sunshiny, horny dreams and determinedly chic comic anarchy, this manic display remains a zingy if slightly dated adaptation of Ann Jellicoe's fascinating original play.

KNIFE IN THE WATER
(NOZ W WODZIE)
1962 94m bw   ★★★★
Drama   /X
Film Polski   (Poland)

Leon Niemczyk (Andrzej), Jolanta Umecka (Christine), Zygmunt Malanowicz (The Young Man)

p, Stanislaw Zylewicz; d, Roman Polanski; w, Roman Polanski, Jerzy Skolimowski, Jakub Goldberg; ph, Jerzy Lipman; m, Krzysztof Komeda

Roman Polanski's first feature immediately established him as a filmmaker to be reckoned with, winning top honors at the Venice Film Festival, a Best Foreign Film Oscar nomination, and a place on the cover of Time in conjunction with the first New York Film Festival. Polanski's career-long fascination with human cruelty and violence is already evident, as is his intense interest in exploring the complex tensions involved in close relations.

When Andrzej (Niemczyk), a successful sportswriter on holiday with his wife, Christine (Umecka), picks up a hitchhiker (Malanowicz), the couple asks the young man (nameless throughout) to join them on a short boating excursion. Jealous of the blonde boy's youth and looks, Andrzej boasts of his physical prowess, faulting his guest's inexperience at sea. Tension between the men intensifies, with the pocket knife that represents the hitchhiker's particular skills lending a continual suggestion of violence and sexuality to the goings-on. Things eventually do get violent.

Filmed in black and white, this film is extremely assured, concise, and telling in its characterizations. KNIFE IN THE WATER is also notable in the career of another Polish filmmaker, coscenarist Jerzy Skolimowski, who had already begun to direct, but emerged internationally in 1982 with the offbeat MOONLIGHTING. Some would argue that KNIFE IN THE WATER is a more interesting movie than any Polanski made in the west after leaving his native land. Brilliantly told and well-acted, Polanski's half tongue-in-cheek, lugubrious and sinister filmic style seemed quite refreshing at the time.

KNIGHT WITHOUT ARMOR
1937 107m bw   ★★★★
Adventure/Romance   /U
Korda/London Films   (U.K.)

Marlene Dietrich (Alexandra Vladinoff), Robert Donat (Ainsley Fothergill), Irene Vanbrugh (Duchess of Zorin), Herbert Lomas (Gen. Gregor Vladinoff), Austin Trevor (Col. Adraxine), Basil Gill (Axelstein), John Clements (Poushkoff), Miles Malleson (Drunken Soldier), Hay Petrie (Station Master), David Tree (Alexis Maronin)

p, Alexander Korda; d, Jacques Feyder; w, Lajos Biro, Arthur Wimperis, Frances Marion (based on the novel Without Armour by James Hilton); ph, Harry Stradling, Bernard Browne, Jack Cardiff; ed, William Hornbeck, A.W. Watkins; m, Miklos Rozsa; fx, Ned Mann; cos, G.K. Benda

"Knight Without Asthma" is what the "gwamowous Miss Dietwich" dubbed costar Wobert Donat upon his return to the set after a particularly nasty bout with chronic asthma. For a time the powers that be considered replacing him, but luckily Dietrich fought to keep Donat. It's a good thing, too, because their teamwork is one of the highlights of this lavish, underrated spectacle.

About to be kicked out of Czarist Russia for writing an article critical of the state, Britisher Ainsley Fothergill (Donat) manages to stay when he is engaged as a spy for his native country. Investigating young radicals trying to overthrow the Czar, he meets one involved in a plot to kill General Gregor Vladinoff (Lomas), father of the Countess Alexandra (Dietrich). Fothergill is arrested along with others connected with the attempt, and spends years languishing in prison until he is set free by the Russian Revolution. He later meets up with the Countess, whose estate has been overrun and who has been taken prisoner herself. Ordered to escort her to Petrograd to stand trial, Fothergill reveals his identity to Alexandra and proceeds to help her escape. The two find an unlikely ally in the form of Poushkoff (Clements, an appealing actor) and must use disguises and their wits to make their way to safety.

KNIGHT WITHOUT ARMOR boasts grand period sets by Lazare Meerson and a thunderous, majestic Rozsa score that captures the spirit of the stirring and cataclysmic events onscreen. Dietrich looks lovely and her performance is generally quite good, even if she is tousled and dirtied up in only the most decorative manner possible amidst the fires of revolution. Once described as having sex without gender, the incredible Marlene spans quite a sexual gamut in this film. One scene offers striking quasi-nudity as the Countess races across the lawn of her estate in a diaphanous white robe upon discovering that she has been abandoned by her servants. Not long afterward, though, she must masquerade as a Cossack during an escape and the Androgyne of the Ages gets to strut her stuff once more. Donat is in fine form, too, full of dash but avoiding the impulse to be too precious. (Not an easy thing to do when you're playing a character named "Ainsley Fothergill"!) He and Marlene play beautifully together; one especially lovely vignette features him reciting an optimistic English poem and her responding with a Russian one full of despair. Moments such as these and Feyder's directorial flair keep KNIGHT WITHOUT ARMOR from drowning in the sea of production values. The politics are naive, but then they never serve as more than a backdrop for boy meets girl. Call this flick a dry run for the more heavy-handed histrionics of DR. ZHIVAGO three decades later.

KNOCK ON ANY DOOR
1949 100m bw   ★★★½
Crime   /A
Santana

Humphrey Bogart (Andrew Morton), John Derek (Nick Romano), George Macready (District Attorney Kerman), Allene Roberts (Emma), Susan Perry (Adele), Mickey Knox (Vito), Barry Kelley (Judge Drake), Dooley Wilson (Piano Player), Cara Williams (Nelly), Jimmy Conlin (Kid Fingers)

p, Robert Lord; d, Nicholas Ray; w, Daniel Taradash, John Monks, Jr. (based on the novel by Willard Motley); ph, Burnett Guffey; ed, Viola Lawrence; m, George Antheil; art d, Robert Peterson; cos, Jean Louis

"Live fast, die young, and have a good-looking corpse." This hard-hitting crime melodrama offers excellent direction from the always interesting Nicholas Ray and a fine performance from Bogart as Andrew Morton a crusading attorney.

Morton's latest crusade involves saving Nick Romano (Derek), an embittered slum youth, from the electric chair. Piecing together the young man's story in flashback, Morton

describes Nick's crooked early life and his brief happiness with Emma (Roberts). Already having difficulty holding down a job, Nick really cracks when Emma tells him she's pregnant. His return to thievery gets worse after Emma commits suicide, and Nick's crime spree climaxes with his murder of a policeman. An expert liar who makes the most of his boyish good looks, Nick has convinced Morton of his innocence, only to crack when district attorney Kerman (Macready) asks about Emma.

Ray really makes us feel the oppressive filth and poverty of slum life, conjuring considerable sympathy for the distinctly dislikable Nick Romano. A problem even he couldn't surmount, however, was John Derek. Making his film debut here, pretty boy Derek constructs his dull performance with scissors, cardboard and library paste. The role could have ignited the screen, but Derek's high-school histrionics make for a pretty wet blanket. Bogart, on the other hand, does quite well, even if principled attorney Morton recalls the actor's fledgling days in MARKED WOMAN more than any of the classic Bogie roles. Straightforward virtue was never his strong suit, but Bogart nevertheless does a great job with his long climactic courtroom speech.

Not as memorable as Bogart's other collaboration with director Ray, the haunting IN A LONELY PLACE, this film still makes for absorbing viewing. Sequel: LET NO MAN WRITE MY EPITAPH.

KNOCK ON WOOD
1954 103m c   ★★★
Spy/Thriller/Comedy   /U
Dena

Danny Kaye (Jerry), Mai Zetterling (Ilse Nordstrom), Torin Thatcher (Langston), David Burns (Marty Brown), Leon Askin (Gromeck), Abner Biberman (Papinek), Gavin Gordon (Car Salesman), Otto Waldis (Brodnik), Steven Geray (Dr. Kreuger), Diana Adams (Princess)

p, Norman Panama, Melvin Frank; d, Norman Panama, Melvin Frank; w, Norman Panama, Melvin Frank; ph, Daniel Fapp (Technicolor); ed, Alma Macrorie; chor, Michael Kidd

An often funny, sight gag variation on Hitchcock's "wrong man" thrillers. Danny Kaye plays Jerry, a ventriloquist with a dummy that talks when he doesn't want it to and insults the customers. His manager (Burns) suggests he see a psychiatrist (Zetterling). Meanwhile, the the plans for a new weapon have been stolen and two rival groups are after them. The blueprints are placed in, you guessed it, the dummy. The spies begin chasing Jerry all over creation and that's where most of the comedy happens.

The entire premise is all an excuse for several of Kaye's best comic set pieces, including his dancing with a Russian ballet troupe to avoid being found by the spies. (Alfred Hitchcock did something similar in THE 39 STEPS when Robert Donat steps in front of a political rally and masquerades as a speaker while the spys look on.) The chase also leads Kaye into a convention of Irishmen, where he sings "The Drastic, Livid History of Monahan O'Han," penned by Kaye's wife, the writer, Sylvia Fine. The versatile Kaye gets the chance to wear several disguises, to sing a few tunes (including a nice ballad "All About You"), and, in general, to do what Danny Kaye does best. It's just that sometimes he's more manic than funny and he often doesn't know when to quit.

KNUTE ROCKNE—ALL AMERICAN
1940 98m bw   ★★½
Biography/Sports   /U
WB

Pat O'Brien *(Knute Rockne)*, Gale Page *(Bonnie Skiles Rockne)*, Ronald Reagan *(George Gipp)*, Donald Crisp *(Father John Callahan)*, Albert Basserman *(Father Julius Nieuwland)*, John Litel *(Committee Chairman)*, Henry O'Neill *(Doctor)*, Owen Davis, Jr. *(Gus Dorais)*, John Qualen *(Lars Knutson Rockne)*, Dorothy Tree *(Martha Rockne)*

p, Robert Fellows; d, Lloyd Bacon; w, Robert Buckner (based on the private papers of Mrs. Knute Rockne); ph, Tony Gaudio; ed, Ralph Dawson; m, Ray Heindorf; art d, Robert Haas; fx, Byron Haskin, Rex Wimpy; cos, Milo Anderson

Corn doesn't grow any higher than this male bonding tribute to testosterone. Pat O'Brien gives a gung-ho performance as the great Notre Dame football coach Knute Rockne in this bland biography that features Reagan as Rockne's most famous player, George Gipp. The film follows Rockne from his Norwegian immigrant beginnings through his playing days at Notre Dame (when he helped invent the forward pass) and on to his glory days as head coach at his alma mater. With the support of Father Callahan (Donald Crisp), Rockne rises from assistant coach and chemistry teacher to the top spot, and revolutionizes the game as he turns out winning team after winning team, blessed with great players like the "Four Horseman" and Gipp, who dies young of pneumonia and provides the inspiration for Rockne's famed "win one for the Gipper" pep talk! Along the way, Rockne even finds time to romance and marry Bonnie Skilles (Gale Page). Four of Rockne's contemporaries play themselves—the grandfather of all coaches, Amos Alonzo Stagg, Howard Jones of USC, William Spaulding, and "Pop" Warner—and much of the football action is culled from newsreel footage. For legal reasons, some of the big scenes—such as the pep talk O'Brien gives in the locker room and the "for the Gipper" speech are missing on television. But it's all there in the home video, sitting in the cobwebs on your video store shelf.

KRAMER VS. KRAMER
1979 105m c   ★★★★
Drama   PG
Columbia

Dustin Hoffman *(Ted Kramer)*, Meryl Streep *(Joanna Kramer)*, Jane Alexander *(Margaret Phelps)*, Justin Henry *(Billy Kramer)*, Howard Duff *(John Shaunessy)*, George Coe *(Jim O'Connor)*, JoBeth Williams *(Phyllis Bernard)*, Bill Moor *(Gressen)*, Howland Chamberlin *(Judge Atkins)*, Jack Ramage *(Spencer)*

p, Stanley R. Jaffe; d, Robert Benton; w, Robert Benton (based on the novel by Avery Corman); ph, Nestor Almendros (Panavision, Technicolor); ed, Jerry Greenberg; m, Henry Purcell, Antonio Vivaldi; prod d, Paul Sylbert; cos, Ruth Morley

For weepie fans, a high class divorce, finely played. KRAMER VS. KRAMER is, essentially, a television movie that was raised into the feature category by the excellence of the execution. With Robert Reed in the Hoffman role and Suzanne Pleshette as his wife, it would have been a typical CBS entry.

Based on a novel by Avery Corman, the story takes place in New York City and shows Streep, an independent woman, leaving husband Hoffman, an art director in an ad agency, for no other reason than that she wants to "find herself." Hoffman is left to care for their young son, Henry. The extra strain of having to be both father and mother to Henry causes Hoffman to make some mistakes at work and lose a major account, which results in his getting fired. On top of that, Streep surfaces and is suing for custody of the child she's abandoned. Streep now has an excellent job and can afford day care for Henry, so she wants him back.

It's the old wash, but so well done that we can overlook Benton's manipulations of our emotions and let our feelings flow. Movies about divorce and the wrenching apart of families have been part of the motion picture scene since the silents. They will always work, however, if the writing is honest and if the acting is sincere.

KRAYS, THE
1990 119m c   ★★★½
Crime   R/18
Fugitive/Parkfield (U.K.)

Billie Whitelaw *(Violet Kray)*, Gary Kemp *(Ronald Kray)*, Martin Kemp *(Reginald Kray)*, Susan Fleetwood *(Rose)*, Charlotte Cornwell *(May)*, Jimmy Jewel *(Cannonball Lee)*, Avis Bunnage *(Helen)*, Kate Hardie *(Frances)*, Alfred Lynch *(Charlie Kray, Sr.)*, Tom Bell *(Jack "The Hat" McVitie)*

p, Dominic Anciano, Ray Burdis; d, Peter Medak; w, Philip Ridley; ph, Alex Thomson; ed, Martin Walsh; m, Michael Kamen; prod d, Michael Pickwoad; fx, Aaron Sherman, Maralyn Sherman; cos, Lindy Hemming

Better than you might think. THE KRAYS begins after identical twins Ronald and Reginald Kray (Gary and Martin Kemp) are born in a working-class slum in London's East End. They are raised amidst the hardship and deprivation of WWII, in a world of women and children—the men being either in the army or draft dodgers like the twins' own father. Brought up by their strong-willed mother, Violet (Billie Whitelaw), and her equally commanding mother and sisters, the boys grow up fiercely devoted to each other and to the women who raised them, admiring strength and cunning and contemptuous of weakness and of the law. Bullies as children, the Krays turn into criminals hardened by stints in prison and the army. Vicious, fearless, and highly conscious of the figure they cut as twins, they begin to build an illegal empire based on gambling and protection rackets. But as their businesses expand, the twins begin to grow apart. Ron, who's homosexual, begins to show signs of mental instability, is prone to fits of irrational violence, and is also determined to dominate his brother. Reg tries to escape Ron's influence by getting married, but his high-strung bride can't take the strain of living as a gangster's wife and commits suicide. After her death, the twins are closer than ever; however, Ron's arrogant savagery eventually brings them down.

Although the real-life Krays—called the "Kings of Crime" during their heyday in the London underworld in the 60s—are genuine celebrities in the UK (where they are still serving time), they're all but unknown elsewhere. THE KRAYS isn't compelling enough to explain the brothers' enduring notoriety to outsiders. The key to their appeal isn't that they were criminal masterminds (they weren't, not by any stretch of the imagination), but that they were *performers*, flash lower-class icons who mixed with celebrities and aristocrats, carefully cultivating their own myth. Twins, they dressed identically, travelled in tandem, and finished each other's thoughts. One homosexual and one heterosexual, one mad and one controlled, both simultaneously brutal and stylish, the Krays were bound by an intricate web of loyalty and love. You couldn't make them up without being charged with lurid sensationalism.

On the other hand, no one could accuse screenwriter Philip Ridley or director Peter Medak of exploiting the story. They've stuck close to the facts of the Krays's lives, but rendered the inherently bizarre material almost lifeless. In concentrating on locating the Krays in a socioeconomic and historical context, Ridley's script winds up being top-heavy with scenes of the twins as children, when they weren't doing anything very interesting. Medak (A DAY IN THE DEATH OF JOE EGG, THE RULING CLASS) vacillates in this film between theatrical stylization and cheerless realism, but the styles don't mesh and neither has any real punch. Nicolas Roeg and Donald Cammell's overwrought PERFORMANCE, which isn't overtly about the Krays at all, captures better the studied decadence of their short, brutal turn in the limelight.

THE KRAYS' one unequivocal asset is the Kemps—brothers, former child actors, and members of the Spandau Ballet—who are extraordinary as the twins. Many rock singers have tried to make the transition to acting, few of them triumphantly. Even such superstars as Mick Jagger (who starred in PERFORMANCE), David Bowie and Madonna have achieved only limited success on the screen. But the Kemps use what they've learned about stage presence and channel it into characterizations. They've got the charismatic performers in the Krays down pat, and they play off one another with authoritative ease. (Even the fact that they aren't twins works for them, since, as adults, Ron and Reg looked significantly different.) The Kemps make THE KRAYS worth watching. And they're supported by a first-rate cast of female monsters and victims, and some compelling seedy bits by strong character actors.

KWAIDAN
(KAIDAN)
1964   125m   c   ★★★★
Horror   /X
Toho   (Japan)

Rentaro Mikuni *(Samurai)*, Michiyo Aratama *(1st Wife)*, Misako Watanabe *(2nd Wife)*, Katsuo Nakamura *(Hoichi)*, Ganjiro Nakamura *(Head Priest)*, Takashi Shimura *(Priest)*, Joichi Hayashi *(Yoshitsune)*, Ganemon Nakamura *(Kannai)*, Noboru Nakaya *(Heinai)*, Tetsuro Tamba

d, Masaki Kobayashi; w, Yoko Mizuki (based on the stories of Lafcadio Hearn); ph, Yoshio Miyajima (Tohoscope, Eastmancolor); m, Toru Takemitsu; art d, Shigemasa Toda

Four short supernatural stories based on the tales of Lafcadio Hearn, an American who settled in Japan in 1890 and eventually became a citizen of that country, comprise KWAIDAN. Directed with an eerie visual sense by Masaki Kobayashi and containing some spectacular art direction by Shigemasa Toda, the stories each involve an encounter with a ghost—in Hearn's tales a supernatural being who appears to be corporeal but is actually one of the dear departed left to wander aimlessly through the real world. "Black Hair" is the tale of a samurai (Rentaro Mikuni) who returns to the wife he deserted years before and, after sleeping with her, discovers her skeletal remains and long black tresses in his bed. "The Woman of the Snow" is a story cut from the US release about a young woodcutter (Tatsuya Nakadai) saved from death by a mysterious snow maiden who swears to kill him should he ever reveal what has occurred. "Hoichi, the Earless" is about a blind musician (Katsuo Nakamura) whose ears are cut off as he sings at the request of a samurai ghost. "In a Cup of Tea" features a guard (Ganemon Nakamura) who sees a samurai's face in his teacup and absorbs the ghost's soul into his body after drinking the tea. A celebration of the marvelous from director Kobayashi, KWAIDAN's haunting poetry is conveyed not only in its beautiful color images, but also through the chilling soundtrack.

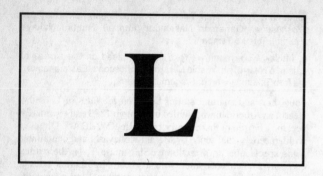

L

L-SHAPED ROOM, THE

1962   142m   bw
Drama   ★★★★
Romulus   (U.K.)   /15

Leslie Caron (Jane Fosset), Anthony Booth (Youth in Street), Avis Bunnage (Doris), Patricia Phoenix (Sonia), Verity Edmett (Jane II), Tom Bell (Toby), Cicely Courtneidge (Mavis), Harry Locke (News Agent), Ellen Dryden (Girl in News Agent's), Emlyn Williams (Dr. Weaver)

p, James Woolf, Richard Attenborough; d, Bryan Forbes; w, Bryan Forbes (based on the novel The L-Shaped Room by Lynne Reid Banks); ph, Douglas Slocombe; ed, Anthony Harvey; m, John Barry; art d, Ray Simm; cos, Beatrice Dawson

An excellent, albeit talky, drama with enough comedy to leaven the heaviness. Caron is a French woman in her late twenties who departs her home in the provinces and moves to London. She spends a sexual weekend and gets pregnant. Rather than have an abortion, she decides to have the baby after meeting a money-hungry gynecologist (Williams) in London's famed Harley Street. By this time, she's moved to a sleazy boarding house in Notting Hill Gate and occupies the small L-shaped room of the title.

The house is filled with characters, and she soon falls for Bell, an out-of-work writer. Since everyone in the small hotel knows everyone else, Caron and Bell's affair is the main topic of conversation, and the tenants are thrilled by what's transpiring. The other people who live there, actresses, hookers, et al., are sentimental about the love that's flourishing, but Bell's best friend, Brock Peters, is incensed. He's a jazz musician with a conservative streak, and when he learns that Caron is pregnant, he tells Bell in an attempt to split the two.

Bell is angered and leaves Caron, who responds by taking some "abortion pills" given to her by Courtneidge, an aging actress who occupies a room below Caron's. The pills fail to work and Caron is actually relieved. Bell returns but cannot accept the fact that Caron is having someone else's baby. Caron goes to the hospital to have the child, and Bell arrives with a copy of a story he's written about their situation. It's called "The L-Shaped Room." Caron returns to France and leaves the story in Bell's room with a note attached to it saying, "It's a lovely story but it has no end."

That's basically what's wrong with the movie. What's right with the film is that we are made to care deeply about Caron and Bell and all the others, and for that reason we want them to succeed. It's a character piece with many sidetracks and incidents and no singular thrust to the story, but Forbes and company do it so well that we must believe the old adage, "If you like the people, you'll like the movie." In treatment, this film is very much like a British version of a Chayefsky story (MARTY, THE BACHELOR PARTY, or MIDDLE OF THE NIGHT). Forbes has seldom done better work.

LA BAMBA

1987   108m   c   ★★★★
Biography   PG-13/15
New Visions

Lou Diamond Phillips (Ritchie Valens), Esai Morales (Bob Morales), Rosana DeSoto (Connie Valenzuela), Elizabeth Pena (Rosie Morales), Danielle von Zerneck (Donna Ludwig), Joe Pantoliano (Bob Keene), Rick Dees (Ted Quillin), Marshall Crenshaw (Buddy Holly), Howard Huntsberry (Jackie Wilson), Brian Setzer (Eddie Cochran)

p, Taylor Hackford, Bill Borden; d, Luis Valdez; w, Luis Valdez; ph, Adam Greenberg (Deluxe Color); ed, Sheldon Kahn, Don Bruchu; m, Carlos Santana, Miles Goodman; prod d, Vincent Cresciman; cos, Sylvia Vega-Vasquez

In the 1950s, when rock 'n' roll was young, novice composer-singers registered high on the musical Richter scale with their revolutionary sound. Among them was a young Mexican-American, Ricardo Valenzuela, better known as Ritchie Valens, whose short life story is told in LA BAMBA.

Beginning with his teenage days as a poor barrio resident in California, the film follows Valens (Lou Diamond Phillips) as he meets Donna Ludwig (Danielle von Zerneck), the love of his life and later the inspiration for his song "Donna," while living with his adoring mother (Rosana De Soto) and irresponsible, violent half-brother, Bob (Esai Morales). Ritchie's natural talent soon makes him the star of the small band he's joined, though his personal popularity causes friction with his jealous sibling.

Soon, a record producer spots Ritchie, leading to his recording "Donna" and "La Bamba," which top the charts to the chagrin of Bob, whose attempts to equal his brother's success fail miserably. After the two get into a fight, Ritchie—still a clean-cut kid who has not let fame go to his head—goes on the road with Buddy Holly (rocker Marshall Crenshaw). Before flying to his next gig, he calls home and patches things up with Bob, and the next day the family learns that Ritchie has died in the famous plane crash that killed Valens, Holly, and the Big Bopper on February 3, 1959.

The film is poignant and rich with period flavor, and Phillips is superb as Valens. Focusing on the real-life, rags-to-riches story of Valens' troubled family, for whom the American Dream, or a slice of it, was momentarily achieved, LA BAMBA is not really a rock 'n' roll movie, although the music is performed well by Los Lobos, who do an excellent job in re-creating Valens' tunes. Carlos Santana provided a top-notch score.

LA BETE HUMAINE

1938   105m   bw   ★★★½
Drama   /PG
Paris   (France)

Jean Gabin (Jacques Lantier), Simone Simon (Severine), Fernand Ledoux (Roubaud, Severine's Husband), Julien Carette (Pecqueux), Blanchette Brunoy (Flore), Jean Renoir (Cabuche, the Poacher), Gerard Landry (Dauvergne's Son), Jenny Helia (Philomene), Colette Regis (Victoire), Jacques Berlioz (Grand-Morin)

p, Robert Hakim, Raymond Hakim; d, Jean Renoir; w, Jean Renoir (based on the novel by Emile Zola); ph, Curt Courant; ed, Marguerite Renoir, Suzanne de Troeye; m, Joseph Kosma

Locomotive engineer Jacques Lantier (Jean Gabin) is infatuated with Severin (Simone Simon), the beautiful but dangerous young wife of assistant stationmaster Roubaud (Fernand Ledoux). When Roubaud learns that Severin secured his job by sleeping with his superior, he goes mad with jealousy. With the aid of Severin, he kills his superior, an act blamed on an innocent poacher but witnessed by Lantier. Roubaud then sends his wife to Lantier as a means of ensuring the engineer's silence. Again Severin's bedroom prowess secures a lover's loyalty, resulting in a romance between the pair, whereupon Severin tries to persuade Lantier to kill Roubaud.

Based on the novel by Emile Zola (whose *Nana* was also adapted by Jean Renoir in 1926), LA BETE HUMAINE features one of Jean Gabin's greatest performances—one with even more force than the locomotive he powers. The catlike Simon is perfect as the persuasive beauty who drives both of the men in her life to their destructive deeds, her unattainable love their tragic downfall. This picture was remade by Fritz Lang as HUMAN DESIRE, Lang's second remake of a Renoir film. The first was SCARLET STREET, a remake of LA CHIENNE.

LA CAGE AUX FOLLES

1979 103m c ★★★½
Comedy R/15
Artistes/Da.Ma. (France/Italy)

Ugo Tognazzi *(Renato)*, Michel Serrault *(Albin/"Zaza")*, Michel Galabru *(Charrier)*, Claire Maurier *(Simone)*, Remi Laurent *(Laurent)*, Benny Luke *(Jacob)*, Carmen Scarpitta *(Madame Charrier)*, Luisa Maneri *(Andrea)*

p, Marcello Danon; d, Edouard Molinaro; w, Marcello Danon, Edouard Molinaro, Francis Veber, Jean Poiret (based on his play); ph, Armando Nannuzzi (Eastmancolor); ed, Robert Isnardon, Monique Isnardon; m, Ennio Morricone; art d, Mario Garbuglia; cos, Piero Tosi, Ambra Danon

In less sure hands, this could have wound up as a disaster, but director Edouard Molinaro was skillfully able to film the long-running play and wring every drop of humor from it. Renato (Ugo Tognazzi) and Albin (Michel Serrault) have been lovers for more than 20 years. Albin is the lead "drag queen" of La Cage aux Folles, a Saint-Tropez nightclub, and Renato, the more masculine of the two, runs the day-to-day operations of the boite. Many years before, Renato stepped out of his gay lifestyle long enough to father Laurent (Remi Laurent) in a one-night stand, and since then both men have raised the boy. Now, Laurent comes home from college with the news that he is engaged to Andrea (Luisa Maneri), whose father, Charrier (Michel Galabru), is the secretary of the blue-nosed Union of Moral Order. As a result, Laurent has lied about his parentage and told his future father-in-law that his father is a cultural attache. From this set-up alone, one can guess that the situations that follow—revolving around Charrier's meeting with Renato—lead to some riotous results. Despite the apparent risk of making a movie with two gay leads, LA CAGE AUX FOLLES is basically an old-fashioned bedroom farce—and tamer than most, at that. Nonetheless, it was a huge international hit, spawning a pair of dreadful sequels and a fabulously successful stage musical.

LA COLLECTIONNEUSE

1967 88m c ★★★
Drama /X
Losange/Rome Paris (France)

Patrick Bauchau *(Adrien)*, Haydee Politoff *(Haydee)*, Daniel Pommereulle *(Daniel)*, Alain Jouffroy *(Writer)*, Mijanou Bardot *(Carole)*, Eugene Archer *(Sam)*, Annik Morice *(Carole's Friend)*, Denis Berry *(Charlie)*, Brian Belshaw *(Haydee's Lover)*, Donald Cammell *(Boy At St. Tropez)*

p, Georges Beauregard, Barbet Schroeder; d, Eric Rohmer; w, Eric Rohmer, Patrick Bauchau, Haydee Politoff, Daniel Pommereulle; ph, Nestor Almendros (Eastmancolor); ed, Jackie Raynal; m, Blossom Toes, Giorgio Gomelsky

This film is the third in a series of six by Rohmer, "The Moral Tales." Adrien (Bachau) is the handsome young man faced with the problem of whether to sleep with Haydee (Politoff), the pretty temptress who is staying at the same boarding house during his vacation in St. Tropez. Listening to her carry on with a number of different men, he attempts to purify himself, avoiding sex and other pleasurable pursuits.

The figure of Woman here provides a vehicle for Rohmer to question notions of moral correctness. The narrative structure follows a pattern that resembles Rohmer's other films, a presentation of a threatened moral stance in which the male always opts out of taking chances for a more secure existence. Bauchau could be criticized for being much too haughty and self-possessed to be very likable, but he is otherwise a perfect subject for Rohmer's experiment. The beautiful temptress played by Politoff is not really required to do much beyond looking nice; the camera does all the work. Almendros captures the beauty of Politoff and the scenery with an acute sense of detail. COLLECTIONEUSE was released belatedly in the US following the tremendous success of MY NIGHT AT MAUD'S, the fourth entry in Romer's series.

LA DOLCE VITA

1960 180m bw ★★★½
Drama /X
Riama/Pathe/Gray (Italy/France)

Marcello Mastroianni *(Marcello Rubini)*, Anita Ekberg *(Sylvia)*, Anouk Aimee *(Maddalena)*, Yvonne Furneaux *(Emma)*, Magali Noel *(Fanny)*, Alain Cuny *(Steiner)*, Nadia Gray *(Nadia)*, Lex Barker *(Robert)*, Annibale Ninchi *(Marcello's Father)*, Walter Santesso *(Paparazzo)*

p, Giuseppe Amato, Angelo Rizzoli; d, Federico Fellini; w, Federico Fellini, Ennio Flaiano, Tullio Pinelli, Brunello Rondi (based on a story by Federico Fellini, Ennio Flaiano, Tullio Pinelli); ph, Otello Martelli (Totalscope); ed, Leo Catozzo; m, Nino Rota; art d, Piero Gherardi; cos, Piero Gherardi

After what we've seen of decadence during the last 25 years, LA DOLCE VITA now seems tamely absurd, but people wasting time in nightclubs, dancing in the fountains of Rome, and just generally hanging out seemed a bit of a shock at the turn of the decade between the 50s and the 60s. If LA DOLCE VITA still works, it's because of Marcello Mastroianni's consistently engaging performance.

The picture begins as Romans are shocked by seeing a large statue of Jesus being carried over the city by a helicopter. Following in a second chopper is Mastroianni, a gossip writer for the local scandal sheets. He aspires to serious writing but never gets beyond what he churns out for *lire*. While visiting a local nightspot, Mastroianni meets Aimee, a wealthy heiress suffering from a huge case of ennui. Everything bores her, and she is constantly on the lookout for new thrills. Together, they pick up hooker Moneta and spend the night as a *menage a trois* in the prostitute's room. When Mastroianni gets home, he finds his regular mistress, Furneaux, has taken an overdose of sleeping pills. He rushes her to the hospital, where he is assured that she'll recover, then races off to cover the arrival of Hollywood starlet Ekberg at the airport. He is soon infatuated with the buxom blonde and takes her for a tour around his Rome, including all the usual spots—Trevi, St. Peter's, the Caracalla Baths, etc. The tour is interrupted violently when Mastroianni is attacked by Ekberg's fiance Barker (who was her husband in real life). Things continue in this mode as Mastroianni takes in a fake vision of the Blessed Virgin by two young children, a visit from his quiet-living father, an infatuation with an innocent young waitress, etc. His crisis about the meaninglessness of his life comes to a head when Cuny, a bohemian intellectual whom he idolizes and envies, inexplicably commits suicide and takes the lives of his two children. True to the spirit of the film, Mastroianni still fails to act on his feelings, continuing with his hollow, glamorous life.

Episodic yet engrossing, LA DOLCE VITA is still worth a look, primarily for the window it offers onto the early days of the jet-set lifestyle. After nearly three hours, though, Fellini's relentlessly enigmatic, non-committal approach leaves you wishing for something more than poignant imagery and moody, self-obsessed characters.

LA FEMME INFIDELE

1969 98m c ★★★★½
Thriller M/AA
Boetie/Cinegai (France/Italy)

Stephane Audran (Helene Desvallees), Michel Bouquet (Charles Desvallees), Maurice Ronet (Victor Pegala), Serge Bento (Bignon), Michel Duchaussoy (Police Officer Duval), Guy Marly (Police Officer Gobet), Stephane Di Napoli (Michel Desvallees), Louise Chevalier (Maid), Louise Rioton (Mother-in-Law), Henri Marteau (Paul)

p, Andre Genoves; d, Claude Chabrol; w, Claude Chabrol; ph, Jean Rabier (Eastmancolor); ed, Jacques Gaillard; m, Pierre Jansen; art d, Guy Littaye

A Chabrol peak. Bouquet plays Charles Desvallees, a middle-aged insurance broker who lives in Versailles with his wife Helene (Audran) and son Michel (Di Napoli). He becomes suspicious that his wife is having an affair and hires a private eye to shadow her. It is soon discovered that she is spending her time with Victor Pegala (Ronet), a Parisian writer. Charles pays a visit to Victor and, after some civilized conversation, bludgeons him with a statuette, though not before commenting on his "ugly mug." Charles then returns to his wife, and as the police close in, their romance reawakens. The finale, simple and quietly underplayed, is quite memorable. A subtle, semi-Hitchcockian murder drama which stresses character more than action.

LA FEMME NIKITA

(NIKITA)
1991 115m c ★★★
Action/Drama R/18
Films du Loup/Cecchi Gori Group/Tiger
Cinematografica/Gaumont Production (France/Italy)

Anne Parillaud (Nikita), Jean-Hugues Anglade (Marco), Tcheky Karyo (Bob), Jeanne Moreau (Amande), Jean Reno (Nikita's Partner), Jean Bouise (Cabinet Chief), Philippe DuJanerand (Ambassador), Roland Blanche (Police Investigator), Phillipe Leroy-Beaulieu (Commander Grosmann), Marc Duret (Rico)

d, Luc Besson; w, Luc Besson; ph, Thierry Arbogast; ed, Olivier Mauffroy; m, Eric Serra; prod d, Dan Weil

A high-gloss thriller from director-writer Luc Besson about the transformation of a sociopathic punk into a beautiful, enigmatic spy.

After casually shooting a policeman during a bungled robbery attempt, Nikita (Parillaud) is tried and sentenced to death. Her nihilism lands her the chance to forego her sentence, in return for agreeing to work as an undercover government agent/hit-person. During several years of training in a mysterious high-tech compound, Nikita begins by exuding attitude—i.e. biting the ear of her karate instructor—but finally shapes up as an operative and is "released" into the world for a series of sleek, if farfetched assignments.

In the tradition of NOTORIOUS and DISHONORED, LA FEMME NIKITA features a morally questionable beauty burnished by a master spy, only to be converted from the secret trade by both a lover and the harsher elements of spycraft. LA FEMME NIKITA has far less substance than either of those films, offering little in the way of character development or verisimilitude. We are never given a rationale for Nikita's missions, and the screenplay never even begins to explain her behavior. Jeanne Moreau's cameo as a woman who instructs our heroine in the art of femininity borders on the ludicrous. For fans of Besson (SUBWAY, THE BIG BLUE), though, that's hardly the point. The director has turned out a supremely slick piece of entertainment where style triumphs over substance. The beautiful Parillaud leads us on a high-tech rollercoaster ride which, if you don't mind the stylized ultra-violence and throwaway plot, can be a lot of fun.

LA GUERRE EST FINIE

(KRIGETAR SLUT)
1967 121m bw ★★★★
Drama /X
Sofracima/Europa (France/Sweden)

Yves Montand (Diego), Ingrid Thulin (Marianne), Genevieve Bujold (Nadine Sallanches), Jean Daste (Chief), Jorge Semprun (Narrator), Dominique Rozan (Jude), Jean-Francois Remi (Juan), Marie Mergey (Madame Lopez), Jacques Wallet (CRS Policeman), Michel Piccoli (1st Customs Inspector)

p, Catherine Winter, Gisele Rebillon; d, Alain Resnais; w, Jorge Semprun; ph, Sacha Vierny; ed, Eric Pluet; m, Giovanni Fusco; cos, Marie Martine

Montand is Diego, a longtime revolutionary who lives in Paris. He has been active against the Spanish government and is now returning from Madrid carrying a false passport. The Guardia Civil stops him at the border and tries to determine his real identity, but a call to his Paris phone number turns up Nadine (Bujold), a student in the revolutionary movement who corroborates his papers. Diego returns to Paris to learn that his pals have been captured in Madrid and that his local contact, Juan (Remi), went back to Spain at the same time he was returning to France. Diego wants to help Juan, but has difficulties enlisting any aid for the mission.

He turns briefly to Nadine for love, but soon goes back to his former mistress Marianne (Thulin), a divorcee who is raising a son on her own. Diego still yearns to go to Madrid to aid the cause, but others in his group forbid their well-known colleague from going and send another (Jean Bouise) in his place. Diego must also contend with the plans of Nadine and her student comrades to terrorize tourists in Spain in order to publicize their political beliefs. Ultimately, though, Diego does head for Madrid, where things go awry almost instantly.

This picture has more tension than action, which is typical of director Resnais, who gave us the endlessly teasing LAST YEAR AT MARIENBAD. Filmed in and around Paris, LA GUERRE EST FINIE never did much at the box office and sank into the sunset all too quickly. Not Resnais' greatest effort, but a provocative portrait of political rebels and a challenging anti-war film just the same.

LA MARSEILLAISE

1938 130m bw   ★★★½
Historical/War   /U
La Marseillaise Society   (France)

Pierre Renoir (Louis XVI), Lise Delamare (Marie Antoinette), Leon Larive (Picard), William Haguet (La Rochefoucald-Liancourt), Louis Jouvet (Roederer), Aime Clariond (M. de Saint-Laurent), Maurice Escande (Le Seigneur du Village), Andre Zibral (M. de Saint Merri), Andrex (Arnaud), Ardisson (Bomier)

d, Jean Renoir; w, Jean Renoir, Carl Koch, N. Martel Dreyfus, Mme. Jean-Paul Dreyfus; ph, Jean Bourgoin, Alain Douarinou, Jean-Marie Maillols, Jean-Paul Alphen, J. Louis; ed, Marguerite Renoir, Marthe Huguet; m, Lalande, Gretry, Jean-Philippe Rameau, Johann Sebastian Bach, Wolfgang Amadeus Mozart, Rouget de l'Isle, Joseph Kosma, Sauveplane; cos, Granier Chanel

LA MARSEILLAISE is essentially a grand march from Marseilles to Paris, contrasting the lives of the commoners with those of the aristocracy. It tells the story of a battalion of 500 volunteers who arrive in time to capture the Tuilleries, leading to the publication of the Brunswick Manifesto and the overthrow of the monarchy of Louis XVI. With this march, of course, came "La Marseillaise," sung energetically here by the peasants—first as a quiet melody and later as an anthem. Jean Renoir does what he does best in providing a naturalistic, nearly documentary portrayal of the characters. In one sense, LA MARSEILLAISE is something of a Western, its march like the progress of a wagon train. Released on the heels of the brilliant GRAND ILLUSION, it's reception suffered from the belief that a director can't make two masterpieces in a row.

LA NOTTE

1961 122m bw   ★★★½
Drama   /X
Nepi/Silver/Sofitedip   (France/Italy)

Marcello Mastroianni (Giovanni Pontano), Jeanne Moreau (Lidia), Monica Vitti (Valentina Gherardini), Bernhard Wicki (Tommaso), Maria Pia Luzi (Patient), Rosy Mazzacurati (Resy), Guido A. Marsan (Fanti), Gitt Magrini (Signora Gherardina), Vincenzo Corbella (Gherardina), Giorgio Negro (Roberto)

p, Emanuele Cassuto; d, Michelangelo Antonioni; w, Michelangelo Antonioni, Tonino Guerra, Ennio Flaiano (based on a story by Michelangelo Antonioni); ph, Gianni Di Venanzo; ed, Eraldo Da Roma; m, Giorgio Gaslini

Marcello Mastroianni and Jeanne Moreau play husband and wife in Antonioni's study of emptiness and sterility in modern life and relationships.

It opens with their visit to a hospitalized friend dying of cancer. They are on their way to a party for the publication of Giovanni's (Mastroianni) new novel, but the celebration is cut short when Lidia (Moreau) informs him, en route, that he disgusts her and she no longer wants to live with him. She leaves the party and wanders the barren streets for the remainder of the night, while Giovanni chases after Valentina (Vitti), the young daughter of an industrialist who has offered him a job. When Lidia and

Giovanni confront one another at home later, the news of a friend's death that night draws them together once again.

Much of Antonioni's greatness is evident in this picture—the seemingly hopeless relationship between a man and a woman, the overwhelming environment which is devoid of emotion, and the quietly observant camerawork. But at the same time Antonioni is sometimes painfully obvious with his use of symbolism. One of the film's major faults lies in its casting of Mastroianni, who simply doesn't fit his role. This problematic film serves more as a transition for Antonioni than anything else, and seems to make even less sense when screened without having seen his previous film, the masterful L'AVVENTURA.

LA NUIT DE VARENNES

1982 135m c   ★★★★
Historical/Comedy   R/15
Gaumont/Columbia   (France/Italy)

Marcello Mastroianni (Casanova), Jean-Louis Barrault (Nicolas Edme Restif), Hanna Schygulla (Countess Sophie de la Borde), Harvey Keitel (Thomas Paine), Jean-Claude Brialy (M. Jacob), Daniel Gelin (De Wendel), Jean-Louis Trintignant (M. Sauce), Michel Piccoli (King Louis XVI), Eleonore Hirt (Queen Marie-Antoinette), Andrea Ferreol (Mme. Adelaide Gagnon)

p, Renzo Rossellini; d, Ettore Scola; w, Ettore Scola, Sergio Amidei; ph, Armando Nannuzzi; ed, Raimondo Crociani; m, Armando Travajoi; art d, Dante Ferretti; cos, Gabriella Pescucci

This fine, often bizarre, historical drama begins with a basis in fact and runs wild with imaginative possibilities. King Louis XVI (Michel Piccoli) and his queen (Eleonore Hirt) flee Paris for the safety of Varennes at the height of the French Revolution. Close behind in a pursuing coach, bickering about life and politics, are Casanova (Marcello Mastroianni, in an excellent performance) and American revolutionary Thomas Paine (Harvey Keitel). All the while, the revolution spreads like wildfire. As with other recent films by Italian director Ettore Scola—LE BAL, MACARONI, THE FAMILY—the exploration of the past becomes a vehicle for understanding today's problems and those of the future.

Besides the benefits of the lush photography and elegant costumes, Scola again works with an excellent cast that reads as a virtual Who's Who of European cinema, including Jean-Louis Barrault, Hanna Schygulla, Jean-Claude Brialy, Jean-Louis Trintignant, Andrea Ferreol and Daniel Gelin. A feast of a film in many ways.

LA RONDE

1950 97m bw   ★★★★★
Drama   /X
Commercial   (France)

Anton Walbrook (Raconteur), Simone Signoret (Leocadie, the Prostitute), Serge Reggiani (Franz, the Soldier), Simone Simon (Marie, the Maid), Daniel Gelin (Alfred), Danielle Darrieux (Emma Breitkopf), Fernand Gravet (Charles, Emma's Husband), Odette Joyeux (The Grisette), Jean-Louis Barrault (Robert Kuhlenkampf), Isa Miranda (The Actress)

p, Sacha Gordine; d, Max Ophuls; w, Max Ophuls, Jacques Natanson (based on the play "Der Reigen" by Arthur Schnitzler); ph, Christian Matras; ed, Leonide Azar; m, Oscar Straus

Released in Paris in 1950, LA RONDE, though quickly hailed as one of Max Ophuls' greatest achievements, was kept from US shores for four years thanks to a judgment of "immoral" by the New York State censorship board. A merry-go-round of romance is detailed in episodic fashion as characters drift from sequence to sequence, switching lovers as they go.

A young prostitute (Signoret) meets a soldier (Reggiani), who leaves her for a maid (Simon). The maid, however, soon meets another (Gelin), who seduces a wealthy married woman (Darrieux), whose husband is involved with a young worker (Joyeux). This woman in turn loves a poet (Barrault) in love with an actress (Miranda). The actress, however, loves an officer (Philipe). Love comes around full circle when he calls on the prostitute from the first episode. Each segment is delightfully introduced by a master of ceremonies (Walbrook), who appears with the metaphorical carousel in each of his scenes.

Originally Ophuls had planned to adapt a novel by Balzac with Greta Garbo in a lead role, but instead he turned his attentions to the heralded Arthur Schnitzler play, which in his hands emphasized the follies of love over the concerns about syphillis the play explored. One of four masterworks Ophuls dashed off in the 1950s before his untimely death, LA RONDE explores his recurrent obsession with circles to dizzying effect. The humor is beguiling, the satire on target, Ophuls legendary camerawork is in fine and restless form, and the acting of a very high order.

Signoret is particularly good, but stealing the show, unexpectedly, is the marvelous Walbrook. Indulging the gentle sentiment of the whole undertaking to just the right degree, he is dapper and alert. The moment where one story is interrupted as he quickly reassembles the broken film is perfection. You're not likely to forget Walbrook's song—a round, of course.

L.A. STORY

1991   95m   c   ★★½
Comedy/Romance   PG-13/15
Carolco Pictures/IndieProd Company/L.A. Films

Steve Martin *(Harris K. Telemacher)*, Victoria Tennant *(Sara)*, Richard E. Grant *(Roland)*, Marilu Henner *(Trudi)*, Sarah Jessica Parker *(SanDeE*)*, Susan Forristal *(Ariel)*, Kevin Pollak *(Frank Swan)*, Sam McMurray *(Morris Frost)*, Patrick Stewart *(Maitre d' at l'Idiot)*, Andrew Amador *(Male News Reporter)*

p, Daniel Melnick, Michael Rachmil; d, Mick Jackson; w, Steve Martin (from his story); ph, Andrew Dunn; ed, Richard A. Harris; m, Peter Melnick; prod d, Lawrence Miller; art d, Charles Breen; cos, Rudy Dillon

In its dream-like sweetness and fairy tale romanticism, L.A. STORY resembles another film written by and starring Steve Martin, ROXANNE. But the comic romance that was that film's *raison d'etre* is not much in evidence here.

During the credit sequence, director Mick Jackson mobilizes his barbs in short vignettes of daily L.A. life, from people walking to work in gas masks to signs designating "Libra Parking Only." The film unfolds from the clear-eyed gaze of Harris K. Telemacher (Martin), who immediately reveals his peculiar malaise by confiding to us: "I was deeply unhappy but I didn't know it because I was happy all the time." As a TV news program's wacky weekend weatherman, Telemacher predicts the predictable, propagating a heaven-on-earth Los Angeles of perfect sunshine and a perpetual temperature of 72 degrees. But pockets of unease quietly begin to undermine his complacency, culminating in an outdoor luncheon with his testy girlfriend Trudi (Henner) and a group of shallow acquaintances. Arriving late is unconventional British reporter Sara (Tennant), to whom Harris is curiously attracted. To further complicate Harris's life, a neon signpost on an L.A. freeway begins to counsel him on his love life. From that moment of epiphany, Harris's relationships undergo an intensified metamorphosis, as he finds himself breaking

up with Trudi, meeting attractive and perky 23-year-old SanDeE* (Parker), and becoming more deeply involved with Sara. Harris ultimately must invoke his strange power over the weather to help him win the woman of his choice.

In L.A. STORY, the romance assumes a supporting role beside the mystical, apocalyptic aura evoked by the city itself. The characters in the film have no past, no future, and are in the grip of the off-balance life of L.A. Unlike Woody Allen's New York City, which becomes a staging area for character angst and transformation, Martin's L.A. stifles the characters, and neither they, screenwriter Martin or director Jackson seem to be aware of it. Instead, Harris and Sara find themselves put through the paces of a Spielbergian fantasy landscape as they gaze upward at the divine white aura of a Hollywood sign before the final clinch. And it is a sad loss, for the filmmakers squandered the opportunity to produce a satiric West Coast MANHATTAN.

Martin has rarely been better, performing with a dancer's grace and a slightly askew obtuseness perfectly suited to a character who roller skates through museums and spouts insights like "I could never be a woman because I'd spend all day at home playing with my breasts." But when filmmakers cover themselves with Industrial Light & Magic tricks and shopworn dramatic formulas, they are afraid to break new ground. When Martin emerged in the mid-70s, he was a genuinely subversive presence. Fifteen years later, he is dead and buried in banality.

LA STRADA

1954   115m   bw   ★★★★★
Drama   /PG
Trans-Lux   (Italy)

Giulietta Masina *(Gelsomina)*, Richard Basehart *(Matto "The Fool")*, Aldo Silvani *(Columbiani)*, Marcella Rovere *(La Vedova)*, Livia Venturini *(La Suorina)*

p, Carlo Ponti, Dino De Laurentiis; d, Federico Fellini; w, Federico Fellini, Tullio Pinelli, Ennio Flaiano (based on a story by Federico Fellini and Tullio Pinelli); ph, Otello Martelli; ed, Leo Catozzo, Lina Caterini; m, Nino Rota; art d, Mario Ravasco, E. Cervelli

Federico Fellini was at the top of his form here, as was his wife and frequent star, Giulietta Masina, whose pantomime in LA STRADA caused her to be dubbed a female Chaplin. She *is* marvelous.

Zampano (Anthony Quinn), a traveling strongman, "buys" the dim-witted but pure of heart Gelsomina (Masina) to help him with his act. The two travel together, with her beating the drum and playing a trumpet to herald his act, and serving as his mistress and slave. Eventually, the pair join a tiny circus and meet il Matto ("The Fool," played by Richard Basehart), a clown and high-wire artist who treats Gelsomina kindly. When the ethereal Fool is accidentally killed by the brutish Zampano, she is devastated and suffers an emotional breakdown, and the strongman abandons her. Many years later, still traveling, Zampano learns of Gelsomina's fate and belatedly realizes his need for her.

Perhaps the simplest and certainly one of the most powerful of Fellini's films, LA STRADA established his international fame while marking a distinct break from neorealism in its poetic, deeply personal imagery (especially the "Felliniesque" circus motif), and religious symbolism. While Masina's unforgettable performance, perfectly combining comedy and pathos, caused the greatest stir, Quinn and Basehart are also excellent, and Nino Rota's music became famous worldwide.

LA TERRA TREMA
1947 160m bw ★★★★★
Drama
Universalia (Italy)

Luchino Visconti, Antonio Pietrangeli (Narrators), Antonio Arcidiacono

p, Salvo D'Angelo; d, Luchino Visconti; w, Luchino Visconti (based on the novel I Malavoglia by Giovanni Verga); ph, G.R. Aldo; ed, Mario Serandrei

With a lyrical, even operatic quality that subtly combines photographic beauty with the cruel plight of its subjects, LA TERRA TREMA is one of the greatest films to emerge from the Italian neorealist movement.

Set in Aci-Trezza, a small Sicilian fishing village, with the entire cast consisting of locals—their weather-beaten faces lending a sense of realism—the film involves the villagers' victimization by the entrepreneurs who control the fishing market. One young man, 'Ntoni (Antonio Arcidiacono), returns home from WWII convinced that the villagers need no longer be subject to such unfairness, that by pulling together they can alter the system and eventually overcome their imposed poverty.

LA TERRA TREMA is a powerful picture that exposes the injustice inherent in a society where the privileged are allowed to ride roughshod over their inferiors. Despite its social import, the film was a terrible failure at the Italian theaters. Its historical significance, however, is immense. The use of non-professional actors, deep-focus cinematography, natural light, and direct sound recording, while rarely seen in Italian films of the day, were all integral to LA TERRA TREMA—products undoubtedly of Visconti's work with Jean Renoir.

Serving as assistant directors on this picture were Francesco Rosi and Franco Zeffirelli, both of whom would eventually become leading directors. LA TERRA TREMA today stands as one of the most brilliant combinations of the realistic with the stylized that Visconti ever achieved.

LA TRAVIATA
1982 105m c ★★★★
Opera G/U
Accent/RA-1 (Italy)

Teresa Stratas (Violetta Valery), Placido Domingo (Alfredo Germont), Cornell MacNeil (Giorgio Germont), Alan Monk (Baron), Axelle Gall (Flora Betvoix), Pina Cei (Annina), Maurizio Barbacini (Gastone), Robert Sommer (Doctor Grenvil), Ricardo Oneto (Marquis d'Obigny), Luciano Brizi (Giuseppe)

p, Tarak Ben Ammar; d, Franco Zeffirelli; w, Franco Zeffirelli (based on the libretto by Francesco Maria Piave from the novel The Lady of the Camelias by Alexandre Dumas); ph, Ennio Guarnieri; ed, Peter Taylor, Franca Sylvi; m, Giuseppe Verdi; prod d, Franco Zeffirelli; art d, Gianni Quaranta; chor, Alberto Testa; cos, Piero Tosi

Franco Zeffirelli's version of the classic Verdi opera stars Teresa Stratas as Violetta and Placido Domingo as her lover, Alfredo. Zeffirelli outdoes himself this time, offering no less than one of cinema's finest opera adaptations. LA TRAVIATA boasts not only the presence of Domingo and the electrifying Stratas but some truly amazing camerawork. The camera dollies, zooms, cranes and pans relentlessly showcase the gigantic, elaborately constructed set. Indeed, cinematographer Ennio Guarnieri and art designer Gianni Quaranta have joined forces with Zeffirelli to present a feast for the eyes—a worthy accompaniment to the brilliant score.

LABYRINTH
1986 101m c ★★★½
Children's/Fantasy PG/U
Tri-Star

David Bowie (Jareth), Jennifer Connelly (Sarah), Toby Froud (Toby), Shelley Thompson (Stepmother), Christopher Malcolm (Father), Natalie Finland (Fairy), Shari Weiser (Hoggle), Rob Mills (Ludo), David Barclay (Didymus), Karen Prell (The Worm/Junk Lady)

p, Eric Rattray; d, Jim Henson; w, Terry Jones (based on a story by Dennis Less, Henson); ph, Alex Thomson; ed, John Grover; m, Trevor Jones; prod d, Elliot Scott; art d, Roger Cain, Peter Howitt, Michael White, Terry Ackland-Snow; fx, George Gibbs; chor, Cheryl McFadden, Charles Augins, Michael Moschen; cos, Brian Froud, Ellis Flyte

Muppet creator Jim Henson, who previously directed THE DARK CRYSTAL, special-effects master George Lucas, screenwriter Terry Jones (of Montey Python fame), and rock star-actor David Bowie combined their talents to produce this fantasy reminiscent of THE WIZARD OF OZ, ALICE IN WONDERLAND and Maurice Sendak's "Outside over There." While baby-sitting, Sarah (Connelly), a suburban teenager, lets her imagination run wild and goes on a magical adventure to rescue her brother from Jareth (Bowie), the goblin king, who is holding the boy in his castle on the other side of an intricate maze. Along the way she meets an array of charming creatures and overcomes great danger, as well as Jareth's deceptions, to learn that the surest route to her brother is both simple and direct.

The finest work that the late Henson had yet produced, LABYRINTH packs enough surprises to captivate an audience of children and provides enough wisecracking to keep adults laughing. Besides acting in the role of the goblin king, Bowie (who was chosen for the role from a group of rock stars that included Mick Jagger, Sting and Michael Jackson) composed and performed a number of songs for the film.

LABYRINTH OF PASSION
(LABERINTO DE PASION)
1990 100m c ★★★★
Comedy
Alphaville (Spain)

Cecilia Roth (Sexilia), Luis Ciges (Her Father), Imanol Arias (Riza Niro), Antonio Banderas (Sadeq), Helga Line (Toraya), Marta Fernandez-Muro (Queti), Angel Alcazar (Eusebio), Agustin Almodovar (Hassan), Pedro Almodovar (Performer)

d, Pedro Almodovar; w, Pedro Almodovar; ph, Angel L. Fernandez; ed, Jose Salcedo; prod d, Pedro Almodovar

Made in 1982, but released in the US in 1990 following the success of WOMEN ON THE VERGE OF A NERVOUS BREAKDOWN, Pedro Almodovar's LABYRINTH OF PASSION is a screwball sex comedy set in a world of unorthodox and baroquely intertwined personal relationships in Madrid. Predicated on mistaken identity and misinterpreted motives, the plot is a tangle that defies simple summary.

Among the some 50 characters is Sexilia (Cecilia Roth), "Sexi" for short, a carefree, heliophobic nymphomaniac whose father (Luis Ciges) is a repressed, world-famous fertility specialist. Hoping to exorcise her fear of sunlight, Sexi consults a therapist, who announces that Sexi's trouble is incestuous attraction to her father. The therapist then confesses her own determination to seduce the fertility expert, whose patients include the manipulative, aristocratic Toraya (Helga Line). Toraya, in turn, has designs on Riza Niro (Imanol Arias), the gay son of the deposed ruler of the Arab nation of Tyran. Riza, who just wants to cruise the Spanish bars and docks incognito, has difficulty maintaining a low profile. Scandal sheets speculate about his activities, revolutionary student terrorists hope to kidnap him, and Toraya is determined to find and seduce him as part of a plot to avenge herself on his father. Blithely unaware of these goings-on, Riza meets Sexi in a discotheque, and they fall head over heels for one another. Needless to say, the course of their love—true though it is—does not run smooth.

Spanish writer-director Almodovar is noted for the slyly subversive power with which he infuses his stylized comedies of sexual error, and this early effort from the director of MATADOR and WHAT HAVE I DONE TO DESERVE THIS? is no exception. Its outlandish plot—which includes such absurdist touches as a cageful of identical test-tube parakeets who refuse to sing and a terrorist who tracks people through his sense of smell—pokes good-natured fun at more traditional romantic comedies even as it's driven by the same fundamental idea: that in the end, love truly conquers all.

What gives the film its revolutionary twist is the breadth of its definition of love. LABYRINTH OF PASSION's sexual landscape is a virtual catalogue of erotic possibility, a pop paean to a multiplicity of forms and desires. Old and young, fat and thin, beautiful and homely pair off and break up according to the whims of outrageous fortune, paying little, if any, attention to conventional notions of appropriate coupling. And in the end, all's well that ends well—an optimistic message delivered with sophisticated, satirical bite.

LACEMAKER, THE
(LA DENTELLIERE)
1977 108m c   ★★★½
Romance   R/AA
Citel/FR-3/Action/Janus (France)

Isabelle Huppert *(Beatrice, "Pomme")*, Yves Beneyton *(Francois)*, Florence Giorgetti *(Marylene)*, Christian Baltauss *(Gerard)*, Renata Schroeter *(Marianne)*, Annemarie Duringer *(Beatrice's Mother)*, Michel de Re *(Painter)*, Monique Chaumette *(Francois' Mother)*, Jean Obe *(Francois' Father)*, Odile Poisson *(Cashier)*

d, Claude Goretta; w, Claude Goretta, Pascal Laine (based on the novel by Laine); ph, Jean Boffety (Eastmancolor); ed, Joele Van Effenterre; m, Pierre Jansen

As carefully spun as fine lace. Huppert plays Beatrice, a shy and passive young woman nicknamed "Pomme" ("Apple") who travels to the Normandy coast with her best friend Marylene (Giorgetti) and meets Francois (Beneyton), a middle-class literature student. He is attracted to the sheepish, freckle-faced Beatrice even though there is an obvious difference in class and education.

They become lovers and get an apartment together in Paris. They are genuinely in love, but their differences begin to surface. Marylene tries to convince Beatrice to do more with her life than be a beautician. She is content, however, with simply loving Francois. When he brings her home to meet the family, he realizes that he should be with a woman who shares his interests in journalism. They soon drift apart, and finally he asks her to leave. Beatrice becomes ill and soon is admitted to a mental hospital. Her mother writes to Francois, asking him to pay her daughter a visit. At the urging of his friends, he agrees. Their bittersweet reunion leads the film to its conclusion.

A delicately wrought yet devastating look at the pain of love, THE LACEMAKER boasts one of the earliest major perfor-

mances from the 22-year-old Huppert, who has gone on to become one of Europe's most breathtakingly prolific actresses, appearing in ENTRE NOUS and two Godard films, EVERY MAN FOR HIMSELF and PASSION.

LACOMBE, LUCIEN
1974 141m c   ★★★★
Drama/War   R/
FOX

Pierre Blaise *(Lucien)*, Aurore Clement *(France)*, Holger Lowenadler *(Albert Horn)*, Therese Gieshe *(Bella Horn)*, Stephane Bouy *(Jean Bernard)*, Loumi Iacobesco *(Betty Beaulieu)*, Rene Bouloc *(Faure)*, Pierre Decazes *(Aubert)*, Jean Rougerie *(Tonin)*, Gilberte Rivet *(Mme. Lacombe)*

p, Louis Malle; d, Louis Malle; w, Louis Malle, Patrick Modiano; ph, Tonino Delli Colli (Eastmancolor); ed, Suzanne Baron; m, Django Reinhardt, Andre Claveau, Irene de Trebert; art d, Ghislain Uhry

A masterful job. Director Louis Malle directs his intellectual focus at the Occupation this time around. Blaise plays Lucien, a young farm boy who tries to join the French Resistance but is rejected because of his youth. The Gestapo, however, is happy to have him and treats the boy royally, supplying him with liquor and anything else he requests. He then makes the mistake of falling in love with a Jewish girl, France (Clement), resulting in her father's deportation. With France and her mother in tow, Lucien sets out for Spain with the Resistance out to kill him.

LACOMBE, LUCIEN represents a turn for the better for Malle, whose sometimes tends to shroud audience sympathy in underdeveloped intellectualizing. Much of Malle's motivation came from his own experiences growing up in France during the German Occupation. Even so, his fellow countrymen did not care very much for this cutting portrayal of the Resistance. Their vocal indictments inspired Malle to migrate to America, where he made such films as ATLANTIC CITY and PRETTY BABY. A great score by Reinhardt helps flesh out this moving, carefully handled film.

LADY AND THE TRAMP
1955 75m c   ★★★½
Animated   /U
Buena Vista

VOICES OF: Peggy Lee *(Darling/Peg/Si/Am)*, Barbara Luddy *(Lady)*, Larry Roberts *(Tramp)*, Bill Thompson *(Jock/Bull/Dachsie)*, Bill Baucon *(Trusty)*, Stan Freberg *(Beaver)*, Verna Felton *(Aunt Sarah)*, Alan Reed *(Boris)*, George Givot *(Tony)*, Dal McKennon *(Toughy/Professor)*

p, Walt Disney; d, Hamilton Luske, Clyde Geronimi, Wilfred Jackson; w, Erdman Penner, Joe Rinaldi, Ralph Wright, Don DaGradi (based on the novel by Ward Greene); ph, (CinemaScope, Technicolor); ed, Donald Halliday; m, Oliver Wallace; anim, Milt Kahl, Franklin Thomas, Oliver M. Johnston, John Lounsbery, Wolfgang Reitherman, Eric Larson, Hal King, Les Clark

This animated Disney classic tells the tale of Lady, a prim and proper cocker spaniel who falls in love with Tramp, a ragged mutt. When Lady runs away from her owner and is pursued by tough dogs in a bad neighborhood, Tramp rescues her. The two dogs spend a night on the town, which includes the memorable spaghetti-eating scene in which both Lady and Tramp eat the same strand, their mouths drawn closer and closer until at last they kiss. Lady is furious with Tramp when they end up in the pound after being caught raiding a chicken coup, but by the finale they are happily raising their own litter of pups. Disney's first

CinemaScope cartoon, LADY AND THE TRAMP cost $4,000,000 and took three years to complete, but it grossed over $25,000,000, making more money than any other film from the 1950s except THE TEN COMMANDMENTS and BEN-HUR.

LADY EVE, THE

1941 97m bw ★★★★★
Comedy/Romance /U
Paramount

Barbara Stanwyck *(Jean Harrington)*, Henry Fonda *(Charles Pike)*, Charles Coburn *("Colonel" Harry Harrington)*, Eugene Pallette *(Mr. Pike)*, William Demarest *(Muggsy-Ambrose Murgatroyd)*, Eric Blore *(Sir Alfred McGlennan Keith)*, Melville Cooper *(Gerald)*, Martha O'Driscoll *(Martha)*, Janet Beecher *(Mrs. Pike)*, Robert Greig *(Burrows)*

p, Paul Jones; d, Preston Sturges; w, Preston Sturges (based on the story "The Faithful Heart" by Monckton Hoffe); ph, Victor Milner; ed, Stuart Gilmore; art d, Hans Dreier, Ernst Fegte; cos, Edith Head

Sturges's chic, sly little masterpiece of comic seduction. Fonda, who is the son of a wealthy brewer (Pallette, whose slogan is "Pike's Pale, the Ale That Won for Yale"), is a rather shy and backward young man whose main interest is in snakes. As the film opens, he has just spent a year with a scientific expedition on the Amazon, looking for undiscovered species of reptiles. He and his bodyguard, Demarest, board a ship in the Atlantic which will take them back to New York. Of course, Fonda, being young, handsome, and the heir to a vast fortune, attracts the attention of virtually every female on the ship, but he shows no interest in the opposite sex.

Also on board is a team of card sharps, father and daughter Stanwyck and Coburn, and Cooper, posing as their butler. They figure Fonda would make an excellent pigeon, and Stanwyck conspires to gain his trust, which she does. Fonda is quickly smitten with her, and sits down to play some cards with her and her father. He considers himself to be quite the card player, but is embarrassed when he wins $600 from these nice people. Of course, he's only being set up to lose, but before the cons can reel in their prey, they hit a snag. Stanwyck has genuinely fallen in love with the man, much to the disgust of her associates.

THE LADY EVE is one of Sturges' best romantic comedies, with just the right blend of satire and slapstick, the laughs coming mostly from his clever, often inspired comedic lines. His direction is flawless, and the cast, from stars to stock players, performs beautifully. Stanwyck, is particular, is an effortless comedienne. She's also such a consummate performer that she can make you *think* she's beautiful, like Bette Davis. But Davis never quite got the hang of comedy, nor did Crawford; Davis had more unpredictable fire, Crawford more glamour and nobility, but Stanwyck's roles show a staggering range the other two lacked. In EVE Stanwyck pitches much of her performance into a kind of hushed, urgent, intimate whisper. When she talks to Fonda, she's constantly toying with him, touching him like an item of fetishism, and she's always in his face, often looking at his lips. Then out snakes a sexy leg—a very sexy leg—and over he topples. There's an unparalleled moment early on, when she narrates his movements, taking his part and every woman's who attempts to trap him in conversation, while watching the action backwards in her compact mirror. It's a daring, roguish display of her talent; one can't imagine any commediene—even Colbert or Russell—bringing it off as she does. Sturges, who began as a contract scriptwriter for Paramount, promised Stanwyck that he would write a great comedy for her some day, and she got it.

Impressed by Sturges' directorial debut, THE GREAT McGINTY, which proved to be a box-office bonanza, Paramount allowed him a big budget for THE LADY EVE. While THE LADY EVE was still in production, Sturges received enthusiastic reviews for another of his films, CHRISTMAS IN JULY, and happily read these accolades to any and all on the set. The raves for THE LADY EVE were even more widespread, and the public loved the film, filling Paramount's coffers with such large profits that the studio realized that it had a "golden boy" in Sturges and gave him a free hand in his subsequent superlative comedies. Later, THE LADY EVE was remade as THE BIRDS AND THE BEES, with George Gobel, Mitzi Gaynor, and David Niven (as the cardsharp father) under the direction of Norman Taurog. Poorly produced and poorly directed—with most of Sturges' funniest lines rewritten—it deservedly bombed at the box office.

LADY FROM SHANGHAI, THE

1948 87m bw ★★★★★
Crime /A
Columbia

Rita Hayworth *(Elsa Bannister)*, Orson Welles *(Michael O'Hara)*, Everett Sloane *(Arthur Bannister)*, Glenn Anders *(George Grisby)*, Ted de Corsia *(Sidney Broome)*, Erskine Sanford *(Judge)*, Gus Schilling *(Goldie)*, Carl Frank *(District Attorney)*, Lou Merrill *(Jake)*, Evelyn Ellis *(Bessie)*

p, Orson Welles; d, Orson Welles; w, Orson Welles (based on the novel *The Lady from Shanghai,* by [Raymond] Sherwood King); ph, Charles Lawton, Jr.; ed, Viola Lawrence; m, Heinz Roemheld; art d, Stephen Goosson, Sturges Carne; fx, Lawrence Butler; cos, Jean Louis

This remarkably inventive if decidedly confusing film noir stars Welles as a wandering Irishman named Michael O'Hara. One evening he saves Elsa Bannister (Hayworth) from a couple of thugs and, as a result, she is drawn to him like a shark to a swimmer. Her husband, famed lawyer Arthur Bannister (Sloane), offers to hire O'Hara as a deckhand for an upcoming cruise. O'Hara—who begins the film by saying, "When I start out to make a fool of myself, there's very little can stop me!"—accepts the offer, trying not to succumb to Elsa's advances along the way. Pretty soon O'Hara is on his way to making an A-1 fool out of himself, entering into an agreement with Bannister's goony, sweat-stained friend George Grisby (Anders), who offers O'Hara a sum of money to stage Grisby's own murder. When things start to misfire, O'Hara becomes, in fatalistic noir fashion, a puppet under the reckless control of everyone around him.

Replete with humorous self-deprecating narration, marvelous performances, and typically Wellesian visuals, THE LADY FROM SHANGHAI dazzles as much as it obfuscates. The most amazing visual effect is the climactic Crazy House/Hall of Mirrors location, which is a wonder of surrealistic set design. With its complex and occasionally incoherent narrative, the film will stump many of those viewers who think they can easily decipher a mystery. Fans of Rita Hayworth, then Welles's wife, were shocked—as was studio mogul Harry Cohn—when they saw her long, luxuriant russet hair cut into a blonde bob. The yacht on which the characters sail belonged to Welles's friend Errol Flynn, and it is Flynn (unseen) who is sailing the vessel during the trip. An uneven film, perhaps, but one which only seems to improve with age.

LADY IN THE DARK

1944 100m c   ★★★
Musical   /U
Paramount

Ginger Rogers (Liza Elliott), Ray Milland (Charley Johnson), Jon Hall (Randy Curtis), Warner Baxter (Kendall Nesbitt), Barry Sullivan (Dr. Brooks), Mischa Auer (Russell Paxton), Mary Philips (Maggie Grant), Phyllis Brooks (Allison DuBois), Edward Fielding (Dr. Carlton), Don Loper (Adams)

p, Richard Blumenthal; d, Mitchell Leisen; w, Frances Goodrich, Albert Hackett (based on the play by Moss Hart, Kurt Weill, Ira Gershwin); ph, Ray Rennahan, Farciot Edouart (Technicolor); ed, Alma Macrorie; m, Robert Emmett Dolan; art d, Hans Dreier, Raoul Pene du Bois; fx, Gordon Jennings, Paul K. Lerpae; chor, Billy Daniels, Don Loper; cos, Edith Head, Mitchell Leisen, Babs Wilomez, Raoul Pene Du Bois

LADY IN THE DARK seemed like a breakthrough musical on Broadway in its day, where it featured Danny Kaye and Victor Mature in support of Gertrude Lawrence. Unfortunately, none of these suitably cast players made it to the screen version, and the loss is evident. Also regrettable is the excising of several wonderful Kurt Weill-Ira Gershwin tunes from the play in favor of new songs that don't advance or enhance the plot. As if all this weren't enough, even the original's book doesn't seem quite as good as its reputation would suggest.

Ginger Rogers (in her first color film) is Liza Elliott, a magazine editor who's on the verge of a nervous breakdown, partly because she has too many men in her life. She seeks help from a psychiatrist (Barry Sullivan), and her sessions with him and some dream sequences provide the material for the film's production numbers. Vying for Liza's attention and threatening her job security are Charley Johnson (Ray Milland), the advertising manager for her magazine; recently divorced Kendall Nesbitt (Warner Baxter); and handsome hunk Randy Curtis (Jon Hall).

This expensive film made a lot of money upon its 1944 release, when audiences were clamoring for something light to relieve wartime anxieties. The story was unusual then, dealing as it did with Liza's position in a high-pressured man's world, her precarious emotional state (presented in Freudian terms that were still fairly novel for most moviegoers), and her inability to make a decision. It's all lavishly presented with glamorous style, but it's almost as if director Leisen cared more about the look of the film than its content.

Rogers has a good (if too distantly filmed) dance number with Don Loper, and she does a fine job singing the amusing "The Saga of Jenny", but her performance is uneven. The same goes for most of the cast, and even the storyline, missing the crucial song "My Ship" (from the heroine's childhood), seems a little out of kilter in retrospect. The result is a glitzy but superficial marriage of musical comedy and pop psychology.

LADY IN THE LAKE

1947 105m bw   ★★★★
Mystery   /A
MGM

Robert Montgomery (Philip Marlowe), Lloyd Nolan (Lt. DeGarmot), Audrey Totter (Adrienne Fromsett), Tom Tully (Capt. Kane), Leon Ames (Derace Kingsby), Jayne Meadows (Mildred Havelend), Morris Ankrum (Eugene Grayson), Lila Leeds (Receptionist), Richard Simmons (Chris Lavery), Ellen Ross (Elevator Girl)

p, George Haight; d, Robert Montgomery; w, Steve Fisher, Raymond Chandler (based on the novel by Chandler, uncredited); ph, Paul C. Vogel; ed, Gene Ruggiero; m, David Snell; art d, Cedric Gibbons, Preston Ames; fx, A. Arnold Gillespie; cos, Irene

"YOU accept an invitation to a blonde's apartment! YOU get socked in the jaw by a murder suspect!" That's how the ads promoted this rugged, inventive film noir, the first to employ a subjective camera. Under Robert Montgomery's clever direction, the viewer is in the film, so to speak, with all the action and characters addressing the camera, which presents the story from the point of view of Raymond Chandler's incorruptible private eye, Philip Marlowe.

The film opens as the camera moves into Montgomery's office where he sits behind a desk. There Montgomery begins to relate the "Lady in the Lake" caper, and the subjective camera takes over, the story unfolding in flashback. Tired of sleuthing for a living, Montgomery has taken up writing and produced a number of detective stories that he has submitted to Kingsby Publications. Having read Montgomery's most recent story, editor Totter asks that he come to see her. When he arrives in the magazine office, Montgomery learns that Totter is not really interested in his story; instead she wants Montgomery to locate Ames' missing wife. Totter plans to wed Ames, and she wants the detective to find the missing wife so Ames can divorce her and marry Totter. The first step in Montgomery's investigation is a visit to wealthy, musclebound gigolo Simmons. At first, Montgomery is welcomed by the handsome young rake, but when the detective asks one sensitive question too many, he is suddenly punched silly.

Montgomery wakes up in the Bay City jail, where tough cop Nolan tells him that he was picked up for drunk driving. Explaining that he was forced to knock out Montgomery when the detective gave the police a hard time, Nolan returns Montgomery's money to him and begins to read Totter's letter to the detective-turned-writer, sarcastically noting the title of the story Montgomery has submitted, "If I Should Die Before I Live." Nolan then escorts Montgomery into his boss's office, and Tully, the captain in charge, lectures Montgomery about drunk driving. Montgomery claims that he was framed—averring that he was knocked out and had booze poured over him before he was thrown into his car, which was then driven wildly down the street and over a curb. Unconvinced, Tully tells him to stop messing around in his district. Nolan threatens Montgomery with a beating and shows him the door.

Montgomery returns to Totter's office and informs her that the $300 he was given to find Ames' wife is not enough compensation for the beating he has taken. Then comes a report that the wife of the caretaker of Ames' retreat at Little Fawn Lake has been murdered, her body found floating in the lake. Believing that the caretaker's wife was murdered by Ames' wife, Totter asks Montgomery to go up to the lake and prove her theory so Ames' wife can be prosecuted for murder. Montgomery returns from the lake with a pin engraved from Simmons to Ames' wife, and tells Totter the murdered woman was not the caretaker's wife. By now, of course, Montgomery has decided to remain on the case.

LADY IN THE LAKE was an experiment Robert Montgomery, actor, had long dreamed of performing as Robert Montgomery, director. However, Montgomery's decision to direct was not well received by his studio, MGM. But when John Ford fractured his leg three weeks before completing THEY WERE EXPENDABLE and Montgomery completed the film for him, he won plaudits from Ford and the studio. MGM agreed to let Montgomery direct a film based on Raymond Chandler's *Lady in the Lake*, the rights to which had been purchased from the author for $35,000 (more money than Paramount had paid Chandler for the screenplays for DOUBLE INDEMNITY and THE BLUE DAHLIA). As early as 1938 Montgomery had been planning to make a film using the subjective camera. He originally wanted to adapt John Galsworthy's *Escape*, but MGM moguls told him that the studio had just purchased the Chandler novel, and he accepted the crime tale.

LADY IN THE LAKE is extremely fluid film; the camera floats from scene to scene, simulating Montgomery's movements. Moreover, much of the $1 million budget that went into making LADY IN THE LAKE was for elaborate "breakaway" sets. In one instance, the camera approaches Montgomery's car and enters it, but the car was actually in two separate pieces and when the camera swung behind the wheel, it merely moved in back of the front part of the car, the rear being swung away to make room for it.

Despite his brief appearances, Montgomery is undoubtedly the most polished, sophisticated and urbane Philip Marlowe to grace the screen. In fact, film historian Philip French averred that Montgomery came closer than any other actor in style and appearance to Chandler's professed ideal casting for the role, Cary Grant. Yet Chandler not only disliked Montgomery's performance but hated the film itself. The author's pessimism was certainly created by the unpleasant experience he endured in attempting to adapt his novel to the screen, the only time Chandler was ever paid to create a screenplay from one of his original works.

LADY IN THE LAKE is no mere curiosity; rather it is a full-blown, well-told, and always arresting story, engulfing the viewer, as it were, into the action, the mystery, and the harrowing finale, despite Chandler's disdain. Aside from a documentary for the US Navy, LADY IN THE LAKE would be Montgomery's last MGM film. The actor would go on to star and direct another offbeat but fascinating film noir entry, RIDE THE PINK HORSE, in which he talked out of the side of his mouth and was a lot tougher than the Philip Marlowe he gently plays here.

LADY IN WHITE

1988 112m c   ★★★★
Thriller   PG-13/15
New Century

Lukas Haas *(Frankie Scarlatti)*, Len Cariou *(Phil)*, Alex Rocco *(Angelo Scarlatti)*, Katherine Helmond *(Amanda)*, Jason Presson *(Geno Scarlatti)*, Renata Vanni *(Mama Assunta)*, Angelo Bertolini *(Papa Charlie)*, Jared Rushton *(Donald)*, Gregory Levinson *(Louie)*, Joelle Jacob *(Melissa)*

p, Andrew G. La Marca, Frank LaLoggia; d, Frank LaLoggia; w, Frank LaLoggia; ph, Russell Carpenter (Deluxe Color); ed, Steve Mann; m, Frank LaLoggia; prod d, Richard K. Hummel; fx, Image Engineering, Fantasy II Film Effects; cos, Jacqueline Saint Anne

Independent filmmaker Frank LaLoggia's (FEAR NO EVIL) long-awaited second feature is an impressive, if overly ambitious, semiautobiographical ghost story that rejects gore in favor of genuine gothic chills.

Surprisingly rich in character, period, and place, LADY IN WHITE begins on Halloween, 1962, as the youngest son of a widower (Alex Rocco), young Frankie (Lukas Haas), is locked in the school cloakroom by pranksters who leave him there for the night. Resigned to his fate, Frankie climbs up on the top shelf and tries to get some sleep. Suddenly he is awakened by the ghost of a little girl (Joelle Jacob) about his age who was murdered in

the cloakroom many years before. To his horror, Frankie watches as the murder of the child is reenacted before his eyes. Then, a real man, whose face is obscured, enters the cloakroom.

It's the killer, and he has returned to the scene of the crime to remove the girl's hair clip, which fell down the heating duct during the murder so many years before (the school plans to install a new heater the very next day). Unfortunately for Frankie, the intruder notices the boy and tries to strangle him. Frankie survives the attack, and the police soon after arrest a drunken janitor and charge him with the attempted murder of Frankie, suspecting him of being the child killer who has plagued the town for several years. Frankie knows the man is innocent and sets out to find the real killer with the help of the little girl's ghost.

An intensely personal film, LADY IN WHITE is an incredibly ambitious low-budget effort that attempts to combine a good ghost story with a childhood reminiscence about growing up during the early 1960s. Fortunately, LaLoggia pulls off this unlikely combination, although his narrative is a bit too diffuse at times. Instead of using encounters with ghosts to escape the realities of everyday life, LaLoggia's film is firmly rooted in the real world—child murders, racism, and cruelty share the spotlight here. Such horrors contrast markedly with the warm, loving and secure family of which Frankie is proud to be a part—he does not want to escape.

What does trouble the youth, however, is the death of his mother. The boy's subconscious longing for her is at the root of his quest, and he fulfills his desire to be with her again by helping to reunite the ghostly little girl with her mother. LaLoggia shares his unique vision with the viewer through an imaginative and innovative visual style that flows skillfully from traditional naturalism into surreal dreamlike fantasies and back again without ever seeming gratuitous or clumsy. A remarkable film.

LADY JANE

1986 142m c   ★★★½
Biography   PG-13/PG
Paramount   (U.K.)

Helena Bonham Carter *(Lady Jane Grey)*, Cary Elwes *(Guilford Dudley)*, John Wood *(John Dudley, Duke of Northumberland)*, Michael Hordern *(Dr. Feckenham)*, Jill Bennett *(Mrs. Ellen)*, Jane Lapotaire *(Princess Mary)*, Sara Kestelman *(Frances Grey, Duchess of Suffolk)*, Patrick Stewart *(Henry Grey, Duke of Suffolk)*, Warren Saire *(King Edward VI)*, Joss Ackland *(Sir John Bridges)*

p, Peter Snell; d, Trevor Nunn; w, David Edgar (based on a story by Chris Bryant); ph, Douglas Slocombe (Technicolor); ed, Anne V. Coates; m, Stephen Oliver; prod d, Allan Cameron; art d, Fred Carter, Martyn Hebert; chor, Geraldine Stephenson, Sheila Falconer; cos, Sue Blane, David Perry

The superb Helena Bonham Carter stars in this biographical look at the life of Lady Jane Grey, the 15-year-old Queen of England whose reign lasted a scant nine days. With the death of Henry VIII in 1547, the throne has passed on to his 16-year-old son, Edward VI (Warren Saire), the favorite cousin of Lady Jane (Carter). Because of the imminent death of Edward, a successor must be chosen. Fearing that the Protestant monarchy will fall into the hands of the rival Catholic faction led by Princess Mary (Jane Lapotaire), the Duke of Northumberland (John Wood) puts into effect his plan—betrothing Jane to his son Guilford (Cary Elwes) and persuading Edward to name Jane as his successor. Young, idealistic love soon overwhelms the couple. Jane tells Guilford of her faith in Catholicism, denouncing the crass materialism of the Protestantism of the day. Together they dream of a reformed England. While Jane is crowned and announces her plans for reform, however, the Catholic Princess Mary plans a takeover.

Gorgeously photographed and elegantly told, LADY JANE remains faithful, if not to the letter of history, at least to the spirit of the young lovers. The direction by Trevor Nunn sparkles with sincerity and a clear understanding of his characters' youthful idealism. The film never feels as long as its 142-minute running time, almost every frame seeming to fit without excess.

LADY SINGS THE BLUES

1972   144m   c   ★★★
Biography/Musical   R/X
Motown/Weston/Furie

Diana Ross (Billie Holiday), Billy Dee Williams (Louis McKay), Richard Pryor (Piano Man), James Callahan (Reg Hanley), Paul Hampton (Harry), Sid Melton (Jerry), Virginia Capers (Mama Holiday), Yvonne Fair (Yvonne), Scatman Crothers (Big Ben), Robert L. Gordy (Hawk)

p, Jay Weston, James S. White; d, Sidney J. Furie; w, Terence McCloy, Chris Clark, Suzanne De Passe (based on the book by Billie Holiday, William Dufty); ph, John A. Alonzo (Panavision, Eastmancolor); ed, Argyle Nelson; m, Michel Legrand; prod d, Carl Anderson; cos, Bob Mackie, Ray Aghayan, Norma Koch

View this film about Billie Holiday as a completely fictional story, and you'll enjoy it far more than you would otherwise. Ostensibly based on Holiday's autobiography, LADY SINGS THE BLUES begins in the early 1930s in Baltimore, where the teenaged Billie (Diana Ross) is raped and then sent to New York to stay with a friend of her mother's. In Harlem she works first as a maid, and later as a whore, in a brothel. With the encouragement of the brothel's "piano man" (Richard Pryor), she begins singing professionally and eventually becomes the lover of gambler Louis McKay (Billy Dee Williams)—actually Holiday's third husband but the sole romantic interest in the film.

"Lady Day's" inimitable style begins to win her notice on the club circuit, and she is invited to tour the South with a band led by white musicians. On tour she's devastated by racist treatment and turns to drugs, becoming an addict—a habit which threatens both her professional and personal success. Things get worse when her mother dies, and Holiday enters a sanitarium in an attempt to get clean. Although she later begins a new life with McKay, her triumph is short-lived, and the film closes by glancing over her remaining, troubled days until her death at age 44.

Perhaps because Holiday's true life story is so well documented, the filmmakers felt they had to alter the facts in order to interest audiences. The dramatized results angered many; jazz critic Leonard Feather, for one, noted that the film made no mention of Lester Young, Jimmy Monroe (to whom Holiday was married), John Hammond, Benny Goodman, Count Basie, Artie Shaw and Teddy Wilson—all important associations for Holiday during the period covered in the film. Taken as pure fiction, however, LADY SINGS THE BLUES is an overdirected but fairly watchable movie, aided by a good if not quite good enough performance by Ross in her dramatic screen debut. Ross's renderings of Holiday's great songs are effective, evocative rather than imitative of Holiday, and the former Supreme received a Best Actress Oscar nomination for her work.

LADY VANISHES, THE

1938   97m   bw   ★★★★★
Mystery/Spy   /U
Gaumont   (U.K.)

Margaret Lockwood (Iris Henderson), Michael Redgrave (Gilbert Redman), Paul Lukas (Dr. Hartz), Dame May Whitty (Miss Froy), Cecil Parker (Eric Todhunter), Linden Travers (Margaret Todhunter), Mary Clare (Baroness), Naunton Wayne (Caldicott), Basil Radford (Charters), Emile Boreo (Hotel Manager)

p, Edward Black; d, Alfred Hitchcock; w, Alma Reville, Sidney Gilliat, Frank Launder (based on the novel The Wheel Spins by Ethel Lina White); ph, Jack Cox; ed, Alfred Roome, R.E. Dearing; m, Louis Levy

Flabbergasting peak suspense, civilized but breathlessly fast. This is one of Hitchcock's finest British films, a classic mystery that manages to combine humor with a genuine sense of menace—not to mention the kinds of characters that everyone dreams of meeting on a Central European train journey.

The film is set into motion when a seemingly innocuous old woman, Miss Froy (Whitty), disappears while on board a train bound for England. An acquaintance, Iris (Lockwood), becomes concerned and sets out to find her. Despite the fact that there are only so many places to hide on a speeding train, Whitty cannot be found. Even more mysteriously, no one else seems convinced that she ever really existed. Each time that Lockwood thinks she has proof of what happened, that proof itself evaporates; and each time she begins to doubt her own memory, some objective fact re-alerts her suspicions. After a series of ingenious developments, Lockwood finally uncovers the truth with the help of music scholar Gilbert (Redgrave).

THE LADY VANISHES begins slowly but picks up speed as it goes along, finally steaming toward a suspenseful denouement. The film was extremely popular in the US and laid the tracks for the great British director's new career in Hollywood. After striking a deal with David O. Selznick, Hitchcock completed one more British picture, JAMAICA INN, and began a love affair with America, returning to England just once more, some 30 years later, for FRENZY.

LADYHAWKE

1985   121m   c   ★★★½
Fantasy/Adventure   PG-13/PG
WB

Matthew Broderick (Phillipe Gaston), Rutger Hauer (Navarre), Michelle Pfeiffer (Isabeau), Leo McKern (Imperius), John Wood (Bishop), Ken Hutchison (Marquet), Alfred Molina (Cezar), Loris Loddi (Jehan), Alessandro Serra (Mr. Pitou), Charles Borromel (Insane Prisoner)

p, Richard Donner, Lauren Shuler; d, Richard Donner; w, Edward Khmara, Michael Thomas, Tom Mankiewicz (based on a story by Edward Khmara); ph, Vittorio Storaro (Technovision, Technicolor); ed, Stuart Baird; m, Andrew Powell; prod d, Wolf Kroeger; art d, Giovanni Natalucci, Ken Court; fx, John Richardson; cos, Nana Cecchi

Phillipe (Matthew Broderick), a pickpocket in 13th-century France, is thrown into a dungeon, but escapes and tries to elude the palace guards in the thick of a nearby forest. Rescued by Navarre (Rutger Hauer), a mysterious knight, Phillipe is eager to be on his way, but the knight refuses to set him free, eventually filling him in on his secret. Navarre, the former chief guard for an evil bishop (John Wood), was involved in a romance with the bishop's mistress Isabeau (Michelle Pfeiffer). When the bishop learned of the affair, he appealed to the gods and had the lovers cursed. As a result the two take on different forms—Navarre, a wolf by night, and Isabeau, a hawk by day—never again able to embrace each other as humans.

Majestically photographed, LADYHAWKE is a joy to look at, employing some beautiful techniques to capture the transformations. Unfortunately, the synthesized soundtrack is drastically out of place and out of character. Hauer, playing a more gentle role than usual, is excellent, but Pfeiffer, who looks stunning, isn't given much to do. While not without faults, LADYHAWKE is much more striking than many of Donner's other films. A poetic, mythic tale of impossible love that was one of the overlooked films of 1985.

LADYKILLERS, THE

1956 96m c ★★★★
Comedy/Crime /U
Ealing (U.K.)

Alec Guinness (*Professor Marcus*), Cecil Parker (*The Mayor*), Herbert Lom (*Louis*), Peter Sellers (*Harry*), Danny Green (*One-Round*), Jack Warner (*Police Superintendent*), Katie Johnson (*Mrs. Wilberforce*), Philip Stainton (*Police Sergeant*), Frankie Howerd (*Barrow Boy*), Fred Griffiths (*The Junkman*)

p, Seth Holt; d, Alexander Mackendrick; w, William Rose (based on his story); ph, Otto Heller (Technicolor); ed, Jack Harris; m, Tristram Cary; art d, Jim Morahan

The last of the comedies produced by the Ealing Studios, and one of the finest, with a supremely dark tone which makes a climactic series of murders as hilarious as they are grotesque.

THE LADYKILLERS pits an implacably dotty landlady (Katie Johnson) against a criminal gang which includes Alec Guinness, as a "mastermind" with hideous teeth; Cecil Parker, as a bumbling military type; Herbert Lom, as an American-style gangster; Peter Sellers, as an inept teddy boy; and Danny Green, as a kind-hearted thug. The gang are using Johnson's house as a base from which to plan an elaborate robbery, but their combined talents evaporate in the face of their landlady's blithe command of her own, idiosyncratic world. In one scene, they are forced to halt their attempted getaway in order to take tea with Johnson and her friends and join in a sing-song around the harmonium!

THE LADYKILLERS was the last comedy produced by Ealing, which was in the process of closing down at the time of the film's release in 1955. Johnson, who was to die two years later, won a British Film Academy Award for her role. Shortly after the film's completion, director Mackendrick left England for the US, where he scored another triumph with SWEET SMELL OF SUCCESS.

L'AGE D'OR

1930 60m bw ★★★★★
Drama /AA
Corinth (France)

Lya Lys (*The Woman*), Gaston Modot (*The Man*), Max Ernst (*Bandit Chief*), Pierre Prevert (*Bandit*), Caridad de Laberdesque, Lionel Salem, Madame Noizet, Jose Artigas, Jacques Brunius

p, Le Vicomte de Noailles; d, Luis Bunuel; w, Luis Bunuel, Salvador Dali; ph, Albert Duverger; ed, Luis Bunuel; m, Richard Wagner, Felix Mendelssohn, Ludwig van Beethoven, Claude Debussy

One of the most controversial films of all time, L'AGE D'OR is a surreal inquiry into the traditions and standards of modern culture that have kept true passion and instinct from being freely expressed.

Modot and Lys, simply called the Man and the Woman, are the lovers who allow nothing to prevent them from demonstrating their feelings for each other. They want to make love, but must first overcome a number of seemingly insurmountable obstacles: the church, bourgeois social etiquette, and their own psychological handicaps. This love is demonstrated through surreal images that are both hilarious (a cow lying on a bed, a frustrated man kicking a socialite's obnoxious poodle into the air) and disturbing (a helpless boy being brutally shot to death), but the overall impact suggests love's transcendent power.

L'AGE D'OR, like many other surrealist and Dadaist works, is more than a piece of art—it is a manifesto. It is not an entertainment but a display of the iconoclasm, rage, wit and passion which Bunuel, Salvador Dali and their contemporaries wanted humanity to embrace. L'AGE D'OR is full of incredible moments: the opening documentary on the savagery of scorpions, Lys obsessively sucking the toes of a statue, the pompous clerics on the rocks. The accompanying program for the film read, "It is LOVE that brings about the transition from pessimism to action: Love, denounced in the bourgeois demonology as the root of all evil. For love demands the sacrifice of every other value: status, family, and honor."

During one of the film's initial showings in Paris, a minor riot broke out as people destroyed paintings by such artists as Man Ray, Max Ernst and Dali. L'AGE D'OR was subsequently banned and became the subject of heated debate in both left- and right-wing newspapers. Although Dali was involved, this film more properly belongs to Bunuel. Many of the themes appearing in his later works are evident here for the first time, though less tempered with his later occasional gentleness.

LANCELOT OF THE LAKE

(LANCELOT DU LAC)
1974 85m c ★★★★½
Historical /A
Mara/Laser/ORTF/Gerico Sound (France)

Luc Simon (*Lancelot*), Laura Duke Condominas (*Queen Guinevere*), Humbert Balsan (*Gawain*), Vladimir Antolek-Oresek (*King Arthur*), Patrick Bernhard (*Modred*), Arthur De Montalembert (*Lionel*)

p, Jean-Pierre Rassam, Francois Rochas; d, Robert Bresson; w, Robert Bresson; ph, Pasqualino De Santis (Eastmancolor); ed, Germaine Lamy; m, Philippe Sarde; prod d, Pierre Charbonnier; cos, Gres

The brilliant French director Robert Bresson applies his intensely personal cinematic vision to the legend of Lancelot and the Knights of the Round Table to create an entirely new rendition of the famous story. These knights are portrayed as anything but noble and conscientious individuals; rather, they are ruthless, greedy men whose main motivation is to obtain their desires. Disillusioned with their inability to find the Holy Grail, the knights on the quest return to England, causing havoc along the way, much of it fighting among themselves. Lancelot (Simon) returns to the love of Guinevere (Condominas), further sparking battles among the knights and leading to Lancelot's dismissal from King Arthur's favor.

The famous legend itself takes on secondary importance in the company of the moody visual style, the low-key performances, and a deliberately obtrusive soundtrack. The romantic substance of the underlying myth is here exposed for the coverup of bourgeois medieval savagery it is often taken to be. The visual and sound elements combine to create an extremely disturbing effect, further proof of Bresson's cinematic genius.

LAND BEFORE TIME, THE

1988   70m   c   ★★★½
Animated/Children's   G/U
Sullivan-Bluth/Amblin

VOICES OF: Pat Hingle *(Narrator/Rooter)*, Helen Shaver *(Littlefoot's Mother)*, Gabriel Damon *(Littlefoot)*, Candice Houston *(Cera)*, Burker Barnes *(Daddy Topps)*, Judith Barsi *(Ducky)*, Will Ryan *(Petrie)*

p, Don Bluth, Gary Goldman, John Pomeroy; d, Don Bluth; w, Stu Krieger (based on a story by Judy Freudberg, Tony Geiss); ed, Dan Molina, John K. Carr; m, James Horner; prod d, Don Bluth; fx, D.A. Lanpher; anim, John Pomeroy, Linda Miller, Ralph Zondag, Dan Kuenster, Lorna Pomeroy, Dick Zondag

In THE LAND BEFORE TIME, created under the tutelage of George Lucas and Steven Spielberg, Don Bluth capitalizes on the renewed interest in dinosaurs among children, setting his tale millions of years ago and creating what has been called a prehistoric BAMBI.

An orphaned brontosaurus named Littlefoot (voiced by Gabriel Damon) is forced to make his way through desolation in order to find the Great Valley, which is lush and green but very far away. Joining Littlefoot on his adventure are a feisty baby triceratops named Cera (Candice Houston); a restless, chatty anatosaurus named Ducky (Judith Barsi); a pterodactyl named Petrie (Will Ryan); and a mute, dull-witted stegosaurus named Spike. A gorgeous production from beginning to end, THE LAND BEFORE TIME contains all the essential elements missing from most of Disney's recent efforts. Bluth, a former Disney animator, understands that the greatest Disney films take us on an emotional journey in which all our hopes and fears are played out in a vivid fantasy world where anything can happen. THE LAND BEFORE TIME continues that great tradition.

LANDLORD, THE

1970   112m   c   ★★★½
Drama/Comedy   R/X
Mirisch

Beau Bridges *(Elgar Enders)*, Pearl Bailey *(Marge)*, Diana Sands *(Fanny)*, Louis Gossett, Jr. *(Copee)*, Lee Grant *(Mrs. Enders)*, Douglas Grant *(Walter Gee)*, Mel Stewart *(Prof. Duboise)*, Walter Brooke *(Mr. Enders)*, Susan Anspach *(Susan)*, Robert Klein *(Peter)*

p, Norman Jewison; d, Hal Ashby; w, Bill Gunn (based on the novel by Kristin Hunter); ph, Gordon Willis (DeLuxe Color); ed, William A. Sawyer, Edward Warschilka; m, Al Kooper; prod d, Robert Boyle; cos, Domingo Rodriguez

This satiric look at racial tensions has sheltered rich kid Elgar Enders (Beau Bridges) buying a ghetto tenement with the intention of kicking the tenants out and remodeling it for his own use. His plans change when he grows attached to the people living in the building—an interesting assortment who spark emotions in Elgar that he never knew he possessed. He falls in love with Lanie (Marki Bey), a black art student, and decides to marry her, but their plans are postponed when he discovers he has gotten his neighbor Fanny (Diana Sands) pregnant. The film offers some fine performances (Lee Grant was nominated for Best Supporting Actress), and Ashby's quirky but skillful direction allows the individual personalities of the characters to shine through. The script has a few uneven moments, none of which damage the overall quality of the film, and Willis captures the atmosphere of both rich and poor New York lifestyles with an impressive visual style.

LANDSCAPE IN THE MIST

1988   127m   c   ★★★★
Drama   /15
Greek Film Center/RAI-TV/Paradis/ET-1
(Greece/France/Italy)

Iania Palaiologou, Michalis Zeke, Stratos Tzortzoglou

d, Theo Angelopoulos; w, Theo Angelopoulos, Tonino Guerra; ph, Georges Arvanitis; m, Helen Karaindrou

A brother and sister (played by 11-year-old Palaiologou and five-year-old Zeke) go to an Athens train station daily to await their father's return from Germany. One day they muster the courage to hop a northbound train, determined to look for him themselves, but learn from an uncaring uncle that their father is not in Germany. The youngsters run away from the police station where they are temporarily being kept, only to be picked up by a rapist who turns their journey into a nightmare. They are helped at various points along the way, however, by a member of a traveling theatre company (Tzortzoglou), a gay man anguishing over his imminent army duty. A minor epiphany involving a tree gives the film a hopeful if ambiguous finale.

Theo Angelopoulos is one of Greece's most successful directors, and this film certainly does nothing to damage his reputation. All of his films concern travels around the Greek countryside, but LANDSCAPE IN THE MIST presents a Greece far different from the one depicted in sunny travel posters. Set during a rainy, miserable winter, the action moves across a bleak landscape, where a gray beach faces a distant factory and tractors drag dying horses through the snow. Operating on a less than literal level that is exemplified by the film's imaginary Greek-German border, this dreamlike affair is punctuated with surreal monologues by the children and a powerfully understated rape scene. LANDSCAPE IN THE MIST is a meticulously crafted production with beautifully composed shots, fine performances (particularly Palaiologou's), and an excellent score.

L'ARGENT

1984   90m   c   ★★★★★
Crime   /PG
Marion's/FR3/EOS   (France/Switzerland)

Christian Patey *(Yvon Targe)*, Sylvie van den Elsen *(Old Woman)*, Michel Briguet *(The Woman's Father)*, Caroline Lang *(Elise Targe)*, Vincent Risterucci *(Lucien)*, Beatrice Tabourin *(Woman Photographer)*, Didier Baussy *(Man Photographer)*, Marc Ernest Fourneau *(Norbert)*, Brune Lapeyre *(Martial)*, Andre Cler *(Norbert's Father)*

p, Jean-Marc Henchoz; d, Robert Bresson; w, Robert Bresson (based on the story "The False Note" by Leo Tolstoy); ph, Emmanuel Machuel, Pasqualino De Santis; ed, Jean Francois Naudon; m, Johann Sebastian Bach; art d, Pierre Guffroy; cos, Monique Dury

Writer-director Robert Bresson's 13th film in 40 years, L'ARGENT is, like so many of his other films, a work of true cinematic genius that stands head and shoulders above most other pictures and seems to defy critical judgment. L'ARGENT begins with young schoolboy Norbert's (Marc Ernest Fourneau) trying unsuccessfully to get money from his parents. An enterprising classmate gives him some counterfeit bills, which Norbert passes on to a worker in a photographic shop. The shop owner (Didier Baussy) is determined to get rid of the phony bills and palms them off to an unsuspecting deliveryman (Christian Patey), who innocently pays a cafe bill with the forged notes and is promptly arrested. The schoolboy's mother pays the shop owner to keep silent about her son's involvement. Throughout the first half-hour of the film (before we are certain that Patey is the leading player), money is the central character. It changes hands from one person to another in extreme close-ups and carries us from one scene to the next, one location to the next. The bills are recognizable, whereas the people passing them are not. The power of money and the effects of one person's impositions upon another eventually lead the feckless deliveryman along an increasingly harrowing life's path to the film's stunning conclusion. Bresson justly won acclaim for this piercing film from the Cannes Film Festival, which voted him Best Director.

LASSIE, COME HOME
1943   90m   c   ★★★★
Adventure/Children's   /U
MGM

Roddy McDowall (Joe Carraclough), Donald Crisp (Sam Carraclough), Edmund Gwenn (Rowlie), Dame May Whitty (Dolly), Nigel Bruce (Duke of Rudling), Elsa Lanchester (Mrs. Carraclough), Elizabeth Taylor (Priscilla), J. Pat O'Malley (Hynes), Ben Webster (Dan'l Fadden), Alec Craig (Snickers)

p, Samuel Marx; d, Fred M. Wilcox; w, Hugo Butler (based on the novel by Eric Knight); ph, Leonard Smith (Technicolor); ed, Ben Lewis; m, Daniele Amfitheatrof; art d, Cedric Gibbons, Paul Groesse; fx, Warren Newcombe

This low-budget effort wasn't expected to do much at the box office, but moviegoers fell in love with the title collie, and many sequels, a radio program, and a long-running TV show followed. In Yorkshire in the dark days after WWI, young Joe Carraclough (Roddy McDowall) is forced to give up Lassie when his parents (Donald Crisp and Elsa Lanchester) can no longer afford to keep the dog. After escaping once from her new owner, the Duke of Rudling (Nigel Bruce), Lassie is taken by him to Scotland, and, freed by the duke's sympathetic granddaughter (Elizabeth Taylor), makes a long, eventful journey back to Joe.

This Lassie, actually a male dog named Pal, was bought for $10 by trainer Rudd Weatherwax, who had worked for MGM training animals for PECK'S BAD BOY and THE CHAMP. The studio wanted a female dog and Weatherwax was chosen to find a good one, but when shooting began the female shed heavily and was replaced by Pal. Contrary to popular belief, this was not Taylor's first film. She had been signed to a brief contract by Universal and appeared in THERE'S ONE BORN EVERY MINUTE the year before. Even more than costar Roddy McDowall, the seductive Taylor has that uncanny quality some child actors possess of looking and sometimes acting quite like an adult, even at a pre-adolescent age. The presence of these kids, and that of the well-trained pooch, quite upstage the endearing and highly professional actors surrounding them. Still, this film is a fairly well-balanced effort, and if you're in the mood for an evening of obvious sentiment, this boy-and-his-dog film works quite well.

LAST AMERICAN HERO, THE
1973   95m   c   ★★★
Sports   PG/AA
Fox

Jeff Bridges (Elroy Jackson Jr.), Valerie Perrine (Marge), Geraldine Fitzgerald (Mrs. Jackson), Ned Beatty (Hackel), Gary Busey (Wayne Jackson), Art Lund (Elroy Jackson Sr.), Ed Lauter (Burton Colt), William Smith, II (Kyle Kingman), Gregory Walcott (Morley), Tom Ligon (Lamar)

p, William Roberts, John Cutts; d, Lamont Johnson; w, William Roberts (based on articles by Tom Wolfe); ph, George Silano (Panavision, DeLuxe Color); ed, Tom Rolf, Robbe Roberts; m, Charles Fox; art d, Lawrence G. Paull

Based on an *Esquire* article by Tom Wolfe, this well-crafted film tells the story of real-life stock car driver Junior Jackson, who served as THE LAST AMERICAN HERO's technical adviser. As a North Carolina youth, Jackson (Jeff Bridges) is a hot-rodding, small-time hoodlum until his father is busted for moonshining and hauled off to prison. He then decides to put his ability behind the wheel to good use, becoming a professional stock car racer to raise money for his father's defense. Starting at a local track, Bridges begins a rise to the stock car big time, where his stubborn independence runs up against the realities of corporate sponsorship. Well written and subtly directed, THE LAST AMERICAN HERO concentrates on the human elements of the story without becoming overly sentimental. Its performances— including Ned Beatty as the local promoter and Valerie Perrine a trackside groupie—are also excellent.

LAST DETAIL, THE
1973   103m   c   ★★★★
Drama   R/18
Columbia

Jack Nicholson (Buddusky SM1), Otis Young (Mulhall GM1), Randy Quaid (Meadows SN), Clifton James (Chief Master-at-Arms), Michael Moriarty (Marine Duty Officer), Carol Kane (Young Whore), Luana Anders (Donna), Kathleen Miller (Kathleen), Nancy Allen (Nancy), Gerry Salsberg (Henry)

p, Gerald Ayres; d, Hal Ashby; w, Robert Towne (based on the novel by Darryl Ponicsan); ph, Michael Chapman (Metrocolor); ed, Robert C. Jones; m, Johnny Mandel; prod d, Michael Haller; cos, Ted Parvin

A grim yet very touching portrait of a trip taken by three men, one of whom is to lose his freedom by journey's end. Two career sailors, Nicholson and Young, are randomly selected to escort Quaid from their West Virginia base to a prison in Massachusetts. Quaid was caught stealing from the polio charity box; since that was the favorite charity of the admiral's wife, he is sentenced to eight years in jail, or a year for every five dollars. Nicholson and Young got a lot more than they bargained for when they were assigned this detail. At first, they think it's just another shore leave with liberty to be enjoyed and lots of carousing. The two hardened sailors are soon won over, however, by Quaid's bumbling ways and the difficulty of his plight. This causes them to take a paternal attitude toward him as they travel from one dim location to another. Only the characters in the film look alive, as everywhere they go appears to have been filtered by pale grays and yellows. Nicholson and Young try to show Quaid a good time before his long stay in the brig. They encounter Anders, who brings them to a Nicheren Shoshu meeting where religious zealots (including Gilda Radner before she became a TV star) chant "Nam-Myoho-Renge-Kyo" and dance happily in their scented environment. Anders next takes Quaid to her room when she learns of his bleak future and tells him that she's going to do something that will be very important. The naive Quaid thinks she's about to seduce him; instead, she begins to chant, which confuses him at first, then leads to a poignant scene later. Nicholson and Young can't make any time with Anders's pals, so it's off to another adventure—this time to a brothel where they offer Quaid a good time with Kane, which they'll pay for. Quaid unsuccessfully tries to escape (while chanting the liturgy Anders taught him), but after an agonizing chase across a frozen park, Nicholson and Young capture him and deliver him to prison. We get the feeling that Nicholson and Young, if their naval careers did not depend on it, would have taken off with Quaid. They try hard not to be emotional as Quaid is escorted up a small staircase to the room where he will spend the rest of his youth.

THE LAST DETAIL is a gritty look at the military life and the people who are attracted to it. It is dark in its message and gray to the eye. Locations are all washed out as though there were a thin membrane of filth spread across everything except the leads, who pop out colorfully like three strawberries in a bowl of Cream of Wheat. This is Nicholson's best work since FIVE EASY PIECES, perhaps because his character seems to be an extension of that film's Bobby DuPea. Ashby's direction is superlative, as is his use of music to help secure the mood. Ashby was able to get Nicholson's least-mannered performance in many a day, after bombs with THE KING OF MARVIN GARDENS; A SAFE PLACE; and DRIVE, HE SAID. Ponicsan also wrote the naval-based novel, *Cinderella Liberty,* which was made into a film the same year. THE LAST DETAIL won no Oscars but did get nominations for Quaid, Nicholson (who lost to Jack Lemmon for SAVE THE TIGER), and Robert Towne for his screenplay.

LAST EMPEROR, THE

1987   160m   c   ★★★★½
Historical/Biography   PG-13/15
Columbia

John Lone *(Aisin-Gioro "Henry" Pu Yi as an Adult),* Joan Chen *(Wan Jung, "Elizabeth"),* Peter O'Toole *(Reginald Johnston),* Ying Ruocheng *(The Governor),* Victor Wong *(Chen Pao Shen),* Dennis Dun *(Big Li),* Ryuichi Sakamoto *(Masahiko Amakasu),* Maggie Han *(Eastern Jewel),* Ric Young *(Interrogator),* Wu Jun Mei *(Wen Hsiu)*

p, Jeremy Thomas; d, Bernardo Bertolucci; w, Mark Peploe, Bernardo Bertolucci, Enzo Ungari; ph, Vittorio Storaro (Technovision, Technicolor); ed, Gabriella Cristiani; m, Ryuichi Sakamoto, David Byrne, Cong Su; prod d, Ferdinando Scarfiotti; art d, Gianni Giovagnoni, Gianni Silvestri, earia Teresa Barbasso; fx, Gianetto De Rossi, Fabrizio Martinelli; cos, James Acheson

Fascinating but passive pageantry, due to an inactive protagonist. But where else can you get some of *these* visuals. After a six-year absence, Italian director Bernardo Bertolucci returned to the screen with this grand and powerful biography of Aisin-Gioro "Henry" Pu Yi, who in 1908, at the age of three, was named emperor of China and by the end of his life was quietly working as a gardener at Peking's Botanical Gardens. Told in an intricate flashback/flashforward narrative that uses Pu Yi's communist "remolding" period as its fulcrum, the film opens in 1950 as Pu Yi, and thousands of others, are returned to their now-communist homeland to face rehabilitation. From that point the story moves to Pu Yi's childhood, his imprisonment in the Forbidden City, his term as Japan's puppet emperor of Manchukuo, and his release into the population of China in 1959. Combining the command of the historical epic he displayed in 1900 with the political intrigue and melodrama of THE CONFORMIST, Bertolucci has, in THE LAST EMPEROR, constructed a beautiful film about the transformation of both a man and a country. A storyteller and not a historian, Bertolucci offers two tales in THE LAST EMPEROR—that of China's change, told through a selective sampling of events; and that of Pu Yi's change, told with an emphasis on myth rather than on fact. Moreover, Vittorio Storaro's carefully constructed lighting schemes and moving camera are unmatched by any cinematographer working today. John Lone, as

the adult Pu Yi, is wholly credible, and Wu Tao, as the adolescent Pu Yi, is every bit Lone's equal. Both actors convey the emperor's innocence, ignorance, and veiled sadistic streak. Joan Chen demonstrates her skill by playing both a radiant teen bride and a rotting opium addict. Peter O'Toole shows more restraint than usual and simply becomes his character, as if he, like Reginald Johnston, would have made an excellent tutor for the emperor. Also worthy of note is the film's score, which combines lush romanticism with traditional Chinese melodies and was written chiefly by Ryuichi Sakamoto (who also scored MERRY CHRISTMAS, MR. LAWRENCE) and David Byrne (of Talking Heads fame). THE LAST EMPEROR made a clean sweep at the Academy Awards, winning an Oscar in every category in which it was nominated: Best Film, Director, Adapted Screenplay, Cinematography, Original Score, Editing, Art Direction, Costumes, and Sound. How we wish the film had used a more red-blooded attack on it's commentary on blue-blooded privelege.

LAST EXIT TO BROOKLYN

1989   102m   c   ★★★★½
Drama   /18
Neue Constantin   (West Germany)

Stephen Lang *(Harry Black),* Jennifer Jason Leigh *(Tralala),* Burt Young *(Big Joe),* Peter Dobson *(Vinnie),* Jerry Orbach *(Boyce),* Stephen Baldwin *(Sal),* Jason Andrews *(Tony),* James Lorenz *(Freddy),* Maia Danziger *(Mary Black),* Cameron Johann *(Spook)*

p, Bernd Eichinger; d, Uli Edel; w, Desmond Nakano (based on the novel by Hubert Selby Jr.); ph, Stefan Czapsky; ed, Peter Przygodda; m, Mark Knopfler; art d, Mark Haack; cos, Carol Oditz

Red Hook, Brooklyn, 1952: Korea-bound conscripts, sadistic teenage gangs, and despondent strikers eke out their desolate existences amidst a frenzied mixture of prostitutes, psychos, winos, and junkies. Based on a collection of short stories by Hubert Selby Jr., which unleashed a storm of controversy upon their publication in 1964, German director Uli Edel's film is a relentlessly bleak account of life in the neighborhood during a brief period in the summer of '52.

The stories of a cross-section of characters is recounted in episodic fashion. Tralala (Jennifer Jason Leigh) is a prostitute who picks up tricks in sleazy bars and lures them to rubble-strewn vacant lots where they are mugged by ex-convict Vinnie (Peter Dobson) and his gang of thugs. Harry (Stephen Lang) is in charge of the local strike office, enjoying his position of power, but troubled by his awakening homosexuality. Georgette (Alexis Arquette) is an effeminate, tormented gay who lusts after Vinnie. Big Joe (Burt Young) is a striking worker who is upset over the pregnancy of his unmarried daughter Donna (Ricki Lake), while his motorcycle-obsessed son Spook (Cameron Johann) pines for Tralala. Tralala, tired of being short-changed by Vinnie, takes up with a handsome soldier (Frank Military), hoping it will lead to a big payoff. But when he ships out, he leaves her with nothing but a love letter, sending her back to her sordid life in Red Hook. During a party, Harry meets transvestite Regina (Zette), and spends the night with him, causing him to be late the next morning when scabs break through factory picket lines. Fired by union boss Boyce (Jerry Ohrbach), Harry is also rejected by Regina, and his world begins to completely unravel. Unable to win the affections of Vinnie, Georgette, high on heroin late one night, charges into the street and is run down and killed by a cab (driven by author Selby). Tommy (John Costelloe), father of Donna's unborn child, agrees to marry her, somewhat mollifying the emotional Big Joe, while Spook's love for Tralala only leads to pain.

In blending the personal worlds of these characters into a complete cosmology of the abyss, director Uli Edel (CHRISTIANE F.) and scriptwriter Desmond Nakano have demonstrated great skill. They have taken the episodic nature of Selby's book and transformed it into an aesthetic whole that is greater than the sum of its parts. Moreover, Edel's and Nakano's efforts are just part of what was clearly the engaged teamwork of a group of gifted people committed to doing justice to Selby's uncompromising artistic vision. Lang and, especially, Jason Leigh, are standouts in a terrific ensemble cast. Producer Bernd Eichinger's LAST EXIT TO BROOKLYN is one of the first great films of the 1990s. An apocalyptic vision packed with soul-shuddering violence and brutality, it is even more successful on all levels than Eichinger's last production, THE NAME OF THE ROSE, and marks his coming of age as an international filmmaker.

LAST HURRAH, THE

1958   121m   bw   ★★½
Political   /U
Columbia

Spencer Tracy *(Frank Skeffington)*, Jeffrey Hunter *(Adam Caulfield)*, Dianne Foster *(Maeve Caulfield)*, Pat O'Brien *(John Gorman)*, Basil Rathbone *(Norman Cass, Sr.)*, Donald Crisp *(The Cardinal)*, James Gleason *(Duke Gillen)*, Edward Brophy *(Ditto Boland)*, John Carradine *(Amos Force)*, Willis Bouchey *(Roger Sugrue)*

p, John Ford; d, John Ford; w, Frank S. Nugent (based on the novel by Edwin O'Connor); ph, Charles Lawton, Jr.; ed, Jack Murray; art d, Robert Peterson

One of John Ford's weakest films. Spencer Tracy breezes through this cliched, sentimental study of a political boss like a college student showing off when asked to recite his multiplication tables. Frank Skeffington (Tracy) rises each morning to put a rose beneath the portrait of his deceased wife. His son (Arthur Walsh), an empty-headed good-for-nothing, does nothing but play jazz and chase women. Though surrounded by cronies and political associates, Skeffington is essentially friendless, except for his young and idealistic nephew Adam (Hunter). Adam works as a reporter for an opposition newspaper run by Amos Force (Carradine), leader of the patrician class which has always been at odds with Skeffington and his minions. Skeffington seeks a loan from banker Cass (Rathbone) to back a new housing project. Cass refuses, and Frank retaliates by making Cass' retarded son (O.Z. Whitehead) acting fire commissioner. Rather than see his childlike son disgrace the family, Cass grants the loan but takes his revenge by financially backing the opposition. Adam records Frank's last political campaign, his "last hurrah" for the city's mayoralty, which is packed with old-time street marches, slogans, and banners. The venerable politico loses, however, and soon after dies in bed after his political pals (Pat O'Brien, James Gleason, Edward Brophy and Frank McHugh among them) make their final farewells.

For Ford, Tracy and most of the veteran cast, this film was like old home week, and Tracy considered making it his final film. It did turn out to be the last film made by veteran character actor Brophy, here giving the film's best performance. The rest of the cast, Tracy included, turn in enjoyably effortless if if not particularly inspired work; the heavily sentimental atmosphere seemed to get the better of the cast and crew. Ford's approach here is rather tedious and somber, despite the comedic aspects of the script, placing emphasis on death; his scenes are deeply

shadowed, and there is a pervasive gloom in almost every scene, heralding Tracy's demise. Some of the humor works well, though the comedy milked at the expense of the mentally retarded Cass Jr. today seems in bad taste.

LAST METRO, THE

(LE DERNIER METRO)
1980   133m   c   ★★★½
War/Romance   R/PG
Carrosse/TF-1   (France)

Catherine Deneuve *(Marion Steiner)*, Gerard Depardieu *(Bernard Granger)*, Jean Poiret *(Jean-Loup Cottins)*, Heinz Bennent *(Lucas Steiner)*, Andrea Ferreol *(Arlette Guillaume)*, Paulette Dubost *(Germaine Fabre)*, Sabine Haudepin *(Nadine Marsac)*, Jean-Louis Richard *(Daxiat)*, Maurice Risch *(Raymond, the Stage Manager)*, Marcel Berbert *(Merlin)*

d, Francois Truffaut; w, Francois Truffaut, Suzanne Schiffman, Jean-Claude Grumberg (based on a story by Truffaut, Schiffman); ph, Nestor Almendros; ed, Martine Barraque; m, Georges Delerue; art d, Jean-Pierre Kohut-Svelko; cos, Lisele Roos

Truffaut's oblique, microcosmic look at the German occupation of France is set almost entirely in a theater building. Marion Steiner (Deneuve, in an arresting performance) is the wife of top stage director Lucas Steiner (Bennent), who is forced to go underground in order to avoid Nazi persecution. Instead of fleeing Paris, Lucas hides in the cellar of the theater, eavesdropping on the rehearsals of his new play, which costars Marion and Bernard Granger (Depardieu). Time passes and the lives of the theater personnel become strained, particulary as Marion and Bernard try to resist a growing mutual attraction.

Politics and romance are placed on parallel tracks in this film through the figure of Marion, who tries to remain as loyal to her husband as she is to her countrymen. Often scolded for not addressing political issues in his pictures, director Francois Truffaut finally found a suitable vehicle in THE LAST METRO, which filters the Nazi occupation through a love story and recognizes the complexities of the situation with a dual, on- and off-stage ending. Truffaut's vision of 1940s Paris is more influenced by mythicized images of the city in films of the period than by historical reality, but the social commentary is vivid nonetheless.

LAST MOVIE, THE

1971   108m   c   ★★½
Drama   R/X
Universal

Julie Adams *(Mrs. Anderson)*, Dennis Hopper *(Kansas)*, Daniel Ades *(Thomas Mercado)*, Rod Cameron *(Pat)*, John Alderman *(Jonathan)*, Michael Anderson, Jr. *(Mayor's Son)*, Rich Aguilar *(Gaffer)*, Donna Baccala *(Miss Anderson)*, Tom Baker *(Member of Billy's Gang)*, Toni Basil *(Rose)*

p, Paul Lewis; d, Dennis Hopper; w, Stewart Stern (based on a story by Dennis Hopper and Stewart Stern); ph, Laszlo Kovacs (Technicolor); ed, Dennis Hopper, David Berlatsky, Antranig Mahakian; m, Kris Kristofferson, John Buck Wilkin, Chabuca Granda, Severn Darden, The Villagers of Chinchero, Peru; art d, Leon Ericksen; fx, Milt Rice; cos, Jerry Alpert

After the success of EASY RIDER, Dennis Hopper was given $1 million by Universal to make a film, and came back with more than 40 hours worth of footage. His final cut, after more than a year of editing, was incomprehensible to the studio and to most of the people who saw the film, except for those at the Venice

Film Festival, who gave it an award. Take a look at the cast list and you'll see that Hopper called in many of his pals to do cameos, but all that talent couldn't help. The picture is supposedly based on some experiences Hopper had while filming THE SONS OF KATIE ELDER in Mexico. He'd hoped to shoot this in Mexico but was refused, so he took the entire company to Peru. The movie begins at the end, flashes back to the beginning, and winds up somewhere in the middle. Hopper plays Kansas, a movie stunt man who stays behind on a film location after the company has moved off. He takes up with a local whore (Stella Garcia) then goes off to find gold with his friend Neville (Don Gordon) who, inexplicably, commits suicide. The local priest (Tomas Milian), meanwhile, makes trouble by blaming movies for the introduction of death and destruction to his naive villagers. Kansas is adopted by the local Peruvian Indians who have made some abandoned movie equipment part of their religion. In the end, the Indians plan to crucify Kansas, as they have cast him as Billy The Kid in their production.

THE LAST MOVIE is filled with such distancing devices as blank frames and inserts that read "Scene Missing." It is also overly pretentious. Cinematographer Kovacs can usually make anything look good, but he comes a cropper in this case. Hopper, to this day, thinks that his film is a masterpiece, and while the film's self-conscious play with the medium of filmmaking does generate some interest, there probably aren't many people out there who agree with the director's evaluation.

LAST OF SHEILA, THE

1973   120m   c   ★★★½
Mystery   PG/AA
WB

Richard Benjamin (*Tom*), Dyan Cannon (*Christine*), James Coburn (*Clinton*), Joan Hackett (*Lee*), James Mason (*Philip*), Ian McShane (*Anthony*), Raquel Welch (*Alice*), Yvonne Romain (*Sheila*), Pierro Rosso (*Vittorio*), Serge Citon (*Guido*)

p, Herbert Ross; d, Herbert Ross; w, Anthony Perkins, Stephen Sondheim; ph, Gerry Turpin (Technicolor); ed, Edward Warschilka; m, Billy Goldenberg; prod d, Ken Adam; art d, Tony Roman

THE LAST OF SHEILA is a superb murder mystery and something of a curio in film history, thanks to a script (by Anthony Perkins and Stephen Sondheim) that is written in the style of a British crossword puzzle. A wealthy Hollywood producer (Coburn) whose wife was killed by a hit-and-run driver at a party a year before, invites six people, all suspects, to his yacht in the south of France, hoping to uncover the culprit. He engages the six—a failed screenwriter (Benjamin); his rich, neurotic wife (Hackett); a movie star (Welch); her manager-husband (McShane); an aging film director (Mason); and a high-powered agent (Cannon)—in a psychological game designed to provoke the murderer into revealing his or her identity. The producer actually succeeds in getting murdered himself, and another death follows before the mystery is solved. If you enjoy puns, anagrams, and wordplay, you will find THE LAST OF SHEILA a positive Joycean delight. Listen for Bette Midler singing "Friends" on the soundtrack.

LAST OF THE MOHICANS, THE

1936   91m   bw   ★★★★
Historical/Adventure/War
Small

Randolph Scott (*Hawkeye*), Binnie Barnes (*Alice Munro*), Heather Angel (*Cora Munro*), Hugh Buckler (*Col. Munro*), Henry Wilcoxon (*Maj. Duncan Heyward*), Bruce Cabot (*Magua*), Robert Barrat (*Chingachgook*), Philip Reed (*Uncas*), Willard Robertson (*Capt. Winthrop*), Frank McGlynn, Sr. (*David Gamut*)

p, Edward Small, Harry M. Goetz; d, George B. Seitz; w, Philip Dunne, John Balderston, Paul Perez, Daniel Moore (based on the novel by James Fenimore Cooper); ph, Robert Planck; ed, Jack Dennis, Harry Marker; art d, John DuCasse Schulze; cos, Franc Smith

Undoubtedly the finest film version of James Fenimore Cooper's classic adventure tale, THE LAST OF THE MOHICANS benefits from fine performances by Randolph Scott as Hawkeye, Henry Wilcoxon as Maj. Duncan Heyward, and Bruce Cabot as the vicious, lascivious Huron Indian, Magua, one of the most hateful roles in film history. During the height of the French and Indian War, Hawkeye escorts Maj. Heyward, Alice (Binnie Barnes), and Cora Munro (Heather Angel), the daughters of the commander of Ft. William Henry, through hostile lines., accompanied by Chingachgook (Robert Barrat) and his son, Uncas (Philip Reed), who are the last survivors of the Mohican tribe, wiped out by the French-allied Hurons. During the course of their dangerous trek to the fort, Alice becomes enamored of Hawkeye, Cora and Uncas fall in love, and Magua makes life miserable for everyone. Before Chingachgook sends Magua to the happy hunting ground, the sadistic Huron brings about the deaths of both Cora and Uncas. What's more, the British are routed at Ft. William Henry and Hawkeye is taken prisoner and tied to a stake by the Hurons before Maj. Heyward comes to his rescue.

Packed with excitement and well-staged battle scenes, this superbly crafted adventure film was masterfully directed by George B. Seitz and magnificently lensed in California's High Sierras by Robert Planck. Cooper's famous tale has been brought to the screen a number of times (including two 1911 one-reelers; Maurice Tourneur and Clarence Brown's smashing 1922 feature-length silent with Wallace Beery as Magua; a ten-chapter 1924 serial version called LEATHERSTOCKING; Mascot Films's 1932 12-chapter serial with Harry Carey; and a 1947 Columbia version, THE LAST OF THE REDMEN, starring Jon Hall, Evelyn Ankers, and Buster Crabbe as Uncas), but none of these other versions matches the scope and wonderful performances of this extraordinary film. The film earned an Oscar nomination for Clem Beauchamp for Best Assistant Director, losing to Jack Sullivan for THE CHARGE OF THE LIGHT BRIGADE.

LAST PICTURE SHOW, THE

1971   118m   bw   ★★★★½
Drama   R/X
BBS

Timothy Bottoms (*Sonny Crawford*), Jeff Bridges (*Duane Jackson*), Cybill Shepherd (*Jacy Farrow*), Ben Johnson (*Sam the Lion*), Cloris Leachman (*Ruth Popper*), Ellen Burstyn (*Lois Farrow*), Eileen Brennan (*Genevieve*), Clu Gulager (*Abilene*), Sam Bottoms (*Billy*), Sharon Taggart (*Charlene Duggs*)

p, Stephen Friedman; d, Peter Bogdanovich; w, Peter Bogdanovich, Larry McMurtry (based on the novel by McMurtry); ph, Robert Surtees; ed, Donn Cambern; prod d, Polly Platt; art d, Walter Scott Herndon

Bogdanovich's finest effort; bleak and beguiling. None of his other films ranks with THE LAST PICTURE SHOW when it comes to dramatic flair and authenticity. He seems comfortable doing period pieces, but, in this, his second feature (preceded by

TARGETS), he captures the era so accurately that the viewer can feel the hopelessness of living in a dying Texas town. Bridges and Timothy Bottoms are the stars of the lackluster local high school football team. Bridges is the aggressive one, and Timothy Bottoms provides the contrasting sensitivity; they are best friends. The story unfolds seamlessly, detailing relationships in a small town. Sam Bottoms is a retarded boy (he got the part after he showed up to watch brother Tim's first day of shooting) who is the butt of cruel jokes by the denizens of the cafe-pool hall-theater owned by Johnson, a one-time cowboy who seems to be every boy's idol and surrogate father. Tim Bottoms takes up the cudgel as Sam Bottom's protector and is soon befriended, then bedded by Leachman, the lonely wife of the school's basketball coach, Thurman. The affair continues for most of the picture, heating up and cooling down a few times. To keep it up, Tim Bottoms ceases dating his regular girl friend, Taggart. Bridges continues dating his girl, Shepherd, but is not happy about her self-centered behavior. She attends a nude bathing party in order to meet the rich Brockette. Her mother, Burstyn, wants her daughter to marry well. Brockette rejects Shepherd because he doesn't want to be bothered with a virgin. Bridges and Tim Bottoms take a short and wild trip to Mexico, and when they return they are saddened to learn that Johnson has died.

THE LAST PICTURE SHOW is a refreshing look backward. While others were outfoxing themselves with multiscreen techniques, Bogdanovich made a movie that could have been shot years before and the result was critically and financially rewarding. The director is an admirer of Ford and Hawks and this is a homage to their styles, as opposed to the kind of ripoffs Colin Higgins and Brian De Palma have done with Hitchcock. The only element that separates this from an early film is the use of frontal nudity and the frank treatment accorded the adult themes. Bogdanovich was hailed as another Orson Welles (another of the director's mentors and friends). This episodic, human story lives and breathes with more power than any Darth Vader or Rocky. There was a time when Bogdanovich considered Jimmy Stewart, among others, for a part in the film. However, he wisely opted against using establlished stars. Johnson and Leachman each won Oscars, and the entire cast is quite fine (especially Ellen Burstyn, seen here like she's never been, before or since). Look for "Magnum's" John Hillerman in a small role as a teacher. THE LAST PICTURE SHOW could have been a tawdry, sleazy soap opera, but the 31-year-old former film critic kept a light, compassionate touch that elevated the story and presented it as a slice of a life that has all but disappeared.

LAST STARFIGHTER, THE

1984   101m   c   ★★★½
Science Fiction   PG
Lorimar

Lance Guest (*Alex Rogan*), Dan O'Herlihy (*Grig*), Catherine Mary Stewart (*Maggie Gordon*), Barbara Bosson (*Jane Rogan*), Norman Snow (*Xur*), Robert Preston (*Centauri*), Kay E. Kuter (*Enduran*), Chris Hebert (*Louis Rogan*), Dan Mason (*Lord Kril*), John O'Leary (*Rylan Bursar*)

p, Gary Adelson, Edward O. DeNault; d, Nick Castle; w, Jonathan Betuel; ph, King Baggot (Panavison, Technicolor); ed, C. Timothy O'Meara; m, Craig Safan; prod d, Ron Cobb; art d, James D. Bissell; fx, Kevin Pike; cos, Robert Fletcher

This very good science fiction film has young Alex Rogan (Lance Guest) stuck in a trailer park in California with his mother (Barbara Bosson) and little brother (Chris Hebert). He longs to leave with his girlfriend Maggie (Catherine Mary Stewart). His only solace is a video game, "Starfighter," at which he breaks the record one evening. Later that night Centauri (Robert Preston) shows up, introduces himself as the inventor of the game, and asks Alex to climb into his unusual car to discuss a business proposition. Within minutes the bewildered youth finds himself hurtling through space to a strange planet, where he's given a uniform and is put into a room with a lot of strange-looking aliens for a briefing on the evil Kodan forces, under the traitor Xur, who are attacking the Star League. It finally dawns on Alex that he's being asked to be a real starfighter. Clever, exciting, and fun, THE LAST STARFIGHTER boasts good performances by Guest and Preston, and a literate, funny script that highlights the real story: not the space war that only Guest can win but the difficulty of leaving home, family, and security for a totally new life when the opportunity presents itself. The special effects, computer-generated rather than STAR WARS-type models, work rather well, giving the film an odd but effective look.

LAST STOP, THE

(OSTATNI ETAP)
1949   110m   bw   ★★★★
War/Drama
Films Polski   (Poland)

Huguette Faget (*Michele*), W. Bartowna (*Helene*), T. Gorecka (*Eugenie*), A. Gorecka (*Anna*), M. Winogradowa (*Nadia*), B. Drapinska (*Marthe*), B. Fijewska (*Agnes*), A. Slaska (*Superintendent*), B. Rachwalska (*Elsa*), H. Drohocka (*Lala*)

p, Wanda Jakubowska; d, Wanda Jakubowska; w, Wanda Jakubowska, Gerda Schneider; ph, Boris Monastirsky; m, R. Palester; art d, J. Rybowski

This grim film focuses on the lives of the women inmates of Auschwitz. Shot on location, THE LAST STOP re-creates the horror of Nazi concentration camps with startling accuracy, focusing on one woman's efforts to survive and her eventual rescue. The results are not easy to watch, but THE LAST STOP is an important work, unsparing in its treatment of humankind's capacity for atrocity. Made only a few years after WWII's end, its creators were themselves women who survived Auschwitz.

LAST TANGO IN PARIS

1973   125m   c   ★★★★
Drama   X/18
UA   (France/Italy)

Marlon Brando (*Paul*), Maria Schneider (*Jeanne*), Jean-Pierre Leaud (*Tom*), Massimo Girotti (*Marcel*), Maria Michi (*Rosa's Mother*), Veronica Lazare (*Rosa*), Gitt Magrini (*Jeanne's Mother*), Darling Legitimus (*Concierge*), Catherine Sola (*TV Script Girl*), Mauro Marchetti (*TV Cameraman*)

p, Alberto Grimaldi; d, Bernardo Bertolucci; w, Bernardo Bertolucci, Franco Arcalli (based on story by Bertolucci); ph, Vittorio Storaro; ed, Franco Arcalli; m, Gato Barbieri

Shattering social and sexual conventions, LAST TANGO IN PARIS stands as one of Bertolucci's finest achievements. Marlon Brando plays Paul, a confused middle-aged American living in Paris whose wife has just, inexplicably, committed suicide. Paul is obsessed with the thought that his wife's death, and her whole life, is a mystery to him. He knew nothing about her, nothing of the secret affair she carried on for years with Marcel (Massimo Girotti). Maria Schneider plays Jeanne, a 20-year-old from a wealthy Parisian family who is engaged to Tom (Jean-Pierre Leaud), a New Wave filmmaker who documents his fiancee's life in an attempt to discover the truth about her. While hunting for an apartment, Jeanne meets Paul. Moments later, the two strangers are wildly making love. Shortly afterwards they leave the empty apartment. When they meet again, it is under Paul's ground rules: "You and I are going to meet here without knowing anything that goes on outside here. We are going to forget everything we knew—everything." All the elements are perfectly synthesized in this film masterpiece—Bernardo Bertolucci's direction; the raw, brave performances of Brando and Schneider; Storaro's lush camerawork; and the psycho-sexual dynamics of the script. Not to be missed.

LAST TEMPTATION OF CHRIST, THE
1988   164m   c   ★★★★
Religious   R/18
Cineplex Odeon

Willem Dafoe (Jesus Christ), Harvey Keitel (Judas Iscariot), Barbara Hershey (Mary Magdalene), Harry Dean Stanton (Saul/Paul), David Bowie (Pontius Pilate), Verna Bloom (Mary, Mother of Jesus), Andre Gregory (John the Baptist), Juliette Caton (Girl Angel), Roberts Blossom (Aged Master), Irvin Kershner (Zebedee)

p, Barbara De Fina; d, Martin Scorsese; w, Paul Schrader (based on the novel by Nikos Kazantzakis); ph, Michael Ballhaus (Technicolor); ed, Thelma Schoonmaker; m, Peter Gabriel; fx, Gino Galliano, Iginio Fiorentini; chor, Lahcen Zinoune

Martin Scorsese's adaptation of Nikos Kazantzakis's controversial novel *The Last Temptation of Christ* seeks to emphasize the human aspects of Jesus Christ, a figure described in the Bible as both fully God and fully man. The film opens with the carpenter Jesus of Nazareth (Willem Dafoe) making crosses upon which the Romans crucify rebellious Jews; it closes with the controversial last-temptation sequence, depicting the human love and gratifications Jesus sacrificed to fulfill his destiny as the savior of humankind. Between these powerful and affecting scenes is a fresh and vivid retelling of the Gospel's familiar events—the assembly of the disciples, the miracles, and so forth. Striving for historical accuracy, Scorsese presents Jerusalem as a flat, arid, harsh land suffering under the oppressive thumb of Roman rule. Cinematographer Michael Ballhaus's and production designer John Beard's evocative vision of the Holy Land combines with Peter Gabriel's musical score (derived mostly from traditional and contemporary Arabic rhythms) to vividly convey Christ's world and time—and it is not the lush, picturesque, sanitized Hollywood version popularized by Cecil B. DeMille. Powerful, haunting, and at times very moving, THE LAST TEMPTATION OF CHRIST presents its fictionalized account of the events and conflicts of Christ's life with a depth of dramatized feeling and motivation that renders them freshly compelling.

LAST TIME I SAW PARIS, THE
1954   116m   c   ★★★½
Romance
MGM

Elizabeth Taylor (Helen Ellsworth), Van Johnson (Charles Wills), Walter Pidgeon (James Ellsworth), Donna Reed (Marie Ellsworth), Eva Gabor (Lorraine Quarl), Kurt Kasznar (Maurice), George Dolenz (Claude Matine), Roger Moore (Paul), Sandy Descher (Vicki), Celia Lovsky (Mama)

p, Jack Cummings; d, Richard Brooks; w, Richard Brooks, Julius J. Epstein, Philip G. Epstein (based on the story, "Babylon Revisited," by F. Scott Fitzgerald); ph, Joseph Ruttenberg (Technicolor); ed, John Dunning; m, Conrad Salinger; art d, Cedric Gibbons, Randall Duell; fx, A. Arnold Gillespie; cos, Helen Rose

F. Scott Fitzgerald's tragic love story was brought to the screen with surprising vitality under Brooks' expert hand. He drew fine performances from Taylor, Johnson, and others in a sumptuous MGM production that captured the flavor of expatriate life in the City of Light. While Fitzgerald set his poignant tale in the 1920s, this film begins just after WWII; Johnson is a GI with literary ambitions who goes to Paris and meets the wealthy Taylor. They fall in love and he settles down there, attempting to write his first novel. All goes well for a while until failure to sell his writing causes Johnson to turn to the bottle. His excessive drinking soon causes the couple to argue and Taylor to be accidentally locked out of their Parisian quarters during a rainstorm. She catches pneumonia and later dies. Their child is raised by Taylor's sister, Reed, who has always disapproved of Johnson. He returns to the US and becomes a successful novelist. Once back in Paris (which is how the film opens, with the Johnson-Taylor love story shown in flashback), Johnson begs for custody of his little girl. Reed relents at the last moment, and the child is reunited with her reformed father.

Taylor was never more lovely and turns in a superior performance as the star-crossed lady in love with Johnson. Johnson, who also turns in a good effort, although he's a bit glib in spots, was first teamed with Taylor in 1950 in THE BIG HANGOVER and got top billing. With THE LAST TIME I SAW PARIS, Taylor received the top slot because she had become one of the big box-office draws for MGM. Producer Lester Cowan had originally purchased the rights from Fitzgerald to this story for $3,000, intending to film it as a Mary Pickford vehicle in the 1920s for Goldwyn. Cowan sold the story to Paramount for a Gregory Peck-William Wyler production that fell through. But MGM purchased the rights from Paramount specifically for Taylor, assigning the clever Epstein twins to write a sparkling script that kept the flavor, if not the brilliance, of Fitzgerald's story intact. MGM shot two weeks on location in Paris and on the Riviera, mostly at Cannes, producing the balance of the film on the Culver City lot.

LAST WAVE, THE
1978   106m   c   ★★★★
Thriller   PG/AA
Ayer/South Australian/Australian Film Commission
(Australia)

Richard Chamberlain (David Burton), Olivia Hamnett (Anne Burton), David Gulpilil (Chris Lee), Frederick Parslow (Rev. Burton), Vivean Gray (Dr. Whitburn), Nanjiwarra Amagula (Charlie), Walter Amagula (Gerry Lee), Roy Bara (Larry), Cedric Lalara (Lindsey), Morris Lalara (Jacko)

p, Hal McElroy, James McElroy; d, Peter Weir; w, Peter Weir, Tony Morphett, Peter Popescu; ph, Russell Boyd (Artlab Color); ed, Max Lemon; m, Charles Wain; art d, Neil Angwin; fx, Neil Angwin, Monty Fieguth; cos, Annie Bleakley

A powerful, yet subtle, picture from Australian director Weir, who has demonstrated quite a flair for mystical themes. Like his earlier work, PICNIC AT HANGING ROCK, this picture involves inexplicable events and their connection with the aboriginal world and the ancient Australian landscape. The picture opens as a raging thunderstorm from a clear blue sky drenches a small desert settlement, and then flashes quickly to Sydney, which is also in the midst of a torrential downpour. A voice over the radio unconvincingly attempts to explain the phenomenon as a reaction to cold winds from the Antarctic. An earlier shot of an aborigine painting on a cave wall lets the viewer know there is something at work here that transcends scientific explanation, setting the mood for the rest of the film. The contrast between the Western viewpoint, which attributes geophysical results to scientific reason, and the aboriginal perspective of a cosmos beyond the grasp of conscious thought, creates a tension that is carried throughout the film. Chamberlain plays a Sydney lawyer who becomes involved in defending a group of aborigines accused of murder (despite his lack of experience with both aborigines and criminal law).

Weir does a fine job of weaving real events with dream sequences, as well as capturing the aboriginal perspective—this is one of few films that does not portray the aborigines as a defeated people, entirely subjugated by white settlers. Chamberlain is convincing as a wealthy lawyer and family man who becomes possessed by a vision beyond his grasp. Although the plot falters in a few instances, it maintains a high level of overall suspense.

LAST YEAR AT MARIENBAD
(L'ANNEE DERNIERE A MARIENBAD)
1961 94m bw   ★★★★★
Drama   /U
Terra/Cormoran/Precitel/Como/Tamara/Silver-Cineriz (France/Italy)

Delphine Seyrig (A/Woman), Giorgio Albertazzi (X/Stranger), Sacha Pitoeff (M/Escort/Husband), Francoise Bertin, Luce Garcia-Ville, Helena Kornel, Francois Spira, Karin Toeche-Mittler, Pierre Barbaud, Wilhelm von Deek

p, Pierre Courau, Raymond Froment; d, Alain Resnais; w, Alain Robbe-Grillet; ph, Sacha Vierny (Dyaliscope); ed, Henri Colpi, Jasmine Chasney; m, Francis Seyrig; art d, Jacques Saulnier; cos, Bernard Evein, Chanel

The cinematic equivalent of the *nouveau roman* ("new novel") and a true landmark in film history. One of the most formally inventive of all feature films, LAST YEAR AT MARIENBAD stretches the limits of film language to the extreme. Scripted by Robbe-Grillet, the movie introduces us to four main characters—A (Seyrig), a lovely, well-dressed woman; X (Albertazzi), a handsome stranger; M (Pitoeff), a man who might be A's husband; and a luxurious estate (important enough to be considered a character) with long, sterile hallways and perfectly manicured grounds. The "plot", if you can call it one, focuses on X's attempt to convince A that they met, possibly last year, at a resort hotel, perhaps in Marienbad, where she may have promised to run away with him this year. A, however, has no recollection of the meeting. . . or else is being coy. . . or dares not recognize X. . . or whatever you care to make of it. The viewer is kept in perpetual doubt as to whether the meeting ever took place, whether it has not yet taken place, or whether it's a hopeful fantasy X has made up. Frustrated? You should be.

LAST YEAR AT MARIENBAD was hailed as a masterpiece at the time of its release, largely thanks to Robbe-Grillet and director Resnais's manipulation of time—past, present, and future—in relation to the subjective realities of the film's characters. Easy to read as a parody of Hollywood love triangles, MARIENBAD also mocks classical cinema's tendency to be redundant by repeating lines, indeed entire scenes, over and over again. All the characters are flat, often nothing but statues in a well-kept mausoleum. This is precisely how they appear in the film's most famous shot, in which the tiny figures amid the large sculpture garden cast shadows, but the starkly groomed bushes do not. A true cinematic puzzle, stunningly shot, MARIENBAD decenters the human subject from its place of primacy in most

narrative cinema, and the result is a provocative study of alienation and bourgeios alienation.

L'ATALANTE
(LE CHALAND QUI PASSE)
1934 89m bw   ★★★★★
Romance   /PG
J.L. Nounez (France)

Michel Simon (Pere Jules), Jean Daste (Jean), Dita Parlo (Juliette), Gilles Margaritis (Peddler), Louis Lefebvre (Cabin Boy), Fanny Clar (Juliette's Mother), Raphael Diligent (Juliette's Father), Maurice Gilles (Office Manager), Rene Bleck (Best Man), Charles Goldblatt (Thief)

p, Jacques-Louis Nounez; d, Jean Vigo; w, Jean Vigo, Albert Riera (based on a scenario by R. de Guichen); ph, Boris Kaufman, Louis Berger; ed, Louis Chavance

Jean Vigo's poetic tale centers on Jean (Daste), captain of the barge L'Atalante, who marries Juliette (Parlo), a young woman from the country. (The early scenes leading up to and including their wedding are marvelous.) Bored with life on the barge, Juliette longs to see the bright lights of Paris. Jean finally gives in to his wife's request and takes her to a Paris cabaret, where a peddler flirts with the young woman. The next day, an angry and jealous Jean leaves the ship without his wife. She is visited by the peddler, who entertains her and then is promptly thrown off the barge upon Jean's return. Juliette then sneaks off to Paris, and Jean purposefully sets sail without her, leaving his penniless wife to take a job in town. The film then concentrates on the lovers' pain before L'Atalante again sails on.

Vigo made only four films (A PROPOS DE NICE, TARIS CHAMPION DE NATATION, ZERO DE CONDUITE, and L'ATALANTE) before his untimely death at age 29. In L'ATALANTE, he treats his simple story both realistically and surrealistically, combining and contrasting styles. Thus, in one scene, Jean dives into the water and sees an image of a smiling Juliette swimming in her wedding gown; in another, a seaman played by Michel Simon (in possibly the greatest role of his distinguished career) displays his odd collection of curios, including a pair of severed hands in a jar. (Surrealist poet Jacques Prevert and his brother, filmmaker Pierre, also make cameo appearances.) L'ATALANTE was poorly received at its initial 1934 screening, prompting its distributors to insert a popular song and re-edit nearly all the scenes. The result was a box-office disaster, and three weeks later Vigo was dead.

Years later, a complete version was finally constructed thanks to the Cinematheque Francais and Henri Langlois. Less iconoclastic and experimental than his earlier films, L'ATALANTE is nonetheless brilliantly idiosyncratic and insightful, the warmest film of this great director's career.

LATE AUTUMN
(AKIBIYORI)
1960 127m c   ★★★
Drama
New Yorker (Japan)

Setsuko Hara (The Mother), Yoko Tsukasa (The Daughter), Chishu Ryu (The Uncle), Mariko Okada (The Daughter's Friend), Keiji Sada (The Young Man)

d, Yasujiro Ozu; w, Kogo Noda, Yasujiro Ozu; ph, Yushun Atsuta (Agfacolor); m, Takanobu Saito; art d, Tatsuo Hamada

One of the final efforts from one of the great masters of Japanese cinema, LATE AUTUMN was originally made in 1960 but not brought to then US until ten years after Ozu's death. Tsukasa plays the daughter of Hara, a recently widowed woman who finds that her late husband's friends are taking an extreme interest in seeing her remarried. Hara herself is not so keen on walking down the aisle quite yet, something that shocks men raised in a tradition that has little place for an unattached woman. Eventually Hara does agree to marry, out of a desire to please the insistent elders, but her ideas of marriage still seem quite obscure to the traditionalists.

Ozu made 54 films in his long career, most marked by a subtle, distinctive directorial style featuring a stationary camera placed only a few feet above the floor. The latter portion of his career saw Ozu extremely concerned about the effects of Westernization upon traditional Japan; in LATE AUTUMN this is reflected in the consternation caused in the elders by Hara's "unorthodox" views.

LATE GEORGE APLEY, THE

1947 93m bw ★★★★
Comedy /A
FOX

Ronald Colman (George Apley), Peggy Cummins (Eleanor Apley), Vanessa Brown (Agnes), Richard Haydn (Horatio Willing), Charles Russell (Howard Boulder), Richard Ney (John Apley), Percy Waram (Roger Newcombe), Mildred Natwick (Amelia Newcombe), Edna Best (Catherine Apley), Nydia Westman (Jane Willing)

p, Fred Kohlmar; d, Joseph L. Mankiewicz; w, Philip Dunne (based on the novel by John P. Marquand and the play by Marquand and George S. Kaufman); ph, Joseph La Shelle; ed, James B. Clark; m, Cyril J. Mockridge; art d, James Basevi, J. Russell Spencer; fx, Fred Sersen; cos, Rene Hubert

After a couple of whopping flops, Colman made it clear that he would only accept the very best material and was not about to make more than one film per year. His desire for quality was more than fulfilled by THE LATE GEORGE APLEY, which had first been a best-selling Pulitzer Prize-winning novel, then was adapted into a play. Colman is Apley, a man who believes his beloved Boston to be the hub of the universe. Moreover, he is convinced that any place not within 10 miles of Beacon Hill is savage as Borneo. Colman demands that his son, Ney, attend Harvard and that his daughter, Cummins, only marry a man who has grown up within earshot of the Charles Street Church. But as fate would have it, Ney falls for Brown, a girl from Worcester, and Cummins begins dating a Yalie (perish the thought!). What's a Brahmin to do? The situation is not hopeless, though, as Cummins's boyfriend, Russell, does show some signs of culture by regularly quoting Emerson, Colman's favorite author. Still, Colman forbids Ney to marry his love and by film's end, it seems likely that Ney will wind up like his father, watching birds and upholding all the moral standards that their ancestors handed down.

There are some similarities between this film and LIFE WITH FATHER in that the central characters in both stories are concerned with the status quo. However, Colman's Apley is basically a sympathetic character underneath all his surface bluster, while William Powell's Clarence Day is more or less the same on the inside as he is on the outside. Moreover, unlike Day, George Apley also demonstrates some openness to change. Reputedly, author Marquand pictured no one but Colman in the role of Apley, and the English actor—who had no problem slipping into the highbrow, quasi-English accent of the Back Bay—gives a wonderful performance. Cummins, another English import in her first American film, is also excellent, and Ney contributes some of his best work. Natwick and Best score in supporting roles, and Haydn is superb as a prissy Boston type. Mankiewicz, who had been known primarily as a writer and producer before directing DRAGONWYCK, handles the directional chores with aplomb and keeps the comedy coming with regularity. Bostonians, notoriously putoff by attempts to spoof them, flocked to the theaters to see THE LATE GEORGE APLEY and laughed their heads off.

LATE SHOW, THE

1977 94m c ★★★½
Crime PG/15
Lion's Gate

Art Carney (Ira Wells), Lily Tomlin (Margo Sperling), Bill Macy (Charlie Hatter), Eugene Roche (Ron Birdwell), Joanna Cassidy (Laura Birdwell), John Considine (Lamar), Ruth Nelson (Mrs. Schmidt), John Davey (Sgt. Dayton), Howard Duff (Harry Regan)

p, Robert Altman; d, Robert Benton; w, Robert Benton; ph, Charles Rosher, Jr.; ed, Lou Lombardo, Peter Appleton; m, Ken Wannberg

This fine, overlooked film stars Carney as Ira Wells, an aging private eye whose former partner, Harry Regan (Duff), is murdered while tracking down a missing cat for Margo Sperling (Tomlin). A sometime dealer in stolen goods, she suspects her pet has been nabbed by an associate whom she's failed to pay. At the urging of Charlie Hatter (Macy), Ira picks up where Regan left off, and he and Margo do a Nick and Nora Charles number as they piece together the complex clues that lead to the cat and climax of this intriguing mystery. Along the way, Margo begins to find herself attracted to Ira, but he doesn't return her affection—at least at first.

THE LATE SHOW was director Benton's second outing, and he showed immense sensitivity and the ability to spin a good yarn. Tomlin, in her second film after NASHVILLE, and Carney, in his return to the screen after his Oscar-winning performance in HARRY AND TONTO, work wonderfully together. Carney's portrayal of a man whose body is beginning to betray him but whose spirit won't throw in the towel is nothing short of elegant.

LAUGHTER

1930 85m bw ★★★★★
Comedy/Drama
Paramount

Fredric March (Paul Lockridge), Nancy Carroll (Peggy Gibson), Frank Morgan (C. Mortimer Gibson), Glenn Anders (Ralph Le Saint), Diane Ellis (Marjorie Gibson), Leonard Carey (Benham), Ollie Burgoyne (Pearl)

d, Harry d'Abbadie D'Arrast; w, Donald Ogden Stewart (based on a story by Douglas Doty, Harry d'Abbadie D'Arrast); ph, George Folsey; ed, Helene Turner

Director and cowriter Harry d'Abbadie D'Arrast had a brief film career that included a stint with Charlie Chaplin, but had he done nothing but work on LAUGHTER, D'Arrast's place in movie history would be secure. This film is a dandy, far ahead of its time in content, photography, and style. Nancy Carroll is a dancer in The Follies, surrounded by amorous stage-door Johnnies. When she falls for multimillionaire Frank Morgan, Carroll gives up all her old suitors, including composer Fredric March, who travels to Paris to forget his rejection. However, Morgan spends too much time watching ticker tapes, so Carroll seeks new ways to relieve her loneliness, limousining to Greenwich Village, where she visits Glenn Anders, another former beau. A sculptor who has had little success, Anders has just destroyed a statue and finished penning a suicide note when Carroll arrives and lifts him from his depression. When Diane Ellis, Morgan's daughter by a former marriage, comes home from Europe, Carroll meets her at the dock, and the two women, who are close in age, become fast friends. Returning from Paris, March seeks to rekindle his relationship with Carroll. She tries to stay away from him at first, but is soon so charmed by March that she begins an affair with him. Noticing that Carroll no longer has her old *joie de vivre*, March encourages her to put some laughter back into her now-barren life.

Meanwhile, Anders and Ellis also meet and are soon attracted to each other. Riding in the country when a sudden rainstorm hits, March and Carroll seek shelter in a small, empty house, where locals see them removing their wet clothes. The village police arrest the twosome for breaking and entering, and when they are taken to the small town's hoosegow, an embarrassed Carroll has to ask Morgan for the needed money to get them out of jail. Back in the city, at a huge ball at the Morgan mansion, Carroll sees Ellis get a phone call, then surreptitiously slip away. Tailing Ellis to Anders's flat, Carroll learns that the lovebirds plan to wed, but, suspecting that Anders is marrying Ellis because he can't have her stepmother, Carroll challenges the sculptor to publicly proclaim his affection for Ellis. Enraged by Carroll's behavior, Ellis storms out of Anders's apartment, followed by her stepmother, who hears a shot as she leaves: Anders has killed himself. Although the cops believe that Anders has taken his own life, the press is waiting for Carroll when she returns home. Naturally, Morgan wants an explanation. Carroll tells her thunderstruck husband that she is leaving him, that love is more important to her than money. That night she and March board an ocean liner, and the last scene shows them sharing champagne on a wide Parisian street with Carroll laughing once more.

LAUGHTER could have been as soapy as a tubful of Tide, but D'Abbadie D'Arrast lends his fast-paced comedy the sort of deft sophisticated touch that would become Ernst Lubitsch's trademark. The script crackles with wit, March is elegant, and Carroll is sweet, as all the elements come together to brilliant effect in this neglected film from an unjustly neglected director. Made when Herbert Hoover was in the White House, LAUGHTER has lost none of its luster over the years. It garnered one Academy Award nomination, for Best Original Story, losing to THE DAWN PATROL.

LAURA
1944 88m bw   ★★★★★
Mystery   /U
FOX

Gene Tierney *(Laura Hunt)*, Dana Andrews *(Mark McPherson)*, Clifton Webb *(Waldo Lydecker)*, Vincent Price *(Shelby Carpenter)*, Judith Anderson *(Ann Treadwell)*, Dorothy Adams *(Bessie Clary)*, James Flavin *(McAvity)*, Clyde Fillmore *(Bullitt)*, Ralph Dunn *(Fred Callahan)*, Grant Mitchell *(Corey)*

p, Otto Preminger; d, Otto Preminger; w, Jay Dratler, Samuel Hoffenstein, Elizabeth Reinhardt, Ring Lardner, Jr., Jerry Cady (based on the novel by Vera Caspary); ph, Joseph La Shelle; ed, Louis Loeffler; m, David Raksin; prod d, Thomas Little, Paul S. Fox; art d, Lyle Wheeler, Leland Fuller; fx, Fred Sersen; cos, Bonnie Cashin

The sleekest of *Noirs*, the chicest of murders, and deliciously twisted—the detective is a necrophiliac, two of the title character's suitors seem gay, and the Laura all the men are vying

for is a corpse with no face. Indeed LAURA, goes the genre one further by taking apart the conventions, then putting them back together, and diving wholeheartedly into them for the finale—a cocktail party denouement to name the killer.

LAURA, based on the novel by Vera Caspary, revolves around the murder of the title character (Tierney)—a shotgun blast completely obliterating the corpse's once-lovely face. Homicide detective Mark McPherson (Andrews) has a trio of suspects—newspaper critic Waldo Lydecker (Webb), who "created" Laura; playboy/parasite and fiance Shelby Carpenter (Price); and Anne Treadwell (Anderson), Laura's socialite aunt who has been carrying on with Shelby. Just as Mark is beginning to fall in love with a vision of the deceased woman—in the form of an oil portrait—in walks the *real* Laura. . .

LAURA is a truly haunting study of obsession, with suitably poignant music provided by David Raksin (lyrics by Johnny Mercer). Originally, Otto Preminger was assigned only as producer, with studio chieftain Darryl Zanuck offering the directing chore to Rouben Mamoulian. Part of the way into production, however, Zanuck fired Mamoulian and handed the reins over to Preminger. Preminger reshot Mamoulian's footage, replaced cinematographer Lucian Ballard with Joseph La Shelle (who won an Academy Award), and scrapped the Mamoulian costumes and sets—including a portrait of Laura which Mamoulian's wife had painted.

LAVENDER HILL MOB, THE
1951 82m bw   ★★★★½
Crime/Comedy   /U
Ealing   (U.K.)

Alec Guinness *(Henry Holland)*, Stanley Holloway *(Pendlebury)*, Sidney James *(Lackery)*, Alfie Bass *(Shorty)*, Marjorie Fielding *(Mrs. Chalk)*, John Gregson *(Farrow)*, Edie Martin *(Miss Evesham)*, Clive Morton *(Station Sergeant)*, Ronald Adam *(Turner)*, Sydney Tafler *(Clayton)*

p, Michael Balcon; d, Charles Crichton; w, T.E.B. Clarke; ph, Douglas Slocombe; ed, Seth Holt; m, Georges Auric; art d, William Kellner

A hilarious tongue-in-cheek crime comedy, one of the finest to come out of the Ealing Studios during their most prolific years. Guinness stars as a mild-mannered transporter of gold bullion who, after 20 years of faithful service, blithely decides to steal one million pounds' worth. He enlists Holloway, an old pal who is a paperweight manufacturer and a bit of a sculptor. They team up with James and Bass, two cockney professional crooks, and the scheme is launched. After a successful hijack, they melt down their booty, mold it into small, souvenir Eiffel Towers, and ship it off to Paris. Guinness and Holloway follow the gold, only to learn that six of the Eiffel Towers have been purchased by a group of daytripping English schoolgirls. . . Much hilarity follows, including a superlative chase scene in which Guinness and Holloway, driving a stolen police car, thwart their pursuers by issuing contradictory messages over the police radio, which ends by broadcasting "Old MacDonald Had a Farm" to all cars! The film had begun, however, with Guinness telling this story to a man in a swank Rio restaurant. The camera returns there for the conclusion, and we see that Guinness is not only having a drink with the other chap—he's handcuffed to him.

Guinness is winning as the last man on earth you'd suspect of being a criminal (he was nominated for an Oscar but lost to Gary Cooper, for HIGH NOON). Clarke's screenplay quite rightly won the award. Many of England's best comic actors are seen in small roles, including Sidney Tafler, Peter Bull, and John Gregson. In a tiny role, you may notice James Fox (brother of Edward), still being billed as William. And in the opening sequence, Guinness hands a cute young woman some money and tells her to buy a little gift. You'll have to look fast to recognize Audrey Hepburn as the little girl.

L'AVVENTURA

1959 145m bw   ★★★★★
Drama   /X
Cino del Duca/Europee/Lyre   (Italy/France)

Monica Vitti (Claudia), Gabriele Ferzetti (Sandro), Lea Massari (Anna), Dominique Blanchar (Giulia), James Addams (Corrado), Renzo Ricci (Anna's Father), Esmeralda Ruspoli (Patrizia), Lelio Luttazzi (Raimondo), Dorothy De Poliolo (Gloria Perkins), Giovanni Petrucci (Young Prince)

p, Cino Del Duca; d, Michelangelo Antonioni; w, Michelangelo Antonioni, Elio Bartolini, Tonino Guerra (based on the story by Antonioni); ph, Aldo Scavarda; ed, Eraldo Da Roma; m, Giovanni Fusco; cos, Adriana Berselli

The title translates as "The Adventure" and this *is* an adventure, if you're willing to take it. A group of wealthy Italians goes yachting to a rocky island near Sicily. After arriving, they notice that Anna (Massari) is missing, and everyone searches for her amidst the endless crevices and wave-battered cliffs. Her best friend, Claudia (Vitti), teams with Anna's lover, Sandro (Ferzetti), in the search, which is eventually abandoned in the hope that Anna simply left the island. Inquiries are made in town as to her whereabouts, and several people claim to have seen her. In the process, Sandro becomes increasingly involved with Claudia, who becomes his lover and substitute for Anna.

L'AVVENTURA is one of Antonioni's finest films, and a landmark in the devlopment of cinematic narrative. The seemingly pressing question raised by the film's opening—"What happened to Anna?"—becomes increasingly irrelevant as we learn that there is no "adventure" of this type, just a shifting, unsettling meditation on contemporary alienation and the opacity of all human relationships. The acting is appropriately minimalist and the blank-faced, passive Vitti is marvelouly Garboesque in the role that deservedly made her an international star. One character will be in deep focus at the "back" of the image, seemingly ready to call out to the person in the foreground, but communication is all but impossible. Even sex is a feeble attempt to escape the oddly charged ennui of this milieu. As with all Antonioni, the cinematography and composition are unsurpassed. He scatters his existential characters over the landscape, brilliantly emphasizing empty space over the trappings of plot. Photographed largely outdoors, shooting took months to complete and sent the original production company, Imeria, into debt. Cino Del Duca came to Antonioni's aid and filming continued, though many of the summer shots actually took place in the winter. Some four months later, the Cannes Film Festival audience greeted the picture with an unparalleled assault of hisses and boos. Several months later, though, L'AVVENTURA set box-office records in Paris; by the time it hit America, it had received a "condemned" rating from the National League of Decency, apparently for its lack of morality.

LAW OF DESIRE, THE

(LA LEY DEL DESEO)
1987 100m c   ★★★★
Comedy   /18
El Deseo/Laurenfilm   (Spain)

Eusebio Poncela (Pablo Quintero), Carmen Maura (Tina Quintero), Antonio Banderas (Antonio Benitez), Miguel Molina (Juan Bermudez), Manuela Velasco (Ada, Child), Bibi Andersen (Ada, Mother), Fernando Guillen (Inspector), Nacho Martinez (Dr. Martin), Helga Line (Antonio's Mother), Fernando G. Cuervo (Policeman, Child)

p, Miguel Angel Perez Campos; d, Pedro Almodovar; w, Pedro Almodovar; ph, Angel Luis Fernandez (Eastmancolor); ed, Jose Salcedo; m, Igor Stravinsky, Dmitri Shostakovich; cos, Jose M. Cossio

Spain's acclaimed director Pedro Almodovar, who scored a huge international success with WOMEN ON THE VERGE OF A NERVOUS BREAKDOWN, has stated he wants to reach audiences through "their hearts, their minds, and their genitals." In LAW OF DESIRE, he more than fulfills this challenge, offering an exhilarating romp detailing the erotic adventures of Pablo (Eusebio Poncela), a gay filmmaker; his bisexual lover, Juan (Miguel Molina); his transsexual "sister," Tina (Carmen Maura), the mother of a teenager fathered by her when "she" was a "he"; and Antonio (Antonio Banderas), who becomes involved with both Pablo and Tina as the story accelerates to its tragic finale.

No one can accuse Almodovar of bashfulness. LAW OF DESIRE works overtime, piling one eccentric plot element atop another. . . and it works. Flashy? Yes. Vulgar? Yes. Impassioned? Thanks to the wonderful Maura and Banderas, definitely. Of Almodovar's early work, the first, FUCK, FUCK, FUCK ME, TIM, a Super-8 feature, has received little exposure outside the filmmaker's native Spain. The others, in chronological order, are PEPI, LUCI, BOM AND OTHER GIRLS ON THE HEAP; LABYRINTH OF PASSIONS; DARK HABITS; WHAT HAVE I DONE TO DESERVE THIS? and MATADOR. In this, his seventh feature, Almodovar reveals himself to be a supremely stylish and self-assured filmmaker, one of the bright lights of international cinema.

LAWRENCE OF ARABIA

1962 220m c   ★★★★★
Biography/Adventure/War   /PG
Horizon   (U.K.)

Peter O'Toole (T.E. Lawrence), Alec Guinness (Prince Feisal), Anthony Quinn (Auda Abu Tayi), Jack Hawkins (Gen. Allenby), Jose Ferrer (Turkish Bey), Anthony Quayle (Col. Harry Brighton), Claude Rains (Mr. Dryden), Arthur Kennedy (Jackson Bentley), Donald Wolfit (Gen. Murray), Omar Sharif (Sherif Ali Ibn El Kharish)

p, Sam Spiegel, David Lean; d, David Lean; w, Robert Bolt, Michael Wilson (based on The Seven Pillars of Wisdom by T.E. Lawrence); ph, Freddie Young; ed, Anne V. Coates; m, Maurice Jarre; prod d, John Box; art d, John Stoll; cos, Phyllis Dalton

David Lean's splendid biography of the enigmatic T.E. Lawrence paints a complex portrait of the desert-loving Englishman who united Arab tribes in battle against the Ottoman Turks in WWI on a sun-drenched 70mm canvas that often seems as large as the Arabian peninsula itself. At the center of Lean's visual symphony is Peter O'Toole's eccentric but magnificent portrayal of the erudite, Oxford-educated lieutenant, who wangles an assignment as an observer with Prince Feisal (Alec Guinness), the leader of the Arab revolt against the Turks. Feisal is resigned to allowing his tribal army to become just another branch of the British forces, but the messianic Lawrence, determined to prevent the Arabs from falling under British colonial domination, undertakes a military miracle. He, Sherif Ali (Omar Sharif)—whom Lean introduces as a tiny dot on the desert horizon that steadily enlarges, in one of the film's most striking scenes—and 50 men traverse the "uncrossable" Nefud Desert; join forces with their traditional tribal enemies, led by Auda Abu Tayi (Anthony Quinn); and rout the Turks at the strategic port city of Aqaba. Given the go-ahead by Gen. Allenby (Jack Hawkins), worshiped by the Arabs he has brought together, and cloaked in their flowing white robes, "El Aurens" leads the Arabs in a brutal guerrilla war that is as much about establishing Arab sovereignty as it is about defeating the Turks. His thrilling exploits are glorified by the Lowell Thomas-like American journalist Jackson Bentley (Arthur Kennedy). In time, however, Lawrence's legions dwindle, he begins to revel sadistically in violence, his grand attempt at overseeing the formation of a united Arab Council in Damascus collapses, and he returns to Britain exhausted. Lean's film is best appreciated on the big screen, and in 1989 a carefully restored version of LAWRENCE was released that reinstated 20 minutes cut for the original roadshow release and another 15 minutes trimmed when it was rereleased in 1970. Moreover, Lean and his original editor, Anne V. Coates, were finally given the chance to do a "fine cut" on the film, now 216 memorable minutes long.

LE BEAU MARIAGE

1982 97m c   ★★★★
Drama/Comedy   PG/
Losanger/Carosse   (France)

Beatrice Romand (Sabine), Andre Dussollier (Edmond), Feodor Atkine (Simon), Huguette Faget (Antique Dealer), Arielle Dombasle (Clarisse), Thamila Mezbah (Mother), Sophie Renoir (Lise), Herve Duhamel (Frederic), Pascal Greggory (Nicolas), Virginie Thevenet (The Bride)

p, Margaret Menogoz; d, Eric Rohmer; w, Eric Rohmer; ph, Bernard Lutic, Romain Winding, Nicolas Brunet; ed, Cecile Decugis, Lisa Heredia; m, Ronan Gure, Simon Des Innocents

The second installment in Eric Rohmer's "Comedies and Proverbs" series, LE BEAU MARIAGE is the charming tale of Sabine (Beatrice Romand), a university student with a Paris flat who decides one day, quite arbitrarily, to get married. All she is lacking is a husband, a minor detail. She leaves her painter boyfriend, quits her antique-store job, and begins pursuing Edmond (Andre Dussollier), a busy lawyer who is friendly to Sabine but clearly not interested in romancing her. This thoroughly enjoyable picture is carried by the spunky, idiosyncratic performance of Romand, who appeared 12 years earlier in Rohmer's "Moral Tale," CLAIRE'S KNEE. Two of her costars in this film would also be rewarded with lead roles in subsequent Rohmer films—Arielle Dombasle, who appears in PAULINE AT THE BEACH, and Sophie Renoir (cast here as Romand's pesty little sister), who stars in Rohmer's final "Comedies and Proverbs" entry, BOYFRIENDS AND GIRLFRIENDS. There's also a fine synthesized pop score that you may find yourself humming long after the film's end. In French with English subtitles.

LE BEAU SERGE

1958 97m bw   ★★★½
Drama   /X
United Motion Picture   (France)

Gerard Blain (Serge), Jean-Claude Brialy (Francois), Bernadette Lafont (Marie), Edmond Beauchamp (Glomaud), Michele Meritz (Yvonne), Jeanne Perez, Claude Cerval, Andre Dino

d, Claude Chabrol; w, Claude Chabrol; ph, Henri Decae; ed, Jacques Gaillard; m, Emile Delpierre

Generally considered the film that put the French New Wave in the history books (though Jacques Rivette's PARIS BELONGS TO US was the first to go into production), LE BEAU SERGE received overwhelming critical approval of its use of non-professional actors, raw black-and-white photography (masterfully executed by Henri Decae), and personal vision. It is the tale of two old friends, Francois (Jean-Claude Brialy), a city dweller who returns to the provincial French village of his childhood, and Serge (Gerard Blain), a successful architect-turned-drunkard. After the birth of a malformed son, Serge's life and marriage go into a tailspin as he collapses under the weight of tremendous guilt. Unfortunately, the film is cluttered with Catholicism, which director Claude Chabrol had the good sense to deemphasize as his career developed. Though highly acclaimed, LE BEAU SERGE was quickly overshadowed by the subsequent success of Francois Truffaut's 400 BLOWS, Jean-Luc Godard's BREATHLESS, and Alain Resnais's HIROSHIMA MON AMOUR. LES COUSINS, a companion piece to LE BEAU SERGE that also starred Brialy and Blain, appeared the following year to an equally enthusiastic reception.

LE BOUCHER

1971 93m c   ★★★
Thriller   GP/18
La Boetie/Euro Intl.   (France/Italy)

Stephane Audran (Helene), Jean Yanne (Popaul), Antonio Passalia (Angelo), Mario Beccaria (Leon Hamel), Pasquale Ferone (Pere Cahrpy), Roger Rudel (Police Inspector Grumbach), William Guerault (Charles)

p, Andre Genoves; d, Claude Chabrol; w, Claude Chabrol; ph, Jean Rabier (Eastmancolor); ed, Jacques Gaillard; m, Pierre Jansen; cos, Joseph Poulard

A calculated, slow-paced thriller set in the French countryside, where schoolteacher Audran begins a new assignment. She is soon romanced by the village butcher, Yanne, though she seems more concerned with her schoolchildren than with finding a lover. In the meantime, the village is stricken with random murders. Audran finds herself directly involved when a young girl's body is found near the schoolyard. During a school outing, she and the children take a lunch break and eat their sandwiches outdoors. One girl, who is sitting next to a cliff, suddenly finds blood dripping onto her bread. Above her is discovered yet another butchered body. Audran's suspicions are raised when she finds Yanne's cigarette lighter next to the body, but the clever, deranged killer is one step ahead of her and buys an identical lighter. By the finale, Audran's concern has turned into deadly fear as she barricades herself inside her house.

LE BOUCHER is a compelling psychological thriller that occasionally gets bogged down and fails to reach the level of suspense that could have been achieved. Like the psychopathic killer of little girls in Fritz Lang's M, Yanne's character is presented in a manner which is calculated to stir a measure of audience sympathy: he is a man with good qualities who is unable to help himself. Audran, the real-life wife of director Chabrol and star of three of his films, gives a compelling performance, but she is simply too sophisticated to come across as a country schoolteacher.

LE DERNIER MILLIARDAIRE

1934 90m bw   ★★½
Comedy
Pathe/Natan   (France)

LE GAI SAVOIR

Max Dearly *(Banco)*, Marthe Mellot *(Queen)*, Renee Saint-Cyr *(Princess)*, Sinoel *(Prime Minister)*, Paul Olivier *(Chamberlain)*, Charles Redgie *(Crown Prince)*, Raymond Cordy *(Valet)*, Jose Noguero *(Band Leader)*, Marcel Carpentier *(Detective)*, Raymond Aimos

d, Rene Clair; w, Rene Clair; ph, Rudolph Mate, Louis Nee; ed, Jean Pouzet; m, Maurice Jaubert; art d, Lucien Aguettand, Lucien Carre

A fictitious country, Casinaria, depends on gambling foreigners to support its economy and finds itself on the verge of bankruptcy. Queen Mellot lures financier Dearly to her country, intending to marry him to her daughter (Saint-Cyr), although the girl loves Noguero, leader of the national band (whose entire repertoire consists of the national anthem played in a variety of tempos). Dearly is appointed dictator and suffers a blow to the head, resulting in some very strange behavior. Saint-Cyr elopes with Noguero and Dearly ends up engaged to the queen before revealing that he is not the millionaire he pretended to be. A major letdown after his earlier successes, this Clair offering provoked riots in France, then in the midst of a wave of conservatism (provoked by the rise of Hitler next door). Although a flop in its native country, the film became a big success in the USSR and Japan. Worth seeing for a number of funny scenes revolving around the collapse of the nation's currency. Clair had originally contracted with Tobis (Les Films Sonores) to make the film, but the German-owned French company rejected his script for obvious reasons; the finished film was banned in Mussolini's Italy and Hitler's Germany. Some of the funniest scenes in the film have to do with the terrible economic conditions of the day in those Depression-torn countries. A farmer pays a waiter for his dinner with a hen and receives as change two chicks and an egg; he leaves the latter as a tip. In another scene which presaged the later craze for aerobic exercise, mad dictator Dearly decrees that all citizens must run for hours around the public square. After this film Clair left France and made the wonderful THE GHOST GOES WEST in England and several excellent features in the US (AND THEN THERE WERE NONE and I MARRIED A WITCH among them) before returning to his homeland after the war.

LE GAI SAVOIR
1968 95m c   ★★★★
Drama   /X
O.R.T.F./Anouchka/Bavaria Atelier   (France)

Juliet Berto *(Patricia Lumumba)*, Jean-Pierre Leaud *(Emile Rousseau)*

d, Jean-Luc Godard; w, Jean-Luc Godard (based on "Emile" by Jean Jacques Rousseau); ph, Georges Leclerc (Eastmancolor); ed, Germaine Cohen

A fascinating film from the master of cinematic discourse, Jean-Luc Godard, in which he makes a profound attempt to dissolve narrative structure to its most basic elements: sound and image. Commissioned by the French government as a television adaptation of Jean Jacques Rousseau's "Emile," LE GAI SAVOIR instead turned out to be a study of language, or, more precisely, film language. It is completely absent of plot and leaves Berto and Leaud (two of the most prominent acting figures in the French New Wave) sitting in the black void of a sound stage, lit only by a single light. Not surprisingly the French government was furious with Godard for his failure to deliver an "acceptable" movie and refused to televise it, allowing him to buy back the rights. What results is a wealth of philosophy relating to Godard's

radical thoughts on filmmaking, delivered in the form of a conversation between Leaud and Berto. Intercut with their thoughts are some compelling word association tests which further exemplify Godard's love of language. It's no CASABLANCA, but for those with adventurous tastes and an interest in questioning the status quo, LE GAI SAVOIR's language deserves the same consideration as the literature of such contemporaries as Jean-Paul Sartre.

LE PETIT THEATRE DE JEAN RENOIR
1974 100m c   ★★★★
Drama   /U
Son et Lumiere/ORTF   (France)

THE LAST NEW YEAR'S EVE: Nino Fornicola *(The Bum)*, Minny Monti *(The Female Bum)*, Roger Trapp *(Max Vialle)*, Roland Martin, Frederic Santaya, Pierre Gulda. THE ELECTRIC FLOOR WAXER: Marguerite Cassan *(Isabelle)*, Pierre Olaf *(The Husband)*, Jacques Dynam *(The 2nd Husband)*, Jean-Louis Tristan *(Agent)*

p, Pierre Long; d, Jean Renoir; w, Jean Renoir; ph, Georges Leclerc (Eastmancolor); ed, Genevieve Winding; m, Joseph Kosma, Jean Wiener; prod d, Gilbert Margerie

An exceptional coda to the long and magnificent career of Renoir, which sums up his world in a personal manner. Divided into four parts, each introduced by the charming 75-year-old director himself, the picture moves from the artificially theatrical to the naturally realistic. The first episode, "The Last New Year's Eve," has Fornicola, a ragged and seemingly lonely bum, standing outside the window of an upper-class restaurant. One of the rich people inside pays to have the bum watch them eat from the outside. Of course, the diners lose their appetites, and as a consolation they have the food given to the bum. One of the rich women also gives her coat to the man. He is then seen returning to his riverside shelter, where he is greeted by his equally ragged wife. Together, during the night, they peacefully die. The segment was shot entirely on a stage, with Renoir paying homage in his narration to Hans Christian Andersen. The second episode, "The Electric Floor Waxer," is an odd little piece for those familiar with Renoir (and for anyone else, for that matter). Based on an earlier project, "It's Revolution," this tale is a satirical opera complete with singing choruses of office workers rising up from the lower depths of the Metro station. They sing repetitive refrains about their offices and their jobs. One woman (Cassan) goes through life obsessed with giving the floor a good waxing, causing heartache among her successive husbands. Dynam, her second, finally saves Cassan from waxing by throwing the vibrating, whirling machine out the window. As it crashes to the ground below, Cassan leaps from the window to join her electric lover. The third episode is hardly an episode at all; in one long dolly in-dolly out Jeanne Moreau sings a little tune called "When Love Dies" (Oscar Cremieux). It is included, as Renoir puts it, to "take us for a little while outside our century of sleazy progress." The fourth episode, "The King of Yvetot," is the most purely realistic, shot entirely on location. At the introduction Renoir shows us his little theater (a miniature model of a stage) and briefly explains the sport of petanque, the values and the rules of this game. He takes a tiny metal ball and rolls it along the little stage, and with one quick edit, we are transported into the world of cinema as a large petanque ball rolls along the ground. An old man is seen playing, then his young wife, and then her younger lover. The conflicts of this triangle are resolved peacefully and with respect to set morals in a final game of petanque, which Renoir "firmly believes to be an instrument of peace." The film's finale is also the end of Renoir's little theater; the members of the cast come out for a closing bow. The actors thank us for watching, and we cannot help but feel thanks for Renoir's humble presentation. What way could be more appropriate for one of filmdom's greatest directors (and probably the greatest in Europe) to wrap up his truly profound career? Originally made for French television in 1969.

LEADBELLY

1976 126m c ★★★½
Musical/Biography PG/AA
Paramount

Roger E. Mosley *(Huddie Ledbetter)*, Paul Benjamin *(Wes Ledbetter)*, Madge Sinclair *(Miss Eula)*, Alan Manson *(Prison Chief Guard)*, Albert Hall *(Dicklicker)*, Art Evans *(Blind Lemon Jefferson)*, James E. Brodhead *(John Lomax)*, John Henry Faulk *(Governor Neff)*, Vivian Bonnell *(Old Lady)*, Dana Manno *(Margaret Judd)*

p, Marc Merson; d, Gordon Parks, Sr.; w, Ernest Kinoy; ph, Bruce Surtees (Eastmancolor); ed, Harry Howard; m, Fred Karlin; prod d, Robert Boyle

Fine biopic of famed black blues/folk singer Huddie Ledbetter, known as Leadbelly, who wrote or adapted such classics as "Goodnight, Irene," "The Midnight Special," "Rock Island Line," and "The Bourgeois Blues." Ledbetter's hard life is related in flashback from his early teens to his last term in prison (he also served twice on chain gangs). The film shows how he was victimized by racism but does not minimize the complexity of his erratic personality—often manifested in outbursts of violence. Though several of his songs are rendered well here by HiTide Harris, backed by Sonny Terry, Brownie McGhee, David Cohen, and Dick Rosmini, LEADBELLY focuses less on the man's musical artistry than one would wish. Still, this is a very informative film, beautifully photographed by Bruce Surtees, with fine performances by almost everyone in the cast, especially Robert E. Mosley in the title role.

LEAGUE OF GENTLEMEN, THE

1961 116m bw ★★★½
Crime/Comedy /A
Allied Film Makers (U.K.)

Jack Hawkins *(Hyde)*, Nigel Patrick *(Peter Graham Race)*, Roger Livesey *(Mycroft)*, Richard Attenborough *(Edward Lexy)*, Bryan Forbes *(Martin Porthill)*, Kieron Moore *(Stevens)*, Robert Coote *(Bunny Warren)*, Terence Alexander *(Rupert Rutland-Smith)*, Melissa Stribling *(Peggy)*, Norman Bird *(Frank Weaver)*

p, Michael Relph; d, Basil Dearden; w, Bryan Forbes (based on the novel *The League of Gentlemen* by John Boland); ph, Arthur Ibbetson; ed, John D. Guthridge; m, Philip Green; prod d, Peter Proud; art d, Peter Proud; cos, Joan Ellacott

Near perfection to the last detail is accorded to THE LEAGUE OF GENTLEMEN. Unfortunately for the perpetrators of the cinematic crime, the same "near perfection" is what does them in. Hawkins is so angry at having been mandatorily retired by the British army that he decides to put his service experience to devious use by masterminding a huge bank robbery. He enlists a group of his old buddies in his plan and promises that each will receive a share of the million-pound heist. Every painstaking phase of the operation, plus the psyches of the miscreants, is shown in a fascinating, even humorous fashion. We, the audience, grow to like these guys and want them to succeed. When the moment of the robbery arrives, the men jump into action with military precision and use all of their expertise to make it a success. Gas masks, smoke bombs, radio jamming—the lot—are

utilized, and they get away with it. However, we've all learned that "crime doesn't pay," and the heist is uncovered when Coote, a drunken pal of Hawkins, arrives unexpectedly. Through his stupidity, the authorities are led to the den of thieves where the crooks are nabbed before they can divvy up the cash.

THE LEAGUE OF GENTLEMEN starts a bit slow as the plot is unraveled but then begins to move like lightning. The film might have been played straight for thrills and intrigue, but the screenplay (by Forbes, who also plays the role of Porthill) and the direction are lighthearted, providing each characterization with some comedic quirk that makes it distinctive from the others.

LEARNING TREE, THE

1969 107m c ★★½
Drama M/AA
Winger Enterprises

Kyle Johnson *(Newt Winger)*, Alex Clarke *(Marcus Savage)*, Estelle Evans *(Sarah Winger)*, Dana Elcar *(Sheriff Kirky)*, Mira Waters *(Arcella Jefferson)*, Joel Fluellen *(Uncle Rob)*, Malcolm Atterbury *(Silas Newhall)*, Richard Ward *(Booker Savage)*, Russell Thorson *(Judge Cavanaugh)*, Peggy Rea *(Miss McClintock)*

p, Gordon Parks, Sr.; d, Gordon Parks, Sr.; w, Gordon Parks (based on his novel); ph, Burnett Guffey (Panavision, Technicolor); ed, George Rohrs; m, Gordon Parks; art d, Edward Engoron; fx, Albert Whitlock

Undoubtedly the biggest surprise among the first 25 films selected in 1989 for inclusion in the National Film Registry, this visually beautiful and moving, if somewhat melodramatic, story of a black teenager growing up in Kansas in the 1920s was the first feature film by a black director to be financed by a major Hollywood studio. Gordon Parks directed, produced, wrote, and composed the score of this adaptation of his semi-autobiographical novel *The Learning Tree* (1963) after a highly successful, 20-year career as an acclaimed photojournalist for *Life* magazine. Essentially a coming-of-age tale, the film focuses on Newt Winger (Kyle Johnson), a black teenager living in a small Kansas town. Like many other movie teens, Newt is shown learning about sex (from a prostitute, Big Mabel, played by Carole Lamond) and death, encountering the latter after he and some friends discover the corpse of a black gambler who was murdered by the local sheriff, Kirby (Dana Elcar). Newt's nemesis is Marcus Savage (Alex Clarke), an embittered, troubled young black who comes from a less-than-loving home, with an absent mother and a negligent, angry father. Newt, by contrast, is supported by his hard-working, understanding, and strong mother (Estelle Evans), who has strived to teach her son to keep to a righteous path despite the hardships and racism he must face, advising him to put life's ups and downs to constructive use as a "learning tree." Marcus has it in for Newt, but is temporarily prevented from acting on his resentment when he is sent to jail for the brutal beating of Kiner (George Mitchell), the benign white farmer for whom Newt works.

Newt falls seriously in love for the first time when he meets the beautiful new girl in town, Arcella Jefferson (Mira Waters), but she is seduced and impregnated by the white, wastrel son of Judge Cavanaugh (Russell Thorson), and moves away with her family in disgrace. Heartbroken, Newt soon faces a crisis of conscience after he sees Marcus's father, Booker (Richard Ward), and a white drunkard, Silas Newhall (Malcolm Atterbury), attempting to steal liquor from Kiner. Kiner catches them and is killed by Booker, who flees, leaving behind Silas, lying unconscious at the scene of the crime. Silas is then arrested and tried for murder. Fearing that the truth of Kiner's killing will cause the whites in town to lynch and attack blacks, torn between racial loyalty and the honesty that compels him to vindicate an innocent man, Newt hesitates to accuse Booker but eventually testifies to the truth, relying on the moral strength that has been instilled by his mother, who dies of a heart attack from the strain of recent events. Booker kills himself, and Marcus, who has been released from jail, determines to murder Newt. Eventually, the two square off in a fight at a carnival. Newt wins and Marcus flees, pursued by the racist Sheriff Kirby. Kirby shoots Marcus in the back, killing the young black man, just as he killed the gambler whose body Newt discovered early in the movie. As the film ends, Newt, sadder and wiser as a result of the hostility, violence, and hypocrisy he has seen, leaves town in search of a brighter future elsewhere.

In tracing the encounters that make up Newt's moral and practical education, Parks depicts the ambiguous racial attitudes of blacks and whites in the Kansas town with an at times ironic complexity rarely found in earlier films dealing with racism. Chauncey (Zooey Hall), the callous seducer of Arcella, also advocates desegregation; his father the judge, though implicated in a system of unequal justice for whites and blacks, is shown angrily denouncing his fellow whites' lynch-mob thirst for vigilante "justice." In another scene, Newt's high-school principal criticizes a teacher for discouraging the young man's dreams of a college education, though he himself will not or cannot dare to allow blacks to play on the school's sports teams. Newt's struggle to adhere to an absolute notion of justice and morality, therefore, is by no means easy or clear-cut.

The fact that he does hold to that standard, however, places THE LEARNING TREE far more in the mainstream, thematically, than Parks's strikingly different second feature, SHAFT, the hugely successful, angry, urban action film that set the tone for the 70s blaxploitation movies. THE LEARNING TREE's potential openness to criticism as a naive, old-fashioned tale is made greater by its occasional sermonizing, sentimental characterizations, relatively slow pace, and melodrama, especially as the film moves toward its wrap-up. On the other hand, Parks and cinematographer Burnett Guffey, who filmed on location in the director's native Fort Scott, beautifully and lovingly capture the period and mood of 1920s Kansas, and Johnson's lead performance is fine. (Most of the other performances from the cast of unknowns, unfortunately, are undistinguished at best.) Especially evocative are the nostalgic scenes of black life, from church services to outdoor barbecues.

Parks's next films—SHAFT, SHAFT'S BIG SCORE, and THE SUPER COPS, which was one of few examples of a film dealing with white characters to be directed by a black—were radical departures from THE LEARNING TREE, being full of violent action, hip, and clearly commercial in intent. With LEADBELLY (1976) Parks returned a more personal and understated style of filmmaking, and to beautifully photographed rural, period detail. A pianist, composer, and former professional basketball player, Parks is also the father of the late Gordon Parks, Jr., who directed SUPERFLY.

LEATHER BOYS, THE
1965 108m bw   ★★★
Drama   /15
Raymond Stross (U.K.)

Rita Tushingham *(Dot)*, Colin Campbell *(Reggie)*, Dudley Sutton *(Pete)*, Gladys Henson *(Gran)*, Avice Landone *(Reggie's Mother)*, Lockwood West *(Reggie's Father)*, Betty Marsden *(Dot's Mother)*,

Martin Matthews *(Uncle Arthur)*, Johnny Briggs *(Boy Friend)*, James Chase *(Les)*

p, Raymond Stross; d, Sidney J. Furie; w, Gillian Freeman (based on the novel by Eliot George); ph, Gerald Gibbs (CinemaScope); ed, Reginald Beck; m, Bill McGuffie; art d, Arthur Lawson

Dot (Rita Tushingham) marries motorcycle buff Reggie (Colin Campbell) to escape from her parents, and the relationship never gets off the ground. She doesn't do any housework, and only cooks cans of beans. Reggie moves out and goes to live with his friend Pete (Dudley Sutton), whom Reggie begins to suspect is a homosexual. He moves back when he hears that Dot is pregnant but discovers that she's sleeping with another man. He and Pete decide to run off to sea, but Pete enjoys himself too much with a gay group of sailors; Reggie is left bereft of bride and friend.

LEFT-HANDED GUN, THE
1958 102m bw   ★★★½
Biography/Western   /PG
WB

Paul Newman *(Billy Bonney)*, Lita Milan *(Celsa)*, John Dehner *(Pat Garrett)*, Hurd Hatfield *(Moultrie)*, James Congdon *(Charlie Boudre)*, James Best *(Tom Folliard)*, Colin Keith-Johnston *(Tunstall)*, John Dierkes *(McSween)*, Robert Anderson *(Hill)*, Wally Brown *(Moon)*

p, Fred Coe; d, Arthur Penn; w, Leslie Stevens (based on the teleplay "The Death of Billy the Kid" by Gore Vidal); ph, Peverell Marley; ed, Folmar Blangsted; m, Alexander Courage; art d, Art Loel; cos, Marjorie Best

A good but disturbing psychological western, well directed by Penn and acted in a strangely fascinating style by Newman. Penn demythologizes Billy the Kid, and Newman plays him more honestly than anyone else ever has. He was a slow-witted illiterate with a streak of sadistic bloodlust in him, fiercely loyal to his few friends and deadly to all who became his enemy. Newman is nothing but a western guttersnipe until John Tunstall (Keith-Johnston), a kindly rancher whom Billy had known in real life, treats him with understanding. Newman reacts as would any loveless human, becoming fanatically devoted to the rancher. When the unarmed Keith-Johnston is shot to death by a deputy and three others in a range war, Newman and his equally empty-headed saddlemates, Best and Congdon, track down the killers and murder them one by one. Pat Garrett (Dehner), the famous lawman who was the harsh, real-life father figure for Billy, vows revenge on the Kid after Newman kills one of the guests—the last of the foursome sought for Keith-Johnston's death—at Dehner's wedding party. Newman is arrested and jailed, but he escapes, murdering his guards in the process. The relentless Dehner then tracks him down and kills the unarmed outlaw with a single shot. Flitting in and out of Newman's life is a neurotic pulp writer, Hatfield, who creates the myth of Billy the Kid and then condemns the outlaw for not living up to his lies. This first film by director Penn stems from Gore Vidal's wacky, self-serving teleplay, "The Death of Billy the Kid," which was helmed by Penn for TV in 1955. Penn toned down Vidal's portrait of the Kid as a rampant homosexual which reflected the author's interests perhaps more than the facts of history. Newman, as he had in SOMEBODY UP THERE LIKES ME, took a role here which was originally coveted by James Dean, who died prematurely in a car accident, but he does a masterful job in portraying the ruthless killer whose reputation existed only beyond the grave.

LENNY
1974 111m bw   ★★★
Biography   R/18
UA

Dustin Hoffman *(Lenny Bruce)*, Valerie Perrine *(Honey Bruce)*, Jan Miner *(Sally Marr)*, Stanley Beck *(Artie Silver)*, Gary Morton *(Sherman Hart)*, Rashel Novikoff *(Aunt Mema)*, Guy Rennie *(Jack Goldstein)*, Frankie Man *(Baltimore Strip Club MC)*, Mark Harris *(San Francisco Defense Attorney)*, Lee Sandman *(San Francisco Judge)*

p, Marvin Worth; d, Bob Fosse; w, Julian Barry (based on the play by Julian Barry); ph, Bruce Surtees; ed, Alan Heim; prod d, Joel Schiller; cos, Albert Wolsky

Harsh, funny, grim, and as truthful a film biography as you will ever see, LENNY received Academy nominations for Hoffman (Art Carney won for HARRY AND TONTO), Perrine (Ellen Burstyn won for ALICE DOESN'T LIVE HERE ANYMORE), Surtees, Fosse, Best Screenplay, and Best Picture (THE GODFATHER, PART II took this honor) but didn't take any Oscars. Produced by onetime gag writer Worth, LENNY proved that it isn't easy to be ahead of your time. By today's liberal standards, much of what comedian Lenny Bruce said on stage would be allowed without police interference. There are those who say he would be just another comic today, but they don't realize that his quest was always to stay ahead of his time; if Bruce were alive, he'd be breaking new ground in the comedy sphere. Bruce was an immensely intelligent commentator on the current scene, who was crushed by the cogs of society's mechanism. Fosse's third picture (after CABARET and SWEET CHARITY) exhibits some of the problems he encountered in making his own biography, ALL THAT JAZZ. At times LENNY looks like an autobiography, as Hoffman becomes the famed comedian and pours his guts out on stage, using many of the very routines Bruce did in real life. The movie is divided into three sections, as a play might be (which is what it actually began as). This a conscious decision on Fosse's part—influenced either by his stage background or his goal of the intimacy of the stage rather than the scope of the screen. The first part shows Hoffman's courtship of Perrine, a stripper with a surprising amount of class and smarts (at least, that's how Perrine portrays her). Hoffman refers to her as his "shiksa goddess"—a reference to her obvious flaxen-haired Gentile-ity. At first Hoffman enjoys a standard kind of popularity as a performer. Then he decides to experiment, opting for more controversial material. After Hoffman and Perrine have an auto accident that nearly costs her life, the comedian is portrayed as, perhaps, a too-loving husband, with an obsession about his wife. His somewhat obsessive personality dogs him all of his life; he never seems to know how to let go of something. He becomes hooked on drugs. Then he becomes obsessed with the various police departments who seek to stop his shows wherever he performs. Rather than pay a fine or do a few days' time, Hoffman determines to fight City Hall, and that takes up about a third of the film. In the end it is his obsession with death that overrides all others, and we never know whether he has a predisposition for his own destruction or not.

The film was a series of interviews and flashbacks conducted by an off-camera party, a la CITIZEN KANE. Perrine, never considered a good actress before this movie, was solid as Hoffman's wife. Miner essayed the role of Sally Marr, mother of the comedian, who in real life is less abrasive than her portrayal here. (Marr is a manager of comedians, an actress in her own right, and a funny woman who adored her son and was his best audience.) Beck, who did a fine job as Hoffman's agent, is a longtime personal friend in real life. The chemistry between his character and Hoffman's worked. The disjointed interviews eventually merge into part of a patchwork quilt whose pattern is the ongoing struggle that an "original" must face in order to become a success. It's interesting to watch the private life of the comic against the public one. In real life, Bruce seldom used foul language and even remonstrated with those who did if there was a woman present. What he wanted was the right to use four-letter words in his act. When the police began to harass him, Hoffman gave his greatest performances—in court, to less-than-receptive audiences, the judges and juries who heard them. The film was shot in atmosphereic black and white. One wonders whether it is Fosse's or the comedian's obsession with death that takes hold at the end, because the director's work in ALL THAT JAZZ, as well as in his STAR 80, is heavily concerned with morbidity. Bruce was generous to many—with money, things, and most of all himself. His daughter, Kitty, married one of Lenny's greatest fans, Freddie Prinze, who later died tragically, the result of a gun accident (some claimed suicide) at the height of his television popularity. Many comedians, such as George Carlin, Richard Pryor, and Eddie Murphy, owe a debt of gratitude to Bruce for his pioneering efforts to get all censorship lifted from the nightclub stage. Without him, one wonders whether other comedians would have made it so quickly. Bruce died as the result of a drug overdose. Hoffman won an Oscar for KRAMER VS. KRAMER, but this is one of his greatest roles. Background music includes some older Miles Davis recordings.

LEO THE LAST
1970 104m c   ★½
Drama   R/X
UA (U.K.)

Marcello Mastroianni *(Leo)*, Billie Whitelaw *(Margaret)*, Calvin Lockhart *(Roscoe)*, Glenna Forster Jones *(Salambo)*, Graham Crowden *(Max)*, Gwen Ffrangcon-Davies *(Hilda)*, David De Keyser *(David)*, Vladek Sheybal *(Laszlo)*, Keefe West *(Jasper)*, Kenneth J. Warren *(Kowalski)*

p, Irwin Winkler, Robert Chartoff; d, John Boorman; w, William Stair, John Boorman (based on the play "The Prince" by George Tabori); ph, Peter Suschitzky (DeLuxe Color); ed, Tom Priestley; m, Fred Myrow; prod d, Tony Woollard; fx, John Richardson; cos, Joan Woollard

Mastroianni is an exiled European monarch who returns to London after many years away. The area where his mansion is located has become a black ghetto, but Mastroianni is oblivious to his surroundings; he is absorbed in bird-watching. In time Mastroianni notices the plight of his neighbors through his telescope, but he moves into action only after Jones is forced into prostitution. He takes her in as his ward and tries to involve himself in the problems of the ghetto. The monarch's royal guardsmen revolt, taking over his house and arming themselves. Mastroianni and the neighborhood folk band together, defeat the guards with fireworks, and burn down the mansion. A pretentious, heavy-handed satire of the class structure and European royalty. Director Boorman tries to say much in this film, but little is clearly stated.

LEOPARD, THE
(IL GATTOPARDO)
1963 165m c   ★★★★½
Historical   PG
Titanus (Italy)

Burt Lancaster (*Prince Don Fabrizio Salina*), Alain Delon (*Tancredi*), Claudia Cardinale (*Angelica Sedara/Bertiana*), Rina Morelli (*Maria Stella*), Paolo Stoppa (*Don Calogero Sedara*), Romolo Valli (*Father Pirrone*), Lucilla Morlacchi (*Concetta*), Serge Reggiani (*Don Ciccio Tumeo*), Ida Galli (*Carolina*), Ottavia Piccolo (*Caterina*)

p, Goffredo Lombardo; d, Luchino Visconti; w, Luchino Visconti, Suso Cecchi D'Amico, Pasquale Festa Campanile, Enrico Medioli, Massimo Franciosa (based on the novel *Il Gattopardo* by Giuseppe Tomasi di Lampedusa); ph, Giuseppe Rotunno (CinemaScope, DeLuxe Color); ed, Mario Serandrei; m, Nino Rota, Giuseppe Verdi; art d, Mario Garbuglia; cos, Piero Tosi, Reanda, Sartoria Safas

Superb, sumptuous epic based on Guiseppe di Lampedusa's novel about the decline of the Italian aristocracy and the rise to power of the bourgeoisie. Financed by 20th Century-Fox and released to critical acclaim in Europe, THE LEOPARD was butchered for its initial, inauspicious U.S. release, finally earning the acclaim it deserved when a restored version was presented in 1983.

Burt Lancaster plays an elderly prince struggling to come to terms with the rapidly changing Italian social structure of the 1860s. He arranges for his nephew, Tancredi (Alain Delon), to marry Angela (Claudia Cardinale), the daughter of a rich merchant, in an attempt to shore up his status and lifestyle and, during a nearly hour-long ball scene with which the film closes, ruminates on his own past and present as well as that of his social class.

This is a gorgeous, fascinating account of the interplay between the personal and the social, directed with the kind of insight that only an aristocrat-turned-Marxist like Visconti could afford. (Lancaster claimed that he actually based his performance on Visconti's character.) The ball scene, at which the aristocrats come to accept that power has passed into the hands of the nouveau riches, is justly regarded as one of the finest set pieces in film history. THE LEOPARD took the Golden Palm as Best Film at Cannes and received an Oscar nomination for Best Costume Design.

LES BICHES
1968 104m c   ★★★½
Drama   R/X
Boetie/Alexandra (Italy/France)

Stephane Audran (*Frederique*), Jacqueline Sassard (*Why*), Jean-Louis Trintignant (*Paul Thomas*), Nane Germon (*Violetta*), Serge Bento (*Bookseller*), Dominique Zardi (*Riais*), Henri Attal (*Robeque*), Claude Chabrol (*Filmmaker*), Henri Frances

p, Andre Genoves; d, Claude Chabrol; w, Paul Gegauff, Claude Chabrol; ph, Jean Rabier (Eastmancolor); ed, Jacques Gaillard; m, Pierre Jansen; cos, Maurice Albray

Claude Chabrol's suspenseful and erotic story of two lesbian lovers—Frederique (Stephane Audran), a wealthy and elegant woman, and Why (Jaqueline Sassard), a young bohemian who earns a living making charcoal drawings on the sidewalks of Paris. Frederique, who has already seduced Why and dragged her off to a lovely St. Tropez villa, upsets the balance when she next seduces architect Paul (Jean-Louis Trintignant). Why loves them both and cannot bear the thought of being left behind when Frederique and Paul run off to Paris together. One of the few Chabrol films available on videotape (under the title BAD GIRLS), LES BICHES features the director's favorite lead actress, Audran (then his wife), in yet another situation of suspense that, while Hitchcockian at its root, is pure Chabrol. The setup is

a familiar one—a love triangle—but Chabrol's delicate treatment and highly controlled direction make this one of his finest efforts.

LES COMPERES
1983 92m c   ★★★½
Comedy/Drama   PG/
Fideline/Efve/D.D. (France)

Pierre Richard (*Francois Pignon*), Gerard Depardieu (*Jean Lucas*), Anne Duperey (*Christine Martin*), Michel Aumont (*Paul Martin*), Stephane Bierry (*Tristan Martin*), Jean-Jacques Scheffer (*Ralph*), Philippe Khorsand (*Milan*), Roland Blanche (*Jeannot*), Jacques Frantz (*Verdier*), Maurice Barrier (*Raffart*)

d, Francis Veber; w, Francis Veber (based on his story); ph, Claude Agostini; ed, Marie-Sophie Dubus; m, Vladimir Cosma; prod d, Gerard Daoudal; cos, Corinne Jorry

Tristan Martin (Stephane Bierry) is a 16-year-old runaway who leaves Paris and hitchhikes to Nice with Michele (Florence Moreau), a tough young girl who hangs out with degenerate bikers. Tristan's middle-class parents (Anne Duperey and Michel Aumont) inform the authorities but receive only the feeble assurance that their son will turn up sooner or later, "like a stolen car." Tristan's mother decides to phone newspaperman and old flame Jean (Gerard Depardieu), convincing him that he is Tristan's real father, in the hope that he will offer to find the boy. When he refuses, she tries the same scheme on another past lover, Francois (Pierre Richard), a suicidal manic-depressive who is thrilled by the request and agrees to help. In the meantime, Jean has reconsidered. Both men eventually meet and discover they have a mutual interest—finding a missing son—but it takes a while for them to realize that they are both looking for the same son. Naturally, the question of the boy's real parentage is at issue, with both men claiming to be the father. A delightful film, LES COMPERES combines healthy doses of comedy, drama, and crime with three superbly sketched characters. Jean's and Francois's reactions to the possibility of fatherhood are fascinating, as is the interaction between the two. LES COMPERES is a film that depends on the chemistry among the actors, and fortunately this doesn't fail for a moment. Depardieu and Richard are both superb, reminiscent of Laurel and Hardy—the hulkish Depardieu playing Hardy to Richard's whimpering Laurel—in their affectionate dislike for each other. The result is a thoroughly enjoyable, entertaining, funny, and touching celebration of fatherhood.

LES ENFANTS TERRIBLES
1950 107m bw   ★★★
Drama   /X
Melville (France)

Nicole Stephane (*Elisabeth*), Edouard Dermit (*Paul*), Jacques Bernard (*Gerard*), Renee Cosima (*Dargelos/Agathe*), Roger Gaillard (*Gerard's Uncle*), Melvyn Martin (*Michael*), Maurice Revel (*Doctor*), Adeline Aucoc (*Mariette*), Maria Cyliakus (*The Mother*), Jean-Marie Robain (*Headmaster*)

p, Jean-Pierre Melville; d, Jean-Pierre Melville; w, Jean-Pierre Melville, Jean Cocteau (based on the novel *Les Enfants Terribles* by Jean Cocteau); ph, Henri Decae; ed, Monique Bonnot; m, Johann Sebastian Bach, Antonio Vivaldi

Two seemingly disparate filmmakers—Jean-Pierre Melville, best known for his dark black-and-white ventures into the criminal underworld, and Jean Cocteau, the poet of the mythical underworld—came together to bring Cocteau's celebrated play of love, death, and incest to the screen. Paul (Edouard Dermit), a young Parisian, is severely injured when hit by a snowball thrown by Dargelos (Renee Cosima), the school bully whom he idolizes. He is cared for by his sister Elisabeth (Nicole Stephane), with whom he shares a bedroom, though both are in their teens. The near-incestuous pair are brought closer together by the death of their ailing mother and are joined by Paul's friend Gerard (Jacques Bernard), who is infatuated with Elisabeth. The trio eventually becomes a quartet when Paul meets his sister's friend Agathe (Cosima, in a dual, cross-gender role). As the relationships intertwine, Elisabeth is forced to admit her attraction to her brother. Melville, who was given the chance to direct this prestigious property after Cocteau saw one of his early 16mm films, shot LES ENFANTS TERRIBLES in his own apartment, which he rented with the intention of using it as a location. The film also unmistakably bears Cocteau's stamp, and he even directed one scene (at the beach) when Melville fell ill.

LES GIRLS

1957   114m   c   ★★★
Musical/Comedy   /A
MGM

Gene Kelly (Barry Nichols), Mitzi Gaynor (Joy Henderson), Kay Kendall (Lady Wren), Taina Elg (Angele Ducros), Jacques Bergerac (Pierre Ducros), Leslie Phillips (Sir Gerald Wren), Henry Daniell (Judge), Patrick MacNee (Sir Percy), Stephen Vercoe (Mr. Outward), Philip Tonge (Associate Judge)

p, Sol C. Siegel; d, George Cukor; w, John Patrick (based on a story by Vera Caspary); ph, Robert Surtees (CinemaScope, Metrocolor); ed, Ferris Webster; m, Cole Porter; art d, William A. Horning, Gene Allen; chor, Jack Cole; cos, Orry-Kelly

Attempting to carry on the tradition of their great musicals of the 1930s and 40s, MGM released this relatively minor effort employing some of the studio's finest creative talents in 1957. Barry (Gene Kelly), Angele (Taina Elg), Joy (Mitzi Gaynor), and Sybil (Kay Kendall) are the former members of "Barry Nichols and Les Girls," a popular European cabaret act. Years after the group has dissolved, Sybil, now Lady Wren, publishes her all-too-candid recollections of what went on romantically behind the scenes among Barry and his partners. Angele is outraged by the revelations and sues Sybil for defamation of character, the case is tried in court, and the picture becomes a musical RASHOMON, with each of the principals telling the story of the act as they remember it—none lying, but all recalling matters very differently. Not surprisingly, Barry (now married to Joy) gives the key testimony, and the picture ends with resumed good relations among the group, after all have had their say and a host of musical numbers have been performed. The script is more complicated than witty and can't sustain what's meant to be a breezy paean to the great MGM musicals; Kelly (in his last MGM appearance before THAT'S ENTERTAINMENT) never quite musters the energy needed for his role; and Cole Porter's last Hollywood score is not one of his best. Among les girls, Kendall stands out, and scored a deservedly blazing success in this, her first US picture. LES GIRLS's failure to make big money signaled the end of the "original musical" for Hollywood. Once the 60s arrived, the studios didn't want to make big musicals unless they were adapted from proven Broadway hits, and even then (as with Gaynor's SOUTH PACIFIC), success was not assured. The tunes include: "Les Girls," "Flower Song," "You're Just Too, Too," "Ca C'est L'Amour," "Ladies in Waiting," "La Habanera," and a delicious satire of Brando's THE WILD ONE entitled "Why Am I So Gone (About That Gal)?" Orry-Kelly's costumes earned

an Oscar and the film was nominated for Best Sound and Best Art Direction.

LES LIAISONS DANGEREUSES

(RELAZIONI PERICOLOSE)
1959   106m   bw   ★★
Drama   /X
Marceau/Cocinor/Laetitia   (France/Italy)

Gerard Philipe (Valmont de Merteuil), Jeanne Moreau (Juliette de Merteuil), Jeanne Valerie (Cecile Volanges), Annette Vadim (Marianne Tourvel), Simone Renant (Mme. Volanges), Jean-Louis Trintignant (Danceny), Nicolas Vogel (Court), Boris Vian (Prevan), Frederic O'Brady, Gillian Hills

d, Roger Vadim; w, Roger Vadim, Roger Vailland, Claude Brule (based on the novel by Choderlos de Laclos); ph, Marcel Grignon; ed, Victoria Mercanton; m, Thelonius Monk, Jack Murray

Philipe and Moreau are a married couple who thrive on extramarital affairs. When Philipe finds himself emotionally involved with Vadim (nee Stroyberg, director Vadim's wife after Brigitte Bardot), his relationship with Moreau falls apart. Eventually Philipe is killed and Moreau disfigured in a fire that she set to burn her husband's incriminating letters.

LES MISERABLES

1935   108m   bw   ★★★★★
Drama   /A
20th Century

Fredric March (Jean Valjean), Charles Laughton (Javert), Cedric Hardwicke (Bishop Bienvenu), Rochelle Hudson (Big Cosette), Marilyn Knowlden (Little Cosette), Frances Drake (Eponine), John Beal (Marius), Jessie Ralph (Mme. Magloire), Florence Eldridge (Fantine), Ferdinand Gottschalk (Thenardier)

p, Darryl F. Zanuck; d, Richard Boleslawski; w, W.P. Lipscomb (based on the novel by Victor Hugo); ph, Gregg Toland; ed, Barbara McLean

Fredric March gives a superb performance as the sensitive, persecuted Jean Valjean who steals a loaf of bread to survive, is captured, and given ten years' hard labor. When he finally escapes the prison galley, March is a hardbitten, unsympathetic character, all compassion hammered out of him by the rigors of confinement. He is taken in by Bishop Bienvenu, played by Cedric Hardwicke, who refuses to prosecute him for stealing two silver candlesticks. Through Hardwicke's kindness and understanding, March regains his sensitive nature and is reformed. He builds a new life for himself under an assumed name and adopts a young child as his own. He becomes a well-to-do businessman, and, moving to another town, becomes so widely liked and respected that he is elected mayor, an office which helps him devote his life to benefiting others. Charles Laughton, as Javert, the town's chief of police, is a cold, unimpassioned official, single-minded in his view that the law is to be upheld and enforced at all costs, with no mercy shown to anyone committing the slightest infraction. Laughton and March clash repeatedly over the interpretation of the law, and the policeman becomes incensed when March intercedes on behalf of a social pariah (Florence Eldridge, March's real-life wife). One day March sees a villager trapped beneath a heavy wagon, and, with what seems to be superhuman strength, he puts his back to the wagon and lifts it so the man can be saved. Laughton watches this feat and is reminded of a galley prisoner he once encountered. He investigates March's past and identifies March as Jean Valjean, the wanted criminal. He is then confused when another prisoner is found, a mindless inmate who amazingly resembles March and who claims to be Jean Valjean. The impostor is put on trial, but the honorable March (who plays both parts) admits that he is the real Jean Valjean. Before he can be jailed, he again escapes with his daughter (Frances Drake) to Paris where he assumes yet another identity. His daughter falls in love with John Beal, a young radical who works for prison reform. Laughton arrives in Paris and is assigned to watch the revolutionaries. He gets onto March's trail once more as March becomes more and more involved with Beal and his revolutionary friends. When Drake comes to her father with the news that Beal has been injured in the fighting, March goes to the barricades. With Laughton on his heels, he escapes into the Paris sewers, carrying the injured young man through treacherous chest-high waters and delivering him to Drake. Once Beal and Drake are reunited, March goes to surrender to Laughton. But having witnessed March's selfless sacrifice, the policeman begins to feel compassion, an emotion that so confuses and vexes him that he is almost willing to break the law to allow the noble March his freedom. Laughton solves his dilemma by hurling himself into the Seine and drowning himself. March is free to rejoin his daughter and Beal and to live out his life with those who love him.

This lavish production is full of meticulous detail, and, with the exception of the ending, faithful to Victor Hugo's novel. (Valjean dies in the original tale.) Richard Boleslawski (RASPU- TIN AND THE EMPRESS, THE PAINTED VEIL), a largely forgotten director today, was masterful in his handling of LES MISERABLES, adhering closely to Hugo's scenes and working diligently from W.P. Lipscomb's compact 108-minute script, which is literate and moving. March gives one of his greatest performances as the hunted victim Jean Valjean, far superior to the rendering of the character in a French version in 1936, or in the crude 1918 silent version (also made by Fox, and starring William Farnum). The film was remade in 1952 with Michael Rennie as Jean Valjean and Robert Newton as Javert, the police- man, but this later version is a pale imitation of the 1935 classic. A number of other actors, including Richard Jordan in a British remake of the film in 1979, portrayed Hugo's great fictional character. But no one has ever approached March's profound performance.

LES MISERABLES

1936   305m   bw   ★★★
Historical
Pathe/Nathan   (France)   /A

Harry Baur (Jean Valjean/M. Madeleine/M. Fauchelevent), Charles Vanel (Javert), Henry Krauss (Bishop Myriel), Charles Dullin (Thenardier), Marguerite Moreno (Mme. Thenardier), Odette Florelle (Fantine), Gaby Triquet (Cosette as a Child), Jean Servais (Marius), Josseline Gael (Cosette as an Adult), Orane Demazis (Eponine)

d, Raymond Bernard; w, Raymond Bernard, Andre Lang (based on the novel by Victor Hugo); ph, Jules Kruger; m, Arthur Honneg- ger

One of many versions of Victor Hugo's classic novel about a thief who tries to make good but who is hounded by a determined detective. At 305 minutes, this version is arguably the most faithful to the novel, but it still doesn't equal the 1935 US adaptation. Upon its release in Paris in 1933, this was shown in three parts—TEMPETE SOUS UN CRANE (120m), LES THE- NARDIERS (90m), LIBERTE, LIBERTE CHERIE (95m)—and in three different theaters. It was later cut to a single 165-minute

version and later edited again into two parts—JEAN VALJEAN (109m) and COSETTE (100m).

LES MISERABLES

1952   105m   bw   ★★★
Historical   /U
FOX

Michael Rennie (Jean Valjean), Debra Paget (Cosette), Robert Newton (Javert), Edmund Gwenn (Bishop), Sylvia Sidney (Fant- ine), Cameron Mitchell (Marius), Elsa Lanchester (Mme. Magloire), James Robertson Justice (Robert), Joseph Wiseman (Genflou), Rhys Williams (Brevet)

p, Fred Kohlmar; d, Lewis Milestone; w, Richard Murphy (based on the novel by Victor Hugo); ph, Joseph La Shelle; ed, Hugh S. Fowler; m, Alex North; art d, Lyle Wheeler, J. Russell Spencer; fx, Ray Kellogg; cos, Dorothy Jeakins

This was the fifth version of Victor Hugo's novel (versions by Fox Film Co. in 1918, Universal in 1927, United Artists in 1935, and a French production in 1936 preceded it). The story of justice and the law is told in three episodes: Rennie's arrest for stealing bread and his imprisonment; his becoming a mayor and adoption of Paget; and Newton's hounding of Rennie. The film ends when Newton lets Rennie go and commits suicide for going against his own principles. Although a well-crafted production, it doesn't hold up as well as the 1935 UA version.

LES MISERABLES

1982   187m   c   ★★
Historical
GEF/CCFC   (France)

Lino Ventura (Jean Valjean), Michel Bouquet (Inspector Javert), Jean Carmet (Thenardier), Francoise Seigner (La Thenardier), Evelyne Bouix (Fantine), Christine Jean (Cosette), Franck David (Marius), Candice Patou (Eponine), Louis Seigner (Monseigneur Myriel), Fernand Ledoux (Guillenormand)

p, Dominique Harispuru; d, Robert Hossein; w, Hossein Decaux, Alain Decaux (adapted from the novel by Victor Hugo); ph, Edmond Richard (Eastmancolor); ed, Martine Baraque-Curie; art d, Francois de Lamothe

This is the sixth French version of Victor Hugo's classic novel and the weakest. The two best French versions are director Henri Fescourt's 1927 silent version (which runs more than seven hours) and Raymond Bernard's 1936 version (six hours and fifteen minutes). This was a French film and TV coproduction (six 52-minute episodes for television) at a cost of $10,000,000. The film is heavy-handed, and because so much of the book has been squeezed in, many scenes aren't given enough time to develop. This makes the film seem forced and many sequences melodramatic.

LES PARENTS TERRIBLES

1948   105m   bw   ★★★★
Drama   /A
Ariane   (France)

Jean Marais (Michel), Yvonne de Bray (Yvonne-Sophie), Gabrielle Dorziat (Aunt Leo), Marcel Andre (Georges), Josette Day (Made- leine), Jean Cocteau (Narrator)

d, Jean Cocteau; w, Jean Cocteau (based on the play by Jean Cocteau); ph, Michel Kelber; ed, Jacqueline Sadoul; m, Georges Auric; art d, Christian Berard, Guy de Gastyne

Cocteau's brilliant domestic drama which many, including Cocteau himself, consider to be his greatest achievement. Based on his stage play (performed ten years earlier with much the same cast) it casts de Bray as the dangerously possessive mother who is wed to Andre, a weak and defeated man. De Bray opposes the marriage of her young son Marais to the beautiful Day. It turns out that Day is the mistress of Andre, who happens to be the object of Marais's aunt's (Dorziat's) desires. When the tangled affairs come into the open, de Bray commits suicide, unable to accept the loss of her magnetic hold over her family. Set in only two locations—de Bray's family's apartment and Day's apartment—the film is, as Cocteau said, a record "of the acting of an incomparable cast." Georges Auric's score is a prime example of sound in perfect unity with the picture. A far-inferior remake, INTIMATE RELATIONS, was released in Britain in 1953. Various lengths exist, with both a 98m and 86m cut being shown in the US.

LESS THAN ZERO

1987 96m c   ★½
Drama   R/18
FOX

Andrew McCarthy (Clay Easton), Jami Gertz (Blair), Robert Downey, Jr. (Julian Wells), James Spader (Rip), Tony Bill (Bradford Easton), Nicholas Pryor (Benjamin Wells), Donna Mitchell (Elaine Easton), Michael Bowen (Hop), Sarah Buxton (Markie), Lisanne Falk (Patti)

p, Jon Avnet, Jordan Kerner, Marvin Worth; d, Marek Kanievska; w, Harley Peyton (based on the novel by Bret Easton Ellis); ph, Ed Lachman (Deluxe Color); ed, Peter E. Berger, Michael Tronick; m, Thomas Newman, Rick Rubin; prod d, Barbara Ling; art d, Stephen Rice; cos, Richard Hornung

Loosely based on the novel by Bret Easton Ellis, LESS THAN ZERO refuses to take the risks necessary to capture the keen social observation of the book. Clay Easton (Andrew McCarthy), a college freshman, returns home to Los Angeles for the Christmas holidays, largely because Blair (Jami Gertz), his old girlfriend, has requested it. Blair and Julian Wells (Robert Downey, Jr.), a former high-school buddy of Clay, have become an item, and now Blair wants Clay to save Julian from the downward spiral of his drug abuse. Julian is being harassed and forced to prostitute himself by the drug dealer (James Spader) to whom he owes $50,000. The filmmakers apparently felt there were no sympathetic characters in the novel, but in sanitizing and simplifying Ellis' downbeat story, in transforming it into a relatively conventional love story and a didactic tragedy, they have diluted the disturbing social reality of the novel. The saving grace of LESS THAN ZERO is Downey, who gave a truly inspired performance. He makes his character a convincing lost cause but one the audience wishes to see saved. Gertz's performance is uneven, and McCarthy, an overrated actor, brings what little he can to his role.

LETHAL WEAPON

1987 110m c   ★★★½
Crime   R/18
WB

Mel Gibson (Martin Riggs), Danny Glover (Roger Murtaugh), Gary Busey (Joshua), Mitchell Ryan (The General), Tom Atkins (Michael Hunsaker), Darlene Love (Trish Murtaugh), Traci Wolfe (Rianne Murtaugh), Jackie Swanson (Amanda Hunsaker), Damon Hines (Nick Murtaugh), Ebonie Smith (Carrie Murtaugh)

p, Richard Donner, Joel Silver; d, Richard Donner; w, Shane Black; ph, Stephen Goldblatt (Technicolor); ed, Stuart Baird; m, Michael Kamen, Eric Clapton; prod d, J. Michael Riva; fx, Chuck Gaspar; cos, Mary Malin

It's drugs again, this time in southern California with cop partners Mel Gibson and Danny Glover chasing sleazy dope dealers in a nonstop crime actioner. Roger Murtaugh (Glover), who is about to turn 50, exercises the kind of life-preserving caution that Martin Riggs (Gibson) has discarded. Riggs's wife has been killed in an accident, and he doesn't care whether he lives or dies, just so long as he can take all the bad guys with him. Murtaugh has a hard time surviving with such a self-destructive partner as they investigate "The General" (Mitchell Ryan), head of an extensive drug smuggling operation. The acceleration of this film, which has a brisk pace at the start, is dizzying at the finale and is accomplished mostly through fantastic editing. It's an effective if not obvious ploy to blind the viewer to the fact that there is not much plot or character development in the predictable script. Gibson is truly frightening as the cop about to go into orbit, and Glover is a standout as the down-to-earth lawman with very much to lose. Director Richard Donner, whose previous efforts include the first SUPERMAN and LADYHAWKE, had another hit with LETHAL WEAPON, which grossed more than $60 million at the box office within three months after its release. A less entertaining sequel, LETHAL WEAPON II, appeared in 1989. Nominated by the Academy for Best Sound.

LETHAL WEAPON 2

1989 113m c   ★★★
Crime/Thriller   R/15
Silver

Mel Gibson (Martin Riggs), Danny Glover (Roger Murtaugh), Joe Pesci (Leo Getz), Joss Ackland (Arjen Rudd), Derrick O'Connor (Pieter Vorstedt), Patsy Kensit (Rika van den Haas), Darlene Love (Trish Murtaugh), Traci Wolfe (Rianne Murtaugh), Steve Kahan (Capt. Murphy), Mark Rolston (Hans)

p, Richard Donner, Joel Silver, Steve Perry, Jennie Lew Tugend; d, Richard Donner; w, Jeffrey Boam (based on a story by Shane Black, Warren Murphy and on the characters created by Black); ph, Stephen Goldblatt (Panavision, Technicolor); ed, Stuart Baird; m, Michael Kamen, Eric Clapton, David Sanborn; prod d, J. Michael Riva; art d, Virginia Randolph, Richard Berger; cos, Barry Delaney

A sequel that stands on its own, LETHAL WEAPON 2 is a well-crafted, rousingly fast-paced action thriller with a first-rate cast. Los Angeles cops Roger Murtaugh (Danny Glover) and Martin Riggs (Mel Gibson) are in hot pursuit of a red BMW as the film gets off to a fender-bending start. After much property destruction, the cops capture the red car, but lose the driver. However, they discover a fortune in South African gold Krugerrands in the trunk. Determined to keep the two hyperactive cops out of further high-priced mayhem, their superior puts them in charge of guarding a government witness in a drug-money laundering case. But when the witness (Joe Pesci) reveals he was laundering for South Africans, Murtaugh and Riggs spring back into action. Those stopping to think about such things may find more than a few holes in LETHAL WEAPON 2's plot. But to question is to quibble in this case; LETHAL WEAPON 2's pluses easily outweigh its minuses. If anything, Gibson and Glover are even better here than they were the first time out. Jeffrey Boam's script polishes and improves their characters. Returning director Richard Donner seems to have smoothed over the few stylistic rough edges remaining from the earlier film to deliver here two hours of pure, breathless, high-impact entertainment.

LET'S TALK ABOUT WOMEN
(SE PERMETTETE)
1964   108m   bw   ★★★
Comedy
Fair/CON   (France/Italy)

Vittorio Gassman (Stranger/Practical Joker/Client/Lover/Impatient Lover/Waiter/Timid Brother/Ragman/Prisoner). FIRST EPISODE: Maria Fiore (Fearful Wife). SECOND EPISODE: Donatella Mauro (His Wife), Mario Lucidi (Son), Giovanna Ralli (Prostitute), Umberto D'Orsi (Old Friend). FOURTH EPISODE: Antonella Lualdi (Fiancee). FIFTH EPISODE: Sylva Koscina (Reluctant Girl), Edda Ferronao (Willing Maid). SIXTH EPISODE: Heidi Stroh (Pick-Up)

p, Mario Cecchi Gori; d, Ettore Scola; w, Ettore Scola, Ruggero Maccari; ph, Sandro D'Eva; ed, Marcello Malvestiti; m, Armando Trovajoli; art d, Arrigo Breschi

A captivating Italian comedy made up of nine episodes about Gassman's encounters with various women. One of the better skits has Gassman visiting a hooker and recognizing a picture of her husband as an old chum. She brings him back to her house for a reunion, during which the husband refuses to let Gassman pay for the wife-hooker's services. In another episode, Gassman is a rag dealer who pays a visit to a wealthy and promiscuous woman, wanting to buy her rag collection. She tries instead to give him her body, but he declines, stating that he prefers material goods.

LETTER, THE
1940   95m   bw   ★★★★
Drama
WB   /PG

Bette Davis (Leslie Crosbie), Herbert Marshall (Robert Crosbie), James Stephenson (Howard Joyce), Gale Sondergaard (Mrs. Hammond), Bruce Lester (John Withers), Elizabeth Inglis (Adele Ainsworth), Cecil Kellaway (Prescott), Victor Sen Yung (Ong Chi Seng), Doris Lloyd (Mrs. Cooper), Willie Fung (Chung Hi)

p, Robert Lord; d, William Wyler; w, Howard Koch (based on the story by W. Somerset Maugham); ph, Tony Gaudio; ed, George Amy; m, Max Steiner; art d, Carl Jules Weyl; cos, Orry-Kelly

As THE LETTER opens, David Newell visits Davis's Malayan rubber plantation while her husband, Marshall, is away on business. Davis shoots him to death, and later claims that Newell, an old family friend, tried to attack her and that she killed him in self-defense. Marshall, ever faithful, believes her absolutely and asks Stephenson, a respected lawyer, to defend her. Stephenson then receives word that Newell's Eurasian widow, Sondergaard, has in her possession a letter Davis wrote to Newell, asking him to come to visit her at the plantation on the night he was killed. When confronted with this information, Davis coldly admits that she murdered Newell and that he was her lover. Taking pity on her, Stephenson agrees to buy the letter for $10,000—Sondergaard's blackmail price—telling Marshall there will be some extra expenses in preparing Davis' case, but not how much money is involved. Sondergaard insists that she will not turn the letter over unless Davis claims it personally, leading to a dramatic scene in which Davis must kneel at her feet to pick up the incriminating document. After Davis is deemed innocent of the murder charge in court and returns home to Marshall, the husband discovers that all his savings have been spent to buy the letter and demands to be told what it contains. Davis admits

everything, but the always forgiving Marshall—now an emotional shambles—tells her he loves her still. As Davis walks into the garden, Sondergaard appears with a henchman and stabs Davis to death. Police stop them when they try to flee.

Though W. Somerset Maugham's story could easily have been filmed as a turgid melodrama, director William Wyler's magnificent handling of the material and Bette Davis's taut and calculated performance converted it into enduring cinematic art. THE LETTER is as good today as it seemed upon its first release. Though Davis's strong performance is the film's center, Herbert Marshall (who had played the lover in an earlier version of the story) is excellent as the long-suffering husband, and James Stephenson actually manages to steal scenes from his costars as the honest lawyer who puts his career in jeopardy for a friend. Jack Warner asked Wyler to test Stephenson for the role, but when Wyler (to his own surprise) recognized the superiority of Stephenson's acting and cast him, the unpredictable Warner balked at the move, worrying about the stock player's lack of name recognition. Wyler insisted upon keeping Stephenson, putting him in the odd position of having to fight to cast an actor Warner had originally suggested.

The famously temperamental Davis sometimes vexed Wyler, but the director persuaded her to play the scenes his way. Though she walked off the set at one point to protest one of Wyler's instructions (he insisted that she tell Marshall that she still loved the dead Newell to his face, while Davis felt that the character could not make such an admission to her devoted husband without turning away), Davis later claimed in Mother Goddam (her autobiographical collaboration with Whitney Stine) that she had full confidence in Wyler after working with him on JEZEBEL and that she had, in fact, prevented Stephenson from walking out on the film. Temperamental or not, Davis wanted to play the lead in THE LETTER in the worst way. Not only was the role meaty and challenging, but it had been played before by an actress who had always fascinated her, the tragic and electric Jeanne Eagels. Eagels had died young of a heroin overdose in 1929, after she had mesmerized Broadway audiences as Sadie Thompson in "Rain" and gone on to a brief but stellar career in films, including the starring role in Paramount's 1929 version of THE LETTER. By the time the heroin-addicted Eagels finished that film, she was nearly crazy; reportedly, she threw a fit after seeing a working print, clawing the screen and demanding that the studio reshoot the film with another leading man. They did, and this bizarre actress was even more macabre in her role. Davis attempted to duplicate this power, for Eagels was her secret idol. She watched Eagels' silent films in utter amazement and found her strangely captivating, emulating some of her gestures and quirky style. Much of it worked its way into Davis's performance in THE LETTER, which earned the actress another Oscar nomination, though she lost to Ginger Rogers for KITTY FOYLE. The film was also nominated for Best Picture (losing to REBECCA), Best Director, Best Cinematography, Best Original Score, and Best Editing. Warner Bros. produced a remake in 1947, THE UNFAITHFUL, starring Ann Sheridan.

LETTER FROM AN UNKNOWN WOMAN
1948   86m   bw   ★★★★★
Drama
Rampart   /A

Joan Fontaine (Lisa Berndle), Louis Jourdan (Stefan Brand), Mady Christians (Frau Berndle), Marcel Journet (Johann Stauffer), John Good (Lt. Leopold von Kaltnegger), Leo B. Pessin (Stefan, Jr.), Art

Smith *(John)*, Carol Yorke *(Marie)*, Howard Freeman *(Herr Kastner)*, Erskine Sanford *(Porter)*

p, John Houseman; d, Max Ophuls; w, Howard Koch (based on the novel *Brief Einer Unbekannten* by Stefan Zweig); ph, Franz Planer; ed, Ted J. Kent; m, Daniele Amfitheatrof; art d, Alexander Golitzen; cos, Travis Banton

An intense and lush romantic film made by the incomparable Ophuls during his often trying sojourn in America in the WWII and immediate postwar years. Fontaine plays Lisa, who has a brief encounter with and falls for her pianist neighbor Stefan (Jourdan). As he heads off on a concert tour, Stefan promises to return for her, but that doesn't happen. Lisa holds out as long as possible but is forced to marry another man when she discovers that she's pregnant with Stefan's child. She meets the pianist some time later, but he doesn't remember her and sets about seducing her all over again. The story is told in flashbacks as Stefan reads a letter from Lisa as she is suffering from typhus, and he finally learns her entire story.

The first film from the production company formed by Fontaine and William Dozier, LETTER FROM AN UNKNOWN WOMAN has an unusually persuasive Continental look to it. Its lyrical, sweet sadness and incredibly lovely *mise en scene* are typical of Ophuls at his best. His meaningful, highly deliberate camera wanderings beautifully capture the sorrows of Lisa's entrapment by cultural norms. The direction and Koch's well-judged screenplay admirably manage to retain an ironic edge despite the potent romanticism of it all. Fontaine has never looked lovelier and gives what is probably the greatest performance of her career. The dashing and persuasive Jourdan and a fine cast ably support her, as does the incredible camerawork of regular Ophuls collaborator Franz Planer. Although CAUGHT and THE RECKLESS MOMENT are films of considerable merit, LETTER is almost certainly Ophuls' greatest American film. Watching it is like finding a locket you thought you had lost, one which contains the picture of someone who once broke your heart.

LETTER TO BREZHNEV

1986 94m c   ★★★½
Romance/Comedy   R/15
Yeardream/Film Four/Palace (U.K.)

Alfred Molina *(Sergei)*, Peter Firth *(Peter)*, Margi Clarke *(Teresa)*, Tracy Lea *(Tracy)*, Alexandra Pigg *(Elaine)*, Susan Dempsey *(Girl in Yellow Pedal Pushers)*, Ted Wood *(Mick)*, Carl Chase *(Taxi Driver)*, Robbie Dee *(Charlie)*, Sharon Power *(Charlie's Girlfriend)*

p, Janet Goddard, Caroline Spack; d, Chris Bernard; w, Frank Clarke; ph, Bruce McGowan; ed, Lesley Walker; m, Alan Gill; prod d, Lez Brothrston, Nick Englefield, Jonathan Swain; cos, Mark Reynolds

LETTER TO BREZHNEV is a low-budget gem. Teresa (Margi Clarke) and Elaine (Alexandra Pigg) are best pals. Teresa works in a frozen-chicken factory and Elaine is unemployed, as are many thousands in the depressed area of Liverpool. One night the two decide to go out on the town. At a local spot Teresa steals a wallet, and the friends head for an upscale disco where they meet Peter (Peter Firth) and Sergei (Alfred Molina), two Russian sailors in Liverpool for some R&R. With the money she stole, Teresa rents a pair of hotel rooms and drags Sergei into hers. The sweeter, gentler Elaine spends the evening talking to Peter. Both are terminally romantic; and in the course of nonstop conversation, they decide that they are in love and would like to get married. This is a simple story on the surface, but the details are

many and the individual moments joyous. It's a mature picture (there is no stinting on the raunchy and often-incomprehensible Liverpudlian dialogue), unabashedly romantic but not sentimental. There are amateurish moments here and there, and one wishes that the production values were better, but all the flaws pale in light of the overall impact of the love story.

LETTER TO THREE WIVES, A

1948 103m bw   ★★★★
Drama   /U
FOX

Jeanne Crain *(Deborah Bishop)*, Linda Darnell *(Lora May Hollingsway)*, Ann Sothern *(Rita Phipps)*, Kirk Douglas *(George Phipps)*, Paul Douglas *(Porter Hollingsway)*, Barbara Lawrence *(Babe)*, Jeffrey Lynn *(Brad Bishop)*, Connie Gilchrist *(Mrs. Finney)*, Florence Bates *(Mrs. Manleigh)*, Hobart Cavanaugh *(Mr. Manleigh)*

p, Sol C. Siegel; d, Joseph L. Mankiewicz; w, Joseph L. Mankiewicz, Vera Caspary (based on the novel by John Klempner); ph, Arthur Miller; ed, J. Watson Webb; m, Alfred Newman; art d, Lyle Wheeler, J. Russell Spencer; fx, Fred Sersen; cos, Kay Nelson

Delicious bites of suburbia, with lucious Darnell a surprising prize plum. This ingeniously constructed film is one of the finest movies ever made about marriage. It focuses on the doubts, fears and recriminations of three lovely wives who believe they are soon to lose their husbands to another woman. Crain, Darnell, and Sothern are about to leave on a boat trip along the Hudson River, escorting a group of youngsters, when a messenger delivers a letter to each of them, all from the same woman, Addie Ross, never shown and played only as an off-screen voice by Holm. Holm has written the same message to all three wives; she has run off with *one* of their husbands but she does not mention which one, leaving them to figure out who has lost out, and subjecting all three to subtle emotional torture. The three wives live in comfortable homes in the Hudson Valley and have ostensibly happy marriages, but the letters cause them to frantically review their relationships.

The acting of the six leading players here is outstanding, with the aforementioned Darnell in particular giving the finest performance of her career (in the film's best sketch) as the supposedly hardhearted lady with only wealth on her mind (Top line—when Thelma Ritter cracks Darnell should dress up, wear beads, Linda retorts, "What I got don't need beads!"). Both Douglases, Ann Southern, Gilchrist and Ritter team, Florence Bates and Jeanne Crain all rise to the occasions. The sharp piquancy of the dialog earned Mankiewicz an Oscar for his script, another for his deft direction. Mankiewicz developed the story from a John Klempner short story first appearing in *Cosmopolitan*, entitled "One of Our Hearts." Klempner later expanded the piece into an overlong, repetitious novel, called *A Letter to Five Wives*. Mankiewicz's screenplay was originally called "A Letter to Four Wives," but Fox boss Zanuck thought the screenplay overworked the idea. On Zanuck's orders Mankiewicz eliminated one story, making for a much tighter dramatic structure. Originally, Zanuck wanted Ernst Lubitsch to direct the film, and gave producer Siegel a fight before he would accept Mankiewicz. The selection of Holm as narrator of the film, the vixen Addie Ross, was a stroke of genius on Mankiewicz's part; she had the perfect voice for such an off-camera role, sweet and sour, kind and bitchy. Mankiewicz and the tragic Darnell began an ill-fated, tempestuous affair during the production of this film, one that did not end for several years. The film was a landmark achievement for

Mankiewicz, who, on the strength of it, became the darling of the Fox lot, earning profound resentment from Zanuck. Years later, Zanuck blamed Mankiewicz personally for almost destroying Fox with his hugely expensive production of CLEOPATRA.

LIANNA

1983   110m   c   ★★★
Drama   R/18
Winwood

Linda Griffiths *(Lianna)*, Jane Hallaren *(Ruth)*, Jon DeVries *(Dick)*, Jo Henderson *(Sandy)*, Jessica MacDonald *(Theda)*, Jesse Solomon *(Spencer)*, John Sayles *(Jerry)*, Stephen Mendillo *(Bob)*, Betsy Julia Robinson *(Cindy)*, Nancy Mette *(Kim)*

p, Jeffrey Nelson, Maggie Renzi; d, John Sayles; w, John Sayles; ph, Austin de Besche (DuArt Color); ed, John Sayles; m, Mason Daring; art d, Jeanne McDonnell; chor, Marta Renzi; cos, Louise Martinez

Lianna (Linda Griffiths) is the unsure wife of a domineering college professor (Jon DeVries). He ridicules her decision to return to school, but she continues to pursue her degree anyway. Ruth (Jane Hallaren), one of her teachers, helps Lianna to cope with her internal struggles. The two women gradually grow closer until their friendship blossoms into a love affair. This is a restrained and caring film that never lapses into preachiness about its lesbian theme. Director-writer John Sayles was noted for writing such films as THE HOWLING and ALLIGATOR, so he could finance his own independent features. The direction and dialog appear completely natural, allowing the characters to tell the story; not a moment in the film seems false or contrived. The two female leads give sensitive performances, and DeVries handles his character's sexual confusions and anger convincingly. There are some technical problems, symptomatic of a low budget, but they don't much hamper this otherwise fine and intelligently told story.

LIBELED LADY

1936   98m   bw   ★★★★
Comedy   /A
MGM

William Powell *(Bill Chandler)*, Myrna Loy *(Connie Allenbury)*, Jean Harlow *(Gladys Benton)*, Spencer Tracy *(Warren Haggerty)*, Walter Connolly *(James B. Allenbury)*, Charley Grapewin *(Hollis Bane)*, Cora Witherspoon *(Mrs. Burns-Norvell)*, E.E. Clive *(Evans, the Fishing Instructor)*, Bunny Beatty *(Babs Burns-Norvell)*, Otto Yamaoka *(Ching)*

p, Lawrence Weingarten; d, Jack Conway; w, Maurine Watkins, Howard Emmett Rogers, George Oppenheimer (based on a story by Wallace Sullivan); ph, Norbert Brodine; ed, Frederick Y. Smith; m, William Axt; art d, Cedric Gibbons, William A. Horning; cos, Dolly Tree

A sparkler from the days when they knew how to do screwball comedy. Tracy plays Warren Haggerty, the managing editor of a newspaper which erroneously prints a story saying that wealthy Connie Allenbury (Loy) is busy nabbing another woman's husband, a British peer. She sues the paper for $5 million. Warren is about to marry Gladys Benton (Harlow), a woman he's left at the altar several times. Now the festivities have to be postponed once again, because Warren must get to the bottom of the story and defuse the lawsuit which could cost him his job. He hires Bill Chandler (Powell), a former co-worker who doesn't like him but needs a job. The task is to marry Gladys (in name only), thus clearing the way for Bill to woo Connie. If that works, Gladys

can sue the heiress for alienation of affection, and then agree to drop that suit if Connie drops hers. What goes wrong in all this confusion is that Gladys isn't entirely crazy about being used like this and Bill and Connie really do start falling in love. (What else would you expect from William Powell and Myrna Loy?) The complications are fast and furious before the expected two-pair finale.

LIBELED LADY combines the talents of four first-rate farceurs with a crackling script and ace direction. They all have a chance to shine, but we give the slightest of edges to Harlow, who shifts into high wisecracking gear for this one. Don't try to make any sense of the plot; you'll find yourself following its daffy logic just fine. Simply relax and enjoy the merry meanderings of a cast that seemed to be having a bang-up time making this movie. The laughs come rolling off the screen in just about every sequence, but Powell's attempt at fishing and the "bride kisses the best man" bit at one wedding are two highlights. Jack Conway, a good director of many fine films, isn't quite a Leo McCarey or a Howard Hawks, and this film doesn't quite equal THE AWFUL TRUTH or BRINGING UP BABY. Still, LIBELED LADY stands as one of the better "screwball" comedies of the 1930s. It earned an Academy Award nomination for Best Picture, but lost to THE GREAT ZIEGFELD.

LICENCE TO KILL

1989   133m   c   ★★★½
Spy   PG-13/15
Eon   (U.K.)

Timothy Dalton *(James Bond)*, Carey Lowell *(Pam Bouvier)*, Robert Davi *(Franz Sanchez)*, Talisa Soto *(Lupe Lamora)*, Anthony Zerbe *(Milton Krest)*, Frank McRae *(Sharkey)*, Everett McGill *(Killifer)*, Wayne Newton *(Prof. Joe Butcher)*, Benicio Del Toro *(Dario)*, Desmond Llewelyn *(Q)*

p, Albert R. Broccoli, Michael G. Wilson; d, John Glen; w, Richard Maibaum, Michael G. Wilson (based on the characters created by Ian Fleming); ph, Alec Mills (Panavision, Deluxe Color); ed, John Grover; m, Michael Kamen; prod d, Peter Lamont; art d, Michael Lamont; cos, Jodie Tillen

Although James Bond purists will no doubt be dismayed by the drastic character change undergone by 007 in his 16th outing, LICENCE TO KILL offers a fresh look at the superspy, a new set of villains, and some of the most spectacular action sequences yet seen in the series. The film finds Bond (Timothy Dalton) in the Florida Keys for the wedding of his CIA buddy Felix Leiter (David Hedison). The happy event is interrupted, however, when Leiter and Bond make a detour to capture Franz Sanchez (Robert Davi), a notorious Colombian drug dealer. But that night Sanchez escapes with the help of a corrupt DEA agent (Anthony Zerbe). Sanchez dispatches his goons to Leiter's home, where they create havoc. Bond vows revenge, ignores his superior's orders to give up his personal vendetta, and is subsequently stripped of his license to kill by M (Robert Brown) himself. In his second outing as Bond, Dalton presents a more serious, harder-edged agent 007 than either the Roger Moore or Sean Connery incarnations. This new spin lends some badly-needed complexity to a character that had become increasingly cartoonish and predictable. As with Bond, the villain here, played superbly by Davi, is much more realistic and complex than the usual exaggerated Bond heavy. Hardcore Bond fans may be dismayed by some of the changes, but no one can deny that the action scenes staged by director John Glen are some of the most spectacular of the entire series and well worth the price of admission.

LIFE AND DEATH OF COLONEL BLIMP, THE

1945 163m c ★★★★½
Drama/War /U
The Archers (U.K.)

Roger Livesey (Clive Candy), Deborah Kerr (Edith Hunter/Barbara Wynne/Johnny Cannon), Anton Walbrook (Theo Kretschmar-Schuldorff), Roland Culver (Col. Betteridge), James McKechnie (Spud Wilson), Albert Lieven (Von Ritter), Arthur Wontner (Embassy Counsellor), David Hutcheson (Hoppy), Ursula Jeans (Frau von Kalteneck), John Laurie (Murdoch)

p, Michael Powell, Emeric Pressburger; d, Michael Powell; w, Michael Powell, Emeric Pressburger; ph, Jack Cardiff, Georges Perinal (Technicolor); ed, John Seabourne; m, Allan Gray

One of the most celebrated films from the extraordinary director-writer partnership of Michael Powell and Emeric Pressburger, THE LIFE AND DEATH OF COLONEL BLIMP is a warm and wise work that displays extraordinary generosity of spirit. It tells the story of Clive Candy (Roger Livesey), a stuffy British soldier whose life is shown in episodes that range from 1902, when he had a dashing career as a young officer in the Boer War, to 1943, when he creaks crankily about in the London blitz, remembering his lost youth and loves. Not at all a war film in any conventional sense, rather it is a life affirming character study that lingers with the viewer long after it's over.

Roger Livesy gives one of the great performances of the British cinema. He fully conveys the sense of a character with a long and complex life as he is transformed by time and experience from the dashing young firebrand of the 1890s to the anachronistic old codger of the World War II era. The great old British warrior virtues of fair play and chivalry become quaint and inappropriate when faced with the modern horrors of war. Deborah Kerr is a joy to watch as she plays three different roles from different eras in the great man's life. Anton Walbrook (who would be even better a few years later in Powell and Pressburger's THE RED SHOES) is splendid as Theo Kretschmar-Schuldorff, the charming Prussian officer whom Clive fights in a duel and who far exceeds the young Briton in sensitivity and understanding.

The title comes from the satiric character created by cartoonist David Low in the London Evening Standard, by which members of Britain's pompous and stiff military upper-crust came to be known as "Colonel Blimps." Part of what makes this film so special is that it never descends to the level of easy caricature. This was the third Powell-Pressburger collaboration (after THE 49TH PARALLEL and ONE OF OUR AIRCRAFT IS MISSING) and the first produced under the banner of their production company, the Archers.

Prime Minister Winston Churchill illegally prohibited the film's exportation for two years, citing its portrayal of a Colonel Blimp as "detrimental to the morale of the Army." Refusing to heed to the advice of the Ministry of Information (which felt his position would do more harm than good), Churchill lifted the ban only after the film became such a smash commercial hit in England that its export could no longer be thwarted. Initially released in America in a butchered 93-minute version, the film was restored to its full length in 1986 by Britain's National Film Archive.

LIFE AND NOTHING BUT

(LA VIE EST RIEN D'AUTRE)
1990 135m c ★★★½
Drama PG
Hachette Premiere/Little Bear/A2 (France)

Philippe Noiret (Maj. Dellaplanne), Sabine Azema (Irene de Courtil), Pascale Vignal (Alice), Maurice Barrier (Mercadot), Francois Perrot (Perrin), Jean-Pol Dubois (Andre), Daniel Russo (Lt. Trevise), Michel Duchaussoy (Gen. Villerieux), Arlette Gilbert (Valentine), Louis Lyonnet (Valentin)

p, Rene Cleitman, Albert Prevost; d, Bertrand Tavernier; w, Bertrand Tavernier, Jean Cosmos; ph, Bruno de Keyzer (Eastmancolor); ed, Armand Psenny; m, Oswald d'Andrea; prod d, Guy-Claude Francois; cos, Jacqueline Moreau

LIFE AND NOTHING BUT, the latest film from Bertrand Tavernier (ROUND MIDNIGHT, COUP DE TORCHON, A SUNDAY IN THE COUNTRY), is a compelling successor to such antiwar movies as Stanley Kubrick's PATHS OF GLORY and Lewis Milestone's ALL QUIET ON THE WESTERN FRONT, focusing, like Kubrick's and Milestone's films, on WWI. Instead of detailing the ongoing carnage and cannon fire of life in the trenches, however, Tavernier paints a harrowing portrait of devastation after the fact. The year is 1920 (almost two years after the Armistice), and the massive task of counting corpses and identifying the missing among the French soldiers remains. Supervising these efforts is Major Dellaplane (Noiret), a career soldier obsessed with logic and detail who turns his responsibility into a personal crusade to justify the sacrifice made by the dead men, believing that by naming the unidentified and humanizing the grim statistics, he can somehow make sense of the horror that has occurred. Noiret's quest to tie up the loose ends of war in peacetime is interwoven with the story of another officer's mission to locate one suitable unknown soldier for ceremonial enshrinement in the Arc de Triomphe, and with vignettes concerning families seeking information about the fate of their relatives. Among those vying for Noiret's attention are Vignal, a young working-class woman looking for her fiance, and Azema, a senator's daughter-in-law traveling throughout Europe in search of her missing husband. Although he locks horns with the latter, a proud aristocrat who's tired of getting the bureaucratic runaround, Noiret also falls in love with her, and the fitful progress of their incongruous affair is played out on the former battlefields. In one scene, during a visit to a body identification center where family members sift through medals and personal belongings in the hope of locating loved ones, the travelers pause from their heart-rending task to picnic on the grass, and an explosion rocks a tunnel where the dead are stored pending identification. It's as if the war's appetite can never be satisfied. When Noiret discovers that Vignal's fiance and Azema's husband are the same man, the knowledge frees each woman to go on with her life. The unknown soldier is interred and the war is officially laid to rest, but it will never be over for Noiret. Allowing Azema to slip out of his life, he can only proclaim his love in letters, after she's moved to America.

Cowritten by Tavernier and Jean Cosmos (a playwright and TV scenarist making his screenwriting debut), LIFE AND NOTHING BUT is a muted, carefully wrought drama about the emotionally shell-shocked survivors of WWI. Somber, handsome, exquisitely produced, and featuring a towering lead performance by Philippe Noiret in what is reportedly his 100th screen role, Tavernier's elegy strikes no false notes. With an extraordinary talent for conveying the bustle of life amidst the stasis of death, Tavernier employs his sweeping camera and his skill in relating characters to their widescreen environment to create an unforgettable mise-en-scene. Despite its brilliant technical accomplishment and its seamless blend of gallows humor and intriguing drama, however, Tavernier's examination of lives held in check by the fortunes of war lacks the full-throttle emotionalism that might have made it a classic pacifist epic. Visually, it couldn't be improved upon (Tavernier's cinematographer, once again, is the superb Bruno de Keyzer), but one does wish it were a little less calculated, a little more reckless. The *chagrin d'amour* of Noiret's unconsummated affair with Azema palls in comparison with Tavernier's moving depiction of war and loss on a larger scale. Somehow the intimate love story fails to move us as much as some of the vignettes, such as the darkly humorous scene in which town officials plead for re-zoning because they don't have any dead war heroes in their district. Even more haunting is the last shot, in which Noiret walks through a cemetery that appears to stretch on forever—remarking that the French victory parade lasted three hours, but a march by all the dead would have taken eleven days.

LIFE BEGINS FOR ANDY HARDY

1941 100m bw   ★★★½
Drama   /U
MGM

Mickey Rooney *(Andy Hardy)*, Lewis Stone *(Judge Hardy)*, Judy Garland *(Betsy Booth)*, Fay Holden *(Mrs. Hardy)*, Ann Rutherford *(Polly Benedict)*, Sara Haden *(Aunt Milly)*, Patricia Dane *(Jennitt Hicks)*, Ray McDonald *(Jimmy Frobisher)*, George Breakston *(Beezy)*, Pierre Watkin *(Dr. Waggoner)*

d, George B. Seitz; w, Agnes Christine Johnston (based on characters created by Aurania Rouverol); ph, Lester White; ed, Elmo Veron; art d, Cedric Gibbons; cos, Robert Kalloch

A serious departure in MGM's highly successful "Andy Hardy" series finds Rooney as the prodigal. The recent high school graduate has a heart-to-heart discussion with his father, Stone, about his future. Not wanting to follow immediately in his father's footsteps, Rooney's ambition is to go off to New York and "find himself." Though they don't agree with him, the Hardys let their son go off to New York City. There he joins his long-suffering friend Garland (in her third and last film in the "Hardy" series, though she continued to work onscreen with Rooney in other films). After much difficulty, Rooney finds a job as an office boy for the paltry sum of $10 a week. He meets McDonald, a struggling dancer, and sneaks the penniless, homeless young man into his hotel room. But Rooney is startled one evening when he comes home to find his new friend dead of a heart attack. He gets a loan on his jalopy so McDonald can have a decent funeral rather than a pauper's grave. Rooney has befriended Dane, an older divorcee—the receptionist in his employer's office—who invites the young man up to her apartment for an evening. The offer is tempting, but Rooney's homespun value system—along with the arrival of his father in the big city—cause him to decline. Looking over the events that have happened since his arrival in New York, Rooney decides that his home town and college are his real future and he returns to Carvel with Stone. Though the critics attacked the film as too much of a departure from the "Andy Hardy" series's normal vein, this is a fine addition. Rooney and Garland both show great maturity with their characters. Garland is a fine counterbalance for Rooney, constantly watching over him like a loving mother and calling his father when things look dark. Though she truly wants to be in love with him, she can circumvent her feelings to help the skittish young man when he really needs her. The National Legion of Decency surprised everyone in the film world by rating this film A-2, an objectional film for children. They felt that Rooney's heart-to-heart talks with Stone were too "daring" for children, to say nothing of his scenes with Dane.

LIFE IS A BED OF ROSES
(LA VIE EST UN ROMAN)

1984 111m c   ★★★
Fantasy   PG
Soprofilm/A2/Fideline/Ariane/Filmedi s   (France)

Vittorio Gassman *(Walter)*, Ruggero Raimondi *(Count Michel Forbek)*, Geraldine Chaplin *(Nora)*, Fanny Ardant *(Livia)*, Pierre Arditi *(Robert)*, Sabine Azema *(Elizabeth)*, Robert Manuel *(Georges)*, Martine Kelly *(Claudine)*, Samson Fainsilber *(Zoltan)*, Nathalie Holberg *(Veronique)*

p, Philippe Dussart; d, Alain Resnais; w, Jean Gruault; ph, Bruno Nuytten (Eastmancolor, Fujicolor); ed, Albert Jurgenson, Jean-Pierre Besnard; m, M . Philippe-Gerard; art d, Jacques Saulnier, Enki Bilal; cos, Catherine Leterrier

A unique and funny film from intellectual French director Resnais that combines a three-part narrative structure with fantasy, comedy, and musical elements. Raimondi is a wealthy turn-of-the-century eccentric who designs a "temple of happiness," in which people who visit revert to a state of infancy. To create a Utopian aura, Raimondi's guests are exposed to only positive sensations—strains of harmonious music fill the air, and blindfolds keep out unpleasant sights—while they lie blissfully in oversized cribs. Raimondi's plan goes awry when Ardant, who never drank the assigned potion, discovers that one of her friends accidentally died because of negligence. The arrival of WW I, however, puts an end to the temple of happiness and to Raimondi's dreams. Intercut with this episode is a present-day symposium on the methods of Raimondi and the possibility of achieving Utopia, attended by teachers, philosophers, anthropologists, and city planners. The gist of the symposium is that the imagination must be nurtured and developed in order for lives to improve. This theory quickly leads to a difference of opinion among those in attendance and results in a flurry of heated arguments. The third tale, which is intercut with the others and is related through the imaginations of a group of children in a forest, is a medieval one in which a warrior must battle a diabolical king. As usual with Resnais, the audience can comprehend part of the film but not another (usually greater) portion, which seems completely out of reach. Instead of simply filming a story, Resnais films a puzzle. The viewer has the choice of whether or not to unravel Resnais's tightly woven structure. Unless one possesses a genius level IQ, it is probably best (for sanity's sake) just to sit back and be bewildered by LIFE IS A BED OF ROSES.

LIFE IS SWEET

1991 102m c   ★★★½
Drama/Comedy   /15
Thin Man Films   (U.K.)

Alison Steadman *(Wendy)*, Jim Broadbent *(Andy)*, Timothy Spall *(Aubrey)*, Claire Skinner *(Natalie)*, Jane Horrocks *(Nicola)*, David Thewlis *(Nicola's Lover)*, Moya Brady *(Paula)*, Stephen Rea *(Patsy)*, David Neilson *(Steve)*, Jack Thorpe Baker *(Nigel)*

d, Mike Leigh; w, Mike Leigh; ph, Dick Pope; ed, John Gregory; m, Rachel Portman; prod d, Alison Chitty; art d, Sophie Becher; cos, Lindy Hemming

Following 1988's HIGH HOPES, a grim portrait of Thatcherite London, comes the latest feature from acclaimed British director Mike Leigh, an unsettling yet compelling look at life in a lower-middle-class household in outer London.

Wendy (Alison Steadman), a brassily attractive, thirtysomething blonde, is constantly involved in one chore or another.

When she isn't dusting the bric-a-brac that clutters her home, she's working in a children's clothing store or teaching aerobics to little girls. Just as she is always "on the move," so, too, is she always chattering, joking and giggling nervously. Her husband, Andy (Jim Broadbent), is a chef employed in a large institutional kitchen. He's a laid-back sort, inclined to tinker at one or another unimportant gadget but never completing any of his initially ambitious projects. He's often found in the shed in back of the house where he examines and reexamines bits and pieces of junk. Sometimes a chum pops in and they talk, have a beer and talk some more.

Wendy and Andy have twin daughters, Natalie (Claire Skinner) and Nicola (Jane Horrocks), who are as unalike as night and day. Natalie is quiet, subdued and focused, an apprentice plumber. Nicola, with her horn-rimmed glasses and straggly hair, is a sullen university dropout intent on letting everyone within earshot know how awful life is and how much she hates living. Refusing to eat anything at the family meals, she has a stock of candy bars on which she privately gorges and purges. A deeply unhappy individual who never leaves the house, Nicola is always spouting vitriol, damning everything and everyone around her.

While hardly plot-driven, LIFE IS SWEET has its share of small events: Andy, intent on finally becoming his own boss, unwisely purchases a dilapidated mobile food stand; Nicola's disgusted lover (David Thewlis) walks out on her; Natalie quietly makes plans for a trip to America; Aubrey (Timothy Spall), a farcically drawn friend of the family, makes last-minute preparations for the opening of his small restaurant, the *Regret Rien*, which will feature such up-scale items as black pudding and camembert soup, pork cyst, liver in lager, and tongues in rhubarb-hollandaise sauce. Good-hearted Wendy promises to help out at the restaurant's opening to which, of course, no one comes, and after which a drunken Aubrey attempts to seduce Wendy before passing out. Perhaps most importantly, Wendy confronts Nicola about her unhappiness, confiding in her that she herself had nearly died of self-starvation as a youth, and urging her to adopt a more positive attitude. Andy suffers an accident at work which, if only temporarily, brings the family together.

A creative force on London's fringe theater scene since the 1960s, Mike Leigh made his feature directorial debut with the acclaimed BLEAK MOMENTS in 1971. This was followed by a 17-year hiatus, during which Leigh focused on TV and stage work, notably *Abigail's Party* and the BBC telemovies HARD LABOUR, HOME SWEET HOME and FOUR DAYS IN JULY. While not to everyone's taste, Leigh's films have been hailed as a kind of "neo-Marxist Dickens." Not surprisingly, his forte is chronicling, with grace and economy, the vicissitudes of daily life among Britain's downtrodden. The well-rounded characters who populate his films stem from extensive one-on-one collaborations with his actors, followed by group improv sessions from which his precisely structured scripts emerge.

LIFE OF EMILE ZOLA, THE
1937 123m bw   ★★★★★
Biography
WB

Paul Muni *(Emile Zola)*, Gale Sondergaard *(Lucie Dreyfus)*, Joseph Schildkraut *(Capt. Alfred Dreyfus)*, Gloria Holden *(Alexandrine Zola)*, Donald Crisp *(Maitre Labori)*, Erin O'Brien-Moore *(Nana)*, John Litel *(Charpentier)*, Henry O'Neill *(Col. Picquart)*, Morris Carnovsky *(Anatole France)*, Louis Calhern *(Maj. Dort)*

p, Henry Blanke; d, William Dieterle; w, Norman Reilly Raine, Heinz Herald, Geza Herczeg (based on the story by Heinz Herald and Geza Herczeg); ph, Tony Gaudio; ed, Warren Low; m, Max Steiner; art d, Anton Grot; cos, Milo Anderson, Ali Hubert

Along with George Arliss, Paul Muni was Hollywood's designated portrayer of historical personages and Great Men. He appeared as Louis Pasteur (an Oscar-winning role), as Benito Juarez, as French explorer Pierre Radisson, as Chopin's teacher Joseph Elsner, as the Capone-based gangster in SCARFACE, and as Napoleon and Schubert (among others) in SEVEN FACES. So it's no surprise to find him playing Emile Zola—and wonderfully—in this fine film. Literate, powerful, and sincere, THE LIFE OF EMILE ZOLA was a huge box-office success, although its subject matter—the French novelist's life and his part in the Dreyfus Affair—hardly seemed promising in that regard. The film introduces Zola (Muni) as an anguished figure surrounded by controversy, censured by the French government and public for his "scandalous" work. After the publication of his novel *Nana* (based on his own experiences with a prostitute, played by O'Brien-Moore), he is roundly condemned for his frank treatment of social themes and realistic portrayal of squalid life, but the book becomes very popular nonetheless. Years pass, and he is increasingly heralded as France's greatest writer and as the champion of those who cannot speak for themselves during France's Second Empire.

One night, Zola is visited by Lucie Dreyfus (Sondergaard), whose husband, army captain Alfred Dreyfus (Schildkraut), has been accused of betraying military secrets. Zola begins to study the case, and soon writes his famous open letter to the president of France, "J'accuse", asserting that Dreyfus has been railroaded and accusing Major Walsin-Esterhazy (Barrat) of the treason with which Dreyfus has been charged. Dreyfus—an easy scapegoat because he is a Jew—is tried, convicted, discharged, and sent to Devil's Island for a life term. Zola, meanwhile, is put on trial for libeling the army, convicted in a room full of officers, and sentenced to a year in prison. Rather than serve time, he goes to England and continues to write about the Dreyfus Affair in exile. The French populace starts believing its laureate, and the final turns of events make for an absorbing finale.

The film's script was originally shown to Ernst Lubitsch at Paramount, who liked what he saw but felt he had no actor in his stable who could do justice to the main character. Generously, he suggested that it be shown to Henry Blanke at Warner Bros., a producer who had the services of Muni, whom Lubitsch felt was the only actor for the part. As on so many other occasions, Lubitsch was right; Muni triumphs completely in this demanding role. As was his custom, Muni steeped himself in his character, reading all of Zola's works, extensively researching the Dreyfus case, and attempting many different makeup variations before settling on his final choice. The other actors are equally fine, with Holden in particular a warm glow as Zola's wife. It's nice to see Sondergaard in such a sympathetic part and, as her husband, the center of the controversy, Schildkraut rivals Muni in effectiveness. Scene after scene of the nervous and later numbed Dreyfus being stripped of his honor haunt this film and Schildkraut was the only possible choice for the year's Supporting Actor Oscar. The movie itself, though it deviates from the facts a bit, is basically faithful to history and well scripted, without extraneous characters or plot lines. The period details are all authentic, with no expense spared to recreate the settings. Director Dieterle, one of Hollywood's best, interprets the screenplay magnificently, especially in the brilliant courtroom scenes, and the anti-Semitic nature of Dreyfus's persecution is also conveyed effectively, though circumspectly. (The word *Jew* is never heard.)

The film also won well-deserved Oscars for Best Picture and Best Screenplay, and Muni, Dieterle, Max Steiner, and the original story were nominated as well. A 1958 remake of the tale, I ACCUSE, had little to recommend it.

LIFE OF OHARU
(SAIKAKU ICHIDAI ONNA)
1952   146m   bw   ★★★½
Drama   /A
Shin Toho   (Japan)

Kinuyo Tanaka *(Oharu)*, Tsukie Matsura *(Tomo, Oharu's Mother)*, Ichiro Sugai *(Shonzaemon, Oharu's Father)*, Toshiro Mifune *(Katsunosuke)*, Toshiaki Konoe *(Lord Tokitaka Matsudaira)*, Hisako Yamane *(Lady Matsudaira)*, Jukichi Uno *(Yakichi Senya)*, Eitaro Shindo *(Kohei Sasaya)*, Akira Oizumi *(Fumikichi, Sasaya's Friend)*, Masao Shimizu *(Kikuno Koji)*

d, Kenji Mizoguchi; w, Yoshikata Yoda, Kenji Mizoguchi (based on the novel *Koshuku Ichidai Onna* by Saikaku Ibara); ph, Yoshimi Kono, Yoshimi Hirano; ed, Toshio Goto; m, Ichiro Saito; art d, Hiroshi Mizutani

LIFE OF OHARU is a later film in the long and brilliant career of masterful director Kenji Mizoguchi. The plot details the painful life of Oharu (Kinuyo Tanaka), a 50-year-old, 17th-century prostitute. In flashback, Oharu's life unfolds, beginning when she, the young daughter of a samurai, falls in love with a lower-class man, Katsunosuke (Toshiro Mifune). As punishment, her lover is decapitated and her family banished from Kyoto. After a failed suicide, Oharu becomes the mistress of a prince, who sends her away after she bears him a son. She is then sold by her father and put to work as a prostitute. A wealthy client buys her, but he is discovered to be a criminal, and she is again forced to sell herself. In time, Oharu meets and marries a merchant and lives with him until his death. Once again, at age 50, she is forced to turn to prostitution. In LIFE OF OHARU, Mizoguchi concentrates on the formal style he developed so successfully in his earlier work—extremely long takes of meticulously composed shots with a minimal amount of cutting. Kinuyo Tanaka is superb as the prostitute whose unceasing degradation Mizoguchi uses to criticize feudal Japan and its treatment of women. The winner of the Silver Lion at the Venice Film Festival.

LIFE WITH FATHER
1947   118m   c   ★★★★
Comedy   /A
WB

William Powell *(Clarence Day)*, Irene Dunne *(Vinnie Day)*, Elizabeth Taylor *(Mary)*, Edmund Gwenn *(Rev. Dr. Lloyd)*, ZaSu Pitts *(Cora)*, James Lydon *(Clarence)*, Emma Dunn *(Margaret)*, Moroni Olsen *(Dr. Humphries)*, Elisabeth Risdon *(Mrs. Whitehead)*, Derek Scott *(Harlan)*

p, Robert Buckner; d, Michael Curtiz; w, Donald Ogden Stewart (based on the play by Howard Lindsay, Russel Crouse and the book by Clarence Day Jr.); ph, Peverell Marley, William V. Skall (Technicolor); ed, George Amy; m, Max Steiner; art d, Robert Haas; fx, Ray Foster, William McGann; cos, Milo Anderson

Based on an autobiographical book by Clarence Day, Jr., and a play that ran for 3,224 performances on Broadway (a total that was eclipsed only by "Fiddler on the Roof"), LIFE WITH FATHER is a son's fond remembrance of his Victorian youth

spent in the home of his authoritarian but lovable father (William Powell). There's really not much of a plot, just a lot of alternately quiet and raucous moments of love and laughter as the family goes about its urban, urbane life. Irene Dunne, playing the mother of the red-headed Day clan, is frequently rankled by Father's sexist ways, but, like the rest of the family, she loves dear old Dad anyway.

Powell is nothing less than magnificent as the mustached philosophizing patriarch, and his performance won him an Academy Award. Elizabeth Taylor, Martin Milner, Jimmy Lydon, and Edmund Gwenn all contribute strong supporting performances; Michael Curtiz (CASABLANCA; YANKEE DOODLE DANDY; THE ADVENTURES OF ROBIN HOOD) provides his usual sure-handed direction; Peverell Marley and William V. Skall earned Oscar nominations for their cinematography, and Max Steiner's score was also nominated. There was an attempt at a sequel, LIFE WITH MOTHER, but it doesn't hold a candle to this. Day's story also inspired a brief TV series in 1955. Look for a very young and beautiful Arlene Dahl in a scene at Delmonico's Restaurant. Older TV fans will also recognize singer Russell Arms as the stock quotation operator.

LIFEBOAT
1944   96m   bw   ★★★★★
Drama/War   /PG
FOX

Tallulah Bankhead *(Connie Porter)*, William Bendix *(Gus)*, Walter Slezak *(The German)*, Mary Anderson *(Alice)*, John Hodiak *(Kovak)*, Henry Hull *(Rittenhouse)*, Heather Angel *(Mrs. Higgins)*, Hume Cronyn *(Stanley Garrett)*, Canada Lee *(Joe)*, William Yetter, Jr. *(German Sailor)*

p, Kenneth MacGowan; d, Alfred Hitchcock; w, Jo Swerling (based on the story by John Steinbeck); ph, Glen MacWilliams; ed, Dorothy Spencer; m, Hugo Friedhofer; art d, James Basevi, Maurice Ransford; fx, Fred Sersen

Alfred Hitchcock's taut wartime thriller concerns a handful of survivors who climb into a lifeboat after their ship is torpedoed by a German U-boat. The captain (Walter Slezak) of the U-boat, which has also sunk, swims to the already crowded boat and is taken aboard by the kind-hearted survivors. Since he is the only man capable of handling the craft in rough weather and navigating it to a safe harbor, he is elected helmsman. The survivors are an odd lot—fashion writer Connie Porter (Tallulah Bankhead), industrial tycoon Rittenhouse (Henry Hull), socially conscious seaman Kovak (John Hodiak), wounded stoker Gus (William Bendix), meek radio operator Stanley Garrett (Hume Cronyn), bewildered nurse Alice (Mary Anderson), a mother in shock (Heather Angel), cradling her child who had just died, and black steward Joe (Canada Lee). Slowly, and with insidious cleverness, the German steers a course not for land, but to a secret rendezvous with a German mother ship. The entire cast is superb, but the standouts are Bankhead, as the spoiled, wealthy dilettante writer whose expensive furs and jewelry are worth more to her than the lives of her fellow survivors, and Bendix, as the compassionate but not-too-bright stoker whose gangrenous leg poses a threat to his dreams of returning home to dance with his sweetheart. John Steinbeck, on whose original story the film was based, was first assigned to pen the script, but reportedly felt too restricted by the film's single set (the lifeboat). Jo Swerling eventually wrote the script, but, as was customary with Hitchcock, the talented Ben Hecht was brought in at the last moment to tighten up scenes and sharpen dialogue.

LIFEGUARD

1976 96m c   ★★★
Drama   PG/15
Paramount

Sam Elliott (*Rick Carlson*), Anne Archer (*Cathy*), Stephen Young (*Larry*), Parker Stevenson (*Chris*), Kathleen Quinlan (*Wendy*), Steve Burns (*Machine Gun*), Sharon Weber (*Tina*), Mark Hall, Scott Lichtig

p, Ron Silverman; d, Daniel Petrie; w, Ron Koslow; ph, Ralph Woolsey (CFI Color); ed, Argyle Nelson; m, Dale Menten

This quickie is a real surprise: a sensitive, thought-provoking story involving a man forced to look at himself. Elliott is the title character, an old-timer in the profession at age 30. Although he enjoys his work, pressure from his parents and peers force Elliott to realize that beach life can't go on forever. His performance is intelligent, with some good support by Archer as Elliott's high school sweetheart and Quinlan as a young girl with a crush on him. Unfortunately, this was marketed as nothing more than another beach movie and consequently had little box office success.

LIGHT THAT FAILED, THE

1939 97m bw   ★★★★
Drama   /A
Paramount

Ronald Colman (*Dick Heldar*), Walter Huston (*Terpenhow*), Muriel Angelus (*Maisie*), Ida Lupino (*Bessie Broke*), Dudley Digges (*The Nilghai*), Ernest Cossart (*Beeton*), Ferike Boros (*Mme. Binat*), Pedro de Cordoba (*M. Binat*), Colin Tapley (*Gardner*), Fay Helm (*Red-Haired Girl*)

p, William A. Wellman; d, William A. Wellman; w, Robert Carson (based on the novel by Rudyard Kipling); ph, Theodor Sparkuhl; ed, Thomas Scott; m, Victor Young; art d, Hans Dreier, Robert Odell

This tragic Kipling tale, from his first novel, displays Wellman's consummate directorial skills in following the story faithfully, unlike earlier versions in which sugar-coated endings are supplied. Colman is a gifted artist who receives a sabre cut during a battle. He returns to England where he becomes a famous painter; his masterpiece is a portrait of a London prostitute, Lupino. She is driven half-mad with desire for him, a part so intensely played that it brought her to stardom. Realizing that her station in life will prevent her from ever having him, she viciously destroys the painting. The old wound has caused him to slowly go blind. In a shattering scene, Colman proudly displays the portrait to his devoted friend Huston, not realizing that Lupino has slashed it. His sight almost gone, Colman bids goodbye to his childhood sweetheart and returns to the Sudan with friend Huston. At the first sound of battle, Colman begs Huston to put him into the fight, and he is sent blindly charging on his white stallion to his death. This moving, haunting film reinforces Kipling's love of honor, male friendship, and nobility of spirit. Wellman handles the story and gaslight era with great care, developing his characters with incisive scenes. This was no easy task for Wellman since he and Colman argued throughout the film, the director refusing Colman's perfectionist demands for endless takes and ignoring the actor's insistence that Vivien Leigh play the slatternly Bessie. Lupino got that emotion-charged part by barging into Wellman's office to tell him that no other woman in the world could play Bessie as well as she and providing an impromptu interpretation right then and there. She got the role, and audiences around the world were stunned by her marvelous portrayal. Of Colman, the director would later comment: "Ronald Colman and Wellman,

an odd combination to say the least. He didn't like me; I didn't like him—the only two things we agreed fully on. [He has] the most beautiful voice in the whole motion picture business."

LIGHTSHIP, THE

1986 89m c   ★★★
Drama   PG-13/15
CBS/Castle Hill

Robert Duvall (*Caspary*), Klaus Maria Brandauer (*Capt. Miller*), Tom Bower (*Coop*), Robert Costanzo (*Stump*), Badja Djola (*Nate*), William Forsythe (*Gene*), Arliss Howard (*Eddie*), Michael Lyndon (*Alex*), Timothy Phillips (*Thorne*)

p, Bill Benenson, Moritz Borman; d, Jerzy Skolimowski; w, William Mai, David Taylor (based on the novel *Das Feuerschiff* by Sigfried Lenz); ph, Charly Steinberger; ed, Barrie Vince; m, Stanley Myers; art d, Holger Gross

Set in 1955, the film takes place almost exclusively aboard a US Coast Guard lightship, an anchored vessel that functions in much the same way as a lighthouse, keeping other ships from crashing into the rocky Virginia shore. The lightship is captained by Brandauer, a German-born American citizen who is haunted by his naval past. During WWII, while commanding a destroyer, Miller chose to go after an enemy U-boat rather than pick up victims from the sea. He was court-martialed, but although acquitted is tormented by his conscience. Living on the lightship with his delinquent teenage son Lyndon and a small crew, Miller spots a stranded speedboat. He brings the boaters aboard—the frightfully effete and evil Duvall and two leather-clad brothers, Forsythe and Howard. An odd trio of unnaturally close fugitives, the men demand that Miller deliver them to their chosen destination. Miller, however, cannot desert the Virginia coast. Director Skolimowski has fashioned an interesting although flawed picture. The screenplay lacks coherence, which necessitated the postproduction addition of narration by Lyndon, but the performances more than make up for it.

LILI

1953 81m c   ★★★½
Drama   /U
MGM

Leslie Caron (*Lili Daurier*), Mel Ferrer (*Paul Berthalet*), Jean-Pierre Aumont (*Marc*), Zsa Zsa Gabor (*Rosalie*), Kurt Kasznar (*Jacquot*), Amanda Blake (*Peach Lips*), Alex Gerry (*Proprietor*), Ralph Dumke (*M. Corvier*), Wilton Graff (*M. Tonit*), George Baxter (*M. Enrique*)

p, Edwin H. Knopf; d, Charles Walters; w, Helen Deutsch (based on the story by Paul Gallico); ph, Robert Planck (Technicolor); ed, Ferris Webster; m, Bronislau Kaper; art d, Cedric Gibbons, Paul Groesse; fx, Warren Newcombe; chor, Charles Walters, Dorothy Jarnac; cos, Mary Ann Nyberg

Leslie Caron plays the title role in this charming film. Sixteen-year-old Lili Daurier runs off to work as a waitress with a carnival and falls in love with Marc (Jean Pierre Aumont), a magician who is more amused by the young innocent than anything else. Fired for paying too much attention to Marc, Lili is comforted by a group of puppets operated by Paul Berthalet (Mel Ferrer), a bitter ex-dancer crippled by a war injury. Though Paul is insanely jealous of Lili's affection for Marc, he is only able to show his tender side through his puppets (in the film's nicest moment, as Lili and the dancing figures sing the famous "Hi-Lili, Hi-Lo"), and Lili thinks of him as a cruel man. When Lili learns that Rosalie (Zsa Zsa Gabor, in a surprisingly good performance) is Marc's wife as well as his assistant, she packs her bags to leave, but love wins out in the end, though it's not the magician who has the final trick up his sleeve. Caron is wonderful as Lili and was nominated for an Academy Award (losing to Audrey Hepburn for ROMAN HOLIDAY), as were Charles Walters for his direction, Robert Planck for his cinematography, Cedric Gibbons and company for the set decoration and Helen Deutsch for her adaptation of Paul Gallico's short story. Bronislau Kaper won an Oscar for his music. LILI was the basis for a hit Broadway musical in 1961 called "Carnival," with Anna Maria Alberghetti in the Caron role.

LILI MARLEEN

1981 120m c   ★★
Drama/War   R/15
Roxy/CIP/Rialto (West Germany)

Hanna Schygulla (Wilkie Bunterberg), Giancarlo Giannini (Robert Mendelsson), Mel Ferrer (David Mendelsson), Karl-Heinz von Hassel (Henkel), Christine Kaufmann (Miriam), Hark Bohm (Tascher), Karin Baal (Anna Lederer), Udo Kier (Drewitz), Erik Schumann (Von Strehlow), Gottfried John (Aaron)

p, Luggi Waldleitner, Enzo Peri; d, Rainer Werner Fassbinder; w, Manfred Purzer, Joshua Sinclair, Rainer Werner Fassbinder (based on the song by Lale Andersen); ph, Xaver Schwarzenberger; ed, Franz Walsch, Juliane Lorenz; m, Peer Raben; prod d, Rolf Zehetbauer; art d, Herbert Stravel; fx, Joachim Schulz; chor, Dr. Dieter Gackstetter; cos, Barbara Baum

Fassbinder was surely one of the world's most prolific filmmakers, producing an enormous body of work before his early death, which ironically occurred as he was editing film. With such a large output there were bound to be a few pictures that fell short of the director's normally high quality, LILI MARLEEN being an example. "The story of a song!" claimed the advertising copy, which is more or less truth in advertising. "Lili Marleen" was a song made famous in Germany by Lale Andersen and later Marlene Dietrich. It was very popular with the German forces during WWII. However, Fassbinder's film has little to do with the true story of the song. The film opens in 1938 with the lovely and accomplished Schygulla, a cabaret singer in Zurich. She discovers that boyfriend Giannini, a Swiss Jew, is not only a musical composer but also a member of the underground resistance movement. During a trip to Germany, her song becomes a hit, and no less than the Fuhrer himself wants to meet her. She becomes a big star, while Giannini's father blocks her return to Switzerland. Giannini sneaks into Berlin and meets once more with his now-famous lover. She becomes blacklisted and is forced to leave the country while Giannini is arrested. After the war, they meet once more, but he is now married and well on his way to success. Though Fassbinder's camerawork is excellent, including some allusions to the famous German studio UFA, his themes are never really developed. The political and social messages so often found in his work give way to more melodramatic storytelling. Schygulla, who is usually a shining performer, is spotty here. Her singing makes one wonder how the song got to be such a hit.

LILIES OF THE FIELD

1963 94m bw   ★★★½
Drama   /U
Rainbow

Sidney Poitier (Homer Smith), Lilia Skala (Mother Maria), Lisa Mann (Sister Gertrude), Isa Crino (Sister Agnes), Francesca Jarvis (Sister Albertine), Pamela Branch (Sister Elizabeth), Stanley

Adams (Juan), Dan Frazer (Father Murphy), Ralph Nelson (Mr. Ashton)

p, Ralph Nelson; d, Ralph Nelson; w, James Poe (based on the novel by William E. Barrett); ph, Ernest Haller; ed, John McCafferty; m, Jerry Goldsmith

LILIES OF THE FIELD is a "feel-good" movie that blazed new trails in the motion picture world. Not that it had any particular special effects or innovations in movies. It had no spectacular action or dance sequences and surely no violence. But it was a trendsetter in that it marked the first time that the Academy of Motion Picture Arts and Sciences ever awarded an Oscar to a black actor, Poitier. It was also nominated for Best Picture, Best Screenplay, Best Cinematography, and Best Supporting Actress. Poitier is an ex-GI roaming around the Southwest, taking odd jobs and seeing what there is to see when he stops at a small farm to refill his car radiator. The farm is run by five German nuns who immediately set upon him to help them with their manual labors. They are new to these shores and don't speak much English but the Mother Superior, Skala, convinces Poitier to stay a while and help work the farm that was willed to them. He fixes their leaky roof and they send up prayers in honor of the man whom "God has sent." Now, Skala asks if he will stay on to help with some other chores. Poitier is a little tired of his aimless wanderings and not much convincing is necessary, even though they prevail on him to do a major project—the building of a chapel. Poitier agrees, as long as they will supply the needed materials. He teams up with Nelson (doing double chores as director and actor), a contractor, and they start to build the chapel. Meanwhile, he donates his small salary back to the nuns to buy food and spends his spare time teaching them how to speak English. When building materials for the chapel run out, Poitier disappears and the nuns think he's abandoned them, but he returns a few weeks later to complete the job he started for the nuns he has come to love. Now, however, he is finally assisted by the local townspeople who refused to help him the first time around. On the night before the sanctification of the chapel, Poitier leaves with as little fanfare as when he first arrived. This was a small, low-budget picture that went straight for the heart and succeeded critically as well as financially. Director Nelson also helmed another Oscar-winning performance when he did Cliff Robertson's CHARLY, and his work on FATHER GOOSE helped screenwriters Frank Tarloff and Peter Stone win Oscars.

LIMELIGHT

1952 145m bw   ★★★★
Drama/Comedy   G/U
Chaplin

Charles Chaplin (Calvero), Claire Bloom (Terry, a Ballet Dancer), Sydney Chaplin (Neville, a Composer), Andre Eglevsky (Harlequin), Melissa Hayden (Columbine), Charles Chaplin, Jr., Wheeler Dryden (Clowns), Nigel Bruce (Postant, an Impresario), Norman Lloyd (Stage Manager), Buster Keaton (Piano Accompanist)

p, Charles Chaplin; d, Charles Chaplin; w, Charles Chaplin; ph, Karl Struss; ed, Joe Inge; m, Charles Chaplin; art d, Eugene Laurie; chor, Charles Chaplin, Andre Eglevsky, Melissa Hayden

Chaplin, as usual, is the whole show, superb in this swansong statement about his own career and the old-style entertainment he best represented. He is a one-time great of the British music halls at the turn of the century (which is exactly where Chaplin himself began), who finds a young dancer, Bloom, depressed over setbacks, attempting suicide in their cheap boarding house. He takes her in, nurses her back to health, and supports her efforts to become a success. As her star rises, his fades, but he bows out with magnificent aplomb in the place he most loves, the theater. Chaplin plays comic and dramatic scenes with great skill. He is simply wonderful in his pantomime routines, particularly so when he tames a flea and when he imagines himself a great lion tamer. Chaplin is a delight as he teaches Bloom his "laughter therapy." He ends his career—and his life—with a hilarious routine with the great comic Keaton, collapsing from exhaustion, falling into the orchestra pit and getting wedged in a large drum, commenting: "Ladies and gentlemen, I would like to say something, but I am stuck." He dies happy, believing that Bloom is in love, not with him, but with a young composer, played by Chaplin's real-life son, Sydney. Other children, from his marriage with Oona O'Neill (daughter of the great American playwright), appear as street urchins. The overlong film is extraordinary in that Chaplin produced, directed, wrote the script, and helped compose the haunting, Oscar winning score (In an unusual occurance, the composers won the Award, not in 1952, but in 1972, which was the first year the picture was ever shown in a Los Angeles theatre). The film's main love theme, "Eternally," became a popular ballad. LIMELIGHT is a direct comment on Chaplin's own fabulous career, one which saw the triumph and decline of physical comedy. He had fallen out of favor with a public that believed him to be a wild-eyed leftist radical, if not an outright communist, and LIMELIGHT suffered as a result, yielding little profit at the box office. LIMELIGHT pays homage to a past in which simple, nuance-free entertainment gave joy and laughter to millions. Bloom, at age 19, became an overnight star with her appearance in the film. (She had debuted in THE BLIND GODDESS at age 16.) She later recalled in her memoirs, *Limelight and After*: "Chaplin was the most exacting director, not because he expected you to produce wonders on your own, but because he expected you to follow unquestioningly his every instruction. I was surprised at how old-fashioned much of what he prescribed seemed—rather theatrical effects that I didn't associate with the modern cinema."

LION IN WINTER, THE

1968 134m c ★★★★
Historical PG/15
Haworth (U.K.)

Peter O'Toole (*King Henry II*), Katharine Hepburn (*Queen Eleanor of Aquitaine*), Jane Merrow (*Princess Alais*), John Castle (*Prince Geoffrey*), Timothy Dalton (*King Philip of France*), Anthony Hopkins (*Prince Richard the Lion-Hearted*), Nigel Stock (*William Marshall*), Nigel Terry (*Prince John*), Kenneth Griffith (*Strolling Player*), O.Z. Whitehead (*Bishop of Durham*)

p, Martin Poll; d, Anthony Harvey; w, James Goldman (based on the play by Goldman); ph, Douglas Slocombe (Panavision, Eastmancolor); ed, John Bloom; m, John Barry; art d, Peter Murton; Gilbert Margerie; cos, Margaret Furse

O'Toole, the all-powerful Henry II, summons his politically ambitious family to a reunion in 1183. This includes his wife, Hepburn, whom he has kept in a remote castle to keep her from meddling with his empire. His three sons—all coveting his wide kingdom—Castle, Terry, and Hopkins are also present, along with O'Toole's mistress Merrow and her brother Dalton, playing King Philip of France. The members of this tempestuous family jockey for position and brutally squabble among each other, rekindling every injury suffered and adding new, Homeric insults to their already bruised reputations.

Hepburn is simply wonderful as the scheming and shrewd Eleanor of Aquitaine. Her verbal duels with the equally impres-

sive O'Toole (here playing a man of 50 behind a beard and heavy makeup) are spellbinding. Hepburn won her third Oscar for this superlative performance, becoming the first actress in history to do so (her previous Oscars were for MORNING GLORY and GUESS WHO'S COMING TO DINNER). O'Toole holds his own with the magnificent Hepburn in a witty, literate, and inventive script. The claim that costume dramas are never successful was mightily disproved by this film, which enjoyed a booming box-office business and the wide respect of the public. Shot on location in Ireland, Wales, and France, the film received additional Oscars for Best Screenplay and Best Original Score. Other nominations included Best Picture (won by OLIVER!), O'Toole (Cliff Robertson took the award for CHARLY), Best Direction, and Best Costume Design.

LIQUID SKY

1982 118m c ★★★½
Science Fiction R/18
Z Films

Anne Carlisle (*Margaret/Jimmy*), Paula Sheppard (*Adrian*), Susan Doukas (*Sylvia*), Otto von Wernherr (*Johann*), Bob Brady (*Owen*), Elaine C. Grove (*Katherine*), Stanley Knapp (*Paul*), Lloyd Ziff (*Lester*), Harry Lum (*Deliveryman*), Roy MacArthur (*Jack*)

p, Slava Tsukerman; d, Slava Tsukerman; w, Slava Tsukerman, Anne Carlisle, Nina V. Kerova; ph, Yuri Neyman (TVC Color); ed, Sharyn L. Ross; m, Slava Tsukerman, Brenda I. Hutchinson, Clive Smith; prod d, Marina Levikova; fx, Yuri Neyman; cos, Marina Levikova

Outrageous fun, this film is New Wave chic, satire, self-parody, science fiction, and certainly one of the more accessible independent features ever made. Aliens are after the heroin-like substance produced by the human brain at the point of orgasm. Anne Carlisle, who cowrote the screenplay, plays a lesbian punk model *and* a male homosexual punk model. As a woman, Carlisle discovers a special sexual power. At orgasm she can make her lover disappear into thin air, courtesy of some wonderful special effects. A subplot involves Otto von Wernherr, a government scientist investigating the UFO on Carlisle's roof. He holes up across the street in the apartment of a horny and hysterically funny socialite, Susan Doukas, whose very vocal expressions of frustration he balances with a great low-key performance. This offbeat film was directed by Slava Tsukerman, a classically trained Soviet-born filmmaker. His observations of modern America, as well as the beautiful New York City photography, are right on the money. LIQUID SKY deservedly became a cult classic shortly after its release.

LIST OF ADRIAN MESSENGER, THE

1963 98m bw ★★★½
Mystery /A
Universal

George C. Scott (*Anthony Gethryn*), Dana Wynter (*Lady Jocelyn Brutenholm*), Clive Brook (*Marquis of Gleneyre*), Gladys Cooper (*Mrs. Karoudjian*), Herbert Marshall (*Sir Wilfred Lucas*), Jacques Roux (*Raoul le Borg*), John Merivale (*Adrian Messenger*), Marcel Dalio (*Anton Karoudjian*), Bernard Archard (*Inspector Pike*), Walter Huston (*Derek*)

p, Edward Lewis; d, John Huston; w, Anthony Veiller (based on the novel by Philip MacDonald); ph, Joseph MacDonald; ed, Terry Morse, Hugh S. Fowler; m, Jerry Goldsmith; art d, Alexander Golitzen, Stephen Grimes, George Webb

This convoluted but absorbing mystery begins when Anthony Gethryn (Scott), a retired British colonel, is given a list of 11 names by his friend Adrian Messenger (Merivale) and asked to check on the whereabouts of those on the list. When Messenger's plane blows up, Gethryn looks into the fates of those on the list and discovers that all have met a similar fate. Gethryn also learns that the killer is a master of disguises—adopting a new identity for every victim—that all the victims were POWs in Burma during WWII, and that they all knew the identity of the traitor in their midst. John Huston directs this film with calculating care, setting up a number of red herrings who are all played by superstars in disguise, including Robert Mitchum, Frank Sinatra, Burt Lancaster, Kirk Douglas, Tony Curtis, and even Huston himself. It was all eerily effective and provided many a scary moment. Location shooting was conducted in Ireland.

LITTLE BIG MAN

1970　147m　c　　　　　　　　　　　　★★½
Western/War　　　　　　　　　　　　PG/15
National General

Dustin Hoffman (Jack Crabb), Faye Dunaway (Mrs. Pendrake), Martin Balsam (Allardyce T. Merriweather), Richard Mulligan (Gen. George A. Custer), Chief Dan George (Old Lodge Skins), Jeff Corey (Wild Bill Hickok), Aimee Eccles (Sunshine), Kelly Jean Peters (Olga), Carol Androsky (Caroline), Robert Little Star (Little Horse)

p, Stuart Millar; d, Arthur Penn; w, Calder Willingham (based on the novel by Thomas Berger); ph, Harry Stradling, Jr. (Panavision, Technicolor); ed, Dede Allen; m, John Hammond; prod d, Dean Tavoularis; art d, Angelo Graham; fx, Dick Smith, Logan Frazee; cos, Dorothy Jeakins

This strange tale of the Old West is recounted in flashback by 121-year-old Jack Crabb (Dustin Hoffman), who claims to be the only survivor of the massacre at the Little Big Horn. As a boy, Jack is taken in by Cheyenne Indians and raised by Old Lodge Skins (Chief Dan George), but later he protests that he is white when his tribe is attacked by the cavalry, beginning a pattern of cultural fence-hopping that dominates the rest of his life. Over the course of a century or so, Jack earns the name Little Big Man for his bravery in battle; is taken in by a preacher and his randy wife (Faye Dunaway); becomes both an assistant to a cure-all-peddling drummer (Martin Balsam) and a less-than-successful gunfighter; nearly dies when Custer (Richard Mulligan) and his troops attack his tribe at the Washita River; turns to alcohol; and guides the Seventh Cavalry into the Little Big Horn massacre. Based on a Thomas Berger novel, Arthur Penn's film wasn't the first movie to revise the cinematic history of the Old West with a sympathetic slant toward the native American point of view, but, given its oddly whimsical tone, it is one of the most unconventional westerns ever made. Unlike HOW THE WEST WAS WON, in which the characters' lives and the history of the West unfold with the certainty of Manifest Destiny, Jack's story is a series of seemingly random occurrences in which history acts *upon* him, almost always with tragic or tragicomic results. Aided by a strong supporting cast (Chief Dan George earned the film's only Oscar nomination), Hoffman gives a fine performance as the bewildered man in the middle in this odd but engaging film.

LITTLE CAESAR

1931　80m　bw　　　　　　　　　　　★★★★
Crime　　　　　　　　　　　　　　　/PG
First National

Edward G. Robinson (Cesare Enrico Bandello/"Little Caesar"), Douglas Fairbanks, Jr. (Joe Massara), Glenda Farrell (Olga Strassoff), William Collier, Jr. (Tony Passa), Ralph Ince (Diamond Pete Montana), George E. Stone (Otero), Thomas Jackson (Lt. Tom Flaherty), Stanley Fields (Sam Vettori), Armand Kaliz (DeVoss), Sidney Blackmer (the Big Boy)

p, Hal B. Wallis; d, Mervyn LeRoy; w, Robert N. Lee, Darryl F. Zanuck (uncredited), Francis Edwards Faragoh (uncredited), Robert Lord (based on the novel by W.R. Burnett); ph, Tony Gaudio; ed, Ray Curtiss; art d, Anton Grot; cos, Earl Luick

This is the classic gangster film of the very early years of talkies. Directed by Mervyn LeRoy, it may seem a bit dated and inelegant to modern viewers but it is an indisputable landmark. Though not the first gangster film, it is responsible for launching the immensely popular classic gangster cycle of the 1930s. It also launched the career of one of the greatest icons of the genre—Edward G. Robinson. Simply, this is the violent story of the rise and fall of an Al Capone-like gangster. This tough film still packs a considerable whallop largely due to the mesmerizing performance of Robinson as the thoroughly vicious Rico Bandello.

Rico Bandello is a dedicated killer and thief right from the opening scene. He disappears into a gas station and, after a flash of gunfire, emerges with the money from the till. His driver, Joe Massara (Douglas Fairbanks, Jr.), nervously wheels the coupe into the darkness. Later, Rico and Joe are in a diner, ordering "spaghetti and coffee for two," telegraphing their ethnicity to the audience. After reading in the newspaper about underworld big shots, Rico informs Joe of his ambition to become a rackets czar. He declares that he's not "just another mug." Rico is a man with a mission. He quickly goes about making his criminal dreams come true.

Caring only about money and power, the dynamic if somewhat frog-like gangster later advises his handsome pal that "dames" will be his downfall, that "having your own way or nothing" is the only real reason for living. Thus he feels incredibly betrayed when he learns that he is losing his buddy to a woman. There seems to be a nascent homoeroticsm at work here on a thematic level but Robinson's interpretation of Rico suggests that he truly has no lust for anything other than power. Still his loyalty to Joe will prove to be his undoing.

LITTLE CAESAR was one of the first sound films to portray the American gangster outside of prison walls, coming after such early prison stories as THE LAST MILE, THE BIG HOUSE, and NUMBERED MEN. Robinson's character is as ruthless as Al Capone, the real-life gangster upon whom Chicago author W.R. Burnett based the novel from which the film is adapted. Capone rose, as does Robinson. through the ranks from goon bodyguard to overall crime czar. The screenplay earned an Oscar nomination for Best Screen Adaptation.

Made for a then-hefty $700,000, the film was a box-office smash and typecast Robinson in the role of the gangster. Given free rein by Zanuck, director Mervyn LeRoy produced a fast-paced film that kept up with its lightning-fast star. Oddly, LITTLE CAESAR contains a minimum of explicit violence, although murderous intent is always lurking in Robinson's menacing face. The 37-year-old Robinson was not new to films; he had been acting in movies since 1923, though he was largely unnoticed. Wallis assigned Robinson the lead, but the sensitive actor found it difficult to adjust to the role of the killer, blinking wildly every time he had to fire a gun. LeRoy solved the problem by affixing little transparent bands of tape to Robinson's upper eyelids, so that when he did blast away, his eyes remained wide open; this trick had the added benefit of giving Robinson an even more menacing, heartless appearance.

LITTLE DORRIT

1988 360m c ★★★★
Comedy/Drama G/U
Sands/Cannon (U.K.)

Alec Guinness (William Dorrit), Derek Jacobi (Arthur Clennam), Cyril Cusack (Frederick Dorrit), Sarah Pickering (Little Dorrit), Joan Greenwood (Mrs. Clennam), Max Wall (Flintwinch), Amelda Brown (Fanny Dorrit), Daniel Chatto (Tip Dorrit), Miriam Margolyes (Flora Finching), Bill Fraser (Mr. Casby)

p, John Brabourne, Richard Goodwin; d, Christine Edzard; w, Christine Edzard (based on the novel by Charles Dickens); ph, Bruno de Keyzer (Technicolor); ed, Olivier Stockman, Fraser Maclean; m, Giuseppe Verdi; cos, Barbara Sonnex, Judith Loom, Joyce Carter, Jackie Smith, Sally Neale, Claudie Gastine, Danielle Garderes

Little Dorrit is one of Charles Dickens's greatest and least-read novels, and this massive, six-hour version by director-screenwriter Christine Edzard, essentially faithful to the work, is one of the finest of all Dickens screen adaptations. The film plays in two three-hour parts. Part I, "Nobody's Fault" (Dickens' original title), is told from the point of view of Jacobi, a middle-aged bachelor returning home to London after 20 years in China. Jacobi becomes interested in the case of Guinness, a man who has been locked in a debtors' prison for the last 25 years, and in his daughter, Pickering, a seamstress who works for Jacobi's forbidding mother. Impressed by their sad story, Jacobi sets out to help the man and his daughter to reclaim a fortune. Part II, "Little Dorrit's Story," told from the seamstress's point of view, begins with her birth in prison and follows her as she assumes the role of mother to her selfish family. When Jacobi arrives in England, she falls in love with him, though she knows he loves another. LITTLE DORRIT is one film in two feature-length parts. Part II is necessarily the stronger, developing themes and filling out the plot, but the two halves are interdependent. In Edzard's version, Dickens' Little Dorrit character takes on a much more forceful consciousness; she becomes, in a sense, the Dickensian conscience provided by the novel's third-person narration. Boasting a 211-member cast, LITTLE DORRIT is packed with fine performances—and best of all is veteran Dickensian Alec Guinness (GREAT EXPECTATIONS, OLIVER TWIST, SCROOGE).

LITTLE FOXES, THE

1941 115m bw ★★★½
Drama /PG
RKO

Bette Davis (Regina Hubbard Giddens), Herbert Marshall (Horace Giddens), Teresa Wright (Alexandra Giddens), Richard Carlson (David Hewitt), Patricia Collinge (Birdie Hubbard), Dan Duryea (Leo Hubbard), Charles Dingle (Ben Hubbard), Carl Benton Reid (Oscar Hubbard), Jessie Grayson (Addie), John Marriott (Cal)

p, Samuel Goldwyn; d, William Wyler; w, Lillian Hellman, Arthur Kober, Dorothy Parker, Alan Campbell (based on a play by Lillian Hellman); ph, Gregg Toland; ed, Daniel Mandell; m, Meredith Willson; art d, Stephen Goosson; cos, Orry-Kelly

Time has proven Bette Davis right—no on could top Tallulah Bankhead's Broadway portrayal of the vituperative Regina Giddens, the central figure of Lillian Hellman's now creaking, but still compelling deep south potboiler. During filming, Wil-

liam Wyler was often heard to say, "We'll have to get Bankhead." Would that he had. Davis, in an impulsive stampede to make the role her own, took an opposite track to the character. Or perhaps Wyler did; every Davis bio tells it differently. Whatever: the important thing is, it's wrong. In her rice powder, with her mouth drawn into a tiny, hard line (it makes her look more beaked and birdlike than ever) she loses the hothouse-flower sensuality that Bankhead brought to her manipulations. And it was precisely that certain quality that justified Regina's ability to manipulate men to high heaven in the turn of the century south. Davis's tightness makes the film look mothballed; her dissatisfaction spills over into how she wears the highnecked costumes—like she's choking with barely contained fury, working so hard in technique and yet feeling it elude her, before Wyler, the man she most wanted to please. As a result, the film loses its passionate, reckless drive and fury. If Bankhead was a thunderstorm on stage (and she certainly sounds like one on the recording we have of her performance), Davis is a duststorm on film—arid and a trifle, dare we say, dull.

FOXES tells the story of a turn-of-the-century southern family, the Hubbards (whose exploits are also detailed in ANOTHER PART OF THE FOREST [1948], from Hellman's dramatic prequel), as greedy a bunch as ever drank juleps and branch water. The plot is set in motion when Davis is asked by her brothers, Dingle and Reid, to loan them money to build a cotton mill. They need $75,000, a not unsubstantial sum, but she recognizes the fact that she can profit greatly by the move, especially through the use of cheap labor. Davis invites the Yankee financier who suggested the enterprise, Hicks, to dinner at her home so she can take a closer look at him. Next, Davis instructs her daughter, Wright, to travel north and fetch Davis's husband (Marshall), who has been recuperating from a heart attack at a Baltimore sanitarium. Marshall comes home with Wright, and Davis begins to nag him about financing the new venture, but he remains firmly against it for several reasons, including moral opposition to the plan to exploit cheap labor and set up a virtual southern sweatshop, as well as distrust of his brothers-in-law. Reid and Dingle realize they'll never be able to coax Marshall into giving them the money, so they get the weak-willed Duryea, Reid's son who works in the family banking business, to rob a handful of negotiable bonds from Marshall's private vault. But the avaricious Davis instantly suspects them of the theft and attempts to blackmail her brothers into giving her a percentage of their business in return for her keeping quiet about their crime. That plan is scotched when Marshall steps forward and says that the bonds weren't stolen at all, protecting Duryea by saying he gave Duryea the money as an interest-free loan. Thus frustrated, the scheming Davis continues to badger and rankle her husband so much that he suffers a coronary seizure. He collapses and pleads for his medicine, but Davis just sits there, coldly ignoring him.

Among the cast of THE LITTLE FOXES—originally scripted by Hellman, but with additional scenes and dialog by Arthur Kober, Dorothy Parker, and Alan Campbell—Patricia Collinge, Carl Benton Reid, Charles Dingle, John Marriott, and Dan Duryea had appeared in the Broadway original. This is the third and last time Davis worked with Wyler, following the triumphs of JEZEBEL and THE LETTER. The furious battles enacted by the two on FOXES are Hollywood legend—a sad farewell to a legendary collaboration. Perhaps the rest of the principals didn't cotton to Davis's tantrums (being from Bankhead's production)—they look like wolves moving in on her acting territory, except for Teresa Wright, in her film debut. The other newcomer— Dan Dureya— does move in; it's overkill that needed slapping down.

We are not, however, discounting FOXES's impressive technical achievement. Many of the sequences directed by Wyler and shot by cinematographer Gregg Toland (famed for his deep-focus work in CITIZEN KANE) have been hailed by film scholars, especially the scene in which the camera stays on Davis in the foreground as Marshall suffers his heart attack in the background. Davis never blinks, never acknowledges her husband's plight. She just sits there, while Marshall struggles out-of-focus, an effect by which Wyler makes the audience concentrate on Davis's (unfortunate Kabuki) face and see just how cold-hearted her character is. The costumes by Orry-Kelly for Davis are either great or wrong. Somehow FOXES feels embalmed instead of lived; still we enjoy the drama done aloud. IT was nominated for nine Oscars; interestingly, it won none.

LITTLE GIRL WHO LIVES DOWN THE LANE, THE

1977 91m c   ★★★½
Thriller   PG/AA
Rank (Canada)

Jodie Foster (Rynn Jacobs), Martin Sheen (Frank Hallet), Alexis Smith (Mrs. Hallet), Mort Shuman (Officer Miglioriti), Scott Jacoby (Mario Podesta), Clesson Goodhue (Bank Manager), Hubert Noel, Jacques Famery (Bank Clerks), Mary Morter, Judie Wildman (Tellers)

p, Zev Braun; d, Nicolas Gessner; w, Laird Koenig (based on novel by Koenig); ph, Rene Verzier (Panavision); ed, Yves Langlois; m, Christian Gaubert; art d, Robert Prevost; cos, Denis Sperdouklis, Valentino

This Canadian-made film, a star vehicle for the then 13-year-old Jodie Foster, is a disturbing, wonderfully acted, well-scripted, and suspenseful study of a murderous 13-year-old girl, Rynn (Foster). Living alone in her father's home, Rynn makes up stories that her father is away when in fact he is dead. She handles the bills, the upkeep, and her own survival, admirably putting into practice what her father taught her. When a snooping neighbor makes a nuisance of herself, Rynn knocks her down the stairs. Matter-of-factly, Rynn lets the cellar door close and gets back to her work. Soon the creepy Frank (Martin Sheen) is making a pest of himself, wanting both answers to his suspicions and Rynn's barely pubescent body. Meanwhile, Rynn becomes genuinely attracted to Mario (Scott Jacoby), a youngster her own age. Frank, knowing that something is odd about Rynn's situation, presses her for answers about her father, his insistence threatening to ruin the private, self-sustaining, child-as-adult world she has created with Mario. This leads to a fatal game of cat-and-mouse between Rynn and Frank. Tautly directed by Nicolas Gessner, the film is a showcase for the young Foster and she does not disappoint, turning in a slyly nuanced performance that is downright creepy and at the same time oddly innocent.

LITTLE MERMAID, THE

1989 82m c   ★★★½
Animated/Children's   G/U
Disney/Silver Screen Partners IV

VOICES OF: Rene Auberjonois (Louis), Christopher Daniel Barnes (Eric), Jodi Benson (Ariel), Pat Carroll (Ursula), Paddi Edwards (Flotsam & Jetsam), Buddy Hackett (Scuttle), Jason Marin (Flounder), Kenneth Mars (Triton), Edie McClurg (Carlotta), Will Ryan (Seahorse)

p, Howard Ashman, John Musker; d, John Musker, Ron Clements; w, John Musker, Ron Clements (based on the fairy tale by Hans Christian Andersen); ed, Mark Hester; m, Robby Merkin, Alan Menken; prod d, Maureen Donley; art d, Michael A. Peraza, Jr., Donald A. Towns; anim, Mark Henn, Glen Keane, Duncan Marjoribanks, Ruben Aquino, Andreas Deja, Matthew O'Callaghan

THE LITTLE MERMAID is Walt Disney Studio's 28th full-length animated feature and its first animated fairy tale since SLEEPING BEAUTY (1958). It is the story of Ariel, a mermaid with a beautiful voice who lives under the sea in a kingdom ruled by her father, Triton the Sea King. Ariel longs to visit the world above the surface, but Triton hates humans for their love of seafood. Not surprisingly, Ariel swims to the surface anyway and saves a prince from a shipwreck, falling in love with him in the process and longing to be with him. Triton learns what has happened and, in a fit of rage, forbids her ever to go to the surface again. Dejected and angry, Ariel seeks help from Ursula the Sea Witch, who secretly longs to rule the sea. Although neither as rich nor as memorable as Disney's earlier efforts, THE LITTLE MERMAID is still an impressive achievement; its animation is exceptionally good. Nearly every character in the film is funny, and cute creatures abound. As entertaining and amusing as this all is (and it is very good family entertainment), some of the Disney magic seems to be missing. THE LITTLE MERMAID lacks the depth and emotional power of so many of the studio's classics. The story, which is full of potentially serious themes, is played strictly for bland emotionless laughs. The result is a movie that is fun to watch but that remains disappointing. Alan Menken's score and the song "Under the Sea" won Academy Awards. Also nominated was the tune "Kiss the Girl."

LITTLE ROMANCE, A

1979 108m c   ★★★★
Romance/Comedy   PG
Pan Arts/Trinacra (U.S./France)

Laurence Olivier (Julius), Diane Lane (Lauren), Thelonious Bernard (Daniel), Arthur Hill (Richard King), Sally Kellerman (Kay King), Broderick Crawford (Brod), David Dukes (George de Marco), Andrew Duncan (Bob Duryea), Claudette Sutherland (Janet Duryea), Graham Fletcher-Cook (Londet)

p, Robert L. Crawford, Yves Rousset-Rouard; d, George Roy Hill; w, Allan Burns (based on the novel E=MC, Mon Amour by Patrick Cauvin); ph, Pierre-William Glenn (Panavision, Technicolor); ed, William Reynolds; m, Georges Delerue; prod d, Henry Bumstead; art d, Francois de Lamothe; cos, Rosine Delamare

Completely charming, this teenage romantic comedy tells the innocent tale of a pair of 13-year-olds who fall in love in Paris. Lauren (Diane Lane) is living in Paris with her understanding stepfather (Arthur Hill) and her floozy mother (Sally Kellerman). While visiting the set of a movie production, Lauren meets Daniel (Thelonious Bernard), a lower-class youngster with a system for playing the horses and a fascination with both Robert Redford and Humphrey Bogart. Daniel becomes "Bogie" to Lauren's "Bacall," and before long they've fallen for each other in the most innocent of ways. Their attachment strengthens when they discover they both have extremely high IQs and interests in philosophy, qualities that usually embarrass them. Their adventures begin when they meet Julius (Laurence Olivier), a friendly old scoundrel who informs them of an age-old romantic legend: If two lovers kiss under Venice's Bridge of Sighs in a gondola at sunset when the bells toll, their love will last forever. The two youngsters are determined to try out the legend for themselves, but they cannot travel without a guardian and must bring along Julius, who isn't quite what he appears to be. This sweet and innocent movie about teen romance won't fail to bring a tear and a smile in its heart-tugging finale. The Oscar-winning score by Georges Delerue is magnificent. The film also received an Oscar nomination for Best Screenplay.

LITTLE SHOP OF HORRORS

1961 70m bw   ★★★
Comedy/Horror   /PG
Filmgroup

Jonathan Haze (Seymour Krelboin), Jackie Joseph (Audrey), Mel Welles (Gravis Mushnick), Jack Nicholson (Wilbur Force), Dick Miller (Fouch), Myrtle Vail (Winifred Krelboin), Laiola Wendorf (Mrs. Shiva)

p, Roger Corman; d, Roger Corman; w, Charles B. Griffith; ph, Arch R. Dalzell; ed, Marshall Neilan, Jr.; m, Fred Katz; art d, Daniel Haller

This is the ultimate Roger Corman super-low-budget cult favorite, also one of the funniest black comedies ever made. The plot details the sorry existence of a dim-witted schlepp, Haze, who works in Welles's Skid Row flower shop. To impress his girl, Joseph, Haze invents a flower he names Audrey, Jr. Soon the plant is all the rage among botanists. The only problem is that the little flower needs human blood to grow. After discovering this gruesome detail, and the fact that the plant can talk (when it's hungry it yells, "Feed me!"), Haze becomes slowly possessed by the flora and commits several murders in order to stop his plant's tummy from growling. With these feedings comes the plant's rapid growth; it soon overgrows the whole flower shop while bellowing "Feeeed meee!" in a monstrously loud and obnoxious voice. Poor Haze finds he can no longer handle his creation. While its story doesn't make for very funny reading, LITTLE SHOP OF HORRORS is a hilarious (and yes, quite silly) film filled to the brim with enough little vignettes and character quirks to sustain laughter throughout its brief 70-minute running time. Shot in two days by Corman, who was challenged by a studio employee to come up with a script and shoot a movie in the brief time remaining before the storefront set was torn down (it had been left standing from another production), LITTLE SHOP OF HORRORS is surprisingly well shot and performed. Corman contacted screenwriter Chuck Griffith from his other camp hit, A BUCKET OF BLOOD, and together they hacked out the killer plant story in less than a week. Aided by on-the-set inspiration, Corman, his crew, and the cast (including a very young Jack Nicholson in a side-splitting cameo as a masochistic dental patient begging for more pain) threw together a small masterpiece of taut, economical filmmaking. The story was revived in the 1980s as a very successful Off-Broadway musical, and a film version of the musical was released in 1986.

LITTLE SHOP OF HORRORS

1986 88m c   ★★★
Comedy/Horror/Musical   PG-13/PG
WB

Rick Moranis (Seymour Krelboin), Ellen Greene (Audrey), Vincent Gardenia (Mushnik), Steve Martin (Orin Scrivello), Tichina Arnold (Crystal), Tisha Campbell (Chiffon), Michelle Weeks (Ronette), James Belushi (Patrick Martin), John Candy (Wink Wilkinson), Christopher Guest (1st Customer)

p, David Geffen; d, Frank Oz; w, Howard Ashman (based on the musical stage play by Howard Ashman); ph, Robert Paynter (Panavision, Technicolor); ed, John Jympson; m, Alan Menken, Miles Goodman; prod d, Roy Walker; art d, Steven Spence; fx, Bran Ferren; chor, Pat Garrett; cos, Marit Allen

This is the multimillion-dollar movie version of the off-Broadway musical, which was based in turn on an old movie conceived and shot in a matter of days by Roger Corman. Although the plots (in which a carnivorous plant feeds on human flesh, causing its creator to kill to satisfy it) are virtually identical, much of the edge was taken off of the material in its transition from screen to stage to screen. The killer plant has been transformed into a being from outer space (rather than a warped hybrid created by the dimwitted Seymour in his basement). Big-budget and bloated, the film has none of the shabby charm of Corman's effort and is memorable only for a couple of decent tunes, a parade of star cameos, some impressive special effects, and a wonderful performance from Greene as Audrey. Conway's special effects involved several generations of Audrey II, from a potted plant to a mammoth 12.5-foot-tall creature that takes over the entire florist shop. It weighed, at the close, more than 2,000 pounds and used almost 12 miles of cable. The most remarkable aspect of the device were the lips, perfectly in sync with the singing and dialog. Although an impressive technical achievement, the film itself is a rather overblown and overhyped affair—which, for all its expensive excess, fails to recapture the spirit of the original. Nominations by the Academy for Best Song, "Mean Green Mother From Outer Space," and Best Visual Effects.

LITTLE THIEF, THE

1989 105m c   ★★½
Drama   R/15
Orly/Renn/Cine Cinq/Carrosse   (France)

Charlotte Gainsbourg (Janine Castang), Didier Bezace (Michel Davenne), Simon de la Brosse (Raoul), Raoul Billerey (Uncle Andre Rouleau), Chantal Banlier (Aunt Lea), Nathalie Cardone (Mauricette), Clotilde de Bayser (Severine Longuet), Philippe Deplanche (Jacques Longuet), Marion Grimault (Kebadian), Erick Deshors (Raymond)

p, Alain Vannier, Claude Berri; d, Claude Miller; w, Claude Miller, Annie Miller, Luc Beraud (based on the story by Francois Truffaut, Claude de Givray); ph, Dominique Chapuis (Fujicolor); ed, Albert Jurgenson; m, Alain Jomy; art d, Jean-Pierre Kohut-Svelko; cos, Jacqueline Bouchard

THE LITTLE THIEF stars Charlotte Gainsbourg as Janine Castang, who, as the film opens, is a rebellious 15-year-old struggling against the provincial strictures of life in her small French village after WWII. Her penchant for petty thievery has aroused the wrath of her aunt and uncle, who have cared for her since her flighty mother deserted them. Removed from school and put to work, Janine finds escape in the local cinemas, where she meets Michel Davenne (Didier Bezace), a mild-mannered, married choirmaster for whom she develops a convulsive passion. THE LITTLE THIEF's main character was originally conceived as part of Francois Truffaut's THE 400 BLOWS, but cut for reasons of length. Truffaut never forgot her, however. After his death, the task of making the film fell to Claude Miller, Truffaut's longtime production manager. The spirit of Truffaut is very much in evidence in THE LITTLE THIEF: the affection for the past, the concern with adolescent angst, the abiding love of cinema. What's lacking is his radiantly omniscient sense of humanity, not to mention his sureness of control with both performances and film technique. The film is diverting and moves along briskly, but is never really moving or compelling. Gangling Gainsbourg, with her hushed, sibilant voice, is the best thing in the film.

LITTLE VERA
(MALENKAYA VERA)
1988 110m c   ★★★½
Drama   /15
Gorky (U.S.S.R.)

Natalya Negoda *(Vera)*, Andrei Sokolov *(Sergei)*, Ludmila Zaitzeva *(Mother)*, Andrei Fomin *(Andrei)*, Alexander Alexeyev-Negreba *(Victor)*, Yuriy Nazarov *(Father)*, Alexandra Tabakova *(Christyakova)*, Alexander Mironov *(Tolik)*, Alexander Linkov *(Mikhail Petrovich)*

d, Vasily Pichul; w, Maria Khmelik; ph, Yefim Reznikov; ed, Elena Zabolockaja; m, Vladimir Matetsky; cos, Natalya Polyakh

Set in a provincial industrial city, LITTLE VERA focuses on the plight of a rebellious teenager (Negoda), who, much to her parents' dismay, seems wholly uninterested in her future after she graduates from secondary school. Both her father, Nazarov, a heavy-drinking truck driver, and her mother, Zaitzeva, a controller at a sewing factory, are anxious for her to begin training as a telephonist. They would also like to see her eventually marry her devoted boyfriend, who is off to join the navy. Negoda, however, isn't interested in either, and—almost always clad in a red-and-white striped jumper, black mini, fishnet stockings, and heels—is instead a good-time girl, hanging out in cafes, partying with friends, and toying with her lustful boyfriend. When a rumble erupts at a local rock concert (with Armenians playing the Sharks to the Russian Jets) and police arrive on the scene, the fleeing Negoda ends up with Sokolov, a handsome metallurgy student whose cooler-than-cool demeanor sweeps her off her feet. Before long they are sleeping together, and her parents, convinced Negoda has become a slut, summon their doctor son (Negreba) from Moscow to straighten out his sister. When he learns that she has taken up with his old friend Sokolov, a legendary ladies' man, Negreba also hits the roof. Negoda refuses to break off the relationship, and when she says she is pregnant (though it's relatively clear that she isn't), Sokolov agrees to marry her and moves in with her family. The problem is that he can't stand them and they don't like him. One night, Nazarov, plastered as usual, takes his abuse of Sokolov too far, and the younger man locks him in a bathroom. When Nazarov is let out, he impulsively stabs Sokolov, sending the latter to the hospital. In the days that follow, the family tries to persuade Negoda to lie to the police about the incident to protect her father, and, after much painful soul-searching, she does. Treated coolly by Sokolov during a hospital bedside visit, Negoda returns home and tries to kill herself. In a climax that is alternately emotionally high-pitched, capricious, and finally melancholy, Negreba happens upon his overdosed sister and saves her.

With an offbeat family-in-the-kitchen finale right out of MOONSTRUCK, LITTLE VERA is a far cry from the stridency of Soviet Realism, yet in its evocation of rank-and-file life it presents its own brand of kitchen-sink verisimilitude. Aided by marvelous performances and Maria Khmelik's well-crafted screenplay, director Vasily Pichul has fashioned an extraordinarily involving film that is as funny as it is poignant. Each of the principal actors establishes a clearly defined personality, transforming situations that are not inherently funny into scenes that are amusing and touching. Although his lighting is occasionally uneven, Pichul's handling of the camera is assured and inventive,

and the moodily photographed shots of the industrial landscape (particularly a slow-motion rendering of the harbor at night) used as a bridge between the story's episodes are particularly evocative. His pacing is equally skilled and the film seems considerably shorter than its more than two-hour length. Likewise, Pichul's direction of his actors is outstanding. When all is said and done, though, the most memorable thing about the film may be Little Vera herself, Natalya Negoda, whose captivating screen presence lingers long after the film has unspooled. Containing a sex scene that is tame by Western standards but that reportedly caused something of a stir in the Soviet Union and generated quite a lot of publicity for the film.

LITTLE WOMEN
1933 117m bw   ★★★★★
Drama   /U
RKO

Katharine Hepburn *(Jo)*, Joan Bennett *(Amy)*, Paul Lukas *(Prof. Fritz Bhaer)*, Edna May Oliver *(Aunt March)*, Jean Parker *(Beth)*, Frances Dee *(Meg)*, Henry Stephenson *(Mr. Laurence)*, Douglass Montgomery *(Laurie)*, John Lodge *(Brooke)*, Spring Byington *(Marmee)*

p, Kenneth MacGowan; d, George Cukor; w, Sarah Y. Mason, Victor Heerman (based on the novel by Louisa May Alcott); ph, Henry Gerrard; ed, Jack Kitchin; m, Max Steiner; art d, Van Nest Polglase; fx, Harry Redmond; cos, Walter Plunkett

This unabashedly sentimental adaptation of Louisa May Alcott's novel remains, to this day, an example of Hollywood's best filmmaking, as it tells the captivating Civil War-era story of four independent New England sisters—Jo (Katharine Hepburn), Amy (Joan Bennett), Meg (Frances Dee), and Beth (Jean Parker) March. Jo, who wants to leave home and become a writer, stays on for the good of the family, but when Meg plans to marry, Jo leaves for New York, fearing that the family will disintegrate. There she meets a professor who helps her with both her anger and her writing. Meanwhile, Amy falls in love with and marries Jo's old sweetheart (Douglass Montgomery). Beth, however, is dying, and Jo returns to be with her during her last days.

Sarah Mason and Victor Heerman's script called for great production values, and RKO provided them, foreshadowing David O. Selznick's opulent treatment of life on the Southern side of the Civil War, GONE WITH THE WIND. The sets, costumes, lighting, and direction by George Cukor all contribute greatly to this magnificent film, but the performances, especially Hepburn's, are what make the simple story so moving. There are laughs and tears aplenty in this movie, which presents a slice of American history in a way that children will find palatable. Released during the depths of the Depression, LITTLE WOMEN buoyed Americans' spirits. It still does.

LIVES OF A BENGAL LANCER, THE
1935 109m bw   ★★★★
Adventure/War   /U
Paramount

Gary Cooper *(Lt. Alan McGregor)*, Franchot Tone *(Lt. John Forsythe)*, Richard Cromwell *(Lt. Donald Stone)*, Guy Standing *(Col. Stone)*, C. Aubrey Smith *(Maj. Hamilton)*, Monte Blue *(Hamzulia Khan)*, Kathleen Burke *(Tania Volkanskaya)*, Colin Tapley *(Lt. Barrett)*, Douglas Dumbrille *(Mohammed Khan)*, Akim Tamiroff *(Emir)* p, Louis D. Lighton; d, Henry Hathaway; w, Waldemar Young, John Balderston, Achmed Abdullah, Grover Jones, William Slavens McNutt (based on the novel by Maj. Francis Yeats-Brown); ph, Charles Lang, Ernest B. Schoedsack; ed, Ellsworth Hoagland; m, Milan Roder; art d, Hans Dreier, Roland Anderson; chor, LeRoy Prinz; cos, Travis Banton

Set in northwest India, this rousing adventure film was hailed by many as the greatest war movie ever made at the time of its release. Under Henry Hathaway's adroit direction, Gary Cooper stars as 41st Bengal Lancers member Lt. McGregor, a seasoned frontier fighter who doesn't hesitate to speak his mind or violate orders—a man first and a soldier second. His commanding officer, Col. Stone (Sir Guy Standing), is his very opposite, a total military man who will soon be retiring. In order to keep alive the name of Stone in the regiment, a fellow officer, Maj. Hamilton (C. Aubrey Smith), has Stone's son (Richard Cromwell) transferred into the unit, along with another new officer, Lt. Forsythe (Franchot Tone). The two new arrivals get a quick initiation, as Col. Stone and British intelligence try to prevent a planned Indian uprising by blocking a local chieftain's attempt to steal two million rounds of ammunition from the friendly Emir of Gopal (Akim Tamiroff).

The script is filled with plenty of humor and builds two strong, honest friendships—McGregor and Forsythe have a great buddy rapport while the cold and stubborn Col. Stone opens up to his cub soldier son. The Indian atmosphere is lovingly captured by Hathaway's direction (his love of the exotic appears to have been heavily influenced by his association with Josef von Sternberg) and by Charles Lang and Ernest B. Schoedsack's photography (incorporating some stock footage previously shot by Schoedsack). While the glorification of British imperialism hangs over the picture, the portrayal of the Indians is fortunately less offensive than in other Hollywood films such as 1939's GUNGA DIN.

LIVING DAYLIGHTS, THE

1987   130m   c   ★★★½
Spy   PG
Eon/UA   (U.K.)

Timothy Dalton (James Bond), Maryam D'Abo (Kara Malovy), Jeroen Krabbe (Gen. Georgi Koskov), Joe Don Baker (Brad Whitaker), John Rhys-Davies (Gen. Leonid Pushkin), Art Malik (Kamran Shah), Andreas Wisniewski (Necros), Thomas Wheatley (Saunders), Desmond Llewelyn (Q), Robert Brown (M)

p, Albert R. Broccoli, Michael G. Wilson; d, John Glen; w, Richard Maibaum, Michael G. Wilson (based on a story by Ian Fleming); ph, Alec Mills (Panavision, Technicolor); ed, John Grover, Peter Davies; m, John Barry; prod d, Peter Lamont; art d, Terry Ackland-Snow; fx, John Richardson; cos, Emma Porteous

Celebrating the 25th year of the Bond series, THE LIVING DAYLIGHTS introduces the fourth actor to take on the role of 007, Timothy Dalton, a 40-year-old veteran of the English stage whose Bond is more human and serious than that of the wry Sean Connery and the droll Roger Moore. Scripters Richard Maibaum and Michael G. Wilson have also shifted the emphasis away from glitz and gadgetry and back to the business of spying. Bond is sent to Czechoslovakia to assist with the defection of Gen. Georgi Koskov (Jeroen Krabbe), a KGB higher-up, whose escape is accomplished in a specially designed vehicle that whisks him through the trans-Siberian natural gas pipeline to Austria. Meanwhile, Bond falls for the beautiful Kara Malovy (Maryam d'Abo), a cellist who is a victim of KGB intrigue, and later he

helps her make a breathtaking escape, ultimately using her priceless cello as a sled. Once in the West, Koskov is seemingly abducted by the KGB, but Bond suspects otherwise and eventually learns that the Soviet is in cahoots with Brad Whitaker (Joe Don Baker), a psychopathic American arms dealer who, unlike the standard Bond villain, is interested in becoming fabulously wealthy but not in ruling the world. Bond's danger-filled attempts to put an end to Whitaker's scheming take him and Kara from Vienna to Tangier and eventually into the middle of the war in Afghanistan. Made for $30 million, this feast for the eyes has more action than any of the other Bond films and is certainly one of the best of them. Dalton is an engaging Bond, d'Abo is coolly alluring, and Krabbe is the epitome of the double-dealing spy master. Only Baker disappoints, hamming up his villain. Director John Glen is an old hand at James Bond films, having worked on three other 007 movies. He knows this popular spy well and does him great service in this well-paced film.

LOCAL HERO

1983   111m   c   ★★★★½
Comedy   PG
Enigma/Goldcrest   (U.K.)

Burt Lancaster (Happer), Peter Riegert (Mac), Fulton Mackay (Ben), Denis Lawson (Urquhart), Norman Chancer (Moritz), Peter Capaldi (Oldsen), Rikki Fulton (Geddes), Alex Norton (Watt), Jenny Seagrove (Marina), Jennifer Black (Stella)

p, David Puttnam; d, Bill Forsyth; w, Bill Forsyth; ph, Chris Menges; ed, Michael Bradsell; m, Mark Knopfler; prod d, Roger Murray-Leach; art d, Richard James, Adrienne Atkinson, Frank Walsh, Ian Watson; fx, Wally Veevers

Charming, whimsical, and practically perfect, LOCAL HERO reminds us of the great pleasures that British comedy used to routinely provide. This is the greatest Ealing comedy never made: a quirky character comedy with a skillful use of location that is sweetly reminiscent of WHISKEY GALORE!. A discerning eye may even spot a wee bit of the magical Powell-Pressburger ethos as expressed in I KNOW WHERE I'M GOING. However the offbeat sensibility on display here is ultimately distinctively that of Scottish filmmaker Bill Forsyth (GREGORY'S GIRL, THAT SINKING FEELING, COMFORT AND JOY, HOUSEKEEPING).

Burt Lancaster gets star billing as the loony head of a huge oil company in Texas, a tycoon so ambivalent about his success that he has a psychiatrist (Norman Chancer) come in regularly and insult him. Bored with business success, astronomy has become his great passion. The true protagonist of the film is Mac (Peter Riegert), an ambitious young executive of the oil company, who is is dispatched to Scotland to buy an entire town so the company can drill for North Sea oil. An important side mission is to keep watching the sky for anything interesting. The utterly charming remote little coastal town is largely controlled by Urquhart (Dennis Lawson), a sharp but good-natured lawyer-innkeeper. Victor (Christopher Rozycki), a Soviet trawler captain, makes regular stops at the village, where Urquhart conducts sundry investments for him in real estate and securities. The obvious plot turn would be to show the Americans as nasty and rapacious, but it turns out that the Scots would be only too happy to depart the area if the price were right. Throughout the film, nothing is quite what it seems to Mac, and the denouement is wonderfully unexpected.

The Scottish landscape is gorgeous, soothing, and handsomely shot. The casting, down to the smallest role, is just right. Lancaster gives one of his best performances in a parody of the role he's played straight so many times before—the blustering industrial mogul. Scottish writer-director Bill Forsyth has outdone himself with this funny, touching, and original film. Don't miss this magical treat. (Incidentally this film served as a MAJOR source of inspiration for the hit CBS television series, "Northern Exposure.")

LODGER, THE
1944 84m bw ★★★★
Thriller /A
FOX

Merle Oberon (Kitty), George Sanders (John Garrick), Laird Cregar (The Lodger), Cedric Hardwicke (Robert Burton), Sara Allgood (Ellen), Aubrey Mather (Supt. Sutherland), Queenie Leonard (Daisy), David Clyde (Sgt. Bates), Helena Pickard (Anne Rowley), Lumsden Hare (Dr. Sheridan)

p, Robert Bassler; d, John Brahm; w, Barre Lyndon (based on the novel by Marie Belloc Lowndes); ph, Lucien Ballard; ed, J. Watson Webb; m, Hugo Friedhofer; art d, James Basevi, John Ewing; fx, Fred Sersen; chor, Kenny Williams

Cregar is absolutely chilling in this Jack the Ripper tale, perhaps the best film made about Bloody Jack. THE LODGER's re-creation of Victorian London is soaked with fog, with cobblestones sweating and gaslights flickering as blood-chilling screams pierce the night air and a dark figure goes running. Oberon is a beautiful singer whose parents, Allgood and Hardwicke, rent a room to Cregar. The mysterious lodger tells them he won't be joining them for breakfast, lunch, or dinner, because he works at night. During the night, Cregar slips out into the fog carrying a little black bag; in the early hours, he can be heard pacing back and forth in his rooms—which are always kept locked, and where he performs what he terms "experiments." Cregar eyes Oberon and fences with her friend Sanders, a Scotland Yard inspector developing new criminology techniques, but, in the end, he cannot resist killing the lovely Oberon, as he has killed so many others. Before he can murder her, however, the police and Sanders interrupt the attack and chase Cregar wildly through a theater. Trapped like a bear, salivating and maniacal, Cregar hurls himself through a huge window and into the Thames to drown rather than surrender.

This ending is not in keeping with that of the film's source material, the superlative novel written by Marie Belloc Lowndes. In addition, THE LODGER, unlike the novel, leaves no doubt that Cregar's character is Jack the Ripper. The huge actor is superb in this grand *film noir*; he and Sanders would almost repeat their parts in the similar HANGOVER SQUARE, also directed by John Brahm. (Only 28 at the time, Cregar longed to be a matinee idol and, shortly after the release of this film, went on a crash water diet and literally starved himself to death.) THE LODGER remakes the Alfred Hitchcock silent film starring Ivor Novello, and is probably better. Brahm's directs with a taut rein, the script is brilliant, the photography by Lucien Ballard (Oberon's husband-to-be) is a marvel of fluid action, and the whole is mightily enhanced by Hugo Friedhofer's strange and unnerving score.

LOLA
(DONNA DI VITA)
1961 90m bw ★★★
Drama /X
Rome-Paris-Euro Intl. (France/Italy)

Anouk Aimee (Lola), Marc Michel (Roland), Elina Labourdette (Mme. Desnoyers), Alan Scott (Frankie), Annie Duperoux (Cecile), Jacques Harden (Michel), Margo Lion (Jeanne, Michel's Mother), Catherine Lutz (Claire, the Waitress), Corinne Marchand (Daisy), Yvette Anziani (Mme. Frederique)

p, Carlo Ponti, Georges de Beauregard; d, Jacques Demy; w, Jacques Demy; ph, Raoul Coutard (Franscope); ed, Anne-Marie Cotret, Monique Teisseire; m, Michel Legrand, Johann Sebastian Bach, Wolfgang Amadeus Mozart, Carl Maria von Weber; art d, Bernard Evein

Free-flowing debut feature from French director Jacques Demy who, with his wife, director Agnes Varda, flourished during the New Wave. Because of its abundance of sweeping camera movement (superbly engineered by Raoul Coutard), the film has often been called a musical without music. (Demy would later go to Hollywood and make a real musical with Gene Kelly.) Aimee plays the title role, a cabaret singer who awaits the return of Harden, her husband who has been away for seven years. In the meantime she has a few affairs, her strongest affections going to childhood friend Michel. Michel has dreams of settling down with Aimee, but those are shattered when Harden returns and sweeps Aimee away in his glaring white Cadillac. The picture is filled with cinematic allusions (a fondness of French New Wave directors) to Robert Bresson, Gary Cooper, Max Ophuls (especially his camerawork), and Josef von Sternberg. Demy received a helping hand from Jean-Luc Godard, who offered his talents as a production consultant.

LOLA
1982 113m c ★★★½
Drama/War R/AA
Rialto/Trio (West Germany)

Barbara Sukowa (Lola), Armin Mueller-Stahl (Von Bohm), Mario Adorf (Schuckert), Mathias Fuchs (Esslin), Helga Feddersen (Hettich), Karin Baal (Lola's Mother), Ivan Desny (Wittich), Karl-Heinz von Hassel (Timmerding), Sonja Neudorfer (Mrs. Fink), Elisabeth Volkmann (Gigi)

p, Horst Wendlandt; d, Rainer Werner Fassbinder; w, Peter Marthesheimer, Pia Frohlich, Rainer Werner Fassbinder; ph, Xaver Schwarzenberger; ed, Juliane Lorenz; m, Peer Raben; art d, Rolf Zehetbauer; cos, Barbara Baum

The third installment of Rainer Werner Fassbinder's war trilogy, which he called "The Entire History of the German Federal Republic" (VERONIKA VOSS and THE MARRIAGE OF MARIA BRAUN being the other two parts), LOLA is set in the 1950s and stars Barbara Sukowa as a steamy cabaret singer who lives a double life. Her straight-arrow lover Armin Mueller-Stahl is a building inspector committed to fighting corruption, especially that of property-developer Mario Adorf. When Von Bohm sees Lola dancing at the Villa Frink, a decadent club/brothel, it's more than he can handle and his conflict threatens their romance. Shot before VERONIKA VOSS (the second part), LOLA was announced as the third installment with more to follow, though none ever did. (Fassbinder completed one other film, QUERELLE, before his untimely death in 1982.) Essentially an update of THE BLUE ANGEL, the film suffers from a skilled but less-than-memorable performance by Sukowa, who has nowhere near the presence of Marlene Dietrich or Fassbinder regular Hanna Schygulla.

LOLA MONTES

1955 110m c   ★★★★★
Drama   /A
Gamma/Florida/Union (France/West Germany)

Martine Carol (Lola Montes), Peter Ustinov (Circus Master), Anton Walbrook (Ludwig I, King of Bavaria), Ivan Desny (Lt. James), Will Quadflieg (Franz Liszt), Oskar Werner (Student), Lise Delamare (Mrs. Craigie), Henri Guisol (Maurice), Paulette Dubost (Josephine), Helena Manson (James' Sister)

d, Max Ophuls; w, Max Ophuls, Jacques Natanson, Franz Geiger, Annette Wademant (based on the unpublished novel La Vie Extraordinaire de Lola Montes by Cecil Saint-Laurent); ph, Christian Matras (CinemaScope, Eastmancolor); ed, Madeleine Gug; m, Georges Auric; art d, Jean d'Eaubonne, Willy Schatz; cos, Georges Annenkov, Marcel Escoffier

Andrew Sarris in 1963 dubbed this film the greatest ever made, and although he's noted for his quirky opinions, he's no fool. A masterpiece, LOLA MONTES is certainly director Max Ophuls' greatest achievement. In flashback, we take a fascinating look at the life of the passionate yet oddly passive title character (Carol, more perfect in the part than she could possibly have fathomed). Introduced by a New Orleans circus master (Ustinov), the aging Lola answers (or has answered for her) personal questions from the audience for a small fee. The ringmaster tells of her many romances throughout Europe, including one with Franz Liszt (Quadflieg) and another with the king of Bavaria (Walbrook). In the last scene, Lola (who throughout has been made to perform various acts like a well-trained seal) stands atop a high platform, preparing for a dangerous jump. Her health is as precarious as her position, yet the ringmaster removes the safety net. The finale is unforgettable.

Along with Michael Powell's BLACK NARCISSUS, this is one of the most gorgeous films ever shot in color. Eastmancolor generally pales beside Technicolor; leave it to Ophuls to make the most of it. Ditto the use of CinemaScope, which Ophuls didn't want and tried to negate by using pillars and curtains at the edges of the frame. The effect is to frame the whole affair as a performance, and Ophuls' innate visual flair makes shot after shot (e.g. the descending chandeliers at the opening) a stunning use of widescreen. He even knows when to ditch both resources, as Lola's most intimate moments are signaled with a ghostly blue monochrome and a tight closeup with most of the frame in black. His customary genius with the camera has rarely been on better display, as he dizzyingly dollies 360 degrees around the trapped, immobile Lola while the exploitative ringmaster spins her platform. Never cutting when camera movement will do, Ophuls tilts, tracks and cranes magnificently, embodying Lola's flashback motto, "For me, life is movement." By contrast, the overwhelmingly cluttered mise en scene of the circus all but smothers the degraded courtesan.

Carol doesn't appear young enough as the teen-aged Lola nor does she look really ravaged at the finale, but her masklike quality allows Ophuls a great chance to project, indulging the French fondness for casting Woman as Cinema. Wolbrook is quietly heartrending as the aging monarch, and Werner, as a young student and sex interlude for Lola, displays the promise he would later fulfill so well. Top honors, though, go to the magnificent Ustinov, who, two Oscars elsewhere notwithstanding, has never done anything better. Both heartless and tender to Lola, abusive and always on the verge of falling in love, his rueful expression and biting wit speak volumes that otherwise never surface. A film whose power is in the image itself, the endlessly

amazing LOLA MONTES explores the magic (and the cost) of illusion as few films have ever done.

LOLITA

1962 152m bw   ★★★★
Drama   /X
Seven Arts/A.A./Anya/Trans World (U.S./U.K.)

James Mason (Humbert Humbert), Sue Lyon (Lolita Haze), Shelley Winters (Charlotte Haze), Peter Sellers (Clare Quilty), Marianne Stone (Vivian Darkbloom), Diana Decker (Jean Farlow), Jerry Stovin (John Farlow), Gary Cockrell (Dick), Suzanne Gibbs (Mona Farlow), Roberta Shore (Lorna)

p, James B. Harris; d, Stanley Kubrick; w, Vladimir Nabokov (based on the novel by Nabokov); ph, Oswald Morris; ed, Anthony Harvey; m, Nelson Riddle; art d, Bill Andrews; cos, Gene Coffin

A fascinating if problematic early film from Stanley Kubrick, perhaps the most obsessive of the great auteurs of the 1960s, made just on the cusp of a run of cinematic masterpieces. Here Vladimir Nabakov adapts his own controversial satirical novel about the obsessive love a British middle aged professor develops for a 12-year-old girl. While the novel outraged many bluenoses, the film advances the age of the "nymphet" to about 15 thereby neutralizing much of of the controversy. It's quite long—too long—possibly as a result of having Nabokov do his own screen adaptation. Nabakov's novels are so intensely concerned with language that one would expect that they would be particularly difficult to translate to the screen. LOLITA, a great grey comedy of the 1950s, succeeds in carefully setting up and knocking down the shibboleths of the silent generation.

James Mason is the smitten professor, Humbert Humbert, in love with the American girl, Lolita (Sue Lyon). Shelly Winters is the vulgar mother with misguided intellectual aspirations who is attracted to Humbert. The ever resourceful Peter Sellers, with a great American accent and a succession of disguises, is a standout as Quilty. The scene in which he explains himself to Mason is a small masterpiece of the acting art. Mason and Winters are less showy but equally impressive while the young Lyons, sadly, is only barely adequate.

The film is not particularly shocking or titillating; the most erotic scene in the film is a pedicure. Kubrick exhibited great subtlety (he had to, or they'd have given this one a hard time in the theaters)—perhaps too much subtlety. The script was nominated for an Oscar.

LONELINESS OF THE LONG DISTANCE RUNNER, THE

1962 104m bw   ★★★★
Drama   /15
Woodfall/Bryanston/Seven Arts (U.K.)

Tom Courtenay (Colin Smith), Michael Redgrave (The Governor), Avis Bunnage (Mrs. Smith), Peter Madden (Mr. Smith), James Bolam (Mike), Julia Foster (Gladys), Topsy Jane (Audrey), Dervis Ward (Detective), Raymond Dyer (Gordon), Alec McCowen (Brown)

p, Tony Richardson; d, Tony Richardson; w, Alan Sillitoe (based on his story); ph, Walter Lassally; ed, Anthony Gibbs; m, John Addison; prod d, Ralph Brinton; art d, Ted Marshall; cos, Sophie Harris

It was considered chic among cinephiles in the 1960s to denigrate British stage and film director Tony Richardson, but on balance he was responsible for as many important British films in these years as anyone else. One of the best of the British Angry Young Man films, THE LONELINESS OF THE LONG DISTANCE

RUNNER concerns Courtenay, an ill-educated youth who is sentenced to a reformatory after robbing a bakery. The borstal's governor, Redgrave, a great believer in the rehabilitative powers of sports, is delighted to learn that Courtenay is a natural distance runner and encourages him to train for a big meet with a local public school, promising him special privileges in exchange for a victory. Most of the film is taken up with Courtenay's training, during which he flashes back to the events and relationships that have brought him to this point in his life. When the big race finally arrives, Courtenay easily outclasses his competitors, but at the finish line he shocks the governor with an unexpected act of defiance. Adapted by Alan Sillitoe from his own short story and masterfully directed by Richardson, this poignant film was also the auspicious film debut of Courtenay, whose excellent performance earned him the British Academy's Most Promising Newcomer award.

LONELY ARE THE BRAVE

1962 107m bw   ★★★★
Western   /A
Universal

Kirk Douglas (Jack Burns), Gena Rowlands (Jerri Bondi), Walter Matthau (Sheriff Johnson), Michael Kane (Paul Bondi), Carroll O'Connor (Hinton), William Schallert (Harry), Karl Swenson (Rev. Hoskins), George Kennedy (Guitierrez), Dan Sheridan (Deputy Glynn), Bill Raisch ("One Arm")

p, Edward Lewis; d, David Miller; w, Dalton Trumbo (based on the novel Brave Cowboy by Edward Abbey); ph, Philip Lathrop (Panavision); ed, Leon Barsha, Edward Mann; m, Jerry Goldsmith; art d, Alexander Golitzen, Robert E. Smith

Dalton Trumbo wrote this elegy to the western. Kirk Douglas gives one of his finest performances as an out-of-place cowboy in the modern west—almost like a time traveller. The theme of the film is eloquently set up by the opening of the film in which we see Douglas reclining beneath a clear and spacious western sky. The peace and quiet is suddenly disrupted by the sound of a jet plane passing overhead. This brings a wry smile to the old cowboy's face. He rides his horse into Albuquerque to visit friends Kane and Rowlands. Rowlands tells him that her husband has been jailed for helping Mexicans enter the US illegally. Douglas starts a brawl in a saloon to get put into jail; there Douglas offers his friend Kane help in breaking out, but Kane tells Douglas that he wants to serve his brief time, intends to play out his hand with the law, and refuses to become a fugitive. Douglas is hurt but undaunted. He breaks out himself and heads for the hills, pursued by the compassionate technocratic sheriff Matthau and a posse.

Douglas is superb as the cowboy who will not yield to the modern world. Miller's direction is excellent, this being the finest film in his generally ineven career. Matthau is also convincing as the understanding sheriff who tries his best to capture a man he does not want to see locked up. Lathrop's sharp black-and-white photography and Goldsmith's evocative score add measurably to this outstanding production. There is one particularly memorable scene as Douglas and his good old horse attempt to cross a busy highway with the eighteen wheelers barrelling by. It will stay with you forever.

LONELY PASSION OF JUDITH HEARNE, THE

1988 110m c   ★★★
Romance   R/15
HandMade (U.K.)

Maggie Smith (Judith Hearne), Bob Hoskins (James Madden), Wendy Hiller (Aunt D'Arcy), Marie Kean (Mrs. Rice), Ian McNeice (Bernard Rice), Alan Devlin (Father Quigley), Rudi Davies (Mary), Prunella Scales (Moira O'Neill), Aine Ni Mhuiri (Edie Marinan), Sheila Reid (Miss Friel)

p, Peter Nelson, Richard Johnson; d, Jack Clayton; w, Peter Nelson (based on the novel by Brian Moore); ph, Peter Hannan (Fuji Color); ed, Terry Rawlings; m, Georges Delerue; prod d, Michael Pickwoad; cos, Elizabeth Waller

In this moving film based on the novel by Moore, Smith plays a lonely, aging Irish spinster whose occasional bouts with the bottle lead her from boardinghouse to boardinghouse. At one such residence, she meets Hoskins, who is middle-aged, single, and—in Judith's eyes—worldly and sophisticated. Her pursuit of him, however, proves to have devastating consequences. Bleak and disquieting, THE LONELY PASSION OF JUDITH HEARNE is nevertheless a finely acted, gripping film. Smith, the epitome of British propriety, is just about perfect as the abandoned woman, and Hoskins is just as effective as the sleazy, alienated loser. The pace may be slow, but the film is both disturbing and thought provoking.

LONG DAY'S JOURNEY INTO NIGHT

1962 174m bw   ★★★★★
Drama   /A
Landau

Katharine Hepburn (Mary Tyrone), Ralph Richardson (James Tyrone, Sr.), Jason Robards, Jr. (James Tyrone, Jr.), Dean Stockwell (Edmund Tyrone), Jeanne Barr (Cathleen)

p, Ely Landau, Jack J. Dreyfus, Jr.; d, Sidney Lumet; w, (based on the play by Eugene O'Neill); ph, Boris Kaufman; ed, Ralph Rosenblum; m, Andre Previn; prod d, Richard Sylbert; art d, Richard Sylbert; cos, Motley

O'Neill's greatest play is brought to the screen with an overpowering wealth of talent: Hepburn, Richardson, and Robards giving magnificent, once-in-a-lifetime performances as members of the doomed Tyrone family. The difference between JOURNEY and other O'Neill is it's heavy claustrophobia is offset by pervading viciousness and a sense of disappointment that is perhaps universal. Everyone has pockets of lost chances in their lives; the playwright described JOURNEY as "a play of old sorrow, written in tears and blood."

The setting is one long, long day and night in the year 1912 at the Tyrone summer home in New London, Connecticut. The senior Tyrone, Richardson, once a fine Shakespearean actor, has in recent years been playing the same role over and over again in a commercial play—simply for the money. Reinforcing his stinginess is his fear, as he enters old age, of dying broke. His wife, Hepburn, has just returned from a sanitarium. She is all lady, an Irish Catholic with strong moral principles, but she is also strangely withdrawn. Elder son Robards has attempted to follow his father into the acting profession but, failing miserably, takes solace in drink. He has by now become an alcoholic cynic who would rather destroy all around him than show the deep affections he feels. Younger son Stockwell is recovering from tuberculosis and has himself spent time in a sanitarium—a second-rate institution that his tightwad father sent him to in order to save money. Stockwell is a budding writer who struggles not only with his craft but with profound, contradictory feelings toward his family. Richardson dwells on the past as he recalls his theatrical triumphs of yesterday, eloquently trying to impress his amused sons with his stature in the theater. Hepburn, meanwhile, spends lengthy periods of time in her room, a fact that clearly is beginning to unnerve Richardson. As the day wears on, Richardson, to spare expense, insists that only a few lights be turned on. He, like his wife and elder son, cannot control his quirks. Each character struggles against his or her secret vice for the sake of a family that exists in name only.

Of the cast, Hepburn takes it. Where she takes it is in her transistion points —from girlish coquette remembering her apple-blossom youth to maddened dope fiend, from loving mother to mindless creature groping for identity. This is where Hepburn departed once and for all from delicious commedienne into legendary tragidienne. Richardson's performance is just right: his spareness as an actor incredibly personifies a miser and for once the camera captures Robards wildness, his lunging danger, before alcohol crabbed him into permanent grit. There's nothing wrong with Stockwell's performance. It's just that we know he's O'Neill, a heavy task for a young actor. Obviously, it's a part for an older performer who looks younger. We can't help but brood that Montgomery Clift was too ruined and prematurely old for the role.

Hepburn took on the role of the addicted mother for a pittance and tried to convince Spencer Tracy to play the father, but he adamantly refused. Tracy was exhausted after working in JUDGMENT AT NUREMBERG and told producer Landau: "Look, Kate's the lunatic—she's the one who goes off and appears at Stratford in Shakespeare—'Much Ado' and all that stuff. I don't believe in that nonsense. I'm a movie actor." The $500,000 he asked for to appear in the movie was, of course, impossible on Landau's limited budget. Richardson was brought in just after Hepburn agreed to play the role. It's probably her finest portrait. The film, shot on location in New York City, followed the superb O'Neill play almost word for word. O'Neill began writing the play in 1939, and finished it the following year. His father, James O'Neill, had once been an accomplished Shakespearean actor but became successful and rich playing "The Count of Monte Cristo," season after season. His wife, O'Neill's mother, was addicted to morphine from the time of O'Neill's birth, and his brother Jamie was a would-be actor who died prematurely of acute alcoholism. According to O'Neill's will, the play was not to be produced until 25 years after his death, which occurred in 1951, but his widow, Carlotta, waited until 1956 to let it be performed. "Long Day's Journey into Night," starring Fredric March, Florence Eldridge, Robards, and Bradford Dillman, became an overnight classic.

To experience the majesty of the film, you must absolutely bypass the shortened 136 minute version, and wait for the uncut 170 minute one. You won't be sorry. Or bored.

LONG GOOD FRIDAY, THE

1982   105m   c   ★★★½
Crime   R/18
Calendar/Black Lion   (U.K.)

Bob Hoskins (Harold), Helen Mirren (Victoria), Eddie Constantine (Charlie), Dave King (Parky), Bryan Marshall (Harris), George Coulouris (Gus), Derek Thompson (Jeff), Pierce Brosnan (1st Irishman), Charles Cork (Eric), Billy Cornelius (Pete)

p, Barry Hanson; d, John Mackenzie; w, Barrie Keefe; ph, Phil Meheux; ed, Mike Taylor; m, Francis Monkman; art d, Vic Symonds

This English gangster thriller stars Bob Hoskins as a mob boss whose world crumbles violently. During the Easter weekend, Hoskins tries to work a massive land deal connected with the 1988 London Olympics with his American counterparts. Business is interrupted when his buildings are bombed and men are

murdered. Hoskins goes after his rival gang bosses only to learn they have had no part in the "hits." The gangster soon finds out the IRA is behind the violence because one of Hoskins' men stole protection money from the organization. Hoskins sets out to get revenge, but soon learns that he has grossly underestimated his opponent. This was the film that brought Hoskins to the attention of American audiences, and he is terrific. His performance as a brutal, bullying mob boss is reminiscent of the American gangster films of the 1930s and 1940s, and his work is equal to James Cagney, Edward G. Robinson, Paul Muni and the other giants of that era. In addition to Hoskins's dynamic performance, the film features a taut, violent story and creates an atmosphere that vividly captures the British criminal milieu. Eddie Constantine makes a welcome appearance as the key US negotiator in the criminal deal.

LONG GOODBYE, THE

1973   112m   c   ★★★
Crime   R/18
UA

Elliott Gould (Philip Marlowe), Nina Van Pallandt (Eileen Wade), Sterling Hayden (Roger Wade), Mark Rydell (Marty Augustine), Henry Gibson (Dr. Verringer), David Arkin (Harry), Jim Bouton (Terry Lennox), Warren Berlinger (Morgan), Jo Ann Brody (Jo Ann Eggenweiler), Jack Knight (Hood)

p, Jerry Bick; d, Robert Altman; w, Leigh Brackett (based on the novel by Raymond Chandler); ph, Vilmos Zsigmond (PanaVision, Technicolor); ed, Lou Lombardo; m, John Williams; cos, Kent James, Marjorie Wahl

Director Robert Altman offended the fans of Raymond Chandler's Philip Marlowe character by completely subverting the role here. Elliott Gould plays the usually hard-boiled detective as something of a well-meaning bumbler, and while it may not be Chandler, it is a moody and entertaining film. The film is set in Los Angeles where Gould's troubles begin when he gives his friend, Bouton (a former baseball pitcher), a ride to Tijuana. Upon his return, he learns that Bouton is wanted by police for the brutal murder of his wife. Convinced of his friend's innocence, Gould begins his own investigation of the crime. His inquiry first leads him to the beautiful Van Pallandt, with whom Bouton was having an affair. Her husband, Hayden, is a once-successful author who is suffering a severe case of writer's block, which has turned him into an alcohlic. Somewhat batty and insanely jealous regarding his wife, Hayden becomes Gould's prime suspect in the killing. Fueling his suspicion is the bizarre relationship Hayden has with the sinister Gibson, an alleged psychologist who has been treating him. The case is complicated further by vicious hood Rydell, to whom Boulton owed a large amount of cash. Rydell is certain Gould has the cash and goes to great lengths to show the detective he better fork it over if he does have it. As Gould sifts through the clues, he is sure he has solved the case—but his instincts are wrong, and the trail leads to a suprising and somewhat improbable conclusion.

Certainly Gould shatters the Marlowe mold in this film, playing the detective as a wisecracking, disheveled eccentric, much the same character he portrayed in other Altman films, M*A*S*H and CALIFORNIA SPLIT. From that viewpoint, Chandler's fans had reason to be upset, but Altman's approach to the *film noir* crime drama is not without its good points. Gould's persona is an amusing counterpoint to the traditional tough-guy detective who always knew exactly what to say and do and who never ran across a situation he couldn't handle. Gould's Marlowe is an often bewildered investigator, who nevertheless maintains the character's strong sense of morality in the midst of a cruel world. Gould gets admirable support from the volcanic Hayden, who superbly conveys a character rendered impotent by the loss of his talent. Also notable is Gibson, whose work for Altman in this film and NASHVILLE revealed an acting talent that sadly was never put to use by other filmmakers. Rydell, who had directed such films as THE REIVERS and THE COWBOYS and would go on to direct ON GOLDEN POND, is chilling as the brutal Augustine. The scene in which, to show Marlowe he means business, he smashes a Coke bottle across the face of his girlfriend (Brody) is startling in its violence and thoroughly depicts the character's ruthlessness. Altman's penchant for offbeat casting is in evidence with appearances of Van Pallandt and Bouton. Van Pallandt achieved much notoriety at the time as the mistress of Clifford Irving, whose faked biography of reclusive billionaire Howard Hughes had landed him in prison. This was her screen debut, and she had a limited career with appearances in other Altman films such A WEDDING and QUINTET, as well as AMERICAN GIGOLO. As for Bouton, he had offended the baseball establishment with his bawdy biography *Ball Four,* and his brief appearance here showed his acting abilities were decidedly slim, which explains why this was his only film appearance. Look for Arnold Schwarzenegger in a small role as one of Rydell's hoods. Billed as Arnold Strong, he had made his film debut in HERCULES IN NEW YORK, this was his second film. In his next film, STAY HUNGRY, he would begin using his real name.

LONG, HOT SUMMER, THE

1958   115m   c   ★★★★
Drama   /15
FOX

Paul Newman *(Ben Quick),* Joanne Woodward *(Clara Varner),* Anthony Franciosa *(Jody Varner),* Orson Welles *(Will Varner),* Lee Remick *(Eula Varner),* Angela Lansbury *(Minnie Littlejohn),* Richard Anderson *(Alan Stewart),* Sarah Marshall *(Agnes Stewart),* Mabel Albertson *(Mrs. Stewart),* J. Pat O'Malley *(Ratliff)*

p, Jerry Wald; d, Martin Ritt; w, Irving Ravetch, Harriet Frank, Jr. (based on "Barn Burning," "The Spotted Horse," and the novel *The Hamlet* by William Faulkner); ph, Joseph La Shelle (CinemaScope, DeLuxe Color); ed, Louis Loeffler; m, Alex North; art d, Lyle Wheeler, Maurice Ransford; fx, L.B. Abbott; cos, Adele Palmer

Filmmakers have often found it difficult to bring William Faulkner's dense novels to the screen, but here director Martin Ritt and writers Harriet Frank, Jr. and Irving Ravetch opted for a less-than-faithful adaptation of the author's work, and the results were excellent. Newman plays a Mississippi man with a bad temper, no doubt inherited from his father who was known to burn down barns to settle disputes. He drifts into a small town which is bossed by Welles, a wealthy landowner. Franciosa is Welles's son, a weak man nothing like his father. Franciosa is married to Remick, who is dedicated to him but openly wishes he would stand up for himself. Rounding out Welles's family is feisty Woodward, already considered to be an old maid by many in the town, but one who stubbornly maintains her independence. Newman becomes a sharecropper on Welles's property and Welles is impressed by the young man's toughness. He begins to think Newman would make a fine son-in-law, a man much better suited to running his empire than his own son. Woodward is seeing Anderson, a man totally dominated by his mother, Albertson. Welles attempts to get his daughter and Newman together, but she rebels. It's not that she doesn't find Newman attractive, she just resents being told what to do. She also thinks that

Newman is beneath her station and finds him a bit vulgar. When Franciosa becomes aware of his father's intentions, he traps the old man in a barn and sets it on fire, thinking Newman will be blamed for the crime. As the fire burns, Franciosa has a change of heart and rescues Welles. Woodward eventually succumbs to Newman's charms, while Lansbury, Welles's long-time mistress, finally coaxes Welles to walk down the aisle with her.

The pairing of Newman, on loan from Warner Bros., and Fox's rising star Woodward, was pure magic. She had already won an Oscar for her work in THE THREE FACES OF EVE, while Newman had impressed in films such as THE LEFT-HANDED GUN and SOMEBODY UP THERE LIKES ME, but wasn't quite a star yet. With this film and CAT ON A HOT TIN ROOF (for which he received his first Oscar nomination), also released in 1958, Newman quickly became one of Hollywood's hottest stars. There was plenty of electricity on the screen in his scenes with Woodward, and, evidently, off screen too, as they were married in 1958. Only 42 at the time, Welles looked much older and, though he overplays the role at times, was well cast as the tyrannical landowner. In fact, the whole cast is worthy of praise. Lansbury, who *always* played characters much older than she was, is delightful as Welles's mistress, tossing off many of the film's best lines. Remick had made her film debut the year before in A FACE IN THE CROWD, and she also got a big boost from this film, following it up with ANATOMY OF A MURDER. Franciosa had the year before been nominated for a Best Actor Oscar for his role in A HATFUL OF RAIN and again received good notices here. However, his film career stalled, and he moved into television, starring in such series as "Valentine's Day" and "The Name of the Game." The script was literate, sharp, and humorous. Ritt and screenwriters Ravetch and Frank would team two more times with Newman, first for HUD, one of Newman's best films, and again for HOMBRE.

LONG RIDERS, THE

1980   99m   c   ★★★★
Western   R/18
UA

David Carradine *(Cole Younger),* Keith Carradine *(Jim Younger),* Robert Carradine *(Bob Younger),* James Keach *(Jesse James),* Stacy Keach *(Frank James),* Dennis Quaid *(Ed Miller),* Randy Quaid *(Clell Miller),* Kevin Brophy *(John Younger),* Harry Carey, Jr. *(George Arthur),* Christopher Guest *(Charlie Ford)*

p, Tim Zinnemann; d, Walter Hill; w, Bill Bryden, Steven Phillip Smith, James Keach, Stacy Keach; ph, Ric Waite (Technicolor); ed, David Holden; m, Ry Cooder; prod d, Jack T. Collis; art d, Peter Romero; chor, Katina Sawidis; cos, Bobbie Mannix

THE LONG RIDERS is a superb, nitty-gritty retelling of the story of the James-Younger gang, the most notorious American bandits of the 19th century. In a unique bit of casting, the Younger, James, Miller, and Ford brothers are played by the brothers Carradine, Keach, Quaid, and Guest. The film opens with the band led by Jesse James (James Keach) and Cole Younger (David Carradine) robbing a bank. In episodic fashion, it then follows the various gang members as they go their separate ways, reuniting later for a disastrous attempt to rob a bank in Northfield, Minnesota. THE LONG RIDERS is one of the last great westerns made in America, directed tautly by Walter Hill from an excellent, well-researched script. The cinematography by Ric Waite is magnificent, the period is beautifully captured, and Ry Cooder's outstanding score nicely incorporates folk music of the era. The whole feeling of this film is one of antiquity, an atmosphere marvelously created by Hill and enhanced by a superb cast. James Keach realistically plays Jesse James; Stacy Keach is perfect as the puzzled, puritanical, but loyal Frank; David Carradine is excellent as the confident, bold Cole Younger; Keith and Robert Carradine are very good as the other Younger brothers; and Nicholas and Christopher Guest epitomize the treacherous Ford siblings. Though THE LONG RIDERS does not spare the violence, this is a must for any adult western fan.

LONG SHOT

1981   85m   c/bw   ★★★
Drama   PG/AA
Mithras   (U.K.)

Charles Gormley (Charlie), Neville Smith (Neville), Ann Zelda (Anne), David Stone (A Distributor), Suzanne Danielle (Sue), Ron Taylor (American Director), Wim Wenders (Another Director), Stephen Frears (Biscuit Man), Jim Haines (Professor of Sexual Politics), Maurice Bulbulian (French-Canadian Director)

p, Maurice Hatton; d, Maurice Hatton; w, Maurice Hatton, Eoin McCann; ph, Michael Davis, Michael Dodds, Ivan Strasburg, Maurice Hatton, Teo Davis; ed, Howard Sharp; m, Terry Dougherty, Antonio Vivaldi

An interesting independent film that deals with business and other hurdles one must go through to make a film. Most of the people acting in the film are nonactors: Gormley, who plays a producer, is a film producer, and directors Wenders and Boorman depict directors. Most of the film was shot during the 1977 Edinburgh Festival using part improvisation and part scripted scenes. Gormley plays a Scottish producer trying to get his so-called commercial film "Gulf and Western" off the ground. A somewhat bleak picture that should be seen by anyone who ever thought they'd like to make a movie.

LONG VOYAGE HOME, THE

1940   105m   bw   ★★★★★
Drama   /A
Argosy

John Wayne (Ole Olsen), Thomas Mitchell (Aloysius Driscoll), Ian Hunter (Smitty), Barry Fitzgerald (Cocky), Wilfrid Lawson (Captain), Mildred Natwick (Freda), John Qualen (Axel Swanson), Ward Bond (Yank), Joe Sawyer (Davis), Arthur Shields (Donkeyman)

p, Walter Wanger; d, John Ford; w, Dudley Nichols (based on the plays "The Moon of the Caribbees," "In the Zone," "Bound East for Cardiff," "The Long Voyage Home," by Eugene O'Neill); ph, Gregg Toland; ed, Sherman Todd; m, Richard Hageman; art d, James Basevi; fx, Ray Binger, R.T. Layton

Based on four one-act plays by Eugene O'Neill, THE LONG VOYAGE HOME is a grim, powerful saga of merchant seamen, their hardscrabble lives, and their hopes for a better future. John Ford's film is a magnificent portrayal of life at sea and of the struggle not only to survive, but also to remain civilized, during the early days of WWII. As the film opens, the crew of the tramp freighter SS Glencairn is enjoying a last night of liberty on a Caribbean island, attending a party with local women that ends in a brawl, after which the men stagger back to the freighter. Only Hunter has remained on board, refusing to join the raucous festivities. At Baltimore, the ship takes on a load of dynamite to be delivered to England, a cargo that makes the crew jumpy; each sailor knows that German U-boats lurk in the waters all around England, and that a single torpedo will blow the Glencairn to bits. Among the crew is Wayne, a good-hearted young Swede whose only ambition is to make enough money to return home and settle down with his family on a small farm. To that end he

is protected by his fellow seamen—especially Mitchell, Bond, Fitzgerald, and Qualen—all inveterate sailors who share Wayne's longing to make a home, but also know they will only briefly return to the land. During the Atlantic crossing, a raging storm engulfs the freighter. Bond is mortally injured in an accident, and dies painfully below deck as his friends stand by to comfort him. Ever-watchful for submarines and increasingly paranoid, the crew members see a light flicker on and off from a porthole below decks and conclude that someone on board is sending signals, perhaps to a U-boat. Investigating, the crewmen find Hunter in their quarters, acting suspiciously. Fitzgerald accuses him of being a spy, telling the others that he has seen Hunter writing in secret and storing his missives in a locked tin box. Over Hunter's protests, Mitchell and the others break into the box and read a letter enclosed therein, discovering—to their acute embarrassment and Hunter's agony—that is written to Hunter's wife, who has left him because of his excessive drinking. Sheepishly, the men leave him to his misery. Later, Hunter is killed when a German plane strafes the ship. Despite this attack, the Glencairn arrives safely in England, where crew members vow to put Wayne on a ship to Sweden, determined that nothing will waylay the youth this time. Qualen, a fellow Swede who has looked after Wayne through this voyage and others, sews Wayne's back pay into the lining of his coat and pins his ticket home to the lining. The crew then goes on its usual pub crawl, with Wayne tagging along, allowed to take one "ginger beer." The seamen become inebriated and fail to notice Natwick, a prostitute, taking Wayne aside and insisting that he join her for a drink. Politely, he complies, sipping another ginger beer, which she has dosed with a knockout drug. She waits, distracted but pretending to listen to Wayne's simple stories about home, until the drug takes effect. Once Wayne is out, Kerrigan—a stooge for the cutthroat owners of the hated ship the Amindra—maneuvers the drugged Wayne on board the vessel, which must shanghai sailors to fill its necessary crew requirements. When Mitchell and the others learn that Wayne has been shanghaied, they storm the Amindra and a savage fight ensues. Wayne is rescued from the sinister ship, but Mitchell is struck over the head and kept on board in Wayne's place, unknown to the others. Wayne is sent safely back home the next day, but a newspaper (unseen by the crew) reports that the Amindra has been sunk by U-boats and all hands on board lost.

THE LONG VOYAGE HOME is one of Ford's masterpieces, a startlingly well-photographed movie taken from four short works by O'Neill (in fact, Mitchell and Bond are essentially playing the same character as two different roles). The contrasting lighting, the wonderful atmospherics at sea and on the land, and the configuration of shots were basically accomplished by cinematographer Gregg Toland. As Wayne later told Maurice Zolotow, author of the Wayne biography Shooting Star, "Usually it would be Mr. Ford who helped the cinematographer get his compositions for maximum effect—bring out what was good in any setup, help him light it—but in this case it was Gregg Toland who helped Mr. Ford. LONG VOYAGE is about as beautifully photographed a movie as there ever has been." The film earned an Oscar nomination for Best Cinematography, along with nominations for Best Picture (losing to REBECCA), Best Screenplay, Best Editing, and Best Special Effects.

Wayne himself initially resisted Ford's instruction that he play his character with a Swedish accent, fearing he would appear comic. But he had the actress Osa Massen help him with the accent, and when he first employed it he was congratulated by Ford for getting it right. (Wayne neglected to tell Ford his coach was Danish.) Wayne gives a reserved and very effective performance, convincingly playing a simple man who is not a simpleton. Mitchell also does a wonderful job as an old salt, and Hunter is moving as the tortured seaman who has ruined his life on land. There is a pervasive air of gloom about THE LONG VOYAGE HOME: the sun is always behind the clouds and the threat of death lurks everywhere (especially on land). Although the seamen yearn for their long-lost homes, they know that, except for Wayne, they will never leave the sea, but will sail on until they are buried beneath the waves. THE LONG VOYAGE HOME was playwright O'Neill's favorite film; Ford gave him a print of the movie and he ran it over and over again until he wore it out.

LONG WALK HOME, THE

1991 97m c	★★★
Drama/Historical	PG/15
New Visions Pictures	

Sissy Spacek *(Miriam Thompson)*, Whoopi Goldberg *(Odessa Cotter)*, Dwight Schultz *(Norman Thompson)*, Ving Rhames *(Herbert Cotter)*, Dylan Baker *(Tunker Thompson)*, Erika Alexander *(Selma Cotter)*, Lexi Faith Randall *(Mary Catherine)*, Richard Habersham *(Theodore Cotter)*, Jason Weaver *(Franklin Cotter)*, Mary Steenburgen *(Narration)*

p, Howard W. Koch, Jr., Dave Bell; d, Richard Pearce; w, John Cork; ph, Roger Deakins; ed, Bill Yahraus; m, George Fenton; prod d, Blake Russell; cos, Shay Cunliffe

A modest but effective period piece, THE LONG WALK HOME takes as its setting the Montgomery, Alabama, bus boycott of 1955-56, in which Dr. Martin Luther King, Jr. successfully led a prolonged campaign to desegregate the city's public transportation system.

The event's racial conflicts are dramatized through the experiences of two families. The Thompsons, Miriam (Sissy Spacek) and Norman (Dwight Schultz), are well-to-do whites whose country-club lives consist of golf, real estate, Junior League and dinner parties. Their immaculate house is kept, and their seven-year-old daughter largely raised, by a black maid, Odessa Cotter (Whoopi Goldberg). Odessa and her husband Herbert (Ving Rhames) must also care for their own three children in the midst of Montgomery's political and racial turmoil.

While Odessa keeps her family in solidarity with the boycott, she also quietly spurs Miriam's *sub rosa* conversion, over Norman's racist objections, to the cause. When the bus boycott keeps her maid from getting to work on time, she rationalizes reasons to drive her to and from home. Across town, blacks, including the Cotters' own children, confront mounting white hostility but meet it with nonviolent resistance. Gradually Miriam's eyes are opened to the social inequities that allow her privileged life to exist. She resolves to join the growing boycott.

Meanwhile, Norman has been politicized in the opposite direction, recruited into the Klan-ish white Citizen's Council by his sleazy brother, Tunker (Dylan Baker). Miriam subverts her husband's orders to stay at home. Family and racial tensions climax when Tunker brings Norman to a vigilante raid on the boycott headquarters only to find Miriam and Odessa there. When she refuses to abandon the scene of the raid, Tunker attacks Miriam along with the blacks gathered there. Norman moves to defend his wife, but, having saved her, still cannot cross over the line to support her moral stand. As the men of the Citizen's Council form a gauntlet and chant, "Walk, nigger, walk," the assembled black women drown out the lynch mob with the singing of a defiant spiritual.

Ironically, at a time when Hollywood was releasing more films from black directors and black viewpoints than ever before,

THE LONG WALK HOME joined a growing list of dramatizations of the civil rights struggle (MISSISSIPPI BURNING, DRIVING MISS DAISY, GLORY) made by white filmmakers and seen through the eyes of white liberal protagonists. The individual works in this new genre, including LONG WALK HOME, are stirring dramas featuring strong African-American characters. In this respect, Whoopi Goldberg's Odessa takes her place alongside the memorable characters in other civil rights films. Yet one wonders why the protagonists in such films must continually be white when they are principally stories of black struggle.

However, in some respects, THE LONG WALK HOME may signal something of a reversal in this trend. Although nominally the story of a white housewife's political awakening, its narrative seems to tug in the direction of making this Odessa's story. It is *her* long walk home every evening of the bus boycott that the title suggests should be the central subject of the film. And, in fact, we see her life at home as much as we see Miriam's. But in this and other recent civil rights dramas it is not so much a matter of who gets screen time but of whose voice gets heard. Quite literally the black heroes of these films are often kept in positions of silence and quiet courage: in MISSISSIPPI BURNING blacks rarely speak at all; in GLORY they march staunchly to their death; and in DRIVING MISS DAISY the hero is placed in a lifelong subservience.

Odessa too is a servant who must hold her tongue in the presence of racial insults. But increasingly she gains a voice, albeit a reserved one, which she uses to teach her employer about the politics of segregation. And in the end, it is the voices of many black women who are heard above the din of racism. This victory of the black voice is primed throughout the film by the repeated sounds of Dr. King's sermons (*the* voice of the era) and the joyful noise of church choirs.

While THE LONG WALK HOME seems able to share the viewpoints of Odessa and Miriam, its structure is somewhat marred by an unnecessary voiceover narration from a third character. Although the voice of Miriam's daughter, now grown, is interjected in only brief instances, she introduces and concludes the film as if it is her story—which it clearly is not. Seeing the civil rights movement as a loss of innocence (she learns there is no Santa Claus just as her mother learns the truth about segregation) is an inappropriate choice of allegory. Fortunately, the narrator's final recollection of what the Montgomery uprising "would mean to my mother and me" does little to disrupt the true power of this story: what the struggle meant to Odessa and her community. Despite its accomodations to history, THE LONG WALK HOME succeeds in presenting a low-key, moving slice-of-life lived in the midst of that turbulent time.

LONGEST DAY, THE

1962 180m bw	★★★★
War	G/PG
FOX	

John Wayne *(Col. Benjamin Vandervoort)*, Robert Mitchum *(Brig. Gen. Norman Cota)*, Henry Fonda *(Brig. Gen. Theodore Roosevelt)*, Robert Ryan *(Brig. Gen. James Gavin)*, Rod Steiger *(Destroyer Commander)*, Robert Wagner, Fabian, Paul Anka, Tommy Sands *(US Rangers)*, Richard Beymer *(Schultz)*

p, Darryl F. Zanuck; d, Andrew Marton, Ken Annakin, Bernhard Wicki, Gerd Oswald; w, Cornelius Ryan, Romain Gary, James Jones, David Pursall, Jack Seddon (based on the novel by Cornelius Ryan); ph, Jean Bourgoin, Henri Persin, Walter Wottitz, Guy Tabary; ed, Samuel E. Beetley; m, Maurice Jarre; art d, Ted Haworth, Leon Barsacq, Vincent Korda; fx, Karl Helmer, Karl Baumgartner, Augie Lohman, Robert MacDonald, Alex Weldon

One of the most ambitious war films ever undertaken, this star-studded depiction of the D-Day invasion was long the pet project of Fox Studios boss Darryl Zanuck, who spared no expense in bringing THE LONGEST DAY breathtaking scope and authenticity, going so far as to insist that the shooting be done only in weather conditions that matched those of the actual event. Based on Cornelius Ryan's compilation of interviews with D-Day survivors, the film is presented in three segments, the first detailing the Allied preparation for the invasion and the wait for the weather to break; the second re-creating the movement of the massive armada across the English Channel and the preliminary, behind-the-lines sallies of paratroops and glider-transported commandos; and the last depicting the assaults on the Normandy beaches. Intercut with the portrayal of the Allied side of the momentous invasion is the German (subtitled) response, including the report to headquarters of the first German officer to spot the armada: "Those thousands of ships you say the Allies don't have—well, they have them!" The work of three credited directors (reportedly, Zanuck helmed all the American and British interiors himself) and no less than eight cameramen, THE LONGEST DAY is visually stunning—its extraordinary camera movement and Cinemascope photography brilliantly augmenting the meticulously reenacted battle scenes. The only thing bigger than the film's scope are its stars, including John Wayne (who received $250,000 for four days' work) as Lt. Col. Benjamin Vandervoort of the 82nd Paratroop Division; Henry Fonda as Brig. Gen. Theodore Roosevelt, Jr.; Robert Mitchum as Brig. Gen. Norman Cota, who finally moves his hard-pressed men off bloody Omaha Beach, where they are being slaughtered by German crossfire; Red Buttons as a paratrooper; Rod Steiger as the captain of one of the armada ships; Peter Lawford as the flamboyant commando leader Lord Lovat (who was present at the shoot); Richard Burton as a wounded pilot; and Curt Jurgens as German general Blumentritt. Made for $10 million, this magnificent film was the most expensive black-and-white production to its date.

LONGEST YARD, THE
1974 121m c   ★★★½
Sports/Comedy   R/X
Paramount

Burt Reynolds (Paul Crewe), Eddie Albert (Warden Hazen), Ed Lauter (Capt. Knauer), Michael Conrad (Nate Scarboro), James Hampton (Caretaker), Harry Caesar (Granville), John Steadman (Pop), Charles Tyner (Unger), Mike Henry (Rassmeusen), Bernadette Peters (Warden's Secretary)

p, Albert S. Ruddy; d, Robert Aldrich; w, Tracy Keenan Wynn (based on a story by Ruddy); ph, Joseph Biroc (Technicolor); ed, Michael Luciano, Frank Capacchione, Allan Jacobs, George Hively; m, Frank DeVol; prod d, James Vance

Part prison film, part football film, this violent but outstanding comedy-drama by gifted action director Robert Aldrich (BIG LEAGUER, ALL THE MARBLES) explores the brutality inherent in both the American penal system and football. Burt Reynolds gives one of his best performances as Paul Crewe, a former

pro who tires of being a kept man, steals his lover's car, and ends up in the prison ruled by Warden Hazen (Eddie Albert). Hazen compels Crewe to put together a team of prisoners to face the crack guard team, offering him parole in exchange for a lopsided loss. Crewe assembles the "Mean Machine" and then does his best to throw the game (which takes up 47 minutes of screen time), leaving it early with an "injury" but returning later to lead the Machine's comeback when the guards' savageness continues unabated. Deftly employing split-screen and slow-motion techniques, Aldrich makes the most of Tracy Keenan Wynn's incisive script, aided by fine cinematography and tight Oscar-nominated editing. Both sides of the line of scrimmage feature former gridiron stars: the guards boast one-time Viking quarterback Joe Kapp and Packer Hall of Famer Ray Nitschke, while among the prisoners are Ernie Wheelwright, Pervis Atkins, and the University of Washington's legendary QB Sonny Sixkiller. No stranger to football himself, Reynolds, an All-Southern Conference halfback at Florida State, also played a pigskin hero in SEMI-TOUGH.

LOOK BACK IN ANGER
1959 115m bw   ★★★
Drama   /PG
Pathe/Associated British   (U.K.)

Richard Burton (Jimmy Porter), Claire Bloom (Helena Charles), Mary Ure (Alison Porter), Edith Evans (Mrs. Tanner), Gary Raymond (Cliff Lewis), Glen Byam Shaw (Cpl. Redfern), Phyllis Neilson-Terry (Mrs. Redfern), Donald Pleasence (Hurst), Jane Eccles (Miss Drury), S.P. Kapoor (Kapoor)

p, Harry Saltzman; d, Tony Richardson; w, Nigel Kneale, John Osborne (based on the play by Osborne); ph, Oswald Morris; ed, Richard Best; m, Chris Barber; art d, Peter Glazier; cos, Jocelyn Richards

In the late 1950s and early 1960s, several films by "Angry Young Men" were written and produced. Osborne, a forerunner of the genre, wrote the play on which this film is based and which had enormous success in London and New York. This lensing was faithful to the original, but it lost a bit in the translation from the intimacy of the stage to the screen. Canadian Harry Saltzman, who made his fortune in England, produced the picture before he decided to make films that had more commercial possibilities (i.e., the James Bond series which he did with Albert Broccoli). He is to be congratulated for taking a chance with an iffy property. Burton, in a no-holds-barred performance, is a university-educated malcontent who currently earns his keep by running a candy stall in a large market run by Pleasence, in yet another of his fine roles. Burton seems to love his wife, Ure, but can't help verbally mistreating her. (She repeats the part she played on the stage. This was one of her very few film appearances. She had been married to playwright Osborne, then married playwright-actor Robert Shaw. She died at 42 after mixing whiskey with barbiturates.) Ure takes about as much as anyone can stand, then leaves Burton when her best friend, Bloom, persuades her that she must to save her sanity. Burton is now alone, with nobody to insult, and he takes up with Bloom, a woman he has despised for most of the first few reels. Ure has been pregnant all along but didn't tell Burton. When she loses the baby, she returns to Burton, and Bloom figures it's time for her to leave. Evans is a sweet old lady who helps Burton set up his business, and Kapoor has a few good scenes as an Indian trader, but most of the picture belongs to Burton's bravura performance.

The major problem of the picture is that Osborne seems to have concocted the slight plot for one reason only: to vent his spleen against the church, society, the rich, the government, and whatever irked him at the time. The dialogue at times is endless and much too flip in the wrong situations. It's as though the author attempted to be a modern-day Oscar Wilde, but with a social conscience, and his message is heard loud, clear, and far too often. Although Burton has the range to be kind, funny, earthy, noble, and passionate, he is given little opportunity to get beyond letting that memorable voice of his bellow and roar. Still, for all the obvious drawbacks, LOOK BACK IN ANGER should be seen by anyone who is interested in learning about the England of that era. Burton had been making films for ten years and had starred as Alexander in ALEXANDER THE GREAT and as Edwin Booth in PRINCE OF PLAYERS. This seamy role, however, was the one that brought him to the attention of many who thought that he could act only when dressed in Biblical clothes, as in THE ROBE, or in doublet and hose. He was only 34 at the time this was made, but the ravages of high living were already beginning to show on his rugged Welsh face.

LOOK WHO'S TALKING

1989 93m c   ★★★
Comedy   PG-13/12
Tri-Star

John Travolta (James), Kirstie Alley (Mollie), Olympia Dukakis (Rosie), George Segal (Albert), Abe Vigoda (Grandpa), Bruce Willis (Voice of Mikey), Twink Caplan (Rona), Jason Schaller, Jaryd Waterhouse, Jacob Haines

p, Jonathan D. Krane; d, Amy Heckerling; w, Amy Heckerling; ph, Thomas Del Ruth (AlphaCine Color); ed, Debra Chiate; m, David Kitay; art d, Reuben Freed; chor, Mary Ann Kellogg; cos, Molly Maginnis

LOOK WHO'S TALKING contains a different kind of explicit sex scene, one presenting an inside view of the action. After Mollie (Kirstie Alley) and Albert (George Segal) fall to the floor in a fit of passion, the next thing on-screen is a school of sperm swimming upstream. Leading the charge is a sperm that wins the race and succeeds in fertilizing the egg, all the while narrating its adventure. The voice belongs to Bruce Willis, the "who" in LOOK WHO'S TALKING, a mildly amusing comedy buoyed by the voiceover gimmick. Mollie is an accountant who has been having an affair with Albert, a married client who can't bring himself to leave his wife. Even Mollie's pregnancy doesn't change his mind. But when Mollie goes into labor, she meets an interesting taxi driver (John Travolta). Writer-director Amy Heckerling takes a clever idea and conveys it superbly. The voiceover works well because the filmmakers use the device for all it's worth, with Willis providing a voice for the child when it's a sperm, a fetus, and a baby. With his sarcastic delivery, Willis has the ideal voice for the part. Alley and Travolta are affable enough, but the story itself is ordinary and merely passes time. Thanks to the ingenious voiceover, however, LOOK WHO'S TALKING rises above the second-rate. It's a genial, entertaining film. The film's enormous popularity led to a dismal sequel in 1990.

LOOKING FOR MR. GOODBAR

1977 135m c   ★★★½
Drama   R/18
Paramount

Diane Keaton (Theresa Dunn), Tuesday Weld (Katherine Dunn), William Atherton (James Morrissey), Richard Kiley (Mr. Dunn), Richard Gere (Tony Lopanto), Alan Feinstein (Professor Engle),

Tom Berenger (Gary Cooper White), Priscilla Pointer (Mrs. Dunn), Laurie Prange (Brigid Dunn), Joel Fabiani (Barney)

p, Freddie Fields; d, Richard Brooks; w, Richard Brooks (based on the novel by Judith Rosner); ph, William A. Fraker (Panavision, Metrocolor); ed, George Grenville; m, Artie Kane; art d, Edward Carfagno; cos, Jodie Tillen

In the hands of a less sure director, this could have been a tawdry mess, but Brooks exercises some good judgment in dealing with the material to create a somewhat satisfying adaptation of the Rossner novel. Keaton is a repressed teacher of deaf-and-dumb children who lives under the thumb of her macho father, Kiley, and her let's-make-everything-nice mother, Pointer. She would love to be free of them, so she sets out to find "Mr. Right" but in all the wrong places. She haunts the singles bars and goes on a sexual voyage, sleeping with Atherton, a befuddled, sweet guy who loves her; Gere, a stud with sadistic tendencies that thrill her; and finally, Berenger, the insane bisexual who eventually takes her life. Keaton is shown existing in two worlds: the safety of school and home versus the madcap life of the swingers who stay up late, drowning their loneliness in stingers and sex. This is the other side of Hoffman and Farrow's JOHN AND MARY; we kept looking hard at the bar scenes to see if Dustin and Mia were in the background. There are many erotic scenes, but they are handled well. Imagine Brian DePalma with the same script, and you'll realize how disgusting it could have been. Feinstein is excellent as Keaton's first lover, and Weld (who earned an Oscar nomination for her supporting performance) is sensational as Keaton's slightly dippy sister who is happy following whatever trend is au courant. LOOKING FOR MR. GOODBAR made lots of money and showed that Keaton, who had just scored in ANNIE HALL, could get out from under Woody Allen's wing and be a star on her own. An added plus is the score by Artie Kane, which evokes the solitude of living in a city with millions of people but still not having anyone with whom to really talk. Fraker's cinematography also earned an Oscar nomination.

LOOKS AND SMILES

1982 104m bw   ★★★
Drama   /15
Black Lion/Kestrel/MK2 (U.K.)

Phil Askham, Pam Darrell, Graham Greene, Tracey Goodlad, Stuart Golland, Patti Nichols, Tony Pitts, Arthur Davies, Cilla Mason, Carolyn Nicholson

p, Irving Teiltelbaum; d, Kenneth Loach; w, Barry Hines; ph, Chris Menges; ed, Stephen Singleton; m, Marc Wilkinson, Richard & The Taxmen; art d, Martin Johnson

Powerful, gritty drama shot in a documentary style about two high school dropouts who are faced with the choice of going into the military or going on public aid. One of the boys enlists and finds himself in Belfast, where he begins terrorizing Catholics; the other stays home and becomes increasingly destitute as he tries to find work. The cast members are all amateurs, and the visual style is stunningly realistic.

LORD JIM

1965 154m c   ★★★★
Adventure   /PG
Columbia (U.K.)

Peter O'Toole (Lord Jim), James Mason (Gentleman Brown), Curt Jurgens (Cornelius), Eli Wallach (The General), Jack Hawkins (Marlow), Paul Lukas (Stein), Akim Tamiroff (Schomberg), Daliah Lavi (The Girl), Ichizo Itami (Waris), Tatsuo Saito (Chief Du-Ramin)

p, Richard Brooks; d, Richard Brooks; w, Richard Brooks (based on the novel by Joseph Conrad); ph, Freddie Young (Super Panavision, Technicolor); ed, Alan Osbiston; m, Bronislau Kaper; prod d, Geoffrey Drake; art d, Bill Hutchinson, Ernest Archer; fx, Cliff Richardson; cos, Phyllis Dalton

This stunningly exotic film of Conrad's classic features O'Toole in the title role. He serves an apprenticeship at sea under the protective eye of Hawkins and later graduates to first officer of a tramp liner, the *Patna*, which carries religious passengers on an awful passage in which the ship is mercilessly lashed by a hurricane. In a moment of desperation, the idealistic O'Toole abandons the ship and leaves its passengers to their fate. The craft survives, although many of its passengers are drowned, and O'Toole loses his license and sinks into waterfront obscurity. To redeem himself, O'Toole agrees to take a shipment of dynamite from Lukas and deliver it to a tribe of natives in uncharted territory. The tribe is in bondage to oppressive warlord Wallach. Surviving ambushes and treachery from his own crew members, O'Toole manages to get the explosives to the settlement and hide the barrels, exploding one to make Wallach and his henchmen believe that the entire shipment has been destroyed. Wallach captures O'Toole and tortures him, but native girl Lavi helps him escape. He joins the natives and organizes an attack on the fortress, a seesaw battle that finally sees O'Toole and the natives triumph and Wallach killed. Jurgens, however, escapes to join river pirate Mason, and they muster their forces to return to the fortress to obtain Wallach's fabulous cache of jewels stolen from the natives. O'Toole greets the thieves with a cannon shot that decimates them, but the son of the native chief is killed in the encounter and, to make up for the death, O'Toole nobly sacrifices his own life at the finish. Beautifully photographed by Young and tightly directed by Brooks, LORD JIM is moving and suspenseful. Shot on location in Cambodia and Hong Kong.

LORD LOVE A DUCK

1966   105m   bw   ★★★
Comedy   /A
Charleston

Roddy McDowall (*Alan "Mollymauk" Musgrave*), Tuesday Weld (*Barbara Ann Greene*), Lola Albright (*Marie Green*), Martin West (*Bob Barnard*), Ruth Gordon (*Stella Barnard*), Harvey Korman (*Weldon Emmett*), Sarah Marshall (*Miss Schwartz*), Lynn Carey (*Sally Grace*), Max Showalter (*Howard Greene*), Donald Murphy (*Phil Neuhauser*)

p, George Axelrod; d, George Axelrod; w, George Axelrod, Larry H. Johnson (based on a novel by Al Hine); ph, Daniel Fapp; ed, William Lyon; m, Neal Hefti; art d, Malcolm Brown; fx, Herman Townsley; cos, Paula Giokaris

A wacky satire/black comedy with high school senior McDowall helping schoolmate Weld get whatever she desires. McDowall's IQ is so high he knows what everyone wants before they speak. He gets Weld into the sorority of her choice and ensures she will get good grades by getting her a secretarial job with the high school principal, Korman. She meets West, a rich college senior, at a sex seminar at a drive-in church. Weld is tested for a beach party movie with West's help, but problems arise when West's mother, Gordon, doesn't approve of Weld. McDowall fixes that by introducing Gordon to booze. Weld's mother, Albright, kills herself when she thinks she has ruined her daughter's relationship and life. Weld and West marry and he becomes a marriage counselor. When he objects to his wife's movie career, McDowall decides to get rid of him. His attempts fail until he

runs him over at the high school graduation with a bulldozer (killing everyone on the speaker's platform as well). The film is told in flashback with McDowall in the prison psychiatric wing telling his story to a tape recorder. Directed by the man who wrote THE SEVEN YEAR ITCH and WILL SUCCESS SPOIL ROCK HUNTER?

LORD OF THE FLIES

1963   90m   bw   ★★
Drama   /PG
Allen/Hogdon/Two Arts   (U.K.)

James Aubrey (*Ralph*), Tom Chapin (*Jack*), Hugh Edwards (*Piggy*), Roger Elwin (*Roger*), Tom Gaman (*Simon*), The Surtees Twins (*Sam and Eric*), Roger Allen, David Brunjes, Peter Davy, Kent Fletcher

p, Lewis Allen; d, Peter Brook; w, Peter Brook (based on the novel by William Golding); ph, Tom Hollyman; ed, Peter Brook, Gerald Feil, Jean-Claude Lubtchansky; m, Raymond Leppard

Poorly directed by Brook, this disappointing rendition of the Golding novel is set in the near future. As war is about to erupt, a plane carrying some wealthy British school boys is flown out of London to the supposed safety of the South Pacific. The plane crashes on a remote island (actually, the film was shot in Puerto Rico and Vieques in the Caribbean), none of the adults makes it to shore, and 40 of the boys are left to fend for themselves. With Aubrey as their leader, the lads begin to set up a subsociety so that they can survive until rescued. Aubrey uses the myopic Edwards' spectacles to ignite a fire in the hope of attracting passing aircraft. Chapin, the toughest of the lot, names himself as the great white hunter and leads the boys on a boar hunt. They catch and kill a pig, putting its head on a stick, and point it toward the "beast" at the top of the mountain—actually the dead body of the pilot who parachuted from the plane and died. Eventually, the boys divide into two different factions, one led by Aubrey, the other by Chapin. The boys in Chapin's group dress up as Indians and paint their faces like savages. These once well-mannered boys become increasingly feral, their dancing frenzied, as they chant and invent rituals. Gaman, one of the quiet lads in the other group, arrives to tell them that the beast is their late pilot, but they refuse to believe his story, turning on him and killing him in a blood-letting ritual. Next, they murder the defenseless, fat Edwards, and also make plans to kill Aubrey to use him as a sacrifice to appease their new god. They pursue him across the island, stopping short of another murder only when a rescue group appears. They stop chasing Aubrey and suddenly realize what they've done. Then, they begin crying, like the little boys they were before all this happened. The film presents a provocative idea, but it is so overwrought that, in the end, it is hardly more than a preteen version of MOST DANGEROUS GAME or THE ISLAND OF DR. MOREAU. In his haste to get to the savagery, Brook neglects to motivate the boys' actions honestly and the result leaves audiences wondering how these youngsters could have become evil so quickly. Even preteenagers, the very group the young actors portray, find little to tell their friends about the picture, which received only moderate box-office success.

LORDS OF FLATBUSH, THE

1974   86m   c   ★★★
Drama   PG/15
Columbia

493

Perry King *(Chico)*, Sylvester Stallone *(Stanley Rosiello)*, Henry Winkler *(Butchey Weinstein)*, Paul Mace *(Wimpy Murgalo)*, Susan Blakely *(Jane Bradshaw)*, Maria Smith *(Frannie Malincanico)*, Renee Paris *(Annie Yuckamanelli)*, Paul Jabara *(Crazy Cohen)*, Bruce Reed *(Mike)*, Frank Steifel *(Arnie)*

p, Stephen Verona; d, Stephen Verona, Martin Davidson; w, Stephen Verona, Martin Davidson, Gayle Gleckler, Sylvester Stallone; ph, Joseph Mangine, Ed Lachman (Technicolor); ed, Stan Siegel, Muffie Meyer; m, Joe Brooks, Paul Jabara, Joseph Nicholas; art d, Glenda Miller

Anyone who grew up in the Brooklyn of the 1950s will recognize the essential honesty of this picture, but it might as well be taking place in Korea for everyone else. The rambling movie with a good mix of drama and comedy served to introduce several actors who went on to much greater fame in other movies. The Lords of Flatbush is the name of a tough street gang but not one of those groups that pillage and vandalize. Rather, it is a social club, one of thousands that once were found in Brooklyn. (The small area of Coney Island alone had at least a dozen, including The Mariners, The Acwans [*A Club without a Name* acronym], the Emanons [*Nonames* backwards], et al). Stallone and King are best pals in Brooklyn's Flatbush area (and is there an uglier name for a neighborhood?). Codirector Verona must like the area because he used it for BRIGHTON BEACH. Stallone gets his girlfriend, Smith, pregnant and then takes her to a local jewelry shop to buy a ring. King's girlfriend is Blakely (while she was still "Susie" and not Susan), but she eventually dumps him. Several small but compelling incidents serve truly to represent life in Brooklyn. The film is a character piece that wanders from place to place with no single impetus, although one gets the feeling that this technique is intentional. The actors who distinguished themselves later include Blakely; Winkler ("Happy Days"); Armand Assante (I, THE JURY); Ray Sharkey (THE IDOLMAKER); Dolph Sweet ("Gimme a Break"); Jabara (who became a songwriter and won an Oscar); and, of course, Stallone, who was making his leading-man debut after an unbilled bit in Woody Allen's BANANAS and a few roles in films that will never reach a Saturday matinee for kids. Codirector Verona eventually became one of the prime movers of music video as well as a best-selling artist in his own right. Brooks did the music with some help from Nicholas and Jabara. Brooks will be best remembered (or forgotten) for scripting, producing, directing, and writing the song for YOU LIGHT UP MY LIFE.

LOS OLVIDADOS

1950   88m   bw   ★★★★★

Drama   /X

Tepeyac   (Mexico)

Estela Inda *(The Mother)*, Alfonso Mejia *(Pedro)*, Roberto Cobo *(Jaibo)*, Jesus Navarro *(The Lost Boy)*, Miguel Inclan *(The Blind Man)*, Alma Fuentas *(The Young Girl)*, Francisco Jambrino *(The Principal)*, Hector Portillo, Salvador Quiros, Victor Manuel Mendoza

p, Oscar Dancigers; d, Luis Bunuel; w, Luis Bunuel, Luis Alcoriza; ph, Gabriel Figueroa; ed, Carlos Savage; m, Gustavo Pittaluga

After a strange interlude of nearly two decades of critical obscurity, one of the great masters of the cinema returned to the public eye with this gripping combination of gritty realism and disorienting surrealism. Set in the slums of Mexico City, this is Luis Bunuel's brutally clear-eyed account of "The Forgotten Ones", the reckless youth whose dismal marginal existence has become a deadly web from which they cannot extract themselves. Bunuel

adopts many of the trappings of the popular form of the liberal social problem drama to tell his story but his goals are different. Rather than blaming all of the misery of these young people on their grim social conditions, he utilizes surrealism to expose the psychological underpinnings of their condition as he zeroes in on their dreams and sexuality. The result is a film that is realistic yet dreamy, heartrendingly sad yet subversively funny. There are no easy heroes or villains in this tough film. Bunuel also deftly avoids the sentimentalism that often afflicts this form.

At the film's core is the relationship between Pedro (Alfonso Mejia) and Jaibo (Roberto Cobo), two youths who live in Mexico's most disease-ridden urban slum. Jaibo, the older of the two, is already set in his ways, his selfish, vicious nature leading him to take advantage of those less fortunate than himself. As the film opens, he has just been released from jail and immediately returns to take control of the gang of boys who hang out in the streets and commit senseless acts of violence—not for money but for the pleasure of seeing the less fortunate suffer. The boy most eager to follow and please Jaibo is the childlike Pedro, whose innocent eyes reveal a spark of goodness lacking in the others.

The roots of this film extend back to LAS HURDES, Bunuel's devastating (yet also peversely amusing) 1932 documentary about the wretched living conditions in Spain's poorest region. There is also a vigorous nod to the Italian neo-realists; LOS OLVIDADOS is, as celebrated French critic Andre Bazin called it, "a film that lashes the mind like a red-hot iron and leaves one's conscience no opportunity for rest." Rarely have such squalor and savagery been displayed so unsentimentally, for Bunuel, who has a deep love for his characters, refuses to judge or pity them. Bunuel was named Best Director at the 1951 Cannes Film Festival, an award richly deserved.

LOST HONOR OF KATHARINA BLUM, THE
(DIE VERLORENE EHRE DER KATHARINA BLUM)

1975   104m   c   ★★½

Drama   R/AA

Orion/WDR/Bioskop/Paramount   (West Germany)

Angela Winkler *(Katharina Blum)*, Mario Adorf *(Beizmenne)*, Dieter Laser *(Werner Toetgess)*, Heinz Bennent *(Dr. Blorna)*, Hannelore Hoger *(Trude Blorna)*, Harald Kuhlmann *(Moeding)*, Karl Heinz Vosgerau *(Alois Straubleder)*, Jurgen Prochnow *(Ludwig Goetten)*, Rolf Becker *(Hach)*, Regine Lutz *(Else Woltersheim)*

p, Eberhard Junkersdorf; d, Volker Schlondorff, Margarethe von Trotta; w, Volker Schlondorff, Margarethe von Trotta (based on the novel by Heinrich Boll); ph, Jost Vacano (Eastmancolor); ed, Peter Przygodda; m, Hans Werner Henze

Codirected by Volker Schlondorff and Margarethe von Trotta, this adaptation of the Heinrich Boll novel capably depicts the author's themes and structure on-screen. Winkler, a waitress and model citizen, suddenly finds herself the victim of an unorthodox police investigation and media assault after a brief affair with a man wanted by the police because of his political affiliations. Before her troubles began, Winkler had been respected by her employers for her efficiency and by her friends for her level head. Her calm and uneventful life is made a shambles, however, by one particularly ruthless reporter who stops at nothing (including a grueling interview with her sickly mother) to find something behind the simple facts, going so far as to label her a Communist conspirator. The story unfolds in a series of bits of information gathered about the suspect, providing various conflicting viewpoints of her character. While this method may be too cold and distancing to evoke much audience empathy, it is effective in creating the oppressive atmosphere the story requires. Winkler's performance is equally cool, exposing a woman who seems incapable of revealing her emotions. An Americanized made-for-TV version, THE LOST HONOR OF KATHRYN BECK, appeared in 1984 starring Marlo Thomas and Kris Kristofferson.

LOST HORIZON

1937 138m bw   ★★★★★
Fantasy/Adventure   /U
Columbia

Ronald Colman (*Robert Conway*), Jane Wyatt (*Sondra*), Edward Everett Horton (*Alexander P. Lovett*), John Howard (*George Conway*), Thomas Mitchell (*Henry Barnard*), Margo (*Maria*), Isabel Jewell (*Gloria Stone*), H.B. Warner (*Chang*), Sam Jaffe (*High Lama*), Hugh Buckler (*Lord Gainsford*)

p, Frank Capra; d, Frank Capra; w, Robert Riskin (based on the novel by James Hilton); ph, Joseph Walker; ed, Gene Havlick, Gene Milford; m, Dimitri Tiomkin; art d, Stephen Goosson; fx, Roy Davidson, Ganahl Carson; cos, Ernest Dryden

Frank Capra's classic romantic fantasy leaves the standard "Capraesque" middle-class milieu of most of his most beloved masterpieces for a vividly realized world of strange adventure and fantasy. Faithfully adapted from James Hilton's popular novel, the film opens as Colman, a gallant British diplomat, author, and Far Eastern historian, comes to the aid of some refugees from a Chinese revolution. The group takes off in a small passenger plane, the motley collection including Colman; his younger, impressionable brother, Howard; a swindler wanted by the law, Mitchell; a prostitute with tuberculosis, Jewell; and a fussy fossil-hunting scientist, Horton. Colman notices that the plane is not headed for safety but climbing into the snow-topped Himalayas and into Tibet, "The Roof of the World." Moreover, the passengers discover that the pilot is not the European they had believed him to be, but an Asian. The plane crashes and the passengers struggle out of it, sinking into deep snow. Just when they are about to give up all hope of surviving, they are rescued by an odd-looking party led by Warner, an ancient Chinese who appears to have been looking for the Europeans. He gives them warm clothing and they join the rescuers' caravan, heading over the terrain to a remote, small pass. Suddenly, as the group crosses over a narrow bridge between towering mountains, the blizzard conditions vanish, and they stand within a beautiful, snowless, sun-filled world known as the Valley of the Blue Moon, looking down upon the majestic landscapes that make up the lamasery of Shangri-La. Taken to a magnificent structure and given luxurious rooms, the Europeans soon discover the marvelous tranquility of this hidden, unknown land where nothing is known of greed, war, hatred, or crime.

LOST HORIZON came to epitomize its audience's image of Utopia. Capra's paradise on earth—with its pure air, bright sun, and untroubled centuries of blissful life—became so entrenched in the public imagination that *Shangri-La* became a household word. Though Hilton wrote the novel (published in 1933) in six weeks, Capra took two years to transfer the tale to celluloid. The magnificent Shangri-La set constructed by art designer Stephen Goosson (who won an Oscar for his work) was the largest ever built in Hollywood. For two months, 150 workmen labored to build the 1,000-foot-long, 500-foot-wide lamasery, with its deep flights of marbled stairs and huge patio, broad terraces, rich gardens, lily-coated pools, and main building influenced by art deco and Frank Lloyd Wright. Little Columbia Studios and its tough boss, Harry Cohn, staggered under the burden of the film's

$2.5 million cost, which amounted to half of the company's entire yearly budget.

All of the painstaking care Capra took with LOST HORIZON shows; the film is directed with swift pace, inventive shots, and evident vitality. Capra was at a high point in his career. Two reels were eliminated after a problematic preview screening. LOST HORIZON was released in a cut version at 118 minutes to universal applause. Columbia had itself a box-office blockbuster which returned many millions to its depleted coffers and remained popular in re-release for decades. Everything about LOST HORIZON reflects quality work, from Robert Riskin's bright and literate script to Dimitri Tiomkin's stirring music, the outstanding special effects, and Joseph Walker's evocative soft-focus photography. In addition to the Oscar the film won for best Interior Decoration, it also won for Best Editing and earned nominations for Best Picture (losing to THE LIFE OF EMILE ZOLA), Best Supporting Actor (Warner), Best Sound, Best Assistant Director (C.C. Coleman, Jr.), and Best Score.

LOST IN AMERICA

1985 91m c   ★★½
Comedy   R/15
Geffen

Albert Brooks (*David Howard*), Julie Hagerty (*Linda Howard*), Tom Tarpey (*Brad Tooley*), Gary K. Marshall (*Casino Manager*), Maggie Roswell (*Patty*), Ernie Brown (*Pharmacist*), Art Frankel (*Employment Agent*), Joey Coleman (*Skippy*), Donald Gibb (*Ex-Convict*), Sylvia Farrel (*Receptionist*)

p, Marty Katz; d, Albert Brooks; w, Albert Brooks, Monica Johnson; ph, Eric Saarinen (Technicolor); ed, David Finfer; m, Arthur B. Rubinstein; prod d, Richard Sawyer; fx, Richard Albain, Jr.; cos, Cynthia Bales

Just when it seemed Albert Brooks had gotten his creative energies under control, along comes this intermittently funny, often overdone comedy that could have been a classic. Brooks is an ad man expecting to get a senior VP stripe. His main worries are how to furnish the new $450,000 house he is about to occupy and how to satisfy his wife, Julie Hagerty, who is complaining that she is bored with the regimentation of their lives. Brooks is shocked when his boss tells him the veep job has gone to someone else and that Brooks will, instead, be transferred to New York. Brooks storms out of the office and then persuades Hagerty to quit her job. They have no children, and they have money saved up; this is their chance to do what everyone wants to do, get lost in America and have a grand time. They sell everything, buy a huge motor home, and leave. It would be a perfect trip except that they get romantically remarried in Las Vegas, and that is the beginning of the end. If a moral exists here, it's that you can't win. Brooks and Hagerty are excellent, and it's good to see Brooks giving someone else a few moments on the screen. Somewhere, underneath all of the indulgence, beats the heart of a filmmaker.

LOST PATROL, THE

1934 74m bw   ★★★½
War   /A
RKO

Victor McLaglen (*The Sergeant*), Boris Karloff (*Sanders*), Wallace Ford (*Morelli*), Reginald Denny (*George Brown*), J.M. Kerrigan (*Quincannon*), Billy Bevan (*Herbert Hale*), Alan Hale (*Cook*), Brandon Hurst (*Bell*), Douglas Walton (*Pearson*), Sammy Stein (*Abelson*)

p, Cliff Reid; d, John Ford; w, Dudley Nichols, Garrett Fort (based on the novel *Patrol* by Philip MacDonald); ph, Harold Wenstrom; ed, Paul Weatherwax; m, Max Steiner; art d, Van Nest Polglase, Sidney Ullman

A strange and fascinating film, John Ford's THE LOST PATROL gives a sense of impending doom from frame to frame, but is nevertheless an absorbing adventure drama. The story concerns a British cavalry patrol in the Mesopotamian desert during WWI. A single shot rings out and their leader, an officer, falls dead from his horse, his face buried in the sand. With him goes the knowledge of their mission's purpose and even the direction in which the patrol is traveling. The unnamed sergeant (Victor McLaglen) who takes over finds nothing in the officer's map case to indicate where they are, and tells his men that the officer kept everything in his head. He leads the group to an oasis, but the men find themselves under occasional sniper fire from the Arabs who have surrounded them and lie in wait, out of sight in the stretching dunes. The soldiers—except for the sergeant—never see the Arabs, and this insidious enemy takes on an almost mythic character as, one by one, the British are picked off until only the sergeant, Morelli (Wallace Ford), and Sanders (Boris Karloff) are left, desperately trying to stay alive. Shot on location in the desert around Yuma, Arizona, THE LOST PATROL is a much superior remake of a like-titled 1929 British silent film that featured Agnew McMaster in Karloff's role and Cyril McLaglen, Victor's brother, as the sergeant.

LOST WEEKEND, THE

1945 101m bw   ★★★★½
Drama   /A
Paramount

Ray Milland *(Don Birnam)*, Jane Wyman *(Helen St. James)*, Phillip Terry *(Nick Birnam)*, Howard Da Silva *(Nat the Bartender)*, Doris Dowling *(Gloria)*, Frank Faylen *(Bim)*, Mary Young *(Mrs. Deveridge)*, Anita Sharp Bolster *(Mrs. Foley)*, Lilian Fontaine *(Mrs. St. James)*, Lewis L. Russell *(Charles St. James)*

p, Charles Brackett; d, Billy Wilder; w, Charles Brackett, Billy Wilder (based on the novel by Charles R. Jackson); ph, John Seitz; ed, Doane Harrison; m, Miklos Rozsa, Giuseppe Verdi; art d, Hans Dreier, Earl Hedrick; fx, Gordon Jennings; cos, Edith Head

THE LOST WEEKEND was the most celebrated of the "problem films" of the 1940s. Though it was hailed in its time as a great advance in screen seriousness and "adult" concerns, this film just barely missed being shelved. The script by the celebrated team of Wilder and Brackett is dispassionate and unrelenting but also ocassionally poetic. The emotional power of the film is greatly abetted by the evocative black-and-white cinematography of John F. Seitz. The visual style is excruciatingly effective as it ranges from unvarnished realism to delirious Expressionism. Finally Milland's virtuoso performance as the hopeless alcoholic is surprising, shocking, and utterly riveting.

Milland is a struggling writer who waters down his writer's block with booze. The film opens with the camera zooming through the window of a New York apartment building which Milland shares with his responsible brother Terry, who is about to go away on a weekend vacation. Terry is somewhat worried about leaving Milland alone, but Milland assures him all will be fine, that he will be settling down to do some serious writing. However we are immediately clued in to the fact that he is already a sneaking, manipulative drunk because we see that he is hiding a bottle of liquor while he is reassuring his brother all will be well. Milland makes a feeble attempt to write but knows from the outset that it's a useless effort. His real ambition is to consume the contents of those bottles he has secreted about the apartment. After Milland disposes of all the booze on the premises, he takes the money his brother has left for the cleaning lady and slips down to his favorite watering hole where bartender Da Silva, a congenial chap, hates to see him coming because he knows Milland is not just a social drinker. Da Silva begins to pour, and Milland sinks deeper into his alcoholic haze. He is at first charming and wonderfully imaginative, spewing forth the literature that he hasn't been able to put down on paper. He is fascinating, and the liquor seems to free up his intelligence and creativity for the beguilement of Da Silva and others. It's a fading charm, however; he runs out of money and Da Silva cuts him off, not because of the money but because he pities him and wants to help him. Da Silva encourages Milland to go home and take care of himself. From there it's all downhill fast.

THE LAST WEEKEND is candid and brilliantly conceived from shot to shot. Wilder slowly builds his scenes and utilizes low-key lighting and deep-focus photography to emphasize objects that suggest the menace of booze. Scenes are shot through whiskey shot-glasses and bottles. Milland is superb as the romantic alcoholic, a masterstroke of casting. Up to the time of THE LOST WEEKEND, he had been a matinee idol who made his mark in light comedy and romances. Milland was initially apprehensive. After reading the stark Jackson novel, he believed that the film might earn some critical praise as a social document but not much else. He also felt that he was not equipped to handle such a serious role, but his wife encouraged him to try it. He was also encouraged also by the fact that Wilder and Brackett had never had a flop. Faylen, though only on screen for a few moments, makes an indelible impact as a cynical and utterly repulsive male nurse in the sanitarium. His is only one of many roles played in the film by fine character actors, of whom Da Silva is the most potent as the sympathetic and conscientious bartender.

Milland's outstanding performance won him an Oscar as Best Actor. THE LOST WEEKEND also took home Oscars for Best Picture, Best Director, and Best Screenplay. Oddly, Paramount executives took one look at the finished film and told Wilder they were seriously considering not releasing it. They had received an avalanche of protest, ironically from temperance advocates, who felt the film would *encourage* drinking. Powerful lobbyists for the liquor industry offered as much as $5 million for the negative of the film so it could be destroyed. But, at Wilder's urgings, Paramount released the film on a limited engagement in New York City, and the critics fell all over themselves praising the magnificent job. The public responded by packing the theater, and the same thing happened in some West Coast theaters. Paramount released the film across the country and it proved to be one of the biggest hits of 1945.

LOVE AFFAIR

1939 87m bw   ★★★★
Comedy/Romance   /U
RKO

Irene Dunne *(Terry McKay)*, Charles Boyer *(Michel Marnet)*, Maria Ouspenskaya *(Grandmother Janou)*, Lee Bowman *(Kenneth Bradley)*, Astrid Allwyn *(Lois Clarke)*, Maurice Moscovich *(Maurice Cobert)*, Scotty Beckett *(Boy on Ship)*, Bess Flowers, Harold Miller *(Couple on Deck)*, Joan Leslie *(Autograph Seeker)* p, Leo McCarey; d, Leo McCarey; w, Delmer Daves, Donald Ogden Stewart (based on a story by McCarey, Daves, Mildred Cram); ph, Rudolph Mate; ed, Edward Dmytryk, George Hively; m, Roy Webb; art d, Van Nest Polglase, Al Herman; fx, Vernon L. Walker; cos, Howard Greer, Edward Stevenson

A superb romantic comedy-drama, the film deftly mixes humor with pathos, passion, and ennui, and takes us on an emotional voyage that never fails to please. Boyer is engaged to Allwyn, and Dunne is engaged to Bowman when the two meet onboard ship, but their mutual attraction is instant. Bowman and Allwyn are both wealthy and would make excellent spouses, yet is that enough? Evidently not. Boyer and Dunne flirt, then realize that this is not merely a shipboard fling; there is much more to their feelings about each other. They resolve to meet in six months at the top of the Empire State Building. If they both still feel the way they do now, they'll jettison their respective spouses-to-be and reactivate their fires. The months pass, and Dunne has a bit of luck working as a nightclub singer while Boyer is content to bide his time as a painter. Neither has married and both count the days until they meet again. On the way to the building, Dunne is hurt in an automobile accident, and it would appear that she's going to be permanently crippled. She doesn't want Boyer to feel sorry for her, so she doesn't get in touch with him. Boyer waits at the rendezvous for hours, then leaves, thinking she must have married Bowman. When they finally are reunited by chance, he understands her motives in staying away, but he feels deep in his heart that he can help her walk again. There are many wonderful moments in the picture, both comedic and touching. As Boyer's mother, Ouspenskaya, is dying, Dunne underplays her farewell to the old woman, and Boyer can't help but fall in love with her.

The first half of the picture is breezy, witty and chic, but, while the second has a decidedly more serious tone, we never have the feeling that they are divided. Reportedly, the writers were scripting new pages every day, and the actors never had a finished script. If that's true, more power to director McCarey who kept it all together and didn't betray the fact with jumpy direction. In the Philadelphia nightclub scene, Dunne gets to warble "Sing My Heart," and, when she briefly works at an orphanage, we hear "Wishing" done by the tykes. Look for veteran TV actor Gerald Mohr in a tiny extra bit and Joan Leslie, in her fourth film, at the age of 14. The picture was nominated for Oscars for Best Picture, Best Screenplay, Best Actress, Best Supporting Actress (Ouspenskaya), Best Original Story, Best Interior Decoration, and Best Song, ("Wishing," by B.G. De Sylva), but this was the year of GONE WITH THE WIND, STAGECOACH, and THE WIZARD OF OZ (among others), so there was no chance. It was remade as AN AFFAIR TO REMEMBER.

LOVE AFFAIR; OR THE CASE OF THE MISSING SWITCHBOARD OPERATOR

(LJUBAVNI SLUCAJ ILI TRAGEDIJA SLUZBENICE P.T.T.)
1967 70m bw   ★★★
Comedy   /X
Avala (Yugoslavia)

Eva Ras *(Isabela)*, Slobodan Aligrudic *(Ahmed)*, Ruzica Sokic *(Ruza, Isabela's friend)*, Miodrag Andric *(Mica, the Postman)*, Aleksandar Kostic *(Sexologist)*, Zivojin Aleksic *(Criminologist)*, Dragan Obradovic

d, Dusan Makavejev; w, Dusan Makavejev; ph, Aleksandar Petkovic; ed, Katarina Stojanovic; m, Hanns Eisler; art d, Vladislav Lazic

It is with great economy that Dusan Makavejev directs this 70-minute feature—his second—which contains a love story, a criminal investigation, lectures by both a sexologist (Dr. Aleksandar Kostic) and a criminologist (Dr. Zivojin Aleksic), a short documentary and a poem about killing rats, an autopsy, a *cinema-verite* scene on how to install a shower, documentary footage of Soviet citizens destroying churches, a lesson in how to make strudel, a Hungarian folk song ("A Man Isn't Made of Wood"), a Communist Party anthem ("Crush to Dust the Rotten Vermin"), and a tender and erotic lovemaking scene. Amid all this is the story, set in Yugoslavia, of a Hungarian switchboard operator, Izabela (Eva Ras), who falls in love with an Arabian rat exterminator, Ahmed (Slobodan Aligrudic). As their affair blossoms, the happy, playful footage of them together is intercut with *cinema-verite*-style shots of a female corpse being extracted from a deep well and the subsequent autopsy. Our fear that this corpse is Izabela is quickly confirmed, and all we can do is await the signs of why and how she died. This, however, seems to concern Makavejev less than the juxtaposition of scenes and sounds. For example, he places the lovemaking next to documentary footage of the destruction of churches, paralleling (as in his WR: MYSTERIES OF AN ORGANISM and SWEET MOVIE) sexuality with politics. He also shocks his audience into a strange distance by comparing, though less obviously, the nude body of Izabela lying on her bed with that of the cold corpse lying in the morgue. Makavejev's cinema is very much a dialectic one, though LOVE AFFAIR is a tender, sweet, and ultimately very sad film.

LOVE AND DEATH

1975 85m c   ★★★½
Comedy/War   PG
UA

Woody Allen *(Boris Dimitrovich Grushenko)*, Diane Keaton *(Sonja)*, Georges Adet *(Old Nehamkin)*, Frank Adu *(Drill Sergeant)*, Edmond Ardisson *(Priest)*, Feodor Atkine *(Mikhail)*, Albert Augier *(Waiter)*, Yves Barsacq *(Rimsky)*, Lloyd Battista *(Don Francisco)*, Jack Berard *(Gen. Lecoq)*

p, Charles H. Joffe; d, Woody Allen; w, Woody Allen; ph, Ghislain Cloquet (Deluxe Color); ed, Ron Kalish, Ralph Rosenblum; m, Sergei Prokofiev; art d, Willy Holt; cos, Gladys DeSegonzac

Woody Allen takes on Russia and just about all its great writers—not to mention Eisenstein, Kierkegaard, and Bob Hope—in this comedy set roughly at the same time as Tolstoy's similarly named *War and Peace*. The plot defies description but involves the aristocratic yet typically nebbish-ish Boris (Allen), who is impressed into the Russian army during the Napoleonic Wars. Boris and his distant (both emotionally and genetically) cousin, Sonja (Diane Keaton), eventually set out to assassinate Napoleon, a la Tolstoy's Pierre. Along the way, the not-so-perfect couple have hilarious philosophical dialogues and numerous comedic adventures in their DR. ZHIVAGO-like hegira across the frozen wastes. The laughs come fast and furious in this film, so if you miss one joke you're likely to pick up on the next. Hailed as one of Allen's best movies at the time of its release, LOVE AND DEATH—with its scattershot mix of silly gags and highbrow satire—seems much weaker in retrospect. Allen's next picture was his breakthrough work, ANNIE HALL. Filmed in France and Hungary.

LOVE AT LARGE
1990 97m c   ★★★½
Comedy/Romance   R/15

Tom Berenger (*Harry Dobbs*), Elizabeth Perkins (*Stella Wynkowski*), Anne Archer (*Miss Dolan*), Ted Levine (*Frederick King/James McGraw*), Annette O'Toole (*Mrs. King*), Kate Capshaw (*Mrs. Ellen McGraw*), Ann Magnuson (*Doris*), Barry Miller (*Marty*), Kevin J. O'Connor (*Art, Farmhand*), Neil Young (*Rick*)

p, David Blocker; d, Alan Rudolph; w, Alan Rudolph; ph, Elliot Davis (Deluxe Color); ed, Lisa Churgin; m, Mark Isham; prod d, Steven Legler; art d, Steve Karatzas; fx, Frank Ceglia; cos, Ingrid Ferrin

When you walk into an Alan Rudolph film, you can be pretty sure of what you are going to see: a dreamy, misty romance—cool but sexy and long on mood. LOVE AT LARGE, a soft-boiled, tongue-in-cheek detective fantasy, is no different. Tom Berenger plays Harry Dobbs, a down-at-heel private eye with a maniacally jealous girl friend (Ann Magnuson). Just as the two are about to have a racy reconciliation after their latest fight, Dobbs receives a call from the mysterious Miss Dolan (Anne Archer), who offers him a case. Mistaking the call for a romantic rendezvous, Doris (Magnuson) gives Dobbs a less-than-loving send-off as he goes out to interview for the job. Miss Dolan, as it turns out, wants her boyfriend, Rick (Neil Young), put under surveillance. He has threatened her life and she, quite reasonably, wants to know where he is so she can make sure to keep out of his way. Working with a sketchy description, Dobbs finds himself trailing the wrong man, Frederick King (Ted Levine), who, as it happens, has some interesting secrets of his own. The "real" Rick, a bad egg with a short temper, doesn't come to dominate the film as he might in a more conventional *film noir*-style gumshoe melodrama. Instead, Rudolph keeps Dobbs on King's trail through most of the film. Dobbs reports to Dolan that, to all appearances, King is a boring business executive with a devoted, picture-perfect wife (Annette O'Toole) and kids. Then comes the day when King loads his luggage into a waiting cab while his wife tearfully bids him farewell. Dobbs follows King to the "north" (Rudolph's films are rarely set in real places), where, Dobbs discovers, King keeps a large ranch under an alias, complete with another wife (Kate Capshaw) and daughter. Through all of this, Dobbs himself is being followed, none too inconspicuously, by another private eye, Stella (Elizabeth Perkins), hired by Dobbs' girl friend to get the goods on Dobbs and Dolan. When Dobbs and Stella are brought together by car trouble, Doris suspects Stella of fooling around with Dobbs, which gets her fired by her detective agency (run by, of all people, Ruby Dee). Dobbs and Stella begin working together on King, finding out, almost too late, Dobbs' mistake, all of which leads to a frantic climax.

Though complicated, the plot outcome is fairly predictable. All who deserve it get their comeuppances and the right couplings occur. But those familiar with past Rudolph films know that plot is of secondary importance in the director's work. Mostly, it's an excuse to get the characters into evocative settings. At the weird, lavish Blue Danube nightclub, where Dobbs and Dolan meet to discuss the case, everybody moves in a slow, deliberate, dreamlike manner. Fittingly, Dolan is herself a creature of gossamer fantasy, living only for love and romance (and to break into song at the oddest moments). The "north," meanwhile, exists mostly as a stark netherland in which Dobbs and Stella come together as two lost souls starved for emotional sustenance.

Beyond its serious moments, LOVE AT LARGE has an appealing playfulness that has been missing in Rudolph's other recent efforts TROUBLE IN MIND and, especially, MADE IN HEAVEN (THE MODERNS, on the other hand, was entirely too fatuous). There is also a looser, more freewheeling flavor to the performances, reminiscent of CHOOSE ME, still Rudolph's best film. Both a visual director and an actor's director, Rudolph has great sympathy for his male performers. Rarely has it been as much fun to watch and listen to Berenger as it is here. But Rudolph also loves his female players. His camera is enchanted by them, zeroing in with a fetishist's fervor on such details as Archer's full, sensuous lips, O'Toole's knees, Perkins' alabaster skin, and Magnuson's severe, masklike face. On the whole, Rudolph might benefit from a good, tough-minded collaborator to sharpen up his plots and characters. Still, even for those uninitiated to Rudolph's sometimes fragile charms, LOVE AT LARGE is a much better than average place to park your eyes for a while.

LOVE AT TWENTY
(L'AMOUR A VINGT ANS)
1963 110m bw   ★★★
Drama   /X
Ulysse/Unitec/Toho/Cinescolo/Towa/Kamera/Film Polski/Beta   (France/Italy/Poland/West Germany/Japan)

FRANCE: Jean-Pierre Leaud (*Antoine Doinel*), Marie-France Pisier (*Colette*), Francois Darbon (*Colette's Father*), Rosy Varte (*Colette's Mother*), Patrick Auffay (*Rene*), Jean-Francois Adam (*Albert Tazzi*). ITALY: Eleonora Rossi-Drago (*Valentina*), Cristina Gajoni (*Christina*), Geronimo Meynier (*Leonardo*). JAPAN: Koji Furuhata (*Hiroshi*)

p, Pierre Roustang; d, Francois Truffaut, Renzo Rossellini, Shintaro Ishihara, Marcel Ophuls, Andrzej Wajda; w, Yvon Samuel, Francois Truffaut, Renzo Rossellini, Shintaro Ishihara, Marcel Ophuls, Jerzy Stefan Stawinski; ph, Raoul Coutard, Mario Montuori, Shigeo Hayashida, Wolf Wirth, Jerzy Lipman; ed, Claudine Bouche; m, Georges Delerue, Toru Takemitsu, Jerzy Matuszkiewicz

An international compilation film best known for its Truffaut episode, "Antoine and Colette," the second installment of his "Antoine Doinel" series begun in THE 400 BLOWS. Conceived by French producer Roustang, the film is built on the theme of being 20 years old or, as he would put it, "the inscrutable youth of the atomic age and technological civilization." Five young filmmakers contributed: Francois Truffaut (France), Renzo Rossellini (Italy), Shintaro Ishihara (Japan), Marcel Ophuls (West Germany), and Andrzej Wajda (Poland). Truffaut's episode has Leaud relocate to across the street from the girl he loves only to discover that her parents like him more than she does. In Rossellini's segment a young man juggles relationships with a young woman and an older one. Ishihara's piece has a love-maddened, working-class lad kill his girlfriend—but fail, because of class differences, to win the wealthy girl he loves. Ophuls' segment is far more optimistic. A photographer on a stopover in Munich gets a girl pregnant. After arriving home he learns what has happened and returns, marries the girl, and soon falls in love with her. Wajda's episode differs from the others; it is told from an older person's point of view (not surprising, considering that at age 35 he was the eldest of the directors). A middle-aged man saves a young girl who has slipped into a polar bear pit in a zoo. Later, at a party to which he is invited by two teenage witnesses, he relates an account of his past as a resistance fighter. The party-goers get him drunk, tease him, and sing him a song about a "sleepy old bear" before they kick him out.

LOVE CRAZY

1941   97m   bw   ★★★★
Comedy   /A
MGM

William Powell (*Steven Ireland*), Myrna Loy (*Susan Ireland*), Gail Patrick (*Isobel Grayson*), Jack Carson (*Ward Willoughby*), Florence Bates (*Mrs. Cooper*), Sidney Blackmer (*George Hennie*), Vladimir Sokoloff (*Dr. Klugle*), Kathleen Lockhart (*Mrs. Bristol*), Sig Rumann (*Dr. Wuthering*), Donald MacBride (*"Pinky" Grayson*)

p, Pandro S. Berman; d, Jack Conway; w, William Ludwig, Charles Lederer, David Hertz (based on a story by David Hertz, William Ludwig); ph, Ray June; ed, Ben Lewis; m, David Snell; art d, Cedric Gibbons

William Powell and Myrna Loy, who made a dozen films together (six as the "Thin Man" characters Nick and Nora Charles), are romantically teamed again in this breakneck farce. This time, they're a happily married couple about to celebrate their fourth wedding anniversary. Unfortunately, their domestic tranquility is shattered when Loy's battleaxe mother (Bates) arrives for a visit, sprains an ankle, and extends her stay a lot longer than had been anticipated. Powell, who has to take care of Bates while Loy goes out on an errand to meet her aunt, is bored by his meddling mother-in-law and decides to have a few drinks with his old flame, Patrick, who lives in the same apartment building and is now married to MacBride. Bates eavesdrops on their conversation, misconstrues it, and fills her daughter's ears with gossip when Loy comes home. Loy, trying to make Powell jealous, also goes to their neighbors' apartment, but mistakenly winds up in the flat of Carson, a nutcase archery champion. Carson tries to show Loy how good he is with a bow and arrow and, when she tries to leave, follows her in the building's halls, stripped to the waist. The two run into Powell, who is less than thrilled to find his lovely wife being pursued by a half-naked madman. An argument ensues when Powell, who is a bit tipsy, tells her that his evening with Patrick was completely innocent. Loy won't hear of it, walks out on him, and soon decides she wants a divorce. Powell initially agrees, then realizes that he loves his wife and would like to renege. His lawyer, Blackmer, advises him to buy time by pretending he's crazy, since the law prohibits Loy from divorcing him if he's of unsound mind. Loy sees through her mate's charade, however, and has Powell committed to a mental institution to teach him a lesson. Stuck in the hospital—where one wonders who is crazier, the patients or the doctors (Rumann and Sokoloff)—Powell has to convince everyone that he is sane, which isn't easy, since patients frequently make this claim. He escapes from the asylum and heads home, avoiding the police by shaving off his trademark mustache, dressing in drag, and pretending to be his own sister. His mother-in-law is taken in by the disguise, and when the reconciled Loy and Powell (the latter still in women's dress) retire to their bedroom, Bates tells them to "sleep well."

Featuring several superb set pieces, LOVE CRAZY has more slapstick than the verbal wit that usually characterized Powell and Loy's films, but there is also enough raillery to satisfy lovers of sophisticated dialogue. Under Jack Conway's deft direction, the scenes go by quickly—you'll be laughing so hard at one that you won't notice that you're halfway through the next.

LOVE FINDS ANDY HARDY

1938   90m   bw   ★★★
Romance   /U
MGM

Lewis Stone (*Judge James Hardy*), Mickey Rooney (*Andy Hardy*), Judy Garland (*Betsy Booth*), Cecilia Parker (*Marian Hardy*), Fay Holden (*Mrs. Hardy*), Ann Rutherford (*Polly Benedict*), Betty Ross Clarke (*Aunt Milly*), Lana Turner (*Cynthia Potter*), Marie Blake (*Augusta*), Don Castle (*Dennis Hunt*)

p, Carey Wilson; d, George B. Seitz; w, William Ludwig (based on stories by Vivian B. Bretherton and characters by Aurania Rouverol); ph, Lester White; ed, Ben Lewis; m, David Snell; art d, Cedric Gibbons, Stan Rogers; cos, Jeanne

Another entry in the "Andy Hardy" series extolling the small-town American virtues that movie mogul Louis B. Mayer loved so much, this picture proved to be one of the highest grossing films for MGM in 1938 and also marked Judy Garland's first appearance in the series. In this episode, Andy (Mickey Rooney) angers his girl friend, Polly Benedict (Ann Rutherford), when he agrees to escort his buddy's "dishy" girl, Cynthia Potter (Lana Turner, in her first MGM appearance), for a fee, so that he can pay off the car he just bought. When Betsy Booth (Judy Garland) pops up to visit her aunt and uncle, Andy quickly dismisses her as nothing but a kid—until he hears her sing at a local dance. She quickly becomes another girl problem for Andy, but she sets him straight, pronto. The entire cast give excellent performances under the skilled direction of George B. Seitz. The wholesome script was written by William Ludwig, a young lawyer from New York who moved west for his health and got a job in MGM's Junior Writing Department. In 1942 the "Andy Hardy" series won an award certificate at the Oscar ceremonies for "Achievement in Representing the American Way of Life."

LOVE FROM A STRANGER

1937   86m   bw   ★★★★
Thriller   /A
Trafalgar   (U.K.)

Ann Harding (*Carol Howard*), Basil Rathbone (*Gerald Lovell*), Binnie Hale (*Kate Meadows*), Bruce Seton (*Ronald Bruce*), Jean Cadell (*Aunt Lou*), Bryan Powley (*Dr. Gribble*), Joan Hickson (*Emmy*), Donald Calthrop (*Hobson*), Eugene Leahy (*Mr. Tuttle*)

p, Max Schach; d, Rowland V. Lee; w, Frances Marion (based on the short story by Agatha Christie and the play by Frank Vosper); ph, Philip Tannura; ed, Howard O'Neill; cos, Samuel Lange

This top-notch thriller provides some brilliant acting by Harding and Rathbone who parry and thrust in a game of deadly wits. Harding is a sweet and unsuspecting lady of beauty and refinement who wins a lottery while on a European vacation. A short time later, she encounters the suave and charming Rathbone who walks her to the altar. Rathbone uses some of Harding's money to buy a luxurious home in the country, and all seems blissful until he quite casually asks Harding to sign a document, claiming it is a mortgage transfer. The document, if signed, would turn over her entire fortune to Rathbone. Up to this point, the viewer has no inkling that he is even dishonest. Seton, a stranger, warns her that Rathbone is a regular bluebeard, that he has killed many women for their money. From that point on, Harding desperately maneuvers to save her own life as her husband tries to kill her in a variety of subtle ways. In the end, he tries poisoning her coffee, but Harding is aware of the ploy and turns the tables on him, or appears to. She finally convinces Rathbone that he is the one who has swallowed the poisoned cup of coffee. His weak heart gives out, and he dies, but without a drop of poison in his veins. Rathbone is both charming and frightening in his sophisticated role, and this film remains one of his finest. Harding is also excellent as the victim desperate to preserve her life. This was the American actress's first British film. All the vagaries and nuances of the original Agatha Christie story remain in tact, and Lee's direction and Marion's script shine.

LOVE ME OR LEAVE ME

1955   122m   c   ★★★★
Musical/Biography   /A
MGM

Doris Day (*Ruth Etting*), James Cagney (*Martin "The Gimp" Snyder*), Cameron Mitchell (*Johnny Alderman*), Robert Keith (*Bernard V. Loomis*), Tom Tully (*Frobisher*), Harry Bellaver (*Georgie*), Richard Gaines (*Paul Hunter*), Peter Leeds (*Fred Taylor*), Claude Stroud (*Eddie Fulton*), Audrey Young (*Jingle Girl*)

p, Joe Pasternak; d, Charles Vidor; w, Daniel Fuchs, Isobel Lennart (based on the story by Fuchs); ph, Arthur E. Arling (Eastmancolor, Cinemascope); ed, Ralph E. Winters; m, Percy Faith (for Doris Day); art d, Cedric Gibbons, Urie McCleary; fx, Warren Newcombe; chor, Alex Romero; cos, Helen Rose

In a departure from the standard musicals of its day, LOVE ME OR LEAVE ME provides a hard-edged love story, augmented with Jazz Age tunes, chronicling the life and times of Prohibition-era torch singer Ruth Etting. This was a once-in-a-lifetime role for Doris Day, who is terrific as Etting in a part unlike any other she played, calling for her to be alternately sizzling in performance and naive offstage. James Cagney is equally sensational as Martin "The Gimp" Snyder, the ruthless gangster who was her Svengali, and normally lightweight Cameron Mitchell excels as Harry Myrl Alderman (called Johnny in the film), Etting's true love. Snyder, a powerful Chicago racketeer, sees Etting at a dime-a-dance club. After she is fired for resisting the advances of a customer, he gets her a job dancing at another club, but she really wants to be a singer, so he pushes the owner into giving her a small singing bit. Club pianist Alderman helps her develop her talents, and, with Snyder's aid, Etting eventually becomes a headliner, going on to radio and a spot in the Ziegfeld Follies in New York. When Etting grows increasingly independent of Snyder, however, he tears up her Ziegfeld contract and takes her on tour, then to movie stardom in Hollywood. There, Alderman resumes subtly courting her, but Snyder has manipulated her into marrying him, and Etting takes to drink over having to live with a man she does not love. When Snyder catches his wife and Alderman kissing, he shoots the latter and is jailed. Alderman survives to marry Etting, who divorces Snyder—although, when Snyder is released, she is headlining in the club he owns as a gesture of gratitude for his help, an act he accepts with some grace. The chemistry between Cagney and Day is electric, Charles Vidor's direction is lively and inventive, and the overall production lavishly and accurately reproduces the 1920s era—though the film distorts some facts of Etting's life. The Jazz Age music is outstanding, superbly performed by Day. MGM paid $50,000 for the song rights alone, as well as substantial but unstated sums to Etting, Alderman, and Snyder for the rights to film their lives. Etting later noted that "they took a lot of liberties with my life, but I guess they usually do with that kind of thing". They made back the money upon the film's release, however, when it was enthusiastically received by both critics and audiences. Cagney was nominated for Best Actor, but lost to Ernest Borgnine for MARTY. Fuchs took home an Oscar for Best Story, and the film was nominated for Best Screenplay, Best Song, Best Sound and Best Score.

LOVE ME TONIGHT

(MAREZ-MOI CE SOIR!)
1932   104m   bw
Musical/Comedy   /A
Paramount

Maurice Chevalier (*Maurice Courtelin*), Jeanette MacDonald (*Princess Jeanette*), Charlie Ruggles (*Vicomte Gilbert de Vareze*), Charles Butterworth (*Count de Savignac*), Myrna Loy (*Countess Vantine*), C. Aubrey Smith (*The Duke*), Elizabeth Patterson, Ethel Griffies, Blanche Frederici (*Aunts*), Joseph Cawthorn (*Dr. Armand de Fontinac*)

p, Rouben Mamoulian; d, Rouben Mamoulian; w, Samuel Hoffenstein, Waldemar Young, George Marion, Jr. (based on the play "Tailor in the Chateau" by Leopold Marchand, Paul Armont); ph, Victor Milner; ed, William Shea; art d, Hans Dreier; cos, Edith Head, Travis Banton

Love it forever. Along with SWING TIME and perhaps one of Busby Berkeley's best, this film stands as the greatest musical of the 1930s and one of the finest ever. Although the film seems very much in a Lubitsch vein, Rouben Mamoulian directed it, and he is perhaps most responsible for its stunning appeal. His earliest period in film (1929-34) was certainly his greatest and in this film he displays such audacity in playing with sound and image that it's no wonder he frightened everyone in Hollywood.

The tale of a romance between Princess Jeanette (MacDonald) and Maurice the tailor (Chevalier), LOVE ME TONIGHT is effervescent frippery to be sure, but it's so inventive as to be downright eerie. The slow-motion retreat from the lovers' cottage still astounds and Jeanette's final ride on horseback to stop a train is dramatically quite striking. One is not likely to forget the dark shadows of Chevalier's "I'm an Apache" number or the cutting and framing of both the title duet and the witty "The Son of a Gun Is Nothing But a Tailor". The Princess' three worrisome aunts could almost be comic variants of the witches in MACBETH and, at one point during their clucking and yowling, they sound like a kennel in an uproar. The film mocks those very conventions the musical genre employs, from the famous traveling rendition of "Isn't It Romantic?" to the sudden thud of a ladder which disrupts Jeanette's balcony reverie.

The cast, too, is quite remarkable, and they make the most of the saucy pre-Code antics afforded by the delightful screenplay. Charlie Ruggles' mad dash in his underwear and Charles Butterworth's "I fell flat on my flute" demonstrate comic diffidence of the highest caliber. In what is almost certainly her most memorable role before achieving stardom, Myrna Loy plies her smooth comic touch and gets to add a naughtiness she usually wasn't allowed later. Her man-crazy Vantine displays great timing and a freshness partly inspired by Mamoulian and Loy's creating the part as they went along. When someone is ill and she is asked, "Could you go for a doctor?" she instantly replies, "Oh, yes, send him in." The starring duo, meanwhile, enjoy one of their greatest partnerings here. Though we like some of her later films with Nelson Eddy, the genial, risque tension between Chevalier and MacDonald works as deliciously as vodka in orange juice. MacDonald is not sufficiently appreciated for her wonderful comic flair and Mamoulian is bold enough to simply toss off her spirited rendition of "Lover" in long shot, knowing that her play with both an uncooperative horse and the ending of the verses will be more hilarious that way. She matches the winking Frenchman innuendo for innuendo and her carefully stylized and sexy performance fits perfectly within the film's magnificent sense of hyperbole. Finally, the incomparable Chevalier knows exactly what he's up to as well here. Not conventional leading man material, he's both beautifully tongue-in-cheek and utterly sincere. His naughtiness completely avoids the puerile and the nasty, yet he can get more out of his signature song "Mimi" than any lyricist can write.

Such a remark, however, intends no slight to the marvelous score by Rodgers and Hart. Is it any wonder that almost every Paramount film from this period uses "Isn't It Romantic?" as background music at some point? Isn't it delightful how you can never get this song out of your head? Best of all, the clever lyrics and lilting melodies are carefully integrated into the film, tying a perky ribbon around an irresistible package. Mamoulian's experiments with musical theatre onstage with his PORGY AND BESS clearly show in his sense of design here. From the brilliant opening sound and image montage of Paris awakening to a final blast of romantic steam, LOVE ME TONIGHT displays a full-blown quality musicals demand but so rarely enjoy.

LOVE ON THE RUN
(L'AMOUR EN FUITE)
1979 94m c   ★★★½
Drama/Comedy   PG/15
Carosse (France)

Jean-Pierre Leaud (Antoine Doinel), Marie-France Pisier (Colette), Claude Jade (Christine), Dani (Liliane), Dorothee (Sabine), Rosy Varte (Colette's Mother), Marie Henriau (Divorce Judge), Daniel Mesguich (Xavier the Librarian), Julien Bertheau (M. Lucien), Jean-Pierre Ducos (Christine's Lawyer)

d, Francois Truffaut; w, Francois Truffaut, Marie-France Pisier, Jean Aurel, Suzanne Schiffman; ph, Nestor Almendros; ed, Martine Barraque; m, Georges Delerue; art d, Jean-Pierre Kohut-Svelko

LOVE ON THE RUN is the fifth and final entry in Francois Truffaut's "Antoine Doinel" series, which began in 1959 with THE 400 BLOWS. By now the young, unpredictable Antoine (Jean-Pierre Leaud) has grown into a man of 34, able to reminisce about his past loves and put them into his new book. The picture opens with the unshaven Antoine and his newest love, Sabine (Dorothee, in a wonderful debut performance), awakening to a sunny morning—the morning that he is to get a divorce from his wife, Christine (Claude Jade, from 1971's BED AND BOARD). Before the day is over Antoine also encounters his first love, Colette (Marie-France Pisier, who appeared years before in Truffaut's episode of LOVE AT TWENTY). There is actually very little in LOVE ON THE RUN that resembles a story. Its chief purpose is simply to look back at the women Antoine has loved. Like so many of Truffaut's characters, Antoine is obsessed with the desire to love, and here he tells how he found a ripped-up, discarded picture of Sabine in a phone booth and set out to find her. In the process, clips are shown from THE 400 BLOWS; LOVE AT TWENTY; STOLEN KISSES; and BED AND BOARD, amounting to an overview of the life of Doinel (as well as those of both Leaud and Truffaut). For those who haven't seen any of the previous "Doinel" pictures, LOVE ON THE RUN will probably be a difficult picture to sit through, but for those who have followed the growth of these characters, the film is a true charmer. In keeping with other Truffaut films, LOVE ON THE RUN includes a superb score from Georges Delerue and a perfectly hummable title song from Alain Souchon.

LOVE PARADE, THE
(PARADE D'AMOUR)
1929 107m bw   ★★★½
Musical/Comedy
Paramount

Maurice Chevalier (Count Alfred Renard), Jeanette MacDonald (Queen Louise), Lupino Lane (Jacques), Lillian Roth (Lulu), Edgar Norton (Major Domo), Lionel Belmore (Prime Minister), Albert Roccardi (Foreign Minister), Carl Stockdale (Admiral), Eugene Pallette (Minister of War), E.H. Calvert (Sylvanian Ambassador)

p, Ernst Lubitsch; d, Ernst Lubitsch; w, Ernest Vajda, Guy Bolton (based on the play "The Prince Consort" by Leon Xanrof, Jules Chancel); ph, Victor Milner; ed, Merrill White; art d, Hans Dreier

Students of film lore will find much to enjoy in THE LOVE PARADE. It was Ernst Lubitsch's first sound film, Jeanette MacDonald's debut, Maurice Chevalier's second picture, and the first of three that the director made with these leads. (The others were ONE HOUR WITH YOU, THE MERRY WIDOW.) The featherweight story takes place in mythical Sylvania, where the queen (MacDonald) is desperately lonely for male companionship. Chevalier, her emissary to France, has been cavorting so conspicuously that she has recalled him to Sylvania. MacDonald reads of Chevalier's adventures with a bevy of beauties and wonders if he could make her happy. She invites him to her chambers to check out for herself what endears him to so many women and is so impressed with his amorous skills that she marries him. Meanwhile, she is trying to borrow cash for the country, and Chevalier, who is sure he could get the job done, stays in the background. Male chauvinist that he is, his subservient position becomes intolerable to him, however, and he begins to balk at her regal demands. Ordered to squire her to the first night of the opera, Chevalier refuses, so she attends alone. Later, to her delight, he shows up, but he's come to tell her that he is tired of feeling like the royal gigolo and plans to leave the next day for Paris, where his attorney will dissolve this mistaken marriage. Late that night, she returns from the opera and goes to his apartment, where she agrees to make him king, and the picture ends as they embrace.

The story could not be less substantial, but the execution is so insouciant and bubbly that we don't care about the frail plot. Chevalier has the distinction of performing the first musical soliloquy in a talking picture with "Nobody's Using It Now." Although this was a sound picture, large stretches were shot silently, then inserted with sound sequences, the result of which is somewhat incoherent. The film was a rarity for its time, when most musicals depicted backstage-Broadway, with wise-cracking chorus girls and songs that stopped, rather than advanced the action. Chevalier earned an Academy Award nomination for his performance, one of two nominations he garnered that year (the other was for THE BIG POND), but lost to George Arliss for DISRAELI. The film earned five other nominations including Best Picture (losing to ALL QUIET ON THE WESTERN FRONT), Best Director, Best Cinematography, Best Decoration, and Best Sound Recording. Songwriter Victor Schertzinger also directed films, from 1917 (THE CLODHOPPER) to 1941 (THE FLEET'S IN, for which he also wrote the music). All the music was written by Schertzinger and Clifford Grey except for the "Valse Tatjana" by O. Potoker. Songs include "Champagne" (sung by Lupino Lane), "Paris, Stay the Same" (sung by Chevalier, Lane, and Jiggs), "Dream Lover" (sung by MacDonald and female chorus), "Anything to Please the Queen" (sung by MacDonald and Chevalier), "Sylvania's Queen" (sung by the chorus), "Let's Be Common" (sung by Lane and Lillian Roth),

"March of the Grenadiers" (sung by MacDonald and male chorus), and "The Queen Is Always Right" (sung by Roth, Lane, and chorus).

LOVE STORY

1970 99m c ★★½
Romance GP/PG
Paramount

Ali MacGraw *(Jenny Cavilleri)*, Ryan O'Neal *(Oliver Barrett IV)*, Ray Milland *(Oliver Barrett III)*, Katharine Balfour *(Mrs. Oliver Barrett III)*, John Marley *(Phil Cavilleri)*, Russell Nype *(Dean Thompson)*, Sydney Walker *(Dr. Shapely)*, Robert Modica *(Dr. Addison)*, Walker Daniels *(Ray)*, Tommy Lee Jones *(Hank)*

p, Howard G. Minsky; d, Arthur Hiller; w, Erich Segal (based on the novel by Erich Segal); ph, Dick Kratina (Movielab Color); ed, Robert C. Jones; m, Francis Lai; art d, Robert Gundlach; cos, Alice Manougian Martin, Pearl Somner

"Love means never having to say you're sorry" was the catch phrase that helped make this a huge grosser. LOVE STORY is a unique picture because it is actually better than Segal's best-seller from whence it sprang. To show how poorly some actors and directors are when it comes to knowing what's best for them, Jon Voight, Beau Bridges, and three Michaels—York, Douglas, and Sarrazin—all nixed the script. Directors Anthony Harvey and Larry Peerce (who may hold the record for consecutive bombs) also rejected the script before Hiller took it on. In other hands, it might have been sentimental slush, but Hiller's work is excellent, and the movie was nominated by the Academy for Best Picture, Best Director, Best Actor, Best Actress, Best Supporting Actor, Best Music, and Best Screenplay from Another Medium. Only the music took the Oscar, as PATTON, AIRPORT, and M*A*S*H dominated the proceedings. O'Neal is at Harvard (where much of this was made) in his final pre-law year, when he meets and falls for MacGraw, a Radcliffe student studying music. She's a poor girl from a lower-class family, and he is one of the Boston Brahmins. O'Neal's father, Milland, won't hear of his son and heir marrying the daughter of an Italian baker and says he'll cut him off without a farthing. Love triumphs over money and O'Neal and MacGraw wed. With no money coming in, O'Neal has to apply for a scholarship to study law, but the dean, Nype, thinks it ludicrous that a millionaire's son is asking for financial aid and decrees O'Neal must pay his own tuition if he wants to have the prestigious Harvard degree. MacGraw has already bypassed a scholarship to study music in France in favor of the wedding. She takes a job as a vocal coach for a school choir and earns a small salary. O'Neal takes a series of jobs to help support them, and they move into an apartment they can barely afford in a poor section of the Hub City. Still, they are ecstatically happy with each other. He graduates high in the class and gets a job with an important New York law firm. They move into a nice apartment and decide it's time to have a baby. Though they try hard, it's not working, so they see a doctor about what to do regarding her barren condition (or is it his fault?). Their physician, Walker, tells O'Neal that MacGraw is dying. O'Neal is reeling with shock but must put on a happy face for his wife, whom he assumes knows nothing about her impending demise. Then he learns that she also knows, and she declines his offer to take her to France, a place she's always wanted to see. She would prefer, instead, to spend her last days with him at home. Time passes. She's taken to the hospital, and O'Neal has to borrow money from his father to pay for the expenses, but he won't tell Milland why. She dies in O'Neal's arms, and Milland comes to the hospital to say he's sorry for his earlier behavior. O'Neal

retorts with the famous line mentioned above, then walks past the old, bald man out into Central Park to think about what might have been. It's touching, well-made, and expertly crafted to wring hankies. Segal's dialog is often sappy and not nearly as good as the actors who must deliver it. The same subject was examined in TERMS OF ENDEARMENT many years later. That picture nailed several awards but was inferior to this one on most levels. A picture that touched everyone who saw it, LOVE STORY can take its place with DARK VICTORY and LOVE AFFAIR in the ranks of the excellent romantic films for which Hollywood is so famous.

LOVE STREAMS

1984 141m c ★★★½
Drama PG-13/15
MGM

Gena Rowlands *(Sarah Lawson)*, John Cassavetes *(Robert Harmon)*, Diahnne Abbott *(Susan)*, Seymour Cassel *(Jack Lawson)*, Margaret Abbott *(Margarita)*, Jakob Shaw *(Albie Swanson)*, Michele Conway *(Agnes Swanson)*, Eddy Donno *(Stepfather Swanson)*, Joan Foley *(Judge Dunbar)*, Al Ruban *(Milton Kravitz)*

p, Menahem Golan, Yoram Globus; d, John Cassavetes; w, Ted Allan, John Cassavetes (based on the play by Allan); ph, Al Ruban (Metrocolor); ed, George Villasenor; m, Bo Harwood; art d, Phedon Papamichael; cos, Jennifer Smith-Ashley

With Israeli filmmakers Golan and Globus watching over him, director John Cassavetes was guilty of less self-indulgence than usual, and the result is one of his best movies ever. Appearing for the first time in a movie that he also directed, Cassavetes and real-life spouse Gena Rowlands team up as a brother and sister, Robert Harmon and Sarah Lawson. The screen exudes their intensity; and despite their apparently different personalities, a oneness of spirit unites them. Robert is a well-known author, who is researching a book on prostitution and becomes the den father to some lively ladies of the evening. His research takes him on nightly forays to the underbelly of town. Sarah is a delicate creature in the throes of a divorce and custody battle against her husband, Jack (Seymour Cassel). The intercutting of the two stories contrasts the tawdriness of Robert's life to the exemplariness of Sarah's. For half the movie we see their separate lives and wonder when and if they will get together. Rowlands is wonderfully convincing in her many opportunities to play unusual scenes. Cassavetes also has his moments. More an amalgam of telling bits and pieces than a real story, this movie (like so many of Cassavetes' works) goes on too long. This time, however, it all seems to work.

LOVE WITH THE PROPER STRANGER

1963 102m bw ★★★★
Comedy/Drama /X
Boardwalk/Rona

Natalie Wood *(Angie Rossini)*, Steve McQueen *(Rocky Papasano)*, Edie Adams *(Barbie, Barbara of Seville)*, Herschel Bernardi *(Dominick Rossini)*, Tom Bosley *(Anthony Colombo)*, Harvey Lembeck *(Julio Rossini)*, Penny Santon *(Mama Rossini)*, Virginia Vincent *(Anna)*, Nick Alexander *(Guido Rossini)*, Augusta Ciolli *(Mrs. Papasano)*

p, Alan J. Pakula; d, Robert Mulligan; w, Arnold Schulman; ph, Milton Krasner; ed, Aaron Stell; m, Elmer Bernstein; art d, Hal Pereira, Roland Anderson; cos, Edith Head

Wood plays a sort of female Marty in this role that netted the actress her third Oscar nomination. She is a quiet, well-brought-up Italian girl in a situation that is more than she can handle. She is so quiet, well-brought-up, and Italian, in fact, that it's hard to imagine how she got into this mess! How does a sweet, traditional type manage to find herself pregnant after a one-night stand with McQueen? It seems that they attended the same party at a summer hotel where he was working as a jazz musician, and one thing led to another. When she realizes her predicament, Wood comes to his union hall to ask McQueen's help in finding a doctor to do the needful. For some reason his regular girlfriend becomes angry when he asks her advice, and she tosses him out. Meanwhile, Wood's family (mama Santon and brothers Bernardi and Lembeck) have no idea she's expecting and are pushing her to marry Bosley, the pudgy, self-effacing owner of a small restaurant. While trying to raise money for the abortion, McQueen takes Wood to meet his parents, who fall under her charm. Then, in the squalid digs of the abortionist, McQueen is gripped by the horror of what Wood is enduring in the next room. He bursts in and drags her out. They decide to find another way—to get to know more about each other. Wood realizes that McQueen is not a great prospect for marriage. Further, Bosley now knows that she is pregnant, has claimed paternity, and is more than willing to marry her. But McQueen and Wood awkwardly explore pursuing the relationship, despite its inauspicious beginnings. The film ends as they embrace.

The theme of unmarried pregnancy had been seen often before (e.g., in BLUE DENIM) but was not usually handled so deftly as in this picture, which has lots of down-to-earth, Italian humor from Bosley, Lembeck, and Bernardi. Adams is outstanding as McQueen's stripper girlfriend, however. She always had a way with comedy and showed it early when playing the foil for her genius husband, Ernie Kovacs. In small roles, look for Richard Mulligan, Arlene Golonka, Vic Tayback, and Richard Dysart, all of whom later achieved success on TV. Oscar nominations went to the screenplay, cinematography, art direction, and costume design as well as to Wood.

LOVED ONE, THE

1965 116m bw   ★★★★
Comedy   /X
MGM

Robert Morse (*Dennis Barlow*), Jonathan Winters (*Wilbur Glenworthy/Harry Glenworthy*), Anjanette Comer (*Aimee Thanatogenos*), Rod Steiger (*Mr. Joyboy*), Dana Andrews (*Gen. Brinkman*), Milton Berle (*Mr. Kenton*), James Coburn (*Immigration Officer*), John Gielgud (*Sir Francis Hinsley*), Tab Hunter (*Guide*), Margaret Leighton (*Mrs. Kenton*)

p, John Calley, Haskell Wexler; d, Tony Richardson; w, Terry Southern, Christopher Isherwood (based on the novel by Evelyn Waugh); ph, Haskell Wexler; ed, Anthony Gibbs; m, John Addison; prod d, Rouben Ter-Arutunian; art d, Sydney Z. Litwack; fx, Geza Gaspar; cos, Nat Tolmach, Rouben Ter-Arutunian, James Kelly, Marie T. Harris

This spoof of morticians and funerals captures much of the macabre hilarity in the Waugh novel but failed to impress critics at the time of release. It often sinks into broad burlesque due to Southern and Isherwood's heavy-handed script, but the laughs are still there. Morse, a naive, rather gawky character from England, visits his uncle, Gielgud, an aging, fussy art director living in a dilapidated Hollywood mansion. When his studio fires him, Gielgud hangs himself. Robert Morley, head of the British community of Hollywood talent, arrives and instructs Morse to arrange to have Gielgud buried at Whispering Glades Memorial Park (the real-life Forest Lawn), the most resplendent funeral

grounds in America, run by Winters. In the process of contacting morticians, Morse obtains a job at a pet cemetery run by Winters' twin brother (also played by Winters), and the various schemes, scams, and lack of concern by morticians for both humans and pets are revealed in all their callous glories. A host of bizarre characters then parade through Morse's life, including Comer, a sultry, naive beauty he covets and who is lusted after by Winters (the one running the high-class mortuary) and Steiger, a crackpot cosmetologist who works with her. Comer is repelled by Steiger's obese and gluttonous mother and is almost won over by Morse who reads poetry (stolen from Steiger) to her. Then Comer's ideals are smashed by Winters, head of Whispering Glades, when he tries to seduce her, and she commits suicide by injecting herself with embalming fluid. A further plot develops when Morse discovers that Winters, in collusion with Andrews, an Air Force general, plans to get rid of all the bodies on his property by sending them into space, so he can transform his cemetery into a luxurious spa for retirees, making even more millions. He is foiled by Morse who replaces the body of a dead astronaut, the first to be shot into space, with Comer's comely corpse. Having exposed Winters and sent him to ruin, Morse returns to England to try to forget his morbid, morose, and strange experience in America. Morse is unappealing, but the supporting players, especially Winters, and bits performed by Stander, Coburn, and Hunter are very funny.

LOVERS, THE
(LES AMANTS)
1959 90m bw   ★★★
Drama   /X
Nouvelle Editions des Films   (France)

Jeanne Moreau (*Jeanne Tournier*), Alain Cuny (*Henri Tournier*), Jean-Marc Bory (*Bernard Dubois-Lambert*), Judith Magre (*Maggy Thiebaut-Leroy*), Jose-Luis de Vilallonga (*Raoul Flores*), Gaston Modot (*Coudray*), Patricia Garcin (*Catherine, Jeanne's Daughter*), Claude Mansard (*Marcelot*), Georgette Lobbe (*Marthe*)

d, Louis Malle; w, Louis Malle, Louise de Vilmorin (based on the novel *Point de Lendemain* by Dominique Vivant); ph, Henri Decae (Dyaliscope); ed, Leonide Azar; m, Johannes Brahms, Alain de Rosnay; prod d, Bernard Evein, Jacques Saulnier

Notorious for its extended seminude love-making scene when first released in 1959, Louis Malle's THE LOVERS seems tame today when compared with average "R" rated films of the decades following it. The film tells the simple tale of Moreau, a bored mother and wife, who meets, falls in love with, and sleeps with young archaeologist Bory—all in the course of one evening. The next morning she abandons her family and runs off with her new lover to an uncertain future. The film was vastly overrated due to the censorship it incurred overseas and in the US. (A suburban Cleveland theater manager was prosecuted for showing an obscene film. The case went to the Supreme Court and was eventually thrown out.) The film is a solid but not great examination of female mid-life crisis, with Moreau in typically fine form.

LOVERS AND OTHER STRANGERS

1970 104m c   ★★★½
Comedy   R/15
ABC

Gig Young (*Hal Henderson*), Bea Arthur (*Bea Vecchio*), Bonnie Bedelia (*Susan Henderson*), Anne Jackson (*Cathy*), Harry Guardino (*Johnny*), Michael Brandon (*Mike Vecchio*), Richard

Castellano *(Frank Vecchio)*, Bob Dishy *(Jerry)*, Marian Hailey *(Brenda)*, Joseph Hindy *(Richie)*

p, David Susskind; d, Cy Howard; w, Renee Taylor, Joseph Bologna, David Zelag Goodman (based on the play by Joseph Bologna, Renee Taylor); ph, Andrew Laszlo (Metrocolor); ed, David Bretherton, Sidney Katz; m, Fred Karlin; prod d, Ben Edwards; cos, Albert Wolsky

A well-done, multifaceted comedy containing several romantic vignettes that take place before and during the wedding of a young couple, Brandon and Bedelia, who have decided to marry after living together for a year and a half. Though both the couple's families are thrilled, the tension and excitement leading up to the wedding and the wedding itself bring out many family squabbles heretofore repressed. Castellano is wonderful (it was his first major role and led to his being cast as a major character in THE GODFATHER) as the groom's father, whose happiness is disturbed by the news that his other son, Hindy, is considering divorcing his wife, Diane Keaton (this was also Keaton's first major role). On the other side of the family, Young, the rich, strict Irish-Catholic father of the bride, finds himself trapped by his longtime mistress, Jackson, who suddenly decides to force him into choosing between her and his wife. Meanwhile, Anne Meara, the bride's sister, is going through the collapse of her marriage because her husband, Guardino, has become more interested in television than sex. The evening before the wedding, Brandon and Bedelia arrange a blind date between her cousin, Hailey, and one of the ushers, Dishy. Dishy, hoping to score with Hailey, finds his efforts at seduction frustrated by the girl's nonstop chatter. The next day all the emotional turmoil works itself out and the wedding proceeds smoothly. LOVERS AND OTHER STRANGERS is a charming, hilarious film that skillfully balances the many divergent storylines into a fascinating, entertaining whole. Well cast (a fine example of ensemble acting), and well paced, it holds up to several viewings. For some mysterious reason the MPAA gave the film an undue "R" rating, but any nudity or foul language is not to be found, and the sexual aspects of the story are handled tastefully. Songs were performed by Country Coalition and Larry Meredith. The tune "For All We Know" won the Oscar for Best Song, and the film was also nominated for Best Supporting Actor (Castellano) and Best Screenplay.

LOVERS, HAPPY LOVERS!
(MONSIEUR RIPOIS)
1954 85m bw   ★★½
Drama
Transcontinental (U.K./France)

Gerard Philipe *(Andre Ripois)*, Natasha Parry *(Patricia)*, Valerie Hobson *(Catherine)*, Joan Greenwood *(Norah)*, Margaret Johnston *(Anne)*, Germaine Montero *(Marcelle)*, Diana Decker *(Diana)*, Percy Marmont *(Catherine's Father)*, Bill Shine, Mai Bacon

p, Paul Graetz; d, Rene Clement; w, Hugh Mills, Raymond Queneau, Rene Clement (based on a novel by Louis Hemon); ph, Oswald Morris; m, Roman Vlad

Philipe stars as an amorous Frenchman who goes off to London to charm a number of women, finally marrying Hobson. Soon after that, boredom sets in and Philipe pursues Parry. When she spurns his advances, he desperately fakes a suicide attempt to gain her sympathy, but the trick goes awry and he plunges off a balcony to his death. An ironic but sympathetic look at some naive women and a genuine knave, a man who is a failed cynic pursuing women almost as an addiction. To achieve authenticity

in background shots, director Clement shot the streets of London with a hidden camera.

LOVES OF A BLONDE
(LASKY JEDNE PLAVOVLASKY)
1965 88m bw   ★★★½
Comedy
Barrandov/Ceskoslovensky (Czechoslovakia)

Hana Brejchova *(Andula)*, Vladimir Pucholt *(Milda)*, Vladimir Mensik *(Vacovsky)*, Ivan Kheil *(Manas)*, Jiri Hruby *(Burda)*, Milada Jezkova *(Milda's Mother)*, Josef Sebanek *(Milda's Father)*, Marie Salacova *(Marie)*, Jana Novakova *(Jana)*, Jana Crkalova *(Jaruska)*

d, Milos Forman; w, Jaroslav Papousek, Ivan Passer, Milos Forman, Vaclav Sasek; ph, Miroslav Ondricek; ed, Miroslav Hajek; m, Evzen Illin; art d, Karel Cerny

This charming and frequently touching romantic comedy, directed by Milos Forman, concerns a young woman, Brejchova, who works in a shoe factory and dreams of love. Dissatisfied with the men in her town, she is forced to suffer the attentions of Blazejovsky, an ardent admirer, but less than what she perceives to be her ideal man. When a dance is held in honor of soldiers stationed in the town, Brejchova looks forward to meeting a handsome military man. To her disappointment, however, the soldiers all turn out to be middle-aged reserves, so she sets her sights on the piano player, Pucholt. After some uneasy introductions, Brejchova spends the night with Pucholt. Now in love, she travels to his parents' home in Prague, where her stay is anything but blissful. An international success, LOVES OF A BLONDE was an important film not only in the career of Forman (who would go to America and direct ONE FLEW OVER THE CUCKOO'S NEST), but also as one of the films (along with THE SHOP ON MAIN STREET and CLOSELY WATCHED TRAINS) that helped give Czech cinema worldwide attention. It received an Oscar nomination for Best Foreign Film, but lost to A MAN AND A WOMAN.

LOVESICK
1983 95m c   ★★
Comedy   PG/15
Ladd

Dudley Moore *(Saul Benjamin)*, Elizabeth McGovern *(Chloe Allen)*, Alec Guinness *(Sigmund Freud)*, Christine Baranski *(Nymphomaniac)*, Gene Saks *(Frantic Patient)*, Renee Taylor *(Mrs. Mondragon)*, Kent Broadhurst *(Gay)*, Lester Rawlins *(Silent Patient)*, Wallace Shawn *(Otto Jaffe)*, Suzanne Barrie *(His Wife)*

p, Charles Okun; d, Marshall Brickman; w, Marshall Brickman; ph, Gerry Fisher (Technicolor); ed, Nina Feinberg; m, Philippe Sarde; prod d, Philip Rosenberg; cos, Kristi Zea

Saul Benjamin (Dudley Moore) is a psychiatrist who falls in love with patient Chloe Allen (Elizabeth McGovern). This second feature from writer-director Marshall Brickman reveals the influence of his friend Woody Allen. Allen's character in PLAY IT AGAIN SAM carries on a dialogue with an apparition of Humphrey Bogart; here, Benjamin talks with a spectral Sigmund Freud. The roles are all neatly done, but Brickman's script is nearly directionless. The film has its cute moments, but in the end, it is a waste of fine talent.

LOVING
1970 89m c   ★★
Comedy/Drama   R/X
Columbia

George Segal (*Brooks Wilson*), Eva Marie Saint (*Selma Wilson*), Sterling Hayden (*Lepridon*), Keenan Wynn (*Edward*), Nancie Phillips (*Nelly*), Janis Young (*Grace*), David Doyle (*Will*), Paul Sparer (*Marve*), Andrew Duncan (*Willy*), Sherry Lansing (*Susan*)

p, Don Devlin; d, Irvin Kershner; w, Don Devlin (based on the novel *Brooks Wilson, Ltd.* by J.M. Ryan); ph, Gordon Willis (Eastmancolor); ed, Robert Lawrence; m, Bernardo Segall; prod d, Walter Scott Herndon; cos, Albert Wolsky

Sometimes funny, sometimes dramatic, LOVING is most times dull. Based on a novel by J.M. Ryan, it's the story of freelance artist Segal and his wife, Saint, as they try to keep their rocky marriage together in suburban Connecticut. Segal is having an in-town affair with Young, and his work situation is teetering. The combination serves to place him on the precipice of a breakdown. He has a chance at a large commission and is supposed to meet with mogul Hayden at a private dining club that caters to admen. Segal drinks too much and gets vicious with the club's prexy. Hayden finds that behavior amusing and says he'll think about giving Segal the business. At a party tossed by his mistress' aunt and uncle, Segal finds out that Hayden liked him enough to award him the art business. He tells neither Saint (who thinks it's time they had a new house) nor Young (who thinks it's time they had a more permanent relationship). When Phillips, the nympho wife of neighbor Doyle, begins to come on to him, Segal falls for it. The two of them go to a child's playroom that has closed-circuit TV (for parents to keep tabs on the kids), and the entire party crowd observes Segal and Phillips as they make love. Saint watches and the crowd howls until Segal realizes what's happening as he spies the camera. He runs outside, not wearing his pants, where Doyle whacks him around. Then Saint pounds him with her purse until her arms get tired, and when Segal tells her he's won Hayden's account, we are left with the feeling she might just stay with him. Roy Scheider has a small role, and Lansing, who later became a film executive and ran FOX studios for years before beginning her own independent company, plays a sexpot. Her business ability was far greater than her acting prowess, and acting's loss became producing's gain when she doffed the sock and buskin in favor of the executive suite.

LUCAS
1986 104m c   ★★★
Comedy/Drama   PG-13/15
Lawrence Gordon

Corey Haim (*Lucas Blye*), Kerri Green (*Maggie*), Charlie Sheen (*Cappie Roew*), Courtney Thorne-Smith (*Alise*), Winona Ryder (*Rina*), Thomas E. Hodges (*Bruno*), Ciro Poppiti (*Ben*), Guy Boyd (*Coach*), Jeremy Piven (*Spike*), Kevin Gerard Wixted (*Tonto*)

p, David Nicksay; d, David Seltzer; w, David Seltzer; ph, Reynaldo Villalobos (Panavision, DeLuxe Color); ed, Priscilla Nedd; m, Dave Grusin; art d, James J. Murakami; cos, Molly Maginnis

After years of sophomoric teenage sex comedies, along came LUCAS, a film that deals with real problems of adolescent love. The title character (Haim) is a 13-year-old eccentric who likes bugs and classical music. Being a short, four-eyed intellectual to boot, he is the victim of all the high school bullies. Offended by the teenage social system that rewards people (especially football players and their cheerleader acolytes) for their physical prowess, Lucas spots a lovely 16-year-old Green. They become friends, and Lucas falls in love with her. His ideal is threatened, however, by Green's attraction to Sheen, a handsome football player. Worse, Green decides to become a cheerleader. LUCAS,

the directorial debut of Seltzer, has more honest teenage scenes than all of John Hughes's films combined. Seltzer's characters are real; and Haim, Green, and Sheen play them wonderfully. As a result LUCAS is not just a film for teenagers but for anyone who has ever been a teenager. The film's greatest fault is its reliance on football heroics at the end; after such wonderfully developed relationships, it is a shame to see LUCAS take a cheap turn.

LUCK OF GINGER COFFEY, THE
1964 100m c   ★★★
Drama   /A
Roth/Kershner/Crawley   (U.S./Canada)

Robert Shaw (*Ginger Coffey*), Mary Ure (*Vera*), Liam Redmond (*MacGregor*), Tom Harvey (*Joe McGlade*), Libby McClintock (*Paulie*), Leo Leyden (*Brott*), Powys Thomas (*Fox*), Tom Kneebone (*Kenny*), Leslie Yeo (*Stan Melton*), Vern Chapman (*Hawkins*)

p, Leon Roth; d, Irvin Kershner; w, Brian Moore (based on his novel); ph, Manny Wynn; ed, Anthony Gibbs; m, Bernardo Segall; prod d, Harry Horner; art d, Albert Brenner

A well-intentioned, noncommercial Canadian-based film starring real-life husband and wife Shaw and Ure as a husband and wife. Shaw is pushing forty and can't hold a job in Dublin, so he and his family emigrate to Montreal in the hope of a new life. His teenage daughter, McClintock, doesn't like the move, but Shaw and Ure hope she'll adjust. Shaw has little success in Canada, and his family asks to return to Ireland. They've had a nest egg for the trip home, but Shaw has spent it, and now they must stay. Ure leaves him, taking McClintock, but soon the girl returns to live with her father. Shaw has apparently settled down and is working as a proofreader at a newspaper under hardhearted Redmond and as a laundry delivery man by day. Shaw thinks he may get a better job as a reporter, so he jettisons his delivery job, despite getting a good offer from the folks who run the laundry. For no apparent reason, he is fired from the newspaper, but it's too late to get back into the laundry. He talks Ure into coming home to help him control McClintock. Shaw can't find work and winds up a drunk. He's soon arrested and tossed in the clink. Kindly judge Legare lets him out with a rap on the knuckles, and Shaw is heartened to see that Ure is standing outside the court waiting for him, open-armed. A nice picture with an interesting look at immigrants who have no language problem, it's about little people in a big predicament and succeeds on its own terms; however, we are left with the thought that if we'd seen another two hours of this, Shaw would have wound up beating his wife and daughter, then stealing a car, and driving drunkenly off a bridge.

LUST FOR LIFE
1956 122m c   ★★★★½
Biography   /A
MGM

Kirk Douglas (*Vincent Van Gogh*), Anthony Quinn (*Paul Gauguin*), James Donald (*Theo Van Gogh*), Pamela Brown (*Christine*), Everett Sloane (*Dr. Gachet*), Niall MacGinnis (*Roulin*), Noel Purcell (*Anton Mauve*), Henry Daniell (*Theodorus Van Gogh*), Madge Kennedy (*Anna Cornelia Van Gogh*), Jill Bennett (*Willemien*)

p, John Houseman; d, Vincente Minnelli; w, Norman Corwin (based on the novel by Irving Stone); ph, Freddie Young, Russell Harlan (CinemaScope, Metrocolor, Ansco Color); ed, Adrienne Fazan; m, Miklos Rozsa; art d, Cedric Gibbons, Hans Peters, Preston Ames; cos, Walter Plunkett

Lust for Life was optioned by MGM in 1947, but it took almost nine years before the studio got around to filming Irving Stone's immensely popular novel, a fictionalized biography of Vincent Van Gogh. Here, Kirk Douglas plays the Dutch painter, who, as the film opens, leaves Holland to give religious instruction to coal miners in a Belgian province in 1878. There, full of pity for the impoverished workers and their families, Van Gogh gives away not only his own worldly goods, but also those belonging to the church. Censured by his superiors in the church for his actions, he denounces them as hypocrites, abandons his evangelical activities, and suffers an emotional and physical decline.

Found living in squalor by his brother, Theo (James Donald), Van Gogh is persuaded to return to Holland and recuperate. Back in his family's home, he begins to pursue his burgeoning interest in painting. His ever-restless nature upsets the Van Gogh household, however, and his sister asks him to leave. In the Hague, Douglas sets up house with Christine (Pamela Brown), a prostitute who becomes his model and mistress. Anton Mauve (Noel Purcell), a successful painter and relative of Van Gogh, tries to help him, but the emotionally volatile, fiercely independent Van Gogh soon rejects Mauve's advice and alienates the better-known painter, losing his economic support and friendship.

After the death of their father, Van Gogh joins Theo in Paris (where Theo is an art dealer), and meets the great artists of the Impressionist movement, including Paul Gauguin (Quinn). Gauguin is nearly as eccentric as Van Gogh, and equally independent in his ideas about painting, and Van Gogh becomes his friend, feeling that Gauguin is the only one would understand his own aims and style. Van Gogh still finds himself commercially unsuccessful and alienated from his fellow artists, however, and he leaves for western Provence to paint the beautiful countryside around Arles. Theo later persuades Gauguin to join his brother but the painters' friendship is contentious at best. The two soon clash in their aesthetic creeds, and Gauguin leaves, unable to put up with his friend's eccentricities and agitated demands. Alone, Van Gogh falls further into emotional isolation and depression.

LUST FOR LIFE tells a tragic story, but it is at the same time inspirational in its portrait of Van Gogh's uncompromised genius. Douglas gives an appropriately fiery performance as Van Gogh, delivering some of the best work of his stellar career, and Quinn, though his appearance is relatively brief, is also excellent as the moody Gauguin, who vainly attempts to befriend his fellow genius. Douglas, a very dedicated actor, threw himself totally into his part, even to the extent of taking intensive instructions in painting from a French artist. He was later nominated for a well-deserved Best Actor Oscar but he lost out to Yul Brynner for THE KING AND I. Quinn, as the truculent, contemplative Gauguin, did win an Oscar for Best Supporting Actor.

Director Vincente Minnelli fought in vain against using CinemaScope for this film, feeling that "the dimensions of the wider screen [bore] little relation to the conventional shape of paintings." Minnelli also felt that the Eastmancolor used by MGM did not offer the soft, subdued tones he thought necessary to reproduce Van Gogh's world and paintings. He described the color process as being "straight from the candy box, a brilliant mixture of blues, reds, and yellows that resembled neither life nor art." Minnelli wanted to use the discontinued Ansco process. With producer Houseman's support, however, Minnelli hounded MGM executives into buying up all the remaining Ansco stock, about 300,000 feet of film. Ansco then opened a special laboratory to process Minnelli's footage. Filming Van Gogh's paintings presented more problems. Houseman agreed that no movie camera could capture the brilliance and subtlety of the work; moreover, the light required by the cameras radiated intense heat that could ruin any painting. Houseman and Minnelli then devised a technical approach that would work when their crew went into the homes of private collectors and museums around the world to put 200 of Van Gogh's masterpieces on film.

In their quest for authenticity, Minnelli and Houseman searched out some surviving contemporaries of the great artist. They also went to many of the actual European locations where Van Gogh lived and worked such as the Hague, Le Borinage, Nuenen, and at Arles. The picture was also nominated for Best Color Art Direction/Set Decoration and Best Adapted Screenplay.

LUSTY MEN, THE

1952 113m bw ★★★★★
Sports/Western /U
RKO

Susan Hayward (*Louise Merritt*), Robert Mitchum (*Jeff McCloud*), Arthur Kennedy (*Wes Merritt*), Arthur Hunnicutt (*Booker Davis*), Frank Faylen (*Al Dawson*), Walter Coy (*Buster Burgess*), Carol Nugent (*Rusty Davis*), Maria Hart (*Rosemary Maddox*), Lorna Thayer (*Grace Burgess*), Burt Mustin (*Jeremiah*)

p, Jerry Wald, Norman Krasna; d, Nicholas Ray; w, Horace McCoy, David Dortort (based on a story by Claude Stanush); ph, Lee Garmes; ed, Ralph Dawson; m, Roy Webb; art d, Albert S. D'Agostino, Alfred Herman; cos, Michael Woulfe

Director Nicholas Ray was a master of the offbeat film, and this brilliant contemporary western, easily the best movie ever made about rodeo (see also JUNIOR BONNER, J.W. COOP and RODEO), is no exception. Washed-up rodeo champion Jeff McCloud (Robert Mitchum) takes a job on the ranch of Wes and Louise Merritt (Arthur Kennedy and Susan Hayward), and, with his guidance, Wes becomes a rodeo star. Meanwhile, Louise leads on the infatuated Jeff to insure his continued training of her husband, but, when Wes gets too big for his britches, Jeff goes head to swelled head with him in rodeo competition, with tragic results. THE LUSTY MEN is full of action and dangerous stunts, photographed beautifully by master cinematographer Lee Garmes. Ray's direction is superb, and all three leads give bravura performances. Based on a *Life* magazine story by Claude Stanush, and coscripted by cowboy David Dortort, its screenplay presents classical situations, full of poetry and destiny. In his search for realism, Ray took his cameras on location, filming rodeos in Tucson, Arizona, Spokane, Washington, Pendleton, Oregon, and Livermore, California, using a host of real rodeo stars such as Gerald Roberts, Jerry Ambler, and Les Sanborn.

M

M
(MORDER UNTER UNS)
1931 117m bw ★★★★★
Crime/Horror /PG
Nero (Germany)

Peter Lorre *(Franz Becker)*, Otto Wernicke *(Inspector Karl Lohmann)*, Gustaf Grundgens *(Schraenker)*, Theo Lingen *(Bauernfaenger)*, Theodor Loos *(Police Commissioner Groeber)*, Georg John *(Blind Peddler)*, Ellen Widmann *(Mme. Becker)*, Inge Landgut *(Elsie)*, Ernst Stahl-Nachbaur *(Police Chief)*, Paul Kemp *(Pickpocket)*

p, Seymour Nebenzal; d, Fritz Lang; w, Fritz Lang, Thea von Harbou, Paul Falkenberg, Adolf Jansen, Karl Vash (based on an article by Egon Jacobson); ph, Fritz Arno Wagner, Gustav Rathje; ed, Paul Falkenberg; m, Edvard Grieg (abstract from "Peer Gynt"); art d, Emil Hasler, Karl Vollbrecht

Fritz Lang's first sound film, his most chilling and provocative work, features Peter Lorre's greatest performance as a child molester and murderer. As the film opens, Berlin is gripped by terror: a child molester is killing little girls, while the police's frantic search has so far turned up no clues to his identity. Frenzied citizens inform on their neighbors; police raids net scores of criminals, but none that can be linked to the killings. To stop this trend, the underworld's leading members resolve to catch the killer themselves, ordering the criminal community to find the murderer and bring him to a tribunal—and the trap to catch the desperate man is set in thrilling motion. Lang tells his grim tale in murky, expressive shadow, and (keeping the murders offscreen) achieves chilling effects through brilliant cinematic strategies: distorted camera angles; expressive shadows; innovative use of sound; and meticulously designed claustrophobic sets. Lang succeeds in conveying the increasing frenzy of various strata of Berlin life as he cross-cuts between wildly different environments to suggest their mutual fear. One particularly interesting and effective manuever was Lang's decision to visually link the police search for the killer with that of the criminals thereby suggesting an equivalence between the two. Lang also makes inspired use of the city of Berlin, its antiquity and squalor, to suggest a deep-seated corruption.

While M offers a truly creepy image of its psychopathic killer, it is all the more effective for its psychological subtlety as it conveys his guilt, despair, and compulsiveness. At that point in his life, Lorre was a rather roly-poly fellow; his plump child-like features adds a poignancy and pathos to the character. The child murderer appears to be a child himself. Lorre was so effective in this role that he would be cast as grotesque psychopaths for the bulk of his long career.

MAJOR AND THE MINOR, THE
1942 100m bw ★★★★½
Comedy /U
Paramount

Ginger Rogers *(Susan Applegate)*, Ray Milland *(Maj. Kirby)*, Rita Johnson *(Pamela Hill)*, Robert Benchley *(Mr. Osborne)*, Diana Lynn *(Lucy Hill)*, Edward Fielding *(Col. Hill)*, Frankie Thomas *(Cadet Osborne)*, Raymond Roe *(Cadet Wigton)*, Charles Smith *(Cadet Korner)*, Larry Nunn *(Cadet Babcock)*

p, Arthur Hornblow, Jr.; d, Billy Wilder; w, Billy Wilder, Charles Brackett (based on the play "Connie Goes Home" by Edward Childs Carpenter and the story "Sunny Goes Home" by Fannie Kilbourne); ph, Leo Tover; ed, Doane Harrison; m, Robert Emmett Dolan; art d, Hans Dreier, Roland Anderson; cos, Edith Head

The LOLITA of the 1940s, and just as sexy. A sparkling farce that marked Billy Wilder's directorial debut after years of writing witty screenplays for other directors, THE MAJOR AND THE MINOR sails along breezily from its very first scenes until its romantic ending. The dialogue is scintillating and full of potentially risque situations, and flies at a pace that punches the laughs out in rapid-fire succession. Rogers is a working girl who has had it with New York City and is eager to return home to the Midwest. When she applies for a ticket at the station, she is shocked to learn that the prices have gone up and she doesn't have enough to cover the fare. When she learns that she does have enough for a half-fare, she dresses up as a 12-year-old child and hopes to pull off the disguise until she reaches her home in Iowa. ("She looks kind of filled out for twelve," notes one of the lunkheaded train conductors.) On board the train she meets Milland, an Army major who is going to a boys' military school for a three day layover. Also on board are several young cadet officers who begin to make eyes at her. Milland, always the gentleman, finds his feelings stirred by this pre-teener and doesn't know how to handle it. Once in Iowa, Milland's fiancee, Johnson, wants to keep him out of active service. Lela Rogers plays Ginger's mother and at one point, Ginger dresses up to impersonate Lela. (Lela Rogers was Ginger's real mother so the resemblance was understandable.) The masquerade is uncovered by Lynn, a teenager, but she keeps mum about it.

All the supporters were good, and special mention should be made of Benchley, who was making a name for himself as an actor after years of writing for *The New Yorker* magazine and starring in a few shorts before he died in 1945. A comic highlight he shares with Rogers is the egg shampoo she gives him at the film's opening. The military school exteriors were filmed in Wisconsin at St. John's Military Academy in Delafield. This was Ginger Rogers's first film for Paramount since SITTING PRETTY. She had been toiling in the RKO vineyards for nine years and her work here ranks among her finest performances. She seemed to have inherited Mary Pickford's gift for playing children and teen-aged types without seeming too ridiculous or coy—except here Wilder takes it one better. Relying on Rogers' formidable talents at mimicry and impersonation, he has her playing someone who plays someone. Almost as delightful is the wonderful Diana Lynn, her pert wisecracking style seemingly an adolescent version of Rogers' style. Milland is in very funny form, too, somehow pulling off the eternally befuddled major whose attraction to a 12 year-old has him concerned. Hilarious from start to finish and featuring the memorable "Maginot Line" sequence, THE MAJOR AND THE MINOR retains its sharpness even amidst today's rather more heavy-handed approaches to sex farce. Dully remade as YOU'RE NEVER TOO YOUNG.

MACARTHUR

1977 128m c   ★★★½
Biography/War   PG/A
Universal

Gregory Peck *(Gen. Douglas MacArthur)*, Ed Flanders *(President Truman)*, Dan O'Herlihy *(President Roosevelt)*, Ivan Bonar *(Gen. Sutherland)*, Ward Costello *(Gen. George Marshall)*, Nicolas Coster *(Col. Huff)*, Marj Dusay *(Mrs. MacArthur)*, Art Fleming *(The Secretary)*, Russell D. Johnson *(Adm. King)*, Sandy Kenyon *(Gen. Wainwright)*

p, Frank McCarthy; d, Joseph Sargent; w, Hal Barwood, Matthew Robbins; ph, Mario Tosi (Technicolor); ed, George Nicholson; m, Jerry Goldsmith; prod d, John J. Lloyd; fx, Albert Whitlock

General of the Army Douglas MacArthur was not a modest man, but he was charismatic, dashing, eloquent, and arguably the most brilliant military strategist of WWII. Gregory Peck captures all those qualities in his magnificent portrayal of the man who symbolized the spirited refusal to accept defeat in the Pacific. Using MacArthur's speech to an assembly of West Point cadets as a framing device, the film traces his illustrious and stormy career—from his retreat from the Philippines and famous promised return, through the success of his controversial island-hopping strategy (bypassing Japanese strongholds and cutting off their supply lines), on to his success as the military governor of a ruined but rebuilding Japan, and finally to his explosive conflict with President Harry Truman over the conduct of the Korean War, which led to the general's retirement. MACARTHUR is an enormous undertaking of a subject much too big to encompass in a single film, and the slices of MacArthur's life sometimes appear disjointed. But Peck is memorable and believable in one of his best parts, capturing the general's eccentricities, vanities, and heroism. Although the film lacks the panache of PATTON, it presents a more introspective look at one of this century's most celebrated warriors. At the time of the film's release, critics found little of the exceptional in MACARTHUR, but Peck's forceful performance and director Joseph Sargent's honest effort to tell an unwieldy story later compelled many to acknowledge the film as a superior production.

MACBETH

1971 140m c   ★★★★
Drama   R/AA
Playboy (U.K.)

Jon Finch *(Macbeth)*, Francesca Annis *(Lady Macbeth)*, Martin Shaw *(Banquo)*, Nicholas Selby *(Duncan)*, John Stride *(Ross)*, Stephan Chase *(Malcolm)*, Paul Shelley *(Donalbain)*, Terence Bayler *(Macduff)*, Andrew Laurence *(Lennox)*, Frank Wylie *(Mentieth)*

p, Andrew Braunsberg, Roman Polanski; d, Roman Polanski; w, Roman Polanski, Kenneth Tynan (based on the play by William Shakespeare); ph, Gilbert Taylor (Todd AO 35, Technicolor); ed, Alastair McIntyre; m, The Third Ear Band; prod d, Wilfred Shingleton; art d, Fred Carter; fx, Ted Samuels; chor, Sally Gilpin; cos, Anthony Mendleson

Roman Polanski's controversial version of the classic Shakespeare play casts Jon Finch and Francesca Annis as the murderously obsessed couple who utilize witchcraft and prophecies as stepping stones to power. Polanski's first film after the murder of his wife, Sharon Tate, by the Manson family, this graphically violent MACBETH could be read as an attempt to exorcise real-life demons. In any case, this version, if not the best Shakespearean adaptation, is certainly the most inspired in its recreation of the cold barbaric spirit of the play's original setting. The vulgarity and gore on the screen is neither exploitative nor irresponsible, but a thoughtful interpretation that is less beholden to conventional theatrical techniques of the time. In accordance with this approach, Polanski elicited naturalistic understated performances from his actors which bolstered the play's realism while bringing the poetry down to earth. Some would argue he brought it too far down.

While Annis's nude sleepwalking scene has been criticized as evidence of Playboy Enterprises' involvement (in fact, the script was written before Playboy agreed to produce the film), it is true to the period. The project was originally offered to Allied Artists and then to Universal but both deals fell through. *Playboy* publisher Hugh Hefner, who was anxious to diversify into film production, felt this would be an ideal project for the growing Playboy Enterprises. However it turned out to be his first major failure. Polanski originally intended to cast Tuesday Weld as Lady Macbeth, but she declined after learning about the nude scene. Photographed in Wales during incessant downpours and fog, the picture was completed way behind schedule and lost about $3.5 million dollars. The original cut received an "X" rating.

MACOMBER AFFAIR, THE

1947 89m bw   ★★★½
Adventure   /A
UA

Gregory Peck *(Robert Wilson)*, Robert Preston *(Francis Macomber)*, Joan Bennett *(Margaret Macomber)*, Reginald Denny *(Capt. Smollet)*, Carl Harbord *(Coroner)*, Earl Smith *(Kongoni)*, Jean Gillie *(Aimee)*, Vernon Downing *(Reporter Logan)*, Frederic Worlock *(Clerk)*, Hassan Said *(Abdullah)*

p, Benedict Bogeaus, Casey Robinson; d, Zoltan Korda; w, Casey Robinson, Seymour Bennett, Frank Arnold (based on the story "The Short Happy Life of Francis Macomber" by Ernest Hemingway); ph, Osmond Borradaile, John Wilcox, Freddie Francis, Karl Struss; ed, Jack Wheeler, George Feld; m, Miklos Rozsa; art d, Erno Metzner; cos, Greta, Jerry Bos

The tough, uncompromising Hemingway story "The Short Happy Life of Francis Macomber" (a title too long for any marquee) was brought to the screen with vitality and invention by the eccentric and talented Zoltan Korda, brother of mogul Alexander, and it was surprisingly effective. Peck, Preston, and Bennett had more to do with that than the script. Preston is Macomber, a wealthy playboy who, with wife Margaret (Bennett) at his side, hires great white hunter Robert Wilson (Peck) to guide them to the African hunting grounds. Margaret has little or no respect for her husband, knowing that he is a weak-willed character with no courage at all, and she makes a play for Robert, whose honor will not permit him to dally with a married woman. At first, Macomber shows his yellow streak on the dangerous safari, but he gradually discovers his courage. In a final hunt, he refuses to run from a charging animal but, before he can bring it down, he is shot by Margaret, who claims she was trying to save his life. She is later tried for murder and acquitted, the jury deciding that the shooting was accidental. The budding romance of Robert and Margaret, however, must still be dealt with.

Peck later stated that everyone in the production had a hand in adjusting the story to make it acceptable to the censor. Hemingway, who had been paid $80,000 for the story, refused to help, ignoring cables for ideas from the studio. The script, though considerably changed from the original story, still retains the direct style Hemingway made so famous. The film, except for background footage shot in Africa, was filmed mostly on Hollywood soundstages, with the hunting scenes staged in the northern part of Baja, California. Despite the compromises and problems which plagued the production, though, (including an ongoing debate about what to name the film) the result is a tense and provocatively adult piece of film fiction, its often steamy material suitably underplayed by the talented star trio.

MAD LOVE

1935 83m bw ★★★★½

Horror

MGM

Peter Lorre (*Dr. Gogol*), Colin Clive (*Stephen Orlac*), Frances Drake (*Yvonne Orlac*), Ted Healy (*Reagan*), Edward Brophy (*Rollo*), Sara Haden (*Marie*), Henry Kolker (*Prefect Rosset*), May Beatty (*Francoise*), Keye Luke (*Dr. Wong*), Isabel Jewell (*Marianne*)

p, John W. Considine, Jr.; d, Karl Freund; w, Guy Endore, P.J. Wolfson, John Balderston (based on the novel *Les Mains d'Orlac* by Maurice Renard); ph, Chester Lyons, Gregg Toland; ed, Hugh Wynn; m, Dimitri Tiomkin

Mad about it. Combining Grand Guignol, surrealism and comedy to great effect, MAD LOVE remains to this day a chilling film. Peter Lorre is Gogol, a doctor who adores Yvonne Orlac (Drake), star of the Parisian Horror Theatre. Although she rebuffs him, Gogol buys a life-size replica of Yvonne that stood in the theater's lobby, harboring a secret wish that perhaps he can bring it to life as Pygmalion did Galatea. Yvonne's husband (Clive), a famous pianist, loses his hands in a railway accident; she goes to Gogol, a brilliant surgeon, and pleads with him to help. The love-crazed doctor grafts the hands of Reagan (Brophy), a recently executed knife-wielding murderer, onto Orlac's stumps. The initially grateful patient finds, though, that while he can't play the piano, he can throw knives only too well. When Gogol kills Orlac's stepfather, the mad doctor brainwashes Orlac into thinking that he did it. Things get even eerier when the dead Reagan ostensibly shows up, claiming that Gogol has sewn his head back on and that he wants his hands back! The truth behind this, as well as how Orlac's new hands ironically help him save his wife from Gogol's clutches, make for an improbable but brilliantly fitting climax.

Three excellent, distinctive cameramen were employed on the film, and the results show it. Director Karl Freund had been behind the lens on many films, and his bringing in Gregg Toland and Chester Lyons adds to the rich mixture of stark semi-Expressionism and dreamy near-surrealism that marks this film. One memorable shot shows Lorre's shaved head half in bright light and half in dark shadow, a striking visual rendering of his psychotic state. Casting the likable Brophy as the killer was admittedly a mistake, although it may have been done because Brophy was the only actor around who somewhat resembled the odd-looking Lorre and was about the same diminutive size. The comic relief by Ted Healy (who used to headline with The Three Stooges) is sometimes unwelcome as it takes too much edge off the film's scare tactics. At other points, though, it provided a much-needed punctuation to the ever-building suspense. Lorre, meanwhile, gives a top-notch performance in his well-written role. His doctor is no mad scientist of the Lugosi-Karloff school, but a man driven crazy by his lust. His character displays recognizable motivations throughout, no matter how bizarre his activities. Though the film is really Lorre's show, Colin Clive deserves praise for pulling off nervousness as few actors can, and Frances Drake brings serenity and vulnerability to the part of the heroine. A film which had a palpable influence on CITIZEN KANE (which Toland shot), MAD LOVE stands today as one of the most compelling horror films of its time.

MAD MAX

1979 90m c ★★★½

Action/Science Fiction R/18

Mad Max (Australia)

Mel Gibson (*Max*), Joanne Samuel (*Jessie*), Hugh Keays-Byrne (*the Toecutter*), Steve Bisley (*Jim Goose*), Roger Ward (*Fifi Macaffee*), Vincent Gil (*Nightrider*), Tim Burns (*Johnny the Boy*), Geoff Parry (*Bubba Zanetti*), Paul Johnstone (*Cundalini*), John Ley (*Charlie*)

p, Byron Kennedy; d, George Miller; w, George Miller, James McCausland (based on a story by George Miller, Byron Kennedy); ph, David Eggby (Todd-AO 35); ed, Tony Paterson, Clifford Hayes; m, Brian May; art d, Jon Dowding; fx, Chris Murray; cos, Clare Griffin

Australia exported this creative, original, exciting, low-budget genre landmark which gave the young Mel Gibson his first starring role. Set in the near future, MAD MAX presents a society descending into chaos. The forces of law and order are barely holding their own. The highways are terrorized by packs of lunatic speed demons. Gibson plays Max, a good cop who's fed up with his job. After chasing crazed criminals for years and seeing so many of his buddies killed in action, he just wants to retire and spend the rest of his days with his wife and child. His chief tries to bribe him with a new, faster police car ("the last of the V-8s"). He attempts to flatter him by telling him that he's the last of the heroes but Max isn't buying. The boss tells him to take a vacation and he does. Spending an idyllic week with his family on the beach, he decides to put away his badge and uniform for good. But this is not to be. A psychotic gang of road rats kills Gibson's wife and child in revenge for the death of one of their members. Left with nothing to live for, Gibson turns avenger, dons his black leather uniform, fuels up his V-8, and hits the road.

Though the plot is that of a simple revenge western, director George Miller infuses the film with a kinetic combination of visual style, amazing stunt work, creative costume design, and eccentric, detailed characterizations that practically jump out of the screen and grab the viewer by the throat. Miller, whose inspiration was comic books, serials, and B westerns, has created some of the most stunning car-chase/crash-and-burn scenes ever put on film (the chase scenes in MAD MAX make films like BULLITT and THE FRENCH CONNECTION look dull in comparison). Miller is a filmmaker who seems to have just discovered the exciting possibilities of composition, camera movement, and editing, and uses them to their most powerful effect, bringing movement back to the movies. Done independently with a laughably small budget (Miller edited most of the film in his bedroom), MAD MAX went on to make more money in Australia than George Lucas's STAR WARS. The American distributors, however, didn't quite know what to do with the film and stupidly dubbed lousy American-sounding voices over the Australians'. An even better sequel, THE ROAD WARRIOR (MAD MAX II in Australia), followed, and a third film, MAD MAX BEYOND THUNDERDOME, was released four years later.

MAD WEDNESDAY

1950 79m bw ★★★½

Comedy /U

California

Harold Lloyd *(Harold Diddlebock)*, Frances Ramsden *(Miss Otis)*, Jimmy Conlin *(Wormy)*, Raymond Walburn *(E.J. Waggleberry)*, Edgar Kennedy *(Jake, the Bartender)*, Arline Judge *(Manicurist)*, Franklin Pangborn *(Formfit Franklin)*, Lionel Stander *(Max)*, Margaret Hamilton *(Flora)*, Alan Bridge *(Wild Bill Hitchcock)*

p, Howard Hughes; d, Preston Sturges; w, Preston Sturges; ph, Robert Pittack; ed, Thomas Neff; m, Werner R. Heymann, Harry Rosenthal; art d, Robert Usher; fx, John P. Fulton

When Preston Sturges was good (THE GREAT MCGINTY, SULLIVAN'S TRAVELS), he was wonderful. When he was bad (THE FRENCH THEY ARE A FUNNY RACE), he could be really off. This film is somewhere in the middle, and when it's good your sides will ache from laughter. It begins with a sequence from Lloyd's classic silent, THE FRESHMAN. Next, we learn that the football hero didn't go on to be a man of industry. Instead, he became a frumpy bookkeeper with no life other than that at the office, with all his glory days behind him. When he's fired from his job after being faithful to the firm for two decades, he goes on a drunken spree, and, in as unlikely a series of events as you'll ever see, wakes up the owner of a moth-eaten and bankrupt circus. Eventually Lloyd winds up reprising the silent comedy scene from SAFETY LAST for which he is perhaps most famous—hanging from a tall building, this time with a huge lion menacing him.

The idea of combining comic aces Lloyd and Sturges sounds highly promising, but both men's careers were on the wane, and the effort they make to milk laughs sometimes shows a bit too much. MAD WEDNESDAY was financed by, of all people, Howard Hughes, a man not usually known for his sense of humor. It includes several excellent character bits by some of Hollywood's best second bananas: Kennedy (master of the slow burn), Stander (who left movies for years due to Red-baiting, then came back as a TV star), Hamilton (the ultimate witch), and Pangborn, who elevated prissiness to an art form. If you can hang on through the long, dead scenes and wait for Lloyd to get going, you'll probably end up satisfied by at least some of the frantic slapstick which transpires. As with many films Hughes made, several versions of this film exist, the 89-minute version going under the title of THE SIN OF HAROLD DIDDLEBOCK.

MADAME CURIE

1943   124m   bw   ★★★★
Biography   /U
MGM

Greer Garson *(Mme. Marie Curie)*, Walter Pidgeon *(Pierre Curie)*, Robert Walker *(David LeGros)*, Dame May Whitty *(Mme. Eugene Curie)*, Henry Travers *(Eugene Curie)*, C. Aubrey Smith *(Lord Kelvin)*, Albert Basserman *(Prof. Jean Perot)*, Victor Francen *(President of University)*, Reginald Owen *(Dr. Henri Becquerel)*, Van Johnson *(Reporter)*

p, Sidney Franklin; d, Mervyn LeRoy; w, Paul Osborn, Paul H. Rameau (based on the book by Eve Curie); ph, Joseph Ruttenberg; ed, Harold F. Kress; m, Herbert Stothart; art d, Cedric Gibbons, Paul Groesse; fx, Warren Newcombe; cos, Irene Sharaff, Gile Steele

This fine film stirs the heart and stays closer to the facts of its subject's life than might be expected for its time. Greer Garson plays Marie, a Polish student studying in Paris near the turn of the century, who shares a lab with scientist Pierre Curie (Walter Pidgeon). The shy Pierre grows not only to respect Marie's scientific knowledge, but also falls in love with her, and the two soon marry. Together they observe the odd behavior of certain samples of pitchblende, eventually leading, after five years of study, to Marie's discovery of radium. Years pass as the Curies struggle to continue financing their work, until finally they extract one decigram of radium from thousands of pounds of pitchblende. The breakthrough makes the couple famous, but tragedy awaits them as well.

MADAME CURIE maintains its dignity throughout and, if this occasionally weighs down the picture a bit, it also lends a certain low-key intensity to scientific research which proves quite gripping. Garson and Pidgeon are fully into the spirit of the film, and their teaming here is much more satisfying than in the more acclaimed MRS. MINIVER. Nominated for five Oscars (including Best Picture, Actor and Actress), MADAME CURIE is an intelligent, interesting, and unusually faithful screen biography.

MADAME ROSA

(LA VIE DEVANT SOI)
1977   105m   c   ★★★½
Drama   PG/AA
Lira   (France)

Simone Signoret *(Mme. Rosa)*, Claude Dauphin *(Dr. Katz)*, Samy Ben Youb *(Mohammed "Momo")*, Gabriel Jabbour *(Mr. Hamil)*, Michal Bat Adam *(Nadine)*, Constantin Costa-Gavras *(Ramon)*, Stella Anicette *(Mme. Lola)*, Bernard Lajarrige *(Mr. Charmette)*, Mohammed Zineth *(Kadir Youssef)*, Genevieve Fontanel *(Maryse)*

p, Jean Bolary; d, Moshe Mizrahi; w, Moshe Mizrahi (based on the novel *Momo* by Romain Gary); ph, Nestor Almendros (Eastmancolor); ed, Sophie Coussein; m, Philippe Sarde, Dabket Loubna

An aging survivor of Auschwitz, Madame Rosa (Simone Signoret) is a Parisian ex-streetwalker who cares for prostitutes' children in the city's poor Arab-Jewish section. Although she is slowly losing her memory, she is still able to care for her charges, especially Momo (Samy Ben Youb), an unruly Arab Muslim boy who, although he tends to be rebellious, reciprocates her love. When Madame Rosa has delusions that the Gestapo is coming for her and makes the boy promise to hide her, he does so, sending a doctor away and maintaining that the dying woman has gone to Israel.

MADAME ROSA handles its underlying conflicts—between Arabs and Jews, between Nazis and Jews—well, and explores its mixed racial and cultural milieu with grace, sensitivity, and subtlety. The film is the first pairing of director-writer Moshe Mizrahi, a Moroccan-born Israeli, and the great Simone Signoret, who won a Cesar for her marvelous and unglamorous performance here. The two would team again for the bittersweet 1981 drama I SENT A LETTER TO MY LOVE. Film director Costa-Gavras has a supporting role in MADAME ROSA, which won the Best Foreign Film Oscar in 1977. The videocassette is dubbed in English.

MADAME SOUSATZKA

1988   122m   c   ★★★
Drama   PG-13/15
Sousatzka/Cineplex Odeon   (U.K.)

Shirley MacLaine *(Mme. Irina Sousatzka)*, Navin Chowdhry *(Manek Sen)*, Peggy Ashcroft *(Lady Emily)*, Twiggy *(Jenny)*, Shabana Azmi *(Sushila Sen)*, Leigh Lawson *(Ronnie Blum)*, Lee Montague *(Vincent Pick)*, Robert Rietty *(Leo Milev)*, Jeremy Sinden *(Woodford)*, Roger Hammond *(Lefranc)*

p, Robin Dalton; d, John Schlesinger; w, Ruth Prawer Jhabvala, John Schlesinger (based on a novel by Bernice Rubens); ph, Nat Crosby (Rank color); ed, Peter Honess; m, Gerald Gouriet; prod d, Luciana Arrighi; cos, Amy Roberts

A fiery, autocratic piano teacher, Madame Sousatzka (Shirley MacLaine) has spent the last 30 years living in a London boardinghouse when she meets Manek Sen (Navin Chowdhry), a gifted 15-year-old Indian student. She believes she can turn him into a brilliant musician, starting from scratch and molding him into a new whole. "I teach not only how to play the piano, but how to live," she claims.

MADAME SOUSATZKA features a cast good enough to sidestep being sunk by the film's pedestrian script and direction. Five years after her Oscar-winning performance in TERMS OF ENDEARMENT, MacLaine attempts to deliver another tour de force here, and while she's often quite good, too often the showiness of her star turn sabotages the sentiment. Newcomer Chowdhry turns in a strong, believable performance as the musical prodigy on the verge of a major breakthrough. The movie's chief fault is its insistence on the trite themes of change versus tradition, commerce versus art, and the general destruction of history and values. MADAME SOUSATZKA is not the great or important film that it tries to be; rather, it is a warm and touching human drama, made so by the often exceptional acting.

MADE FOR EACH OTHER

1971 104m c   ★★★
Comedy   GP/PG
Fox

Renee Taylor (Pandora Gold), Joseph Bologna (Gig Pinimba), Paul Sorvino (Gig's Father), Olympia Dukakis (Gig's Mother), Helen Verbit (Pandora's Mother), Louis Zorich (Pandora's Father), Norman Shelley (Dr. Furro), Ron Carey, Peggy Pope, Susan Brockman

p, Roy Townshend; d, Robert B. Bean; w, Renee Taylor, Joseph Bologna; ph, William Storz (DeLuxe Color); ed, Sonny Mele; m, Trade Martin; art d, Robert Ramsey; cos, Elaine Mangel

Charming, offbeat, if rather slight comedy written by Taylor and Bologna and starring them as two perennial losers who meet and fall in love at a group-therapy session. They then struggle to make a go of the relationship. Semi-autobiographical (Taylor and Bologna are married in real life), the film is moving, human, and real, with a fine touch of romance. The underrated Bologna again shows a wonderful comic talent. Shot in New York City, this watchable little film is very much of its period.

MADIGAN

1968 101m c   ★★★½
Crime   /X
Universal

Richard Widmark (Detective Daniel Madigan), Henry Fonda (Commissioner Anthony X. Russell), Inger Stevens (Julia Madigan), Harry Guardino (Detective Rocco Bonaro), James Whitmore (Chief Inspector Charles Kane), Susan Clark (Tricia Bentley), Michael Dunn (Midget Castiglione), Steve Ihnat (Barney Benesch), Don Stroud (Hughie), Sheree North (Jonesy)

p, Frank P. Rosenberg; d, Don Siegel; w, Howard Rodman, Abraham Polonsky, Harry Kleiner (based on the novel The Commissioner by Richard Dougherty); ph, Russell Metty (Techniscope, Technicolor); ed, Milton Shifman; m, Don Costa; art d, Alexander Golitzen, George Webb

Action-packed cops-and-robbers film cowritten by longtime television vet Howard Rodman, who evidently didn't like the way it turned out (he used his pseudonym, Henri Simoun). In the Spanish Harlem section of Manhattan, detectives Madigan and Bonaro (Widmark and Guardino) arrest Barney Benesch (Ihnat), a wanted hoodlum who is hiding out in a tacky flat to avoid an indictment by the Brooklyn courts. Benesch is in bed with a naked woman when they break in, which distracts the two cops from their quarry long enough for him to pull a gun on them and escape. Police commissioner Russell (Fonda) dresses the two men down for allowing Benesch to get away in such an inglorious manner and gives them 72 hours to nail the killer. Russell has a lot of other woes as well: he's having an affair with a married woman (Clark), his colleague (Whitmore) has accepted bribes to keep a brothel operating, and he must contend with a black minister (St. Jacques) whose activist son was badly beaten by racist cops. Aggravating this hornet's nest for Madigan is his socialite wife (Stevens), who urges him to give up his career in law enforcement. Although Benesch proves an even more painful thorn for the detectives after he kills two police officers with Madigan's gun, the duo eventually track him down again in Spanish Harlem. A standoff ensues until an enraged Madigan gets fed up. The film ends with a consideration of whether Madigan is "just another lousy cop."

Very documentarian in approach, MADIGAN successfully reworks standard genre material into a realistic, hard-hitting portrait which deliberately sticks pins in the police department hierarchy. Writer Polonsky had been blacklisted by the Red-baiters in the 1950s and his partner Rodman kept his status active with a local construction union even while working in the Hollywood community. The acting is good throughout, all the characters lurking in the background fine character sketches of urban types. It's unfortunate that many people inadvertently confused this picture with ELVIRA MADIGAN, the Swedish film that came out just before this one.

MAEDCHEN IN UNIFORM

1931 110m bw   ★★★★★
Drama   /A
Deutsch/Gemeinschaft (Germany)

Emilia Unda (The Principal), Dorothea Wieck (Fraulein von Bernburg), Hedwig Schlichter (Fraulein von Kesten), Hertha Thiele (Manuela von Meinhardie), Ellen Schwannecke (Ilse von Westhagen)

p, Carl Froehlich; d, Leontine Sagan; w, Christa Winsloe, F.D. Andam (based on the play "Gestern und Heute" by Christa Winsloe)

Late Weimar Germany produced a number of fine anti-authoritarian films, perhaps the best of which was MAEDCHEN IN UNIFORM, the story of a girl's struggles within the rigid discipline of a boarding school for daughters of poor military officers. New student Manuela (Thiele) is homesick, introspective, and alienated. The headmistress (Unda) disapproves of such individualism, and rules her students with the Prussian dictum "Through discipline and hunger, hunger and discipline, we shall rise again." Manuela becomes attached to one teacher (Wieck), who sees in the sensitive new student a reflection of her former, nonconformist self. But Manuela's dependence on her mentor grows into obsessive love, testing the headmistress' tolerance.

Though MAEDCHEN IN UNIFORM's symbolism can seem heavy-handed (like Murnau's THE LAST LAUGH, it invests much in the uniform as an image of German social consciousness), this film displays remarkable emotional, narrative, and visual assurance. It is particularly sensitive in its treatment of female bonding and a lesbian love. Written (by Christa Winsloe and F.D. Andam, from the former's play) and directed (Leontine Sagan) by women, with an all-female cast, MAEDCHEN IN UNIFORM suggested for future generations of aspiring women filmmakers the importance of their ambitions. Historically, this film represents a finality: within a few years the Nazis would control the film studios, replacing the thoughtful messages of many films like MAEDCHEN IN UNIFORM with propaganda.

MAGIC BOX, THE
1952 118m c   ★★★★
Biography   /U
Festival   (U.K.)

Renee Asherson (Miss Tagg), Richard Attenborough (Jack Carter), Robert Beatty (Lord Beaverbrook), Martin Boddey (Sitter in Bath Studio), Edward Chapman (Father in Family Group), John Charlesworth (Graham Friese-Greene), Maurice Colbourne (Bride's Father at Wedding), Roland Culver (1st Company Promoter), John Howard Davies (Maurice Friese-Greene), Michael Denison (Connaught Rooms Reporter)

p, Ronald Neame; d, John Boulting; w, Eric Ambler (based on the book Friese-Greene, Close-Up of an Inventor by Ray Allister); ph, Jack Cardiff (Technicolor); ed, Richard Best; m, William Alwyn; prod d, John Bryan; art d, Hopewell Ash; cos, Julia Squire

Nearly every actor who ever appeared in British movies worked in this feature. Robert Donat plays William Friese-Greene, the pioneer who patented the first motion picture camera. The film shows his beginnings as a photographer's assistant and his days as a society lenser in London, spending all his resources on his new invention (patented two years before Edison's). His first wife (Maria Schell) shares his triumphs while his second wife (Margaret Johnston) shares his failures. In between, viewers are treated to the sight of at least 50 of England's finest actors, all playing tiny bits. (Laurence Olivier, for example, is quite amusing as a police officer who is an early witness to the moving pictures.) Friese-Greene is hardly remembered now and had already been dead more than 30 years when THE MAGIC BOX was made, but the filmmakers' conviction that his story should be told convinced all of the actors (who agreed to alphabetical billing) to devote their talents to this good-looking, well-directed film. Donat is excellent, holding his own among the industry's finest.

MAGICIAN, THE
(ANSIKTET)
1958 102m bw   ★★★★½
Drama   /X
Svensk   (Sweden)

Max von Sydow (Vogler), Ingrid Thulin (Manda Aman), Gunnar Bjornstrand (Vergerus), Naima Wifstrand (Grandmother), Bengt Ekerot (Spegel), Bibi Andersson (Sara), Gertrud Fridh (Ottilia), Lars Ekborg (Simson), Toivo Pawlo (Starbeck), Erland Josephson (Egerman)

d, Ingmar Bergman; w, Ingmar Bergman; ph, Gunnar Fischer, Rolf Halmquist; ed, Oscar Rosander; m, Erik Nordgren; art d, P.A. Lundgren

In THE MAGICIAN, Ingmar Bergman takes two favorite motifs—masks and magic—and explores them on a number of different levels. Albert Emanuel Vogler (Max von Sydow), a 19-century magician, brings a troupe of traveling illusionists to a small Swedish town where the people don't believe in magic.

Led by Vogler, the troupe proceeds to play with the townspeople's minds, and director Bergman, in turn, makes imaginative use of editing, lighting, and special effects to toy with audience expectations. Things are never quite what they seem, either narratively or cinematically. The film's mysterious nature is further enhanced by the dark, rich, gothic look of Bergman's mise-en-scene. Though at times the story is overwhelmed by its theme and symbols (especially in its final third), THE MAGICIAN is still fascinating, presenting a myriad of challenging ideas about magic, reality, and the nature of film itself. The acting, as in typical in Bergman, is exceptionally good, with Bjornstrand a standout. The videocassette is available in both dubbed and subtitled (Swedish into English) versions.

MAGNIFICENT AMBERSONS, THE
1942 88m bw   ★★★★★
Drama   /U
Mercury Theatre

Joseph Cotten (Eugene Morgan), Dolores Costello (Isabel Amberson Minafer), Anne Baxter (Lucy Morgan), Tim Holt (George Amberson Minafer), Agnes Moorehead (Fanny Amberson), Ray Collins (Jack Amberson), Richard Bennett (Maj. Amberson), Erskine Sanford (Benson), J. Louis Johnson (Sam the Butler), Donald Dillaway (Wilbur Minafer)

p, Orson Welles; d, Orson Welles, Freddie Fleck, Robert Wise; w, Orson Welles (based on the novel by Booth Tarkington); ph, Stanley Cortez, Russell Metty, Harry Wild; ed, Robert Wise, Jack Moss, Mark Robson; m, Bernard Herrmann, Roy Webb; art d, Mark-Lee Kirk; fx, Vernon L. Walker; cos, Edward Stevenson

Though mutilated by studio cuts and wholly misunderstood at the time of its original release, THE MAGNIFICENT AMBERSONS, based on the Booth Tarkington novel and set during the twilight of the 19th century, remains Orson Welles's second great masterpiece.

Young George Amberson (Tim Holt), the spoiled, insufferable scion of the wealthy Amberson family, is first seen, to the consternation of his neighbors, whipping his buggy horse through the streets of Indianapolis. Eugene Moran (Joseph Cotten) is a struggling inventor who loves George's mother, Isabel Amberson (Dolores Costello), but loses her to the wealthy Wilbur Minafer (Donald Dillaway). After an absence of several years, Eugene returns, now successful, having invented an automobile, an instrument of the future that many of the old school find repulsive, especially the haughty George. Wilbur dies, and Eugene, a widower with an attractive daughter, Lucy (Anne Baxter), attempts to rekindle his love affair with Isabel, but George interferes. Lucy, in turn, rejects Isabel's idle son when he refuses to enter a profession. George and Isabel then depart on an extended European tour to rid themselves of painful memories. Meanwhile, Eugene's auto factory prospers. Isabel has a heart attack in Paris and is brought back to recuperate, but the old Amberson mansion has fallen into disrepair and the family fortune nearly evaporated.

Though more controlled, subtle and cinematically exciting than CITIZEN KANE, Welles's earlier masterpiece, it's a wonder that THE MAGNIFICENT AMBERSONS survived at all. Alarmed by the negative reaction at the film's premiere screening, RKO president George J. Schaefer instructed Robert Wise, a respected editor, to shorten the film's running length. Welles had already reduced the film from 148 minutes to 131 minutes, but Wise cut the film down to 88 minutes, and this even included adding an optimistic ending, the hospital scene, tacked on by a nameless studio writer and directed by Freddie Fleck. This presumptuous and dictatorial savaging of Welles's work, according to the great director-writer himself, destroyed "the whole heart of the picture, really." Yet, THE MAGNIFICENT AMBERSONS survives nonetheless.

The film is so rich in innovative technique that it takes several viewings to note even the most essential elements. The "Welles sound" permeates every frame of the film, with his overlapping dialogue giving a natural feel to the words spoken; the volume of the words diminishing as characters recede from the camera; speeches fading; others increasing in volume as the camera picks them up; other voices mixed with street sounds; and groups of citizens talking, their words meshing. (Welles rehearsed the actors before each scene, then allowed them to improvise and add or delete their words, trusting in their ability to interpret what their characters would or would not say.) In crowd scenes he allows a host of gossips to function as a Greek chorus in estimating the worth of the Amberson and Morgan families. At times the voices of the characters boom and bellow, and, at others, they are so hushed that the words are barely discernible.

Many of the modern devices and photographic tricks Welles initally used in CITIZEN KANE are refined in THE MAGNIFICENT AMBERSONS, showing in split-second frames his people reflected in mirrors, highly glossed furniture, sometimes in a glare of light, most in half-shadow, as if the blackness of time were shutting out the light of the living. Through his great visual gifts, Welles was able to express the true nature of the characters through their relevant actions: Fanny Amberson (Agnes Moorehead) peering over a railing to eavesdrop on those far below in the Amberson mansion's main foyer; George methodically spooning down strawberry shortcake at the enormous dining-room table, indifferently listening to aunt Fanny pour out her heart; Eugene standing mute and stunned at the front door of the Amberson mansion, which has been closed in his face by George, who stands behind the frosted glass panes.

The look of THE MAGNIFICENT AMBERSONS was modeled on the low-key lighting used by photographers at the turn-of-the-century, and Stanley Cortez's deep-focus lensing is arresting, dwelling upon set scenes only Welles could have framed—notably, 10-minutes soliloquies that are saved from tedium by the unique framing. Dolly and truck shots keep the film fluid, and some crane shots capture the changing architecture from Victorian to modern, from resplendent to mundane, as Welles graphically and eloquently shows the passing of an age.

MAGNIFICENT OBSESSION

1954 107m c   ★★★½
Drama   /U
Universal

Jane Wyman *(Helen Phillips)*, Rock Hudson *(Bob Merrick)*, Barbara Rush *(Joyce Phillips)*, Agnes Moorehead *(Nancy Ashford)*, Otto Kruger *(Rudolph)*, Gregg Palmer *(Tom Masterson)*, Sara Shane *(Valerie)*, Paul Cavanagh *(Dr. Giraud)*, Judy Nugent *(Judy)*, George Lynn *(Williams)*

p, Ross Hunter; d, Douglas Sirk; w, Robert Blees, Wells Root (based on the novel by Lloyd C. Douglas and the screenplay by Sarah Y. Mason, Finley Peter Dunne, Jr., Victor Heerman); ph, Russell Metty (Technicolor); ed, Milton Carruth; m, Frank Skinner; art d, Bernard Herzbrun, Emrich Nicholson; fx, David S. Harsley; cos, Bill Thomas

Not quite as heart-wrenching as the original version, this remake is still pretty good and does benefit from being filmed in color. Wyman is Helen Phillips, a blind woman, and Hudson is Bob Merrick, the cad who becomes her savior. Merrick is partly responsible for the accidental death of Helen's husband, a man who was revered in the community as a combination of Dr. Kildare, Ben Casey, and every other angel of mercy ever seen. After the doctor's demise, Bob attempts to apologize, and Helen, avoiding him, is blinded in an accident. With Rudolph (Kruger), a friend of the late, great physician, egging him on, Bob forsakes his wastrel ways and decides to dedicate himself to medicine. Without revealing his true identity, he contacts Helen, and their relationship soon becomes a loving one. When she finds out who he is, she departs. Much later, though, Bob is given an incredible opportunity to save Helen and redeem himself for his past peccadilloes.

A film requiring as many Kleenex as you can spare, this unabashed appeal to the tear ducts does not fail in its efforts. Director Douglas Sirk made only a few more films before retiring to Munich in 1959, just before he turned 60. He brings to this effort the same combination of overblown, indulgent melodramatics and distanced perspective which would mark his masterpiece, IMITATION OF LIFE. Notable also as the film which really put Rock Hudson on top and gave the first inklings that he might be able to act if sufficiently prodded, MAGNIFICENT OBSESSION really relies on Wyman's womanly, Oscar-nominated assurance to put this stuff over.

MAGNIFICENT SEVEN, THE

1960 128m c   ★★★★
Western   R/PG
Mirisch/Alpha

Yul Brynner *(Chris)*, Eli Wallach *(Calvera)*, Steve McQueen *(Vin)*, Horst Buchholz *(Chico)*, Charles Bronson *(O'Reilly)*, Robert Vaughn *(Lee)*, Brad Dexter *(Harry Luck)*, James Coburn *(Britt)*, Vladimir Sokoloff *(Old Man)*, Rosenda Monteros *(Petra)*

p, John Sturges; d, John Sturges; w, William Roberts, Walter Newman, Walter Bernstein (based on THE SEVEN SAMURAI); ph, Charles Lang (Panavision, DeLuxe Color); ed, Ferris Webster; m, Elmer Bernstein; art d, Edward Fitzgerald; fx, Milt Rice

Very nearly a classic, this Americanization of Akira Kurosawa's THE SEVEN SAMURAI does a good job of mirroring the major themes and attitudes of the original while re-creating that monumental film in an occidental setting. However, Sturges's film fails to present its heroes with the style, grace, and dignity that Kurosawa accords his samurai warriors. Nevertheless THE MAGNIFICENT SEVEN is an excellent film and deserves the accolades it has received through the years. A small Mexican village is pillaged regularly by Wallach and his cutthroats. The quaking townsfolk don't have the courage to take on Wallach and his desperadoes so they decide to hire seven of the toughest hombres on that side of the Rio Grande: Brynner, McQueen, Bronson, Vaughn, Dexter, Coburn, and Buchholz. The Seven train the fearful townspeople to fight alongside them and set a trap for the wily Wallach and his group.

There's not a weak performance in the film but that's to be expected with this cast, although Brynner, who had already won an Oscar for THE KING AND I, was the only "name" at the time the film was made. Although Coburn has little dialogue, his presence is strongly felt. It wouldn't be long before screenwriters were giving him plenty to say. In fact, the only member of the Seven who didn't rise in the acting ranks after this film was Dexter, who made a few more movies, then retired from the biz.

Sturges's direction is the key to the film's quality. Just as he did in BAD DAY AT BLACK ROCK and THE GREAT ESCAPE, Sturges assembled a superb cast and skillfully put them through their paces. Bernstein's score also plays a major role in the film's success, and his main theme became an even more familiar part of American popular culture as the signature music for Marlboro cigarettes. The film spawned a number of sequels: RETURN OF THE MAGNIFICENT SEVEN; GUNS OF THE MAGNIFICENT SEVEN; and THE MAGNIFICENT SEVEN RIDE. Perhaps the ultimate testimony to the excellence of THE MAGNIFICENT SEVEN is the sword that Kurosawa presented to Sturges after seeing the film.

MAGNIFICENT YANKEE, THE

1950 89m bw ★★★★
Biography /U
MGM

Louis Calhern *(Oliver Wendell Holmes, Jr.)*, Ann Harding *(Fanny Bowditch Holmes)*, Eduard Franz *(Judge Louis Brandeis)*, Philip Ober *(Mr. Owen Wister)*, Ian Wolfe *(Mr. Adams)*, Edith Evanson *(Annie Gough)*, Richard Anderson *(Reynolds)*, Herbert Anderson *(Baxter)*, James Lydon *(Clinton)*, Robert Sherwood *(Drake)*

p, Armand Deutsch; d, John Sturges; w, Emmett Lavery (based on the book *Mr. Justice Holmes* by Francis Biddle and the play by Emmett Lavery); ph, Joseph Ruttenberg; ed, Ferris Webster; m, David Raksin; art d, Cedric Gibbons, Arthur Lonergan; fx, A. Arnold Gillespie, Warren Newcombe; cos, Walter Plunkett

An excellent cinematization of Emmett Lavery's long-running Broadway play (which also starred Louis Calhern), THE MAGNIFICENT YANKEE is the story of Oliver Wendell Holmes, Jr. (Calhern), and his rise to the acme of American jurisprudence. In following his career, the movie charts contemporary history, but without neglecting Holmes' personal life, particularly his touching relationship with his wife Fanny (Ann Harding, in one of the few good roles she enjoyed at this stage of her career). Also portrayed are Louis Brandeis (Eduard Franz) and Holmes's close friend, author Owen Wister (Philip Ober), whose literate narration never intrudes upon the drama. MGM producers were not surprised at the film's critical success, but they were surprised that the film, made largely as a favor to Calhern, also appealed to an unexpectedly large audience and turned a mild profit. Calhern was justly nominated for a Best Actor Oscar but lost to Jose Ferrer in CYRANO DE BERGERAC. The picture was also nominated for Best Costume Design.

MAHABHARATA, THE

1990 171m c ★★★★
Historical /PG
Les Prods. du 3eme Etage (U.K./France/U.S.)

Robert Langton-Lloyd *(Vyasa)*, Antonin Stahly-Vishwanadan *(Boy)*, Bruce Myers *(Ganesha/Krishna)*, Vittorio Mezzogiorno *(Arjuna)*, Andrzej Seweryn *(Yudhishthira)*, Mamadou Dioume *(Bhima)*, Jean-Paul Denizon *(Nakula)*, Mahmoud Tabrizi-Zadeh *(Sahadeva)*, Miriam Goldschmidt *(Kunti)*, Mallika Sarabhar *(Draupadi)*

p, Michel Propper; d, Peter Brook; w, Jean-Claude Carriere, Peter Brook, Marie-Helene Estienne; ph, William Lubtchansky; ed, Nicolas Gaster; m, Djamchid Chemirani, Toshi Tsuchitori, Kudsi Erguner, Kim Menzer, Mahmoud Tabrizi-Zadeh; prod d, Chloe Obolensky; art d, Emmanuel de Chauvigny, Raul Gomez; cos, Pippa Cleator

In adapting the 100,000-stanza Sanskrit poem that is roughly India's equivalent to the Bible, renowned stage director Peter Brook has created a work that is more filmed theater than fluid moviemaking. (In fact, Brook first tackled this material in a nine-hour stage production). This version, the result of trim-mings from other stage and television presentations, runs just under three hours. In spite of all this cutting and pasting, THE MAHABHARATA manages to be both overlong—a byproduct both of its staginess and of its emphasis on talk over action—and underdeveloped. Yet the cumulative power of this 2,000-year-old tale is undeniable, and Brook's approach, if debatable on an artistic level, is nevertheless respectful without being overly reverential.

THE MAHABHARATA tells the story of two warring families, the Pandavas, descendants of King Pandu, and the Kaurava family, the offspring of Pandu's blind brother, Dhritharashtra. That the above synopsis covers only a small part of what actually occurs in THE MAHABHARATA is indicative of the film's main problem, the overcomplexity of its plot. It takes a tremendous effort just to follow the story, let alone to savor its subtleties. Moreover, the talky script—co-authored by Brook, Jean-Claude Carriere, and Marie-Helene Estienne—and staginess of the action are added distractions. Nonetheless, what Brook, his collaborators, and the uniformly excellent cast are able to accomplish in THE MAHABHARATA far outweighs the film's weaknesses. Brook manages to emphasize what is uniquely Indian in the epic poem that provides the film's basis without neglecting its points of contact with other enduring works of spiritual enlightenment. As much as possible, the international cast, many of whom appeared in the stage version, also labor to give the characters a human realism, imbuing the tale with a poignant intimacy to match its epic sweep. Though filmed at minimal cost, THE MAHABHARATA is a story for the ages.

MAJOR BARBARA

1941 121m bw ★★★★½
Comedy /A
Pascal/Rank (U.K.)

Wendy Hiller *(Maj. Barbara Undershaft)*, Rex Harrison *(Adolphus Cusins)*, Robert Morley *(Andrew Undershaft)*, Emlyn Williams *(Snobby Price)*, Robert Newton *(Bill Walker)*, Sybil Thorndike *(The General)*, Deborah Kerr *(Jenny Hill)*, David Tree *(Charles Lomax)*, Penelope-Dudley Ward *(Sarah Undershaft)*, Marie Lohr *(Lady Brittomart)*

p, Gabriel Pascal; d, Gabriel Pascal, Harold French, David Lean; w, Anatole de Grunwald, George Bernard Shaw (based on his play); ph, Ronald Neame; ed, Charles Frend; m, William Walton; prod d, Vincent Korda

One of Shaw's most amusing comedies, excitingly performed by a brilliant cast, though Shaw's monologues sometimes get boggy with verbiage and the direction (largely by Pascal) isn't very spritely. Hiller plays the idealistic title role, a socialist major in the Salvation Army who busies herself with attacks on wealthy capitalists, chiefly her munitions magnate father (Morley). A young professor of Greek history and literature (Harrison) is hopelessly in love with the major, but she's too busy saving the poor from the wealthy. Pop Undershaft is a calm, benevolent tycoon who believes that the impoverished can be helped only through the careful manipulation of funds. Barbara throws her father's philosophy in his face, and he responds by donating 50,000 pounds to the Salvation Army. An Army general (Thorndike), to Barbara's surprise, gratefully accepts the gift and the disillusioned major quits the Army. Touring her father's factories, she witnesses the humane treatment the workers receive and converts to her father's viewpoint: "I am a millionaire. That is my religion." But her perspective is tempered with the Shavian belief that "the greatest of all our evils and the worst of our crimes is poverty."

Shaw's 1905 social comedy was brought to the screen by Pascal, who had talked the curmudgeonly playwright into allowing him in 1938 to film (with great success) PYGMALION, starring Hiller and Leslie Howard. MAJOR BARBARA, however, was not as well received by audiences who found it too sophisticated and couldn't relate to its socialist preachings. One can argue with Shaw's ideas, but his thought that it's better to give the poor jobs than to give them charity is still a provocative one. The cast is uniformly marvelous, with the dry radiance of Hiller (reminiscent of Katharine Hepburn's, but uniquely all her own) firing scene after scene. Harrison has a great way with flip dialogue, yet still manages to convey his passion for Barbara. Newton is delightfully wicked as a money-grubbing slum dweller. The rest of the cast (Emlyn Williams, Sybil Thorndike, Marie Lohr, David Tree, Donald Calthrop, Miles Malleson, Felix Aylmer, Stanley Holloway, Kathleen Harrison) reads like a who's who of British character actors and they keep the rather stodgy, unimaginative direction constantly on the go. They help make this a film where you engage the issues rather than merely resist its "photographed play" quality. Special mention must go to the touching Kerr, just starting her career, and the wonderful Morley. (You almost have to look twice to recognize him behind that beard.) The 32-year-old actor is not only convincing as the father of the 28-year-old Hiller but also a worthy and likable mouthpiece for many of Shaw's ideas. Valuable as a fine performance of an important and delightful play, MAJOR BARBARA makes for bracingly intelligent cinema.

MAKE WAY FOR TOMORROW

1937 91m bw   ★★★★
Drama   /U
Paramount

Victor Moore (*Barkley Cooper*), Beulah Bondi (*Lucy Cooper*), Fay Bainter (*Anita Cooper*), Thomas Mitchell (*George Cooper*), Porter Hall (*Harvey Chase*), Barbara Read (*Rhoda Cooper*), Maurice Moscovich (*Max Rubens*), Elisabeth Risdon (*Cora Payne*), Minna Gombell (*Nellie Chase*), Ray Mayer (*Robert Cooper*)

p, Leo McCarey; d, Leo McCarey; w, Vina Delmar (based on the novel *The Years Are So Long* by Josephine Lawrence and the play by Helen Leary, Nolan Leary); ph, William Mellor; ed, LeRoy Stone; m, Victor Young, George Antheil; art d, Hans Dreier, Bernard Herzbrun; fx, Gordon Jennings

MAKE WAY FOR TOMORROW is a melancholy tear-jerker that, amazingly, never once goes over the edge into false or maudlin sentimentality. But a sensitive script and flawless acting and direction didn't help at the box office because the issue of "what to do with the old folks" was not attractive to audiences still suffering the aftermath of the Depression. Give Paramount credit, however, for making the film, and Leo McCarey credit for the same skill with sentiment which distinguished GOING MY WAY and LOVE AFFAIR. Victor Moore and Beulah Bondi play Barkley and Lucy Cooper, a poor elderly couple whose home is being taken away. None of their children has the space or the wherewithal to take in both parents, so the couple must be split up. Several scenes depict the difficulties which arise in both houses. In the end, the couple share a beautifully restrained, realistic and moving farewell at the railway station from which they embarked on their honeymoon decades ago.

Stage and screen comedian Moore was already 60 when he accepted this unaccustomed dramatic role, and he was simply brilliant. Bondi was only 46, but Wally Westmore's makeup convinces the eye that she is two decades older. Critics loved it, and MAKE WAY FOR TOMORROW made many of the Best

Film lists, although it was nominated for no awards by the Oscar crowd. Thomas Mitchell, as a son, and Fay Bainter as his wife were both just 16 years younger than Moore, although no one noticed. It was a timely motion picture then, and is if anything even more relevant today as life expectancies continue to increase. Bring several hankies for this one. The one song, "Make Way For Tommorow," had about as much acceptance as the film.

MALA NOCHE

1985 78m c/bw   ★★★★
Drama   /18
Northern Film

Tim Strecter (*Walt Curtis*), Doug Cooeyate (*Johnny*), Ray Monge (*Roberto Pepper*), Nyla McCarthy (*Betty*)

p, Gus Van Sant, Jr.; d, Gus Van Sant, Jr.; w, Gus Van Sant, Jr. (based on the novella by Walt Curtis); ph, John Campbell; ed, Gus Van Sant, Jr.; m, Creighton Lindsay, Karen Kitchen, Peter Daamaan

The often maddening perversity of love and desire is captured most effectively in director Gus Van Sant's MALA NOCHE, which was released theatrically after DRUGSTORE COWBOY proved one of the year's biggest independent successes.

Shot in 1985 on a miniscule budget, this gritty, poetic 16mm feature concerns Walt Curtis (Tim Streeter), an amiable skid-row liquor-store clerk in Portland, Oregon, who falls madly in love with 18-year-old Johnny (Doug Cooeyate), an illegal Mexican immigrant. When Johnny turns out to be much more interested in Walt's sister, Betty (Nyla McCarthy), than he is in Walt, the rejected suitor settles for the more amenable, if less desirable, Roberto (Ray Monge).

The fluidly imaginative technique that Van Sant displayed in DRUGSTORE COWBOY is much in evidence in this earlier feature—the highly graphic, grainy black-and-white camerawork making ingenious use of partly blacked out frames, vertiginous angles, tight close-ups, and time-lapse photography. Van Sant's frequently astonishing script is funny and passionate, his editing savvy, and his choice of music perfect as he freely and unapologetically celebrates Walt's love of Mexican boys.

MALE ANIMAL, THE

1942 101m bw   ★★★★
Comedy   /A
WB

Henry Fonda (*Tommy Turner*), Olivia de Havilland (*Ellen Turner*), Joan Leslie (*Patricia Stanley*), Jack Carson (*Joe Ferguson*), Eugene Pallette (*Ed Keller*), Herbert Anderson (*Michael Barnes*), Hattie McDaniel (*Cleota*), Ivan Simpson (*Dr. Damon*), Don DeFore (*Wally*), Jean Ames (*"Hot Garters" Garner*)

p, Wolfgang Reinhardt; d, Elliott Nugent; w, Julius J. Epstein, Philip G. Epstein, Stephen Morehouse Avery (based on the play by James Thurber, Elliott Nugent); ph, Arthur Edeson; ed, Thomas Richards; m, Heinz Roemheld

Charming adaptation of the comic play by Thurber and Nugent (who also directed the film) about a stuffy midwestern college professor who plans to read a letter written by Vanzetti (of Sacco and Vanzetti infamy) to his students. The trustees, lead by Pallette, say that Fonda will be fired if he dares read the missive that was penned a few days before the alleged anarchists were executed. At the same time, Carson arrives in town. He's an old flame of Fonda's wife, de Havilland, and she is, once again, taken by his dubious charm. Carson has come home for "the big game," and Fonda thinks he's just a big, beefy bore. Anderson is the editor of the school paper who writes an editorial in which he applauds Fonda for his decision to read the controversial letter. The editorial also states that the school seems to have a bias against liberal teachers. Simpson, the dean, is irate and warns Fonda that his job is in jeopardy. Matters come to a head when de Havilland suggests that Fonda forget about reading the letter. He refuses and cites the First Amendment. She gets angry, they quarrel, and she exits to join Carson at a cocktail party. Fonda and Anderson meet and get drunk together, and this infusion of whiskey courage causes Fonda to say he will never let his wife be stolen by another man. When Carson and de Havilland return to the Fonda home, they find Fonda smashed so badly that he attempts to fight the bigger Carson and only manages to knock himself unconscious. Carson lifts Fonda, puts him to bed, and realizes that he may be in the middle of a separation. Although he likes de Havilland, that's as far as it goes; there's no way that he is about to steal her away. On the following day, Fonda reads the letter in the school auditorium. He's slightly hung over from the drinking the night before, and, as he reads the real letter, the trustees and other members of the faculty relax visibly when they hear it. The letter contains no politics whatsoever; in fact, it's a lovely plea that calls for humanity to understand. Tears are seen at the corners of some eyes, and de Havilland and Fonda are reunited.

Director Nugent not only cowrote the play, he also starred in it on Broadway. He insisted that Fonda was the only person who could do it justice on screen. The remake, SHE'S WORKING HER WAY THROUGH COLLEGE, was terrible. Fonda eventually played it on the stage in the 1950s, when he accepted an offer from his onetime stock company to do the role. (One of the supporting parts in this stage version was essayed by an up-and-coming actress who had a hugging relationship with Fonda. It was his daughter, Jane.) In small roles, note Gig Young, David Willock, and Audra Lindley as students, as well as Raymond Bailey and William Hopper as reporters.

MALTESE FALCON, THE

1941 100m bw   ★★★★★
Mystery   /PG
WB

Humphrey Bogart (*Sam Spade*), Mary Astor (*Brigid O'Shaughnessy*), Gladys George (*Iva Archer*), Peter Lorre (*Joel Cairo*), Barton MacLane (*Detective Lt. Dundy*), Lee Patrick (*Effie Perine*), Sydney Greenstreet (*Kasper Gutman the Fat Man*), Ward Bond (*Detective Tom Polhaus*), Jerome Cowan (*Miles Archer*), Elisha Cook, Jr. (*Wilmer Cook*)

p, Henry Blanke; d, John Huston; w, John Huston (based on the novel by Dashiell Hammett); ph, Arthur Edeson; ed, Thomas Richards; m, Adolph Deutsch; art d, Robert Haas; cos, Orry-Kelly

A rare bird, the prized one and only. This third film version of the Dashiell Hammett novel was propelled into the ranks of popular classic by a stunning directorial debut from screenwriter John Huston. This was also Bogart's big chance as a star/leading man and he is peerless as private eye Sam Spade, a cynical rebel-hero tangled in a labyrinthe of hissing vipers.

While trying to investigate the murder of his partner, Miles Archer (Cowan), Spade finds himself surrounded by a number of eccentric characters: the mysterious Brigid O'Shaughnessy (Astor), the effeminate Joel Cairo (Lorre), the huge Kasper Gutman (Greenstreet), and Gutman's psychotic gunsel Wilmer (Cook)—all greedily fighting for possession of a statue of a falcon containing priceless jewels. From the superb casting (it was the 61-year-old Greenstreet's film debut) to the textbook

perfect direction, every aspect of THE MALTESE FALCON revealed the surprisingly assured hand of its novice director. A seminal moment in the development of what would come to be known as film noir, Huston's faithful adaptation helped establish the cynicism, corruption, and moral ambiguity that would mark the genre, while his visuals—although not nearly as dark as what would follow—showed a cramped, stifling, claustrophobic world from which there was no escape. Huston has a field day laughing at greedy corruption and treating the plot with the insolence a man has for a discarded mistress; often it's funny to us, too. Lorre's gardenia-scented little crook versus Cook's tough sissy gigolo; fat, obsequious sugar daddy (to Cook) Greenstreet meeting Bogie's snarls—these make us laugh. Mary Astor has one howler bit when she kicks Lorre, but otherwise she embodies the plot's dark, bottomless center. Piling lie on top of lie, Astor's portrayal of sociopathic nymphomania has never been equalled. It's pitched at an underplayed sob that keeps us guessing right up to the end with Bogart. Gladys George is the classic noir widow—you've seen this bit parodied countless times—here's the real thing. Ditto Patrick's doggedly devoted secretary (it's nice to see her playing a dame that's not cheap for once). And that's Walter Huston, John's distinguished father, who delivers the bird to Bogie. While film historians may argue over the relative virtues of the work (actually a waste of everyone's time), there is no denying its entertainment value. Two flaws? The rise of Adolph Deutsch's music in the last clinch, and the fact that Patrick's character (unlike in Hammett's book) doesn't realize the essential darkness of Bogart. But perhaps the latter explains the film's continued success. The audience can participate in Sam Spade's fear of intimacy, homophobia, privately relished victories and laughs at the expense of greed. Spade is Huston himself, even though the script has been faithfully rendered by the director. What makes FALCON a delight on each viewing is that it doesn't shift from its arch, nasty attitude. Compare it to the present little faux noirs crawling out from rocks, and you'll really have a laugh—or a cry. The only caution: don't watch it "colorized", which means, like every other bastardized project treated thus, it looks like it's been schmeared with dijon and old barbecue. The hell with Ted Turner.

MAMMA ROMA

1962 110m bw   ★★★★
Drama   /X
Arco (Italy)

Anna Magnani (*Mamma Roma*), Ettore Garofalo (*Ettore*), Franco Citti (*Carmine*), Silvana Corsini (*Bruna*), Luisa Loiano (*Blancofiore*)

p, Alfredo Bini; d, Pier Paolo Pasolini; w, Pier Paolo Pasolini; ph, Tonino Delli Colli; ed, Nino Baragli; m, Carlo Rustichelli

Pasolini's second film after ACCATTONE (1961) stars Magnani as a prostitute who tries to start a new life. She and her son (Garofalo) move to a different part of town where she tries to make a living legitimately, but her past keeps popping up. She is eventually forced to occasionally go back to the red-light district when money becomes scarce. Her son becomes a thief and soon things go from bad to worse for the pair.

The mood of this film is grim throughout and lingers long after the closing credits roll. Bolstered by yet another powerhouse performance from Magnani, MAMMA ROMA is strongly realistic and remains one of Pasolini's most accessible if not most important films.

MAN AND A WOMAN, A
(UN HOMME ET UNE FEMME)
1966   102m   c/bw   ★★★½
Drama   /X
Films 13   (France)

Anouk Aimee *(Anne Gauthier)*, Jean-Louis Trintignant *(Jean-Louis Duroc)*, Pierre Barouh *(Pierre Gauthier)*, Valerie Lagrange *(Valerie Duroc)*, Simone Paris *(Head Mistress)*, Antoine Sire *(Antoine Duroc)*, Souad Amidou *(Francoise Gauthier)*, Yane Barry *(Mistress of Jean-Louis)*, Paul Le Person *(Garage Man)*, Henri Chemin *(Jean-Louis' Codriver)*

p, Claude Lelouch; d, Claude Lelouch; w, Claude Lelouch, Pierre Uytterhoeven (based on a story by Claude Lelouch); ph, Claude Lelouch (Eastmancolor); ed, Claude Lelouch, G. Boisser, Claude Barrois; m, Francis Lai; art d, Robert Luchaire

Effusively romantic, visually stunning, slightly bland. A MAN AND A WOMAN has been condemned by some as an exercise in style for style's sake and by others for its lack of emotional complexity. Yet for many viewers this Claude Lelouch-directed film is as magical a love story as any brought to the screen. Widowed film studio script girl Anne Gauthier (Anouk Aimee) and auto racer Jean-Louis Duroc (Jean-Louis Trintignant), whose wife has committed suicide, meet at the boarding school attended by his son and her daughter. When Jean-Louis gives Anne a ride back to Paris, friendship and then love blossom, though the specter of her much-loved late husband confuses their romance. At one point it looks like the end, but Lelouch still has a dazzling scene on the beach at Deauville up his sleeve.

Pulling out all the stops, Lelouch employs a wide variety of filmmaking techniques (swirling cameras, slow motion, switches from color to black and white, flashforwards and flashbacks) to tell his simple but effective love story. Although not the equal of the work of Lelouch's French contemporaries, A MAN AND A WOMAN demonstrated that a wide American audience was interested in stylish films, provided their stories hit home. The film won Academy Awards for Best Story/Screenplay and Best Foreign-Language Film, Aimee was justly nominated as Best Actress and Lelouch as Best Director, but for many viewers Francis Lai's catchy score remains their dominant memory.

MAN AND A WOMAN: 20 YEARS LATER, A
(UN HOMME ET UNE FEMME: VINGT ANS DEJA)
1986   108m   c   ★★★
Romance   PG/15
Films 13   (France)

Anouk Aimee *(Anne Gauthier)*, Jean-Louis Trintignant *(Jean-Louis Duroc)*, Evelyne Bouix *(Francoise)*, Marie-Sophie Pochat *(Marie-Sophie)*, Philippe Leroy *(Prof. Thevenin)*, Charles Gerard *(Charlot)*, Antoine Sire *(Antoine)*, Andre Engel *(Film Director)*, Richard Berry, Patrick Poivre d'Arvor

p, Claude Lelouch; d, Claude Lelouch; w, Claude Lelouch, Pierre Uytterhoeven, Monique Lange, Jerome Tonnerre; ph, Jean-Yves Le Mener (Eastmancolor); ed, Hugues Darmois; m, Francis Lai; art d, Jacques Bufnoir; fx, Georges Demetreau; cos, Emanuel Ungaro, Mic Cheminal

Two decades after the smashing success of A MAN AND A WOMAN, director Claude Lelouch, stars Anouk Aimee and Jean-Louis Trintignant, and Francis Lai's unforgettable theme song came together again for this relatively satisfying sequel. Twenty years older, no longer a racing-car driver, and involved with a considerably younger woman (Marie-Sophie Pochat), Jean-Louis (Trintignant) organizes a Paris-to-Dakar rally; Anne

(Aimee), his love in the original film, has risen from script girl to producer and, searching for a hit, has chosen to make a musical about her affair with Jean-Louis starring Richard Berry (playing himself). As the film continues, several stories interweave: the real-life reunion between Jean-Louis and Anne; the on-screen tale she is filming; the rally, during which Jean-Louis and his young girlfriend are stranded in the desert; and a seemingly unrelated subplot about a madman who escapes from a mental hospital. Despite Lelouch's attempt to cram too many stories into one movie, A MAN AND A WOMAN: 20 YEARS LATER is an enjoyable, often funny effort, though those who've seen and liked the original are bound to appreciate this more than other viewers. Trintignant and Aimee, who look older and wiser, give fine performances, and the feeling of being with old friends is heightened by the presence of Antoine Sire, who played Jean-Louis's son in the original and does so again here. Just in case our memories needed further jogging, Lelouch also uses liberal amounts of footage from the first film.

MAN CALLED PETER, A
1955   119m   c   ★★★★
Political/Biography/Religious   /U
FOX

Richard Todd *(Peter Marshall)*, Jean Peters *(Catherine Marshall)*, Marjorie Rambeau *(Miss Fowler)*, Jill Esmond *(Mrs. Findlay)*, Les Tremayne *(Sen. Harvey)*, Robert Burton *(Mr. Peyton)*, Gladys Hurlbut *(Mrs. Peyton)*, Gloria Gordon *(Barbara)*, Billy Chapin *(Peter John Marshall)*, Sally Corner *(Mrs. Whiting)*

p, Samuel G. Engel; d, Henry Koster; w, Eleanore Griffin (based on the book by Catherine Marshall); ph, Harold Lipstein (CinemaScope, DeLuxe Color); ed, Robert Simpson; m, Alfred Newman; art d, Lyle Wheeler, Maurice Ransford; fx, Ray Kellogg; cos, Renie

One of the rare Hollywood films about religion not to drown in piety, A MAN CALLED PETER is a fine biography of Peter Marshall, the Scotsman who became the US Senate's chaplain. Marshall appealed to young and old in his sermons, as will this picture, a good yarn combining interesting sentiments and solid production values. Richard Todd is captivating as Marshall, as is Jean Peters as his wife, upon whose memoirs the film was based. She must cope with Marshall's tuberculosis and derives her strength from his sermons, as does Sen. Harvey (Les Tremayne), who resolves to clean up politics in his home state. There are struggles along the way, most of which arise from Marshall's unconventional treatment of religion as a living thing rather than as a repository of dead tradition. The message is never blatant, however, even in Marshall's fascinating sermons, and the performances are all excellent under Henry Koster's typically smooth direction. Shot in and around Washington, DC, the movie looks as good as it sounds, with preachiness put aside in favor of the very down-to-earth story of two people who are devoted to each other. Cinematographer Lipstein earned an Oscar nomination for his fine work here.

MAN ESCAPED, A
(UN CONDAMNE A MORT S'EST ECHAPPE)
1957   102m   bw   ★★★★★
Drama   /U
Gaumont   (France)

Francois Leterrier *(Lt. Fontaine)*, Charles Le Clainche *(Francois Jost)*, Roland Monod *(De Leiris the Pastor)*, Maurice Beerblock *(Blanchet)*, Jacques Ertaud *(Orsini)*, Roger Treherne *(Terry)*, Jean-

Paul Delhumeau (Hebrard), Jean-Philippe Delamare (Prisoner No. 110), Jacques Oerlemans (Chief Warder), Klaus Detlef Grevenhorst (German Intelligence Officer)

p, Jean Thuillier, Alain Poire; d, Robert Bresson; w, Robert Bresson (based on articles by Andre Devigny); ph, L.H. Burel; ed, Raymond Lamy; m, Wolfgang Amadeus Mozart ("Kyrie" from "Mass in C Minor"); art d, Pierre Charbonnier

One of the most important films from a cinema giant. The very spare plot features Leterrier playing a Resistance hero captured by the Nazis and imprisoned in Fort Montluc. Most of the film shows him and his cellmate (Le Clainche) attempting to successfully scale the prison walls and escape. Based on a published account of Andre Devigny, a Resistance fighter who was sentenced to be executed in 1943, A MAN ESCAPED is one of Bresson's finest works, particularly notable for his creative use of sound. Even after the success of THE DIARY OF A COUNTRY PRIEST, Bresson had to wait five years to get this project underway. The two films have in common a faith in God which is made most obvious in this picture's alternate title, THE WIND BLOWETH WHERE IT LISTETH, and in the music (Mozart's "Mass in C Minor"). As in many of Bresson's films, the cast is made up of non-professionals such as Leterrier, a philosophy graduate and a lieutenant in the military. Bresson's experience as a POW at the start of WWII, Devigny's contribution as a technical adviser, and the use of his actual cell for the location make for an grippingly authentic and detailed account. In an unanimous decision, Bresson received the "Best Director" prize from the Cannes Film Festival in 1957 for this film. In a surprisingly similar, but less successful manner, Don Siegel detailed a prison break in ESCAPE FROM ALCATRAZ, with Clint Eastwood in the starring role.

MAN FACING SOUTHEAST
(HOMBRE MIRANDO AL SUDESTE)
1986   105m   c   ★★★★½
Drama   R/
Cinequanon   (Argentina)

Lorenzo Quinteros (Dr. Dennis), Hugo Soto (Rantes), Ines Vernengo (Beatriz), Cristina Scaramuzza (Nurse), Rubens W. Correa (Dr. Prieto), David Edery, Rodolfo Rodas, Jean Pierre Requeraz

p, Lujan Pflaum; d, Eliseo Subiela; w, Eliseo Subiela; ph, Ricardo de Angelis; ed, Luis Cesar D'Angiolillo; m, Pedro Aznar; art d, Abel Facello

Argentine director Eliseo Subiela takes an allegorical approach to the story of Christ in this enigmatic parable. A jaded mental asylum psychiatrist, Dr. Dennis (Lorenzo Quinteros), becomes fascinated with Rantes (Hugo Soto), who suddenly appears in his ward. Upon questioning, Rantes explains he is a holographic being from another planet, which transmits to him from the southeast. As the two men grow closer, it begins to appear that Rantes' mission is something beyond an intergalactic visit; eventually, his inexplicable influence on the other patients incurs the displeasure of authorities who demand that Dennis take severe measures to counteract his friend and patient's delirium.

Writer-director Subiela incorporates a wide variety of influences to create a fascinating, multifaceted work of art. The reworking of the Gospels is evident, but the biblical references are a basis for convincing contemporary characters and open questions, with the film clearly participating in and reconsidering the mystical tradition in Latin American literature. Subiela also incorporates a variety of references to paintings in the film's design. Soto's performance is remarkable, with Quinteros providing an excellent counterpart. Their natural, often affectionate, and unique relationship becomes the heart of this profound and highly personal film.

MAN FOR ALL SEASONS, A
1966   120m   c   ★★★★★
Drama   /U
Highland   (U.K.)

Paul Scofield (Sir Thomas More), Wendy Hiller (Alice More), Leo McKern (Thomas Cromwell), Robert Shaw (King Henry VIII), Orson Welles (Cardinal Wolsey), Susannah York (Margaret More), Nigel Davenport (Duke of Norfolk), John Hurt (Richard Rich), Corin Redgrave (William Roper), Colin Blakely (Matthew)

p, Fred Zinnemann; d, Fred Zinnemann; w, Robert Bolt, Constance Willis (based on the play by Robert Bolt); ph, Ted Moore (Technicolor); ed, Ralph Kemplen; m, Georges Delerue; prod d, John Box; art d, Terence Marsh; cos, Elizabeth Haffenden, Joan Bridge

This film adaptation of Robert Bolt's hit play is a rare film that was both prestigious and commercial. Studio executives were unsure whether the regular folks would show up for the story of Sir Thomas More, a Catholic statesman in England who rebelled against Henry VIII's self-proclaimed status as the head of the Church of England and paid for his religious beliefs by having his head exhibited on London Bridge.

Scofield as More is appointed to be the Cardinal's (Welles's) successor as Lord Chancellor. More is a highly religious man, devoted to his beliefs. He comes to grips with Shaw, as Henry VIII, who wants to divorce his wife and take a new bride. Since the sacrament of marriage is to be upheld at all costs, Scofield objects to Shaw's plan. Shaw can objectively appreciate Scofield's beliefs, but he will not allow them to stand in the way of shedding his barren wife to marry Redgrave (Boleyn), who was dispatched in a different fashion and in a different film (ANNE OF THE THOUSAND DAYS). Scofield is bound to serve his king but makes no bones about his feelings regarding the divorce. The Pope also refuses Shaw's request, so Shaw, believing that, as king, he is just as infallible as the Catholic leader, makes himself the spiritual ruler of his country.

Scofield won the Oscar in this, his first major film role, after having played the part on stage in London and on Broadway. The decision to keep him, rather than cast some big name like Burton or O'Toole, was a wise and brave one. Hurt showed some of the talent he was to demonstrate in later years when he stepped out to become a star; Shaw also scored in a multidimensional performance as the most outrageous monarch in British history. Director Zinnemann never allows his primarily stage-trained actors to indulge in theatrical over-emoting. Scofield was strong yet restrained, showing his inner fortitude with the smallest facial expression. Oscar-nominated Hiller is good as Scofield's wife, as is York, their daughter. Shaw also received an Oscar nomination for Best Supporting Actor.

This absorbing film features inventive camera work and superior production values. Well-paced at two hours, A MAN FOR ALL SEASONS neither drags nor races. The film won Oscars for Best Picture, Best Actor, Best Director, Best Screenplay (from another medium), Best Color Cinematography, Best Color Costume Design, and seven awards from the British Film Academy for all the aforementioned categories as well as Best British Film.

MAN FROM LARAMIE, THE
1955 104m c   ★★★★
Western   /U
Columbia

James Stewart (Will Lockhart), Arthur Kennedy (Vic Hansbro), Donald Crisp (Alec Waggoman), Cathy O'Donnell (Barbara Waggoman), Alex Nicol (Dave Waggoman), Aline MacMahon (Kate Canaday), Wallace Ford (Charley O'Leary), Jack Elam (Chris Boldt), John War Eagle (Frank Darrah), James Millican (Tom Quigby)

p, William Goetz; d, Anthony Mann; w, Philip Yordan, Frank Burt (based on a Saturday Evening Post story by Thomas T. Flynn); ph, Charles Lang (Technicolor); ed, William Lyon; m, George Duning; art d, Cary Odell

The westerns of director Anthony Mann revitalized the genre in the 1950s because they were derived from classic struggles inspired by such works as the Bible and Shakespeare. His westerns weren't just action-packed chases; they were adult dramas which illustrated the psychological and moral dilemmas regarding the family, hatred, revenge, the land, and the nature of savagery versus civilization. In addition to being skillfully shot, acted, and scripted, Mann's westerns have an intelligence and conviction which compares well even with those by John Ford. Stewart leaves his home in Laramie, Wyoming, on a mission to find the men responsible for selling automatic rifles to the Apaches who had killed his brother in the cavalry. He enters the town of Coronado, New Mexico, and soon learns that most of the territory is ruled by Crisp, an aging, almost blind, megalomaniacal rancher who has been waging a long war against rival female rancher MacMahon. While riding through some salt flats owned by Crisp, Stewart is confronted by the powerful rancher's psychotic son, Nicol. Unaware that he has done anything wrong, Stewart finds himself beaten and dragged through his camp-fire. It looks as though Nicol is going to beat Stewart to death until the violence is interrupted by Kennedy, the foreman of the ranch and Crisp's adopted son. Stewart is brought back to the ranch where Crisp pays for the damages and advises the stranger to leave town. Determined to find the men responsible for his brother's death, Stewart ventures to MacMahon's ranch and is hired by the woman rancher. He learns that Crisp has become increasingly concerned with who will take over his empire, and although Kennedy has been running things smoothly for years, the rancher is likely to pick Nicol, his blood heir. Finally Crisp, blind to his real son's failings, chooses Nicol to take over the ranch; Kennedy is enraged. Stewart, still digging for clues, is once again caught by Nicol and his men. After a brutal fight, the crazed cowboy has his men subdue the stranger while he fires a bullet through Stewart's hand at point blank range. Nicol's men, disgusted by their participation in this cowardly act, help the crippled Stewart onto his horse and send him on his way. Still angry over the inheritance of the ranch, Kennedy starts an argument with Nicol regarding the guns and kills him. Stewart, of course, is blamed for the murder. Soon after, Crisp discovers that his sons have been selling rifles to the Apaches. He confronts Kennedy on the trail and a fight ensues. To keep their evil deeds a secret, Kennedy pushes the old man off a jagged cliff. Stewart learns the truth about the guns and confronts Kennedy. The emotionally charged final confrontation has Stewart on one side and the Apaches on ther other, with Kennedy in the middle awaiting his fate.

At the time of his death in 1967, director Mann had announced his plan to adapt Shakespeare's King Lear as a western (much the same way Japanese director Akira Kurosawa did with RAN).

One can see that THE MAN FROM LARAMIE was something of a dress rehearsal for this project. Crisp, as Lear, frets over the continuation of his empire and is blind to the fact that it is Kennedy who loves him most. His guilt feelings regarding his ruthless life (and having turned his former lover into an enemy) cloud his mind and move him to make bad decisions that ensure his downfall. This is the stuff of tragedy, and it does not often surface in westerns. THE MAN FROM LARAMIE came at the end of a cycle of collaboration between director Mann and actor Stewart which produced such fine Westerns as WINCHESTER '73, BEND OF THE RIVER, THE NAKED SPUR, and THE FAR COUNTRY. Their creative teamwork stands equal to those of John Ford-John Wayne and Budd Boetticher-Randolph Scott collaborations, and helped establish the western genre as a true American art form.

MAN FROM SNOWY RIVER, THE
1983 102m c   ★★★
Western/Adventure   R/PG
Hoyts/Cambridge   (Australia)

Kirk Douglas (Harrison/Spur), Jack Thompson (Clancy), Tom Burlinson (Jim Craig), Terence Donovan (Henry Craig), Tommy Dysart (Mountain Man), Bruce Kerr (Man in Street), David Bradshaw (A. B. "Banjo" Paterson), Sigrid Thornton (Jessica), Tony Bonner (Kane), June Jago (Mrs. Bailey)

p, Geoff Burrowes; d, George Miller; w, John Dixon, Fred Cullen (based on the poem by A.B. "Banjo" Paterson); ph, Keith Wagstaff (Panavision, Eastmancolor); ed, Adrian Carr; m, Bruce Rowland; art d, Leslie Binns; cos, Robin Hall

Kirk Douglas plays two brothers, the one, Harrison, an aristocratic landowner, the other, Spur, a one-legged, scraggly prospector. The pair experience a falling out, though this is not addressed until the latter half of the picture. More important than the plot are the characters of the brothers. The film was one of Australia's top-grossing pictures, though the producers took a chance in casting an American in the roles. (Robert Mitchum and Burt Lancaster also were considered.) A fine directorial debut from George Miller, who, not surprisingly, tends to be confused with the director of MAD MAX and THE ROAD WARRIOR, also named George Miller.

MAN HUNT
1941 105m bw   ★★★★½
Spy   /A
FOX

Walter Pidgeon (Capt. Thorndike), Joan Bennett (Jerry), George Sanders (Quive-Smith), John Carradine (Mr. Jones), Roddy McDowall (Vaner the Cabin Boy), Ludwig Stossel (Doctor), Heather Thatcher (Lady Risborough), Frederic Worlock (Lord Risborough), Roger Imhof (Capt. Jensen), Egon Brecher (Whiskers)

p, Kenneth MacGowan; d, Fritz Lang; w, Dudley Nichols (based on the novel Rogue Male by Geoffrey Household); ph, Arthur Miller; ed, Allen McNeil; m, Alfred Newman; art d, Richard Day, Wiard Ihnen; cos, Travis Banton

One of the best-loved of Lang's spy dramas, MAN HUNT is an exciting, tightly constructed, atmospheric picture which stars Pidgeon as a big-game hunter who packs up his rifle for a vacation in the Bavarian Alps. While walking through a forest near Adolf Hitler's Berchtesgaden retreat in the aftermath of the Munich Pact, Pidgeon spots the dictator in his gun sight. He pulls the trigger, but only a click is heard. Then he puts a bullet in the empty chamber and prepares to shoot, but is apprehended by the Gestapo. Gestapo leader Sanders pressures him into signing a confession, and when he refuses he is mercilessly beaten. Unconscious, he is dumped into an abyss in order to make the beating look like an accident. Stumbling through the forest and wading through murky swamps, Pidgeon makes his way to a rowboat in the harbor. With the help of a friendly youngster, McDowall, he stows away on a Danish steamer. Also on board, however, is the mysterious Carradine, who has found Pidgeon's passport and has taken his identity. Hiding in the shadows of London streets, Pidgeon tries to reach safety while being pursued by Sanders and his thugs. Pidgeon meets Bennett, a friendly cockney prostitute who helps him find a hiding place. Pidgeon becomes enamored of Bennett and buys her a handsome arrow-shaped hatpin for her tam-o'-shanter, telling her, "every soldier needs a crest for his cap." A confrontation finally occurs between Pidgeon and Carradine, resulting in a furious chase through London's underground. The darkness obscures their hand-to-hand battle, which climaxes when one of them is pushed into the path of an oncoming train. The following day, Bennett reads a newspaper story which reports that a body, mangled beyond recognition, was found and could be identified as Pidgeon only by his passport. Bennett and Pidgeon are reunited, but not for long. Their teary parting takes place on London Bridge and is interrupted by a bobby. Fearing that Pidgeon may be identified by the bobby, Bennett plays the prostitute and is taken away, creating the necessary diversion. Returning to her flat, Bennett is met by Sanders and his men and killed when she fails to cooperate with them. Pidgeon's countryside cave hideout proves ineffective, and he is discovered by Sanders. He is trapped inside with only a single small air shaft, and Sanders informs him of Bennett's murder, producing the arrow hatpin as evidence. Being a resourceful hunter, Pidgeon constructs a makeshift bow-and-arrow and kills Sanders through the airshaft. After a series of newsreel shots depicting the advancement of the war and the raging battles between the Germans and the Royal Air Force, Pidgeon is seen parachuting into Germany with a rifle slung over his back as a narrator says: "And from now on somewhere within Germany is a man with a precision rifle and the high degree of intelligence and training that is required to use it. It may be days, months, or even years—but this time he clearly knows his purpose."

Based on the best-selling novel, *Rogue Male*, MAN HUNT was scripted by the immensely talented Dudley Nichols and intended as a John Ford picture. Ford, however, disliked the subject matter and the film was offered, by Darryl Zanuck, to Lang. Lang encountered, as he often did, some problems on the set involving both the Hays Code and financial restraints by Zanuck. Lang, a great lover of complex female characters, had cast Bennett as a compassionate, honest girl who happened to be a prostitute. The Hays Code, however, disagreed with the idea of casting prostitutes in a "glamorous light" and forced some scenes to be emended. According to Lang, "We had to prominently show a sewing machine in her apartment; thus she was not a whore, she was a 'seamstress.' Talk about authenticity!" Most objectionable to Zanuck was the parting scene between Pidgeon and Bennett which was to take place on London Bridge. Zanuck was distressed by the fact that a "decent" girl (such as Bennett's character) had to play the whore in front of Pidgeon, the man she loved. Zanuck refused to allow any money in the budget for this scene, a scene which Lang felt essential. Regardless of Zanuck's sentiments, Lang, his cameraman, Miller, and unit manager Benny Silvi planned to go ahead with the scene. Digging among the studio's props, they found a single bridge railing. Two were

needed, however, so Lang dug into his pockets, pulled out $40, and paid to have a second one constructed. Without the aid of studio workers (whose unions would not allow such defiance), Lang, Miller, and Silvi stole into the studio at 4 a.m. They painted the backdrop, hung light bulbs in a manner of diminishing perspective to create depth, and then obscured the whole thing in a blanket of fog. The result was a beautifully atmospheric set.

MAN IN LOVE, A
(UN HOMME AMOUREUX)
1987 108m c   ★★★½
Romance   R/18
Camera One/Alexandre/JMS   (France)

Greta Scacchi *(Jane Steiner)*, Peter Coyote *(Steve Elliott)*, Peter Riegert *(Michael Pozner)*, Claudia Cardinale *(Julia Steiner)*, John Berry, Jr. *(Harry Steiner)*, Vincent Lindon *(Bruno Schlosser)*, Jamie Lee Curtis *(Susan Elliott)*, Jean Pigozzi *(Dante Pizani)*, Elia Katz *(Sam)*, Constantin Alexandrov *(De Vitta)*

p, Marjorie Israel, Armand Barbault, Roberto Guissani; d, Diane Kurys; w, Diane Kurys, Olivier Schatzky, Israel Horovitz; ph, Bernard Zitzermann (Eastmancolor); ed, Joele Van Effenterre; m, Georges Delerue; art d, Dean Tavoularis; cos, Brigitte Nierhaus

A MAN IN LOVE is romantic melodrama on a grand, international scale. Set mostly in Italy's Cinecitta film studio, it stars Peter Coyote as Steve Elliott, a temperamental American actor playing the lead in a film biography of Cesare Pavese, the Italian Communist writer who committed suicide in 1950 at age 41. The film's stereotypically obsessive director (Jean Pigozzi) has cast a relatively unknown English-speaking actress, Jane Steiner (Greta Scacchi), in a minor role as one of the many women Pavese loved, and her first visit to the set results in an explosive confrontation with the difficult star, offering a hint of things to come. An unpredictable, sexually charged romance develops between the two actors both on-and offscreen, putting Steve's acting ability and his feelings for his wife (Jamie Lee Curtis) to the test. Diane Kurys's first film in English transcends borders. Displaying remarkable adroitness, she interweaves various languages and locales, shows her characters to be a unique group of people involved in a fiction-making process that overlaps with and confuses real life, and maintains a complex plot in which the simple act of choosing a supporting actress nearly sinks the film-within-the-film and upsets two relationships. Badly underrated by critics, especially in comparison with Kurys's ENTRE NOUS, A MAN IN LOVE firmly establishes that Kurys is one of the most compelling filmmakers to emerge from France in recent years.

MAN IN THE GRAY FLANNEL SUIT, THE
1956 152m c   ★★★½
Drama   /A
FOX

Gregory Peck *(Tom Rath)*, Jennifer Jones *(Betsy Rath)*, Fredric March *(Ralph Hopkins)*, Marisa Pavan *(Maria)*, Ann Harding *(Mrs. Hopkins)*, Lee J. Cobb *(Judge Bernstein)*, Keenan Wynn *(Caesar Gardella)*, Gene Lockhart *(Hawthorne)*, Gigi Perreau *(Susan Hopkins)*, Portland Mason *(Janie)*

p, Darryl F. Zanuck; d, Nunnally Johnson; w, Nunnally Johnson (based on the novel by Sloan Wilson); ph, Charles Clarke (CinemaScope, DeLuxe Color); ed, Dorothy Spencer; m, Bernard Herrmann; art d, Lyle Wheeler, Jack Martin Smith; fx, Ray Kellogg; cos, Charles LeMaire

This is a story of middle-class middle-America seen through the eyes of one young businessman, Peck, who had served with distinction in WWII and is now in a mortgaged house (for $10,000) with a wife, Jones, and three children whose futures are uncertain if he does not land a better job. Moreover, there is a claim on the house Peck inherited from his grandmother made by Joseph Sweeney, a vicious, old, and greedy caretaker who, as events later prove, falsifies his claims to the old estate. While commuting back and forth to his job in New York City, Peck remembers vividly his days in the service. A man sits in front of him wearing a heavy winter coat with a fur-lined collar. He recalls how, when freezing, he knifed a young German soldier to death to take his coat during WWII. On another occasion he recalls how, while fighting the Japanese, he had thrown a grenade and accidentally killed his best friend. He also remembers Pavan, a beautiful girl he loved but never returned to after the war. Instead, he married Jones, who is anything but a forward-looking, vibrant helpmate. She is a spoiled, nagging, neurotic woman who never seems to be pleased with her better-than-average lot in life. Lockhart, one of Peck's fellow commuters, tells Peck of a new, well-paying job at UBC, and he applies as a speechwriter for its dynamic president, March. First he is interviewed by dry, clinical Arthur O'Connell, who does everything to discourage his application, as does his superior, Henry Daniell, a softspoken but insidious character who revels in his position as top aide to March. Meanwhile, trying to solve the claims against Peck's small estate is Cobb, a Jewish judge in Westport, Connecticut, where Peck and Jones reside. Peck finally gets the job at UBC and meets March, the man at the top, an impeccable, brilliant, and well-meaning man who has sacrificed his personal life, as he explains to Peck in a moment of candor, for the respected role of tycoon. Peck later learns what that sacrifice entails: a wife who has no use for March and a daughter, Perreau, who is utterly spoiled and has no respect for her father as she squanders her life with a wastrel who, in the words of her mother, "is right out of the F. Scott Fitzgerald era." March relies more and more on Peck, insisting he help him with an important speech, even if it consumes his off hours. The extra time Peck spends at work causes stress with his wife, and Jones really gets hysterical after Peck tells her that he has just learned that he has an illegitimate child in Italy, and that Pavan has written to him asking for some minimum support. Jones tells him she wants a divorce and he is to leave the house. When Peck tries to reason with her, Jones gets even more hysterical. Peck is on the brink of getting promoted to a top position at UBC but, at the last minute, refuses to work on March's speech over a weekend, telling the boss that he's "one of those nine-to-five" men. He risks his position, but the understanding March respects him for his stand, and it appears he will get that top job anyway. By this time, Jones has calmed down and goes with Peck to Cobb. They ask the humanitarian judge, who has dismissed the suit by the avaricious Sweeney, to help them out with Peck's sexual *faux pas*. Cobb admires the couple, particularly Jones, who suggests that they send money to Pavan regularly and asks him to arrange the payments. "This is a day, I'm sure," intones Cobb, "that inspired the poet to say that God is in His heaven and all is right with the world."

Peck does a fine job with a rather shallow story, as does that consummate actor March. All the supporting players play well their Madison Avenue stereotypes. Wynn is particularly effective as the elevator operator who spots Peck going to work and gives him the information about Pavan and their child. Cobb, though registering his typical hysterics, is very effective as the emotional judge. Jones, however, misreads her role and does a job of flagrant overacting, turning her part into pure soap, an unbeliev-

able and embarrassing performance accented by the obvious fact that Jones is much too old for her part. Johnson's script and direction have some flair but bog down midway. Peck, always the professional, researched his role by going to New York City and immersing himself in the advertising world. He was never recognized. The actor felt that the film "was spotted," but that it "had some good sequences," particularly those flashbacks depicting the war and his time with Pavan. This was Zanuck's last personally produced film before he left Fox. When Peck and Jones had appeared together in DUEL IN THE SUN a decade earlier, the reserved Peck was simply overwhelmed by the flamboyant, raven-haired actress, vowing never to act with her again. He nevertheless holds his own in THE MAN IN THE GREY FLANNEL SUIT, despite the fact that Jones's husband, mogul David O. Selznick, bombarded director Johnson with memos on how to shoot his wife, how to dress her, and how to have her makeup done.

MAN IN THE IRON MASK, THE

1939   110m   bw   ★★★★
Historical/Adventure   /PG
UA

Louis Hayward (*Louis XIV/Philippe*), Joan Bennett (*Maria Theresa*), Warren William (*D'Artagnan*), Joseph Schildkraut (*Fouquet*), Alan Hale (*Porthos*), Miles Mander (*Aramis*), Bert Roach (*Athos*), Walter Kingsford (*Colbert*), Marion Martin (*Mlle. de la Valliere*), Montagu Love (*Spanish Ambassador*)

p, Edward Small; d, James Whale; w, George Bruce (based on the novel by Alexandre Dumas); ph, Robert Planck; ed, Grant Whytock; m, Lucien Moraweck; art d, John DuCasse Schulze; fx, Howard Anderson

James Whale's high quality version of Dumas's classic tale of twin brothers, one the king of France and the other a prisoner at Isle St. Marguerite (Hayward, very fine in a dual role). William, as musketeer D'Artagnan, comes to the aid of the imprisoned brother, who is mercilessly forced to wear an iron mask to prevent anyone from realizing he is heir to the throne. Whale directed this elaborately costumed adventure with the greatest of verve and flair, though his career came to a halt in 1941. (He died mysteriously in his swimming pool 16 years later.) This film also marked the first screen appearance of Peter Cushing. The film's original score was nominated for an Oscar.

MAN IN THE WHITE SUIT, THE

1952   85m   bw   ★★★★★
Comedy   /U
Ealing   (U.K.)

Alec Guinness (*Sidney Stratton*), Joan Greenwood (*Daphne Birnley*), Cecil Parker (*Alan Birnley*), Michael Gough (*Michael Corland*), Ernest Thesiger (*Sir John Kierlaw*), Howard Marion-Crawford (*Cranford*), Duncan Lamont (*Harry*), Henry Mollison (*Hoskins*), Vida Hope (*Bertha*), Patric Doonan (*Frank*)

p, Michael Balcon; d, Alexander Mackendrick; w, Roger MacDougall, John Dighton, Alexander Mackendrick (based on the play by Roger MacDougall); ph, Douglas Slocombe; ed, Bernard Gribble; m, Benjamin Frankel; art d, Jim Morahan; fx, Sydney Pearson, Geoffrey Dickinson; cos, Anthony Mendleson

A sharp satirical comedy with serious undertones that indict the British industrial system, THE MAN IN THE WHITE SUIT offers a tour de force by master comic Guinness. He plays Sidney Stratton, an eccentric inventor believed crazy by most except for Daphne Birnley (Greenwood), daughter of a millionaire textile king (Parker). Stratton manages to finagle access to Birnley's elaborate development laboratory, supplied with all the chemicals and equipment he requires. Although Birnley and his associates have to deal with lab explosions and the eerie gurgling of Stratton's setup, Sidney eventually comes through, creating a fabric that never wears out and which repels dirt completely. He fashions a pristine white suit of the material and is as first hailed as a genius. Soon enough, though, the problems with the miracle material become evident. Labor dislikes poor Sidney because they'll all be put out of work once people buy enough of these wonder suits, and management changes its attitudes when they realize they'll be put out of business by Sidney's new fashion line. Although the two opposing forces do seem to get the better of Sidney in the memorable finale, his last-second knowing smile suggests an even greater discovery just around the corner.

THE MAN IN THE WHITE SUIT, besides offering consistent humor and often hilarious scenes, is another minor masterpiece of acting on Guinness' part: he shows marvelous restraint that gives way to brief hysteria, emphasizing again the complete versatility of this astounding actor. Greenwood, meanwhile, with her striking eyes, haughty yet vaguely haunted manner and that one-of-a-kind voice, is at her peak, parrying comic thrusts with great aplomb. The reliable Parker shines yet again as the worried capitalist and, on the proletariat side, the forceful Vida Hope and the adorable Edie Martin are especially outstanding. Special mention should also be made of Ernest Thesiger, that unique comic talent from several James Whale masterworks of the 1930s. He is wonderful here as the decrepit but all-powerful industrial czar who decrees Sidney's fate for the sake of business. In addition to the laughs, this film also indicts the ruthless and manipulative ways of businessmen. The acerbic social criticism lacing the film, however, does not exclude union representatives either, and the result is an intelligently rounded satire. Director Mackendrick's considerable gifts are on vivd display here, and he was nominated, along with MacDougall and Dighton, for an Oscar for their splendid screenplay.

MAN OF A THOUSAND FACES

1957 122m bw   ★★★½
Biography   /A
Universal

James Cagney (Lon Chaney), Dorothy Malone (Cleva Creighton Chaney), Jane Greer (Hazel Bennet), Marjorie Rambeau (Gert), Jim Backus (Clarence Logan), Robert Evans (Irving Thalberg), Celia Lovsky (Mrs. Chaney), Jeanne Cagney (Carrie Chaney), Jack Albertson (Dr. J. Wilson Shields), Roger Smith (Creighton Chaney at Age 21)

p, Robert Arthur; d, Joseph Pevney; w, Ivan Goff (based on a story by Ralph Wheelwright); ph, Russell Metty; ed, Ted J. Kent; m, Frank Skinner; art d, Alexander Golitzen, Eric Orbom; fx, Clifford Stine; cos, Bill Thomas

Other than Douglas Fairbanks, Jr., Rudolph Valentino, and Charlie Chaplin there were few who approached the star status in the silent film era of Lon Chaney, the master of disguise, a makeup genius who specialized in roles inspiring terror. He was the heart of horror during the glorious days of the silents, and Cagney's rendering of this great artist is spectacular. Cagney is the son of deaf-mute parents (he himself is free of these impairments). He becomes a successful vaudeville entertainer, offering magical performances as a mime, a juggler, and a man of many routines and characters, all creatively constructed through inventive makeup. Cagney meets beautiful but neurotic Malone and makes her his assistant. They fall in love and marry, but when Malone

is taken home by Cagney to meet his gentle but speechless parents, she becomes hysterical and then glumly resigned to the belief that any children they might have will be congenitally afflicted. Nothing Cagney can say or do will convince her otherwise. Malone remains terrified of having a deaf-and-dumb baby. When their child is born, she will not even look at him, until Cagney brings the child to her and loudly claps his hands close to the boy's ears, causing him to scream and Malone to become overjoyed. But Malone begins to resent her husband's rising popularity and, when he becomes a headliner, she competes with his fame by taking on a lover, then abandoning him and their son, Creighton (later Lon Chaney, Jr.), who is soon put into a home because Cagney lacks funds to support him.

Hurt and embittered, Cagney goes to Hollywood in 1913 to become a film extra. He works like a man possessed, answering every call for actors, his makeup box constantly at his side. Rambeau, who plays noble ladies in bit parts, becomes his friend but she is puzzled by his whirlwind work schedule. One hour he is playing a spearman, the next a pirate, changing his face constantly into a whole new character. When Rambeau quizzes him about his frantic schedule, Cagney replies: "I've got to get my kid out of hock." Cagney becomes so much in demand as a versatile character actor that he soon begins to earn substantial money in the movies and is able to have his little boy join him, especially after he meets and falls in love with Greer, a loving and generous woman who supports him and treats his son as her own. Cagney goes on to superstardom, enacting horrific figures such as The Hunchback of Notre Dame, The Phantom of the Opera, and strange, compelling, and almost always sinister characters in such films as WEST OF ZANZIBAR, THE PENALTY, THE UNHOLY THREE, and LONDON AFTER MIDNIGHT, all Chaney smash hits. Cagney, Greer, and the boy live a tranquil life; the star enjoys his mountain retreat, where he fishes and teaches his son his lifestyle and principles. One of the many great little scenes involves Cagney trying to get his son to sleep by making his face up to resemble a funny little grandmotherly type who stitches her fingers together. Then Malone comes back into Cagney's life, having lost her voice, ironically, from illness, and demanding to have the boy returned to her. Cagney is adamant, refusing to even allow her to visit the child. But persuaded by the compassionate Greer, he ultimately allows the boy to visit his mother. Malone's utter helplessness causes the teenage Creighton to stay with her, and, in young manhood, played by Smith, he continues to live with Malone, supporting her with his own acting work. Cagney disowns Smith for his loyalty to a woman who had earlier deserted both of them, but, when dying of throat cancer at the height of his fantastic career, Cagney reconciles with his son.

Cagney is riveting as Chaney, who died in 1930 at the age of 47, enacting the many great roles the silent star made famous in startling cameo performances. Some of the facts in Chaney's life were altered, but this did not affect a top-notch production. Cagney was ever mindful of Chaney's credo: "Unless I suffer, how can I make the public believe me?" when making this film. He acts with serene dignity, plumbing the tortuous life of a great artist, showing restraint and fully developing the sensitive, withdrawn character that was Lon Chaney. When playing the on-camera Chaney, fully understanding the tormented man he was playing, Cagney gives vent to his agony, slobbering mindlessly in the bell tower as the deformed hunchback or weeping unconsolably as the phantom over his hideous appearance. Cagney studied the actor's life and came to a deep understanding about why Chaney chose to play misfits and freaks: it was a way of expiating his own remorse over a miserable personal life. (Coincidentally, Cagney had, in these years, played a number of characters who were physically or psychologically crippled, like Martin "the Gimp" Snyder in LOVE ME OR LEAVE ME and the unbalanced Arthur Cody Jarrett in WHITE HEAT.) Chaney's unforgettable makeup tricks could not be exactly duplicated since the actor's secrets of disguise died with him, but makeup artists Bud Westmore and Jack Kevan did a great job in coming close. Cagney acted his heart out in this film and certainly deserved an Oscar nomination, which he did not receive. (The film was captioned for the deaf by the US Department of Health, Education, and Welfare.)

Malone gives a strong but strange performance as the weird first Mrs. Chaney, and Greer is outstanding as the second wife. Lovsky, as Cagney's deaf-mute mother, is superb and also deserved an Oscar nomination for supporting actress. MGM mogul Irving Thalberg is played unconvincingly by Evans, who was "discovered" sitting at poolside by Thalberg's widow, Norma Shearer; as an actor, he proved to be just another pretty boy without a tad of talent. Ironically, Evans later became a real-life mogul, heading Paramount from 1966 to 1976. Pevney's direction lags in spots and he sometimes overplays the tearjerking scenes but is mostly effective. Smith, playing the 21-year-old Creighton Chaney, is rather stoical. The real Creighton, who became Lon Chaney, Jr., and gleaned some fame in performing horror roles for Universal (THE WOLF MAN in particular), was himself a rather pathetic figure. The battle between his mother and father scarred his memories and troubled him throughout his own tormented life. As a teenager, Creighton Chaney searched widely for the mother who had abandoned him, finally tracking her down to a small ranch in the desert. He knocked on the door and a thin woman with haunted, hollow eyes answered. "My name is Creighton Chaney and I'm looking for Mrs. Cleva Fletcher," he said. "I'm sorry," she said, "no one here by that name," and began to close the door. Then someone inside the house shouted out, "Who is it, Cleva?" Oscar nominated for Best Screenplay.

MAN OF FLOWERS

1984 91m c   ★★★½
Drama   /18
Flowers   (Australia)

Norman Kaye (*Charles Bremer*), Alyson Best (*Lisa*), Chris Haywood (*David*), Sara Walker (*Jane*), Julia Blake (*Art Teacher*), Bob Ellis (*Psychiatrist*), Barry Dickins (*Postman*), Patrick Cook (*Coppershop Man*), Victoria Eagger (*Angela*), Werner Herzog (*Father*)

p, Jane Ballantyne, Paul Cox; d, Paul Cox; w, Paul Cox, Bob Ellis; ph, Yuri Sokol (Fujicolor); ed, Tim Lewis; m, Gaetano Donizetti; art d, Asher Bilu; cos, Lirit Bilu

Charles Bremer (Norman Kaye) is a sexually repressed, middle-aged artist who sublimates his desires into paintings of flowers and impassioned organ playing. He hires artist's model Lisa (Alyson Best) for $100 a week to come to his house and take off her clothes for him on a makeshift altar while he plays "The Love Duet" from Donizetti's "Lucia di Lammermoor," after which he rushes to church and vents his emotions on a pipe organ. Charles finally goes to a psychiatrist, who, in the tradition of movie shrinks, is kinkier than his patients.

An interesting, sometimes funny film about loneliness and emotional isolation, MAN OF FLOWERS boasts a literate script, a lush, sensual texture and, best of all, a silent cameo by German director Werner Herzog as Bremer's domineering father.

MAN OF IRON

(CZLOWIEK Z ZELAZA)
1981 140m c   ★★★★
Historical   PG/A
Film Polski/Film Unit X   (Poland)

Jerzy Radziwilowicz (*Tomczyk*), Krystyna Janda (*Agnieszka*), Marian Opania (*Winkiel*), Irene Byrska (*Anna Hulewicz' Mother*), Boguslaw Linda (*Radio-TV Technician Dzidek*), Wieslawa Kosmalska (*Anna*), Andrzej Seweryn (*Capt. Wirski*), Krzysztof Janczar (*Kryszka*), Boguslaw Sobczuk (*TV Editor*), Frantiszek Trzeciak (*Badecki*)

d, Andrzej Wajda; w, Aleksander Scibor-Rylski; ph, Edward Klosinski, Janusz Kalicinski; ed, Halina Prugar; m, Andrzej Korzynski; art d, Allan Starski, Maja Chrolowska; cos, Wieslawa Starska

Andrzej Wajda's sequel to MAN OF MARBLE in which he uses the same scriptwriter and leading players to once again trace its story through interviews. This film is a realistic portrayal of Gdansk from the student reform movement of 1968 to the Solidarity strikes in 1980. Strike leader Tomczyk (Jerzy Radziwilowicz) is harassed by the government and by a journalist (Marian Opania). The latter conducts a smear campaign against the young labor activist, but his own loyalties are tested during the strike. Wajda's superb amalgam of fictional characters and historical fact not only entertains but also documents a tense period in Polish history. Solidarity leader Walesa is among the real-life figures who appear. Made under censorious political pressures, MAN OF IRON was finished only hours before its premiere at the Cannes Film Festival, where it won top honors.

MAN OF MARBLE

(CZLOWIEK Z MARMURU)
1979 160m c   ★★★★½
Drama   /U
Enterprise de Realization/Ensemble X   (Poland)

Jerzy Radziwilowicz (*Mateusz Birkut/His Son Maciek Tomcyzyk*), Michal Tarkowski (*Wincenty Witek*), Krystyna Zachwatowicz (*Hanka Tomcyzyk*), Piotr Cieslak (*Michalak*), Wieslaw Wojcik (*Jodia*), Krystyna Janda (*Agnieszka*), Tadeusz Lomnicki (*Jerzy Burski*), Jacek Lomnicki (*Young Burski*), Leonard Zajaczkowski (*Leonard Frybos*), Jacek Domanski (*Sound Man*)

p, Andrzej Wajda; d, Andrzej Wajda; w, Aleksander Scibor-Rylski; ph, Edward Klosinski (Eastmancolor); ed, Halina Pugarowa, Maria Kalinciska; m, Andrzej Korzynski; prod d, Allan Starski, Wojciech Majda, Maria Osiecka-Kuminek; cos, Lidia Rzeszewska, Wieslawa Konopelska

A fine example of political art. The events which culminated in the workers' revolt and eventual martial law crackdown in Poland in 1982 are foreshadowed by one of Poland's highest-ranking directors in this black satire. Director Wajda follows film student Janda who wants to make a documentary about a former worker as her graduation requirement. Radziwilowicz is to be her subject, a man who had been lauded for his brick-laying skills before vanishing into total obscurity. Previously the subject of a film that showed what a great worker he was, Radziwilowicz became something of a star. But when he began believing the publicity himself and started interfering in worker politics, the government quickly stifled him, disgracing his name, and banishing him into historical obscurity. This is the story Janda discovers through interviews with Radziwilowicz's contemporaries and family and through old newsreels. Using an expository style similar to that of CITIZEN KANE, Wajda has fashioned a sophisticated indictment of Poland's communist regime, with all of its warts clearly exposed. Wajda followed this with MAN OF IRON, using similar storytelling methods to portray the rise of Poland's Solidarity movement and its leader Lech Walesa.

MAN OF THE WEST

1958   100m   c   ★★★★★
Western   /A
UA

Gary Cooper (Link Jones), Julie London (Billie Ellis), Lee J. Cobb (Dock Tobin), Arthur O'Connell (Sam Beasley), Jack Lord (Coaley), John Dehner (Claude), Royal Dano (Trout), Bob Wilke (Ponch), Jack Williams (Alcutt), Guy Wilkerson (Conductor)

p, Walter M. Mirisch; d, Anthony Mann; w, Reginald Rose (based on the novel The Border Jumpers by Will C. Brown); ph, Ernest Haller (CinemaScope, DeLuxe Color); ed, Richard Heermance; m, Leigh Harline; art d, Hilyard Brown; cos, Yvonne Wood

This is the last western directed by Anthony Mann, and it is his most powerful and disturbing foray into the genre. Working this time with Cooper instead of Jimmy Stewart, Mann once again tells a tale of Shakespearian proportions in which the heroes are complicated men struggling against their own worst instincts. The film opens as Cooper, a seemingly pleasant and somewhat guileless bumpkin, leaves his wife and two children and boards a train. He has been entrusted by the people of his small Texas town to travel to Ft. Worth and hire a new schoolteacher with the large sum of money he has been given. On the train he meets O'Connell, a nervous con man who enlists beautiful saloon singer London in a scheme to fleece Cooper, though she is rather hesitant. Telling Cooper that London is a schoolteacher, O'Connell almost succeeds in his con, but the train is halted by bandits before the transaction takes place. The robbers turn out to be the notorious Tobin gang, a psychotic band of thieves prone to extreme violence. After the robbery, Cooper, London, and O'Connell are stranded when the train leaves without them. Luckily, Cooper grew up in the area and takes his companions to a nearby cabin. There they find the Tobin gang, led by the grizzled and cruel Cobb. Surprisingly, it is revealed that Cobb is Cooper's uncle and that this unassuming man from a small Texas town used to be a member of the brutal gang. Cooper's unplanned homecoming is somewhat strained. Although Cobb is very glad to see his favorite nephew, Cooper's sadistic cousins, Lord, Dano (who is a mute), and Wilke, resent and distrust him. Thinking that Cooper has returned to rejoin the gang, Cobb happily relates a few bone-chilling reminiscences about the old days when he and his nephew would kill and rob. Lord, meanwhile, has become very excited by the presence of London, and he forces her to strip naked while holding a knife to Cooper's throat. The tension builds as London disrobes. Though it is obvious she has probably worked as a prostitute in the past, Cooper cannot stand to see this woman degraded in this way. Before she removes her undergarments, Cobb stops the depraved Lord by yelling at him for ruining the train robbery. To ensure that no further sexual molestations occur, Cooper tells Cobb that London is his woman. Cobb promises to enforce Cooper's request, but he takes the money intended to pay for the schoolteacher. He then allows his "guests" to stay in the barn. London begins to fall in love with Cooper, and in a scene charged with sexuality, a tempted Cooper begins telling the singer of his wife and family in a herculean effort to suppress his desire for her.

Soon after, Cooper's cousin Dehner, the smartest gang member who had replaced Cooper as second-in-command, rides up to the cabin. He and Cooper have a grudging respect for one another, perhaps because they recognize that they are two sides of the same coin. Cobb declares that there is a bank to rob in Lassoo, a town that represents the glory days of the gang, and the robbers pack up and ride off, accompanied by their guests. At their first encampment, Cooper has it out with Lord and there is a brutal fight. Cooper wins the battle and then strips Lord of his clothes in front of London. The crazed Lord grabs his pistol and tries to shoot Cooper, but O'Connell takes the bullet instead. Disgusted by his son's cowardly act, Cobb shoots Lord dead. Depressed over the incident, Cobb agrees to let Cooper ride into Lassoo to scout the bank. Accompanied by the mute Dano, Cooper discovers that Lassoo is now a ghost town. The only thing in the bank is a lone Mexican woman. In an inexplicable fit of rage, Dano shoots the woman. Shocked, Cooper kills Dano. Worried when Cooper and Dano haven't returned, Cobb sends Dehner and Wilke to Lassoo to search for them. When they arrive, Cooper manages to kill Wilke easily, but he and Dehner have a long and brutal gun battle. Eventually Cooper kills Dehner, but he does so regretfully, because it is like shooting a mirror image of himself. Before he leaves, Cooper sadly folds Dehner's arms to cover his chest as a sign of respect. Cooper rides back to the camp to fetch London and settle things with Cobb. Upon his return he discovers that Cobb has raped London and run off into the mountains. Cobb stands atop the rocks and watches as his favorite nephew comes to serve justice. Cooper tells Cobb that he has killed all his sons. His madness now completely out of control, Cobb taunts Cooper ("Kill me—you've lost your taste for it.") and fires wildly in the air, forcing his nephew to shoot him. Cobb tumbles down the rocks and falls dead in a crumpled heap. Cooper takes his money from Cobb's corpse and, accompanied by London, rides out of the wilderness.

As in Mann's other westerns with Stewart, there is an air of epic tragedy to MAN OF THE WEST. Cooper, a man whose past is as vicious and sordid as that of the other members of the Tobin gang, somehow managed to reject that life and start anew as a respectable man of the community. His accidental reentry into the gang causes his base instincts to once again boil to the surface after years of conformity, and Cooper is again able to be cold, hard, brutal, and lethal. He also understands that Cobb and the gang's time is up. The Old West they once knew is now a ghost town. These savages no longer have a place. Dehner and Cobb understand this. Cobb, in his raving madness, realizes that Cooper, who represents the new world, must kill him. He forces Cooper to shoot by violating what he believed to be his nephew's woman. Offering only token resistance, the true "Man of the West" dies in a crumpled heap after falling from a great height. Mann ended his stunning series of westerns most appropriately. His western heroes and villains do not wear white and black hats to tell good from evil. They are real people who suffer from anxiety, guilt, hatred, and self-doubt. Some succumb to these savage impulses and are destroyed after having outlived their epoch. The others (Stewart's characters, Cooper), all who have sinned, manage to overcome their dark sides and attain some sort of grace. MAN OF THE WEST was Mann's last western, and his importance to the genre cannot be overstated. While others would come to test the same waters and make significant contributions to the western (most notably Sam Peckinpah, Sergio Leone, and Clint Eastwood), Mann was one of the last consistently superior directors to leave his unique stamp on the genre.

MAN ON A TIGHTROPE

1953   105m   bw   ★★★★
Drama   /A
FOX

Fredric March *(Karel Cernik)*, Terry Moore *(Tereza Cernik)*, Gloria Grahame *(Zama Cernik)*, Cameron Mitchell *(Joe Vosdek)*, Adolphe Menjou *(Fesker)*, Robert Beatty *(Barovic)*, Alex D'Arcy *(Rudolph)*, Richard Boone *(Krofta)*, Pat Henning *(Konradin)*, Paul Hartman *(Jaromir)*

p, Robert L. Jacks; d, Elia Kazan; w, Robert E. Sherwood (based on the story "International Incident" by Neil Paterson); ph, Georg Krause; ed, Dorothy Spencer; art d, Hans Kuhnert, Theo Zwiersky; cos, Ursula Maes

March, in another powerful role, is the manager of a little Czech circus that is trying to get across the border through the Iron Curtain to freedom. March's family has owned the circus for generations. When the communists take over Czechoslovakia, his young performers are drafted into the service and his equipment sadly goes to seed without proper repair and replacement parts, which the new regime denies him. Moreover, he is told he no longer owns the circus but operates it for the benefit of the state. His troupers are instructed to perform their routines so that the communist credo is emphasized, which rankles the fiercely independent March. He nevertheless plays a waiting game, until his circus nears the Bavarian border. Meanwhile, he tries to keep his willful daughter Moore from becoming entangled with a worthless, shiftless lion tamer, Mitchell. Grahame, his young wife, believes March is a coward, especially after she sees him buckling under to instructions from communist cop Menjou. March learns that there is a spy in the circus and suspects Mitchell, but he later learns that it's the brawny Boone, the man in charge of the equipment. At the border, March parades his circus in full regalia, distracting guards, then unleashes dogs the guards believe to be wolves and stampedes his elephants while the performers race pell-mell across a bridge in their wagons and into free Germany. March is shot to death by Boone, who in turn is killed by a circus dwarf. With March dead, Grahame, now proud of her dead husband, vows to carry on in his shoes. Kazan's direction is flawless, and the story, written with great style and sharp dialogue by Sherwood, is superb. Shot on location in Bavaria, Germany, authentic acts were used, and the entire Birnbach Circus was employed for this excellent production.

MAN ON THE EIFFEL TOWER, THE

1949   97m   c   ★★★★
Mystery   /A
RKO

Charles Laughton *(Inspector Maigret)*, Franchot Tone *(Radek)*, Burgess Meredith *(Huertin)*, Robert Hutton *(Bill Kirby)*, Jean Wallace *(Edna Wallace)*, Patricia Roc *(Helen Kirby)*, Belita *(Gisella)*, George Thorpe *(Comelieu)*, William Phipps *(Janvier)*, William Cottrell *(Moers)*

p, Irving Allen; d, Burgess Meredith; w, Harry Brown (based on the story "A Battle of Nerves" by Georges Simenon); ph, Stanley Cortez (Ansco Color); ed, Louis Sackin; m, Michel Michelet; art d, Rene Renoux

Georges Simenon's famous sleuth, Inspector Maigret, was never better enacted than by the shrewd, slow, and sure Charles Laughton, who pursues a thrill killer-for-hire in this superb film noir production. The nephew of a rich woman hires Radek (Tone) to kill his aunt, and Maigret investigates. After dismissing a blind knife-grinder (Meredith, who also directed) as too obvious a suspect, Maigret unearths Tone, a psychopathic murderer who enjoys killing and baiting the police. Cop and killer play an intense cat-and-mouse game until one of them finally cracks under the psychological strain, with a superb chase up the Eiffel Tower as the exciting finale. The acting is outstanding in this film, and Franchot Tone actually overcomes Laughton's masterful mannerisms in their scenes together. Burgess Meredith both adroitly performs his red-herring role and directs with a sure hand. The lensing by Stanley Cortez, in rich Ansco color, lovingly shows a majestic Paris while sharply capturing the thrilling story. Michelet's score is also exceptional.

MAN ON THE FLYING TRAPEZE, THE

1935   65m   bw   ★★★★
Comedy   /A
Paramount

W.C. Fields *(Ambrose Wolfinger)*, Mary Brian *(Hope Wolfinger)*, Kathleen Howard *(Leona Wolfinger)*, Grady Sutton *(Claude Neselrode)*, Vera Lewis *(Mrs. Cordelia Neselrode)*, Lucien Littlefield *(Mr. Peabody)*, Oscar Apfel *(President Malloy)*, Lew Kelly *(Adolph Berg)*, Tammany Young *("Willie" the Weasel)*, Walter Brennan *("Legs" Garnett)*

p, William LeBaron; d, Clyde Bruckman; w, Ray Harris, Sam Hardy, Jack Cunningham, Bobby Vernon (based on a story by Sam Hardy and Charles Bogle); ph, Alfred Gilks; ed, Richard Currier

Another W.C. Fields gem, THE MAN ON THE FLYING TRAPEZE reprises the "prisoner of middle-class life" routine that he delineated so hilariously in IT'S A GIFT. Here Fields is seen brushing his teeth late at night—four times—and gargling from a flask in the bathroom until his wife, Kathleen Howard, complains about the noise. He trundles to bed and falls asleep snoring, only to be awakened by Howard, who has heard sounds of burglars singing. Howard insists that Fields go downstairs to investigate, taking his gun. But the gun goes off by accident, and Howard faints. The shot brings Howard's mother (Vera Lewis) and son (Grady Sutton) on the run. Then Fields's daughter (Mary Brian) comes in and chastises her stepbrother Sutton for refusing to go downstairs to face the burglars with her father. Fields goes alone, tripping at the head of the basement stairs and sailing downward, landing on his backside. The two burglars, Walter Brennan and Tammany Young, are tipsy, having broken into Fields's barrel of applejack. After he introduces himself, they genially offer him a drink. Soon they are all drinking together and singing "On the Banks of the Wabash." A cop shows up, but instead of arresting Young and Brennan, he takes a noggin and joins the group to make a singing quartet. Then the four go down to the courthouse, where the intruders are released, but Fields is thrown in jail for manufacturing spirits without a license. Fields appeals to his wife, but it is left to Brian to bail him out with the last of her savings. Fields assumes that Brian was sent by Howard and the daughter does not correct his error. The next morning at breakfast, most of the food goes to the insufferable Sutton, and Howard spears the last piece of sausage. Fields is left to eat cold toast, which he crunches into with a martyred speech and a sour look on his face. Howard is elated to find one of her avant-garde poems in the morning paper and begins reading it aloud, Fields suffering through it, crunching loudly on his hard toast. Sutton exclaims that he has found a $15 front-row ticket to a wrestling match; it's Fields's ticket, but he cannot admit that he spent so much money on an extravagance like that so he grins in impotent rage and bears Sutton's obvious theft of his prized possession. Late for work, Fields is greeted affably by his secretary, Carlotta Monti (who was Fields's real-life secretary and mistress and wrote a book about the comedian, *W.C. and Me*). His boss, Oscar Apfel, is annoyed at his being late but puts up with it because the firm needs Fields's photographic memory. Fields later succeeds in getting the day off, hinting that his mother-in-law, Lewis, has died. Before Fields takes off for the wrestling match, he gets four parking tickets—all in the same parking space—and tries to fix a flat on a steep hill. Meanwhile, funeral flowers arrive at Fields's home, and Howard thinks her husband has been killed. Then an office mate (Mickey Bennett) who hates Fields calls and asks how Lewis died. Howard tells him that her mother is very much alive. Fields arrives at the wrestling arena to find the place sold out, and the ticket window is slammed in his face just as he begins to pay for a ticket. As he views the match through a knothole, one wrestler tosses the other out of the ring and the arena. Fields rushes to the door but is flattened by the wrestler's flying body. The crowd pours out of the arena, including secretary Monti who helps her boss to his feet. Sutton, also emerging, thinks Fields is drunk and carrying on with Monti; he rushes home gleefully to break the news. When Fields arrives home, Howard, Lewis, and Sutton lambast him for lying about Lewis's death, for losing his job over the lie, and for having an affair while drunk. When Brian defends her father and Sutton threatens to hit her, Fields finally explodes, knocks Sutton cold, and leaves with his daughter to go live in their own apartment. Apfel, meanwhile, needs his memory expert, and tells Bennett to get him back. When Bennett calls, Brian answers and, hearing that Fields's old job is again available, says that her father has just been offered a position for twice his old salary—and gets him hired back at double what he was making. Howard returns to him, but now he calls the shots. He is in the driver's seat, literally and figuratively, and takes the family out for a drive in his new luxury roadster, his daughter and wife beside him, and in the rumble seat the obnoxious Sutton and Lewis. When a sudden rainstorm begins, Fields puts up the top, but Sutton and Lewis get the drenching of their lives, the much-desired comeuppance.

THE MAN ON THE FLYING TRAPEZE had nothing to do with circuses, other than depicting the circus of life as Fields so humorously saw it. This is one of Fields's most entertaining movies, full of ordinary mishaps that produce wonderful physical disasters, the characters and situations providing consistent laughs. The story mirrors Fields's career at Paramount, where he had been fired, then hired back at a fabulous salary, after IT'S A GIFT and other films had brought him fame. Howard was his favorite on-screen wife, and he never tired of telling reporters what an accomplished actress she was. She had been a singer with the Metropolitan Opera before becoming a fashion writer; she was asked to take a part in the movie DEATH TAKES A HOLIDAY while visiting the set. Afterwards she stayed on in Hollywood to become a regular character actress. Brian got her part in this movie because she was Fields's neighbor, and he liked the looks of her for the part.

MAN WHO CAME TO DINNER, THE

1942 112m bw ★★★★
Comedy /U
WB

Bette Davis (*Maggie Cutler*), Ann Sheridan (*Lorraine Sheldon*), Monty Woolley (*Sheridan Whiteside*), Richard Travis (*Bert Jefferson*), Jimmy Durante (*Banjo*), Reginald Gardiner (*Beverly Carlton*), Billie Burke (*Mrs. Stanley*), Elisabeth Fraser (*June Stanley*), Grant Mitchell (*Ernest Stanley*), George Barbier (*Dr. Bradley*)

p, Jerry Wald, Jack Saper; d, William Keighley; w, Julius J. Epstein, Philip G. Epstein (based on the play by George S. Kaufman, Moss Hart); ph, Tony Gaudio; ed, Jack Killifer; m, Frederick Hollander; art d, Robert Haas; cos, Orry-Kelly

This smash hit Broadway comedy became a smash hit movie due to a superb adaptation and the retention of Woolley, who played the lead on the stage. Davis had seen the play and wanted to take the secondary role as the "Great Man's" secretary. It was originally to star John Barrymore, but he had trouble with the lines, so Woolley was paged to repeat his role. The studio paid the then unheard-of price of a quarter of a million dollars for the rights and their investment paid off many times. It's a very thinly veiled account of some real people in an unlikely situation. Alexander Woollcott, Harpo Marx, and Noel Coward were all part of the Algonquin Hotel crowd who met for regular lunches. Hart and Kaufman took what they knew of the lunchers, placed them in a "fish-out-of-water" situation, and the result was a funny, acerbic, and successful play and film. Woolley (as Woollcott) is on a lecture tour across the US when he arrives in Ohio and accepts a dinner invitation from one of the leading families of a small town. As he is arriving with Davis, his tolerant secretary, he slips on the ice outside the home. He is carried inside as he shouts insults and says he will sue them for everything they have. Mitchell and Burke, who own the house and are the essence of Midwest respectability (which makes them everything Woolley dislikes), are frightened by the thought of the lawsuit and attempt to make Woolley comfortable as he waits for Barbier, the family doctor, to complete the examination. The doctor concludes that Woolley has been hurt badly and must stay in a wheelchair until he is well enough to leave. This throws the Mitchell-Burke household into chaos as Woolley malevolently decides to have a bit of amusement by making everyone around conform to his wishes. He charms the servants and advises the home's children, Russel Arms and Fraser, to flee immediately and seek to make their own ways apart from this stifling Ohio existence. Meanwhile, Davis is falling for local newsman-playwright Travis, and Woolley sees that he may lose her services, so he calls Sheridan, a sexy actress living in Palm Beach luxury as the mistress of a titled Englishman, and persuades her to come to cold Ohio with the promise of a leading role in a new play by Travis. His plan is to have Sheridan vamp Travis and get him away from Davis. Sheridan arrives, but Davis is hip to Woolley's plan, so she threatens to leave his employ. Woolley gets rid of Sheridan by packing her inside a mummy case to Philadelphia. Four penguins arrive from Admiral Byrd, as well as a live octopus from another admirer. Now Woolley finds out that his leg isn't badly hurt at all, as Barbier admits he diagnosed the injury incorrectly. But by this time, Woolley has laid many plans and he can't leave, so he convinces Barbier to keep mum with the promise that he'll have published the doctor's memoirs, surely a best-seller. Woolley is to make his annual Christmas radio broadcast from the Ohio location, so a full boys' choir and a large radio crew descend upon the house. In the meantime, he is also visited by Durante (as Harpo Marx) and Gardiner (as a Noel Coward type). Mitchell finally learns that Woolley is faking it and orders him out of the house in an attempt to quash the children's dreams of escaping. Now Woolley recognizes Mitchell's oddball sister, Ruth Vivian, as an alleged axe murderess who was tried and acquitted of killing her parents. With this fodder for his cannon, Woolley remains in the house, fixes up Davis's romance with Travis, and sends Arms and Fraser out into the world. His work done, Woolley exits the home only to truly break his leg on the ice. As he is carried bodily for the second time, a call from Eleanor Roosevelt comes in and the picture ends.

Witty lines, wonderful performances, and top-notch characterizations are delivered all around. Chester Clute and Laura Hope Crews, although billed as Mr. and Mrs. Gibbons, never appear in the final print. There was no mistaking the originals upon whom the story was based. Others might have sued, but Woollcott and company were apparently delighted at having been enshrined in the Comedy Hall of Fame by Kaufman and Hart's writing.

MAN WHO FELL TO EARTH, THE

1976 140m c   ★★★½
Science Fiction   R/18
Cinema 5 (U.K.)

David Bowie (Thomas Jerome Newton), Rip Torn (Nathan Bryce), Candy Clark (Mary-Lou), Buck Henry (Oliver Farnsworth), Bernie Casey (Peters), Jackson D. Kane (Prof. Canutti), Rick Riccardo (Trevor), Tony Mascia (Arthur), Linda Hutton (Elaine), Hilary Holland (Jill)

p, Michael Deeley, Barry Spikings; d, Nicolas Roeg; w, Paul Mayersberg (based on the novel by Walter Tevis); ph, Anthony Richmond (Panavision); ed, Graeme Clifford; fx, Paul Ellenshaw

Nicolas Roeg's cult classic about an alien, Bowie, who arrives on Earth in search of water for his drought-stricken planet where his wife and children are dying of thirst. Bowie takes an Earth name, arrives at the office of gay patent attorney Henry, and offers him a number of invention designs with which they can make a great deal of money, enough for Bowie to build a vehicle for him to return to his home planet. In almost no time Bowie and Henry are running a huge financial empire, one of the world's largest corporations. Torn is a professor of chemistry who spends his off hours seducing his students. He wants to know more about Bowie's company, especially how it is that they have become a $300 million company in three years. Bowie is hiding out in New Mexico when he meets hotel clerk Clark, who encourages him to drink gin and watch television. Not a person to do things halfway, Bowie is soon guzzling the booze and watching several television sets simultaneously as he continues his plan to start his own space project. Bowie continues to drink, watch television, and, in general, become more and more human in his lifestyle. Thus are the seeds of his ruin planted as an otherworldy innocent is corrupted by American culture.

The film looks wonderful, and cultists have named it one of their favorites. The soundtrack helps establish the near-future mood, although Bowie doesn't sing much at all. Roeg began his career as a cameraman (he worked second-unit on LAWRENCE OF ARABIA) and progressed to become a director of photography (THE MASQUE OF THE RED DEATH, A FUNNY THING HAPPENED ON THE WAY TO THE FORUM, FAHRENHEIT 451). Clearly Roeg's very practiced eye determined the memorable imagery on display here. The sets are very stylish, and all technical credits are first quality. Bowie proves he isn't just another beautiful and androgenous face with his performance in this film. This was the beginning of his interesting if ultimately minor career as an actor/icon.

There is no question that the more crowdpleasing E.T. has a similar premise: i.e., an alien stranded on Earth who wants to get back to his home planet. However, Newton becomes a far more dedicated couch potato. Of course, Roeg's dreamily downbeat handling of the subject matter could not be more different from the quasi-religious uplift of Steven Spielberg's method. In some ways, the Roeg film is more comforting for jaded adults and adolescents aspiring to coolness because it is nowhere near as emotionally calculating or overwhelming. Indeed some viewers will undoubtedly find it find it annoyingly vague and drawn out. There are many changes from the Tevis novel, not all of them for the better. Roeg enjoys using singers as actors and cast Mick Jagger (PERFORMANMCE) and Art Garfunkel (BAD TIM-

ING) in films that also have devoted followers. This film is essentially a science-fiction movie with a touch of social commentary and modern music tossed in to add spice to the stew. In the final analysis, images are everything here; it's a sensual experience in which narrative takes a backseat. Eddy Arnold sings "Make the World Go Away" in addition to the rock tunes.

Originally released at 140 minutes, the US distributor, Cinema 5, edited the film down to versions of 117, 120, and 125 minutes, before restoring it to its original length in 1980.

MAN WHO KNEW TOO MUCH, THE

1935 75m bw   ★★★★
Mystery
Gaumont (U.K.)

Leslie Banks (Bob Lawrence), Edna Best (Jill Lawrence), Peter Lorre (Abbott), Frank Vosper (Ramon Levine), Hugh Wakefield (Clive), Nova Pilbeam (Betty Lawrence), Pierre Fresnay (Louis Bernard), Cicely Oates (Nurse Agnes), D.A. Clarke-Smith (Binstead), George Curzon (Gibson)

p, Michael Balcon; d, Alfred Hitchcock; w, A.R. Rawlinson, Charles Bennett, D.B. Wyndham-Lewis, Emlyn Williams, Edwin Greenwood (based on a story by Charles Bennett and D.B. Wyndham-Lewis); ph, Curt Courant; ed, Hugh Stewart; m, Arthur Benjamin; art d, Alfred Junge, Peter Proud

Married couple Bob and Jill Lawrence (Banks and Best) are vacationing in Switzerland with daughter Betty (Pilbeam), when Louis Bernard (Fresnay), a Frenchman who befriends them, is found murdered. Before dying, however, Louis Bernard whispers a secret—that a diplomat will be assassinated at great embarrassment to the British government. To keep Bob's lips sealed, Betty is kidnapped—to be held until after the assassination by hired killer Abbott (Lorre), scheduled to take place during a concert at London's Albert Hall. Bob must follow his duty as a Englishman and prevent the assassination, but at the same time he must do all in his power to insure the safety of his child. It is in this film that Hitchcock showed his development of a theme he would repeat in films to come—the innocent victim suddenly caught up in a terrifying situation with apparently no way out, coupled with breathless chases in popular public places. This was Lorre's first English-speaking part; he had been brought to England at Hitchcock's request after the director saw him in Fritz Lang's impressive M. Hitchcock, who was not known to favor child actors, got along so well with the young Pilbeam that he gave her her first adult leading role in his film YOUNG AND INNOCENT, three years later.

MAN WHO KNEW TOO MUCH, THE

1956 120m c   ★★★★
Mystery   PG/A
Paramount

James Stewart (Dr. Ben McKenna), Doris Day (Jo McKenna), Brenda de Banzie (Mrs. Drayton), Bernard Miles (Mr. Drayton), Ralph Truman (Buchanan), Daniel Gelin (Louis Bernard), Mogens Wieth (Ambassador), Alan Mowbray (Val Parnell), Hillary Brooke (Jan Peterson), Christopher Olsen (Hank McKenna)

p, Alfred Hitchcock; d, Alfred Hitchcock; w, John Michael Hayes, Angus Macphail (based on a story by Charles Bennett, D.B. Wyndham-Lewis); ph, Richard Mueller (VistaVision, Technicolor); ed, George Tomasini; m, Bernard Herrmann; art d, Hal Pereira, Henry Bumstead; fx, John P. Fulton; cos, Edith Head

The original version of this film so appealed to Hitchcock that he felt it could take a remake and survive. He also believed that he could improve upon it—an opinion open to debate. Though the director altered some locales (Switzerland became Morocco), he kept the original story fairly much intact, enhanced the production values, and added 45 minutes to its running time. Dr. Ben and Jo McKenna (Stewart and Day) are sweetly innocent and unsuspecting tourists whose vacation in French Morocco turns into a nightmare. Traveling with their son Hank (Olsen) they are enjoying their holiday when they meet Mr. and Mrs. Drayton (Miles and de Banzie), a friendly British couple, and Louis Bernard (Gelin), a suspicious but friendly Frenchman. Later, while Ben and Jo are shopping in the bazaar, an Arab runs frantically up to them, having been stabbed in the back. Ben grabs the man as he falls and finds, to his horror, that it is Louis Bernard in disguise. Before he dies, Louis Bernard whispers something to Ben, thereby tossing him into a tangle of international intrigue that only he can unravel. Though there is obviously more polish and a lavish budget in this remake, the 1956 version of THE MAN WHO KNEW TOO MUCH has no more or less impact than the first version. Again, Hitchcock's scenes are beautifully framed and tautly directed—especially the double climax of the assassination attempt at the Albert Hall and the Embassy search for the kidnapped Hank. Day delivers the only musical number in a Hitchcock film, singing "Que Sera, Sera"—a song good enough to win an Oscar as Best Song and to become a smash hit. Hitchcock makes his customary cameo, as does his composer Bernard Herrmann.

MAN WHO LOVED WOMEN, THE
(L'HOMME QUI AIMAIT LES FEMMES)
1977   119m   c   ★★★
Drama/Comedy   /X
Carrosse/Artistes   (France)

Charles Denner (Bertrand Morane), Brigitte Fossey (Genevieve Bigey), Nelly Borgeaud (Delphine Grezel), Leslie Caron (Vera), Genevieve Fontanel (Helene), Nathalie Baye (Martine Desdoits), Sabine Glaser (Bernadette), Valerie Bonnier (Fabienne), Martine Chassing (Denise), Roselyne Puyo (Nicole)

d, Francois Truffaut; w, Francois Truffaut, Michel Fermaud, Suzanne Schiffman; ph, Nestor Almendros; ed, Martine Barraque; m, Maurice Jaubert

Truffaut's swiftly paced, light-hearted exercise concerns a man whose very existence is devoted to women—a man perhaps not unlike Truffaut himself. Denner is the amorous title male, a well-off researcher who is surely one of the most woman-crazy men ever to appear on film. He can't keep his mind off women; a mere glance at one femme dressed in black silk stockings sends him on a long journey toward love. All the while that Denner chases skirts, he remains charming and innocent, never believing he is doing anything wrong or harmful. Unlike those men who abuse women, Denner adores them—all of them. THE MAN WHO LOVED WOMEN is filled with Truffaut's ironic sense of humor, always charming, and never in any way offending. As in all of Truffaut's romantic comedies, what appears as flippant and sugary is actually a cover for some very complex statements about the nature of love, Truffaut himself, and the cinema. In this sense THE MAN WHO LOVED WOMEN can be viewed, along with THE STORY OF ADELE H. and THE GREEN ROOM, as part of a trilogy about unrequited love and frustrating obsessions. A Hollywood remake of this film appeared in 1983, directed by Blake Edwards and starring Burt Reynolds.

MAN WHO PLAYED GOD, THE
1932   81m   bw   ★★½
Drama
WB

George Arliss (Montgomery Royale), Violet Heming (Mildred Miller), Ivan Simpson (Battle), Louise Closser Hale (Florence Royale), Bette Davis (Grace Blair), Andre Luguet (The King), Donald Cook (Harold Van Adam), Charles E. Evans (The Doctor), Oscar Apfel (The Lip Reader), Paul Porcasi (French Concert Manager)

p, Jack L. Warner; d, John G. Adolfi; w, Julien Josephson, Maude Howell (based on a short story by Gouverneur Morris, and the play "The Silent Voice" by Jules Eckert Goodman); ph, James Van Trees; ed, William Holmes; m, Salvatore Santaella

Concert pianist Arliss performs a private concert for king Luguet but loses his hearing when an anarchist throws a bomb into the palace in an assassination attempt. Depressed and at the end of his career, Arliss returns to his hometown of New York with his fiancee Davis. After a suicide attempt, Arliss discovers that he can read lips. He spends all of his time staring into nearby Central Park, eavesdropping on people's conversations. He becomes generous, bestowing upon the unfortunate various gifts. When he "overhears" a conversation between Davis and Cook, the man she really loves, Arliss allows her to break off the engagement, knowing that she is staying only to serve him. Arliss then donates a pipe organ to a church where he proceeds to play hymns that he cannot hear, but feels. The religious overtones are excessive, but the subject matter allows for them and diminishes any feeling of intrusion. Arliss does a fine job, returning to the role he first played in the 1922 silent version. Davis makes her first Warner Brothers appearance, and there are also bits from Hedda Hopper and a young Ray Milland. Remade as SINCERELY YOURS with Liberace.

MAN WHO SHOT LIBERTY VALANCE, THE
1962   123m   bw   ★★★
Western   /U
Ford

James Stewart (Ransom Stoddard), John Wayne (Tom Doniphon), Vera Miles (Hallie Stoddard), Lee Marvin (Liberty Valance), Edmond O'Brien (Dutton Peabody), Andy Devine (Link Appleyard), Ken Murray (Doc Willoughby), John Carradine (Maj. Cassius Starbuckle), Jeanette Nolan (Nora Ericson), John Qualen (Peter Ericson)

p, Willis Goldbeck; d, John Ford; w, Willis Goldbeck, James Warner Bellah (based on a story by Dorothy M. Johnson); ph, William Clothier; ed, Otho Lovering; m, Cyril J. Mockridge, Alfred Newman; art d, Hal Pereira, Eddie Imazu; cos, Edith Head

This is a solid, if overrated, Ford western, one with its share of cliches and predictability. It's still fascinating to watch Wayne and Stewart deal with hellion Marvin in a fast-changing West. The movie opens after the story is all over, when Stewart, a US senator, and his wife, Miles, return to the western town of Shinbone in 1910. They have come unannounced and unexpected to attend Wayne's funeral, which piques the interest of a local reporter who quizzes them about their interest in this obscure dead rancher. With Miles's approval, Stewart begins to tell the reporter exactly how he came to know Wayne, as the movie goes into flashback to a time when Shinbone was in its wild and woolly days. At that time Stewart is a fledgling lawyer who has no place to practice and no clients interested in any kind of law other than what comes out of a six-gun. The man with the most deadly gun is Marvin, the dreaded Liberty Valance, who goes nowhere without two killer nitwits, Lee Van Cleef and Strother Martin. Stewart is waylaid by Valance and his men just as he enters Shinbone territory; they believe he is an agitator for statehood, exactly what a group of powerful businessmen do not want. Marvin is the western thug working for this clique, and he brutally beats up Stewart and leaves him for dead. Wayne finds him on the trail and takes him to town, finding him a restaurant where he can take shelter and recuperate. When Stewart goes to work in the restaurant, owned by Qualen and where Miles is the cook, he is ridiculed for his awkward efforts as a waiter, with Marvin and his boys tripping and insulting him at every turn. Stewart sleeps in the kitchen and continues to practice law by lamplight, ignoring challenges from the drunken cowboys who vex him. Miles is attracted to him, and it's obvious to everyone, especially Wayne, that she will be his wife. Wayne and O'Brien, a drunken editor of a little newspaper, are the only people who have ever stood up to Marvin. He fears Wayne and hates O'Brien, who is constantly printing unkind remarks about him. In one scene inside the restaurant, Wayne orders a steak and when Stewart tries to serve it, Marvin trips him and the steak goes flying onto the floor. Marvin and Van Cleef guffaw like the cretinous goons they are, and Marvin revels in Stewart's refusal to face him with a gun over the repeated insults, calling the lawyer "yellow." Wayne marches over to Marvin and tells him to pick up the steak. Marvin sneers and stands up, his hand twitching toward his gun, but he thinks twice about it. He picks up the steak but intends to deal with Wayne later. Stewart lobbies for statehood, and he wins an election, with Wayne's help, as a delegate to the convention to ratify statehood. This causes Marvin to explode, and he tells Stewart he will return to Shinbone and kill him. Stewart tries to learn how to use a six-gun, but even Wayne cannot teach him the fine art of gunfighting. Stewart puts his trust in his lawyer's shingle, hanging it out in O'Brien's newspaper office. O'Brien prints one editorial too many, and Marvin and his goons pay him a visit, pistol-whipping him and wrecking his press. Marvin also orders Stewart to face him that night in the streets of Shinbone. It is dark when the two men meet, and several shots are fired. Marvin falls dead; Stewart is hailed as a hero and, on the strength of his shootout with outlaw Marvin, is elected US senator and marries Miles. When Wayne hears that Miles, the girl he has always taken for granted as his girl, will be Stewart's wife, he returns to his ranch and sets it on fire, almost burning with it. He is saved at the last moment by his trusty friend and worker, Woody Strode. Stewart cannot stand the fact that he is being elected to office for killing a man and is about to walk out on the nomination when Wayne takes him aside and tells him that he, not Stewart, shot the outlaw from the shadows. Wayne did it, he says, because Miles came to him and asked him to save Stewart's life, and he did it only for her. Stewart now must continue to take the credit for the killing for Miles's sake, Wayne tells him, which Stewart does. Later, Stewart is about to become governor and begins to back down from the undeserved reputation he has earned in the Marvin shooting as a law-and-order candidate. Wayne appears again, as Stewart's conscience, and tells him he must go on fighting for the right and for the belief Miles has in him. Stewart goes on to become governor and later serves with great distinction in Washington. Wayne lives in obscurity until his death, which brings the film fully around to the present again. The reporter listening to the story begins to tear up the notes he has taken. Stewart says, "You're not going to use the story?" The reporter replies, quoting his late, great editor, O'Brien, "It ain't news. This is the West. When the legend becomes the fact, print the legend."

Starkly photographed and often heavily screened for nighttime shots, Ford's picture of the West here is a gloomy one, murky and often pitch black when the only thing that comes out of it is beast Marvin. Many cliches and stereotypes people the film; the crusading newspaper editor, for example, had been used in many an earlier western, notably DODGE CITY. Oddly Ford, the master of great western exterior scenes, shot the entire film on two Paramount sound stages. Auteur critics and others read much into this rather routine Ford film but the insights and value judgments existed only in their inventive and superlative-clutching minds. The movie is certainly above average, thanks to the performances by Stewart and Wayne, but Marvin is so flamboyant a badman that he is simply a caricature, more than his outlandish Oscar-winning performance in CAT BALLOU. On the whole, this picture was simply a quick reworking of a standard western yarn. Nominated by the Academy for Best Costume Design.

MAN WHO WOULD BE KING, THE

1975 129m c   ★★★★★
Adventure   PG
Allied Artists   (U.K.)

Sean Connery *(Daniel Dravot)*, Michael Caine *(Peachy Carnehan)*, Christopher Plummer *(Rudyard Kipling)*, Saeed Jaffrey *(Billy Fish)*, Karroum Ben Bouih *(Kafu-Selim)*, Jack May *(District Commissioner)*, Doghmi Larbi *(Ootah)*, Shakira Caine *(Roxanne)*, Mohammed Shamsi *(Babu)*, Paul Antrim *(Mulvaney)*

p, John Foreman; d, John Huston; w, John Huston, Gladys Hill (based on the story by Rudyard Kipling); ph, Oswald Morris (Panavision, Technicolor); ed, Russell Lloyd; m, Maurice Jarre; prod d, Alexander Trauner; art d, Tony Inglis; cos, Edith Head

That this picture did not win one Oscar is evidence of the shortsightedness and chauvinism of the Motion Picture Academy. It was nominated for Screenplay, Editing, Production Design, Art Direction, and Costumes but was trampled by ONE FLEW OVER THE CUCKOO'S NEST. THE MAN WHO WOULD BE KING is one of those films that inspire the question "Why don't they make films like that anymore?" The director is John Huston, a man who made many pictures "like they don't make anymore," and this ranks as one of his greatest achievements in a career chock-a-block with brilliant work. The film is based on Rudyard Kipling's short story, which Huston read when he was a lad. The director intended to make the film for years, first with Clark Gable and Humphrey Bogart, then with Richard Burton and Peter O'Toole. But he did not undertake the project until producer Foreman got $8 million from Manny Wolf at the struggling Allied Artists company. In later years both Caine and Connery sued Allied Artists for a share in the profits. It's a vast parable that vaguely and metaphorically intimates some of the colonial injustices visited upon the various natives by the avaricious British Empire of the era. Kipling's message is that if you walk into another man's land and look only to take what is rightfully his, you will pay a mortal price.

Plummer, playing Kipling, is in his Lahore, India, office one night when an aged beggar, Caine, enters. The unrecognizable man is old and a bit mad, and his voice is raspy. Caine begins to spin an incredible yarn that Plummer can hardly believe, and we flash back to another Kipling office. Caine, now young and vibrant and a bit of a boorish braggart, and Connery ask Plummer to witness a document attesting to what they have told him. They are British army officers in India who have supplemented their service incomes by engaging in various conniving schemes. At this point they have very little left of their booty, having lavished it all on high living and low women. They are undaunted by their empty pockets and have concocted a new plan: They will sojourn into the hills of Kafiristan (a province in eastern Afghanistan now called Nuristan) where they intend to set up themselves as rulers. Plummer is taken by these two brash explorers-to-be and secures an appointment for them with the man in charge of the district, May. May is not at all impressed with them and goes so far as to call the pair "detriments" to the British cause in India. Caine and Connery respond by duck-walking out the door of May's office. They return to Plummer's office, not the least bit daunted by May's rejection. Plummer believes in them, though Caine had once stolen his pocket watch and returned it later when he saw the Masonic sign on the timepiece and, being a Mason as well, thought it was his duty to return it. Caine and Connery endure several hardships as they trek over hill and dale, through the storied Khyber Pass, and down into the glorious valley of Kafiristan. With the aid of a few renegades, they attack the city of Sikandergul, an ancient, holy place once ruled by Alexander the Great. During the course of events an arrow strikes Connery in the chest, but does not kill him. In full view of the amazed battlers he does not fall mortally wounded. Instead, he blithely pulls the arrow out of his chest. The natives think he is a god who cannot be killed by the weapons of mere humans. What they do not know is that the arrow hit his Freemason pendant and failed to penetrate his flesh. The natives immediately throw down their arms and prostrate themselves before Connery because they believe, as had been prophesied in their rituals, that he is the incarnation of Alexander and has come back to lead them. Connery is somewhat jolted by this. He had meant to steal a lot of gems and gold and get the heck out of there, but the prospect of being a living god appeals to him. Caine says it might be best for them to take the money and run, but Connery rapidly is becoming corrupted by all this adulation and decides to stay awhile. (One wonders how the story would have turned out if Caine's character had been the lucky so-and-so.) Connery accepts all of the plaudits and begins to think that, perhaps, he is the second coming of Alexander. Caine wants no part of it and plans to leave before a tragedy occurs. Connery has decided to take himself a wife (Shakira Caine, Michael's real-life spouse at the time), and Connery urges his old friend to remain for the nuptials. Shakira shows up at the wedding, terrified at the prospect of marrying a god, and bites Connery's face, thereby drawing blood. The natives, who do know that gods have no blood, advance on the men because they now understand that Connery is human. Connery and Caine run for it, but Connery is killed when he falls into a deep gorge, and Caine is caught, crucified, and left for dead. Back to the present in Plummer's office, Caine reveals himself to be Connery's partner, and the tale he is telling is not fiction, it is a memory. The picture ends in the office, and we have been treated to slightly more than two hours of high adventure in the genre of GUNGA DIN and BEAU GESTE.

The film, is of the kind Huston, John Ford, and Howard Hawks did so well so long ago. Plummer, who did his best acting since THE SOUND OF MUSIC, was amazing in his portrayal of Kipling and took great pains to prepare for his brief, though important, role. To achieve reality, Plummer secured a tape of Kipling's voice from the British Broadcasting offices and several photographs of the late story-teller and thoroughly immersed himself into the persona of Kipling. What came out was worth all the effort. Made on location in Morocco because of the costs and dangers of shooting in Afghanistan, the picture had niggling flaws. Caine might have gone over the top a bit, but that was necessary to separate the natures of the two men. Jarre's music was, surprisingly, not an asset to the film, as it did not have the feeling of the setting. Still, it did not detract from what was happening on-screen. Jaffrey, playing Connery and Caine's interpreter in the early scenes who sacrifices himself for the men, gave a good performance in a small part. Connery also appeared in another adventure film in 1975, the pretentious THE WIND AND THE LION, which was a midget compared to the grandeur of THE MAN WHO WOULD BE KING. The movie's underlying message, though never stated, was that the sun was beginning to set on the British Empire. This is a remarkable movie with more adventure than all of Steven Spielberg's and George Lucas's films put together and with characterizations that live on in our memories.

MAN WITH BOGART'S FACE, THE

1980 106m c   ★★★½
Comedy/Mystery   PG/A
FOX

Robert Sacchi *(Sam Marlow)*, Franco Nero *(Hakim)*, Michelle Phillips *(Gena Anastas)*, Olivia Hussey *(Elsa Borsht)*, Misty Rowe *(Duchess)*, Victor Buono *(Commodore Anastas)*, Herbert Lom *(Mr. Zebra)*, Sybil Danning *(Cynthia)*, Richard Bakalyan *(Lt. Bumbera)*, Gregg Palmer *(Sgt. Hacksaw)*

p, Andrew J. Fenady; d, Robert Day; w, Andrew J. Fenady (based on his novel); ph, Richard C. Glouner (CFI Color); ed, Eddie Saeta; m, George Duning; prod d, Robert Kinoshita; cos, Oscar Rodriguez, Jack Splangler, Vou Lee Giokaris

THE MAN WITH BOGART'S FACE is a deliciously funny sendup of hard-boiled detective films. It stars Robert Sacchi—an actor who, when he combs his hair just right, bears a remarkable resemblance to Humphrey Bogart. Sam Marlow (Sacchi) undergoes plastic surgery so that he will look like (three guesses) Bogie, and when he opens a small detective agency, he is called upon by a goofy assemblage of clients, all of whom want him to find the Eyes of Alexander. Among those seeking these famous gems are Hakim (Nero), a Turkish mogul, Greek shipping millionaire Commodore Anastas (Buono, in a parody of Sydney Greenstreet), Mr. Zebra (Lom, doing Peter Lorre), Wolf Zinderneuf (Jay Robinson), a Nazi war criminal, and Gena (Phillips), a mysterious Mary Astor type. Action, murder, and laughs follow as the film goes from yachts to mansions and winds up on a boat docked at the island of Santa Catalina, where Marlow (his name is a combination of Sam Spade and Philip Marlowe) lays bare the motives of the jewel-hungry bunch. It is all wonderfully silly, but played totally straight by everyone, and therein lies the fun. Six well-known radio and newspaper reporters play themselves in the picture, including onetime *Hollywood Reporter* editor Frank Barron. Former football player Joe Theismann is seen briefly.

MAN WITH THE GOLDEN ARM, THE

1955 119m bw   ★★½
Drama   /15
Carlyle

Frank Sinatra *(Frankie Machine)*, Kim Novak *(Molly)*, Eleanor Parker *(Zosch Machine)*, Arnold Stang *(Sparrow)*, Darren McGavin *(Louie)*, Robert Strauss *(Schwiefka)*, George Mathews *(Williams)*, John Conte *(Drunky)*, Doro Merande *(Vi)*, George E. Stone *(Sam Markette)*

p, Otto Preminger; d, Otto Preminger; w, Walter Newman, Lewis Meltzer (based on the novel by Nelson Algren); ph, Sam Leavitt; ed, Louis Loeffler; m, Elmer Bernstein; prod d, Joseph Wright; cos, Mary Ann Nyberg

This was a pioneering film in that it defied the Production Code with its depiction of dope addiction. There had been other dope operas before but none had gone so far in showing the pain and despair of heroin addiction. In any of several other directors' hands, this might have been a classic, but Preminger overplays his hand. Nelson Algren's book was deservedly a best seller and the film made a few dollars, mostly because of Sinatra's excellent acting in the lead, as a professional card dealer struggling with the torment of drugs. Sinatra has just come home from half a year in Kentucky, where he was supposedly cured of his addiction. He arrives in his old Chicago neighborhood where he is welcomed by Stang, a slightly retarded street person whom he loves, and McGavin, a drug pusher who happily offers Sinatra a fix, just for old times' sake. Sinatra says "no thanks" and goes home to his wife, Parker, an angry woman confined to a wheelchair. Sinatra has great plans to become a jazz drummer but Parker wants him to return to his old job, dealing cards at Strauss's illegal poker game. Sinatra does not want to but she points out it was he who crippled her when he crashed a car while drunk. Sinatra does what Parker wants and moves into his old slot with Strauss. At Strauss's club, Sinatra meets Novak, a professional B-girl who gets the men to buy her drinks at inflated prices and then does not come across. Sinatra falls hard for Novak but cannot bring himself to leave his helpless wife. Still desiring a new career as a drummer, he attempts to practice at home but Parker keeps carping about all that noise so he stops and begins practicing at Novak's apartment. It pays off and he is rewarded by an audition so he quits his job with Strauss. But there is a big poker game coming up and Strauss prevails on him for one last deal. It is a two-day poker game and Sinatra succumbs to McGavin's offer of a fix. The game goes on and Sinatra pushes the audition off but when he is caught cheating, he is beaten up. By the time he gets to the audition, he is totally strung out on drugs and in need of a shot so badly that he cannot perform.

Meanwhile, McGavin walks into Sinatra's apartment and finds Parker standing up and walking around. Now he knows that she had been using her "crippled" status to hold on to Sinatra. McGavin means to tell Sinatra about this but Parker, in desperation, pushes McGavin down the long, dark stairwell and he dies in the fall. Sinatra learns from Novak that he is McGavin's suspected killer and he knows that he must talk to the police but he will not do it on drugs so he agrees to go "cold turkey" in Novak's apartment. It's a brutal sequence as he screams, cries, pounds walls, etc. until he rises, three days later, weak but clean. He goes to his apartment to tell Parker that he is going away with Novak but he will continue to support her. She jumps up from the wheelchair and follows him after he walks out the door. Then she sees cops in the hall and leaps out the window to her death. Sinatra is at her side when she dies as Novak watches in the background.

The movie has a slickness to it that works against the grittiness of the story. Stang stood out in his role, a rare dramatic outing for a man who spent most of his life as a comic flunky, beginning with his work on Henry Morgan's radio show in the 1940s. Novak did not have much to do except look pretty and act concerned. Parker never hit the right mixture of self-hate and pity. It was Sinatra's movie all the way (he received an Oscar nomination for Best Actor, but lost to Ernest Borgnine for MARTY) despite the clumsy script, the obvious sets, and Preminger's hammering direction. Although ostensibly set in Chicago, there is absolutely no feeling for location and it might as well have taken place in Fresno. Oscar nominations went to Wright and Silvera for Art Direction/Set Decoration and to Bernstein for his score.

MAN WITH TWO BRAINS, THE
1983 93m c ★★
Comedy R/15
Aspen

Steve Martin (Dr. Michael Hfuhruhurr), Kathleen Turner (Dolores Benedict), David Warner (Dr. Necessiter), Paul Benedict (Butler), Richard Brestoff (Dr. Pasteur), James Cromwell (Realtor), George Furth (Timon), Peter Hobbs (Dr. Brandon), Earl Boen (Dr. Conrad), Bernie Hern (Gun Seller)

p, David V. Picker, William E. McEuen; d, Carl Reiner; w, Carl Reiner, Steve Martin, George Gipe; ph, Michael Chapman (Technicolor); ed, Bud Molin; m, Joel Goldsmith; prod d, Polly Platt; art d, Mark Mansbridge; fx, Allen Hall, Clay Pinney, Robert Willard; cos, Kevin Brennan

Following their parody of film noir, DEAD MEN DON'T WEAR PLAID, comedian Steve Martin and director Carl Reiner took on the mad-scientist films of the 1940s in this film, though with mixed results. Dr. Michael Hfuhruhurr (Martin), a famed neurosurgeon, travels to Vienna with his beautiful-but-frigid wife, Dolores (Kathleen Turner), in an attempt to revive their romance. There he meets fellow scientist Dr. Alfred Necessiter (David Warner), who has devised a method to keep disembodied brains alive. This, in turn, allows Hfuhruhurr to communicate telepathically with the brain of a very sweet woman who was brutally murdered and with whom he falls hopelessly in love. Desperate to consummate his love, Hfuhruhurr decides to plant his beloved's brain in Dolores's body, thus creating the perfect woman. The premise of this comedy sounds good on paper, but is lost somewhere in its transition to the screen. Martin and Reiner are never really in control of their wacky style of humor. While THE MAN WITH TWO BRAINS certainly has its moments, overall it's a disappointment. The brain's voice is provided by Oscar winner Sissy Spacek.

MANCHURIAN CANDIDATE, THE
1962 126m bw ★★★★★
Political/Thriller /PG
MC/Essex

Frank Sinatra (Bennett Marco), Laurence Harvey (Raymond Shaw), Janet Leigh (Rosie), Angela Lansbury (Raymond's Mother), Henry Silva (Chunjin), James Gregory (Sen. John Iselin), Leslie Parrish (Jocie Jordon), John McGiver (Sen. Thomas Jordon), Khigh Dhiegh (Yen Lo), James Edwards (Cpl. Melvin)

p, George Axelrod, John Frankenheimer; d, John Frankenheimer; w, George Axelrod (based on the novel by Richard Condon); ph, Lionel Lindon; ed, Ferris Webster; m, David Amram; prod d, Richard Sylbert; art d, Richard Sylbert, Philip Jefferies; fx, Paul Pollard; cos, Moss Mabry

A nerve-beating masterpiece, and more timely now than then. Frankenheimer's tightrope walk between political satire and suspenser is flawlessly rendered; based on Richard Condon's uneasily prophetic novel.

Harvey returns from the Korean War a superhero and holder of the Congressional Medal of Honor, but those in his platoon—including his own commanding officer, Sinatra—are vague about how Harvey actually won the medal, just stating that he is a great hero. Sinatra and another soldier, however, begin to have recurring nightmares about Korea, and when this is reported, Sinatra conducts an investigation into Harvey and his present activities. Piece by sinister piece, Sinatra and others put the story together. Sinatra, Harvey, and the entire platoon received mass brainwashing until all came to believe Harvey was a hero when, in truth, he had been programmed as a killer. But whom is he to kill? Upon his return from service Harvey leaves his overly protective mother (Lansbury) and her husband (Gregory), a dominated fascist-oriented senator. Harvey goes to work as a journalist, but when his control contacts him with the code, he becomes a robot, killing without guilt or memory of his crime. A liberal columnist-publisher becomes his first victim. Harvey, now married, is next sent to kill his own wife and his father-in-law, a liberal senator. Sinatra's brainwashing wears off so that Sinatra is able to determine just how Harvey is controlled. It turns out that the controller is Lansbury, the top Communist spy in the US. She orders her robotlike son to kill the presidential nominee; her husband, who is the vice-presidential running mate, will then take control of the White House.

THE MANCHURIAN CANDIDATE takes aim at both the Left and the Right, rendering them both dangerous fraternal twins—an outrageous, terrifying premise to contend with. The entire cast is first-rate. This is Harvey's best work—for once the unlovable quality he built a career on emerges sympathetically. But it is Angela Lansbury's incestuous, power-mad mother who makes your blood run cold. This was the peak of the first part of her career, which depended upon these hardbitten kind of characters. Forget Hitchcock—here's the monster mother of all time.

THE MANCHURIAN CANDIDATE is political fiction—we hope—at its finest, certainly at its most forceful on the screen. It earned distinction as one of the first of a genre that mixed reality, symbolism, and the fantastic, alternating caprice and grim fact so that the view is jarred from one scene to the next as it would be riding on a speeding train constantly being rerouted. Have a wild ride.

MANDABI
(LE MONDAT)
1970 90m c   ★★
Comedy
Domireve/Comptoir Francais   (France/Senegal)

Mamadou Gueye (Ibrahim Dieng), Ynousse N'Diaye (1st Wife), Issa Niang (2nd Wife), Serigne N'Diayes (Imam), Serigne Sow (Maissa), Moustapha Toure (Shopkeeper), Farba Sarr (Businessman), Moudoun Faye (Mailman), Moussa Diouf (Nephew), Christophe M'Doulabia (Water Seller)

p, Jean Maumy; d, Ousmane Sembene; w, Ousmane Sembene (based on a story by L.S. Senghor); ph, Paul Soulignac (Eastmancolor); ed, Gil Kikoine

Gueye tries to cash a money order from his nephew, but finds he can't because he doesn't have an identity card. He can't get an identity card without a birth certificate, and he can't get a certificate without a photograph. Everywhere he goes he must have something else-either identification or money. After a series of misfortunes and setbacks, Gueye realizes his nephew is ripping him off.

MANHATTAN
1979 96m bw   ★★★★
Comedy/Romance   R/15
UA

Woody Allen (Isaac Davis), Diane Keaton (Mary Wilke), Michael Murphy (Yale), Mariel Hemingway (Tracy), Meryl Streep (Jill), Anne Byrne (Emily), Karen Ludwig (Connie), Michael O'Donoghue (Dennis), Victor Truro, Tisa Farrow

p, Charles H. Joffe; d, Woody Allen; w, Woody Allen, Marshall Brickman; ph, Gordon Willis (Panavision); ed, Susan E. Morse; m, George Gershwin; prod d, Mel Bourne; cos, Albert Wolsky, Ralph Lauren

Deft tragi-comedy and a neurotic town. People may argue about the relative merits of ANNIE HALL (which took Oscars for Best Picture, Best Direction, Best Actress, and Best Screenplay) vis-a-vis MANHATTAN, which won nothing but is a better and more realized film. By this time Allen had forsworn the glib one-liner and spent more time developing rich, round characters about whom we could care. As the title indicates, the action takes place on that small island that the Dutch bilked out of the Manhattan Indians for a pittance. Allen is a well-known and wealthy television scribe who has had it with the medium and wants to use his talent to amuse in another fashion, perhaps even with something serious. He knows how to make people laugh but can he move them? Allen sometimes lives with the teenage Hemingway, who is studying drama at her high school. He is more than twice her age, and it weighs on his mind and contributes to his already full capacity for guilt. Hemingway adores him and wants nothing more than to please him, but he begins pushing her away and opting for an end to their relationship. He talks about his dreams of becoming an important writer and shares his angst about Hemingway with his best friend, Murphy, who admits that he is not having an easy time of it in his domestic relationship with his wife, Byrne (who had been married to Dustin Hoffman offscreen). Ennui has set in on the Murphy-Byrne marriage, and Murphy has taken up with Keaton, a bright but apparently pseudo-intellectual woman. Murphy is also suffering in his work and would like to toss aside his frippery in favor of something more challenging. Murphy introduces Keaton to Allen, and Allen finds her annoying, aggressive, and, underneath that, fascinating. In a while, Allen realizes that her behavior is all a sham and she is, in truth, a lovely person who is acting the way she thinks people should act in Manhattan. They become friends, though not lovers. Not yet. Allen visits his ex-wife, Streep, who has taken their young son, Damion Sheller, and moved in with a lesbian, Ludwig, with whom she is deliriously happy. Streep is writing a book about her life with Allen, her divorce, and her ultimate happiness as a lesbian entitled Marriage, Divorce and Selfhood. Allen tries to persuade her not to publish it, but she does and it's a huge hit; everyone in America now knows how weird Allen is.

MANHATTAN is funny, though not as funny as some of Allen's earlier work. But it has such insight, such depth that his other films seem as shallow as pie plates by comparison. The music, by that most Manhattan of all composers, George Gershwin, is the perfect accompaniment for the film. Allen's camera direction is as unobtrusive as a British butler, and as he grows more mature, he seems to feel that the least direction is the best. Shooting the film in black and white was also a benefit because Manhattan is a black and white city (as opposed to Los Angeles, which looks as good as it's going to look in color). Of the actors, MANHATTAN is stolen by the appealing and lovely Hemingway. In a small role, note Wallace Shawn, who has since distinguished himself as a writer for the stage and screen (MY DINNER WITH ANDRE) as well as an actor in several other films (ATLANTIC CITY). The producers petitioned to change the "R" rating to a "PG" but were turned down, mostly because of the content concerning the older man and the teenage girl. If he never made another movie, this would be Woody Allen's masterpiece. The music is performed by the New York Philharmonic conducted by Zubin Mehta and the Buffalo Philharmonic conducted by Michael Tilson Thomas. Allen and Brickman received Oscar nominations for their screenplay.

MANHATTAN MELODRAMA

1934 93m bw ★★★★
Crime /A
Cosmpolitan

Clark Gable (*Blackie Gallagher*), William Powell (*Jim Wade*), Myrna Loy (*Eleanor*), Leo Carrillo (*Father Joe*), Nat Pendleton (*Spud*), George Sidney (*Poppa Rosen*), Isabel Jewell (*Anabelle*), Muriel Evans (*Tootsie Malone*), Claudelle Kaye (*Miss Adams*), Frank Conroy (*Blackie's Attorney*)

p, David O. Selznick; d, W.S. Van Dyke, II; w, Oliver H.P. Garrett, Joseph L. Mankiewicz (based on the story "Three Men" by Arthur Caesar); ph, James Wong Howe; ed, Ben Lewis; art d, Cedric Gibbons, Joseph C. Wright; fx, Slavko Vorkapich; cos, Dolly Tree

This is a splendid film, packed with action and the kind of tuxedo sophistication that marked the 1930s. W.S. Van Dyke, who would later make SAN FRANCISCO, one of the great disaster films of the decade, begins this movie with another real-life disaster, the burning of the *General Slocum,* a tour boat that caught fire on June 15, 1904, in the middle of the East River, killing 1,021 persons before it was beached. (Its captain, Van Schaick, later went to prison for negligence.) Two boys, Mickey Rooney and Jimmy Butler, are on the boat with their families and a priest played by Leo Carrillo. Both boys lose their families but are rescued by Carrillo. George Sidney, a kindly Jewish merchant who has lost his family in the catastrophe, takes both boys as his own and raises them. Butler is a fine student and an upstanding youth; Rooney is a ne'er-do-well who spends his time shooting craps and cutting school. Nevertheless, the boys share a deep affection for each other.

As adults they are Clark Gable, one of New York City's slickest gamblers and racketeers, and William Powell, a noble prosecuting attorney who can't be bullied, bribed, or bought. Slinky, sultry Myrna Loy is Gable's girl, but she doesn't care too much for her lover's manners and morals. No common gangster's moll, she is educated, refined, beautiful, and full of wit. She believes he is decent at heart, but when she asks him to give up the rackets, he only smiles. When Gable wins a yacht, he takes Loy aboard, promising that he will name it after her, but she tells him she's more interested in marriage, children, and a home. Then Powell is elected district attorney of New York City. Gable is unable to celebrate with him, so he sends Loy to entertain Powell. The pair go to the Cotton Club and enter into a bantering conversation that was to be the hallmark of their on-screen relationship for the next two decades. Meanwhile, Gable is having trouble with Noel Madison, a high-stepping gambler who has welched on a wager. Gable and his sidekick, Nat Pendleton, pay Madison a visit, and Gable shoots him when he goes for a gun. Pendleton, however, leaves behind a coat he has picked up at Gable's apartment, one left by Powell when depositing Loy. When the coat is found by police, Powell can't believe his pal would murder someone in cold blood, so he tells his assistant, Thomas Jackson, that Gable is innocent, but Jackson insists otherwise. (Madison's character is loosely based on Arnold Rothstein, the infamous Manhattan gambler murdered in 1928. The crime was never solved.) When Gable learns what Pendleton has done, he has an exact copy of the coat made and plants a souvenir from the Cotton Club which Powell had left behind in the pocket. Just as Powell is about to reluctantly indict Gable for the Madison killing, the new coat is delivered with a note claiming that it had been left behind when Powell took Loy

out on the town. Powell discovers that the coat fits perfectly, and the souvenir is the clincher.

A short time later Loy breaks up with Gable and begins to see Powell. They marry and she settles down to the life she's always wanted. During the campaign for governor, Jackson, who has been fired for taking bribes, tries to blackmail Powell, threatening to make public that his wife was once Gable's lover, and thus prove collusion in the Madison killing. Loy overhears this threat and goes to Gable for help. Gable helps by cornering Jackson in the men's room of Madison Square Garden and killing him. Outside the restroom, a blind beggar squats on the floor. Gable tosses a dollar into the man's hat and walks away, whereupon the beggar lifts his dark glasses and looks after him. (This scene duplicates one appearing in Fritz Lang's M.) Some time later, Gable is indicted based on the blind man's testimony, and prosecuted by Powell. When Gable's lawyer attempts to put up some sort of defense, Gable stops him. Loy is beside herself: she visits Gable and begs him to tell Powell that it was she who put him up to confronting Jackson. He refuses to sully her marriage or destroy Powell's chance to be governor. The prosecutor's summation is impassioned and eloquent. Gable is found guilty and is sentenced to the electric chair, and Powell is elected governor on the strength of the conviction. Loy begs Powell to commute Gable's sentence to life imprisonment but he refuses to show favoritism. However, when she reveals that she told Gable about Jackson's blackmail, Powell goes to the prison and tells Gable that he can't allow him to go to the chair. Gable tells him to forget it; he is resigned to death. Powell quits his post as governor, telling the New York state legislature that Gable killed a man for his benefit, even though he had no knowledge of the crime. Loy is waiting for him when he leaves the chamber, and they go off together.

Gable and Powell are excellent as the polarized pals, even though they appear on screen together in only a few scenes. This was Loy's first starring role, although she had appeared cast as vamps and Orientals since silent days. The teaming of Powell and Loy for the first time was electric; they would do thirteen more films together, most of them in the delightful THIN MAN series. The film, shot in Van Dyke's whirlwind style, was completed in 24 days on a budget of $355,000. It was very popular and earned more than $400,000 its first time around, as well as an Oscar for Best Original Story. The theme of two close friends going separate ways would be used countless times over in movies, notably in ANGELS WITH DIRTY FACES with James Cagney and Pat O'Brien. Future mogul David Selznick produced this film and, despite protests from MGM executives, insisted upon using Powell, who had been a matinee idol since 1922. This appearance not only saved his career but made him a superstar all over again. This was the film that John Dillinger reportedly watched before he was killed outside the Biograph Theatre in Chicago on the evening of July 22, 1934. MANHATTAN MELODRAMA was reprised on "Lux Radio Theatre," with Don Ameche playing Gable's role, on September 9, 1940.

MANHUNTER

1986 119m c ★★★
Crime/Thriller R/18
DEG

William Petersen (*Will Graham*), Kim Greist (*Molly Graham*), Joan Allen (*Reba*), Brian Cox (*Dr. Lektor*), Dennis Farina (*Jack Crawford*), Stephen Lang (*Freddie Lounds*), Tom Noonan (*Francis Dollarhyde*), David Seaman (*Kevin Graham*), Benjamin Hendrickson (*Dr. Chilton*), Michael Talbott (*Geehan*) p, Richard Roth; d, Michael Mann; w, Michael Mann (based on the book *Red Dragon* by Thomas Harris); ph, Dante Spinotti (Technicolor); ed, Dov Hoenig; m, The Reds, Michel Rubini; prod d, Mel Bourne; art d, Jack Blackman; fx, Joseph DiGaetano, II; cos, Colleen Atwood

A grim stylish thriller from the creator of television's "Miami Vice." Based on Thomas Harris's gripping novel *Red Dragon*, MANHUNTER introduces us to the Behavioral Science Unit of the FBI and its top agent, Will Graham (William Petersen). The secret of Graham's success is his uncanny ability to duplicate the twisted thought processes of serial killers and thereby predict their actions. Brought out of early retirement by his friend and colleague Jack (Dennis Farina), Graham launches an investigation of a serial killer who operates on a "lunar cycle," killing entire families only when the moon is full. Graham's peculiar talent of adopting a criminal's mindset extracts a heavy emotional toll and nearly destroyed him on his last case when he captured Dr. Hannibal Lektor (Brian Cox), a brilliant psychiatrist turned brutal killer. Lektor is in prison and though Graham clearly still fears him, he visits him in an effort to get insights on his new case. He only succeeds in putting himself and his family in great danger.

Writer-director Michael Mann wrote a superior script and assembled an incredible cast for MANHUNTER making one of the most underrated outstanding thrillers of the 1980s. Mann knows how to construct an intense movie. As in his earlier THIEF, he presents the viewer with a fascinating amount of procedural detail—both law-enforcement and criminal. Petersen is superb as the obsessive investigator who risks madness each time he takes on a case, and Tom Noonan is absolutely chilling as the psycho killer. Cox is also frightening as the complex Lektor, a character who would be memorably embodied by Anthony Hopkins in Jonathan Demme's adaptation of Harris's quasi-sequel, *The Silence of the Lambs*.

MANIFESTO

1988 96m c	★★★
Comedy/Political	R/18
Golan-Globus	

Camilla Soeberg (*Svetlana Vargas*), Alfred Molina (*Avanti*), Simon Callow (*Police Chief Hunt*), Eric Stoltz (*Christopher*), Lindsay Duncan (*Lily Sacher*), Rade Serbedzija (*Emile*), Svetozar Cvetkovic (*Rudi Kugelhopf*), Chris Haywood (*Wango*), Patrick Godfrey (*Dr. Lombrosow*), Linda Marlowe (*Stella Vargas*)

p, Menahem Golan, Yoram Globus; d, Dusan Makavejev; w, Dusan Makavejev (based on a story by Emile Zola); ph, Tomislav Pinter (Rank Color); ed, Tony Lawson; m, Nicola Piovani; prod d, Veljko Despotovic; cos, Marit Allen

Having returned to Yugoslavia after 17 years in exile, director Dusan Makavejev (MONTENEGRO [1981]; THE COCA-COLA KID [1985]) has also returned to political satire. The film takes place in 1920 in a fictional Eastern European town called Waldheim, "where nothing is what it seems." Arriving in Waldheim are Svetlana (Camilla Soeberg), a beautiful young woman who is involved in a plot to assassinate a visiting king, and Avanti (Alfred Molina), a secret policeman driven by secret lust. Although everyone in town has an interest in the king—in protecting him or assassinating him—they all seem more intent on getting into one another's knickers. MANIFESTO treats both political revolution and eroticism in a comic light; instead of making an "art film" that preaches only to the converted few,

Makavejev has created an entertainment that may just tweak the minds of the masses.

MANON OF THE SPRING
(MANON DES SOURCES)

1986 113m c	★★★½
Drama	R/PG
Renn/RAI-TV/DEG/A2 (France)	

Yves Montand (*Cesar "Le Papet" Soubeyran*), Daniel Auteuil (*Ugolin Soubeyran*), Emmanuelle Beart (*Manon Cadoret*), Hyppolite Girardot (*Bernard Olivier*), Elisabeth Depardieu (*Aimee Cadoret*), Gabriel Bacquier (*Victor*), Armand Meffre (*Philoxene*), Andre Dupon (*Pamphile*), Pierre Nougaro (*Casimir*), Jean Maurel (*Anglade*)

p, Pierre Grunstein; d, Claude Berri; w, Claude Berri, Gerard Brach (based on the novel by Marcel Pagnol); ph, Bruno Nuytten (Technovision, Eastmancolor); ed, Genevieve Louveau, Herve de Luze; m, Jean-Claude Petit, Giuseppe Verdi; prod d, Bernard Vezat; cos, Sylvie Gautrelet

The continuation of JEAN DE FLORETTE resumes the story and follows its characters to their fates. Ten years have passed, and Manon (played by newcomer Emmanuelle Beart), the daughter of the hunchbacked farmer Jean (Gerard Depardieu in Part I), has grown into a beautiful young shepherdess who tends her flock deep in the hills of Provence. In the years since Jean's death, Le Papet (Yves Montand) and his nephew, Ugolin (Daniel Auteuil), have worked Jean's land into a profitable carnation farm by unplugging the underground spring they had kept secret from the hard-working farmer. Ugolin's vibrant red carnations now blossom in full glory, enabling him to save a small fortune. Le Papet, now old and withered, pushes his nephew toward marriage. Unless Ugolin takes a wife and begins a family, the name of Soubeyran (once the most powerful family in the region) will cease to exist. Ugolin, however, has no desire to marry—until, one day, he sees Manon bathing in a small spring and falls instantly in love.

Like its predecessor, MANON OF THE SPRING is filled with marvelous photography, gorgeous rolling landscapes, and spectacular performances. While Part I favors Depardieu's character and his struggles against both man and nature, Part II concentrates on the tragic end of Montand and his final reconciliation with the higher forces of fate. Montand, always brilliant, turns in a performance that ranks with his best work; Auteuil is also excellent as the manipulated young fool. Beart, while easy on the eyes, is given very little to do besides play the object of desire. This is an admirable though traditional piece of entertainment. MANON surpasses JEAN DE FLORETTE in its portrayal of the villagers, a necessary element virtually absent from the earlier picture. Together JEAN DE FLORETTE and MANON OF THE SPRING earned a total of eight Cesars (the French Oscar): Best Film, Best Director, Best Actor (Auteuil), Best Actress, Best Screenplay, Best Score, Best Cinematography, and Best Sound (Pierre Gamet, Dominique Hennequin).

MAN'S FAVORITE SPORT?

1964 120m c	★★½
Comedy	/U
Universal	

Rock Hudson (*Roger Willoughby*), Paula Prentiss (*Abigail Page*), Maria Perschy (*Isolde "Easy" Mueller*), Charlene Holt (*Tex Connors*), John McGiver (*William Cadwalader*), Roscoe Karns (*Maj.*

Phipps), Forrest Lewis *(Skaggs)*, Regis Toomey *(Bagley)*, Norman Alden *(John Screaming Eagle)*, Don Allen *(Tom)*

p, Howard Hawks; d, Howard Hawks; w, John Fenton Murray, Steve McNeil (based on the story "The Girl Who Almost Got Away" by Pat Frank); ph, Russell Harlan (Technicolor); ed, Stuart Gilmore; m, Henry Mancini; art d, Alexander Golitzen, Tambi Larsen; fx, Ben McMahon; cos, Edith Head

Director-producer Hawks here returned to the comic formulas that worked so well for him in BRINGING UP BABY and I WAS A MALE WAR BRIDE but achieved only limited success. Cary Grant had been able to carry the earlier films with a characteristic charm that leading man Hudson was unable to match. Hudson is the star fishing-supplies salesman of a large sporting goods store, but he knows nothing about fishing. Publicity agent Prentiss convinces Hudson's boss, McGiver, that Hudson should enter a fishing contest. With a little luck and assistance from a bear, Hudson wins. Acknowledging that his win is a fluke, he forfeits the prize and subsequently gets fired. In the end, Hudson gets his job back and lands Prentiss as well. Hawks delivers his usual heavy-handed direction, but the film's premise is too flimsy to spread over two hours. The script is marred by tired comic routines and slow pacing. The cast, though, with the exception of Hudson, offers very good performances—Prentiss in particular.

MAN'S HOPE
(SIERRA DE TERUEL)
1947 78m bw   ★★★★
War
Lopert   (Spain)

Majuto *(Capt. Munoz)*, Nicolas Rodriguez *(Pilot Marquez)*, Jose Lado *(The Peasant)*

p, Andre Malraux; d, Andre Malraux; w, Andre Malraux (based on the novel *Espoir* by Andre Malraux); ph, Louis Page; m, Darius Milhaud

This film was shot in Spain during the Spanish Civil War and later smuggled into Occupied France, where screening was postponed until after the Liberation. As a result, it was eight years before the public was allowed to view MAN'S HOPE. When the film finally was screened, it received the Louis Delluc Award, one of the highest honors the French could bestow on a film. In adapting his own novel for the screen, Andre Malraux creates a powerful, sweepingly realistic film through the use of actual combat footage. The story focuses on a Loyalist air squadron's attempt to destroy a bridge. To succeed, the Loyalists must neutralize a new airfield. The only one who can locate the field is a peasant who can't read a map, so he is taken along on the air raid. Although the narrative structure of MAN'S HOPE is unconventional and the film is otherwise flawed, these problems pale next to the overwhelming realism of Malraux's depiction of life during wartime.

MARAT/SADE (PERSECUTION AND ASSASSINATION OF JEAN-PAUL MARAT AS PERFORMED BY THE INMATES OF THE ASYLUM OF CHARENTON UNDER THE DIRECTION OF THE MARQUIS DE SADE, THE)
1967 115m c   ★★★
Historical   /X
Marat Sade   (U.K.)

Clifford Rose *(M. Coulmier)*, Brenda Kempner *(Mme. Coulmier)*, Ruth Baker *(Mlle. Coulmier)*, Michael Williams *(Herald)*, Freddie Jones *(Cucurucu)*, Hugh Sullivan *(Kokol)*, Jonathan Burn

(Polpoch), Jeanette Landis *(Rossignol)*, Robert Lloyd *(Jacques Roux)*, Glenda Jackson *(Charlotte Corday)*

p, Michael Birkett; d, Peter Brook; w, Peter Weiss, Geoffrey Skelton, Adrian Mitchell (based on the play by Peter Weiss); ph, David Watkin (DeLuxe Color); ed, Tom Priestley; m, Richard Peaslee; prod d, Sally Jacobs; art d, Ted Marshall; chor, Malcolm Goddard; cos, Gunilla Palmstierna Weiss

Peter Brook directed this film of his seminal stage production of the play-within-a-play by Peter Weiss. In combining Brechtian techniques with some of the lessons of theatrical philosopher Antonin Artaud, Weiss's play was a landmark of the 60s that seemed to be exploiting everything the theater could do that film could not. Brecht suggested distancing audiences; Artaud demanded the opposite—total involvement. Many fans of the play went to see the film only to prove that this stuff couldn't work on celluloid. It does. Brook is a filmmaker as well as a master of the modern theater and he, perhaps uniquely, understood how to translate something so stagey and theatrical onto celluloid. MARAT/SADE is, in fact, a musical with more than a dozen songs, and remains an important record of a turning point in western theater.

Geoffrey Skelton and Adrian Mitchell translated Weiss's play, which opened in Berlin in April 1964. The members of the Royal Shakespeare Company, who did the London stage production, are used again here. Patrick Magee plays the Marquis de Sade, holed up in the mental hospital where he will spend his last days; Ian Richardson plays Marat, who figures in a play that de Sade has written and that is being performed by the inmates of the hospital. Glenda Jackson makes her screen debut. When the play ran in London, the actors had a good time counting the number of walkouts between the acts. The same happened with the film version, but the production costs were so low (just over $500,000) that the distributors rightly thought they could recover their investment in the art-house market.

MARATHON MAN
1976 125m c   ★★★★
Spy/Thriller/War   R/18
Paramount

Dustin Hoffman *(Babe Levy)*, Laurence Olivier *(Szell)*, Roy Scheider *(Doc Levy)*, William Devane *(Janeway)*, Marthe Keller *(Elsa)*, Fritz Weaver *(Prof. Biesenthal)*, Richard Bright *(Karl)*, Marc Lawrence *(Erhard)*, Allen Joseph *(Babe's Father)*, Tito Goya *(Melendez)*

p, Robert Evans, Sidney Beckerman; d, John Schlesinger; w, William Goldman (based on his novel); ph, Conrad Hall (Metrocolor); ed, Jim Clark; m, Michael Small; prod d, Richard MacDonald; art d, Jack DeShields; fx, Richard E. Johnson, Dick Smith, Charles Spurgeon; cos, Robert de Mora

A truly harrowing film, MARATHON MAN is a clever series of accidents that produce a nightmare thriller with an unrelenting attack on the viewer's nerves. Babe Levy (Dustin Hoffman), a Columbia University graduate student who runs whenever possible, dreaming of the Olympic marathon, is haunted by the memory of his father's suicide, brought about by the McCarthy witchhunts. Babe's brother, Doc (Roy Scheider), an American secret agent, helps sneak Szell (Laurence Olivier), an old Nazi, into the US from South America. Szell's brother, who has watched over a fortune in jewels taken from Jewish concentration camp victims, has died, and Szell has come to New York to collect the booty. After killing Doc, Szell uses the tools of his dentist's trade to torture Babe for information the student doesn't possess. Putting his marathon training to use, Babe escapes Szell, and eventually the pursuer becomes the pursued. Hoffman is excellent as the crazed Szell's victim, and Olivier is the essence of evil, his sadistic acts so expertly enacted that the film has a deeply disturbing quality. John Schlesinger's direction is highly stylized and more than effective, jammed with action and offering unforgettably terrifying scenes. Scheider is good as the errant older brother, and William Devane is his usual tricky self as the double-dealing intelligence chief. William Goldman's script, based on his novel, is literate and full of surprises.

MARGIE
1946 94m c ★★★★
Musical/Comedy /U
FOX

Jeanne Crain (*Margie McDuff*), Glenn Langan (*Prof. Ralph Fontayne*), Lynn Bari (*Miss Isabelle Palmer*), Alan Young (*Roy Hornsdale*), Barbara Lawrence (*Marybelle Tenor*), Conrad Janis (*Johnny Green*), Esther Dale (*Grandma McSweeney*), Hobart Cavanaugh (*Angus McDuff*), Ann Todd (*Joyce*), Hattie McDaniel (*Cynthia*)

p, Walter Morosco; d, Henry King; w, F. Hugh Herbert (based on stories by Ruth McKinney, Richard Bransten); ph, Charles Clarke (Technicolor); ed, Barbara McLean; m, Alfred Newman; art d, James Basevi, J. Russell Spencer, Lyle Wheeler; fx, Fred Sersen

A sweet nostalgia piece that evokes memories of the 1920s, MARGIE unfolds in flashback as Margie McDuff (Jeanne Crain) tells her teenage daughter, Joyce (Ann Todd), the way it was way back when. Margie is a typical flapper, pursued by boy friend Roy Hornsdale (Alan Young), but she has her eyes on Prof. Ralph Fontayne (Glenn Langan), a handsome young French teacher who sets coeds' hearts aflutter. Margie's school rival is Maybelle Tenor (Barbara Lawrence), though they are friendly, not bitter, enemies. In the end, Margie winds up with Ralph, who, of course, turns out to be Joyce's father. Despite its slight plot, consisting mainly of Margie's crush on Ralph and a brief sequence showing her on the debating team, MARGIE is filled with humorous situations that almost all pay off. While it is definitely a "high school" movie, it aims for the heart and funny bone with none of the smarminess of so many recent films of its ilk. Moreover, MARGIE is a fine depiction of the way life was for the teens in the 20s, replete with the madness of raccoon coats, Charleston dancing, rouged knees, and peroxided hair. Ruth McKinney, the coauthor of the story on which the film is based, was also responsible for MY SISTER EILEEN.

MARIE
1985 112m c ★★★½
Biography/Political PG-13/15
DEG

Sissy Spacek (*Marie Ragghianti*), Jeff Daniels (*Eddie Sisk*), Keith Szarabajka (*Kevin McCormack*), Morgan Freeman (*Charles Traughber*), Lisa Banes (*Toni Greer*), Fred Thompson (*Himself*), Trey Wilson (*FBI Agent*), John Collum (*Deputy Attorney General*), Don Hood (*Gov. Blanton*), Graham Beckel (*Charlie Benson*)

p, Frank Capra, Jr.; d, Roger Donaldson; w, John Briley (based on the book *Marie, A True Story* by Peter Maas); ph, Chris Menges (Joe Dunton Camera, Technicolor); ed, Neil Travis; m, Francis Lai; art d, Ron Foreman; cos, Joe I. Tompkins

The true story of Marie Ragghianti, a woman who fought corruption in Tennessee, is a powerful film from a book by Peter Maas with a screenplay by Oscar-winner John Briley and a first

US assignment for New Zealand director Roger Donaldson. Marie (Sissy Spacek) leaves home in 1968 after being brutalized by her husband. A mother of three, she must struggle as she stays at her mother's home, works as a waitress, and puts herself through Vanderbilt University. An old pal, Eddie Sisk (Jeff Daniels), helps her get a job with the state. He's the governor's legal counsel and not without power in the hierarchy, so her job as extradition director is an excellent first rung for her. It's not long before she rises in the state bureaucracy and becomes a member of the parole board and finally the chairperson of that board. It's not too long before Marie realizes that the governor (Don Hood) is using his influence to get some powerful criminals released. The movie could have become a cliched investigatory picture, as did so many after Watergate. Director Donaldson keeps matters moving. Spacek is superb and so is Daniels, unaccustomed as he is to the villain's role. But the acting surprise is the work of Fred Thompson, playing himself as the real-life attorney who handled the case for Marie Ragghianti.

MARIE ANTOINETTE
1938 160m bw ★★★★
Biography/Historical/Romance /A
MGM

Norma Shearer (*Marie Antoinette*), Tyrone Power (*Count Axel de Fersen*), John Barrymore (*King Louis XV*), Gladys George (*Mme. Du Barry*), Robert Morley (*King Louis XVI*), Anita Louise (*Princess DeLamballe*), Joseph Schildkraut (*Duke of Orleans*), Henry Stephenson (*Count Mercey*), Reginald Gardiner (*Artois*), Peter Bull (*Gamin*)

p, Hunt Stromberg; d, W.S. Van Dyke, II, Julien Duvivier (uncredited); w, Claudine West, Donald Ogden Stewart, Ernest Vajda, F. Scott Fitzgerald (based on a book by Stefan Zweig); ph, William Daniels; ed, Robert J. Kern; m, Herbert Stothart; art d, Cedric Gibbons, William A. Horning; fx, Slavko Vorkapich; chor, Albertina Rasch; cos, Adrian, Gile Steele

Although it has its admirers, this lavish, lengthy but consistently gripping film remains an underrated historical biopic done in the grand Hollywood manner. It also remains an uncannily appropriate showcase for Norma Shearer, and along with PRIVATE LIVES, SMILIN' THROUGH and THE WOMEN, stands as one of the best things she ever did. Long the queen of MGM's lot, Shearer had won some major battles with MGM just before the film was shot, but, as in the film, her decline was linked to the death of her husband. True, Marie Antoinette was executed and Shearer lost interest in her career and retired a wealthy and happy woman, but that sense of art imitating life permeates the film. Shearer's choosing to do two light, silly comedies in the early 1940s helped diminish her long starring career just as Marie Antoinette's indulgences helped put an end to her life. Started as early as 1933 by Shearer's husband, the famous Irving Thalberg, boy genius of the studio, it was halted when Thalberg died in 1936. Planned as Shearer's triumphant return to the screen after a two-year absence, it's amazing that the film turned out as well as it did.

In the title role, Shearer is married off to Louis Auguste, the Dauphin of France (Morley) and heir to the throne, by her calculating mother, the Empress of Austria (Alma Kruger). Marie is repelled by her first meeting with her new husband, who is surly, dullwitted, and unattractive. Further distressing her are the sneering, jeering King Louis XV (Barrymore, in a role parallel to his real-life condition as well), Morley's scheming cousin, the Duke of Orleans (Schildkraut), and the conspiratorial Madame Du Barry (George), the king's notorious mistress.

(Shearer and Morley share an excellent scene early on as Louis admits he is incapable of performing his marital duties—an adult, well-handled scene for the Hollywood of the day.) Du Barry, feeling threatened by the future queen, forms intrigues against her, and Marie quickly becomes a pariah at the court of Versailles. She takes Orleans's advice and gains attention and solace from lavish parties and expensive gowns. In one sumptuous casino, Marie meets the dashing, handsome Count Axel de Fersen (Power), a rich Swedish nobleman, and begins a quiet love affair with him. The Austrian ambassador (Stephenson) begs Marie to strengthen his country's alliance with France by giving a huge ball and recognizing Du Barry as a "woman of royal position," but Marie winds up insulting the haughty former laundress (a great scene). The enraged King threatens to annul Marie's marriage and send her back to Austria in disgrace. But Louis XV suddenly dies, and his son and Marie are now King and Queen of France. Fersen tells his love that her duties must come before their affair, and he sails off for a new life in America. Marie buckles down and develops an affectionate relationship with Louis, who also gathers his wits enough to manage as King and to produce two children. The Duke of Orleans, however, who had refused to help Marie at her low ebb, is now an outcast at court and incites the people to revolt against their rulers. After an abortive escape attempt, the King and Queen are arrested, and though Fersen returns to plan a rescue, the guillotine beckons the rulers of France.

After Thalberg's death, MGM mogul Louis B. Mayer tried to make a flat settlement with his estate. Shearer, however, fought this move and managed to hold the studio to an agreement giving Thalberg's estate a percentage of all the profits the studio made since Mayer and Thalberg consolidated it in the early 1920s. The handling of MARIE ANTOINETTE ended up being not only an attempt to control the costs of the one of the priciest pictures the studio had made to date, but also perhaps a subtle revenge on the victorious Shearer. La Norma, meanwhile, also had to contend with the enmity of William Randolph Hearst, who had wanted both MARIE ANTOINETTE and the earlier Shearer vehicle THE BARRETTS OF WIMPOLE STREET for his mistress-protege Marion Davies. (In all fairness Shearer was more suitable for these roles.) Mayer continued to make life unpleasant for Shearer. He removed her favored director, Sidney Franklin, and replaced him with Van Dyke, a quick, no-nonsense helmsman who didn't like to make more than one or two takes for each scene, much loved by the cost-conscious Mayer. According to Morley's autobiography, "Franklin had worked on the picture for two years. Van Dyke had never seen the script before he started shooting and knew apparently nothing whatever about the French or their revolution."

Morley was not Thalberg's original choice for the role of Louis XVI; the production chief wanted Charles Laughton for the role, but he and his wife Elsa Lanchester, whom Thalberg wanted to play the role of Princess De Lamballe, were unavailable when the film finally went into production. Maureen O'Sullivan was the next candidate to play Princess De Lamballe, but she was pregnant when the film finally got underway, so the part went to Anita Louise (who played Marie Antoinette in MADAME DU BARRY, produced by Warner Bros.). Morley disliked the whole production and referred to it as "Marie and Toilette." Shearer had more reason than Morley to dislike the treatment she received. Van Dyke refused to accord her the status of reigning queen of the lot and balked at her requests for more takes. In one instance, she walked off the set, though she returned the next day and apologized. The technicians were aware that her power at MGM was declining fast, so they showed her no special

respect: when she tripped over a wire and fell flat on her backside, the hoops of her magnificent dress billowing upward, they roared with laughter, something that would never have happened in the Thalberg era. Shearer surprised them, however, by laughing along with them. She was nominated for an Oscar for her exceptional performance but lost out to Bette Davis for JEZEBEL. Although a few scenes show her fluttering or hamming it up a bit too much (something which mars many of her performances), there's a lot of excellent stuff here, especially as Marie awaits death. The superlative Morley lost out as Best Supporting Actor to Walter Brennan for KENTUCKY. The film was also nominated for Best Interior Decoration and Best Score.

Almost totally ignored throughout the lavish production was Power, then the reigning king of 20th Century-Fox. His part was almost that of a supporting player, which caused Fox's boss, Darryl Zanuck, to explode. Mayer had loaned out Spencer Tracy to Fox for the making of STANLEY AND LIVINGSTON. In return, Zanuck gave Mayer his prized star, Power. Seeing that all the publicity and major scenes went to Shearer and that his man was treated like a handsome prop, Zanuck vowed he would never again loan out his studio's top box-office draw. Power would not again be available for 15 years. Despite all the infighting and the whopping $1.8 million cost, everything about MARIE ANTOINETTE was so awesome that it turned into a huge money-maker for MGM. Its budget showed in every stunning scene. Gibbon's sets were magnificent, crammed with authentic French artifacts of the period culled from Parisian antique stores by set designer Willis, who spent three months and a fortune abroad in his foraging expedition for MGM. Costumers Adrian and Steele designed period gowns and male attire for thousands of extras and lavished particular care on costumes for the 152 actors with lines. No less than 200 dancers appeared in ballroom scenes choreographed by Rasch, and Stothart's score is both tender and rousing, perfectly suited to the scenes and the period. Daniels' camera work is exceptional, and Van Dyke makes this long film move like a short one. The flamboyant Barrymore (not looking at all well) and the sly and unctuous Schildkraut (with a terrific makeup job) steal many scenes, but this is above all a showcase for the glamour and regal qualities audiences had come to love in La Norma. Van Dyke's directorial job keeps the tonnage moving and what we have is MGM at its production zenith, a rich, ornate, and wholly satisfying film.

MARIUS

1931 103m bw ★★★½
Drama
Joinville/Paramount (France)

Raimu (Cesar Olivier), Orane Demazis (Fanny), Pierre Fresnay (Marius), Fernand Charpin (Honore Panisse), Alida Rouffe (Honorine Cabanis), Robert Vattier (Mon. Brun), Paul Dullac (Felix Escartefigue), Alexandre Mihalesco (Piquoiseau), Edouard Delmont (2nd Mate), Milly Mathis (Aunt Claudine Foulon)

p, Marcel Pagnol; d, Alexander Korda; w, Marcel Pagnol (based on the play by Marcel Pagnol); ph, Ted Pahle; ed, Roger Mercanton; m, Francis Gromon; prod d, Alfred Junge, Vincent Korda

MARIUS is the first of the "Marseilles Trilogy" penned by Marcel Pagnol, and was followed by FANNY and CESAR. Marius (Pierre Fresnay), toils at the Bar de la Marine in Marseilles and yearns for the sea. The bar is owned by his father, Cesar (Raimu), a widower who prates about Marius's lack of drive, though he truly adores the boy. Cesar spends his time consorting with his patrons—the wealthy Panisse (Fernand Charpin), ferry captain Felix Escartefigue (Paul Dullac), and customs inspector Brun (Robert Vattier). Marius loves Fanny (Orane Demazis), though he is unable to make a lasting commitment to her—the call of the sea is too strong. When the elderly Panisse asks for Fanny's hand, Fanny sees this as her opportunity to work on Marius's jealousy, a ploy which works and results in their eventually becoming engaged. But despite her powerful love for Marius, Fanny is aware that he loves only the sea and cannot be happy as long as he lives in Marseilles. MARIUS is a touching and deeply affecting movie with an excellent cast (Raimu, a stage actor and silent screen comedian, is wonderful as Cesar and carried his role to even higher levels in the sequels), a rich record of life in Marseilles. Writer and producer Marcel Pagnol stayed on the set and watched carefully, then allowed Marc Allegret to direct FANNY and took over that chore himself for CESAR.

MARK OF ZORRO, THE

1940 93m bw ★★★★
Adventure /U
FOX

Tyrone Power *(Don Diego Vega)*, Linda Darnell *(Lolita Quintero)*, Basil Rathbone *(Capt. Esteban Pasquale)*, Gale Sondergaard *(Inez Quintero)*, Eugene Pallette *(Fra Felipe)*, J. Edward Bromberg *(Don Luis Quintero)*, Montagu Love *(Don Alejandro Vega)*, Janet Beecher *(Senora Isabella Vega)*, Robert Lowery *(Rodrigo)*, Chris-Pin Martin *(Turnkey)*

p, Raymond Griffith; d, Rouben Mamoulian; w, John Taintor Foote, Garrett Fort, Bess Meredyth (based on the novel *The Curse of Capistrano* by Johnston McCulley); ph, Arthur Miller; ed, Robert Bischoff; m, Alfred Newman; art d, Richard Day, Joseph C. Wright; cos, Travis Banton

A smashing swashbuckler, the finest of the many Zorro films, this remarkable film owes everything to its inventive and action-minded director Mamoulian. This was Fox's answer to Warner Bros.' THE ADVENTURES OF ROBIN HOOD. Power is marvelous as the fop by day and brave avenger by night. He is the son of Love, the onetime Alcalde of early 19th-century Los Angeles, who returns from Europe at his father's request to find that Bromberg has replaced his benevolent father and that the people are now energetically oppressed by the new Alcalde's tax collectors, led by cruel captain Rathbone. The area nobles, the caballeros, are powerless to resist the newly appointed governor Bromberg, whose rule is studded with torture, humiliation, and death. Bromberg is himself without compassion, obsessed with the accumulation of gold. His vain and pompous wife, Sondergaard, longs only for the glories of the European courts. Into this shaky world struts Power, a perfumed and boorish aristocrat full of little magic tricks, gossip, and a disdainful air—or, at least, that is what he appears to be. Rathbone, Bromberg, and their minions consider him a harmless popinjay. Then, to the surprise of the tyrants and the relief of the peons and caballeros, a masked rider appears, demanding in proclamations that Bromberg either resign his post or face his vengeance; he carves his signature with his sword, a "Z" to signify his name: Zorro. The avenger, dressed all in black, proves to be an amazing swordsman, attacking and defeating Rathbone's soldiers, stealing tax money, and upsetting Bromberg's plans at every turn. He even visits Bromberg in his lodgings, terrifying him before disappearing through a secret panel. Rathbone persuades Bromberg to hold on to his power and begins to investigate the identity of the masked intruder. No one but the viewer realizes that Zorro and Love's foppish son are one and the same. Still playing the repulsive fop, Power visits Bromberg and meets his wife, Sondergaard, flattering her mercilessly. He also meets Bromberg's ravishingly beautiful niece, Darnell, and utterly charms her while they dance. Sondergaard, who is having an affair with Rathbone, goes riding with the young caballero to learn of social events in Spain; Power ingratiates himself to her only to learn more of Bromberg's plans. Rathbone, ever the intriguer, advises the rather dull-witted Bromberg that a marriage between Power and his niece Darnell would help unite the caballeros and his tyrannical government. Power agrees, since he is really in love with the beautiful girl, but Darnell is glum over the prospect of marrying an ineffectual idler. She quickly changes her mind when Power reveals his identity as the daring Zorro. The masked avenger continues to steal back the tax money squeezed from the peons; he hands it over to a courageous priest, Pallette, who in turn distributes the money to the starving people. Rathbone finds some of the money in the priest's mission and imprisons Pallette. Meanwhile, Power visits Bromberg in the office of his Alcalde mansion, terrifying the man. Just before Bromberg is about to put a shaky signature to his resignation, his protector, the evil Rathbone, bursts into the office, and he and Power duel to the death (Rathbone's, of course). Bromberg is not a complete fool, however, and realizes that only a former occupant of the mansion would know its secret passageways. He rightfully deduces that Power is Zorro and has him thrown into jail. Love arrives and protests, telling Bromberg that his "worthless son," whom he has all but disinherited, could never be the daring Zorro. He is quickly convinced by Power, however, that he is indeed the legendary Zorro, and the two lead the caballeros in open revolt against Bromberg. With the help of the peons, they overthrow the cruel regime, and Love is reinstated as the governor. Power and Darnell plan to marry and raise a large family, according to Power's last charming remarks at the fadeout.

Power cuts a stylish and convincing Zorro, vigorously playing the brilliant swordsman, although his more strenuous routines are performed by stunt double Albert Cavens. Mamoulian cleverly cuts in and out of his terse scenes to suggest more action than really occurs. The final deadly confrontation between Rathbone and Power is a magnificent and thrilling duel no less exciting than the final contretemps between Errol Flynn and Rathbone in THE ADVENTURES OF ROBIN HOOD. Rathbone is terrific as the villain, always fondling his sword, prepared at any moment to draw blood for sport or sadistic amusement. "Most men have objects they play with," Rathbone remarks in one scene. "Churchmen have their beads; I toy with a sword." When this film was released much comparison went on between the Power movie and the 1921 Zorro production directed by Fred Niblo and starring the amazingly energetic Douglas Fairbanks, Sr. But the silent film pales before the lavish, elegant, and intelligent Mamoulian production. Alfred Newman's excellent score was nominated for an Academy Award. Power would go on to more swashbuckling films, such as THE BLACK SWAN, CAPTAIN FROM CASTILE, PRINCE OF FOXES, THE BLACK ROSE, but none ever quite equaled the early and electric impression he made with the public in THE MARK OF ZORRO, much enhanced by a dynamic and memorable score from Newman. Though he did not perform all his swordplay stunts, his adversary Rathbone paid Power a supreme compliment: "Power was the most agile man with a sword I've ever faced before a camera. Tyrone could have fenced Errol Flynn into a cocked hat." This was high praise, and generous at that, since Rathbone received two fairly severe cuts in the forehead during his riveting duel with Power. There were other Zorros. Yakima Canutt, the great stuntman, played the role in 1937 in ZORRO RIDES AGAIN; Frank Langella had a swipe at the dashing role in 1974. But none would ever equal Power's role. He looked and acted like a man who could, with bold acts and brave heart, change the course of history. And, of course, for the burgeoning coffers of Fox, he did.

MARKETA LAZAROVA

1968 180m bw ★★★★
Adventure
Barrandov (Czechoslovakia)

Magda Vasaryova (*Marketa Lazarova*), Frantisek Velicky (*Mikolas*), Michal Kozuch (*Lazar*), Pavla Polaskova (*Alexandria*), Josef Kemr (*Kozlik*), Ivo Paluch (*Adam Jednorucka*), Harry Studt (*Old Count Christian*), Vlastimil Harapes (*Young Count Christian*), Vladimir Mensik (*Wandering Monk Bernard*), Karla Chadimova (*Prioress*)

d, Frantisek Vlacil; w, Frantisek Vlacil, Frantisek Pavicek (based on the novel *Marketa Lazarova* by Vladislav Vancura); ph, Bedrich Batka; ed, Miroslav Hajek; m, Zdenek Liska

Based on 13th-century Czechoslovakian legend, this epic follows the adventures of a clan of feudal lords that uses robbery and kidnapping to meet its desired goals. The film is a convincing portrayal of a people fearful of mystic power and controlled by superstition. The clans are shown as cruel and barbarian, thinking nothing of raping a woman or beheading a man in grotesque fashion, as this is the only existence they know. Director Vlacil does not try to romanticize medieval knighthood but creates an atmosphere of mysticism and superstition, with excellent results.

MARNIE

1964 120m c ★★★★
Thriller/Romance PG/X
Universal

Tippi Hedren (*Marnie Edgar*), Sean Connery (*Mark Rutland*), Diane Baker (*Lil Mainwaring*), Martin Gabel (*Sidney Strutt*), Louise Latham (*Bernice Edgar*), Bob Sweeney (*Cousin Bob*), Milton Selzer (*Man at the Track*), Alan Napier (*Mr. Rutland*), Henry Beckman (*1st Detective*), Edith Evanson (*Rita*)

p, Alfred Hitchcock; d, Alfred Hitchcock; w, Jay Presson Allen (based on the novel by Winston Graham); ph, Robert Burks (Technicolor); ed, George Tomasini; m, Bernard Herrmann; prod d, Robert Boyle; cos, Edith Head

Hitchcock's most liberated and poetic film, MARNIE is a masterpiece of psychological mystery that encompasses all of the director's obsessions—the unleashing of suppressed female sexuality, duplicitous personalities and false identities, childhood trauma leading to a disturbed and warped reality in adulthood, and the director's own love of cool-looking blondes and "pure cinema." Its characters are possessed by psychological demons similar to those in VERTIGO or PSYCHO. Hedren plays a kleptomaniac whose compulsion to steal springs from her need to be loved. Using various identities and disguises, she moves from one job to the next, each time running off with a cache of cash and leaving behind no clues. Connery, a business associate of one of Marnie's previous victims, recognizes Marnie when she comes to work for him, and confronts her with his information. Rather than turn her in, however, Mark blackmails her into marriage—discovering her deep-seated fears of men, sex, thunderstorms, and the color red. Met with a less-than-enthusiastic response, MARNIE was one of Hitchcock's 1960s films (THE BIRDS, TORN CURTAIN, and TOPAZ were the others) that raised suspicions among some critics of the master's having lost his touch, unable to adjust to the times. In retrospect, MARNIE

emerges as prime Hitchcock—its tone and subtext as revealing as that of VERTIGO, although more desperate and disquieting (perhaps because of Hitchcock's deep obsession with Hedren during production). Of interest is Hitchcock's uncharacteristic use of a technique that makes the audience actually *feel* Hedren's traumas. Seeing Hedren against abstract backdrops and "poor" rear-screen projections makes her world seem disturbingly unreal. The ever-changing weather conditions, in which thunderstorms conveniently brew and night changes rapidly to day, and the use of a few frames of red shock the audience into experiencing Hedren's fear (a technique Hitchcock had attempted as early as 1935 in SECRET AGENT).

MARRIAGE OF A YOUNG STOCKBROKER, THE

1971 95m c ★★★½
Comedy R/X
FOX

Richard Benjamin (*William Alren*), Joanna Shimkus (*Lisa Alren*), Elizabeth Ashley (*Nan*), Adam West (*Chester*), Patricia Barry (*Dr. Sadler*), Tiffany Bolling (*Girl in the Rain*), Ed Prentiss (*Mr. Franklin*), William Forrest (*Mr. Wylie*), Johnny Scott Lee (*Mark*), Bill McConnell (*Charlie McGuire*)

p, Lawrence Turman; d, Lawrence Turman; w, Lorenzo Semple, Jr. (based on the novel by Charles Webb); ph, Laszlo Kovacs (DeLuxe Color); ed, Fredric Steinkamp; m, Fred Karlin; prod d, Pato Guzman; fx, Howard A. Anderson and Company; cos, Doris Rambeau, Ed Wynigear

Benjamin plays a happily married but bored husband who takes to innocent voyeurism for kicks. His wife Shimkus is upset and confused by her husband's behavior. Spurred on by her overbearing sister, Ashley, who recently dropped her alcoholic husband, Shimkus heads for the west coast. The couple discover how much they mean to each other and are quickly reunited. Benjamin and Shimkus deliver fair performances, supported by a cast who keep the story interesting. What the script lacks in its approach to story construction, it makes up for in well-structured direction.

MARRIAGE OF MARIA BRAUN, THE

(DIE EHE DER MARIA BRAUN)
1978 120m c ★★★★
Drama/War R/15
Albatros/Trio/Westdeutscher/Autoren (West Germany)

Hanna Schygulla (*Maria Braun*), Klaus Lowitsch (*Hermann Braun*), Ivan Desny (*Oswald*), Gottfried John (*Willi*), Gisela Uhlen (*Mother*), Gunter Lamprecht (*Hans*), Hark Bohm (*Senkenberg*), George Byrd (*Bill*), Elisabeth Trissenaar (*Betti*), Rainer Werner Fassbinder (*Peddler*)

p, Michael Fengler; d, Rainer Werner Fassbinder; w, Peter Marthesheimer, Pia Frohlich, Rainer Werner Fassbinder (based on an idea by Rainer Werner Fassbinder); ph, Michael Ballhaus (Fujicolor); ed, Juliane Lorenz, Franz Walsch; m, Peer Raben; art d, Norbert Scherer, Helga Ballhaus, Claud Kottmann, Georg Borgel; cos, Barbara Baum, Susi Reichel, George Kuhn, Ingeborg Proller

She eludes you, even if she does start—and finish—with a bang. The first in Rainer Werner Fassbinder's trilogy about women in post-WWII Germany (followed by VERONIKA VOSS and LOLA), this was also the film that solidified Fassbinder's reputation abroad and in Germany. In the opening sequence, a German city is being torn apart by Allied bombs while Maria (Hanna Schygulla) and her soldier fiance, Hermann Braun (Klaus Lowitsch), are getting married. Immediately afterwards, the new husband is sent to the Russian front, leaving Maria with her mother and sister, impoverished and waiting for her husband, visiting the train station every day with the hope of hearing news about him. After receiving word that he has died, Maria takes work as a barmaid in a cafe that caters to American soldiers. There she meets Bill (George Byrd), a hefty black soldier who, despite the fact the they can barely converse, becomes her lover. Just when she has nearly forgotten about her husband, however, the starving and emasculated Hermann turns up while Maria and Bill are beginning to make love. The highly stylized, deliberate structure of THE MARRIAGE OF MARIA BRAUN owes much to such Douglas Sirk 1950s Hollywood melodramas as IMITATION OF LIFE and WRITTEN ON THE WIND. For both Sirk and Fassbinder, the director remains distanced from the heart-wrenching dramatics of the story in order to comment on certain societal ills, but Fassbinder is even further removed from his material—a product of the alienation prominent in a postwar Germany striving to rebuild itself into an industrial power, yet failing to account for the human bonds that make a society healthy. The effect is one of helplessness; we can only watch as the beautiful, young Maria Braun places herself in an emotional vacuum.

Schygulla is quite powerful in perhaps the best role of her career, remaining cold and aloof, yet evoking a strong sense of pity. Though THE MARRIAGE OF MARIA BRAUN is not always an easy film to understand, the stark atmosphere, icy performances, and poignant revelations make it one of the most important films to emerge from Germany in the 1970s, and one of Fassbinder's best.

MARRIED TO THE MOB

1988   103m   c   ★★★
Comedy/Crime   R/15
Mysterious Arts

Michelle Pfeiffer (Angela Demarco), Matthew Modine (Mike Downey), Dean Stockwell (Tony "The Tiger" Russo), Mercedes Ruehl (Connie Russo), Oliver Platt (Ed Benitez), Alec Baldwin (Frank "The Cucumber" DeMarco), Anthony J. Nici (Joey DeMarco), Sister Carol East (Rita Harcourt), Paul Lazar (Tommy Boyle), Trey Wilson (Franklin)

p, Kenneth Utt, Edward Saxon; d, Jonathan Demme; w, Barry Strugatz, Mark R. Burns; ph, Tak Fujimoto (Duart Color); ed, Craig McKay; m, David Byrne; prod d, Kristi Zea; fx, Efex Specialists, Inc.; cos, Colleen Atwood

Aa pleasant trifle. Lacking the disturbing edge of director Demme's previous effort SOMETHING WILD, MARRIED TO THE MOB is a gangster film with a twist and the idiosyncratic Demme touch. There is plenty to amuse and delight here, including fine performances from Michelle Pfeiffer, Matthew Modine, and Dean Stockwell.

The movie begins on Long Island, where the homes are full of gilded Mediterranean furniture, the men dress in pin-striped suits, and the women spend most of their time getting their hair teased at the local beauty salon. Angela DeMarco (Pfeiffer), wife of up-and-coming hit man Frank "The Cucumber" DeMarco (Alec Baldwin), is tired of the criminal mentality of everyone around her and wants out. After Frank is caught by his boss, Mafia don Tony "The Tiger" Russo (Stockwell), with the boss's mistress and "iced," a couple of FBI agents (Modine and Oliver Platt) assume that Angela and Tony are lovers. Angela packs up with her son (Anthony J. Nici) and moves into a seedy apartment on Manhattan's Lower East Side, only to have the Feds follow and keep her embroiled in the mob's doings. Of course, romance

eventually blooms between Angela and agent Mike Downey (Modine).

The wonderfully tacky production design by Kristi Zea, the bizarre costumes by Colleen Atwood, the clash of musical styles in the score by David Byrne, and the eccentric performances of the entire cast combine to create a dizzying array of forces swirling around Pfeiffer. She plays her part fairly straight, thus making everyone else seem that much more bizarre. Stockwell received an Oscar nomination for his supporting role, and he is wonderful as the tyrannical hood. This was the last film appearance for veteran character actor Joe Spinell (TAXI DRIVER, ROCKY, NIGHT SHIFT), who has a small role as one of Stockwell's henchmen. He appeared in 40 films in the 70s and 80s before his death in 1989.

MARRIED WOMAN, THE

(UNE FEMME MARIEE)
1964   94m   bw   ★★★½
Drama
Anouchka/Orsay   (France)

Macha Meril (Charlotte), Bernard Noel (Robert, the Lover), Philippe Leroy (Pierre, the Husband), Rita Maiden (Mme. Celine), Margaret Le Van, Veronique Duval (Girls in Swimming Pool), Chris Tophe (Nicolas), Georges Liron (The Physician), Roger Leenhardt (Himself), Jean-Luc Godard (Narrator)

d, Jean-Luc Godard; w, Jean-Luc Godard; ph, Raoul Coutard; ed, Agnes Guillemot, Francoise Collin; m, Claude Nougaro; art d, Henri Nogaret; cos, Laurence Clairval

Meril is a Parisian housewife with both a husband, airplane pilot Leroy, and a lover, Noel. When she becomes pregnant, she realizes either man could be the father. She debates whether she should stay with her husband or leave him for Noel; she gets no help from either in making her decision. Subtitled "Fragments of a film made in 1964," THE MARRIED WOMAN is a fragmented, distanced film that dissects Meril's character and morally situates her between the two men in her life. Even at the film's opening, Meril is represented as a disembodied figure—in separate shots we are shown, against a white bed sheet, her hands, legs, feet, torso. Taking place over a 24-hour period, even THE MARRIED WOMAN's time frame is cut apart into almost Resnaisian divisions. Heavily under the influence of the distancing devises of Brecht, director Jean-Luc Godard makes use of the written word, magazine advertisements and billboards, allusions to other artists (Racine, Apollinaire, Hitchcock, Resnais, Beethoven), visual references to film technique (the use of negative film images), and interviews in a cinema-verite mode.

MARTIN

1978   95m   c   ★★★★
Horror   R/X
Laurel

John Amplas (Martin), Lincoln Maazel (Cuda), Christine Forrest (Christina), Elayne Nadeau (Mrs. Santini), Tom Savini (Arthur), Sarah Venable (Housewife Victim), Fran Middleton (Train Victim), Al Levitsky (Lewis)

p, Richard P. Rubinstein; d, George Romero; w, George Romero; ph, Michael Gornick; ed, George Romero; m, Donald Rubinstein; fx, Tom Savini

There's something happening in Pittsburgh-based independent filmmaking. Something rich, strange, and frightening. Considered by many to be George Romero's greatest work, this superb and shocking film is a thoughtful and relevant reworking of the vampire myth set in a dying modern American steel town. Martin (John Amplas) is a shy, alienated 17-year-old who thinks he may be a vampire, a theory which seems to be confirmed by the opening scene. Aboard a Pittsburgh-bound train, Martin waylays a female passenger, injects her with sodium pentothal, and while she is in a stupor, violates her. Lacking fangs, he then cuts her wrist with a razor blade and drinks her blood. (The gruesomely realistic special makeup effects are by Tom Savini, the Wizard of Gore, here working on the first of his many films for Romero.) When Martin arrives in Pittsburgh, he is confronted with his elderly Old World cousin, Tata Cuda (Lincoln Maazel), a religious zealot who is convinced that the boy is an 84-year-old vampire, the product of a family curse. Calling Martin "Nosferatu," Tata Cuda is determined both to save the boy's soul and to destroy him. Martin has no friends in his new life; he only gets to experience a sense of community by becoming a regular caller to a radio talk show. He spills his guts (figuratively) over the air but the host assumes he's just another colorful kook. However Martin becomes popular and earns a playful nickname: "The Count."

Writer-director Romero leaves Martin's true status up in the air. At times the boy is convinced that he is the monster Tata Cuda believes him to be, seeing himself in Universal horror movie-type flashbacks as a Count Dracula-like vampire eluding angry villagers. Other times he seems able to differentiate fantasy from reality as he tells his grandfather "There's no magic." For the most part, Martin is shown to be a severely troubled teenager with deadly psychosexual problems. He's a painfully shy boy who can only relate to attractive women by drinking their blood. He's the nightmare version of the quiet kid next door. At times Martin's vampirism is compared to drug addiction. However the horror of vampirism is shown to pale by comparison to the brutality of a police raid on a den of drug dealers. Romero all of his socially satirical barbs in a gut-wrenching psychological horror film that is both meaningful and moving. Combining vampire legend and Old World beliefs with the harsh realities of life in a depressed and depressing Pittsburgh, Romero creates a resonant, multifaceted, and, at times, surprisingly lyrical film that works both as insightful social commentary and as a fascinating rumination on horror film conventions. MARTIN deserves to be considered one of the key films in the genre and, as such, essential viewing for fans. But let the squeamish beware!

MARTY

1955 91m bw   ★★★★
Drama   /U
UA

Ernest Borgnine *(Marty)*, Betsy Blair *(Clara)*, Esther Minciotti *(Mrs. Pilletti)*, Karen Steele *(Virginia)*, Jerry Paris *(Thomas)*, Frank Sutton *(Ralph)*, Walter Kelley *(the Kid)*, Robin Morse *(Joe)*, Augusta Ciolli *(Catherine)*, Joe Mantell *(Angie)*

p, Harold Hecht; d, Delbert Mann; w, Paddy Chayefsky (based on a television play by Chayefsky); ph, Joseph La Shelle; ed, Alan Crosland, Jr.; m, Roy Webb; art d, Ted Haworth, Walter M. Simonds; cos, Norma

Dowdy but winning and poignant, and Ernie's Oscar. Borgnine is a burly, lonely, good-natured man living with his mother, with no prospects for any other kind of future. The heavy-set Bronx butcher runs in a small world populated by his Italian relatives and fast-aging male friends, chiefly Mantell. When Borgnine and Mantell meet after work, they stand about mindlessly thinking of ways to fill their lives with something interesting to do. Their soon predictable, groping interchange never varies: "So, what do you wanna do tonight, Marty?" "I dunno, Angie. What do you wanna do?" At home, Borgnine is totally dominated by his love-smothering mother, Minciotti, who fusses and worries over him. When Borgnine attempts to step outside of his world he's roundly rejected as a bumbling, unattractive person. He attends a dance with Mantell and others and tries to pick up some girls but strikes out. Then he spots homely Blair, a schoolteacher whose life is excruciatingly similar to his, dull, hopeless, inching into loveless middle-age. Borgnine asks Blair to dance, and not long afterward they begin to date. But Borgnine runs into a brick wall when he introduces Blair to his mother and male friends. His pals call her a "dog," and Minciotti is downright hostile to her, considering Blair a threat to her life with her son. Borgnine, not a courageous man, backs away from Blair. He doesn't call her as he promised, leaving her to sit miserably at home alone watching TV, while he agonizes over ignoring the woman he has grown to love.

MARTY, coming in the mid-1950s, in an era of epics and extravagant films designed to stifle upstart television, was all the more startling in that it was a movie expanded from an original television drama (with Rod Steiger in the lead), written brilliantly by Chayefsky, one of the leaders of what came to be known as "kitchen sink" or "clothesline" dramas. Besides Borgnine, Oscars also went to Chayefsky for Best Screenplay and to Mann for Best Direction, and it was named Best Picture.

Before doing this film Borgnine was nothing more than an uninteresting heavy. But here he showed the world the great depths of his own character. Mantell also gives a solid performance as the pal addicted to the more bloody passages of Mickey Spillane, constantly asserting: "Boy, he sure can write." Blair is less effective, and Minciotti is not much more than a prop mother. UA executives were not enthusiastic about the production and almost cancelled the movie; they, along with the rest of Hollywood's elite, were amazed at the movie's universal success, and MARTY soon set a trend toward the small-budgeted, prosaic films to come.

MARY POPPINS

1964 140m c   ★★★★
Musical/Comedy   /U
Disney

Julie Andrews *(Mary Poppins)*, Dick Van Dyke *(Bert/Mr. Dawes, Sr.)*, David Tomlinson *(Mr. Banks)*, Glynis Johns *(Mrs. Banks)*, Hermione Baddeley *(Ellen)*, Reta Shaw *(Mrs. Brill)*, Karen Dotrice *(Jane Banks)*, Matthew Garber *(Michael Banks)*, Elsa Lanchester *(Katie Nanna)*, Arthur Treacher *(Constable Jones)*

p, Walt Disney, Bill Walsh; d, Robert Stevenson; w, Bill Walsh, Don DaGradi (based on the *Mary Poppins* books by P.L. Travers); ph, Edward Colman (Technicolor); ed, Cotton Warburton; m, Irwin Kostal; art d, Carroll Clark, William H. Tuntke; fx, Peter Ellenshaw, Eustace Lycett, Robert A. Mattey; chor, Marc Breaux, Dee Dee Wood; cos, Tony Walton; anim, Milt Kahl, Oliver M. Johnston, Jr., John Lounsbery, Hal Ambro, Franklin Thomas, Ward Kimball, Eric Larson, Cliff Nordberg, Hamilton Luske

One of the greatest children's films ever, MARY POPPINS is as perfect and inventive a musical as anyone could see, with a timeless story, strong performances, a flawless blend of live action and animation, wonderful songs, and a sterling script with all the charm of the P.L. Travers books upon which it is based. The film begins when a remote father and mother (Tomlinson and Johns) decide to advertise for a nanny to care for their rowdy children, Michael and Jane Banks (Garber and Dotrice). The children write their own ad, and when their father tears it up and burns it in the fireplace, the pieces miraculously reassemble and go up the flue. Next day, Mary Poppins (Andrews) appears, gliding down from on high with an umbrella as her parachute. This is no ordinary nanny, the children soon learn, as she leads them on a series of delightful escapades, all the while teaching them lessons in proper behavior. Among the wonderful new friends Mary introduces the children to are Bert the chimney sweep (Van Dyke). He accompanies them on holiday to a world inhabited by animated penguins, who serve them tea on a carousel having strangely willful horses, and Uncle Albert (Wynn), whose infectious laughter leads to strange consequences. In retrospect, we consider Andrews a trifle young for the role; she lacks the wisdom of, say, an Irene Dunne, our ideal vision of the role. Look for the magnificent Jane Darwell, as the Bird Lady, in her final role. The movie won Academy Awards for Best Actress, Best Film Editing, Best Original Score, Best Song, and Best Special Visual Effect. MARY POPPINS was producer Walt Disney's crowning achievement in a career that had earned him more Oscars than anyone else. The memorable songs by Disney writers Richard and Robert Sherman include "Super-califragilisticexpialidocious," "Chim Chim Cheree," and "A Spoonful of Sugar."

MASCULINE FEMININE
(MASCULIN FEMININ)
1966 103m bw ★★★★
Drama /X
Anouchka/Argos/Svensk/Sandrews (France/Sweden)

Jean-Pierre Leaud (Paul), Chantal Goya (Madeleine), Marlene Jobert (Elisabeth), Michel Deborb (Robert), Catherine Duport (Catherine), Eva-Britt Strandberg (Lavinia), Birger Malmsten (Actor), Elsa Leroy (Miss 19), Francoise Hardy (Woman with the American Officer), Chantal Darget (Woman on Metro)

d, Jean-Luc Godard; w, Jean-Luc Godard (based on the stories "The Signal" and "Paul's Mistress" by Guy de Maupassant); ph, Willy Kurant; ed, Agnes Guillemot, Marguerite Renoir; m, Francis Lai, Jean-Jacques Debout

Jean-Luc Godard visited the world of young folk to create his most humane film. This is Godard's fifteen-point inquiry into the generation he refers to as the "children of Marx and Coca-Cola," the 1960s youth culture. Paul (Jean-Pierre Leaud), a confused young romantic in search of perfect love, meets pop singer Madeleine (Chantal Goya) in a cafe and eventually moves in with her. Paul copes with his changing views by taking a job for a market research firm, gathering data, and interviewing people (including a young woman voted "Miss Nineteen"). While Madeleine pursues her career, Paul tries to coexist with her and her two roommates, Elisabeth and Catherine (Marlene Jobert and Catherine-Isabelle Duport). Leaud's character—practically an extension of the Antoine Doinel character he played for Francois Truffaut (he even adopts the name Doinel at one point in the film)—wants to live for love, but the ideal becomes problematic in a detached and increasingly consumer-oriented society.

With MASCULINE FEMININE, Godard began a string of increasingly political pictures, leading eventually to his self-imposed exile from commercial cinema. His interest in the synthesis of fiction and documentary is already in full evidence here, with long static shots of people being interviewed included as a means of bringing to the screen an everyday chronicle of Parisian youth in the winter of 1965. (Contrary to the director's intentions, the picture was banned in France for those under 18.) Charming, innovative, provocative, and prophetic, MASCULINE FEMI-

NINE is a Godard film that even appeals to people who think they don't like Godard films. One of Godard's masterpieces.

M*A*S*H
1970 116m c ★★★★½
Comedy/War R/15
Aspen

Donald Sutherland (Hawkeye Pierce), Elliott Gould (Trapper John McIntyre), Tom Skerritt (Duke Forrest), Sally Kellerman (Maj. Hot Lips Houlihan), Robert Duvall (Maj. Frank Burns), Jo Ann Pflug (Lt. Hot Dish), Rene Auberjonois (Dago Red), Roger Bowen (Col. Henry Blake), Gary Burghoff (Radar O'Reilly), David Arkin (Sgt. Major Vollmer)

p, Ingo Preminger; d, Robert Altman; w, Ring Lardner, Jr. (based on the novel by Richard Hooker); ph, Harold Stine (Panavision, Deluxe Color); ed, Danford B. Greene; m, Johnny Mandel; art d, Jack Martin Smith, Arthur Lonergan; fx, L.B. Abbott, Art Cruickshank

Set during the Korean War but made at the height of the war in Vietnam, Robert Altman's exceptional antiwar comedy-drama follows the fortunes of a MASH (Mobile Army Surgical Hospital) unit. Hawkeye Pierce (Donald Sutherland), Trapper John (Elliott Gould), and Duke Forrest (Tom Skerritt) are the martini-swilling, prank-playing, but compassionate and capable battlefield surgeons who make life miserable for chief nurse Hot Lips Houlihan (Sally Kellerman) and fellow surgeon Maj. Frank Burns (Robert Duvall), a by-the-book prig. Among the terrible trio's shenanigans are the broadcast of a Burns-Houlihan lovemaking session over the camp public address system and the collapse of the women's shower to reveal the naked Maj. Houlihan. At the root of all this foolishness, however, is the attempt to mitigate the otherwise overwhelming bleakness of the war, to distract the doctors and nurses from the terrible waste of life they witness. The film's climactic football game, one of Hollywood's funniest (featuring a number of onetime pro players), pits the MASH unit against a crack team brought in by a general who has been investigating the unit.

Clever camera setups, Altman's patented overlapping dialogue, wonderful sight gags and situations, and universally fine ensemble performances combine to make this one the most enjoyable war-themed films ever. What makes M*A*S*H so extraordinary, however, is that beyond its hilarious antics and rich characters, the film offers a poignant portrait of the madness of war. Ring Lardner, Jr. wrote the Oscar-winning screenplay. Nominations also went to Altman for Best Direction, Kellerman for Best Supporting Actress, and Danford Green for Best Film Editing. It was also nominated for Best Picture but lost to another fine if more conventional war film, PATTON. This film was Altman's first major hit; the strength of this film made his subsequent career over the next decade possible.

MASK OF DIMITRIOS, THE
1944 95m bw ★★★★★
Crime/Spy /A
WB

Sydney Greenstreet (Mr. Peters), Zachary Scott (Dimitrios), Faye Emerson (Irana Preveza), Peter Lorre (Cornelius Latimer Leyden), George Tobias (Fedor Muishkin), Victor Francen (Wladislaw Grodek), Steven Geray (Bulic), Florence Bates (Mme. Chavez), Eduardo Ciannelli (Marukakis), Kurt Katch (Col. Haki) p, Henry Blanke; d, Jean Negulesco; w, Frank Gruber (based on the novel *A Coffin For Dimitrios* by Eric Ambler); ph, Arthur Edeson; ed, Frederick Richards; m, Adolph Deutsch; art d, Ted Smith

One of the great film noir classics to come out of the 1940s, THE MASK OF DIMITRIOS boasts no superstars, just uniformly fine talents, a stupendous script full of intrigue, surprises, and subtle turns, and Negulesco's exciting and innovative direction. It's an edge-of-the-seat thriller all the way. Lorre is a Dutch mystery writer vacationing in Istanbul. At a party he meets one of his most ardent fans, Katch, head of the secret police, who tells him that the body of arch criminal Dimitrios Makropoulous (Scott), a man he has sought for years, has washed up on the nearby beach, murdered, stabbed to death. What fascinates Lorre about the dead man is Katch's obsession with Scott, a man who practiced "murder, treason, and betrayal" as a way of life. Katch so piques Lorre's morbid curiosity that the writer accompanies the police chief to the morgue to view the body. Following this grim visit, Lorre decides to write a novel about the sinister Scott and begins to delve into the criminal's sordid past. In his search for the real Scott, Lorre travels through Smyrna, Athens, Sofia, Belgrade, and finally to Paris. "What is it about a man like that?" Lorre asks Katch at the beginning of his quest. "Why does anyone trust him in the first place?" While Lorre books passage, portly, calculating Greenstreet enters Lorre's Istanbul hotel, picks up a paper announcing the discovery of Scott's body, and crushes the newspaper angrily. On the train to Sofia, Greenstreet suddenly joins Lorre in his compartment. The fat man ingratiates himself to Lorre, telling him as he settles back on the train couch opposite the pensive Lorre: "There's not enough kindness in the world. If only men would live as brothers without hatred, seeing only the beautiful things. But no, there are always people who look on the black side." Lorre goes to sleep while Greenstreet eyes him over a book he is reading entitled *Pearls of Everyday Wisdom*. When the train reaches Sofia, Greenstreet recommends a hotel where Lorre will be comfortable. In Sofia, Ciannelli, a journalist friend of Lorre's, takes him to a murky, smoky cabaret run by Emerson, once Scott's lover. She tells him, after some reluctance, about how Scott, down and out in Sofia, starving in an apartment next to hers without being able to pay the rent, observed her as she alighted from a carriage with a wealthy merchant at her side. Shown in flashback to 1923, Scott begs some food from Emerson and also borrows some money. He promises to pay her back and does, with interest. Scott is now well-dressed and admits that he blackmailed Emerson's merchant-lover for the money. She falls in love with Scott, who promises her jewels, furs, and a fine apartment. At dinner, police pick Scott up for questioning when they identify him as a member of a Bulgarian patriotic society. Later he is shown with a rich patron from whom he seeks more money for an unspecified chore; he's turned down. Later, a diplomat is assassinated (in a rainy scene reminiscent of the assassination in Alfred Hitchcock's FOREIGN CORRESPONDENT). Scott takes refuge in Emerson's apartment, telling his lover to lie to police should they come, to say he's been with her all day. She does. Then he leaves, after taking almost all her money, promising to pay her back. He vanishes and she never again sees him or the money.

It's back to the present, and Lorre departs the club and returns to his hotel room, which he finds ransacked. The fat man is present; Greenstreet holds a gun on him and asks him to close the door. Greenstreet sits down with a smug smile on his face and tells him that he is interested in Scott; he wants to know what Lorre has learned about the evildoer. When he learns that Lorre has seen the body of Scott in the Turkish mortuary, Greenstreet

becomes confused. He tells Lorre that he should not go to Belgrade, that he will find out nothing and will get into trouble with the authorities. He tells him that Francen, a rich and powerful political intriguer in Geneva, will help him, and he proposes an alliance to determine the authenticity of Scott's death. He tells Lorre that, after Lorre sees Francen, he should travel to Paris to see him and promises some spoils, a half million French francs. Lorre goes to Geneva, where Francen, a retired master spy, tells him how Scott was employed by him to obtain military secrets in Yugoslavia for Italy in 1926. In a flashback to Belgrade, Scott is shown befriending Geray, a clerk in the government. He allows Geray to win large amounts in fixed games but then arranges for him to lose an enormous amount of money. Scott tells Geray that he will make good his debts only if he steals the new secret plans for the minefields of the Otranto Strait. To stave off ruination and save his sluttish wife disgrace, Geray complies but later commits suicide. Scott steals the plans from Francen and sells them elsewhere. In another flash forward, Lorre, now thoroughly disgusted with the truth about the conniving Scott, goes to Paris to see Greenstreet, who is living in a lavish apartment hidden away in a deserted building. There Greenstreet tells Lorre exactly what piece of information he possesses that is worth a half million French francs, his own memory of what the dead man in Istanbul looked like. Greenstreet tells Lorre that he was part of a smuggling ring which Scott betrayed; that the dead man found in Istanbul was another member of the ring, Konstantin Gollos; and that Scott is very much alive. Greenstreet intends to blackmail Scott, using Lorre as the man who can identify the dead man as someone other than Scott. The price tag is one million francs. Scott later delivers the money but attempts to kill both Greenstreet and Lorre. He wounds Greenstreet, but Lorre knocks the gun out of his hands and Greenstreet picks it up. Lorre, at Greenstreet's request, steps outside, while Scott begs him to come back. A shot rings out and Scott is killed. Police arrive at Lorre's summons, and Greenstreet steps outside, helped down the stairs by gendarmes. As the police take the bulky smuggler away, he turns to Lorre and tells him to send him a copy of the novel he will write about Scott, saying: "I'll have a lot of time to read it where I'm going." He adds at the fadeout: "You see, there's not enough kindness in the world."

Other than Ambler's American title for his novel and the fact that the mystery-detective writer in it is English, almost nothing was changed from the original novel. Ambler's despicable antihero is most certainly based upon one of the world's greatest intriguers, Basil Zaharoff, billionaire munitions king, whose early career is unmistakably that of the scheming Dimitrios Makropoulos. The character of the writer was changed from English to Dutch to account for Lorre's accent. Though Lorre performs one of his few sympathetic roles, and does it with fascinating aplomb, Greenstreet, whom Lorre affectionately called "the old man" after they had become close personal friends during their appearance together in THE MALTESE FALCON, dominates their scenes together. The entire film fits with the murky intrigue of the era, its stylized sets, its low-key lighting, and a literate, witty script working to enchance the wonderful character actors in their segmented roles. Francen is particularly effective as the suave master spy. Greenstreet matches Lorre's enigmatic character with his own girthsome mystique, and newcomer Scott is a properly loathsome creature without remorse or compassion for his myriad victims. Emerson, as the deserted tart, is also very good, as is the hapless, trusting Geray. This film, under Negulesco's superb guidance, remains a superlative espionage yarn that artfully blends fact with fiction.

MASQUE OF THE RED DEATH, THE
1964 86m c   ★★★★
Horror   /15
Alta Vista/Anglo-Amalgamated (U.S./U.K.)

Vincent Price (Prince Prospero), Hazel Court (Juliana), Jane Asher (Francesca), David Weston (Gino), Patrick Magee (Alfredo), Nigel Green (Ludovico), Skip Martin (Hop Toad), John Westbrook (Man in Red), Gaye Brown (Senora Escobar), Julian Burton (Senor Veronese)

p, Roger Corman; d, Roger Corman; w, Charles Beaumont, R. Wright Campbell (based on "The Masque of the Red Death" and "Hop-Frog, or the Eight Chained Orang-outangs" by Edgar Allan Poe); ph, Nicolas Roeg (Panavision/Pathecolor); ed, Ann Chegwidden; m, David Lee; prod d, Daniel Haller; art d, Robert Jones; fx, George Blackwell; chor, Jack Carter; cos, Laura Nightingale

One of the best and most ambitious of the Roger Corman Edgar Allan Poe series, this is a colorful symphony of the macabre loosely based on two Poe stories. It boasts a magnificent performance from the always wonderful (and often hammy) Vincent Price. Price is Prince Prospero, a 12th-century Italian despot who lives for his one true love. . . Satan! After jailing two locals, Ludovico (Nigel Green) and Gino (David Weston) for defying his harsh tax laws, Prospero meets the beautiful Francesca (Jane Asher), daughter of Ludovico and the fiancee of Gino. She comes to him to plead for mercy. Prospero tells her that only one will be spared and toys with her emotions for his private amusement. When Prospero learns that the Red Death is sweeping the village, he locks himself and his followers in his castle where they continue their decadent parties. Soon a mysterious figure dressed in red robes arrives but he bides his time outside the castle, playing solitaire in the graveyard.

Weird and extremely downbeat, this is Corman's most sustained attempt at producing an Art Film. It even selfconsciously echoes the work of Ingmar Bergman and Luis Bunuel—two directors Corman greatly admires. The script by Charles Beaumont and R. Wright Campbell is among the most intelligent and literate of the Poe series. With photography by future director Nicolas Roeg (DON'T LOOK NOW, THE MAN WHO FELL TO EARTH), the film is also one of Corman's best-looking. It features incredible sets and costumes and a brilliant use of color. Best of all, however, is Price's inspired performance as the wicked Prospero. While Corman may veer dangerously close to pretention, his crisp staging and confident visual style keep the film from collapsing under its own weight.

MASS IS ENDED, THE
(LA MESSA E FINITA)
1988 96m c   ★★★½
Comedy
Faso (Italy)

Nanni Moretti (Don Giulio), Margarita Losanno (Mother), Ferrucio De Ceresa (Father), Enrica Maria Modugno (Valentina)

p, Achille Manzotti; d, Nanni Moretti; w, Nanni Moretti, Sandro Petraglia; ph, Franco Di Giacomo; ed, Mirco Garrone; m, Nicola Piovani

An insightful, moving, and often hilarious comedy-drama directed by and starring Nanni Moretti, THE MASS IS ENDED tells of a young priest, Don Giulio, struggling to maintain his faith. Having been a radical college student in the 1960s, Don Giulio has now rejected his long hair and liberal ideals in favor of the church. He has himself transferred to his home parish, only to discover the church empty and the town indifferent. Meanwhile, Don Giulio's friends from his radical days begin popping up with their lives in serious disarray. Don Giulio seeks solace with his beloved family, but his family too is in chaos. THE MASS IS ENDED is a wonderful film that examines one man's struggle to escape the difficult realities of everyday life by becoming a priest. As director, Moretti presents his characters in loving detail. He does not condescend to their craziness and instead embraces them as sympthetic people trapped in an insane world.

MATA HARI
1931 91m bw   ★★★½
Romance/Biography/Spy   /A
MGM

Greta Garbo (Mata Hari), Ramon Novarro (Lt. Alexis Rosanoff), Lionel Barrymore (Gen. Serge Shubin), Lewis Stone (Andriani), C. Henry Gordon (Dubois), Karen Morley (Carlotta), Alec B. Francis (Caron), Blanche Frederici (Sister Angelica), Edmund Breese (Warden), Helen Jerome Eddy (Sister Genevieve)

p, Irving Thalberg; d, George Fitzmaurice; w, Benjamin Glazer, Leo Birinski, Doris Anderson, Gilbert Emery; ph, William Daniels; ed, Frank Sullivan

The subject of Mata Hari, the WWI Javanese-Dutch spy, was not new to film, but when Greta Garbo agreed to play the role of the beautiful exotic dancer who traded sex for secrets, it was not only news but also cause for MGM to produce a lavish and memorable film. We first see the German spy in Paris, posing as a dancer. Her spymaster, Lewis Stone, directs her to intercept certain Russian messages involving Allied troop movements. For some time Garbo has been having an affair with Lionel Barrymore, an indiscreet general, but she meets Ramon Novarro, a lowly lieutenant, and truly falls in love with him. Then she learns that Novarro has the messages she is seeking and she betrays her love for him to serve her country, taking him to bed while her associates copy his messages. Barrymore learns of the tryst and explodes, threatening to turn Garbo in as an agent and implicate Novarro. To save herself and her unwitting lover, Garbo shoots and kills Barrymore. When Novarro begins to seek out Barrymore, Garbo compels him to leave. The pilot flies to Russia where he is shot down and blinded. Learning of this, Garbo follows her passion rather than her military orders and goes to Novarro to tell him of her devotion to him. Stone orders an agent to kill her, but the man is foiled by local police. Garbo is then unmasked and is brought to trial. Rather than involve Novarro in testimony that will expose her black past to him, she pleads guilty so that his memory of her will be pure. Just before her execution, Novarro is brought to her—Garbo's last request—thinking her prison is a hospital and that she is dying of an illness. They meet briefly, declare their love, and then she is led from her cell, accompanied by nuns, to the firing squad. Garbo is stunning, full of her special mystique as the exotic dancer-spy, in one scene wearing a revealing costume and snaking her body around a lascivious-looking, many-armed Buddha-like statue in an odd, interpretive dance. George Fitzmaurice directs with great style here and makes the most of the lavish production techniques available to him. Both Garbo and Novarro had accents that later caused some critics to sneer, particularly at one of Novarro's lines which sounded like "What's the mata, Mata?" Of course, little shown here is based on real events. The historical figure, Gertrud Margarete Zelle MacLeod, 1876-1917, danced in Paris and stole secrets from the French for the Germans, low-level secrets at that, until she was uncovered as a spy and shot, not in Russia, but at

Saint-Lazare in France on October 15, 1917. No mention is made in the film of Mata Hari's little girl, who was being raised in a Dutch convent at the time of the spy's execution. Mata Hari, a Dutch pseudonym meaning "Eye of the Dawn," was portrayed by Asta Nielsen in a German production, DIE SPIONIN, by Magda Sonja in MATA HARI, DIE ROTE TANZERIN, and by Jeanne Moreau in MATA HARI, but none compared with the fabulous Garbo interpretation. Although this film lacks the violence that permeated the spy's real world, it captures the actual hazards awaiting any agent who faltered, particularly in the scene where Karen Morley, a hesitant German spy, is murdered by agents. At the insistence of British censors, Mata Hari's execution was cut and it did not appear in any American prints after the film's initial release. Also softened were two love scenes where Novarro and Garbo clinch and then turn out the lights. Of particular annoyance to the British was the scene where Garbo reclines on a couch and Novarro stands over her, looking up to an icon of The Virgin Mary, and then sinking into the arms of the alluring spy. In the British version, the icon was changed to a portrait of somebody's mother with a vigil light beneath it. This was Garbo's 18th movie, the second with Barrymore, the fifth with Stone, and the one and only with Novarro, then Hollywood's greatest heartthrob and matinee idol. Garbo had earlier played a spy in THE MYSTERIOUS LADY, but with less impact than her performance in this film.

MATCH KING, THE

1932 70m bw ★★★½
Biography/Crime /A
First National

Warren William (Paul Kroll), Lily Damita (Marta Molnar), Glenda Farrell (Babe), Harold Huber (Scarlatti), Spencer Charters (Oscar), John Wray (Foreman), Murray Kinnell (Nyberg), Hardie Albright (Erik Borg), Juliette Compton (Sonia), Claire Dodd (Ilse Wagner)

p, Hal B. Wallis; d, Howard Bretherton, William Keighley; w, Houston Branch, Sidney Sutherland (based on the novel by Einar Thorvaldson); ph, Robert Kurrle; ed, Jack Killifer

This is an unabashed biography of spectacular international swindler Ivar Kreuger, made hot on the heels of Kreuger's suicide in Paris after he was exposed as a giant fraud, having bilked thousands of investors out of millions by selling worthless stock in his many bogus European companies. The film begins in Paris as Warren William (playing Paul Kroll, the fictionalized Krueger character) realizes he is about to be revealed as a swindler and contemplates suicide. He thinks back to his beginnings and, in flashback, is shown as a street cleaner in Chicago, where he plans a murder in his fantastic scheme to monopolize the common kitchen match. He swindles bankers into pumping money into his phony firms, using and discarding women as if they were burned-out matches. Along the way, the suave William attracts a famous European film star, Lily Damita, who dresses, acts, and talks like Greta Garbo, and for good reason. Garbo was reportedly duped into investing substantial funds in Kreuger's bogus schemes. Director Howard Bretherton deftly, and at a startling pace, details a sinister career of murder, blackmail, and forgery that is no more fanciful than Kreuger's actual machinations. (Kreuger built his fortune by offering some Italian bonds, which he had masterfully forged, as collateral for his multi-million-dollar loans; only when these bonds were exposed as fake did his career end.) The overall production of this film is superior. William is a wonder to behold, handling his conniving role with marvelous restraint. Damita is a bit campy as the Garbo-like actress who dumps her lover-entrepreneur after suspecting his

empire is about to collapse. All in all, THE MATCH KING is an intriguing artifact of the early talkie era.

MATCHMAKING OF ANNA, THE

(TO PROXENIO TIS ANNAS)
1972 87m c ★★★★
Romance
Katsourides (Greece)

Anna Vaguena (Anna), Stavros Kalarogiou (Kosmas), Smaro Veaki (Anna's Mistress), Ketty Panou (Mistress' Daughter), Costas Regopoulos (Mistress' Son-in-law)

p, Dinos Katsourides; d, Pantelis Voulgaris; w, Menis Koumantareas, Pantelis Voulgaris; ph, Nikos Kavoudikis

This simple, well-told story of love among the working class features Vaguena as the longtime maid of Veaki. A marriage between Kalarogiou and Vaguena is arranged by Veaki's daughter Panou. The young couple goes out for a walk, and though they feel awkward, they gradually get to know each other and feel the beginnings of love. Not realizing the time, Vaguena returns to her mistress's home quite late. Kalarogiou is blamed and considered to be not good enough for the girl. In addition, the family realizes they cannot do without her maid services and try to break up the marriage. Even the girl's mother agrees, as she needs the money her daughter gives her. Reluctantly Vaguena subordinates her feelings in favor of practicality and accepts her fate. This is an especially sensitive and well-made film. The direction is straightforward, nicely portraying the maid's boring existence and giving a magical quality to her brief love affair. Vaguena is marvelous, giving a natural and effective performance. The supporting cast is equally fine, and the overall production values are excellent.

MATEWAN

1987 132m c ★★★★
Drama PG-13/15
Red Dog

Chris Cooper (Joe Kenehan), Will Oldham (Danny Radnor), Jace Alexander (Hillard), Ken Jenkins (Sephus Purcell), Bob Gunton (C.E. Lively), Gary McCleery (Ludie), Kevin Tighe (Hickey), Gordon Clapp (Griggs), Mary McDonnell (Elma Radnor), James Earl Jones ("Few Clothes" Johnson)

p, Peggy Rajski, Maggie Renzi; d, John Sayles; w, John Sayles; ph, Haskell Wexler (DuArt Color); ed, Sonya Polonsky; m, Mason Daring; prod d, Nora Chavooshian; art d, Dan Bishop; cos, Cynthia Flynt

Made for $4 million but looking as if it cost three times that, this is an excellent offering from one of America's best-known independent filmmakers, John Sayles (THE BROTHER FROM ANOTHER PLANET; EIGHT MEN OUT). As the film opens, Danny Radnor (Will Oldham), a 15-year-old coal miner, spreads the news that the Stone Mountain Coal Company of Matewan, West Virginia, has decided to lower the tonnage rate paid the miners—again. A strike is called. Joe Kenehan (Chris Cooper), a pacifist and former Wobbly, is sent by the United Mine Workers to coordinate the action and to keep it from becoming violent; however, a group of Italian immigrants continues to work, as do the black miners whom the company has brought from Alabama. A battle seems inevitable; but slowly the three factions grow into a community, and the strike spreads like wildfire. In MATEWAN Sayles captures the feel of a 1930s "people united" film but grounds it in the complex reality of a world that refuses to present easy choices. With Oscar winner Haskell Wexler acting as cinematographer, MATEWAN is beautifully shot, and there is not a weak performance in the film. Jones is a tower of dignity; Cooper is the epitome of quiet strength; and Oldham glows with the passion of a zealot, first for God, then for the union.

MATILDA

1978   105m   c   ★★★½
Sports/Comedy   G/U
AIP

Elliott Gould (*Bernie Bonnelli*), Robert Mitchum (*Duke Parkhurst*), Harry Guardino (*Uncle Nono*), Clive Revill (*Billy Baker*), Karen Carlson (*Kathleen Smith*), Roy Clark (*Wild Bill Wildman*), Lionel Stander (*Pinky Schwab*), Art Metrano (*Gordon Baum*), Larry Pennell (*Lee Dockerty*), Roberta Collins (*Tanya Six*)

p, Albert S. Ruddy; d, Daniel Mann; w, Albert S. Ruddy, Timothy Galfas (based on the book by Paul Gallico); ph, Jack Woolf (Movielab Color); ed, Allan Jacobs; prod d, Boris Levin; fx, Jerry Endler; cos, Jack Martell, Donna Roberts Orme

Far from a routine boxing film, MATILDA is a charming family picture that bounces along as happily as the kangaroo (actually a man in a kangaroo suit) that fights for the world championship in it. Despite the objections of animal lover Carlson the title marsupial earns a shot at the heavyweight championship, and by the end of the big bout in Lake Tahoe everyone is smiling except gangland chief Guardino. The excellent cast includes Mitchum as a sportswriter, Gould as a two-bit promoter, Stander as the champ's nominal manager, and several real-life ring announcers, most notably Don Dunphy.

MAURICE

1987   140m   c   ★★½
Drama   /15
Cinecom/Merchant Ivory/Film Four   (U.K.)

James Wilby (*Maurice Hall*), Hugh Grant (*Clive Durham*), Rupert Graves (*Alec Scudder*), Denholm Elliott (*Dr. Barry*), Simon Callow (*Mr. Ducie*), Billie Whitelaw (*Mrs. Hall*), Ben Kingsley (*Lasker-Jones*), Judy Parfitt (*Mrs. Durham*), Phoebe Nicholls (*Anne Durham*), Mark Tandy (*Risley*)

p, Ismail Merchant; d, James Ivory; w, Kit Hesketh-Harvey, James Ivory (based on the novel by E.M. Forster); ph, Pierre Lhomme (Technicolor); ed, Katherine Wenning; m, Richard Robbins; prod d, Brian Ackland-Snow; art d, Peter James; cos, Jenny Beavan, John Bright

Following the enormous success of A ROOM WITH A VIEW, the producer-director team of Ismail Merchant and James Ivory undertook another E.M. Forster adaptation, MAURICE, the story of a young man's homosexual awakening. Maurice Hall (James Wilby) is a wide-eyed Cambridge underclassman in 1910 where his elder classmates espouse the glories of classical civilization. Maurice and Clive Durham (Hugh Grant), an aristocratic music student, grow increasingly closer, until one day Clive tells Maurice that he loves him. Confused, Maurice initially rebuffs him and then confesses his love, too, and attempts to consummate it physically. This time Clive is reticent. They remain in love but do not become lovers. As time passes, Maurice attempts to put his desires behind him. In the Merchant-Ivory tradition, MAURICE captures the look and spirit of Edwardian England in exquisite detail. At its best, the film is moving and thought-provoking, but at other moments it is unintentionally silly. It is not the story but the telling of it that is the problem; at 140 minutes, MAURICE simply goes on too long. Nonetheless,

the performances are generally convincing. Nominated by the Academy for Best Costume Design.

MAYERLING

1936   96m   bw   ★★★★★
Historical/Romance   /15
Concordea   (France)

Charles Boyer (*Archduke Rudolph of Austria*), Danielle Darrieux (*Marie Vetsera*), Suzy Prim (*Countess Larisch*), Jean Dax (*Emperor Franz Joseph*), Gabrielle Dorziat (*Empress Elizabeth*), Jean Debucourt (*Count Taafe*), Marthe Regnier (*Baroness Vetsera/Helene*), Yolande Laffon (*Stephanie*), Vladimir Sokoloff (*Chief of Police*), Andre Dubosc (*Loschek, the Valet*)

d, Anatole Litvak; w, Joseph Kessel, Irma Von Cube (based on the novel *Idyl's End* by Claude Anet); ph, Armand Thirard; ed, Henri Rust; m, Arthur Honegger

MAYERLING is one of the greatest love stories ever brought to the screen, the bittersweet, painfully poignant romance between the star-crossed Crown Prince Rudolph of Austria and his adoring mistress, Marie Vetsera. Charles Boyer, in a riveting performance, is Rudolph, son of the powerful Franz Joseph, Emperor of Austria-Hungary. A free spirit who associates with radicals and gypsies, Rudolph is also a prisoner of his royal blood. Everywhere there are court spies assigned to track and trail the errant heir to the throne. Eluding his followers at a fair, he meets 17-year-old Marie Vetsera (Danielle Darrieux), and it's love at first sight, although Marie has no idea that he is the prince as the couple enjoys such little pleasures as tossing rings around a swan's neck and watching a puppet show. The following night, Marie attends the opera and is startled to see the handsome young man from the fair sitting in the royal box. Though she comes from an aristocratic family, she has no hope of reaching so high. Instead, Rudolph reaches out to her, meeting secretly with the beautiful young woman. Only in Marie's presence does Rudolph find joy and peace; she responds to him with an innocence he has never encountered. When their liaison is discovered, however, the lovers must depart to a country hunting lodge from which they will never return. Based on fact, this story of an impossible love is told on a grand, exquisite scale by Anatole Litvak, and represents one of the high points of the director's spotty career. Filled with dreamy dissolves and fluid, nearly waltzlike camera movements, the film is a brilliant technical achievement, further enhanced by the wonderful performances of the two leads—the debonair Boyer and the ravishing Darrieux, who was then just 21 years old.

MAYTIME

1937   132m   bw   ★★★★½
Romance/Musical   /U
MGM

Jeanette MacDonald (*Marcia Morney/Miss Morrison*), Nelson Eddy (*Paul Allison*), John Barrymore (*Nicolai Nazaroff*), Herman Bing (*August Archipenko*), Tom Brown (*Kip Stuart*), Lynne Carver (*Barbara Roberts*), Rafaela Ottiano (*Ellen*), Charles Judels (*Cabby*), Paul Porcasi (*Composer Trentini*), Sig Rumann (*Fanchon*)

p, Hunt Stromberg; d, Robert Z. Leonard; w, Noel Langley (based on the operetta by Rida Johnson Young, Sigmund Romberg); ph, Oliver T. Marsh; ed, Conrad A. Nervig; art d, Cedric Gibbons, Frederic Hope; chor, William von Wymetal, Val Raset; cos, Adrian

A very fragile lace valentine, admittedly but performed with more than enough conviction and style to make it work. Based on a Sigmund Romberg-Rida Johnson Young operetta that was so popular that two productions of it ran simultaneously on Broadway in 1917, MAYTIME returned five times its $1.5 million price tag en route to becoming the 1937 box-office champion. The third Nelson Eddy-Jeanette MacDonald pairing, it was also reputedly the actress's personal favorite, because the famed duo had so much more to do than sing and were finally able to prove their depth as actors. At a May Day celebration in 1906, Miss Morrison (MacDonald), an aged woman, meets Kip (Tom Brown), whose fiancee, Barbara (Lynn Carver), yearns for a singing career. The elderly woman explains that she was once a famous opera star, and the film flashes back to France, 1865, where Marcia Mornay (MacDonald) accepts a marriage proposal from Nicolai Nazaroff (John Barrymore, very potent here), the architect of her success. Later, she is swept off her feet by Paul Allison (Eddy), a handsome young American singer, but remains true to her promise to marry Nazaroff. Several years pass, and when Marcia and Paul costar in American production, their love is rekindled, but when Marcia asks Nazaroff for a divorce, he responds by killing Paul. A flash forward then brings events full circle as the now enlightened Barbara contemplates the future of her own career and love life, while Miss Morrison dies and the ghostly images of Marcia and Paul reprise, for the umpteenth time, "Will You Remember?" Perhaps MAYTIME's most intriguing sidelight is the faked opera "Czaritza," written from Tchaikovsky music with French lyrics by Giles Guilbert, created in the tradition of such other great phony movie operas as CITIZEN KANE's "Salammbo," and CHARLIE CHAN AT THE OPERA's "Carnival." Despite critical and popular success, MAYTIME only received one Oscar nomination for Herbert Stothart's excellent musical direction.

MAZE, THE
1953 81m bw ★★½
Horror /X
Allied Artists

Richard Carlson (Gerald McTeam), Veronica Hurst (Kitty Murray), Katherine Emery (Mrs. Murray), Michael Pate (William), John Dodsworth (Dr. Bert Dilling), Hillary Brooke (Peggy Lord), Stanley Fraser (Robert), Lilian Bond (Mrs. Dilling), Owen McGiveney (Simon), Robin Hughes (Richard Roblar)

p, Richard Heermance; d, William Cameron Menzies; w, Dan Ullman (based on a story by Maurice Sandoz); ph, Harry Neumann (3-D); ed, John C. Fuller; m, Marlin Skiles; prod d, William Cameron Menzies; art d, David Milton

This strange piece features Carlson and Hurst as a couple about to be married. He is summoned back to his ancestral home in Scotland and does not return. Worried, Hurst follows her love, accompanied by Emery, her aunt and constant chaperone. They find Carlson at his family's castle but are shocked to discover him prematurely grey and refusing to speak to them. They walk about the castle until coming onto a hedge maze. Entering, Emery spots something unusual at the center. Closer investigation proves the unusual thing to be a hideous man-frog. It is revealed that the amphibious humanoid is Carlson's 200-year-old ancestor. Its climactic death frees the man from a curse, and he marries Hurst. Though somewhat hampered by its minuscule budget, this 3-D nightmare is fascinating to look at. The direction moves the story suspensefully through its eerie sets (designed by the director). The man-frog practically leaps out at the audience with the 3-D effects. The actors take their roles seriously, making this a cut above average.

MCCABE AND MRS. MILLER
1971 120m c ★★★★½
Western R/X
WB

Warren Beatty (John McCabe), Rene Auberjonois (Sheehan), John Schuck (Smalley), Bert Remsen (Bart Coyle), Keith Carradine (Cowboy), Julie Christie (Constance Miller), William Devane (The Lawyer), Corey Fischer (Mr. Elliott), Shelley Duvall (Ida Coyle), Michael Murphy (Sears)

p, David Foster, Mitchell Brower; d, Robert Altman; w, Robert Altman, Brian McKay (based on the novel McCabe by Edmund Naughton); ph, Vilmos Zsigmond (Panavision, Technicolor); ed, Lou Lombardo; m, Leonard Cohen; prod d, Leon Ericksen; art d, Philip Thomas, Albert J. Locatelli; fx, Marcel Vercoutere; cos, Erickson

A grim and dirty slice of bleak frontier life rendered with extraordinary beauty. Robert Altman cast a decidedly deglamourized Warren Beatty and Julie Christie together with his stock company in this richly textured anti-Western. It's an atmospheric and resonant exploration of a small northwestern settlement in the middle of winter. Christy is the thoroughly modern madam of a bordello and Beatty is the smaller than life hero. Perhaps Altman's most thoughtful genre critique, MCCABE AND MRS. MILLER offers a cynical vision of the settling of the West than is the antithesis of traditional Hollywood myth. MCCABE is an acquired taste for many; it's a film that inspires passionate attacks and defenses. Admittedly it can be offputting at first—seeming like a jumbled, mumbling, fumbling film—but with patience (and a second viewing or two) this is a richly rewarding experience.

It's shortly after the turn of the century when McCabe (Beatty), a man with a mysterious past, rides into a raw snow-covered northwestern wilderness settlement called Presbyterian Church. Here he gambles his way to some winnings and then establishes the community's first whorehouse. Initially a slapdash collection of tents, it becomes a smoothly running business when the feisty Mrs. Miller (Christie) comes aboard as the madam and chief prostitute. She uses McCabe's money to construct a whorehouse that becomes the communal center of the growing town. Miners pour into the brothel-bathhouse, and McCabe's success does not go unnoticed by the region's mining operators, who offer him $6,250 to sell out. McCabe, a business neophyte grown cocky with commercial triumph, refuses their offer. He's holding out for $15,000. Mrs. Miller warns her smart-talking partner that the company employs hired guns to get its way but he intends to settle before things reach that state. This turns out to be a tragic miscalculation.

This is a sad and beautiful film that sides with the losers and dreamers. Beatty, in a courageous anti-star turn, is bearded, blustery, and ignorant as McCabe but finally endearing. Christie is at least as good as the tough-talking, opium-smoking lady from the Continent who's smart enough to know the real score. Altman makes extensive and effective use of Leonard Cohen's haunting ballads throughout the film. Vilmos Zsigmond provides sublime muted images of icy landscapes and warm interiors. Christie received a Best Actress Oscar nomination, but she lost to Jane Fonda for KLUTE. This is not an easy film for everyone, but it is a great one.

MC KENZIE BREAK, THE

1970 108m c   ★★★½
War   PG/AA
UA (U.K.)

Brian Keith *(Capt. Jack Connor)*, Helmut Griem *(Kapitan Schluetter)*, Ian Hendry *(Maj. Perry)*, Jack Watson *(Gen. Kerr)*, Patrick O'Connell *(Sgt. Maj. Cox)*, Horst Janson *(Neuchl)*, Alexander Allerson *(Von Sperrle)*, John Abineri *(Kranz)*, Constantin de Goguel *(Lt. Hall)*, Tom Kempinski *(Schmidt)*

p, Jules Levy, Arthur Gardner, Arnold Laven; d, Lamont Johnson; w, William Norton (based on the novel *The Bowmanville Break* by Sidney Shelley); ph, Michael Reed (DeLuxe Color); ed, Tom Rolf; m, Riz Ortolani; prod d, Frank White; fx, Thomas "Knobby" Clark; cos, Tiny Nicholls

This well executed, taut drama deals with German prisoners in an Allied POW camp, a rare subject in American films. Keith is an Irish intelligence agent sent to Camp McKenzie in Scotland. After a prison riot is quelled with fire hoses, Keith suspects it was merely a ruse to distract attention from an escape plot. This theory is proven to be true after Janson, a homosexual prisoner ostracized by his fellow inmates and severely beaten during the riot, mumbles something about an escape. But Janson is mysteriously strangled before regaining consciousness and Keith is forced into a cat-and-mouse game with Griem, a captured U-Boat captain the Irishman suspects is behind the plan. He allows the prisoners to break free in hopes of capturing the U-Boat sent to pick up the men, but his plans go awry, and all but two of the Germans escape. Keith is left facing disciplinary action for his failure. Suspense is nicely sustained throughout the film, thanks to the particularly strong characterizations by Keith and Griem. Though the character played by Keith is a hard drinking, unorthodox soldier, he is highly intelligent, a nice complement to Griem's more calculating but equally brainy character.

ME

(L'ENFANCE NUE)
1970 83m c   ★★½
Drama
Athos/Parc/Stephan/Renn/Carrosse   (France)

Michel Terrazon *(Francois)*, Marie-Louise Thierry *(Mme. Minguet)*, Rene Thierry *(Minguet)*, Marie Marc *(Meme)*, Henri Puff *(Raoul)*, Pierrette Deplanque *(Josette)*, Linda Gutemberg *(Simone)*, Raoul Billery *(Roby)*, Maurice Coussoneau *(Letillon)*

p, Francois Truffaut, Claude Berri, Mag Bodard, Guy Benier; d, Maurice Pialat; w, Maurice Pialat, Arlette Langmann; ph, Claude Beausoleil (Eastmancolor)

Terrazon is a 10-year-old boy who is abandoned by his mother and goes through a number of foster parents before he is taken in by one family he learns to love. He develops a special relationship with the family's grandmother, but when she dies, he has a hard time adjusting. He drops a cat down a flight of stairs in order to prove that cats land on their feet, and then nurses the cat back to health. Then he causes a serious accident when he drops bars from a bridge. This results in the young boy being sent to a special school, but he knows that upon his release he can return to the family.

MEAN STREETS

1973 110m c   ★★★★
Crime   R/X
TPS

Harvey Keitel *(Charlie)*, Robert De Niro *(Johnny Boy)*, Amy Robinson *(Teresa)*, David Proval *(Tony)*, Richard Romanus *(Michael)*, Cesare Danova *(Giovanni)*, Victor Argo *(Mario)*, George Memmoli *(Joey Catucci)*, Lenny Scaletta *(Jimmy)*, Jeannie Bell *(Diane)*

p, Jonathan T. Taplin; d, Martin Scorsese; w, Martin Scorsese, Mardik Martin; ph, Kent Wakeford (Technicolor); ed, Sidney Levin

MEAN STREETS is the film that launched the career of one of the finest American filmmakers of his generation: Martin Scorsese. After making the interesting WHO'S THAT KNOCKING AT MY DOOR? and working for Roger Corman on BOXCAR BERTHA, Scorsese exploded onto the scene with this remarkably assured low budgeter about the lives of some small-time hoods in New York's Little Italy. Shot on location in New York and Los Angeles—with the same crew used on BOXCAR BERTHA—MEAN STREETS comes vividly to life. The film centers on the struggles of four residents of Little Italy, all men in their mid-20s who aspire to be gangsters, loan sharks or just plain hoods. There is Tony (David Proval), the big friendly one who runs the neighborhood bar; Mike (Richard Romanus), a small-time loan shark who likes to rip off naive teenagers from Brooklyn; Johnny Boy (Robert De Niro), a crazy, irresponsible hood, who has a penchant for blowing up mail boxes and borrowing money from loan sharks he never intends to pay back; and Charlie (Harvey Keitel), the well-dressed nephew of the local mafia boss (Cesare Danova), who wants nothing more than to run his own restaurant. Charlie is torn between the life of the streets (and trying to keep Johnny Boy out of trouble) and the life his uncle can give him. He is also deeply religious, patterning himself after St. Francis of Assisi—testing his faith and seeking penitence for his sins on the streets. The testing of this faith takes the form of Johnny Boy and his sister Teresa (Amy Robinson). Charlie's uncle doesn't want Charlie to keep company with either of these people—Johnny Boy because he seems to be so unstable, and Teresa because she is an epileptic. Charlie is determined to "save" Johnny Boy and sees this challenge as a way to bring his two worlds together and achieve sainthood.

Virtually plotless, MEAN STREETS offers a series of vignettes detailing life in Little Italy. The natural progression of the situations is so lifelike that no plot is necessary, and the characters are so realistic that the film is fascinating. The focus of the film—like the focus of many of Scorsese's movies—is the conflict within the central character, an outsider whose views on life are a little different from those around him. (The "outsider" or "loner" is usually the hero of Scorsese's work: Travis in TAXI DRIVER, Paul in AFTER HOURS, and Rupert in KING OF COMEDY are all prime examples.) Keitel is brilliant as Charlie, combining the street-smarts of a local boy with the higher aspirations of a saint. His conflict of faith is so strongly and assuredly brought to the screen that this is easily the most religious of all of Scorsese's work (including THE LAST TEMPTATION OF CHRIST), and provides an interesting and provocative subtext which is fully explored. Charlie is not unlike Willem Dafoe's Christ of THE LAST TEMPTATION. He, too, is tempted by the flesh and by the warped values of humanity, and must find a way to appease himself and his god. Charlie's own philosophy—which is that you pay for your sins on the street, not in church—is tested to the limits when he takes on the challenge of Johnny Boy. De Niro, with the more flamboyant role, is simply astounding, and his scenes with Keitel (most of which were improvised or developed through improvisation) are absolutely brilliant, ringing of complete truth and natural progression. The supporting cast is also impressive with Romanus and Danova being particularly strong, and, in smaller roles,

Harry Northup (as a disturbed Vietnam vet) and George Memmoli (as the owner of a pool hall) are outstanding.

With this film, Scorsese first gave evidence that he was a master of the medium. MEAN STREETS is a terrifically well-made film, sharply photographed, and crisply edited, with the usual assured visual flair Scorsese puts into all of his films. Some of the stand-out moments include an extended fight scene in a pool hall (the fight starts amusingly enough, over someone being called a "mook"—the guys aren't quite sure what it means, but they fight anyway), in which Scorsese uses long takes to emphasize the chaos, and employs a wild tracking shot to follow a pair fighting throughout the room. Another creative moment comes when Charlie gets drunk at a party. By attaching a camera to Keitel, using a wide angle lens and employing a swinging stedicam, Scorsese almost perfectly recreates the feeling of intoxication. All of this flashy style never interferes with the characters or detracts from the story, which remains powerful, funny and ultimately tragic. There are enough wonderfully inspired moments to fill a year's worth of films. MEAN STREETS is worth seeing simply for those moments: Northup's breakdown at his coming home party; the guys at a movie theatre watching THE SEARCHERS; Johnny Boy shooting a gun from a roof; or the striking moment when Teresa has a seizure and Charlie chooses to chase after Johnny instead of staying with his girlfriend (he leaves her in the care of an elderly woman played by Scorsese's mother). The hilarious scene in which Charlie and Johnny Boy argue about Johnny Boy's debts in the backroom of a bar (a scene that was improvised) is alone worth the price of admission. The banter is genuine, the atmosphere thickly realistic and the people are alive (Scorsese did, after all, grow up on Canal Street).

MEDIUM COOL

1969 110m c   ★★★★½
Political   R/X
H and J

Robert Forster (John Cassellis), Verna Bloom (Eileen Horton), Peter Bonerz (Gus), Marianna Hill (Ruth), Harold Blankenship (Harold Horton), Sid McCoy (Frank Baker), Christine Bergstrom (Dede), Robert McAndrew (Pennybaker), William Sickinger (News Director Karlin), Beverly Younger (Rich Lady)

p, Jerrold Wexler, Haskell Wexler, Tully Friedman; d, Haskell Wexler; w, Haskell Wexler (based on the novel The Concrete Wilderness by Jack Couffer); ph, Haskell Wexler (Technicolor); ed, Verna Fields; m, Mike Bloomfield; art d, Leon Ericksen

A classic from the 1960s time capsule. During the summer of 1968, sentiment against the war in Vietnam was growing daily, and a host of Hippies, Yippies, and representatives of various other counterculture groups descended on Chicago to make those gathering for the Democratic Convention aware of their feelings. It was a tense time that led to numerous skirmishes and all-out riots as police and demonstrators battled in parks and on the streets. Haskell Wexler, the celebrated left-wing cinematographer, directed this Godardian essay in the meaning of movies on location in Chicago during the Democratic Convention of 1968. Robert Forster is a television cameraman, Peter Bonerz is his soundman, Verna Bloom is the woman from the Kentucky hills he meets and Harold Blankenship is her son. While "the whole world is watching," Forster remains unmoved by the politics or human drama of the situation. He's the ultimate artist divorced from society. "God, I love to shoot film," he declares, and it doesn't matter if the subject of his filming is an auto accident or the dramatic riots that took place in Lincoln Park that year. Through his contact with Bloom and even more so with her

son, who trains pigeons, he opens up a little only to be caught in a surrealistic web of his own design at the end. At the end Wexler turns his camera on us. We're responsible, too. Spectators are just as immoral as artists. This is an extraordinary, powerful, and meaningful movie whose effects has never been duplicated. Wexler captured an unusual balance between feelings and intelligence.

The noted cinematographer of such films as THE THOMAS CROWN AFFAIR and IN THE HEAT OF THE NIGHT, Wexler took on directorial duties for the first time with this film, something he would not do again until LATINO. Filmed on location in Chicago, Minnesota, Washington, and Kentucky, the film is an inventive and provocative drama that did very little box-office business on its release. Certainly it's heavy-handed at times—as when Forster interviews a wealthy Lake Shore Drive resident who babbles about needing to get out of the city in the summer just before the film cuts to the a scene of squalid tenements. But mixing footage of real chaotic events with a fictitious drama proves to be compelling.

MEET JOHN DOE

1941 135m bw   ★★★★
Political   /U
WB

Gary Cooper ("John Doe"/Long John Willoughby), Barbara Stanwyck (Ann Mitchell), Edward Arnold (D.B. Norton), Walter Brennan (Colonel), James Gleason (Henry Connell), Spring Byington (Mrs. Mitchell), Gene Lockhart (Mayor Lovett), Rod La Rocque (Ted Sheldon), Irving Bacon (Beany), Regis Toomey (Bert Hansen)

p, Frank Capra; d, Frank Capra; w, Robert Riskin (based on a story "The Life and Death of John Doe" by Robert Presnell, Richard Connell); ph, George Barnes; ed, Daniel Mandell; m, Dimitri Tiomkin; art d, Stephen Goosson; fx, Jack Cosgrove; cos, Natalie Visart

Dark, oddball Capra, but a worthwhile watch with a tail ending wagging the dog. The film opens as Stanwyck, a struggling journalist, is fired from her job when a new managing editor, Gleason, takes over her newspaper. She angrily writes her last piece about a mythical idealist she calls John Doe and through him rants about the little guy being punished and mistreated by tycoons, moguls, magnates, and captains of industry. To make good his protest, Doe states, in Stanwyck's fabricated letter to the paper, that he will leap off the top of City Hall on Christmas Eve. The public response is enormous, and Gleason demands that Stanwyck turn over the letter she has received from this so-called John Doe. She confesses that there is no letter, that she made up the whole story. But then, to keep the job she values above all else, Stanwyck suggests they find a phony hero from the ranks of the great unemployed and continue the story to sell more papers. When another paper jeeringly labels the story a fraud, Gleason, to save his newspaper's image, orders Stanwyck to pick out a stewbum and make him into her real-life John Doe. The man selected is Cooper, called Long John Willoughby, a onetime minor league pitcher whose arm has gone bad and put him out of work and on the bum. He wolfs down a free meal and is persuaded to play the John Doe role for money that will go toward an operation to heal his arm.

The ending of MEET JOHN DOE has been accused by some critics of being tacked on to provide a happy ending (the original authors sued). Since there is a suicide undercurrent here (as in IT'S A WONDERFUL LIFE), it would be interesting to know if Capra, an ultimate idealist, struggled with the issue. The performances are all of a generous repertory, but somehow you feel compromised after watching JOHN DOE. The film, developed by Riskin and Capra in story form, stems from a Harry Langdon comedy, LONG PANTS, which Capra directed in 1927, but is much more in message and content.

MEET JOHN DOE was Capra's first independent film production done away from his home studio Columbia and beyond the tyrannical reach of its boss, Harry Cohn. It's basically an answer to the fascist elements then in America, notably the German-American Bund which was pro-Nazi. Capra wanted to warn Americans about the powerful fascist influences in their midst and did so mightily with this film. Though MEET JOHN DOE reportedly profited Capra and Riskin's independent company $900,000 on its initial release, Capra later reported that the tax bite was so heavy that he dissolved the company after a few months. So great had Capra's reputation become that all the leading players in MEET JOHN DOE agreed to do the film without reading the script. Actually, they had no script to read, since Capra, Riskin, and others were just putting the idea together. It mattered not to Barbara Stanwyck, who is quoted in *Stanwyck* by Jane Ellen Wayne as saying about her feet-first appearance in MEET JOHN DOE: "There is no one like Frank Capra. He is in a class all by himself. It is a joy watching him work every day. You make other pictures to live, but you live to make a Capra picture."

MEET ME IN LAS VEGAS

1956   112m   c   ★★★
Musical   /U
MGM

Dan Dailey *(Chuck Rodwell)*, Cyd Charisse *(Maria Corvier)*, Agnes Moorehead *(Miss Hattie)*, Lili Darvas *(Sari Hatvani)*, Jim Backus *(Tom Culdane)*, Oscar Karlweis *(Loisi)*, Liliane Montevecchi *(Lilli)*, Cara Williams *(Kelly Donavan)*, George Kerris *(Young Groom)*, Betty Lynn *(Young Bride)*

p, Joe Pasternak; d, Roy Rowland; w, Isobel Lennart; ph, Robert Bronner (CinemaScope, Eastmancolor); ed, Albert Akst; m, George Stoll; art d, Cedric Gibbons, Urie McCleary; fx, Warren Newcombe; chor, Hermes Pan, Eugene Loring; cos, Helen Rose

Rancher Chuck Rodwell (Dan Dailey) is a roulette addict, but he doesn't become a big winner until he hooks up with Maria Corvier (Cyd Charisse), a lovely, leggy ballerina who becomes his good luck charm. Every time he holds her hand the numbers come up for Chuck—not only at the casino but on his ranch, where the chickens lay a record-breaking number of eggs and an oil well gushes. The center of activity is the Sands casino, but Chuck and Maria, who form a 50-50 partnership, saunter through many other glamorous spots in America's foremost gaming gulch before deciding to extend their partnership into the arena of romance. Between spins of the wheel, lots of great tunes and dance numbers are presented. Among the guest stars who pop up in clever scenes are Frank Sinatra, Debbie Reynolds, Vic Damone, and Pier Angeli, and the film also offers a wonderful 10-second shot of Peter Lorre sitting at a blackjack table and snapping to dealer Oscar Karlweis, "Hit me, you creep." Songs by Nicholas Brodszky and Sammy Cahn include: "The Girl with the Yaller Shoes" (sung and danced by Dailey and Charisse), "If You Can Dream" (sung over the credits by the Four Aces, reprised by Lena Horne), "Hell Hath No Fury" (sung by Frankie Laine), "Lucky Charm" (sung by Jerry Colonna), "I Refuse to Rock 'n' Roll" (sung by Cara Williams), "Rehearsal Ballet," "Sleeping Beauty Ballet" (danced by Charisse), "Frankie and Johnny" (new lyrics by Sammy Cahn, sung by Sammy Davis,

Jr., danced by Charisse). Stoll and Green's scoring earned the picture an Oscar nomination.

MEET ME IN ST. LOUIS

1944   113m   c   ★★★★★
Musical   /U
MGM

Judy Garland *(Esther Smith)*, Margaret O'Brien *("Tootie" Smith)*, Mary Astor *(Mrs. Anne Smith)*, Lucille Bremer *(Rose Smith)*, June Lockhart *(Lucille Ballard)*, Tom Drake *(John Truett)*, Marjorie Main *(Katie)*, Harry Davenport *(Grandpa)*, Leon Ames *(Mr. Alonzo Smith)*, Hank Daniels *(Lon Smith, Jr.)*

p, Arthur Freed; d, Vincente Minnelli; w, Irving Brecher, Fred Finklehoffe (based on the stories by Sally Benson); ph, George Folsey (Technicolor); ed, Albert Akst; art d, Cedric Gibbons, Lemuel Ayers; chor, Charles Walters; cos, Irene Sharaff

Perfection: a Valentine to the good old days, and all they stood for. Near-peak Judy Garland under the stylish direction of her future husband, Vincente Minnelli, in this wonderful period musical. It opens in 1903 in St. Louis, where Alonzo Smith (Leon Ames), a well-to-do businessman, lives with his wife (Mary Astor), daughters (Garland, Lucille Bremer, Joan Carroll, and Margaret O'Brien), son (Hank Daniels), capricious Grandpa (Harry Davenport), and maid (Marjorie Main). Daughter Rose (Bremer) is courted by one beau at home and corresponds with another away at college, while Esther (Garland) becomes engaged to the new boy next door. Little sisters Agnes (Joan Carroll) and Tootie (Margaret O'Brien) represent the timeless mischief of childhood. Trouble arises when Alonzo is promoted and ordered to New York, a move no one in the family wants to make.

This is a peerless portrayal of America at the turn of the century and one family's struggles to deal with progress, symbolized by the 1904 World's Fair in St. Louis (beautifully re-created for the film). Minnelli proves his eye for detail and captures the era and its values in richly colored, gentle images, displaying a startling balance of emotions from scene to scene, song to song. Among the songs included in this triumph of Americana are "The Boy Next Door," "Meet Me in St. Louis," the marvelous production number "The Trolley Song," and Garland's evergreen "Have Yourself a Merry Little Christmas". An almost unbeatable musical. Note Garland's beauty in this film: a tribute to the overhaul given her by Dottie Pondell, whose services Garland had snatched from under the noses of every major star in Hollywood, upon the death of Carole Lombard.

MEETING VENUS

1991   119m   c   ★★★½
Comedy/Romance/Musical   PG-13/12
Enigma Productions   (U.K.)

Glenn Close *(Karin Anderson)*, Niels Arestrup *(Zoltan Szanto)*, Marian Labuda *(Von Schneider)*, Maite Nahyr *(Maria Krawiecki)*, Victor Poletti *(Stefano Del Sarto)*, Johara Racz *(Dancer)*, Rita Scholl *(Delfin Van Delf)*, Michael Kroecher *(Cashier)*, Andre Chameau *(Etienne Tailleur)*, Jay O. Sanders *(Stephen Taylor)*

p, David Puttnam; d, Istvan Szabo; w, Istvan Szabo, Michael Hirst; ph, Lajos Koltai; ed, Jim Clark; m, Richard Wagner; prod d, Attila Kovacs; art d, Lorand Javor; cos, Catherine Leterrier

Splendidly directed by Istvan Szabo, who co-wrote the screenplay with Michael Hirst, and lavishly photographed by Lajos Koltai, MEETING VENUS utilizes the petty squabbling that lies behind a major opera company's efforts to stage *Tannhauser* as a metaphor for contemporary Europe.

Zoltan Szanto (Niels Arestrup), a virtually unknown Hungarian conductor, receives his big break when he's engaged to conduct Wagner's *Tannhauser* at the Opera Europa in Paris. What's more, the production will be broadcast by satellite to 27 countries around the world, assuring Szanto overnight celebrity. Heading a stellar international cast is the *prima donna* Karin Anderson (Glenn Close). A superstar in every sense, she isn't particularly happy about working with Szanto, having vaguely recalled a disparaging remark he made against her.

Things do not begin well in Szanto's preparations for rehearsals, despite his dream of creating a blend of singers, musicians, dancers and stagehands united under his baton. It seems that music is next to the last thing on everyone's mind. Management bickers for position and power; the set designer has created a post-modernist nightmare; the dancers' union calls a strike; the singers squabble over petty jealousies; the chorus is determined to gain advantage from the chaos; Szanto can't even collect living expenses or his conducting fee; and as a final straw, environmental action groups are arranging to picket the opera house. And on top of all this turmoil, there remains the ice barrier between the diva and the conductor. Then, quite miraculously, a love affair develops between Szanto and Anderson and it turns life upside down because, all of a sudden, they can and do laugh and cavort.

MEETING VENUS, with its robust, often comedic interplay and delicious love story, is an exciting and gratifying film. The music is superbly sung by a stellar cast. Glenn Close is radiantly luminous as Karin. Her arias are sung by Kiri Te Kanawa and the synchronization is flawless. As for Niels Arestrup, his is a magnetic aura that will charm audiences and serve to infatuate every woman who experiences him here.

What is of special note about this film which, in great part, is based on the personal experiences of its writer-director, is that for the first time in film we are privy to the netherworld of backstage shenanigans—dealing with unions, dissident groups, casts interested in self-aggrandizement, bloated egos that must be appeased. In short, everything and more that we read about in the press but never really fathom. And if screenwriters Szabo and Hirst have used the Opera Europa's troubled staging of *Tannhauser* as a metaphor for contemporary Europe, it is worth noting that Wagner used his opera in much the same way—to reflect the move for religious and political freedom in Germany in the mid-1880s.

MEETING VENUS was filmed on location in Budapest, using the city's hundred-year-old State Opera House before moving to Paris to complete principal photography. The State Opera House was built in 1884 for one million forints in gold, donated by Franz Joseph, Emperor of the Austro-Hungarian empire. Both Gustav Mahler and Otto Klemperer were at one time its music directors.

MELO

1988   110m   c   ★★★★★
Romance   /PG
MK2/CNC/A2   (France)

Sabine Azema (*Romaine Belcroix*), Pierre Arditi (*Pierre Belcroix*), Andre Dussollier (*Marcel Blanc*), Fanny Ardant (*Christiane Levesque*), Jacques Dacqmine (*Dr. Remy*), Hubert Gignoux (*Priest*), Catherine Arditi (*Yvonne*)

p, Marin Karmitz; d, Alain Resnais; w, Alain Resnais (based on the play "Melo" by Henri Bernstein); ph, Charlie Van Damme (Agfa-Gevaert Color); ed, Albert Jurgenson; m, Johannes Brahms, Johann Sebastian Bach, Philippe Gerard; prod d, Jacques Saulnier; cos, Catherine Leterrier

Since his brilliant HIROSHIMA, MON AMOUR, Alain Resnais's experiments with nonlinear structure and the relationship between memory and the past have placed him among the ranks of the greatest directors. In light of these experiments, MELO comes as a shock, a traditionally constructed linear narrative adapted from a 1929 Parisian stage melodrama written by Henry Bernstein. Deceptively simple in appearance, MELO is the story of two musicians, Marcel Blanc and Pierre Belcroix (Andre Dussollier and Pierre Arditi), whose friendship dates back to their days at the conservatory. Marcel has gone on to international fame as a soloist while Pierre has settled down in a Parisian suburb to lead a simple life with his wife, Romaine (Sabine Azema). After a quiet evening of drink and reminiscence, Marcel and Romaine begin a passionate affair. Romaine plots to gradually poison the unsuspecting and good-natured Pierre. Masterfully directed, MELO is both an entertaining romantic melodrama and an extension of Resnais's ideas about memory and imagination, reality and fiction. As in HIROSHIMA, MON AMOUR, Resnais gives us characters whose present is haunted by the past. Only rarely is a film this simple *and* this complex.

MELODY TIME

1948   75m   c   ★★★½
Animated/Musical   /U
Disney

VOICES OF: Roy Rogers, Luana Patten, Bobby Driscoll, Ethel Smith, Bob Nolan, The Sons of the Pioneers, Buddy Clark, The Andrews Sisters, Fred Waring and His Pennsylvanians, Frances Langford

p, Walt Disney; d, Clyde Geronimi, Wilfred Jackson, Hamilton Luske, Jack Kinney; w, Winston Hibler, Erdman Penner, Harry Reeves, Homer Brightman, Ken Anderson, Ted Sears, Joe Rinaldi, Art Scott, William Cottrell, Bob Moore, Jesse Marsh, John Walbridge, Hardie Gramatky; ph, Winton C. Hoch (Technicolor); ed, Donald Halliday, Thomas Scott; anim, Harvey Toombs, Cliff Nordberg, John Sibley, Ken O'Brien, Judge Whitaker, Marvin Woodward, Hal King, Don Lusk, Rudy Larriva, Bob Cannon, Hal Ambro, Edwin Aardal

This last musical compilation film from the Disney studios was also one of the best, and Disney's animators display their entire creative range, from the irrepressible comedy of Donald Duck to more refined work reminiscent of FANTASIA. The sequences include the story of a young couple's quarrel, told in flashback after they are a long-married pair; a marvelously surreal piece, dubbed "an instrumental nightmare," in which a befuddled bee buzzes about in a frenzied effort to escape a variety of musical perils to the accompaniment of a jazzy "Flight of the Bumble Bee"; a retelling of the Johnny Appleseed folktales; the charming "Little Toot," in which the title tugboat is always getting into trouble in its attempts to emulate its father; "Trees," a version of Joyce Kilmer's poem that is Disney animation at its best; "Blame It on the Samba," which once more teams Donald Duck with his pal Joe Carcioca from the popular cartoon "The Three Caballeros"; and a final segment featuring cowboy king Roy Rogers and the Sons of the Pioneers crooning "Blue Shadows on the Trail" against a series of desert night scenes. Essentially a compendium of unrelated shorts, the delightful MELODY TIME incorporates visual styles as varied as the subjects of its segments.

MELVIN AND HOWARD

1980 93m c ★★★½
Biography/Comedy R/AA
Universal

Jason Robards, Jr. *(Howard Hughes)*, Paul LeMat *(Melvin Dummar)*, Elizabeth Cheshire *(Darcy Dummar)*, Mary Steenburgen *(Lynda Dummar)*, Chip Taylor *(Clark Taylor)*, Melvin E. Dummar *(Bus Depot Counterman)*, Michael J. Pollard *(Little Red)*, Denise Galik *(Lucy)*, Gloria Grahame *(Mrs. Sisk)*, Pamela Reed *(Bonnie Dummar)*

p, Art Linson, Don Phillips; d, Jonathan Demme; w, Bo Goldman; ph, Tak Fujimoto (Technicolor); ed, Craig McKay; m, Bruce Langhorne; prod d, Toby Rafelson; art d, Richard Sawyer

After churning out CAGED HEAT and CRAZY MAMA for Roger Corman's New World Pictures, Jonathan Demme (STOP MAKING SENSE, SOMETHING WILD, THE SILENCE OF THE LAMBS) finally broke through the ranks of B-movie directors with this pungent fable about the elusiveness of the American Dream.

Based on a real-life incident, Melvin Dummar (Paul LeMat) is an amiable milkman and perpetual also-ran who, while driving along a lonesome stretch of Nevada highway early one morning, picks up a grizzled tramp (Jason Robards) headed for Las Vegas. He's nice to the eccentric codger, who claims to be Howard Hughes, and even gives him two bits at the end of the ride.

Melvin quickly dismisses the incident and goes about his life, remarrying his ex-wife, Lynda (Mary Steenburgen), and chasing success with typically poor results. Even when Lynda wins $10,000 tap dancing to the Rolling Stones's "Satisfaction" on a television game show, the Dummars are unable to turn the situation to their advantage. Life remains a struggle for the embattled couple until Melvin discovers that the bum he befriended earlier really was Howard Hughes—and that the recently deceased billionaire has made him the beneficiary of $156 million via the so-called Morman will.

Like the earlier, underrated HANDLE WITH CARE, Demme displays an affinity for Preston Sturges-like tales that portray a system which places a premium on material success, but MELVIN AND HOWARD never quite lives up to its satiric or dramatic potential, suffering from a somewhat sidelong approach to Melvin's odyssey that renders the film more engaging than truly compelling.

MEMBER OF THE WEDDING, THE

1952 91m bw ★★★
Drama /A
Columbia

Ethel Waters *(Berenice Sadie Brown)*, Julie Harris *(Frankie Addams)*, Brandon de Wilde *(John Henry)*, Arthur Franz *(Jarvis)*, Nancy Gates *(Janice)*, William Hansen *(Mr. Addams)*, James Edwards *(Honey Camden Brown)*, Harry Bolden *(T. T. Williams)*, Dickie Moore *(Soldier)*, Danny Mummert *(Barney MacKean)*

p, Stanley Kramer; d, Fred Zinnemann; w, Edna Anhalt, Edward Anhalt (based on the novel and play by Carson McCullers); ph, Hal Mohr; ed, Harry Gerstad, William Lyon; m, Alex North; prod d, Rudolph Sternad; art d, Cary Odell

Harris is a 12-year-old girl who is quickly approaching that awkward time known as adolescence. She imagines herself a member of her brother's wedding party, and then tries to tag along for the honeymoon. Dejected at being refused, she runs away, but returns home after a sensuous brush with a drunken soldier pushes her further toward womanhood. Upon her return home, she receives the tragic word that her cousin, de Wilde, has died suddenly. After a passage of time, the picture ends with her entering the dating stage of teenhood. Director Fred Zinnemann would follow this up with SHANE, making the wide-eyed de Wilde a household name. The photography is obviously the work of a master, and it adds a certain atmosphere, which becomes a life-support for the film's sometimes slow-moving drama. Cameraman Mohr, approaching the end of his long career, had previously shot such films as THE JAZZ SINGER, THE WEDDING MARCH, A MIDSUMMER NIGHT'S DREAM, and RANCHO NOTORIOUS. Five people from the award-winning Broadway play (Harris, Waters, de Wilde, Hansen, and Bolden) repeat their roles in this film. The stage role of the 12-year-old girl made Julie Harris (she was 25 years old at the time) a Broadway leading light, and earned her a Best Actress Oscar nomination (she lost to Shirley Booth for COME BACK, LITTLE SHEBA). De Wilde won the stage's Donaldson Award for his debut effort.

MEN, THE

1950 85m bw ★★★★
Drama/War /PG
Kramer

Marlon Brando *(Ken)*, Teresa Wright *(Ellen)*, Everett Sloane *(Dr. Brock)*, Jack Webb *(Norm)*, Richard Erdman *(Leo)*, Arthur Jurado *(Angel)*, Virginia Farmer *(Nurse Robbins)*, Dorothy Tree *(Ellen's Mother)*, Howard St. John *(Ellen's Father)*, Nita Hunter *(Dolores)*

p, Stanley Kramer; d, Fred Zinnemann; w, Carl Foreman; ph, Robert de Grasse; ed, Harry Gerstad; m, Dimitri Tiomkin; prod d, Rudolph Sternad

This was Marlon Brando's film debut and, as such, set standards not only for his fellow actors but for himself. Brando gives a tremendous performance as Ken, a WWII veteran who has been left a paraplegic as a result of a sniper's bullet in the lower back. In the hospital, Ken is angry, resentful, and uncooperative with his doctors and nurses. His girlfriend, Ellen (Teresa Wright), visits him, but the embittered Ken turns her away. Dr. Brock (Everett Sloane) slowly breaks through Ken's mental wall, however, convincing him to begin his exercise program, through which Ken strengthens his upper torso, later learning to expertly manipulate his wheelchair and to drive a specially equipped auto. Ellen will not give up on him and soon Ken agrees to marry her, but despite the progress he has made, the vet is still consumed with doubt, anger, and self-pity. Producer Stanley Kramer earlier produced such message-filled films as CHAMPION and HOME OF THE BRAVE, the first concerning the corruption of the blood sport of prizefighting, the second dealing with racism and bigotry. Here Kramer, aided by the steady direction of Fred Zinnemann, studies the adjustment of severely wounded men with little hope of complete recovery. Zinnemann rarely steps over the line into mawkishness or bathos, and Carl Foreman's witty, sensitive script was the reason Brando agreed to step off the stage to appear in this film. Brando worked hard at his role, actually moving into a 32-bed ward with real paraplegics and observing their day-to-day agonies, research that resulted in a finely nuanced performance.

MEN
(MANNER)
1985   99m   c   ★★★½
Comedy   /15
Olga/Second German TV   (West Germany)

Heiner Lauterbach *(Julius Armbrust)*, Uwe Ochsenknecht *(Stefan Lachner)*, Ulrike Kriener *(Paula Armbrust)*, Janna Marangosoff *(Angelika)*, Marie-Charlott Schuler *(Marita Strass)*, Dietmar Bar *(Lothar)*, Edith Volkmann *(Frau Lennert)*

d, Doris Dorrie; w, Doris Dorrie; ph, Helge Weindler; ed, Jorg Neumann; m, Claus Bantzer

Taking an age-old situation and turning it on its head, this wonderful farce is brimming with unique twists, wit, and style. Julius Armbrust (Heiner Lauterbach) is an advertising executive about to celebrate his 12th year of wedded bliss with wife Paula (Ulrike Kriener). His world suddenly falls apart, however, when he discovers she has been cheating on him with Stefan Lachner (Uwe Ochsenknecht), a young, long-haired bohemian who meanders about town on his bicycle. Julius decides on revenge, not through blackmail or murder but in a manner he knows will bring Paula back to him. After ingratiating himself with Stefan on the sly, Julius begins work on his scheme, transforming Paula's artist-lover into a carbon copy of himself. MEN is a sharp satire, playing off gender roles and male bonding with some real insight. Made by female director Doris Dorrie, the film wisely carries no obtrusive social message that might undermine the wonderful humor. Dorrie does rely rather heavily on slapstick (there is a silly bit involving a gorilla suit), but fortunately her inventive storytelling overcomes the film's lesser elements. Shot in 25 days on a budget of only $360,000, MEN grossed in excess of $15 million in international box-office receipts.

MEN DON'T LEAVE
1990   115m   c   ★★★★
Drama   PG-13/15
Paul Brickman-Jon Avnet/Geffen

Jessica Lange *(Beth Macauley)*, Chris O'Donnell *(Chris Macauley)*, Charlie Korsmo *(Matt Macauley)*, Arliss Howard *(Charles Simon)*, Tom Mason *(John Macauley)*, Joan Cusack *(Jody)*, Kathy Bates *(Lisa Coleman)*, Corey Carrier *(Winston Buckley)*, Jim Haynie *(Mr. Buckley)*, Belita Moreno *(Mrs. Buckley)*

p, Jon Avnet; d, Paul Brickman; w, Barbara Benedek (based on the film LA VIE CONTINUE written by Moshe Mizrahi); ph, Bruce Surtees (CFI Color); ed, Richard Chew; m, Thomas Newman; prod d, Barbara Ling; art d, John Mark Harrington; fx, John E. Gray; cos, J. Allen Highfill, Susan Becker

MEN DON'T LEAVE is an unabashed, four-hanky family melodrama. But it's also an unexpectedly poignant slice of life, the best film of its type since THE ACCIDENTAL TOURIST. Jessica Lange plays Beth Macauley, who is widowed as the film begins by an accident that claims the life of her construction contractor husband. Besieged by leftover debts from his last unfinished project, she is forced to sell the family home, over the loud objections of her teenage son, Chris (Chris O'Donnell). To cut expenses, she relocates her family, which also includes younger son Matt (Charlie Korsmo), to an apartment in Baltimore. There, she takes a job as assistant manager of a gourmet food market run by the acerbic Lisa (Kathy Bates, star of Rob Reiner's film adaptation of Stephen King's *Misery*).

Despite its familiar premise, reminiscent of films like PLACES IN THE HEART and Lange's own COUNTRY, MEN DON'T LEAVE is not just another tale about a strong mother

holding her family together through hardships and calamities. Its characters are more believably flawed and frail than those generally found in films of this ilk, and therefore more interesting. Through much of the film it seems as if Beth's family is dissolving around her. Chris almost immediately becomes involved with an "older" woman, Jody (Joan Cusack), a twentysomething X-ray technician who lives in the same building as the Macauleys. Matt, meanwhile, takes up with Winston (Corey Carrier), a pint-sized, knife-carrying schoolyard terror who makes money on the side by stealing VCRs and selling them to a video porno freak. More important to Matt, Winston comes from a solid upper-middle-class family, complete with a dad who becomes a surrogate father for Matt. Only Beth is unable to adjust to her new life. Her budding relationship with likable musician Charles (Arliss Howard) falls victim to her preoccupation with supporting her family. Then, a show of temper costs her job. Finding herself in an empty apartment and feeling all but abandoned by her wandering brood, Beth plunges into a depression and winds up falling back on the kindnesses of strangers to pull herself back together.

Notwithstanding Beth's breakdown, MEN, like THE ACCIDENTAL TOURIST, isn't really about its big crises. Instead, it's about how people live from one day to the next, and the hard choices and compromises they make to survive. Beth swallows her pride to get her job back at Lisa's store and tentatively revives her relationship with Charles. Chris also continues his involvement with Jody, though he stops wearing the laughably garish, country club clothes she buys for him. Nevertheless, the film ends with Jody and Charles left waiting on shore while Beth, Chris, and Matt enjoy a "family day" boat ride, alone and together. While the crises, especially those faced by Beth and Matt, give MEN DON'T LEAVE its dramatic shape, it is in its small, beautifully observed details that the film really comes to life. A fine screenplay by Barbara Benedek is painstakingly directed by Paul Brickman, who elicits meticulous ensemble performances from his cast. As she did in her scripts for THE BIG CHILL and IMMEDIATE FAMILY, Benedek compellingly examines how average people cope with extraordinary changes in their lives. Once again she demonstrates a rare talent for writing characters that eloquently express her themes yet remain utterly believable people. Brickman—directing his first film since his remarkable debut, RISKY BUSINESS—deftly maintains a precarious emotional balance between the script's joys and heartaches and laughter and tears. Visually, MEN DON'T LEAVE is as expressive as any film in recent years, its subtle shifts from light to darkness richly conveying the inner states and outer realities of its characters.

Lange complained in interviews at the time of MEN's release that Brickman kept pushing her to give a more comic performance despite what she saw as the script's straight dramatic focus. However, it is clear that what Brickman was after wasn't out-and-out comedy, but a feeling of unpredictability in the performances that proves to be one of the film's greatest assets. Newcomers O'Donnell and Korsmo struggle to establish their authority as actors just as their characters struggle for identity. The rest of the more experienced cast play interestingly against type. As the secure mom suddenly thrust into an insecure world, Lange seems to have been allowed to give a "dramatic" performance, but the slight uncertainty in her acting helps to convey the uncertainty of her character. Similarly, Howard, best known for more physical roles in films like FULL METAL JACKET, and Cusack, who added ditzy comic relief to BROADCAST NEWS, WORKING GIRL, and SAY ANYTHING, find themselves in unfamiliar territory—he as a sensitive, intelligent artist, and she as a woman of depth and compassion—but turn this unfamiliarity to their advantage. The overall result is a film that is refreshingly realistic and spontaneous, a work of consummate craft from all involved. MEN DON'T LEAVE is a rare film that can be equally savored as rich, offbeat entertainment and admired for its sheer artistry.

MEN OF THE FIGHTING LADY

1954 79m c   ★★★★
War   /A
MGM

Van Johnson (Lt. Howard Thayer), Walter Pidgeon (Cmdr. Kent Dowling), Louis Calhern (James A. Michener), Dewey Martin (Ensign Kenneth Schechter), Keenan Wynn (Lt. Cmdr. Ted Dodson), Frank Lovejoy (Lt. Cmdr. Paul Grayson), Robert Horton (Ensign Neil Conovan), Bert Freed (Lt. Andrew Szymanski), Lewis Martin (Cmdr. Michael Coughlin), George Cooper (Cyril Roberts)

p, Henry Berman; d, Andrew Marton; w, Art Cohn (based on stories appearing in The Saturday Evening Post entitled "The Forgotten Heroes of Korea" by James A. Michener and "The Case of the Blind Pilot" by Cmdr. Harry A. Burns, USN); ph, George Folsey (Ansco Color); ed, Gene Ruggiero; m, Miklos Rozsa; art d, Cedric Gibbons

This top-flight action film features an all-male cast of aircraft carrier pilots during the Korean War and chronicles their heroic flights and tragic deaths. Johnson is the lead pilot around whom the stories revolve. The storie are all told to Calhern, playing the role of writer James A. Michener, by Martin, Wynn, Lovejoy, and others. There are a lot of landings and takeoffs from the carrier and some thrilling dogfights between American- and Russian-made jets, but the most exciting sequence, which was based on a story by another writer, Burns, is one in which Johnson "talks down" a blinded Martin so that he can land on the deck of their carrier. Here the whistling wind and the talk between the pilots would have sufficed to heighten the drama, but these are almost drowned out by Rozsa's overwhelming, rich score. Marton's direction is swift and economical, and Ruggiero's editing is adroit and clever as he intercuts the dramatic and action scenes. (Ruggiero went to Washington and procured a great deal of black and white footage, along with some color stock footage shot during WWII and the Korean War, to be used in the film. He found one spectacular 16mm black-and-white scene of a plane crashing on a carrier and, when he returned to Hollywood, had backdrop specialist Warren Newcomb paint this sequence, no more than 30 feet of film, in color for a $5,000 fee. Then he spliced this scene to some live-action footage.) Pidgeon, as the ship's surgeon, is a standout, as are Johnson, Martin, and, in particular, Lovejoy, the commander who advocates low-level bombing to achieve his objectives. Freed provides some burly laughs as a much harassed repair officer putting together the broken pieces of the jets aboard the carrier. This was a heavy box-office winner for MGM at the time of its release, coming just as the Korean War ended.

MEPHISTO

1981 144m c   ★★★★
War/Drama   /15
Mafilm/Objectiv/Manfred Durniok/Analysis (Hungary/West Germany)

Klaus Maria Brandauer (Hendrik Hofgen), Krystyna Janda (Barbara Bruckner), Ildiko Bansagi (Nicoletta Von Niebuhr), Karin Boyd (Juliette Martens), Rolf Hoppe (The General), Christine Harbort (Lotte Lindenthal), Gyorgy Cserhalmi (Hans Miklas), Christiane

Graskoff (Cesar Von Muck), Peter Andorai (Otto Ulrichs), Ildiko Kishonti (Dora Martin)

p, Manfred Durniok; d, Istvan Szabo; w, Istvan Szabo, Peter Dobai (based on the novel by Klaus Mann); ph, Lajos Koltai (Eastmancolor); ed, Zsuzsa Csakany; m, Zdenko Tamassy; art d, Jozsef Romvari

The winner of 1981's Academy Award for Best Foreign Language Film, MEPHISTO is an inspired update of the Faust legend featuring a tour de force performance by Klaus Maria Brandauer. Critically acclaimed stage actor Hendrik Hofgen (Brandauer) tires of the "entertaining" theatrical forms and attempts something more revolutionary, more Brechtian. Despite his groundbreaking ideas, he does not rise to fame—they cannot even spell his name correctly on posters. Desperate, Hendrik sells his soul—not to the Devil, but to the Nazis—his desire for fame more urgent than his hatred of the oppressor. It is only later, after he is indebted to the Third Reich, that he realizes his mistake. Based on a novel by Klaus Mann (son of Thomas) and exquisitely photographed, MEPHISTO bubbles over with the energy of Brandauer's bravura performance, which quickly attracted the attention of Hollywood. Brandauer and director Istvan Szabo would team again to make COLONEL REDL and HANUSSEN.

MERRY ANDREW

1958 103m c   ★★½
Musical/Comedy   /U
MGM

Danny Kaye (Andrew Larabee), Pier Angeli (Selena), Salvatore Baccaloni (Antonio Gallini), Noel Purcell (Matthew Larabee), Robert Coote (Dudley Larabee), Patricia Cutts (Letitia Fairchild), Rex Evans (Gregory Larabee), Walter Kingsford (Mr. Fairchild), Peter Mamakos (Vittorio Gallini), Rhys Williams (Constable)

p, Sol C. Siegel; d, Michael Kidd; w, Isobel Lennart, I.A.L. Diamond (based on the story "The Romance of Henry Menafee" by Paul Gallico); ph, Robert Surtees (CinemaScope, Metrocolor); ed, Harold F. Kress; m, Saul Chaplin; art d, William A. Horning, Gene Allen; chor, Michael Kidd; cos, Walter Plunkett

Kaye, an instructor at a stuffy boys' school in England, sets out on an archaeological dig and finds himself befriended by a circus performer. He travels with the girl (Angeli) to the big top, where he dons some clown makeup and gets into the act. Pretty tame in comparison to Kaye's early efforts, but still enjoyable. Includes the tunes: "Pipes of Pan," "Salud," "Chin Up Stout Fellows," "Everything Is Tickety Boo," "You Can't Always Have What You Want," "Square of the Hypotenuse," and "Here's Cheers" (Saul Chaplin, Johnny Mercer).

MERRY CHRISTMAS, MR. LAWRENCE

1983 124m c   ★★★★
Prison/War   R/15
Recorded Picture/Cineventure TV/Asashi/Oshima (U.K./Japan)

David Bowie (Celliers), Tom Conti (Col. John Lawrence), Ryuichi Sakamoto (Capt. Yoni), Takeshi (Sgt. Hara), Jack Thompson (Hicksley-Ellis), Johnny Okura (Kanemoto), Alistair Browning (DeJong), James Malcolm (Celliers' Brother), Christopher Brown (Celliers at Age 12), Yuya Uchida p, Jeremy Thomas; d, Nagisa Oshima; w, Nagisa Oshima, Paul Mayersberg (based on the novel *The Seed and the Sower* by Laurens Van Der Post); ph, Toichiro Narushima (Eastmancolor); ed, Tomoyo Oshima; m, Ryuichi Sakamoto; prod d, Shigemasa Toda; art d, Andrew Sanders

Japanese director Nagisa Oshima's first film in English stars Tom Conti as the title character, a British colonel in a Japanese-run POW camp during WWII.

Colonel Lawrence is an astute observer of the cultural codes of his captors and even forms a friendship of sorts with one Japanese officer (Takeshi). He is also witness to the strange dynamics between new camp commandant Yoni (Ryuichi Sakamoto) and a new prisoner, Jack Celliers (David Bowie), with whom Lawrence served in Libya. Yoni is fascinated by Celliers, and plans to make him the prisoners' CO, replacing Hicksley-Ellis (Jack Thompson).

Oshima's ambitious film is not without faults, but these are overshadowed by its emotional power. Many of the characters' actions and impulses are apparently contradictory, but their motivation can generally be found buried in Oshima's complex story. (The Yoni-Celliers relationship, which needs greater development, is a notable exception.) Fine performances by Conti, Takeshi (brilliant in his first dramatic role), Sakamoto (a Japanese pop star in his film acting debut who also contributed the memorable score), and Bowie enhance this provocative film.

MERRY WIDOW, THE

1934 99m bw ★★★★★
Musical/Comedy /A
MGM

Maurice Chevalier *(Prince Danilo)*, Jeanette MacDonald *(Sonia)*, Edward Everett Horton *(Ambassador Popoff)*, Una Merkel *(Queen Dolores)*, George Barbier *(King Achmed)*, Minna Gombell *(Marcelle)*, Ruth Channing *(Lulu)*, Sterling Holloway *(Mischka)*, Henry Armetta *(Turk)*, Barbara Leonard *(Maid)*

p, Irving Thalberg; d, Ernst Lubitsch; w, Samson Raphaelson, Ernest Vajda (based on the operetta "Die Lustique Witwe" by Franz Lehar, Victor Leon, Leo Stein); ph, Oliver T. Marsh; ed, Frances Marsh; m, Franz Lehar; art d, Cedric Gibbons, Frederic Hope; chor, Albertina Rasch; cos, Adrian, Ali Hubert

One of the greatest of the screen operattas. After a smashing debut in Austria, Franz Lehar's operetta "The Merry Widow" was brought to the US in 1907, became a silent two-reeler in 1912, then, in 1925, Erich von Stroheim directed Mae Murray and John Gilbert in an opulent, controversial version in which Clark Gable appeared as an extra. This version, however, is by far the best of the lot. Jeanette MacDonald, at the peak of her career, is Sonia, an immensely wealthy widow whose spending keeps the small country of Marshovia afloat economically. When she decides to move to Paris to find a suitable husband, the king (George Barbier) dispatches Danilo (Maurice Chevalier), whom he has caught dallying with Queen Dolores (Una Merkel), to the City of Light to woo the widow and bring her home. Failing to recognize Sonia in a cafe, Danilo falls in love with her, then tries to persuade her that his affection is real when she learns the nature of his mission. Unable to convince her, Danilo is called back to Marshovia and put on trial; however, Sonia becomes the star witness for the defense, the two are trapped in a jail cell, and matters end happily and romantically.

The best musical helmed by the great Ernst Lubitsch, THE MERRY WIDOW is frothy, funny, and tuneful from start to finish. MacDonald more than holds her own in the comedy department, snapping off lines with Carole Lombard-like expertise. Star Chevalier had played with newcomer MacDonald at Paramount, and though he reputedly never liked her, their pairing here is near perfection. The dancing, choreographed by Albertina Rasch, is as good as it comes and the huge waltz in the embassy ball ranks among the best large ensemble pieces ever filmed. Enjoy the opening sequence where Marshovia is found on the map or the "There's a limit to every widow" scene. "The Merry Widow" is one of 30 operettas penned by Lehar, and here his music was given new lyrics by Lorenz Hart, Gus Kahn, and an uncredited Richard Rodgers.

METROPOLITAN

1990 98m c ★★★★
Comedy /15
Westerly Film

Carolyn Farina *(Audrey Rouget)*, Edward Clements *(Tom Townsend)*, Christopher Eigeman *(Nick Smith)*, Taylor Nichols *(Charlie Black)*, Allison Rutledge-Parisi *(Jane Clarke)*, Dylan Hundley *(Sally Fowler)*, Isabel Gillies *(Cynthia McClean)*, Bryan Leder *(Fred Neff)*, Will Kempe *(Rick Von Sloneker)*, Elizabeth Thompson *(Serena Slocum)*

p, Whit Stillman, Brian Greenbaum, Peter Wentworth; d, Whit Stillman; w, Whit Stillman; ph, John Thomas; ed, Chris Tellefsen; m, Mark Suozzo; cos, Mary Jane Fort

METROPOLITAN is a film about a strata of the young and privileged it would be easy to despise. Yet as a result of terse direction, urbane writing, and beguiling performances by a number of new actors, the young, privileged characters at the heart of this film are surprisingly disarming. It's the Christmas season in Manhattan and the rush is on. The rush, in this case, refers to the heady round of debutante balls and get-togethers that are the highlight of the social season for an Upper East Side bunch still in the thrall of arcane rituals. This determinedly proper crew, the self-dubbed SFRP (Sally Fowler Rat Pack), includes Nick (Christopher Eigeman), its arrogantly dissolute leader; Audrey (Carolyn Farina), a sweet young thing trying to uphold the ideals of Jane Austen in an increasingly unkind world; Charlie (Taylor Nichols), an uptight stutterer paralyzed by his love for Audrey; Cynthia (Isabel Gillies), a *femme fatale*-in-training; and pudgy, narcoleptic Fred (Bryan Leder). One snowy eve, Tom Townsend (Edward Clements), a proletarian radical, stumbles into their exalted midst from truly alien territory—the West Side. With Nick as his Mephistophelian guide, Tom gradually becomes caught up in such life-and-death matters as whether to buy his tux from Brooks Brothers or Paul Stuart. Although Audrey is infatuated with Tom, he is still weathering the after-effects of a fatal crush on the notorious heartbreaker Serena Slocum (Elizabeth Thompson). Also threatening the welfare and happiness of the clique is Nick's special enemy, Rick von Sloneker (Will Kempe), a meretricious, pony-tailed Lothario over whom an alarming number of debs have committed suicide. The film climaxes with a pursuit and rescue of virtue in Southampton, and ends on a sweet note of comradeship.

Exhibiting a prodigy's control over his cleverly devised material, Whit Stillman has made an updated drawing-room comedy that takes place largely at deb-party postmortems, with the SFRP endlessly jawing about honor and position. Only occasionally does METROPOLITAN indulge in more earthy pursuits involving Truth games, mescaline, and strip poker. Yet, surprisingly, the film is so adroitly written and played that there is nothing claustrophobic about the proceedings—who wants to leave the room with such stimulating talk going on?

METROPOLITAN is a party-night dream vision of New York, with roots in Astaire-Rogers musicals, screwball comedies, and Woody Allen films. But most notably, it brings to mind George Cukor's elegant masterpiece, HOLIDAY. Like Cary Grant's outsider in that film, Tom wins the heart of an aristocratic rebel, and Christopher Eigeman invests his Nick with some of the pixilated omniscience of Lew Ayres' character in the 1938 film. In the process, Nick emerges as the most engaging of METROPOLITAN's characters, with his easy hypocrisy in carnal matters and propensity for spreading scandalous stories about his rivals. "When you are an egotist, none of the harm you do is intentional. . . I'm about to go upstate to a stepmother of untrammeled malevolence," he explains, with aplomb worthy of Clifton Webb or George Sanders. Epigrams like these and visual touches like the silly Lester Lanin hats the boys wear in one scene should give some idea of the real joy of METROPOLITAN. Stillman is a careful observer with an obvious love of language, and his wonderful, fresh cast handles the script with ease, conveying just the right measure of deadpan, *jejune* super-seriousness.

The limited budget obviously precluded any actual footage of deb balls; instead, Stillman provides graceful suggestions of these *fetes* with montages outside the Plaza Hotel. John Thomas' mellow cinematography captures a magical, wintry Manhattan in all its landmark glory and is especially alert to the beautifully detailed interiors. (The filmmakers managed to get a serendipitous shot of a holiday window display of *The Collected Works of Jane Austen* in the legendary Scribner's Bookstore.) The choice of music is also skillful, Philadelphia Soul ballads alternating with cha-chas and melancholy themes.

Clements is amusingly sobersided as the opinionated Tom, who carries on weighty conversations about books although he only reads criticism of them. He makes his seduction by high society both convincing and touchingly desperate, a portrayal that is reminiscent of *The Great Gatsby*'s Nick Carraway, but with less angst. As a would-be sophisticate, Farina has an appealing, demure ruefulness, like a brainier Molly Ringwald. She can say a line like, "There's something dubious about Tom," and get away with it. In just a few scenes, Alice Connorton, as Tom's mother, completely and emphatically captures the character of a slightly harried single parent. Nichols is very funny as the intense Charlie, whose smug beliefs are forever being shattered. The scene in which he gracefully bows out, leaving the field romantically open for Tom and Audrey in the finale, is far superior to similar scenes in most other farces dealing with romantic triangles; utterly devoid of malice, this scene provides METROPOLITAN with a lovely, perfect ending. The film earned an Oscar nomination for its screenplay.

MIAMI BLUES

1990 97m c   ★★★
Crime   R/18
Tristes Tropiques

Fred Ward (*Sgt. Hoke Moseley*), Alec Baldwin (*Frederick J. "Junior" Frenger*), Jennifer Jason Leigh (*Susie "Pepper" Waggoner*), Nora Dunn (*Ellita Sanchez*), Obba Babatunde (*Blink Willie*), Charles Napier (*Sgt. Bill Henderson*), Shirley Stoler (*Edie Wulgemuth*), Paul Gleason (*Sgt. Frank Lackley*), Gary Goetzman (*Hotel Desk Manager*), Ron Bozman (*Senor Lerner*)

p, Jonathan Demme, Gary Goetzman; d, George Armitage; w, George Armitage (based on the novel *Miami Blues* by Charles Willeford); ph, Tak Fujimoto; ed, Craig McKay; prod d, Maher Ahmad

Frederick Frenger, Jr. (Alec Baldwin), an amoral con man and killer fresh out of prison, arrives in Miami with a dead man's wallet and a powerful, if impractical, urge to remake his life along more prosaic lines. In the airport he is annoyed by a Hare Krishna, whose finger he breaks out of instinctive viciousness, shocking the weak-hearted religious zealot to death. When Frenger checks into a hotel, he sends for a hooker. Pepper (Jennifer Jason Leigh), the naive, not particularly smart young woman who answers the summons, harbors a secret wish to be an ordinary housewife. And the two see in each other an opportunity to live out their fantasies of conventionality. Detective Hoke Moseley (Fred Ward) is called in to investigate the death of the Hare Krishna and quickly catches up with Frenger. A grizzled, pragmatic loner, Moseley recognizes Frenger as real trouble and tries to persuade the guileless Pepper to turn him in. Despite his promise to Pepper to abandon his criminal ways, Frenger breaks into Moseley's hotel room, beats him, and steals his badge, gun, and as a spiteful afterthought, his false teeth. With Moseley hospitalized, Frenger and Pepper move to Coral Gables and play house: she trades in her high heels for housework, while he, equipped with Moseley's gun and badge, becomes a one-man crime wave. Battered and angry, Moseley tracks Frenger, facing off with him during the aborted robbery of a pawn shop, after the store's owner (Shirley Stoler) chops off Frenger's fingers with a machete she keeps behind the cash register. Pepper, who now knows Frenger has broken his promise to her, abandons him. Moseley then trails Frenger home and kills him.

Adapted from a novel by Charles Willeford, MIAMI BLUES toys with hard-boiled crime-film cliches and keeps the viewer constantly off balance. Its plot is minimal and straightforward, and no attempt is made to explain the psychology of the sociopath who murders casually and yet yearns for the security of a middle-class life. But the movie's details are fascinating and often surprising. Director George Armitage, a Roger Corman protege, exposes a collection of idiosyncratic characters to Florida's hot sun and the effect is startling.

Unlike the television series MIAMI VICE, Armitage's film does not portray Florida's largest city as a surreal, neon wonderland of high-stakes depravity; instead, it focuses on pastel seediness and petty criminality. Even the character of Frenger lacks psychotic grandeur; he is a dangerous cipher with some endearing quirks (after his death, Pepper observes wistfully that there were good things about him: he never hit her and always ate everything she cooked).

MIAMI BLUES suffers from a number of basic structural problems. Awkwardly paced, it alternates sharp, compact scenes with aimless ones that neither advance the plot nor illuminate the characters. Time passes erratically, without logic and without any visual cues to keep the viewer clear on the story's development. Moreover, the characters never deviate far from their initial notes: Frenger is crazy, Pepper is dumb, and Moseley has seen it all. In a slam-bang action picture in which something is blown up every 10 minutes, these would be minor complaints, but MIAMI BLUES's overt quirkiness promises more without delivering. Often on the verge of wearing out its welcome, MIAMI BLUES is nevertheless redeemed by its offbeat sensibility and sporadic, intense set pieces.

MICKI & MAUDE

1984 118m c   ★★★½
Comedy   PG-13/PG
Delphi III/Blake Edwards Entertainment/Columbia

Dudley Moore (*Rob Salinger*), Amy Irving (*Maude Salinger*), Ann Reinking (*Micki Salinger*), Richard Mulligan (*Leo Brody*), George Gaynes (*Dr. Eugene Glztszki*), Wallace Shawn (*Dr. Elliot Fibel*), John Pleshette (*Hap Ludlow*), H.B. Haggerty (*Barkhas Guillory*), Lu Leonard (*Nurse Verbeck*), Priscilla Pointer (*Diana Hutchison*)

p, Tony Adams; d, Blake Edwards; w, Jonathan Reynolds; ph, Harry Stradling, Jr. (Panavision, Metrocolor); ed, Ralph E. Winters; m, Lee Holdridge; prod d, Rodger Maus; art d, Jack Senter; fx, Roy Downey; cos, Patricia Norris

Rob Salinger (Dudley Moore) is the host of a typically inane TV talk show in Los Angeles. He's happily married to a busy and competent attorney, Micki (Ann Reinking), and yearns to be a father, but her breakneck schedule keeps them from having enough time to even try for a child. Rob meets Maude (Amy Irving), a seductive cellist who sets her sights on him. She has no idea that he's married, and he manages to carry off the deception until she announces that she's pregnant. Rob does the proper thing and marries Maude, believing that bigamy is the only answer to his problem. When Micki gets pregnant, too, and starts consulting the same gynecology team as Maude, the fun heats up. For all his character's shoddy behavior, Moore is so engaging in the role that he can't be faulted—he persuades us that he has been trapped by fate. The denouement is less than satisfying but does come as a mild surprise. MICKI & MAUDE has some very funny scenes and excellent acting from all the performers. It begins a bit slowly but builds well and winds up in a comic celebration.

MIDNIGHT

1939 94m bw ★★★★★
Comedy /A
Paramount

Claudette Colbert (*Eve Peabody/"Baroness Czerny"*), Don Ameche (*Tibor Czerny*), John Barrymore (*George Flammarion*), Francis Lederer (*Jacques Picot*), Mary Astor (*Helene Flammarion*), Elaine Barrie (*Simone*), Hedda Hopper (*Stephanie*), Rex O'Malley (*Marcel*), Monty Woolley (*Judge*), Armand Kaliz (*Lebon*)

p, Arthur Hornblow, Jr.; d, Mitchell Leisen; w, Charles Brackett, Billy Wilder (based on a story by Edwin Justus Mayer, Franz Shulz); ph, Charles Lang; ed, Doane Harrison; m, Frederick Hollander; art d, Hans Dreier, Robert Usher; fx, Farciot Edouart; cos, Irene

A witty, well-paced comedy, the story is set in Paris where Colbert is a struggling showgirl. Wealthy Barrymore believes gigolo Lederer is paying too much attention to his wife Astor, so he hires Colbert to keep Lederer occupied. Ameche plays a taxi driver who has fallen in love with Colbert. When the group goes to Barrymore's chateau in Versailles, Colbert is constantly in danger of being exposed, and the plot is further complicated when Ameche arrives, posing as her husband. Eventually, Barrymore and Astor solve their problems, and Ameche and Colbert plan to wed.

Astor's appearance here was cleverly designed to hide a thickening body. The actress's waistline was hidden from view by costumer Head who encased her in furs. She was shown seated behind tables having lunch or playing bridge, and, in a scene where Astor was to lead a conga line, she was unexpectedly called to the phone. It was a sad reunion with Barrymore, who had been her lover 15 years earlier when they appeared in BEAU BRUMMELL. "He was sick and old," she recalled in *A Life on Film*, "He was vague and quiet and sat on the set barely talking to anyone." Barrymore could not remember his lines, so he worked off cue cards. "Even with cue cards," added Astor, "and

only a faint idea of what the picture was all about, he had enough years of experience behind him to be able to act rings around anyone else." Another woman in Barrymore's life, his wife Barrie, was also in the cast. At one point Astor, sitting next to Barrymore on the set, reached over to touch his hand and he pulled away, saying, "Don't. . . My wife—ah—Miss Barrie—is very jealous." She watched the Great Profile brush away tears, then laugh at his brimming emotions.

MIDNIGHT COWBOY

1969 119m c ★★★★
Drama R/18
UA

Dustin Hoffman (*Enrico "Ratso" Rizzo*), Jon Voight (*Joe Buck*), Sylvia Miles (*Cass*), John McGiver (*Mr. O'Daniel*), Brenda Vaccaro (*Shirley*), Barnard Hughes (*Towny*), Ruth White (*Sally Buck*), Jennifer Salt (*Annie*), Gil Rankin (*Woodsy Niles*), Gary Owens

p, Jerome Hellman; d, John Schlesinger; w, Waldo Salt (based on the novel by James Leo Herlihy); ph, Adam Holender (DeLuxe Color); ed, Hugh A. Robertson; m, John Barry; prod d, John Robert Lloyd; fx, Dick Smith; cos, Ann Roth

MIDNIGHT COWBOY was the only "X"-rated picture ever to win an Oscar as Best Movie of the year. The rating was later changed to an "R" and, by today's standards, might almost be considered a "PG-13." Director Schlesinger also took an Academy Award, as did screenwriter Salt. The film presents a seamy look at the vile side of New York and some of the denizens who haunt the streets and abandoned houses of Manhattan. The picture moves between the city's high and low spots, with one very funny parody of the Andy Warhol crowd inserted for comic relief, but it is essentially a movie that is depressing almost to the point of being unbearable. Voight, a restless, frustrated dishwasher in a tiny Texas burg, is convinced that he can use his sexual prowess to satisfy all of the rich New York women who don't know what real loving from a real man is like. He bids farewell to his Lone Star pals (including Salt, the screenwriter's daughter) and heads for the Big Apple. On the trip he waxes reminiscent about his past, and in a flashback we see his history: the uncaring father who deserted his slatternly mother; his grandmother, White, and all of her "gentlemen callers"; and a recounting, apparently, of every sexual experience he ever had. Voight arrives in New York and checks into a second-rate hotel and then cruises the streets until he meets Miles, a blowsy blonde. Voight makes love to the loudmouthed woman in her expensive apartment, but when the time comes for him to extract his fee, she has no money—he even has to give her taxi fare. Voight wanders into a tacky bar and meets Hoffman, a street hustler who steals for a living—when he isn't coughing (he has a tubercular condition). When Hoffman learns why Voight is in town, he offers his services as the Texan's manager and sends him on a job to the room of McGiver, a homosexual Christian. Voight and Hoffman argue over the assignment but then smooth out their differences, and Hoffman invites Voight to crash with him in an abandoned building where Hoffman makes his drafty home. The two men become as close as George and Lenny in OF MICE AND MEN, talking about how it's going to be when they make their big score. They want to settle in sunny Florida and never have to face a New York winter again.

Based on the novel by Herlihy, the screenplay is an excellent example of how a novel can be translated into a screenplay that deserved the Oscar it received. After the success of THE GRADUATE and the disaster of MADIGAN'S MILLIONS (which was made before THE GRADUATE but was released afterwards),

Hoffman was very picky about his roles and refused several parts that were not unlike the young man who was seduced by Mrs. Robinson. He wanted a part that was unique—and surely found that in the role of Ratso Rizzo. Voight had appeared on Broadway in "The Sound of Music" and a couple of less-than-memorable films (HOUR OF THE GUN, FEARLESS FRANK, OUT OF IT) before soaring to the heights with this role. Englishman Schlesinger had an unerring eye for capturing the grimy reality of New York. Sometimes it takes a foreigner to see the US in a new light—Czech Milos Forman did with TAKING OFF and Britisher Michael Apted with COAL MINER'S DAUGHTER. The subject matter was so depressing that no one anticipated its becoming the hit that it did. Besides New York, other locations were in Texas and Florida; cinematographer Holender captured all the atmosphere possible from each area. In a small role as one of the party-goers, notice songwriter Jabara, who later won an Oscar for "The Last Dance" for the forgettable THANK GOD IT'S FRIDAY. Good work by jazz harmonicist Jean "Toots" Theilemans helps the mood immensely. Several songs provided background, and one of them—"Everybody's Talking" (Fred Neil, sung by Harry Nilsson)—was a hit. Other tunes included "A Famous Myth," "Tears and Toys" (Jeffrey Comanor, sung by the Group), "He Quit Me" (Warren Zevon, sung by Lesley Miller), "Old Man Willow," (Stan Bronstein, Michael Shapiro, Myron Yules, Richard Sussman, sung by Elephants Memory), "Jungle Jim at the Zoo" (Bronstein, Sussman, Richard Frank, sung by Elephants Memory), and "Crossroads of the Stepping Stones" (Shapiro, Bronstein, sung by Elephants Memory).

MIDNIGHT EXPRESS

1978 120m c   ★★★★
Prison/Biography   R/18
Casablanca (U.K.)

Brad Davis (Billy Hayes), Randy Quaid (Jimmy Booth), Bo Hopkins (Tex), John Hurt (Max), Paul Smith (Hamidou), Mike Kellin (Mr. Hayes), Norbert Weisser (Erich), Irene Miracle (Susan), Paolo Bonacelli (Rifki), Michael Ensign (Stanley Daniels)

p, David Puttnam, Alan Marshall; d, Alan Parker; w, Oliver Stone (based on the book by Billy Hayes, William Hoffer); ph, Michael Seresin (Eastmancolor); ed, Gerry Hambling; m, Giorgio Moroder; prod d, Geoffrey Kirkland; art d, Evan Hercules; cos, Milena Canonero, Bobby Lavender

MIDNIGHT EXPRESS will rivet the viewer from the first instant it flashes onscreen. The acting is superb, the direction is excellent, and Moroder's score is exhilarating. The picture won two Oscars, for Best Music and Best Script from Another Source, and was nominated for four others, for Best Movie (it lost to THE DEER HUNTER), Best Direction, Best Film Editing and Best Supporting Actor (Hurt). Like many Alfred Hitchcock films, MIDNIGHT EXPRESS is the story of an innocent person being thrust into a situation beyond his control. Based on the true life story of Billy Hayes (now working as an actor in Hollywood), it begins as Davis (playing Hayes) and girlfriend Miracle are about to leave for home after a trip to Turkey. Davis is seen taping blocks of hashish to his body before climbing aboard the airplane. Miracle is totally unaware of his attempt at smuggling, and when Davis is caught with the goods at the airport, she is bypassed and allowed to leave Turkey. The Turkish government was on the alert for drug smugglers, and we never know if this was a tipoff or just a coincidence that Davis was caught. In a brilliantly tense scene Davis is herded at gunpoint to a room where he is stripped and interrogated. From here, he is taken to a fierce Turkish prison. Here the prisoners must fend for themselves, as human rights do

not exist. Comfort means a night when someone isn't brutally raped, beaten, or otherwise abused. Davis meets many of the other inmates, including a few Westerners who are all in there for the same drug raps. Quaid is the American, Hurt is the dope-smoking Englishman, and Weisser is a gay Scandinavian with whom Davis has a brief sexual liason. (How much of what is truth and what is fiction cannot be discerned unless one has read the book by Hayes and Hoffer.) The prisoners are shown to be wayward sheep rather than the smugglers and criminals they are, so they come off as sympathetic characters. Davis' father, Kellin, attempts to get his son out of jail by hiring a local attorney, Jeffrey, to defend him. But the Turkish legal system is bent on making Davis an example to other potential smugglers. In a sensational courtroom moment Davis berates his captors with an obscene lambasting of the judges, most of whom don't speak English and have no idea what he's saying. The court sentences him to more years than he thought he'd get, and once remanded to the jail, he makes plans to take the "midnight express" out of there (the euphemism for escape). Davis and Quaid try to get out by burrowing, but Smith, the behemoth sadist who runs the security department for the jail, catches them and beats them badly; Davis is shipped to the insane ward. One of the prisoners, Franco Diogene, makes life easier for himself by selling goods to the other prisoners and by being a fink for the guards. When he is to be released, he is beaten by the others, and Davis bites the man's tongue out. Now Smith takes Davis to the torture room and is about to whack him around again, probably until he dies. But Davis fights back, sending the 300-pound Smith up against the wall, where a clothes spike impales and kills him. Davis puts on a guard's uniform and walks out the door of the jail into the dusk. The final sequence is a series of snapshots chronicling the happy reunion of Davis and family, not an altogether prudent choice on the part of the creators, but the film was so dour and downbeat that they must have felt the audience needed their hearts to be lightened before strolling up the aisles.

All the performances in the picture are top-notch. Quaid's portrayal of the slightly deranged American is outstanding; Hurt, as the addicted Englishman, is a study in understatement; Weisser is totally believable; and Smith must rank a close second to Hume Cronyn's Captain Munsey in BRUTE FORCE for sheer evil in a prison official. But the standout is Davis, who is given the task of displaying just about every emotion known to man, and he succeeds. MIDNIGHT EXPRESS is often a bit too stylish for its own good, something that may have been an indulgence on the part of Parker, who also showed the same zealous adherence to style over substance with BUGSY MALONE and BIRDY. It is, however, most effective. Parker and editor Hambling both won British Film Academy Awards for their work. The picture was shot in Greece and on the island of Malta, where Fort St. Elmo doubled as the Turkish prison. This movie probably did more to discourage amateur dope smugglers than all the US government's warnings. Extremely violent and sadistic; not for youngsters.

MIDNIGHT RUN

1988 122m c   ★★★½
Comedy/Crime   R/15
City Lights

Robert De Niro (Jack Walsh), Charles Grodin (Jonathan Mardukas), Yaphet Kotto (Alonzo Mosely), John Ashton (Marvin Dorfler), Dennis Farina (Jimmy Serrano), Joe Pantoliano (Eddie Moscone), Richard Foronjy (Tony Darvo), Robert Miranda (Joey), Jack Kehoe (Jerry Geisler), Wendy Phillips (Gail) p, Martin Brest; d, Martin Brest; w, George Gallo; ph, Donald Thorin (Astro Color, Metrocolor); ed, Billy Weber, Chris Lebenzon, Michael Tronick; m, Danny Elfman; prod d, Angelo Graham; fx, Roy Arbogast; cos, Gloria Gresham

A thoroughly engaging action film, MIDNIGHT RUN boasts a superb cast that transforms its rather mundane story line into something memorable, funny, and moving. Tough, foul-mouthed bounty hunter Jack Walsh (Robert De Niro) is hired by bail bondsman Eddie Moscone (Joe Pantoliano) to bring back Mafia accountant Jonathan Mardukas (Charles Grodin), who has embezzled $15 million from the Los Angeles mob, given the money to charity, and skipped bail. In an extended cross-country chase, Walsh, flat broke, drags Mardukas on board nearly every modern mode of transportation available in an effort to avoid their pursuers and get back to LA so Walsh can collect his money. As the plot takes a series of complicated twists and turns, the two men's personalities and relationship develop. BEVERLY HILLS COP director Martin Brest has allowed the actors to improvise, and their resulting interaction is more realistic, funny, and surprising than that of any buddy film released in the last several years. The characters in MIDNIGHT RUN feel real—not only as if they existed before we met them, but also as if they will continue after the movie ends.

MIDSUMMER NIGHT'S DREAM, A

1935 132m bw   ★★★½
Fantasy/Comedy   /U
WB

James Cagney (Bottom), Dick Powell (Lysander), Joe E. Brown (Flute), Jean Muir (Helena), Hugh Herbert (Snout), Ian Hunter (Theseus), Frank McHugh (Quince), Victor Jory (Oberon), Olivia de Havilland (Hermia), Ross Alexander (Demetrius)

p, Max Reinhardt; d, Max Reinhardt, William Dieterle; w, Charles Kenyon, Mary C. McCall, Jr. (based on the play by William Shakespeare); ph, Hal Mohr; ed, Ralph Dawson; m, Felix Mendelssohn; art d, Anton Grot; fx, Fred Jackman, Byron Haskin, H.F. Koenekamp; chor, Bronislava Nijinska, Nini Theilade; cos, Max Ree

When Jack Warner suddenly put aside $1.5 million for the Reinhardt production of A MIDSUMMER NIGHT'S DREAM, all of Hollywood was amazed because Warner Bros. was always known as "the working class" studio. The film involves creatures of the forest, chiefly fairies and artisans, who plan to put on a play to amuse the royal court. Egeus (Grant Mitchell) demands that Hermia (Olivia de Havilland) marry Demetrius (Ross Alexander) despite her love for Lysander (Dick Powell). Unless she goes through with the nuptials, Theseus, Duke of Athens (Ian Hunter), will severely punish her. Meanwhile, Theseus is preparing to marry Hippolyta, Queen of the Amazons (Verree Teasdale). Hermia and Lysander elope, escaping to the forest, and Demetrius pursues them. He, in turn, is pursued by Helena (Jean Muir) who is in love with Demetrius. The local artisans, Bottom (James Cagney), Quince (Frank McHugh), Snout (Hugh Herbert), Flute (Joe E. Brown) and others, enter the forest to rehearse the play they intend to perform for Theseus' wedding. The rulers of the forest, the fairies, come to life. Their monarchs, Oberon (Victor Jory) and Titania (Anita Louise), are quarreling, when in a fit of pique he orders the mischievous Puck (Mickey Rooney) to squeeze the juice of a passion flower into her eyes so that she will fall madly in love with the first creature she sees on awakening. To complicate matters, Puck playfully turns Bottom's head into that of an ass. When Titania awakens, Bottom is the first creature she spots and she instantly adores him. Puck also uses the magic potion to alter the affections of the four lovers, so Hermia and Lysander begin to hate each other. Not until Oberon, Titania, Puck, and the scores of fairies depart the forest do things get back to normal. Bottom and company then go on to perform an awkward play for the edification of Hunter and his court.

Max Reinhardt (1873-1943) had successfully staged the play in Europe and was thought to be one of the great theatrical geniuses of the early 20th Century. He insisted A MIDSUMMER NIGHT'S DREAM was ideal for film because the fairy sequences offered the proper magic for celluloid. He demanded that Erich Korngold, with whom he had worked in Europe, be brought in to do the score based on the music Mendelssohn created in 1843 for the play. Reinhardt had no idea of how to film this masterpiece, and it soon became apparent that he would lead the production to ruin if steps weren't taken. Cinematographer Ernest Haller, following Reinhardt's obtuse instructions, filmed forest scenes that were blurred. The foliage was so dense that the actors could not be distinguished from the trees. Haller was fired and Hal Mohr brought in to replace him. Mohr had half the forest cut down and Anton Grot's elaborate sets thinned out, but the forest still appeared dense. Ultimately, the photography emerged as stunning. Mohr won an Oscar for his work, and one went to editor Dawson as well. The studio threw all of its best talent into the movie, even crooner Powell whose Arkansas accent was still somewhat pronounced. (In later years, Powell would state that he never really understood the lines he mouthed in the film.) Cagney overcame a background deficient in Shakespeare by turning his role of Bottom into an energy-packed performance that is more acrobatic than theatrical. During a production break midway during shooting, Rooney went tobogganing at a winter resort, broke his leg and had to be wheeled quickly through the forest's foliage by stagehands as he rode an unseen bicycle. Only Hunter and a few others with classical backgrounds were comfortable with their roles, but the film is nevertheless convincing. The delicate ballet sequences by Bronislava Nijinska and Nini Theilade (the latter playing the leading ballerina in the film) were thought to be ineffective and were rechoreographed in the Busby Berkeley mold.

MIDSUMMER NIGHT'S SEX COMEDY, A

1982 88m c   ★★½
Comedy   PG/15
Orion

Woody Allen (Andrew), Mia Farrow (Ariel), Jose Ferrer (Leopold), Julie Hagerty (Dulcy), Tony Roberts (Maxwell), Mary Steenburgen (Adrian), Adam Redfield (Student Foxx), Moishe Rosenfeld (Mr. Hayes), Timothy Jenkins (Mr. Thompson), Michael Higgins (Reynolds)

p, Robert Greenhut; d, Woody Allen; w, Woody Allen; ph, Gordon Willis (Technicolor); ed, Susan E. Morse; m, Felix Mendelssohn; prod d, Mel Bourne; art d, Speed Hopkins; cos, Santo Loquasto

Woody Allen is among a very few people in the history of film who have provided audiences with really intelligent humor. But even Homer nods, and never has Allen more obviously fallen down on the job than in A MIDSUMMER NIGHT'S SEX COMEDY, a trifle that owes much to Ingmar Bergman in style and to Groucho Marx in content. The setting is a weekend houseparty at a farmhouse in upstate New York at the turn of the century. Andrew (Allen) and his wife, Adrian (Mary Steenburgen), are joined by Leopold (Jose Ferrer), a pretentious intellectual, and his promiscuous fiancee, Ariel (Mia Farrow); the party is completed by Maxwell (Tony Roberts), a womanizing doctor, and his current fling, Dulcy (Julie Hagerty). Andrew is preoccupied with trying to get his sexually unavailable wife to bed him; his frustration is exacerbated by the presence of Ariel, with whom he had a chaste relationship in the past, and who he now realizes to his chagrin was among the most sexually accessible of women. The stage is set for comedy, but the film doesn't have the wallop, the belly-laughs, or the wry comments usually found in Allen's work. While *bons mots* pepper the screenplay, Allen is prevented by the period setting from exercising his wit on contemporary sexual mores, which have always provided one of his richest comic sources. The pastoral setting is beautifully photographed by Gordon Willis.

MIKEY AND NICKY

1976 119m c   ★★½
Drama   R/15
Paramount

Peter Falk *(Mikey)*, John Cassavetes *(Nicky)*, Ned Beatty *(Kinney)*, Rose Arrick *(Annie)*, Carol Grace *(Nell)*, William Hickey *(Sid Fine)*, Sanford Meisner *(Dave Resnick)*, Joyce Van Patten *(Jan)*, M. Emmet Walsh *(Bus Driver)*, Sy Travers *(Hotel Clerk)*

p, Michael Hausman; d, Elaine May; w, Elaine May; ph, Victor J. Kemper (Panavision, Movielab Color); ed, John Carter, Sheldon Kahn; m, Johann Strauss; prod d, Paul Sylbert

There is much to enjoy in this movie, but just as much to yawn over. One has the feeling that this was a play that was never produced on stage but went directly to the screen from the typewriter. Since so much of it is dialogue with very little cinematic action, it just feels stagebound. Cassavetes and Falk are two small-time thugs who have been friends since their youth. Cassavetes is going to be killed by Beatty, the unlikely hit man in the service of boss Meisner (who was just about everyone's acting coach in New York at one time). Cassavetes gets in touch with Falk after trying to get help from his estranged wife, Van Patten, and his current amour, Grace. Falk is apparently going to help Cassavetes get away from the potential assassin, though we are often struck by Falk's words and actions and not sure if he is friend or foe. Some very touching scenes punctuate the camaraderie, but the film is essentially far too long, self-indulgent, and talky to elicit much emotional response. It's a character study that would be at home in an East Village theater. It's hard to say where the script ends and the improvisation begins, as in so many of Cassavetes's films. The executive producer was veteran TV executive Bud Austin, who had run Paramount Television before moving into feature production. Very foul language and some painful sequences make this hardly fit for anyone with a priggish attitude. This was the third film directed by May and the most experimental. Her first two were A NEW LEAF (which she also wrote and costarred in) and THE HEARTBREAK KID, with a script by Neil Simon and some terrific performances by Jeannie Berlin, Charles Grodin, and Cybill Shepherd.

MILDRED PIERCE

1945 111m bw   ★★★★★
Drama   /A
WB

Joan Crawford *(Mildred Pierce)*, Jack Carson *(Wally Fay)*, Zachary Scott *(Monte Beragon)*, Eve Arden *(Ida)*, Ann Blyth *(Veda Pierce)*, Bruce Bennett *(Bert Pierce)*, George Tobias *(Mr. Chris)*, Lee Patrick *(Maggie Binderhof)*, Moroni Olsen *(Inspector Peterson)*, Jo Ann Marlowe *(Kay Pierce)*

p, Jerry Wald; d, Michael Curtiz; w, Ranald MacDougall (based on the novel by James M. Cain); ph, Ernest Haller; ed, David Weisbart; m, Max Steiner; art d, Anton Grot; fx, Willard Van Enger; cos, Milo Anderson

Impeccable, bleak gloss with supreme Crawford engineering the greatest comeback of them all. MILDRED PIERCE is one of the finest noir soap operas ever made, with the queen of pathos, Crawford, shouldering the storm alone; her efforts snagged the golden statuette as 1945's Best Actress. It's quite a story.

To begin with, MILDRED PIERCE was lefovers: Barbara Stanwyck, Bette Davis and Ann Sheridan turned down the lead part, but producer Jerry Wald gambled on MGM-bounced, unemployed Crawford, and the film swept the box offices, returning $5 million to Warner Bros. and putting Crawford back on top as the hottest star in town.

Crawford is married to Bennett in a marriage that has gone sour. While she dotes on their two daughters, chiefly the oldest, Blyth, Bennett finds pleasant company with Lee Patrick. As the marriage breaks up, Crawford takes pennyante jobs to keep vicious Blyth in good schools and nice clothes. Then she gets a job as a waitress, with the help of wisecracking Arden. She becomes so good at the job and is so full of ideas on how to provide better service and good but inexpensive food that real estate jerk Carson agrees to help her open her own restaurant. Slimy playboy Scott, rich in real estate but poor in cash, gives her the property on which she builds her new place. The restaurant not only prospers but Crawford soon branches out until she has a lucrative chain of eateries and is in the big money. She marries Scott so that his social prestige and position will rub off on her daughter Blyth, but the plan backfires when Scott begins to pay more attention to Blyth than to Crawford. She mistakenly makes Scott a business partner, and he goes through Crawford's hard-earned fortune like a plague of locusts, forcing her into bankruptcy. The crushing blow comes when Crawford learns that Scott has been having an affair with Blyth behind her back.

Everything about MILDRED PIERCE is top rate, from stellar production values to Curtiz's marvelously paced direction where he refuses to allow sentiment to rule the story. The Ranald MacDougall script, adapted from James M. Cain's terse novel is sharp, literate, and innovative, with plenty of fast dialogue. The Curtiz string-pulling is greatly aided by Grot's imposing sets, Haller's lush, moody photography and Steiner's haunting score. Bravely cresting the waves of disaster, is a mature, neurotic Crawford in a real tour de force, defying the industry to write her off as washed up. She's matched every slap of the way by Blyth, here giving the performance of *her* career.

After 18 years at Metro as third in demand among screen queens (after Garbo and Shearer; her box-office is said to have paid for the other two's films and to have built the writer's building), Crawford and Mayer came to a parting. Her appeal was waning, and she refused to stagnate in bad properties that were ruining her career, while newer actresses (Turner, Garland, Garson and Lamarr) received their pick of scripts. She signed with Warner Bros., but refused clinkers, and was taken off salary, surprising Jack Warner by agreeing to no wages while she waited for a strong property. It was a gamble: these years of stagnation at MGM up until MILDRED would cement Crawford's demons of drink and domestic abuse, as she began to crack under the strain of being broke and unwanted. A year later, Wald brought the MILDRED PIERCE script to her. She flew through it and called the producer to say that it was *exactly* what she'd been waiting for. But Curtiz, Jack Warner's favored helmsman on the studio lot, was not in love with directing Joan Crawford. Crawford was told about Curtiz's reluctance to direct her, but so eager was she to make the film that she stooped to begging a screen test for Curtiz. He agreed, and, after seeing Crawford as Mildred, he told Wald he would work with her. Universal contract player Blyth, then only 16 years old, was also rejected by the picky Curtiz, but Crawford took the youngster aside and rehearsed and then did a test with her, as she did with most of the other character actors, amazing one and all at Warners that such a luminous star would deign to perform such mundane chores.

The first day on the set proved nearly disastrous. Curtiz, sitting high up on a boom chair, looked down to see Crawford come forth simply coiffed and made up. But his famed Hungarian temper flared when he riveted on her housedress costume's broad shoulders. "You and your goddamn shoulder pads!", he is said to have fumed. Literally tearing at her dress, he found upon inspection that she wasn't wearing any. Crawford took Curtiz's abuse until the director realized that she would suffer humiliation to make a good film. Then he began to appreciate her devotion and slavish work habits in connection with MILDRED.

Crawford astounded the Warner Bros. technical people who had never worked with her by her professionalism (in contrast to fit-throwing Bette Davis, then reigning queen of the lot). A new Crawford emerged from MILDRED: less warm than MGM Joan, defensive, unhappy, but hopeful and willing to suffer for a last shot at love. Styled in the postwar mode, the mature Crawford (in MILDRED, 41 years old) was still stunning, but less resilient to hard knocks. Word spread from the soundstages of her excellence, and the front office began to lobby for the Best Actress Oscar. Columnists, publicists and the press jumped on the bandwagon, sniffing an unequaled industry comeback.

Upon completion, Crawford and Curtiz met at a post-production party, where the actress jokingly gave the director a gargantuan pair of shoulder pads designed by Adrian. Then MILDRED opened; the critics raved about her performance and millions poured into the theaters to see the great movie queen, believing she had just given the finest performance of her life.

Hard-boiled Cain sent her a leather-bound copy of *Mildred Pierce* enscribed thus: "To Joan Crawford, who brought Mildred to life as I had always hoped she would be, and who has my lifelong gratitude." Crawford's bravura performance in the film was not matched by such an attendance at the Academy Awards ceremonies. She called Wald and other studio bosses and told them she could not appear, that she felt she would not win, or, if she did, she would make an ass of herself in her acceptance speech. On the night of the Oscars she was physically ill according to her personal physician, who reported that she had a temperature of 104 and that she could not attend. Her home was filled with photographers who poured into her lavish bedroom, where, on the bed, she listened to the ceremonies on the radio. When Charles Boyer announced she had won the Oscar, the bedroom exploded in a sea of blinding flashbulbs. Wald called from the ceremonies to congratulate Crawford, and Blyth appeared to embrace her. Celebrities, headed by Van Johnson, her most ardent fan, poured into the Crawford home to pay homage. The great star had regained her regal status, indeed, surpassed it.

The supporting troupers in MILDRED are without reservation an expert team. Arden, who turned in a definitive job as Crawford's pal and remained the leading lady's friend long after making the film, thought the script for MILDRED PIERCE was "fairly interesting," but, as she stated in her autobiography, *Three Phases of Eve*: "I would never have guessed that it would bring Crawford her only Oscar and me a nomination in the supporting category, and become a classic." Peak scene among afficionados of Saint Joan: Mildred calls the police. Unforgettable.

MILESTONES

1975 195m c/bw   ★★★
Drama
Stone

Grace Paley (*Helen*), David C. Stone (*Joe*), John Douglas (*John*), Laurel Berger (*Laurel*), Mary Chapelle (*Mama*), Bobby Buechler (*Jamie*), Liz Dear (*Liz*), Jay Foley (*Terry*), Suey Hagadorn (*Suey*), Harvey Quintal (*Harvey*)

p, David C. Stone, Barbara Stone; d, Robert Kramer, John Douglas; w, Robert Kramer, John Douglas; ph, John Douglas, Robert Kramer; ed, Robert Kramer, John Douglas

A huge independent undertaking by Robert Kramer and John Douglas. The film takes the audience on a journey across the United States, with characters interwoven through the film via their interrelationships. One couple travels state to state, bickering all the way. Another man tries to relate to his son, who is now on his own. The film also focuses on Vietnam vets and ex-radicals in their attempts to adjust to the changing times. The film works well because the directors avoid heavy-handedness and allow the audience to judge the characters. An insightful examination of the transition from the 1960s to the 1970s.

MILKY WAY, THE

(LA VIA LATTEA)
1969 105m c   ★★★½
Religious   PG/A
Greenwich/Fraia   (France/Italy)

Paul Frankeur (*Pierre*), Laurent Terzieff (*Jean*), Alain Cuny (*Man with Cape*), Edith Scob (*Virgin Mary*), Bernard Verley (*Jesus*), Francois Maistre (*French Priest*), Claude Cerval (*Brigadier*), Muni (*Mother Superior*), Julien Bertheau (*Maitre d'Hotel*), Ellen Bahl (*Mme. Garnier*)

p, Serge Silberman; d, Luis Bunuel; w, Luis Bunuel, Jean-Claude Carriere; ph, Christian Matras (Eastmancolor); ed, Louisette Hautecoeur; m, Luis Bunuel; art d, Pierre Guffroy; cos, Jacqueline Guyot, Francoise Tournafond

The most overtly religious film in Luis Bunuel's *oeuvre*, THE MILKY WAY is an allegorical journey through the history of Catholicism that follows a pair of travelers—the somewhat pious Pierre (Paul Frankeur) and the younger, more skeptical Jean (Laurent Terzieff)—as they undertake a pilgrimage across Spain to the tomb of Saint James. En route, they meet any number of religious figures, including a caped, God-like figure (Alain Cuny) with a midget, the Virgin Mary (Edith Scob), Jesus (Bernard Verley), a bishop (Jean-Claude Carriere, Bunuel's screenwriting collaborator), a sadistic Marquis (Michel Piccoli), a prostitute (Delphine Seyrig), and even the Devil (Pierre Clementi). This comical film will make any viewer question his beliefs—from religious fanatic to rabid atheist. While it may seem strange that Bunuel, a lifetime surrealist and professed atheist, would produce such a work, the filmmaker remarked in his autobiography, *My Last Sigh*, that THE MILKY WAY "evokes the search for truth, as well as the necessity of abandoning it as soon as you've found it." If that doesn't shed some light on Bunuel's intent, then perhaps his most famously ambiguous statement will: "Thank God I'm an atheist."

MILLER'S CROSSING

1990 115m c   ★★★★
Crime   R/18
Circle Films/Ted and Jim Pedas-Ben Berenholtz-Bill Durkin

Gabriel Byrne *(Tom Reagan)*, Marcia Gay Harden *(Verna)*, John Turturro *(Bernie Bernbaum)*, Jon Polito *(Johnny Caspar)*, J.E. Freeman *(Eddie Dane)*, Albert Finney *(Leo)*, Mike Starr *(Frankie)*, Al Mancini *(Tic-Tac)*, Richard Woods *(Mayor Dale Levander)*, Thomas Toner *(O'Doole)*

p, Ethan Coen; d, Joel Coen; w, Joel Coen, Ethan Coen; ph, Barry Sonnenfeld (Duart Color); ed, Michael R. Miller; m, Carter Burwell; prod d, Dennis Gassner; art d, Leslie McDonald; fx, Image Engineering, Peter Chesney; cos, Richard Hornung

The plot isn't the main event in MILLER'S CROSSING. After all, guns, booze, broads—they're timeworn gangster film cliches. Fortunately, this offering from Joel and Ethan Coen is anything but cliched.

A gang war is brewing in the anonymous town run by Leo (Albert Finney), a tough but sentimental Irishman, and his acerbic right-hand man, Tom Reagan (Gabriel Byrne). The Italians are the new kids on the block, and they're sensitive about it. Johnny Caspar (Jon Polito) is particularly thin-skinned, and he's mad as hell because small-time chiseler Bernie Bernbaum (John Turturro) is cutting in on his gambling action. Caspar wants Bernie murdered, but Leo won't hear of it; he's promised Bernie's tough-as-nails sister, Verna (Marcia Gay Harden), that he'll look out for her brother. Verna is the love of Leo's life, but she's also sleeping with Tom. Meanwhile, Tom, a drinker and gambler, is deeply in debt to his bookie, who's putting the screws to him. When Leo and Tom have a falling out over Verna, Tom offers his services to Caspar. Forced to prove his loyalty by killing Bernie, Tom fakes the murder, only to have Bernie turn around and attempt to blackmail him.

MILLER'S CROSSING represents a remarkable advance over the first two Coen brothers efforts, BLOOD SIMPLE and RAISING ARIZONA. Though the nature of their style changes from film to film, the Coens are consistently stylish: BLOOD SIMPLE was new wave noir; RAISING ARIZONA gave new meaning to the term larger than life. MILLER'S CROSSING is no exception. Richly colored and painstakingly composed, its images are punchy without being cartoonish.

What differentiates MILLER'S CROSSING from the Coens' first two films is its astonishing emotional complexity. Neither less witty nor less ironic than their earlier work, it resonates long after the novelty of its presentation has worn off. MILLER'S CROSSING tackles big issues—the nature of love, loyalty, friendship, and responsibility—without putting any of them in the foreground. Never does the film resort to didacticism. Still more surprising, the Coens resisted the Hollywood dictum that the protagonist must be sympathetic.

Byrne's Tom is a man of principles, smart, loyal and willing to gratify his own ambitions through Leo. But he's also a drunk, and he gambles compulsively. What's more, he sleeps with Verna and murders her brother. Tom has his reasons, and they're eminently reasonable, but what's remarkable is that the Coens trust their audience to understand him. They also assume moviegoers can follow a fairly convoluted plot devoid of deadening expository interludes, and they proceed from a position of absolute confidence in the evocative power of language.

After opening in the woods, with a man's fedora swirling in the breeze, the film cuts to a lengthy scene in which Caspar propounds his self-serving theory of ethics. A study in contrast—between silence and sound, light-filled woods and darkened rooms, action and verbiage—these two scenes introduce the film's major themes with an economy and style that the Coens maintain throughout the film.

MILLER'S CROSSING takes place in an artificial world constructed largely from the mythology of other movies, but its internal structure is so seamless that the film possess its own veracity. While several contemporary filmmakers are capable of constructing a movie as well as Joel and Ethan Coen—Martin Scorsese, Francis Ford Coppola, Jonathan Demme, and Spike Lee come immediately to mind—none of them can do it better.

MILLION, THE
(LE MILLION)
1931 83m bw ★★★★★
Comedy
Tobis (France)

Annabella *(Beatrice)*, Rene Lefevre *(Michel)*, Paul Olivier *("Father Tulipe" Crochard, a Gangster)*, Louis Allibert *(Prosper)*, Constantin Stroesco *(Sopranelli)*, Odette Talazac *(La Chanteuse)*, Vanda Greville *(Vanda)*, Raymond Cordy *(Taxi Driver)*

d, Rene Clair; w, Rene Clair (based on a musical play by Georges Berr, M. Guillemaud); ph, Georges Perinal, Georges Raulet; m, Armand Bernard, Philippe Pares, Georges Van Parys; art d, Lazare Meerson

Perhaps Rene Clair's most appealing film, and an extremely inventive one in the bargain. One of the string of superb films this fine French director made in the 1920s and 1930s, this is a nonstop comic chase through a studio set of Paris (designed by Clair's collaborator Lazare Meerson) to find a winning lottery ticket left in the pocket of a discarded jacket. Generally considered Clair's masterpiece (though A NOUS LA LIBERTE also has its supporters), the film is a sustained comic delight. As in the previous UNDER THE ROOFS OF PARIS and his subsequent A NOUS LA LIBERTE, Clair creates a wholly original world of song and sound that completely defies realism. He also manages quite a few satiric touches which belie his background in the Surrealist and Dada movements of the 1920s. Although such uses of sound effects as the noise of a football game dubbed in over one particularly frantic chase have since been repeated, they still enchant today. The camerawork too, is amazingly supple for a period in which bulky sound recording devices turned so many films into stagy bores, and the story simply floats along as a result. Annabella and Rene Lefevre are immensely winning in the leading roles, and are backed by a solid supporting cast. One of the truly great early sound films, it was an international success with both critics and public.

MILLIONAIRE, THE
1931 82m bw ★★★
Comedy/Drama /U
WB

George Arliss *(James Alden)*, Evalyn Knapp *(Barbara Alden)*, David Manners *(Bill Merrick)*, James Cagney *(Schofield, Insurance Salesman)*, Bramwell Fletcher *(Carter Andrews)*, Florence Arliss *(Mrs. Alden)*, Noah Beery, Sr. *(Peterson)*, Ivan Simpson *(Dr. Harvey)*, Sam Hardy *(McCoy)*, J. Farrell MacDonald *(Dan Lewis)*

d, John G. Adolfi; w, Julien Josephson, Maude Howell, Booth Tarkington (based on the story "Idle Hands" by Earl Derr Biggers); ph, James Van Trees; ed, Owen Marks

An interesting comedy-drama that was remade 16 years later (and not nearly as well) as THAT WAY WITH WOMEN. Arliss is a Henry Ford type, the immensely wealthy and overworked head of his own enormous automobile company. His wife, Arliss (his real wife as well), wishes he'd slow down. Cagney, a brash, fast-talking insurance man, makes a pitch in one scene for

Arliss's business. The old fella is just this side of total exhaustion and considering the advice of his doctor, J.C. Nugent, to take off a half-year or find himself pushing up daisies. Cagney tells Arliss that if he stays inactive and has no reason to get up in the morning, one day he just won't get up. Arliss can't stand not doing anything, so he masquerades as a poor man and buys a half-interest in a gas station with Manners, who just happens to be in love with Arliss' daughter, Knapp, but doesn't know that his crotchety partner is one of the richest men around. Manners works at the station while studying architecture. Later, when Manners comes to call and asks for the hand of Knapp, he is shocked to see that his partner is her father. It's all improbable, but so what? The young lovers get together, the old man realizes that he can be happy despite being rich, everyone winds up smiling, and, after all, how much more can be asked of a movie? The screenplay is sharp and pointed and may have sired the television show of the same name, although no credit seems to have been given to Biggers on the program which starred Marvin Miller. Biggers is the same man who invented Charlie Chan, who first appeared in films in 1926. Simpson, a longtime pal of Arliss, usually worked in the same movies with him and this time plays the magnate's valet.

MILLIONS LIKE US
1943 103m bw   ★★★
Drama
Gainsborough (U.K.)   /U

Eric Portman (*Charlie Forbes*), Patricia Roc (*Celia Crowson*), Gordon Jackson (*Fred Blake*), Anne Crawford (*Jennifer Knowles*), Joy Shelton (*Phyllis Crowson*), Megs Jenkins (*Gwen Price*), Terry Randall (*Annie Earnshaw*), Basil Radford (*Charters*), Naunton Wayne (*Caldicott*), Moore Marriott (*Jim Crowson*)

p, Edward Black; d, Frank Launder, Sidney Gilliat; w, Frank Launder, Sidney Gilliat; ph, Jack Cox, Roy Fogwell

Roc is an aircraft factory worker during WWII who falls in love with and marries air gunner Jackson. Though Jackson is killed in action, the film never becomes melodramatic. Everything is staged and acted so simply and to the point that the action seems realistic, perhaps because the film was shot at the height of the war when all involved in the production were directly connected to the conflict raging around them in a way their American counterparts were not. The film was reissued in 1947.

MIN AND BILL
1930 66m bw   ★★★★
Drama/Comedy
MGM

Marie Dressler (*Min Divot*), Wallace Beery (*Bill*), Dorothy Jordan (*Nancy Smith*), Marjorie Rambeau (*Bella Pringle*), Donald Dillaway (*Dick Cameron*), DeWitt Jennings (*Groot*), Russell Hopton (*Alec Johnson*), Frank McGlynn, Sr. (*Mr. Southard*), Gretta Gould (*Mrs. Southard*), Jack Pennick (*Merchant Seaman*)

d, George Hill; w, Frances Marion, Marion Jackson (based on the novel *Dark Star* by Lorna Moon); ph, Harold Wenstrom; ed, Basil Wrangell; art d, Cedric Gibbons; cos, Rene Hubert

One of the most unlikely romantic duos ever to stroll across a screen was the pairing of 62-year-old Marie Dressler and big-bellied, 55-year-old Wallace Beery. Yet they made such a lovable couple in MIN AND BILL that they were teamed again in a sequel, TUGBOAT ANNIE, in 1933, and acted together in DINNER AT EIGHT that same year. Although MIN AND BILL is a heartfelt drama, most viewers recall its hilarious comedy

sequences and the noisy relationship between Dressler and Beery. Dressler is the rough-and-tumble owner of a cheap waterfront hotel on the California coast; Beery is the local fisherman who is the object of her affections when Dressler isn't doting on Dorothy Jordan, a sweet young girl whose mother deserted her several years previously. Dressler minces no words with the girl, but Jordan realizes that the older woman is the only person who has ever cared deeply about her. Nevertheless truant officers want Jordan living in a better environment and attending school regularly. Furthermore, local prohibition officers have been observing the cafe and appear ready to close it up. In a tearful scene, Jordan reluctantly leaves Dressler to live with the school's principal (Frank McGlynn) and his wife (Gretta Gould). To make matters worse, Jordan's drunken, slatternly mother (Marjorie Rambeau) appears on the scene, but Dressler persuades her to leave town so as not to complicate Jordan's life further. In the meantime, Dressler scrapes up enough money to take Jordan out of the principal's home and sends her to an exclusive boarding school, where the girl falls in love with the wealthy Donald Dillaway (in his film debut). In no time, the two are talking about marriage; however, when Rambeau learns that her daughter is marrying into money, the unscrupulous woman tells Dressler that she wants a share of the booty or she'll resort to blackmail, revealing her daughter's sordid lineage. During an argument, Rambeau burns Dressler's face with a hot iron, forcing Dressler to pull a gun and shoot Rambeau. A sailor who dislikes Dressler (Hank Bell) goes to the cops, and as Jordan and Dillaway sail off on their honeymoon, Dressler is taken away by the police. Dressler won an Oscar for her role in MIN AND BILL over such sexpots as Marlene Dietrich for MOROCCO, Irene Dunne for CIMARRON, Ann Harding for HOLIDAY, and Norma Shearer for A FREE SOUL (the last of whom had won the year before for THE DIVORCEE and presented Dressler with the statuette). A huge star in the silent era, Dressler watched her career wane until she made a triumphant return in ANNA CHRISTIE earlier in 1930. As a result of her success in MIN AND BILL, she was to spend her last years as the biggest star at MGM. In 1940, six years after Dressler's death, a second sequel to MIN AND BILL, TUGBOAT ANNIE RIDES AGAIN, was released with Rambeau in the Dressler role.

MINISTRY OF FEAR
1945 84m bw   ★★★★
Mystery/Spy
Paramount

Ray Milland (*Stephen Neale*), Marjorie Reynolds (*Carla Hilfe*), Carl Esmond (*Willi Hilfe*), Hillary Brooke (*Mrs. Bellane*), Percy Waram (*Inspector Prentice*), Dan Duryea (*Cost/Travers*), Alan Napier (*Dr. Forrester*), Erskine Sanford (*Mr. Rennit*), Thomas Louden (*Mr. Newland*), Aminta Dyne (*1st Mrs. Bellaire*)

p, Seton I. Miller; d, Fritz Lang; w, Seton I. Miller (based on the novel by Graham Greene); ph, Henry Sharp; ed, Archie Marshek; m, Victor Young; art d, Hans Dreier, Hal Pereira

Uncertainty and fear of the unknown are the hallmarks of this classic film noir by master director Lang, which, until the last revelation, is guaranteed to puzzle and chill the viewer. Milland gives a spellbinding performance as a man recently released from an insane asylum who finds that the real madness is all around him in the outside world. Milland has been an asylum inmate for two years for ostensibly murdering his wife. She was ill, and he brought poison home to perform euthanasia but could not bring himself to go through with it; while his back was turned she took the fatal dose and he was convicted nevertheless. But the terrors of the asylum are nothing compared to the wartime England into which Milland steps. He waits for a train to London and then follows a crowd to a local carnival sponsored by a Nazi front organization called "Mothers of the Free Nations." He is mistaken for a Nazi agent, and it is arranged for him to win a large cake, which he carries back to the depot. As he turns to get on the train, he hears the ominous sound of a tapping cane, and then, through the thick cloud of steam from the train's engines emerges a blind man, Eustace Wyatt, who joins Milland in his compartment. Milland offers him a piece of cake, which he takes with groping fingers. (The camera shows in close-up the vacant stare of Wyatt, but the so-called blind man suddenly focuses, for a brief, chilling moment, on Milland, then resumes his sightless look.) Wyatt begins to crumble the cake in his hands, until it goes to little pieces. He suddenly grabs the cake, leaves the compartment, and runs wildly across a marsh, where he is blown to pieces by a bomb planted in the cake. Milland, who has been mechanically chasing the man, stands staring in horror. Once in London, Milland goes to the "Mothers of the Free Nations" organization, where he is met by sympathetic Reynolds and Esmond, brother and sister. Esmond takes Milland to see Brooke, one of the sponsors of the carnival where he received the strange, exploding cake, to see if she can offer some kind of explanation. Dyne, a medium who told Milland's fortune at the carnival, is about to hold a seance at this time, and Milland is asked to participate. He does but is instantly accused by a so-called spirit voice of killing his wife. Before he can protest, a shot rings out and when the lights go on, another guest, Duryea, is found dead on the floor. Police arrive and accuse Milland of murdering the man. The medium in the room is not really the woman he first met at the fair, although she insists she is. She is Rita Johnson, not Dyne, which perplexes Milland no end. Before he can be arrested, Milland escapes. He briefly employs a seedy, middle-aged private detective, Sanford, a weird little man who drinks alcohol out of teacups and puffs on a stubby cigar. The eccentric detective is more trouble than help, especially when he gets himself killed. Fleeing the seance murder, Milland goes to the only person he knows, Reynolds. She takes him to a small London bookshop, where the owner agrees to hide him. In return, she asks that Milland deliver a suitcase full of books to Napier, but the hotel room to which he is directed is empty and the phone is dead. The hallway outside is strangely deserted. Milland begins to open the suitcase but his instincts suddenly tell him to leap aside. As he does, the suitcase goes off with a terrific explosion. Milland wakes in a hospital. He hears the creaking of a rocking chair and sees a man from the back all dressed in black. The man, Waram, is a Scotland Yard inspector, and he tells Milland he's wanted for murder. Milland tells him he doesn't know how the man at the seance was shot, and Waram tells him he doesn't know what he's talking about, that he's a suspect in the murder of private detective Sanford, adding: "They shouldn't have let you out of that asylum." Now Milland doubts even his memory, as well as the soundness of his own mind. Milland persuades police to go to the marsh where the blind man was blown up, and they accompany him to the site, where Milland finds—in a ruined shed in the marsh—some fragments of the cake and inside this a piece of microfilm. Upon examining this, police realize that it shows part of some important minefield charts. Now Milland and the police realize that they are dealing with enemy agents and they soon trace the Nazis to a haberdashery store. Milland and Waram pretend to be fitted for new suits and spot tailor Duryea, the man Milland was accused of murdering at the seance. Duryea goes to a phone and dials a number with a pair of lethal-looking scissors, telling his customer: "I think you'll find that when you've worn

it once the shoulders will settle." Next, knowing he is exposed, Duryea goes into a fitting room and drives the scissors into his stomach while standing before three mirrors. The telephone call is traced, however, to Esmond, and Duryea's message becomes clear to police: a suit delivered to Esmond contains microfilm in its lining. Milland gets to Esmond before the police and struggles with the Nazi agent, who is about to kill him when Reynolds, who really loves Milland, shoots her brother. But Nazi agents then attack the pair and drive them up onto the roof, where they hide in the darkness. The door leading to the roof is open, but Milland and Reynolds can see nothing but blackness on the stairway. They wait for their own grim ends. All is silence; then some slight movement is heard as the Nazi agents start to approach. There is a blaze of gunfire, then more silence. Suddenly, appearing on the roof are Scotland Yard detectives, not Nazis. Milland and Reynolds are saved.

The suspense in this thriller espionage yarn is terrific as Lang, ever the careful craftsman, shows only what is necessary to the confusing plot; the viewer sees only what Milland sees and is as perplexed as the hero. Like the fragments of an intricate crossword puzzle, Lang puts together one piece after another until the riddle is solved, but almost at the cost of Milland's life. The low-key lighting and moody cinematography by Sharp are perfectly suited to the chilling tale. Never before did Lang present such an elaborate structure in any film, with a Kafka-like approach wherein shadow, silence, and normally pedestrian movements, shown out of context, take on the air of the sinister. There is a pervasive atmosphere of doom to the entire film which the director attempted to relieve with a brief epilog showing Milland and Reynolds driving to their honeymoon in a world bright with sunshine. Reynolds talks about their wedding and mentions a wedding cake. Milland shudders and says: "Cake? No! No cake!" Milland is excellent as the victimized man who endures the tortures of most of the film before he realizes that he's been sane all along. Lang had accepted the directorial chore of this film before reading the script. He received a call from his agent and, as soon as he learned the film would be based upon Graham Greene's novel, he accepted this assignment. But he did not like the script written by producer Miller and was much pained years later when he viewed the film on television "where it was cut to pieces."

MINNIE AND MOSKOWITZ

1971 114m c   ★★
Drama/Comedy   PG/
Universal

Gena Rowlands (Minnie Moore), Seymour Cassel (Seymour Moskowitz), Val Avery (Zelmo Swift), Tom Carey (Morgan Morgan), Katherine Cassavetes (Sheba Moskowitz), Elizabeth Deering (Girl), Elsie Ames (Florence), Lady Rowlands (Georgia Moore), Holly Near (Irish), Judith Roberts (Wife)

p, Al Ruban; d, John Cassavetes; w, John Cassavetes; ph, Arthur J. Ornitz, Alric Edens, Michael D. Margulies (Technicolor); ed, Robert Heffernan, Frederic Knudtson; cos, Helen Colvig

Having provided a starring vehicle for himself and colleagues Peter Falk and Ben Gazzara in 1970's HUSBANDS, director John Cassavetes showcased both his talented wife, Gena Rowlands, and frequent collaborator Seymour Cassel in MINNIE AND MOSKOWITZ the following year.

Minnie Moore (Rowlands) is a lonely former prom queen who's about to turn 40. She's been having an unsatisfactory affair with Jim (John Cassavetes), a married man, and spends the rest of her spare time time with Florence (Elsie Ames), her best friend and movie-going companion. Jim is cruel to Minnie, but she puts up with it until Jim's wife threatens suicide and he's forced to end the affair. They meet for a last time at the museum where Minnie works; he's brought his two kids with him, at the request of his wife, to corroborate the cessation of the affair.

Minnie, lonely and desperate for male companionship, accepts a blind date with Zelmo Swift (Val Avery), a noisy boor who never once notices Minnie's delicate condition. They have lunch at a restaurant, and Zelmo proposes marriage but Minnie, realizing that he's mentally unbalanced, demurs and tries to get away. In the parking lot Zelmo begins to harass Minnie, but this is witnessed by Seymour Moskowitz (Cassel), a thirtyish, aging hippy and parking lot attendant, who comes to her rescue. He gets Zelmo out of the picture, then gets Minnie into his pickup truck and rides away with her. In less than a minute, Moskowitz decides that he is madly in love with Minnie. She leaps out of the pickup truck, but Moskowitz follows her until she agrees to go on a date.

For 35 years, John Cassavetes held a unique position in American film, maintaining dual careers as a highly regarded actor in mainstream features and as a director of independent films which themselves explored the art of acting. With MINNIE AND MOSKOWITZ, Cassavetes took a break from the decidedly somber mood of FACES and HUSBANDS. Unfortunately, although the scenes of Rowlands and Cassel wandering from hot dog stand to hot dog stand are touching and funny, the film ultimately suffers from narrative aimlessness.

MIRACLE IN MILAN

(MIRACOLO A MILANO)
1951 100m bw ★★★★
Fantasy
ENIC (Italy)

Branduani Gianni (*Little Toto at Age 11*), Francesco Golisano (*Good Toto*), Paolo Stoppa (*Bad Rappi*), Emma Gramatica (*Old Lolatta*), Guglielmo Barnabo (*Mobbi, the Rich Man*), Brunella Bovo (*Little Edvige*), Anna Carena (*Signora Marta Altezzosa*), Alba Arnova (*The Statue*), Flora Cambi (*Unhappy Sweetheart*), Virgilio Riento (*Sergeant*)

p, Vittorio De Sica; d, Vittorio De Sica; w, Cesare Zavattini, Vittorio De Sica, Suso Cecchi D'Amico, Mario Chiari, Adolfo Franci (based on the story "Toto Il Buono" by Cesare Zavattini); ph, Aldo Graziati; ed, Eraldo Da Roma; m, Alessandro Cicognini; art d, Guido Fiorini; fx, Ned Mann

The writing-directing team of Cesare Zavattini and Vittorio De Sica produced this picture shortly after they received international acclaim for THE BICYCLE THIEF. Though not as popular as that masterwork, MIRACLE IN MILAN is an equally touching look into human nature that concentrates on the plight of the poor in post-WWII Italy. The story is essentially a fairy tale, packed with a strong moral implications. The Good Toto (Francesco Golisano), a young orphan, finds refuge in a colony of beggars and helps to organize them, generating happiness among the otherwise distressed members of the group. When a wealthy landowner decides to kick the beggars off his land, Toto is given a magic dove by a fairy. Not only are the landowner's attempts thwarted, but the magical powers of the dove also allow Toto to grant wishes to the beggars. Unable to deny them anything, he grants their greedy requests, until eventually the dove is stolen. As in other neo-realist films, the performers in MIRACLE IN MILAN are a combination of professional actors and actual denizens of the street, and all the players give realistic and humane portrayals. De Sica handles his fantastic material subtly and with simplicity, yielding an original mix of sharp satire and poetic fable that extended the limits of the neo-realist style.

MIRACLE MILE

1989 87m c ★★★½
Romance/Science Fiction R/15
Hemdale

Anthony Edwards (*Harry Washello*), Mare Winningham (*Julie Peters*), John Agar (*Ivan Peters*), Lou Hancock (*Lucy Peters*), Mykel T. Williamson (*Wilson*), Kelly Minter (*Charlotta*), Kurt Fuller, Danny De La Paz, Robert DoQui, Denise Crosby

p, John Daly, Derek Gibson; d, Steve DeJarnatt; w, Steve DeJarnatt; ph, Theo Van de Sande; ed, Stephen Semel, Kathie Weaver; m, Tangerine Dream; prod d, Claire Gaul, Jerry Casillas; cos, Shay Cunliffe

An uneven apocalyptic thriller from young writer/director Steve DeJarnatt. MIRACLE MILE begins harmlessly enough as Harry (Anthony Edwards), a shy young musician, falls in love at first sight with Julie (Mare Winningham). They set up a rendezvous for midnight, but Harry oversleeps and is several hours late. He tries to call Julie from a phone booth to apologize, but winds up talking to her answering machine. When the phone suddenly rings, Harry impulsively answers it. On the other end of the line is a desperate young soldier who works at a missile silo. Thinking he is talking to his father, the hysterical soldier announces that American nuclear missiles have been launched and only 70 minutes remain before the retaliatory strike hits. It is a tribute to DeJarnatt's skills that he is able to keep the audience dangling on a string of hope throughout MIRACLE MILE's grim proceedings. The quirky combination of dizzy romance and apocalyptic horror doesn't always work, but there's enough to keep you hooked until the. . . climax?

MIRACLE OF MORGAN'S CREEK, THE

1944 99m bw ★★★★★
Comedy /A
Paramount

Eddie Bracken (*Norval Jones*), Betty Hutton (*Trudy Kockenlocker*), Diana Lynn (*Emmy Kockenlocker*), Brian Donlevy (*Governor McGinty*), Akim Tamiroff (*The Boss*), Porter Hall (*Justice of the Peace*), Emory Parnell (*Mr. Tuerck*), Alan Bridge (*Mr. Johnson*), Julius Tannen (*Mr. Rafferty*), Victor Potel (*Newspaper Editor*)

p, Preston Sturges; d, Preston Sturges; w, Preston Sturges; ph, John Seitz; ed, Stuart Gilmore; m, Leo Shuken, Charles Bradshaw; art d, Hans Dreier, Ernst Fegte; cos, Edith Head

Miraculously mad masterpiece. The marvel of THE MIRACLE OF MORGAN'S CREEK is how the film ever got made in the first place. This onslaught against American morals in small towns, against the wartime romances of servicemen, against just about everything that the country held sacred during WWII was reckless, exaggerated, and very funny. Sturges at his irreverent best with his screenplay and direction of this most unlikely story. Hutton is a man-crazy blonde who lives in the tiny town of Morgan's Creek with her bitchy sister, Lynn, and her policeman father, Demarest. She allows herself to get just a tad careless during one wild and passionate night with a soldier, whom she thinks she may have married, and becomes pregnant. The soldier, who she recalls is named something like "Ratsky-Watsky," vanishes, and since being pregnant in a small town without being married is the worst thing that can happen in a girl's life, Hutton's sometime bank clerk boyfriend, Bracken, is tapped to be the father of whatever she's carrying. Bracken would love to be in the service but is too nervous to be inducted and sees spots before his eyes whenever he is under too much stress. Bracken dresses in a uniform (from WWI) to marry Hutton under another name, the one she opines belongs to the sire of her future progeny. In one mix-up after another, Bracken winds up being sought by authorities for impersonating a soldier, corrupting the morals of a minor, kidnapping, forgery, and bank robbery, and he has to get out of town in a hurry. It looks mighty bad for the young couple, and the only thing that can save them is a miracle. It does.

Every role is handled with deftness, and Sturges even gets in a few holdovers from an earlier success, THE GREAT McGINTY, by having Brian Donlevy and Akim Tamiroff stop by for a few well-chosen words. The idea of having squeaky-clean Hutton shown as a (shudder) girl with loose morals was a sensation that somehow eluded the censor's scissors. Some say that the plot managed to escape snipping because the picture was so funny that no one could take it seriously, but the truth is that this movie kept a tight grip on reality and that's what made it so hilarious. Hutton's enormous energy radiated in every frame, and Bracken and Demarest were never better.

Later that same year, Bracken was to repeat his comedic success under Sturges's baton with his work in HAIL THE CONQUERING HERO, another satirical barb at the mores of the day; he never came close to either film in any of his subsequent work. Bracken at first refused to play in another Hutton film, since he felt he was being used to build up her career at the expense of his own. Every time he went to see a film in which he appeared with Hutton, four or five of her singing numbers had been inserted into the film without his knowledge. When Sturges reassured Bracken that there would be no singing numbers for Hutton in THE MIRACLE OF MORGAN'S CREEK, Bracken finally agreed to appear in the film. Hutton went on to make several sensational musicals, including ANNIE GET YOUR GUN, before suffering an injury to her shoulder, then a series of personal problems. She was only 23 years old in THE MIRACLE OF MORGAN'S CREEK, and her youthful exuberance leapt off the screen and grabbed audiences' hearts. As early as 1942 Hutton was a Sturges groupie, begging him to write a role for her. He wrote this one, which was perfect for the boisterous blonde. Sturges, who had begun his movie career as a screenwriter, was one of the most influential director-writers of the 1940s, with one hit after another, including THE GREAT McGINTY, CHRISTMAS IN JULY, THE LADY EVE, SULLIVAN'S TRAVELS, THE PALM BEACH STORY, HAIL THE CONQUERING HERO, THE GREAT MOMENT, MAD WEDNESDAY, UNFAITHFULLY YOURS, and THE BEAUTIFUL BLONDE FROM BASHFUL BEND. Sturges earned an Oscar nomination for his screenplay for this film, giving him a double nomination in that category since he was also nominated for his script for HAIL THE CONQUERING HERO. MIRACLE AT MORGAN'S CREEK was (sort of) remade by Paramount in 1958 as ROCK-A-BYE BABY.

MIRACLE ON 34TH STREET

1947   96m   bw   ★★★½
Fantasy   /U
FOX

Maureen O'Hara (Doris Walker), John Payne (Fred Gailey), Edmund Gwenn (Kris Kringle), Gene Lockhart (Judge Henry X. Harper), Natalie Wood (Susan Walker), Porter Hall (Mr. Sawyer), William Frawley (Charles Halloran), Jerome Cowan (Thomas Mara), Philip Tonge (Mr. Shellhammer), James Seay (Dr. Pierce)

p, William Perlberg; d, George Seaton; w, George Seaton (based on a story by Valentine Davies); ph, Charles Clarke, Lloyd Ahern; ed, Robert Simpson; m, Cyril J. Mockridge; art d, Richard Day, Richard Irvine; fx, Fred Sersen

A touch labored but lovable. THE MIRACLE ON 34TH STREET opens during Manhattan's Christmas Parade as Macy's executive Doris Walker (Maureen O'Hara) finds the Santa Claus for the store float so drunk he can't stand up. Chiding Doris for employing such a derelict is a kindly, white-bearded man who, when she asks his name, tells her it's "Kris Kringle." Ignoring this, she pleads with him to replace the drunk, and he proves such a crowd-pleaser that she hires him as Macy's resident Santa for the holiday rush. This sets in motion a series of events in which Kris touches the lives of many, teaching them a lot about faith and the true meaning of Christmas. Among those touched are Doris, her sophisticated little girl, Susan (Natalie Wood), who thinks the very idea of Santa Claus is ridiculous, Doris's suitor Fred Gailey (John Payne), and dozens of Macy's customers who are pleasantly surprised when Kris directs them to competitors to get the gifts they seek. Unfortunately all are not smitten with this kindly man, particularly the store's amateur psychologist whose contention that Kris is unbalanced leads to a trial in which the court must decide the weighty matter of whether or not there is a Santa Claus. Gwenn won an Oscar for his role, and for many, his charming, endearing performance has been identified with the spirit of the Christmas season ever since the completion of this sentimental production. Wood is wonderful in MIRACLE; it's interesting to ponder what happened along the way to transform her into a usually synthetic actress.

MIRACLE WOMAN, THE

1931   90m   bw   ★★★½
Religious
Columbia

Barbara Stanwyck (Florence "Faith" Fallon), David Manners (John Carson), Sam Hardy (Bob Hornsby), Beryl Mercer (Mrs. Higgins), Russell Hopton (Sam Welford), Charles Middleton (Simpson), Eddie Boland (Collins), Thelma Hill (Gussie), Aileen Carlyle (Violet), Al Stewart (Brown)

p, Harry Cohn; d, Frank Capra; w, Dorothy Howell, Jo Swerling (based on the play "Bless You Sister" by John Meehan, Robert Riskin); ph, Joseph Walker; ed, Maurice Wright; art d, Max Parker

The subject of phony evangelists is a tricky one, entailing the risk of offending believers. Barbara Stanwyck is convincing as the daughter of a pastor who has just been discharged from his parish and, as a result, has died of a broken heart. Stanwyck goes in front of the congregation and delivers a stinging denunciation of their hypocrisy. Sam Hardy, a two-bit promoter and con man, realizing that Stanwyck is mighty handy with her mouth, talks her into becoming an evangelist. Soon she is one of the most important pulpit pounders in the land, and, caught up in the furor of phony cripples "healed" and testifying to the pigeons, Stanwyck is too successful to stop. David Manners, a blind ex-pilot who is about to kill himself by leaping out a window, hears Stanwyck preaching on the radio and decides that she might be able to cure him. He goes to the tent and volunteers to step inside a lion's cage. His faith brings him closer to Stanwyck, and she is soon in love with him. Russell Hopton, the press agent for the group, wants a larger piece of the spoils, but Hardy won't hear of it and knocks Hopton off. Helped by his love for Stanwyck, Manners overcomes his shyness enough to declare himself through his ventriloquist's dummy. When Hardy sees that Manners and Stanwyck are getting close, he arranges a trip to the Holy Land to get her away from the blind lad. Stanwyck is beginning to understand that her faith healing is a lot of nonsense and that the people whom she has really healed just needed something—anything—to believe in. All of her ravings don't help Manners recover his sight. (To the credit of the authors and director, there is no miracle recovery for the blind man.) Hardy sets the tent ablaze as Stanwyck is about to confess to all that she is a sham. Later Stanwyck, who has become a member of the Salvation Army, receives a wire from Manners, opening the possibility that the two young people will get together. Riskin, who became Frank Capra's favorite screenwriter, went on to write such classics as IT HAPPENED ONE NIGHT, MR. DEEDS GOES TO TOWN, LOST HORIZON, YOU CAN'T TAKE IT WITH YOU and and MEET JOHN DOE. THE MIRACLE WOMAN was an expensive film for its day, and every penny shows on the screen. There's hardly a wasted word or frame of film in the movie. It is a fine film, although it would have been even better had Capra and the writers had the freedom to attack their subject with sabers instead of pins.

MIRACLE WORKER, THE

1962   106m   bw   ★★★★★
Biography   /X
Playfilms

Anne Bancroft (*Annie Sullivan*), Patty Duke (*Helen Keller*), Victor Jory (*Capt. Keller*), Inga Swenson (*Kate Keller*), Andrew Prine (*James Keller*), Kathleen Comegys (*Aunt Ev*), Beah Richards (*Viney*), Jack Hollander (*Mr. Anagnos*), Peggy Burke (*Helen at Age 7*), Mindy Sherwood (*Helen at Age 5*)

p, Fred Coe; d, Arthur Penn; w, William Gibson (based on the play by William Gibson and the book *The Story of My Life* by Helen Keller); ph, Ernesto Caparros; ed, Aram Avakian; m, Laurence Rosenthal; art d, George Jenkins, Mel Bourne; cos, Ruth Morley

An amazing work, with Arthur Penn repeating his Broadway triumph, directing Duke and Bancroft, the two stage leads. This remarkable story of Helen Keller, one of the 20th century's great individuals, began as a book by Keller, then became a play on Broadway in October 1959, from the script by William Gibson. When the time came to make the film, Penn, Gibson, and producer Coe insisted that Bancroft and Duke be retained, with resulting Oscars for both stars. Duke had riveted Broadway audiences with the role as Keller, and, at age 16, became the youngest recipient of the Best Supporting Actress Oscar. (In 1973, Tatum O'Neal eclipsed that achievement by winning the award at age 10 for PAPER MOON.)

THE MIRACLE WORKER is a powerful picture, even as the credits roll. Duke is groping, lost and angry in her silent world when Bancroft arrives in Tuscumbia, Alabama, on a mission to teach the girl how to communicate through sign language. The task seems impossible, since Duke is blind as well as deaf. Bancroft, we learn, was blind at birth and still must wear very thick glasses in order to see images. Her own life had been brutalized by many years in institutions and the loss of the one person she cared about, a crippled brother who died young. Bancroft senses that the only way she can make any progress with Duke is to separate the child from her doting mother, Swenson, and her overbearing father, Jory.

The film is a harrowing, painfully honest, sometimes violent journey, astonishingly acted and rendered. Penn and cinematographer Caparros use short dissolves to great advantage, and Rosenthal's score heightens every nuance of the drama. The interiors were shot in New York and the exteriors in New Jersey,

which doubled for Alabama. The eight-minute sequence featuring a physical fight between Bancroft and Duke as the teacher attempts to teach the pupil some manners stands as one of the most electrifying and honest ever committed to film. What is most incredible about the film is Penn's ability to get performances out of his two leads that feel totally fresh. The rest of the cast perform their roles flawlessly.

In real life, Keller had lost her sight and hearing at the age of 19 months. Alexander Graham Bell asked the Perkins Institution (founded in 1829) to send someone to work with the child, and they assigned 26-year-old Sullivan, who arrived in Alabama and began her teaching on March 2, 1887. After the first breakthrough, the child began to read by feeling the words on raised cardboard and then made her own sentences by arranging the letters in a frame. In 1904, Keller graduated magna cum laude from Radcliffe College. She learned how to speak at the Horace Mann School for the Deaf in Boston by feeling the position of the tongue and lips of others with her fingers. She began to lip-read by putting her fingers on the lips of others while the words were being tapped out on her hand by an interpreter. In 1902, her book *The Story of My Life* was published, followed by another book, *Optimism*. Keller began lecturing in 1913 to raise funds for the American Foundation for the Blind, and Sullivan stayed with Keller until the teacher died in 1936. In 1920, Keller joined with Clarence Darrow, Upton Sinclair, Jane Addams, Norman Thomas, Felix Frankfurter, and others to form the American Civil Liberties Union (ACLU). She spent the rest of her life in the service of the handicapped and died in 1968. The rest of her life would make a wonderful movie. Unfortunately, the only sequel to THE MIRACLE WORKER thus far was a dismal flop—a stage play years later called "Monday after the Miracle," written by Gibson and starring Jane Alexander as Sullivan and Karen Allen as Keller.

In an hilarious Hollywood footnote, Joan Crawford picked up Bancroft's Oscar as the actress was working on Broadway at the time and could not attend the Academy ceremonies. It was understood that Crawford positioned herself to accept for absent Best Actress nominees in a successful attempt to upstage rival Bette Davis, nominated for WHATEVER HAPPENED TO BABY JANE?.

MIRAGE

1965   108m   bw   ★★½
Mystery   /18
Universal

Gregory Peck (*David Stillwell*), Diane Baker (*Sheila*), Walter Matthau (*Ted Caselle*), Kevin McCarthy (*Josephson*), Jack Weston (*Lester*), Leif Erickson (*Maj. Crawford*), Walter Abel (*Charles Calvin*), George Kennedy (*Willard*), Robert H. Harris (*Dr. Broden*), Anne Seymour (*Frances Calvin*)

p, Harry Keller; d, Edward Dmytryk; w, Peter Stone (based on the novel *Fallen Angel* by Walter Ericson); ph, Joseph MacDonald; ed, Ted J. Kent; m, Quincy Jones; art d, Alexander Golitzen, Frank Arrigo; cos, Jean Louis

MIRAGE is a mystery in the truest sense because it is just as baffling at the end as at the beginning. The film is held together by the firm direction of Dmytryk and a good performance by Peck. It was shot on location in New York City, so it is a visual feast if not an intellectual one. During an unexplained blackout at a major Gotham skyscraper, Abel, a prominent man of peace, falls out of a 27th-story window to his death. Peck races down the stairwells (the elevators are out of commission) to the street below. When he emerges, he is met by several people who know him, including Baker. When he reenters the building, he is stunned to find that the offices and business he recalled being there, aren't there at all. He is confused, goes to his apartment, and is met by Weston, who holds a gun on him, insisting that they must see a man Weston refers to as "the Major." Peck knocks out Weston and goes straight to the police to explain his plight. They listen but don't believe a word of it, as he cannot provide them with even the most mundane information about his own life, like his birthday. Peck thinks he may be going mad, so he visits psychiatrist Harris, who refuses to get involved because the story sounds fishy and might involve the frightened shrink with the cops. One detective, Matthau, believes Peck is telling the truth, but he is soon murdered by unknown killers. Further, Peck is now being tailed by Weston and Kennedy, two gunmen who are intent on finding out what Peck is up to, even though Peck himself has no idea of that. Peck returns to Harris, and they begin to work out Peck's problem together. Their conclusion is that Peck is a physiochemist who lost his memory after he saw his friend, Abel, fall to his death. They also deduce that Peck had discovered a new way to neutralize radiation and had taken the findings to Abel, who had wanted to bring it to his associate, Erickson, a tycoon. When Peck refused to give the discovery to anyone for business reasons (preferring to give it to the world as a donation), Abel attempted to take the formula away from Peck by force as Peck was burning the paper on which it was written. In his zealousness to get the formula, Abel slipped and went out the window. It all comes back to Peck in a flash, and he goes to Erickson's office to confront him. When Peck's life is threatened by the shadowy businessman (Erickson's alliance with the supposedly peaceful Abel is also not firmly demonstrated), Peck is saved by Baker, who walks in and out of scenes with aplomb and no rhyme or reason.

Though the picture flits around like a tsetse fly in Upper Volta, it is still fun to watch—most of the time. Screenwriter Stone (who also wrote CHARADE and cowrote FATHER GOOSE just before this assignment) may have bitten off more than he could chew with this adaptation from Ericson's original material. There are no questions answered and no cogent arguments to drive the film forward from scene to scene. This is in sharp contrast to the Hitchcock-type stories Stone and Ericson were likely attempting to emulate. Peck is good as the enigmatic protagonist who is seldom actually threatened except by his own self-doubt. Matthau does well in his brief bit as the detective, but he isn't around long enough to be appreciated. Dmytryk, a vastly underrated director, brought forth another one of his inventive techniques with this film. To show flashbacks, he discarded the usual oil dissolves in which the effect is an undulating, out-of-focus image to suggest dream or memory sequences. He instead went to straight cuts touched off with a short lead-in line, and audiences still grasped the sequence of events. The technique has been used ever since, although not always effectively. Remade by James Goldstone as JIGSAW.

MISERY

1990 107m c   ★★½
Horror   R/18
Castle Rock/Nelson

James Caan (*Paul Sheldon*), Kathy Bates (*Annie Wilkes*), Richard Farnsworth (*Buster, Sheriff*), Frances Sternhagen (*Virginia*), Lauren Bacall (*Marcia Sindell*), Graham Jarvis (*Libby*), Jerry Potter (*Pete*), Tom Brunelle (*Anchorman*), June Christopher (*Anchorwoman*), Wendy Bowers (*Waitress*)

p, Rob Reiner, Andrew Scheinman, Steve Nicolaides, Jeffrey Stott; d, Rob Reiner; w, William Goldman (based on the novel by Stephen King); ph, Barry Sonnenfeld; ed, Robert Leighton; m, Marc Shaiman; prod d, Norman Garwood; art d, Mark Mansbridge; fx, Phil Cory, KNB EFX Group; cos, Gloria Gresham

In the "Kill the Bitch" tradition of FATAL ATTRACTION, this adaptation of Stephen King's misogynist fable about a "serious" (male) author trapped by his own "frivolous" (female) commercial creation isn't quite satisfying either as a flat-out horror screamer or a psychological thriller. Curiously, it derails itself on a combination of a lack of conviction behind the camera and a show-stopping performance in front of the camera.

It's doubtful anyone but the most diehard fans would actually want to read a "serious" novel by King. But King, when writing from his own solid-gold bondage in the horror genre, retains his genius for physicalizing subconscious fears. And Paul Sheldon (James Caan) has a fan in Annie Wilkes (Kathy Bates) who is willing to die hard for him. Trouble is, she wants to take him with her. At first, Wilkes is an angel of mercy, rescuing Sheldon from a car wreck in the midst of a Colorado blizzard. Sheldon, the creator of the fabulously successful romance-novel heroine Misery Chastain, has just killed her off in the final book of the series and gone on to complete his first serious novel, which he is delivering to his agent when his car runs off a remote mountain road. Severely injured, with both legs broken, he becomes Wilkes' unwilling, though not uncomfortable guest. Wilkes is a former nurse who expertly splints his legs while stroking his ego with her worshipful admiration for the man and his work. In return, Sheldon lets her sneak a peak at his newest book. And that's where the trouble starts. Annie has an extreme reaction, bordering on hysteria, to the gutter language in Sheldon's new work, an autobiographical novel about the gritty lives of ghetto street kids. And much worse is yet to come when Annie gets through her just-published copy of the latest and last "Misery" novel. Having lived vicariously through the character since her invention, Annie becomes livid at the tragic ending of the new installment. She, or rather, God decides, "speaking" directly to Annie, to help Sheldon purge himself of his unhealthy impulse to turn serious novelist and to set him back on the course of his true calling. After forcing Sheldon to put the match to his new manuscript, she sits him at a table with his assignment from above to resurrect Misery Chastain and write a new final chapter that has the heroine finding happiness. What gradually becomes apparent to Sheldon is that Misery's final chapter will also be his. Sheldon confirms his suspicions when, getting out of his room when Annie is away from the house, he discovers that she is a serial killer of some repute, and more than a match for Sheldon's anxious agent (Lauren Bacall) and the wily local sheriff (Richard Farnsworth) who bring the state police in on the search for the missing author.

Not surprisingly for the director of the comedies THIS IS SPINAL TAP, THE SURE THING, and WHEN HARRY MET SALLY, as well as an earlier, non-horror, King adaptation, STAND BY ME, Rob Reiner is clearly more comfortable with the humor and humanity than the gory horror in King's grisly tale. The script by William Goldman (BUTCH CASSIDY AND THE SUNDANCE KID, ALL THE PRESIDENT'S MEN) is also at its strongest early on when Sheldon faces off in a test of artistic mettle against the toughest editor of his life in Wilkes. As a result, when the horror comes, it feels forced, unoriginal, and unconvincing. In part, the lack of originality comes from the source work. The plot element of the writer driven into a murderous rage is derived from King's *The Shining* (and was much better handled in Stanley Kubrick's filming of that work). The climactic battle between Sheldon and Annie degenerates into yet another recycling of the unkillable killer movie gimmick of "Friday the 13th" ilk.

However, what is most ironic is the effectiveness of Bates' Oscar-winning performance in rendering MISERY ineffective as a horror tale. Her work is a subtle mixture of wit, energy, psychological realism, and, most of all, a weird empathy which winds up all but upending the possibility of a pat, bloodthirsty resolution. In the end, it is Caan's Sheldon who becomes the monster, a civilized man of words who allows himself to be driven to barbaric violence in response to a woman whose real offense in relation to Sheldon was to believe what he had written. King, Reiner, Goldman, and Caan don't demonstrate much interest in exploring Sheldon's culpability in creating his own predicament. Yet, Bates' performance demands it. As a result, MISERY is about as entertaining as any film made from King's work as far as it goes. But its ending leaves a sour taste. As a result, instead of succeeding as a "Kill the Bitch" movie, it works best as an inadvertent critique of horror-movie misogyny, which, on the whole, comes as a welcome relief from the real thing.

MISFITS, THE
1961 124m bw   ★★★
Western   /15
Seven Arts

Clark Gable (*Gay Langland*), Marilyn Monroe (*Roslyn Taber*), Montgomery Clift (*Perce Howland*), Thelma Ritter (*Isabelle Steers*), Eli Wallach (*Guido*), James Barton (*Old Man in the Bar*), Estelle Winwood (*Church Lady*), Kevin McCarthy (*Raymond Taber*), Denis Shaw (*Young Boy in Bar*), Philip Mitchell (*Charles Steers*)

p, Frank E. Taylor; d, John Huston; w, Arthur Miller; ph, Russell Metty; ed, George Tomasini; m, Alex North; art d, Stephen Grimes, William Newberry; fx, Cline Jones; cos, Jesse Munden

A disturbing but captivating film about modern cowboys who have lost their purpose in a world that has robbed them of the West into which they were born. THE MISFITS was Gable's last film. That the strenuous stunts and bronc-busting feats he performed killed Gable is still in debate but it is certain that he gave one of the finest performances of his career for the fade-out. This was also Monroe's last film, one that ended a glittering but tortuous career. Gable and sidekicks Wallach and Clift are cowboys without saddles, driving a pickup about the West in search of odd jobs, but mostly following the rodeo circuits, living on the fringe of the rope-and-tie action. Their talk is laced with thin bravado, and they have more of the past to discuss than the future. In Reno, they meet recently divorced blond voluptuary Monroe, who left her successful businessman husband. She is a one-time stripper who is seeking truth and a meaningful relationship with anyone who can relate to her idealistic notions. Gable is twice Monroe's age, has no noble purpose, and intends to round up "misfit" horses, those wild mustangs too small for rodeo or ranch work, so they can be ground up for dog food. His partners are Wallach, a one-time bombardier, and Clift, a troubled rodeo rider who hates his stepfather. Both men take a liking to the neurotic Monroe and try to persuade her to leave Gable and go with either of them, but she remains steadfast to the old cowboy, believing he has a heart of gold if she can only discover the shaft leading to it. When Monroe learns the truth of the trio's horse-catching mission, she denounces Gable and his buddies, which incenses Gable. After all, he's only trying to make a living. The group traps a small herd of horses and Monroe pleads with Clift and

Wallach to let the feisty leader go, but Gable is adamant. No woman will tell him his business, even though it's a business he knows is rotten to the core. He breaks the wild stallion and then, showing the compassion Monroe always knew was there, lets the horse go. He and Monroe drive off to make some sort of life together.

This is an awkward film, even though it has many fine moments, most of them Gable's—when he gets drunk and begins calling for his long-lost children, his spirited horse-breaking scenes (he did not employ a double and the strain undoubtedly caused him to have a fatal heart attack shortly thereafter), and some of his nostalgic scenes with Monroe. The actress is weak and directionless in her part, trying to adopt Actor's Studio methods and deadpanning her scenes while belying her altruistic lines with a jiggling, tight-skirted image. She's unbelievable and hardly the Monroe of old. Miller's presence at the on-location scenes in Reno and Dayton, Nevada, undoubtedly inhibited director Huston, who fails to develop anyone's character except Gable's. Huston could not control Monroe, who seemed to be on the verge of a nervous breakdown; she did not show up in time for her scenes and, when she did show up, she could not remember a line of dialog until heavy coaching jarred her memory. Much has been said about this film being a brilliant mood piece of a dying Old West, but that is not enough to make it a masterpiece. Gable had misgivings about performing the part and suspected Miller's script of being too arty, but he took on the introspective role and did much more with it than even Miller expected; the playwright-screenwriter initially believed that the one-time matinee idol was unsuitable for the part. Gable received $750,000 for his part, plus ten percent of the gross and an overtime rate of $48,000-a-week. Gable, instead of being upset with the drug-taking, sick-to-the-stomach Monroe, treated her with great consideration and kindness, working with her and never complaining when she appeared late for scenes. He was the same with Clift, but resented Wallach and his "method" school of acting, often quipping to Wallach that they would be having "boiled ham" for lunch after their scenes. Wallach would retort with: "Hey, king, can you lower my taxes?" Huston and Gable got along, although the director unnerved the actor by losing great amounts of money at the Reno gambling dens and then bragging about it. Miller grew to admire Gable greatly, later stating: "He was, of course, more glamorous than the real Gay, the one I wrote—any actor would be, the acting dimension does this. But the gallant essence he did not enlarge on or overdo. He was a gent." Clift was also on the razor's edge when the film was made, drinking heavily and never fully recovering from a car accident that had scarred him. He does have one poignant scene in a phone booth wherein he tries to communicate with an indifferent mother, but for the most part he is merely hanging on to his neurotic role. Early in the film technicians made the mistake of having Clift bare-hand the ropes he used in handling the horses and, since much footage had been shot without gloves, the actor had to go on using his bare hands until they were completely raw and rope-burned. Clift received $200,000 for his performance. The film was begun on July 18, 1960 and was completed on November 24, 1960; Gable had died eight days earlier and the following March his wife Kay gave birth to his one and only child. The picture was also Monroe's last completed feature film. After filming was finished, Monroe went into production with SOMETHING'S GOT TO GIVE, a comedy costarring Dean Martin. Her death from a sleeping-pill overdose occurred in the middle of the production.

MISHIMA

1985   120m   c   ★★★½
Biography   R/15
Zoetrope/Filmlink/Lucasfilm

Ken Ogata (Yukio Mishima), Masayuki Shionoya (Morita), Hiroshi Mikami (Cadet No. 1), Junya Fukuda (Cadet No. 2), Shigeto Tachihara (Cadet No. 3), Junkichi Orimoto (Gen. Mashita), Eimei Exumi (Ichigaya Aide-de-Camp), Minoru Hodaka (Ichigaya Colonel), Go Riju (Mishima, Age 18-19), Yuki Nagahara (Mishima, Age 5)

p, Mata Yamamoto, Tom Luddy; d, Paul Schrader; w, Paul Schrader, Leonard Schrader (conceived in collaboration with Jun Shiragi, literary executor of the Mishima estate); ph, John Bailey (Technicolor); ed, Michael Chandler, Tomoyo Oshima; m, Philip Glass; prod d, Eiko Ishioka; art d, Kazuo Takenaka; cos, Etsuko Yagyu

"Never in physical action had I discovered the chilling satisfaction of words. Never in words had I experienced the hot darkness of action. Somewhere there must be a higher principle which reconciles art and action. That principle, it occurred to me, was death." These words, written by Japanese author Yukio Mishima and spoken in a voice-over narration by Roy Scheider, eloquently state what writer-director Paul Schrader tried to convey in this ambitious, unique undertaking. Though MISHIMA contains much biographical material, it doesn't claim to be a definitive biography of the controversial writer. Instead, the film concentrates on Mishima's art, attempting to piece together a complicated puzzle by examining his work and its relation to his personal obsessions. Perhaps Japan's best-known author, Mishima wrote 35 novels, 25 plays, 200 short stories, and 8 volumes of essays before his ritual suicide at age 45. One of his driving concerns was his perception of Japan's post-WWII rejection of its rich history of tradition, ritual, honor, and religion in favor of the Western world's pursuit of money. He formed his own private army, called the Shield Society, whose purpose was to restore Japan to the emperor. Schrader approaches his subject with taste and intelligence, juxtaposing Mishima's suicide with flashbacks from his life and dramatizations of his novels *Temple of the Golden Pavilion*, *Kyoko's House,* and *Runaway Horses*. Separated into four chapters ("Beauty," "Art," "Action," and "Harmony of Pen and Sword"), the film skillfully integrates the novels and real events, slowly dissecting Mishima's obsessions. MISHIMA's most stunning aspect is the visual style employed in the dramatizations of the novels. With colorful, theatrical sets by famed Japanese designer Eiko Ishioka, the sequences are quite unique and impressive in their own right, and the entire film is photographed beautifully by John Bailey. The visuals are enhanced by Philip Glass's haunting score.

MISS FIRECRACKER

1989   102m   c   ★★
Comedy/Romance   PG
Corsair

Holly Hunter (Carnelle Scott), Mary Steenburgen (Elain Rutledge), Tim Robbins (Delmount Williams), Alfre Woodard (Popeye Jackson), Scott Glenn (Mac Sam), Veanne Cox (Tessy Mahoney), Ann Wedgeworth (Miss Blue), Trey Wilson (Benjamin Drapper), Amy Wright (Missy Mahoney), Bert Remsen

p, Fred Berner; d, Thomas Schlamme; w, Beth Henley (based on her play "The Miss Firecracker Contest"); ph, Arthur Albert (Duart color); ed, Peter C. Frank; m, David Mansfield, Homer Denison; prod d, Kristi Zea; art d, Maher Ahmad; cos, Molly Maginnis

The town of Yazoo City, Mississippi, is agog over the annual Fourth of July Miss Firecracker Contest, and no one is more obsessed with winning this honor than Carnelle Scott (Holly Hunter). But Carnelle has more than a few obstacles to overcome if she is to win the title. Adding to the hubbub are the simultaneous arrivals of her cousins, Elain Rutledge (Mary Steenburgen) and Delmount Williams (Tim Robbins). A former contest winner, Elain has always been Carnelle's idol. Delmount, a poetic wildman, has had a less easy time of it: a recent stay at an insane asylum and a stint as a highway maintenance worker have not tamed his manic exuberance. But Carnelle pursues her dream with relentless fervor. Playwright-scriptwriter Beth Henley specializes in this type of cloying Southern Gothic whimsy. But what might once have seemed refreshingly quirky and a good actors' workout on the stage has become a desperate struggle for melodramatic laughs. Moreover, director Thomas Schlamme's unsure handling of scenes and indiscriminate use of unappealing close-ups of actors emoting at full steam only emphasize the material's weakness.

MISSING

1982   122m   c   ★★★★
Drama/War   PG/15
Polygram

Jack Lemmon (Ed Horman), Sissy Spacek (Beth Horman), Melanie Mayron (Terry Simon), John Shea (Charles Horman), Charles Cioffi (Capt. Ray Tower), David Clennon (Consul Phil Putnam), Richard Venture (US Ambassador), Jerry Hardin (Col. Sean Patrick), Richard Bradford (Carter Babcock), Joe Regalbuto (Frank Teruggi)

p, Edward Lewis, Mildred Lewis; d, Constantin Costa-Gavras; w, Donald Stewart, Constantin Costa-Gavras (based on *The Execution of Charles Horman* by Thomas Hauser); ph, Ricardo Aronovich (Technicolor); ed, Francoise Bonnot; m, Vangelis; prod d, Peter Jamison; art d, Agustin Ytuarte, Luceoro Isaac; fx, Albert Whitlock; cos, Joe I. Tompkins

With MISSING, Costa-Gavras (Z; STATE OF SEIGE; THE CONFESSION), one of cinema's most political filmmakers, turned his attention to the alleged US involvement in the coup that led to the death of socialist Chilean president Salvador Allende in 1973. Based on Thomas Hauser's *The Execution of Charles Horman*, Costa-Gavras's first Hollywood-produced film presents an only slightly fictionalized account of the disappearance of American expatriate writer Charles Horman (John Shea) in Santiago (though neither the city nor Chile are ever mentioned) just after a military coup. His wife, Beth (Sissy Spacek), and his conservative father, Ed (Jack Lemmon), who has traveled from the US, become a political odd couple as they search for Charles, growing closer as they run into the official stonewalling of American embassy and Chilean authorities who insist there is no trace of Charles. Costa-Gavras pulled so few punches in this powerful, provocative thriller that then-Secretary of State Alexander Haig felt compelled to issue categorical denials of the film's allegations. Few films fuse the personal and the political as successfully as MISSING, and Lemmon and Spacek bring tremendous feeling to their portrayals. Though Costa-Gavras clearly has a political axe to grind, he manages to do so without haranguing the viewer, keeping the film's focus on his characters and masterfully building tension as the story moves toward its stinging resolution.

MISSION, THE

1986 126m c ★★★
Historical PG
Enigma/Goldcrest/Kingsmere (U.K.)

Robert De Niro *(Mendoza)*, Jeremy Irons *(Gabriel)*, Ray McAnally *(Altamirano)*, Liam Neeson *(Fielding)*, Aidan Quinn *(Felipe)*, Ronald Pickup *(Hontar)*, Charles Low *(Cabeza)*, Cherie Lunghi *(Carlotta)*, Bercelio Moya *(Indian Boy)*, Sigifredo Ismare *(Witch Doctor)*

p, Fernando Ghia, David Puttnam; d, Roland Joffe; w, Robert Bolt; ph, Chris Menges (JDC Widescreen, Rank Color); ed, Jim Clark; m, Ennio Morricone; prod d, Stuart Craig; art d, George Richardson, John King; fx, Peter Hutchinson; cos, Enrico Sabbatini

In South America, circa 1750, Gabriel (Jeremy Irons) is a Jesuit priest sent to build a mission for the Guarani Indians. There he encounters Mendoza (Robert De Niro), a ruthless slave trader who kills several Guaranis and captures many more, taking them back to town as slaves. Mendoza also kills his handsome young brother Felipe (Aidan Quinn) in a duel over Mendoza's fiancee, but because he is an aristocrat, he isn't punished for his crime. But the slave trader has a conscience and feels that he must do penance; accordingly, Gabriel arranges for Mendoza to join him back at the mission where Mendoza committed so many sins. In time, the mission faces serious trouble, brought on by a dispute among Spain, Portugal, and the Church. Ambitious, moving, and visually stunning, THE MISSION falls right in step with other high-quality British historical epics, but also fails to escape the pitfalls that typically plague such projects. While an impressive production, THE MISSION tries to do so much that little is explored fully. Irons's character is really more an icon than a man, as is De Niro's. Perhaps most distressing is the fact that THE MISSION is yet another film made by Europeans or Americans that, while sympathetic to the plight of South American Indians, portrays them as an indistinguishable mass of childlike innocents just waiting to be exploited by outsiders. The film won an Oscar for Best Cinematography, and was nominated for Best Picture (won by PLATOON), Best Direction, Best Original Score, Best Art Direction, Best Film Editing, and Best Costume Design.

MISSISSIPPI BURNING

1988 128m c ★★
Historical R/18
Frederick Zollo

Gene Hackman *(Rupert Anderson)*, Willem Dafoe *(Alan Ward)*, Frances McDormand *(Mrs. Pell)*, Brad Dourif *(Deputy Pell)*, Lee Ermey *(Mayor Tilman)*, Gailard Sartain *(Sheriff Stuckey)*, Stephen Tobolowsky *(Townley)*, Michael Rooker *(Frank Bailey)*, Pruitt Taylor Vince *(Lester Cowens)*, Badja Djola *(Agent Monk)*

p, Frederick Zollo, Robert F. Colesberry; d, Alan Parker; w, Chris Gerolmo; ph, Peter Biziou (Duart Color); ed, Gerry Hambling; m, Trevor Jones; prod d, Geoffrey Kirkland, Philip Harrison; fx, Stan Parks; cos, Aude Bronson Howard

Using the shocking murders of three civil rights workers by the Ku Klux Klan in Mississippi on June 21, 1964, as its inspiration, MISSISSIPPI BURNING presents a fictionalized version of the events and turns them into another cop-buddy movie. Alan Ward and Rupert Anderson (Willem Dafoe and Gene Hackman) are two very different FBI agents sent to Mississippi to investigate the disappearance of the young men. Ward is morally outraged by the racism he finds in the South and is determined to do something about it, while Anderson wanders the streets like a good ol' boy, chatting with the townsfolk to ferret out clues.

MISSISSIPPI BURNING is visually splendid. From the sets, costumes, props, and Mississippi locations to the gorgeous cinematography of Peter Biziou, director Alan Parker and his crew have created a film that is unquestionably watchable. But despite all the attention to the images, something essential is missing here, something that can be found in the faces of the local Mississippians cast as extras—genuine human experience. Biziou won an Oscar for his cinematography. Other nominations include Best Picture (won by RAIN MAN), Best Actor (Hackman losing to Dustin Hoffman for RAIN MAN), Best Supporting Actress (McDormand), Best Direction, Best Sound, and Best Film Editing.

MISSISSIPPI MERMAID

(LA SIRENE DU MISSISSIPPI)
1969 123m c ★★★½
Mystery GP/AA
Carrosse/Artistes/Delphos (France/Italy)

Jean-Paul Belmondo *(Louis Mahe)*, Catherine Deneuve *(Julie Roussel/Marion)*, Michel Bouquet *(Comolli)*, Nelly Borgeaud *(Berthe Roussel)*, Marcel Berbert *(Jardine)*, Martine Ferriere *(Landlady)*, Roland Thenot *(Richard)*, Yves Drouhet

p, Marcel Berbert; d, Francois Truffaut; w, Francois Truffaut (based on the novel *Waltz into Darkness* by Cornell Woolrich); ph, Denys Clerval (Dyaliscope, DeLuxe Color); ed, Agnes Guillemot; m, Antoine Duhamel; art d, Claude Pignot

Belmondo is a millionaire tobacco planter who becomes engaged to Deneuve through a personal column. He is taken by her beauty and they soon marry, but she leaves with his bank account. He hires a private detective to track her down, but eventually discovers her himself, or so he thinks. The girl he finds is not his wife, but bears an uncanny resemblance to her (not surprising, since Deneuve plays both roles). Eventually Belmondo learns that his new companion is trying to kill him. As he is about to be poisoned, he professes his love for Deneuve, who promptly knocks the cup from his hand and shamefully vows to love him forever. This is Truffaut's most successful attempt to blend a complex, Hitchcockian genre film with his own personality. It was also his first chance to work with superstars, ensuring success at the box office. The film is full of references to cinema—a clip from LA MARSEILLAISE (the picture is dedicated to Jean Renoir, whose film LA CARROSSE D'OR [THE GOLDEN COACH] was the inspiration for the name of Truffaut's production company), and homages to Humphrey Bogart, Nick Ray, Honore de Balzac, Jean Cocteau, and a *Cahiers Du Cinema* editor who bore the same name as this film's detective, Comolli.

MISSOURI BREAKS, THE

1976 126m c ★★★
Western PG/15
UA

Marlon Brando *(Lee Clayton)*, Jack Nicholson *(Tom Logan)*, Randy Quaid *(Little Tod)*, Kathleen Lloyd *(Jane Braxton)*, Frederic Forrest *(Cary)*, Harry Dean Stanton *(Calvin)*, John McLiam *(David Braxton)*, John Ryan *(Si)*, Sam Gilman *(Hank Rate)*, Steve Franken *(Lonesome Kid)*

p, Elliott Kastner, Robert M. Sherman; d, Arthur Penn; w, Thomas McGuane; ph, Michael Butler (DeLuxe Color); ed, Jerry Greenberg, Stephen A. Rotter, Dede Allen; m, John Williams; prod d, Albert Brenner; art d, Steve Berger; cos, Patricia Norris

In the 1970s westerns started to come a little weird, and this one was downright eccentric, although Brando, as a nutty gunfighter, and Nicholson, as a leader of rustlers, are fascinating to watch, if not believable in their disjointed roles. The film opens as a rustler, on ranch baron McLiam's orders, is hanged, no little example for Nicholson, who heads a gang of vicious horse thieves. The hanged man, Hunter Von Leer, was Nicholson's friend, and Nicholson intends to avenge the death; but he falls for Lloyd, daughter of the cattle baron, and somehow is persuaded to settle down to the mundane chores of farming, much to the disgust of his gang. The rustlers carry on without Nicholson's help, raiding McLiam's herds and driving the cattle baron half crazy. He sends for a top gun bounty hunter, Brando, who turns out to be the most unpredictable and outright strangest creature to ever visit a western movie. To capture one outlaw he takes to wearing a bonnet and dress, and when Nicholson goes to kill him he finds Brando taking a bubble bath, a sight that so jars him that he misses his opportunity to kill him. Brando continues his rampage, destroying all the rustlers except Nicholson, who manages to finish off the weirdo in the end. The whole thing, script, acting, and especially Penn's heavy-handed direction, is bizarre. Yet there's a perverse joy in watching Brando and Nicholson try to compete with each other in mugging, switching accents, and mannerisms that could only be found elsewhere in institutions like the Bellevue Insane Asylum. The erratic and exotic behavior of the stars is infectious, with Quaid, Forrest, Stanton, and others mimicking them with slavish devotion.

MR. AND MRS. BRIDGE

1990 124m c   ★★★½
Drama   PG-13/PG
Merchant Ivory/Robert Halmi

Paul Newman *(Walter Bridge)*, Joanne Woodward *(India Bridge)*, Robert Sean Leonard *(Douglas Bridge)*, Margaret Welsh *(Carolyn Bridge)*, Kyra Sedgwick *(Ruth Bridge)*, Blythe Danner *(Grace)*, Simon Callow *(Dr. Sauer)*, Malachy McCourt *(Dr. Forster)*, Austin Pendleton *(Mr. Gadbury)*, Diane Kagan *(Julia)*

p, Ismail Merchant; d, James Ivory; w, Ruth Prawer Jhabvala (based on the novels *Mrs. Bridge* and *Mr. Bridge*, by Evan S. Connell); ph, Tony Pierce-Roberts (Technicolor); ed, Humphrey Dixon; m, Richard Robbins; prod d, David Gropman; cos, Carol Ramsey

Everything's up-to-date in Kansas City, but then the clock stops circa the early 40s for Walter and India Bridge, the leads of this gem of a period piece and finely wrought drama of an American marriage. Actually, life for the provincial upper middle class couple—played brilliantly by the long-married Paul Newman and Joanne Woodward—hasn't stopped or even settled in. More precisely, it has congealed. As if frozen in time, their stolidly conservative, predictable existence is clearly stultifying. Still, boring lives don't necessarily make for boring films, and the cumulative impact onscreen is anything but. The main characters are indelibly set in their ways with an almost foolish consistency. *He* is a prosperous lawyer who is hopelessly intractable. Archly self-satisfied and authoritarian, he patronizes his wife (*all* women, for that matter), votes straight Republican, and confines his actions to the very narrow channels he deems acceptable. *She* is a relic of Victorian sensibilities, a living embodiment of the antique aphorism, "children should be seen, not heard" grown to maturity. So hungry for affection and desperate to please, she has long since lost any individual identity and emerges as a mass of repression.

So what happens? Not much. But then that's just the point of the film, derived almost literally from both of Evan S. Connell's best-selling novels (*Mrs. Bridge* was written in 1959; *Mr. Bridge* in 1967). What fills the screen is not heightened melodrama, but a series of stark, sometimes painfully poignant vignettes that reflect the oppressive stasis of their lives. The events depicted are episodic in nature. India is rebuffed by her son when he refuses to kiss her at a Boy Scout ceremony. One daughter, the rebellious, sexually charged Ruth (Kyra Sedgwick), opts for the arty, Bohemian life in New York, and is tolerantly bankrolled by her father. Her younger, more conventional sister, Carolyn (Margaret Welsh) makes an impulsive marriage to a college beau. Mrs. Bridge is ordered by her husband to ignore tornado warnings during a dinner at their club, and despite entreaties from fellow members and the staff that she head for shelter, fearfully obeys him until the storm subsides. Her best friend Grace (Blyth Danner), a banker's wife (and closet heretic), conforms to the ultraconservative codes expected of her until the strain grows too much to bear. Another friend, Mabel (Gale Garnett), who fancies herself a rebel, turns to a psychoanalyst for help. Mr. Bridge ignores the feelings of his secretary of 20 years, a spinster who has long been in love with him. And so on. Everything leads up to the final scene, which seems to synthesize the very essence of the film. One ordinary winter day, India dresses for a trip to town, gets into her car and starts backing out of the garage when the motor conks out. The garage is too narrow for her to open the car door and get out, so she is trapped, and sits waiting for her husband to come home and rescue her.

As India Bridge, Woodward (who earned a Best Actress Oscar nomination for her performance) eloquently recreates an emotional dishrag that's been squeezed dry. She perceptively portrays a naive, totally guileless mother of three, a suburban matron and country club member whose inner dreams have been put on permanent hold. Her utterly respectable, lackluster life remains defined by what everyone else—especially her husband—expects of her. She wouldn't think of making a decision without his input. Though Newman does an excellent job as Mr. Bridge—his low-keyed interpretation of the highly controlled, highly controlling patriarch is a powerful example of emotional restraint——the kudos must go to his wife. But to both their credit, they play the parts with enough humor and compassion to avoid reducing their roles to caricatures. You might not quite exactly like them as individuals, but as a film, you will. This was another entertaining collaboration from the long-time producing/directing/writing team of Ismail Merchant, James Ivory, and Ruth Prawer Jhabvala, whose previous efforts have included THE BOSTONIANS, A ROOM WITH A VIEW, and MAURICE.

MR. AND MRS. NORTH

1941 68m bw   ★★½
Comedy/Mystery   /A
MGM

Gracie Allen *(Pamela North)*, William Post, Jr. *(Gerald P. North)*, Paul Kelly *(Lt. Weigand)*, Rose Hobart *(Carol Brent)*, Virginia Grey *(Jane Wilson)*, Tom Conway *(Louis Berex)*, Porter Hall *(George Reyler)*, Millard Mitchell *(Mullins)*, Lucien Littlefield *(Barnes, Postman)*, Inez Cooper *(Mabel Harris)*

p, Irving Asher; d, Robert B. Sinclair; w, S.K. Lauren (based on the play by Owen Davis, Sr., from a story by Richard and Frances Lockridge); ph, Harry Stradling; ed, Ralph E. Winters

Mystery spoof has Allen and Post as a married couple who come home to their apartment after a weekend absence to find a corpse in the closet. The couple wind up with all their friends as suspects and try to solve the crime. The script is overly talky, but Allen, who carries the majority of the lines, and without George Burns for a change, gives the script some life. The direction does a good job in keeping a level of suspense going in the midst of all the comedy.

MR. BLANDINGS BUILDS HIS DREAM HOUSE
1948 94m bw   ★★★
Comedy   /U
RKO

Cary Grant (Jim Blandings), Myrna Loy (Muriel Blandings), Melvyn Douglas (Bill Cole), Reginald Denny (Simms), Sharyn Moffett (Joan Blandings), Connie Marshall (Betsy Blandings), Louise Beavers (Gussie), Harry Shannon (W.D. Tesander), Ian Wolfe (Smith), Tito Vuolo (Mr. Zucca)

p, Norman Panama, Melvin Frank; d, H.C. Potter; w, Norman Panama, Melvin Frank (based on the novel by Eric Hodgins); ph, James Wong Howe; ed, Harry Marker; m, Leigh Harline; art d, Albert S. D'Agostino, Carroll Clark; fx, Russell A. Cully; cos, Robert Kalloch

The novel upon which this film was based was very funny and timely. This movie suffered in the translation to the screen, although it did have enough humor to make it a hit. The years have not been gentle to MR. BLANDINGS BUILDS HIS DREAM HOUSE and there are many tedious stretches in the film that feel leaden. This was the third duet for Grant and Loy, and a weak triangular plot-turn with Douglas was added in order to put some spice in the one-joke premise. Grant and Loy are married Manhattanites who must give up their apartment and find new lodgings for themselves and their daughters, Moffett and Marshall. As in the Kaufman and Hart play "George Washington Slept Here," the leads are seduced by the dream of having their own suburban home in the greenery of the country. A sharp real estate agent, Wolfe, sells them a house that's nearly 200 years old and they pay an incredible sum for the privilege of living in a drafty, dilapidated home. The rest of the movie is a series of incidents (somewhat interminable) that looks like just another segment of TV's "Green Acres." Grant tries to deal with architect Denny, who's brought in to raze the old house and start from scratch. There are several gags we've all seen (or heard) before, such as the jam-packed hall closet that disgorges everything each time the door is opened (a running joke on the old "Fibber McGee and Molly" radio series), water rising in the cellar, windows that don't fit flush and allow the elements to invade, and all of the expected jokes that come with the territory. Whatever fun one gets in is in watching Grant's frustration as he deals with the problems of being a home builder. Douglas's comedic talents are totally wasted as the couple's attorney, who is their close friend and upon whom the screenwriters have attempted to place the mantle of "other man." In a small role, note Lex Barker, one-time movie TARZAN.

MR. DEEDS GOES TO TOWN
1936 115m bw   ★★★★★
Comedy   /U
Columbia

Gary Cooper (Longfellow Deeds), Jean Arthur (Babe Bennett), George Bancroft (MacWade), Lionel Stander (Cornelius Cobb), Douglas Dumbrille (John Cedar), Raymond Walburn (Walter), Margaret Matzenauer (Madame Pomponi), H.B. Warner (Judge Walker), Warren Hymer (Bodyguard), Muriel Evans (Theresa)

p, Frank Capra; d, Frank Capra; w, Robert Riskin (based on the story "Opera Hat" by Clarence Budington Kelland); ph, Joseph Walker; ed, Gene Havlick; art d, Stephen Goosson; fx, Roy Davidson; cos, Samuel Lange

Peak inspired lunacy. Here is a shamelessly simple story with a populist point of view, but it is handled with such charm and charisma and acted so well by Gary Cooper and Jean Arthur, that it has become another Frank Capra classic. Cooper, a rural rube from Vermont, inherits his uncle's vast fortune and becomes national news overnight. The whole town turns out at the train station to see Cooper, tuba player and local poet, off to New York, where he will assume the responsibilities of his uncle's business and move into an enormous mansion. But cynical news editor George Bancroft does not fall for Cooper's image of a simple, honest man. Bancroft assigns Arthur to interview Cooper, with explicit instructions not to spare the ridicule, but the aggressive and devious reporter cannot corral Cooper. When she fakes a faint in front of his residence, the gallant Cooper picks her up and takes care of her. She tells him she's unemployed, and then begins wheedling information from him.

Capra directs flawlessly as he captures the prosaic character of Longfellow Deeds; Cooper is tailor-made for the role, natural and authentic. Both he and Arthur remained favorites of Capra, who would use Cooper again in MEET JOHN DOE, Arthur in YOU CAN'T TAKE IT WITH YOU, and MR. SMITH GOES TO WASHINGTON. Capra never had any doubt in casting Cooper for the role of Longfellow Deeds—his first and only choice—but he was in a quandary over the female lead until he spotted Arthur in a minor western. The director was at his high-water mark at Columbia, allowed by Columbia studio chief Harry Cohn to function as he pleased without front office interference. Capra insisted that only Cooper play the lead in the film, causing the production to be delayed for six months while Cooper fulfilled other duties and costing Columbia $100,000. Cohn did not want any more postponements so he okayed Arthur and the production got under way. Arthur literally shook with nerves before each scene, believing she could not pull it off. Yet she was an original in front of the cameras.

The supporting cast is extraordinary, notably Dumbrille, Bancroft, and that venerable character player Warner, who had appeared in many a Capra film and played Christ in DeMille's classic KING OF KINGS. The film achieved immense popularity and gleaned a fortune for Columbia chiefly because of the gangling, rumpled, taciturn Cooper, who was one of the most durable film stars in history and ranked in the top-10 list for 15 years. In 1939 he made almost $500,000, making him the highest paid American actor that year, and would earn more than $10 million throughout his long career. MR. DEEDS won Capra an Academy Award for Best Director.

MISTER 880
1950 90m bw   ★★★½
Drama/Comedy   /U
FOX

Burt Lancaster (Steve Buchanan), Dorothy McGuire (Ann Winslow), Edmund Gwenn (Skipper Miller), Millard Mitchell (Mac), Minor Watson (Judge O'Neil), Howard St. John (Chief), Hugh Sanders (Thad Mitchell), James Millican (Olie Johnson), Howland Chamberlin (Duff), Larry Keating (Lee)

p, Julian Blaustein; d, Edmund Goulding; w, Robert Riskin (based on the *New Yorker* article "Old Eight Eighty" by St. Clair McKelway); ph, Joseph La Shelle; ed, Robert Fritch; m, Sol Kaplan, Lionel Newman; art d, Lyle Wheeler, George W. Davis; fx, Fred Sersen; cos, Travilla

This enchanting comedy stars Edmund Gwenn as the cheery Skipper Miller, an aging counterfeiter who prints dollar bills to support himself. Although he breaks the law, he is such a harmless, whimsical criminal that he defies censure, counterfeiting bills because he needs money to live and out of love for his old-fashioned printing press, which he calls "Cousin Henry." Miller proves an embarrassment to the federal agents who have been after him for 10 years, but a new man on the case, Steve Buchanan (Burt Lancaster), comes closer than any other agent to nabbing Miller. He traces one of the bills to an apartment where he meets a pretty United Nations translator (Dorothy McGuire) with whom he falls in love, and soon afterwards he discovers that the elusive counterfeiter is his girlfriend's neighbor. But identifying the "crook" proves to be only half the battle as Buchanan and his colleagues find it difficult to prosecute this charming little man. Lancaster and McGuire perform admirably, but Gwenn, who earned a Best Supporting Actor Oscar nomination for his work, steals the show with one of his most memorable performances (along with his role in MIRACLE ON 34TH STREET and his endearing presence in THE TROUBLE WITH HARRY).

MR. HULOT'S HOLIDAY
(LES VACANCES DE MONSIEUR HULOT)

1953 85m bw   ★★★★½
Comedy   /U
Cady/Gaumont   (France)

Jacques Tati *(Mr. Hulot)*, Nathalie Pascaud *(Martine)*, Louis Perrault *(Fred)*, Michelle Rolla *(The Aunt)*, Andre Dubois *(Commandant)*, Suzy Willy *(Commandant's Wife)*, Valentine Camax *(Englishwoman)*, Lucien Fregis *(Hotel Proprietor)*, Marguerite Gerard *(Strolling Woman)*, Rene Lacourt *(Strolling Man)*

p, Jacques Tati, Fred Orain; d, Jacques Tati; w, Jacques Tati, Henri Marquet, Pierre Aubert, Jacques Lagrange; ph, Jacques Mercanton, Jean Mousselle; ed, Suzanne Baron, Charles Bretoneiche, Jacques Grassi; m, Alain Romans; prod d, Henri Schmitt; art d, R. Brian Court, Henri Schmitt

Director Jacques Tati turned his attention to those French who wrongly believe that a coastal holiday will be a time of rest and relaxation with this delightful film. Featuring the first appearance of M. Hulot (played by Tati himself, in the tradition of the great silent comedians), MR. HULOT'S HOLIDAY takes place at a coastal resort in Brittany. Chaos seems to follow Hulot wherever he goes, but he somehow makes it through life without ever really noticing. Like all vacationers, Hulot (and director Tati) spends a great deal of time observing other vacationers. There is the comely Martine (Nathalie Pascaud), whom Hulot would like to get to know better, but is too shy to confront directly; the workaholic businessman (Jean-Pierre Zola, later seen in MY UNCLE) who cannot stop to relax; the burly British old maid (Valentine Camax); the besieged waiter (Raymond Carl); the former military man who still thinks he's leading a battalion (Andre Dubois); the beachcombing couple (Rene Lacourt and Marguerite Gerard), and countless other unidentified persons who are equally important to the scenery. There is no plot (as the prologue warns us), only a seemingly endless stream of events—with and without Hulot—that carry the film through to the end. With very little dialogue and a creative use of sound, Tati (the

actor and director) gives us an entirely new way of looking at a very familiar landscape.

MR. MOM

1983 91m c   ★★½
Comedy   PG
Sherwood

Michael Keaton *(Jack)*, Teri Garr *(Caroline)*, Frederick Koehler *(Alex)*, Taliesin Jaffe *(Kenny)*, Courtney White, Brittany White *(Megan)*, Martin Mull *(Ron)*, Ann Jillian *(Joan)*, Jeffrey Tambor *(Jinx)*, Christopher Lloyd *(Larry)*

p, Lynn Loring, Lauren Shuler; d, Stan Dragoti; w, John Hughes; ph, Victor J. Kemper (Metrocolor); ed, Patrick Kennedy; m, Lee Holdridge; prod d, Alfred Sweeney; cos, Nolan Miller

Jack (Michael Keaton) loses his position in a Detroit auto plant and must take over at home while his wife, Caroline (Teri Garr), goes out to earn their daily bread. He must cope with hassles with the kids, supermarket coupons and other predictable material. MR. MOM could have been a telling look at the plight of the middle class during the economically depressed early 80s, but it soon becomes just another television-style sitcom that is only partly redeemed by the superior work of the actors. Despite its striking lack of originality, MR. MOM did well at the box office, due, in part, to the meteoric rise of Keaton after his fine performance in NIGHT SHIFT.

MISTER ROBERTS

1955 123m c   ★★★★
War/Comedy/Drama   /U
Orange

Henry Fonda *(Lt. Doug Roberts)*, James Cagney *(Captain)*, Jack Lemmon *(Ens. Frank Thurlowe Pulver)*, William Powell *(Doc)*, Ward Bond *(C.P.O. Dowdy)*, Betsy Palmer *(Lt. Ann Girard)*, Philip Carey *(Mannion)*, Nick Adams *(Reber)*, Harry Carey, Jr. *(Stefanowski)*, Ken Curtis *(Dolan)*

p, Leland Hayward; d, John Ford, Mervyn LeRoy; w, Joshua Logan, Frank S. Nugent (based on the play by Logan and Thomas Heggen and the novel by Heggen); ph, Winton C. Hoch (CinemaScope, WarnerColor); ed, Jack Murray; m, Franz Waxman; art d, Art Loel; cos, Moss Mabry

The movie version of one of the most beloved American stage plays is wholly entertaining, with wonderful performances from the entire cast—notably Henry Fonda (who created the title role) and Jack Lemmon (who won a Best Supporting Actor Oscar for his work)—but the story behind the film is a turbulent one, the production going through three directors (John Ford, Mervyn LeRoy, and Josh Logan) before its completion. In the Pacific, during WWII, we meet Lieutenant Roberts (Fonda), the cargo officer of the USS *Reluctant*, a toothpaste and toilet paper supply ship aimlessly sailing the South Pacific. Roberts feels that the war is passing him by and he yearns to be a part of it. His captain (James Cagney) is a megalomaniac who abuses his crew with asinine orders and who dotes on a small palm tree sitting outside his quarters, lavishing more attention and compassion on the plant than he does on his own men. Roberts, normally a calm and kind man, is driven to outrage by the insensitive captain and acts as a buffer between him and the restless crew. While Roberts takes the brunt of the captain's wrath, the young and immature Ensign Pulver (Jack Lemmon) does his part by constantly pulling pranks on the captain in the hope of driving him mad. As Roberts grows more desperate for a transfer—a request that must be approved by the captain—the captain has the troublesome lieutenant right where he wants him and continues to make life miserable for the crew at Roberts's expense.

Fonda had abandoned Hollywood for the Broadway stage, and studio bosses felt his marquee value was dubious, despite the fact that he had created the role of Mr. Roberts onstage. Producer Leland Hayward wanted either Marlon Brando or William Holden to play Roberts, but director Ford insisted that Fonda be given the part. Unfortunately, it wasn't long before Ford and Fonda clashed, mostly because Fonda had some fixed ideas as to how to play Roberts, having done it so many times before. The dispute grew heated and led to Ford's assaulting Fonda, causing a rift between them that never healed, despite the director's attempts to apologize. Shortly thereafter, Ford suffered a gall-bladder attack and was hospitalized. Having completed only the exterior scenes, Ford was replaced by Warners veteran LeRoy, who finished the picture. Later, playwright and screenwriter Logan (who also directed the Broadway original) was brought in to direct some additional scenes. The resulting effort is a bit of a mess, with Ford's scenes instantly recognizable by their distinctive style (actor Ward Bond's removing his work glove to handle a letter from Roberts at the climax is a definite "Fordian" bit of business), while LeRoy's scenes—mostly interiors—suffer from static, stagy direction. (The exact nature of Logan's contributions has never been made clear, but some sources credit him with some of the comedic scenes, such as the making of the bootleg scotch and Pulver's blowing up the laundry.) Luckily, the sparkling script and terrific cast make up for the schizophrenic cinematic treatment, and the film is, overall, a success. MR. ROBERTS was shot aboard the USS *Hewell* at the South Pacific island of Midway before moving to Kaneoke Bay in Hawaii for the final filming. It also garnered nominations for Best Picture (it lost to MARTY) and Best Sound.

MR. SMITH GOES TO WASHINGTON
1939 125m bw   ★★★★★
Political   /U
Columbia

Jean Arthur *(Saunders)*, James Stewart *(Jefferson Smith)*, Claude Rains *(Sen. Joseph Paine)*, Edward Arnold *(Jim Taylor)*, Guy Kibbee *(Gov. Hubert Hopper)*, Thomas Mitchell *(Diz Moore)*, Eugene Pallette *(Chick McGann)*, Beulah Bondi *(Ma Smith)*, H.B. Warner *(Sen. Fuller)*, Harry Carey *(President of the Senate)*

p, Frank Capra; d, Frank Capra; w, Sidney Buchman (based on the novel *The Gentleman from Montana* by Lewis R. Foster); ph, Joseph Walker; ed, Gene Havlick, Al Clark; m, Dimitri Tiomkin; art d, Lionel Banks; cos, Robert Kalloch

Stellar Capra-corn Americana. This great film works on the premise that all that is necessary for evil to triumph is the inaction of good men. Against this danger, director Frank Capra shows a naive everyman to be the true guardian of democratic ideals. James Stewart gives the performance that made him a star as Jefferson Smith, an innocent bumpkin selected by cynical politicians to replace a recently deceased senator in the belief that he can be manipulated by the state's esteemed senior senator, Joseph Paine (Claude Rains). Smith sets off for Washington full of ideals and dreams of working with his idol, Paine, little realizing that he is expected to be a rubber stamp for a crooked scheme to finance a new dam that will profit only Paine and his cronies. The Washington press immediately sizes Smith up as a gullible novice, getting him off to a rocky start, but his idealism captivates Saunders (Jean Arthur), his cynical new secretary. Saunders proves to be a valuable mentor as the innocent Smith slowly comes to realize that his altruistic view of the world doesn't

necessarily jibe with reality, and he sets out to expose those who make a mockery of the country he loves so dearly.

While MR. SMITH GOES TO WASHINGTON is the most moral of films, it is so artfully filled with real emotion that it never becomes heavy-handed. Capra supervised every element of the production and used a variety of techniques to accelerate the story line without disrupting it, making every move by every player meaningful and illustrating his credo of "one man, one film." This inspiring masterpiece received 11 Oscar nominations but won only for Best Original Story. Stewart is tops and the rest of the much-loved cast, featuring such familiar veterans as Thomas Mitchell, Edward Arnold, William Demarest and especially Harry Carey, provides unforgettable support.

MIXED BLOOD
1984 98m c   ★★★½
Drama   /18
Sef Satellite

Marilia Pera *(Rita La Punta)*, Richard Ulacia *(Thiago)*, Linda Kerridge *(Carol)*, Geraldine Smith *(Toni)*, Angel David *(Juan the Bullet)*, Ulrich Berr *(The German)*, Marcelino Rivera *(Hector)*, Rodney Harvey *(Jose)*, Ignazio Spalla *(Commanche)*, Carol Jean Lewis *(Woman Cop)*

p, Antoine Gannage, Steven Fierberg; d, Paul Morrissey; w, Paul Morrissey, Alan Browne; ph, Stefan Zapasnik (Eastmancolor); ed, Scott Vickrey; m, Andy Hernandez; art d, Stephen McCabe

An engaging mix of off-the-wall black humor and obdurate violence presents Rita La Punta (Marilia Pera), a Brazilian woman running a drug-pushing outfit in New York City's Lower East Side. Her gang consists of neighborhood teenagers, whom she sincerely loves as her own, living in a squalid apartment. When her gang intercepts a shipment intended for a rival group, a 14-year-old is tossed off a rooftop in retaliation. Instead of intimidating Rita, the action results in an all-out war between her gang and the rival group. Pera's performance is wacky and believable. This is a story steeped in violence, which happens as casually and frequently as spitting on a sidewalk. Unlike director Paul Morrissey's films for Andy Warhol or some of his 1970s underground work, this is not a comic gorefest. Despite the often-hysterical proceedings, the work is steadfastly rooted in realism. It captures the heart and soul of a neighborhood in one of the more unique slice-of-life pictures in a long time.

MOBY DICK
1956 116m c   ★★★½
Adventure   /U
Moulin (U.K.)

Gregory Peck *(Capt. Ahab)*, Richard Basehart *(Ishmael)*, Leo Genn *(Starbuck)*, Harry Andrews *(Stubb)*, Bernard Miles *(Manxman)*, Orson Welles *(Father Mapple)*, Mervyn Johns *(Peleg)*, Noel Purcell *(Carpenter)*, Frederick Ledebur *(Queequeg)*, James Robertson Justice *(Capt. Boomer)*

p, John Huston, Vaughan N. Dean; d, John Huston; w, John Huston, Ray Bradbury (based on the novel by Herman Melville); ph, Oswald Morris (Technicolor); ed, Russell Lloyd; m, Philip Stainton; art d, Ralph Brinton, Stephen Grimes; fx, Gus Lohman; cos, Elizabeth Haffenden

Not too sea-worthy. John Huston gives a passionate and faithful rendering of Herman Melville's novel in MOBY DICK, aided by a stellar cast. The film opens as a man (Richard Basehart) enters the whaling town of New Bedford in 1840, and, in voiceover, makes the famous declaration "Call me Ishmael." He signs on board the *Pequod*, commanded by peg-legged Capt. Ahab (Gregory Peck). Once under way, the wild-eyed, stony, horribly scarred Ahab assembles his crew to tell them that this will be no routine whaling expedition but a mission of vengeance against the great white whale Moby Dick, which tore off his leg and scarred him for life. He whips them into a frenzy, and when Moby Dick is finally sighted, the crew is as obsessed with killing it as Ahab is. Filmed at considerable danger to cast and crew, MOBY DICK, under Huston's strong direction, is one of the most historically authentic, visually stunning, and powerful adventures ever made. Inevitably, many critics disagreed with Huston's interpretation of Melville's classic. Two fishbones to pick: Peck and Genn's miscasting. But there's Welles in rare form, fine whaling scenes, the first glimpse of Moby Dick, good use of color (akin to old whaling prints) and a literate adaptation by Ray Bradbury. When MOBY is good, it's a whale of a time. Huston received the New York Film Critics Best Director Award.

MODERN ROMANCE

1981 93m c   ★★★½
Comedy   R/15
Columbia

Albert Brooks *(Robert Cole)*, Kathryn Harrold *(Mary Harvard)*, Tyann Means *(Waitress)*, Bruno Kirby *(Jay)*, Jane Hallaren *(Ellen)*, Karen Chandler *(Neighbor)*, Dennis Kort *(Health Food Salesman)*, Bob Einstein *(Sporting Goods Salesman)*, Virginia Feingold *(Bank Receptionist)*, Thelma Leeds *(Mother)*

p, Andrew Scheinman, Martin Shafer; d, Albert Brooks; w, Albert Brooks, Monica Johnson; ph, Eric Saarinen (Metrocolor); ed, David Finfer; m, Lance Rubin; prod d, Edward Richardson

Albert Brooks directed, cowrote, and stars in this brilliantly funny and at times uncomfortably perceptive comedy. Brooks plays Robert, a film editor trapped in an on-again, off-again relationship with Mary (Kathryn Harrold). After breaking up (again) with Mary, Robert is torn between freedom and love. Attempting to forget her, he invests hundreds of dollars in jogging clothes and vitamins, ventures into the LA singles scene (pre-AIDS), mopes, and buries himself in his work (editing a really bad science fiction film for an exploitation studio). None of it works, and soon he's pursuing Mary again in the hope of winning her back—which he does, until anxiety, paranoia, and doubt return to threaten the relationship once again. In addition to being one of the most realistic, insightful romantic comedies ever made, MODERN ROMANCE also offers a detailed and uproarious glimpse into the technical side of the movie business. A progressive, innovative comic filmmaker, Brooks began to find the large audience he deserves with LOST IN AMERICA.

MODERN TIMES

1936 85m bw   ★★★★½
Comedy   /U
Chaplin

Charles Chaplin *(A Worker)*, Paulette Goddard *(Gamine)*, Henry Bergman *(Cafe Owner)*, Tiny Sandford *(Big Bill/Worker)*, Chester Conklin *(Mechanic)*, Hank Mann, Louis Natheaux *(Burglars)*, Stanley Blystone *(Sheriff Couler)*, Allan Garcia *(Company Boss)*, Sammy Stein *(Foreman)*

p, Charles Chaplin; d, Charles Chaplin; w, Charles Chaplin; ph, Roland Totheroh, Ira Morgan; m, Charles Chaplin; art d, Charles D. Hall, J. Russell Spencer

Known as "the last of the great silent feature comedies," this picture reflects holdout Charlie Chaplin's resistance to the changing times; synchronous dialogue was everywhere ascendant by the time of the film's release, yet MODERN TIMES contains mostly sound effects, synchronous music, and a pattern song with nonsense syllables. The film's opening shows a seemingly endless number of sheep racing across the screen, an image followed by its corollary—factory-bound workers streaming from a subway train. Chaplin, numbered among the laborers, tightens nuts on an interminable stream of steel plates coursing along a conveyor belt. Armed with two wrenches, he nips spasmodically at the bolts as they speed on their way. Momentarily diverted, Chaplin pursues a plate he has missed down the conveyor line, decking his coworkers in his frantic flight to tighten the fastenings that have evaded him. Finally catching the errant hardware, Chaplin returns to his normal tempo, only to have boss Allan Garcia, in a fit of boredom, speed up the assembly section. Chaplin's labors become a frenzied jazz ballet. Sneezing, he misses a bolt, then frantically dives onto the conveyor line, hoping to catch it. As his coworkers attempt to hold him back, Chaplin is borne by the moving belt into a chute, to emerge among great cogs and gears, tightening every available nut in his transit. A worker operates the mechanism that reverses the belt's direction and Chaplin emerges, still madly tightening. Taking a brief break, Chaplin sneaks a cigarette in the washroom. Suddenly, one entire wall of the room becomes a giant TV screen bearing the image of boss Garcia, screaming at the little man to get back to work, a portent of the "Big Brother" later to appear in George Orwell's novel *1984*.

This remarkable picture—three years in the making, like most of Chaplin's feature pictures—was hardly novel in its theme of Luddite disaffection with the mechanized society of the times. Following the film's release, Chaplin was sued for plagiarism by the French production company Films Sonores Tobis, producer of Rene Clair's A NOUS LA LIBERTE, whose representatives cited similarities in the conveyor belt sequences of the two films. The lawsuit was dropped after director Clair pointed out that he would be honored and flattered to find that he had been able to render such assistance to the wonderful Chaplin. There seems little doubt that Chaplin's social consciousness had been formed years before, during his impoverished London childhood. The man-eaten-by-machine theme reportedly came to the 12-year-old Chaplin in 1901, when he was apprenticed as a printer's devil and found himself dwarfed by an enormous Wharfedale printing press. Further ideas for the factory sequence of the film came from verbal reports of the Detroit automotive assembly lines and from an enormous automatic dishwashing machine—complete with conveyor belt—Chaplin saw in a Los Angeles restaurant. As early as 1931, two years before production started, Chaplin expressed his concern about the social issues of the Great Depression, stating that things had been badly managed if five million men were out of work in the richest country in the world. And again, speaking of his own adulation by an adoring public, he wondered what kind of a world makes people lead such wretched lives that, if anybody makes them laugh, they want to kneel down and touch his overcoat, as though he were Jesus Christ.

Chaplin's resistance to synchronous dialogue was legend, even though this picture is the first to contain such dialogue by the comic master himself (in a sort of parody, a patter song in gibberish). Chaplin *had* spoken for the cinema before—in a newsreel filmed in Vienna in 1931 during a world tour, in which he said *"Guten Tag, guten Tag"* into the microphone—but dialogue simply was not his way, even as late as 1936. For one thing, he was accustomed to the silent-screen technique of cranking the camera at different rates of speed to modify the tempo of the picture; synchronous dialogue had to be shot at a fixed rate of 24 frames per second. For another, he felt that he had no need of dialogue (as early as 1922, Chaplin had compared sound in films with painting statues). Chaplin's view echoed the anti-mechanistic theme of the film. Still, with all his reservations about the talkies, Chaplin fudged the issue, viewing synchronized dialogue as, perhaps, "an addition, not as a substitute" for the visuals on the screen. Indeed, in November of 1934, Chaplin and Goddard made sound tests at the studio to hear how they might sound should dialogue be decided on for the film. Both had good voices, and Chaplin ordered a dialogue script prepared. The script was choppy and failed to follow the tempo Chaplin wanted for the film, so he trashed it, going with his first instinct instead. Music and sound effects were a different matter altogether; Chaplin felt that these belonged, and he took infinite pains with them. He handled many of the sound effects for MODERN TIMES personally; the stomach-rumbling sounds made by the hungry job-seeker in the film were created by Chaplin blowing bubbles in a pail of water. Work on the musical score took months, with Chaplin and his musical collaborators screening and re-screening sequences of the film.

MODERN TIMES was costar Goddard's first big break in pictures. Chaplin had met the actress aboard cinemogul Joseph Schenck's yacht when she was doing bit parts in Hal Roach comedies. He formed a close personal relationship with the young actress—22 years his junior—who was to live with him as his wife. Goddard is a perfect gamine in the picture, as she was in life—a charmer, lovely, vibrant, and active, with a fine sense of humor and a compassionate nature. Many of Chaplin's features had him similarly befriending a homeless girl, including THE VAGABOND, THE CIRCUS, CITY LIGHTS, and, later, LIMELIGHT. He never befriended a more appealing waif than Goddard, who was unique among Chaplin's adoptive waifs in many ways. She was less distanced from him than most of the other orphans of a stormy, unsettled society. Indeed, the gamine is very like her protector; their stories parallel one another in many ways, even prior to their first meeting. This affinity surely contributes to Chaplin's close relationship with his likable costar, who served as mother to his children.

Unlike many of his previous films, Chaplin was able to do the planning and much of the scripting of MODERN TIMES in privacy, away from his hectic, acolyte-ridden home, aboard the "Panacea," the 38-foot Chris-Craft motor cruiser he purchased in 1933. MODERN TIMES was enormously successful in the US. It was less so in the USSR (where the Stakhanovites were interested in speeding up production, not slowing it) and was banned completely as Communist propaganda in Fascist Italy and in Nazi Germany (whose Fuehrer was soon to be parodied in Chaplin's next film, THE GREAT DICTATOR). Still, the film was not a novel departure into social criticism for Chaplin—all his pictures had their share of that, even the old two-reelers. Indeed, one critic said of MODERN TIMES that it was really just four two-reelers strung together: "The Shop," "The Jailbird," "The Watchman," and "The Singing Waiter." It is true enough that each of the four sequences can stand on its own; its creator inflexibly followed the muse that had served him so well in his earlier work. This is the film that truly marked the passing of an era. Despite its sound-on-film technology, it is the last of the great silent feature pictures. Although he retained much of his silent style—and all of his talent—when he created his later films, the master of mime was finally forced to adapt to modern times. Other songs and musical numbers used in the film include

"Hallelujah, I'm a Bum," "Prisoner's Song" (C. Massey), "How Dry Am I" and "In the Evening by the Moonlight" (Bland).

MODERNS, THE

1988 126m c   ★★★★
Drama   R/15
Alive

Keith Carradine (Nick Hart), Linda Fiorentino (Rachel Stone), Genevieve Bujold (Libby Valentin), Geraldine Chaplin (Nathalie de Ville), Wallace Shawn (Oiseau), John Lone (Bertram Stone), Kevin J. O'Connor (Ernest Hemingway), Elsa Raven (Gertrude Stein), Ali Giron (Alice B. Toklas), Charl Elie Couture (Charley)

p, Carolyn Pfeiffer, David Blocker; d, Alan Rudolph; w, Alan Rudolph, Jon Bradshaw; ph, Toyomichi Kurita (CFI color); ed, Debra T. Smith, Scott Brock; m, Mark Isham; prod d, Steven Legler; cos, Renee April

With THE MODERNS, visionary Alan Rudolph completed his long-standing project about the spirit of Paris in the 1920s. Nick Hart (David Carradine) is an American who earns a living as an illustrator, though his heart lies in painting. Into Hart's favorite cafe walks Stone (John Lone), a proud American businessman who has amassed a fortune in the prophylactic business and who now wants to buy the best collection of modern art in Paris. With Stone is his wife, Rachel (Linda Fiorentino) who, unknown to Stone, had a few years earlier married (and never divorced) Hart. It's not long before Hart and Stone are embroiled in a brutal struggle for art and romance. Displaying a vision of the world uniquely his own, Rudolph has succeeded in making a very modern period film that can be viewed as a documentary—not of an actual time or place, but of a feeling. Better than any piece of newsreel footage or recorded documents, THE MODERNS re-creates the spirit of Paris in the 1920s, a spirit that is the most important aspect of that era and the essence of all art of that period.

MOGAMBO

1953 115m c   ★★★★
Adventure/Romance
MGM

Clark Gable (Victor Marswell), Ava Gardner (Eloise Y. Kelly), Grace Kelly (Linda Nordley), Donald Sinden (Donald Nordley), Philip Stainton (John Brown Pryce), Eric Pohlmann (Leon Boltchak), Laurence Naismith (Skipper), Denis O'Dea (Father Josef), Asa Etula (Young Native Girl)

p, Sam Zimbalist; d, John Ford; w, John Lee Mahin (based on the play "Red Dust" by Wilson Collison); ph, Robert Surtees, Freddie Young (Technicolor); ed, Frank Clarke; art d, Alfred Junge; cos, Helen Rose

A remarkable and action-packed remake of RED DUST (directed by Victor Fleming), this is one of Ford's more stylish and unpredictable films, lacking his stock company and the so-called "Fordian elements" that go to make up the director's unmistakable signature. Yet MOGAMBO is solid and exciting, dealing subtly with a love triangle involving white safari leader Gable, showgirl Gardner, and cool, married Kelly. Gardner visits Gable in his African quarters; he learns that she has arrived to be the guest of a rich maharaja, who never appears. While waiting for the steamer to arrive to take her away, she spends her time with Gable, exchanging barbs and mild insults but falling in love with the virile, self-confident white hunter. She betrays the fact that she's pleased when hearing that the steamer has broken down and her visit must be prolonged. Then Sinden and Kelly arrive, representatives of various zoos. Sinden is an anthropologist seeking to capture gorillas in order to study their habits. He hires Gable to lead a safari to capture gorillas and Gardner goes along. Gardner sees that Gable is attracted to beautiful, blonde Kelly and tries to persuade him not to tamper with her. Gable, however, believes he is in love with Kelly and takes Sinden aside to tell him the truth, but he stops short when he realizes how deeply he will hurt the kind and faithful husband. Gable has the opportunity to let Sinden be killed but saves the Englishman. To shut off the affection flowing from Kelly, Gable meets with Gardner, drinking with her in her tent. When Kelly comes to investigate the noise, she sees them embracing and kissing. Kelly raises a pistol and shoots Gable in the shoulder. When Sinden comes on the run, Gardner proves she is noble, too, and tells the anthropologist that she, Gardner, shot Gable for making improper advances. Sinden and Kelly leave, and Gable is left with Gardner, a woman he realizes he truly loves. He asks her to stay with him and she does.

MOGAMBO lacks the lusty story of the original RED DUST and the wild banter between Gable and his then-costar Jean Harlow, who had been dead 16 years when this film was made. Gable is no longer the rough-and-tumble young plantation manager, but a seasoned, somewhat weary white safari guide and hunter. Here his female costars Kelly and Gardner, diametric opposites, exchange the verbal sparring. Gardner is sensual, earthy, and often vulgar, while Kelly is refined, distant, and even prudish. Ford provides action all the way, trekking his cameras through Kenya, Tanganyika, and Uganda. Instead of using a traditional bravura score for the film, Ford insisted that the sounds of Africa would be more effective on the sound track. He had scores of animal and bird sounds and dozens of native shouts recorded and interspersed throughout the sound track, punctuating the dialogue and action to lend authenticity to the exotic locales his cameras captured. The absence of the lush sound track was a rarity for an MGM production; executives thought such devices too experimental for their "family" audience, but they deferred to the great Ford. There are scenes—reminiscent of Ford's great westerns—in which he visually exploits the lavish African landscape. In one scene, Gable stoically marches through a gauntlet of spear-holding tribesmen, coming resolutely toward the camera, facing danger, while the horizon spreads to infinity beyond him, a scene not unlike the finale of MY DARLING CLEMENTINE, in which Henry Fonda (as Wyatt Earp) rides away from the camera, down a road stretching into infinity. Ford does not ignore the torrid scene of the outdoor shower, one of the highlights of RED DUST, wherein bombshell Harlow bathed in the altogether. Here it's Gardner behind the wooden stall with Gable handing her the towel. Where RED DUST was bawdy and brawling and unsophisticated, MOGAMBO (meaning "to speak") is cultured, despite the primitive surroundings, and its characters operate on a more educated, literate level. Their emotions, however, are as earthbound as those in RED DUST. Ford spoke little of this taut production, commenting: "I never saw the original picture. I liked the script and the story. I liked the setup and I'd never been to that part of Africa—so I just did it." With the enormous success of its 1950 production of KING SOLOMON'S MINES, MGM was only too happy to allow Ford a free hand in producing another super adventure-romance film on the Dark Continent.

Gardner arrived in Africa with her secretary and then-husband, Frank Sinatra, on hand. The Gardner-Sinatra romance was falling apart because the singer's career was on the skids. While in Africa, Sinatra got wind of the fact that Columbia was about to cast FROM HERE TO ETERNITY and he pleaded with his wife to ask her friend Columbia chief Harry Cohn to give him a part. She did, and Sinatra left to secure the role with a screen test. Meanwhile, according to later reports, Gardner left for London midway through the production to have Sinatra's child but lost the baby in a miscarriage. Gable's life was altered much by this film. He became an ardent flier and even halted the production so he could fly back to the US to have his teeth fixed (trusting only his American dentist). The actor enjoyed hunting and, when the production was stalled for one technical reason or another, he went on hunting expeditions by himself and, before their falling out, sometimes with Ford. He killed a crocodile that had been menacing a river tribe and became a local hero; the natives thereafter called Gable "Bwana." Kelly, however, called Gable "Ba," which is Swahili for "father." Gable liked Gardner but he was emotionally drawn to Kelly, giving her a party on location when the beautiful blonde actress celebrated her 24th birthday. The budding romance ended when Kelly decided that the relationship was impossible since Gable was twice her age. Gable was then suffering from slight palsy, and his hands shook during some takes which Ford patiently reshot. But the director lost his patience with Gable when the actor asked for another take with Gardner because he felt the scene was not right. Ford ignored him and walked away, causing a breach between the actor and director which was not patched up until the cast and crew went to England to finish some interior scenes.

MOGAMBO proved to be a box-office bonanza for MGM, returning almost $5 million from its initial release. Gable finished BETRAYED for the studio the next year and then departed forever as executives wrung their hands in financial anguish. They had formerly wanted to get rid of the salary-heavy star, but MOGAMBO and BETRAYED so shored up Gable's image and box office appeal that he was again rising to mainstream popularity. He refused to discuss another contract and went off to make films elsewhere, taking with him his $400,000 in pension money. The story was used one other time, when Gable reprised his RED DUST role in 1940 for a "Gulf Screen Guild" radio production, also featuring Ann Sothern (playing the Harlow role) and Jeffrey Lynn. Gardner was nominated for Best Actress, but lost to Audrey Hepburn for ROMAN HOLIDAY, while Best Supporting Actress nominee Kelly lost to Donna Reed for FROM HERE TO ETERNITY.

MOLLY MAGUIRES, THE

1970   124m   c   ★★★
Historical   PG
Tamm

Richard Harris *(James McParlan/McKenna)*, Sean Connery *(Jack Kehoe)*, Samantha Eggar *(Mary Raines)*, Frank Finlay *(Davies)*, Anthony Zerbe *(Dougherty)*, Bethel Leslie *(Mrs. Kehoe)*, Art Lund *(Frazier)*, Anthony Costello *(Frank McAndrew)*, Philip Bourneuf *(Father O'Connor)*, Brendan Dillon *(Mr. Raines)*

p, Martin Ritt, Walter Bernstein; d, Martin Ritt; w, Walter Bernstein (based on the book *Lament for the Molly Maguires* by Arthur H. Lewis); ph, James Wong Howe (Panavision, Technicolor); ed, Frank Bracht; m, Henry Mancini; art d, Tambi Larsen; fx, Willis Cook; cos, Dorothy Jeakins

As depicted in this biased but absorbing film, the Molly Maguires were members of a secret union organization made up of malcontent coal miners in eastern Pennsylvania, circa 1876. In order to improve working conditions and correct the inhuman treatment members received from cruel mine owners, the Mollies dynamited or sabotaged mines and killed bosses. They were a formidable and often lethal underground force that struck terror into the heart of the government itself. The leader of the Mollies is Jack Kehoe (Connery), a tough and shrewd adversary. The owners hire Harris, a Pinkerton detective, to infiltrate the Mollies and report on their activities so they can eradicate the Irish menace. Harris rents a room in the home of a disabled miner and promptly begins to court his daughter, Eggar. He also lets it be known that he is wanted for murder. Connery, though he is given in-depth reports about Harris confirming that he is an enemy of the owners, is skeptical about the man and delays recruiting him into the Mollies. To prove his loyalty, Harris helps Connery's football team defeat a Welsh group on the field and later, savagely beats a sadistic policeman. These actions win over Connery and Harris is tentatively admitted into the secret society. To further convince Connery of his sincerity, Harris votes to murder a mine boss and even rescues one of the Mollies involved in the killing. When Eggar's father dies, Connery and Harris—now fast allies—break into a company store to steal a suit for the burial, then set fire to the place. Later, Connery and Costello plan to blow up a mine, but when Harris gets wind of the plan he turns them over to police. Private policemen lead raids against the society's leaders, many of whom are shot to death while in bed with their wives. Connery is captured and Harris's testimony condemns him to death. Harris meets with Connery as he waits to be hanged. He seeks absolution from the Irish leader, but there is only hatred as Connery brands him a traitor. Eggar also rejects Harris, calling him a Judas. The Pinkerton detective leaves to head the agency office in Denver as Connery is led to his execution.

This film cost more than $11 million. It was shot almost wholly on location in eastern Pennsylvania in Eckley, Llewelyn, Wilkes-Barre, Bloomsburg, and other nearby towns. The period is superbly recreated in the crude mining town sets (the film earned an Oscar nomination for Best Art Direction-Set Decoration), the homes, and the music which includes such traditional Irish songs as "Gary Owen," "Eileen Aroon," and "Cockles and Mussels." Ritt's direction, however, is airless and sluggish and, when scenes are set in the mines, outright claustrophobic. Camerman Howe—normally an outstanding cinematographer—dwells on long shots, and the lighting is so dim, it's next to impossible to discern many of the scenes in the mines. In his attempt to reach authenticity and use only available torch and helmet light (the weak candles affixed to the miner's helmets), Howe pitched the production into dismal darkness. Connery and Harris turn in good performances, but Ritt allows them to sink into dialects that are sometimes difficult to understand. The script is decidedly prejudiced in favor of Pinkerton and the owners of the mines. The awful plight of the miners at the time—having no job protection whatsoever, and wholly at the mercy of the owners—is given little attention. Instead, the miners are portrayed as savage, murderous, and unfeeling creatures, not worthy of empathy or understanding. The film cannot compare with John Ford's masterpiece about coal miners, HOW GREEN WAS MY VALLEY. However, it does offer some memorable moments of quality and passion. It failed miserably at the box office, returning only $1.5 million in its initial release.

MON ONCLE D'AMERIQUE
(LES SOMNAMBULES)

1978 125m c ★★★★½

Drama PG/A

Andrea/TF-1 (France)

Gerard Depardieu (Rene Ragueneau), Nicole Garcia (Janine Garnier), Roger-Pierre (Jean Le Gall), Nelly Borgeaud (Arlette Le Gall), Marie Dubois (Therese Ragueneau), Pierre Arditi (Zambeaux),

Gerard Darrieu (Leon Veestrate), Philippe Laudenbach (Michel Aubert), Alexandre Rignault (Jean's Grandfather), Guillaume Boisseau (Jean as a Child)

p, Philippe Dussart; d, Alain Resnais; w, Jean Gruault (based on the works of Prof. Henri Laborit); ph, Sacha Vierny (Eastmancolor); ed, Albert Jurgenson; m, Arie Dzierlatka

Alain Resnais's greatest, and most unlikely, commercial success is an offbeat, humorous case study of three characters—manager Rene (Gerard Depardieu), actress Janine (Nicole Garcia), and executive Jean (Roger-Pierre). Their pasts are quickly, and simultaneously, accounted for, allowing the focus to be placed on the pursuit of their careers. This action is intercut with segments of a lecture from Prof. Henri Laborit, a behavioral scientist speaking in a pure documentary fashion (Resnais had, in fact, attempted to do a short documentary project with Laborit), who contributes his theories on memory. Resnais also intercuts footage from other movies, featuring the film personae that serve as inspiration for the three main characters—for Rene, Jean Gabin; for Janine, Jean Marais; for Roger-Pierre, Danielle Darrieux. The (somewhat inexplicable) commercial and (less baffling) critical success of this film experiment was phenomenal, for it defies viewer pigeonholing. If you're interested in films that stretch the limits of narrative structure, MON ONCLE D'AMERIQUE is essential viewing. It won numerous awards, including six French Cesars and an Academy Award nomination for screenwriter Jean Gruault.

MONA LISA

1986 104m c ★★★½

Crime R/18

Palace (U.K.)

Bob Hoskins (George), Cathy Tyson (Simone), Michael Caine (Mortwell), Clarke Peters (Anderson), Kate Hardie (Cathy), Robbie Coltrane (Thomas), Zoe Nathenson (Jeannie), Sammi Davies (May), Rod Bedall (Terry), Joe Brown (Dudley)

p, Stephen Woolley, Patrick Cassavetti; d, Neil Jordan; w, Neil Jordan, David Leland; ph, Roger Pratt (Technicolor); ed, Lesley Walker; m, Michael Kamen; prod d, Jamie Leonard; art d, Gemma Jackson; cos, Louise Frogley

With MONA LISA, Irish director Neil Jordan (THE COMPANY OF WOLVES) continues to breathe new life into the staid British film industry with a "Hollywood-ready" blend of slick visual style and a fairly standard genre narrative. This film has the quality of an outstanding audition.

George (Bob Hoskins), a recently released convict, has just served a seven-year sentence after taking the fall for his mob boss, Mortwell (Michael Caine). Looking to collect his due, George meets with Mortwell and is informed that he's been assigned a job chauffeuring a high-class Black call girl, Simone (Cathy Tyson). George and Simone take an intense dislike to each other at first, but gradually their relationship warms up. Nearly every night, Simone has George drive her through an area where the streetwalkers gather to ply their trade. Here Simone searches for her only friend, Cathy (Kate Hardie), a 15-year-old whore who once worked for the same pimp (Clarke Peters). Eventually George agrees to descend into the underworld to bring back the young woman, a plot device in the grand tradition of TAXI DRIVER and HARDCORE.

Hoskins is tremendous, giving a sensitive, multi-faceted performance that infuses the film with an inner life. Tyson is perfect as Simone, bringing an enigmatic and exotic air to the role that captures the essence of the title. The ever-reliable Caine is terrifying as the sometimes charming villain. The plot's similarity to Martin Scorsese's TAXI DRIVER is not lost on director Jordan, who pays homage to Scorsese frequently by simulating shots from the earlier film. Still this is no slavish tribute. The film often has a rather charming offbeat quality that is quite distinctive particularly in scenes featuring the delightful Robby Coltrane as Thomas, George's gentle giant of a roommate. MONA LISA is a detailed, thoughtful film that sensitively explores the emotions within its seedy, exploitative milieu. Jordan's next stop was Hollywood where things have not gone to well to date (HIGH SPIRITS, WE'RE NO ANGELS) but a talent like his may yet surprise us. He returned to Great Britain (temporarily?) in 1991 to make a nice little personal film called THE MIRACLE.

MONKEY BUSINESS

1931 77m bw   ★★★★
Comedy   /U
Paramount

Groucho Marx (Groucho), Harpo Marx (Harpo), Chico Marx (Chico), Zeppo Marx (Zeppo), Thelma Todd (Lucille), Tom Kennedy (Gibson), Ruth Hall (Mary Helton), Rockliffe Fellowes (Joe Helton), Harry Woods ("Alky" Briggs), Ben Taggart (Capt. Corcoran)

d, Norman Z. McLeod; w, Arthur Sheekman (based on a story by S.J. Perelman, W.B. Johnstone, Roland Pertwee); ph, Arthur Todd

The Marx Borthers are the McDonald's of movies in that you always know that you're going to have consistency in one of their films just as you know, ahead of time, what a Big Mac is going to taste like. (The Brothers are, however, much tastier.) It was the first Marx Brothers picture written directly for the screen and it had all of the quips and situations for which they have become world famous. The boys have stowed away on an ocean liner and race from stateroom to stateroom in order to keep from being clapped in the brig. Harpo gets involved with a Punch and Judy show and delights all of the kids on the vessel (as well as all the adults in the audience). Naturally, there are the heavies and the Marxes become embroiled with Fellowes and Woods, a pair of well-dressed and well-heeled gangsters. The Marx Brothers split up with two of them siding with each of the crooks. Hall, the daughter of a hoodlum, is kidnapped and winds up in a barn after being at a masquerade ball. In the finale, Zeppo, the "straight" brother, goes after the tough hoodlum, while Groucho leaps from one bale of hay to another, offering one-liners as punctuation to the punches. Sorely missing is Margaret Dumont, the best mature female foil in movies around that time. It slows down a bit when Chico tickles the ivories and Harpo plucks the harp. This is either a concession to their reputations or it might have been because of a plea from the Marxes' mother, Minnie, who didn't want all that money she'd spent for piano and harp lessons to go to waste. Thelma Todd handles the female ingenue work well enough and dances the tango well with Groucho. All members of the supporting cast are as effective as they can be in the midst of the comedic cyclone known as the Marx Brothers. In later years, Zeppo would step out and leave the acting to the other three, but there was a fifth brother, Gummo (Milton), who left the act early and was replaced by Zeppo. Their career began with COCOANUTS in 1929 and ended, as a team, with LOVE HAPPY in 1950. They did work in THE STORY OF MANKIND but in unrelated episodes.

MONKEY SHINES: AN EXPERIMENT IN FEAR

1988 113m c   ★★★★
Horror   R/18
Orion

Jason Beghe (Allan Mann), John Pankow (Geoffrey Fisher), Kate McNeil (Melanie Parker), Joyce Van Patten (Dorothy Mann), Christine Forrest (Maryanne Hodges), Stephen Root (Dean Burbage), Stanley Tucci (Dr. John Wiseman), Janine Turner (Linda Aikman), William Newman (Doc Williams), Tudi Wiggins (Esther Fry)

p, Charles Evans; d, George Romero; w, George Romero (based on the novel by Michael Stewart); ph, James A. Contner (DeLuxe Color); ed, Pasquale Buba; m, David Shire; prod d, Cletus Anderson; fx, Tom Savini, Steve Kirshoff; cos, Barbara Anderson

George Romero further bolstered his reputation as America's preeminent horror film writer-director with this terrifying psychological horror film. Allan Mann (Jason Beghe), a handsome young track star and law student who is hit by a truck and paralyzed from the neck down, participates in an experimental health care program in which a small, trained capuchin monkey named Ella becomes an extension of the quadriplegic's immobile limbs. Unknown to Allan, Ella is also the main participant in a scientific experiment conducted by Allan's best friend, Geoffrey (John Pankow), an idealistic med student who has tried to increase the primate's intelligence by injecting it with a serum made from human brain tissue. Gradually, as Allan grows more and more dependent on Ella, Ella becomes an extension of Allan's mind as well as his limbs, acting out his repressed anger in the most violent ways. In MONKEY SHINES, as in most of his best films, George Romero poses the question, What does it mean to be human? This notion has also been the overriding concern of his "Living Dead" trilogy. In DAY OF THE DEAD, the catalyst for Romero's inquiry was an incredibly intelligent zombie named Bub, and the parallels between Bub and Ella are strong—both are nonhuman, posited as the missing link between pure animal instinct and civilized human behavior. The character of Allan, on the other hand, is the opposite of Romero's zombies; they are brainless mobility, while he is immobile intellect. Claustrophobic, gripping, and incredibly intense throughout, MONKEY SHINES is an extremely complicated emotional drama that taps into the dark side of family ties, friendship, dependency, nurturing, and love—the last emotion represented by the four very different females (his mother, the nurse, his new girlfriend, and especially Ella) who all compete to care for Allan. After trying for years to finance MONKEY SHINES independently, Romero was forced to turn to Hollywood, which led to a lack of control over the project. The studio imposed a sappy happy ending after test audiences were dissatisfied with Romero's dark sociopolitical conclusion (entailing an army of killer monkeys). The new ending didn't make a bit of difference commercially, since the film was ineptly marketed and was yet another box-office flop for the better-deserving Romero.

MONSIEUR HIRE

1989 81m c   ★★★★
Thriller   /15
Cinea/Hachette/FR3   (France)

Michel Blanc (M. Hire), Sandrine Bonnaire (Alice), Luc Thuillier (Emile), Andre Wilms (Inspector)

p, Philippe Carcassonne, Rene Cleitman; d, Patrice Leconte; w, Patrice Leconte, Patrick Dewolf (based on the novel Les Fiancailles de Monsieur Hire by Georges Simenon); ph, Denis Lenoir; ed, Joelle Hache; m, Michael Nyman

A superb thriller containing the ugliest portrait of French provincialism since Henri-Georges Clouzot's LE CORBEAU, Patrice Leconte's MONSIEUR HIRE is set in a Parisian suburb in which conformity reigns supreme, and anyone who doesn't behave like everyone else is apt to be viewed suspiciously. Based on *Les Fiancailles de Monsieur Hire*, the Georges Simenon novel that also inspired Julien Duvivier's PANIQUE, MONSIEUR HIRE is a penetrating psychological portrait of a warped, love-starved outsider who, by the film's end, arouses the audience's protective instincts. When a lovely young girl is murdered, a dogged police investigator (Wilms) immediately suspects Blanc, a loner distrusted and hated by his neighbors. Tormented by children who play vicious pranks and singled out for suspicion by his neighbors, Blanc is hounded mercilessly by the detective. Blanc resembles his tormenter in that he is an ever-vigilant soul, if in a less acceptable form—for the outcast is a voyeur who spies on Bonnaire, the country-fresh girl who has moved in across the way, when he is not toiling away joylessly at his tailor's shop. Watching Bonnaire—whose innocent look recalls that of the murdered girl—as she undresses or as she makes love to her handsome, ne'er-do-well boy friend (Thuillier), Blanc becomes infatuated with her. Eventually, she spots her secret admirer and, surprisingly, pays him a visit rather than reporting him to the police. An uninhibited free spirit, she is drawn to Blanc and allows him to share the simple pleasures of his life with her. Despite continual harassment from Wilms, Blanc even makes plans to move to Switzerland with Bonnaire—who, despite her apparent attraction to the rabbitlike Blanc, remains loyal to Thuillier, no matter how much he may take her for granted or what he may have done. It would destroy the film's suspenseful climax to reveal further plot developments, but the denouement provides a heart-rending exploration of duplicity and betrayal, with a particularly effective freeze-frame halting the action just before it flows into the twist ending.

Rather than jazz up the suspense through the conventional device of cross-cutting, director Leconte works within the frame to create a sense of inexorable doom. MONSIEUR HIRE doesn't move at a fast clip; instead, it involves the viewer in a downward spiral by making us covoyeurs with the title character, whose life has been a study in self-protective detachment. The audience is implicated in this point of view, eyeing Bonnaire hungrily through her window as Leconte's camera pulls back to an over-the-shoulder shot of Blanc doing the same. In another dazzling, sexually provocative sequence that puts the same motif to very different purposes, the film cuts from an over-the-shoulder shot of Bonnaire watching Thuillier as he enjoys a brutal boxing match to a shot of Blanc fondling her sensually—connecting Blanc and Bonnaire at last, and irrevocably.

Anchored by a haunting performance from Michel Blanc (Gerard Depardieu's diminutive lover in Bertrand Blier's MENAGE) as the Peeping Tom who throws years of self-control to the winds, MONSIEUR HIRE is a study of blindness on two levels: that of prejudice and that of love. As a result of this blindness, both the deceiver and the deceived become victims of fate in this icily compelling film.

MONSIEUR VERDOUX

1947 102m bw   ★★★★
Crime   /PG
Chaplin

Charles Chaplin (*Henri Verdoux/Varney/Bonheur/Floray/Narrator*), Mady Correll (*Mona Verdoux, His Wife*), Allison Roddan (*Peter Verdoux, Their Son*), Robert Lewis (*Maurice Bottello*), Audrey Betz (*Martha Bottello*), Martha Raye (*Annabella Bonheur*), Ada May (*Annette, Her Maid*), Isobel Elsom (*Marie Grosnay*), Marjorie Bennett (*Marie's Maid*), Margaret Hoffman (*Lydia Floray*)

p, Charles Chaplin; d, Charles Chaplin; w, Charles Chaplin (based on an idea by Orson Welles); ph, Roland Totheroh, Curt Courant, Wallace Chewing; ed, Willard Nico; m, Charles Chaplin; art d, John Beckman

Chaplin, that master comedian, cannot seem to decide here which way to go, either into straight drama or farcical crime, but his black humor is in force nevertheless and he has produced a compelling film about the notorious Landru, better known as "Bluebeard." Instead of WWI—when Landru was busy wooing and murdering scores of women, mostly rich spinsters bereft of the males who had gone to fight at the front—Chaplin sets his tale during the late 1930s, when France was on the brink of war with Germany. Though happily married, with a young son, Chaplin feels the need to murder after losing his bank-clerk job. To support his family he romances rich widows and women with savings and is quickly supplied with a countless stream of victims. Raye is exceptional as the one woman who proves his nemesis, and Chaplin is mesmerizing as the droll little methodical killer who becomes especially eccentric and scary when being tried for mass murder. Chaplin attempts to lift this depressing little film out of the pitch darkness of nightmare with little touches that sometimes fail to amuse. He falls into a lake and is rescued by his intended drowning victim; his little boy pulls a cat's tail and he wonders where the child learned such cruelty. Little of it is funny, even though the great silent comedian subtitled this effort "A Comedy of Murders." Had Chaplin played the role straight rather than reaching too far for empathy and some bizarre black laughs, it might have been a minor masterpiece. As it is, MONSIEUR VERDOUX is a curiosity with flashes of brilliance, but definitely not one of Chaplin's best. It is not recommended for children, and to say that about any Chaplin film ought to indicate how frightening this sinister little picture really is. Later Chaplin stated that he made this film to protest the A-bomb. The film was utterly rejected by audiences worldwide when released, although it has gained some critical admirers and cult status since.

MONTE CARLO

1930 90m bw   ★★★★
Musical/Comedy   /PG
Paramount

Jack Buchanan (*Count Rudolph Falliere*), Jeanette MacDonald (*Countess Vera von Conti*), ZaSu Pitts (*Maria, Vera's Maid*), Claud Allister (*Prince Otto von Seibenheim*), Lionel Belmore (*Duke Gustave von Seibenheim, His Father*), Tyler Brooke (*Armand, Rudolph's Friend*), John Roche (*Paul, the "Real" Hairdresser*), Albert Conti (*Prince Otto's Companion/M.C.*), Helen Garden ("*Lady Mary" in Stage Opera*), Donald Novis ("*M. Beaucaire" in Stage Opera*)

p, Ernst Lubitsch; d, Ernst Lubitsch; w, Ernest Vajda, Vincent Lawrence (based on the play *The Blue Coast* by Hans Muller and the novelette "Monsieur Beaucaire" by Booth Tarkington and Evelyn Sutherland); ph, Victor Milner; ed, Merrill White; m, Richard Whiting, W. Franke Harling; cos, Travis Banton

MONTE CARLO did much to advance the role of the sound film, still very much in its infancy when this musical comedy was made in 1929. The immensely talented Ernst Lubitsch was able to so integrate the fluid cinematic techniques he'd used in silents with the new-found discovery of sound that the outcome here is delightful. On the verge of marrying a prince (Claude Allister), countess Jeanette MacDonald dumps the Teutonic twit and boards the "Blue Express" train for Monte Carlo. In Monaco, with little money left, MacDonald checks into a posh hotel, and is spotted immediately in the casino by a wealthy count (Buchanan) who believes that touching MacDonald's golden tresses will bring him good luck. But when Buchanan strokes MacDonald's hair, it's the countess who begins winning magically, and, not knowing the count's true station in life, she hires him as her hairdresser-chauffeur-valet. Playing along just to be close to her, Buchanan calls MacDonald nightly, and, without identifying himself, sings his love for her. As her money again begins to run out and she is forced to reconsider marrying Allister, MacDonald grows increasingly frustrated. While attending "Monsieur Beaucaire" (an opera about a gentleman who poses as a commoner to be near the woman he loves), MacDonald spots Buchanan in a box seat and realizes that he is anything but common. When she confronts him, Buchanan admits that he is also the mysterious caller, and the two live happily and wealthily forever. Very sweet but not too much so, MONTE CARLO is a charming musical comedy generously blessed with the famous Lubitsch touch. MacDonald looks ravishing and is in wonderful voice; her comic skills are also on prominent display here, especially when she frizzes her hair in frustration. Costar Buchanan, who wasn't give the chance to transfer his legendary stage charisma to the screen often enough, fares less well. (He wouldn't appear in another American feature until THE BAND WAGON [1953].) Musical selections include: "Day of Days," "Give Me a Moment, Please," "This is Something New to Me," "Women, Just Women," "She'll Love Me and Like It," "Always in All Ways."

MONTY PYTHON AND THE HOLY GRAIL

1975 89m c ★★★★
Historical/Comedy PG/15
Python (U.K.)

Graham Chapman *(King Arthur/Hiccoughing Guard/Three-Headed Knight)*, John Cleese *(Second Soldier with a Keen Interest in Birds/Large Man with Dead Body/Black Knight/Mr. Newt, a Village Blacksmith Interested in Burning Witches/A Quite Extraordinarily Rude Frenchman/Tim the Wizard/Sir Lancelot)*, Terry Gilliam *(Patsy/Arthur's Trusty Steed/The Green Knight/Soothsayer/Bridgekeeper/Sir Gawain, the First to be Killed by the Rabbit)*, Eric Idle *(The Dead Collector/Mr. Blint, a Village Ne'er-Do-Well Very Keen on Burning Witches/Sir Robin/The Guard Who Doesn't Hiccough but Tries to Get Things Straight/Concorde, Sir Lancelot's Trusty Steed/Roger the Shrubber, a shrubber/Broth)*, Neil Innes *(The First Self-Destructive Monk/Robin's Least Favourite Minstrel/The Page Crushed by a Rabbit/The Owner of a Duck)*, Terry Jones *(Dennis's Mother/Sir Bedevere/Three-Headed Knight/Prince Herbert)*, Michael Palin *(1st Soldier with a Keen Interest in Birds/Dennis/Mr. Duck, a Village Carpenter Who Is Almost Keener Than Anyone Else to Burn Witches/Three-Headed Knight/Sir Galahad/King of Swamp Castle/Brother Maynard's Roommate)*, Connie Booth *(The Witch)*, Carol Cleveland *(Zoot and Dingo)*, Bee Duffell *(Old Crone to Whom King Arthur Said "Ni—")*

p, Mark Forstater; d, Terry Gilliam, Terry Jones; w, Graham Chapman, John Cleese, Terry Gilliam, Eric Idle, Terry Jones, Michael Palin; ph, Terry Bedford; ed, John Hackney; m, Neil Innes, De Wolfe; prod d, Roy Smith

A zany, hysterically funny, and sometimes brilliant if sometimes sophomoric send-up of every medieval movie ever made, brought to you by the wacky six-member cast of BBC-television's "Monty Python's Flying Circus." Superior to their first film, AND NOW FOR SOMETHING COMPLETELY DIFFERENT (which was only a series of their televison vi-

gnettes released for the theaters), HOLY GRAIL is told in a straight (well all right, fairly straight) narrative structure that follows King Arthur (Chapman) and his knights in their search for the legendary Holy Grail. What transpires in the next 90 minutes is nearly impossible to describe to those unfamiliar with the lunacy of the Python bunch (the six male actors play nearly all the parts, including women's roles), but some of the highlights are well worth mentioning (this film must be seen to be understood). Due to the lack of horses in the kingdom (and a low budget), Chapman and his knights are followed throughout the movie by their servants, who smack two coconuts together to simulate the sound of hoofbeats. One of Chapman's first battles is against the Black Knight (Cleese), who refuses to let the king pass. A reluctant Chapman is then forced to cut the man limb from limb until all that is left of Cleese is a torso that yells at the King to come back and fight like a man. Meanwhile, Sir Lancelot (once again Cleese) rushes into a castle and hacks up several wedding guests in a bloody frenzy in an attempt to rescue an effeminate prince who really doesn't need to be rescued. After Cleese calms down and surveys the carnage, he manages a feeble, "I just get carried away" as an apology. Of course, every fan of this film has his favorite moment (the Trojan Rabbit, the Knights Who Say "Ni", Robin and his Minstrels, the killer rabbit, the Holy Hand Grenade and the crazed bridgekeeper). But, all the insanity finally leads to a climactic battle scene populated with hundreds of costumed extras, which is stopped before it really gets started by a few carloads of policemen who interrupt the shooting and grab the camera. Not only is HOLY GRAIL a strange, occasionally sidesplitting film, but it paints a grubby, muddy, and vile portrait of life in the middle ages. The set design and visual style are detailed and rich, lending such credence to the film that at the end, when modern-day police arrive to break things up, it is a real shock. A must see.

MONTY PYTHON'S LIFE OF BRIAN

1979 93m c ★★★½
Religious/Comedy R/15
WB/Orion (U.K.)

Terry Jones *(The Virgin Mandy/The Mother of Brian, a Ratbag/Colin/Simon the Holy Man/Saintly Passer-By)*, Graham Chapman *(1st Wise Man/Brian Called Brian/Biggus Dickus)*, Michael Palin *(2nd Wise Man/Mr. Big Nose/Francis a Revolutionary/Mrs. A. Who Casts the Second Stone/Ex-leper/Ben, an Ancient Prisoner/Pontius Pilate, Roman Governor/A Boring Prophet/Eddie/Nisus Wettus)*, John Cleese *(3rd Wise Man/Reg, Leader of the Judean People's Front/Jewish Official at the Stoning/Centurion of the Yard/Deadly Dirk/Arthur)*, Kenneth Colley *(Jesus the Christ)*, Gwen Taylor *(Mrs. Big Nose/Woman with Sick Donkey/Young Girl)*, Eric Idle *(Mr. Cheeky/Stan Called Loretta, a Confused Revolutionary/Harry the Haggler, Beard and Stone Salesman/Culprit Woman, Who Casts the First Stone/Intensely Dull Youth/Otto, the Nazarene Jailer's Assistant/Mr. Frisbee III)*, Terence Bayler *(Gregory/Revolutionaries and Masked Commandos/Dennis)*, Carol Cleveland *(Mrs. Gregory/Elsie)*, Charles McKeown *(Man Further Forward/Revolutionaries and Masked Commandos/Roman Soldier Stig/Giggling Guard/A False Prophet/Blind Man)*

p, John Goldstone; d, Terry Jones; w, Graham Chapman, John Cleese, Terry Gilliam, Eric Idle, Terry Jones, Michael Palin; ph, Peter Biziou; ed, Julian Doyle; m, Geoffrey Burgon, Andre Jacquemin, David Howman, Eric Idle; art d, Roger Christian; cos, Hazel Pethig, Charles Knode; anim, Terry Gilliam

"Monty Python's" follow-up to MONTY PYTHON AND THE HOLY GRAIL, MONTY PYTHON'S LIFE OF BRIAN, is intellectually amusing in spots. The story begins as the three wise men travel to the manger where Chapman is born. Mistaking the child for the Messiah, the wise men give the baby gifts, only to take them back when they realize that the real Messiah is located in the next manger. This case of mistaken identity is one that plagues Chapman throughout his life. The film follows him from one strange adventure to another (including a ride in a spaceship) until he is eventually brought before Pontius Pilate (played by Palin with a silly, but funny, speech impediment) and mistakenly sent to be crucified. This leads to the film's conclusion, also its funniest scene, in which Chapman and his fellow "crucifixees" happily sing "Always Look on the Bright Side of Life" while nailed to the cross.

MONTY PYTHON'S THE MEANING OF LIFE

1983   107m   c   ★★★
Comedy   R/18
Celandine/Python   (U.K.)

Graham Chapman, John Cleese, Terry Gilliam, Eric Idle, Terry Jones, Michael Palin, Carol Cleveland, Judy Loe, Simon Jones, Andrew MacLachlan

p, John Goldstone; d, Terry Jones; w, Graham Chapman, John Cleese, Terry Gilliam, Eric Idle, Terry Jones, Michael Palin; ph, Peter Hannan (Technicolor); ed, Julian Doyle; m, Eric Idle, John Du Prez; prod d, Harry Lange; art d, Richard Dawking; chor, Arlene Phillips; cos, James Acheson; anim, Terry Gilliam

For their fourth film, the "Monty Python" troupe reverted to the vignette structure used in their first (and weakest) feature, AND NOW FOR SOMETHING COMPLETELY DIFFERENT. While the sketches are loosely structured to convey elements of life (e.g., birth, education, sex, food, the military, and death), the film is uneven and disconnected. It gets off to a promising start with a marvelous pre-credit sequence depicting a British financial building being raided by swashbuckling pirates and turned (literally) into a giant ship. Many of the sketches show the Pythons' deranged, offbeat humor at its best, but the film begins to pale long before the end and relies on some revolting bits such as a "live" organ transplant and the spectacular (and graphic) explosion of an obese glutton. This is definitely not for anyone with delicate sensibilities.

MOON AND SIXPENCE, THE

1942   89m   c/bw   ★★★★
Drama   /A
UA

George Sanders (Charles Strickland), Herbert Marshall (Geoffrey Wolfe), Steven Geray (Dirk Stroeve), Doris Dudley (Blanche Stroeve), Eric Blore (Capt. Nichols), Albert Basserman (Doctor Coutras), Molly Lamont (Mrs. Strickland), Elena Verdugo (Ata), Florence Bates (Tiara Johnson), Heather Thatcher (Rose Waterford)

p, David L. Loew; d, Albert Lewin; w, Albert Lewin (based on a novel by W. Somerset Maugham); ph, John Seitz; ed, Richard L. Van Enger; m, Dimitri Tiomkin; prod d, Gordon Willis; art d, F. Paul Sylos

Though Marshall is the svelte-voiced narrator of this riveting story, it is Sanders as the relentless cad and heartless artist who makes this film a standout. He is a stockbroker who decides he will take up this film's secret passion, painting, and discard his former life. To that end he convinces Geray, a successful but mediocre painter, to aid him in developing his art and, during the process,

when Geray takes Sanders into his home as a protege, he seduces Geray's wife and ruins Geray himself. Marshall, who is Sanders's friend, narrates the rake's progress from broker to painter to homewrecker and exile in Tahiti where Sanders comes to grips with his own personality and discovers his great talent, producing one masterpiece after another until dying tragically. The Maugham story on which this film is based unabashedly profiles the profligate career of the brilliant Paul Gauguin and Sanders plays this introspective, brilliant, and cruel-streaked genius to the hilt. Lewin's direction is terse, swift, and often magnificent as he chronicles Sanders's meteoric career and love life, the best part of the film being that set in the tropical islands toward the end. Here a sepia tone is employed to capture some of the illustrative flavor of the paintings shown and, during the life-consuming fire of Sanders's Tahitian hut—one which destroys his masterpiece and himself—color is lavishly and correctly employed. Seitz's camerawork is terrific and the supporting cast, especially Geray, and Blore, as a drunken Englishman, is excellent. The film earned an Oscar nomination for its score.

MOON IN THE GUTTER, THE

(LA LUNE DANS LE CANIVEAU)
1983   126m   c   ★★★
Drama   R/18
TF-1/Opera/SFPC/Gaumont   (France/Italy)

Gerard Depardieu (Gerard), Nastassja Kinski (Loretta), Victoria Abril (Bella), Vittorio Mezzogiorno (Newton Channing), Dominique Pinon (Frank), Bertice Reading (Lola), Gabriel Monnet (Tom), Milena Vukotic (Frieda), Bernard Farcy (Jesus), Anne-Marie Coffinet (Dora)

p, Lise Fayolle; d, Jean-Jacques Beineix; w, Jean-Jacques Beineix, Olivier Mergault (based on the novel by David Goodis); ph, Philippe Rousselot, Dominique Brenguier (Panavision, Eastmancolor); ed, Monique Prim, Yves Deschamps; m, Gabriel Yared; prod d, Hilton McConnico, Sandro dell'Orco, Angelo Santucci, Bernard Vezat; cos, Claire Fraisse

Jean-Jacques Beineix's follow-up to DIVA is an obscure, poetic, dreamlike mystery based on a novel by cult favorite David Goodis. This visually awe-inspiring production tells the story of Gerard (Gerard Depardieu), a riverfront dock worker tormented by the need to find out who raped his sister, causing her to commit suicide while lying in a gutter. During his search, Gerard becomes attracted to Loretta (Nastassia Kinski), the stunning mystery woman who cruises the waterfront in her blazing red convertible. The billboard in front of Gerard's house reads "Try Another World," and that is precisely what he decides to do. Where DIVA overpowered with bright romanticism, MOON IN THE GUTTER stuns with obsession. The script is often embarrassingly indulgent, but, for every failed line, action, and camera swirl, there is another that is astoundingly effective.

MOON IS BLUE, THE

1953   99m   bw   ★★½
Comedy   /PG
UA

William Holden (Donald Gresham), David Niven (David Slater), Maggie McNamara (Patty O'Neill), Tom Tully (Michael O'Neill), Dawn Addams (Cynthia Slater), Fortunio Bonanova (Television Announcer), Gregory Ratoff (Taxi Driver), Hardy Kruger (Sightseer), Johanna Matz (His Wife)

p, Otto Preminger, F. Hugh Herbert; d, Otto Preminger; w, F. Hugh Herbert (based on his play); ph, Ernest Laszlo; ed, Ronald Sinclair, Otto Ludwig; m, Herschel Burke Gilbert; prod d, Nicolai Remisoff; cos, Don Loper;

This pleasant trifle received more publicity, and, therefore, more business than it deserved. It was a Broadway farce with what was, for New York, mild to spicy dialogue. However, in the eyes of the movie censors who handed out the Production Code seal of approval, it was far too risque for movies because it dealt with the seduction of a virgin and used the words "virgin", "mistress", "seduction" and "pregnant" in a cavalier fashion. The newspaper space accorded the brouhaha was truly a tempest in a teapot, and the people who flocked to see this "hot" movie were disappointed by the tepidity. Niven's career had been in a downward spiral when Preminger, over the objections of the releasing company, hired the Englishman, whose flagging business life went soaring after the movie hit the theaters. Niven won the Golden Globe for his work in THE MOON IS BLUE, which was Preminger's first independent movie for the company he started with playwright Herbert. Preminger had staged the Broadway version of Herbert's farce with a cast that included Barbara Bel Geddes, Barry Nelson, and Donald Cook in the roles later played by McNamara, Holden, and Niven. At the same time he was directing this, Preminger was also making a version in German, DIE JUNGFRAU AUF DEM DACH (THE VIRGIN ON THE ROOF), with translated dialogue by Carl Zuckmayer. That one starred Hardy Kruger in the Holden role, with Matz as the sweet young thing. This version begins atop the Empire State Building on Fifth Avenue at 34th Street in New York. Holden, an up-and-coming architect, meets McNamara, a young actress who accepts his invitation to have dinner. They stop at Holden's apartment for a moment on their way to a restaurant, and she tells him that she is a wonderful cook and that if he has the fixings, she would be delighted to make them a meal right there. Holden tells her to relax and he will be back in a flash with enough food for them to dine upon. While he's gone, Addams arrives. She is Holden's onetime fiancee and more than a bit surprised to see McNamara. Now Niven, Addams' roue father, arrives and is instantly taken by McNamara's naivete. She invites him to stay for dinner, and he accepts. McNamara spills something on her dress and goes to Holden's bedroom, where she dons his dressing gown. While Holden is trying to calm down Addams somewhere else, Niven moves in on McNamara, who has already stated publicly that she's not against heavy necking but remains firm about her virginity, which must stay intact until she weds. Niven proposes marriage to McNamara and offers her a gift of $600, no strings attached. McNamara declines the marriage offer but happily accepts the $600, and she gives the old man a daughterly kiss as Holden enters and becomes enraged at the sight of this rakehell with the young girl in a dressing gown. Now Tully, McNamara's beefy father, enters and is angered when he finds his daughter in a bachelor pad in a state of semiclothedness. He knocks Holden for a loop, and despite Niven's attempts to reconcile matters, the romance goes out the window. The next day, Holden and McNamara are again both drawn to the top of the then-tallest building in New York. They meet Kruger and Matz, see each other on the observation deck, and Holden promptly asks for her hand as the movie ends. McNamara, the film editor, Otto Ludwig, and the title song received Oscar nominations. She made only three other films, THREE COINS IN THE FOUNTAIN; PRINCE OF PLAYERS; and THE CARDINAL, before committing suicide in February, 1978.

MOONLIGHTING

1982   97m   c   ★★★★
Drama   PG
Miracle   (U.K.)

Jeremy Irons *(Nowak)*, Eugene Lipinski *(Banaszak)*, Jiri Stanislav *(Wolski)*, Eugeniusz Hackiewicz *(Kudaj)*, Dorothy Zienciowska *(Lot Airline Girl)*, Edward Arthur *(Immigration Officer)*, Denis Holmes *(Neighbor)*, Renu Setna *(Junk Shop Owner)*, David Calder *(Supermarket Manager)*, Judy Gridley *(Supermarket Supervisor)*

p, Mark Shivas, Jerzy Skolimowski; d, Jerzy Skolimowski; w, Jerzy Skolimowski, Boleslaw Sulik, Barry Vince, Danuta Witold Stok; ph, Tony Pierce-Roberts; ed, Barrie Vince; m, Stanley Myers, Hans Zimmer; prod d, Tony Woollard; cos, Jane Robinson

One month after martial law was declared in Poland in the wake of the Solidarity uprising, Jerzy Skolimowski began work on this political allegory about a group of four Polish workers in London. Led by the only English speaker among them, their foreman, Nowak (Jeremy Irons), the group arrives to renovate a flat for their Polish boss. Working illegally at what by English standards are cut rates, they must live on the site under uncomfortable living arrangements. When Soviet troops roll into Warsaw, Nowak learns of the events, but, driven by private anxieties and determined to avoid dissent, schemes to conceal the news from his men. As budgetary and scheduling pressures mount, he must take increasingly drastic and draconian measures to do so. MOONLIGHTING contains no manifestos or crude symbols. Its politics are almost entirely limned in the actions and thoughts of Nowak, who is beautifully portrayed by Irons in the performance that made him one of the most respected actors of the decade. The better-educated and more highly paid Nowak is sympathetically characterized even as he mirrors the actions of the Polish authorities, cutting off his men's access to information and family ties, the workers' hierarchy (including the bosses back home) serving as a microcosm of Polish society. Director-cowriter Skolimowski never fails to truly dramatize his themes, however—creating that rarity, a "political film" that is also deeply personal, true to life, and morally and emotionally complex.

MOONRAKER

1979   126m   c   ★★★
Spy/Adventure   PG
UA   (U.K.)

Roger Moore *(James Bond)*, Lois Chiles *(Holly Goodhead)*, Michel Lonsdale *(Drax)*, Richard Kiel *(Jaws)*, Corinne Clery *(Corinne Dufour)*, Bernard Lee *("M")*, Geoffrey Keen *(Frederick Gray)*, Desmond Llewelyn *("Q")*, Lois Maxwell *(Miss Moneypenny)*, Emily Bolton *(Manuela)*

p, Albert R. Broccoli; d, Lewis Gilbert; w, Christopher Wood (based on the novel by Ian Fleming); ph, Jean Tournier (Panavision); ed, John Glen; m, John Barry; prod d, Ken Adam; art d, Max Douy, Charles Bishop; fx, Derek Meddings, John Evans, John Richardson; cos, Jacques Fonteray

A space-age James Bond (Moore) pursues evil to the final frontier in this big-budget entry that cost as much as the first eight Bond films put together. Bond is assigned to search for a missing space shuttle, and along the way he discovers a plot by Drax (Lonsdale) to take over the world by replacing its population with the super race he has bred in the huge space station to which Bond comes for their final battle. Richard Kiel, a dentist's dream, repeats his role from THE SPY WHO LOVED ME as the indestructible, steel-toothed Jaws. Lois Chiles plays the manda-

tory Bond love interest, and the film marks the last appearance
of Lee as M. The gadgets are up to the usual Bond standards, but
fancy effects do not a movie make, and 007 is less satisfying
floating around in space than when his feet are more or less firmly
planted on the ground. John Barry and Hal David collaborated
on the theme song, which was sung by Shirley Bassey. The film
picked up an Oscar nomination for Best Costume Design.

MOONSTRUCK

1987   102m   c   ★★★★
Romance/Comedy   PG
MGM

Cher *(Loretta Castorini)*, Nicolas Cage *(Ronny Cammareri)*, Vin-
cent Gardenia *(Cosmo Castorini)*, Olympia Dukakis *(Rose
Castorini)*, Danny Aiello *(Johnny Cammareri)*, Julie Bovasso *(Rita
Cappomaggi)*, John Mahoney *(Perry)*, Louis Guss *(Raymond
Cappomaggi)*, Feodor Chaliapin, Jr. *(Loretta's Grandfather)*, Anita
Gillette *(Mona)*

p, Patrick Palmer, Norman Jewison; d, Norman Jewison; w, John
Patrick Shanley; ph, David Watkin; ed, Lou Lombardo; m, Dick
Hyman; prod d, Philip Rosenberg; chor, Lofti Travolta

Oscar-nominated for Best Picture in 1987, this delightful roman-
tic comedy directed by Norman Jewison and deftly scripted by
John Patrick Shanley features excellent ensemble performances
and an acting tour de force from Cher. A 38-year-old widow,
Loretta Castorini (Cher), works as a bookkeeper and lives in
Brooklyn with her very Italian-American family: her father,
Cosmo (Vincent Gardenia), a prosperous plumber; her mother,
Rose (Olympia Dukakis); and her grandfather (Feodor
Chaliapin). Her longtime boyfriend, Johnny Cammareri (Danny
Aiello), proposes to her; although not passionately in love with
him, she accepts. However, Johnny must travel to his mother's
deathbed in Sicily before the wedding. Meanwhile, Loretta meets
Ronny (Nicholas Cage), Johnny's brother, to whom Johnny
hasn't spoken in five years, and they are instantly attracted to
each other. MOONSTRUCK brilliantly captures its Italian-
American milieu. Director Jewison and screenwriter Shanley
have fashioned a charming, funny tale of infidelity and transcendent love whose cultural setting provides both content and context. A symbol of the undeniable power and unpredictability of
passionate love, the moon that glows magically over the Manhattan skyline as the events in the film transpire is there not only
for Cher and Cage but also for Gardenia and Dukakis. Cher turns
in an outstanding performance that deservedly won her an Academy Award for Best Actress. Although Cage stumbles at points,
the supporting performances are all superb and wonderfully
nuanced. The moon and the whole of the film are beautifully
photographed by Oscar winner David Watkin. Simply stated, it
is difficult not to be swept up by this charming picture.

MORGAN!

1966   97m   bw   ★★★
Comedy/Drama   /A
Quintra   (U.K.)

Vanessa Redgrave *(Leonie Delt)*, David Warner *(Morgan Delt)*,
Robert Stephens *(Charles Napier)*, Irene Handl *(Mrs. Delt)*, New-
ton Blick *(Mr. Henderson)*, Nan Munro *(Mrs. Henderson)*, Bernard
Bresslaw *(Policeman)*, Arthur Mullard *(Wally)*, Graham Crowden
(Counsel), Peter Cellier *(2nd Counsel)*

p, Leon Clore; d, Karel Reisz; w, David Mercer (based on the
television play "A Suitable Case for Treatment" by David Mercer);
ph, Larry Pizer, Gerry Turpin; ed, Victor Proctor, Tom Priestley; m,
John Dankworth; art d, Philip Harrison

In the late 1950s and early 1960s, British films were densely
populated with angry young men. In MORGAN! the young man
is not only angry, he's crazier than a bedbug in Bedlam. By
altering the nature of the role from the original television play,
the creators of this film seem to be saying that anything is
possible if the leading character is deranged. With that premise,
all normalcy is tossed out the window and we are asked to accept
the lead as he is, crazy or not. By today's standards, this picture
is somewhat dated. The technique often overwhelms the story,
with innumerable slow-motion shots, freeze frames, and surrealistic scenes. Warner is a London artist married to Redgrave,
a woman considerably above his working-class standing. He
spends his time daydreaming about swinging through the jungle.
(Clips of KING KONG and TARZAN movies are used in the
dream sequences.) His mother, Handl, an ardent old communist,
spends lots of time at Karl Marx's grave in Highgate Cemetery.
Handl adores her son but feels he has betrayed his role in "The
Great Revolution" by marrying Redgrave. Redgrave secures a
divorce, and Warner, who was supposedly in Greece, shows up
on the day it is to be granted. He asks to be taken back and is
upset that she wants to leave him to marry priggish Stephens, an
art dealer who is closer to her in social status. Redgrave still
adores Warner but she is tired of being Jane to his Tarzan. Warner
will stop at nothing to get Redgrave to return to him. He hides in
her car, installs a buzzer in their house that erupts whenever
Redgrave and Stephens hug, puts a real skeleton in her bed, and
draws the hammer and sickle insignia on the furniture. He also
puts a bomb under the bed to try to get Stephens out of her life.
None of it seems to help. He goes as far as to sleep with her one
night when she wavers on her pledge to leave him. Eventually,
with the help of Mullard, a wrestler, he kidnaps Redgrave, but
she is saved by her parents, Munro and Blick. Warner is put in
jail on Redgrave's testimony and released on the same day she
is to wed Stephens. Warner puts on a gorilla suit, crashes the
wedding reception, and winds up on fire. He is then pursued as
he rides a motorcycle and winds up at the Thames. In his ravings,
he thinks that he's being put up against a wall to face a firing
squad made up of Redgrave, Stephens, and Handl. Finally, he is
committed to an asylum and Redgrave, very pregnant, comes to
visit him. He wonders if the child she's carrying is the result of
their one brief liaison. She smiles enigmatically, gives the most
subtle of nods, and walks away. Warner turns back to the garden
he's been tending. It's all been reshaped into the form of a
hammer and sickle.

The director's attempt to blend reality and fantasy is sometimes successful, but the humor is strained as a result and doesn't
always work. The truth is that Warner's character is certifiable;
he deserves to be incarcerated before he harms himself or someone else. It's a bizarre film, too heavy in places and not light
enough in others. The picture was released in England as MOR-
GAN; A SUITABLE CASE FOR TREATMENT. Czech director
Reisz has made some fascinating films, such as SATURDAY
NIGHT AND SUNDAY MORNING; THE GAMBLER; and
WHO'LL STOP THE RAIN. But in this one, he tries so hard to
be interesting that the effort shows in every frame. Oscar nomi-
nations went to Redgrave for Best Actress (won by Elizabeth
Taylor for WHO'S AFRAID OF VIRGINA WOOLF?) and
Rickards for Best Costume Design.

MORNING GLORY

1933 74m bw   ★★★
Drama   /A
RKO

Katharine Hepburn (Ada Love/"Eva Lovelace"), Douglas Fairbanks, Jr. (Joseph Sheridan), Adolphe Menjou (Louis Easton), Mary Duncan (Rita Vernon), C. Aubrey Smith (Robert Harley Hedges), Don Alvarado (Pepe Velez, the Gigolo), Fred Santley (Will Seymour), Richard Carle (Henry Lawrence), Tyler Brooke (Charles Van Dusen), Geneva Mitchell (Gwendolyn Hall)

p, Pandro S. Berman; d, Lowell Sherman; w, Howard J. Green (based on a play by Zoe Akins); ph, Bert Glennon; ed, William Hamilton; m, Max Steiner; art d, Van Nest Polglase, Charles Kirk; cos, Walter Plunkett

Hepburn received her first Oscar nomination for this, her third film, won the Oscar for her role, and was three times as good as the picture itself. The story paralleled Hepburn's own real-life experience so there was an undeniable streak of reality in her performance. Hepburn leaves a tiny burg in New England. She enters New York City as stagestruck as is humanly possible, but she soon learns that there are a lot of worms in the Big Apple and it's not the most hospitable place to seek fame and fortune. She encounters veteran actor Smith, who has been around since stages were lit by candles, and he takes an interest in her, teaches her a few tricks about acting, and squires her to the right parties. He brings her to a cocktail bash tossed by Duncan, a successful actress and neurotic woman in the Margo Channing (Bette Davis's role in ALL ABOUT EVE) mold. Hepburn hasn't eaten anything so she gets very drunk on champagne and performs two Shakespearean soliloquies for the sake of the startled partygoers. Later, Hepburn takes up with slick Menjou, a manager, then tosses him aside in favor of young playwright Fairbanks, who has written a new show that Duncan is to star in. When the actress goes off the deep end and leaves the show on opening night, guess who steps in, does the role, and is an overnight sensation?

By the story outline, it's easy to see where ALL ABOUT EVE got some of its characters and inspiration. The young actress, the older and temperamental star, the playwright, the manager should be evident. The picture was remade as STAGE STRUCK with Susan Strasberg as the aspiring hopeful and Henry Fonda and Christopher Plummer as the men in her life. That film was not as successful as this one, which was raised in entertainment value by Hepburn's glowing performance. By 1933, the combination of backstage manipulations and overnight success was already a cliche that had been covered many times before. Merian C. Cooper served as the executive producer, and if that seems familiar, it's because he was also responsible for such films as THE FOUR FEATHERS, KING KONG, FORT APACHE, MIGHTY JOE YOUNG, THE QUIET MAN, and many more.

MOROCCO

1930 90m bw   ★★★★
Romance/War
Paramount

Gary Cooper (Tom Brown), Marlene Dietrich (Amy Jolly), Adolphe Menjou (Mons. Le Bessiere), Ullrich Haupt (Adjutant Caesar), Juliette Compton (Anna Dolores), Francis McDonald (Cpl. Tatoche), Albert Conti (Col. Quinnevieres), Eve Southern (Mme. Caesar), Michael Visaroff (Barratire), Paul Porcasi (Lo Tinto)

p, Hector Turnbull; d, Josef von Sternberg; w, Jules Furthman (based on the novel Amy Jolly by Benno Vigny); ph, Lee Garmes, Lucien Ballard; ed, S.K. Winston; m, Karl Hajos; art d, Hans Dreier; cos, Travis Banton

Timeless romantic exotica; and that fadeout. . . That mistress of illusion, Marlene Dietrich, in her first American film—this stylish, poetic, and atmospheric tale of love during wartime, directed by the brilliant Josef von Sternberg. Amy Jolly (Dietrich), a German singer, arrives in North Africa and is hired as the lead act in a cabaret frequented by members of the Foreign Legion. She is pursued by Le Bessier (Adolphe Menjou), a worldly gentleman, but finds herself attracted to Tom Brown (Gary Cooper), a handsome Legionnaire, a man who ultimately tests the strength of her love. An intelligent story of devotion, MOROCCO is slim on plot but heavy on atmosphere. The movie exists solely to give von Sternberg the opportunity to create a poetic world of his own, peopled with characters (specifically Dietrich) and situations that do not exist in the real world, especially in a Moroccan desert city. Although MOROCCO is set during wartime and is populated with members of the Foreign Legion, von Sternberg is concerned with a different legion—"a foreign legion of women," in the director's words, as devoted to their men as the men are to the military. Includes the Dietrich number "What Am I Bid for My Apples?" by Leo Robin and Karl Hajos. MOROCCO would go a long way in establishing Dietrich as a new star (THE BLUE ANGEL was held up in release, until this Americanized Dietrich could be presented). Grooming for superstardom was severe for Dietrich—she was massaged hourly, her ankles wrapped in tight surgical bandages to re-deposit fat (thus the reliance on slacks to hide them, creating an international fashion fad) and she dieted severely. It may be true that her back molars were pulled to produce the cavernous cheekbones (likewise Joan Crawford); certainly this would remove part of the pleasure of eating. Her brows were shaved and wide, arching "wings" were drawn to open up her face, and give her an expression of remote impassiveness. Here was a new continental vamp, who didn't suffer like Garbo—American audiences were bowled over.

Camera wizard Lee Garmes was ordered by von Sternberg to shoot Dietrich only from one side, an idea cloned from screening Garbo films. But Dietrich's features were more irregular. Garmes came up with a "north light" for Dietrich; above her and slightly forward. It hollowed the cheeks, shadowed her heavy eyelids and burned out the dimensions of her wide though ingenious nose. Dietrich would refuse to be photographed or lit for public performance any other way for the length of her career (her concert career involved very little movement once she slunk to the microphone).

Von Sternberg and Cooper didn't get on. Cooper resented the director often using German on the set. Watch how he often blocks scenes so Dietrich stands above Cooper, and he must look up to her. Cooper's angry resignation resulted inadvertently in a fey, effective performance. His slightly effete reactions—tucking a rose behind his ear, smoking with a limp wrist, kissing behind a fan—balanced perfectly Dietrich's androgeny (the latter most apparent when she kisses a woman on the mouth in a nightclub scene) and the two had a rather torrid affair (with time out for Dietrich to tangle with fading John Gilbert; former flame Garbo got incensed and snatched him back, sending Dietrich snaking back to her recent costar).

The film is monochromatic expressionism—all the performances are pitched in the same straight line—explaining its appeal as a timeless piece. The slight story was based on Amy

Jolly, by Berlin newsman Benno Vigny, supposedly chronicling his experiences in the French foreign legion. You can bet it was never as beguiling as this.

MOSCOW ON THE HUDSON

1984 115m c   ★★★½
Comedy/Drama   R/15
Columbia

Robin Williams *(Vladimir Ivanoff)*, Maria Conchita Alonso *(Lucia Lombardo)*, Cleavant Derricks *(Lionel Witherspoon)*, Alejandro Rey *(Orlando Ramirez)*, Savely Kramarov *(Boris)*, Elya Baskin *(Anatoly)*, Oleg Rudnik *(Yury)*, Alexander Beniaminov *(Vladimir's Grandfather)*, Ludmila Kramarevsky *(Vladimir's Mother)*, Ivo Vrzal *(Vladimir's Father)*

p, Paul Mazursky; d, Paul Mazursky; w, Paul Mazursky, Leon Capetanos; ph, Don McAlpine (Metrocolor); ed, Richard Halsey; m, David McHugh; prod d, Pato Guzman; art d, Michael Molly, Peter Rothe; cos, Albert Wolsky

A loving, dramatic comedy that resembles early Frank Capra in its patriotism and sentiment, this movie just misses on several levels but has enough humor to make you smile and enough corn to warm anyone's heart. Vladimir Ivanoff (Robin Williams) is a saxophonist with a Russian circus visiting the US on a tour. Just before leaving New York, Vladimir is in Manhattan's trendiest department store, Bloomingdale's, when he makes the decision to defect. He races around the store, chased by KGB men, and hides under a counter handled by Lucia Lombardo (Maria Conchita Alonso). After the cops come in and Vladimir tells them he's defecting, he is taken to Harlem by security guard Lionel Witherspoon (Cleavant Derricks), whose family welcomes him. It isn't long before Vladimir and Lucia are an item, and she tries to help him get official status in the US through an immigration attorney (Alejandro Rey). There is no great story to speak of, just the adjustments Vladimir must make to become an American. Although uneven, Williams's performance here is a harbinger of the excellent work he would do in GOOD MORNING, VIETNAM and DEAD POETS SOCIETY.

MOSQUITO COAST, THE

1986 117m c   ★★★½
Adventure   R/PG
WB

Harrison Ford *(Allie Fox)*, Helen Mirren *(Mother)*, River Phoenix *(Charlie)*, Jadrien Steele *(Jerry)*, Hilary Gordon *(April)*, Rebecca Gordon *(Clover)*, Jason Alexander *(Clerk)*, Dick O'Neill *(Mr. Polski)*, Alice Sneed *(Mrs. Polski)*, Tiger Haynes *(Mr. Semper)*

p, Jerome Hellman; d, Peter Weir; w, Paul Schrader (based on the novel by Paul Theroux); ph, John Seale (Technicolor); ed, Thom Noble; m, Maurice Jarre; prod d, John Stoddart; art d, John Wingrove; fx, Larry Cavanaugh; cos, Gary Jones

A courageous and serious film featuring a tour de force performance by Harrison Ford. The print advertising campaign provided a succinct summary of the themes of THE MOSQUITO COAST: "How far should a man go to follow his dream? Allie Fox went to the Mosquito Coast. He went too far." In this beautifully photographed film, director Peter Weir (THE LAST WAVE, PICNIC AT HANGING ROCK, WITNESS, DEAD POETS' SOCIETY) considers the toll the untamed jungle can take on an already unbalanced mind.

Allie Fox (Harrison Ford) is an eccentric inventor, a wildly optimistic can-do kind of guy. Disgusted with what he perceives to be a dying America, Fox takes his wife (Helen Mirren) and

four children, including 15-year-old Charlie (River Phoenix), to an unsettled area near Honduras called the Mosquito Coast. Fox buys the deed to an isolated town that turns out to be only a few shacks and a handful of residents. But he pushes himself, his family, and the residents of the town into building a thriving community. His dream world is shaken, though, when three gun-toting terrorists show up. Unfortunately as Fox's dreams and sanity begin to fall apart so does the film but it's a pretty intense ride up to that point. The strong suggestion here is that the very qualities that allow people or nations to achieve greatness can be the very same ones that plant the seeds of future destruction.

Paul Theroux's novel, the film's source material, was long considered a property that was untranslatable to the screen. Consequently one can forgive many of the film's flaws. While Ford is terrific for much of the film, one cannot help but speculate what Jack Nicholson, an even greater actor who was originally sought for the lead, would have done with the character of Allie Fox. Nicholson excels at portraying morally ambiguous characters while it is difficult to vanquish the image of Indiana Jones from our heads as Ford battles the jungle. Speaking of Dr. Jones, River Phoenix, quite good here as Ford's son, would play the young Indiana Jones in the prologue to INDIANA JONES AND THE LAST CRUSADE. The ambitious screenplay for this film was written by Paul Schrader, a frequent collaborator with Martin Scorsese (screenplays for TAXI DRIVER, RAGING BULL, THE LAST TEMPTATION OF CHRIST)and a significant director (and often a director-writer) in his own right (BLUE COLLAR, HARDCORE, AMERICAN GIGOLO, PATTY HEARST, MISHIMA).

MOST DANGEROUS GAME, THE

1932 63m bw   ★★★
Thriller/Adventure
RKO

Joel McCrea *(Bob Rainsford)*, Fay Wray *(Eve Trowbridge)*, Leslie Banks *(Count Zaroff)*, Robert Armstrong *(Martin Trowbridge)*, Steve Clemente, Noble Johnson *(Tartar Servants)*, Hale Hamilton

p, Merian C. Cooper, Ernest B. Schoedsack; d, Ernest B. Schoedsack, Irving Pichel; w, James Ashmore Creelman (based on a story by Richard Connell); ph, Henry Gerrard; ed, Archie Marshek; m, Max Steiner

This is a grim and morose film with strong undertones of sadism and, toward the end, brutality. It is also a genuinely frightening film involving Banks as a mad Russian count who lords over a mist-enshrouded island and waits like a vicious spider for wayward ships to wreck themselves on the dangerous reefs surrounding his sinister domain. One of the sinking ships delivers up flotsam in the form of McCrea, Wray, and Armstrong, who are, at first, warmly welcomed to Banks's lavish estate. But slowly, as Banks describes his passion for hunting the wild beasts on the island, he begins to finger a scar on his forehead, one caused by a lion. Before they can realize their horrible situation, the shipwrecked survivors are compelled to flee into the thorny wilderness of the island with their host hunting them as he would animals, armed with bow and arrows, to give them a sporting chance. With Banks are his henchmen and a pack of the most vicious dogs ever unleashed in any film. Directors Schoedsack and Pichel dwell on the hunt, showing the victims fleeing madly through the brush and forests, narrowly missing death at the claws of wild animals or plunging into bottomless gorges. The hounds are shown in quick closeups that are terrifyingly abrupt, and telescopic shots cutting from the hunter to the hunted heighten the tension. Banks is relentless in his pursuit, crazily blowing his hunting horn and drawing his bow with an accuracy that proves deadly. He finally meets the grim fate he has designed for the others, plunging to his death while his own bloodthirsty hounds close in on him. There are wonderful atmospherics to this film—the count's looming, black castle, the primeval forests of the island—the same kind of environment producers Cooper and Schoedsack would create for their horror masterpiece, KING KONG, a year later. The studio thought that showing some decapitated heads, victims of Banks's unnatural hunts, might upset viewers, so these scenes were later cut. Wray, Armstrong, and Steiner, who composed the eerie score, would all be effectively used in KING KONG. The dark theme of this movie would be employed in countless films to come, as well as in radio and television programs. RKO would remake this film as A GAME OF DEATH and United Artists would explore the idea in RUN FOR THE SUN. Also that year, Rod Steiger would undergo the torment of being hunted by vicious Indians in RUN OF THE ARROW.

MOTHER AND THE WHORE, THE

(LA MAMAN ET LA PUTAIN)
1973 210m bw   ★★★★
Drama   /X
Losange/Elite/Cine Qua Non/Simar/V-M (France)

Bernadette Lafont (Marie), Jean-Pierre Leaud (Alexandre), Francoise Lebrun (Veronika), Isabelle Weingarten (Gilberte), Jacques Renard (Friend), Jean-Noel Picq, Jessa Darrieux, Marinka Matuszewski, Genevieve Mnich, Berthe Grandval

p, Pierre Cottrell; d, Jean Eustache; w, Jean Eustache; ph, Pierre Lhomme, Jacques Renard, Michel Cenet; ed, Jean Eustache, Denise de Casabianca

If any film signified that the French New Wave had come to an end, it was THE MOTHER AND THE WHORE, a grueling three-and-a-half hour study that may be one of the more enlightening works the cinema has ever produced. Set against a background of Paris cafes and tiny one-room apartments, it traces the amorous adventures of Leaud, an irresponsible young man who pretends to be a leftist intellectual. He is really little more than a victim of the postwar existentialist thought that paved the way for the materialistic attitudes of the early 1970s and a generation filled with empty ideals. One morning, Leaud feels an extraordinary need to marry. Leaving the small flat he shares with Lafont, his lover and willing meal ticket, he sets out to pop the question to his old girlfriend. Leaud brings the girl to a cafe where he engages in a long pseudo-intellectual monologue while asking for her hand. She flatly refuses, responding, "What novel are you being a character in?" (Leaud characteristically perceives himself in such terms.) Later that same day, he passes by a cafe where he spots the vampirish-looking Lebrun staring at him. He gets her phone number and agrees to meet her later. After several failed attempts to meet her, the two eventually arrange to meet at a cafe. Lebrun works as a nurse, a job that allows her enough money to pay for her dingy room, to buy pretty clothes, and to keep herself numbed with alcohol. Other than this, the only thing that interests her is sex, and she has no qualms about sleeping with any passing stranger. Leaud and Lebrun start a shaky affair that consists mainly of meeting in cafes and long monologues on Leaud's part. To Lebrun, he has become much more than her usual casual fling. She even calls him while he is spending the evening with Lafont, then sleeps with both of them. Lafont attempts suicide and the tension created by the triangle continually mounts until a gruesome climax in which Lebrun, who has seemed aloof and unaffected to this point, delivers a tear-filled

soliloquy revealing her self-perception as a sexual object. Leaud follows her to her room and asks her to marry him. She accepts while vomiting into a bucket which he holds.

Prior to THE MOTHER AND THE WHORE, director Eustache had worked as an assistant for New Wave directors, most notably Jean-Luc Godard. (He even appeared briefly in WEEK-END). His first two solo efforts were medium-length features that were of some interest, but this picture proved he was a perceptive filmmaker. However, Eustache's career was very short. After THE MOTHER AND THE WHORE won both the Grand Prix and the International Critics Award at Cannes, he made only one more feature before his suicide in 1980. THE MOTHER AND THE WHORE captures a sense of realism rare in any type of film, for it brings us deep beneath the surface of the characters's exteriors.

MOULIN ROUGE

1952 123m c   ★★★★
Biography   /PG
Romulus (U.K.)

Jose Ferrer (Henri de Toulouse-Lautrec/The Comte de Toulouse-Lautrec), Colette Marchand (Marie Charlet), Suzanne Flon (Myriamme Hayem), Zsa Zsa Gabor (Jane Avril), Katherine Kath (La Goulue), Claude Nollier (Countess de Toulouse-Lautrec), Muriel Smith (Aicha), Georges Lannes (Patou), Walter Crisham (Valentin Dessosse), Mary Clare (Mme. Loubet)

p, John Huston; d, John Huston; w, Anthony Veiller, John Huston (based on the novel by Pierre La Mure); ph, Oswald Morris (Technicolor); ed, Ralph Kemplen; m, Georges Auric; art d, Paul Sheriff; cos, Marcel Vertes, Juliaes Squire, Schiaparelli

Nominated for Best Picture, Best Direction, Best Actor, Best Supporting Actor, and Best Film Editing, MOULIN ROUGE won none of those Oscars (Best Picture went to THE GREATEST SHOW ON EARTH, Best Actor went to Gary Cooper for HIGH NOON, and Best Director went to John Ford for THE QUIET MAN), and only managed to take two statuettes; Marcel Vertes's Best Costume Design (Color) and Vertes and Paul Sheriff's Art Direction. The shame of it is that Oswald Morris's work was not even nominated and should have won an Oscar as it was, by far, the best color cinematography of 1952 and much better than that of the winning film, THE QUIET MAN. Ferrer was making his mark with portrayals of real or famous fictional characters (CYRANO DE BERGERAC, the Dauphin in JOAN OF ARC) and his role here was a combination of the two as Huston's adaptation took many liberties with the truth. Ferrer, in a magnificent job that must have been painful, as he played much of the film on his knees, is Toulouse-Lautrec, the son of wealthy Parisians. As a child, he had suffered an accident and his legs ceased to grow. He becomes a painter and his works glorify the colorful Montmartre area of Paris, filled with raucous music clubs, including the title bistro. He sits night after night at the club, painting its scenes and enagaging in banter with its star singer, Jane Avril (Gabor). Lautrec falls for a prostitute (Marchand) but she only uses him to get money for her boyfriend, so Lautrec becomes increasingly bitter, easing his pain by consuming excessive amounts of cognac. His posters promoting the Moulin Rouge have turned it into a major attraction, but he finds it lacks the earthy charm it had when it was less successful. He seems to have little to live for until he meets the beautiful Myriamme Hayem (Flon) and is smitten by her but does his best to hide his feelings lest he be crushed again. He sees her often, escorting her to numerous social functions. She loves him but does not think her feelings are returned, and she eventually leaves him for another. Hayem sends him a last letter in which she declares her love for him and Lautrec is now completely shattered to know that he has forever lost this woman. He begins drinking even more heavily, which takes its toll as the artist dies at the age of 37.

The drama is so depressing sometimes (against the brilliant use of color) that one wonders if the fellow were really that unhappy all the time. Surely, his works do not reflect that dour attitude and so much of his art indicates the *joie de vivre* of the period and the area better than any photography (a medium that was just beginning). MOULIN ROUGE was filmed in France and England and had a few interesting people in small roles. Look hard for horrorists Christopher Lee and Peter Cushing, as well as a young Tutte Lemkow (British choreographer/actor who was the Fiddler in FIDDLER ON THE ROOF). The first 25 minutes of the movie are outstanding as a cancan sequence sets the tone for what is to come. Much of the drama is, in fact, quite fine. Unfortunately, some of what follows the opening pales by comparison and the picture begins to wallow in sentimentality and self-pity, something that Toulouse-Lautrec never betrayed in his art. The dance sequences, with the traditional cancan steps, eclipse Jean Renoir's FRENCH CANCAN and Walter Lang's CAN CAN.

MOUSE THAT ROARED, THE

1959 83m c ★★★★
Comedy/War /U
Open Road (U.K.)

Peter Sellers (*Tully Bascombe/Grand Duchess Gloriana XII/Prime Minister Count Mountjoy*), Jean Seberg (*Helen*), David Kossoff (*Prof. Kokintz*), William Hartnell (*Will*), Timothy Bateson (*Roger*), MacDonald Parke (*Snippet*), Monty Landis (*Cobbley*), Leo McKern (*Benter*), Harold Kasket (*Pedro*), Colin Gordon (*BBC Announcer*)

p, Jon Penington, Walter Shenson; d, Jack Arnold; w, Roger MacDougall, Stanley Mann (based on the novel *The Wrath of the Grapes* by Leonard Wibberley); ph, John Wilcox (Eastmancolor); ed, Raymond Poulton; m, Edwin Astley; art d, Geoffrey Drake; cos, Anthony Mendleson

THE MOUSE THAT ROARED is the outlandish, sidesplitting tale of the fortunes of the Duchy of Grand Fenwick, a mythical land on the verge of bankruptcy because its one export, a fine wine, has been copied and undercut by a US company. Grand Fenwick's prime minister (Peter Sellers) and female monarch (Sellers again) cook up a scheme to solve the problem: they will declare war on the States, lose immediately, then get back in the black with all the aid that the US usually bestows upon its beaten foes. They send out an "army" of 20, clad in armor and carrying bows and arrows, led by Tully Bascombe (Sellers once more). Of course, the arrival of these ragtag warriors in New York leads to a series of very funny situations, including the group's inadvertent acquisition of the "Q-bomb," a weapon that makes them a genuine threat. In the meantime, Bascombe meets and falls in love with Helen (Jean Seberg), the daughter of a scientist. Besides the wonderful Sellers, there are fine performances from all, especially Leo McKern as the pompous leader of Grand Fenwick's "loyal opposition." An inferior sequel, MOUSE ON THE MOON, was directed by Richard Lester.

MOVIE CRAZY

1932 81m bw ★★★½
Comedy
Paramount

Harold Lloyd (*Harold Hall*), Constance Cummings (*Mary Sears*), Kenneth Thomson (*Vance, a Gentleman Heavy*), Sidney Jarvis (*The Director*), Eddie Fetherston (*Bill, the Assistant Director*), Robert McWade (*Wesley Kitterman, the Producer*), Louise Closser Hale (*Mrs. Kitterman, His Wife*), Spencer Charters (*J.L. O'Brien*), Harold Goodwin (*Miller, a Director*), Lucy Beaumont (*Mrs. Hall, Harold's Mother*)

p, Harold Lloyd; d, Clyde Bruckman; w, Vincent Lawrence (based on a story by Agnes Christine Johnston, John Grey, Felix Adler); ph, Walter Lundin; ed, Bernard W. Burton; art d, William MacDonald, Harry Oliver

Silent comedian Harold Lloyd's best sound effort, MOVIE CRAZY is partly autobiographical. Lloyd plays a Kansas boy who is enamored of the movies. In imitation of the screen dramas that thrill him, he performs elaborate, dramatic scenes for the amusement of his mother and to the chagrin of his father. Lloyd sends a letter to Hollywood offering to appear in any film of their choosing. Through a mixup, a photograph of an extremely handsome lad is substituted for Lloyd's with the letter, and soon Hollywood calls him for a screen test. Ecstatic, Lloyd hustles off to Hollywood to begin a career as a movie actor. Unfortunately, Hollywood gets more than it bargained for when Lloyd, a bumbling Kansas clod, shows up and gets himself in all sorts of slapstick trouble on the set. While the studio heads decide just what to do with him, Lloyd falls for actress Constance Cummings when he sees her made up as a Mexican girl for a scene. When he meets her again, sans makeup, he doesn't realize that it's the same woman and falls in love with her again. Cummings allows the confusion to continue, just to have fun with Lloyd. Eventually the powers-that-be in the studio decide Lloyd would be perfect for comedy pictures and they sign him to a lucrative contract. Filled with creative gags and funny bits, MOVIE CRAZY is not only a successful comedy but a fascinating behind-the-camera look at the studio system in the early days of talkies.

MOVIE MOVIE

1978 105m c/bw ★★★★
Comedy PG
WB

George C. Scott (*Gloves Malloy/Spats Baxter*), Trish Van Devere (*Betsy McGuire/Isobel Stuart*), Red Buttons (*Peanuts/Jinks Murphy*), Eli Wallach (*Vince Marlowe/Pop*), Jocelyn Brando (*Mama Popchik/Mrs. Updike*), Barry Bostwick (*Johnny Danko/Dick Cummings*), Art Carney (*Dr. Blaine/Dr. Bowers*). DYNAMITE HANDS: Harry Hamlin (*Joey Popchik*), Ann Reinking (*Troubles Moran*), Michael Kidd (*Pop Popchik*)

p, Stanley Donen; d, Stanley Donen; w, Larry Gelbart, Sheldon Keller; ph, Bruce Surtees, Charles Rosher, Jr.; ed, George Hively; m, Ralph Burns, Buster Davis; art d, Jack Fisk; chor, Michael Kidd; cos, Patty Norris

Two movies in one (hence the title), with many of the same actors appearing in both halves, this funny Stanley Donen-directed sendup of film cliches takes an affectionate look at an era when lawmen were "coppers" and people could say "swell" without smirking. Shot in both black-and-white and color, it is intended as a whole evening of entertainment and includes a coming-at-tractions trailer for "Zero Hour," a war movie that obviously was never made. After a George Burns prolog we plunge into the first movie, "Dynamite Hands," which parodies 1930s fight films, following the fortunes of a poor law student, Harry Hamlin, who takes to the ring to pay for an operation to save his sister's eyesight, then completes his studies to use the legal system to get even with a crooked promoter. In "Baxter's Beauties of 1933," which obviously was inspired by 42ND STREET, George C. Scott is a Flo Ziegfeld type who is trying to put on a big show. You know the story: An unknown girl gets the chance to star when the leading lady breaks her leg. Trish Van Devere (Scott's real-life wife) is the leading lady, Rebecca York is the ingenue, and Barry Bostwick is her beau. Choreographer Michael Kidd effects a passable imitation of Busby Berkeley, despite a small budget for chorines and cameras. The satire gets a bit heavy at times, and you have to know a lot about the movies upon which this is based to glean the most out of the humor; still, there's lots of nostalgic fun here and the tunes and cast are exceptional, even when removed from their satirical context.

MRS. MINIVER

1942 134m bw ★★★
Drama/War /U
MGM

Greer Garson (Mrs. Kay Miniver), Walter Pidgeon (Clem Miniver), Teresa Wright (Carol Beldon), Dame May Whitty (Lady Beldon), Henry Travers (Mr. Ballard), Reginald Owen (Foley), Miles Mander (German Agent's Voice), Henry Wilcoxon (Vicar), Richard Ney (Vin Miniver), Clare Sandars (Judy Miniver)

p, Sidney Franklin; d, William Wyler; w, Arthur Wimperis, George Froeschel, James Hilton, Claudine West (based on the novel by Jan Struther); ph, Joseph Ruttenberg; ed, Harold F. Kress; m, Herbert Stothart; art d, Cedric Gibbons, Urie McCleary; fx, A. Arnold Gillespie, Warren Newcombe; cos, Robert Kalloch

Frightfully nice, it's like war at teatime. MRS. MINIVER tells of the British people's will to survive the German bombing raids and fight to the end for their own human dignity. Director William Wyler achieves his goal by concentrating on the inhabitants of the country village of Belham, especially the middle-class Miniver family—lovely Kay Miniver (Greer Garson), gallant husband Clem (Walter Pidgeon), brave eldest son Vin (Richard Ney) and adorable younger children Toby and Judy (Christopher Severn and Clare Sandars). As the country slips into war, Vin falls in love with noble Carol (Teresa Wright), the teenage daughter of crotchety village matriarch Lady Beldon (Dame May Whitty). As romance grows and the village prepares for its annual flower-growing competition, German bombs begin to decimate the once-peaceful countryside and a downed German aviator seeks refuge with the Minivers. Villagers die, the Miniver home is bombed, and the church is reduced to rubble, but the people's spirit is strengthened when the vicar (Henry Wilcoxon) delivers a powerful speech, and the flower show goes on.

When Winston Churchill saw the film, he maintained that MRS. MINIVER would prove more valuable than the combined efforts of six divisions. At Oscar time, this heavy-handed film was named Best Picture; statuettes were also given to Garson, Wyler, Wright, cinematographer Ruttenberg and the screenwriters. Garson gave the longest (5½ minute) speech in Oscar history; never mind she didn't deserve the award. Ponder her as an actress: totally ordinary, though lovely. Just when you've settled into that opinion, she does something brilliant. Resigned to being wrong, you watch as she settles back into self-satisfied mediocrity. Did that. Quite right. Lovely.

MUMMY, THE

1932 72m bw ★★★★★
Horror /15
Universal

Boris Karloff (Im-Ho-Tep/Ardeth Bey), Zita Johann (Helen Grosvenor/Princess Anck-es-en-Amon), David Manners (Frank Whemple), Edward Van Sloan (Professor Muller), A.S. Byron (Sir Joseph Whemple), Bramwell Fletcher (Norton), Noble Johnson (the Nubian), Leonard Mudie (Professor Pearson), Katherine Byron (Frau Muller), Eddie Kane (Doctor)

p, Carl Laemmle, Jr.; d, Karl Freund; w, John Balderston (based on a story by Nina Wilcox Putnam, Richard Schayer); ph, Charles Stumar; ed, Milton Carruth; art d, Willy Pogany; fx, John P. Fulton

Absolutely marvelous. Following his triumph as the monster in FRANKENSTEIN, Boris Karloff created yet another unforgettable horror character with the help of makeup man Jack Pierce and ace cinematographer-turned-director Karl Freund. THE MUMMY opens at an Egyptian archeological dig in 1921 as a group of scientists examine their most recent finding—a sarcophagus in an unmarked grave. The coffin in which the mummy rests has been stripped of all religious markings that would have ensured an afterlife for the deceased, proof that the 3700-year-old corpse was buried in disgrace. Interred with the mummy is a large box upon which is written a warning to those who would dare open it—this, however, is a horror movie, and were no one to open the box we would never be treated to Karloff's magnificent wrappings. THE MUMMY was the directorial debut of the brilliant German cinematographer, Freund, who had photographed such classic German silents as THE LAST LAUGH; VARIETY; and METROPOLIS, as well as DRACULA in the US. Though THE MUMMY is not an overtly terrifying film (with the exception of the mummy's revival at the beginning), Freund creates an uneasy atmosphere of dread and foreboding. His camera is remarkably mobile, with impressive tracking and crane shots that float through the action, creating an eerie mood. Although made during a time when many films suffered from a lack of music, THE MUMMY has a full score, an effectively muted collection of themes perfectly suited to the carefully paced, mystical feel of the film. Though the technical credits are excellent, it is Karloff who carries the film. Makeup genius Pierce once again molded his magic to the actor, and the combination of linen, fuller's earth, and clay used to create the recently discovered mummy took over eight hours a day to apply. The effect is startling, though Karloff only appears as the mummy briefly. Perhaps more impressive is the more subtle makeup Pierce created for Karloff in his reincarnated state. The mass of delicate wrinkles on Karloff's face and hands, combined with the actor's deliberately gentle, flowing movements, creates a being who looks as if he may fall apart at any moment. It is a tribute to Karloff's immense skill that he can lend dignity and conviction to such a role. The supporting roles are also well-handled, with Johann making an appealingly offbeat heroine and Van Sloan crusading against yet another movie monster. The relationship between Karloff's mummy and Johann, whom he believes to be the reincarnation of his lost love, lends the film conviction and a certain sadness amidst the horror. The re-creation of the days of the pharaohs is also quite effective, and the scene wherein Karloff is wrapped alive, eyes going wider as his mouth is covered, is unforgettable. One of the rare horror films to somehow include a touch of the poetic, this stately yet brilliantly absorbing film stands the test of time beautifully today. Four inferior, shlocky sequels followed: THE MUMMY'S HAND; THE MUMMY'S TOMB; THE MUMMY'S GHOST; and THE MUMMY'S CURSE. Hammer Films of England revived the series beginning with THE MUMMY.

MUMMY, THE

1959   86m   c   ★★★
Horror   /X
Hammer   (U.K.)

Peter Cushing (*John Banning*), Christopher Lee (*Kharis, the Mummy*), Yvonne Furneaux (*Isobel Banning/Princess Ananka*), Eddie Byrne (*Inspector Mulrooney*), Felix Aylmer (*Stephen Banning*), Raymond Huntley (*Joseph Whemple*), George Pastell (*Mehemet, Priest*), John Stuart (*Coroner*), Harold Goodwin (*Pat*), Denis Shaw (*Mike*)

p, Michael Carreras; d, Terence Fisher; w, Jimmy Sangster (based on the screenplays "The Mummy" by Nina Wilcox Putnam, and "The Mummy's Tomb" by Griffin Jay); ph, Jack Asher (Technicolor); ed, James Needs, Alfred Cox; m, Franz Reizenstein; prod d, Bernard Robinson; art d, Bernard Robinson

Doesn't come unravelled. This lively Hammer reworking of the classic mummy material stars Peter Cushing as John Banning, one of three British archaeologists who desecrate the tomb of an Egyptian princess, awakening Kharis (Lee), her mummified lover, who was buried alive with the princess when she died. Kharis follows the archaeologists back to England and is about to kill Banning when he sees his victim's beautiful wife, Isobel (Furneaux), the spitting image of Kharis's lover, Princess Ananka. Stylishly directed by Terence Fisher (the action scenes, in particular, are breathtakingly choreographed), THE MUMMY features a surprisingly energetic performance from Christopher Lee, whose mummy moves swiftly and with strength, unlike his slow, shuffling 1940s predecessors. By playing the Mummy, Lee completed something of a trilogy of terror, having already starred as Frankenstein's Monster and Dracula. This remake really can't compare with the 1932 original and Lee is given no chance to flesh out his character in the haunting manner that Boris Karloff did, but for fairly standardized movie horror, this flick isn't half bad.

MUPPET MOVIE, THE

1979   98m   c   ★★★
Musical/Children's   G/U
ITC   (U.K.)

GUEST STARS: Charles Durning (*Doc Hopper*), Austin Pendleton (*Max*), Scott Walker (*Frog Killer*), Mel Brooks (*Prof. Krassman*), Carol Kane (*Miss.*). MUPPET PERFORMERS: Jim Henson (*Kermit the Frog/Rowlf/Dr. Teeth/Waldorf*), Frank Oz (*Miss Piggy/Fozzie Bear/Animal/Sam the Eagle*), Jerry Nelson (*Floyd Pepper/Crazy Harry/Robin the Frog/Lew Zealand*), Richard Hunt (*Scooter/Statler/Janice/Sweetums/Beaker*), Dave Goelz (*The Great Gonzo/Zoot/Dr. Bunsen Honeydew*)

p, Jim Henson; d, James Frawley; w, Jerry Juhl, Jack Burns; ph, Isidore Mankofsky (CFI color); ed, Christopher Greenbury; m, Paul Williams; prod d, Joel Schiller; art d, Les Gobruegge; cos, Calista Hendrickson (Muppets), Gwen Capetanos

This charming children's film was the first to star the successful television puppets (two sequels followed). The loose plot follows Kermit the Frog and Fozzie Bear as they travel cross-country on their way to fame and fortune in Hollywood. On the road they pick up a variety of passengers (muppet and human) and sing a dozen songs. The special effects are handled very well; highlights feature Kermit riding a bicycle and rowing a boat. Cute without being insipid, funny without being childish, THE MUPPET MOVIE contains enough magic to please all ages. Nominated for two Oscars: Best Song Score and Best Song ("The Rainbow Connection" by Paul Williams and Kenny Ascher).

MUPPETS TAKE MANHATTAN, THE

1984   94m   c   ★★½
Children's/Comedy   G/U
Tri-Star

Juliana Donald (*Jenny*), Lonny Price (*Ronnie*), Louis Zorich (*Pete*), Art Carney, James Coco, Jim Henson (*Kermit/Rowlf/Dr. Teeth/Swedish Chef, Waldorf*), Frank Oz (*Miss Piggy/Fozzie/Animal*), Dave Goelz (*Gonzo/Chester/Rat/Bill/Zoot*), Steve Whitmire (*Rizzo the Rat/Gil*), Richard Hunt (*Scooter/Janice/Statler*)

p, David Lazer; d, Frank Oz; w, Frank Oz, Tom Patchett, Jay Tarses (based on a story by Patchett, Tarses); ph, Robert Paynter (Technicolor, Metrocolor); ed, Evan Lottman; m, Ralph Burns; prod d, Stephen Hendrickson; art d, W. Steven Graham, Paul Eds; fx, Ed Drohan; chor, Chris Chadman; cos, Karen Roston, Calista Henrickson, Polly Smith

This follow-up to THE MUPPET MOVIE and THE GREAT MUPPET CAPER is not as good or as hip as its predecessors, but the Muppet gang remains charming. The plot follows the old "Hey kids, let's put on a show" story line—except that this time the barn is Broadway and the "kids" are a frog, a chicken, a pig, and other assorted creations of executive producer and Muppet master Jim Henson. Kermit and the gang are presenting a revue called "Manhattan Melodies" at a college campus. They feel that the show is good enough to take to New York, so everyone goes off to conquer the Big Apple. There they find the doors of all the reputable producers firmly closed, although one unsavory character (Dabney Coleman) is interested, providing they kick in $300 each. Crestfallen, they all go off in different directions to raise money for their show, with various adventures and encounters with the film's guest stars (making for some fun celebrity spotting) on the way. The film's song score was nominated for an Oscar.

MURDER

1930   92m   bw   ★★★★
Mystery   /PG
British Intl.   (U.K.)

Herbert Marshall (*Sir John Menier*), Norah Baring (*Diana Baring*), Phyllis Konstam (*Dulcie Markham*), Edward Chapman (*Ted Markham*), Miles Mander (*Gordon Druce*), Esme Percy (*Handel Fane*), Donald Calthrop (*Ion Stewart*), Amy Brandon Thomas (*Defence*), Marie Wright (*Miss Mitcham*), Hannah Jones (*Mrs. Didsome*)

p, John Maxwell; d, Alfred Hitchcock; w, Alma Reville, Walter C. Mycroft, Alfred Hitchcock (based on the novel and play *Enter Sir John* by Clemence Dane and Helen Simpson); ph, Jack Cox; ed, Emile De Ruelle, Rene Harrison; m, John Reynders; art d, John Mead

An atypical Hitchcock film which depends on the element of surprise rather than his usual building of suspense. Diana (Baring), a young actress, is accused of killing one of her friends, tried, and sentenced to death by a jury. Jury member Sir John Menier (Marshall), an actor-manager and gentleman knight, remains unconvinced of her guilt and makes an attempt to locate the actual murderer. Visually astonishing, MURDER also makes creative use of sound by recording a character's spoken thoughts on the soundtrack. While the innocent person accused became a staple of Hitchcock's later films, the director would expand on this idea of theatricality in his mystery STAGE FRIGHT. Hitchcock also directed a German version of MURDER, entitled MARY, starring Alfred Abel.

MURDER BY DEATH

1976 94m c   ★★★★
Mystery/Comedy   PG
Rastar

Eileen Brennan (*Tess Skeffington*), Truman Capote (*Lionel Twain*),
James Coco (*Milo Perrier*), Peter Falk (*Sam Diamond*), Alec Guin-
ness (*Butler Bensonumum*), Elsa Lanchester (*Jessica Marbles*),
David Niven (*Dick Charleston*), Peter Sellers (*Sidney Wang*),
Maggie Smith (*Dora Charleston*), Nancy Walker (*Yetta the Maid*)

p, Ray Stark; d, Robert Moore; w, Neil Simon; ph, David M. Walsh
(Panavision); ed, Margaret Booth, John F. Burnett; m, Dave Grusin;
prod d, Stephen Grimes; art d, Harry Kemm; fx, Augie Lohman;
cos, Ann Roth

This spoof of the great fictional-film detectives offers consistently funny, often hysterical scenes sparked by Falk, Niven,
Sellers, and Guinness. Wealthy Lionel Twain (Capote, in his film
debut), invites the world's greatest detectives to his eerie castle-
like home. These counterparts to Miss Marple, Nick and Nora
Charles, Sam Spade, Hercule Poirot, and Charlie Chan, tumble
and fumble into the dungeonlike fortress full tilt and off tilt. They
soon discover that Twain is holding them prisoner in a home
suddenly covered with bars and steel doors, rooms that lead
nowhere and everywhere, leaving them with the clue that a
murder is about to be committed by one among them. Falk is
terrific as the fiercely posturing Humphrey Bogart-Sam Spade
prototype, with the other leading players not far behind him in a
race for the insane asylum. Capote is so bad an actor that he's
funny, which may or may not be the point. This one is also the
film debut of director Moore and he does a fine job of presenting
so many twists and turns that no viewer will be able to sort it all
out, even at the finale. Producer Ray Stark, director Moore,
screenwriter Neil Simon, and stars Falk, Coco, and Brennan
teamed again two years later in the less successful parody THE
CHEAP DETECTIVE.

MURDER, HE SAYS

1945 91m bw   ★★★★
Comedy
Paramount

Fred MacMurray (*Pete Marshall*), Helen Walker (*Claire Mathews*),
Marjorie Main (*Mamie Johnson*), Jean Heather (*Elany Fleagle*),
Porter Hall (*Mr. Johnson*), Peter Whitney (*Mert Fleagle/Bert Flea-
gle*), Mabel Paige (*Grandma Fleagle*), Barbara Pepper (*Bonnie
Fleagle*), Walter Baldwin (*Vic Hardy*), James Flavin (*Police Officer*)

p, E.D. Leshin; d, George Marshall; w, Lou Breslow (based on a
story by Jack Moffitt); ph, Theodor Sparkuhl; ed, LeRoy Stone; m,
Robert Emmett Dolan; art d, Hans Dreier, William Flannery; fx,
Gordon Jennings, Paul K. Lerpae

It's goodbye to logic and sanity in this one, a zany laugh riot in
which MacMurray shines as a statistics-gathering insurance
salesman in the Ozarks who must deal with hillbilly mentality
and crazy twin killers, both played brilliantly by Whitney.
MacMurray discovers, much to his chagrin, that the only sane
person in the entire community is Walker, who is trying to
vindicate her father, wrongly imprisoned for a robbery committed by female bandit Pepper. Meanwhile the Fleagle family
members, who would just as soon kill a stranger as say hello, are
frantically searching for Pepper's hidden $70,000 in stolen loot.
"Ma" Main, doing something like her Ma Kettle routine but with
sinister overtones, is splendid as she confuses MacMurray, already perplexed, in his quest for statistics. Further complicating
matters is Pepper, who gets out of prison and is now looking to

pick up her buried money. The chases—awkward, narrow escapes by MacMurray and Walker—are, granted, larded with
slapstick, but the antics are so zany and Marshall's clever direction so swift that the laughs are delivered rapid-fire. A truly
hilarious, fun-filled movie in the then-popular vein of the fatal
farce (epitomized in ARSENIC AND OLD LACE). MacMurray
is in his element here and is nothing less than terrific.

MURDER, MY SWEET

1945 95m bw   ★★★★★
Mystery   /PG
RKO

Dick Powell (*Philip Marlowe*), Claire Trevor (*Velma/Mrs. Grayle*),
Anne Shirley (*Ann*), Otto Kruger (*Amthor*), Mike Mazurki (*Moose
Malloy*), Miles Mander (*Mr. Grayle*), Douglas Walton (*Marriott*), Don
Douglas (*Lt. Randall*), Ralf Harolde (*Dr. Sonderborg*), Esther How-
ard (*Mrs. Florian*)

p, Adrian Scott; d, Edward Dmytryk; w, John Paxton (based on the
novel *Farewell, My Lovely* by Raymond Chandler); ph, Harry Wild;
ed, Joseph Noriega; m, Roy Webb; art d, Albert S. D'Agostino,
Carroll Clark; fx, Vernon L. Walker; cos, Edward Stevenson

Near perfect, my sweet. Hard-boiled detective Philip Marlowe
(Powell) is hired by ex-con Moose Malloy (Mazurki) to find his
missing girlfriend Velma. Shortly thereafter, Marlowe is hired by
socialite Mrs. Grayle (Trevor) to find a valuable jade necklace
that has been stolen from her. Dividing his time between the
seedy underworld and the ritzy digs of the upper class, Marlowe
finds blackmail, doublecrosses, corruption, and murder on both
sides of the tracks. Much to Marlowe's surprise, both cases
dovetail into one. Considered one of the quintessential film noir
films, this tough, sardonic, and unusually witty film brought
one-time movie crooner Powell back from the brink of career
catastrophe and made him a superstar. Not even Humphrey
Bogart's portrayal of Marlowe in THE BIG SLEEP could match
Powell's portrayal of the down-and-out gumshoe. Director Edward Dmytryk uses every cinematic trick in the book here,
creating a truly bleak and disorienting netherworld populated by
a variety of sordid characters. Here's Mazurki's best in his
catalogue of hoods, our fave Shirley performance, but it's Miss
Trevor who rises to the top, like a dangerous cup of posioned
cream, viewing after viewing.

MURDER ON THE ORIENT EXPRESS

1974 128m c   ★★★½
Mystery   PG
Paramount (U.K.)

Albert Finney (*Hercule Poirot*), Lauren Bacall (*Mrs. Hubbard*),
Martin Balsam (*Bianchi*), Ingrid Bergman (*Greta Ohlsson*), Jacque-
line Bisset (*Countess Andrenyi*), Jean-Pierre Cassel (*Pierre Paul
Michel*), Sean Connery (*Col. Arbuthnot*), John Gielgud (*Beddoes*),
Wendy Hiller (*Princess Dragomiroff*), Anthony Perkins (*Hector
McQueen*)

p, John Brabourne, Richard Goodwin; d, Sidney Lumet; w, Paul
Dehn (based on the novel by Agatha Christie); ph, Geoffrey Un-
sworth (Panavision, Technicolor); ed, Anne V. Coates; m, Richard
Rodney Bennett; prod d, Tony Walton; art d, Jack Stephens; cos,
Tony Walton

With a cast as dazzling as this film's, it doesn't really matter if
the story is good or bad. Fortunately, this one is elegant and
stylish in the best Agatha Christie tradition—a thoroughly entertaining and classy whodunit. Hercule Poirot (Finney) is aboard
the luxurious Orient Express in 1934, traveling across Asia and

Europe to Paris. When an American financier (Richard Widmark) is found dead—stabbed a dozen times—Finney is prevailed upon by railway executive Bianchi (Balsam) to solve the case. Through an elaborate re-creation of the crime, Finney is able to determine, in a surprise ending, exactly who the killer is. For years Agatha Christie refused to have this story filmed, but MURDER ON THE ORIENT EXPRESS was worth the wait. A box-office smash, the film grabbed six Oscar nominations: Best Actor (Finney, who lost to Art Carney for HARRY AND TONTO), Best Cinematography, Best Costume Design, Best Original Score, Best Adapted Screenplay and Bergman, in a sentiment decision took home the Best Supporting Actress Award. Very enjoyable, but frankly, too many stars for its own good.

MURIEL
(MURIEL, OU LE TEMPS D'UN RETOUR)
1963   115m   c   ★★★★★
Drama   /A
Argos/Alpha/Eclair/Pleiade/Dear   (France/Italy)

Delphine Seyrig (Helene), Jean-Pierre Kerien (Alphonse), Nita Klein (Francoise), Jean-Baptiste Thierree (Bernard), Claude Sainval (de Smoke), Laurence Badie (Claudie), Jean Champion (Ernest), Jean Daste (The Goat Man), Martine Vatel (Marie-Dominique), Philippe Laudenbach (Robert)

p, Anatole Dauman; d, Alain Resnais; w, Jean Cayrol (based on the story by Cayrol); ph, Sacha Vierny (Eastmancolor); ed, Kenout Peltier, Eric Pluet, Claudine Merlin; m, Hans Werner Henze; art d, Jacques Saulnier

Alain Resnais's third feature and first color film once again concerns memory. Helene (Delphine Seyrig) is a widow who sells antiques from her Boulogne-sur-Mer apartment. She shares the place with her eccentric filmmaker stepson, Bernard (Jean-Baptiste Thierree), a 22-month veteran of the Algerian War, during which he took part in the torture and murder of a young woman named Muriel. Bernard is haunted by the memory of Muriel, spending much time watching a grainy 8mm film of her and filming the surroundings in his neighborhood. He talks of Muriel to Helene, who assumes the woman is a girl friend she has yet to meet. Helene, meanwhile, is reunited with a past lover, Alphonse (Jean-Pierre Kerien), another veteran of Algeria, but they cannot recapture what they once had, if they had anything at all. Alphonse arrives at Helene's with his mistress, Francoise (Nita Klein), whom he introduces as his niece. While Helene, her present lover, de Smoke (Claude Sainval), and Alphonse try to sort out their emotions, Francoise shows an attraction to Bernard, who is involved with Marie-Dominique (Martine Vatel). MURIEL marked the second time Resnais worked with screenwriter Jean Cayrol, who previously contributed the commentary for Resnais's short documentary masterpiece NIGHT AND FOG. Their collaboration here produced a technical and thematic masterpiece that makes brilliant and confounding use of montage, sound construction, overlapping dialogue, and color photography. With MURIEL, Resnais' true filmmaking style had finally begun to emerge, employing characters who are real people (not named after cities or designated by letters) with memories that cut deeply into their personalities and relationships. The videotape is in French with English subtitles, though in most of the washed-out prints of the film the reportedly excellent use of color is hardly evident.

MURMUR OF THE HEART
(LE SOUFFLE AU COEUR)
1971   118m   c   ★★★★
Drama/Comedy
Nouvelles Editions/Marianne/Vides/Franz Seitz
(France/Italy/West Germany)

Lea Massari (Clara Chevalier), Benoit Ferreux (Laurent Chevalier), Daniel Gelin (the Father), Marc Winocourt (Marc), Fabien Ferreux (Thomas), Michel Lonsdale (Father Henri), Ave Ninchi (Augusta), Gila von Weitershausen (Freda), Micheline Bona (Aunt Claudine), Henri Poirier (Uncle Leonce)

p, Vincent Malle, Claude Nedjar; d, Louis Malle; w, Louis Malle; ph, Ricardo Aronovich (Eastmancolor); ed, Suzanne Baron; m, Charlie Parker, Sidney Bechet, Gaston Freche, Henri Renaud; art d, Jean-Jacques Caziot, Philippe Turlure

Among the French New Wave directors, Louis Malle is one of the most versatile and accessible. He isn't afraid to handle delicate issues and he approaches his subjects with sensitivity and wit. Incest, perhaps the most unspeakable of all taboos, was the subject of MURMUR OF THE HEART. Malle's comic look at the subject makes for a wonderful, tender film which accurately portrays all the joys and agonies of adolescent sexuality. Ferreux is the 14-year-old son of a French gynecologist. His mother (Massari), who had married her father when she was 16, is perhaps his closest confidante. They are two kindred spirits because they both enjoy the lively things in life. It is easy to see how the surroundings of their bourgois life trap the pair and force them to turn to one another for relief. Ferreux's two older brothers take him to a prostitute for his first sexual experience, but the drunken boys interrupt the tentative beginnings. When Ferreux contracts scarlet fever, which leaves him with a heart murmur, his mother takes him to a mountain health spa to recuperate. It is here that Massari sees a chance to break away from the suffocating atmosphere of her home life. While she flirts with another patient, Ferreux tries his own hand at love by attempting to pick up a pair of girls his own age. Mother and son are both rejected by their prospective lovers at a Bastille Day celebration. The pair return to their hotel room, get drunk, then fall into bed. Their mutual comforting leads to lovemaking. Massari is sensitive to her son's adolescent psyche and explains that this will be their own special experience that will never be repeated or discussed. Ferreux later leaves the room and makes love with one of the teenage girls. Upon returning to his room, he's surprised to find his father and brothers waiting for him. The older boys realize what their brother has just come back from and they break out laughing. At first Massari feels a pang of rejection, but then joins in the laughter.

This is a film alive with energy. One never forgets those terrible moments of early adolescence, and this film recaptures the feelings with honesty and real sensitivity. Backed by a wonderful jazz score, the drama is made believable by its characters. Massari and Ferreux have a marvelous natural chemistry that makes their relationship honest and understandable. Their lovemaking is treated in a subtle manner. Malle never dwells upon it, nor does he make it seem like a moment of depraved abandon. Instead, this is a special moment for two people who cannot explain their actions to outsiders. Malle stated that this film, while not a biography, did have a certain basis in truth. At 14 he did have a heart murmur, and he did visit a prostitute. The mother-son relationship was taken from the lives of several friends for whom the experience was not painful but as special a relationship as portrayed here. Rather than create a paean to incest, Malle has created a song of life. The film's comedy works because of the director's insight into adolescents and the pain they go through in discovering themselves. The script earned the film a Best Original Screenplay Oscar nomination.

MURPHY'S ROMANCE

1985 107m c   ★★½
Romance   R/15
Fogwood

Sally Field (*Emma Moriarity*), James Garner (*Murphy Jones*), Brian Kerwin (*Bobby Jack Moriarity*), Corey Haim (*Jake Moriarity*), Dennis Burkley (*Freeman Coverly*), Georgann Johnson (*Margaret*), Dortha Duckworth (*Bessie*), Michael Prokopuk (*Albert*), Billy Ray Sharkey (*Larry Le Beau*), Michael Crabtree (*Jim Forrest*)

p, Laura Ziskin; d, Martin Ritt; w, Harriet Frank, Jr., Irving Ravetch (based on the novella by Max Schott); ph, William A. Fraker (Panavision); ed, Sidney Levin; m, Carole King; prod d, Joel Schiller; fx, Dennis Dion; chor, Ken Rinker; cos, Joe I. Tompkins

In an age in which screen romance inevitably means teenagers in various states of undress, MURPHY'S ROMANCE is a welcome relief, a warm—if not entirely successful—portrait of two people falling in love. Emma Moriarity (Sally Field) is a divorced woman who moves with 13-year-old son Jake (Corey Haim) to a ranch on the outskirts of a rural Arizona town where she hopes to start her own horse-training business. When Emma meets the town pharmacist, Murphy Jones (James Garner), the two gradually build a comfortable friendship until she is unhappily surprised by a visit from her irresponsible ex-husband, Bobby Jack (Brian Kerwin). As Bobby Jack becomes increasingly annoying to Emma, she finds herself turning more and more to Murphy. MURPHY'S ROMANCE builds the friendship between Field and Garner in a slow and wholly natural manner, a refreshing change from the "instant" love stories that abound in modern cinema. Garner's performance is thoroughly likable and earned him a well-deserved Oscar nomination. Field, though she gives a spirited performance, is not entirely believable. Director Martin Ritt and screenwriters Harriet Frank, Jr., and Irving Ravetch rely too heavily on little vignette sequences to move the narrative, a technique that quickly becomes tedious and predictable. William Fraker also received an Oscar nomination for his cinematography.

MUSIC BOX

1989 124m c   ★★★★
Drama   PG-13/15
Carolco

Jessica Lange (*Ann Talbot*), Armin Mueller-Stahl (*Michael Laszlo*), Frederic Forrest (*Jack Burke*), Lukas Haas (*Michael "Mikey" Talbot*), Donald Moffat (*Harry Talbot*), Michael Rooker (*Karchy Laszlo*), Cheryl Lynn Bruce (*Georgine Wheeler*), Mari Torocsik (*Magda Zoldan*), J.S. Block (*Judge Erwin Silver*), Sol Frieder (*Istvan Boday*)

p, Irwin Winkler; d, Constantin Costa-Gavras; w, Joe Eszterhas; ph, Patrick Blossier; ed, Joele Van Effenterre; m, Philippe Sarde; prod d, Jeannine Claudia Oppewall; art d, Bill Arnold; chor, Eva Nemeth, Karoly Nemeth; cos, Rita Salazar

As they did with BETRAYED, critics took director Costa-Gavras to task for not approaching the subject of MUSIC BOX (the prosecution of WWII Nazi war criminals residing in the United States) in a more high-pitched, emotional manner. Yet, what MUSIC BOX arguably loses by keeping its emotions reined in is more than made up for by a deliberately detailed, deeply disturbing realism. As he did with THE JAGGED EDGE, writer

Joe Eszterhas (who also wrote BETRAYED) starts with a sharp female defense lawyer facing a crisis of conscience when confronted with indisputable evidence of the guilt of a client with whom she has a deep emotional bond. Jessica Lange plays Ann Talbot, the troubled attorney who helps her father, Michael Laszlo, played by Armin Mueller-Stahl, with what she first assumes to be a case of mistaken identity. A Hungarian immigrant after the war, Mueller-Stahl claimed on his application for citizenship to have been a farmer. After decades of raising a family in America on a steelworker's pay, Mueller-Stahl is now faced with deportation on the nominal charge of having lied about his former occupation. In fact, he is being sent back to Hungary to be tried for wartime atrocities he is accused of committing as part of that country's Nazi collaborationist police force. He admits to having been with the police but claims innocence on the atrocity charges, saying he left the force in reaction to the very brutality of which he is accused. Up against badgering prosecutor Forrest, who is fueled by righteous rage, Lange is nevertheless able to puncture the testimony of key government witnesses. Masterfully she then builds her own case, presenting the deportation as a revenge-motivated sham orchestrated by the Hungarian communist government against Mueller-Stahl for his disruption of a cultural exchange with the US several years earlier (he threw garbage during a performance of a Hungarian dance company in Chicago, where the film is set, and caused the company's nationwide tour to be cancelled in the wake of the ensuing publicity). While preparing her case, the only irregularity Lange is able to find in her father's life is a series of large payments—Mueller-Stahl dismisses them as loans—to a fellow immigrant subsequently killed in a hit-and-run accident. Only in her later investigation does she discover blackmail, at the heart of which lies the hideous truth about the man who raised her. At first, she is fierce and cunning in the defense of her father. Later, she's finally forced to see him as a man who, at one time, is said to have sadistically raped and tortured a 16-year-old girl while his friend, later to become his blackmailer, took photos. At this point Lange takes the only course of action open to her as a woman who has chosen the pursuit of justice as her life's work, but she does so at the cost of destroying her family. Similarly, the people from Mueller-Stahl's neighborhood, including nuns and priests, initially rally to his support, unable to conceive of a good, old patriotic family man like Laszlo and the brutal Nazi torturer "Mishka" as being the same man. Later, when Holocaust survivors terrorize Mueller-Stahl's family at home, throwing rocks through his window, the media get involved. Appearing on his front porch brandishing a baseball bat, Mueller-Stahl is photographed, the photos used this time to fuel the false image of Mike Laszlo, proud American, rather than Mishka, fugitive from justice. The manipulations, lies, and distortions extend to corporate suites, where Lange's ex-father-in-law, Moffat, a high-powered business attorney, perpetuates the "revisionist" view of the Holocaust, secretly teaching his grandson, Haas, to think of the murder of millions as nothing more than Semitic propaganda.

Throughout the film, Costa-Gavras chooses not to chastise or harangue. There is nothing shrill about his style here, nor about the performances he elicits from the uniformly excellent cast he has assembled. Rather, MUSIC BOX conveys a feeling of sadness and dread over American innocence, so easily turned to willful ignorance. Costa-Gavras defines Ann Talbot's dilemma as one shared by the nation. The main focus of MUSIC BOX is not on the trial itself, the outcome of which, to be honest, is never much in doubt. Rather, mirroring the ongoing debate in American politics, Costa-Gavras' real concern is showing the potential consequences of accepting easily digested images without examining the unsavory realities slick imagery is too often meant to conceal. Far from a hot-headed diatribe, MUSIC BOX is more a plaintive plea to America to leave its illusions behind even if it means, as it does in Ann Talbot's case, starting from scratch to build a braver new world. In the wake of films like MUSIC BOX and BETRAYED, it's little wonder that so much of mainstream American culture has become obsessed with escapism. Costa-Gavras stubbornly insists on confronting us with those things we wish to escape, and it's not a pretty picture. Lange was Oscar-nominated for Best Actress, but lost to Jessica Tandy for DRIVING MISS DAISY.

MUSIC MAN, THE

1962 151m c   ★★★★
Musical   /U
WB

Robert Preston (Harold Hill), Shirley Jones (Marian Paroo), Buddy Hackett (Marcellus Washburn), Hermione Gingold (Eulalie MacKechnie Shinn), Paul Ford (Mayor Shinn), Ewart Dunlop, Oliver Hix, Jacey Squires, Olin Britt (The Buffalo Bills), Pert Kelton (Mrs. Paroo)

p, Morton Da Costa; d, Morton Da Costa; w, Marion Hargrove (based on the musical by Meredith Willson, Franklyn Lacey); ph, Robert Burks (Technirama, Technicolor); ed, William Ziegler; m, Meredith Willson; art d, Paul Groesse; chor, Onna White, Tom Panko

THE MUSIC MAN is a nostalgic mix of corn, laughs, exuberance, and infectious songs. Robert Preston reprises his greatest Broadway role as Prof. Harold Hill, a traveling salesman/con man who arrives in River City, Iowa, in 1912 and persuades its citizens that the town is headed for moral ruin because of its new pool room. The way to keep the town youth from being corrupted is to start a band, says Preston, adding that he will sell the instruments and teach the kids how to play. His real plan is to take the money and run before the instruments arrive. Prim librarian Marian Paroo (Shirley Jones) questions Hill's credentials, but he sells her on his revolutionary "Think System," by which all one has to do is think a tune to be able to play it. As he attempts to swindle the townsfolk, Hill alternately charms and exasperates its citizens, including the mayor (Paul Ford at his befuddled best), his wife (Hermione Gingold), and the members of the town council (played by the barbershop quartet, the Buffalo Bills, who provide some of the film's most delightful musical interludes).

Preston is a true joy in this film, perhaps as ideally suited for the role as Yul Brynner was for the King of Siam. Though the charming rogue has long been a staple in the entertainment world, few played the role as engagingly as Preston does here. Though it's Preston's film all the way, the other performances are also notable, particularly the lovely Jones, the delightful Gingold and Ford, and little, lisping Ron Howard. Splendid, but this is, and will always be, Preston's picture. Absurdly, Preston didn't even get a *nomination* for Best Actor, though the film was nominated for Best Picture, losing to LAWRENCE OF ARABIA. It won an Oscar for Best Score Adaptation, and also gleaned nominations for Best Sound, Best Color Art Direction, Best Editing, and Best Color Costume Design. Meredith Willson's songs, which are among the best ever to grace a musical production, include "Trouble," "Till There Was You," "If You Don't Mind," "The Wells Fargo Wagon," "Being in Love," "Goodnight, My Someone," "Rock Island," "Iowa Stubborn," "Sincere," "The Sadder but Wiser Girl," "Gary, Indiana," "Marian, the Librarian," "Lida Rose," "Will I Ever Tell You?" "Shipoopi," "Pick a Little,"

"Goodnight, Ladies," "It's You," "My White Knight," "The Piano Lesson," and the stirring "76 Trombones," which provides an unforgettable climax for the movie.

MUSIC ROOM, THE

(JALSAGHAR)
1963 95m bw   ★★★★½
Drama   /U
Edward Harrison (India)

Chhabi Biswas (Huzur Biswambhar Roy), Padma Devi (His Wife), Pinaki Sen Gupta (Khoka, His Son), Tulsi Lahari (Manager of Roy's Estate), Kali Sarkar (Roy's Servant), Ganga Pada Basu (Mahim Ganguly), Akhtari Bai, Salamat Khan (Singers), Roshan Kumari (Kathak Dancer), Pratap Mukhopdhya

p, Satyajit Ray; d, Satyajit Ray; w, Satyajit Ray (based on a novel by Tarashankar Banerjee); ph, Subrata Mitra; ed, Dulal Dutta; m, Dakhin Mohan Takhur, Asis Kumar, Robin Majumder; art d, Bansi Chandragupta

One of Satyajit Ray's finest works, THE MUSIC ROOM is also one of the most meditative and lyrical. Its basic concern is the demise of an aristocratic household led by Biswas. Feeling a growing resentment toward his neighbors' elaborate parties, Biswas decides to hold his own and sells his wife's jewels to finance it. Shortly afterward his wife and son die at sea during a thunderstorm, which sends Biswas into seclusion. Four years later, when his neighbor plans a party in his newly built music room, Biswas decides to have his own party. He scrounges together all the money he has left and throws an elegant party. He loses his sanity, however, and takes off on his son's horse. He is thrown from the animal and dies in the arms of his servants. Beautifully photographed, THE MUSIC ROOM is a fine example of Ray's directorial mastery. Released in India in 1958, shortly before the completion of his Apu trilogy.

MUTINY ON THE BOUNTY

1935 132m bw   ★★★★★
Adventure   /A
MGM

Charles Laughton (Capt. William Bligh), Clark Gable (1st Mate Fletcher Christian), Franchot Tone (Roger Byam), Herbert Mundin (Smith), Eddie Quillan (Ellison), Dudley Digges (Bacchus), Donald Crisp (Burkitt), Henry Stephenson (Sir Joseph Banks), Francis Lister (Capt. Nelson), Spring Byington (Mrs. Byam)

p, Irving Thalberg; d, Frank Lloyd; w, Talbot Jennings, Jules Furthman, Carey Wilson (based on the novels Mutiny On The Bounty and Men Against the Sea by Charles Nordhoff, James Norman Hall); ph, Arthur Edeson; ed, Margaret Booth; m, Herbert Stothart; art d, Cedric Gibbons, Arnold Gillespie

A bounty for viewers. Few adventure epics can approach MUTINY ON THE BOUNTY for its action-filled dramatization of the conflict of good against evil. A great film in every important respect, the picture made box office history and established Clark Gable in the minds of cinema audiences as the epitome of everything manly and noble. It also established Charles Laughton as an arch-villain, for his convincingly hateful interpretation of a role that would be linked forever to his amiable real-life person. Adding substantially to the power of the high-seas action tale was the film's basis in fact, presenting as it did the historical mutiny on board the British ship *Bounty* in the year 1788.

The film opens in December, 1787, as the ship sails from Portsmouth, England, for Tahiti, to gather breadfruit trees and take them back to England. Before it sets sail, idealistic midshipman Roger Byam (Franchot Tone) raises his glass in an eloquent and optimistic toast to the voyage ahead. For Tone and the rest of the crew, the future looks bright and promising, but as the vessel heads across the Pacific to the tropical paradise of Tahiti, shipboard life evolves as a nightmare, a series of desperate confrontations between Laughton's vicious, bullying Captain Bligh and the courageous first mate, Fletcher Christian, played by Gable. In the weeks to come, the crew would endure torture, an historic mutiny, shipwrecks, a record survival in an open boat, and a manhunt that does not cease for decades. Right from the beginning, Laughton establishes his regime of fear and punishment, ordering floggings, keelhaulings, and other savage disciplines for the slightest infraction of the rules. He is not above cheating the men out of their rations, early on in the voyage ordering Gable to witness the disappearance of several large cheeses, implying these have been stolen by his worthless crew. Gable objects, having learned that the food was taken off the ship before it sailed, and delivered to Laughton's home. Laughton's reign of terror subsides when the *Bounty* reaches Tahiti. Here the crew leisurely collect breadfruit trees and consort with gentle Polynesian women. Laughton jealously tries to sabaotage Gable's love affair with the chief's daughter, Tehani (Movita Castaneda), but the chief (William Bambridge) makes Gable's freedom a condition of gathering the breadfruit trees. Laughton seethes with an even deeper hatred for his first mate. After six months, the *Bounty* is loaded with breadfruit trees and Laughton orders his crew aboard to make the return trip. As the men say their goodbyes to their Polynesian sweethearts, Gable promises that he will return to Castaneda, but they both believe this is wishful thinking.

On the homeward voyage, Laughton's actions become even more barbaric. He orders sick men sent aloft into the masts, and others, for sneaking a drink of precious water, locked in chains in the ship's brig. Dudley Digges, the elderly alcoholic ship's doctor, is gravely ill, yet Laughton orders him topside to witness a flogging. When Digges does manage to struggle to the deck, he dies from the effort. This is the last straw for Gable. He goes to the brig, where one of Laughton's men is beating seaman Donald Crisp. Gable knocks down the captain's henchman, and calls members of the crew he knows are bent on mutiny, telling them that he's taking over the ship.

Expertly crafted and brilliantly acted, MUTINY ON THE BOUNTY was one of the most durable and engrossing adventure films ever made. For the first and only time in motion-picture history, three actors from the same film—Gable, Laughton, and Tone—were nominated for Oscars in the Best Actor division. The film walked off with the Best Picture Oscar. Frank Lloyd's rich direction captures the exotic South Sea island of Tahiti and the rigors of the hardscrabble voyage, while developing wonderful characterizations, not only in the leads but also in many of the supporting players. Lloyd had had a long-standing fascination with the *Bounty* incident and, with his agent Edward Small, bought the rights to the Nordhoff-Hall novel (actually a trilogy published in 1932, *Mutiny on the Bounty*, *Men Against the Sea*, and *Pitcairn Island*), paying only $12,500 for the screen rights. Lloyd had directed the silent adventure film THE SEA HAWK (1924) and had ample experience in handling the unwieldy problems attendant on epic productions. Lloyd and Small then took the property to MGM—not to Irving Thalberg, the chief of studio production, but to the overall boss, Louis B. Mayer. Mayer decided that the entire project was out of the question, that nobody would be interested in a hero who was a mutineer, that there was a lack of romantic interest, and that the film would be

excessively expensive. Besides, Mayer reasoned, Australian producer Charles Chauvel had already produced a film dealing with the basic story in 1932, IN THE WAKE OF THE BOUNTY, starring a 23-year-old novice actor from Tasmania named Errol Flynn as Fletcher Christian. Lloyd and Small then went to Thalberg, who was enthusiastic about the project. Thalberg wielded heavy clout, having produced one great film after another, and Mayer bowed to his wishes, but the studio boss expected MUTINY ON THE BOUNTY to eat up a fortune in costs and flop at the box office.

From the beginning, Thalberg had only one actor in mind for the role of Fletcher Christian, MGM's hottest male star, Clark Gable. But Gable was concerned about his image, reluctant to appear in costume, and afraid that his voice would sound flat in comparison with the accents of the British actors appearing in the film. But his character comes off seeming full of integrity, decision, and courage, even capable of tenderness in his brief romantic scenes with Castaneda (though there's an undercurrent of bisexuality to his scenes in Tahiti). Laughton was another matter. His role as Captain Bligh, which ranks as one of the all-time portrayals of complete villainy, almost went to Wallace Beery, but Beery was too "American" for the role, Thalberg concluded, and Lloyd and company looked elsewhere, finally selecting Laughton because of his success in unsympathetic roles such as the tyrannical monarch of THE PRIVATE LIFE OF HENRY VIII and the harsh and unfeeling father in THE BARRETTS OF WIMPOLE STREET. Laughton himself was not eager to portray the loathsome Bligh. He felt that taking the top billing, as Thalberg insisted, would immediately put him at odds with Gable. The great character actor nevertheless threw himself into the role with such vigor that he became identified with the hated Bligh, and his oft-repeated line "Mr. Christian—come here!" chilled the spines of generations of moviegoers.

The production was dogged by problems of all kinds, from dissension between Laughton and Gable, to director and studio warring about costs. Franchot Tone, who had taken the part of the luckless Midshipman Byam after Robert Montgomery turned it down, spent much of his time off-camera trying to settle quarrels between warring stars and a director battling executives. The cost of the production, which took almost two years, soared out of sight, until the studio discovered it had spent almost $2 million, then a whopping amount. (The film would prove, however, to be one of the big money-makers of the 1930s, returning a gross of $4,460,000 the first time out.) Much of the overhead went into Lloyd's insistence upon authentic locations and the lifesize reproductions of the ships *Bounty* and *Pandora*. These ships were actually sailed 14,000 miles to Tahiti and back. In Tahiti, the second-unit crew shot miles of film, using 2,500 native extras. The ships, which had to battle severe storms, were repaired at additional expense. When they returned, it was found that the film had been ruined by the tropical humidity and was useless. The second unit set sail again for Tahiti to get the necessary background shots. Most of the principal shooting was done on Catalina Island, but even in this normally tranquil area, hazards abounded. A camera barge sank with $50,000 in vital equipment, and a technician drowned trying to save it. Two more technicians almost drowned on an 18-foot model of the *Bounty*, which was hurled out to sea in a storm and lost for several days. Other problems—and expenses—emerged in the writing of the script. Among the many writers employed on the film was Carey Wilson, who started the script alone but stalled in getting down to work on it until MGM executives grew alarmed at the infrequency of his manuscript deliveries. (It turned out he was moonlighting for producer Walter Wanger.)

The film has been criticized for presenting an inaccurately harsh portrait of Bligh. But history seems to bear out Laughton's characterization of a self-important, vindictive brute. Following the mutiny, Bligh fought in naval battles and was cited for bravery, but by 1805, as governor of New South Wales in Australia, he was back to ordering men's backs whipped to the bone. His tyranny caused another revolt, this time among the land garrison, and he was shipped back to England in disgrace, although he was again vindicated by his ruling-class peers. MUTINY ON THE BOUNTY was weirdly remade in 1962 (with Marlon Brando's infamous avant-garde take on Fletcher Christian), and again (more reasonably) in 1984 as THE BOUNTY, but never as successfully as here.

MY AIN FOLK
1974 54m bw   ★★
Drama   /AA
British Film Institute   (U.K.)

Stephen Archibald, Hughie Restorick, Jean Taylor-Smith, Bernard McKenna

d, Bill Douglas; w, Bill Douglas; ph, Gale Tattersall; ed, Peter West

A short piece that has some delightful moments but is ultimately unsatisfying. A nine-year-old boy lives with his maternal grandmother in England during the 1940s. When she dies, he is passed to his paternal grandmother, who eventually sends him to an orphanage. The photography offers some nice compositions and an interesting use of black and white, but the film can't seem to follow through on the situations it builds up. This was the second film in a planned trilogy by the director; the first, MY CHILDHOOD, won the Golden Hugo Award at the 1972 Chicago International Film Festival.

MY BEAUTIFUL LAUNDRETTE
1986 93m c   ★★★★★
Drama   R/15
Working Title/SAF/Channel 4   (U.K.)

Daniel Day Lewis (Johnny), Saeed Jaffrey (Nasser), Roshan Seth (Papa), Gordon Warnecke (Omar), Shirley Ann Field (Rachel), Rita Wolf (Tania), Richard Graham (Genghis), Winston Graham, Dudley Thomas (Jamaicans), Derrick Branche (Salim)

p, Sarah Radclyffe, Tim Bevan; d, Stephen Frears; w, Hanif Kureishi; ph, Oliver Stapleton; ed, Mick Audsley; m, Ludus Tonalis; prod d, Hugo Luczyc-Whyhowski; cos, Lindy Hemming

An offbeat winner. Director Stephen Frears and screenwriter Hanif Kureishi have fashioned a wonderfully fresh examination of the political and racial climate of Margaret Thatcher's Britain. Omar (Gordon Warnecke) is a young Pakistani living in London with his father (Roshan Seth), a drunk who was previously one of Pakistan's leading intellectuals. When Papa asks his brother Nasser (Saeed Jaffrey), an underworld crime boss, to find work for Omar, Nasser makes him the manager of a run-down laundrette, and Omar enterprisingly employs Johnny (Daniel Day Lewis), a London street punk and boyhood friend whom he has not seen since Johnny joined a fascist group. In addition to becoming work partners, Omar and Johnny also become lovers. In the meantime, Johnny's friends have turned against him, baffled by his devotion to the "Pakis." Kureishi has come up with at least a half-dozen complex characters whose lives are brilliantly woven together in the film's relatively short 93 minutes. Amidst all the conflicts of racism, sexuality, bigotry, violence, and politics, MY BEAUTIFUL LAUNDRETTE still manages to be humorous and entertaining, largely because of Frears's skill

as a director and marvelous performances all round. Beautifully handled, warmly intelligent and insightful, extremely entertaining.

MY BLUE HEAVEN
1990 97m c   ★★★
Comedy/Crime   PG-13/PG
Hawn-Sylbert

Steve Martin (Vinnie Antonelli), Rick Moranis (Barney Coopersmith), Joan Cusack (Hannah Stubbs), Melanie Mayron (Crystal Rybak), Carol Kane (Shaldeen), Bill Irwin (Kirby), William Hickey (Billy Sparrow), Daniel Stern

p, Herbert Ross, Anthea Sylbert; d, Herbert Ross; w, Nora Ephron; ph, John Bailey (Technicolor); ed, Stephen A. Rotter; m, Ira Newborn; prod d, Charles Rosen; art d, Richard Berger; chor, Lynne Taylor-Corbett; cos, Joseph G. Aulisi

As we zoom in on this so-perfect-it-must-be-a-set vision of suburbia, we see an unlikely new neighbor: gangster Vincent Antonelli (Steve Martin). Vinnie, with his spiky black hair, shiny suits and New York accent, is not here by choice; he's a mob informant who's been plunked down in this land of barbecue grills and picket fences as part of the government's witness relocation program. FBI agent Barney Coopersmith (Rick Moranis) is in charge of Vinnie, and must ensure that the gangster stays out of trouble until he can testify at two important mob trials in New York. But Vinnie still can't resist swiping the occasional car or ripping off a supermarket here and there, which brings him to the attention of District Attorney Hannah Stubbs (Joan Cusack). Hannah refuses to be won over by the charming though conniving Vinnie and is even less amused when Barney informs her that as a government-protected witness Vinnie cannot be prosecuted for his crimes. To further complicate matters, Vinnie has also encountered a number of his old Mafia pals, all of whom are apparently living in the same suburb under assumed names. Naturally, this gang plans a new crime spree. But thanks to his quick thinking and cunning, Vinnie outwits both Stubbs and the gunmen who are after him, and by the time the film ends he's a local hero, with a Little League stadium named after him, and a couple of wives and girlfriends to boot.

For a film with as many missed plot opportunities as this one, MY BLUE HEAVEN is actually fairly amusing. The notion of a gangster adjusting to anonymity in suburbia is funny, but the film pays scant attention to this idea; instead, MY BLUE HEAVEN is really about Vinnie and Barney and their differing ideas of law and order. Still, the film manages to work about two-thirds of the time, largely due to the efforts of the cast. Moranis is well-suited to his role as the repressed Barney, and Cusack, like a high-school teacher from hell, with her pulled-back hair and stern, unflinching demeanor is wonderful as Hannah. (She's also one of the few actresses whose look can change from goofy to striking within a single film.) As Moranis's partner, performance artist Bill Irwin gets to show off his unique dance style; however, Carol Kane is wasted, given only about five lines as a woman Vinnie picks up in a supermarket and marries a few scenes later. As for Martin, he may not be the most likely actor for the part of Vinnie, but his exaggerated mannerisms aren't that out of place in a film that's basically an extended sketch. Although the script seems to lose track of the story in the second half of the film, when the plot is stretched a little thin, for the most part, this is an amiable comedy with some unexpected laughs.

MY BODYGUARD

1980 96m c   ★★★★
Drama   PG
FOX

Chris Makepeace (Clifford), Adam Baldwin (Linderman), Matt Dillon (Moody), Paul Quandt (Carson), Joan Cusack (Shelley), Dean R. Miller (Hightower), Tim Reyna (Koontz), Richard Bradley (Dubrow), Denise Baske (Leilani), Hank Salas (Mike)

p, Don Devlin; d, Tony Bill; w, Alan Ormsby; ph, Michael D. Margulies (CFI Color); ed, Stu Linder; m, Dave Grusin; prod d, Jackson DeGovia

This is essentially a tale of revenge, but not along the lines of some mindless vigilante movie; this is revenge with intelligence and sensitivity. Young Makepeace moves to Chicago with his motel manager father, Mull, and grandmother, Ruth Gordon (doing her wisecracking, randy old lady bit). His new high school is ruled by Dillon, who extorts money from classmates ostensibly so they won't be pummeled by Baldwin, a huge, reclusive hulk whom everyone fears. Makepeace tries to befriend Baldwin and finds him to be a very troubled young man. This is a heartwarming film, superbly directed by ex-actor Tony Bill. Makepeace is excellent as the slight protagonist, and Baldwin is perfect as the brooding, misunderstood mammoth. Dave Grusin's score adds immeasurably to the tone.

MY BRILLIANT CAREER

1980 98m c   ★★★★
Drama   G/U
New South Wales/GUO/Analysis   (Australia)

Judy Davis (Sybylla Melvyn), Sam Neill (Harry Beecham), Wendy Hughes (Aunt Helen), Robert Grubb (Frank Hawdon), Max Cullen (Mr. McSwat), Patricia Kennedy (Aunt Gussie), Aileen Britton (Grandma Bossier), Peter Whitford (Uncle Julius), Carole Skinner (Mrs. McSwat), Alan Hopgood (Father)

p, Margaret Fink; d, Gillian Armstrong; w, Eleanor Witcombe (based on the novel by Miles Franklin); ph, Don McAlpine (Eastmancolor); ed, Nicholas Beauman; m, Nathan Waks; prod d, Luciana Arrighi; cos, Anna Senior

Late in the 19th century in the Australian outback everyone in a small farming community knows his or her place and what is expected. All except Sybylla Melvyn (Judy Davis), that is, a headstrong young woman who wants a career—an idea that shocks her family and friends. Resisting the rigid codes of society and the marriage proposal of a wealthy man, Harry Beecham (Sam Neill, in a fine portrayal), Sybylla plows ahead with pluck and charm.

Davis gives a lively and humanistic performance, and the direction by Gillian Armstrong (MRS. SOFFEL, HIGH TIDE), in her feature debut, matches her heroine's character: strong, with a good sense of wanting to get something done and then doing it. The mise-en-scene is well composed, and the story is well told in this wonderful Australian work. Based on a true story, MY BRILLIANT CAREER was one of the key films in the resurgence of Australian cinema in the late 1970s and early 80s.

MY DARLING CLEMENTINE

1946 97m bw   ★★★★★
Western   /A
FOX

Henry Fonda (Wyatt Earp), Linda Darnell (Chihuahua), Victor Mature (Doc Holliday), Walter Brennan (Old Man Clanton), Tim Holt (Virgil Earp), Cathy Downs (Clementine), Ward Bond (Morgan Earp), Alan Mowbray (Granville Thorndyke), John Ireland (Billy Clanton), Roy Roberts (Mayor)

p, Samuel G. Engel; d, John Ford; w, Samuel G. Engel, Winston Miller (based on a story by Sam Hellman from the novel Wyatt Earp, Frontier Marshall by Stuart N. Lake); ph, Joseph MacDonald; ed, Dorothy Spencer; m, Cyril J. Mockridge, David Buttolph; art d, James Basevi, Lyle Wheeler; fx, Fred Sersen; cos, Rene Hubert

Perhaps the best orchestrated western of all time, courtesy the modest Mr. Ford. No western figure inspired more cinematic lore and created more romantic legend in print than the indomitable Wyatt Earp. He was the courageous champion of the law and defender of decency, if the Old West myths are to be believed. Fonda, recently returned from WWII and four years in the Navy, gives a definitive and restrained portrayal of the famous frontier lawman. He and his brothers, Bond, Holt, and Don Garner, have driven a small herd of cattle to the outskirts of rough-and-tumble Tombstone, Arizona, in the year 1882 (the events portrayed actually took place in 1881). Coming upon their campsite is Brennan, leader of the outlaw Clanton clan, and his oldest son, Grant Withers. Brennan offers Fonda a cut-rate price for the cattle, but Fonda rejects the offer, stating that they intend to get a better price in town. He mentions he'll be going into Tombstone that night with his brothers, Bond and Holt, leaving young Garner to mind the cattle. When Fonda arrives in Tombstone, he sees it's a wide open hellhole with the saloons roaring. He goes to the barber shop with his brothers, but just as he is about to have a shave the barber shop is riddled with bullets that narrowly miss Fonda and his brothers. He walks outside to see Charles Stevens, a drunken Indian, recklessly firing his pistol from the now emptied Oriental Saloon. Fonda, indignant, his face still lathered, marches up to the town mayor, Roberts, and sees the local marshal resigning on the spot. Incensed, Fonda goes to the building housing the saloon, enters at the second floor level, and then drags an unconscious Stevens out of the saloon. He drops him next to the mayor and says with disgust: "What kind of town is this, serving liquor to Indians?" Roberts offers Fonda the job of town marshal, but he refuses. When he and his brothers return to their camp they find Garner killed and their cattle stolen. Fonda rides back into town, wakes up Roberts, and takes the marshal's job, making his brothers deputies.

Dramatic and wonderfully brooding, with shadows at night and blinding light at day under a sky that never ends, MY DARLING CLEMENTINE is Ford's homage to legend. The film doesn't follow history exactly, but it's close; there was no Old Man Clanton at the O.K. Corral, Virgil Earp was not killed before the fight but was wounded in it, Doc Holliday was not killed in the gun battle, and no mention of the McLowery Brothers is made in the film, among other pertinent facts of the most famous gunfight in the Old West. Fonda's wonderfully simple, direct lawman has a heart and more than a little humor as he embodies Ford's staunch theme of law and order. Mature is also outstanding, acting out his doomed gunslinger role with amazing restraint. Bond, Brennan, and Holt are true grit Westerners, while Darnell's luscious noir persona is effective, in yet another doomed portrayal. Downs is more a refined and pretty statue than a flesh and blood girl, and only during the delightful church dance does she become recognizably human. Beyond the legendary leads, the most hateful character of this film is the vile Brennan, who prefers to raise his sons as beasts instead of men.

Ford, who reportedly did not want to make this film, owed Fox one more film on his contract before beginning independent production with his own company, Argosy Pictures. He shot the entire film in 45 days in his favorite location site, Monument Valley, in northern Arizona, not in the south where the real Tombstone is located. When Fox mogul Darryl Zanuck viewed the film, he decided that it was too long and some of it lacked cohesion, so he arbitrarily cut 30 minutes from the original. Yet he did it with loving care since he believed Ford to be the greatest director of the sound era. Almost every scene in this splendidly constructed film is a visual treat. As with other films by Ford, there is no sustained and dynamic score; Newman merely provides haunting little variations of the title song on a harmonica, and other western folk ballads played on fiddles, a guitar, and sung by a cowboy chorus. Engel and Miller cut a simple story but provide wry, ironic, and down-home dialogue. And throughout is the startlingly grand photography of Joseph MacDonald, who followed the pointing finger of Ford, the consummate film artist, in providing graphics so broad and sweeping that the whole of the West seems to be captured in his frames. Although other films about Wyatt Earp and the fabulous gunfight at the O.K. Corral have been made, none captures the visual grimness, the impromptu nature of that bullet-ridden moment, with the possible exception of the excellent GUNFIGHT AT THE O.K. CORRAL. Other films depicting Earp in or out of Tombstone include LAW AND ORDER, with Walter Huston, FRONTIER MARSHAL, with George O'Brien, Randolph Scott in FRONTIER MARSHAL, TOMBSTONE, THE TOWN TOO TOUGH TO DIE, with Richard Dix, Joel McCrea in WICHITA, Burt Lancaster in GUNFIGHT AT THE O.K. CORRAL, HOUR OF THE GUN, and DOC, the latter being nothing more than a psychodrama.

MY DINNER WITH ANDRE

1981 110m c   ★★★
Drama   PG/A
Andre

Wallace Shawn (Wally), Andre Gregory (Andre), Jean Lenauer (Waiter), Roy Butler (Bartender)

p, George W. George, Beverly Karp; d, Louis Malle; w, Wallace Shawn, Andre Gregory; ph, Jeri Sopanen (Movielab Color); ed, Suzanne Baron; m, Allen Shawn; prod d, David Mitchell; art d, Stephen McCabe; cos, Jeffrey Ullman

Louis Malle's somewhat overrated MY DINNER WITH ANDRE is a filmed conversation between two theatrical acquaintances, and whether you find the movie profound, entertaining or merely pretentious will depend on how interesting you find the talk.

The main raconteur is Andre (Andre Gregory), a theatre director and self-styled seeker of enlightenment who details his sometimes-bizarre quest as he dines with his old friend, Wally (Wallace Shawn), a playwright and actor. Wally is more concerned with creature comforts than with quixotic spiritual searches and serves as Andre's philosophical foil as the two men talk and eat at a fancy New York restaurant. Although Malle provided the minimalist direction, the film really belongs to Shawn and Gregory, who cowrote the script.

MY FAIR LADY

1964 170m c   ★★★
Musical/Comedy   /U
WB

Audrey Hepburn (Eliza Doolittle), Rex Harrison (Prof. Henry Higgins), Stanley Holloway (Alfred P. Doolittle), Wilfrid Hyde-White (Col. Hugh Pickering), Gladys Cooper (Mrs. Higgins), Jeremy Brett (Freddy Eynsford-Hill), Theodore Bikel (Zoltan Karpathy), Isobel Elsom (Mrs. Eynsford-Hill), Mona Washbourne (Mrs. Pearce), John Alderson (Jamie)

p, Jack L. Warner; d, George Cukor; w, Alan Jay Lerner (based on a musical play by Alan Jay Lerner, Frederick Loewe and the play Pygmalion by George Bernard Shaw); ph, Harry Stradling (Super Panavision 70, Technicolor); ed, William Ziegler; m, Frederick Loewe; prod d, Cecil Beaton; art d, Gene Allen; chor, Hermes Pan; cos, Cecil Beaton

Just fairly fair; call it the revenge of Mary Poppins. Audrey's effortless swan can't redeem the fact that she's a Givenchy mannequin picturesquely dusted with Jack Warner's cigar ashes, when we meet her "playing" an ugly duckling. Hepburn specialized in Cinderella variations (ROMAN HOLIDAY, SABRINA) but was getting too mature, too sophisticated to play the waif bit without outside plot stimuli (danger—CHARADE, broken heart—BREAKFAST AT TIFFANY'S, etc.). Anyway, Shaw's original Eliza is not quite as waifish as she is raffish. Hepburn can't summon up the guts to guttersnipe, and when she opens her mouth wide to presumably sing (dubbed by Marni Nixon, who deserves a special Oscar for all the stars she made look good) like she's never even seen a singer in her entire life, it's a shock and a laugh at the same time.

Otherwise, the Lerner and Lowe musical emerges as an overly long, sometimes enjoyable dinosaur. Perhaps there is truthfully no way to liberate Shaw—his writing is heavy, obtuse. Adding music makes it come up heavily trimmed, like a fancy Christmas turkey. The film makes you feel bloated and tired. But it made a fortune at the box office and undeservedly took Oscars in almost every category—with the exception of Best Actress, which ironically went to MARY POPPINS's Julie Andrews, who costarred with Rex Harrison in the Broadway hit.

Henry Higgins (Harrison) bets fellow linguist Col. Hugh Pickering (Wilfrid Hyde-White) that he can turn Cockney flower girl Eliza Doolittle (Hepburn) into a lady with elocution so pure no one will suspect her origins. The two men work hard with Eliza until they feel she is ready to be tested at Ascot, where she meets and charms the handsome young Freddy Eynsford-Hill (Jeremy Brett). Then they take her to a huge ball where even a famous linguist takes her for royalty. Back home, Higgins and Pickering congratulate each other but disregard Eliza, who departs in anger to carry on with Freddy. Only then does confirmed bachelor Higgins realize that he has fallen in love with his "creation."

Yes, Harrison is mechanically expert, like a graduate with honors from the Lord Olivier School of Going through the Motions (we think, belatedly, we'd have preferred orignal choice Cary Grant opposite Andrews). But film always pointed up his hatefulness. It's hard not to think of dead Carole Landis lying on her bathroom floor when he waxes sentimental. Frankly, we hate this damned thing. The songs include "The Rain in Spain," "I Could Have Danced all Night," "On the Street Where You Live," "Get Me to the Church on Time," and "I've Grown Accustomed to Her Face."

MY FAVORITE BLONDE

1942 78m bw   ★★★½
Spy/Comedy   /A
Paramount

Bob Hope (*Larry Haines*), Madeleine Carroll (*Karen Bentley*), Gale Sondergaard (*Mme. Stephanie Runick*), George Zucco (*Dr. Hugo Streger*), Lionel Royce (*Karl*), Walter Kingsford (*Dr. Faber*), Victor Varconi (*Miller*), Otto Reichow (*Lanz*), Charles Cane (*Turk O'Flaherty*), Crane Whitley (*Ulrich*)

p, Paul Jones; d, Sidney Lanfield; w, Don Hartman, Frank Butler (based on a story by Melvin Frank and Norman Panama); ph, William Mellor; ed, William O'Shea; m, David Buttolph; art d, Hans Dreier, Robert Usher

Carroll is a beautiful spy who posesses plans involving the shipment of war planes to England and is being chased by Nazis who want the plans for themselves. While in New York, she escapes from them by ducking into a small dressing room at a theater. Coincidentally this is the dressing room of Hope, a wisecracking ladies' man who's preparing his performing penguin for its debut. Without much pleading, the lovely Carroll convinces Hope to aid her escape. From there it's a comic cross-country chase with lots of disguises and silliness. Hope is wonderful, with something smart to say no matter what the situation. His smug behavior is very funny (far and away superior to anything he ever did in the television work that made him rich) and the pacing is as good as it usually is in these Hope comedies. His old partner from the ROAD films, the wonderfully laid back Bing Crosby, makes a cameo (as he so often did in Hope's solo comedies) as a man giving the two travelers directions. "No, it can't be," mutters Hope after the benefactor leaves. Some good fun, but the poor penguin is treated like a toy rather than an animal. Penguins are inherently funny animals (as television's "Monty Python's Flying Circus" proved time and again), and there was no need for the knockabout treatment of the bird.

MY FAVORITE BRUNETTE
1947 87m bw   ★★★★
Mystery/Comedy   /PG
Paramount

Bob Hope (*Ronnie Jackson*), Dorothy Lamour (*Carlotta Montay*), Peter Lorre (*Kismet*), Lon Chaney, Jr. (*Willie*), Charles Dingle (*Maj. Simon Montague*), Reginald Denny (*James Collins*), Frank Puglia (*Baron Montay*), Ann Doran (*Miss Rogers*), Willard Robertson (*Prison Warden*), Jack LaRue (*Tony*)

p, Daniel Dare; d, Elliott Nugent; w, Edmund Beloin, Jack Rose; ph, Lionel Lindon; ed, Ellsworth Hoagland; m, Robert Emmett Dolan; art d, Hans Dreier, Earl Hedrick; fx, Gordon Jennings; cos, Edith Head

In what ranks as one of his best comedies, Hope plays a harried baby photographer who is asked by his private-eye pal to watch his detective business for a few days while he goes on vacation. Hope agrees and finds himself getting involved with a lot more than watching dust settle. Believing Hope to be the real private eye, Lamour hires him to search for her uncle, a wealthy baron who has vanished, and gives the dubious detective a map, warning him to guard it with his life. Hope goes off to the palatial estate of a former associate of the missing man, Dingle, who introduces Hope to a wheelchair-bound man who is supposedly Lamour's uncle. Hoyt, a doctor who is present, insists that Lamour has a few screws loose. Hope is just about convinced of the veracity of Dingle and Hoyt's story until he is about to leave and spots the "disabled" baron walking about. When Hope snaps a quick picture, Dingle gets one of his crazed henchmen (Lorre in a wonderful self-parody) to knock out Hope and recover the film. In an effort to determine the importance of the map, Hope and Lamour pay a visit to the geologist who drew it, but Lorre

has killed him, framing Hope for the murder. Minutes before Hope is to be executed, fresh evidence is discovered by Lamour, and the executioner, furious that his day has been ruined, takes off his hood and reveals himself to be none other than Hope's offscreen (and sometimes onscreen) pal Bing Crosby. "Boy," says Hope as he turns to the camera, "he'll take any kind of a part!" This is a classic Hope film, with one gag following another in rapid succession. Particularly good is Lorre, who was known at this stage in his career for doing films that approached this genre seriously. And Chaney's characterization of a dumb sanitarium guard so tough he cracks walnuts with his eyelids is great fun. Alan Ladd is equally amusing in his cameo role of the vacationing detective.

MY FAVORITE WIFE
1940 88m bw   ★★★★
Comedy   /U
RKO

Irene Dunne (*Ellen Arden*), Cary Grant (*Nick Arden*), Randolph Scott (*Stephen Burkett*), Gail Patrick (*Bianca*), Ann Shoemaker (*Ma*), Scotty Beckett (*Tim Arden*), Mary Lou Harrington (*Chinch Arden*), Donald MacBride (*Hotel Clerk*), Hugh O'Connell (*Johnson*), Granville Bates (*Judge*)

p, Leo McCarey; d, Garson Kanin; w, Sam Spewack, Bella Spewack (based on a story by Leo McCarey, Sam Spewack, and Bella Spewack); ph, Rudolph Mate; ed, Robert Wise; m, Roy Webb; art d, Van Nest Polglase, Mark-Lee Kirk; cos, Howard Greer

After Grant and Dunne made such a success of THE AWFUL TRUTH, they were reteamed for this up-to-date version of the "Enoch Arden" story. Producer McCarey was supposed to direct, but he had a terrible auto accident just before shooting, so Kanin was handed the task and came through with a fast-moving, often amusing film. Dunne has supposedly been dead for seven years, the result of having been shipwrecked, when Grant, now able to remarry, takes Patrick as his lawful wedded wife. In a twinkling, Dunne shows up. She's been rescued after having spent all those years on an island with the burly Scott, the other survivor. Grant takes Patrick on their honeymoon to Yosemite National Park, and Dunne follows them there. When Grant spots her, he can't tell Patrick what's happened, so he avoids it and takes Patrick back to their home. Dunne left two small children behind when she took the ill-fated South Seas voyage, and they don't recognize her. At the Grant-Patrick house, Dunne is already in residence when the lovebirds return, and she pretends to be a friend. When Grant learns that Dunne had been on the island with a man all that time, he becomes concerned that she may have been compromised. She circumvents that by hiring a shoe salesman, a much older man, to pretend to have been her island companion. Grant buys that for a while, then learns it was handsome Scott all the while. Grant takes Dunne to lunch with Scott, and there is the cliche scene where she falls into the swimming pool at Scott's hotel-apartment building. Meanwhile, Patrick is getting mentally disturbed, so she begins to consult psychiatrist Pedro de Cordoba. In the end, Grant realizes that he still loves Dunne, and, after a riotous scene in a courtroom with Bates presiding, the second marriage is annulled and Grant and Dunne are free to resume their lives together. Lots of laughs for the first three-quarters of the film but then it peters out for the expected finale. The film earned Oscar nominations for Best Original Story, Best Interior Decoration, and Best Original Score. Remade, not as well, as MOVE OVER, DARLING, which starred Doris Day and James Garner in the Dunne and Grant roles.

MY FAVORITE YEAR

1982 92m c ★★★★
Comedy PG
Brooksfilms

Peter O'Toole (Alan Swann), Mark Linn-Baker (Benjy Stone), Jessica Harper (K.C. Downing), Joseph Bologna (King Kaiser), Bill Macy (Sy Benson), Lainie Kazan (Belle Carroca), Anne DeSalvo (Alice Miller), Basil Hoffman (Herb Lee), Lou Jacobi (Uncle Morty), Adolph Green (Leo Silver)

p, Michael Gruskoff; d, Richard Benjamin; w, Norman Steinberg, Dennis Palumbo (based on a story by Dennis Palumbo); ph, Gerald Hirschfeld (Metrocolor); ed, Richard Chew; m, Ralph Burns; prod d, Charles Rosen; cos, May Routh

A delightful film presenting a poignant portrait of television in the early 1950s. Benjy Stone (Mark Linn-Baker) is a fledgling writer for a live comedy television show hosted by zany, tough, yet soft-hearted King Kaiser (Joseph Bologna). Benjy is assigned to chaperone the unpredictable, boozing, onetime Hollywood swashbuckler Alan Swann (Peter O'Toole), who is to appear on television in a Kaiser skit. Arriving in Manhattan drunk and uncontrollable, Swann begins to lead Stone in a wild night of revelry, and over the next several days, the famous guest is involved in a series of escapades. On the show itself he staggers about with the near-DTs, forgetting his lines and getting into a fight with a bunch of union goons invading the set over Kaiser's past insults. O'Toole is superb as the former matinee idol, and Bologna is outstanding as the brusque and brawling comic. Linn-Baker, who would later go on to his own television series in 1986, is excellent, playing out a real-life incident where novice comedy writer Mel Brooks was assigned to chaperone the colorful Errol Flynn before he appeared on Sid Caesar's "Your Show of Shows." Cameron Mitchell plays a union crime boss with lead-foot accuracy and deadpan deadliness. Richard Benjamin's direction surprisingly provides a dizzy pace and inventive set-ups, aided greatly by cinematographer Gerald Hirschfeld and editor Richard Chew.

MY FIRST WIFE

1985 96m c ★★★★
Drama /15
Dofine (Australia)

John Hargreaves (John), Wendy Hughes (Helen), Lucy Angwin (Lucy), David Cameron (Tom), Julia Blake (Kirstin), Anna Jemison (Hilary), Charles Tingwell (Helen's Mother), Robin Lovejoy (John's Father), Lucy Uralov (John's Mother), Xenia Groutas (John's Sister)

p, Paul Cox, Jane Ballantyne; d, Paul Cox; w, Paul Cox, Bob Ellis; ph, Yuri Sokol; ed, Tim Lewis; prod d, Santhana Naidu; art d, Asher Bilu

Cox, a Dutch-born director working in Australia, took the pain of his own divorce and turned it into an honest cinematic account of the end of a marriage, exposing painfully raw nerve endings with care and compassion. Hargreaves is a disc jockey for a classical music station, working also on his own musical compositions. Hughes, his wife, is sick of being ignored while her husband devotes himself to his work, and subsequently she begins a most indiscreet affair. Only Hargreaves is unaware of what is really happening, but eventually he learns the truth and separates from Hughes. Hargreaves refuses to tell his parents, who disapproved of the marriage in the first place. Lovejoy, Hargreaves's Russian emigrant father, is dying, and though his own marriage was far from happy, he lectures his son on the importance of matrimony. Hargreaves gives an emotional performance, a man who has no understanding of what is happening to his life. The cold indifference he displays toward Hughes early in the story is a sad but accurate portrait of a man for whom work means everything. Cox presents his story without redemption at the conclusion, leaving characters in pain and confusion. Though a bleak view of life, this is a frank and compelling film. MY FIRST WIFE was submitted as an Australian entry to the Venice Film Festival, but surprisingly it was rejected by this prestigious gathering. The film garnered three Australian Film Awards—Best Actor for Hargreaves, Best Director for Cox, and Best Original Screenplay for Cox and Ellis.

MY FRIEND FLICKA

1943 89m c ★★★★
Children's /U
FOX

Roddy McDowall (Ken McLaughlin), Preston Foster (Rob McLaughlin), Rita Johnson (Nell), James Bell (Gus), Jeff Corey (Tim Murphy), Diana Hale (Hildy), Arthur Loft (Charley Sargent), Jimmy Aubrey

p, Ralph Dietrich; d, Harold Schuster; w, Lillie Hayward, Francis Edwards Faragoh (based on the novel by Mary O'Hara); ph, Dewey Wrigley (Technicolor); ed, Robert Fritch; m, Alfred Newman; art d, Richard Day, Chester Gore; cos, Herschel

A wonderful film, beautifully photographed and sensitively told. McDowall is a young boy who longs for a colt of his own. His rancher father finally gives in and is displeased when the boy chooses the foal from an unruly mare. But through painstaking work by McDowall, the colt is trained and nurtured, eventually growing to become a fine mare and a loyal companion. The performances and direction are as fine as they come. The humanistic qualities within the film come through well, without being the least bit overbearing or overly sentimental. The color photography is wonderful, capturing all the grandeur of the Rocky Mountains. Perfect for the whole family. A sequel was made with almost the same cast: THUNDERHEAD, SON OF FLICKA. Later a series on television.

MY LEFT FOOT

1989 98m c ★★★★½
Biography R/PG
Granada (Ireland)

Daniel Day-Lewis (Christy Brown), Ray McAnally (Mr. Brown), Brenda Fricker (Mrs. Brown), Ruth McCabe (Mary Carr), Fiona Shaw (Dr. Eileen Cole), Eanna MacLiam (Old Benny), Alison Whelan (Old Sheila), Declan Croghan (Old Tom), Hugh O'Conor (Young Christy), Cyril Cusack (Lord Castlewelland)

p, Noel Pearson; d, Jim Sheridan; w, Shane Connaughton, Jim Sheridan (based on the book by Christy Brown); ph, Jack Conroy (Technicolor); ed, J. Patrick Duffner; m, Elmer Bernstein; prod d, Austin Spriggs; cos, Joan Bergin

Thank god, an insolent hoof. Stories about people overcoming devastating handicaps have long been grist for the filmmaker's mill. The title of this screen adaptation of Christy Brown's best-selling autobiography refers to the only limb over which Brown, crippled since birth by a severe case of cerebral palsy, ever had any control. Daniel Day-Lewis plays the acclaimed Irish-born artist and author, as the film intercuts flashbacks of his formative years with scenes at a stately Dublin home in 1959. There, the wheelchair-bound Brown, guest of honor at a benefit dinner for a cerebral palsy foundation, first meets Mary (Ruth

McCabe), a young nurse assigned to care for him for the evening. Presented with a copy of Brown's book, Mary leafs through its pages, and the author's life is re-created on the screen, beginning with his early years as the ninth of 13 surviving children (out of 22) in a close-knit, working-class Irish Catholic family. That MY LEFT FOOT succeeds as well as it does is in large part due to a superb supporting cast and the virtuoso performances of Hugh O'Conor and Day-Lewis, who play Brown as child and adult, respectively. Undoubtedly, MY LEFT FOOT begs comparison with GABY, A TRUE STORY, the depiction of another cerebral palsy victim. Indeed, the films are like two sides of the same coin. While the less satisfying GABY focuses on the dour aspects of its subject's plight, the better-scripted, more entertaining MY LEFT FOOT is filled with wit and unselfconscious humor. To Brown's credit, his portrayal is unerringly tough, sometimes surprisingly sensual. It keeps FOOT from maudlin static. A rich cinematic experience, this uplifting British production will leave you in awe of the extraordinary Christy Brown.

MY LIFE AS A DOG
(MITT LIV SOM HUND)
1985 101m c   ★★★
Comedy/Drama   PG-13/PG
AB/Svensk (Sweden)

Anton Glanzelius (Ingemar Johansson), Anki Liden (His Mother), Tomas von Bromssen (Uncle Gunnar), Manfred Serner (Erik), Melinda Kinnaman (Saga), Ing-Marie Carlsson (Berit), Kicki Rundgren (Aunt Ulla), Lennart Hjulstrom (Konstnaren), Leif Erickson (Farbor Sandberg), Christina Carlwind (Fru Sandberg)

p, Waldemar Bergendahl; d, Lasse Hallstrom; w, Lasse Hallstrom, Reidar Jonsson, Brasse Brannstrom, Per Berglund (based on the novel by Jonsson); ph, Jorgen Persson, Rolf Lindstrom (Fujicolor); ed, Christer Furubrand, Susanne Linnman; m, Bjorn Isfalt; art d, Lasse Westfelt; cos, Inger Pehrsson, Susanne Falck

This critically acclaimed Swedish film, which also won kudos for its talented star, Anton Glanzelius, is a tragicomic, sensitive portrayal of adolescence set in 1959. The film centers on 12-year-old Ingemar Johansson (Glanzelius), who lives with his abusive brother (Manfred Serner) and terminally ill mother (Anki Liden). He is not discouraged, however—sure, he has it bad, but not as bad as Laika, the Soviet spacedog who starved to death while in orbit and whose fate haunts the boy. Ingemar's life has begun to spin out of control, and, like Laika, there's little he can do to stop it. When Ingemar is sent away for the summer to stay with relations, he meets a menage of eccentric—and sexually intimidating—villagers; eventually, these experiences give him a sustaining inner strength. Writer-director Lasse Hallstrom's tale is an episodic rite of passage, a story in which the emotions are touching but never sappy, the main character has the integrity and complexity of a real child with real troubles, and the glimpses of village life are rich and engaging. Not just another charming film about growing up, but an expertly directed tale that takes a small, simple subject and colors it with invention and inspiration. Released in the US in 1987, the film earned Oscar nominations for Best Direction and Best Screenplay.

MY LIFE TO LIVE
(VIVRE SA VIE)
1962 85m bw   ★★★★★
Drama
Pleiade (France)

Anna Karina (Nana), Sady Rebbot (Raoul), Andre Labarthe (Paul), Guylaine Schlumberger (Yvette), Gerard Hoffman (the Cook), Monique Messine (Elizabeth), Paul Pavel (A Journalist), Dimitri Dineff (A Youth), Peter Kassowitz (A Young Man), Eric Schlumberger (Luigi)

p, Pierre Braunberger; d, Jean-Luc Godard; w, Jean-Luc Godard; ph, Raoul Coutard; ed, Agnes Guillemot; m, Michel Legrand

An early stunner from Jean-Luc Godard and one of the seminal films of the French New Wave. The filmmaker's fourth feature stars his then-wife, Anna Karina, as Nana, a Parisian sales clerk who, after separating from her husband, Paul (Labarthe), tries to make it as an actress. After seeing Dreyer's silent classic THE PASSION OF JOAN OF ARC, she abandons the idea and turns to prostitution. The film is divided into 12 tableaux, which take place in cafes, in a record store, at a police station, and on the streets of Paris. The scenes and the issues raised range from prostitution (with quoted facts and figures on the subject) to experiments with narration and autobiographical elements (Godard narrating, Karina starring). In Godard's typically dense and provocative style, we also have many allusions to films and literature (Renoir's NANA, Zola's Nana, Truffaut's JULES AND JIM, Dreyer and Falconetti, and Edgar Allen Poe's "The Oval Portrait"), as well as an absorbing discussion on linguistic philosophy with Brice Parain).

Through this complex and intriguing network we have an abundance of humor and many uniquely touching vignettes. Karina is considerably more at home in front of the camera than in her earlier films, and Godard has by this point clearly learned how to bring out the very best that's in her. MY LIFE TO LIVE represents an interesting mix of those facets Godard has explored more individually in his earlier films—the genre elements of BREATHLESS, the politics of LE PETIT SOLDAT, and the narrative experimentation of A WOMAN IS A WOMAN. Technically MY LIFE TO LIVE was (and perhaps still is) far ahead of its time, knocking down the traditional walls of sound recording. Godard refused to mix the sound in the studio (except for Michel Legrand's barely used score), instead applying the same rule for sound and image—to capture them directly—and amended his "jump-cut" style of editing by allowing shots to last from six to eight minutes as the camera wandered through the set. MY LIFE TO LIVE also contains one of Godard's greatest and most personal scenes—a reading of Charles Baudelaire's translation of "The Oval Portrait," the story of an artist whose wife dies just as he finishes her portrait. Although Godard does not play Nana's lover in this scene, he does provide the character's voice. As we hear Godard reading Poe's words, we see the face of his wife, Anna Karina as Nana, and realize that, like Poe, Godard is painting a portrait of his wife. The finale is memorable and puts a suitable spin on this early mix of cinematic experimentation and the sociological concerns which would continue to distinguish's this great filmmaker's work as the decade progressed.

MY LITTLE CHICKADEE
1940 83m bw   ★★½
Comedy/Western   /A
Universal

W.C. Fields (Cuthbert J. Twillie), Mae West (Flower Belle Lee), Joseph Calleia (Jeff Badger, The Masked Bandit), Dick Foran (Wayne Carter, Editor), Margaret Hamilton (Mrs. Gideon), George Moran (Clarence), Si Jenks (Deputy), Gene Austin (Himself), Russell Hall (Candy), Otto Heimel (Coco)

p, Lester Cowan; d, Edward F. Cline; w, Mae West, W.C. Fields; ph, Joseph Valentine; ed, Edward Curtiss; m, Frank Skinner; art d, Jack Otterson; cos, Vera West

MY LITTLE CHICKADEE should have been a lot funnier than it was. Although both West and Fields get credit for the script, it was essentially by her, with a few insertions by Fields, mostly after West had finished her work on the movie. She was a perfectionist who honed every punch line as though it were a diamond and he was a man to whom a script was a place to put his martini, much preferring to let the camera roll and have his ad-lib way with the scene. As a team, they were far less amusing than they were apart, and situations come one after another without the guffaws to go with them. It was shot on the western lot at Universal and the studio-bound sets show that. They didn't go on location because the stars were getting a lot of money; West received $300,000 for writing and acting, while Fields, who was under contract to the Valley lot, got $25,000 for writing and $125,000 for acting. That was very heavy money in those days and corners had to be cut. Directed by ex-Keystone Kop Cline, this was expected to be a wrestling match between the two volatile stars but the expected battles never came off and the shooting went smoothly, if not hilariously. West had been off the screen for two years and audiences eagerly flocked to see MY LITTLE CHICKADEE, which was a weird western satire punctuated with a few of Fields' polished skits. West is a woman of medium-to-loose morals who has been romanced by a masked bandit. The women of her town find that unpalatable and she is dispatched aboard the train to Greasewood City. While on the train, she meets Fields, a con man, and thinks that his suitcase is filled with money (actually coupons) which impresses her. When the train is attacked by Indians, she displays amazing shooting skills. West knows that she can't arrive in the new town as a single woman because her reputation is likely to have preceded her there, so she arranges to marry Fields aboard the train and the service is performed by professional card-cheater Donald Meek. They arrive in the small town and check into a hotel but she won't consummate the marriage and switches places with a goat in the nuptial bed. Fields says, "Darling, have you changed your perfume?" as his famed proboscis sniffs the air. West goes out on the town and meets Calleia, owner of the local watering spot, and it isn't a few minutes before these two are madly in love. Now Fields is made sheriff of the town and shortly thereafter, while wearing a cloak and mask to impress West, he's mistaken for the masked bandit, hauled into his own jail, and prepared for a necktie party. West asks that the real bandit make his presence known in order that the innocent Fields be released. It turns out to be Calleia, who returns all the money he's stolen. Foran is the crusading newspaper editor who wants to nail Calleia. He would also like to see the man out of the way because he loves West. Near the film's conclusion, West tells Fields that their marriage is a sham. He gets ready to depart, with the question of who gets her, Calleia or Foran, not yet determined. Fields is going east to sell shares in hair-oil wells. He tells her "Come up and see me sometime" as she mounts the stairs at their hotel. She replies that she will and calls him "my little chickadee."

Fields and West never could connect in the movie. After the film was completed West told newsmen: "There's no one in the world like Bill [Fields]. Thank God!" She stipulated in her contract that he was not allowed to drink or smoke on the set. According to film lore, he got drunk only once during the shooting, but he did get some flak for encouraging some children who were near the soundstage door to go out and play in traffic, although that may be only hearsay. The poker scene in the bar is a classic if only for the moment when Fuzzy Knight asks, "Is this a game of chance?" and Fields replies, "Not the way I play it." One song: "Willie of the Valley" (Ben Oakland, Milton Drake).

MY MAN GODFREY

1936 94m bw   ★★★★½
Comedy   /A
Universal

William Powell (Godfrey Parke), Carole Lombard (Irene Bullock), Alice Brady (Angelica Bullock), Eugene Pallette (Alexander Bullock), Gail Patrick (Cornelia Bullock), Alan Mowbray (Tommy Gray), Jean Dixon (Molly, Maid), Mischa Auer (Carlo), Robert Light (Faithful George), Pat Flaherty (Mike)

p, Gregory La Cava; d, Gregory La Cava; w, Morrie Ryskind, Eric Hatch, Gregory La Cava (based on the story "1101 Park Avenue" by Eric Hatch); ph, Ted Tetzlaff; ed, Ted J. Kent; m, Charles Previn; art d, Charles D. Hall; cos, Brymer, Travis Banton

A silvery romp. The flaw is that it never delivers on the satire it starts with, dissolving into romantic comedy along the way. But the leads are so impeccable that the seam never shows and the greatly underrated La Cava directs with precision. Of all the great comediennes, Lombard's innocently unflappable center was unique. She's like an eternal playmate—a quality only Harlow shared. It's a pity the two never played sisters.

Anyway, MY MAN GODFREY is comedy with a social conscience, although the message's subtlety has to be unearthed from all the humor. Carole Lombard and Gail Patrick are two Park Avenue spoiled brats in the midst of a scavenger hunt that is part of a gala evening. They have a list of odd items that includes tennis racquets, goldfish, and the nabbing of a "forgotten man" from one of Manhattan's hobo jungles. Lombard is flaky—sweet as can be—but dancing to a different drummer, and Patrick is her calculating sister, dark and sensuous. They wind up at a location near the East River and locate Powell, who is living with the other survivors of the Depression in a village of knocked-together lean-to's. When Patrick approaches him to be her forgotten man, Powell, incensed at the callousness of this charade, forces the elegantly dressed young woman back into a heap of debris. Patrick is angered by Powell's response and leaves, but Lombard, intrigued by Powell, remains, telling him that Patrick, who is accustomed to winning everything she's ever attempted, will probably find some other bum to take back to the posh hotel where the hunt's winner will be decided. Rather than allow the snobby Patrick to take the banner, Powell agrees to act as Lombard's forgotten man. He accompanies Lombard to the hotel, where he delivers a punchy speech to the bejeweled and tuxed crowd about the silliness of their quest—a speech that wins the hunt for Lombard.

Thrilled at having beaten Patrick for a change, Lombard also finds herself attracted to Powell, so she offers him the job of butler to her immensely wealthy family in their Park Avenue digs.

The rich are made to look very foolish and the poor appear very noble in this film, something that Depression audiences must have appreciated. Two years later, a film inspired by this one, MERRILY WE LIVE, was released, but it and the 1957 remake of MY MAN GODFREY were inferior attempts at recreating the chemistry of this film. Powell and Lombard, had been married in 1931 and divorced in 1933, remaining friendly enough to make this marvelous movie together. MY MAN GODFREY must be listed as one of the best of the screwball comedies and stands as an excellent example of witty scripting, direction, and editing. With Eugene Palette (growling some of the best lines, and certainly one of the strangest, funniest men ever), Alice Brady (second only to Billie Burke in these roles), Mischa Auer (doing the monkey imitation), among the congress of nitwits. Look fast—there's Janie Wyman in the party scene.

MY NAME IS IVAN
(IVANOVO DETSTVO)
1962 97m bw   ★★★★
Drama/War   /PG
Mosfilm   (U.S.S.R.)

Kolya Burlyayev *(Ivan)*, Valentin Zubkov *(Capt. Kholin)*, Ye. Zharikov *(Lt. Galtsev)*, S. Krylov *(Cpl. Katasonych)*, Nikolai Grinko *(Col. Gryaznov)*, D. Milyutenko *(Old Man)*, V. Malyavina *(Masha)*, I. Tarkovskaya *(Ivan's Mother)*, Andrei Konchalovsky, Ivan Savkin

d, Andrei Tarkovsky; w, Vladimir Osipovich Bogomolov, Mikhail Papava (based on the short story "Ivan" by Vladimir Osipovich Bogomolov); ph, Vadim Yusov; ed, L. Feyginova; m, Vyacheslav Ovchinnikov; art d, Ye. Chernyayaev; fx, V. Sevostyanov, S. Mukhin

This first feature from Soviet director Andrei Tarkovsky, an intense cinematic poem about war and childhood, presents the most horrific account of war's ravaging effect on a child's innocence since Roberto Rossellini's GERMANY, YEAR ZERO. Like Rossellini's Edmund, Tarkovsky's Ivan (Kolya Burlyayev) is a 12-year-old man/boy who has known little else but war—war that has forced him to become an adult and (in the irony of the actual translated title) robbed him of his childhood. When first seen, Ivan might be assumed to be an average youngster until he is shown trekking, neck-deep, through a murky swamp. This swamp is at the enemy's front line, to which Ivan, a member of a WWII Russian military intelligence unit, has been sent to gather information on troop movements. Ivan has only a cause and a country; his town has been overrun by the Germans, his father murdered, his mother shot and killed, his sister blown apart by a bomb. Although his superiors are pleased with his efforts, they protectively transfer him to the rear, but Ivan rebels at this and is allowed to go on one more mission. Much more than a war film about a young boy, MY NAME IS IVAN is a pure film experience. Tarkovsky fills the frame with beautiful images composed in extreme high, low, or tilted angles; uses an unpredictable editing style that alternates between rapid, jarring cuts and carefully composed long takes; employs a stark black-and-white contrast, which often turns natural scenery into abstract imagery; and constructs a soundtrack that is as inventive as his visuals. Complementing Tarkovsky's vision is the performance of Burlyayev, whose face expresses both determination and tenderness. Highly praised upon its release—it won awards at the Venice Film Festival for Best Film, Director, and Actor—MY NAME IS IVAN has found a new audience with the rising international recognition of Tarkovsky.

MY NIGHT AT MAUD'S
(MA NUIT CHEZ MAUD)
1969 105m bw   ★★★★
Drama   GP/12
F.F.P./Losange/Carrosse/Renn/Deux
Mondes/Gueville/Simar/Pleiade   (France)

Jean-Louis Trintignant *(Jean-Louis)*, Francoise Fabian *(Maud)*, Marie-Christine Barrault *(Francoise)*, Antoine Vitez *(Vidal)*, Leonide Kogan *(Concert Violinist)*, Anne Dubot *(Blonde Friend)*, Guy Leger *(Preacher)*, Marie Becker *(Marie, Maud's Daughter)*, Marie-Claude Rauzier *(Student)*

p, Pierre Cottrell, Barbet Schroeder; d, Eric Rohmer; w, Eric Rohmer; ph, Nestor Almendros; ed, Cecile Decugis; art d, Nicole Rachline

Tantalizingly witty, beautifully shot. The third of Eric Rohmer's "Six Moral Tales," MY NIGHT AT MAUD'S stars Jean-Louis Trintignant as Jean-Louis, a devout Catholic in love with Francoise (Marie-Christine Barrault), a pretty student he sees in church but is too shy to approach. When Jean-Louis runs into Vidal (Antoine Vitez), an old friend, Vidal invites him to dinner at the home of his bohemian lover, Maud (Francoise Fabian). There, Maud, Vidal (a Marxist professor), and Jean-Louis become involved in a lively conversation about the philosophy of Pascal and freedom of choice. In light of the bad snowstorm outside and the heavy drinking inside, Jean-Louis is persuaded to stay overnight at Maud's, but despite his hostess's advances does not make love to her. Later, he finally meets, and then marries, Francoise, only to find years later that she is the former mistress of Maud's husband. As in all of Rohmer's films, there is little "action" in MY NIGHT AT MAUD'S, but there is a great deal of intelligent and fascinating conversation as the characters question, expose, and explain their motivations and feelings (hence the "morality" of the tale). In Jean-Louis's case, his belief in premarital chastity is at issue. Photographed in black-and-white by Nestor Almendros, the film nicely captures the snowbound mood of the Christmas season, and the ensemble acting is excellent. The film was nominated for Best Foreign-Language Film and Best Original Screenplay Oscars, and won the New York Film Critics Best Screenwriting award.

MY OWN PRIVATE IDAHO
1991 102m c   ★★★★
Drama   R/18
Idaho Productions

River Phoenix *(Mike Waters)*, Keanu Reeves *(Scott Favor)*, James Russo *(Richard Waters)*, William Richert *(Bob Pigeon)*, Rodney Harvey *(Gary)*, Chiara Caselli *(Carmella)*, Michael Parker *(Digger)*, Jessie Thomas *(Denise)*, Flea *(Budd)*, Grace Zabriskie *(Alena)*

p, Laurie Parker; d, Gus Van Sant; w, Gus Van Sant; ph, Eric Alan Edwards, John Campbell; ed, Curtiss Clayton; prod d, David Brisbin; art d, Ken Hardy; cos, Beatrix Aruna Pasztor

The most shocking thing about Gus Van Sant's third feature is its firm resolve to show us beauty and tenderness—rare commodities in contemporary American movies. A genuine poetic voice is at work in MY OWN PRIVATE IDAHO, and it fascinates us with its strength and clarity.

Taking the form of a road movie, blended with elements borrowed from Shakespeare's *Henry IV Part 1*, the film chronicles the misadventures of Mike Waters (River Phoenix), a lonesome young hustler who suffers from narcolepsy—he passes out at stressful moments and must literally depend on strangers to protect him. After one such fit at the opening of the film, Mike awakens in a Seattle flophouse, being fellated by a balding, overweight john. Later, he's picked up and taken to the home of a rich matron. There he meets Scott Favor (Keanu Reeves), the rebellious son of the mayor of Portland, who is slumming among hustlers before he comes into his inheritance. After Mike has another fit, Scott carries him to a safe place to sleep it off. The next day Mike meets Hans (Udo Kier), a rich German, falls asleep again, and ends up in Portland with Scott. Led by the Falstaffian Bob Pigeon (William Richert), Mike, Scott and several other hustlers take over a derelict building, only to be cleared out by a police raid. The police are searching for Bob, but they also let Scott know that he must go to see his disapproving father, which he does before setting off with Mike on a motorbike to look for Mike's mother.

The search takes the pair to Idaho, where they meet Mike's brother—also, it turns out, his father—Richard (James Russo); Snake River, where they re-encounter Hans; and Italy, where they find out the elusive Mom has returned to the US, and where Scott abandons Mike in favor of a beautiful young farmer's daughter, Carmella (Chiara Caselli). Back in Portland, Scott becomes an elegant, upright young citizen after the death of his father. Bob follows Scott into a swank restaurant and accosts him, but Scott refuses to acknowledge his former mentor; Bob dies of a fever the same night. The end of the film finds Mike again on the road, falling asleep and being bundled into a car by a stranger.

Van Sant (MALA NOCHE, DRUGSTORE COWBOY) combines a realistic grasp of the underside of urban life with a visual sense that is by turns playful and elegiac. In one scene, a group of real-life hustlers exchange stories in a dingy coffee bar, with the director perfectly capturing the aimlessness and pathos which pervade their lives. In a more light-hearted set piece, the covers of a rack of gay porn magazines come to life with pop-art brio (a similar sensibility is evident in the screens of bright, 60s colors which divide up the film's sections.) Perhaps most memorably, Waters's narcoleptic trances are accompanied by fleeting images of extraordinary beauty: leaping fish in a silver stream; a lonely road; a bank of quickly moving clouds; a wooden house falling from the heavens.

Van Sant's attempt to impose a Shakespearean conceit on his material is much less successful. Though Richert brings an enjoyable Falstaffian swagger to the *Henry IV* sequences, most of the other actors seem ill at ease with Van Sant's self-consciously theatrical blend of Shakespearean dialogue and contemporary street slang. All these sequences pale in comparison to the understated pathos of the quiet scenes. In the most moving of these—a nighttime, roadside confession by Mike of his love for Scott—Van Sant casts a gently hypnotic spell that is not easily forgotten.

MY PAL TRIGGER
1946 79m bw   ★★★½
Western   /U
Republic

Roy Rogers (Roy Rogers), George "Gabby" Hayes (Gabby Kendrick), Dale Evans (Susan), Jack Holt (Brett Scoville), LeRoy Mason (Carson), Roy Barcroft (Hunter), Sam Flint (Sheriff), Kenne Duncan (Croupier), Ralph Sanford (Auctioneer), Francis McDonald (Storekeeper)

p, Armand Schaefer; d, Frank McDonald; w, Jack Townley, John K. Butler (based on a story by Paul Gangelin); ph, William Bradford; ed, Harry Keller; art d, Gano Chittenden; fx, Howard Lydecker, Theodore Lydecker

Roy Rogers named this as his favorite of all his films, and one can see why. It's well plotted, with lively direction and much better camera work than most of the Singing Cowboy's films. Rogers plays a horse trader planning to mate a prize mare with a stallion belonging to his pal Gabby Kendrick (Gabby Hayes). A gambler (Jack Holt) with similar plans for his own mare tries to steal the stallion, which escapes and mates with Rogers's mare. When the gambler catches up to the horse, he shoots it. Rogers is blamed, but he and his now-pregnant mare escape capture and leave town, with Roy determined to return to clear his name and unmask the real villain. This is the quintessential Rogers film, with some fine acting (undoubtedly some of the best the genre

would produce) and, of course, musical numbers by the Sons of the Pioneers and duets by Rogers and Dale Evans.

MY SISTER EILEEN
1955 108m c   ★★★½
Musical/Comedy   /U
Columbia

Janet Leigh (Eileen Sherwood), Betty Garrett (Ruth Sherwood), Jack Lemmon (Bob Baker), Bob Fosse (Frank Lippencott), Kurt Kasznar (Appopolous), Dick York ("Wreck"), Lucy Marlow (Helen), Tommy Rall (Chick Clark), Barbara Brown (Helen's Mother), Horace MacMahon (Lonigan)

p, Fred Kohlmar; d, Richard Quine; w, Blake Edwards, Richard Quine (based on the play by Joseph Fields, Jerome Chodorov from the stories by Ruth McKenney); ph, Charles Lawton, Jr. (CinemaScope, Technicolor); ed, Charles Nelson; m, George Duning; art d, Walter Holscher; chor, Bob Fosse; cos, Jean Louis

This musical version of the hit Broadway play has virtually the same story as the 1942 film. The actors this time include Bob Fosse, who also choreographs and dances, and Jack Lemmon, charming in the first of several films he was to do with director Richard Quine. The plot once again follows a series of incidents and complications in the lives of a pair of sisters (Betty Garrett and Janet Leigh) who come to New York from Ohio and wind up in what must be the busiest apartment in the city. It's a fast-moving version of the play with songs that add greatly to the fun provided by the crackling dialogue and good performances.

MY SON, MY SON!
1940 115m bw   ★★★★
Drama   /A
UA

Madeleine Carroll (Livia Vaynol), Brian Aherne (William Essex), Louis Hayward (Oliver Essex), Laraine Day (Maeve O'Riorden), Henry Hull (Dermont O'Riorden), Josephine Hutchinson (Nellie Essex), Sophie Stewart (Shella O'Riorden), Bruce Lester (Rory O'Riorden), Scotty Beckett (Oliver as a Child), Brenda Henderson (Maeve as a Child)

p, Edward Small; d, Charles Vidor; w, Lenore Coffee (based on the novel by Howard Spring); ph, Harry Stradling; ed, Grant Whytock, Fred R. Feitshans, Jr.; art d, John DuCasse Schultze; fx, Howard Anderson

A superb drama has Aherne in one of his best roles as a gentle and considerate writer of romantic novels, a man who sacrifices most of his life for others, chiefly an ungrateful, hurtful son, Hayward. Aherne is a product of the Manchester slums but he struggles heroically and becomes a famous novelist. He is devoted to his son, played first by Beckett, then, as an adult, by Hayward. The boy and then the young man prove, over 25 years, to be thoroughly rotten. Hayward makes fun of his father's writing, brings tragedy to his childhood girlfriend Day, and even tries to seduce artist Carroll, the woman his widowed father loves and plans to marry. Yet Aherne cannot bring himself to condemn the boy he has given his heart to. Both wind up in the trenches during WWI, with Aherne covering the war as a correspondent and his son a young officer. Aherne meets his son for the last time and begs him to reform, telling him he still loves him and that he forgives him for breaking his heart. Hayward tells him that his father has loved him too much, but in the end, Hayward redeems himself by dying a hero's death, leaving Aherne to cry out in agony: "My son, my son!" Carroll is beautiful and Day is pure springtime in this poignant and powerful film but it is coldhearted

Hayward and his merciless inhuman ways who steals this film which Vidor directs with great care and innovative style. The film was Oscar-nominated for Best Interior Decoration.

MY 20TH CENTURY

1989   104m   bw   ★★★★
Comedy/Drama
Mafilm/Friedlander/ICAIC   (Hungary/Canada)

Dorotha Segda *(Dora/Lili/Mother)*, Oleg Jankowski *(Z)*, Peter Andorai *(Thomas Alva Edison)*, Gabor Mathe *(X)*, Paulus Manker *(Weininger)*, Gyula Kery, Andrei Schwartz, Sandor Tery, Sandor Czvetko, Endre Koronszi

d, Ildiko Enyedi; w, Ildiko Enyedi; ph, Tibor Mathe; ed, Maria Rigo; m, Laszlo Vidovszky; prod d, Zoltan Labas; cos, Agnes Gyarmathy

Filmed in shimmering black and white that suggests a fairy tale, this film is so breathtakingly lovely to look at it makes one mourn the fact that black-and-white cinematography has fallen into disfavor. This is a dazzling celebration of feminism, mechanical progress, unbreakable familial ties, and the early history of the 20th century. Despite some occasionally slack pacing, it is a magical achievement that creates its own universe.

Taking the form of a fable, the film outlines a world of unlimited possibilities. In Hungary in 1880, identical twin girls are separated while selling matches. The different paths of the girls, Lili and Dora (both played by Dorotha Segda) are then followed over many years before they serendipitously cross once more. Aglow with revolutionary fervor, Lili has become a radical determined to free the masses and willing to employ a bomb to get her point across. Accustomed to trading her favors to support her lifestyle, Dora leans toward the pleasures of the flesh. To his total confusion, a man known as Z (Oleg Jankowski) meets both women while traveling on the Orient Express, believing them to be one fascinating creature. Intercut with this dual romance are depictions of technological breakthroughs of the time, including the tale of a laboratory dog who outsmarts his scientist keepers, and commentary by Thomas Alva Edison (Peter Andorai). Somehow the fanciful comedy of errors which forms the film's basic plotline seems to be a logical extension of the progress-driven world in the early 1900s; the characters exist in a shining new world where anything can happen. Since creativity charges the air, the ingenuity of the characters in getting themselves out of scrapes seems only natural. At the film's climax, Lili (en route to eliminate the minister of the interior) encounters her long-lost sister in a hall of mirrors where the women are held rapt by their endless reflections. Abandoning her revolutionary goals, Lili links up with Dora, who casts off her need to be protected by men. Freed of their dependencies, both women dump Z. Blending an intellectual political bent with a sexual nature, the women combine their best qualities and find they are now free to be themselves.

In his directorial debut, Ildiko Enyedi dexterously unfolds a fanciful tale layered with whimsical and historical segments that touch tangentially on the main storyline. Never tied to a linear structure, it is full of delightful asides, such as the story of the monkey whose naivete about human beings lands him in captivity. In this enchanting fairy tale, the narrative doesn't proceed as expected, but all the side roads link up with Enyedi's destination. The best way to enjoy MY 20TH CENTURY is to approach it as a fantastic cavalcade in which human truths are revealed by accident. Despite the fact that the characters wander through a technological wonderland, the most magical proposition of the film lies not in inventiveness but in the capacity of the spirit to reinvent itself. At the end of the fairy tale the little match girls find a happy ending for themselves, rather than waiting around for a man to impose his idea of a happy ending on them. Watching the film is a liberating experience and a joyful occasion for movie lovers in search of a fresh filmmaking visionary.

MY UNCLE

(MON ONCLE)
1958   110m   c   ★★★★
Comedy   /U
Specta/Gray/Alter/Cady   (France)

Jacques Tati *(Mons. Hulot)*, Jean-Pierre Zola *(Mons. Arpel)*, Adrienne Servantie *(Mme. Arpel)*, Alain Becourt *(Gerald Arpel)*, Lucien Fregis *(Mons. Pichard)*, Betty Schneider *(Betty, Landlord's Daughter)*, Yvonne Arnaud *(Georgette, Arpel's Maid)*, Dominique Marie *(Neighbor)*, J.F. Martial *(Walter)*, Andre Dino *(Sweep)*

p, Jacques Tati; d, Jacques Tati; w, Jacques Tati, Jacques Lagrange, Jean L'Hote; ph, Jean Bourgoin (Eastmancolor); ed, Suzanne Baron; m, Franck Barcellini, Alain Romans; art d, Henri Schmitt, Pierre Etaix

Tati, France's most loved director, follows MR. HULOT'S HOLIDAY with this impressive satire on technological gadgetry and the people who devote their lives to technological convenience. Tati has described his own comedy as "laughter born of a certain fundamental absurdity. Some things are not funny of themselves but become so on being dissected." It is this quality that Tati's films share with such satires as Rene Clair's A NOUS LA LIBERTE, Charles Chaplin's MODERN TIMES, and even Albert Brooks's LOST IN AMERICA. Like Chaplin (MODERN TIMES) and Rene Clair (A NOUS LA LIBERTE) before him, Jacques Tati delivered here a comic satire on the ills of the technological age. Tati again casts himself in the role of Mons. Hulot, a lanky fellow with a raincoat and umbrella who stumbles through life, but just barely. Content to live in his neglected quarters, Hulot is in direct contrast to the very modern Arpel family, comprising his sister (Adrienne Servantie), brother-in-law (Jean-Pierre Zola), and nephew, Gerald (Alain Becourt). The Arpels live in a stylized, modernized, desensitized suburb, their angular brick-and-glass house hidden from the street by a clanging metal gate, and fronted by a fountain with an obscene upright metal fish spurting water from its mouth. Inside are a number of gadgets that are meant to save time but do nothing but waste it—and make noise. Hulot's humble, simple life attracts young Gerald, whose mischievous enthusiasm has no place in the modern world. As much as Hulot and Gerald would like to escape from their high-tech environment, however, they cannot; it's here to stay, and they must contend with it. Less a condemnation of technology than of its worshippers, MY UNCLE is (like all of Tati's work) a rare example of comedy that is simultaneously entertaining, intelligent, and technically inventive. Of all Tati's films, it is the most accessible—the Hulot character taking center stage here instead of remaining in the background. MY UNCLE also contains one of the greatest shots in all of film, as Mme. and Mons. Arpel are each seen, from outside, walking back and forth before their round bedroom windows, giving the impression that the house is rolling its eyes. Winner of the 1958 Academy Award for Best Foreign-Language Film.

MY UNCLE ANTOINE

(MON ONCLE ANTOINE)
1971   110m   c   ★★★½
Drama
Natl. Film Board of Canada   (Canada)

Jean Duceppe *(Uncle Antoine)*, Olivette Thibault *(Aunt Cecile)*, Claude Jutra *(Fernand, Clerk)*, Jacques Gagnon *(Benoit)*, Lyne Champagne *(Carmen)*, Lionel Villeneauve *(Joe Poulin)*, Helene Loiselle *(Mme. Poulin)*, Mario Dubuc, Lise Burnelle, Alain Legendre

p, Marc Beaudet; d, Claude Jutra; w, Claude Jutra, Clement Perron (based on a story by Clement Perron); ph, Michel Brault (Eastmancolor); ed, Claude Jutra, Claire Boyer; m, Jean Cousineau; art d, Denis Boucher, Lawrence O'Brien

Though a boy's coming of age has been given innumberable screen treatments, MY UNCLE ANTOINE must rank as one of the best of the genre. Gagnon is a 14-year-old orphan living in a small French Canadian mining town during the 1940s. Under the care of aunt and uncle Thibault and Duceppe, who run the local general store, Gagnon participates in the annual Christmas celebration by flirting with Champagne, his foster sister, but the adults put a stop to this. That evening the townspeople gather at the store for the annual holiday gathering. A phone call interrupts the festivities when Loiselle needs Duceppe's services. (In addition to running the store, he is also the local undertaker.) Loiselle's son has just died, and with her husband away at a logging camp, she needs the man to remove the body. Gagnon accompanies his uncle on the sleigh ride to the home. On the way back, the old man reflects on his life while slowly getting drunk. The sleigh goes out of control and the casket falls off. Since his uncle is too drunk to help recover it, Gagnon must rush back to the store for help. There he finds his aunt and a store clerk locked in a tight embrace. The clerk (Jutra) goes to help, but they discover the casket missing. Arriving at the deceased boy's home, Gagnon looks through the window and sees the family sadly standing over the body. Apparently the father had found the body and taken it back home. Gagnon is left alone with his thoughts, learning much about human nature and its foibles on this Christmas Eve.

This sad heart-felt drama avoids cliches and shows genuine sensitivity for its subject. Gagnon carries his load well, giving the kind of sincere performance that other actors take years to achieve. The story had some basis in truth. Screenwriter Perron had grown up in the French Canadian mining areas and used his childhood memories to fashion the screenplay. The direction, though for the most part strong, has an annoying predilection for the zoom lens, using it more often than needed. Occasionally the zooming defeats its own purpose, imposing false drama where it should simply have allowed characters and actions to speak for themselves. Overall, though, this is a beautiful piece and took the Gold Hugo at the 1971 Chicago Film Festival.

MYSTERIOUS DR. FU MANCHU, THE
1929   80m   bw   ★★★
Mystery
Paramount

Warner Oland *(Dr. Fu Manchu)*, Jean Arthur *(Lia Eltham)*, Neil Hamilton *(Dr. Jack Petrie)*, O.P. Heggie *(Nayland Smith)*, William Austin *(Sylvester Wadsworth)*, Claude King *(Sir John Petrie)*, Charles Stevenson *(Gen. Petrie)*, Noble Johnson *(Li Po)*, Evelyn Selbie *(Fai Lu)*, Charles Giblyn *(Weymouth)*

d, Rowland V. Lee; w, Florence Ryerson, Lloyd Corrigan (based on the story by Sax Rohmer); ph, Harry Fischbeck; ed, George Nichols, Jr.

The first of the popular Sax Rohmer (Arthur Sarsfield Ward) mystery novels to be made into a talking feature is a fairly good job, reaching the same level of chilling suspense as the novels and later radio shows. Benevolent looking, overweight Oland

(known for his renditions of Charlie Chan) is the evil green-eyed Chinese doctor bent on revenge against the British officer who commanded forces during the Boxer rebellion. It was during this time that Oland's wife and son were killed, warping the doctor's mind to the extent that all he can think about is vengeance. To assist him, he uses the daughter of an English official killed during the Rebellion. The girl is put into a trance and forced to do Oland's dirty work. After having killed several of the British officers he is after, Oland then attempts to gain vengeance against King and son Hamilton. But before this can happen, Scotland Yard is aware of Oland's pattern, and warns King before he meets with a disastrous end. Oland is quite convincing in the title role that would later be shared by such greats as Boris Karloff and Christopher Lee. The eerie atmosphere and steadily building suspense make this early entry in the series as frightening as those made in the 1960s.

MYSTERY OF THE WAX MUSEUM, THE
1933   73m   c   ★★★★
Horror   /A
WB

Lionel Atwill *(Ivan Igor)*, Fay Wray *(Charlotte Duncan)*, Glenda Farrell *(Florence Dempsey)*, Frank McHugh *(Jim)*, Gavin Gordon *(Harold Winton)*, Edwin Maxwell *(Joe Worth)*, Holmes Herbert *(Dr. Rasmussen)*, Arthur Edmund Carewe *(Sparrow)*, Allen Vincent *(Ralph Burton)*, Monica Bannister *(Joan Gale)*

p, Henry Blanke; d, Michael Curtiz; w, Don Mullaly, Carl Erickson (based on a play by Charles Belden); ph, Ray Rennahan (Technicolor); ed, George Amy; art d, Anton Grot

Lionel Atwill and Fay Wray are teamed here for the second time in a Michael Curtiz-directed, Warner Brothers-produced two-strip Technicolor horror film (their first pairing was in DR. X in 1932). The film opens in London, in 1921, as the brilliant sculptor Ivan Igor (Atwill) is hard at work on his latest creation, surrounded by beautiful wax sculptures of female historical figures. Having eschewed the more sensational—and, therefore, more lucrative—figures of killers like Jack the Ripper in favor of these beautiful creations, Ivan finds his wax museum on the brink of bankruptcy. A fight over finances between Ivan and his partner, Joe Worth (Edwin Maxwell), results in the museum's destruction by fire, the "death" of the wax figures, and Ivan's near death. The scene then shifts to New York City, 1933, where the grey-haired Ivan is confined to a wheelchair, his hands crippled from the fire. When a wealthy socialite dies and her corpse is stolen from the morgue, tough-talking female reporter Florence Dempsey (Glenda Farrell) investigates the case. The strange disappearance of the corpse coincides suspiciously with Ivan's preparation for the opening of his new museum, in which the wax beauties have a remarkably lifelike appearance. Feared to be lost for many years, THE MYSTERY OF THE WAX MUSEUM gained a mighty reputation when film historians' memories of the movie were jogged by the 1953 3-D remake, HOUSE OF WAX. When a print of the original film surfaced in the late 1960s, however, many critics were disappointed with it, shrugging it off as a silly mystery picture, though their initial reaction was entirely unfounded. An amazing film filled with stunning sets (by Anton Grot), exceptional moments, and perhaps Atwill's greatest performance, THE MYSTERY OF THE WAX MUSEUM is also a surprisingly adult picture that deals explicitly with drug addiction, necrophilia, and insanity. Notably, it was also one of the first horror films to be set in the everyday reality of modern-day New York and not in a mystical foreign land.

MYSTERY TRAIN

1989   113m   c   ★★★½
Comedy   R/15
MTI

Masatoshi Nagase *(Jun)*, Youki Kudoh *(Mitzuko)*, Screamin' Jay Hawkins *(Night Clerk)*, Cinque Lee *(Bellboy)*, Nicoletta Braschi *(Luisa)*, Elizabeth Bracco *(Dee Dee)*, Sy Richardson *(News Vendor)*, Tom Noonan *(Man in Diner)*, Stephen Jones *(The Ghost)*, Rufus Thomas *(Man in Station)*

p, Jim Stark; d, Jim Jarmusch; w, Jim Jarmusch; ph, Robby Muller; ed, Melody London; m, John Lurie; prod d, Dan Bishop; cos, Carol Wood

New York-based filmmaker Jim Jarmusch continues his deadpan Cook's Tour of America with MYSTERY TRAIN, a trio of tangentially relatedu stories set in Memphis, Tennessee.

All three tales center on the run-down Arcade Hotel, where every room is a shrine to Memphis's favorite son, Elvis Aron Presley. A candidate for the wrecking ball, the Arcade is staffed by two dedicated souls (legendary rhythm & blues performer Screamin' Jay Hawkins and Cinque Lee, Spike's younger brother) who seem to have no existence beyond the front desk. As the film's first episode, "Far from Yokohama," opens, Jun (Masatoshi Nagase) and Mitzuko (Youki Kudoh), two teenaged devotees of American culture, check into the Arcade, where they argue over rock 'n' roll favorites, make love, listen to Elvis on the hotel radio, and remain undisturbed by everything that occurs—even the gunshot they hear near checkout time. The Arcade also plays host to Luisa (Nicoletta Braschi), an Italian woman visiting the States to bring her dead husband back to Italy. The focus of the second episode, "A Ghost," Luisa is harassed by a low-life who promises her she will be visited by visions of Elvis. The third episode, "Lost in Space," involves Dee Dee (Elizabeth Bracco), her alcohol-crazed lover (Joe Strummer), her nervous-wreck brother (Steve Buscemi), and their fast-talking pal (Rick Aviles) as they get involved in a shooting. At checkout time, all the characters go their separate ways.

As with STRANGER THAN PARADISE and DOWN BY LAW, Jarmusch focuses his offbeat sensibility on urban iconoclasts, small-town oddballs, and bewildered strangers. Not surprisingly, MYSTERY TRAIN will work best for those who share Jarmusch's fondness for America's pop culture junkyard; he's a true original, but Jarmusch's originality lies in a quirky viewpoint that may leave some audience members cold. Others who abandon themselves to his deadpan drollery and Robby Muller's witty cinematography, which makes squalor look festive, will be rewarded with a cockeyed valentine to the cradle of rock 'n' roll.

NAKED CITY, THE

1948 96m bw   ★★★★
Crime   /A
Universal

Barry Fitzgerald *(Lt. Dan Muldoon)*, Howard Duff *(Frank Niles)*, Dorothy Hart *(Ruth Morrison)*, Don Taylor *(Jimmy Halloran)*, Ted de Corsia *(Garzah)*, House Jameson *(Dr. Stoneman)*, Anne Sargent *(Mrs. Halloran)*, Adelaide Klein *(Mrs. Batory)*, Grover Burgess *(Mr. Batory)*, Tom Pedi *(Detective Perelli)*

p, Mark Hellinger; d, Jules Dassin; w, Albert Maltz, Malvin Wald (based on a story by Malvin Wald); ph, William Daniels; ed, Paul Weatherwax; m, Miklos Rozsa, Frank Skinner; art d, John DeCuir; cos, Grace Houston

This superlative film set the pattern for myriad documentary-type dramas to come. Its producer, Hellinger, patterned the tale after the tabloid newspaper stories he wrote in his youth, and he narrates the picture with the same kind of terse but poignant vitality that was the hallmark of his sensational prose. Though basically a crime story—with, oddly, only character actor Fitzgerald as its star—the film is also a romance with the city itself, one where Hellinger embraces soiled urchins and immaculate society ladies with equal passion. The story opens with the bathtub murder of a beautiful blonde playgirl. The police are left with no clues. Fitzgerald and his brash young assistant, Taylor, are assigned the case and spend most of their time running down weak leads that reveal nothing. In the process, the routine of their lives is detailed, as the various suspects and would-be witnesses who make up much of the story are presented. Fitzgerald, a cop for 30 years, is relentless in his pursuit of criminals. Taylor, who lives in a modest home and kisses his wife good-bye every morning on his way to headquarters, tries to please his superiors and cover up his lack of experience, but he slowly learns the wily ways of the cop under Fitzgerald's expert tutelage. Their tedious procedures are summed up by narrator Hellinger: "Ask a question, get an answer, ask another." But the dogged Fitzgerald finally gets enough right answers to lead him to playboy Duff, who is trapped by the cop into admitting that he is broke and got the blonde killed for money, the deed actually being performed by de Corsia, a strong-arm goon and friend of Duff. Police take Duff into custody without a struggle but de Corsia, a strutting, egocentric, one-time wrestler, is another matter. He flees for his life, with the police hot in pursuit through the streets and on the elevated trains of Manhattan, a spectacular chase that culminates on the high girders of the Brooklyn Bridge, where the cops are forced to shoot the killer to death.

Shot completely on location in New York City, THE NAKED CITY chronicles the grim urban landscape and depicts its everyday life and citizens, embracing swank Fifth Avenue, Broadway,

kids playing hop-skip-and-jump in the streets, straphangers en route to work and back on the crowded subways. Dassin's direction is as taut and telling as the tale he relates with such visual punch and panache, much like his other starkly realistic films, BRUTE FORCE, NIGHT AND THE CITY, and THIEVES' HIGHWAY. His association with Hellinger (who also produced BRUTE FORCE) drew heavily upon the one-time newspaperman's visual sensibility for historical sensationalism. Hellinger's THE ROARING TWENTIES, for example, a 1939 crime production starring James Cagney and Humphrey Bogart, interspersed—among the dramatic scenes—newsreel clips of the excesses of the Jazz Age. Influencing the tendency toward total on-location shooting were such films as THE HOUSE ON 92ND STREET and CONFESSIONS OF A NAZI SPY. More than 100 location sites were employed in the filming of THE NAKED CITY, with the brilliant cameraman Daniels shooting most of his scenes from inside a van parked along the streets, using a one-way mirror and tinted windows so that passersby were oblivious to the camera's presence. In the late 1950s and early 1960s, a long-running TV series on ABC used this film's title to show the "slice-of-life" style of drama the original film typified, and also employed Hellinger's postscript in this, his last feature production, a line which became a household phrase: "There are eight million stories in the naked city. This has been one of them."

NAKED GUN, THE

1988 85m c   ★★½
Comedy   PG-13/15
Paramount

Leslie Nielsen *(Lt. Frank Drebin)*, George Kennedy *(Capt. Ed Hocken)*, Priscilla Presley *(Jane Spencer)*, Ricardo Montalban *(Vincent Ludwig)*, O.J. Simpson *(Nordberg)*, Nancy Marchand *(Mayor)*, John Houseman *(Driving Instructor)*, Reggie Jackson *(Right Fielder)*, Jeannette Charles *(Queen Elizabeth II)*, Curt Gowdy

p, Robert K. Weiss; d, David Zucker; w, Jerry Zucker, Jim Abrahams, David Zucker, Pat Proft; ph, Robert Stevens (Technicolor); ed, Michael Jablow; m, Ira Newborn; prod d, John J. Lloyd; cos, Mary Vogt

The Zucker, Abrahams, and Zucker writing-directing team, who made a huge splash with AIRPLANE!, based THE NAKED GUN on their hilarious but short-lived television show "Police Squad." Leslie Nielsen reprises his role as the bumbling police lieutenant Frank Drebin, who becomes embroiled in a case involving suave heroin smuggler Vincent Ludwig (Ricardo Montalban). Drebin falls for Ludwig's assistant, Jane (Priscilla Presley), who is just as dim and clumsy as he is. Meanwhile, Drebin's boss (George Kennedy) learns that there will be an assassination attempt on Queen Elizabeth (played by look-alike Jeannette Charles) during her visit to Los Angeles. Merely recounting the plot of any ZAZ comedy utterly fails to convey the lunacy of the production and, therefore, its charm. From the credits sequence, which has the camera mounted on top of a police car that drives through the city streets, into a house, and finally into a girls' locker room and shower; to the sight of the villain falling off a tier at the ballpark and being crushed by a bus, a steamroller, and then a marching band, THE NAKED GUN throws the gags at the viewer fast and furious. Unfortunately, what worked in the half-hour television format can't be sustained through a full-length feature, and for every gag that works there are 10 that don't.

NAKED GUN 2½: THE SMELL OF FEAR, THE

1991 85m c ★★★

Comedy PG-13/12

Zucker Brother Productions/Paramount

Leslie Nielsen (Lieutenant Frank Drebin), Priscilla Presley (Jane Spencer), George Kennedy (Ed Hocken), O.J. Simpson (Nordberg), Robert Goulet (Quentin Hapsburg), Richard Griffiths (Dr. Meinheimer/Earl Hacker), Jacqueline Brookes (Commissioner Brumford), Anthony James (Hector Savage), Lloyd Bochner (Baggett), Peter Mark Richman (Dunwell)

p, Robert K. Weiss; d, David Zucker; w, David Zucker, Pat Proft (from the characters created by Zucker for the TV series "Police Squad!"); ph, Robert Stevens; ed, James Symons, Chris Greenbury; m, Ira Newborn; prod d, John J. Lloyd; cos, Taryn Dechellis

---

THE NAKED GUN 2½: THE SMELL OF FEAR spins and whirls like the Tasmanian devil, gags and jokes swirling like crazed mites around it, engulfing all criticism and plot descriptions before it.

That indefatigable nincompoop, Lieutenant Frank Drebin (Leslie Nielsen) of Police Squad, happens to be in Washington, D.C., at a state dinner and finds himself investigating an explosion at the offices of Dr. Meinheimer (Richard Griffiths), set to deliver recommendations on energy policy to President George Bush (John Roarke). In a nefarious attempt to lead Bush down the garden path, a group of energy czars, headed by oily, yet suave, Quentin Hapsburg (Robert Goulet), kidnap the real Dr. Meinheimer and place a double in his place in order to deliver a pro-energy-abuse recommendation to the President the following day. Unfortunately for Drebin, during his investigation he comes upon old flame Jane Spencer (Priscilla Presley), now working for Dr. Meinheimer.

The past comes back to haunt Drebin and seeing Jane attracted to Quentin makes him feel both jealous and depressed. When Drebin discovers Quentin is connected to the Meinheimer bombing, Jane thinks Drebin is merely resentful until a hired goon tries to kill her while she's taking a shower. Then Jane realizes that Meinheimer has been acting differently and not only begins to believe Drebin, but falls in love with him all over again.

The night of Meinheimer's speech to Bush, after a few absurd complications, Drebin literally exposes the phony Meinheimer to a distinguished assembly and defuses a bomb set by Quentin, who falls through a window of a high-rise and lands unharmed on the street below, only to be mauled to death by a passing lion. Bush asks Drebin to head a federal bureau of Police Squad, Drebin tells reporters he wants to be known as "the environmental police lieutenant," and Jane embraces him.

Like the previous "Police Squad!" film, THE NAKED GUN, the sight gags, jokes, puns, parodies, double-entendres and cheap laughs assault you at every turn. The jokes are so dense as to be almost Escheresque—TV cop-show parodies within film parodies within slapstick within nonsensical word-play within visual puns. As the laughs subside involving Drebin's incompetence, you discover yourself to be in takeoffs on PSYCHO, GHOST or GOLDFINGER. And as you find yourself trapped in this loop of jokes and parodies, THE NAKED GUN 2½ taunts you with obviously phony slapstick gags as in the long-shot dance routine by two eccentric tango dancers who are supposed to be Jane and Drebin, or in the GHOST parody where, in true FLASHDANCE form, Nielsen's 65-year-old form suddenly transforms in close-ups to the well muscled torso of a Chippendale dancer. It is in this rapid-fire joke explosion, where to blink is to miss a gag, that the film, like its predecessor, succeeds most joyously.

THE NAKED GUN 2½ also spreads the base of gleeful rip-offs from the first film. From the brazen homages to the sultans of bad comedy, the Three Stooges, the film proceeds to borrow from films as diverse as Woody Allen's BANANAS, Blake Edwards's circumstantial slapstick disasters and Mack Sennett. Most surprising are the audacious borrowings from Jerry Lewis, particularly a scene in which Drebin and Meinheimer are stuck in his out-of-control wheelchair and O.J. Simpson's mad careening through the streets on a flatbed, reminiscent of the climax of THE DISORDERLY ORDERLY. David Zucker is not even ashamed of pillaging his own "Police Squad!," many jokes in the film having made their initial appearances on that irreverent TV series.

Leslie Nielsen, invigorated by a second career disemboweling his first as a drab, one-note television actor, accepts the promise held in THE NAKED GUN and becomes an all-out comic riot in the manner of an Americanized Inspector Clouseau. Watching Nielsen play top banana is as bracing as having ice cubes shoved down your pants, and he can seemingly do everything right—wrong, that is—from making senseless threats to singing in a mariachi band.

The one fault that prevents NAKED GUN 2½ from being as hilarious as its predecessor is its propensity to telescope the gags, permitting one character to look puzzled at the absurd mouthings of another character. Doing so draws attention to the comedy and stops the film cold. In a film like THE NAKED GUN 2½, to single out one bit of business as peculiar when everything around it is out of control is the height of madness.

NAKED LUNCH

1991 115m c ★★★½

Science Fiction/Fantasy/Drama R/18

Naked Lunch Productions/Recorded Picture Co.
(U.K./Canada)

Peter Weller (William Lee), Judy Davis (Joan Frost/Joan Lee), Ian Holm (Tom Frost), Julian Sands (Yves Cloquet), Roy Scheider (Dr. Benway), Monique Mercure (Fadela), Nicholas Campbell (Hank), Michael Zelniker (Martin), Robert A. Silverman (Hans), Joseph Scorsiani (Kiki)

p, Jeremy Thomas; d, David Cronenberg; w, David Cronenberg (from the novel by William S. Burroughs); ph, Peter Suschitzky; ed, Ronald Sanders; m, Howard Shore; prod d, Carol Spier; art d, James McAteer; fx, Chris Walas Inc; cos, Denise Cronenberg

---

Filmmaker David Cronenberg has been quoted as saying that a completely faithful translation of William S. Burroughs's Naked Lunch would have cost hundreds of millions of dollars to make and would have resulted in a film that virtually nobody would want to see. The film that Cronenberg has made can hardly be considered a crossover, feel-good hit. But it is a respectful tribute to Burroughs that, partly because it's also a typical piece of Cronenbergiana, is not entirely inaccessible to those unfamiliar with the writer's work.

Cronenberg has come a long way since his early films, like 1979's THE BROOD, played their premiere New York engagements in 42nd Street grindhouses—usually on double-bills with x-rated epics starring Marilyn Chambers, who gave her only "mainstream" performance in Cronenberg's 1976 feature RABID. But, along the way, something has been lost as well as gained.

1953. New York City. Struggling writer Bill Lee (Peter Weller) is making a living as an exterminator, but his professional zeal is impeded by his wife Joan's (Judy Davis) addiction to the bug powder he uses. She steals it from his applicator when he comes home at night, which leaves Bill short in the middle of a job and gets him in hot water with his boss. Confronting his wife, Lee shoots up some of the bug powder and becomes addicted himself, leading to his arrest by the police, who allege that the bug powder in Lee's possession is really an illegal drug. To prove their point, the cops interrogating Lee try his powder on a huge insect they keep in a box in their office. Instead of dying, however, the bug swoons on the stuff and begins talking to Lee through an anus-like orifice on its back after the cops have left the room.

The bug identifies itself as Lee's case officer and says Lee is an unwitting agent in the covert war against Interzone. This corporation, headquartered in a city-state of the same name on the North African coast, is involved in mind control using powerful drugs developed by the evil Dr. Benway (Roy Scheider). Lee's case officer orders Lee to kill his wife, an Interzone agent, then go to Interzone and write a report about it. Lee refuses, smashing the bug to a pulp and escaping from the police, only to walk in on his wife having sex with one of his best friends. Later, playing a game of "William Tell," Lee attempts to shoot an apple balanced on his wife's head, but misses and kills her (the scene is based on a real-life accident in which Burroughs did, in fact, mortally wound his wife). Using a cruise ticket slipped to him in a gay bar by a mugwump—a lizard-like creature with appendages atop its head that ooze an addictive jism—Lee flees to Interzone, which is a kind of hallucinatory version of the Tangiers inhabited by expatriate American writers in the 1950s. There, he becomes addicted to another drug, made from ground-up South American black centipedes, and tries to write his report on an old typewriter that metamorphoses into the bug-officer, which gets sexually aroused when Lee types on it. As this frequently stomach-turning take on the bohemian life continues, Lee encounters figures based on real-life Burroughs contemporaries including Paul Bowles (Ian Holm) and his wife Jane (Judy Davis again), with whom he has an affair of sorts.

NAKED LUNCH's ad campaign proclaimed "Exterminate all rational thought"; however, that's precisely what the film itself does *not* do. For all its surreal imagery and themes, NAKED LUNCH is not the work of a surrealist sensibility. Surrealism exposes the strangeness inherent in the familiar; Cronenberg does the opposite, revealing the familiar humanity in the twisted and grotesque.

The strategy he employs in NAKED LUNCH is to imply that Lee never actually leaves New York City and that the bugs, mugwumps, Interzone itself and everything in it are actually nothing more than the products of Lee's fevered, drug-addled imagination, with the reports eventually taking form as *Naked Lunch*, the novel. By reassuring us that the horrors within Burroughs' mind have no basis in reality, Cronenberg may be trying to make things more acceptable for a mainstream audience. But in so doing, he runs the risk of diminishing the impact of Burroughs' work; rather than tapping into the dark core of reality, the writer's fantasies can be safely explained away as drug-induced ravings.

Nevertheless, Cronenberg remains one of the few true originals making films today. Like the novel that served as its inspiration, NAKED LUNCH defies generic definition. It's funny, horrifying, inspirational, and disturbing. More a literary labor of love than a cinematic masterpiece, NAKED LUNCH is no DEAD RINGERS, but it is a worthy, compelling work from one of modern cinema's sanest mad geniuses.

NAKED PREY, THE

1966 96m c ★★★½
Adventure /PG
Theodora/Sven Persson (U.S./South Africa)

Cornel Wilde *(Man)*, Gert Van den Bergh *(2nd Man)*, Ken Gampu *(Warrior Leader)*, Patrick Mynhardt *(Safari Overseer)*, Bella Randels *(Little Girl)*, Jose Sithole, Richard Mashiya, Eric Sabela, Joe Diaminl, Frank Mdhluli

p, Cornel Wilde; d, Cornel Wilde; w, Clint Johnston, Donald A. Peters; ph, H.A.R. Thomson (Panavision, Eastmancolor); ed, Roger Cherrill; cos, Freda Thompson

In the South African bush near the end of the 19th century, Wilde is a safari guide leading Van den Bergh, Mynhardt, and others on an ivory hunting expedition. Despite Wilde's warnings and recommendations, Van den Bergh offends local tribesmen. In an ambush, the natives kill all but six of the party, who are taken back to the tribesmen's village for ritual torture and execution. One victim is caked with mud, has hollow breathing tubes inserted in his nostrils, then is put on a spit and roasted alive, screaming all the while. Another is feathered, hobbled, then butchered like a chicken. Van den Bergh is staked out with his head at the only opening in a ring of fire that surrounds a deadly cobra. Wilde, presumably because the natives have some respect for him, is offered "The Chance of the Lion." Stripped naked, he is given a head start of a few hundred yards. Then six warriors, each of whom has killed 10 lions, set out to hunt him down. One impetuous warrior runs out in front of the others and hurls his spear, but Wilde dodges it and then uses it to kill the pursuer. Before the others can catch up, he has taken the dead man's sandals, loincloth, and water bottle. The chase continues as Wilde evades not only the men hunting him, but natural hazards such as scorpions, spike-covered lizards, and thorns five inches long on the trees. He kills two more of the warriors, then manages to lose the others for a few days by cutting off their chase with a brush fire he sets. From a hiding place he watches a slavery raid on a peaceful village and briefly befriends a young girl who escapes. The two travel together for a few days, then part. Soon, the remaining hunters begin to draw nearer to their prey, and Wilde again has to run for his life. Finally he breaks out of the bush into a clearing where a British fort stands. He dashes across the open ground, and the leader of the warriors runs out to make a final attempt to kill him. The warrior is about to throw his spear when a red-coated soldier marching on duty shoots him dead. As the exhausted Wilde is taken into the stockade, he turns to look at the remaining warriors. They show their respect for him with a salute, much the way the Zulu armies salute the British defenders of Rorke's Drift in ZULU (1963).

Wilde's fourth directorial outing was easily his best, tightly constructed and featuring a rapid pace. (Fewer than 15 minutes pass between the credits and Wilde's being set out into the bush for the chase.) Wilde took the idea from a radio show about fur trappers chased across the American West by hostile Indians and transposed it to South Africa and the Zulus. Production, though inexpensive, was arduous—at one point a lizard latched onto Wilde's leg and had to be killed before it would let go. The unit manager was bitten by a cobra. Five crew members were hospitalized after a swarm of bees attacked. Wilde contracted tick fever, a debilitating malady similar to malaria, but took advantage of his less-than-healthy appearance to look even more exhausted and pressed as the tribesmen pursued him. At one point in the shooting, Wilde shocked a native chief by turning down the chief's generous offer of a 15-year-old girl for a wife. Chief Shwasa, with six wives himself, couldn't understand how Wilde could be happy with only one. The film was fairly successful both critically and at the box office, receiving an Oscar nomination for Best Story.

NAKED SPUR, THE
1953 91m c   ★★★★
Western   /A
MGM

James Stewart (*Howard Kemp*), Janet Leigh (*Lina Patch*), Robert Ryan (*Ben Vandergroat*), Ralph Meeker (*Roy Anderson*), Millard Mitchell (*Jesse Tate*)

p, William H. Wright; d, Anthony Mann; w, Sam Rolfe, Harold Jack Bloom; ph, William Mellor (Technicolor); ed, George White; m, Bronislau Kaper; art d, Cedric Gibbons, Malcolm Brown

Another superb western from director Anthony Mann who, along with Budd Boetticher, created an outstanding series of engrossing, thoughtful, and challenging films that helped keep the genre fresh and vital during the 1950s. Stewart is excellent as the obsessed, disillusioned Civil War veteran who returns home to find that he has lost his land. To raise the money needed to regain his land, Stewart decides to become a bounty hunter and enters the Colorado Territory in search of escaped killer Ryan, who has a $5,000 reward on his head. Ryan is accompanied by Leigh, a lonely young woman who wants to escape to California. While searching for Ryan, Stewart picks up a pair of companions. The first is Mitchell, a grizzled prospector, the second Meeker, a Union soldier who was dishonorably discharged. The two drifters believe Stewart to be a lawman and they agree to help him capture Ryan. They corner Ryan and Leigh on a rugged hillside and take them prisoner. Soon after, Mitchell and Meeker learn that Stewart is no lawman and they demand an equal share of the reward. Stewart refuses. Ryan sees that his only means of escape is to divide the three men, so, with Leigh's help, he begins a clever campaign to pit the men against each other. During the seven-day trip through dangerous Indian territory back to Abilene, Ryan baits the men by encouraging each to kill the other two and take the reward solo. Leigh, meanwhile, flirts with both Stewart and Meeker, which further erodes the uneasy partnership. Seeking to eliminate his competition, Meeker causes an Indian uprising in the hopes that the Indians will massacre the group. Stewart is wounded in the attack, but the Indians are defeated and the group pushes on. As they near Abilene, Ryan talks Mitchell into helping him escape. The old prospector does so and Ryan murders him. The crazed killer then sets a trap for Stewart and Meeker. Leigh, who has fallen in love with Stewart, foils Ryan's plot, but not before Meeker and Ryan lie dead. Stewart, by now almost insane with his obsession over the bounty, retrieves Ryan's body and puts it head down over a horse. Leigh, disturbed and disgusted by the whole experience, persuades an unwilling Stewart to abandon the body and go off to California with her. Exhausted and defeated, Stewart finally allows his repressed humanity to surface and rides off with Leigh to start a new life.

Mann's protagonists are men who allow their desire for vengeance to consume their inherent qualities of honor and decency. Their quests through rugged landscapes are enlightening journeys of near-religious revelation that see these men finally come to grips with themselves and their lives. The characters in THE NAKED SPUR form a highly volatile family unit that can explode into chaos at any moment. Each of them is in varying degrees of mental unbalance, with Ryan's killer at one extreme and Leigh at the other. When the smoke clears, the unforgiven die, giving the repentant Stewart a new lease on life.

THE NAKED SPUR actually found some support among the Academy of Motion Picture Arts and Sciences (rare for a western, especially a low-budget one) and the screenplay was nominated for an Academy Award.

NAME OF THE ROSE, THE
1986 130m c   ★★
Mystery   R/18
Bernd Eichinger/Bernd Schaefers/Neue
Constantin/Cristaldifilm/Ariane

Sean Connery (*William of Baskerville*), F. Murray Abraham (*Bernardo Gui*), Christian Slater (*Adso of Melk*), Elya Baskin (*Severinus*), Feodor Chaliapin, Jr. (*Jorge de Burgos*), William Hickey (*Ubertino de Casale*), Michel Lonsdale (*The Abbot*), Ron Perlman (*Salvatore*), Volker Prechtel (*Malachia*), Helmut Qualtinger (*Remigio de Varagine*)

p, Bernd Eichinger; d, Jean-Jacques Annaud; w, Andrew Birkin, Gerard Brach, Howard Franklin, Alain Godard; ph, Tonino Delli Colli (Technicolor); ed, Jane Seitz; m, James Horner; prod d, Dante Ferretti; art d, Giorgio Giovannini, Rainer Schaper; fx, Adriano Pischiutta; cos, Gabriella Pescucci

Based on the witty, somewhat scholarly first novel by noted Italian semiotician and journalist Umberto Eco, this medieval murder mystery is a little slow-moving at 130 minutes but is ultimately rewarding for the patient. At an Italian monastery in 1327, the Franciscans, who live in religious poverty, and the Dominicans, who enjoy a life of luxury, meet to debate whether the Catholic church should be in the business of accruing wealth. William of Baskerville (Connery), a brilliant English monk (whose Holmesian manner is reinforced by his name, taken from *The Hound of the Baskervilles*), and his teenage novice, Adso of Melk (Slater), arrive early, and when murders begin occurring, the abbot (Lonsdale) requests that they begin an investigation. But even as William begins looking into the matter, the murders continue, seemingly following the prophecy of the Apocalypse. The more rational clues lead to the monastery's extraordinary library, but before the Englishman can find the truth, the Dominicans and, most important, his old rival Bernardo Gui (Abraham), the Inquisitor, arrive and matters become even more complicated as Gui sees the Devil's hand in the murders. Gifted cinematographer Tonino Delli Colli has given the film an appropriately dark look, and the many odd-looking monks appear as if they have stepped from the set of a Federico Fellini picture. Much of the $18 million production was shot at Kloster Eberbach, a 12th-century monastery near Frankfurt, West Germany.

NAPOLEON
1955 190m c   ★★
War/Biography/War
Filmsonor/CLM/Francinex   (France)

Jean-Pierre Aumont (*Renault de Saint-Jean d'Angely*), Jeanne Boitel (*Mme. de Dino*), Pierre Brasseur (*Barras*), Gianna Maria Canale (*Pauline Borghese*), Daniel Gelin (*Bonaparte*), Raymond Pellegrin (*Napoleon*), Danielle Darrieux (*Eleonore Denuelle*), Sacha Guitry (*Talleyrand*), Lana Marconi (*Marie Walewska*), Michele Morgan (*Josephine de Beauharnais*)

d, Sacha Guitry; w, Sacha Guitry; ph, Pierre Montazel (Eastmancolor); ed, Raymond Lamy; m, Jean Francaix

The life, loves, and military campaigns of Napoleon are brought to the screen in this opus from French stage and screen director-writer-actor Sacha Guitry. Not the masterpiece that Abel Gance's silent NAPOLEON is, Guitry's retelling is just that—Guitry, as

Talleyrand, telling his friends about various episodes in Napoleon's life. Guitry re-creates the period with the help of legendary art director Eugene Lourie and a cast that includes two of the cinema's greatest directors, Orson Welles (as Sir Hudson Lowe) and Erich von Stroheim (as Beethoven, whose "Eroica" symphony is said to have been originally dedicated to Napoleon). As expected, most of the highlights of Napoleon's career are here—the campaigns of Italy, Austria, and Egypt; his rise to emperor; his return from Elba and the Battle of Waterloo; and his involvement with both Josephine and Desiree (affairs fictionalized in the 1954 Marlon Brando film DESIREE). Originally released at 190 minutes, the videocassette version has been reduced to 115 minutes and dubbed into English.

NARROW CORNER, THE
1933 71m bw   ★★★
Adventure   /A
WB

Douglas Fairbanks, Jr. (Fred Blake), Patricia Ellis (Louise Frith), Dudley Digges (Dr. Saunders), Ralph Bellamy (Eric), Arthur Hohl (Capt. Nichols), Henry Kolker (Fred's Father), Willie Fung (Ah Kay), Reginald Owen (Frith), William V. Mong (Swan), Josef Swickard (Dutch Constable)

p, Hal B. Wallis; d, Alfred E. Green; w, Robert Presnell (based on a novel by W. Somerset Maugham); ph, Tony Gaudio; ed, Bert Levy

An engrossing film adaptation of Somerset Maugham's novel featuring an outstanding cast of supporting players. Fairbanks plays a young Englishman who commits a murder in Australia and is sent out to sea by his powerful father, Kolker, in the hopes that the furor over the crime will die down. Kolker entrusts his son to craggy old skipper Hohl, who drinks heavily to numb the pain of the cancer that slowly consumes him. Fairbanks and Hohl become friends, and at one port of call they acquire Digges, an opium-smoking defrocked physician who comes along for the ride. After braving some violent South Seas storms, the trio stop at a tiny island and are invited to dinner by an eccentric British family that lives there. At dinner Fairbanks falls in love with the daughter, Ellis, despite the fact that she is engaged to Bellamy (the eternal doomed fiance of the 1930s). Seeing that his sweetheart has fallen for the seafaring stranger, Bellamy commits suicide, leaving behind enough evidence to throw suspicion of murder on Fairbanks once again. THE NARROW CORNER is a solid adventure film, which contains some surprisingly intense and effective scenes of sea storms while etching a memorable array of characterizations. The wandering misfits (Fairbanks, Hohl, and Digges) are vividly portrayed, each with his own endearing character quirks. Hohl is especially fine as the gruff, drunken, and slowly dying captain. The film was remade as ISLE OF FURY, an early Humphrey Bogart vehicle, but the original version remains the better of the two.

NARROW MARGIN, THE
1952 71m bw   ★★★
Thriller   /PG
RKO

Charles McGraw (Walter Brown), Marie Windsor (Mrs. Neall), Jacqueline White (Ann Sinclair), Gordon Gebert (Tommy Sinclair), Queenie Leonard (Mrs. Troll), David Clarke (Kemp), Peter Virgo (Densel), Don Beddoe (Gus Forbes), Paul Maxey (Jennings), Harry Harvey (Train Conductor)

p, Stanley Rubin; d, Richard Fleischer; w, Earl Fenton (based on a story by Martin Goldsmith, Jack Leonard); ph, George E. Diskant; ed, Robert Swink; art d, Albert S. D'Agostino, Jack Okey

A competent B movie from RKO that takes place almost entirely on board a train from Chicago to Los Angeles. Walter Brown (McGraw) is a hard-boiled detective who, with his partner, Gus Forbes (Beddoe), is assigned to escort a racketeer's widow (Windsor) to a West Coast court where she will give testimony before a grand jury. However, three thugs aboard the train are trying to shut her up—permanently. Unfortunately for the gang members, they do not know what the widow looks like, so they bump off anyone they suspect might be their quarry. While far from a masterpiece, THE NARROW MARGIN is a well-executed programmer that turned a fantastic profit for RKO, considering its meager $230,000 budget. Audiences loved the film—thrilling at the plot twists, the characters, and the trick train photography—making it into one of the studio's most profitable B movies.

NASHVILLE
1975 159m c   ★★★★★
Drama   R/AA
Paramount

David Arkin (Norman Chauffeur), Barbara Baxley (Lady Pearl), Ned Beatty (Delbert Reese), Karen Black (Connie White), Ronee Blakley (Barbara Jean), Timothy Brown (Tommy Brown), Keith Carradine (Tom Frank), Geraldine Chaplin (Opal), Robert DoQui (Wade), Shelley Duvall (LA Joan)

p, Robert Altman; d, Robert Altman; w, Joan Tewkesbury; ph, Paul Lohmann (Panavision, Metrocolor); ed, Sidney Levin, Dennis M. Hill; m, Richard Baskin

NASHVILLE is Robert Altman's triumph; it's the best movie made in the 1970s and one of the most complex pictures ever. Sprawling over two and one-half hours and never flagging, it successfully introduces and exposes 24 different characters so wonderfully that we never have the feeling we're watching a corn whiskey version of Tin Pan Valley soap opera. It isn't easy to single out performances because every actor has his or her moment to strut on stage, and each one scores. Although apparently a melange of sights and sounds, everything miraculously comes together at the conclusion, and we sit at the finale, limp from having been pushed, dragged, uplifted, and wrung out by Altman's direction and Tewkesbury's script (although the actors spent a great deal of time improvising, even writing their own songs in character). The music is more a part of NASHVILLE than it is in most films, and even if you do not cotton to country sounds, you'll enjoy the documentary effect achieved with it. Altman cuts back and forth between the characters, but with such aplomb that the audience never loses track of the narrative, which all takes place on one climactic weekend in the Country Music Capital of America. A huge music festival is taking place in Nashville, and at the same time a political rally is slated to promote the candidacy of the never-seen presidential hopeful Hal Phillip Walker, who leads a new entity known as the Replacement Party. Though Walker's politics are not deeply plumbed, he sounds vaguely like George Wallace did when he was running on his third-party ticket. Walker's aides, Michael Murphy and Beatty, know what kind of people the candidate appeals to, and they prevail upon several of the top country music singers to help their cause. Henry Gibson, playing a veteran performer who appears to be patterned after Hank Snow, is the gray eminence whom most of the younger performers venerate. Despite his down-home smile as he sings, Gibson is a mean, rotten, self-serving man who would sell his mother for a gold record. Also in the top echelon is Blakley, a country music queen and authentic folk artist (said to be based on Loretta Lynn, who was angry about it) who has just recovered from a mental breakdown and is teetering on the edge of another. The festival has attracted singers from all over the country, each hoping to have a moment in the sun, be discovered, and take a place in the pantheon of pickin' and grinnin'. Carradine is one of a trio of folk singers. He's nothing more than skin stretched over lechery and is currently sleeping with partner Allan Nicholl's wife, Cristina Raines. That doesn't stop him from plucking favors from Lily Tomlin, Beatty's neglected wife, and Chaplin, an hilariously irritating BBC correspondent who is covering the festival for the listeners in the British Isles. Blakley's first concert is a flop, as she can't handle appearing in front of a crowd after such a long layoff, and her husband-manager, Allan Garfield, tells the annoyed assemblage that she will give them all a free concert in a couple of days to make up for this one. And to keep her crown from being stolen by Karen Black, doing a posionous turn as a combo Tammy Wynette-Lynn Anderson, Beatty comes to Blakley and Garfield and asks her to appear for Walker at the rally, and she agrees. Beatty and Murphy stage a small fund-raising stag party and hire waitress Gwen Welles to sing, knowing she's so desperate for fame that they can force her to strip. (The leering men at the stag were actually played by some members of the Nashville Chamber of Commerce who were totally convincing.) After she finishes, Beatty vainly attempts to bed Welles. On the day of the rally, David Hayward, whom we've seen flit in and out of the film carrying a violin case, comes to the stage and shoots Gibson and Blakley after their singing has stopped the show.

There are other rich characterizations: Barbara Harris, a dearranged white trash runaway out for her big break; Baxley, as Johnson's longtime cynical, bullshit mistress; Keenan Wynn as a Bible Belt family man, with Duvall as an eternal groupie; Tim Brown (magnificently playing a character based on Charlie Pride) is the black singer who has crossed over to become a success in the white world; Scott Glenn is the faithful puppy-dog serviceman who is entranced by Blakley; Jeff Goldblum is the local freak; Arkin as a chauffeur who witnesses everything; and David Peel is Gibson's son, a boy who does whatever his father asks and hates every minute of it. On top of all that, Elliott Gould and Julie Christie come in to do cameos as themselves, two movie stars tub-thumping a new project, and Richard Baskin (the film's music arranger and supervisor) also does a bit.

Amazingly, this movie was shot for about $2 million in less than 45 days. To do that, all the stars accepted a clause that they would receive the same amount of money for their roles. With no economic jealousy, they worked closely with each other and, when not called before the cameras, spent their off-hours honing their scenes and getting prepared for the snappy shooting schedule. Tewkesbury and Altman were quite willing to allow the script to be altered by the actors if they felt it could be improved. Made on location in Nashville, the final concert scenes used many cameras and were shot in one day. On the final morning of shooting a rainstorm moved over the area, but legend has it that Altman stepped outside, looked up at the gray skies, and shouted "Stop!" and it did. Susan Anspach was supposed to be in the film, but because of some trouble about her contract Altman decided instead to hire Blakely, Anspach's vocal coach, who later married German director Wim Wenders and continued her acting career after debuting in NASHVILLE. If we had to pick out the film's brightest stars, they'd be Blakey, Harris, Tomlin, and, most surprising of all, Gibson, as the man who holds it all together.

Gibson's career soared when he created the meek poet character that put him on television's "Laugh-In," but he is an actor of enormous range and does a wonderful job here.

The film includes some fine songs, including: "Two Hundred Years," "Keep A' Goin'" (Richard Baskin, Henry Gibson), "One, I Love You," "Let Me Be the One" (Baskin), "The Day I Looked Jesus in the Eye" (Baskin, Robert Altman), "For the Sake of the Children" (Baskin, Richard Reicheg), "I Never Get Enough" (Baskin, Ben Raleigh), "It Don't Worry Me," "I'm Easy," "Honey" (Keith Carradine), "Down to the River," "Tapedeck in His Tractor [the Cowboy Song]," "Bluebird," "My Idaho Home," "Dues" (all by Ronee Blakley), "Sing a Song" (Joe Raposo), "The Heart of a Gentle Woman" (Dave Peel), "Rose's Cafe" (Allan Nicholls), "Old Man Mississippi" (Juan Grizzle), "Since You've Gone" (Gary Busey), "Trouble in the USA" (Arlene Barnett), "My Baby's Cookin' in Another Man's Pan" (Jonnie Barnett), "Swing Low, Sweet Chariot" (traditional, arranged by Millie Clements), "Yes, I Do" (Baskin, Lily Tomlin), "Memphis," "I Don't Know If I Found It in You," and "Rolling Stone" (all by Karen Black). Jonnie Barnett, Sue Barton, Vassar Clements and the Misty Mountain Boys also appeared as themselves. This was an ambitious project, a bold idea, and a perfect realization of Altman's dream. Unfortunately, after making this film Altman turned out some dreadful exercises, including HEALTH; A WEDDING; and QUINTET. Carradine's tune, "I'm Easy," won the Oscar, and the movie, Altman, Tomlin, and Blakley were nominated as well, but that was the year ONE FLEW OVER THE CUCKOO'S NEST won it all. Gibson was wrongfully overlooked, but the Academy must have had a hard time deciding who was a leading performer and who was a supporter in a movie in which everyone was a star who supported the others.

NATIONAL LAMPOON'S ANIMAL HOUSE

1978 109m c   ★★★½
Comedy   R/15
Universal

John Belushi *(John "Bluto" Blutarsky)*, Tim Matheson *(Eric "Otter" Stratton)*, Peter Reigert *(Donald "Boon" Schoenstein)*, John Vernon *(Dean Vernon Wormer)*, Tom Hulce *(Larry "Pinto" Kroger)*, Cesare Danova *(Mayor Carmine DePasto)*, Mary Louise Weller *(Mandy Pepperidge)*, Stephen Furst *(Kent "Flounder" Dorfman)*, James Daughton *(Greg Marmalard)*, Bruce McGill *(Daniel "D-Day" Simpson)*

p, Matty Simmons, Ivan Reitman; d, John Landis; w, Harold Ramis, Douglas Kenney, Chris Miller; ph, Charles Correll (Panavision, Technicolor); ed, George Folsey, Jr.; m, Elmer Bernstein; art d, John Lloyd; fx, Henry Millar; cos, Deborah Nadoolman

Rude, rough, tasteless, but often hilarious, this movie was a huge hit with young audiences and grossed more than $80 million as it grossed out the older viewers. Supposedly based on the actual college experiences of the screenwriters (specifically Miller's year at Dartmouth), it served to introduce to films the anarchistic talents of Belushi as he played off the fine work by Hulce, Matheson, and others. The story takes place in the early 1960s, before the Vietnam War had heated up. Hulce and the rotund Furst attempt to join fraternities on their Faber College campus, but they are turned away and wind up at Delta House, a pig sty where they are welcomed by Matheson. The school's dean, Vernon, is keeping an eye on this particular house because its boozing members all have rotten grades and break nearly every school edict with their raucous "toga parties," in which the revelers dress up in bed sheets. Vernon, who would like to shut down the place, enlists Daughton, the head of the conservative Omega House, in his scheme. Daughton's fraternity brother Mark Metcalf leads Faber's ROTC unit. One day after field drills he attempts to break the spirit of Furst, who is now a Delta pledge, by making him do pushups in a pile of manure in the horses' stable. To get even for that, Furst, egged on by Belushi and McGill, late one night takes Metcalf's prized horse to Vernon's office, where he is supposed to shoot the beast. However, the plan is all an initiation stunt concocted by his companions, as Belushi has loaded the gun with blanks. When Furst pulls the trigger, however, the gunshot causes the animal to have a heart attack and it dies. The pranksters hastily evacuate the premises, leaving the horse for the dean to deal with when he arrives for work in the morning. The college pranks continue as Belushi sneaks over to comely Weller's sorority house and peeks through a window as she doffs her clothing after coming back from a date with her boyfriend, Daughton. At the next school lunch Belushi begins a "food fight," and the Omegas are hit hard by anything that can be thrown. Vernon, monitoring all of Delta's indiscretions, thinks he can get the house closed if the boys fail their midterms, but Belushi steals the exams and gives them to his fraternity brothers. The only trouble is that he stole the wrong exams, and the result is that everyone in the house fails their tests. The Deltas are depressed and decide the only way to get out of their doldrums is to throw a toga party. At the party Matheson seduces Vernon's wife, the nymphomaniacal Verna Bloom. When Vernon finds that booze was offered at the party, that's enough to bring the house up for discipline in front of a committee stacked against it. The house is closed and all members of the frat are forbidden to march in the annual parade that traditionally ends the school year. The Deltas wreak revenge by wrecking the parade, using a car they have altered as an attack vehicle, and, in the end, they are all allowed to return to school because Vernon fears any further action from them. The epilogue includes snapshots of the characters and what they did in later years. Belushi marries Weller and becomes a US senator, Metcalf is killed in Vietnam (by his own men), and Daughton becomes an assistant to President Nixon and gets raped in prison.

Though this was the first of these crazy-college-antics films, it was not the best. REVENGE OF THE NERDS not only had funnier scenes, but it also had more to say. Landis's penchant for crashing cars came to a head with his disastrous movie THE BLUES BROTHERS, and he still hasn't come close to the fun he managed to engender in this one. In a small role, note composer Stephen Bishop. The costumer, Deborah Nadoolman, was Landis's girlfriend. Fans of raunch will love it, but some scenes try so hard to be outrageous that they feel forced. The film was shot on location in Oregon at Eugene and Cottage Grove. Songs: "Animal House," "Dream Girl" (Stephen Bishop, sung by Bishop), "Shout," "Shama Lama Ding Dong," "Louie, Louie" (sung by the Kingsmen), "Money" (sung by Belushi), "Hey Paula" (sung by Paul and Paula), "Wonderful World," "Twistin' the Night Away" (sung by Sam Cooke), "Let's Dance" (sung by Chris Montez), "Who's Sorry Now?" (sung by Connie Francis), "Tossin' and Turnin'" (sung by Bobby Lewis).

NATIONAL LAMPOON'S EUROPEAN VACATION

1985 95m c   ★★★
Comedy   PG-13/15
WB

Chevy Chase (*Clark W. Griswald*), Beverly D'Angelo (*Ellen Griswald*), Dana Hill (*Audrey Griswald*), Jason Lively (*Rusty Griswald*), John Astin (*Game Show Host*), Sheila Kennedy, Trisha

Long (*Game Show Hostesses*), Paul Bartel (*Mr. Froeger*), Cynthia Szigeti (*Mrs. Froeger*), Malcolm Danare (*The Froegers' Son*)

p, Matty Simmons, Stuart Cornfeld; d, Amy Heckerling; w, John Hughes, Robert Klane (based on a story by Hughes); ph, Robert Paynter; ed, Pembroke J. Herring; m, Charles Fox; prod d, Robert Cartwright; art d, Leslie Tomkins, Alan Tomkins; fx, Richard Richtsfeld; chor, Gillian Lynne; cos, Graham Williams

A low and often hilarious comedy that serves as a sequel to NATIONAL LAMPOON'S VACATION. This time Clark Griswald (Chevy Chase) and family take on Europe, and that entire continent may never by the same. Clark and wife Ellen (Beverly D'Angelo) win a European holiday on a silly game show called "Pig in a Poke." They're expecting the 1980s version of "The Grand Tour," but it turns out to be a cut-rate economy ride. Few incidents are related, but most are funny; so this movie is actually somewhat better than the original, which took great pleasure in being bizarre for its own sake. Director Amy Heckerling is gentler than Harold Ramis was, and the result is a slightly more cohesive picture that is far less mean-spirited. Lighthearted fun, pretty scenery, lots of chuckles, a few guffaws, and a lilting score by Charles Fox all contribute to making this movie a pleasant surprise.

NATIONAL VELVET

1944 125m c   ★★★★
Drama   /U
MGM

Mickey Rooney (*Mi Taylor*), Donald Crisp (*Mr. Brown*), Elizabeth Taylor (*Velvet Brown*), Anne Revere (*Mrs. Brown*), Angela Lansbury (*Edwina Brown*), Juanita Quigley (*Malvolia Brown*), Jackie "Butch" Jenkins (*Donald Brown*), Reginald Owen (*Farmer Ede*), Terry Kilburn (*Ted*), Alec Craig (*Tim*)

p, Pandro S. Berman; d, Clarence Brown; w, Theodore Reeves, Helen Deutsch (based on the novel by Enid Bagnold); ph, Leonard Smith (Technicolor); ed, Robert J. Kern; m, Herbert Stothart; art d, Cedric Gibbons, Urie McCleary; fx, Warren Newcombe; cos, Irene

Perhaps the only time Elizabeth Taylor's costar matched her visual scene stealing. He's a horse, albeit a gelding. One of MGM's most beloved films, NATIONAL VELVET was the picture that made a star out of Taylor. The place is Sussex, England, where radiant Velvet Brown (Taylor) wins a horse that she names Pie and plans to enter in the Grand National. With the help of Mi Taylor (Rooney) she begins to rigorously train the animal, though she hasn't the money to enter the National. But Velvet's mother (Anne Revere, who won a Best Supporting Actress Oscar for her performance) has been saving money she won as a young girl by swimming the English Channel, and she parts with it so Velvet can enter the race. Velvet, Mi and the horse then go off on their adventurous quest for the Grand National title. The movie features one of the best horse racing sequences ever filmed, as well as a host of winning performances. Although Taylor had already made her mark in four films, this was the one that really thrust her into the spotlight. Surprisingly she was not the first choice for the role, as Katharine Hepburn, Shirley Temple, and Margaret Sullavan were all candidates to play it. Angela Lansbury finally got one young role that wasn't opportunistic—here she's dreamy and romantic—English peaches and cream. And Jackie "Butch" Jenkins is an outstanding little brother, so ugly his cuteness makes you smile even hours after the movie. The film was remade as INTERNATIONAL VELVET starring Tatum O'Neal, and we grow ashen whenever we think of it.

NATIVE LAND

1942 80m bw ★★½
Drama
Frontier

Fred Johnson *(The Farmer)*, Mary George *(His Wife)*, John Rennick *(His Son)*, Amelia Romano *(Slavey)*, Houseley Stevenson, Louis Grant *(Sharecroppers)*, James Hanney *(Union President)*, Howard da Silva *(Stool Pigeon)*, Art Smith *(Vice President)*, Richard Bishop *(Spy Executive)*

p, Paul Strand, Leo Hurwitz; d, Paul Strand, Leo Hurwitz; ph, Paul Strand; ed, Leo Hurwitz

Based on US Senate Civil Liberties Commission records and other public documents, this is American propaganda at its finest. Paul Robeson narrates this drama which is designed to instill patriotism in the little man. Encouraging the American worker to perform at top efficiency while producing munitions, it rightly knocks the Ku Klux Klan, labor spies, and land barons—almost anyone considered a threat to the working man. NATIVE LAND presents a series of violations of the Bill of Rights through reenactments. One scene depicts an assault on a Michigan farmer who dares to raise his voice at a farmers' association meeting; another shows the murders of two sharecroppers by vigilantes.

NATURAL, THE

1984 134m c ★★★
Sports PG
Natural

Robert Redford *(Roy Hobbs)*, Robert Duvall *(Max Mercy)*, Glenn Close *(Iris)*, Kim Basinger *(Memo Paris)*, Wilford Brimley *(Pop Fisher)*, Barbara Hershey *(Harriet Bird)*, Robert Prosky *(The Judge)*, Richard Farnsworth *(Red Blow)*, Joe Don Baker *(The Whammer)*, John Finnegan *(Sam Simpson)*

p, Mark Johnson; d, Barry Levinson; w, Roger Towne, Phil Dusenberry (based on the novel by Bernard Malamud); ph, Caleb Deschanel (Technicolor); ed, Stu Linder; m, Randy Newman; prod d, Angelo Graham, Mel Bourne; art d, James J. Murakami, Speed Hopkins; fx, Roger Hensen; cos, Bernie Pollack, Gloria Gresham

Transforming Bernard Malamud's fabulist first novel into a mythical morality play, THE NATURAL follows the fortunes of Roy Hobbs (Robert Redford) as the 19-year-old farm boy makes his way to try out with the Cubs. En route, he wins a bet by striking out the Whammer (Joe Don Baker), a slugger of Ruthian proportions, proving greatness is in his future. But in Chicago, a mysterious women (Barbara Hershey) lures Roy to her hotel room and shoots him with a silver bullet. Fifteen years later, in 1939, Roy joins the hapless New York Knights and literally knocks the cover off the ball, leading the team back into contention. The Knights' owner (Robert Prosky), who is betting against his own team, sends Roy a beautiful temptress (Kim Basinger) so that he falls into a terrible slump, but his virtuous former girlfriend (Glenn Close) appears to revive his hitting. Without using his familiar "Wonderboy" bat for the big game, Roy still blasts an awe-inspiring home run into the lights, setting off a magical shower of fireworks to the strains of Randy Newman's evocative score. Somewhat overly sentimental, lacking the novel's subtlety, and less interesting when the action leaves the ball park, Barry Levinson's beautifully shot film is nonetheless a charming fairy tale. Redford, who played baseball at the University of Colorado, gives an appropriately iconic performance as Roy Hobbs—part Shoeless Joe Jackson (EIGHT MEN OUT), part Joe Hardy (DAMN YANKEES)—and the supporting roles are also well handled, especially Wilford Brimley as the manager. Filmed partly in Buffalo's War Memorial Stadium, a minor league park built in the 1930s, THE NATURAL also offers an appearance by "Super" Joe Charboneau, who had his own miracle season with the Cleveland Indians before disappearing from the big leagues. Nominated by the Academy for Best Supporting Actress (Close), Best Cinematography, Best Original Score, and Best Art Direction.

NAUGHTY MARIETTA

1935 106m bw ★★★★
Musical /A
MGM

Jeanette MacDonald *(Princess Marie de Namours de la Bonfain, "Marietta Franini")*, Nelson Eddy *(Capt. Richard Warrington)*, Frank Morgan *(Governor Gaspard d'Annard)*, Elsa Lanchester *(Mme. d'Annard)*, Douglas Dumbrille *(Prince de Namours de la Bonfain)*, Joseph Cawthorn *(Herr Schuman)*, Cecilia Parker *(Julie)*, Walter Kingsford *(Don Carlos de Braganza)*, Greta Meyer *(Frau Schuman)*, Akim Tamiroff *(Rudolpho, Puppet Master)*

p, Hunt Stromberg; d, W.S. Van Dyke, II; w, John Lee Mahin, Frances Goodrich, Albert Hackett (based on the operetta by Victor Herbert, Rida Johnson Young); ph, William Daniels; ed, Blanche Sewell; art d, Cedric Gibbons; cos, Adrian

Nelson Eddy made his full-fledged debut in this, the first of eight films in which he costarred with Jeanette MacDonald. Rita Johnson Young and Victor Herbert's hoary operetta was dusted off, given a new screenplay, new lyrics by Gus Kahn, and the result was a neatly paced (by "One-Take" Woodie Van Dyke) Best Picture nominee that only slightly belies its stage origins. Fleeing an arranged marriage to a Spanish grandee (Walter Kingsford), French princess Marie de Namours de la Bonfain (MacDonald) switches places with her maid and boards a ship bound for Louisana, where its female passengers are to become colonial brides. En route the ship is attacked by pirates, but the women are soon rescued by a group of soldiers led by Capt. Richard Warrington (Eddy), with whom the princess, now calling herself Marietta, falls in love. In New Orleans, she continues to conceal her identity, avoiding marriage by claiming to be a woman of ill repute. Eventually Capt. Warrington comes to the realization that he is in love with Marietta, but several hurdles stand in the way of their happiness, including arrest and the appearance of the princess' father (Douglas Dumbrille), who is determined to take his daughter back to her marital obligations in France. A much underrated if not great film, NAUGHTY MARIETTA features some particulary amusing supporting work by Harold Huber and Edward Brophy. Eddy is actually much better than most would have it, and his singing *is* quite stirring. MacDonald, though, is really the one in excellent form here, whether blasting the lengthy final high C of the "Italian Street Song" right in Nelson Eddy's face or doing an hilarious impersonation of a gluttonous, bespectacled woman on board the ship. One should admit, though, that the film isn't nearly as good some of her others, most notably THE MERRY WIDOW, where her comedic talents are in full bloom.

NAVIGATOR, THE

1989 92m c/bw ★★½
Adventure/Fantasy PG/U
Arenafilm/Film Investment Group (Australia)

Bruce Lyons *(Connor)*, Chris Haywood *(Arno)*, Hamish McFarlane *(Griffin)*, Marshall Napier *(Searle)*, Noel Appleby *(Ulf)*, Paul Livingston *(Martin)*, Sarah Pierse *(Linnet)*, Mark Wheatley *(Tog 1)*, Tony Herbert *(Tog 2)*, Jessica Cardiff-Smith *(Esme)*

p, John Maynard, Gary Hannam; d, Vincent Ward; w, Vincent Ward, Kely Lyons, Geoff Chapple; ph, Geoffrey Simpson; ed, John Scott; m, Davood A. Tabrizi; prod d, Sally Campbell; art d, Mike Becroft; cos, Glenys Jackson

THE NAVIGATOR is a singular experience, a time-warp, Chinese-box puzzle of a film that bespeaks the obsessed vision of Vincent Ward, its writer-director.

It takes place in 1348 in Cumbria, New Zealand, where a psychic young boy, Griffin (Hamish McFarlane), dreams of a way to save his village from the advancing black plague, later leading his brother, Conner (Bruce Lyons), and four other men on a quest that somehow transports them to the present time. But Griffin has envisioned that along the way one of their number will be betrayed and another will die.

With its simplistic parallels to the Christ story and the AIDS crisis, THE NAVIGATOR is compelling in a dumb kind of way. Ward obviously sees it as an extension of Spielbergian fantasy-adventure with heavy mystic and sociological overtones—not the most alluring of premises.

In a strenuous effort *not* to tell his story as simply as possible, Ward engages a battery of film-school cinematic effects—the mixed use of black and white with color, time-lapse views of clouds scampering across ominous skies, dizzying tracking shots up spiral staircases, superimpositions galore—and all of this in the first 10 minutes. To a man, the actors lay it on as thick as the medieval mummers out of Breughel they're made up to resemble.

NEAR DARK
1987 95m c   ★★★½
Horror   R/18
F/M

Adrian Pasdar *(Caleb)*, Jenny Wright *(Mae)*, Lance Henriksen *(Jesse)*, Bill Paxton *(Severen)*, Jenette Goldstein *(Diamondback)*, Tim Thomerson *(Loy)*, Joshua Miller *(Homer)*, Marcie Leeds *(Sarah)*, Kenny Call *(Deputy Sheriff)*, Ed Corbett *(Ticket Seller)*

p, Steven-Charles Jaffe, Eric Red; d, Kathryn Bigelow; w, Eric Red, Kathryn Bigelow; ph, Adam Greenberg (CFI Color); ed, Howard Smith; m, Tangerine Dream; prod d, Stephen Altman; art d, Dian Perryman; fx, Steve Galich, Dale Martin; cos, Joseph Porro

An auspicious solo directing debut from Kathryn Bigelow, NEAR DARK combines such diverse genres as horror, western, crime, and romance into what may be the first vampire road movie.

Set in the contemporary American Southwest, the film begins as Caleb (Adrian Pasdar), a bored farm boy, spots the beguiling Mae (Jenny Wright) at his usual Friday night hangout. By the break of dawn, Caleb has been bitten in the neck by Mae and befriended by a bizarre "family" of vampires—led by Jesse (Lance Henriksen), undead since before the Civil War—who travel across the country in a Winnebago. To his horror, Caleb learns that he has been "nipped" (i.e., he's almost a full-fledged vampire), and to graduate he must kill and drink blood. Sensing that Mae is in love with the boy, Jesse gives Caleb a week to perform his first kill.

Although several movie genres are represented here, NEAR DARK is most obviously based on Nicholas Ray's feature debut, THEY LIVE BY NIGHT (Bigelow's characters literally *must* live by night). Both films focus on a young couple desperately in love but trapped in a lifestyle they detest by their surrogate

families (bank robbers and vampires, respectively). Bigelow, who codirected THE LOVELESS with Monty Montgomery in 1982, and coscreenwriter Eric Red (THE HITCHER) demonstrate a keen understanding of the history of American cinema and create a unique film that explores the conventions of the vampire movie while moving it from dank European castles to modern-day Southwestern America. Bigelow sees the vampire (the word is never used in the film) as a nomadic outlaw, much like the fabled gunslingers of the Old West or the bands of bank robbers that roved the landscape during the Depression.

The weak ending, while disappointing, should not deter anyone from witnessing the development of a talent who may prove to be one of the most exciting and valuable new American filmmakers of the future.

NETWORK
1976 120m c   ★★★★
Drama   R/15
MGM

Faye Dunaway *(Diana Christensen)*, William Holden *(Max Schumacher)*, Peter Finch *(Howard Beale)*, Robert Duvall *(Frank Hackett)*, Wesley Addy *(Nelson Chaney)*, Ned Beatty *(Arthur Jensen)*, Arthur Burghardt *(Great Ahmed Kahn)*, Bill Burrows *(TV Director)*, John Carpenter *(George Bosch)*, Jordan Charney *(Harry Hunter)*

p, Howard Gottfried; d, Sidney Lumet; w, Paddy Chayefsky; ph, Owen Roizman (Panavision, Metrocolor); ed, Alan Heim; m, Elliot Lawrence; prod d, Philip Rosenberg; cos, Theoni V. Aldredge

Finch's posthumous Oscar, one of four that included Dunaway (Best Actress), Beatrice Straight (Best Supporting Actress) and Chayefsky (Best Original Screenplay). This time Chayefsky takes on television (his first true love) which is making us all idiots. Truth to tell, it informs and entertains some of us—all television can do is reinforce idiocy, not create it. This is hollow stuff, so hollow it's more timely now than then—all it's missing is Madonna. The self-congratulating postulation has an uneasy time—it strains in its mix of realism and satire. NETWORK is more a tribute to shallow people getting older, losing power, than anything. Emotional honesty gets equated with notoriety and sexual athleticism; the only centered character is Straight's. But among the empty landscapes, there's an amazing display of acting talent (though Lumet doesn't do much to tie the loose threads together). Finch's washed-up bull-spouting fool *is* expert, but somehow we prefer Holden's sardonic edge, even if his big speeches seem the most predictably written in the film. For Dunaway runaways, there are some great moments: Faye zipping up her briefcase in a state of mania, and that rattling teacup. But watching her now there are already signs that she's haunted by Joan Crawford; she's like a jingoisitc Joan, all broad ideas, putting people in their place and work mania. But with her strangely undersized mouth of yellow baby teeth, she's a believable media carnivore.

Finch, a veteran newsman for the mythical United Broadcasting System, is sent over the mental edge when he is told that he will be fired after a quarter of a century on the air. He can't handle the situation and tells his audience that he intends to commit suicide on his final broadcast the following week. Ratings go straight through the roof, and his fan mail comes in by the carload. On the night he plans to put a gun to his head, Finch relents, apologizes to the millions watching (it's his largest audience ever), and stands up like an electronic Messiah to shout "go to your nearest window and yell as loud as you can, 'I'm mad as hell and I'm not going to take it anymore!'" And his audience does just that. The words rattle across hill and dale, valley and mountain, in and out of the city's concrete canyons. Dunaway, a programming executive at UBS, knows how to make capital of this, so she signs Finch to a weekly show in which he can let it all hang out. This idea is opposed by Holden, the man in charge of network news and an old pal of Finch. He can see that Finch is on the edge of insanity and he can't stand the thought of the news being used to further ratings. Dunaway's bosses like the idea and fire Holden for his disagreement. Finch's program, a melange of various items, goes on and is a smash hit, with Finch closing each program like a latter-day Jesus as he regales the audience with the Gospel according to Finch. Dunaway, now a star at the network, has other innovations in mind. She intends doing a show about urban guerrillas, but instead of hiring actors, she wants the terrorists to play themselves. Holden and Dunaway meet again and are soon involved; Holden then leaves his wife, Straight, in the most moving (and least gimmicky) scene in the film, as he tells her why he is departing.

There are several superb scenes, including one in which the communist guerrillas' lawyers argue with the network's representatives over the ancillary rights and syndication money that will accrue from their show. Every small role is well cast, and Jordan Charney, who also appeared in HOSPITAL, is a standout. Darryl Hickman, who actually became a television network executive, was playing one in this, his first film in 17 years. Ken Kercheval went on to have a large career on television in "Dallas." Marlene Warfield is superior as the communist who brings in terrorist Burghardt. For any students considering a career in television, NETWORK will probably send them quickly to medical or dental school.

NEVER CRY WOLF

1983 91m c   ★★★½
Adventure   PG
Amarok

Charles Martin Smith (Tyler), Brian Dennehy (Rosie), Zachary Ittimangnaq (Ootek), Samson Jorah (Mike), Hugh Webster (Drunk), Martha Ittimangnaq (Woman), Tom Dahlgren, Walker Stuart (Hunters)

p, Lewis Allen, Jack Couffer, Joseph Strick; d, Carroll Ballard; w, Curtis Hanson, Sam Hamm, Richard Kletter, C.M. Smith, Eugene Corr, Christina Luescher (based on the book by Farley Mowat); ph, Hiro Narita (Technicolor); ed, Peter Parasheles, Michael Chandler; m, Mark Isham; art d, Graeme Murray; fx, John Thomas

This is the haunting story of a scientist who is sent to the Arctic to study the behavior of wolves. Unfamiliar with the wilderness, Tyler (Charles Martin Smith) finds himself unprepared for his stay in the frozen desolation. Near death, he is rescued by a mysterious Eskimo who builds him a shelter and then leaves without waiting for thanks. Forced to rely on his ingenuity and common sense, Tyler survives until the spring and sets up camp near a small pack of wolves, building mutual trust with the leader of the pack. His now-idyllic surroundings are threatened when a group of caribou hunters arrives. Based on Farley Mowat's study of wolves for the Ottawa Wildlife Service, this beautifully photographed wilderness film is as fine as director Carroll Ballard's previous film, BLACK STALLION. Capturing the changes a man goes through as he learns about life in the wilds, NEVER CRY WOLF is very informative, but it is Smith's performance that makes the film a resounding success.

NEVER GIVE A SUCKER AN EVEN BREAK

1941 71m bw   ★★★
Comedy   /U
Universal (U.S./France)

W.C. Fields (The Great Man), Gloria Jean (His Niece), Leon Errol (The Rival), Billy Lenhart (Butch), Kenneth Brown (Buddy), Anne Nagel (Mlle. Gorgeous), Franklin Pangborn (The Producer), Mona Barrie (The Producer's Wife), Margaret Dumont (Mrs. Hemogloben), Susan Miller (Ouliotta Delight Hemogloben)

d, Edward F. Cline; w, John T. Neville, Prescott Chaplin (based on a story by W.C.); ph, Charles Van Enger; ed, Arthur Hilton; m, Frank Skinner; art d, Jack Otterson, Richard H. Riedel; cos, Vera West

The great W.C. is at his wild antics again, this time spoofing Hollywood and the eccentricities of filmmaking or the insanity of producing films as Fields perceived them. He was later accused of biting the hand that fed him, but W.C. gnawed on anything that moved anyway, while providing one belly laugh after another, and this film is no exception. Fields is shown en route to Esoteric Studios to sell a producer a new script he has written. He stops near the studio and admires a huge billboard advertising his last movie (THE BANK DICK, starring, of course, W.C. Fields), and catches two young boys denigrating his latest film. He runs them off, then spots a cutie and makes a pass at her. The girl's burly boyfriend arrives and immediately lands a haymaker on Fields's kisser, driving him over a hedge. Fields requires some refreshment before continuing and drops into a lunchroom for a small snack. A fat, obnoxious waitress, Jody Gilbert, begins to cross off every entree on the menu as Fields mentions the dish, until there's nothing left but eggs. Gilbert carps that Fields is too free with his hands and he tells her that he was "only trying to guess your weight." For his caprice, Fields receives some ice water down the back of his neck, poured unceremoniously by Gilbert. After flirting with the studio receptionist (Carlotta Monti, Fields's real-life mistress), the comedian is shown into producer Pangborn's office where he relates the tale of his proposed movie. He has little luck in persuading Pangborn of its possiblilities and Fields is then seen meeting with his niece, Gloria Jean, who is in a shooting gallery operated by Errol, father of the two boys who earlier were taunting Fields. Nagel, Gloria Jean's mother, a trapeze artist, is killed in a fall and Fields becomes the young girl's guardian. He and the child immediately leave for Mexico where Fields believes he will become rich by selling wooden nutmegs to Russian immigrants who have established a colony there. While in flight on a plane that offers sleeping berths like that of a train and has an open-air observation deck, Fields drops a bottle of booze and immediately dives after it. He catches up with the bottle in mid-air, screws a cap back on it, and then falls onto a giant mattress. He next meets Russian expatriate Miller and is smitten by her beauty, but before he can properly pitch his woo, Dumont, Miller's mother, appears and is so aggressive that Fields promptly retreats. Fields learns just how much money Dumont has, but when he again visits the man-eating matron he finds Errol embracing her. Thoroughly defeated, Fields is resigned to failure and he withdraws. At that point Fields is shown back in Pangborn's office and it is evident that the whole Mexican adventure is a filming of the very story he has been trying to sell to Pangborn, who thinks the tale so impossible that he has an apoplectic attack before kicking Fields out of his office. The dejected comedian then begins driving home and stops to help an obese woman who tells him she must get to the maternity hospital pronto. He drives madly through downtown Los Angeles, caroming his car off other autos; he even gets entangled in the careening ladder of a fast-moving fire engine but manages to deliver the heavyset woman, and then wrecks his car. Gloria Jean arrives on the crash site to see Fields stagger forth, holding the steering wheel of his car. She smiles adoringly at her uncle and says: "My Uncle Bill. . . but I still love him."

Of course, there is no sense whatever to this utterly plotless film which was Fields's last feature-length movie. Yet the great comedian provides so many crazy scenes and offbeat laughs that it makes little difference. Oddly, this spoof of Hollywood realistically capped Fields's own movie career. The great comedian had pretty much run out his options in Hollywood by the time of NEVER GIVE A SUCKER AN EVEN BREAK and knew that Universal was planning to sidetrack his career in favor of the more slapstick Abbott and Costello, the dynamic duo who would dominate comedy at the studio through the 1940s. In this film Fields thumbs his considerable nose at the industry that was ousting him. Fields had insisted that this film be called THE GREAT MAN but Universal nixed the idea; he had tried to title his previous film the same way but the studio had entitled the film THE BANK DICK. Fields was not happy about the title of NEVER GIVE A SUCKER AN EVEN BREAK, commenting: "It doesn't matter anyway. Their title won't fit on a marquee, so they'll cut it down to 'W.C. Fields—Sucker.'" The title used by Universal was close to one employed by MGM in 1933, NEVER GIVE A SUCKER A BREAK, which was an alternate for the official release title for THE NUISANCE, directed by Jack Conway and starring Lee Tracy, Madge Evans, and Frank Morgan. The motto, not to be confused with P.T. Barnum's "there's a sucker born every minute," has been credited to writer-con man Wilson Mizener. Yet Fields himself ad-libbed the line in the play "Poppy" in 1924, and in titles for his silent film IT'S THE OLD ARMY GAME. The two little boys in SUCKER, Lenhart and Brown, goaded Fields off the set and he muttered threats in their direction. Their chaperone loudly demanded that Fields not drink during the production of NEVER GIVE A SUCKER AN EVEN BREAK and the studio hounded the comedian, assigning detectives to follow him about. They cornered him outside his dressing room one day as he was lifting a small bottle of dark-hued liquid to his smiling lips. They yelled in the middle of his swig and Fields sneered and then gave them a wry smile as he removed his hand from the bottle's label, saying: "Just Listerine." But Fields did not abandon drinking altogether, even though he proclaimed that he had given up swilling rum and pineapple juice, his favorite libation. He went to straight gin and this caused his feet to swell drastically, he claimed, and he was forced to regularly retreat to his dressing room to soak his feet before propping them up on thick pillows. Fields wrote the script in about four months and it brought a wrathful response from the Hollywood censor at that time, the Breen Office, which labeled the screenplay "vulgar and suggestive" and claimed that Fields made too many references to drinking and liquor. Out came the scissors, but Fields got revenge of sorts. In one scene in the film he turns directly to the camera and whines: "This scene was supposed to be in a saloon but the censor cut it out. It'll play just as well." Beyond the cameras the comedian kept carping, telling reporters that the censors committed rapine on his script: "Why, those guys won't let me do anything. They find double meaning in commas and semicolons in my scripts. As an example, they made me cut a line out about a drunk. The line reads, 'He's tighter than a dick's hat band.' Now what's wrong with that? They also won't let me look at a girl's legs. I'm just looking, not saying anything, and they censor me." The script was badly tampered with by a bevy of hack writers assigned by Universal to clean up and clarify the screenplay. "They produced the worst script I ever

read. I was going to throw it in their faces," Fields stated, "when the director (Cline) told me not to. He said: 'We'll shoot your own script. They won't know the difference.' We did—and they didn't."

NEVER ON SUNDAY
(POTE TIN KYRIAKI)

1960 97m bw	★★★
Comedy/Drama	/X
Melina (Greece)	

Melina Mercouri *(Ilya)*, Jules Dassin *(Homer)*, George Foundas *(Tonio)*, Titos Vandis *(Jorgo)*, Mitsos Liguisos *(The Captain)*, Despo Diamantidou *(Despo)*, Dimos Starenios *(Poubelle)*, Dimitris Papamichael *(A Sailor)*, Alexis Salomos *(Noface)*

p, Jules Dassin; d, Jules Dassin; w, Jules Dassin; ph, Jacques Natteau; ed, Roger Dwyre; m, Manos Hadjidakis; cos, Denny Vachlioti

Filmed in Greece for a pittance (under $200,000), this colorful art-house comedy broke through to the mainstream market and made a ton of money. NEVER ON SUNDAY is the brainchild of Jules Dassin, an American writer-director who ran afoul of Red-baiters in the 1950s and had to go to Europe to earn a living. He helmed RIFIFI, then went to Greece, where he met and married Melina Mercouri, NEVER ON SUNDAY's star. Although the film is a standard "hooker with a heart of gold" story, audiences were very much taken with its unfamiliar locale. Dassin not only wrote, produced, and directed, but also costarred as Homer, a tweedy American Grecophile who comes to Piraeus and encounters the local peasantry, who are slightly taken aback by his open ways. Homer loves Greece and everything about it. He soon meets Ilya (Mercouri), a prostitute who takes pride in her work and sees nothing immoral about the way she earns her living. Ilya takes customers six days a week and reserves Sunday for seeing the great Greek plays, none of which she actually comprehends. Homer intends to reform Ilya, but old habits are hard to break. The title song won an Oscar, and nominations also went to Dassin's script and direction, Mercouri's performance (Mercouri fared a bit better at Cannes, where she won top honors), and Vachlioti's costumes. Most of the dialogue is in English with a few speeches in Greek with titles.

NEVER SAY NEVER AGAIN

1983 137m c	★★½
Spy	PG
Woodcote/Taliafilm (U.K.)	

Sean Connery *(James Bond)*, Klaus Maria Brandauer *(Largo)*, Max von Sydow *(Blofeld)*, Barbara Carrera *(Fatima Blush)*, Kim Basinger *(Domino)*, Bernie Casey *(Felix Leiter)*, Alec McCowen *(Q/Algy)*, Edward Fox *(M)*, Pamela Salem *(Miss Moneypenny)*, Valerie Leon *(Lady in Bahamas)*

p, Jack Schwartzman; d, Irvin Kershner; w, Lorenzo Semple, Jr. (based on a story by Kevin McClory, Jack Whittingham and Ian Fleming); ph, Douglas Slocombe (Panavision, Technicolor); ed, Robert Lawrence, Ian Crafford; m, Michel Legrand; prod d, Philip Harrison, Stephen Grimes; art d, Leslie Dilley, Michael White, Roy Stannard; fx, David Dryer, Ian Wingrove; cos, Charles Knode

Sean Connery returns to action after a 12-year absence from his role as 007. The title is based on his comment that he would never do a James Bond film again following DIAMONDS ARE FOREVER. Basically a remake of THUNDERBALL, the film opens with an aging Bond trying to get back in shape at a special clinic. When SPECTRE psycho Largo (Brandauer) hijacks a couple of

American cruise missiles, Bond is assigned the case. Fatima Blush (Carrera), a gorgeous but deadly SPECTRE agent, does her best bring an end to Bond's illustrious career, but, surviving the requisite high-speed chase, he eventually catches up with Largo and his beautiful companion Domino (Basinger) on the villain's yacht. Connery delivers his usual charming performance, and Brandauer (MEPHISTO, OUT OF AFRICA) makes a great Bond villain. Gone is the excessive gadgetry that mars Bond films, and, as a result, the characters are more prominent and colorful. This was director Irvin Kershner's first film following the huge success of THE EMPIRE STRIKES BACK. Lani Hall croons the title song, written by Alan and Marilyn Bergman.

NEVERENDING STORY, THE

(DIE UNENDLICHE GESCHICHTE)
1984 94m c   ★★★½
Fantasy   PG/U
Neve Constantin/WDR   (West Germany)

Barret Oliver (Bastian), Gerald McRaney (Bastian's Father), Drum Garrett, Darryl Cooksey, Nicholas Gilbert (Bullies), Thomas Hill (Koreander), Deep Roy (Teeny Weeny), Tilo Pruckner (Night Hob), Moses Gunn (Cairon), Noah Hathaway (Atreyu)

p, Bernd Eichinger, Dieter Geissler; d, Wolfgang Petersen; w, Wolfgang Petersen, Herman Weigel (based on the novel by Michael Ende); ph, Jost Vacano (Technivision, Technicolor); ed, Jane Seitz; m, Klaus Doldinger, Giorgio Moroder; prod d, Rolf Zehetbauer; art d, Gotz Weidner, Herbert Strabel, Johann Iwan Kot; fx, Brian Johnson; cos, Diemut Remy; anim, Steve Archer

Only a certified grump could dislike this engaging fantasy that wends its way into the imagination and is a delight on most levels. Bastian (Barret Oliver) is a troubled lad who has just lost his mother. He lives with his father (Gerald McRaney), who lectures Bastian about the boy's penchant for daydreaming. The lad has to fend off school bullies and is having difficulty adjusting to being motherless. One day, instead of going to school, he wanders into a weird bookstore and borrows a book called *The Neverending Story*. As Bastian turns the pages, the story comes to life. A childlike empress (Tami Stronach), who is not well, lives in a land called "Fantasia" and fears that it will be taken over if she dies. So she sends Atreyu (Noah Hathaway), a young warrior, off to find a cure for her lingering illness. What menaces Fantasia is a plague of "nothing": when the inhabitants of Earth lose hope and forget their aspirations, Fantasia is due to crumble as a direct result. Atreyu's voyage is fraught with peril, and he meets a cast of fantastic characters. Bastian is so enthralled by the story that he is plunged into it as a character. Made on a budget of more than $27 million, the film features state-of-the-art puppetry, animation, opticals, and makeup. THE NEVERENDING STORY owes much to ALICE IN WONDERLAND and THE DAY THE EARTH STOOD STILL in some sequences, but director Wolfgang Petersen combines the elements into a charming film that is excellent for children and won't put any adults to sleep, either.

NEW JACK CITY

1991 97m c   ★★½
Crime/Action   R/18
Jacmac Films Inc

Wesley Snipes (Nino Brown), Ice-T (Scotty Appleton), Allen Payne (Gee Money), Chris Rock (Pookie), Mario Van Peebles (Detective Stone), Michael Michele (Selina), Bill Nunn (Duh Duh Duh Man), Russell Wong (Kim Park), Bill Cobbs (Old Man), Christopher Williams (Kareem Akbar)

p, Doug McHenry, George Jackson; d, Mario Van Peebles; w, Barry Michael Cooper, Thomas Lee Wright; ph, Francis Kenny; ed, Steven Kemper; m, Michel Colombier; prod d, Charles C. Bennett; art d, Barbra Matis, Laura Brock; cos, Bernard Johnson

1991 will go down in movie history as the year African-American films finally came into their own. Buoyed by Spike Lee's success, studios and investors embraced young black *male* filmmakers, and the predominance of a paternalistic, condescending, white view of black life seems to be ebbing. Of course, not every young black filmmaker is Spike Lee. The year's output has varied tremendously, both in quality and in popularity.

One of the bigger-budgeted films, Mario Van Peebles's NEW JACK CITY, attracted lots of publicity upon release due to rioting at theatres where it screened. This gave the movie an aura of provocativeness that the publicists could never have dreamed of, especially for what is, in the end, a cliche-ridden, sloppy piece of work. The public who hadn't seen the film worried that it was pro-drug and encouraged gang warfare. Ironically, NEW JACK CITY is preachy to a fault, letting the story stall often to mandate its anti-drug message.

As gang leader and cocaine dealer Nino Brown (Wesley Snipes) brutally gains power on the mean streets of New York in 1986, he first learns about the next big thing—crack. Meanwhile, Scotty Appleton (Ice-T), an unorthodox, streetwise cop, arrests young Pookie (Chris Rock). By 1989, Brown has become immensely powerful in the neighborhood, and the police are at a loss as to how to deal with him. Detective Stone (Mario Van Peebles) talks his chief into bringing two rougher ex-cops back onto the force, Appleton and tough, slightly racist, ex-junkie Nick Peretti (Judd Nelson). They despise each other instantly.

As Brown cannily distributes food to the poor at Christmastime, winning their loyalty, Pookie, now a crackhead, is dragged into rehab by Appleton, who stays with him throughout. Once he's cleaned up, Pookie offers to help bring Brown down. He gets hired as a lookout in Brown's apartment building, and informs the cops of the huge production and distribution set-up. Meanwhile, Brown, drunk with power, takes his best friend Gee Money's (Allen Payne) girlfriend for himself. The cops hook Pookie up with a camera, unaware that the stress has made him revert to substance abuse. He gets inside, but acts silly and is caught and killed. The cops move in, but the gang destroys all their files before the shootout begins.

At Pookie's funeral, Detective Stone lets Appleton and Peretti know they're a liability now and are fired. Though still hating each other, they decide to bring Brown down themselves. Appleton wins the confidence of Gee Money, and gets him to introduce him to Brown as a connection. Brown is untrusting, but Appleton proves himself by protecting Brown from the angry, ranting Old Man (Bill Cobbs), a neighborhood fixture, and a Mafia attack. Stone rehires Peretti and Appleton. When Appleton tries to make a sale to Brown, a cohort recognizes him from an earlier arrest, and all hell breaks loose. Appleton and Peretti save each other's life, but Brown gets away, and kills Gee Money. Appleton and Peretti track Brown down and Appleton beats him up in front of a crowd. In court, Brown blames society, names some names, and gets one year in prison. But on his way out of the courtroom, he's killed by the Old Man.

One must assume that Van Peebles was sincere in his desire to make The Ultimate Crack Movie. But in trying to do so, he instead created a pastiche of anti-drug montages, held together by a series of cliches from gangster and older black films (this becomes most obvious and laughable when a long scene is played out in front of a TV screen showing De Palma's SCARFACE, switching to Melvin Van Peeble's SWEET SWEETBACK'S BAADASSSSS SONG, for no apparent reason. The casting is generally fine—Snipes having the star power to carry the movie forward, and Ice-T making a terrifically simmering debut—with two major exceptions.

First of all, what idiot thought of casting bratpacker Judd Nelson as a tough, streetsmart ex-junkie cop? Maybe they needed a white name actor for financing, but was Gary Busey too busy? But Nelson's problems pale next to Van Peebles himself, whose ego insists on showing himself only in glamorous shots. And while he was clearly trying to inspire kids to emulate his good-cop character, that doesn't mean he has to dress better than the drug dealers in every scene, and be carrying an unexplained baby during a meeting with his undercover cops!

Despite its preachiness, we all know NEW JACK CITY is making the right statement on drugs, racism, the system, etc. But the fact is it's not very good. If it had come out a few years ago, perhaps it would have been a revelation. But in comparison to DO THE RIGHT THING and BOYZ N THE HOOD it seems merely slick and phony. Van Peebles shows talent, and may someday prove to be a fine filmmaker, when, like his character in HEARTBREAK RIDGE, he stops being so childish and egotistical, and starts to become a real soldier in this new Hollywood army.

NEW LAND, THE

(NYBYGGARNA)

1973	161m c	★★★
Drama		PG/AA
Svensk	(Sweden)	

Max von Sydow (Karl Oskar), Liv Ullmann (Kristina), Eddie Axberg (Robert), Hans Alfredson (Jonas Petter), Halvar Bjork (Anders Mansson), Allan Edwall (Danjel), Peter Lindgren (Samuel Nojd), Pierre Lindstedt (Arvid), Oscar Ljung (Petrus Olausson), Karin Nordstrom (Judit)

p, Bengt Forslund; d, Jan Troell; w, Bengt Forslund, Jan Troell (based on the novel The Emigrants by Vilhelm Moberg); ph, Jan Troell (Technicolor); ed, Jan Troell; m, Bengt Ernryd, George Oddner; art d, P.A. Lundgren; cos, Ulla-Britt Soderlund

This touching sequel to THE EMIGRANTS follows the struggle of von Sydow and Ullmann during their first decade in America. The story includes a futile trek to the Southwest to search for gold. The film is a subtle depiction of the hardships people face as they try to find a niche for themselves. The story moves slowly at times, but this helps to focus on the changes that the characters undergo. Nominated for Best Foreign Film in 1972. Edited for television under the title THE IMMIGRANT SAGA.

NEW LEAF, A

1971	102m c	★★★
Comedy		G/U
Howard W. Koch/Hillard Elkins		

Walter Matthau (Henry Graham), Elaine May (Henrietta Lowell), Jack Weston (Andrew McPherson), George Rose (Harold Henry, Graham's Butler), William Redfield (Beckett), James Coco (Uncle Harry), Graham Jarvis (Bo), Doris Roberts (Mrs. Traggert), Rose Arrick (Gloria Cunliffe), Renee Taylor (Sally Hart)

p, Joe Manduke; d, Elaine May; w, Elaine May (based on the short story "The Green Heart" by Jack Ritchie); ph, Gayne Rescher (Movielab Color); ed, Fredric Steinkamp, Don Guidice; prod d, Richard Fried; art d, Warren Clymer; cos, Anthea Sylbert

An often funny film that might have been funnier had anyone seen the original version. May, who was tripling as history's first female star/writer/director, attempted to have her credits removed from the picture since, after the studio recut it, she felt that it did not reflect her work. In her movie Matthau gets away with murder, disposing of Weston and William Hickey, a blackmailer, who was entirely cut from the movie. Another scene that was cut showed May fantasizing herself as a sexy woman whom men cannot leave alone. The film she handed in ran over 180 minutes, and since this one is only 102 minutes, we can only guess what was excised. Nevertheless, and despite her rancor, the picture was delightful and did well with critics and audiences alike. Matthau is a ne'er-do-well who has exhausted the huge trust fund he was left at his father's death. When his attorney, Redfield, tells him that, Matthau is understandably shaken and wonders how he can maintain his high-flying lifestyle, which includes a plush Manhattan town house and a live-in man, Rose. There is only one solution, proposed by Rose, and that is to marry a rich woman. Matthau is against it but soon acquiesces when he sees that it's the only way out. Since he has no money to stay in the swim of things, Matthau borrows several thousand from his hated uncle, Coco, who insists that Matthau pledge everything he owns as collateral for the loan. Matthau strives to find a suitable wife but has no success until he is at a tea with his pal, Jarvis, and meets ungainly and myopic May, a botanist with no sense of style or grace, but who is the heir to a huge fortune. Matthau begins wooing the woman, and she agrees to marry him despite the pleas of her attorney, Weston, who is a crook in his own right. May pays off Coco before the service, and they are wed. Once ensconced in her huge estate, Matthau sees why Weston was against the union. The poor, naive May is being bilked by Weston, who is in cahoots with her servants, led by Roberts as the mansion's major domo. Matthau has the servants fired and takes over her financial dealings. His plan is to kill May when they make their yearly trip to the mountains. She found a unique fern on their honeymoon and named it after her adoring husband, but that doesn't stop him from continuing with his plot to get rid of her. They go off to the mountains and the canoe they are in is overturned. She is not a swimmer and hangs on to a jutting rock as he swims to safety on the shore. He tells her that if she lets go, the rapids will take her to a safe pool below where he'll rescue her. (The truth is, of course, that she'll probably drown once she takes her hands off the rock.) She believes him and is soon being rushed to her death. Then Matthau sees a fern on the shore, the same kind of plant life that she named after him, and he is overcome with guilt about what he's done. He dives into the rolling water and saves May. They get to the shore and he realizes that he has now put himself into her hands forever. It's a throwback to the screwball comedies of the 1930s and often surpasses many of them in comic invention and wit. Lots of laughs and several excellent observations on greed. There is no music credit; the score of OH DAD, POOR DAD, MAMA'S HUNG YOU IN THE CLOSET AND I'M FEELIN' SO SAD was transferred, almost entirely, to this movie. That score was written by Neal Hefti and worked better here than it did there.

NEW YORK, NEW YORK

1977 155m c ★★★½
Musical PG
UA

Robert De Niro *(Jimmy Doyle)*, Liza Minnelli *(Francine Evans)*, Lionel Stander *(Tony Harwell)*, Mary Kay Place *(Bernice)*, George Memmoli *(Nicky)*, Murray Moston *(Horace Morris)*, Barry Primus *(Paul Wilson)*, Georgie Auld *(Frankie Harte)*, Dick Miller *(Palm Club Owner)*, Leonard Gaines *(Artie Kirks)*

p, Irwin Winkler, Robert Chartoff; d, Martin Scorsese; w, Earl Mac Rauch, Mardik Martin (based on a story by Rauch); ph, Laszlo Kovacs (Panavision, Deluxe Color); ed, Irving Lerner, Marcia Lucas, Tom Rolf, Bert Lovitt, David Ramirez; m, Ralph Burns; prod d, Boris Leven; art d, Harry Kemm; fx, Richard Albain; chor, Ron Field; cos, Theadora Van Runkle

Martin Scorsese's attempt at making an old-fashioned musical, NEW YORK, NEW YORK never found much of an audience, but remains a visually fascinating rumination on the genre.

New York City. 1945. USO singer Francine Evans (Liza Minnelli) and aspiring sax player Jimmy Doyle (Robert De Niro) meet cute during the V-J Day revelry, audition for a job together, and later end up in the employ of big band leader Frankie Harte (Georgie Auld, who dubbed De Niro's sax playing), falling deeply in love and marrying. Jimmy eventually takes over Harte's band, and when Francine returns to New York to have their baby, he becomes involved with her replacement singer (Mary Kay Place). Francine and Jimmy have a son, but in time their marriage disintegrates as Francine becomes a hit recording artist (singing the kind of tunes her husband despises) and film star, while Jimmy turns to jazz and later opens his own club, en route to the film's distinctly downbeat ending.

NEW YORK, NEW YORK cost almost $9 million, and it's uneven in spots—the result of being drastically edited from its original four-hour length (among the slashes was the 12-minute, $300,000 "Happy Endings" production number, later reinserted for the film's 1981 rerelease). Nevertheless, the film is a treat for the ears as well as the eyes. De Niro gives an outstanding performance, masterfully conveying Jimmy's vanity, selfishness, and egotism. Minnelli is nothing less than brilliant, more than deserving of an Oscar nomination that never came her way. Place (THE BIG CHILL, television's "Mary Hartman, Mary Hartman") got her first big break here, and longtime Roger Corman favorite Miller, comic Gaines, and rotund Memmoli all contribute fine work.

NEWSFRONT

1979 110m c/bw ★★★
Drama /A
Palm Beach (Australia)

Bill Hunter *(Len Maguire)*, Gerard Kennedy *(Frank Maguire)*, Angela Punch-McGregor *(Fay Maguire)*, Wendy Hughes *(Amy McKenzie)*, Chris Hayward *(Chris Hewett)*, John Ewart *(Charlie)*, Don Crosby *(A.G. Marawood)*, John Dease *(Ken)*, John Clayton *(Cliff)*, Bryan Brown *(Geoff)*

p, David Elfick; d, Phillip Noyce; w, Phillip Noyce, Bob Ellis (based on an idea by David Elfick, Phillipe Mora); ph, Vincent Monton (Panavision); ed, John Scott; m, William Motzing; art d, Lawrence Eastwood; fx, Kim Hilder; cos, Norma Moriceau

A creative combination of color and black and white photography helps to establish a unique atmosphere for this story of two brothers, Hunter and Kennedy, who are newsreel cameramen for competing companies. The story takes place between the years 1949 and 1956, a period of great social and political change in Australia, depicted not only in the stories the brothers cover but also in the changes that occur in their own lives. Hunter is unwilling to adapt to changes, preferring to remain at home with his camera recording events. Kennedy is more aggressive, always striving to better himself and eventually leaving for Hollywood as television destroys the newsreel business. Realistic and fictional events are intermingled in a way that moves the narrative in a compelling manner, showing how the changes in the social climate of Australia affect individual lives. Hunter gives a powerful performance as a cynical man and maintains a skillful command of the film. This was the feature debut for director Noyce, who proves adept at intermingling narrative and events into a working whole. Technical credits and supporting case are all top-notch.

NEXT OF KIN

1989 105m c ★★★½
Action/Crime R/15
Lorimar

Patrick Swayze *(Truman Gates)*, Liam Neeson *(Briar Gates)*, Adam Baldwin *(Joey Rosseleni)*, Helen Hunt *(Jessie Gates)*, Andreas Katsulas *(John Isabella)*, Bill Paxton *(Gerald Gates)*, Ben Stiller *(Lawrence Isabella)*, Michael J. Pollard *(Harold)*, Ted Levine *(Willy)*, Del Close *(Frank)*

p, Les Alexander, Don Enright; d, John Irvin; w, Michael Jenning; ph, Steven Poster (Metrocolor); ed, Peter Honess; m, Jack Nitzsche; prod d, Jack T. Collis; cos, Donfeld

Neither a buddy-buddy action-comedy nor a pyrotechnical showcase of explosions and stunts, NEXT OF KIN—an intelligently made and moodily atmospheric action melodrama—provides solid, satisfying entertainment while demonstrating just how effective a fully realized genre film can be. Chicago cop Truman Gates (Patrick Swayze) has alienated his rural Kentucky kinfolk, especially older brother Briar (Liam Neeson), by moving to the big city and convincing younger brother Gerald (Bill Paxton) to do so also. But then Gerald runs afoul of Chicago's Mafia organization, led by John Isabella (Andreas Katsulas). While the plot mechanics of NEXT OF KIN are not appreciably better (or worse) than those of many other films of the same genre, the movie's meticulous execution make it a particularly accomplished effort. Major themes, characters, and milieus are explored in fascinating detail. The assured, painstaking direction of John Irvin fixes upon the parallel of the two families, lending their inner workings and rituals an almost epic quality that propels the film. Michael Jenning's screenplay provides well-motivated action, emotion, and humor. Swayze offers a solid, low-key performance. The other actors also contribute fine characterizations, but Neeson impresses most with his intense portrayal of the brooding older brother.

NEXT STOP, GREENWICH VILLAGE

1976 111m c ★★★★
Comedy R/X
FOX

Lenny Baker *(Larry Lapinsky)*, Shelley Winters *(Mrs. Lapinsky)*, Ellen Greene *(Sarah)*, Lois Smith *(Anita)*, Christopher Walken *(Robert)*, Dori Brenner *(Connie)*, Antonio Fargas *(Bernstein)*, Lou Jacobi *(Herb)*, Mike Kellin *(Mr. Lapinsky)*, Michael Egan *(Herbert)*

p, Paul Mazursky, Tony Ray; d, Paul Mazursky; w, Paul Mazursky; ph, Arthur J. Ornitz (Deluxe Color); ed, Richard Halsey; m, Bill Conti; prod d, Philip Rosenberg; cos, Albert Wolsky

Anyone who spent time in New York's Greenwich Village in the early 1950s will attest to the accuracy of this wonderful and nostalgic look at that era. It's essentially Mazursky's own story, and he manages to capture the time and the people with a loving touch. Mazursky, it is alleged, walked into a session at Brooklyn College and announced he was changing his name. The others there nodded and understood his desire until he said that he was altering it from Irwin Mazursky to Paul Mazursky. Baker is the young man who graduates from Brooklyn College in 1953 and makes the decision to leave his family, Kellin and Winters, and switch boroughs to Manhattan. Winters, the ultimate Jewish mother, is totally against it, but he leaves anyway and takes up residence in the Village, where he takes a job at a health food place, then starts his acting lessons with Egan, a proponent of the "Method." He is soon part of "the scene," and his pals include nutty Brenner (who later married Andre Previn and became an important songwriter); Smith, who is always teetering on the brink of suicide; Walken, the WASPish poet who speaks in epigrams; and Fargas, a black homosexual with a Jewish name. The tight-knit group members are symbiotic and help each other when needed, so when Smith tries suicide, they pour coffee into her. When Baker's sweetheart, Greene, becomes pregnant they arrange an abortion. Baker is out of money and due to be tossed out of his apartment, so the others stage a "rent party" to raise the cash. Baker learns that a major studio wants to cast some juvenile delinquents and he hopes to get one of the parts. (In real life, Mazursky was in THE BLACKBOARD JUNGLE as "Stoker." It was an MGM picture, although he uses the name of Fox here because this film was produced by that lot.) Winters and Kellin come to see how Baker is living, and Winters is shocked when she learns that Baker and Greene are sleeping together. Before she can faint, Kellin takes Winters home to Brooklyn. The group is saddened to learn that Smith's customary suicide attempt worked this time, and they share their grief with each other. Baker gets a chance at the role, then Greene announces that she is going off to Mexico with Walken, Fargas, and Brenner. Baker and Greene make love for the last time and she takes this opportunity to inform him that she is also Walken's lover. An argument erupts as Winters and Kellin enter the apartment surreptitiously. Greene leaves, and Baker understands that this part of his life is now finished. Baker bids his pals farewell, goes to his job, and gets the call about the role. He is to report to Hollywood within the week. At the last supper with Winters and Kellin, she reminds him to never forget where he came from.

Baker was simply marvelous in the leading role. He went on to play in the Broadway hit musical, "I Love My Wife," before dying of cancer. Mazursky's real acting career began in Stanley Kubrick's first feature, FEAR AND DESIRE, which was followed by THE BLACKBOARD JUNGLE. Co-producer Tony Ray, director Nicholas Ray's son, later married his father's ex-wife, Gloria Grahame. In a small role, look for Jeff Goldblum. Conti's music is outstanding and evokes the period without parodying it.

NIAGARA

1953 92m c   ★★★★
Thriller   /PG
FOX

Marilyn Monroe (*Rose Loomis*), Joseph Cotten (*George Loomis*), Jean Peters (*Polly Cutler*), Casey Adams (*Ray Cutler*), Denis O'Dea (*Inspector Sharkey*), Richard Allan (*Patrick*), Don Wilson (*Mr. Kettering*), Lurene Tuttle (*Mrs. Kettering*), Russell Collins (*Mr. Qua*), Will Wright (*Boatman*)

p, Charles Brackett; d, Henry Hathaway; w, Charles Brackett, Walter Reisch, Richard Breen; ph, Joseph MacDonald (Technicolor); ed, Barbara McLean; m, Sol Kaplan; art d, Lyle Wheeler, Maurice Ransford; fx, Ray Kellogg; cos, Dorothy Jeakins

A rivalry of resplendent scenery between the force of nature in the film title, and the marvel that is Marilyn Monroe, here at the peak of her wolf whistle period of fame. Later, she would become ethereal, almost more a nature symbol than a sex symbol, but NIAGARA, a tidy little noir, presents her as magnetically scheming. Yet beneath the siren song suggested by the suggestiveness gurgles the definitive fears, longing and loneliness that the camera captures as it gapes at her beauty. She becomes a star here. Never before or since has anyone been so sensual. Never before or since has anyone seemed so needy for fame. So talented without hindrance. Or so doomed.

Everyone's honeymoon haven at one time, Niagara Falls, is the deceptive setting for this offbeat, absorbing film with bow-string-tight direction from Hathaway and superb performances from Cotten as a jealous husband and Monroe as his neurotic wife. Newlyweds Peters and Adams arrive at their Niagara honeymoon cottage and meet another couple, Cotten and Monroe. Monroe, from the beginning, confides about her husband being considerably older than she; he is depressed, and has just been released from a mental institution. Peters later sees Monroe kissing a young man, Allan, and learns that the couple plans to murder Cotten.

The film is breathtakingly photographed, in lurid Technicolor that heightens the sensual energy of the Monroe persona. Jean Peters is lovely and effective in a difficult part; the script calls for her to be in Monroe's shadow, yet she's the stronger of the two. Peters is often the film's protagonist who moves the action forward with her insights or discovery. Her performance in NIAGARA underlines what a shame it is that her career was short-circuited by Howard Hughes. Here was an actress of classic leading lady potential. Just contrast her here with PICK-UP ON SOUTH STREET; you'll think you're looking at two different actresses. Peters is teamed with the ridiculous, hopelessly sissy Adams, and Don Wilson and Lurene Tuttle are irritating, identikit boss and wife. But Cotten makes a marvelous antihero; here's another largely forgotten actor deserving of worthy career analysis. And Richard Allan's dark, macho seductiveness strikes an exciting contrast to Monroe.

Darryl Zanuck never had any trouble exploiting Monroe in roles unworthy of her, but he never liked her, either. The difficult side of Monroe was fostered during these years by Fox management, largely because Zanuck saw her as right for only unsympathetic tramp roles, like NIAGARA's Rose Loomis. It's amazingly to her credit that she infuses her role with sympathy. Certainly, it is easy to be swayed by her physicality. Only Monroe can wear a tailored suit in a way that suggests nudity beneath it, or has hips that curve out from the waist, then curve out again before reaching the upper thigh. There are two memorable walking scenes in this film. One is when Monroe wears the aforementioned suit—it's only a glimpse of pale blue—but never was a wobble so gravity-defying. Later, in a red jacket and black skirt, the camera, in a long tracking shot, follows her for the longest walk in motion picture history. As she moves away from us into infinity, in that curious vertical bounce, the hips moving horizontially, there's something strange going on, something indefinable. Other stars were more beautiful, but none had Monroe's impact. When NIAGARA shows in a theatre, audiences always gasp at this scene. It's not just the display of abandon. It's something sad and moving; though early in her career, with her star years ahead of her, it's a warning, a goodbye. It's there in the film when she waits for a call from her lover, there when she has a nightmare, there when she looks one way, then the other, lost in fear and indecision. No wonder contemporary culture still carries a torch for Monroe. She was the most fabulous star of them all.

NICHOLAS AND ALEXANDRA

1971 183m c ★★★½
Biography/War GP/PG
Horizon (U.K.)

Michael Jayston (*Nicholas II*), Janet Suzman (*Alexandra*), Roderic Noble (*Alexis*), Ania Marson (*Olga*), Lynne Frederick (*Tatiana*), Candace Glendenning (*Marie*), Fiona Fullerton (*Anastasia*), Harry Andrews (*Grand Duke Nicholas*), Irene Worth (*the Queen Mother*), Tom Baker (*Rasputin*)

p, Sam Spiegel; d, Franklin J. Schaffner; w, James Goldman, Edward Bond (based on a book by Robert K. Massie); ph, Freddie Young (Panavision, Eastmancolor); ed, Ernest Walter; m, Richard Rodney Bennett; prod d, John Box; art d, Jack Maxsted, Ernest Archer, Gil Parrondo; fx, Eddie Fowlie; cos, Yvonne Blake, Antonio Castillo

This lavish, overlong production chronicles the downfall of the last Russian czar Nicholas II (Michael Jayston), and his wife Alexandra (Janet Suzman). The film concentrates on their troubled family life, especially the affliction of their only son, Alexis (Roderic Noble), with hemophilia. Nicholas's preoccupation with this tragedy influences state decisions and increases his disengagement from his starving people, while Alexandra falls completely under the influence of the profligate peasant monk Rasputin (Tom Baker), believing that his mystic powers can heal her son. Rasputin's power increases in the Imperial Court despite Nicholas's weak efforts to maintain authority; meanwhile, hundreds are slaughtered at the Winter Palace, fueling Lenin (Michael Bryant) and Trotsky's (Brian Cox) crusade to overthrow "Bloody Nicholas." As the tide of assassination and unrest rises, an ill-prepared Russia suffers terrible losses in WWI, setting the stage for revolution in 1917 and the execution of the deposed czar and family in July 1918. While it remains a treat for the eyes, NICHOLAS AND ALEXANDRA suffers from the filmmakers' attempts to tell too much. Its overview of more than two decades of tumultuous, epochal history develops few of its famous figures beyond caricature (although Baker, of "Dr. Who" fame, plays Rasputin with flamboyance and verve), and the failure to bring Nicholas and Alexandra to life—despite the script's intimate and sympathetic treatment of the pair—is especially critical. Shot on location in Spain and Yugoslavia, the film won Oscars for Best Art Direction, Set Decoration, and Costumes. It was also nominated for Best Picture (losing to THE FRENCH CONNECTION), Best Actress (Suzman, who lost to Jane Fonda for KLUTE), Best Score, and Best Cinematography.

NICHOLAS NICKLEBY

1947 108m bw ★★
Drama /U
Ealing (U.K.)

Cedric Hardwicke (*Ralph Nickleby*), Stanley Holloway (*Vincent Crummles*), Alfred Drayton (*Wackford Squeers*), Cyril Fletcher (*Alfred Mantalini*), Bernard Miles (*Newman Noggs*), Derek Bond (*Nicholas Nickleby*), Sally Ann Howes (*Kate Nickleby*), Mary Merrall (*Mrs. Nickleby*), Sybil Thorndike (*Mrs. Squeers*), Vera Pearce (*Mrs. Crummles*)

p, Michael Balcon; d, Alberto Cavalcanti; w, John Dighton (based on the novel by Charles Dickens); ph, Gordon Dines; ed, Leslie Norman; m, Lord Berners; art d, Michael Relph; fx, Lionel Banes, Cliff Richardson; cos, Marion Horn

Following within a year of the release of David Lean's popular and highly regarded GREAT EXPECTATIONS, it was inevitable that this adaptation of a Dickens novel would be compared to the earlier effort. It was, and it came up lacking. Bond is the young man who toils in a boys' school in Yorkshire where he has been apprenticed by his thoroughly reprehensible uncle, played by Hardwicke. Conditions at the school are appalling, and Bond befriends one of the students, Aubrey Woods, who has been the victim of much of the brutality at the school. They escape, join a traveling theatrical troupe, and enjoy a series of adventures, with Bond meeting and falling in love with Jill Balcon. Their relationship is complicated by the fact that Hardwicke has provided testimony that sent Balcon's father to debtor's prison as part of an an attempt to force Balcon to marry him. Drayton, Hardwicke's henchman, kidnaps Woods and, though he is rescued by Bond, he dies from the abuse he has been subjected to by Hardwicke. Bond discovers that Woods was Hardwicke's son, and that Hardwicke had abandoned the boy at an early age to acquire a fortune that rightfully belonged to Woods. When Bond reveals his discovery, the shamed Hardwicke kills himself, and Bond and Balcon find happiness together. Casting couldn't be better and Cavalcanti has created an authentic Dickensian mood, but too much story is compressed into the film, making it difficult to follow. The producer's daughter, Jill, made her screen debut here, as did Woods, both coming from the British stage. Neither would make much of a mark in the movie world, however.

NICKELODEON

1976 121m c ★★
Comedy PG/U
Columbia

Ryan O'Neal (*Leo Harrigan*), Burt Reynolds (*Buck Greenway*), Tatum O'Neal (*Alice Forsyte*), Brian Keith (*H.H. Cobb*), Stella Stevens (*Marty Reeves*), John Ritter (*Franklin Frank*), Jane Hitchcock (*Kathleen Cooke*), Harry Carey, Jr. (*Dobie*), James Best (*Jim*), George Gaynes (*Reginald Kingsley*)

p, Irwin Winkler, Robert Chartoff; d, Peter Bogdanovich; w, Peter Bogdanovich, W.D. Richter; ph, Laszlo Kovacs (Metrocolor); ed, William Carruth; m, Richard Hazard; art d, Richard Berger; cos, Theadora Van Runkle

An attempt by director Bogdanovich to capture his great love of early movies in a full-length motion picture. Based on anecdotes Bogdanovitch gleaned from his interviews with John Ford, Howard Hawks, Raoul Walsh, Allan Dwan, and other directors, the picture is a somewhat true account of what the motion picture industry was like before the moguls turned movie-making into a big business. According to NICKELODEON, stars and directors got their starts more through convenience and accessibility than through any great talent or drive to make movies. The results were a haphazard mixture that served as a great form of entertainment for millions. NICKELODEON begins with Reynolds and Ryan O'Neal landing jobs on a production, Reynolds as the leading man and O'Neal, a struggling lawyer, as a director. The first half of the picture is more or less a number of slapstick incidents as the untalented filmmakers try to make movies, while O'Neal and Reynolds fight for the affection of leading lady Hitchcock. The tone gets serious as the industry starts to grow, and the players go their separate ways only to be reunited in a somewhat sappy "happy" ending.

Though the fine cast delivers good performances, they are never allowed to show much depth. As an homage to the start of the film industry, this extravaganza is quite a tribute, but as a motion picture it's sadly lacking. Scenes are shown from BIRTH OF A NATION (with a red tint), with D.W. Griffith actually taking a bow on the movie theater stage while O'Neal and Reynolds cheer him. This signifies the end of the one-reelers and the beginning of feature films. Reynolds reportedly had a hard time with Tatum O'Neal, later stating: "I like children, but she ain't no kid."

NIGHT AND THE CITY

1950 95m bw   ★★★½
Crime
FOX (U.K.)

Richard Widmark (*Harry Fabian*), Gene Tierney (*Mary Bristol*), Googie Withers (*Helen Nosseross*), Hugh Marlowe (*Adam Dunn*), Francis L. Sullivan (*Phil Nosseross*), Herbert Lom (*Kristo*), Stanislaus Zbyszko (*Gregorius*), Mike Mazurki (*Strangler*), Charles Farrell (*Beer*), Ada Reeve (*Molly*)

p, Samuel G. Engel; d, Jules Dassin; w, Jo Eisinger (based on the novel by Gerald Kersh); ph, Mutz Greenbaum; ed, Nick De Maggio, Sidney Stone; m, Franz Waxman; art d, C.P. Norman; cos, Oleg Cassini, Margaret Furse

A dark, brooding, almost clammy production, NIGHT AND THE CITY is terrific *film noir* and Widmark is a riveting standout as a hustling promoter who sinks into the quagmire of his own ambitions. The film is set in London where Widmark works for obese Sullivan, owner of a sleazy dive. Widmark steers suckers to the joint on the promise of witnessing some racy shows. But it's all very tame and even proper Tierney sings there, she being a disapproving girlfriend of wily Widmark. Tierney keeps after Widmark to get a decent job, but the con is in his blood and he is obsessed with developing a big money scheme. He overhears famed wrestler Zbyszko talking to his protege Ken Richmond in a huge sports arena owned by Zbyszko's son, Lom. Before Widmark is thrown out of the arena for hustling customers to Sullivan's club, he learns that Zbyszko is disgusted by the fake wrestling matches his son offers to the public. Zbyszko believes that only his traditional Greco-Roman wrestling is a pure sport. Widmark later goes to Zbyszko and cons him into believing that he will promote the long-neglected Greco-Roman wrestling and bring it back to the popularity it once enjoyed. The legendary wrestler agrees to lend his name to the enterprise, which incenses the powerful Lom, who threatens to kill Widmark if he misuses Lom's father. On the other hand, if he truly promotes Greco-Roman wrestling, Lom tells Widmark, he can go ahead.

Widmark goes to Withers, Sullivan's two-timing wife and Widmark's sideline paramour. He asks her for the money to establish his wrestling matches since Sullivan refuses to make a loan. Withers tells him yes, but only on the condition that he bribe authorities into giving her a nightclub license so she can leave her dominating husband. Widmark provides Withers with a forged license and she leaves Sullivan. Sullivan is furious, and he now believes Widmark has been having an affair with his wife. He goes to Lom and they work out a deal to ruin Widmark. Sullivan tells Widmark he will back the matches if Widmark uses big, murderous, phony wrestler Mazurki, the very man Zbyszko hates the most as the epitome of modern, fake wrestling. Trapped, Widmark has Mazurki come to the gym where he insults Zbyszko and the two go at each other in earnest in the ring. The older

Zbyszko wins but the effort is too much for him and he has a stroke. Lom arrives to see his father die and Widmark, knowing he's to blame, flees.

Widmark first goes to Withers for help, but she ignores him. He then tries Sullivan, who laughs at him, revealing he was the one who set him up. Widmark runs through the dark streets of London, panting, sweating, afraid of every shadow as a thousand killers hunt him. He has nowhere to turn and nowhere to go and he knows it. He finally remembers an old barge lady, Maureen Delaney, who has dealt with him in black marketeering. He sits with her in a small cabin on her barge anchored on the Thames and pours out his fears, shaking, stating in a quavering voice, "How close I came. . . The things I did." Widmark is not remorseful about his conniving ways and merely uses the barge lady as an emotional sop, much the same way he has used everyone in his life, including Tierney, his one true love, who tracks him down at the barge. She tries to save him, but Lom's henchmen close in on him. He tries to escape but runs right into Mazurki, who kills him and dumps his body into the murky waters of the Thames.

NIGHT AND THE CITY is an uncompromising, exciting, but thoroughly anxious film that is seen through Widmark's desperate viewpoint. Director Dassin relentlessly displays London without charm and grace, showing only the seamy side where Widmark and his unsavory kind, except the lovely Tierney, dwell and live out their unscrupulous lives without thought of love or compassion. Everything is cold and calculating, one character greedily using another for human control. The world Widmark desires to enter is that controlled by the Loms and Sullivans—who belong to a very exclusive club. They are as crooked and immoral as Widmark, but they have the money and the connections, and Widmark only aspires to be a loftier version of his own venal self. Despite the feeling of lonely helplessness that pervades the film, the story proceeds at such a frenetic pace that it's utterly captivating. Widmark's performance is nothing short of remarkable. Greene's camerawork captures the stark reality of London's tawdry side and Waxman's score is pulsating and emotionally powerful. The wrestling scene between Zbyszko, a former heavyweight wrestling champion, and Mazurki is one of the most heart-pounding matches ever filmed.

NIGHT AT THE OPERA, A

1935 90m bw   ★★★★
Comedy   /U
MGM

Groucho Marx (*Otis B. Driftwood*), Chico Marx (*Fiorello*), Harpo Marx (*Tomasso*), Kitty Carlisle (*Rosa Castaldi*), Allan Jones (*Riccardo Baroni*), Walter Woolf King (*Rodolfo Lassparri*), Sig Rumann (*Herman Gottlieb*), Margaret Dumont (*Mrs. Claypool*), Edward Keane (*Captain*), Robert Emmett O'Connor (*Detective Henderson*)

p, Irving Thalberg; d, Sam Wood; w, George S. Kaufman, Morrie Ryskind, Al Boasberg, Bert Kalmar, Harry Ruby (based on a story by James Kevin McGuinness); ph, Merritt Gerstad; ed, William LeVanway; m, Herbert Stothart; art d, Cedric Gibbons, Ben Carre; chor, Chester Hale; cos, Dolly Tree

The Marx Brothers' most popular film and Groucho's favorite, before MGM queered their joyful anarchy. (Groucho must have loved the money which started rolling in; actually, the Marx Bros. were far more at home at Paramount.) Groucho, Chico, and Harpo join forces to disrupt the stuffy world of opera by wreaking havoc on the music, stage, and audience. Otis B. Driftwood (Groucho) tries to con rich Mrs. Claypool (Margaret Dumont, in fabulous form) into investing her money in an opera company, while Tomasso (Harpo) and Fiorello (Chico) join the fray and take it upon themselves to help advance the careers of two struggling young singers, Allan Jones and Kitty Carlisle—both begging for a stagehand to drop twin sandbags and kill the misery they subject an audience to. OPERA is their first at MGM, in case you hadn't guessed, after being dropped by Paramount and the first without Zeppo. Producer Irving Thalberg had faith in them but thought their films for Paramount lacked cohesive stories and enough time to work out the routines, so he prevailed upon them to take a 50-minute precis of the best scenes on the road. They toured four cities with writers George S. Kaufman and Morrie Ryskind in the audience for 24 days and polished the gags until they were ready to film. The result was a huge success and the picture was a hit. Today it is fondly remembered for such classic comedy bits as Groucho and Chico drafting a contract, the stateroom scene, and the hilarious climax where the brothers make a shambles of "Il Trovatore." Sans DUCK SOUP, we'll watch this any day.

'NIGHT, MOTHER

1986 96m c   ★★★½
Drama   PG-13/15
Universal

Sissy Spacek (Jessie Cates), Anne Bancroft (Thelma Cates), Ed Berke (Dawson Cates), Carol Robbins (Loretta Cates), Jennifer Roosendahl (Melodie Cates), Michael Kenworthy (Kenny Cates), Sari Walker (Agnes Fletcher)

p, Aaron Spelling, Alan Greisman; d, Tom Moore; w, Marsha Norman (based on the play by Norman); ph, Stephen Katz (Deluxe Color); ed, Suzanne Pettit; m, David Shire; prod d, Jackson DeGovia; art d, John R. Jensen; cos, Robert Blackman

Deceptively complex, this adaptation of the 1983 Pulitzer Prize winner hews closely to the grim line of the stage play and seldom compromises. It's early evening in a small house in the Midwest. Jessie Cates (Sissy Spacek), a woman in her late 30s, is going about what seems to be a normal routine, as though she is about to take a trip. She cleans the refrigerator, cancels the newspaper delivery, packs and labels her clothes for the Salvation Army, and does a few other chores. After 10 minutes or so have elapsed, she tells her mother (Anne Bancroft) that she is going to kill herself later that evening. Jessie is an epileptic; she has an ex-husband and a son who is on his way to becoming a criminal. The only person she ever loved, her father, has died and now she is living with her mother. Her life has spun out of control and she is apparently exercising her only remaining option by ending it. Director Tom Moore, who also directed the play, makes a fairly good debut in a difficult task. Spacek and Bancroft have the only speaking roles, but brief glimpses of some of the other family members are provided in an effort to keep the picture from seeming totally stagebound, which it is. Marsha Norman's script had many levels, switching sympathies for both actresses at the turn of a phrase. It is to her credit that it works.

NIGHT MUST FALL

1937 117m bw   ★★★★
Thriller   /A
MGM

Robert Montgomery (Danny), Rosalind Russell (Olivia), Dame May Whitty (Mrs. Bransom), Alan Marshal (Justin), Merle Tottenham (Dora), Kathleen Harrison (Mrs. Terence), Matthew Boulton (Belsize), Eily Malyon (Nurse), E.E. Clive (Guide), Beryl Mercer (Saleslady)

p, Hunt Stromberg; d, Richard Thorpe; w, John Van Druten (based on a play by Emlyn Williams); ph, Ray June; ed, Robert J. Kern; m, Edward Ward; art d, Cedric Gibbons; cos, Dolly Tree

Due primarily to an amazing performance by Robert Montgomery, this superb, nerve-tingling thriller improves on Emlyn Williams's already shocking stage hit "Night Must Fall." Whitty is a fussy, domineering grande dame living in a cottage in Essex, England, with niece Russell and several cowed servants. Just after Russell and Whitty hear that a "very flashy" woman guest in a nearby inn has vanished, Montgomery appears, claiming that he has been working as a page boy at the inn but is now looking for new job. Montgomery brings with him a heavy hatbox that he places in a closet after being hired as a handyman by the wheelchair-bound Whitty. He waits hand and foot upon her, flattering Whitty at every opportunity, but exchanges barbs with Russell, who distrusts him. When asked about the missing woman, Montgomery describes her in chilling detail, revealing his psychopathic personality and further arousing Russell's suspicion. As soon as Montgomery finds the family's safe, he puts in motion a plan to kill Whitty. By then Russell has learned of Montgomery's murderous background, but she, like the 72-year-old Whitty, is mesmerized by the killer and does nothing. Forced to leave suddenly, Russell returns to find Whitty's corpse and correctly assumes that her aunt has been murdered by Montgomery. After Russell narrowly escapes becoming Montgomery's next victim, he is arrested by police. As he is being hauled away, Montgomery insists upon taking his hat box with him. Inside it, of course, is the severed head of the woman from the inn.

NIGHT MUST FALL is directed with great care by Richard Thorpe, who evokes every bit of suspense intended by playwright Williams (who played the role of the killer on stage, though not nearly as subtly as Montgomery does). Producer Hunt Stromberg saw the play in London and insisted on making it into a film. Although MGM boss Louis B. Mayer thought it was an awful idea, he reluctantly agreed to allow Stromberg, his most successful producer, to undertake the project. However, Mayer was outraged when Stromberg cast Montgomery, the popular star of frothy MGM comedies, in the role of the killer. Of course, Montgomery went after the part right from the start, insisting he play the spine-tingling killer to prove that he was an actor of the first rank. Montgomery added all sorts of mannerisms to his weird character, opting for a slight Irish accent that provides the boyish charm that bedazzles Whitty and Russell. His performance earned him a Best Actor Academy Award nomination, though he lost to Spencer Tracy for CAPTAINS COURAGEOUS, also produced at MGM.

The studio converted one of its back lots for the English country setting, and Mayer kept a tight hold on the budget, trying to starve the film out of existence. Mayer felt NIGHT MUST FALL projected the wrong image for his studio and reputedly cringed in his chair during the film's Grauman's Chinese Theater premiere on the night of May 4, 1937. He had taken extraordinary measures to disassociate MGM and himself from NIGHT MUST FALL, seeing that handbills that more or less disclaimed the film were distributed to all theatergoers that night and during the following weeks. Moreover, Mayer personally supervised the making of a trailer in which the studio admitted making the film but asked audiences to think of it as nothing more than an experimental product. When the rave reviews poured in, Mayer cancelled the handbills and cut the prelude to the film.

Montgomery's performance won him praise as a startlingly gifted actor and garnered an Oscar nomination. Montgomery and Rosalind Russell had been teamed before in FORSAKING ALL

OTHERS and TROUBLE FOR TWO, and they would later appear together in LIVE, LOVE AND LEARN and FAST AND LOOSE. Dame May Whitty's marvelous performance in NIGHT MUST FALL earned her a Supporting Actress Oscar nomination. (She lost to Alice Brady for IN OLD CHICAGO.) Rumors later had it that Mayer got back at the film he so disliked by instructing his people not to vote for Oscars of any kind for NIGHT MUST FALL.

The film was remade by the studio neerly 20 years later, starring Albert Finney, Susan Hampshire, and Mona Washbourne, but the remake lacked the tautness and dramatic impact of the powerful original.

NIGHT OF THE COMET

1984 95m c   ★★★½
Science Fiction   PG-13/15
Atlantic 9000

Robert Beltran (Hector), Catherine Mary Stewart (Regina), Kelli Maroney (Samantha), Sharon Farrell (Doris), Mary Woronov (Audrey), Geoffrey Lewis (Carter), John Achorn (Oscar), Michael Bowen (Larry), Ivan E. Roth (Willy), Raymond Lynch (Chuck)

p, Andrew Lane, Wayne Crawford; d, Thom Eberhardt; w, Thom Eberhardt; ph, Arthur Albert; ed, Fred Stafford; m, David Campbell; prod d, John Muto; fx, Wizard Court

A comet is approaching the Earth, and all over California people are celebrating even though, as the narrator points out, the last time the comet passed was coincidental with the overnight extinction of the dinosaurs. Sisters Regina (Catherine Mary Stewart) and Samantha (Kelli Maroney) for different reasons spend the night in steel-lined rooms and come out in the morning to find nothing left of humanity but piles of empty clothes and some fine red dust. Those taking the full effects of the comet's rays have evaporated, while those only partly exposed have been turned into flesh-eating zombies. Together they make their way to a radio station that is still on the air, but all they find there is an automated tape. They soon discover another survivor, Hector (Robert Beltran), likewise attracted to the radio station. But a group of soldiers from a secret government agency are around, too, and they want to use some immune blood to save their own lives. This is a terrifically witty, refreshingly unpretentious science-fiction film with the least likely and most likable heroines in memory. All the performers are excellent, especially Maroney, who can veer from petulant to heroic in the blink of an eye. Lost in the shuffle of bloated big-budget sci-fi epics released at the same time (DUNE; 2010), this movie received almost universally favorable reviews but failed to find an audience.

NIGHT OF THE HUNTER, THE

1955 93m bw   ★★★★½
Thriller   /PG
UA

Robert Mitchum (Preacher Harry Powell), Shelley Winters (Willa Harper), Lillian Gish (Rachel), Evelyn Varden (Icey Spoon), Peter Graves (Ben Harper), Billy Chapin (John), Sally Jane Bruce (Pearl), James Gleason (Birdie), Don Beddoe (Walt Spoon), Gloria Castillo (Ruby)

p, Paul Gregory; d, Charles Laughton; w, James Agee (based on the novel by Davis Grubb); ph, Stanley Cortez; ed, Robert Golden; m, Walter Schumann; art d, Hilyard Brown; fx, Jack Rabin, Louis DeWitt; cos, Jerry Bos

Actor Charles Laughton's only directorial effort is a brilliantly eerie tale of religious madness, greed, innocence, and murder set in the rural South during the Great Depression. Harry Powell (Mitchum), a psychopathic preacher with the word "Love" tattooed on the fingers of his right hand and "Hate" tattooed on the left, is driven by repressed sexual desires to murder women. While in jail for driving a stolen car, Powell meets young Ben Harper (Graves), a bank robber condemned to death for killing a man during a heist. Powell is certain Harper has stashed the loot ($10,000) from the robbery somewhere, but is unable to get Harper to reveal where. Powell is released shortly after Harper is executed, and the mad preacher tracks down his cellmate's widow, Willa (Winters). Powell soon persuades the idiotic Willa to marry him—much to the dismay of her son, John (Chapin), who senses what the preacher is really after and knows that the money is hidden inside one of the dolls of his sister, Pearl (Bruce). Powell soon becomes frustrated with the ignorant Willa and murders her, turning his attention to the children. John and Pearl take the doll and flee into the countryside with the murderous Powell always one step behind them. Working from a script by James Agee (THE AFRICAN QUEEN), Laughton created what he called "a nightmarish sort of Mother Goose tale," employing an eclectic mix of visual styles (German expressionism, D.W. Griffith) to convey both the horror of Powell's quest and the idyllic flight of the children to the safety of the farm of an old spinster (Gish). In addition to Stanley Cortez's stunning cinematography, the film boasts Robert Mitchum's greatest performance—a chilling essay that would unfortunately typecast him for much of his career. Beautiful, haunting, poetic, and intensely personal, THE NIGHT OF THE HUNTER is a unique, terrifying masterpiece. The adaptation of the Davis Grubb novel was the last film work by James Agee. Audiences didn't know *what* to make of this one; it bombed, and the great Laughton never directed again.

NIGHT OF THE IGUANA, THE

1964 125m bw   ★★½
Drama   /X
Seven Arts

Richard Burton (Rev. T. Lawrence Shannon), Ava Gardner (Maxine Faulk), Deborah Kerr (Hannah Jelkes), Sue Lyon (Charlotte Goodall), James Ward (Hank Prosner), Grayson Hall (Judith Fellowes), Cyril Delevanti (Nonno), Mary Boylan (Miss Peebles), Gladys Hill (Miss Dexter), Billie Matticks (Miss Throxton)

p, Ray Stark; d, John Huston; w, Anthony Veiller, John Huston (based on the play by Tennessee Williams); ph, Gabriel Figueroa (CinemaScope); ed, Ralph Kemplen; m, Benjamin Frankel; art d, Stephen Grimes; cos, Dorothy Jeakins

Based on the Williams play that won the New York Drama Critics Award for 1961-62, THE NIGHT OF THE IGUANA is alternately fascinating and boring. It served to put the sleepy little village of Puerto Vallarta on the Mexican vacation map, and visitors to the town are still shown the rotting sets for the movie as part of their "official" tour. Hall, cinematographer Figueroa, and art director Grimes were nominated for Oscars but were bypassed by their rivals in ZORBA THE GREEK. However, Dorothy Jeakins did receive an Oscar for her costume design. Burton is a defrocked Episcopalian priest who now earns his living as a tour guide. He's taking a group of schoolteachers around. Lyon, the junior member of the group, finds him attractive, so he squires her to his ratty hotel room, where they are discovered by Hall. The older woman threatens to have him sacked for his dalliance with Lyon unless he ceases. The group are supposed to be quartered in a plush inn, but Burton takes them to a run-down place owned by friend Gardner, who has just been widowed. The teachers balk, but they are stranded while Burton tinkers with their bus and must now remain at the seedy hotel. Burton falls ill with fever and tells Gardner that Hall means to have him fired, so Gardner won't let Hall use the phone to call Burton's employers. Kerr, a poor artist, and her grandfather, Delevanti, a poorer poet, have been working their way across Mexico by selling her sketches and arranging readings by him, and they arrive at the hotel broke. Ward, the tour's bus driver, soon becomes Lyon's suitor. He repairs the bus and leaves, as tour leader, with the teachers. Kerr, Burton, Delavanti, and Gardner remain at the hotel, and Kerr and Burton become friends. But Burton's mind seems to be on the verge of crumbling. Gardner loves Burton although she sees that his existence might be better served by Kerr and offers her hotel to the two of them. Meanwhile Delavanti, who has been working on the same poem for 20 years, finally finishes it and dies. Kerr leaves, after burying her grandfather, and Burton and Gardner stay on at the shuttered hostelry as the picture ends. We're never certain whether Hall's jealousy of the relationship, if it can be called that, between Lyon and Burton, stems from her attraction to Burton or to Lyon. Gardner is depicted as an aging nymphomaniac, whose two hotel boys, Fidelman Duryan and Roberto Leyva, meet a number of her needs.

The offscreen conduct of cast and crew was almost as weird as the film itself. Burton's wife, Elizabeth Taylor, was on hand throughout the filming, sticking like glue to Burton's side, reportedly to make sure her husband's eyes didn't turn too far in Gardner's direction. Gardner, on the other hand, spent most of her time driving a sports car wildly through the surf along the beach. Director Huston cultivated paranoia by providing guns for the leading players with which to protect themselves from unknown dangers. Lyon, who began her career as the title character in LOLITA, was making her second film appearance chaperoned by her mother. Her movie life was, at best, erratic (TONY ROME, SEVEN WOMEN, etc.), and she later retired to become a teacher in Los Angeles. The iguana mentioned in the title refers to a long lizard that can be seen roaming the streets and hotels of Puerto Vallarta—and looks far more ferocious than it is.

NIGHT OF THE LIVING DEAD

1968 90m bw ★★★★
Horror /18
Image Ten

Judith O'Dea (Barbara), Russell Streiner (Johnny), Duane Jones (Ben), Karl Hardman (Harry Cooper), Keith Wayne (Tom), Judith Ridley (Judy), Marilyn Eastman (Helen Cooper), Kyra Schon (Karen), Bill Heinzman, Charles Craig

p, Russell Streiner, Karl Hardman; d, George Romero; w, John A. Russo (based on a story by Romero); ph, George Romero; ed, George Romero; prod d, Vincent Survinski; fx, Regis Survinski, Tony Pantanello

Pittsburgh-based industrial filmmaker George Romero gathered together a loyal cast and youthful crew from the local talent, scrounged up enough money to shoot on weekends, and made motion picture history. The first truly modern horror film, NIGHT OF THE LIVING DEAD is the most influential work to emerge in the genre since PSYCHO. It shattered most of the revered conventions of the genre and led the way for other ambitious genre filmmakers who would follow in his wake such as Wes Craven, David Cronenberg, Tobe Hooper, and Sam Raimi. Despite mostly unprofessional acting, near nonexistent production values, homemade special effects, and cheap grainy black-and-white film stock, the film is a triumph. What could

have been just dreadful succceeds in creating and sustaining a genuine sense of dread. The cheap-looking imagery gives the film a dreamy authenticity like that of old black-and-white television news footage. This is a film of its time—the era of the Vietnam War abroad and social upheaval at home—in which good does not triumph over evil and likable people die just as brutally and unexpectedly as the despicable ones. The violence of the film, which was extreme in its day, reflects the horrors Americans saw each night on the evening news. The values and institutions of patriarchy are shown to be outmoded and are depicted in a critical and pessimistic manner. The genre would never be the same again.

Barbara (O'Dea) and her brother, Johnny (Streiner), have driven many miles at the behest of their mother to honor their dead father by placing a wreath on his grave. Neither is enthusiastic about the annual task. Johnny reminisces about how he used to frighten his sister when they were children. "They're coming to get you, Barbara!" he intones ominously in his best Boris Karloff fashion. Though now grown up and ostensibly too mature to be affected by such juvenile scare tactics, Barbara is still unnerved by her brother's creepy performance. Johnny sees an odd-looking fellow lurching unsteadily in the distance. "Look, there's one of them now!" The fun and games abruptly stop, however, when the weird man savagely grabs Barbara. Johnny leaps to his sister's defence but he's knocked down by the maniac. His head strikes a tombstone, apparently killing him. Barbara races for her life back to the car, leaps in, and discovers that the keys are in Johnny's pocket. The maniac bangs on the windows desperate to get at her. Barbara releases the emergency brake and the car rolls down a hill away from her clumsy pursuer. She gets out and runs to an old farmhouse where she is soon joined by Ben (Jones), a young Black man. Ben informs Barbara that the recently dead have been returning to life to eat the living. He sets about fortifying the house by nailing boards over doors and windows without much help from Barbara who has gone catatonic.

Thus the stage is set for one of the most nightmarish films ever made. It's hard to laugh off even today. Things get a bit talky once all the characters gather in the farmhouse but the film remains gripping much in the manner of a Rod Serling allegory on "The Twilight Zone". The gore effects for the most part are not all that gross by modern standards but it is extremely intense. Produced for less than $150,000, the film was booked in a haphazard manner—rejected by Columbia because it wasn't in color and by American International Pictures because it had no romance and a downbeat ending—turning up at kiddie matinees, scaring the daylights out of the unprepared youngsters. NIGHT OF THE LIVING DEAD then found its niche on the midnight movie circuit and went on to become one of the most successful independent films of all time. The film's underlying premise is horror at its most basic: a group of strangers trapped together in a small house being attacked by the living dead. Once friends, relatives, and neighbors, they are now mindless flesh-eating machines. With his zombies, Romero hit upon a subject that is rich in metaphor and meaning, and he continued to explore the implications of his concept in two fascinating (and far bloodier) sequels: DAWN OF THE DEAD and DAY OF THE DEAD. All three are essential viewing for anyone with a serious interest in the horror film.

NIGHT OF THE SHOOTING STARS, THE

1981 106m c ★★★
Drama/War R/A
RAI-TV/Ager/Premier (Italy)

Omero Antonutti (Galvano), Margarita Lozano (Concetta), Claudio Bigagli (Corrado), Massimo Bonetti (Nicole), Norma Martelli (Ivana), Enrica Maria Modugno (Mara), Sabina Vannucchi (Rosanna), Dario Cantarelli (Priest), Sergio Dagliana (Olinto), Giuseppe Furia (Requiem)

p, Giuliani G. De Negri; d, Paolo Taviani, Vittorio Taviani; w, Vittorio Taviani, Paolo Taviani, Giuliani G. De Negri, Tonino Guerra; ph, Franco Di Giacomo (Agfacolor); ed, Roberto Perpignani; m, Nicola Piovani; art d, Gianni Sbarra

On the night of San Lorenzo (a magical evening during which many Europeans believe wishes may become fulfilled), a shooting star darts across the sky, sending a grown woman into a recollection of her childhood. As the star passes her window, she relates the events that took place in her small town during the last days of WWII: With the advancing Allies pushing the last remnants of the German army out of Italy, the Nazis enact sick and desperate revenge on the Italian civilians, staging vicious attacks on the old men, women, and children left in the villages. The members of the small town of San Miniato are divided in their opinions as to whether to remain in their village and risk dealing with the Germans, or to attempt traveling across the back roads, dodging attacks from sadistic Blackshirts, in an effort to meet the advancing Allies. One group made up of various segments of the town's population sets out on the journey, with all the old prohibitions breaking down as the people pull together in an effort to survive. An elderly peasant man with natural leadership ability is chosen to guide the group to safety. Despite a few voices of dissent, the old man brings ingenuity to his assignment and keeps the group's spirits up by showing a humane concern for all and encouraging them to watch out for one another. During the journey, he develops a romantic relationship with an aristocratic woman who has always admired him but could never let him know because of their difference in class. Once he has guided the group out of danger, however, the townspeople immediately resume the societal roles that previously divided them. The Taviani brothers, who gained international attention with 1977 Cannes Film Festival Golden Palm winner PADRE PADRONE, approached this film in much the same way as they did their earlier effort—using an imaginative combination of events and showing them as remembered by the narrator as she reminisces about the magical moments of her childhood—and came up with a dazzling, immensely popular film that earned them the Special Jury Prize at Cannes.

NIGHT SHIFT

1982 105m c   ★★★
Comedy   R/15
Ladd

Henry Winkler (Chuck Lumley), Michael Keaton (Bill Blazejowski), Shelley Long (Belinda Keaton), Gina Hecht (Charlotte Koogle), Pat Corley (Edward Koogle), Bobby Di Cicco (Leonard), Nita Talbot (Vivian), Basil Hoffman (Drollhauser), Tim Rossovich (Luke), Clint Howard (Jefferey)

p, Brian Grazer; d, Ron Howard; w, Lowell Ganz, Babaloo Mandel; ph, James Crabe (Technicolor); ed, Robert J. Kern, Daniel Hanley, Michael Hill; m, Burt Bacharach; prod d, Jack T. Collis; art d, Pete Smith; fx, Allen Hall

This surprisingly tasteful and funny comedy stars Henry Winkler as Chuck Lumley, a dippy morgue attendant whose mundane life changes when he is assigned to work the night shift with crazed schemer Bill Blazejowski (Michael Keaton). Chuck, who secretly longs for some excitement in his life, becomes embroiled

in Bill's wild get-rich-quick plans. When the two meet nice-girl hooker Belinda (Shelley Long), who has just lost her pimp, the boys turn the morgue into a nighttime brothel using Belinda's prostitute pals. Ron Howard's direction is carefully balanced, and he treats his characters with humanity and respect. Winkler turns in the best performance of his career, and Keaton is wonderful.

NIGHT TO REMEMBER, A

1958 123m bw   ★★★★
Disaster   /PG
Rank (U.K.)

Kenneth More (Herbert Lightoller), Ronald Allen (Clarke), Robert Ayres (Peuchen), Honor Blackman (Mrs. Lucas), Anthony Bushell (Capt. Rostron), John Cairney (Murphy), Jill Dixon (Mrs. Clarke), Jane Downs (Mrs. Lightoller), James Dyrenforth (Col. Gracie), Michael Goodliffe (Thomas Andrews)

p, William McQuitty; d, Roy Ward Baker; w, Eric Ambler (based on the book by Walter Lord); ph, Geoffrey Unsworth; ed, Sidney Hayers; m, William Alwyn; art d, Alex Vetchinsky; cos, Yvonne Caffin

The sinking of the great luxury liner Titanic is the subject of this spectacular, well-acted, and brilliantly directed film. The night all the world remembers is April 14, 1912, when the great ship struck an iceberg and sank, taking to the bottom with her 1,513 passengers and crew members (out of a total complement of 2,224 on board), sinking on the fifth day of her maiden voyage from Southampton to New York. Although Kenneth More is ostensibly the star of this film, the production is the result of a great team effort with more than 200 speaking parts. The story, based on Lord's popular book, recounts the sailing of the Titanic, billed as the "unsinkable ship," and its inevitable voyage toward the Grand Banks of Newfoundland and doom. Brief scenes of the passengers are shown—those in first class, those in steerage—as well as the crew members, from officers to stewards and seamen, with the central figure being More. As second officer Lightoller, More's perspective is the focal point of the events surrounding the mammoth tragedy. He witnesses the passengers settling into their quarters and the routine operations of the ship's progress as it ploughs across the tranquil Atlantic. We see the rich in their luxurious suites, the second-class passengers envying them, and the steerage travelers just happy to be making the voyage to America despite their cramped quarters below decks. Early on, the communications cabin is swamped with messages from the wealthy passengers asking for stock prices and arranging for their receptions in Manhattan. Ominously, the wireless operator is so swamped with these messages that he falls behind in sending to the bridge the all-important weather reports, particularly those sightings of icebergs drifting south from the polar regions to the sea lanes. "Slices of life" show David McCallum as the ship's radio operator, Naismith as the ship's captain, Goodliffe as the ship's designer, Tucker McGuire as the robust, "unsinkable Molly Brown," and Bushell as the heroic captain of the ancient Carpathia, who drove his ship near destruction to cover the 58 miles between it and the Titanic after receiving the SOS signal. (The Carpathia almost burst its boilers in steaming to the rescue in four-and-a-half hours to pluck 711 passengers from their lifeboats.) Most of the film depicts in detail exactly how the disaster occurred, with the 46,000-ton liner striking the iceberg and having a 300-foot gash made through three of her four watertight boiler rooms by an underwater spur of the iceberg which ripped the vessel open like a tin can. Fast cuts show how the passengers are calmly roused and taken to the lifeboats—of which there were too few—so that only the women and children and crew members needed to man the boats are lowered while paupers and millionaires remain on board. Those remaining heroically sing along with the ship's band the tunes of the day, particularly an old hymm, "Nearer My God to Thee."

Using the facts of the event, Baker constructed a brilliant and startling film and Ambler's script is uncluttered with fictional side episodes; here the facts are as dramatic as any imagined tale. The film received a small budget, only $1,680,000, but it suggests a much more expensive price tag. All the acting is superb and underplayed. Costumes, settings, and special effects are outstanding. A NIGHT TO REMEMBER is superior to the Fox production TITANIC of 1953. A weaker effort was made by the British in 1929 in a film called ATLANTIC. A NIGHT TO REMEMBER was a critical success but received only lukewarm box-office support.

NIGHT TRAIN

1940 90m bw   ★★★★
Spy/War   /A
Gaumont (U.K.)

Margaret Lockwood (Anna Bomasch), Rex Harrison (Gus Bennett), Paul Henreid (Karl Marsen), Basil Radford (Charters), Naunton Wayne (Caldicott), James Harcourt (Axel Bomasch), Felix Aylmer (Dr. John Fredericks), Wyndham Goldie (Dryton), Roland Culver (Roberts), Eliot Makeham (Schwab)

p, Edward Black; d, Carol Reed; w, Sydney Gilliat, Frank Launder (based on a story by Gordon Wellesley); ph, Otto Kanturek; ed, R.E. Dearing; art d, Alex Vetchinsky

One of the finest spy films ever, NIGHT TRAIN reflects the immense talents of its brilliant director, Carol Reed, and of scripters Frank Launder and Sydney Gilliat. After Hitler's conquest of Czechoslovakia, Anna Bomasch (Margaret Lockwood) is arrested. Her father, Axel (James Harcourt), who possesses technical information the Nazis want, has fled to England, but Anna is interred in a concentration camp. There, she meets Karl Marsen (Paul Henreid), with whom she manages to escape to England, and in London she contacts music hall performer Gus Bennett (Rex Harrison)—who is actually a British secret agent—to get in touch with her father. In short order the Bomasches, duped by Marsen—who is himself a Gestapo plant—are taken to Germany, where the Nazis threaten Anna to secure Axel's cooperation. Bennett follows, infiltrates the Naval Ministry in Berlin, and discovers that the Bomasches are on the night train to Munich. With the help of two comedic cricketers played by Naunton Wayne and Basil Radford (who performed the same service in Alfred Hitchcock's THE LADY VANISHES), Bennett boards the train and is able to free father and daughter, leading to the trio's final flight to Switzerland, with Marsen and the SS in hot pursuit. Though action-packed with one harrowing scene after another, the film is not broadly played, and Reed employs subtlety over bravado. Its portrayal of the Germans, too, is fairly balanced, without the propagandistic characterizations that would mark films made later in the war. Harrison is perfect as the daring, suave British spy; Lockwood is fine as his love interest; and Henried is appropriately subtle as the deceiving Marsen in this gripping, razor-edged melodrama that mounts to a stunning climax.

NIGHT WATCH, THE

(LE TROU)
1964 118m bw   ★★★★
Prison
Playart/FS/Titanus (France/Italy)

Michel Constantin (Geo Cassid), Jean Keraudy (Roland Darban), Philippe Leroy (Manu Borelli), Raymond Meunier (Monseigneur), Marc Michel (Claude Gaspard), Andre Bervil (Warden), Eddy Rasimi (Guard Bouboule), Jean-Paul Coquelin (Guard Grinval), Catherine Spaak (Nicole)

p, Georges Charlot; d, Jacques Becker; w, Jacques Becker, Jose Giovanni, Jean Aurel (based on the novel Le Trou by Giovanni); ph, Ghislain Cloquet; ed, Marguerite Renoir, Geneviève Vaury; fx, Philippe Arthuys

This outstanding drama was the last film to be directed by Becker, who died shortly after its completion. While awaiting trial for the attempted murder of his wife, Michel is moved into a cell with Keraudy, Constantin, Leroy, and Meunier, who decide to include him in their elaborate escape plan. The film goes into great detail about the mechanics of the escape. Dummies are made, a tunnel is dug, the men build a periscope out of a mirror and a toothbrush to watch for guards, a medicine bottle filled with sand is used as an hourglass so the conspirators can time their shifts, and eventually the tunnel connecting to the city's sewer system is complete. On the day they are to make their escape, Michel is called into the warden's office. There he is informed that his wife has dropped the charges against him. He relates the news to his cellmates, who eye him suspiciously, but he intends to go through with the escape anyway because he still faces a five-year term. As the men are about to make their way down the tunnel, alarms ring and guards appear to stop them. The men then realize that Michel has betrayed them in exchange for a lighter sentence. Using a cast of nonprofessionals, Becker paints a powerful portrait of men in desperate circumstances forced, against their better instincts, to trust one another. The film, shot in a documentary style, contains no music, using only the natural sounds of the prison to convey suspense and tension. American director Don Siegel was surely influenced by THE NIGHT WATCH when he made ESCAPE FROM ALCATRAZ, starring Clint Eastwood.

NIGHTHAWKS

1981 99m c   ★★★½
Crime   R/18
Universal

Sylvester Stallone (Deke DaSilva), Billy Dee Williams (Matthew Fox), Lindsay Wagner (Irene), Persis Khambatta (Shakka), Nigel Davenport (Peter Hartman), Rutger Hauer (Wulfgar), Hilarie Thompson (Pam), Joe Spinell (Lt. Munafo), Walter Mathews (Commissioner), E. Brian Dean (Sergeant)

p, Martin Poll; d, Bruce Malmuth; w, David Shaber (based on a story by David Shaber and Paul Sylbert); ph, James A. Contner (Technicolor); ed, Christopher Holmes; m, Keith Emerson; prod d, Peter Larkin; fx, Ed Drohan, Walter Tatro, Dick Smith, Nick Allder; cos, Robert DeMora, John Falabella

Deke DaSilva (Sylvester Stallone) and Matthew Fox (Billy Dee Williams) are New York cops assigned to track down terrorist Wulfgar (Rutger Hauer). In London, Wulfgar planted a bomb in a London department store, killing several children and incurring the wrath of terrorist leaders. He resumes his career with financing from Shakka (Persis Khambatta). Soon DaSilva and Wulfgar are engaged in a violent battle of wits, while DaSilva struggles to save his marriage to Irene (Lindsay Wagner). This very effective thriller features a chilling performance by Hauer as the emotionless killing machine. Stallone and Williams are also credible, and the film makes good use of its New York locations.

NIGHTMARE ALLEY

1947 111m bw ★★★★
Crime /A
FOX

Tyrone Power *(Stanton Carlisle)*, Joan Blondell *(Zeena)*, Coleen Gray *(Molly)*, Helen Walker *(Dr. Lilith Ritter)*, Taylor Holmes *(Ezra Grindle)*, Mike Mazurki *(Bruno)*, Ian Keith *(Pete)*, Julia Dean *(Mrs. Peabody)*, James Flavin *(Clem Hoatley)*, Roy Roberts *(McGraw)*

p, George Jessel; d, Edmund Goulding; w, Jules Furthman (based on the novel by William Lindsay Gresham); ph, Lee Garmes; ed, Barbara McLean; m, Cyril J. Mockridge; art d, Lyle Wheeler, J. Russell Spencer; fx, Fred Sersen; cos, Bonnie Cashin

Power is simply terrific as the sideshow hustler who makes it to the big time through underhanded methods that ultimately bring about his horrific ruination. Power gets a menial job with a cheap carnival and becomes fascinated with a mind-reading act performed by Keith and Blondell. Becoming the show's barker, Power entices carnival patrons to see the mind readers in action. Another of the carnival's attractions is an illegal geek show featuring a "half-man, half-beast" who works in a pit and bites the heads off live chickens. (Geek shows were prevalent in midwestern country carnivals circa 1900-1935 and featured human derelicts who not only chewed the heads off chickens but also of live snakes.) Here the geek is a fallen carney performer, a dipsomaniac who conducts his ghastly routines so he can be paid off with a quart of booze each evening. In no time, Power is made a part of the mind-reading act; collecting questions audience members have written on pieces of paper, he switches these questions with blank pieces of paper that are given to the blindfolded Blondell—billed as "Miracle Woman of the Ages"—who burns them in a vase. The real questions are slipped to Keith, who is hiding beneath the stage, and he writes the questions on a blackboard that is reflected through mirrors into Blondell's crystal ball. Blondell simply reads off the questions and gives ambiguous answers that sound as if they have meaning. A pretty sideshow artist, Gray, who is in love with Power, tells him that the mind-reading bit is good but that it's no match to the spectacular act Blondell and Keith used to perform as big-time vaudevilleans. In that act Keith stayed in the audience and merely held up the written question, which Blondell would answer, a never-miss system that was controlled by a secret word code. Power goes to Keith and begins to feed liquor to him, pumping him for information about the old act. Keith shows Power the ease with which universal human experiences can be manipulated in mind-reading and explains that the great act he and his wife had went to pieces after he began drinking. Power keeps after Keith to teach him the secret word code, but he mistakenly gives Keith some wood alcohol and the drunk dies the next day. Then Power goes to work on the promiscuous Blondell, beginning an affair with her, and eventually learning the secret word code. Together they revive the old act, with Power in the audience holding up items given to him by patrons and Blondell accurately describing them even though she is blindfolded. When Power cheats on Blondell by seducing Gray, he incurs the wrath of the carnival people, who insist that the scoundrel marry the poor girl. Power and Gray wed and then move to Chicago, where Power installs himself as a great spiritualist in a swanky nightclub, with Gray assisting him. He mesmerizes audiences and becomes the

city's sensation. He meets psychologist Walker, who is enamored of him, and they strike a deal. In exchange for confidential information about her clients, the richest people in town, she will share in 50 percent of the profits. Through Walker's high-society contacts, Power becomes rich by giving rigged seances, putting magnates and tycoons in touch with their dead loved ones. Holmes is so moved by seeing a vision of his deceased sweetheart that he promises to give the sharpster $150,000 to build a spiritual temple, and Power makes plans to establish a religious cult that will make him millions. Reluctantly, Gray poses as the spirit of Holmes's dead girlfriend, but when Holmes falls to his knees pathetically praying to God, Gray breaks down and admits to the hoax to the outraged Holmes. Power goes to Walker, but she tells him to leave her alone, threatening to go to the police with the story of Keith's death, which she has learned from Blondell. Ruined, Power takes to the road, loses all his money, and begins to drink heavily—living in cheap rooming houses, then in hobo jungles—until he is nothing more than an alcoholic derelict. He appears filthy and gaunt at a tawdry carnival, begs for work, and is given a job as a geek. After performing the hideous act the first day, Power is seen screaming as he runs hysterically through the carnival grounds. Gray, who is a performer in the same carnival, steps from a trailer and stops Power, comforting him and taking him in, suggesting that she will rehabilitate her errant husband. (This scene was added to the powerful film at the insistence of the Hays Office—then Hollywood's censoring board—which demanded that the film be softened and that Power be redeemed from his disgusting fate.)

Although it could not include all of the terrifying details of Gresham's shocking novel, Furthman's script is potent and revealing as it examines the sleazy world of the spiritual con artist. Carefully constructing Power's rise and fall, director Goulding is merciless in his inspection of a character who is rotten through and through. Power, who asked to play the part and had Fox buy the rights of the novel for him, gives the performance of his career, proving that he was not merely a matinee idol but a player who could dig deep inside himself and produce a characterization that was both memorable and telling. Goulding was then Power's favorite director; they had worked together in the 1946 production of THE RAZOR'S EDGE, presenting a stunning version of the Somerset Maugham tale. Goulding was noted for eliciting excellent performances from actors thought to be one-dimensional or routine, as he did in such such films as GRAND HOTEL, DARK VICTORY, THE GREAT LIE, and CLAUDIA.

Walker is a standout as the cold-blooded psychologist and Blondell excels as the frowzy but calculating spritualist, the essence of cheapness. Gray is also fine as the stupid but loving wife who can forgive any crime. Mockridge's score is eerie and perfectly suited to the shadowy images captured in Garmes' photography.

NIGHTMARE ON ELM STREET, A

1984 91m c ★★★½
Horror R/18
New Line

John Saxon *(Lt. Thompson)*, Ronee Blakley *(Marge Thompson)*, Heather Langenkamp *(Nancy Thompson)*, Amanda Wyss *(Tina Gray)*, Nick Corri *(Rod Lane)*, Johnny Depp *(Glen Lantz)*, Robert Englund *(Fred Krueger)*, Charles Fleischer *(Dr. King)*, Joseph Whipp *(Sgt. Parker)*, Mimi Meyer-Craven *(Nurse)* p, Robert Shaye, Sara Risher; d, Wes Craven; w, Wes Craven; ph, Jacques Haitkin (Deluxe Color); ed, Rick Shaine; m, Charles Bernstein; prod d, Gregg Fonseca; fx, Jim Doyle; cos, Dana Lyman

"One, two; Freddy's comin' for you/Three, four; better lock your door/Five, six; grab your crucifix/Seven, eight; gonna stay up late/Nine, ten; never sleep again." A NIGHTMARE ON ELM STREET, one of the most intelligent and terrifying horror films of the 1980s, begins and ends with this haunting children's song. This was the film that introduced the world to Freddy Krueger, the horribly scarred man with the ragged slouch hat, dirty red-and-green striped sweater, and metal gloves with knives at the tips. Freddy (Robert Englund), a genius of a monster who exists in his victims' dreams and preys on them in the vulnerability of sleep, has returned to the town where years before he was burnt alive as a child killer by locals who took the law into their own hands. Now he's back to take revenge on their kids. In an era in which the horror film has become little more than a mindless exercise in gratuitous high-tech bloodletting, A NIGHTMARE ON ELM STREET (like most of Wes Craven's films) brought some hope to those concerned about the fate of the genre. This movie intelligently probes into the audience's terror of nightmares and combines it with another horrific element—the very real fear of killers in one's own neighborhood. The teenagers in the film, who are paying for the sins of their parents, are not simply fodder for the special-effects crew but have distinct personalities and are independent and intelligent. The initial success of the movie was based on the audience's insecurity: we are never sure whether the characters are dreaming because the line between nightmare and reality is blurred, and, as a result, the terror is almost nonstop. The success of the sequels, while still based in the dream-versus-reality premise, has become increasingly dependent on the heroic pose of Freddy Krueger, played with energy and humor by Robert Englund.

As the film opens, teenaged Tina Gray (Amanda Wyss) wanders in a dark boiler room. A horribly scarred man stalks her. On his hands are crude gloves outfitted with knives that he scrapes on the pipes to make a spine-chilling screech. Just as we think she may have lost him, he pops up behind her and grabs her. She wakes up screaming in her bed. It was just a dream. The next morning Tina learns that her friends Nancy (Heather Langenkamp) and Rod (Nick Corri) have had the same dream. Afraid to sleep alone the next night while her mother is out of town, Tina invites Nancy and her boyfriend, Glen (Johnny Depp), to stay over, and Rod drops by as well. After falling asleep, Tina has another dream where she is being chased by the same man (Robert Englund). Suddenly Rod wakes up in bed to hear Tina screaming next to him. He looks under the covers and sees the man attacking her. Tina has been murdered, and this time it's no dream. It's often not clear whether the characters are dreaming, therefore the tension is constant. Craven fills the film with so many imaginative, unexpected ways to terrify that the viewer is afraid to relax during the lulls in action. The result is one of the best and most financially successful horror films of the 1980s. See it at your own peril.

NIGHTS OF CABIRIA
(LE NOTTI DI CABIRIA)
1957 110m bw   ★★★★½
Drama   /15
Marceau   (Italy)

Giulietta Masina *(Cabiria)*, Francois Perier *(Oscar D'Onofrio, Accountant)*, Amedeo Nazzari *(Alberto Lazzari, Movie Star)*, Aldo Silvani *(Hypnotist)*, Franca Marzi *(Wanda Cabiria's Friend)*, Dorian

Gray *(Jessy Lazzari's Girl Friend)*, Mario Passante *(Cripple in the "Miracle" Sequence)*, Pina Gualandri *(Matilda the Prostitute)*, Polidor *(The Monk)*, Enio Girolami

p, Dino De Laurentiis; d, Federico Fellini; w, Federico Fellini, Ennio Flaiano, Tullio Pinelli, Pier Paolo Pasolini; ph, Aldo Tonti, Otello Martelli; ed, Leo Catozzo; m, Nino Rota; art d, Piero Gherardi; cos, Piero Gherardi

Masina's finest film performance, perhaps husband Fellini's as well. NIGHTS OF CABIRIA lacks the lyrical simplicity that made LA STRADA such a magical experience, but is an impressive enough display of Fellini's fascinating visual style to have warranted the Academy Award for Best Foreign-Language Film. Set in a district on the outskirts of Rome, the film focuses on Cabiria (Masina), a near-perfect embodiment of the prostitute with a heart of gold. She's the type who understands misfortune to be part and parcel of life, but never loses faith in the value of life itself. When misfortune does come her way, Cabiria shrugs it off and continues walking the streets for money. A handsome movie star picks her up during a brawl with his girlfriend. He takes her to his fabulous home, but quickly discards her when he is through with her services. Eventually someone does fall in love with Cabiria—the shy and withdrawn Oscar D'Onofrio (Francois Perier)—or at least she believes this to be the case. Perhaps the most difficult aspect of NIGHTS OF CABIRIA is accepting Masina as a prostitute: this sweet and naive-looking woman, who stole audiences' hearts with her childlike innocence in LA STRADA, isn't at all typical of women selling themselves on the streets, but does express the dismal point that fate makes no exceptions. Her Cabiria is a sucker for a sob story, and this very flaw gives her a saving grace. As in the majority of Fellini's films, the emphasis here is on visual elements rather than on straight narrative form, relying on small details and eccentricities to breathe life into Cabiria. The film was the basis for the Broadway and film version of *Sweet Charity*.

NIKKI, WILD DOG OF THE NORTH
1961 74m c   ★★★½
Children's   /U
Disney/Cangary/West   (U.S./Canada)

Jean Coutu *(Andre Dupas)*, Emile Genest *(Jacques Lebeau)*, Uriel Luft *(Makoki)*, Robert Rivard *(Durante)*, Nikki the Dog *("The Malemute Wonder Dog")*, Taao the Dog *(Old Champion Fighting Dog)*, Neewa the Bear *(Himself)*, Jacques Fauteux *(Narrator)*, The Nomads *(Performers of French-Canadian Folk Songs)*

p, Walt Disney, Winston Hibler; d, Jack Couffer, Donald Haldane; w, Winston Hibler, Ralph Wright, Dwight Hauser (based on the novel *Nomads of the North* by James Oliver Curwood); ph, Lloyd Beebe, Jack Couffer, Ray Jewell, William W. Bacon, III, Don Wilder (Technicolor); ed, Grant K. Smith; m, Oliver Wallace; cos, Jan Kemp

Andre Dupas (Jean Coutu) is a trapper in the Canadian wilderness whose dog Nikki runs off and returns with a new friend, Neewa, a bear cub. Andre ties the two animals together, loads them into his canoe, and heads downstream; however, they are separated from him when the canoe overturns in the rapids. The animals, still leashed together, have to learn to fend for themselves under their unusual constraint. The rope finally breaks, but Nikki and Neewa stick together for further adventures. Unlike many films of this type, NIKKI, WILD DOG OF THE NORTH is a well-made and exciting animal-action piece. Nikki and Neewa are quite a team, and some sequences will have the viewer wondering how the Disney folks ever got these surprising animal actors to behave so naturally. Perfect for the kids (though one fight scene may be a little too much for the youngest in the family), and the adults will be charmed as well.

9/30/55

1977 101m c ★★★½
Drama PG/
Universal

Richard Thomas (*Jimmy J.*), Susan Tyrrell (*Melba Lou*), Deborah Benson (*Charlotte*), Lisa Blount (*Billie Jean*), Tom Hulce (*Hanley*), Dennis Quaid (*Frank*), Mary Kai Clark (*Pat*), Dennis Christopher (*Eugene*), Collin Wilcox (*Jimmy J.'s Mother*), Ben Fuhrman (*Coach*)

p, Jerry Weintraub; d, James Bridges; w, James Bridges; ph, Gordon Willis (Technicolor); ed, Jeff Gourson; m, Leonard Rosenman; art d, Robert Luthardt; cos, Kent Warner, Patricia Zinn, Mina Mittleman

Fine and sensitive drama features Thomas (John-Boy of television's "The Waltons") as a teenager who is crushed on September 30, 1955, when his hero, James Dean, is killed in a car crash. Blount is his wild friend who goes into hysterics over the teen idol's death. The pair join with other Dean-worshiping friends for an occult-mystical ceremony honoring their hero. The liquor-infested ceremony results in the accidental disfiguring of Blount's face. Themes of hero worship and death are well handled in this unusual film. Thomas breaks from his nice-guy television image, giving a powerfully effective performance. Unlike so many films of this sort, teenagers are treated as human beings. What's more, the adults are also well handled, being given fine characterizations to work with. The excellent score is by Rosenman, who wrote the music for Dean's first two films as well. This film unfortunately never saw wide release and ironically was put out at the time of the death of another 1950s teen idol, Elvis Presley.

NINE TO FIVE

1980 110m c ★★★
Comedy PG/15
IPC

Jane Fonda (*Judy Bernly*), Lily Tomlin (*Violet Newstead*), Dolly Parton (*Doralee Rhodes*), Dabney Coleman (*Franklin Hart, Jr.*), Sterling Hayden (*Tinsworthy*), Elizabeth Wilson (*Roz*), Henry Jones (*Hinkle*), Lawrence Pressman (*Dick*), Marian Mercer (*Missy Hart*), Ren Woods (*Barbara*)

p, Bruce Gilbert; d, Colin Higgins; w, Colin Higgins, Patricia Resnick (based on a story by Patricia Resnick); ph, Reynaldo Villalobos (Deluxe Color); ed, Pembroke J. Herring; m, Charles Fox; prod d, Dean Edward Mitzner; art d, Jack G. Taylor, Jr.; fx, Chuck Gaspar, Matt Sweeney; cos, Ann Roth

Recently divorced Jane Fonda takes an office job and soon becomes pals with fellow secretaries Dolly Parton (in a sensational movie debut) and Lily Tomlin. Their boss is male chauvinist Dabney Coleman, who is trying to land Parton in bed. While smoking dope one night the women hatch a plan to take revenge on their cruel boss. Lots of laughs, little sense, and pure fantasy. Produced by Fonda's company, NINE TO FIVE is an amusing way to spend 110 minutes, but hardly memorable. Later made into a short-lived TV series. The title song received an Oscar nomination.

1918

1985 91m c ★★★½
Drama
Guadalupe

William Converse-Roberts (*Horace Robedaux*), Hallie Foote (*Elizabeth Robedaux*), Rochelle Oliver (*Mrs. Vaughn*), Michael Higgens (*Mr. Vaughn*), Matthew Broderick (*Brother*), Jeanne McCarthy (*Bessie*), Bill McGhee (*Sam*), L.T. Felty (*Mr. Thatcher*), Horton Foote, Jr. (*Jessie*), Tom Murrel (*Stanley*)

p, Lillian V. Foote, Ross Milloy; d, Ken Harrison; w, Horton Foote (based on his play); ph, George Tirl (Duart Color); ed, Leon Seith; art d, Michael O'Sullivan; cos, Van Broughton Ramsey

This thoughtful and carefully detailed story examines life on the WWI homefront in a rural Texas town that, in its own way, is forever changed by the war's far-reaching effects. Horace (William Converse-Roberts) and Elizabeth Robedaux (Hallie Foote) are a young married couple with an 8-month-old daughter. Their home, where much of the film's action takes place, has been paid for by Elizabeth's wealthy parents (Michael Higgens, Rochelle Oliver), who exert a domineering influence over the two. Horace has claimed he would fight in the war if he could be assured his wife and baby would be properly taken care of. His father-in-law promises to care for the family and leaves Horace no excuse. Elizabeth is furious with her husband and father, but matters take a sudden turn when the flu epidemic sweeps the country. 1918 is a multilayered work that delves deeply into the complexities of its characters and how they cope with the encroaching specter of death both at home and abroad. Foote gives a strong central performance that anchors the film with honest, deeply felt emotions. The screenplay, by her father, Horton Foote, is based on family experiences. The direction by Ken Harrison is thoughtful, allowing the events to unfold naturally in long takes. The small moments of everyday life are as prominent as the war in Europe, an important factor 1918 reflects with care and intelligence, complemented by its exact period detail.

1984

1956 94m bw ★★½
Drama/Science Fiction /15
Holiday (U.K.)

Michael Redgrave (*Gen. O'Connor*), Edmond O'Brien (*Winston Smith*), Jan Sterling (*Julia*), David Kossoff (*Charrington the Junk Shop Owner*), Mervyn Johns (*Jones*), Donald Pleasence (*Parsons*), Carol Wolveridge (*Selina Parsons*), Ernest Clark (*Outer Party Announcer*), Patrick Allen (*Inner Party Official*), Ronan O'Casey (*Rutherford*)

p, N. Peter Rathvon; d, Michael Anderson; w, William Templeton, Ralph Gilbert Bettinson (based on the novel by George Orwell); ph, C. Pennington-Richards; ed, Bill Lewthwaite; m, Malcolm Arnold; art d, Terence Verity; fx, B. Langley, George Blackwell, N. Warwick; cos, Barbara Gray

Great liberties were taken with the story written by Orwell and published in 1949, a year before Orwell passed away. Those liberties were to the detriment of one of the most powerful and depressing books ever written. The year is, of course, 1984, and London is the capital of one of three world communities of Oceania. It's after the first atomic war, and everyone in London (and everywhere else) is constantly watched by TV cameras (which are also screens) and by "Big Brother" and his faceless aides. The surroundings are drab, and no individuality will be tolerated. The walls are festooned with posters which read "War Is Peace," "Freedom Is Slavery," and "Big Brother Is Watching

You." And he is. O'Brien works for the state and finds that he cannot handle the stultifying atmosphere of being ruled by the Minsitry of Love because he is falling for Sterling. They begin to have a clandestine affair which will be life-threatening if ever uncovered by the Anti-Sex League or the Thought Police. Sterling and O'Brien make plans to overthrow Big Brother and they are joined in their cabal by Redgrave, but he is, in reality, a member of the Government who eventually informs on them. Since there are two-way microphones in every residence, the deepest fears of every citizen have been audiotaped and are known to the authorities. When someone is brought in, they are taken to Room 101, where they have to confront their innermost fears. In the case of O'Brien, it's rats, and when he must face the little furry things, he breaks. The end of the movie is varied, depending on which country you see it in. The British version has Sterling and O'Brien killed. The American version has O'Brien betraying Sterling and so successfully brainwashed that he shouts for the love of Big Brother rather than "down with Big Brother," the words he screams as his last epithet in England. The last words of the book are also different. After O'Brien's character is bumped off, the comment is made that "he loved Big Brother." Another version of the film was made in the 1980s which was equally depressing and ultimately unsuccessful with the critics and the public. Perhaps this is one of those novels that defies cinematization and must be savored in one's brain, rather than with the ears and eyes. The same could be said for Huxley's *Brave New World.*

1984

1984   117m   c   ★★★
Drama/Science Fiction   R/X
Umbrella/Rosenblum/Virgin   (U.K.)

John Hurt *(Winston Smith)*, Richard Burton *(O'Brien)*, Suzanna Hamilton *(Julia)*, Cyril Cusack *(Charrington)*, Gregor Fisher *(Parsons)*, James Walker *(Syme)*, Andrew Wilde *(Tillotson)*, David Trevena *(Tillotson's Friend)*, David Cann *(Martin)*, Anthony Benson *(Jones)*

p, Simon Perry; d, Michael Radford; w, Michael Radford, Jonathan Gems (based on the novel by George Orwell); ph, Roger Deakins (Eastmancolor); ed, Tom Priestley; m, The Eurythmics, Dominic Muldowney; prod d, Allan Cameron; art d, Martyn Hebert, Grant Hicks; cos, Emma Porteous

In this admirable attempt at bringing George Orwell's classic novel to the screen, director Michael Radford is perhaps too faithful to his source material. This is the well-known story of Winston Smith (John Hurt), a citizen of Oceania whose job it is to rewrite history for Big Brother, the autocratic symbol of a repressive regime that has forbidden such things as freedom of thought and expression—including sex. Winston becomes involved in an illicit love affair with Julia (Suzanna Hamilton), a young woman who works in the Ministry of Truth. Unfortunately for Winston, a high-ranking member of the government, O'Brien (Richard Burton), who has looked upon him as a protege, discovers the rebellion. Orwell wrote his novel in 1948, and his vision of the future is unrelentingly bleak. Radford chooses to present a view of the future as it might have looked to Orwell in 1948. This is not a future made up of colorful blinking lights and high-tech manufacturing; it is a gray, dull, stark, depressing world possessed of little visual stimulation. The performances in the film are excellent, and its look is entirely appropriate and mesmerizing—but only for a while. The basic flaw in 1984 is that it is just too painful, too depressing, and too slow to watch.

1900

(NOVECENTO)
1976   245m   c   ★★★½
Drama   R/18
PEA/Artistes Associes   (Italy)

Burt Lancaster *(Alfredo Berlinghieri, Grandfather)*, Romolo Valli *(Giovanni)*, Anna-Maria Gherardi *(Eleonora)*, Laura Betti *(Regina)*, Robert De Niro *(Alfredo Berlinghieri, Grandson)*, Paolo Pavesi *(Alfredo as a Child)*, Dominique Sanda *(Ada)*, Sterling Hayden *(Leo Dalco)*, Gerard Depardieu *(Olmo Dalco)*, Roberto Maccanti *(Olmo as a Child)*

p, Alberto Grimaldi; d, Bernardo Bertolucci; w, Franco Arcalli, Bernardo Bertolucci, Giuseppe Bertolucci; ph, Vittorio Storaro (Technicolor); ed, Franco Arcalli; m, Ennio Morricone; art d, Ezio Frigerio; cos, Gitt Magrini

Like a delicious pasta salad, ruined with intermittent slabs of Velveeta cheese. It's the portable Bernardo Bertolucci film, but it's too heavy to lift. The director wanted to make a collective memory, "popular" film—there's no denying some brilliant, definitive moments in this homage to how communism preserves the pastoral peasant life—if that's your thing. But somewhere Bertolucci got popular culture confused with pulp. Sometimes, this looks like animated Harold Robbins.

1900 captures everything that characterizes the director: his concern with the class dialectic and the battle between Marxism and Fascism, his painterly images of Italy, his historical scope, and his "divided hero" (to borrow a phrase from critic Robin Wood). While it may be a masterpiece at its original length of 320 minutes, 1900's American, British, and videocassette release is a shortened, somewhat erratic 245-minute version. The plot is about as grand and baroque as one can get, entailing the history of the Italian people and politics in the first half of the 1900s, from the organization of the peasant class to the rise of socialism to the fall of Fascism. This political dialectic is personified in Bertolucci's two central characters (the "divided hero"), Alfredo (Robert De Niro), born into a bourgeois clan of landowners, and Olmo (Gerard Depardieu), born into a peasant family, who share the same birthday, January 27, 1901 (the day Verdi died, another point of homage). Although they grow up the best of friends, their friendship turns into a love/hate relationship. As an adult, the weak Alfredo is put in charge of his family's property but is merely a puppet controlled by his evil foreman, Attila (Donald Sutherland), while the Marxist Olmo becomes a leading union organizer. Even in its shortened version, 1900 is an achievement of considerable genius, directed by Bertolucci but made possible by the combined efforts of collaborator-cinematographer Vittorio Storaro, composer Ennio Morricone, art director Enzo Frigerio, costumer Gitt Magrini, and a phenomenal cast that includes an international Who's Who of performers. But if this was an American work would we think so? Ahhh—there's the arrogant rub.

Bertolucci's clearly left-wing politics and the populism of his directing style have made him a subject of controversy, but his work is an interesting and important contrast to the radical techniques of Jean-Luc Godard, whose looming genius has long haunted Bertolucci, but whose triumph of content over style has mostly eluded him.

NINOTCHKA

1939   110m   bw   ★★★★★
Comedy   /U
MGM

Greta Garbo (*Lena Yakushova, "Ninotchka"*), Melvyn Douglas (*Count Leon Dolga*), Ina Claire (*Grand Duchess Swana*), Sig Rumann (*Michael Ironoff*), Felix Bressart (*Buljanoff*), Alexander Granach (*Kopalski*), Bela Lugosi (*Commissar Razinin*), Gregory Gaye (*Count Alexis Rakonin*), Richard Carle (*Vaston*), Edwin Maxwell (*Mercier*)

p, Ernst Lubitsch; d, Ernst Lubitsch; w, Charles Brackett, Billy Wilder, Walter Reisch (based on a story by Melchior Lengyel); ph, William Daniels; ed, Gene Ruggiero; m, Werner R. Heymann; art d, Cedric Gibbons, Randall Duell; cos, Adrian

---

Garbo laughs. So read the advertising for the star's first outright comedy, and it brilliantly sums up the appeal of this remarkable film. Director Ernst Lubitsch has La Divina (as the Europeans call her) gracefully step down from her pedestal as the stern Communist who warms to the appeal of Paris champagne and playboy Melvyn Douglas. Combining farce, romance and satire, yet still maintaining moments of that soaring Garbo intensity which make us treasure many of her otherwise mediocre films, NINOTCHKA is special indeed.

When three Soviet emissaries (Bressart, Rumann, Granach, whose work could not possibly be bettered) arrive in Paris on a mission, it's not long before Paris arrives on them instead. And so, super efficient Comrade Ninotchka (Garbo) appears to retrieve jewelry in the possession of the former Grand Duchess Swana (Claire). It is the Soviet government's contention that the property of the aristocrats properly belongs to the people. The two women's tussle over the goods becomes complicated, however, when Swana's swain Leon (Douglas) becomes infatuated with the frosty commissar.

Many of Garbo's films rely on her presence alone for their appeal. That's not the case here. Working from a brittle, witty script by no less than Wilder, Brackett, and Reisch, the gifted Lubitsch brings his patented "touch" to scene after scene. From the bumbling emissaries' arithmetic about ringing for hotel maids to Ninotchka's hilarious "execution scene" the film bubbles merrily throughout. Garbo rarely had a paramour as adroit as Douglas, who wears a dinner jacket with the flair of Astaire and the polish of Powell. He plays the gushy romantic dialogue early on with the perfect combination of conviction and playfulness, and one of the film's beauties is watching Garbo shift gears into this mode herself. The lovely scene in a cafe where Douglas cracks Ninotchka up only when he falls off his chair remains a highlight of both film comedy and screen romance. How wonderful that at this moment (and others) Garbo is less than our blue moon goddess, our tragic enchantress. Yet there's a dreamy closeup later on of her leaning again a sofa that lets us know that she is still all those mystical things as well. Garbo's scenes with Ina Claire are electric and lend edge to a film already deeper than most of its kind. In real life Claire (once married to silent screen idol John Gilbert) may not have been crazy about La Sphinx, a lingering love in Gilbert's life. And here they fight over a man again! It's almost too creepy.

An adroit satire of both Communism and capitalism, NINOTCHKA still manages a healthy heartiness and a sweet sadness rarely duplicated in film. Its success inspired pallid imitations from COMRADE X with Lamarr and Gable to THE IRON PETTICOAT with Hepburn and Hope. A musical remake, SILK STOCKINGS, featured some good Fred Astaire-Cyd Charisse dancing and a show-stealing turn by Janis Paige, but had little sparkle and even less depth. Garbo would attempt to repeat this film's magic with her next, TWO-FACED WOMAN, with George Cukor (at one point slated for NINOTCHKA) directing. The script lacked subtlety, Cukor was not at his best,

and it was all so "we've seen it already". Its overextended drunk scene can't hold a candle to the one in this beauty. Extremely funny, beautifully put together and surprisingly intense, NINOTCHKA needs no candles. It shines brightly enough on its own.

NO GREATER GLORY
1934 117m bw ★★★★
Drama /U
Columbia

George Breakston (*Nemecsek*), Jimmy Butler (*Boka*), Jackie Searl (*Gereb*), Frankie Darro (*Feri Ats*), Donald Haines (*Csonakos*), Rolf Ernest (*Ferdie Pasztor*), Julius Molnar (*Henry Pasztor*), Wesley Giraud (*Kolnay*), Beaudine Anderson (*Csele*), Bruce Line (*Richter*)

d, Frank Borzage; w, Jo Swerling (based on the novel *The Paul Street Boys* by Ferenc Molnar); ph, Joseph August; ed, Viola Lawrence

---

This is a fine and honest film with excellent performances by its youthful cast. George Breakston plays a frail youngster who idolizes gang leader Jimmy Butler. The gang is modeled after an army, complete with uniforms and a flag. Breakston's ill health makes him something of an outcast, but he is allowed to join up as a private, the only enlisted soldier in an army otherwise composed of officers. Butler despises him for his weakness, but Breakston cannot see this, so great is his admiration and his need to belong. When their flag is stolen by a rival gang of older boys called "The Red Shirts," Breakston takes it upon himself to retrieve the banner. He invades the enemy camp in a driving rain and confronts their leader Frankie Darro, who repeatedly shoves the younger boy's head under water. Darro cannot break the boy's spirit and gradually comes to respect his pluck. Breakston catches pneumonia and is forced to remain in bed but, when he learns that Butler's gang is taking on the Red Shirts, he sneaks off to join the battle. The excitement is too much for him and he dies fighting for his cause. Butler, realizing the true meaning of strength and courage, tearfully watches as Breakston's mother carries away the limp body of her son.

Breakston is all heart and innocent emotion, the epitome of admiring, loyal youth. Butler, whose career was tragically cut short by his death in World War II, is equally fine. His portrayal of the handsome, serious-minded idol is believable and moving. This film also serves as an allegory of the futility of war and what it does to the best of men. The film is based on an autobiographical novel by noted Hungarian playwright Ferenc Molnar. Sensitive adaptation and direction bring out the honesty and spirit of the book.

NO SURRENDER
1986 100m c ★★★½
Comedy R/15
Dumbarton/National Film Finance/Film Four/William Johnston/Ronald Lillie/Lauron (U.K.)

Michael Angelis (*Mike*), Avis Bunnage (*Martha Gorman*), James Ellis (*Paddy Burke*), Tom Georgeson (*Mr. Ross*), Bernard Hill (*Bernard*), Ray McAnally (*Billy McCracken*), Mark Mulholland (*Norman*), Joanne Whalley-Kilmer (*Cheryl*), J.G. Devlin (*George Gorman*), Vince Earl (*Frank*)

p, Mamoun Hassan; d, Peter Smith; w, Alan Bleasdale; ph, Michael Coulter (Panavision); ed, Kevin Brownlow, Rodney Holland; m, Daryl Runswick; prod d, Andrew Mollo; cos, Emma Porteous

---

Seldom has the world's bleakness and humankind's small-mindedness provided such as a romping good time as this black comedy from writer Alan Bleasdale. Set on New Year's Eve at a rundown nightclub on the outskirts of Liverpool, NO SURRENDER ruthlessly takes jabs at the situation in Northern Ireland, the gross unemployment of England's industrial cities, and corrupt businessmen/mobsters who take advantage of the less fortunate. Arriving for his first day's work as manager of the Charleston Club, Mike (Michael Angelis) is faced with a complicated situation stemming from the outgoing manager's plans for revenge against the crooked owner. For the New Year's celebration three vastly different groups have been booked into the club: Irish Catholic pensioners prepared for a costume ball, their longtime Protestant adversaries, and a group of helplessly senile inmates of a nursing home. Complications increase when an untalented magician (Elvis Costello), a quarreling punk-rock band, and an unfunny gay comedian are discovered to be the evening's entertainment, booked as a last laugh by the former manager. The bizarre caricatures combined with Bleasdale's witty dialogue give NO SURRENDER its air of lighthearted mirth despite the seriousness of its themes. Like any good satire, this film makes us laugh at events that normally make us sad, a credit to the finesse of Bleasdale in highlighting the absurdities of the world in a Liverpudlian microcosm.

NO TIME FOR SERGEANTS

1958 111m bw   ★★★½
Comedy   /U
WB

Andy Griffith *(Will Stockdale)*, Myron McCormick *(Sgt. King)*, Nick Adams *(Ben Whitledge)*, Murray Hamilton *(Irvin Blanchard)*, Howard Smith *(Gen. Bush)*, Will Hutchins *(Lt. Bridges)*, Sydney Smith *(Gen. Pollard)*, James Millhollin *(Psychiatrist)*, Don Knotts *(Manual Dexterity Corporal)*, Jean Willes *(WAF Captain)*

p, Mervyn LeRoy; d, Mervyn LeRoy; w, John Lee Mahin (based on the play by Ira Levin from the novel by Mac Hyman); ph, Harold Rosson; ed, William Ziegler; m, Ray Heindorf; art d, Malcolm Brown; fx, Louis Lichtenfield

Mac Hyman's hilarious novel, which then became a television special, which then became a Broadway smash (script by Ira Levin), now comes to the screen with all of the fun intact. Andy Griffith played the role on television and the stage and gets his chance to show how humorous he is in this, his second film, after a sensational debut in A FACE IN THE CROWD. He's a Georgia backwoods boy who is inducted into the peacetime Air Force when his country sends him "Greetings." His sergeant is McCormick (also repeating his Broadway role), a man who thinks that being in the service is a fine way to spend one's life, as long as nobody creates a ruckus. But that's exactly what Griffith does, as his warm naivete and questioning ways throw a monkey wrench into the sedate peacetime service. It's an episodic farce with one bright scene after another and some terrific acting by everyone. Griffith is sent to psychiatrist Millhollin and totally confounds the doctor. After he and Adams fall out of a plane and are posted as "missing, presumed dead," they turn up at their own funeral in a scene reminiscent of Mark Twain's *Tom Sawyer*.

Griffith's characterization as he faces the constantly fuming McCormick may well be the inspiration for television's "Gomer Pyle" and the way Jim Nabors worked with his sergeant, Frank Sutton. The story works so well that we're surprised no one has done it yet as a musical. Roddy McDowall was also in the Broadway play, but he declined the chance to appear in the movie, and his role was taken by Adams, who had a meteoric career in television as "The Rebel" and was nominated for a Best Supporting Actor in TWILIGHT OF HONOR before dying at 37

of an accidental overdose of the drugs he was taking to correct a medical problem. Service comedies have long been popular as the basis for movies, and this one must rank up there with STALAG 17 and MR. ROBERTS as being one of the best. Note Don Knotts and veteran Benny Baker in small roles, as well as a man who went on to star in television's M*A*S*H after he changed his name from Jameel Farah to Jamie Farr.

NO WAY OUT

1987 114m c   ★★★
Crime/Thriller   R/15
Neufeld, Ziskin, Garland

Kevin Costner *(Lt. Cmdr. Tom Farrell)*, Gene Hackman *(David Brice)*, Sean Young *(Susan Atwell)*, Will Patton *(Scott Pritchard)*, Howard Duff *(Sen. Willy Duvall)*, George Dzundza *(Dr. Sam Hesselman)*, Jason Bernard *(Maj. Donovan)*, Iman *(Nina Beka)*, Fred Dalton Thompson *(Marshall)*, Leon Russom *(Kevin O'Brien)*

p, Laura Ziskin, Robert Garland; d, Roger Donaldson; w, Robert Garland (based on the novel *The Big Clock* by Kenneth Fearing); ph, John Alcott (Metrocolor); ed, Neil Travis; m, Maurice Jarre; prod d, J. Dennis Washington, Kai Hawkins; art d, Anthony Brockliss; fx, Jack Monroe, Terry Frazee, Ken Durey

Tom Farrell (Costner) is a Naval officer working in the Pentagon who discovers that his lover, Susan (Young), is also the mistress of his boss, Secretary of Defense Brice (Hackman). When Brice arrives unexpectedly at Susan's lavish duplex, Tom sneaks out a side door, and although Brice sees Tom in the dark street outside, he cannot identify him. Brice then explodes with jealousy, and he and Susan get into a fierce argument that leads to Susan's accidental fall over a railing to her death. A shaken Brice returns to his offices in the Pentagon and there seeks the help of another aide, the ruthlessly ambitious Scott Prichard (Patton), who goes to Susan's duplex, wipes away fingerprints, and removes all traces of his boss. Next, to throw off investigators, he introduces a theory that the killer is a KGB mole long rumored to be operating in the Pentagon. Ironically, Tom, who knows that Brice is the real culprit, is then put in charge of ferreting out the fictitious enemy agent. A worthy remake of the film noir classic THE BIG CLOCK, NO WAY OUT is nearly undone by an unbelievable and unnecessary twist ending, which betrays the entire film. Before the unfortunate coda, however, director Roger Donaldson presents a taut, stylish thriller with good performances from a strong cast.

NOBODY WAVED GOODBYE

1965 80m bw   ★★
Drama   /A
Natl. Film Board of Canada (Canada)

Peter Kastner *(Peter)*, Julie Biggs *(Julie)*, Claude Rae *(Father)*, Toby Tarnow *(Sister)*, Charmion King *(Mother)*, Ron Taylor *(Boy Friend)*, Robert Hill *(Patrolman)*, Jack Beer *(Sergeant)*, John Sullivan *(Probation Officer)*, Lynne Gorman *(Julie's Mother)*

p, Roman Kroiter, Don Owen; d, Don Owen; w, Don Owen; ph, John Spotton; ed, John Spotton, Donald Ginsberg; m, Eldon Rathburn

Kastner plays a rebellious high schooler. He refuses to listen to his mother and gets in trouble with the law after he drives away in a demonstrator model from his father's car dealership. The only person he can talk to is his girlfriend, Biggs. Though more mature, she admires his reckless ways and tries to emulate him. Kastner finally leaves his parents and moves into a rooming house. His parents insist he return home and go to college. Their provisions also forbid him to ever see Biggs again. After she runs away as well, the two of them steal a car. When she realizes that nothing good will ever come of this, she asks to go back. She reveals that she is pregnant, gets out of the car, and Kastner rides off alone. NOBODY WAVED GOODBYE is a mixed bag. The story and script are routine, often dipping to a soap opera level. The direction is simplistic and predictable, with pretentious camerawork. The acting, however, is competent. The two leads are good despite their inexperience, and Rae and King as Kastner's parents are excellent counterpoints to the teenagers, giving the film some intelligence.

NONE BUT THE LONELY HEART

1944 113m bw   ★★★★
Drama   /A
RKO

Cary Grant (Ernie Mott), Ethel Barrymore (Ma Mott), Barry Fitzgerald (Twite), June Duprez (Ada), Jane Wyatt (Aggie Hunter), George Coulouris (Jim Mordiney), Dan Duryea (Lew Tate), Konstantin Shayne (Ike Weber), Eva Leonard Boyne (Ma Chalmers), Morton Lowry (Taz)

p, David Hempstead; d, Clifford Odets; w, Clifford Odets (based on the novel by Richard Llewellyn); ph, George Barnes; ed, Roland Gross; m, Hanns Eisler; prod d, Mordecai Gorelik; art d, Albert S. D'Agostino, Jack Okey; fx, Vernon L. Walker; cos, Renie

This was a daring and inventive film in its day, and Grant, playing the dedicated outsider, and Barrymore, as his cockney mother, are superb. The time is just prior to WWII and the place is Whitechapel in the East End of London. Through these mean streets wanders Grant, a shiftless but lighthearted young man whose mother, Barrymore, runs a dingy second-hand furniture store. Grant and his mother exchange barbs whenever they meet; however, Grant is seldom home to occupy his room above the store. Instead, he vagabonds his way through the area, cadging cigarettes and food from friendly shopkeepers who have known him since boyhood. Particularly concerned about Grant and protective of his mother is the local pawnbroker, Shayne, who dispenses wisdom and wit, as does family friend Fitzgerald, a drifter. Though cellist Wyatt is in love with Grant, he forsakes her for sultry Duprez, the divorced wife of British underworld leader Coulouris. The gangster persuades Grant to join his band of thieves, knowing that Grant will spend his ill-gotten gain on the high-living Duprez. Feeling guilty because of his participation in some robberies, Grant withdraws from Coulouris' evil gang, but Duprez demands more and more luxuries. Learning from Shayne that his mother has been concealing cancer and is on the brink of death, Grant becomes a dutiful son, though he doesn't let on that he knows about the cancer. Working all hours, repairing furniture and clocks, Grant tries to cheer up Barrymore whenever he can. Never close, mother and son now form a strong bond. Barrymore knows that Grant is impoverished and cannot even contemplate his future without a nest egg, so, hoping to leave him a legacy, she begins to receive stolen property. Arrested and imprisoned for her law-breaking, Barrymore dies in a prison hospital, leaving Grant to make his way alone and to become—as the opening narration suggests—the unknown soldier of WWII.

Odets' powerful script and direction do well by the Llewellyn novel, and the film is unyielding, uncompromising in its portrayal of slum life and fragile dreams lost in the gutter. It does not shrink from the depressing and sordid; only in Grant's indomitable spirit is there hope. Nevertheless, NONE BUT THE LONELY HEART was not a box-office winner, yet it has remained a film classic, enhanced by a dedicated cast. To get

Barrymore into the film during its hurried production schedule, RKO paid the expenses of closing the long-running play "The Corn Is Green," in which the actress was starring. She ended up winning the Best Supporting Actress Oscar for her performance, while Grant earned a Best Actor nomination (losing to Bing Crosby for GOING MY WAY). The film also earned nominations for its score and its editing.

NORMA RAE

1979 110m c   ★★★★
Drama   PG
FOX

Sally Field (Norma Rae), Beau Bridges (Sonny), Ron Leibman (Reuben), Pat Hingle (Vernon), Barbara Baxley (Leona), Gail Strickland (Bonnie Mae), Morgan Paull (Wayne Billings), Robert Broyles (Sam Bolen), John Calvin (Ellis Harper), Booth Colman (Dr. Watson)

p, Tamara Asseyev, Alexandra Rose; d, Martin Ritt; w, Irving Ravetch, Harriet Frank, Jr.; ph, John A. Alonzo (Panavision, Deluxe Color); ed, Sidney Levin; m, David Shire; prod d, Walter Scott Herndon; art d, Tracy Bousman

Sally Field won her first Oscar for her performance in the title role, a complex portrayal of an ill-educated southern woman who matures into a complete person when she is faced with labor woes and must grow up or fall by the wayside. Field is one of many overworked and underpaid workers at a cotton mill where management doesn't seem to realize that the days of slavery are over. Her father, Hingle, dies for lack of proper medical attention, while her mother, Baxley, is rapidly going deaf from the incessant din of the factory's equipment. The place is functioning without a union, and when New York labor organizer Leibman arrives to establish one, the workers fear for their jobs. When Field and Leibman first meet, his aggressive personality irritates her, while her lack of ambition does the same to him; but as the film progresses, so does their mutual respect. A divorced woman with two children (one of whom is illegitimate), Field marries Bridges, who becomes jealous of her relationship with Leibman once she decides to to join the union organizer in his efforts to unite the workers. Field begins undermining management from within and eventually manages to rally the workers into a strike. Production at the mill ceases, and management must capitulate in order to keep production rolling.

The simple story is enlivened by an intelligent, compassionate screenplay, whose sole deficiency is that it makes no attempt to represent the management point of view. Field's performance is flawless. Shire's song "It Goes Like It Goes" took an Oscar; the screenplay was nominated, as was the picture, but it lost on both counts to KRAMER VS. KRAMER. Audiences thronged to see NORMA RAE, which made more money than just about any other union movie with the possible exception of ON THE WATERFRONT. (NORMA RAE grossed well over $10 million on initial release.) The film's technical excellence is at least partly due to director Ritt's using the same crew he used on many of his films about the south; Alonzo, Levin, and Herndon have a history of working well with each other and with Ritt.

NORTH BY NORTHWEST

1959 136m c   ★★★★
Spy   /PG
MGM

Cary Grant (George Kaplan), Eva Marie Saint (Eve Kendall), James Mason (Phillip Vandamm), Jessie Royce Landis (Clara

Thornhill), Leo G. Carroll *(Professor)*, Philip Ober *(Lester Townsend)*, Josephine Hutchinson *(Handsome Woman)*, Martin Landau *(Leonard)*, Adam Williams *(Valerian)*, Edward Platt *(Victor Larrabee)*

p, Alfred Hitchcock; d, Alfred Hitchcock; w, Ernest Lehman; ph, Robert Burks (VistaVision, Technicolor); ed, George Tomasini; m, Bernard Herrmann; prod d, Robert Boyle; art d, William A. Horning, Merrill Pye; fx, A. Arnold Gillespie, Lee LeBlanc

One of Hitchcock's most famous, NORTH BY NORTHWEST has everything—thrills, suspense, intrigue, mystery, humor—revealing the director at his most giddy and playful. Roger Thornhill (Grant, in perennially spectacular form) is a successful advertising executive in New York City who is lunching with mother (Landis, the exact same age as Grant) at Plaza Hotel's Oak Room when he answers the wrong page, one for a George Kaplan, and is mistaken for Kaplan. It becomes an identity which Thornhill cannot shake and one that drags him across the country in the face of death with the pretty Eve Kendall (Saint, who plays her part in awe to be opposite Grant) at his side. The great suspense director was at his most entertaining (if not sexy—NOTORIOUS—or original—THE LADY VANISHES or STRANGERS ON A TRAIN), creating a helter skelter action film where the hero is propelled from one breathless situation to the next. It is filled with classic scenes—the two most memorable being the crop-dusting sequence in which Thornhill is terrorized by an aerial menace, and the chase across the face of Mt. Rushmore. The title of the film stems from a line appearing in "Hamlet," in which Hamlet states: "I am but mad north-north-west; when the wind is southerly I know a hawk from a handsaw," an implication that neither Thornhill, Hitchcock, nor Hamlet is mad. Although NORTH BY NORTHWEST is available on videotape, no small screen viewing can match the Technicolor, VistaVision experience of seeing this one in the theater. With James Mason, a study in velvet villany, but looking dowdy for once, next to Grant and Landau as one of Hitch's homophobic weaklings.

NORTH DALLAS FORTY

1979   119m   c   ★★★½
Sports   R/18
Paramount

Nick Nolte *(Phillip Elliott)*, Mac Davis *(Maxwell)*, Charles Durning *(Coach Johnson)*, Dayle Haddon *(Charlotte)*, Bo Svenson *(Jo Bob Priddy)*, Steve Forrest *(Conrad Hunter)*, G.D. Spradlin *(B.A. Strothers)*, Dabney Coleman *(Emmett)*, Savannah Smith *(Joanne)*, Marshall Colt *(Art Hartman)*

p, Frank Yablans; d, Ted Kotcheff; w, Frank Yablans, Ted Kotcheff, Peter Gent (based on the novel by Gent); ph, Paul Lohmann (Panavision, Metrocolor); ed, Jay Kamen; m, John Scott; prod d, Alfred Sweeney; cos, Dorothy Jeakins

Pro football fans may be disillusioned by this excellent, honest, and often brutal expose of the play-for-pay game. Phillip Elliott (Nick Nolte) is a veteran pass-catcher for the North Dallas Bulls, who bear a strong resemblance to the Dallas Cowboys—not surprising given that the film is based on a novel by former Cowboy wide receiver Pete Gent. The coaches (G.D. Spradlin and Charles Durning) and team owner (Steve Forrest) feel the fiercely independent Elliott has an attitude problem because of his blatant cynicism and his awareness of how he and his teammates are constantly being manipulated by management. Cast aside after being callously used to motivate a fellow player, the receiver comes to realize there is more to life than football, but

that he loves the game just the same. Country singer Mac Davis, making his film debut, is quite good as the quarterback who is Elliott's best friend and knows how to play the game both on and off the field and Bo Svenson is effective as a big, dumb defensive lineman. The National Football League refused to help with the production of this film in any way, so the action is kept to a minimum (though what *is* shown is brutal), but the locker room atmosphere and the off-the-field drama smack of authenticity in NORTH DALLAS FORTY, as telling a depiction of pro football as any to be found. Note the presence of one-time Oakland Raider behemoth John Matuszak, who went on to appear in films such as CAVEMAN and THE GOONIES before his death in 1989.

NORTHWEST PASSAGE

1940   125m   c   ★★★★★
Adventure   /A
MGM

Spencer Tracy *(Maj. Robert Rogers)*, Robert Young *(Langdon Towne)*, Walter Brennan *(Hunk Marriner)*, Ruth Hussey *(Elizabeth Browne)*, Nat Pendleton *(Capt. Huff)*, Louis Hector *(Rev. Browne)*, Robert Barrat *(Humphrey Towne)*, Lumsden Hare *(Gen. Amherst)*, Donald MacBride *(Sgt. McNott)*, Isabel Jewell *(Jennie Coit)*

p, Hunt Stromberg; d, King Vidor, Jack Conway (uncredited); w, Laurence Stallings, Talbot Jennings (based on the novel by Kenneth Roberts); ph, Sidney Wagner, William V. Skall (Technicolor); ed, Conrad A. Nervig; m, Herbert Stothart; art d, Cedric Gibbons, Malcolm Brown

One of the greatest adventure films of all time, this Vidor classic owes much of its success to the rugged Tracy, who plays celebrated Indian fighter Robert Rogers, leader of Rogers' Rangers. Tracy is earthy, eloquent, and utterly awesome as the frontier leader who knows no fear in a wilderness rife with terror and bloodshed. Set in 1759, the film opens with talented artist Young arriving home in Portsmouth, New Hampshire, to sheepishly explain to his family that he has been expelled from Harvard because of the snide political comments he has inserted into his cartoons. Naturally, his criticism is aimed at the British, which alienates finacee Hussey's Tory family. Young and his roughneck sidekick, Brennan, get drunk in a pub one night and tell off Hussey's stuffed-shirt father, Hector. As a result, Young's arrest is ordered, but he and Brennan escape into the wilderness, later stopping at a wayside inn, where they meet Tracy. After a night of hard drinking, Young and Brennan wake up outside the military post at Crown Point, headquarters of Tracy's rangers. Tracy entices Young to join the Rangers as a mapmaker, and Brennan tags along. Soon Young and Brennan are boating along with hundreds of other leather-clad veterans of many an Indian war. Their goal is St. Francis, the headquarters of the vicious, French-backed Abernaki tribe, which has conducted bloody raids into colonial territory under British control. Tracy has been ordered to annihilate the Abernakis and then escape by an uncharted route. The Rangers work their way through the wilderness but disaffected Indian guides cause trouble, and some of the powder carried by the Rangers accidentally explodes, wounding several dozen men. Tracy sends a quarter of his force back to Crown Point with the Indians and proceeds with the rest of his men. The Rangers portage their huge boats over impossible hills and through woods until they find waterways feeding Lake Champlain, which is controlled by the French. When they can no longer row, the Rangers hide their boats and slog through swamps to cover their tracks. The men who fall ill or are injured are left behind to face the merciless enemy. Regis Toomey is one of these casualties; having broken a leg in the swamp, he positions himself on a tree limb just above water level, takes a long chaw of tobacco, and is grateful for the extra ammunition and food Tracy leaves with him.

Young is stunned by the harsh realities of Tracy's campaign, but he soon learns the lessons of survival in the wilderness. At one point, a wild river blocks the path of the Rangers, but they form a human chain, stretching from one river bank to the other. (This is only one of many spectacular scenes in a film packed with extraordinary physical feats.) When the Rangers arrive at St. Francis, they follow Tracy's carefully constructed battle plan, attacking the French and Indians from four sides, slaughtering the enemy. After discovering that the main French force is away but will soon return, Tracy orders that the white captives be brought along with the Rangers. Among those taken prisoner is Jewell, who has been with the Abernakis so long that she is half-savage herself. In the wake of the battle, Young is found wounded, a bullet in his stomach. Knowing that he must either motivate Young to stay on his feet or leave him behind, Tracy orders Jewell to tend to the wounded Ranger. The mapmaker improves as he moves, his bleeding stops, and he slowly regains his strength. With the French hot on their trail, the Rangers flee through the wilderness. Splitting into smaller groups, they head for Lake Memphremagog but find no food or British troops waiting for them as expected. Starving and exhausted, the Rangers push on toward old Fort Wentworth, going solely on Tracy's promise that the British will be waiting for them with great stores of food. When they finally do stumble on the fort, they find it abandoned. All seems lost, but the fifes and drums of an approaching British relief force are heard. Tracy and his skeletal force stand bravely at attention as the British march in bearing armloads of food. Back in Portsmouth, recuperating from their ordeal, the Rangers are ordered to prepare for an adventure that will make their recent exploit seem like "a duck hunt." Tracy explains to his men that they are going to Fort Detroit and then push westward to find a northwest passage to the Pacific. Young, however, decides to stay behind and pursue his art.

Based on Kenneth Roberts's well-researched novel about Rogers's exploits, NORTHWEST PASSAGE is a rousing adventure all the way, full of thundering action. Its depiction of the colonial era is amazingly convincing, thanks to the perfectionist techniques of director King Vidor, who went at the $2 million production with the vigor and relentless energy of Robert Rogers himself. Vidor, who began working on the film with an incomplete script (new portions of which were flown daily to the production's Idaho location), believed that he was shooting a prologue for a film that would also include Rogers's search for the Northwest Passage. However, producer Hunt Stromberg and MGM decided to confine the film to Rogers's adventures during the Indian Wars. As a result Jack Conway was brought in to shoot an ending to the film when Vidor was called to New York. To make his "prologue," Vidor took his almost all-male cast into the wilds of Idaho, around Lake Payette, which resembled the New England terrain of 200 years earlier. There, for 70 days, Vidor drove his cast and crew nonstop. In the river-crossing sequence, which was shot in two days (with additional footage later filmed in the studio tank), no doubles were employed and Tracy wore out two pairs of leather pants as he anchored himself to a tree next to the river to begin the human chain. The more than 300 native Americans hired as warriors and extras in the film actually had less to do than the white actors and were under less strain, yet the local Indians hired for the film refused to act for the $5-a-day fee Vidor was offering, insisting upon $10. With dubious reasoning, Tracy told Vidor to tell them they were only

playing half-breeds and therefore not entitled to full pay. He did and the Indians surprisingly accepted the $5-a-day fee.

Originally, MGM had slated the colossal adventure tale for Tracy, Robert Taylor, Wallace Beery, and Franchot Tone, but only Tracy actually took part, with Young and Brennan brought in for support. Tracy got along with Vidor but reportedly later refused to work with him again because of the director's slave-driving techniques. Still, Vidor was always uncompromising in his praise for Tracy. Splintered tale though it might be, NORTHWEST PASSAGE is nevertheless a powerful and moving picture, Vidor's first in Technicolor. He made good use of the verdant location sites; Wagner and Skall's cinematography is absolutely breathtaking, capturing the rich blues of the lakes and the deep greens of the forests, although they had some trouble with the drab greens of the ranger costumes, until special dyes were ordered to tone down the kelly green hues. Wagner and Skall were nominated for an Oscar for their work, but lost to George Perinal for THE THIEF OF BAGHDAD. The film was a great box-office and critical success and is considered to be one of Vidor's true masterworks. The story was remade in a TV series in 1959-60 for NBC, starring Keith Larsen as Rogers, Buddy Ebsen as Mariner, and Don Burnett as Towne.

NOSFERATU, THE VAMPIRE
(NOSFERATU, PHANTOM DER NACHT)
1979 107m c   ★★★
Horror   PG/15
FOX   (France/West Germany)

Klaus Kinski *(Count Dracula)*, Isabelle Adjani *(Lucy Harker)*, Bruno Ganz *(Jonathan Harker)*, Roland Topor *(Renfield)*, Walter Ladengast *(Dr. Van Helsing)*, Dan Van Husen *(Warden)*, Jan Groth *(Harbormaster)*, Carsten Bodinus *(Schrader)*, Martje Grohmann *(Mina)*, Rijk de Gooyer *(Town Official)*

p, Werner Herzog; d, Werner Herzog; w, Werner Herzog (based on the novel *Dracula* by Bram Stoker and the film script NOSFERATU by Henrik Galeen); ph, Jorg Schmidt-Reitwein (Eastmancolor); ed, Beate Mainka-Jellinghaus; m, Popol Vuh, Florian Fricke, Richard Wagner, Charles Gounod; prod d, Henning von Gierke, Ulrich Bergfelder; art d, Henning von Gierke; fx, Cornelius Siegel; cos, Gloria Storch

After capturing the attention of American critics and public with ambitious, unique, and powerful films, German director Werner Herzog remade what he considers to be the most visionary and important of all German films, a remake of F.W. Murnau's 1922 silent masterpiece, NOSFERATU. Held together by the sheer power of Klaus Kinski's performance as the vampire, NOSFERATU, THE VAMPIRE evokes several scenes (practically shot-for-shot) from the Murnau classic while slightly altering some of the original's thematic structures. In Murnau's film, the vampire is pure evil invading a small German community (Herzog feels that the 1922 film adumbrated the rise of Nazism in Germany). Herzog's vampire is much more sympathetic. An outcast from society (as are all of Herzog's protagonists), Kinski's Nosferatu longs for contact, acceptance, and even love from the humans who fear and revile him. Sadly, his curse and death's-head appearance forever prevent this. The vampire's undead state and need for blood seem to be presented as a horrible, irreversible *disease*, rather than an inherently evil harbinger of hell. While this isn't exactly an innovation in the development of the horror film (Tod Browning's DRACULA, 1931, starring Bela Lugosi, had moments of pathos, as does George Romero's MARTIN), Herzog and Kinski succeed here because they convey a sense of pity for a creature so visually repulsive it's hard to look at him.

As with most of Herzog's films, the story behind the production is almost more interesting than the film itself. Unable to shoot in Bremen, as Murnau did in 1922, Herzog prepared to settle for the Dutch town of Delft. Still bitter over their occupation by the Nazis during WWII, the citizens of Delft were less than enthusiastic about this small army of German filmmakers invading their town. When Herzog announced his plan to release 11,000 rats into the streets of Delft for the scene in which Nosferatu arrives (the director wanted grey rats but could only obtain white ones, which his crew painted grey), the Delft *burgermeister* categorically refused and told the apparently insane German that his town had just spent months clearing the canals of their own home-grown rats and had no intention of reinfesting the area with laboratory rats from Hungary. Nonplussed, Herzog moved his rats to a more accommodating city, Schiedam, where he was allowed to shoot, albeit on a smaller scale.

NOSTALGHIA

1984 120m c/bw ★★★★
Drama /15
Sovin/RAI-TV/Opera (U.S.S.R./Italy)

Oleg Yankovsky *(Andre Gortchakov)*, Domiziana Giordano *(Eugenia)*, Erland Josephson *(Domenico)*, Patrizia Terreno *(Gortchakov's Wife)*, Delia Boccardo *(Domenico's Wife)*, Laura De Marchi *(Chambermaid)*, Milena Vukotic *(Civil Servant)*, Alberto Canepa *(Farmer)*

d, Andrei Tarkovsky; w, Andrei Tarkovsky, Tonino Guerra; ph, Giuseppe Lanci (Technicolor); ed, Amedeo Salfa, Erminia Marani; m, Ludwig van Beethoven, Giuseppe Verdi; prod d, Andrea Grisanti; fx, Paolo Ricci; cos, Lina Nerli Taviani

A meditative film by visionary Soviet filmmaker Tarkovsky that lures viewers into its mysterious, mystical world and completely envelops them for a two-hour stretch. Yankovsky is a Soviet architecture professor who travels to northern Italy's Tuscan Hills to research an exiled 18th-century Russian composer who committed suicide there. Away from his homeland, Yankovsky becomes nostalgic suffering with his unfulfilled desire to return to a home that is out of reach. The melancholy Yankovsky becomes involved with Giordano, his volatile, strong-minded interpreter. Their relationshop, however, is never consummated and gradually deteriorates. Their romance is strained even further by Yankovsky's growing friendship with Josephson, a batty Italian professor who years ago locked his family inside their house and awaited Armageddon—for seven years. Josephson proves too much for Giordano, who makes plans to return to her lover in Rome. Yankovsky finds Josephson living among the rain-soaked ruins of a 16th-century spa. In this ancient crumbling structure is a large, placid mineral bath that Josephson unsuccessfully tries to wade across (its waters are chest-high) while holding a lit candle. His crazy belief is that to save mankind he must cross the bath without letting the candle flame extinguish. Having once again failed, Josephson makes a public proclamation. He climbs atop Michelangelo's statue of Marcus Aurelius in Rome, plays Beethoven's "Ode to Joy" on a portable turntable, and shouts prophetic doomsday messages to those who'll listen. At the same time, Yankovsky has taken up Josephson's plight to cross the bath. His first two attempts fail, each time the candle flame flickering out in the swirling drafts of hot air. Back atop the statue, Josephson soaks himself with kerosene and sets himself ablaze. As he burns to death, Yankovsky completes a

successful trip across the waters. The candle burns, but Yankovsky's energy is extinguished. Struggling at the water's edge to stay alive, Yankovsky envisions his homeland as the snow covers its grassy hills.

The final sequence of NOSTALGHIA is one of the most captivating ever put on film. The viewer becomes completely swept away by Tarkovsky's world where the elements reign supreme—fire and water are everywhere. The atmosphere Tarkovsky creates is one of constantly dripping water, unsettling mists, and dew seeping through the eternally damp walls. Coupled with these memorable visuals is a remarkable highlighting of sounds (a job admirably performed by Remo Ugolinelli) such as the echoing drip of water or the swirling of the drafts. NOSTALGHIA is not a film for everyone—if it is fast-paced action you desire, then you will quickly be snoring. Instead of excitement, the feeling one gets after seeing NOSTALGHIA is one of utter relaxation that makes us long for the world we left behind in the theater.

NOTHING BUT A MAN

1964 95m bw ★★★
Drama /A
Du Art

Ivan Dixon *(Duff Anderson)*, Abbey Lincoln *(Josie Dawson)*, Gloria Foster *(Lee)*, Julius Harris *(Will Anderson)*, Martin Priest *(Driver)*, Leonard Parker *(Frankie)*, Yaphet Kotto *(Jocko)*, Stanley Greene *(Rev. Dawson)*, Helen Lounck *(Effie Simms)*, Helene Arrindell *(Doris)*

p, Robert Young, Michael Roemer, Robert Rubin; d, Michael Roemer; w, Michael Roemer, Robert Malcolm Young; ph, Robert Young; ed, Luke Bennett; prod d, William Rhodes; cos, Nancy Ruffing

A well-intentioned, independently made film describing the life of a black man in the 1960s South. Basically, all the title character (Dixon) wants to do is live simply. While working for the railroad in Alabama, he falls in love with Lincoln, the daughter of the minister (Greene). Greene does not like Dixon, so the couple goes to Birmingham to see Dixon's father, a dying alcoholic. Dixon also visits his illegitimate son, who has been abandoned by his mother and left in the care of a woman not related to him. Lincoln wants to marry, but Dixon does not want to assume the responsibility. The couple finally weds, and Dixon gets a job at the town sawmill. When he won't ingratiate himself to his racist white employers, he is fired and labeled a troublemaker. He then finds work at a gas station but is still harassed by the townspeople. After beating and berating his wife, out of frustration, he returns to Birmingham to watch his father die. Facing the situation is a step toward manhood, and he begins to come to terms with his responsibilities. He gets his son and goes back to Lincoln to try to live in peace and dignity. The film garnered a great deal of praise, at the time of its release, for its realistic recounting of the life of a black laborer in the South and for refusing to sentimentalize the subject matter.

NOTHING BUT THE BEST

1964 99m c ★★
Comedy /A
Domino (U.K.)

Alan Bates *(Jimmy Brewster)*, Denholm Elliott *(Charlie Prince)*, Harry Andrews *(Mr. Horton)*, Millicent Martin *(Ann Horton)*, Pauline Delany *(Mrs. March)*, Godfrey Quigley *(Coates)*, Alison Leggatt

(*Mrs. Brewster*), Lucinda Curtis (*Nadine*), Nigel Stock (*Ferris*), James Villiers (*Hugh*)

p, David Deutsch; d, Clive Donner; w, Frederic Raphael (based on the short story "The Best of Everything" by Stanley Ellin); ph, Nicolas Roeg (Eastmancolor); ed, Fergus McDonell; m, Ron Grainer; art d, Reece Pemberton

Ellin wrote some of the best and most chilling short stories , including the famous "Specialty of the House" that was made into an eerie Alfred Hitchcock half-hour. He is not given his due in this spotty adaptation by Raphael, who is usually much better than he is here. Bates is a lower-class real estate clerk who aspires to move up the ladder. He will stop at nothing to achieve social status and hires Elliott, a degenerate character, to teach him manners and deportment suitable for the upper-crust society that Bates means to crack. Elliott instructs Bates (the way Higgins did with Eliza) in all the niceties, and Bates moves in on his boss's daughter, Martin. Her father, Andrews, watches carefully as Bates makes his calculated approach. Martin sees right through Bates, but Bates is handsome and is lots more fun than the twits who surround the girl. After Elliott wins a bundle at the races, he is of a mind to blow the whistle on Bates, who puts an end to those thoughts by putting an end to Elliott. He strangles Elliott with his necktie and, with the help of landlady Delany (who is smitten by Bates), stows the body in a huge trunk and hides it in her basement. With Elliott out of the way, Bates continues to woo Martin and soon marries her. While the couple is honeymooning, Delany sells her property and takes a trip to South Africa. Bates and Martin return—Bates confident that he has achieved everything he set out to do, as he has been made Andrews's partner as well as his son-in-law. The smile soon dissolves when he sees that Delany's house is being razed by workmen, and the picture ends as Bates watches and winces and worries about the discovery of Elliott's body. This picture aspires to be a comedy in the grand tradition of KIND HEARTS AND CORONETS, but Bates has neither the comedic skill nor the kind of sex appeal required to pull it off. Martin is beautiful and does what she can with the slim material given her. Good cinematography from Roeg who went on to be a confusing director.

NOTHING SACRED

1937 75m c   ★★★★★
Comedy   /A
Selznick

Carole Lombard (*Hazel Flagg*), Fredric March (*Wally Cook*), Charles Winninger (*Dr. Enoch Downer*), Walter Connolly (*Oliver Stone*), Sig Rumann (*Dr. Emile Egglehoffer*), Frank Fay (*MC*), Maxie Rosenbloom (*Max Levinsky*), Margaret Hamilton (*Drug Store Lady*), Troy Brown (*Ernest Walker*), Olin Howlin (*Baggage Man*)

p, David O. Selznick; d, William A. Wellman; w, Ben Hecht, Ring Lardner, Jr., Budd Schulberg (based on the story "Letter to the Editor" by James H. Street); ph, W. Howard Greene (Technicolor); ed, Hal C. Kern, James E. Newcom; m, Oscar Levant; art d, Lyle Wheeler; fx, Jack Cosgrove; cos, Travis Banton, Walter Plunkett

A marvelous black comedy full of wit and journalistic wisdom in the grand and capricious style of Hecht (who co-authored, with Charles MacArthur, THE FRONT PAGE), this film is all the more stunning thanks to the outrageous and hilarious performance of super comedienne Lombard. This was one of the first of the screwball comedies, a classic of the genre which is just as funny today as when it was first filmed. March is an ambitious newsman who gets into big trouble when he tries to pass off a New York Negro as the "Sultan of Marzipan," a potentate who is about to donate $500,000 to establish an art institute. The Negro is actually penniless and doesn't know Marzipan from Manhattan. When Connolly, the editor of March's sensation-seeking tabloid, finds out about the impersonation, he becomes livid and demotes March to writing obituaries. Meanwhile, Lombard, a working girl in Warsaw, Vermont, who longs to visit New York City, is routinely examined by her less than competent doctor, Winninger; the bumbling doctor sadly tells Lombard that she has radium poisoning and will only live a short while. News of this tragedy reaches March and he sets out to write a great sob story, but by the time he reaches Lombard, Winninger has changed his diagnosis: Lombard will live a long time since she isn't poisoned after all. March won't hear of it; he has a great story and refuses to allow the truth to ruin his fabulous tale. He persuades Lombard to go through with the charade, promising that she will not only see New York but will enter the great city in style. She agrees, and by the time March begins grinding out the tragedy in daily installments in his paper, New York is weeping loudly. Lombard arrives, is given the key to the city and is installed in one of Manhattan's most lavish hotels, her suite and every convenience, including expensive clothes, jewels, nonstop service, provided for by Connolly, Rumann, and other magnates wishing to look good to the world. March takes Lombard out dining and she gets drunk, passing out. The shocked sob sisters are quickly informed that Lombard has had a relapse due to her deadly illness and this causes another rash of city-wide bawling. Everywhere Lombard goes, women weep and men gulp down sorrow. At public events, such as a wrestling match in Madison Square Garden, her appearance causes authorities to demand "minutes of respect," where crowds stand in sorrowful silence for the soon-to-be-deceased Lombard. But the beautiful blonde continues to thrive, and her condition appears much too robust for editor Connolly's liking. Suspicious of his star reporter March, Connolly orders a team of expert physicians to examine Lombard. Just before the medical people arrive in her suite, March arranges to rough up the now disgusted Lombard, so she'll be properly run-down. He not only bruises and pummels her but lands a terrific right cross to her face. (This lady-beating scene became one of the most famous and hilarious sequences in Hollywood history.) Still, Lombard cannot conceal her good health forever, and a group of her financial backers, suddenly wise to her ruse, ask her, please, to find a way to die and save them all further spiritual mortification. March and Lombard prepare an elaborate but fake suicide for the lady and then they sail away in disguise, wearing sunglasses, en route to a new life together.

Hecht had a great deal of fun writing NOTHING SACRED for the screen, plucking the background from his own newspaper experiences. The fake sultan, for instance, was based upon a prank Hecht himself had concocted, one in which his eccentric poet friend Maxwell Bodenheim, then unknown, pretended to be a foreign potentate visiting Chicago where Hecht was working as a spectacular journalist. Like the fake poisoning shown in NOTHING SACRED, Hecht himself had "created" many a news story during his days in Chicago as a journalist, sprucing up slow news days with reports of nonexistent earthquakes, fires, and untraceable tragedies. Of course, the role of the errant reporter is based on his incredible exploits. Lombard is wonderfully funny in NOTHING SACRED, playing a role that was made for her madcap talent, and March, one of the fine serious actors, showed his considerable flair for comedy in this delightful farce. Director Wellman squirmed with delight with Hecht's spoofing script and his amused attitude affected every aspect of the film production.

He was overheard by Lombard and March to say that "a little fun is the best tonic between scenes," and the leading lady and man jumped on that line. Lombard was vexed when she tried to talk to Wellman about her scenes; he would only shake his head and walk away. She fixed Wellman by having several technicians grab him one day, slip him into a straightjacket and tie him to his director's chair so she could have his undivided attention. She even infected March with her penchant for zany antics and the two of them spent their off-camera hours driving madly about the Selznick lot in a rented fire engine. The pace of this great film is so brisk that the viewers will have to remind themselves just what scene caused the laughter to start, and it's a film with a laugh a minute throughout. Frank Capra borrowed some of this story line for MEET JOHN DOE, and the film would be remade as a Broadway musical entitled HAZEL FLAGG. Dean Martin and Jerry Lewis appeared in the 1954 remake, LIVING IT UP.

NOTORIOUS

1946   101m   bw   ★★★★★
Thriller/Spy   /U
RKO

Cary Grant (Devlin), Ingrid Bergman (Alicia Huberman), Claude Rains (Alexander Sebastian), Louis Calhern (Paul Prescott), Mme. Konstantin (Mme. Sebastian), Reinhold Schunzel (Dr. Anderson), Moroni Olsen (Walter Beardsley), Ivan Triesault (Eric Mathis), Alexis Minotis (Joseph), Wally Brown (Mr. Hopkins)

p, Alfred Hitchcock; d, Alfred Hitchcock; w, Ben Hecht; ph, Ted Tetzlaff; ed, Theron Warth; m, Roy Webb; art d, Albert S. D'Agostino, Carroll Clark; fx, Vernon L. Walker, Paul Eagler; cos, Edith Head

This brilliant Hitchcock offering combines romance, suspense, and international intrigue with unforgettable performances from Grant and Bergman. Okay, there's more complex Hitch to be had elsewhere, but for us diehard romantics, this is the swoon supreme. The thriller trappings are merely trim: what's really at hand is a sado-masochistic, twisted love affair between Grant and Bergman. He's untrusting, passive and unsympathetic. She's shady, agressive and an alcoholic. The gloss is all trim, too: underneath lies exploitation of women, co-dependence upon men, both in the name of true love. It's a dangerous chocolate box of posioned candy, Hitchcock's ode to the dementia of passion. Dig in.

Alicia Huberman (Bergman), the daughter of a convicted Nazi spy, has an international jet set reputation as a playgirl, causing American agent Devlin (Grant) to fall in love with her. Devlin, in an effort to uncover a Nazi plot, enlists Alicia's aid in Rio de Janeiro. They contact Nazi agent Alexander Sebastian (Rains), whom Alicia must eventually marry. Meanwhile, Devlin and she must discover how the Sebastian plot is being engineered. With the blistering onscreen romance between Grant and Bergman—two of the most popular stars in Hollywood—and the creation of one of Hitchcock's greatest "MacGuffins"—the secret uranium shipments—NOTORIOUS emerges as one of Hitchcock's most masterful and sophisticated efforts. The passionate kissing scene in which the lovers devour themselves instead of their chicken dinner still retains all of its power. Ingrid Bergman was certainly never sexier: here's the woman who scandalized America with her torrid, extramarital affair. Next to the protagonists, Rains's expert villany as mama's boyism gone awry. And no wonder. With Mdme. Leopold Konstantin chomping cigars, Hitch really flails away at motherhood. The camera swoons right slong with us in a dizzying manner. Best shot: the key. You can't miss it.

NOW, VOYAGER

1942   117m   bw   ★★★★
Drama   /PG
WB

Bette Davis (Charlotte Vale), Paul Henreid (Jerry D. Durrance), Claude Rains (Dr. Jaquith), Gladys Cooper (Mrs. Henry Windle Vale), Bonita Granville (June Vale), John Loder (Elliott Livingston), Ilka Chase (Lisa Vale), Lee Patrick ("Deb" McIntyre), James Rennie (Frank McIntyre), Charles Drake (Leslie Trotter)

p, Hal B. Wallis; d, Irving Rapper; w, Casey Robinson (based on the novel by Olive Higgins Prouty); ph, Sol Polito; ed, Warren Low; m, Max Steiner; art d, Robert Haas; fx, Willard Van Enger; cos, Orry-Kelly

Now, Bette: A glittering, slushy take on the ugly duckling transformation. It's Olive Higgins Prouty, at it again (she also penned Stella Dallas, the durable soap opera from which three films, including the Barbara Stanwyck classic, were made), with a title lifted from Walt Whitman's Leaves of Grass, a conceit enough to raise a dead poet. Irving Rapper directs as if he wants to stay out of the way of Davis and Cooper—perfectly understandable.

As usual, Davis has to overplay her hand at Jekyll/Hyde transformation. Beforehand, she's got unplucked eyebrows like last spring's dead caterpillars, hair like a mudpuddle with a net over it, and glasses and shoes borrowed from the first continental congress. It sets a satisfyingly camp feeling of self-sacrifice over the entire proceedings. Later she is artfully styled; you have the feeling Davis is shedding her own New England repression, which is exactly what she means for you to feel.

Davis plays the dowdy, frustrated daughter of Cooper, with whom she lives in the oppressive Boston mansion. Davis is close to a nervous breakdown because she can't get any love from Cooper, who also forces her to dress "sensibly." Chase, Davis's sister-in-law, worries about Davis's mental condition and enlists the services of famed psychiatrist Rains, who sees that Davis is near collapse and recommends that she leave her lonely home and take refuge at his sanitarium. There, Davis begins a regimen that begins to restore her mental and physical health; she drops pounds and gains confidence daily, transforming into a self-assured swan within three months (a feat none of us can seem to master so quickly). At Rains's suggestion, Davis boards a liner for South America. On the cruise, she meets Henreid, whose wife pretends to be in bad health to keep her unhappy husband from ending their marriage. On a stopover in Rio, Davis and Henreid enjoy a wonderful day and night together, then wake up to discover that their ship has already left the port. They stay in Rio for a few days and Davis experiences passionate love for the first time in her life, although she understands from the start that Henreid will never leave his wife.

Though VOYAGER is best remembered for the scene in which Henreid lights two cigarettes simultaneously and then hands one to Davis, this pleasurable, popular tearjerker is Davis's show all the way. She claimed to have worked extensively on the screenplay, deleting some of Casey Robinson's hard work in favor of Prouty's original words. Cooper is an excellent choice for the matriarchal dowager; Davis always stood in awe (or angry envy) of stage actors, and their scenes have a weight the rest of the picture lacks. Henreid and Rains, both great friends of Davis's (and supposedly Rains a lover) contribute smooth work. The marvelous Ilka Chase is wasted here, and Bonita Granville's take on irritant is grating and overacted. The Polito camerawork finally settles down to Davis-devotion and Steiner's Oscar-winning score clings to her like lush flypaper. It's Grade-A schlock at its most maudlin, classic soapflakes—you just add the tears. And if it's not the moon, at least you have one hell of a star.

NUMBER TWO
(NUMERO DEUX)
1975 88m c ★★
Drama /X
Sonimage/Bela (France)

Sandrine Battistella *(Wife)*, Pierre Dudry *(Husband)*, Alexandre Rignault *(Grandpa)*, Rachel Stefanopoli *(Grandma)*

d, Jean-Luc Godard; w, Jean-Luc Godard

Announced by Godard as a remake of BREATHLESS (a ploy to get financing), this video project has almost nothing to do with his 1959 masterpiece. Battistella and Dudry are a dissatisfied couple who suffer from physical ailments. Battistella is stricken with chronic constipation, and her husband is unable to perform sexually. They teach their children about sex by showing them, and the grandparents, naked, speak directly to the camera. As Richard Roud writes, "although NUMERO DEUX is a frustrating film about frustration, a constipated film about constipation, it is not entirely without a sense of hope." Shot on videotape (and later transferred to film), the majority of the picture uses only a portion of the screen, usually the upper-left and the lower-right portions. The finish, however, relieves the tension this creates by opening up the entire screen. To further his interests in video, Godard built a studio in Grenoble where his tape experiments for French television continued until 1980 with the release of EVERY MAN FOR HIMSELF, marking his much-awaited return to commercial filmmaking and international distribution.

NUN'S STORY, THE
1959 149m c ★★★★★
Religious/Biography /U
WB

Audrey Hepburn *(Sister Luke/Gabrielle Van Der Mal)*, Peter Finch *(Dr. Fortunati)*, Edith Evans *(Mother Emmanuel Superior General)*, Peggy Ashcroft *(Mother Mathilde)*, Dean Jagger *(Dr. Van Der Mal)*, Mildred Dunnock *(Sister Margharita)*, Beatrice Straight *(Mother Christophe)*, Patricia Collinge *(Sister William)*, Eva Kotthaus *(Sister Marie)*, Ruth White *(Mother Marcella)*

p, Henry Blanke; d, Fred Zinnemann; w, Robert Anderson (based on the book by Kathryn C. Hulme); ph, Franz Planer (Technicolor); ed, Walter Thompson; m, Franz Waxman; art d, Alexander Trauner; cos, Marjorie Best

It's hard to believe that this rare and moving film did not win one single Oscar of the six for which it was nominated. The film, the direction, the screenplay, the photography, the music, and Miss Hepburn were all in the running, but 1959 saw the emergence of another religion-based film, BEN-HUR, which took most of those awards, with the others going to Simone Signoret and the screenplay for ROOM AT THE TOP. The story begins with the autobiographical bestseller by a one-time nun who chose to let the world know what it was like inside the walls of a convent. Several years later, a satirical film, NASTY HABITS, was made about the subject. Dame Edith Evans played the Abbess in that film, as she did in this one. Less knowledgeable handling of this story might have resulted in an overly sentimental or even melodramatic telling, but director Zinnemann and screenwriter Anderson resisted all temptation and have presented the eye and the soul with one of the best pictures ever made about the subject of man's struggle to understand God. Zinnemann chose his shots carefully and with an accent on simplicity, rather than resorting

to any cinematic tricks, and we must be grateful, for at no time does the style overcome the story. Hepburn is radiant and gives one of her best performances ever, and every role, no matter how miniscule, has been cast and played with excellence.

Hepburn is the daughter of Belgian surgeon Jagger, and she has the desire to become a nursing nun in the Congo, which was still overseen by Belgium at the time, several years prior to WWII. She enters a convent, and the first 30 minutes or so becomes an uneditorialized documentary segment about the young novitiate's experiences and her development from postulant to nun. The Order, which is never identified, is run by Evans, who admits that the life of a nun is, in many ways, a life against nature, but if one is willing to adhere to the principles, there are rewards to be found on earth as well as in Heaven. After watching the rigors of the cloistered existence, Hepburn is finally a nun and goes off to a school where she learns tropical medicine. Her desire to go to the Congo is sidetracked when she is first assigned to a mental hospital in Belgium where she is almost killed by a maniacal patient whom she thought she could handle. The authorities had asked her to stay away from the person, but she was guilty of the sin of pride and believed that she was capable of taking care of the patient. Eventually, she travels to the Congo where she is disappointed by her assignment. She'd hoped to do her nursing with natives, but is, instead, sent to a hospital for Europeans where she meets crusty Finch, a dedicated surgeon who has no room in his life for women or religion and devotes himself to his medical work. Hepburn understands that she must shed her old ways and plunges her life into work. The result is that she is stricken with a mild case of tuberculosis, although she is cured after her brief bout with it. Hepburn wants to be one with God and thinks that by staying in Africa she will expunge her brain of the memories she has and achieve that exalted state. Finch reckons she wants to remain in the Congo because she fears going back to the rigidity of the convent. He thinks that's the reason why she came down with TB.

Her next assignment is to squire a Belgian official back to the motherland, and she arrives there just as the war is beginning. Travel restrictions force her to stay in Europe and she's sent to a hospital near Holland. She sees what kind of people the invading Nazis are, but she is told to turn the other cheek to the enemies of Belgium and maintain her Christian attitude when dealing with them. When Jagger is killed by Nazis as he's helping refugees escape, she makes the conscious decision to involve herself in the struggle and joins the underground. It doesn't take much time before she realizes that she is incapable of keeping her dispassionate attitude and that she must leave the convent in order to fight against the oppressors. With her superior's permission, she goes through the steps necessary to unbind her from her vows and the picture fades out as Hepburn is walking away from the convent, totally alone.

This was perhaps the only movie from this studio (Warners) in which there was no music over the final titles. No one could decide if Waxman should write an upbeat or a downbeat theme because the choice would imply an editorial decision on the part of the filmmakers, something that Zinnemann zealously and successfully avoided all the way through. Jack Warner fought against that viewpoint, but Zinnemann prevailed, and the end credits are accompanied by silence. Assistant director Piero Mussetta used 70 members of Rome's Royal Opera Ballet to stage a sequence in which nuns are involved in various rituals. That sequence should be viewed by every film student as an exercise in how to handle a large group. Hepburn is Belgian-born of a Dutch mother and a British father. She spent the war in Holland, where she and her mother were caught at the start of the battles, and so she could identify with the plight of the character she played. THE NUN'S STORY has it all—warmth, drama, humor, and a sense of taste that is hard to find these days.

NUTS

1987 116m c	★★½
Drama	R/18
Barwood	

Barbra Streisand (*Claudia Draper*), Richard Dreyfuss (*Aaron Levinsky*), Maureen Stapleton (*Rose Kirk, Claudia's Mother*), Karl Malden (*Arthur Kirk*), Eli Wallach (*Dr. Herbert A. Morrison, Psychiatrist*), Robert Webber (*Francis MacMillan, Prosecuting Attorney*), James Whitmore (*Judge Stanley Murdoch*), Leslie Nielsen (*Allen Green*), William Prince (*Clarence Middleton*), Dakin Matthews

p, Barbra Streisand; d, Martin Ritt; w, Tom Topor, Darryl Ponicsan, Alvin Sargent (based on the play by Topor); ph, Andrzej Bartkowiak (Technicolor); ed, Sidney Levin; m, Barbra Streisand; prod d, Joel Schiller; art d, Eric Orbom; cos, Joe I. Tompkins

Claudia Draper (Barbra Streisand) is a high-priced prostitute. She has been arrested for killing one of her johns (Leslie Nielsen), and her erratic behavior and frequent outbursts would lead one to believe she is crazy. Her mother (Maureen Stapleton) and stepfather (Karl Malden) have conspired with their attorney (William Prince) to have Claudia committed to a mental institution rather than have her go on trial for manslaughter. Claudia knows that if she is committed, she may never get out of her hospital gown. She wants a sanity hearing and wishes to stand trial, believing she can prove the killing was in self-defense. After Claudia physically attacks her parents' attorney, he immediately asks to be taken off the case. A hapless public defender, Aaron Levinsky (Richard Dreyfuss), is given the task of dealing with the wild woman. There are holes galore in the script. As a story, it's thin. As cinema, it's static. There is enough in all the performances to make it a diversion, but little more. For a fleeting moment, there is just a scintilla of attraction between Dreyfuss and Streisand; but that's tossed aside in favor of the bare-bones plot. Although he costars, Dreyfuss has fashioned more of a Best Supporting Actor performance and seems happy to stand outside the glow of Streisand's histrionics. Despite all of her emoting, the picture seldom catches fire. All of the secondary roles are well cast, and Martin Ritt's direction is as good as it can be, considering the script's limitations.

NUTTY PROFESSOR, THE

1963 107m c	★★★½
Comedy	/PG
Paramount	

Jerry Lewis (*Prof. Julius Ferris Kelp/Buddy Love*), Stella Stevens (*Stella Purdy*), Del Moore (*Dr. Hamius R. Warfield*), Kathleen Freeman (*Millie Lemmon*), Med Flory, Skip Ward, Norman Alden (*Football Players*), Howard Morris (*Father Kelp*), Elvia Allman (*Mother Kelp*), Milton Frome (*Dr. Leevee*)

p, Jerry Lewis, Ernest D. Glucksman; d, Jerry Lewis; w, Jerry Lewis, Bill Richmond (based on a story by Lewis); ph, W. Wallace Kelley (Technicolor); ed, John Woodcock; m, Walter Scharf; art d, Hal Pereira, Walter Tyler; fx, Paul K. Lerpae; cos, Edith Head

Jerry Lewis's best film stars the often moronic comic as Julius F. Kelp, a bumbling professor of chemistry at a small college who falls hopelessly in love with one of his more popular students, Stella Purdy (Stella Stevens). Seeking to improve his looks, Kelp whips up a chemical potion and is transformed into an overbearing and obnoxious but dashing singer who calls himself Buddy Love. Though totally conceited, Buddy Love (Lewis in a dual role) succeeds in winning over Stella. Unfortunately, his formula has a way of wearing off at the wrong times. Although only tangentially related to horror films, THE NUTTY PROFESSOR can be seen as a strange companion piece to the *Dr. Jekyll and Mr. Hyde* films, in which the dark, menacing side of an otherwise harmless character seeps through to the forefront. Much has been made of Buddy Love's resemblance to Lewis's former partner, Dean Martin, but the person Love really resembles is the pompous, self-important and bitter Jerry Lewis of talk shows and telethons.

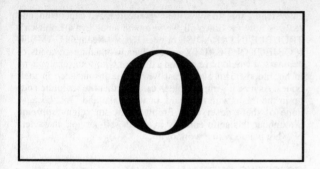

O LUCKY MAN!

1973 186m c ★★★★

Comedy R/15

Memorial/Sam (U.K.)

Malcolm McDowell (*Mick Travis*), Ralph Richardson (*Monty/Sir James Burgess*), Rachel Roberts (*Gloria Rowe/Mme. Paillard/Mrs. Richards*), Arthur Lowe (*Mr. Duff/Charlie Johnson/Dr. Munda*), Helen Mirren (*Patricia Burgess*), Dandy Nichols (*Tea Lady/Neighbor*), Mona Washbourne (*Sister Hallett/Usher/Neighbor*), Michael Medwin (*Army Captain/Power Station Technician/Duke of Belminster*), Mary McLeod (*Mrs. Ball/Vicar's Wife/Salvation Army Woman*), Vivian Pickles (*Welfare Lady*)

p, Michael Medwin, Lindsay Anderson; d, Lindsay Anderson; w, David Sherwin (based on an idea by Malcolm McDowell); ph, Miroslav Ondricek (Technicolor); ed, David Gladwell, Tom Priestley; m, Alan Price; prod d, Jocelyn Herbert; art d, Alan Withy; fx, John Stears; cos, Elsa Fennell

This film is an awesome achievement in many ways. It is unlike anything you have ever seen with the exception of IF. . ., which was also directed by Anderson and also starred McDowell. Thirteen of the actors play multiple roles, which would ordinarily confuse, but they are so good at what they do, there is no mistaking what is going on. McDowell is a young salesman for a coffee company, an adherent to the Protestant work ethic. He is a smiling, guileless innocent, qualities which soon attract Roberts, a public relations executive who promptly seduces him and gives him a position as a supervisor. While driving to his new assignment, he witnesses an accident in which two drivers are killed. When he attempts to give a statement to the two policemen on the scene, he is ordered to leave at once and observes that the cops are more interested in looting the sports car and van which were involved in the fatal crash. McDowell checks in at a small hotel operated by McLeod. Then he meets Lowe, a lecherous customer of the coffee company, who takes him to a wild party where the entertainment consists of X-rated films as well as women performing various sexual acts. When he returns to his room, McLeod awaits him in his bed. They make love, and McDowell gets a call from Roberts informing him that he has been named to run the company's operations in Scotland. He's about to depart the following morning when Richardson, an aged resident of the hotel, gives him the gift of a gold suit with the warning, "Try not to die like a dog." McDowell discovers that the suit fits him well and takes off for Scotland. He gets to the address he was given, is immediately arrested by uniformed guards, and is taken to a research facility where he is tortured until he signs a confession admitting several crimes of which he is entirely innocent. Just then, a warning siren sends his guards running. He gets away through the aid of Nichols, a tea lady, and

watches as the factory blows up in an atomic blast which levels the surrounding area as well. He finds what's left of his car, grabs the gold suit, and roams through the afflicted area until coming upon a peaceful valley and walking into a church where he falls asleep. He is awakened by the vicar's wife (also McLeod), and her children take him to a road where he hitches a ride with a male nurse (Warren Clarke). On the ride, Clarke talks McDowell into becoming a guinea pig for medical research and promises that he will be paid handsomely. Once at the lab, McDowell learns that the doctor, Graham Crowden, wants to sterilize him. McDowell also sees the result of one of Crowden's earlier experiments: a huge pig with the head of a young man. McDowell escapes and is picked up by a rock band and their groupie, Mirren. They travel to London, and he spends the night with Mirren. Next day, he learns that she is the daughter of one of the richest and vilest men in England (Richardson again), whom McDowell finally meets and goes to work for as an assistant. When one of Richardson's crooked deals is exposed, McDowell takes the rap and gets five years in jail. Meanwhile, Mirren decides to marry Medwin, a young peer. In prison, McDowell finds God and decides to devote himself to religion upon his release. He begins lecturing for the Salvation Army and has his pockets picked by a couple of thieves. In his attempt to save the life of would-be suicide Roberts (in one of her three roles), she dies, and he nearly does so as well. McDowell seeks to aid a group of drunks and drug addicts with food and advice, and he is shocked to find Mirren and Medwin, now poverty stricken, among them. McDowell sees a poster advertising for an unknown to play the lead in a new film. Hundreds show up at the audition hall, but McDowell is instantly picked by director Anderson (as himself) to be the star. When McDowell finds it difficult to smile (at Anderson's request), the director whacks him across the face with the script. The picture is made, and it becomes a hit. At a fete for the cast and crew, McDowell wears his gold suit, dances with the others, and is now a Lucky Man.

As black as this synopsis makes the film sound, it's every bit that hilarious. They cut 20 minutes from the original and, even at the ultimate U.S. length of 166 minutes, many felt it was short and wished the entire picture were shown. The cuts came largely in the Salvation Army sequence and Roberts' suicide. Anderson pulls out all the technical stops, but, since this is essentially a fantasy, the gimmickry never gets in the way.

O. HENRY'S FULL HOUSE

1952 117m bw ★★★½

Comedy/Drama

FOX

Jeanne Crain (*Della*), Farley Granger (*Jim*), Anne Baxter (*Joanna*), Jean Peters (*Susan*), Charles Laughton (*Soapy*), Marilyn Monroe (*Streetwalker*), David Wayne (*Horace*), Richard Widmark (*Johnny Kernan*), Fred Allen (*Sam*), Oscar Levant (*Bill*)

p, Andre Hakim; d, Henry Hathaway, Henry Koster, Henry King, Howard Hawks, Jean Negulesco; w, Lamar Trotti, Richard Breen, Ben Roberts, Ivan Goff, Walter Bullock, Nunnally Johnson (based on the stories by O. Henry); ph, Lloyd Ahern, Lucien Ballard, Joseph MacDonald, Milton Krasner; ed, Nick De Maggio, Barbara McLean, William B. Murphy; m, Alfred Newman; art d, Lyle Wheeler, Chester Gore, Joseph C. Wright, Richard Irvine, Addison Hehr

This hearty and entertaining compendium of O. Henry's best stories features some energetic performances and, in a few cases, marvelous direction. The first tale, "The Cop and the Anthem," is about a haughty tramp who, with the onset of winter, tries to get arrested so he can enjoy the warmth of a jail cell. But, try as he might, he simply cannot offend the law. "The Clarion Call" is a terse slice of life in which a decent cop must arrest an old friend. In "The Last Leaf," a dying woman watches autumn leaves wither, and comes to believe that when the last leaf blows away, she, too, will die. Winter comes and the leaves vanish, one by one, until a single leaf remains, stubbornly clinging to the wall and giving the woman hope. There's a laugh a minute in "The Ransom of Red Chief," the story of a boy so bad that his parents couldn't care less when he's kidnapped. The rowdy kid makes life so miserable for his abductors that *they* bribe the parents to take the insufferable brat back. In the famous "The Gift of the Magi," a pair of impoverished young newlyweds sacrifice their most cherished possessions to buy each other Christmas gifts. The direction and writing in all these sequences are good, and the entire film is a great treat, enhanced by John Steinbeck's narration—an homage to the mysterious O. Henry.

OBJECT OF BEAUTY, THE

1991   101m   c   ★★½
Comedy   R/15
Avenue Entertainment/BBC Films

John Malkovich *(Jake)*, Andie MacDowell *(Tina)*, Lolita Davidovich *(Joan)*, Rudi Davies *(Jenny)*, Joss Ackland *(Mr. Mercer)*, Bill Paterson *(Victor Swayle)*, Ricci Harnett *(Steve)*, Peter Riegert *(Larry)*, Jack Shepherd *(Mr. Slaughter)*, Rosemary Martin *(Mrs. Doughty)*

p, Jon S. Denny; d, Michael Lindsay-Hogg; w, Michael Lindsay-Hogg; ph, David Watkin; ed, Ruth Foster; m, Tom Bahler; prod d, Derek Dodd; cos, Les Lansdown

THE OBJECT OF BEAUTY is not a joy forever. To watch Andie MacDowell and John Malkovich flounder in roles that might once have gone to Cary Grant and Irene Dunne or William Powell and Myrna Loy is to experience true movie-going misery.

For Jake (Malkovich) and Tina (MacDowell), two expatriate Americans in a luxury London hotel, life is one long, languorous round of room service and lovemaking. When rich boy Jake's latest business scheme flounders, the temporarily strapped duo toys with the idea of an insurance scam. Could they get away with pretending that Tina's Henry Moore sculpture has been stolen from their rooms? Before they can finalize their scheme, a deaf and dumb maid, Jenny (Rudi Davies), pilfers the objet d'art because she's mesmerized by its beauty, not by its market value.

When the sculpture disappears, Jake and Tina suspect each other of larceny-for-one. As their relationship deteriorates, they continue barraging insurance agents with demands and lambasting the hotel manager, Mr. Mercer (Joss Ackland). When Jenny's brother Steve (Ricci Harnett) steals the sculpture but can't find anyone to fence it, he disposes of his sister's treasure in a garbage dump. Steve's theft infuriates Jenny and then incites the greed of Frankie (Roger Lloyd Pack), a thuggish fence who has learned that the insurance company is offering a hefty reward for the sculpture's recovery. Convinced that Tina has double-crossed him, Jake sleeps with her best friend Joan (Lolita Davidovich) and searches Joan's flat. Although Jenny returns the sculpture after retrieving it from the trash heap, she must re-steal it in order to protect her brother from the unscrupulous Frankie, who beats Steve to a pulp.

Finally, with the intervention of the insurance company, the sculpture is returned to its rightful owners. Steve and Jenny are spared criminal charges; spoiled brats Jake and Tina can now sell the Henry Moore piece to the highest bidder and live off their windfall—as long as the money lasts.

Watching this thinly written, intellectualized caper film, one realizes how far downhill we've come since Ernst Lubitsch's TROUBLE IN PARADISE or even Ronald Neame's GAMBIT. If OBJECT OF BEAUTY were to have worked as a comedy of manners, it would have needed a director with some champagne in his bloodstream and a cast with some insouciance in their bones. As it is, it's impossible to care whether the sculpture ends up in the trash, with the maid, or with Jake and Tina, because none of them deserve it. Empty cynicism reigns supreme throughout this serio-comedy in which self-serving characters play hot potato with a work of art.

OBJECTIVE, BURMA!

1945   142m   bw   ★★★★
War   /PG
WB

Errol Flynn *(Maj. Nelson)*, James Brown *(Sgt. Treacy)*, William Prince *(Lt. Sid Jacobs)*, George Tobias *(Gabby Gordon)*, Henry Hull *(Mark Williams)*, Warner Anderson *(Col. Carter)*, John Alvin *(Hogan)*, Mark Stevens *(Lt. Barker)*, Richard Erdman *(Nebraska Hooper)*, Anthony Caruso *(Miggleori)*

p, Jerry Wald; d, Raoul Walsh; w, Ranald MacDougall, Lester Cole (based on a story by Alvah Bessie); ph, James Wong Howe; ed, George Amy; m, Franz Waxman; art d, Ted Smith; fx, Edwin DuPar

This is one of the finest WWII films made during the war, and Errol Flynn, discarding his usual impudent and pranksterish style, is terrific as the straightforward and very human leader of 50 American paratroops who drop behind enemy lines to destroy a Japanese radar station. The commandos complete their mission successfully, but while waiting to rendezvous with the rescue planes they are attacked by a force of Japanese and have to fight their way out of the Burmese jungle on foot. Flynn gives one of his most convincing and powerful performances, and Raoul Walsh's direction is nothing less than excellent, with the great action director maintaining a harrowing pace, providing a wealth of interesting military detail, and delivering one thrilling scene after another. Alvah Bessie, who would later become one of the "Hollywood Ten" writers indicted by HUAC, provided the engrossing story, marked by its relative lack of patriotic speechifying and some marvelously entertaining banter between the experienced commandos. Exceptional, too, is the dynamic, masterful score by Franz Waxman, which fits the mood and menace of the mysterious jungle and incorporates the sounds of wild animals and exotic birds. James Wong Howe's splendid photography, with its naturalistic lighting, lends a great deal of authenticity to the jungle scenes, especially when one considers that the film was shot almost entirely on the "Lucky" Baldwin Santa Anita ranch outside Pasadena. The film received rave reviews and heavy box-office support in the US, but when OBJECTIVE, BURMA! was released in England, the British press exploded, claiming that the film minimized the efforts of the British in Burma by giving the impression that an American commando team liberated the area by themselves. The film was banned in Britain until 1952, when prints were reissued with a prologue extolling the British contribution to the campaign.

ODD COUPLE, THE

1968   105m   c   ★★★★
Comedy   G/15
Paramount

Jack Lemmon *(Felix Ungar)*, Walter Matthau *(Oscar Madison)*, John Fiedler *(Vinnie)*, Herb Edelman *(Murray)*, David Sheiner *(Roy)*, Larry Haines *(Speed)*, Monica Evans *(Cecily)*, Carole Shelley *(Gwendolyn)*, Iris Adrian *(Waitress)*, Heywood Hale Broun *(Sportswriter)*

p, Howard W. Koch; d, Gene Saks; w, Neil Simon (based on the play by Simon); ph, Robert B. Hauser (Panavision, Technicolor); ed, Frank Bracht; m, Neal Hefti; art d, Hal Pereira, Walter Tyler; fx, Paul K. Lerpae; cos, Jack Bear

Neil Simon has the unique ability of depicting life, enhancing it a bit, and winding up with gold. His older brother, Danny (a successful writer in his own right who toiled on many TV shows), was divorced and living with Roy Gerber, a veteran agent, and, occasionally, with Les Colodny, a writer, then a TV studio executive, and later an advertising man. Danny Simon is a self-confessed fussbudget who insists on neatness, and Gerber and Colodny couldn't care less. They lived in a house above Hollywood that Danny attempted, with little success, to keep neat, as the debris kept piling up. Danny considered writing a play about the experience and told his brother some of the incidents. When Neil made him an offer he couldn't refuse (a piece of the action), Danny okayed it and the rest is stage, film, and TV history. Neil realized that doing "The Odd Trio" might be a bit unwieldy, so he made it into a couple instead. His honest screenplay adaptation of his stage play is even better and adds to the more than 250 laughs (by actual count) in the play's script. Matthau and Art Carney did it on the stage (with Carney being replaced from time to time by Paul Dooley), but Paramount paged Lemmon for the coveted role of Felix. Billy Wilder had wanted to do the direction, but his price was allegedly higher than that of Saks, who directed the stage version. The other actors were all from the stage play, with the addition of Adrian, Broun, John C. Becher, and the ballplayers who played themselves.

Lemmon's wife has left him, and he wants nothing more than to end his life. He's a TV newswriter and is so depressed that he is forever building dungeons in the air. After failing at his first suicide attempt, he goes to his regular Friday night poker game, which is being held at the huge apartment of his friend, Matthau, a divorced sportswriter for whom cleanliness is next to impossible. The others in the game—Fiedler, Sheiner, Haines, and Edelman (who also appeared as the phone repairman in the play and movie BAREFOOT IN THE PARK)—all fear for Lemmon's life, so Matthau allows the distressed man to move in with him. What the heck, it's a big apartment and they won't get on each other's nerves, will they? Well, you *know* they will: Lemmon's obsessive-compulsive behavior is soon gnawing on Matthau's nerves. The apartment is turned into a model of attractiveness, but Matthau is thinking that perhaps Lemmon's wife had a good idea when she left him. The riotous domestic quarrels sound like a typical husband-and-wife battle, as Lemmon nags Matthau about the overflowing cigarette butts, footprints in the kitchen, a souffle that falls, etc. Before Matthau throttles Lemmon, he suggests that they double-date two English women who live in the building, Evans and Shelley. Lemmon doesn't feel he is ready to talk to anyone with a voice higher than his, but he finally agrees when Matthau allows him to cook dinner. Lemmon's dinner is a shambles: his meat loaf burns, everything goes wrong, and he disintegrates into a river of sobs when the sisters ask about his wife and he tearfully recalls his lost marriage. Matthau is seething at the destruction of the sexy mood he was trying to create, but Evans and Shelley do their best to comfort Lemmon and are soon in tears themselves. When Lemmon won't take the sisters back to their apartment (Matthau was hoping for some action up

there), Matthau finally cracks and begins breaking things and putting his now-immaculate apartment back in the original sloppy condition it was in when Lemmon first arrived. Lemmon leaves, and when the poker cronies come by and no one has heard from him, they fear the worst and go around the city looking for him, to no avail. Later, at the Matthau apartment, Lemmon enters to gather his remaining possessions and tells them all that he is moving upstairs with the two sisters while he contemplates his next decision. Lemmon exits, and the men sit down to play cards while Matthau carps at them for spilling some of their ashes on the table as the picture ends. The barrage of one-liners that snap off the screen are all to the point and never out of character. Typical of the socko jokes is the one where one of the sisters asks Lemmon what he does for a living, and he replies that he writes the news for television. She responds, "Isn't that interesting. Where on earth do you get all your ideas?" So funny and character-oriented are these gages that many of them would mean nothing without the framework that surrounds them. Other than the few scenes they added to take the action out of the stifling atmosphere of the apartment, this picture is essentially a filmed version of the play. The TV series that came from this movie is a rare example of a film being transferred to the little screen without losing the flavor.

ODD MAN OUT

1947   116m   bw   ★★★★★
Drama   /PG
Two Cities   (U.K.)

James Mason *(Johnny McQueen)*, Robert Newton *(Lukey)*, Kathleen Ryan *(Kathleen)*, Robert Beatty *(Dennis)*, William Hartnell *(Barman)*, F.J. McCormick *(Shell)*, Fay Compton *(Rosie)*, Beryl Measor *(Maudie)*, Cyril Cusack *(Pat)*, Dan O'Herlihy *(Nolan)*

p, Carol Reed; d, Carol Reed; w, F.L. Green, R.C. Sherriff (based on the novel by F.L. Green); ph, Robert Krasker; ed, Fergus McDonell; m, William Alwyn; prod d, Roger Furse; art d, Ralph Brinton; fx, Stanley Grant, Bill Warrington

Reed man in. One of Britain's finest directors set himself on top with this haunting, lyrical masterpiece about a doomed fugitive. In perhaps the greatest performance of his illustrious career, Mason plays Johnny, an IRA leader who breaks out of jail and then plans a payroll holdup of a mill in Belfast to fund his underground operations. Though he abhors violence, Johnny accidentally kills a man during the holdup, and is himself critically wounded. Left behind by the panicky driver of the getaway car, Johnny stumbles away, descending into a nightmare as he becomes more and more delirious from his wound. He is harbored by a bunch of strange people who either want to help him or sell him to the British authorities. Sweetheart Kathleen (Ryan) and Johnny's IRA pals are in the meantime searching frantically for him. The man is hidden in deserted buildings and even in a junkyard bathtub for a while. On another occasion, two spinsters take him in, serve him tea, and then discover he is wounded, bandaging him before he departs. He finally falls into the clutches of an eccentric painter (Newton), who wants to catch the look of death in Johnny's eyes before it's too late. Struggling free from this madman, Johnny makes his way toward the docks in a final desperate effort to escape. Kathleen finally finds him there, but so do the police. The finale is very powerful.

Mason's performance as the dying fugitive, enhanced by that unique voice, is nothing less than great. Johnny's escalating pain, his lingering pride and the desperate look he gives an uncomprehending child searching for a ball are searingly intense. Ryan, who debuted here, never had the chance to impact like this again, and marvelous performances are contributed by Cusack and O'Herlihy as Mason's chief lieutenants. The fascinating McCormick steals most of his scenes as a rag-picking bum who hides Johnny, and Newton positively gorges himself on the scenery in a wild portrait of the artist as a crazed man.

Early on, Reed, aided by Krasker's gritty cinematography, establishes a deeply somber mood in this modern odyssey to doom and death in an uncaring world. Each frame is another lethal step for Johnny as Reed poetically captures his last moments on earth. The plot and character development are touchingly constructed and enhanced by a magnificent score by Alwyn. Though Mason is initially presented as a culprit, his agonizing plight slowly transfigures him into a Christ-like figure. Visually reminiscent of John Ford's THE INFORMER, ODD MAN OUT also shares thematic concerns with Ford's THE FUGITIVE, insofar as both films depict an intolerable fate for a man who is basically decent but is condemned for his own altruistic beliefs. A great work of art, ODD MAN OUT is a painting on celluloid, evoking the best canvases of Goya and Velasquez. (Check out the weird shot of what manifests itself in Johnny's beer bubbles.) Although it was not popular at the box office, the film quickly won worldwide plaudits and established Reed as a great director.

ODDS AGAINST TOMORROW

1959 95m bw   ★★★
Crime   /A
Harbel

Harry Belafonte (Johnny Ingram), Robert Ryan (Earl Slater), Shelley Winters (Lorry), Ed Begley (Dave Burke), Gloria Grahame (Helen), Will Kuluva (Bacco), Richard Bright (Coco), Lew Gallo (Moriarity), Fred J. Scollay (Cannoy), Carmen de Lavallade (Kitty)

p, Robert Wise; d, Robert Wise; w, John O. Killens, Nelson Gidding (based on the novel by William P. McGivern); ph, Joseph Brun; ed, Dede Allen; m, John Lewis; art d, Leo Kerz; cos, Anna Hill Johnstone

A crackling crime caper that includes an overlay of racial tension, ODDS AGAINST TOMORROW was the first film out of Belafonte's own producing entity and proved that he wasn't just another pretty face and froggy voice. Robert Ryan, who was a liberal in real life, again plays a psychotic racist, nearly the same character he did in CROSSFIRE as a vicious anti-Semite. Belafonte is a gambling junkie, a man whose love for the horses has caused his marriage to fall apart. He's a childish nightclub singer and is now in danger from the harassment of Kuluva, a gay gangster in the employ of the people who hold Belafonte's IOUs. Ryan is an ex-con looking for a big score and Begley is a former cop who has been cashiered from the force for illegal dealings. This unlikely trio unite to rob an upstate New York bank of $150,000. Belafonte desperately needs his share of the swag to call off Kuluva, who is now threatening to kill Belafonte's wife and daughter. Ryan is married to Winters, though dallying with Grahame, who gets vicarious thrills before they make love when she pleads with Ryan to tell her how it feels to murder someone. Ryan's anti-black feelings are overcome by Begley and the robbery takes place. But everything goes awry. A gas station jockey spots Ryan. Belafonte witnesses an accident and must give his version of the incident; then he switches places with the food delivery man who brings the bank's night workers their refreshments. The regular guy shows up and so do the cops. Begley is shot, and when he can't get the getaway car's keys to his buddies, he takes his own life, rather than suffer the ignominy of arrest. Ryan and Belafonte escape and flee to an oil storage

area not unlike the one in the final scenes of WHITE HEAT. By this time, the black-white tension has reached an apex; the two men shoot at each other and the oil tanks blow up, incinerating Ryan and Belafonte. After the resulting fire has cooled, the two charred corpses are found and cannot be told apart, an indication that in death there is no color differential. In small roles, note Cicely Tyson, Wayne Rogers, and Zohra Lampert. This film noir picture had the added twist of race relations and didn't get the kind of box-office attention it deserved, perhaps due to that element. Terrific jazz score by John Lewis, pianist for the Modern Jazz Quartet.

OF HUMAN BONDAGE

1934 83m bw   ★★★★
Drama   /A
RKO

Leslie Howard (Philip Carey), Bette Davis (Mildred Rogers), Frances Dee (Sally Athelny), Reginald Owen (Thorpe Athelny), Reginald Denny (Harry Griffiths), Kay Johnson (Norah), Alan Hale (Emil Miller), Reginald Sheffield (Dunsford), Desmond Roberts (Dr. Jacobs), Tempe Pigott (Landlady)

p, Pandro S. Berman; d, John Cromwell; w, Lester Cohen (based on the novel by W. Somerset Maugham); ph, Henry Gerrard; ed, William Morgan; m, Max Steiner; art d, Van Nest Polglase, Carroll Clark; fx, Vernon L. Walker; cos, Walter Plunkett

Cautious, forced adaptation of Somerset Maugham's tragic tale features the electric performance by Bette Davis that made her a star. Today, it looks a trifle much, but given time and circumstance—the stylized acting of the early sound era, and her desire to be noticed—it's a blistering job. When she unleashes the full force of her venom, it feels like the camera framework may not contain her. She threatens to burn a hole in the screen—it's naked acting like you rarely ever see.

The club-footed Howard studies painting in Paris but realizes that his work will never be more than second-rate, so he returns to England and begins to study medicine. Davis is a blond tart whom he meets in the restaurant where she works as a waitress. She manipulates his affection cruelly, breaking a date with him to go out with loutish salesman Alan Hale and later telling him that she could never love a cripple. Even after she tells him she intends to marry Hale, and Howard later meets Kay Johnson, a sophisticated and decent lady who aggressively courts him, he can only think of Davis. When she appears at his apartment and explains that she is pregnant and Hale has deserted her, Howard promises to marry her. But Davis is no more faithful to Howard than she ever was, and she runs off with Reginald Denny, one of Howard's fellow students. And yet she returns one last time. . .

Despite John Cromwell's stilted treatment, thanks to the wonderful performances by the leads, this version of the Maugham story is certainly the finest. Howard's quiet, studied performance is just right. Davis came by her role the hard way. After RKO acquired the novel for production, studio executives were shocked to learn that none of their leading ladies wanted the part of the sluttish Mildred. Katharine Hepburn, Ann Harding, and Irene Dunne all rejected the role. Davis, however, was languishing in unimportant roles at Warner Bros., and she began to lobby Jack Warner to loan her to RKO for the part. He finally agreed, though he confided to friends that he was doing her no favor, that the part would drain her emotionally and damage her image. Cromwell was not concerned, however; he knew well the depth of Davis's talent.

The actress threw herself into the role, adopting a Cockney accent which she refused to discard when off-camera. She supervised her own makeup so that it would convey the gradual disintegration of her character right up to the last scene in which she is dying of syphilis, appearing emaciated and ghost-white save for eyes blackened by the illness. Davis's natural tendency to slouch worked very well for Mildred; within a few years this tendency would be gone for good.

Davis and Howard did not get on. Howard looked down upon Davis, had no confidence that she could portray an English part and joked about her to other cast members between scenes. Halfway through filming he realized that not only was she expert, but she was taking the picture out from under his cultivated nose. Howard bucked up, but it was too late to undo the damage done to their working relationship.

At the premiere, RKO executives were horrified to hear members of the audience laughing at the most poignant and dramatic scenes, but they later reasoned that this happened because the music evoked the wrong emotions. Max Steiner's revised score did the trick, so by the time OF HUMAN BOND-AGE went into general release, it received universally favorable reviews with the laurels going to Davis. She was profoundly disappointed when she failed to win the 1934 Academy Award for Best Actress, but this film was her watershed picture.

OF MICE AND MEN

1939   107m   bw   ★★★★
Drama   /A
Hal Roach
_____

Burgess Meredith *(George)*, Betty Field *(Mae)*, Lon Chaney, Jr. *(Lennie)*, Charles Bickford *(Slim)*, Roman Bohnen *(Candy)*, Bob Steele *(Curley)*, Noah Beery, Jr. *(Whit)*, Oscar O'Shea *(Jackson)*, Granville Bates *(Carlson)*, Leigh Whipper *(Crooks)*

p, Lewis Milestone; d, Lewis Milestone; w, Eugene Solow (based on the novel by John Steinbeck); ph, Norbert Brodine; ed, Bert Jordan; m, Aaron Copland; art d, Nicolai Remisoff; fx, Roy Seawright
_____

John Steinbeck's moving and power-packed story of two ranch hands trying to find a safe haven in a hostile world comes to the screen with penetrating compassion under the deft hand of director Milestone. Right from the opening credits, where Meredith and Chaney are shown fleeing a posse, the pace of the film is set and is maintained by Milestone, who discarded overlaps and controlled his cameras with the precision of a bombardier. Having escaped the clutches of the law, Meredith and Chaney wander about the rural West, looking for work during the Depression era. They find odd jobs and hostility everywhere they go, until they reach the San Joaquin Valley in California, where a meanminded barley ranch owner hires them as hands. They live in the bunkhouse with the other workers, who soon realize that Chaney is dimwitted to the point of being *non compos mentis*, and that Meredith has appointed himself Chaney's guardian. The two fantasize about owning their own small ranch, and Chaney brightens at the thought of Meredith's promise that he can tend the rabbits and stroke their soft furry bodies. Meanwhile, the son of the owner, cruel and vicious Steele, begins bullying the much larger Chaney, even though Bickford, the decent foreman, tries to shield the half-wit from Steele's sadistic attacks. The seething hatred deep inside Steele has been implanted by his sexy wife, Field, who has dallied with some of his ranch hands in the past and, he suspects, even with foreman Bickford. Bohnen, another ranch worker, is missing a hand and is followed about by an ancient, smelly dog. He overhears Meredith and Chaney talking about how they will live off the land and begs them to take him along with them when they get their little ranch. Bickford asks

about Chaney's mental state and is told that the big fellow has a clouded brain "on accounta he'd been kicked in the head by a horse." The brawny Chaney does not know his own strength. He finds little animals and tries to keep them as pets but his affectionate strokes often turn to crushing and killing blows as his mind drifts. At the beginning Meredith finds him carrying about a dead mouse he has crushed to death and he later crushes a little puppy without knowing what he has done. But usually the giant is gentle and cannot comprehend violence. Realizing that his wife has been looking for a healthy farm hand to satisfy her, and that Field has been flirting with Chaney, Steele barges into the bunkhouse and confronts the big man. He yells at the dumbfounded Chaney and then begins to punch him viciously. Chaney does nothing but take one slashing punch after another from the vindictive Steele. Chaney looks to Meredith for guidance, and Meredith shouts to his friend: "Fight him, Lennie, fight him!" Steele is like a windmill, throwing an avalanche of punches against the seemingly defenseless man, but finally Chaney scowls and grabs Steele's gloved hand in midswing, crushing it so that the sound of the cracking bones is heard by Meredith, Bickford, and the others. Steele screams in agony and then drops to the floor after Meredith tells Chaney to let him go. Later, when Field approaches the baffled Chaney in the barn, trying to seduce him, the giant begins stroking her hair, much the way he has stroked the puppy's fur, and, trying to keep her from screaming as she struggles to get away, he accidentally kills her.

Though grim and offbeat, OF MICE AND MEN is a noble morality tale that can be appreciated for its simplicity. The acting is faultless and Copland's score is magnificent. Steinbeck's THE GRAPES OF WRATH was brought to the screen under John Ford's masterful direction in the same year as this picture, but neither suffered from the other's presence. This was Chaney's finest acting ever; equally impressive are Meredith, Bickford, Field and even B-film cowboy star Steele. Indeed, today the fine acting elevates the simplistic human philosophy that would have dated in clumsier hands.

OF STARS AND MEN

1961   53m   c   ★★★★
Animated/Fantasy
Storyboard
_____

Dr. Harlow Shapley, Mark Hubley, Hamp Hubley *(Commentators)*

p, John Hubley, Faith Hubley; d, John Hubley; w, John Hubley, Faith Hubley, Harlow Shapley (based on the book *Of Stars and Men* by Shapley); ph, John Buehre (Eastmancolor); ed, Faith Hubley; anim, Bill Littlejohn, Gary Mooney
_____

Evolution and man's place in the universe are explored in this charming animated fable created by John and Faith Hubley. Using Dr. Harlow Shapley's book *Of Stars and Men* as a basis (a volume written "to tell the people in simple language what man is and where he is in the universe of atoms, protoplasm, stars, and galaxies"), the Hubleys begin by showing the evolution of the earth and animal life. Man is introduced in the form of an arrogant boy who slowly comes to realize he's not alone in the universe. Though the ideas expressed in the story are familiar, the presentation is pure visual delight. The stylized pictures are brimming with humor and also carry a touch of pathos. The soundtrack is well suited to the images, using Hubley's children, Mark and Hamp, along with Dr. Shapley, as commentators on the action. OF STARS AND MEN is another standout in John Hubley's productive career. He worked with Disney on such films as SNOW WHITE and DUMBO before leaving to help form UPA Productions, where he created such memorable cartoon characters as Gerald McBoing Boing and the irrepressible Mr. Magoo.

OFFICER AND A GENTLEMAN, AN

1982 126m c	★★★½
Romance/War	R/15
Lorimar	

Richard Gere (Zack Mayo), Debra Winger (Paula Pokrifki), David Keith (Sid Worley), Robert Loggia (Byron Mayo), Lisa Blount (Lynette Pomeroy), Lisa Eilbacher (Casey Seeger), Louis Gossett, Jr. (Sgt. Emil Foley), Tony Plana (Emiliano Della Serra), Harold Sylvester (Perryman), David Caruso (Topper Daniels)

p, Martin Elfand; d, Taylor Hackford; w, Douglas Day Stewart; ph, Donald Thorin (Metrocolor); ed, Peter Zinner; m, Jack Nitzsche; prod d, Philip Jefferies; art d, John V. Cartwright

Lou Gossett, Jr., won a much-deserved Best Supporting Actor Oscar for his stellar portrayal of a drill instructor in this story of determination and love set against the backdrop of a Naval Aviation Officer Candidate School. Richard Gere plays Zack Mayo, a would-be flyer with a tough-luck background who, like his classmates, must survive the rigors of training under draconian Marine sergeant Emil Foley (Gossett) before moving on to flight school. Sgt. Foley singles out Zack for special derision, and though he pushes his charge to the limit, the feisty Zack refuses to give up, eventually tangling with the DI in martial-arts battle. Meanwhile, Zack and classmate Sid Worley (David Keith), the film's tragic figure, become involved with a couple of local girls, millworkers Paula Pokrifki (Debra Winger, who received a Best Actress nomination for her fine performance) and Lynette Pomeroy (Lisa Blount). Paula becomes convinced that Zack is like all the other officer candidates who do their training, take advantage of local women, and then disappear forever once they've earned their white uniform. Douglas Day Stewart's Oscar-nominated screenplay is generally involving (if a little overheated), but it is ultimately compromised by its sexism, particularly in the finale, which leaves Paula with only one hope for happiness—to be carried off by a dashing knight. Nonetheless, the performances are uniformly strong, with Gere offering some of his best work—though it pales in comparison with Gossett's tour de force as the tough, principled Sgt. Foley, which he patterned after real-life army DI Bill Dower (familiar to some from his appearances in Miller Lite commercials). The film's memorable theme song, "Up Where We Belong" (sung by Joe Cocker and Jennifer Warnes), also won an Academy Award.

OFFICIAL STORY, THE

(LA HISTORIA OFICIAL)

1985 112m c	★★★½
Drama	/15
Historias Cine (Argentina)	

Hector Alterio (Roberto), Norma Aleandro (Alicia), Chela Ruiz (Sara), Chunchuna Villafane (Ana), Hugo Arana (Enrique), Patricio Contreras (Benitez), Guillermo Battaglia (Jose), Maria-Luisa Robledo (Nata), Jorge Petraglia (Macci), Analia Castro (Gaby)

p, Marcelo Pineyro; d, Luis Puenzo; w, Luis Puenzo, Aida Bortnik; ph, Felix Monti; ed, Juan Carlos Macias; m, Atilio Stampone; prod d, Abel Facello; art d, Abel Facello; cos, Tiky Garcia Estevez

The first important film to emerge from Argentina after the fall of its military regime, THE OFFICIAL STORY is a deeply moving drama examining one of the saddest chapters in that country's history. The tranquil lives of Alicia (Norma Aleandro), a history professor; her husband, Roberto (Hector Alterio), a high-powered businessman; and their five-year-old daughter, Gaby (Analia Castro), are thrown into turmoil when an old friend who was tortured and exiled by the military reveals that, under the junta, babies were taken from political prisoners and sold to well-connected adoptive parents. Realizing that Gaby may be one of these children, Alicia begins to investigate her daughter's background and meets Sara (Chela Ruiz), one of the women who march each day at the Plaza de Mayo to protest the disappearance of loved ones in the junta's "dirty war." Coming to grips with her political naivete, Alicia confronts Alterio, who proves to be deeply involved with the reprehensible junta. An impressive feature debut by Luis Puenzo, who invests his scenes with tremendous emotional impact, THE OFFICIAL STORY won the 1986 Oscar for Best Foreign-Language Film. Poignantly political, its power derives from the depiction of the junta's tragic effect on individual lives. The screenplay was written with Aleandro (a political exile who returned to her native Argentina after the change of government) in mind, and she delivers a tour de force performance that won her the Best Actress Award at Cannes, as well as an Academy Award nomination. Originally, Puenzo intended to shoot the film in secret, using hidden 16mm cameras, but the junta was voted out of office just after cowriter Aida Bortnik completed the screenplay.

OH! WHAT A LOVELY WAR

1969 144m c	★★★½
War/Musical	G/PG
Accord (U.K.)	

Ralph Richardson (Sir Edward Grey), Meriel Forbes (Lady Grey), Wensley Pithey (Archduke Franz Ferdinand), Ruth Kettlewell (Duchess Sophie), Ian Holm (President Poincare), John Gielgud (Count Berchtold), Kenneth More (Kaiser Wilhelm II), John Clements (Gen. von Moltke), Paul Daneman (Czar Nicholas II), Pamela Abbott (Czarina)

p, Brian Duffy, Richard Attenborough, Len Deighton (uncredited); d, Richard Attenborough; w, Len Deighton (based on Joan Littlewood's stage production of Charles Chilton's play The Long, Long Trail); ph, Gerry Turpin (Panavision, Technicolor); ed, Kevin Connor; m, Alfred Ralston; prod d, Don Ashton; art d, Harry White; fx, Ron Ballanger; chor, Eleanor Fazan; cos, Anthony Mendleson

Richard Attenborough's directorial debut is a sprawling, highly stylized musical satire of WWI featuring some of Britain's very finest actors—Ralph Richardson, Laurence Olivier, Michael Redgrave, John Mills, Jack Hawkins, Ian Holm, and Vanessa Redgrave among them. After an opening that finds Europe's heads of state choosing up sides when Archduke Franz Ferdinand is killed during a royal photo session, OH, WHAT A LOVELY WAR traces WWI through a series of surreal set pieces, alternating between the front lines in France and the English homefront, where generals and diplomats conduct a distant war that is actually waged by the young and poor. In particular, the film focuses on the Smith family, whose sons, seduced into the service in the carnival atmosphere of Brighton, all end up dying for their country. Meanwhile, the sacrifices of the British aristocracy, as embodied by Eleanor (Susannah York) and Stephen (Dirk Bogarde), are limited to boycotting German wine. Against a backdrop that includes flashing neon messages and a cricket scoreboard that keeps tally of the war's casualties, a series of musical numbers from 1914-18 are performed and given a distinctly antiwar slant that won considerable support from the British Left for this film and its inspiration, Joan Littlewood's 1963 stage adaptation of Charles Chilton's radio play "The Long, Long Trail." The rights to the play were purchased by producer

Brian Duffy and novelist Len Deighton, the latter of whom had his name taken off the film before its release because of differences with Attenborough. OH, WHAT A LOVELY WAR is not a flawless film but is thoughtful and enthralling.

OKLAHOMA!
1955 145m c ★★★★
Western/Musical G/U
Magna

Gordon MacRae (Curly), Gloria Grahame (Ado Annie), Gene Nelson (Will Parker), Charlotte Greenwood (Aunt Eller), Shirley Jones (Laurey), Eddie Albert (Ali Hakim), James Whitmore (Carnes), Rod Steiger (Jud Fry), Barbara Lawrence (Gertie), Jay C. Flippen (Skidmore)

p, Arthur Hornblow, Jr.; d, Fred Zinnemann; w, Sonya Levien, William Ludwig (based on the musical by Richard Rodgers, Oscar Hammerstein II, from the play Green Grow the Lilacs by Lynn Riggs); ph, Robert Surtees (Todd-AO, Eastmancolor); ed, Gene Ruggiero; m, Richard Rodgers; prod d, Oliver Smith; art d, Joseph C. Wright; chor, Agnes De Mille; cos, Orry-Kelly, Motley

This paean to Oklahoma's "Sooner" pioneers is one of Hollywood's most inventive musicals despite its rudimentary plot: boys (Gordon MacRae and Gene Nelson) meet girls (Shirley Jones and Gloria Grahame); Boys almost lose girls, all complicated by the anti-romantic efforts of villainous Jud Fry (Rod Steiger). Until the stage version of Oklahoma! dared to be different, the traditional Broadway opening had a line of high-stepping chorus girls with razzle-dazzle outfits. Here the set is quiet until MacRae extols the pleasures of "Oh, What a Beautiful Morning," and we realize right away that we're in for something special. Although the score is, by now, deeply imbedded in the minds of anyone who has ears, it is the creative and, in some cases, offbeat casting that makes OKLAHOMA! so constantly surprising. Jones, only 19 at the time and making her film debut, leaves the most lasting impression, and became an instant star after the release of the film, while MacRae, in fine voice, gives an equally fine performance. In the Dream Ballet, choreographer Agnes DeMille replaced Jones and MacRae with dancers Bambi Linn and James Mitchell, respectively, setting a precedent that would allow other filmmakers to substitute for leads whose dancing wasn't up to par. The first film to be based on a Rodgers and Hammerstein stage musical, OKLAHOMA! was actually shot outside of Nogales, Arizona, where the cast and crew put in nearly eight months of work, delayed by heavy rains and flash floods, one of which washed away a car containing a week's worth of film.

OLD DARK HOUSE, THE
1932 70m bw ★★★★★
Horror /PG
Universal

Boris Karloff (Morgan), Melvyn Douglas (Roger Penderell), Charles Laughton (Sir William Porterhouse), Gloria Stuart (Margaret Waverton), Lilian Bond (Gladys DuCane), Ernest Thesiger (Horace Femm), Eva Moore (Rebecca Femm), Raymond Massey (Philip Waverton), Brember Wills (Saul Femm), Elspeth Dudgeon (Sir Roderick Femm)

p, Carl Laemmle, Jr.; d, James Whale; w, Benn W. Levy, R.C. Sherriff (based on the novel Benighted by J.B. Priestley); ph, Arthur Edeson; ed, Clarence Kolster; art d, Charles D. Hall; fx, John P. Fulton

"No beds! They can't have beds!" A uniquely bizarre, wonderfully funny and exciting haunted house film with an all-star cast directed by the brilliant James Whale. Loosely based on J.B. Priestley's novel Benighted, the story has a group of stranded travelers forced to seek refuge at the strange house of the Femm family. Philip Waverton (Massey), his wife Margaret (Stuart) and their friend Roger Penderell (Douglas) arrive first. Inside lurks a "home" presided over by the 102 year-old bedridden patriarch Sir Roderick (Elspeth Dudgeon, an actress billed in the credits as "John Dudgeon" and brilliant in the role). Also featured are his atheist son Horace (Thesiger), his religious fanatic daughter Rebecca (Moore), and their older brother Saul (Wills), a crazed pyromaniac kept locked in his room upstairs. Hovering around the action is the house's hulking, mute, scarred, and slightly psychotic butler Morgan (Karloff, in his first starring role). Two more stranded travelers, Sir William Porterhouse (Laughton) and his "companion" Gladys DuCane (Bond), arrive soon after, and then the fun starts. The horrors here are not supernatural and arise solely from the madnesses of the Femm household, particularly when Morgan gets drunk and lets Saul loose. The suspense builds incredibly in the final showdown between Penderell and the mad Saul.

Handled in the uniquely theatrical manner that makes James Whale's work instantly recognizable, THE OLD DARK HOUSE is nonetheless never "stagy," benefitting as it does from Edeson's wonderful camerawork. The first glimpse of the foreboding house is still among the best of its kind, and the lighting of the stark indoor sets quite stunning. The marvelous screenplay is full of memorable bits, such as the harsh Rebecca's retelling of past family debaucheries or Saul's genuinely creepy conversation with Penderell near the end. The dialogue is often hilarious, but it takes a cast as brilliant as this one to make the most of it. Massey's early speech about the water trickling down his neck or his remarks about seeing the house ("Perhaps it might be wiser to push on") are beautifully handled. With his typically demonstrative aplomb, Whale gives us these moments as we see an extreme close-up of Massey's neck or just after the house stands illuminated by flashes of lightning. Douglas can shift from glib wisecracks to a warm and touching romance with Bond in moments, and she and Stuart are appealing leading ladies here. Laughton affects a marvelous Lancashire accent as a hearty, bluff man, and yet he can also touch the heart when speaking about his deceased wife. Karloff may not speak here but his acting is as effective as ever and he and Wills demonstrate a remarkable rapport together. His final embrace of the crazed man is unexpectedly powerful. If we had to reserve top honors, though, they would have to go to Thesiger and Moore, whose work is absolutely flawless. When Ernest Thesiger can make "Have a potato" a classic highlight of a film, you know you're in the presence of a rare comic talent. His sinister yet snobbish air, his cowardice, his snide contempt (as when he tosses a bouquet of fresh flowers into the fireplace) all make Horace Femm a character among characters. Ditto Moore as a remnant from Victorian days, with her cluttered, dusty room and hunched shoulders. Her intrusion on Stuart's game of making shadows on the wall is genuinely surprising, and watching her eat her dinner at light-warp speed is a lesson in acting.

As historian William K. Everson has noted, former stage actor and director Whale knows how to emphasize an actor's entrances and exits, or to delay them as needed (as in the case of Saul). His striking flair for composition and editing works an audience over thoroughly, and he adds to the film's impact by deliberately playing with the buildup of suspense. At times very serious, the film is so tongue-in-cheek as to be delightfully deceptive. A quiet film whose merits are subtle, THE OLD DARK HOUSE is the kind of film you'll love best on the tenth viewing. Brilliantly performed, staged and timed, a sly parody on the English household, THE OLD DARK HOUSE stands alongside THE BRIDE OF FRANKENSTEIN and ONE MORE RIVER as one of Whale's most sublime achievements.

OLD MAN AND THE SEA, THE

1958 86m c   ★★★
Drama   /U
WB

Spencer Tracy *(The Old Man)*, Felipe Pazos *(The Boy)*, Harry Bellaver *(Martin)*, Don Diamond, Don Blackman, Joey Ray, Richard Alameda, Tony Rosa, Carlos Rivera, Robert Alderette

p, Leland Hayward; d, John Sturges; w, Peter Viertel (based on the novella by Ernest Hemingway); ph, James Wong Howe, Floyd Crosby, Tom Tutwiler, Lamar Boren; ed, Arthur Schmidt; m, Dimitri Tiomkin; art d, Art Loel, Edward Carrere; fx, Arthur S. Rhoades

This was an impossible film to make, but Warner Bros. and Sturges tackled the job, and, with Tracy giving a virtuoso, bravura performance, the picture became a minor classic. Tracy plays a semi-literate old Cuban fisherman, a man who has been a toiler on the seas all his life. His only possessions are a shack and a small boat, and he has not had any luck at catching anything significant for years. Tracy's pedantic efforts to remain a fisherman only cause snickers of derision from his Spanish community, where he is thought of as an old, simple-minded fool. Only a small boy, Pazos, believes in Tracy and admires him, bringing him his coffee in the morning to get him started for the ritual of the sea. Tracy is up before dawn and moves out with the other men, carrying the mast to his boat on his shoulder, then shoving off into an azure ocean. Once at sea, he makes ready for the day's catch, hoping that he will have luck, putting out his lines, and introspectively thinking back on his life, from the few women he has known to such prosaic but exultant experiences as winning an arm-wrestling contest that took hours to finish. During his wistful daydreams, Tracy comments about the high principles of fishing and, while dreaming and thinking, doesn't realize that he has gone too far beyond his usual limit into the Gulf Stream. A little bird alights on his small craft, and he talks to it, telling it to take a short rest but then reminding it that it must soon fly off and take its chances with nature, as is the case with all living things. Then, with his lines out, Tracy hooks a huge marlin that puts up a titanic struggle with the old man, who uses up all his line to catch it, his back straining as a brace for the line and his hands turned to bloody pulp as the line whirs through them. The battle between the fish and the old man is Homeric, legendary, unthinkable. Yet, after many hours of painful struggle, Tracy wins the battle, killing the fish and tying it next to his boat. He sets sail for home, but he is out very far and the voyage is now fraught with peril. Many sharks are beckoned to the boat, following the trail of the marlin's blood, and they attack the dead fish as Tracy again puts up a fight to save his miraculous catch, slashing at the sharks with his knife and spearing them and slamming them with his oars as they make constant runs at the marlin, tearing it apart piece by piece until only its skeletal remains drift pathetically next to the boat in which the old man sits exhausted, defeated. "You went out too far, old man," Tracy tells himself, as a way of finding a reason for his great triumph turned to tragedy. He has overextended himself and made himself vulnerable to the very elements of nature he had always believed he understood and could control. He had lived all his life for this victory and now he sits vanquished, apologizing to the magnifi-

cent marlin for bringing it to disgraceful mutilation. "Fish, I respect you and I love you," he says and weeps for its miserable fate, which is his own. He drifts homeward, and by the time he sees the lights of Havana, there is hardly anything left of the marlin, only its head and part of its tail and a long, hideous skeleton, so grim and grisly that the old man cannot bear to look at it. He leaves his boat next to a seaside cafe (where tourists gape at the skeleton the next day) and struggles home to his shack, his mast so heavy on his back that Tracy sinks to the ground, exhausted physically and mentally. The boy finds him the next morning, a dying wreck.

THE OLD MAN AND THE SEA is an allegorical tale providing Tracy with his greatest one-man show, and he delivers powerful impact, humor, and an overwhelming image of stoic heroism as only Tracy could. Sturges's direction, given the confining nature of the settings, is masterful, and the cinematography headed by Howe and pieced together by many others is largely eye-popping. (The contribution of much of the footage by many sources, however, has a tendency to present alternating and inconsistent color patterns from scene to scene.) Schmidt's clever editing of Howe's basic photography and that of others is a superb job of integrating and crosscutting shots without interrupting the visual plot. The responsibility for bringing Hemingway's classic novella to the screen wholly rests with Broadway producer Hayward, who visited his old friend Hemingway at his home outside Havana in 1952 and, after Hemingway's wife Mary, was the first person to read *The Old Man and the Sea*. Hayward was so impressed with the tale that he personally hand-carried the manuscript to Hemingway's publisher, Scribner's, in New York. *Life* magazine serialized the novella in September, 1952, and the entire issue was sold out the very day it was issued, all on the strength of the great book. By the time the Book-of-the-Month Club grabbed the novella, Warner Bros., through Hayward, was already arranging to buy the film rights, paying Hemingway $175,000. Hemingway was asked for his choice of screenwriters and suggested that his friend Viertel adapt the tale for the screen. Hayward and Hemingway actually formed a partnership concerning the film, and both men selected Tracy to star as the old man.

Howe began initial photography in 1955, shooting background shots of the Cuban coast. Many fishing parties, including one with Hemingway which sailed as far as Peru's Capo Blanco, made desperate excursions into deep water to try and hook a huge marlin and get footage for the film, but all were unsuccessful in landing a fish anywhere near as big as that described in the novella (indeed, if there ever could be a marlin that big). Fred Zinnemann was hired by Hayward to direct the film, but after four months only a little footage had actually been shot, with Tracy lounging around a huge villa in Cuba with scores of servants to wait on him. He was restless and complained of nothing to do. Moreover, it was rumored that Hayward and Zinnemann had run into great difficulties concerning the Viertel script, which was utterly faithful to the novella. Zinneman reportedly wanted to change the story but producer Hayward wouldn't hear of it. Suddenly, Zinnemann was fired by Hayward; the director stated that it was over a "technical" problem. Meanwhile, enormous costs on the lingering production kept mounting as more and more fishing footage was obtained. Backround footage was obtained from the Disney studio and from private sportsmen like Houston's Alfred Glassnell. Tons of equipment was called for, with more than $400,000 in additional cameras and other technical devices shipped from Warner Bros. The overall production would exceed $6 million, and Sturges would wind up shooting most of the film in five weeks in the Warner

Bros. tank. Since Hemingway and scores of other big-time fishermen came up emptyhanded, Sturges opted for a huge, mechanically operated, rubber fish to pass for the giant marlin. The tank used at Warners contained more than 750,000 gallons of water which had to pass for the sea. Tracy cropped his hair and dyed it snowy white for the role but by the time the film was completed, his hair had turned stark white anyway. Hemingway became disillusioned with the film and began to criticize Tracy, blaming him for the delays when it was really a matter of technical problems. "This picture is becoming my life's work," complained Tracy in 1957. "By now there isn't a chance to make back all the money we will spend, so we're just concentrating on making it worthwhile." Later he was widely quoted as saying he would sell his interest in the film for 15 cents. "This is for the birds," he added. When the film was released, Tracy received kudos from almost all the critics, but Hemingway grouched that the film looked like the work of "a rich, fat actor," a remark that forever tore apart the relationship between the actor and writer. Hemingway's problems with THE OLD MAN AND THE SEA continued after its release. He was sued by a 70-year-old Cuban fisherman, Miguel Ramirez, for reportedly stealing Ramirez' tale and reaping a fortune on a film that rightly belonged to the Cuban. The suit was eventually dismissed as ludicrous.

OLD YELLER

1957 83m c ★★★½
Children's/Drama G/U
Disney

Dorothy McGuire (*Katie Coates*), Fess Parker (*Jim Coates*), Tommy Kirk (*Travis Coates*), Kevin Corcoran (*Arliss Coates*), Jeff York (*Bud Searcy*), Beverly Washburn (*Lisbeth Searcy*), Chuck Connors (*Burn Sanderson*), Spike the Dog (*Old Yeller*)

p, Walt Disney; d, Robert Stevenson; w, Fred Gipson, William Tunberg (based on the novel by Fred Gipson); ph, Charles P. Boyle (Technicolor); ed, Stanley Johnson; m, Oliver Wallace; art d, Carroll Clark; cos, Chuck Keehne, Gertrude Casey

Set in Texas in 1869, Disney Studios' first and best attempt at a boy-and-his-dog film tells the story of a farm family whose head, Jim Coates (Fess Parker), must go on a cattle drive for three months, leaving his 15-year-old son, Travis (Tommy Kirk), in charge. When Travis's younger brother, Arliss (Kevin Corcoran), finds a stray yellow dog and decides to adopt him, Travis is frustrated by this breach of his authority. But his mother (Dorothy McGuire) approves of the dog's presence and reminds Travis that his little brother is lonely. Soon the dog, Old Yeller, has won the hearts of the whole family. Their attachment to the dog will serve as a test for their strength and love in this powerful and moving film. The movie is not afraid to confront issues that all children must eventually face—the loss of a pet and the transformation from child into adult. It is a film which will undoubtedly sadden children (and adults), but its redemptive and educational qualities will also lead young viewers to think about things that have previously gone unnoticed. Sequel: SAVAGE SAM.

OLIVER!

1968 153m c ★★★★
Musical G/U
Warwick/Romulus (U.K.)

Ron Moody (*Fagin*), Shani Wallis (*Nancy*), Oliver Reed (*Bill Sikes*), Harry Secombe (*Mr. Bumble*), Mark Lester (*Oliver Twist*), Jack Wild (*The Artful Dodger*), Hugh Griffith (*The Magistrate*), Joseph

O'Conor (*Mr. Brownlow*), Peggy Mount (*Widow Corney*), Leonard Rossiter (*Mr. Sowerberry*)

p, John Woolf; d, Carol Reed; w, Vernon Harris (based on the play by Lionel Bart from the novel *Oliver Twist* by Charles Dickens); ph, Oswald Morris (Panavision, Technicolor); ed, Ralph Kemplen; m, Lionel Bart; prod d, John Box; art d, Terence Marsh; fx, Allan Bryce; chor, Onna White; cos, Phyllis Dalton

Sweetened Dickens, a contradiction in kind. If the works of Charles Dickens have their moments of sentiment, they're well-earned, thanks to the savagry and deprivation abundant in the master storyteller's plots. Here, Carol Reed tries to balance the story elements by rendering the story as a fable; the moments of tenderness are intellectualized. Given that *Oliver!* could easily get that perfunctory cuteness that packs the matinees with old ladies, it's a wise move. But being English himself and probably knowing Dickens better than we do, why didn't Carol Reed restore the Dickensian flavor that could give OLIVER! some bite? OLIVER! is the familiar story of young Oliver Twist (strongly played by Mark Lester), an orphan who prefers life on the streets to the hard labor of a foster family or life in a vile orphanage. One day he meets another street urchin, the Artful Dodger (Jack Wild, in an equally strong performance), who tells him of a group of young hooligans that will consider him "part of the family." All Oliver has to do is learn to pickpocket and give his earnings to Fagin (Ron Moody), the crusty criminal gang leader; in return he'll have a "family" and a place to stay.

OLIVER! is one of the better example of 1960s musicals, a period when oversize musicals, poorly rendered, did themselves in. The score, while hardly immortal, is well served by the actors and Oliver Reed for once found a character he could sink his loathsome self into.

OLIVER TWIST

1951 105m bw ★★★★½
Drama /U
Cineguild (U.K.)

Robert Newton (*Bill Sikes*), Alec Guinness (*Fagin*), Kay Walsh (*Nancy*), Francis L. Sullivan (*Mr. Bumble*), Henry Stephenson (*Mr. Brownlow*), Mary Clare (*Mrs. Corney*), John Howard Davies (*Oliver Twist*), Josephine Stuart (*Oliver's Mother*), Henry Edwards (*Police Official*), Ralph Truman (*Monks*)

p, Ronald Neame, Anthony Havelock-Allan; d, David Lean; w, David Lean, Stanley Haynes (based on the novel by Charles Dickens); ph, Guy Green; ed, Jack Harris; m, Arnold Bax; fx, Joan Suttie, Stanley Grant; cos, Margaret Furse

David Lean's version of Charles Dickens's *Oliver Twist* is not as enthralling as his GREAT EXPECTATIONS, but it is a fine film in its own right. This time Alec Guinness (EXPECTATIONS was his first film) plays Fagin, Anthony Newley is the Artful Dodger, and the then-unknown and now-forgotten John Howard Davies is Oliver Twist. (Actually, some may recognize Davies as the British television producer responsible for "Monty Python's Flying Circus" and "Fawlty Towers.") Guinness's performance ran into some trouble from Jewish pressure groups—seven minutes of his performance was excised—and the film finally entered the country in 1951. Many of the novel's characters have been excised or compressed to fit the time frame of the film, but only the most die-hard Dickensians will protest. The sets are as much a part of the story as the dialogue, and set designer John Bryan's work is effectively photographed by Guy Green. All the acting is first-rate, and there is not a false note from the cast.

OMEN, THE

1976 111m c   ★★
Horror   R/18
FOX

Gregory Peck (Robert Thorn), Lee Remick (Katherine Thorn), David Warner (Jennings), Billie Whitelaw (Mrs. Baylock), Leo McKern (Bugenhagen), Harvey Stevens (Damien), Patrick Troughton (Father Brennan), Martin Benson (Father Spiletto), Anthony Nicholls (Dr. Becker), Holly Palance (Young Nanny)

p, Harvey Bernhard; d, Richard Donner; w, David Seltzer; ph, Gilbert Taylor (Panavision, DeLuxe Color); ed, Stuart Baird; m, Jerry Goldsmith; art d, Carmen Dillon; fx, John Richardson

This silly and bloody, but at times very effective, horror film takes THE EXORCIST one step further by concentrating, not on possession by the Devil, but on the Antichrist himself. Robert Thorn (Gregory Peck) is a highly respected American ambassador to England whose wife, Katherine (Lee Remick), gives birth to a stillborn child. Thorn is encouraged by a priest to switch his dead child with the living baby of a mother who died during childbirth. Five years later, strange things begin happening in the Thorn household, all of which can be traced to their boy, Damien (Harvey Stevens), who, unbeknownst to his surrogate parents, is the Antichrist. Regardless of its rather questionable premise, execution (unintentionally funny dialogue abounds), or taste, THE OMEN is a fairly entertaining horror picture that made an obscene amount of money and spawned two sequels, DAMIEN—OMEN II and THE FINAL CONFLICT, neither of which was very good. The films were originally conceived as four parts, tracing Damien's rise to power from his childhood through adulthood and eventually to Armageddon, but patron interest slacked off considerably after the second film, forcing the producers to cut the saga short at three.

ON GOLDEN POND

1981 109m c   ★★★★
Comedy/Drama   PG
ITC/IPC/AFD/Universal

Katharine Hepburn (Ethel Thayer), Henry Fonda (Norman Thayer, Jr.), Jane Fonda (Chelsea Thayer Wayne), Doug McKeon (Billy Ray), Dabney Coleman (Bill Ray), William Lanteau (Charlie Martin), Christopher Rydell (Sumner Todd)

p, Bruce Gilbert; d, Mark Rydell; w, Ernest Thompson (based on his play); ph, Billy Williams; ed, Robert Wolfe; m, Dave Grusin; prod d, Stephen Grimes; cos, Dorothy Jeakins

Retired professor Norman Thayer, Jr. (Henry Fonda), and his wife Ethel (Katharine Hepburn) are spending the summer at their New England cottage, just as they have done for nearly 50 years. The Thayers' daughter Chelsea (Jane Fonda) arrives at the cottage with her fiance Bill Ray (Dabney Coleman) and Billy (Doug McKeon), his son from a previous marriage. They plan for Billy to stay at the cottage while Jane Fonda and Coleman head for a summer in Europe. The gruff Norman and the irritating Billy are immediately at odds—much as the father and daughter have always been. The two come to a better understanding of one another over the course of the summer, however, while Fonda also tries to come to terms with his mortality. A beautifully photographed movie filled with poignancy, humor, and (of course) some superb acting. Henry Fonda was 75 when this picture was made and must have known he didn't have much time. There could have been no finer final curtain for him than this. He died nine months after receiving his first Oscar, for this film. Hepburn also won an Oscar, her fourth. Jane Fonda and

director Mark Rydell received Oscar nominations for their work in the film dedicated to editor Robert L. Wolfe, who died shortly after its completion.

ON HER MAJESTY'S SECRET SERVICE

1969 140m c   ★★★½
Spy   M/PG
UA (U.K.)

George Lazenby (James Bond), Diana Rigg (Tracy Draco), Telly Savalas (Ernst Stavro Blofeld), Ilse Steppat (Irma Bunt), Gabriele Ferzetti (Marc Ange Draco), Yuri Borienko (Gruenther), Bernard Horsfall (Campbell), George Baker (Sir Hilary Bray), Bernard Lee ("M"), Lois Maxwell (Miss Moneypenny)

p, Albert R. Broccoli, Harry Saltzman; d, Peter Hunt; w, Richard Maibaum, Simon Raven (based on the novel by Ian Fleming); ph, Michael Reed, Egil Woxholt, Roy Ford, John Jordan, Willy Bogner, Alex Barbey, Ken Higgins (Panavision, Technicolor); ed, John Glen; m, John Barry; prod d, Syd Cain; art d, Robert Laing; fx, John Stears; cos, Marjorie Cornelius

This might have been the best of the James Bond series if it had starred Sean Connery instead of Australian model George Lazenby, whom the producers grabbed after a frantic talent search when Connery turned down the role. When Bond is ordered to cease his pursuit of old nemesis Blofeld (played by Savalas this time), 007 turns in his license to kill and returns to Portugal to pick up the trail. There he falls for Tracy (Rigg), the ravishing daughter of Draco (Ferzetti), an organized crime kingpin. Draco helps Bond locate the Swiss mountaintop stronghold from which Blofeld plans to engineer universal sterilization unless he is granted a title of nobility and amnesty for his past crimes. After rescuing Tracy from Blofeld's clutches and seemingly doing away with him once and for all, Bond marries her and they *almost* live happily ever after. Based on one of the best of Ian Fleming's Bond novels, ON HER MAJESTY'S SECRET SERVICE benefited from an extremely well-written script that finally revealed a bit more of Bond's character. Lazenby, however, had no previous acting experience, and his lackadaisical performance limits the whole production, yet it still manages to remain one of the more entertaining Bond films.

ON THE BEACH

1959 133m bw   ★★½
Drama/War   /A
Kramer

Gregory Peck (Dwight Towers), Ava Gardner (Moira Davidson), Fred Astaire (Julian Osborn), Anthony Perkins (Peter Holmes), Donna Anderson (Mary Holmes), John Tate (Adm. Bridie), Lola Brooks (Lt. Hosgood), John Meillon (Swain), Lou Vernon (Davidson), Guy Doleman (Farrel)

p, Stanley Kramer; d, Stanley Kramer; w, John Paxton, James Lee Barrett (based on the novel by Nevil Shute); ph, Giuseppe Rotunno, Daniel Fapp; ed, Frederic Knudtson; m, Ernest Gold; prod d, Rudolph Sternad; art d, Fernando Carrere; fx, Lee Zavitz; cos, Joe King, Fontana Sisters

Based on Nevil Shute's popular novel, this flawed but moving end-of-the-world drama is set in Australia in 1964, after nuclear war has eliminated life in the northern hemisphere. While the folks down under await the nuclear fallout that will eventually kill them, the US *Sawfish*, a submarine commanded by Dwight Towers (Gregory Peck), ventures to California, only to learn that the radio signal still being transmitted from San Diego is being produced by a soda bottle—everyone at home is dead (dramatically reinforced by some extraordinary shots of a deserted San Francisco). Back in Australia, the principal characters deal with their imminent deaths in their own way: scientist Julian Osborn (Fred Astaire) enters and wins an auto race, then asphyxiates himself; Australian naval officer Peter Holmes (Anthony Perkins) and his wife, Mary (Donna Anderson), take their child's and their own lives; good-time girl Moira Davidson (Ava Gardner) tries to drink her fears away, then falls for Towers, who eventually returns with his crew to the US to die at home. Produced and directed by Stanley Kramer, this unremittingly bleak message film was intended to have a big impact and premiered simultaneously in 18 cities on all seven continents. And though it occasionally goes over the top with its melodrama and lacks some technical credibility, ON THE BEACH remains a powerful, well-acted, deftly photographed film in the tradition of THE WORLD, THE FLESH AND THE DEVIL; FAIL SAFE; DR. STRANGELOVE; and TESTAMENT. Its effective use of "Waltzing Matilda" also contributed to making that most Australian of songs a hit in the US.

ON THE TOWN

1949 98m c   ★★★★
Musical   /U
MGM

Gene Kelly *(Gabey)*, Frank Sinatra *(Chip)*, Betty Garrett *(Brunhilde Esterhazy)*, Ann Miller *(Claire Huddesen)*, Jules Munshin *(Ozzie)*, Vera-Ellen *(Ivy Smith)*, Florence Bates *(Mme. Dilyovska)*, Alice Pearce *(Lucy Shmeeler)*, George Meader *(Professor)*, Bern Hoffman *(Worker)*

p, Arthur Freed; d, Gene Kelly, Stanley Donen; w, Adolph Green, Betty Comden (based on the musical play by Comden, Green and Leonard Bernstein, from the ballet *Fancy Free* by Jerome Robbins); ph, Harold Rosson (Technicolor); ed, Ralph E. Winters; m, Leonard Bernstein, Roger Edens, Saul Chaplin, Conrad Salinger; art d, Cedric Gibbons, Jack Martin Smith; fx, Warren Newcombe; chor, Gene Kelly, Stanley Donen; cos, Helen Rose

Just a trifle forced, like Gene Kelly. And stolen by a tapping whirlwind named Annie Miller, flying through the Museum of Natural History in a blaze of green gingham. But New York City never looked more beautiful or exciting on screen than in ON THE TOWN, a breakthrough film that, for the first time, took the musical out of the claustrophobic sound stages and onto the streets for on-location shooting. Perfectly fusing story, songs, and dances, with no production number staged merely for its own sake, ON THE TOWN is so energetic and vital that the screen barely contains it; the actors seem ready to leap off and dance up the aisles. The slim story follows sailors Gabey (Gene Kelly), Chip (Frank Sinatra), and Ozzie (Jules Munshin) during their 24-hour pass in New York. In the subway, they note the picture of this month's "Miss Turnstiles," with whom Gabey is especially taken; later they meet Miss Turnstiles—one Ivy Smith (Vera-Ellen)—in the flesh, but she vanishes into the rush-hour crowd. Chasing after her, they enlist the help of cabbie Brunhilde Esterhazy (Betty Garrett), who takes a fancy to Chip. Continuing their search, they meet anthropologist Claire Huddesen (Ann Miller), who sets her sights on Ozzie. The group splits into three units—Brunhilde and Chip, Claire and Ozzie, and Gabey—to look for Ivy, agreeing to meet on the Empire State Building's observation deck that night. After a day of romantic adventures and misadventures, they rendezvous at the appointed site, Gabey squiring Ivy, whom he mistakenly believes to be a big star in her position as Miss Turnstiles. By the time she gets around to telling him she's really just a no-name dancer from a tiny town (as it happens, the same tiny town *he's* from), it makes no difference to the smitten Gabey, and, after a run-in with the cops that forces the gobs to pretend they're girls, they return to their ship exactly 24 hours from the time they left.

Louis B. Mayer disliked the original play, but producer Alan Freed managed to get his permission to film on a $2 million budget, including $110,000 to Betty Comden and Adolph Green for rewrites and new lyrics to the music by associate producer Roger Edens (Freed disliked Leonard Bernstein's stage score). Mayer didn't want the film to go on location, while Kelly wanted to shoot the entire picture in New York, leading to a compromise in which Kelly was allowed one frantic week of location shooting, filming the Bronx, the Battery, Coney Island, Brooklyn, the Empire State Building, Times Square, the Statue of Liberty, Fifth Avenue, Radio City, the Bronx Zoo, Central Park, Carnegie Hall, the subway, Wall Street, Grant's Tomb, and the Brooklyn Navy Yard. Perhaps it was the short shooting schedule that contributed to the frantic pace of the film, a jampacked tour without a wasted second. ON THE TOWN was the first of Kelly and Stanley Donen's codirecting triumphs (SINGIN' IN THE RAIN and IT'S ALWAYS FAIR WEATHER would follow), with Kelly helming the dance sequences. (For one ballet, Kelly adopted the strategy of Agnes DeMille in OKLAHOMA, substituting more balletically proficient dancers for the leads.) There may have been better songs and even better performances in other musicals, but for effervescent energy nothing has yet come close to the joyous, influential ON THE TOWN.

ON THE WATERFRONT

1954 108m bw   ★★★★½
Drama   /PG
Columbia

Marlon Brando *(Terry Malloy)*, Karl Malden *(Father Barry)*, Lee J. Cobb *(Johnny Friendly)*, Rod Steiger *(Charley Malloy)*, Pat Henning *("Kayo" Dugan)*, Eva Marie Saint *(Edie Doyle)*, Leif Erickson *(Glover)*, James Westerfield *(Big Mac)*, Tony Galento *(Truck)*, Tami Mauriello *(Tillio)*

p, Sam Spiegel; d, Elia Kazan; w, Budd Schulberg (based on a story suggested by a series of articles by Malcolm Johnson); ph, Boris Kaufman; ed, Gene Milford; m, Leonard Bernstein; art d, Richard Day; cos, Anna Hill Johnstone

A *tour de force* both for director Elia Kazan and actor Marlon Brando, ON THE WATERFRONT is a gritty, no-holds-barred drama about the corruption-glutted New York docks. It is also the story of the dock workers' excruciating struggle to make a living and of the awesome power of the unions that control them. Lee J. Cobb is the gangster union boss, Johnny Friendly, and Rod Steiger his crooked lawyer, Charley Malloy. Charley's brother, Terry (Brando), an ex-prizefighter, hangs around the docks and runs errands for Johnny, who gives handouts to those who do his bidding. Already a has-been as a young man, Terry keeps pigeons on a rooftop and dreams about his days as an up-and-coming fighter. Johnny tells Terry to ask a truculent union worker who is holed up in his apartment to meet him on the roof of his tenement building. The worker goes to the roof, and two of Johnny's goons push him off to his death as Terry watches in shock. Later, Terry tells some of Johnny's other thugs, "I thought they were only gonna lean on him a little," to which Truck (onetime heavyweight boxer "Two-ton" Tony Galento) replies, "The canary could sing but he couldn't fly!" Terry later meets pretty Edie Doyle (Eva Marie Saint), the murdered man's sister, and begins to feel responsible for the death. She introduces him to Father Barry (Karl Malden), who tells Terry that the dead man was killed because he was going to expose racket boss Johnny and his brutal henchmen. The gritty priest then exhorts Terry to provide the crime commission with information that will smash the dock racketeers.

ON THE WATERFRONT is nonstop drama and Brando is spectacular as the ex-fighter who finds his conscience and risks his life for his newfound principles. The realistic dialogue is poetic in its simplicity, and the grimy, seedy tenements and clammy docks are strikingly captured. Kazan sets every scene with menace and suspense, evoking a pitiless, steel-gray world where tough hope is requisite for survival. Cobb is a great villain, exercising his power with a payoff, a sneering smile, and a booming voice, and his goons are really frightening characters, many of them former real-life boxers with faces scarred by years in the ring. Saint is an island of sanity and decency, but an attempt to use Malden as a symbol of good in a troubled world is awfully pat.

The film is a draining experience from beginning to end, relentless in its portrayal of inhumanity. And it is all the more grim and hard-hitting because of the startling documentary approach of cinematographer Boris Kaufman. It is also extremely violent and bloody.

Accused of being anti-American and denounced by union leaders, ON THE WATERFRONT was mired in controversy at the time of its release, but it has stood the test of time and has emerged as a great portrait of a nonconformist who is not an informer but rather a man who experiences a moral transformation for the good of his fellow man. Budd Schulberg's literate, uncompromising screenplay makes sure that no one can mistake Terry Malloy's intentions. Presumably this is because both Schulberg and Kazan squealed during the McCarthy witch-hunt trials. After crusading against corruption in professional boxing in the novel that became THE HARDER THEY FALL, Schulberg was the logical choice to write the screenplay for ON THE WATERFRONT, which he based on a fascinating and heroic series of articles written by Malcolm Johnson for the *New York Sun*. (Oddly, Schulberg had earlier refused to ever write another film for studio mogul Harry Cohn, but here he agreed to contract with independent producer Sam Spiegel, whose arrangement with Columbia guaranteed no interference from Cohn.) What Johnson unearthed in his investigation of waterfront crime and later published in a 24-part series—following the murder of a New York hiring boss in April 1948—shocked America. The hard-hitting series, which won Johnson a Pulitzer Prize, described in detail the killings, bribery, kickbacks, thievery, shakedowns, and extortion that were everyday occurrences along New York's waterfront. Unfortunately, in real life there was no moralistc, happy ending.

Courageously, Columbia decided to make a film on a subject that Hollywood had always considered taboo—labor unions. Studio head Cohn was not originally in favor of doing the film, but since his New York office had made the production deal with producer Spiegel, he did not interfere. He did view the film at his private screening room in his home, however, with Kazan at his side, and only commented on one scene, wherein Brando tells priest Malden to "go to hell." Snorted Cohn to Kazan: "Boy, are you going to have trouble with the Breen Office (the then official Hollywood censor) over that 'go to hell' scene. They'll never pass it." Cohn was so shocked when the Breen Office didn't object to the scene that he barraged the censor with angry questions regarding other Columbia films that had been censored for what he thought were lesser offenses.

Kazan, who had taken cast and crew to Stamford, Connecticut, to film BOOMERANG in 1947 and made the tense drama

PANIC IN THE STREETS in New Orleans in 1950, was noted for shooting on location to achieve a thoroughly authentic look. He insisted on doing the same for ON THE WATERFRONT, with almost every scene shot in Hoboken, New Jersey, much to the dismay of Cohn, who thought it better to make the film on his back lot in California. Kazan's first choice for the role of the ex-fighter was Brando, but the actor reportedly could not make up his mind whether he wanted to play the part, so Kazan offered it to Frank Sinatra, who had just made a memorable comeback in FROM HERE TO ETERNITY and was one of the hottest actors on the scene. Before that deal was finalized, however, Brando decided he wanted to play Terry Malloy after all, and Sinatra later loudly complained, according to one report, that he had been misled by Kazan. Brando's decision proved to be an excellent one, and his dynamic, Oscar-winning performance is one of the most memorable in his distinguished career. (This would be the last film Brando would do with Kazan, although the director would offer him roles for BABY DOLL, A FACE IN THE CROWD and THE ARRANGEMENT.)

Though Harry Cohn had prophesied doom for ON THE WATERFRONT, a film that cost only $902,000 to make, the picture was a whopping success, grossing $9.5 million in its initial release. Moreover, it went on to win eight Academy Awards in 1954. In addition to Brando's Best Actor Oscar, the film was honored as Best Picture, Saint was named Best Supporting Actress, Kazan won Best Director, Schulberg got Best Screenplay, Kaufman won for his cinematography, Day for his art direction and Milford for his film editing.

ON VALENTINE'S DAY

1986 106m c   ★★★½
Drama   PG/
Guadelupe/Hudson/Lumiere

Hallie Foote (*Elizabeth Robedaux*), Michael Higgins (*Mr. Vaughn*), Richard Jenkins (*Bobby Pate*), William Converse-Roberts (*Horace Robedaux*), Jeanne McCarthy (*Bessie*), Steven Hill (*George Tyler*), Irma Hall (*Aunt Charity*), Rochelle Oliver (*Mrs. Vaughn*), Matthew Broderick (*Brother Vaughn*), Carol Goodheart (*Miss Ruth*)

p, Lillian V. Foote, Calvin Skaggs; d, Ken Harrison; w, Horton Foote (based on the play *Valentine's Day* by Horton Foote); ph, George Tirl (DuArt Color); ed, Nancy Baker; m, Jonathan Sheffer; art d, Howard Cummings; cos, Van Broughton Ramsey

Adapted from one of Horton Foote's nine loosely autobiographical plays, 1918 (1985) follows the residents of a rural Texas town during the early 20th century. ON VALENTINE'S DAY is 1918's prequel. Elizabeth (Hallie Foote) and Horace Robedaux (William Converse-Roberts) have eloped, despite the disapproval of her wealthy parents. The couple now live in a small house with Bobby Pate (Richard Jenkins), an alcoholic whose wife has left him, and a lonely spinster (Carol Goodheart). Horace's cousin George (Steven Hill), an unhappy man slowly losing his mind over love for a long-dead woman, is a frequent visitor. A few months pass, but the troubles surrounding this household remain and fester. Bobby's alcoholism gets worse, while George's mind completely snaps. The story is told in a low-key manner, and this understated style deepens the complex emotions of the characters. Foote and Converse-Roberts are excellent as the struggling couple bound by a love that overcomes the tragedies surrounding their union. Supporting roles are perfectly cast, and, as in its predecessor, the period detail is exquisite. ON VALENTINE'S DAY moves at a slow, almost lyrical tempo, allowing its characters and themes to develop without affectation.

ONCE UPON A TIME IN AMERICA

1984 227m c   ★★★★
Crime   R/18
Ladd

Robert De Niro *(Noodles)*, James Woods *(Max)*, Elizabeth McGovern *(Deborah)*, Treat Williams *(Jimmy O'Donnell)*, Tuesday Weld *(Carol)*, Burt Young *(Joe)*, Joe Pesci *(Frankie)*, Danny Aiello *(Police Chief Aiello)*, Bill Forsythe *(Cockeye)*, James Hayden *(Patsy)*

p, Arnon Milchan; d, Sergio Leone; w, Leo Benvenuti, Piero De Bernardi, Enrico Medioli, Franco Arcalli, Franco Ferrini, Sergio Leone, Stuart Kaminsky (based on the novel *The Hoods* by Harry Grey); ph, Tonino Delli Colli (Technicolor); ed, Nino Baragli; m, Ennio Morricone; art d, Carlo Simi, James Singelis; cos, Gabriella Pescucci, Nino Baragli

Italian director Sergio Leone returned to the screen after a 12-year absence, and the result is this ambitious, sprawling, insightful, frustrating, and ultimately challenging gangster film. Its structure is incredibly complex, flashing back and forth from the 20s to the 30s, to the 60s, basically following a group of Jewish boys who meet in the 1920s on Manhattan's Lower East Side. The story concentrates on the mercurial, borderline psychotic Max (James Woods) and Noodles (Robert De Niro), who has loved Deborah (Elizabeth McGovern) since they were children. The gang is virtually destroyed in 1933, but Noodles escapes and goes into hiding for 35 years, returning to New York in 1968 after receiving a mystifying letter. Though it's a confusing movie that has sparked debate and criticism, ONCE UPON A TIME IN AMERICA is visually stunning, rich in detail, and filled with outstanding performances.

ONCE UPON A TIME IN THE WEST

1969 165m c   ★★★★★
Western   M/15
Rafran/San Marco   (U.S./Italy)

Henry Fonda *(Frank)*, Claudia Cardinale *(Jill McBain)*, Jason Robards, Jr. *(Cheyenne)*, Charles Bronson *(The Man "Harmonica")*, Frank Wolff *(Brett McBain)*, Gabriele Ferzetti *(Morton)*, Keenan Wynn *(Sheriff)*, Paolo Stoppa *(Sam)*, Marco Zuanelli *(Wobbles)*, Lionel Stander *(Barman)*

p, Fulvio Morsella; d, Sergio Leone; w, Sergio Leone, Sergio Donati (based on a story by Dario Argento, Bernardo Bertolucci, Leone); ph, Tonino Delli Colli (Techniscope, Technicolor); ed, Nino Baragli; m, Ennio Morricone; art d, Carlo Simi; cos, Carlo Simi

Simply stated, this is Sergio Leone's masterpiece. In ONCE UPON A TIME IN THE WEST, Leone pulls together all the themes, characterizations, visuals, humor, and musical experiments of the three "Dollars" films and comes up with a true epic western. It is a stunning, operatic film of breadth, detail, and stature that deserves to be considered among the greatest westerns ever made. Although the original release in America was a severely edited version (Paramount wanted to cram an extra show in every night to sell more popcorn), the film was rereleased in 1984 uncut. The videotape is uncut as well, and it is this version that will be described here. ONCE UPON A TIME IN THE WEST's credit sequence is perhaps one of the most famous in cinema history. It unfolds slowly, deliberately, as Leone lingers on the strange behavior of Fonda's three hired killers (two of whom are Elam and Strode in unforgettable cameos) who await the arrival of a train carrying Bronson, a stranger who has asked for an audience with Fonda. The slow, rhythmic squeak of a rusty windmill provides an eerie accompaniment to the scene as the three gunmen occupy themselves while they wait. The set

piece—water dripping on Strode's bald head, Elam trying to shoo a pesty fly, and the third member of the gang cracking his knuckles—brings to the scene vital, detailed life accompanied by an almost unbearable sense of anticipation. Suddenly the sound of a shrill train whistle cuts through the tension like a knife, heralding the arrival of Bronson. When the train pulls out, Bronson is standing on the opposite side of the tracks, playing a tuneless, mournful song on his harmonica. When Bronson realizes that these men have no intention of bringing him to a meeting with Fonda, he guns them down without batting an eye. From this opening, the film shifts to the lonely McBain farm where Wolff prepares himself and his three children for the arrival of his new wife, Cardinale, a whore whom he met in New Orleans. Before Wolff's eldest son has a chance to go to the station, a shot rings out and the farmer's daughter falls dead. In a matter of seconds the entire family is wiped out by unseen assassins—with the exception of Wolff's nine-year-old son, who comes running out of the house to investigate. Accompanied by the chilling electric guitar chords of composer Ennio Morricone, the killers emerge from the brush, dust swirling around them. The men are dressed in tan-colored, ankle-length dusters, and as they approach the scene of their carnage, we see that their leader is none other than Henry Fonda. He stares at the small boy coolly. One of his henchman asks, "What do we do with this one, Frank?" Fonda spits, glances at his men, and calmly says, "Now that you called me by name," gives the boy a reassuring smile, and shoots him.

From this point on, the film explores a land war between widow Cardinale (aided by Bronson and charming outlaw Robards) and Fonda, who is employed by crippled railroad magnate Ferzetti to "clear the tracks." Cardinale inherits the land from her murdered husband and learns that he intended to build a lucrative train station on the property to take advantage of the requisite water. Ferzetti, of course, wants the land gratis. Whereas Robards helps Cardinale because he admires (or loves?) her, Bronson's motives are darker and more mysterious. Fonda, however, has ambitious plans, and Bronson's pursuit of him is a mild annoyance. An aging gunfighter, Fonda becomes fascinated with Ferzetti's money and power, and he decides to become a businessman by slowly pushing the crippled railroad man out of the picture. Unfortunately for Fonda, he fails to understand that, in the new America, money is more powerful than the gun. When Ferzetti realizes that Fonda is trying to take over, he buys off some of Fonda's own men to assassinate him. Bronson, of course, sees that Fonda's men are about to ambush him, so he helps the gunfighter survive. Seeing the cat-and-mouse game for what it is finally pushes Fonda over the brink, and he determines to abandon his grandiose ambitions in order to pursue Bronson. Meanwhile, Robards has gathered his men and has slaughtered Fonda's henchmen—a massacre in which Ferzetti is included. The film's major characters finally all assemble at the McBain farm, near Cardinale's train station. Robards, wounded in the confrontation, visits Cardinale for the last time, and they both watch the standoff between Fonda and Bronson from the house. Fonda admits to Bronson, "Morton (Ferzetti) once told me I could never be like him. Now I understand why. It wouldn't have bothered him knowing you were around somewhere alive." Bronson responds, "So you found out you weren't a businessman after all." Fonda replies, "Just a man." Who is Bronson? he finally asks, and what does he want? Bronson says that Fonda will only know "at the point of dyin'." In the long-standing Leone tradition, the men square off against each other in a circular area. Just as they are about to draw, the film cuts to a flashback in which a much-younger Fonda grins malevolently at a man with a noose around his neck, standing on the shoulders of a boy who is struggling mightily to support the man. Fonda shoves a harmonica in the boy's mouth and says, "Keep your lovin' brother happy." Fonda's henchmen laugh. The older brother looks at his torturers with disgust, utters a final epithet, and purposely kicks his brother out from under him, sending the boy face down in the dust and hanging himself. Obviously the young boy is Bronson. Leone cuts to Bronson shooting Fonda once in the heart before the evil man can even draw his gun. As Fonda lies dying, Bronson takes the harmonica he has carried since that day so many years ago and shoves it in Fonda's mouth. Fonda finally understands and breathes his last breath into the harmonica. Having satisfied his long-standing vendetta, Bronson enters Cardinale's house to get his gear. It is obvious that she would like him to stay, but she lets him go. Robards leaves as well and joins Bronson. Not far from the house, Robards's wounds prove too much for him, and he falls off his horse. He tells Bronson to go away and let him die alone, and Bronson honors Robards's last request. After Robards has died, he rides off into the desert with his friend's body hanging head down over a saddle, leaving Cardinale to serve water to the thirsty workers bringing the railroad to the West.

The paths Leone was struggling to develop in his previous three westerns finally merge and take shape in one of the most unusual, stunning westerns ever made. Called a "dance of death" by some critics, the film is an operatic eulogy for the western hero. Leone's men are titans of mythic stature—"an ancient race," as Bronson says at one point—and ONCE UPON A TIME IN THE WEST deals with their demise. By the end of the film, all the major male characters are dead (except for Bronson, but one gets the impression he is riding off to his own death somewhere), and a woman, Cardinale, is left to build this brave new world. From this point on guns are not to be the means of survival; money, the railroad, and water are the new currency. From the beginning, Leone wanted to make a western that was different from the "Dollars" films. United Artists offered Leone such major stars as Kirk Douglas, Gregory Peck, and Charlton Heston, but the director was already feeling some pressure from the studio, and he really wanted to work with Henry Fonda, so he took his picture to Paramount. Leone had been courting Fonda since A FISTFUL OF DOLLARS because he wanted to exploit the underlying hardness he found in the actor's performances, especially in the westerns of John Ford. Unfortunately all the scripts Leone submitted to Fonda were badly translated from Italian to English and were a nightmare to read. Fonda's reaction was the same to the script for ONCE UPON A TIME IN THE WEST, but on a hunch he called his friend Eli Wallach, who had worked with Leone on THE GOOD, THE BAD, AND THE UGLY. Wallach advised Fonda to ignore the script and do the film because Leone was a "genius." Soon Fonda arranged for a private screening of Leone's previous work and sat through all three "Dollars" films in one afternoon. Excited by the uniqueness and humor he found in the films, Fonda agreed to play the villain for Leone. In the weeks before Fonda was due on the set, the actor acquired a set of contact lenses that would turn his blue eyes to brown, and he grew a thick, dark mustache so that he would appear more villainous. When Fonda arrived on the set, Leone took one horrified look at Fonda and insisted that the brown eyes and mustache be taken off immediately. He wanted the Fonda face that the moviegoing public throughout the world loved so well.

Besides the casting of Fonda as a cold-blooded killer, one of the other major distinctions of ONCE UPON A TIME IN THE WEST is its brilliant musical score. Composed by Morricone

(who had also written the memorable music for the director's other westerns), the score contains distinct themes for each of the four main characters (tuneless harmonica for Bronson, biting electric guitar for Fonda, humorous banjo for Robards, and a lush, romantic score for Cardinale). Perhaps the most unusual aspect of the score is the fact that Morricone based his composition on the script, before one frame of film was exposed. Leone was so taken with the score that he played it on the set so that the actors could adapt their body rhythms to the music to be be played over their performance. By using this rather unorthodox method of scoring a film (or perhaps one should say filming a score), Leone and Morricone created perhaps the best integration of music, movement, and visual imagery to be found in Hollywood films. Despite the undeniably brilliant result of his visuals, themes, casting, and music, Leone's epic western was dumped by an American studio system that didn't understand it. Cutting the film to pieces in order to shorten it, the editing rendered the original US release almost unintelligible—confusing to critics and ensuring a bomb at the box office. In Europe, however, where the film was released intact, it did exceptionally well, breaking box-office records in Paris, where it played continuously for *four years*. (The film even started a fashion craze—everyone in Paris wanted the western dusters worn by Fonda's and Robards's men.) Finally, in 1984, Paramount rereleased the uncut version, and the film is only now getting the respect from American critics that it truly deserves.

ONE-EYED JACKS

1961   141m   c   ★★★½
Western   /PG
Pennebaker

Marlon Brando *(Rio)*, Karl Malden *(Dad Longworth)*, Katy Jurado *(Maria)*, Pina Pellicer *(Louisa)*, Slim Pickens *(Lon)*, Ben Johnson *(Bob Amory)*, Sam Gilman *(Harvey)*, Larry Duran *(Modesto)*, Timothy Carey *(Howard Tetley)*, Miriam Colon *(Redhead)*

p, Frank P. Rosenberg; d, Marlon Brando; w, Guy Trosper, Calder Willingham (based on the novel *The Authentic Death of Hendry Jones* by Charles Neider); ph, Charles Lang (VistaVision, Technicolor); ed, Archie Marshek; m, Hugo Friedhofer; art d, Hal Pereira, Joseph MacMillan Johnson; fx, John P. Fulton, Farciot Edouart; chor, Josephine Earl; cos, Yvonne Wood

This offbeat western is almost as strange as the Brando opus THE MISSOURI BREAKS, which he made a decade and a half later, but it packs a wallop and quite a few surprises. Brando and Malden are bandits who rob a Mexican bank in 1880. Both men ride the same horse after fast-approaching possemen shoot one of their mounts; Malden is also without shoes since the lawmen rousted the pair while he was pitching woo at a curvy Latin lady, and he had to leave sans boots. The bandits stop on top of a hill, realizing that they cannot outdistance the posse while riding one horse, and it is decided that Malden will ride off and return for Brando with another mount. He goes, leaving Brando on the hilltop, duelling with the lawmen below. Coming to a small ranch, Malden tries to buy a horse and then figures that by the time he rides back for Brando, he will undoubtedly become a prisoner, too. He rides away to safety with all the gold he and Brando have stolen. Brando is slowly surrounded on the hilltop and taken prisoner after running out of ammunition. He spends five years being brutalized in the stinking Sonora prison and then joins forces with Duran in a daring escape. Later, Brando and Duran meet Johnson and Gilman, two mean-streaked desperadoes, and the four travel—wary of each other—to Monterey, California to rob a bank. The town, however, is controlled by none other than Malden, who has gone straight and is now the town sheriff, having married Jurado and adopted her grown Mexican daughter, Pellicer. Brando and his associates arrive in Monterey just as the town is to have a fiesta, and the outlaw tells a surprised Malden that he escaped the posse five years earlier and has been moving aimlessly around the West. But he seethes with vengeance and spitefully seduces the virginal Pellicer as a way of getting back at Malden. Meanwhile, he and the others plot to rob the bank, but Brando gets sidetracked when sitting in a bar with Duran and watching drunken bully Carey abuse a whore. He beats Carey up and then kills him when Carey tries to shoot him. For this act of self-defense, the wily Malden takes Brando to a hitching post, publicly whips him, and then smashes his shooting hand, just to make sure Brando has no plans to draw on him in the future. While his hand mends, Brando can think only of killing Malden. Johnson and Gilman can think only of robbing the bank and grow insultingly impatient with Brando as they wait for his hand to heal. They finally set out to rob the bank, killing Duran and later, when looting, they accidentally kill a little girl. The innocent Brando is grabbed by Malden and held for the crime. Brando is thrown in the Monterey jail; he asks Malden if he'll get a fair trial. "Sure," Malden says smilingly, "you'll get a fair trial—and then I'm gonna hang you!" Brando stares at Malden and tells him: "You're a real one-eyed Jack in this town, Dad, but I seen the other side of your face." Brando is insulted and abused by fat-gutted Pickens, a sadistic deputy, but he turns the trick on the deputy, shoots him, and escapes. He and Malden then shoot it out in the town square and Malden is killed. Brando, before riding away, embraces Pellicer and promises to come back for her.

ONE-EYED JACKS is Brando's only directorial achievement. The star took over the film from the famous Stanley Kubrick after he and Kubrick disagreed on character development. The story draws heavily upon the legend of Billy the Kid (the father-son relationship between Malden and Brando is almost identical to that between lawman Pat Garrett and the outlaw William Bonney; the escape from jail and the abusive guard are obviously drawn from the Kid's own experiences). It is also fraught with too many pensive moments in which Brando, unlike any real outlaw on the dodge in the Old West, broods and ponders instead of naturally going for his gun or mounting his horse. But the ever-careful and painfully exacting Brando took all the time in the world when assuming the mantle of director. Producer Rosenberg didn't like the idea, but by the time the star and Kubrick had clashed, too much money had already been spent on preproduction, and Paramount's front office was screaming for completion. The film was supposed to be shot on a 60-day shooting schedule, but Brando used six months to get the film in the can. Brando exposed more than one million feet of film which Rosenberg considered "a new world's record." The company—Brando produced under his own production company, Pennebaker Productions—printed about 250,000 feet of film (the normal total exposed footage is about 150,000 feet for any major film, of which 40,000 feet are printed for rushes). Marshek and others edited the huge film down to 141 minutes but it was still overlong, with scenes that played up Brando's martyr-like character (the whipping scene is almost a duplication of the Crucifixion but is oddly sadistic and, like a lot of the film, crammed with gratuitous violence). The film was completed on June 2, 1959, but Brando went back for one day's shooting, on October 14, 1960, to reshoot the final scene, before the film was released that year.

Lang's Oscar-nominated photography of the spectacular Monterey Peninsula, the windswept, ocean-lapped coast and rocky coastline, is outstanding, and Brando's performance, weird or not, is dynamic and intriguing. Malden is a classic study in guile, but Jurado is only a prop, and Pellicer, reportedly a Rosenberg discovery, is unconvincing and unattractive as the naive girl. (This was Pellicer's only US film; after a short-lived career in Mexican pictures, she committed suicide at the age of 24.) The film was not a financial success, costing Paramount more than $6 million (with an original budget of only $1.8 million); it returned, in its initial release, only $4.3 million. This tale of basic revenge shows man as vile and contemptuous of his fellow man, a view repeatedly seen through the eyes of the often smug but never boring Brando.

ONE FLEW OVER THE CUCKOO'S NEST

1975 129m c   ★★★★
Drama   R/18
Fantasy

Jack Nicholson (*Randle Patrick McMurphy*), Louise Fletcher (*Nurse Mildred Ratched*), William Redfield (*Harding*), Michael Berryman (*Ellis*), Brad Dourif (*Billy Bibbit*), Peter Brocco (*Col. Matterson*), Dean R. Brooks (*Dr. John Spivey*), Alonzo Brown (*Miller*), Scatman Crothers (*Turkle*), Mwako Cumbuka (*Warren*)

p, Saul Zaentz, Michael Douglas; d, Milos Forman; w, Lawrence Hauben, Bo Goldman (based on the novel by Ken Kesey and the play by Dale Wasserman); ph, Haskell Wexler, William A. Fraker, Bill Butler (DeLuxe Color); ed, Richard Chew, Lynzee Klingman, Sheldon Kahn; m, Jack Nitzsche; prod d, Paul Sylbert; art d, Edwin O'Donovan; cos, Aggie Guerard Rodgers

A deeply disturbing film, this is a compelling romp through a lunatic ward with the energetic and wisecracking Nicholson. Doing time on a prison farm, Nicholson gets out of work detail and escapes the rigors of prison life by pretending to be crazy. Shipped to a mental asylum, he becomes the prisoner of a much more hateful system, presided over by a quietly sadistic head nurse, Fletcher. To his amazement Nicholson finds his fellow inmates are "no crazier than any other SOB on the street," and he finds that all have distinctive personalities with strange and pathetic quirks, although a few have retreated into entirely monistic states. To bring life to the dead atmosphere, Nicholson introduces card games (with pornographically illustrated cards), organizes basketball games, and even conducts a field trip for his fellow inmates, but at every turn Fletcher is there to administer vicious punishment, attempting to break Nicholson's spirit. At one point Nicholson smuggles two girlfriends, Marya Small and Louisa Moritz, into the ward and passes out a cache of booze, giving a wild midnight party for the inmates and initiating the emotionally disturbed Dourif into sex. Fletcher finds Dourif in bed with one of the girls the next morning and vindictively tells the impressionable youth that she will inform his mother. Dourif commits suicide and Nicholson goes berserk, trying to strangle Fletcher.

Beyond jarring and electrifying drama, ONE FLEW OVER THE CUCKOO'S NEST is a naked study in rebellion and mistreatment, wonderfully enacted by a mostly nonprofessional cast. But to totally buy it, you have to agree with it—that mental patients should have sex and alcohol. Forman's that type of director; his literal approach feels leaden here. Attempting to enliven a basically flabby storyline, all he achieves are alternating moods of goofiness—equating disturbance with cute incompetence—and shrieking emptiness.

Nicholson is in his usual mold (FIVE EASY PIECES; THE LAST DETAIL) as a cagy antihero ready to jab the system at every opportunity, even knowing he cannot win against it.

Fletcher appears in her only effective role. (The woman as an actress is close to catatonic herself—speaking in a monotone, her face immobile, her body as rigid as the starch in her immaculate uniform. Why did she win an Oscar? Everyone mistook her peculiarity for acting. Quick—name the last three Louise Fletcher movies *you* saw). Nicholson, who won the Oscar for Best Actor, gives his frankest performance to date. Actor Kirk Douglas acquired the rights to Wasserman's play (originally written by Kesey as a novel) and had a great success acting in it on Broadway in the 1960s, but by the time this film was made in 1975, he was too old to play the lead and turned the property over to his son Michael, who brought in Forman as director. In addition to Nicholson's and Fletcher's Oscars, the movie swept the top 1975 Academy Awards, winning Oscars for Best Picture, Best Director (Forman) and Best Screenplay (Hauben, Goldman). This picture marked the screen debuts of gigantic Creek Indian painter Will Sampson, of Dourif and Christopher Lloyd, and of Brooks (who was superintendent of the Oregon State Hospital in Salem, where the picture was filmed). Tim McCall, a former governor of Oregon, played the news commentator.

ONE FOOT IN HEAVEN
1941 106m bw   ★★★½
Drama   /U
WB

Fredric March *(William Spence)*, Martha Scott *(Hope Morris Spence)*, Beulah Bondi *(Mrs. Lydia Sandow)*, Gene Lockhart *(Preston Thurston)*, Grant Mitchell *(Clayton Potter)*, Moroni Olsen *(Dr. John Romer)*, Harry Davenport *(Elias Samson)*, Elisabeth Fraser *(Eileen Spence at 17)*, Frankie Thomas *(Hartzell Spence at 18)*, Laura Hope Crews *(Mrs. Thurston)*

p, Robert Lord; d, Irving Rapper; w, Casey Robinson (based on the biography by Hartzell Spence of his father); ph, Charles Rosher; ed, Warren Low; m, Max Steiner

In one of his finest performances, Fredric March plays Rev. William Spence, a Methodist minister who devotes his life to transforming wavering parishes into strong pillars of faith. Episodic in form, ONE FOOT IN HEAVEN begins in Canada in 1904. After listening to an evangelist, Spence and his devoted wife, Hope (Martha Scott), decide to move to a small Iowa community desperately in need of spiritual guidance. Trying to fit in, Spence and Hope live at poverty level, forgoing the luxuries to which they are accustomed. After their work in one parish is complete, they move on to the next, adding to their family in the process. Over the next 20 years, Spence and Hope fight a number of uphill battles, and when it finally appears as if the Spence family is going to settle down, word reaches them of another troubled parish. A huge audience pleaser, ONE FOOT IN HEAVEN was based on the real-life exploits of Rev. William Spence, whose story was told in a book written by his son. Adding to its authenticity was the presence of Rev. Dr. Norman Vincent Peale as technical advisor. What makes the film so enjoyable, however, isn't its religious message, but March's portrayal of Spence as a real man—one with morals and common sense, who can also be aggressive when necessary.

ONE HUNDRED AND ONE DALMATIANS
1961 79m c   ★★★½
Children's/Animated   G/U
Disney

VOICES OF: Rod Taylor *(Pongo)*, Lisa Davis *(Anita)*, Cate Bauer *(Perdita)*, Ben Wright *(Roger Radcliff)*, Frederic Worlock *(Horace)*, J. Pat O'Malley *(Jasper/Miscellaneous Dogs)*, Betty Lou Gerson *(Cruella De Vil/Miss Birdwell)*, Martha Wentworth *(Nani/Goose/Cow)*, Tom Conway *(Collie)*, George Pelling *(Great Dane)*

p, Walt Disney; d, Wolfgang Reitherman, Hamilton Luske, Clyde Geronimi; w, Bill Peet (based on a book by Dodie Smith); ed, Donald Halliday, Roy M. Brewer, Jr.; m, George Bruns; prod d, Ken Anderson; art d, Ken Anderson; anim, Milt Kahl, Marc Davis, Oliver M. Johnston, Jr., Franklin Thomas, John Lounsbery, Eric Larson, Hal King, Cliff Nordberg, Eric Cleworth, Art Stevens, Hal Ambro, Bill Keil, Dick Lucas, Les Clark, Blaine Gibson, John Sibley, Julius Svendsen

Three hundred artists worked on this project for three years and came up with one of the best feature cartoons ever produced by Disney Studios. The story, a romance with an interesting detective twist, is combined with exquisite caricatures of both humans and dogs. The plot revolves around a dog, Pongo, and his master, Roger, who fall for Anita and her dog, Perdita. Roger and Anita marry, allowing Pongo and Perdita to be together and produce a litter of 15 Dalmatian puppies. Wicked Cruella De Vil is overly persistent in her desire to have all 15 puppies, but Roger refuses her, prompting the wealthy woman to hire a pair of cockney crooks to steal the pups. Roger and Anita try everything to locate them, but to no avail, so Pongo resorts to the "twilight bark," a system of dog signals that locates the puppies in a deserted mansion on the outskirts of London. Pongo, assisted by a dog named the Colonel, a horse, and a cat, then sets out to rescue the puppies, discovering in the process a total of 99 Dalmatians that the evil Cruella has gathered to make herself a rare coat. Throughout the story are subtle visual elements creating an atmosphere that transcends mere cartoon reality. The characters are also evocatively voiced by a cast that includes Rod Taylor as Pongo. For fun, note the physical resemblance between many of the dogs and their masters.

100 MEN AND A GIRL
1937 85m bw   ★★★★
Musical
Universal

Deanna Durbin *(Patricia Cardwell)*, Leopold Stokowski *(Himself)*, Adolphe Menjou *(John Cardwell)*, Alice Brady *(Mrs. Frost)*, Eugene Pallette *(John R. Frost)*, Mischa Auer *(Michael Borodoff)*, Billy Gilbert *(Garage Owner)*, Alma Kruger *(Mrs. Tyler)*, Jack Smart *(Marshall, the Doorman)*, Jed Prouty *(Tommy Bitters)*

p, Joe Pasternak; d, Henry Koster; w, Bruce Manning, Charles Kenyon, James Mulhauser, Hans Kraly (based on a story by Hans Kraly); ph, Joseph Valentine; ed, Bernard W. Burton

Charming, still. There are many child stars who have been horrors to work with, but that was not the case with Deanna Durbin, who was a delight for everyone and surely one of the most agreeable tykes ever to don greasepaint. She began her career with Judy Garland in an MGM short, EVERY SUNDAY, but the studio dropped her and kept Garland. It wasn't that her voice wasn't resonant; it was merely that the studio felt there was only room for one teen singer and opted for Judy. Durbin was signed by Universal, cast in THREE SMART GIRLS, and did so well that they top-lined her in this one, which turned out to be a box-office winner that took the studio from the brink of bankruptcy. Menjou is a trombonist without a place to blow. The problem is shared by many of his musician friends. Durbin, realizing the difficulty, forms an orchestra and convinces the eminent Leopold Stokowski to conduct the aggregation in a concert. The orchestra is a hit and all ends well.

Many of Durbin's films (and Durbin herself) have been long underrated as being just too sweet for words, but this is far from the truth, partly because Durbin herself adds an agreeable touch of spunk and spice to her standard "nice girl" roles. Her first dozen films for Universal play delightfully today. 100 MEN AND A GIRL, for instance, is smoothly entertaining from start to finish, with an excellent mix of classical and pop music. The songs include: "Hungarian Rhapsody No. 2" (Franz Liszt), the drinking song from "La Traviata" (Verdi), excerpts from "Lohengrin" (Wagner), "Symphony No. 5" (Tschaikovsky), "Alleluja" (Mozart), "It's Raining Sunbeams" (Sam Coslow, Frederick Hollander), "A Heart That's Free" (Alfred G. Robyn, Thomas T. Railey). An Oscar went to Charles Previn for the musical score, plus nominations for the Best Sound, Best Editing and Best Original Story. Best of all, it was even named as one of the finalists for Best Picture, along with THE AWFUL TRUTH, DEAD END, IN OLD CHICAGO, CAPTAINS COURAGEOUS, LOST HORIZON, STAGE DOOR, and A STAR IS BORN. Pretty stiff competition for the ultimate winner, THE LIFE OF EMILE ZOLA.

ONE MORE RIVER

1934   85m   bw   ★★★★★
Drama
Universal

Diana Wynyard (Lady Clare Corven), Frank Lawton (Tony Croom), Mrs. Patrick Campbell (Lady Mont), Jane Wyatt (Dinny Cherrell), Colin Clive (Sir Gerald Corven), Reginald Denny (David Dornford), C. Aubrey Smith (Gen. Charwell), Henry Stephenson (Sir Lawrence Mont), Lionel Atwill (Brough), Alan Mowbray (Forsyte)

d, James Whale; w, R.C. Sherriff (based on the novel by John Galsworthy); ph, John Mescall

Classical Hollywood's finest and most convincing representation of contemporary Great Britain. A superb screen adaptation of John Galsworthy's last novel, ONE MORE RIVER represents a rare melding of the sensibilities of the theatre and the possibilities of cinema. Brilliantly directed by Whale, the story centers around Lady Clare Corven (Wynyard), who has been badly mistreated by her sadistic husband, Sir Gerald (Clive). Leaving home, she begins a platonic friendship with young Tony Croom (Lawton), who falls madly in love with her. Using a detective to spy on the couple, Sir Gerald soon brings the conflict to the divorce court, a move still capable of causing a scandal at that time. Setting much of the latter part of the film in an English court of law, Whale grippingly brings the story to its conclusion.

Although the subject matter of this wonderful film might seem slightly dated to an age used to divorce, ONE MORE RIVER is an exceptionally well-observed portrait of England at a specific historical moment. Lovingly rendered vignettes are everywhere, from the elderly man who has refused to vote ever since the death of Prime Minister Gladstone, to the marvelous theatrics of Clare's aunt (the legendary Mrs. Patrick Campbell). The cast is uniformly superb, with the luminous Wynyard bringing grace and insight to her victimized wife and Clive in wonderful lipcurling form as her nasty spouse. Lawton is also quite touching, and the supporting cast includes gems from Denny, Smith, Wyatt, Stephenson, Atwill, Mowbray, Gilbert Emery and E.E. Clive. In some ways this quietly splendid effort seems an Anglicized parallel to DODSWORTH as it keenly explores the sadnesses of both love's birth and marriage's twilight. Full of beautiful camerawork and gleaming with warm understanding, ONE

MORE RIVER is a mature, sadly forgotten beauty from one of Hollywood's greatest directors.

ONE NIGHT OF LOVE

1934   84m   bw   ★★½
Musical   /U
Columbia

Grace Moore (Mary Barrett), Tullio Carminati (Giulio Monteverdi), Lyle Talbot (Bill Houston), Mona Barrie (Lally), Jessie Ralph (Angelina, Housekeeper), Luis Alberni (Monteverdi's Assistant), Andres de Segurola (Galuppi), Rosemary Glosz (Frappazini), Nydia Westman (Muriel), Jane Darwell (Mary's Mother)

p, Sara Risher; d, Victor Schertzinger; w, S.K. Lauren, James Gow, Edmund H. North (based on a story by Dorothy Speare and Charles Beahan); ph, Joseph Walker; ed, Gene Milford; m, Louis Silvers; art d, Stephen Goosson; fx, John Hoffman; cos, Robert Kalloch

Moore is a struggling opera singer who goes to Europe after losing a radio talent contest. Singing teacher Carminati is impressed after hearing her sing in a cafe. He takes her on as a student and develops her voice, while she falls in love with him. She becomes jealous when he takes on another female singer as a pupil, which almost ruins her opening night. She is triumphant, however, proving her star talent at the New York Metropolitan Opera House. It's all rather cliche-ridden, but the film was a box office hit and earned Academy Award nominations for Best Picture, Best Actress (Moore), and Best Director, losing on all counts to IT HAPPENED ONE NIGHT. However, the film did win Oscars for Best Sound and Best Score.

ONE OF OUR AIRCRAFT IS MISSING

1942   90m   bw   ★★★½
War   /U
Archers/British National   (U.K.)

Godfrey Tearle (Sir George Corbett), Eric Portman (Tom Earnshaw), Hugh Williams (Frank Shelley), Bernard Miles (Geoff Hickman), Hugh Burden (John Glyn Haggard), Emrys Jones (Bob Ashley), Googie Withers (Jo de Vries), Pamela Brown (Else Meertens), Joyce Redman (Jet van Dieren), Hay Petrie (Burgomeister)

p, Michael Powell, Emeric Pressburger; d, Michael Powell, Emeric Pressburger; w, Michael Powell, Emeric Pressburger; ph, Ronald Neame; ed, David Lean; art d, David Rawnsley

During WWII, squadrons of heavy Wellington bombers take off from Britain at dusk and cross the English Channel for a raid on Stuttgart. On the return flight, six crewmen on one plane are forced to bail out over German-occupied Holland. Some Dutch children help them evade a German patrol; then, disguised, they are aided by an underground network that enables them to reach the coast and to return to Britain in a small boat. Almost immediately after being reunited with their squadron they are back in the air, flying even more dangerous missions into Germany. The second Michael Powell-Emeric Pressburger collaboration (the first on which Pressburger was codirector), this film does not reach the heights of their previous, similarly plotted picture, THE INVADERS. The best sequences are the opening ones, precisely detailing the raid as the men concentrate on their duties, adjusting instruments while their planes shake under the anti-aircraft fire all around them. The performances—of the stiff-upper-lip variety—are all good, especially Godfrey Tearle's as the aircraft commander, Googie Withers's as an important link in the chain of rescuers, and Scottish character actor Hay Petrie's as an apoplectic burgomeister. The film's worth as a propaganda piece was considerable, but too many long-winded speeches about people uniting to fight the Germans date the film somewhat now.

ONE, TWO, THREE
1961   115m   bw   ★★★½
Comedy   /U
Mirisch/Pyramid

James Cagney (C.R. MacNamara), Horst Buchholz (Otto Ludwig Piffl), Pamela Tiffin (Scarlett Hazeltine), Arlene Francis (Phyllis MacNamara), Lilo Pulver (Ingeborg), Howard St. John (Hazeltine), Hanns Lothar (Schlemmer), Lois Bolton (Mrs. Hazeltine), Leon Askin (Peripetchikoff), Peter Capell (Mishkin)

p, Billy Wilder; d, Billy Wilder; w, Billy Wilder, I.A.L. Diamond (based on the play Egy, Ketto, Harom by Ferenc Molnar); ph, Daniel Fapp (Panavision); ed, Daniel Mandell; m, Andre Previn; art d, Alexander Trauner; fx, Milt Rice

James Cagney left the movie business for more than 20 years after finishing his role in ONE, TWO, THREE and it's no wonder; he needed at least that much time to rest up after the fastest-moving comedy made in the 1960s, and surely one of the funniest. This film begins at mach one and gets somewhere near the speed of light by the time it finishes. As a matter of fact, it's often too furiously quick for its own good as the dialogue comes at the ears with Uzi-like speed. Cagney is the fast-talking, hard-driving, self-made man who heads up Coca-Cola's bottling interests in Germany. His attitude is similar to the man who once ran General Motors and said, "What's good for General Motors is good for America." And since there is nothing in Europe more American than Coca-Cola, Cagney is determined to bring it to everyone with two lips and a gullet. Cagney would like to become chief of all the European operations and is working toward that end when Tiffin, the teenage daughter of St. John—one of the heavyweights at Coca-Cola's Georgia headquarters—arrives, and Cagney has to baby-sit her for two weeks as she makes her way through a tour of the Continent. Cagney does his best to squire the dippy Tiffin, in the hope that his behavior will get him his desired promotion, but things go awry when she falls hard for Buchholz, a dedicated East Berlin Communist hippy. Cagney learns that St. John is coming to Germany at the same time he discovers Tiffin has married Buchholz. He plants a copy of that most capitalistic of papers, The Wall Street Journal, on Buchholz, figuring the youth will be clapped in irons and an annulment can be secured. Then he learns that Tiffin is expecting Buchholz's baby, so he has to get the kid out of jail and train him to be a capitalist in order to make him a suitable son-in-law for St. John. Cagney successfully springs Buchholz, spends a few bucks to purchase a royal title for him, and gives him a crash course in American business. Buchholz impresses St. John so much that the pleased father-in-law hands the plum job of running Europe to his new relation, the father of his unborn grandchild. Cagney winds up going back to Atlanta with wife Francis. He did his job too well and lost the promotion he'd hoped for.

Cagney plays this part with such verve and energy that he seems to be a much younger man than he was (62) and even appears to be a new actor eager to impress the studio with his abilities. But that was always the way Cagney played things—to the hilt. Many of the jokes were taken right from the period's headlines and were already dated by the time the film was released. It was based on a one-act play by the master farceur Molnar and expanded beautifully by Wilder and Diamond. Filmed on location in West Berlin and at the studios in Munich (where Wilder had been before the war), it won no awards except the laughter of those who saw it. Fapp got an Oscar nomination

for his cinematography. Previn's score was perfect, and the use of several old ditties was excellent, including "Yes, We Have No Bananas" (Frank Silver, Irving Cohn). It would be better to watch this alone as the sound of chuckling in a theater will drown out many of the clever lines.

ONION FIELD, THE
1979   122m   c   ★★★
Crime   R/18
Avco Embassy

John Savage (Karl Hettinger), James Woods (Greg Powell), Franklyn Seales (Jimmy Smith), Ted Danson (Ian Campbell), Ronny Cox (Pierce Brooks), David Huffman (District Attorney Phil Halpin), Christopher Lloyd (Jailhouse Lawyer), Diane Hull (Helen Hettinger), Priscilla Pointer (Chrissie Campbell), Beege Barkett (Greg's Woman)

p, Walter Coblenz; d, Harold Becker; w, Joseph Wambaugh (based on the book by Wambaugh); ph, Charles Rosher, Jr.; ed, John W. Wheeler; m, Eumir Deodato; prod d, Brian Eatwell

After have some of his earlier works unacceptably altered, Wambaugh decided to write the screenplay himself for this version of his true story about two Los Angeles cops and the killers of one of them. Danson and Savage, a pair of plainclothes officers working the Hollywood beat, go after two lowlifes in a car, Woods and Seales, and are shocked when a gun is put in their faces. The cops are disarmed, kidnapped, and taken to a field some distance from Los Angeles where Danson is assassinated. Savage gets away, and with his accurate description the killers are soon nabbed. The rest of the picture concerns the judicial system and how it favors the felon over the victim. Both killers are willing to cooperate in return for a deal from the DA's office, and each claims it was the other who pulled the trigger on Danson. Meanwhile, Savage is so wracked with guilt for his partner's death that he begins to break down mentally. An authentic look at police work (and that is where it shines), the picture gets confused in the court scenes and can't sustain the power of its opening sequences. Good acting and careful direction by Becker make it worth seeing, but the violence and the language may be too graphic for some tastes. Although Wambaugh himself was a cop with the Los Angeles Police Department, he had technical assistance on this from Richard Falk. Advice on courtroom procedures came from Phillip Halpin and Dino Fulgoni, who were portrayed by Huffman and Pataki. The crime took place in 1963 and Smith (Seales) was released in the 1980s, over strenuous objections.

ONLY ANGELS HAVE WINGS
1939   121m   bw   ★★★★
Drama   /A
Columbia

Cary Grant (Geoff Carter), Jean Arthur (Bonnie Lee), Richard Barthelmess (Bat McPherson), Rita Hayworth (Judith McPherson), Thomas Mitchell (Kid Dabb), Sig Rumann (Dutchman), Victor Kilian (Sparks), John Carroll (Gent Shelton), Allyn Joslyn (Les Peters), Don "Red" Barry (Tex Gordon)

p, Howard Hawks; d, Howard Hawks; w, William Rankin (uncredited), Eleanore Griffin (uncredited), Jules Furthman (based on a story by Howard Hawks); ph, Joseph Walker, Elmer Dyer; ed, Viola Lawrence; m, Dimitri Tiomkin, Manuel Maciste, M.W. Stoloff; art d, Lionel Banks; fx, Roy Davidson, Edwin C. Hahn; cos, Robert Kalloch

An amazing adventure film in which the adventure is primarily confined to a shabby saloon, this Grant-Arthur vehicle clearly bears the mark of director Howard Hawks. Grant, the head of a broken-down air freight company, sends courageous pilots over the treacherous Andes Mountains in Peru. Arthur becomes involved with one such pilot, Noah Beery, Jr., then quickly switches her attention to the hardboiled Grant. Several other pilots (Joslyn, Carroll, and Barry) are much taken with Arthur, but she only has eyes for the all-business Grant, who fails to return her affection. Enter Barthelmess, a pilot who tarnished his reputation in an accident years earlier in which another flier was killed. The guilt-ridden Barthelmess is washed up as a pilot, but Grant gives him a job anyway. Hayworth, Barthelmess's sexy, cuckolding wife, tries to seduce Grant and almost succeeds before Grant realizes he really loves the smart-talking Arthur. Although the other pilots have made a pariah of Barthelmess, he proves that he's made of courageous stuff by volunteering to take on the most hazardous missions. Meanwhile, Mitchell—an elderly pilot who acts as surrogate father to Grant and whose brother was killed in the accident that ruined Barthelmess's reputation—is losing his sight but won't admit it. Grant keeps him on the ground to protect him. But when Grant prepares to undertake a dangerous flight himself, Mitchell goes in his place and is killed. The hard-boiled exterior Grant has maintained throughout the film disintegrates with the death of his dearest friend, and Arthur finally sees his human side. At the film's close it seems likely that Grant and Arthur will end up together, but that their life will continue to be hectic.

ONLY ANGELS HAVE WINGS is a powerful character study, and director Hawks and his fine, predominantly male cast carefully develop the personalities of an interesting collection of characters. Though much of the dialogue is predictable, the story is strong, the acting is outstanding, and Hawks's cameras move with fluid grace through the confining sets. A number of earlier films covered ground to similar to that flown over here—including CEILING ZERO; THE DAWN PATROL; and NIGHT FLIGHT—but this picture's true predecessor is the surprisingly good low-budget FLIGHT FROM GLORY, with Chester Morris and Van Heflin. Made two years earlier, FLIGHT FROM GLORY bears an uncanny resemblance to Hawks's film; focusing on another isolated company of men that is disrupted by a beautiful woman, the earlier film also features a valiant pilot supervisor, as well as a brash flier who is thought to be cowardly. What's more, the strained love story between Grant and Arthur is nearly identical to the one at the center of RED DUST, yet it has wonderfully poignant moments, including an ending right out of THE FRONT PAGE.

Rita Hayworth gives a notable performance as a vamp, and supporting players Allyn Joslyn and John Carroll are jaded, sardonic live wires. Richard Barthelmess, as the film's most complex character, plays his role stoically, failing to invest his washed-up flier with the necessary emotional depth. This was an important comeback attempt for Barthelmess, who had experienced lean years since his days as a silent screen star. Regrettably, the meaty part he was given was left on the kitchen table, half-eaten, and Barthelmess never again appeared in a major film as a lead. The special effects, particularly the fine aerial sequences, earned Roy Davidson and Edwin C. Hahn an Oscar nomination in a category recognized for the first time by the Academy. The film was also nominated for Best Black-and-White Cinematography. It's interesting to note that Thomas Mitchell, who had a supporting role in this fine film, in 1939 also appeared in GONE WITH THE WIND, MR. SMITH GOES TO WASHINGTON, THE HUNCHBACK OF NOTRE DAME,

and STAGECOACH, for which he won an Oscar. It's unlikely any actor has ever had a more impressive year.

ONLY WHEN I LAUGH
1981 120m c ★★★
Comedy/Drama R/15
Columbia

Marsha Mason (Georgia), Kristy McNichol (Polly), James Coco (Jimmy), Joan Hackett (Toby), David Dukes (David), John Bennett Perry (Lou the Actor), Guy Boyd (Man), Ed Moore (Dr. Komack), Byron Webster (Tom), Peter Coffield (Mr. Tarloff)

p, Roger M. Rothstein, Neil Simon; d, Glenn Jordan; w, Neil Simon (based on the play The Gingerbread Lady by Neil Simon); ph, David M. Walsh (Metrocolor); ed, John Wright; m, David Shire; prod d, Albert Brenner; art d, David M. Haber; cos, Ann Roth

Neil Simon's play The Gingerbread Lady was not a huge success, and neither was this film version of it. Georgia (Marsha Mason, who received an Oscar nomination for her role) is a divorced actress just released from an alcohol-treatment program. She is trying to reestablish her relationship with her teenage daughter Polly (Kristy McNichol) after having neglected the child in favor of booze for several years. She also has a chance to get her career back on track by starring in a play by her former lover (David Dukes), and as the pressure mounts, so does her desire for liquor. It's all pretty predictable, but there are some sincere moments, especially between Mason and McNichol. James Coco, playing a gay actor who never hit the big time, and Joan Hackett, who gets all the best lines as a tart-tongued egotist, received Oscar nominations for their supporting work.

OPEN CITY
(ROMA, CITTA APERTA)
1945 105m bw ★★★★
War/Drama /A
Excelsa (Italy)

Anna Magnani (Pina), Aldo Fabrizi (Don Pietro Pellegrini), Marcell Pagliero (Giorgio Manfredi), Maria Michi (Marina), Harry Feist (Maj. Bergmann), Francesco Grandjacquet (Francesco), Giovanna Galletti (Ingrid), Vito Annichiarico (Marcello Pina's Son), Carla Revere (Lauretta), Nando Bruno (Agostino)

p, Roberto Rossellini; d, Roberto Rossellini; w, Sergio Amidei, Federico Fellini, Roberto Rossellini (based on a story by Amidei and Alberto Consiglio); ph, Ubaldo Arata; m, Renzo Rossellini

One of the most important achievements in the history of cinema, OPEN CITY is the first great fusion of documentary and melodrama. Filmed on the streets, without the use of sound recorders (dialog was dubbed in later), during the months just after the Allies liberated Italy from the grip of Fascism, the film has the appearance of a documentary. The actors, except for Anna Magnani (then a sometime dance-hall girl), were all nonprofessionals. The backgrounds were not constructions on a Cinecitta lot, but actual apartments, shops, and streets—a change for those used to sets and costumes. Set in Rome, 1943-44, the story brings together two enemy forces—the Communists and the Catholics—and unites them in the fight for their country's liberation. Manfredi (Marcello Pagliero) is a Resistance leader wanted by the Germans who must deliver some money to his compatriots. Hiding out in the apartment block of Francesco (Francesco Grandjacquet) and his pregnant fiancee, Pina (Magnani), Manfredi plans to let a Catholic priest, Don Pietro (Aldo Fabrizi), make the delivery. When their building is raided, Francesco is arrested and hauled away. Pino chases after him, screaming, and is gunned down in the middle of the street. Manfredi takes refuge in the apartment of his mistress, Marina (Maria Michi), a lesbian drug addict who, unknown to him, is an informant whose drug supplier is an outrageous lesbian Gestapo agent (Giovanna Galleti). As excellent as OPEN CITY is, it has often been criticized for its black-and-white division of characters into Good and Evil, and the emotional manipulation of Renzo Rossellini's score as well as its use of comic devices—these attributes apparently weakening the objective aims of neorealist cinema. Director Roberto Rossellini, however, cannot be criticized for stirring emotions rather than intellect, since objectivity is not possible here. In OPEN CITY one can see, above all else, the honesty and morality of Rossellini's direction, and, while his result may not wholly comply with the accepted definition of neorealism, his intent—to bring reality to the screen—most certainly does. Most videotape copies offer prints of mediocre quality and often unreadable subtitles. For us, the brief time Magnani is on the screen is more than enough.

OPERATION MAD BALL

1957   105m   bw   ★★★
War/Comedy   /U
Columbia

Jack Lemmon (Pvt. Hogan), Kathryn Grant (Lt. Betty Bixby), Ernie Kovacs (Capt. Paul Locke), Arthur O'Connell (Col. Rousch), Mickey Rooney (M/Sgt. Yancy Skibo), Dick York (Cpl. Bohun), James Darren (Pvt. Widowskas), Roger Smith (Cpl. Berryman), William Leslie (Pvt. Grimes), Sheridan Comerate (Sgt. Wilson)

p, Jed Harris; d, Richard Quine; w, Jed Harris, Blake Edwards, Arthur Carter (based on the play by Arthur Carter); ph, Charles Lawton, Jr.; ed, Charles Nelson; m, George Duning; art d, Robert Boyle

Lemmon received his first starring role in this military comedy which also served as the screen debut of the brilliant television comedian Ernie Kovacs. Based on a play, OPERATION MAD BALL centers on a group of bored WWII GIs stationed at an Army medical unit in France who try to improve morale by throwing a "Mad Ball" for the nurses. Unfortunately, all the nurses are officers and the enlisted men are forbidden to fraternize with them. The mastermind behind this plan is Lemmon, a fast-talking private who sneaks around behind the back of his by-the-book captain, Kovacs. Lemmon arranges for the party to be held at a hotel run by Jeanne Manet, a shifty French local out to make a fast buck off the GIs.

Rooney shines as the clever master sergeant who can dig up anything Lemmon needs at a moment's notice, and Grant (Mrs. Bing Crosby) is likable as Lemmon's disapproving girlfriend. The film is filled with some funny rapid-fire dialogue adapted by playwright Carter and producer Harris with help from a young Blake Edwards. OPERATION MAD BALL was the obsession of actor Richard Quine, who saw the property as his ticket into directing. Quine brought the screenplay to Columbia studio chief Harry Cohn and refused to sell it unless he could direct. Cohn balked at first but gave in with the proviso that Cohn and Jed Harris, who produced the show on Broadway and whom Cohn hated, would never meet. At one point in the shooting, Quine decided to film the climactic party scene at night and served the cast real alcohol so that everyone would be relaxed and in a party mood. When Cohn learned of the costly overtime shoot, he stormed onto the set and demanded an explanation. Quine explained his logic and invited the mogul to stay, have a drink, and watch the shooting. This seemed to appease Cohn, and he sat out of camera range sipping a drink and had a good time.

Lemmon fondly remembers the shooting of OPERATION MAD BALL and cites it as one of his personal favorites. He greatly enjoyed working with both Rooney and Kovacs (he would make two more films with Kovacs, BELL, BOOK AND CANDLE and IT HAPPENED TO JANE), but Rooney had him laughing so much that 30 takes were required for one scene. Director Quine says in Don Widener's biography of the actor, Lemmon, "Mickey never did the scene twice the same way and every time he'd add a new touch, Jack would just fall over backwards. It was the only time I ever saw Lemmon unable to handle an acting chore. He had only one line in the scene and I don't think he ever got it out." As for Kovacs, he grabbed eagerly at the chance to work his special magic on the big screen. He tackled the role of Capt. Paul Locke with verve and a malevolent zest and garnered good reviews. Unfortunately, Hollywood didn't really know what to do with Kovacs and typecast him in the role for much of his brief movie career. Of the nine movies Kovacs appeared in, he played a captain four times (OPERATION MAD BALL, OUR MAN IN HAVANA, WAKE ME WHEN IT'S OVER, and SAIL A CROOKED SHIP). Frustrated by this short-sighted casting which handcuffed his creativity, Kovacs took out an ad in Variety which simply read, "No more [*] [!!] captains."

OPERATION PETTICOAT

1959   124m   c   ★★★½
Comedy/War   /U
Granarte

Cary Grant (Adm. Matt Sherman), Tony Curtis (Lt. Nick Holden), Joan O'Brien (Lt. Dolores Crandall), Dina Merrill (Lt. Barbara Duran), Arthur O'Connell (Sam Tostin), Gene Evans (Molumphrey), Dick Sargent (Stovall), Virginia Gregg (Maj. Edna Hayward), Robert F. Simon (Capt. J.B. Henderson), Robert Gist (Watson)

p, Robert Arthur; d, Blake Edwards; w, Stanley Shapiro, Maurice Richlin (based on a story by Paul King, Joseph Stone); ph, Russell Harlan, Clifford Stine (Eastmancolor); ed, Ted J. Kent, Frank Gross; m, David Rose; art d, Alexander Golitzen, Robert E. Smith; cos, Bill Thomas

After the end of WWII, Adm. Matt Sherman (Cary Grant) reads over his log from the USS Sea Tiger, the submarine he captains. Sherman is about to turn over the command of the sub to Lt. Nick Holden (Tony Curtis), who is assigned to squire it until it is destroyed and replaced by a nuclear vessel. The movie unwinds in flashback as Sherman recalls some of the events in the sub's life—particularly how that life was renewed when he became determined to raise the Sea Tiger in the wake of an attack in Manila Bay. It's December 1941 and, with help from Holden, who secures the supplies and gear to help restore the badly damaged sub, Sherman and his crew take to the waters. Along the way, they are joined by five stranded nurses, a couple of Filipino families, and a goat. The sailors ferry them out of harm's way, especially enjoying the presence of the nurses—a chesty bunch who always seem to be passing the hot young sailors in the sub's very narrow corridors. They also paint the sub pink. There's not much story to speak of, and the jokes are more than a bit sexist, but the gags are bright and Blake Edwards's direction adroit enough to make OPERATION PETTICOAT an enjoyable time. A TV series was later attempted, but never came close to the energy of the movie.

ORCHESTRA WIVES
1942 98m bw   ★★★★
Musical   /A
FOX

George Montgomery (Bill Abbott), Ann Rutherford (Connie), Glenn Miller (Gene Morrison), Cesar Romero (Sinjin), Lynn Bari (Jaynie), Carole Landis (Natalie), Virginia Gilmore (Elsie), Mary Beth Hughes (Caroline), Brothers Nicholas (Specialty), Tamara Geva (Mrs. Beck)

p, William LeBaron; d, Archie Mayo; w, Karl Tunberg, Darrell Ware (based on a story by James Prindle); ph, Lucien Ballard; ed, Robert Bischoff; art d, Richard Day, Joseph C. Wright

Among the many cinematic looks behind the scenes in the 1940s, ORCHESTRA WIVES may be the finest example of the genre, due in great part to the presence of Glenn Miller (in his final appearance before his ill-fated flight over the English Channel). The plot concerns Connie (Ann Rutherford), the new wife of trumpeter Bill Abbott (George Montgomery). Connie accompanies Bill as he tours with Gene Morrison's (Miller) orchestra; meanwhile, the other wives cattily speculate as to how long the union can last, especially considering sensuous band singer Jaynie's (Lynn Bari, whose singing is dubbed by Pat Friday) fondness for other women's men. Sure enough, Jaynie sets her sights on Bill, and the sniping among the wives nearly breaks up the band, but all ends happily as the ensemble's dapper pianist (Cesar Romero) manages to keep both the newlyweds and the orchestra together. The picture swings with Miller music from start to finish, with songs provided by those aces of movie tunes, Harry Warren and Mack Gordon.

ORDET
1954 126m bw   ★★★★½
Drama
Palladium   (Denmark)

Henrik Malberg (Morten Borgen), Emil Hass Christensen (Mikkel Borgen), Preben Lerdorff-Rye (Johannes Borgen), Cay Kristiansen (Anders Borgen), Birgitte Federspiel (Inger Mikkel's Wife), Ejner Federspiel (Peter Skraedder), Ove Rud (Pastor), Ann Elisabeth Rud (Maren Borgen Mikkel's Daughter), Susanne Rud (Lilleinger Borgen Mikkel's Daughter), Gerda Nielsen (Anne Skraedder)

p, Carl-Theodor Dreyer; d, Carl-Theodor Dreyer; w, Carl-Theodor Dreyer (based on the play by Kaj Munk); ph, Henning Bendtsen; ed, Edith Schussel; m, Poul Schierbeck; art d, Erik Aaes

Based on the play by Kaj Munk, this inspirational drama focuses on one of director Dreyer's favorite themes, the conflict between institutional religion and personal faith.

Set in a staunchly God-fearing Danish village, ORDET tells the story of Morten Borgen (Malberg) and his three sons. Mikkel (Christensen) is filled with religious doubt. Anders (Kristiansen), meanwhile, is involved in a romance complicated by differences of faith. The central character, Johannes (Lerdorff-Rye), has the biggest problem of all: He believes he is Christ and his extreme faith is viewed as madness. Things change when he is visited by the Holy Spirit and Mikkel's wife is resurrected at her funeral.

Although any plot summary of ORDET would border on the ludicrous, the film is nothing of the kind. This is an overwhelming emotional and intellectual experience, thanks both to its subject matter and its austere yet potent presentation. Dreyer's rigorously spare visual style (the film contains only 114 shots in 126 minutes) perfectly conveys his metaphysical themes and creates a meditative and genuinely inspirational mood. Not to be

missed, certainly by anyone who loved his great THE PASSION OF JOAN OF ARC.

ORDINARY PEOPLE
1980 124m c   ★★½
Drama   R/15
Wildwood

Donald Sutherland (Calvin), Mary Tyler Moore (Beth), Judd Hirsch (Berger), Timothy Hutton (Conrad), M. Emmet Walsh (Swim Coach), Elizabeth McGovern (Jeannine), Dinah Manoff (Karen), Fredric Lehne (Lazenby), James B. Sikking (Ray), Basil Hoffman (Sloan)

p, Ronald L. Schwary; d, Robert Redford; w, Alvin Sargent (based on the novel by Judith Guest); ph, John Bailey (Technicolor); ed, Jeff Kanew; art d, Phillip Bennett, Michael Riva; cos, Bernie Pollack

Depressingly ordinary. It's your basic therapy for the masses, with falling leaves suggesting chilling emotions: it wants to be Chekhov directed by Bergman, and it runs as long as if it were. Mary Tyler Moore is a big part of the problem. Her portrait of repressed mommie love is strictly TV. The producers must have hoped for this kind of headline in the trades: "Sitcom Queen Wows 'em in High Water Drama!" Handling her, Redford gets cautionary. His camera keeps backing down and away. And Moore hasn't the guts to go ahead and play it up without him. When we think of original choice Ann-Margret, whom the producers wouldn't okay because they didn't believe she was actress enough to play unsympathetic, we could cry about lost opportunities. Donald Sutherland playing opposite her is eerily Dick Van Dyke-like (Dick having a very depressing day). Judd Hirsch—ever warm, ever ethnic—is on hand as the Jewish therapist who can open up repressed WASPS to—we don't know—Valerie Harper, maybe? Love those cardigan sweaters though. Yet with the young actors, Redford gets something going that draws out innocent emotions. Perhaps the story wasn't "pure" enough for his first effort. The WASP repressiveness comes across as something Redford still suffers from.

The teenage Conrad (Hutton) is an emotionally disturbed young man from a well-to-do family who attempted suicide after the drowning death of his brother. His father, Calvin (Sutherland) is a caring but passive man; his mother, Beth (Moore), has become distant since the death of the son on which she doted. A psychiatrist (Hirsch) and a fellow student (Elizabeth McGovern, surprisingly good) help Calvin cope with emotional distress, while his parents' relationship crumbles. And not a second too soon.

ORGANIZER, THE
(LES CAMARADES)
1964 126m bw   ★★★
Drama   /A
Lux/Vides/Mediterranee/Avala   (France/Italy/Yugoslavia)

Marcello Mastroianni (Prof. Sinigaglia), Renato Salvaroti (Raoul), Annie Girardot (Niobe), Gabriella Giorgelli (Adele), Bernard Blier (Martinetti), Folco Lulli (Pautasso), Francois Perier (Maestro Di Meo), Vittorio Sanipoli (Baudet), Giuseppe Cadeo (Cenerone), Elvira Tonelli (Cesarina)

p, Franco Cristaldi; d, Mario Monicelli; w, Agenore Incrocci, Furio Scarpelli, Mario Monicelli; ph, Giuseppe Rotunno; ed, Ruggero Mastroianni; m, Carlo Rustichelli; art d, Mario Garbuglia; cos, Piero Tosi

A coproduction of several companies, this powerful labor film won a number of awards, including four at the Argentina Film Festival in 1964, and a nomination by the Academy for Best Screenplay. Workers are toiling an ungodly number of hours at a Turin textile plant in the late 1800s. A worker is hurt because of his weariness, and three of his fellows (Tonelli, Lulli, and Blier) approach the company's bosses for some relief; but Sanipoli, the foreman, spurns them. The workers plan to retaliate by leaving work an hour before quitting time. Lulli gives the order, but Sanipoli won't let the workers go, and Lulli is rewarded for his attempted rebellion by suspension from his job without pay for a fortnight. The workers turn to Mastroianni, a professor who has come to stay in Turin with his pal, Perier, a schoolteacher. Mastroianni has made some political noises and is in semihiding, but he surfaces long enough to help the workers plan a strike. The bosses agree to lift Lulli's suspension and rescind any fine, but that's all they'll do, so the strike takes place. Management calls in the goons, but the angered workers meet the scabs at the train station, and violence follows during which Lulli is killed. Newspapers get the story and make it a cause celebre. Then the commissioner of the Turin police force tells the scabs that they must leave the city before any more deaths occur. Management, realizing that Mastroianni is behind the uprising, uses coercion to get the police to arrest the professor. He escapes the long arm of the law by staying with Girardot, a local lady of the evening. Sanipoli manages to talk Blier into going back to the mill for the good of all. At that, Mastroianni emerges from Girardot's apartment to make an impassioned speech that galvanizes the other mill employees. As one, they descend on the factory, where they are met by waiting soldiers who fire on the workers, killing a young teenager. Mastroianni is taken in by the police, and the workers go back to their labors. In the end the workers' plight seems the same, but they have made their presence felt, and unionism is the next step. Excellent film with good performances, although 20 minutes could have been cut out easily. Directed by the man who did what may be the best Italian comedy ever, BIG DEAL ON MADONNA STREET.

ORPHANS

1987 115m c   ★★★★
Drama   R/15
Lorimar

Albert Finney (Harold), Matthew Modine (Treat), Kevin Anderson (Phillip), John Kellogg (Barney), Anthony Heald (Man in Park), Novella Nelson (Mattie), Elizabeth Parrish (Rich Woman), B. Constance Barry (Lady in Crosswalk), Frank Ferrara (Cab Driver), Clifford Fearl (Doorman)

p, Alan J. Pakula, Susan Solt; d, Alan J. Pakula; w, Lyle Kessler (based on the play by Lyle Kessler); ph, Don McAlpine (Technicolor); ed, Evan Lottman; m, Michael Small; prod d, George Jenkins; art d, John J. Moore; chor, Lynnette Barkley; cos, John Boxer

After the dismal failure of 1986's DREAM LOVER, director Alan J. Pakula has returned to top form with the screen version of the popular 1985 Lyle Kessler play Orphans. Basically a three-man show, ORPHANS deals with a pair of orphaned brothers, Treat (Matthew Modine) and Phillip (Kevin Anderson), who live in a dilapidated old house in a seedy part of Newark, New Jersey. Treat, a potentially dangerous petty thief, is the dominant sibling. Fearing that he will lose his brother just as he lost his parents, Treat keeps Phillip imprisoned in his own home. Harold (Albert Finney) is brought home by Treat as a potential kidnapping victim, but he quickly begins to take control of the

situation. It's not often that a play can survive the transition from stage to screen without suffering some loss. ORPHANS, however, does. Kessler (who wrote both the stage play and the screenplay) worked his claustrophobic, prisonlike setting to the film's advantage. More important to the success of ORPHANS is the brilliant acting by all three leads. Finney turns in a spectacular performance. Modine displays another facet of his acting ability as the violent, emotionally confused Treat. Anderson, whose image changes as his character becomes readied for the outside world, keeps pace with (and often surpasses) his costars. It is perhaps because of its deceptively simple emotions and themes that ORPHANS (both the play and the film) has been such a widespread success. Part fairy tale and part heightened reality, it manages to strike an emotional chord with almost everyone who sees it.

ORPHEUS

(OPRHEE)
1950 112m bw   ★★★★½
Fantasy   /PG
Andre Paulve (France)

Jean Marais (Orpheus), Maria Casares (The Princess), Marie Dea (Eurydice), Francois Perier (Heurtebise), Juliette Greco (Aglaonice), Edouard Dermit (Cegeste), Henri Cremieux (Friend in Cafe), Pierre Bertin (Police Commissioner), Roger Blin (Writer), Jacques Varennes

p, Emil Darbon; d, Jean Cocteau; w, Jean Cocteau (based on the play by Jean Cocteau); ph, Nicolas Hayer; ed, Jacqueline Sadoul; m, Georges Auric, Christophe Willibald Gluck; art d, Jean d'Eaubonne

A compelling cinematic allegory from one of the great artists of the twentieth century, ORPHEUS is the perfect example of magical filmmaking. Updating the Greek myth and adding an autobiographical element—the story is now set in in contemporary Paris—Cocteau casts his longtime companion Jean Marais as Orpheus, a famous poet married to Eurydice (Marie Dea). When a fellow poet, the handsome young Cegeste (Edouard Dermit), is hit by a passing motorcyclist in front of a popular cafe, Orpheus is invited by an elegant and mysterious Princess (Maria Casares) to accompany her and the dead poet to her chalet. There, the Princess brings Cegeste "back to life" (by ingeniously running the film backwards for that one shot, Cocteau was able to perform such magic) and disappears through a liquescent mirror into the Underworld. Later, after being chauffeured home by the Princess's servant, the angel Heurtebise (Francois Perier), Orpheus devotes himself to his poetry, scribbling down indecipherable messages transmitted to him over a car radio. He ignores everything but the radio and fails to even notice when Eurydice is killed. Heurtebise, who has fallen in love with Eurydice during Orpheus's preoccupation with poetry, comes to suspect that the Princess overstepped her authority as an Angel of Death by killing Eurydice in order to make room for herself in Orpheus's life. Together, Heurtebise and Orpheus pass through the mirror and journey into the Underworld to find the Princess and Eurydice.

Awarded the top prize at the 1950 Venice Film Festival, ORPHEUS was instantly heralded as a masterpiece. It was blessed with perfect casting (though Cocteau had considered both Greta Garbo and Marlene Dietrich for Casares's role), photographic innovation, indelible imagery and an exceptional score by Georges Auric. The film is as much about the creative process as it is about death, but even those who miss its many meanings will still be hypnotized by its style and beauty. As with all Cocteau's films, the written word cannot adequately describe the visual sensations he creates, sensations that do not diminish with the passage of time.

OSSESSIONE

1942 112m bw ★★★½
Drama /PG
ICI Roma (Italy)

Clara Calamai (Giovanna), Massimo Girotti (Gino), Juan De Landa (The Husband), Elia Marcuzzo (Lo Spagnuolo), Dhia Cristani (Anita), Vittorio Duse (The Lorry Driver), Michele Riccardini, Michele Sakara

p, Libero Solaroli; d, Luchino Visconti; w, Mario Alicata, Antonio Pietrangeli, Gianni Puccini, Giuseppe De Santis, Luchino Visconti (based on the novel The Postman Always Rings Twice by James M. Cain); ph, Aldo Tonti, Domenico Scala; ed, Mario Serandrei; m, Giuseppe Rosati; art d, Gino Rosati

The first directorial effort in the brilliant, though sporadic, career of Luchino Visconti was made in 1942 but not shown in the US until 1959 because of copyright problems. Based on the James M. Cain novel The Postman Always Rings Twice, the film is a sizzling love story set against a background of murder and adultery along the backroads of the Italian countryside. The nomadic Gino (Massimo Girotti), a man living under the illusion that attachments only act as a hindrance, happens upon the roadside inn run by Giovanna (Clara Calamai) and her older, grotesque-looking husband (Juan de Landa). One look at this couple tells their entire story: she is young, beautiful, and full of passion, married to a man unequal to her in all areas except one—money. Giovanna soon takes a romantic interest in the visitor, discovering the spark that never ignited with her husband. It's a potentially murderous situation.

Despite its exquisitely hardboiled source material and film noir plot, OSSESSIONE is often cited as the first harbinger of neorealism. The film was shot in the Italian countryside (as opposed to the studios—a technique favored by Jean Renoir, with whom Visconti apprenticed) and showed the Italian people living in their natural environs. Because the Fascist government of 1942 had complete control over film production in Italy, Visconti had to have his script okayed before shooting. The government saw nothing wrong with the script he presented, but was quite shocked with the final product, which displayed an Italy in contrast to the stylized depiction common to Italian films of the time. Fearful of political overtones, the government temporarily shelved the film, only to put it back into circulation after Mussolini saw and enjoyed it. As a portrayal of the conflict between moral conscience and uncontrollable passion, between the need to maintain a secure existence and the desire to remain free of any confining forces, OSSESSIONE is a powerful statement, and a remarkable first film from Visconti.

OTELLO

1986 120m c ★★★½
Musical PG/U
RAI-TV (Italy)

Placido Domingo (Otello), Katia Ricciarelli (Desdemona), Justino Diaz (Iago), Petra Malakova (Emilia), Urbano Barberini (Cassio), Massimo Foschi (Lodovico), Edwin Francis (Montano), Sergio Nicolai (Roderigo), Remo Remotti (Brabanzio), Antonio Pierfederici (Doge)

p, Menahem Golan, Yoram Globus; d, Franco Zeffirelli; w, Franco Zeffirelli (based on Arrigo Boito's libretto for Giuseppe Verdi's Otello); ph, Ennio Guarnieri (Eastmancolor); prod d, Gianni Quaranta; cos, Anna Anni, Maurizio Millenotti

Serious opera enthusiasts will be appalled by the cuts made in this cinematic version of the opera that Shakespeare inspired. But when Verdi and librettist Boito united to bring the Moor's tale to the musical stage in 1887, they had to make many alterations in the Bard's story, and director Franco Zeffirelli made similar cuts and pastes in order to make it work for the screen. It's near the end of the 15th century on the isle of Cyprus. Otello (Placido Domingo), the governor of the island, is returning from a successful campaign against the Turks. Desdemona (Katia Ricciarelli) awaits his return and pledges her love upon seeing him. Otello's friend, Iago (Justino Diaz), is angry because Cassio (Urbano Barberini) had been promoted over him, so he begins his treacherous behavior against Cassio and Otello. There is no question that Zeffirelli pulled out all stops in order to get the story off a stage and make it feel like a movie. This $9 million production is fabulous to look at, and the acting is superb, but the picture is weak in the music department, mainly because some of the best music has been excised to make the movie zip along. On balance, it's still a good introduction to the work of Verdi, although it's more a series of highlights than the entire opera. The acting is so uniformly good that the English subtitles are hardly needed.

OTHELLO

1952 90m bw ★★★½
Drama /U
Mercury (U.S./France/Italy)

Orson Welles (Othello), Michael MacLiammoir (Iago), Suzanne Cloutier (Desdemona), Robert Coote (Roderigo), Hilton Edwards (Brabantio), Michael Laurence (Cassio), Fay Compton (Emilia), Nicholas Bruce (Lodovico), Jean Davis (Montano), Doris Dowling (Bianca)

p, Orson Welles; d, Orson Welles; w, Orson Welles (based on the play by William Shakespeare); ph, Anchisi Brizzi, G.R. Aldo, Georges Fanto, Oberdan Trojani, Alverto Fusi; ed, Jean Sacha, John Shepridge, Renzo Lucidi, William Morton; m, Angelo Francesco Lavagnino, Alberto Barberis; art d, Alexander Trauner; cos, Maria De Matteis

Orson Welles's version of the Shakespearean tragedy, with the director also turning in a magnificent performance as the title character. Though he had spent only three weeks shooting his MACBETH, Welles devoted four years to this picture, a production that proceeded by fits and starts as he struggled to scrape together cash from various sources. (As part of his fund-raising efforts, Welles did acting duties in Henry King's PRINCE OF FOXES, Henry Hathaway's THE BLACK ROSE, and Carol Reed's THE THIRD MAN.) Though the final result cannot disguise its on-again, off-again production history—sloppy sound synchronization, cutaways to hide absent actors, lines dubbed by performers other than those onscreen—it nonetheless stands as an important part of the Welles canon, and one of the finest screen adaptations of Shakespeare. The text of the original play has been slashed to its bare bones, with bravura cinematography and editing also helping make this a taut, visceral experience. Michael MacLiammoir, an old Abbey Theatre friend of Welles's, makes a truly devious and convincing Iago, and Suzanne Cloutier is a serenely beautiful Desdemona. OTHELLO co-won the Best Feature Film prize at Cannes in 1952, but enjoyed little commercial success in the US at the time. A fully restored version was released to considerable critical acclaim in 1992.

OTHELLO

1956 108m c ★★½
Drama /U
Mosfilm (U.S.S.R.)

Sergei Bondarchuk (Othello), Andrei Popov (Iago), Irina Skobtseva (Desdemona), Vladimir Soshalsky (Cassio), E. Vesnik (Roderigo), A. Maximova (Emilia), E. Teterin (Brabantio), M. Troyanovsky (Doge of Venice), A. Kelberer (Montano), N. Brilling (Lodovico)

d, Sergey Yutkevich; w, Sergey Yutkevich (based on the play by William Shakespeare); ph, E. Andrikanis; ed, G. Mariamov; m, Aram Khachaturian; art d, A. Vaisfeld, V. Dorrer, M. Karykin; cos, O. Kruchinina

Released in the USSR in 1955, this version of the Shakespearean play is inexcusably damaged by Universal's insistence on dubbing the picture instead of using subtitles. This botched dubbing detracts from the beautiful Soviet landscape, which releases the story from the usually confining quarters of the stage. Bondarchuk's performance and Khachaturian's score are the film's prime assets.

OUR DAILY BREAD

1934 74m bw ★★★
Drama /A
Viking

Karen Morley (Mary Sims), Tom Keene (John Sims), John Qualen (Chris), Barbara Pepper (Sally), Addison Richards (Louie), Harry Holman, Billy Engle, Frank Minor, Henry Hall, Ray Spiker

p, King Vidor; d, King Vidor; w, King Vidor, Elizabeth Hill, Joseph L. Mankiewicz; ph, Robert Planck; ed, Lloyd Nosler; m, Alfred Newman

This was part of an intended film trilogy by Vidor, and a film that he always considered equal in quality to his majestic silent classic THE CROWD. It is not, but it has a certain poignancy, quaintness, and simplicity that make it a strong document of hard times in the early 1930s. During the depth of the Depression, Morley and Keene, down and out like most Americans, inherit a dilapidated farm and seek to save it and themselves by inviting homeless but hard-working people to join them in a farm collective, or loosely organized commune. While everyone slaves away at tilling the soil and eking out a few meals a day, Keene grows restless and depressed. Then Pepper—a slovenly, slatternly city girl—arrives and quickly seduces Keene, persuading him to run away with her. He deserts Morley and his fellow workers and heads for the city in the middle of a drought, the wheat withering under a blazing sun. As he makes his way with Pepper, Keene suddenly discovers a hidden stream and his thoughts go back to the needy people of his farm. He cannot desert them after all and races back to tell one and all that water is at hand and, if they all work like demons, they might be able to divert the stream and irrigate the crops, saving their future. Men, women, and children pour forth with tools and form a chain of workers who run ahead of the diverted stream, furiously digging a ditch and shoring it up with boulders, chopping down trees and bushes, anything in the water's path, until it flows freely downhill into the valley, where the farm and thirsty crops await. The jubilant farm workers (some so excited that they cartwheel across the screen) are saved and so, too, is Morley's marriage. The ever-faithful wife is reunited with her errant husband and the world is once more bearable, if not overly hopeful. The film was shot on a shoestring after Irving Thalberg, production chief at MGM, told Vidor that he wanted no part of a film dealing with farm communes (or any kind of picture offering a strong socialist message). Vidor nevertheless went ahead and produced a film of sincerity and powerful emotions, even though his actors, except for Morley and a few others, were amateurs. One report stated that Vidor was compelled to use Pepper—a thoroughly inept actress—at the insistence of one of Vidor's financial backers. She nevertheless is surprisingly convincing as the city tramp and has become a minor cult-film figure. Most of the film reflects Vidor's great vitality, especially the spectacular irrigation scenes at the end, some of the most dramatic and dynamic moments ever put on celluloid. Yet much of the film lacks the overall polish and professionalism that a first-rate budget would have given it. It is obvious that Vidor was inspired by the Soviet film THE EARTH THIRSTS (1930) by Yuli Rayzman; it is also true that the scenes showing crowds of Chinese farmers massing to ward off the locusts in THE GOOD EARTH (1936) were inspired by this Vidor production.

OUR HITLER, A FILM FROM GERMANY

(HITLER, EIN FILM AUS DEUTSCHLAND)
1977 450m c ★★★
Drama
OMNI Zoetrope (West Germany)

Heinz Schubert, Peter Kern, Helmut Lange, Rainer von Artenfels, Martin Sperr, Peter Moland, Johannes Buzalski, Alfred Edel, Amelie Syberberg, Harry Baer

d, Hans-Jurgen Syberberg; w, Hans-Jurgen Syberberg; ph, Dietrich Lohmann; ed, Jutta Brandstaedter; m, Richard Wagner; art d, Hans Gailling; cos, Barbara Gailling, Brigitte Kuhlenthal

German director Hans-Jurgen Syberberg, who was born in 1935 and grew up under Nazi rule, presents an epic nightmare ruminating on the effect Adolf Hitler had and continues to have on Germany and on humankind. Originally presented on German television in four parts, OUR HITLER's American release (at seven and a half hours) is generally shown in two parts. Syberberg presents a simple theme: Such evil as occurred in Hitler could never have existed without the support, however unwitting, of the rest of humanity. (The word "our" was added to the American title by its distributor, Francis Ford Coppola, driving the point home further.) The presentation is the stuff of nightmares. The music of Hitler's beloved Richard Wagner is included to suggest a sort of decadent, modern Wagnerian opera. Syberberg's vision is not an optimistic one; it is forthright and brutal in its honesty, a vision of humanity's dark, unsettling dreams.

OUR MAN IN HAVANA

1960 111m bw ★★★
Comedy /A
Kingsmead (U.K.)

Burl Ives (Dr. Hasselbacher), Alec Guinness (Jim Wormold), Brul Ives (Dr. Hasselbacher), Maureen O'Hara (Beatrice Severn), Ernie Kovacs (Capt. Segura), Noel Coward (Hawthorne), Ralph Richardson ("C"), Jo Morrow (Milly Wormold), Paul Rogers (Hubert Carter), Gregoire Aslan (Cifuentes)

p, Carol Reed; d, Carol Reed; w, Graham Greene (based on his novel); ph, Oswald Morris (CinemaScope); ed, Bert Bates; m, Hermanos Deniz; art d, John Box; cos, Phyllis Dalton

As hilarious as it is absurd, this droll comedy about spies in Cuba stars the prodigiously talented Guinness. The real world of espionage is ridiculous enough, but director Reed manages to make it seem even sillier by putting an innocuous vacuum cleaner salesman (Guinness) in the the middle of all the clandestine goings-on. Guinness, the owner of a small store in Havana, is approached by Coward, a master spy who enlists him as an agent. Realizing he will be making good money for every tidbit of information he passes along to headquarters in London, and wanting that money to be able to buy the good things in life for his daughter (Morrow), but knowing there is no real information to gather, Guinness begins to invent information. Kovacs, the reportedly brutal chief of police, who has cast a covetous eye on Morrow, gets reports that Guinness has been acting in a furtive manner. Kovacs spies on Guinness, while Guinness spies on Kovacs, and the whole affair begins to expand crazily. However, the intrigue ceases to be phony when Guinness is forced to dispatch a very real enemy. Nevertheless, Guinness eventually has to admit to the fabricated nature of the information he has been providing to British intelligence, and he is ordered back to London, where he meets an unexpected fate. Mixing subtle comedy with sinister consequences, OUR MAN IN HAVANA is probably Guinness' drollest film. Guinness is superb as the greedy but imaginative shop owner, but Kovacs, as the posturing police chief, and Coward, as the British master spy, steal the film, which was shot in Havana shortly after the Cuban Revolution.

OUR RELATIONS

1936 65m bw ★★★★
Comedy /U
Stan Laurel/Hal Roach

Stan Laurel *(Himself/Alfie Laurel)*, Oliver Hardy *(Himself/Bert Hardy)*, Sidney Toler *(Captain of the S.S. Periwinkle)*, Alan Hale *(Joe Groagan, the Waiter)*, Daphne Pollard *(Mrs. Daphne Hardy)*, Betty Healy *(Mrs. Betty Laurel)*, Iris Adrian *(Alice, the Beer Garden Girl)*, Lona Andre *(Lily, the Other Cafe Girl)*, James Finlayson *(Finn, the Chief Engineer)*, Arthur Housman *(Inebriated Stroller)*

p, Stan Laurel, L.A. French; d, Harry Lachman; w, Richard Connell, Felix Adler, Charles Rogers, Jack Jevne (based on the short story "The Money Box" by William Jacobs); ph, Rudolph Mate; ed, Bert Jordan; m, LeRoy Shield; art d, Arthur I. Royce, William Stevens; fx, Roy Seawright

Perhaps the best Laurel and Hardy feature, OUR RELATIONS marked Stan Laurel's first credit as a producer, and he does an excellent job in this elaborate picture that owes a great deal to Shakespeare's "Comedy Of Errors." Stan and Ollie, sailors on shore leave, have a valuable diamond ring to deliver. Knowing that in the past they've spent all their money while on liberty, they give their cash to Sidney Toler, their captain, telling him to hold it in safekeeping and not to return it until after their ship has sailed. The town they are visiting is the same place where their twin brothers now live in domestic harmony with their henpecking wives, Daphne Pollard and Betty Healy. Stan and Ollie meet two girls, Iris Adrian and Lona Andre, in a local waterfront dive, while nearby, their twins are quaffing beer with their mates in another tavern. Need we say that the duos are soon mixed? The diamond ring turns up missing, and when Stan and Ollie can't locate the jewel, gangsters Ralf Harolde and Noel Madison trap the pair in cement blocks and leave them on a pier where they will soon fall into the water. Naturally, it all comes together in the end with the right husbands re-matched with the correct wives and the twins reunited after a long separation. Several funny scenes include Laurel and Hardy attempting to convince Toler to give them back their money; a set-piece in a hotel room where they have been placed without clothing; and their difficulty (as the married men) to make beer-hall owner Alan Hale, Sr., understand that they had not been there earlier with Adrian and Andre. Amidst all the fun, there is real danger to the boys when they come up against the villains. This was the first and only time they worked with director Harry Lachman, who was not known for his comedic skills. (His most famous feature was DANTE'S INFERNO, 1935; he also did a couple of CHARLIE CHAN films.) He seems to just turn on Rudolphe Mate's camera and let the boys have their way with the humor. A standout comedy role was played by Arthur Housman as a drunk, and Stanley Sandford, one of the wharf rats, was appearing in his final film of the 23 he made with Laurel and Hardy. In one of her first roles, Iris Adrian was developing the character she would play for the next several decades, the brash blonde with a heart of gold. Despite the excellence of this film, other Laurel and Hardy movies are better remembered.

OUR TOWN

1940 90m bw ★★★★
Drama /A
Principal Artists

Frank Craven *(Mr. Morgan, the Narrator)*, William Holden *(George Gibbs)*, Martha Scott *(Emily Webb)*, Fay Bainter *(Mrs. Gibbs)*, Beulah Bondi *(Mrs. Webb)*, Thomas Mitchell *(Dr. Gibbs)*, Guy Kibbee *(Editor Webb)*, Stuart Erwin *(Howie Newsome)*, Philip Wood *(Simon Stinson)*, Doro Merande *(Mrs. Soames)*

p, Sol Lesser; d, Sam Wood; w, Thornton Wilder, Frank Craven, Harry Chandlee (based on the play by Thornton Wilder); ph, Bert Glennon; ed, Sherman Todd; m, Aaron Copland; prod d, William Cameron Menzies, Harry Horner

Sam Wood directed this version of Thorton Wilder's Pulitzer Prize-winning play about the multiple relationships among the folks in a small New England town. The "our town" genre—studies of the relationships that mold a community—became a welcome staple of the movies. Wilder must be given credit for establishing such an important form.

Our Town is brought to the screen with wonderful characterizations by an inspired cast. Small-town America is typified by Craven, the down-home narrator who profiles the lives of citizens of Grover's Corners. Scott is the idealistic but hard-working daughter of the local newspaper editor, and Holden is the son of the local physician who falls in love with Scott, goes through a difficult courtship, and finally wins her hand in marriage. Life in this quaint small town is shown in three periods—1901, 1904, and 1913—with the attention basically focused upon two families, those of Holden and Scott. The result is a moving portrait of small-town America before WWII.

Remaining faithful to Wilder's script, director Wood skillfully conveys the laughter, love, and pain in the lives of Wilder's heartwarming characters. And the techniques Wood employs to tell their stories are marvelous to behold: a dazzling series of dissolves, evocative lighting, and montages that effectively capture the flavor of the periods depicted. Scott, appearing in her first film, is splendid, as is Holden. Mitchell as the physician, Kibbee as the editor, and their wives, played by Bainter and Bondi, all provide sturdy supporting performances. Wood's outstanding direction is enhanced by a stirring score by Copland and lovely sets by Menzies, who is a genius at capturing any locale.

OUR VINES HAVE TENDER GRAPES

1945   105m   bw   ★★★★

Drama   /U

MGM

Edward G. Robinson *(Martinius Jacobson)*, Margaret O'Brien *(Selma Jacobson)*, James Craig *(Nels Halverson)*, Agnes Moorehead *(Bruna Jacobson)*, Jackie "Butch" Jenkins *(Arnold Hanson)*, Morris Carnovsky *(Bjorn Bjornson)*, Frances Gifford *(Viola Johnson)*, Sara Haden *(Mrs. Bjornson)*, Louis Jean Heydt *(Mr. Faraassen)*, Francis Pierlot *(Minister)*

p, Robert Sisk; d, Roy Rowland; w, Dalton Trumbo (based on the novel *For Our Vines Have Tender Grapes* by George Victor Martin); ph, Robert Surtees; ed, Ralph E. Winters; m, Bronislau Kaper; art d, Cedric Gibbons, Edward Carfagno; fx, A. Arnold Gillespie, Danny Hall; cos, Irene, Kay Carter

Few films touch the heart so deeply as this one and fewer still present such moving performances. Robinson is terrific as the Norwegian-born Wisconsin farmer and father of O'Brien; he's a widower who is strict with his precocious offspring but also loving and tender. In O'Brien's world there are daily tragedies, such as the time she accidentally kills a squirrel, but her understanding father is always there to comfort her. Robinson hears that a huge circus is passing through town on a train; since his daughter will not have the opportunity to see the circus in performance, Robinson drives with O'Brien in the middle of the night to the train station and offers one of the foremen of the circus a few dollars if he'll only bring one of the elephants off the train for a few minutes. O'Brien is filled with wonder at the sight of the great, gentle beast. When attractive Gifford arrives in Benson Junction to teach school, a great deal of excitement ensues, especially among the children and gossipy neighbors, who observe how handsome town editor Craig is drawn to her. Craig proposes after a while, but Gifford draws back, fearing that she will be bored to death in the small farming community. Craig is called to serve in WWII and asks Gifford to wait for him, but she cannot make such a commitment. Later, a near tragedy almost consumes the town when O'Brien and her cousin, Jenkins, disappear. The community is in an uproar as a frantic search for the children is conducted during torrential spring rains. They are found alive but soaking wet in a bathtub that has taken them on a perilous journey through the swollen waters of a nearby stream. Robinson doesn't know whether to spank or hug his adventurous child and opts for the latter. But he is severe with O'Brien when she refuses to let Jenkins borrow her skates. Robinson is the personification of a man who knows when to display emotion, such as explaining to his daughter, upset at Craig's induction into the service, that to preserve "peace on earth," one must be willing to fight for peace. All of the lessons taught by Robinson come to fruition when the town gathers to hear that a neighbor's farm has been struck by lightning and that the resultant fire has wiped him out. O'Brien is the first to stand up in church and offer her prize calf to the destitute farmer, which starts a run of charity through the parishioners. Robinson beams in pride at his daughter and then forgoes his own plans for a new barn to help the stricken neighbor. This wonderful outpouring of neighborly generosity and compassion is witnessed by schoolteacher Gifford, who then and there decides that Benson Junction is not a dull place after all but one of the grandest spots on earth in which to live. She resolves to stay there and wait for Craig to return from the war.

Supporting Robinson with marvelous performances are O'Brien, who furthered her juvenile career in films mightily with this entry, as did Jenkins, one of Louis B. Mayer's favorite child actors. Moorehead is excellent and sports a mild Norwegian accent in an underplayed part, and Morris, as the retarded neighbor who dies, displays fine talent. Craig and Gifford made such convincing and gentle lovers that MGM teamed them again in SHE WENT TO THE RACES (1945) and LITTLE MR. JIM (1946). Released just after V-J Day, OUR VINES HAVE TENDER GRAPES was written with great care by the talented Trumbo, whom Robinson had earlier befriended (he was later criticized for this friendship by citizens siding with HUAC during the Sen. Joseph McCarthy era, when Trumbo was part of the "Hollywood Ten").

OUT OF AFRICA

1985   150m   c   ★★½

Romance   PG

Universal

Meryl Streep *(Karen Blixen-Finecke)*, Robert Redford *(Denys Finch Hatton)*, Klaus Maria Brandauer *(Baron Bror Blixen-Finecke)*, Michael Kitchen *(Berkeley)*, Malick Bowens *(Farah)*, Joseph Thiaka *(Kamante)*, Stephen Kinyanjui *(Kinanjui)*, Michael Gough *(Delamere)*, Suzanna Hamilton *(Felicity)*, Rachel Kempson *(Lady Belfield)*

p, Sydney Pollack; d, Sydney Pollack; w, Kurt Luedtke (based on *Out of Africa* and other writings by Isak Dinesen, *Isak Dinesen: The Life of a Storyteller* by Judith Thurman, and *Silence Will Speak* by Errol Trzebinski); ph, David Watkin (Technovision, Rank Color); ed, Fredric Steinkamp, William Steinkamp, Pembroke J. Herring, Sheldon Kahn; m, John Barry, Wolfgang Amadeus Mozart; prod d, Stephen Grimes; art d, Herbert Westbrook, Colin Grimes, Clifford Robinson; fx, David Harris; cos, Milena Canonero

There was very little to begin with here—a delicate, lyrical, autobiographical tale written by an austere, refined woman who brought an opera glass instead of a microscope to her life. The author, Isak Dinesen, recounts the tale of lost loves and old imperial Africa. Karen (Meryl Streep) is the well-born woman who marries Baron Bror Blixen-Finecke (Klaus Maria Brandauer), a playboy who bestows a title upon her, promises her eternal bliss on an African plantation in 1914, and then leaves her alone to run things. Bror is nothing more than a drinker, spendthrift, and womanizer. Denys Finch Hatton (Robert Redford) is an enigmatic white hunter who falls in love with the plantation-bound Karen. Streep, affecting the most inarticulate and cumbersome accent in any film within the last three decades, strives mightily to bring reason and substance to a role that has neither. To make up for the lack of real story here, director Sydney Pollack shoots endless travelogue footage in soft light and pleasing colors. The movie is not drama and far from a compelling romance.

OUT OF THE PAST

1947   97m   bw   ★★★★★

Mystery   /A

RKO

Robert Mitchum *(Jeff Bailey)*, Jane Greer *(Kathie Moffett)*, Kirk Douglas *(Whit Sterling)*, Rhonda Fleming *(Meta Carson)*, Richard Webb *(Jim)*, Steve Brodie *(Fisher)*, Virginia Huston *(Ann)*, Paul Valentine *(Joe)*, Dickie Moore *(The Kid)*, Ken Niles *(Eels)*

p, Warren Duff; d, Jacques Tourneur; w, James M. Cain (uncredited), Frank Fenton (uncredited), Geoffrey Homes (based on the novel *Build My Gallows High* by Geoffrey Homes); ph, Nicholas Musuraca; ed, Samuel E. Beetley; m, Roy Webb; art d, Albert S. D'Agostino, Jack Okey; fx, Russell A. Cully; cos, Edward Stevenson

This quintessential film noir catapulted contract player Robert Mitchum into superstardom and set the standard for the genre for years to come. Boasting a typically confusing and convoluted plot line, the film follows laconic private eye Jeff Bailey (Mitchum) as he is lured into a fateful quagmire when hired by notorious gangster Whit Sterling (Douglas) to find his mistress, Kathie Moffett (Greer), who shot him and ran off with $40,000. Jeff traces Kathie to Mexico, but when he meets the seductive *femme fatale* he falls in love with her and willingly becomes involved in an increasingly complicated web of double-crosses, blackmail, and murder. Directed with supreme skill by Jacques Tourneur (CAT PEOPLE, I WALKED WITH A ZOMBIE) and brilliantly photographed by Nicholas Musuraca, this is an unrelentingly gloomy film set in a dark world of greed and deceit where love is just another device to ensnare the gullible. It was here that Mitchum created what became his iconographic screen persona: the droopy-eyed cynic who accepts fate with a studied nonchalance. Jane Greer is equally superb, perfecting the role of the *femme fatale* with a combination of erotic fire and cool detachment. Her first appearance in the film—cutting a sultry silhouette as she enters a dark cantina from the bright white outdoors—is one of the great entrances in film history. A seminal genre film, certainly among the greatest whose influence is still felt today, OUT OF THE PAST was remade as the distinctly inferior AGAINST ALL ODDS.

OUT-OF-TOWNERS, THE

1970 98m c   ★★★★
Comedy   G/U
Jalem

Jack Lemmon *(George Kellerman)*, Sandy Dennis *(Gwen Kellerman)*, Milt Kamen *(Counterman)*, Sandy Baron *(TV Man)*, Anne Meara *(Woman in Police Station)*, Robert Nichols *(Man in Airplane)*, Ann Prentiss *(Airline Stewardess)*, Ron Carey *(Boston Cab Driver)*, Philip Bruns *(Officer Meyers)*, Graham Jarvis *(Murray)*

p, Paul Nathan; d, Arthur Hiller; w, Neil Simon; ph, Andrew Laszlo (Movielab Color); ed, Fred Chulack; m, Quincy Jones; art d, Charles Bailey, Walter Tyler; cos, Forrest T. Butler, Grace Harris

If playwrighting success were gaged solely on money in the bank, Neil Simon would likely be tops in his field; having brought laughter to so many, he probably deserves that status. In his script for THE OUT-OF-TOWNERS, he mines gold from a field that had been virtually tapped out. Lemmon is an Ohio businessman on his way to New York with his wife, Dennis, to talk about taking a job in the Big Apple. Anticipating dining in one Manhattan's fine restaurants, they refuse an in-flight meal. Their intention is to sup, check into a good hotel, have the appointment the following morning, and return to Dayton. But things don't work out the way they were planned. The plane cannot land in New York because of fog, so it's shunted to Boston. In Beantown, Lemmon and Dennis learn that their luggage is missing; then they have to take a crowded, foodless train to New York. Arriving in a driving rainstorm, they learn that the city has been crippled by a number of strikes, including walkouts by the transit workers and the garbage collectors. They walk a distance to the Waldorf only to learn that the hotel has cancelled their reservation. Jarvis, an apparently sweet man, says he can find them a room; instead, he steals all of their money. With no cash, they decide to try the police, who tell them they can be put up at a local armory for the night. On their way there, the police car is hijacked by crooks, and Lemmon and Dennis are tossed out in Central Park, where they spend the night. The next morning, Lemmon is taken to be a rapist by two joggers, who beat him up. Then he is chased by a police officer on a horse who thinks Lemmon is a child molester. In an attempt to get to his interview, Lemmon hitches a ride in the car of a Cuban official, Carlos Montalban, but the auto is sidetracked by angry anti-Castro demonstrators. When he finally gets to his appointment, Lemmon looks seedy and totally unpresentable, but the company offers him the job anyway. Lemmon decides that New York is no place for him and Dennis, and he turns the job down, preferring to stay in quiet, tranquil Ohio. Lemmon and Dennis happily board their plane back to Ohio and it is promptly hijacked to Cuba as the film ends.

While it's implausible that all of these mishaps would befall a couple in 24 hours, none of these occurrences is beyond the realm of belief, and Simon has cleverly strung them together in one of his best screenplays. Director Hiller happily keeps Dennis' quirky mannerisms to a minimum and lets Lemmon do his thing (and a wonderful thing it is), with all secondary roles well cast. The picture did well at the box office and enhanced Lemmon's reputation as one of Hollywood's finest comedic actors. Many of Simon's plays have not transferred well to the screen (with the notable exceptions of THE ODD COUPLE and BAREFOOT IN THE PARK), perhaps because he writes differently for the stage. But when Simon has written directly for the screen, he has done much better, as he did with this film, THE GOODBYE GIRL, and THE HEARTBREAK KID.

OUTLAND

1981 109m c   ★★
Science Fiction   R/15
Ladd/WB (U.K.)

Sean Connery *(O'Niel)*, Peter Boyle *(Sheppard)*, Frances Sternhagen *(Lazarus)*, James B. Sikking *(Montone)*, Kika Markham *(Carol)*, Clarke Peters *(Ballard)*, Steven Berkoff *(Sagan)*, John Ratzenberger *(Tarlow)*, Nicholas Barnes *(Paul O'Niel)*, Manning Redwood *(Lowell)*

p, Richard A. Roth; d, Peter Hyams; w, Peter Hyams; ph, Stephen Goldblatt (Panavision, Technicolor); ed, Stuart Baird; m, Jerry Goldsmith; prod d, Philip Harrison; art d, Malcolm Middleton; fx, John Stears; chor, Anthony Van Laast; cos, John Mollo

HIGH NOON in outer space. Connery is the marshal on Io, Jupiter's third moon, home for a mining colony. His investigation of some strange outbreaks of violence uncovers a plot involving the managing company, led by Boyle, and a drug that increases productivity but has dangerous side effects. Connery wants to bring the culprits to justice, but no one else on Io wants anything to do with the battle, so he is left to face company henchmen alone. Connery and Boyle are fine, but the wholesale lifting of HIGH NOON's plot (there's even an on-screen digital readout periodically displayed, counting down the minutes until the big confrontation) certainly undermines interest. The film has an appealing look to it, although many of the visuals bear a striking resemblance to those seen in ALIEN.

OUTLAW JOSEY WALES, THE

1976 135m c   ★★★★★
Western   R/18
Malpaso

Clint Eastwood *(Josey Wales)*, Chief Dan George *(Lone Watie)*, Sondra Locke *(Laura Lee)*, Bill McKinney *(Terrill)*, John Vernon *(Fletcher)*, Paula Trueman *(Grandma Sarah)*, Sam Bottoms *(Jamie)*, Geraldine Keams *(Little Moonlight)*, Woodrow Parfrey *(Carpetbagger)*, Joyce Jameson *(Rose)*

p, Robert Daley; d, Clint Eastwood; w, Philip Kaufman, Sonia Chernus (based on the book *Gone to Texas* by Forrest Carter); ph, Bruce Surtees (Panavision, DeLuxe Color); ed, Ferris Webster; m, Jerry Fielding; prod d, Tambi Larsen

This superb Western is not only a memorable achievement by Eastwood, it's an important step in the development of the Western hero. The film opens as Missouri farmer and family man Eastwood plows his field, aided by his young son. Later in the day his farm is attacked by a vicious band of Union guerrillas, known as "Redlegs" because of their red boots. Left for dead, Eastwood awakens to find that his house has been burned to the ground, with the charred corpses of his family in the rubble. Sitting alone near the fresh graves of his family, Eastwood's brooding is interrupted by a dozen men on horseback who ride up out of the woods. They are men led by "Bloody" Bill Anderson, a brutal Confederate guerrilla leader. Surveying the ruined farm, the rebel leader asks, "Redlegs?" Eastwood nods. "You'll find 'em up in Kansas. They're with the Union. And we're goin' up there and set things right." Eastwood looks up at the ragtag group of men, the gash on his face hardening into a scar. "I'll be comin' with ya," he replies.

Several years later, the war over, we watch as Vernon, now in command of the Confederate guerrillas, is tricked into surrendering his men—save for Eastwood, who refuses to go alone—to the Union. McKinney, the man responsible for the murders of Eastwood's family, presides over their surprise execution. Out of the mist rides Eastwood. Singlehandedly he kills many Union soldiers and rescues a young rebel, Bottoms, who has been severely wounded. The Union sends McKinney and the reluctant Vernon south in pursuit of Eastwood and the dying Bottoms.

Continuing his journey, Eastwood next encounters an old Cherokee Indian, George, a young Cherokee woman (Keams), and even a stray dog. The following day, this ragtag caravan witnesses the abduction of an old woman (Trueman) and her granddaughter (Locke) by a group of outlaws who promptly sell them to the Comanches. Soon after, George accidentally gets himself captured by the Comanches and is imprisoned alongside Trueman and Locke. Eastwood attacks the convoy and rescues them. Grateful for the help, Trueman invites Eastwood and his small troupe of travelers to live with her and Locke at the farmhouse her son built. En route, the voyagers discover a ghost town inhabited only by a bartender (Matt Clark), an aging prostitute (Jameson), an old Mexican (John Verros), and a gambler (Royal Dano). His enlarged band of travelers then heads for the ranch where Eastwood is struck by how similar the farm is to his own. Trueman declares that they all can live together and make a go of it.

Their troubles are far from over, however, as it seems certain Sampson and his Comanches will attack the settlers. Eastwood prepares them for the attack, then rides off to Sampson's camp. There he tells the Indian he's prepared to fight, if that's what is called for, but suggests that maybe they could just leave one another alone. "Dyin' ain't so hard for men like you and me," he says. "It's the livin' that's hard. . . I'm sayin' that men can live together without butcherin' one another." It is obvious that both men are tired of violence and killing. "It shall be life," declares Sampson, and Eastwood returns to the ranch.

As dawn breaks the following day, Eastwood, with great regret, saddles his horse and prepares to leave. His departure is interrupted by the arrival of McKinney and his Redlegs. McKinney gloats and smiles, "You're all alone now." "Not quite," replies George, as a dozen rifles appear from the windows of the farmhouse. A full-scale battle ensues, and while the farmers defeat the Redlegs, Eastwood chases McKinney back to the ghost town for a final confrontation.

Whereas Eastwood's homage to director Sergio Leone, HIGH PLAINS DRIFTER, was bleak from start to finish, with no alternatives to damnation, THE OUTLAW JOSEY WALES begins with life (Eastwood and his family) and ends with life (the communal family). In between is a long period of healing and rebuilding. Eastwood re-examines the "man-with-no-man" screen persona he developed with director Leone, that of an unattached, uncivilized avenger who possesses mystical gunfighting skills. Likewise, the classic Western hero is typically a man with a dark, pained past who, although he may have become briefly involved in the lives of others, can never settle down and reap the fruits of society. THE OUTLAW JOSEY WALES, however, is a cautiously optimistic epic, deeply rooted in the history of America.

Eastwood, despite his efforts, is not a loner. The viewer has witnessed the great tragedy that brought him to this cold, hard, violent existence. We understand his pain and see that deep down he seeks to heal and start a new life. Eastwood changes both his image and the image of the Western hero by making himself more vulnerable. Though his skills in the art of killing are frequently demonstrated, his companions save his life more than once. Instead of surrendering and assimilating into the "rebuilt" postwar society full of carpetbaggers, Klansmen, and dishonor, Eastwood and his group head out on their own. They create their own society, steeped in honor, mutual respect and love.

The cinematography by Bruce Surtees is magnificent, as is Jerry Fielding's musical score—his work received an Oscar nomination. Acting honors must go to Chief Dan George, who nearly steals the film from the star and serves as the emotional center of the film. His dry wit and dignified, loving presence serves to remind Eastwood's Josey Wales that life is always better than death.

OUTSIDER, THE

1980 128m c ★★★½
Drama R/AA
Cinematic Arts

Craig Wasson (*Michael Flaherty*), Patricia Quinn (*Siobhan*), Sterling Hayden (*Seamus Flaherty*), Niall Toibin (*Farmer*), Elizabeth Begley (*Mrs. Cochran*), T.P. McKenna (*John Russell*), Frank Grimes (*Tony Coyle*), Bosco Hogan (*Finbar Donovan*), Niall O'Brien (*Emmet Donovan*), Joe Dowling (*Pat*)

p, Philippe Modave; d, Tony Luraschi; w, Tony Luraschi (based on the novel *The Heritage of Michael Flaherty* by Colin Leinster); ph, Ricardo Aronovich; ed, Catherine Kelber; m, Ken Thorne; art d, Franco Fumagalli; cos, Judy Dolan

One of the finest films concerning the tensions in Northern Ireland, THE OUTSIDER stars Craig Wasson as a young Irish-American inspired by his grandfather's patriotic tales of fighting the British years ago. He arrives in Belfast and discovers he is the target of an IRA plot. The IRA is planning to arrange his death so that it appears to be the work of the British army, thereby turning him into an American martyr and raising funds from sympathetic Irish-Americans. The occupying British are no more flatteringly portrayed than the IRA. The production (which came in at under $3 million) begins and ends in Detroit, but most of it was shot in Dublin, substituting for Belfast.

OUTSIDERS, THE

1983 91m c ★★★
Drama PG/15
Zoetrope

Matt Dillon (*Dallas Winston*), Ralph Macchio (*Johnny Cade*), C. Thomas Howell (*Ponyboy Curtis*), Patrick Swayze (*Darrel Curtis*), Rob Lowe (*Sodapop Curtis*), Emilio Estevez (*Two-Bit Matthews*), Tom Cruise (*Steve Randle*), Glenn Withrow (*Tim Shephard*), Diane Lane (*Cherry Valance*), Leif Garrett (*Bob Sheldon*)

p, Fred Roos, Gray Frederickson; d, Francis Ford Coppola; w, Kathleen Rowell (based on the novel by S.E. Hinton); ph, Stephen H. Burum (Panavision, Technicolor); ed, Anne Goursaud; m, Carmine Coppola; prod d, Dean Tavoularis; cos, Marge Bowers

In the early 1980s, after his "Godfather" films (1972, 1974) and APOCALYPSE NOW (1979), works of epic scale, Francis Ford Coppola began choosing small projects that he proceeded to blow up to preposterous proportions. Such is the case with THE OUTSIDERS, a film based on the fine teenage novel by S.E. Hinton (who makes a cameo appearance here as a nurse). The story is about the conflict between a group of "greasers" and their more affluent high school peers, the "Socs." Dallas Winston (Matt Dillon) leads his rebellious punk buddies on a variety of typical teenage "adventures," but when two fellow gang members (Ralph Macchio and C. Thomas Howell) have a run-in with their rivals, events take a violent turn. Dillon is a believable rebel, and gets solid support from a cast that went on to populate some of the best teenage films in the years to come. The fault lies in Coppola's unduly reverent interpretation of the story, which resulted in a film steeped in artistic pretension. Set in the 1950s, it attempts to evoke REBEL WITHOUT A CAUSE, but it is without any of the beautiful roughness found in Nicholas Ray's classic work. Coppola's grandiose vision pays off in stunning photography, but visual pleasures are not enough to make this anything but a modest, small-scale teenage drama.

OX-BOW INCIDENT, THE

1943 75m bw ★★★★★
Western /A
FOX

Henry Fonda (*Gil Carter*), Dana Andrews (*Donald Martin*), Mary Beth Hughes (*Rose Mapen*), Anthony Quinn (*Juan Martines*), William Eythe (*Gerald Tetley*), Harry Morgan (*Art Croft*), Jane Darwell (*Ma Grier*), Matt Briggs (*Judge Daniel Tyler*), Harry Davenport (*Arthur Davies*), Frank Conroy (*Maj. Tetley*)

p, Lamar Trotti; d, William A. Wellman; w, Lamar Trotti (based on the novel by Walter Van Tilburg Clark); ph, Arthur Miller; ed, Allen McNeil; m, Cyril J. Mockridge; art d, Richard Day, James Basevi; cos, Earl Luick

The finest indictment of lynching ever made, and we're not forgetting LeRoy's THEY WON'T FORGET or Lang's FURY either. THE OX-BOW INCIDENT is powerful portrait of mob violence that rises to the level of Greek tragedy. Based on an event that occurred in 1885 in Nevada, this William Wellman-directed masterpiece brilliantly penetrates the psyche of its characters.

Fonda and Morgan play two travelers who ride into Bridger's Wells, Nevada, a dying town, and head for the local saloon after finishing a cattle drive. Soon thereafter someone races in to announce that a popular local rancher has been shot by rustlers. Although a storekeeper (Davenport) cautions against rash action in the absence of the local sheriff, many locals form a posse anyway. Under the leadership of a pompous ex-Confederate officer (Conroy) who suddenly appears in his old Civil War uniform, the posse rides off. The strangers join the posse largely to keep the townspeople from unfairly suspecting them.

The gallery of characters involved include the former officer's sensitive son (Eythe), brought along to be made "into a man"; a robust boarding house shrew with an iron will (Darwell); an adventure-seeking bartender (Paul Hurst); a man seeking vengeance (Marc Lawrence); and a mild-mannered sort (Leigh Whipper) who joins the group to pray for the victims. The posse eventually finds three exhausted homesteaders (Andrews, Quinn and Francis Ford) and, although the evidence against them is largely circumstantial, they are convicted of the crime on the spot. The three are given no real trial, just enough time to write farewell letters to loved ones and to "make their peace with God". The men, are of course, innocent, and the memorable finale has Fonda reading aloud the letter Andrews wrote to his family.

Fonda gives a compassionate performance as the observer in this powerful anti-lynching film, the man through whose eyes the story unfolds. Stunning performances are also given by Darwell, Davenport, Hurst, and Conroy. Quinn only has a small role as one of the victims, but he is terrific as the indignant lynch candidate who is about to be hanged not for past crimes but for something he did not do. Wellman's direction of this superb cast is nothing less than awesome; he coaxes subtle performances from some of his players, properly bombastic renderings from others. In keeping with its somber subject matter, the whole film has a gritty, worn-out look, right down to the threadbare costumes on the actors. Much of the credit for the film's tone is due to Miller's outstanding photography, supported by a downbeat score from Mockridge. Although scenes at the beginning and the end of the film offer realistic-looking western exteriors, Wellman insisted that the bulk of the film be shot on a set with painted backdrops, mostly since the bulk of the story occurs at night. On the set he could better control the nuances of lighting he wanted. Some critics complained about the "claustrophobic" look and feel of the picture because of its set-bound image, but it is exactly that atmosphere that helps to create the mood of pervasive doom and maniacal intent of the two dozen "average citizens" to commit a capital crime.

A personal favorite of Wellman's and a film he campaigned long and hard to do, THE OX-BOW INCIDENT more than justifies his extended efforts. Although lynchings in America had dropped drastically by the time the film came out (only three in 1943 compared to a record high of 231 in 1892), the film's message speaks even today to all kinds of prejudice and rash judgment. A surprisingly gloomy non-war film to be made in the middle of WWII, it proved stunningly cathartic for those few who appreciated it at the time.

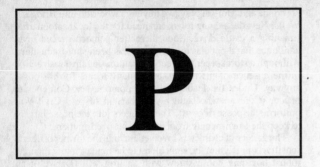

P

PADDY, THE NEXT BEST THING

1933 75m bw ★★★
Comedy /U
Fox Films

Janet Gaynor (*Paddy Adair*), Warner Baxter (*Lawrence Blake*), Walter Connolly (*Maj. Adair*), Harvey Stephens (*Jack Breen*), Margaret Lindsay (*Eileen Adair*), Mary McCormick (*Herself*), J.M. Kerrigan (*Collins*), Fiske O'Hara (*Mr. Davy*), Merle Tottenham (*Maid*), Roger Imhof (*Micky*)

d, Harry Lachman; w, Edwin Burke (based on the novel by Gertrude Page); ph, John Seitz

This is a simplistic, amiable comedy about the problems of an Irish family. Connolly is an impoverished landowner with two daughters. He insists that the elder (Lindsay) marry local rich man Baxter. The money will help Connolly and he'll have one less daughter to worry about. But Lindsay loves Stephens and is caught in a quandary. Leave it to her tomboy sister (Gaynor) to save the day. Gaynor busts up the budding romance and wins Baxter for herself. Gaynor is an utter delight, making this marshmallow-soft story work. The locales are nicely used, and there's some fine Irish music on the soundtrack.

PADRE PADRONE

1977 114m c ★★★½
Drama /18
Radio Italiano (Italy)

Omero Antonutti (*Gavino's Father*), Saverio Marconi (*Gavino*), Marcella Michelangeli (*Gavino's Mother*), Fabrizio Forte (*Gavino as a Child*), Marino Cenna (*Servant/Shepherd*), Stanko Molnar (*Sebastiano*), Nanni Moretti (*Cesare*)

p, Giuliani G. De Negri; d, Paolo Taviani, Vittorio Taviani; w, Vittorio Taviani, Paolo Taviani (based on a book by Gavino Ledda); ph, Mario Masini (Eastmancolor); ed, Roberto Perpignani; m, Egisto Macchi; art d, Gianni Sbarra

This is the simple story of a boy's growth into manhood under the despotism of his father. At age six, Gavino (played as a child by Fabrizio Forte) is pulled out of school and taken by his father (Omero Antonutti) into the mountains to become a shepherd. His father tries to control his son's life in every respect, with a comportment bordering on the sadistic. As he grows to manhood, Gavino (played as a young man by Saverio Marconi) begins to discover things for himself and rebel against his father's authority, eventually escaping from the patriarch's rule but encountering his changed father one last time in the film's denouement. Originally filmed by the Taviani brothers for Italian television, PADRE PADRONE is a fine example of a strong ensemble telling a story naturally, without intrusion by the directors. Using

both professional actors and untrained locals from the Sardinian countryside, this story of the virtual imprisonment of young Sardinians by the sheep and pastures of their land unfolds simply and yet with great power. The winner of the grand prize at the Cannes Film Festival of 1977, the tale is based in truth: the real-life Gavino underwent similar experiences before escaping at age 20, going on to become a linguistics professor, and writing a book about his experiences.

PAISAN

(PAISA)
1946 120m bw ★★★★★
War /A
Organizational Films/Foreign Film (Italy)

Carmela Sazio (*Carmela*), Robert Van Loon (*Joe*), Alfonsino Pasca (*Boy*), Maria Michi (*Francesca*), Renzo Avanzo (*Massimo*), Harriet White (*Harriet*), Dotts Johnson (*MP*), William Tubbs (*Capt. Bill Martin*), Dale Edmonds (*Dale*), Carlo Piscane (*Peasant in Sicily Story*)

p, Roberto Rossellini, Rod E. Geiger, Mario Conti; d, Roberto Rossellini; w, Sergio Amidei, Federico Fellini, Roberto Rossellini, Annalena Limentani (based on stories by Victor Haines, Marcello Pagliero, Amidei, Fellini, Rossellini, Klaus Mann, Vasco Pratolini); ph, Otello Martelli; ed, Eraldo Da Roma; m, Renzo Rossellini

PAISAN, perhaps Rossellini's greatest achievement, is one of those rare segmented films that never loses steam as it moves through six chronologically ordered sequences beginning with the Allied invasion of Sicily in 1943 and concluding with liberation in 1945. In addition to moving across time, the film transports the viewer northward throughout Italy, each episode observing a slice of regional life. In the first, a New Jersey soldier (Van Loon) gets the job of guarding a young Sicilian woman (Sazio) who refuses to say anything or betray any emotion. The story details his attempts to win her over with no knowledge of Italian. In Naples, meanwhile, a black MP (Johnson) falls into a drunken sleep and has his shoes stolen by a street urchin. He finds the boy living in a cavern with a horde of homeless Neapolitans and decides that others need his shoes more than he. In the Roman tale, an American soldier (Gar Moore) meets Francesca (Michi), a streetwalker. He drunkenly reminisces about a woman he met as his tank rolled into the city. Francesca recognizes him—she was that woman, but he is too drunk to know it. On to Florence, where an American nurse (White) and an Italian partisan (Gigi Gori) scramble through German lines in a suspensful episode which shows that John Sturges has nothing on Rossellini. In the fifth episode, three army chaplains (Catholic, Protestant, and Jewish) have an amusing yet telling ecumenical encounter with Franciscan monks at a rural monastery. And the final episode brings action: a shootout with the Germans against a group of OSS and British. The shot with the baby is stunning.

A film unlike any other the world had seen, PAISAN is OPEN CITY without the melodrama. Rossellini doesn't have De Sica's ability to coax brilliant dramatic performances out of nonprofessionals, yet there's an amazing honesty about the actors' sometimes awkward presence in this film. Despite the film's slice-of-life approach, it is anything but a flat, uninvolving newsreel. Rossellini in fact uses newsreel techniques precisely to point out the propaganda inherent in their purportedly "objective" style. PAISAN is instead a wartime portrait full of humor, pathos, romance, tension, and warmth. Handled in a seemingly direct manner, free of ornamental flourishes, PAISAN highlights the power of the neorealist style better than almost any other film.

PAJAMA GAME, THE

1957 101m c ★★★★
Musical /U
WB

Doris Day *(Kate "Babe" Williams)*, John Raitt *(Sid Sorokin)*, Carol Haney *(Gladys Hotchkiss)*, Eddie Foy, Jr. *(Vernon Hines)*, Reta Shaw *(Mabel)*, Barbara Nichols *(Poopsie)*, Thelma Pelish *(Mae)*, Jack Straw *(Prez)*, Ralph Dunn *(Hasler)*, Owen Martin *(Max)*

p, George Abbott, Stanley Donen; d, George Abbott, Stanley Donen; w, George Abbott, Richard Bissell (based on the Broadway musical by Bissell, Abbott and the novel *Seven and a Half Cents* by Bissell); ph, Harry Stradling (Warner Color); ed, William Ziegler; art d, Malcolm Bert; chor, Bob Fosse; cos, William, Jean Eckart

A terrific movie comes out of this simple idea: Katie "Babe" Williams (Doris Day) works in a pajama factory. She and her coworkers want a 7.5-cent raise, but management refuses, so she leads a grievance committee and takes their complaints to shop superintendent Sid Sorokin (John Raitt), spoiling the whole movement when she falls in love. Day is an utter delight in the role, funny and intelligent even in pajamas, and the choreography by Bob Fosse is energetic. The dancing isn't just left to the actors, however; the camera moves are carefully planned to give the hoofing the best look possible, and the inventive pans and tracking shots seem wonderfully natural and add to the fun. The camera even serves as an additional dance partner, doing a unique, comic tango with Carol Haney. This is a movie that knows how to move! Codirectors George Abbott and Stanley Donen lift the film from its Broadway roots to produce a cinematic musical that everyone will enjoy, with a smash-hit score. Excellent second banana work from Haney, Eddie Foy, Jr., Barbara Nichols, and Thelma Pelish.

PAL JOEY

1957 111m c ★★★★
Musical/Comedy /PG
Essex/George Sidney

Rita Hayworth *(Vera Simpson)*, Frank Sinatra *(Joey Evans)*, Kim Novak *(Linda English)*, Barbara Nichols *(Gladys)*, Bobby Sherwood *(Ned Galvin)*, Hank Henry *(Mike Miggins)*, Elizabeth Patterson *(Mrs. Casey)*, Robin Morse *(Bartender)*, Frank Wilcox *(Col. Langley)*, Pierre Watkin *(Mr. Forsythe)*

p, Fred Kohlmar; d, George Sidney; w, Dorothy Kingsley (based on the *New Yorker* stories by John O'Hara, the musical play by O'Hara, Richard Rodgers, Lorenz Hart); ph, Harold Lipstein (Technicolor); ed, Viola Lawrence, Jerome Thoms; m, Nelson Riddle; art d, Walter Holscher; chor, Hermes Pan; cos, Jean Louis

PAL JOEY's original source was John O'Hara's series of fictional "letters," published in the *New Yorker*, from a mythical dancer who signed all the missives, "Your Pal Joey." O'Hara was approached by producer George Abbott, who talked him into adapting the stories into a book for a musical. Rodgers and Hart came aboard and the play was a success, with sensational, sexy tunes. In this bowdlerized film adaptation, Joey is not a dancer but a singer. Sinatra does a bang-up job as Joey, a saloon singer who arrives in San Francisco with a gleam in his eye, a tuxedo in his suitcase, and not a penny in his pocket. He gets a job at a nightclub, and soon has his way with most of the club chorines, the hold-out being Linda (Kim Novak), a sweet ingenue. When Joey and the band (led by real-life bandleader Bobby Sherwood) are booked for a private soiree at the posh home of wealthy widow Vera (Rita Hayworth), Joey recognizes her as a former stripper. Vera has eyes for Joey, who is himself rapidly falling for Linda, and decides to finance him in his own nightspot, the Chez Joey. Noting, however, that there is more between Joey and Linda than a professional relationship, she holds back the money and tells Joey he cannot open the club if Linda remains with the establishment. Turning over a new leaf, erstwhile heel Joey won't give in, but Linda begs Vera to go ahead with the deal. Vera says she'll do so if Linda will get lost, and offers to end Joey's years of poverty by marrying him, a tempting prospect—but Joey makes the right choice. Some of Rodgers and Hart's best songs ever are in this score, including Sinatra's classic rendition of "The Lady Is a Tramp." (Novak and Hayworth's singing voices are dubbed.) Add gorgeous costumes, excellent choreography by Hermes Pan, and snappy direction by George Sidney to the tunes and what you have is a don't-miss picture.

PALE RIDER

1985 115m c ★★★½
Western R/15
Malpaso

Clint Eastwood *(Preacher)*, Michael Moriarty *(Hull Barret)*, Carrie Snodgress *(Sarah Wheeler)*, Christopher Penn *(Josh LaHood)*, Richard Dysart *(Coy LaHood)*, Sydney Penny *(Megan Wheeler)*, Richard Kiel *(Club)*, Doug McGrath *(Spider Conway)*, John Russell *(Stockburn)*, Charles Hallahan *(McGill)*

p, Clint Eastwood; d, Clint Eastwood; w, Michael Butler, Dennis Shryack; ph, Bruce Surtees (Panavision, Technicolor); ed, Joel Cox; m, Lennie Niehaus; prod d, Edward Carfagno; fx, Chuck Gaspar; cos, Glenn Wright

The quiet calm of a beautiful autumn day is broken by the thundering sound of hooves coming down the hillside. A cadre of men employed by powerful strip-miner Coy LaHood (Richard Dysart) rides into a small mining encampment and begins shooting up the place. One of the terrorists kills the dog of young Megan Wheeler's (Sydney Penny). As Megan buries her pet, she says a prayer, begging the Lord to send someone to defend them. Later Megan sits with her widowed mother (Carrie Snodgress) and reads from the Bible: "And I saw, and behold, a pale horse, and its rider's name was death, and hell followed him." Then a lone horseman (Clint Eastwood), dressed as a preacher, rides into camp. From its breathtaking opening, PALE RIDER heralds the return of the western. Although PALE RIDER is definitely a step down from producer-director Eastwood's masterpiece, THE OUTLAW JOSEY WALES and even from HIGH PLAINS DRIFTER (which it most resembles), it had been so long since a quality western had hit America's screens that it appears as if Eastwood purposely set out to remind audiences of all the elements that make the genre work. Eastwood has a deep love and understanding for the genre, and it shows in every frame of PALE RIDER. The supernatural elements of the story are incidental and handled in a restrained, subtle manner that does not distract from the story but enhances it, bringing another dimension to the oft-told tale. Eastwood the director has finely honed his talents and delivers a thought-provoking, well-crafted western.

PALM BEACH STORY, THE

1942 90m bw ★★★★
Comedy /U
Paramount

Claudette Colbert *(Gerry Jeffers)*, Joel McCrea *(Tom Jeffers)*, Mary Astor *(Princess Centimillia)*, Rudy Vallee *(J.D. Hackensacker III)*, Sig Arno *(Toto)*, Robert Warwick *(Mr. Hinch)*, Arthur Stuart Hull *(Mr. Osmond)*, Torben Meyer *(Dr. Kluck)*, Jimmy Conlin *(Mr. Asweld)*, Victor Potel *(Mr. McKeewie)*

p, Paul Jones; d, Preston Sturges; w, Preston Sturges; ph, Victor Milner; ed, Stuart Gilmore; m, Victor Young; art d, Hans Dreier, Ernst Fegte; cos, Irene

Preston Sturges at full tilt, with Claudette Colbert and Joel McCrea, Rudy Vallee, and Mary Astor. Joel is a crazy young architect who has dreams of building a magnificent airport. Claudette is his adoring wife who, in search of investment money for her beloved's dreams, runs away to Palm Beach with the Ale and Quail Club and meets Rudy the incredibly normal zillionaire J.D. Hackensacker III who of course falls in love with her. Rudy's sister, Mary, falls for Joel. In the end all's set right again and each Jack has his Jill. It's hard to describe Sturges' special brand of comedy. Perhaps it's realistic farce. He takes a perfectly natural action and lets it run on just too long to the point of slight but affectionate absurdity.

McCrea and Sturges had just come off the wonderful SULLIVAN'S TRAVELS which took many potshots at Hollywood. They teamed again to snipe at the idle rich with this hysterically funny fairy tale. The war was raging in 1942 and nearly every Hoolywood movie set in contemporary times seemed to involve that conflict in some way. Sturges reasoned that what the country really needed was some laughter. THE PALM BEACH STORY delivers the goods as it pokes fun at how sex and money rule our lives.

Colbert was never lovelier or more energetic than when she blithely delivers Sturges's sophisticated dialogue. Vallee is delightful as the somewhat naive and eccentric billionaire, carefully cataloging every cent he spends. As his sister, Astor is wickedly caustic, especially when dealing with her incomprehensible lover, Arno. As in SULLIVAN'S TRAVELS, McCrea is again well-cast, adeptly playing off the film's wild collection of characters. All the other roles are carefully cast and virtually anyone who walks on screen delivers a memorable witticism. You won't soon forget these actors and you'll be surprised to discover what a nice fellow Rudy Vallee apparently was.

Though this film may lack the satirical bite of Sturges's great comedies such as SULLIVAN'S TRAVELS or MIRACLE AT MORGAN'S CREEK, it remains a delight that is sure to entertain again and again.

PAPER CHASE, THE
1973 112m c   ★★½
Comedy/Drama   PG
FOX

Timothy Bottoms *(Hart)*, Lindsay Wagner *(Susan Kingsfield)*, John Houseman *(Prof. Kingsfield)*, Graham Beckel *(Ford)*, Edward Herrmann *(Anderson)*, Bob Lydiard *(O'Connor)*, Craig Richard Nelson *(Bell)*, James Naughton *(Kevin)*, Regina Baff *(Asheley)*, David Clennon *(Toombs)*

p, Robert C. Thompson, Rodrick Paul; d, James Bridges; w, James Bridges (based on the novel by John Jay Osborn Jr.); ph, Gordon Willis (Panavision, DeLuxe Color); ed, Walter Thompson; m, John Williams; art d, George Jenkins

John Houseman had already distinguished himself as a writer (JANE EYRE), a producer (EXECUTIVE SUITE, THE BAD AND THE BEAUTIFUL) and the story editor of CITIZEN

KANE before winning the Best Supporting Actor Oscar for this, his second role. Bottoms is a Minnesota-bred law student who comes to Harvard and the lecture hall of Houseman, an instructor who seemingly takes great pleasure in puncturing his students' egos. Bottoms falls in love with Wagner. Essentially, this is a military school plot with a change of venue. Bridges secured an Oscar nomination for his adaptation of the novel, and the film was also nominated for Best Sound.

PAPER MOON
1973 102m c   ★★★½
Comedy/Drama   PG/A
Saticoy

Ryan O'Neal *(Moses Pray)*, Tatum O'Neal *(Addie Loggins)*, Madeline Kahn *(Trixie Delight)*, John Hillerman *(Sheriff Hardin/Jess Hardin)*, P.J. Johnson *(Imogene)*, Jessie Lee Fulton *(Miss Ollie)*, James N. Harrell *(Minister)*, Lila Water *(Minister's Wife)*, Noble Willingham *(Mr. Robertson)*, Bob Young *(Gas Station Attendant)*

p, Peter Bogdanovich; d, Peter Bogdanovich; w, Alvin Sargent (based on the novel *Addie Pray* by Joe David Brown); ph, Laszlo Kovacs; ed, Verna Fields; prod d, Polly Platt; fx, Jack Harmon; cos, Pat Kelly, Sandra Stewart

Driving a Model-T roadster in the Depression year of 1936, O'Neal stops to pay his respects at the funeral of one of his former girlfriends. Neighbors explain that the woman's death has left an "adorable" 9-year-old daughter an orphan and beg him to take the child to relatives in St. Joseph, Missouri. O'Neal takes Tatum O'Neal along with him and almost instantly regrets his generosity. The little girl smokes, swears, and exhibits altogether unchildlike behavior. After taking sly vengeance on the brother of the man who caused the death of Tatum's mother in a car accident by defrauding him of $200, O'Neal buys a new car and then takes Tatum to a train station, buying her a ticket for St. Joseph. Rather than get on the train, she creates a scene in the station restaurant, screaming that O'Neal owes her $200. Since he got it from the family that inadvertently caused her mother's death, she asserts, it is therefore her rightful inheritance—and he's probably her father to boot. O'Neal denies this last loudly, but she continues to yell "we got the same jaw!" Finally, O'Neal takes her along on his roadway adventures through Kansas and Missouri. He works a variety of con games on the gullible rurals. For example, he sells monogrammed Bibles at steep prices to widows, claiming that they were ordered by their recently deceased spouses as gifts for their wives. Tatum joins O'Neal in swindling busy department store cashiers in a money switch involving $20 bills. At a country carnival the amorous O'Neal picks up Kahn, a slatternly, buxom tart, and she and her black teenage maid accompany Tatum and O'Neal, the black girl becoming Tatum's friend. Tatum learns that Kahn is a prostitute and resolves to get rid of her. She arranges O'Neal's discovery of a hotel clerk in Kahn's bedroom, causing him to abandon the woman. In a small town O'Neal swindles a bootlegger out of $625, but he is later jailed by sheriff Hillerman—who is also the bootlegger's brother. After the ensuing excape, O'Neal asks Tatum to aid him in a "big score," but Hillerman shows up with his goons and O'Neal is beaten to a pulp. Later, driving a dilapidated truck, O'Neal manages to deliver Tatum to her relatives. He starts to leave, but Tatum insists that he take her along, still believing that O'Neal is her real father. The pair ride off together.

PAPER MOON offers brilliant, bittersweet images and an entertaining story, despite Tatum's forced performance. Ryan O'Neal is quite good, but he fails to take his role much beyond that of an adult constantly being victimized on an emotional level by a 9-year-old. Kahn is excellent as the hippy, bosomy slut. Her annoying high-pitched voice and forward-leaning posture, coupled with her absurd dialogue, wholly capture the part she is playing. Hillerman, however, is too hammy to be convincing. Bogdanovich's direction is fast, furious, and full of fun. As with THE LAST PICTURE SHOW, the director opted for black-and-white cinematography (beautifully done by Kovacs) in a world swimming in color celluloid, to achieve an historical feel. "I have more affection, more affinity for the past," Bogdanovich later stated. "Since I am more interested in it, it comes easier for me." Originally, John Huston was to direct this film, Paul Newman was to play the Ryan O'Neal role and Newman's daughter, Nell Potts, was to play Tatum O'Neal's part. Critics were mixed about the film, many endorsing it as a minor classic that almost perfectly recreated the 1930s, while others thought the film preposterous and insincere. It returned $16 million at the box office in the initial U.S. release. This was Tatum O'Neal's film debut, and no one would ever forget it, especially Tatum O'Neal, who won a Best Supporting Actress Oscar for her performance (over costar Kahn). For Bogdanovich, the grown-up little girl provided "one of the most miserable experiences of my life." The picture was filmed on location near Hays, Kansas, and St. Joseph, Missouri. The highly effective musical backdrop for the picture is a procession of nostalgia from the record collection of Rudi Fehr. Included are 1930s classics such as "A Picture of Me Without You," "Mississippi Mud" (performed by Paul Whiteman and His Orchestra), "About A Quarter To Nine" (performed by Ozzie Nelson and His Orchestra), "Georgia On My Mind" (performed by Hoagy Carmichael and His Orchestra), "After You've Gone" (performed by Tommy Dorsey and His Orchestra), and "The Music Goes Round and Round" (performed by Nat Gonella and His Orchestra). The film also earned Oscar nominations for Best Screenplay and Best Sound.

PAPERHOUSE

1989   92m   c   ★★
Horror   PG-13/15
Working Title   (U.K.)

Charlotte Burke (Anna Madden), Elliott Spiers (Marc), Glenne Headly (Kate), Ben Cross (Dad), Gemma Jones (Dr. Sarah Nichols), Sarah Newbold (Karen), Samantha Cahill (Sharon), Jane Bertish (Miss Vanstone), Gary Bleasdale (Policeman), Steven O'Donnell (Dustman)

p, Sarah Radclyffe, Tim Bevan; d, Bernard Rose; w, Mathew Jacobs (based on the novel Marianne Dreams by Catherine Storr); ph, Mike Southon (Technicolor); ed, Dan Rae; m, Hans Zimmer, Stanley Myers; prod d, Gemma Jackson; art d, Frank Walsh, Anne Tilby; cos, Nic Ede

PAPERHOUSE opens on the 11th birthday of Burke, whose relationship with her mother (Headly) is strained and whose father (Cross) is away on business, as he often is. At school, Burke passes out and, dreaming, finds herself in the middle of large grassy field that leads to a house like one that she has drawn in her notebook. When Burke is revived, Headly arrives to take her to the doctor, but Burke claims that she faked the fainting spell and her mother makes her go back to school. Burke's vivid dreaming continues, however, with a young boy (Spiers) playing a key role in them, and Burke soon recognizes a relationship between her notebook drawings and her dreams. With PAPER-HOUSE, producers Tim Bevan and Sarah Radclyffe, the founders of Working Title Productions (MY BEAUTIFUL LAUNDRETTE; PERSONAL SERVICES; SAMMY AND ROSIE GET LAID), and director Bernard Rose have arrived at an extremely inventive premise for what is essentially a horror film. Unfortunately, their execution is not the equal of their conceptual inventiveness. Eschewing standard gore and violence, opting for less sensational situations, and refusing to round up the usual suspects, they have explored the troubled subconscious of a young girl through a horror film approach. The film offers plenty of tension in the early going, but after the initial shock of the approach wears off, it becomes less frightening. Although Charlotte Burke—chosen from 1,500 would-be Annas and making her acting debut—is convincingly innocent and confused, the other actors contribute less to the proceedings. Glenne Headly (MAKING MR. RIGHT; DIRTY ROTTEN SCOUNDRELS) is hampered by a post-filming decision to make her erstwhile American character English and to have her loop her character's dialogue in two days. Still, she is far more successful than Ben Cross (CHARIOTS OF FIRE), who appears to be sleepwalking even when he's not. In the final analysis, the makers of PAPERHOUSE deserve a great deal of credit for the risks they took, but the idea of the film is more interesting than the film itself.

PAPILLON

1973   150m   c   ★★★★
Prison   PG/18
Corona/General Production

Steve McQueen (Henri Charriere Papillon), Dustin Hoffman (Louis Dega), Victor Jory (Indian Chief), Don Gordon (Julot), Anthony Zerbe (Toussaint Leper Colony Chief), Robert Deman (Maturette), Woodrow Parfrey (Clusoit), Bill Mumy (Lariot), George Coulouris (Dr. Chatal), Ratna Assan (Zoraima)

p, Robert Dorfmann, Franklin J. Schaffner; d, Franklin J. Schaffner; w, Dalton Trumbo, Lorenzo Semple, Jr. (based on the autobiographical novel by Henri Charriere); ph, Fred Koenekamp (Panavision, Technicolor); ed, Robert Swink; m, Jerry Goldsmith; prod d, Tony Masters; art d, Jack Maxsted; cos, Anthony Powell

A grim, authentically brutal film about the escape of notorious French felon Henri "Papillon" Charriere (Steve McQueen) from the supposedly inescapable prison fortress of Devil's Island. The story begins in the streets of Marseilles in the 1930s, with French soldiers escorting a large group of prisoners to the docks. Among them are McQueen, a convicted murderer, and Hoffman, a big-time stock swindler who still has a lot of money hidden. During the ensuing voyage, a couple of brutal murderers attempt to kill Hoffman but McQueen saves him. Once in Cayenne McQueen thinks only about escape. He attacks a guard who abuses Hoffman, and makes a break, only to be later recaptured. McQueen spends most of his time in solitary confinement for repeated escape attempts. Here he staves off starvation, madness, and disease while his body deteriorates. He and William Smithers, the commandant of the solitary confinement compound, engage in a contest of wills and slowly age together, their hair turning white over the years. Finally returned to the main prison, McQueen is received warmly by Hoffman, who is now living a (relatively) cushy life, paying off the guards and the warden for favorable treatment. Hoffman tries to persuade McQueen to serve out his time and wait for parole, but eventually joins him in an escape attempt just as harrowing as life on the inside.

PAPILLON was produced with consummate technical skill and offers brilliant acting by McQueen and Hoffman. Schaffner, who expertly captured the gritty story of PATTON, does not flinch from showing every conceivable horror of the French penal system. Excellent supporting performances are provided by Zerbe, as the compassionate leader of a leper colony, Jory, as a stoic Indian chief, and Coulouris, as a venal prison doctor. Even scriptwriter Trumbo, who had become a cult figure by the time of this film, gets into the act, appearing as the commandant of the penal colony at the beginning of the film. Shot on location in Spain and Jamaica, PAPILLON was a costly film, with McQueen's salary a reported $2 million and Hoffman's $1,250,000; Schaffner, according to one report, received $750,000 for his directorial efforts. The overall price tag for this excellent prison saga exceeded $13 million, with distributor Allied Artists contributing $7 million. The movie gleaned $22 million through U.S. release. PAPILLON was originally rated R by the MPAA for its extreme violence, but Allied Artists appealed and the rating was changed to PG.

PARALLAX VIEW, THE

1974   102m   c   ★★★½
Thriller   R/15
Paramount

Warren Beatty (Joseph Frady), Hume Cronyn (Editor Edgar Rintels), William Daniels (Austin Tucker), Paula Prentiss (Lee Carter), Kelly Thordsen (Sheriff L.D.), Earl Hindman (Deputy Red), Chuck Waters (Busboy-Assassin), Bill Joyce (Sen. Carroll), Bettie Johnson (Mrs. Carroll), Bill McKinney (Art, an Assassin)

p, Alan J. Pakula; d, Alan J. Pakula; w, David Giler, Lorenzo Semple, Jr. (based on the novel by Loren Singer); ph, Gordon Willis (Panavision, Technicolor); ed, John W. Wheeler; m, Michael Small; prod d, George Jenkins; art d, George Jenkins; cos, Frank Thompson

A popular senator is shot by a waiter at the Seattle Space Needle. Three years later Lee (Prentiss), a television reporter who was on the scene, goes to newspaper reporter Joe Frady (Beatty) frightened for her life. Assassination witnesses have been systematically killed, she says, and Lee knows that she's next. Frady discounts her fears as irrational paranoia, but after her supposed suicide, doubt creeps into his mind. He begins investigating the story and uncovers a huge conspiracy involving the mysterious "Parallax Corporation," a secret company that recruits assassins to eliminate troublemakers on their "list." Alan J. Pakula's taut direction maintains a neat balance between the real and the perceived; things are not what they appear to be. He presents disorienting shots and editing patterns with characters often filmed behind glass or curtains, allowing only a partial look at the whole scene. The most compelling aspects are of course the political and historical overtones. The fictional assassination was a deliberate attempt to suggest a possible explanation for the John F. Kennedy assassination. Using historical parallels (the photographs implying a second gunman at Dallas; the fact that many of the assassination witnesses died mysteriously in the years following 1963), Pakula created a possible, though fictional, explanation in a film steeped in American symbolism. The film was released in June 1974, after the studio had let the controversial work sit for several months. This is one of the best political thrillers of the 1970s.

PARDON MON AFFAIRE

(UN ELEPHANT CA TROMPE ENORMEMENT)
1976   105m   c   ★★★½
Comedy/Romance   PG/X
Gaumont/La Gueville   (France)

Jean Rochefort (Etienne), Claude Brasseur (Daniel), Guy Bedos (Simon), Victor Lanoux (Bouly), Daniele Delorme (Marthe), Anny Duperey (Charlotte), Martine Sarcey (Esperanza), Marthe Villalonga (Mouchy)

p, Alain Poire, Yves Robert; d, Yves Robert; w, Jean-Loup Dabadie (based on the story by Robert, Dabadie); ph, Rene Mathelin; ed, Gerard Pollicand; m, Vladimir Cosma

Yves Robert, the director responsible for THE TALL BLONDE MAN WITH ONE BLACK SHOE and its sequel, struck again with this pleasant, enjoyable mixture of comedy and drama about husbands and their affairs. Etienne (Jean Rochefort) is a Parisian civil servant who, while in his company parking lot, gazes at the bright red dress of a pretty young woman (Anny Duperey) as it is blown up above her waist by a rush of air. Although he is happily married to Marthe (Daniele Delorme, wife of director Robert) and has never even thought of having an affair, Etienne becomes enamored of this mystery woman. In the meantime, he and his three best friends witness the result of years of dalliances when one of them, Bouly (Victor Lanoux), comes home one day to find that his wife has left him, taking along his children and every last possession. Robert successfully creates a number of believable characters with honest emotions and places them in lightly humorous situations, and the result falls somewhere between broad comedy (one memorable scene has a character pretending to be blind and causing havoc in an elegant restaurant) and heartfelt drama (Bouly's reaction to his wife's departure), as if Robert was attempting a farcical French version of John Cassavetes's HUSBANDS. Many of the same names reunited for the less successful sequel, PARDON MON AFFAIRE, TOO! Remade in Hollywood as THE WOMAN IN RED.

PARENTHOOD

1989   124m   c   ★★★½
Comedy   PG-13/15
Imagine

Steve Martin (Gil Buckman), Tom Hulce (Larry Buckman), Rick Moranis (Nathan), Jason Robards, Jr. (Frank Buckman), Martha Plimpton (Julie), Mary Steenburgen (Karen Buckman), Dianne Wiest (Helen), Keanu Reeves (Tod), Harley Kozak (Susan), Leaf Phoenix (Garry)

p, Brian Grazer; d, Ron Howard; w, Lowell Ganz, Babaloo Mandel (based on a story by Lowell Ganz, Babaloo Mandel, Ron Howard); ph, Don McAlpine (Deluxe Color); ed, Michael Hill, Daniel Hanley; m, Randy Newman; prod d, Todd Hallowell; art d, Christopher Nowak; cos, Ruth Morley

Occasionally corny, yet thoroughly entertaining, PARENTHOOD is a movie by, for, and about parents. Four generations are portrayed by an all-star cast, delivering a lesson in child-rearing worthy of Dr. Spock. Jason Robards plays Frank, the head of the Buckman clan. Gil (Steve Martin), Helen (Dianne Wiest), Susan (Harley Kozak), and Larry (Tom Hulce) are his children; all of them have kids of their own. Gil tries to balance his career with being the attentive father Frank never was; divorcee Helen has her hands full with son Garry (Leaf Phoenix), who is badly in need of a male role model, rebellious teenage daughter Julie (Martha Plimpton), and burn-out son-in-law Tod (Keanu Reeves). Susan does her best to give her toddler a childhood while husband Nathan (Rick Moranis) has the precocious kid studying karate, long division, and Kafka. With his own illegitimate son in tow, prodigal son Larry has returned home deeply in debt to some very rough customers. All of these situations get worse before they get better, but by film's end the family is closer than ever. PARENTHOOD's coscreenwriters Ron Howard, Lowell Ganz, and Babaloo Mandell—the fathers of 14 children in all—have produced a funny, poignant script with very contemporary humor. It is the acting, though, that shines brightest in the movie. Rarely has such a formidable array of talent been assembled for one film, and theirs is truly an ensemble effort. While PARENTHOOD crosses the border into schmaltz a number of times, the movie runs the gamut of realistic emotions, and one scene or another is bound to hit home with the parents who see the film.

PARENTS
1989 82m c   ★★★
Comedy/Horror   R/18
Great American

Randy Quaid (Nick Laemle), Mary Beth Hurt (Lily Laemle), Sandy Dennis (Millie Dew), Bryan Madorsky (Michael Laemle), Juno Mills-Cockell (Sheila Zellner), Kathryn Grody (Miss Baxter), Deborah Rush (Mrs. Zellner), Graham Jarvis (Mr. Zellner), Helen Carscallen (Grandmother), Warren Van Evera (Grandfather)

p, Bonnie Palef-Woolf; d, Bob Balaban; w, Christopher Hawthorne; ph, Ernest Day, Robin Vidgeon (Filmhouse Color); ed, Bill Pankow; m, Jonathan Elias, Angelo Badalamenti, Sherman Foote; art d, Andris Hausmanis; cos, Arthur Rowsell

In his directorial debut actor Bob Balaban uses a fantastic plot metaphorically to study a repressed young boy's exposure to his parent's sexuality. Having settled into their home in the suburbs during the late 1950s, Nick and Lily Laemle (Randy Quaid and Mary Beth Hurt) offer young son Michael (Bryan Madorsky) a continual display of their ravenous sexual appetites, but pay little attention to him, except to wonder why he won't eat his meat. In time, Michael comes to suspect that his folks are making their meals out of corpses Nick brings home from the workplace. When Michael tells the school psychologist (Sandy Dennis) about his homelife, she determines to show him the reality behind his "hallucinations," but ends up as steak herself, as the film becomes increasingly bizarre. PARENTS concentrates heavily on Michael's Freudian pathology; however, in its emphasis on psychological themes, the film loses sight of its story and becomes a confused collection of isolated vignettes. In adopting the boy's single-minded perspective, it prevents its characters from developing, so that Quaid hovers and glowers, Hurt giggles and flirts, and Madorsky lurks in dark recesses without variation from beginning to end. Nevertheless, Balaban clearly demonstrates a talent for visuals; his swooping, gliding camera movements indicate a sure and promising directorial hand.

PARIS BELONGS TO US
(PARIS NOUS APPARTIENT)
1962 120m bw   ★★★
Mystery
Ajym/Carrosse   (France)

Betty Schneider (Anne Goupil), Giani Esposito (Gerard Lenz), Francoise Prevost (Terry Yok), Daniel Crohem (Philip Kaufman), Francois Maistre (Pierre Goupil), Jean-Claude Brialy (Jean Marc), Jean-Marie Robain (De Georges), Brigitte Juslin, Noelle Leiris, Monique Le Poirier

p, Roland Nonin; d, Jacques Rivette; w, Jacques Rivette, Jean Gruault; ph, Charles Bitsch; ed, Denise de Casabianca; m, Philippe Arthuys

Schneider, after overhearing a discussion on the suicide of a young Spaniard, is compelled to learn why the youth's life ended so tragically. She gets involved with Esposito, a theater director, and takes a part in his production of Shakespeare's "Pericles." She becomes worried for Esposito's life when he tells her that the Spaniard was part of a worldwide conspiracy and that he is targeted for murder by the same organization. She also meets Crohem, an American victim of McCarthyism, who is responsible for informing the Spaniard and Esposito of the organization. Eventually it is revealed that Crohem made the whole thing up, but not before Esposito's paranoia gets the better of him and he commits suicide.

Along with Claude Chabrol's LE BEAU SERGE, this first feature by Jacques Rivette kindled the flame that became known as the French New Wave. Production began in the early summer of 1958 with money borrowed from the magazine Rivette (and his New Wave counterparts) worked for, Cahiers du Cinema. Technicians, actors, and lab fees were all on credit, with no money exchanged until the film's release in 1960. Without so much as a car, Rivette and his entourage of film enthusiasts worked whenever they could, spending Sundays trying to raise enough money to begin filming again on Mondays. With the help of Chabrol and Truffaut, whose first films were already receiving acclaim at the Cannes Film Festival, PARIS was finally released—a stepping stone toward French cinema's rebirth.

PARIS, TEXAS
1984 150m c   ★★★★
Drama   R/15
Road Movies/Argos/Westdeutscher/Channel 4/Pro-Ject
(France/West Germany)

Harry Dean Stanton (Travis Clay Henderson), Nastassja Kinski (Jane), Dean Stockwell (Walt Henderson), Aurore Clement (Anne), Hunter Carson (Hunter), Bernhard Wicki (Dr. Ulmer), Viva Auder (Woman on TV), Socorro Valdez (Carmelita), Tommy Farrell (Screaming Man), John Lurie (Slater)

p, Don Guest; d, Wim Wenders; w, Sam Shepard (based on a story adapted by L.M. Kit Carson); ph, Robby Muller; ed, Peter Pryzgodda; m, Ry Cooder; art d, Kate Altman; cos, Birgitta Bjerke

Epic but intimate, PARIS, TEXAS combines the European sensibility of director Wim Wenders with the expansive locations of the American West.

Amid the desert and brilliant sky of Big Bend, Texas, Travis Clay Henderson (Harry Dean Stanton) aimlessly wanders under the boiling sun. He stops in a tavern and promptly collapses, awakening in the care of a German doctor (Bernhard Wicki). Assuming the catatonic Travis is mute, the doctor calls a number in his wallet and reaches Travis's brother, Walt (Dean Stockwell), who lives in Los Angeles with his French wife (Aurore Clement) and Hunter (Hunter Carson), Travis's seven-year-old son by his estranged wife, Jane (Nastassia Kinski). It turns out Travis has been missing and assumed dead for four years. Walt brings him back to L.A. for a reunion with Hunter, who subsequently joins his father on a quixotic quest for family, true love, and Jane.

PARIS, TEXAS features neither sweeping themes, grandiose sets, nor a cast of thousands, but from its opening shots one senses its uniquely epic quality. The vast landscapes recall those of John Ford, but instead of John Wayne it's Stanton who wanders across the frame, a modern American father in suit and tie, displaced, aimless, and emotionally dead, on an odyssey to find himself. He knows where he began—in Paris, Texas—but not where he is going. Although based on stories by Sam Shepard, the film's vision of America is wholly that of Wenders, a

PARIS WHEN IT SIZZLES

German director deeply fascinated by Americana. As the title suggests, Wenders' America is a by-product of the European imagination.

Superbly scripted, the film features wonderful performances from all its major players. Equally brilliant, especially in a film that emphasizes script and character, is the cinematography by Robby Muller, perfectly capturing the notion of "America." A final factor in PARIS, TEXAS's success is the remarkably haunting score by blues musician Ry Cooder.

PARIS WHEN IT SIZZLES

1964   110m   c   ★★
Romance/Comedy   /A
Quine/Charleston

William Holden (*Richard Benson*), Audrey Hepburn (*Gabrielle Simpson*), Gregoire Aslan (*Police Inspector*), Raymond Bussieres (*Gangster*), Christian Duvallex (*Maitre d'Hotel*), Noel Coward (*Alexander Meyerheimer*), Tony Curtis (*2nd Policeman*), Marlene Dietrich, Mel Ferrer (*Guest Stars*), Fred Astaire

p, Richard Quine, George Axelrod; d, Richard Quine; w, George Axelrod (based on the story by Julien Duvivier, Henri Jeanson); ph, Charles Lang (Technicolor); ed, Archie Marshek; m, Nelson Riddle; art d, Jean d'Eaubonne; fx, Paul K. Lerpae; cos, Hubert de Givenchy, Christian Dior

Paris when it fizzles. A remake of the 1953 French picture HENRIETTE'S HOLIDAY (directed by Julien Duvivier), this movie pairs Holden and Hepburn for the first time since SABRINA, in 1954. Holden is a screenwriter under pressure from movie producer Coward to finish his latest script, "The Girl Who Stole the Eiffel Tower." Coward gives him 48 hours to finish, unaware that the writer has yet to begin. Hoping to hurry the process along, Holden hires a secretary, Hepburn. She moves in with him, and during her short stay they fall madly in love, while confusing their own lives with those of the script's characters. They imagine themselves in various scenes from the film—a western, a musical, a spy drama, a romance, a comedy—with their fantasies taking precedence over their work. When the 48-hour time limit has expired, they still have no script. Distraught, Holden tells Hepburn that he is not good enough for her, and she leaves. But an unhappy ending is not in the cards.

The couple's relationship takes off with the promise of a Hollywood-style romance. Unfortunately, PARIS WHEN IT SIZZLES falls as flat as "The Girl Who Stole the Eiffel Tower." Although the locations and Hepburn both photograph brilliantly, the relationship between Hepburn and Holden never comes to life. This is not surprising, since Holden and Hepburn were on rather shaky ground in real life. During the filming of SABRINA Holden had found himself falling uncontrollably in love with Hepburn. Ten years after her refusal to marry him, the two paired in PARIS WHEN IT SIZZLES. Holden's biography reports that Holden once told Ryan O'Neal, "I remember the day I arrived at Orly Airport for PARIS WHEN IT SIZZLES. I could hear my footsteps echoing against the walls of the transit corridor, just like a condemned man walking the last mile. I realized that I had to face Audrey and I had to deal with my drinking. And I didn't think I could handle either situation." Hepburn tried her best to make Holden comfortable (which only made Holden want her more) and to ease tensions on the set. After the first day's "rushes," however, Hepburn was extremely dissatisfied with how she had been photographed. She demanded that Renoir be fired (a gross insult to the highly respected family name in Paris). Franz Planer was the first-choice replacement; but when his schedule was found to be too busy, Lang was picked. After that

delay another, more-major setback followed. Holden's drinking binges alternated with a clinic dryout and then a bout with minor injuries sustained in a car accident. (With only one more scene to complete, he had bought a Ferrari, driven to Switzerland for Bastille Day—ignoring the pleas of Quine and Axelrod—and crashed into a brick wall.) In what seemed like a desperate attempt to add some stronger box office potential to the film, Quine enlisted a number of big names to appear in a party scene, among them Dietrich (who reportedly got to keep the limousine and the fur coat in which she arrives in the film), Ferrer (Hepburn's husband at that time), Curtis, and the singing voices of Sinatra and Astaire. All of this box office artillery, however, couldn't raise PARIS WHEN IT SIZZLES to anything more than an average piece of entertainment.

PARTING GLANCES

1986   90m   c   ★★★
Drama   /15
Rondo

Richard Ganoung (*Michael*), John Bolger (*Robert*), Steve Buscemi (*Nick*), Adam Nathan (*Peter*), Kathy Kinney (*Joan*), Patrick Tull (*Cecil*), Yolande Bavan (*Betty*), Richard Wall (*Douglas*), Jim Selfe (*Douglas' Sidekick*), Kristin Moneagle (*Sarah*)

p, Yoram Mandel, Arthur Silverman; d, Bill Sherwood; w, Bill Sherwood; ph, Jacek Laskus (DuArt Color); ed, Bill Sherwood; prod d, John Loggia; art d, Daniel Haughey, Mark Sweeney; cos, Sylvia Heisel

Unlike several major studio productions, in which homosexuality is used either as an issue or as comic relief, PARTING GLANCES takes an inside look at New York's gay community. The pain and joys of love, unspoken cultural rules, and the specter of AIDS are all dealt with in an energetic manner that balances the story's varying shades of emotion.

Michael (Richard Ganoung) is a pleasant young man about to end a six-year relationship with his live-in lover, Robert (John Bolger). Robert is preparing to leave for Africa, ostensibly to accept an employment opportunity, but also to give himself a little breathing room from Michael's steady companionship. Before going to a dinner to be hosted by Robert's boss, Cecil (Patrick Tull), and his wife, Michael drops by the apartment of Nick (Steve Buscemi), a cynical New Wave musician who is dying of AIDS. Later, as the evening of farewells continues, Michael becomes more despondent.

The plot is fairly simple, but the affection displayed by PARTING GLANCES's marvelous ensemble makes these everyday events something more than commonplace. At the center of it all is Ganoung, who handles his key role well. Buscemi's performance as the dying musician is another standout. Writer-director Bill Sherwood shows marvelous talent in his feature debut. He deals with touchy issues in a forthright manner and doesn't allow these events to unfold without a well-aimed sense of humor. Sadly, Sherwood himself succumbed to AIDS complications in early 1990.

PASSAGE TO INDIA, A

1984   163m   c   ★★★½
Drama   PG
John Heyman/Edward Sands/HBO   (U.K.)

Judy Davis (*Adela Quested*), Victor Banerjee (*Dr. Aziz*), Peggy Ashcroft (*Mrs. Moore*), James Fox (*Richard Fielding*), Alec Guinness (*Godbole*), Nigel Havers (*Ronny Heaslop*), Richard Wilson

(Turton), Antonia Pemberton (Mrs. Turton), Michael Culver (McBryde), Art Malik (Mahmoud Ali)

p, John Brabourne, Richard Goodwin; d, David Lean; w, David Lean (based on the play by Santha Rama Rau and the novel by E.M. Forster); ph, Ernest Day (Metrocolor); ed, David Lean; m, Maurice Jarre; prod d, John Box; art d, Leslie Tomkins, Clifford Robinson, Ram Yedekar, Herbert Westbrook; cos, Judy Moorcroft

At 75, David Lean, whose epics THE BRIDGE ON THE RIVER KWAI, LAWRENCE OF ARABIA, and DOCTOR ZHIVAGO garnered 19 Oscars, returned to work after a 14-year absence with this adaptation of the E.M. Forster novel about sexual repression and racial prejudice in 1924 India. Set in the fictional town of Chandrapore, the story concerns Adela Quested (Judy Davis) who has settled in India and is to marry Ronny Heaslop (Nigel Havers), a town magistrate. She is befriended by the charming Dr. Aziz (Victor Banerjee), but it's a friendship that ultimately leads to tragedy. Lean does an excellent job of conveying the repressive nature of British society captured in the novel. Although the story makes for a movie that is often slow going, it is also a beautiful and evocative film fueled by an excellent performance from Davis. Also a marvel is the performance of Peggy Ashcroft, who deservedly won a Best Supporting Actress Oscar for this role.

PASSAGE TO MARSEILLE

1944 110m bw   ★★★½
Drama/War   /PG
WB

Humphrey Bogart (Matrac), Claude Rains (Capt. Freycinet), Michele Morgan (Paula), Philip Dorn (Renault), Sydney Greenstreet (Maj. Duval), Peter Lorre (Marius), George Tobias (Petit), Victor Francen (Capt. Patain Malo), Helmut Dantine (Garou), John Loder (Manning)

p, Hal B. Wallis; d, Michael Curtiz; w, Casey Robinson, John C. Moffitt (based on the novel Men Without a Country by Charles Nordhoff, James Norman Hall); ph, James Wong Howe; ed, Owen Marks; m, Max Steiner; art d, Carl Jules Weyl; fx, Jack Cosgrove, Edwin DuPar, Byron Haskin, Roy Davidson, Rex Wimpy; cos, Leah Rhodes

With adventurer Humphrey Bogart as his lead, director Michael Curtiz here offers a slam-bang action film, one with a tricky plot whose narrative unfolds through a complicated series of flashbacks-within-flashbacks and flash forwards, but that is nevertheless exciting and absorbing all the way. A group of prisoners who have escaped the dreaded prison at Cayenne in French Guiana are picked up by a passing French freighter, commanded by Malo (Victor Francen), who is loyal to Free France but who hides his sympathies from the fascistic Maj. Duval (Sydney Greenstreet), a French officer sympathetic to the Vichy government. The rescued men claim they are survivors of a torpedoed ship, but eventually their true identities are learned. They are Matrac (Bogart), a French journalist who opposed the Nazi takeover of his country from within, and his criminal comrades Marius (Peter Lorre), Garou (Helmut Dantine), Renault (Philip Dorn), and Petit (George Tobias). All are loyal to the Free French, and when Maj. Duval plans to turn the ship over to the Vichy government, Matrac and his comrades fight to keep the ship from the clutches of the collaborators. Although Curtiz draws superb performances from his great cast, many of whom (Bogart, Lorre, Greenstreet, Dantine, Claude Rains, Corinna Mura, and Louis Mercier) appeared in Warner Bros.' recent smash hit CASABLANCA, which was also directed by Curtiz, the story is more than a little

confusing because of the unwieldy flashbacks used to tell the tale. Yet the great action director packs the film with marvelous adventure and exciting scenes, not to mention stirring patriotism. Warners attempted to time PASSAGE TO MARSEILLE's release to coincide with what the studio thought would be the invasion of southern France, but when this failed to take place the film was distributed without an international news event to boost the production (as had been the case with CASABLANCA, released just after American troops landed in Africa and Allied leaders met in that African city for top-level conferences). James Wong Howe's gritty photography helps set the mood, and Max Steiner's music dynamically establishes patriotic fervor.

PASSENGER, THE
(PASAZERKA)
1970 60m bw   ★★★½
Drama   /PG
Kamera   (Poland)

Aleksandra Slaska (Liza), Anna Ciepielewska (Marta), Jan Kreczmar (Walter), Marek Walczewski (Tadeusz), Maria Koscialkowska (Inga), Irena Malkiewicz ("Ober"), Leon Pietraszkiewicz (Commandant), Janusz Bylczynski (Kapo), A. Golebiowska (Female Commandant), John Rees (English Narrator)

d, Andrzej Munk; w, Zofia Posmysz-Piasecka, Andrzej Munk (based on the book Pasazerka by Posmysz-Piasecka); ph, Krzysztof Winiewicz (Dyaliscope); ed, Zofia Dwornik, Witold Lesiewicz; m, Tadeusz Baird; art d, Jerzy Possack; cos, Wieslawa Chojkowska

Slaska, a former overseer at Auschwitz and an SS member, is reunited with Ciepielewska, a prisoner in the concentration camp. The two had become friendly when Slaska arranged for the prisoner to meet with her lover, a fellow prisoner. Slaska also reveals the jealousy she felt over the woman's relationship, and how she used her power to control the prisoner. Before the film was completed, director Andrzej Munk was killed in an auto accident. The unfinished picture, later pieced together by his associates, might have been a masterpiece had Munk lived. It received the International Critics Award at Cannes in 1964, a year after its Polish release.

PASSENGER, THE
1975 123m c   ★★★★
Drama   PG/A
CIC/Concordia/C.I.P.I/Champion   (Italy)

Jack Nicholson (David Locke), Maria Schneider (Girl), Jenny Runacre (Rachel Locke), Ian Hendry (Martin Knight), Steven Berkoff (Stephen), Ambroise Bia (Achebe), Jose Maria Caffarel (Hotel Keeper), James Campbell (Witch Doctor), Manfred Spies (German Stranger), Jean Baptiste Tiemele (Murderer)

p, Carlo Ponti; d, Michelangelo Antonioni; w, Mark Peploe, Peter Wollen, Michelangelo Antonioni (based on a story by Peploe); ph, Luciano Tovoli (Metrocolor); ed, Franco Arcalli, Michaelangelo Antonioni; art d, Piero Poletto; cos, Louise Stjernsward

In this visually stunning adventure David Locke (Jack Nicholson) is a reporter sent to northern Africa on a mission to interview a band of guerrillas. After a battle with a Jeep that refuses to travel through sand, Locke winds up in a blisteringly hot, rundown hotel. There he is confused with another hotel guest, Robertson (Chuck Mulvehill), to whom he bears a striking resemblance. When he discovers Robertson dead in his room, Locke is presented with a perfect opportunity to escape his hell of a life. He switches passport photos and personal belongings and places the corpse in his own room. Looking through "his" daily planner, he finds a number of women's names and various appointments. Curious, he decides to keep a rendezvous and discovers that Robertson was a gun runner who supplied foreign governments with plans and documents. In the meantime he meets an enigmatic young woman (Maria Schneider) to whom he is magnetically drawn, causing him to ignore and avoid the efforts of his wife and best friend to locate him. THE PASSENGER could probably be analyzed until the end of time, each viewing uncovering a different path to understanding the film as a whole. What is more interesting than the "whys" and "hows" of the plot however, are the "where" and "when." Locke and the girl are very much a part of their environment, whether it's the sandy wastelands of northern Africa or the exquisitely organic Gaudi architecture of Barcelona. The girl has no history—she just is—a state of being to which Locke also aspires.

PASSION

1983 88m c ★★★½

Drama R/15

Sara/Sonimage/A2/Film et Video/SSR (France/Switzerland)

Jerzy Radziwilowicz, Hanna Schygulla, Isabelle Huppert, Michel Piccoli, Laszlo Szabo, Sophie Loucachevski, Patrick Bonnel, Myriem Roussel, Magaly Campos, Jean-Francois Stevenin

p, Alain Sarde; d, Jean-Luc Godard; w, Jean-Luc Godard; ph, Raoul Coutard (Eastmancolor); ed, Jean-Luc Godard; art d, Serge Marzolff, Jean Bauer

Radziwilowicz (MAN OF MARBLE) plays a cigar-smoking director (much like Godard) from Poland who is filming in the style of the great painters—Rembrandt, Delacroix, Goya, and El Greco. The film he is making is a study of light and image, but he is far behind schedule because he can never get the lighting right. A noisy parody of an Italian filmmaker keeps asking what the story is. The director places his faith in the Americans, who always come through. Schygulla is a motel owner whose image on a video screen becomes an obsession with Radziwilowicz. Huppert plays a stuttering factory worker who is trying to stir up a revolt among her coworkers. A commercial failure, PASSION is the second film from the "new" Godard after his self-imposed exile into Marxist filmmaking and French television. It is, however, a superb film with more narrative than one usually expects from Godard and a surprising amount of humor. PASSION also boasts an excellent international cast. In addition to Radziwilowicz, it includes Rainer Werner Fassbinder regular Hanna Schygulla in perhaps her most visually striking screen appearance ever, Isabelle Huppert, whom Godard perviously cast in his EVERY MAN FOR HIMSELF, and Michel Piccoli, who starred opposite Brigitte Bardot in Godard's CONTEMPT. Equal credit must go to Raoul Coutard, whose camerawork and lighting are the center of the entire film.

PASSION OF ANNA, THE

(EN PASSION)

1969 100m c ★★★

Drama R/AA

Cinematograph (Sweden)

Liv Ullmann (Anna Fromm), Bibi Andersson (Eva Vergerus), Max von Sydow (Andreas Winkelman), Erland Josephson (Elis Vergerus), Erik Hell (Johan Andersson), Sigge Furst (Verner), Svea Holst (Verner's Wife), Annika Kronberg (Katarina), Hjordis Pettersson (Johan's Sister), Lars-Owe Carlberg

d, Ingmar Bergman; w, Ingmar Bergman; ph, Sven Nykvist (Eastmancolor); ed, Siv Kanalv; prod d, P.A. Lundgren; fx, Ulf Nordholm; cos, Mago

Max von Sydow, an ex-convict who lives alone in an island farmhouse, is visited one day by the crippled Ullmann, who requests to use the phone. Ullmann soon leaves, but forgets to take her purse with her. Von Sydow looks through it, finds her name, address, and a letter from her husband which discusses their unhappy marriage. He returns the purse and is introduced to Josephson and Andersson, friends of Ullmann's. Eventually Ullmann moves into von Sydow's farmhouse. Tensions between the two begin to rise, partially due to reports of a crazed murderer who is on the loose. In a fit of anger, von Sydow goes after Ullmann with an ax. Later, the *real* maniac strikes at von Sydow's farm, setting his barn on fire. Ullmann rescues von Sydow from the scene of the blaze, and drives frantically down the road. Von Sydow accuses Ullmann of trying to kill him, perhaps as she killed her husband and son years earlier in the auto accident that left her crippled. Hailed by many as a masterpiece, THE PASSION OF ANNA (only Bergman's second film in color) employs some interesting techniques, such as interviews with each of the four main actors and also sheds some light on many of the baroque mannerisms and symbols that have come to be associated with Bergman. It still contains, however, that element of coldness which has turned many viewers against Bergman. Filmed on the island of Faro, a one-time home for Bergman.

PASSPORT TO PIMLICO

1949 84m bw ★★★

Comedy /U

Ealing/Eagle-Lion (U.K.)

Stanley Holloway (Arthur Pemberton), Hermione Baddeley (Eddie Randall), Margaret Rutherford (Prof. Hatton-Jones), Paul Dupuis (Duke of Burgundy), Basil Radford (Gregg), Naunton Wayne (Straker), Jane Hylton (Molly), Raymond Huntley (Mr. Wix), Betty Warren (Connie Pemberton), Barbara Murray (Shirley Pemberton)

p, Michael Balcon; d, Henry Cornelius; w, T.E.B. Clarke; ph, Lionel Barnes, Cecil Cooney; ed, Michael Truman; m, Georges Auric; art d, Roy Oxley; cos, Anthony Mendleson

A light British comedy about an unexploded bomb that suddenly goes off and unearths documents stating that part of London belongs to Burgundy, France. Halloway becomes the head of the new government; new borders are drawn and new customs barriers are put into effect. A fresh comedy with some well-aimed satirical arrows from producer Balcon's Ealing Studios, famous for their sophisticated, irreverent comedies.

PAT AND MIKE

1952 95m bw ★★★★

Comedy /U

MGM

Spencer Tracy (Mike Conovan), Katharine Hepburn (Pat Pemberton), Aldo Ray (Davie Hucko), William Ching (Collier Weld), Sammy White (Barney Grau), George Mathews (Spec Cauley), Loring Smith (Mr. Beminger), Phyllis Povah (Mrs. Beminger), Charles Bronson (Hank Tasling), Frank Richards (Sam Garsell)

p, Lawrence Weingarten; d, George Cukor; w, Ruth Gordon, Garson Kanin; ph, William Daniels; ed, George Boemler; m, David Raksin; art d, Cedric Gibbons, Urie McCleary; fx, Warren Newcombe; cos, Orry-Kelly

After playing a sports-hating character 10 years earlier in WOMAN OF THE YEAR, Katharine Hepburn essays the role of an all-around athlete not unlike the great Babe Didrikson Zaharias (who plays herself here) in this marvelous romantic comedy, which paired her again with real-life companion Spencer Tracy. Pat (Hepburn), a perky PE instructor at a southern California college and gifted athlete, falls apart whenever her professor fiance, Collier (William Ching), comes to watch her compete. Mike (Tracy), a somewhat shady sports promoter, recognizes her talent and persuades her to turn pro. Despite his unsuccessful attempt to get her to throw a match, she begins winning golf and tennis tournaments under his guidance, and gradually they fall for each other. What did you expect? Still, the point isn't what happens, but how it happens, and under the direction of George Cukor—working from an Oscar-nominated script by Garson Kanin and Ruth Gordon—Tracy and Hepburn turn in unforgettable performances. Shot mostly at the Riviera Country Club in Pacific Palisades, PAT AND MIKE gave Hepburn an opportunity to display her authentic athletic ability amidst a cast that included pro golfers Helen Dettweiler and Betty Hicks, as well as tennis professionals Don Budge and Pancho Gonzales. Chuck Connors, on loan from his job as the Triple A Los Angeles Angels's first sacker, makes his film debut as a police captain. Oscar nominated for Best Screenplay.

PAT GARRETT AND BILLY THE KID

1973 106m c ★★
Western R/18
Gordon Carroll/Sam Peckinpah

James Coburn (Pat Garrett), Kris Kristofferson (Billy the Kid), Bob Dylan (Alias), Jason Robards, Jr. (Gov. Lew Wallace), Richard Jaeckel (Sheriff Kip McKinney), Katy Jurado (Mrs. Baker), Slim Pickens (Sheriff Baker), Chill Wills (Lemuel), John Beck (Poe), Rita Coolidge (Maria)

p, Gordon Carroll; d, Sam Peckinpah; w, Rudy Wurlitzer; ph, John Coquillon (Panavision, Metrocolor); ed, Roger Spottiswoode, Garth Craven, Robert Wolfe, Richard Halsey, David Berlatsky, Tony De Zarraga; m, Bob Dylan; art d, Ted Haworth; fx, Augie Lohman

After director Sam Peckinpah handed in his final cut of PAT GARRETT AND BILLY THE KID, which he considered his finest film, the hierarchy at MGM saw fit to radically reedit it. The approximately 15 minutes cut from the film so drastically altered Peckinpah's structure and pacing that the incensed director tried to get his name removed from the credits. A restored version of Peckinpah's original film was given a very limited rerelease in 1990, but the initial-release version remains the one that most viewers will be able to see and it is a very choppy affair. James Coburn is Pat Garrett; Kris Kristofferson is Billy the Kid. Feeling that the time has come for him to settle down, aging desperado Garrett switches sides of the law and puts on a badge. Duty-bound to protect the interests of the railroad and wealthy cattlemen, he is assigned to hunt down his old friend Billy. Despite his aversion to his task, Garrett searches for Billy and finds him in the New Mexico territory. Billy, bursting with the confidence of youth, ignores Garrett's warning to clear out, and forces his old buddy to take him off to jail. Billy is sentenced to be the guest of honor at a necktie party but shoots his way out of jail with a gun he finds in the prison outhouse. In doing so, he kills two deputies (Matt Clark, R.G. Armstrong). Billy then hits the trail, accompanied by a former printer, Alias (rock 'n' roller Bob Dylan, who contributed the film's score and whose knowing looks and existential one-liners act as kind of Greek chorus).

Back in New Mexico, Billy puts a gang together. Meanwhile, Garrett hires Alamosa Bill (Jack Elam), another former criminal, to help him, and the territorial governor, Lew Wallace (Jason Robards), engages Poe (John Beck) to bring Billy to justice. (In addition to cleaning up the New Mexico territory, Wallace was the author of the best-seller that became the basis for BEN HUR.) The manhunt begins. Billy reluctantly kills Poe; Garrett guns down Billy's best pal, Black Harris (L.Q. Jones). As his friends are eliminated one by one, Billy considers going to Mexico to escape. However, he dismisses this notion when he comes across the body of one of his cohorts (Emilio Fernandez) who was tortured and murdered while attempting to flee to his home south of the border. Beginning to wonder whether his fate may already be sealed, Billy holes up at Harris's ranch, but it isn't long before Garrett gets word of his quarry's whereabouts. Garrett, Poe, and another lawman, Sheriff Kip McKinney (Richard Jaeckel), make their way to the ranch, where Billy is making love with Maria (singer Rita Coolidge, Kristofferson's one-time real-life wife) when they arrive. Garrett, who has peered in on the lovers through a window, allows them to finish, then shoots Billy when he comes outside. Later, in a fit of guilt over having killed his old compadre, Garrett shoots at his own reflection in a mirror.

Among the important scenes cut from the initial release of film was an epilogue that reveals Garrett to have been killed by the same man who ordered the outlaw-turned-lawman to shoot Billy. A prologue was also cut, as were a scene between Garrett and his wife, and the roles of Barry Sullivan, Elisha Cook, Jr., and Dub Taylor. Indeed, at those moments when the film begins to hit its stride, awkward edits undermine its development. Nevertheless the film is visually stunning, and Peckinpah makes great use of his Durango, Mexico, locations. He and screenwriter Rudy Wurlitzer (TWO-LANE BLACKTOP; WALKER) also make cameo appearances.

Billy the Kid (William Bonney) has been fodder for several films. Wallace Beery and Johnny Mack Brown played Garrett and Bonney, respectively, in BILLY THE KID, and a 1941 film by the same name featured Brian Donlevy and Robert Taylor. The story was told again in MY DARLING CLEMENTINE and THE LEFT-HANDED GUN, and was even touched upon in films like BILLY THE KID VERSUS DRACULA. More recently, Billy and Garrett have come to the screen in the "Young Guns" series.

PATHER PANCHALI

1955 112m bw ★★★★★
Drama /U
West Bengal Government (India)

Kanu Banerji (Harihar the Father), Karuna Banerji (Sarbojaya the Mother), Subir Banerji (Apu), Runki Banerji (Durga as a child), Umas Das Gupta (Durga as a young girl), Chunibala Devi (Indirtharkun the Old Aunt), Reva Devi (Mrs. Mookerji), Rama Gangopadhaya (Ranu Mookerji), Tulshi Chakraborty (Schoolmaster), Harimoran Nag (Doctor)

p, Satyajit Ray; d, Satyajit Ray; w, Satyajit Ray (based on the novel by Bibhutibhusan Bandopadhaya); ph, Subrata Mitra; ed, Dulal Dutta; m, Ravi Shankar; art d, Banshi Chandra Gupta

Satyajit Ray's debut film, and the first installment in his "Apu Trilogy," quietly and intently studies a family living in the grip of poverty in a Bengal village. This was the first film of a great body of work characterized by visual beauty, humor, and emotional generosity, and announced the arrival of a major new director on the world scene, as well as the debut of Indian cinema in the West.

The father, a struggling writer, sets off to seek his fortune in the city, leaving his wife to take care of the children and an elderly aunt. Mere survival is a struggle for the poor family and the mother worries about how much the old lady eats. What follows is a series of perfectly ordinary events with a cumulative emotional power which may make some western viewers forever question the way Hollywood tells our stories. It's a powerful, unforgettable experience to watch characters whose lives are so different from our own, but whose concerns are ultimately universal. The remaining two films of the trilogy, APARAJITO and THE WORLD OF APU, follow the son, Apu (here played by Subir Banerji), into manhood and fatherhood.

Commissioned in 1945 to illustrate a children's version of the popular novel *Pather Panchali*, Ray became interested in bringing the novel to the screen, even though he had no previous film experience (nor did most of his crew). The production began sporadically on weekends, and was often interrupted by cash shortages before the Bengal government helped finish the picture. Like all Ray's best films, PATHER PANCHALI is influenced by the work of Jean Renoir (Ray visited the set of THE RIVER during its production in India) and of the Italian neorealists.

PATHS OF GLORY

1957 86m bw ★★★★★
War /PG
Bryna

Kirk Douglas (*Col. Dax*), Ralph Meeker (*Cpl. Paris*), Adolphe Menjou (*Gen. Broulard*), George Macready (*Gen. Mireau*), Wayne Morris (*Lt. Roget*), Richard Anderson (*Maj. Saint-Auban*), Joseph Turkel (*Pvt. Arnoud*), Timothy Carey (*Pvt. Ferol*), Peter Capell (*Col. Judge*), Susanne Christian (*The German Girl*)

p, James B. Harris; d, Stanley Kubrick; w, Stanley Kubrick, Calder Willingham, Jim Thompson (based on the novel by Humphrey Cobb); ph, Georg Krause; ed, Eva Kroll; m, Gerald Fried; art d, Ludwig Reiber

Stanley Kubrick's first great film established the epic style that has served him so well since. This is a harrowing and still very effective antiwar film that ranks with Lewis Milestone's epic ALL QUIET ON THE WESTERN FRONT in its power. The split between officers and men has never been so sharply delineated. The film was banned in France when it first appeared for eighteen years because of its anti-militarist stance.

Col. Dax (Kirk Douglas) is the commander of the battle-decimated 701st Infantry Regiment of the French Army during WWI, dug in along the Western Front in a brutally stalemated war. It is 1916, and the Allies have been struggling to overcome an equally determined German war machine for two years. Dax's hope that his regiment will be relieved from front-line duty is destroyed when corps commander Gen. Broulard (Adolphe Menjou) orders Gen. Mireau (George Macready), the divisional general in charge, to make an all-out attack against an impregnable German position nicknamed "the Ant Hill." The battle scenes showing the suicidal attack on the Ant Hill are devastating and brutally authentic, the barrage through which Dax leads his men (Kubrick's camera moving inexorably through the carnage) is a hurricane of death. Three soldiers are selected to be court-martialed unjustly to serve as scapegoats for the military humiliation. Dax is the officer charged with their defense but the powers-that-be confound his efforts.

This is a director's film: Kubrick profiles naked power and the effects thereof with a visual excitement seldom seen on the screen; his attitude toward the actions he portrays is always felt.

One particularly striking and effective strategy is the tendency to utilize mesmerizing but inhuman tracking shots for the trenches and battlegrounds while using elegant circling camera movements for the comfortable surroundings of the officers' chateau.

Though its condemnation of war is overwhelming, PATHS OF GLORY offers more optimism than is usual for the pessimistic Kubrick. The film may be read as a testament to human courage, compassion, and spirit that battles valiantly for survival despite the efforts of tyrants to vanquish principle and humanity.

PATTERNS

1956 83m bw ★★★★
Drama
UA

Van Heflin (*Fred Staples*), Everett Sloane (*Walter Ramsey*), Ed Begley (*William Briggs*), Beatrice Straight (*Nancy Staples*), Elizabeth Wilson (*Marge Fleming*), Joanna Roos (*Miss Lanier*), Eleni Kiamos (*Sylvia Trammel*), Shirley Standlee (*Miss Hill*), Ronnie Welsh, Jr. (*Paul Briggs*), Sally Gracie (*Ann*)

p, Michael Myerberg; d, Fielder Cook; w, Rod Serling (based on his television play); ph, Boris Kaufman; ed, David Kummins, Carl Lerner; art d, Richard Sylbert; cos, Mary Merrill

There wasn't one note of music in PATTERNS, and the absence wasn't felt; Serling's words had a music of their own. It began as a television play for the "Kraft Theatre" and, like MARTY and other TV plays, it was turned into a film. The limited use of film technique (much of the movie takes place in the offices of a huge conglomerate and it is basically an interior story) does not work against this film since the characters are so fascinating and the performances are universally superior. Heflin is brought in from Ohio to serve at a company's New York office. The boss of all bosses is Sloane, a ruthless company man who runs the firm like a tyrant. Begley is an executive who has seen better days and is being eased out by Sloane, who intends Heflin to be Begley's replacement. There is no room in Sloane's mind for old loyalties, and the company's interests must be above all feelings. Heflin truly likes Begley, who is always excusing Sloane's behavior and shrugging off the boss's insults. There are a few cutaways as Heflin discusses matters with his wife, Straight, but most of the action is strictly in the "executive suite," which was the name of a movie not unlike this one. Anyone who has ever worked in a large company will recognize the people and the situations depicted in the screenplay, but some of the Machiavellian tactics may be lost on others. Brilliantly directed by another TV veteran, Cook, this picture did not garner any awards and didn't do much business, which was a shame. Sloane's work as the corporation chief is sensational, a portrait of a driven man who rules his roost like an emperor. Begley, who came out of radio, where he appeared in more than 10,000 programs, was one of the most versatile actors in show business and proved so when he played the William Jennings Bryan role in Broadway's "Inherit the Wind" for more than 700 performances, then turned around and did Clarence Darrow after Paul Muni left the show.

PATTON

1970 170m c ★★★★½
War/Biography PG
FOX

George C. Scott *(Gen. George S. Patton, Jr.)*, Karl Malden *(Gen. Omar N. Bradley)*, Michael Bates *(Field Marshal Sir Bernard Law Montgomery)*, Edward Binns *(Maj. Gen. Walter Bedell Smith)*, Lawrence Dobkin *(Col. Gaston Bell)*, John Doucette *(Maj. Gen. Lucian K. Truscott)*, James Edwards *(Sgt. William George Meeks)*, Frank Latimore *(Lt. Col. Henry Davenport)*, Richard Muench *(Col. Gen. Alfred Jodl)*, Morgan Paull *(Capt. Richard N. Jenson)*

p, Frank McCarthy, Frank Caffey; d, Franklin J. Schaffner; w, Francis Ford Coppola, Edmund H. North (based on the books *Patton: Ordeal and Triumph* by Ladislas Farago and *A Soldier's Story* by Gen. Omar N. Bradley); ph, Fred Koenekamp (Dimension 150, CinemaScope, Deluxe Color); ed, Hugh S. Fowler; m, Jerry Goldsmith; art d, Urie McCleary, Gil Parrondo; fx, L.B. Abbott, Art Cruickshank

What PATHS OF GLORY attempted to show about the relationships between officers and men of the first World War, PATTON in part attempts to do for the second. Patton, of course, is best remembered as the general who slapped a soldier. But George C. Scott, under the direction of Franklin Schaffner, creates a much more colorful and ambiguous portrait. This WWII spectacle is immense but Scott's virtuoso performance looms larger than any of its battles. His characterization can appeal to both hawks and doves; it can appreciated either as a critique or a paean. He's insensitive to his men's plight on some occasions, gentle as a loving father on others. Patton's eccentricity may very well have been an important ingredient of victory. PATTON is a war movie of unusual depth and a landmark in screen biographies.

Beginning with a classic six-minute speech by Patton about the fighting spirit of Americans, the film traces the legendary WWII exploits of "Old Blood and Guts" from his defeat of Rommel's *Afrika Korps* at El Guettar to the invasion of Sicily, during which he disobeys orders and beats rival Field Marshal Montgomery (Michael Bates) to Messina. We also see his loss of command for slapping a battle-fatigued soldier because he has been hospitalized but has no wounds. Then, after sitting out D-Day as a decoy, Patton is given command of the 3rd Army, winning one mighty battle after another with his armored troops and eventually speeding to the rescue of the encircled 101st Airborne Division at Bastogne, ending Hitler's last great counteroffensive in the Battle of the Bulge. Following the war, Patton is sent into involuntary retirement after his highly vocal criticism of the Soviet Union, and the film ends with his farewell to his faithful staff.

Scott won a richly deserved Academy Award (which he refused) for his performance. Sturdy support is provided by Karl Malden as Gen. Omar Bradley, Edward Binns as Maj. Gen. Walter Bedell Smith, John Doucette as Maj. Gen. Lucian K. Truscott, and Bates as Montgomery. Franklin J. Schaffner's direction is majestic particularly in his masterful handling of complex battle scenes; shot in 70-millimeter, Dimension 150, these broad, impersonal spectacles have a macabre beauty that gives the viewer a serene God's-eye-view of modern warfare. Fox hoped to duplicate the success of its black-and-white blockbuster, THE LONGEST DAY, by spending a fortune on this spectacular film, which was shot on location in England, Spain, Morocco, and Greece. In addition to Scott's award, the film picked up Oscars for Best Direction, Best Screenplay (Francis Ford Coppola and Edmund L. North), Best Art Direction, Best Sound and Best Film Editing. It was also nominated for Best Cinematography, Best Original Score and Best Special Effects.

PAULINE AT THE BEACH
(PAULINE A LA PLAGE)
1983 94m c ★★★½
Drama/Comedy R/15
Losange/Ariane (France)

Amanda Langlet *(Pauline)*, Arielle Dombasle *(Marion)*, Pascal Greggory *(Pierre)*, Feodor Atkine *(Henry)*, Simon de la Brosse *(Sylvain)*, Rosette *(Louisette)*

p, Margaret Menegoz; d, Eric Rohmer; w, Eric Rohmer; ph, Nestor Almendros; ed, Cecile Decugis; m, Jean-Louis Valero

For the third in Eric Rohmer's series of "Comedies and Proverbs," the director shifts from Paris to the coast of Normandy. Pauline (Amanda Langlet) is a teenager on vacation with her older, recently divorced cousin, Marion (Arielle Dombasle). They become involved with three men during a beachside vacation. Marion carries on with a writer, Henry (Feodor Atkine), and tries to ignore the advances of an old friend, Pierre (Pascal Greggory), while Pauline meets a boy her own age, Sylvain (Simon De La Brosse), and has her first sexual experiences. This film is close in spirit to the work of Jean Renoir. Rohmer confines much of it to the beach and a vacation home, turning his directorial attention to the interplay among the five main characters as they move in and out of rooms, spied through windows and doors and forced to become masters of romantic deception. Instead of characteristically following one determined individual, Rohmer intertwines his characters and lets their paths overlap. Pauline, though singled out in the title, tends to function more as an observer caught in the whirlwind of love and romance. Rohmer was named Best Director at the Berlin Film Festival for PAULINE.

PAWNBROKER, THE
1965 114m bw ★★★★
Drama/War /X
Landau/Unger/Pawnbroker

Rod Steiger *(Sol Nazerman)*, Geraldine Fitzgerald *(Marilyn Birchfield)*, Brock Peters *(Rodriguez)*, Jaime Sanchez *(Jesus Ortiz)*, Thelma Oliver *(Ortiz's Girl)*, Marketa Kimbrel *(Tessie)*, Baruch Lumet *(Mendel)*, Juano Hernandez *(Mr. Smith)*, Linda Geiser *(Ruth Nazerman)*, Nancy R. Pollock *(Bertha)*

p, Roger Lewis, Philip Langner; d, Sidney Lumet; w, David Friedkin, Morton Fine (based on the novel by Edward Lewis Wallant); ph, Boris Kaufman; ed, Ralph Rosenblum; m, Quincy Jones; art d, Richard Sylbert; cos, Anna Hill Johnstone

Although there have been numerous films about the post-Vietnam era and the war's psychological aftereffects on the soldier returning home, very few pictures have dealt with the similar predicament of those who lived through WWII (or WWI, for that matter). THE PAWNBROKER, one of the seminal American films of the 1960s, focuses on Sol Nazerman (Rod Steiger), a middle-aged concentration camp survivor who lost his entire family to the Nazis and now runs a pawnshop in Harlem. That he remained alive is a source of bewilderment and pain. He has lost faith in God and man; he is emotionless and totally removed from the world that surrounds his run-down shop. Shop assistant Jesus Ortiz (Jaime Sanchez) and social worker Marilyn Birchfield (Geraldine Fitzgerald) try to get through Sol's icy exterior, but to no avail. Instead, Sol becomes increasingly cruel and offensive. Meanwhile, he conducts an affair with Tessie (Marketa Kimbrell), a fellow camp survivor whose husband was a victim of Nazi atrocities.

Directed by Sidney Lumet in a gritty, raw style that was fashionable at the time, THE PAWNBROKER is memorable today for its innovative use of flashbacks—in this case quick cuts lasting only a fraction of a second—to represent the disturbing, unrelenting flashes of Sol's memory. Also unforgettable is Steiger's towering performance as the volatile survivor, a powder keg of hateful remembrances. The soundtrack was composed by Quincy Jones.

PAYDAY

1972 102m c ★★★★
Drama R/X
Cinerama

Rip Torn (Maury Dann), Anna Capri (Mayleen), Elayne Heilveil (Rosamond), Michael C. Gwynne (Clarence), Jeff Morris (Tally), Cliff Emmich (Chauffeur), Henry O. Arnold (Ted), Walter Bamberg (Bridgeway), Linda Spatz (Sandy), Eleanor Fell (Galen Dann)

p, Martin Fink, Don Carpenter; d, Daryl Duke; w, Don Carpenter; ph, Richard C. Glouner (CFI Color); ed, Richard Halsey

Torn is a fading country singer in this excellent, overlooked drama. The film chronicles the last 36 hours of Torn's life, as he travels from one honky-tonk to the next. Torn is a cruel, egotistical performer who knows his career is on the skids. Screenwriter Carpenter and director Duke capture in unglamorized fashion the grind of being on the road, the groupies, the payoffs, and the drugs. The film has no heroes or villains, and every character is three-dimensional. Gwynne is Torn's ruthless manager, Capri is the singer's mistress, and Heilveil makes her debut as an innocent groupie. Torn's brilliant performance deserves more recognition, as does the film, which examines the dark side of the music business and the struggle for success and fame.

PEDESTRIAN, THE

(DER FUSSGANGER)
1974 97m c ★★★½
Drama/War PG/
Cinerama (West Germany)

Gustav Rudolf Sellner (Heinz Alfred Giese), Ruth Hausmeister (Inge Maria Giese), Maximilian Schell (Andreas Giese), Manuel Sellner (Hubert Giese), Elsa Wagner (Elsa Giese), Dagmar Hirtz (Elke Giese), Michael Weinert (Michael Giese), Peter Hall (Rudolf Hartmann), Alexander May (Alexander Markowitz), Christian Kohlund (Erwin Gotz)

p, Maximilian Schell, Zev Braun; d, Maximilian Schell; w, Maximilian Schell; ph, Wolfgang Treu, Klaus Koenig (Eastmancolor); ed, Dagmar Hirtz; m, Manos Hadjidakis

A powerful and revealing film about death, guilt, and Germany's involvement in wartime atrocities, THE PEDESTRIAN focuses on an aging industrialist, Heinz Alfred Giese (Gustav Rudolf Sellner), who prefers not to remember the events of WWII. In fact, he prefers to be involved with life as little as possible. Since the death of his son Andreas (Maximilian Schell) in an auto accident in which Giese was driving (resulting in the loss of his license, hence the title), his whole life has centered around his grandson, Hubert (Manuel Sellner). Although Giese would rather forget his past, Alexander Markowitz (Alexander May), the senior editor of a newspaper, begins a probe into Giese's involvement in the massacre of a Greek village. With the help of two witnesses—a survivor of the attack (Fani Fotinou) and a former German soldier (Walter von Varndal)—Markowitz discovers that Giese was involved in the massacre and could have pre-

vented it. When the story is printed, Giese becomes the target of moral outrage and violence. This strong indictment of his generation's complacency is especially damning because its villain is not a monster but a well-respected businessman and a loving grandfather. Produced, directed, and written by Maximilian Schell, THE PEDESTRIAN received a Golden Globe award for Best Film and an Oscar nomination for Best Foreign Film.

PEE-WEE'S BIG ADVENTURE

1985 90m c ★★★★½
Comedy PG/U
Aspen/Shapiro

Pee Wee Herman (Himself), Elizabeth Daily (Dottie), Mark Holton (Francis), Diane Salinger (Simone), Judd Omen (Mickey), Irving Hellman (Neighbor), Monte Landis (Mario), Damon Martin (Chip), David Glasser, Gregory Brown

p, Robert Shapiro, Richard Gilbert Abramson; d, Tim Burton; w, Phil Hartman, Paul Reubens, Michael Varhol; ph, Victor J. Kemper (Technicolor); ed, Billy Weber; m, Danny Elfman; prod d, David L. Snyder; fx, Chuck Gaspar; cos, Aggie Guerard Rodgers; anim, Rich Heinrichs

Pee-Wee Herman is not like the other boys. "I'm a loner. . . a rebel," he announces to his would-be girlfriend. He's a comic rebel without a pause. Inspired lunacy, PEE-WEE'S BIG ADVENTURE is one of the most inventive films in recent memory. This clever and wholly original work incorporates a wide variety of cinematic tools with a fresh and unique sense of style. Pee-Wee Herman, a creation of writer-comedian Paul Reubens, is a great comic creation on a par with Chaplin's Little Tramp. Somewhat reminiscent of the most popular Jerry Lewis screen persona, Pee-Wee is a magical, happy-go-lucky, occasionally mischievous little boy living in an adult body. What makes this seemingly moronic character work on an intelligent level is the cartoonlike environment he inhabits. In both structure and content, PEE-WEE'S BIG ADVENTURE often resembles a Warner Brothers cartoon. Like those classic animations, this film thrives on easily identifiable characterizations, simple plot motivations, throwaway gags, and an often surreal sense of logic, all mixed together with talent and ingenuity. The story gets started when the pride and joy of Pee-Wee's life, his shiny red bicycle, is stolen. The police are of no help, so a crazed Pee-Wee consults a fraudulent fortune-teller who tells him his bike is in the basement of the Alamo in Texas. Naturally, Pee-Wee takes to the road.

The episodic plot is a perfect format for Reuben's comedy. For many this character was rather hard to take prior to this marvelous movie. In his nightclub act and numerous appearances on "Late Night with David Letterman," Pee-Wee was bit too disturbingly manic, regressive, and grotesquely fey for some genteel sensibilities. He's just as frenetic and sexually ambiguous here but he is so thoroughly contextualized within his own beautifully realized world that he allows even the most traditional among us to get the joke. The smart and wacky script by Rubens and Phil Hartman (of television's "Saturday Night Live" and "The Simpsons") is given added vibrance by director Tim Burton (BEETLEJUICE, BATMAN, EDWARD SCISSORHANDS, and FRANKENWEENIE). Burton's background as a Disney animator is perfect for the film; he gives PEE-WEE'S BIG ADVENTURE a wonderfully cartoonish look through design, lighting, and camera angles. Two stars were born with the release of this film—one in front of the camera and one behind it. One could also make a case for a third star here: Soundtrack composer Danny Elfman from the rock group Oingo Bongo provides a witty and manic score that bolsters every scene.

PEEPING TOM

1960   109m   c   ★★½
Thriller   /X
Anglo-Amalgamated   (U.K.)

Karl Boehm (Mark Lewis), Moira Shearer (Vivian), Anna Massey (Helen Stephens), Maxine Audley (Mrs. Stephens), Esmond Knight (Arthur Baden), Bartlett Mullins (Mr. Peters), Shirley Ann Field (Diane Ashley), Michael Goodliffe (Don Jarvis), Brenda Bruce (Dora), Martin Miller (Dr. Rosan)

p, Michael Powell; d, Michael Powell; w, Leo Marks; ph, Otto Heller (Eastmancolor); ed, Noreen Ackland; m, Brian Easdale; art d, Arthur Lawrence; chor, Wally Stott

With its incredibly complex structure—which continually accuses the audience of sharing the central character's sickness—PEEPING TOM is a remarkable examination of the psychology of filmmaking and film viewing, and one of the most disturbing films ever made.

Mark Lewis (Karl Boehm), a focus-puller at a film studio, works part-time at a corner cigar store taking pornographic photos of women. One night, he approaches a prostitute on the street, goes to her apartment, and stabs her with the sharpened leg of the tripod of the 16mm camera he uses to record the whole affair. The next morning, he films the police investigation of her murder.

Mark rents out most of the house he owns, and Helen Stephens (Anna Massey), a young woman who lives there with her blind mother (Maxine Audley), takes a liking to Mark, and the two become friendly. When he lets Helen watch home movies of him as a young boy, she is horrified to see that the films show his father (Michael Powell) scientifically torturing the boy—part of the psychologist's studies in fear, Mark explains. (One reel captures the young Mark being awakened by the lizard his father has thrown on his bed.) It is not long, however, before Mark kills again.

This time his victim is Vivian (Moira Shearer), a dancer-actress working at his film studio. He promises her a screen test, but as the camera rolls, he places the pointy tripod at her throat, and as she watches her reflection in a mirror connected to the camera, she is killed. Increasingly attracted to Helen, Mark tries to repress his cinematic obsession by leaving his camera at home when they go out, but his perverted impulses begin to get the best of him, especially after Helen's mother confronts him.

Michael Powell, who, along with partner Emric Pressburger, was one of the cornerstones of the British film industry during the 1940s, was vilified by the British press following PEEPING TOM's release in 1960. The director of THE LIFE AND DEATH OF COLONEL BLIMP, STAIRWAY TO HEAVEN, BLACK NARCISSUS, and THE RED SHOES had made a rich and provocative psychological horror film, but critics in his homeland found it completely repugnant. The film was quickly butchered by the studio and was shown briefly in US second-run houses. It wasn't until 1979, however, that a restored version was released due to the efforts of director Martin Scorsese, a devout fan of the picture. Sadly, Powell's career never recovered from the critical attacks, and he made only a handful of features and shorts before his death in 1990.

PEGGY SUE GOT MARRIED

1986   104m   c   ★★★
Fantasy/Comedy   PG-13/15
Rastar

Kathleen Turner (Peggy Sue), Nicolas Cage (Charlie Bodell), Barry Miller (Richard Norvik), Catherine Hicks (Carol Heath), Joan Allen (Maddy Nagle), Kevin J. O'Connor (Michael Fitzsimmons), Barbara Harris (Evelyn Kelcher), Don Murray (Jack Kelcher), Maureen O'Sullivan (Elizabeth Alvorg), Leon Ames (Barney Alvorg)

p, Paul R. Gurian; d, Francis Ford Coppola; w, Jerry Leichtling, Arlene Sarner; ph, Jordan Cronenweth (Deluxe Color); ed, Barry Malkin; m, John Barry; prod d, Dean Tavoularis; art d, Alex Tavoularis; cos, Theadora Van Runkle

A bittersweet cross between OUR TOWN and IT'S A WONDERFUL LIFE, PEGGY SUE GOT MARRIED tells the poignant story of Peggy Sue Bodell (Kathleen Turner). She's a 43-year-old housewife on the verge of a divorce from Charlie (Nicholas Cage), an obnoxious philanderer who is locally famous for his tacky TV commercials for his retail appliance business. Peggy Sue squeezes into her old prom dress and goes to her 25th high school reunion to meet all her old friends from James Buchanan High. Subsequently named queen of the reunion, she ascends the podium to accept her crown, and passes out. Tossed into a time warp, she awakens in 1960, a 43-year-old consciousness in an ostensibly 17-year-old body. This feat requires a suspension of disbelief on the part of the audience but Turner pulls it off admirably. The film asks a powerful question: If we had a chance to go back and do it all again, would we do it the same way? Or would we rewrite our lives to create a new outcome?

Released the year after BACK TO THE FUTURE, there were inevitable comparisons. However, PEGGY SUE GOT MARRIED is a more grown up and fatalistic film (even if it is ultimately inferior) that eschews cartoonish exaggeration for a more realistic approach to its subject matter. The film features good acting from almost everyone, the one notable exception being the annoying Cage who adopts a grating constricted voice for the role. Turner was Oscar-nominated for her role and justly so. The movie has many lovely moments and just as many dead spots, but its strengths make this atypical film from Francis Coppola a worthwhile viewing experience.

PEKING OPERA BLUES

(DAO MA DAN)
1986   104m   c   ★★★½
Action/Comedy
Cinema City   (Hong Kong)

Lin Ching Hsia, Sally Yeh, Cherie Chung, Mark Cheng, Ling Pak Hoi

p, Tsui Hark, Claudie Chung; d, Tsui Hark; w, To Kwok Wai; ph, Poon Hung Seng; ed, David Wu; m, James Wong; art d, Vicent Wai, Ho Kim Sing, Leung Chi Hing; fx, Cinefex Workshop; chor, Ching Sui Tung; cos, Ng Po Ling

A delightfully frenetic comedy-adventure, PEKING OPERA BLUES serves as a terrific introduction to the energetic popular cinema of Hong Kong. Set in China circa 1913, the fast-paced and complicated story centers on three young women from different social classes who become embroiled in a revolutionary plot to overthrow the military government. Surprisingly, one of the key players in the revolution is the beautiful Lin Ching Hsia, the daughter of China's most powerful general. She and a male accomplice are ordered to steal some secret documents from her father's safe. Through a series of slapstick circumstances, a winsome but dim-witted street performer, a disaffected soldier, and the attractive daughter of the local opera house owner become involved in the plot and wind up comrades of the revolutionaries. Together, the five do battle with the army, the generals, and the secret police, with most of the zany action revolving around the colorful opera house. After a series of nonstop seductions, disguises, gunfights, kung-fu skirmishes, gymnastics, chases, double crosses, separations and reunions, the heroes succeed in getting the valued documents to the revolutionary leaders. The film ends with the five on horseback vowing to meet again someday before going their separate ways.

In an era in which most American films are either lifeless bores or cynical exercises in mass marketing (or both), PEKING OPERA BLUES is a welcome burst of manic energy that never fails to please. The skillful combination of breathtaking action and slapstick comedy in this film is nearly indescribable. Martial arts coordinator Ching Sui Tung's innovative choreography of the film's numerous action scenes is superb and he continually manages to thrill and surprise. The cast, boasting three of Hong Kong's most popular actresses, is also marvelous; Lin Ching Hsia, Cherie Chung, and Sally Yeh are all vivacious, beautiful, and charming. They make a splendidly entertaining team and their comedic timing together is flawless. Tsui Hark directs with a verve and style little seen on American screens, and while he always entertains, he also slips in some genuinely touching scenes and loads of relevant social observations.

A massive box-office hit in Hong Kong, the film proved popular with festival audiences in Europe and North America. The only American film to even approach the kind of energy and comedy found in PEKING OPERA BLUES is BIG TROUBLE IN LITTLE CHINA. However, John Carpenter's loving *hommage* to the wild and rambunctious popular films of Hong Kong never found an audience and sunk like a stone.

PELLE THE CONQUEROR
(PELLE EROVRAREN)
1987   160m   c   ★★★
Drama   PG-13/15
Svensk/Danish Film Institute/Swedish Film Institute/
DR TV/SID   (Denmark/Sweden)

Max von Sydow *(Pappa Lasse)*, Pelle Hvenegaard *(Pelle, His Son)*, Erik Paaske *(Farm Foreman)*, Bjorn Granath *(Farmhand Erik)*, Axel Strobye *(Kongstrup)*, Astrid Villaume *(Mrs. Kongstrup)*, Troels Asmussen *(Rud)*, John Wittig *(Schoolteacher)*, Anne Lise Hirsch Bjerrum *(Karna)*, Sofie Grabol *(Miss Sine)*

p, Per Holst; d, Bille August; w, Bille August (based on volume one of a novel by Martin Andersen Nexo); ph, Jorgen Persson (Fujicolor); ed, Janus Billeskov Jansen; m, Stefan Nilsson; prod d, Anna Asp; cos, Kicki Ilander, Gitte Kolvig, Birthe Qualmann

Bille August, the director of TWIST AND SHOUT (1986), the most commercially successful Danish film ever, followed that teen drama with this Swedish-Danish coproduction set in the 1890s and starring Max von Sydow as an impoverished Swedish widower who moves to Bornholm, a Danish island in the Baltic, hoping to improve his lot in life. He takes along his seven-year-old son, Hvenegaard, but instead of finding a better life, they are reduced to virtual slavery. A grim story of deprived and depraved humanity unfolds, focusing on both the oppressed and the oppressors. An Oscar winner for Best Foreign Film, this is an often brutal tale which is boosted by a powerful performance from Von Sydow. He earned a Best Actor Oscar nomination, losing to Dustin Hoffman for RAIN MAN.

PENN & TELLER GET KILLED
1989   89m   C   ★★★½
Comedy   R/
Lorimar

Penn Jillette *(Penn)*, Teller *(Teller)*, Caitlin Clarke *(Carlotta)*, David Patrick Kelly *(Fan)*, Leonardo Cimino *(Ernesto)*, Christopher Durang *(Jesus Freak)*, Alan North *(Old Cop)*, Jon Cryer

p, Arthur Penn, Timothy Marx; d, Arthur Penn; w, Penn Jillette, Teller; ph, Jan Weincke; ed, Jeffrey Wolf; m, Paul Chihara; prod d, John Arnone; cos, Rita Ryack

Although some critics have found PENN & TELLER GET KILLED unworthy of the talents of director Arthur Penn (BONNIE AND CLYDE), he and comedy magicians Penn & Teller (playing themselves) have made a deeply subversive film, a disillusionist work in an era when illusion permeates American culture, a comedy that plays for keeps. During a television interview, Penn confesses that life has gotten a little dull lately and irresponsibly wishes that someone would liven things up by trying to kill him. Naturally, things get livelier as Penn and Teller each hatch elaborate plots against the other, with the gags that follow escalating in scale and potential violence. Then the action takes a darker turn when it seems that someone really is trying to kill Penn. During its early sections, PENN & TELLER GET KILLED recalls the films of W.C. Fields and The Marx Brothers, acting as a showcase for the illusionist comedians, but the film's covert subject—the way in which our culture has turned violence into entertainment—lends even the early passages an odd gravity, and the film turn ominous by following its premise to its logical conclusion—that our cultural fascination with violence represents a kind of a national death wish. Like Arthur Penn, Penn & Teller are loved by some and hated by others, but their power to provoke is undeniable. Their movie, like their act, is very serious fun.

PENNIES FROM HEAVEN
1936   80m   bw   ★★★
Musical   /U
Columbia

Bing Crosby *(Larry)*, Madge Evans *(Susan)*, Edith Fellows *(Patsy)*, Donald Meek *(Gramps)*, John Gallaudet *(Hart)*, Louis Armstrong *(Henry)*, Tom Dugan *(Crowbar)*, Nana Bryant *(Miss Howard)*, Charles Wilson *(Warden)*, Harry Tyler *(Concessionaire)*

p, Emanuel Cohen; d, Norman Z. McLeod; w, Jo Swerling (based on the story "The Peacock's Feather" by Katherine Leslie Moore); ph, Robert Pittack; ed, John Rawlins; m, Arthur Johnston; art d, Stephen Goosson

An amusing musical, notable mainly for its fine selection of songs, including the Academy Award-nominated title tune penned by Johnny Burke and Arthur Johnston. The film opens with Crosby serving a jail sentence for smuggling (for which he has been wrongly convicted). Before he is released he is given a note by a murderer who is about to meet his end in the gas chamber. The killer's note contains the name and address of his victim's relatives. As a final request, he asks Crosby to locate the relatives and move them into his abandoned family estate. Crosby finds the relatives—a 10-year-old girl, Fellows, and her grandfather, Meek—living in squalor. At Crosby's urging, Fellows and Meek pack their bags and head for their new home, only to find that it looks haunted. To make the place more inviting, Crosby comes up with the idea of turning it into a restaurant called the Haunted House Cafe. To draw the crowds he croons a number of Johnston and Burke tunes, with the title tune being nominated for an Oscar for Best Song. Other numbers include "One, Two, Button Your Shoe," "So Do I," "Let's Call a Heart a Heart," "Now I've Got Some Dreaming to Do," "What This Country Needs," and "Skeleton in the Closet."

PENNIES FROM HEAVEN

1981 108m c	★★½
Musical	R/15
MGM	

Steve Martin (*Arthur*), Bernadette Peters (*Eileen*), Christopher Walken (*Tom*), Jessica Harper (*Joan*), Vernel Bagneris (*Accordion Man*), John McMartin (*Mr. Warner*), John Karlen (*Detective*), Jay Garner (*Banker*), Robert Fitch (*Al*), Thomas Rall (*Ed*)

p, Herbert Ross, Nora Kaye; d, Herbert Ross; w, Dennis Potter (based on the television series by Dennis Potter); ph, Gordon Willis (Metrocolor); ed, Richard Marks; m, Marvin Hamlisch, Billy May; art d, Fred Tuch, Bernie Cutler; chor, Danny Daniels; cos, Bob Mackie

MGM mistakenly thought Dennis Potter's acclaimed British television miniseries "Pennies from Heaven" could be condensed into a feature, so they cast Martin in the role originated by Bob Hoskins and asked Martin's flame at the time, Peters, to costar. Costing more than $20 million and barely recovering $4 million, PENNIES FROM HEAVEN is a musical in which the singing is done to old records by famed performers. Martin plays a Depression-era sheet-music salesman who falls for Peters, even though he's married to Harper. The movie is just too big—with incredible sets, mammoth dance sequences, and a weird underlying aura of discontent—and was consequently berated by just about everyone when it came out. So much time is devoted to style and songs that there is hardly a moment left for character development. The movie deserved better, however, if only for attempting something different—even if telescoping several hours of a television miniseries into 108 minutes was a mistake. The movie also contains profanity and some sex, which lost whatever family audience it might have acquired. The film is unquestionably beautiful to look at, though, and Martin displays dancing talent that should be used in another film. Potter's script, Mackie's costumes, and the sound team were nominated for Oscars.

PENTHOUSE

1933 90m bw	★★★
Crime	
Cosmpolitan	

Warner Baxter (*Jackson Durant*), Myrna Loy (*Gertie Waxted*), Charles Butterworth (*Layton, Durant's Butler*), Mae Clarke (*Mimi Montagne*), Phillips Holmes (*Tom Siddall*), C. Henry Gordon (*Jim Crelliman*), Martha Sleeper (*Sue Leonard*), Nat Pendleton (*Tony Gazotti*), George E. Stone (*Tim Murtoch*), Robert Emmett O'Connor (*Lt. Stevens*)

p, Hunt Stromberg; d, W.S. Van Dyke, II; w, Frances Goodrich, Albert Hackett (based on the novel by Arthur Somers Roche); ph, Lucien Andriot, Harold Rosson; ed, Robert J. Kern; m, William Axt; art d, Alexander Toluboff; cos, Adrian

Pendleton shines as a powerful but sympathetic gangland chief, a pragmatist with a sense of humor, whose self-constructed empire is threatened by rival gangster Gordon. Baxter is a successful corporation lawyer who, bored with the legalistic doings of the high and mighty, craves the company of criminal clients. He takes on the defense of Pendleton, who has been accused of murder. He wins the case, but as a result loses both his prestigious position with a firm of Harvard attorneys and his fiancee, Clarke. Pendleton—fearful that his new-found barrister buddy's life may be in jeopardy as a result of his successful courtroom battle—appoints two goons, Raymond Hatton and Arthur Belasco, to safeguard his legal savior. Clarke's new high-society romantic attachment is the victim of a murder frame-up at the instigation of bad gangster Gordon, and so Baxter defends his rival in romance. When Clarke is killed also, Baxter tries to solve the continuing series of crimes, this time with the help of Gordon's wisecracking moll, Loy. Wise to her betrayal, Gordon abducts his ex-mistress, holding her in his hideout. Baxter races to Loy's defense, arriving at the hideout to a tune of machine gun fire. He is greeted by his smiling hoodlum pal Pendleton, who has raided the place and pulled off the rescue. Pendleton then slumps to the floor, mortally wounded, having given his life on behalf of his new high-society friend. This interesting melding of bourgeoisie and *lumpenproletariat* presaged things to come in the THIN MAN series which began a year later, featuring the same director, W.S. "One-shot Woody" Van Dyke, the same team of scriptwriters, and the same leading lady. Loy was just breaking away from her ethnic "you touch me, I keel you" roles, which had her using her universal ethnic accent for every characterization ranging from East Indian to Egyptian. From now on, she would play high-society roles herself, albeit still with wisecracks.

PEOPLE WILL TALK

1951 110m bw	★★★★
Comedy	/A
FOX	

Cary Grant (*Dr. Noah Praetorius*), Jeanne Crain (*Annabel Higgins*), Finlay Currie (*Shunderson*), Hume Cronyn (*Prof. Elwell*), Walter Slezak (*Prof. Barker*), Sidney Blackmer (*Arthur Higgins*), Basil Ruysdael (*Dean Lyman Brockwell*), Katherine Locke (*Miss James*), Will Wright (*John Higgins*), Margaret Hamilton (*Miss Pickett*)

p, Darryl F. Zanuck; d, Joseph L. Mankiewicz; w, Joseph L. Mankiewicz (based on the play "Dr. Praetorius" by Curt Goetz); ph, Milton Krasner; ed, Barbara McLean; m, Johannes Brahms, Richard Wagner; art d, Lyle Wheeler, George W. Davis; fx, Fred Sersen; cos, Charles LeMaire

Joseph L. Mankiewicz had just won two Oscars for ALL ABOUT EVE (writing, directing) and the year before that two more for the same tasks on A LETTER TO THREE WIVES. He took on a big challenge here, adapting Curt Goetz's play, "Dr. Praetorius," making it into an odd amalgam of wit, satire, high drama, and glistening dialog. Grant is an early crusader in the medical profession who thinks that the mind can cure just as well, if not better, than massive doses of medicine. He believes in treating the patient rather than the disease, a practice that delights his charges but horrifies his colleagues, who are far more traditional and hidebound in their diagnoses. Grant is teaching at a medical school and living what is thought to be a strange life. His servant and best friend is Currie, a murderer who has been sent to jail twice. His other friend is Slezak, a rotund scientist who loves model trains and knockwurst, not necessarily in that order. Grant's enemy at the school is Cronyn, a sourpuss anatomy instructor who feels more at home dissecting corpses than talking to humans. One day, while Grant is teaching his students, Crain, an aspiring young doctor, faints during the lecture. Grant is soon aware that she's newly pregnant, and when she tries to kill herself, he says that his first diagnosis was wrong, then marries her. Crain's father is Blackmer, a drunk and a loser, but a man with what Tennessee Williams called "the charm of the defeated." In between his classes, Grant conducts the school's orchestra in Wagner and Brahms. Out of spite, Cronyn contacts the dean, Ruysdael, and brings up a few interesting things about Grant's medical background, obliging Grant to defend himself to the school's board of directors. He explains his philosophy of medicine and eventually wins over the listeners. While all this is going on, Grant is spending his time at home convincing Crain that he really does love her and didn't marry her out of pity for her plight. The designation "sophisticated" applies well to PEOPLE WILL TALK, and Grant gives one of his best performances, a carefully controlled job of acting that never becomes farce. The movie is mature and frank, and Mankiewicz uses the opportunity to take a few potshots at academic hypocrisy.

PEPE LE MOKO

1937 90m bw ★★★★½
Crime/Romance /PG
Hakim/Paris (France)

Jean Gabin (Pepe le Moko), Mireille Balin (Gaby Gould), Line Noro (Ines), Lucas Gridoux (Inspector Slimane), Gabriel Gabrio (Carlos), Fernand Charpin (Regis), Saturnin Fabre (Grandfather), Gilbert Gil (Pierrot), Roger Legris (Max), Gaston Modot (Jimmy)

p, Robert Hakim, Raymond Hakim; d, Julien Duvivier; w, Julien Duvivier, Henri Jeanson, Henri La Barthe, Jacques Constant (based on the book by Henri La Barthe); ph, Jules Kruger, Marc Fossard; ed, Marguerite Beauge; m, Vincent Scotto, Mohamed Yguerbouchen; prod d, Jacques Krauss

Based on the life of a real criminal who hid in the Casbah under the protection of his pals, PEPE LE MOKO stars Jean Gabin as the title thief, brigand, and charmer, who has surrounded himself with loyal gang members and keeps them in line through the sheer force of his personality, never resorting to violence. Tired of life with his moll, Ines (Line Noro), and of being on the run, Pepe yearns for his old days in Paris. He falls in love with a gorgeous tourist, Gaby Gould (Mireille Balin), but in the process lets his guard down and gives Algerian police inspector Slimane (Lucas Gridoux) the opportunity to finally nab him.

PEPE LE MOKO owes a thematic and stylistic debt to the early Hollywood gangster films, most notably Howard Hawks' SCARFACE, but director Julien Duvivier took the conventional mix of love and bullets and made it into dark poetry.Indeed this film is cited as a prime example of the Poetic Realism movement in France. The camera undulates through dingy realistic sets cloaked in deep shadow. The performances are so naturalistic that the actors don't seem to be acting, and the lack of sentimentality deserves special praise.

The film's success and the universality of its themes can be attested to by the fact that a Hollywood version, ALGIERS, was made immediately after PEPE LE MOKO and released in the States before the original could be imported. Charles Boyer turned the part of Pepe down when it was offered by Duvivier, then starred in the US version when Gabin refused to make the trip to Hollywood, explaining that he, like French wine, "didn't travel well." When WW II started, the French government banned the film as too depressing and demoralizing, especially since the news from the front was also bleak. The Germans took over and their puppet government retained the ban, but the moment the war ended, PEPE LE MOKO was again shown and hailed as a classic.

PEPPERMINT SODA

(DIABOLO MENTHE)
1977 97m c ★★★½
Drama/Comedy PG/
Alma/Alexandre/Gaumont (France)

Eleonore Klarwein (Anne Weber), Odile Michel (Frederique Weber), Coralie Clement (Perrine Jacquet), Marie Veronique Maurin (Muriel Gazau), Valerie Stano (Martine Dubreuil), Anne Guillard (Sylvie Le Garrec), Corinne Dacla (Pascal Carimil), Veronique Vernon (Evelyne Delacroix), Francoise Berlin (Mlle. Sassy), Arlette Bonnard (Mme. Poliakoff)

d, Diane Kurys; w, Diane Kurys; ph, Philippe Rousselot (Eastmancolor); ed, Joele Van Effenterre; m, Yves Simon

A thoroughly charming picture which brings to life the loves and fears of two teenaged sisters. Kurys marks her directing debut with a semi-autobiographical story starring Klarwein as the 13-year old Anne (Kurys's age in 1963—the setting of the film) and Michel as her 15-year old sibling. Living with their divorced mother, Ferjac, the girls discover and talk about the things that interest teenage girls—boys, sex, school, and politics (they are French). Lacking a boyfriend, Klarwein steams open her older sister's love letters from her boyfriend. Klarwein's confused reaction to men is further illustrated by her dislike for her mother's boyfriend. It is only from her father that she gets what she wants (a ski trip), but not until she shows her disapproval at his leaving home.

A sensitive portrayal of teens which compares with Truffaut's Antoine Doinel series (THE 400 BLOWS through LOVE ON THE RUN) and George Roy Hill's A LITTLE ROMANCE. Kurys continued exploring her growing years with ENTRE NOUS and C'EST LA VIE. For the curious, the film's title refers to an "adult" drink that Klarwein nearly gets a chance to taste.

PERFECT COUPLE, A

1979 110m c ★★½
Comedy/Romance PG/AA
Lion's Gate

Paul Dooley (Alex Theodopoulos), Marta Heflin (Sheila Shea), Titos Vandis (Panos Theodopoulos), Belita Moreno (Eleousa), Henry Gibson (Fred Bott), Dimitra Arliss (Athena), Allan Nicholls (Dana 115), Ann Ryerson (Skye 147 Veterinarian), Poppy Lagos (Melpomeni Bott), Dennis Franz (Costa)

p, Robert Altman; d, Robert Altman; w, Robert Altman, Allan Nicholls; ph, Edmond Koons (Panavision, DeLuxe Color); ed, Tony Lombardo; m, Allan Nicholls

Though it isn't completely successful, this is an entertaining film, far more successful than the Altman projects which immediately preceded it, A WEDDING and QUINTET. Dooley is a lonely middle-aged man who is completely dominated by autocratic Greek father, Vandis. Through a computer dating service, Dooley meets Heflin and is attracted to her. She's a rather insecure woman who is part of a rock band led by Neeley (who starred in JESUS CHRIST, SUPERSTAR). Neeley rules his extended family of musicians, singers, and hangers-on every bit as autocratically as Vadnis controls his more traditional family. Vadnis would never approve of his son dating Heflin, while Neeley so drives his people they barely have time for a social life. The film focuses on these two people as the attempt to deal with their "family" problems and come to terms with one another.

Dooley, an Altman favorite, is quite good as a man torn between traditional responsibilities and his desire to become independent, while Heflin is winsome as the object of his desire. Moreno does a nice turn as Dooley's sister who encourages him to stand up to the old man, while Vadnis is properly filled with bluster. Neeley and the "Keepin' 'Em Off the Streets" band provide some worthwhile music, including the songs "Hurricane" (Tom Berg, Ted Neeley, Allan Nicholls) and "Fantasy" (Nicholls).

PERFORMANCE

1970 105m c   ★★★
Drama   R/X
Goodtimes Enterprises   (U.K.)

James Fox (Chas Devlin), Mick Jagger (Turner), Anita Pallenberg (Pherber), Michele Breton (Lucy), Ann Sidney (Dana), John Bindon (Moody), Stanley Meadows (Rosebloom), Allan Cuthbertson (The Lawyer), Anthony Morton (Dennis), Johnny Shannon (Harry Flowers)

p, Sanford Lieberson; d, Nicolas Roeg, Donald Cammell; w, Donald Cammell; ph, Nicolas Roeg; ed, Antony Gibbs, Brian Smedley-Aston; art d, John Clark

Visually dazzling, finely acted investigation into such diverse matters as identity, sexuality, violence, power, and underground culture in late 1960s London.

James Fox stars as Chas, a sadistic petty gangster who has trouble fitting in, even with his hoodlum cohorts. Chas gets into trouble with the mob after carrying out a murder for personal—as opposed to business—reasons, and hides out in the basement of "retired" rock star Turner while he waits to skip the country. Turner has secluded himself in the house in order to lament the loss of his powers of "incantation," which seems primarily to mean that he indulges in a lot of drug-taking and sex with two female companions. Soon, Turner senses a connection between Chas's brutally violent nature and his own dried-up creative powers, and he draws the young hood into his world. Introduced to hallucinogenic drugs, Chas begins wearing androgynous clothes and even admits he is sexually attracted by Turner, before the mob shows up again and things turn sour.

Uneven, dated, and—at least during the first half-hour—too frantically paced, PERFORMANCE is nevertheless a haunting meditation on human identity from co-directors Donald Cammel and Nicolas Roeg (Roeg had previously worked as a cinematographer on films including FAHRENHEIT 451 and FAR FROM THE MADDING CROWD). Questions of role-playing, imagery and individuality are explored in uniquely visual terms, particularly by the directors' intriguing use of mirror shots. Mick Jagger's performance is a pleasant surprise, and his presence in the film accounted for most of the limited commercial success it enjoyed at the time of its initial release. PERFORMANCE has since become a much-discussed cult classic. Originally released with an "X" rating in the U.S., the film was subsequently re-edited and re-catalogued as an "R."

PERSONA

1966 81m bw   ★★★★★
Drama   /X
Svensk (Sweden)

Bibi Andersson (Nurse Alma), Liv Ullmann (Actress Elisabeth Vogler), Gunnar Bjornstrand (Mr. Vogler), Margareta Krook (Dr. Lakaren), Jorgen Lindstrom (The Boy)

p, Ingmar Bergman; d, Ingmar Bergman; w, Ingmar Bergman; ph, Sven Nykvist; ed, Ulla Ryghe; m, Lars-Johan Werle; prod d, Bibi Lindstrom; art d, Bibi Lindstrom; fx, Evald Andersson; cos, Mago

This is Ingmar Bergman's chaste exploration of psychosis. It's not a horror story but a poem, and remarkable for that. This is one of the director's masterworks. Opening with a sequence that includes a bare bulb projecting onto a screen, the countdown leader of the first reel, and short film clips from slapstick comedies and cartoons, Bergman reminds us that we are in the act of watching a film. Gradually, however, the story gets underway. Ullmann plays an actress who mysteriously stops speaking after a performance of "Electra" and is sent by a psychiatrist to a seaside cottage where she is looked after by nurse Andersson. Using light and shadow masterfully, Bergman and his cinematographer, Sven Nykvist, accentuate the resemblance between the two women, drawing the viewer into a psychodrama that is more the nurse's story than the patient's, as Andersson pours her soul out to the silent Ullmann. She gradually appears to be just as troubled as her patient, whose personality she seems to be assuming. The shot of their two faces merged near the end of the film is one of the great images of cinema.

PERSONA has variously been interpreted as an exploration of the role of the artist, an embodiment of the psychoanalytic process, and as a meditation on Bergman's favorite existential themes. In any case, it is a film of great emotional intensity that benefits from the superlative performances of Ullmann—who reacts only with facial and body gestures—and Andersson, who speaks for both of them as she slips into a kind of subtle madness.

PERSONAL BEST

1982 124m c   ★★★
Sports   R/18
Geffen

Mariel Hemingway (Chris Cahill), Scott Glenn (Terry Tingloff), Patrice Donnelly (Tory Skinner), Kenny Moore (Denny Stites), Jim Moody (Roscoe Travis), Kari Gosswiller (Penny Brill), Jodi Anderson (Nadia "Pooch" Anderson), Maren Seidler (Tanya), Martha Watson (Sheila), Emily Dole (Maureen)

p, Robert Towne; d, Robert Towne; w, Robert Towne; ph, Michael Chapman, Allan Gornick, Jr. (Technicolor); ed, Ned Humphreys, Jere Huggins, Jacqueline Cambas, Walt Mulconery, Bud Smith; m, Jack Nitzsche, Jill Fraser; prod d, Ron Hobbs; fx, Dale Newkirk; cos, Linda Henrikson, Ron Heilman

Oscar-winning screenwriter Robert Towne (CHINATOWN; SHAMPOO) made his directorial debut with this uneven but affecting study of romantic and athletic commitment set against the background of women's track and field. At the 1976 Olympic trials, pentathlete Tory Skinner (onetime track star Patrice Donnelly in her film debut) and hurdler Chris Cahill (Mariel Hemingway) meet after the former qualifies for the US team, while the latter runs badly. The two become lovers, and Tory persuades her reluctant coach, Terry Tingloff (Scott Glenn), to allow Chris to train with her under his guidance. Eventually, Tingloff convinces Chris to train for the pentathlon, creating a rivalry between Chris and Tory that leads to the breakup of their relationship. Later, Chris falls for Denny (Kenny Moore), a onetime Olympic medalist in swimming; then, against Tingloff's wishes, Chris renews her friendship with Tory during the 1980 Olympic trials.

Although Towne's script is a little talky and heavy-handed, he nonetheless captures the essence of the competitive impulse, exploring both the "killer instinct" and the inner drive to compete only with oneself. The lesbian love story at the film's center is less well developed, but still engaging, its poignancy heightened by the well-cast Hemingway's understated performance. Visually, PERSONAL BEST is frequently interesting, if occasionally studied. Towne's over-reliance on slow motion ultimately undercuts the poetry of motion he seeks to convey, but his camera placement during the track and field action is almost always inventive, as is the film's editing. Moreover, PERSONAL BEST offers a detailed, believable insider's portrait of the world of track and field. This very different sports film isn't for everyone, but patient viewers should find many small pleasures in it. Olympic marathoner Frank Shorter and veteran sportscaster Charlie Jones provide the commentary during the Olympic trials.

PETER PAN

1953 76m c	★★★★
Animated/Children's	G/U
Disney	

VOICES OF: Bobby Driscoll *(Peter Pan)*, Kathryn Beaumont *(Wendy)*, Hans Conried *(Capt. Hook/Mr. Darling)*, Bill Thompson *(Mr. Smee)*, Heather Angel *(Mrs. Darling)*, Paul Collins *(Michael Darling)*, Tommy Luske *(John)*, Candy Candido *(Indian Chief)*, Tom Conway *(Narrator)*

p, Walt Disney; d, Hamilton Luske, Clyde Geronimi, Wilfred Jackson; w, Ted Sears, Bill Peet, Joe Rinaldi, Erdman Penner, Winston Hibler, Milt Banta, Ralph Wright (based on the play by James M. Barrie); ph, (Technicolor); m, Oliver Wallace, Edward Plumb; anim, Milt Kahl, Franklin Thomas, Wolfgang Reitherman, Ward Kimball, Eric Larson, Oliver M. Johnston, Marc Davis, John Lounsbery, Les Clark, Norman Ferguson

PETER PAN is a wonderful movie. Patriarch Mr. Darling (whose voice is provided by Hans Conried) is annoyed that daughter Wendy (voiced by Kathryn Beaumont) insists on telling stories to the other children about a mythical boy known as Peter Pan. When Mr. and Mrs. Darling leave for a night on the town, Peter Pan (voiced by Bobby Driscoll) and fairy sidekick Tinker Bell magically appear in Wendy's room. They all take a magical trip to Never Never Land, where they get involved in a series of adventures that include a confrontation with the evil Captain Hook (Conried, in a dual role). Lots of laughs, fabulous animation, and excellent voicing by the actors. The picture cost more than $4 million to make, a huge amount for a film in 1953. Lest you wonder why it came in so high, you should know that Disney filmed a live-action version of the movie first in order to give his artists something to base their sketches upon.

PETRIFIED FOREST, THE

1936 83m bw	★★★★
Crime	/A
WB	

Leslie Howard *(Alan Squier)*, Bette Davis *(Gabrielle Maple)*, Genevieve Tobin *(Mrs. Chisholm)*, Dick Foran *(Boze Hertzlinger)*, Humphrey Bogart *(Duke Mantee)*, Joe Sawyer *(Jackie)*, Porter Hall *(Jason Maple)*, Charley Grapewin *(Gramp Maple)*, Paul Harvey *(Mr. Chisholm)*, Eddie Acuff *(Lineman)*

p, Henry Blanke; d, Archie Mayo; w, Charles Kenyon, Delmer Daves (based on the play by Robert E. Sherwood); ph, Sol Polito; ed, Owen Marks; m, Bernhard Kaun; art d, John Hughes; fx, Warren Lynch, Fred Jackman, Willard Van Enger; cos, Orry-Kelly

One of the variants on the GRAND HOTEL theme halfway between the pleasant comings and goings at that hostelry and the

screaming disasters of, say, THE POSEIDON ADVENTURE. This screen version of Robert E. Sherwood's smash play is handled with great care by director Archie Mayo and a sterling cast. This was the film that catapulted Humphrey Bogart to fame, but without Leslie Howard's insistence on Bogart for the part of Duke Mantee, Bogart might never have gotten his big movie break.

This film is really about the confrontation between intellectualism and brute force. Howard, an idealistic writer and world traveler who has grown weary of life's cruelties, finds himself penniless and hitchhiking through the Arizona desert. As he passes the renowned Petrified Forest, it occurs to him that he is like it, an ossified relic of the past. Stopping at a dilapidated service station restaurant run by grumpy Porter Hall, Howard meets and falls in love with poet Bette Davis, Hall's daughter. She dreams of studying in Paris. Dick Foran, a college halfback who pumps gas for Hall, is in love with Davis, and therefore jealous of Howard; but Howard assures him that he has little to worry about. When a rich couple, Paul Harvey and Genevieve Tobin, arrive at the station, Davis persuades them to take Howard along with them to California. After Howard departs, Hall, Davis, Foran, and Charley Grapewin, Hall's ancient father, hear on the radio that the ruthless gangster Duke Mantee and his henchmen, on the run after committing murders in Oklahoma, are headed into Arizona. On the road, Mantee (Bogart) and his gang are stalled by a broken down car. When Harvey's car comes along, they order the occupants out and drive off with the rich man's auto. Bogart then storms into Hall's service station cafe and holds everyone prisoner, waiting to join up with another carload of henchmen and his gun moll. When Howard, Harvey, Tobin, and their chauffeur, John Alexander, return to the cafe, Bogart holds them hostage as well. Howard challenges Bogart with words Bogart doesn't understand, calling the gangster "the last great apostle of rugged individualism." Howard makes a quiet pact with Bogart, requesting that Bogart shoot him before leaving.

Howard was born for the role of the fatalistic lover and lapsed idealist of THE PETRIFIED FOREST. He had played it to the hilt on Broadway, as did Bogart with the Mantee role in the 1935 stage play. But when it came to casting the film, Jack Warner wanted no part of Bogart, who had appeared in small roles in B films some years earlier. He selected Edward G. Robinson to play Duke Mantee. When Howard heard this, he went to Warner, telling him that if Bogart did not get the role of gangster, he (Howard) would drop out of the picture. Warner needed Howard, so he cast Bogart, who went on to become one of the studio's greatest stars. Bogart's gangster was clearly based on Public Enemy No. 1, John Dillinger (as was Sherwood's original character). Coincidentally, Bogart closely resembled Dillinger, and after studying films of the gangster to perfect his mannerisms, he was a sensation. Yet the Duke Mantee role was also a curse, typecasting Bogart for years to come in the ruthless gangster mold, until 1941 when he appeared as a sympathetic gangster in HIGH SIERRA and, in the same year, as Sam Spade in THE MALTESE FALCON. Davis, too, is outstanding as the culture-hungry girl who yearns to escape the desert and the ominous Petrified Forest. This success of this film would soon land her meatier roles. The film was remade as ESCAPE IN THE DESERT. In 1955, Bogart, Lauren Bacall, and Henry Fonda would reenact the original play in an excellent television production.

PETULIA

1968 105m c ★★★

Drama/Comedy R/X

Petersham (U.S./U.K.)

Julie Christie *(Petulia Danner)*, George C. Scott *(Archie Bollen)*, Richard Chamberlain *(David Danner)*, Arthur Hill *(Barney)*, Shirley Knight *(Polo)*, Pippa Scott *(May)*, Kathleen Widdoes *(Wilma)*, Roger Bowen *(Warren)*, Richard Dysart *(Motel Receptionist)*, Ruth Kobart

p, Raymond Wagner; d, Richard Lester; w, Larry Marcus, Barbara Turner (based on the novel *Me and the Arch Kook Petulia* by John Haase); ph, Nicolas Roeg (Technicolor); ed, Anthony Gibbs; m, John Barry; prod d, Tony Walton; art d, Dean Tavoularis; cos, Tony Walton, Arlette Nastat

By the time PETULIA was released, audiences were tiring of the quick-cutting gimmickry used by Lester, a veteran of TV commercials, to tell his stories. Had he spent more time on content and less on sheer style, this film might have had greater impact. To be sure, there are many wonderful, satirical potshots taken, but they are such throwaways that they get lost in the maelstrom. Scott is a middle-aged doctor who truly cares about his patients in his San Francisco practice. He has just left his wife, Knight, and their children but maintains a jealous attitude toward Knight's new beau, Bowen. Scott is not finding it easy to learn how to be single in the swinging scene. He goes to a party and meets Christie, a married woman who comes on very strong. She falls quickly for him and predicts that they will eventually marry. Scott is fascinated by her, as she is totally different from every woman he's ever met before. They make love, but that's the smallest part of their relationship, as Scott begins to feel younger and more energized by their affair. Scott doesn't know it but she had planned to meet him after having seen an operation he performed on Vincent Arias, a Mexican youth whom she subsidizes. Christie is married to Chamberlain, the weak-willed son of millionaire Joseph Cotten. They've been wed for six months, but he was impotent on the wedding night so she has since refused to share the marital bed with him, something that causes him to beat her regularly. Christie is at Scott's apartment one day, but he's not there. Chamberlain arrives, beats her bloody, and leaves. When Scott does arrive home, he takes Christie to the hospital and supervises her treatment and recovery. Near the end of her stay, Scott comes to the hospital to check on her welfare and is shocked to learn that she's left with Chamberlain and moved back in with him at the family's huge home. Scott goes to the mansion, but Christie opts to stay with Chamberlain, something Scott cannot understand one bit. Chamberlain swears he will never again hurt Christie and asks that she be patient with him and not expect miracles. He has a problem and hopes she will help him get over it. A year goes by and Christie is in the hospital again, this time for a more pleasant reason: she is about to have Chamberlain's child. Scott visits her and asks that she go away with him. She agrees, then, with all the unpredictability demonstrated earlier, changes her mind. Chamberlain arrives just after Scott has left, and she is put under sedation for the delivery. Her last word before the anesthesia takes effect is Scott's name. It's a strange movie that reflects the era of the 1960s in the characters' inability to make commitments, other than Scott, who is a Dr. Kildare-Ben Casey combination. Lots of laughs are in between the tears, including good barbs pointed at such things as topless waitresses, artificial flowers, Catholic hospitals, "hot pillow" motels, 24-hour supermarkets, and, most of all, the way people have become inured to the horrors of war and can engage in banal conversation as the television news blares the latest body count in the background. Nick Roeg did the slick cinematography. Producer Wagner had been an executive for many years at Universal Studios before striking out as an independent. Shot in San Francisco and Tijuana.

PEYTON PLACE

1957 162m c ★★★½

Drama /15

FOX

Lana Turner *(Constance MacKenzie)*, Hope Lange *(Selena Cross)*, Lee Philips *(Michael Rossi)*, Lloyd Nolan *(Dr. Matthew Swain)*, Diane Varsi *(Allison MacKenzie)*, Arthur Kennedy *(Lucas Cross)*, Russ Tamblyn *(Norman Page)*, Terry Moore *(Betty Anderson)*, Barry Coe *(Rodney Harrington)*, David Nelson *(Ted Carter)*

p, Jerry Wald; d, Mark Robson; w, John Michael Hayes (based on the novel by Grace Metalious); ph, William Mellor (CinemaScope, DeLuxe Color); ed, David Bretherton; m, Franz Waxman; art d, Lyle Wheeler, Jack Martin Smith; fx, L.B. Abbott; cos, Adele Palmer, Charles Le Maire

Peyton Place was one of the best-selling novels of all time, and no one thought it could be made into a decent movie. The subject matter was so steamy it was feared that it might be truncated and done as a pale soap opera. But the pundits were mistaken. Hayes's masterful adaptation of the book managed to keep all of the stories going on such a high level of taste that the Catholic Legion of Decency gave it their "A" rating, which meant it was "acceptable to all." Filmed in the small town of Camden, Maine, it's a terrific example of Hollywood's professionalism on all counts. The lives of seemingly "ordinary people" were examined in a small-town community, and the result was a box-office smash that became one of the biggest hits of the year. Set in the 1940s, it paved the way for a sequel, RETURN TO PEYTON PLACE, and a very successful television series that was seen three nights per week in prime time. Mildred Dunnock, a loving teacher of the children at Peyton Place's high school, is overlooked by the powers-that-be for the job of principal, and Philips, a sharp Ph.D., is brought in for the job. He has many new ideas for educational advances and the town wants fresh blood. In no time at all, he meets Turner, a widow with a teenage daughter, Varsi. Since he is such a dashing type, Philips is surprised when Turner spurns his amorous advances and he retaliates by sniping at her for the way she treats Varsi, specifically when the teen's birthday party turns into an innocent-enough petting fest. Varsi and her pals are due to graduate this semester. Wealthy Coe marries Moore, a sensuous young woman, despite his father's annoyance. Meanwhile, Varsi is having a sincere friendship with Tamblyn, whose mother, Erin O'Brien-Moore, is a domineering woman who resents his friendship with anyone. At the same time, Lange, the stepdaughter of the school's drunken caretaker, Kennedy, is raped by Kennedy, and she later kills him accidentally. The war begins, and things begin to change rapidly in the town. Varsi finds she must flee Turner's influence and goes to New York, where she becomes the person who writes about life in the slow lane of Peyton Place. When Lange goes on trial for Kennedy's death, Varsi comes home to cover, is reunited with Turner, and learns her mother is finally going to marry Philips. The reason for her reluctance to marry and her doting attitude toward Varsi is that Varsi was born out of wedlock and Turner didn't want her daughter to go the same way.

PEYTON PLACE is a jewel of a soap opera and manages to make all its points without ever becoming maudlin. The Academy gave it nine Oscar nominations, but it won none. The kudos went for Best Picture (it lost to THE BRIDGE ON THE RIVER

KWAI), Best Actress (Turner, who lost to Joanne Woodward for THE THREE FACES OF EVE), Best Director, Best Script, Best Cinematography, and four nominations in supporting roles for Tamblyn, Kennedy, Lange, and Varsi. Only THE GODFATHER, PART II garnered that many Best Supporting nominations. The details of the story are what make it exciting. Lange gets pregnant by Kennedy and has an abortion by kindly doctor Nolan; Field, Kennedy's wife, kills herself over the anguish; Coe joins the service and is one of the first soldiers to be killed; Tamblyn finally escapes his mother's forceful ways; the Lange trial ends when Nolan produces a document he's forced Kennedy to sign, admitting the parenthood of his stepdaughter's baby, and so on. In later years, another small town would be examined in THE LAST PICTURE SHOW, and there are several similarities between the two. If someone had judiciously pruned 20 minutes out of this, it would have been even better, but since so many millions had bought the book (someone figured it out to be one out of every 37 people in the US), they feared a bad reaction from those who'd loved Metalious's work.

PHANTOM LADY

1944   87m   bw   ★★★★½
Mystery   /A
Universal

Franchot Tone (Jack Marlow), Ella Raines (Carol "Kansas" Richman), Alan Curtis (Scott Henderson), Aurora Miranda (Estela Monteiro), Thomas Gomez (Inspector Burgess), Fay Helm (Ann Terry), Elisha Cook, Jr. (Cliff March), Andrew Tombes (Bartender), Regis Toomey, Joseph Crehan (Detectives)

p, Joan Harrison; d, Robert Siodmak; w, Bernard C. Schoenfeld (based on the novel by Cornell Woolrich); ph, Elwood Bredell; ed, Arthur Hilton; m, H.J. Salter; art d, John B. Goodman, Robert Clatworthy; cos, Vera West, Kenneth Hopkins

A superb thriller, and the first American film by German director Siodmak to enjoy any significant success. Alan Curtis plays an innocent man accused of murdering his wife, with Ella Raines, as his secretary, and Thomas Gomez, as an off-duty copy, engaging in a search for the man's female alibi, a mysterious woman (Fay Helm) whose existence is denied by every witness. Adapted from a novel by Cornell Woolrich, with suitably Expressionistic camera angles and moody lighting.

PHANTOM OF LIBERTY, THE

(LE FANTOME DE LA LIBERTE)
1974   104m   c   ★★★★
Drama   R/X
Greenwich   (France)

Jean-Claude Brialy (Mr. Foucauld), Monica Vitti (Mrs. Foucauld), Milena Vukotic (Nurse), Michel Lonsdale (Hatter), Michel Piccoli (2nd Prefect), Claude Pieplu (Commissioner), Paul Frankeur (Innkeeper), Julien Bertheau (1st Prefect), Adriana Asti (Prefect's Sister), Adolfo Celi (Dr. Legendre)

p, Serge Silberman; d, Luis Bunuel; w, Luis Bunuel, Jean-Claude Carriere; ph, Edmond Richard (Eastmancolor); ed, Helene Plemiannikov

An uproarious summary of Luis Bunuel's surrealistic concerns in a collection of anecdotes starring Jean-Claude Brialy, Michel Piccoli, and Monica Vitti. THE PHANTOM OF LIBERTY jumps from place to place and time to time in a manner that follows the (il)logic of dreams. The film opens in the Napoleonic era with Spanish patriots urging on the firing squad that's about

to execute them with shouts of things like "Down with Liberty!" and "Up with Chains!" Following this is a scene of a maid reading to a child the story we have just witnessed. Again the scene changes to show a man selling supposedly pornographic postcards that are actually shots of entirely non-pornographic French tourist attractions. A nurse then makes the mistake of wandering into a poker game played by a group of monks. A man with a rifle kills passers-by from the top of a Montparnasse building and is hailed as a hero. A missing girl helps the police fill out a report on her disappearance. And, in perhaps the most memorable sequence, a group of elegantly dressed dinner guests sit on toilet seats as they converse around a dining room table. They sheepishly request to be excused when hunger strikes and then creep off to a room containing a private little stall where they may dine.

This is a crazy, subversively funny film about convention-bound characters who have a hard time dealing with sexuality and freedom. It's heartening to see that Bunuel could still ruffle as many feathers at age 75 as he did in 1928 and 1930 with UN CHIEN ANDALOU and L'AGE D'OR.

PHANTOM OF THE OPERA, THE

1929   93m   c/bw   ★★★★
Horror   /PG
Universal

Lon Chaney (The Phantom), Mary Philbin (Christine Daae), Norman Kerry (Raoul de Chagny), Snitz Edwards (Florine Papillon), Gibson Gowland (Simon), Edward Martindel (Philippe de Chagny), Virginia Pearson (Carlotta), Arthur Edmund Carewe (Ledoux), Edith Yorke (Mama Valerius), Anton Vaverka (Prompter)

p, Carl Laemmle; d, Rupert Julian, Edward Sedgwick, Ernst Laemmle (sound sequences); w, Raymond L. Schrock, Elliott Clawson, Tom Reed, Frank M. McCormack (based on the story "Le Fantome de l'Opera" by Gaston Leroux); ph, Virgil Miller, Milton Bridenbecker, Charles Van Enger; ed, Maurice Pivar; prod d, Charles D. Hall, Ben Carre

One of the most famous horror movies of all time, THE PHANTOM OF THE OPERA still manages to frighten after more than 60 years. The legendary Lon Chaney is magnificent as Erik, the horribly disfigured maniac composer known only as the "Phantom," who takes an interest in Christine (Mary Philbin), an understudy at the Paris Opera. Hidden in secret passages, he coaches her, perfecting her art until she is a star. Then he forces the company's leading soprano to step down by unleashing a series of horrors, including sending an enormous chandelier crashing down on the audience during a performance. Eventually the masked Phantom lures Christine to his subterranean lair, where he professes his love for her. He also agrees to let her return to the stage on the condition that she break off her relationship with Raoul (Norman Kerry). Christine agrees, but once she is free rushes to her lover, and they make plans to flee to England following her performance. The Phantom overhears them, however, and kidnaps Christine. As he sits and plays his huge pipe organ, curiosity overwhelms Christine and she creeps up behind the Phantom and pulls off his mask, revealing the terrible skull-like visage beneath. Eventually, Raoul and a mysterious foreign agent set out to capture the Phantom, as does an enraged mob led by the brother of one of the Phantom's victims.

A much stronger film than THE HUNCHBACK OF NOTRE DAME (1923), THE PHANTOM OF THE OPERA further cemented Chaney's reputation as a superstar and made Universal synonymous with horror. From the point of view of the studio's management, however, THE PHANTOM OF THE OPERA was horrific in more ways than one, taking more than two years to reach the theaters after its initial completion in 1923. When it was originally previewed in California, critics told Carl Laemmle that he would have a turkey on his hands unless he offset the scary aspects with plenty of comedy relief, so the studio head brought in Chester Conklin from the Sennett lot and additional footage was shot. These additions, however, necessitated a new set of titles, and the expensive Walter Anthony was hired to provide them. When the picture, which Universal hoped would achieve "prestige" status, was then screened in San Francisco, the consensus was that it had some wonderful moments but failed to make sense. So the whole production was turned over to a new staff of title writers and editors who *really* tore it apart. Out came the comedy, as well as a whole subplot involving Ward Crane and a lot of sword play, until finally studio execs felt they had their "big picture." With its play of light and shadow, its secret passageways, masked ball (filmed in two-strip Technicolor), and the still-chilling unmasking scene, THE PHANTOM OF THE OPERA deserves its revered place in horror film history.

PHANTOM OF THE OPERA

1943 92m c ★★★
Horror /A
Universal

Nelson Eddy (Anatole Garron), Susanna Foster (Christine DuBois), Claude Rains (Enrique Claudin), Edgar Barrier (Inspector Raoul de Chagny), Leo Carrillo (Signor Feretti), Jane Farrar (Biancarolli), J. Edward Bromberg (Amiot), Fritz Feld (Lecours), Frank Puglia (Villeneuve), Steven Geray (Vercheres)

p, George Waggner; d, Arthur Lubin; w, Eric Taylor, Hans Jacoby, Samuel Hoffenstein (based on the novel Le Fantome de l'Opera by Gaston Leroux); ph, Hal Mohr, W. Howard Greene (Technicolor); ed, Russell Schoengarth; m, Edward Ward (operatic score), George Waggner; art d, John B. Goodman, Alexander Golitzen; cos, Vera West

Universal Studios' elaborate and expensive remake of their classic 1925 silent horror film THE PHANTOM OF THE OPERA boasts fabulous sets, gorgeous costumes, and stunning Technicolor photography—but fails in the horror department, because of an excess of music and low comedy. Draining much of the fear, suspense, and mystery out of the original Gaston Leroux material, this remake posits Enrique Claudin (Claude Rains)—the future "Phantom"—as a somewhat frail, middle-aged violinist with the Paris Opera who is in love from afar with Christine DuBois (Susanna Foster), a pretty and talented singer in the chorus. Although Christine doesn't even know the violinist exists, Enrique devotes his entire life to her, sacrificing his musical future just to make her happy. Universal spent $1.5 million on PHANTOM OF THE OPERA and every dollar is on the screen. While the opera house set is the same one used in the original, many additional sets were constructed and dressed up with elaborate and expensive wares. Rains, who had just finished playing what would later become his best-remembered role—that of Capt. Louis Renault in CASABLANCA—managed to bring a sense of pathos and menace to the Phantom. The sparse and briefly seen makeup of the disfigured violinist is merely serviceable; wisely, no attempt was made to duplicate or surpass Lon Chaney's amazing visage in the original. While this version can be quite entertaining at times, it is frustrating that the horror elements are used merely as a plot device to propel the story along to the next elaborate opera scene—a structure that pleased neither horror fans nor opera buffs. PHANTOM OF THE OPERA won Oscars for Best Color Cinematography and Best Color Interior

Decoration (John B. Goodman, Alexander Golitzen, R.A. Gausman, Ira S. Webb), receiving nominations for Best Sound Recording and Best Musical Score.

PHANTOM OF THE OPERA, THE

1962 84m c ★★★
Horror /A
Hammer (U.K.)

Herbert Lom (The Phantom), Heather Sears (Christine Charles), Thorley Walters (Lattimer), Edward De Souza (Harry Hunter), Michael Gough (Lord Ambrose D'Arcy), Martin Miller (Rossi), Miles Malleson (Philosophical Cabby), Miriam Karlin (Charwoman), John Harvey (Vickers), Harold Goodwin (Bill)

p, Anthony Hinds; d, Terence Fisher; w, Anthony Hinds (based on a story by Gaston Leroux); ph, Arthur Grant (Technicolor); ed, Alfred Cox; m, Edwin Astley; prod d, Bernard Robinson; art d, Don Mingaye

Following successful reinterpretations of such horror film icons as Frankenstein, Dracula, the Mummy, and the Wolfman, Hammer Studios turned its attention to the classic tale of THE PHANTOM OF THE OPERA. Fully aware that its small-budget efforts would be closely compared with the two previous big-budget American versions (in 1925 starring Lon Chaney, Sr., and again in 1943 starring Claude Rains), Hammer bravely forged ahead and managed to produce a film that, while no classic, stands as a well-crafted thriller with some chilling, memorable moments. Shifting the action from Paris to London, the film opens during the first performance of "Saint Joan," a new opera written by the wealthy and influential lord, Gough. In the middle of a scene, the body of a hanged stagehand swings into view from the wings. The audience is thunderstruck, as is the prima donna, Aukin, who immediately quits. The producers soon replace the skittish singer with a new discovery, Sears. Sears refuses to knuckle under to Gough's lecherous advances, and the powerful benefactor rejects her for the role. Sears's tribulations continue when she is kidnapped by a strange dwarf, Ian Wilson, and brought into the bowels of the opera house. There she meets Lom, a bizarre man whose face is hidden behind a crudely crafted, one-eyed mask. Lom admires Sears's vocal talents and decides to train her to sing an opera he has written. The mysterious composer vows that she soon will be given the lead in a new show. Meanwhile, Sears's fiance, De Souza, has discovered that Gough had stolen his opera from an obscure composer who was believed to have drowned in the Thames. Curious about the dead man, De Souza traces the composer's last hours and discovers a sewer tunnel that leads underneath the opera house. There he finds Sears with Lom, and he unmasks the composer. Beneath the mask is a badly scarred visage. When confronted by De Souza, Lom admits that he is the composer whose work was stolen by Gough. Lom discovered that the copyright to his opera had been made in Gough's name. A struggle broke out between the men and during the fight, Lom's face was horribly burned by acid. Screaming in pain, Lom had run to the river and thrown himself in. There he found the sewer tunnel and decided to take up residence beneath the opera. Because he did not resurface, police assumed he had drowned. Sympathetic to Lom's plight, De Souza agrees to let Sears's vocal training continue. Sears is eventually given the lead in the opera, and during the opening night performance, De Souza notices the dwarf Wilson watching from the catwalk above the stage. Others see Wilson, and in his attempt to escape he knocks loose the huge chandelier that hangs directly above Sears. Seeing that she is about to be killed, Lom pulls off his mask, leaps onto the stage, and pushes Sears out of the way before the chandelier crushes him.

Hammer's THE PHANTOM OF THE OPERA was originally to have starred the studio's favorite Dracula, Christopher Lee, but a last-minute switch was made in favor of Lom. While he could not hope to equal Chaney's classic tour-de-force or even Rains's memorable portrayal, Lom succeeded admirably in creating an alternately malevolent, sympathetic, and even tragic character. Hammer had hired professional maskmakers to create the phantom's mask, but they failed to come up with a suitable design. Director Fisher tried to shoot around Lom's masked scenes while awaiting the result of the maskmaker's work, but he finally grew impatient and had Hammer's makeup man, Roy Ashton, construct a crude mask out of cloth, tape, and gauze. The effect is perfect because the mask looks like something the Phantom would have made for himself while combing the dank sewers beneath the opera house. Despite the film's low budget, the production has the usual Hammer eye for detail and looks as if it had an expensive treatment. Gough turns in his usual fine performance as the evil opera benefactor, while Sears (whose singing was dubbed by opera singer Pat Clark) and De Souza are serviceable as the standard heroine and hero.

PHANTOM TOLLBOOTH, THE

1970 90m c	★★★½
Animated/Children's/Fantasy	G/U
MGM	

Butch Patrick *(Milo).* VOICES OF: Mel Blanc, Daws Butler, Candy Candido, Hans Conried, June Foray, Patti Gilbert, Shepard Menken, Cliff Norton, Larry Thor

p, Chuck Jones, Abe Levitow, Les Goldman; d, Chuck Jones, Abe Levitow, David Monahan; w, Chuck Jones, Sam Rosen (based on the book by Norton Juster); ph, Lester Shorr (Metrocolor); ed, Jim Faris; m, Dean Elliott; prod d, Maurice Noble; art d, George W. Davis, Charles K. Hagedon; anim, Irv Spence, Bill Littlejohn, Richard Thompson, Tom Ray, Philip Roman, Alan Zaslove, Edwin Aardal, Ed DeMattia, Xenia, Lloyd Vaughan, Carl Bell

This fine adaptation of the children's book by Norton Juster was Chuck Jones's and MGM's first animated feature. Butch Patrick stars (in the live-action sequences) as Milo, a bored youngster who cannot maintain an interest in anything. One day the "phantom tollbooth" appears in his bedroom and Milo drives his toy car into it. He is then transported through the magic of animation into a strange and wonderful world broken up into two camps, letters and numbers. Unfortunately, letters and numbers are at war with each other (each thinking they are more important to society), and Milo soon finds himself caught in the middle. Aided by a dog called Tock, Milo strives mightily to restore the land to peace, in a charming film that combines some fairly sophisticated ideas (demons from the "Mountains of Ignorance" cause much of the trouble, and Milo tries to restore "Rhyme and Reason" to the land) with cute and likable characters that are sure to grab a child's attention.

PHAR LAP

1984 107m c	★★★½
Sports	PG
FOX (Australia)	

Tom Burlinson *(Tommy Woodcock),* Ron Leibman *(Dave Davis),* Martin Vaughan *(Harry Telford),* Judy Morris *(Bea Davis),* Celia De Burgh *(Vi Telford),* Richard Morgan *("Cashy" Martin),* Robert Grubb *(William Neilsen),* Georgia Carr *(Emma),* James Steele *(Jim Pike),* Vincent Ball *(Lachlan McKinnon)*

p, John Sexton; d, Simon Wincer; w, David Williamson (based on the book *The Phar Lap Story* by Michael Wilkinson); ph, Russell Boyd (Panavision); ed, Tony Paterson; m, Bruce Rowland; prod d, Lawrence Eastwood; art d, David Bowden; cos, Anna Senior

Another story of a boy and his horse, this time a factual one set in Australia in the early 1930s. The film opens as the horse lies dying in a Mexican stable after winning the biggest race of its career, the Agua Caliente, in April 1932. The cause of Phar Lap's death goes unexplained, as it has to this day, although blame is clearly directed toward the gamblers who consistently lost money as the horse won race after race. From this point the narrative moves backward, showing how the young horse was purchased in New Zealand by Harry Telford (Martin Vaughan), a trainer whose experienced eye spots potential in the animal despite its lack of pedigree. His partner in the purchase is Dave Davis (Ron Leibman), a fast-talking American Jew who suffers greatly at the hands of anti-Semites in Australia as his horse triumphs over their horses. The horse is extremely skittish, though, and loses its first four races, even as Telford tries ever more brutal methods of snapping it into line. Finally Tommy Woodcock (Tom Burlinson), a stable boy, establishes a bond with the horse through kindness, and from that time on it wins every race. Phar Lap today is remembered in Australia in the same way as Man O' War in the US or Red Rum in Britain—as the greatest horse of its day and a symbol of national pride. Although the film plays a little too heavily on this patriotic theme, its simple boy-and-his-horse story is beautifully effective.

PHILADELPHIA STORY, THE

1940 112m bw	★★★★
Comedy	/PG
MGM	

Cary Grant *(C.K. Dexter Haven),* Katharine Hepburn *(Tracy Lord),* James Stewart *(Macauley Connor),* Ruth Hussey *(Elizabeth Imbrie),* John Howard *(George Kittredge),* Roland Young *(Uncle Willie),* John Halliday *(Seth Lord),* Mary Nash *(Margaret Lord),* Virginia Weidler *(Dinah Lord),* Henry Daniell *(Sidney Kidd)*

p, Joseph L. Mankiewicz; d, George Cukor; w, Donald Ogden Stewart, Waldo Salt (based on the play by Philip Barry, uncredited); ph, Joseph Ruttenberg; ed, Frank Sullivan; m, Franz Waxman; art d, Cedric Gibbons, Wade B. Rubottom; cos, Adrian

George Cukor directed this classic comedy talkfest that offers special pleasures for fans of Katherine Hepburn, James Stewart, and Cary Grant. Hepburn, the daughter of a super-wealthy family living in a ritzy suburb of Philadelphia, is slated to marry stuffed-shirt coal company executive Howard. Previously she had been married to Grant in a stormy short-lived relationship that ended largely because Hepburn couldn't deal with Grant's drinking and irresponsible ways. As her wedding nears, Grant shows up at the estate, ostensibly to attend the nuptials, but really to protect the reputation of his ex-in-laws. Grant has learned that publisher Daniell plans to run an expose about Hepburn's stagedoor Johnny father, Halliday, revealing in his *Spy* magazine details of Halliday's chronic womanizing. To mollify the publisher, Grant, who works for Daniell, arranges for the magazine's chief scandal reporter, Stewart, and a photographer, Hussey, to report on the wedding for the magazine. Stewart is a cynical tough talking reporter with a healthy skepticism about the ways of rich folks until he gets smitten by Hepburn, who grows more unsure of her desires as her wedding approaches. Indeed most of the major characters must decide whom they really love before the film is over. Of course, all must end happily even if unexpectedly.

With such a stellar cast, a fine director working in the type of picture he did best, and some genuinely witty dialogue, this film has all the ingredients for a great comedy. And it is great though there have been many funnier comedies. The film has an unfortunate tendency to take itself too seriously for long stretches. Stewart's shameless adoration of Hepburn and the cloying speeches he's forced to deliver in her praise try our credulity and patience. A very strong case is being made here for the sheer irresistibility of the film's female star. The film also strenuously drives home the point that people born poor aren't necessarily noble while men born rich aren't necessarily cads. No need to stop the presses for this little news bulletin!

This was a project especially dear to Hepburn. Two years prior to the release of THE PHILADELPHIA STORY, Hepburn had been branded "box-office poison" by a leading exhibitor thus prompting her to storm out of town in a huff. She decided to look for a Broadway show suitable for her talents. Playwright Barry wrote the lead in "The Philadelphia Story" expressly for Hepburn who starred in the smash Broadway hit before making the film. She covered 25 percent of the play's cost and took no salary, shrewdly opting to take 45 percent of the profits and these were considerable. Joseph Cotten played the Cary Grant role while Van Heflin originated the role that Stewart would play in the film. Hepburn intended to return to Hollywood in style. She owned the film adaptation rights to the play and shrewdly encouraged Louis B. Mayer to deal with her. Hepburn not only succeeded in getting Mayer to pay her $250,000 for the rights but also won the right to select her own director, screenwriter, and costars. She picked her favorite director, Cukor, and Donald Ogden Stewart, a close friend, as the writer. Grant accepted his role only on the proviso that he receive top billing, which he did. He then demanded a then-whopping salary of $137,000 for the film and got it. (Grant donated his entire salary from THE PHILADELPHIA STORY to the British War Relief Fund.) Hepburn particularly wanted James Stewart, who was suddenly one of the most important young actors around since his smash success in MR. SMITH GOES TO WASHINGTON a year earlier (for which he had received an Oscar nomination).

The film became a box-office smash. It broke all records at Radio City Music Hall with a return of almost $600,000 in six weeks. Stewart received an Oscar as Best Actor. Donald Ogden Stewart received an Oscar for his screenplay. Other nominations went to Best Picture, Hepburn as Best Actress, Hussey as Best Supporting Actress, and Cukor as Best Director. Hepburn, who won the coveted New York Film Critics Award, was defeated by Ginger Rogers for her role in KITTY FOYLE. The film was remade as a musical, HIGH SOCIETY, in 1956, starring Bing Crosby, Frank Sinatra, and Grace Kelly.

PICKPOCKET
1963 75m bw   ★★★★
Crime   /A
Lux (France)

Martin Lassalle *(Michel)*, Marika Green *(Jeanne)*, Pierre Leymarie *(Jacques)*, Jean Pelegri *(Police Inspector)*, Kassagi *(Master Pickpocket)*, Pierre Etaix *(Accomplice)*, Dolly Scal *(Michel's Mother)*, Cesar Gattegno *(Detective)*

p, Agnes Delahaie; d, Robert Bresson; w, Robert Bresson (based on the novel *Crime and Punishment* by Feodor Dostoyevsky); ph, L.H. Burel; ed, Raymond Lamy; m, Jean-Baptiste Lully; art d, Pierre Charbonnier

Using Dostoyevsky's *Crime and Punishment* as a point of departure, director Bresson has created a wonderful study of a criminal on the road to redemption in PICKPOCKET (released in Paris in 1959). Lassalle stars as a lonely young man who resigns himself to the fate of becoming a pickpocket. An initial attempt is unsuccessful, and he is easily caught. It is during his arrest that Lassalle's consciousness is raised on the rights and wrongs of theft. When his sickly mother dies, Green and Leymarie, his two closest friends, offer advice and solace. Lassalle, however, chooses to return to crime, taking lessons from master pickpocket Kassagi. The police inspector observes Lassalle's criminal life but fails to arrest him, partly because of flimsy evidence and partly because he is intrigued with Lassalle's ideas. When Lassalle's partners in crime are arrested, the pickpocket flees France, leaving behind Green, who has by now fallen in love with him. When he returns years later he finds Green unmarried and with a child. Again he resorts to stealing and again he is caught. Green visits him in his cell, and for the first time he realizes that he loves her. In the memorable final moments, Green and Lassalle embrace through the bars of the cell as he tells her, "What a strange way I have traveled to find you at last." As Bresson has so often done in his films, PICKPOCKET details a man's struggle between his inner feelings and his attempt to survive in society. What separates PICKPOCKET from so many other films is Bresson's use of Lassalle's inner voice (which corresponds to the written words in his diary) as a narrative element. Those familiar with the work of screenwriter-director Paul Schrader will note a few similarities in style and thought, which comes as no surprise since Schrader wrote a book entitled *Transcendental Style on Film: Ozu, Bresson, and Dreyer*. Elements of TAXI DRIVER's narrative (voiceover and diary passages corresponding) are lifted from PICKPOCKET, as in the final line of AMERICAN GIGOLO. While Schrader's transcendental style has failed to achieve the status of Bresson or Ozu or Dreyer (TAXI DRIVER, his finest achievement, comes closest), he has, at least, brought an interesting philosophical element into American film.

PICKUP ON SOUTH STREET
1953 80m bw   ★★★★
Crime/Spy   /A
FOX

Richard Widmark *(Skip McCoy)*, Jean Peters *(Candy)*, Thelma Ritter *(Moe)*, Murvyn Vye *(Capt. Dan Tiger)*, Richard Kiley *(Joey)*, Willis Bouchey *(Zara)*, Milburn Stone *(Winoki)*, Henry Slate *(MacGregor)*, Jerry O'Sullivan *(Enyart)*, Harry Carter *(Dietrich)*

p, Jules Schermer; d, Samuel Fuller; w, Samuel Fuller (based on the story "Blaze of Glory" by Dwight Taylor); ph, Joseph MacDonald; ed, Nick De Maggio; m, Leigh Harline; art d, Lyle Wheeler, George Patrick; fx, Ray Kellogg; cos, Travilla

A brutal melodrama set against a backdrop of New York's seedy underworld, PICKUP ON SOUTH STREET delves into the shadowy world of federal agents and communist spies. Widmark is a petty crook, a three-time loser whose actions are motivated solely by greed. When he steals a wallet from the purse of Peters, he finds himself in deeper trouble than he ever imagined. Inside the wallet is top-secret microfilm that Peters is unwittingly transporting for her lover, Kiley, a communist spy she believes to be a patent lawyer. When Kiley discovers that the microfilm has been stolen, he demands that Peters find Widmark and get the film back. Also on Widmark's track are two federal agents who have been shadowing Peters. Both the agents and Peters get information on Widmark's whereabouts from Ritter, an aging ex-pickpocket who supplements her scant income from tie peddling by selling information on underworld criminals. Peters tries to use sex to get the microfilm from Widmark but fails. The agents appeal to Widmark's sense of patriotism, but this, too, fails since Widmark doesn't care about the effect of communism on the American way of life. With all the interest that has been shown in the microfilm, Widmark knows that it is worth a great deal of money, so he holds out for an offer from Kiley. By now Peters has fallen for Widmark, and has turned against Kiley, whom she sees as un-American. Kiley attempts to buy Widmark's address from Ritter, but she proudly refuses to sell to a communist—at any price. Enraged, Kiley kills Ritter. Widmark now has a reason to keep the microfilm out of Kiley's hands—not because Kiley is a communist but because the spy killed a friend of Widmark's. Kiley then returns to Peters (who by now has obtained the film) and mercilessly beats her when he learns of her part in the scheme. After discovering that some of the microfilm is missing and obtaining Widmark's waterfront address, Kiley pays the thief a visit. Widmark eludes Kiley and follows him to a subway station, where Widmark manages to steal back the microfilm. In retaliation for the death of Ritter and the attack on Peters, Widmark pounds Kiley into the pavement and turns him over to the federal agents. Only after Kiley is killed is it revealed that his contact is none other than the federal agent who has been heading up the search for the spy. Having assisted the feds, Widmark is left to finish his romance with Peters and to return to his gutter life.

This provocative film from Sam Fuller is is based on "Blaze of Glory," a straightforward story about drug pushers written by Dwight Taylor. Although this original story line was retained in the dubbed version of the film released in France under the title LA PORTE DE LA DROGUE, Fuller decided to politicize the American version of the film. Unfortunately, PICKUP ON SOUTH STREET has been viewed by some as rabidly anti-communist, an assessment that ignores the depth and complexity that Fuller brings to the film. Like so many of Fuller's heroes, Widmark's Skip McCoy fights to retain his individuality in the face of societal pressures. Yet McCoy doesn't foil the communist scheme because of his devotion to the American ideal but because Kiley, who just happens to be a communist spy, has done McCoy wrong. Both Widmark and Peters are superb, but it is Ritter, as the seedy but much-loved Moe, who gives the film its emotional punch, and her performance earned an Oscar nomination for Best Supporting Actress—something of an oddity for a Fuller-directed B movie.

PICNIC

1955 115m c ★★★★
Drama /A
Columbia

William Holden (Hal Carter), Rosalind Russell (Rosemary Sydney), Kim Novak (Madge Owens), Betty Field (Flo Owens), Susan Strasberg (Millie Owens), Cliff Robertson (Alan), Arthur O'Connell (Howard Bevans), Verna Felton (Mrs. Helen Potts), Reta Shaw (Linda Sue Breckenridge), Nick Adams (Bomber)

p, Fred Kohlmar; d, Joshua Logan; w, Daniel Taradash (based on the play by William Inge); ph, James Wong Howe (CinemaScope, Technicolor); ed, Charles Nelson, William Lyon; m, George Duning; prod d, Jo Mielziner; art d, William Flannery; chor, Miriam Nelson; cos, Jean Louis

Joshua Logan's faithful screen adaptation of William Inge's Pulitzer Prize-winning play about small-town America features a bravura performance by Holden as a drifter come to a small Kansas town just as the community is preparing to celebrate Labor Day. Seeking out old college friend Robertson in the hope of landing a job with Robertson's father, the richest man in the county, Holden is invited to join in the festivities. What's more, Robertson insists that Holden meet his fiancee, the beautiful Novak, and she and the drifter fall in love at first sight. Holden struts about the town flexing his muscles, and most of the local ladies, including Novak's naive younger sister, Strasberg, and schoolmarm Russell, fall for the handsome stranger. Holden brags about his adventures, and Russell gets drunk while admiring him, thrusting aside her reliable date, O'Connell, and losing control, ripping Holden's shirt right off his back in her seizure of lust. Along with this humiliation, Holden is forced into a fight with Robertson so that he beats up his old friend and then must run from the law, dragging Novak with him. He finally persuades her to return home, confessing that he's nothing but a bum and a liar. Novak does go home, and Holden exits the way he arrived, by hopping a freight train. Novak, however, realizes that her love for Holden is stronger than the security of home and she takes a bus heading in the same direction as the train, intending to catch up with the love of her life.

The love scenes between Holden and Novak steam up the screen, and the sequence showing their dance together is as sensual as any recorded on film. PICNIC was Holden's last film for Columbia. He initially refused to play Hal—believing that at 37 he was too old for the role—but he turned out a brilliant performance. This was Novak's first major role. Reputedly, she was terrified of botching the job and became something of a recluse during the shooting, decling dinner offers from fellow cast members and regularly going to church to pray for success. Hollywood lore also has it that Holden didn't believe he was up to the famous slow dance with Novak. Logan, who rubbed every scene in the film to high gloss, took Holden to roadhouses and compelled him to dance with choreographer Nelson to jukebox songs until the actor was confident he could perform his dance with Novak. Still, Holden is said to have almost backed out at the last moment, and he persuaded Columbia mogul Cohn to pay him an extra $8,000 for the "stunt." Cinematographer Howe circled the two dancers with his camera, showing them mostly from the waist up, their eyes riveted to each other, capturing the love scene in one take. That scene became one of the most famous of the 1950s and it made "Moonglow" a sensational hit; women coast to coast dreamed of dancing with Holden on a clammy night atop a boat landing somewhere in Kansas. The film was shot in Hutchinson, Kansas, and in Columbia's Burbank Studio. Nominated for six Academy Awards, it won two: Best Art Direction and Best Film Editing. The other nominations were for Best Picture (MARTY won that year), Best Supporting Actor (O'Connell), Best Direction and Best Score.

PICNIC AT HANGING ROCK

1975 110m c ★★★
Drama PG/A
Atlantic (Australia)

Rachel Roberts (Mrs. Appleyard), Dominic Guard (Michael Fitzhubert), Helen Morse (Dianne De Poiters), Jacki Weaver (Minnie), Vivean Gray (Miss Greta McGraw), Kirsty Child (Dora Lumley), Anne Lambert (Miranda), Karen Robson (Irma), Jane Vallis (Marion), Christine Schuler (Edith Horton)

p, Jim McElroy, Hal McElroy; d, Peter Weir; w, Cliff Green (based on the novel by Joan Lindsay); ph, Russell Boyd (Eastmancolor); ed, Max Lemon; m, Bruce Smeaton; art d, David Copping; cos, Judy Dorsman

The critical recognition of Australia's film industry in the late 1970s can, to a large degree, be credited to the works of Peter Weir. After his first feature, THE CARS THAT ATE PARIS, films such as PICNIC AT HANGING ROCK and THE LAST WAVE exhibited a peculiar and fascinating mystical quality that revealed a distinctive sensibility. Unfortunately Weir's decidedly personal vision is often rather murky.

PICNIC AT HANGING ROCK recounts the strange story of four girls and their teacher from a boarding school in Victoria who go for a picnic at nearby Hanging Rock on a beautiful St. Valentine's Day in 1900. One of the girls, Edith (Christine Schuler), takes a nap and wakes to find that the other three have removed their shoes and stockings to climb higher. They vanish. The police are called in but they are unsuccessful in their search. A young Englishman conducts a search of his own with odd and inconclusive results.

An exceedingly beautiful film, PICNIC AT HANGING ROCK seems to aspire to be an existential thriller of some sort. At times the film seems to thread in BLACK NARCISSUS territory with its depiction of barely controlled sexual hysteria and its eccentric lyrical quality. It's all pretty overheated and underexplained but this arty vague and possibly supernatural movie lingers on in the memory.

PICTURE OF DORIAN GRAY, THE

1945 110m c/bw ★★★½
Horror /A
MGM

George Sanders (Lord Henry Wotton), Hurd Hatfield (Dorian Gray), Donna Reed (Gladys Hallward), Angela Lansbury (Sybil Vane), Lowell Gilmore (Basil Hallward), Peter Lawford (David Stone), Richard Fraser (James Vane), Reginald Owen (Lord George Farmoor), Lydia Bilbrook (Mrs. Vane), Morton Lowry (Adrian Singleton)

p, Pandro S. Berman; d, Albert Lewin; w, Albert Lewin (based on the novel by Oscar Wilde); ph, Harry Stradling; ed, Ferris Webster; m, Herbert Stothart; art d, Cedric Gibbons, Hans Peters

This subtle and frightening adaptation of the classic Oscar Wilde novel allows the audience's imagination to do most of the scaring. Hurd Hatfield stars as the title character—a young aristocrat in 19th-century London whose gentle, angelic appearance is dangerously deceptive. Coaxed by the manipulative and hedonistic Lord Henry Wotton (George Sanders), Dorian grows as evil and scandalous as his mentor, becoming a philandering louse who entertains sadistic and perverse thoughts, alluding to (unseen) orgies and unspeakable evils. At the height of his vanity, Dorian has his portrait painted, and, in a Faustian pact, trades his soul for eternal youth. As a result, the portrait ages hideously, while Dorian's appearance never changes. In much the same manner as Val Lewton's horror films, THE PICTURE OF DORIAN GRAY frightens the audience by mere suggestion, without

ever resorting to distracting visual representations of the horrible. All the infamy of Hatfield's character is implied, resulting in a building up of evil so horrible that it becomes unspeakable. The only visual shock the audience is subjected to is the portrait itself (which one never expects to see when it pops onto the screen in Technicolor with a violent musical crash), painted in a brilliantly grotesque style by Ivan Albright. THE PICTURE OF DORIAN GRAY not only frightened many viewers, it also earned the respect of the Motion Picture Academy, which bestowed upon the film two Oscar nominations—one to Angela Lansbury (as Dorian's jilted fiancee) for Best Supporting Actress and another to Cedric Gibbons and Hans Peters for Best Black-and-White Art Direction—and one statuette for the deep-focus camerawork of Harry Stradling.

PIERROT LE FOU

1968 110m c ★★★★
Crime/Romance /A
Rome/Paris/SNC/DEG (France/Italy)

Jean-Paul Belmondo (Ferdinand Griffon, "Pierrot"), Anna Karina (Marianne Renoir), Dirk Sanders (Fred, Marianne's Brother), Raymond Devos (Man on the Pier), Graziella Galvani (Ferdinand's Wife), Roger Dutoit, Hans Meyer (Gangsters), Jimmy Karoubi (Dwarf), Krista Nell (Mme. Staquet), Pascal Aubier (2nd Brother)

p, Georges de Beauregard; d, Jean-Luc Godard; w, Jean-Luc Godard (based on the novel Obsession by Lionel White); ph, Raoul Coutard (Techniscope, Eastmancolor); ed, Francoise Collin; m, Antoine Duhamel, Antonio Vivaldi; art d, Pierre Guffroy

Like BAND OF OUTSIDERS before it and the incomprehensible MADE IN USA afterward, Jean-Luc Godard's PIERROT LE FOU is based on a pulp detective novel, providing the filmmaker with a simple story on which to hang his personal, artistic and philosophical beliefs.

Ferdinand Griffon (Jean-Paul Belmondo) leaves behind his Parisian wife and child during a party and takes off on an adventure with Marianne Renoir (Anna Karina), the family baby-sitter with whom he had an affair five years earlier. The following morning a man is found in Marianne's apartment with scissors sticking out of his throat. They set out for the Riviera (heading south, as the characters in Godard's previous film, ALPHAVILLE, hoped to do) in the hope of locating Marianne's gunrunner brother. Ferdinand spends his time writing a journal, but Marianne grows increasingly impatient and gets herself involved once more in gangster activities. Again the result is a mobster—a dwarf—being found with scissors in his throat.

The pair is separated when Ferdinand is kidnapped and tortured by gangsters who are interested in finding Marianne. Ferdinand eventually meets up with her and learns that her brother is really her lover. A double cross follows, and Ferdinand ends up shooting them both. Having had enough of the adventure, Ferdinand phones his wife in Paris but cannot get through to her. He goes to the top of a hill, paints his face blue, ties red and yellow sticks of dynamite to his head, and lights the fuse. He makes an effort to put out the fuse as he changes his mind about the suicide, but from a distance we see a devastating explosion.

PIERROT LE FOU was Godard's tenth film in six years (not including four sketches that he contributed to compilation films) and perhaps the first to contain all the elements that have been called "Godardian." He combined everything that came before—the romanticism of BREATHLESS, the inner monologue externalized in LE PETIT SOLDAT, the structural divison of MY LIFE TO LIVE, and the epic odyssey of CONTEMPT—with the linguistic diary format that would overpower some of his later films.

Working from the outline provided by Lionel White's novel *Obsession*, Godard was able to proceed without a script and create what he called "a completely spontaneous film." Spontaneous or not, PIERROT LE FOU is arguably one of the few Godard pictures to have the desired balance of romance, adventure, violence, and humor on one side, and philosophy, literary and cinematic allusion, and Brechtian distancing on the other.

Because of the personal nature of his pictures, is difficult to judge Godard on the basis of one film; his body of work is brilliant, but each of his films serves more as a component of the whole than an entity in itself. PIERROT LE FOU, which was lensed quickly in May, June, and July 1965 and then edited even more rapidly for a showing at the Venice Film Festival at the end of August, is the exception, a film that stands on its own. Despite the mixed reaction that inevitably accompanies a new Godard film, it was soon elevated to the position of runner-up in the prestigious *Sight and Sound* poll of 1972.

PILLOW TALK

1959   105m   c   ★★★½
Comedy   /A
Arwin

Rock Hudson (*Brad Allen*), Doris Day (*Jan Morrow*), Tony Randall (*Jonathan Forbes*), Thelma Ritter (*Alma*), Nick Adams (*Tony Walters*), Julia Meade (*Marie*), Allen Jenkins (*Harry*), Marcel Dalio (*Pierot*), Lee Patrick (*Mrs. Walters*), Mary McCarty (*Nurse Resnick*)

p, Ross Hunter, Martin Melcher; d, Michael Gordon; w, Stanley Shapiro, Maurice Richlin (based on a story by Russell Rouse, Clarence Greene); ph, Arthur E. Arling (CinemaScope, Eastmancolor); ed, Milton Carruth; m, Frank DeVol; art d, Alexander Golitzen, Richard Riedel; cos, Bill Thomas, Jean Louis

PILLOW TALK was the first of the witty, well-produced sex comedies featuring Day and Hudson. Hudson, a playboy songwriter, and Day, a successful, independent interior designer, learn to loathe each other when they are forced to share a party line during a Manhattan phone-line shortage. Day gets increasingly angry every time she tries to make a call and hears Hudson coming on to yet another unsuspecting woman he's trying to bed. After listening to enough of his suave baloney, Day begins causing trouble. Naturally, Hudson thinks she's an uptight old hag, and eventually they agree to take turns using the phone every half-hour. Coincidentally, Hudson's buddy, Randall, is in love with Day and the phone-sharers finally meet when Randall brings her to see the progress of a Broadway show he's funding and for which Hudson is writing the tunes. Surprised by Day's good looks, Hudson pretends to be a dopey Texan and begins to work his charms on her. Day quickly realizes who Hudson is and puts an end to the romance. Now hooked, Hudson seeks advice from Day's maid, Ritter (who nearly steals the movie), and she suggests that Hudson let Day decorate his apartment. This ploy backfires, however, when the not-to-be-fooled Day gets her licks in by doing over Hudson's pad in a hideous manner. Frustrated because he can get her no other way, Hudson does some quick thinking and states that he hopes his apartment will be to her liking when they get married. Day finally gives in and agrees to marry Hudson.

Though PILLOW TALK is silly and at times overly "cute," it was the first time Day was allowed to show a more sexually frank side to her character, and Hudson was able to prove he was more than just a good-looking hunk. The combination clicked, leaving Hudson and Day among the most popular stars of the next five years. PILLOW TALK garnered five Academy Award nominations (Best Actress [Day lost to Simone Signoret for ROOM AT THE TOP], Best Supporting Actress [Ritter], Best Original Screenplay, Best Art Direction, and Best Music) and won the award for Best Screenplay. It was also among the bigger box-office successes of its day, taking in $7.5 million in domestic distribution. Songs include: "Pillow Talk" (Buddy Pepper, Inez James, sung by Day, Hudson), "Possess Me" (Joe Lubin, I.J. Roth, sung by Day), "Inspiration" (Lubin, Roth, sung by Hudson), "I Need No Atmosphere," "You Lied" (Lubin, Roth, sung by Perry Blackwell), "Roly Poly" (Elsa Doran, Sol Lake, sung by Day, Hudson, Blackwell).

PIMPERNEL SMITH

1942   100m   bw   ★★★½
Spy/War   /U
British National   (U.K.)

Leslie Howard (*Prof. Horatio Smith*), Francis L. Sullivan (*Gen. von Graum*), Mary Morris (*Ludmilla Koslowski*), Hugh McDermott (*David Maxwell*), Raymond Huntley (*Marx*), Manning Whiley (*Bertie Gregson*), Peter Gawthorne (*Sidimir Koslowski*), Allan Jeayes (*Dr. Beckendorf*), Dennis Arundell (*Hoffman*), Joan Kemp-Welch (*Teacher*)

p, Leslie Howard; d, Leslie Howard; w, Anatole de Grunwald, Roland Pertwee, Ian Dalrymple (based on a story by A.G. MacDonnell, Wolfgang Wilhelm); ph, Mutz Greenbaum; ed, Douglas Myers; m, John Greenwood

Leslie Howard more or less reprises his most famous swashbuckling role, that of THE SCARLET PIMPERNEL, as that tale of disguise and rescue is transplanted from Paris during the Reign of Terror to Germany under the Nazis. Prof. Horatio Smith (Howard), an absent-minded professor of archaeology, is supposedly involved in the search for Aryan artifacts near Switzerland, but secretly he runs refugees over the border to safety while disguising himself in a bewildering variety of get-ups. Meanwhile, Gen. von Graum (Francis L. Sullivan), a corpulent Gestapo officer, sets out to stop the elusive "Pimpernel." Eventually Smith's students figure out what their professor is up to and help him smuggle a large group of persecuted scientists across the border. Smith then goes back one more time, all the way to Berlin, to free Ludmilla Koslowski (Mary Morris), a young woman being held by the Gestapo. This was Howard's first solo directorial effort (he codirected PYGMALION earlier) and he does a creditable job, keeping the film moving with the right mixture of action and suave, stiff-upper-lip heroism; however, his relaxed acting and immensely likable screen presence are what carry the film.

PINK FLOYD—THE WALL

1982   99m   c   ★★
Musical   R/15
Tin Blue/Goldcrest   (U.K.)

Bob Geldof (*Pink*), Christine Hargreaves (*Pink's Mother*), James Laurenson (*Pink's Father*), Eleanor David (*Pink's Wife*), Kevin McKeon (*Young Pink*), Bob Hoskins (*Rock 'n' Roll Manager*), David Bingham (*Little Pink*), Jenny Wright (*American Groupie*), Alex McAvoy (*Teacher*), Ellis Dale (*English Doctor*) p, Alan Marshall; d, Alan Parker; w, Roger Waters (based on the album "The Wall" by Pink Floyd); ph, Peter Biziou (Metrocolor); ed, Gerry Hambling; prod d, Brian Morris; art d, Chris Burke, Clinton Cavers; fx, Martin Gutheridge, Graham Longhurst; anim, Gerald Scarfe

This overlong, tedious film based on the multimillion-selling record album by Pink Floyd stars Boomtown Rats singer and "Live Aid" organizer Bob Geldof as Pink, a successful, narcissistic, and wholly unsympathetic rock star on the verge of burnout. Driven to the edge by the news that his wife has left him for another man, Pink spirals into a neurotic conglomeration of flashbacks and fantasies detailing his life. A child of WWII, he grows up amidst the horrors and ruins of wartime Britain. Eventually he becomes a star singer, in the process discovering his power to manipulate a crowd for his own satisfaction (much as his own schoolteachers manipulated and dehumanized him when he was a boy). Cut off from human feeling, Pink slowly builds a wall around himself to deflect suffering. While the music may be interesting and effective on vinyl, on film it becomes repetitious and pretentious, despite director Alan Parker's flair for flashy visuals. Thematically the film is banal, and even its simple themes of alienation, loneliness, and paranoia are muddled and sapped of relevancy by the overblown treatment. Geldof is effective in the lead, and the animation sequences by political cartoonist Gerald Scarfe are interesting and well executed, though too long. Rabid Pink Floyd fans have supported this film enthusiastically since its inception and look upon it as one of the greatest rock 'n' roll films of all times (it isn't).

PINK PANTHER, THE

1964 113m c   ★★★½
Comedy   /PG
Mirisch/G&E

David Niven (Sir Charles Lytton), Peter Sellers (Inspector Jacques Clouseau), Robert Wagner (George Lytton), Capucine (Simone Clouseau), Claudia Cardinale (Princess Dala), Brenda de Banzie (Angela Dunning), Fran Jeffries (Greek "Cousin"), Colin Gordon (Tucker), John Le Mesurier (Defense Attorney), James Lanphier (Saloud)

p, Martin Jurow; d, Blake Edwards; w, Blake Edwards, Maurice Richlin; ph, Philip Lathrop (Technirama, Technicolor); ed, Ralph E. Winters, Marshall M. Borden, David Zinnemann; m, Henry Mancini; art d, Fernando Carrere; fx, Lee Zavitz; chor, Hermes Pan; cos, Yves Saint-Laurent

Writer-director Blake Edwards hit paydirt with the character of Inspector Clouseau, a Tati-like police inspector in an over-large trenchcoat who is sublimely indifferent to the physical realities that surround him. Peter Sellers brought magnificent life to the character and it lasted through a number of movies until Sellers' death. (Clouseau has occasionally been played by others.) This was the first of the long-running series. What most people don't recall is that the "Pink Panther" referred to in the film titles was not Sellers but the name of a legendary jewel. When the cartoon-series shorts based on the movie featured a panther as the title character, however—and the classic Mancini theme caught the ear of the public—Sellers and the title became confused in the minds of viewers. The sequel movies traded on the mix-up and always used the same cartoon treatment for the titles.

Niven, in a role not unlike his RAFFLES character (or the part played by Cary Grant in TO CATCH A THIEF almost a decade before), is a famous jewel thief who is suave beyond belief, fairly dripping with sophistication. He is vacationing at the Alpine resort of Cortina D'Ampezzo, where all the skiers are swathed in clothes by famous French designers. One of the guests is Cardinale, an Indian princess who owns the famous "Pink Panther" gem, a bauble of immeasurable price. Niven wants the jewel and will stop at nothing to get it. He has been the scourge of Interpol for the previous 15 years, as he's pulled off one daring robbery after another. All that time, Niven has been tailed by Sellers, a French inspector, who also wants to nail Niven's female accomplice. The fact that Sellers can never seem to catch up with Niven must have something to do with the fact that his wife, Capucine, is Niven's lover and is therefore able to alert Niven before Sellers can nab him. Meanwhile, Niven's American-born nephew, Wagner, is being supported by his uncle under the pretext that he is a college student. Wagner seems, however, to have inherited a predisposition for his uncle's "occupation." Niven is moving in on Cardinale and the gem when Wagner arrives, also intent on purloining the "Panther."

Though he has less time on screen than the other principals, Sellers stole the film. The ensuing follow-up pictures proved his staying power. Gorgeous photography and sets, huge guffaws, and lots of fun. Sequels included A SHOT IN THE DARK, INSPECTOR CLOUSEAU (Alan Arkin in the lead), THE RETURN OF THE PINK PANTHER, THE REVENGE OF THE PINK PANTHER, THE PINK PANTHER STRIKES AGAIN. Mancini stuck around to do the music for all and took an Oscar nomination for this one, his first in the series.

PINK PANTHER STRIKES AGAIN, THE

1976 103m c   ★★★
Comedy   PG
Amjo (U.K.)

Peter Sellers (Inspector Jacques Clouseau), Herbert Lom (Ex-Chief Inspector Dreyfus), Colin Blakely (Alex Drummond), Leonard Rossiter (Quinlan), Lesley-Anne Down (Olga), Burt Kwouk (Kato), Andre Maranne (Francois), Richard Vernon (Dr. Hugo Fassbender), Michael Robbins (Jarvis), Briony McRoberts (Margo Fassbender)

p, Blake Edwards; d, Blake Edwards; w, Blake Edwards, Frank Waldman; ph, Harry Waxman (Panavision, DeLuxe Color); ed, Alan Jones; m, Henry Mancini; prod d, Peter Mullins; art d, John Siddall; fx, Kit West

Director Edwards and co-author Maurice Richlin created the Clouseau character in the first PINK PANTHER picture, and in 1974 THE RETURN OF THE PINK PANTHER took in huge amounts at the theaters. Consequently, this one was rushed out to take advantage of the wave, and it looks it. That's not to say that there aren't plenty of laughs in the picture, but it lacks a credible story, something that was present in the earlier ones. Lom, the head of the French police, has been driven mad by Sellers's behavior and is now incarcerated, with Sellers in his fourth Clouseau movie, sitting in the chief's seat. Lom escapes, kidnaps scientist Vernon, who has invented a "death ray," and he threatens to use it to end the world unless the authorities see fit to turn over Sellers to Lom. With the future of the world at stake, the US and the USSR are consulted. Byron Kane and Dick Crockett are Henry Kissinger and Gerald Ford, while Down plays a Soviet spy who is put on the case but defects, NINOTCHKA-style, because she falls in love with Sellers. There are some marvelous sight gags, but the film goes over the top into mindless farce at times, destroying much of the Chaplinesque believability that Sellers had earlier engendered. Mancini and Don Black teamed on "Come To Me" (sung by Tom Jones) to get an Oscar nomination, the only notice the picture had from the Academy. Nevertheless, it took in almost $20 million, even more than THE RETURN OF THE PINK PANTHER, which was a better film. The titles were again cartoons and including the names of Jackie Cooper, Howard K. Smith, and Marne Maitland, all of whom were cut from the final release print. Omar Sharif does a cameo as an Egyptian killer.

PINKY

1949   102m   bw   ★★★★
Drama   /A
FOX

Jeanne Crain *(Pinky, Patricia Johnson)*, Ethel Barrymore *(Miss Em)*, Ethel Waters *(Granny Dysey Johnson)*, William Lundigan *(Dr. Thomas Adams)*, Basil Ruysdael *(Judge Walker)*, Kenny Washington *(Dr. Canady)*, Nina Mae McKinney *(Rozelia)*, Griff Barnett *(Dr. Joe McGill)*, Frederick O'Neal *(Jake Walters)*, Evelyn Varden *(Melba Wooley)*

p, Darryl F. Zanuck; d, Elia Kazan; w, Philip Dunne, Dudley Nichols (based on the novel *Quality* by Cid Ricketts Sumner); ph, Joseph MacDonald; ed, Harmon Jones; m, Alfred Newman; art d, Lyle Wheeler, J. Russell Spencer; cos, Charles LeMaire

Producer Darryl F. Zanuck, who had attacked anti-Semitism in GENTLEMAN'S AGREEMENT in 1947, tackled the subject of prejudice against African Americans in this film. Crain plays the eponymous Pinky (a term used in the black community to described those whose complexions are light enough that they can pass for white), a bright young woman who has been studying nursing at a school in New England. Lundigan, a white physician, would like to marry her, but Crain believes the interracial union could never work, suspects Lundigan of being more "tolerant" than committed, and is unwilling to be absorbed into the white world. Sadly, she leaves and returns to the southern town of her birth. Crain's grandmother, Waters, works for feisty dowager Barrymore, and when the old woman becomes ill, Crain becomes her nurse and stays on until her death. Barrymore leaves her estate to Crain, but her family contests the legacy because Crain is black, claiming that Crain exerted undue influence on the dying Barrymore. The dispute is taken to court, where Crain wins the estate. Afterwards, she turns it into a nursing home and school for blacks. Zanuck initially asked John Ford to direct PINKY, but he was reportedly relieved, nevertheless, when Ford (who didn't get along with actress Waters and felt little enthusiasm for the story) asked to be taken off the picture two weeks into shooting, since Zanuck had misgivings about Ford's ability to create credible black characters. After Ford's exit, Zanuck immediately called in Elia Kazan; eight weeks later the film was completed, Ford's footage totally scrapped. Today, PINKY is still remarkable for its sincerity and directness, especially when one considers its date of origin. This is a mature film, with great respect for the humanity of people who are able to transcend social barriers and care for one another. Crain, Waters, and Barrymore all received Oscar nominations for their performances.

PINOCCHIO

1940   88m   c   ★★★★★
Children's/Fantasy/Animated   /U
Disney

VOICES OF: Dick Jones *(Pinocchio)*, Christian Rub *(Geppetto)*, Cliff Edwards *(Jiminy Cricket)*, Evelyn Venable *(The Blue Fairy)*, Walter Catlett *(J. Worthington Foulfellow)*, Frankie Darro *(Lampwick)*, Charles Judels *(Stromboli the Coachman)*, Don Brodie *(Barker)*

p, Walt Disney; d, Ben Sharpsteen, Hamilton Luske; w, Ted Sears, Otto Englander, Webb Smith, William Cottrell, Joseph Sabo, Erdman Penner, Aurelius Battaglia (based on the story by Carlo Collodi); m, Paul J. Smith; art d, Charles Philippi, Hugh Hennesy, Dick Kelsey, Terrell Stapp, John Hubley, Ken Anderson, Kendall O'Connor, Thor Putnam, McLaren Stewart, Al Zinnen; anim, John Lounsbery, Charles A. Nichols, Art Palmer, Fred Moore, Eric Larson, Milt Kahl, Ward Kimball, Franklin Thomas, Vladimir Tytla, Arthur Babbitt, Wolfgang Reitherman

This was Disney's second full-length animated feature and it may well the greatest of the studio's cartoon classics. A technical tour de force, PINOCCHIO was brilliantly crafted with an awesome attention to detail and verisimilitude. This film showcased all of Disney's innovative techniques when they were still fresh. The episodic story of the wooden puppet who earns real life by learning to be a good person was an unusual but inspired choice for adaptation. Emotionally rich, humorous, and periodically terrifying, the film offers images so startling and memorable that generations of children have been enthralled by it.

This timeless story focuses on a wooden puppet that wants nothing more than to be a real boy, a wish echoed by his creator, Geppetto. One night, the Blue Fairy descends from the skies and promises to turn Pinocchio into a flesh-and-blood little boy if he swears to be brave and unselfish and to learn right from wrong. The Blue Fairy even assigns Pinocchio a conscience, in the form of Jiminy Cricket. This is, of course, the film that features what would become the Disney theme song, "When You Wish upon a Star," sung by the inimitable Cliff Edwards, the voice of Jiminy Cricket. Pinocchio must undergo many harrowing life lessons before his dream comes true.

PINOCCHIO boasts the first extensive use of the Disney-developed multiplane camera. This allows for a convincing illusion that the animation camera is actually moving in three dimensions through different planes of action in the way a dolly or tracking shot functions in a live action film. The animators have further refined their animation of human figures which had still been a bit shaky in their first feature, SNOW WHITE. With both FANTASIA and PINOCCHIO in release in 1940, the future must have seemed bright and interesting at the Disney studios. Then came DUMBO, BAMBI, the studio strike, WWII, and a long stretch of declining success with animated features from which Disney was not able to recover artistically. Some would argue did this recovery finally occured with the release of THE LITTLE MERMAID but this film and BEAUTY AND THE BEAST were, at best, a return to form rather than new plateaus for the animated feature. See PINOCCHIO again and again. A marvel and a joy to behold, it's the real thing. It's the stuff that dreams—and nightmares—are made of.

PIRATE, THE

1948   102m   c   ★★★½
Musical   /U
MGM

Judy Garland *(Manuela)*, Gene Kelly *(Serafin)*, Walter Slezak *(Don Pedro Vargas)*, Gladys Cooper *(Aunt Inez)*, Reginald Owen *(The Advocate)*, George Zucco *(The Viceroy)*, The Nicholas Brothers *(Specialty Dancers)*, Lester Allen *(Uncle Capucho)*, Lola Deem *(Isabella)*, Ellen Ross *(Mercedes)* p, Arthur Freed; d, Vincente Minnelli; w, Albert Hackett, Frances Goodrich, Joseph L. Mankiewicz (uncredited), Joseph Than, Lillian Braun, Anita Loos, Wilkie Mahoney (based on a play by S.N. Behrman); ph, Harry Stradling (Technicolor); ed, Blanche Sewell; m, Cole Porter; art d, Cedric Gibbons, Jack Martin Smith; chor, Robert Alton, Gene Kelly; cos, Tom Keogh, Barbara Karinska

The story is wearisome and the acting fever-pitched, but the music and dancing in this colorful film are spectacular. The setting is the Caribbean Island of San Sebastian in the 1820s, where young Manuela (Judy Garland) fantasizes about the notorious pirate Macoco, better known as "Mack the Black." Serafin (Gene Kelly), a strolling minstrel, falls in love with Manuela, and tries to win her heart by impersonating Macoco. Meanwhile, Don Pedro (Walter Slezak), the mayor of the town and Manuela's fiance by arrangement, schemes against Serafin, who nonetheless persists in his charade, boldly demanding that the town hand Manuela over to him or he will let loose his fierce pirates. Manuela discovers his fraud, however, and a knock-down, drag-out fight between the fiery lovers takes place while they sing/shout Cole Porter's "Love of My Life." To his peril, Serafin learns that Don Pedro is *really* Macoco incognito; Manuela, however, has never known this and is by now hopelessly in love with the street performer. Eventually, she joins his troupe of players, ending the film with a reprise of "Be a Clown" in which Garland and Kelly sing and dance with several of their teeth blackened and big red noses gleaming. THE PIRATE is an old-fashioned lavish MGM musical, dripping with lush color and peppered with wonderful numbers. Little care is given to the script and the dramatics, but the film is a scenic treat, offering magnificent sets and a frenetic pace typical of director Vincente Minnelli (then Garland's husband). Filming was slowed down considerably by Garland's emotional illness; she was on the verge of a breakdown and delayed the proceedings with paranoiac attacks directed at Minnelli, Kelly, and Porter. Though THE PIRATE cost MGM $3,768,000 and earned back only $2,290,000 in its initial release, it ranks high among movie cultists today, chiefly for its extravagant choreography, especially in the sweeping "Nina" and "Mack the Black" numbers, danced energetically by Kelly. A special treat is the appearance of the Nicholas Brothers, who dance with Kelly in the first "Be a Clown" number; they were edited out of this scene in southern theaters at the time of release. Other songs: "You Can Do No Wrong" (Porter), "Sweet Ices, Papayas, Berry Man," "Sea Wall," "Serafin" (Roger Edens), "The Ring," "Judy Awakens," "Not Again," "The Tight Rope" (Lennie Hayton), "Gene Meets Mack the Black," "The Mast" (Conrad Salinger), "Voodoo" (Porter, deleted), "Manuela" (Porter, not used).

PIT AND THE PENDULUM, THE

1961 85m c   ★★★½
Horror   /15
Alta Vista

Vincent Price *(Nicholas Medina)*, John Kerr *(Francis Barnard)*, Barbara Steele *(Elisabeth Barnard Medina)*, Luana Anders *(Catherine Medina)*, Anthony Carbone *(Dr. Charles Leon)*, Patrick Westwood *(Maximillian the Butler)*, Lynn Bernay *(Maria)*, Larry Turner *(Nicholas as a Child)*, Mary Menzies *(Isabella)*, Charles Victor *(Bartolome)*

p, Roger Corman; d, Roger Corman; w, Richard Matheson (based on a story by Edgar Allan Poe); ph, Floyd Crosby (Panavision, Pathe Color); ed, Anthony Carras; m, Les Baxter; prod d, Daniel Haller; art d, Daniel Haller; fx, Pat Dinga; cos, Marjorie Corso

The second and one of the best films in Roger Corman's Edgar Allan Poe series stars Vincent Price as Nicholas Medina, owner of a large and spooky castle with an elaborate torture chamber built by his father during the Spanish Inquisition. Stricken with grief after the death of his wife, Elisabeth (Barbara Steele, in her American film debut), Nicholas becomes obsessed with the notion that he accidentally buried her alive. Elisabeth's brother, Francis Barnard (John Kerr), suspects foul play and travels to the castle looking for answers. He finds Nicholas slowly going mad and claiming to hear Elisabeth's voice calling to him. Eventually it is revealed that Elisabeth is not dead at all, but has conspired with her lover, family doctor Charles Leon (Anthony Carbone), to drive her husband insane. Corman brought in THE PIT AND THE PENDULUM on a 15-day shooting schedule, and the result is a very entertaining horror film with chills, humor, and a bravura performance by Price, who was just beginning to finely hone his wickedly delightful, villainous characters. Shot in lush and almost garish color by cinematographer Floyd Crosby (who also shot Corman's previous Poe film, THE HOUSE OF USHER), the picture includes some impressive techniques and camera movement. Screenwriter Richard Matheson did a fine job of adapting Poe's rather limited (for films) short story by saving the dungeon sequences for the climax and then creating a rather interesting plot line to lead up to it. One of Corman's and AIP's best.

PIXOTE

1981 127m c   ★★★★½
Drama   /18
Embrafilm (Brazil)

Fernando Ramos da Silva *(Pixote)*, Marilia Pera *(Sueli)*, Jorge Juliao *(Lilica)*, Gilberto Moura *(Dito)*, Jose Nilson dos Santos *(Diego)*, Edilson Lino *(Chico)*, Zenildo Oliveira Santos *(Fumaca)*, Claudio Bernardo *(Garatao)*, Tony Tornado *(Cristal)*, Jardel Filho *(Sapatos Brancos)*

p, Paulo Francini; d, Hector Babenco; w, Hector Babenco, Jorge Duran (based on the novel *Infancia Dos Martos* by Jose Louzeiro); ph, Rodolfo Sanchez; ed, Luiz Elias; m, John Neschling; art d, Clovis Bueno

This grim, disturbing, and engrossing Brazilian film set in the slums of Sao Paulo tells the disheartening tale of Pixote (da Silva), a boy abandoned by his parents, who becomes a streetwise pimp and eventually a murderer by the age of 10. One of the most powerful films ever made about children in the city, PIXOTE depicts a life of unrelenting violence and hopelessness. Director Babenco does not flinch from the squalor of these boys' lives: the violence in the reformatory; an aborted baby in a bucket in a bathroom; the young hero suddenly reverting to near-infancy, suckling at the breast of a momentarily sympathetic prostitute. This film obviously draws on famous earlier films in which the innocence of youth is brutally stripped from their very beings. Rossellini (GERMANY YEAR ZERO) and Truffaut (THE 400 BLOWS), for example, have explored aspects of this social phenomenon. In PIXOTE, Babenco successfully combines neorealism's documentary approach with an often surreal visual context. In this respect his closest stylistic inspiration is Bunuel, whose brilliant LOS OLVIDADOS was the most obvious influence on this film. What separates an extremely fine film from a great one is that Babenco pulls back in ways that Bunuel never does. The framing of the story is the perhaps the most notable example, but also consider the brief vignette at the prison in which the children gaze at a statue of the Virgin Mary. Babenco doesn't take it anywhere; he just lets the moment hang in midair.

PIZZA TRIANGLE, THE

He see religion as a moment of respite but really doesn't seem to think it would help matters much, and yet he's not critical either. One can find other such scenes in which Babenco substitutes the impact of the moment for a sustained critical and cultural examination. This is precisely what prevents PIXOTE from achieving its formidable potential. That said, this overwhelming film should be required viewing for everyone who thinks she or he has any idea of how children are forced to live in most of the world today. What is most ironic is that the tragedy of PIXOTE is not make-believe: in 1986, da Silva was killed in a shootout with police after allegedly resisting arrest for an assault.

PIZZA TRIANGLE, THE
(DRAMMA DELLA GELOSIA—TUTTI I PARTICOLARI IN CRONACA)
1970 99m c ★★½
Comedy/Drama R/
Dean/Jupiter Generale/Midega (Italy/Spain)

Marcello Mastroianni (Oreste), Monica Vitti (Adelaide), Giancarlo Giannini (Nello), Manuel Zarzo (Uto), Marisa Merlini (Silvana), Hercules Cortes (Ambleto Di Meo), Fernando Sanchez Polack (District Head of Communist Party), Gioia Desideri (Adelaide's Friend), Juan Diego (Antonia's Son), Bruno Scipioni (Pizza Maker)

p, Pio Angeletti, Adriano De Micheli; d, Ettore Scola; w, Furio Scarpelli, Agenore Incrocci, Ettore Scola (based on the story "Jealousy Italian Style" by Agenore Incrocci, Furio Scarpelli); ph, Carlo Di Palma (Panavision, Technicolor); ed, Alberto Gallitti; m, Armando Trovajoli; art d, Luciano Ricceri; cos, Ezio Altieri

Despite the fact that Mastroianni won Best Actor at the Cannes Film Festival for his performance here, THE PIZZA TRIANGLE is just another dreary Italian sex farce. Vitti plays a beguiling flower vendor with whom bricklayer Mastroianni falls in love. After a few blissful weeks, Vitti strikes up a torid affair with the bricklayer's friend, Giannini, a pizza baker. When this affair is discovered, the former friends come to blows and Vitti attempts suicide because she cannot decide between the two men. But failing to kill herself, she goes off to live in seclusion with kindly butcher Cortes. When she learns that Giannini has also attempted suicide, Vitti rushes back to tell him that they will marry. Upon leaving the hospital, the couple bumps into Mastroianni, who is now a bum. Another fight breaks out between the men, but this time Vitti is accidentally killed by Mastroianni with her own flower shears.

PLACE IN THE SUN, A
1951 122m bw ★★★★
Drama /A
Paramount

Montgomery Clift (George Eastman), Elizabeth Taylor (Angela Vickers), Shelley Winters (Alice Tripp), Anne Revere (Hannah Eastman), Keefe Brasselle (Earl Eastman), Fred Clark (Bellows), Raymond Burr (Marlowe), Herbert Heyes (Charles Eastman), Shepperd Strudwick (Anthony Vickers), Frieda Inescort (Mrs. Vickers)

p, George Stevens; d, George Stevens; w, Michael Wilson, Harry Brown (based on the novel An American Tragedy by Theodore Dreiser and the play by Patrick Kearney); ph, William Mellor; ed, William Hornbeck; m, Franz Waxman; art d, Hans Dreier, Walter Tyler; fx, Gordon Jennings; cos, Edith Head

Ponderous version of Dreiser's An American Tragedy transfers the mood of intent to murder for upward mobility, to intent to murder for prettier girlfriend. That said, we think he deserves to fry. Clift, whom we almost unreservedly admire, may have been just a touch callow for the role—but Stevens knows how this quality can be used to read opportunistic. Elizabeth Taylor, here at the peak of her MGM-sorority, debutante beauty, is so startlingly lovely and Shelley Winters so actressed in loser drabness that the issues get too black and white. Indeed, this small town has no middle class. It's depression cartoony—but without the depression setting which made it potent. Stevens fills in with 1950s psychobabble touches, enhanced by the sun disappearing for good behind a cloud, and the lurching, lonely cry of loons.

The film opens with Clift on a highway trying to hitch a ride. Taylor drives past him in a shiny sports car, beeps her horn in a flirtatious manner, and keeps going. Clift gapes after her, awed by her stunning beauty. When Clift arrives in the city looking for a job in his uncle's bathing-suit factory, he is amazed to discover that Taylor is his cousin. The uncle, Heyes, puts Clift to work in the factory, giving him a menial job, but providing the young man with the security Clift's doting mother, Revere, has prayed for. Clift looks from afar at the grand life style, the foreign cars, clothes, and the estate of Heyes and Taylor and, goaded by unbridled ambition, decides to reach upward into a forbidden caste system for acceptance. Meanwhile, he combats his loneliness by getting involved with Winters, who works in the factory. As his affair with low-life Winters deepens, so does Clift's association with Heyes and his upper-crust family. Clift is invited to a party at Heyes's mansion where he meets and instantly falls in love with the ravishing Taylor, and she with him. In a whirlwind of torrid trysts, Clift and Taylor fall so deeply in love that they plan to wed. Clift is on the verge of elevating himself from the lower class into the super rich, a poor boy about to make good, but Winters dashes his plans by telling Clift that she is pregnant and insisting that he marry her.

This powerful examination of a man's soul was first filmed in 1931 by Josef von Sternberg, who presented the story in a stark and realistic manner. However, through some of the most stunning visuals ever created, Stevens has gone beyond the story and encompassed a have-not generation in the form of Clift. The closeup love scenes—enormous blowups of Clift and Taylor kissing passionately—are so intimate they drown the viewer's emotions. Stevens does not shrink from the story or any of the characters, and his cameras continually draw closer, revealing innermost emotions. Clift is both sensitive and so greedy for love that he is pitiable. His characterization is less calculating than the initial filmic portrayal of that character by Phillips Holmes in the 1931 version.

The cumulative impact of the Stevens film is overwhelming (even if the overly long treatment gets you restless). Mellor's restless cameras fully capture the starkly realistic mood and ambiance of the story and background, while Waxman's score superbly complements the overall production. Stevens filmed A PLACE IN THE SUN at Lake Tahoe during the winter months and, to get rid of snow for summer scenes, expensive melting machines were brought in. Though the weather was very cold, Taylor swam in the lake, water skied, and appeared sultry in a skimpy bathing suit. She was only 17 when Stevens cast her in her rich-girl role, but the studio tried to promote a romance between the young actress and Clift. That romance didn't require much prompting, however; Clift fell in love with his leading lady and helped her through her most difficult scenes. Their performances, especially when they're on screen together, are breathtaking, like watching incestous fraternal twins make love.

Winters, as the poor girl scorned, began her journey from B-bombshell to character actress. When Winters was first suggested for the role, Stevens refused to consider her. Then Winters lobbied for the rejected lover role through powerful friends; even writer Norman Mailer sent Stevens a letter asking him to consider the actress. Stevens agreed to meet Winters at a restaurant and when he walked in, there she sat, drab, plainly dressed, no makeup on, so shy and retiring that the director didn't at first recognize the woman who had played brassy blondes for years. He said he would give her the part if she would do a screen test. Winters agreed, but every time the test was to be shot, she found some excuse to be absent. Stevens steamed but gave Winters the part anyway and during the production the director so hounded her into playing the distasteful, vulgar, repulsive other woman that Winters refused to talk to him. This role became so indelibly linked to Winters that directors for years to come would have her play no other kind of role.

Stevens made the film in his usual painstaking fashion, spending more than $2.5 million and using more than 400,000 feet of film. Yet the film was a huge box-office success and received universal critical acclaim. This was Paramount's prestige film of 1951, and it has since become a classic. Stevens won an Oscar for Best Direction, and the movie also took Oscars for Best Screenplay, Best Cinematography, Best Editing, Best Musical Score, and Best Costume Design. Revere, as the coddling but dominating mother to the troubled Clift, made her last screen appearance with A PLACE IN THE SUN. She was branded a communist by the House Un-American Activities Committee and her career disintegrated.

Like Dreiser's extraordinary novel, the film was based on the murder of Grace Brown by her social-climbing boyfriend Chester Gillette, at Big Moose Lake, New York, in 1906. Dreiser personally sat through Gillette's macabre trial and noted that while the killer awaited execution, he sold photos of himself to admiring young ladies so he could have catered meals brought to his cell.

PLACES IN THE HEART
1984 112m c ★★★½
Drama PG
Tri-Star

Sally Field (Edna Spalding), Lindsay Crouse (Margaret Lomax), Ed Harris (Wayne Lomax), Amy Madigan (Viola Kelsey), John Malkovich (Mr. Will), Danny Glover (Moze), Yankton Hatten (Frank), Gennie James (Possum), Lane Smith (Albert Denby), Terry O'Quinn (Buddy Kelsey)

p, Arlene Donovan; d, Robert Benton; w, Robert Benton; ph, Nestor Almendros (Technicolor); ed, Carol Littleton; m, John Kander, Howard Shore; prod d, Gene Callahan; art d, Sydney Z. Litwack; fx, Bran Ferren; cos, Ann Roth

Set in Texas in 1930, this film stars Sally Field as Edna Spalding, a mother of two whose lawman-husband has just been killed by a drunk. Near penniless, she is stunned to learn that the bank is about to foreclose on her property, which includes a 40-acre cotton field. Determined to keep her home, she decides to plant and harvest the cotton, though she's ill equipped to do so. She hires wandering laborer Moze (Danny Glover) to help and takes in blind boarder Mr. Will (John Malkovich) to generate some cash, and the little group struggles to make a go of it. Director Robert Benton (KRAMER VS. KRAMER) effectively re-creates depression-era Texas in this moving tale that landed the second Oscar for Field (her first came for NORMA RAE). Malkovich's terrific performance generated an Oscar nomina-

tion, while Benton was nominated for Best Director and Best Screenplay, winning the latter. The film was also nominated as Best Picture but lost to AMADEUS.

PLANES, TRAINS AND AUTOMOBILES
1987 93m c ★★★
Comedy R/15
Paramount

Steve Martin (Neal Page), John Candy (Del Griffith), Laila Robins (Susan Page), Michael McKean (State Trooper), Kevin Bacon (Taxi Racer), Dylan Baker (Owen), Carol Bruce (Joy Page), Olivia Burnette (Marti), Diana Douglas (Peg), William Windom (Boss)

p, John Hughes; d, John Hughes; w, John Hughes; ph, Don Peterman (Technicolor); ed, Paul Hirsch; m, Ira Newborn; prod d, John W. Corso; art d, Harold Michelson; cos, April Ferry

The guru of teenager movies, John Hughes, enters the world of adults with this seasonal comedy based on the horrors of transportation in America. Two days before Thanksgiving, yuppie marketing consultant Neal Page (Steve Martin) races from Manhattan to catch a plane home to Chicago, only to find that his flight has been delayed. Hours later, he boards the plane and ends up next to Del Griffith (John Candy), a huge slob wearing a polyester suit. When the flight is detoured to Wichita, it's just the beginning of Page's trip and his association with Griffith. With a concept as thin as this, PLANES, TRAINS AND AUTOMOBILES could have easily become a repetitious bore. Instead, producer-director-writer Hughes infuses his film with an appealing sense of sentiment and humanity—not to mention many hilarious scenes. Candy finally has a bravura role and proves himself to be not only a superb comedian but also a fine actor. Martin, in the less flamboyant of the two roles, is excellent as well. Hughes's insistence on cramming the film with a glut of pop songs (which in most cases do nothing to complement the action) is unfortunate.

PLANET OF THE APES
1968 112m c ★★★★
Science Fiction G/PG
Apjac

Charlton Heston (George Taylor), Roddy McDowall (Cornelius), Kim Hunter (Dr. Zira), Maurice Evans (Dr. Zaius), James Whitmore (President of the Assembly), James Daly (Honorius), Linda Harrison (Nova), Robert Gunner (Landon), Lou Wagner (Lucius), Woodrow Parfrey (Maximus)

p, Arthur P. Jacobs; d, Franklin J. Schaffner; w, Michael Wilson, Rod Serling (based on the novel Monkey Planet by Pierre Boulle); ph, Leon Shamroy (Panavision, Deluxe Color); ed, Hugh S. Fowler; m, Jerry Goldsmith; art d, Jack Martin Smith, William Creber; fx, John Chambers, L.B. Abbott, Art Cruickshank, Emil Kosa, Jr.; cos, Morton Haack

An outstanding science-fiction film that spawned four sequels (BENEATH THE PLANET OF THE APES, ESCAPE FROM THE PLANET OF THE APES, CONQUEST OF THE PLANET OF THE APES, and BATTLE FOR THE PLANET OF THE APES), an animated cartoon series, a live-action television series, bubble-gum cards, Halloween masks, plastic models, bendable toys, etc. Massive marketing notwithstanding, the original film is still quite an artistic achievement. Heston plays the commander of a lengthy outer-space mission that is interrupted when the spaceship crashes on an unknown planet. The three survivors, Heston, Gunner, and Jeff Burton, make their way through an arid wasteland into a lush forest where they observe what appears to be a tribe of human beings in the throes of the Stone Age. The astronauts join the speechless humans and forage for food. Suddenly a bizarre horn cries, and the sounds of hoofbeats and gunfire are heard, sending the savage humans running into the woods. The confused astronauts are shocked to see that the armed horsemen are actually gorillas wearing strange-looking pseudomilitary gear. The apes employ nets to gather up dozens of the humans and lock them in large cages. While attempting to escape, Heston is shot in the throat, rendering him as speechless as the primitive people. Captured, Heston is brought to the ape town along with the rest of the trapped humans and thrown into a cage. His comrades have not fared as well. Jeff Burton was killed in the hunt, and Gunner, who could still speak, was given a lobotomy by the orangutan scientist and leader, Evans, to silence him. While in his cage, Heston is befriended by peaceful chimpanzee scientists Hunter and McDowall, who are convinced that the astronaut's frustrated pantomimes are a sure sign of superior intelligence. Evans knows the truth, however, and blocks their efforts to study Heston more closely. At one point, Heston tries to escape and is recaptured, but he manages to yell, "Take your stinking paws off me, you damn dirty ape!" This vocal outburst sends shock waves throughout the ape community, and soon Evans moves to have Heston destroyed. With the help of Hunter and McDowall, Heston escapes and ventures into the Forbidden Zone where McDowall began an archeological dig yielding some strange evidence regarding the evolution of "ape-kind." Pursued by Evans and his gorilla soldiers, Heston manages to nab the ape leader and hold him hostage in the dig site. There, Heston forces Evans to reveal that humans once did rule the planet, but their stupid, animalistic tendencies led to a war that destroyed them, leaving the apes to take over. Since then the wiser apes have desperately tried to prevent the violent humans from taking over again. Having extracted the truth from Evans, Heston steals a horse and rides off into the Forbidden Zone alone, despite warnings from Evans that he won't like what he'll find. A few miles up the beach Heston sees something that makes him drop to his knees and pound on the sand in a frustrated rage, yelling, "You bastards! You finally did it! You blew it up! Damn you all to hell!" The camera pans up to reveal the battered Statue of Liberty, waist-deep in sand. Heston has been on Earth all along.

PLANET OF THE APES is a success on all levels. The script by Rod Serling is a marvel of twisted logic containing insightful moments of social parody and grim forebodings regarding the future of mankind. The production values are superb. The set design and costumes were something that audiences had never seen before and created a unique, detailed world that helped audiences accept the odd premise of the film. Most praised, and rightly so, was Chambers's special makeup that transformed human actors into living apes. By using a special latex application, Chambers allowed the actors a full range of facial expressions that aided greatly in creating the illusion of an ape society. He received an Oscar for his special process, becoming one of the few makeup artists ever honored by the Academy. These production elements, combined with Shamroy's stunning cinematography, Goldsmith's Oscar-nominated haunting musical score, and a wonderful cast of performers who rose to the occasion, captured the imaginations of moviegoers throughout the world. Unfortunately, the sequels to PLANET OF THE APES (except the fairly interesting BENEATH THE PLANET OF THE APES and CONQUEST OF THE PLANET OF THE APES) are pretty lame and lack the spark of imagination that fueled the original. Perhaps because of the unparalleled marketing push, the

"Apes" series spiraled into gross self-parody that made even rabid fans a bit sick of the whole thing. One cannot deny, however, that the original film is a superlative example of fantasy filmmaking.

PLATOON
1986 111m c ★★★★
War R/15
Hemdale

Tom Berenger *(Sgt. Barnes)*, Willem Dafoe *(Sgt. Elias)*, Charlie Sheen *(Chris)*, Forest Whitaker *(Big Harold)*, Francesco Quinn *(Rhah)*, John C. McGinley *(Sgt. O'Neill)*, Richard Edson *(Sal)*, Kevin Dillon *(Bunny)*, Reggie Johnson *(Junior)*, Keith David *(King)*

p, Arnold Kopelson; d, Oliver Stone; w, Oliver Stone; ph, Robert Richardson (CFI Color); ed, Claire Simpson; m, Samuel Barber; prod d, Bruno Rubeo; art d, Rodel Cruz, Doris Sherman Williams; fx, Yves De Bono

Chris (Charlie Sheen), a green recruit and child of privilege who dropped out of college and enlisted, finds himself in Vietnam as a member of a platoon divided against itself. On one side is Sgt. Barnes (Tom Berenger), a horribly scarred veteran of several tours of duty—a morally corrupt, remorseless killing machine. The men who follow him seek clear-cut solutions to the complicated realities they face. On the other side is veteran sergeant Elias (Willem Dafoe), who, though equally skilled in the ways of death, still retains some semblance of humanity and attempts to impose a sense of compassion and responsibility on his men. Chris is caught between these two in what he describes as a "battle for possession of my soul."

PLATOON is a shattering experience. Writer-director Stone, a Vietnam veteran, used his first-hand knowledge to create one of the most realistic war films ever made, one whose success lies in the mass of detail Stone brings to the screen, bombarding the senses with vivid sights and sounds that have the feel of actual experience. Stone captures the heat, the dampness, the bugs, the jungle rot, and, most important, the confusion and fear experienced by the average soldier. The men in PLATOON do perform heroic acts on occasion, but the heroism isn't motivated by love of country or idealism—it is motivated by pure terror, by desperation, by a desire to end the madness one way or another. Never before in a war film has stark terror among soldiers been such a tangible, motivating force. There is nothing appealing in Stone's war; it doesn't have a "recruitment flavor." However, while PLATOON has no equal when it comes to capturing the reality of the combat experience, it falters when Stone attempts to apply greater meaning to his vision. The film's battle between the forces of good and evil as represented by the two sergeants is heavy-handed, as is Sheen's totally unnecessary voice-over narration, which dilutes the power of Stone's visuals. On an incredibly low budget of $6.5 million, Stone brought his cast and crew to the Philippines and shot PLATOON in a swift 54 days. To everyone's surprise, the film was a massive hit with the critics and the public, and won Best Picture, Best Director, Best Editing, and Best Sound Academy Awards.

PLAY IT AGAIN, SAM
1972 85m c ★★★½
Comedy PG/15
Apjac/Rollins-Joffe

Woody Allen *(Allan Felix)*, Diane Keaton *(Linda Christie)*, Tony Roberts *(Dick Christie)*, Jerry Lacy *(Humphrey Bogart)*, Susan Anspach *(Nancy Felix)*, Jennifer Salt *(Sharon)*, Joy Bang *(Julie)*,

Viva *(Jennifer)*, Mari Fletcher *(Fantasy Sharon)*, Diana Davila *(Girl in Museum)*

p, Arthur P. Jacobs; d, Herbert Ross; w, Woody Allen (based on the play by Allen); ph, Owen Roizman (Technicolor); ed, Marion Rothman; m, Billy Goldenberg, Max Steiner; prod d, Ed Wittstein; cos, Anna Hill Johnstone

A true film buff's film about a film buff, Allen, who is obsessed with CASABLANCA. The impish, neurotic Allen patterns his personality after Humphrey Bogart but has nothing of the actor's tough guy image. When Allen's wife, Anspach, leaves him she explains that she wants a new life. "You're one of life's great watchers," she tells him. "I'm not like that, I'm a doer." While the distressed Allen laments over his lack of "cool," he is visited by Bogart (Lacy), who sits in a dark corner of the room, wearing his usual trenchcoat and smoking a cigarette. Bogart gives him advice: "Dames are simple. I never met one that didn't understand a slap in the mouth or a slug from a forty-five." To boost his spirits Allen's married friends, Roberts and Keaton, try to fix him up with another girl. They first try the genuinely friendly Salt, who is turned off by Allen's excessive machismo. Next Allen is paired with nymphomaniac Viva, whom he somehow succeeds in turning off. Finally his date with the naive Bang ends with him being beaten by two grizzly bikers, who abduct the girl. After striking out with every girl he meets Allen becomes more and more desperate. When Roberts goes away on his umpteenth business trip Keaton is once again left alone and neglected. She agrees to come over to Allen's apartment and cook dinner. Allen, who is now entertaining thoughts of romance with Keaton, sets the mood with candlelight and champagne. When he gets an opportunity to kiss her, however, he loses courage. Again Bogart appears from nowhere to coach the nervous Allen. On Bogart's urging Allen finally makes his move. Keaton becomes confused, however, and leaves while Allen is professing his love to her. A moment later she returns, and they spend the night together in bed. The following morning a guilt-stricken Keaton struggles with the thought of telling Roberts. Unexpectedly, Roberts returns from a business trip, sensing that Keaton is involved with another man. He tells Allen of his suspicions and confides that he truly loves Keaton. He also threatens to kill her lover if he ever finds out who he is. Keaton realizes she needs Roberts and follows him to the airport, where he is about to leave on another business trip. Allen also rushes to the airport (driven by Bogart, who coaches him along the way) determined to keep his best friend's marriage together. On a fog-filled runway reminiscent of that in CASABLANCA, all three characters stand dressed in their trenchcoats. Realizing that this is a rare chance to act out the finale of CASABLANCA in real life, Allen paraphrases that film's dialogue. He confesses to Roberts that he loves Keaton, but then orders her to get on the plane with her husband. Afterward Bogart commends Allen on his style. Allen learns to believe in himself without relying on Bogart, and the two bid farewell in the fog. As Allen walks away, Bogart delivers his immortal lines, "Here's looking at you, kid."

Based on Allen's Broadway play (Allen, Roberts, Keaton, and Lacy all appeared in the stage version, which opened on February 12th, 1969, and ran for 453 performances), PLAY IT AGAIN, SAM differs somewhat from Allen's previous pictures, TAKE THE MONEY AND RUN and BANANAS. Having helmed those previous films, Allen handed over the directorial reins here to Herbert Ross, a craftsman, but a director who has no recognizable style of his own. What Ross brings to Allen's play is a sense of control and drama as opposed to the slapstick vignettes of TAKE THE MONEY AND RUN and BANANAS. Though Ross's name is in the credits, PLAY IT AGAIN, SAM is clearly Allen's film. (Atypical, however, for an Allen film is the location. A strike in New York caused filming to move to San Francisco.) Though his character, Allan Felix, is the typical neurotic Allen hero (most clearly seen in ANNIE HALL), he strikes a common chord with film audiences. What Allen hits on in PLAY IT AGAIN, SAM is a cultural phenomenon unique to the movie era—audiences living their lives as a movie. However, instead of relying on that crutch, Allan Felix, at the film's end, learns that he has a style of his own and that he doesn't need Bogart to help him anymore. What makes PLAY IT AGAIN, SAM such a success is this universal appeal. While not every audience can relate to the New York intellectual idiosyncracies of ANNIE HALL, they can relate on a gut emotional level to an average man idolizing a movie star. For film buffs, Allen has included countless film references (Erich von Stroheim, Francois Truffaut, Ida Lupino), film posters (ACROSS THE PACIFIC, SAN QUENTIN, THE JUNGLE PRINCESS, ALL THROUGH THE NIGHT, and MARCH OF THE WOODEN SOLDIERS, among others) and, of course, clips and music from CASABLANCA. Composer Goldenberg borrows heavily from the themes of Max Steiner, which are heard throughout, as is the unforgettable "As Time Goes By" (Herman Hupfeld, sung by Dooley Wilson) and an Oscar Peterson composition titled "Blues for Allan Felix." Also deserving special mention is Lacy's flawless portrayal of Bogart, which consistently makes one feel as if Allen somehow got the real Bogart for this film.

PLAY MISTY FOR ME
1971   102m   c   ★★★½
Thriller   R/18
Malpaso

Clint Eastwood *(Dave Garland)*, Jessica Walter *(Evelyn Draper)*, Donna Mills *(Tobie Williams)*, John Larch *(Sgt. McCallum)*, Jack Ging *(Dr. Frank Dewan)*, Irene Hervey *(Madge Brenner)*, James McEachin *(Al Monte)*, Clarice Taylor *(Birdie)*, Don Siegel *(Murphy the Bartender)*, Duke Everts *(Jay Jay)*

p, Robert Daley; d, Clint Eastwood; w, Jo Heims, Dean Riesner (based on a story by Jo Heims); ph, Bruce Surtees (Technicolor); ed, Carl Pingitore; m, Dee Barton; art d, Alexander Golitzen; cos, Helen Colvig, Brad Whitney

This was Clint Eastwood's directorial debut and it far surpasses other attempts in the genre, such as the popular FATAL ATTRACTION, for thrills, suspense, and insight into sexual obsession. Dave Garland (Eastwood) is a Carmel, California, disc jockey who gets a call every night from a mysterious woman listener who requests that he play the Erroll Garner classic "Misty." After breaking up with his girlfriend Tobie (Mills), Dave looks for action in the local bars and meets Evelyn (Walter), a rather high-strung but seductive woman who, he learns, is the mysterious voice that requests "Misty." The lustful pair adjourn to Evelyn's apartment and they sleep together with the understanding that it will be a one-night stand. Unfortunately for Dave, Evelyn is quite mad and absolutely refuses to leave him alone despite the fact that he has patched up his relationship with Tobie. Evelyn's jealous rage is at first suicidal, then quite murderous. A superior thriller, PLAY MISTY FOR ME proved that popular actor Eastwood could direct himself in a film, concentrate on every aspect of the production from the visuals to the performances, and complete the shooting ahead of schedule and under budget. What he delivered was an engrossing study of how loneliness and longing can be transformed into irrational rage after a thoughtless act of selfish indulgence. Much of the credit must go to Jessica Walter for her outstanding performance which somehow manages to be chilling while at the same time sympathetic.

PLAYTIME
(LA RECREATION)
1967   87m   bw   ★★★
Drama   /U
General/Elite   (France)

Jean Seberg *(Kate Hoover)*, Christian Marquand *(Philippe)*, Francoise Prevost *(Anne de Limeuil)*, Evelyne Ker *(Kate's Friend)*, Paulette Dubost *(Anne's Maid)*

p, Herve Messir; d, Francois Moreuil, Fabien Collin; w, Francois Moreuil, Daniel Boulanger (based on a story by Francoise Sagan); ph, Jean Penzer; ed, Rene Le Henaff; m, Georges Delerue

Interesting drama in which Seberg plays a lonely and bored American student in Versailles who becomes fascinated by sculptor Marquand. He lives next-door to her dorm with his patron, the wealthy Prevost. One day, near his house, she witnesses a hit-and-run accident in which a pedestrian is killed, but she can't see the driver of the car. Later, she meets Marquand and he is attracted to her. They begin an affair, but she soon realizes that he was the hit-and-run driver. Appalled by her discovery, she quickly brings the relationship to an end.

PLAZA SUITE
1971   114m   c   ★★★★
Comedy   GP/PG
Paramount

Walter Matthau *(Sam Nash/Jesse Kiplinger/Roy Hubley)*, Maureen Stapleton *(Karen Nash)*, Jose Ocasio *(Waiter)*, Dan Ferrone *(Bellhop)*, Louise Sorel *(Miss McCormack)*, Barbara Harris *(Muriel Tate)*, Lee Grant *(Norma Hubley)*, Jenny Sullivan *(Mimsey Hubley)*, Tom Carey *(Borden Eisler)*

p, Howard W. Koch; d, Arthur Hiller; w, Neil Simon (based on the play by Neil Simon); ph, Jack Marta (Technicolor); ed, Frank Bracht; m, Maurice Jarre; art d, Arthur Lonergan; cos, Jack Bear

To his credit, Neil Simon never stops trying to expand. With several solid successes in the comedy genre behind him, he attempted something here that wasn't merely a pack of one-liners but had an underlying pathos and humanity. George C. Scott and Maureen Stapleton opened on Broadway in the show, which ran more than 1,000 performances with Mike Nichols directing. Stapleton returns to do one of the three vignettes, as does Lee Grant, who did the Road Show version playing another of the parts, and Barbara Harris in the middle segment. Simon's plays are almost always one-set jobs, and the task of adapting them for the screen is not an enviable one, since movie fans will often carp that they are photographed stage plays of people talking with no cinematic value. Since this picture takes place in one suite at New York's Plaza Hotel, its staginess was all the more evident. The only unifying force in the trio of stories is Matthau in a tour-de-force job as three very different men. There were to be four stories in the original, and the one that was dropped was used as the basis for Simon's original screenplay of THE OUT-OF-TOWNERS. Director Hiller had just come off LOVE STORY, and there was some doubt as to whether he could direct a comedy.

The first segment has Stapleton and Matthau in what she believes is the same suite they'd occupied 24 years before on their honeymoon night. He is a very successful businessman with little time for sentiment, and Stapleton senses that their marriage

may be on the rocks. She is hoping that a return to the place where they spent their first night together may have some influence on his attitude. She has room service bring his favorite meal, lean roast beef and champagne. Then, upon his arrival from the office, he tells her that their anniversary is on the following day, that they are in the wrong suite, and that they are celebrating their 23rd, not their 24th anniversary. After the roast beef is delivered (far too fatty), Matthau says he will have to get back to his office to work, which destroys Stapleton's plans for a romantic tryst. His secretary, Sorel, arrives to leave some important documents, and Stapleton sees right through their charade. Sorel leaves, and Stapleton accuses Matthau of having an affair with the attractive Sorel; Matthau doesn't deny it. He's getting older, wonders if he's still got any sex appeal, and is doing his best to confirm that with an office affair. She pleads with him to remain, but he heads for the door and exits as the waiter brings the champagne. There is some indication, though, that Matthau will come to his senses and eventually return to this good woman who loves him. In the 33-minute second segment Matthau is the ultimate Hollywood producer, a man given to gold chains and lots of "babies" and "sweethearts" in his speech. He's in New York on business and has two hours to kill, so he calls an oldgirl friend from 15 years before, Harris, who is now a married woman living in Tenafly, New Jersey. Harris, who has followed her high school crush's career over the years, races into town. Matthau pours vodka cocktails down her, but Harris resists his advances, insisting all along that she has a terrific marriage. Matthau tries everything to seduce her, even lying about his "loneliness" at the top. Nothing seems to work until Matthau discovers that she is a movie junkie, one of those fans who reads every word about all the stars and who lives vicariously through the pages of the rags one finds at supermarket checkout stands. As he promises to tell her all the dirt about Sinatra and several other names he drops, he leads her into the bedroom and she giggles as she falls onto the bed. The 37-minute third and final episode has Matthau and wife Grant in the suite as guests are gathering downstairs for the wedding of their daughter, Sullivan, and her groom, Carey. Sullivan has locked herself in the suite's bathroom and won't come out despite all the pleading by Matthau and Grant. Since the wedding is already paid for and the guests are getting restless, Matthau's frustration hits a peak; he attempts to break down the door and only succeeds in hurting his shoulder and ripping his formal clothing. He crawls out on the window ledge, is attacked by pigeons, drenched in a rainstorm, and defeated by Sullivan's refusal to unlock the bathroom window. Carey arrives, walks to the door, yells "Cool It!" and tells Matthau and Grant that everything will be all right now. And it is. Sullivan comes out, the wedding goes off a bit later than expected, and the couple ride off on a motorcycle. Matthau's character in the final sketch is similar to the man he played in the first, but the wives are quite different. Of the female roles, Harris steals the picture. Critics were divided in their assessment of PLAZA SUITE, but we have to stand in the "pro" corner, although Simon has had some terrible adaptations (STAR SPANGLED GIRL) and even some bummer screenplays of his own, as in THE SLUGGER'S WIFE.

PLENTY
1985   125m   c   ★★★
Drama/War   R/15
FOX

Meryl Streep *(Susan Traherne)*, Charles Dance *(Raymond Brock)*, Tracey Ullman *(Alice Park)*, John Gielgud *(Sir Leonard Darwin)*, Sting *(Mick)*, Ian McKellen *(Sir Andrew Charleson)*, Sam Neill

(Lazar), Burt Kwouk (Mr. Aung), Pik Sen Lim (Mme. Aung), Andre Maranne (Villon)

p, Edward R. Pressman, Joseph Papp; d, Fred Schepisi; w, David Hare (based on his play); ph, Ian Baker (Panavision, Technicolor); ed, Peter Honess; m, Bruce Smeaton; prod d, Richard MacDonald; art d, Tony Reading, Adrian Smith; cos, Ruth Myers

Adapted by playwright-director David Hare ("A Map of the World", WETHERBY) from his own play, PLENTY follows the fortunes of Englishwoman Susan Traherne (Meryl Streep) from her thrilling days as a courier behind the lines in occupied France through the boredom she experiences in her postwar life. During the war, in France, she has a brief but passionate affair with a dashing young British agent called Lazar (Sam Neill). When she returns to England after the war, she is unable to forget him. Taking a stab at bohemian life, she becomes involved in a calculated relationship with Mick (Sting), a working-class gent she's decided will make a suitable father for her child. When they fail to produce a baby, however, Susan drops Mick and eventually marries Raymond Brock (Charles Dance), a patient, polished foreign service officer she follows around the globe. But the life of a diplomat's wife is hardly satisfying for the increasingly frustrated and neurotic Susan, and her cruelty to her husband worsens as the years pass. On its face, director Fred Schepisi's film concerns a woman whose warped personality becomes less rational and more malicious as she realizes she will never recapture the excitement of her life during wartime; however, Hare's well-crafted screenplay also uses Susan as a symbol of the squandered hopes for a better postwar Britain. Middle-class Susan and working-class Mick's inability to produce a child is symbolic of postwar Labor governments' failure to eliminate class division and inequity from British society, even in a time of economic "plenty." Intriguing and generally overlooked, PLENTY works on both levels. Employing yet another flawless accent, Streep delivers an excellent, restrained but edgy performance, well supported by Dance, Sting, and Ullman, who plays her best friend.

PLOT AGAINST HARRY, THE

1990 81m bw   ★★★
Comedy   /PG

Martin Priest (Harry Plotnick), Ben Lang (Leo), Maxine Woods (Kay), Henry Nemo (Max), Jacques Taylor (Jack), Jean Leslie (Irene), Ellen Herbert (Mae), Sandra Kazan (Margie)

p, Michael Roemer, Robert Young; d, Michael Roemer; w, Michael Roemer; ph, Robert Young; ed, Terry Lewis, Georges Klotz; m, Frank Lewin; art d, Howard Mandel; cos, Lily Partridge

Released 20 years after it was made, this hilarious tale of a small-time hood who can't get a break stars Martin Priest as the infamous Harry Plotnick, whose bad luck starts the moment he is freed after a nine-month prison term, when Max (Henry Nemo), his faithful driver and not-too-bright sidekick, is late meeting him. On the way home, they have an car accident, not just with anyone, but with Harry's ex-brother-in-law, Leo (Ben Lang), whose passengers include Harry's ex-wife, Kay (Maxine Woods), and the grown daughter Harry didn't know he had. Just as Harry is starting to settle into life on the outside, he becomes ill, prompting visits from his overprotective sister, Mae (Ellen Herbert), and an entourage of assorted relatives bearing fruit baskets and vaporizers. While reporting to his parole officer, Harry faints from anxiety and is taken to the hospital, where he learns he has an enlarged heart. His woes continue when he checks out of the hospital and returns to his hotel only to discover

that there has been a fire, set by Max, who, panicking over an impending IRS audit, torched Harry's accounting books. Naturally, everybody—including Max—contends that Harry put the driver up to the dirty deed. To complicate matters further, Harry's daughter becomes pregnant, and Kay informs Harry's parole officer about one of her ex-husband's parole violations. Later, Harry is invited to the Heart Foundation's "Have a Heart" marathon, during which he becomes drunk, walks onto the set, and has a heart attack on national television. Thinking he's not long for this world, Harry pledges $20,000 to the Heart Foundation, and claims that he did, in fact, tell Max to burn "the books." Eventually, Harry ends up where he began, in prison.

Michael Roemer and his talented cast have created an extremely funny film, which, unlike Woody Allen's overtly neurotic comedies, conveys the problems and anxieties of its characters with great subtlety. As interesting as this well-crafted film is, the story behind its long-delayed release is even more fascinating. After garnering critical praise for their low-budget feature NOTHING BUT A MAN (1965), Roemer, a professor of Film and American Studies at Yale, and former Harvard classmate Robert Young (director of the acclaimed SHORT EYES) received financing from the Seattle-based King Screen Productions to make another film. Made on a budget of $680,000, written and directed by Roemer with Young again acting as the cinematographer, that film, THE PLOT AGAINST HARRY, was completed in 1969; however, Roemer was unable to find a distributor. Shelving THE PLOT AGAINST HARRY, Roemer continued to teach and made a number of documentaries and features, mostly for public television, the best-known being the fiction film "Haunted," which was aired on PBS's "American Playhouse" series in 1984. Twenty years after his original attempt to distribute THE PLOT AGAINST HARRY, Roemer decided to transfer the film to videotape so that, as he explained to the New York Times, his kids could see it. In the process of reworking the soundtrack, he decided to make new 35 mm prints of the film and sent them off to the New York and Toronto film festivals, where THE PLOT AGAINST HARRY was extremely well received, leading to the film's general release.

A period film that was not intended to be a period film, THE PLOT AGAINST HARRY is a wonderful document of the sights and sounds of the late 1960s. Well-acted, deftly written and directed, and expertly shot by Young, this darkly comic tale of a hapless small-time gangster is an engaging cinematic artifact that remains as fresh today as the day it was made.

PLOUGHMAN'S LUNCH, THE

1984 107m c   ★★★★
Drama   R/15
Greenpoint (U.K.)

Jonathan Pryce (James Penfield), Tim Curry (Jeremy Hancock), Rosemary Harris (Ann Barrington), Frank Finlay (Matthew Fox), Charlie Dore (Susan Barrington), David De Keyser (Gold), Nat Jackley (Mr. Penfield), Bill Paterson (Lecturer), William Maxwell, Paul Jesson

p, Simon Relph, Ann Scott; d, Richard Eyre; w, Ian McEwan; ph, Clive Tickner; ed, David Martin; m, Dominic Muldowney; prod d, Luciana Arrighi; art d, Michael Pickwoad; cos, Luciana Arrighi

BBC radio journalist and would-be historian James Penfield (Jonathan Pryce) is an unbridled opportunist and self-promoter. He is at work on a book about the 1956 Suez Canal crisis in which his aim is to interpret events in a politically popular manner that will enhance his career. He pursues television-documentary researcher Susan Barrington (Charlie Dore), mainly because her mother (Rosemary Harris) is an expert on Suez. As he gets more involved with these characters and his work, it becomes more difficult to determine just who is using whom. First-time director Richard Eyre has created a gripping film that honestly explores political morality in the 1980s. Pryce is superb as the self-interested corporate-social climber, and the entire film plays like THE GRADUATE stood on its head.

POCKETFUL OF MIRACLES

1961   136m   c   ★★★½
Crime/Comedy   /U
Franton

Glenn Ford (Dave, the Dude, Conway), Bette Davis (Apple Annie, "Mrs. E. Worthington Manville"), Hope Lange (Elizabeth "Queenie" Martin), Arthur O'Connell (Count Alfonso Romero), Peter Falk (Joy Boy), Thomas Mitchell (Judge Henry G. Blake), Edward Everett Horton (Hutchins, the Butler), Mickey Shaughnessy (Junior), David Brian (Governor), Sheldon Leonard (Steve Darcey).

p, Frank Capra; d, Frank Capra; w, Hal Kanter, Harry Tugend, Jimmy Cannon (based on the story "Madame La Gimp" by Damon Runyon and the screenplay LADY FOR A DAY by Robert Riskin); ph, Robert Bronner (Panavision, Technicolor); ed, Frank P. Keller; m, Walter Scharf, Peter Ilich Tchaikovsky; art d, Hal Pereira, Roland Anderson; fx, Farciot Edouart; chor, Nick Castle; cos, Edith Head, Walter Plunkett

This was Frank Capra's swan song as a producer-director, and although it was not well received upon initial release, it's still a good movie with some outstanding performances. New York gangster Dave "the Dude" Conway (Glenn Ford) is a superstitious type who believes he can't come to any harm as long as he continues to buy his daily apple from Apple Annie (Bette Davis), a drunken fruit vendor. In essence, Dave's belief is that "an apple a day keeps the Mafia away," and although his bodyguard, Joy Boy (Peter Falk), and chauffeur, Junior (Mickey Shaughnessy), think it's a lot of hooey, his girlfriend (Hope Lange) goes along with whatever Dave wants. When Apple Annie isn't at her usual street corner one morning, Dave goes looking for her. He finds her in deep depression because her daughter, Louise (Ann-Margret, in her first role), who thinks her mother is a wealthy matron, is coming to pay a visit. With Dave's help, Apple Annie is able to pull off her charade as "Mrs. E. Worthington Manville," even receiving help from the mayor, the governor, and a horde of real socialites. A remake of Capra's picture LADY FOR A DAY.

POIL DE CAROTTE

1932   80m   bw   ★★★★
Drama
Legrand Majestic   (France)

Harry Baur (M. Lepic), Robert Lynen (Francois, "Poil de Carotte"), Catherine Fontenay (Mme. Lepic), Louis Gouthier (Uncle), Simone Aubry (Ernestine Lepic), Maxime Fromiot (Felix Lepic), Colette Segall (Mathilde), Marthe Marty (Honorine), Christiane Dor (Annette)

d, Julien Duvivier; w, Julien Duvivier (based on the novels Poil de Carotte and La Bigote by Jules Renard); ph, Armand Thirard; ed, Marthe Poncin; m, Alexandre Tansman

Julien Duvivier's second attempt to film the popular stories of Jules Renard, which he first brought to the screen in a 1925 silent, is a lyrical story of the unhappy childhood of the preadolescent Francois (Robert Lynen). Better known as "Poil de carotte," the red-haired Francois is a victim of the hatred between his mother (Catherine Fontenay) and her husband (Harry Baur)—a marriage that exists only for appearance sake. Francois is actually his mother's illegitimate child, the result of an affair with a man who has the same glowing red hair as the boy. The mother treats her son with spite and cruelty, blaming him for her isolation; the stepfather, for the most part, treats Francois with indifference, but through the course of the film the two develop a close friendship based on mutual respect. One of the prolific Duvivier's most memorable films (he made 19 in the 1930s alone), POIL DE CAROTTE succeeds chiefly because of the characterization of Francois, who is a victim of other people's inconsiderateness, but is never idealized or treated as a saint. Rather, he is a normal child—at times irrational, at times loving, and often mischievous. Much credit goes to young Lynen, who was encountered by Duvivier while walking along a street. After appearing in a number of films in the 1930s, Lynen was killed by the Nazis for his involvement in the French underground.

POINT BLANK

1967   92m   c   ★★½
Crime
Bernard/Winkler

Lee Marvin (Walker), Angie Dickinson (Chris), Keenan Wynn (Fairfax, "Yost"), Carroll O'Connor (Brewster), Lloyd Bochner (Frederick Carter), Michael Strong (Stegman), John Vernon (Mal Reese), Sharon Acker (Lynne), James B. Sikking (Hired Gun), Sandra Warner (Waitress)

p, Judd Bernard, Robert Chartoff; d, John Boorman; w, Alexander Jacobs, David Newhouse, Rafe Newhouse (based on the novel The Hunter by Donald E. Westlake); ph, Philip Lathrop (Panavision, Metrocolor); ed, Henry Berman; m, Johnny Mandel; art d, George W. Davis, Albert Brenner; fx, Virgil Beck, J. McMillan Johnson; cos, Margo Weintz

John Boorman's second film (after HAVING A WILD WEEKEND) and his first US production is a confusing effort in which style overcomes substance. Boorman showed fantastic attention to details and forgot about flesh and blood, with a few exceptions, but that didn't seem to hurt the picture, as it did well in theaters. Marvin has just been involved with a heist of the mob's money, a feat he accomplished with Vernon. They have nailed the cash and are hiding on the deserted island of Alcatraz when Vernon shoots Marvin point-blank. As Marvin begins to go under, he notes that Vernon has his arm around Acker, Marvin's wife, and it dawns on him that he has been gulled in two departments. Acker and Vernon leave Marvin for dead, but he is tougher than they think and eventually swims to shore (something countless escapees could not manage). Some time later, Marvin meets Wynn while both are taking a guided tour of Alcatraz. Wynn says he knows about the robbery and offers to help Marvin wreak revenge on Vernon and Acker as well as get his hands on his share of the loot, a tidy sum near $100,000. Marvin goes south to Los Angeles, finds Acker's apartment, and shoots the place up but doesn't kill her. She's been deserted by Vernon and is now taking drugs; later she commits suicide without revealing Vernon's whereabouts. Marvin next uses Acker's sister, Dickinson, to get into Vernon's heavily guarded residence. Dickinson seduces Vernon while Marvin sneaks into the penthouse, but before he can shoot Vernon, the man falls to his death. So where is the money? Wynn appears again and says that it's in the hands of Bochner, who is married to Haynes and is a member of the mob. Bochner and his buddy Strong know that Marvin is gunning for them, but they are hoisted by their own petards and die in the trap they've prepared. Marvin gets to the boss's right-hand man, O'Connor, who wants to take over the top spot, occupied by a man named Fairfax. The plan is to pull another heist of the gang money. O'Connor and Marvin go back to San Francisco to effect the robbery, but O'Connor is shot dead by Wynn who, it turns out, is not the mob's bookkeeper but the top dog. Wynn is happy that Marvin has helped him ferret out the rats in his organization and now offers him a job. Marvin thinks about it, then decides it might be a trap and exits. This is a bloodbath filled with gunshots, torture, fights, crashes—everything the devoted sadist might enjoy—presented in flashbacks, flash-forwards, and instant replays.

POLLYANNA

1960   134m   c   ★★★★
Comedy   /U
Buena Vista

Hayley Mills (Pollyanna), Jane Wyman (Aunt Polly Harrington), Richard Egan (Dr. Edmund Chilton), Karl Malden (Reverend Paul Ford), Nancy Olson (Nancy Furman), Adolphe Menjou (Mr. Pendergast), Donald Crisp (Mayor Karl Warren), Agnes Moorehead (Mrs. Snow), Kevin Corcoran (Jimmy Bean), James Drury (George Dodds)

p, Walt Disney; d, David Swift; w, David Swift (based on the novel by Eleanor H. Porter); ph, Russell Harlan (Technicolor); ed, Frank Gross; m, Paul J. Smith; art d, Carroll Clark, Robert Clatworthy; fx, Ub Iwerks; cos, Walter Plunkett, Chuck Keehne, Gertrude Casey

Ever since Mary Pickford filmed the silent version of this book in 1920, the name "Pollyanna" has become English vernacular meaning someone who is a die-hard optimist. This time Pollyanna (Hayley Mills) is an orphan who comes to live with her Aunt Polly (Jane Wyman), a wealthy woman in a small 1912 town. The village is filled with nay-sayers and depressing townsfolk, but Pollyanna soon changes matters by always managing to find something good in every situation, seeing the bright side of even the blackest occurrences. Although the townspeople are initially reluctant to share in her optimism, they are eventually won over, even coming to Pollyanna's aid when she is temporarily paralyzed and can no longer find any good in life. Another fine Disney entry, this one earning Hayley Mills a special Oscar for Outstanding Juvenile Performance.

POLTERGEIST

1982   114m   c   ★★
Horror   PG/15
MGM-UA

Craig T. Nelson (Steve), JoBeth Williams (Diane), Beatrice Straight (Dr. Lesh), Dominique Dunne (Dana), Oliver Robins (Robbie), Heather O'Rourke (Carol Anne), Zelda Rubinstein (Tangina), Martin Casella (Marty), Richard Lawson (Ryan), Michael McManus (Tuthill)

p, Steven Spielberg, Frank Marshall; d, Tobe Hooper; w, Steven Spielberg, Michael Grais, Mark Victor; ph, Matthew F. Leonetti (Panavision, Metrocolor); ed, Michael Kahn; m, Jerry Goldsmith; prod d, James H. Spencer; cos, L.J. Mower

A vapid, silly horror movie with occasional moments of promise that ultimately fails due to an overdose of cuteness. Steve and Diane (Craig T. Nelson and JoBeth Williams) are a happy suburban couple who suddenly find that their perfect house in the perfect neighborhood has begun acting funny, scaring their perfect children. They really sit up and take notice, however, when

wide-eyed young daughter Carol Anne (Heather O'Rourke) becomes possessed by late-night television and gets sucked into limbo by God knows what. Enter clairvoyant Tangina (Zelda Rubinstein), who surmises that the subdivision was built on a sacred Indian burial ground and that the gods aren't happy. POLTERGEIST is frustrating because one gets a hint of what director Tobe Hooper *really* wanted to do, but it's obvious that he was restrained by producer Steven Spielberg. The problem is, some of the truly horrifying moments slip through the censorship cracks, scaring little kids (and their parents), leaving POLTERGEIST a very disjointed, uneven movie. Nominated by the Academy for Best Visual Effects and Best Sound Effects Editing.

POOR COW

1968   101m   c   ★★★
Drama   /15
Vic/Fenchurch   (U.K.)

Carol White (Joy), Terence Stamp (Dave), John Bindon (Tom), Kate Williams (Beryl), Queenie Watts (Aunt Emm), Geraldine Sherman (Trixie), James Beckett, Billy Murray (Tom's Friends), Simon King (Johnny, Age 1-1/2), Stevie King (Johnny, Age 3)

p, Joseph Janni; d, Kenneth Loach; w, Kenneth Loach, Nell Dunn (based on her novel); ph, Brian Probyn (Eastmancolor); ed, Roy Watts; m, Donovan; art d, Bernard Sarron

A complex and poignant look at a woman left to fend for herself and her newborn child after her husband has been jailed, with her attempts to grab survival and even happiness despite her situation. White is married to bullying thief Bindon, who treats her in a gruff, even brutal manner while living in their dingy London flat. When he is sent to jail, White moves in with Stamp, a fellow thief and friend of her husband, but a gentle and caring man who treats her son affectionately. Her brief happiness with Stamp ends when he is also arrested. Though White promises to be faithful to Stamp, left on her own she makes a living as a nude model and as a barmaid, treating herself to an occasional affair. She begins divorce proceedings against Bindon, but when he is released he attempts to revive their marriage for the benefit of their son. White gives an excellent performance as a woman who finds herself in many squalid situations. The production relies effectively on improvisational techniques to get the proper emotional levels for certain sequences.

PORGY AND BESS

1959   138m   c   ★★★½
Musical   /A
Goldwyn

Sidney Poitier (Porgy), Dorothy Dandridge (Bess), Sammy Davis, Jr. (Sportin' Life), Pearl Bailey (Maria), Brock Peters (Crown), Leslie Scott (Jake), Diahann Carroll (Clara), Ruth Attaway (Serena), Clarence Muse (Peter), Everdinne Wilson (Annie)

p, Samuel Goldwyn; d, Otto Preminger; w, N. Richard Nash (based on the operetta by George Gershwin, Ira Gershwin, DuBose Heyward, the play by DuBose Heyward, Dorothy Heyward, and the novel by DuBose Heyward); ph, Leon Shamroy (ToddAO/Technicolor); ed, Daniel Mandell; m, George Gershwin; prod d, Oliver Smith; art d, Serge Krizman, Joseph C. Wright; chor, Hermes Pan; cos, Irene Sharaff

Wuth a budget of over $6 million, why wasn't this classic American operetta a classic American movie? Perhaps the fault lies in Samuel Goldwyn's decision to fire director Rouben Mamoulian in favor of Otto Preminger—if anyone could muddle a great saga, it was Preminger. The crippled Porgy (Sidney Poitier) loves Bess (Dorothy Dandridge), a floozy adored by many men, including Crown (Brock Peters), a tough stevedore, and Sportin' Life (Sammy Davis, Jr.), who supplies her with heroin and who is always trying to take her away from life in Catfish Row. After Crown kills a man in an argument over a game of craps and must flee the police, Bess settles in with Porgy. When Crown returns, wanting Bess back, Porgy kills him in turn, then hides out, while Bess agrees to follow Sportin' Life to New York. Porgy comes back to Catfish Row, learns that she's left, and is determined to follow her as the film ends—a simple story carried into the stratosphere by the glorious music. Poitier, not yet a star, initially accepted the role of Porgy, then declined, reportedly because of feeling within the black community that the story was racist, until producer Goldwyn and Mamoulian again convinced him to do the project. His singing voice and Dandridge's are dubbed; Davis, Pearl Bailey (as Maria), and Peters all do their own singing. (As Clara, Diahann Carroll, a wonderful nightclub singer lacking operatic range, also has her voice looped.) Shooting was delayed when fire decimated the Goldwyn lot, and in the month it took to rebuild everything, Goldwyn and Mamoulian began to have "creative differences." Thus Preminger was called in to replace Mamoulian, with rather heavy-handed results. The brilliant score by the Gershwins and DuBose Heyward, however, will last forever, while Preminger's veteran cameraman, Leon Shamroy, did a wonderful job and the art direction by Serge Krizman and Joseph Wright was sensational. Previn and Darby took home Oscars for their scoring, and the film was also nominated for Best Cinematography, Best Sound and Best Costume Design.

PORK CHOP HILL

1959 97m bw   ★★★★
War   /PG
Melville

Gregory Peck (Lt. Clemons), Harry Guardino (Forstman), Rip Torn (Lt. Russell), George Peppard (Fedderson), James Edwards (Cpl. Jurgens), Bob Steele (Kern), Woody Strode (Franklin), George Shibata (Lt. O'Hashi), Norman Fell (Sgt. Coleman), Robert Blake (Velie)

p, Sy Bartlett; d, Lewis Milestone; w, James R. Webb (based on a story by S.L.A. Marshall); ph, Sam Leavitt; ed, George Boemler; m, Leonard Rosenman; prod d, Nicolai Remisoff; cos, Edward Armand

A grim, harrowing film detailing a single brutal Korean War battle, PORK CHOP HILL was directed by veteran helmsman Lewis Milestone and is the third entry in his informal trilogy devoted to 20th-century military conflict (ALL QUIET ON THE WESTERN FRONT was set during WWI, and A WALK IN THE SUN during WWII). Gregory Peck plays the commander of an Army company that is ordered to take Pork Chop Ridge, an inconsequential tactical objective. Compounding the seeming pointlessness of the assignment are the Panmunjom peace talks, which the troops believe may end the war at any minute, so that they are reluctant to participate in what may be its final battle. PORK CHOP HILL is an ode to the common American infantryman, soldiers who manage to retain their honor and dignity despite being ordered into an insane action by a top brass unwilling to lose face to the enemy, even though the conflict's end appears imminent. Peck is outstanding as the resolute but compassionate commander, and Rip Torn, Harry Guardino, Woody Strode, James Edwards (veteran of Sam Fuller's excellent Korean War film THE STEEL HELMET), and Robert Blake

provide solid support. Moreover, Milestone employs his considerable technical skills to create an authentic and memorable cinematic experience, projecting a grim realistic air that captures the forlorn atmosphere of the meaningless mission. Sam Leavitt's photography is topnotch and depicts this heroic battle in such stark detail that the viewer can almost smell the acrid fumes of cordite and taste the dust blown from the dead ridge. This powerful movie and HAMBURGER HILL, which deals similarly with an assault during the Vietnam War, would make a very interesting double bill.

PORT OF SHADOWS

(LE QUAI DES BRUMES)
1938 91m bw   ★★★★
Drama
Gregor Rabinovitch   (France)

Jean Gabin (Jean), Michele Morgan (Nelly), Michel Simon (Zabel), Pierre Brasseur (Lucien Laugardier), Robert Le Vigan (Michel Krauss), Jenny Burnay (Lucien's Friend), Marcel Peres (Chauffeur), Rene Genin (Doctor), Edouard Delmont (Panama), Raymond Aimos (Quart-Vittel)

p, Gregor Rabinovitch; d, Marcel Carne; w, Jacques Prevert (based on the novel Le Quai Des Brumes by Pierre Mac Orlan); ph, Eugene Schuftan, Louis Page; ed, Rene Le Henaff; m, Maurice Jaubert; prod d, Alexander Trauner

This fantastic film mirroring the prevailing mood in prewar France was the first feature to win critical acclaim for the directing-writing team of Marcel Carne and Jacques Prevert (who had collaborated on JENNY and BIZARRE, BIZARRE, and who would later create the much-heralded CHILDREN OF PARADISE). Gabin plays a deserter who comes to the port of Le Havre looking for passage to a distant country. In a local dive he becomes attracted to Morgan, ward of the owner of a shop that is a front for illicit dealing. When Gabin comes to Simon's shop to buy a gift for Morgan, the evil Simon promises Gabin a passport and money if he will kill one of Simon's enemies. Gabin refuses. But hope for Gabin's escape comes when visionary artist Le Vigan gives the deserter his own passport before walking out on the quay and drowning himself. Later, Simon confesses that jealousy has led him to murder Morgan's boyfriend; then when Simon tries to rape Morgan, Gabin smashes Simon's head with a brick. On his way to the ship to gain passage to South America, Gabin is gunned down by mysterious gangster Brasseur.

This classic of French Poetic Realism conveys a deeply fatalistic belief that humankind is at the mercy of malevolent fate, a message that is communicated both through the simple story line and through the superb fog-shrouded sets and forbidding locations. The mood of hopelessness that pervades this gray masterpiece so perfectly paralleled the prevailing feeling in prewar France that a Vichy government spokesman reputedly blamed the film for his country's misfortune during the war.

Ironically, PORT OF SHADOWS was originally to have been a German production. Carne was introduced to the Mac Orlan novel on which the picture is loosely based by Raoul Ploquin, then head of French productions at UFA in Berlin. Nazi propaganda minister Josef Goebbels turned thumbs down on the project, however; he considered this story of a deserter to be decadent. The rights were sold to French producer Gregor Rabinovitch, who envisioned a lighter, happier film, and so quarreled constantly with Carne. Carne also had political problems within his own country, primarily with the French minister of war, who would not permit the word "deserter" to be used and insisted that Gabin's soldier's uniform be treated respectfully. As a result, writer Prevert was forced to deviate from the novel in almost every respect. Notably, in the book, Morgan's heroine is no tempest-tossed innocent; she is a prostitute who murders her pimp and ends up wealthy. During the Nazi occupation of France, this remarkable picture was totally banned in that country.

PORTRAIT OF JENNIE

1948 86m c/bw   ★★★★
Romance
Vanguard

Jennifer Jones (*Jennie Appleton*), Joseph Cotten (*Eben Adams*), Ethel Barrymore (*Miss Spinney*), Cecil Kellaway (*Mr. Matthews*), David Wayne (*Gus O'Toole*), Albert Sharpe (*Mr. Moore*), Florence Bates (*Mrs. Jekes the Landlady*), Lillian Gish (*Mother Mary of Mercy*), Henry Hull (*Eke*), Esther Somers (*Mrs. Bunce*)

p, David O. Selznick; d, William Dieterle; w, Paul Osborn, Peter Berneis, Leonardo Bercovici (based on the novel by Robert Nathan); ph, Joseph August (Technicolor sequence); ed, William Morgan; m, Dimitri Tiomkin (based on themes of Claude Debussy); prod d, J. McMillan Johnson; art d, Joseph B. Platt; fx, Clarence Slifer, Paul Eagler, J. McMillan Johnson; cos, Lucinda Ballard, Anna Hill Johnstone

An eerie love story, PORTRAIT OF JENNIE offers superb performances from Cotten, as a struggling painter, and Jones, as a girl from the past with whom he falls in love. It is 1932, the nadir of the Depression, and Cotten, a young painter who feels that his work lacks depth, sits glumly in New York City's Central Park, contemplating his not-so-bright future. A beautiful young girl, Jones, approaches him and begins to speak with him, using strange words that belong to a previous era, mentioning that she attends a convent school and that her parents are trapeze artists at Hammerstein's Opera House. She sings Cotten a haunting song (with the provocative lyrics, "Where I come from nobody knows / And where I'm going everything goes. / The wind blows, the sea flows / And nobody knows"), then disappears as abruptly as she appeared. Afterwards, Cotten struggles on with his art, encouraged by wealthy art dealer Barrymore, who takes a motherly interest in him, buying his water colors even though she knows they are poor, and suggesting that he try a new medium. Jones turns up periodically throughout that winter, while Cotten finds work painting a mural on the wall of an Irish saloon, a commisssion arranged by Cotten's good friend Wayne, a cab driver. Each time Jones reappears through the following spring and summer, she seems older by years, growing up from adolescence to young womanhood. Cotten asks her to sit for a portrait and finishes it just as she tells him she's about to graduate from college. When Barrymore and her associate, Kellaway, see the portrait of Jones, they hail it as a startling, innovative work by the hitherto unpromising Cotten that will surely establish his artistic reputation. Yet Cotten is haunted by Jones and begins to look into her background, discovering that her parents were killed in a highwire accident. Moreover, he finds out from Gish, the mother superior at an all-girl college, that Jones was in fact killed during a hurricane in New England in the 1920s. Cotten refuses to believe that the girl he painted is a ghost, but on the eve of the hurricane's anniversary, he rushes to New England. There, Jones comes to him during a raging storm and tells him that their love will live across the barriers of time, then vanishes for good. Eventually, Cotten begins to doubt he ever really met the beautiful girl, but when he finds her scarf, he begins to believe that he will meet his true love again in the afterlife after all.

Dieterle's direction is sensitive and the sequences are wonderfully constructed, with no scene bruising the next. He draws forth stellar performances, especially from Cotten; Jones is seen too briefly, but projects a genuinely ethereal quality during her moments on the screen. August's photography is stunning, and Tiomkin's lyrical score, drawn from Claude Debussy's themes (principally "The Afternoon of a Faun") is highly memorable. The foreword of the film, written by Ben Hecht, sums up the story's effect: "Out of the shadows of knowledge, and out of a painting that hung on a museum wall, comes our story, the truth of which lies not on our screen but in your heart." (A similar story of love that crosses mortal boundaries is at the core of a Hecht romance of considerable note, MIRACLE IN THE RAIN.)

PORTRAIT OF LENIN

(LENIN V POLSHE)
1967 98m bw   ★★
Biography
Mosfilm/Studio Film Unit/Polski   (Poland/U.S.S.R.)

Maksim Shtraukh (*Vladimir Ilich Lenin*), Anna Lisyanskaya (*Krupskaya, Lenin's Wife*), Antonina Pavlycheva (*Krupskaya's Mother*), Ilona Kusmierska (*Ulka*), Edmund Fetting (*Hanecki*), Krysztof Kalczynski (*Andrzej*), Tadeusz Fijewski (*Secretary of the Prison*), Gustaw Lutkiewicz (*Investigator*), Kazimierz Rudzki (*Priest*), Zbigniew Skowronski (*Matyszezuk*)

d, Sergey Yutkevich; w, Sergey Yutkevich, Yevgeniy Gabrilovich; ph, Jan Laskowski (Sovscope); m, Adam Walacinski; art d, Jan Grandys; fx, Boris Travkin, A. Rudachenko

Biography of the events of the Bolshevik leader prior to the Russian revolution. The story concentrates mainly on his exile in Poland where he befriends a peasant girl and her boyfriend. She is a strong believer in the nationalist cause. Shtraukh, as Lenin, learns later that the girl was killed when she withheld information about him.

POSTCARDS FROM THE EDGE

1990 101m c   ★★★
Comedy/Drama   R/15
Columbia

Meryl Streep (*Suzanne Vale*), Shirley MacLaine (*Doris Mann*), Dennis Quaid (*Jack Falkner*), Gene Hackman (*Lowell*), Richard Dreyfuss (*Dr. Frankenthal*), Rob Reiner (*Joe Pierce*), Mary Wickes (*Grandma*), Conrad Bain (*Grandpa*), Annette Bening (*Evelyn Ames*), Simon Callow (*Simon Asquith*)

p, Mike Nichols, John Calley; d, Mike Nichols; w, Carrie Fisher (based on her novel); ph, Michael Ballhaus (Technicolor); ed, Sam O'Steen; m, Carly Simon; prod d, Patrizia Von Brandenstein; art d, Kandy Stern; cos, Ann Roth

Adapted by Carrie Fisher from her first novel, POSTCARDS FROM THE EDGE is yet more proof that Hollywood makes its best films about what it knows best—making films in Hollywood. But while POSTCARDS is entertaining and observant of the world of moviemaking—with a casual command of mood, character, and *mise en scene*—too much of its running time is taken up with the predictable, cliched mother-daughter drama at the film's center. Continuing in the dark comedy vein she began with SHE DEVIL, Meryl Streep, playing actress Suzanne Vale, starts at rock bottom. While working on a film, Suzanne is so addled by a cocaine habit that her director, Lowell (Gene Hackman), finds it necessary to threaten her life just to get her focused. When she then overdoses on sedatives while in the bed of Jack

Falkner (Dennis Quaid), the womanizing producer anonymously wheels her into a hospital emergency room. There her stomach is pumped by a doctor (Richard Dreyfuss) who sends her a card and flowers and asks her out on a date. During her rehabilitation, Suzanne must contend with a therapist (C.C.H. Pounder of BAGDAD CAFE fame) whose grab-bag of what Suzanne calls "bumper-sticker" self-help slogans is enough to drive a patient back to drugs. Upon completing her clinical rehab, Suzanne finds her career in need of resuscitation. She has developed a "reputation" and is only able to find work on a mediocre B-grade cop movie. As a stipulation of her employment on even this lowly project, Suzanne must submit to random drug testing. During the production she is also required to live with her domineering, alcoholic, entertainer-mom, Doris (Shirley MacLaine), the too-obvious cause of Suzanne's problems. Suzanne can't open her mouth without finding herself in a battle of oneupmanship with Doris, who matches her daughter's tales of drug addiction with fondly overwrought reminiscences of her own nervous breakdown and who responds to Suzanne's anguish with adroit guilt-mongering. Even a casual singing performance at a party becomes a show-biz battle-to-the-death between mother and daughter. Suzanne finds that being drug-free poses new challenges on other fronts as well. On the set, she is forced to sit still for her hack producers' unsolicited advice on her performance. She also listens in secrecy while her director (Simon Callow) and wardrobe mistress (Dana Ivey) casually discuss how they will shoot around Suzanne's weight gain in close-up love scenes—which actually makes no sense, since Streep, notwithstanding the can of cola and bag of corn chips permanently grafted to her hands, looks as trim as ever. Then Suzanne has to endure the return of Falkner, who professes his love for her, though his main interest is in adding notches to his "gun."

However, the film never resolves its on-the-set subplot, letting it fall by the wayside as MacLaine's Doris bulldozes into the action, finally appearing, sans wig and balding, in a hospital room after wrapping her Mercedes around a tree and getting cited for driving under the influence. Talk about upstaging! Ultimately, Hackman's bullying director makes a climactic reappearance to give Suzanne permission to break away from her mom and build her own life. Beyond its sexist implications and the fact that it deprives Suzanne of a victory that is solely her own, this scene is just plain implausible. How exactly has Hackman's Lowell, who has been absent since the beginning of the film, come into all this intimate knowledge of Suzanne's personal crises? While there is no easy answer to that question, Lowell's dispensation and Suzanne's response do echo Mike Nichols's previous film, WORKING GIRL, in which Melanie Griffith's strong heroine irrationally requires the endorsement of Harrison Ford's hunky hero to be complete.

If the foreground action is predictable, Nichols and Fisher nevertheless manage to slip a few provocative ideas into the background, much as Nichols did with WORKING GIRL. Notably, Suzanne's return to sobriety is anything but rewarding; instead it provides her with a new sensitivity to the callousness and treachery of agents, producers, directors, lovers, and, most importantly, of her mother. Suzanne's personal struggle is also contrasted throughout with Doris's nonstop, unrepentant boozing. On her way to a dubbing session for the film she made with Lowell, Suzanne finally backslides, popping enough tranquilizers to make her woozy. Although she pulls over to throw up along the way, the point is made that sedation is not an unreasonable response to a life as grueling and crazy as the one Suzanne leads. Because she is caught up in a world of constant role-playing, events that happen off the set seem even less "real" than those

enacted before the cameras. The movie winds up with Suzanne's triumphant country-and-western singing debut, but Nichols gives her success a double edge; behind the crowd of madly cheering extras is a less-than-enthusiastic "real" audience, the moviemaking crew—bored grips and gaffers marking time until lunch.

If for no other reason, POSTCARDS deserves praise for giving movie audiences their first real exposure to Streep's singing voice, much lauded by those familiar with her stage work. Her performance here isn't riveting, but she does a good job of belting out a tune. The performance earned her a Best Actress Oscar nomination, while the song, "I'm Checking Out" (Shel Silverstein), also was nominated. What sabotages POSTCARDS are the extended screaming scenes between Streep and MacLaine, who seem to be acting in two different films—MacLaine in some sort of MOMMIE DEAREST-like show-business horror story and Streep in a far more delicate modern comedy of bad manners, LA-style (which is more in keeping with Fisher's largely plotless novel). Instead of sending off either dramatic or comedic sparks, they wind up highlighting each others' weaknesses, with MacLaine's scene-gobbling stridency steamrollering Streep's technical polish and emotional reserve.

In the final analysis, POSTCARDS is a mixed bag. There are a number of entertaining moments; however, potentially interesting characters and situations wither from lack of development for the sake of the central relationship, which is never wholly convincing—the idea of MacLaine mothering Streep never gets past its initial bizarreness. While Fisher shows some potential as a screenwriter, her script here is mostly an exercise in technique, its pieces fitting neatly together. But though no Screenwriting 101 teacher could fail to give her an A, the script never comes to life under Nichols's direction, which remains irritatingly self-conscious; again he has carefully and condescendingly packaged sophistication for a mass audience. If anything holds the film together, it is Streep's comic flair. But she's almost as stranded here as she was in SHE DEVIL, with material that rarely allows her to call upon her strengths as an actress. She deserves better, and so does the audience.

POSTMAN ALWAYS RINGS TWICE, THE
1946   113m   bw   ★★★★★
Crime   /PG
MGM

Lana Turner *(Cora Smith)*, John Garfield *(Frank Chambers)*, Cecil Kellaway *(Nick Smith)*, Hume Cronyn *(Arthur Keats)*, Leon Ames *(Kyle Sackett)*, Audrey Totter *(Madge Gorland)*, Alan Reed *(Ezra Liam Kennedy)*, Jeff York *(Blair)*, Charles Williams *(Jimmie White)*, A. Cameron Grant *(Willie)*

p, Carey Wilson; d, Tay Garnett; w, Harry Ruskin, Niven Busch (based on the novel by James M. Cain); ph, Sidney Wagner; ed, George White; m, George Bassman; art d, Cedric Gibbons, Randall Duell; cos, Irene, Marion Herwood Keyes

The best version of James M. Cain's hard-hitting, sex-obsessed, tangled romance comes to startling life under Garnett's shrewd direction, surprisingly at MGM. This was the moment the studio threw in the towel on Turner's ladylike, sweet parts and let her turn on the blowtorch and expose the seething passions. Although 1946 censors assured some downplaying of the heat between the leads, from the moment surly Garfield sees the "Man Wanted" sign, and Turner's lipstick rolls tauntingly across the floor, we know we're in for dangerous, pulp romance. By the time the camera swings from Turner's foot to the top of her white-hot visage, we know what the goods are and that Garfield's horny drifter is sold. If Turner is more infantile than Stanwyck in DOUBLE INDEMNITY, we also know it's a ruse she already knows works with men. This is art imitating Turner imitating life.

Drifter Garfield stops at a California roadside cafe owned by the amiable Kellaway, who offers him a job as a handyman. Garfield is disinclined toward such menial work until he catches a glimpse of Turner, Kellaway's siren wife. He immediately takes the job and then begins making advances to a most receptive lady. The two become lovers, and Turner tells Garfield that she married the goodhearted Kellaway to escape a life of poverty but wound up with a life of boredom, living in another trap, having a loveless marriage and a cafe in which she has no financial interest. Kellaway gives no sign of detecting the torrid trysting of his wife with Garfield and goes on his jovial way, treating both of them as if they were his cherished children. Garfield cannot get enough of the voluptuous Turner, telling her at one point, "Give me a kiss or I'll sock ya!" The couple sit guilt-ridden in Kellaway's presence; he seems to be everywhere, smothering them in their claustrophobic romance until—as Garnett's careful direction suggests—there is no way for them to breathe except to eliminate Kellaway. The lovers' first plan is to run away together, but Turner cannot bear to lose the security of Kellaway's cozy nest egg. She suggests to Garfield that they murder Kellaway, but their initial attempt to kill the kindly cafe owner fails in a twist of fate. If they want each other, they have to try again.

THE POSTMAN ALWAYS RINGS TWICE is narrated by Garfield from his death cell from beginning to end, a technique employed in DOUBLE INDEMNITY, where Fred MacMurray narrates his damned relationship with scheming Barbara Stanwyck, which also led to murder. Except for two scenes in which Turner wears black (one when she contemplates suicide and the other when she goes to her mother's funeral), the alluring platinum blond actress wears nothing but white in the film. Though she is a *femme fatale* here, Turner is a softer, more emotionally vulnerable Lucrezia Borgia than her sisterly counterparts in other Cain stories. Even at the end she is seeking love, not revenge, telling Garfield after the murder that she wants "kisses that come from life, not death." Cain's narrow, common stories always dealt with sordid love triangles and featured repressed sexuality, but never was this theme better exploited than in this film, and no soiled heroine better exemplified his characters than that played by Turner. So impressed was Cain with Turner's performance that he presented her with a leather-bound first edition of the novel, inscribing it, "For my dear Lana, thank you for giving a performance that was even finer than I expected."

This film was long in the making. MGM acquired the rights to the novel in 1934 after its sensational release, but there was no way a script could be prepared that would appease the severe restrictions of the Hollywood censors. It was adapted as a play in 1936 and this production, short-lived, starred Mary Philips, Richard Barthelmess, and Joseph Greenwald. In 1939 a French film version, LE DERNIER TOURNANT, starred Michel Simon, Fernand Gravet, and Cortinne Luchaire. Then in 1942 Luchino Visconti ignored the copyright on this property and blatantly and illegally made his own film from the Cain story, OSSESSIONE, starring Clara Calamai, Massimo Girotti, and Elio Marcuzzo, but MGM was quick to retaliate, blocking all prints from American release. (It would not be seen in the US until 1977 and even then only in a brief and limited release in American art houses.) By early 1945, writer-producer Wilson had developed a script that would be acceptable to the censors, and the film was cast with Garfield and Turner in the leading

roles, an inspired selection as it turned out. The two were electric on screen. Garfield almost missed being in the film because he was inducted into the service. Cameron Mitchell was tested for the role and almost got the part, but Garfield was released from service with a bad heart and went into the production. Director Garnett caught the actor playing handball and asked him to stop it. "I've got a tricky ticker, so what?" replied the hard-boiled Garfield. "Don't get me wrong," Garnett said. "I don't want to louse up your fun, but I've got to finish this picture." Garfield promised to stop playing handball until the film was completed. The censor was always looking over Garnett's shoulder during the production, and the director later complained: "It was a real chore to do POSTMAN under the Breen Office, but I think I managed to get the sex across. I think I like it better that way. I'm not a voyeur, and I don't like all the body display that you get in pictures nowadays. I think that it's just a crutch for untalented directors and writers." The idea of dressing Turner all in white was Wilson's; he thought that by adorning her in such clothes her sexy image would be downplayed. What it did was propell further her haughty phospherent steaminess; this angelically venal little trollop begged to be dirtied up.

The critical and public response to THE POSTMAN ALWAYS RINGS TWICE was enormous. Turner and Garfield won kudos from the critics, and the supporting players, especially Ames and Cronyn, received plaudits (with Kellaway's simpleton cuckold the only jarring note). Cronyn was exceptional as the conniving criminal lawyer and he parlayed his snide lines for all they were worth. After the murder of Kellaway he delivers one of the most caustic quips ever delivered on screen, sneering at Garfield and Turner, who have just been married, and saying, "I can only think of 15 or 20 reasons why you shouldn't be happy." More than $4 million poured into MGM from the initial box-office receipts. The studio announced in 1972 that it would remake this *film noir* classic, but delays in casting and directing stalled the production until 1980 when Bob Rafelson took over the chore of directing Jack Nicholson and Jessica Lange. The remake was an utter disaster, played strictly for sex with such scenes as Nicholson ravishing Lange on the kitchen table in the cafe. But for all the heaving and pawing, the 1946 version is light years more suggestive.

POURQUOI PAS!
1979 93m c ★★★
Drama
Dimage (France)

Sami Frey *(Fernand)*, Mario Gonzalez *(Louis)*, Christine Murillo *(Alexa)*, Nicole Jamet *(Sylvie)*, Michel Aumont *(Inspector)*, Mathe Souverbie *(Sylvie's Mother)*, Marie-Therese Saussure *(Mme. Picaud)*, Alain Salomon *(Roger)*, Jacques Rispal *(Louis's Father)*, Bernard Crommbe *(Roger's Colleague)*

p, Michele Dimitri; d, Coline Serreau; w, Coline Serreau; ph, Jean-Francois Robin (Eastmancolor); ed, Sophie Tatischeff; m, Jean-Pierre Mas; art d, Denis Martin-Sisteron

A sensitive look at the relationship among three people, Frey, Gonzalez, and Murillo. Frey and Murillo are recent victims of disastrous marriages, finding relief with the bisexual Gonzalez. Frey leaves the setup, creating temporary friction between the other two, but he returns with Jamet, who has conventional values and who, after some internal conflict, decides to join them for a *menage a quatre*. Complex theme is given a nice treatment by Serreau in her first feature. Attempting to explain her purpose in making this offbeat film, Serreau says that her characters, whom she finds likable, "have found a way of life convenient for them—not necessarily for everyone."

PRAISE MARX AND PASS THE AMMUNITION

1970 90m c   ★★
Political/Comedy   /X
Mithras (U.K.)

John Thaw *(Dom)*, Edina Ronay *(Lucy)*, Luis Mahoney *(Julius)*, Anthony Villaroel *(Arthur)*, Helen Fleming *(Clara)*, David David *(Lal)*, Tanya *(Paraguayan Girl)*, Eva Enger *(Swedish Girl)*, Tandy Cronyn *(American Girl)*, Tina Packer *(Air Hostess)*

p, Maurice Hatton; d, Maurice Hatton; w, Maurice Hatton (based on an idea by Maurice Hatton, Michael Wood); ph, Charles Stewart (Eastmancolor); ed, Eduardo Guedes, Tim Lewis; m, Carl Davis; art d, Nick Pollock

Thaw stars as a Marxist who travels around Britain trying to start a revolution but who spends most of his time in bed with the women willing to listen to his political rambling. Suspected by party leaders of not being a "true" revolutionary, Thaw is captured and brought before a tribunal located in a warehouse. College-level theoretical political discourse is thrown back and forth until the cops come and break things up. Pretty tedious unless one enjoys pretentious counterculture nostalgia.

PRANCER

1989 103m c   ★★★½
Drama   G/U
Raffaella/Nelson/Cineplex Odeon

Sam Elliott *(John Riggs)*, Rebecca Harrell *(Jessica Riggs)*, Cloris Leachman *(Mrs. McFarland)*, Rutanya Alda *(Aunt Sarah)*, John Joseph Duda *(Steve Riggs)*, Abe Vigoda *(Dr. Orel Benton)*, Michael Constantine *(Mr. Stewart/Santa)*, Ariana Richards *(Carol Wetherby)*, Mark Rolston *(Herb Drier)*, Johnny Galecki *(Billy Quinn)*

p, Raffaella De Laurentiis, Greg Taylor, Mike Petzold; d, John Hancock; w, Greg Taylor (based on his story); ph, Misha Suslov; ed, Dennis O'Connor; m, Maurice Jarre; prod d, Chester Kaczenski; art d, Marc Dabe; cos, Denny Burt

Plucky nine-year-old Jessica Riggs (Rebecca Harrell) resolutely believes in Santa Claus even though her schoolmates think she's a baby. When she finds Prancer, one of Saint Nick's famous reindeer, injured in nearby forest, Jessica secretly nurses the reindeer back to health, aided by an elderly veterinarian (Abe Vigoda). However, her attempts to help Prancer are complicated when she confides in a shopping-mall Santa (Michael Constantine), who spills the beans to the press, and by her father (Sam Elliott), who sells the reindeer to a merchant for use as part of a promotional stunt. When children's films are released for the holidays, one's heart sinks at the memory of such saccharine seasonal "gems" as SANTA CLAUS: THE MOVIE, and television's "It Came upon a Midnight Clear"; however, PRANCER marches to the beat of a different little drummer boy. Sensitively directed by John Hancock and filmed in the Indiana area where he grew up, the movie benefits from an authentic atmosphere, fleshed-out characters who behave as if they live in the real world, and an especially charming performance by Harrell. Good family films are as rare as flying reindeer, but PRANCER deserves to join the select ranks of those Christmas movies we return to again and again.

PREDATOR

1987 107m c   ★★
Thriller/Science Fiction   R/18
Gordon/Silver/Davis/American Entertainment Partners

Arnold Schwarzenegger *(Maj. Alan "Dutch" Schaefer)*, Carl Weathers *(Dillon)*, Elpidia Carrillo *(Anna)*, Bill Duke *(Mac)*, Jesse Ventura *(Sgt. Blain)*, Sonny Landham *(Billy)*, Richard Chaves *(Pancho)*, R.G. Armstrong *(Gen. Phillips)*, Shane Black *(Hawkins)*, Kevin Peter Hall *(Predator)*

p, Lawrence Gordon, Joel Silver, John Davis; d, John McTiernan; w, Jim Thomas, John Thomas; ph, Don McAlpine (Deluxe Color); ed, John F. Link, II, Mark Helfrich; m, Alan Silvestri; prod d, John Vallone; art d, Frank Richwood, Jorge Saenz, John K. Reinhart, Jr.; fx, R/Greenberg, Joel Hynick, Stuart Robertson, Dream Quest Images, Al Di Sarro, Laurencio Cordero, Stan Winston

Never look to Arnold Schwarzenegger for any kind of film that doesn't muscle its way through impossible odds, absurd characters, and pygmy-brained scripts. This film, however, has a great deal of suspense and is technically above average, although its premise is just as ludicrous as Schwarzenegger's earlier films. The menace, an other-world creature, is established early on in PREDATOR, but the muscle-flexing Maj. Dutch Schaefer (Schwarzenegger) and his fellow soldiers-of-fortune (including Carl Weathers) have to learn the hard way in dense Central American jungles that they are not up against the usual human enemies. When these fly-by-night military men undertake to rescue some captured American soldiers, the predator, an alien from outer space, begins to prey on them. Technically, this film is well done, and the special effects in creating the alien are top-notch, garnering an Oscar nomination. But the improbability of such a creature living in a jungle just to kill humans (the movie offers no explanation for its presence) undermines the project.

PRESIDENT'S ANALYST, THE

1967 103m c   ★★★½
Spy/Comedy   /A
Panpiper

James Coburn *(Dr. Sidney Schaefer)*, Godfrey Cambridge *(Don Masters)*, Severn Darden *(Kropotkin)*, Joan Delaney *(Nan Butler)*, Pat Harrington, Jr. *(Arlington Hewes)*, Barry Maguire *(Old Wrangler)*, Jill Banner *(Snow White)*, Eduard Franz *(Ethan Allan Cocket)*, Walter Burke *(Henry Lux)*, Will Geer *(Dr. Lee Evans)*

p, Stanley Rubin; d, Theodore J. Flicker; w, Theodore J. Flicker; ph, William A. Fraker (Panavision, Technicolor); ed, Stuart Pappe; m, Lalo Schifrin; prod d, Pato Guzman; art d, Hal Pereira, Al Roelofs; cos, Jack Bear

Though it's now badly dated, at the time of its release this picture was a mostly on-the-mark satire of American culture and international politics in the 1960s. Coburn plays a psychiatrist who serves his country as the analyst for the president of the United States. It isn't long before some in the government become concerned about what Coburn has learned in this position, and he's marked for assassination. However, other nations figure Coburn might be able to supply them with valuable information, and soon agents from around the globe are tracking the hapless psychiatrist. Among those in pursuit are American agent Cambridge, his longtime friend and adversary Russian agent Darden, and Arte Johnson and Martin Horsey as a couple of humorless "FBR" agents. Mindless bureaucracy, Cold War mentality, blind liberalism, and psychoanalysis are spoofed in this fast-paced comedy.

PRESUMED INNOCENT

1990　127m　c　　　　　　　　　★★★½
Crime/Mystery　　　　　　　　　　R/15
Mirage

Harrison Ford *(Rusty Sabich)*, Brian Dennehy *(Raymond Horgan)*, Raul Julia *(Sandy Stern)*, Bonnie Bedelia *(Barbara Sabich)*, Paul Winfield *(Judge Larren Lyttle)*, Greta Scacchi *(Carolyn Polhemus)*, John Spencer *(Detective Lipranzer)*, Joe Grifasi *(Tommy Molto)*, Tom Mardirosian *(Nico Della Guardia)*, Anna Maria Horsford *(Eugenia)*

p, Sydney Pollack, Mark Rosenberg; d, Alan J. Pakula; w, Frank Pierson, Alan J. Pakula (based on the novel by Scott Turow); ph, Gordon Willis (Du Art Color); ed, Evan Lottman; m, John Williams; prod d, George Jenkins; art d, Bob Guerra; fx, C5, Inc.; cos, John Boxer

If they gave an Oscar for the year's most claustrophobic film, PRESUMED INNOCENT could win it in a walk. Everything about this film is as cramped, clenched, and constricted as Harrison Ford's face, which looks like a tightly balled-up fist here. Even in his love scenes he manages to look more like he's withdrawing than advancing, kissing with his lips pressed tightly together against both the dazzling Greta Scacchi and the exquisite Bonnie Bedelia. However, Ford's perpetually coiled-up state also makes him the perfect murder suspect in this adaptation of attorney Scott Turow's best-selling novel, which presents a perversely fascinating view of the beleaguered American criminal justice system and the flawed people who run it. Finishing the novel, the reader wonders how anything of merit is accomplished amid the crosscurrents of ambition, greed, and lust that fill the courtrooms of mythical Kindle County. Coming away from the movie, the viewer is likely to feel as drained as Gordon Willis' trademark monochromatic cinematography and Ford's desiccated performance.

Ford plays prosecuting attorney Rusty Sabich, the quintessential good soldier right down to his absurd Roman Centurion haircut. But Sabich serves a degraded master, District Attorney Raymond Horgan (Brian Dennehy), a soured idealist whose principles have been compromised by years of deals made to keep the wheels of justice from grinding to a halt. As the film begins, Horgan is making a halfhearted run at re-election, but his campaign is fatally rocked by the sordid rape-murder of his star prosecutor in the sex-crimes division, the brilliant, beautiful, and ambitious Carolyn Polhemus (Scacchi). Initially, the list of suspects is extensive, a grim tribute to Polhemus' enviable conviction rate, if not her rapacious sex life. But that list narrows to a single name when Sabich's fingerprints are found on a beer glass five feet from Polhemus' body and when tests reveal that the killer's blood type also matches that of Sabich, who had an affair with Polhemus that ended messily. That affair damaged but failed to destroy Sabich's marriage to his wife Barbara (Bedelia), a frustrated academic. Now it has come back to haunt his career. Ever the good soldier, and despite a clear conflict of interest, Sabich takes charge of the investigation after being practically begged to do so by Horgan, who is himself one of Polhemus' former lovers. Not content with having driven Horgan from office in disgrace and embarrassment, the newly elected county DA, Nico Della Guardia (Mardirosian), seizes upon the Sabich case, which he handles personally, in an effort to thoroughly discredit Horgan's tenure. To save his new career in private practice, Horgan is content to shift the blame to Sabich. Furious because Sabich failed to disclose his tryst with Polhemus to him, Horgan is even willing to commit perjury on the witness stand. As the film progresses it becomes clear that truth and justice are the real victims here. Seeing that justice is done is not the object—winning a case is. To that end, Sabich engages top defense lawyer Sandy Stern (Raul Julia), whose stock strategy is to weave a web of doubt around seemingly expert and unimpeachable witnesses. (Stern was the real hero of Turow's novel, a character so rich and vivid that the author placed him at the center of *The Burden of Proof*, his follow-up to *Presumed Innocent*.) While the other characters, including Sabich, scramble to conceal and confuse, Stern succeeds by exposing human frailty and remorseless self-interest in the cold light of the courtroom. So thorough is his demolition of the prosecution that he never has to present anything so mundane as a defense. The case is dismissed by the judge (Paul Winfield) before Stern can place any of his own witnesses on the stand. And a good thing, too. As it turns out, his first witness was fully prepared to confess to the crime.

The solution to this whodunit will hardly surprise any of the millions who have read Turow's novel. However, neither the book nor the movie hinges on the killer's disclosure. Instead the mystery serves to pull readers and viewers deeply into the world of characters whose lives and careers are taken up by the endlessly fascinating business of placing inhuman acts in a human perspective for their evaluation and punishment. In these characters—who have one foot planted outside society and one within—the most civilized ideals mix freely with the most base instincts and motivations.

Despite Turow's contributions, the controlling sensibilities behind the film are those of director Alan J. Pakula, who cowrote the script, and cinematographer Willis. Sabich is repeatedly and implausibly seen poring over legal documents in near-complete darkness for the sake of an expressive photographic effect from Willis, known for his artful use of shadows and darkness in films like THE GODFATHER and its sequels. Meanwhile, Pakula at times seems overly attuned to the weary, overstressed quality that dominated the characters in Turow's book. Forget the dashing, physical Ford of STAR WARS and Indiana Jones fame. Here, we rarely see him walk, much less crack whips or punch out bad guys. Mostly—almost too often—we see him sitting and moping.

However, in the end, along with its strong basic story line, there are simply too many powerful themes, ideas, and characters in PRESUMED INNOCENT to make it anything less than absolutely engrossing whatever its incidental flaws. Though Pakula and company have abridged Turow's work, they wisely haven't altered it in any important way. Turow's familiarity with the world of the law and its personalities cannot be disputed. But, like any lawyer, he also knows how to weave the "physical evidence" into a persuasive narrative rich with nuance. And those qualities carry over easily into PRESUMED INNOCENT, aided by a uniformly fine cast and Pakula's best work since he turned out Oscar winners such as KLUTE, SOPHIE'S CHOICE, and ALL THE PRESIDENT'S MEN.

PRETTY BABY

1978　109m　c　　　　　　　　　★★★½
Drama　　　　　　　　　　　　　R/18
Paramount

Keith Carradine *(E.J. Bellocq)*, Susan Sarandon *(Hattie)*, Brooke Shields *(Violet)*, Frances Faye *(Mme. Nell Livingston)*, Antonio Fargas *(Professor, Piano Player)*, Gerrit Graham *(Highpockets)*, Mae Mercer *(Mama Mosebery)*, Diana Scarwid *(Frieda)*, Barbara Steele *(Josephine)*, Matthew Anton *(Red Top)* p, Louis Malle; d, Louis Malle; w, Polly Platt (based on a story by Platt and Malle, from the book *Storyville, New Orleans: Being an Authentic Account of the Notorious Redlight District* by Al Rose); ph, Sven Nykvist (Metrocolor); ed, Suzanne Baron, Suzanne Fenn; prod d, Trevor Williams; fx, Maureen Lambray; cos, Mina Mittleman

Everyone knows that jazz came up the river from New Orleans, but few people know the reason. Many of the musicians worked for brothels in Storyville, that area which seemed to have been built for one reason only: pleasure. When the US Secretary of the Navy thought that too many of his men were spending too much time in the neighborhood, he ordered the place shuttered, and since the musicians had no place else to work, they came north to establish their music in the Midwest and, later, New York. Malle's look at life in a Storyville brothel annoyed many people because he refused to take a stand, just presenting the facts as he knew them through the original material by Al Rose. The story is seen through the eyes and memory of a 12-year-old prostitute, Shields, the daughter of Sarandon. Because there had been such a brouhaha about child pornography and child abuse, the film was banned in a few venues, but the picture is mild by comparison to many others. Faye runs a plush brothel, and one of her favorite girls is Sarandon. She gives birth to a son, much to the delight of all the other women and of her daughter, Shields, who has grown up in the house and has no idea who her father is. Sarandon tells the "johns" that Shields is her sister, a virgin, because she wants to get out of the profession and eventually marry. Shields takes everything around her with a sweet naivete. When that's the only life you know, it doesn't seem all that unusual. She becomes both friend and surrogate child to all the other women: Scarwid, Steele, Seret Scott, Cheryl Markowitz, and Laura Zimmerman. She watches Graham do her voodoo and loves to hear Fargas play his barrelhouse piano (in an imitation of Jelly Roll Morton). Shields is not the only child living in the large house, and her best pal among the others is Anton. Carradine (playing a real-life character named E.J. Bellocq) is a photographer who uses the women as models for his prints. He loves Shields, thereby causing Sarandon some pain. Carradine is not at all desirous of their wares, just contents himself with taking photographs. (The truth was that Bellocq was barely five feet tall, had a pointed head, and may have been totally asexual.) Since Shields is as yet unsullied, her virginity is a valuable possession, and when the moment arrives for it to end, she is sold for a huge amount, $400, to Don Lutenbacher. After she has pretended to have fainted from the experience, Lutenbacher leaves hurriedly and Faye keeps selling Shields as a first-timer. Hood is a regular customer of Sarandon and loves her enough to propose marriage. Sarandon leaves with her infant son and Shields stays behind, a gesture Shields resents bitterly. Shields begins to act up, then runs away from the brothel to Carradine's home where they are soon lovers and she becomes the focus for his camera. Soon enough Shields is making childish demands, and Carradine tosses her out. By this time Storyville has been shuttered and Faye's mind has cracked. Fargas takes his 10 talented fingers to Chicago, and Shields has no place to live. Carradine proposes marriage and they tie the knot in the presence of the other women. No sooner is the license signed, when Shields begins her old tricks and her spoiled attitude annoys Carradine. Sarandon and Don Hood return to New Orleans with the baby and ask Shields to move in with them and make something of herself by attending school. Shields wants to stay with Carradine and is torn by the offer of having her marriage annulled and living a straight life. In the end Shields chooses to be with her mother and Carradine is destroyed by her departure. The final shot is a family portrait, taken by Hood, of Sarandon, Shields, and the baby, and looking at it, no one would ever know where they came from and how they spent their lives.

The subject matter is shocking, but Malle and his brilliant Swedish cinematographer, Nykvist, handle it with such taste in such a matter-of-fact fashion that it never goes over the edge. The photography is lush and warm; each shot looks like a painting. The movie is slow in places and takes a bit too long establishing moods, but you'll remember it long after you've forgotten many others. Shields' mother was attacked for allowing her 12-year-old model-daughter to pose in the nude and to be exploited. But Shields has grown up to be a well-balanced young woman, albeit an ordinary actress. So far PRETTY BABY has been her best work. Wexler earned an Oscar nomination for his musical direction.

PRETTY IN PINK
1986 96m c   ★★★
Comedy/Drama   PG-13/15
Paramount

Molly Ringwald (*Andie Walsh*), Harry Dean Stanton (*Jack Walsh*), Jon Cryer (*Phil "Duckie" Dale*), Andrew McCarthy (*Blane McDonough*), Annie Potts (*Iona*), James Spader (*Steff McKee*), Jim Haynie (*Donnelly*), Alexa Kenin (*Jena*), Kate Vernon (*Benny*), Andrew Dice Clay (*Bouncer*)

p, Lauren Shuler; d, Howard Deutch; w, John Hughes; ph, Tak Fujimoto (Technicolor); ed, Richard Marks; m, Michael Gore; prod d, John W. Corso; chor, Kenny Ortega

Andie Walsh (Molly Ringwald) is a kid from the wrong side of the tracks. She's a self-confident high-school senior who dresses in handmade clothes, works in a record store, and lives in a modest home with her unemployed father (Harry Dean Stanton). Times are tough for Andie in school, where she and her friends are tormented by the wealthy students who make up the majority of the student body, and where her worst fear is that she won't get invited to the senior prom. Her best friend, "Duckie" (Jon Cryer), talks matter-of-factly with her father about marrying Andie, but he never thinks of taking her to the prom—a social event that most of the poor kids avoid. To her surprise, she is asked to go to the dance by the charming Blaine (Andrew McCarthy), who's not as snobbish as the rest of his elitist friends. As in all of John Hughes's films, PRETTY IN PINK touches a chord with today's teens (as well as anyone who has been that age), but at the same time seems to pander somewhat to the audience's expectations. Interestingly, however, the finest moments in PRETTY IN PINK come not from the script by Hughes, but from Howard Deutch's careful direction. While the script contains trite and unbelievable dialogue, the superbly convincing performances make up for these faults.

PRETTY POISON
1968 89m c   ★★★½
Thriller   /15
Lawrence Turman/Molino

Anthony Perkins (*Dennis Pitt*), Tuesday Weld (*Sue Ann Stepanek*), Beverly Garland (*Mrs. Stepanek*), John Randolph (*Azenauer*), Dick O'Neill (*Bud Munsch*), Clarice Blackburn (*Mrs. Bronson*), Joe Bova (*Pete*), Ken Kercheval (*Harry Jackson*), Don Fellows (*Detective*), Parker Fennelly (*Night Watchman*) p, Marshal Backlar, Noel Black; d, Noel Black; w, Lorenzo Semple, Jr. (based on the novel *She Let Him Continue* by Stephen Geller); ph, David Quaid (DeLuxe Color); ed, William Ziegler; m, Johnny Mandel; art d, Jack Martin Smith, Harold Michelson; fx, Ralph Winigar, Billy King; cos, Ann Roth

A fascinating thriller that was mostly ignored at the time of its release, this is a fine film with a terrific performance by Tuesday Weld. Perkins is again a mentally unstable young man. As a youth, after a fight with his aunt, he kills the woman by burning down her house, though he claims he didn't know she was inside. As the film opens, he's recently been released from prison and is being watched carefully by parole officer Randolph. He gets a job with a lumber company and meets Weld, a pert high-school student. To impress her, he tells her he's with the CIA and in town to investigate nasty business at the lumber company. The two soon begin a relationship, though Weld's domineering mother, Garland, thinks Perkins is a nut and tells her daughter to stay away from him. It isn't long before Perkins finds that Weld's sweet face hides a killer's psyche, and he finds himself caught in a murder wrap as he is cleverly manipulated by the calculating Weld. It's up to the wily Randolph to figure out what really happened. This was Noel Black's directorial debut, and he maintains a brisk pace and a necessary level of tension throughout. Perkins, of course, is fine in the kind of role he excels at, but it's Weld's performance that really makes the film something special. She is superb as the pretty young thing whose exterior cloaks an ice-cold killer. With this film and her fine performances in such movies as SOLDIER IN THE RAIN; THE CINCINNATI KID; and WHO'LL STOP THE RAIN?, she consistently proved herself to be an actress of depth who is much more than a pretty face and a silly name. The picture was made in Great Barrington, Massachusetts.

PRETTY WOMAN

1990 119m c   ★★½
Comedy/Romance   R/15
Silver Screen Partners/Touchstone

Richard Gere *(Edward Lewis)*, Julia Roberts *(Vivian Ward)*, Ralph Bellamy *(James Morse)*, Jason Alexander *(Philip Stuckey)*, Laura San Giacomo *(Kit De Luca)*, Alex Hyde-White *(David Morse)*, Amy Yasbeck *(Elizabeth Stuckey)*, Elinor Donahue *(Bridget)*, Hector Elizondo *(Hotel Manager)*, Judith Baldwin *(Susan)*

p, Arnon Milchan, Steven Reuther; d, Garry Marshall; w, J.F. Lawton; ph, Charles Minsky; ed, Priscilla Nedd; m, James Newton Howard; prod d, Albert Brenner; art d, David M. Haber; fx, Gary Zink; cos, Marilyn Vance-Straker

Director Garry Marshall tips his hand in this lackluster film when he shows Julia Roberts, as Hollywood hooker Vivian Ward, gleefully watching Audrey Hepburn and Cary Grant kissing at the end of a Stanley Donen romantic comedy. Though the man who gave the world "Laverne and Shirley" strives in PRETTY WOMAN for a sophistication that is beyond his grasp, he is right about one thing: Roberts radiates a sprightly, Hepburnish star quality that goes a long way towards making PRETTY WOMAN tolerable entertainment. She is a nonstop delight to watch and demonstrates an astounding maturity in her performance here.

Richard Gere costars as Roberts's love interest, hard-driving corporate takeover specialist Edward Lewis, who, as the film begins, is at a high-powered Hollywood Hills party. But he is without his girlfriend, who is in the process of moving out of their New York apartment. Leaving the party to head back to his Beverly Hills hotel, Lewis winds up in Hollywood instead.

Meanwhile, Vivian is getting ready to hit the streets because her roommate, Kit (SEX, LIES AND VIDEOTAPE's Laura San Giacomo), has spent the household nest egg and the rent is due. On the street, Vivian meets the lost Lewis, who pays her $20 for directions back to Beverly Hills, and even lets her drive his car. On an impulse, he invites her up to his penthouse suite to spend the night—harboring only the purest of intentions, of course. Stripping down to her silky lingerie, however, Vivian manages to loosen up the staid Lewis. The next morning, saying he needs a social partner during his week in LA, Lewis hires Vivian to fill the role. This being a romantic comedy, emotions and nature then take their course.

While only some viewers may find it unlikely that a hooker would be named Vivian, most will agree that the chances are considerably slimmer that two cover girl knockouts like Roberts and San Giacomo would be plying their trade on the boulevard. All right, so PRETTY WOMAN is supposed to be a fairy tale. But whose? It's hard to tell, because the script fails to make the film the street-smart "Pygmalion" it wants to be. Vivian is hardly more than a stereotype, little more than a pneumatic fantasy whore. It's never even completely clear why Lewis hires her, because most of his working week is taken up with business meetings with James Morse (Ralph Bellamy), whose company Lewis is bidding to take over (since when do you bring dates to business meetings?). Between meetings, Lewis seems to have a lot of time on his hands, and he spends it hanging out with Vivian while his evil lawyer, Stuckey (Jason Alexander), plays hardball with Morse. Not many lawyers try to rape their clients' girlfriends, but so many illogical events occur in this film that Stuckey's attempted rape of Vivian becomes just one more bizarre development in a script full of implausibilities.

Still, if Marshall knows anything, it's how to cast a film. Roberts is on the screen most of the time because she deserves to be there (and needs to be there, to provide a distraction from the script and ham-handed direction). Her performance earned a Best Actress Oscar nomination. Yet surprisingly, most of the overt sexual titillation is contributed by Gere, whose physique is on display more than that of Roberts or San Giacomo. Although Gere seems to have phoned in his performance, he nevertheless displays a potential flair for comedy (though that potential may never be realized unless Gere works with a director who finds the key to waking him up). San Giacomo, on the other hand, gives the film's funniest performance in her brief role as the gum-cracking Kit. The other actors comprise a solid ensemble. Alexander, Bellamy, and Marshall regular Hector Elizondo, as the hotel's indulgent manager, all contribute fine performances. Had the producers just been able to lure Stanley Donen out of retirement—and George Bernard Shaw back from the dead—they might have had a good movie on their hands.

PRICK UP YOUR EARS

1987 111m c   ★★★½
Biography   R/18
Civilhand Zenith   (U.K.)

Gary Oldman *(Joe Orton)*, Alfred Molina *(Kenneth Halliwell)*, Vanessa Redgrave *(Peggy Ramsay)*, Wallace Shawn *(John Lahr)*, Lindsay Duncan *(Anthea Lahr)*, Julie Walters *(Elsie Orton)*, James Grant *(William Orton)*, Janet Dale *(Mrs. Sugden)*, Dave Atkins *(Mr. Sugden)*, Margaret Tyzack *(Mme. Lambert)*

p, Andrew Brown; d, Stephen Frears; w, Alan Bennett (based on the biography by John Lahr); ph, Oliver Stapleton (Eastmancolor); ed, Mick Audsley; m, Stanley Myers; prod d, Hugo Luczyc-Wyhowski; art d, Philip Elton; cos, Bob Ringwood

Stephen Frears's PRICK UP YOUR EARS chronicles the rise and tragic demise of Joe Orton, the gay playwright whose brief but dazzling career spawned the brilliant farces *Loot, Entertaining Mr. Sloan* and *What the Butler Saw* and made a lasting contribution to the English-language theater.

Born John Orton in Leicester, England, Orton died at age 34 in 1967 when his longtime lover, Kenneth Halliwell, crushed his skull with a hammer before downing two handfuls of Nembutal to take his own life. PRICK UP YOUR EARS opens with this grisly event, then unfolds in flashbacks as biographer John Lahr (Wallace Shawn) researches Orton's brief life.

At 17, Orton (Gary Oldman) arrives in London to attend the Royal Academy of Dramatic Art, where he meets the hulking Halliwell (Alfred Molina), who is several years older and has an independent income. The attractive, impressionable Orton is quickly taken under the latter's wing and they soon move into a squalid bed-sitter in North London—their home for the next 16 years. Under Halliwell's tutelage, the two attempt a few novels with no success. Halliwell eventually settles into the role of long-suffering spouse while Orton increasingly indulges his taste for anonymous sexual encounters. When their novels are summarily rejected, the now impoverished duo wreak revenge by defacing books in a local library. They are eventually caught and incarcerated. Separated from Halliwell for the first time in many years, Orton uses his six-month sentence to write a radio play, *The Ruffian on the Stair*, which, upon his release, gives him entree into London's literary world; Orton's incarceration has given his work a scathing, provocative edge previously lacking in his collaborations with Halliwell. He's soon snapped up by Peggy Ramsay (Vanessa Redgrave), a leading agent, who guides Orton's professional career but not his increasingly strained personal life.

This is director Frears's second film with an openly homosexual theme, the first being 1986's acclaimed MY BEAUTIFUL LAUNDRETTE, and he attempts to delve deeply into the relationship between the two protagonists. In real life, however, Halliwell was not the bearish brute that Molina's physical presence indicates; those who knew him say that he had a certain charm of his own as well as a Svengali influence over Orton. Other than the unfortunate miscasting of Molina, an otherwise superb actor, and Wallace Shawn's grating performance, everyone else is right on the money. Oldman, fresh from his triumph as Sex Pistol Sid Vicious in SID AND NANCY, is the key and holds it all together with a performance that confirms his stature as Britain's great new acting hope.

PRIDE AND PREJUDICE

1940 117m bw ★★★★★
Drama /U
MGM

Greer Garson (*Elizabeth Bennet*), Laurence Olivier (*Mr. Darcy*), Mary Boland (*Mrs. Bennet*), Edna May Oliver (*Lady Catherine de Bourgh*), Maureen O'Sullivan (*Jane Bennet*), Ann Rutherford (*Lydia Bennet*), Frieda Inescort (*Miss Caroline Bingley*), Edmund Gwenn (*Mr. Bennet*), Karen Morley (*Charlotte Lucas*), Heather Angel (*Kitty Bennet*)

p, Hunt Stromberg; d, Robert Z. Leonard; w, Aldous Huxley, Jane Murfin (based on the play by Helen Jerome and the novel by Jane Austen); ph, Karl Freund; ed, Robert J. Kern; m, Herbert Stothart; art d, Cedric Gibbons, Paul Groesse; chor, Ernst Matray; cos, Adrian, Gile Steele

We may be prejudiced, but MGM can be proud. A remarkable example of Hollywood's not choking on the prestige adorning

the filming of a classic, PRIDE AND PREJUDICE is an unusually successful adaptation of the nearly inimitable Jane Austen's most famous novel. Although the satire is slightly reduced and coarsened and the period advanced in order to use more flamboyant period costumes, the spirit is entirely in keeping with Austen's sharp, witty portrait of rural 19th century social mores. The film tells the familiar story of Mr. and Mrs. Bennet (Gwenn and Boland) and their five marriageable daughters. Jane (O'Sullivan) falls for the wealthy Mr. Bingley (Bruce Lester) but, unsure of her love and discouraged by his snooty sister (Inescourt) and his haughty friend Mr. Darcy (Olivier), he leaves town without any promises. The middle daughter, Mary (Marsha Hunt) is goofy and bookish, the fourth child Kitty (Angel) insecure and suggestible and the youngest, Lydia (Rutherford), overly flirtatious. Troubles really brew when Lydia runs off with a caddish officer (Edward Ashley) and when Darcy, who feels himself too "proud" to fall for just any woman, flips for the second Bennet daughter, the independent Elizabeth (Garson). She, however, "prejudiced" against him because of his arrogance, will have none of him. Her mother, though, plans for her to wed their foppish cousin, Mr. Collins (Melville Cooper). How scandals are avoided and the appropriate couples paired up makes for marvelous storytelling.

The screenplay, by old hand Jane Murfin and no less than Aldous Huxley, retains much of the novel's famous dialogue (e.g., the open conversation between Mr. and Mrs. Bennet). They have also added a few scenes to "open up" the action a bit; our favorites are the hilarious carriage race and the enchanting archery lesson. The sets and costumes are lovingly rendered and the cinematography by ace Freund evokes a glorious sense of period. PRIDE AND PREJUDICE may represent the finest directorial work by MGM perennial Robert Z. Leonard. Liked by actors whom he indulged, Leonard generally crafts his work smoothly but it often lacks personality, imagination or even a strong sense of control. Here, however, the pacing is perfect and the sense of detail gleams with both modesty and precision. The ball, for example, artfully suggests both the intrigues afoot and the romances burgeoning. For personality, all one has to do is turn to that amazing cast. Garson never did anything better in her entire career than her Elizabeth Bennet. Genteel but not precious, witty yet not forced, spirited but never vulgar, Garson's Elizabeth is an Austen heroine incarnate. She doesn't look younger than the charming O'Sullivan (playing her elder sister) but this lovely actress manages a wide range of emotions as her intelligent heroine realizes her grievous errors. Olivier, too, has rarely been better in a part requiring the passion of his Heathcliff from WUTHERING HEIGHTS but strapping it into the straitjacket of snobbery. Neither actor has ever looked better, either. (It's a real toss-up who's prettier.) Elizabeth's sisters are all fine, though we prefer Inescourt's incredibly frosty performance as Bingley's sister. As Mr. Bennet, Gwenn makes a wonderfully wry and composed foil for his wife's antics, and Cooper rarely had the chance to huff and fluff quite so amusingly again. Biggest laugh-getters, though, are Boland as the matchmaking mother and Oliver as Darcy's insufferable aunt. Neither seems really British, but you'll be laughing so hard it hardly matters. Boland's devastating timing and vocal range lead her flighty character from death's door to aggressive man-hunting in mere moments. Oliver, meanwhile, is priceless arranging the parade into dinner or declaring that uncooperative chickens must be immediately "killed and boiled". It is precisely a cast as golden as this one which both indulges and transcends the Hollywoodisms of the production to create a memorable period romantic comedy.

PRIDE OF THE MARINES

1945　119m　bw　　　　　　　　★★★★
War　　　　　　　　　　　　　　　　/A
WB

John Garfield (Al Schmid), Eleanor Parker (Ruth Hartley), Dane Clark (Lee Diamond), John Ridgely (Jim Merchant), Rosemary DeCamp (Virginia Pfeiffer), Ann Doran (Ella Merchant), Warren Douglas (Kebabian), Don McGuire (Irish), Tom D'Andrea (Tom), Rory Mallinson (Doctor)

p, Jerry Wald; d, Delmer Daves; w, Albert Maltz, Marvin Borowsky (based on a story by Roger Butterfield); ph, Peverell Marley; ed, Owen Marks; m, Franz Waxman; art d, Leo K. Kuter; fx, L. Robert Burgs

A grand and emotional study in heroism, PRIDE OF THE MARINES is a tour de force for rugged Garfield and a film that allowed director Daves to introduce some startling psychological techniques which made this film exceptional. Based on the true story of Al Schmid, the film shows us Garfield as a workingman in Philadelphia who falls in love with Parker. They have a rough-and-tumble courtship, then marry on the eve of WW II. Garfield is one of the first to join up, enlisting in the Marines and being sent to Guadalcanal where, in 1942, American troops had their first significant confrontation with invading Japanese troops. Garfield and his small machine gun crew receive orders to be on the alert for a massive Japanese attack one night, and when it comes the defenders are almost overwhelmed. Machine gunners Anthony Caruso and Clark are put out of action, and Garfield takes over the gun, literally mowing down hundreds of Japanese storming his position. One enemy soldier hurls a grenade at the gun, and Garfield is blinded. But even blinded, Garfield draws his pistol and fires, sightless, at the enemy. Returned to a San Diego hospital, Garfield undergoes intense medical treatment along with psychological preparation to face the world without eyesight. But he cannot bring himself to reenter society a cripple and fears rejection by his wife, Parker. He not only fights treatment but becomes embittered and insists that he will see again. Some light can be seen by Garfield in one eye, but it is only a milky blur and doctors tell him not to hold out too much hope. Finally it is time for him to return to Philadelphia, and he is escorted by Clark who encourages him to face the future. Garfield has nightmare visions of himself standing in a train station and Parker walking away from him after seeing that he is blind. He nevertheless goes home, awkwardly attempting to fit into society. He resents his now clumsy, unsure movements and is embarrassed at bumping into a Christmas tree. Slowly Garfield adjusts, and by the time he is decorated with the Navy Cross for his heroism on Guadalcanal (credited with killing 200 enemy soldiers), the "Pride of the Marines" displays equal courage in facing life with Parker.

　　Garfield is brilliant in his portrayal of Schmid, and Daves's direction is superb, utilizing remarkable techniques such as double printings, negative images, and telescopic shots which all add to the eerie and unnerving experience Garfield is undergoing in his rehabilitation. The battle scenes in this film are some of the most harrowing ever shot. The idea for the film was largely Garfield's. He read an article about Schmid in Life magazine and contacted writer Maltz, suggesting a script be written about the man. Maltz had worked on the film DESTINATION TOKYO, also directed by Daves, and Garfield felt he would be the ideal writer to handle the project. Daves was brought into the project a short time later. This film, along with AIR FORCE and DESTINATION TOKYO, was one of Garfield's favorite films made at Warner Bros. PRIDE OF THE MARINES was a box office smash, released just as WWII came to a close, timed perfectly with the public's curiosity about rehabilitating a generation of wounded American servicemen. Co-author Maltz later became one of the "Hollywood Ten," and some of the dialogue in PRIDE OF THE MARINES was later recalled by the House Un-American Activities Committee, particularly those lines dealing with social consciousness and working class arguments (mostly expressed by Clark), as an example of communistic philosophy insidiously inserted into movies. The film nevertheless remains a deeply moving, sensitive production, and one of the finest war films ever made.

PRIDE OF THE YANKEES, THE

1942　127m　bw　　　　　　　　★★★★½
Biography/Sports　　　　　　　　　/U
RKO

Gary Cooper (Lou Gehrig), Teresa Wright (Eleanor Gehrig), Walter Brennan (Sam Blake), Dan Duryea (Hank Hanneman), Babe Ruth (Himself), Elsa Janssen (Mom Gehrig), Ludwig Stossel (Pop Gehrig), Virginia Gilmore (Myra), Bill Dickey (Himself), Ernie Adams (Miller Huggins),

p, Samuel Goldwyn; d, Sam Wood; w, Jo Swerling, Herman J. Mankiewicz (based on a story by Paul Gallico); ph, Rudolph Mate; ed, Daniel Mandell; m, Leigh Harline; prod d, William Cameron Menzies; art d, Perry Ferguson, McClure Capps; fx, Jack Cosgrove; cos, Rene Hubert

Eloquently written (by Herman Mankiewicz and Jo Swerling from a story by Paul Gallico), stunningly photographed, and directed with great sensitivity, THE PRIDE OF THE YANKEES is the sweet, sentimental, and utterly American story of Lou Gehrig, the "Iron Man" first baseman of the indefatigable New York Yankees of the 1920s and 30s. Gary Cooper is exceptional as Gehrig and Teresa Wright marvelous as his sweetheart (and later wife), Eleanor.

　　Gehrig is first shown as a Columbia student, playing baseball whenever possible but dedicated to his studies. Determined to become an engineer to please his mother (Elsa Janssen), who has slaved to pay his tuition, he turns down a contract offer from the Yankees. When she requires surgery, however, Gehrig signs with the team to pay for her medical expenses, beginning his spectacular career in June 1925 and meeting his future wife during his first game, as he stumbles on a pile of bats, much to her amusement. Soon Gehrig has helped lead the Yankees to the World Series, becoming one of the best ever to play the game, until, in 1939, he learns that he has a lethal neurological disease (amyotrophic lateral sclerosis, since known as Lou Gehrig's disease) and has only a short time to live. He retires from baseball and makes a dramatic farewell at Yankee Stadium (perhaps the most famous scene in any sports film), standing at home plate and stating, "Some people say I've had a bad break, but I consider myself to be the luckiest man on the face of the earth." As the crowd gives him a deafening ovation, Gehrig walks from the field, into the dugout, and up a passageway, exiting into legend. THE PRIDE OF THE YANKEES is the story of a simple man with extraordinary talent and a soaring spirit that made him the idol of every American schoolboy. Although the film keeps the on-field action to a minimum, Cooper, a righthander, spent many weeks under the tutelage of Lefty O'Doul learning to bunt and throw lefthanded like Gehrig. To complete the illusion, Cooper wore a uniform with the numbers reversed and ran to third base instead of first so that when the film was processed, in reverse, he would appear to be swinging from the left side of the plate. Among the real-life Bronx Bomber teammates who appear in

THE PRIDE OF THE YANKEES are Babe Ruth, Bill Dickey, Mark Koenig, and Bob Meusel. In 1938, Gehrig made his own acting debut, playing himself in RAWHIDE, wherein he trades in his bat for life on a ranch and ends up combating racketeers who are making life miserable for local ranchers.

PRIME CUT

1972 88m c   ★★★
Crime   R/18
Cinema Center

Lee Marvin (Nick Devlin), Gene Hackman ("Mary Ann"), Angel Tompkins (Clarabelle), Gregory Walcott (Weenie), Sissy Spacek (Poppy), Janit Baldwin (Violet), William Morey (Shay), Clint Ellison (Delaney), Howard Platt (Shaughnessy), Les Lannom (O'Brien)

p, Joe Wizan; d, Michael Ritchie; w, Robert Dillon; ph, Gene Polito (Panavision, Technicolor); ed, Carl Pingitore; m, Lalo Schifrin; art d, Bill Malley; fx, Logan Frazee; cos, Patricia Norris

Hackman is a degenerate Kansas City cattleman who sells as many girls as he does cows. Chicago gangster Marvin is sent to teach him a lesson on behalf of factory owners who are fed up with Hackman's insolence. Some of the more interesting aspects of this violent film from director Michael Ritchie are an unlikely setting for a gangster film (a country fair), a wheatfield chase scene (a la NORTH BY NORTHWEST), and a switch in casting (Hackman playing the louse and Marvin playing the relatively good guy). Ritchie breaks tradition by portraying the rural population as far more despicable than the city folk, referring to Chicago as being "as peaceful as anyplace anywhere." Sissy Spacek makes her film debut as one of Hackman's commodities.

PRIME OF MISS JEAN BRODIE, THE

1969 116m c   ★★★★
Drama/Comedy   M/15
FOX (U.K.)

Maggie Smith (Jean Brodie), Robert Stephens (Teddy Lloyd), Pamela Franklin (Sandy), Gordon Jackson (Gordon Lowther), Celia Johnson (Miss MacKay), Diane Grayson (Jenny), Jane Carr (Mary McGregor), Shirley Steedman (Monica), Lavinia Lang (Emily Carstairs), Antoinette Biggerstaff (Helen McPhee)

p, Robert Fryer; d, Ronald Neame; w, Jay Presson Allen (based on the play by Allen from the novel by Muriel Spark); ph, Ted Moore (DeLuxe Color); ed, Norman Savage; m, Rod McKuen; prod d, John Howell; art d, Brian Herbert; cos, Elizabeth Haffenden, Joan Bridge

Prime, indeed. Lying back for a good wallow in Smith's Oscar-winning performance makes you feel as if you're participating in a guilty pleasure. The book had been a mild success; then Allen turned it into a play in 1966 starring Vanessa Redgrave in London and Zoe Caldwell in New York. The ensuing attention warranted acquiring it for a feature production (Lucky moviegoers were spared Redgrave's blazing humorless nobility).

In the Edinburgh of 1932, Smith teaches in an upscale private girls' school. She inspires her students with her ideas on art, music, and politics—the latter based on romantic notions that lead her to express admiration for the *fascisti* in Italy. Smith has assembled a small coterie of adoring students—including Carr, Grayson and Franklin—who follow her around. She even arranges to take them with her on one of her occasional visits to the country home of Jackson, a fellow teacher who is more interested in her than she is in him. Actually, she is romantically involved with Stephens, another teacher and a sometime painter,

whose jealousy she hopes Jackson's attentions will arouse. Stephens, however, a married Catholic with children, balks at breaking up his marriage to make a commitment to Smith. Dour headmistress Johnson, meanwhile, takes a dim view of Smith's influence and has her suspicions about the impropriety of the teacher's actions. Young follower Franklin, annoyed by Smith's evaluation of her as scholarly and practical—and of Grayson as a romantic beauty—determines to seduce Stephens away from Smith.

Celia Johnson makes a formidible adversary for Smith, and Smith's then-husband Stephens is dead-on right as the art professor. Pamela Franklin, accomplished and lovely, does the best she can with the film's most difficult plot-fulcrum role. The movie loses some steam when it turns to romantic melodrama, but Smith keeps you watching to see how she works with it. Work she does, managing at the same time to make her unique brand of magic look easy as breathing.

Rod McKuen's song "Jean" gained some attention here and there. The interiors were shot at London's Pinewood studios and Edinburgh itself served for all location shooting.

PRINCE AND THE PAUPER, THE

1937 120m bw   ★★★½
Adventure   /U
WB/First National

Errol Flynn (Miles Hendon), Claude Rains (Earl of Hertford), Henry Stephenson (Duke of Norfolk), Barton MacLane (John Canty), Billy Mauch (Tom Canty), Bobby Mauch (Prince Edward), Alan Hale (Captain of the Guard), Eric Portman (1st Lord), Montagu Love (Henry VIII), Robert Warwick (Lord Warwick)

p, Robert Lord; d, William Keighley; w, Laird Doyle (based on the novel by Mark Twain and the play by Catherine Chisholm Cushing); ph, Sol Polito; ed, Ralph Dawson; m, Erich Wolfgang Korngold; art d, Robert Haas; fx, Willard Van Enger, James Gibbons; cos, Milo Anderson

This Mark Twain doppelganger tale of rags and royalty in 16th-century England is sumptuously produced and full of high drama and adventure, with Errol Flynn swashbuckling between the precocious Mauch twins—Bill and Bobby. The look-alikes decide that they will switch roles as a lark, one being Prince Edward (later King Edward VI), the other a beggar boy. Despite the beggar boy's outlandish behavior in his new station, the royal court and advisors accept him as the heir to the throne. The true Edward, however, is submerged in low-life London and, when he decides he's had enough of the game, asserts that he is the real prince. Miles Hendon (Flynn), a soldier of fortune, meets the real Edward and is amused by his claims to the throne, thinking him mad until he begins to believe the emphatic urchin just as the impostor is about to be crowned king. Enemies at court send an assassin (Alan Hale) after the boy, but he is prevented from carrying out his evil task by Miles, who saves the real king-to-be at the last moment.

PRINCE AND THE SHOWGIRL, THE

1957 117m c   ★★★½
Comedy   /PG
Marilyn Monroe/L.O.P. (U.K.)

Marilyn Monroe (Elsie Marina), Laurence Olivier (Charles), Sybil Thorndike (Queen Dowager), Richard Wattis (Northbrooke), Jeremy Spenser (King Nicholas), Esmond Knight (Hoffman), Paul Hardwick (Major Domo), Rosamund Greenwood (Maud), Aubrey Dexter (The Ambassador), Maxine Audley (Lady Sunningdale)

p, Laurence Olivier; d, Laurence Olivier; w, Terence Rattigan (based on the play *The Sleeping Prince* by Rattigan); ph, Jack Cardiff (Technicolor); ed, Jack Harris; m, Richard Addinsell; chor, William Chappell; cos, Beatrice Dawson

By combining the light comic skills of Monroe and the grand acting ability of Olivier, THE PRINCE AND THE SHOWGIRL manages to succeed not only as pleasant entertainment but also as a wonderful mixture of two very different screen personalities. It's 1911 in London, and Monroe plays a flighty American showgirl who catches the eye of the prince regent of Carpathia, Olivier, who is in town for the coronation of George V. Traveling with the prince is his partially deaf mother-in-law, Thorndike, and his son, Spenser. Olivier, who has very little time for courtship, invites Monroe to dinner in his room at the embassy with the hope of seducing her. Monroe rejects Olivier's romantic overtures, greatly frustrating the prince. After drinking an excess of liquor, Monroe falls asleep. When she awakens the next morning, she realizes that she is in love with Olivier. He, however, wants nothing more than to see her leave. In between Monroe's attempts to renew Olivier's interest, she becomes a mediator in a feud between the prince and his son. She discovers that Spenser is impatiently awaiting the day, 18 months away, when he comes of age and inherits the throne of Carpathia. Upset with his father's habit of treating him like a child, Spenser plots to take control as soon as possible. Monroe manages to bring the two together and helps them overcome their differences. Eventually, Olivier is won over by Monroe's beauty and charm, but must return to his country until the end of the 18-month period. Olivier travels to Carpathia and promises to return to Monroe, who lovingly agrees to wait.

Produced and directed by Olivier and financed by Monroe's newly formed production company (she reportedly was to receive a phenomenal 75 percent of the profits), THE PRINCE AND THE SHOWGIRL shows both actors in fine form. Monroe—in this, her 25th picture—had turned 30 and was as beautiful as ever, delivering a comic performance which is among her very finest. She is thoroughly endearing in her scatterbrained but well-mannered way and ably holds her own opposite her accomplished costar. Olivier had already familiarized himself with the role on the British stage in the Rattigan play "The Sleeping Prince," which costarred his terribly miscast wife, Vivien Leigh. Initially Rattigan had expressed reservations about having an actor of Olivier's stature playing a character the author had envisioned as a mundane bureaucrat. But Rattigan needn't have worried; after much ballyhoo in the press, the play opened to rave reviews. What's more, the casting of Monroe in place of Leigh brought the film a remarkable balance between two of film's most arresting screen personalities.

PRINCE OF FOXES
1949 107m bw   ★★★★
Adventure/Historical   /A
FOX

Tyrone Power (*Andrea Corsini*), Orson Welles (*Cesare Borgia*), Wanda Hendrix (*Camilla Verano*), Everett Sloane (*Mario Belli*), Marina Berti (*Angela Borgia*), Katina Paxinou (*Mona Zeppo Constanza*), Felix Aylmer (*Count Marc Antonio Verano*), Leslie Bradley (*Don Esteban*), Joop van Hulzen (*D'Este*), James Carney (*Alphonso D'Este*)

p, Sol C. Siegel; d, Henry King; w, Milton Krims (based on the novel by Samuel Shellabarger); ph, Leon Shamroy; ed, Barbara McLean; m, Alfred Newman; art d, Lyle Wheeler, Mark-Lee Kirk; fx, Fred Sersen; cos, Vittorio Nino Novarese

Great adventure, a literate script, and fine performances combine in PRINCE OF FOXES to produce splendid entertainment, directed with marvelous briskness by Henry King. Set during the Italian Renaissance, the film opens with Welles, as the notorious Cesare Borgia, outlining his plans for the domination of Italy to his trusted aide, Power. Welles tells Power that the city-state cannot be taken of Ferrara by force, its fortress being too well-manned and well-defended by the Duke Alfonso D'Este (van Hulzen), cannon-maker extraordinaire. He assigns Power to persuade van Hulzen to marry Welles's sister, the scheming Lucrezia Borgia. This Power does, with considerable guile and brass, after which he is instructed by Welles to seduce the young Hendrix—wife of the elderly Aylmer, who presides over a neighboring duchy—and then to turn over Aylmer's mountain fortress to Welles. En route to Aylmer's duchy, Power, an aspiring painter, stops to visit his mentor, art dealer Eduardo Ciannelli, and arranges to have one of his own works on display when Hendrix inspects Ciannelli's collection. She spots Power's work and admires it, after which the artist makes a gift of it to her. Hendrix, in turn, invites Power to visit her and Aylmer. However, having thus inveigled his way into Aylmer's court, Power soon realizes that the old duke is an honorable, decent man whose deep love for Hendrix is more paternal than sexual, and he cannot bring himself to betray Hendrix and Aylmer's trust. Deciding he can no longer wait for Power to deliver the duchy, Welles orders his men to march against the mountain fortress. Power offers his sword to Aylmer and Hendrix, betraying his master to join in the heroic defense of the stronghold. Welles's troops eventually overcome the defenders, however, and Aylmer is dead by the time Hendrix and Power surrender the duchy. After Sloane, Power's erstwhile friend and advisor, reports to Welles that he has discovered that Power's mother (Paxinou) is a peasant, Welles realizes that his former aide, now his prisoner, has not only betrayed him but is not of noble birth, and allows Sloane to gouge out Power's eyes before a dinner party at which Hendrix begs for Power's life. However, Sloane has really crushed two grapes over Power's eyes and offered this gore up as the real thing, whispering to Power to scream in feigned pain. Power is led away, but soon organizes a plot to retake Citta del Monte and free Hendrix. He appears magically, slaying his former captors, and, with Sloane's help and that of the local citizenry, routs Welles's overconfident army. Afterwards, the low-born Power is officially elevated to a lordship and weds Hendrix.

Beautifully photographed on location in Italy by cinematographer Leon Shamroy, this Fox production is both tasteful and lavish, with Power exceptional in his portrait of an ambitious but honorable Renaissance man. Unfortunately, the exquisite costuming suffers somewhat as a result of Fox's decision to shoot in black and white, even though King had begged for color. Welles, who makes a wholly sinister Cesare Borgia, took the role because he was desperately in need of cash to fuel his own projects. But he couldn't resist the urge to direct, and reportedly infuriated King when, during his scenes, he would upbraid his fellow actors for not reacting correctly to his evil, powerful character.

PRINCE OF THE CITY

1981 167m c   ★★★½
Crime   R/15
Orion

Treat Williams *(Daniel Ciello)*, Jerry Orbach *(Gus Levy)*, Richard Foronjy *(Joe Marinaro)*, Don Billett *(Bill Mayo)*, Kenny Marino *(Dom Bando)*, Carmine Caridi *(Gino Mascone)*, Tony Page *(Raf Alvarez)*, Norman Parker *(Rick Cappalino)*, Paul Roebling *(Brooks Paige)*, Bob Balaban *(Santimassino)*

p, Burtt Harris; d, Sidney Lumet; w, Jay Presson Allen, Sidney Lumet (based on the book by Robert Daley); ph, Andrzej Bartkowiak (Technicolor); ed, John J. Fitzstephens; m, Paul Chihara; prod d, Tony Walton; art d, Edward Pisoni; cos, Anna Hill Johnstone

PRINCE OF THE CITY is an excellent, if overlong, fictional treatment of a true story, set in the 1960s. New York cop Daniel Ciello (Treat Williams) reluctantly turns informer on his pals and colleagues after being recruited by the US Justice Department to expose police corruption, especially the involvement of the cops in the drug trade. Williams gives a fine performance, the rest of the cast is also excellent, and director Sidney Lumet's eye for detail is sure throughout this authentic look at the dirtier side of police work. Lumet's and Jay Presson Allen's screenplay was nominated for an Oscar.

PRINCE OF TIDES, THE

1991 132m c   ★★★½
Drama/Romance   R/15
Barwood Films/Longfellow Productions/Columbia

Nick Nolte *(Tom Wingo)*, Barbra Streisand *(Dr. Susan Lowenstein)*, Blythe Danner *(Sallie Wingo)*, Kate Nelligan *(Lila Wingo Newbury)*, Jeroen Krabbe *(Herbert Woodruff)*, Melinda Dillon *(Savannah Wingo)*, George Carlin *(Eddie Detreville)*, Jason Gould *(Bernard Woodruff)*, Brad Sullivan *(Henry Wingo)*, Maggie Collier *(Lucy Wingo)*

p, Barbra Streisand, Andrew Karsch; d, Barbra Streisand; w, Becky Johnston, Pat Conroy (from the novel by Conroy); ph, Stephen Goldblatt; ed, Don Zimmerman; m, James Newton Howard; prod d, Paul Sylbert; art d, W. Steven Graham; cos, Ruth Morley

THE PRINCE OF TIDES is melodrama of a high order, crammed with lyrical sequences and featuring some inspired performances, especially by Nick Nolte and Kate Nelligan. Directed with obvious loving care by Barbra Streisand, this eagerly awaited film adaptation of Pat Conroy's best-seller also boasts a serious flaw: Streisand herself.

Narrated by Tom Wingo (Nolte) in flashbacks intercut with present-day sequences, THE PRINCE OF TIDES tells the story of his family, a poor white clan from the South Carolina tidewater. They've been emotionally crippled by a horrendous, never-talked-about event which took place during Tom's childhood. Only years later, following yet another suicide attempt by Tom's twin sister Savannah (Melinda Dillon), a poet living in Manhattan's Greenwich Village, is the "truth" exhumed and the Wingo family demon exorcised.

Hospitalized in intensive care, Savannah, now a borderline catatonic who has lost her will to live, has entirely censored out her youth and does not respond to therapy. At the request of Savannah's psychoanalyst (Streisand), Tom flies north to help shed light on his sister's troubled psyche.

A lovable loser, Tom, too, has been left emotionally scarred by the mysterious childhood event. Though he makes light of it, his present situation is far from ideal. An unemployed high-school English teacher and football coach, the father of three, he spends depressing days as house-husband to dissatisfied wife Sallie (Blythe Danner), a doctor who's thinking of leaving leave him for her lover. Tom's life is a mess, but he hides his misery with self-deprecating humor.

Over a six-week period with Dr. Lowenstein, Tom explores the disconnected fragments of the Wingo past, all of which are colored by a debilitating, elusive sense of terror. Finally, the truth comes out. Years before, Tom's mother Lila (Nelligan) and both twins were raped by three escaped convicts, two of whom were shot and killed by Tom's older brother, Luke (Grayson Fricke). Lila stabbed the third. Obsessed with appearances and with her standing in the community, Lila insisted the incident be kept a secret, forbidding her children to ever mention what happened—not even to their abusive father, a redneck shrimper. That night, dinner went on as usual, but the long-term effects of denial and repression on her family have proved disastrous.

As the summer continues, Tom's confidence slowly returns—partly thanks to a soft-focus love affair with Lowenstein, partly thanks to his successful coaching of her withdrawn, preppy son Bernard (Jason Gould) in football. Bernard, a promising violinist on school vacation, has been thoroughly undermined by his father, Herbert (Jeroen Krabbe), an arrogant violin virtuoso who treats most people—including his wife and son—with disdain. (For their simulated onscreen solos, both Gould and Krabbe spent months learning correct violin technique to complement concert violinist Pinkas Zuckerman's soundtrack recordings.)

By the end of the summer—and of the film—all wrongs have been righted. Bernard has developed muscles and self-esteem; Lowenstein, a neglected wife, has dumped her cheating husband; Savannah is on her way to recovery; and Tom, his ego fully restored, has returned to the loving arms of his wife in South Carolina. For the first time, he feels he has something to give back to the women in his life, and his last words (here, as in the novel) say it all: "I am a teacher, a coach, and a well-loved man."

Therapists will be scornful of Lowenstein's quick cure for the Wingo family's trauma (i.e. remember the past, and all neurosis will immediately disappear), especially since she dispenses her expertise *gratis*—not to mention the fact that she tumbles into bed with her "client." Most moviegoers, though, are probably willing to let this slip by.

What *doesn't* wash is Streisand's one-note characterization of the sophisticated New York shrink. As the film's star, director and co-producer, Streisand was able to change the story as she saw fit, and she did, shifting the book's focus from the depraved past of the Wingo clan to the Tom-Susan love affair. This could have worked if Streisand had directed herself better—if, indeed, she had directed herself at all. Instead of a performance, we get smirks, poses, shots that linger on her outrageously long mani-cured fingernails, and radiant, cloying smiles.

Streisand's inadequacies are more than compensated for by Nolte's compelling portrayal of Tom. He brings conviction and depth to the role, treading a fine line between self-pity and self-respect and exposing his frailties with a rare sensitivity. (He also manages to keep a straight face during a restaurant scene where Susan orders dinner in French—now *that's* acting.)

Streisand works well with the rest of the cast, who might have been lifted directly off the novel's pages: Brad Sullivan (TIN MEN, TRUE COLORS), as Henry Wingo, the sullen family patriarch; Dutch actor Jeroen Krabbe (THE FOURTH MAN, KAFKA) as Herbert; Blythe Danner (THE GREAT SANTINI, MR. AND MRS. BRIDGE) as Nolte's troubled wife; and Kate Nelligan (THE EYE OF THE NEEDLE, FRANKIE &

JOHNNY) as Lila. Nelligan in particular makes an impressive transition from an iron-willed, ambitious young mother trapped by her marriage to a shrimp-boat captain, to an elderly society matron determined to maintain appearances at all costs.

Though not a faithful adaptation of Conroy's spellbinding family saga, THE PRINCE OF TIDES whets the appetite for the best-selling novel, which more thoroughly fleshes out the Wingo's eccentric and complex familial history. Both are a cathartic experience.

PRINCESS BRIDE, THE

1987 98m c ★★★½
Adventure/Children's/Comedy PG
Act III

Cary Elwes (Westley), Mandy Patinkin (Inigo Montoya), Chris Sarandon (Prince Humperdinck), Christopher Guest (Count Rugen), Wallace Shawn (Vizzini), Andre the Giant (Fezzik), Fred Savage (The Grandson), Robin Wright (Buttercup, the Princess Bride), Peter Falk (The Grandfather), Peter Cook (The Impressive Clergyman)

p, Arnold Scheinman, Rob Reiner; d, Rob Reiner; w, William Goldman (based on his novel); ph, Adrian Biddle (Deluxe Color); ed, Robert Leighton; m, Mark Knopfler; prod d, Norman Garwood; art d, Keith Pain, Richard Holland; fx, Nick Allder; cos, Phyllis Dalton

A hilarious mixture of Errol Flynn swashbuckler and Monty Python send-up, THE PRINCESS BRIDE works as love story, as adventure, and as satire. In the framing story, a sick 10-year-old (Fred Savage) is visited by his grandfather (Peter Falk), who reads him *The Princess Bride*, a "kissing" story set in a medieval make-believe land. In it, the beautiful Buttercup (Robin Wright) reluctantly becomes engaged to a prince (Chris Sarandon) when her true love, Westley (Cary Elwes), disappears. Soon, however, she is kidnapped by a crafty Sicilian (Wallace Shawn) and his hirelings, Spanish swordsman Inigo Montoya (Mandy Patinkin) and gargantuan Fezzik (Andre the Giant). Buttercup is rescued by a mysterious man in black, who turns out to be Westley; but after surviving the Dreaded Fireswamp, they are apprehended by the prince. Buttercup agrees to marry the prince when he promises to free Westley, but the dashing lad is actually tortured to death—or is he? With the help of a wizened miracle maker (Billy Crystal), Inigo and Fezzik join forces with Westley to fight the forces of evil. With tongues in cheeks and hearts on sleeves, director Rob Reiner and scripter William Goldman create a dazzling adventure for younger viewers, while at the same time hilariously satirizing the same genre. Goldman's screenplay, adapted from his own novel, made the rounds for 14 years before finally making it to the screen. The wait was worth it. When it comes to pleasing both kids and adults, you can't do much better than THE PRINCESS BRIDE.

PRISONER OF SECOND AVENUE, THE

1975 98m c ★★★
Comedy PG
WB

Jack Lemmon (Mel), Anne Bancroft (Edna), Gene Saks (Harry), Elizabeth Wilson (Pauline), Florence Stanley (Pearl), Maxine Stuart (Belle), Ed Peck (Man Upstairs), Gene Blakely (Charlie), Ivor Francis (Psychiatrist), Stack Pierce (Detective)

p, Melvin Frank; d, Melvin Frank; w, Neil Simon (based on the play by Simon); ph, Philip Lathrop (Panavision, Technicolor); ed, Bob Wyman; m, Marvin Hamlisch; art d, Preston Ames; cos, Joel Schumacher

"The Prisoner of Second Avenue" was not one of Simon's best plays, nor was the film adaptation one of his better screenplays. Actually, Simon may have been stealing from himself, as this story bears a resemblance to his earlier original THE OUT-OF-TOWNERS. In that one, Lemmon was a man from Ohio to whom every possible problem of being a tourist occurred. This story might just be what happened to Lemmon if he'd accepted the job in the former film and stayed in New York instead of going home to the Midwest. Parallels can also be drawn between this and THE APARTMENT, in which Lemmon is a junior executive. In this movie Lemmon is living life near the top. He's married to Bancroft, and they dwell in a small, fashionable, expensive, and well-furnished cheese box on the East Side of Manhattan. Lemmon, an ad man, loses his job, has his apartment robbed, and then must suffer the embarrassment of his wife going out to win the bread. That brings him to the edge of a nervous collapse. It's not a very funny subject, and the picture wavers between comedy and drama. Lemmon's ego is shattered, he feels worthless, and he takes it all out on Bancroft, who loves him dearly and understands that it's a temporary setback, but he must have his brains in order before he goes back into the advertising jungle. In the end, the two of them are united in their defiance of the system that brought him teetering. The film has lots of one-liners and plenty of pathos.

On the stage, the couple was played by Peter Falk and Lee Grant, who may have been better suited to the roles. Simon's favorite stage director, Gene Saks, makes an acting appearance as Lemmon's brother, with Wilson and Stanley doing bits as the concerned sisters. In the play, the "Man Upstairs" was named "Jacoby" and was never seen. The filmmakers decided to hire deep-voiced Ed Peck (who has made a living doing commercials with his booming throat) in the role but neglected to delete one of the play's lines which was then out of place. Lemmon yells to the ceiling, "You think I don't know what you look like but I do." That's wrong because we've just seen Lemmon looking up at Peck when Peck drenches Lemmon. (That scene was shot earlier on the real balcony in New York, but the color didn't match, so it was shot again on the set at Warner Brothers studios in Burbank.) Director Frank, amazed by Peck's timbre, hired him because of it, but someone thought it was just too powerful and Peck was later looped by Joseph Turkel (one of Stanley Kubrick's pets, having appeared in PATHS OF GLORY; THE SHINING; etc.). Turkel, a friend of Peck's, had just days earlier recommended Peck for a voice job at Fox. Strange but true, and a good indication of what happens in Hollywood. Costumer Schumacher soon gave up sewing and measuring to become a writer-director. Sylvester Stallone does a tiny bit in Central Park.

PRISONER OF SHARK ISLAND, THE

1936 95m bw ★★★★
Prison/Biography /A
FOX

Warner Baxter (Dr. Samuel A. Mudd), Gloria Stuart (Mrs. Peggy Mudd), Joyce Kay (Marth Mudd), Claude Gillingwater (Col. Jeremiah Dyer), Douglas Wood (Gen. Ewing), Fred Kohler, Jr. (Sgt. Cooper), Harry Carey (Commandant of Fort Jefferson "Shark Island"), Paul Fix (David Herold), John Carradine (Sgt. Rankin), Francis McDonald (John Wilkes Booth) p, Darryl F. Zanuck; d, John Ford; w, Nunnally Johnson (based on the life of Dr. Samuel A. Mudd); ph, Bert Glennon; ed, Jack Murray; art d, William Darling; cos, Gwen Wakeling

Warner Baxter is smashing as a doctor who treats the ankle of fugitive assassin John Wilkes Booth, played by Francis McDonald. Arrested shortly thereafter, Baxter is charged with being part of the conspiracy to murder President Abraham Lincoln. Dragged away from his wife, Gloria Stuart, and their small child, Baxter is convicted on scant evidence and sent to prison for life at Fort Jefferson on Shark Island in the Dry Tortugas. There he is considered, even by the black guards, to be a worthy "southern gentleman" doctor determined to care for prisoners and their captors alike when they fall sick. When a yellow fever epidemic breaks out, Baxter, risking his own life, saves the lives of many. For this heroic act, Baxter's case is reopened; exonerated of being part of the Lincoln conspiracy, he returns to his family. This based-on-fact story about the injustice meted out to one man is handled beautifully by director John Ford, whose cameras, under Bert Glennon's expert guidance, starkly depict the horrors of prison life. Baxter underplays his role superbly, eliciting viewer sympathy early on. Ford leaves no doubt as to the man's innocence by stating the facts of the case right at the beginning of the film. The good doctor's sympathies are revealed when Baxter, while treating Booth, refers to Abraham Lincoln as the only salvation Southerners can look to. There are some slight similarities between this film and I AM A FUGITIVE FROM A CHAIN GANG and LES MISERABLES, but THE PRISONER OF SHARK ISLAND is a distinctive Ford film with his imprint on every frame, offering a taut, believable script by Nunnally Johnson. Typical of the reverential Ford is the scene depicting the assassination. Frank McGlynn, who played Lincoln many times, is shown seated in his box; when the shot that ends his life rings out, only McGlynn's hand is shown slumping, then a quick full shot of the lifeless body dissolves into a magnificent portrait of the President.

PRISONER OF ZENDA, THE
1937 101m bw   ★★★★★
Romance/Adventure   /U
Selznick

Ronald Colman (Rudolph Rassendyl/King Rudolf V), Madeleine Carroll (Princess Flavia), Douglas Fairbanks, Jr. (Rupert of Hentzau), Mary Astor (Antoinette De Mauban), C. Aubrey Smith (Col. Zapt), Raymond Massey (Black Michael), David Niven (Capt. Fritz von Tarlenheim), Eleanor Wesselhoeft (Cook), Byron Foulger (Johann), Montagu Love (Detchard)

p, David O. Selznick; d, John Cromwell, George Cukor, W.S. Van Dyke, II (uncredited); w, John Balderston, Wells Root, Donald Ogden Stewart (based on the novel by Anthony Hope and the play by Edward Rose); ph, James Wong Howe; ed, Hal C. Kern, James E. Newcom; m, Alfred Newman; art d, Lyle Wheeler; fx, Jack Cosgrove; cos, Ernest Dryden

This meticulous Selznick production is about as posh as movies come. The viewer, in addition to being dazzled by marvelous sets, costumes, and splendid technical details, is treated to exceptional performances by Colman, Carroll, Fairbanks, Smith, Astor, and Massey. The great Hope adventure is created for the screen with loving loyalty to the story, and Cromwell's helmsmanship is decisive and full of affection for the tale. Colman plays the doppelganger roles of Rassendyl and King Rudolf V of the mythical Ruritanian kingdom in Central Europe. (In fact, this film presents *the* Ruritanian tale which all others would emulate.)

The film opens by showing Colman arriving in Strelsau (a mythical city). He startles officials and citizens, who immediately note his likeness to the royal prince about to be crowned king; in fact, many believe him to be the prince traveling in disguise. He wears a goatee where the prince sports a mustache. Colman, in the country to do some fishing, is found by Niven and Smith, aides to the prince. The Prince, also played by Colman, comes upon the English visitor and invites his lookalike, a distant cousin, they discover, to dine with him in the royal hunting lodge. At dawn, Colman is rudely awakened by having a pitcher of water dashed in his face by Smith, who asks what he and the prince had been drinking the night before. The prince has been drugged and is in a coma. Smith proposes that Colman substitute for the prince at the coronation by shaving his goatee and, until the prince has recovered, playing his part. They take the prince to a cellar room of the royal hunting lodge while Smith learns that the housekeeper was responsible for giving the prince the drugged wine. He forces the woman to drink the drugged wine, then has Niven tie and gag her at the entrance to the cellar room, entrusting the safety of the prince to a faithful valet. Smith vows to his unconscious prince that he will see him crowned, through the impostor Colman, and that "Black Michael," the prince's evil brother, Massey, will never sit on the throne.

In his distant palace Massey sits smugly looking at a message that his brother will not live to be crowned and receives congratulations from his aides, who tell him he will be the next king. Yet Massey is cautious, not having heard it confirmed that his brother is dead, and he warns his minions that their enthusiasm might be "premature." On a train bound for the capital, Strelsau, Colman sits in regal uniform inside the royal train coach with Niven and Smith, struggling to memorize his coronation speech. As Colman emerges from the coach when arriving at Strelsau, someone cries, "God save the king!" Says Smith as they emerge from the coach, "God save them *both!*" As Colman arrives, Massey almost goes into shock, ordering his scheming henchman, Fairbanks, to go to the royal lodge and "find out what went wrong." Massey then receives Colman as he marches into the royal court. Dressed in black, squinting through a monocle, Massey looks over his so-called brother, and Colman looks apprehensively back at him. Massey then bows obediently, accepting the impostor, and offers his arm, leading Colman to the throne where he is crowned king. Carroll, the beautiful princess betrothed to the prince, arrives and swears her allegiance to him. Colman, unnerved at this beautiful blonde woman kneeling before him, whispers to Smith, "Do I kiss her?" Smith nods and Colman leans forward and kisses Carroll on the cheek, leading her outside to cheering citizens, getting into the royal coach for the grand parade. Both Colman and Carroll nod to the cheering subjects, and he learns that the prince has neglected her terribly, sending her "two picture postcards in three years." He tells her she's the loveliest girl in Europe. That night, at the grand ball, Colman falls in love with Carroll, and she discovers that the once indifferent prince who has mistreated her is charming, warm, and utterly romantic. He has already slighted Massey by spending his time with Carroll. Colman tells Massey later that his impetuous manner is caused by "the excitement, the first time I've ever been crowned." He then taunts Massey by telling him that he had an excellent wine the night before, knowing it was Massey's agents who drugged the real prince. Colman then yawns in Massey's face and Massey withdraws, telling Colman, "I see that I bore your majesty." Carroll later warns Colman against Massey and tells him that his life means much to "your country, your friends, and. . . your cousin and most loving servant." He begs her to stay, but she promises to see him the next day. That night Smith and Colman sneak out of the palace to go to the hunting lodge to reinstate the prince to his true identity. Niven is ordered to stay behind, and if Massey insists upon seeing the king, he is to draw his sword. Colman and Smith find the lodge empty, the prince gone, and the prince's valet dead. They find a note, ostensibly from Fairbanks, which reads: "One king is enough for any kingdom." Later Smith tells Colman that the kidnapers cannot speak unless they "denounce themselves," and cannot expose Colman as the impostor without admitting that they have kidnaped the true prince. He asks that Colman continue his charade, that the kidnapers cannot kill the real prince and leave him on the throne. "Rudolf is my king," Smith says, "I have a feeling for my king." He then tells Colman that if he quits his impersonation, Massey will be crowned king and Carroll will be compelled to marry him. "But you can't let that happen to her," Colman says. "Can you?" replies Smith wisely, knowing Colman is in love with Carroll. Colman goes on with the impersonation, taking Carroll to a great royal ball, marching down an enormous staircase to a huge ballroom where hundreds of distinguished visitors accord him honor. Colman and Carroll begin waltzing but when he stops to talk to her, the hundreds of dancers abruptly stop. Colman stops the dance and refuses to resume dancing, causing all of the others to stop, until Carroll promises to step out on the terrace with him. In a marvelous garden setting, Colman and Carroll stroll past lagoons filled with swans. He tells her, "I love you. . . I love you more than truth or life or honor." They kiss, and Carroll tells him that she loves him. He asks her if she could love him if he were not the king. "In my heart," Carroll tells him, "there is no king, no crown, only you." Colman is about to tell Carroll his true identity, but the ever alert Smith interrupts him, telling Colman that he must bid his important guests goodnight. Colman later tells Smith that he is in love with Carroll and is thinking of remaining on the throne to have her. He tells Smith to find the real king "before it's too late."

Fairbanks by then has met with Massey, explaining that there are *two* kings, doppelgangers. Massey proposes that they kill Colman and bury him as the real king and then murder the king who is being held by Fairbanks in his castle at Zenda. The way will then be paved for Massey to assume the crown. Fairbanks tries to entice Colman to his death by sending a message to meet Astor, Massey's mistress, with a promise that she will tell him where the real king is being hidden. The two meet in a remote spot and Astor tells Colman that three men are en route to kill him. Next she tells him that the king is a prisoner at Zenda castle. She promises to help him free the king to protect Massey against Fairbanks. Fairbanks arrives with two henchmen and asks for a truce, offering Colman a fortune to depart the country. Colman refuses and escapes the trap, returning to the palace. He tells Carroll that he's going hunting but will come for her soon. Colman then sets off for Zenda with Niven, Smith, and loyal troops to rescue the king. At first they meet Fairbanks, who tries to barter with Colman, telling him that Massey will give him 100,000 pounds to leave the country. When he refuses, Fairbanks tells him he will betray Massey if he, Fairbanks, receives Massey's estates. Colman laughs at him, and Fairbanks throws a knife in the impostor's direction that barely misses him, then escapes into his lair. Meanwhile, the true king languishes in a dank cell at Zenda castle while Astor tends to the sick man. Fairbanks gloats over the stricken king, showing him a trap door, and telling him that, if there is any attempt to rescue him, his guards will shove him through the trapdoor to a watery death below. Massey arrives and tries to get the king to sign his abdication. "I will not disgrace a crown I never wore," the king tells Massey, proving his noble spirit. An agent for Astor, Foul-

ger, goes to Colman and Smith, giving them a map of the castle and a promise that he will lower the drawbridge. One man must enter the castle and prevent the guards from drowning the true king until Smith and his troops enter. Colman insists that he be the one to penetrate the castle and save the king. "I've been an impostor for your sake," he tells Smith. "I won't be one for my own." Colman slips into the castle through a secret entrance. At the same time Fairbanks enters Astor's room, but Massey finds the two together and struggles with Fairbanks, who kills him. Fairbanks then finds Foulger trying to lower the drawbridge and crushes his skull with a pike. Colman goes to the king, kills two guards, and is about to take the real king to safety when Fairbanks confronts him with a gun. Colman challenges Fairbanks to a duel, tricking him into swordplay. The pair fight with blades through the castle in a terrific struggle. They thrust and parry back and forth, barbing each other with words. When Fairbanks sees that Colman is trying to work himself toward the rope that holds the drawbridge, attempting to cut it, he says, "I just killed a man for trying that." "An unarmed man, of course," retorts Colman. Colman manages to sever the rope holding the drawbridge, and Smith and Niven lead their cavalrymen across it, many being shot down by the castle guards who are overwhelmed and hacked to death with sabers wielded by the king's loyal troops. (Here is the symbolism of the old nobility against the modern assassin, men on horseback with swords facing gun-firing thugs in uniform.) Fairbanks, realizing that the game is over, leaps through a window, dives into the moat, and escapes after wounding Colman. The true king thanks his savior and tells him that he "would have been my best and dearest friend," had they known each other earlier and that "you taught me how to be a king." Colman later confronts Carroll, who knows the truth. She admits that she loves him, but when he begs her to go away with him, Carroll tells him that she is honor-bound to remain loyal to her king and her vows. Colman is escorted to the border by Niven and Smith. "We'll meet again, Fritz," Colman tells Niven. "Fate doesn't always make the right men kings," Niven says. Colman rides to the crest of a ridge, turns, waves, and then vanishes over the horizon, his adventure ended.

Director Cromwell does a marvelous job in extracting great performances from his leading players, as well as carefully developing the Colman-Carroll romance, which is touched with gentility and poetic grace thanks to the elegant appearances of the lovers, as well as their wonderfully modulated voices and deliveries of dialog. Cromwell was brought in by Selznick because the producer knew that this director would bring out the best from the cast and that he would stay within his budget. Selznick nevertheless hedged his bets and had George Cukor, famed as a "woman's director," helm the final scene between Colman and Carroll. This shows in Carroll's departure from her pose as the soft and gentle Princess Flavia, as she becomes abruptly assertive and much more expressive, her voice rising to tell Colman that she must do her duty and not run away with him. Action director W.S. Van Dyke was also called in to direct the exciting and dashing duel between Colman and Fairbanks. Selznick was repeatedly warned not to revive this Ruritanian adventure-romance story, his advisors telling him that the production was doomed. The Hope story had been filmed several times before, as early silents in 1912 and 1915, and a major silent in 1922, ornately costumed and directed by Rex Ingram, starring Lewis Stone as the commoner-king, Alice Terry as Flavia, and Ramon Novarro as Rupert. Selznick, however, rightly reasoned that he could capture the public interest in the film, highlighting the coronation scenes, since the public was already keyed to the upcoming coronation of Britain's King Edward VIII. He was right. The film was a smash, enhancing the careers of all involved in the production.

Colman was not really a swashbuckling actor, although he retained some of that image after appearing in A TALE OF TWO CITIES; CLIVE OF INDIA; LOST HORIZON; and playing the daring French poet Francois Villon in IF I WERE KING. The fabulous duel staged between Fairbanks and Colman in THE PRISONER OF ZENDA suggests more than really happens. Brilliant cameraman Howe advised Cromwell that Colman, Selznick's all-time favorite actor, who received $200,000 for his work here, had a "bad side," and had to be photographed carefully. When the beautiful but patrician Carroll heard about this, she went to Cromwell and said she too had a bad side and wanted special consideration in the camera angles. Her bad side, according to Cromwell, was the same side as Colman's and it would be impossible to shoot the pair by accenting only their best profiles. When Howe was asked by Cromwell if Carroll had a bad side, Howe said she couldn't be faulted if she were stood on her head; Cromwell passed this opinion along to Carroll, who responded by not speaking to him for the rest of the picture. Carroll was also upset because Selznick ordered her not to use her usual heavy makeup, desiring a "fresh scrubbed" look to suggest virginity. Yet, years later, Carroll never tired of telling everyone that her role in THE PRISONER OF ZENDA was her favorite.

Beyond the flawless visual elegance provided by Cromwell, the script by Balderston, Root, and Stewart is witty, literate, and lyrical to the point of poetry, and Newman's sweeping, stirring, memorable score was one of the composer's finest. The design of the picture is often stunning and earned an Oscar nomination for Lyle Wheeler for Best Interior Decoration. Fairbanks is superb as the rascally, lethal Rupert, and Massey is the perfect scheming Prince Michael, while Astor does commendable work as his ill-fated mistress. Smith is charming, quaint, and heroically stalwart as the king's aide, and Niven is superb as his brave protege. Though some critics delivered some fun-poking asides at the film for its grand style, they nevertheless endorsed the film, and the public loved it worldwide, making it an enormous box-office success. The venerable C. Aubrey Smith, so memorable as Colonel Zapt, was the dean of the British acting community in Hollywood. He had long developed the habit of sitting regally in a captain's chair off set, waiting to play his part, his hearing aid turned off (he was almost completely deaf during the sound film era) and reading a copy of the London *Times*. Massey, who was having some difficulty with his role of "Black Prince Michael," sought out Smith and found him reading his paper. The knighted Smith turned on his hearing aid, and Massey tried to explain his problems with the role. Smith listened with great patience and then said, "Ray, in my time I've played every part in ZENDA except Princess Flavia." He paused, and Massey leaned forward, expecting to hear a helpful secret. "And I've always had trouble with Black Michael," concluded Smith. He then switched off his hearing aid and snapped open the paper before his deep-socketed eyes. The amazing special effects achieved in this film in showing two Ronald Colmans shaking hands, talking to each other, and drinking together in the royal lodge were achieved through carefully disguised split screen processes. Doubles were used with over-the-shoulder shots and when Colman shook hands with himself one of the hands was that of a stunt man with his arm masked. The remake, produced in 1952, with Stewart Granger as the commoner-king (he is wooden throughout, but his duel with Rupert is much more energetic and impressive than the 1937 encounter), Deborah Kerr as Flavia, and James Mason as a much more pensive Rupert, was a lavish picture that fell far short of the Cromwell film. Author

Hope, a barrister by profession, wrote only one blockbuster, *The Prisoner of Zenda*, published in 1894, but it made him world famous and fabulously rich. He wrote a sequel, *Rupert of Hentzau*, published in 1898, which was filmed as a silent, ironically produced in 1923 by Lewis Selznick, David Selznick's father, and starring Lew Cody as villain Rupert. In this sequel Rupert returns to kill the king and is killed by Rudolph Rassendyl. Flavia abdicates and marries Rassendyl, going to England to live in bliss.

PRIVATE BENJAMIN

1980 109m c   ★★½
Comedy/War   R/15
WB

Goldie Hawn *(Judy Benjamin)*, Eileen Brennan *(Capt. Doreen Lewis)*, Armand Assante *(Henri Tremont)*, Robert Webber *(Col. Clay Thornbush)*, Sam Wanamaker *(Teddy Benjamin)*, Barbara Barrie *(Harriet Benjamin)*, Mary Kay Place *(Pvt. Mary Lou Glass)*, Harry Dean Stanton *(Sgt. Jim Ballard)*, Albert Brooks *(Yale Goodman)*, Alan Oppenheimer *(Rabbi)*

p, Nancy Meyers, Charles Shyer, Harvey Miller; d, Howard Zieff; w, Nancy Meyers, Charles Shyer, Harvey Miller; ph, David M. Walsh (Technicolor); ed, Sheldon Kahn; m, Bill Conti; prod d, Robert Boyle; art d, Jeff Howard; fx, Robert Peterson; cos, Betsy Cox

Goldie Hawn brings that old standby, the service comedy, into the 1980s in this funny tale of a Jewish girl who decides to be all that she can be in the all-new Army. After her second husband (wonderfully played by Albert Brooks) dies while they are making love, Hawn enlists in the Army, much to the chagrin of her well-to-do parents, Sam Wanamaker and Barbara Barrie. The reality of Army life under demanding commanding officer Eileen Brennan turns out to be a far cry from Hawn's notion that she'll have her own room to decorate and the opportunity to visit exciting locales. The pampered Hawn's reactions to rigorous training exercises, her interactions with her superiors, and a not-quite-successful love affair with French physician Armand Assante while on duty in Europe inspire plenty of laughs. Hawn makes the most of the Oscar-nominated script, written by Nancy Meyers, Charles Shyer, and Harvey Miller, providing many funny moments in a performance that earned her an Academy Award nomination as Best Actress (she lost to Sissy Spacek in COAL MINER'S DAUGHTER). Brennan, as her lesbian-leaning CO, received a Best Supporting Actress nomination from the Academy, and Robert Webber (as the unit commander) and Mary Kay Place (as Judy's sidekick) also provide strong support.

PRIVATE FUNCTION, A

1985 93m c   ★★★
Comedy   R/15
Hand Made   (U.K.)

Michael Palin *(Gilbert Chilvers)*, Maggie Smith *(Joyce Chilvers)*, Denholm Elliott *(Dr. Swaby)*, Richard Griffiths *(Allardyce)*, Tony Haygarth *(Sutcliff)*, John Normington *(Lockwood)*, Bill Paterson *(Wormold)*, Liz Smith *(Mother)*, Alison Steadman *(Mrs. Allardyce)*, Jim Carter *(Inspector Noble)*

p, Mark Shivas; d, Malcolm Mowbray; w, Alan Bennett (based on a story by Bennett, Mowbray); ph, Tony Pierce-Roberts; ed, Barrie Vince; m, John Du Prez; prod d, Stuart Walker; art d, Judith Lang, Michael Porter; cos, Phyllis Dalton

To sum up this movie in two words, one would have to flip a coin to decide whether it is "hysterically tasteless" or "tastelessly hysterical." It is surely one or the other, and perhaps both. The time is 1947. England is just recovering from the war, and there are still many restrictions on the inhabitants of the Yorkshire town where the action takes place. There could be a brisk trade in black market items, but Wormold (Bill Paterson), the local inspector from the Food Ministry, keeps tabs on everyone, making certain that nobody is growing food or breeding livestock illegally. Gilbert (Michael Palin) and Joyce Chilvers (Maggie Smith) are a married couple with little in common. He's a quiet podiatrist, and she is a lower-class hoyden who wants to move up to the middle class. When Joyce learns that some village big shots have bribed a local farmer to keep an unlicensed pig for them and fatten it up, she convinces Gilbert that they should abduct the animal. Once they have a supply of sausages and chops, there is no question they will be welcomed into the town's fanciest homes. Now the trouble begins. This movie is a vicious satire of class distinctions mixed with some of the grossest humor ever seen on-screen. But the British love their scatology and their sociology, so the two seem to blend. The result is a film that you don't have to be British to enjoy, just brutish.

PRIVATE LIFE OF HENRY VIII, THE

1933 97m bw   ★★★★
Biography   /U
London Films   (U.K.)

Charles Laughton (Henry VIII), Robert Donat (Thomas Culpepper), Lady Tree (Henry's Old Nurse), Binnie Barnes (Katherine Howard), Elsa Lanchester (Anne of Cleves), Merle Oberon (Anne Boleyn), Wendy Barrie (Jane Seymour), Everley Gregg (Catherine Parr), Franklin Dyall (Thomas Cromwell), Miles Mander (Wriothesley)

p, Alexander Korda, Ludovico Toeplitz; d, Alexander Korda; w, Lajos Biro, Arthur Wimperis; ph, Georges Perinal; ed, Harold Young, Stephen Harrison; m, Kurt Schroeder; art d, Vincent Korda; chor, Espinosa; cos, John Armstrong

An admirable glutton. And a resurrection for England's film industry, with palms going to Korda, and French cinematograper Georges Perinal. How the film came to be has been discussed for many years. Some say that Korda was searching for something for Charles Laughton and his wife, Elsa Lanchester, and when he saw a statue of the king, spotted the resemblance and ordered a script written. The other tale maintains that Korda heard the old British folk song "I'm 'Enery the Eighth, I Am, I Am" (later to become a rock 'n' roll hit by Herman's Hermits) and came up with the idea. Many costume epics were made in the silent years and some even touched upon the life of the monarch, but this is the one that will be remembered. Laughton's performance was outstanding and won the first Oscar ever for a British-made movie. Korda called upon his brother Vincent to be set designer and the nepotism was worthwhile, as Vincent managed to make this picture look far more expensive than the 60,000 pounds it cost to produce it in just five weeks. The attitude taken was to dispense with the public utterances and show the intimate side of the monarch, a technique Korda was to use again in the less fulfilling THE PRIVATE LIFE OF DON JUAN.

There was a great deal of humor in this picture, which details the life of Henry VIII and five of his six wives. The first wife, Catherine of Aragon, is dispensed with by a prologue that explains that she was far "too respectable to be included." Merle Oberon is his first spouse pictured (Anne Boleyn; it's like seeing Zsa Zsa Gabor play Margaret Thatcher) and is soon beheaded. Wendy Barrie plays Jane Seymour and dies giving birth. Henry

next marries Lanchester (Anne of Cleves), wearing an odd wig and doing her best to look terrible in order to justify the film's most famous line, uttered by Laughton with a regal sigh as he enters the bedroom, "The things I've done for England." Lanchester, using a German accent, is the only performer to come close to Laughton in scene-stealing, nearly swiping their sequences entirely. That marriage leads to divorce, and Henry next marries Binnie Barnes, who loses her head after losing her heart to Laughton's pal, Robert Donat. At the finale, after raving and roaring and ranting, eating like an animal, ruling his roost like a cock of the walk, Laughton is shown to be a tranquil, almost whipped man at the hands of his last mate, Everley Gregg, a sharp-faced shrew.

Laughton was only 33 at the time this film was made but already a veteran of nine movies and many stage productions. There are several standout scenes, not the least of which are the "eating" sequences with Laughton chewing on a chop, then tossing the remains over his shoulder. Actually, the eating bits are sexier than the bedroom scenes, and one wonders if Tony Richardson didn't study them for his directing of TOM JONES. Until this movie was released, there had been a mild recession in costume epics, but they came back with a flurry when the totals were in on the profits, about 10 times the cost. Korda's sets, which were poverty-stricken at best, were photographed so well by Perinal that no one realized how frail they were. Barnes sings a song in the film that was reputedly written by King Henry VIII himself, just another side to this amazing historical character.

PRIVATE LIFE OF SHERLOCK HOLMES, THE

1970 125m c   ★★★½
Comedy/Mystery   GP/PG
Phalanx/Mirisch   (U.S./U.K.)

Robert Stephens (Sherlock Holmes), Colin Blakely (Dr. John H. Watson), Irene Handl (Mrs. Hudson), Stanley Holloway (1st Gravedigger), Christopher Lee (Mycroft Holmes), Genevieve Page (Gabrielle Valladon), Clive Revill (Rogozhin), Tamara Toumanova (Petrova), George Benson (Inspector Lestrade), Catherine Lacey (Old Lady)

p, Billy Wilder; d, Billy Wilder; w, Billy Wilder, I.A.L. Diamond (based on the characters created by Sir Arthur Conan Doyle); ph, Christopher Challis (Panavision, DeLuxe Color); ed, Ernest Walter; m, Miklos Rozsa; prod d, Alexander Trauner; art d, Tony Inglis; fx, Wally Veevers, Cliff Richardson; chor, David Blair; cos, Julie Harris

This unjustly forgotten Billy Wilder film takes on the much-loved character of Sherlock Holmes and attempts to humanize him by examining his vulnerabilities: his ambiguous sexuality and his cocaine addiction. Told via an unpublished manuscript by Dr. Watson (Blakely), the story begins with a bored, frustrated Sherlock Holmes (Stephens), who turns to cocaine between cases. One evening a beautiful Belgian woman, Gabrielle Valladon (Page), turns up at 221B Baker Street asking Holmes to find her missing husband. Although warned by his mysterious brother, Mycroft (Lee), to abandon the case, Holmes persists and the trail leads to Scotland's Loch Ness, where Holmes and Watson come face to face with the legendary monster. Although the film was cut by more than 30 minutes by United Artists, what is left of this satirical, intimate look at the revered character is intriguing and wholly entertaining. Nevertheless it it bombed at the box office. The sets were designed under the direction of Alexander Trauner, who re-created, in detail, the Victorian atmosphere of Holmes's London residence, including a massive backlot reproduction of Baker Street. The score by Miklos Rozsa is one of his most impressive, and he can be seen conducting it during the ballet sequence. Robert Stephens is an excellent, never-before-seen Holmes, one with wild mood swings which veil his insecurities. Colin Blakely's Dr. Watson is loyal, humorous, and energetic, while Christopher Lee as Mycroft is excellent, making him the only actor in Holmes screen history to play both the detective (in the German-made SHERLOCK HOLMES AND THE NECKLACE OF DEATH) and his brother.

PRIVATE LIVES

1931   92m   bw   ★★★★½
Comedy   /A
MGM

Norma Shearer (Amanda Chase Paynne), Robert Montgomery (Elyot Chase), Reginald Denny (Victor Paynne), Una Merkel (Sibyl Chase), Jean Hersholt (Oscar), George Davis (Bellboy)

d, Sidney Franklin; w, Hans Kraly, Richard Schayer, Claudine West (based on the play by Noel Coward); ph, Ray Binger; ed, Conrad A. Nervig; art d, Cedric Gibbons; cos, Adrian

PRIVATE LIVES is one of those enduring scripts that can't be hurt, even by ordinary actors; in the case of this film, the acting is excellent, and the result is charming. Norma Shearer and Robert Montgomery play Amanda and Elyot, a once-married couple who have divorced and wed other mates. He's now married to Sibyl (Merkel) and she to Victor (Denny). Both Sibyl and Victor are conservative sorts, devoid of the joy and madness that once attracted Amanda and Elyot to one another. By a coincidence, both couples are honeymooning at the French hotel where Amanda and Elyot had spent their first two weeks of marriage years before. For a time we see the divorced pair struggling to show affection to their new spouses, a tall order when considering the surpassingly bland Sibyl and the stuffed-shirt Victor. Since their suites are next to each other, it isn't long before our fireball lovers meet on their balconies, at once delighted and stunned to see one another. In no time, the newlyweds are quarreling; the formerly-weds, convinced that they are still in love, leave their fresh spouses behind and go to a mountain chalet to have another honeymoon. Of course, their passion is as volatile as it ever was, and they are soon arguing viciously between romantic interludes. The words become blows, and when Sibyl and Victor finally catch up with the elopers they are in the midst of a battle royale. Amanda and Elyot reconcile with Victor and Sibyl, but when the latter two get into an argument over breakfast, the true lovers realize that even the most placid types get into scrapes. What the impish pair do and how the word "Sollochs" helps them make for an amusingly sweet finale.

Noel Coward wrote and starred in PRIVATE LIVES onstage with Gertrude Lawrence in a 1930 London production, then brought it to New York with Laurence Olivier and Jill Esmond in the secondary roles. Producer Irving Thalberg, Shearer's husband, made a film record of this production to aid cast and crew in bringing its unique flavor to the cinema. One of the film's joys is that it achieves a faithful reproduction of the original without seeming a mere copy. The actors don't convince as British (only Denny was), but that really doesn't matter. Shearer and Montgomery attack their roles with such zest and comic elan that we don't miss the spirits of Noel and Gertie hanging around. La Norma rarely had the chance to play farce, and though she has a few overplayed, chirpy moments early on, she's so good on the whole that one regrets that all her later prestige roles didn't allow for much high comedy. Her timing (as on "Does he drink?" "Yes, gallons") is splendid and her delivery pacy and tongue-in-cheek ("I must see those dear flamingos"). Her most hilarious moment comes during the great fight scene. As she runs screaming out of the room, she lets out a final yelp while struggling with a door, and we witness one of those great moments when a Hollywood glamour queen has totally let herself go. Montgomery matches her step for step with an incredibly polished and well-judged performance. His dapper manner and feather-light diffidence lend his line readings great style and wit. In verbal repartee with Shearer he's great losing his temper over whether adders snap or sting and his rendition of "Yes, slattern and fishwife" during a name-calling bout could not possibly be bettered. Opening up the play for a spot of mountain climbing (and a very pre-Code sleeping scene), director Franklin does a fine job in preventing his film from becoming stagy. He carefully guides his leads through such key moments as their marvelous balcony scene and his unobtrusive helming of the camera and the editing adds considerably to this glossy and enchanting film's overall finesse.

PRIZZI'S HONOR

1985   129m   c   ★★★★½
Romance/Comedy/Crime   R/15
ABC

Jack Nicholson (Charley Partanna), Kathleen Turner (Irene Walker), Robert Loggia (Eduardo Prizzi), John Randolph (Angelo "Pop" Partanna), William Hickey (Don Corrado Prizzi), Lee Richardson (Dominic Prizzi), Michael Lombard (Filargi "Finlay"), Anjelica Huston (Maerose Prizzi), George Santopietro (Plumber), Lawrence Tierney (Lt. Hanley)

p, John Foreman; d, John Huston; w, Richard Condon, Janet Roach (based on the novel by Condon); ph, Andrzej Bartkowiak (Panavision, DeLuxe Color); ed, Rudi Fehr, Kaja Fehr; m, Alex North; prod d, J. Dennis Washington; art d, Michael Helmy, Tracy Bousman; fx, Connie Brink; cos, Donfeld

Director John Huston, one-time master of film noir, returns to the form with a black comedy about the Mafia. The benefits from some stellar performances from Jack Nicholson, Kathleen Turner, and William Hickey. This was the penultimate film from the ailing great director. It is also one of his best.

Charley Partanna (Nicholson) is an aging dopey hit man who works for a powerful New York Mafia family. He spots luscious Irene Walker (Turner) at a gangster wedding and loses his heart. She's ostensibly a tax consultant living in Los Angeles, and soon Charley finds himself flying westward to court her. Then he discovers that she is really a hit woman for the mob. With this, at least, Charley can identify, but when he learns that Irene has cheated his own Mafia family—the Prizzis—out of a great sum of money, his loyalties are painfully divided. The finale is a shocker finish few viewers will ever forget. It's all good and funny in a cynical, bleak sort of way, reflecting the then 78-year-old Huston's perspective of the world. A lesser-known director might have been pilloried for bad taste. Huston was not only tolerated but cheered.

The film received a host of Oscar nominations, including Best Picture, Best Actor (Nicholson), Best Supporting Actor (Hickey), Best Costume Design, Best Direction, Best Editing, and Best Screenplay from Another Medium (Richard Condon, Janet Roach). Anjelica Huston (the director's daughter) won an Oscar as Best Supporting Actress.

PRODUCERS, THE

1967   88m   c   ★★★★
Comedy   /PG
Springtime/Crossbow

Zero Mostel *(Max Bialystock)*, Gene Wilder *(Leo Bloom)*, Dick Shawn *(Lorenzo St. Du Bois)*, Kenneth Mars *(Franz Liebkind)*, Estelle Winwood *(Old Lady)*, Christopher Hewett *(Roger De Bris)*, Andreas Voutsinas *(Carmen Giya)*, Lee Meredith *(Ulla)*, Renee Taylor *(Eva Braun)*, Michael Davis *(Production Tenor)*

p, Sidney Glazier; d, Mel Brooks; w, Mel Brooks; ph, Joseph Coffey (Pathe Color); ed, Ralph Rosenblum; m, John Morris; art d, Charles Rosen; chor, Alan Johnson; cos, Gene Coffin

Without taste, but not without laughs. An often hilarious farce that spoofs upper-crust Broadway theater as well as its fickle audiences, THE PRODUCERS has become a cult film, a surprisingly better work than most of what director-writer Brooks would create later (except for THE TWELVE CHAIRS). But forewarned is forewarned: Mostel, genius that he is, doesn't scale his performances down at all for film. The first half hour you feel you're in the presence of comedy's king. After that, you gradually begin to feel bludgeoned by shrill overkill.

Mostel is a down-and-out but still pompous theater producer who desperately wants to regain his former glory. Wilder is his new, meek accountant who finds his books an utter disaster. He tells Mostel that the only way he will ever recover is to produce an enormous hit or, he whimsically suggests, to collect a lot of money from investors for a play guaranteed to fail. That way Mostel could keep most of the investors' money. Of course, Wilder points out, he's only talking in theoretical terms. Mostel's eyes bulge as his greed ratio goes out of control, and he avalanches Wilder with cajoling, threats, and prospects of untold wealth to finally get the shy accountant not only to doctor the books but to go into the production scheme with him. They celebrate their venal union by going to the Lincoln Center fountain that night, with Wilder dancing wildly about the fountain, thoroughly committed to larceny, shouting, "I want. . . I want. . . everything I've ever seen. . . in the movies!" The pair exhaust themselves soliciting and reading the worst scripts ever penned. Finally, they hit upon a play that is a surefire flop, "Springtime for Hitler," written by Mars, a Nazi fanatic living in Yorkville. They find this loony on top of his tenement building tending to his pigeons (he still wears his German helmet from WWII), and they sign him to a contract. Next, Mostel woos and wins the backing of every spinster in New York, taking in hundreds of thousands of dollars to back his doomed play. To further assure failure, Mostel hires an inept tranvestite director, Hewett—assisted by Voutsinas, as swishy a gay as ever to glide across a screen—to helm Mars's montrosity. The role tryouts are disastrous with the worst talent on Broadway turning out, and Mostel selects for the lead a mindless, drug-bombed hippie, Shawn, who believes he is trying out for another role in another theater. He belches out a song called "Love Power," a tune he wrote describing how he was clubbed on the head by a cop, his girlfriend was stuffed into a garbage can, and his landlord took his most cherished flower and flushed it down the toilet (ostensibly for nonpayment of rent), where it ends up "in the sewer with the yuck runnin' through 'er" and then as "the water that we drink." "Perfect!" yells Mostel, and the play goes on.

THE PRODUCERS, Brooks's first film, is utterly preposterous and so outlandish as to provide one belly laugh after another. Nothing is too gauche or crude for Brooks in his merciless burlesque of legitimate theater as he expands every cliche and pun. Though it is gross, vulgar, and stereotyped on all levels, the film appeals for these very reasons. It is comedy by reason of planned insanity, and that's what makes this movie a near classic of the absurd, almost pure Dada. Mostel and Wilder are *dedicated* lunatics who are harmless and disarming in their oddball antics

and therefore somehow lovable. This film raised Mostel to new heights of zany appeal and made a star of Wilder (who went on playing his original role too many times). Shot on location in New York City. Our favorite among the investors: Estelle Winwood, as "Touch Me, Feel Me"—she takes the material and runs with it. Highlight: The opening number, opening night.

PROJECTIONIST, THE

1970 88m c   ★★★½
Drama/Comedy   PG/A
Maglan

Chuck McCann *(Projectionist/Captain Flash)*, Ina Balin *(The Girl)*, Rodney Dangerfield *(Renaldi/The Bat)*, Jara Kohout *(Candy Man/Scientist)*, Harry Hurwitz *(Friendly Usher)*, Robert Staats *(TV Pitchman)*, Robert King *(Premiere Announcer)*, Stephen Phillips *(Minister)*, Clara Rosenthal *(Crazy Lady)*, Jacquelyn Glenn *(Nude on Bearskin)*

p, Harry Hurwitz; d, Harry Hurwitz; w, Harry Hurwitz; ph, Victor Petrashevic (Technicolor); ed, Harry Hurwitz; m, Igo Kantor, Erma E. Levin

Long before ZELIG; THE PURPLE ROSE OF CAIRO; and DEAD MEN DON'T WEAR PLAID, there was THE PROJECTIONIST, a film made for the pittance of $160,000 and, in its own way, better than any of those three films because it was the first to utilize the superimposition technique. Hurwitz wrote, produced, directed, edited, and even played a small role in this film, which received a limited release but now has a large cult audience and is part of the permanent collection at the Museum of Modern Art. Anyone who loves movies will love THE PROJECTIONIST, the story of a man (McCann) who makes his living running motion pictures in a sleazy theater then goes home to watch even more films on television. the line between reality and fantasy begins to blur for McCann and he imagines himself as part of every movie he's ever seen, including newsreels. A lovable schlemiel, McCann lives for those moments when he imagines himself to be super-hero known as Captain Flash. As this fearless defender of the downtrodden, McCann does battle with the Bat, the embodiment of evil, who is played in McCann's dreamworld by Dangerfield (appearing in his first film), his real-life boss. When McCann meets Balin, an attractive young woman, she immediately becomes part of his flights of fancy, cast as a dark-haired, imperiled Pauline, whom McCann must save with regularity from the clutches of Dangerfield. A quarrel with Dangerfield prompts McCann to picture the coming attractions trailer for "The Terrible World of Tomorrow," a film about the end of civilization. When McCann sees a poster for BARBARELLA, his imagination takes him to "The Wonderful World of Tomorrow," where everything is sweet and the good guys always triumph over the bad guys. One night, McCann finds himself in Rick's Cafe, Humphrey Bogart's bar in CASABLANCA, where he observes Syney Greenstreet, Peter Lorre, and Conrad Veidt (by the magic of cinema, he is actually *in* the bar), and hears a remark that leads him to the *Thugee* hiding place of Eduardo Ciannelli in GUNGA DIN. Later, after work, McCann is walking down the street and sees an ad for the premiere of STAR! Suddenly he is part of the festivities as a movie personality surrounded by adoring fans. In yet another of his mind movies, McCann most do battle not only with constant nemesis Dangerfield but also with Hitler and Mussolini. In taking on these imposing foes, McCann enlists the help of Sam Jaffe (as Gunga Din), John Wayne, Gary Cooper, John Garfield, Errol Flynn, and Buster Crabbe (the latter of whom Hurwitz and McCann would work with again in the less-successful THE

COMEBACK TRAIL). These vaunted movie heroes marshal their strength, smash Dangerfield and his cohorts—who now include a horde of Nazi soldiers and aliens from outer space—and plant the US flag atop Mount Suribachi. After McCann belts Dangerfield, the projectionist/super hero squires Balin into the quiet movie theater, where the finale has them flanked by everyone in DAMES, including Ruby Keeler and Dick Powell, with an additional appearance by Fred Astaire and Ginger Rogers.

Among the other stars who grace the screen in THE PROJECTIONIST are Marilyn Monroe and Clark Gable. At one point, Hurwitz intercuts FORT APACHE with THE BIRTH OF A NATION, so that John Wayne seems to be leading a charge against the KKK. THE PROJECTIONIST was made in four weeks, but took 18 months to edit. While DEAD MEN DON'T WEAR PLAID seemed like an overlong TV sketch, this picture, aside from its war scenes and some depictions of urban violence, remains consistently interesting throughout. After years of delighting New York TV audiences with his daily mix of old movies and new satire, McCann had demonstrated his ability as a dramatic actor in THE HEART IS A LONELY HUNTER. Here he gives an absolutely delightful performance. Kohout was a refugee making his first film after years of being known as "the Charlie Chaplin of Czechoslovakia."

PROMISED LAND

1988 102m c   ★★★
Drama   R/15
Wildwood

Jason Gedrick (Davey Hancock), Tracy Pollan (Mary Daley), Kiefer Sutherland (Danny Rivers), Meg Ryan (Bev), Googy Gress (Baines), Deborah Richter (Pammie), Oscar Rowland (Mr. Rivers), Sandra Seacat (Mrs. Rivers), Jay Underwood (Circle K Clerk), Herta Ware (Mrs. Higgins)

p, Rick Stevenson; d, Michael Hoffman; w, Michael Hoffman; ph, Ueli Steiger, Alexander Gruszynski; ed, David Spiers; m, James Newton Howard; prod d, Eugenio Zanetti; fx, Bob Riggs; cos, Victoria Holloway

Following the fortunes of four young adults, this third picture from the producer-director team of Rick Stevenson and Michael Hoffman seeks to examine the unfulfilled promises of the American Dream. High school basketball star Davey Hancock (Jason Gedrick) is bound for college on an athletic scholarship. His friend, Danny Rivers (Kiefer Sutherland), drops out of school and leaves the little town of Ashville, Utah. Two years later, Davey is an Ashville policeman, having failed to make the grade in college ball, who is trying to hold onto his girlfriend, Mary (Tracy Pollan), whose horizons have been broadened by college. In Nevada, Danny marries Bev (Meg Ryan), an impetuous hellraiser whom he has known for only three days, and heads back to Ashville to visit his parents. As the four young people converge, Bev, drugged, drunken, and psychotic, precipitates disaster. PROMISED LAND is a well-intentioned film, but despite strong performances, an engaging plot, and some arresting photography, its ambitious reach exceeds its grasp. Instead of being shown as the stuff of which American Dreams are made, the picture's symbolism has a grafted-on quality. However, Hoffman still delivers an intriguing, well-paced story that draws the viewer in as it builds to its tragic climax. The photography of the mountains, plains, and huge Western skies is gorgeous, and Hoffman's use of the camera is occasionally dazzling.

PROSPERO'S BOOKS

1991 120m c   ★★★½
Drama/Fantasy   R/15
Allarts/Cinea/Camera One/Penta Film/Elsevier Vendex Film/Film Four International/VPRO Television/Canal Plus/Nippon Hoso Kyokai (U.K./Netherlands/France/Italy)

John Gielgud (Prospero), Michael Clark (Caliban), Michel Blanc (Alonso), Erland Josephson (Gonzalo), Isabelle Pasco (Miranda), Tom Bell (Antonio), Kenneth Cranham (Sebastian), Mark Rylance (Ferdinand), Gerard Thoolen (Adrian), Pierre Bokma (Francisco)

p, Yoshinobu Numano, Katsufumi Nakamura; d, Peter Greenaway; w, Peter Greenaway (adapted from the play The Tempest by William Shakespeare); ph, Sacha Vierny; ed, Marina Bodbyl; m, Michael Nyman; prod d, Ben Van Os, Jan Roelfs

Idiosyncratic and offbeat, British director Peter Greenaway usually finds himself in the heat and heart of controversy. As much as any filmmaker today, he's simultaneously praised and vilified for his unorthodox abandon in such films as A ZED AND TWO NOUGHTS, IN THE BELLY OF AN ARCHITECT, DROWNING BY NUMBERS and THE COOK, THE THIEF, HIS WIFE AND HER LOVER. He's envied and admired, but nobody always likes Greenaway—his stylish indulgences often divisively get between him and his audience. PROSPERO'S BOOKS is no exception. True to form and with id unbound, Greenaway virtually startles the senses with his egocentric deconstruction of Shakespeare's The Tempest.

Actually, it's The Tempest plus. Beginning with its opening sequence of a urinating angel, PROSPERO'S BOOKS is a remarkable celebration of excess. Literate as it is, with its abundant nudity, it will never receive an imprimatur. Penises, especially, proliferate like so many pairs of socks dangling from a clothesline. Naked bodies in all sizes and shapes fill the screen. It's Shakespeare's work, though certainly not as originally envisioned. No matter. Throughout, Greenaway has superlative control of the film's content and structure.

The story—before Greenaway dissected and reframed it—concerns Prospero, the rightful Duke of Milan. A magician and Renaissance philosopher, he lives in exile on an enchanted island with his beautiful young daughter Miranda (Isabelle Pasco). They're the only humans in a fantasy world inhabited by otherworldly creatures including his slave Caliban (Michael Clark), a misshappen monster with gentian violet genitals, and his servant Ariel (Greenaway gives us four of them, portrayed by Paul Russell, James Thierree, Emil Wolk and Orpheo), a lively sprite, and the pair, metaphysically, represent the basic elements of all physical matter: water and air, earth and fire.

Twelve years before, Prospero's brother Antonio (Tom Bell) seized his dukedom with the help of Alonso (Michel Blanc), King of Naples, and set him and his daughter adrift in a leaky boat. They survived because Gonzalo (Erland Josephson), the king's honest advisor, had secretly stocked the craft with food, clothing and the things Prospero valued most: his books. There were 24 of them. And it is these books that figure most deeply in Greenaway's reinterpretation.

Shakespeare never named them. Greenaway does. Rather, he conjectures what they would have been: books about science, about art and architecture, about raising a child, about plant and animal life, about magic, pornography, mathematics, and so on. Then he gives form to those fantasies in creative, phantasmagoric, cinematic renderings. And we, the audience, are the beneficiaries of his splendid visions. In rapid succession, all 24 volumes are recreated before our eyes in mind-boggling revisionist-Renaissance, Greenaway style.

But to continue with the tale, Prospero's wisdom is tainted by an almost-tragic flaw: he is consumed by thoughts of vengeance. Through his magical arts, he learns his brother and the King are on a nearby ship, and creates a tempest, causing it to capsize. All aboard—including the King's handsome son Ferdinand (Mark Rylance), the King's brother Sebastian (Kenneth Cranham) and Gonzalo—are safely washed ashore, singly or in groups.

Miranda and Ferdinand meet and fall in love. (Apart from her father's, his is the only human face she can remember seeing.) Other subplots include conspiracies between Caliban and some of the King's men to usurp the crown and take over the island. Eventually, the various cabals are thwarted. (They're no match for Prospero's magical powers.) Both Antonio and the King repent their cruel deeds, and Prospero finally embraces the one noble quality eluding him throughout his long exile: forgiveness. He throws his magical books into the sea, gives Ariel his freedom, and makes peace with his enemies, promising them safe passage home to Naples and Milan. (He'll follow later, to reclaim his lost dukedom and witness his daughter's marriage to the prince.) The film—as in the play—ends with Prospero, willingly having given up his magical powers, once more becoming a benign mortal. Remorseful and penitent, he begs us, the audience, to pardon him for his frailties and misdeeds, and grant him the forgiveness that will set him free, as he forgave his own enemies.

That's the general plot, but Greenaway's typically atypical interpretation plays havoc with Shakespeare's scenario. He has Gielgud vocally assuming *all* the parts until the film's very end. The film's noted cast of fine actors—especially Blanc and Josephson—are almost wasted. They're no more than silent presences, seen but not heard till the finale.

Sir John Gielgud at 86, in a virtuoso performance as a most regal Prospero, the master manipulator of people and events, is a wonder. Age has not withered him. It's *his* film all the way. Mellifluously, resonantly, speaking some of the most famous lines in the history of theater, Gielgud functions as a sort of onscreen chorus—an intermediary between the action and audience to give form and fabric to the film. Throughout, Gielgud also portrays the Bard who, like the veteran actor himself, is nearing the end of his long career. (*The Tempest* was Shakespeare's 36th and final play.) In a triple conceit of Greenaway's, we see Gielgud-Shakespeare-Prospero writing the play in elegant Elizabethan script. Concurrently, he conjures onscreen the images and characters he has just created on paper. He recites all their dialogue. Their voices are dimly overlaid with his, as if by echo. Only at the film's very end, when Prospero has given up all thoughts of revenge and reconciled with his enemies, are the other characters allowed to speak for themselves in their own voices. Symbolically, revenge made them fictional, forgiveness makes them real.

Gielgud breathes life into a difficult role and makes it look natural and easy. Richly garbed in embroidered cowl and cloak, looking like a cross between a Venetian doge and Dame Edith Sitwell, it's as if he were born to it. ("The most difficult part," he jested, "was the cloak—beautiful to look at but extraordinarily heavy to wear. It took four people to put it on me.") Actually, it was at his suggestion that Greenaway undertook the project, designing the film for him in that role. He even used some ideas Gielgud jotted down years before—observations made as a result of the many times he's performed the role on stage. As Gielgud noted: "For example, I had the idea that the long dialogue between Prospero and Miranda, often so boring on the stage, could be enormously heightened by showing some of the events leading up to his exile. I think Peter achieved this to great dramatic effect."

This film is so complex, so esoteric, so visually exciting, that to best appreciate it you should take a refresher course in *The Tempest* and then watch the movie at least twice. It's worth the effort. There's too much going on for the intellect to absorb in one sitting.

PROVIDENCE

1977   104m   c   ★★★★
Drama   R/X
Action/SFP   (France/Switzerland)

John Gielgud *(Clive Langham)*, Dirk Bogarde *(Claude Langham)*, Ellen Burstyn *(Sonia Langham)*, David Warner *(Kevin Woodford)*, Elaine Stritch *(Helen Weiner/Molly Langham)*, Denis Lawson *(Dave Woodford)*, Cyril Luckham *(Dr. Mark Eddington)*, Kathryn Leigh-Scott *(Miss Boon)*, Milo Sperber *(Mr. Jenner)*, Anna Wing *(Karen)*

p, Yves Gasser, Yves Peyrot, Klaus Hellwig; d, Alain Resnais; w, David Mercer; ph, Ricardo Aronovich (Eastmancolor); ed, Albert Jurgenson; m, Miklos Rozsa; art d, Jacques Saulnier; cos, Catherine Leterrier, Yves Saint-Laurent, John Bates

Alain Resnais's PROVIDENCE is truly a breakthrough film, a provocative attempt to synthesize past and future, literature and cinema, into a disarming but totally compelling present tense.

The film takes place on the eve of the 78th birthday of Clive Langham (John Gielgud), a dying novelist. He lives alone in his country estate in Providence, Rhode Island, battling alcoholism, the memory of his dead wife, and a chronic rectal disorder. At night, he struggles to write what appears to be his last novel, basing the characters on his own children. In this malevolent fiction, his son, Claude (Dirk Bogarde), and daughter-in-law, Sonia (Ellen Burstyn), are unhappily married and constantly—if wittily—sparring. Another, illegitimate son, Kevin Woodford (David Warner) is a former soldier on trial, prosecuted by Claude, for killing an old man who turned into a werewolf. Claude is the prosecuting attorney, but the defendant is acquitted, and soon falls in love with Sonia. This, however, does not upset Claude as much as it disgusts him.

The increasingly inebriated Clive decides to give Claude a mistress, but the character he creates, Helen (Elaine Stritch), is the image of his dead wife—an older woman with a terminal disease, whom Clive continually mistakes for her prototype. As he labors to complete his retributive narrative, characters disintegrate further and further, delivering each other's dialogue and hopelessly confusing the story. Settings, too, change inexplicably. The next morning, Clive's children pay a birthday visit and prove a far cry from the ailing novelist's representations of them.

Director Alain Resnais—who collaborated with novelists Marguerite Duras in HIROSHIMA MON AMOUR, Alain Robbe-Grillet in LAST YEAR AT MARIENBAD, and Jorge Semprun in LA GUERRE EST FINIE—joined forces here with playwright David Mercer, best known for his *A Suitable Case for Treatment* (filmed by Karel Reisz as MORGAN!). PROVIDENCE should put those who attack Resnais for being pretentious and cold at ease, especially in light of Gielgud's virtuoso performance. Filled with brilliant wit, PROVIDENCE is a superb instance of inventive filmmaking with a comic touch and an intellectual theme.

PSYCHO

1960 109m bw ★★★★★
Horror /15
Paramount

Anthony Perkins (Norman Bates), Janet Leigh (Marion Crane), Vera Miles (Lila Crane), John Gavin (Sam Loomis), Martin Balsam (Milton Arbogast), John McIntire (Sheriff Chambers), Lurene Tuttle (Mrs. Chambers), Simon Oakland (Dr. Richmond), Frank Albertson (Tom Cassidy), Patricia Hitchcock (Caroline)

p, Alfred Hitchcock; d, Alfred Hitchcock; w, Joseph Stefano (based on the novel by Robert Bloch); ph, John L. Russell, Jr.; ed, George Tomasini; m, Bernard Herrmann; prod d, Joseph Hurley, Robert Clatworthy; fx, Clarence Champagne; cos, Helen Colvig

The most successful film ever directed by the Master of Suspense is the mother of all modern horror films. Perhaps no other film changed Hollywood's perception of the horror film so drastically as did PSYCHO. Not until George A. Romero's NIGHT OF THE LIVING DEAD eight years later would any horror film so radically revise the rules of the game. Nowadays when any psychological thriller featuring a loony with a knife is designated "Hitchcockian" in some quarters, it's easy to forget just what a dramatic change of pace this was for Hitchcock. Though renowned for stories of murder, intrigue, and high adventure, Hitchcock's Hollywood films of the 1950s generally boasted top drawer production values, big stars, picturesque surroundings, and, more often than not, Technicolor. In comparison to the likes of NORTH BY NORTHWEST, TO CATCH A THIEF, VERTIGO, and THE MAN WHO KNEW TOO MUCH, PSYCHO seemed unusually sleazy and cheap both in look and subject matter. In a sense, this was an accurate perception. This stark black-and-white thriller bore a strong family resemblance to an episode of Hitchcock's modestly budgeted television series, "Alfred Hitchcock Presents." Indeed he utilized many members of his television crew for the feature. However this is a case in which every production constraint worked to enhance the integrity of the film.

The now familiar plot concerns Norman Bates (Anthony Perkins), a nervous, bird-like motel proprietor who lives under the domineering influence of his aged invalid mother. Norman takes care of Mother, and, in return, she protects the disturbingly boyish man from temptation and corruption, particularly in the form of attractive single women who come to stay at the motel. Marion Crane (Janet Leigh) stops at the Bates Motel after impulsively fleeing from her workplace with a large sum of stolen money. She had hoped this cash would allow her married lover, Sam Loomis (John Gavin), to divorce his wife and marry her. After chatting with Norman, Marion appears to resolve to return the money. However Mother intervenes, leaving a bloody mess for Norman to clean up. After he's scrubbed down the bathroom, the dutiful son places the corpse in the trunk of Crane's rented car and sinks all the evidence in a nearby swamp. The situation gets tense for Norman when Marion's sister, Lila (Vera Miles), Marion's lover, Sam, and private investigator Milton Arbogast (Martin Balsam) arrive to ask some questions.

Here's a Pandora's Box: this masterpiece has spawned so much dreck—and sadistic dreck at that—during the last thirty-odd years that delicate souls might almost wish that it had never been made. So many people have been slashed, sliced and diced in the generic vein that PSYCHO seems to have established, that Hitchcock must bear some guilt. Wherever he is, he probably appreciates the guilt and the irony of it. But PSYCHO itself is not at all like the many movies that tried to imitate it. It's got a jet black sense of humor that becomes increasingly apparent

upon repeated viewings and there's no doubt that it is masterful filmmaking. Hitchcock himself approached it almost as a technical joke: he wanted to see what would happen to audiences if you killed off the star in the first reel. The film is a textbook example of audience manipulation as Hitchcock shifts our identification from character to character with the alacrity of a magician. Though darkly funny, the film is thematically serious as it critiques the power the dead have over the living, the irrationality of American mother worship, the casual cruelty of everyday life and the emotional failings that make intimacy so difficult.

Inspired by the life of the demented, cannibalistic Wisconsin killer Ed Gein (whose gruesome acts would also inspire THE TEXAS CHAIN SAW MASSACRE and DERANGED), PSYCHO's importance to the genre cannot be overestimated. The influence comes not only from the Norman Bates character (who has since been reincarnated in a staggering variety of forms), but also from Hitchcock's use of pop psychological themes (the probable cause of the mayhem stems from the character's perverse familial and sexual history rather than an outside supernatural agency), Bernard Herrmann's famed all-string instruments score (his innovative nerveracking violin "screams" have been oft-mimicked), and new levels of screen violence. One intriguing difference between PSYCHO and the horror films of today is in the age of the characters. There isn't a teenager in sight in the Hitchcock classic—a revealing sign of the subsequent evolution of the genre *and* the downward shift in the age of moviegoing audiences.

PUBLIC ENEMY, THE

1931 83m bw ★★★★½
Crime /A
WB

James Cagney (Tom Powers), Jean Harlow (Gwen Allen), Edward Woods (Matt Doyle), Joan Blondell (Mamie), Beryl Mercer (Ma Powers), Donald Cook (Mike Powers), Mae Clarke (Kitty), Mia Marvin (Jane), Leslie Fenton (Nails Nathan), Robert Emmett O'Connor (Paddy Ryan)

p, Darryl F. Zanuck; d, William A. Wellman; w, Kubec Glasmon, John Bright, Harvey Thew (based on the original story Beer and Blood by John Bright); ph, Dev Jennings; ed, Ed McCormick; art d, Max Parker; cos, Earl Luick, Edward Stevenson

Grapefruit, anyone? Fascinating, brutally realistic, THE PUBLIC ENEMY, along with LITTLE CAESAR, set the gangster genre for the 1930s, making a star of its pugnacious, volatile leading man, James Cagney, and establishing director William A. Wellman as a major helmsman of talkies. Where LITTLE CAESAR had its share of violence, this film portrays the underworld in even seedier terms, taking on the most gruesome situations and portraying sex and violence liberally for its time (THE PUBLIC ENEMY was made before the Hays Office established its rigid codes).

The film opens with two young Irish boys, Frank Coghlan and Frankie Darro, growing up in the shantytown South Side of Chicago, circa 1909, hanging around pool halls and saloons and visiting a so-called boys' club run by the sinister Murray Kinnell, fencer of the stolen goods the boys bring to him. Coghlan (playing Cagney as a youngster), the ill-used son of Chicago cop Purnell Pratt, spends his time playing brutal pranks on the girls of his run-down neighborhood and leading Darro (playing Woods as a boy) into crime.

The boys soon grow to be young men, earning their living during the day as delivery men, while at night planning robberies with Kinnell, who gives them guns and outlines their first big heist, the robbery of a fur warehouse. As the thieves enter the warehouse, Cagney is startled by a huge stuffed bear's head and impulsively fires several shots into it. The thieves panic, open a window, and slide down a drain pipe to the street. Police descend upon the site at the sound of the shots, killing one of the thieves, while Cagney and Woods kill a cop in return before escaping. Running breathlessly back to Kinnell's seedy club, the boys find that Kinnell has left town. Deserted by their underworld guide, Cagney and Woods go to saloon owner Robert Emmett O'Connor, a wheeling-dealing criminal operator, who tells them that the coming Prohibition will mean a million-dollar racket for anyone selling illegal booze and beer. He intends to organize a mob to control such an enterprise in his district, and promises the boys that he will distribute what they steal. Their first job, the robbery of a federal warehouse for impounded liquor, nets the boys more money than they've ever seen before. With newly purchased tailor-made clothes and a flashy car, Cagney and Woods go to a nightclub, roaring up to the place in their new roadster. They enter and pick up two floozies; Cagney takes Mae Clarke, while Woods pairs off with Joan Blondell.

The four move into an apartment, while Cagney goes home to lavish his bootleg dollars on his good-hearted mother, Beryl Mercer, a widow still taking in washing to make ends meet. She tells him that his older brother, Donald Cook, has ordered her not to take any money. Later, at a family party, Woods and Cagney place a huge keg of beer in the middle of the table; when Woods asks Cook why he isn't drinking any beer, the older brother explodes, smashing the keg against a wall and shouting: "You think I don't know what you two have been up to? That's not just beer in that keg, but blood and beer!" Back at his apartment next morning, Cagney walks sleepily to the breakfast table, where moll Clarke greets him without a smile. When she provokes him with the suggestion that he has found someone he likes better, Cagney smashes a grapefruit into Clarke's face to end their relationship. Later, when Cagney and Woods are driving down Michigan Avenue, Cagney spots a voluptuous blonde, Jean Harlow, and orders Woods to stop the car. Cagney picks her up, and before getting out, she asks for *his* phone number. Afterwards, Cagney, Harlow, Woods, Blondell, and their new crime boss, Leslie Fenton, all enter a nightclub, where they spot the long-missing Kinnell. Fenton goads the boys with a reminder of how Kinnell once set them up and then disappeared. Cagney and Woods excuse themselves, follow Kinnell from the club, and trail him to his apartment. There the old crook, realizing that Cagney and Woods are out for revenge, begs for his life, asking the boys to remember their youth and how he used to play dirty songs for them. He sits down at the piano and begins to play an old ditty. Off-camera, Cagney shoots his mentor, whose body is heard collapsing on discordant piano keys; on-camera, Woods stares mutely at the scene. Cagney visits his mother once more, trying to shove thousands of dollars into her hand, but she again refuses, saying Cook will get angry. Cook appears, telling Cagney to leave and never again to offer "blood money" to them. Cagney tries to take a punch at his brother, but Cook slugs him first. Shoving his mother out of the way, the gangster leaves.

Later, Cagney learns from Woods that their boss, Fenton, has been kicked to death on a bridle path by a spirited horse. Cagney and Woods visit the stable and shoot the horse. With Fenton dead, gang war breaks out, and O'Connor's saloon is bombed. Now the nominal leader of the gang, O'Connor orders Cagney, Woods, and other gang members to go into hiding. He takes their guns and money so they will stay in the apartment he has selected for their hideout. When Cagney wakes up in the apartment to discover that he was seduced by a whore during the night while in a drunken stupor, he angrily shoves her aside and leaves the building, followed closely by Woods. Across the street, a rival gang has set up a machine gun in a second-story window, and the gun traces the steps of Cagney and Woods as they leave the building. As the two reach the edge of the building, the machine gun opens up and cuts Woods down. Cagney slips behind the corner of the building, looking back to see Woods reach out for his lifelong friend before flopping over dead.

THE PUBLIC ENEMY is one of the most realistic gangster films ever produced. Wellman's direction is a frontal attack on the subject; other than handling a number of violent deaths off-screen, he spares no brutality of emotion, no ruthlessness of action or thought in his grim portrayal of a lethal criminal. Cagney is *the* gangster of his day, cocky, seemingly invulnerable, and utterly without conscience, a character obviously predisposed toward evil from childhood. In this character Wellman shows us his philosophy that the environment creates the man. We see only the criminal world, with police barely in the background. The one cop shown in detail, Pratt, is a brute who walks around his house dressed in a half-uniform, communicating with his unruly youngster by means of a razor strop. Photographer Dev Jennings shot this film with sharp contrasts: glaring sunlit exteriors, grainy gray interiors that fade to black alleyways and gutters.

Cagney shot to fame with this international hit, typecasting himself for almost a decade as a ruthless hoodlum, an image that would carry him through the 1930s in such hell-raising films as G-MEN, ANGELS WITH DIRTY FACES, THE ROARING TWENTIES, and EACH DAWN I DIE. He was a human wolf with an insatiable appetite for violence in THE PUBLIC ENEMY, displaying original screen mannerisms that captivated the viewing public. His character is based upon the colorful Chicago gangster Charles Dion "Deanie" O'Bannion, archrival to Al Capone. Fenton acts the part of Samuel J. "Nails" Morton, a decorated lieutenant of WWI, formerly in command of a machine-gun company, who later used that deadly weapon with great and devastating effect in the gangland wars of Chicago in the early 1920s. The scenes involving Cagney and Woods killing the horse that killed Fenton are, surprisingly, based on actual fact. The most remembered scene of this film, of course, is the one in which Cagney smashes the grapefruit in Clarke's face. Everyone connected with the grapefruit scene remembered it differently. According to Cagney, the incident was concocted for the film after the writers, John Bright and Kubec Glasmon, learned that Chicago gangster Earl "Hymie" Weiss, incensed with his gun moll's endless talk, slammed an omelet into her face; Wellman thought the omelet too messy, so he opted for a grapefruit half. At one time, Cagney claimed that Wellman and he cooked up a conspiracy that involved the notorious grapefruit. He was to pick it up and then push it *past* Clarke's face, along the profile unseen by the camera, not touching the flesh. But he and Wellman decided to actually slam the grapefruit into Clarke's incredulous countenance without telling her in order to capture genuine shock. This it did, if the story be true; the blow hurt Clarke physically, and she showed all the pain and embarrassment in that memorable, if crude, scene. Clarke later stated that no grapefruit was to be used, that Cagney did the smashing impulsively instead of shouting at her. Still later, Clarke told interviewer Richard Lamparski that Wellman made one take where Cagney was merely to insult her verbally, then asked to do another "gag" take for a laugh. The gag involved Cagney shoving the grapefruit into Clarke's face. The actress forgot about the gag, and was shocked when she saw the film. Women's groups rose up in protest over such brutal abuse of a woman on-screen. Of course, Cagney and Clarke were ever after associated with that grapefruit scene. For years after the release of the film, when Cagney entered a restaurant, he was likely to receive a half grapefruit from some customer in the place.

Wellman finished THE PUBLIC ENEMY in a short 26 days and for only $151,000. Although the film would yield millions in reissues as a classic gangster picture, Wellman had to fight for Cagney as well as the picture itself. Cagney had appeared in only four films for Warner Bros. and was thought of only as an engaging young supporting player. Woods, ironically enough, had been cast in the lead. Wellman viewed early rushes of the film and concluded that he had the wrong man playing the tough Tom Powers. Proving his toughness many times over in THE PUBLIC ENEMY, Cagney actually stood only a foot away from the wall of a building while a WWI veteran machine gunner hired by the studio sprayed the wall with live ammunition. In one scene, Cook, called upon to hit Cagney in the face, did not pull the punch, but landed the blow squarely on Cagney's jaw, breaking a tooth in the process. Just as he would in other films, Cagney brought his indelible mannerisms to THE PUBLIC ENEMY. In several scenes he lightly taps Mercer's jaw affectionately, a gesture Cagney's own father used on him. Harlow, the sexy blonde bombshell of the decade, has really a small role in the film, playing the part of a call girl whose favors are available for money, but who practices her own strange perversions by indulging herself in men of violence. She was only 20 years old at the time, and her inexperience shows drastically. It would take another year before Harlow hit upon the formula for comic seduction that skyrocketed her to success in RED-HEADED WOMAN. This was Harlow's only film with Cagney and her only lead role at Warner Bros. The film received one Academy Award nomination, for Best Original Story.

PUMPKIN EATER, THE

1964 118m bw   ★★★★
Drama   /X
Romulus   (U.K.)

Anne Bancroft *(Jo Armitage)*, Peter Finch *(Jake Armitage)*, James Mason *(Bob Conway)*, Janine Gray *(Beth Conway)*, Cedric Hardwicke *(Mr. James, Jo's Father)*, Rosalind Atkinson *(Mrs. James, Jo's Mother)*, Alan Webb *(Mr. Armitage, Jake's Father)*, Richard Johnson *(Giles)*, Maggie Smith *(Philpot)*, Eric Porter *(Psychiatrist)*

p, James Woolf; d, Jack Clayton; w, Harold Pinter (based on the novel *The Pumpkin Eater* by Penelope Mortimer); ph, Oswald Morris; ed, James B. Clark; m, Georges Delerue; art d, Edward Marshall; cos, Motley

Bancroft, in an Oscar-nominated performance, plays a twice-married mother of six. She divorces her second husband (Johnson) and takes up with Finch, a highly successful screenwriter. The two marry; it seems like a perfect marriage until Bancroft realizes her philandering husband will never buckle down to her notions of marital fidelity. She gives birth to her seventh child and suffers a nervous breakdown. This, along with an encounter with an unbalanced woman at her hairdresser's, sends Bancroft to a psychiatrist (Porter). He is not much help. Bancroft's father dies, and she discovers that she is once more expecting a baby. She refuses to accompany Finch to a film location in Morocco but agrees to his arguments for sterilization. Later she runs into Mason, a man who once made a pass at her. Mason reveals that Finch has been having an affair with his wife (Gray), who is now

expecting a child. In an ugly scene Bancroft confronts Finch and returns to Johnson. After she spends the night with her former husband, Johnson gets a phone call from old-friend Finch, whose father has just died. Bancroft goes to the funeral, but Finch pretends not to notice her. As she chases him, she slips and falls in the mud. Demoralized once more, she goes to their unfinished country house and spends the night alone. In the morning she wakes to the sound of her children as Finch leads them up a hill. Bancroft resigns herself to life, for good or ill, with the man. This is a fine film, encompassing the joys and tragedies of life: birth and death, marriage and divorce, love and hate. The leads give their characters life. They seem to be real people on the screen, not actors in a drama. Bancroft lends her role real depth, switching moods with eerie and wonderful believability. Mason, in a small supporting role, is nothing short of excellent. The script, by noted playwright Pinter, is complex and painful but often exhibits a good sense of the comic as well. The direction, slow and even-handed, allows the story to develop at its own pace, gradually building in speed as the story's intensity grows. This is a fine and sensitive work, a truthful portrait of human foibles and complexities. The film was charismatic character-actor Hardwicke's final one; he died the year of its release.

PUNCHLINE

1988 128m c   ★★★½
Comedy   R/15
Columbia

Sally Field *(Lilah Krytsick)*, Tom Hanks *(Steven Gold)*, John Goodman *(John Krytsick)*, Mark Rydell *(Romeo, Comedy Club Owner)*, Kim Greist *(Madeline Urie)*, Paul Mazursky *(Arnold)*, Pam Matteson *(Utica Blake)*, George Michael McGrath *(Singing Nun)*, Taylor Negron *(Albert Emperato)*, Barry Neikrug *(Krug)*

p, Daniel Melnick, Michael Rachmil; d, David Seltzer; w, David Seltzer; ph, Reynaldo Villalobos (DeLuxe Color); ed, Bruce Green; m, Charles Gross; prod d, Jackson DeGovia; cos, Dan Moore, Aggie Lyon

PUNCHLINE, the first major release to hit on this subculture of comedy clubs and struggling comedians, is both funny and sad. Tom Hanks plays Steven Gold, a callous down-and-out comedian who spends more time delivering routines than studying for medical exams. Lilah Krytsick (Sally Field) is a New Jersey housewife who tells dirty Polish jokes about her husband and even resorts to buying jokes on the black market. After 18 months in stand-up, Steven is broke, has been kicked out of his apartment and dropped from med school, and seems not to have any friends. Then he learns that talent scout Madeline Urie (Kim Greist) is planning a television comedy contest, the winner of which will receive a guest shot with Johnny Carson. A surprisingly dark film, PUNCHLINE is a success because it doesn't try to glorify its surroundings. It presents instead a world in which far more get laughed *at* than get laughs. Along with strong performances, the movie is brimming with "moments." Writer-director David Seltzer is not afraid to stop his narrative and let a scene linger. Although PUNCHLINE occasionally falters—in its contrived contest ending and saccharine tendencies—it is still an engaging and honest achievement.

PURPLE HEART, THE

1944 99m bw   ★★★★
War   /A
FOX

Dana Andrews *(Capt. Harvey Ross)*, Richard Conte *(Lt. Angelo Canelli)*, Farley Granger *(Sgt. Howard Clinton)*, Kevin O'Shea *(Sgt. Jan Skvoznik)*, Don "Red" Barry *(Lt. Peter Vincent)*, Trudy Marshall *(Mrs. Ross)*, Sam Levene *(Lt. Wayne Greenbaum)*, Charles Russell *(Lt. Kenneth Bayforth)*, John Craven *(Sgt. Martin Stoner)*, Tala Birell *(Johanna Hartwig)*

p, Darryl F. Zanuck; d, Lewis Milestone; w, Jerry Cady (based on a story by Zanuck); ph, Arthur Miller; ed, Douglas Biggs; m, Alfred Newman; art d, James Basevi, Lewis Creber; fx, Fred Sersen

Wildly overrated at the time of its release, THE PURPLE HEART has not aged well, and viewers today may have trouble with its leering racism, overwrought patriotic speechifying, and terribly bombastic musical score. The story concerns two bomber crews captured by the Japanese after the 1942 air raid against Tokyo. Capt. Harvey Ross (Dana Andrews) is the ranking American officer of the eight bomber crew members who are imprisoned in Japan and brought to trial, not as prisoners of war, but as war criminals. The false charge against them is that they purposely dropped bombs on schools, hospitals, and other nonmilitary targets. When none of the Americans will admit to such atrocities, they are taken from their cells one by one and tortured by Gen. Mitsubi (Richard Loo), the sadistic military intelligence officer, not so much to gain confessions but so that their Japanese interrogators can learn the base from which the bombers flew. The bombers, unbeknownst to the Japanese, launched their planes from the US carrier *Hornet* while at sea—a secret the men must keep from the enemy no matter what. Directed by veteran helmsman Lewis Milestone, who seems to have shed the pacifism he so movingly extolled in ALL QUIET ON THE WESTERN FRONT (1930), THE PURPLE HEART was based on an actual kangaroo trial conducted by the Japanese in which some American pilots were condemned as war criminals and later beheaded. Although based on fact and obviously designed as propaganda to fuel patriotic fervor at the height of WWII, the film is a bit hard to take now because of the overt racism embodied by Loo, who specialized in the sort of devious, sneering, buck-toothed portrayals of the Japanese common in those days. Racism aside, the film is not without cinematic interest. Milestone brings his trademark visual style to the proceedings, especially in the courtroom scenes, in which the camera constantly prowls through the space. Cinematographer Arthur Miller's use of light and shadow is almost expressionistic, and is especially effective as the prisoners are led down the long hallway from their cells to the courtroom. The filmic highlight occurs when news comes that Corregidor has fallen to the Japanese and Milestone conveys the triumph of the enemy through an impressive Eisensteinian montage.

PURPLE ROSE OF CAIRO, THE

1985   84m   c/bw   ★★★
Comedy/Fantasy   PG
Jack Rollins/Charles H. Joffe

Mia Farrow *(Cecilia)*, Jeff Daniels *(Tom Baxter/Gil Shepherd)*, Danny Aiello *(Monk)*, Dianne Wiest *(Emma)*, Van Johnson *(Larry)*, Zoe Caldwell *(The Countess)*, John Wood *(Jason)*, Milo O'Shea *(Fr. Donnelly)*, Deborah Rush *(Rita)*, Irving Metzman *(Theater Manager)*

p, Robert Greenhut; d, Woody Allen; w, Woody Allen; ph, Gordon Willis (Deluxe Color); ed, Susan E. Morse; m, Dick Hyman; prod d, Stuart Wurtzel; art d, Edward Pisoni; cos, Jeffrey Kurland

The premise here is unique, but it wears thin after the first reel, even though directer-writer Woody Allen strives mightily to keep things humming. Cecilia (Mia Farrow) is married to loutish, womanizing Monk (Danny Aiello) and lives a miserable life as a diner waitress. Her only escape from the woes of the depression is in the local movie house. Cecilia is particularly absorbed by a film (fictional) entitled "The Purple Rose of Cairo" starring a simon-pure hero (Jeff Daniels). She watches the same movie over and over, and then the miracle occurs. The hero suddenly faces the camera on-screen and begins to talk to Cecilia in the audience, then he startles the rest of the on-film actors by stepping out of the screen and into the theater, asking Cecilia to show him what real life is all about. He falls in love with her and she with him, but Monk and the Hollywood moguls are concerned. It's all a clever gimmick, of course, and Allen pulls it off well technically, but the story is as one-dimensional as the fictional Daniels. Where Allen succeeds is in his re-creation of the old studio programmers of the 1930s, something he had done briefly before in ZELIG. Allen has done better than this, but THE PURPLE ROSE OF CAIRO is a sweet little film and an interesting diversion for his legion of followers. Allen was nominated for an Oscar for his screenplay.

PURSUED

1947   101m   bw   ★★★½
Mystery/Western   /PG
United States

Teresa Wright *(Thorley Callum)*, Robert Mitchum *(Jeb Rand)*, Judith Anderson *(Medora Callum)*, Dean Jagger *(Grant Callum)*, Alan Hale *(Jake Dingle)*, Harry Carey, Jr. *(Prentice McComber)*, John Rodney *(Adam Callum)*, Clifton Young *(The Sergeant)*, Ernest Severn *(Jeb, Age 8)*, Charles Bates *(Adam, Age 10)*

p, Milton Sperling; d, Raoul Walsh; w, Niven Busch; ph, James Wong Howe; ed, Christian Nyby; m, Max Steiner; art d, Ted Smith; fx, William McGann, Willard Van Enger; cos, Leah Rhodes

An offbeat, film noir western/murder mystery which stars Robert Mitchum as Jeb Rand, a man pursued for his entire life by unseen (by him) assailants. Told in flashback, the film tells Jeb's story beginning when, as a young boy, his entire family was slaughtered—a vision that haunts him into adulthood. When the killers discover that Jeb was the only family member to survive, they vow to kill him too. He spends his life trying to find out who is responsible and why his adopted mother agreed to raise him. While not a mystery in the truest sense, PURSUED is one of darkest films ever made—one in which the main character spends his entire life (and the duration of the film) being victimized by everyone around him. Although some of the motives are made clear in an early scene, Mitchum's character knows nothing of the mysterious events which envelop him. It's not completely a western (it's merely a western location) and it's not completely a mystery, but it is a film which stretches the parameters of both genres.

PURSUIT OF D.B. COOPER, THE

1981   100m   c   ★★½
Crime   PG/AA
Polygram

Robert Duvall *(Bob Gruen)*, Treat Williams *(D.B. Cooooper/Jim Meade)*, Kathryn Harrold *(Hannah Meade)*, Ed Flanders *(Brigadier Meade)*, Paul Gleason *(Remson)*, R.G. Armstrong *(Dempsey)*, Dorothy Fielding *(Denise)*, Nicolas Coster *(Avery)*, Cooper Huckabee *(Homer)*, Howard K. Smith *(Himself)* p, Dan Wigutow, Michael Taylor; d, Roger Spottiswoode; w, Jeffrey Alan Fiskin (based on the book *Free Fall* By J.D. Reed); ph, Harry Stradling, Jr. (Metrocolor); ed, Robbe Roberts, Allan Jacobs; m, James Horner; prod d, Preston Ames

On November 4, 1971, a man identifying himself as D.B. Cooper boarded a Northwest Airlines Portland, Oregon to Seattle, Washington flight. In flight, he threatened to detonate a bomb unless he was given $200,000 and four prachutes. His demands were met in Seattle and he directed the plane to head for Reno, Nevada. While in flight somewhere over Washington, the man bailed out of the plane with the money and the case has never been solved. This film offers a fictionalized musing on Cooper and his travails after bailing out of the plane, with Williams starring as the daring thief. Once on the ground, Williams makes his way out of the woods to reunite with his wife (Harrold) whom he left some six months earlier. Meanwhile, Duvall, an insurance investigator who was Williams's sergeant in the Army, comes to the conclusion that Williams is D.B. Cooper, and he heads to Harrold's place. Rounding out the foursome is Gleason, Williams's sleazy ex-Army buddy, who also comes to the conclusion that Williams was the hijacker and wants to get a piece of the action. This sets up a seemingly endless series of captures and escapes as Williams and Harrold attempt to elude their captors while heading for Mexico.

The repetition of events wears a little thin after awhile, and Duvall's amazing ability to continually find the fugitives in the vast West borders on the absurd, but overall it's an entertaining, fast-moving film. Duvall, as always, is wonderful, as are Williams and Harrold—who always turns in solid performances and is so attractive one wonders why her career never got untracked. Universal's publicity scheme for the film promised anyone who could come up with information leading to the capture of the real Cooper a possible $1 million reward. No one got the money.

PYGMALION
1938 96m bw ★★★★★
Comedy /U
MGM (U.K.)

Leslie Howard (*Prof. Henry Higgins*), Wendy Hiller (*Eliza Doolittle*), Wilfrid Lawson (*Alfred Doolittle*), Marie Lohr (*Mrs. Higgins*), Scott Sunderland (*Col. Pickering*), Jean Cadell (*Mrs. Pearce*), David Tree (*Freddy Eynsford-Hill*), Everley Gregg (*Mrs. Eynsford-Hill*), Leueen MacGrath (*Clara Eynsford-Hill*), Esme Percy (*Count Aristid Karpathy*)

p, Gabriel Pascal; d, Anthony Asquith, Leslie Howard; w, George Bernard Shaw, W.P. Lipscomb, Cecil Lewis, Ian Dalrymple, Anthony Asquith (based on the play by George Bernard Shaw); ph, Harry Stradling; ed, David Lean; m, Arthur Honegger; art d, Laurence Irving; cos, Prof. Czettell, Worth, Schiaparelli

Shaw's magnificent comedy, a 1913 smash on the London stage, was never better served than in this flawless Pascal production with Howard and Hiller perfectly matched as thoroughly mismatched lovers. Howard is Henry Higgins, a wealthy phonetics professor who encounters Cockney flower seller Eliza Doolittle (Hiller) and bets with his friend Col. Pickering (Sunderland) that he can transform the uncouth, uneducated, and thick-accented woman ("a squashed cabbage leaf," as he calls her) into a grand lady within three months. Eliza is only too happy to move into Henry's elegant home until she endures the rigorous routines

Henry subjects her to as his education of this "lowly guttersnipe." Best of all he has her talk with marbles in her mouth to perfect her elocution. (When she swallows one, he calmly notes, "That's all right. We have plenty more.") He also drills his would-be duchess on courtly manners and knowledge until she is ready to drop. And yet when the big test comes, Eliza enchants the ball guests with her lovely speaking, perfect manners and restrained grace. Congratulating himself alone on his achievement, Higgins entirely ignores Eliza, who ponders her now-awkward condition. What becomes of this odd couple leads to the film's famous final line.

The film, which Howard codirected with Asquith, is delightful from beginning to end, and Hiller is splendid in her impossible role, making an amazing transformation from illiterate to lady. The closest Britain ever got to having their own Katharine Hepburn, Hiller nevertheless projects a charm, energy and talent entirely her own. What a pity she didn't work in films more often, for she is quite perfect here. Her first public test, when Henry invites Eliza to take tea with his mother (Lohr, marvelous) is sidesplittingly funny. You may have tears in your eyes when Hiller goes on about her father's drinking and the fate of her deceased aunt's lovely straw hat. A great line: "Them what pinched it, done her in." The curmudgeonly Shaw, who needed considerable persuading from Pascal to allow the film to be made, wanted Charles Laughton for Higgins, but later gave in and agreed that Howard would have a broader appeal in America, where he had scored many film successes. Howard went beyond the playwright's dour expectations, however, and delivered one of his most effective performances, becoming the epitome of the intellectual tyrant (undoubtedly studying and emulating Shaw's own personality). Sunderland is excellent as the kindly Col. Pickering, and Lawson, as Doolittle the dustman, whose life is suddenly enriched with the discovery of his uneducated daughter, is stupendous. Lawson's speeches, despite Pascal's promise to Shaw, along with many other philosophical diatribes, were cut. The clever Pascal got around Shaw by having the dramatist write many of the scenes, especially the Ambassador's Ball scene, which is not present in the play, thus making Shaw a culpable party to the truncating of his own work.

Asquith, who has the lion's credit for direction, and deservedly so, moves the ethereal tale along at a fast clip and gets wonderful performances from his stunning cast. The film was an international success, especially in America, but Hiller did not heed the siren call of Hollywood, preferring to stay on the British stage. The play of course later inspired the famous stage musical MY FAIR LADY, which was filmed in 1964. What a pity that this version was taken out of circulation for nearly a decade as a result. The greatest filming of a Shaw play ever, PYGMALION easily eclipses its rather pallid musical remake. Audrey Hepburn can play the swan but not the "cabbage leaf" and, for our money, Harrison simply can't touch Howard's brilliant work in the original. The Oscar votes fouled up yet again on this one, nominated the film for Picture, Actor and Actress, but saw fit to bypass Howard in favor of Spencer Tracy's unimpressive work in BOYS TOWN and the film itself in favor of the rather sticky YOU CAN'T TAKE IT WITH YOU. (Hiller admittedly had stiffer competition, though the choice between her and winner Bette Davis sure is a hard one.) At least the film won Best Screenplay for Shaw and company. Prepare yourself for a stimulating night of that *rara avis*, intelligent comedy.

Q

1982   100m   c   ★★★½
Horror   R/15
United Film Distribution

Michael Moriarty (*Jimmy Quinn*), Candy Clark (*Joan*), David Carradine (*Detective Shepard*), Richard Roundtree (*Sgt. Powell*), James Dixon (*Lt. Murray*), Malachy McCourt (*Police Commissioner*), Fred J. Scollay (*Capt. Fletcher*), Peter Hock (*Detective Clifford*), Ron Cey (*Detective Hoberman*), Mary Louise Weller (*Mrs. Pauley*)

p, Larry Cohen; d, Larry Cohen; w, Larry Cohen; ph, Fred Murphy; ed, Armond Lebowitz; m, Robert O. Ragland; fx, Steve Neill, David Allen, Randall William Cook, Peter Kuran

Larry Cohen once again proves himself to be among the most creative, original, and intelligent American horror film directors in this bizarre masterwork, which successfully combines a *film noir* crime story with a good old-fashioned "giant monster" movie. Michael Moriarty turns in a brilliant performance as Jimmy Quinn, an ex-con, former junkie, and small-time hood looking to make one big score. After robbing a Manhattan diamond center, he hides out in the tower of the Chrysler Building and discovers a large hole in the dome of the structure, containing a huge nest with an equally large egg and several partially devoured human corpses. Meanwhile, the New York City police have been plagued by a bizarre string of deaths, and Detective Shepard (David Carradine) and Sgt. Powell (Richard Roundtree) have been investigating reports of people being snatched off rooftops. What all soon find out is that the Aztec god Quetzalcoatl, the winged serpent, is flying over Manhattan. Though Q's premise seems fairly silly (so does KING KONG's), Cohen's handling of the material is superior; he really convinces us that the idea of a giant bird living in a nest at the top of the Chrysler building isn't as implausible as it sounds. Cohen packs the film with stunning visuals and makes the most of New York City's architecture, capitalizing on its dozens of facades with birds and birdlike carvings. Q bombed at the box office because it was nearly impossible to package into a nice, simple ad campaign, but the film is a skillful combination of genres, sporting some fine acting and a literate, fascinating script with dashes of biting humor, that is well worth seeing.

Q&A

1990   134m   c   ★★½
Crime/Drama   R/18
Regency International Pictures-Odyssey Distributors Ltd.

Nick Nolte (*Lt. Mike Brennan*), Timothy Hutton (*Al Reilly*), Armand Assante (*Bobby Texador*), Patrick O'Neal (*Kevin Quinn*), Lee Richardson (*Leo Bloomenfeld*), Luis Guzman (*Detective Luis Valentin*),

Charles Dutton (*Detective Sam Chapman*), Jenny Lumet (*Nancy Bosch*), Paul Calderon (*Roger Montalvo*), International Chrysis (*Jose Malpica*)

p, Arnon Milchan, Burtt Harris; d, Sidney Lumet; w, Sidney Lumet (based on the book by Edwin Torres); ph, Andrzej Bartkowiak (Technicolor); ed, Richard Cirincione; m, Ruben Blades; prod d, Philip Rosenberg; art d, Beth Kuhn; cos, Ann Roth, Neil Spisak

Director Sidney Lumet has depicted the world of the New York City policeman in two very successful films, SERPICO and PRINCE OF THE CITY. Forceful exposes that delve into the dark and complex world of police corruption, they remain two of the director's finest works. After a string of commercially and artistically unsuccessful efforts, Lumet returns to SERPICO's terrain with Q&A, but the results are not nearly as good; in fact, they're pretty bad. Widespread corruption of body and soul (and its effect on the judicial system and police force of New York City) are again at the center of Lumet's film. The embodiment of that corruption is Lt. Mike Brennan (Nick Nolte), hailed by his peers as one of the finest cops in New York. "The first through any door, window, or skylight," he has taken a bullet for a fellow officer on several occasions. But, unknown to most, Brennan is also one of the dirtiest cops on the force. In the film's opening scene, he kills an unarmed Latino drug dealer in cold blood, then plants a gun on him. When more officers arrive on the scene, it appears that Brennan simply shot the dealer in self-defense. Still, this incident requires an investigation by the DA's office, and ex-cop turned assistant DA Al Reilly (Timothy Hutton) is assigned to the case. This being Reilly's first investigation, chief of homicide Kevin Quinn (Patrick O'Neal) briefs him on how to go about it: Reilly will ask questions regarding the incident, a stenographer will record Brennan's answers (the Q&A of the title), and after a few interviews with some witnesses, the whole matter will be neatly cleared up. In their initial meeting, Brennan explains his side of the story in suspiciously thorough detail; then Reilly learns his own former girlfriend, Nancy (Jenny Lumet, the director's daughter), is now romantically involved with Bobby Texador (Armand Assante), a drug dealer who is also a witness. The young assistant DA decides to launch a full investigation of this seemingly simple matter and events take a dangerous turn. The trail of corruption leads from drug dealers to Brennan and ultimately directly to Quinn's office. Assisted by an African-American cop (Charles Dutton), a Hispanic officer (Luis Guzman), and Jewish district attorney and mentor Leo Bloomenfeld (Lee Richardson), Reilly discovers plenty of dirt on Brennan and Quinn. In the process, Reilly makes enemies of both Brennan and Texador, the latter failing to appreciate Reilly's attempt to win back Nancy's love. While Brennan is killing all those who might incriminate him (most of whom are homosexuals), Reilly struggles with the truth about the system and about himself. Tellingly, we learn that Nancy broke up with him after his negative reaction upon learning that her father is African-American. As the film moves to its close, big questions remain to be answered. Is the system that corrupt? (With Reilly's case on the rocks, Brennan and all the witnesses dead, and Quinn's freedom imminent, Reilly asks Leo if it is really possible to cover up something so big. "Bigger," Leo responds.) Is Reilly truly a racist? Will he ever get Nancy back? By the closing credits we know that the investigation has been aborted, and that Reilly catches up with Nancy on an island, announces that he is a changed man, and declares his love for her. What we don't learn is whether she will take him back.

The true subject of this film seems to be the nature of corruption and racism, both very real problems within the police community. Unquestionably, there are many racist policeman, but in Q&A *every* character has notable racist tendencies (the words "spic," "nigger," and "guinea" are used regularly). While it is clear that the film's dramatic conflict centers on Reilly's coming to terms with his prejudice, Q&A is neither enlightening nor sure of its message. Lumet, whose recent FAMILY BUSINESS is also loaded with racial stereotypes and slurs, has mistaken the trading of racial insults for camaraderie, and stereotypes for atmosphere (straining for a "melting pot" ambiance, he creates the least authentic New York in recent memory). The result is an uncomfortably nasty picture. The disturbing subtext of Lumet's last two pictures is especially surprising coming from this director. Lumet was once married to an African-American woman, Lena Horne's daughter (Jenny is one of their two children), and it is odd that he fails to demonstrate a greater awareness of the sensitive nature of his subject matter. Instead the screenplay abounds with overtones of bigotry. It is unfathomable why any director would choose to have a hispanic character tell a black character to "quit eating watermelons" in what is supposedly a friendly exchange. In addition to racist slurs, the film is jam-packed with insulting depictions of homosexuals and with gay-bashing scenes. Brennan strangles two transvestites and nearly emasculates another; gay characters are referred to as "fags" and Lumet photographs them in the most unflattering ways possible.

All of this could be forgiven had the film followed through on its ideas. But while trying to create a dark, seedy world (which the film's glossy photography works against), Lumet overstuffs Q&A with plot. Providing little or no character motivation, he reduces the film's central concerns (racism and corruption) to an offensive subplot. Clearly, Lumet wanted to present a serious look at racism, but his naive and superficial treatment of his subject both prevents him from making a good film and insults the viewer. The film's shifting point of view doesn't help matters, either. Is this Reilly's story or Brennan's? Is it a police expose or a character study? This lack of focus goes a long way toward sinking the film. In addition, although Lumet's strongest talent has always been his handling of actors, Q&A is full of below-par performances. Nolte is particularly bad, giving a performance that is as weak as his turn in FAREWELL TO THE KING. Completely out of his element as the hulking Irish cop, he overplays his hand on several occasions. And it doesn't help that his character's motivation is a complete mystery (notably, there are unanswered questions concerning his drinking and possible latent homosexuality). Hutton, complete with a shaky Brooklyn accent, is too restrained and flat-out boring to be the central character of the film. Making her film debut, Jenny Lumet is absolutely terrible; she fails to convince in any of the three emotionally challenging scenes in which she appears. Not surprisingly, O'Neal and Richardson ham it up tirelessly. Although at times he, too, is painfully over-the-top, Assante at least adds life to the proceedings. Despite his homophobia and racism, Assante's Bobby Texador is the only character in the film that is almost likable.

Even on the technical level Q&A is a disappointment, its screenplay forgettable, its music ridiculous (at the most inappropriate moments, the film's lame theme song comes thudding over the soundtrack). Lumet's boring editing style and immobile camera are more appropriate for television than the big screen. Moreover, his obsession with introducing plot twists reaches absurd heights when the film *ends* with a new plot development. But the main problem with the movie is its lack of likable characters. In PRINCE OF THE CITY and SERPICO, Lumet's focus was on one tortured character, and the effect in both films

was powerful. In Q&A, Reilly is too transparent and Brennan too repellent to hold the viewer's interest. Aside from two or three effective scenes (all of which include Assante), the film is a tremendous disappointment.

QUACKSER FORTUNE HAS A COUSIN IN THE BRONX

1970 90m c   ★★★
Comedy/Drama   R/A
UMC (Ireland)

Gene Wilder *(Quackser Fortune)*, Margot Kidder *(Zazel Pierce)*, Eileen Colgan *(Betsy Bourke)*, Seamus Ford *(Mr. Fortune)*, May Ollis *(Mrs. Fortune)*, Liz Davis *(Kathleen Fortune)*, Caroline Tully *(Vera Fortune)*, Paul Murphy *(Damien)*, David Kelly *(Tom Maguire)*, Tony Doyle *(Mike)*

p, Mel Howard, John H. Cushingham; d, Waris Hussein; w, Gabriel Walsh; ph, Gilbert Taylor (Eastmancolor); ed, Bill Blunden; m, Michael Dress; art d, Herbert Smith

This picture was made before Wilder began fancying himself an *auteur* and fell into bad acting habits, and consequently offers one of his best, most controlled performances. An offbeat story and the lovely Dublin locations also add to the mix. Wilder has chosen to earn his living by following delivery horses through the streets, picking up their droppings and selling them to housewives as fertilizer. He makes a good living at what he does, and, unlike his father (Ford), who works long, hard hours in a foundry, Wilder gets plenty of exercise and fresh air, and enjoys his independence. His job also provides perks like his continuing affair with one of his regular customers, Colgan. Enter Kidder, a pretty American student at Trinity College whose whose parents are apparently wealthy. She is in love with Dublin and its history, which she knows much more about than most of the residents. Kidder is attracted to Wilder, and the two travel around the city together. When the Trinity students have a fancy ball, Kidder invites Wilder as her date. However, by this point, she is tiring of Wilder and pays little attention to him at the ball, preferring to be with her wealthy pals. The other students cruelly make fun of Wilder, prompting him to lash out. Wilder hastily exits with Kidder, who takes him to bed at a posh hotel. After their lovemaking, Kidder leaves. When Wilder wakes up and finds her gone, he hurries to Trinity College and learns that Kidder has departed, leaving no forwarding address. To add to Wilder's woes, Dublin has enacted a new law banishing horses from the streets. When it looks as though the animals will be sent to rendering plants, Wilder sets them free on the streets, making it impossible for all of them to be rounded up. Next, he drinks himself into near-oblivion, but his fortunes change when he learns that his cousin, who lives in the Bronx, has died and left him a small inheritance. With that money, Wilder buys a bus and uses the knowledge imparted to him by Kidder to take tourists around the city he loves so much. Kidder is excellent and succeeds in making us believe that she could actually find something intriguing in Wilder. The humor is much subtler here than in most of Wilder's other efforts.

QUADROPHENIA

1979 120m c   ★★★★
Drama   R/X
Who Films (U.K.)

Phil Daniels *(Jimmy Michael Cooper)*, Mark Wingett *(Dave)*, Philip Davis *(Chalky)*, Leslie Ash *(Steph)*, Garry Cooper *(Pete)*, Toyah Wilcox *(Monkey)*, Sting *(The Ace Face)*, Trevor Laird *(Ferdy)*, Gary Shail *(Spider)*, Kate Williams *(Mrs. Cooper)*

p, Roy Baird, Bill Curbishley; d, Franc Roddam; w, Dave Humphries, Martin Stellman, Franc Roddam, Pete Townshend; ph, Brian Tufano; ed, Mike Taylor; m, The Who; prod d, Simon Holland; chor, Gillian Gregory

In 1964 London, Jimmy (Phil Daniels) and his pals are Mods, dividing their time between dancing and brawling with Rockers. QUADROPHENIA episodically depicts Jimmy's struggles with his seemingly empty existence, alleviated only by his relationships with his pals, most of whom are in the same grim boat. Adapted from a double album written by Pete Townshend and performed by the Who (who also acted as executive producers for the film), QUADROPHENIA is one of the best films about youth ever made, beautifully illustrating the frustrations of being young and bright but still having no future. First-time director Franc Roddam does a fine job with his young cast and his re-creation of period detail is nearly perfect. Daniels gives an amazing performance as the confused Jimmy, looking for an identity and coming literally to the brink of self-destruction—so intense and full of divergent emotions, he seems ready to explode at any moment.

QUARTET

1949 120m bw   ★★★★
Drama/Comedy   /A
Gainsborough/Eagle-Lion/Rank   (U.K.)

Basil Radford *(Henry Garnet)*, Naunton Wayne *(Leslie)*, Ian Fleming *(Ralph)*, Jack Raine *(Thomas)*, Angela Baddeley *(Mrs. Garnet)*, James Robertson Justice *(Branksome)*, Jack Watling *(Nicky)*, Nigel Buchanan *(John)*, Mai Zetterling *(Jeanne)*, Dirk Bogarde *(George Bland)*

p, Antony Darnborough; d, Ken Annakin, Arthur Crabtree, Harold French, Ralph Smart; w, R.C. Sherriff (based on the stories of W. Somerset Maugham); ph, Ray Elton; ed, Charles Knott, Jean Baker; m, John Greenwood; art d, George Provis

Few segmented films are successful, generally because the sequences are not of consistent quality. In QUARTET, however, the wit and poignancy of the W. Somerset Maugham stories upon which the segments are based are in full force throughout, each tale holding its own in the hands of a different director and through the talents of the performers. In "The Facts of Life," the conservative Radford cautions his apparently naive son, Watling, to avoid gambling, lending money, or trusting women while on his tennis tour of Monte Carlo. Indeed, Watling does seems to be as gullible as they come, winning big at roulette only to be duped by an adventuress, Zetterling. But can he be so dumb? "The Alien Corn" stars Bogarde, in one of his early and most memorable roles, as an aspiring musician who is in love with Honor Blackman, but also obsessed with becoming a world-class talent. After studying for two years in Paris, he returns to England to be bluntly and cruelly informed by a famous composer that he will never make the grade. In "The Kite," George Cole is dominated by a shrewish mother, Baddeley, and marries the same kind of woman, Susan Shaw. But he escapes this cycle when Shaw destroys his prized kite. The final entry, "The Colonel's Lady," features Nora Swinburne as a woman who becomes famous after a collection of her love poems is published. Her husband, Cecil Parker, is driven to distraction by the fact that this sonnet sequence is addressed to a younger, dashing man. Unable to stand

it any longer, he finally confronts his wife and demands to be told the identity of the young lover, with whom he suspects her of having an affair. All of these ironic tales are excellent, disproving the notion that segmented films cannot sustain interest. This one does it all the way.

QUEEN CHRISTINA

1933 97m bw   ★★★★★
Historical/Romance   /U
MGM

Greta Garbo *(Queen Christina)*, John Gilbert *(Don Antonio De la Prada)*, Ian Keith *(Magnus)*, Lewis Stone *(Chancellor Oxenstierna)*, Elizabeth Young *(Ebba Sparre)*, C. Aubrey Smith *(Aage)*, Reginald Owen *(Prince Charles)*, Georges Renavent *(French Ambassador)*, Gustav von Seyffertitz *(General)*, David Torrence *(Archbishop)*

p, Walter Wanger; d, Rouben Mamoulian; w, H.M. Harwood, Salka Viertel, S.N. Behrman (based on a story by Salka Viertel, Margaret R. Levino); ph, William Daniels; ed, Blanche Sewell; m, Herbert Stothart; art d, Alexander Toluboff, Edwin B. Willis; cos, Adrian

Garbo rules. A revelation, wrung from the usual MGM Bio identikit, but given shape by Mamoulian's painterly eye, and immortality by Garbo's ability to transcend. Even when the script serves up great clumps of unleavened bread, Garbo's strange majesty imbues it with living emotion. She really *is* divine. Although the same cannot be said of still-handsome Gilbert's Spanish Ambassador, their love scenes capture the depth of overwhelming emotion in an unparalleled, perfectly beautiful way. If some of Garbo's other performances have dated, this one remains a documentary of her magical strangeness that time itself cannot challenge.

Garbo's CHRISTINA is a decisive queen, ruling Sweden with wisdom and compassion. Her former lover, Ian Keith, attempts to arrange a marriage between Garbo and a dashing prince, but she will have nothing to do with political unions. Sweden has been waging a bloody war of attrition; Garbo is elated, however, when she manages to obtain a peace treaty. Then, while out riding, she encounters Gilbert, the newly appointed ambassador from Spain. Intrigued by the handsome, gallant Spaniard, Garbo decides to discover his real nature by disguising herself as a male. Pretending to be a wealthy youth in search of adventure, Garbo goes to an inn where she knows Gilbert is staying. He befriends her, advising her to be wary of strangers and always to follow a virtuous path. Gilbert, still unaware that she is not only female but also the queen, invites Garbo to spend the night in his room. She eventually reveals her identity and the two fall in love, spending two glorious days and nights together. Their idyll over, Garbo returns to her court and receives Gilbert officially, pretending she knows him only as an official representative of a foreign power. He is there, he informs her, to ask for her hand in marriage—for the king of Spain. She does not respond, but instead continues to meet him secretly. When the manipulative Keith discovers their secret meetings, he rouses the public against Gilbert, labeling him a trifling interloper.

In QUEEN CHRISTINA, Garbo had her way, making use of an iron-clad contract that paid her $250,000 a film, gave her the choice of director, cameraman, leading man, and, in fact, the entire cast, if she cared to select the extras. Garbo did not, as popularly thought, immediately select Gilbert to play opposite her in QUEEN CHRISTINA. She had seen a young British actor, Laurence Olivier, in WESTWARD PASSAGE and liked him. Olivier was signed to play the Spanish ambassador and came to the studio to rehearse with Garbo, at Mamoulian's suggestion.

The rehearsal was a disaster, as Garbo froze up. Olivier was told to forget about appearing in a Garbo film, and Mamoulian immediately called Gilbert, asking the then- seldom-employed actor to help out, to warm up the woman he had starred with in the heyday of the silent era. Gilbert happily agreed and within hours was wearing Olivier's costume, standing before Garbo. The effect he had on her was amazing. Still, Gilbert was only helping out. The studio had proposed other leading players, *anyone* but Gilbert, but Garbo refused anyone else. Much has been said about Garbo's magnanimous insistence that Gilbert, the fallen star, join her in a major film to rescue his almost lost career. She was reportedly no longer in love with him but was returning the favor he had extended to her at the beginning of *her* career when he demanded she costar with him in the silent classic FLESH AND THE DEVIL, which launched Garbo's movie reign. But not until Gilbert signed his contract to do QUEEN CHRISTINA did Mayer give up trying to replace him. Chief of production Irving Thalberg and Garbo hoped for a comeback for Gilbert, but even though he was touching in his role, the public was no longer interested, having bought the myth, sponsored by Mayer, about the actor's inadequacies in talkies.

QUEEN CHRISTINA received major advertising and publicity from MGM, and its New York premiere featured a three-story-high electric sign showing Garbo's face with only the name GARBO circling it like a halo. But it wasn't enough. The film, shot in 68 days and costing $1,444,000, gleaned only $632,000 in its initial release. Although the film was beautifully acted and directed, and sumptuously mounted with wonderful baroque sets, the public in this Depression year found it a strain to pay the $2 top price to see Garbo, even at her finest. Though the critics lauded the film, Garbo *and* Gilbert, it would be many years before the film earned back its investment. Perhaps the public felt abandoned by their legendary star. Garbo had not appeared in a film in 18 months and was living in Sweden most of the time. In fact she was residing in Sweden when her good friend Salka Viertel suggested she read up on the mysterious Queen Christina (1626-1689), giving Garbo two highly romanticized versions of that monarch's life. When the actress told Viertel that she felt she had an affinity for Queen Christina, Viertel and Margaret R. Levino wrote a screenplay about the monarch and sent it to Garbo. She liked it enough to wire MGM, telling her studio that it would be her next vehicle (her 21st film). The real Queen Christina of Sweden worried the Hollywood censors, who knew her gay sexual orientation and insisted on seeing the script before approving the Garbo production. They breathed a sigh of relief and even allowed the trysting in the inn scenes in preference to the truth. The film later may have reminded the actress of the idea of abdicating her Hollywood throne, for Garbo would disappear from the screen in eight years. QUEEN CHRISTINA was disastrously remade in 1974 as ABDICATION, starring Liv Ullmann.

QUEEN OF HEARTS

1989 112m c   ★★★★
Comedy/Romance   PG
Enterprise/TVS/Nelson   (U.K.)

Vittorio Duse *(Nonno)*, Joseph Long *(Danilo)*, Anita Zagaria *(Rosa)*, Eileen Way *(Mama Sibilla)*, Vittorio Amandola *(Barbariccia)*, Roberto Scateni *(Falco)*, Stefano Spagnoli *(Young Eddie)*, Alec Bregonzi *(Headwaiter)*, Ronan Vivert *(Man in Pig Scene)*, Matilda Thorpe *(Woman in Pig Scene)*

p, John Hardy; d, Jon Amiel; w, Tony Grisoni; ph, Mike Southon; ed, Peter Boyle; m, Michael Convertino; prod d, Jim Clay; art d, Philip Elton; cos, Lindy Hemming

A jewel of a film from director Jon Amiel, who directed Dennis Potter's award-winning "The Singing Detective." QUEEN OF HEARTS is a mystical fable of love and revenge, seen through the imaginative eyes of a child. Now grown, Eddie (Ian Hawkes) narrates the flashback story of his close-knit Italian family, who emigrate to England after WWII, when his father, Danilo (Joseph Long), and mother, Rosa (Anita Zagaria), elope, escaping her arranged marriage to the wealthy Barbariccia (Vittorio Amandola). On the advice of a talking pig, Danilo makes enough money gambling to become the proprietor of a London restaurant, the Lucky Cafe, supporting his family until Barbariccia, who has also emigrated and become the owner of several gambling houses, wins everything Danilo owns in a card game. The stage is then set for the STING-like scam the family works to get even with Barbariccia. There may be a few Italian immigrant family cliches along the way, but the characters in QUEEN OF HEARTS are treated sensitively, with much humor and warmth—never patronized. Much credit has to go to the film's wonderful cast, handpicked by director Amiel from what he called "a treasure trove" of relative unknowns.

QUEST FOR FIRE

1982 97m c   ★★★
Adventure/Historical   R/15
ICC/Cine-Trail/Belstar   (France/Canada)

Everett McGill *(Naoh Ulam Tribe Member)*, Ron Perlman *(Amoukar Ulam Tribe Member)*, Nameer El-Kadi *(Gaw Ulam Tribe Member)*, Rae Dawn Chong *(Ika Ivaka Tribe Member)*, Gary Schwartz, Frank Olivier Bonnet, Jean-Michel Kindt, Kurt Schiegl, Brian Gill, Terry Fitt

p, John Kemeny, Denis Heroux, Jacques Dorfmann, Vera Belmont; d, Jean-Jacques Annaud; w, Gerard Brach (based on the novel *La Guerre de Feu* by J.H. Rosny, Sr.); ph, Claude Agostini (Panavision, Bellevue-Pathe Color); ed, Yves Langlois; m, Philippe Sarde; prod d, Brian Morris, Guy Comtois; art d, Clinton Cavers; fx, Martin Malivoire; cos, John Hay, Penny Rose

A fascinating look at what the life of early man may have been like, QUEST FOR FIRE stars Everett McGill, Ron Perlman, and Nameer El-Kadi as members of a prehistoric tribe, the Ulams, who are sent out to find fire after their only source is accidentally extinguished. They find another, barbarous tribe, the Ivakas, who to the amazement of the Ulams can create fire using flint and sticks. The three rescue Ika (Rae Dawn Chong) from the cruel Ivakas and take her along, with the secret of firestarting. The characters register humor, grief, happiness, anxiety, and other everyday emotions, creating realistic personalities that the audience can identify with. Desmond Morris, author of "The Naked Ape," created a body language for the film based on actual simian gestures, while famed novelist Anthony Burgess created a primitive language. Although occasionally bleak, the film affords many pleasurable moments, showing early man learning to laugh and expressing delight and amazement at the sight of fire. The film received an Academy Award for Best Make-Up.

QUESTION OF SILENCE, A

(DE STILTE ROND CHRISTINE M.)
1983 92m c   ★★★½
Crime   R/15
Sigma   (Netherlands)

Cox Habbema *(Dr. Janine Van Den Bos)*, Edda Barends *(Christine M.)*, Nelly Frijda *(Waitress)*, Henriette Tol *(Secretary)*, Eddy Brugman *(Rudd)*, Dolf DeVries *(Boutique Manager)*, Kees Coolen *(Police Inspector)*, Onno Molenkamp *(Pathologist)*, Hans Croiset *(Judge)*, Eric Plooyer

p, Matthijs van Heijningen; d, Marleen Gorris; w, Marleen Gorris; ph, Frans Bromet; ed, Hans Van Dongen; m, Lodewijk De Boer, Martijn Hasebos; prod d, Harry Ammerlaan

This controversial film focuses on three women—housewife Christine M. (Edda Barends), waitress Annie (Nelly Frijda), and secretary Andrea (Henriette Tol)—who, though unacquainted, spontaneously kill a male boutique owner when he catches one of them shoplifting. They are arrested and assigned a female psychiatrist, Dr. Janine Van Den Bos (Cox Habbema), who prepares a plea of insanity. Christine appears to be the most deeply affected of the threesome, slipping into a state of shock and refusing to utter a word. As Dr. Van Den Bos talks with Annie and Andrea, she begins to have her doubts about the insanity plea, and the murder makes increasingly more sense to her. Each of the three women was dealing with her own frustrations with men: the housewife was a slave to housekeeping duties and a victim of a thoughtless husband; the waitress subjected to rude comments by male customers; and the secretary constantly treated as a subordinate at the executive office where she worked. Instead of confirming the expected insanity pleas, Dr. Van Den Bos tells the courtroom that the women are fully responsible for the crime against the patronizing shopkeeper. But to the surprise of the males in the courtroom, all the women present unite in a grand show of female solidarity. QUESTION OF SILENCE is the first feature from writer-director Marleen Gorris, who hit upon the idea after reading an article about a working-class woman's arrest for shoplifting. Instead of putting three murderesses on trial, this superb, disturbing feminist film turns the tables and puts male society on the stand—which will undoubtedly anger as many viewers as it thrills.

QUIET MAN, THE
1952 129m c ★★★★★
Romance/Comedy /U
Argosy

John Wayne *(Sean Thornton)*, Maureen O'Hara *(Mary Kate Danaher)*, Barry Fitzgerald *(Michaeleen Flynn)*, Ward Bond *(Fr. Peter Lonergan)*, Victor McLaglen *(Red Will Danaher)*, Mildred Natwick *(Mrs. Sarah Tillane)*, Francis Ford *(Dan Tobin)*, Eileen Crowe *(Mrs. Elizabeth Playfair)*, May Craig *(Woman at Railway Station)*, Arthur Shields *(Rev. Cyril Playfair)*

p, Merian C. Cooper, John Ford, Michael Killanin (uncredited); d, John Ford; w, Frank S. Nugent, Richard Llewellyn (based on the story by Maurice Walsh); ph, Winton C. Hoch, Archie Stout (Technicolor); ed, Jack Murray; m, Victor Young; art d, Frank Hotaling; cos, Adele Palmer

Epic romantic comedy, but so thick on the blarney, that it helps to be Irish, at least to a degree. Otherwise, it may be hard to get a grasp on the turbulent traditions, fiesty sentimentality and burning coldness that exists in the Irish soul. That understood, cook a corned beef and invite the neighbors over.

THE QUIET MAN is Ford's sentimental journey into the past of Ireland, his ancestral home, a journey enacted by Ford's onscreen alter ego, John Wayne. The story begins in the 1920s, when the American Wayne, a quiet fellow but a former fighter with a brutal past, arrives in Innisfree. He is greeted by the elfin, capricious, witty Fitzgerald, the village cabman, matchmaker,

and mentor, who grabs Wayne's bags at the train station and places them in his pony cart. Wayne hops onto the seat and the two are off to a little cottage—Wayne's birthplace, White O'Mornin'—which Wayne has purchased from Natwick, a rich local widow. En route, he sees in the distance a beautiful, red-haired woman framed by a stand of trees, a soft wind rippling her skirts and hair. She seems a vision of another, lost world, and Wayne asks Fitzgerald, "Is that real?" (Quips the coachman, "Only a mirage brought on by your terrible thirst!") Wayne is really asking about the scene itself, rather than the lovely woman inhabiting it, and recalls the voice of his dead mother as she described Innisfree to him when he was a child. Arriving at his cottage, he tells Fitzgerald, "I'm Sean Thornton and I was born in that little cottage. I'm home and home I'm going to stay." It's almost a declaration of war, war against the vicissitudes of the present in favor of the security and stability of the past.

In buying his property, Wayne has alienated the richest, toughest man in the area, McLaglen, who is doubly angered over the fact that widow Natwick has sold the property to "a dirty Yank." Wayne moves into the small cottage, a stranger in a land he loves, where he is considered a foreigner even though he was born in Innisfree. Though his land appears green and fertile, Wayne turns up nothing but rocks when he tries to plough it for planting. He battles the present for the illusion of the past at every turn, and is even upbraided for his romanticism when he proudly shows off his cottage to a neighbor, who inspects its trim thatched roof and immaculately painted walls, remarking that "It looks the way all Irish cottages should, and seldom do. And only an American would think of painting it emerald green." One day, Wayne enters his cottage to find his neighbor O'Hara there. She has been cleaning the place for him, a gesture that seems to indicate more than communal fellowship. Just as she is about to flee, Wayne grabs hold of her arm and attempts to kiss her. She gives him a stiff-armed slap, but, before escaping the cottage, encourages him with a light kiss of her own. Later, Wayne meets O'Hara's brutish brother, McLaglen, in the local pub. McLaglen seethes with hate for him, believing him to be an interloper upsetting his plans and "backdealing" him out of his property. When Wayne extends his hand, the powerful McLaglen squeezes it with all his might and the ex-boxer responds with his own pressure, until both men let loose, wincing with pain.

Witnessing this first confrontation between the two giants is a group of local men—most of whom hate McLaglen and side with Wayne—including members of the IRA and the priests Bond and Lilburn. Wayne has already befriended Bond, in a meeting during which the priest recalls Wayne's family, including his wayward father, who died in Australia in a penal colony, and his mother—"brave soul"—who struggled to raise the little boy who has now returned a strapping man with a mysterious past. In fact, Wayne goes out of his way to say nothing of his background. But the local Protestant clergyman, Shields, knows Wayne's dark secret and tells him so privately. Shields, a onetime amateur boxer, has kept a scrapbook about boxers the world over. He shows Wayne clippings concerning the American boxer "Trooper Thorn," who retired from the ring forever after he accidentally killed a man during a match, and, discredited, moved with his prize money to Ireland to find the peace, happiness, and beauty of his boyhood.

A love story that packs a fearsome punch, THE QUIET MAN is a passionate, full-blooded film. Ford constructs the picture carefully, and lavishes the tale with some of the most visually extraordinary scenes ever filmed. Some of these, such as the idealistic vision of O'Hara in the glen herding her sheep, are presented in muted, diffused tones that suggest an ethereal world—into which Wayne has barged. THE QUIET MAN is Ford's symbolic homecoming, in which he shapes his own longing and memories in the form of living, full-blooded characters, who are at the same time representative types. Wayne is Ford's youth; O'Hara his great love, as well as all the women of Ireland; McLaglen, the sentimental bully; Fitzgerald, the local conscience and historian; Bond, the priest who would rather fish than pray, though fishing is also a form of prayer; Shields, the patient outsider; Natwick, the typical Irish spinster. The wonderful lead and supporting performances by Ford's stock company in these roles further contribute to make THE QUIET MAN an utterly moving and fascinating portrait of rural life in Ireland.

THE QUIET MAN is truly an Irish family film. The character of Feeney (Abbey Player Jack McGowran)—a toady to McLaglen who writes down the names of all McLaglen's enemies in a little black book—is given the Anglicized version of Ford's real surname, and the main character's last name, Thornton, was also that of Ford's real-life cousins. Wayne's children appear in the picture, as do two of O'Hara's brothers; Fitzgerald and Shields were also siblings. Moreover, Ford's own brother, Francis Ford, who was a wonderful mime and early silent screen star, plays the old man who refuses to die until he sees the herculean fight between Wayne and McLaglen. Although this marked Francis' 29th appearance in his brother's films, the two did not socialize. They had mysteriously fallen out years earlier, when Francis was a top star and John just coming up as a director. Rumor had it that they had had a terrible fight over a woman or that, in their cups, they had gone at each other in much the same way Wayne and McLaglen battle here. But the rift was never spoken of after Ford became the preeminent American film director. Francis received his assignments by mail, appeared on the set or at the location promptly, did his wonderful little bits, and then walked off and waited for John to call him back. The actor and director hardly spoke to each other, only nodded in each other's direction after a completed scene. Brothers by birth, they never achieved the blood brothership of the combatants in THE QUIET MAN. Winner of two Academy Awards: Best Cinematography and Best Direction. The best line goes to Fitzgerald, seeing the broken bed on the morning after the wedding: "Impetuous! Homeric!"

QUILOMBO
1984 114m c   ★★★★
Historical
CDK (Brazil)

Antonio Pompeo (Zumbi), Zeze Motta (Dandara), Tony Tornado (Ganga Zumba), Vera Fischer (Ana de Ferro), Antonio Pitanga (Acaiuba), Mauricio do Valle (Domingos Jorge Velho), Daniel Filho (Carrilho), Joao Nogueira (Rufino), Jorge Coutinho (Sale), Grande Otelo (Baba)

p, Augusto Arraes; d, Carlos Diegues; w, Carlos Diegues; ph, Lauro Escorel Filho; ed, Mair Tavares

This is a spectacular, brilliantly colored historical epic that explores the beginnings of Quilombo de Palmares, the Brazilian slave nation in the mid-1600s. Director Diegues described the nation as "the first democratic society that we know of in the Western hemisphere." The picture begins as the slaves revolt and violently murder their Portuguese owners. Taking to the forests of northeastern Brazil, the slaves form a nation, free from the oppression of slave owners. They are soon joined by other oppressed peoples such as Jews and poor white farmers. A government is created and a leader elected—Ganga Zumba, played by Tornado. The Portuguese, however, retaliate and at-

tempt to conquer the nation. Diegues previously scored on American art-house screens with BYE BYE BRAZIL and XICA. Here, he successfully manages to mix history with folklore. Exquisitely photographed and lavishly produced, the film has a great deal of action, culminating with some intense battle sequences, but it often loses sight of its story. More than examining a historic period, QUILOMBO, like Diegues's other films, comments on the present state of Brazil as well as the nation's possible future.

QUO VADIS
1951 171m c   ★★★½
Historical   /PG
MGM

Robert Taylor (Marcus Vinicius), Deborah Kerr (Lygia), Leo Genn (Petronius), Peter Ustinov (Nero), Patricia Laffan (Poppaea), Finlay Currie (Peter), Abraham Sofaer (Paul), Marina Berti (Eunice), Buddy Baer (Ursus), Felix Aylmer (Plautius)

p, Sam Zimbalist; d, Mervyn LeRoy; w, John Lee Mahin, S.N. Behrman, Sonya Levien (based on the novel by Henryk Sienkiewicz); ph, Robert Surtees, William V. Skall (Technicolor); ed, Ralph E. Winters; m, Miklos Rozsa; art d, William McCoy, Cedric Gibbons, Edward Carfagno; fx, Thomas Hayward, A. Arnold Gillespie, Donald Jarnhaus; chor, Madi Obolensky, Auriel Millos; cos, Herschel McCoy

One of MGM's biggest box-office hits, the epic QUO VADIS offers a spectacular cast to match its overwhelming production. Over it all looms a loony Ustinov as Emperor Nero, despite director LeRoy's best efforts to keep him from chewing the scenery as he steals the show. Robert Taylor is the nominal star, playing a Roman army commander who returns victorious to the Eternal City in the 1st Century AD. After receiving a hero's welcome from the empress (Laffan), Taylor meets Kerr, a hostage who is the Christian daughter of a defeated king. Taylor lusts after Kerr, but is put off by her protector, the giant Baer, and further rejected by Kerr because he is a pagan. Angered, Taylor makes Kerr his slave, but is still unable to make her his mistress. He subsequently frees her, then follows her to a secret Christian meeting at which the sermon is preached by Currie (as the apostle Peter). Now Taylor begins to soften toward Kerr—who, in turn, falls in love with the handsome soldier and decides to marry him, against the advice of her friends. He cannot reconcile himself to her beliefs, however, and leaves her when she adamantly clings to her religion.

Meanwhile, Ustinov succumbs further to his megalomania, and torches Rome so that he can build a new white city of his own design, blaming the Christians for the fire. (The film shows him playing his lyre and reciting his poems while the city burns and thousands perish.) Taylor rushes to Kerr and saves her from the fire, only to be rounded up with the Christians who are to be punished for the disaster. Taken to a dungeon with the rest, Kerr and Taylor are married by Currie, then selected to die by the mad Ustinov. Currie is released and crucified (though in deference to his Savior he asks to be crucified upside down, a task carried out with malicious relish by his Roman guards). At the arena, Kerr is tied to a stake and Taylor—to make an example of the Roman officer who has betrayed his emperor for the love of a hated Christian—is tied in the royal box so that he will be forced to watch Kerr's end. Ustinov plays a vicious game, however, promising the crowd to free the Christian beauty if her faithful servant, the mammoth Baer, can kill the wild bull he orders sent into the arena. In a titanic struggle, Baer does kill the bull, but Ustinov goes back on his word and orders the execution of both Kerr and

Baer. At this Taylor, in a superhuman effort, breaks free of his bonds and leads the crowd—as well as the Roman soldiers guarding Ustinov—to turn against the distrusted and hated tyrant. Ustinov and Laffan are executed.

The performances are fine, especially those of Kerr, Taylor, and Genn (as the gentle advisor to the emperor), but it's the wild Ustinov who scoops up every scene he's in, giving one of the most outlandish performances ever filmed. Ustinov was tested for the role of Nero by MGM as early as 1949, and the studio chiefs liked what they saw, but the film was slow to develop. A year later, MGM wired Ustinov that they were still interested in him for the part but they were worried that he might be too young for the role. Ustinov wired back, "If you wait much longer I shall be too old. Nero died at thirty-one." (Tony Thomas, *Ustinov in Focus*.) To play the scene in which the mad emperor sings some of his poems while plucking his lyre and watching Rome burn with gimlet eye, Ustinov asked a tutor at the Rome Opera House to give him voice lessons, and was offered some arcane advice by the maestro, including "breathe with the forehead," "think with the diaphragm," and "in all circumstances. . . sing with the eye." (Peter Ustinov, *Dear Me*.) As Ustinov prepared to step out onto Nero's balcony and survey the fiery city, he received more advice from Mervyn LeRoy, who urged his Nero, "Don't forget, you're responsible for all this!" Ustinov later noted dryly that LeRoy "was never a director to leave anything to chance" (*Dear Me*).

LeRoy inherited the QUO VADIS project, which had long been in the making, and almost wasn't made at all when MGM chieftains fell to squabbling over its commercial viability. The story had been filmed as early as 1902 as a 12-minute one-reeler in France; then as an Italian opus in 1912 that ran 12 reels, road-showing as a high-ticket epic in the US the following year; and again in 1924 as another Italian feature, which would run as a silent in the US in 1925 and be revamped with sound effects in 1929. MGM's Hunt Stromberg planned to make an all-talkie adaptation of the chestnut in the mid-1930s, and plans went so far as to schedule director Robert Z. Leonard for a trip to Italy to scout locations, but when WWII broke out the production was abandoned, only to be reinstated in 1949, with John Huston selected to direct a mammoth version of the tale. Huston, producer Arthur Hornblow, and stars Gregory Peck and Elizabeth Taylor went to Italy and began shooting, but the post-WWII Italian movie industry was in such a chaotic state that the film soon bogged down in delays and costs that exceeded $2 million. Huston's version was to be a rather modern interpretation of the tale sanctioned by Dore Schary, who was then in mortal combat with Louis B. Mayer for control of MGM production. The project fell through, much to the delight of Mayer, who had argued all along that the traditional approach he favored would be better accepted by the viewing public. Mayer launched his own production of QUO VADIS in 1950, naming Sam Zimbalist as its producer and entrusting the direction to LeRoy.

But LeRoy soon discovered that filmmaking in Italy was still a haphazard process. QUO VADIS was the Roman Cinecitta Studio's first color production, and the Italian technicians did not realize how much light was necessary for color photography. Consequently, they ruined many of LeRoy's setups with the wrong lighting arrangements. His crowd scenes were especially hard to manage, particularly the one featuring 120 lions. The beasts were let loose into an arena crowded with 6,000 extras, among whom stood lion tamers with loaded guns, ordered to shoot any lion that tried to eat an extra. But when the lions were let through the gate into the arena from the tunnel area where they had been kept, they looked up at the bright sun and then retreated back into the tunnels. The lion tamers advised LeRoy to starve the animals for two weeks. LeRoy did, but had sleepless nights worrying about how to prevent the hungry beasts from devouring his extras. When he did let the lions loose again, they merely looked up at the glaring sun again, and again retreated into their tunnels. The director finally conceived the idea of stuffing dummies dressed like the Christians with raw meat and letting the hungry animals loose once more, and the results were better, though never to LeRoy's satisfaction (Thomas).

The most difficult scene of all, however, was the burning of Rome. Workmen labored for months to construct a four-block area of authentic-looking building facades, and to lay two miles of iron pipe through more than 100 doors and windows in the huge set, eventually sending thousands of gallons of gasoline, fuel oil, butane, and naphthalene through the pipe to conduct the fire and re-create the infamous conflagration. As MGM promotional materials noted at the time, it took LeRoy and his technicians 24 nights to burn Rome, compared to Nero's six days. LeRoy, a master at handling crowds, moved his 2,000 extras through the fires without a single mishap.

Shot in six months at a cost of almost $7 million, QUO VADIS was an enormous box-office success, gleaning $25 million in world rentals and becoming the second all-time grosser after GONE WITH THE WIND. It led the way to even greater spectacles, including other mighty MGM epics starring Taylor, among them IVANHOE and KNIGHTS OF THE ROUND TABLE. Its success inspired Columbia to produce SALOME and 20th Century Fox to make DAVID AND BATHSHEBA, THE ROBE, and DEMETRIUS AND THE GLADIATORS. (William Wyler's BEN-HUR, set in the same period and shot in Italy, would finally top QUO VADIS in box-office receipts.) Enhancing the epic's success was the fine score by Miklos Rozsa, who, along with MGM librarian George Schneider, located all the known instruments of the period and then, although no clear record of the era's music remained, pieced his score together through slave songs, Christian hymns, marches, and fanfares played on modern instruments (using the Scottish clarsach to approximate the sound of the ancient lyre, for example). QUO VADIS was nominated for seven Oscars: Best Picture (losing out to AN AMERICAN IN PARIS), Best Cinematography, Best Art Direction, Best Score, Best Film Editing, Best Costume Design and two nominations for Best Supporting Actor (Genn and Ustinov). Oddly, it didn't win a single statuette.

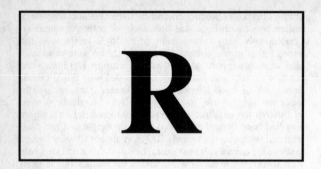

R

RABID

1976 91m c ★★

Science Fiction/Horror R/

Cinepix/Dibar (Canada)

Marilyn Chambers (Rose), Frank Moore (Hart Read), Joe Silver (Murray Cypher), Howard Ryshpan (Dr. Dan Keloid), Patricia Gage (Dr. Roxanne Keloid), Susan Roman (Mindy Kent), Roger Periard (Lloyd Walsh), Lynne Deragon (Nurse Louise), Terry Schonblum (Judy Glasberg), Victor Desy (Claude LaPointe)

p, John Dunning; d, David Cronenberg; w, David Cronenberg; ph, Rene Verzier (Panavision, Eastmancolor); ed, Jean LaFleur; art d, Claude Marchand; fx, Joe Blasco, Al Griswold; cos, Erla Gliserman

A virtual remake of THEY CAME FROM WITHIN, RABID finds director David Cronenberg more in control of his narrative and his visual style than in his previous films, but the results are still somewhat uneven. Once again Cronenberg explores sexually transmitted horror, but this time through none other than hardcore porno starlet Marilyn Chambers, who makes her legitimate debut here as Rose, a woman seriously injured in a motorcycle accident. A local plastic surgeon uses the opportunity to experiment with some new skin grafts he's been developing, but somehow the surgery goes awry and soon Rose sports a grotesque, phallus-like organ in her armpit that sucks blood out of her unsuspecting lovers (the original treatment of the film was entitled "Mosquito"). This soon leads to an epidemic that turns the citizens of Montreal into rabid, blood-seeking, sex-crazed monsters that drool green slime.

Once again, Cronenberg has made a rather frustrating film. Although RABID is full of interesting ideas, they are not particularly well developed or presented by Cronenberg's unfocused script. And while the film has an uneasy sense of humor, Cronenberg again overplays his most visceral sequences, including the well-shot but pointless car crash. As with THEY CAME FROM WITHIN, the performances are weak, and while Chambers does add some resonance to the film as a sexual icon, her acting ability is decidedly limited.

RACHEL, RACHEL

1968 101m c ★★★½

Drama R/X

Kayos

Joanne Woodward (Rachel Cameron), James Olson (Nick Kazlik), Kate Harrington (Mrs. Cameron), Estelle Parsons (Calla Mackie), Donald Moffat (Niall Cameron), Terry Kiser (Preacher), Franco Corsaro (Hector Jonas), Bernard Barrow (Leighton Siddley), Geraldine Fitzgerald (Rev. Wood), Nell Potts (Rachel as a Child)

p, Paul Newman; d, Paul Newman; w, Stewart Stern (based on the novel A Jest of God by Margaret Laurence); ph, Gayne Rescher (Technicolor); ed, Dede Allen; m, Jerome Moross, Erik Satie, Robert Schumann; art d, Robert Gundlach; cos, Domingo Rodriguez

Woodward, Parsons, Stern (screenwriter), and the picture itself were all nominated for Oscars, and Newman and Woodward both won awards from the New York Film Critics. While other directors were impressing with their flash and technique in the 1960s, Newman chose to make a small, understated, and very sensitive film as his directorial debut. It was sometimes halting and quite spare, but the overall effect was excellent and business was meritorious, something no one expected. Newman had trouble securing the financing and was saved by then-production chief Ken Hyman, a man with some foresight who recognized the need for this kind of story. Shot on location at various Connecticut sites, the film was a departure for Woodward, who had been made into a glamour girl in her early years and resented it. In her thirties at this point, she began an entirely new career and proved that her Oscar for THE THREE FACES OF EVE was not a fluke. Woodward is a 35-year-old spinster who lives with her widowed mother, Harrington, in a small apartment above the funeral parlor once owned by her late father and now run by Corsaro. She is a teacher who feels that there is nothing left to live for and constantly questions why she was ever born. (This is more covert than overt.) Every day is like the day before. She has to look after Harrington and teach the snot-noses at the school; there is virtually no fun in her life. Woodward's best friend is Parsons, another old maid in much the same circumstance. Searching for a meaning in life, Parsons asks Woodward to accompany her to a revival meeting run by Fitzgerald. When a visiting evangelist, Kiser, takes the pulpit and pounds it, Woodward is surprised to find herself caught up in the emotionalism of the moment. Later, Parsons makes what has to be termed a "pass" at Woodward, which makes her realize that she had better find out what men are like before she falls into a homosexual pattern. Woodward is sexually naive, frustrated, and willing to learn, so when Olson, a childhood friend, comes back to the small town to visit his parents, she is easy for him to seduce. Woodward doesn't know the difference between lust and love, and her brief sexual freedom with Olson causes her to become emotionally involved. He is frightened by her intensity and lies, telling her that he's married. When that doesn't matter to her, he ends the relationship. Woodward thinks she may be pregnant and is secretly delighted and plans to have the child. When her pregnancy turns out to be a minor ovarian cyst (which is the reason for the book's title, A Jest of God), Woodward is disappointed but pulls herself together, intending to make a new start. Woodward and Harrington take off for Oregon where Woodward hopes she can get out of her doldrums and begin again.

The film's double-word title is made more intriguing because Newman uses his and Woodward's daughter, Nell Potts, as the young Rachel; and Woodward is occasionally replaced by Potts to indicate that the child in her still remains. In the final scene, for example, as Woodward climbs on the bus to Oregon, she waves farewell to Potts, finally bidding good-bye to the child she's been. In later years, a horde of "women's pictures" would appear, but this one was the first in the cycle and one of the best. It could have been a drab, weepy story, but Stern and Newman collaborated to make it an inspiring one that proves one is never too old to change one's life.

RACING WITH THE MOON

1984 108m c   ★★½
Comedy/Drama   PG/15
Paramount

Sean Penn *(Henry "Hopper" Nash)*, Elizabeth McGovern *(Caddie Winger)*, Nicolas Cage *(Nicky)*, John Karlen *(Mr. Nash)*, Rutanya Alda *(Mrs. Nash)*, Max Showalter *(Mr. Arthur)*, Crispin Glover *(Gatsby Boy)*, Barbara Howard *(Gatsby Girl)*, Bob Maroff *(Al)*, Dominic Nardini *(Soldier with Annie)*

p, Alain Bernheim, John Kohn; d, Richard Benjamin; w, Steve Kloves; ph, John Bailey (Movielab Color); ed, Jacqueline Cambas; m, Dave Grusin; prod d, David L. Snyder; fx, Garry J. Elmendorf; cos, Patricia Norris

In this slight film about two boys about to be drafted into WWII, everyone tries hard, but the movie is essentially superficial and has difficulty sustaining audience interest. Hopper (Sean Penn) and Nicky (Nicolas Cage) have six weeks before they are due to be marines. Nicky is a street youth who gets his girlfriend (Suzanne Adkinson) pregnant and has to raise the money for her abortion. Hopper, in the meantime, has fallen for a new girl in town, Caddie Winger (Elizabeth McGovern). She lives in a mansion, so Hopper assumes she is wealthy. But when Nicky asks Hopper to ask Caddie for money for the abortion, Hopper learns that her parents are the servants in the mansion, not the owners. RACING WITH THE MOON offers good period evocation, excellent costumes, and a few funny scenes. A nice little movie—perhaps too nice—with none of the edge that was apparently needed to sell tickets in the 1980s.

RACKET, THE

1951 88m bw   ★★★★
Crime   /A
RKO

Robert Mitchum *(Capt. McQuigg)*, Lizabeth Scott *(Irene)*, Robert Ryan *(Scanlon)*, William Talman *(Johnson)*, Ray Collins *(Welch)*, Joyce MacKenzie *(Mary McQuigg)*, Robert Hutton *(Ames)*, Virginia Huston *(Lucy Johnson)*, William Conrad *(Turck)*, Walter Sande *(Delaney)*

p, Edmund Grainger; d, John Cromwell, Nicholas Ray; w, William Wister Haines, W.R. Burnett (based on the play by Bartlett Cormack); ph, George E. Diskant; ed, Sherman Todd; m, Paul Sawtell, Roy Webb; art d, Albert S. D'Agostino, Jack Okey; cos, Michael Woulfe

This hard-hitting melodrama was the second film adaptation of Bartlett Cormack's popular 1920s play from Howard Hughes, who released a version in 1928 and updated the story here to tie it in with the then-controversial Kefauver crime hearings, which had captured the TV viewing audience of the day. Mitchum (in a switch from his usual casting) plays a tough, honest police captain in a midwestern city who, on the eve of an important election, battles to wrest control of the city's government from crime boss Ryan. However, Mitchum's superior, prosecuting attorney Collins, is in Ryan's pocket, as is police inspector Conrad, forcing Mitchum to fight city hall as well as the underworld. Ryan runs a plush nightclub that showcases torch singer Scott, and this headquarters of corruption becomes the focal point of Mitchum's investigations. A throwback to the days when gunmen shot first and reasoned later, Ryan is under pressure to assume a more businesslike style, abandon violence, and clean his organization of trigger-happy goons. Finding that Ryan's weak spot is his kid brother (Brett King), Mitchum arrests the punk for carrying an unlicensed gun and puts him in jail, then

brings Scott in to testify against him as a material witness. When Scott agrees to talk, Ryan issues orders to have her killed. Mitchum learns of this plan and, with the help of honest cop Talman, thwarts the killers, though only at the cost of Talman's life. Mitchum then captures Ryan (after a rooftop battle) and tricks him into confessing to an earlier murder. Though Collins and other bigwigs are content to let Ryan stew in a cell until the elections are over, the crime boss compels them to bail him out. He is then told to make his choice: run or be killed. Mitchum, who has set up the whole situation to trap Conrad and Collins, nabs the grafters in the end; Ryan is killed by hit men, ridding the city of a lethal menace.

Director Cromwell does a fine job of keeping up a lightning pace here, and elicits a great performance from Ryan, who is truly sinister and disturbingly psychotic in his profile of the gang boss striving to change his unalterably violent character. Mitchum is solid if not enthusiastic in his role as an honest cop, and the rest of the cast (particularly Collins and Conrad) is excellent, though Scott, while appropriately sultry and attractive, is little more than window dressing in her role. After taking over RKO in 1948, Hughes immediately scheduled THE RACKET for production, banking on the success of the 1928 film version, though the remake is more faithful to Cormack's play (in which Cromwell had appeared as an actor). The city profiled, of course, is Chicago and its corrupt politics of the 1920s. Cromwell had been directing films on and off at RKO since 1932; this picture marked his last such assignment for the studio.

RADIO DAYS

1987 85m c   ★★★½
Comedy   PG
Orion

Woody Allen *(Narrator)*, Seth Green *(Little Joe)*, Julie Kavner *(Mother)*, Michael Tucker *(Father)*, Dianne Wiest *(Aunt Bea)*, Josh Mostel *(Uncle Abe)*, Renee Lippin *(Aunt Ceil)*, William Magerman *(Grandpa)*, Leah Carrey *(Grandma)*, Joy Newman *(Ruthie)*

p, Robert Greenhut; d, Woody Allen; w, Woody Allen; ph, Carlo Di Palma (Duart Color); ed, Susan E. Morse; prod d, Santo Loquasto; art d, Speed Hopkins; cos, Jeffrey Kurland

Writer-director Woody Allen draws on his own past in this nostalgic piece, cross-cutting between the Brooklyn of his youth, in this case the Rockaway area, and the uptown life being led by radio personalities. Allen gives us a typical yet intriguing family in Rockaway. Joe (Seth Green) is the youthful protagonist who lives with his parents (Julie Kavner and Michael Tucker), grandparents (Willian Magerman and Leah Carrey), maiden aunt Bea (Dianne Wiest), uncle Abe (Josh Mostel, son of Zero), Abe's wife Ceil (Renee Lippin), and their daughter Ruthie (Joy Newman). In voice-over, Allen (who doesn't appear in the film) relates stories about members of this household. While life goes on in Brooklyn, Allen intercuts stories about radio and its personalities, many of the tales focusing on Sally White (Mia Farrow), a cigarette girl with a dreadful "Noo Yawk" accent who dreams of radio stardom. If this summary sounds disjointed, so is the film. There is no real story, just a succession of funny and nostalgic interludes. Allen presents a host of anecdotes and remembrances of things past, but one wishes it could have been slightly more cohesive. One of the joys in this picture is the soundtrack of songs of the period that will delight anyone who lived in those radio days.

RAFFLES

1930 70m bw ★★★½
Crime/Romance /U
UA

Ronald Colman *(A.J. Raffles)*, Kay Francis *(Lady Gwen Manders)*, Bramwell Fletcher *(Bunny Manders)*, Frances Dade *(Ethel Crowley)*, David Torrence *(McKenzie)*, Alison Skipworth *(Lady Kitty Melrose)*, Frederick Kerr *(Lord Harry Melrose)*, John Rogers *(Crawshaw)*, Wilson Benge *(Barraclough)*, Virginia Bruce *(Blonde)*

p, Samuel Goldwyn; d, Harry d'Abbadie D'Arrast, George Fitzmaurice (uncredited); w, Sidney Howard (based on the novel *the Amateur Cracksman* by Ernest William Hornung and the play "Raffles, The Amateur Cracksman" by E.W. Hornung, Eugene Wiley Presbrey); ph, George Barnes, Gregg Toland; ed, Stuart Heisler; art d, William Cameron Menzies, Park French

After being adapted for the stage, Ernest William Hornung's novel *The Amateur Cracksman* came to the screen twice in the silent era, with John Barrymore and House Peters cast as the roguish A.J. Raffles in the 1914 and 1925 versions, respectively. In this first sound version of the story, Ronald Colman is the famed British cricket player who spends his evenings as "The Amateur Cracksman," an equally famous criminal who consistently eludes Scotland Yard. Colman falls in love with beautiful socialite Kay Francis and manages to wangle an invitation to a weekend bash thrown by royal couple Frederick Kerr and Alison Skipworth. Also in attendance is Scotland Yard investigator David Torrence, who has a hunch that Colman is "The Cracksman." Both Colman and Torrence know that Alison Skipworth is the owner of an extremely valuable necklace, which Colman is planning to steal to help a suicidal friend (Bramwell Fletcher) through a financial crisis. Torrence watches Colman like a hawk, but the criminal still manages to sneak into Skipworth's boudoir. Another criminal (John Rogers) has the same idea, but Colman ends up with the necklace while Rogers is carted away by Scotland Yard. However, when no necklace turns up, Torrence decides to use Rogers as bait to locate Colman. As Scotland Yard breathes down Colman's neck, he manages to give the necklace to Fletcher, who then receives a sizable reward. Taking advantage of a grandfather clock with a secret panel, Colman sneaks out of his apartment and past a horde of detectives. With his freedom won, he plans to continue his romance with Francis in Paris.

Having established himself with moviegoers as Bulldog Drummond, Colman found himself in another crowd-pleasing role as the lovable Raffles. Opening to almost unanimously favorable reviews, RAFFLES marked a farewell to silent films for Sam Goldwyn's production company. A firm believer in the future of sound films, Goldwyn quickly made the transition, and this picture was the last that his company produced in both silent and sound versions. Goldwyn's faith in sound recording resulted in an Oscar nomination for sound recordist Oscar Lagerstrom. The picture was begun under the direction of Harry d'Abbadie D'Arrast (LAUGHTER), but he was fired and his name struck from the credits by Goldwyn after endless disagreements between the two. His replacement, George Fitzmaurice, an able craftsman, had been responsible for bringing D'Arrast to Hollywood from France eight years earlier. RAFFLES was remade, practically scene for scene, in 1939 with David Niven and Olivia de Havilland in the leads, and again in 1960 as EL RAFFLES MEXICANO, a Spanish-language picture with Rafael Bertrand as The Amateur Cracksman.

RAGGEDY MAN

1981 94m c ★★★
Drama PG/15
Universal

Sissy Spacek *(Nita)*, Eric Roberts *(Teddy)*, Sam Shepard *(Bailey)*, William Sanderson *(Calvin)*, Tracey Walker *(Arnold)*, R.G. Armstrong *(Rigby)*, Henry Thomas *(Harry)*, Carey Hollis, Jr. *(Henry)*, Ed Geldart *(Mr. Calloway)*, Bill Thurman *(Sheriff)*

p, Burt Weissbourd, William D. Wittliff; d, Jack Fisk; w, William D. Wittliff; ph, Ralf D. Bode (Technicolor); ed, Edward Warschilka; m, Jerry Goldsmith; art d, John Lloyd; cos, Joe I. Tompkins

A compelling but oddly empty film, RAGGEDY MAN stars Spacek as a young divorcee who struggles to raise her two sons in Texas during WWII. Since her divorce, she has been harassed by local low-lifes who believe that all divorced women are looking for stand-in husbands. Two men in particular (Sanderson and Walker) have refused to leave her alone. Another local character, Shepard, a mysterious down-and-outer, also haunts Spacek's existence. Her life changes dramatically when Roberts, a young sailor, arrives on the scene and captivates both Spacek and her sons. His eventual departure, however, sends the story rushing toward a disturbing climax that isn't completely in keeping with everything that has preceded it. Fine performances by Spacek and Roberts, combined with able direction from Spacek's husband, Fisk (directing his first feature), make this one well worth a look.

RAGING BULL

1980 129m c/bw ★★★★½
Biography/Sports R/18
UA

Robert De Niro *(Jake LaMotta)*, Cathy Moriarty *(Vickie LaMotta)*, Joe Pesci *(Joey)*, Frank Vincent *(Salvy)*, Nicholas Colasanto *(Tommy Como)*, Theresa Saldana *(Lenore)*, Frank Adonis *(Patsy)*, Mario Gallo *(Mario)*, Frank Topham *(Toppy/Handler)*, Lori Anne Flax *(Irma)*

p, Irwin Winkler, Robert Chartoff; d, Martin Scorsese; w, Paul Schrader, Mardik Martin (based on the book by Jake LaMotta with Joseph Carter, Peter Savage); ph, Michael Chapman (Technicolor); ed, Thelma Schoonmaker; prod d, Gene Rudolf; art d, Alan Manser, Kirk Axtell, Sheldon Haber

RAGING BULL is an uncompromisingly brutal and emotionally devastating movie based on the life of middleweight boxing champion Jake LaMotta. The film chronicles the life of the fighter from 1941 until the mid-1960s and is chiefly concerned with the irrational and violent LaMotta's struggle to find peace within himself. Loosely based on LaMotta's autobiography and filmed in gorgeous black and white, the story begins in 1941 and follows LaMotta (Robert De Niro), who is managed by his brother, Joey (Joe Pesci), as he pursues the middleweight championship. During his rise to the crown the hostile LaMotta is distracted by both the local mafia's efforts to control his career and his romance with 15-year-old Vickie (Cathy Moriarty). Eventually LaMotta divorces his first wife to marry Vickie, but the extremely paranoid and insanely jealous boxer abuses both his wife and his brother when he unjustly suspects them of wrongdoing. LaMotta eventually wins the championship (in a bout with Frenchman Marcel Cerdan), but quickly relinquishes it to his nemesis, Sugar Ray Robinson (Johnny Barnes), who defeated LaMotta five out of the six times they met. The collapse of his boxing career coincides with the destruction of his personal life, and, estranged from both his brother and his wife, the now-bloated boxer begins the long road back to personal salvation.

Fueled by Martin Scorsese's brilliant direction and a magnificent Oscar-winning performance by De Niro—who gained nearly 50 pounds to play the older, fatter LaMotta—RAGING BULL is one of the most powerful boxing films ever made. Often unpleasant and painful to watch, the film is a no-holds-barred look at a violent man in a brutal sport, in which, amazingly, the wholly unsympathetic LaMotta attains a state of grace at the end that is inspiring. As usual, the director is examining maleness in this film, and RAGING BULL has a way of zeroing in on masculine values and codes, and how they weigh men down. The film's senseless feel for violence forces you to consider its place in the male idenity—it's easier for most men to retreat into than honest emotion. Many people feel BULL was the best movie of the 80s; like the decade, it leaves a sour taste that lingers long after.

RAGTIME
1981   155m   c   ★★★
Historical   PG/15
Sunley   (U.S./U.K.)

James Cagney (Police Commissioner Waldo), Brad Dourif (Younger Brother), Moses Gunn (Booker T. Washington), Elizabeth McGovern (Evelyn Nesbit), Kenneth McMillan (Willie Conklin), Pat O'Brien (Delmas), Donald O'Connor (Evelyn's Dance Teacher), James Olson (Father), Mandy Patinkin (Tateh), Howard E. Rollins, Jr. (Coalhouse Walker, Jr.)

p, Dino De Laurentiis; d, Milos Forman; w, Michael Weller (based on the novel by E.L. Doctorow); ph, Miroslav Ondricek (Todd-AO, Technicolor); ed, Anne V. Coates, Anthony Gibbs, Stanley Warnow; m, Randy Newman; prod d, John Graysmark; art d, Patrizia von Brandenstein, Tony Reading; chor, Twyla Tharp; cos, Anna Hill Johnstone

Although more than $32 million were pumped into this kaleidoscopic portrait of American life in 1906, RAGTIME is too long, too splintered in its characterizations, and too much of a good thing squeezed dry. The most impressive aspect of the film is the return, after a 20-year hiatus, of top-billed Cagney, at age 81, to play a feisty NYC police commissioner. Based on Doctorow's novel, the film balances two themes and two families—one factual, one fictional. The more compelling story is that of the infamous Thaw-White murder case, in which mad millionaire Harry K. Thaw (Robert Joy) kills famed architect Stanford White (Norman Mailer) over the affections of Thaw's showgirl wife Evelyn Nesbit (Elizabeth McGovern). This story was better told in THE GIRL IN THE RED VELVET SWING. The fictional tale, which is far less interesting, shows the disintegration of an upper-class American family after a wife and mother (Mary Steenburgen) leaves her family to dally with an emigre Russian film director. Her husband (Olson) then winds up being held hostage by black revolutionaries. An exploration of the down side of the American Dream, RAGTIME is not always convincing, and under Forman's occasionally heavy-handed direction, its performances are hardly universally satisfying. Despite the confusion at its core, however, the film is ambitious and sporadically engaging. RAGTIME received eight Oscar nominations: Rollins, Jr. and McGovern for their supporting roles, Best Screenplay, Best Cinematography, Best Art Direction, Best Song, "One More Hour," Best Original Score, and Best Costume Design.

RAIDERS OF THE LOST ARK
1981   115m   c   ★★★★½
Adventure   /PG
Lucasfilm

Harrison Ford (Indiana Jones), Karen Allen (Marion Ravenwood), Paul Freeman (Belloq), Ronald Lacey (Toht), John Rhys-Davies (Sallah), Denholm Elliott (Brody), Wolf Kahler (Dietrich), Anthony Higgins (Gobler), Alfred Molina (Satipo), Vic Tablian (Barranca)

p, Frank Marshall; d, Steven Spielberg; w, Lawrence Kasdan (based on a story by George Lucas, Philip Kaufman); ph, Douglas Slocombe, Paul Beeson (Panavision, Metrocolor); ed, Michael Kahn; m, John Williams; prod d, Norman Reynolds; art d, Leslie Dilley; fx, Richard Edlund, Kit West; cos, Deborah Nadoolman; anim, John Van Vliet, Kim Knowton, Garry Waller, Lording Doyle, Scott Caple, Judy Elkins, Sylvia Keuler, Scott Marshal

The old 1930s adventure serial was never better served than in this spectacular cliffhanger to end all cliffhangers. Indeed RAIDERS OF THE LOST ARK totally transcends its modest source material. Packed with astounding action setpieces, this movie was crafted with such polish, humor, and elan that it became an instant classic. This was the film that Spielberg made while still smarting from the massive flop of 1941, his large scale period slapstick comedy about invasion paranoia in southern California on the eve of WWII. Not a personal project, Spielberg describes it as "work for hire" for his old pal executive producer George Lucas. In any event, it is clearly a labor of love.

Harrison Ford went stellar with this perfect portrayal of archeologist Dr. Indiana Jones, a distinguished scholar who sheds his spectacles to live a life of high adventure outside of the classroom. Ford's performance is an underrated but remarkable achievement; he succeeds in fully embodying a comic-book style hero without ever descending into camp. It's a brilliantly stylized portrayal that is now burned into our pop culture memory.

Set in 1936, the film follows Jones on his US intelligence mission to find the Ark of the Covenant which reputedly still contains the Ten Commandments. The catch is that the Ark is also being sought by agents of Adolf Hitler, who resort to all manner of treachery to stop our hero. Aided by Marion Ravenwood, his tough, beautiful, hard-drinking ex-flame (Karen Allen), however, Indy escapes one outrageous life-threatening situation after another in the quest that takes him from Nepal to Cairo.

RAIDERS is such an overwhelming experience that most viewers are powerless to resist the kinetic pleasures of this endlessly inventive action adventure. Some naysayers have correctly pointed out that the film gave new life to late and unlamented racial stereotypes—cowering natives of color and all that—and the that initially proto-feminist Marion is all-too-soon reduced to screeching for Indy to rescue her. It is difficult to resuscitate dead genres without bringing back their offensive aspects and assumptions but RAIDERS OF THE LOST ARK could have been far worse on these counts. Nonetheless this is great filmmaking, warts and all.

The action, though fairly intense, is extremely witty and playful. The violent setpieces have the imaginatively stylized quality of the progressively escalating gags in a vintage 1940s Tex Avery cartoon. Spielberg demonstrates a delightfully oblique approach to action. He also has a sharp eye for simultaneous movement on several planes of action. On a purely visual level, this young master of the cinema has never done better work. The supporting performances are outstanding as are the stuntwork and special effects. Shot in Hawaii, France, Tunisia, and at Elstree Studios in England—in just 73 days for $22.8 million—

this perpetual motion machine has made more than $200 million and inspired two sequels (INDIANA JONES AND THE TEMPLE OF DOOM and INDIANA JONES AND THE LAST CRUSADE).

Oscars were awarded for Best Art Direction, Best Sound, Best Film Editing, and Best Visual Effects. Nominations included Best Picture (won by CHARIOTS OF FIRE), Best Direction, Best Cinematography, and Best Original Score. After the extraordinary success of this blockbuster, Spielberg decided to take a chance on finally making his intimate personal film about childhood—a somewhat popular trifle called E.T. THE EXTRA-TERRESTRIAL.

RAILROAD MAN, THE
(IL FERROVIERE)
1965 105m bw   ★★½
Drama
Ponti/ENIC/DEG   (Italy)

Pietro Germi (Andrea Marcocci), Luisa Della Noce (Sara Marocci), Sylva Koscina (Giulia), Saro Urzi (Liverani), Renato Speziali (Renato), Carlo Giuffre (Marcello), Edoardo Nevola (Sandrino), Amedeo Trilli

p, Carlo Ponti; d, Pietro Germi; w, Pietro Germi, Alfredo Giannetti, Luciano Vincenzoni, Ennio De Concini (based on a story by Giannetti); ph, Leonida Barboni, Aiace Parolin; ed, Dolores Tamburini; m, Carlo Rustichelli; art d, Carlo Egidi; cos, Mirella Morelli

The heartfelt story of an easygoing railroad engineer, Germi, whose unruly family starts to take its toll on him. It starts with his daughter, Koscina, becoming pregnant and refusing to marry her lover, instead running off with another man. Further trouble erupts when Germi drives a train over a suicide victim; shaken by the event, he messes up on the job and is demoted to driving a freight. The whole world seems to be against Germi, except for his faithful son. His spirit broken by the unhappy turn of events, Germi heads to the pub where he had once enjoyed the company of his many friends only to suffer a stroke when he receives a warm welcome. A simple tale of the ironies of life.

RAILWAY CHILDREN, THE
1971 108m c   ★★★
Historical/Children's   G/U
EMI   (U.K.)

Dinah Sheridan (Mother), Bernard Cribbins (Perks Railway Porter), William Mervyn (Old Gentleman), Iain Cuthbertson (Father), Jenny Agutter (Bobbie), Sally Thomsett (Phyllis), Peter Bromilow (Doctor), Ann Lancaster (Ruth), Gary Warren (Peter), Gordon Whiting (Russian)

p, Robert Lynn; d, Lionel Jeffries; w, Lionel Jeffries (based on a novel by E. Nesbit); ph, Arthur Ibbetson (Technicolor); ed, Teddy Darvas; m, Johnny Douglas; art d, John Clark; fx, Pat Moore, John Richardson; cos, Elsa Fennell

An effective children's film set in Britain during the Edwardian period and starring Sheridan as the wife of a British Foreign Office employee who is falsely accused of treason and imprisoned. Forced by disgrace and lack of income to move from their lush surroundings to the Yorkshire moors, Sheridan sells the idea to her children as sort of a game (they "pretend" to be poor). The kids take to their new surroundings quickly, and it is only a matter of time until they have made new friends and sunk roots in the area. The village they now live in is located near a railway, and much of their play time is spent among the trains. Among their

new friends is a wealthy resident of the area who volunteers to help them clear their father's name. Well acted, nicely scripted, and produced with the right amount of heart and sentiment.

RAIN MAN
1988 128m c   ★★★½
Drama   R/15
Guber-Peters

Dustin Hoffman (Raymond Babbitt), Tom Cruise (Charlie Babbitt), Valeria Golino (Susanna), Jerry Molen (Dr. Bruner), Jack Murdock (John Mooney), Michael Roberts (Vern), Ralph Seymour (Lenny), Lucinda Jenney (Iris), Bonnie Hunt (Sally Dibbs), Kim Robillard

p, Mark Johnson; d, Barry Levinson; w, Ronald Bass, Barry Morrow (based on a story by Morrow); ph, John Seale (DeLuxe Color); ed, Stu Linder; m, Hans Zimmer; prod d, Ida Random; cos, Bernie Pollack

Well written, smartly directed, and sensitively performed, RAIN MAN depicts the one-sided relationship between two brothers, self-centered Los Angeles hustler Charlie Babbitt (Tom Cruise) and the older Raymond (Dustin Hoffman), an autistic resident of a home for the mentally disabled. Their father's estate, worth $3 million, has been left in trust to Raymond, and figuring he can force the trustee to turn over half of the inheritance, Charlie abducts Raymond and attempts to fly him back to Los Angeles. Raymond—an *idiot savant* who can cite airline crash statistics and other bizarre facts and figures in astounding detail—refuses to fly, however, forcing the pair to drive from Cincinnati to LA in their father's car. As they make their way across the country, the emotionally unreachable Raymond becomes the catalyst for Charlie's transformation from a self-absorbed character incapable of intimacy into a caring and sympathetic adult. RAIN MAN rises above the banality of its concept—another buddy movie crossbred with a road picture—to become a genuinely moving and intelligent look at what it means to be human. Hoffman delivers a magnificent stunt of a performance; Cruise brings depth and conviction to the emotional development of his character; and Valeria Golino (as Charlie's girlfriend) gives the film an extra spark.

RAIN PEOPLE, THE
1969 101m c   ★★★
Drama   R/AA
WB

James Caan (Jimmie "Killer" Kilgannon), Shirley Knight (Natalie Ravenna), Robert Duvall (Gordon), Marya Zimmet (Rosalie), Tom Aldredge (Mr. Alfred), Laurie Crewes (Ellen), Andrew Duncan (Artie), Margaret Fairchild (Marion), Sally Gracie (Beth), Alan Manson (Lou)

p, Bart Patton, Ronald Colby; d, Francis Ford Coppola; w, Francis Ford Coppola (based on his story "Echoes"); ph, Wilmer C. Butler (Technicolor); ed, Blackie Malkin; m, Ronald Stein; art d, Leon Ericksen

This is one of those "better luck next time" pictures—and, of course, next time meant THE GODFATHER for Coppola. He'd already directed four films without much success: TONIGHT FOR SURE, DEMENTIA 13, YOU'RE A BIG BOY NOW, and FINIAN'S RAINBOW. Although studios felt sure of his screenwriting ability (he'd also cowritten THIS PROPERTY IS CONDEMNED and had collaborated with Gore Vidal on IS PARIS BURNING?), his directorial work was seriously in question. This odd odyssey was not a hit, even though over the years it has been regarded as one of Coppola's more personal pictures and has attained a limited following. Knight is a childless Long Island housewife married to a decent man, Robert Modica. She learns she's pregnant and can't decide what to do, so she bolts, early one rainy morning, while Modica snores. Once on the road, she phones and tells him that she needs some time to herself away from him and will probably come back eventually. She has no idea where she's going; she just wants to go. During the movie she calls Modica from time to time to let him know she's all right, to admit that she hasn't been a very good wife, and to let him know she's expecting and is not certain that she wants to have the child. Modica, who is seen solely in the first sequence and is thereafter only a voice on the phone, is irate when she talks about an abortion but calms down and says she can do what she wishes as long as she returns to him. Knight is a sexually naive woman, eager to find another partner, so when she picks up Caan on the road, he is elected. Then she learns that he is a brain-damaged football player, who wears a plate in his head, the result of a gridiron accident for which the school gave him $1,000 when he signed away any future claims. He wants to go to West Virginia, where he thinks he has a job promised by Duncan, the father of his former girlfriend, Crewes. When he and Knight get there, Duncan is shocked to see that Caan is no longer the macho young man he was but shows definite signs of brain damage. Knight doesn't know what to do with Caan, as he now has no place to stay in West Virginia. She takes him to Tennessee and tries to drop him off; but that doesn't work, so they go to Nebraska, where she manages to find him work as a handyman at one of those roadside reptile farms that put up colorful signs along the highway. She leaves and is soon stopped for speeding by Duvall, a widowed cop who lives with his 12-year-old daughter, Zimmet, in a small trailer. She is taken to a justice of the peace, Tom Aldredge, who rules the town and also owns the reptile farm. He fines her, and she stays on to dally with Duvall. Meanwhile, Caan feels sorry for the caged creatures he is in charge of and sets them free. Aldredge exacts most of Caan's savings for that action and fires him. In Duvall's trailer the cop is putting pressure on Knight, while Caan is watching through a window. At first Knight seems ready to cooperate; but then she has second thoughts, and Duvall begins to force his attentions on her. Caan breaks in and battles with Duvall, beating the cop badly. Zimmet, who has also observed the situation, grabs her daddy's gun and shoots Caan. Knight cradles Caan's head in her arms, tearfully telling him that he won't have to worry any more, that she and husband Modica will take care of him. Her words fall on Caan's lifeless ears as the picture ends.

Too many flashbacks spoil the narrative, and Knight's character is confused, not very sympathetic, and not clearly motivated. Caan, who had played football and basketball players in a few films, is convincingly wooden here. His next film was RABBIT, RUN, where he played an ex-basketball player in a small Pennsylvania town. THE RAIN PEOPLE—shot in Colorado, Tennessee, Nebraska, New York, and West Virginia—was one of the first "road" pictures done. It was also way ahead of its time as a "feminist" movie, predating STAND UP AND BE COUNTED and AN UNMARRIED WOMAN in the 1970s. The title is from a line by Caan that is hardly right for the retarded youth—"The rain people are made of rain, and when they cry, they disappear altogether"—whatever that means. The movie races all over the place in a hurry to make points, to illuminate the "little people" who live in quiet desperation. The film is a bit too noisy for that, and yet there is enough about it to warrant attention.

RAINMAKER, THE

1956 121m c ★★★
Comedy /A
Paramount

Burt Lancaster (*Starbuck*), Katharine Hepburn (*Lizzie Curry*), Wendell Corey (*File*), Lloyd Bridges (*Noah Curry*), Earl Holliman (*Jim Curry*), Cameron Prud'Homme (*H.C. Curry*), Wallace Ford (*Sheriff Thomas*), Yvonne Lime (*Snookie*), Dottie Bee Baker (*Belinda*), Dan White (*Deputy*)

p, Hal B. Wallis; d, Joseph Anthony; w, N. Richard Nash (based on the play by N. Richard Nash); ph, Charles Lang (VistaVision, Technicolor); ed, Warren Low; m, Alex North; art d, Hal Pereira, Walter Tyler; fx, John P. Fulton; cos, Edith Head

THE MUSIC MAN may have owed something to this story, since both concern confidence men who come to small towns to peddle their scams, then fall for spinsters. Nash wrote the film as a television play then expanded it to work on the Broadway stage, where it ran 124 performances with Geraldine Page in the Hepburn role and Prud'Homme as her father, under the direction of Anthony, who also did this film and, later, the musical version, "110 in the Shade." Composer North garnered an Oscar nomination, as did Hepburn, her seventh. The main problem is that the film is far too talky, and the leads are somewhat grizzled for the situation. Hepburn is a hick-town spinster in an arid area of the Southwest. (She never really convinces anyone that she's a country girl because that New England accent and her flighty mannerisms constantly intrude.) Lancaster is a brash, lively con artist who comes to the burg claiming that he can bring rain to the drought-ravaged locale for the sum of $100. He is taken into Prud'Homme's house and allowed to live in one of the outbuildings. Hepburn's brothers are Bridges, who never quite buys Lancaster's spiel, and Holliman, an oafish young man who is wooing town beauty Lime. Once Lancaster is ensconced, he begins to change things around. Hepburn is being courted, albeit reluctantly, by the town's lawman, Corey, but he doesn't seem to be able to pop the question, and time is a-wasting in her old maid life. Lancaster convinces the plain Hepburn that she is gorgeous, and once she feels that's true, her attitude about herself begins to alter. She's been told for years by everyone, mostly her brother Bridges, that she is, at best, plain, but the intrusion of Lancaster works a minor miracle on her self-confidence. She now has a duo of suitors in Lancaster and Corey, who suddenly awakens to the fact that she is a terrific woman. At the end, there is a coincidental downpour, and Lancaster, it should go without saying, takes all the credit before departing for his next conquest. Behind him, he has left a changed woman, and his visit has been the most exciting thing to happen to the tiny village in its history. Lancaster does one of his ELMER GANTRY bravura performances and was a perfect selection, although a little timeworn at 43. Hepburn was pushing 50 and Corey was 7 years younger. The difference in all their ages was revealed by the close-ups and worked against the believability of the story. Still, it's a pleasant movie with more than many laughs.

RAISIN IN THE SUN, A

1961 127m bw ★★★★
Drama /A
Paman/Doris

Sidney Poitier (*Walter Lee Younger*), Claudia McNeil (*Lena Younger*), Ruby Dee (*Ruth Younger*), Diana Sands (*Beneatha Younger*), Ivan Dixon (*Asagai*), John Fiedler (*Mark Lindner*), Louis Gossett,

RAISING ARIZONA

Jr. *(George Murchison)*, Stephen Perry *(Travis)*, Joel Fluellen *(Bobo)*, Roy E. Glenn, Sr. *(Willie Harris)*

p, David Susskind, Philip Rose; d, Daniel Petrie; w, Lorraine Hansberry (based on the play by Lorraine Hansberry); ph, Charles Lawton, Jr.; ed, William Lyon, Paul Weatherwax; m, Laurence Rosenthal; art d, Carl Anderson

Hansberry's lovely adaptation of her 1959 Broadway hit reunies unites seven of the original cast in the film version. The plot concerns a black family questioning the difficulties of their existence. But especially given the economic difficulties today for most people struggling to get by in the inner city, there are enough universalities to touch any audience member.

McNeil is the matriarch of a family living in cramped quarters on Chicago's south side (where all the location shots were done). Her husband has just died and she receives a check for $10,000 from the insurance company, a bonanza back then. McNeil has practical notions for the cash. She wants to get out of the dangerous slum in which they live and buy a decent house, then use the other money to pay for medical school for her daughter, Sands. Poitier, her son, has other ideas. He's a chauffeur and longs for the day when he can have his own business and be his own boss, so he asks if he can have the money to invest in a liquor store, which he feels is a money-making machine. McNeil won't hear of Poitier's scheme and she promptly puts $3,500 down on a house in a white neighborhood. Poitier is angered, quarrels with McNeil and his wife, Dee, and leaves the apartment, disappearing for three days from the residence as well as from his job. McNeil finally finds him in a local tavern and offers him $6,500, with the proviso that $3,500 be held for Sands's education. Fiedler, the only white person in the cast, arrives. He's a member of an "improvement association" and on its behalf offers the family more than what they paid for the house. They can turn a profit without even moving. They decline. Now it's learned that Poitier took all of the cash, including the college fund, and put it into the liquor store deal, which turns out to be a fraud, and they are out the entire sum.

The performances without reservation are excellent, with Poitier's role allowing him an opportunity to explore the limitations society places on black men. McNeil's handling of the matriarch is unflinching in its emotional honesty. Look for Gossett in a small part as a black youth fixiated by WASP values. Since much of the action takes place in the tiny apartment, director Petrie had to pull out all the stops to keep it from being stage-bound, and, with the help of cinematographer Lawton, he succeeded. The poignancy that RAISIN packs more than compensates for any stagebound conventions that remain.

RAISING ARIZONA

1987   94m   c   ★★★
Comedy   PG-13/15
Circle

Nicolas Cage *(H.I. McDonnough)*, Holly Hunter *(Edwina)*, Trey Wilson *(Nathan Arizona, Sr.)*, John Goodman *(Gale)*, William Forsythe *(Evelle)*, Sam McMurray *(Glen)*, Frances McDormand *(Dot)*, Randall "Tex" Cobb *(Leonard Smalls)*, T.J. Kuhn *(Nathan Arizona, Jr.)*, Lynne Dumin Kitei *(Florence Arizona)*

p, Ethan Coen, Mark Silverman; d, Joel Coen; w, Ethan Coen, Joel Coen; ph, Barry Sonnenfeld (Duart Color); ed, Michael R. Miller; m, Carter Burwell; prod d, Jane Musky; art d, Harold Thrasher; cos, Richard Hornung

The promise that was evident in BLOOD SIMPLE, the Coen brothers' remarkably assured debut, is fulfilled in RAISING ARIZONA, an entertaining, energetic, and stylish comedy about a simple but loving couple who long to be parents.

H.I. "Hi" McDonnough (Nicholas Cage) is a hopelessly inept petty crook who attempts to go straight after he marries prison officer Edwina (Holly Hunter), and they settle down in a trailer in the middle of the Arizona desert. They long for a normal family life, but are childless and unable to adopt due to Hi's criminal past. When Hi and Edwina read that the wife of wealthy furniture dealer Nathan Arizona (Trey Wilson) has given birth to quintuplets, they decide to steal one for themselves.

RAISING ARIZONA is populated with excellent performances, especially from its two leads. Cage creates a homey and thoroughly likable character who earns the respect of the audience, but Hunter is the real surprise. Appearing in her first starring role, the stage veteran displays so much energy that she forces the audience to pay attention. The supporting cast is equally impressive, particularly John Goodman and William Forsythe as a couple of escaped convicts who pay a visit to their old friend Cage. Former professional boxer Randall "Tex" Cobb is also memorable as a thoroughly bizarre and very menacing bounty hunter.

RAMBLING ROSE

1991   112m   c   ★★★★
Drama/Romance/Comedy   R/15
Carolco Pictures

Laura Dern *(Rose)*, Robert Duvall *(Daddy Hillyer)*, Diane Ladd *(Mother Hillyer)*, Lukas Haas *(Buddy Hillyer)*, John Heard *(Willcox "Buddy" Hillyer)*, Kevin Conway *(Doctor Martinson)*, Robert Burke *(Police Chief Dave Wilkie)*, Lisa Jakub *(Doll Hillyer)*, Evan Lockwood *(Waski Hillyer)*, Matt Sutherland *(Billy)*

p, Renny Harlin; d, Martha Coolidge; w, Calder Willingham (from his novel); ph, Johnny Jensen; ed, Steveny Cohen; m, Elmer Bernstein; prod d, John Vallone; art d, Christiaan Wagener; cos, Jane Robinson

Directed by Martha Coolidge from a screenplay by Calder Willingham based on his autobiographical novel, RAMBLING ROSE is a humorous coming of age story with a barbed central message.

When Rose (Laura Dern) becomes part of the eccentric Hillyer household in 1935, she proves more of a disruptive element than anyone could have anticipated. A tall country girl with flowing golden hair, carrying a cardboard suitcase tied with string, she comes to work at the house and quickly captivates 5-year-old Waski (Evan Lockwood), 11-year-old Doll (Lisa Jakub) and, especially, 13-year-old Buddy (Lukas Haas). Rose, in turn, is awed by the genteel, learned Mother (Diane Ladd) and courtly Daddy (Robert Duvall), a Southern gentleman who makes Rose feel welcome with these words: "You are as graceful as the capital letter 'S'. You will adorn our house. You will give a glow and a shine to these old walls."

The film is narrated by an adult Buddy (John Heard), who is looking back to a time when he was on the brink of adolescence. He recalls that Rose created "one damnable commotion" in the Hillyer family and elsewhere, though not through any malicious intent on her part. Rose's failing is that she. . . rambles. Beautiful, naive, and sexually uninhibited, she has an overriding need for emotional—and physical—affection. She begins by declaring her unrequited love for Daddy, and rapidly moves on to stirring Buddy's adolescent ardor, leading to a piquant bedroom scene in which she only half-heartedly fends off his inquisitive fumblings.

Rose's first appearance in town creates a minor sensation, and she soon becomes the target of many a local Lothario. Daddy, meanwhile, is less than delighted at having to deal with young men sloping about outside the house and even finding their way into Rose's bedroom. The central scene comes when the misogynistic Doctor Martinson (Kevin Conway) suggests the only way to deal with Rose's "condition" is to have her sterilized. He goes some way toward convincing Daddy of his case, but the two men are humiliated by a powerhouse speech in which Mother defends Rose's—and every woman's—right to be herself and to express her own sexuality. Eventually Rose must move on, but the memory of her stay lingers with the Hillyers for the rest of their lives.

Coolidge does a supremely assured job of bringing the period to life, handling her story with a charm that does not blunt the edge of its message. In the central role of Rose, Laura Dern gives an impeccable performance as a heroine whose unbridled sexuality is matched only by her complete lack of guile, and Robert Duvall is superb as a Southern gentleman completely nonplussed by the combination. Lukas Haas gives a winning performance as young Buddy, and Diane Ladd paints a finely observed portrait of a compassionate, intellectual Southern matron.

RAMBLING ROSE deals with cultural misogyny and sexual oppression in a human, comic way accessible to all. An intelligent, witty screenplay, deft direction, excellent production values and top-flight performances make this a quietly compelling gem.

RAN
1985   160m   c   ★★★★★
Historical/War   R/15
Herald Ace/Nippon Herald/Greenwich   (France/Japan)

Tatsuya Nakadai *(Lord Hidetora Ichimonji)*, Akira Terao *(Tarotakatora Ichimonji)*, Jinpachi Nezu *(Jiromasatora Ichimonji)*, Daisuke Ryu *(Saburonaotora Ichimonji)*, Mieko Harada *(Lady Kaede)*, Yoshiko Miyazaki *(Lady Sue)*, Kazuo Kato *(Ikoma)*, Masayuki Yui *(Tango)*, Peter *(Kyoami)*, Hitoshi Ueki *(Fujimaki)*

p, Masato Hara, Serge Silberman; d, Akira Kurosawa; w, Akira Kurosawa, Hideo Oguni, Masato Ide (based on "King Lear" by William Shakespeare); ph, Takao Saito, Masaharu Ueda, Asakazu Nakai; ed, Akira Kurosawa; m, Toru Takemitsu; prod d, Yoshiro Muraki, Shinobu Muraki; art d, Yoshiro Muraki; cos, Emi Wada

At age 75, Akira Kurosawa, Japan's greatest living director, created one more magnificent work that will surely stand the test of time. In RAN, Kurosawa turned to Shakespeare for inspiration—as he had in THRONE OF BLOOD nearly 30 years before—and chose to film a Japanese adaptation of "King Lear." Set in 16th-century Japan, RAN (the Japanese character for fury, revolt, and madness—chaos) begins as Hidetora Ichimonji (Tatsuya Nakadai), an aging warlord who has acquired power through 50 years of ruthless bloodshed, announces his intention to divide his kingdom among his three sons, each of whom will live at one of three outlying castles. While the elder sons thank him for the honor, the youngest calls his father senile and mad, noting—prophetically—that it will only be a matter of time until the ambitious brothers begin battling for possession of the whole domain. In the process, Hidetora and his kingdom are consigned to a tragic and spectacular end. For more than 10 years, Kurosawa wanted desperately to make RAN, and, on the strength of KAGEMUSHA's success, he was finally able to obtain funding for this, the most expensive film ever made in Japan (though the $11 million budget is small by Hollywood standards). Partly shot at two of that country's most revered landmarks (the ancient castles at Himeji and Kumamoto; the third castle was constructed of plastic and wood on the slopes of Mount Fuji), RAN is a visually stunning epic, containing some of the most beautiful, colorful, breathtaking imagery ever committed to celluloid. As he grew older, Kurosawa began to shoot his films in a more traditionally Japanese style (static takes, little camera movement, no flamboyant editing). Here, especially in the battle scenes, he adopts a detached, impassive camera, heightening the tragedy by giving the audience a godlike but powerless perspective on all the madness and folly unfolding onscreen. At the same time, Kurosawa infuses the film with deep human emotion, aided by uniformly superb performances. The work of a mature artist in complete control of his medium, RAN is a true cinematic masterwork of sight, sound, intelligence, and—most important—passion.

RANCHO DELUXE
1975   93m   c   ★★½
Western/Comedy   R/
UA

Jeff Bridges *(Jack McKee)*, Sam Waterston *(Cecil Colson)*, Elizabeth Ashley *(Cora Brown)*, Charlene Dallas *(Laura Beige)*, Clifton James *(John Brown)*, Slim Pickens *(Henry Beige)*, Harry Dean Stanton *(Curt)*, Richard Bright *(Burt)*, Patti D'Arbanville *(Betty Fargo)*, Maggie Wellman *(Mary Fargo)*

p, Elliott Kastner; d, Frank Perry; w, Thomas McGuane; ph, William A. Fraker (DeLuxe Color); ed, Sidney Katz; m, Jummy Buffett; art d, Michael Haller

McGuane's script for RANCHO DELUXE must have been better than the final picture because, every now and again, the film has some terrific lines, good-natured humor, and lovely touches. Overall, however, Perry's attempt at directing a comedy falls short. Bridges and Waterston are best friends who make a living rustling a few head from the ranch of James, who is married to pneumatic Ashley, a woman who is love-starved by her conservative husband. Bridges is divorced from Cooke, and when he goes back to see her and, perhaps, effect a reconciliation, her attitude only sends him right back to being a happy-go-lucky drifter. Waterston is an Indian and returns to his tribe for a brief visit, but the other Indians are so hidebound and stuffy that he wants no part of them. So the two men decide that these little thefts are not enough; they want a big one. They enlist two of James's workers, Bright and Stanton, into a huge heist. Meanwhile, James has employed a crochety private detective, Pickens, to track down those responsible for these Montana misdemeanors. Stanton takes up with Dallas (who claims she is Pickens' niece, but is, in reality, his daughter), and she blows the whistle on the plot to steal a herd of cattle. D'Arbanville and Wellman are rustler "groupies" who hang around with Bridges and Waterston and add little to the episodic plot. The best parts of the movie are little details that are shown, with no comment, for the eyes to catch. These elements give the film an odd charm, and it's often enjoyable when it's not preaching about the fate of the Old West. Nothing much happens and it just ambles along from set-piece to set-piece with occasional harsh language and glimpses of enough flesh to put it into the category of "don't let the kids see this." One of Kastner's better films.

RANCHO NOTORIOUS
1952   89m   c   ★★★★
Western   /PG
Fidelity

Marlene Dietrich (*Altar Keane*), Arthur Kennedy (*Vern Haskell*), Mel Ferrer (*Frenchy Fairmont*), Lloyd Gough (*Kinch*), Gloria Henry (*Beth*), William Frawley (*Baldy Gunder*), Lisa Ferraday (*Maxine*), John Raven (*Chuck-a-Luck Dealer*), Jack Elam (*Geary*), George Reeves (*Wilson*)

p, Howard Welsch; d, Fritz Lang; w, Daniel Taradash (based on the story "Gunsight Whitman" by Sylvia Richards); ph, Hal Mohr (Technicolor); ed, Otto Ludwig; m, Emil Newman; prod d, Wiard Ihnen; cos, Joe King, Don Loper

The last of Fritz Lang's three westerns, following THE RETURN OF JESSE JAMES and WESTERN UNION, RANCHO NOTORIOUS is a bizarre, strangely poetic, and highly personal ballad of one man's transformation from an innocent, loving cowhand to a man obsessed with avenging his fiancée's murder. Kennedy plays the cowhand who, at the film's opening, is wooing his sweetheart, Henry. After exchanging hugs and kisses with his lady love, fantasizing about the children they will have when married, and discussing the name of their new ranch, Kennedy presents her with a brooch and goes off to work, leaving her behind in the general store where she works. A couple of outlaws, Gough and John Doucette, ride into town soon after and stop at the store to empty out the safe. Gough gets rough with the girl, and (as the camera moves to an outside vantage point) a gunshot is heard. The outlaws take off as Gough fires a shot at a young boy who witnessed the crime. When Kennedy returns to the store, he is greeted by a crowd of onlookers and a doctor who, after declaring Henry dead, tells Kennedy that "She wasn't spared anything," pointedly implying that she was also raped. As the camera moves down to her hand, clawed in rigor mortis, Kennedy, along with a posse, begins his search for the killer. The posse soon backs down, however, leaving Kennedy to set out alone, as a reprise of the song "The Legend of Chuck-a-Luck" (Ken Darby, sung by William Lee) is heard: "Listen to the legend of the Chuck-a-Luck, Chuck-a-Luck; listen to the wheel of fate, as round and round with a whispering sound it spins, it spins the old, old story of hate, murder, and revenge." Kennedy follows the trail through the woods until he comes across the dying Doucette, who has been shot in the back by Gough. Doucette's last words, "Chuck-a-Luck," provide Kennedy with his first clue. After making countless inquiries, Kennedy learns that *chuck-a-luck*, a vertical gambling wheel, is also the name of a criminal hideout run by a tough but beautiful barroom singer named Altar Keane, played marvelously by Dietrich. As we see in flashback, her past, like Kennedy's, ties in with the Chuck-a-Luck legend as well. The gambling wheel netted her a sizable winning, with the help of much-feared gunman Ferrer, who subsequently became her lover.

After hearing the story, Kennedy decides that he must make contact with Ferrer in order to locate the Chuck-a-Luck hideout. The trail leads to a town that is in the process of overthrowing its corrupt officials and electing a new law-and-order party. There, in the local jail, Ferrer is behind bars. To get himself arrested, Kennedy causes a ruckus in a saloon and is thrown into jail, where he makes friends with Ferrer and joins him in a jailbreak. To show his appreciation, Ferrer invites Kennedy to Chuck-a-Luck, an unassuming horse ranch nestled in an obscure valley. Dietrich, the only woman there, runs a tight ship, wielding an all-powerful hand over the nine or ten outlaws who share her roof. She also has rigid house rules, the most important stipulating that no one ask questions. In return for shelter, food, and her confidence, Dietrich receives a five-percent share of the take on any job the outlaws pull. As Dietrich introduces Kennedy to everyone, he hones in on Reeves, a sleazy ladies' man with a

hideous scar on his face, which Kennedy assumes was put there by Henry. Although Dietrich clearly belongs to Ferrer, the subtle attraction between her and Kennedy inspires a lament for her wasted youth, which she sings to the boys: "Get Away, Young Man" (Ken Darby). Kennedy, however, still bent on "hate, murder, and revenge," continues to make a play for Dietrich in order to elicit the information he needs. Then he recognizes the pin Dietrich is wearing as the one he gave his fiancée and tries to convince Dietrich to reveal where she got it. (Naturally, he assumes it came from Ferrer.)

When the sheriff's men come to the ranch, Dietrich orders her men to escape to a nearby hideout until further notice. Kennedy pretends to have become separated from the group and returns to the ranch. When the sheriff's aide notices the large number of horses that have recently left the ranch, Kennedy allays the aide's suspicions by inventing a story about some strays Kennedy has supposedly just rounded up. The sheriff leaves, convinced that there has been no foul play. Kennedy makes his play for Dietrich, pulling her into his arms and kissing her. After the kiss, to which Dietrich responds, she says, "That was for trying." She then does an about face and slaps Kennedy's face twice, saying "That was for trying too hard." When the gang returns to Chuck-a-Luck, they begin planning a big bank robbery, but their enthusiasm is undercut by Dietrich's demand for a 10 percent share. Although she gives as her reason the high risk involved, her real concern is keeping Ferrer and Kennedy out of trouble. Dissent begins to brew when Kennedy finally learns that the brooch was given to Dietrich, as part of her share, by Gough. When Kennedy confronts Gough, the gang feels betrayed. Kennedy tries to goad Gough into drawing his gun, but Gough refuses, realizing that his opponent has by this time acquired Ferrer's superb gunslinging ability. Then the sheriff arrives, and Kennedy sees his chance to expose Gough and have him arrested. The gang, however, is not pleased and breaks Gough from jail. The group then heads back to Chuck-a-Luck to settle with Dietrich. A blazing battle breaks out; when the gunsmoke settles, Gough is dead and Dietrich lies dying, having stepped between Kennedy and a bullet meant for him. Kennedy has ridden out the wave of fate. He has settled the score of "hate, murder, and revenge." As he rides off with Ferrer, however, the scene suggests a sense of loss, with its implication that Kennedy can never return to his former, innocent life, untouched by hatred.

RANCHO NOTORIOUS combines the quintessential Lang theme of a man ruled by fate with the generic elements of the western. Although set in the West, with western sets and costumes, it is not a classic western in the style of John Ford. Whereas Ford, along with other western-movie pioneers, has a sense of American myth making, Lang is still absorbed in his German heritage, with its outward expression and physical representation of inner turmoil. Like Dave Bannion (played by Glenn Ford) in THE BIG HEAT, RANCHO NOTORIOUS's hero Vern Haskell is a basically good man turned inside out by thoughts of revenge. In Bannion's case it is the death of his wife that triggers the action; in Haskell's it is the death of his fiancée. From this crucial point on, a trail—seemingly dictated by the unwritten fate of the gods—leads each man to express his dark side. In each film a *femme fatale* (Gloria Grahame in THE BIG HEAT and Dietrich in this film) is destroyed in the process. RANCHO NOTORIOUS is on the surface a western, but (in much the same way as Nicholas Ray's nonwestern JOHNNY GUITAR) it expresses no western themes or ideals.

The original title, "Chuck-a-Luck," fell victim to the blind power of RKO head Howard Hughes, who arbitrarily decided that Lang's reference to the chuck-a-luck wheel would have no meaning in Europe, so he changed it to the even less meaningful, though more appealing, RANCHO NOTORIOUS. Lang's troubles with RKO were not limited to the film's title, however. Even though Lang was to have been consulted before any reediting was undertaken, the film was recut under producer Welsch's orders. The recutting removed much of the ambiance. Lang also had troubles with Dietrich, who for the first time was being cast as an aging woman instead of the glamorous, glowing beauty of her youth. Like her Altar Keane character, Dietrich could not accept the effects of mortality, begging cameraman Mohr (who at one point was asked to be relieved of his duties but was refused) to make her look as lovely as he had years earlier (in 1939) for DESTRY RIDES AGAIN. The tensions between Dietrich and Lang drew close to the breaking point, although the two had been romantically linked for a brief period in 1934, after Lang had left Germany to film LILIOM in France. The working relationship between director and actress was not helped by Dietrich's suggestion that Lang try certain methods and techniques used by her mentor and charisma-creator Josef von Sternberg. By film's end Lang and Dietrich were not even speaking.

None of those problems, however, come out in the film. Dietrich's mature performance is superb (especially memorable is her first scene, in which she rides a man, as if on horseback, in a drunken barroom contest). Her portrayal of a woman torn between two men and between youth and old age is a revelation. The role of Altar Keane also marks a very different *femme fatale*: one who, instead of causing a lover's death, brings about her own while saving his. In addition to the number "Get Away, Young Man," Dietrich also sings another Ken Darby tune, "Gypsy Davey." Missing from the credits on the film was actor Lloyd Gough who, because he refused to testify before the House Un-American Activities Committee, was blacklisted and had his name removed by Hughes.

RANDOM HARVEST

1942 125m bw ★★★½
Drama /U
MGM

Ronald Colman (*Charles Rainier*), Greer Garson (*Paula*), Philip Dorn (*Dr. Jonathan Benet*), Susan Peters (*Kitty*), Reginald Owen ("*Biffer*"), Edmund Gwenn (*Prime Minister*), Henry Travers (*Dr. Sims*), Margaret Wycherly (*Mrs. Deventer*), Bramwell Fletcher (*Harrison*), Arthur Margetson (*Chetwynd*)

p, Sidney Franklin; d, Mervyn LeRoy; w, Claudine West, George Froeschel, Arthur Wimperis (based on the novel by James Hilton); ph, Joseph Ruttenberg; ed, Harold F. Kress; m, Herbert Stothart; art d, Cedric Gibbons, Randall Duell; chor, Ernst Matray; cos, Robert Kalloch

Amnesia, that standard movie plot device, was never used better than in this filmed adaptation of James Hilton's popular 1940 novel *Random Harvest*. The setting is England, where WWI has just ended. Colman, a soldier from a wealthy family, is hospitalized for shell shock, having lost his memory in battle. When the armistice is declared, Colman wanders out of the hospital during a joyous celebration and winds up in the town of Medbury, where he meets Garson, a dancer in a local club. Garson quickly realizes Colman is an amnesiac and takes him to a country village to help him put his life back together. There, Colman is unable to regain his memory, but he does regain his full faculty of speech and, as he builds a new identity, discovers that he has a talent for writing. In time, he and Garson fall in love, marry, and have a child.

This idyll is ended when Colman, whose writing abilities are quickly developing, goes to Liverpool to sell one of his stories and is hit by a car. This restores his old memories, but wipes out his last three years with Garson. He returns to his relatives and works in the family industrial business; meanwhile, Garson goes through much hardship, including the loss of their child. After Dorn, a psychiatrist, helps her find her husband, Garson gets a job as Colman's secretary. Colman is pleased with her work, but doesn't recognize Garson—who, on Dorn's advice, doesn't let on who she is, to avoid subjecting her husband to further severe psychological trauma. Peters, Colman's fiancee, senses that there is a woman in his past with whom she cannot compete and calls off the engagement, leaving Colman increasingly depressed. He throws himself into his work, coming to rely more and more on Garson, and eventually proposes to her. But theirs is at first a marriage in name only, though Garson tries to renew the forgotten spark. Meanwhile, Colman embarks on an increasingly notable political career. Since Colman still fails to recognize her, a despairing Garson decides to go on holiday to lift her spirits. First, however, she returns to Medbury, and stays at the cottage she had shared with Colman. Colman is summoned to Medbury at the same time to settle a labor strike, and, upon his arrival, is jarred by the strange familiarity of his surroundings. Slowly his lost years come back to him, and he finally returns to the cottage for an emotional reunion with Garson.

RANDOM HARVEST is a deeply moving film, marked by superb direction of its intricate story from Mervyn LeRoy, and by the strong performances of Greer Garson and Ronald Colman. Their scenes together are sensitive and heartfelt, giving a depth to the implausible plot that allows the proceedings to transcend soap opera. Colman was nominated for an Oscar for his work (as was supporting actress Susan Peters); Garson did win Best Actress honors, but for MRS. MINIVER rather than RANDOM HARVEST. The film also earned nominations for Best Picture, Best Director, Best Screenplay, Best Interior Decoration, and Best Score. Made at a cost of $2 million, RANDOM HARVEST brought in $4.5 million at the box office, made record receipts for Radio City Music Hall, and became one of the top 25 money-making films of its year. On the strength of its success, Colman won renewed respect in Hollywood and Garson's future at MGM was assured.

RASHOMON

1950 90m bw ★★★★★
Drama /X
Daiei (Japan)

Toshiro Mifune (*Tajomaru*), Machiko Kyo (*Masago*), Masayuki Mori (*Takehiro*), Takashi Shimura (*Firewood Dealer*), Minoru Chiaki (*Priest*), Kichijiro Ueda (*Commoner*), Fumiko Homma (*Medium*), Daisuke Kato (*Policeman*)

p, Jingo Minoura; d, Akira Kurosawa; w, Shinobu Hashimoto, Akira Kurosawa (based on the short story "Yabu no Naka" and the novel *Rasho-Mon* by Ryunosuke Akutagawa); ph, Kazuo Miyagawa; m, Fumio Hayasaka; art d, So Matsuyama

One of the most brilliantly constructed films of all time, RASHOMON is a monument to Akira Kurosawa's greatness, combining his well-known humanism with an experimental narrative style that has become a hallmark of film history. The central portion of the film revolves around four varying points of view of the rape of a woman and the death of her husband in a forest. Set in the 11th century, the film opens with a framing device, the conversation between three men—a woodcutter (Takashi Shimura), a priest (Minoru Chiaki), and a commoner (Kichijiro Ueda)—who have taken refuge from a rainstorm under the ruins of the stone Rashomon Gate. The priest relates the details of a trial he witnessed in a prison courtyard involving the rape of Masago (Machiko Kyo) and the murder of her samurai husband Takehiro (Masayuki Mori). As he explains, the audience is shown the four main defendants: Masago; the bandit Tajomaru (Toshiro Mifune); the spirit of Takehiro, which has been conjured by a medium; and the woodcutter, who admits that he witnessed the murder. Each of their viewpoints is depicted, the "truth" changing with each new defendant's explanation. Based on two short stories by Japanese author Ryunosuke Akutagawa ("In the Grove," the inspiration for the central crime story, and "Rashomon," the basis for the framing scenes), RASHOMON is a reflection of Kurosawa at his most Eisensteinian. Here he uses a juxtaposition of shots and a varying sequence of events to tell an essentially visual story. Although the film has been described by some as being about the search for truth, it is much more than that, as the framing story hints. Like the ruins of the Rashomon Gate (the film is after all named RASHOMON and not IN THE GROVE), the humanity Kurosawa depicts is crumbling and in danger of completely collapsing. While philosophers contend there are many truths, logic asserts there is only one, and, therefore, three of the four testifying characters in this film must be lying. Since Kurosawa's interests lie chiefly in human nature (and not philosophy or narrative structure), it follows that RASHOMON is not about truth but human fallibility, dishonesty, and selfishness. Like so many Kurosawa films, RASHOMON also contains some of the most amazing performances you are likely to find anywhere, especially that of the wildly fascinating Toshiro Mifune as the bandit. The videocassette is available in both dubbed and subtitled versions.

RASPUTIN AND THE EMPRESS

1932 135m bw ★★★★
Historical /A
MGM

John Barrymore *(Prince Paul Chegodieff)*, Ethel Barrymore *(Empress Alexandra)*, Lionel Barrymore *(Rasputin)*, Ralph Morgan *(Emperor Nikolai)*, Diana Wynyard *(Natasha)*, Tad Alexander *(Alexis)*, C. Henry Gordon *(Grand Duke Igor)*, Edward Arnold *(Doctor)*, Gustav von Seyffertitz *(Dr. Wolfe)*, Anne Shirley *(Anastasia)*

p, Bernard H. Hyman; d, Richard Boleslawski, Charles Brabin (uncredited); w, Charles MacArthur; ph, William Daniels; ed, Tom Held; m, Herbert Stothart; art d, Cedric Gibbons, Alexander Toluboff; cos, Adrian

This superb historical epic gathers the royal family of the American stage, the only film in which the three dynamic Barrymores appeared together. It was a production feast for the eyes as the last royal court of the czars, the tragic Romanovs of Russia, made its final glittering bow. A greater treat is to see the magnificent Barrymores vie with each other for every frame of this memorable film.

John Barrymore, playing Prince Paul Chegodieff, arrives at court to warn the weak Czar Nicholas II (Ralph Morgan) and his strong-willed Czarina, the Empress Alexandra (Ethel Barrymore), that peasants and revolutionaries are in the streets demanding food and freedom. He urges quick reforms before a full-scale revolution breaks out. The royal couple's son, Prince Alexis (Tad Alexander), suffers a fall and, being a hemophiliac, begins to bleed to death. No doctor can stop the bleeding, but a lady-in-waiting (Diana Wynyard) tells the desperate Empress that she knows of a mystical holy man who may save the young prince. Rasputin, the Mad Monk, played by Lionel Barrymore, arrives at court and, using a single burning candle and riveting

the boy's gaze to his own intense stare, hypnotizes the child and causes the bleeding to stop. To Alexandra, the monk is a miracle man and she insists that Rasputin remain at court, close to her son in case he is needed. Rasputin, a perverse, crude peasant who claims to embody great spiritual powers, agrees only because he sees his opportunity to seize power. He uses Alexandra's dependency on him to assume authority and slowly begins to take control, naming his own graft-paying cronies to high office, stealing a fortune from the public treasury, and casting a covetous eye on the older royal daughters.

Director Richard Boleslawsky does an admirable job in moving the story along at a brisk pace. Writer Charles MacArthur's screenplay displays deep sympathy for the royal couple and their afflicted son, and shows the revolutionaries as unthinking brutes—a stance that did not endear the film to the new Communist government headed by Stalin; in fact, although factually accurate, based on the best known sources regarding Rasputin and his diabolical activities, the film was banned in the USSR. Producing this particular story was an inspiration of MGM production chief Irving Thalberg, whose special pet project the film became. It was also his idea to star the three Barrymores in the lead roles. He had no trouble signing John (at $150,000) and assigning Lionel, who was then an MGM contract player. But Ethel was a different matter. She was now a grand dame of Broadway theater. However, she agreed that for $100,000 she would play the Empress, but only if production could be completed in Hollywood within an eight-week period during the summer months so she could return to a Broadway commitment in the fall. Thalberg agreed and Ethel traveled to the West Coast to join her brothers in their first effort together since they had appeared in *Camille* in Baltimore, circa 1916. True to her stubborn word, Ethel marched off the set at the end of her time as stipulated by her contract, leaving Boleslawsky (who had replaced Charles Brabin) to shoot around her. The resulting film stands as a fine historical piece, a minor classic, enhanced by the histrionic Barrymores.

RATS, THE
(DIE RATTEN)
1955 91m bw ★★★
Drama /18
CCC (West Germany)

Maria Schell *(Pauline Karka)*, Curt Jurgens *(Bruno Mechelke)*, Heidemarie Hatheyer *(Anna John)*, Gustav Knuth *(Karl John)*, Ilse Steppat *(Frau Knobbe)*, Fritz Remond *(Harro Hassenreuter)*, Barbara Rost *(Selma Knobbe)*

d, Robert Siodmak; w, Jochen Huth (based on the play by Gerhardt Hauptmann); ph, Goran Strindberg; m, Werner Eisbrenner

This very depressing look at postwar Germany stars Schell as a pregnant girl from East Germany who has been abandoned by her lover. When the baby is born, she gives it to another woman, who has wanted a child for a long time, but has been unable to conceive. This sets the stage for a conflict between the two women over the child. The acting, production, and script are fine, yielding a very bleak and realistic view of the plight of the German people after the war.

RAW DEAL
1948 79m bw ★★★
Crime /18
Reliance/Eagle-Lion

Dennis O'Keefe *(Joe Sullivan)*, Claire Trevor *(Pat)*, Marsha Hunt *(Ann Martin)*, John Ireland *(Fantail)*, Raymond Burr *(Rick Coyle)*, Curt Conway *(Spider)*, Chili Williams *(Marcy)*, Richard Fraser, Whit Bissell, Cliff Clark *(Men)*

p, Edward Small; d, Anthony Mann; w, Leopold Atlas, John C. Higgins (based on a story by Arnold B. Armstrong, Audrey Ashley); ph, John Alton; ed, Al DeGaetano; m, Paul Sawtell; art d, Edward L. Ilou; fx, George J. Teague

A hard-hitting gangster film with lots of action, good dialog, and fine performances by all, especially Trevor as a gun moll. O'Keefe is serving time for a crime of which he was innocent. His one-time associates arranged a frame, and O'Keefe is determined to get even with them when he breaks out of jail. With the aid of Trevor, his lover and pal, O'Keefe flees prison and is on his way to wreak revenge. While inside he was visited by Hunt, a social worker; he decides that she would be a good hostage in case the cops close in, so he kidnaps her. The three begin a trip to get Burr and his gang, the men responsible for O'Keefe's stint in prison. It isn't long before O'Keefe begins to fall for Hunt, much to the jealous consternation of Trevor, who has risked her life and her freedom for O'Keefe. Hunt, a heretofore legal and solid citizen, finds this all very exciting, and when O'Keefe has a battle with Ireland, one of the thugs, and loses, O'Keefe pleads with Hunt to save him, which she does by shooting Ireland in the back. Now she's a full part of the underworld. Hunt thinks she is in love with O'Keefe, but he wants her out of this hard life, so he temporarily sends her off while he goes to execute Burr—playing a pyromaniacal part in the best Laird Cregar style. O'Keefe bursts into the hideout as Burr is experimenting with some flames, and Burr shoots O'Keefe. Then the place goes up in a conflagration, and Burr leaps out the window to escape the heat and smoke and falls to his death. As O'Keefe is dying from the gunshot wound, Hunt holds him in her arms, and Trevor watches. A *film noir* picture in the best tradition, with fast-paced direction by Mann and superior photography by Alton. Whit Bissell (still known at the time as "Whitner") does a small role as a hood.

RAZOR'S EDGE, THE
1946 146m bw   ★★★★
Drama/War   /15
FOX

Tyrone Power *(Larry Darrell)*, Gene Tierney *(Isabel Bradley)*, John Payne *(Gray Maturin)*, Anne Baxter *(Sophie Nelson)*, Clifton Webb *(Elliott Templeton)*, Herbert Marshall *(Somerset Maugham)*, Lucile Watson *(Mrs. Louise Bradley)*, Frank Latimore *(Bob MacDonald)*, Elsa Lanchester *(Miss Keith)*, Fritz Kortner *(Kosti)*

p, Darryl F. Zanuck; d, Edmund Goulding; w, Lamar Trotti (based on the novel by W. Somerset Maugham); ph, Arthur Miller; ed, J. Watson Webb; m, Alfred Newman; art d, Richard Day, Nathan Juran; fx, Fred Sersen; chor, Harry Pilcer; cos, Charles LeMaire, Oleg Cassini

Larry Darrell (Tyrone Power) is an idealistic youth, a former WW I pilot whose experiences in battle have caused him to question the moral values and the very fiber of his society. Returning to Chicago, Larry disturbs his high-society fiancee, Isabel (Gene Tierney), with his inexplicable urge to seek out the real meaning of life. He balks at the thought of joining the social *creme de la creme*, and instead embarks on a quest to find intellectual and spiritual freedom, journeying to Paris and Nepal, where he finds an elderly Hindu mystic who brings peace to his troubled mind and spirit. Ten years later, Larry is reunited with Isabel and his

former friends, all of whom have undergone various degrees of suffering—physically, emotionally, and financially. More melodrama and romance than war film, THE RAZOR'S EDGE—based on the classic novel by Somerset Maugham—depicts a generation of people affected by war, by the senselessness of battlefield deaths and war's constant reminders of mortality. The film examines the possible futility of life, including the certain futility of war, and provides an intelligent and thoughtful counterpoint to the many films that celebrate glory in battle.

RE-ANIMATOR
1985 86m c   ★★½
Horror   /18
Re-Animated

Jeffrey Combs *(Herbert West)*, Bruce Abbott *(Dan Cain)*, Barbara Crampton *(Megan Halsey)*, David Gale *(Dr. Carl Hill)*, Robert Sampson *(Dean Halsey)*, Gerry Black *(Mace)*, Carolyn Purdy-Gordon *(Dr. Harrod)*, Peter Kent *(Melvin the Re-Animated)*, Barbara Pieters *(Nurse)*, Ian Patrick Williams *(Swiss Professor)*

p, Brian Yuzna; d, Stuart Gordon; w, Dennis Paoli, William J. Norris, Stuart Gordon (based on the story "Herbert West, The Re-Animator" by H.P. Lovecraft); ph, Mac Ahlberg (DeLuxe Color); ed, Lee Percy; m, Richard Band; art d, Robert Burns; fx, Anthony Doublin, John Naulin; cos, Robin Burton

H.P. Lovecraft, a Rhode Island native and recluse, wrote a large number of short stories, most of which were published only in lurid pulp magazines like *Weird Tales*. He has since been acclaimed as the most important and influential writer of horror and fantasy to appear post-Poe and pre-King. Several attempts to film Lovecraft's eerie tales of monsters and madness have been made, ranging from DIE, MONSTER, DIE to THE DUNWICH HORROR. RE-ANIMATOR is the latest effort to bring Lovecraft to the big screen. While it fails as a faithful adaptation of Lovecraft, it is an incredibly demented movie in its own right that combines a plethora of downright disgusting grand guignol with disturbing black humor. Herbert West (Jeffrey Combs) is an intense young med student determined to make a scientific breakthrough and bring the dead back to life. He works at home on mysterious experiments and finally, using the glowing green fluid he has developed, revivifies a dead cat. The next stop is the med school morgue, where Herbert reanimates a human corpse. Of course, this and every other cadaver he brings to life becomes a bit difficult to subdue. A major-league splatterfest, RE-ANIMATOR has a number of horrifying moments, made even more macabre by the grisly humor evident in almost every unforgettable scene (the most memorable and bizarre being the sex scene with a cadaver's detached head). Perhaps the film's only drawback is the somewhat arch self-consciousness of the performers, who are constantly winking at the viewer as the horrible is defused into the safely ludicrous. Director-coscreenwriter Stuart Gordon again turned his attention to Lovecraft in FROM BEYOND.

REACH FOR THE SKY
1957 123m bw   ★★★
War   /U
Pinnacle (U.K.)

Kenneth More *(Douglas Bader)*, Muriel Pavlow *(Thelma Bader)*, Lyndon Brook *(Johnny Sanderson)*, Lee Patterson *(Stan Turner)*, Alexander Knox *(Mr. Joyce)*, Dorothy Alison *(Nurse Brace)*, Michael Warre *(Harry Day)*, Sydney Tafler *(Robert Desoutter)*, Howard Marion-Crawford *("Woody" Woodhall)*, Jack Watling *(Peel)* p, Daniel M. Angel; d, Lewis Gilbert; w, Lewis Gilbert, Vernon Harris (based on the book *Story of Douglas Bader* by Paul Brickhill); ph, Jack Asher; ed, John Shirley; m, John Addison; art d, Bernard Robinson

Moving account of the true story of a British aviator who, after losing both his legs, rejoins the Royal Air Force and becomes a war hero. More plays the cocky flyer who, through agony and determination, masters a set of artificial limbs and takes to the air again at the outset of WWII. In the midst of the Battle of Britain, he is forced to bail out of a plane and is captured by the Germans. After he makes three escape attempts, his captors imprison him in an impregnable castle. Handled in an effective and subtle manner, with convincing performances all the way around, the picture is a dissertation on the power of individual determination and courage. Tighter editing could have helped to move the story along.

REAL GLORY, THE

1939 95m bw   ★★★½
War   /PG
UA

Gary Cooper *(Dr. Bill Canavan)*, Andrea Leeds *(Linda Hartley)*, David Niven *(Lt. McCool)*, Reginald Owen *(Capt. Steve Hartley)*, Broderick Crawford *(Lt. Swede Larson)*, Kay Johnson *(Mabel Manning)*, Charles Waldron *(Padre Rafael)*, Russell Hicks *(Capt. George Manning)*, Roy Gordon *(Col. Hatch)*, Benny Inocencio *(Miguel)*

p, Samuel Goldwyn; d, Henry Hathaway; w, Jo Swerling, Robert Presnell (based on the novel by Charles L. Clifford); ph, Rudolph Mate; ed, Daniel Mandell; art d, James Basevi; fx, Ray Binger, Paul Eagler; cos, Jeanne Beakhurst

In the Philippines shortly after the US capture of the islands in the Spanish-American war, an uprising of Moslem Moro tribesmen terrorizes the occupying Yanks. Most of the islands are evacuated of Americans, and only a small cadre of Army officers is left to lead Filipino soldiers against the rebels, who attack the soldiers headlong with machetes, seemingly impervious to bullets. (In fact, the resistance of the Moros to the .38-caliber bullets of the Army pistols led to the development of the .45-caliber automatic, a gun designed to stop a man in his tracks.) The commander of the base, Hicks, soon falls victim to one of these attacks, killed in front of his wife. Owen takes command although he is gradually going blind, and forbids physician Cooper to go into the hills with a Moro boy to check out the situation. Cooper goes anyway and sees the rites the Moros perform. He gathers valuable information, but when he returns to the base, he is arrested and locked up. The Moros dam the river that provides the base with water and cholera breaks out. Released to treat the sick, Cooper accompanies Owen, now completely blind, as he leads an attack on the dam, leaving Niven in charge of the fort. This is exactly what the Moros have been waiting for, and they mount a furious assault on the outpost, launching themselves over the wall with catapults made from bent-over trees. The dam is breached with dynamite, and as the water rushes down from the hills, Cooper rides on a log to the fort and helps save the day, heaving sticks of dynamite over the walls at the attackers in one of the bloodiest battles ever staged for the camera.

This exciting film is filled with amazing action scenes highlighting the seeming invincibility of the Moros. Henry Hathaway, who also directed the stirring Cooper vehicle THE LIVES OF A BENGAL LANCER, does a magnificent job here, giving Cooper one of his best action roles. All the performances are good, particularly Cooper's, and David Niven has a terrific death scene after the final battle.

Reportedly the Philippine government objected to the film on the grounds that it portrayed the native soldiers as cowards, though the Filipinos seem no more afraid than the Americans—everyone is afraid of men who don't die when they are shot. The movie year 1939 was one of the best ever, boasting the release of GONE WITH THE WIND, THE WIZARD OF OZ, and STAGECOACH. While THE REAL GLORY isn't in that league, it still holds up well as a classic war-adventure film.

REAL LIFE

1979 99m c   ★★★★★
Comedy   PG
Paramount

Dick Haynes *(Harris)*, Albert Brooks *(Himself)*, Matthew Tobin *(Dr. Howard Hill)*, J.A. Preston *(Dr. Ted Cleary)*, Mort Lindsey *(Himself)*, Joseph Schaffler *(Paul)*, Phyllis Quinn *(Donna)*, James Ritz *(Jack)*, Clifford Einstein, Harold Einstein

p, Penelope Spheeris; d, Albert Brooks; w, Albert Brooks, Monica Johnson, Harry Shearer; ph, Eric Saarinen (Panavision); ed, David Finfer; m, Mort Lindsey; art d, Linda Spheeris, Linda Marder

Comedian-filmmaker Albert Brooks established himself as a major force in American film comedy with this devastating look at how the media has dominated and nearly destroyed family life in the United States. Brooks plays himself, an obnoxious documentary filmmaker who sets out to find a "typical American family" and then film their lives for a year. After exhaustive behavioral testing, two families are still in the running for the honor, each being deemed perfectly "typical." One lives in Wisconsin, the other in Arizona. With clinical scientific precision, Brooks decides which family would be best suited to spend a year with—opting out of winter in Wisconsin. Charles Grodin and Frances Lee McCain, the parents of the chosen Arizona family, are star-struck with their newfound fame, but soon things turn sour. Normal family problems are blown up by filmmaker Brooks into crises of disastrous proportions. McCain's simple trip to her gynecologist becomes an expose on her doctor. Eventually the family members start to come apart at the seams and soon stop talking to each other. Needing an *active* family to film, Brooks desperately tries to manipulate the family members so that they will do *something* in front of the cameras. He decides to bribe the parents and children with gifts and emotional support. Meanwhile, other problems threaten the success of Brooks' project. The psychologists who have been monitoring the project become disgusted with Brooks and dissociate themselves from him. The head of the studio Brooks works for (who attends meetings via a speaker phone) laments that there are no "stars" in the film: "Albert, I have two words for you. . . James Caan." Brooks, pushed to the brink as he watches a year's worth of work going down the drain, begins to crack. The last straw comes when Grodin and McCain decide that to save their marriage they will have to abandon the project. Half-crazed, Brooks decides to pull one last stunt to gain some usable footage—he sets the house on fire. ("What are they gonna do? Put me in movie jail?")

REAL LIFE was obviously inspired by the PBS television documentary "American Family," which followed the lives of the Loud family and led to the couple's divorce. At the time of that program's airing, critics and psychologists debated whether the presence of cameras in the household contributed to the collapse of the family, and whether the documentary merely *recorded* the events, or, in fact, *caused* them. Brooks borrowed the basic premise and took it one step further by having a

Hollywood lunatic in charge of the project. Not only is REAL LIFE a pointed and insightful look at the influence of media on our lives, it is also one of the most hysterical looks at filmmaking ever put on screen. Dozens of bits regarding the shooting of Brooks's film hit home. His cameramen wear diving-bell-type head gear containing cameras and microphones, which transforms the men into bug-eyed robots whose faces no one ever sees. At the beginning of the film, Brooks introduces Grodin's family to nearly 20 members of the film crew (makeup, lighting, grip, Teamsters), all of whom are unnecessary due to advanced technology: "But the union says we have to pay these people anyway, so have a nice vacation. See you guys at the premiere!" With REAL LIFE, Brooks pushed his way into the forefront of American comedy and his two subsequent films, MODERN ROMANCE and LOST IN AMERICA, are both just as insightful and funny as his first.

REAR WINDOW

1954 112m c ★★★★★
Thriller /PG
Paramount

James Stewart (L.B. "Jeff" Jeffries), Grace Kelly (Lisa Carol Fremont), Wendell Corey (Detective Thomas J. Doyle), Thelma Ritter (Stella), Raymond Burr (Lars Thorwald), Judith Evelyn (Miss Lonely Hearts), Ross Bagdasarian (Songwriter), Georgine Darcy (Miss Torso), Sara Berner (Woman on Fire Escape), Frank Cady (Fire Escape Man)

p, Alfred Hitchcock; d, Alfred Hitchcock; w, John Michael Hayes (based on the story "It Had to Be Murder" by Cornell Woolrich); ph, Robert Burks (Technicolor); ed, George Tomasini; m, Franz Waxman; art d, Hal Pereira, Joseph MacMillan Johnson; fx, John P. Fulton; cos, Edith Head

This much-loved Hitchcock picture, based on the Cornell Woolrich story "It Had to Be Murder," is a superb example of suspense filmmaking, especially when one considers the technical limitations of its single set. Magazine photographer Stewart has a broken leg and is confined to a wheelchair in his Greenwich Village apartment, where he has nothing to do but passively sit back and watch the mundane day-to-day activities that take place in the courtyard outside his rear apartment window. His neighbors are conspicuously unconscious of their own vulnerability to Stewart's constant gaze. He watches housewives, newlyweds (the only persons who actually draw the shades on *their* rear windows), a composer in a posh apartment, a lonely woman he dubs Miss Lonely Hearts, a Broadway ballerina, and, of particular interest, Lars Thorwald (Burr). After playing the voyeur for some time, Stewart begins to suspect that Thorwald has murdered his wife. Since Stewart is immobile, he enlists the aid of Kelly, a cool, blonde fashion model (here at her loveliest and most beguiling) who, because she is desperately in love with him, agrees to do his dangerous "legwork".

This, of all Hitchcock films, is an exercise in voyeurism, in which the audience has no choice but to assume the role of voyeur. It's like being Hitchcock for 112 minutes. "Look out the window, see things you shouldn't see," says Stewart's nurse Ritter, and look out the window the viewer does, having the same single and mounting terrifying perspective as does Stewart. One of the film's early ad campaigns read, "If you do not experience delicious terror when you see REAR WINDOW, then pinch yourself—you are most probably dead."

REBECCA

1940 130m bw ★★★★
Thriller /PG
Selznick

Laurence Olivier (Maxim de Winter), Joan Fontaine (Mrs. de Winter), George Sanders (Jack Favell), Judith Anderson (Mrs. Danvers), Nigel Bruce (Maj. Giles Lacy), C. Aubrey Smith (Col. Julyan), Reginald Denny (Frank Crawley), Gladys Cooper (Beatrice Lacy), Philip Winter (Robert), Edward Fielding (Frith)

p, David O. Selznick; d, Alfred Hitchcock; w, Robert E. Sherwood, Joan Harrison (based on the novel by Daphne du Maurier, adapted by Philip MacDonald, Michael Hogan); ph, George Barnes; ed, James Newcom, Hal C. Kern; m, Franz Waxman; art d, Lyle Wheeler

A landmark: Hitchcock's Oscar, his first Hollywood film and his second Daphne du Maurier adaptation in a row (JAMAICA INN preceded). REBECCA is women's gothic melo-romance, but Hitchcock makes it a film about his distrust and dislike for women. He must have enjoyed a private chuckle over the women he knew would flood theaters to see it.

Fontaine stars as the unnamed narrator and shy, young, second wife of the urbane and handsome Maxim de Winter (Olivier). They meet and fall in love while vacationing on the Riviera. Following their quick marriage, they return to Maxim's vast English estate, Manderley. His wife is introduced to an army of servants who immediately, though subtly, display hostility toward her, as they all adored Rebecca, Maxim's first wife, whose death is shrouded in secrecy. As the servants become more hostile, the second wife grows more fearful, until she finally learns what happened to Rebecca. REBECCA was a prestige project for producer David O. Selznick, who was still coming down off the high of GONE WITH THE WIND. As with that 1939 classic, Selznick surrounded REBECCA with publicity including a massive talent hunt for this film's leads. Loretta Young, Margaret Sullavan, Olivia de Havilland, Vivien Leigh (Olivier's intended bride and GONE WITH THE WIND star), and Anne Baxter were all mentioned, but it was the 22-year-old Fontaine who was ultimately selected for the part.

Depending on your own feelings, you will find Fontaine either endearing or totally maddening. Whichever, she's right in the part; and Hitchcock's relentless camera seems to luxuriate in her emotional masochism. Olivier seems oddly out of command here—perhaps he and Welles should have switched off acting chores on REBECCA and JANE EYRE. The supporting roles are rendered quite well indeed. Anderson, Sanders, and Florence Bates all reveled in nasty roles; they look delighted sharpening their talons on Fontaine's little brown wren.

REBEL WITHOUT A CAUSE

1955 111m c ★★★★½
Drama /PG
WB

James Dean (Jim), Natalie Wood (Judy), Sal Mineo (Plato), Jim Backus (Jim's Father), Ann Doran (Jim's Mother), Corey Allen (Buzz), William Hopper (Judy's Father), Rochelle Hudson (Judy's Mother), Virginia Brissac (Jim's Grandma), Nick Adams (Moose)

p, David Weisbart; d, Nicholas Ray; w, Stewart Stern (based on Irving Shulman's adaptation of "The Blind Run", a story by Dr. Robert M. Lindner); ph, Ernest Haller (CinemaScope, Warner Color); ed, William Ziegler; m, Leonard Rosenman; prod d, William Wallace; art d, Malcolm Bert; cos, Moss Mabry

In this pensive, powerful study of juvenile violence, Dean gives a riveting performance as a teenager groping for identity and love from parents, peers, and an adult society he believes to be alien and oppressive. This is the film that forever linked Dean to the issue of the restless 1950s generation; it's the best of the school. Dean is a troublemaker who has caused his parents to move from one town to another before settling in Los Angeles. The boy is soon picked up by police for being drunk and disorderly. A patient cop, Edward Platt, learns from him that he is smothered at home by superficial love from his parents, Backus and Doran, but that neither ever listens to him or gives him advice. Moreover, he resents his mother because she so thoroughly dominates his weak-willed father. While Dean is waiting at the police station for his parents, who must break off a dinner date at their swanky country club to bail him out, he notices Wood, a lonely girl who has been picked up for walking the streets after curfew, and Mineo, a disturbed rich kid whose family is always traveling and who has been brought in for killing a litter of puppies. Upon entering his new high school for the first time the next day, Dean spots Wood and asks her for a date. She rejects him flatly as she gets into a car driven by her hot-rodding, leather-jacketed boy friend, Allen. Allen is surrounded by a group of followers, all sporting the zippered, black-leather jackets of the day. The gang makes fun of Dean and speeds off. Later, when the class attends a lecture at the planetarium, Allen confronts Dean, picking a fight. Knives are drawn and Dean bests Allen, but the fight isn't over. Dean accepts Allen's challenge of a "chickie run," in which both boys are to drive beat-up cars at breakneck speed to the edge of a coastal cliff, diving out before their cars carry them over the edge to certain death. Whoever jumps from the car first is, of course, a chicken, a coward not worthy of recognition by the group or a share in its activities.

The nothing much plot is somehow made forceful and compelling in this directorial gem. Director Ray, always a perfectionist, spent endless hours researching hundreds of teenage police cases before filming. He shot the CinemaScope movie in black and white for a few weeks during preproduction to get the mood and feeling for the muted color patterns he would later use in the final color print. Transcending what might have been merely a teenage exploitation film, REBEL draws heavily upon the presence of the intense and fascinating Dean. The young actor's appearance here electrified audiences, especially teenagers who went on to identify with this powerful symbol of their alienated generation. There is much of Marlon Brando's character from THE WILD ONE (1953) in Dean's supercharged performance. Critics accused Dean of mimicking Brando's early brooding, mumbling delivery, but Dean was later recognized as an actor of singular stature, particularly after completing EAST OF EDEN and GIANT. Wood and Mineo, although fine in their roles, serve mainly as dramatic foils for Dean's brooding exploration of self. What has now become a cult picture was originally genuinely disturbing to adults. They saw it as promoting violence, indicting parents for spoiling their children, and dwelling on madness, the morose, and death. With this picture the clean-cut juvenile ideal of the past moved into the adult world of film noir. Dean did not anticipate a cycle of youth films; he began it—although much of what followed in the next decade, with the exception of THE BLACKBOARD JUNGLE, was of questionable merit at best. When Ray first suggested this film to Warner Bros., executives enthusiastically supported the idea but proposed as stars, of all people, Tab Hunter and Jayne Mansfield (it would have been a classic, but another kind). Ray rejected this recommendation and refused to make the film without Dean and Wood. After a struggle, he got them. He had been particularly impressed by Dean's performance in EAST OF EDEN, and drove Dean mercilessly to produce the scenes he wanted.

The tragedy of the film was relived in real life. All three of the principals met sad, premature fates. Mineo was murdered in West Hollywood. He had spent money crazily on clothes, fast cars, and even a $250,000 estate for his parents in Long Island, New York. In his impressive home in Hollywood, Mineo gave one expensive party after another and became one of the stars of a chic gay set. On the eve of the Academy Awards, he was so convinced that he would win an Oscar for his role in REBEL that he gave an enormous and costly party at which a huge banner was strung across the facade of his home that read: "Congratulations, Sal!" He did not win, and the banner was yanked down and burned before dawn the next day. When Mineo was murdered, returning to his apartment in West Hollywood from a play rehearsal, little was left of his fortune. His formerly expensive apartment had few furnishings, Mineo having sold most of his possessions. On the wall, however, in an expensive frame, was a prized possession he could not part with in life. It was a poster advertising REBEL WITHOUT A CAUSE that was captioned ironically: "Teenage terror torn from today's headlines."

Wood drowned in a still-mysterious accident while boating off Catalina Island with her husband, Robert Wagner, and Christopher Walken. Dean himself was killed just as his career began to expand toward greatness. He died much the same way Allen did in REBEL WITHOUT A CAUSE, speeding at more than 100 mph in a racing car on a public highway in California. Besides killing himself, he seriously injured two other people. Only two hours before his death, Dean was stopped by a traffic cop and given a ticket for driving 75 mph in a 45 mph zone. He took the ticket with a smirk and remarked flippantly, "So what?" before gunning his sports car down the road toward doom. REBEL WITHOUT A CAUSE is still a powerful film today, but its indictment of parents seems a little anachronistic.

RED BADGE OF COURAGE, THE

1951 69m bw ★★★★★
War/Western /U
MGM

Audie Murphy *(Henry Fleming the Youth)*, Bill Mauldin *(Tom Wilson the Loud Soldier)*, Douglas Dick *(Lieutenant)*, Royal Dano *(Tattered Man)*, John Dierkes *(Jim Conlin the Tall Soldier)*, Arthur Hunnicutt *(Bill Porter)*, Andy Devine *(Fat Soldier)*, Robert Easton *(Thompson)*, Smith Ballew *(Captain)*, Glenn Strange *(Colonel)*

p, Gottfried Reinhardt; d, John Huston; w, John Huston, Albert Band (based on the novel by Stephen Crane, adapted by Band); ph, Harold Rosson; ed, Ben Lewis; m, Bronislau Kaper; art d, Cedric Gibbons, Hans Peters

John Huston always insisted that this Civil War battle picture examining the fine line between cowardice and bravery, "could have been" his greatest film, and certainly it is among the director's best, despite the tampering of studio executives. Audie Murphy, the most decorated hero of WWII, *is* Henry Fleming, a youth who joins the Union army and grows restless waiting for the orders that will take him into battle. When news finally comes that his unit is to join others for an impending battle, he turns braggart. But faced with the enemy, Murphy runs in terror, only to confront his fear later and return to his unit for another battle. Huston's direction is vivid in every scene; the film's battle sequences, however, are its most impressive element. In more pensive moments, THE RED BADGE OF COURAGE is a moving study of Americans fighting Americans, and the reluctance many of them bring to this awful task. Much of the credit for the overall visual effect of the film goes to cameraman Harold Rosson, who lends it a gritty, hardscrabble feel, marvelously capturing the period. Huston left the production immediately after its completion to fly across the world to make THE AFRICAN QUEEN, leaving his film in the hands of studio chiefs who cut it as they saw fit. They removed much of the director's questioning of the necessity for warfare (unacceptable during the Cold War), adding narration by James Whitmore and reducing the running time to a scant 69 minutes. Because the film didn't play well with premiere audiences, MGM sent it out without fanfare, offering it as a second feature on double bills— hardly a way to recoup production costs. Audiences failed to identify with the film's grim realism and its mostly unknown cast, and the classic Crane story wasn't enough of a draw to insure box-office success. Huston maintained that the movie as he filmed it was one of his favorites, and in the 1970s an attempt was made to revive the uncut version. To Huston's knowledge, however, a print of his original cut no longer existed, so the idea was dropped.

RED DESERT
(IL DESERTO ROSSO)

1964 116m c   ★★★★★
Drama   /X
Film Duemila/Federiz/Francoriz   (France/Italy)

Monica Vitti *(Giuliana)*, Richard Harris *(Corrado Zeller)*, Carlo Chionetti *(Ugo)*, Xenia Valderi *(Linda)*, Rita Renoir *(Emilia)*, Aldo Grotti *(Max)*, Valerio Baroleschi *(Valerio)*, Giuliano Missirini *(Workman)*, Lili Rheims *(Workman's Wife)*, Emanuela Paola Carboni *(Girl in Fable)*

p, Antonio Cervi; d, Michelangelo Antonioni; w, Michelangelo Antonioni, Tonino Guerra; ph, Carlo Di Palma (Eastmancolor); ed, Eraldo Da Roma; m, Giovanni Fusco, Vittorio Gelmetti; art d, Piero Poletto; fx, Franco Freda; cos, Gitt Magrini

A masterpiece of color cinematography, RED DESERT uses its carefully rendered color scheme to heighten the emotional impact of Michelangelo Antonioni's portrayal of the alienating effect of the modern world on one woman. Giuliana (an atypically brunette Monica Vitti in a marvelous performance) lives in the northern Italian town of Ravenna with her husband, Ugo (Carlo Chionetti), a factory engineer who fails to appreciate the depth of her despair, and with her young son, Valerio (Valerio Bartoleschi), upon whom she dotes. The city's grim industrial landscape weighs heavily on Giuliana. Corrado (Richard Harris), who has come to recruit workers for a South American project, is attracted to her and understands her depression, realizing that the auto accident ostensibly responsible for her malaise was really a suicide attempt. Giuliana's struggle to come to terms with her environment is not easily resolved. As the film ends and her son asks her why birds don't fly through the poisonous yellow smoke of factory, she is able to tell him it's "because they have learned to fly around it," illustrating the separate peace she must make with technology.

An extremely disturbing film, RED DESERT captures a rare beauty that extends the boundaries of film art in its use of color and setting. In attempting to depict Giuliana's perception of the destructive influence of technology on the natural environment, Antonioni went so far as to enhance the bleakness of his industrial wasteland by literally painting the marshlands gray, and Giuliana's sense of isolation is further reenforced by a frightening electronic soundtrack. Not an easy film to watch because of its very deliberate pacing, but well worth the effort.

RED RIVER

1948 125m bw   ★★★★★
Western   /U
UA

John Wayne *(Tom Dunson)*, Montgomery Clift *(Matthew Garth)*, Joanne Dru *(Tess Millay)*, Walter Brennan *(Groot Nadine)*, Coleen Gray *(Fen)*, John Ireland *(Cherry Valance)*, Noah Beery, Jr. *(Buster McGee)*, Harry Carey *(Mr. Millville)*, Harry Carey, Jr. *(Dan Latimer)*, Paul Fix *(Teeler Yacy)*

p, Howard Hawks; d, Howard Hawks; w, Borden Chase, Charles Schnee (based on the novel *The Chisholm Trail* by Borden Chase); ph, Russell Harlan; ed, Christian Nyby; m, Dimitri Tiomkin; art d, John Datu Arensma; fx, Don Steward

There have been many classic westerns but this Hawks masterpiece certainly ranks among the best of the genre. It's probably the best of all the 1940s westerns—an unforgettable sweeping spectacle with the kind of grandeur few westerns achieved.

Wayne is shown as a young, determined man at the opening of RED RIVER, taking his wagon out of the line of a train heading west. He and his companion, Brennan, intend to head south, toward Texas and the Red River. The youthful, pretty Gray, Wayne's sweetheart, tries to persuade him to go west with her, but he is adamant. He gives her a snake bracelet, kisses her, and tells her that he will send for her when he is settled. Hours later, Wayne and Brennan turn around to see in the far distance black smoke curling skyward, and they know that Indians have attacked the wagon train. Brennan suggests that they turn back, but Wayne tells him it's useless. Later that night, a band of Indians attacks Wayne and Brennan. The two men defeat the Indians, and Wayne finds the snake bracelet on the body of one of the attackers and knows Gray was killed.

The next day, they find a survivor from the wagon train massacre, young Micky Kuhn, and decide to take him along with them on their journey to Texas. They continue south and cross the Red River to find sweeping horizonless plains rich with grazing. Wayne unties his bull and Kuhn's cow and lets them free. "They'll get away," Kuhn says. "Wherever they go they'll be on my land," Wayne says, declaring his ranch to be as far as the eye can see and beyond. At that moment, two Mexican wranglers approach on horseback and warn Wayne that he is on land owned by a wealthy Mexican. Wayne kills one of the men and then tells the other to return to his boss and let him know the land has a new owner. Wayne then kneels in the dirt and draws his Red River brand, two lines to indicate the river and a large D to indicate his last name, Dunson. Kuhn notes that since he's contributed his cow to the ranch his name should be included in the brand. Wayne tells him it will be added when he earns it.

Years pass, and Wayne owns a sprawling cattle empire. He has more cattle than anyone in Texas, and his ranch is so wide and deep that it takes his many cowhands weeks to cross it. The boy he brought along to Texas is now grown (played by Clift). He has returned from the Civil War and is Wayne's righthand man. The cattle baron is white-haired but still as tough as ever. In need of cash, Wayne decides to drive a herd of cattle north and sell them. He rounds up thousands of steers and then pushes the entire herd northward. Along on the drive are Clift, his newfound friend and fellow gunman Ireland, and Brennan driving the chuck wagon. The herd heads north, Wayne uncertain where he might be able to reach the railhead, but intending to follow the old trail to Missouri. Ireland tells him there's a shorter route, to Kansas, where the railhead has already extended its line, but Wayne refuses to alter his plan and the drive pushes on through sandstorms and rainstorms, heading for Missouri. But the trek is long and hard, and food grows short. The men grumble and grow to dislike Wayne, who shows them no mercy when it comes to work, driving them relentlessly. Three of the men finally have a showdown with Wayne, telling him they are quitting. They reach for their guns, but Wayne, with Brennan and Clift's help, shoots them down. Ireland then tells Clift that by taking the Chisholm Trail, they could shortcut the disastrous Missouri trip and take the herd to Kansas, but Clift isn't quite ready to confront Wayne. That changes when three of the best men desert, and Ireland tracks two of them down. Wayne announces that he is going to hang the men for desertion, and Clift finally can take no more of Wayne's madness. Clift tells Wayne he can't hang the men and Wayne goes for his gun, but Ireland shoots it out of his hand. It is apparent that all have lined up against Wayne, even Brennan, who tells his old friend that he is clearly in the wrong. The next day Clift leaves the wounded Wayne a horse and supplies and tells him *he's* taking the herd to Kansas. Wayne's only response is to tell Clift that he will hunt him down and kill him.

Hawks fills every frame of this movie with action and drama. Around the sturdy plot, Hawks constructs his characters so that there is no doubt in the mind of any viewer as to how they will react, except at the end where the director saved both characters. (In the original story by Chase, Dunson is mortally wounded in the fight and taken back by wagon to Texas so that he can die on the other side of the Red River and be buried in the empire he created. The author was always resentful of Hawks for changing that ending.) Wayne gives a terrific performance, certainly one of the best of his career. Clift, too, given the opportunity to make his first major film here, is a perfect counterpoint to Wayne's ruthlessness in his gentle but determined manner. Brennan is fine in a definitive role. It was Hawks who insisted that Brennan remove his false teeth for the running gag with Chief Yowlachie. At first the 42-year-old balked at the idea, but he quickly remembered that it was Hawks who had expanded his role in COME AND GET IT, which earned Brennan an Oscar for Best Supporting Actor. He played mostly without his teeth and was excellent. All of the supporting players, especially Ireland, Beery, the Careys, and Fix, are memorable. Harlan's photography is stunning, sweeping through the horizonless plains and covering the vast territory the cowboys must travel in their odyssey: storms, rivers, canyons, distant buttes all encompassed beautifully. Matching the elegance of the cinematography is Tiomkin's stirring score.

At this point in his career, Hawks was already an established master of the directorial craft, highly regarded for his versatility. His work had included comedies (HIS GIRL FRIDAY), war films (AIR FORCE), and mysteries (THE BIG SLEEP), all classics. This was his first western, and he quickly exhibited his mastery of that genre as well. It was promoted with the majestic claim: "THE COVERED WAGON, CIMARRON, and now RED RIVER." The film deserved such company. It was just as great as the best of the genre that had gone before. RED RIVER, which would gross almost $5 million in its initial release, was seen by the public and critics alike as a classic, and it remains so today.

RED SHOES, THE

1948   133m   c   ★★★★★
Dance   /U
Archers   (U.K.)

Anton Walbrook *(Boris Lermontov)*, Moira Shearer *(Victoria Page)*, Marius Goring *(Julian Craster)*, Leonide Massine *(Grischa Ljubov)*, Robert Helpmann *(Ivan Boleslawsky)*, Albert Basserman *(Sergei Ratov)*, Esmond Knight *(Livy)*, Ludmilla Tcherina *(Irina Boronskaja)*, Jean Short *(Terry)*, Gordon Littman *(Ike)*

p, Michael Powell, Emeric Pressburger; d, Michael Powell, Emeric Pressburger; w, Michael Powell, Emeric Pressburger, Keith Winter; ph, Jack Cardiff (Technicolor); ed, Reginald Mills; m, Brian Easdale; art d, Hein Heckroth, Arthur Lawson; chor, Robert Helpmann; cos, Hein Heckroth

Magical. Although THE RED SHOES is the ultimate ballet film, you don't have to be a balletomane to enjoy this backstage love story distinguished by glorious dancing, superb acting, and masterful direction. After the successful staging of a new ballet, impresario Boris Lermontov (Walbrook, obviously modeled on Serge Diaghilev) admits two new members to his company: Victoria Page (Shearer), a gifted young ballerina, and Julian Craster (Goring) an equally talented composer. After Julian acquits himself well as an arranger, Boris gives him a chance to collaborate on a new ballet, "The Red Shoes," with Victoria. A breathtaking 20-minute ballet based on Hans Christian Anderson's story about a pair of magical shoes that permit their wearer to dance gloriously but tragically prevent her from stopping, it brings great acclaim to both Julian and Victoria, who have fallen in love. When Julian leaves the company, Victoria follows, marrying him over the objections of the jealous Boris, who avers that she is ruining her brilliant future. Owning the rights to "The Red Shoes," Boris prevents her from dancing her greatest role until, much later, he gives her one more opportunity to perform in Monaco. Doing so, however, means she will miss the premiere of Julian's new work. The three principals confront one another just before the performance as the film builds to its memorable climax.

THE RED SHOES began as a Pressburger script commissioned by producer Alexander Korda for wife Merle Oberon, whose dancing was to have been done by a double. (We sometimes like La minx Merle, the Eurasian faux pearl, but here?!) Pressburger and collaborator Powell then bought the script back from Korda and co-helmed this extraordinary tale of romance and artistic obsession. According to Lermontov, there is hardly the time to be both a ballerina and a loving wife. While some may quibble with this, the film's tension becomes such that you totally understand why dancing or composing becomes the most important thing in the world to those gifted and dedicated enough to do them. The parallels between Victoria's story and that of the ballet are obvious without being too heavy-handed. The ballet, meanwhile, is so engrossing that it flies breathlessly by. Full of audacious lighting, dance modernisms and swirling plastic, it is gloriously unafraid of its own pretensions. The always impassioned but usually more subdued Walbrook does a magnificent job essaying the driven impresario, and the unusual-looking Goring is convincing and compelling as well. Shearer, whose gorgeous red hair is beautifully rendered by Cardiff's opulent Technicolor photography, was a Sadler's Wells ballerina who proved to be a much better actress than anyone had dreamed. This bewitching performer covers the emotional gamut quite skillfully and would ever after be identified with this role. Praise should also go to the other dancers in the cast—Massine, Tcherina, and Helpmann (who also did the choreography). They all perform with great assurance and grace, onstage or off. The film's backstage detail remains intoxicating and when it comes to the more melodramatic aspects of the film, Powell and Pressburger let the naysayers be damned. As visually incredible as all the best Michael Powell, THE RED SHOES deservedly won Oscars for its art direction and scoring and was nominated for Best Screenplay and Picture.

RED SORGHUM
(HONG GAOLIANG)

1988 91m c ★★★★

Drama /15

Xi'an (China)

Gong Li *(Nine, the Grandmother)*, Jiang Weng *(Yu, the Grandfather)*, Jiu Ji *(Their Son)*, Ji Cun Hua *(Sanpao, the Bandit Chief)*, Teng Rujun *(Luohan)*, Cui Cun-Hua

d, Zhang Yimou; w, Chen Jianyu, Zhu Wei, Mu Yan; ph, Gu Changwei; ed, Du Yuan; m, Zhao Jiping; prod d, Yang Gang

RED SORGHUM is a devastating and visually arresting first feature from Zhang Yimou, one of the "Fifth Generation" new wave of Chinese filmmakers, best known in the West as the cinematographer of Chen Kaige's THE BIG PARADE and YELLOW EARTH and as the lead actor in Wu Tianming's OLD WELL. It won the Golden Bear at the Berlin Film Festival and a selection at the New York Film Festival, where it was undeservedly pounced upon by local critics who were too involved with festival politics to see clearly. RED SORGHUM opens in the 1930s, though for the first hour the period could be any time over the last few hundred years. In northwest China—a landscape exotic and desolate to Western eyes—an ocean of red sorghum (a tall, grasslike grain) flows in the gusts and swirls of the wind. An unseen narrator informs us that this story is about his grandparents. The grandmother (Gong Li) is a pretty 18-year-old whose name means "Nine," called thus because she was the ninth child, born on the ninth day of the ninth month. She is being prepared for an upcoming wedding to Li, a winemaker who lives in seclusion at his distillery and who suffers from leprosy. The bride-to-be, whose peasant father has sold her to the winemaker in exchange for a donkey, is carried by bearers in her bridal sedan chair across the barren landscape, accompanied by a group of musicians. While the party passes through a field of sorghum, they are attacked by a masked bandit. The bandit tries to rape the young woman, but the chair-bearers, led by the strong Jiang Weng, attack him and kill him. Jiang Weng and Gong Li exchange a quiet, romantic glance before the young woman returns to her sedan chair. Before the wedding ceremony is completed, however, two events occur: Gong Li and Jiang Weng make love deep in the sorghum fields, and later the leprous winemaker is found murdered. The narrator tells us that he believes his grandfather, Jiang Weng, committed the murder. With the leper dead, Gong Li takes charge of the distillery, enlisting the aid of the chair-bearers and musicians. The working atmosphere is one of a pre-Communist cooperative, in which everyone works together and Gong Li, reflecting her peasant origins, treats her men like equals, expecting like treatment in return. Time passes, and the story resumes after nine years: Gong Li and Jiang Weng have married and have a young son (the narrator's father). China is in the midst of a war, and invading Japanese soldiers have recruited the winemakers to trample the sorghum fields in order to make way for a new road. The Chinese are treated savagely by the Japanese and forced to flay alive leaders of the rebellion. When one man, an elderly Chinese butcher, refuses to commit such an atrocity, he is gunned down. Another, the butcher's assistant, submits to the Japanese commander's demands and is later seen laughing maniacally, covered with blood, as he sits in the middle of a sorghum field. Eventually, Gong Li and Jiang Weng organize an attack on the road. After much bloodshed, only Jiang Weng, caked in blood and mud, and his young son are left standing. In the sky above, a solar eclipse turns the sky and the sorghum field a deep red.

Although the visual style of RED SORGHUM is one of resounding natural beauty—wide-screen horizon shots, flowing sorghum fields, heavenly sunsets—and the directorial style invokes myth and legend, the film does incorporate a certain level of realism. Shown in great detail are the distilling of the sorghum, the preparation of a dead animal and an ox-head meal at the butcher's, the trampling of the sorghum fields, and the bloody butchering and flaying of an ox during the Japanese attack—all of which contrast with the sense of fable Zhang Yimou creates. While the film essentially seems a sentimental ballad to the director's grandparents (and, on a larger scale, to the grandparents of his generation), these other elements strike another chord, by which we cannot even be sure if the film really is about Zhang Yimou's family. In one sense, RED SORGHUM is a documentary on the color red—the red of sorghum, of wine, of a bridal robe, of blood, of the Communist victory, of solar eclipses, of camera filters.

Obviously inspired to some extent by Hollywood films, RED SORGHUM is directed with a certain amount of manipulation and a great deal of humor, emphasized through contrast with sadness or violence. At the film's very start, for example, the male bearers transporting the young bride-to-be make her trip as bumpy as possible. They also playfully sing a raucous, vulgar song called "Jolting the Sedan Chair" as they switch the bars from shoulder to shoulder. In the chair, Gong Li looks alternately sick and suicidal. When the men finally stop, they hear her terrible sobbing from inside, realize their mistake, and carry on ceremoniously. Much of the film's humor comes from Jiang Weng, a large, tall man, bare-chested and bald, who recalls some of Toshiro Mifune's clownish antics. Gong Li's character is equally compelling—a powerful, independent woman who drinks and works like a man but who has a coy, girlish sexuality. (It's especially interesting that none of the men [save for Jiang Weng] make any sort of sexual advances toward her, instead treating her with respect and friendship.) Released in a very limited art-house run at the end of 1988, RED SORGHUM is yet another of the great achievements of the new wave in Chinese film—one of the most vital national cinemas in the world today.

REDS

1981 200m c ★★★½

Historical/Biography/War PG/15

Paramount

Warren Beatty *(John Reed)*, Diane Keaton *(Louise Bryant)*, Edward Herrmann *(Max Eastman)*, Jerzy Kosinski *(Grigory Zinoviev)*, Jack Nicholson *(Eugene O'Neill)*, Paul Sorvino *(Louis Fraina)*, Maureen Stapleton *(Emma Goldman)*, Nicolas Coster *(Paul Trullinger)*, M. Emmet Walsh *(Speaker at the Liberal Club)*, Ian Wolfe *(Mr. Partlow)*

p, Warren Beatty; d, Warren Beatty; w, Warren Beatty, Trevor Griffiths; ph, Vittorio Storaro (Technicolor); ed, Dede Allen, Craig McKay; m, Stephen Sondheim, Dave Grusin; prod d, Richard Sylbert; art d, Simon Holland; cos, Shirley Russell

Produced, directed, and cowritten by Warren Beatty, who also stars as radical journalist John Reed, REDS is a sprawling yet highly personal epic. Focusing on Reed's tempestuous relationship with feminist Louise Bryant (Diane Keaton), the $45-million production also encompasses a capsule history of the American Left in the early 20th century and depicts the Russian Revolution, which Reed chronicled in *Ten Days That Shook the World*. Punctuated by the reminiscences of a number of Reed's real-life contemporaries (shot in stark black and white and unidentified, although they include Rebecca West, Henry Miller, and Hamilton Fish) the three-hour-plus marathon shifts the action among a variety of American locales and from the States to the Soviet Union. Among the larger-than-life figures given the personal treatment are Louise's one-time lover Eugene O'Neill (Jack Nicholson), Emma Goldman (magnificently portrayed by Maureen Stapleton, who won a Best Supporting Actress Oscar for her work), Communist party chief Grigory Zinoviev (novelist Jerzy Kosinski), and Max Eastman (Edward Herrmann). Beatty, who won the Academy Award for Best Director and was nominated as Best Actor, has created a film of DOCTOR ZHIVAGO-like scope and majesty, yet REDS succeeds best in its smallest moments, focusing on the interaction among its carefully drawn characters. Keaton fails to bring the necessary depth to her portrayal and relies too much on her familiar, quirky film persona; but Beatty gives a highly nuanced, appropriately energized performance, and the supporting players are uniformly excellent. The film's chief attribute, however, is also one of its major flaws. In presenting an up-close, personal look at the lives of its famous figures—particularly Reed and Bryant in their love affair and marriage—the film sometimes gives short shrift to the world-shaking events that are its unique subject. Nonetheless, the brilliantly designed and photographed REDS is a beautiful, passionate film, both in its stunningly recreated action scenes and its quietest moments.

REGARDING HENRY

1991 107m c ★★
Drama
Scott Rudin Productions/Paramount PG-13/12

Harrison Ford *(Henry Turner)*, Annette Bening *(Sarah Turner)*, R.M. Haley *(Court Clerk)*, Stanley H. Swerdlow *(Mr. Matthews)*, Julie Follansbee *(Mrs. Matthews)*, Rebecca Miller *(Linda)*, Bruce Altman *(Bruce)*, Elizabeth Wilson *(Jessica)*, Donald Moffat *(Charlie)*, Mikki Allen *(Rachel)*

p, Scott Rudin, Mike Nichols; d, Mike Nichols; w, Jeffrey Abrams; ph, Giuseppe Rotunno; ed, Sam O'Steen; m, Hans Zimmer; prod d, Tony Walton; art d, Dan Davis, William Elliott; cos, Ann Roth

Directed with embarrassing ineptness by Mike Nichols, REGARDING HENRY concerns a ruthless coporate lawyer's rehabilitation and redemption. There's much amiss here, with a long catalog of artless, contrived situations and implausible behavior that make this film a tough act to swallow.

You could swear you're in the wrong movie. As the camera pans the richly panelled courtroom, you hear Harrison Ford before you see him, declaiming with deadpan monotony on justice just as he did in PRESUMED INNOCENT. Deja vu? But wait! You notice slight differences. A sleek Armani suit. Dark, slicked-back hair. Perhaps a tinge of smugness as Harrison ever so adroitly convinces a jury the plaintiff is in the wrong. No, it's not Rusty Sabich; it's Henry Turner, counsel for the defense, and as slippery a character as you could hope to meet.

The apotheosis of 80s greed in New York's fast lane, Henry cheats on his beautiful wife Sarah (Annette Bening), bullies his adorable, precocious pre-teen daughter Rachel (Mikki Allen), and treats his underlings—secretary, doorman, maid—like dirt. Late one night, in a quest for cigarettes, Henry leaves his swank Fifth Avenue apartment and interrupts a robbery in progress at his local deli, miraculously surviving gunshot wounds to his head and shoulder. As a result, he loses his motor skills and memory, becoming a Hollywood innocent in the style of Dustin Hoffman in RAINMAN or Robert De Niro in AWAKENINGS.

Back home after intensive therapy, Henry walks around with a permanent gee-whiz expression on his face, hugging his door-

man, speaking gently to his maid, liking everything he had formerly claimed to detest. All of this endears him to his family, who treat him like a new-found puppy. (At one point, he even brings home a puppy for his daughter—something she'd always wanted and he'd always denied her.) Henry's appearance changes, too. His hair is lightened and parted down the middle like a hayseed's, and he takes to wearing baggy pants and floppy sweaters. Utterly childish, he becomes his daughter's perfect playmate. In one scene in a library, Henry tosses balled-up wads of paper at Rachel while she tries to study; seems he's bored.

In one particularly precious, overlong interval, Henry plods his way phonetically through a Dr. Seuss primer with Rachel's help. After painfully deciphering the word "mother," he prances about with fatuous glee exclaiming "I can read! I can read!" then proceeds to read everything in sight—including a nearby can of Ajax. Sarah returns home, and all three hug, kiss and literally jump for joy in an ecstatic frenzy.

In an even less convincing turn of events, Henry is welcomed back into the fold of his high-powered law firm—even after he haltingly says, in an awkward after-dinner speech, that he can't remember any of them. He then proceeds to pore through the records of his old cases, coming to the conclusion he's been a liar, a cheat, and has dishonestly withheld evidence—not bad for a guy who's just learned the word "mother."

As 24-year-old screenwriter Jeffrey Abrams would have us believe, a mugger's bullet transforms Henry from the Gordon Gekko of the legal profession to a 90s flower child. Unfortunately, Henry's new-found simple-mindedness is matched by that of the script and direction. Though the talents of Ford and Bening are wasted in this patronizing attempt at a contemporary parable, there are a couple of bright spots. Bill Nunn, as Henry's physical therapist Bradley, and Mikki Allen, as Henry's emotionally deprived daughter, both manage to bring some life and substance to their roles. Without them, Henry would be almost completely disregardable.

REMARKABLE MR. KIPPS

1942 86m bw ★★
Comedy /U
FOX (U.K.)

Philip Frost *(Arthur Kipps as a boy)*, Michael Redgrave *(Arthur Kipps)*, Diana Wynyard *(Helen Walshingham)*, Diana Calderwood *(Ann Pornick as a girl)*, Phyllis Calvert *(Ann Pornick as a woman)*, Arthur Riscoe *(Chitterlow)*, Max Adrian *(Chester Coote)*, Helen Haye *(Mrs. Walshingham)*, Michael Wilding *(Ronnie Walshingham)*, Lloyd Pearson *(Shalford)*

p, Edward Black; d, Carol Reed; w, Frank Launder, Sidney Gilliat (based on the novel by H.G. Wells); ph, Arthur Crabtree; ed, R.E. Dearing

A very good cast, an able director (Carol Reed, better known for THE THIRD MAN), a slick production, and an H.G. Wells story should add up to a fairly good movie, but something went wrong in this story about shop clerk Redgrave who remains a virtual nonentity until he becomes the heir to a vast fortune. He is hoodwinked by society girl Wynyard into marrying her, but at the last minute he backs out and runs off with his childhood sweetheart, Calvert. The two marry, but their marriage is marred when Calvert demands a simple existence while Redgrave is still flirting with the rich ways he's acquired. However, Redgrave loses all his money which causes him and Calvert to lead a humble life ever after. The story takes place in a rural English community at the turn of the century which may be the problem with the picture: the characters are all so smug, it's hard to generate any form of feeling for them.

REMBRANDT

1936 84m bw   ★★★★
Biography   /A
London Films   (U.K.)

Charles Laughton (Rembrandt van Rijn), Gertrude Lawrence (Geertje Dirx), Elsa Lanchester (Hendrickje Stoffels), Edward Chapman (Fabrizius), Walter Hudd (Banning Cocq), Roger Livesey (Beggar Saul), John Bryning (Titus van Rijn), Allan Jeayes (Dr. Tulp), John Clements (Gavaert Flink), Raymond Huntley (Ludvig)

p, Alexander Korda; d, Alexander Korda; w, Carl Zuckmayer, Lajos Biro, June Head, Arthur Wimperis; ph, Georges Perinal, Richard Angst; ed, William Hornbeck, Francis D. Lyon; m, Geoffrey Toye; prod d, Vincent Korda; fx, Ned Mann; cos, John Armstrong

This box-office failure wonderfully exposes the creative process of the artist and presents an unromanticized look at one of art's geniuses. The film confines itself to the final 27 years of the Dutchman's life, beginning shortly after the death of Rembrant's first wife, with Rembrandt, played by Charles Laughton, busily at work on "The Night Watch." The men who appear in the famous painting, all of whom have paid a fee for the privilege of sitting for the master, are unhappy with the way they have been painted, but Rembrandt, true to his vision, will not allow them to criticize his work. With his first wife buried, he turns to the female closest to him, Geertje (Gertrude Lawrence), his house-keeper and sometime model, a vulgar woman he might never have noticed were he still happily married. The moment he begins his alliance with Geertje, things go rotten. First, he must sell his regal house and most of his assets in order to satisfy his outstanding bills. Then, when he turns his attentions on the maid, Hendrickje (Elsa Lanchester), Geertje leaves him. Hendrickje is soon pregnant, and they are married after she gives birth. When Hendrickje dies, Rembrandt becomes almost instantly old, a doddering old fool on the brink of total senility. Producer-director Alexander Korda, an art collector, teamed up with his brother in designing a marvelous "look" to the movie, each scene looking as though it were taken from one of Rembrandt's own paintings. Laughton did his research by traveling to Holland, studying the art and whatever biographical material he could lay hands on, then steeped himself in the information and entered into the persona of the painter, offering a superb, complex characterization that must rank among his best, and, perhaps, one of the best biographical roles in film history. Laughton dominated the film in the title role, as he'd done before in the roles of Henry, Nero, Javert, and Bligh. He was in every scene but one, giving such a restrained performance that audiences expecting his thespian fireworks were disappointed. That the movie was not a hit does not detract from the achievements of the Kordas, Laughton, and everyone associated with this tasteful, mostly accurate, and satisfying motion picture.

REMEMBER LAST NIGHT?

1935 81m bw   ★★★★
Comedy/Mystery   /A
Universal

Edward Arnold (Danny Harrison), Constance Cummings (Carlotta Milburn), Sally Eilers (Bette Huling), Robert Young (Tony Milburn), Robert Armstrong (Fred Flannagan), Reginald Denny (Jack Whitridge), Monroe Owsley (Billy Arliss), George Meeker (Vic Huling), Edward Brophy (Maxie), Jack LaRue (Baptiste Bouclier)

p, Carl Laemmle, Jr.; d, James Whale; w, Doris Malloy, Harry Clork, Louise Henry, Dan Totheroh (based on the novel Hangover Murders by Adam Hobhouse); ph, Joseph Valentine; ed, Ted J. Kent

Effervescent comedy/whodunnit about a murder that takes place during a night of heavy drinking by a bunch of wealthy socialites, including Constance Cummings and Robert Young. It actually develops into a string of murders, all dealt with in sublimely light-hearted fashion. Edward Arnold plays a light-hearted detective who enlists the aid of a hypnotist to try and jog the memories of the hungover revellers; naturally enough, the hypnotist is himself dispatched just on the point of disclosure. This is screwball comedy at its finest, with imaginatively outrageous gags, superb character players, and direction that perfectly blends parody and suspense.

REMEMBER THE NIGHT

1940 86m bw   ★★★½
Comedy/Romance   /A
Paramount

Barbara Stanwyck (Lee Leander), Fred MacMurray (John Sargent), Beulah Bondi (Mrs. Sargent), Elizabeth Patterson (Aunt Emma), Willard Robertson (Francis X. O'Leary), Sterling Holloway (Willie), Charles Waldron (Judge, New York), Paul Guilfoyle (District Attorney), Charles Arnt (Tom), John Wray (Hank)

p, Mitchell Leisen; d, Mitchell Leisen; w, Preston Sturges; ph, Ted Tetzlaff; ed, Doane Harrison; m, Frederick Hollander; art d, Hans Dreier, Roland Anderson; cos, Edith Head

You'd have to be a grump not to like this funny, sentimental blend of pathos, drama and zaniness. It may have been former art director Leisen's best directorial effort, mainly due to the superior Sturges script. Sturges had a way with designing a picture so it could get right to the brink of syrup, then pull back with an hysterical comedy sequence. Conversely, just as the humor was about to disintegrate into chaotic slapstick, Sturges would throw a curve that put the story back onto a firm, dramatic footing. Stanwyck is a tough cookie with a shoplifting habit. Christmas is approaching and she decides to give herself a present, a bracelet of diamonds. She's caught by the security people and sent to jail to await trial. She's been in twice before for the same sort of crime and the judge decides to deal with her after the Christmas holidays. MacMurray is to prosecute her in his job as assistant district attorney. He's going home to Indiana for the holiday and when he learns that Stanwyck is also from the same state, he gets her out of jail in his custody. He takes her to her home, but her mother, Georgia Caine, wants nothing to do with her. MacMurray takes her to his home to meet his mother, Bondi, his aunt, Patterson, and their handyman, Holloway. Stanwyck has never been part of such a loving family and is struck by the closeness. She and MacMurray are soon in love but she holds back, fearing that it could never be permanent. She considers fleeing, then changes her mind and returns to New York for the trial. Her defense attorney, Robertson (who usually played the stern judge or vicious no-nonsense prosecutor) makes an impassioned and funny plea on Stanwyck's behalf, but that all goes out the window when she pleads guilty and accepts the brief jail term. It goes without saying that MacMurray will be waiting for her when she is released. It could have been maudlin and dreary in many other hands but Leisen and Sturges have made this a wonderful Yuletide movie that's good watching any time of year. Three songs: "Easy Living" (Ralph Rainger, Leo Robin, sung by

Martha Mears in a nightclub sequence), "Back Home in Indiana" (James F. Hanely, Ballard MacDonald, performed by Mears and the King's Men), and "End of a Perfect Day" (Carrie Jacobs Band, sung by Holloway as Stanwyck plays the piano).

REPENTANCE
(POKAYANIYE)

1987 150m c	★★★★
Fantasy/Political	PG
Gruziafilm (U.S.S.R.)	

Avtandil Makharadze *(Varlam Aravidze/Abel Aravidze)*, Iya Ninidze *(Guliko, Varlam's Daughter-in-law)*, Merab Ninidze *(Tornike, Varlam's Grandson)*, Zeinab Botsvadze *(Katevan Barateli, Sandro's Daughter)*, Ketevan Abuladze *(Nino Baratelli, Sandro's Wife)*, Edisher Giorgobiani *(Sandro Baratelli, Painter)*, Kakhi Kavsadze *(Mikhail Korisheli)*, Nino Zakariadze *(Elena Korisheli)*, Nato Otijigava *(Ketevan as a Child)*, Dato Kemkhadze *(Abel as a Child)*

d, Tengiz Abuladze; w, Nana Djanelidze, Tengiz Abuladze, Rezo Kveselava; ph, Mikhail Agranovich (Orwo Color); ed, Guliko Omadze; m, Nana Djanelidze; prod d, Georgi Mikeladze

Written in 1981 and okayed under the Brezhnev administration by Eduard Shevardnadze, REPENTANCE was filmed in Soviet Georgia, the homeland of Stalin, as a television project. It was shelved from 1984 until 1987, when, under Gorbachev, the Union of Cinematographers liberated it from state censorship. Before 1987 came to a close, REPENTANCE had won a Special Jury Prize at the Cannes Film Festival and was named as the Soviet Union's official entry in the Academy Awards' Foreign-Language Film category. As the film opens, Ketevan Barateli (Zejnab Botsvadze), a cake decorator, learns of the death of the aged Varlam Aravidze (brilliantly played by Avtandil Makharadze, who also plays the deceased man's son), a highly revered Georgian mayor whose physical appearance and personality is a composite of Stalin, Mussolini, Hitler, and Lavrenti Beria, Stalin's chief of secret police. Later that evening, after the dignitary's funeral, the freshly buried corpse keeps reappearing in his family's garden, despite all attempts at reinterment. The grave robber turns out to be the cake decorator, who is apprehended and tried. As she explains her actions to the court, the film flashes back to the Stalinist era, and a terrible history for which the living are still culpable is laid bare. A powerful, intelligent, and visually poetic picture, REPENTANCE condemns not only Stalinism but those who try to bury it. The film is also a plea for religious freedom, filled with religious iconography. Many of its dreamy images (such as that of the painter and his wife buried, except for the faces, under a pile of rocks while the mayor sings an aria) are unforgettable, although Abuladze's use of them sometimes becomes too generous. Still, REPENTANCE stands as one of the finest films to be released as a result of *glasnost*.

REPO MAN

1984 92m c	★★★½
Science Fiction/Comedy	R/18
Edge City	

Harry Dean Stanton *(Bud)*, Emilio Estevez *(Otto)*, Tracey Walter *(Miller)*, Olivia Barash *(Leila)*, Sy Richardson *(Lite)*, Susan Barnes *(Agent Rogers)*, Fox Harris *(J. Frank Parnell)*, Tom Finnegan *(Oly)*, Del Zamora *(Lagarto)*, Eddie Velez *(Napo)*

p, Jonathan Wacks, Peter McCarthy; d, Alex Cox; w, Alex Cox; ph, Robby Muller (Deluxe Color); ed, Dennis Dolan; m, Tito Larriva, Steven Hufsteter; art d, J. Rae Fox, Lynda Burbank; fx, Robby Knott, Roger George; cos, Theda Deramus

The youth cult film of 1984, REPO MAN marked the auspicious debut of writer-director Alex Cox, born in Britain and educated as a lawyer at Oxford before relocating to Los Angeles to study at UCLA Film School on a Fulbright scholarship.

Otto (Emilio Estevez) is a disaffected youth in Los Angeles who loses his supermarket stock boy job as the film opens. He spends the night wandering through the punk underground before he encounters Bud (Harry Dean Stanton), who tells him that his wife left her car in a bad neighborhood and offers Otto $25 to drive it out for him. Otto accepts but is indignant when he learns that Bud lied to him and that he has just helped repossess a car. Later, however, he listens to offers of big money and sets off to learn the trade under Bud's tutelage. Meanwhile, a nuclear physicist (Fox Harris), who has had himself lobotomized to stop guilt feelings about his work on the neutron bomb, has stolen something dangerous and glowing and put it in the trunk of his 1964 Chevy Malibu. Variously it is a nuclear device of some sort or the decomposing body of an alien with spectacular powers. Several government agencies are after the car and offer a $20,000 reward for whoever finds it, a prize that makes it the most sought-after car in the city.

REPO MAN looks at the neon-lit, horizontal sprawl of Los Angeles in a way that no one had before, and a great deal of credit for the film's distinctive look goes to German cinematographer Robby Muller, who'd already distinguished himself via numerous collaborations with Wim Wenders. Cox's familiarity with the punk milieu is impressive, and he would continue in this vein for his follow-up, SID AND NANCY. The performances vary wildly in their quality, with Stanton and Estevez taking top honors and most of the other characters little more than cartoons. Still, REPO MAN is one of the most original films of recent memory, with an edge of black humor and punk sensibility—wickedly funny, ceaselessly inventive, and never boring.

REPULSION

1965 104m bw	★★★★★
Horror	/18
Compton/Tekli (U.K.)	

Catherine Deneuve *(Carol Ledoux)*, Ian Hendry *(Michael)*, John Fraser *(Colin)*, Patrick Wymark *(Landlord)*, Yvonne Furneaux *(Helen Ledoux)*, Renee Houston *(Miss Balch)*, Helen Fraser *(Bridget)*, Valerie Taylor *(Mme. Denise)*, James Villiers *(John)*, Hugh Futcher *(Reggie)*

p, Gene Gutowski; d, Roman Polanski; w, Roman Polanski, Gerard Brach, David Stone; ph, Gilbert Taylor; ed, Alastair McIntyre; m, Chico Hamilton; art d, Seamus Flannery

One of the most frightening and disturbing pictures ever made, REPULSION contains a scene in which a man's face is slashed with a razor until he dies, captured by Polanski's camera with a clinical expertise that pushes the viewer's nervous system to the edge. REPULSION has often been compared to PSYCHO, but Polanski's film, rather than presenting a portrait of a psychotic killer from outside, pulls the audience into the crazed individual's mind.

Deneuve plays a Belgian manicurist working in London and living in an apartment with her sister, Furneaux. She becomes increasingly unhinged, apparently due to her feelings about sex, which simultaneously repulses and attracts her, and about which she is constantly reminded by the presence of Furneaux's lover. When her sister goes on holiday, Deneuve is left to fend for herself and becomes the victim of terrifying, destructive hallucinations within the confines of the apartment. REPULSION tells a simple story, but Polanski turns it into something undeniably brilliant. The director-writer took great pains in creating the proper composition and details for his nightmarish black-and-white visuals, extracting maximum hallucinatory effect from the apartment set. A powerfully engrossing film that owes much to the realistic, nearly silent performance of Deneuve, REPULSION was Polanski's first English-language feature. The director makes a cameo appearance as a spoons player.

REQUIEM FOR A HEAVYWEIGHT

1962 85m bw   ★★★½
Sports   /A
Columbia

Anthony Quinn (*Mountain Rivera*), Jackie Gleason (*Maish Rennick*), Mickey Rooney (*Army*), Julie Harris (*Grace Miller*), Stanley Adams (*Perelli*), Madame Spivy (*Ma Greeny*), Herbie Faye (*Bartender*), Jack Dempsey (*Himself*), Muhammad Ali (*Ring Opponent*), Steve Belloise (*Hotel Desk Clerk*)

p, David Susskind; d, Ralph Nelson; w, Rod Serling (based on his TV play); ph, Arthur J. Ornitz; ed, Carl Lerner; m, Laurence Rosenthal; art d, Burr Smidt; cos, John Boxer

Six years after Jack Palance brilliantly essayed the character of Mountain Rivera on television's "Playhouse 90," Anthony Quinn took on the role of the battered boxer for this big-screen adaptation of Rod Serling's Emmy-winning teleplay. As the film begins, Rivera, a veteran of 17 years in the ring, is beaten senseless by a younger, faster opponent (played by Cassius Clay, soon to be Muhammad Ali), going down for the count in the seventh round. His longtime manager, Gleason, who assured mobster Spivy that his fighter wouldn't last past the first few rounds, is given three weeks to compensate her for her betting losses—or else. Rivera has been told that he may go blind if he fights again, so he tries to get a job to come up with the money with the help of Harris, a caring employment counselor. Gleason, however, sabotages his interview for a position at a summer camp. Disappointed with Gleason but ever loyal, Rivera compromises his dignity by donning an Indian war bonnet and entering the professional wrestling ring to save his manager's life. Quinn, Gleason, and Rooney, as Rivera's erstwhile trainer, turn in magnificent performances in this unforgettable drama of abiding friendship and the abuse of trust. However, director Ralph Nelson, who also helmed the original 1956 television production, asked that his name be removed from the credits when nonessential scenes that had been cut from the original release print were reinstated to make the feature longer. Although those scenes, which slow down the narrative, certainly work against the film, REQUIEM FOR A HEAVYWEIGHT remains a thoroughly engaging movie.

RESCUERS, THE

1977 76m c   ★★★
Animated/Children's   G/U
Disney

VOICES OF: Bob Newhart (*Bernard*), Eva Gabor (*Miss Bianca*), Geraldine Page (*Mme Medusa*), Joe Flynn (*Mr. Snoops*), Jeanette Nolan (*Ellie Mae*), Pat Buttram (*Luke*), Jim Jordan (*Orville*), John McIntire (*Rufus*), Michelle Stacy (*Penny*), Bernard Fox (*Chairman*)

p, Wolfgang Reitherman; d, Wolfgang Reitherman, John Lounsbery, Art Stevens; w, Ken Anderson, Vance Gerry, Larry Clemmons, David Michener, Burny Mattinson, Frank Thomas, Fred Lucky, Ted Berman, Dick Sebast (based on the stories "The Rescuers" and "Miss Bianca" by Margery Sharp); ph, (Technicolor); ed, Jim Melton, Jim Koford; m, Artie Butler; art d, Don Griffith; anim, Oliver M. Johnston, Franklin Thomas, Milt Kahl, Don Bluth

Four years in the making, costing nearly $8 million, THE RESCUERS is a beautifully animated film that showed the Disney studio still knew a lot about making quality children's fare even as their track record was weakening. The story concerns two mice, Bernard and Miss Bianca (their voices provided by Newhart and Gabor), who set out to rescue a girl named Penny (Stacy) from the evil Mme Medusa (Page). The girl is held captive in a swamp, which offers the setting for some genuinely frightening action. Comic relief is provided by a bird named Orville, who transports the mice as they search for the girl. The voices are all well suited to the characters, and the film is a delight for children as well as adults who appreciate good animation and brisk storytelling. The tune "Someone's Waiting for You" by Sammy Fain, Carol Connors, and Ayn Robbins, received an Oscar nomination for Best Song.

RETURN OF MARTIN GUERRE, THE

1982 111m c   ★★★½
Historical   /15
La Societe Francaise/France Region 3/Marcel Dassault/Roissi/Palace (France)

Gerard Depardieu (*Martin Guerre*), Bernard-Pierre Donnadieu (*Martin Guerre*), Nathalie Baye (*Bertrande de Rols*), Roger Planchon (*Jean de Coras*), Maurice Jacquemont (*Judge Rieux*), Isabelle Sadoyan (*Catherine Boere*), Rose Thiery (*Raimonde de Rols*), Maurice Barrier (*Pierre Guerre*), Stephane Peau (*Young Martin*), Sylvie Meda (*Young Bertrande*)

p, Daniel Vigne; d, Daniel Vigne; w, Daniel Vigne, Jean-Claude Carriere; ph, Andre Neau (Fujicolor); ed, Denise de Casabianca; m, Michel Portal; art d, Alain Negre; cos, Anne-Marie Marchand

Set in 16th-century France, this engrossing period piece is based on existing records of an actual court case tried in a small village. Two youngsters, Martin Guerre and Bertrande de Rols, enter into a marriage of convenience at the behest of their peasant families. After a number of years, the strangely distant Martin disappears from the village, leaving behind his chaste, love-starved wife (Nathalie Baye). When Martin (Gerard Depardieu) returns, nine years later, he receives a warm welcome from the townsfolk and Bertrande, who has remained faithful to him. However, when Martin experiences occasional lapses of memory and fails to recognize faces, accusations fly—some of the villagers accusing him of being an impostor in the belief that the real Martin lost a leg in combat. Bertrande grows increasingly confused, at times defending her husband who has discovered a newfound affection for her, but on other occasions condemning him with her silence. The matter becomes even more confused when another man claiming to be Martin Guerre (Bernard Pierre Donnadieu) arrives in the village. One of the most successful art-house films of the 1980s, THE RETURN OF MARTIN GUERRE relies on two powerful performers—Depardieu, who is perfectly cast as the mysterious peasant, and Baye, whose demanding role calls for carefully measured silence and reserve. In his second cinematic outing, television director Daniel Vigne realized that he need only stick to the original facts to create a captivating film.

Anne-Marie Marchand's costumes received an Oscar nomination.

RETURN OF THE JEDI

1983   133m   c   ★★★½
Science Fiction   PG/U
Lucasfilm

Mark Hamill *(Luke Skywalker)*, Harrison Ford *(Han Solo)*, Carrie Fisher *(Princess Leia)*, Billy Dee Williams *(Lando Calrissian)*, Anthony Daniels *(See Threepio (C-3PO))*, Peter Mayhew *(Chewbacca)*, Sebastian Shaw *(Anakin Skywalker)*, Ian McDiarmid *(Emperor Palpatine)*, Frank Oz *(Yoda)*, David Prowse *(Darth Vader)*

p, Howard Kazanjian, Robert Watts, Jim Bloom; d, Richard Marquand; w, Lawrence Kasdan, George Lucas (based on a story by Lucas); ph, Alan Hume, Jack Lowin, James Glennon (Panavision, Rank Color); ed, Sean Barton, Marcia Lucas, Duwayne Dunham, Arthur Repola; m, John Williams; prod d, Norman Reynolds; art d, Fred Hole, James Schoppe, Joe Johnston; fx, Roy Arbogast, Kit West, Richard Edlund, Dennis Muren, Ken Ralston; chor, Gillian Gregory; cos, Aggie Guerard Rodgers, Nilo Rodis-Jamero; anim, James Keefer

This final segment of the trilogy that began with STAR WARS and THE EMPIRE STRIKES BACK is the most spectacular installment, at least in terms of the special-effects mastery of George Lucas and his cohorts at the Industrial Light and Magic Company. Darth Vader (acted by David Prowse, with voice by James Earl Jones) is building a new Death Star that cannot be destroyed. Han Solo (Harrison Ford) has been imprisoned in carbonite. Luke Skywalker (Mark Hamill) has sent robot pals C-3PO (Anthony Daniels) and R2-D2 (Kenny Baker) to rescue Solo, and Princess Leia (Carrie Fisher) masquerades as a bounty hunter, accompanied by Chewbacca (Peter Mayhew). There is also the adorable Yoda (Frank Oz) and a collection of cuddly critters called Ewoks. The space battles are overwhelming photographically, and every technical credit is first rate, although dialogue and characterization are minimal. The film won the 1983 Oscar for Special Visual Effects, and was nominated for Best Art Direction, Best Sound, Best Original Score, and Best Sound Effects Editing.

RETURN OF THE PINK PANTHER, THE

1975   115m   c   ★★★½
Mystery/Comedy   PG
UA   (U.K.)

Peter Sellers *(Inspector Jacques Clouseau)*, Christopher Plummer *(Sir Charles Litton)*, Catherine Schell *(Claudine Litton)*, Herbert Lom *(Chief Inspector Dreyfus)*, Peter Arne *(Col. Sharki)*, Burt Kwouk *(Cato)*, Andre Maranne *(Francois)*, Gregoire Aslan *(Chief of Police)*, Peter Jeffrey *(Gen. Wadafi)*, David Lodge *(Jean Duval)*

p, Blake Edwards; d, Blake Edwards; w, Frank Waldman, Blake Edwards; ph, Geoffrey Unsworth (Panavision, DeLuxe Color); ed, Tom Priestley; m, Henry Mancini; prod d, Peter Mullins; art d, Peter Mullins; fx, John Gant; cos, Bridget Sellers

This was the third in the "Pink Panther" series, which starred Sellers. Alan Arkin and director Bud Yorkin had attempted their version with INSPECTOR CLOUSEAU, but it couldn't compare to the comedy engendered by Sellers under Edwards's direction. This sequel took in more than $30 million and earned every cent. The famous diamond named in the title has been stolen from the museum where it had been residing for the past several years. Blame is laid at the feet of retired jewel thief Plummer (doing the David Niven role established in THE PINK PANTHER), though he is innocent. Plummer is married to Schell and is in danger of being arrested for a crime he didn't commit, so he must find out who the real crook is. Lom, again Sellers's boss, reluctantly gives Sellers the task of solving the crime. A series of sight gags and misplaced-word jokes follows, with Sellers playing off Aslan and Arne, two Middle Eastern cops; Victor Spinetti and Mike Grady, employees at a Gstaad resort; and all of the villains, led by Eric Pohlmann in an imitation of Sydney Greenstreet. The picture comes to life only when Sellers is onscreen, and the rest of the time it's just vamping. The locations were visually satisfying with scenes being shot at Gstaad, Switzerland, the French Riviera, Marrakesh, and Casablanca. The picture races along like a "Road Runner" cartoon with occasional stops to catch its breath. Try to see it on television in a room alone because the laughter in a full-theater audience might cause you to miss some good lines. Julie Andrews, who is Edwards's wife, did a small cameo as a chambermaid, but the scene was cut out in the final print. Edwards comes from directorial genes, as his grandfather, J. Gordon Edwards, was in charge of the lensing of many films.

RETURN OF THE SECAUCUS SEVEN

1980   110m   c   ★★★½
Drama   R/AA
Salsipuedes

Mark Arnott *(Jeff)*, Gordon Clapp *(Chip)*, Maggie Cousineau *(Frances)*, Brian Johnston *(Norman Gaddis)*, Adam LeFevre *(J.T.)*, Bruce MacDonald *(Mike)*, Jean Passanante *(Irene)*, Maggie Renzi *(Kate)*, John Sayles *(Howie)*, David Strathairn *(Ron)*

p, William Aydelott, Jeffrey Nelson; d, John Sayles; w, John Sayles; ph, Austin de Besche (DuArt Color); ed, John Sayles; m, Mason Daring

After scripting low-budget horror films such as PIRANHA and BATTLE BEYOND THE STARS for Roger Corman, acclaimed novelist and short story writer John Sayles made an auspicious directorial debut with THE RETURN OF THE SECAUCUS SEVEN, a more authentic and charming portrait of the same territory explored in the glossier THE BIG CHILL.

In the late 1960s seven friends were arrested in Secaucus, New Jersey, on their way to a march on the Pentagon. Ten years after graduating from college, the forgotten "Secaucus Seven" and a few companions come together at the New Hampshire home of Mike (Bruce MacDonald) and Kate (Maggie Renzi, coproducer of LIANNA, THE BROTHER FROM ANOTHER PLANT, MATEWAN). Over the course of the few days they spend together, much is revealed about their past and present lives and romances.

Shot in 1978 on a miniscule budget (reportedly $40,000) and using inexperienced actors, Sayles succeeds in creating an intelligent and often compelling study of former 1960s political activists coming to grips with their lives. Though that's about all THE RETURN OF THE SECAUCUS SEVEN offers, it is nevertheless an honest examination of the characters and their relationships. Fans of Sayles's work will note the presence of Gordon Clapp and David Strathairn, both of whom appear in the director's MATEWAN and EIGHT MEN OUT.

REVENGE OF THE NERDS

1984   90m   c   ★★★½
Comedy   R/18
Interscope Communications

Robert Carradine (Lewis), Anthony Edwards (Gilbert), Timothy Busfield (Poindexter), Andrew Cassese (Wormser), Curtis Armstrong (Booger), Larry B. Scott (Lamar), Brian Tochi (Takashi), Julie Montgomery (Betty), Michelle Meyrink (Judy), Ted McGinley (Stan)

p, Ted Field, Peter Samuelson; d, Jeff Kanew; w, Steve Zacharias, Jeff Buhai (based on a story by Tim Metcalfe, Miguel Tejada-Flores, Zacharias, Buhai); ph, King Baggot (Deluxe Color); ed, Alan Balsam; m, Thomas Newman; prod d, James Schoppe; fx, Joe Unsinn; chor, Dorain Grusman; cos, Radford Polinsky, Deborah Hopper

This funny movie is about 10 rungs above the usual teenage-college films. Lewis (Robert Carradine) and Gilbert (Anthony Edwards) are the essential nerds, in that Gilbert is a shy computer genius and Lewis is a boy with an annoying laugh and a huge overbite. When they arrive at Adams College and try to join fraternities, they are turned aside as they are so nerdy. In desperation, they join with other nerds to start their own branch of Lambda Lambda Lambda, an all-black fraternity that is functioning on other campuses. All the while, they are being closely watched by the jock contingent led by Stan (Ted McGinley), who is also the chairman of the Greek council. The jocks begin to make life miserable for the nerds, but revenge is on its way. This picture is hipper than NATIONAL LAMPOON'S ANIMAL HOUSE; PORKY'S; and all of the other teenage films lumped together. It's engaging, hysterically funny at times, wildly satiric, and has fewer lapses of good taste than most.

REVERSAL OF FORTUNE

1990 120m c   ★★★½
Drama   R/15
Edward R. Pressman/Shochiku Fuji/Sovereign

Jeremy Irons (Claus von Bulow), Glenn Close (Sunny von Bulow), Ron Silver (Alan M. Dershowitz), Anabella Sciorra (Carol), Uta Hagen (Maria), Fisher Stevens (David Marriott), Christine Baranski (Andrea Reynolds), Mano Singh, Felicity Huffman, Alan Pottinger

p, Edward R. Pressman, Oliver Stone; d, Barbet Schroeder; w, Nicholas Kazan (based on the book by Alan Dershowitz); ph, Luciano Tovoli; ed, Lee Percy; m, Mark Isham; prod d, Mel Bourne; cos, Judianna Makovsky, Milena Canonero

Having plunged into the lower depths of humanity with BARFLY, director Barbet Schroeder now explores the very upper strata of Newport society with this cool, quirky adaptation of lawyer Alan Dershowitz's book about his successful appeal of Claus von Bulow's conviction for the attempted murder of his wife, Martha "Sunny" von Bulow. Neither docudrama nor out-and-out fiction, REVERSAL OF FORTUNE is, in the words of screenwriter and coproducer Nicholas Kazan, "some kind of fiction based on fact." It is also, as all good courtroom dramas should be, a drama about the clash between absolutes of truth, justice, and judgement and the ambiguity of the human animal. As a result, it is one of the best and most intriguing films of its kind since Otto Preminger's classic of the genre, ANATOMY OF A MURDER.

As in BARFLY, Schroeder reveals himself as a director as interested in extremes as he is disinterested in the middle ground. The film begins with its most extreme character of all, Sunny (Glenn Close), who becomes the film's narrator from the vantage point of her "persistent vegetative state," not too unlike William Holden's narration of SUNSET BOULEVARD from the vantage point of being face-down dead in a swimming pool. She supplies a quick summary of Claus's (Jeremy Irons's) first trial, which ended in his sentencing to a 30-year term and his release on $1

million bail. FORTUNE really begins with Claus approaching Dershowitz (Ron Silver) to file his appeal. Dershowitz is reluctant to accept Claus as a client at first. Claus displays a tinge of anti-Semitism, and, as an arrogant, elitist, decadent multi-millionaire, he generally represents everything Dershowitz hates. Yet, the lawyer finally accepts on the basis of his recurring "Hitler dream," in which Hitler approaches Dershowitz to defend him. Instead of making a choice between acquitting him or killing him, Dershowitz decides to first acquit him, then kill him. Dershowitz has no special desire to kill Claus von Bulow, but, as he would be with Hitler, he is stimulated by the challenge of defending the indefensible.

The remainder of FORTUNE becomes a review of the evidence, from depositions to the characters of Claus and Sunny themselves. In the process, Dershowitz, working with what amounts to an army recruited from his classes at Harvard Law School, manages to pretty much demolish the prosecution case, which had Claus injecting Sunny with enough insulin to bring about her coma. Yet, Dershowitz can't supply a theory of what really happened until he comes to see Claus as an average man instead of a symbol, like most average people, neither completely culpable nor entirely innocent. His chastening comes about in one of the film's more intriguing subplots, in which Dershowitz personally involves himself in the investigation of a witness (Fisher Stevens) who, it turns out, is aiming to destroy Dershowitz and his case. Dershowitz is taken in by the witness because he is the only one in the film who fully confirms his contemptuous view of the rich, seducing him by telling him what he wants to hear.

But it is Irons's performance that dominates the film and Claus's character that seems to have captivated Schroeder's camera. Claus is finally the odd man out. Too old world and old money to make a comfortable fit with Dershowitz's world view, he's also out of place in his own milieu, even his own family. Sunny calls him a "prince of perversion" not for the obvious reasons but because he wants to work as a member of a class that simply does not work. In the face of Sunny's tirades and neuroses, Claus reacts with an odd devotion. He is unabashedly adulterous, but when Sunny insists on sleeping with the windows wide open in the middle of winter, Claus simply wears heavy clothes and a ski hat to bed without complaint. We believe him when he tells Dershowitz that he loves her as he loves all the women in his life, though of the two mistresses we see, one is a traitor and the other seems more concerned with getting back Claus's million-dollar bail than seeing him exonerated. With Sunny's children from her first marriage, he has to compete with Burt Lancaster and THE CRIMSON PIRATE on television while trying to tell them of the likelihood of their own divorce. Irons's plays the role with a frankness and a quiet dignity rather than with melodramatic villainy. Schroeder's camera virtually always frames him in isolation to convey his dramatic bleakness and isolation. As a result he remains enigmatic. The single trait that finally stands out most in him is a kind of willful, self-destructive childishness that drives him to revel in his naughty public image but that also drives him to childish extremes of devotion and loyalty. Sunny's millions become his solace, rather than his motivation for a crime.

Whether any of this has anything to do with the real people portrayed is finally anybody's guess. But, in essence, that is the whole point. The movie finally "guesses" that Claus neither meant to kill Sunny nor that Sunny necessarily meant to commit suicide. The truth, like so much else in REVERSAL OF FORTUNE, is somewhere inbetween. Schroeder is finally not nearly the visually expressive director that Preminger was, and FOR-

TUNE suffers for it. His sensitivity to the von Bulows seems at times too insistent. The telemovie visual flatness with which he treats Dershowitz's bright-eyed, bushy-tailed legal forces keeps threatening to edge over into under-served derision. But what saves FORTUNE is what is usually fatal to good filmmaking—Schroeder's own honest indecision about his plot and his characters. He doesn't seem sure of who is right and who is wrong, whether he was making a film about the banality of evil or the evil of banality. It finally doesn't make for as luridly flashy drama as FORTUNE easily could have been, but it does make for a fascinating one, a strange and compelling tragicomedy of ill manners. Irons won the Best Actor Oscar, and the film earned nominations for its director and its screenplay.

REVOLT OF JOB, THE

(JOB LAZADASA)
1983 98m c   ★★★½
Drama/War
Mafilm Tarsulas/Starfilm/Macropus/ZDF/Hungarian TV
(Hungary/West Germany)

Ferenc Zenthe (Job), Hedi Temessy (Roza), Gabor Feher (Lacko), Peter Rudolf (Jani), Leticia Caro (Ilka)

d, Imre Gyongyossy, Barna Kabay; w, Imre Gyongyossy, Barna Kabay, Katalin Petenyi; ph, Gabor Szabo (Eastmancolor); ed, Katalin Petenyi; m, Zoltan Jeny

Set in a small Hungarian farming village in 1943, THE REVOLT OF JOB stars Ferenc Zenthe and Hedi Temessy as Job and Roza, an elderly Jewish couple who have outlived all their children. Wishing for an heir, the couple schemes with an adoption center to gain custody of a seven-year-old Christian boy, Lacko (Gabor Feher), by trading two calves for him. Lacko is at first rebellious and cannot be reached by his loving "parents," choosing instead to play with a dog he has befriended, but eventually he warms to Job and Roza. All the while, the advance of Hitler's troops threatens Job and Roza's safety, and the couple prepares for the worst, arranging for a Gentile family to take care of their bewildered, now-loving adopted son while teaching him all they can about their endangered culture. Wisely concentrating its examination of religious and historical themes in a simple, small story, THE REVOLT OF JOB is a moving and intelligent film. As told from the boy's point of view, the film is dependent on Feher's performance as Lacko, and, thankfully, he is superb in his debut role. The script and direction by Imre Gyongyossy and Barna Kabay are fine, but it is the young star—selected from more than 4,000 hopefuls by the filmmakers—who remains the picture's brightest point. The movie received a Best Foreign-language Film Oscar nomination.

REVOLUTIONARY, THE

1970 101m c   ★★★½
Political   GP/A
Pressman/Williams   (U.K.)

Jon Voight (A), Jennifer Salt (Helen Peret), Seymour Cassel (Leonard), Robert Duvall (Despard), Collin Wilcox-Horne (Anne), Lionel Murton (Professor), Reed de Rouen (Mayor), Warren Stanhope (A's Father), Mary Barclay (A's Mother), Richard Pendry (NCO)

p, Edward R. Pressman; d, Paul Williams; w, Hans Koningsberger (based on the novel by Hans Koningsberger); ph, Brian Probyn (DeLuxe Color); ed, Henry Richardson; m, Michael Small; prod d, Disley Jones

Well-made Kafkaesque story with undertones of 1984. Although THE REVOLUTIONARY was shot in London, its locale is never specified, and most of the lead actors are American. Voight is a radical student who feels that he has been betrayed by the political group to which he belongs because they are establishing a policy of cooperation while he thinks more violent actions must be taken in order to alter the system. Voight and his lover, Wilcox-Horne, quit the student organization and join forces with Duvall, a tough factory worker who leads a local communist group. In his new role, Voight becomes part of a general strike, which the authorities seek to quell. Once Voight is known to be a leader, he is forced to seek a hiding place to avoid being arrested for his activities. When he receives a draft notice, he goes into the service, then learns that his first assignment is to squash the very strike he helped organize. Rather than battle against his political beliefs, Voight goes AWOL and stays with Salt, an attractive woman he'd met earlier who is somewhat sympathetic to him, if not his cause. With Duvall's group under surveillance and soft-pedaling themselves to avoid arrest, Voight decides that he must move on. He becomes involved with Cassel, an extremist who wants to kill Reginald Cornish to punish the judge for his anti-labor rulings. Cassel plans to place a bomb in the courtroom, and Voight's job is to set off a second explosive if the first one is a dud. Cornish sentences some of the workers to jail for their activities, Cassel's bomb doesn't go off, and Voight is left holding the second bomb as he stands in front of Cornish. Although full of ideas, THE REVOLUTIONARY doesn't stop to cram them down our throats. Instead, the film moves at a quick clip while still managing to provide insights into Voight's carefully drawn character.

RHAPSODY IN BLUE

1945 139m bw   ★★★½
Musical/Biography   /U
WB

Robert Alda (George Gershwin), Joan Leslie (Julie Adams), Alexis Smith (Christine Gilbert), Charles Coburn (Max Dreyfus), Julie Bishop (Lee Gershwin), Albert Basserman (Prof. Frank), Morris Carnovsky (Poppa Gershwin), Rosemary DeCamp (Momma Gershwin), Anne Brown (Bess), Herbert Rudley (Ira Gershwin)

p, Jesse L. Lasky; d, Irving Rapper; w, Howard Koch, Elliot Paul (based on a story by Sonya Levien); ph, Sol Polito; ed, Folmar Blangsted; m, George Gershwin; art d, John Hughes, Anton Grot; fx, Ray Davidson, Willard Vanenger; chor, LeRoy Prinz

George Gershwin died before he was 40, but his music continues to be a source of delight and inspiration. Like NIGHT AND DAY and WORDS AND MUSIC—film biographies about Cole Porter and Rogers and Hart, respectively—RHAPSODY IN BLUE has little to do with the real life of its subject, but, as is the case with those films, its subject's wonderful songs are the main attraction. In telling its story of the Gershwin Brothers' rise to fame from Manhattan's Lower East Side, RHAPSODY IN BLUE offers the usual scenes of song-plugging, struggle, failure, rehearsals, and backstage life; episodes in New York, London, and Paris; goes so far as to invent a character who never existed (played by Joan Leslie); and alters others to the point of laughability. In his second film, Robert Alda won't be confused for Laurence Olivier, but he does contribute a relatively convincing portrayal of George Gershwin, while Herbert Rudley, as Ira, looks very much like the master wordsmith at the same age and carries off his part well. There are many celebrity impersonations, as well as appearances by several stars playing themselves, but the film's best lines belong to Gershwin's good friend Oscar Levant (as himself), who contributes piano solos along with Ray Turner. Max Steiner did the musical adaptation with orchestrations by Ray Heindorf and

Ferde Grofe, composer of the "Grand Canyon Suite." Given this lineup and Gershwins' timeless tunes, it would be possible to remove all the talk, leave the music, and still have a good movie; and, of course, in the age of remote-control "mute" buttons, that's an option.

RHYTHM ON THE RIVER

1940 92m bw   ★★★½
Musical/Comedy   /U
Paramount

Bing Crosby (Bob Summer), Mary Martin (Cherry Lane), Basil Rathbone (Oliver Courtney), Oscar Levant (Billy Starbuck), Oscar Shaw (Charlie Goodrich), Charley Grapewin (Uncle Caleb), Lillian Cornell (Millie Starling), William Frawley (Mr. Westlake), Jeanne Cagney (Country Cousin), Charles Lane (Mr. Bernard Schwartz)

p, William Le Baron; d, Victor Schertzinger; w, Dwight Taylor (based on a story by Billy Wilder, Jacques Thery); ph, Ted Tetzlaff; ed, Hugh Bennett; m, Victor Young; art d, Hans Dreier, Ernst Fegte; cos, Edith Head

The "river" of the title is the Hudson, and the "rhythm" is provided by Bob Somers (Crosby), a talented but unmotivated tunesmith, and Cherry Lane (Mary Martin), a clever lyricist—both of whom ghost write for Oliver Courtney, a famous songwriter whose inspiration left him when his wife ran off with another man, though he prefers to think of her as dead. After meeting at a quiet resort owned by Bob's uncle, the songwriters decide to make a go of it on their own, but Oliver warns them its a tough road for unknowns, which they discover soon enough. Cherry turns to singing in a nightclub and Bob returns to the farm. Pressured to come up with material for a new big-budget musical, however, Oliver uses a very personal love song by Bob and Cherry that they have forbidden him to appropriate, but by the film's end credit is given where credit is due and all ends justly. The script, written by Dwight Taylor, from a story by Billy Wilder and Jacques Thery, is full of funny lines, and Rathbone is marvelous in his comedic role as the egomaniacal, burnt-out composer. Crosby and Martin also contribute solid performances and the film has plenty of strong tunes, including the Oscar-nominated "Only Forever" and "I Don't Want to Cry Anymore," the latter composed by the film's director, Victor Schertzinger.

RICH KIDS

1979 96m c   ★★★
Drama/Comedy   PG/AA
Lion's Gate

Trini Alvarado (Franny Phillips), Jeremy Levy (Jamie Harris), Kathryn Walker (Madeleine Philips), John Lithgow (Paul Philips), Terry Kiser (Ralph Harris), David Selby (Steve Sloan), Roberta Maxwell (Barbara Peterfreund), Paul Dooley (Simon Peterfreund), Diane Stilwell (Stewardess), Dianne Kirksey (Ralph's Secretary)

p, George W. George, Michael Hausman; d, Robert M. Young; w, Judith Ross; ph, Ralf D. Bode (Panavision, Technicolor); ed, Ed Beyer; m, Craig Doerge; art d, David Mitchell; cos, Hilary Rosenfeld

This clever story is a look through the eyes of a child at a divorce in an upper-class New York family. Alvarado plays the 12-year-old daughter of Walker and Lithgow, whose marriage is on its last legs. Alvarado knows that the blow is coming and can only wait for the final showdown. Levy plays the brainy friend whose family has already gone through a breakup. An old hand at this stuff, he coaches Alvarado as she copes with the emotional trauma, emphasizing the freedom he has achieved as a result of his parents' split. Maintaining a sense of humor toward its touchy

subject, the film is a refreshing look at those people—the children—who are the real victims of divorce, but who are seldom given a voice in the matter. The young actors give convincing performances (although Levy is perhaps a little too smug), and are handled effectively through the well-paced direction of Young.

RICHARD III

1956 158m c   ★★★½
Historical/War   /U
Big Ben/London Films   (U.K.)

Laurence Olivier (King Richard III), Ralph Richardson (Buckingham), Claire Bloom (Lady Anne), John Gielgud (Clarence), Cedric Hardwicke (King Edward IV), Mary Kerridge (Queen Elizabeth), Pamela Brown (Jane Shore), Alec Clunes (Hastings), Stanley Baker (Henry Tudor), Michael Gough (Dighton)

p, Laurence Olivier; d, Laurence Olivier, Anthony Bushell; w, Alan Dent, Laurence Olivier, Colley Cibber, David Garrick (based on the play by William Shakespeare); ph, Otto Heller (VistaVision, Technicolor); ed, Helga Cranston; m, William Walton; prod d, Roger Furse; art d, Carmen Dillon; fx, Wally Veevers; cos, H. Nathan, L. Nathan

Laurence Olivier's third Shakespeare film—the first two were HENRY V and HAMLET, the latter earning him an Oscar—and RICHARD III is arguably the best of the three. For once, Olivier's coldness finds a part he can invest magnetic chill in. He makes you almost rejoice in his villany, whether you consider his interpretation amazing high camp or just amazing.

The picture begins with the coronation of Edward IV (Cedric Hardwicke), in a scene borrowed from the end of "Henry IV, Part III," with Richard (Olivier) watching jealously in the background. Edward is soon drowned in a vat of wine and Richard is the king, engaging in a series of back-stabbings and duplicities that eventually bring him to the Battle of Bosworth, where he is unseated from his steed, screams "A horse, a horse! My kingdom for a horse!" and is then set upon by the minions of Henry Tudor (Stanley Baker). The battle scene was the first shot (in Spain); during shooting Olivier was accidentally pierced by a bolt from the film's stunt archer that was supposed to hit the protected horse (an animal that had been trained to fall and play dead on command). Olivier continued the scene until a natural break in the action was called for, then asked for medical aid. (The limp he sports as Richard is real, a result of the accident.) It took three hours each day to put on Olivier's complex makeup—the same prosthetics he wore on stage, including a false nose, hunched back, false hand, and black pageboy wig. Olivier and screenwriter Alan Dent added to Shakespeare's story the two monks who act as a silent Greek chorus as they view the intrigues.

RICHARD III was not a hit when it was released in England, so the producers made a unique deal with the NBC television network in the US in which the networks acquired the rights to broadcast the film for the sum of $500,000 (in later years it was re-released to resounding success, and has been the most financially rewarding of Olivier's Shakespeare films).

But the rest of RICHARD's cast play the meter, not the characters; they weigh Olivier down. It serves him right—he was directing them. And there's the rub: Olivier was a poor director, approaching everything with the same clinical, timid little mouse approach, save his own big moments. They string the dullness together; yet when they try to transcend the storybook setpiece staidness, they look too brazen, almost parodistic.

Olivier and Alexander Korda had hoped to film a version of "Macbeth," with Vivien Leigh as Lady Macbeth, but Korda died a year after RICHARD III was made, and lack of interest in the project caused it to be tabled. The British Film Academy gave RICHARD III Best British Film, Best Film, and Best Actor awards. Olivier was nominated for a Best Actor Academy Award, but lost to Yul Brynner for THE KING AND I.

RIDE THE HIGH COUNTRY

1962   94m   c   ★★★★★
Western
MGM

Randolph Scott *(Gil Westrum)*, Joel McCrea *(Steve Judd)*, Mariette Hartley *(Elsa Knudsen)*, Ronald Starr *(Heck Longtree)*, R.G. Armstrong *(Joshua Knudsen)*, Edgar Buchanan *(Judge Tolliver)*, John Anderson *(Elder Hammond)*, L.Q. Jones *(Sylvus Hammond)*, Warren Oates *(Henry Hammond)*, James Drury *(Billy Hammond)*

p, Richard E. Lyons; d, Sam Peckinpah; w, N.B. Stone, Jr.; ph, Lucien Ballard (CinemaScope, Metrocolor); ed, Frank Santillo; m, George Bassman; art d, George W. Davis, Leroy Coleman

One of the best-loved and most fondly remembered westerns of all time, director Sam Peckinpah's second feature film proved to be a bittersweet swan song for the Old West and a classy farewell to the screen for actors Scott and—for some years—McCrea. Set at the turn of the century, the film opens in the town of Hornitos, which is in the midst of a celebration. Down the crowded main street rides McCrea, an aging, somewhat haggard former lawman who has fallen on hard times but still manages to maintain an undeniable air of dignity. He hears the cheers of the crowd and, pleasantly surprised at being recognized, tips his hat to the people. His reverie is interrupted by a policeman who tells him to get out of the way because he is blocking the path of a race being run down the street. Embarrassed, McCrea realizes that the cheers from the crowd were actually jeers for him to clear the road. The race turns out to be a vulgar display of a horse against a camel. Slightly befuddled by the whole thing, McCrea is then nearly run over by an automobile as he tries to cross the street. (The automobile is a recurring image in Peckinpah's westerns and also plays significant roles in THE WILD BUNCH and THE BALLAD OF CABLE HOGUE.) McCrea enters the local bank and announces that he is the man the owner hired to escort a shipment of gold from the mountainous mining town of Coarse Gold back to the bank. The banker is a bit taken aback by McCrea's age and expresses doubt that he can do the job. McCrea tries to hide his frayed cuffs, and then he goes to the bathroom with the contract so that he can read it without the banker having to see him use his spectacles. The old lawman is finally given the job, and he sets out to hire a second man to help him on the trip. In town he runs into Scott, an old friend and fellow former lawman. Scott has learned to survive by selling out his heroic image, dressing up as the "Oregon Kid," a ridiculous looking "Wild West" sharpshooter with a carnival patter. Almost unrecognizable in his huge cowboy hat, long-haired wig, phony beard, and frilly outfit, Scott agrees to have dinner with McCrea after the show. At a Chinese restaurant McCrea offers the job to Scott and his young sidekick, Starr. The two accept the offer, with Scott planning to steal the gold at the first opportunity.

In RIDE THE HIGH COUNTRY, director Peckinpah began what was to be an obsession with men who have lived past their era in history and find it difficult to adapt to changing times (THE WILD BUNCH; THE BALLAD OF CABLE HOGUE; and PAT GARRETT AND BILLY THE KID all share the identity-crisis theme). Integral to this theme are the emotional and moral dilemmas Peckinpah's very human main characters undergo. These are men wracked with guilt, for they have made bad decisions, misjudgments, and have sometimes failed to live up to the standards they have set for themselves. Each protagonist serves as a mirror image of the other, reflecting what their lives would have been like if they had made different choices. What separates them from the scoundrels they invariably encounter is a personal code of honor they try to uphold. Eventually, these tortured souls attain a sort of grace because in the end, they do what it takes to regain their self-respect (with the exception of Coburn, who sells out in PAT GARRETT AND BILLY THE KID, Peckinpah's bleakest western). Producer Lyons acquired a screenplay about two aging lawmen written by N.B. Stone, Jr., called "Guns in the Afternoon" that was subsequently rewritten by William S. Roberts (who was never credited). The producer eventually persuaded McCrea (who was a friend) and Scott to star in his movie. Soon after, McCrea—who had originally agreed to play the part of Gil Westrum, the lawman gone bad—felt uncomfortable with the role (he had never played a villain before, albeit, here, a sympathetic one) and asked Lyons if he could see how Scott felt about switching parts. Later that same afternoon, Lyons received a call from Scott who confessed that he was feeling insecure about his role and wondered if McCrea would mind a swap. Much to the actors' relief, the roles were switched.

Searching for a director, Lyons was told of Peckinpah, a young television writer-director who had written for "Gunsmoke" (13 episodes) and created "The Rifleman" and "The Westerner." Lyons viewed several episodes of "The Westerner" and was duly impressed. Conscious of MGM's negative attitude toward television people, Lyons had the episodes screened for the studio's head of production, Sol Siegel. Siegel was also impressed and gave Lyons the go-ahead to hire Peckinpah. Peckinpah accepted the project with the provision that he be allowed to rewrite the script—which was granted. The director then improved the dialog and brought much of his own personal experience into the story. The Peckinpah family included true westerners. Peckinpah mountain in California near the real Coarse Gold was bought by the director's grandfather in 1883, and as a child the director was taken by his father, a judge, to a mining town much like the one in the film. Garner Simmons, in his book on the director entitled *Peckinpah*, quotes Peckinpah's sister Fern Lea: "We went to see RIDE THE HIGH COUNTRY at a sneak preview," she said, "and when it was over, I went to the ladies' room and cried and cried because the character played by Joel McCrea reminded me so much of my father who had just died the year before." (The famous line "All I want is to enter my house justified" was often uttered by Peckinpah's father). The director also changed the ending of the script. The original draft had Scott's character dying in the end, thus receiving salvation for his wicked ways, but Peckinpah thought it more effective to have Scott's character survive and let McCrea "enter his house justified." Both Scott and McCrea thought Peckinpah's improvements brilliant. Now that the project had a good script, enthusiastic stars, and an eager director, the only problem was to decide who would receive top billing. Scott and McCrea agreed to a public coin toss at the Brown Derby restaurant, and Scott won.

Shooting was planned on location at Mammoth Lake in the High Sierras, but after four days it began to snow, and cost-conscious MGM insisted the production be moved to a more workable area. Peckinpah was upset, but the film continued shooting at Bronson Canyon in Hollywood where soap suds were used to simulate snow. Other money-saving efforts saw art director Davis stealing sails from the *Bounty* (used in the remake of MUTINY ON THE BOUNTY) to make the miners' tents, and cast and crew sneaking onto the set of HOW THE WEST WAS

WON at night to shoot the confrontation scene between McCrea and Scott. Shooting was completed in an astounding 26 days, and that's when things turned for the worst. After a well-received rough cut of the film was completed, a shake-up at MGM saw Siegel ousted (he supported Peckinpah) and replaced by Joseph R. Vogel. Peckinpah was barred from the studio, leaving his editor and sound mixers to finish the film without him. To keep Peckinpah involved, the technicians played the daily sound mixes over the phone to him for approval. Vogel promptly fell asleep during the screening of the final cut, and when it was over he awoke and called it the worst film he had ever seen. This, of course, did not endear Peckinpah to Vogel or vice versa. Despite the director's and producer's protests, RIDE THE HIGH COUNTRY was dumped on the market on the lower half of ludicrous double bills with films like BOYS' NIGHT OUT, a comedy starring Kim Novak and James Garner, and THE TARTARS, a medieval drama produced in Italy starring Victor Mature and Orson Welles. The film was a commercial disaster in America, despite favorable reviews, but abroad it became a major hit. RIDE THE HIGH COUNTRY won First Prize at the Cannes Film Festival, the Grand Prize at the Brussels Film Festival (beating out Federico Fellini's 8½), and the Silver Goddess from the Mexican Film Festival for Best Foreign Film. The film went on to become one of MGM's biggest grossing films in Europe. Over the years European and American critics have kept the praise for RIDE THE HIGH COUNTRY flowing.

Peckinpah's attention to detail, realistic settings, and total understanding of character makes this film a multifaceted jewel to be studied and enjoyed again and again. Peckinpah went on to gain an infamous reputation for his strong-willed, highly personal brand of filmmaking, but he proved himself one of the most interesting, albeit inconsistent, directors in America. The honest, subtle, and consummately skillful performances by Scott and McCrea continue to draw viewers in. Scott never made another film. While McCrea has made a few screen appearances since, most consider RIDE THE HIGH COUNTRY his finest effort. Not only did producer Lyons and director Peckinpah create one of the greatest westerns ever made in RIDE THE HIGH COUNTRY, they also made it possible for two of America's most popular and beloved actors to bid a moving, passionate, and memorable farewell to the silver screen.

RIDER ON THE RAIN
(LE PASSAGER DE LA PLUIE)

1970	119m	c		★★★½
Thriller				GP/18
Greenwich/Medusa	(France/Italy)			

Marlene Jobert (Melancolie "Mellie" Mau), Charles Bronson (Col. Harry Dobbs), Annie Cordy (Juliette), Jill Ireland (Nicole), Gabriele Tinti (Tony), Jean Gaven (Toussaint), Marc Mazza (The Stranger), Corinne Marchand (Tania), Jean Piat (M. Armand), Marika Green (Hostess at Tania's)

p, Serge Silberman; d, Rene Clement; w, Sebastien Japrisot, Lorenzo Ventavoli; ph, Andreas Winding (Eastmancolor); ed, Francoise Javet; m, Francis Lai; art d, Pierre Guffroy; cos, Rosine Delamare

A young woman (Jobert) who lives in a small seaside resort in France happens to see a stranger exit from a bus. While trying on a dress the next day at Ireland's boutique, she sees the stranger watching her. That evening the stranger breaks into Jobert's home after her husband (Tinti), a jealous airline pilot, has left. The stranger rapes Jobert and knocks her unconscious. Upon waking she hears the man in the basement. Frightened, she grabs

a shotgun and kills the man in two blasts as he tries to attack her once more. She throws his body into the sea, fearful of what could happen should she report the incident to the authorities. After a few days the stranger's body washes up on the beach, and this occurrence makes newspaper headlines. Jobert goes to a wedding reception and there is confronted by another stranger, Bronson, an American who accuses her of murdering a sex fiend who escaped from prison and stole $60,000 from the US Army. He demands that Jobert return the airline bag that held the money, but Jobert ignores his threats. Bronson continues to harass her, sparking childhood memories for Jobert: when she discovered that her mother had a lover, her father badgered a confession out of the confused girl. Once he learned the truth, Jobert's father ran out on the family. Eventually, Jobert finds the bag in question and goes to Bronson's hotel to return it. She gets into his room and, upon searching Bronson's luggage, learns he is a colonel in the US Army. Suddenly Bronson bursts into the room, and informs Jobert that another woman has been arrested for the stranger's murder. She goes to Paris and meets with the suspect's sister, the operator of a brothel. Later, Jobert is attacked by a trio of crooks who think she knows more than she should about the crime. Bronson rescues her, and the two return to the resort town, where they are informed by the police that the body washed ashore is not the man Bronson wants. The stranger's corpse eventually turns up with a button from Jobert's dress clutched in his hand. Bronson, satisfied to get back the money, decides against causing Jobert any further problems.

RIDER ON THE RAIN is a tightly plotted, well-executed thriller. And Bronson handles his character's ambivalent nature with great skill. For once the actor's three stock expressions are put to good use. The location work on the French coast and in Paris is used effectively; combined with careful cinematography, the scenery adds greatly to the story's inherent tension. This stylish, Hitchcock-like thriller was filmed in French and dubbed into English for American distribution. But unlike many similar projects, the dubbing for RIDER ON THE RAIN is extremely well done.

Bronson, who had starred in several American television series, didn't catch on with film audiences in the US in the 1960s. It wasn't until after he became a hit in Europe that he achieved enormous popularity stateside. In just one year he scored with ONCE UPON A TIME IN THE WEST; FAREWELL, FRIEND; and this film. These three films, along with the French gangster film BORSALINO, broke all previous box-office records in France, a remarkable achievement that gave Bronson real clout. Ireland, Bronson's wife, had a minor role in this film and played her husband's leading lady in the majority of his films in the 1970s.

RIDERS OF THE PURPLE SAGE

1931	58m	bw	★★½
Western			/U
Fox Films			

George O'Brien (Jim Lassiter), Marguerite Churchill (Jane Withersteen), Noah Beery, Sr. (Judge Dyer), Yvonne Pelletier (Bess), James Todd (Venters), Stanley Fields (Oldring), Shirley Nails (Fay Larkin), Lester Dorr (Judkins), Frank McGlynn, Sr. (Jeff Tull)

d, Hamilton MacFadden; w, John Goodrich, Philip Klein, Barry Connors (based on the novel by Zane Grey); ph, George Schneiderman; ed, Al DeGaetano

O'Brien plays a cowboy out to rescue his kidnapped sister (Nails) in this adaptation of the noted Grey novel. Though a bit creaky as far as dialogue goes, there are several sequences that feature topnotch action. A wide-angle lens was used in the photography with great effect. O'Brien is fine as the hero and fits the characterization of the strong, silent type. This first sound version was followed by a sequel, THE RAINBOW TRAIL, in 1932. Two silent versions were also filmed, the first in 1918 with William Farnum and the second in 1925 with silent legend Tom Mix. Mix also made a sequel to his version. A second sound version, starring George Montgomery, was produced by Fox in 1941. *Riders of the Purple Sage* was the first really successful novel by noted western writer Grey, who formerly caught fish for a living.

RIDING HIGH

1950 112m bw ★★★½
Musical/Comedy/Sports
Paramount

Bing Crosby *(Dan Brooks)*, Coleen Gray *(Alice Higgins)*, Charles Bickford *(J.L. Higgins)*, William Demarest *(Happy McGuire)*, Frances Gifford *(Margaret Higgins)*, Raymond Walburn *(Prof. Pettigrew)*, James Gleason *(Racing Secretary)*, Ward Bond *(Lee)*, Clarence Muse *(Whitey)*, Percy Kilbride *(Pop Jones)*

p, Frank Capra; d, Frank Capra; w, Robert Riskin, Melville Shavelson, Jack Rose (based on the story "Broadway Bill" by Mark Hellinger); ph, George Barnes, Ernest Laszlo; ed, William Hornbeck; art d, Hans Dreier, Walter Tyler; fx, Farciot Edouart; cos, Edith Head

Frank Capra directed both BROADWAY BILL and its remake, RIDING HIGH, and the 1950 film is one of the rare instances in which the remake is as good as the original. BROADWAY BILL stars Myrna Loy and Warner Baxter are replaced here by Coleen Gray and Bing Crosby, who, not surprisingly, contributes a few tunes to the proceedings. Dan Brooks (Crosby) is devoted to both a racehorse and to wealthy meal ticket Alice Higgins (Gray), whose jealousy of the quadruped forces Dan to choose between them. Naturally, he chooses the horse, who repays his love by winning the big race and making Dan rich, then dying. One-time heavyweight champion Max Baer makes a cameo appearance as the man with whom Alice seeks solace; Oliver Hardy, in a rare Laurel-less appearance, also does a brief bit.

RIFIFI

1955 117m bw ★★★★★
Crime /X
Indus/Pathe/Prima (France)

Jean Servais *(Tony le Stephanois)*, Carl Mohner *(Jo Le Suedois)*, Robert Manuel *(Mario)*, Jules Dassin *(Cesar)*, Magali Noel *(Viviane)*, Marie Sabouret *(Mado)*, Janine Darcey *(Louise)*, Pierre Grasset *(Louis Grutter)*, Robert Hossein *(Remi Grutter)*, Marcel Lupovici *(Pierre Grutter)*

p, Rene G. Vuattoux; d, Jules Dassin; w, Jules Dassin, Rene Wheeler, Auguste Le Breton (based on the novel by Le Breton); ph, Philippe Agostini; ed, Roger Dwyre; m, Georges Auric; art d, Auguste Capelier

This landmark caper film shows the robbery of a Parisian jewelry store and the complications that follow for the thieves—mastermind Tony (Jean Servais), a recently released ex-con who may or may not have a terminal respiratory problem; Jo (Carl Mohner), whom Tony served time to protect; safecracker Cesar (the film's director, Jules Dassin, acting under the pseudonym Perlo Vita); and Mario (Robert Manuel)—all of them surprisingly decent men. The film's centerpiece is a 28-minute sequence that captures the robbery itself in fascinating detail, employing neither dialogue nor music, allowing only the actual sounds of the thieves at work to be heard. Once the heist is accomplished, life doesn't get any easier for the crooks, as Tony's gangster rival (Marcel Lupovici) and cohorts get violently greedy after learning about the robbery through Cesar's indiscretion. The kidnapping of Jo's son and plenty of shooting follow before RIFIFI (French slang for "trouble") is over.

This was the second European-made film for writer-director-actor Dassin, an American who plied his trade abroad after the House Un-American Activities Committee made life difficult at home. Dassin, whose wonderful you-are-there direction won him a share of the Best Director award at Cannes, also manages to inject more than a little humor into this tension-filled genre classic, preceded by the likes of THE ASPHALT JUNGLE and followed by films like BIG DEAL ON MADONNA STREET and Dassin's own TOPKAPI.

RIGHT STUFF, THE

1983 192m c ★★★★
Biography PG/15
Ladd

Sam Shepard *(Chuck Yeager)*, Scott Glenn *(Alan Shepard)*, Ed Harris *(John Glenn)*, Dennis Quaid *(Gordon Cooper)*, Fred Ward *(Gus Grissom)*, Barbara Hershey *(Glennis Yeager)*, Kim Stanley *(Bancho Barnes)*, Veronica Cartwright *(Betty Grissom)*, Pamela Reed *(Trudy Cooper)*, Scott Paulin *(Deke Slayton)*

p, Irwin Winkler, Robert Chartoff; d, Philip Kaufman; w, Philip Kaufman (based on the book by Tom Wolfe); ph, Caleb Deschanel (Technicolor); ed, Glenn Farr, Lisa Fruchtman, Stephen A. Rotter, Tom Rolf, Douglas Stewart; m, Bill Conti; prod d, Geoffrey Kirkland; art d, Richard Lawrence, Stewart Campbell, Peter Romero; fx, Gary Gutierrez, Jordan Belson

Funny, trenchant account, based on Tom Wolfe's book, of the dawn of the space age, seen as both a shameless piece of media mythmaking, and as an act of genuine courage on the part of the first astronauts. The movie spans about 15 years, beginning with Chuck Yeager (Sam Shepard) breaking Mach 1, and concluding with a huge barbecue at the Astrodome at which President Johnson (Donald Moffat) hosts the astronauts. In between, it depicts their arduous training and complex personal lives, and the absurd lengths to which they have to go to satisfy the public's demand for real-life heroes. Director-writer Philip Kaufman's script brings a wealth of humor to a faithful retelling of the astronauts' fascinating stories, the actors fit smoothly into their roles and even physically resemble their characters, and the direction is well-paced and visually exciting. The film garnered three Academy Award nominations: Best Picture; Shepard for Best Supporting Actor; and Caleb Deschanel for Best Cinematography.

RING-A-DING RHYTHM

1962 73m bw ★★½
Musical/Comedy
Amicus (U.K.)

Helen Shapiro *(Helen)*, Craig Douglas *(Craig)*, Felix Felton *(Mayor)*, Arthur Mullard *(Police Chief)*, Timothy Bateson *(Coffeeshop Owner)*, Hugh Lloyd *(Usher)*, Ronnie Stevens, Frank Thornton *(TV Directors)*, Derek Nimmo *(Head Waiter)*, Mario Fabrizi *(Spaghetti Eater)*

p, Richard Lester; d, Richard Lester; w, Milton Subotsky; ph, Gilbert Taylor; ed, Bill Lenny; m, Ken Thorne; prod d, Al Marcus; art d, Maurice Carter; cos, Gamp Ferris, Maude Churchill

Richard Lester's first feature proved to be an effective springboard for his highly stylized direction, employing techniques (unusual camera angles, quick cuts) that he polished further in the Beatles' A HARD DAY'S NIGHT. The plot here is not unlike a number of 50s films in which a town's upstanding citizens react vehemently to the corrupting spread of demon rock 'n' roll, forcing the kids to stand up for their rights. In this case, the mayor of an English town, Felton, goes so far as to take away one coffeeshop's license for having a jukebox. A pair of crafty local teens, Shapiro and Douglas, counterattack by trying to put together a festival that will demonstrate the merits of traditional jazz (then an important part of British counterculture) and rock 'n' roll, traveling to a London TV studio to try to persuade some big-name performers to appear. This plot gives Lester an opportunity to creatively showcase a number of pop, rock, and trad jazz stars—including Del Shannon, Chubby Checker, Gary "U.S." Bonds, Gene Vincent, Chris Barber's Jazz Band, and the Temperance Seven. Songs include "Space Ship to Mars" (Norrie Paramor, Milton Subotsky, sung by Gene Vincent), "Tavern in the Town" (Paramor, Subotsky, sung by Terry Lightfoot), "Nineteen-Nineteen March" (Paramor, Subotsky, sung by Kenny Ball), "Double Trouble" (Geoff Brook, Ricky Brook, sung by the Brook Brothers), "Everybody Loves My Baby" (Jack Palmer, Spencer Williams, sung by the Temperance Seven), "Dream Away Romance" (Paul McDowell, Clifford Beven, sung by the Temperance Seven), "Bellissima" (Subotsky, performed by Bob Wallis and His Storyville Jazzmen), "In a Persian Market" (Albert Ketelbey, Mack David, performed by Mr. Acker Bilk and His Paramount Jazz Band), "Lonely City" (Geoffrey Goddard, sung by John Leyton), "High Society" (Clarence Williams, A.J. Piron, performed by the Bilk Jazz Band), "Frankie and Johnny" (Subotsky, performed by the Bilk Jazz Band), "Aunt Flo" (Bob Wallis, performed by Wallis and His Jazzmen), "Rainbows" (Paramor, Bunny Lewis, sung by Craig Douglas), "Let's Talk About Love" (Paramor, Lewis, sung by Helen Shapiro), "Sometime Yesterday" (Clive Westlake, sung by Shapiro), "My Maryland" (arranged by Lightfoot, sung by Lightfoot), "Beale Street Blues" (W.C. Handy, sung by Kenny Ball), "Yellow Dog Blues" (Handy, performed by Chris Barber's Jazz Band), "Down by the Riverside" (Chris Barber, sung by Ottilie Patterson), "When the Saints Go Marching In" (arranged by Barber, performed by Barber's Jazz Band), "Ring-a-Ding" (Paramor, Lewis, sung by Shapiro), "Seven Day Weekend" (Doc Pomus, Mort Shuman, sung by Gary "U.S." Bonds), "What Am I to Do?" (Pomus, Shuman, sung by the Paris Sisters), "Another Tear Falls" (Hal David, Burt Bacharach, sung by Gene McDaniels), "Lose Your Inhibition Twist" (Kal Mann, Dave Appell, performed by Chubby Checker), "By and By" (performed by the Dukes of Dixieland), "You Never Talk About Me" (Pomus, Shuman, sung by Del Shannon).

RING OF BRIGHT WATER

1969 107m c   ★★★
Comedy/Drama   G/U
Brightwater/Palomar   (U.K.)

Bill Travers (Graham Merrill), Virginia McKenna (Mary MacKenzie), Peter Jeffrey (Colin Wilcox/Colin Clifford), Jameson Clark (Storekeeper), Helena Gloag (Mrs. Flora Elrich), W.H.D. Joss (Lighthouse Keeper), Roddy McMillan (Bus Driver), Jean Taylor-Smith (Mrs. Sarah Chambers), Archie Duncan (Road Mender), Kevin Collins (Fisherman)

p, Joseph Strick; d, Jack Couffer; w, Jack Couffer, Bill Travers (based on the book by Gavin Maxwell); ph, Wolfgang Suschitzky (Technicolor); ed, Reginald Mills; m, Frank Cordell; prod d, Terry Lens; art d, Ken Ryan; cos, Ernie Farrer

Film depiction of the autobiography of Maxwell, focused on his adventures with a playful otter. The semidocumentary flavor was heightened by the presence of Travers and McKenna (then recently of BORN FREE fame, another animal story). Travers plays an increasingly distraught London clerk who decides to purchase the otter he sees in the pet shop that he passes every day on his way to work. When the otter's antics get him evicted from his apartment, Travers takes to the Scottish Highlands, intending to devote himself to writing about Arabia; but the otter, whom he names Mij, takes up a great deal of Travers's attention, and he's unable to spend much time writing. When Travers leaves Mij in the local veterinarian's care while he returns to London for a business trip, Mij is killed in a road accident. Despite this depressing news, Travers takes solace in the appearance of a female otter and her three cubs, spotted near Mij and Travers's favorite hangout. Travers is convinced that they must be Mij's family and decides to write about his experiences with his otter. The lush photography of the Scottish Highlands provides a pleasant background to this delightful and moving tale.

RIO BRAVO

1959 141m c   ★★★★
Western   /PG
Armada

John Wayne (John T. Chance), Dean Martin (Dude), Ricky Nelson (Colorado Ryan), Angie Dickinson (Feathers), Walter Brennan (Stumpy), Ward Bond (Pat Wheeler), John Russell (Nathan Burdette), Pedro Gonzalez-Gonzalez (Carlos), Estelita Rodriguez (Consuelo), Claude Akins (Joe Burdette)

p, Howard Hawks; d, Howard Hawks; w, Jules Furthman, Leigh Brackett (based on a story by Barbara Hawks McCampbell); ph, Russell Harlan (Technicolor); ed, Folmar Blangsted; m, Dimitri Tiomkin; art d, Leo K. Kuter; cos, Marjorie Best

Annoyed that the critically acclaimed and immensely popular western HIGH NOON portrayed a sheriff so afraid of his adversaries that he spends most of the movie asking the townsfolk for help, director Howard Hawks—whose first western, RED RIVER, stands as a masterpiece of the genre—decided to make a filmed response, namely RIO BRAVO. Hawks and his star, John Wayne, both felt that a frontier professional would never seek help from those he has been assigned to protect, and that a sheriff should face danger only with those skilled enough to do the job and take care of themselves; amateurs would get in the way. A lengthy, leisurely paced film, RIO BRAVO is set in a small Texas border town, Rio Bravo, that is under the control of evil cattle baron Russell and his dim-witted brother, Akins. The film begins as Martin, a former deputy who has become a pathetic alcoholic because of a tragic love affair, enters the back door of the local saloon and begs for a drink. Akins, who is enjoying a drink and a card game with his men, tosses a coin in Martin's direction, but it lands in a full spittoon—which is what he was really aiming for. Desperate for alcohol, Martin gets on his hands and knees and is about to reach into the spittoon for the coin when the spittoon is violently kicked away. Martin looks up and sees the sheriff, Wayne, staring down at him. Angered, Martin conks Wayne on the head and then goes after Akins. Akins and his men restrain Martin and then begin beating on the sheriff. When a bystander tries to stop them, Akins calmly draws his pistol and kills the man at point-blank range. Wayne gathers himself, arrests Akins for murder, throws him in a cell, and tells him he'll sit there until the US marshal comes to get him. Akins brags that Wayne won't be able to keep him in jail long because his brother, Russell, will come with their men and bust him out. Wayne concedes that that may be true, but that Akins will be the first to die in the confrontation.

Aware that he's outnumbered 40 to 1, Wayne wonders if his former deputy can be relied upon to do his share. Wayne's only other help is a toothless, cranky old cripple named Stumpy (Brennan), good only for standing at the cell door with a shotgun. Enter wagonmaster Bond, an old friend of Wayne's who's come through town with his crew. At the saloon Bond offers to help, but Wayne tells him that he's not "good enough" to take on Russell's men. Wayne does notice that Bond has hired a new hand, a young, confident gunslinger of few words, Nelson. Wayne would like to enlist the youngster's aid because "he's so good he doesn't feel like he's got to prove it." Bond asks Nelson if he wants to help out, but Nelson declines, saying that he doesn't want to stick his nose into other people's business. This reponse only confirms Wayne's good opinion of the gunslinger. ("He made sense. I'd like to have him.") During the discussion, Wayne has been keeping his eye on a beautiful young stranger who has been playing cards, Dickinson. He suspects she's been cheating and takes her upstairs to question her. But she puts the shy Wayne off his guard by demanding that he search her if he's so smart. Wayne is taken aback by her aggressiveness—but also intrigued. At the same time, Nelson has come to suspect another man at the poker table of doing the cheating, and proves it. With Dickinson cleared, Wayne retracts his demand that she "get outa town."

That night, Bond is shot in the back and killed by one of Russell's men. Martin manages to wound the culprit and sees him run off into the saloon. Wayne and Martin enter the bar—which is filled with Russell's men—and Martin makes them drop their gunbelts to the floor and show him their boots (the killer stepped in a muddy puddle during his escape). None of the men is the killer, and the villainous group's taunts at Martin begin to unnerve him. While standing at the bar, Martin notices blood dripping into a beer glass. Though he has been on the wagon for a few days now, he walks to the far end of the bar and orders a drink. As he brings the drink to his lips, he suddenly whirls around and shoots into the rafters. The killer falls to the floor—dead. Afterwards, with renewed self-confidence and approval from Wayne, Martin buys a new set of clothes and once again proudly wears his deputy's badge. The next day, battle stations are assigned. Martin stands at the entrance to town and collects guns from Russell and his men before they go to the jail to visit Akins. Brennan stays by the cell with his shotgun—thus allowing Wayne freedom of movement. Nelson, who has stayed in town to avenge Bond despite Wayne's order that he leave, stays in the background but watches carefully. While Russell goes to the jail to visit Akins, Martin keeps an eye on his men. Unfortunately, they get the drop on him and knock him cold. One of the men dons Martin's clothes and gun, and the group heads off in the direction of Wayne, who is standing in front of the hotel, his rifle leaning against a post on the porch. Thinking the villains are accompanied by Martin, Wayne drops his guard and the men draw on him. Nelson, who is in the hotel, tells Dickinson to throw a flower pot through the window after he wanders out to the porch. Pretending to be a stranger, Nelson then innocently walks outside and asks what's going on, at which moment the pot comes crashing through the window. Nelson uses the diversion to toss Wayne his rifle and draw his own pistol, and Russell's men are gunned down in short order.

Now Wayne allows Nelson to stay on in town as his deputy. Once again, however, Russell's men get the drop on Wayne and Martin and both are held hostage. While Martin is kept under wraps, two of Russell's men take Wayne to the jail and force him to tell Brennan to release Akins. Despite the danger, Brennan answers with a blast from his shotgun and kills both men. Wayne is freed, but is forced to arrange a swap of Akins for Martin. When morning comes, Wayne and Nelson prepare to make the swap at the building where Martin is being held, on the far side of town. Brennan makes ready to come with them, but Wayne flatly forbids this, because Brennan is crippled and will only get in the way. Wayne and Nelson arrive at the exchange point and send Akins toward the house, while Russell sends Martin toward them. As the hostages pass each other, Martin tackles Akins and drags him behind the ruins of an adobe hut. After a vicious fistfight, Martin manages to subdue Akins. A full-scale gun battle ensues, and at one point three of Russell's men manage to escape the house and get behind Nelson, Wayne, and Martin. Because of their position, there is nothing the lawmen can do to stop the outlaws from getting the drop on them. But suddenly shots ring out and the three assailants fall dead, felled by Brennan, who has disobeyed Wayne's orders and tagged along. Nelson sees that the old man is standing next to one of Bond's wagons, which is filled with dynamite. A stray bullet could blow him to kingdom come. Wayne runs over and tells Brennan of the danger, but Brennan goes back and pulls a case of dynamite off the truck and throws a stick at the house while Wayne shoots it in the air to make it explode. The trick works, and after several huge explosions rock the hideout, Russell's men give themselves up.

Now that peace has returned to Rio Bravo, Wayne goes to the hotel to visit Dickinson. He is shocked to find her in a skimpy dance-hall outfit, but, as she tells the sheriff, if she's to sing in the saloon for a living she needs all the help she can get. Wayne's failure to respond to this infuriates Dickinson, who then admits that she put on the outfit to make Wayne jealous, hoping he'd tell her not to wear it. He answers that he'll arrest her if she wears it in public, and Dickinson beams at the threat—which is as close as Wayne is going to get to telling her he loves her—changes her clothes, and kisses him. Wayne tosses her sexy tights out the window; they land next to Martin and Brennan, who happen to be walking by. Brennan picks up the tights and looks up at the window, and both men laugh as they walk off.

With its simple plotline, familiar characters, songs, and frequent humor, RIO BRAVO is outstanding entertainment. However, the film has been overrated by some zealous critics, who either ignore its weak points or defend them as praiseworthy oddities. As enjoyable as the film is, it has flaws that prevent it from reaching the classic status of RED RIVER—particularly the casting. Pop star Ricky Nelson was cast on the basis of his great popularity with teenagers rather than because of any acting talent, a decision that ensured additional box office from young girls who wouldn't normally think of going to see a western. Despite his moneymaking potential, however, Nelson simply couldn't act, and Hawks must have known it. The singer is given the fewest lines possible for a third-billed actor, and he is physically restricted to the background or alongside the other leads. He is never given center stage alone—this is no Montgomery Clift (Wayne's costar in RED RIVER). Also somewhat weak is Angie Dickinson. While she is given all the right Hawksian dialog and her character is the quintessential Hawks woman, tough enough to stand up to any man who comes her way, she doesn't possess the spunkiness of a Jean Arthur or the sultriness of a Lauren Bacall. Wayne, however, turns in a fine performance (though not as good his work in RED RIVER), and Walter

Brennan is superb as the grouchy, nasty old man who is undyingly loyal to his friends. The real revelation, however, is Dean Martin. His role as the drunken deputy who redeems himself is crucial to the film, and the singer-actor handles his part with skill. Hawks enjoyed working with Martin, whom he found eager and willing to take direction. Martin was so intent to please Hawks that on the first day of shooting he showed up on the set, as the director described it in an interview, "dressed like a musical comedy cowboy. I said, 'Dean, look, you know a little about drinking. You've seen a lot of drunks. I want a *drunk*. I want a guy in an old dirty sweatshirt and an old hat.' He went over, and he came back with the outfit he wore in the picture. He must have been successful because Jack Warner said to me, 'We hired Dean Martin. When's he going to be in this picture?' I said, 'He's the funny-looking guy in the old hat.' 'Holy smoke, is that Dean Martin?'" (Joseph McBride, *Hawks on Hawks*.)

RIO BRAVO was very successful commercially, and Hawks later used two variations of the story (with the same character types, similar situations, sometimes even the same sets) in his last two westerns, EL DORADO and RIO LOBO. All cowritten by Leigh Brackett, the films form a sort of informal trilogy, although they become successively weaker. Though Hawks was inspired to make RIO BRAVO as a rebuttal to HIGH NOON, his daughter, Barbara Hawks McCampbell, an aspiring writer, came up with the basic plotline that later became the film's climax— outlaws holed up in a house, while the heroes explode sticks of dynamite by shooting them like clay targets—and was paid and given screen credit for the story. Overall, RIO BRAVO is an excellent film featuring strong, proud, but very human characters who fight against their various handicaps and pull together to do a job and do it right. The people in RIO BRAVO have the same kind of deep affection and understanding for one another as do close family members who are not afraid to speak truthfully for fear of hurting each other's feelings, and it is that aspect of the film that is so appealing. Director John Carpenter's second feature, ASSAULT ON PRECINCT 13, is an updated remake of RIO BRAVO.

RIO GRANDE

1950   105m   bw   ★★★★
Western/War   /U
Argosy

John Wayne *(Lt. Col. Kirby Yorke)*, Maureen O'Hara *(Mrs. Kathleen Yorke)*, Ben Johnson *(Trooper Tyree)*, Claude Jarman, Jr. *(Trooper Jeff Yorke)*, Harry Carey, Jr. *(Trooper Daniel "Sandy" Boone)*, Chill Wills *(Dr. Wilkins)*, J. Carrol Naish *(Gen. Philip Sheridan)*, Victor McLaglen *(Sgt. Maj. Quincannon)*, Grant Withers *(Deputy Marshal)*, Peter Ortiz *(Capt. St. Jacques)*

p, John Ford, Merian C. Cooper; d, John Ford; w, James Kevin McGuinness (based on the story "Mission with No Record" by James Warner Bellah); ph, Bert Glennon; ed, Jack Murray; m, Victor Young; art d, Frank Hotaling; fx, Howard Lydecker, Theodore Lydecker; cos, Adele Palmer

This fine portrait of the US Cavalry was the third in John Ford's magnificent trilogy about the troopers of the Old West, following FORT APACHE and SHE WORE A YELLOW RIBBON. Lt. Col. Kirby Yorke (John Wayne) is a tough commanding officer at a remote cavalry post whose hard edge is softened when his only son, Jeff (Claude Jarman, Jr.), reports for duty. After dropping out of West Point, the shamed Jeff has enlisted in the Cavalry and now wants to prove himself to his father. Kirby is cool toward the boy, promising no favoritism, and explains what Army life is really about: "Put out of your mind any romantic ideas that it's

a way of glory. It's a life of suffering and hardship, an uncompromising devotion to your oath and your duty." Jeff is taken under the wings of fun-loving troopers Tyree (Ben Johnson) and Boone (Harry Carey, Jr.), who keep an eye on the young man, and the arrival of Kathleen Yorke (Maureen O'Hara), Kirby's estranged wife and Jeff's mother, adds some tension to the scene. She is determined to buy back Jeff's enlistment, and in the process rekindles Kirby's love for her. An excellent post-Civil War tale with romance (Wayne and O'Hara), humor (Johnson, Carey, and Victor McLaglen), and music (a few tunes by the Sons of the Pioneers), RIO GRANDE is one of Ford's great achievements. As in FORT APACHE and SHE WORE A YELLOW RIBBON, Ford creates a powerful portrait of the wild, remote Southwest during the Indian wars, presenting the traditions and exploits of the old cavalry in very realistic terms, showing them in action as tired, dirty, wounded men performing their assignments in pain and discomfort and emphasizing the real glory of these soldiers as typified by their leader Kirby. The director's camera angles, broadly encompassing whole lines of riding cavalrymen, accentuate their prosaic nobility and dedication to taming the frontier. Much of the score nicely supports the story, indicating the cavalrymen's Irish background and sentimentality, especially in the inclusion of the fine Sons of the Pioneers song "I'll Take You Home Again, Kathleen."

RIO LOBO

1970   114m   c   ★½
Western   G/PG
Malabar/Cinema Center

John Wayne *(Col. Cord McNally)*, Jorge Rivero *(Capt. Pierre Cordona)*, Jennifer O'Neill *(Shasta Delaney)*, Jack Elam *(Phillips)*, Victor French *(Ketcham)*, Susana Dosamantes *(Maria Carmen)*, Christopher Mitchum *(Tuscarora)*, Mike Henry *(Sheriff Tom Hendricks)*, David Huddleston *(Dr. Jones)*, Bill Williams *(Sheriff Pat Cronin)*

p, Howard Hawks; d, Howard Hawks; w, Leigh Brackett, Burton Wohl (based on a story by Burton Wohl); ph, William Clothier (Technicolor); ed, John Woodcock; m, Jerry Goldsmith; prod d, Robert Smith; fx, A.D. Flowers, Cliff Wenger; cos, Luster Bayless, Ted Parvin

This is probably the hardest film to watch that either Howard Hawks or John Wayne ever took part in, surpassing even Wayne's early days in Republic's "Three Mesquiteer" series for forced acting and situations. The 1930s pictures are more forgivable because the budgets were limiting and the outings were approached routinely. But for such a refined director as Hawks to end his career on a note like this, having made some of the finest films in the history of American cinema, is an atrocity not worth the silver used in the negative. The story isn't so bad, taking place soon after the Civil War. Union captain Wayne teams up with two Confederate soldiers to track down the man responsible for stealing a shipment of gold. Their efforts land them in the middle of a town being terrorized by a crooked sheriff. Wayne and company put an end to the sheriff's tyranny by rallying the townspeople to stand up for their rights. Witty lines are injected that would normally provide a chuckle but are so poorly delivered here that veiwers are left sighing. The common Hawksian theme of male comradeship can be found in the relationship between Wayne and his Confederate cohorts, but the way Wayne and his supporting cast walk through their roles is ridiculous. Rivero and O'Neill face the Duke like beginning stars in the shadow of a great master, something Wayne is aware of and can't seem to shake. Only the performance of Elam remains lively, but it is the type of characterization he has done dozens of times. A sad finale to Hawks's magnificent career.

RISE OF LOUIS XIV, THE
(LA PRISE DE POUVOIR PAR LOUIS XIV)

1966 100m c ★★★
Biography G/U
O.R.T.F. (France)

Jean-Marie Patte *(King Louis XIV)*, Raymond Jourdan *(Jean Baptiste Colbert)*, Silvagni *(Cardinal Mazarin)*, Katherina Renn *(Queen Anne of Austria)*, Dominique Vincent *(Mme. du Plessis)*, Pierre Barrat *(Nicolas Fouquet)*, Fernand Fabre *(Michel Le Tellier)*, Francoise Ponty *(Louise de la Valliere)*, Joelle Langeois *(Marie Therese)*, Jacqueline Corot *(Mme. Henrietta)*

d, Roberto Rossellini; w, Philippe Erlanger, Jean Gruault; ph, Georges Leclerc (Eastmancolor); ed, Armand Ridel; art d, Maurice Valay; cos, Christiane Coste

This is Roberto Rossellini's sparse, near-documentary look at the young Sun King (Jean-Marie Patte) and at how he codified and choreographed an empire, framing fashions to ensure absolute obedience. No detail of the artful young king's designs and graces—which culminated in the structured elegance of the court at Versailles—is too small to be captured by the camera, while the big events, the executions and rebellions, are, quite properly, trivialized. What won obeisance for playboy Louis was fashion, carefully crafted for conquest. Rossellini's pans and zooms follow these strategies of manners and mores intimately: Louis's dying mentor Mazarin (Silvagni) rouges his pallid cheeks prior to his audience with the young king; Louis demands more height to his wigs to enhance his stature and more lace to his jacket to gain attention; the king choreographs the rituals attendant on funerals, cabinet meetings, banquets. The complexities of Louis's life-structurings consolidate his previously shaky power—all eyes are on the young king, hoping to spot each new nuance, each fad-to-be—and intrigues and plots are forgotten in this atmosphere of utter attendance: the Sun King is all-powerful. A revival of sorts for Rossellini, this picture would set the standard for its genre, playing as important a part in film history as did his earliest Neo-Realist films. Like PAISAN, its predecessor of 20 years, the film is constructed of episodes, each giving the observer a chance to bear witness to a reality, a view of history not of battles and bravado, but of guile, manipulation, and role-playing charisma.

RISKY BUSINESS

1983 98m c ★★★½
Comedy R/18
Geffen

Tom Cruise *(Joel)*, Rebecca De Mornay *(Lana)*, Joe Pantoliano *(Guido)*, Richard Masur *(Rutherford)*, Bronson Pinchot *(Barry)*, Curtis Armstrong *(Miles)*, Nicholas Pryor *(Joel's Father)*, Janet Carroll *(Joel's Mother)*, Shera Danese *(Vicki)*, Raphael Sbarge *(Glenn)*

p, Jon Avnet, Steve Tisch; d, Paul Brickman; w, Paul Brickman; ph, Reynaldo Villalobos (Technicolor); ed, Richard Chew; m, Tangerine Dream; prod d, William J. Cassidy; cos, Robert de Mora

One of the key films of the 1980s, it proved that a teen sex comedy could also be a superior film. Smart, stylish, and cynical about the values of its time, this movie aspires to be THE GRADUATE for its generation and it comes pretty darn close. The affluent teenaged hero is poised on the brink of manhood eager for the promised pleasures of maturity and fearful of the

responsibilities. One wrong step could destroy a potentially bright future. The title refers to both sex and capitalist endeavor; this film documents a time in which everything has become a commodity.

Like Fellini's 8½, RISKY BUSINESS begins with a revealing dream of its stymied protagonist. "The dream is always the same": a steamy sexual encounter is nightmarishly transformed into a crucial college entrance examination to which Joel (Tom Cruise) has arrived too late. There will no future for our young protagonist. Joel lives in a fashionable Chicago suburb with his alarmingly straight parents (Nicholas Pryor and Janet Carroll). They are going off on a trip leaving their outwardly model son in charge. Munching on frozen TV dinners and raiding his Dad's liquor cabinet, Joel lives out an adolescent rock 'n' roll fantasy. Clad in a button-down shirt and Jockey briefs, he plays air guitar and dances wildly to Bob Seeger's anthem, "Old Time Rock 'n' Roll." This was a star-making scene for the young Tom Cruise. Of course, his thoughts soon turn to sex and the "adult" ads in a local newspaper. After an unsettling initial encounter with a Black transvestite prostitute, Joel is referred to the services of the spectacular Lana (Rebecca De Mornay) who visits his home and rocks his world. The morning after, the kittenish hooker surveys her upscale surroundings and proposes to Joel a plan that could net them a lot of money. She and her associates have something that the neighborhood boys want and Joel has an empty house where they can all gather. What sounds like a risky but potentially profitable plan is complicated by the intervention of Guido the Killer Pimp (Joe Pantoliano) and the equally frightening interviewer from Princeton University, Mr. Rutherford (Richard Masur).

Cruise is likable and credible in the lead. His youthful nervousness and exuberance in early part of the film is joyous to behold. De Mornay is exceedingly sexy and touching as the woman who changes a young man's life. This film should have instantly catapulted her to stardom but that turned out to be a much more gradual process. Bronson Pinchot and Curtis Armstrong are also memorable in supporting roles. Paul Brickman wrote a rich and darkly satirical screenplay. One wonders if his true inspiration for this sexy cynical movie was actually the beloved Dr. Seuss children's story, "The Cat in the Hat" in which a mysterious feline enters the ho-hum lives of two innocent children. In the course of their adventurous day, he thoroughly disrupts their household and they have to scramble to get everything back to normal before their mother returns home. Who knows? In any event, Brickman does a slick professional job with his first directorial effort. Tangerine Dream provided the dreamy electronic score.

RITA, SUE AND BOB TOO!

1987 95m c ★★★
Comedy R/18
Film Four/Umbrella/British Screen (U.K.)

Michelle Holmes *(Sue)*, Siobhan Finneran *(Rita)*, George Costigan *(Bob)*, Lesley Sharp *(Michelle, Bob's Wife)*, Willie Ross *(Sue's Father)*, Patti Nicholls *(Sue's Mother)*, Kulvinder Ghir *(Aslam)*, Paul Oldham *(Lee)*, Bryan Heeley *(Michael)*

p, Sandy Lieberson, Patsy Pollock; d, Alan Clarke; w, Andrea Dunbar (based on her plays "The Arbor," "Rita, Sue and Bob Too"); ph, Ivan Strasburg (Eastmancolor); ed, Stephen Singleton; m, Michael Kamen; art d, Len Huntingford; cos, Cathy Cook

Sue (Michelle Holmes) and Rita (Siobhan Finneran) are hefty teenage girls who live in a deteriorating housing project in economically depressed north England. As the film opens, they trek across town to baby-sit for Bob (George Costigan) and Michelle (Lesley Sharp), a middle-class suburban couple. Instead of driving the baby-sitters home at the end of the evening, George takes them out on the darkened moors, where he produces a condom for their inspection and then proposes they put it to use. After a bit of glib demurring, the girls accept. All three are more or less delighted by the experience and repeat it frequently. But their cozy arrangement runs into problems. Based on two plays by Andrea Dunbar, this is a sex comedy in which the on-screen sex (which is limited) is far less important than the idea of that sex. With their *menage a trois*, the girls are capable of bringing some excitement to their lives even if the surrounding world wallows in hopeless inertia. Although there are some slow sections, RITA, SUE AND BOB TOO! provides a number of good laughs and also more than a few empathetic winces.

RIVER, THE

1951 99m c   ★★★½
Drama   /U
UA

Nora Swinburne *(The Mother)*, Esmond Knight *(The Father)*, Arthur Shields *(Mr. John)*, Thomas E. Breen *(Capt. John)*, Suprova Mukerjee *(Nan)*, Patricia Walters *(Harriet)*, Radha *(Melanie)*, Adrienne Corri *(Valerie)*, Richard Foster *(Bogey)*, Penelope Wilkinson *(Elizabeth)*

p, Kenneth McEldownery; d, Jean Renoir; w, Jean Renoir, Rumer Godden (based on the novel by Godden); ph, Claude Renoir, Ramananda Sen Gupta (Technicolor); ed, George Gale; m, M.A. Partha Sarathy

Before returning to France after his stay in Hollywood, director Jean Renoir stopped over in India, where he had the creative license to explore his feeling for nature. The colorful life along the Ganges River proved the perfect setting for this exploration, resulting in a lively, yet subtle, vision of the beautiful environment—which is wholly romanticized, but nonetheless captivating. The simple story centers on a British family whose routine life is interrupted by Breen, a visiting war veteran who has come to claim his cousin's daughter. The teenage daughters of the family fall deeply in love with the soldier, the eldest believing that her Prince Charming has come to take her away. Renoir brings out the best from his child actors, presenting their complex emotions in a fair and mature manner.

RIVER, THE

1984 122m c   ★★★
Drama   PG-13/PG
Universal

Mel Gibson *(Tom Garvey)*, Sissy Spacek *(Mae Garvey)*, Shane Bailey *(Lewis Garvey)*, Becky Jo Lynch *(Beth Garvey)*, Scott Glenn *(Joe Wade)*, Don Hood *(Sen. Neiswinder)*, Billy "Green" Bush *(Harve Stanley)*, James Tolkan *(Howard Simpson)*, Bob W. Douglas *(Hal Richardson)*, Andy Stahl *(Dave Birkin)*

p, Edward Lewis, Robert Cortes; d, Mark Rydell; w, Robert Dillon, Julian Barry (based on a story by Dillon); ph, Vilmos Zsigmond (Technicolor); ed, Sidney Levin; m, John Williams; prod d, Charles Rosen; art d, Norman Newberry; fx, Ken Pepiot, Stan Parks; cos, Joe I. Tompkins

A good film for the viewer who isn't interested in being entertained but is willing to be thrown into the muck of the problems facing hard-working American farmers. Strong, stubborn Tom Garvey (Mel Gibson) has been working his family farm since his youth. He and Mae (Sissy Spacek), his "stand by your man" wife,

are struggling to maintain their way of life against terrible odds. The elements are not on their side, and neither is local kingpin Joe Wade (Scott Glenn), who wants to build a dam on the river that runs through the Garvey acreage. Wade intends to use his clout to buy out all the farmers who stand in his way, then flood their lands in order to make a reservoir for his own use. The background story is that Garvey and Wade were once friends, and Wade had also been Mae's lover before she chose Garvey and the hard life she now leads. The script barely manages to keep the characters from being caricatures, since everyone does, more or less, exactly what is expected. Good performances, especially from Glenn as "Mr. Greed" and Spacek as "Earth Mother." Gibson is somewhat rigid, although his is not an easy role to portray. The Southern dialects are well handled, and the special effects are excellent. What is missing is any attempt to show political or organizational solutions to the farm problems and the woes farmers face. Instead, we are shown the strong individualist who goes deeply into himself in order to outwit the forces of profit. Nominations for Academy Awards: Spacek for Best Actress (losing to Sally Field for PLACES IN THE HEART), Best Cinematography, and Best Sound.

RIVER'S EDGE

1987 99m c   ★★★½
Drama   R/18
Hemdale

Crispin Glover *(Layne)*, Keanu Reeves *(Matt)*, Ione Skye *(Clarissa)*, Daniel Roebuck *(Samson "John" Tollette)*, Dennis Hopper *(Feck)*, Joshua Miller *(Tim)*, Roxana Zal *(Maggie)*, Josh Richman *(Tony)*, Phil Brock *(Mike)*, Tom Bower *(Bennett)*

p, Sarah Pillsbury, Midge Sanford, David Streit; d, Tim Hunter; w, Neal Jimenez; ph, Frederick Elmes (Metrocolor); ed, Howard Smith, Sonya Sones; m, Jurgen Knieper; prod d, John Muto; art d, Mick Muhlfriedel; cos, Claudia Brown

One of the most haunting films of the 1980s, RIVER'S EDGE looks at a suburban, postpunk generation which has no causes, no morals, no feelings, and, worst of all, no future.

This controversial film, based on a notorious 1981 murder case profiled in *Rolling Stone*, opens with John Tollette (Daniel Roebuck), a hulking teenager who strangles his girlfriend Jamie (Danyi Deats, in the ultimate thankless role) and then matter-of-factly tells his friends about it. Matt (Keanu Reeves) and Clarissa (Ione Skye), the murdered girl's best friend, are disturbed, but Layne (Crispin Glover), a speed freak, views the situation differently. In his eyes, Jamie was a friend, but now she's dead; John is also their friend, but he's still alive and needs their help. As tensions within the group escalate, John and Layne take refuge with Feck (Dennis Hopper), a burned-out biker from the 1960s who had killed his own beloved girlfriend and has now given his heart to a blow-up sex doll named Ellie.

RIVER'S EDGE owes its success, in large part, to Neal Jimenez's superb screenplay, which digs beneath the facades that contemporary teenagers hide behind and yields honest and complex portraits. This generation's postpunk worldview is rooted in nihilism, detachment, fear of nuclear annihilation, and the belief that there is no future. As a result the concepts of life and death become blurred, if not altogether irrelevent, since nothing matters except friends, rock 'n' roll, and getting stoned.

The film also boasts the best cast of unknowns since Francis Ford Coppola's THE OUTSIDERS. Reeves and Skye are superb as the moral centers of the film, Roebuck is great as the killer, and the supporting performaces are also impressive. Glover's performance is a peculiar caricature that doesn't fit comfortably with the rest of the film's acting, but it is one of such intensity that it cannot be forgotten. Cast as a symbol of the 1960s is Hopper, whose free-wheeling, pot-smoking EASY RIDER character is the role model for the RIVER'S EDGE kids. Hopper is excellent, playing his part somewhere between lunacy and honesty.

While RIVER'S EDGE is disturbing—it contains numerous scenes of drinking, pill popping, and driving combined; is filled with profanity; and often cuts back to a young girl's naked, lifeless body—it deals with issues of profound importance to parents and teenagers alike. Not since Luis Bunuel's portrait of youth in Mexico City's slums, LOS OLVIDADOS, has a film so perfectly captured a generation's lack of hope and direction.

ROAD HOUSE

1948 95m bw   ★★★
Thriller   /A
FOX

Ida Lupino (Lily Stevens), Cornel Wilde (Pete Morgan), Celeste Holm (Susie Smith), Richard Widmark (Jefty Robbins), O.Z. Whitehead (Arthur), Robert Karnes (Mike), George Andre Beranger (Lefty), Ian MacDonald (Police Captain), Grandon Rhodes (Judge), Jack G. Lee (Sam)

p, Edward Chodorov; d, Jean Negulesco; w, Edward Chodorov (based on a story by Margaret Gruen, Oscar Saul); ph, Joseph La Shelle; ed, James B. Clark; m, Cyril J. Mockridge; art d, Lyle Wheeler, Maurice Ransford; fx, Fred Sersen; cos, Kay Nelson

A stylish and perverse film noir which stars Widmark as the owner of a roadhouse near the Canadian border and Wilde as his best friend and manager. When they hire Lupino as the joint's singer and piano player, the friendship takes a strange turn. Widmark becomes obsessed with Lupino, who in turn finds herself attracted to Wilde. Wilde, however, also the object of cashier Holm's desires, remains aloof. When Widmark goes away on a hunting trip, Wilde finally gives in to Lupino and the two become lovers. When Widmark returns and is told by Wilde of the new situation, Widmark's dark side comes to light. He stages a robbery which points to Wilde as the guilty party. Rather than watch the framed Wilde go to jail, however, he persuades the judge to release the "criminal" into his custody. Widmark's form of imprisonment is a psychological one—forcing Wilde to stay on at the roadhouse but keeping him from Lupino and, ultimately, his freedom. To further torment him, Widmark arranges for a trip to a lodge nestled in the woods, placing Wilde even closer to the border than before. Widmark hopes that his "prisoner" will make an attempt to escape across the border, thereby giving Widmark the chance to shoot him. Meantime, Holm, who has come along to the lodge, is still silently in love with Wilde. A chance finally comes to escape, and Wilde and Lupino run off into the woods. Holm tries to warn them that Widmark is on their trail, hunting them with a psychotic vengeance, but in the process she is wounded by the crazed hunter. A battle follows between Widmark and Wilde. Lupino, determined to fight for her man, intervenes and guns down Widmark for the animal he is. A strong movie scattered with land mines of psychotic characters, ROAD HOUSE has a disturbing quality of psychological torture to it—a quality magnified by the claustrophobic atmosphere of the stylized diner and the false outdoors of the studio's sound stage. Wilde does fine as the victimized lover, Widmark plays his archetypal villain with his usual intensity, and Lupino is remarkable in her raw toughness. Holm, however, is the one who keeps ROAD HOUSE from going over the edge by playing a normal girl with a foothold on reality. Adding to the

film's atmosphere is Lupino's delivery of a few bluesy numbers including "Again," (Dorcas Cochran, Lionel Newman), "One for My Baby" (Johnny Mercer, Harold Arlen), and "The Right Time."

ROAD TO MOROCCO

1942 83m bw   ★★★★
Comedy/Musical   /U
Paramount

Bing Crosby (Jeff Peters), Bob Hope (Turkey Jackson), Dorothy Lamour (Princess Shalmar), Anthony Quinn (Mullay Kasim), Dona Drake (Mihirmah), Mikhail Rasumny (Ahmed Fey), Vladimir Sokoloff (Hyder Khan), George Givot (Neb Jolla), Andrew Tombes (Oso Bucco), Leon Belasco (Yusef)

p, Paul Jones; d, David Butler; w, Frank Butler, Don Hartman; ph, William Mellor; ed, Irene Morra; art d, Hans Dreier, Robert Usher; chor, Paul Oscard; cos, Edith Head

The third, and best, in the "Road" series, ROAD TO MOROCCO has everything going for it. Bob Hope and Bing Crosby were not yet tired of the formula, and their breezy acting wafts the picture along in a melange of gags, songs, thrills, and calculated absurdities. The duo had already sent up adventure movies in ROAD TO SINGAPORE and jungle films in ROAD TO ZANZIBAR—the next target was the Arabian Nights. Jeff Peters (Crosby) and Turkey Jackson (Hope) are the lone survivors of a Mediterranean shipwreck. They land on a beach, mount a passing camel, and go off toward Morocco, where they learn that things aren't swell. The area is parched, the people poor, and foreigners looked upon with scorn. The two are penniless and hungry when a local merchant offers Jeff money to sell Turkey into slavery as the personal plaything of Princess Shalmar (Dorothy Lamour). Jeff makes the deal, Turkey is forcibly removed to the palace, and life in Morocco gets increasingly difficult for everyone thereafter. The picture is filled with great gags and one-liners, including Hope's lament for the Oscar he might have won; the camel's complaint that "this is the screwiest picture I've ever been in!"; Hope's appearance in drag; and the backfire of the "patty cake" routine, after which it's remarked, "Hmmm. That gag sure got around." And there are countless more, delivered at a pace that never lets up.

ROAD TO RIO

1947 100m bw   ★★★½
Comedy/Musical   /U
Paramount

Bing Crosby (Scat Sweeney), Bob Hope (Hot Lips Barton), Dorothy Lamour (Lucia Maria De Andrade), Gale Sondergaard (Catherine Vail), Frank Faylen (Trigger), Joseph Vitale (Tony), Frank Puglia (Rodrigues), Nestor Paiva (Cardoso), Robert Barrat (Johnson), Jerry Colonna (Cavalry Captain)

p, Daniel Dare; d, Norman Z. McLeod; w, Edmund Beloin, Jack Rose; ph, Ernest Laszlo; ed, Ellsworth Hoagland; art d, Hans Dreier, Earl Hedrick; fx, Gordon Jennings, Paul K. Lerpae; chor, Bernard Pearce, Billy Daniel; cos, Edith Head

The fifth "Road" picture was a more standard comedy than most of the others and paid off at the box office, becoming the top-grossing film of the year. Gone were the talking animals and some of the zany humor of the earlier entries. In their place was a more conventional story, sans Hollywood in-jokes, in which Hot Lips Barton (Bob Hope) and Scat Sweeney (Bing Crosby) are musicians who accidentally cause a fire at a carnival. To avoid being arrested for arson, they jump on an ocean liner headed for

Rio and stow away. On the ship, they meet Lucia Maria De Andrade (Dorothy Lamour), who is friendly, then chilly, smiling, then frowning, so that the boys can't figure her out. Upon investigation, they discover she has been hypnotized by the evil Catherine Veil (Gale Sondergaard) and is to marry a man she doesn't love once they reach Rio. Of course, the pair decide they must interfere and prevent the marriage, going so far as to crash the wedding party dressed as a pirate (Crosby) and a Latin American bombshell (Hope in drag) in order to expose the hypnotist's deceit. Lots of laughs.

ROAD TO UTOPIA

1945   90m   bw   ★★★½
Comedy/Musical   /PG
Paramount

Bing Crosby (Duke Johnson/Junior Hooton), Bob Hope (Chester Hooton), Dorothy Lamour (Sal Van Hoyden), Hillary Brooke (Kate), Douglas Dumbrille (Ace Larson), Jack LaRue (LeBec), Robert Barrat (Sperry), Nestor Paiva (McGurk), Robert Benchley (Narrator), Will Wright (Mr. Latimer)

p, Paul Jones; d, Hal Walker; w, Norman Panama, Melvin Frank; ph, Lionel Lindon; ed, Stuart Gilmore; m, Leigh Harline; art d, Hans Dreier, Roland Anderson; fx, Farciot Edouart; chor, Danny Dare; cos, Edith Head; anim, Jerry Fairbanks

This addition to the "Road" series is told in flashback, as a wealthy couple, Chester Hooton (Bob Hope) and Sal Van Hoyden (Dorothy Lamour), recall how they got rich. They'd gained control of a Klondike gold mine but lost their best friend, Duke Johnson (Bing Crosby), in the process. While they reminisce, he suddenly pops in, very much alive. The three begin to talk about the old days, and the film goes back in time to show Chester and Duke as a couple of failed vaudevillians who try to make a shady deal in San Francisco and then must flee the city. They board a northbound ship and purloin the deed to a gold mine in Alaska from a pair of vicious murderers. Considering this theft and the fact that they are running from the cops, the vaudevillians pretend to be the tough guys they just scammed. But, in keeping with tradition, the duo get in deep trouble and find themselves vying for the affections of Sal before the final credits roll. Lots of excellent gags punctuate the story, including one in which Hope and Crosby are in the boiler room of the steamer when a formally dressed gentleman walks in looking for a match. Hope and Crosby want to know if he's supposed to be in the movie, and the man replies with a shrug, "Nope, I'm taking a shortcut to stage 10." Once again, animals talk, sight gags abound, and the complementing temperaments of Hope and Crosby are mined to great advantage.

ROAD TO ZANZIBAR

1941   92m   bw   ★★★½
Comedy/Musical   /PG
Paramount

Bing Crosby (Chuck Reardon), Bob Hope (Hubert "Fearless" Frazier), Dorothy Lamour (Donna Latour), Una Merkel (Julia Quimby), Eric Blore (Charles Kimble), Iris Adrian (French Soubrette in Cafe), Lionel Royce (Mons. Lebec), Buck Woods (Thonga), Leigh Whipper (Scarface), Ernest Whitman (Whiteface)

p, Paul Jones; d, Victor Schertzinger; w, Frank Butler, Don Hartman (based on the story "Find Colonel Fawcett" by Don Hartman, Sy Bartlett); ph, Ted Tetzlaff; ed, Alma Macrorie; m, Victor Young; art d, Hans Dreier, Robert Usher; chor, LeRoy Prinz; cos, Edith Head

Tarzan movies had been around for years when ROAD TO ZANZIBAR, the second of the "Road" pictures, took the opportunity to satirize every jungle picture lensed up to that time. The script was funny, although much of the humor reportedly derived from on-set improvisations. Connivers Fearless Frazier (Bob Hope) and Chuck Reardon (Bing Crosby) must blow town because they sold a bogus diamond mine to Mons. Lebec (Lionel Royce), a criminal type who doesn't take well to being fleeced. Rather than face Lebec, Chuck and Hubert (as Fearless is known) light out for Zanzibar, where they meet a pair of Brooklynite entertainers, Donna Latour (Dorothy Lamour) and Julia Quimby (Una Merkel), who are in Africa to find Donna's brother. The girls convince Chuck and Hubert to put up the money for a safari into the interior, but the boys soon realize that they've been duped. It's not Donna's brother they're after, but a British millionaire she hopes to marry. Things only get worse after that, but that's as expected. The lyrics of "On the Road to Zanzibar" are banal compared to Sammy Cahn's words for "Road to Morocco," but it's a funny routine, with cannibals chanting a nonsense background.

ROAD WARRIOR, THE

1982   94m   c   ★★★★
Science Fiction/Action   R/X
WB   (Australia)

Mel Gibson (Max), Bruce Spence (Gyro Captain), Vernon Wells (Wez), Emil Minty (Feral Kid), Mike Preston (Pappagallo), Kjell Nilsson (Humungus), Virginia Hey (Warrior Woman), Syd Heylen (Curmudgeon), Moira Claux (Big Rebecca), David Slingsby (Quiet Man)

p, Byron Kennedy; d, George Miller; w, Terry Hayes, George Miller, Brian Hannat; ph, Dean Semler (Panavision, Technicolor); ed, David Stiven, Tim Wellburn, Michael Chirgwin; m, Brian May; art d, Graham Walker; fx, Jeffrey Clifford, Kim Priest; cos, Norma Moriceau

Director George Miller, whose film MAD MAX set new standards of kinetic, visceral excitement, has surpassed himself with this sequel, THE ROAD WARRIOR. Both are set in a post-apocalypse savage world devoted solely to the pursuit of gasoline and oil with which to fuel the vehicles. In THE ROAD WARRIOR, Max (Mel Gibson), whose wife and child were killed in MAD MAX, has become an alienated drifter. He is led by the Gyro Captain (Bruce Spence) to a small oil refinery populated by the "good" people under the leadership of Pappagallo (Mike Preston). Their precious encampment is constantly attacked by an army of grotesque, nomadic desert rats led by a massive bodybuilder known as the Humungus (Kjell Nilsson), who wants their gasoline. In one of the most spectacular chase scenes ever put on film, Max and his comrades fight off a series of vicious high-speed attacks from a convoy of bizarre vehicles. While the plot line is that of a simple B western, director Miller brings every visual trick in the book into play, creating a stunningly detailed, vibrant new world that never ceases to amaze. He pulls all the fresh and original elements of MAD MAX together, and straightens out his earlier muddled narrative style into a strict linear plot that rips along at a breathtaking pace.

ROARING TWENTIES, THE

1939   104m   bw   ★★★★
Crime   /PG
WB

James Cagney *(Eddie Bartlett)*, Priscilla Lane *(Jean Sherman)*, Humphrey Bogart *(George Hally)*, Jeffrey Lynn *(Lloyd Hart)*, Gladys George *(Panama Smith)*, Frank McHugh *(Danny Green)*, Paul Kelly *(Nick Brown)*, Elisabeth Risdon *(Mrs. Sherman)*, Edward Keane *(Pete Henderson)*, Joe Sawyer *(Sgt. Pete Jones)*

p, Samuel Bischoff; d, Raoul Walsh, Anatole Litvak; w, Jerry Wald, Richard Macaulay, Robert Rossen (based on a story by Mark Hellinger); ph, Ernest Haller; ed, Jack Killifer; m, Heinz Roemheld, Ray Heindorf; art d, Max Parker; fx, Byron Haskin, Edwin DuPar; cos, Milo Anderson

This slick, whirlwind-paced crime melodrama is another tour de force for James Cagney, oozing nostalgia and providing a companion piece to ANGELS WITH DIRTY FACES. It was the brainchild of journalist-turned-producer Mark Hellinger, who assures audiences in voice-over during the opening credits that what they are about to see is based upon real characters and events he covered as a newsman during the 1920s when the gangster was king and Prohibition was nothing more than a bad law that elevated the gangster to his dangerous throne. The film is also the story of three men, Cagney, Bogart, and Lynn, all of them doughboys.

The picture opens with Bogart in a bomb crater during a battle in France. As a barrage sends up smoke and dirt, another soldier, Cagney, comes tumbling into the crater, landing right on Bogart's head. "You always come into a hole like that?" carps Bogart. "What did you want me to do, knock?" replies Cagney. Later, in a trench, Cagney, Lynn, and Bogart talk about what they will do when the war is over. Lynn intends to be a lawyer when he is mustered out, and Cagney plans on going back to repairing cabs, a job he enjoys, but Bogart explains that he is determined to put his Army weapons training to good use. It's clear that Bogart is the real criminal of the lot.

When the war ends Cagney goes back to his old garage, but the owner tells him he's hired mechanics to replace him. So insulting are two of the mechanics who now hold his old job that Cagney punches one of them, knocking him and the other mechanic to the floor. Cagney's old friend, taxi driver McHugh, puts him up in his little room, and Cagney lives like thousands of returning veterans in those days, hand to mouth, getting and losing menial jobs. Finally he gets a job driving a cab. Asked by one of his fares to deliver a package, Cagney enters a store, asks for George, as he has been told to do, and is sent through a secret door and into a speakeasy, where George takes the package (which contains bonded whiskey). She asks Cagney to stay a few minutes and he does, ordering a glass of milk. She tells him that there is golden opportunity for him in distributing booze. Sure it's breaking the law, she says, but Prohibition is a bad law and everyone ignores it, except Temperance fanatics and do-gooder cops. As if emphasizing her point, a policeman enters the secret saloon and asks who has a car parked outside. When a man nervously admits to ownership of the car, the cop tells him to move it or get a ticket for illegal parking. Cagney watches, surprised, as the cop steps up to the bar and is served a free shot of booze. Cagney accepts George's proposition and begins distributing booze, but he is arrested and thrown into jail. George bails him out and Cagney goes into the bootlegging business in a big way, first making his own bathtub gin with McHugh, then producing his synthetic gin on an assembly-line basis, becoming rich and powerful.

Meanwhile, Cagney hooks up with pert blonde Lane, who had written him when he was overseas, though they had never met. She is only a teenager, and though Cagney tells her to look him up when she grows up, he later helps her land a singing job. Later,

Cagney escorts Lane to her small hometown; however, she turns a cold shoulder to Cagney's romantic interest in her.

Blocking the expansion of Cagney's business is rival bootlegger Kelly, who operates his large gangster enterprises from his Italian restaurant. When Cagney learns that Kelly is smuggling whiskey into the country by disguising ships as Coast Guard vessels, Cagney and his men board a freighter at sea, and confiscate its cargo of liquor. The boss of the ship turns out to be Bogart, who doesn't like working for Kelly and agrees to be Cagney's junior partner. While visiting George, who is now a hostess at a swanky nightclub (modeling her role on the famous Texas Guinan, who greeted all patrons with a brassy "hello, sucker!"), Cagney spots old flame Lane in the chorus. When the proprietor complains about Lane, Cagney buys the place and makes Lane the star singing attraction, much to the chagrin of George, who is in love with Cagney. He has also taken good care of Army buddy Lynn, now a lawyer, turning over all his legal work to him, giving him tens of thousands of dollars to buy fleets of taxicabs, Cagney's first love.

Bootlegger Kelly sees his empire eroding and Cagney becoming more and more powerful. When Cagney realizes that gang war between him and Kelly is about to break out, he tries to effect a truce, meeting with Kelly in the gangster's Italian restaurant, but to no avail. Later, Kelly kidnaps McHugh and delivers his corpse to Cagney's club with a note reading: "Leave me alone and I'll leave you alone." Cagney explodes and rounds up his men, telling Bogart that he's going to have a showdown with Kelly. But Bogart, who is seething by this time at having to play second fiddle to Cagney, refuses to participate in the gun battle to come and even warns Kelly that Cagney and his boys are coming. (Ever the snarling gangster, Bogart expresses his disaffection with a wonderfully funny line: "First you ask me, then you tell me, then you don't tell me anything at all. My feeling's is *hoit*.") When Cagney enters Kelly's restaurant, the gangster and his henchmen are lying in wait, and a gun battle is on, with Kelly's men shot to pieces and Cagney dispatching Kelly.

This confrontation marks the beginning of the end of Cagney's reign as crime boss. And his love life also plummets when he finds Lynn and Lane (who have been in love with each other all along) kissing. Cagney slugs Lynn, but later realizes that he's wrong in insisting upon Lane's love and apologizes to Lynn. Slowly, Cagney's rackets are smashed by the law; he loses millions in the stock market crash and even sells off his fleets of cabs to Bogart, who leaves him just one taxi.

At the end of the wild decade Cagney is reduced to driving that cab and spending most of his time drinking, hanging out in a dive where George sings. Lynn, who by this time has become one of the city's top prosecuting attorneys, has been going after big-shot Bogart, now the town's top crime kingpin. Bogart sends his men to warn Lane that if her husband doesn't stop he will be killed. Lane finds Cagney in an alcoholic state in George's club and begs him to stop Bogart. He refuses to lift a finger to save Lynn, but when a broken-hearted Lane leaves, Cagney thinks it over and, still hopelessly in love with Lane, decides he'll talk to Bogart. He goes to Bogart's mansion, and there Bogart's army of killers makes fun of the shabby Cagney before he is allowed to see the big shot. Cagney tries to persuade Bogart to lay off Lynn, but Bogart tells him he intends to kill their one-time Army buddy, just as ruthlessly as Bogart earlier killed Sawyer, a sergeant he hated during the war and later shot while robbing a booze warehouse. Bogart then decides that he must also kill Cagney because he knows too much about his operation and might help Lynn destroy his empire. He motions for a goon, Biberman, to take Cagney "for a ride" home. Cagney realizes he has received a death sentence and, while being ushered out, grabs Biberman's gun and knocks him down, turning to Bogart, who begs for mercy. But Cagney shows him no more mercy than Bogart was going to show to Lynn and his family, and shoots the mobster to death. Then, using Biberman as a shield, Cagney makes his way downstairs. There Bogart's gang, massed in the living room (all wearing tuxedos, since it is New Year's Eve), fire at Cagney as he moves toward the front door, killing Biberman. Outside, as the snow falls, Cagney makes his dash for life. Several gangsters shoot at him, and he is hit twice but continues his escape. While police close in on the mansion, George, who had been waiting for Cagney in his cab, runs after Cagney. Now mortally wounded, he attempts to climb the steps of a church, but his wobbly legs give out and he tumbles down the steps. Weeping, George embraces the dead gangster. "Who was he?" a cop asks. "His name is Eddie Bartlett," George says tearfully. "What did he do?" the cop says. "He used to be a big shot," George replies as the camera pulls back slowly to show George cradling Cagney's head, the cop leaning over them, the huge and sweeping steps and the snow falling like a blanket, covering not only a dead gangster, but also his reckless era.

Raoul Walsh's direction of this third and last film in which Cagney and Humphrey Bogart appeared together is awesomely swift, encompassing an entire decade in slick episodes, interspersed with newsreel footage of gangsters, rumrunning, and booze being made on an assembly line. Cagney is shown to be a good man ruined by the excesses of the times, a forgotten man of the day, like so many millions of returning servicemen who were forgotten. Though Cagney is a good man gone bad, strains of decency are apparent in his relationship with Lynn and Lane, and in his self-sacrificing attempt to save them from the violence of Bogart, a truly bad man bent on the destruction of society.

Cagney is a dynamo whose performance is akin to an electrical storm, and he is marvelous in every frame, particularly when he is down-and-out and acting the role of a drunk in a stupor. In reality, Cagney was a teetotaler of sorts, his father having been an alcoholic, and he looked back upon the boyhood image of his father to dredge up his shocking portrayal of a man in an alcoholic daze. Bogart is all ice, a sinister creature without human kindness or human affection, while Gladys George is terrific as the loyal saloon gal who will go to the Devil for her man. Priscilla Lane and Jeffrey Lynn are almost too good and pure to be spending so much time with Cagney, but the point is well made that it was the good people who went along with the gangsters that allowed them to flourish.

The clever use of 1920s music, especially some well-chosen jazz numbers, does much to invest THE ROARING TWENTIES with the mood of the era. The film, which Hellinger had long planned to make, was originally to be titled "The World Moves On." It was also originally to be directed by Anatole Litvak, but Walsh replaced him at the last minute. The director and the supercharged Cagney, with whom Walsh was working for the first time, got along famously, especially when Walsh encouraged Cagney to drop his own little bits and pieces of business and dialogue into the film. Though the tragic hero of this stellar film dies splendidly, closing out the year with a salary of $368,333, and ranking second to Gary Cooper at the box office. This would be the last gangster film Cagney would make until he took on the psychotic gangster role in WHITE HEAT almost a decade later, working again with his good friend Walsh.

Cagney's role in THE ROARING TWENTIES is based upon the spectacular rise and fall of New York gangster Larry Fay, a colorful and enigmatic underworld character who promoted the career of Texas Guinan and who reputedly provided the inspiration for F. Scott Fitzgerald's *The Great Gatsby*. The role of the Guinan-type hostess was all-important since it set the whole tenor of the film. At first Ann Sheridan was selected to play this role, but she was replaced by Lee Patrick, who was in turn replaced by Glenda Farrell. But, at the last minute, Gladys George was given the part and she was perfect as the brassy blonde who mistreated customers right and left and was loved for it.

ROBE, THE

1953 135m c   ★★★½
Religious   /U
FOX

Richard Burton *(Marcellus Gallio)*, Jean Simmons *(Diana)*, Victor Mature *(Demetrius)*, Michael Rennie *(Peter)*, Jay Robinson *(Caligula)*, Dean Jagger *(Justus)*, Torin Thatcher *(Sen. Gallio)*, Richard Boone *(Pilate)*, Betta St. John *(Miriam)*, Jeff Morrow *(Paulus)*

p, Frank Ross; d, Henry Koster; w, Philip Dunne (based on the novel by Lloyd C. Douglas); ph, Leon Shamroy (CinemaScope, Technicolor); ed, Barbara McLean; m, Alfred Newman; art d, Lyle Wheeler, George W. Davis; fx, Ray Kellogg

This was the film with which Fox answered the upstart television by employing its heavy gun, CinemaScope, a new widescreen process that could project films on an enormous screen, with a panoramic visual power television could never equal. CinemaScope's debut was a success; audiences (especially Catholic schoolchildren brought by their teachers) flocked to see this majestic, stirring treatment of Lloyd C. Douglas's novel. Richard Burton gained an Oscar nomination for his lead performance (he lost to William Holden for STALAG 17) as a young Roman officer ordered to crucify Christ. He goes about his chore coldly, even rolling dice with his fellow soldiers for the rich red robe worn by their victim. As Christ perishes on the cross, a storm comes up and Burton, who has won the robe, is suddenly startled and perplexed by strange emotions. His Greek slave, Mature, sweeps up the robe and presses it to his tearful face, then vanishes, only to meet the apostle Peter (Rennie), who converts Mature to Christianity. The earthy Burton goes on with his pagan life, participating in military campaigns and—when not lopping off the heads of Rome's enemies—indulging himself in various orgies and revels, as well as wooing his childhood sweetheart (Simmons), who has become interested in Christianity. When the mad Roman emperor Caligula, who cannot abide Christians, hears that the robe possesses magical powers, he demands that Burton secure it for him. But the emperor (played with sustained hysteria and campy gestures by Robinson) is not able to use the robe for his own evil ends and explodes in wrath. Learning that Burton, one of his favorite tribunes, has become sympathetic to the Christians because of the influence of Simmons (now a devout convert to the faith), he demands that Burton and Simmons renounce Christ. Burton defies Robinson, who orders that the lovers be put to death. Both walk blissfully to their doom, but en route to the executioner Burton hands the all-powerful robe to Mature—a gesture that assured Fox of a sequel starring Mature, who would go on to further adventures with the robe in DEMETRIUS AND THE GLADIATORS.

THE ROBE was already under production when Fox mogul Darryl F. Zanuck saw a demonstration of what CinemaScope, with its anamorphic lens created by Prof. Henri Chretien, could do. The problem was that there was only one lens. Zanuck, always a risk-taker, stopped production of THE ROBE and ordered another lens made so that this film would be the first to use the new process, then had the lens guarded night and day to assure Fox's dominance in widescreen experiments. Fox money man Spyros Skouras, convinced that CinemaScope would be the answer to TV's threat, went about cajoling and pressuring theater owners across the US to tear down their old screens and put up the new wide screens necessary for the process. To make sure that the theater owners converted to the wide screens, Zanuck called a meeting of Hollywood studio heads to see a spectacular short in the CinemaScope process, hoping to lease the new lens to the other studios. They were impressed at the process and signed up, except Paramount, which later developed its own widescreen process, Panavision. CinemaScope became the only process used at Fox, but it was an expensive proposition, and to meet the cost the studio cut its film output in half, figuring it would make up the difference in overall box-office receipts by charging a higher ticket price for its CinemaScope offerings. The concept worked for a while, until the process became commonplace; later, Zanuck was forced to admit that Panavision was the superior process, better proportioned to the human eye. Nonetheless, when THE ROBE premiered the novelty of CinemaScope was an immense success. In its first week at the Roxy Theater in New York, THE ROBE grossed a whopping $264,000, and within a few months the film had more than made up its reported $8 million price tag and was on its way to establishing box-office records.

Burton, though by then an accomplished Shakespearean actor, had relatively little film experience—with only a few British films and two unreleased Hollywood movies to his credit—when production of THE ROBE began. Zanuck gambled on him, however, and Burton proved his mettle by doing fine work in his difficult role, appearing in 96 percent of the movie's scenes and delivering numerous speeches. Burton threw himself wholeheartedly into the film and hardly slept throughout the entire production, wearing his togas and tribune uniforms home and often sleeping in them. He proclaimed to friends that this was the opportunity of his lifetime and he would not fail Fox, Zanuck, or CinemaScope, an ambition that proved well-founded when THE ROBE made him an international star and one of Fox's hottest film properties. Critics hailed Burton's performance as stunning, though the actor privately told friends that he considered the part of Marcellus "a prissy role" (John Cottrell, Fergus Cashin, *Richard Burton: Very Close Up*). Nevertheless, the actor was on his way to superstardom, having helped make THE ROBE a watershed picture, best summed up by the *Variety* reviewer who proclaimed, "All roads should lead to THE ROBE—and Fort Knox—for a long time to come." Winner of two Academy Awards: Best Color Art Direction/Set Decoration and Best Color Costume Design. In addition to Burton's nomination, the film was also nominated for Best Picture (losing to FROM HERE TO ETERNITY) and Best Color Cinematography.

ROBERTA
1935 105m bw ★★★★★
Musical/Comedy /U
RKO

Irene Dunne *(Stephanie)*, Fred Astaire *(Huck Haines)*, Ginger Rogers *(Countess Scharwenka/Lizzie Gatz)*, Randolph Scott *(John Kent)*, Helen Westley *(Roberta/Aunt Minnie)*, Victor Varconi *(Ladislaw)*, Claire Dodd *(Sophie)*, Luis Alberni *(Voyda)*, Ferdinand Munier *(Lord Delves)*, Torben Meyer *(Albert)*

p, Pandro S. Berman; d, William A. Seiter; w, Jane Murfin, Sam Mintz, Allan Scott, Glenn Tryon (from the musical play *Roberta* by Jerome Kern and Otto Harbach based on the novel *Gowns By Roberta* by Alice Duer Miller); ph, Edward Cronjager; ed, William Hamilton; m, Jerome Kern; art d, Van Nest Polglase, Carroll Clark; chor, Fred Astaire, Hermes Pan; cos, Bernard Newman

The least-seen and appreciated of the magical Astaire-Rogers series at RKO, this now seems, along with TOP HAT and SWING TIME, as one of the three wonder films of the series. Astaire and Rogers persistently upstage the romantic leads, Irene Dunne and Randolph Scott, and they simply fly, largely unburdened by the plot. And yet Dunne is luminous and appealing, lending a sense of humor and an approachability to all the princess nonsense, and Scott's prudish hick abroad is mocked in a good-natured way. He's much easier to take here than in a similar role in the later FOLLOW THE FLEET. Seiter's direction is deliciously light, and the film never loses its pace or good humor.

John Kent (Scott) is a former football star touring Europe with a swing band led by his pal Huck Haines (Astaire, in a role that combined those performed by Bob Hope and George Murphy in the Broadway original). In Paris they visit the salon of noted designer Mme. Roberta, actually John's Aunt Minnie (a marvelous Westley), where they encounter Stephanie (Dunne), a Russian princess employed there since Revolution times. They also meet Countess Scharwenka (Rogers), who, as with the other women, is not what she seems. She's an old girlfriend of Huck's using an aristocratic Polish stage name. John becomes involved with Stephanie, Huck and his old flame rekindle their passion, and together the four see to it that the fashion show goes on at the finale.

What's hung on this frivolous plot are some of Jerome Kern's most beautiful tunes and a set of dances that leave audiences waiting impatiently for the return Astaire and Rogers. Thankfully they return frequently. "I'll Be Hard to Handle" remains one of their greatest ever, partly because it firmly establishes the personas of "Fred and Ginger" in the popular imagination. Astaire, a great light comedian, makes the most of his many savage wisecracks, and a hilarious Rogers steals practically every scene in which she appears. Her flair for mimicry and parody is in full throttle here, whether imitating stage predecessor Lyda Roberta's accented scat singing or seductively flirting with the awkward John. Astaire does one of his all-time greatest solos to "I Won't Dance," a brilliantly choreographed and performed routine. No wonder Ballanchine was so nuts about this incomparable performer. Two other brief duets, a touchingly simple yet dramatic romantic turn to "Smoke Gets in Your Eyes," and a blistering final recap of "I Won't Dance" make this film dance-happy to the max. Check it out, and you may be surprised to find it touching when appropriate, frequently hilarious, and glisteningly performed, with Fred and Ginger at an early peak.

ROBIN AND MARIAN
1976 106m c ★★★
Romance/Adventure PG
Columbia (U.K.)

Sean Connery *(Robin Hood)*, Audrey Hepburn *(Maid Marian)*, Robert Shaw *(Sheriff of Nottingham)*, Richard Harris *(King Richard)*, Nicol Williamson *(Little John)*, Denholm Elliott *(Will Scarlett)*, Kenneth Haigh *(Sir Ranulf de Pudsey)*, Ronnie Barker *(Friar Tuck)*, Ian Holm *(King John)*, Bill Maynard *(Mercadier)* p, Denis O'Dell; d, Richard Lester; w, James Goldman; ph, David Watkin (Technicolor); ed, John Victor Smith; m, John Barry; prod d, Michael Stringer; art d, Gil Parrondo; fx, Eddie Fowlie; cos, Yvonne Blake

What might have been a wonderful movie is only so-so due to Lester's unnecessarily frantic direction and a ponderous script by James Goldman, who had so much success with THE LION IN WINTER that some of his lines for this seem like bon mots he may have cut from that screenplay. It's ROMEO AND JULIET for the gray-haired set. Twenty years have passed since the bandit who robbed from the rich to give to the poor ran off to fight in the Crusades with his beloved king. He's now back, in the form of wizened Connery, and in the two decades since he left much has transpired. His love, Hepburn, is now a nun; his king, Harris, has become a madman man dedicated to amassing a fortune, etc. The one thing remaining constant in Connery's life is that the sheriff of Nottingham, Shaw, is still eager to see him hang. Connery is traveling in France with Harris when they pass an old seedy castle occupied by a crazed ancient man, Esmond Knight, as well as several women and children. Harris thinks there might be something of value inside the ramshackle structure, so he orders Connery to go in and take it. Connery refuses, and the two men get into an argument. Knight sends an arrow into Harris, who is mortally wounded. Before dying, Harris has his loyal men destroy the castle, but his death stops his chastisement of Connery. Williamson (a slight "Little John" if there ever was one) and Connery are now free to leave Europe and finally go home to England. They immediately return to Sherwood Forest and look with nostalgia at the old landmarks. Two of their old friends, Elliott and Barker, appear, and smiles are in order. The two gang members tell Connery that he is now a hero, celebrated in song by men like their late friend, Alan-a-Dale, who used to sing folk tunes. Harris's heinous brother, Holm, now rules the area with Shaw, while Hepburn is now running a nearby nunnery. Connery goes off to see her and notes that she is no longer the twittering maid of so many years ago. Rather, she is one tough cookie who is risking her life by staying in England because Holm has decreed that anyone loyal to Rome must be exiled. Hepburn steadfastly remains, true to her faith and willing to go to jail or even death to uphold it. Connery thinks that's foolish, so he knocks her unconscious and carts her off. Williamson and Connery masquerade as sellers of goods, fight the soldiers inside Nottingham Castle, and save the nuns who have already been incarcerated (Julio, Sanguino, and Minguillon). Later, Hepburn admits that she tried killing herself when he departed twenty years before and she wishes he would finally sheath his sword, since she could not bear his death at this point. Meanwhile, Haigh, one of Holm's nobles, thinks it would be quite a feather in his cap if he captured Connery, so he sets a trap in Sherwood Forest. The battle commences, and all of Haigh's men are killed by Connery's band. Haigh, barely escaping with his life, goes to Holm and gets a battalion of two hundred to come back and finish off Connery. Meanwhile, Hepburn and Connery are spending a peaceful few days in the quiet woods. Soon enough, the story about Connery returning has been shouted around the countryside and he is beset with many who want to join him. Unfortunately, the prospective Merry Men are mostly underage lads and overage grandfathers. Nevertheless, Connery thinks he can forge a fighting force out of them. Shaw's men and Haigh's small army are already descending on Sherwood Forest, and it looks as though a bloody battle will ensue. Hepburn pleads with Connery to back off and tries to get Williamson to intervene. Connery has an idea. Why kill so many when this dispute is really

between two men, himself and Shaw? He suggests that they fight each other, with a mutual promise that no matter who wins, no other blood will be shed. Shaw agrees, and the two men have a go at it with axes and swords. It's a long, cruel fight, and Connery eventually vanquishes Shaw but is badly wounded in the fray. Hepburn kneels beside the dying Connery, and Haigh orders his men to attack. The fight they tried to avoid takes place and many are slain. Williamson kills Haigh, and Connery, who doesn't have much time, is taken to the abbey where they will attempt to stanch the flow of blood. Hepburn is well aware that Connery doesn't have much time left. She puts some poison in a wine glass and drinks it, then hands it to him. Connery sips, then asks why she's done what she's done. Hepburn replies that she could not live without him and loves him more than God. Williamson walks in and Connery, with his last bit of strength, shoots an arrow out the window and instructs Williamson to bury them both where the arrow has landed. A touching conclusion to a spotty picture that was satirical, sometimes pretentious, often slow, but occasionally exciting. If they'd decided to shoot an all-out comedy that showed Connery creakily trying to recapture his old derring-do, it might have made more sense. Hepburn came back to movies after a nine-year absence to accept this role and had nothing but praise for Lester's quick direction. Her only reservation was about the love scenes with Connery, where she would have liked more time. Connery and Hepburn personally raised the stature of the movie above the script. Ray Stark presented the film, and it is presumed that it was his personal appeal to all that got this movie made.

ROBIN HOOD: PRINCE OF THIEVES

1991 143m c   ★★½
Action/Adventure/Historical   PG-13/PG
Morgan Creek Productions/Trilogy Entertainment Group

Kevin Costner (Robin of Locksley/Robin Hood), Morgan Freeman (Azeem), Mary Elizabeth Mastrantonio (Maid Marian), Christian Slater (Will Scarlett), Alan Rickman (Sheriff of Nottingham), Geraldine McEwan (Mortianna), Michael McShane (Friar Tuck), Brian Blessed (Lord Locksley), Michael Wincott (Guy of Gisborne), Nick Brimble (Little John)

p, Richard B. Lewis, Pen Densham, John Watson; d, Kevin Reynolds; w, Pen Densham, John Watson (from the story by Densham); ph, Doug Milsome; ed, Peter Boyle; m, Michael Kamen; prod d, John Graysmark; art d, Alan Tomkins, Fred Carter, John F. Ralph; cos, John Bloomfield

Though Fox Television's ROBIN HOOD, released theatrically overseas, is in many ways the more successful presentation of the material, ROBIN HOOD: PRINCE OF THIEVES is the more elaborate production and by far the bigger hit. It also tries desperately to make the legend relevant to contemporary audiences.

With the help of Azeem (Morgan Freeman), young nobleman Robin of Locksley (Kevin Costner) escapes from a hellish prison in the Holy Land and makes his way home to England, where a rude surprise awaits him. His father has been murdered, King Richard the Lionhearted (Sean Connery) is in exile and the wicked Sheriff of Nottingham (Alan Rickman), who rules with the guidance of a cackling witch, has laid siege to the countryside. While traveling through Sherwood Forest, Robin is set upon by a gang of thieves. He defeats their leader Little John (Nick Brimble) in hand-to-hand combat, and learns that they're not desperados, but honest men and women driven from their homes by Nottingham's cruelty. Robin wins their trust and becomes their commander—though impetuous young Will Scarlett (Christian Slater) remains aloof.

The newly christened Robin Hood trains them in the arts of war and leads them in a guerrilla battle against the Sheriff's army. Robin also strikes up a romance with the lovely, strong-willed Maid Marian (Mary Elizabeth Mastrantonio). Marian, who is related to King Richard and works secretly for his cause, has little use for the vain, spoiled Robin of Locksley she remembers from childhood. But Robin Hood, man of the people, appeals to her. There is, however, a complication: the Sheriff of Nottingham is determined to marry her in order to link his family to royalty. He orders Robin Hood killed and coerces Marian into marrying him, but Robin and his men disrupt the wedding and save the day.

If nothing else, ROBIN HOOD: THE PRINCE OF THIEVES is resolutely politically correct, positing a feminist Marian, adding women to the band of merry men, and battling racism and religious intolerance by pairing Robin with Azeem, who is both black and a Muslim. Costner's surprisingly portly Robin is less a dashing force of justice than a decent kind of guy forced by circumstance to do the right thing because the wrong thing—embodied in the flamboyantly wicked Sheriff of Nottingham—is so obviously unacceptable. He's a Robin Hood for an age when no one believes in heroes.

PRINCE OF THIEVES falls somewhere between the idealized historical romps of yore and more current, aggressively revisionist films that emphasize the violence, ignorance and squalor of the past; it takes place neither in the fantasy Sherwood Forest of Michael Curtiz's THE ADVENTURES OF ROBIN HOOD, starring a supremely confident Errol Flynn, nor in the delirious squalor of Paul Verhoeven's FLESH + BLOOD.

Director Kevin Reynolds (FANDANGO) seems to have made no effort to unify the cast, so accents and styles of acting vary wildly from individual to individual—in particular, one notices the difference between the American stars and the British supporting cast. Costner is lifeless and speaks strangely (he was said to have attempted a British accent, then abandoned it during shooting), Mastrantonio is a vivacious Marian, and Slater an anachronistic Will Scarlett, whose performance, once again, recalls his work in HEATHERS. Connery's walk-on as King Richard was a closely guarded secret during production, and reviewers were asked not to spoil the surprise for movie-goers; surprisingly, most complied. As the Sheriff of Nottingham, Alan Rickman, swaggering through his scenes in sinister black, hissing one-liners and basically acting up a storm, is so theatrically vile that he seems to be in another movie altogether, and one can't help but think that it's a more entertaining movie than ROBIN HOOD: PRINCE OF THIEVES.

ROBOCOP

1987　103m　c　　　　　　　　　★★★½
Crime/Science Fiction　　　　　　R/18
Orion

Peter Weller (Alex J. Murphy/Robocop), Nancy Allen (Anne Lewis), Ronny Cox (Richard "Dick" Jones), Kurtwood Smith (Clarence J. Boddicker), Miguel Ferrer (Robert Morton), Robert DoQui (Sgt. Reed), Dan O'Herlihy (The Old Man), Ray Wise (Leon Nash), Felton Perry (Johnson), Mario Machado

p, Arne L. Schmidt; d, Paul Verhoeven; w, Edward Neumeier, Michael Miner; ph, Jost Vacano (DuArt Color); ed, Frank J. Urioste; m, Basil Poledouris; prod d, William Sandell; art d, Gayle Simon; fx, Dale Martin, Rob Bottin, Craig Davies, Peter Ronzani; cos, Erica Edell Phillips

A first-rate production full of nonstop action and inventive special effects but what truly makes ROBOCOP spellbinding is a superior script. Intelligent and satirical, it has the quality of cutting-edge British comic books such as the "Judge Dred" series. Kudos to the screenwriting team of Michael Miner and Edward Neumeir.

It's the not-too-distant future in crime-ridden Old Detroit. A corporate conglomerate is running the city and, under the direction of Richard Jones (Ronny Cox), has developed a huge metal android to combat rampant street crime. When this creation demonstrates a murderous "glitch," Robert Morton (Miguel Ferrer) sees an opportunity to advance his company position by building a better cop machine. He gets his chance when cop Alex Murphy (Peter Weller) is brutally killed by a gang of sadistic hoodlums. Murphy's body is reconstructed by technicians and dubbed RoboCop. It proves to be more than effective against street criminals thereby elevating Morton to top corporate management. This motivates the scheming Jones to make a pact with supervillain Boddicker (Kurtwood Smith) to destroy RoboCop.

Though extremely violent, ROBOCOP showcases an invigorating style even in its goriest scenes. Paul Verhoeven makes every scene sparkle with tilted angles, oddball twists, and special-effects wonders. ROBOCOP effectively conveys a combination of reality and fantasy in a hard-boiled world of humane robots and unfeeling humans.

ROCCO AND HIS BROTHERS
(ROCCO ET SES FRERES)
1960　175m　bw　　　　　　　　　★★★★
Drama　　　　　　　　　　　　　　　　/15
Titanus/Marceau　(France/Italy)

Alain Delon (Rocco Parondi), Renato Salvatori (Simone Parondi), Annie Girardot (Nadia), Katina Paxinou (Rosaria Parondi), Roger Hanin (Morini), Paolo Stoppa (Boxing Impresario), Suzy Delair (Luisa), Claudia Cardinale (Ginetta), Spiros Focas (Vincenzo Parondi), Max Cartier (Ciro Parondi)

p, Giuseppe Bordogni; d, Luchino Visconti; w, Luchino Visconti, Suso Cecchi D'Amico, Pasquale Festa Campanile, Massimo Franciosa, Enrico Medioli (based on the novel The Bridge of Ghisolfa by Giovanni Testori); ph, Giuseppe Rotunno; ed, Mario Serandrei; m, Nino Rota; art d, Mario Garbuglia; cos, Piero Tosi

Luchino Visconti's episodic prize-winning study of five brothers and their widowed mother transplanted from rural Sicily to industrial Milan in northern Italy is violent, deliberately operatic, and makes ambiguous social statements. The characters' relationships are explored over a period of 12 years, with concentration chiefly on Delon and Salvatori as they alternately enjoy and abuse the affections of Girardot, a prostitute who yearns to be free. She loves Delon, but he sacrifices her to the brutal Salvatori because the latter seems to have greater need of her love. Unable to return Salvatori's affection or to put up with his possessiveness, she returns to her former profession. Enraged, he stabs her to death (the 13 on-screen stabbings in European versions are cut to three for American audiences). ROCCO exists in a variety of running times. The American premiere audience found the 175-minute version overlong and began walking out before the film's final scene ended; but the raped 95-minute version should be avoided.

ROCK AROUND THE CLOCK
1956　77m　bw　　　　　　　　　★★★
Musical　　　　　　　　　　　　　　/U
Columbia

Bill Haley and the Comets, The Platters, Tony Martinez and His Band, Frankie Bell and His Bellboys *(Themselves)*, Alan Freed *(Himself)*, Johnnie Johnston *(Steve Hollis)*, Alix Talton *(Corinne Talbot)*, Lisa Gaye *(Lisa Johns)*, John Archer *(Mike Dennis)*, Henry Slate *(Corny LaSalle)*

p, Sam Katzman; d, Fred F. Sears; w, Robert E. Kent, James B. Gordon; ph, Benjamin Kline; ed, Saul A. Goodkind, Jack Ogilvie; art d, Paul Palmentola; chor, Earl Barton

The rock 'n' roll movie. Producer Sam Katzman and director Fred Sears again pooled their exploitative talents to deliver a film not so much *about* rock 'n' roll, but a film that *was* rock 'n' roll. The story is barely evident—legendary rock deejay Alan Freed discovers Bill Haley and the Comets in a mountain village and brings them back to New York, where they quickly become a musical phenomenon. Katzman was correct in assuming that if rock concerts could cause youth riots, so could a movie. In England, soon after a couple of screenings, young rockers were tearing up the seats and dancing up a storm. Of course all their moms and dads were bowled over with shock and banned the film from the theaters. Even now it can still make the feet move to the beat. Haley's tunes include "Razzle Dazzle," "Happy Baby," "See You Later, Alligator," "Rudy's Rock," and the greatest rocker of them all "Rock around the Clock." And then there's "The Great Pretender," "Only You" (The Platters), "Codfish and Potatoes," "Sad and Lonely," "Cuero," "Mambo Capri" (Tony Martinez), and "Giddy Up, Ding Dong," "We're Gonna Teach You to Rock" (Freddie Bell).

ROCK 'N' ROLL HIGH SCHOOL

1979 93m c   ★★★★
Musical/Comedy   PG/15
New World

P.J. Soles *(Riff Randell)*, Vincent Van Patten *(Tom Roberts)*, Clint Howard *(Eaglebauer)*, Dey Young *(Kate Rambeau)*, Mary Woronov *(Evelyn Togar)*, Dick Miller *(Police Chief Klein)*, Paul Bartel *(Mr. McGree)*, Alix Elias *(Coach Steroid)*, Don Steele *(Screamin' Steve Stevens)*, Loren Lester *(Fritz Hansel)*

p, Michael Finnell; d, Allan Arkush; w, Richard Whitley, Russ Dvonch, Joseph McBride (based on a story by Arkush, Joe Dante); ph, Dean Cundey (Metrocolor); ed, Larry Bock, Gail Werbin; m, The Ramones; art d, Marie Kordus; chor, Siana Lee Hall; cos, Jack Buehler

When tickets for an upcoming concert by her favorite rock band, the Ramones, go on sale, aspiring teenage songwriter Riff Randell (P.J. Soles) skips school to be the first in line, enraging Evelyn Togar (Mary Woronov), the no-nonsense principal of Vince Lombardi High School, who has dedicated herself to putting an end to her charges' obsession with rock 'n' roll. Aided by a couple of aggressive henchmen (Loren Lester and Daniel Davies), Togar does everything in her power to see that no backbeat bopping deters her students from their studies, including confiscating all of the Ramones' concert tickets Riff has purchased. Meanwhile, under the guidance of the school's resident operator, Eaglebauer (Clint Howard), Tom Roberts (Vince Van Patten), a handsome but hopelessly unhip football player, pursues Riff, while smart but not particularly sexy Kate Rambeau (Dey Young) tries to win Tom's affections. The action heats up—both in Tom's van and between Togar and the students—and after an attempted record burning, Riff, the kids, *and* the Ramones prove once again that winning isn't everything, it's the only thing, turning Lombardi High into Rock 'n' Roll High School. Written by Joe Dante and directed by Allan Arkush, this

refreshingly wacky teenage film is filled with warped humor (including mice exploding to Ramones music), and makes wonderful use of the "so dumb they're smart" Ramones, who stepped to the fore when Cheap Trick backed out of the project. Nothing is taken seriously and nothing should be—it's only rock 'n' roll.

ROCKY

1976 119m c   ★★★★
Sports   PG
UA

Sylvester Stallone *(Rocky Balboa)*, Talia Shire *(Adrian)*, Burt Young *(Paulie)*, Carl Weathers *(Apollo Creed)*, Burgess Meredith *(Mickey)*, Thayer David *(Miles Jergens)*, Joe Spinell *(Tom Gazzo)*, Jimmy Gambina *(Mike)*, Bill Baldwin *(Fight Announcer)*, Aldo Silvani *(Cut Man)*

p, Irwin Winkler, Robert Chartoff; d, John G. Avildsen; w, Sylvester Stallone; ph, James Crabe (Technicolor); ed, Richard Halsey, Scott Conrad; m, Bill Conti; prod d, William J. Cassidy; art d, James H. Spencer; fx, Garrett Brown; chor, Sylvester Stallone; cos, Robert Cambel, Joanne Hutchinson

Better films have been made about the world of sports, but for many ROCKY is *the* sports movie. As drenched in sentiment as it is in sweat, as much love story as fight film, this classic tale of a tireless "bum" who makes good is one of the most uplifting films ever made. Set primarily in working-class Philadelphia, it follows the fortunes of Rocky Balboa (Sylvester Stallone), a 30-year-old club fighter who earns his living as a collections man for a loan shark. His boxing career has hit bottom, but Rocky's love life is looking up. He clumsily but endearingly woos Adrian (Talia Shire), the shy, repressed sister of Paulie (Burt Young), Rocky's friend who engineers their strange first date, and in no time, Rocky and Adrian are deeply in love. When a challenger's injury leaves the Ali-like world heavyweight champion Apollo Creed (ex-Oakland Raider linebacker Carl Weathers) without an opponent for his upcoming title defense, the boisterous champ decides to give a nobody a chance and chooses Rocky, "the Italian Stallion." Urged on by Mickey (Burgess Meredith), his crotchety old manager, and to the accompaniment of Bill Conti's rousing theme "Gonna Fly Now," Rocky undergoes grueling training for his title long shot: doing one-armed push-ups, pounding slabs of meat in a slaughterhouse freezer, making his now-famous run through the Philadelphia streets and up the steps of its art museum. Come fight time, Rocky wants only to go the distance with Creed, to prove he isn't "just another bum from the neighborhood." Surprising everyone, he gives Creed the fight of his life, narrowly losing a split decision. Amid the post-fight hubbub, Rocky and Adrian meet in a loving mid-ring clinch. Establishing a formula that would be duplicated over and over (especially in its own sequels—see ROCKY series), the film slowly draws the audience into Rocky's struggle, until his triumph becomes that of every "little guy" who's dreamed of making it big. Reminiscent of Marlon Brando's Terry Malloy (ON THE WATERFRONT) and Paul Newman's Rocky Graziano (SOMEBODY UP THERE LIKES ME), Stallone's Rocky is magnificent, mirroring the actor's own battle for Hollywood success. As a struggling actor and screenwriter known mainly for THE LORDS OF FLATBUSH, Stallone, inspired by New Jersey club boxer Chuck Wepner's courageous loss to Muhammad Ali (a 15th-round TKO), wrote ROCKY's screenplay in three days. Determined to star in it himself, he turned down a quarter-million-dollar offer for his script, won the part, and, under John Avildsen's Oscarwinning direction, gave the screen one of its most memorable characters. What's more, both his performance and screenplay were nominated for Academy Awards, and the film won for Best Picture and Best Editing. Shire, who is wonderful as the gradually blooming Adrian, and Meredith also earned nominations. The fairy-tale championship match is generally well choreographed (by Stallone), and the training montage, in its originality, remains more gripping than the many glossier imitations it inspired. Expertly paced, benefiting from well-drawn characters and an evocative, often funny script, ROCKY simply pushes all the right buttons. Former heavyweight champ and Philly homeboy Joe Frazier appears as himself.

ROCKY II

1979   119m   c   ★★★½
Sports   PG
UA

Sylvester Stallone (*Rocky Balboa*), Talia Shire (*Adrian*), Burt Young (*Paulie*), Carl Weathers (*Apollo Creed*), Burgess Meredith (*Mickey*), Tony Burton (*Apollo's Trainer*), Joe Spinell (*Gazzo*), Leonard Gaines (*Agent*), Sylvia Meals (*Mary Anne Creed*), Frank McRae (*Meat Foreman*)

p, Irwin Winkler, Robert Chartoff; d, Sylvester Stallone; w, Sylvester Stallone; ph, Bill Butler (Panavision, Technicolor); ed, Danford B. Greene, Stanford C. Allen, Janice Hampton, James Symons; m, Bill Conti; art d, Richard Berger; chor, Sylvester Stallone; cos, Tom Bronson, Sandra Berke

Considerably less satisfying than the original ROCKY, but head and shoulders above the later installments, ROCKY II picks up the saga of "the Italian Stallion" during the last two rounds of his gutsy loss to world champ Apollo Creed (Carl Weathers). After the bout, Rocky (Sylvester Stallone) and Adrian (Talia Shire), his no-longer-mousy sweetheart, marry and use his fight purse to buy a car and condo. Soon Rocky learns that if he enters the ring again he runs the risk of being blinded in the eye he injured fighting Apollo. He does his best to provide for Adrian but is laid off by the slaughterhouse where he works with his brother-in-law, Paulie (Burt Young). Worried about the future—which is about to include a new baby—Rocky accepts a rematch with Apollo, who is anxious to prove Rocky's showing in their first bout was a fluke. Adrian doesn't want her husband to fight, and without her support Rocky is unable to immerse himself in training, much to the chagrin of his manager, Mickey (Burgess Meredith). When Adrian falls into a coma after giving birth to their son, a despondent Rocky stops training completely. However, after his revived wife tells Rocky to *win*, he trains again in earnest (followed up the steps to the museum by a legion of running kids) and does just that, surprising Apollo by boxing right-handed for most of the fight and switching back to his natural southpaw style only for the decisive final round.

All the endearing characters from the original are back, as is Bill Conti's familiar music. This time Stallone both wrote and directed the film, and though his handling of the actors and camera is less assured than John Avildsen's in ROCKY, he keeps things moving at a good pace and delivers another charming performance himself. Again the characters and relationships are engaging—Rocky and Adrian's center-stage love still touching—and though the main plot differs little from the first film, audiences will have a hard time not becoming involved in Rocky's quixotic quest all over again. Unfortunately, the big fight is a letdown, ending preposterously as both exhausted fighters fall to the canvas, with Rocky clambering back to his feet to take the title.

ROCKY HORROR PICTURE SHOW, THE

1975   100m   c   ★★
Comedy/Horror/Musical   R/15
Adler/White   (U.K.)

Tim Curry (*Dr. Frank N. Furter*), Susan Sarandon (*Janet Weiss*), Barry Bostwick (*Brad Majors*), Richard O'Brien (*Riff Raff*), Jonathan Adams (*Dr. Everett Scott*), Nell Campbell (*Columbia*), Peter Hinwood (*Rocky Horror*), Patricia Quinn (*Magenta*), Meatloaf (*Eddie*), Charles Gray (*Criminologist*)

p, Michael White, John Goldstone; d, Jim Sharman; w, Jim Sharman, Richard O'Brien (based on the stage musical by O'Brien); ph, Peter Suschitzky (Eastmancolor); ed, Graeme Clifford; m, Richard O'Brien; prod d, Brian Thomson; art d, Terry Ackland Snow; fx, Wally Veevers; chor, David Toguri; cos, Sue Blane, Richard Pointing, Gillian Dods

This film has become the official definition of a cult movie—so much so that the audience watching (or more accurately, participating in) the picture is the most interesting element. Depending on the quality of the audience's performance, ROCKY HORROR can be a fantastic viewing experience or just a really fun experience. But the movie alone—blah, what a waste! The audiences around the country that line up every Friday and Saturday at midnight are *the* show. What happens on the screen is secondary.

Based on a British musical stage play by O'Brien (who also appears in the film and wrote all the music), RHPS eventually made it to the screen with the help of Lou Adler and Michael White. After a short run in New York it closed, but soon was revived on the midnight circuit. It is the story of Brad and Janet (Bostwick and Sarandon) whose car breaks down during a rainstorm in Ohio. They look for shelter in a mansion, which turns out to be the residence of Dr. Frank N. Furter, wildly played by Curry. They soon find themselves in the middle of a convention of alien transsexuals from the planet Transsexual in the galaxy Transylvania. Curry is ready to reveal his Frankenstein-esque creation—a monster named Rocky who is to be the ultimate sexual male. What follows, in a nutshell, is sex, cannibalism (Meatloaf is appropriately eaten), murder, seduction, more sex, people being turned into statues, RKO Radio Pictures being spoofed, and Brad and Janet (dammit!) escaping before everything is blown up. The film itself is trash—its script and direction poor, its music mediocre—but audience participation has taken Bertolt Brecht into the twilight zone. Weird to the maximum. Songs: "The Time Warp," "Science Fiction Double Feature," "Wedding Song," "Sweet Transvestite," "The Sword of Damocles," "Charles Atlas Song," "What Ever Happened to Saturday Night," "Touch-a Touch-a Touch-a Touch Me," "Eddie's Teddy," "Planet Schmanet," "Over at the Frankenstein Place," "It Was Great When It All Began," "I'm Going Home," and "Superheroes." SHOCK TREATMENT was a sequel of sorts.

ROLLERBALL

1975   129m   c   ★★★
Sports/Science Fiction   R/15
UA

James Caan (*Jonathan E.*), John Houseman (*Bartholomew*), Maud Adams (*Ella*), John Beck (*Moonpie*), Moses Gunn (*Cletus*), Pamela Hensley (*Mackie*), Barbara Trentham (*Daphne*), Ralph Richardson (*Librarian*), Shane Rimmer (*Team Executive*), Alfred Thomas (*Team Trainer*)

p, Norman Jewison; d, Norman Jewison; w, William Harrison (based on his story "Rollerball Murders"); ph, Douglas Slocombe (Technicolor); ed, Anthony Gibbs; m, Andre Previn, Johann Sebastian Bach, Peter Ilich Tchaikovsky, Dmitri Shostakovich, Tomaso Albinoni; prod d, John Box; art d, Robert Laing; fx, Sass Bedig, John Richardson, Joe Fitt; cos, Julie Harris

It is the year 2018 and society is rid of war and poverty, and the only violence left is supplied by the political corporation-controlled rollerball teams, who fight to the bloody finish with spikes and motorcycles in a sport combining roller derby, football, and hockey. When champion rollerball player Caan is asked to retire because the corporate executives who rule the world are fearful that he has become too popular with the masses, he fights the move. To get rid of him, the corporate executives decide to change the rollerball rules and make it a fight to the death. Produced and directed by Norman Jewison, this science-fiction film envisions a time when major corporations will control the populace by offering them a brutal and compelling entertainment to distract from the real social issues at hand and act as a funnel for their frustrations, hatred, and resentment. While the questions raised about the relationship between corporate power and sporting events are valid and intriguing, ROLLERBALL is, unfortunately, hopelessly heavy-handed and ponderous. From its gloomy and solemn air to the overbearing use of baroque music, the film is far too self-important for its own good. Luckily, the performances of Caan and Richardson are excellent, and the rollerball sequences are fast-paced and interesting.

ROMA

1972 119m c ★★★½
Drama R/
Ultra/Artistes (Italy/France)

Federico Fellini (Himself), Peter Gonzales (Fellini, Age 18), Stefano Majore (Fellini As a Child), Pia De Doses (Princess), Renato Giovanneli (Cardinal Ottaviani), Fiona Florence (Young Prostitute), Marne Maitland (Underground Guide), Galliano Sbarra (Music Hall Compere), Alvaro Vitali (Tap Dancer Imitating Fred Astaire), Britta Barnes

p, Turi Vasile; d, Federico Fellini; w, Federico Fellini, Bernardino Zapponi; ph, Giuseppe Rotunno (Technicolor); ed, Ruggero Mastroianni; m, Nino Rota; prod d, Danilo Donati; fx, Adriano Pischiutta; chor, Gino Landi; cos, Danilo Donati

ROMA, a confounding picture that is as much a documentary as it is a story, was Fellini's attempt to blend reality, fantasy, dreams, and pain. He succeeded, but he divided audiences and critics with the result. The story begins in Rimini, where young Fellini, played by Majore, was born. Majore learns early he wants to leave this seaside village on the Adriatic. He takes a trip with his classmates to the Eternal City in 1931, then finally moves there in 1938, just before war breaks out. Majore gives way to Gonzales as Fellini. The youth is treated to a panorama of Roman customs, as he moves in with a family in a tenement and watches as the gregarious citizens live out their rich, noisy lives. Jump to the early 1970s and Fellini, as himself, is now a renowned director making a picture. He's shooting a scene in a traffic jam during a heavy rainstorm, and Fellini's memory is jogged back to his early days in the city when he attended a vaudeville show during the war. The show features dreadful entertainment punctuated by various projectiles thrown at the stage, including a dead cat. Back in the present Fellini is shooting the construction of the subway that has been in the process of being built for decades. Every time workers dig in the streets, another archaeological find

is made and the area becomes off-limits to the builders. They find an ancient villa under the city, and when they attempt to bring out the priceless frescoes they fall apart upon hitting Rome's fetid air. Fellini sees a young couple in love and goes back in reverie to a visit to a bordello where the girls walked up and down shamelessly in front of their ogling prospects. Then another, more upscale whorehouse is seen, and the young Fellini thinks he is truly in love with Florence, one of the hookers. Back in the present we see a hysterical scene of a clerical fashion show set in the home of De Doses, an elderly princess who is entertaining a cardinal, Giovanelli. Priests on roller skates and nuns in neon habits parade for the assemblage. At a street festival in Trastevere (a section of Rome that means "across the Tiber") the cops besiege the local hippies. Fellini begins interviewing people on camera: Anna Magnani, Gore Vidal, Alberto Sordi, and Marcello Mastroianni, among others. (The latter two were cut from the US print.) Darkness descends, the city begins to snore, and the silence is overwhelmed by a horde of motorcyclists careening through the city past the old relics and winding up at the Colosseum, as they appear to be just one of the many groups that have sacked Rome since time began. What does it all mean? Who knows?

Fellini made two movies about people with writer's block: LA DOLCE VITA, in which Mastroianni is a journalist who can't write, and 8½, in which he is a director with no ideas. Here Fellini has too many ideas and uses several that he's used before in other films, so it appears to be a remake of those pictures, albeit with several other actors and more scenes added. It's episodic and enigmatic and almost a grotesque parody of Fellini's other movies, as though the master was making fun of his own work. Two versions were released, in English and with subtitles. The dubbed version is excellent and loses nothing unless one is an Italian scholar. Rome has never looked so inviting and depressing as seen in this $3 million paean to the city Fellini loves and hates so much. Many laughs and just as many winces.

ROMAN HOLIDAY

1953 119m bw ★★★★
Romance/Comedy /U
Paramount

Gregory Peck (Joe Bradley), Audrey Hepburn (Princess Anne), Eddie Albert (Irving Radovich), Hartley Power (Mr. Hennessy), Laura Solari (Hennessy's Secretary), Harcourt Williams (Ambassador), Margaret Rawlings (Countess Vereberg), Tullio Carminati (Gen. Provno), Paolo Carlini (Mario Delani), Claudio Ermelli (Giovanni)

p, William Wyler; d, William Wyler; w, Ian McLellan Hunter, John Dighton (based on a story by Hunter); ph, Franz Planer, Henri Alekan; ed, Robert Swink; m, Georges Auric; art d, Hal Pereira, Walter Tyler; cos, Edith Head

Delicious, and delectable Audrey's Oscar-winning American debut. But not such a difficult feat with William Wyler backing you up. The secret is in the way Wyler, who had been away from comedy for about 18 years, builds an atmosphere of charm that leads us to her. And it didn't hurt Hepburn at all that she came along during a time when Monroe's sex doll influence had Hollywood brimming over with sex bombs from all over; or that Wyler cast her opposite dependable, protective Gregory Peck. The film gained 10 Academy Award nominations—amazing for a comedy—with Oscars awarded (beside Hepburn) to costumer Edith Head, and Ian McClellan Hunter, who wrote the story. Charming, wistful, and frothy, it earned strong receipts at the box office. Hepburn, who had previously appeared in six European movies and in "Gigi" on Broadway (selected for her role in that play by author Colette herself, who met the actress in the south of France and was immediately struck by her gamine beauty.), ROMAN HOLIDAY auspiciously presents her. She *is* infectious as Anne, a princess on holiday in Rome, where her ever-present coterie includes Rawlings, her chaperon, and Carminati, an aide. Overprotected all her life, she hasn't the vaguest idea of what the world outside her castle and her small country is like. Now in her teenage years, she is beginning to rebel against the formality and constrictions of her royal position and, seeing her chance to see how the other half lives, escapes her claustrophobic entourage. While they conduct a frantic search for her, she falls asleep on a park bench and meets Peck, one of the many reporters who have been trying to interview the princess, who has hitherto been shielded from the world's press corps by her aides. Peck knows he has a major scoop in meeting Hepburn, but initially pretends not to know who she is, taking her on a sightseeing tour of Rome while Albert, a news photographer, secretly snaps pictures of her as she plays hookey. For 24 hours, Peck shows Hepburn the famous sights, as well as some that are less familiar, since it is necessary to evade the police who are looking everywhere for the missing princess. Peck takes her on a motorcycle, they go dancing, and the pair land in some minor scrapes; all the while, the hard-boiled reporter falls harder for the guileless, beautiful Hepburn.

The film also has enough adventure and excitement to satisfy, and the faintly bittersweet note of the ending is made deliciously palatable by its artistic rightness. ROMAN HOLIDAY inspired several imitations, but none came close to the charming insouciance of the original. Rumor has it that Hunter, picking up his Oscar, may have been fronting for blacklisted Dalton Trumbo.

ROMAN SCANDALS

1933 85m bw ★★★½
Musical/Comedy /PG
UA

Eddie Cantor (*Eddie*), Ruth Etting (*Olga*), Gloria Stuart (*Princess Sylvia*), David Manners (*Josephus*), Verree Teasdale (*Empress Agrippa*), Edward Arnold (*Emperor Valerius*), Alan Mowbray (*Majordomo*), Jack Rutherford (*Manius*), Grace Poggi (*Slave Dancer*), Willard Robertson (*Warren F. Cooper*)

p, Samuel Goldwyn; d, Frank Tuttle; w, William Anthony McGuire, George Oppenheimer, Arthur Sheekman, Nat Perrin (based on a story by George S. Kaufman, Robert E. Sherwood); ph, Gregg Toland; ed, Stuart Heisler; art d, Richard Day; chor, Busby Berkeley; cos, John Harkrider

This was Eddie Cantor's fourth of six films for Samuel Goldwyn and second only to THE KID FROM SPAIN in popularity. Goldwyn had originally hoped to star Cantor in a musical version George Bernard Shaw's "Androcles and the Lion," but that failing, he hired Robert Sherwood and George S. Kaufman to fashion a story that would take Cantor to ancient Rome. Disappointed with their effort (so much so that Sherwood and Kaufman had to sue to collect their promised fee), Goldwyn hired Nat Perrin, George Oppenheimer, Arthur Sheekman, and William Anthony to punch up the screenplay. This time too many cooks didn't spoil this broth, and ROMAN SCANDALS is one of the best, funniest Cantor-Goldwyn associations. It opens with Cantor as a delivery boy in West Rome, Oklahoma, then shifts to the long dream sequence that makes up most of the film and finds him as the official food taster for the evil Emperor Valerius (Edward Arnold) in ancient Rome. The slim plot includes a love story between Princess Sylvia (Gloria Stuart) and Josephus

(David Manners), Eddie proving the emperor to be a fraud, and a satire of BEN HUR's chariot race, shot by Ralph Cedar. Busby Berkeley, in his last choreographic job before going on to Warner Bros. and into film history, provides one scene wherein The Goldwyn Girls (Lucille Ball among them) are totally nude except for long blonde wigs. Ruth Etting, who contributes but one song here, later had a film made of her life, LOVE ME OR LEAVE ME, starring Doris Day and James Cagney.

ROMAN SPRING OF MRS. STONE, THE

1961 103m c ★★★½
Drama /X
Seven Arts/Anglo-Amalgamated (U.S./U.K.)

Vivien Leigh (*Karen Stone*), Warren Beatty (*Pablo di Leo*), Coral Browne (*Meg*), Jill St. John (*Bingham*), Lotte Lenya (*Contessa Magda Terribili-Gonzales*), Jeremy Spenser (*Young Man*), Stella Bonheur (*Mrs. Jamison-Walker*), Josephine Brown (*Lucia*), Peter Dyneley (*L. Greener*), Carl Jaffe (*Baron*)

p, Louis de Rochemont; d, Jose Quintero; w, Gavin Lambert, Jan Read (based on the novel by Tennessee Williams); ph, Harry Waxman (Technicolor); ed, Ralph Kamplen; m, Richard Addinsell; prod d, Roger Furse; art d, Herbert Smith; cos, Pierre Balmain, Bumble Dawson

This picture, like some French wines, grows better with age and is a good example of Beatty's acting ability, a talent that was really there, before he became a matinee idol. Leigh was 48, and her husband, Olivier, had just left her for a younger woman. Beatty was 23, eager, ambitious, and sincerely wanting to change his image after SPLENDOR IN THE GRASS. Based on Williams's only novel (he'd written many books of short stories, some of which became plays, and others, films), the screenplay by Lambert became far more explicit in many ways than the subtlety of the short book. Leigh was making her first appearance in six years and would only do one more film, SHIP OF FOOLS, before her death. Williams loved Leigh's work in the film but never said a thing about Beatty, perhaps because he was, at first, against the man in the role. But he changed his mind when Beatty arrived in Puerto Rico masquerading as an Italian and totally fooled him. After Beatty admitted it was only an accent he acquired for the role, Williams shrugged and gave his blessing. Beatty's Italian accent was occasionally spotty, but it was actually fairly good when one considers Beatty's Virginia heritage. The film is filled with Williams's bon mots, many of which are quotable and most of which went right over the heads of the people who decried the movie.

Leigh is a fading actress who has just failed in a role tailored for her but which should have gone to a younger actress. She decides that it's time for a vacation in Europe with husband John Phillips, a wealthy man in poor health who adores her. Phillips dies on the way to Italy, but she continues to Rome, where she makes an attempt to enjoy herself. Browne is Leigh's friend and confidante. When the widow admits that she misses being with a man, journalist Browne arranges for her to meet Lenya, a pimp who specializes in romance for anyone who has the money to buy. Lenya's newest find is Beatty, an Italian youth who takes Lenya's orders. It's not long before Beatty is making love to this woman more than twice his age, and Leigh rewards him with expensive gifts and folderol which annoy Lenya. She would prefer that Leigh pay Beatty real money, so a percentage could be cut from the cash. Lenya decides that it's time to break this up, so she introduces Beatty to rich movie star St. John. When Leigh learns of this, there is a bitchy confrontation between her and the younger actress. While all of this is going on, Spenser, a mysterious young man, has been tailing Leigh from the minute she arrived in Rome. Leigh pleads with Beatty to return to her arms, but he shows her contempt and sneers that she is now the object of all Rome's derision because she has thrown herself so completely at him. She follows Beatty to St. John's hotel, and when there is no longer any question that the two of them are having an affair, Leigh sadly returns to her home, still followed by Spenser. Once there, she removes Beatty's photo from its frame. Then she wraps her keys in a handkerchief, goes to the open window, and tosses them to the furtive Spenser, still not knowing who he is or what he wants. The few glimpses we've had of Spenser are enough to know that he is homicidal. Leigh sits in a chair, lights a cigarette, sighs, and looks up as Spenser enters the room and walks toward her, his coat filling the frame, like the Angel of Death who has come to claim his latest victim.

The lines are pure Williams. When Lenya has a complaint, Leigh retorts: "The beautiful make their own laws." Beatty mentions a middle-aged woman he knows of who died in bed with her throat cut. Leigh, who has been concentrating on her card hand, looks up and says, "After three more years of this, assassination would be a convenience." Lenya was superb and received an Oscar nomination but lost to Rita Moreno in WEST SIDE STORY. The great German actress never had much success in US movies, although she will always be remembered as the villainess in FROM RUSSIA WITH LOVE. Married for years to Kurt Weill (who wrote "The Threepenny Opera" among other things), she became widely familiar because her name appears in the song her husband penned with Bertolt Brecht, "Mack the Knife." The assistant director, who went on to great fame, was Peter Yates.

ROMANCING THE STONE

1984   105m   c   ★★★½
Adventure/Romance   PG
FOX

Michael Douglas (Jack Colton), Kathleen Turner (Joan Wilder), Danny DeVito (Ralph), Zack Norman (Ira), Alfonso Arau (Juan), Manuel Ojeda (Zolo), Holland Taylor (Gloria), Mary Ellen Trainor (Elaine), Eve Smith (Mrs. Irwin), Joe Nesnow (Super)

p, Michael Douglas; d, Robert Zemeckis; w, Diane Thomas; ph, Dean Cundey (Panavision, Deluxe Color); ed, Donn Cambern, Frank Morriss; m, Alan Silvestri; prod d, Lawrence G. Paull; art d, Augustin Ituarte; chor, Jeffrey Hornaday; cos, Marilyn Vance

A rousing, good old-fashioned romantic adventure about Joan Wilder (Kathleen Turner), an author of successful romantic fiction who sits in her New York City apartment banging out novel after novel. The picture opens as Joan is embroiled in her latest literary fantasy. She is snapped out of her reverie by the arrival of a strange package that contains some sort of treasure map showing the way to a glorious green jewel. This is followed by a frantic phone call from her sister who is being held captive by an evil art dealer, Ira (Zack Norman), and his snarling cousin, Ralph (Danny DeVito). Her sister's husband has disappeared in Colombia, and it was he who sent Joan the map. Ira and Ralph threaten to kill Joan's sister unless the treasure map is turned over to Ralph in Colombia. So timid Joan takes off for the jungles of South America only to discover that Zolo (Manuel Ojeda), a corrupt military official, is also after the map. Luckily, she is rescued by a handsome, American soldier-of-fortune, Jack Colton (Michael Douglas), and together they go after the treasure. ROMANCING THE STONE moves like lightning through its 105-minute running time, barely giving viewers a chance to catch their breath. Although comparisons with Steven Spielberg's

RAIDERS OF THE LOST ARK are inevitable, it is the interplay between Turner and Douglas that gives the film its real charm. Norman and DeVito score strongly in roles that would have been played by Sydney Greenstreet and Peter Lorre 30 years ago, and the whole film has the feel of a Warner Bros. thriller with broadly comic overtones. An inferior sequel, THE JEWEL OF THE NILE, was released the following year.

ROMANTIC ENGLISHWOMAN, THE

1975   115m   c   ★★★½
Comedy/Romance   R/15
Dial/Meric/Matalon   (U.K./France)

Glenda Jackson (Elizabeth Fielding), Michael Caine (Lewis Fielding), Helmut Berger (Thomas), Marcus Richardson (David Fielding), Kate Nelligan (Isabel), Rene Kolldehoff (Herman), Michel Lonsdale (Swan), Beatrice Romand (Catherine), Anna Steele (Annie), Nathalie Delon (Miranda)

p, Daniel M. Angel; d, Joseph Losey; w, Tom Stoppard, Thomas Wiseman (based on the novel by Wiseman); ph, Gerry Fisher (Eastmancolor); ed, Reginald Beck; m, Richard Hartley; art d, Richard MacDonald; cos, Ruth Myers

Caine is a successful writer whose imagination becomes increasingly vivid when his wife, Jackson, travels to Europe. Separated by hundreds of miles and angry emotions, Jackson forgets about her husband and becomes attracted to German drug-smuggler Berger. She returns home to Caine in Britain, and the pair invite Berger to stay with them. Caine is intent on having the fellow help do some writing, but instead finds him fondling his wife. Jackson runs away with Berger, but Caine pursues and retrieves his wife. This intelligent film (a comedy, of sorts) from Joseph Losey explores Luigi Pirandello's concept of characters being under control of the author.

ROMEO AND JULIET

1936   127m   bw   ★★★★
Romance/Historical   /U
MGM

Norma Shearer (Juliet), Leslie Howard (Romeo), Edna May Oliver (Nurse to Juliet), John Barrymore (Mercutio), C. Aubrey Smith (Lord Capulet), Basil Rathbone (Tybalt), Andy Devine (Peter), Henry Kolker (Friar Lawrence), Violet Kemble-Cooper (Lady Capulet), Ralph Forbes (Paris)

p, Irving Thalberg; d, George Cukor; w, Talbot Jennings (based on the play by William Shakespeare); ph, William Daniels; ed, Margaret Booth; m, Herbert Stothart; art d, Cedric Gibbons; chor, Agnes De Mille; cos, Oliver Messel, Adrian

MGM production chief and lover of the classics Irving Thalberg spared no expense in this superb filming of Shakespeare's famous tragedy/romance, starring the queen of the MGM lot, Norma Shearer (Thalberg's wife) and the sensitive Leslie Howard. The story opens in Verona, where Romeo and Juliet meet and fall in love, despite the mortal enmity of their families, the Montagues and the Capulets, who have been feuding for decades. Their brief bliss is shattered when Tybalt (Basil Rathbone), Juliet's truculent cousin, duels with and kills the ebullient Mercutio (John Barrymore), Romeo's close friend. The incensed Romeo kills Tybalt, causing himself to be banished from Verona. Juliet's family, unaware that she is secretly wed to Romeo, arranges for a marriage between her and Paris (Ralph Forbes). Desperate and alone, Juliet consults with her confessor, Friar Lawrence (Henry Kolker), who devises a plan by which she can escape her marriage to Paris. The friar gives her a sleeping potion that will give the appearance of death, then has her body placed in the family vault; when Romeo returns, she will awaken, and they will flee to Mantua to live happily. But the plan goes awry. The message from the friar to Romeo explaining that Juliet is only in a deep sleep is waylaid, and Romeo, discovering his beloved and thinking her really dead, stabs himself to join her in eternity; Juliet awakens, finds to her horror that Romeo is dead, and drinks poison. Finding the young lovers dead, the warring families sorrowfully settle their feud.

The eternal Romeo and Juliet story has never been brought to the screen with such verve and lavish production values as in this picture. George Cukor was the perfect director for this romance, a man of genuine emotion, who was able to communicate to his cast his own passion for the characters. Although Howard and Shearer are technically too old for their roles (the characters were teenagers), they perform splendidly, rendering their parts with great sensitivity. She flutters girlishly a bit too much early on and is not quite right in the balcony scene; her reading of the famous potion speech is, however, superb. Howard, meanwhile, though he is more reticent and less passionate than one would often like, nonetheless performs with considerable grace and sensitivity. Shearer was 34 when she did the film; Howard was 46 and refused the part at first, saying that he was too old. Barrymore gives a spritely, excellent performance in the role of Mercutio, delivered with a slight Irish brogue. When on the set, Barrymore vexed the gentle Cukor no end by inserting foul words into the beautiful Shakespearean lines.

To do the film, Thalberg had to promise Mayer that he would bring it in for $800,000, not the $1.5 million originally planned. Thalberg supervised the costumes and sets down to the last balcony. He instructed Shakespeare experts William Strunk, Jr., and James Tucker Murray to supervise the script, which was not to have one line in it that was not Shakespeare's. Thalberg met endlessly with director Cukor, urging him to complete the film with taste and speed at the same time. Thanks to production delays, to which the illustrious Barrymore made no small contribution, ROMEO AND JULIET went over $2 million, and when released, the film barely recouped its investment. The film was nominated for Academy Awards for Best Picture (losing to THE GREAT ZIEGFELD), Best Actress, Best Supporting Actor (Rathbone), and Best Interior Decoration.

ROMEO AND JULIET
1954 138m c ★★★★
Historical/Romance /U
Verona (U.K.)

Laurence Harvey (*Romeo*), Susan Shentall (*Juliet*), Flora Robson (*Nurse*), Mervyn Johns (*Friar Laurence*), Bill Travers (*Benvolio*), Enzo Fiermonte (*Tybalt*), Aldo Zollo (*Mercutio*), Giovanni Rota (*Prince of Verona*), Sebastian Cabot (*Capulet*), Lydia Sherwood (*Lady Capulet*)

p, Sandro Ghenzi, Joseph Janni; d, Renato Castellani; w, Renato Castellani (based on the play by William Shakespeare); ph, Robert Krasker (Technicolor); ed, Sidney Hayers; m, Roman Vlad; chor, Madi Obolensky; cos, Leonor Fini

A British production shot entirely on location in Italy, this version of Shakespeare's play is particularly distinguished by the visual beauty brought to it by director-screenwriter Renato Castellani. Castellani gives the film a painterly look, composed and costumed (by surrealist painter Leonor Fini) after the model of various Italian painters of the early Renaissance. The 26-year-old Laurence Harvey, still early in his career, stars as Romeo; Juliet is played by 20-year-old Susan Shentall in her only film appear-

ance. (Discovered in a restaurant by Castellani, she soon gave up acting to get married.) Castellani's desire to convey an accurate medieval Italian setting led him to film in various locations, but his unerring eye for detail allowed him to intercut his footage seamlessly, so that it's impossible to tell what was shot in Venice, Siena, or elsewhere; all blends convincingly into the film's 15th-century Verona. Further enhancing the authenticity is the casting of nonprofessionals and unfamiliar faces, including a crew member in the role of Friar John, a Veronese architect as Mercutio, a Venetian canal worker as Montague, and more than 200 extras culled from the local population. Castellani's adaptation of Shakespeare is necessarily somewhat abridged, and the sequence of some scenes is altered, but the film is generally a sensitive treatment of the play, and the gorgeous images do much to compensate for its literary shortcomings. Although it was not a popular success, it won the Venice Film Festival's Grand Prix Award, nosing out such films as LA STRADA and ON THE WATERFRONT.

ROMEO AND JULIET
1968 138m c ★★★★
Historical/Romance PG
British Home Entertainment/Verona/DEG (U.K./Italy)

Olivia Hussey (*Juliet*), Leonard Whiting (*Romeo*), Milo O'Shea (*Friar Laurence*), Murray Head (*The Chorus*), Michael York (*Tybalt*), John McEnery (*Mercutio*), Pat Heywood (*The Nurse*), Natasha Parry (*Lady Capulet*), Robert Stephens (*Prince of Verona*), Keith Skinner (*Balthazar*)

p, Anthony Havelock-Allan, John Brabourne; d, Franco Zeffirelli; w, Franco Zeffirelli, Masolino D'Amico, Franco Brusati (based on the play by William Shakespeare); ph, Pasqualino De Santis (Technicolor); ed, Reginald Mills; m, Nino Rota; prod d, Lorenzo Mongiardino; art d, Luciano Puccini, Emilio Carcano; cos, Danilo Donati

This beautiful version of the Veronese love story was by far the most successful at the box office, although Zeffirelli took a huge chance casting two unknowns in the leads. Whiting was 17 and Hussey was 15, the closest any actors have actually come to the ages of the characters. It's a visually stunning adaptation with more action, more broad humor, and surely more sexiness than had ever been seen for the tale. The Italian director had made THE TAMING OF THE SHREW the year before with Elizabeth Taylor and Richard Burton. Although that film was not a big hit, his backers felt that his assured direction merited another attempt at Shakespeare. Filmed in Tuscany at Pienza, Gubbio, Artena, and in the palace once owned by the Borgias, ROMEO AND JULIET won an Oscar for Best Photography (De Santis), with nominations for Best Picture and Best Director as well. In order to take the onus off the relatively inexperienced leads, Zeffirelli trimmed some of the longer speeches, used reaction shots to break matters up, and gave the actors bits of business to do so they wouldn't seem like talking heads. That technique was successful, although both leads did betray their youth on several occasions. Also, one can only wonder how he could ever manage to cut Juliet's potion speech. (This is only the most unforgivable of several major excisions.) Laurence Olivier was around to lend his mellifluous voice as a narrator, a definite plus, but the director is the true star here as he gives us rousing crowd scenes, vicious fights, and a look at Romeo's nudity and the partial nakedness of Juliet. It was that flesh that caused British censors not to allow teenagers under 16 to see the film without an adult. The sets are magnificent, the supporting actors excellent, and the costumes attractive enough to warrant an Oscar for Donati, beating out another period piece that year, OLIVER! Young people have been turned off by some Shakespearean films because they could not identify with them. By casting these teenagers in the starring roles, Zeffirelli brought millions of youngsters into the theater who had been born and bred on a diet of BEACH PARTY pictures.

ROOM AT THE TOP

1959 115m bw   ★★★★½
Drama   /15
Romulus (U.K.)

Laurence Harvey *(Joe Lampton)*, Simone Signoret *(Alice Aisgill)*, Heather Sears *(Susan Brown)*, Donald Wolfit *(Mr. Brown)*, Ambrosine Phillpotts *(Mrs. Brown)*, Donald Houston *(Charles Soames)*, Raymond Huntley *(Mr. Hoylake)*, John Westbrook *(Jack Wales)*, Allan Cuthbertson *(George Aisgill)*, Mary Peach *(June Samson)*

p, John Woolf, James Woolf; d, Jack Clayton; w, Neil Paterson (based on the novel by John Braine); ph, Freddie Francis; ed, Ralph Kemplen; m, Mario Nascimbene; art d, Ralph Brinton

A ruthless indictment of the British class system, ROOM AT THE TOP is a hallmark, seminal film in the social realist British "kitchen sink" movement, which produced such movies as SATURDAY NIGHT AND SUNDAY MORNING; A TASTE OF HONEY; and THIS SPORTING LIFE. But ROOM set the trend and lured adults back into theaters in droves, thanks to its frank treatment of sexuality and the blaze of energy brought to it by the magnificence and suffering of the incomparable Signoret. You may not agree, but we think (because of *her*) it stands the test of time. Laurence Harvey is the film's ruthless main character, a former POW turned romantic bastard, hoping to gatecrash past his working-class origins. Arriving in Warnley, a bleak industrial town in Yorkshire, he secures a low-paying job as a government accountant, but soon realizes all the professional ability in the world will never elevate his status. Accordingly, he sets his cap for Sears, the naive young daughter of Warnley's most powerful citizen, millionaire industrialist Wolfit. Wolfit recognizes a bit of himself in the calculating, cold Harvey—who clearly does not love Sears, only the social prestige (and social revenge) that marriage to her would provide—and tries to break up the romance by shipping Sears off to the Continent until her genuine passion for Harvey cools. Harvey then begins an affair with Signoret, the star of the local theater group, who is 10 years older than he and unhappily married to Cuthbertson. With Signoret, Harvey begins for the first time to show some genuine warmth, but he stifles his feelings in his constant quest for position. Signoret, meanwhile, falls in love with the young climber, but everything works against her: Cuthbertson refuses to divorce, and Sears returns to Warnley.

Based on the Angry Young Man novel by John Braine, ROOM AT THE TOP broke new ground in its realistic dialogue, sexual frankness (it received an X certificate in Britain), and bitter condemnation of provincialism and class-consciousness. Director Jack Clayton, who had previously directed only the mid-length THE BESPOKE OVERCOAT, was hailed as an important new voice in British cinema on its strength, while screenwriter Neil Paterson and Simone Signoret both won Oscars for their work. It also took Best Picture and Best Foreign Actress (Signoret) British Film Academy awards, as well as another Best Actress for Signoret at Cannes. Among the supporting performers Wolfit and Phillpotts (as Harvey's wealthy future in-laws) are especially good. Aside from its reputation for explicitness, ROOM AT THE TOP conveys the snobbism, the poverty, the desperation, and the politics of class in provincial England. A

sequel, LIFE AT THE TOP, also starred Harvey, but otherwise failed to live up to the standard of its original.

ROOM SERVICE

1938 78m bw   ★★
Comedy   /U
RKO

Groucho Marx *(Gordon Miller)*, Chico Marx *(Harry Binelli)*, Harpo Marx *(Faker Englund)*, Lucille Ball *(Christine)*, Ann Miller *(Hilda Manney)*, Frank Albertson *(Leo Davis)*, Donald MacBride *(Gregory Wagner)*, Clifford Dunstan *(Joseph Gribble)*, Philip Loeb *(Timothy Hogarth)*, Philip Wood *(Simon Jenkins)*

p, Pandro S. Berman; d, William A. Seiter; w, Morrie Ryskind (based on the play by John Murray and Allen Boretz); ph, J. Roy Hunt; ed, George Crone; art d, Van Nest Polglase, Al Herman; cos, Renie

The hit Broadway comedy by Allen Boretz and John Murray was not given a great treatment by the Marx Brothers and the production team. Harpo didn't play the harp, Chico didn't play the piano, Groucho didn't have Margaret Dumont to play off, and there were no songs other than "Swing Low, Sweet Chariot." It cost more than a quarter of a million dollars for the stage rights, and despite the fact that the budget was low, the movie still cost almost $400,000 the first time around. Scenarist Ryskind did what he could to adapt the farce for the unique talents of the Marxes, but the result was just another comedy. Groucho and Chico are living at a Broadway hotel. They are planning a new stage show and are waiting for the financing to come through. Their room is packed with members of the cast, and the hotel bill is now well over $1,000, which rankles MacBride, an executive of the hotel, and Dunstan, the inn's manager. Since this debt is outstanding and results in the hotel's books being on the debit side, MacBride tells Dunstan that the time has come to evict the guests in room 920. Albertson, the play's author, arrives. He hasn't a dime, so he moves into the already-crowded room. Miller, a secretary, has come to see Groucho to set up a reading for Alexander Asro, a Russian waiter who wants to be in the show. The moment Miller and Albertson set eyes on each other, bells clang. The following morning, Ball enters the room to announce that she has a potential angel who is willing to sink some money into the show, if they can just hold out for one more day in the room. Albertson is tapped to fake a case of measles, so they have to be quarantined and no one can be tossed out. However, his passion for Miller causes him to slip out of the room and go to the lobby to see her. Dunstan and MacBride spot him. Meanwhile, Harpo fakes being ill, and Ball pretends to be his nurse. When Halton, an outside doctor, is called in to diagnose the illness of Harpo, he spots the fraud, and, rather than have him tell the management, they tie him up and put him in the bathroom. Wood enters with the check from his client but changes his mind about the deal. They think that they have talked him into it, Wood signs the check, and Groucho gives it to MacBride to pay for the bills run up by the cast and crew. Albertson learns that Wood only signed the check so he could get out of the room and will stop payment on it as soon as he can call his bank. Groucho realizes he must work fast, so he sets up the show to open in the hotel's theater right away. MacBride tries to cash the check and learns that there is a stop payment on it. While the play is being presented on stage, MacBride has the hotel cops keep the Marxes and Albertson in the room. Albertson pretends to commit suicide, and Miller, seing that it's a fake, goes downstairs to see the show so she can report back to him. Albertson "expires," and MacBride is desperately attempting to get the body out of the hotel because the resultant publicity might cost him his job. Harpo now fakes having been assaulted with a knife and he is taken down the back way to an alley. Albertson has slipped inside the theater with Miller and the show is getting laughs in all the right places. MacBride walks into the theater, sees the "dead" Albertson, and responds by fainting dead away. The play's script calls for a dead man, and Harpo is carried on in that capacity. The show is a smash, and the picture ends on a high note. In 1944, it was turned into the musical, STEP LIVELY, with Frank Sinatra in the lead. Holdovers from the Broadway show include Wood, Asro, Dunstan, MacBride, and Loeb. The play was, and still is, an excellent vehicle for stock companies, and, when directed with pace, as funny as it was in the 1930s. The picture, however, is not that good.

ROOM WITH A VIEW, A

1986   115m   c   ★★★★
Comedy/Drama   PG-13/PG
Cinecom   (U.K.)

Maggie Smith (Charlotte Bartlett), Helena Bonham Carter (Lucy Honeychurch), Denholm Elliott (Mr. Emerson), Julian Sands (George Emerson), Daniel Day Lewis (Cecil Vyse), Simon Callow (Rev. Beebe), Judi Dench (Miss Lavish), Rosemary Leach (Mrs. Honeychurch), Rupert Graves (Freddy Honeychurch), Patrick Godfrey (Mr. Eager)

p, Ismail Merchant; d, James Ivory; w, Ruth Prawer Jhabvala (based on the novel by E.M. Forster); ed, Humphrey Dixon; m, Richard Robbins; prod d, Gianni Quaranta, Brian Ackland-Snow; cos, Jenny Beavan, John Bright

Made for only $3 million, this Merchant-Ivory production was nominated for eight Oscars and won three. The droll comedy of manners and morals begins in 1907, when Lucy Honeychurch (Helena Bonham Carter) goes off to Italy in the company of Charlotte Bartlett (Maggie Smith), her maiden cousin and spinster chaperone. They arrive in Florence and take up residence at the Pensione Bertolini, where they meet the charming Mr. Emerson (Denholm Elliott) and his son, George (Julian Sands). It's evident from the start that George finds Lucy pleasing to gaze upon, and on a visit to Fiesole, the town high above Florence, he takes the opportunity to kiss the young girl. Charlotte witnesses the kiss and insists they leave for England at once. Back in Surrey, where Lucy lives with her mother (Rosemary Leach) and ne'er-do-well brother, Freddy (Rupert Graves), Lucy settles into her relationship with Cecil (Daniel Day Lewis), the twit to whom she is engaged. But the Emersons move into a vacant villa in the area, and uninhibited passion again enters Lucy's safe world. It's hard to believe A ROOM WITH A VIEW cost so little; the costumes and sets are dazzling and the acting is superb—from two-time Oscar-winner Smith to the smallest role, there's not a false note.

ROPE

1948   80m   c   ★★★
Thriller   /PG
Transatlantic

James Stewart (Rupert Caldell), John Dall (Shaw Brandon), Farley Granger (Philip), Joan Chandler (Janet Walker), Cedric Hardwicke (Mr. Kentley David's Father), Constance Collier (Mrs. Atwater), Edith Evanson (Mrs. Wilson the Governess), Douglas Dick (Kenneth Lawrence), Dick Hogan (David Kentley)

p, Sidney Bernstein, Alfred Hitchcock; d, Alfred Hitchcock; w, Arthur Laurents, Hume Cronyn, Ben Hecht (based on the play "Rope's End" by Patrick Hamilton); ph, Joseph Valentine, William V. Skall (Technicolor); ed, William Ziegler; m, David Buttolph; art d, Perry Ferguson; cos, Adrian

Exhibiting the mastery of cinema's greatest craftsman, Alfred Hitchcock, ROPE is famous for being the first, and thus far only, film which appears to be one continuous shot. Based on a 1929 stage play, which in turn was drawn from the infamous Leopold and Loeb murder case of 1924, ROPE tells the story of two young, intelligent, collegiate homosexuals, Dall and Granger, who murder a weak-willed friend, Hogan, simply for the thrill of it. In their New York penthouse apartment, safely hidden behind the drawn window shades, Dall and Granger strangle the life out of Hodges with a length of rope and then stuff his corpse into an antique chest. After hiding the rope in a kitchen drawer, the pair celebrate their gruesome feat with champagne. The apartment is then prepared for the evening's cocktail party; included among the guests are Hardwicke, the murdered boy's father, Chandler, the victim's fiancee, and Stewart, a college professor whose philosophical discussions of Friedrich Nietzsche's "superman" theory have inspired the murderers. Dall, the more arrogant of the killers, enjoys toying with the crime he just committed, insisting that dinner be served from the chest and making veiled references to the crime such as "I could kill you" and "Knock 'em dead." Granger, on the other hand, appears not to enjoy the game, reacting nervously to such purposely ironic comments. As the night wears on, the guests become concerned with Hogan's absence, fearing that something may have happened to him. The dinner party begins to take on a more morbid tone when Dall pulls Stewart into a conversation about murder. Stewart speaks on an abstract level of man's right and moral duty to rid the world of the weak. This philosophy, which disgusts most of the guests, excites Dall who tries to bring the conversation into more concrete terms. By this point, Granger has gotten himself quite drunk and becomes carelessly emotional, arousing Stewart's suspicions. Dall pushes the proceedings too far when he gives Hardwicke some books tied together with the piece of rope used in the murder. An hour after the party has begun, with Hogan still unaccounted for, the guests leave, and it looks as if Dall and Granger have succeeded. Stewart, however, returns and presses the issue of their earlier conversation about murder. When he puts the facts together and finds the body, he calls the police. As the three wait, Stewart realizes that he taught his pupils too well and assumes a measure of the guilt for the murder.

Although the story of the murder and its discovery is intriguing, it is not what people remember ROPE for, nor is it top-drawer Hitchcock in terms of storytelling, complexity, and structure. Like LIFEBOAT before it, Rope is an experiment in overcoming technical barriers and restrictions—a task which always thrilled Hitchcock. Known for his deliberate and meticulous preproduction planning of a film, Hitchcock is widely believed to have thought of his actors in a secondary light. Here, this is most clear since all of his energies go into technique, but, paradoxically, ROPE, with its long takes, can be seen as favorable to the actors since their performances are closer to theater than film. The construction of ROPE is simple—eight 10-minute takes cut together to appear as one continuous shot. Feature films have an average of about 600 shots. (Hitchcock's THE BIRDS had over 1,300 and just the shower scene in PSYCHO had dozens.) ROPE appears to be one continuous take, exclusive of a separate shot which opens the film and a couple of direct reverse angle cuts within the film, which are often forgotten. Since the maximum length for a reel of 35mm film is around 10 minutes, the reels were joined inconspicuously by stopping the camera behind a character with his back filling the entire frame. Not surprisingly, there were many other hurdles for Hitchcock and his crew to overcome. Together with cameraman Valentine, art director Ferguson, set designers Kuri and Bristol, and editor Ziegler, Hitchcock outlined specific plans for the production. Ziegler's job was to choreograph the actors' movements with a small scale model of the set. Valentine's camera needed the freedom to travel through the set without crashing into things, so breakaway walls were built, which were suspended from ceiling beams and rolled along by technicians to allow camera passage. The furniture and the chest which hid the corpse were also on rollers. Because dialogue was being recorded, the movement of the walls and the props had to be done silently, so the tracks on which they moved were coated with petroleum jelly. The floors of the sound stage were specially built with one-inch tongue-and-groove lumber, soundproofing, and felt-lined carpeting to prevent any creaking. Even a special camera dolly was invented (by head grip Morris Rosen) to allow for greater freedom of movement. Countless lights were hung overhead, as were microphones. On some occasions there were as many as five boom operators recording sound at the same time, adding to the already crowded sound stage.

Because of the number of people and the number of things that could go wrong, many takes were needed for each scene. One perfectly good take was ruined when, after the 10-minute reel was nearly done, an electrician was spotted in the background. Valentine, in a 1948 interview with *American Cinematographer* magazine, said: "My biggest problem was the lighting, especially the job of eliminating mike and camera shadows. In the reel in which we had 10 mikes in operation we had to have electricians operating five dimmer panels." This was Hitchcock's first film in color, and Valentine was experienced only with black-and-white photography, so he was unable to capture the color Hitchcock needed during sundown. Technicolor advisor Skall was brought in and, after Valentine left the production due to illness, reshot the final five reels (over half of the film). Special care was also taken on the New York City skyline which is seen outside the penthouse window. Since the film took place in real time, night had to fall over the city. A set was built which encompassed 35 square miles of skyline, including such landmarks as the Empire State Building and the Chrysler Building. Six thousand flashing miniature lights, 200 miniature neon signs, 26,000 feet of wire, 150 transformers, and 126,000 watts of electricity were controlled by an electrician operating 47 different switches. (The skyline included a neon sign which advertised a product called Reduco, featuring a before and after silhouette of Hitchcock—a gag also seen in a newspaper ad in LIFEBOAT.) Everything outside the window was constructed in diminishing perspective and in a semicircle to keep the constantly mobile camera from accidentally photographing part of a bare set. Technically correct cloud formations were constructed from spun glass and chickenwire, under the expert instructions of a specially hired advisor, meteorologist Dr. Dinsmore Alter.

Budgeted at $1.5 million, ROPE was scripted first by Hitchcock's friend, actor Hume Cronyn, from Hamilton's play. Playwright Laurents was then brought in to improve on Cronyn. Even Ben Hecht (who had previously written SPELLBOUND and NOTORIOUS) added some uncredited lines to the final climactic scene. Rehearsals began on January 12, 1948, to perfect the interplay between camera, cast, and crew. Numbers were placed on the floor marking everyone's specific spots, each of which corresponded with the actors' dialogue cues. Filming commenced on January 22 and finished on February 21. Hitchcock later said, "I undertook ROPE as a stunt; that's the only way I know how to describe it." As a result, ROPE is chiefly of interest to filmmakers curious to learn how things were achieved; it lacks much of the flair and audience manipulation that Hitchcock has become famous for. Stewart's performance is competent, but never reaches the level of disturbance or authority that it should have. Dall and Granger (whom Hitchcock spotted after screening Nicholas Ray's first picture, THEY LIVE BY NIGHT) are both superb. Their characters and their thinly shrouded homosexuality were based on the murderous exploits of Richard A. Leopold, the 18-year-old son of a multi-millionaire shipping magnate, and Nathan F. Loeb, the 17-year-old son of a wealthy Sears, Roebuck and Company vice president. Together, in 1924, they kidnapped and killed 14-year-old Bobbie Franks of Chicago just for the thrill of trying to get away with murder. Because of the underlying homosexuality in ROPE, the film was initially banned in Chicago (perhaps as a reaction to the raking up of the memory of the real murder case), Spokane, Memphis, Seattle, and morally condemned in many other towns. Only after an "adults only" policy was enacted in Chicago, and the opening murder scene deleted in Sioux City, Iowa, could the film be shown in those cities. ROPE was one of five Hitchcock films—REAR WINDOW, THE TROUBLE WITH HARRY, VERTIGO, and the 1956 version of THE MAN WHO KNEW TOO MUCH were the others—held from distribution for many years until their re-release in 1983.

ROSALIE GOES SHOPPING

1989 94m c ★★★
Comedy PG-13/15
Pelemele (West Germany)

Marianne Sagebrecht *(Rosalie)*, Brad Davis *(Liebling Ray)*, Judge Reinhold *(Priest)*, Willy Harlander *(Rosalie's Father)*, Erika Blumberger *(Rosalie's Mother)*, Patricia Zehentmayr *(Barbara)*, John Hawkes *(Schnuki)*, Alex Winter *(Schatzi)*, Courtney Kraus *(April)*, David Denney

p, Percy Adlon, Eleonore Adlon; d, Percy Adlon; w, Eleonore Adlon, Christopher Doherty, Percy Adlon; ph, Bernd Heinl; ed, Heiko Hindkers; m, Bob Telson; cos, Elizabeth Warner Nonkin

The third (and final) part in Percy Adlon's "Marianne" trilogy, ROSALIE GOES SHOPPING is a respectable attempt to maintain the runaway success of Adlon's last feature, BAGDAD CAFE. It's always hard to follow a hit, but Adlon certainly hasn't missed the mark this time. Marianne Sagebrecht, as chubbily charming as ever, stars as Rosalie, a German peacetime bride residing in her GI husband's hometown of Stuttgart, Arkansas. Although she has lived in Arkansas many years and raised her ridiculously harmonious family there, she still yearns for Bavaria, for Bad Tolz, and—even more—to spend, spend, spend. . . but not her own money. With her collection of 37 credit cards, skill at fraud and forgery, and her ability to wheedle husband Davis' pay packet from his boss weeks before it's due, Sagebrecht indulges all her own and her family's whims and fancies. Each time she commits another act of embezzlement, she rushes off to confession to clear her soul of guilt. The day Sagebrecht gives a megacomputer to her daughter is the day her life changes for good, the stakes becoming much higher. As a bold, canny computer hacker, Sagebrecht begins to shuffle stocks around the markets and to move cash around bank accounts. One day, her friendly postman gives her a tip—"If you owe the bank

$100,000, it's your problem; if you owe them a million, it's theirs"—and from that point on she never looks back.

Adlon's film plays off its cute love-hate relationship with materialism, in which Sagebrecht's practical Bavarian acquisitiveness meets childlike American consumer decadence. This satiric marriage is a happy one—a fantasy in which the client rips off the bank and not vice versa.

ROSE, THE
1979 134m c   ★★★
Musical   R/15
FOX

Bette Midler (Rose), Alan Bates (Rudge), Frederic Forrest (Dyer), Harry Dean Stanton (Billy Ray), Barry Primus (Dennis), David Keith (Mal), Sandra McCabe (Sarah), Will Hare (Mr. Leonard), Rudy Bond (Monty), Don Calfa (Don Frank)

p, Marvin Worth, Aaron Russo; d, Mark Rydell; w, Bo Goldman, Bill Kerby, Michael Cimino (based on the story by Kerby); ph, Vilmos Zsigmond (DeLuxe Color); ed, Robert Wolfe; m, Paul A. Rothchild; prod d, Richard MacDonald; art d, James Schoppe; chor, Toni Basil; cos, Theoni V. Aldredge

Bette Midler turns in a magnificent performance as a dissipated, Janis Joplin-like rock singer. Exhausted from touring, Rose (Midler) tells her manager (Alan Bates) that she wants a year off to rest, and when he resists, the singer goes into a tailspin. One night she picks up Dyer (Frederic Forrest), a chauffeur, and embarks on the most fulfilling romance of her life. Dyer cannot deal with the penalties of fame that come with Rose's success, however, and eventually he leaves her to her music. A triumphant performance before a hometown audience turns out to be her last as the troubled singer resorts to a fatal combination of booze and drugs. Midler successfully brings her charged stage persona to the screen, presenting a convincing portrait of the backstage life of a rock 'n' roll performer. Forrest, as the chauffeur, and Harry Dean Stanton, in a cameo as a country singer, add an earthy contrast to the glamorous aspects of rock stardom. Only Bates is wasted in a relatively minor role as the manager whose hunger for success is greater than Rose can handle. Nominated for three Oscars: Best Actress (Midler, who lost to Sally Field for NORMA RAE), Best Supporting Actor (Forrest) and Best Sound. A number of hard-hitting tunes are featured: "Fire down Below" (Bob Seger), "I've Written a Letter to Daddy" (Larry Vincent, Harry Tobias, Mo Jaffe), "Let Me Call You Sweetheart" (Leo Friedman, Beth Slater Whitson), "The Rose" (Amanda McBroom), "Stay with Me" (Jerry Ragavoy, George Weiss), "Camellia" (Stephen Hunter), "Sold My Soul to Rock 'n' Roll" (Gene Pistilli), "Keep on Rockin'" (Sammy Hagar, John Carter), "When a Man Loves a Woman" (C. Lewis, A. Wright), "Whose Side Are You On?" (Kenny Hopkins, Charley Williams), "Midnight in Memphis" (Tony Johnson), "The Night We Said Goodbye" (Bill Elliott), and "Evil Lies" (Greg Prestopino, Carol Locatell).

ROSE MARIE
1936 110m bw   ★★★★½
Musical/Comedy   /U
MGM

Jeanette MacDonald (Marie de Flor), Nelson Eddy (Sgt. Bruce), James Stewart (John Flower), Reginald Owen (Myerson), George Regas (Boniface), Robert Greig (Cafe Manager), Una O'Connor (Anna), Jimmy Conlin (Joe the Piano Player), Lucien Littlefield (Storekeeper), Dorothy Gray (Edith)

p, Hunt Stromberg; d, W.S. Van Dyke, II; w, Frances Goodrich, Albert Hackett, Alice Duer Miller (based on the operetta by Otto Harbach, Oscar Hammerstein II, Rudolf Friml, Herbert Stothart); ph, William Daniels; ed, Blanche Sewell; m, Rudolf Friml, Herbert Stothart; art d, Cedric Gibbons, Joseph C. Wright, Edwin B. Willis; chor, Chester Hale, William von Wymetal; cos, Adrian

Of all the Jeanette MacDonald-Nelson Eddy films, ROSE MARIE made the most money and is the best remembered. Grace Moore was to star but due to a schedule conflict, MacDonald, coming off her smash hit collaboration with Eddy, NAUGHTY MARIETTA, replaced her. As opera star Marie de Flor, she pleads with the Canadian priemer (Alan Mowbray) to release convicted bank robber John Flower (James Stewart, in his second film), but when he kills a man during a breakout, Marie leaves the opera (five acts of Charles Gounod's "Romeo et Juliette" amazingly compressed into roughly six minutes) and hires Boniface (George Regas), a half-breed guide, to take her into the wilderness in search of Flower. After Boniface double-crosses Marie, stealing all her money, she survives by becoming a saloon singer. Enter handsome Sgt. Bruce (Eddy) of the Mounties, whose mission it is to bring in Flower and who falls for the lovely Marie, then learns of her connection with the escapee. However, a Mountie always gets his man, and so does Sgt. Bruce, though by film's end he's also gotten his woman. A few laughs, excellent singing, and gorgeous photography all contribute to making this a must-see for Eddy-MacDonald fans. Her opening impersonation of a pampered prima donna is hilarious, an ample reminder of MacDonald's formidable if not always utilized comic talents. Although composer Rudolf Friml is always remembered for ROSE MARIE, it was actually MGM musical director Herbert Stothart who wrote many of the tunes. Under no circumstances confuse this offering, retitled INDIAN LOVE CALL for television showings, with the remake, which is inferior, despite its wide-screen, color treatment.

ROSE TATTOO, THE
1955 117m bw   ★★★★
Drama   /A
Paramount

Anna Magnani (Serafina Delle Rose), Burt Lancaster (Alvaro Mangiacavallo), Marisa Pavan (Rosa Delle Rose), Ben Cooper (Jack Hunter), Virginia Grey (Estelle Hohengarten), Jo Van Fleet (Bessie), Sandro Giglio (Father De Leo), Mimi Aguglia (Assunta), Florence Sundstrom (Flora), Dorrit Kelton (Schoolteacher)

p, Hal B. Wallis; d, Daniel Mann; w, Tennessee Williams, Hal Kanter (based on the play by Williams); ph, James Wong Howe (VistaVision); ed, Warren Low; m, Alex North; art d, Hal Pereira, Tambi Larsen; cos, Edith Head

Tennessee Williams wrote "The Rose Tattoo" as a play vehicle for Anna Magnani several years before this film appeared, but at that time she was still struggling with English and declined the role. Five years later, after a fairly successful run, Williams did the screenplay and Mann, the director of the stage production, handled the directing. Magnani, by this time, had enough confidence in her command of the language (plus the added convenience of being able to shoot again and again until she got it right) to take the role, her first US job. The result was a hit. Oscars were given to Magnani, cinematographer Howe, Pereira and Larsen for their art direction (black-and-white), Comer and Krans for their black-and-white set decoration, and nominations went to the picture (it lost to MARTY), costume designer Edith Head, film editor Low, supporting actress Pavan, and composer North.

Magnani is a Sicilian-born widow with a 15-year-old daughter, Pavan. She cremates her dear husband, who she'd always felt was totally faithful to her, so she can keep his ashes—a violation of the Catholic religion in which she was raised. Cooper, a young sailor, makes eyes at Pavan in the little Louisiana town, and Magnani forces him to promise not to lay a hand on her until they are married. Lancaster enters, a banana hauler like her late husband. He also has a rose tattoo on his chest, just as the late mister did. The tattoo is a superstitious indication of great sexual virility, and she is drawn to Lancaster but reveres her husband's memory so much that she holds her emotions in check. It's only when Magnani learns that the dead mate was cheating with Grey that she realizes she is free to accept Lancaster as her lover at the conclusion.

Magnani is not an attractive woman to look at. She's earthy, robust, and doesn't mind being harshly photographed. Lancaster is grossly miscast, as he was opposite Shirley Booth in COME BACK, LITTLE SHEBA. Magnani later appeared opposite Marlon Brando in THE FUGITIVE KIND, another Williams piece, but never came close in any of her other US pictures to the dynamic performance she gave in THE ROSE TATTOO. North's excellent music helped the mood enormously. North was honored at the 1985 Oscars (in March, 1986) and came on television to accept his award with an impassioned plea to put good taste back in films, something he's always shown. Pavan, the sister of the tragic Pier Angeli, later married Jean-Pierre Aumont.

ROSELAND

1977   103m   c   ★★★
Drama   PG/A
Merchant Ivory

Teresa Wright *(May)*, Lou Jacobi *(Stan)*, Don de Natale *(Master of Ceremonies)*, Louise Kirtland *(Ruby)*, Geraldine Chaplin *(Marilyn)*, Helen Gallagher *(Cleo)*, Joan Copeland *(Pauline)*, Christopher Walken *(Russel)*, Conrad Janis *(George)*, Lilia Skala *(Rosa)*

p, Ismail Merchant; d, James Ivory; w, Ruth Prawer Jhabvala; ph, Ernest Vincze; ed, Humphrey Dixon, Richard Schmiechen; m, Michael Gibson; chor, Patricia Birch; cos, Dianne Finn Chapman

The setting serves as the central character in this threefold tale of dancers who spend their time at New York's Roseland ballroom. The three main characters are Wright, a widow whose memories flow when on the dance floor with Jacobi; Walken, a gigolo involved with the dying Copeland and the pesty Chaplin; and Skala, the film's one treasure as an elderly German lady who works as a cleaning woman in order to pay for her night out. Technically careless and below par, but this is due unfortunately to a meager three-week shooting schedule. The stories that surface from the technical problems, however, are filled with liveliness and charm. Some of the dance classics on the soundtrack are "Baubles, Bangles and Beads," "Stranger in Paradise" (George Forrest, Robert Wright), "Moon of Manakoora" (Alfred Newman, Frank Loesser), "On a Slow Boat to China" (Loesser), "Rockin' Chair" (Hoagy Carmichael), and "Super Cool."

ROSEMARY'S BABY

1968   136m   c   ★★★★
Horror   R/18
Paramount

Mia Farrow *(Rosemary Woodhouse)*, John Cassavetes *(Guy Woodhouse)*, Ruth Gordon *(Minnie Castevet)*, Sidney Blackmer *(Roman Castevet)*, Maurice Evans *(Hutch)*, Ralph Bellamy *(Dr.*

Sapirstein), Victoria Vetri *(Terry Fionoffrio)*, Patsy Kelly *(Laura-Louise)*, Elisha Cook, Jr. *(Mr. Nicklas)*, Charles Grodin *(Dr. Hill)*

p, William Castle; d, Roman Polanski; w, Roman Polanski (based on the novel by Ira Levin); ph, William A. Fraker (Technicolor); ed, Sam O'Steen, Bob Wyman; m, Krzysztof Komeda; prod d, Richard Sylbert; art d, Joel Schiller; fx, Farciot Edouart; cos, Anthea Sylbert

Roman Polanski's first American movie and his second masterpiece of horror (REPULSION was released in 1965) is set under the sunny skies of modern-day New York City. There are no creepy characters and no eerie locations, just a happy young couple expecting their first child. Newlyweds Rosemary (Mia Farrow) and unemployed actor Gus (John Cassavetes) have just moved into their new apartment in a gothic Central Park building (shot in the famous Dakota, home of the late John Lennon). Their neighbors, the elderly Minnie (Ruth Gordon) and Roman Castevet (Sidney Blackmer), are friendly but a bit intrusive. Rosemary learns that she is pregnant but feels a strange sense of anxiety. She seems to remember a vague dream in which she was raped by a savage beast. She has mysterious scratches on her stomach. Her doctor prescribes a curious elixir. It's perhaps not surprising that Rosemary becomes fixated by the idea that she has been impregnated by Satan and is now carrying his unholy child in her womb while living among a coven of witches.

Truly frightening because so much of it is so plausible, ROSEMARY'S BABY is one of the finest examples of modern horror, a milestone in the evolution of the genre. Although the subject matter is ultimately supernatural, the treatment is very realistic. Perhaps the film's most disturbing aspect is that the fears and anxiety that Rosemary experiences initially seem like an understandable response for a neurasthenic young woman to have when an "alien" being is growing within her. The brilliance of the film is that it takes this realistic basis and builds upon it with supernatural metaphors that make pregnancy a rich and strange condition. Ruth Gordon won the Oscar for Best Supporting Actress.

ROTTEN TO THE CORE

1965   89m   bw   ★★½
Comedy/Crime   /A
Tudor   (U.K.)

Eric Sykes *(Hunt)*, Ian Bannen *(Vine)*, Dudley Sutton *(Jelly)*, Kenneth Griffith *(Lenny)*, James Beckett *(Scapa)*, Avis Bunnage *(Countess)*, Anton Rodgers *(Duke)*, Charlotte Rampling *(Sara)*, Victor Maddern *(Anxious)*, Thorley Walters *(Preston)*

p, Roy Boulting; d, John Boulting; w, John Warren, Len Heath, Jeffrey Dell, Roy Boulting (based on a story by Warren and Heath, Dell, Roy Boulting and an idea by Warren and Heath); ph, Freddie Young (Panavision); ed, Teddy Darvas; m, Michael Dress; art d, Alex Vetchinsky; fx, Wally Veevers

A trio of petty criminals fresh out of the slammer search for their boss, Rodgers, who has been holding onto their cut of the robbery for which they were doing time. They are first told that he is dead but discover that he is hiding out in a health clinic, plotting to undertake a major robbery. The trio soon become part of the operation, which results in Rodgers being reduced to a petty criminal, while the others get off scot-free, but without the loot. Charlotte Rampling made her film debut in a sizable role as Rodgers's girlfriend.

ROUND MIDNIGHT

1986   133m   c   ★★★★
Drama   R/PG
PECF/Little Bear   (France/U.S.)

Dexter Gordon *(Dale Turner)*, Francois Cluzet *(Francis Borier)*, Gabrielle Haker *(Berangere)*, Sandra Reaves-Phillips *(Buttercup)*, Lonette McKee *(Darcey Leigh)*, Christine Pascal *(Sylvie)*, Herbie Hancock *(Eddie Wayne)*, Bobby Hutcherson *(Ace)*, Pierre Trabaud *(Francis's Father)*, Frederique Meininger *(Francis's Mother)*

p, Irwin Winkler; d, Bertrand Tavernier; w, Bertrand Tavernier, David Rayfiel (based on incidents in the lives of Francis Paudras and Bud Powell); ph, Bruno de Keyzer (Panavision, Eastmancolor); ed, Armand Psenny; m, Herbie Hancock; prod d, Alexander Trauner; art d, Pierre Duquesne; cos, Jacqueline Moreau

ROUND MIDNIGHT might easily be called the best jazz film ever made, and not only because, aside from 1988's BIRD, the competition is so weak. The film's greatness lies not just in its vivid portrayal of the bebop milieu, but also in its sensitive examination of the turbulent forces within an artist compelled to create on a nightly basis, despite personal consequences. Dedicated to jazz greats Lester Young and Bud Powell, the film begins in 1959 as black bebop jazzman Dale Turner (Dexter Gordon), "the greatest tenor saxophone player in the world," leaves New York City for Paris. Alcoholic, ill, and apparently a former heroin addict, Turner plays nightly at Paris' famous Blue Note club to adoring fans, who appreciate his and his fellow expatriates' music. One of his most fervent admirers, Francis (Francois Cluzet), forms a close friendship with Turner, who moves in with him. Together the two try to bring Turner's self-destructive impulses under control, until Turner decides to risk a return to the US. The irony of ROUND MIDNIGHT—a sadly familiar one recognized in the plot—is that it took a Frenchman, director-cowriter and jazz lover Betrand Tavernier, to make this most accurate and intelligent film about the distinctly American art of jazz. Casting musicians (including Wayne Shorter, Tony Williams, Ron Carter, and Herbie Hancock, who did the Oscar-winning score) as his actors and insisting that the music be recorded live on the set with cameras rolling, Tavernier captures the complex relations among the players at work; the process has never been shown so well in a narrative film. Turner (an amalgam of various figures, including Young, Powell, and Gordon himself) is brilliantly played by the great Gordon, who contributed much of the dialogue, suggested changes in the script, and eventually received a Best Actor Oscar nomination. With Gordon's performance and the wonderful musical numbers to provide the heart of his film, Tavernier captures not only jazz, but passion—for music, for art, for life itself.

ROXANNE

1987   107m   c   ★★★½
Comedy/Romance   PG
Columbia

Steve Martin *(Charlie "C.D." Bales)*, Daryl Hannah *(Roxanne Kowalski)*, Rick Rossovich *(Chris McDonell)*, Shelley Duvall *(Dixie)*, John Kapelos *(Chuck)*, Fred Willard *(Mayor Deebs)*, Max Alexander *(Dean)*, Michael J. Pollard *(Andy)*, Shandra Beri *(Sandy)*, Brian George *(Dr. David Schepisi)*

p, Michael Rachmil, Daniel Melnick; d, Fred Schepisi; w, Steve Martin (based on the play "Cyrano de Bergerac" by Edmond Rostand); ph, Ian Baker (Deluxe Color); ed, John Scott; m, Bruce Smeaton; prod d, Jackson DeGovia; art d, David Fischer; fx, Bill Orr; cos, Richard Bruno, Tish Monaghan

Unlike many of his comedic contemporaries, Steve Martin likes to take risks. Martin served as executive producer and wrote the screenplay for this modernization of Edmond Rostand's "Cyrano de Bergerac," which stars Martin as C.D. Bales, the fire chief in a small northwestern town, a much beloved and witty man who happens to have a huge nose. C.D. has hired Chris McDonell (Rick Rossovich), a handsome dimwit who knows his way around hoses but not around women. Roxanne Kowalski (Daryl Hannah) is an astronomer who has rented a local house for the summer, and in scant moments we see that C.D. is mad about Roxanne. But Roxanne gets a look at Chris and falls for him, whereupon Chris asks C.D. for help in wooing her. C.D. agrees, albeit reluctantly. Many wonderful jokes dot the picture, but it is, in essence, a love story and most satisfying in that respect. The bright, literate screenplay sometimes descends into slapstick but stays close enough to its source that it pays homage without sacrificing originality. Martin makes his character amiable and downright lovable; Hannah shows a fire she hadn't demonstrated in previous efforts. In an era when romance seems to have taken second place to sex, it's heartwarming to see a film like ROXANNE bring back the loveliness of love.

ROYAL FAMILY OF BROADWAY, THE

1930   68m   bw   ★★★★
Drama/Comedy   /U
Paramount

Ina Claire *(Julia Cavendish)*, Fredric March *(Tony Cavendish)*, Mary Brian *(Gwen Cavendish)*, Henrietta Crosman *(Fanny Cavendish)*, Charles Starrett *(Perry Stewart)*, Arnold Korff *(Oscar Wolff)*, Frank Conroy *(Gilbert Marshall)*, Royal C. Stout *(Joe)*, Elsie Edmond *(Della)*, Murray Alper *(McDermott)*

d, George Cukor, Cyril Gardner; w, Herman J. Mankiewicz, Gertrude Purcell (based on the play *The Royal Family* by George S. Kaufman and Edna Ferber); ph, George Folsey; ed, Edward Dmytryk

When George S. Kaufman and Edna Ferber's thinly veiled parody of the acting Barrymores, "The Royal Family," opened in Los Angeles, Fredric March took on the role Otto Kruger had played on Broadway. Paramount studio bosses were so impressed by March's performance that they cast him in the lead in their film version of the play, THE ROYAL FAMILY OF BROADWAY (the name was changed to prevent confusion), and he responded by gaining an Oscar nomination and a huge following. Adapters Herman Mankiewicz and Gertrude Purcell wisely jettisoned some extraneous subplots and hammered out a tight script that George Cukor snappily directed, with assistance from Cyril Gardner.

Henrietta Crosman, matriarch of the famous acting Cavendishes, lives in a fabulous apartment and talks of her ancient theatrical triumphs. When son March arrives, with the press and various process servers in hot pursuit, he is not welcomed. By leaving the stage and going to California to become a movie matinee idol, he has incurred the wrath of the purists in the family. Meanwhile, a Polish actress is trying to get a couple of hundred thousand out of March, claiming he's reneged on his promise of marriage. March is also being sought by a film director he decked in a fit of pique. What's more, as the biggest star in pictures, he is the target of many eager young women who would gladly become his wife. As a result, the family apartment is the only place March can find any rest, and he has stopped there for a brief visit before continuing on to the Continent. His sister, Ina Claire (in a role that enraged Ethel Barrymore), has been dating wealthy Frank Conroy, but prefers to keep their relationship platonic, and

Conroy is willing to bide his time. Claire's daughter by a previous marriage, Mary Brian, is an immensely gifted actress, and, of course, the family expect her to follow in their footsteps; however, she is totally against it, hates the idea of the theater, and intends to marry Charles Starrett, a vapid society type.

With March in the movies, Claire semi-retired, and Brian unwilling to carry on the family tradition, Crosman decides to carry the torch herself and accepts an offer to go on tour with a repertory company, despite the fact that she is old and not feeling well. The tour proves too much for her and she suffers a heart attack while performing, dying later with her family gathered around her. Substituting for her mother on the tour, Claire finally decides to choose the family acting tradition over marriage, as does Brian.

Even though March is on screen less than the other leads, his presence is extraordinarily powerful in the film's flashiest role. His impression of John Barrymore is nearly flawless, capturing every gesture, every raised eyebrow, every sneer perfectly. Although the film's humor is tempered by the drama of Crosman's demise, the screenwriters crafted her death so skillfully that even this heart-tugging scene has funny moments. A must-see for anyone who loves the theater, THE ROYAL FAMILY OF BROADWAY was edited by Edward Dmytryk, later the director of such films as THE JUGGLER, RAINTREE COUNTY, and WALK ON THE WILD SIDE.

ROYAL FLASH
1975 98m c   ★★★
Historical/Comedy/Adventure   PG/15
FOX   (U.K.)

Malcolm McDowell *(Harry Flashman)*, Alan Bates *(Rudi von Sternberg)*, Florinda Bolkan *(Lola Montez)*, Oliver Reed *(Otto von Bismarck)*, Britt Ekland *(Duchess Irma)*, Lionel Jeffries *(Kraftstein)*, Tom Bell *(de Gautet)*, Joss Ackland *(Sapten)*, Christopher Cazenove *(Hansen)*, Roy Kinnear *(Old Roue)*

p, David V. Picker, Denis O'Dell; d, Richard Lester; w, George MacDonald Fraser (based on the novel by Fraser); ph, Geoffrey Unsworth (Technicolor); ed, John Victor Smith; m, Ken Thorne; prod d, Terence Marsh; art d, Alan Tomkins

Richard Lester's patented brand of comedy is again put to good use in this satirical adventure picture. McDowell is a cowardly swashbuckler who worms his way into European high society, where he meets Reed and Bates. They use McDowell for a plan to advance their political cause, by which he must pose as a Prussian nobleman and wed a duchess, Ekland. Lester's energetic direction pushes along the film's twisting plot. One of the best of author Fraser's series of novels featuring the grown-up braggart-bully of Thomas Hughes's novel *Tom Brown's School Days*, with smatterings of history and real period characters such as Bismarck and Lola Montez, ROYAL FLASH is loosely based on Anthony Hope Hawkins's novel *The Prisoner of Zenda*. The latter was made into one of the all-time great action films THE PRISONER OF ZENDA, starring Ronald Colman, with Douglas Fairbanks, Jr., in a terrific performance as Rudi.

ROYAL WEDDING
1951 93m c   ★★★★
Musical/Comedy   /U
MGM

Fred Astaire *(Tom Bowen)*, Jane Powell *(Ellen Bowen)*, Peter Lawford *(Lord John Brindale)*, Sarah Churchill *(Anne Ashmond)*, Keenan Wynn *(Irving Klinger/Edgar Klinger)*, Albert Sharpe *(James Ashmond)*, Viola Roache *(Sarah Ashmond)*, Henri Letondal *(Purser)*, James Finlayson *(Cabby)*, Alex Frazer *(Chester)*

p, Arthur Freed; d, Stanley Donen; w, Alan Jay Lerner; ph, Robert Planck (Technicolor); ed, Albert Akst; art d, Cedric Gibbons, Jack Martin Smith; fx, Warren Newcombe; chor, Nick Castle

On the eve of the royal wedding of then-Princess Elizabeth and Philip Mountbatten, an American brother and sister vaudeville act, Ellen (Jane Powell) and Tom Bowen (Fred Astaire), ventures to London to perform. There Tom falls in love with Anne Ashmond (Sarah Churchill, daughter of Sir Winston Churchill, making her only US film appearance) a music hall dancer, while Ellen becomes involved with an English lord (Peter Lawford). The picture ends with couples married, after the usual misunderstandings and rocky romantic plot twists. That's about it for the story, but what shines here are the great songs by Alan Jay Lerner and Burton Lane (among them the Oscar-nominated "Too Late Now"), the singing, and the dancing, including two of the most spectacular Astaire routines ever devised. In the first, he dances with a hat rack that nearly comes alive as his partner; in the second and most celebrated, the legendary hoofer seems to be dancing on the walls and ceiling of a room—accomplished by building the room so it could be rotated at the same speed as the camera, with the camera operator strapped in and shooting upside down. Although Nick Castle is listed as choreographer, it seems likely that it was Astaire's genius that inspired these dazzling routines. When all is said and done, Stanley Donen's first solo directorial assignment, after his work with Gene Kelly, is a lovely bit of frou-frou.

RUGGLES OF RED GAP
1935 76m bw   ★★★★
Comedy   /U
Paramount

Charles Laughton *(Marmaduke Ruggles)*, Mary Boland *(Effie Floud)*, Charlie Ruggles *(Egbert Floud)*, ZaSu Pitts *(Mrs. Judson)*, Roland Young *(George Van Bassingwell)*, Leila Hyams *(Nell Kenner)*, Maude Eburne *(Ma Pettingill)*, Lucien Littlefield *(Charles Belknap-Jackson)*, Leota Lorraine *(Mrs. Belknap-Jackson)*, James Burke *(Jeff Tuttle)*

p, Arthur Hornblow, Jr.; d, Leo McCarey; w, Walter DeLeon, Harlan Thompson, Humphrey Pearson (based on the play and novel by Harry Leon Wilson); ph, Alfred Gilks; ed, Edward Dmytryk; m, Ralph Rainger, Sam Coslow; art d, Hans Dreier, Robert Odell; cos, Travis Banton

RUGGLES OF RED GAP is one of the great comedies of all time, a wonderful source of pleasure. Charles Laughton is brilliantly cast as Marmaduke Ruggles, the ultimate valet. His aristocratic, impoverished English master (Roland Young) loses him in a poker game in Paris to a rough-and-ready visiting American rancher, played by actor Charlie Ruggles. Laughton, Ruggles, and one of Ruggles's buddies have a hysterically funny night on the town before Laughton packs up everything and goes to Red Gap, a brawling frontier town in the West. The locals there take Laughton for a British aristocrat, and he decides that since he is here in the land of the free, he no longer has to be an indentured servant. He falls for and marries ZaSu Pitts, and leaves Ruggles and his wife (Mary Boland) to open a restaurant with Pitts. Eventually, Young comes to visit the small town, meets Maude Eburne, falls in love with her, and decides to stay in Red Gap. Seventy-six fast-moving minutes directed with an eye toward huge laughs, RUGGLES OF RED GAP ends with a startling scene where the slightly tipsy Laughton recites

Lincoln's "Gettysburg Address," his masterful reading and palpable sincerity overcoming the incongruity of the scene to win over on-screen listeners and generations of audiences.

Laughton had already shown himself to be a superb dramatic actor in MUTINY ON THE BOUNTY and HENRY VIII, but few knew that he could be funny as well as pompous, underplay as well as emote, and show a subtle comedic side, which he did masterfully in this film. The versatile Leo McCarey deftly directs the picture, making it one his best films. Harry Leon Wilson's 1915 novel was first done by Essanay as a silent starring Taylor Holmes in 1918, and again by Paramount in 1923, with a youthful Edward Everett Horton in the lead. The picture was remade as FANCY PANTS, starring Bob Hope, but the remake was a tepid imitation of McCarey's hilarious version.

RULES OF THE GAME
(LA REGLE DU JEU)
1939   110m   bw   ★★★★★
Drama
N.E.F.   (France)

Marcel Dalio *(Robert de la Chesnaye)*, Nora Gregor *(Christine de la Chesnaye)*, Roland Toutain *(Andre Jurieu)*, Jean Renoir *(Octave)*, Mila Parely *(Genevieve de Marrast)*, Paulette Dubost *(Lisette)*, Gaston Modot *(Schumacher)*, Julien Carette *(Marceau)*, Odette Talazac *(Charlotte de la Plante)*, Pierre Magnier *(The General)*

d, Jean Renoir; w, Jean Renoir (in collaboration with Carl Koch, Camille Francois, and the cast); ph, Jean Bachelet; ed, Marguerite Renoir; m, Camille Saint-Saens, Salabert, E. Rose, Vincent Scotto, Wolfgang Amadeus Mozart, Johann Strauss, Frederic Chopin, Monsigny, G. Claret, Camille Francois, Delonnel Garnier; cos, Chanel

One of cinema's most monumental achievements, Renoir's RULES OF THE GAME passionately tackles the pre-WWII French class system, and succeeds in bringing forth the complexities and frailties underlying bourgeois civility. When aviator Andre Jurieu (Toutain) is met by his friend Octave (director Renoir) and ecstatic reporters after a record-setting flight, he tells the radio audience that he undertook the adventure for the love of a woman—who failed to greet him at the airport. This woman, Christine (Gregor), is in the meantime preparing for an evening out with her husband, Robert de la Chesnaye (Dalio), who knows of his wife's affair and doesn't want to lose her. Toward this end, he tries to end his relationship with his adoring mistress (Parely). Octave, the character with the clearest understanding of his environment, admits to Andre that he too cares for Christine (although, like the others, he has difficulty distinguishing love from "friendship"), and maintains that Andre will never win her because he doesn't heed "the rules" of society. Later the two are among the guests at a weekend shooting party at de la Chesnaye's country estate (a remarkably beautiful location evoking the works of the director's father, Auguste Renoir, and that is greatly enhanced by the gorgeous deep-focus photography). Everyone, servants included, brings along their own little drama, to be played out during and after the hunt—a brutal game complete with its own rigid rules threatening to spill over into the domestic, "civilized" sphere.

RULES OF THE GAME has a flavor like no other film, its tone covering farce, satire, and tragedy alike. Renoir extracts great power from sequences such as the slaughter of the rabbits, an act done with the utmost cool by the aristocrats partying in the country. Later Robert displays his latest mechanical toy for his guests, and a stunning dolly shot carries us into several planes of action, as seductions and murderous chases occur among both servants and masters. So many things here unfold with the beauty of inevitability (e.g. what Christine sees through a set of binoculars during the hunt) and yet the film breathes surprise, improvisation, reversal. No stone is left unturned as Renoir explores the follies of love, the contradictory class relations and the casual anti-Semitism inhabiting these barren people.

The acting is great, with Dalio and Carette giving perhaps the performances of their careers as the self-indulgent host and the hilarious and sneaky poacher of rabbits and wives alike. Toutain, Parely, and Modot, meanwhile, as would-be lover, mistress, and cuckold respectively, superbly cover a range of types frustrated by love. Dubost manages to be both very appealing and appropriately vague as the blithe and careless maid, and the actors embodying the guests and servants are perfectly cast. (Could Magnier's marvelously fading military man have inspired, if only by osmosis, Richard Bennett's character in THE MAGNIFICENT AMBERSONS?) Renoir, as the hapless, compassionate yet insightful friend to all, proves himself a terrific actor, leaving one to regret that he didn't act more often. His Octave, the most likable character in the film, is appropriately its emotional center. And finally Gregor (a real-life aristocrat and sometime actress who would commit suicide in the late 1940s), carefully coached by Renoir, gives perhaps her most impressive performance. Interested in her at the time, Renoir realizes her limitations and turns them into strengths. The Austrian actress's flawed French and slightly remote quality are well-nigh perfect for the role of an outsider tossed amidst a rampaging sea of desire.

The ending is one of incredible poignancy, and if anything brilliantly highlights the film's already intense reflexivity. A labor of love and passion, RULES OF THE GAME was borne of Renoir's discontent with the complacency of his French contemporaries as the country faced occupation. Relentlessly booed at its 1939 Paris premiere and banned by both the French and Vichy governments, the film is a classic example of audience revulsion to a perceptive critique of their world. Renoir aimed to create "an exact description of the bourgeoisie of our time" and he evidently struck a very raw nerve. It wasn't until 1959 that the film was restored to its nearly original form at 110 minutes. The Venice Film Festival premiere of the restored version quickly put the film onto nearly every list of greatest films ever made, a position it has justly retained. Alain Resnais considered this film the most overwhelming experience he had ever had at the cinema, and while those knowledgeable in French history may pick up on more, several dozen viewings of this unique film (what it takes) will get you hooked too.

RULING CLASS, THE
1972   148m   c   ★★★½
Comedy   R/X
Keep   (U.K.)

Peter O'Toole *(Jack, 14th Earl of Gurney)*, Alastair Sim *(Bishop Lampton)*, Arthur Lowe *(Tucker)*, Harry Andrews *(13th Earl of Gurney)*, Coral Browne *(Lady Claire Gurney)*, Michael Bryant *(Dr. Herder)*, Nigel Green *(McKyle)*, William Mervyn *(Sir Charles Gurney)*, Carolyn Seymour *(Grace Shelley)*, James Villiers *(Dinsdale Gurney)*

p, Jules Buck, Jack Hawkins; d, Peter Medak; w, Peter Barnes (based on the play by Barnes); ph, Ken Hodges (DeLuxe Color); ed, Ray Lovejoy; m, John Cameron; prod d, Peter Murton; fx, Roy Whybrow; chor, Eleanor Fazan; cos, Ruth Myers

Overly long, controversial comedy with plenty of tragedy mixed in, this was adapted by the playwright, Peter Barnes, for the screen and would have been better with a crueler set of fingers at the typewriter to remove some of the indulgences. Still, it has many wonderful moments and mixes satire with farce and pain to create a movie with many faults, though it remains memorable.

Andrews is a member of the House of Lords. He comes back to the family manse after having delivered a scathing speech to Parliament, and his alcoholic butler, Lowe, helps him prepare for what is apparently his nightly ritual. He dons long underwear, a tutu, and a Napoleonic hat; puts a silken noose around his neck; and will swing a few times before landing on the ladder top that gives him safety. This night he inadvertently kicks the ladder over and dies of strangulation, thus leaving his membership in the House of Lords and his estate to his insane son, O'Toole. The sum of 30,000 pounds has been bequeathed to Lowe, but the rest of the family, Mervyn (Andrews's brother), Browne (Mervyn's wife), and Villiers (their dotty son), are shocked upon hearing the will read by Sim, their local bishop. Lowe chooses to stay in the family's service, but now that he is rich, his attitude changes. He begins spouting communist slogans, drinking in public, and telling everyone in the family exactly what he thinks of them. O'Toole has been in a mental hospital for the last several years and returns dressed as Jesus, a role he insists he is playing for real. He admits that when he prays to God, he finds that he's talking to himself. O'Toole spends many of his hours on a huge cross in the living room and distributes the family's wealth to the meek and downtrodden, something that infuriates the others in the family. They decide they have only one means by which to rectify matters: have O'Toole sire a child, then toss him back into the looney bin so the family can assume control of the money by becoming the unborn child's guardians. Mervyn has been keeping a woman on the side, Seymour, and his plan is to get O'Toole and her wed as soon as possible. O'Toole, however, keeps telling everyone that he's already married to the Lady of the Camellias. Seymour arrives, dressed as Camille, sings a snatch from "La Traviata," and O'Toole is convinced that she is who she says she is. They get married, but Seymour falls in love with O'Toole and admits that this is all Mervyn's plan.

Hardly a segment of British society comes out of this film unscathed: the public school system, the Houses of Parliament, snobbism, religion, homosexuals, servants, the upper classes, and just about everything else that can be decried. It's caustic and funny, but often goes too far and stays too long in making its points. O'Toole was nominated for an Oscar as the mad earl and bites off Barnes's speeches with Shavian diction. Lowe, playing an irascible butler much like the one in TV's "Benson," steals every scene he is in. Sim's role as the aged bishop is one of his best in a long career. A lot of money was spent on this movie, making it one of the best-produced British films of the year. Interiors were done at Twickenham with locations shot in Buckinghamshire, Lincolnshire, Surrey, Hampshire, and London.

RUMBLE FISH

1983   105m   c   ★★★★½
Drama   R/18
Zoetrope

Matt Dillon (Rusty James), Mickey Rourke (Motorcycle Boy), Diane Lane (Patty), Dennis Hopper (Father), Diana Scarwid (Cassandra), Vincent Spano (Steve), Nicolas Cage (Smokey), Christopher Penn (B.J.), Larry Fishburne (Midget), William Smith (Patterson)

p, Fred Roos, Doug Claybourne; d, Francis Ford Coppola; w, S.E. Hinton, Francis Ford Coppola (based on a novel by S.E. Hinton); ph, Stephen H. Burum (Technicolor); ed, Barry Malkin; m, Stewart Copeland; prod d, Dean Tavoularis; chor, Michael Smuin; cos, Marge Bowers

Here's an instance of a quirky career move. After gaining notoriety as a director of genre blockbusters (THE GODFATHER films, APOCALYPSE NOW), small "serious" films (THE CONVERSATION, THE RAIN PEOPLE), and the ocassional controversial grand folly (ONE FROM THE HEART), Coppola decided to turn to what initially seemed like a most unlikely sub-genre for an artist of his stature—the teenpic. The GODFATHER grosses helped finance Coppola's studio, American (later Omni) Zoetrope. However the chaotic and costly (though ultimately profitable) APOCALYPSE NOW put the studio on shaky financial footing and ONE FROM THE HEART finally sank it. He next decided to make two modestly budgeted teen-oriented movies filmed back-to-back. Both were based on S.E. Hinton novels for young adults and starred Matt Dillon. The two films were THE OUTSIDERS and RUMBLE FISH. THE OUTSIDERS was the crowdpleaser of the two, filmed in gloriously old-fashioned color and starring a wide assortment of future young stars (Dillon, C. Thomas Howell, Ralph Macchio, Emilio Estevez, Patrick Swayze, Tom Cruise, Rob Lowe, and Diane Lane). The film simultaneously (and fitfully) worked as a tribute to GONE WITH THE WIND and REBEL WITHOUT A CAUSE. Not surprisingly it was a minor hit. Coppola likened THE OUTSIDERS to his biggest success, THE GODFATHER. If that film was like a GODFATHER for teens, he reasoned, then RUMBLE FISH was APOCALYPSE NOW.

Filmed in dreamy black-and-white with an ocassional dab of color, RUMBLE FISH is an unabashed art film. Deliriously expressionistic visually and aurally, it owes at least as much to the work of Jean Cocteau, Kenneth Anger, and F.W. Murnau as to the juvenile delinquent sagas of the 1950s. Set in Tulsa, Oklahoma, RUMBLE FISH is the story of a somewhat slow-witted but charismatic teenager, Rusty James (Matt Dillon), who idolizes his elder brother, the Motorcycle Boy (Mickey Rourke), a former gang leader. He is entranced by the spurious gang mystique and fancies himself a tough guy to be reckoned with. The Motorcycle Boy has repudiated his own gang past and disapproves of Rusty James's fighting but he really has no practical advice to offer his younger sibling. He's intelligent enough to know that he has done nothing admirable to earn his local notoriety. He's just a very cool dude ("He's like royalty in exile," observes an admiring Black pool player) in a way that his hot-headed and increasingly dopey younger brother can never hope to match. This is readily apparent to everyone but Rusty James himself. He's too blinded by hero-worship and addled by injury-induced deliriums and booze to see things clearly. The advertising line for the film offers an apt summary for their situation: "Rusty James can't live up to his brother's reputation. His brother can't live it down." The person most annoyed by the former gang leader's lofty reputation is Officer Patterson (William Smith) who ominously watches the Motorcycle Boy from behind his jet black shades.

Many of the characters in RUMBLE FISH seem trapped in some way either through circumstance or enigmatic quirks of character and dissatisfied with their dreary lives. They turn to various avenues of escape—alcohol, heroin, sex, and artistic expression—with various degrees of success. The boys' father (Dennis Hopper) was once a successful lawyer but now lives on welfare as a hardcore drunk. Like the Motorcycle Boy (with whom he always seems to be sharing a private joke), he is prone to making classical allusions that mystify Rusty James.

Coppola has never made a more beautiful film. The rumble sequence alone is a rousingly choreographed frenzy that deserves to be studied by generations of film students. Hinton collaborated with the director in adapting her eccentric but profoundly moving novel for the screen. The resulting film is an amazingly sensitive recreation of the sensibility of the literary work. Stephen Burum's black-and-white cinematography is exquisite particularly when he utilizes deep focus and time-lapse photography to create expressionistic effects that reflect the peculiar point-of-view of the protagonists. The fighting fish to which the title refers are in color though they float in a black-and-white pet shop window. The innovative impressionistic score from Stewart Copeland (drummer for the Police) plays a major part in creating the unique mood of the film. The percussive music blends perfectly with Coppola's striking images. Often it sounds like ticking clocks thereby heightening the sense that time is running out for these characters. Clocks are also a recurring visual motif.

RUMBLE FISH is much more than beautiful sounds and pictures; the film contains some truly outstanding performances. Rourke gives what may be his most satisfying performance as the impossibly cool Motorcycle Boy. One never knows whether he is truly insane, as several characters assert, or just suffers from what his father calls "acuteness of the senses." Dillon shines through with a heartbreaking portrayal of a vulnerable and confused teen who gets increasingly lost in a mental fog. Dillon may be a pretty boy star but he is also a fine and serious actor. Diane Lane is quite touching and believable as Patty, Rusty James' long-suffering girlfriend. Vincent Spano, who plays Rusty's somewhat nerdy friend, Steve, shows great range in a character totally unlike those for which he is best known (e.g. OVER THE EDGE, BABY, IT'S YOU, ALPHABET CITY). Dennis Hopper is superb in one of his series of performances on the "comeback trail". Here he has the ravaged but still beautiful facial features of a fallen angel. Diana Scarwid is memorable as Cassandra, a substitute teacher who used to date the Motorcycle Boy and has become a junkie by the time of this story. Intriguingly she seems to be one of the few people who understands the local hero's odd world view. Nicholas Cage is less irritating than usual while Larry Fishburne and singer/songwriter Tom Waits excell in small but indelible roles. S.E. Hinton herself turns up in a cameo as a streetwalker.

While THE OUTSIDERS made a hefty profit and spawned a short-lived FOX television series, RUMBLE FISH died at the box office. Clearly this is not a film for all audiences, indeed it is difficult to imagine to what audience it is targeted. Some wags even had the temerity to christen this film as "Mumble Fish." This may well be a minority opinion but to us, it's some kind of masterpiece. Give it a try. It might change your life.

RUN SILENT, RUN DEEP

1958 93m bw	★★★
War	/U
Hecht/Hill/Lancaster	

Clark Gable (Cmdr. Richardson), Burt Lancaster (Lt. Jim Bledsoe), Jack Warden (Mueller), Brad Dexter (Cartwright), Don Rickles (Ruby), Nick Cravat (Russo), Joe Maross (Kohler), Mary LaRoche (Laura), Eddie Foy, III (Larto), Rudy Bond (Cullen)

p, Harold Hecht; d, Robert Wise; w, John Gay (based on a novel by Cmdr. Edward L. Beach); ed, George Boemler; m, Franz Waxman; art d, Edward Carrere; fx, A. Arnold Gillespie

After his lucrative teaming with Gary Cooper in VERA CRUZ, Burt Lancaster and his partners, Harold Hecht and James Hill, decided to pair Lancaster with the fading but still popular Clark Gable. Gable plays Commander Richardson, the only survivor when the submarine he commands is sunk by a Japanese destroyer dubbed "Bongo Pete." Back at Pearl Harbor, he is given command of another submarine, the Nerka, but on it he encounters much dissension. Lt. Bledsoe (Lancaster), the sub's executive officer, is upset because he expected to get the command, and the crew refuses to trust a commander who is the sole survivor of a sunken vessel. Richardson battles frequently with Bledsoe, who is just short of mutinous, and drills the crew repeatedly in a tricky maneuver designed to torpedo "Bongo Pete" head on, an operation he calls the "down the throat shot." Ordered to stay well clear of Japan's dangerous Bongo Straits, the obsessed commander disobeys and pursues the destroyer. Gable, two years and three films away from death, is plainly too old for his role, but he makes the most of it with a very good performance. The entire film, in fact, is one of the better submarine dramas ever made, tense and claustrophobic, with a minimum of dalliances back at the base (in defiance of the Hollywood dictum that no movie without a love interest can succeed). On the set, things were rather tense, with Lancaster and his two partners arguing over the script, while Gable worried about what was going to happen to his character when the dust settled. Although reasonably successful at the box office, RUN SILENT, RUN DEEP was ultimately overshadowed by another film that put an old star and a new star in a submarine, OPERATION PETTICOAT, with Cary Grant and Tony Curtis.

RUNAWAY TRAIN

1985 111m c	★★★½
Prison/Thriller	R/18
Northbrook	

Jon Voight (Manny), Eric Roberts (Buck), Rebecca De Mornay (Sara), Kyle T. Heffner (Frank Barstow), John P. Ryan (Ranken), T.K. Carter (Dave Prince), Kenneth McMillan (Eddie MacDonald), Stacey Pickren (Ruby), Walter Wyatt (Conlan), Edward Bunker (Jonah)

p, Menahem Golan, Yoram Globus; d, Andrei Konchalovsky; w, Djordje Milicevic, Paul Zindel, Edward Bunker (based on the screenplay by Akira Kurosawa, Ryuzo Kikushima, Hideo Oguni); ph, Alan Hume (Rank Color); ed, Henry Richardson; m, Trevor Jones; prod d, Stephen Marsh; art d, Joseph T. Garrity; fx, Keith Richins, Rick H. Josephsen, Bob Riggs, Tassilo Baur, Ray Brown; cos, Katherine Dover

The action in this superlative film is relentless and gripping from beginning to end. Manny (Jon Voight) is a hard-as-nails prison inmate who, with vicious punk Buck (Eric Roberts), escapes from a brutal Alaskan prison. They emerge into a blizzard and grope their way toward the train tracks, clambering aboard a passing train. They are unaware that the engineer has just suffered a fatal heart attack. Frantic passenger Sara (Rebecca De Mornay), a railroad employee, encounters the hiding convicts and begs them to save the train and her. The tough cons make it to the engineer's cab, and then their brutal ordeal to stop this train begins—an exercise in raw courage and chilling perils that drives both convicts to the brink of madness. What's more, Ranken (John P. Ryan), the prison warden who has a long-standing vendetta with Manny, is after the train as well. Voight is powerful and absorbing, and Roberts gives a fascinating performance as his cretinous sidekick. This is the second American-made film by Russian director Andrei Konchalovsky, and he does an outstanding job with his material and actors.

RUNNING ON EMPTY

1988 116m c   ★★★
Drama   PG-13/15
Lorimar/Double Play

Christine Lahti *(Annie Pope)*, River Phoenix *(Danny Pope)*, Judd Hirsch *(Arthur Pope)*, Martha Plimpton *(Lorna Phillips)*, Ed Crowley *(Mr. Phillips)*, L.M. Kit Carson *(Gus Winant)*, Steven Hill *(Mr. Patterson)*, Augusta Dabney *(Mrs. Patterson)*, David Margulies *(Dr. Jonah Reiff)*, Lynne Thigpen *(Contact at Eldridge St.)*

p, Amy Robinson, Griffin Dunne; d, Sidney Lumet; w, Naomi Foner; ph, Gerry Fisher (Technicolor); ed, Andrew Mondshein; m, Tony Mottola; prod d, Philip Rosenberg; cos, Anna Hill Johnstone

Sidney Lumet fuses the personal with the political in RUNNING ON EMPTY, dramatizing the conflicts in a family on the run from the FBI. Arthur and Annie Pope (Judd Hirsch and Christine Lahti) are former student radicals who have been underground for 15 years, moving from town to town with their two children and changing identities whenever the law begins to catch up. Their son, Danny (River Phoenix), a gifted musician, is ready to graduate from high school and is being encouraged by his music teacher (Ed Crowley) to apply to Julliard. To do so, however, Danny would have to produce a transcript, which would mean leaving the underground and separating permanently from his family. At the same time, the boy falls in love with the music teacher's daughter, Lorna (Martha Plimpton), further straining familial bonds. RUNNING ON EMPTY is about an age-old dilemma: the difficulties that arise when the time comes for children to leave the nest. Lumet develops his story at a leisurely but effective pace, allowing the dynamics of a family in transition—not the sudden appearance of the FBI or an action-paced chase—to give the film its tension. Though Arthur and Annie are center stage very nearly as much as Danny, RUNNING ON EMPTY is Danny's story, seen from his perspective. Phoenix delivers a convincing, serious performance, and the rest of the cast, save for the miscast Hirsch, is also strong. Phoenix was Oscar-nominated for his supporting role, as was the film's original screenplay.

RUSH

1991 120m c   ★★★
Crime/Drama   R/18
The Zanuck Company/MGM-Pathe

Jason Patric *(Jim Raynor)*, Jennifer Jason Leigh *(Kristen Cates)*, Sam Elliott *(Larry Dodd)*, Max Perlich *(Walker)*, Gregg Allman *(Will Gaines)*, Tony Frank *(Chief Donald Nettle)*, William Sadler *(Monroe)*, Special K. McCray *(Willie Red)*, Dennis Letts *(Senior District Attorney)*, Dennis Burkley *(Motorcycle Guy)*

p, Richard D. Zanuck; d, Lili Fini Zanuck; w, Pete Dexter (from the novel by Kim Wozencraft); ph, Kenneth MacMillan; ed, Mark Warner; m, Eric Clapton; prod d, Paul Sylbert; cos, Colleen Atwood

Producer-turned-director Lili Fini Zanuck and novelist-screenwriter Pete Dexter have largely de-fanged ex-narcotics cop Kim Wozencraft's semi-autobiographical thriller, turning RUSH into a melodramatic, if gritty, Hollywood muddle.

Jim Raynor (Jason Patric) is an undercover Texas cop ordered to "sacrifice a virgin" by his supervisor, Larry Dodd (Sam Elliott), as part of establishing a cover to bring down suspected big-time drug dealer Will Gaines (Gregg Allmann). Over Dodd's objections, Raynor chooses fresh-scrubbed police recruit Kristen

Cates (Jennifer Jason Leigh). Unbeknownst to Kristen, Raynor has already succumbed to substance abuse and part of her own cover will include snorting, smoking or shooting up *anything* that is put in front of her to establish her credibility on the street. But, fueled by idealism and Raynor's false promises to keep her from any real danger, she accepts the assignment.

In the small town lorded over by Gaines, Raynor and Cates set themselves up as a couple in the market for any and all kinds of drugs. They also become lovers and move in together, to the chagrin of Dodd and puritanical police chief Donald Nettle (Tony Frank), who is obsessed with bringing down Gaines to further his career. Raynor and Cates make their initial buys from Walker (Max Perlich), an aimless, likeable car thief who puts them in touch with low-level drug dealers and manufacturers. But they remain unable to pin anything on Gaines, while becoming broken-down addicts as a result of their undercover activity.

After hitting bottom, they clean themselves up, coercing Walker into working with them in exchange for immunity from prosecution. They themselves are then coerced by Nettle into falsifying a case against Gaines, who is one of those taken into custody during a mass arrest. Walker, unable to come to terms with having betrayed all his friends, hangs himself.

Shortly after Gaines is freed on bail, Raynor and Cates are attacked in the middle of the night by a shotgun-wielding invader, who kills Raynor. At Gaines's trial, Kristen confesses to falsifying the evidence against him, and he is freed. In the final scene, Gaines is killed in his car with a shotgun by an unseen assailant who may or not be Cates taking revenge for Gaynor's death.

RUSH is a prime example of Hollywood's tendency to buy up hot literary properties, only to sanitize them of whatever qualities made them hot in the first place. What made Wozencraft's novel more than a standard crime thriller was her inside perspective on abuses within the government's "war on drugs." In Wozencraft's bitterly ironic tale, Raynor and Cates risk life, limb and sanity, only to become pawns in a personal vendetta being waged by Nettle against Gaines for producing porn videos starring the daughter of a prominent town official. When they realize they have been duped, the pair turn state's evidence and wind up serving time for their efforts, after an extended period in hiding to protect them as much from Nettle's vengeance as from Gaines's.

Gutted of the novel's irony, the film becomes little more than an updated LOST WEEKEND before turning into a routine revenge melodrama in its final moments. Zanuck and Dexter employ an elliptical narrative style, stringing together vaguely connected scenes that nervously cut away before their full, depressing implications can sink in. The result is a lack of any meaningful character development or narrative drive.

Along the way, Patric and Leigh do highly compelling work, but the film's last-minute reversion into vigilante violence seems especially repellant, considering that Wozencraft triumphed over her own setbacks by putting violence aside. There's a kind of depressing commercial logic to resolving the plot with a loaded shotgun rather than by the inherently less cinematic process of going back to school and turning devastation into redemption.

RUSSIA HOUSE, THE

1990 123m c   ★★★★
Romance/Spy   R/18
Pathe

Sean Connery *(Barley Blair)*, Michelle Pfeiffer *(Katya)*, Roy Scheider *(Russell)*, James Fox *(Ned)*, John Mahoney *(Brady)*, Klaus Maria Brandauer *(Dante)*, Ken Russell *(Walter)*, J.T. Walsh *(Quinn)*, Michael Kitchen *(Clive)*, David Threlfall *(Wicklow)*

p, Fred Schepisi, Paul Maslansky; d, Fred Schepisi; w, Tom Stoppard (based on the novel by John le Carre); ph, Ian Baker; ed, Peter Honess; m, Jerry Goldsmith; prod d, Richard MacDonald; cos, Ruth Myers

The so-called a "adult audience" inexplicably stayed away from this finely crafted, thoroughly absorbing, and beautifully acted adaptation of John le Carre's glasnost-era espionage novel, making it an undeserving victim of the HOME ALONE juggernaut, as that film crushed all its competition in the latter part of 1990. A movie as good as this will certainly find new life on video and cable, but audiences will still be the losers. This is an epic of the heart that demands to be seen in a theater. Directing on an expansive, wide-screen canvas, Fred Schepisi (PLENTY, ROXANNE) and his regular cinematographer Ian Baker constantly startle and enrapture the eye, making expressive use of their settings in the first entirely US-produced film to be substantially filmed on location in the Soviet Union, primarily Moscow and Leningrad. Indeed, if THE RUSSIA HOUSE has a fault, it is that it needs to be seen twice, once to be overwhelmed by the scenery and once to appreciate the outstanding work of the cast and the rich intricacies of the plot, which Schepisi and screenwriter Tom Stoppard keep in constant motion through the two-hour plus running time.

The film opens at a Moscow audio-book fair where a furtive Russian woman, Katya (Michelle Pfeiffer), is seeking a British publisher named Barley Blair. Katya has an important manuscript she wishes to deliver to Blair, but he has elected not to attend the fair. Desperate, she enlists the aid of another exhibitor at the fair, Niki Landau (Nicholas Woodeson), imploring him to help her by smuggling the manuscript out of Moscow and giving it to Blair in London. Landau agrees to help, but when he arrives in London, he turns the manuscript over to British intelligence. A cover letter, though signed by Katya, was clearly written by an unidentified Soviet scientist who indicates he has met Blair and urges him to publish the manuscript, which contains a detailed analysis of Russian defense systems. Naturally, intelligence authorities want to know more about the entire matter, and they search for Blair (Sean Connery), finding him in his apartment in Lisbon, where he indulges in his favorite activities: drinking and playing the saxophone in seedy jazz clubs. Cynical and weary, Blair has little interest in being involved in espionage games, but he does reveal that he met the author, whom he knew only as "Dante" (Klaus Maria Brandauer) at a writers' retreat in the Soviet Union months earlier. British intelligence agents Ned (James Fox) and Walter (played with expected flamboyance by director Ken Russell) want Blair to become involved in a plan to establish the identity of the author and, thereby, the credibility of the manuscript, but Blair is unwilling to cooperate. That is, until he sees a photograph of Katya and is quickly smitten with her. Blair then agrees to become a pawn in the scheme, which grows more sticky when the British reveal the entire affair to the American intelligence community. Led by CIA agent Russell (Roy Scheider), the Americans run roughshod over Ned's delicate operation. While bickering among themselves, both the British and Americans wind up underestimating Blair, who turns out to have an agenda of his own that is entirely unrelated to the sordid matters of international politics.

With the onset of glasnost and the fall of the Berlin Wall, there was a great deal of doubt as to whether a spy film such as this would have any audience appeal at the time of its release. Yet what is remarkable is how perceptively and poetically Stoppard and Schepisi have honed in on some of the potential problems facing the West's reconciliation with the USSR. THE RUSSIA HOUSE is a profound study in miscommunication and misinterpretation, contrasting a jaded West, made complacent by its long history of freedom, and the East, passionate and sincere as it tests the bounds of that same freedom it is only beginning to taste. What sets the action in motion is Dante's initial mistake in accepting Barley's drunken ramblings at the writers' retreat as a genuine expression of his ideals and intentions to act. Katya inserts Dante's key phrases in the cover letter to Barley to remind him of Dante's identity, which is misconstrued by Ned as a straight love letter to Blair. Ned takes to and trusts Blair immediately, while being suspicious of Dante, when, as the plot revolves, it's apparent he should have done the opposite. Then, when the Americans jump into the fray, they suspect a homosexual affair between Blair and Dante. And so it goes throughout the film. All these plot turns and diversions are superbly handled by the excellent cast. Connery is in top form as the apparent cynic who at his heart is a true romantic, while Pfeiffer is thoroughly credible as the idealistic Katya. Brandauer makes good use of his limited screen time, Fox is excellent as the intelligence professional who is wise enough to recognize the foibles of the game, and Scheider convincing as the CIA man who is as much a politician as he is an expert on international intrigue.

A good thriller puts its characters in physical peril and has them use their intelligence and stealth to survive. A great thriller also puts its characters in spiritual peril, drawing its thrills from the makeup of the characters and the extent to which they act, or fail to act, on their ideals. On that criteria, THE RUSSIA HOUSE has to be judged as a great thriller and one of the year's best films.

RUTHLESS PEOPLE
1986 93m c   ★★★½
Comedy   R/18
Touchstone/Silver Screen Partners II

Danny DeVito *(Sam Stone)*, Bette Midler *(Barbara Stone)*, Judge Reinhold *(Ken Kessler)*, Helen Slater *(Sandy Kessler)*, Anita Morris *(Carol)*, Bill Pullman *(Earl)*, William Schilling *(Police Commissioner)*, Art Evans *(Lt. Bender)*, Clarence Felder *(Lt. Walters)*, J.E. Freeman *(Bedroom Killer)*

p, Michael Peyser; d, Jim Abrahams, David Zucker, Jerry Zucker; w, Dale Launer; ph, Jan De Bont (DeLuxe Color); ed, Arthur Schmidt; m, Michel Colombier; art d, Don Woodruff; cos, Rosanna Norton; anim, Sally Cruikshank

This is a wacky, tasteless, hilarious reworking of O. Henry's classic short story "The Ransom of Red Chief." The movie begins as millionaire garment manufacturer Sam Stone (Danny DeVito) is having dinner with Carol (Anita Morris), his sultry mistress. He is planning to murder Barbara (Bette Midler), his overweight and shrewish wife, unaware that Carol is cheating on him with her hunky, clunky beau, Earl (Bill Pullman). Before Sam can kill Barbara, however, she is kidnapped by a sweet young couple, Ken (Judge Reinhold) and Sandy (Helen Slater), who are seeking revenge against Sam for using an idea of Sandy's to make a fortune without paying her one cent in royalties. They tell Sam that Barbara will be tortured and killed if he breathes one word of the kidnapping to the police or the press. Naturally, Sam thinks his troubles are over, but he's wrong. Everyone in the movie seems to have a comic moment, because the laughs are piled on top of each other. Call it rude, crude, and lewd, but you also have to call it very funny.

RYAN'S DAUGHTER

1970 192m c ★★½
Romance/War R/15
Faraway (U.K.)

Robert Mitchum *(Charles Shaughnessy)*, Sarah Miles *(Rosy Ryan)*, Trevor Howard *(Father Collins)*, Christopher Jones *(Randolph Doryan)*, John Mills *(Michael)*, Leo McKern *(Tom Ryan)*, Barry Foster *(Tim O'Leary)*, Archie O'Sullivan *(McCardle)*, Marie Kean *(Mrs. McCardle)*, Evin Crowley *(Moureen)*

p, Anthony Havelock-Allan; d, David Lean; w, Robert Bolt; ph, Freddie Young (Super/Panavision, Metrocolor); ed, Norman Savage; m, Maurice Jarre; prod d, Stephen Grimes; art d, Roy Walker; fx, Robert MacDonald; cos, Jocelyn Rickards

The best thing about this much-vaunted, overlong Irish epic love triangle is its gorgeous photography by Young. The rest is an expensive potboiler (costing more than $12 million) in which Mitchum saunters through his role as a schoolteacher, cuckolded by trampy wife Miles. The marriage between Miles, the daughter of saloon-keeper McKern, and Mitchum is passionless, the result of Mitchum's lack of interest in sex. Troubled by this absence of lovemaking, Miles consults the parish priest, Howard, who tells her that she should be thankful she's married to such a saint of a man. Then shell-shocked British officer Jones arrives, assigned to suppress associations between the IRA and German spies (it's 1916 and WWI is raging). Miles and Jones are much taken with each other and make wild love in empty buildings and open meadows. Halfwit Mills finds a button ripped off Jones' uniform during one of the love scenes between Miles and Jones and parades around the village square with it, offering it up as evidence against the sinful Miles. Mitchum does not respond to the resulting gossip, preferring to let the romance dissipate. IRA leader Foster then arrives with a boatload of guns sent by the Germans, but, believing the British will make fierce reprisals against the town, Mitchum informs on the gun-runners and the British swoop in. Believing that it was Miles who told her British lover about the weapons, the townspeople swarm into Mitchum's house, strip Miles, and shave her head. Knowing now that he has lost Miles, Jones blows himself up with a hand grenade. Miles and Mitchum pack their things and head for a new life in Dublin.

Directed by fine craftsman Lean, RYAN'S DAUGHTER is self-indulgent and dull, a long-winded period piece that is so introspective that its love scenes, presented in a frenetic style, appear out of place. Miles is only vaguely interesting, Jones boring, and Mitchum so detached that he appears to be thinking about anything but this film. Only Mills, essaying the village idiot, provides a spark to an otherwise aimless and lifeless film. The whole thing is a great disappointment from a great director. Lean and Bolt—actress Miles' husband, and the director's frequent collaborator—spent five years making the picture, which was photographed on location on the Dingle Peninsula, Ireland's rainiest area. Cast and crew spent a full year there, once shooting only a minute of screen time in a 10-day period because of the awful weather. Mills received an Oscar as Best Supporting Actor for his work in the film, and cinematographer Young justly won an Oscar for his fine work. Miles was nominated, but lost to Glenda Jackson for WOMEN IN LOVE. The film was also nominated for Best Sound.

SABOTAGE

1936   76m   bw   ★★★½
Thriller/Spy   /PG
Gaumont   (U.K.)

Sylvia Sidney *(Sylvia Verloc)*, Oscar Homolka *(Karl Verloc)*, John
Loder *(Sgt. Ted Spencer)*, Desmond Tester *(Steve)*, Joyce Barbour
(Renee), Matthew Boulton *(Supt. Talbot)*, S.J. Warmington
(Hollingshead), William Dewhurst *(A.S. Chatman)*, Austin Trevor
(Vladimir), Torin Thatcher *(Yunct)*

p, Michael Balcon, Ivor Montagu; d, Alfred Hitchcock; w, Charles
Bennett, Ian Hay, Alma Reville, Helen Simpson, E.V.H. Emmett
(based on the novel *The Secret Agent* by Joseph Conrad); ph,
Bernard Knowles; ed, Charles Frend; m, Louis Levy

Terrorist Karl Verloc (Homolka) is engaged in a bombing spree
in London using a trusting young boy Stevie (Tester), the little
brother of his wife Sylvia (Sidney), as the one who delivers the
packages of destruction without knowing what they contain.
Meanwhile, neighborhood grocer Ted Spencer (Loder), actually
an undercover Scotland Yard detective, is investigating Verloc's
activities. A tense and chilling espionage picture which contains
one sequence which Hitchcock would never make the mistake
(as he views it) of repeating. The young Stevie, while delivering
a package, takes his time, stopping on occasion along the way
like any curious youngster would. While the later, more experienced, Hitchcock would have devised a way to save the boy, in
SABOTAGE he blows the child to smithereens. As a result, he
violated the trust an audience places in a director—a trust which
Hitchcock values perhaps above all else in his films. SABO-
TAGE was banned in several countries which viewed it as a
handbook to terrorism. Based on a Joseph Conrad novel entitled
The Secret Agent, the film's title was changed to SABOTAGE to
avoid confusion with Hitchcock's previous picture SECRET
AGENT. The confusion came later, however, in 1942, when
Hitchcock directed SABOTEUR. If you're not confused yet, the
US title of SABOTAGE is THE WOMAN ALONE.

SABOTEUR

1942   108m   bw   ★★★★
Spy/War   /A
Universal

Priscilla Lane *(Patricia Martin)*, Robert Cummings *(Barry Kane)*,
Otto Kruger *(Charles Tobin)*, Alan Baxter *(Freeman)*, Clem Bevans
(Neilson), Norman Lloyd *(Frank Fry)*, Alma Kruger *(Mrs. Henrietta
Sutton)*, Vaughan Glaser *(Phillip Martin)*, Dorothy Peterson *(Mrs.
Mason)*, Ian Wolfe *(Robert, the Butler)*

p, Frank Lloyd, Jack H. Skirball; d, Alfred Hitchcock; w, Peter
Viertel, Joan Harrison, Dorothy Parker (based on an original story
by Hitchcock); ph, Joseph Valentine; ed, Otto Ludwig; m, Charles
Previn, Frank Skinner; art d, Jack Otterson

This film, Hitchcock's first contribution to wartime American
propaganda, is as polished and suspenseful as any the great
director would make. A forerunner to NORTH BY NORTH-
WEST, SABOTEUR tells a similar story of an innocent man
accused of murder and chasing a bunch of insidious spies across
the country. Barry Kane (Robert Cummings) is a simple factory
worker in an airplane plant whose best friend is killed in a fire.
It turns out the extinguisher Kane handed him was filled with
gasoline, engulfing his friend in flames before burning the whole
factory. An investigation points to Kane as the saboteur, forcing
him to flee across the country to find the real fifth columnist.
Along the way he meets Pat Martin (Priscilla Lane), the only one
who believes his story. SABOTEUR is no doubt best remembered for its harrowing Statue of Liberty (actually a Universal
backlot) finale, in which Cummings chases his man to the Lady's
torch. Hitchcock had originally hoped to cast Gary Cooper and
Barbara Stanwyck in the leads, with Harry Carey, Sr., in the role
of master spy Charles Tobin.

SABRINA

1954   112m   bw   ★★★★
Romance/Comedy   /U
Paramount

Humphrey Bogart *(Linus Larrabee)*, Audrey Hepburn *(Sabrina
Fairchild)*, William Holden *(David Larrabee)*, Walter Hampden
(Oliver Larrabee), John Williams *(Thomas Fairchild)*, Martha Hyer
(Elizabeth Tyson), Joan Vohs *(Gretchen Van Horn)*, Marcel Dalio
(Baron), Marcel Hillaire *(The Professor)*, Nella Walker *(Maude
Larrabee)*

p, Billy Wilder; d, Billy Wilder; w, Billy Wilder, Samuel Taylor, Ernest
Lehman (based on the play "Sabrina Fair" by Taylor); ph, Charles
Lang; ed, Arthur Schmidt; m, Frederick Hollander; art d, Hal
Pereira, Walter Tyler; fx, John P. Fulton, Farciot Edouart; cos, Edith
Head

Three recent Oscar winners and the sure guidance of Wilder
helped make this familiar Cinderella story into something more
than it might have been under other auspices. Holden was 36 at
the time, a bit ancient to convince us he was a dissolute playboy.
Further, he was more than eclipsed by Bogart's performance as
his older brother, an unaccustomed comedy role that showed
Bogie could play for laughs as well as sneers. Wilder had already
won an Oscar, and co-author Lehman was to be the recipient of
the coveted statuette later, so this was a formidable team. The
story isn't much, but it's the treatment and the witty dialogue that
set it apart from the ordinary. Holden and Bogart are the sons of
Hampden and Walker, two very rich people in the Long Island
horsey set. Holden is the devilish one who lives for fast cars and
faster women, while Bogart is the hard-headed businessman who
has inherited his father's acumen. Also living on the estate (which
was the real Glen Cove acreage owned by Barney Balaban, the
president of Paramount) are Williams, the chauffeur, and his
young, impressionable daughter, Hepburn. Hepburn is mad
about Holden, who only thinks of her as a slightly addled
adolescent and pays just enough attention to make her think there
might be a chance. When Hepburn realizes that Holden is only
toying with her, she attempts suicide by turning on the ignitions
of eight of the family cars in the garage and inhaling the exhaust.
After she is rescued, Williams sends her to France, where she

attends a Parisian school to learn the chef's trade. Once in France, Hepburn meets Dalio, an aged and kindly baron who finds her naivete charming and performs a Pygmalion to her Galatea, thereby transforming the sweet young thing into a sophisticated woman who knows the right clothes to wear, the right wine to drink, and automatically says the right things for all occasions.

In the US, Bogart seeks to enhance the family's wealth by marrying Holden off to Hyer, an heiress to yet another huge fortune overseen by her father, Francis Bushman. Hepburn returns to Long Island, and once Holden gets a look at and listens to this new version, he falls madly in love with her, despite his engagement to Hyer. Hepburn is determined to win Holden, who has been the man of her dreams for so long, but Bogart and Hampden are adamant that in the family's best interest Holden marry Hyer. Bogart tells Hepburn she would be wise to keep out of Holden's grasp, but she won't hear of it. In order to get her mind off Holden, bachelor Bogart pretends to be courting her. Bogart has been concentrating on business for so many years that Hampden wonders if his eldest son can still hold a conversation with a woman that's not about loans or debentures. Bogart assures him that he can and reverts to his youth by donning an old Yale sweater and reaching for a phonograph and the one record he owns, a copy of "Yes, We Have No Bananas" (Frank Silver, Irving Cohn). Bogart manages to talk Hepburn aboard an ocean liner and promises her that he'll be on board. What he really wants to do is get her out of the way so she won't foul up the marriage plans of Holden and Hyer. It's only when Holden points out to his older brother the truth—that Bogart loves Hepburn and should admit it—that Bogart wakes up. He races to the dock, hires a tugboat, and makes it to the ocean liner before it clears the port. Bogart and Hepburn are united much to the surprise of anyone who thought the younger, more handsome brother would nab the female star.

A charming, if often-seen, tale, paced with alacrity by Wilder from the adaptation of Taylor's hit play which had starred Margaret Sullavan, SABRINA was a resounding hit at the box office and with the critics and proved that silk purses were still possible from less than perfect sources. Bogart had been making movies for more than two decades, but this was his first effort for Paramount. He and Wilder did not get along and had differing views of what was funny. Whoever won those battles will never be known, but the results were satisfying, as Bogart played drawing-room comedy with aplomb. Edith Head's costumes won an Oscar, and the film was nominated for Best Screenplay, Best Cinematography and Best Art Direction.

SACCO AND VANZETTI
(SACCO E VANZETTI)
1971   120m   c   ★★★
Historical   GP/AA
Jolly/Unidis/Theatre Le Rex   (Italy/France)

Gian Maria Volonte (Bartolomeo Vanzetti), Riccardo Cucciolla (Nicola Sacco), Cyril Cusack (Frederick Katzmann), Milo O'Shea (Fred Moore), Geoffrey Keen (Judge Webster Thayer), William Prince (William Thompson), Rosanna Fratello (Rosa Sacco), Claude Mann (Journalist), Edward Jewesbury, Armenia Balducci

p, Arrigo Colombo, Giorgio Papi; d, Giuliano Montaldo; w, Giuliano Montaldo, Fabrizio Onofri, Ottavio Jemma; ph, Silvano Ippoliti (Technicolor); ed, Nino Baragli; m, Ennio Morricone; art d, Aurelio Crugnola; cos, Enrico Sabbatini

The American judicial system has a long and spotted history of convicting and executing those whose political views defy the status quo. One most notorious such trial was that of Sacco and Vanzetti, two Italian immigrants and admitted anarchists who were convicted and sent to the electric chair as a result of the 1920s red scare. This English-dubbed version of the tale accurately portrays the facts, with clear sympathy shown towards the two defendants. Cucciolla and Volonte (the latter from A FISTFUL OF DOLLARS and FOR A FEW DOLLARS MORE) portray the duo, who are brought up on charges of murder when two employees of a shoe store are killed in a robbery. After a sham trial in which Cucciolla and Volonte are tried more for their politics than for the actual crime, they are found guilty and sentenced to death. The case causes worldwide commotion as literally thousands of people rally behind them over the course of the next six years. However, despite overwhelming evidence of their innocence, Cucciolla and Volonte are executed on August 23, 1927. Though overall an impressive and accurate retelling of this miscarriage of justice, the film is not without its faults. The major problem is length. Considering the scope of actual time and the myriad events that took place over those seven years, two hours is simply insufficient for the story. Worst of all is an annoying theme song by Joan Baez which is packed with such insincere (and ultimately condescending) lyrics as, "Here's to you, Sacco and Bart/Something, something forever in my heart." The film is at its strongest when allowed to simply speak for itself. This is a story fraught with natural emotion, portrayed with sincerity and genuine sympathy for its doomed protagonists. In the end, SACCO AND VANZETTI becomes an eloquent portrait of two simple men swept up in the fury of political self-righteousness, a portrait which is not flattering to the American way of justice, to say the least.

SACRIFICE, THE
(OFFRET-SA CRIFICATIO)
1986   145m   c   ★★★★
Drama   PG/15
Swedish Film Institute/Argos/Film Four/Josephson & Nykvist/Swedish Television/SVT 2/Sandrew/French Ministry of Culture   (France/Sweden)

Erland Josephson (Alexander), Susan Fleetwood (Adelaide), Valerie Mairesse (Julia), Allan Edwall (Otto), Gudrun Gisladottir (Maria), Sven Wollter (Victor), Filippa Franzen (Marta), Tommy Kjellqvist (Little Man)

d, Andrei Tarkovsky; w, Andrei Tarkovsky; ph, Sven Nykvist (Eastmancolor); ed, Andrei Tarkovsky, Michal Leszczylowski; m, Johann Sebastian Bach, Watazumido Shuoo; art d, Anna Asp; fx, Svenska Stuntgruppen, Lars Hoglund, Lars Palmqvist, Richard Roberts, Johan Toren; cos, Inger Pehrsson

The final film from one of Russia's greatest filmmakers, Andrei Tarkovsky, was also his first to receive any widespread recognition in the US. Like all of Tarkovsky's work, it tackles complex themes and concerns that most directors would never approach. THE SACRIFICE is about a number of things, none obvious and none remaining wholly consistent from one viewing to the next; it is a poetic vision, filled with the symbolism peculiar to Tarkovsky's imagination. It is also a visually stunning, hauntingly beautiful, brilliant piece of art. THE SACRIFICE opens as Alexander (Erland Josephson) and his six-year-old son are busily planting a tree along the sandy, barren shore of the small island where the family is vacationing. During this vacation, it is announced on the radio that WWIII has begun—and the complete destruction of Europe by nuclear arms is certain. Later, when Alexander is alone, he gets down on his hands and knees to ask forgiveness from his creator, begging for the terrible events that are transpiring to be undone. He promises to do anything—give up all his possessions, even part with his son—if only things will be returned to normal. More than a beautiful film, THE SACRIFICE is a hopeful message to future generations to live in harmony with nature and with one another (which only gains in power by virtue of its dedication to the filmmaker's son). By December 29, 1986, less than a year after this movie was completed, Tarkovsky would fall victim to the cancer that he already knew would kill him. Aware that this would probably be his last film, Tarkovsky makes a conscious plea that we consider the damage done to the planet before it's too late, and seems to be saying that for all the modern world's astounding scientific progress, there is nothing to compensate for the loss of our spiritual essence—creating a dangerous gap between human consciousness and the natural world. While perhaps not the most typical of Tarkovsky's works (the Swedish cast, Sven Nykvist's photography, and the Faro location occasionally lend it a Bergmanesque quality), THE SACRIFICE is a brilliant picture that should not be missed.

SAHARA

1943   97m   bw   ★★★★★
War   /PG
Columbia

Humphrey Bogart (Sgt. Joe Gunn), Bruce Bennett (Waco Hoyt), Lloyd Bridges (Fred Clarkson), Rex Ingram (Sgt. Tambul), J. Carrol Naish (Giuseppe), Dan Duryea (Jimmy Doyle), Richard Nugent (Capt. Jason Halliday), Patrick O'Moore (Ozzie Bates), Louis Mercier (Jean Leroux), Carl Harbord (Marty Williams)

p, Harry Joe Brown; d, Zoltan Korda; w, John Howard Lawson, Zoltan Korda, James O'Hanlon (based on a story by Philip Mac-Donald); ph, Rudolph Mate; ed, Charles Nelson; m, Miklos Rozsa; art d, Lionel Banks, Eugene Lourie

One of the most exciting and entertaining propaganda films to come out of WWII, SAHARA features Humphrey Bogart as Sgt. Joe Gunn, an American tank commander who, along with his crew (Bruce Bennett and Dan Duryea), is separated from his unit just after the fall of Tobruk. As the tank, nicknamed *Lulubelle*, slowly makes its way through the desert, Sgt. Gunn and his crew pick up a number of stragglers: several British soldiers (Patrick O'Moore, Lloyd Bridges, Richard Nugent, Carl Harbord), a Sudanese corporal (Rex Ingram) with an Italian prisoner (J. Carrol Naish) in tow, a Free Frenchman (Louis Mercier), a South African volunteer (Guy Kingsford), and a downed Nazi pilot (Kurt Kreuger). As the small rag-tag unit advances, the search for an oasis becomes their primary mission; however, they soon discover that a large German force in the area has the same objective. Blessed with a great cast and smart direction by Zoltan Korda, SAHARA remains one of the most appealing films of WWII. Although the constant speechifying, especially by Naish's repentant Italian, may strike some as passe and overbearing, the basic humanity of the entire affair is a pleasant change from the xenophobic posturing found in most films of the era. Sadly, scriptwriter John Howard Lawson's humane outlook would come back to haunt him when, in the 1950s, he became one of the Hollywood Ten. However, when McCarthyite government officials tried to pressure Columbia Pictures boss Harry Cohn into firing Lawson, he refused, much to his credit.

SAINT JACK

1979   112m   c   ★★½
Crime   R/X
Playboy/Shoals Creek/Copa de Oro

Ben Gazzara (Jack Flowers), Denholm Elliott (William Leigh), James Villiers (Frogget), Joss Ackland (Yardley), Rodney Bewes (Smale), Mark Kingston (Yates), Lisa Lu (Mrs. Yates), Monika Subramaniam (Monika), Judy Lim (Judy), George Lazenby (Senator)

p, Roger Corman; d, Peter Bogdanovich; w, Peter Bogdanovich, Howard Sackler, Paul Theroux (based on the novel by Theroux); ph, Robby Muller; ed, William Carruth; art d, David Ng

In Singapore circa 1971, Gazzara is an American pimp who tries to become an independant operator. This arouses the anger of the local mobsters who want to put him out of business. He finally knuckles under after heavy pressure and goes to work for an American mobster (played by director Bogdanovich in a good quirky performance). He's forced to photograph an important senator in the arms of a young male prostitute, but eventually Gazzara's conscience catches up with him. The film uses the locations well and Gazzara's performance is an actor's dream. But SAINT JACK never quite becomes the "important" film it seems to aspire to be. The story is told in too meandering a style and the many well-acted characterizations never mesh together. This was Bogdanovich's first film in many years. After a promising early career, he got sidetracked creating films for his various mistresses and trying to recapture dead genres (DAISY MILLER and AT LONG LAST LOVE are massive disappointments considering they were made by the director of THE LAST PICTURE SHOW). SAINT JACK helped Bogdanovich regain his critical strength, but it wasn't until 1985's MASK that he was accepted by the public again. SAINT JACK was produced by Roger Corman, who had given the director his start in 1964 with THE WILD ANGELS. Serving as executive producer was Playboy's Hugh Hefner, which may explain some of the film's unnecessary steamier moments.

SAINT STRIKES BACK, THE

1939   67m   bw   ★★★½
Mystery   /A
RKO

George Sanders (Simon Templar), Wendy Barrie (Val Travers), Jonathan Hale (Inspector Henry Fernack), Jerome Cowan (Cullis), Neil Hamilton (Allan Breck), Barry Fitzgerald (Zipper Dyson), Robert Elliott (Chief Inspector Webster), Russell Hopton (Harry Donnell), Edward Gargan (Pinky Budd), Robert Strange (Police Commissioner)

p, Robert Sisk; d, John Farrow; w, John Twist (based on the novel Angels of Doom by Leslie Charteris); ph, Frank Redman; ed, Jack Hively; art d, Van Nest Polglase, Albert S. D'Agostino; cos, Renie

George Sanders plays the Robin Hood-like sleuth in this second installment in "The Saint" series, having taken over the role from Louis Hayward. In this one, the Saint and Inspector Henry Fernack (Hale, reprising his role from THE SAINT IN NEW YORK) are bound for San Francisco to prove that the murdered father of Val Travers (Barrie) was not the brains behind a series of clever murders. Sanders, on loan from 20th Century-Fox, takes the role and makes it his own. Until this film he had been slowly working his way into the Hollywood system after coming from England. Wendy Barrie does a nice job as the female lead, good support is provided in the secondary roles, and spine-tingling direction makes the most of a clever script. After this film The Saint was a guaranteed winner in the public eye and RKO had a monster hit on its hands.

SALAAM BOMBAY!

1988 113m c ★★★★
Drama /15
Mirabai (India)

Shafiq Syed (Krishna/Chaipau), Sarfuddin Qurrassi (Koyla), Raju Barnad (Keera), Raghubir Yadav (Chillum), Nana Patekar (Baba), Aneeta Kanwar (Rekha), Hansa Vithal (Manju), Mohanraj Babu (Salim), Chandrashekhar Naidu (Chungal), Ramesh Deshavani

p, Mira Nair; d, Mira Nair; w, Sooni Taraporevala (based on a story by Nair, Sooni Taraporevala); ph, Sandi Sissel; ed, Barry Alexander Brown; m, L. Subramaniam; prod d, Mitch Epstein

The feature debut for documentary filmmaker Mira Nair, SALAAM BOMBAY! is the story of an 11-year-old boy abandoned by his family after they suspect him unjustly of stealing money.

Unable to read or write, unsure even of the name of his native village, Krishna (Shafiq Syed) arrives in the Bombay slums where he hopes to raise enough money to return to his family. He makes a few rupees a day delivering an opium-like tea, and in the process he comes into contact with a variety of seedy characters: a pimp (Nana Patekar), his prostitute wife (Aneeta Kanwar), a drug-addicted pusher (Raghubir Yadav) who works for the pimp, the pimp's daughter (Hansa Vithal), and a peasant girl called "Sweet Sixteen" (Chanda Sharma), a prostitute-to-be whose virginity is being auctioned off to the highest bidder. Despite the poverty and violence, there are moments of joy, such as a visit to the local cinema in which all the children mimic a ridiculous matinee idol. As time wears on, however, the youngster's surrogate family collapses around him.

Shot in the slums of Bombay with child actors recruited by Nair from the street, SALAAM BOMBAY! is a riveting and uncompromising tale of urban deprivation in the tradition of Bunuel's LOS OLVIDADOS and Hector Babenco's PIXOTE. It received the prestigious Camera d'Or for best first feature at the 1988 Cannes Film Festival, as well as a 1988 Academy Award nomination for Best Foreign Language Film.

SALOME'S LAST DANCE

1988 89m c ★★★½
Comedy/Religious R/18
Vestron (U.K.)

Glenda Jackson (Herodias/Lady Alice), Stratford Johns (Herod/Alfred Taylor), Nickolas Grace (Oscar Wilde), Douglas Hodge (John the Baptist/Lord Alfred "Bosie" Douglas), Imogen Millais-Scott (Salome/Rose), Denis Ull (Tigellenus/Chilvers), Russell Lee Nash (Pageboy), Alfred Russell (Cappadocem), Ken Russell (Kenneth), David Doyle (A. Nabda)

p, Penny Corke, Robert Littman; d, Ken Russell; w, Ken Russell (based on the play Salome by Oscar Wilde); ph, Harvey Harrison (Technicolor); ed, Timothy Gee; chor, Arlene Phillips; cos, Michael Arrals

Ken Russell's most impressive offering in years presents Oscar Wilde's Salome as a play within a film. Wilde (Nickolas Grace) and his lover, Lord Alfred Douglas (Douglas Hodge), visit a local bordello, where a performance of his banned play Salome is to be staged. Playing Herod, the gluttonous king, is the bordello's proprietor (Stratford Johns). Other bordello residents fill out the remaining roles, including a Cockney servant girl (Imogen Millais-Scott) in the role of Salome, and Lord Alfred plays the prophet, John the Baptist. The play dramatizes an ancient biblical tale: Salome tries to seduce the imprisoned prophet and is repulsed. As a reward for performing the titillating "Dance of the Seven Veils" for her sexually besotted stepfather, Herod, she

demands the prophet's head on a silver platter. The events that take place off the stage, however, are as important as what occurs on it. The play-within-a-film structure achieves a synthesis of real-life decadence, historical decadence, and that particular decadence that flowed from Wilde's pen. In an effort to stretch these boundaries even further, director Russell casts himself as a photographer who captures and frames the images, and as the stagehand who creates the sound effects—the aural counterpart to the imagemaker. Despite what are often called "excesses" in Russell's style, SALOME'S LAST DANCE is a film of emotional depth and warmth.

SALT OF THE EARTH

1954 94m bw ★★★★
Docu-drama /A
Intl. Union of Mine, Mill and Smelter Workers

Rosaura Revueltas (Esperanza Quintero), Will Geer (Sheriff), David Wolfe (Barton), Melvin Williams (Hartwell), David Sarvis (Alexander), Juan Chacon (Ramon Quintero), Henrietta Williams (Teresa Vidal), Ernest Velasquez (Charley Vidal), Angela Sanchez (Consuelo Ruiz), Joe T. Morales (Sal Ruiz)

p, Paul Jarrico, Sonja Dahl Biberman, Adolfo Barela; d, Herbert Biberman; w, Michael Wilson, Michael Biberman; ph, Leonard Stark, Stanley Meredith; ed, Ed Spiegel, Joan Laird; m, Sol Kaplan; prod d, Sonja Dahl Biberman, Adolfo Barela

Landmark semi-documentary account of a strike by Mexican-American mineworkers in the American Southwest which was released at the height of McCarthyism and led to the imprisonment and/or blacklisting of several of the key figures involved. This was one of the first films to deal with the rights of Chicanos and to depict women as playing a central role in the labor movement.

SALT OF THE EARTH was filmed using actual participants of the real-life struggle on which it is based (Chacon, a non-professional actor, does an amazing job in his real-life role). The film rises above the level of agitprop by avoiding sloganeering and using the real words of real people to tell its story. Its feminism, too, is real and unforced, with women simply being shown struggling alongside—and when necessary defying—their male counterparts.

Naturally a film with such liberal leanings became a source of controversy in the 1950s; SALT OF THE EARTH was doubly cursed, for its content and its background. Producer Paul Jarrico had been banned from Hollywood, but this could not stop him. He joined with director Herbert Biberman, a member of the "Hollywood Ten," who had served a 5-month prison sentence for being an uncooperative House Un-American Activities Committee (HUAC) witness. They wanted to create a film company which would give work to blacklisted members of the film industry. Their intent was to create stories, as the two wrote 20 years later, "drawn from the living experiences of people long ignored in Hollywood—the working men and women of America." As it turns out, this was their only production, made in association with the International Mine, Mill, and Smelter Workers. They were lucky to make the film at all; shortly after production began in early 1953 the pro-McCarthy establishment press sought to discredit the film and filmmakers. Hollywood actor Walter Pidgeon, then president of the Screen Actors Guild, upon receiving a letter from a New Mexico schoolteacher warning of "Hollywood Reds. . . shooting a feature-length anti-American racial-issue propaganda movie" alerted his contacts in government, ranging from members of HUAC to officials of the FBI and CIA. Donald Jackson, a member of HUAC, claimed he would do everything he could to prevent the screening of "this communist-made film," citing non-existent scenes as examples of the film's Red leanings. Even billionaire Howard Hughes, head of RKO, got on the bandwagon and came up with a plan to stop the film's processing and distribution. The local population near the shooting site also got into the act. Vigilante groups took action, picking fights with crew members and setting fire to real union headquarters. Local merchants refused to do business with anyone in the production. One group threatened to take out the company "in pine boxes," and finally the New Mexico State Police had to come in to protect the filmmakers.

Problems were compounded when Revueltas, a Mexican actress, was arrested by immigration officials for a minor passport violation. She returned to Mexico, and the film had to be completed with a double. Some of her scenes were also shot in her native country on the pretext of being test shots for a future production. (Sadly, the Red fever of this country spilled over into Mexico, and Revueltas was blacklisted there for her work in this film. The talented actress would never work again.) SALT OF THE EARTH enjoyed critical acclaim in Europe but, due to continued blacklisting, did not enjoy wide US release until 1965, when it became a rallying point for the political activism of that decade.

SALVADOR

1986   123m   c   ★★★★
Drama/War   R/18
Hemdale   (U.K.)

James Woods (Richard Boyle), James Belushi (Dr. Rock), Michael Murphy (Ambassador Thomas Kelly), John Savage (John Cassady), Elpidia Carrillo (Maria), Tony Plana (Maj. Max), Colby Chester (Jack Morgan), Cynthia Gibb (Cathy Moore), Will MacMillian (Col. Hyde), Valerie Wildman (Pauline Axelrod)

p, Gerald Green, Oliver Stone; d, Oliver Stone; w, Oliver Stone, Richard Boyle; ph, Robert Richardson; ed, Claire Simpson; m, Georges Delerue; prod d, Bruno Rubeo; art d, Melo Hinojosa; fx, Yves De Bono; cos, Kathryn Morrison

The first, and, so far, the best major film about the war in El Salvador, this Oliver Stone effort is as good as his Oscar-winning Vietnam film PLATOON but never received the recognition it deserved from critics or the public. Although there have been other major films dealing with conflict in Latin America (Chile in MISSING, and Nicaragua in UNDER FIRE), none has conveyed the chaos, tension, and fear within the region as vividly as SALVADOR. Based on the experiences of real-life journalist Richard Boyle, the film begins in 1980, as the unemployed veteran reporter (played brilliantly by James Woods) heads down to El Salvador with his buddy, Dr. Rock (James Belushi), an out-of-work disc jockey. Promising drink, drugs, and an endless supply of inexpensive virginal whores, Boyle cons his friend into coming along to a place where he can make some quick money covering a "little guerrilla war." Once they cross the border, however, things begin to get dangerous as Boyle becomes embroiled in the devastating civil war. A scant plot synopsis cannot fully convey the vivid events that explode in every frame of SALVADOR. Not only does director Stone successfully convey the turmoil and horror of life in El Salvador, he also shows us the rebirth of the conscience of a cynical, self-absorbed journalist whose problems pale in comparison with the atrocities suffered by the Salvadoran people, for whom he genuinely cares. Woods is superb as the journalist who recovers his lost humanity, and it is a tribute to his considerable skills as an actor that he is able to engage the viewer throughout the film with his basically

repugnant character. While Woods's character is one of the most challenging and fascinating to hit the screen in some time, it is Stone's vivid portrayal of El Salvador that gives the film its disturbing tone. In his simple-but-detailed portrayal of the chaotic events of 1980-81, Stone successfully conveys the confusion, terror, senselessness, and despair felt by Salvadorans, while jaded Americans—government, military, and press—blithely ignore the realities of the country's predicament. Stone's camera is like a photojournalist, always on the move, running, swirling, probing, trying to get close to the truth of the tragedy in El Salvador.

SALVATORE GIULIANO

1962   125m   bw   ★★★
Biography/Crime   /X
Lux/Vides/Galatea   (Italy)

Frank Wolff (Gaspare Pisciotta), Salvo Randone (President of Viterbo Assize Court), Federico Zardi (Pisciotta's Defense Counsel), Pietro Cammarata (Salvatore Giuliano), Fernando Cicero (Bandit), Sennuccio Benelli (Reporter), Bruno Ekmar (Spy), Max Cartier (Francesco), Giuseppe Calandra (Minor Official), Cosimo Torino (Frank Mannino)

p, Franco Cristaldi; d, Francesco Rosi; w, Francesco Rosi, Suso Cecchi D'Amico, Enzo Provenzale, Franco Solinas; ph, Gianni Di Venanzo; ed, Mario Serandrei; m, Piero Piccioni; art d, Sergio Canevari, Carlo Egidi; cos, Marilu Carteny

This film is based on the true story of Salvatore Giuliano, an important Sicilian Mafia chieftain who was found shot full of holes on July 5, 1950. The film opens with the bullet-ridden remains found in a sunny courtyard. After his wake and funeral begin, the mobster's career is portrayed in flashbacks. Cammarata is the gangster who becomes involved with some guerrilla activities in postwar Sicily. When the group breaks up, a number of his men continue to follow Cammarata as he stages a minor war against legal authorities. He has a group of peasants slaughtered at a Communist rally, which triggers violent confrontations between gangsters and the law. Slowly, his men grow disillusioned with him and they abandon the man. Wolff, Cammarata's second-in-command, also abandons his boss but, like many of the outlaws, is tried and thrown in jail. There, Wolff is poisoned by members of the Mafia, a group he joined after leaving Cammarata. This is an interesting gangster picture, made in the heart of the Mafia's birthplace. The use of camera technique is excellent, coupled with a strong sense of direction. The acting is equally good, making full use of the cast's respective talents. Non-professional actors, as well as professionals, were used with fine results. However, the film is severely hampered for American audiences by the confusing plot line that was clearly designed with more local audiences in mind. The political, historical, and social references are not always clear, which can be distracting, yet this still works and works well.

SAMMY AND ROSIE GET LAID

1987   100m   c   ★★★½
Drama   R/18
Cinecom/Film Four   (U.K.)

Shashi Kapoor (Rafi Rahman), Claire Bloom (Alice), Ayub Khan Din (Sammy), Frances Barber (Rosie Hobbs), Roland Gift (Danny/Victoria), Wendy Gazelle (Anna), Suzette Llewellyn (Vivia), Meera Syal (Rani), Badi Uzzaman (Ghost)

p, Tim Bevan, Sarah Radclyffe; d, Stephen Frears; w, Hanif Kureishi; ph, Oliver Stapleton; ed, Mick Audsley; m, Stanley Myers; prod d, Hugo Luczyc-Whyowski; cos, Barbara Kidd

Director Stephen Frears and screenwriter Hanif Kureishi, the team that produced the splendid MY BEAUTIFUL LAUNDRETTE, join forces again to provide a cynically humorous and apocalyptic portrait of life in Prime Minister Margaret Thatcher's England. Sammy (Ayub Khan Din) and Rosie (Frances Barber), a young interracial married couple, lead a bohemian existence in a marginal London neighborhood. Theirs is a relationship based on "freedom plus commitment," meaning that they sleep with whomever they want but still love each other. Into this genially amoral world comes Sammy's father, Rafi Rahman (Shashi Kapoor, a huge star in India), a charming rogue who has not seen his son in years. Having made a fortune in his murderous political dealings in Pakistan, Rafi has returned to transfer his wealth into his son's account on the condition that Sammy and Rosie buy a house in a respectable part of England and that they supply him with a grandson. Though he has blood on his own hands, Rafi is appalled by the violence, squalor, and social unrest. The beloved London of his youth has become a living hell in his eyes. Sammy and Rosie's friends disapprove of Rafi's political sins while he is revolted by their "perverted" sexuality and left wing views. Only the strikingly handsome mulatto street person named Danny (Roland Gift, lead singer for the Fine Young Cannibals)— but who prefers to be called "Victoria"—looks up to Rafi and follows him around town. However, before long, the charismatic scoundrel's old crimes come back to haunt him.

SAMMY AND ROSIE GET LAID is a biting satire that does its best to achieve screenwriter Kureishi's stated aim to "get as much filth and anarchy into the cinema as possible." In addition to literate hardhitting scripting and smooth direction, the movie is features excellent performances. However, this is a case where a film is simply too ambitious. Kureishi does an admirable job of juggling numerous balls in the air for the first half of the film—dealing with issues of politics, class, drugs, and interracial strife and attraction—but he becomes less graceful in the film's second half after a bravura triple split screen sex scene. Matters become increasingly contrived as the film collapses in exhaustion from thematic overload. Still it's a fairly impressive achievement as a whole.

SAMSON AND DELILAH
1949   131m   c   ★★★½
Religious   /U
Paramount

Hedy Lamarr (Delilah), Victor Mature (Samson), George Sanders (Saran of Gaza), Angela Lansbury (Semadar), Henry Wilcoxon (Ahtur), Olive Deering (Miriam), Fay Holden (Hazel), Julia Faye (Hisham), Russ Tamblyn (Saul), William Farnum (Tubal)

p, Cecil B. DeMille; d, Cecil B. DeMille; w, Vladimir Jabotinsky, Harold Lamb, Jesse Lasky, Jr., Fredric M. Frank (based on the story in the Bible and the book Judge and Fool by Vladimir Jabotinsky); ph, Dewey Wrigley, George Barnes (Technicolor); ed, Anne Bauchens; m, Victor Young; art d, Hans Dreier, Walter Tyler; fx, Gordon Jennings, Paul K. Lerpae, Devereaux Jennings; chor, Theodore Kosloff; cos, Edith Head, Gus Peters, Dorothy Jeakins, Gwen Wakeling, Elois Jenssen

Late but classic Cecil B. DeMille blockbuster, and one of the director's top money-makers, about biblical strong man Samson (Victor Mature), vanquished by the soft curves of the vixen Delilah (Hedy Lamarr).

SAMSON AND DELILAH was tried and true ground for the great DeMille, best remembered for his spectacular interpretations of the Bible (KING OF KINGS, SIGN OF THE CROSS, THE TEN COMMANDMENTS) and other extravagant historical recreations (CLEOPATRA, THE CRUSADES). Here DeMille, the master of the crowd scene, is in top form managing thousands of extras, particularly in the savage battle scenes in which Samson destroys the Philistine army with the jawbone of an ass. DeMille spent $3 million to film the Old Testament story, but the movie gained enormous and immediate returns, filling Paramount's coffers with more than $12 million from its initial release, the largest box-office take the studio had enjoyed to date. Hans Dreier and Walter Tyler won Oscars for Best Art Direction; Edith Head and her assistants took home a deserved Oscar statuette for the fabulous costumes. The film was also nominated for Best Cinematography, Best Special Effects and Best Score.

SAN FRANCISCO
1936   115m   bw   ★★★★
Romance/Disaster   /A
MGM

Clark Gable (Blackie Norton), Jeanette MacDonald (Mary Blake), Spencer Tracy (Father Tim Mullin), Jack Holt (Jack Burley), Ted Healy (Matt), Margaret Irving (Della Bailey), Jessie Ralph (Maisie Burley), Harold Huber (Babe), Al Shean (Professor), William Ricciardi (Baldini)

p, John Emerson, Bernard H. Hyman; d, W.S. Van Dyke, II, D.W. Griffith (uncredited); w, Anita Loos, Erich von Stroheim (based on a story by Robert E. Hopkins); ph, Oliver T. Marsh; ed, Tom Held; m, Edward Ward; art d, Cedric Gibbons, Arnold Gillespie, Harry McAfee; fx, A. Arnold Gillespie, James Basevi; chor, Val Raset; cos, Adrian

This film left no doubt that MGM was the omnipotent studio of Hollywood. Star power, a great, rowdy story, and one of the most awesome special effects sequences in the history of film made SAN FRANCISCO a blockbuster. The pairing of Gable and Tracy here is historic: Tracy envied Gable's roguish charm and romantic image; Gable thought Tracy the finest actor on screen.

Gable stars as the brassy, colorful boss of the infamous Paradise beer garden, who ensnares starving MacDoanld into a contract singing for him, although she also gains fame with Nob Hill patrons of the San Francisco Opera and amazingly finds time to inspire churchgoers, trilling in priest Tracy's choir. Yes, Jeanette overdoes it a bit, and why not? She's The Belle of San Francisco. Until the special effects, this is a Lifetime Achievement period piece for McDonald, with the rough 'n ready leads battling over her soul and other extremities. It almost holds the picture together while we're waiting for the Big Rumble.

And rumble it does: the great old historic sites of San Francisco are shown breaking to pieces under the strain of the tremendous earthquake. City Hall collapses, fountains disintegrate, and office and residential buildings sway and tumble as the quake grips the entire city. Everywhere people are looking for lost loved ones. A long view of the city shows widespread fires breaking out, and a series of quick shots show firemen helpless to combat them because the water mains are broken. A second tremor begins, and this time the very streets split. But when The King finds Jeanette, she's still in concert.

SAN FRANCISCO is the biggest film Van Dyke ever directed, a work he maintains at a fantastic pace, hustling along his actors to keep time with the gaudy, bawdy era he presented in the background. Although Van Dyke certainly earned the credit for his astounding, technically flawless film, his mentor and the father of American silent film (and creator of almost all the techniques used thereafter in the sound era), D.W. Griffith, appeared at MGM one day and Van Dyke asked "the master" if he cared to direct any of the scenes in the film. He did, but just which scene the great Griffith directed is still in debate. One report had it that he directed one of MacDonald's operatic scenes, another one of the mob scenes at the Paradise club. But it was also rumored that the great Griffith directed the gem of this golden film, the incredible 20-minute earthquake and fire sequence, or at least that portion which was not achieved by the special effects of Gillespie and the uncredited James Basevi.

Van Dyke did not forget others of the silent era and tried to put to work many of the silent stars who were then unemployed and suffering during that year of the Great Depression, including Flora Finch; one-time Vitagraph star Naomi Childers; Jean Acker, who had been Rudolph Valentino's first wife and a leading lady in her own right during the silent days; King Baggot and Rhea Mitchell, whom Van Dyke had directed in the 1918 silent film THE HAWK'S LAIR. Even silent film director Erich von Stroheim got into the act, writing some additional dialog for Loos's script.

SAND PEBBLES, THE
1966   195m   c   ★★★★
Adventure/War   M/A
Argyle/Solar

Steve McQueen *(Jake Holman)*, Richard Attenborough *(Frenchy Burgoyne)*, Richard Crenna *(Capt. Collins)*, Candice Bergen *(Shirley Eckert)*, Marayat Andriane *(Maily)*, Mako *(Po-han)*, Larry Gates *(Jameson)*, Charles Robinson *(Ens. Bordelles)*, Simon Oakland *(Stawski)*, Ford Rainey *(Harris)*

p, Robert Wise; d, Robert Wise; w, Robert Anderson (based on the novel by Richard McKenna); ph, Joseph MacDonald (Panavision, Deluxe Color); ed, William Reynolds; m, Jerry Goldsmith; prod d, Boris Leven; fx, Jerry Endler; cos, Renie

A powerful and spectacular film, featuring Steve McQueen at his finest and director Robert Wise at his most persuasive, THE SAND PEBBLES is the panoramic story of a US Navy gunboat cruising China's Yangtze River in 1926 amidst the Nationalist rebellion led by Chiang Kai-Shek. In an Oscar-nominated performance, McQueen plays Jake Holman, the lone wolf sailor who keeps the cranky engines of the USS *San Pablo* running while Collins (Richard Crenna), its captain, negotiates tricky political waters. Ordered to remain neutral in the Chinese conflict despite the abuse heaped upon them, the crew, who call themselves the "Sand Pebbles," become restive. When Chinese authorities, anxious to create an international incident, frame Jake for the murder of the Chinese wife of a dead shipmate (Richard Attenborough), Collins refuses to hand over the engineer, though the crew is reluctant to back him up. However, when US Marines land in Shanghai, the Sand Pebbles are finally given a chance to fight back, the gunboat battling its way through a blockade to evacuate American missionaries Jameson (Larry Gates), who resents the US involvement in Chinese affairs, and Shirley Eckert (Candice Bergen), with whom Jake has fallen in love. The final rescue, like the rest of this long but involving film, is carefully unfolded by Wise, building in intensity towards a heroic but tragic conclusion. Beautifully photographed (by Joseph MacDonald) and designed, THE SAND PEBBLES earned Academy Award nominations for Best Picture, Art Direction, Color Cinematography, Editing, Musical Score and Sound. Mako (nominated for Best Supporting Actor for his portrayal of Jake's Chinese assistant), Crenna, Attenborough, and Bergen are all

excellent, but McQueen (who actually learned how to run the engines of the 150-foot gunboat replica built for the $12-million film) steals the show. Released in 1966, THE SAND PEBBLES offered parallels to the controversial US involvement then taking place in Vietnam. Although it has undergone several edits, THE SAND PEBBLES is available on videocassette at its original 195-minute running time.

SANDS OF IWO JIMA
1949   110m   bw   ★★★★
War   /PG
Republic

John Wayne *(Sgt. John M. Stryker)*, John Agar *(Pfc. Peter Conway)*, Adele Mara *(Allison Bromley)*, Forrest Tucker *(Pfc. Al Thomas)*, Wally Cassell *(Pfc. Benny Regazzi)*, James Brown *(Pfc. Charlie Bass)*, Richard Webb *(Pfc. Shipley)*, Arthur Franz *(Cpl. Robert Dunne/Narrator)*, Julie Bishop *(Mary)*, James Holden *(Pfc. Soames)*

p, Edmund Grainger; d, Allan Dwan; w, Harry Brown, James Edward Grant (based on a story by Brown); ph, Reggie Lanning; ed, Richard L. Van Enger; m, Victor Young; art d, James Sullivan

Unlike John Wayne's many WWII films in which he single-handedly destroys whole Japanese battalions, SANDS OF IWO JIMA presents him as a believable, vulnerable human being. Sgt. John M. Stryker (Wayne), a battle-toughened Marine, prepares a group of recruits for combat, driving them hard without worrying about making friends, although he is hurt when Pfc. Peter Conway (John Agar) hopes aloud that his newborn son won't be anything like Stryker. Later, in combat on Tarawa, Stryker's men grow furious with him when he refuses to rescue a Marine who has been separated from the squad, because to do so would give away their position. After Tarawa, they go to Hawaii for some R & R, where Stryker shows his heart of gold to a young mother forced into prostitution. The Marines' biggest test comes on Iwo Jima, and Stryker's men perform magnificently as they inch their way up Mt. Suribachi, but their leader is killed and Conway, now his disciple, must try to fill Stryker's big shoes. This is one of Wayne's finest performances, earning him an Oscar nomination. Directed with marvelous restraint by old hand Allan Dwan, SANDS OF IWO JIMA features appearances by three of the Marines who actually participated in the famous flag-raising on Mt. Suribachi—Ira Hayes, Rene Gagnon, and John Bradley.

SANSHO THE BAILIFF
(SANSHO DAYU)
1954   125m   bw   ★★★★½
Drama
Daiei/Kyoto   (Japan)

Yoshiaki Hanayagi *(Zushio)*, Kyoko Kagawa *(Anju)*, Kinuyo Tanaka *(Tamaki)*, Eitaro Shindo *(Sansho)*, Akitake Kono *(Taro)*, Masao Shimizu *(Masauji Taira)*, Ken Mitsuda *(Prime Minister Morozane Fujiwara)*, Chieko Naniwa *(Ubatake)*, Kikue Mori *(Priestess)*, Kazukimi Okuni *(Norimura)*

p, Masaichi Nagata; d, Kenji Mizoguchi; w, Yahiro Fuji, Yoshikata Yoda (based on the story "Sansho Dayu" by Ogai Mori); ph, Kazuo Miyagawa; ed, Mitsuji Miyata; m, Fumio Hayasaka, Kanahichi Odera, Tamekichi Mochizuki; art d, Kisaku Ito

A classic of Japanese and world cinema, SANSHO THE BAILIFF, set in the 11th century, tells the story of Zushio (Yoshiaki Hanayagi) and his struggle within the limits of feudal society. The film begins as family members—mother Tamaki (Kinuyo Tanaka), sister Anju (Kyoko Kagawa), and Zushio—travel through the woods in search of their exiled patriarch. They are soon assaulted by kidnappers, and Tamaki is sold into prostitution and exiled to Sado Island, while the children are sold as slaves to a powerful and cruel bailiff, Sansho (Eitaro Shindo). Ten years pass, and Zushio has become as evil as Sansho, for whom he now works as an overseer at a labor compound. Haunted by thoughts of his dead father and his exiled mother, Zushio prepares his escape, planning to leave with Anju. She, however, in order to keep from burdening her brother or from revealing his whereabouts, drowns herself. When Zushio reaches his destination, Kyoto, he discovers that his father has become a folk hero immortalized in song. In recognition of his father's stature, Zushio is granted the post of governor, and he takes it upon himself to abolish slavery and to banish the bailiff from his land. Having performed his service to humanity, he resigns, resumes his search for his mother, and finds her, now blind, facing the sea. Perhaps Kenji Mizoguchi's greatest achievement, SANSHO THE BAILIFF is a visually mesmerizing picture that pays great and careful attention to the smallest details of nature and environment, highlighted by Mizoguchi's use of the long take and deep-focus shots. In an attempt to film life as he sees it, Mizoguchi and his cinematographer, Kazuo Miyagawa, capture images much as a painter might—using the entire palette of contrasts and colors to create a richly textured atmosphere. The film was not released in the US until 1969.

SANTA FE TRAIL

1940 110m bw   ★★★½
Historical/Adventure   /U
First National

Errol Flynn *(Jeb Stuart)*, Olivia de Havilland *(Kit Carson Holliday)*, Raymond Massey *(John Brown)*, Ronald Reagan *(George Armstrong Custer)*, Alan Hale *(Barefoot Brody)*, Guinn "Big Boy" Williams *(Tex Bell)*, Van Heflin *(Rader)*, Henry O'Neill *(Cyrus Holliday)*, William Lundigan *(Bob Holliday)*, John Litel *(Harlan)*

p, Robert Fellows; d, Michael Curtiz; w, Robert Buckner; ph, Sol Polito; ed, George Amy; m, Max Steiner; art d, John Hughes; fx, Byron Haskin, H.F. Koenekamp; cos, Milo Anderson

Despite its misleading title, this roaring, action-packed film, directed with great vigor by Curtiz, is not a western and has little to do with the Santa Fe Trail. And though it purports to deal with a serious segment of American history, even that is inaccurate.

Flynn is his ever-dashing self as he appears at West Point, playing the southern-born J.E.B. Stuart, who later became the South's greatest cavalryman during the Civil War. He arrives, along with mule and dog, wearing an outlandish uniform of his own design which so confuses the sentinels at the post that they mistakenly call out an honor guard to salute what appears to be a high-ranking officer of a foreign power. This auspicious arrival is soon ended when it is learned that Flynn is nothing more than a new cadet reporting to the Point for training. Other than his academic studies, Flynn's real enemy at the Point is Heflin, a wild-eyed radical abolitionist who is out to change the class and caste system of America. He is a secret follower of the fanatic John Brown, and his political activities finally get Heflin cashiered from the Point. Flynn and his friends (Reagan, playing George Armstrong Custer; David Bruce, essaying Phil Sheridan; Wilcox, playing Longstreet; William Marshall, enacting the role of George Pickett; and George Haywood, playing John Hood) all graduate from the Point in 1854 and are assigned to a western post in Kansas where they must combat the illegal activities of the dreaded Brown, played by Massey. A travesty of history, SANTA FE TRAIL is nonetheless a rousing adventure yarn,

offering a great romp for Flynn and providing a bevy of colorful characterizations. De Havilland is at her feisty, attractive best, while Reagan has the "best friend" role, losing her to the handsome Flynn. Massey, who overacts frantically as Brown, would play him again in SEVEN ANGRY MEN in 1955. The film's gratuitous patriotism is countered by the tentative sympathies Reagan and a few others utter on behalf of Massey, stating that he may be misdirected but that his ambition to free the slaves is a worthy one.

SAPPHIRE

1959 92m c   ★★★
Mystery   /A
Artna   (U.K.)

Nigel Patrick *(Supt.)*, Yvonne Mitchell *(Mildred)*, Michael Craig *(Inspector Learoyd)*, Paul Massie *(David Harris)*, Bernard Miles *(Ted Harris)*, Olga Lindo *(Mrs. Harris)*, Earl Cameron *(Dr. Robbins)*, Gordon Heath *(Paul Slade)*, Jocelyn Britton *(Patsy)*, Harry Baird *(Johnny Fiddle)*

p, Michael Relph; d, Basil Dearden; w, Janet Green, Lukas Heller (based on the screenplay by Green); ph, Harry Waxman (Eastmancolor); ed, John D. Guthridge; m, Philip Green; art d, Carmen Dillon

Good detective yarn starring Patrick and Craig as detectives of Scotland Yard who are investigating the murder of a young black woman whose light-colored skin allowed her to pass as white. Suspects range from Massie, as the girl's white boyfriend, and his parents, who feared for their son's career, to the black youths the girl tosses aside when she is accepted by whites. Craig's prejudice, as well as just about everyone else's, adds a good deal of tension to the sleuthing, which Patrick pursues in a highly dignified, professional manner despite the additional obstacles. Material stays on safe ground about shedding light on the problem of racial prejudice which was rampant in England in the late 1950s. The picture was made shortly after race riots occurred in London and Nottingham.

SARATOGA

1937 94m bw   ★★★½
Comedy   /A
MGM

Jean Harlow *(Carol Clayton)*, Clark Gable *(Duke Bradley)*, Lionel Barrymore *(Grandpa Clayton)*, Walter Pidgeon *(Hartley Madison)*, Frank Morgan *(Jesse Kiffmeyer)*, Una Merkel *(Fritzi O'Malley)*, Cliff Edwards *(Tip O'Brien)*, George Zucco *(Dr. Beard)*, Jonathan Hale *(Frank Clayton)*, Hattie McDaniel *(Rosetta)*

p, Bernard H. Hyman; d, Jack Conway; w, Anita Loos, Robert E. Hopkins; ph, Ray June; ed, Elmo Veron; m, Edward Ward; art d, Cedric Gibbons, John S. Detlie; cos, Dolly Tree

Jean Harlow gave her last screen performance—one of her best—in this sharp-witted and charming trackside comedy that pairs the actress with Clark Gable. Harlow, who died before the film's completion, stars as Carol Clayton, the daughter of a horse breeder (Jonathan Hale) who through gambling loses his Saratoga farm to his bookmaker friend Duke Bradley (Clark Gable). After her father dies of a heart attack, Carol forbids her stockbroker fiance, Hartley Madison (Walter Pidgeon), to make any more trackside wagers—much to the chagrin of Duke, who had planned to win back the money he lost to Hartley at Belmont. While Carol and Duke carry on a love-hate flirtation, the bookmaker schemes with his old friend Fritzi (Una Merkel) to recoup his losses, persuading top jockey Dixie Gordon (Frankie Darro) to ride Fritzi's horse in an upcoming race against Hartley's steed. By now Carol has fallen for Duke and broken off her engagement, but Duke nobly ends their budding romance, respecting her late father's wishes that she be sheltered from the wicked ways of the track. Heartbroken, Carol purchases Frankie's contract from Fritzi, and the stage is set for Duke's ruin until kind-hearted Fritzi saves the day. After Harlow died in June 1937, it was decided to use a stand-in for her remaining scenes, in which Mary Dees and Geraldine Dvorak are photographed from behind while wearing a large floppy hat, with Paula Winslow speaking for the character (whom screenwriters Anita Loos and Robert Hopkins gave a cold and cough).

SATURDAY NIGHT AND SUNDAY MORNING

1961 90m bw	★★★★
Drama	/PG
Woodfall (U.K.)	

Albert Finney *(Arthur Seaton)*, Shirley Ann Field *(Doreen Gretton)*, Rachel Roberts *(Brenda)*, Hylda Baker *(Aunt Ada)*, Norman Rossington *(Bert)*, Bryan Pringle *(Jack)*, Robert Cawdron *(Robboe)*, Edna Morris *(Mrs. Bull)*, Elsie Wagstaffe *(Mrs. Seaton)*, Frank Pettitt *(Mr. Seaton)*

p, Tony Richardson; d, Karel Reisz; w, Alan Sillitoe (based on his novel); ph, Freddie Francis; ed, Seth Holt; m, John Dankworth; art d, Ted Marshall

In a scant 89 minutes, Sillitoe and Reisz create a world, plunge the viewer into it, and make the audience members feel happy they can walk away from the movie house and not have actually been a part of the dismal existence of one young man in the Midlands area of England. This was 23-year-old Finney's first major film (he'd done a bit in THE ENTERTAINER earlier that year) and the resulting performance remains a fresh revelation. It's another of the "angry young men" pictures like ROOM AT THE TOP and this is another one that lingers. Sillitoe, who also wrote THE LONELINESS OF THE LONG DISTANCE RUNNER, adapted his own novel here with major results.

Finney is a lathe operator in a small town near Nottingham. He is a lively young man devoted to pleasure and thumbing his nose at authority. As he says, "All I want is a good time. The rest is propaganda." To that end, he spends his weekends boozing and brawling and bedding down any woman he can. He makes a good wage; he has plenty of discretionary money to spend. He hates his job but is willing to put in his week at the lathe in return for the fun he can have with his pay envelope. He's having an affair with Roberts, who is married to his fellow worker, Pringle. Finney enjoys the sexual liaisons with Roberts, but that's as far as he will go with her; she wants more. At the same time, Finney meets Field, a beautiful, old-fashioned young woman with strict morals. Finney finds himself falling in love with Field, but she won't sleep with him unless there is a commitment, something Finney cannot bear to make. Then Roberts announces that she's pregnant.

The story seems slim at best, but Reisz's sharp direction and the superb editing combine with Sillitoe's grasp of the argot to make this a compelling, if somewhat difficult to understand, movie. The accents in that area of England are almost impossible for US ears (and even many London auricles) to fathom, so it had to be looped in places where the words blurred. Sillitoe, who used to work in a Midlands factory, captures the nuances perfectly in his script, and Reisz, who was in his early thirties at the time, does a smashing job in his first feature after having worked in the documentary field. SATURDAY NIGHT FEVER owes a great deal to this brilliant film. There are so many similarities

that it seems to be a New York remake. Despite Finney's youth, he was already a veteran Shakespearean actor and had once taken over for Olivier when Sir Larry was felled by injury on the eve of a performance of *Coriolanus* at Stratford. It was a sensational outing for Finney, and great things were in store. Roberts was excellent and her performance (not unlike that of Simone Signoret in ROOM AT THE TOP), like Finney's, was also honored with a BFA award. One of the best of the "kitchen sink" pictures of the era, SATURDAY NIGHT AND SUNDAY MORNING has more than its share of humor to temper the highly charged drama, and it stands out in every department—the sex is steamy, the language is raw, the emotions are strong. Still a must-watch.

SATURDAY NIGHT FEVER

1977 119m c	★★★½
Drama	R/PG
Paramount	

John Travolta *(Tony Manero)*, Karen Lynn Gorney *(Stephanie)*, Barry Miller *(Bobby C.)*, Joseph Call *(Joey)*, Paul Pape *(Double J)*, Donna Pescow *(Annette)*, Bruce Ornstein *(Gus)*, Julie Bovasso *(Flo)*, Martin Shakar *(Frank)*, Sam Coppola *(Fusco)*

p, Robert Stigwood; d, John Badham; w, Norman Wexler (based on the *New York* magazine article "Tribal Rites of the New Saturday Night" by Nik Cohn); ph, Ralf D. Bode (Panavision, Movielab Color); ed, David Rawlins; m, Barry Gibb, Robin Gibb, Maurice Gibb, David Shire; prod d, Charles Bailey; chor, Lester Wilson (Lorraine Fields); cos, Patrizia Von Brandenstein, Jennifer Nichols

Reminiscent of both MARTY and SATURDAY NIGHT AND SUNDAY MORNING, this hugely popular picture and its even more popular soundtrack album (more than 27 million copies of which have been sold) raked in nearly $200 million. Moreover, John Travolta's heartfelt portrayal of Tony Manero, a directionless young clerk in a Brooklyn paint store, earned him an Oscar nomination as Best Actor and catapulted him to stardom. Refusing to compete with his seminarian brother (Martin Shakar) for his father's approval, Tony lives for the weekend, strutting his stuff on the disco dance floor with his girlfriend, Annette (Donna Pescow), whom he shuns after meeting Stephanie (Karen Lynn Gorney), an upwardly mobile, smart-stepping miss who becomes his partner for a big dance contest. Tony's tempestuous relationship with Stephanie, his desertion of Annette, and the pleasures and problems of his neighborhood buddies make up the rest of the film, which reaches its tragic climax in a scene at the Verrazano Bridge, where the spurned Annette offers herself sexually to Tony's friends, and Bobby C. (Barry Miller), overcome with worries about the baby he has fathered out of wedlock, precariously scales the bridge. The story here is really secondary to character and milieu, however, as director John Badham and his actors create a convincing portrait of frustrated 1970s working-class youth and the escape that the swirling lights and pulsing rhythms of the disco offered. Although technically not a musical—in that no one in the cast sings—this highly energized film has more songs than most musicals proper (most prominently the eminently danceable contributions of the Bee Gees, who reached their creative and popular apex here) and features some great dancing by Travolta. The sequel, STAYING ALIVE is nowhere near as involving.

SAVE THE TIGER

1973 100m c	★★★
Drama	R/AA
Filmways/Jalem/Cirandinha	

Jack Lemmon (*Harry Stoner*), Jack Gilford (*Phil Greene*), Laurie Heineman (*Myra the Hitchhiker*), Norman Burton (*Fred Mirrell*), Patricia Smith (*Janet Stoner*), Thayer David (*Charlie Robbins*), William Hansen (*Meyer*), Harvey Jason (*Rico*), Liv von Linden (*Ula*), Lara Parker (*Margo the Prostitute*)

p, Steve Shagan; d, John G. Avildsen; w, Steve Shagan; ph, James Crabe (Movielab Color); ed, David Bretherton; m, Marvin Hamlisch; art d, Jack Collis

Director John Avildsen has a knack for using small budgets to make "big" movies. First it was JOE, then this film, then his triumph with ROCKY.

The action of SAVE THE TIGER takes place in about a day and a half in the life of a man who is trapped by his own indulgences. Businesss is rotten, and Lemmon, the managing partner of Capri Casuals, a Los Angeles garment manufacturing company, finds himself daydreaming about his youth. After a nightmare-filled night, he rises in his sumptuous Beverly Hills home; says goodbye to his wife, Smith, who is on her way to a relative's funeral; and gets into his Lincoln for the long drive downtown. On the street, he picks up Heineman, a liberated young woman who proposes that they go to bed together. Lemmon balks. At the office, he and partner Gilford try to figure a way out of their dire financial straits (they owe a bundle and there isn't a bank in town willing to give them a loan). Lemmon suggests torching the company's Long Beach warehouse to collect insurance money, but Gilford won't hear of it. When Burton, a conservative out-of-town client who lets his hair down in LA, arrives to see the new line from Capri, Lemmon arranges for him to be entertained by call girl Parker. Later, in a porno movie house, Lemmon meets with David, who is willing to burn down the warehouse for a price. Outside the theater, Bif Elliott is raising funds to protect wildlife, particularly lions and tigers—hence the film's title. Things continue in this vein, with the increasingly pressured Lemmon eventually breaking down in front of the audience at a fashion show, convinced that the assembled clients are his dead comrades-in-arms from WWII.

SAVE THE TIGER is an uneven but engaging look at a man whose lust for success has bankrupted not only his company but his conscience. Yet despite his illegal and immoral practices, we are drawn to Lemmon's Harry Stoner. Never better, Lemmon delivers a magnificent performance that won him a Best Actor Oscar (he beat an especially distinguished field: Brando for LAST TANGO IN PARIS, Pacino in SERPICO, Redford in THE STING, and Nicholson in THE LAST DETAIL.) Gilford's outstanding supporting work was recognized with a Best Supporting Actor nomination, and the screenplay by producer-screenwriter-novelist Shagan (*The Formula*) was also honored with a nomination. In her screen debut, Heineman is excellent, but the great career that her work here seemed to promise never materialized.

SAY ANYTHING

1989 100m c   ★★★★
Comedy/Drama   PG-13/15
Gracie/Cameron Crowe

John Cusack (*Lloyd Dobler*), Ione Skye (*Diane Court*), John Mahoney (*James Court*), Lili Taylor (*Corey*), Amy Brooks (*D.C.*), Pamela Segall (*Rebecca*), Jason Gould (*Mike Cameron*), Loren Dean (*Joe*), Joan Cusack (*Constance*), Glenn Walker Harris, Jr. (*Jason*)

p, Polly Platt; d, Cameron Crowe; w, Cameron Crowe; ph, Laszlo Kovacs (Deluxe Color); ed, Richard Marks; m, Richard Gibbs, Anne Dudley, Nancy Wilson; prod d, Mark Mansbridge; cos, Jane Ruhm

A far cry from the standard Hollywood teen romance, SAY ANYTHING is the extraordinary directorial debut of Cameron Crowe (who adapted his own novel for the hilariously inventive FAST TIMES AT RIDGEMONT HIGH). Set in Seattle, Crowe's wonderfully nuanced screenplay develops a complex triangular relationship involving a gifted and ambitious high-school graduate, Diane Court (Ione Skye), her doting father, James (John Mahoney), and Lloyd Dobler (John Cusack), the likable, underachieving classmate who falls for her. The relationship of father and daughter is tested when Diane is wooed by Lloyd, an Army brat who lives with his unmarried sister (real-life sibling Joan Cusack) and her young son (Daniel Will-Harris). His best friends, Corey and D.C. (Lili Taylor and Amy Brooks) know just how sensitive, creative, and loving Lloyd is. Diane, too, is won over by Lloyd's generosity of spirit, but her father wants nothing to stand in the way of her success, and pressures her to break up with Lloyd. Seldom have such complexity, emotional depth, honesty, and realism been invested in what is ostensibly a teen love story. Crowe's script is full of careful observations, and his camera unobtrusively serves the spot-on production design, the witty but believable dialog, and especially the outstanding performances by Skye (RIVER'S EDGE; A NIGHT IN THE LIFE OF JIMMY REARDON), Mahoney (MOONSTRUCK; SUSPECT; BETRAYAL), and Cusack, whose Lloyd Dobler is an exceedingly winning portrayal.

SAYONARA

1957 147m c   ★★★★
War/Drama   /PG
Goetz/Pennebaker

Marlon Brando (*Maj. Lloyd Gruver*), Ricardo Montalban (*Nakamura*), Red Buttons (*Joe Kelly*), Patricia Owens (*Eileen Webster*), Martha Scott (*Mrs. Webster*), James Garner (*Capt. Mike Bailey*), Miiko Taka (*Hana-ogi*), Miyoshi Umeki (*Katsumi*), Kent Smith (*Gen. Webster*), Douglas Watson (*Col. Craford*)

p, William Goetz; d, Joshua Logan; w, Paul Osborn (based on the novel by James A. Michener); ph, Ellsworth Fredricks (Technirama, Technicolor); ed, Arthur Schmidt, Philip W. Anderson; m, Franz Waxman; art d, Ted Haworth; chor, LeRoy Prinz; cos, Norma Koch

This beautifully photographed and often moving story of racial prejudice features Marlon Brando as Lloyd Gruver, an Army major reassigned to a Japanese air base in the midst of the Korean conflict. In Japan, Gruver sees the US military's racism against the Japanese, which goes so far as to forbid servicemen from marrying Japanese women. Although at first indifferent to the situation, Gruver is forced to take a stand when his buddy Joe Kelly (Red Buttons) falls in love with a local woman, Katsumi (Miyoshi Umeki), and becomes determined to marry her, going over the heads of the military high command and petitioning Congress for permission. Sticking by his comrade, Gruver risks the wrath of his superiors when he agrees to be Kelly's best man at the ceremony. What's more, Gruver himself falls in love with a beautiful Japanese dancer, Hana-ogi (Miiko Taka), and finds himself in the same predicament as Kelly. SAYONARA is a sensitive work, sparing neither Americans nor Japanese in condemning prejudice. This updating of the "Madame Butterfly" theme is a powerful, well-told story, with a statement on racism that remains timeless. It was certainly topical: when filming began, in 1956, more than 10,000 American servicemen had defied extant regulations and married Japanese women (as the novel's author, James A. Michener, had done earlier). The film received 10 Academy Award nominations, including Best Picture (it lost to THE BRIDGE ON THE RIVER KWAI), Best Director,

Best Actor (Brando lost to Alec Guinness for RIVER KWAI), Best Cinematography, Best Screenplay, and Best Editing. Oscars went to the film for Sound, Art Direction, and Set Decoration, as well as to Buttons and Umeki for their supporting performances.

SCANDAL

1989   114m   c   ★★★
Biography/Political   R/18
Palace/British Screen   (U.K.)

John Hurt (Stephen Ward), Joanne Whalley-Kilmer (Christine Keeler), Bridget Fonda (Mandy Rice-Davies), Ian McKellen (John Profumo), Leslie Phillips (Lord Astor), Britt Ekland (Mariella Novotny), Roland Gift (Johnnie Edgecombe), Jeroen Krabbe (Eugene Ivanov)

p, Stephen Woolley; d, Michael Caton-Jones; w, Michael Thomas; ph, Mike Molloy (Technicolor); ed, Angus Newton; m, Carl Davis; prod d, Simon Holland; art d, Chris Townsend

Michael Caton-Jones's SCANDAL peeks under the bedsheets of Britain's ruling class with a rehashing of the Profumo Affair, the early 60s sex scandal that eventually toppled the Conservative Party from power. Minister of War John Profumo (Ian McKellan) is romantically linked to accused prostitute Christine Keeler (Joanne Whalley-Kilmer), who, as it happened, was also involved with Soviet attache Eugene Ivanov (Jeroen Krabbe), an alleged spy. Keeler met both men through Dr. Stephen Ward (John Hurt), a high-society osteopath. Meanwhile, teenage beauty Mandy Rice-Davies (Bridget Fonda), another Ward protegee, was bedhopping with the high and mighty of two continents, and the whole crew were reported to be frequent participants at extravagant orgies. Instead of sleaze, director Caton-Jones and screenwriter Michael Thomas deliver a vindication of the affair's chief scapegoats—Ward and Keeler—in the form of a two-hour nostalgia trip (complete with imitation Beatles), with some complex and powerful performances. The screen is filled with memorabilia of 1960s London: miniskirts, smoke-filled dens of West Indians, rows of tenements, opportunistic newsmen from tabloids. Overall, however, the direction is uninspired. One problem with SCANDAL is that, compared to scandals of the 80s, the Profumo affair is rather tame. If it's a poke at England's Conservatives you're looking for, the honest fiction of Mike Leigh's HIGH HOPES did more to make them bleed than the pointless fact of SCANDAL.

SCANNERS

1981   102m   c   ★★★
Horror   R/18
Filmplan   (Canada)

Stephen Lack (Cameron Vale), Jennifer O'Neill (Kim), Patrick McGoohan (Dr. Paul Ruth), Lawrence Dane (Keller), Charles Shamata (Gaudi), Adam Ludwig (Crostic), Michael Ironside (Darryl Revok), Victor Desy (Dr. Gatineau), Mavor Moore (Trevellyan), Robert Silverman (Pierce)

p, Claude Heroux; d, David Cronenberg; w, David Cronenberg; ph, Mark Irwin (CFI Color); ed, Ronald Sanders; m, Howard Shore; art d, Carol Spier; fx, Dick Smith, Gary Zeller, Henry Pierrig, Dick Smith, Chris Walas

SCANNERS is a nifty science fiction comic-book of a movie that makes excellent use of its low budget and hastily-written script. The film boasts a few extraordinary set pieces and some inspiredly gory special effects, as well as some resonant visual metaphors for the telepathic condition.

Ephemerol, an experimental tranquilizer, was tested on pregnant women during the 1940s and produced some severe long range side effects. Before the drug was taken off the market, 236 babies were born to the women tested. They were found to possess the ability to read minds. Dubbed "scanners," these powerful telepaths spread out through North America for decades until many were sought and rounded up by two mysterious and competing corporations: Consec, headed by Dr. Paul Ruth (McGoohan), and Biocarbon Amalgamated, headed by the deadly Darryl Revok (Ironside), a scanner assassin. Cameron Vale (Lack) is a homeless drifter with the gift. He is abducted from the street and ends up in the healing hands of Dr. Ruth, who gives him medication that allows him to control his power. Vale is informed that Revok plans to take over the world with an army of evil scanners. He must link up with his farflung "brethren" so they can determine their own futures.

Notorious for the scene in which Ironside uses his awesome scanning power to literally explode the head of another man, SCANNERS is relatively conventional by Cronenberg standards—though wildly imaginative by normal ones. Despite the loose ends and inconsistencies, SCANNERS is a memorable and absorbing genre entertainment that has spawned several direct-to-video sequels. Cronenberg displays more confidence as a visual stylist here than in his previous films, but his storytelling abilities are not much in evidence. Matters aren't helped by Lack's weak lead performance, though his large, emotive eyes add poignance to his predicament. Fortunately McGoohan (of television's "Secret Agent" and "The Prisoner") is on hand to provide an eccentrically entertaining performance as the fatherly Dr. Ruth. Ironside is fantastic as the lethal Revok, helping make this a popular cult favorite.

SCARECROW

1973   112m   c   ★★★
Drama   R/18
WB

Gene Hackman (Max), Al Pacino (Lion), Dorothy Tristan (Coley), Ann Wedgeworth (Frenchy), Richard Lynch (Riley), Eileen Brennan (Darlene), Penny Allen (Annie), Richard Hackman (Mickey), Al Cingolani (Skipper), Rutanya Alda (Woman in Camper)

p, Robert M. Sherman; d, Jerry Schatzberg; w, Garry Michael White; ph, Vilmos Zsigmond (Panavision, Technicolor); ed, Evan Lottman; m, Fred Myrow; prod d, Albert Brenner; cos, Jo Ynocencio

This is a good look at a pair of losers that is a bit too episodic. Hackman has recently been released from San Quentin where he did some hard time for assault. He's on his way to Pittsburgh where he hopes to open a car wash on the modest savings he's accumulated. Pacino is a seaman who has just completed a voyage. The two men hit it off and decide to go east together. On the trip, they have adventures in bars, diners, and various residences belonging to former loves and old pals. As they near their destinations, Pacino becomes nervous about seeing his wife, Allen, whom he left while she was pregnant. Hackman does his best to encourage him, but Pacino is beginning to crumble. He's never seen his child, and, when he phones ahead to Detroit and talks to Allen (in a very sensitive portrayal), she lies, telling him that the child he'd thought she had was never born. She says she miscarried early and all of his trepidation about meeting his child was for naught. Pacino goes into a violent form of nervous breakdown. The final scenes show Hackman using his savings to pay for Pacino's hospital care, his hopes of opening his own business tossed aside in favor of helping his only friend. Hackman gives another splendid, compelling performance. Pacino's characterization is rather weak, however. His roles in DOG DAY AFTERNOON and THE GODFATHER are better indications of his talents. There are points where writer White has created unrealistic lines for Pacino instead of allowing the character to emerge subtly and become part of the story. Brennan does well as a barroom floozie, and Tristan scores as one of Hackman's ex-girlfriends. The picture looks wonderful and captures the grittiness of the road. Schatzberg had been a photographer and his collaboration with Zsigmond is fruitful in that respect for much of the film, though they are both occasionally guilty of gratuitous Hollywood gloss. The ending is not consistent with Hackman's behavior all the way through. Given the box office potency of the two stars, the receipts were disappointing, although the movie eventually did make a small profit. No four-letter word seems to have been omitted.

SCARFACE

1932 99m bw   ★★★★★
Biography/Crime   /15
Caddo

Paul Muni (*Tony Camonte*), Ann Dvorak (*Cesca Camonte*), Karen Morley (*Poppy*), Osgood Perkins (*Johnny Lovo*), Boris Karloff (*Gaffney*), George Raft (*Guino Rinaldo*), Vince Barnett (*Angelo*), C. Henry Gordon (*Inspector Guarino*), Inez Palange (*Tony's Mother*), Edwin Maxwell (*Commissioner*)

p, Howard Hughes; d, Howard Hawks; w, Ben Hecht, Seton I. Miller, John Lee Mahin, W.R. Burnett, Fred Pasley (based on the novel by Armitage Trail); ph, Lee Garmes (additional scenes for censor), L.W. O'Connell; ed, Edward Curtiss; m, Adolph Tandler, Gus Arnheim; prod d, Harry Olivier

Hawks' undisputed masterpiece, and a landmark in the screen depiction of gangsters. Though the gangster genre had begun with a tremendous explosion of films such as LITTLE CAESAR and PUBLIC ENEMY, it was SCARFACE (originally called "Scarface, the Shame of a Nation") that depicted the professional hood as a murderous beast. In earlier films of the genre, a great deal of attention was paid to developing the background of the criminal and placing the blame for his antisocial activities on his environment. But with SCARFACE, all of that was dispensed with to give audiences for the first time an adult, fully developed monster who thrived on murder and power.

The first scene of SCARFACE shows Paul Muni only in shadow, whistling a few bars of an Italian aria before shooting a victim and then walking calmly away. The remainder of the film shows Muni's rise from gunman to crime boss of the city, obviously Chicago.

It's also obvious that the career shown on screen is that of the notorious Al Capone. Muni is honestly portrayed as the typical gangster of the era; he is brutal, arrogant, and stupid (Truffaut believes Hawks directed Muni to make him look and move lika an ape; it's likely), a homicidal maniac who revels in gaudy clothes, fast cars, and machine guns, because their rapid fire allows him to kill more people at a single outing. (The number of deaths recorded in this ultra-violent film is 28, with many more reported as occurring off-camera.) But Muni is also insanely jealous of his slinky sister, Ann Dvorak, to the point where his feelings toward her are obliquely incestuous, though he is too stupid to know it. Muni works for Osgood Perkins, a more sophisticated and clever hoodlum who, in turn, is the chief lieutenant of Harry J. Vejar, the city's nominal crime boss. (Perkins' role is based on Johnny Torrio, the creator of organized crime in America, and Vejar is a duplicate of Chicago's old-time crime czar, Big Jim Colosimo.) Muni is arrested for the murder

shown in the opening scene, but the mob lawyer soon has him freed on a special writ. Muni manipulates the thugs and bosses to achieve his own ends, encouraging Perkins to kill the old-time boss Vejar, since Vejar will not take advantage of the new Prohibition law and go into bootlegging liquor. After Vejar has been killed in his lavish restaurant, Perkins calls a meeting of all the mob bosses in the city and lectures them about the wild shootouts that have drawn too much attention from the press and heat from the police. When Perkins tells Muni to leave North Side boss Boris Karloff alone, Muni says he'll take care of Karloff. Later, Perkins has the ambitious Muni come to his swanky apartment, where the bodyguard gets a good look at cool blonde Karen Morley, Perkins's sexy mistress. It's obvious that the ruthless thug covets her, and she is ready to reciprocate. Perkins warns Muni to curb his strong-arm methods, and Muni gives him an empty promise, continuing to go his own way, strong-arming and killing at will.

SCARFACE was the most violent, bloody film the genre had seen. Hawks excelled himself, running his cameras with the action in truck and dolly shots that were mostly unheard of in the early talkie period. Aiding the director was cameraman Lee Garmes, whose sharp contrasts created some of the starkest and most brutal images ever captured on screen. Producer Howard Hughes spared no expense, but he also interfered with Hawks (as he did with other directors), insisting that Hawks present all decisions for his approval. In fact, the production was almost cancelled because of the incessant squabbling between the producer and director.

Almost nothing was used of the Armitage Trail novel on which the film is based, except the title. Profiling the gangster and his tempestuous sister as modern-day Borgias was Hawks' idea, with the incest relationship as the emotional weakness that destroys the unthinking gangster. Hecht had been offered $20,000 by Hawks to write the script, but wanted instead $1,000 a day in cash—not a particularly advantageous deal since he finished the script in 11 days.

Muni is superb in his role of the maniac killer, and Morley is perfect as his ice-cool moll. Karloff's performance is marred by an oddball interpretation of how a Chicago gangster is supposed to talk. He plays a part based on Chicago's George "Bugs" Moran and he looks his part, with his staring deep-socketed eyes and stiff, lethargic movements. Raft, with his tuxedo and pomaded hair parted in the middle, is excellent as Muni's right-hand man, a killer who does Muni's bidding without question. Muni and Raft became stars overnight because of SCARFACE, and both received lucrative long-term contracts from studios, Muni at Warners where he would see enormous success with such films as I AM A FUGITIVE FROM A CHAIN GANG, JUAREZ, THE GOOD EARTH, THE LIFE OF EMILE ZOLA, and THE STORY OF LOUIS PASTEUR, for which he would win an Oscar as Best Actor. Raft, on the other hand, appeared for Paramount in a host of rather mediocre films, but was nevertheless a solid leading man for two decades to come.

Raft had hung around several New York gangs in the 1920s, including the Dutch Schultz mob. He had been fascinated by one of Schultz's lieutenants, Bo Weinberg, who had a habit of flipping a coin just before he shot someone, a trick Raft incorporated into his portrayal.

Several underworld types were used to supply additional information on how the gangs operated. Capone himself, according to the director, later gave Hawks a special party in Chicago, honoring him for making SCARFACE. (Not only did Capone, according to Hawks, see SCARFACE five or six times, but he had his own print of it. He thought it was great.)

SCARFACE

1934 170m c ★★★★
Crime   R/18
Universal

Al Pacino *(Tony Montana)*, Steven Bauer *(Manny Ray)*, Michelle Pfeiffer *(Elvira)*, Mary Elizabeth Mastrantonio *(Gina)*, Robert Loggia *(Frank Lopez)*, Miriam Colon *(Mama Montana)*, F. Murray Abraham *(Omar)*, Paul Shenar *(Alejandro Sosa)*, Harris Yulin *(Bernstein)*, Angel Salazar *(Chi Chi)*

p, Martin Bregman, Peter Saphier; d, Brian De Palma; w, Oliver Stone (based on the 1932 film script by Ben Hecht); ph, John A. Alonzo (Panavision, Technicolor); ed, Jerry Greenberg, David Ray; m, Giorgio Moroder; art d, Ed Richardson; fx, Ken Pepiot, Stan Parks; cos, Patricia Norris

Yes, it's violent. Yes, it's full of profanity. Yes, it's long. And yes, Al Pacino's performance is wildly over-the-top. But Brian DePalma's SCARFACE is also a terrific example of modern filmmaking. A beautiful, at times poetic exercise in excess, its flights of violent fancy are not only justifiable, but absolutely necessary. The whole point of this film is to be excessive. In depicting the lifestyle of a crazed drug lord, DePalma refuses to back off and creates a seductive, wholly original vision that succeeds in both entertaining and shocking the viewer.

Based on the classic Howard Hawks 1932 gangster film of the same name, the screenplay (written by Oliver Stone) follows the plot of its source almost to the letter. A Cuban refugee with a violent streak is unstoppable in his quest for the American dream. Fresh off the boat from Cuba, two-bit hood Tony Montana (Pacino) lies his way into the country and into a spot in Freedom Town (a camp in Florida for refugees to live in while they wait for their green cards). It's not long before he and his right-hand man Manny (Stephen Bauer) enter the world of crime. They murder a political figure for drug dealer Frank Lopez (Robert Loggia) to get their green cards and are soon on his payroll. They make a drug buy at a Miami Beach motel, but the deal goes sour, and one of Montana's cohorts is chopped up with a chainsaw by a group of fanatical Columbians. After nearly being killed himself, Tony kills the Columbians and brings both the money and the cocaine to Lopez. This gives Tony a more prominent role in the organization. His duties include serving as chauffeur to Lopez's beautiful but cocaine-addicted wife, Elvira (Michelle Pfeiffer). Tony tries to make peace with his long-suffering mother and sister, whom he has not visited for sometime. One night he shows up at their doorstep flashing money, but his mother (Miriam Colon) wants nothing to do with him. His sister Gina (Mary Elizabeth Mastrantonio) is seduced by the money, however. Tony's feelings for his sister are a bit on the incestuous side, and he dominates the girl, refusing to let her date. After a bad business deal and an argument over Elvira, Lopez attempts to have Tony killed. In a brilliant sequence, Tony and two assassins shoot it out in a crowded club. After killing the assassins, Tony murders Lopez, marries Elvira and becomes the most powerful drug lord in Florida. He makes deals with Bolivian drug kingpin Sosa (Paul Shenar) and lives in a mansion with bodyguards and surveillance equipment. However, Manny is secretly dating Gina (though warned not to), Elvira has become increasingly zombie-like, and his money is not earning the interest it should. Moreover, he also has become an extremely selfish, paranoid drug addict. He is setup by the cops and arrested. To avoid prison, Tony agrees to assassinate an anti-drug politician who is exposing Sosa's business practices. Tony travels to New York with Sosa's chief assassin Hector (Al Isreal), but the target shows up with his wife and kids. Tony refuses to go through with

the hit and shoots Hector. When he returns home, Sosa threatens to kill him for backing out of the deal, and Tony challenges him to "go to war," though his gang of bodyguards is pathetic compared to the army of goons Sosa has at his disposal. Meanwhile, Elvira has left him, and he discovers that Manny and his sister have secretly married. In what is probably the most shocking scene in the film, Tony kills his best friend, leaving Gina a widow. As he waits for Sosa's gang to arrive, he uses large amounts of cocaine until Gina wanders into his office with a gun and shoots him in the ensuing confrontation. Wounded, he hides behind a chair as she contiues to fire. An assassin enters and kills Gina. After killing the gunman, Tony sees dozens of armed killers on his grounds. After wiping out countless men (and taking several bullets himself), his body falls into a fountain located beneath a globe encircled by the words, "The World is Yours."

Jammed with action sequences and unbearably tense moments, the film depicts the seediest aspects of America. Stone's screenplay twists gangster movie conventions, and DePalma demonstrates an unusual understanding of the genre. The latter's skill with the camera is certainly his strongest talent. Although not as flashy as some of his work (such as DRESSED TO KILL or CARRIE), it is a showboat of cinematic style. His unique full screen compositions are quite arresting (the most memorable of which is an overhead shot of Pacino soaking in an obscenely large bath tub), and his sweeping shots and cutting style powerfully draw the viewer into the action. In addition to excelling with the action sequences, this film offers the best acting of any De Palma effort. Al Pacino is absolutely brilliant. The supporting players are all strong. Bauer and Pfeiffer are excellent, and Robert Loggia turns in the best performance of his career. The film is complemented by extraordinary art direction (by Ed Richardson) and wonderfully rich photography (by John A. Alonzo). The film remains DePalma's best work and is an undeniably effective, visceral experience.

SCARLET EMPRESS, THE

1934 110m bw ★★★★★
Biography/Historical   /A
Paramount

Marlene Dietrich *(Sophia Frederica)*, John Lodge *(Count Alexei)*, Sam Jaffe *(Grand Duke Peter)*, Louise Dresser *(Empress Elizabeth)*, Maria Sieber *(Sophia as a Child)*, C. Aubrey Smith *(Prince August)*, Ruthelma Stevens *(Countess Elizabeth)*, Olive Tell *(Princess Johanna)*, Gavin Gordon *(Gregory Orloff)*, Jameson Thomas *(Lt. Ostvyn)*

d, Josef von Sternberg; w, Manuel Komroff (based on the diary of Catherine the Great); ph, Bert Glennon; ed, Josef von Sternberg; m, Felix Mendelssohn, Peter Ilich Tchaikovsky, Richard Wagner, Josef von Sternberg; art d, Hans Dreier, Peter Ballbusch, Richard Kollorsz; fx, Gordon Jennings; cos, Travis Banton

For lovers of cinema, this film is practically a religious experience. Like Griffith's INTOLERANCE, Von Stroheim's GREED or Ophuls's LOLA MONTES, this is one of those masterpieces which contemporaries just couldn't grip. Josef von Sternberg's name was scarlet in Hollywood after he made this costly, indulgent box-office failure, but his work has been entirely vindicated by the passing of time. A highly romanticized rendering of the life of Catherine the Great, from her childhood through her arranged married to the half-witted Peter (Jaffe) and her later usurping of the throne of Russia, THE SCARLET EMPRESS represents Sternberg's ultimate recreation of a world from his own eccentric mind. Marlene Dietrich exists in this never-never-land like some incredible goddess who manifests various aspects of human personality and desire, from wide-eyed, open-mouthed innocence through cynical worldliness to political ambition. It's a real credit to Dietrich that she's both credible throughout these changes and ironically distanced in a way that she alone could pull off. The crazed intensity of the film pits her aggressive seduction of the entire Russian army versus Peter's rights as heir and his manic desires. Jaffe matches Dietrich in brilliance with his remarkable facial expressions, whispered lunacies and childishly temperamental displays. Stealing much of the film is Louise Dresser as the queen who regrets passing her throne onto Peter and who attempts to prime Catherine to be a baby machine. She plays the role like a pushy, middle-aged matchmaking mother from the windy Midwest, and it works beautifully. Also worthy of mention is the stunningly handsome John Lodge (who later gave up acting for politics) as the emissary who brings the young princess to the Russian court and later becomes her lover. Delivering his suggestive lines through clenched teeth, he makes an ideal object of desire in the lavish Russian court. As his large dark uniform covers the frame during one seduction of Catherine, we get a striking visual rendering of her initiation into court politics.

In terms of visuals, THE SCARLET EMPRESS is a symphony verging on insanity. From the cuckoo clock of the woman who exposes herself to the long roving shots surveying a grotesque wedding dinner, Sternberg paints a rich tapestry of decadence. Most memorable of all is the statuary of deformed gargoyles and slaughtered people decorating most of the palace. But it's not just the sets which tell the story here. The staging, frame composition and camera movement produce moments of great beauty as well. Consider the shot showing a locket Catherine discards as it bounces down from one tree branch to another, or the scene where Catherine is being hairdressed and garbed for her wedding. Or, for a saucier moment, notice how Sternberg tilts his camera slightly after Peter strips one of Catherine's soldier lovers of his rank. As critic Charles Silver has noted, with the men's groins now in frame as well, we realize that the soldier wears other medals which distinguish him in the Russian court. Sternberg loves to clutter his frame, using veils, smoke and shadows to distance us from his characters. A portrait of Catherine lounging on her bed as she fingers a screen drawn around her focuses so intently on the netting that Catherine becomes an inscrutable blur enmeshed in her own reverie. Greatest of all, though, in their combination of photography, lights and editing, are three moments whose emotional impact comes from the filming and not the writing. As a child Catherine is told of the powers and horrors of ruling, and she envisions an incredible montage of torture scenes, climaxing with the unforgettable shot of a man being used as a clapper inside a giant bell. (The dissolve which links this scene to the next is unforgettable.) The finale, meanwhile, done largely without dialogue to the strains of the "The Ride of the Valkyries", builds great momentum as Catherine rides her horse up the palace steps to declare her ultimate triumph. But the scene of scenes is Catherine's wedding to Peter. A frame jammed with crosses; powerful cuts between the pleased Queen, the helpless emissary, the eccentric Peter and the desperate Catherine; the lingering, increasingly tight closeups of Dietrich behind yet another veil—what can one say? See this film on a large screen and in 35 mm if at all possible. The film does justice to the visual possibilities of cinema as few others have done, so do justice to the film when watching it.

SCARLET LETTER, THE

1934 70m bw ★★
Drama G/A
Darmour

Colleen Moore (Hester Prynne), Hardie Albright (Arthur Dimmesdale), Henry B. Walthall (Roger Chillingworth), William Farnum (Gov. Billingham), Alan Hale (Bartholomew Hockins), Virginia Howell (Abigail Crakstone), Cora Sue Collins (Pearl), William Kent (Samson Goodfellow), Betty Blythe, Al C. Henderson

d, Robert Vignola; w, Leonard Fields, David Silverstein (based on the novel by Nathaniel Hawthorne); ph, James S. Brown, Jr.; ed, Charles Harris

Ye olde curiousity, and a big mistake for Moore, trying to make the transistion to talkies and deep dramatic waters. She had built her silent career on being a comedic, perfect moderne, and what looked like a turnaround chance became an epic piece of miscasting. There were numerous other actresses around who could have improved on her—Colbert or even Loretta Young spring to mind. The script, probably to ease the bind the star found herself in, had a dimension of comedy added—god knows why, because LETTER, as you probably know, is an early American classic by Hawthorne about a woman forced to wear a letter on her chest in order to set her apart from the community outraged by her illegitimate pregnancy. Vignola directed with sluggishness and Walthall reprised his role from the 1926 version as Roger Prynne. Speaking of which, that's the version you should concern yourself with seeing—a four-star job starring the immortal Lillian Gish, who was born to play these classical heroines.

SCARLET PIMPERNEL, THE

1935 85m bw ★★★★
Adventure /U
London Films (U.K.)

Leslie Howard (Sir Percy Blakeney), Merle Oberon (Lady Marguerite Blakeney), Raymond Massey (Chauvelin), Nigel Bruce (The Prince of Wales), Bramwell Fletcher (The Priest), Anthony Bushell (Sir Andrew Ffoulkes), Joan Gardner (Suzanne de Tournay), Walter Rilla (Armand St. Just), Mabel Terry-Lewis (Countess de Tournay), O.B. Clarence (Count de Tournay)

p, Alexander Korda; d, Harold Young, Rowland V. Brown (uncredited), Alexander Korda (uncredited); w, S.N. Behrman, Robert E. Sherwood, Arthur Wimperis, Lajos Biro (based on the novel by Baroness Orczy); ph, Harold Rosson; ed, William Hornbeck; m, Arthur Benjamin; prod d, Vincent Korda; fx, Ned Mann; cos, John Armstrong, Oliver Messel

Classic Korda adventure. THE SCARLET PIMPERNEL is based on a romantic novel about deposed French aristocrats, written by the daughter of deposed Hungarian aristocrats; this powerful film secured lasting fame for Leslie Howard.

Sir Percy Blakeney (Howard) is a mild-mannered aristocrat in the court of the Prince of Wales. While large numbers of aristocrats in France are guillotined in the Reign of Terror, Blakeney loses the respect of his wife, Lady Marguerite (Merle Oberon), for being so ineffectual, and he in turn believes that she has been responsible for the arrest of some old friends of hers. Meanwhile, Robespierre (Ernest Milton) and the rest of the French revolutionary government are troubled by a series of daring rescues of condemned nobles, pulled off by the mysterious agency of a man who leaves behind him a small red flower—a pimpernel—for which he comes to be named. The Scarlet Pimpernel adopts a variety of disguises as he saves the gentry from the guillotine. Suspecting English involvement, the French send one of their most capable individuals, Chauvelin (Raymond Massey), to London, ostensibly to serve as ambassador, but really to discover the identity of the Pimpernel. Chauvelin persuades Lady Marguerite to help bait a trap for the Pimpernel, in return for the lives of her arrested friends.

Although directed by Harold Young, the film is much more the work of its producer, Alexander Korda, another transplanted Hungarian (Howard too, for that matter, was the son of Hungarian immigrants). The first director hired was Rowland Brown, director of QUICK MILLIONS, BLOOD MONEY, and author of several respected screenplays. He also had a reputation for getting fired, however, and on the first day of shooting he butted heads with Korda and lost. The producer took over directing for that day, hired Young the next day, and kept a tight rein on him throughout the production. Much of the film was shot outdoors, contrary to the general practice in England at the time. The impressive production resources of Korda's studio are very much in evidence. Korda imported Hal Rosson from Hollywood to shoot the film, and the cinematographer was ecstatic at the varied English skies. Howard gives a wonderful performance, languid and almost effeminate as Sir Percy, and richly deserving of his wife's contempt, but dashing and daring as the Pimpernel. He is supported by Massey in fine form as the villain, and Merle Oberon, as empty as ever.

The novel served as the basis of several silent films, and was remade in 1950 as THE ELUSIVE PIMPERNEL, with David Niven in the title role. The sequel suffers from having been originally shot as a musical; the way it's edited, you can see where the numbers were cut.

The best remembered thing about the original classic adventure is the little bit of doggerel that Howard makes up to throw off suspicion: "They seek him here, they seek him there / The Frenchies seek him everywhere / Is he in Heaven? Is he in Hell? / That damned elusive Pimpernel."

SCARLET STREET

1945 103m bw ★★★★★
Crime /A
Diana

Edward G. Robinson (Christopher Cross), Joan Bennett (Kitty March), Dan Duryea (Johnny Prince), Margaret Lindsay (Millie), Rosalind Ivan (Adele Cross), Jess Barker (Janeway), Arthur Loft (Dellarowe), Samuel S. Hinds (Charles Pringle), Vladimir Sokoloff (Opo Lejon), Charles Kemper (Patcheye)

p, Fritz Lang; d, Fritz Lang; w, Dudley Nichols (based on the novel and play La Chienne by Georges de la Fouchardiere, Mouezy-Eon); ph, Milton Krasner; ed, Arthur Hilton; m, H.J. Salter; art d, Alexander Golitzen, John B. Goodman; fx, John P. Fulton; cos, Travis Banton

Fritz Lang brings his eye for the bleak to this grim but brilliant noir (done before in a 1931 French film, LA CHIENNE, which featured Michel Simon and director Jean Renoir). Robinson, a cashier for a large New York city clothing retailer, spends his spare time painting. At a company banquet held in his honor for two decades of employment, he is characterized as one of those faceless people who make things tick but never receive their due, except at dinners like this. When Robinson leaves the party, he finds Bennett being attacked in the street. He fends off the mugger by using his umbrella as a saber and takes Bennett to have a quiet drink at a bar. Robinson finds this young woman fascinating and can't bear to tell her what he really does for a living, so he lies about it and lets her think he is a renowned artist. Robinson is married to Ivan, a shrewish woman who heckles him

unmercifully for his lack of ambition. It isn't long before he thinks he is in love with Bennett, who continues to lead him on and doesn't make him aware of her relationship with Duryea, a hoodlum living on the edge of legality. Since they reckon that Robinson is a good mark, Bennett and Duryea conspire to have him rent a studio where he can meet Bennett for their trysts. Robinson does that and hauls several of his art works to the studio. Duryea brings in a professional critic, Barker, to look at the work; he is impressed. The cost of maintaining the separate residence is cutting into Robinson's savings, and he is at a loss to figure how to pay for his passion. Duryea removes Robinson's name from the art and puts Bennett's signature on the work. Robinson is annoyed at this, but when the pictures are acknowledged to be the work of a talented person, Robinson takes solace in the fact that someone appreciates him. Robinson begins to embezzle cash from his company, then learns that Ivan's first husband, long thought dead, is actually still alive. That means he can divorce Ivan and marry Bennett. When he races to the studio to tell Bennett the good news, he finds her and Duryea in each other's arms. He watches surreptitiously until Duryea exits, then walks in and has a confrontation with Bennett. When she taunts him with the news that he's been a patsy all along, he does something he (even more, perhaps, than Duryea) will regret the rest of his days.

One of the quintesstial expressions of the noir sensibility, SCARLET STREET does not flinch from the harsher aspects of its sordid story. Robinson, Bennett and Duryea are all in splendid form, and the incredible visuals entrap the feckless Robinson long before plot circumstances do. The paintings for the film were done by John Decker, the artist who palled around with such luminaries as Errol Flynn, John Barrymore, and W.C. Fields.

SCENES FROM A MARRIAGE

1973 168m c ★★★
Drama PG/15
Cinematograph (Sweden)

Liv Ullmann (Marianne), Erland Josephson (Johan), Bibi Andersson (Katarina), Jan Malmsjo (Peter), Anita Wall (Mrs. Palm), Gunnel Lindblom (Eva), Barbro Hiort af Ornas (Mrs. Jacobi)

p, Ingmar Bergman; d, Ingmar Bergman; w, Ingmar Bergman; ph, Sven Nykvist (Eastmancolor); ed, Siv Lundgren; cos, Inger Pehrsson

One of the finest of Ingmar Bergman's late-period films, SCENES FROM A MARRIAGE was in its original form a six-episode, 300-minute Swedish television series; Bergman cut it for US release. Here the director-writer again proves that he is one of film's best, and most theatrical, directors of actresses, giving the inimitable Ullmann a superb script that casts her in the role of an abandoned wife forced to deal with her weak husband Josephson's involvement with a younger woman. Filmed almost entirely in extreme close-ups by the masterful Sven Nykvist, Ullmann's face conveys a variety of expressions reminiscent of Renee Falconetti in Carl Dreyer's silent THE PASSION OF JOAN OF ARC. The film is not without its faults, especially a certain choppiness resulting from the paring of the television version. (Its made-for-television visual content, however, should be admirably suited to videocassette.) There is little plot to speak of—the film's chief force lying in its dramatization of marital trauma—but viewers will be deeply moved by the marvelous acting and the honesty of Bergman's screenplay.

SCHOOL FOR SCOUNDRELS
1960 94m bw   ★★★★
Comedy   /U
Guardsman (U.K.)

Ian Carmichael *(Henry Palfrey)*, Terry-Thomas *(Raymond Delauney)*, Alastair Sim *(Stephen Potter)*, Janette Scott *(April Smith)*, Dennis Price *(Dunstan Dorchester)*, Peter Jones *(Dudley Dorchester)*, Edward Chapman *(Gloatbridge)*, John Le Mesurier *(Headwaiter)*, Irene Handl *(Mrs. Stringer)*, Kynaston Reeves *(General)*

p, Hal E. Chester, Douglas Rankin; d, Robert Hamer; w, Hal E. Chester, Patricia Moyes, Peter Ustinov (based on the books *Theory and Practice Gamesmanship, Same Some Notes on Lifemanship* and *Oneupmanship* by Stephen Potter); ph, Erwin Hillier; ed, Richard Best; m, John Addison; art d, Terence Verity

Reminiscent of HOW TO SUCCEED IN BUSINESS WITHOUT REALLY TRYING, this nonstop British comedy, subtitled "How to Win Without Cheating," is a delicious satire of self-improvement strategies. Henry Palfrey (Ian Carmichael) is one of life's real losers. He'd like to win the heart of April Smith (Janette Scott), but she's already spoken for by boorishly successful Raymond Delauney (Terry-Thomas). Determined to change his fortunes, Henry enrolls in the College of Lifesmanship, run by Stephen Potter (Alastair Sim). After immersing himself in such courses as "woomanship," "partymanship," and "oneupmanship," Henry returns to London to get the best of those who have taken advantage of him in the past, most notably—and hilariously—Delauney. Not surprisingly, Henry also ends up with April. Based on the satirical how-to-get-ahead books written by the real Stephen Potter, SCHOOL FOR SCOUNDRELS features a terrific cast of comic actors who play the whole affair straight, netting laugh after laugh.

SCOTT OF THE ANTARCTIC
1948 111m c   ★★★½
Historical/Adventure/Biography   /U
Ealing/Eagle-Lion (U.K.)

John Mills *(Capt. Robert Falcon Scott)*, Derek Bond *(Capt. L.E.G. Oates)*, Harold Warrender *(Dr. E.A. Wilson)*, James Robertson Justice *(Petty Officer Taffy Evans)*, Reginald Beckwith *(Lt. H.R. Bowers)*, Kenneth More *(Lt. Teddy Evans)*, James McKechnie *(Lt. Atkinson)*, John Gregson *(Petty Officer Green)*, Norman Williams *(Stoker Lashley)*, Barry Letts *(Apsley Cherry-Garrard)*

p, Michael Balcon; d, Charles Frend; w, Walter Meade, Ivor Montagu, Mary Hayley Bell; ph, Jack Cardiff, Osmond Borradaile, Geoffrey Unsworth (Technicolor); ed, Peter Tanner; m, Ralph Vaughan Williams; art d, Arne Akermark, Jim Morahan; fx, Richard Dendy, Norman Ough, Geoffrey Dickinson, Sydney Pearson; cos, Anthony Mendleson

Although Capt. Robert Scott failed to be the first to reach the South Pole (the Norwegians, under Roald Amundsen, won that prize), and although all five members of Scott's expedition died on the way back—as much due to faulty planning as to bad luck and bad weather—Scott has been revered as a hero of the British Empire. This film is a fairly accurate account of his doomed expedition of 1911-1912, opening with Mills (as Scott) trying to raise money for a second expedition after his first failed to reach its goal. He finally gets the money from the British government and sets about organizing his expedition, which will use motor sledges, Siberian ponies, and dogs. From the start, though, misfortunes plague the expedition. One of the motor sledges falls through the ice; the ponies prove too frail for the Antarctic rigors.

Racing to beat Amundsen to the pole, the expedition, led by Mills, loses time due to these and other delays, and slowly its mission becomes more and more impossible. Finally, through superhuman efforts, five men make it to the pole, where they are heartbroken to find Amundsen's Norwegian flag already flying. They set out on the return journey, but more disasters befall them as the weather turns very bad. Two men die along the way as the party makes less and less distance every day. A blizzard confines them to their tent for some days, during which Bond, suffering from frostbite and holding up the expedition, makes the famous statement, "I am just going outside and may be some time," after which he exits the tent into the raging blizzard, never to be seen again. His sacrifice is in vain, though, and the men are still unable to travel. Eventually they all freeze to death in their tent, not to be found until a relief expedition arrives months later. (The men were buried under a cairn of ice on the spot where they died; it is calculated that eventually Scott and his compatriots will break off in an iceberg and drift north.)

SCOTT OF THE ANTARCTIC was a major success and was the royal-commmand performance of 1948. The cast is good, in the stiff-upper-lip style of British heroics, and the actors were partly chosen on the basis of their resemblance to the real participants in the events. Current counsel holds that Scott's party might have made the mere 11 miles back to its base camp but for the public-school pride that prevented its upper-caste members from eating their sled dogs (the method of preventing starvation and subsequent frostbite employed by Amundsen's men), and the actors represent these hidebound attitudes well.

Scott's log, discovered nearly a year after his death, was loaned, along with many of the personal effects of the real-life explorers, to the film's producers by the British Museum, adding to the authenticity of this faithful near-documentary. (Mills carried Scott's own pocket watch and played the gramophone the explorer took with him.) Producer Michael Balcon also recruited the assistance of composer Ralph Vaughan Williams, who was initially reluctant to do the film's score, by deluging the famed composer with photographs of expedition members and memorabilia, finally gaining Vaughan Williams's interest. Eventually, the composer transmuted his fine score into his seventh symphony, the "Sinfonia Antarctica."

Later, actor Christopher Lee—in his first film role of any great moment, before he became Hammer Films's resident horror menace—recounted some of the difficulties of the production, which had the befurred actors sweating in the studio in the heat of summer while choking on artificial snow crafted of salt and plastic, propelled at them by an engine-driven propeller. Much of the filming was done in the Swiss Alps, where Mills had a narrow brush with disaster. The company could not rehearse many scenes beforehand because of the danger of leaving footprints in the snow, so they would simply receive directions, then carry them out. Mills was instructed to pull his sled a short distance, then turn to wave the others along. When he turned back around to keep walking, he fell through a snow bridge and into a chasm hundreds of feet deep. Only the harness attached to the sled and some other actors kept him from meeting the same kind of fate that befell several real Antarctic explorers.

SCOUNDREL, THE
1935 76m bw   ★★★½
Drama/Comedy   /A
Paramount

Noel Coward *(Anthony Mallare)*, Julie Haydon *(Cora Moore)*, Stanley Ridges *(Paul Decker)*, Rosita Moreno *(Carlotta)*, Martha Sleeper *(Julia Vivian)*, Hope Williams *(Margie)*, Ernest Cossart *(Jimmy Clay)*, Everley Gregg *(Mildred Langwiter)*, Eduardo Ciannelli *(Maurice Stern)*, Helen Strickland *(Mrs. Rollinson)*

p, Ben Hecht, Charles MacArthur; d, Ben Hecht, Charles MacArthur; w, Ben Hecht, Charles MacArthur; ph, Lee Garmes; ed, Arthur Ellis; art d, Walter E. Keller

This is a smart-set literati piece starring Noel Coward as a New York publisher who is a marionette master, pulling the strings of everyone around him while scattering *bons mots* like rose petals. He is a charming heel who loves 'em, leaves 'em, and remains the main topic of conversation at swank hotels, various watering spots, and brittle cocktail parties. Julie Haydon, a young author, is in love with Stanley Ridges, and Coward means to break them up and make her his own. Meanwhile, he meets his female counterpart in Hope Williams, who is just as world-weary, cynical, and cunning as he is. Coward gets aboard a Bermuda-bound flight which crashes, killing everyone aboard. But he gets a new lease on life and is allowed to return to this world, never to rest until he finds someone, anyone, who mourns his passing. In the end, Coward makes peace with his Maker and is allowed to have eternal salvation. The metaphysical conclusion left many in the audience wondering what it all meant, and some of the actors were mystified as well. The picture is mostly talk with very little action. Coming off their sensational debut as co-authors-directors-producers of CRIME WITHOUT PASSION, Ben Hecht and Charles MacArthur made the virtually unreleasable ONCE IN A BLUE MOON. (It was held for a year before it was let slip out.) They followed up with this movie, which must be one of the earliest existential films produced. Hecht and MacArthur were not true directors who knew how to make the screen dance with images, and their lack of expertise is evident throughout. Yet the wonderful words spoken by almost everyone in the cast keep the movie afloat. To star in their original work, which owes a bit to the Hecht novel *Fantazius Mallare* and to his well-known *A Jew In Love*, they chose Noel Coward, who was making his talking picture debut after having done a silent juvenile bit in Griffith's HEARTS OF THE WORLD in 1918. This movie was made at the Astoria, Long Island, lot and was a favorite of sophisticates, pseudo-sophisticates, and anyone who could recognize the real-life people upon whom the screenplay was based.

SCROOGE

1970 118m c   ★★★½
Fantasy/Musical   G/U
Waterbury (U.K.)

Albert Finney *(Ebenezer Scrooge)*, Alec Guinness *(Jacob Marley's Ghost)*, Edith Evans *(Ghost of Christmas Past)*, Kenneth More *(Ghost of Christmas Present)*, Laurence Naismith *(Fezziwig)*, Michael Medwin *(Nephew)*, David Collings *(Bob Cratchit)*, Anton Rodgers *(Tom Jenkins)*, Suzanne Neve *(Isabel)*, Frances Cuka *(Mrs. Cratchit)*

p, Robert H. Solo; d, Ronald Neame; w, Leslie Bricusse (based on the novel *A Christmas Carol* by Charles Dickens); ph, Oswald Morris (Panavision, Technicolor); ed, Peter Weatherley; m, Leslie Bricusse; prod d, Terence Marsh; art d, Robert Cartwright; fx, Wally Veevers, Jack Mills; cos, Margaret Furse

At the center of this musical adaptation of Charles Dickens's *A Christmas Carol* is Albert Finney, singing, dancing, and "Bah, humbug"-ing his way through the familiar title role. Guiding him on his journey to moral reawakening are Edith Evans as the Ghost

of Christmas Past, Kenneth More as the Ghost of Christmas Present, and Paddy Stone as the Ghost of Christmas Yet to Come. Director Ronald Neame's well-paced film captures the period beautifully, and the acting is superb, with Finney and Alec Guinness, as Marley's ghost, real standouts. Richard Harris was originally slated to star, then was replaced by Rex Harrison, who also dropped out, and Finney stepped in just three weeks before shooting began. SCROOGE received Oscar nominations for Best Song ("Thank You Very Much"), Best Art Direction, Best Score, and Best Costumes. If you like your Dickens set to music, this (like OLIVER!) is just the ticket; if you prefer the story played a little straighter, see A CHRISTMAS CAROL or the 1935 version of SCROOGE.

SEA HAWK, THE

1940 126m bw   ★★★★★
Romance/Adventure/War   /U
WB

Errol Flynn *(Capt. Geoffrey Thorpe)*, Brenda Marshall *(Donna Maria Alvarez de Cordoba)*, Claude Rains *(Don Jose Alvarez de Cordoba)*, Flora Robson *(Queen Elizabeth)*, Donald Crisp *(Sir John Burleson)*, Henry Daniell *(Lord Wolfingham)*, Alan Hale *(Carl Pitt)*, Una O'Connor *(Martha)*, William Lundigan *(Danny Logan)*, James Stephenson *(Abbott)*

p, Henry Blanke; d, Michael Curtiz; w, Howard Koch, Seton I. Miller; ph, Sol Polito; ed, George Amy; m, Erich Wolfgang Korngold; art d, Anton Grot; fx, Byron Haskin, H.F. Koenekamp; cos, Orry-Kelly

First class, rousing adventure with the inimitable Flynn swashing away, aided by top Curtiz direction and bracing Korngold score. Everything else clicks, too: the cinematography of Sol Polito, terrific Warners production values and a cast of character actors hard to match in any era.

As the film opens, Spain's King Philip II (Montagu Love) instructs his advisors to devise a plan to conquer England and continental Europe. To placate England's Queen Elizabeth (Flora Robson), he sends Don Jose Alvarez de Cordoba (Claude Rains), his crafty ambassador, to soothe the Virgin Queen's fears and disguise Spain's intentions. En route, the Spanish galleon carrying Don Jose and his niece, Donna Maria (Brenda Marshall), is sunk by a British ship commanded by Geoffrey Thorpe (Flynn). The dashing captain takes the indignant ambassador and Maria on board, bringing them safely to England. Despite his fine manners, Thorpe is a dedicated "Sea Hawk," one of a half-dozen British sea captains who foresee war and have been raiding Spanish coastal forts and seizing Philip's treasures to fund a British fleet, all with Elizabeth's unofficial approval. Although Thorpe's gallantry soon wins over Maria, Don Jose intrigues to capture him in Panama, where Spanish forces waylay the Englishman.

Warners lavished a then-staggering $1.7 million on THE SEA HAWK, with gorgeous results. The 31-year-old Flynn, at the peak of his spectacular career, is magnificent in his swashbuckling role; Marshall was never more radiant; Rains is deliciously evil; and Robson makes a wonderfully witty and intelligent Elizabeth. Eschew shortened versions; you want all 127 minutes.

SEA OF LOVE

1989 113m c   ★★★½
Mystery/Thriller   R/18
Martin Bregman

Al Pacino *(Frank Keller)*, Ellen Barkin *(Helen)*, John Goodman *(Sherman)*, Michael Rooker *(Terry)*, William Hickey *(Frank Keller, Sr.)*, Richard Jenkins *(Gruber)*, Paul Calderon *(Serafino)*, Gene Canfield *(Struk)*, Larry Joshua *(Dargan)*, John Spencer *(Lieutenant)*

p, Martin Bregman, Louis A. Stroller; d, Harold Becker; w, Richard Price; ph, Ronnie Taylor (Deluxe Color); ed, David Bretherton; m, Trevor Jones; prod d, John Jay Moore; cos, Betsy Cox

A thriller featuring a mysterious femme fatale, an involving plot, believable characters, and some nice offbeat twists, SEA OF LOVE owes a good deal to Hitchcock, and to such recent efforts as FATAL ATTRACTION and JAGGED EDGE, though it can claim plenty of originality as well. Several men who have responded to the personals in a popular New York magazine have been found murdered in their beds. Twenty-year veteran cop Frank Keller (Al Pacino), a stressed-out borderline alcoholic, and Sherman (John Goodman), a jolly family man, team up to track the killer, planting an ad and "dating" the respondents. Breaking the first rule of investigation, Keller gets deeply involved with one respondent, a tough and savvy single mother (Ellen Barkin). He becomes caught in a web of infatuation and rough, steamy sex, despite signs that she might be the killer. Beyond its slight (though satisfying) plot, SEA OF LOVE's strength lies in the realism of its characterizations. Writer Richard Price is a master at contriving sympathetic, believable characters. His dialogue here, the skewed, elliptical jargon of urban social maneuvering, is dead on. Director Harold Becker (THE ONION FIELD; TAPS) skillfully and unobtrusively supports the drama with just the right lighting, details, and mood. Pacino gives perhaps his best film performance since DOG DAY AFTERNOON; Barkin matches him well as the hard-bitten, voraciously carnal suspect. SEA OF LOVE captures the emotional risk and false hope of the urban singles scene so accurately it's almost painful to watch.

SEA WOLF, THE
1941 100m bw   ★★★★
Drama   /PG
WB

Edward G. Robinson *(Wolf Larsen)*, John Garfield *(George Leach)*, Ida Lupino *(Ruth Webster)*, Alexander Knox *(Humphrey Van Weyden)*, Gene Lockhart *(Dr. Louie Prescott)*, Barry Fitzgerald *(Cooky)*, Stanley Ridges *(Johnson)*, Francis McDonald *(Svenson)*, David Bruce *(Young Sailor)*, Howard da Silva *(Harrison)*

p, Henry Blanke; d, Michael Curtiz; w, Robert Rossen (based on the novel by Jack London); ph, Sol Polito; ed, George Amy; m, Erich Wolfgang Korngold; art d, Anton Grot; fx, Byron Haskin, H.F. Koenekamp

After a ferryboat capsizes in a fog-shrouded sea, the scavenger ship the *Ghost* picks up two survivors: Knox, an author and scholar, and the sad, sick Lupino. Captained by the brutal, callous Robinson—who rules his seagoing fiefdom both by physical might and strategic cunning—the *Ghost* is manned by shanghaied sailors who have been pressed into service with belaying pins and Mickey Finns in the old British way, except for Garfield, a surly young sailor who has signed on to escape the clutches of the law. Robinson refuses to take Knox and Lupino to shore. Instead, he presses them both into service, telling the reluctant but somewhat fascinated Knox, "You're soft, like a woman. This voyage ought to do you a lot of good." To humiliate the scholar, but also to gain his company—for the cruel captain is a secret intellectual who, when closeted in his cabin, reads poetry and philosophy—Robinson makes Knox the cabin boy for the dura-

tion of the voyage. In this servitude, Knox functions as a captive intellectual audience of one for Robinson as the captain elucidates his Nietzschean superman theories. During one of these discourses, Robinson is suddenly seized with a headache that is literally blinding. He attempts to hide this fact, both because he despises weakness and because his condition threatens his absolute control over his crew. Robinson exerts authority over his men more in the manner of a chess master than a ship's master, manipulating them mentally, divining their weaknesses, and dividing them in order to conquer them. As his condition worsens, however, he becomes locked into a relationship of mutual dependence and fascination with Knox which becomes the ultimate test of each man's character.

THE SEA WOLF contains little of the prolixity of Jack London's philosophically oriented novel, yet it is true to the spirit of the book. The megalomania of the ship's master is wonderfully expressed in Edward G. Robinson's fine portrayal of the contemptuous captain. Alexander Knox's reserve makes a perfect foil for Robinson's sneering bombast; in his screen debut, this fine stage actor is beautifully restrained. Ida Lupino, in her role as a loser, gives one of her best screen performances; John Garfield is also fine as her masculine counterpart; and a laudable assemblage of Warner Bros. stock-company character actors ably supports the leads. Required to work a romance into London's all-male work to satisfy studio formula, screenwriter Robert Rossen did very well with the unenviable task. He added the characters played by Garfield and Lupino, which help flesh out the story, substituting for the novel's uncinematic dialogue. Warner's all-purpose director, Michael Curtiz, performed up to par, shooting all the seafaring scenes in studio tanks. THE SEA WOLF earned an Oscar nomination for Best Special Effects. Erich Wolfgang Korngold's score melds well with the excellent sound effects—the constant creaking of timbers under stress, the whipping of ratlines—that create the ambience of a ship at sea.

SEANCE ON A WET AFTERNOON
1964 115m bw   ★★★★
Crime   /A
Beaver/Allied (U.K.)

Kim Stanley *(Myra Savage)*, Richard Attenborough *(Billy Savage)*, Mark Eden *(Charles Clayton)*, Nanette Newman *(Mrs. Clayton)*, Judith Donner *(Amanda Clayton)*, Patrick Magee *(Supt. Walsh)*, Gerald Sim *(Sgt. Beedle)*, Margaret Lacey *(Woman at 1st Seance)*, Maria Kazan *(Other Woman at Seance)*, Lionel Gamlin *(Man at Seances)*

p, Richard Attenborough, Bryan Forbes; d, Bryan Forbes; w, Bryan Forbes (based on the novel by Mark McShane); ph, Gerry Turpin; ed, Derek York; m, John Barry; art d, Ray Simm

In this eerie tale, Myra Savage (Kim Stanley), a medium, claims contact with "the other side" through her late son Arthur, a stillborn child whose death Myra cannot come to accept. Myra's husband, Billy (Richard Attenborough, the British actor who would later direct MAGIC, CRY FREEDOM and GANDHI), does his best to keep her happy, knowing well that she is walking a tightrope between insanity and rationality. He is a weak man and adores Myra, so he can deny her nothing. Myra would like some publicity for her flagging business, so she concocts a plan to have Billy kidnap a wealthy child and collect his ransom. Myra will then offer the services of her psychic powers to the bereaved family and, of course, "find" the child. An atmospheric film, SEANCE ON A WET AFTERNOON succeeds because of Bryan Forbes' excellent direction and the superb performances of both Kim Stanley (in a rare film appearance) and Attenborough (who also produced). While the film can be slow going in spots, Stanley's portrayal of the emotionally unfit Myra Savage is riveting as she gradually loses her grip on reality and slips into a dark psychological abyss.

SEARCH, THE

1948 105m bw ★★★★
Drama /U
Prasens

Montgomery Clift *(Ralph Stevenson)*, Aline MacMahon *(Mrs. Murray)*, Jarmila Novotna *(Mrs. Malik)*, Wendell Corey *(Jerry Fisher)*, Ivan Jandl *(Karel Malik)*, Mary Patton *(Mrs. Fisher)*, Ewart G. Morrison *(Mr. Crookes)*, William Rogers *(Tom Fisher)*, Leopold Borkowski *(Joel Makowsky)*, Claude Gambier *(Raoul Dubois)*

p, Lazar Wechsler; d, Fred Zinnemann; w, Richard Schweizer, David Wechsler, Paul Jarrico; ph, Emil Berna; ed, Hermann Haller; m, Robert Blum

Clift was making his first movie, RED RIVER, when he was approached by Zinnemann to read the first draft of the script by Peter Viertel, and he liked it enough to commit to making THE SEARCH (which, as it turned out, was released before RED RIVER). When Swiss producer Wechsler hired his son to help rewrite the screenplay, Clift became angered and began to substitute his own words for those in the script. Attorneys were called in to mediate, and, in the end, the younger Wechsler and co-author Schweizer won an Oscar for a screenplay that contained many of Clift's words. As THE SEARCH begins, children who have been left orphaned and homeless by WWII have been taken to a camp for displaced children in Germany. Among them is Jandl, a 9-year-old Czech who hasn't seen his mother since he was torn from her arms at the age of 5. He is wary of everyone at the camp; his terrible experiences have left him an amnesiac. All he can do is mutter "I don't know." Jandl and some of the others fear that they will be harmed, so they escape from a Red Cross ambulance. (Some of them recall how their parents were ferried to gas chambers on trains and in buses.) When Jandl's hat is later found floating in the river, the authorities believe he must have drowned, but he is actually living like a frightened animal in the burnt-out houses of the city, foraging for food in trash cans. He is nearly starved when Clift, an American soldier, finds him and takes him home. Jandl is hostile, fearful, and makes attempts to leave, but Clift begins to convince the boy of his good intentions, injecting as bit of humor as he teaches him some English. (A pretty girl, for example, is a "tomato.") Clift is very patient and relaxed with the boy, and they are soon like father and son. Clift attempts to trace Jandl's history with the help of his pal Corey, but it's a brick wall. Meanwhile, Jandl's mother, Novotna, continues her search of several years for the boy, visiting various camps for displaced children. When she arrives at the one where Jandl had been and is told that he has drowned, she won't accept his death without proof, so she continues her search. Clift would like to arrange to take Jandl to the US with him because he presumes the boy has no living relatives. He is about to go home, so he arranges to place Jandl in the camp until he can finish the paperwork needed to officially adopt the boy. MacMahon, a worker at the camp, recognizes the boy from Novotna's description, locates her, and mother and son are soon reunited.

The rather saccharine ending mars the believablity of the plot, and audiences might have liked it better if Novotna's character were not so wonderful and Jandl had gotten a new lease on life by going to the US with Clift. Zinnemann and Clift received Oscar nominations and Jandl won a special juvenile Oscar for

his haunting portrayal of the tragic child. Jandl was discovered singing with a youth choir in Prague, and, after this picture, it was just assumed that he would stay in films, but his parents refused, and he disappeared from sight. Zinnemann had been with MGM, but they dropped his contract while he was shooting this film, so he signed with RKO. However, after the picture was released, Zinnemann's star again rose, so they re-signed him for a great deal more money. THE SEARCH was shot entirely in the American Occupied Zone of Germany, the first movie to be made there after the war. With THE SEARCH and RED RIVER released the same year, Clift became a huge star and was given a *Life* magazine cover. Only 27, he received $75,000 for this film. He brought along his friend and mentor, Mira Rostova, who stood behind the camera and gave her approval on each scene. Zinnemann objected to this, so she stayed away but spent almost every night before shooting going over each nuance of the next day's pages. Only four professional actors appeared in the movie: Clift, who was under contract to Howard Hawks; Corey, on loan from Hal Wallis; Novotna, an opera star at the Met; and MacMahon. The others were locals, and their unfamiliar presence lent an air of credibility to the project. This superior movie made the world aware of the plight of these children and money poured in to the UNRRA to help their plight.

SEARCHERS, THE

1956 119m c ★★★★★
Western /PG
WB

John Wayne *(Ethan Edwards)*, Jeffrey Hunter *(Martin Pawley)*, Vera Miles *(Laurie Jorgensen)*, Ward Bond *(Capt. Rev. Samuel Clayton)*, Natalie Wood *(Debbie Edwards)*, John Qualen *(Lars Jorgensen)*, Olive Carey *(Mrs. Jorgensen)*, Henry Brandon *(Chief Scar)*, Ken Curtis *(Charlie McCorry)*, Harry Carey, Jr. *(Brad Jorgensen)*

p, Merian C. Cooper, C.V. Whitney; d, John Ford; w, Frank S. Nugent (based on the novel by Alan LeMay); ph, Winton C. Hoch (VistaVision, Technicolor); ed, Jack Murray; m, Max Steiner; art d, Frank Hotaling, James Basevi; fx, George Brown; cos, Frank Beetson, Ann Peck

"What makes a man to wander?/What makes a man to roam?/What makes a man leave bed and board and turn his back on home?/Ride away, ride away, ride away."

This sad and beautiful song accompanies the opening credits of what may be the finest and most ambitious film from director John Ford, America's premier poet of the Western. Part of what makes this classic film so remarkable is that these questions are never answered directly—an oddity for a product of Hollywood where loose ends are rarely allowed. This is the ultimate cult film for the new Hollywood. It is quoted and alluded to in numerous films such as HARDCORE, TAXI DRIVER, CLOSE ENCOUNTERS OF THE THIRD KIND, and STAR WARS.

As THE SEARCHERS begins, we hear the extraordinarily beautiful strains of Max Steiner's score over darkness. A cabin door opens to reveal the harsh beauty of the arid Monument Valley in the distance. The silhouette of a frontier woman moves into the doorway. Far beyond we see a tiny figure on horseback approaching. "Ethan?" queries the woman uncertainly. The figure dismounts and walks toward the house. The woman is Martha Edwards (Dorothy Jordan), the wife of Ethan's brother. She is joined on the porch by her husband, Aaron (Walter Coy), their teenaged daughter, Lucy (Pippa Scott), 10-year-old Debbie (Lana Wood), and teenaged Ben (Robert Lyden). Ethan's clothes are filthy and he wears a faded Confederate coat. The children chant "Uncle Ethan! Uncle Ethan!" Ethan Edwards has finally come home—three years after the end of the Civil War.

John Wayne gives the performance of his career as Ethan Edwards, one of the most intriguing characters the American cinema has given us. Ethan is a mysterious obsessive man who rides in from the wastelands of Monument Valley into a small frontier farm settled by his brother years earlier. He has been missing since the end of the Civil War in which he fought for the Confederacy. He never turned up at the surrender to give up his sword and saber. He is also inexplicably carrying a large quantity of gold and, in the words of the local captain of the Texas Rangers, Reverend Samuel Clayton (Ward Bond), Ethan "fits a lot of descriptions."

The last family member to arrive is Martin Pawley (Jeffrey Hunter). Now nearly grown, Martin was saved years ago by Ethan when his parents were slaughtered by Indians. Ethan left him in the care of Aaron, who has raised him as his own son, but because Martin is one-eighth Cherokee, Ethan now treats him as a boarder rather than as one of the family.

The tranquility of the Edwards' lives is shattered when the local Commanche tribe goes on the warpath. Most of the men are lured away from the farm and the Edwards' farm is attacked. Most of the family is brutally murdered and the two daughters are abducted. The men form a search party and go off in hot pursuit. The ravaged body of the older girl is found and buried while the search for Debbie continues. When the winter snows come, most of the men turn back. Ethan is undaunted by this temporary setback. He and Martin resolve to continue the search and they do—for seven years. As the months drag on, Martin is amazed by Ethan's knowledge of the Indians' ways and his ability to read their signs and speak their language, but comes to realize that his guide is also a fanatical racist who intends to kill Debbie when they find her because she has become a "squaw."

THE SEARCHERS is an extremely rich film that continues to reveal new nuances with each viewing. The genre's traditional opposition between "Civilization" and "Wilderness" has rarely been as powerfully represented dramatically or visually. Ethan sees himself as an agent of civilization but his skills ally him with the forces of wilderness. He can find nowhere where he can be at peace and accepted. His difficulty in accepting a Native American as part of his family mirrors America's tensions regarding civil rights and integration in the 1950s. In a genre that has often be justly condemned for its racism, THE SEARCHERS—while hardly politically correct by modern standards—was a major breakthrough for Ford, Wayne, and the genre. The traditional Western hero and the Cavalry is shown in an unusually critical light. Furthermore the Native American point of view is considered for a change. By balancing points of view, Ford deepens and informs our understanding of the story. Equally well managed is the film's balance of drama and humor. THE SEARCHERS is essentially a tragedy, and without its humorous passages the film would have been almost too grim to bear (as was Alan LeMay's novel). The humor grows out of and illuminates character; even the hard-driven Ethan reveals a sense of irony and wit.

Ford's poetic visual sensibility has never been more richly demonstrated. The film provides an opportunity for numerous striking portraits of John Wayne set against the western vistas in color and widescreen. If you had to pick an ultimate Western still, it would probably come from this film. THE SEARCHERS is also that rare sound film in which more is revealed through facial expression, physical stance, and subtle gesture than through dialogue. Deep and complex insights into characters are all beautifully conveyed by body language. All in all, this is about

as good as Hollywood filmmaking gets. A deeply emotional experience that is also a grand entertainment, THE SEARCHERS is a true American masterpiece.

SECONDS
1966 106m bw   ★★★
Mystery/Thriller   /X
Paramount

Rock Hudson (Antiochus "Tony" Wilson), Salome Jens (Nora Marcus), John Randolph (Arthur Hamilton), Will Geer (Old Man), Jeff Corey (Mr. Ruby), Richard Anderson (Dr. Innes), Murray Hamilton (Charlie Evans), Karl Swenson (Dr. Morris), Khigh Dhiegh (Davalo), Frances Reid (Emily Hamilton)

p, Edward Lewis; d, John Frankenheimer; w, Lewis John Carlino (based on the novel Seconds by David Ely); ph, James Wong Howe; ed, Ferris Webster, David Webster; m, Jerry Goldsmith; art d, Ted Haworth

This film was savaged by critics at the time of its release but is not without its redeeming factors. Frankenheimer's direction is self-conscious and flashy, but the narrative is undeniably absorbing.

A middle-aged banker, Randolph, is followed through Grand Central Station in New York. He is making the routine trip to his Scarsdale home and his boring, aging wife, Reid. An unknown man slips him a note at the station. He rides home, Reid picks him up in the family car, and they exchange banalities. Randolph later receives a call from Hamilton, a man who he thought was dead. Hamilton's call takes Randolph to the headquarters of a mysterious company headed by Geer, an old, sly Southerner. For the sum of $32,000, this company offers select individuals a second chance in life. They will arrange for an individual's "death," make certain that any survivors are taken care of, have a corpse that has been either burned or disfigured enough so identification will prove impossible, and settle the prospect into a new life, after suitable plastic surgery has altered the person's appearance. Corey is the guidance counselor who leads Randolph through until he becomes, through the miracle of medical science, a taller, trimmer Hudson. Hudson emerges as a painter with a Malibu, California home, after Randolph is conveniently burned beyond recognition in a hotel fire. Hudson moves into the house with Addy as his valet, to help him adjust to the new surroundings, and a horde of paintings (executed by artist John Hunter) provided by Geer's company. He is soon part of the local scene. Hudson finds it difficult to step outside the house wearing his new face and persona. He meets Jens on the beach, not knowing that she has been sent by the company. With Jens and Addy to prod him, Hudson tosses a party to meet everyone in the neighborhood. It turns into a disaster as he drinks too much. Now he learns that all of the guests, who have been chosen by Addy, are also "seconds" and they are fearful that Hudson will betray the secret. Hudson returns to Scarsdale to see Reid, tells her that he's an old pal of Randolph's and he is surprised to see that her grieving is over, though she is content to remain in widow's weeds. Hudson returns to the headquarters of the company and says that he is uncomfortable in his new face and body and he wants to be restored to the boring, though contented, life he had before. He is told that in order to have that happen, he must recommend another client, the way Hamilton did in reel one.

The film has a fascinating premise, and Hudson gives one of his best performances. Howe's Oscar-nominated camerawork is somewhat mannered, no doubt as a result of Frankenheimer's prodding. Howe was 66 at the time and had been working in movies since 1923, when he was DeMille's "slate boy" at this very same studio. The main problem with the picture is the failure to motivate Hudson's disappointment with his new existence. SECONDS was treated so poorly at the Cannes Film Festival that Frankenheimer, who was shooting GRAND PRIX nearby, refused to attend, leaving Hudson to face the blistering press alone.

SECRET AGENT

1936   83m   bw   ★★★½
Spy   /U
Gaumont   (U.K.)

Madeleine Carroll (Elsa Carrington), John Gielgud (Edgar Brodie/Richard Ashenden), Peter Lorre (The General), Robert Young (Robert Marvin), Percy Marmont (Caypor), Florence Kahn (Mrs. Caypor), Lilli Palmer (Lilli), Charles Carson ("R"), Michel Saint-Denis (Coachman), Andreas Malandrinos (Manager)

p, Michael Balcon, Ivor Montagu; d, Alfred Hitchcock; w, Charles Bennett, Ian Hay, Jesse Lasky, Jr., Alma Reville (based on the play by Campbell Dixon, from the stories "Triton" and "The Hairless Mexican" in the book Ashenden by W. Somerset Maugham); ph, Bernard Knowles; ed, Charles Frend; cos, Joe Strassner

One of a string of British espionage thrillers Hitchcock directed in the mid-1930s (THE 39 STEPS preceded it in 1935 and SABOTAGE followed in 1936), this one begins in England, 1916, with the funeral of war hero and famed novelist Edgar Brodie (Gielgud). The funeral is a ruse, however, with Brodie still very much alive and in the service of British Intelligence. He is given a new identity, Richard Ashenden, and sent to Switzerland to terminate an enemy agent—although no one knows the identity or description of the agent. Also assigned to the mission are agents Elsa Carrington (Carroll), who is undercover as Ashenden's wife, and The General (Lorre), a demented, sexually charged, professional killer, and together they chase through the Swiss Alps to carry out their operation. SECRET AGENT bursts with not-so-hidden sexual innuendos and a heavy dose of comic dialogue, as well as Lorre's unrestrained lunatic comic performance. Based on two Somerset Maugham stories (for the espionage angle) and a Campbell Dixon play (for the romance), SECRET AGENT did not perform at the box office as well as Hitchcock had hoped. Although the director has cited this film among his favorites, he felt that its fault was in having a main character with whom the audience could not identify. London-based animator Len Lye (who had, in 1934, invented a technique for painting directly on film) had created, for the climactic train crash scene, a piece of brightly colored film which was to make it appear as if the film itself had burst into flames. Proving too much of a distraction, the effect was eliminated in the film's preview screenings.

SECRET LIFE OF WALTER MITTY, THE

1947   105m   c   ★★★★
Fantasy/Comedy   /U
Goldwyn

Danny Kaye (Walter Mitty), Virginia Mayo (Rosalind van Hoorn), Boris Karloff (Dr. Hugo Hollingshead), Fay Bainter (Mrs. Mitty), Ann Rutherford (Gertrude Griswold), Thurston Hall (Bruce Pierce), Konstantin Shayne (Peter van Hoorn), Florence Bates (Mrs. Griswold), Gordon Jones (Tubby Wadsworth), Reginald Denny (RAF Colonel)

p, Samuel Goldwyn; d, Norman Z. McLeod; w, Ken Englund, Everett Freeman (based on the story by James Thurber); ph, Lee Garmes (Technicolor); ed, Monica Collingwood; m, David Raksin; art d, George Jenkins, Perry Ferguson; fx, John P. Fulton; cos, Irene Sharaff

Though James Thurber offered to give producer Sam Goldwyn $10,000 not to film his classic short story, the rights to which Goldwyn had purchased, THE SECRET LIFE OF WALTER MITTY is still an outstanding production and undoubtedly the best film Kaye ever made. Thurber's tale about a middle-aged man who escapes reality by imagining himself in all sorts of heroic situations doesn't lose much in the film adaptation. Kaye, who is hilarious throughout, is single but still henpecked by his dominating mother Bainter and by his grasping fiancee, Rutherford. He works as proofreader for a company that publishes pulp magazines full of crime stories that terrify the timid Kaye. In an uproariously funny scene, the publisher, Hall, storms into Kaye's office and holds up a mock-up cover of a forthcoming magazine edition, showing someone being brutally attacked in lurid color. Kaye lets out a little scream of terror just looking at the graphic gore, but Hall goes on to complain that the cover isn't gory enough. "I don't want this fellow merely killed," says Hall. "I want him stabbed from the front, from the side, from the back!" Like Bainter and Rutherford, Hall acts as another oppressor in the milquetoast's miserable life. Kaye is forever running errands for Bainter, and in Rutherford's pushy presence he is only able to stammer and awkwardly stumble about. To escape his predicament, Kaye envisions himself a confident, heroic figure in a number of very funny sequences. These imaginary adventures are sprinkled throughout the film, supporting a main plot that involves spies and jewel thieves. Kaye's zany imagination thrusts him into the role of a sea captain bravely navigating his ship through a typhoon, a fast-drawing western gunslinger called "The Perth Amboy Kid," a gambler on a Mississippi riverboat who bets against the villain to save the honor of a southern belle, a brilliant surgeon performing an incredible operation to save the life of a patient, and a dashing pilot in the RAF who shoots down countless Nazi fighters. As a rather effeminate fashion designer, Anatole of Paris, he presents one of his famous sing-song numbers.

In all his daydreams, the same luscious blonde heroine appears, leggy Mayo, the girl with whom Kaye is subconsciously seeking to spend the rest of his humdrum life. Lo and behold, Mayo appears in Kaye's real life, asking the confused proofreader to help her escape a villainous character who has been following her. Mayo explains that she is an heiress and that the fabulous jewels she has inherited, entrusted to her uncle, Denny, are now being sought by an infamous gang of international jewel thieves. Kaye aids Mayo and soon the thieves are chasing him around Manhattan and into the country. At one point his chief antagonist even climbs the skyscraper in which Kaye works and appears outside his office window. With danger lurking everywhere, Kaye's offbeat behavior becomes so strange that Bainter and Rutherford convince Hall that Kaye is going crazy, and the dreamer is taken to psychiatrist Karloff. The psychiatrist, however, turns out to be the head of the jewel thieves, and, to throw Kaye off the track, Karloff convinces his "patient" that his recent experiences with Mayo have been nothing more than his usual fantasies. Believing Karloff, Kaye goes ahead with his plans to marry Rutherford. But at the altar Kaye reaches into his pocket and finds a memento that proves Mayo is part of his real life. Rushing to Denny's estate, Kaye manages to round up Karloff and gang and win the heart of his blonde goddess.

Though it slips into slapstick toward the end, THE SECRET LIFE OF WALTER MITTY is enjoyable and presents more genuinely funny scenes than most comedies. Goldwyn sank more than $3 million into this sumptuous showcase for Kaye, parading his statuesque Goldwyn Girls through some of the star's big musical numbers. Mayo is alluring, Bainter is terrific as the overbearing mom, and Hall stands out as the ghoulish publisher. Without the aid of makeup, Karloff also does a great burlesque of himself as the monster from FRANKENSTEIN. And through- out the film there is that memorable sound of Kaye's imaginary life-saving machine—"pucketa, pucketa, pucketa."

SECRET OF NIMH, THE

1982 82m c   ★★★
Animated/Children's   G/U
MGM-UA

VOICES OF: Derek Jacobi (Nicodemus), Elizabeth Hartman (Mrs. Brisby), Arthur Malet (Ages), Dom DeLuise (Jeremy), Hermione Baddeley (Auntie Shrew), John Carradine (Great Owl), Peter Strauss (Justin), Paul Shenar (Jennar), Tom Hattan (Farmer Fitzgibbons), Shannen Doherty (Teresa)

p, Don Bluth, Gary Goldman, John Pomeroy; d, Don Bluth; w, Don Bluth, Gary Goldman, John Pomeroy, Will Finn (based on the novel Mrs. Frisby and the Rats of N.I.M.H. by Robert C. O'Brien); ph, Joe Jiuliano, Charles Warren, Jeff Mellquist (Technicolor); ed, Jeffrey Patch; m, Jerry Goldsmith; fx, D.A. Lanpher, Tom Hush

This superbly animated (but weakly scripted) tale was produced by Don Bluth, who left Disney Studios when he became dissat- isfied with the quality of their animated films in the 1970s, taking a dozen of Disney's best animators with him. The result is a return to the lush, finely detailed animation seen in the best Disney features. This is the story of a mother mouse's desperate attempt to move her family to a new location before they are killed by the farmer who is soon to plow his field. Although hindered by her son's illness, the mother mouse gets help from some escaped laboratory rats with superior intelligence. Among the actors who lend their vocal talents to the proceedings are Dom DeLuise and the fine British stage actor Derek Jacobi.

SECRETS OF WOMEN

(KVINNORS VANTAN)
1952 114m bw   ★★★½
Drama/Comedy
Svensk   (Sweden)

Anita Bjork (Rakel), Karl-Arne Holmsten (Eugen Lobelius), Jarl Kulle (Kaj), Maj-Britt Nilsson (Marta), Eva Dahlbeck (Karin), Gunnar Bjornstrand (Fredrik Lobelius), Birger Malmsten (Martin), Gerd Andersson (Maj), Bjorn Bjelvenstam (Henrik), Aino Taube (Annette)

p, Allan Ekelund; d, Ingmar Bergman; w, Ingmar Bergman; ph, Gunnar Fischer; ed, Oscar Rosander; m, Erik Nordgren; art d, Nils Svenwall

This mostly light-hearted comedy, made by Ingmar Bergman in 1952 but not released in the US until nine years later, was written by the director during what he considered a dark time in his life—which seems strange, considering how much fun the film is. Divided into three parts, SECRETS OF WOMEN is told in flashback as the wives of the Lobelius brothers converse about past romantic experiences. The first section (based on a Bergman play) relates the tale of Rakel's (Anita Bjork) infidelity with an old lover, the second depicts Marta's (Maj-Britt Nilsson) Parisian affair and subsequent marriage to Martin (Birger Malmsten), and

the last takes place in a broken elevator that strands Karin (Eva Dahlbeck) and husband Fredrik (Gunnar Bjornstrand). At the conclusion of these three stories, a fourth Lobelius wife (Aino Taube) decides to keep her story to herself. Although this is one of several well-received comedies that Bergman somewhat grudgingly turned out at the request of the Swedish film industry in the 1950s, it still shows a deliberate attempt on the director's part to advance his cinematic style. In the elevator sequence especially, Bergman, under the influence of Alfred Hitchcock, tried primarily to let images tell his story, keeping the dialogue to a minimum.

SEDUCED AND ABANDONED

(SEDUITE ET ABANDONNEE)
1964 118m bw   ★★
Drama   /X
Lux/Ultra/Vides/C.C.F. Lux   (France/Italy)

Stefania Sandrelli (Agnese Ascalone), Aldo Puglisi (Peppino Califano), Saro Urzi (Vincenzo Ascalone), Lando Buzzanca (Anto- nio Ascalone), Leopoldo Trieste (Baron Rizieri), Rocco D'Assunta (Orlando Califano), Lola Braccini (Amalia Califano), Paola Biggio (Matilde Ascalone), Umberto Spadaro (Cousin Ascalone), Oreste Palella (Police Chief Potenza)

p, Franco Cristaldi; d, Pietro Germi; w, Pietro Germi, Luciano Vincenzoni, Agenore Incrocci, Furio Scarpelli (based on an original idea by Germi and Vincenzoni); ph, Aiace Parolin; ed, Roberto Cinquini; m, Carlo Rustichelli; art d, Carlo Egidi; cos, Angela Sammacciccia, Carlo Egidi

Complications aplenty arise when Puglisi seduces Sandrelli, the 15-year-old sister of his fiancee, Biggio. The girls' father, Urzi, puts an end to Peppino's engagement to his older daughter and demands that the unscrupulous Lothario marry the younger, when it is revealed that she is pregnant. When Puglisi has other ideas, the angry father decides to do away with this plague on his kin, but the police intercede and present Puglisi with their own ultimatum: marry Sandrelli or serve time for seducing a minor. Reluctantly, Puglisi chooses a figurative ball and chain over a literal one, although Sandrelli has some thoughts of her own about the matter. Meanwhile, Urzi has found a new fiancee for Biggio—the ne'er-do-well Trieste. Mixing fantasy and reality, shifting from present to past, and moving in and out of his characters' minds, director Germi (whose script for DIVORCE ITALIAN STYLE was nominated for an Oscar) creates an occasionally amusing but generally undistinguished slice of Si- cilian life here.

SEDUCTION OF JOE TYNAN, THE

1979 107m c   ★★★½
Political   R/15
Universal

Alan Alda (Joe Tynan), Barbara Harris (Ellie), Meryl Streep (Karen Traynor), Rip Torn (Sen. Kittner), Melvyn Douglas (Sen. Birney), Charles Kimbrough (Francis), Carrie Nye (Aldena Kittner), Michael Higgins (Sen. Pardew), Blanche Baker (Janet), Adam Ross (Paul Tynan)

p, Martin Bregman; d, Jerry Schatzberg; w, Alan Alda; ph, Adam Holender (Technicolor); ed, Evan Lottman; m, Bill Conti; art d, David Chapman; cos, Jo Ynocencio

A fine political drama with lots of comedy on the order of THE CANDIDATE, THE BEST MAN, and several others in the genre. Alda proved himself a good writer with this intelligent and observant screenplay loosely based on the supposed life of Ted

Kennedy. The seduction of the title refers to the corrupting potential of political power. Alda is a liberal senator married to Harris, with two children, Ross and Baker. Harris hates being in the limelight, while Alda revels in it. His basically nice nature is seen to change as he rises higher in the national scene. He dallies with labor lawyer Streep but recognizes the affair as basically dishonest and returns to Harris. The performances are fine. Harris especially is sensational, conveying more with a look than many actresses can with 10 pages of dialogue. Torn is vigorous and compelling as a powerful lawmaker. Douglas, who made a career out of portraying public figures near the end of his life (he was the President's adviser in BEING THERE), is superb as a man who's seen his best days and is now looking forward bleakly to his last. The film delves beneath the phony smiles, hearty handshakes, and false sentiment that politics engenders. Viewers may never believe a candidate's speech again. The language and some of the sex are too raw for kids' viewing.

SEDUCTION OF MIMI, THE
(MIMI METALLURGICO FERITO NELL'ONORE)

1972 92m c ★★★½

Drama R/

Vera/Euro-International (Italy)

Giancarlo Giannini (Carmelo "Mimi" Mardocheco), Mariangela Melato (Fiore), Agostina Belli (Rosalia), Elena Fiore (Signora Finocchiaro), Turi Ferro (Tricarico), Agostina Belli, Luigi Diberti, Tuccio Musumeci, Ignazio Pappalardo, Rosaria Rapisarda

p, Daniele Senatore, Romano Cardarelli; d, Lina Wertmuller; w, Lina Wertmuller; ph, Dario Di Palma; ed, Franco Fraticelli; m, Piero Piccioni

This early film by Lina Wertmuller earned her the Best Director prize at the Cannes Film Festival and stars Giancarlo Giannini as a Sicilian metallurgist named Mimi. After refusing to vote for the Mafia candidate in a local election, Mimi loses his factory job and decides to head north for work. Although professing to be communist, he is eager to get rich, enjoy a life of luxury, and step on his fellow workers. Leaving behind his wife, Rosalia (Agostina Belli), whom he cruelly dominates and castigates for her infertility, Mimi finds work in Turin. There, he falls in love with Fiore (Mariangela Melato), a virgin anarchist who bears him a child. Mimi's idyllic life in the north is sabotaged, however, by the menacing Mafia-controlled authorities who transfer him back to Sicily. A clever examination of the bonds between sexual and political power, and the differences between the "civilized" northern Italians and the "barbaric" southerners, Wertmuller's film comes to life through Giannini's bravura performance; a macho brute and philistine, his Mimi is still a sympathetic character, more victim than victimizer. The videocassette is dubbed in English though, as in LOVE AND ANARCHY, the image appears to have been squeezed into the television format.

SEMI-TOUGH

1977 108m c ★★★

Comedy/Sports R/15

UA

Burt Reynolds (Billy Clyde Puckett), Kris Kristofferson (Shake Tiller), Jill Clayburgh (Barbara Jane Bookman), Robert Preston (Big Ed Bookman), Bert Convy (Friedrich Bismark), Roger E. Mosley (Puddin), Lotte Lenya (Clara Pelf), Richard Masur (Phillip Hooper), Carl Weathers (Dreamer Tatum), Brian Dennehy (T.J. Lambert)

p, David Merrick; d, Michael Ritchie; w, Walter Bernstein (based on the novel by Dan Jenkins); ph, Charles Rosher, Jr.; ed, Richard A. Harris; m, Jerry Fielding; prod d, Walter Scott Herndon; cos, Theoni V. Aldredge

Set against the backdrop of professional football, SEMI-TOUGH is both a three-cornered romantic comedy and a scathing satire of self-help movements. Reynolds and Kristofferson are teammates on a fictitious Super Bowl-bound Miami football team owned by Preston, a recent convert to BEAT, the est-like way to a better life "gurued" by Convy. Recently returned from Africa, Preston's twice-divorced daughter, Clayburgh, reappraises her longtime friends, Reynolds and Kristofferson, and finds the latter, whom Convy has led to BEAT, not only a changed man but a suitable fiance. The trouble is Reynolds is in love with Clayburgh; however, being a resourceful guy, he manages to poke a hole in Convy's BEAT bubble, pull off some Super Bowl magic, and make sure that the right guy ends up with Preston's daughter. Based on a book by Dan Jenkins, SEMI-TOUGH is periodically funny and frequently on target in its satire, and it boasts a strong performance from Reynolds (who also starred in the football-themed THE LONGEST YARD). Jenkins's novel did not include the self-help lampooning, which was introduced into the story by screenwriter Bernstein at the insistence of director Ritchie (THE BAD NEWS BEARS; DOWNHILL RACER). Several sportscasters and former football players appear in the film in character or as themselves, including Joe Kapp, Carl Weathers (ROCKY), Paul Hornung, and Lindsay Nelson.

SENATOR WAS INDISCREET, THE

1947 81m bw ★★★½

Political/Comedy

Universal

William Powell (Sen. Melvin G. Ashton), Ella Raines (Poppy McNaughton), Peter Lind Hayes (Lew Gibson), Arleen Whelan (Valerie Shepherd), Ray Collins (Houlihan), Allen Jenkins (Farrell), Charles D. Brown (Dinty), Hans Conried (Waiter), Whit Bissell (Oakes), Norma Varden (Woman at Banquet)

p, Nunnally Johnson; d, George S. Kaufman; w, Charles MacArthur (based on a story by Edwin Lanham); ph, William Mellor; ed, Sherman A. Rose; m, Daniele Amfitheatrof; art d, Bernard Herzbrun, Boris Levin; fx, David S. Horsley; cos, Grace Houston

This broad political satire, George S. Kaufman's directorial debut, is a fine film, but it would have been a much better one had its barbs been aimed at more specific targets. Moreover, the jokes might have worked better had Kaufman contributed to the writing. Myrna Loy and William Powell make their last appearance together here, though her role is just a small cameo. Powell is a pompous boor of a senator who is too dumb to be true. After two decades of fooling his constituents, Powell thinks that he might make a fine President, so he begins a campaign for the nation's highest office, with Hayes as his press agent. The political bosses of his party, led by Brown, would like Powell to go away, but Powell has an ace up his sleeve, a diary he's kept over the years that will ruin the party if it ever gets into a journalist's hands. Powell makes a slew of nonsensical campaign promises, including a three-day work week with eight days' pay, Harvard educations for all Americans, and the introduction of malted milk-producing cows. When Powell's hot diary suddenly disappears, politicians begin booking flights to the Antarctic, Patagonia, and anywhere else that doesn't have an extradition treaty with the US. Hayes finds the diary and can't make up his mind about what to do with it. If he gives it back to Powell, he'll be doing the country a disservice. If he gives it to his sweetheart, newspaperwoman Raines, Hayes will be out of a job when the spit hits the fan. Choosing to do the decent thing, Hayes hands the diary to Raines, who prints the truth. Predictably, all the party members flee, with Powell and his wife, Loy, leading the way.

Among the funny scenes to be found in the film is one in which candidate Powell is inducted into an Indian tribe by Cody. A few years after the release of THE SENATOR WAS INDISCREET, the studios began taking bigger risks with political comedies, pulling fewer punches and leaving less doubt as to the identities of those lampooned.

SEPARATE TABLES

1958 98m bw   ★★★★½
Drama   /PG
Clifton/Joanna

Deborah Kerr *(Sibyl Railton-Bell)*, Rita Hayworth *(Ann Shankland)*, David Niven *(Maj. Pollack)*, Wendy Hiller *(Miss Pat Cooper)*, Burt Lancaster *(John Malcolm)*, Gladys Cooper *(Mrs. Railton-Bell)*, Cathleen Nesbitt *(Lady Matheson)*, Felix Aylmer *(Mr. Fowler)*, Rod Taylor *(Charles)*, Audrey Dalton *(Jean)*

p, Harold Hecht; d, Delbert Mann; w, Terence Rattigan, John Gay (based on the play by Rattigan); ph, Charles Lang; ed, Marjorie Fowler, Charles Ennis; m, David Raksin; prod d, Harry Horner; art d, Edward Carrere; cos, Edith Head, Mary Grant

Superb drama, marred by an unexpected eyesore among the brilliant cast. No, not Hayworth or Lancaster—this is a combination of star chemistry that should have happened long before. It's Deborah Kerr, overacting a repressed spinster almost to the point of retardation. That Delbert Mann could pull such fine work from the rest of the ensemble makes the usually strong Kerr all the more curious, for here is a career built on underacting. Why? Terence Rattigan's original play consisted of two one-acts set in the same Bournemouth, England locale. It was a tour de force for Eric Portman and Margaret Leighton, who played it successfully in London, then in New York during the fall of 1956. Rattigan collaborated with John Gay to blend the two stories into one that used four leads instead of two. TABLES won Oscars for Niven as Best Actor and Hiller as Best Supporting Actress.

The title refers to the practice of seating solo guests at their own dining tables. The small hotel is at the seashore, and the dining room is filled with a host of lonely people. Niven is the ultimate Englishman, peppering his dialogue with cliches like "I say," and "Good show"—he's a one-time military man who waxes on about his experiences in the war's North African campaign, but his stories have the ring of prevarication about them. An aura of panic seems apparent in his eyes. Cooper is a stern and forceful matriarch (a Cooper specialty; was anyone ever better at these roles?) with daughter, Kerr, a mousey spinster fascinated by Niven but far too shy to let him know. Third at the Cooper table is Cooper's friend, Nesbitt, a peeress of the realm. Aylmer is a former schoolteacher who talks about his glory days when he guided young persons' lives. Hallatt is a racing enthusiast, and Taylor and Dalton are unmarried lovers. The hotel is run by Hiller, who devotes herself to the comfort of others. It distracts her from the rejection she feels from her lover, Lancaster, a reclusive American writer who drinks more than he creates and spends much of his time in his room (with his macho bluster, Lancaster brings a Hemingway feeling to the role). Hayworth, Lancaster's former wife, an aging socialite, battered by too many late nights and a succession of ill-fated affairs, arrives unexpectedly at the hotel. And everyone's lives begin to unravel simultaneously.

This is adult, intelligent stuff, marvelously shaded by the amalgamation of talents. That Niven and Hiller are sublime is almost to be expected. But one watches Hayworth with genuine surprise, as the poignant divorcee watching her beauty slip away. These kind of parts are usually the province of Englishwomen— Vivien Leigh, for example. It's the only strong mature role she ever got to play. Lancaster, cast against two women whose talents have an air of gentility, is able to tone down his trademark bravura. Besides Miss Kerr, wouldn't it have been lovely to have been spared Vic Damone's insistent croon over the opening credits?

SEPTEMBER

1987 82m c   ★★★★
Drama   PG
Orion

Denholm Elliott *(Howard)*, Dianne Wiest *(Stephanie)*, Mia Farrow *(Lane)*, Elaine Stritch *(Diane)*, Sam Waterston *(Peter)*, Jack Warden *(Lloyd)*, Ira Wheeler *(Mr. Raines)*, Jane Cecil *(Mrs. Raines)*, Rosemary Murphy *(Mrs. Mason)*

p, Robert Greenhut; d, Woody Allen; w, Woody Allen; ph, Carlo Di Palma (DuArt color); ed, Susan E. Morse; prod d, Santo Loquasto; art d, Speed Hopkins; cos, Jeffrey Kurland

Set entirely in one location—a country home somewhere in Vermont—SEPTEMBER is more than a look at a family; it is a look at a small universe of people. Diane (Elaine Stritch) is an aging sex symbol who has survived the traumas of her past by letting them bounce off her tough veneer. Her daughter, Lane (Mia Farrow), is still struggling with an incident that occurred years before when, as a 14-year-old, she allegedly shot and killed her mother's gangster boyfriend. Diane and her most recent love, Lloyd (Jack Warden), are visiting Lane, who is in love with her neighbor, Peter (Sam Waterston). But Peter loves Stephanie (Dianne Wiest), Lane's good friend, a mother and wife who seeks an escape but doesn't have the courage to pursue it to its conclusion. Rounding out the group is Howard (Denholm Elliott), a neighbor who has helped Lane through a nervous breakdown, growing very close to her in the process. Despite the excellent acting and direction, many critics found little worth in SEPTEMBER. Still infatuated with the language of cinema, Allen has tried to make a film with commercial and artistic appeal. SEPTEMBER is a beautiful, carefully composed work, with Wiest and Stritch creating the most powerful characters. Farrow shines, too, in a difficult role.

SERGEANT YORK

1941 134m bw   ★★★★
War/Biography   /U
WB

Gary Cooper *(Alvin C. York)*, Walter Brennan *(Pastor Rosier Pile)*, Joan Leslie *(Gracie Williams)*, George Tobias *(Michael T. "Pusher" Ross)*, Stanley Ridges *(Maj. Buxton)*, Margaret Wycherly *(Mother York)*, Ward Bond *(Ike Botkin)*, Noah Beery, Jr. *(Buck Lipscomb)*, June Lockhart *(Rose York)*, Dickie Moore *(George York)*

p, Jesse L. Lasky, Hal B. Wallis; d, Howard Hawks; w, Abem Finkel, Harry Chandlee, Howard Koch, John Huston (based on *War Diary of Sergeant York* by Sam K. Cowan, *Sergeant York and His People* by Cowan, and *Sergeant York—Last of the Long Hunters* by Tom Skeyhill); ph, Sol Polito, Arthur Edeson (war sequences); ed, William Holmes; m, Max Steiner; art d, John Hughes

Predictable, a trifle slow, but ultimately winning. Gary Cooper won his first Oscar for his strong portrayal here of WWI hero Alvin C. York, who single-handedly captured 132 German soldiers during the Meuse-Argonne offensive and became one of America's most decorated and beloved heroes. Beginning in 1916, Howard Hawks' masterfully directed film follows the man from the hills of East Tennessee as he falls in love with Gracie Williams (Joan Leslie) and struggles to hold onto his land. When lightning strikes his rifle, York views it a sign from God and, becoming a pacifist, tries to avoid service in WWI. Eventually he does fight in France, however, and the rest is spectacular military history. Hawks brings the life of this incredible hero to the screen with forceful integrity, and Cooper is wonderful as the country fellow who gets religion and holds onto it, even through the nightmare of war. Technically, the film is faultless, with Hawks keeping his cameras fluid and employing Sol Polito's magnificent photographic skills at every turn.

Jesse Lasky, who saw York in the 1919 Armistice Day Parade, spent years trying to convince the modest Tennessean to allow his story to be filmed, finally winning York's approval provided that the proceeds go to charity and that Gary Cooper play him. At first Cooper refused, but he changed his mind after visiting York. Warner Bros. had hoped to have Michael Curtiz direct SERGEANT YORK, but Cooper wouldn't work with him, and when several others couldn't take the job, Hawks was hired, to the lasting pleasure of all who see this magnificent film. That's Robert Porterfield as Zeb Andrews; he established Barter Theater, Virginia's state theater, the oldest repertory still running in the United States.

SERIAL

1980 91m c   ★★★
Comedy   R/18
Paramount

Martin Mull (Harvey), Tuesday Weld (Kate), Jennifer McAllister (Joan), Sam Chew (Bill), Sally Kellerman (Martha), Anthony Battaglia (Stokeley), Bill Macy (Sam), Nita Talbot (Angela), Pamela Bellwood (Carol), Barbara Rhoades (Vivian)

p, Sidney Beckerman; d, Bill Persky; w, Rich Eustis, Michael Elias (based on the novel by Cyra McFadden); ph, Rexford Metz (Movielab Color); ed, John W. Wheeler; m, Lalo Schifrin; art d, William Sandell

Nothing is sacred in this scathingly funny film that sends up California lifestyles of the 1970s. Martin Mull and Tuesday Weld star as a husband and wife struggling to save their marriage while all around them seems to be in trendy chaos. Much of the comedy comes from the interaction between Mull's family and that of his neighbor, Bill Macy. Director Bill Persky, who previously worked strictly in television, made the switch to the big screen with no problem.

SERPENT AND THE RAINBOW, THE

1988 98m c   ★★★
Horror   R/18
Universal

Bill Pullman (Dennis Alan), Cathy Tyson (Marielle), Zakes Mokae (Dargent Peytraud), Paul Winfield (Lucien Celine), Brent Jennings (Mozart), Conrad Roberts (Christophe), Badja Djola (Gaston), Theresa Merritt (Simone), Michael Gough (Schoonbacher), Paul Guilfoyle (Andrew Cassedy)

p, David Ladd, Doug Claybourne; d, Wes Craven; w, Richard Maxwell, Adam D. Rodman (based on the book by Wade Davis); ph, John Lindley (Duart color); ed, Glenn Farr; m, Brad Fiedel; fx, Gary Gutierrez

The moviegoing public has been fascinated with voodoo and zombies since the release of the Halperin brothers' WHITE ZOMBIE. The incredible success of that film spawned a rash of inferior imitations and comedies, until producer Val Lewton and director Jacques Tourneur resuscitated the genre with the lyrical and haunting masterpiece, I WALKED WITH A ZOMBIE. Ever since, cinematic zombies have been detached from their religious roots (voodoo) and made the marauding, cannibalistic hordes popularized by the "Living Dead" films of George Romero. With THE SERPENT AND THE RAINBOW, director Wes Craven returns the zombie to the Caribbean, exploring the culture from which it sprang in this ambitious tale of Haitian voodoo. Dennis Alan (Bill Pullman) is a young scientist hired by an American pharmaceutical company to go to Haiti and uncover the secrets of zombification. Recent studies have proven the existence of actual zombies, and scientists suspect a drug or potion (the discovery of which could mean a fortune to drug manufacturers looking for a new anesthetic) is involved in the process. Dennis' trip, however, happens to coincide with the collapse of the Duvalier government, and he finds himself tossed into the resulting violent social upheaval. In Haiti Dennis teams up with beautiful local psychiatrist Marielle (Cathy Tyson), who introduces him to the mysterious world of voodoo. The more he probes into voodoo rituals, however, the greater the opposition from voodoo priests, who attempt to invade his mind and transform him into a zombie.

An ambitious mix of pop anthropology, scientific exploration, political observation, and good old-fashioned Lewtonesque horror, THE SERPENT AND THE RAINBOW succeeds more often than it fails. Writer-director Craven sees Haiti as a vital, mysterious society where harsh economic reality and belief in the supernatural walk hand in hand, and where the elite has corrupted deep traditional religious beliefs to oppress the masses through fear of violence, death, or, even worse, zombification. From this vivid sociopolitical morass emerges a chilling horror story in which the dead appear to walk and people are possessed by spirits regularly. In conveying this sense of unease and dread, Craven combines the terrifying dream sequences of A NIGHTMARE ON ELM STREET with the subtle and evocative atmospherics of Val Lewton.

SERPICO

1973 129m c   ★★★★
Biography/Crime   R/18
Artists Entertainment/DEG

Al Pacino (Frank Serpico), Tony Roberts (Bob Blair), John Randolph (Chief Sidney Green), Jack Kehoe (Tom Keough), Biff McGuire (Capt. McClain), Barbara Eda-Young (Laurie), Cornelia Sharpe (Leslie), John Medici (Pasquale Serpico), Allan Rich (D.A. Tauber), Norman Ornellas (Rubello)

p, Martin Bregman; d, Sidney Lumet; w, Waldo Salt, Norman Wexler (based on the book by Peter Maas); ph, Arthur J. Ornitz (Technicolor); ed, Dede Allen, Richard Marks; m, Mikis Theodorakis; prod d, Charles Bailey; art d, Douglas Higgins; cos, Anna Hill Johnstone

In 1970, police officer Frank Serpico electrified the Knapp Commission investigating the New York City Police Department by testifying that there were as many cops taking payoffs as there were crooks. Peter Maas's biography of Serpico formed the basis of an Oscar-nominated script by Waldo Salt (MIDNIGHT COWBOY) and Norman Wexler (SATURDAY NIGHT FEVER), and Al Pacino earned an Academy Award nomination—he lost to Jack Lemmon for SAVE THE TIGER—for his portrayal of the title character, an honest cop who refuses to go on the take. One of Pacino's fellow officers, Kehoe, doesn't trust cops who don't take payoffs, and his attitude is representative of most of the officers with whom Pacino works. Several times Pacino is told he cannot remain above the corruption and that if he insists on staying clean, his life won't be worth much. Pacino stays aloof, keeps doing his job, and refuses his share of the booty. However, the corruption that surrounds him begins to stick in his craw, and his life away from work is also disintegrating. His affair with Sharpe comes to an end, and he has more romantic woes with another woman, Eda-Young. When he can no longer abide the double-dealing of his cohorts on the force, Pacino talks with his friend, Roberts, a cop with close ties to the mayor's investigating committee. Encouraged by inspector Ed Grover, Pacino tries to inform police commissioner White of the corruption within the department. He makes his report to McGuire, one of the men who handles internal investigations, but when nothing happens there, Pacino goes to the *New York Times* editors, who print the story. Until this point, Pacino has been transferred from precinct to precinct, but regardless of his assignment, the other officers have given him no support, since they are all, in one way or another, suspect. After the corruption investigation begins, Pacino is sent to Brooklyn to work on the Narcotics Squad. Although he welcomes the change of venue, he is seriously wounded by an unseen sniper when the officers who were supposed to cover him vanish. While recovering from his wounds, Pacino is offered a detective's job, but he realizes it's little more than a bribe, so he quits the force and completes his testimony.

All of the actors contribute excellent performances under the assured direction of Sidney Lumet, who replaced John Avildsen on the project. It's a particular pleasure to see Tony Roberts working in a film that *wasn't* directed by Woody Allen, and he is outstanding as Pacino's trusted pal. Oscar-winner F. Murray Abraham (AMADEUS), Mary Louise Weller (ANIMAL HOUSE), M. Emmet Walsh (STRAIGHT TIME), and Hank Garrett (THREE DAYS OF THE CONDOR) also appear in small but telling roles. But when all is said and done, Pacino is the riveting presence that makes the movie work and it is difficult to imagine any other actor in the part. His stellar portrayal of Serpico, with whom Pacino spent many weeks while preparing for the part, proved that the actor's unforgettable performance in THE GODFATHER was anything but a fluke. Prior to his first film roles—in ME, NATALIE, then PANIC IN NEEDLE PARK—Pacino won an Obie for his work in "The Indian Wants the Bronx" and a Tony for "Does a Tiger Wear a Necktie?".

SERVANT, THE

1964 115m bw ★★★
Drama /15
Springbok (U.K.)

Dirk Bogarde (*Hugo Barrett*), Sarah Miles (*Vera*), Wendy Craig (*Susan*), James Fox (*Tony*), Catherine Lacey (*Lady Mounset*), Richard Vernon (*Lord Mounset*), Ann Firbank (*Society Woman*), Doris Knox (*Older Woman*), Patrick Magee (*Bishop*), Jill Melford (*Younger Woman*)

p, Joseph Losey, Norman Priggen; d, Joseph Losey; w, Harold Pinter (based on the novel by Robin Maugham); ph, Douglas Slocombe; ed, Reginald Mills; m, John Dankworth; prod d, Richard MacDonald; art d, Ted Clements; cos, Beatrice Dawson

Pinter, Losey, and Bogarde had a bit of difficulty getting this interesting but flawed examination of the master-servant relationship in modern England off the ground. Losey, an American, had been in England since the early 1950s, having run afoul of the various witch-hunters who were at that time finding Communists under every bed. Based on Robin Maugham's novel, this movie was overlooked at Oscar time, but it did manage to garner awards from the British Film Academy, which named Bogarde as the Best Actor, Fox as the Most Promising Newcomer, and Slocombe as producer of the Best Cinematography. Fox plays a bored, rich, and lazy playboy who, like Miniver Cheevy, yearns for the days of yore. He comes home from a long holiday in Europe, buys a magnificent Georgian townhouse, and decides that he needs a Jeeves to his Bertie Wooster. He meets Bogarde, a cockney valet, and hires him to run the house. Fox is engaged to Craig, a woman of his own caste, but a marriage date has yet to be set. Under Bogarde's prodding, Fox spends a fortune furnishing the house, and it is soon a posh, elegant place. Craig sees through Bogarde's influence over Fox and resents her fiance's coming to rely more and more upon Bogarde. Craig feels that Bogarde's insidious core will ultimately manifest itself, despite his apparently impeccable behavior. Bogarde realizes that his job is in danger if Craig ever succeeds in undermining his hold over Fox. To forestall such undermining, Bogarde brings in his mistress, Miles (who had won a great deal of approval for her earlier role as the student, opposite Laurence Olivier in TERM OF TRIAL). He introduces her as his sister and offers her services as a maid. Bogarde's plan is to push Craig out of the way, and to that end he sends Miles to seduce the naive Fox, something she manages quite easily. Then Fox comes home one night to discover Bogarde and Miles making love and, shocked by this incestuous behavior, learns that the two are not related at all. Enraged by the ruse, Fox discharges both Bogarde and Miles. Before long, the house begins to run down without the efficient Bogarde to manage things. Further complicating matters, Craig walks out on Fox. Just as his life seems rapidly to be disintegrating, Fox meets Bogarde in a pub (in a seemingly chance encounter that has actually been carefully contrived by Bogarde). Fox is only too happy to bring Bogarde back into the house. Once Bogarde is inside, the balance of power changes, and Fox becomes subservient to his "man." Fox begins drinking, and his already weak spine starts to disintegrate as Bogarde continues his manipulation. (If this domination represents an incipient homosexual situation, it is suggested rather than demonstrated.) Craig comes back in an attempt to repair her life with Fox; but by this time, the youth has retreated far into a dream world of drugs, booze, and debauchery. The servant has become the master, and the corruption—including the erasure of the class distinction between the two men—complete. Pinter's adaptation employed his usual melange of wit and silence. His cameo as a society man proved him a worthy actor. After appearing in PERFORMANCE and THE SERVANT, Fox experienced a religious conversion and retired from movies for a while, before returning in the 1980s. He is the younger brother of Edward Fox (DAY OF THE JACKAL and A BRIDGE TOO FAR among others), with whom he is often confused, so strong is the physical resemblance.

SET-UP, THE

1949 72m bw   ★★★★
Sports   /PG
RKO

Robert Ryan *(Bill "Stoker" Thompson)*, Audrey Totter *(Julie)*, George Tobias *(Tiny)*, Alan Baxter *(Little Boy)*, Wallace Ford *(Gus)*, Percy Helton *(Red)*, Hal Baylor *(Tiger Nelson)*, Darryl Hickman *(Shanley)*, Kenny O'Morrison *(Moore)*, James Edwards *(Luther Hawkins)*

p, Richard Goldstone; d, Robert Wise; w, Art Cohn (based on the poem by Joseph Moncure March); ph, Milton Krasner; ed, Roland Gross; art d, Albert S. D'Agostino, Jack Okey

One of the most realistic and gripping boxing films ever made, THE SET-UP is a tautly constructed, emotionally charged examination of one night in the life of an aging boxer, Stoker Thompson (Robert Ryan). Played out in real time as 72 uninterrupted minutes of Stoker's life, the movie begins as a crowd gathers in front of the arena in anticipation of the evening's bouts. Although almost washed up, Stoker is convinced he'll be back on the road to the top, "just one punch away" from being able to collect a big purse, open his own tavern, and retire. Meanwhile, his seedy manager (George Tobias) has taken $50 from a hood in return for Stoker's throwing the fight. Since, as of late, Stoker has been getting knocked out regularly after the second round, the manager simply doesn't tell the fighter about the setup. Back in the locker room, Stoker watches as the fighters—ranging from fresh-out-of-high-school talent to punchy veterans—prepare for their bouts, while he awaits the fight of his life. THE SET-UP is an amazingly powerful film. Within a very simple format (the screenplay was based on a poem), director Robert Wise and his performers present a myriad of criticisms and emotions, making for one of the most brutal condemnations of boxing ever filmed. The fighting is shown as dehumanizing and cruel, the audience as a mass of animalistic maniacs who live vicariously through the boxers. Everyone, from trainers to promoters to gangsters, is a seedy, uneducated opportunist; only the fighters themselves are shown to have any self-respect. Ryan gives the best performance of his career as the quiet, inarticulate fighter who is determined to stick with the game because he feels that he's "just one punch away" from success. Ryan, who actually boxed for four years undefeated while at Dartmouth College, handles his role with great subtlety: always soft-spoken and sincere, Stoker clings to his simple beliefs and will take whatever punishment is necessary to retain his self-respect and dignity. The fight scenes in THE SET-UP are among the best ever filmed, surpassed only by those in Martin Scorsese's incredible RAGING BULL.

SEVEN BEAUTIES

(PASQUALINO SETTEBELLEZZE)
1976 115m c   ★★★★
Comedy/Drama   R/18
Medusa (Italy)

Giancarlo Giannini *(Pasqualino Frafuso)*, Fernando Rey *(Pedro)*, Shirley Stoler *(Commandant)*, Elena Fiore *(Concettina)*, Enzo Vitale *(Don Raffaele)*, Mario Conti *(Totonno)*, Piero Di Orio *(Francesco)*, Ermelinda De Felice *(Mother)*, Francesca Marciano *(Carolina)*, Lucio Amelio *(Lawyer)*

p, Lina Wertmuller, Giancarlo Giannini, Arrigo Colombo; d, Lina Wertmuller; w, Lina Wertmuller; ph, Tonino Delli Colli (Eastmancolor); ed, Franco Fraticelli; m, Enzo Iannacci; art d, Enrico Job

Memorable, but nasty. The grotesque casting, the surrealistic shooting, and the entire production make one think that Federico Fellini was in charge. But it was Wertmuller who handled the writing and directing (and garnered Oscar nominations for both). Giannini is a small-time crook in Naples during the dark days of WW II. He has seven ugly sisters, none of whom is ever likely to get married, and he is busily supporting them doing whatever he can do to keep their fat bodies and souls together. Giannini is subjected to the terrors of a German prison camp, where gross matron Shirley Stoler forces him to do unspeakable things to her body. In an all-out attempt to survive, Giannini does whatever it is that's necessary to keep from being killed and, finally, manages to live through the war. Wertmuller seems to be saying that Italians are a race willing to do anything to hang on; she strips them of pride and their natural dignity. Giannini's character is a facistic Little Tramp who swallows whatever bull is thrown at him. The picture made a lot of money, proving desensitized audiences were looking for goofball black comedy pratfalls, mixed in with a soupcon of peversion and cruelty. Things haven't changed much since then.

SEVEN BRIDES FOR SEVEN BROTHERS

1954 102m c   ★★★★½
Musical   G/U
MGM

Jane Powell *(Milly)*, Howard Keel *(Adam Pontabee)*, Jeff Richards *(Benjamin Pontabee)*, Russ Tamblyn *(Gideon Pontabee)*, Tommy Rall *(Frank Pontabee)*, Howard Petrie *(Pete Perkins)*, Virginia Gibson *(Liza)*, Ian Wolfe *(Rev. Elcott)*, Marc Platt *(Daniel Pontabee)*, Matt Mattox *(Caleb Pontabee)*

p, Jack Cummings; d, Stanley Donen; w, Albert Hackett, Frances Goodrich, Dorothy Kingsley (based on the story "The Sobbin' Women" by Stephen Vincent Benet); ph, George Folsey (CinemaScope, Ansco Color); ed, Ralph E. Winters; art d, Cedric Gibbons, Urie McCleary; chor, Michael Kidd; cos, Walter Plunkett

Close to perfect. A magical blend of the right story, a great score, and the astonishing choreography of Michael Kidd, SEVEN BRIDES FOR SEVEN BROTHERS is one the big screen's most entertaining musicals. The action takes place in Oregon, where Adam (Howard Keel), the oldest of the Pontabee brothers, who live on a ranch high in the mountains, decides to find a bride. In town, he meets Milly (Jane Powell), a waitress, and woos, marries, and takes her back to the homestead, which is considerably less civilized than she'd expected. Soon Adam's brothers decide they, too, would like some female company, and, taking their inspiration from the story of the "Sobbin' Women" (Sabine women), they kidnap some local beauties, who have to winter at the ranch when an avalanche prevents the townspeople from rescuing them. Come spring, wedding bells ring for all. Based on Stephen Vincent Benet's "The Sobbin' Women," SEVEN BRIDES FOR SEVEN BROTHERS is a rollicking film with a breathless pace, well-defined characters, and incredible vitality under Stanley Donen's direction, marred marginally by an overlying patina of corny Americana. Adolph Deutsch and Saul Chaplin's scoring won an Oscar. The dynamo dancing is mostly due to the terrific male dancers, whose standouts include the barn-raising and the "Lonesome Polecat Lament" ballet. Keel and Powell have an adorable chemistry; neither would ever be this well-matched again, which reminds us we would have preferred Powell in for Kathryn Grayson in KISS ME, KATE. Look for ripe Julie Newmar (then Newmeyer) among the other brides, whom we always found sexier as a wild-maned brunette. The score is by Gene dePaul and Johnny Mercer.

SEVEN DAYS IN MAY

1964 120m bw ★★★★
Thriller/Political/War /U
Seven Arts/Joel

Burt Lancaster *(Gen. James M. Scott)*, Kirk Douglas *(Col. Martin "Jiggs" Casey)*, Fredric March *(President Jordan Lyman)*, Ava Gardner *(Eleanor Holbrook)*, Edmond O'Brien *(Sen. Raymond Clark)*, Martin Balsam *(Paul Girard)*, George Macready *(Christopher Todd)*, Whit Bissell *(Sen. Prentice)*, Hugh Marlowe *(Harold McPherson)*, Bart Burns *(Arthur Corwin)*

p, Edward Lewis; d, John Frankenheimer; w, Rod Serling (based on the novel by Fletcher Knebel, Charles Waldo Bailey II); ph, Ellsworth Fredricks; ed, Ferris Webster; m, Jerry Goldsmith; art d, Cary Odell

The surprising revelations of the Iran-Contra scandal have given new meaning to this gripping, well-acted political thriller based on Charles Waldo Bailey II's and Fletcher Knebel's 1962 bestseller. SEVEN DAYS IN MAY begins as the President of the United States, Jordan Lyman (Fredric March), signs a nuclear disarmament treaty with the Soviets, outraging the military establishment, particularly Gen. James M. Scott (Burt Lancaster), head of the Joint Chiefs of Staff, who conspires with other Joint Chiefs to stage a coup d'etat. His aide, Marine Col. "Jiggs" Casey (Kirk Douglas), stumbles onto evidence of the plot, including a secret Air Force base, and approaches the president. With only days left before the coup is to take place, Lyman swings into action, but trusted friends Sen. Raymond Clark (Edmond O'Brien) and Paul Girard (Martin Balsam), whom the president has sent to secure the proof needed to expose Scott and his cohorts, are captured and killed in a plane crash, respectively. Armed with incriminating letters from Scott's former mistress (Ava Gardner), Lyman confronts the general, and though the president cannot bring himself to use blackmail he eventually triumphs over Scott. Filmed in stark black and white, unraveling its complicated plot at a rapid clip, this exciting film from John Frankenheimer, the director of the similarly taut THE MANCHURIAN CANDIDATE, packs a grim warning about the military's potential abuse of power. Douglas, who, like Lancaster and March, contributes an outstanding performance, initiated the project after reading galleys of the novel. Given the enthusiastic cooperation of the Kennedy administration (though not of the Pentagon, whom the filmmakers understandably never approached), SEVEN DAYS IN MAY smacks of realism, from its skillfully realized sets to its wholly believable supporting performances by O'Brien, Balsam, and John Houseman. Sure to keep you on the edge of your seat.

SEVEN FACES OF DR. LAO

1964 100m c ★★★½
Fantasy
Galaxy/Scarus

Tony Randall *(Dr. Lao/Merlin the Magician/Pan/The Abominable Snowman/Medusa/The Giant Serpent/Apollonius of Tyana)*, Barbara Eden *(Angela Benedict)*, Arthur O'Connell *(Clint Stark)*, John Ericson *(Ed Cunningham)*, Noah Beery, Jr. *(Tim Mitchell)*, Lee Patrick *(Mrs. Howard T. Cassan)*, Minerva Urecal *(Kate Lindquist)*, John Qualen *(Luther Lindquist)*, Frank Kreig *(Peter Ramsey)*, Peggy Rea *(Mrs. Peter Ramsey)*

p, George Pal; d, George Pal; w, Charles Beaumont (based on the novel *The Circus of Dr. Lao* by Charles G. Finney); ph, Robert Bronner (Metrocolor); ed, George Tomasini; m, Leigh Harline; art d, George W. Davis, Gabriel Scognamillo; fx, Paul Byrd, Wah Chang, Jim Danforth, Ralph Rodine, Robert R. Hoag

Set in the Old West, this is a wonderful fantasy from puppeteer George Pal, whose futurist fancies have delighted many. When Dr. Lao (Tony Randall), an Oriental magician, rides into Abalone with his strange circus, he finds the good citizens threatened by the land-grabbing activities of villainous Clint Stark (Arthur O'Connell). Calling upon his mysterious powers and the services of the bizarre characters who populate the strange circus (all played by Randall), Lao comes to the aid of the crusading young newspaper editor (John Ericson) who tries to prevent Stark's takeover of the town. In the film's most fantastic sequence, Lao's pet fish becomes a seven-headed monster to chase down one of Stark's henchmen. Randall gives a virtuoso multiple-character performance, and the special effects are dazzling, including a few scenes from Pal's ATLANTIS, THE LOST CONTINENT. Makeup man William Tuttle won the first of only two special Academy Awards for his work on this film—before the category was permanently established in 1981.

SEVEN LITTLE FOYS, THE

1955 95m c ★★★½
Musical/Biography /U
Paramount

Bob Hope *(Eddie Foy)*, Milly Vitale *(Madeleine Morando)*, George Tobias *(Barney Green)*, Angela Clarke *(Clara)*, Herbert Heyes *(Judge)*, Richard Shannon *(Stage Manager)*, Billy Gray *(Brynie)*, Lee Erickson *(Charley)*, Paul De Rolf *(Richard Foy)*, Lydia Reed *(Mary Foy)*

p, Jack Rose; d, Melville Shavelson; w, Melville Shavelson, Jack Rose; ph, John F. Warren (VistaVision, Technicolor); ed, Ellsworth Hoagland; art d, Hal Pereira, John B. Goodman; chor, Nick Castle; cos, Edith Head

Funny and heartwarming, though a little on the cute side, this engaging musical biography of vaudevillian Eddie Foy, Sr. features a socko cameo by multitalented James Cagney, reprising his Oscar-winning role as George M. Cohan. Bob Hope plays Foy, who declares that he'll always do a "single," both onstage and in life, but who, in short order, is married and has seven kids. When his wife (Milly Vitale) dies, Foy has problems adjusting to single parenthood, but before long the kids are not only in the act, but stealing the show. With Eddie, Jr., Foy's real-life son, doing the narrating, we are taken through the various episodes of the family's life. The highlight of the film comes at a Friars Club dinner for Foy, when he and his great pal Cohan get on stage, throw some fast and furious jokes back and forth, and wind up in a splendid dance routine. Cagney reportedly did the role for no pay, even though he and Hope rehearsed their dancing for 10 days. Melville Shavelson (making his directorial debut) and Jack Rose were Oscar-nominated for the script. A must see for Hope and Cagney fans.

SEVEN-PER-CENT SOLUTION, THE

1977 113m c ★★★
Mystery PG/15
Universal (U.K.)

Alan Arkin *(Sigmund Freud)*, Vanessa Redgrave *(Lola Deveraux)*, Robert Duvall *(Dr. Watson)*, Nicol Williamson *(Sherlock Holmes)*, Laurence Olivier *(Prof. Moriarty)*, Joel Grey *(Lowenstein)*,

Samantha Eggar (*Mary Watson*), Jeremy Kemp (*Baron von Leinsdorf*), Charles Gray (*Mycroft Holmes*), Georgia Brown (*Mrs. Freud*)

p, Herbert Ross; d, Herbert Ross; w, Nicholas Meyer (based on his novel); ph, Oswald Morris (Panavision, Technicolor); ed, Chris Barnes; m, John Addison; prod d, Ken Adam; art d, Peter Lamont; cos, Alan Barrett

A hit at the box office, this revisionist Sherlock Holmes film is based on the best seller by Nicholas Meyer and places a historical figure (Sigmund Freud) and a fictitious one (Sherlock Holmes) from the late 19th century together in a hypothetical situation. The result is a fascinating film that sees the loyal Dr. Watson (Duvall) scheme to trick his friend Holmes (Williamson) into seeking a cure for his cocaine addiction from the soon-to-be-famous Freud (Arkin). The criminologist and the psychologist come to respect each other's considerable deductive talents, and they team up to rescue one of Arkin's patients (Redgrave) who has been kidnapped. Williamson is a Holmes unlike any other, a man of genius but also a man tormented by things he cannot recall. His obsession with the completely innocent Professor Moriarty (Olivier) is actually a reaction to a long-buried secret in the sleuth's subconscious. Williamson's Holmes actually cries at one point, something Basil Rathbone would never have done. Duvall is a breath of fresh air as well; far from the Nigel Bruce bumbler, he is a capable man and a devoted friend. Production design is nothing short of marvelous, conveying the gentility of the late Victorian era in splendid detail. The music was originally to be composed by Bernard Herrmann, but he died before completing it and was replaced by John Addison. Stephen Sondheim, a mystery buff, contributed a witty saloon song.

SEVEN SAMURAI, THE
(SHICHININ NO SAMURAI)
1954   200m   bw   ★★★★★
Drama   /15
Toho   (Japan)

Takashi Shimura (*Kambei*), Toshiro Mifune (*Kikuchiyo*), Yoshio Inaba (*Gorobei*), Seiji Miyaguchi (*Kyuzo*), Minoru Chiaki (*Heihachi*), Daisuke Kato (*Shichiroji*), Ko Kimura (*Katsushiro*), Kuninori Kodo (*Gisaku*), Kamatari Fujiwara (*Manzo*), Yoshio Tsuchiya (*Rikichi*)

p, Shojiro Motoki; d, Akira Kurosawa; w, Shinobu Hashimoto, Hideo Oguni, Akira Kurosawa; ph, Asakazu Nakai; ed, Akira Kurosawa; m, Fumio Hayasaka; art d, So Matsuyama

Much imitated, unsurpassed. Simply one of the best movies ever made, THE SEVEN SAMURAI covers so much ground, assaults so many emotions, and is so totally satisfying that it emerges as a picture that can be viewed over and over again. The film is set in the 1600s during the Sengoku era, when the once-powerful samurai were coming to the end of their rule. A small, unprotected village, which is regularly pillaged by murderous thieves, comes under the protection of a band of these samurai. Kambei (Takashi Shimura) is a veteran warrior who has fallen on hard times and who answers the villagers' appeal for help by gathering six comrades to help defend the town. (Each of the samurai is quickly limned to show us who they are, what they do, and whatever personal quirks they may have.) In return for three small meals daily, the men drill the town on how to fight, but the parties are battling for different reasons. The townspeople are desperate to keep their lives and property intact; the warriors are in it for honor alone. The last of the samurai to join is Kikuchiyo (Toshiro Mifune), a loudmouth who pretends that he is qualified

but who is, in reality, a farmer's son who hopes to be accepted by the others. The 40 bandits arrive, and a huge battle takes place. In the end, only three of the warriors survive. Akira Kurosawa's classic tells a simple tale, but one so rich with underlying meaning and cinematic technique that no synopsis can do justice to the film's power. Those viewers under the misconception that foreign films are boring should be thrilled by the staging of this film's brutal action sequences, such as the raid on the town, the violent hand-to-hand combat in the pouring rain, and the epic horseback battles. The action is never shown strictly for its own sake, however. All the characters are so carefully etched that we sincerely grieve when they are killed. One of the most successful of all Japanese films, and surely the most accessible. Nominated for two Oscars: Best Art Direction/Set Decoration and Best Costume Design.

SEVEN THIEVES
1960   102m   bw   ★★★★
Crime   /A
Fox

Rod Steiger (*Paul Mason*), Edward G. Robinson (*Theo Wilkins*), Joan Collins (*Melanie*), Eli Wallach (*Poncho*), Michael Dante (*Louis*), Alexander Scourby (*Raymond Le May*), Berry Kroeger (*Hugo Baumer*), Sebastian Cabot (*Director of Casino*), Marcel Hillaire (*Duc di Salins*), John Beradino (*Chief of Detectives*)

p, Sydney Boehm; d, Henry Hathaway; w, Sydney Boehm (based on the novel *Lions at the Kill* by Max Catto); ph, Sam Leavitt (CinemaScope); ed, Dorothy Spencer; m, Dominic Frontiere; art d, Lyle Wheeler, John De Cuir; cos, Bill Thomas

There have been many copies of RIFIFI since the early 1950s, some of which have been awful and some excellent. This film falls into the latter category. Robinson was beginning his fourth decade as a hoodlum star, and not many actors could play tough guys better than he could. This time he's a former scientist who realizes he doesn't have much time left and wants to commit the perfect crime. Robinson enlists six accomplices to help him carry out his plan. Prominent among them is Steiger, a recently released crook and old acquaintace of Robinson's. Meeting on the French Riviera, Robinson and Steiger spar verbally in a funny scene that shows both men jockeying for position. Once Steiger is committed to the project—the robbery of millions from the casino at Monte Carlo—the crew of criminals is rounded out by Collins, a sexpot chorine; Wallach, her boyfriend; Dante, a jumpy safe-cracker; Kroeger, an expert wheel man; and Scourby, the insider who works as the right-hand man to the boss of the casino, Cabot. The first half of the film is devoted to gathering the conspirators and planning the robbery. The second half depicts the robbery itself and the plot-twist ending. Collins supposedly seduces Scourby; Wallach fakes a suicide in the casino to divert the security guards. While this goes on, Steiger and Dante make their way to the rooms where the money is kept. The heist is successful, but the cash is in huge denominations that are registered, so the crooks can not do anything with their take. Robinson is so thrilled by having pulled off the job that his heart gives out, and when the other six realize that there is no way they can spend the money, they return it to the casino. The ending is a bit of a disappointment because the characters are so engaging that we want them to succeed, especially since they don't hurt or kill anyone. Until the conclusion, SEVEN THIEVES is a tight, taut, and superior heist film with well-drawn characters. Well-directed by Hathaway and beautifully photographed by Levitt, the film would have benefitted greatly by being shot in color. (It was nominated by the Academy for Best Costume Design for a black-and-white film.) Frontiere's score adds nicely to the tension. The chief of detectives was played by John Beradino, who went on to great success in "General Hospital" but whom sports fans may remember as being the light-hitting infielder for the St. Louis Browns.

SEVEN YEAR ITCH, THE
1955 105m c   ★★★
Comedy   /PG
FOX

Marilyn Monroe (The Girl), Tom Ewell (Richard Sherman), Evelyn Keyes (Helen Sherman), Sonny Tufts (Tom McKenzie), Robert Strauss (Kruhulik), Oscar Homolka (Dr. Brubaker), Marguerite Chapman (Miss Morris), Victor Moore (Plumber), Roxanne (Elaine), Donald MacBride (Mr. Brady)

p, Charles K. Feldman, Billy Wilder; d, Billy Wilder; w, Billy Wilder, George Axelrod (based on the play by Axelrod); ph, Milton Krasner (CinemaScope, DeLuxe Color); ed, Hugh S. Fowler; m, Alfred Newman; art d, Lyle Wheeler, George W. Davis; fx, Ray Kellogg; cos, Travilla, Charles LeMaire

Entertaining Billy Wilder outing, adapted—and toned down—by George Axelrod from his hit Broadway play. This is probably Monroe's best known film, largely thanks to the scene in which a rush of air from a subway grating sends her skirt flying up around her shoulders.

Tom Ewell plays a book publisher who has been married for seven years, and who stays behind in Manhattan for the summer when his wife (Keyes) and son (Bernard) leave on vacation. Ewell's small building has an upstairs apartment which has been sublet to Monroe, a flighty commercial actress/model who becomes the object of his (mostly imaginary) amorous advances. Ewell's lively imagination sends him into flights of fancy involving both his conquest of Monroe, and the humiliation which would result from the exposure of his infidelity (Monroe appearing on a local TV show to openly discuss his proclivities, etc.). The picture ends with no adultery having been committed, except in Ewell's mind.

This was Monroe's 23rd movie and Ewell's eighth, since he broke in opposite Judy Holliday in ADAM'S RIB. Monroe was falling in and out of depression during filming, as her marriage to Yankee slugger Joe DiMaggio was ending. Oscar Homolka has a bit part as a psychiatrist.

SEVENTH SEAL, THE
(DET SJUNDE INSEGLET)
1956 105m bw   ★★★★★
Drama   /15
Svensk (Sweden)

Max von Sydow (Antonius Block), Gunnar Bjornstrand (Jons), Nils Poppe (Jof), Bibi Andersson (Mia), Bengt Ekerot (Death), Ake Fridell (Blacksmith Plog), Inga Gill (Lisa), Maud Hansson (Tyan), Gunnel Lindblom (Girl), Inga Landgre (Block's Wife)

p, Allan Ekelund; d, Ingmar Bergman; w, Ingmar Bergman (based on his play "Tramalning"); ph, Gunnar Fischer; ed, Lennart Wallen; m, Erik Nordgren; fx, Evald Andersson; chor, Else Fischer; cos, Manne Lindholm

The film that gained Ingmar Bergman an international reputation, THE SEVENTH SEAL is a all-out religious allegory addressing that most-contemplated question, "Does God exist?" Set during a single day in the Middle Ages, the film concerns the philosophical quandary of a knight, Antonius Block (von Sydow), who returns from the Crusades to find his country at the mercy of plague and witchhunts. In the midst of his moral and religious confusion, Antonius is visited by Death (Ekerot), a black-cloaked figure who is ready to call the knight from this earth. Antonius strikes a deal with Death, winning a brief reprieve by inviting him to play a game of chess. Since Death apparently has a soft spot for chess, he agrees. Over the next several hours, Antonius is confronted by some who are unconvinced of God's existence (the Knight's agnostic squire, played by Bjornstrand) and some who are (a wandering band of performers). Who survives the plague and who doesn't propels the narrative; the issues, however, are what really matter here.

Long hailed as a masterpiece of cinema, the status of THE SEVENTH SEAL (and, more generally, Bergman's place in the pantheon of great filmmakers) has steadily declined over the years. Still, we must admit to really liking this one. It is most powerful on its first viewing, when the opening burst of light through the sky, the incredible parade of flagellants through the town, and the memorable finale with Death and his conquests have their greatest impact for a viewer. On later viewings the craft of the film remains bracing and its greater concerns stay provocative without becoming heavy-handed. Whatever one thinks of Bergman's philosophical debates on good and evil or God and the Devil, the film nevertheless deserves one's respect. As with so much of this filmmaker's cinema, the acting is of a very high order. Von Sydow's long face makes a perfect portrait of stoicism, and the incredibly versatile Bjornstrand scores again in a change of pace role. Poppe would never again achieve a performance quite as good as this one, his Jof a combination of artlessness and winning grace. Andersson and Lindblom are equally fine, and the details and dignity of the acting throughout render an incredibly effective sense of period. What's most important here is that THE SEVENTH SEAL, for all its downbeat aspects, is so gripping as to be entertaining in an enlightening way. Less austere and more visually unforgettable than some of Bergman's later films, THE SEVENTH SEAL remains an ideal introduction to a thinking person's cinema.

SEVENTH VEIL, THE
1946 95m bw   ★★★★
Drama   /PG
Theatrecraft/Ortus (U.K.)

James Mason (Nicholas), Ann Todd (Francesca Cunningham), Herbert Lom (Dr. Larson), Hugh McDermott (Peter Gay), Albert Lieven (Maxwell Leyden), Yvonne Owen (Susan Brook), David Horne (Dr. Kendal), Manning Whiley (Dr. Irving), Grace Allardyce (Nurse), Ernest Davies (Parker)

p, Sydney Box; d, Compton Bennett; w, Muriel Box, Sydney Box; ph, Reginald Wyer; ed, Gordon Hales; m, Benjamin Frankel; art d, James Carter; cos, Dorothy Sinclair

An intelligent and absorbing psychological drama that took the Oscar for Best Screenplay, THE SEVENTH VEIL was shot in under three months on a modest budget of less than 100,000 pounds and proved that a polished movie could be made for a reasonable price. Todd, in her best performance of an up-and-down career in which she never got the acclaim she deserved, is a concert pianist who suffers from fits of depression and attempts suicide. Her hands were once hurt in an accident and she fears that she will lose their use. The picture unreels in flashback as Todd checks into a mental hospital and puts herself in the care of psychiatrist Lom, who guides her through her past and lifts the veils of her memory. With the aid of drugs and hypnosis, Todd goes back to the time when she was brutally caned by a cruel headmistress the night before she was to take her final exams in music. The result was that she failed the test. Todd is an orphan put in the care of crippled and charismatic Mason, a bachelor who dedicates himself to cultivating her talents. When Todd attempts romance with bandleader McDermott, Mason takes her to Paris where she plays brilliantly and delights crowds and critics. Then she falls for Lieven, an artist; in an attempt to put an end to that attachment, Mason steals a car and crashes it with Todd inside; her hands are burned. Now that Todd has discovered why she feels the way she does, she becomes aware that her talent remains, and the recognition of her personal history causes her to race to the arms of the man she truly loves, Mason.

It's a complex picture that only skims the surface of mental illnes, but the attempt was admirable, if a bit simplistic. Still, for the time, praise must be given to the Boxes for their story and to former film editor Bennett for his direction. The producers showed it to audiences on a sneak-preview basis and let them decide the ending. At first, no one was quite sure how to conclude it. But when the cards came in, it was indicated that the audiences felt Todd should wind up with Mason, and so that is implied at the conclusion. Pianist Eileen Joyce did the solos for Todd. Two years before this, Todd electrified London with her stage work in "Lottie Dundass," in which she played opposite Sybil Thorndike. She began her professional career in 1931 in KEEPERS OF YOUTH and eventually became a producer and director of travel films. Czech-born Lom, who later was seen as Peter Sellers's boss in the "Pink Panther" films, was making his fifth film.

SEVENTH VICTIM, THE

1943   71m   bw   ★★★★★
Horror   /A
RKO

Tom Conway (*Dr. Louis Judd*), Kim Hunter (*Mary Gibson*), Jean Brooks (*Jacqueline Gibson*), Hugh Beaumont (*Gregory Ward*), Erford Gage (*Jason Hoag*), Isabel Jewell (*Frances Fallon*), Chef Milani (*Mr. Romari*), Marguerita Sylva (*Mrs. Romari*), Evelyn Brent (*Natalie Cortez*), Mary Newton (*Mrs. Redi*)

p, Val Lewton; d, Mark Robson; w, DeWitt Bodeen, Charles O'Neal; ph, Nicholas Musuraca; ed, John Lockert; m, Roy Webb; art d, Albert S. D'Agostino, Walter E. Keller; cos, Renie

"I runne to death and death meets me as fast/And all my pleasures are like yesterday." This epigraph from the first "Holy Sonnet" by John Donne sets the tone for what is perhaps producer Val Lewton's most personal film, and certainly one of his greatest. While very little in the way of horrific action takes place in THE SEVENTH VICTIM, the film has a haunting, lyrical, overwhelming sense of melancholy and despair to it—death is looked upon as a sweet release from the oppression of a cold, meaningless existence. Kim Hunter makes her film debut as Mary Gibson, an orphan attending a gloomy Catholic boarding school. Informed by the nuns that her older sister, Jacqueline (Jean Brooks), has disappeared and stopped sending tuition money, Mary is forced to go to New York City and find her. With the help of Jacqueline's husband, Gregory (Hugh Beaumont), Mary discovers that her sister has fallen in with a group of satanists who meet in secret and virtually control the lives of their members. No plot description can fully convey the uneasy sense of dread that pervades every frame of this film. Although Mark Robson, who made his directorial debut here, is no Jacques Tourneur, his direction is restrained and effective. Lewton ensured this by seeing to it that all the delicate nuances of mood and character were written into the screenplay. The film includes a number of unforgettable moments: the scene in which Mary persuades Jacqueline's landlord to open up her room—only to

find a noose hanging from the ceiling and a chair placed beneath it, Mary watching in horror as the body of a murder victim is transported by its killers on the subway, a precursor to the shower scene in PSYCHO that must have been seen by Hitchcock, and the film's final moment—without a doubt the bleakest ending to any film ever made in Hollywood.

SEVENTH VOYAGE OF SINBAD, THE

1958   87m   c   ★★★½
Fantasy   /U
Morningside

Kerwin Mathews (*Capt. Sinbad*), Kathryn Grant (*Princess Parisa*), Richard Eyer (*Baronni the Genie*), Torin Thatcher (*Sokurah the Magician*), Alec Mango (*Caliph*), Danny Green (*Karim*), Harold Kasket (*Sultan*), Alfred Brown (*Harufa*), Nana de Herrera (*Sadi*), Nino Falanga (*Gaunt Sailor*)

p, Charles H. Schneer; d, Nathan Juran; w, Ken Kolb; ph, Wilkie Cooper (Dynamation, Technicolor); ed, Edwin Bryant, Jerome Thoms; m, Bernard Herrmann; art d, Gil Parrendo; fx, Harryhausen

Stop-motion animation master Ray Harryhausen's first color film is also one of the greatest achievements in fantasy filmmaking since KING KONG. For the first time Harryhausen ventures into the realm of myth and legend (his previous films were the modern-day giant monster variety), resuscitating the Sinbad adventure, long thought to be box-office poison. The film opens as Sinbad (Kerwin Mathews) sails to Baghdad, accompanied by Princess Parisa (Kathryn Grant), his future bride. A violent storm blows the ship off course, and the travelers land on the island of Colossa, where they find the sorcerer Sokurah (Torin Thatcher) being chased by a monstrous cyclops from whom he has stolen a magic lamp. Sinbad fends off the cyclops, but only with help from the lamp's genie are they able to escape. During their retreat, the lamp falls into the sea and is recovered by the angry cyclops. Despite the sorcerer's pleas to return for the lamp, Sinbad sails for Baghdad. Sokurah, however, shrinks the princess to miniature size to force Sinbad to see things his way. The rest of the film is an assault of the visually fantastic: Sinbad and his crew battle a baby roc and its giant mother, another cyclops, a fire-breathing dragon, and in the most memorable scene of all, Sinbad has a thrilling sword fight with a living skeleton. Harryhausen would make more magic in such outstanding fantasy features as MYSTERIOUS ISLAND, JASON AND THE ARGONAUTS, and CLASH OF THE TITANS.

SEX, LIES AND VIDEOTAPE

1989   101m   c   ★★★½
Drama   R/18
Outlaw

James Spader (*Graham Dalton*), Andie MacDowell (*Ann Millaney*), Peter Gallagher (*John Millaney*), Laura San Giacomo (*Cynthia Bishop*), Ron Vawter (*Therapist*), Steven Brill (*Barfly*), David Foil (*John's Colleague*), Earl Taylor (*Landlord*), Alexandra Root (*Girl on Tape*)

p, Robert Newmyer, John Hardy; d, Steven Soderbergh; w, Steven Soderbergh; ph, Walt Lloyd (CFI Color); m, Cliff Martinez; art d, Joanne Schmidt; cos, James Ryder

Like its title, SEX, LIES AND VIDEOTAPE sneaks by quietly, in subtle increments, gradually accumulating force. Graham Dalton (James Spader) arrives at the upscale home of his old college friend John Millaney (Peter Gallagher) and the friend's wife, Ann (Andie MacDowell). The two men have little in common any more: Graham is jobless and alienated; John is an aggressive yuppie attorney. He is also having an affair with his wife's sister, Cynthia (Laura San Giacomo), who's a troublemaker. Graham and Ann become friendly, and he reveals that he is impotent. They have a falling out over his collection of videotapes, which contain conversations with women who've consented to speak intimately about sex before his camera. Then Cynthia pays him a visit and makes a tape, precipitating a series of emotional revelations. An unusually mature and self-assured fiction-feature debut for director Steven Soderbergh, SEX, LIES AND VIDEOTAPE was the winner of the Cannes Film Festival's top prize, the Palme d'Or, scoring a rare double win when Spader was named Best Actor as well. Notwithstanding the fervency of its reception, this is a quiet film, relying on talk rather than scenes of sex or nudity to make its points, and in the process establishing a far more intimate tone than many more explicit pictures. Soderbergh coaxes remarkably well-nuanced performances from the four principals. Beautifully edited by Soderbergh, the film is evenly paced, its subtleties accreting slowly, and by the end it gathers powerful emotional momentum.

SHADOW OF A DOUBT

1943 108m bw ★★★★½
Thriller /A
Universal

Teresa Wright (Young Charlie), Joseph Cotten (Uncle Charlie), Macdonald Carey (Jack Graham), Henry Travers (Joseph Newton), Patricia Collinge (Emma Newton), Hume Cronyn (Herbie Hawkins), Edna May Wonacott (Ann Newton), Wallace Ford (Fred Saunders), Irving Bacon (Station Master), Charles Bates (Roger Newton)

p, Jack H. Skirball; d, Alfred Hitchcock; w, Thornton Wilder, Sally Benson, Alma Reville (based on a story by Gordon McDonnell); ph, Joseph Valentine; ed, Milton Carruth; m, Dimitri Tiomkin; art d, John B. Goodman, Robert Boyle

Deathly Americana; not as fun or spine-tingling as others, but who's complaining? Alfred Hitchcock's favorite among his own films (until he made STRANGERS ON A TRAIN) was based on the case of the real-life "Merry Widow Murderer," Earle Leonard Nelson, a mass strangler of the 1920s. The sly Hitchcock made this chiller all the more frightening by having his crafty homicidal maniac intrude into the tranquility of a warm, middle-class family living in a small town, deeply developing his characters and drawing from the soft-spoken Joseph Cotten one of the actor's most remarkable and fascinating performances.

At the beginning of the film, Cotten is shown wooing and then murdering a woman for her riches. He barely escapes the police detectives who chase him through the back alleys of an eastern city, then boards a train, having wired his sister (Collinge) in Santa Rosa, California, that he is coming for an extended stay with the only family he has. (On board the train, as a passenger in his cameo appearance, is director Hitchcock.) In Santa Rosa Cotten's niece, Wright, a vivacious and warm-hearted young lady, is delighted to hear that her urbane, witty, and adventurous uncle will be visiting her family. She, her father (Travers), and her young brother and sister (Wonacott and Bates) greet Cotten at the train station, but are shocked to see him limping on a cane, being helped by porters. He claims to be ill, and the family quickly takes him home, where Collinge pampers him. Wright is totally charmed by the suave Cotten, who compliments her on her wit and attractiveness, and accompanies him about the little town of Santa Rosa. Cotten stops at a bank and makes a scene while depositing $40,000, but his strange behavior is explained

as an idiosyncracy by the adoring Wright. Back home, Collinge, who looks up to her younger brother as the family intellectual, tells her middle-class brood that the young Cotten was "such a quiet boy, always reading." She also relates an anecdote about her brother, who, after being given a bicycle, accidentally hit a streetcar and nearly died. Afterwards, while he was getting well, "There was no holding him. It was just as though all the rest he had was too much and he had to get into mischief to blow off steam." (Hitchcock himself wrote this passage and it is reportedly based on an incident of his own life, but it faithfully recalls an accident that befell Earle Leonard Nelson, whose head was opened when he was struck by a streetcar as a child. It was later thought that he suffered brain damage, the accident making him a lunatic from childhood.) This nostalgic talk warms Cotten's heart, and he fondly and sadly recalls "the old world." In fact, as Wright is to learn later, Cotten hates the world of today and all the women in it (except his sister, a surrogate mother).

Meanwhile, Travers carries on a running dialog with oddball next-door neighbor Cronyn. Both of them are obsessed with murder, a typical preoccupation in their drab small town, and are constantly proposing means of committing the "perfect murder" to each other, then figuring out ways to solve the crimes. Here Hitchcock parades a number of ingenious killings before the viewer, mostly the crimes of 19th-century British killers who fascinated him. The director also inserts a humorous, off-beat autobiographical detail when the younger daughter, Wonacott, complains to Travers about her mother's misuse of the telephone—like Hitchcock's own mother, after whom he named Collinge's character—saying, "Really, Papa, you'd think Mama had never seen a phone. She makes no allowance for science. She thinks she has to cover the distance by sheer lung power!" In fact, both of the smaller children are absorbed by science, Wonacott being a voracious reader and the small boy, Bates, totally obsessed with mathematics. But into this tranquil backwater setting the world and Cotten's awful past begin to intrude. Carey, a detective, comes upon the scene and begins asking Wright about Cotten, arousing her suspicions. Battling the thought that her beloved uncle could be the mass killer Carey has suggested he is, she tries to get closer to Cotten, hoping to learn about his past and allay her fears.

This is Hitchcock's most penetrating analysis of a murderer— a masterful profile, aided by Cotten's superb performance, of a subtle killer who cannot escape his dark passions, despite a superior intellect. The film's construction is adroit and perfectly calculated, letting the viewer know early on just what kind of man Cotton really is, but providing tension through Cotten's devious charade as a gentle, kind man deserving of his family's love—a tension which fuels the chilling cat-and-mouse game between Cotten and Wright that provides the film's suspenseful center.

Hitchcock took his time in making SHADOW OF A DOUBT, and the care shows. The director got Thornton Wilder to write the screenplay, assuming that the playwright who created "Our Town" would be the perfect scenarist to provide the right kind of ambience and characterization to the film's small, close-knit Santa Rosa. After consulting briefly with Hitchcock, Wilder wandered about Hollywood with a notebook, writing bits and pieces of the screenplay when he could. He and the director took their time developing the intricate story, and Wilder had not finished the screenplay when he enlisted to serve in the Psychological Warfare Division of the Army. To finish the script, Hitchcock boarded a cross-country train to Florida (where Wilder was to begin his training) with the writer, and patiently sat in the next compartment as Wilder periodically emerged to give him another few pages of copy. The great playwright finished the last page of SHADOW OF A DOUBT just as the train was coming to his stop, and he used the train upon which he and Hitchcock traveled as his model in creating the setting for Cotten and Wright's final struggle.

The film earned an Oscar nomination for its original story and was remade in 1958 as STEP DOWN TO TERROR.

SHADOWS

1960 81m bw ★★★★
Drama /X
Lion

Hugh Hurd (Hugh), Lelia Goldoni (Lelia), Ben Carruthers (Ben), Anthony Ray (Tony), Dennis Sallas (Dennis), Tom Allen (Tom), David Pokitillow (David), Rupert Crosse (Rupert), David Jones (David), Pir Marini (Pir)

p, Maurice McEndree; d, John Cassavetes; ph, Erich Kollmar; ed, Maurice McEndree, Len Appelson; m, Charlie Mingus, Shifi Hadi

While on a radio talk show during the late 1950s, actor John Cassavetes casually mentioned his desire to film an improvisatory project and was soon surprised to receive public donations totaling nearly $20,000. Inspired, Cassavetes scraped together additional funds and, armed with a 16mm camera, he shot the powerful and moving SHADOWS, heralding a vital new era in independent American filmmaking.

Based on a series of improvisations created by members of the Variety Arts Studio, of which Cassavetes was the director, the film depicts the struggle of three black siblings to survive in the mean streets of Manhattan. Hugh (Hugh Hurd), the oldest and a would-be jazz musician, watches over Ben (Ben Carruthers) and Lelia (Lelia Goldoni), both of whom can, and do, pass for white. Darker-skinned than his younger siblings, Hugh has grown increasingly embittered due to the limited opportunities open to him; his artistic potential is being wasted in the dives and strip joints he's forced to play trumpet in just to survive.

Meanwhile, Lelia hooks up with the pretentious New York art crowd and moves among them, teasing and flirting. She has an affair with Tony (Anthony Ray), a young white man, and loses her virginity to him. However, when Tony learns that Lelia is a mulatto, he leaves her. Ben leads a carefree life, hanging out with his friends Tom (Tom Allen) and Dennis (Dennis Sallas), drinking, carousing and getting into trouble. One night the three young men become involved in a vicious street fight. By the film's end, Hugh grows more determined to win over one of the catatonic strip joint audiences, Lelia has taken refuge with friends, and Ben is abandoned by his buddies and left alone to lick his wounds.

Failing to interest American distributors—who, in addition to the obvious issue of content, were put off by the fact that the film was technically spotty and directed by a man heretofore known only as an actor—Cassavetes took SHADOWS to the 1960 Venice Film Festival, where it won the prestigious Critics Award. Shortly thereafter, the film was picked up for British distribution by Lion International. Finally, it made its way to the States and, to Hollywood's surprise, created a minor sensation.

Cassavetes was promptly hailed as a genius by critics and in no time began receiving offers to direct from major studios. The new director accepted Hollywood's embrace, but after making only two films (TOO LATE BLUES and A CHILD IS WAITING) he became frustrated by the limitations imposed on him by producers and returned to independent filmmaking, which allowed him complete control over his art.

While SHADOWS has become somewhat dated over the years and Cassavetes went on to greater heights as a filmmaker, its importance in the development of the American independent movement cannot be overstated, nor can the unique power it still retains. The film perfectly captured a specific time and place, illuminating simple truths regarding the human condition, while unveiling an important, powerful, and visionary new force in the American cinema.

SHAFT

1971 98m c ★★★
Crime R/15
Stirling Silliphant/Roger Lewis

Richard Roundtree (John Shaft), Moses Gunn (Bumpy Jonas), Charles Cioffi (Lt. Vic Androzzy), Christopher St. John (Ben Buford), Gwenn Mitchell (Ellie Moore), Lawrence Pressman (Sgt. Tom Hannon), Victor Arnold (Charlie), Sherri Brewer (Marcy), Rex Robbins (Rollie), Camille Yarbrough (Dina Greene)

p, Joel Freeman; d, Gordon Parks, Sr.; w, John D.F. Black, Ernest Tidyman (based on the novel by Tidyman); ph, Urs Furrer (Metrocolor); ed, Hugh A. Robertson; m, Isaac Hayes; art d, Emanuel Gerard; cos, Joseph Aulisi

This was the second feature of the longtime still photographer Parks, in which he brought together talent for capturing an image and personal knowledge of life on the streets to create a hard-hitting action thriller. Roundtree plays a private detective hired by Harlem mobster Gunn to find his kidnapped daughter. This requires infiltrating the mob before finding the girl. St. John plays the black militant who assists Roundtree, and Cioffi is the cop who helps keep a gangland war from escalating. Although obvious racial tensions are created, these are kept under check by Parks, who concentrated on the humanistic elements in his character. Isaac Hayes's theme song won an Academy Award and his score was also nominated.

SHAKESPEARE WALLAH

1966 115m bw ★★★
Drama /A
Continental Distributing (India)

Shashi Kapoor (Sanju), Felicity Kendal (Lizzie Buckingham), Madhur Jaffrey (Manjula), Geoffrey Kendal (Mr. Tony Buckingham), Laura Liddell (Mrs. Carla Buckingham), Utpal Dutt (Maharaja), Praveen Paul (Didi), Jim D. Tytler (Bobby), Prayag Raaj (Sharmaji), Pincho Kapoor (Guptaji)

p, Ismail Merchant; d, James Ivory; w, Ruth Prawer Jhabvala, James Ivory (based on a story by Jhabvala); ph, Subrata Mitra; ed, Amit Bose; m, Satyajit Ray

Diverting piece about a bedraggled theatrical troupe engaged in a valiant effort to keep the spirit of Shakespeare alive in post-Independence India. English actress Felicity Kendal stars, and much of the material is based on the experiences of her real-life theatrical family. Kendal gets involved in an interracial romance with a rich playboy (Shashi Kapoor); Madhur Jaffrey, an Indian actress also known for her books on Indian cuisine, turns in a colorful performance as a movie star. A wryly humorous film from the directing/producing/writing team of James Ivory, Ismail Merchant and Ruth Prawer Jhabvala.

SHALL WE DANCE

1937 101m bw ★★★★
Romance/Musical/Comedy /U
RKO

Fred Astaire *("Petrov"/Peter P. Peters)*, Ginger Rogers *(Linda Keene)*, Edward Everett Horton *(Jeffrey Baird)*, Eric Blore *(Cecil Flintridge)*, Jerome Cowan *(Arthur Mille—Linda's Manager)*, Ketti Gallian *(Lady Denise Tarrington)*, William Brisbane *(Jim Montgomery)*, Harriet Hoctor *(Harriet Hoctor)*, Ann Shoemaker *(Mrs. Fitzgerald)*, Ben Alexander *(Rooftop Bandleader)*

p, Pandro S. Berman; d, Mark Sandrich; w, Allan Scott, Ernest Pagano, P.J. Wolfson (based on the story "Watch Your Step" by Lee Loeb, Harold Buchman); ph, David Abel; ed, William Hamilton; m, George Gershwin; art d, Van Nest Polglase, Carroll Clark; fx, Vernon L. Walker; chor, Hermes Pan, Harry Losee; cos, Irene

Shall we dance some more, please? For the seventh time in four years, Fred Astaire and Ginger Rogers team up for another frolicsome romp, though this effort doesn't amount to much more than a rehash of their previous films, replete with the usual romantic screw-ups, people pretending to be what they aren't, and too few stylized dances. Thank goodness for Astaire and Rogers and especially for a sensational Gershwin brothers score. Astaire is Petrov, a Russian ballet dancer; Rogers is Linda Keene, a high-powered musical-comedy star. To keep Linda from retiring to marry, Linda's agent (Cowan) suggests that she's already married to Petrov, to the surprise of the breathless press. Petrov and Linda ultimately decide to get married so they can get a very public divorce and clear the air, but true love does blossom amid the many plot complications.

SHALL WE DANCE might have made more of an impact on moviegoers, who, judging from the still huge but slowly declining boxoffice appeal of the Astaire-Rogers efforts, were growing tired of the formula. The film itself still has plenty of shine, but deficiencies exist. The peerless pair enjoy one of their best-ever tap duets with "They All Laughed", one which includes jokes, challenges, hard and soft tap, changes in tempo, a lovely merging of his ballet and her tap and a snappy close. But it's the only duet that measures up. Astaire and Rogers croon "Let's Call the Whole Thing Off" ("you say ee-ther, and I say eye-ther") quite agreeably, but neither quite pulls off the roller-skating routine which follows. Astaire's solo to "Slap That Bass" has some great moments and a blistering finale, but the fuel it provides really doesn't last. The finale, meanwhile, although it offers a clever resolution to the plot, seems more than a bit forced, with Rogers falling back in love with Astaire at the sight of duplicates of herself dancing onstage. The ballet surrounding this climax is a mess, with chorines and ballerinas ambling about in clumps, Astaire looking uncomfortable, and sideshow freak Harriet Hoctor bollixing any impact the number may have. A ballerina-cum-contortionist, Hoctor stops the show dead (and we mean *dead*) when she performs her signature move: kicking herself in the head while bent backwards like a human croquet wicket. Please be sure to share this moment with someone you love, for things like this don't appear in films everyday. The supporting cast (except for the awkward Ketti Gallian) is as expert as it was in earlier RKO musicals, even if the hilarious and gifted duo of Horton and Blore really have to work overtime to put over some of the thin material. Although it didn't initially appear to be hit-laden, George and Ira Gershwin's unfailingly marvelous score ultimately produced a number of standards, including the haunting, Oscar-nominated "They Can't Take That Away From Me." (What a glorious romantic duet that song would have made for Fred and Ginger!) Maybe we've been harsh, because there's still plenty to enjoy in this typically exhilarating Astaire-Rogers effort, but the lack of invention and the slight dearth of dancing do make this a lesser entry in the duo's joint canon.

SHAME
(SKAMMEN)

1968 103m bw ★★★½
Drama R/15
Svensk (Sweden)

Liv Ullmann *(Eva Rosenberg)*, Max von Sydow *(Jan Rosenberg)*, Gunnar Bjornstrand *(Col. Jacobi)*, Sigge Furst *(Filip)*, Birgitta Valberg *(Mrs. Jacobi)*, Hans Alfredson *(Lobelius)*, Ingvar Kjellson *(Oswald)*, Raymond Lundberg *(Jacobi's Son)*, Frank Sundstrom *(Chief Interrogator)*, Willy Peters *(Elder Officer)*

d, Ingmar Bergman; w, Ingmar Bergman; ph, Sven Nykvist; ed, Ulla Ryghe; art d, P.A. Lundgren, Lennart Blomkvist; fx, Evald Andersson; cos, Mago

A stark, chilling film of incredible despair by Ingmar Bergman, taking place in an unnamed country during a civil war. Concert musicians Ullmann and von Sydow are a husband and wife who avoid the atrocities gripping the rest of their country by fleeing to a small isolated island. But their peace is short-lived, as the island becomes a virtual battleground, forcing the pair to face horrors they have been trying to evade. As the fighting intensifies and their situation worsens, the marriage between Ullmann and von Sydow also changes. Never having to really fend for themselves to remain alive, they find the strains give them a different perspective. Ullmann sleeps with a friend of von Sydow to get out of jail. The jealous von Sydow, refusing to help the friend after he's arrested, allows the man to be killed. But this is just the beginning of the depths to which von Sydow sinks. He goes so far as to kill an innocent soldier just for his boots. Ullmann becomes more distressed, and, upon leaving the island on a small boat, the two travel through a sea literally filled with floating dead bodies. This scene is almost dreamlike in its stark and vivid imagery. SHAME effectively illustrates the depths to which civilized humans can descend when their comfort is taken away. Both Ullmann and von Sydow do an excellent job of portraying personalities taken to the limits of emotional perseverance.

SHAMPOO

1975 109m c ★★★
Drama/Comedy R/18
Columbia

Warren Beatty *(George Roundy)*, Julie Christie *(Jackie Shawn)*, Goldie Hawn *(Jill)*, Lee Grant *(Felicia Carr)*, Jack Warden *(Lester Carr)*, Tony Bill *(Johnny Pope)*, Carrie Fisher *(Lorna Carr)*, Jay Robinson *(Norman)*, George Furth *(Mr. Pettis)*, Ann Weldon *(Mary)*

p, Warren Beatty; d, Hal Ashby; w, Robert Towne, Warren Beatty; ph, Laszlo Kovacs (Panavision, Technicolor); ed, Robert C. Jones; m, Paul Simon; prod d, Richard Sylbert; art d, Stewart Campbell; cos, Anthea Sylbert

Pleasantly satirical romp in which Beatty mercilessly lampoons his own off-screen image. He plays a popular hairdresser for the wealthy women of Beverly Hills, but he does more than cut hair for his clients. The film, which takes place on November 4, 1968 (the day Richard Nixon was elected President), opens as Beatty is engaged in an affair with Grant, an attractive older woman who is married to Warden. Their lovemaking is interrupted by a phone call from Hawn, another of Beatty's client-lovers. He rushes over to her home and ends up spending the rest of the night with her. Later Beatty, who wants to escape from his nagging boss, Robinson, talks to a bank loan officer, hoping to get the money to open his own hair salon. The loan officer thinks Beatty is a poor risk, and the angered hairdresser retaliates by screaming, "I've got the heads!" Grant suggests Beatty approach her husband and borrow the money from him. Warden is currently having an affair with Christie, an old lover (as well as customer) of Beatty's. Warden agrees to consider Beatty's request, assuming that Beatty is a homosexual because of his profession. Warden also asks Beatty to escort Christie to an election night party, since he must take his wife. Beatty reluctantly agrees, and the party proves to be a fiasco. Christie gets angry when Warden ignores her, and subsequently gets drunk. She makes a scene at a dinner table by virtually attacking Beatty in a lustful frenzy. Beatty is instructed to take her home, but instead Beatty and Christie head off to another Beverly Hills party. Warden gets drunk as well, and he is separated from his wife when the building is evacuated because of a bomb threat. He gets a lift from Hawn and her escort, producer Bill, ending up at the same party Beatty and Christie have gone to. Warden, along with Hawn and Bill, surprises Beatty and Christie as they make love. Hawn is furious and Beatty goes chasing after her. The next morning Beatty, after being threatened by Warden who has learned of his indiscretions with both Grant and Christie, races his motorcycle to catch up with Christie. He wants to marry her, but she turns him down, explaining that Warden is leaving Grant to marry her. From a hilltop Beatty watches as Grant and Warden drive off.

SHAMPOO offended many with its amoral characters and frank sexual nature. However, these are the targets of its satire, showing the ugly foundations that lie beneath the beautiful people of Beverly Hills. These are shallow people, concerned only with gratifying themselves, caring not a whit for the consequences of their actions. Surface appearance is everything, and one of the funniest moments has Christie and Grant discovering to their mutual horror that Beatty has given them the same hairstyle. The lines of sexual entanglements turn into a weblike mess and occasionally get out of hand, straying from the film's theme. Beatty, who produced SHAMPOO and cowrote the script (reportedly working for six years on it), is marvelous as the not-too-bright Romeo. Beatty's off-screen romances were well chronicled, and in SHAMPOO he attacks this public image with venom. His character is empty and juvenile, claiming he wants only to please his customers when all he wants is to satisfy his own libido. His proposal to Christie is more out of desperation for stability than for love. Hawn sums up his character nicely when she shouts at him: "You never stop moving! You never go anywhere!" The film's use of television election returns during the election night party is effective. Though history is changing before their very eyes, the party guests remain oblivious to it, instead caught up in the drama of their own sexual politics. Though SHAMPOO's pace is uneven, the satire works, and the cast is marvelous. Grant received an Oscar for Best Supporting Actress, while Beatty's skills as a screenwriter (along with Towne) earned a nomination for the script. Warden also received a nomination as Best Supporting Actor. Simon's music is one of the film's biggest detriments, an annoying guitar accompanied by the popular singer's humming. It intrudes on the action, injecting saccharine where the actors' talents are strong enough to carry the material. The best use of music comes over the closing credits. The Beach Boys' popular song "Wouldn't It Be Nice" plays as the credits roll, a final black-humored punch line to the film. Fisher made her film debut here as Grant's feisty daughter who seduces Beatty in record time. Reportedly Fisher's mother, Debbie Reynolds, was furious with her daughter for taking the part. SHAMPOO was an enormous success at the box office, taking in some $60 million during its initial release.

SHANE
1953 118m c ★★★★
Western /PG
Paramount

Alan Ladd *(Shane)*, Jean Arthur *(Marion Starrett)*, Van Heflin *(Joe Starrett)*, Brandon de Wilde *(Joey)*, Jack Palance *(Wilson)*, Ben Johnson *(Chris)*, Edgar Buchanan *(Lewis)*, Emile Meyer *(Ryker)*, Elisha Cook, Jr. *(Torrey)*, Douglas Spencer *(Shipstead)*

p, George Stevens; d, George Stevens; w, A.B. Guthrie, Jr., Jack Sher (based on the novel by Jack Schaefer); ph, Loyal Griggs (Technicolor); ed, William Hornbeck, Tom McAdoo; m, Victor Young; art d, Hal Pereira, Walter Tyler; fx, Gordon Jennings; cos, Edith Head

Self-important, overly solemn, middlingly paced—all harbingers of what would become Stevens's later style. It's the western styled as Arthurian legend, flawlessly cast, undeniably splendid. The thematic attempt really takes off when the Black Knight himself, Jack Palance, arrives, or when a dog mourns the passing of his master. And Brandon de Wilde had a very special line in children's roles—an ability to bring complexity and individual humor to the realm of childhood's longing. We love him very much.

SHANE stars Alan Ladd in the title role of the gunslinger who becomes a young boy's idol. Joe and Marion Starrett (Van Heflin and Jean Arthur) and their adventurous young son Joey (Brandon de Wilde) are struggling to survive on their Wyoming frontier homestead. One day, Shane (Alan Ladd) approaches on horseback and asks for water for himself and his mount. Joe obliges, and before long Shane is helping the family protect its land from villainous cattle baron Ryker (Emile Meyer). Shane stays on as a ranch hand and, in the process, becomes a friend and hero to young Joey. Shane's presence, however, proves to be too much of an obstacle for Ryker, and the inevitable showdown occurs. SHANE is a powerful drama in which the old West of gunslingers and cattle barons bows to the new era of the homesteader and the family. Ladd, who was never better as the doomed hero, and who gives one of the best performances ever seen in *any* western, knows he is a creature of the past and that he cannot escape his reputation as a hired gun. Although the film is often brutal, there is such a positive sense of morality displayed here that SHANE should be seen by the whole family. Winner of a Best Cinematography Oscar for Loyal Griggs. How many Academy members knew Paramount had sliced the top and bottom off Griggs's compositions, to accomodate the then-new, wide screen, and therefore had lost some of the color? Ladd learned a bitter lesson from SHANE. Then in the process of leaving Paramount for Warners, the former did no lobbying to earn him a Best Actor nomination. Yet the legacy of character he left behind gave this lonely, taciturn man immortality among children who see this movie.

SHANGHAI EXPRESS
1932 80m bw ★★★★★
Drama /A
Paramount

Marlene Dietrich *(Shanghai Lily)*, Clive Brook *(Capt. Donald "Doc" Harvey)*, Anna May Wong *(Hui Fei)*, Warner Oland *(Henry Chang)*, Eugene Pallette *(Sam Salt)*, Lawrence Grant *(Rev. Carmichael)*, Louise Closser Hale *(Mrs. Haggerty)*, Gustav von Seyffertitz *(Eric Baum)*, Emile Chautard *(Maj. Lenard)*, Claude King *(Albright)* d, Josef von Sternberg; w, Jules Furthman (based on a story by Harry Hervey); ph, Lee Garmes; m, W. Franke Harling; art d, Hans Dreier; cos, Travis Banton

The fourth of the Josef von Sternberg-Marlene Dietrich collaborations (following THE BLUE ANGEL, MOROCCO, and DISHONORED), SHANGHAI EXPRESS is a mystical and exotic story of love and destruction, a film for which both star and director became legends. The film begins at the Peking Railroad as China's great train, the Shanghai Express, is being boarded and loaded with baggage. En route to Shanghai is a mixed assortment of characters, including Dietrich, a lady of questionable reputation known as "the White Flower of the Chinese coast;" Clive Brook, a British Medical Corps officer; Warner Oland, a shady half-caste merchant with a penchant for carrying a cane; and Anna Mae Wong, an American-bred Chinese prostitute with plans for starting anew in marriage. The time of the journey is one of great political unrest, with the possibility of bands of rebels attacking the train looming large. Before the train even leaves the station, arrests are made. Brook is surprised to find that he is traveling with Dietrich, a past love of his whom he deserted. Because of his constant work and busy schedule, he has never heard of her reputation as a glamorous prostitute and seductress. But he soon begins to understand Dietrich and the power she holds over men. In the meantime, it becomes clear to everyone on board that Oland is a rebel leader, desperate over the arrest of his aides. Along the way, Oland orders the train stopped at an old station that has been taken over for use as rebel headquarters, while he makes plans to take hostages from among his fellow first-class passengers. Oland, like Brook, is strongly attracted to the elusive Dietrich, but when the rebel leader asks Dietrich to be his mistress, she turns him down flat. But Oland pressures Dietrich by threatening to torture Brook. Only then—in order to save Brook—does Dietrich give in. Brook, however, is unaware of what she has done. Oland's fate is sealed, however, not by Dietrich or Brook, but by Wong, the prostitute in search of redemption, who has earlier been raped by the insatiable rebel leader. As Oland returns to his room, Wong stabs him to death, thereby freeing herself, the Shanghai Express, and the love between Dietrich and Brook.

Though von Sternberg insisted the film was based on a one-page treatment handed him by Harry Hervey, the story of THE SHANGHAI EXPRESS is clearly drawn from Guy de Maupassant's classic short story of a French prostitute during the Franco-Prussian war, "Boule de Suif." The final film, however, is all von Sternberg, his enigmatic creation, Dietrich, filling the screen with her stunning persona. Dietrich, as always, gave von Sternberg the exact performance he had envisioned, but feuds and hard feelings ran rampant between the director and the remainder of the cast. Von Sternberg was something of a tyrant on the set, and actors received the brunt of his wrath. Lending further credence to his tyrannical image on the set, von Sternberg, who had nearly lost his voice from shouting, dismissed a suggestion from Sam Jaffe to use a megaphone, instead hooking up a public address system. This enthusiasm and complete control over the production paid off for the director and for SHANGHAI EXPRESS come Oscar time. The film was nominated for Best Picture (losing to GRAND HOTEL), von Sternberg received a nomination for Best Director (his second in a row), and Lee Garmes walked away with a statuette for his cinematography.

SHARKY'S MACHINE

1981 122m c   ★★★
Crime   R/18
Deliverance/Orion

Burt Reynolds (Sharky), Vittorio Gassman (Victor), Brian Keith (Papa), Charles Durning (Friscoe), Earl Holliman (Hotchkins), Bernie Casey (Arch), Henry Silva (Billy Score), Richard Libertini (Nosh), Darryl Hickman (Smiley), Rachel Ward (Dominoe)

p, Hank Moonjean; d, Burt Reynolds; w, Gerald Di Pego (based on the novel by William Diehl); ph, William A. Fraker (Technicolor); ed, William Gordean; m, Snuff Garrett, Al Capps; prod d, Walter Scott Herndon; cos, Norman Salling

Burt Reynolds proves himself a capable director in this effort in which he plays Sharky, a tough cop out to uncover a gangster kingpin (Gassman). After his cover is blown during an investigation, Reynolds is demoted to the vice squad, but he manages to mold his new coworkers into a force that is every bit a match for the gangsters. In an interesting twist on the standard romantic formula, Reynolds falls in love with the high-class hooker he's been staking out (Ward). Loaded with violence and nonstop action, SHARKY'S MACHINE features one of the most complex and dangerous stunts ever attempted: the 16-floor fall by stuntman Dar Robinson.

SHE DONE HIM WRONG

1933 66m bw   ★★★★★
Comedy   /A
Paramount

Mae West (Lady Lou), Cary Grant (Capt. Cummings), Owen Moore (Chick Clark), Gilbert Roland (Serge Stanieff), Noah Beery, Sr. (Gus Jordan), David Landau (Dan Flynn), Rafaela Ottiano (Russian Rita), Dewey Robinson (Spider Kane), Rochelle Hudson (Sally Glynn), Tammany Young (Chuck Connors)

p, William Le Baron; d, Lowell Sherman; w, Mae West, Harvey Thew, John Bright (based on the play "Diamond Lil" by Mae West); ph, Charles Lang; ed, Al Hall; art d, Robert Usher; chor, Harold Hecht; cos, Edith Head

Marvelously crude melodrama dished up with generous portions of undiluted West in her first starring vehicle. Re-creating her bediamonded demimonde, Diamond Lil, for the screen (the character name is now Lady Lou—the bluenoses were hot on West's heels already), she wriggles her way through some low-down dirty blues ditties, seduces young Cary Grant's righteous Salvation Army crusader, kicks asses and takes names. This is the closest evocation of the Gay '90s we can think of; Sherman did a fine job of evoking the gaudy squalor of the denizens of New York's famed Bowery district, and West established herself as a persona happiest squabbling among the chiselers and money-lenders.

West had been on the stage since eight years of age, and had reigned supreme with Lil on Broadway, before Hollywood beckoned her at around age 40 (West was hazy about age) to support George Raft in NIGHT AFTER NIGHT. With SHE DONE HIM WRONG, West became an enormous star. She made 12 movies altogether, 10 of which she wrote either alone or with collaborators. Amazingly, SHE DONE HIM WRONG was shot in 18 days, plus one week of rehearsal, as West fiddled with the lines to mislead the censors. Paramount was teetering on the brink of bankruptcy when they invested $200,000 in this movie. SHE DONE HIM WRONG returned more than 10 times that amount domestically and another $1 million in foreign release, despite having been banned in Austria after the first night's showing.

SHE WORE A YELLOW RIBBON

West's Lou must rank as one of the first truly liberated women ever seen onscreen as she runs a Bowery saloon, fronting for owner Noah Beery, Sr. Cary Grant, a captain at the local mission, spends more than the usual amount of time in the bar in what seems to be an attempt to save her immortal soul; before long the buxom West is in love with the youthful Grant. Having been the mistress of Beery, who plies her with diamonds, West knows she's in trouble when her heart begins to obscure the glow of the gems. But Beery is discovered to be running a counterfeiting ring and, as a sideline, sending young women to San Francisco to be pickpockets. Gilbert Roland and Rafaela Ottiano have been passing the bogus money that Beery needs to pay for West's diamonds. Then, in a jealous battle with West, Ottiano gets herself killed.

Remember what we said about crude melodrama? Scenes like the latter obviously recall the touring shows West herself must have seen growing up as a tyke in turn of the century Brooklyn. West's original character of Lil was derived from her mother, a former French corset model whose husband (West's Irish prize-fighter father) referred to her affectionately as "Champagne Til". There may also have been a real Lil who lived on the Bowery (said to have a tooth with a diamond in it—so there, Mick Jagger). And some of Lil was undoubtedly West herself: as a child, West's mother spoiled her outrageously, always dressing her in miniature versions of her own elaborate gowns. West never lost her taste for long skirts, fancy fabrics, wasp waists and cornucopic picture hats.

Between clinches and sass, West wows us in her inimitable way with "Maizie," "A Guy What Takes His Time," "Haven't Got No Peace of Mind" (Leo Robin, Ralph Rainger), "I Wonder Where My Easy Rider's Gone" (Shelton Brooks), "Silver Threads Among the Gold" (Egbert Van Alstyne), and her signature, "Frankie and Johnnie" (traditional).

She had spotted Grant on the Paramount lot and asked to have him in the picture, a request that pleased director Lowell Sherman, who liked Grant's work with Marlene Dietrich in BLONDE VENUS. But West, who never saw other women's movies, didn't know that. Eyeing Grant up and down, West said to Sherman, "If he can talk, I'll take 'im." In the years to come, West always played variations on this "Diamond Lil" role in everything she did, tacking on other character names. "Why should I go good, when I'm packin' 'em in 'cause I'm bad?", West once asked. In Hollywood's community of unique personalities, West stood out even among these. Forever unmarried, West remained no man's woman: "I was always too busy, concentratin' on m'self," she explained.

SHE WORE A YELLOW RIBBON
1949   103m   c   ★★★★
Western/War   /U
Argosy

John Wayne *(Capt. Nathan Brittles)*, Joanne Dru *(Olivia Dandridge)*, John Agar *(Lt. Flint Cohill)*, Ben Johnson *(Sgt. Tyree)*, Harry Carey, Jr. *(Lt. Ross Pennell)*, Victor McLaglen *(Sgt. Quincannon)*, Mildred Natwick *(Mrs. Abby Allshard)*, George O'Brien *(Maj. Mack Allshard)*, Arthur Shields *(Dr. O'Laughlin)*, Francis Ford *(Barman)*

p, John Ford, Merian C. Cooper; d, John Ford; w, Frank S. Nugent, Laurence Stallings (based on the stories "War Party" and "The Big Hunt" by James Warner Bellah); ph, Winton C. Hoch, Charles P. Boyle (Technicolor); ed, Jack Murray; m, Richard Hageman; art d, James Basevi; fx, Jack Cosgrove, Jack Caffee; cos, Michael Meyers, Ann Peck

The second film in John Ford's "Cavalry Trilogy" features John Wayne at his best and boasts some incredible, Oscar-winning Technicolor photography of Monument Valley. Capt. Nathan Brittles (Wayne) is a career officer in the US Cavalry marking the final days before his forced retirement from the service. In the wake of the massacre of Custer and the Seventh Cavalry, the local Indians are becoming agitated, and, worse, confident. Brittles is assigned to escort two women (Joanne Dru and Mildred Natwick) from the fort to the stagecoach stop at Sudrow's Wells, but the Indians are on the warpath and there is little chance now to evacuate the women from the area. Wayne gives one of the finest performances of his career here, in the first serious role Ford gave him. (Wayne himself later said that Ford never respected him as an actor until he made RED RIVER.) As Capt. Brittles—the character a full generation older than the actor—Wayne is at his most human, a man who has made the Army his whole life, even sacrificing the lives of his family to its service, and now having to watch his Army career end on a note of failure. The passing of time is the film's recurring theme, suggested as Brittles arrives late with his troops, is forced to retire because of his age, leaves a dance to speak to his dead wife; even the inscription on the watch the troopers give him, "Lest we forget," plays on this theme of time lost and recalled. Ford's main inspiration for the film's scenic look was the western paintings of Frederic Remington. On the set, the director clashed with cinematographer Winton Hoch, a technical perfectionist who would endlessly fiddle with his camera while the cast baked in the sun. One day in the desert, when a line of threatening clouds darkened the horizon, indicating a thunderstorm, Hoch started to pack up his equipment. Ford ordered him to continue shooting, and Hoch did so, but filed an official protest with his union. The shot that emerged, of a fantastic purple sky with jagged streaks of lightning reaching toward earth in the distance, was breathtaking and helped Hoch win an Oscar for his work on the film. After decades of terribly washed-out color prints of SHE WORE A YELLOW RIBBON, the film has recently been restored to its original glory and may soon be available on home video in pristine condition.

SHENANDOAH
1965   105m   c   ★★★½
War   /PG
Universal

James Stewart *(Charlie Anderson)*, Doug McClure *(Sam)*, Glenn Corbett *(Jacob Anderson)*, Patrick Wayne *(James Anderson)*, Rosemary Forsyth *(Jannie Anderson)*, Phillip Alford *(Boy Anderson)*, Katharine Ross *(Ann Anderson)*, Charles Robinson *(Nathan Anderson)*, James McMullan *(John Anderson)*, Tim McIntire *(Henry Anderson)*

p, Robert Arthur; d, Andrew V. McLaglen; w, James Lee Barrett; ph, William Clothier (Technicolor); ed, Otho Lovering; m, Frank Skinner; art d, Alexander Golitzen, Alfred Sweeney; cos, Rosemary Odell

An offbeat performance from James Stewart as Virginia farmer Charlie Anderson makes SHENANDOAH an involving and entertaining look at one family's attempt to deal with the Civil War. A prosperous farmer with six sons and one daughter, Charlie is a widower whose wife died during the birth of Boy (Phillip Alford). Charlie, who is opposed to slavery, tries to maintain a neutral stance in the conflict between North and South. However, a number of events threaten to change his pacifist leanings: 16-year-old Boy is captured by Union soldiers; Confederate son-in-law Sam (Doug McClure) is called to duty; son James

(Patrick Wayne) and his wife, Ann (Katharine Ross), are murdered by Confederate looters; and another son, Jacob (Glenn Corbett), is killed by a Confederate guardsman. Andrew V. McLaglen's excellent direction and carefully crafted battle scenes successfully combine with one of the best supporting casts you're likely to find outside of a John Ford film, including Harry Carey, Jr., Warren Oates, Strother Martin, Denver Pyle, George Kennedy, Paul Fix, and Bob Steele.

SHE'S GOTTA HAVE IT

1986   84m   c/bw   ★★★
Comedy/Drama   R/18
Spike Lee Joint/Forty Acres and a Mule

Tracy Camila Johns (Nola Darling), Tommy Redmond Hicks (Jamie Overstreet), John Canada Terrell (Greer Childs), Spike Lee (Mars Blackmon), Raye Dowell (Opal Gilstrap), Joie Lee (Clorinda Bradford), Epatha Merkinson (Dr. Jamison), Bill Lee (Sonny Darling), Cheryl Burr (Ava), Aaron Dugger (Noble)

p, Shelton J. Lee; d, Spike Lee; w, Spike Lee; ph, Ernest Dickerson; ed, Spike Lee; m, Bill Lee; prod d, Wynn Thomas; art d, Ron Paley; cos, John Michael Reefer

Combining a lively, topical theme with stylish filmmaking techniques, NYU Film School alum Spike Lee won instant recognition for SHE'S GOTTA HAVE IT, his promising but flawed feature debut.

Nola Darling (Tracy Camila Johns) is a young, black Brooklyn woman whose bed is a shrine visited with great frequency by three very different boyfriends. She can't, however, pick the one she likes the best. First there's Jamie Overstreet (Tommy Redmond Hicks), a sensitive, well-mannered sort who smothers Nola with his overpossessiveness. Then there's Greer Childs (John Canada Terrell), a self-absorbed fashion model. The most likable character is the third beau, Mars Blackmon (director Lee), an unemployed bicycle messenger who always manages to make Nola—and audiences—laugh.

Combining humor, drama, and documentary techniques, Lee has created an energetic film that takes an unflinching look at modern sexuality—specifically black sexuality. The film is filled with scenes of the main characters speaking to the camera, commenting on the story and their rival characters—adding a sense of authenticity it might otherwise lack. Although the film's small budget and tight shooting schedule (lensed in 15 days on Super 16mm) is betrayed by sloppy editing, unpolished sound and an occasional flat performance, particularly Johns in the lead role, SHE'S GOTTA HAVE IT still bursts with the energy and technical command that have quickly established Lee as a major force in American cinema.

SHINING, THE

1980   146m   c   ★★★
Horror   R/18
WB   (U.K.)

Jack Nicholson (Jack Torrance), Shelley Duvall (Wendy Torrance), Danny Lloyd (Danny), Scatman Crothers (Halloran), Barry Nelson (Ullman), Philip Stone (Grady), Joseph Turkel (Lloyd), Anne Jackson (Doctor), Tony Burton (Durkin), Lia Beldam (Young Woman in Bathtub)

p, Stanley Kubrick; d, Stanley Kubrick; w, Stanley Kubrick, Diane Johnson (based on the novel by Stephen King); ph, John Alcott; ed, Ray Lovejoy; m, Bela Bartok, Wendy Carlos, Rachel Elkind, Gyorgi Ligeti, Krzysztof Penderecki; prod d, Roy Walker; art d, Leslie Tomkins; cos, Milena Canonero

THE SHINING perversely retains the skeletal outline of Stephen King's superior American Gothic novel while exorcising its soul. Carefully constructed motivations are ignored and some key elements are inexplicably jettisoned, though this nevertheless remains a powerful exercise in (sometimes campy) horror.

Jack Torrance (Nicholson) is a former schoolteacher hoping to find the solitude necessary to write a novel, so he accepts a position as the off-season caretaker of a Colorado resort, the Overlook Hotel. Because the winter storms are so fierce in this isolated mountain region, the hotel is often cut off from the rest of civilization. When he accepts the job, Jack is warned that the isolation can be devastating (some years earlier the caretaker axed his wife and two daughters to death). Jack and his wife, Wendy (Duvall), and their son, Danny (Lloyd), journey by car to the Overlook. Danny possesses the psychic gift that the hotel's chef (Crothers) calls "the shining"—he can "see" events from the future and the past. He can also project his thoughts into the minds of others. Danny senses something evil about the hotel and, while riding his bike through its labyrinthine halls, has visions of the carnage of past murders. His only playmate in this lonely environment is his "imaginary" friend, Tony. The emotionally vulnerable Jack—he's a recovering alcoholic with a history of violent episodes—is bedeviled by visions as well. Before long he begins to succumb to the hotel's supernatural forces and becomes possessed by thoughts of chopping up his family.

While Kubrick does an admirable job of sustaining a mood of unease throughout, the film begins to feel like a cruel tease as it offers scene after elegant scene of slow buildup with no real payoff. The film begins with astounding aerial footage of the Torrances' car driving through breathtaking mountain landscapes, accompanied by Wendy Carlos' mournful electronic score. There's also some impressive Steadicam work as the camera follows directly behind Danny, riding his Big Wheel bike through the winding corridors of the hotel. Cinematographer John Alcott (A CLOCKWORK ORANGE, BARRY LYNDON) does his usual outstanding job in each of these sequences. The film is rich thematically as well as visually—it's interesting to see how well the themes of the novel coincide with Kubrick's ongoing obsessions—but dramatically unsatisfying; it seems to have been conceived as a horror film for people who have contempt for the genre. Duvall and Lloyd are excellent, while Nicholson's performance is completely over the top, complete with rolling eyes and hyperactive eyebrows. By the time of the climactic chase, he's lurching around like a cut-rate Quasimodo.

Wholeheartedly recommended to hardcore Kubrick fans and to those who don't particularly care for horror movies; everyone else should stick with the book.

SHIP OF FOOLS

1965   148m   bw   ★★★★
Drama   /A
Columbia

Vivien Leigh (Mary Treadwell), Simone Signoret (La Condesa), Jose Ferrer (Rieber), Lee Marvin (Tenny), Oskar Werner (Dr. Schumann), Elizabeth Ashley (Jenny), George Segal (David), Jose Greco (Pepe), Michael Dunn (Glocken), Charles Korvin (Capt. Thiele)

p, Stanley Kramer; d, Stanley Kramer; w, Abby Mann (based on the novel by Katherine Anne Porter); ph, Ernest Laszlo; ed, Robert C. Jones; m, Ernest Gold; prod d, Robert Clatworthy; fx, Albert Whitlock, Farciot Edouart, John Burke; cos, Bill Thomas, Jean Louis

GRAND HOTEL at sea. It's the early 1930s, and an oceanliner peopled with a cross-section of society is leaving Vera Cruz for Bremerhaven. In the high class section are several well-to-do people, while below decks are a horde of sugar field workers returning to Spain after a season of work in Cuba. There are several wealthy Germans on the ship, and all are asked to sit at the captain's table, save two. Korvin, the captain of the ship, thinks it might be best if Heinz Ruhmann, a Jew, and Dunn, a dwarf, not dine with the others in view of Hitler's theory of Aryan purity. Alf Kjellin, another German, leaves the table and sits with Dunn and Ruhmann when it is learned that Kjellin's wife is Jewish. Werner, the ship's doctor and a man with a bad heart, spends a great deal of his time with Signoret, a Spaniard being shipped back to Europe for having engaged in political activities. She is facing prison and takes solace in drugs. Werner finds her fascinating, and the two fall in love. Marvin is a failed baseball player whose career went awry because he couldn't hit the outside curve ball. Marvin is a satyr, a drunk, and has an hysterical scene when he attempts to explain his hitting problem to Dunn, who is as familiar with baseball as Marvin is with teetotaling. Also on the ship are Segal and Ashley. They are unmarried lovers, and he resents the fact that he can't make a living as an artist; but they are so sexually magnetized to each other that their arguments usually end up in a passionate embrace. Leigh is a divorcee who flirts with everyone and enjoys leading men on and then shoving them aside. (This was her final screen appearance before she died in 1967.) Wengraf is a religious evangelist who goes down into the hold and preaches to the sugar workers, stirring them into a free-for-all brawl. John Wengraf is aboard the ship with his young nephew, Charles de Vries, who has a roll in the hay with a hooker traveling with Jose Greco's dance group. Greco not only runs the troupe, he is also a panderer. Gila Golan is a young woman who despairs because she feels she's ugly and is only brought out of her self-doubt through the help of Ashley and the fact that Ruhmann thinks she's charming and beautiful. The ship stops, and Signoret is taken off to jail; then it goes on to Bremerhaven, where Werner dies of a heart attack and the others get off to face whatever is their future. All of the above stories are interwoven, soap opera style, so we never follow any single story for any lengthy period of time. It's an adult picture with graphic language and important themes, the main one being Nazism. Ferrer is the principle espouser of Hitler's words and a hated creature throughout the film. Superb acting in a script that seldom descends into bathos. Included are three tunes from Ernest Gold (who wrote the score for EXODUS) and Jack Lloyd, a German-American lyricist. The tunes were: "Heute Abend," "Geh'n Wir Bummelin Auf Der Reeperbahn," and "Irgendwie, Irgendwo, Irgendwanh." Producer-director Kramer made many films focusing on Nazism and racism, including JUDGMENT AT NUREMBERG, THE JUGGLER, PRESSURE POINT, and THE DEFIANT ONES, and the themes crept into much of his other work.

SHOCK CORRIDOR

1963   101m   c/bw   ★★★½
Drama   /15
Allied Artists

Peter Breck (*Johnny Barrett*), Constance Towers (*Cathy*), Gene Evans (*Boden*), James Best (*Stuart*), Hari Rhodes (*Trent*), Larry Tucker (*Pagliacci*), William Zuckert (*Swanee*), Philip Ahn (*Dr. Fong*), Neyle Morrow (*Psycho*), John Matthews (*Dr. Cristo*)

p, Samuel Fuller; d, Samuel Fuller; w, Samuel Fuller (based on his scenario); ph, Stanley Cortez, Samuel Fuller (Technicolor); ed, Jerome Thoms; m, Paul Dunlap; art d, Eugene Lourie; fx, Charles Duncan, Lynn Dunn; chor, Jon Gregory; cos, Einar Bourman

Good example of Fuller's "tabloid" filmmaking style, displaying the contradictory politics and pugnacious visual style that earned him the label "American primitive."

A self-serving reporter (Breck) has himself confined to an asylum so he can uncover a murder and win a Pulitzer Prize. He is sucked into the maelstrom of the asylum, which is presented as a microcosm of contemporary society, and eventually loses his mind. Fuller plays cinematic bully here, forcefully confronting us with unpleasant characters and situations in a way that makes us rethink our preconceptions about insanity and civilization. The bravura camerawork, by Stanley Cortez, is a marvel. Original release prints included some color sequences the director had shot in Japan and Africa as early as 1955. Fuller followed this piece with what was probably one of his best works, THE NAKED KISS.

SHOESHINE

(SCIUSCIA)
1946   93m   bw   ★★★½
Prison   /A
Lopert   (Italy)

Rinaldo Smordoni (*Giuseppe*), Franco Interlenghi (*Pasquale*), Aniello Mele (*Raffaele*), Bruno Ortensi (*Arcangeli*), Pacifico Astrologo (*Vittorio*), Francesco de Nicola (*Ciriola*), Antonio Carlino (*L'Abruzzese*), Enrico de Silva (*Giorgio*), Antonio Lo Nigro (*Righetoo*), Angelo D'Amico (*Siciliano*)

p, Paolo W. Tamburella; d, Vittorio De Sica; w, Cesare Zavattini, Sergio Amidei, Adolfo Franci, Cesare Viola, Vittorio De Sica (based on a story by Zavattini); ph, Anchise Brizzi; m, Alessandro Cicognini

Along with THE BICYCLE THIEF and UMBERTO D, this film is one of the three neorealist masterpieces produced through the collaborative efforts of director Vittorio De Sica and screenwriter Cesare Zavattini. Like so many of the films of the neorealist movement, SHOESHINE is simply real life projected on a screen. After spying on a pair of shoeshine boys for a year in war-torn Rome, De Sica and Zavattini decided to bring their story to the screen with two nonprofessionals in the lead roles. Giuseppe (Rinaldo Smordoni) and Pasquale (Franco Interlenghi) are waifs who survive by harassing American soldiers—the only ones in postwar Italy with spare change—into spending a few lire to have their boots cleaned. Despite their bleak surroundings, these shoeshine boys still have innocent dreams and hopes, and, in fact, are saving their earnings to buy a handsome white horse. When Giuseppe's brother approaches them with a black market opportunity to make some quick money, they jump at the chance, buy their dream horse, and refuse to let it out of their sight, even going so far as to sleep in the stable with it. This brief moment in paradise is short-lived, however, and they are arrested, taken to a reformatory, and locked away. The longer they stay in their damp, vermin-infested cells, the more hardened the youngsters become. A powerful indictment of the Italian penal system and, on a larger scale, the brutal inevitability of the loss of innocence.

SHOOT THE MOON

1982   124m   c   ★★
Drama   R/15

Albert Finney (*George Dunlap*), Diane Keaton (*Faith Dunlap*), Karen Allen (*Sandy*), Peter Weller (*Frank Henderson*), Dana Hill

(Sherry), Viveka Davis (Jill), Tracey Gold (Marianne), Tina Yothers (Molly), George Murdock (French DeVoe), Leora Dana (Charlotte DeVoe)

p, Alan Marshall; d, Alan Parker; w, Bo Goldman; ph, Michael Seresin (Metrocolor); ed, Gerry Hambling; prod d, Geoffrey Kirkland; art d, Stewart Campbell; cos, Kristi Zea

A patently phony attempt to cash in on the yuppie lifestyle, SHOOT THE MOON features Albert Finney as George Dunlap, a successful writer, and Diane Keaton as his wife, Faith. Married 15 years, they have four young daughters and live in trendy Marin County, just north of San Francisco. Ennui has replaced passion in their marriage and they split up. George starts an affair with Sandy (Karen Allen), while Faith finds solace with Frank (Peter Weller), the contractor for the tennis court the Dunlaps are building, and the four kids do their best to try and get their parents together. Finney and Keaton each have their heavy dramatic moments, but there is nothing in writer Bo Goldman's script that hasn't been seen and heard in a thousand other films.

SHOOT THE PIANO PLAYER
(TIREZ SUR LE PIANISTE)
1960   80m   bw   ★★★★★
Crime   /X
Pleiade   (France)

Charles Aznavour (Charlie Kohler/Edouard Saroyan), Marie Dubois (Lena), Nicole Berger (Theresa), Michele Mercier (Clarisse), Albert Remy (Chico Saroyan), Jacques Aslanian (Richard Saroyan), Richard Kanayan (Fido Saroyan), Claude Mansard (Momo), Daniel Boulanger (Ernest), Serge Davri (Plyne)

p, Pierre Braunberger; d, Francois Truffaut; w, Francois Truffaut, Marcel Moussy (based on the novel Down There by David Goodis); ph, Raoul Coutard (Dyaliscope); ed, Cecile Decugis, Claudine Bouche; m, Georges Delerue; art d, Jacques Mely

A marvelously funny movie about sadness. For his follow-up to THE 400 BLOWS (1959), Francois Truffaut chose not to deliver another episode of his autobiography, nor to study childhood, but to pay homage to Hollywood gangster films. Deciding to adapt David Goodis's pulp novel Down There, Truffaut chose Charles Aznavour, one of France's most popular singers and songwriters, to play the role of Charlie Kohler, a honky-tonk cafe piano player who has given up his life as the famed concert pianist Edouard Saroyan. He becomes mixed up in the underworld affairs of his brother, Remy, and fears not only for his own safety, but for that of his adolescent brother, Kanayan. In the process he falls in love with Dubois but has trouble mustering the courage to court her. As he gets entangled deeper and deeper in the underworld and in romance, Aznavour reveals who he really is, how he got "down there," and why he doesn't ever want to go back.

SHOOT THE PIANO PLAYER is a magnificent picture, not because of its debt to the gangster genre, but because of Truffaut's personal approach to that genre. Truffaut doesn't concern himself with plot mechanisms—since those have been provided for him countless times by Hollywood—but instead uses the conventions as a frame upon which to hang his own ideas (in much the same way the science-fiction genre served him in FAHRENHEIT 451), which burst out into all kinds of witty explorations. Said Truffaut, "The idea behind SHOOT THE PIANO PLAYER was to make a film without a subject, to express all I wanted to say about glory, success, downfall, failure, women, and love by means of a detective story. It's a grab bag." More than anything, it is a collection of beautifully scripted and photographed moments, many of which do nothing to further the narrative, but

give the film a soul. One such moment lasts only a split second: A heartless club owner swears that he is telling the truth and proclaims, "If I am lying, may my mother drop dead." At that instant, Truffaut cuts to a shot of a decrepit old woman dropping to the floor. The casting of Aznavour is brilliant, the actor combining the proper blend of cafe piano man and classical pianist—a figure who loses everything he has ever loved, except his music.

SHOOTING, THE
1971   82m   c   ★★★★
Western   R/A
Proteus/Favorite

Jack Nicholson (Billy Spear), Millie Perkins (Woman), Warren Oates (Willett Gashade), Will Hutchins (Coley), B.J. Merholz (Leland Drum), Guy El Tsosie (Indian), Charles Eastman (Bearded Man)

p, Monte Hellman, Jack Nicholson; d, Monte Hellman; w, Adrien Joyce; ph, Gregory Sandor (DeLuxe Color); ed, Monte Hellman; m, Richard Markowitz

In the bleakness of a desert setting a group of bounty hunters has made camp. When Oates returns to camp after being out in the desert, he finds out that his brother has gotten drunk in town and run down a little boy. In addition, his brother's partner was shot in the back by an unknown gunman. Hutchins, fearful of the goings-on, gives equally paranoid Oates his guns. The next day, the two hear a shot and see Perkins near her camp. Perkins, who has just killed her horse, offers Oates $1,000 to take her to the town of Kingsley. He agrees, even though he dislikes her. The three head off, constantly arguing along the trail. After passing a small town, Oates learns his brother has been seen there. Upon reaching the desert, Perkins starts flirting with Hutchins but is stopped by Oates, who realizes she is sending some sort of signal to an unknown person following them. Nicholson finally appears and joins up with the trio. He and Hutchins don't get along and constantly threaten one another. Oates tells his partner to cool it. Given the chance, Nicholson would like nothing better than to kill Hutchins. When Perkins's new horse dies on the trail, Hutchins gives up his and rides with Oates. Nicholson then orders his nemesis to dismount and forces him to remain in the desert. The others soon meet an acquaintance of Perkins who is stranded in the desert with a broken leg. The stranger tells the three that they are close to Perkins's destination. She gives him some water and the party moves on. Later Hutchins gets the man's horse and uses it to charge on Nicholson. Nicholson kills Hutchins, which angers Perkins and saddens Oates. He buries his friend, and the tedious journey begins a catastrophic denouement. Water runs out and the horses all die. Then Oates and Nicholson get into a fight. Oates wins by crushing Nicholson's shooting hand with a large rock. Perkins runs up to some rocks, and Oates follows her. She spots a man she believes killed her child. He turns around, and they discover it is Oates's brother. Perkins and Oates engage in a gun battle with the man and are killed. Nicholson, whose death is inevitable, is left to wander aimlessly in pain around the desert.

This unusual, existential western is highly effective, playing with various levels of character and ideas. At times it approaches a sort of quasi-surrealism, particularly during the climactic battle between Oates and his look-alike brother. Only bits of information are revealed to the audience, leaving much left to mull over when the film is over. The sparse dialogue and dramatic, disorienting use of close-ups are highly effective. The bleak location shooting in the Utah desert is perhaps the best ingredient of all, allowing the audience to almost feel the heat and sense the impending doom symbolized by the barren land. Black comedy is found as well: at one point the man dying from his broken leg is offered some candy. The ensemble is uniformly excellent. Oates's character is fascinating and most expressive in his simple facial gestures. Perkins (a minor starlet in the 1950s) and Nicholson are equally good in their unusual roles. THE SHOOTING was filmed back-to-back with RIDE THE WHIRLWIND during a six-week period in 1965. Both films were produced on minuscule budgets by Nicholson and director Hellman, with an uncredited Roger Corman serving as executive producer. Nicholson also wrote the script for WHIRLWIND, whose sparse dialogue and thematic material is strikingly similar to THE SHOOTING. (The script for THE SHOOTING was by Joyce, who later wrote Nicholson's classic FIVE EASY PIECES). No distributor would touch either film despite excellent reviews at the Montreal Film Festival and an out-of-competition screening at Cannes. Nicholson finally sold the rights to a French producer, who soon went bankrupt. The two films gathered dust for a couple of years before being dumped on a few TV late, late shows. Through word of mouth a few screenings took place, and, with the success of EASY RIDER, THE SHOOTING was given a limited release. It's a real pity that this film is so little known; it is a fine western stylization that should not be missed.

SHOOTIST, THE

1976   100m   C   ★★★★
Western   PG
DEG

John Wayne *(John Bernard Books)*, Lauren Bacall *(Bond Rogers)*, Ron Howard *(Gillom Rogers)*, James Stewart *(Dr. Hostetler)*, Richard Boone *(Sweeney)*, Hugh O'Brian *(Pulford)*, Bill McKinney *(Cobb)*, Harry Morgan *(Marshall Thibido)*, John Carradine *(Beckum)*, Sheree North *(Serepta)*

p, M.J. Frankovich, William Self; d, Don Siegel; w, Miles Hood Swarthout, Scott Hale (based on the novel by Glendon Swarthout); ph, Bruce Surtees (Panavision, Technicolor); ed, Douglas Stewart; m, Elmer Bernstein; prod d, Robert Boyle; fx, Augie Lohman; cos, Moss Mabry, Luster Bayless, Edna Taylor

Eloquent last hurrah for a man who superseded mere movie-star status to become an icon of American culture, with Wayne playing aging, legendary gunfighter J.B. Brooks. Opening with a black-and-white montage of scenes from Wayne's earlier westerns, the film traces Brooks's career from 1871 to 1901, when THE SHOOTIST is set. As we move through scenes from RED RIVER, HONDO, RIO BRAVO and EL DORADO, Wayne ages before our eyes until he rides up before the camera and the film turns to color. During this sequence a voice-over spoken by Howard tells us that Wayne has killed 30 men in 30 years but was never an outlaw—he even spent time as a lawman. Wayne's credo: "I won't be wronged, I won't be insulted, and I won't be laid a hand on. I don't do these things to other people and I expect the same from them." Wayne rides into Carson City, Nevada, where he is informed by the doctor (James Stewart) that his cancer. The drama of his life's end is complicated by the presence of a beautiful widow, played by Lauren Bacall, and a host of young gunfighters looking to prove their worth by going up against him.

THE SHOOTIST is an uneven, elegiac tribute to a great career. The script leaves a lot to be desired, but is compensated for by some fine performances (especially Wayne's), Bruce Surtees' poignant cinematography, and Don Siegel's carefully paced direction.

SHOP AROUND THE CORNER, THE

1940   97m   bw   ★★★★★
Comedy/Romance   /U
MGM

James Stewart *(Alfred Kralik)*, Margaret Sullavan *(Klara Novak)*, Frank Morgan *(Hugo Matuschek)*, Joseph Schildkraut *(Ferencz Vadas)*, Sara Haden *(Flora)*, Felix Bressart *(Pirovitch)*, William Tracy *(Pepi Katona)*, Inez Courtney *(Ilona)*, Charles Halton *(Detective)*, Charles Smith *(Rudy)*

p, Ernst Lubitsch; d, Ernst Lubitsch; w, Samson Raphaelson (based on the play "Parfumerie" by Nikolaus Laszlo); ph, William Daniels; ed, Gene Ruggiero; m, Werner R. Heymann; art d, Cedric Gibbons, Wade B. Rubottom

Delectable Hungarian pastry, served up by masters all around. This may be the best comedy of a romance ever made. The great Ernst Lubitsch handles his "small" theme brilliantly in THE SHOP AROUND THE CORNER, bringing the lives of everyday people to the screen as he had never done before and sounding a common chord in his audience. In contrast to such Lubitsch heroes as Jack Benny's anti-Nazi character in TO BE OR NOT TO BE, Don Ameche's rich playboy in HEAVEN CAN WAIT, or Greta Garbo's Soviet agent in NINOTCHKA, James Stewart's everyman sales clerk in THE SHOP AROUND THE CORNER is as prosaic as they come. Working in a leather goods shop in Budapest, Stewart is the top clerk and a trusted friend of the owner, Morgan. Stewart is considered a merchandising "genius" by Morgan and hence is an invaluable employee. Morgan even goes so far as to invite him home to meet the wife, who is duly charmed. Together, Morgan and Stewart head a tightly knit force of workers, all eager to please. Among them is Stewart's closest ally, Bressart, an aging clerk who leads a simple life and avoids confrontation; Schildkraut, a braggart who flashes his newly acquired wealth; and Tracy, an aspiring clerk who is constantly being bossed around. Trouble brews when the unemployed Sullavan enters the shop and begs Morgan to hire her as Christmas help. He rudely refuses and tells the pouting girl to go away. Before she leaves, however, she manages to sell a musical cigar box to a rotund woman for use as a candy box. Convinced of her ability to sell, Morgan gives her a job, much to Stewart's consternation.

But Stewart has another distraction, as he confides to Bressart: through a lonely-hearts ad, Stewart has met a most wonderful girl, though he knows only by her box number. After exchanging a number of increasingly romantic letters with the charming lady of box 237, Stewart makes a date to meet her in the flesh at a cafe. To ensure recognition, he will be wearing a red carnation, while she will be using one as a bookmark in a copy of *Anna Karenina*. Stewart plans to propose marriage to his correspondent. Also expecting a proposal is Sullavan, herself carrying on an epistolary romance with a man she's never met and whose name she doesn't know—Stewart, of course. While Sullavan and Stewart may love each other in their anonymous letters, however, they feel only an increasing mutual dislike at the shop, where Stewart reprimands Sullavan about everything, including the way she dresses.

While THE SHOP AROUND THE CORNER lacks the immediate impact of the more spectacular TO BE OR NOT TO BE or HEAVEN CAN WAIT, this late entry from Lubitsch touches viewers deeply because its characters reflect those viewers' lives so perfectly. Such fidelity is a rare occurrence in film, making THE SHOP AROUND THE CORNER's achievement all the more admirable. In the characters who work at Matuschek's, one can see a broad array of human emotions and basic traits—happiness, love, devotion, anger, duplicity, jealousy, sorrow. In a letter to Herman G. Weinberg, author of the directorial study *The Lubitsch Touch*, Lubitsch listed what he felt were the best pictures of his career. After citing TROUBLE IN PARADISE as his best film stylistically and NINOTCHKA as his sharpest satire, he said of THE SHOP AROUND THE CORNER: "As for human comedy, I think I never was as good as in THE SHOP AROUND THE CORNER. Never did I make a picture in which the atmosphere and the characters were truer than in this picture." This is a Stewart many of us have forgotten once existed—his touch is delicate and precise. He's perfectly matched by Sullavan, a forgotten genius who never gave a bad performance. And this is perhaps Morgan's finest portrayal. These three had also completed Borzage's THE MORTAL STORM the same year. SHOP was later turned into a musical for Judy Garland and Van Johnson, IN THE GOOD OLD SUMMERTIME—one of Garland's most formulaic efforts.

SHOP ON MAIN STREET, THE

(OBCH OD NA KORZE)
1965   128m   bw   ★★★★★
War/Drama   /A
Barrandov   (Czechoslovakia)

Jozef Kroner (*Tono Brtko*), Ida Kaminska (*Rozalie Lautmann*), Hana Slivkova (*Evelina Brtko*), Frantisek Zvarik (*Marcus Kolkotsky*), Helena Zvarikov (*Rose Kolkotsky*), Martin Holly (*Imro Kuchar*), Martin Gregory (*Katz*), Adam Matejka (*Piti Baci*), Mikulas Ladizinsky (*Marian Peter*), Eugen Senaj (*Blau*)

p, Jaromir Lukas, Jordan Balurov; d, Jan Kadar, Elmar Klos; w, Jan Kadar, Elmar Klos, Ladislav Grosman (based on the story "Obchod No Korze" by Grosman); ph, Vladimir Novotny; ed, Jaromir Janacek, Diana Heringova; m, Zdenek Liska; art d, Karel Skvor

In dramatic terms perhaps one of the most powerful films ever made. Among the most highly praised Eastern European films of the 1960s, THE SHOP ON MAIN STREET is a profoundly moving tragicomedy set against a WWII backdrop of racial hatred and fascism. Tono Brtko (Kroner) seemingly walks through life without any guiding morals or principles. He is content just to get by—though his domineering wife, Evelina (Slivkova), who longs for a more comfortable existence, tries to force him into working for her fascist brother-in-law, Marcus (Zvarik). One night Marcus brings news that Tono has been appointed Aryan comptroller of a Jewish button shop, a job that will bring money and status. Tono visits the shop the next day, informing the aged, frail, and rheumatic proprietress, Rozalie (Kaminska), that he is now in charge. She, however, too deaf to understand and too blind to read his authorization, begins bossing him around. Only later does Tono learn that the shop is completely bankrupt, and that the old woman is supported by her fellow Jewish merchants. He eventually agrees to the charade of working as Rozalie's assistant and forms a strong friendship with her that transcends racial, religious, and political divisions. But the Nazis soon appear and several ironic and stunning dramatic climaxes take place.

Codirected by the team of Kadar and Klos, THE SHOP ON MAIN STREET is a relatively straightforward narrative, without the stylistic virtuosity of so many other films by young Eastern European filmmakers. What the film lacks in flash, however, it makes up for in craftsmanship, intelligence, and universality. The acting is excellent throughout, and Kroner and Kaminska are both spellbinding. When Tono must decide between turning Rozalie over to the Nazis or trying to hide her, the film's careful buildup begins to pay off. When the elderly woman finally

realizes what is happening around her and Tono desperately tries to shut her up, you may feel your guts wrenching in awe, terror and pity. Mixing a comic tone with a tragic subject, the film paints a uniquely vivid portrait of wartime persecution and enforces the view that the greatest, most inhumane of tragedies can strike anyone at any time. A film of unforgettable power, it received a Best Foreign-Language Film Oscar in 1965 and a Best Actress nomination for Kaminska in 1966.

SHOT IN THE DARK, A

1964   103m   c   ★★★★
Mystery/Comedy   /PG
Mirisch/Geoffrey   (U.S./U.K.)

Peter Sellers (*Inspector Jacques Clouseau*), Elke Sommer (*Maria Gambrelli*), George Sanders (*Benjamin Ballon*), Herbert Lom (*Chief Inspector Charles Dreyfus*), Tracy Reed (*Dominique Ballon*), Graham Stark (*Hercule Lajoy*), Andre Maranne (*Francois*), Douglas Wilmer (*Henri Lafarge*), Vanda Godsell (*Mme. Lafarge*), Maurice Kaufmann (*Pierre*)

p, Blake Edwards; d, Blake Edwards; w, Blake Edwards, William Peter Blatty (based on plays by Harry Kurnitz, Marcel Achard); ph, Christopher Challis (Panavision, De Luxe Color); ed, Bert Bates; m, Henry Mancini; prod d, Michael Stringer; cos, Margaret Furse

This picture, the second in the Inspector Clouseau series starring Sellers, was drawn from a French play, "L'idiote," by Marcel Achard, which opened in Paris in the fall of 1960. About a year later Kurnitz presented his adaptation, "A Shot in the Dark," on Broadway, and it is from both these plays that the screenplay was fashioned. Sommer is a chambermaid, in the Parisian residence of Sanders and Reed, who has been accused of murdering her boyfriend. Sellers is mistakenly assigned to the case. His superior, Lom, would like to get him off it because he knows the havoc the man can wreak. ("Give me 10 men like Clouseau and I could destroy the world.") On the surface it would seem that all the clues point to Sommer's having done the Spaniard in, but Sellers believes she is innocent because there are just too many bits of evidence against her. Lom succeeds in pulling Sellers away from the case and has Sommer taken to jail. Then Lom is chagrined to learn that his superiors want Sellers back on the case, and they overrule him. Sommer, released and soon discovered with another corpse, is arrested again. Still sure of her innocence, Sellers springs her from prison and trails her to a nudist camp. Here still another body, this time that of Sanders' first maid (Ann Lynn) is found. Again, the eye of suspicion focuses on Sommer. Now Wilmer, another employee at the Sanders residence, is killed. Lom, who sees Sommer as a modern-day Lucreta Borgia because death seems to follow wherever she goes, insists that Sommer be arrested once more and that Sellers be taken off the case. Still under pressure from above, Lom is forced to put Sellers back on the case and to allow Sommer to leave jail. Sellers squires Sommer for an evening of Parisian *boite* hopping, and there are a number of attempts on Sellers's life, none of which he notices. The result of these assassination attempts is that innocent victims seem to drop like flies (four bite the dust) around the addled Sellers. In a THIN MAN-type conclusion Sellers assembles the suspects in the Sanders residence and lets things happen. All six of the potential murderers begin accusing each other. The lights are suddenly doused, and they all flee, leaving Sellers and Sommer alone. Now the whole group squeezes into one car, in which a bomb, meant to do in Sellers, has been planted. While Sommer and Sellers watch open-mouthed, the car explodes, and all of the suspects are killed. Sellers has, in effect, put an end to the murders. Lom goes mad because he is, in fact, the real killer and was planning to knock off everyone in order to heap shame upon Sellers, who is now being acclaimed a sleuthing genius. The picture is filled with one sight gag after another, many familiar to anyone old enough to remember the glory days of silent comedy. The funniest sustained sequence occurs when Sellers attempts to bed down Sommer, and his aide (Burt Kwouk) leaps into the room ready to conduct the violent judo lesson that was to punctuate many of the later comedies. The original Achard-Kurnitz plays had the lead character a nutty judge, but that was altered in this screenplay to fit the character Sellers played in the first PINK PANTHER film. In the movies that followed, Lom continued as the boss, despite having murdered all of the victims in this one.

SHOUT, THE

1978 87m c   ★★★
Horror   R/15
Recorded Picture   (U.K.)

Alan Bates (Crossley), Susannah York (Rachel), John Hurt (Anthony), Robert Stephens (Medical Man), Tim Curry (Robert), Julian Hough (Vicar), Carol Drinkwater (Wife), Nick Stringer (Cobbler), John Rees (Inspector), Susan Wooldridge (Harriet)

p, Jeremy Thomas; d, Jerzy Skolimowski; w, Michael Austin, Jerzy Skolimowski (based on a story by Robert Graves); ph, Mike Molloy; ed, Barrie Vince; m, Rupert Hine, Tony Banks, Michael Rutherford; art d, Simon Holland

THE SHOUT is a strange, disturbing, and elusive tale of a mental patient, Bates, who, having once lived with a tribe of Aborigines, has learned the secret of "the shout," which has the power to kill. Told in flashback during a cricket match that takes place on the grounds of a mental asylum, the film follows Bates's relationship with experimental composer Hurt and his wife, York. Bates moves in with the couple, and gradually his disturbing presence takes its toll. He tells the couple that he killed his own children, demonstrates his ability to kill with his shout, seduces York, and tries to destroy Hurt. Directed by Polish director Jerzy Skolimowski (MOONLIGHTING), THE SHOUT has a certain compelling element that both mystifies and involves the viewer, its unusual story told with equal amounts of obscurity and skill. It has no tidy conclusions or explanations, leaving the audience as baffled at the end as they were at the start, but the film is definitely worth experiencing. Tony Banks and Mike Rutherford of the rock group Genesis contributed to the electronic score, and ROCKY HORROR star Tim Curry has a supporting role.

SHOW BOAT

1936 110m bw   ★★★★½
Musical   /U
Universal

Irene Dunne (Magnolia Hawks), Allan Jones (Gaylord Ravenal), Charles Winninger (Capt. Andy Hawks), Helen Westley (Parthy Hawks), Paul Robeson (Joe), Helen Morgan (Julie), Donald Cook (Steve), Sammy White (Frank Schultz), J. Farrell MacDonald (Windy), Arthur Hohl (Pete)

p, Carl Laemmle, Jr.; d, James Whale; w, Oscar Hammerstein, II (based on the novel by Edna Ferber and the play by Hammerstein, Jerome Kern); ph, John Mescall; ed, Ted J. Kent, Bernard W. Burton; m, Jerome Kern, Oscar Hammerstein, II; art d, Charles D. Hall; fx, John P. Fulton; chor, LeRoy Prinz; cos, Vera West, Doris Zinkeisen

This time around, Universal got it right. Carl Laemmle, Jr., whose father produced the 1929 version of SHOW BOAT that

owed more to Edna Ferber's novel than to the 1927 Hammerstein and Kern musical, took over the reins here and the result is splendid. It's still the same romance between gambler Gaylord Ravenal (Jones) and Magnolia Hawks (Dunne), daughter of showboat captain Andy Hawks (Winninger). The stars of this mobile 19th century theatre, Julie (Morgan) and Steve (Cook), must leave the showboat when it is found out that Julie is half-black. Gaylord and Magnolia step in and play their romance onstage and off, but an unlucky gambling streak spells trouble for the young couple.

SHOWBOAT's many-tiered plot is secondary to its extraordinary score, but it does make for some beguiling romance, delightful comedy and potent dramatics. Master director Whale, here essaying his first musical, does some typically marvelous things with the camera and *mise-en-scene* and gets wonderful performances from his cast. Many of them had essayed their roles previously onstage, so their dazzling assurance should come as no surprise. Dunne's lilting soprano does full justice to such favorites as "Make Believe" and "You Are Love" and she is sidesplittingly funny acting the role of a schoolteacher in a barnstorming melodrama aboard the showboat. Although her "Gallivantin' Around" number in blackface is awkward today, it does suggest period minstrelsy. Luckily, the comedy behind the set upstages the number, as Capt. Andy and sidekick Rubberface handle the number's special effects. We should be grateful that Winninger's legendary performance has been captured on film. His greatest moment comes when, with incredible dexterity and panache, he enacts the entire finale of a play before an audience. Jones, too, a likable actor-singer underused by Hollywood, does excellent work as a roguish but loving gambler. His rendition of "I Have the Room Above Her" is light and lovely, and he plays extremely well opposite Dunne. The rest of the supporting cast, including the ever-marvelous Westley and the one-and-only Hattie McDaniel, are in grand form, but Robeson and Morgan must be singled out for special praise. These stage stars were born to play the proud but laid-back Joe and the tragic Julie. Robeson's immortal rendition of "Ol' Man River" is stunningly staged by Whale, as a 270 degree pan sweeps around him and the lyrics are enacted with Expressionistic vignettes. The film really suffers when Robeson is no longer around, but his presence haunts even the last reels. The same goes for Helen Morgan, whose decline at this point in her brief life and career is clearly apparent. She makes Julie almost unbearably poignant. Her tremulous voice and slight gestures convey volumes, and one is so grateful when she briefly turns up again in Magnolia's life at just the right moment. When Morgan sings "Bill" (with that amazing close-up near the end), one feels privileged to witness one of the greatest filmed performance of a song in the history of cinema. If you doubt that two minutes of a woman singing can break your heart, guess again.

Universal really poured its money into this film, and it shows in Hall's lovely set designs, Mescall's sumptuous cinematography and the actual riverboat built for the film. Whale's trademark theatricality lends itself perfectly to this film, and he plays the famous miscegenation scene for all it's worth. The film is only really flawed in the last third, as we are rushed into the 1930s while Magnolia's daughter becomes a stage star herself. It's quite improbable that Capt. Andy and Parthy would still be alive, and other contrivances mar the impact of what has come before. The producing Laemmles, in fact, found out how much they had overdone things: Not only did they have to chop out most of the Broadway stuff near the end, they also couldn't benefit from the film's huge profits in time to hang onto the studio they founded. The company passed into other hands, but this version of SHOW

BOAT, blessed with one of the most memorable scores (and books) in musical theatre history and lovingly performed by many gifted people, has passed into collective memory as a job extremely well done. We're grateful to have a record of a stage landmark that's so successful as a film.

SHOW BOAT

1951 107m c ★★★½

Musical /U

MGM

Kathryn Grayson (*Magnolia Hawks*), Ava Gardner (*Julie LaVerne*), Howard Keel (*Gaylord Ravenal*), Joe E. Brown (*Capt. Andy Hawks*), Marge Champion (*Ellie May Shipley*), Gower Champion (*Frank Schultz*), Robert Sterling (*Stephen Baker*), Agnes Moorehead (*Parthy Hawks*), Adele Jergens (*Cameo McQueen*), William Warfield (*Joe*)

p, Arthur Freed; d, George Sidney; w, John Lee Mahin (uncredited), George Wells, Jack McGowan (based on the musical by Jerome Kern and Oscar Hammerstein II from the novel by Edna Ferber); ph, Charles Rosher (Technicolor); ed, John Dunning; m, Jerome Kern; art d, Cedric Gibbons, Jack Martin Smith; fx, Warren Newcombe, Peter Ballbusch; chor, Robert Alton; cos, Walter Plunkett

Greatly enhanced by its deft use of color, this third film version of Hammerstein and Kern's classic musical is nearly as good as the superlative second and much better than the lackluster first (1936 and 1929, respectively). Yet, as was the case with the 1936 version, the Motion Picture Academy barely acknowledged the film's excellence, nominating only Charles Rosher's cinematography and Adolph Deutsch and Conrad Salinger's musical direction. This time out the story is considerably altered and compressed, with Kathryn Grayson in the role of Magnolia and Ava Gardner as Julie, the much-wronged mulatto who helps save Magnolia's marriage to gambler-turned-entertainer Gaylord Ravenal (Howard Keel). The action is again played out on a Mississippi riverboat, *The Cotton Blossom*, piloted by Magnolia's father, Capt. Andy Hawks (Joe E. Brown, whom Edna Ferber reputedly had in mind when she created the character of Capt. Andy for the novel whence the musical sprang). Agnes Moorehead plays Capt. Andy's tough cookie spouse and Leif Erickson is the deckhand who reveals Julie's miscegenation to the authorities when she rebuffs his advances. After planning to shoot the film on location in Mississippi, MGM decided it would be more cost effective to keep the cast at home and, like the 1936 production, went to great lengths to create a realistic riverboat, constructing one from scratch that was over 170 feet long, nearly 60 feet high, and cost more than $125,000. Among the film's fine performances are those of Grayson, who had already played Magnolia in a segment of the fanciful biopic of Kern, TILL THE CLOUDS ROLL BY, and Gardner, who did her own singing but had her voice dubbed by Annette Warren after preview audiences reacted coolly to the beautiful leading lady's vocalizing. Although the film's musical numbers are almost entirely the Kern-Hammerstein originals, the finale, "After the Ball," was penned by Charles K. Harris, while P.G. Wodehouse and Guy Bolton wrote new lyrics for "Bill."

SHY PEOPLE

1988 119m c ★★★½

Drama R/15

Golan-Globus

Jill Clayburgh (*Diana Sullivan*), Barbara Hershey (*Ruth Sullivan*), Martha Plimpton (*Grace Sullivan*), Merritt Butrick (*Mike Sullivan*),

John Philbin (*Tommy Sullivan*), Don Swayze (*Mark Sullivan*), Pruitt Taylor Vince (*Paul Sullivan*), Mare Winningham (*Candy*), Michael Audley (*Louie*), Brad Leland (*Larry*)

p, Menahem Golan, Yoram Globus; d, Andrei Konchalovsky; w, Gerard Brach, Andrei Konchalovsky, Marjorie David (based on a story by Konchalovsky); ph, Chris Menges (Rank color); ed, Alain Jakubowicz; fx, Cal Acord

The fourth American film from Soviet emigre Andrei Konchalovsky (MARIA'S LOVERS; RUNAWAY TRAIN; and DUET FOR ONE preceded), SHY PEOPLE is about a meeting of two people, and two worlds, who initially appear to be diametrically opposed but who, we learn by the film's end, have more in common than we imagined. The film opens in Manhattan, where *Cosmopolitan* reporter Diana Sullivan (Jill Clayburgh) lives with her teenaged coke-sniffing daughter, Grace (Martha Plimpton). At her editor's suggestion, Diana has traced her own roots back to the Louisiana Bayou and talks her bored daughter into accompanying her on a visit to the relatives. As Diana and Grace reveal their urban dependencies, the Cajun cousins reveal their backwoods, superstitious ways. Ruth Sullivan (Barbara Hershey) informs her guests that the family is watched over by her former husband, the outlaw Joe, though he hasn't been seen for over 15 years. The film is full of strange and wonderful events, and in the course of the action the two women grow and change as a result of their exposure to one another. As in his 1985 RUNAWAY TRAIN, Konchalovsky here presents powerful characterizations, beautiful imagery, and philosophical content as entertainment that can appeal to the average filmgoer but that also still has enough depth to stand up to critical analysis.

SID AND NANCY

1986 111m c ★★★★

Biography R/18

Zenith/Initial (U.K.)

Gary Oldman (*Sid Vicious*), Chloe Webb (*Nancy Spungen*), Drew Schofield (*Johnny Rotten*), David Hayman (*Malcolm McLaren*), Debbie Bishop (*Phoebe*), Tony London (*Steve*), Perry Benson (*Paul*), Anne Lambton (*Linda*), Kathy Burke (*Brenda*), Mark Monero (*Clive*)

p, Eric Fellner; d, Alex Cox; w, Alex Cox, Abbe Wool; ph, Roger Deakins; ed, David Martin; m, Pray for Rain, The Pogues, Joe Strummer; prod d, Andrew McAlpine; art d, J. Rae Fox, Lynda Burbank; cos, Cathy Cook, Theda De Ramus

The sordid, pathetic lives of Sex Pistols bassist Sid Vicious and his groupie girlfriend Nancy Spungen might strike some as unsuitable material for a movie romance, but British filmmaker Alex Cox brings their embattled relationship and tragic end to powerful cinematic life.

SID AND NANCY opens in 1978, as police arrive at New York's Chelsea Hotel to find the body of Nancy (Chloe Webb) in the couple's bathroom and zombie-like Sid (Gary Oldman) staring at the wall and holding a knife. The film then flashes back to 1977 when the couple first meet at the home of Linda (Anne Lambton), a friend of Sid's and Johnny Rotten's (Drew Schofield). Nancy is a loud, whining, American rock 'n' roll groupie who's wound up in London at the height of the punk rock movement. She's impressed when she learns that Linda's guests are members of the infamous Sex Pistols, the brainchild of young entrepreneur Malcolm McLaren (David Hayman). (Sid, born John Ritchie, abandoned his role as drummer for the nascent Siouxsie and the Banshees to replace original Sex Pistol bassist Glen Matlock.) That night, she goes to hear the band, riding high on the British charts with "God Save the Queen," their second single, and later tries to seduce Rotten, but he declares sex "boring" and leaves her to Vicious.

A few days later Sid spots Nancy in a pub and follows her when she runs out yelling and crying; another rocker has absconded with her heroin money. Angry and frustrated, Spungen scrapes her knuckles on a brick wall. "That looks like it hurts," Sid tells her sympathetically. "So does this," he continues, and brutally slams his head into the brick wall, a gesture which Nancy seems to understand and appreciate. Sid then gives Nancy money to buy heroin for both of them; although she's already a full-blown junkie, Sid has never done hard drugs.

SID AND NANCY does not canonize Sid Vicious and Nancy Spungen, the Sex Pistols or the punk movement itself, nor does it glamorize the couple's horrible self-destruction. (Sid died of a heroin overdose on February 2, 1979, before his case could be tried.) Although Cox, abetted by co-screenwriter Abbe Wool, often displays a black, quirky sense of humor, the horror of drug addiction is always at the forefront and never made light of.

The performances of Oldman and Webb, both stage-trained veterans, are simply astonishing. SID AND NANCY will certainly be tough going for viewers unfamiliar with the punk movement and unprepared for the extraordinary amount of cynicism, ignorance, anger, and self-abuse that went hand-in-hand with it, but the film's value lies in its honest, unflinching gaze at a social phenomenon.

SILENCE OF THE LAMBS, THE

1991 118m c   ★★★★½
Thriller/Mystery   R/18
Strong Heart Productions/Orion

Jodie Foster (Clarice Starling), Anthony Hopkins (Dr. Hannibal Lecter), Scott Glenn (Jack Crawford), Ted Levine (Jame Gumb), Anthony Heald (Dr. Frederick Chilton), Brooke Smith (Catherine Martin), Charles Napier (Sergeant Boyle), Diane Baker (Senator Ruth Martin), Kasi Lemmons (Ardelia Mapp), Roger Corman (FBI Director Hayden Burke)

p, Edward Saxon, Kenneth Utt, Ron Bozman; d, Jonathan Demme; w, Ted Tally (from the novel by Thomas Harris); ph, Tak Fujimoto; ed, Craig McKay; m, Howard Shore; prod d, Kristi Zea; art d, Tim Galvin; cos, Colleen Atwood

One of the most talked-about movies of 1991, multiple Academy Award-winner THE SILENCE OF THE LAMBS was actually the second "Hannibal Lecter" film, Michael Mann having previously adapted the character from Thomas Harris's novel *Red Dragon* in 1986's MANHUNTER. But Jonathan Demme's taut thriller proved to have a much greater impact on the public imagination.

FBI trainee Clarice Starling (Jodie Foster) is recruited by the Bureau's behavioral sciences unit to help track down one serial killer by getting inside the head of another who's already behind bars—the notorious Hannibal "the Cannibal" Lecter (Anthony Hopkins), a brilliant but psychopathic psychiatrist. In a series of riveting interviews, Starling reveals personal details about her past to Lecter, in exchange for information that may snare "Buffalo Bill," the murderer who flays his female victims. Tensions escalate when Bill kidnaps the overweight daughter of a U.S. senator.

When it becomes clear that Lecter knows the identity of the killer, the powers-that-be strike a deal: the doctor will be given better prison conditions if he helps the FBI get to Bill before he kills again. The devilish psychiatrist, though, proves less than cooperative and pulls off a clever but gruesome escape while

being transferred. Meanwhile, Starling and her boss Jack Crawford (Scott Glenn) have uncovered enough clues to identify Buffalo Bill themselves. While Crawford's crew mistakenly raids an empty house, Starling finds herself tracking down the killer, Jame Gumb (Ted Levine), alone in his dungeon-like hideaway. She rescues the senator's daughter after a suspenseful shootout, though Lecter, her true nemesis, remains at large.

While the suspenseful pursuit of the killer is handled well by Demme, the film's principle attraction stems not from the thrill of the hunt, but from the spellbinding skull sessions between Jodie Foster's heroine and Anthony Hopkins's brilliant, menacing villain. Hopkins plays the cannibalistic doctor with a quiet, controlled erudition, lacing his performance with moments of black humor. His Lecter is a sort of satanic Sherlock Holmes whose spasms of violence are all the more terrifying because they erupt from beneath such an intelligent and refined mask.

Although not as overwhelming, Foster's performance is equally impressive. Her strong-yet-vulnerable interpretation of the rookie FBI agent projects a quietly convincing feminism. Although she remains the pupil of the benign patriarch Crawford, Starling rises above the pettiness of her male colleagues. Unlike the self-serving prison doctor, Frederick Chilton (Anthony Heald), and the geeky entomologists who hit on her during the investigation, she is a scientist with a strong moral sense. And, unlike the macho cops who are uncomfortable answering to a woman, she proves equal to any test of her skills or physical endurance. Foster's own off-screen image as an intelligent, well-spoken Yale graduate contributes greatly to the resonance of Starling's character. Unfortunately, another aspect of Foster's past fame—the public's association of her image with that of TAXI DRIVER's Travis Bickle and real-life assassin John Hinckley—also adds to the visceral tension when Clarice confronts Lecter and Buffalo Bill.

Despite the cinematic and dramatic triumphs of SILENCE OF THE LAMBS, the film's accomplishments cannot be endorsed without reservation. While behavioral scientists within the film offer much psychoanalytical reading of character, the movie itself fails to separate Buffalo Bill's sexual confusion from his homicidal psychopathy. While not central to the story, such a depiction threatens to demonize sexual ambiguity as criminal. Finally, while the amount of violence in this thriller is not unusual, the disturbingly bizarre nature of Lecter's face-eating cannibalism and the misogyny of Buffalo Bill's *modus operandi* may be sufficient reason for many would-be viewers to forego the film's gripping drama.

SILENT MOVIE

1976 86m c   ★★★½
Comedy   PG
FOX

Mel Brooks (Mel Funn), Marty Feldman (Marty Eggs), Dom DeLuise (Dom Bell), Bernadette Peters (Vilma Kaplan), Sid Caesar (Studio Chief), Harold Gould (Engulf), Ron Carey (Devour), Carol Arthur (Pregnant Lady), Liam Dunn (Newsvendor), Fritz Feld (Maitre d')

p, Michael Hertzberg; d, Mel Brooks; w, Mel Brooks, Ron Clark, Rudy DeLuca, Barry Levinson (based on a story by Clark); ph, Paul Lohmann (DeLuxe Color); ed, John C. Howard, Stanford C. Allen; m, John Morris; prod d, Albert Brenner; fx, Ira Anderson, Jr.; chor, Rob Iscove; cos, Patricia Norris

Technically this is what it says it is, a silent movie. However, it does have John Morris's music, sound effects, and one word, uttered by that man of no words, mime Marcel Marceau, who says "non" at one point (the French word for "no"). Writer Ron Clark conceived the film and thought that there would be only two directors who could make such a bold idea work, Brooks and Woody Allen. Since Brooks was local in Los Angeles, he took it to him at Fox, and a deal was made on the spot. Brooks wanted some help with the script, and Clark suggested two men he'd worked with in the past, DeLuca and Levinson. They were hired, and all four contributed to the outcome. (Both Levinson and DeLuca would eventually become directors. DeLuca did TRANSYLVANIA 6-5000 in 1985 and Levinson scored with DINER. Clark got into the directing act after having been production consultant on this film. He returned to his native Canada to helm his original, FUNNY FARM.) Brooks is a film director who has seen better days. In an attempt to quell nagging doubts about his talents and his dubious future, Brooks turns to alcohol. Two of his pals, Feldman and DeLuise, rescue him from his despair and try to convince Brooks that there's more to life than a whiskey bottle. Brooks is not convinced but agrees to try making a silent movie. The trio, who seem to be a modern version of Curly, Larry, and Moe, go off to find some bankable stars who will agree to appear in the picture, then visit Caesar, the "Current Studio Chief" (which is what it says on the sign on his desk), who is worried about the future of the studio because it is about to be bought by the huge conglomerate of Engulf & Devour (a swipe at Gulf & Western, which bought Paramount), which is helmed by Gould. If Gould gets his talons into the studio, it would be the end of the studio, and Caesar is desperate to keep that from happening. Brooks, Feldman, and DeLuise next visit a host of stars in their natural and unnatural habitats. They find James Caan in his trailer, Anne Bancroft doing her nightclub act (which leads to a tango routine by the three men and Bancroft), and Burt Reynolds in his shower. They manage to convince several actors to be in the movie, including Paul Newman, Marceau, and Liza Minnelli, and are about to commence production when Brooks begins to drink again. He is again saved by his cronies and his girlfriend, Peters. The movie is made, turns out to be a huge smash (in real life, SILENT MOVIE grossed well over $20 million), and disaster is averted.

Sight gags take the place of the absent dialogue and they come with the rapidity of machine-gun fire. Not all are wonderful, and some are in the toilet humor category, but if you don't like one of the funnies, wait a few seconds and there will be several more that you will like. The list of superb comic actors is a Who's Who of mirth. Chuck McCann is the perfect Studio Guard, a dictator in a uniform. Riley, who surely must be the radio voice of the 1980s because he seems to be on every radio commercial, joins writers Levinson and DeLuca, along with TV's Howard Hesseman, Lee Delano, and Al Hopson, as executives. Henny Youngman does a brief bit with a fly, and on and on. A very funny movie, done with surprising restraint on the part of Brooks. It is that restraint which makes this funnier than many of his other films, which seemed to stop at nothing to get a laugh. Author Clark said: "The whole idea came to me at once, the set pieces, the plot, even the notion of the cameos from stars. I made a list of their names and we got every single one of them to appear. In order to secure the services of Marceau, I called upon Jacques Fabbri, a French actor who appeared for five years in the Gallic version of 'Norman, Is That You?' (which Clark wrote with Sam Bobrick), and he contacted Marceau for me, who immediately agreed to do the film, thereby breaking his vow of show business silence."

SILENT RUNNING
1972 89m c   ★★★½
Science Fiction   PG/U
Universal

Bruce Dern (*Freeman Lowell*), Cliff Potts (*Wolf*), Ron Rifkin (*Barker*), Jesse Vint (*Keenan*), Steven Brown, Mark Persons, Cheryl Sparks, Larry Whisenhunt (*Drones*)

p, Michael Gruskoff; d, Douglas Trumbull; w, Deric Washburn, Steven Bochco, Michael Cimino; ph, Charles F. Wheeler (Technicolor); ed, Aaron Stell; m, Peter Schickele; fx, Douglas Trumbull, John Dykstra, Richard Yuricich, Richard O. Helmer, James Rugg, Marlin Jones, Richard Helmer, Vernon Archer

In the year 2008, all of Earth's natural plant and animal life has been destroyed by nuclear forces. A group of space stations orbiting Saturn function as outer-space greenhouses, waiting for a time when the planet *may* again be able to support life. When the project is terminated and orders given for the greenhouses to be destroyed, Freeman Lowell (Bruce Dern) kills his three colleagues and takes off in one of the stations, to preserve the potential for life in some other place or time. Lowell is aided in his efforts by three cute robots, known as Huey, Louie and Dewey.

This was a directorial debut for Trumbull, who had previously worked with Stanley Kubrick on the special effects for 2001: A SPACE ODDYSSEY. Like that film, SILENT RUNNING concentrates heavily on special effects, resulting in some stunning imagery. Dern gives an engaging, against-type performance, though the script is stretched out very thin to support a feature-length film. The unusual score is by Peter Schickele, best known for his classical music parodies written under the pseudonym P.D.Q. Bach. Despite the presence of some very dated Joan Baez songs on the soundtrack, SILENT RUNNING has built up a deserved cult status over the years. The writing team of Washburn, Bochco, and Cimino would go on to make the Vietnam drama THE DEER HUNTER.

SILK STOCKINGS
1957 117m c   ★★★★
Musical/Comedy   /U
MGM

Fred Astaire (*Steve Canfield*), Cyd Charisse (*Ninotchka*), Janis Paige (*Peggy Dainton*), Peter Lorre (*Brankov*), Jules Munshin (*Bibinski*), Joseph Buloff (*Ivanov*), George Tobias (*Commissar Vassili Markovich*), Wim Sonneveld (*Peter Ilyitch Boroff*), Belita (*Dancer Vera*), Ivan Triesault (*Russian Embassy Official*)

p, Arthur Freed; d, Rouben Mamoulian; w, Leonard Gershe, Harry Kurnitz (uncredited), Leonard Spigelgass (based on the musical play by George S. Kaufman, Leueen McGrath, Abe Burrows and the screenplay by Billy Wilder, Charles Brackett, Walter Reisch from *Ninotchka* by Melchior Lengyel); ph, Robert Bronner (CinemaScope, Metrocolor); ed, Harold F. Kress; m, Cole Porter; art d, William A. Horning, Randall Duell; chor, Hermes Pan, Eugene Loring; cos, Helen Rose

Great light entertainment that paid heavy dividends at the box office, SILK STOCKINGS is the delightful film version of the George S. Kaufman-Leueen McGrath-Abe Burrows-Cole Porter Broadway musical based on Ernst Lubitsch's classic screen comedy NINOTCHKA (1939). Fred Astaire is Hollywood film producer Steve Canfield, who comes to Paris to make a movie, meets touring Soviet composer Peter Ilyitch Boroff (Wim Sonneveld), and persuades him to remain in France to score his film, prompting Commissar Vassili Markovitch (George Tobias, who appeared in both the stage version and in NINOTCHKA) to dispatch of trio of underlings to retrieve the revered composer. In short order, Brankov (Peter Lorre, who is very funny but struggles vainly as a dancer), Bibinski (Jules Munshin), and Ivanov (Joseph Buloff) are contentedly indulging in the pleasures of life in the West. Ninotchka (Cyd Charisse, in the role Greta Garbo essayed so brilliantly), the exemplary Communist sent by Commissar Markovitch to retrieve the retrievers, is not so easily seduced by Western ways or by Steve, who falls in love with her. Despite Steve's marriage proposal, Ninotchka and the others return to the USSR; however, when Brankov, Bibinski, and Ivanov, sent again to Paris as representatives of the Soviet film industry, become partners in a nightclub with Steve, Ninotchka returns to collect her errant comrades, but this time love wins out. Hermes Pan oversaw Astaire's dancing, some of the last really dazzling terping he would do, while Eugene Loring handled the rest of the choreography. Charisse, a great dancer in her own right, gives a terrific performance (vocally looped by Carol Richards). Rouben Mamoulian's direction is brisk but not brilliant; Cole Porter's songs are witty, airy, and tuneful, though not as memorable as many of the renowned tunesmith's other works; and because the chemistry between Charisse and Astaire isn't the equal of that of Garbo and Melvyn Douglas, SILK STOCKINGS lacks NINOTCHKA's warmth. It does, however, have some wonderful musical moments and is the kind of picture that anyone of any age will enjoy.

SILKWOOD

1983   131m   c   ★★★★
Biography   R/15
Fox

Meryl Streep (Karen Silkwood), Kurt Russell (Drew Stephens), Cher (Dolly Pelliker), Craig T. Nelson (Winston), Diana Scarwid (Angela), Fred Ward (Morgan), Ron Silver (Paul Stone), Charles Hallahan (Earl Lapin), Josef Sommer (Max Richter), Sudie Bond (Thelma Rice)

p, Mike Nichols, Michael Hausman; d, Mike Nichols; w, Nora Ephron, Alice Arlen; ph, Miroslav Ondricek (Technicolor); ed, Sam O'Steen; m, Georges Delerue; prod d, Patrizia von Brandenstein; art d, Richard James; cos, Ann Roth

Karen Silkwood, a worker at the Kerr-McGee nuclear materials plant in Cimarron, Oklahoma, died in 1974 in a suspect auto accident on her way to meet a New York Times reporter to present evidence she had gathered concerning safety violations at her workplace. Based on that story, SILKWOOD is a sensational expose of big business seen through the eyes of average working people. Meryl Streep, in another brilliant portrayal, is the title character, a tough, hard-drinking woman who lives with her boyfriend (Kurt Russell), and a lesbian friend (an engagingly low-key Cher). In the course of her dull, dangerous job at Kerr-McGee, Silkwood is repeatedly contaminated. She begins to suspect a management cover-up of safety measures violations at the plant, and undertakes to get proof of her suspicions for the union brass in Washington. Though her relationship with her boyfriend deteriorates as she plugs more and more of her energy into her spying, she gathers evidence that she intends to give to the reporter, and heads out for the meeting that never took place. The clear implication is that Silkwood was silenced to prevent her from making trouble for the plant. Mike Nichols, in his first venture into movies since THE FORTUNE (1975), elicited superlative performances from the actors, particularly Streep and stage veteran Sudi Bond.

SILVER STREAK

1976   113m   c   ★★½
Thriller/Comedy   PG
FOX

Gene Wilder (George Caldwell), Jill Clayburgh (Hilly Burns), Richard Pryor (Grover Muldoon), Patrick McGoohan (Roger Devereau), Ned Beatty (Sweet), Clifton James (Sheriff Chauncey), Ray Walston (Mr. Whiney), Stefan Gierasch (Johnson/Prof. Schreiner), Len Birman (Chief), Valerie Curtin (Plain Jane)

p, Thomas L. Miller, Edward K. Milkis; d, Arthur Hiller; w, Colin Higgins; ph, David M. Walsh, Ralph Woolsey (DeLuxe Color); ed, David Bretherton; m, Henry Mancini; prod d, Alfred Sweeney; fx, Fred Cramer; cos, Phyllis Garr, Michael Harte

A derivative farce from one of the masters of derivation, Colin Higgins, who has made a career of studying Hitchcock, transforming some of the plots to comedies, and riding the crest of the wave to success. This picture earned well over $30 million due, in great part, to Pryor's brief but hysterical appearance. He and Wilder would team up again for STIR CRAZY. Wilder is a meek book executive who wants to take a leisurely train ride from Los Angeles to Chicago aboard the Silver Streak train. Instead, his trip turns out to be a nightmare. He meets and romances Clayburgh, an art professor's assistant who is traveling in an adjoining compartment. Clayburgh tells Wilder that her boss is about to expose a pack of art forgers. Wilder witnesses Clayburgh's boss falling off the speeding train. He races around the Silver Streak attempting to tell people what he's seen, but nobody will believe him, with the exception of Beatty, an undercover agent masquerading as a traveling salesman. McGoohan, the leader of the villains, is on to Beatty and instructs his thugs to get rid of him, which they do. Meanwhile, McGoohan and Walston continue to attempt to kill Wilder, which results in a series of Harold Lloyd-type stunts as they keep throwing him off the train. Somehow he manages to get back on each time in a comical fashion. About halfway into the story Wilder is joined by Pryor, and the movie takes a sudden turn to excellence. Wilder and Pryor have one funny scene in which Pryor, in order to disguise him, blackens Wilder's face and teaches him how to walk like a hipster. The final scene has the train derailed and crashing through the Chicago station. This smash-up appears to have been tossed in for no other reason than to provide a spectacular ending.

Clayburgh, who was coming off the disastrous GABLE AND LOMBARD and had since licked her critical wounds, delivers a believable performance, but she is no Grace Kelly or Audrey Hepburn. Still, her work stands out as an oasis of characterization in a Sahara of madcap, antic, frenzied performances. It's almost as though she was acting in CHARADE while the others were in ABBOTT AND COSTELLO MEET THE MARX BROTHERS. Mancini's score is a bit too elegant and sophisticated for the goings-on. SILVER STREAK is a throwback to the screwball comedies of the 1930s but with none of the verve or the motivation needed to get an audience to swallow the shenanigans. What Higgins apparently did was to study STRANGERS ON A TRAIN, then THE LADY VANISHES, and figure a way to combine the two with a bit of laughter. McGoohan, whom most believe is British because of his success on TV in "The Prisoner" and his many films in England, was actually born in the US and acquired the accent later in his life. When director Hiller lays his hands on a good script, as in THE IN-LAWS and HOSPITAL, he does well, but all his talents could not overcome all the cliches in this film.

SILVERADO

1985 132m c ★★
Western PG-13/PG
Columbia

Kevin Kline *(Paden)*, Scott Glenn *(Emmett)*, Rosanna Arquette *(Hannah)*, John Cleese *(Sheriff Langston)*, Kevin Costner *(Jake)*, Brian Dennehy *(Cobb)*, Danny Glover *(Mal)*, Jeff Goldblum *(Slick)*, Linda Hunt *(Stella)*, Raymond Baker *(McKendrick)*

p, Lawrence Kasdan; d, Lawrence Kasdan; w, Lawrence Kasdan, Mark Kasdan; ph, John Bailey (Super Techniscope, Technicolor); ed, Carol Littleton, Mia Goldman; m, Bruce Broughton; prod d, Ida Random; fx, Roy Arbogast; cos, Kristi Zea

Jammed with enough characters and plot elements to fill at least 10 films, SILVERADO is a big stampede of a movie with ideas and scenes thundering off in dozens of directions. Without things getting out of hand, the plot here sees four unlikely heros—Paden (Kevin Kline), Emmett (Scott Glenn), Jake (Kevin Costner), and Mal (Danny Glover)—team up to rescue the town of Silverado from nasty sheriff Cobb (Brian Dennehy) and his army of goons. The basics are simple enough and definitely the stuff of 1940s westerns, but then writer-director Lawrence Kasdan bloats the plot with dozens of side stories that, in painfully predictable detail, show how each of our heroes has a reason for being in Silverado and why they decide to stick their necks out. Though much of the running time is devoted to these expository passages, it's all very basic and shallow. Between the gratuitous climaxes that seem to occur every 10 minutes, Kasdan parades a myriad of stereotypes before us and never develops them (Rosanna Arquette as the pretty young widow; Jeff Goldblum as the slimy, dandified gambler; Linda Hunt as the tough saloon owner). In fact, he never really explores any of his characters but only provides them with enough motivation to justify the slaughter of dozens of people. The sound team and Broughton's score were nominated for Academy Awards.

SIN OF MADELON CLAUDET, THE

1931 74m bw ★★★★
Drama
MGM

Helen Hayes *(Madelon Claudet)*, Lewis Stone *(Carlo Boretti)*, Neil Hamilton *(Larry)*, Robert Young *(Dr. Claudet)*, Cliff Edwards *(Victor)*, Jean Hersholt *(Dr. Dulac)*, Marie Prevost *(Rosalie)*, Karen Morley *(Alice)*, Charles Winninger *(Photographer)*, Alan Hale *(Hubert)*

d, Edgar Selwyn; w, Charles MacArthur (based on the play *The Lullaby* by Edward Knoblock); ph, Oliver T. Marsh; ed, Tom Held; art d, Cedric Gibbons

Helen Hayes made her sound-film debut in this well-acted soaper scripted by her husband, Charles MacArthur. Jean Hersholt narrates in flashback the story of Hayes, a French girl who falls in love with Neil Hamilton, an American artist. The two move in together without marrying, but their idyllic life is ruined when Hamilton leaves and marries another woman. Hayes then becomes involved with Lewis Stone, but, arrested on jewel theft charges, he kills himself rather than face the law; Hayes, charged as his accomplice, is sentenced to 10 years in prison. On her release, she becomes a streetwalker to support her illegitimate son, Robert Young, sending the money to Hersholt, a doctor tutoring Young in medicine. Young is suspicious about the money because of the irregular sums and sporadic deliveries; however, Hayes lies, telling Young the money is from the estate of his late mother. Eventually Young becomes a successful doctor, setting

Hayes up in a Parisian apartment. The film ends as Hersholt finishes his narration. He has been telling the story to Young's wife, a woman upset by Young's devotion to his career. She had been considering leaving him, but after hearing Hayes' story, the woman reconsiders.

Hayes won a well-deserved Oscar for this performance, taking her character from young girl to old woman with astonishing believability. The story piles twist upon emotional twist, coming close to self-parody, but audiences of the day loved the picture. The story had been made numerous times under the title MADAME X. Two silent versions were made in 1915 and 1920, while sound versions were made in 1929, 1937, 1948, 1960 (as THE TRIAL OF MADAME X), 1966, and 1981 as a television film.

SINCE YOU WENT AWAY

1944 172m bw ★★★★
War/Drama /U
UA

Claudette Colbert *(Anne Hilton)*, Jennifer Jones *(Jane)*, Shirley Temple *(Bridget "Brig" Hilton)*, Joseph Cotten *(Lt. Anthony Willett)*, Monty Woolley *(Col. Smollett)*, Robert Walker *(Cpl. William G. Smollett II)*, Lionel Barrymore *(Clergyman)*, Hattie McDaniel *(Emily Hawkins)*, Agnes Moorehead *(Emily Hawkins)*, Guy Madison *(Harold Smith)*

p, David O. Selznick; d, John Cromwell; w, David O. Selznick (based on the book *Together* by Margaret Buell Wilder, adaptation by Wilder); ph, Stanley Cortez, Lee Garmes, Jack Cosgrove; ed, Hal C. Kern, James E. Newcom, Don DiFaure, Arthur Fellows, Wayland M. Hendrys; m, Max Steiner, Louis Forbes; prod d, William L. Oereira; fx, Jack Cosgrove, Clarence Slifer; chor, Charles Walters

Focusing on the plight of those left behind when the soldiers went off to fight in WWII, SINCE YOU WENT AWAY was a smash hit with audiences on the home front, grossing well over $4 million at a time when movie ticket prices were as low as 25 cents. Based on a collection of letters written by Ohio newspaper columnist Margaret Buell Wilder to her husband fighting overseas, which Wilder first published in her column, then collected in a book, and finally rewrote as a screen story, SINCE YOU WENT AWAY is a long, episodic, but always interesting film scripted by producer David O. Selznick from Wilder's adaptation. The film focuses on the wartime life of Colbert and her two daughters (Jones and a teenaged Temple, the latter making her first screen appearance after a layoff of a couple of years) after Colbert's husband leaves his family and his job in the advertising business to go off to fight in the war. Jones is in love with a soldier—Walker, a corporal, who returns from the service to romance her. (Jones and Walker were married in real life at the time, and, though they divorced a year later, their off-screen love is still evident here). Also figuring in the proceedings are Cotten, a family friend and Navy lieutenant who lends his moral support to Colbert and never takes advantage of her loneliness; Wooley, Colbert's acerbic boarder, whose sarcasm provides the film's lighter moments; and Soda, the family's scene-stealing English bulldog.

SINCE YOU WENT AWAY unfolds its loosely structured story realistically—even the battle scenes lack the phony heroics common in WWII films—and the film's three hours pass quickly, sped by its interesting assortment of characters, touchingly portrayed by the cast, its well-written script by Selznick, and its high level of technical accomplishment.

SING YOU SINNERS

1938 88m bw   ★★★½
Musical   /U
Paramount

Bing Crosby (Joe Beebe), Fred MacMurray (David Beebe), Donald O'Connor (Mike Beebe), Elizabeth Patterson (Mrs. Beebe), Ellen Drew (Martha), John Gallaudet (Harry Ringmer), William Haade (Pete), Paul White (Filter), Irving Bacon (Lecturer), Tom Dugan (Race Fan)

p, Wesley Ruggles; d, Wesley Ruggles; w, Claude Binyon; ph, Karl Struss; ed, Alma Macrorie; art d, Hans Dreier, Ernst Fegte

Until this picture, Bing Crosby had been playing cliched light comedy roles that made him popular but did nothing to show his acting talent. Here he was able to present another side of his character and audiences loved it. Joe Beebe (Crosby) is a 35-year-old wastrel who spends most of his time concocting plans to make money without toil. His mother (Elizabeth Patterson) wishes he would be more like his brother David (Fred MacMurray), a hardworking garage mechanic. Mom also wants Joe to set a better example for her youngest son, 13-year-old Mike (Donald O'Connor, in only his second film role). The three brothers, all musicians, make a few extra bucks working at a small nightclub, but Joe, not content with barely squeezing out an existence, leaves for Los Angeles. He promises his poor but loving family that as soon as he gets a good job he'll send them money for the fare. Time passes and Mom hears from Joe that he's now in a new business and doing well. That's encouragement enough for her to sell the family home and go to Los Angeles—only to find that Joe has purchased a racehorse, and is hardly prosperous. They scrape by on almost nothing, and little Mike is pressed into service as a jockey for the Big Race that rounds off the film with a big finish.

SINGIN' IN THE RAIN

1952 103m c   ★★★★★
Musical   /U
MGM

Gene Kelly (Don Lockwood), Donald O'Connor (Cosmo Brown), Debbie Reynolds (Kathy Selden), Jean Hagen (Lina Lamont), Millard Mitchell (R.F. Simpson), Rita Moreno (Zelda Zanders), Douglas Fowley (Roscoe Dexter), Cyd Charisse (Dancer), Madge Blake (Dora Bailey), King Donovan (Rod)

p, Arthur Freed; d, Gene Kelly, Stanley Donen; w, Adolph Green, Betty Comden (suggested by the song "Singin' in the Rain"); ph, Harold Rosson (Technicolor); ed, Adrienne Fazan; m, Nacio Herb Brown; art d, Cedric Gibbons, Randall Duell; fx, Warren Newcombe, Irving G. Ries; cos, Walter Plunkett

Very likely the greatest musical MGM or anyone else ever produced, SINGIN' IN THE RAIN has everything—great songs, great dances, a wonderful, nostalgic story, and a dependable cast, although we're beginning to find Kelly and O'Connor a trifle overanimated in scenes they needn't be (but then whenever we see the talented yet obsequious Mr. Kelly play modest, we get a strange olfactory sensation—that of ham baking). It's admittedly directed (by Gene Kelly and Stanley Donen) with a dazzling pace equal to the speed-crazy era the film profiles, the Roaring Twenties. Asked to create a story that would tie together numbers from the best of MGM's musical output, many of which were penned by Nacio Herb Brown and Arthur Freed, screenwriters Adolph Green and Betty Comden found that some of the finest of those tunes appeared in films made during the transition from silents to talkies, and so they decided to focus their tale on that dynamic

period when new stars replaced old; bright, shiny faces took the places of heavily rouged vamps and mascared lotharios.

As the film opens in 1927, dashing Don Lockwood (Kelly) and blonde bombshell Lina Lamont (Jean Hagen) are one of Hollywood's favorite romantic teams, though Lina mistakenly believes their on-screen love is for real. Don and his less famous former partner, song-and-dance man Cosmo Brown (Donald O'Connor), have worked their way to the top the hard way (vaudeville, stuntwork, etc.), and when THE JAZZ SINGER changes the cinematic rules, making a pleasant voice a necessity, Don is ready. Not so Lina, whose shrill voice makes a mockery of the musical their most recent film has been transformed into, despite the best efforts of a stuffy diction coach which are wonderfully lampooned by Don and Cosmo in "Moses Supposes" (written by Comden and Green and Roger Edens). Kathy Selden (Debbie Reynolds, who makes a great flapper—like UNSINKABLE MOLLY BROWN, here's a character with Reynolds's energy level), an aspiring "serious" actress whose life Don enters quite unexpectedly and with whom he falls in love, saves the film when her voice is dubbed for Lina's (ironically, Reynolds's own singing was looped by Betty Royce—her own voice hadn't much training yet). Although it seems at first that Kathy is destined to remain behind the scenes indefinitely, the film's ending sees to it that fair is fair as true love triumphs.

Contributing some of the most captivating choreography ever filmed, Kelly, more than anyone, is responsible for the delightful ambience of this spectacular musical. His *tour de force* dance to the classic title song (which first appeared in HOLLYWOOD REVUE OF 1929) alone makes the film a must-see; bounding through a rain-clogged street, swinging around a lamppost, splashing and jumping in joy over having fallen in love with Kathy, he creates one of the cinema's most unforgettable moments. Nearly as engaging are the hilarious, highly energized comic dance O'Connor performs with props and sets on a soundstage to "Make 'Em Laugh" and the marvelous "Broadway Ballet" sequence with a wonderful guest appearance by surly Cyd Charisse and her "crazy veil," a 25-foot long piece of white China silk that streamed about her, kept afloat by three airplane motors whirring off-camera. This sequence took a month to rehearse, two weeks to shoot, and cost $600,000, almost a fifth of the overall budget of this superlative musical, one of the most popular films ever. Interestingly, SINGIN' was only nominated for two Oscars: Best Supporting Actress (Hagen, one of the 1950s' most versatile, accomplished talents; her versatility may be why Hollywood—which coasted on typecasting—never gave her the big star treatment she deserved) and Best Scoring of a Musical Picture. Look for Madge Blake as a saccharine sob sister columnist and Rita Moreno as a flapper actress.

SINK THE BISMARCK!

1960 97m bw   ★★★★
War/Historical   /U
FOX   (U.K.)

Kenneth More (Capt. Jonathan Shepard), Dana Wynter (Anne Davis), Carl Mohner (Capt. Lindemann), Laurence Naismith (First Sea Lord), Geoffrey Keen (A.C.N.S.), Karel Stepanek (Adm. Lutjens), Michael Hordern (Commander on King George), Maurice Denham (Cmdr. Richards), Michael Goodliffe (Capt. Banister), Esmond Knight (Captain, Prince of Wales)

p, John Brabourne; d, Lewis Gilbert; w, Edmund H. North (based on the book by C.S. Forester); ph, Christopher Challis (CinemaScope); ed, Peter Hunt; m, Clifton Parker; art d, Arthur Lawson; fx, Howard Lydecker, Bill Warrington

Screenwriter Edmund North knows how to write about war, as he proved with his Oscar-winning screenplay for PATTON. Here, he has fashioned a taut, tense wartime drama out of the real story of how the Germans' most powerful naval fighting machine was destroyed. The film starts with actual newsreel footage as the *Bismarck* is launched in Hamburg to the cheers of the Nazi chiefs in 1938. Flash ahead to 1941 and the War Room of the British Admiralty, where More, still stunned by the death of his wife in an air raid, begins to conduct the campaign to blow the German battleship out of the water. Wynter, a WREN (the British equivalent of a WAVE), is at More's side in the War Room. No sooner does More take over the job when word comes in that the *Bismarck* has left its hiding place and is now steaming toward the battle zone. More has to figure some way to make th most of his sparse fleet, and the news is bad when the *Bismarck* sinks the *Hood*, one of Britain's best, then cripples the cruiser *Prince of Wales*. More's son is a gunner on the *Ark Royal*, a carrier More sends to fight the *Bismarck*. Rushing from Gibraltar, *Ark Royal* damages the behemoth enough to cause it to seek shelter on the French coast. Once the *Bismarck* is slowed down, the British ships *King George V* and *Rodney* are able to catch up with it and finally destroy it in a huge sea battle. The film is a marvel of intercutting, shifting repeatedly from More and Wynter in the War Room, to action aboard the German battleship, to all the other British ships as they begin to tighten the noose. More spends countless hours plotting the destruction of the *Bismark*, grabbing a nap here and there, sharing his personal woes with Wynter, who is always at his side. Although there's a bit of caricature in the portrayal of the Germans, the film is still evenhanded enough in its portrayal of the enemy that the villains remain interesting characters. Actual battle footage is combined with flawless miniature work by Howard Lydecker and Bill Harrington and the effect is stunningly convincing. SINK THE BISMARK is a first-class war drama that ranks with IN WHICH WE SERVE and COCKLESHELL HEROES as examples of how to create excitement with a great script. The most impressive part of North's screenplay is that we are almost able to look inside More's head to see why he does what he does.

SISTERS OF THE GION
(GION NO SHIMAI)
1936 70m bw   ★★★★
Drama
Daiichi Eiga (Japan)

Isuzu Yamada *(Umekichi)*, Yoko Umemura *(O-Mocha)*, Eitaro Shindo, Benkei Shiganoya, Namiko Kawahima, Fumio Okura, Taizo Fukami, Reido Aoi

p, Masaichi Nagata; d, Kenji Mizoguchi; w, Yoshikata Toda (based on a story by Mizoguchi); ph, Minoru Miki

This is one of two excellent films (the other being THE OSAKA ELEGY) that director Kenji Mizoguchi made in 1936. Both were made possible by Daiichi Eiga, the failing studio for whom the director was employed, which gave him complete control before it was shuttered. Like so many of Mizoguchi's works, SISTERS OF THE GION focuses on female characters, in this case two sisters, both of whom are geishas. Umekichi (Isuzu Yamada) is the elder, an experienced prostitute who has become romantically involved with one of her former clients, a bankrupt merchant. Omocha (Yoko Umemura), the younger sister, has different ideas about men and relationships. Having seen the way men treat women, especially her sister, she decides to take the upper hand, manipulating, and ultimately to destroying, a young kimono clerk. In a twist of fate that seems to suggest that gender roles are irreversible, both sisters are victimized by the film's end. This elegant, carefully directed tale shows Mizoguchi's early talents. He manages to elicit beautiful performances from his actresses, establishing himself as one of the great directors of women, and embarking on his career as the greatest cinematic interpreter of the lives of Japanese women. From SISTERS OF THE GION's very beginning, with its rollicking jazz score, Mizoguchi demonstrates his unique mastery of the film frame, moving through the expansive space of a merchant's home in which every last piece of furniture is auctioned off—a masculine material defeat that neatly contrasts with the female romantic defeat at the film's end. (In Japanese; English subtitles.)

SITTING DUCKS
1979 90m c   ★★★
Crime/Comedy   R/AA
International Rainbow/Sunny Side Up

Michael Emil *(Simon)*, Zack Norman *(Sidney)*, Patrice Townsend *(Jenny)*, Irene Forrest *(Leona)*, Richard Romanus *(Moose)*, Henry Jaglom *(Jenny's Friend)*

p, Meira Attia Dor; d, Henry Jaglom; w, Henry Jaglom; ph, Paul Glickman (Metrocolor); m, Richard Romanus

Two small-timers decide to go for the big time by stealing money from gangsters. Once they have the money they intend to head to Central America and live it up. Emil and Norman have a marvelous chemistry in this great zany comedy. After they meet Townsend and Forrest along the way, all four play nicely off one another. The comedy here is grounded in well-constructed characters and a simple premise. The result is a rollicking good time, directed with style and a sense of fun.

SITTING PRETTY
1948 84m bw   ★★★★
Comedy   /U
Fox

Robert Young *(Harry)*, Maureen O'Hara *(Tacey)*, Clifton Webb *(Lynn Belvedere)*, Richard Haydn *(Mr. Appleton)*, Louise Allbritton *(Edna Philby)*, Randy Stuart *(Peggy)*, Ed Begley *(Hammond)*, Larry Olsen *(Larry)*, John Russell *(Bill Philby)*, Betty Lynn *(Ginger)*

p, Samuel G. Engel; d, Walter Lang; w, F. Hugh Herbert (based on the novel *Belvedere* by Gwen Davenport); ph, Norbert Brodine; ed, Harmon Jones; m, Alfred Newman; art d, Lyle Wheeler, Leland Fuller; fx, Fred Sersen; cos, Kay Nelson

If ever an actor was born to play a part, it was Clifton Webb in his Oscar-nominated role as Lynn Belvedere, a prissy genius who takes a job as a babysitter. The scene is Hummingbird Hill, a typical suburban community where the three sons of Harry and Tacey (Robert Young and Maureen O'Hara) are so bratty that the family has lost a trio of maids, with little hope of finding another replacement. Tacey advertises in the local paper and in walks Mr. Belvedere, a self-proclaimed genius with definite ideas about raising children. He is stern but fair and it's not long before the boys knuckle under to his discipline. When the baby tosses oatmeal at Belvedere, his response is to toss the goop right back at the baby, thereby establishing his superiority. The neighborhood is filled with gossips and busybodies, and they are all shocked when the real reason for Belvedere's presence is unveiled: he's a writer (besides being a doctor, lawyer, philosopher, and everything else) who has been researching the community. The town is then exposed when Belvedere's book is published and becomes a best-seller. The two sequels to this successful film, MR. BELVEDERE GOES TO COLLEGE and MR. BEL-

VEDERE RINGS THE BELL, were not nearly as witty or biting as the original. In 1985, a TV series was also attempted based on the Webb character.

SIX IN PARIS
(PARIS VU PAR. . .)
1968 96m c   ★★★
Comedy/Drama
Losange/Barbet Schroeder   (France)

SAINT-GERMAIN-DES-PRES: Barbara Wilkin (*Katherine*), Jean-Francois Chappey (*Jean*), Jean-Pierre Andreani (*Raymond*). GARE DU NORD: Nadine Ballot (*Odile*), Barbet Schroeder (*Jean-Pierre*), Gilles Queant (*Stranger*). RUE SAINT-DENIS: Micheline Dax (*Prostitute*), Claude Melki (*Leon*). PLACE DE L'ETOILE: Jean-Michel Rouziere (*Jean-Marc*), Marcel Gallon (*Victim*)

p, Barbet Schroeder; d, Jean Douchet ("Saint-Germain-des-Pres"), Jean Rouch ("Gare du Nord"), Jean-Daniel Pollet ("Rue Saint-Denis"), Eric Rohmer ("Place de L'Etoile"), Jean-Luc Godard ("Montparnasse-Levallois"), Claude Chabrol ("La Muette"); w, Jean Douchet, Jean Rouch, Georges Keller, Jean-Daniel Pollet, Eric Rohmer, Jean-Luc Godard, Claude Chabrol; ph, Nestor Almendros, Etienne Becker, Alain Levent, Albert Maysles, Jean Rabier (Ektachrome); ed, Jackie Reynal; art d, Eliane Bonneau

This six-part compilation film, which opened in Paris in October 1965, is notable for the talent that worked on some of the segments; many of these directors, actors and cinematographers would go on to become central figures of the French New Wave.

In "Saint-Germain-des-Pres," Chappey brings American student Wilkin to his flat for the night. He gets rid of her the next day, announcing that he's flying to Mexico to join his father. Wilkin is later disillusioned when Chappey turns up as a model in her art class. She then allows Andreani to pick her up, only to discover that this boy had loaned his apartment to Chappey for the original affair. The photographer was Almendros, who became a celebrated cinematographer during the 1970s.

In "Gare du Nord," Ballot runs out on her husband (Schroeder) after a fight. She's almost run down by Queant, a handsome stranger in a fancy car. He says he's going to kill himself but will change his mind if Ballot goes away with him. She refuses, and he takes a plunge off a railway bridge.

"Rue Saint-Denis" depicts shy, young Melki bringing prostitute Dax back to his place for a night of fun. His incessant conversation leads to Dax's staying for dinner before they can get to bed.

"Place de l'Etoile," directed by Rohmer, has salesman Rouziere bumping into Gallon, a street person, on his way to work. He hits the poor man with his umbrella during the confrontation, and Gallon falls down. Rouziere is convinced he's killed the derelict and looks for news of his death in the papers. A few weeks later, he sees Gallon engaged in a similar argument with another person at the same place.

"Montparnasse-Levallois" was directed by the bad boy of the *Nouvelle Vague*, Godard, and photographed by noted American documentary filmmaker Maysles. This story has Joanna Shimkus serving as a lover for two men. She sends each a note telling the site of their respective rendezvous but panics when she thinks she mistakenly switched the notes. She goes to each lover to explain away her mistake and is surprised when each man throws her out, then realizes the mistake was all in her mind.

The last segment, "La Muette," was written and directed by Chabrol. He also plays a man who constantly fights with his wife (Stephane Audran) about money and who flirts with the housemaid. His son, tired of the noise, buys some earplugs for himself.

The earplugs end up doing more harm than good when his mother falls down the stairs, and the boy doesn't hear her cry out for help.

SIX OF A KIND
1934 62m bw   ★★★
Comedy   /U
Paramount

Charlie Ruggles (*J. Pinkham Whinney*), Mary Boland (*Flora Whinney*), W.C. Fields (*Sheriff "Honest John" Hoxley*), George Burns (*George Edwards*), Gracie Allen (*Gracie De Vore*), Alison Skipworth (*Mrs. "Duchess" K. Rumford*), Bradley Page (*Ferguson*), Grace Bradley (*Trixie*), William J. Kelly (*A.B. Gillette*), James Burke (*Sparks*)

d, Leo McCarey; w, Walter DeLeon, Harry Ruskin (based on a story by Keene Thompson, Douglas MacLean); ph, Henry Sharp; ed, LeRoy Stone; m, Ralph Rainger; art d, Hans Dreier, Robert Odell

A veritable smorgasbord of comedy was served up by Paramount in SIX OF A KIND, which features not one, but six veteran comedy performers. Ruggles and his wife, Boland, decide to travel to California for their second honeymoon. To defray costs, Boland puts an ad in the paper asking for another couple to join them and share expenses. Much to the honeymooners' dismay, none other than Burns and Allen answer the ad, accompanied by a huge Great Dane. The couples pile their belongings, including the slobbering hound, into the car and speed off for California. Unbeknownst to Ruggles, however, a clerk in the bank where he works has stolen $50,000 and hidden it in one of the suitcases bound for California. The crooked clerk then intends to rob Ruggles out on the open road. Luckily, Allen insists on traveling a different route than planned and the evil clerk is left to wait in vain. Unfortunately, their luck is short-lived for highwaymen accost the travelers, causing the giant attack dog to flee in panic. Once again the travelers escape harm because the robbers overlook the $50,000 and depart. Meanwhile, detectives have discovered the theft and Ruggles becomes their main suspect. The detectives attempt to head off the vacationers and warn sheriff Fields in Nuggetville, Nevada. Determined to capture the scoundrels, Fields and innkeeper Skipworth team up to arrest the travelers. After much craziness Ruggles is cleared of any wrongdoing, leaving the obnoxious Burns and Allen to find another unsuspecting traveling couple to leech onto. Finally alone, Ruggles and Boland look forward to what is left of their second honeymoon. Directed by Leo McCarey, a man who knew how to let the cameras roll and not interfere with great comedians doing their stuff (see the Marx Brothers in DUCK SOUP), SIX OF A KIND offers up a variety of good laughs, but the highlight is definitely W.C. Fields and his billiards routine. The hilariously complicated act, developed and fine-tuned during his years in vaudeville, became one of Fields' best-loved bits. In fact, Fields's very first movie, POOL SHARKS, was supposed to capture the act on film, but in the end very little of the routine was actually used. Nearly 20 years later the classic act was faithfully recreated in SIX OF A KIND. While telling a stranger how he got the name "Honest John" (he returned a man's lost glass eye), sheriff Fields attempts to play some pool. After fussing with several distorted pool cues, indulging in an elaborate chalking-up procedure, and finding just the right spot to set his hat, Fields attempts to break. Unfortunately, while lining up the shot he loses control of his pool cue and struggles to grasp it as the chalked end floats away from his fingers as if weightless. After several attempts to recapture the business end of the pool cue, Fields finally succeeds and makes his shot. The cue ball misses the break, speeds to the opposite end of the table, ricochets off the bumper, flies through the air, and makes a beeline for Fields' forehead. The ball smacks him in the head, bounces straight up, and while Fields clutches his head in agony with one hand, he catches the cue ball in the air with the other and places it back on the pool table—all without any evidence of camera trickery. Grimacing in pain, Fields once again attempts a break, this time by employing a fancy trick shot which sees the pool cue held perpendicular to the cue ball. Fields makes the shot, misses the cue ball, and drives the entire pool cue through the table, making a large hole. While struggling to pull the long stick out of the expensive pool table, Fields glances furtively about, making sure that the owner hasn't seen him ruin the table. Finally freeing the cue stick, Fields places a flower basket over the gaping hole and makes a hasty escape. This hysterical scene has to be seen to be believed. Several viewings are required to catch every subtle nuance that Fields employs to make the brief routine such an amazing display of skilled comedic craftsmanship. The attention to little details and bits of business during the routine is pure genius, as is the endlessly interrupted story about the man with the glass eye. It is one of the most brilliant moments in Fields's undeniably brilliant career and moviegoers throughout the world should say a silent prayer of thanks to director Leo McCarey for having the intelligence and foresight to let his performers perform unhindered by a heavy directorial hand.

SIXTEEN CANDLES

1984 93m c   ★★★
Comedy   PG/15
Channel

Molly Ringwald (*Samantha*), Justin Henry (*Mike Baker*), Michael Schoeffling (*Jake*), Haviland Morris (*Caroline*), Gedde Watanabe (*Long Duk Dong*), Anthony Michael Hall (*Ted, the Geek*), Paul Dooley (*Jim Baker*), Carlin Glynn (*Brenda Baker*), Blanche Baker (*Ginny*), Edward Andrews (*Howard*)

p, Hilton A. Green; d, John Hughes; w, John Hughes; ph, Bobby Byrne (Technicolor); ed, Edward Warschilka; m, Ira Newborn; prod d, John W. Corso; cos, Mark Peterson, Marla Denise Schlom

This funny, unpretentious film marked writer John Hughes's first time out as a director. The premise is ordinary, but the film is distinguished by funny gags and excellent performances by Molly Ringwald and Anthony Michael Hall. Samantha (Ringwald) is a high-school sophomore about to turn 16, and her life is dominated by her love for Jake (Michael Schoeffling), a senior and the school heartthrob. In turn, she is followed around by Ted (Hall), a younger boy who is acknowledged to be a nerd. Nothing seems to be going right for Samantha. Her older sister is about to be married, and her parents are overlooking Samantha's birthday, a major moment in her young life. Her grandparents move into her room, and her relationship with her smart-alecky brother (Justin Henry) gets tense. Simultaneously, Samantha has to be kind and caring to Long Duk Dong (Gedde Watanabe), a loony but sweet Japanese exchange student staying at her home. The situations are predictable, but Hughes saves them from being cliches with his attention to detail. Hall and Ringwald became part of the Hollywood "Brat Pack" with this film, and Hughes emerged as a hot director.

SKIPPY

1931 85m bw   ★★★½
Children's   /U
Paramount

Jackie Cooper (*Skippy Skinner*), Robert Coogan (*Sooky Wayne*), Mitzi Green (*Eloise*), Jackie Searl (*Sidney*), Willard Robertson (*Dr. Herbert Skinner*), Enid Bennett (*Mrs. Ellen Skinner*), David Haines (*Harley Nubbins*), Helen Jerome Eddy (*Mrs. Wayne*), Jack Clifford (*Dogcatcher Nubbins*), Guy Oliver (*Dad Burkey*)

p, Louis D. Lighton; d, Norman Taurog; w, Joseph L. Mankiewicz, Norman Z. McLeod, Don Marquis, Percy Crosby, Sam Mintz (based on the comic strip by Crosby); ph, Karl Struss

A charming children's picture that doesn't neglect adults, SKIPPY was good enough to merit Oscar nominations for Best Picture, Best Director, Best Story, and for Jackie Cooper as Best Actor. Based on a comic strip by Percy Crosby, it's a simple, adorable tale of boys and girls and their dogs. When a dog belonging to Sooky Wayne (Robert Coogan, younger brother of Jackie Coogan) is captured by the local dogcatcher, Sooky and his friend Skippy Skinner (Jackie Cooper) try to raise money to buy a license for the pooch. In order to get the necessary $3, they try everything. One of their plans is to stage a show, for which they sell tickets, lemonade, etc. They also try smashing Skippy's unbreakable bank by putting it under the wheels of a truck. There are many wonderful moments in the picture, and watching Cooper cry is worth the price of admission. There have been few child actors who have been as convincing as he could be. The sequel was SOOKY.

SLACKER

1991 97m c   ★★★½
Comedy   R/18
Detour Filmproduction

Richard Linklater, Rudy Basquez, Jean Caggeine, Jan Hockey, Stephan Hockey, Mark James, Samuel Dietert, Bob Boyd, Terrence Kirk, Keith McCormack

p, Richard Linklater; d, Richard Linklater; w, Richard Linklater; ph, Lee Daniel; ed, Scott Rhodes

An original, narratively innovative, low-budget film from the fringe, SLACKER is a perfectly plotless work that tracks incidental moments in the lives of some one hundred characters who have made the bohemian side of Austin, Texas, their hangout of choice.

Because it lacks any conventional storyline, or even a central character, SLACKER is impossible to synopsize or categorize. The film's organizing sensibility is perhaps best explained by director Richard Linklater himself, who appears onscreen in his film's opening scene. On his way into town, he free-associates to his cab driver: "You know in THE WIZARD OF OZ where Dorothy meets the Scarecrow. . . and they think about going in all those directions and they end up going in that *one* direction? All those other directions, just because they thought about them, became separate realities. . . entirely different movies." SLACKER consists of all those other different movies. Its camera follows one character, splinters off to follow another, then another, never spending more than a few minutes with any one and never returning to a place or person from preceding scenes.

The two forces that hold the film together are its clear sense of place (specifically Austin, more generally college towns) and its intimate knowledge of a certain character type: the "slacker." The term is slang that refers loosely to any number of young underemployed residents of college communities who either lack direction in life or choose an alternative direction. In an hour and a half we meet dozens of these street musicians, espresso czars, co-op kids, sidewalk psychics, paranoid hitchhikers, disgruntled grad students, cafe philosophers, anti-artists, petty thieves, anarchists, post-modernists, dropouts and freaks—slackers all.

While many appear to be lazy and indulgent drags on society, what emerges is a portrait of a collective of creative malcontents. In the clubs, coffeehouses, streets and unfurnished apartments near campus they each spin their idiosyncratic conspiracy theories about modern life, UFOs, Elvis, Madonna, George Bush, popular culture, JFK, Oswald, Marx and various forms of cosmic consciousness. Although there is little action as they practice the fine art of hanging out, their constant talk is full of energy, humor, eccentricity and a warped but discernable intelligence.

Produced on a budget of only $23,000, SLACKER became a surprise hit on the festival circuit. At age 29, director Richard Linklater obtained a major distribution deal from Orion Classics, which blew the original 16mm print up to 35mm and remixed its soundtrack. Such treatment was exceptional for a self-taught, first-time filmmaker who used mostly unpaid amateur talent to create an experiment in cinematic form. But the film's improvisatory, meandering style is actually carefully constructed.

While much of the actual dialogue and monologue were worked out during production (from the hitchhiker who says "I may live badly, but at least I don't have to work to do it," to the anarchist who recalls the 1966 University of Texas tower massacre by sniper Charles Whitman as the town's "finest hour"), the shooting of the film was carefully set out beforehand. The many incidental vignettes are not logically or narratively tied together, but each is visually linked to the next as characters seemingly pass the camera like a baton from one situation to the next. Finally, the camera—the home-movie variety—is literally passed around by a bunch of daytrippers on a joyride who conclude this day-in-the-life of Slackerville by hurling their super-8 camera off a mountain top.

The strength of SLACKER is its refreshing and obvious intention to escape all narrative expectations about filmmaking. The film's character sketches are often funny, sometimes charming, and occasionally flat, but its inventive, exploratory structure keeps things interesting throughout. Ultimately, SLACKER may be a better idea for a movie than its actual finished product. The pace, wit and tone of the film, which drag at times, could certainly have been spiced up if anything more than the barest resources had been available to its inspired producer. Still, Linklater's affectionate comedy of unconventional characters remains an impressive debut and one of the best no-budget features ever made.

SLAP SHOT
1977   123m   c   ★★★
Sports   R/18
Universal

Paul Newman (Reggie Dunlop), Strother Martin (Joe McGrath), Michael Ontkean (Ned Braden), Jennifer Warren (Francine Dunlop), Lindsay Crouse (Lily Braden), Jerry Houser ("Killer" Carlson), Andrew Duncan (Jimm Carr), Jeff Carlson (Jeff Hanson), Steve Carlson (Steve Hanson), David Hanson (Jack Hanson)

p, Robert J. Wunsch, Stephen Friedman; d, George Roy Hill; w, Nancy Dowd; ph, Victor J. Kemper (Panavision, Technicolor); ed, Dede Allen; m, Elmer Bernstein; art d, Henry Bumstead; cos, Tom Bronson

Funny, frank, and violent, George Roy Hill's absorbing film about minor league hockey offers a wonderful comic performance from Newman as the aging player-coach of the Charleston Chiefs. Mired in a long losing streak and deserted by their fans, the Chiefs learn that the franchise is to fold at the end of the

season because the steel mill that employs most of their Pennsylvania town's populace is closing. Refusing to give up, Newman encourages his team in no-holds-barred play. Surprisingly, three recently acquired, bespectacled brothers (Carlson, Carlson, and Hanson) prove to be the ultimate monsters of high-sticking mayhem, leading the Chiefs to victory after violent victory and filling the stands. This doesn't sit well with leading scorer Ontkean, a Princeton grad committed to "old-fashioned" hockey. Meanwhile, Newman plants stories that the Chiefs' unknown owner is negotiating to sell the club and tries to reconcile with his beautician-wife, Warren. The team is destined to become a tax write-off, but with pride on the line, they take on a club composed of the league's roughest players for the championship—a game with a bizarre finish unlike that of any other sports film. Upon its release, SLAP SHOT gained instant notoriety for its locker-room language, which may offend some but is perfect for its milieu. In fact, screenwriter Dowd based the diction on tape recordings her brother, a minor league hockey player, made in the locker room and on the team bus. In addition to Newman's masterful work, the film includes excellent supporting performances by Martin as the Chiefs' general manager, Duncan as a sportscaster, and Crouse as Ontkean's most unhappy wife. The on-ice violence is hyperreal, the emotions believable, and the laughs plentiful in this slightly off-the-wall comedy.

SLEEPER
1973   88m   c   ★★★½
Science Fiction/Comedy   PG
Rollins-Joffe

Woody Allen (Miles Monroe), Diane Keaton (Luna Schlosser), John Beck (Erno Windt), Marya Small (Dr. Nero), Bartlett Robinson (Dr. Orva), Mary Gregory (Dr. Melik), Chris Forbes (Rainer Krebs), Peter Hobbs (Dr. Dean), Spencer Milligan (Jeb Hrmthmg), Stanley Ralph Ross (Sears Wiggles)

p, Jack Grossberg; d, Woody Allen; w, Woody Allen, Marshall Brickman; ph, David M. Walsh; ed, Ralph Rosenblum; m, Woody Allen; prod d, Dale Hennesy; art d, Dianne Wager; fx, A.D. Flowers, Jerry Endler; cos, Joel Schumacher

Like most of Allen's movies, this one is better than the box-office receipts would indicate; it still looks good many years after it was shot. Allen never lets his actors see a full script while they are shooting, so no one, except Allen, knows what's happening in the film. Consequently, many of the performers were confused by their roles.

A Greenwich Village health food store owner who dabbles in Dixieland jazz, Allen reluctantly goes to the hospital for an ulcer operation in 1973. The operation fails, and the doctors quickly put him into the deep freeze. He awakens two hundred years later. The two doctors who revive him, Robinson and Gregory, want to enlist his help to overthrow the "Big Brother" leader who rules the world. The Leader isn't a whole person, just a nose, and his aides propose to clone the tissue from that nose to build a new order. Allen gets out of the hospital disguised as a domestic robot and is brought to Keaton, a wealthy woman who has ordered a new robot for her home. Once she is aware that he's actually human, the two of them get to like each other, and she reluctantly joins him, although she is so rich that there's no reason why she should become a revolutionary. The police begin to chase them, and they wind up at the home of two gay men, Milligan and Ross, who have a swishy domestic robot, Rydbeck. Sex is a no-no in the new world, so people either rub a metal ball known as "The Orb" or climb into a phonebooth-like device called "The Orgasmatron." Allen and Keaton flee again and are captured. Allen is brainwashed in a very funny scene, and Keaton is allowed to leave. She contacts the underground and joins with their chief, Beck. The Leader has a new project in mind, and the Revolutionaries send Keaton to get Allen out of the clutches of the police.

There is one sight gag after another, in a physical, Buster Keaton-like fashion, and many barbs puncture contemporary targets. When someone asks what happened to Norman Mailer, Allen says that he donated his ego to science. The McDonald's signs show trillions of hamburgers sold, etc. SLEEPER is a highly inventive science fiction parody that is typical of Allen's tight, well-edited movies, which usually come in under 90 minutes. Costumes by Joel Schumacher are excellent; he later gave up sewing for writing (CAR WASH) and then directing. Both Milligan and Rydbeck eventually starred in their own Saturday morning TV shows. In years to come, Allen got better and better, winning the Oscar for ANNIE HALL's direction and script and making one unique film after another, not all of them successful, but every one an attempt at broadening his own horizons.

SLEEPING BEAUTY

1959   75m   c   ★★★½
Children's/Animated   G/U
Disney

VOICES OF: Eleanor Audley (Maleficent), Verna Felton (Flora), Vera Vague (Fauna), Barbara Luddy (Merryweather), Taylor Holmes (King Stefan), Bill Thompson (King Hubert), Candy Candido (Goons), Mary Costa (Princess Aurora), Bill Shirley (Prince Phillip)

p, Walt Disney; d, Clyde Geronimi, Eric Larson, Wolfgang Reitherman, Les Clark; ph, (Technirama, Technicolor); ed, Roy M. Brewer, Jr., Donald Halliday; m, George Bruns (from Pyotr Illich Tchaikovsky's Sleeping Beauty Ballet); prod d, Donald Da Gradi, Ken Anderson; anim, Hal King, Hal Ambro, Don Lusk, Blaine Gibson, John Sibley, Bob Carson, Ken Hultgren, Harvey Toombs, Fred Kopietz, George Nicholas, Bob Youngquist, Eric Cleworth, Henry Tanous, John Kennedy, Ken O'Brien

One of the most ambitious projects ever undertaken by Disney, SLEEPING BEAUTY opens as the king and queen decide to throw a gala celebration announcing the birth of their daughter, Aurora, and her immediate betrothal to the infant Prince Phillip. Unfortunately, the overjoyed parents neglect to invite the evil fairy Maleficent, causing the angry denizen of the forest to place a curse on the infant girl that ensures she will prick her finger on a spindle upon her 16th birthday and die. The curse, however, is altered by a good fairy who changes the promise of death to sleep. Hoping to circumvent this prophecy, three good fairies named Flora, Fauna, and Merryweather take the baby into the forest where they can raise her away from the prying eyes of Maleficent. The fairies keep the girl's royal identity a secret from her, and she grows up to be a normal young woman. One day she meets Prince Phillip in the forest, and though both are unaware that they have been betrothed since birth, they fall in love. Tragedy soon strikes despite the three good fairies' precautions; on Aurora's 16th birthday the curse is fulfilled and she falls into a deep sleep which can only be broken by the kiss of a brave prince. This was the most expensive animated film to date, and every penny was on the screen. The attention to movement and detail is stunning, with multiple layers of action filling the frame. The highlight of the film, the fight with the dragon, is terrifying, exciting, and brilliantly executed, though some youngsters may find it a bit too scary. George Bruns garnered an Oscar nomination for his scoring.

SLEEPING CAR MURDER, THE

(COMPARTIMENT TUEURS)
1966   92m   bw   ★★★½
Mystery/Thriller   /X
PECF/Seven Arts   (France)

Yves Montand (Inspector Grazzi), Simone Signoret (Eliane Darres), Pierre Mondy (Commissioner), Catherine Allegret (Bambi), Pascale Roberts (Georgette Thomas), Jacques Perrin (Daniel), Michel Piccoli (Cabourg), Jean-Louis Trintignant (Eric), Charles Denner (Bob), Claude Mann (Jean-Lou)

p, Julien Derode; d, Constantin Costa-Gavras; w, Constantin Costa-Gavras, Sebastien Japrisot (based on the novel Compartiment Tueurs by Japrisot); ph, Jean Tournier; ed, Christian Gaudin; m, Michel Magne; art d, Rino Mondellini

Costa-Gavras (Z, STATE OF SIEGE, MISSING) made his directorial debut with this tightly constructed suspense thriller. Montand portrays a French police inspector investigating the murder of a woman who was sleeping in a lower berth on a moving train. Aided by his assistant Mann, Montand begins to track down all the passengers who were in the train compartment where the murder took place. Piccoli, an office worker who was on the train, volunteers information but afterward is found murdered. At the same time, two other passengers, Allegret and Perrin, attempt to avoid the police because the latter is a runaway who will be taken back to his parents if found. Perrin was hiding from the conductor in a berth and was aided by Allegret, a young woman traveling to a new job in Paris. After the murder, the pair stumble across the wallet of Signoret, an aging actress who also was a passenger on the train that night. They then go to her home to return it. Before knocking at her door, they notice she is being interrogated by Montand. Perrin and Allegret hide nearby and watch as a young man, Trintignant, slips out the back door of Signoret's house. During the interrogation, Signoret reveals that Perrin was hiding in an upper berth of the compartment. Soon after Montand leaves, Signoret is murdered. Eventually, the police determine that Trintignant was Signoret's lover, and when interrogated, the young man provides an airtight alibi. Meanwhile, Perrin overhears a plot by two men to kill Allegret and he tells the girl to hide out in a hotel. The young runaway then goes to Montand and spills everything he knows. When the police arrive, they thwart the murder attempt on Allegret and capture Trintignant. The suspect reveals that he was only an accomplice; the real killer is Montand's assistant Mann, who masterminded the whole scheme in order to pilfer Signoret's large bank account. Trintignant then goes on to state that Mann is out in the streets of Paris now, seeking to kill Perrin. Montand immediately sets out after Mann and following a thrilling chase, he saves Perrin and captures the killer. THE SLEEPING CAR MURDERS was sort of a family affair for Montand and Signoret, who were married, and for the beautiful Allegret, who is Signoret's daughter by writer director Yves Allegret. While the subject matter of this film is less political than those he would go on to make, Costa-Gavras' taut direction, coupled with a superb cast of foreign actors, propels this somewhat impenetrable mystery along at breakneck speed. It is an intriguing, highly entertaining thriller.

SLEEPING WITH THE ENEMY

1991   99m   c   ★★★
Thriller/Romance   R/15
Fox

Julia Roberts *(Laura Burney/Sara Waters)*, Patrick Bergin *(Martin Burney)*, Kevin Anderson *(Ben Woodward)*, Elizabeth Lawrence *(Chloe)*, Kyle Secor *(Fleishman)*, Claudette Nevins *(Dr. Rissner)*, Tony Abatemarco *(Locke)*, Marita Geraghty *(Julie)*, Harley Venton *(Garber)*, Nancy Fish *(Woman on Bus)*

p, Leonard Goldberg; d, Joseph Ruben; w, Ronald Bass (from the novel by Nancy Price); ph, John W Lindley; ed, George Bowers; m, Jerry Goldsmith; prod d, Doug Kraner; art d, Joseph P. Lucky; cos, Richard Hornung

With its timeless theme of domestic violence, SLEEPING WITH THE ENEMY is both contemporary fairy tale and Hollywood hokum of the highest grade, its sturdy prototype the "woman's picture" of the 40s and 50s.

A perfect young beauty named Laura (Julia Roberts) lives with her perfect businessman husband Martin Burney (Patrick Bergin) in their perfect high-tech home by the sea. Laura dutifully conforms to her husband's lifestyle, which is excruciatingly controlled and formal. He has trained her to wear clothes that will complement his handsome suits; to keep the towels symetrically aligned on the rack; and to keep the kitchen cupboard organized with military precision. He also beats her up periodically—a tasteful sadist. The high-tech home begins to resemble a prison tower and the handsome businessman an evil wizard. Laura, with her trailing red tresses, devises a way to escape her tormentor.

Laura seizes her opportunity during a stormy yacht excursion where she jumps into the ocean and fakes her own death. Swimming to safety, she catches the first departing bus and escapes into the heartland of America. She settles in a baseball and apple pie North Carolina town and begins a new life as Sara Waters. No sooner has she redecorated her new home, a Victorian cottage, when new love comes a-knocking. Sara's new suitor is Ben Woodward (Kevin Anderson), a bearded natural-man drama instructor at the local college. They fall blandly in love. Meanwhile Martin has put two and two together and begins to track his wife down with a bitter vengeance.

SLEEPING WITH THE ENEMY teeters constantly on the verge of silliness but director Joseph Ruben keeps the cornball melodrama scaled down to a pleasant lull. Nothing is overplayed and there's an admirable restraint in the story telling. The scenes speed along at a confident pace. Everything is designed to show off the movie's best asset: Julia Roberts. As Laura/Sara, Roberts gives an appealingly straightforward performance. She's likable because she displays a complete lack of show biz technique. Roberts seems home-grown, organic without preservatives. It's a gift that isn't going to last long and the movie thrives on it.

Unfortunately Roberts has been given a drip of a hero to rescue her. As Ben, Kevin Anderson makes his voice sincere and breathy and tries his darndest to act nurturing. He gets more and more annoying. The only thing Laura might see in Ben is someone who's so ineffectual she could belt him one if they ever got into an argument. He's so lame you start feeling nostalgic for the wife beater. But the scenes don't go on long enough for anything to become boring or offensive. The movie just glides by good-naturedly and shows off Julia Roberts's doe-eyed beauty. And by the time the whole thing is over you realize you haven't gone anywhere special but the ride was smooth and amiable.

SLEUTH
1972 138m c   ★★★★
Mystery   PG/15
Palomar (U.K.)

Laurence Olivier *(Andrew Wyke)*, Michael Caine *(Milo Tindle)*, Alec Cawthorne *(Inspector Doppler)*, Margo Channing *(Marguerite)*, John Matthews *(Detective Sgt. Tarrant)*, Teddy Martin *(Police Constable Higgs)*

p, Morton Gottlieb; d, Joseph L. Mankiewicz; w, Anthony Shaffer (based on his play); ph, Oswald Morris (DeLuxe Color); ed, Richard Marden; m, John Addison; prod d, Ken Adam; art d, Peter Lamont; cos, John Furniss

This stylish, intelligent mystery is full of delightfully unexpected twists, and boasts extraordinary performances from Michael Caine and Laurence Olivier. Caine, the owner of a chain of hair salons, is invited to the 16th-century country home of Olivier, a well-known detective novelist with a passion for elaborate games. Olivier reveals that he knows Caine is having an affair with his estranged wife, but instead of being angry, he is delighted and proposes a scheme that will profit both men. Olivier's idea is for Caine to put on a clown disguise and steal his wife's jewels, thereby allowing Olivier to collect the insurance money and Caine to fence the gems and support his lover in the style to which she is accustomed. The film goes through a number of shocking reversals on its way to the surprising but satisfying end. The script, written by Anthony Shaffer from his own stage play, is an actor's dream, and the two stars whip up their roles with relish, pulling the mystery back and forth in this deadly cat-and-mouse game. Director Joseph L. Mankiewicz was determined to keep the unusual nature of his mystery a secret to the audience throughout. Listed in the closing credits as playing Olivier's wife (who appears in the film only as a portrait on Olivier's wall for which actress Joan Woodward posed) is Margo Channing, which film buffs will recognize as the name of Bette Davis's famed character in Mankiewicz's classic film ALL ABOUT EVE.

SLIGHT CASE OF MURDER, A
1938 85m bw   ★★★★
Comedy/Crime   /A
WB

Edward G. Robinson *(Remy Marco)*, Jane Bryan *(Mary Marco)*, Willard Parker *(Dick Whitewood)*, Ruth Donnelly *(Mora Marco)*, Allen Jenkins *(Mike)*, John Litel *(Post)*, Eric Stanley *(Ritter)*, Harold Huber *(Giuseppe)*, Edward Brophy *(Lefty)*, Paul Harvey *(Mr. Whitewood)*

p, Samuel Bischoff; d, Lloyd Bacon; w, Earl Baldwin, Joseph Schrank (based on the play by Damon Runyon, Howard Lindsay); ph, Sid Hickox; ed, James Gibbon; art d, Max Parker

In this marvelous parody of gangster films, Robinson plays a beer baron who has made his fortune during Prohibition. He doesn't realize that his brew is wretched and that it only sold because alcohol was illegal. When the 21st Amendment opens up the market, Robinson's booming business begins losing money. Undaunted, he decides to retire and attempts to make his way into high society. Driving out to his new country estate, he picks up Bobby Jordan, a streetwise kid the old gangster wants to tutor in business. Robinson's daughter Bryan falls for Parker, the unemployed son of a millionaire. Bryan refuses to marry Parker unless he finds a job, so the eager young man hits the pavements. To his future father-in-law's horror, Parker is hired to be a motorcycle cop! Robinson's problems are compounded when he finds some corpses strewn around his new home. Some rival mobsters held up a racetrack, then went to Robinson's home in an effort to frame him for the crime. The gangsters ended up in an argument and consequently killed each other in a gun battle. One gangster (Joseph Downing) manages to survive the fray and hides out in Robinson's home with the $500,000 racetrack booty. Bryan and Parker arrive and the newly deputized lawman shoots all the dead gangsters. Jordan finds Downing, along with the loot. Since the bank has been threatening Robinson with foreclosure, this instant revenue couldn't come at a better time. Robinson takes the cash, while Parker takes credit for the arrest. In the end, Robinson finally samples his brew and realizes why its popularity has suddenly declined. He has the formula changed to save his business, while Parker is made a hero for his seemingly brave actions.

Though Robinson is probably best remembered for LITTLE CAESAR, this marvelous romp (along with the similar THE LITTLE GIANT) was a perfect vehicle for his marvelous comic talents. Robinson successfully spoofs his own image, yet balances out the comic performance with enough serious touches to make the character believable. The film, adapted from a failed play by Runyon and Lindsay, is delightfully Runyonesque in character and plot development. The cast give their characterizations some marvelous personal quirks, taking each crazy turn well in hand. The farce is nicely paced by Bacon's direction, giving the proceedings a genuine sense of fun. A SLIGHT CASE OF MURDER was popular with both critics and filmgoers and was later remade as STOP, YOU'RE KILLING ME in 1952, with Broderick Crawford in the Robinson role. Robinson, in his autobiography *All My Yesterdays*, said of the film, "I had absolutely no fault to find with the script because it was beautifully constructed and written and it was very funny." An admirer of Runyon's work, Robinson claimed that the writer "was absolutely unlike the characters he invented; he was soft-spoken, reserved, and never once did he utter a Runyonism."

SLIPPER AND THE ROSE, THE
1976 146m c   ★★★
Musical/Children's   G/U
Paradine (U.K.)

Richard Chamberlain (*Prince Edward*), Gemma Craven (*Cinderella*), Annette Crosbie (*Fairy Godmother*), Edith Evans (*Dowager Queen*), Christopher Gable (*John*), Michael Hordern (*King*), Margaret Lockwood (*Stepmother*), Kenneth More (*Lord Chamberlain*), Julian Orchard (*Montague*), Lally Bowers (*Queen*)

p, Stuart Lyons; d, Bryan Forbes; w, Bryan Forbes, Richard M. Sherman, Robert B. Sherman; ph, Tony Imi (Panavision, Technicolor); ed, Timothy Gee; m, Richard M. Sherman, Robert B. Sherman; prod d, Ray Simm; art d, Bert Davey; chor, Marc Breaux; cos, Julie Harris

This modernized version of the fairy tale "Cinderella" stars Richard Chamberlain as the suave prince and Gemma Craven as the young servant girl with whom he falls in love. The dialog is translated into more up-to-date language, and an undercurrent of wit should keep adults as engaged as youngsters will be. The scenic Austrian background, for the outdoor sequences, adds the appropriate atmosphere.

SLITHER
1973 97m c   ★★★
Crime/Comedy   PG/15
MGM

James Caan (*Dick Kanipsia*), Peter Boyle (*Barry Fenaka*), Sally Kellerman (*Kitty Kopetzky*), Louise Lasser (*Mary Fenaka*), Allen Garfield (*Vincent J. Palmer*), Richard B. Shull (*Harry Moss*), Alex Rocco (*Man With Ice Cream*), Alex Henteloff (*Man at Phone Booth*), Garry Goodrow (*Man with Camera*), Len Lesser (*Jogger*)

p, Jack Sher; d, Howard Zieff; w, W.D. Richter; ph, Laszlo Kovacs (Metrocolor); ed, David Bretherton; m, Tom McIntosh; art d, Dale Hennesy; fx, John Coles; cos, Lambert Marks, Janet Strong

Feature film debut for director Zieff, a respected veteran of TV commercials who'd won every major advertising award, and screenwriter/associate producer Richter, who went on to become one of the most expensive, though not necessarily commercial, writers in the movie world.

Caan is an ex-con just out of jail after a two-year stint for grand theft auto. He and fellow parolee Shull are happy to be free and go to Shull's tacky California shed where the latter is gunned down by snipers. With his final words, Shull tells Caan that he can have lots of money if he finds Boyle and just mentions the name Garfield. Caan is confused by this, but there is no time to explain. Using his last strength, Shull orders Caan into the basement, then blows the farmhouse up so that anyone watching will believe both men are dead. Later, Caan thumbs a ride with Kellerman, a speed freak. They arrive at a roadside luncheonette, and she pulls out a gun and fires it, then holds up the cashier. Caan doesn't want any part of this woman and gets away. He eventually locates Boyle, who admits that he and the late Shull had stolen over $300,000 from a show business agency and gave the money to investment counselor Garfield. Neither man trusted the other, so each had one half of the information needed to get the cash. Shull knew Garfield's name, and Boyle had the correct address. For the past seven years, Boyle has made his living peddling trailers and working as a comedian at meetings of the local Polish fraternal order. Boyle's wife, Lasser, recalls Caan from the days when he was the football hero at her high school. The trio take off for Garfield's place in Boyle's expensive Airstream motor home. Garfield (posing as someone else) tells them he has divested himself of their holdings and moved north to Pismo Beach. Caan, Boyle and Lasser go back on the road and again encounter Kellerman, who becomes part of the entourage. The mobile home is being tailed by a big van with dark windows. They arrive at Pismo Beach and note that another van has joined the chase. There is no information regarding Garfield in the coastal town and Caan, stretching his legs on the street, is suddenly surrounded by a quartet of business types, all dressed in conservative clothing. He escapes into a trailer park bingo parlor where Virginia Sale is doing the calling. Kellerman sees that Caan is in danger and starts a fight among the players, under cover of which Caan flees. Lasser tells Caan that Boyle has vanished and that she fears for his life. Caan thinks that his associate must be in one of the vans, so he goes after them in the Airstream. Every possible type of collision follows, ending with the vans out of commission and the sleek trailer bubbling at the bottom of a lake. Caan sees Garfield running away from the vans and catches up to him. Soon Garfield reveals that he is the man they've been searching for. It seems he lost the money by putting it into what he thought was a good, solid investment scheme, a children's camp. The vans had been bought for the camp, and the four men in suits weren't hoods at all; they were the accountants who'd been stung. Caan disgustedly eyes the wreckage and walks away, happy that he wasn't killed in the carnage.

SLITHER features some very funny moments and benefits from fine editing by Bretherton and assured camera work by Kovacs. Zieff later made THE MAIN EVENT, HOUSE CALLS and HEARTS OF THE WEST.

SMALL CHANGE
(L'ARGENT DE POCHE)
1976 105m c ★★★★
Drama/Comedy PG/A
Carrosse/Artistes (France)

Geory Desmouceaux (Patrick), Philippe Goldman (Julien), Claudio Deluca (Mathieu Deluca), Franck Deluca (Franck), Richard Golfier (Richard), Laurent Devlaeminck (Laurent Riffle), Bruno Staab (Bruno Rouillard), Sebastien Marc (Oscar), Sylvie Grezel (Sylvie), Pascale Bruchon (Martine)

d, Francois Truffaut; w, Francois Truffaut, Suzanne Schiffman; ph, Pierre-William Glenn (Eastmancolor); ed, Yann Dedet; m, Maurice Jaubert; art d, Jean-Pierre Kohut-Svelko; cos, Monique Dury

Chiefly a collection of vignettes, this sentimental homage to children and their innocent ways focuses on two young boys, Patrick (Geory Desmouceaux) and Julien (Philippe Goldman). Patrick is a shy, slightly plump boy who looks after his paralyzed father and who is infatuated with a schoolmate's mother. His desire for romance is finally satisfied by the film's end, when he gets his first kiss from schoolgirl Martine (Pascale Bruchon). Julien's life is the polar opposite of Patrick's. Long-haired and neglected, he is a present-day "wild child" (see Truffaut's 1972 film, THE WILD CHILD) living in a hovel with his hateful mother and grandmother, who are not beyond physically abusing him. At the center of the children's lives is a schoolteacher (Jean-Francois Stevenin), a thoughtful, fatherly man who eventually becomes a parent himself. The film is filled with adorable youngsters: Sylvie, a seven-year-old with two pet fish and a fuzzy elephant purse that her parents won't let her bring to a restaurant; the Deluca brothers, who offer to play barber to save a classmate some money; and little Gregory, a mischievous tyke too charming to incur ire. Director Francois Truffaut worked his screenplay around the children, using them as his inspiration rather than forcing a script on them. The result is a collection of some of the most natural sequences ever filmed. Although the cast is made up of children, parents will appreciate SMALL CHANGE far more than kids will.

SMART MONEY
1931 90m bw ★★★½
Crime /A
WB

Edward G. Robinson (Nick "The Barber" Venizelos), James Cagney (Jack), Evalyn Knapp (Irene Graham), Ralf Harolde (Sleepy Sam), Noel Francis (Marie), Margaret Livingston (District Attorney's Girl), Maurice Black (The Greek Barber), Boris Karloff (Sport Williams), Morgan Wallace (District Attorney Black), Billy House (Salesman-Gambler)

d, Alfred E. Green; w, Kubec Glasmon, John Bright, Lucien Hubbard, Joseph Jackson (based on the story "The Idol" by Hubbard, Jackson); ph, Robert Kurrle; ed, Jack Killifer

After the smashing success of LITTLE CAESAR, Warner Bros. decided to team its two hottest stars, Edward G. Robinson and James Cagney, in a crime picture guaranteed to do big business—it was the only time the two "tough guys" would ever appear on film together. Robinson plays a barber-shop owner in a small town. He has a penchant for gambling, booze, and women, and he exercises his vices by running a gambling den in the back room. Cagney, a barber in Robinson's shop, also serves as his enthusiastic right-hand man. One day, Boris Karloff, a seedy gambler, shows up to try his luck at Robinson's poker table. Despite Karloff's cheating, Robinson wins and then kicks the bum out. The barber's friends marvel at his luck and skill in games of chance and, with Cagney's encouragement, they raise $10,000 to stake Robinson in a big-time syndicate poker game in the city. Robinson decides to try his hand against the big boys, and on his way to the train station he is met by Karloff, who gives him an additonal $1,000 to gamble with. In the city, Robinson is wooed by a pretty girl, Noel Francis, who steers him to a game run by Ben Taggart—a disaster in which Robinson loses everything. Realizing the whole thing was a setup engineered by Francis, Taggart, and one of the gamblers, Ralf Harolde, Robinson vows revenge. He sends for Cagney, and they both get barbering jobs in the city and work out their scheme.

When they have enough money, Robinson tries his luck at the racetrack and begins winning big. Paul Porcasi, a wealthy Greek, notes Robinson's luck and offers to stake the gambler with big money. Soon the money pours in and Robinson begins his revenge. He ensnares Francis and forces her to live with him. He then bankrupts both Taggart and Harolde and sets up his own massive gambling den, using the familiar barber shop as a front. But he attracts the attention of District Attorney Morgan Wallace, who sets out to destroy Robinson through the gambler's main weakness—women. One day Robinson saves a beautiful blonde, Evalyn Knapp, from suicide, and the two begin a romance. Cagney, ever wary, suspects Knapp is an informant, and sure enough, she eventually plants some incriminating evidence in Robinson's coat pocket so that when the police raid the gambling den, he is caught red-handed. The frame means a six-month jail term for Robinson. Cagney, who saw Knapp plant the incriminating evidence, slaps her across the face and calls her a stool pigeon. Robinson comes to her defense and accidentally kills Cagney. Knapp confesses that she did indeed frame Robinson, but that the District Attorney forced her to because she was facing a blackmail charge. Robinson takes pity on the girl; she promises to wait for him. Sentenced to 10 years for the killing, Robinson tells reporters, "Two to one I'm out in five."

The SMART MONEY script provided Robinson and Cagney with a fast-paced story a bit different from the ones they had previously starred in (more humor and much less violence—the original story was nominated for an Oscar). The film shows the studio's commitment in its top-notch production values. The supporting cast is solid, with an appearance by Karloff, who would soon go on to do FRANKENSTEIN for Universal and reach superstardom of his own. Robinson was a proven star by the time SMART MONEY went before the cameras, and Warner Bros. knew just by watching the rushes from THE PUBLIC ENEMY that Cagney would score big with moviegoers. (Cagney worked on both films at the same time, running from one soundstage to the other.) This isn't to say that Warner Bros. wasn't hedging its bet on the young actor. His role in SMART MONEY is relatively small when compared with Robinson's, and he is totally absent from the middle of the film. THE PUBLIC ENEMY proved to be a smash when released—it's too bad that Cagney's part isn't bigger in SMART MONEY. Meanwhile, Robinson, who still hadn't fully comprehended his popularity in the wake of LITTLE CAESAR, was sent by the studio to New York to attend the premiere of SMART MONEY at the Winter Garden Theater. There his star status became abundantly clear to him when, in order to get into the theater, he had to hide on the floor of the car from throngs of his overzealous fans.

SMASH PALACE
1982 100m c ★★★
Drama R/18
Aardvark/NZ Film Commission (New Zealand)

Bruno Lawrence *(Al Shaw)*, Anna Jemison *(Jacqui Shaw)*, Greer Robson *(Georgie Shaw)*, Keith Aberdein *(Ray Foley)*, Desmond Kelly *(Tiny)*, Margaret Umbers, Sean Duffy, Bryan Johnson, Terence Donovan, Dick Rello

p, Roger Donaldson; d, Roger Donaldson; w, Peter Hansard, Roger Donaldson, Bruno Lawrence; ph, Graeme Cowley (Eastmancolor); ed, Michael Horton; m, Sharon O'Neill; art d, Reston Griffiths; cos, Annabel Blackett

Former racing champ Al Shaw (Bruno Lawrence) returns to his native New Zealand to take over his father's old auto junk shop. Accompanying him is his pregnant European wife, Jacqui (Anna Jemison), who through the years grows tired of her husband and goes to live with his best friend, police officer Ray Foley (Keith Aberdein). The crazed Shaw attempts reconciliation by kidnapping his daughter and running off into the bush, forcing a widespread hunt for the missing child. Although the plot is fairly thin, the concentration is on the characters and on the growing tension between the married couple. The result is a pointed look into the formation and dissolution of a relationship where neither person is to blame. Lawrence is outstanding as the self-absorbed man whose personality undergoes massive changes in the course of the film.

SMILE

1975 113m c   ★★★½
Comedy   PG/A
UA

Bruce Dern *("Big Bob" Freelander)*, Barbara Feldon *(Brenda DiCarlo)*, Michael Kidd *(Tommy French)*, Geoffrey Lewis *(Wilson Shears)*, Nicholas Pryor *(Andy DiCarlo)*, Colleen Camp *(Connie Thompson/"Miss Imperial County")*, Joan Prather *(Robin Gibson/"Miss Antelope Valley")*, Denise Nickerson *(Shirley Tolstoy/"Miss San Diego")*, Annette O'Toole *(Doria Houston/"Miss Anaheim")*, Maria O'Brien *(Maria Gonzales/"Miss Salinas")*

p, Michael Ritchie; d, Michael Ritchie; w, Jerry Belson; ph, Conrad Hall (DeLuxe Color); ed, Richard A. Harris; m, Daniel Osborn, Leroy Holmes, Charles Chaplin; chor, Jim Bates; cos, Patricia Norris

Director Ritchie does a fine job handling a huge cast, with many first-timers, in this satirical glimpse of a real beauty pageant staged in Santa Rosa, California. The original script, written by TV veteran Belson, supplies plenty of laughs, but the picture has so many characters we never get to truly know any of them, and the result, while often hilarious, is ultimately skin-deep, just as the beauty contestants are. Dern is a mobile-home dealer in the town and the chief judge of the contest. His son, Eric Shea, is a pre-teener with an eye toward female flesh and money so he takes some surreptitious shots of the nude beauties and means to sell them to his pals. When that's discovered, father and son have to see a court-ordered psychiatrist, George Skaff, to allow the boy to go back to school. Kidd is a tired choreographer who has received this second-rate assignment and hopes it might lead to a rekindling of his flagging career. The president of the beauty pageant is Lewis, and the prudish female chief of the proceedings is Feldon, who is married to Pryor and is as cold as an Arctic night to him. Cutting between all of these people and the many contestants, Ritchie tries to give us a picture like NASHVILLE with multiple stories going at the same time. The final scenes were staged at the actual pageant, and no one, except Belson and Ritchie, knew the winner, so the conclusion seems realistic. The best of the beauty contestants is Prather, who has to alter her character from naive waif to win-at-any-cost contestant. Pryor

eventually shoots her out of frustration, thus reducing the film's level to something near "Tom and Jerry." Before that, however, the picture is superior in many ways. In 1986 a stage musical based on the movie was being financed, with music by Marvin Hamlisch. The music for SMILE was based on Charles Chaplin's original song "Smile," which became a hit for Nat "King" Cole. Osborn's incidental music was appropriate, and some pop tunes by Neil Sedaka, Shirley and Lee, and the Beach Boys were also used. Like many of Ritchie's films, it was sharp but not good-natured, and people stayed away from it in droves. Most of the beauty contest participants were exactly that, and it's a tribute to Ritchie's ability with actors that he gets them to come off as nonactors, which is one of the most difficult things an actor can do.

SMILES OF A SUMMER NIGHT

(SOMMARNATTENS LEENDE)
1955 108m bw   ★★★★½
Comedy   /X
Svensk   (Sweden)

Ulla Jacobsson *(Anne Egerman)*, Eva Dahlbeck *(Desiree Armfeldt)*, Margit Carlqvist *(Charlotte Malcolm)*, Harriet Andersson *(Petra the Maid)*, Gunnar Bjornstrand *(Fredrik Egerman)*, Jarl Kulle *(Count Malcolm)*, Ake Fridell *(Frid the Groom)*, Bjorn Bjelvenstam *(Henrik Egerman)*, Naima Wifstrand *(Mrs. Armfeldt)*, Gull Natrop *(Malla)*

p, Allan Ekelund; d, Ingmar Bergman; w, Ingmar Bergman; ph, Gunnar Fischer; ed, Oscar Rosander; m, Erik Nordgren; art d, P.A. Lundgren; cos, Mago

A heavenly boudoir farce, alternately sardonic to it's inhabitants, then surprisngly tender, this is easily Bergman's finest comedy.

SMILES OF A SUMMER NIGHT is set in turn-of-the-century Sweden and takes place primarily at an old country estate, where love permeates the summer air. As a result of the scheming of actress Desiree Armfeldt (Eva Dahlbeck), a group of former, present, and would-be lovers gathers at her mother's country home, including Desiree's one-time lover Fredrik Egerman (Gunnar Bjornstrand); Anne (Ulla Jacobsson), his 20-year-old, still-virgin wife of two years; Fredrik's son, Henrik (Bjorn Bjelvenstam), a theology student a little younger than his stepmother; Desiree's current lover, Count Malcolm (Jarl Kulle); and his wife, Charlotte (Margit Carlqvist). In the course of this midsummer's eve, Anne runs off with her stepson, Fredrik rekindles his romance with Desiree, and Count Malcolm and Charlotte reconcile their marriage—while the maid, Petra (Harriet Andersson), literally rolls in the hay with a coachman.

SMILES OF A SUMMER NIGHT is erotic and lyrical, full of blithe spirits brilliantly evoked. Though Bergman's staging of the affair occasionally suggests a proscenium is just beyond the frame, the ensemble brings joyful veracity to the romantic complications and well-drawn characters. Influenced by Shakespeare's *A Midsummer Night's Dream*, Bergman's film provided the inspiration for the Broadway musical *A Little Night Music* and Woody Allen's A MIDSUMMER NIGHT'S SEX COMEDY. A film of opalescent, quicksilver beauty.

SMILING LIEUTENANT, THE

1931 102m bw   ★★★★½
Musical/Comedy   /A
Paramount

Maurice Chevalier *(Niki)*, Claudette Colbert *(Franzi)*, Miriam Hopkins *(Princess Anna)*, George Barbier *(King Adolf)*, Charlie Ruggles *(Max)*, Hugh O'Connell *(Orderly)*, Robert Strange *(Adjutant von Rockoff)*, Janet Reade *(Lily)*, Lon MacSunday *(Emperor)*, Elizabeth Patterson *(Baroness von Schwedel)*

p, Ernst Lubitsch; d, Ernst Lubitsch; w, Ernest Vajda, Samson Raphaelson, Ernst Lubitsch (based on the operetta *A Waltz Dream* by Leopold Jacobson and Felix Doermann, and the novel *Nux der Prinzgemahl* by Hans Muller); ph, George Folsey; ed, Merrill White; m, Oscar Straus; art d, Hans Dreier

Only six years after the release of EIN WALZERTRAUM, the 1925 German silent based on the operetta inspired by Hans Muller's novel *Nux, der Prinzgemahl*, Ernst Lubitsch gathered Maurice Chevalier, Claudette Colbert and Miriam Hopkins, moved them into Paramount's Astoria, Long Island, studios, and made this musical as well as a French-language version, LE LIEUTENANT SOURIANT, with the same cast working from a new French script by Jacques Bataille-Henri. The delightful story is set in Vienna, where Niki (Chevalier), an officer of the Royal Guards, shares romance and an apartment with Franzi (Claudette Colbert), a violinist. During a state visit to the Austrian capital by King Adolf (George Barbier), his desperately plain daughter, Princess Anna (Miriam Hopkins), mistakenly believes that the smile Niki has intended for Franzi was actually directed in her royal direction, but is convinced the handsome soldier is only being kind. When Niki protests that he finds the princess attractive, she falls in love with him, and in no time, bound by his duty to his country, he finds himself married to her. Niki refuses to consummate their marriage, however—that is, until Franzi does a makeover job on Anna that sends the guardsman's head reeling.

The operetta plot bears little resemblance to reality, but the players are so good, the dialogue (by Lubitsch, Ernest Vajda and Samson Raphaelson) so witty, and the direction so skillful that no one minds the logic lapses. The music is delightful, and the songs include such bon-bons as "Spruce Up Your Lingerie." Made and released during the Depression, THE SMILING LIEUTENANT offered welcome escapism for a public reeling under too real economic woes. Colbert—warm, sweet, with touches of sadness—is in wonderful form, and proves to be a fine singer to boot. Hopkins, meanwhile, enjoyed her first major opportunity to display her considerable comic prowess as the princess in need of a makeover, and Chevalier is in his best and most typical form. This was the noted French entertainer's first work together with master director Lubitsch after their successful collaboration on THE LOVE PARADE two years earlier, and the result is an utterly charming film that was box-office hit and was nominated for an Oscar for Best Picture.

SMOKEY AND THE BANDIT

1977 96m c   ★½
Comedy   PG
Rastar

Burt Reynolds *(Bandit)*, Jackie Gleason *(Sheriff Buford T. Justice)*, Sally Field *(Carrie)*, Jerry Reed *(Cledus Snow)*, Mike Henry *(Junior Justice)*, Paul Williams *(Little Enos Burdette)*, Pat McCormick *(Big Enos Burdette)*, Alfie Wise *(Traffic Jam Patrolman)*, George Reynolds *(Sheriff Branford)*, Macon McCalman *(Mr. B)*

p, Mort Engelberg; d, Hal Needham; w, James Lee Barrett, Charles Shyer, Alan Mandel (based on a story by Needham and Robert L. Levy); ph, Bobby Byrne (Panavision, Technicolor); ed, Walter Hannemann, Angelo Ross; m, Bill Justis, Jerry Reed; art d, Mark Mansbridge; fx, Art Brewer

The first in the series and the best of a lousy lot. Depending on whom you believe, the movie grossed anywhere between $40 million and $70 million; that must be some sort of new record for fooling the public. It was the first picture directed by Needham, one of the highest-paid stuntmen in movies, and is one long, stupid car chase punctuated by four-letter words in a live-action version of the "Roadrunner" cartoons.

The plot is premised on the fact that it once was illegal for Coors to sell their Colorado beer east of Texas unless a special permit was secured. McCormick and Williams play a father-son team of filthy-rich Texans who have a car entered in an Atlanta stock race, which they fully expect to win. In order to celebrate, they'd like to have enough Coors around for themselves and their guests, but the race is the following day and there doesn't seem to be any means to get the beer there in time. Reynolds makes an $80,000 wager that he can drive to Texas and back in the needed 28 hours, and the obligatory chases and stunts ensue.

The stunts in SLITHER are excellent but the comedy is numbing, and the acting is on a par with a junior high school production of *Our Town*. Even Gleason comes across badly, and that's a major feat. Adolph Coors and Sons must have been very happy to have a 97-minute commercial for their brew.

SNAKE PIT, THE

1948 108m bw   ★★★½
Drama   /A
FOX

Olivia de Havilland *(Virginia Stuart Cunningham)*, Mark Stevens *(Robert Cunningham)*, Leo Genn *(Dr. Mark Kirk)*, Celeste Holm *(Grace)*, Glenn Langan *(Dr. Terry)*, Helen Craig *(Miss Davis)*, Leif Erickson *(Gordon)*, Beulah Bondi *(Mrs. Greer)*, Lee Patrick, Isabel Jewell

p, Anatole Litvak, Robert Bassler; d, Anatole Litvak; w, Frank Partos, Millen Brand (based on the novel by Mary Jane Ward); ph, Leo Tover; ed, Dorothy Spencer; m, Alfred Newman; art d, Lyle Wheeler, Joseph C. Wright; cos, Bonnie Cashin

Produced under the aegis of 20th Century-Fox studio head Darryl F. Zanuck, this remains one of the best screen explorations of mental illness and its treatment.

In a bravura performance, de Havilland is a disturbed young woman who is put into a mental institution by her husband, Stevens. While he loves his wife, he realizes that she needs more help than he can give her. Luckily, de Havilland's case comes to the attention of Genn, a patient, thoughtful, and caring doctor who devotes much of his time to her. Though the hospital is overcrowded and understaffed, Genn manages to concentrate on her case while desperately trying to keep his hospital from becoming the "snake pit" which most people believe mental institutions to be.

Though the portrayal of the causes and cures of mental illness remains Hollywood-simplistic here, THE SNAKE PIT was one of the first films to seriously examine the subject and treat it with—sometimes harrowing—realism. Producer-director Litvak saw the galley pages to Mary Jane Ward's fictionalized autobiography and immediately paid $75,000 for the film rights. After trying to sell the idea to every other studio in town, Litvak went to his friend Zanuck as a last resort. (Fox rarely took on independent productions.) The studio head was a bit leery about the subject matter, but he felt that films should deal with important subjects, so he agreed to finance the project. Zanuck worked closely with Litvak to tighten the script so that its "suspense and urgency" would cause viewers to accept the more unpleasant passages. Litvak spent three months in preproduction researching mental facilities and procedures, and he required his cast and crew to accompany him. De Havilland gave a subtle, passionate performance and was deservedly nominated for a Best Actress Oscar (though she lost to Jane Wyman for JOHNNY BELINDA). THE SNAKE PIT turned out to be a critical and financial success for Zanuck, and the film called such attention to the treatment of mental illness that 26 states passed new legislation pertaining to procedures in state institutions.

SNOW WHITE AND THE SEVEN DWARFS

1937   83m   c   ★★★★★
Children's/Animated   G/U
Disney

VOICES OF: Adriana Caselotti (Snow White), Harry Stockwell (Prince Charming), Lucille La Verne (The Queen), Moroni Olsen (Magic Mirror), Billy Gilbert (Sneezy), Pinto Colvig (Sleepy/Grumpy), Otis Harlan (Happy), Scotty Mattraw (Bashful), Roy Atwell (Doc), Stuart Buchanan (Humbert)

p, Walt Disney; d, David Hand, Perce Pearce, Larry Morey, William Cottrell, Wilfred Jackson, Ben Sharpsteen; w, Ted Sears, Otto Englander, Earl Hurd, Dorothy Ann Blank, Richard Creedon, Dick Richard, Merrill De Maris, Webb Smith (based on the fairy tale by the Brothers Grimm); m, Frank Churchill, Leigh Harline, Paul J. Smith, Larry Morey; art d, Charles Philippi, Hugh Hennesy, Terrell Stapp, McLaren Stewart, Harold Miles, Tom Codrick, Gustaf Tenggren, Ken Anderson, Kendall O'Connor, Hazel Sewell; anim, Hamilton Luske, Vladimir Tytla, Fred Moore, Norman Ferguson

"The only film that made money in 1937 was SNOW WHITE AND THE SEVEN DWARFS," said Mae West. "And that would have made more money if they woulda let *me* play Snow White." She wasn't far from wrong. Consider Snow White, living with seven devoted, worshipful little men. Obviously, Disney was as naive in ways as the children in his audiences. Maybe that's the secret to his animated successes, or one of them. SNOW WHITE softens the Grimms's fairytale, but then there are the sequences of terror. Timeless they are, and here Expressionistic. Indeed, Disney always seemed to pull the stops out for the moments evoking evil in his animated features. And for all the bird trills of Snow White (never again would Walt's heroine have such a fantasy singing voice, and for that reason, she's the favorite heroine of many animation *auteurs*; certainly, we could all agree she's the most surreal of the sisterhood), and the cuteness of the comic relief inspired by the little men, our nod goes to Eleanor Audley (who would supply the voice for all Disney's memorable villainesses through SLEEPING BEAUTY) and the animated rendering of the Wicked Queen. Did Mr. Disney and Mr. Hitchcock have more than love of terror in common?

Dubbed "Disney's Folly" by its detractors, this masterpiece was a personal success for Walt Disney—the fulfillment of his dream to pioneer animation of unimagined scope. The film opens on a storybook, and as "Some Day My Prince Will Come" plays in the background, the turning pages explain how the orphaned Snow White has been brought up as a servant of a wicked queen. The queen, an icily beautiful woman with piercing eyes, stands before her Magic Mirror and poses her vain, oft-asked question: "Mirror, mirror, on the wall, who is the fairest of them all?" She is shocked when the mirror gives an unexpected answer: "Snow

White." The nasty queen then orders that the innocent young woman be killed. Snow White, however, has eight things going for her—Prince Charming and seven dwarfs named Doc, Happy, Sleepy, Sneezy, Bashful, Grumpy, and Dopey.

This is animation as it had never before been experienced. Disney wisely realized the film could only work if it was full of believable characters, and each personality is distinct, from the purity of Snow White to the absolute evil of the queen. This film classic also features some unforgettable songs, including "Whistle While You Work," "Heigh Ho" and "Some Day My Prince Will Come."

SNOWS OF KILIMANJARO, THE

1952   117m   c   ★★★½
Adventure   /PG
FOX

Gregory Peck (Harry), Susan Hayward (Helen), Ava Gardner (Cynthia), Hildegarde Neff (Countess Liz), Leo G. Carroll (Uncle Bill), Torin Thatcher (Johnson), Ava Norring (Beatrice), Helene Stanley (Connie), Marcel Dalio (Emile), Vincente Gomez (Guitarist)

p, Darryl F. Zanuck; d, Henry King; w, Casey Robinson (based on the short story by Ernest Hemingway); ph, Leon Shamroy (Technicolor); ed, Barbara McLean; m, Bernard Herrmann; art d, Lyle Wheeler, John De Cuir; fx, Ray Kellogg; chor, Antonio Triana; cos, Charles LeMaire

One of the more successful attempts to bring Hemingway material to the screen, this story of a writer who has lost his intellectual and emotional bearings after enjoying early commercial success works splendidly under King's sure directorial hand, and is enacted with power and conviction by Peck. Scriptwriter Robinson expanded the origina Hemingway story to incorporate several elements from the writer's own life and, despite some carping from Hemingway purists, the film was an immense box-office success.

As the story begins, Peck is shown half delirious with fever, lying on a cot in an African campsite, his leg infected with gangrene. A rich and popular author, he finds himself with little left to live for as he drifts in and out of consciousness, with his wealthy wife Hayward at his side. The writer thinks back on his colorful life, seeing himself at age 17 in the Midwest; as a young writer living in Paris and falling in love with Gardner, on whom he bases the heroine of his first novel; traveling around Africa oblivious to Gardner's pregnancy, which is terminated when she falls down a flight of stairs; finally being abandoned by Gardner in Spain, when she realizes he will never settle down with her; re-encountering her during the Spanish Civil War but then being separated from her again; and finally marrying Hayward, whom he initially mistakes for Gardner when he is drunk one night in Paris. The movie ends with him coming to realize the depth of his love for Hayward, and vowing to return to serious work.

This beautifully photographed film, King's favorite, combines many Hemingway tales to make its point, and it features a magnificent score by Herrmann that captures all the exotic locales profiled. Gardner is excellent as the star-crossed lover, but Hayward has a part that is mostly lost inside the flashbacks featuring Gardner. Peck had played a Hemingway hero in THE MACOMBER AFFAIR five years earlier, portraying a white hunter in Africa, and that film had also been written by Robinson. Although the script for SNOWS OF KILIMANJARO is a seamless blend of Robinson's and Hemingway's style, Hemingway didn't like the film, calling Fox mogul Zanuck personally to say that it was a compilation of his stories and that it should have been called "the Snows of Zanuck."

SO DEAR TO MY HEART

1949   82m   c   ★★★★
Children's/Musical   /U
Disney

Burl Ives (Uncle Hiram), Beulah Bondi (Granny Kincaid), Harry Carey (Judge), Luana Patten (Tildy), Bobby Driscoll (Jeremiah Kincaid), Raymond Bond (Storekeeper), Daniel Haight (Storekeeper's Son), Walter Soderling (Villager), Matt Willis (Horse Trainer), Spelman B. Collins

p, Walt Disney, Perce Pearce; d, Harold Schuster; w, John Tucker Battle, Maurice Rapf, Ted Sears (based on the book Midnight and Jeremiah by Sterling North); ph, Winton C. Hoch; ed, Thomas Scott, Lloyd L. Richardson; m, Paul J. Smith; art d, John Ewing

SO DEAR TO MY HEART is a lovely, heartwarming live-action film with several superb animation sequences perfectly blended in. Set around the turn of the century in Indiana, the film is the story of young Jeremiah Kincaid (Bobby Driscoll), who yearns to own a horse. Jeremiah lives with his grandmother (Beulah Bondi) and lovingly raises a pet lamb, although the adventurous animal is sometimes a problem. Uncle Hiram (Burl Ives), the local blacksmith, supports Jeremiah's love for his pet, and thinks the lamb just might be championship caliber, encouraging the boy to enter it in the county fair. It will cost a few bucks to get to the fair and pay the entry fee, but Jeremiah is determined to showcase his lamb, so he takes a job gathering honey. This simple tale is often funny, always intelligent, and never overly sentimental. The animated sequences illustrate Jeremiah's fantasies as he pores over his scrapbook and a wise owl comes to life to demonstrate the importance of following one's dream; in another animated scene, a souvenir program from the fair comes to life.

SO FINE

1981   91m   c   ★★★
Comedy   R/15
WB

Ryan O'Neal (Bobby), Jack Warden (Jack), Mariangela Melato (Lira), Richard Kiel (Eddie), Fred Gwynne (Chairman Lincoln), Mike Kellin (Sam Schlotzman), David Rounds (Prof. McCarthy), Joel Stedman (Prof. Yarnell), Angela Pietro Pinto (Sylvia), Michael Lombard (Jay Augustine)

p, Michael Lobell; d, Andrew Bergman; w, Andrew Bergman; ph, James A. Contner (Technicolor); ed, Alan Heim; m, Ennio Morricone; prod d, Santo Loquasto; art d, Paul Eads; chor, Grover Dale; cos, Rose Trimarco, Bill Christians

By turns sophisticated and satirical, SO FINE runs the comedy gamut from high camp to low farce, but ultimately it is a disappointing directorial debut from writer-director Bergman (BLAZING SADDLES, THE IN-LAWS). O'Neal again proves himself to be a skillful light comedian as the English-professor son of a clothing manufacturer (Warden) menaced by a gargantuan loan shark Kiel, Jaws of Bond film fame. Leaving the groves of academe to help out his father, Bobby becomes involved with the hot-to-trot Melato. There's just one problem: she happens to be Kiel's wife. Warden is outstanding in another of his patented second-banana roles, Kiel proves that he's more than just another ugly face, and Morricone's score greatly enhances the film's pace—but Bergman's reach exceeds his grasp, and SO FINE never completely comes together.

SO PROUDLY WE HAIL

1943   126m   bw   ★★★★
War/Drama   /A
Paramount

Claudette Colbert (Lt. Janet Davidson), Paulette Goddard (Lt. Joan O'Doul), Veronica Lake (Lt. Olivia D'Arcy), George Reeves (Lt. John Summers), Barbara Britton (Lt. Rosemary Larson), Walter Abel (Chaplain), Sonny Tufts (Kansas), Mary Servoss (Capt. "Ma" McGregor), Ted Hecht (Dr. Jose Bardia), John Litel (Dr. Harrison)

p, Mark Sandrich; d, Mark Sandrich; w, Allan Scott; ph, Charles Lang; ed, Ellsworth Hoagland; m, Miklos Rozsa; art d, Hans Dreier, Earl Hedrick; fx, Gordon Jennings, Farciot Edouart, George Dutton

SO PROUDLY WE HAIL is a surprisingly unglamorous Hollywood depiction of the lives of three Army nurses (Goddard, Lake, and Colbert) who survive the battles at Bataan and Corregidor in WWII. The film begins as they arrive back home in the US, then relates their story in flashback, beginning in December 1941. After the attack on Pearl Harbor, the trio's Hawaii-bound ship is diverted to Bataan and finally to Corregidor. Along the way, the women witness the fighting at its most brutal, but also find time for relaxation and romance. Never, however, does SO PROUDLY WE HAIL succumb to pinup star glamour; rather, Mark Sandrich's direction and Allan Scott's screenplay concentrate on the ugly realities of war, the painful scenes including a sequence in which a mother stands by while her son's legs are amputated. All three leads are superbly cast in their nicely balanced characters. Colbert is the mother-hen nurse who avoids romance but eventually winds up married to Reeves; Lake fights a private battle against the Japanese, who killed her boyfriend at Pearl Harbor; and the showy Goddard evenly divides her time between the war and her romance with happy-go-lucky Kansas lad Tufts.

Because of the popularity of its stars, the patriotic spirit of the film, and the novelty of female combat nurses, SO PROUDLY WE HAIL made a sizable dent in the box office. The critics praised its authenticity, which Sandrich went to great lengths to achieve. Having read a news item about 10 nurses who escaped the fall of Corregidor in May 1942, Sandrich, together with Scott, tracked them down. He hired one of them, Lt. Eunice Hatchitt, as a technical advisor and, after receiving permission from the government to tell the nurses' story, began filming. However, although certain to hit box-office gold with Paramount's Claudette Colbert, Veronica Lake, and Paulette Goddard as the stars, Sandrich was also destined to have a battle of egos on his hands. The feuding began when Goddard told a reporter that she preferred working with Lake because "after all, we are closer in age." Colbert was naturally upset at the implication that she was over the hill (and, in fact, Goddard was wrong—her own birth date is usually cited as 1911, making her seven years younger than Colbert and eight years older than Lake). There were also arguments over how they were photographed and rivalry over their respective technical skills. (Goddard and Lake were considered screen personalities, while only Colbert was viewed as an actress.) Often Sandrich would have to retake scenes many times to accommodate Lake's and Goddard's deficiencies, while Colbert needed no more than a couple of takes. Fans of Lake and her famous peek-a-boo hairstyle should be forewarned that she wears her hair short in this picture. Reportedly, the government asked that she not appear as a servicewoman with that hairstyle because there were a number of women factory workers whose long, Lake-inspired hair was getting tangled in the machinery.

SOFT SKIN, THE
(LA PEAU DOUCE)
1964 120m bw   ★★½
Drama
Carrosse/SEDIF (France)

Jean Desailly *(Pierre Lachenay)*, Francoise Dorleac *(Nicole Chomette)*, Nelly Benedetti *(Franca Lachenay)*, Daniel Ceccaldi *(Clement)*, Laurence Badie *(Ingrid)*, Jean Lanier *(Michel)*, Paule Emanuele *(Odile)*, Philippe Dumat *(Reims Cinema Manager)*, Pierre Risch *(Canon)*, Dominique Lacarriere *(Pierre's Secretary)*

d, Francois Truffaut; w, Francois Truffaut, Jean-Louis Richard; ph, Raoul Coutard; ed, Claudine Bouche; m, Georges Delerue; cos, Renee Rouzot

One of Truffaut's least-successful, most-derivative films, THE SOFT SKIN was a response to the resounding impact of JULES AND JIM. While the latter concentrates on love in the country, Truffaut's aim in THE SOFT SKIN was, as he put it, to create "a violent answer to JULES AND JIM. It's as though someone else had made JULES AND JIM. . . [THE SOFT SKIN shows] a truly modern love; it takes place in planes, in elevators; it has all the harassments of modern life." From its opening, THE SOFT SKIN surely does not seem like a Truffaut film. It is distant, restrained—as the title implies, a "surface" film in which emotions run only skin deep. The story concerns Desailly as Lachenay (named after Truffaut's friend), a literary critic with a wife (Benedetti) and a child, who falls in love with a stewardess (Dorleac) after a trip to Lisbon. Although THE SOFT SKIN is perhaps Truffaut's weakest film, it can also be considered his most daring. Rather than present a conventionally melodramatic love triangle, Truffaut chooses for his leading man a common, albiet somewhat bookish, individual (not nearly so romantic as the characters in the Balzac novels on which the critic is an authority). When fate intervenes and Pierre gets his beautiful dream girl, he begins his downward Hitchcockian spiral, an innocent caught up in a situation he cannot control. In THE SOFT SKIN Balzac (a personal favorite of Truffaut) meets Hitchcock, and the film frame becomes an arena in which Truffaut's two greatest influences do battle.

SOLARIS
1972 165m c   ★★★½
Science Fiction   PG
Mosfilm/Magna (U.S.S.R.)

Nathalie Bondarchuk *(Harey)*, Yuri Yarvet *(Snaut)*, Donatas Banionis *(Kris)*, Anatoli Sonlonitsin *(Sartorius)*, Vladislav Dvorjetzki *(Burton)*, Nikolai Grinko *(Father)*, Sos Sarkissian *(Gibarian)*

d, Andrei Tarkovsky; w, Andrei Tarkovsky, Friedrich Gorenstein (based on the novel by Stanislaw Lem); ph, Vadim Jusov (Sovcolor); m, Eduard Artemyer; art d, Mikhail Romadin

This superb science fiction film was directed by Andrei Tarkovsky, very possibly the finest director to come out of the Soviet Union since the earliest days of its cinematic history. The story concerns a cosmonaut who travels to the distant space station on Solaris. Not an ordinary planet, Solaris is also a superintelligent being that materializes into human form for communication purposes. The cosmonaut is there to investigate a phenomenon in which his fellow space travelers have recurring visions of quiet home lives back on Earth. Tarkovsky, who eventually would leave the USSR in search of cinematic freedom, went on to explore the concept of nostalgia and history in NOSTALGHIA and ANDREI ROUBLOV.

SOLDIER OF ORANGE
1977 165m c   ★★★½
War/Drama   R/
Rank (Netherlands)

Rutger Hauer *(Erik)*, Jeroen Krabbe *(Gus)*, Peter Faber *(Will)*, Derek De Lint *(Alex)*, Eddy Habbema *(Robby)*, Lex Van Delden *(Nico)*, Edward Fox *(Col. Rafelli)*, Belinda Meuldijk *(Esther)*, Susan Penhaligon *(Susan)*, Andrea Domburh *(Queen Wilhelmina)*

p, Rob Houwer; d, Paul Verhoeven; w, Paul Verhoeven, Gerard Soeteman, Kees Holierhoek (based on the autobiography of Erik Hazelhoff Roelfzema); ph, Jan De Bont, Jost Vacano (Eastmancolor); ed, Jane Speer; m, Rogier Van Otterloo; art d, Roland De Groot; cos, Elly Claus

Carefully crafted by veteran Dutch director Paul Verhoeven (ROBOCOP, THE FOURTH MAN), this WWII drama details the effects of Nazi occupation on a group of Dutch students. Erik (Rutger Hauer) is at first hesitant to join the resistance effort, but after escaping to England he becomes deeply involved, courageously transporting supplies to his comrades in Holland. After the war, he returns home to find that most of his fellow students and resistance fighters have been killed, including onetime student leader Gus (Jeroen Krabbe), while others have come through the war barely affected. An exceptional character study, SOLDIER OF ORANGE is also beautifully photographed by Peter De Bont—the shots of Hauer on the supply boat's windy prow as he travels between Britain and Holland linger long after the film is over. Verhoeven would again work with Krabbe and screenwriter Gerard Soeteman in his haunting THE FOURTH MAN.

SOLDIER'S STORY, A
1984 101m c   ★★★½
Mystery   PG/15
Columbia

Howard E. Rollins, Jr. *(Capt. Davenport)*, Adolph Caesar *(Sgt. Waters)*, Art Evans *(Pvt. Wilkie)*, David Alan Grier *(Cpl. Cobb)*, David Harris *(Pvt. Smalls)*, Dennis Lipscomb *(Capt. Taylor)*, Larry Riley *(C.J. Memphis)*, Robert Townsend *(Cpl. Ellis)*, Denzel Washington *(Pfc. Peterson)*, William Allen Young *(Pvt. Henson)*

p, Norman Jewison, Ronald L. Schwary, Patrick Palmer; d, Norman Jewison; w, Charles Fuller (based on his stage play "A Soldier's Play"); ph, Russell Boyd (Metrocolor); ed, Mark Warner, Caroline Biggerstaff; m, Herbie Hancock; prod d, Walter Scott Herndon; cos, Chuck Velasco, Robert Stewart

Gripping, thanks to spotless direction and Rollins's inspired work, but nothing new to relay. Charles Fuller's powerful play (a Pulitzer Prize-winner, based on Melville's *Billy Budd*) was adapted by Fuller himself for the screen, and the power of the stage presentation is not diminished (which means it's not particularly cinematic, either).

The action takes place at Fort Neal, Louisiana, a base for black soldiers during WWII. Sgt. Waters (Adolph Caesar), a tough African-American topkick and manager of the baseball team, is coming back to the base drunk one night when he is shot to death by a .45-caliber weapon. That's the only clue to his death. Capt. Davenport (Howard E. Rollins, Jr.) is the black Army attorney who is sent to investigate the murder. The white officers on the base, as well as the black soldiers, are astounded at the choice, and Davenport finds that he's not getting any help in his search for the truth. Some of the black troops blame the Klan, while others suggest it might have been one of the white soldiers who rankled at Waters's attitude. A series of flashbacks establishes

Waters and the relationship he had with all those around him as Davenport begins his interrogations. What makes this such a good film is the multilayered complexity of the script. Fuller has taken a basic Agatha Christie-type plot and bathed it in social issues; A SOLDIER'S STORY is an insightful period drama as well as a totally engaging character study. The picture does become a trifle talky at times, thus betraying its stage origin, but Fuller's words are almost always interesting and powerful and make worthwhile listening. Caesar's performance stands out. With the addition of two musical treats: "The St. Louis Blues March," one of our favorites, over the credits, and Patti Labelle in a cameo as Big Mary, wailing away and tearing down the house as usual.

SOLID GOLD CADILLAC, THE

1956   99m   bw   ★★★★
Comedy   /U
Columbia

Judy Holliday (*Laura Partridge*), Paul Douglas (*Edward L. McKeever*), Fred Clark (*Clifford Snell*), John Williams (*John T. Blessington*), Hiram Sherman (*Harry Harkness*), Neva Patterson (*Amelia Shotgraven*), Ralph Dumke (*Warren Gillie*), Ray Collins (*Alfred Metcalfe*), Arthur O'Connell (*Jenkins*), Richard Deacon (*Williams*)

p, Fred Kohlmar; d, Richard Quine; w, Abe Burrows (based on the play by George S. Kaufman and Howard Teichmann); ph, Charles Lang; ed, Charles Nelson; m, Cyril J. Mockridge; art d, Ross Bellah; cos, Jean Louis

A charming, often hysterically funny poke at big business, government, and the plight of the underdog. The script was by Abe Burrows, based on the hit Broadway play starring a much older Josephine Hull, written by Kaufman and Teichmann. Burrows would later be involved with another successful comedy on the same general subject entitled HOW TO SUCCEED IN BUSINESS WITHOUT REALLY TRYING. The original play was to have had a younger woman, but when Hull, who was so delicious in ARSENIC AND OLD LACE, became available, she was paged for the part. In the film Holliday has the role, and a love story was added to fill the romantic gaps. She plays her patented daffy blonde with a heart of gold who owns 10 shares in a massive company. The board of directors of the organization are a panel of stern-visaged prigs including Clark, Williams, Sherman, Collins, and Dumke. Holliday shows up at a stockholders meeting and protests some of the shenanigans of the board. At first, she is a mere fly in their gargantuan ointment, but her presence is duly noted by the press, and things begin to happen. The former head of the company is Douglas, a hard-driving tycoon who has given up his role as top man on that totem pole in order to donate his services to the government, for which he is functioning as a "dollar-a-year" man. Holliday meets the bombastic Douglas and enlists him in her quest to secure representation for the small stockholders. When Douglas learns that his former aides have stabbed him in the back in their running of the company he started and nurtured, he joins with Holliday to get proxy votes from all the little people and to regain his position with the firm. O'Connell is the "don't rock the boat" office manager who is Holliday's boss, and Patterson is the secretary who aids and abets Holliday's mischief. George Burns handles the narrating chores in the same way Fred Allen did it (pre-recorded) on Broadway. The narration provides a few funny lines and bridges some of the gaps. The title stems from Holliday's fervent wish to own a solid gold cadillac. At the film's conclusion, with Douglas and Holliday united and running the company, she gets her desire.

The humor in the screenplay seldom derives from one-liners. Rather, it is in the situations, the caricatures that are the targets for its darts, and the unflagging energy of Holliday and Douglas as two utterly different people who find love with each other and blend to defeat the pompous executives. Kaufman, who was known as the "Great Collaborator," wrote with more people than the average sit-com scribe. His partners included Moss Hart (YOU CAN'T TAKE IT WITH YOU, among others), Edna Ferber (THE ROYAL FAMILY OF BROADWAY), Marc Connelly (MERTON OF THE MOVIES), Morrie Ryskind (A NIGHT AT THE OPERA), Ring Lardner, Sr., and many more. His sole effort for the stage was *The Butter and Egg Man*.

SOME CAME RUNNING

1959   137m   c   ★★★½
Drama   /A
MGM

Frank Sinatra (*Dave Hirsh*), Dean Martin (*Bama Dillert*), Shirley MacLaine (*Ginny Moorhead*), Martha Hyer (*Gwen French*), Arthur Kennedy (*Frank Hirsh*), Nancy Gates (*Edith Barclay*), Leora Dana (*Agnes Hirsh*), Betty Lou Keim (*Dawn Hirsh*), Larry Gates (*Prof Robert Haven French*), Steven Peck (*Raymond Lanchak*)

p, Sol C. Siegel; d, Vincente Minnelli; w, John Patrick, Arthur Sheekman (based on the novel by James Jones); ph, William Daniels (CinemaScope, Metrocolor); ed, Adrienne Fazan; m, Elmer Bernstein; art d, William A. Horning, Urie McCleary; cos, Walter Plunkett

Author James Jones wrote one of the definitive books about WWII, *From Here To Eternity*, which benefited greatly from the brilliant editing of Maxwell Perkins. Sinatra won an Oscar for his part in that 1953 epic and came back to appear in Jones's next book's movie adaptation, a postwar tale that rambled on and on. The novel took Jones seven years and ran better than 1,200 pages, so trimming it to filmable length was a difficult task. The screenwriters succeeded partially. Sinatra, a veteran, comes back to his home town of Parkman, Illinois, after trying his luck and failing as a writer. Sinatra carries a new manuscript he's just completed under one arm and a funny floozy, MacLaine, draped over the other. She is in love with him, and the appearance of the two creates a minor sensation in the small town. Sinatra's brother is Kennedy, a rigid businessman married to Dana but having an affair with his assistant, Nancy Gates. Dana doesn't much like Sinatra and turns her nose up at him. Hyer teaches at the local college and finds Sinatra intriguing; she's never been out of that tiny burg and is not accustomed to this kind of spirited person. She reads Sinatra's work and thinks that it has merit. The one local "character" is Martin, a loose gambler who finds in Sinatra a kindred spirit. The two men enjoy reveling with each other, running after women, drinking too much, and playing endless games of cards. Martin is suffering from diabetes and on his last legs. Since he is superstitious and his luck is going well for now, he never removes his hat. Sinatra hates Kennedy because the older brother sent him to an orphanage when their parents died. He also hates Kennedy for his disdain for MacLaine despite the fact that Kennedy's affair with Gates is an open secret. Sinatra finds himself falling for Hyer, who remains aloof to his entreaties. MacLaine remains on the scene and makes herself available whenever Sinatra wants her. Sinatra finally proposes to Hyer and still she refuses him. He is depressed by this rejection, grabs hold of MacLaine and Martin, and they drive off to have a wild time. They arrive in Terre Haute, meet Kennedy's teenage daughter Keim, who fled the town with her young boyfriend, John Brennan, when she found out about her father's dalliance with Gates. Sinatra brings Keim back to the Kennedy-Dana home and tells them off for the lying lives they lead. Later, he informs a disbelieving Martin that he intends to marry MacLaine. Martin doesn't know why anyone would want to marry such a trollop. After the wedding, Peck, one of MacLaine's many ex-lovers, enters. He tries to kill Sinatra for taking her away, but MacLaine takes the bullet meant for Sinatra. At her funeral, Martin is so moved that he lifts the hat he never would lift for anyone else.

The title is from the Gospel According to St. Mark and the picture is from the novel according to Minnelli. He made many concessions to Sinatra, who is notorious for disliking more than one take and who refuses to work regular hours, preferring a noon to 8 p.m. schedule over the usual start at 7. It was a large grosser for MGM, perhaps due to the Oscar nominations accorded MacLaine (losing to Susan Hayward for I WANT TO LIVE!), Hyer, Kennedy, and the tune "To Love and Be Loved" by Sammy Cahn and Jimmy Van Heusen. Though MacLaine remembers this as her favorite role, it was Hyer who stole the picture as the frosty teacher. While on location in Madison, MacLaine palled around with Sinatra and Martin and became part of the "Rat Pack," which included Peter Lawford, Sammy Davis, Jr., and, occasionally, Joey Bishop. Martin's easy-going gambler was also effective, and he proved here, as he did in THE YOUNG LIONS, that he was more than able to function without Jerry Lewis.

SOME LIKE IT HOT
1959 120m bw   ★★★★★
Crime/Comedy   /PG
Ashton/Mirisch

Marilyn Monroe (Sugar Kane), Tony Curtis (Joe/Josephine), Jack Lemmon (Jerry/Daphne), George Raft (Spats Columbo), Pat O'Brien (Mulligan), Joe E. Brown (Osgood E. Fielding III), Nehemiah Persoff (Little Bonaparte), Joan Shawlee (Sweet Sue), Billy Gray (Sig Poliakoff), George E. Stone (Toothpick Charlie)

p, Billy Wilder; d, Billy Wilder; w, Billy Wilder, I.A.L. Diamond (based on Robert Thoeren and M. Logan's screenplay for the film FAN-FARES OF LOVE); ph, Charles Lang; ed, Arthur Schmidt; m, Adolph Deutsch; art d, Ted Haworth; cos, Orry-Kelly, Milt Rice

A master comedy that revels in inventive effervescence. Unemployed musicians (Lemmon and Curtis) witness St. Valentine's Day Massacre in Chicago, flee in drag to Miami with all-girl band. Dazzling work by Lemmon and Monroe, memorable Curtis (his drag voice was dubbed), unforgettable supporting work from Brown, Shawlee, Raft, et al. The best authentic capturing of roaring twenties atmosphere ever put on film, with flawless script by director Wilder and I.A.L. Diamond. HOT was the most commercially successful of Monroe's films, and if she was hell to work with (Curtis compared kissing her to kissing Hitler; to her credit, she was pregnant and would lose the baby soon after filming was completed), it doesn't show on film. Brown's closing line may be the funniest closing tag in the history of motion pictures. SOME LIKE IT HOT inspired a Broadway musical, *Sugar*, and remains a tremendously popular film with both audiences and critics.

SOMEBODY UP THERE LIKES ME
1956 113m bw   ★★★½
Sports/Biography   /A
MGM

Paul Newman (Rocky Graziano), Pier Angeli (Norma), Everett Sloane (Irving Cohen), Eileen Heckart (Ma Barbella), Sal Mineo (Romolo), Harold J. Stone (Nick Barbella), Joseph Buloff (Benny), Sammy White (Whitey Bimstein), Arch Johnson (Heldon), Robert Lieb (Questioner)

p, Charles Schnee; d, Robert Wise; w, Ernest Lehman (based on the autobiography of Rocky Graziano written with Rowland Barber); ph, Joseph Ruttenberg; ed, Albert Akst; m, Bronislau Kaper; art d, Cedric Gibbons, Malcolm Brown

After pulling no punches in his brilliant study of the downside of professional boxing, THE SET-UP, director Robert Wise presents a much more upbeat picture of the fight game in this entertaining biography of one-time middleweight champion Rocky Graziano. Paul Newman plays the New York slum-bred fighter, the son of a boxer whose career was stifled by the bottle. In and out of trouble for most of his young life, Rocky drifts from petty crime to reform school, from a dishonorable discharge from the Army to Leavenworth Prison. In the joint, however, Rocky is encouraged to develop his boxing talents, and when he is released he is taken under the wing of small-time manager Irving Cohen (Everett Sloane). Under Cohen's guidance, Rocky begins winning fights, but it isn't until he meets and marries Norma (Pier Angeli) that Rocky becomes a big winner. In time, he battles Tony Zale (brilliantly boxed by Courtland Shepard) for the championship, losing their first fight, but taking the title in the second. Newman, who spent time with Graziano and observed his speech patterns, mannerisms, movements, and boxing style, worked himself into peak condition for the role, lifting weights and sparring with top professionals, and his portrayal of the scrappy, often tongue-tied, but wholly likable boxer is superb. Although the role was originally intended for James Dean, Newman makes it his own, delivering such memorable lines as "I'll drink from the bottle like the rest of the boys" when asked if he needs a cup to complete his boxing garb.

SOMEONE TO LOVE
1988 110m c   ★★★★
Comedy   R/15
Rainbow

Orson Welles (Danny's Friend), Henry Jaglom (Danny Sapir), Andrea Marcovicci (Helen Eugene), Michael Emil (Mickey Sapir), Sally Kellerman (Edith Helm), Oja Kodar (Yelena), Stephen Bishop (Blue), Dave Frishberg (Harry), Geraldine Baron, Ronee Blakley

p, M.H. Simonson; d, Henry Jaglom; w, Henry Jaglom; ph, Hanania Baer (DeLuxe Color); ed, Ruth Wald

Written and directed by Henry Jaglom, SOMEONE TO LOVE is an autobiographical film that also features Jaglom as a character, Danny Sapir, who happens to direct movies identical to Jaglom's own. Danny throws a Valentine's Day party for his lonely friends. The guests arrive at the old movie palace where the party is held. Among them is a mysterious presence that appears at the back of the movie theater, Danny's friend, played by Orson Welles. Accompanied by a camera crew, Danny asks his guests a series of questions about being alone, childhood dreams, and love. An introspective film about films, SOMEONE TO LOVE is a brilliant example of a filmed diary, but there is much in it that will turn away viewers. Jaglom's probing is often abrasive and inconsiderate; musical interludes are thrown into the film sporadically to alleviate audience tension. Notwithstanding Jaglom's vision and honesty, the reason most viewers will see SOMEONE TO LOVE is the presence of Welles in his final film appearance. He sits in the back of the theater declaring his beliefs, serving as Jaglom's mentor, guiding him from the first frame to the last. Like the theater facing demolition, Welles is a part of the past.

SOMEONE TO WATCH OVER ME
1987 106m c   ★★★
Thriller/Romance   R/15
Columbia

Tom Berenger *(Mike Keegan)*, Mimi Rogers *(Claire Gregory)*, Lorraine Bracco *(Ellie Keegan)*, Jerry Orbach *(Lt. Garber)*, John Rubinstein *(Neil Steinhart)*, Andreas Katsulas *(Joey Venza)*, Tony DiBenedetto *(T.J.)*, James Moriarty *(Koontz)*, Mark Moses *(Win Hockings)*, Daniel Hugh Kelly *(Scotty)*

p, Thierry de Ganay, Harold Schneider; d, Ridley Scott; w, Howard Franklin; ph, Steven Poster (Deluxe Color); ed, Claire Simpson; m, Michael Kamen; prod d, Jim Bissell; art d, Chris Burian-Mohr, John J. Moore; cos, Colleen Atwood

Hot on the heels of FATAL ATTRACTION came SOMEONE TO WATCH OVER ME, another film about a happily married man who strays from the marital bed. Mike Keegan (Tom Berenger) is a New York police detective who lives in Queens with his ex-cop wife, Ellie (Lorraine Bracco), and their young son. When wealthy socialite Claire Gregory (Mimi Rogers) witnesses a murder, Keegan is assigned to protect her from the killer. Cold and aloof at first, Claire begins to warm to the handsome, shy, and somewhat dim-witted detective. Although SOMEONE TO WATCH OVER ME has some major problems with plot plausibility, its emphasis is properly on the people involved in the romantic triangle and not the machinations of a contrived story line. Much of the credit for what works in the film should go to the excellent cast. Berenger is superb, and Rogers proves here that she can handle a lead role with class and aplomb. Bracco, however, steals the picture with a refreshing energy and wit.

SOMETHING WILD
1986 113m c   ★★★½
Drama/Comedy   R/18
Religioso Primitiva

Jeff Daniels *(Charles Driggs)*, Melanie Griffith *(Audrey Hankel)*, Ray Liotta *(Ray Sinclair)*, Margaret Colin *(Irene)*, Tracey Walter *(The Country Squire)*, Dana Preu *("Peaches")*, Jack Gilpin *(Larry Dillman)*, Su Tissue *(Peggy Dillman)*, Kristin Olsen *(Tracy)*, John Sayles *(Motorcycle Cop)*

p, Jonathan Demme, Kenneth Utt; d, Jonathan Demme; w, E. Max Frye; ph, Tak Fujimoto (DuArt Color); ed, Craig McKay; m, John Cale, Laurie Anderson; prod d, Norma Moriceau; art d, Stephen J. Lineweaver

One bright Friday afternoon in lower Manhattan, Charles Driggs (Jeff Daniels), a successful young tax consultant, capriciously skips out of a tiny diner without paying his lunch check. Just outside, he is stopped by Audrey Hankel (Melanie Griffith), a Louise Brooks-clone in black wig and vaguely African attire. She calls herself "Lulu," presumably a reference to Brooks' character in PANDORA'S BOX. She tells Charles that she saw him walk out on the check and threatens to turn him in. Declaring that Charles is actually a "closet rebel," she decides instead that he'd be game for a road trip. Before he knows what is happening, Charles finds himself in Audrey's convertible being driven to New Jersey. Through Audrey he is temporarily freed from his normal bourgeois restraints. They have a little adventure on the road as they engage in some petty theft, mildly kinky sex, and finally attend Audrey's high school reunion. This modern screwball comedy takes a frightening dark turn when they encounter

Audrey's psychotic ex-husband, Ray (Ray Liotta), who has just gotten out of jail.

Since his early films, director Jonathan Demme has demonstrated a sharp eye for the American landscape and its people. With a keen wit and an optimistic compassion, Demme has creates vividly human characters whose quirks have the ring of truth about them. With a screenplay from first-time screenwriter E. Max Frye and superior performances from his principal cast, Demme has created a unique and likable film in SOMETHING WILD. John Cale and Laurie Anderson compiled the film's rousing rock soundtrack which features nearly 50 songs.

Some viewers were alarmed at the dark violent turn the story takes more than halfway through but close viewing reveals that the audience is subtly being prepared for this tonal shift from early on. This is a film that benefits greatly from a second screening. Demme keeps his quirky narrative twisting and turning so that the viewer can never predict what will happen next. He draws us in with humor and then grabs us by the throat, bringing us face-to-face with the failures of the American dream. A filmmaker with a small but devoted following, he would not have a major popular hit until the 1991 blockbuster, THE SILENCE OF THE LAMBS.

SON OF FRANKENSTEIN
1939 95m bw   ★★★★
Horror   /H
Universal

Basil Rathbone *(Baron Wolf von Frankenstein)*, Boris Karloff *(The Monster)*, Bela Lugosi *(Ygor)*, Lionel Atwill *(Inspector Krogh)*, Josephine Hutchinson *(Elsa von Frankenstein)*, Donnie Dunagan *(Peter von Frankenstein)*, Emma Dunn *(Amelia)*, Edgar Norton *(Thomas Benson)*, Perry Ivins *(Fritz)*, Lawrence Grant *(Burgomaster)*

p, Rowland V. Lee; d, Rowland V. Lee; w, Willis Cooper (based on characters created by Mary Shelley); ph, George Robinson; ed, Ted J. Kent; m, Frank Skinner; art d, Jack Otterson; fx, John P. Fulton; cos, Vera West

The third film in the Universal "Frankenstein" series and the last feature film appearance by Boris Karloff as the monster, SON OF FRANKENSTEIN boasts some stunning set design by Russell Gausman, a good script, and a magnificent cast. Set 25 years after the end of THE BRIDE OF FRANKENSTEIN, the film begins as the late Baron von Frankenstein's son, Wolf (Basil Rathbone), returns to his homeland and receives a weak welcome from the burgomaster, who presents him with a box containing his father's papers. Once safe in his castle, Wolf is visited by Inspector Krogh (Lionel Atwill), who warns him that he is not welcomed by the villagers, who fear that he will continue his father's experiments. Wolf laughs off their suspicions, but the next day, while wandering the ruins of his father's laboratory, he meets Ygor (Bela Lugosi). The deceased Baron's assistant now hides among the ruins, guarding his "friend"—the comatose Frankenstein monster (Karloff) laid out on a slab, immobile, but very much alive. Wolf becomes obsessed with the idea of bringing the monster back to full power, then vindicating his father by teaching the creature to behave. SON OF FRANKENSTEIN is a rousing, memorable addition to the series, and features a collection of superb portrayals from Lugosi (who delivers the performance of his career and nearly steals the film), Rathbone (in a part originally planned for Peter Lorre), and Lionel Atwill (who milks his false arm for all it's worth), though Karloff is a bit of a disappointment—his beloved monster turned into little more than a mute robot. Dwight Frye, who had been

Frankenstein's assistant in the first two films, unfortunately had his entire role as one of the villagers cut out. While the offbeat vision and humor of James Whale (the director of the first two FRANKENSTEIN films) are missing, Rowland Lee manages to create a memorable world all his own. The series would go downhill from here and end with a rousing parody of the whole genre in ABBOTT AND COSTELLO MEET FRANKENSTEIN.

SON OF PALEFACE

1952 95m c   ★★★½
Western/Comedy   /U
Paramount

Bob Hope *(Junior)*, Jane Russell *(Mike)*, Roy Rogers *(Himself)*, Bill Williams *(Kirk)*, Lloyd Corrigan *(Doc Lovejoy)*, Paul E. Burns *(Ebenezer Hawkins)*, Douglas Dumbrille *(Sheriff McIntyre)*, Harry von Zell *(Stoner)*, Iron Eyes Cody *(Indian Chief)*, Wee Willie Davis *(Blacksmith)*

p, Robert L. Welch; d, Frank Tashlin; w, Frank Tashlin, Robert Welch, Joseph Quillan; ph, Harry Wild (Technicolor); ed, Eda Warren; m, Lyn Murray; art d, Hal Pereira, Roland Anderson; fx, Gordon Jennings, Paul K. Lerpae, Farciot Edouart; chor, Josephine Earl

A very funny sequel to THE PALEFACE that took four years to put on the screen while Hope made a few other pictures. This time, Hope plays his own son. The original character of the pioneer dentist was played by Hope, and now he comes back, again with Russell, as the Harvard graduate who goes west to claim the inheritance left by his father. Russell is a bandit who sings in a saloon known as "The Dirty Shame." Hope teams with Rogers and Trigger (playing themselves) to nab a crook who has been robbing various gold shipments. They suspect that the criminal may be Russell. She thinks Rogers is a handsome guy and has the warms for him, but he would rather kiss his horse, so, rarity of rarities, Hope gets the girl.

SON OF PALEFACE is a satire of every cowboy cliche, with Hope getting the chance to rattle off one-liners while the action takes in Indian uprisings, lynch mobs, posses, ghost towns, mirages, deserts, quick-draws, saloon brawls—in other words, everything that John Wayne ever did for real. Tashlin was receiving his first directorial credit; he had co-directed THE LEMON DROP KID with Sid Lanfield but was not credited. He'd written THE PALEFACE with Ed Hartmann and was rewarded with this assignment, a job he didn't muff. It's fast and witty, and all the rootin' tootin' shootin' cannot be taken seriously for a moment. Tashlin was a one-time cartoonist, and it shows as he sets up the scenes like animated sequences, much to the picture's benefit. In the original, Ray Evans and Jay Livingston wrote the Oscar tune "Buttons and Bows" and they wisely bring it back for another go-around with new lyrics, as sung by Hope, Rogers, and Russell.

Rogers had been the king of the small western movies for over a decade, but after this movie, began to limit his appearances. He did a small guest bit in ALIAS JESSE JAMES, then a role in MACKINTOSH AND T.J. Other than those, he spent most of his time tending his huge real estate investments which are worth over $100 million.

SONG OF BERNADETTE, THE

1943 156m bw   ★★★★
Religious/Biography   /U
FOX

Jennifer Jones *(Bernadette Soubirous)*, William Eythe *(Antoine)*, Charles Bickford *(Peyremaie)*, Vincent Price *(Dutour)*, Lee J. Cobb *(Dr. Dozous)*, Gladys Cooper *(Sister Vauzous)*, Anne Revere *(Louise Soubirous)*, Roman Bohnen *(Francois Soubirous)*, Mary Anderson *(Jeanne Abadie)*, Patricia Morison *(Empress Eugenie)*

p, William Perlberg; d, Henry King; w, George Seaton (based on the novel by Franz Werfel); ph, Arthur Miller; ed, Barbara McLean; m, Alfred Newman; art d, James Basevi, William Darling; fx, Fred Sersen; cos, Rene Hubert

This film depicts the stirring true story of the woman who had a vision of the Virgin Mary in a grotto at Lourdes in 1858. Jennifer Jones is Bernadette Soubirous, a peasant girl whose family lives in the town jail because they have no place of their own. One morning, Bernadette is gathering sticks of wood near the grotto when she is visited by the Virgin (Linda Darnell). Bernadette is directed to dig at the grotto for a healing water with curative power for the lame and the halt. Everyone scoffs at her except her devout mother and, eventually, Peyremaie (Charles Bickford), a local priest. He helps her get into a convent, and, after many years of defending her vision, Bernadette is canonized by the Catholic Church. Since that time, millions have flocked to Lourdes to bathe in the Holy Water. Jones is touching in an Oscar-winning performance.

SONG OF THE SOUTH

1946 94m c   ★★★★
Animated/Children's   /U
Disney

Ruth Warrick *(Sally)*, Bobby Driscoll *(Johnny)*, Luana Patten *(Ginny)*, Lucile Watson *(Grandmother)*, Hattie McDaniel *(Aunt Tempy)*, Glenn Leedy *(Toby)*, James Baskett *(Uncle Remus)*, George Nokes, Gene Holland *(The Favers Boys)*, Erik Rolf *(John)*

p, Walt Disney; d, Harve Foster (live action), Wilfred Jackson (animated); w, Dalton Raymond, Morton Grant, Bill Peet, George Stallings, Ralph Wright, Maurice Rapf (based on *Tales of Uncle Remus* by Joel Chandler Harris); ph, Gregg Toland (Technicolor); ed, William Morgan; m, Daniele Amfitheatrof, Paul J. Smith; art d, Perry Ferguson; fx, Ub Iwerks; cos, Mary Wills; anim, Milt Kahl, Erick Larson, Oliver M. Johnston, Jr., Les Clark, Marc Davis, John Lounsbery, Don Lusk, Tom Massey, Murray McClellan, Jack Campbell, Hal King, Harvey Toombs, Ken O'Brien, Al Coe, Hal Ambro, Cliff Nordberg, Rudy Larriva

This Disney charmer is also the studio's most controversial production. Set in the Reconstruction South, it stars Bobby Driscoll as Johnny, a white little boy who goes to live on his grandmother's plantation after his parents separate. Upset by things he can't understand, Johnny runs away and meets former slave Uncle Remus (James Baskett). Uncle Remus decides to trick Johnny into going home, telling the boy he would also like to run away, but must stop home for a few things. As Uncle Remus packs, he tells Johnny a story, and the film moves into a marvelous combination of live action and animation in a bright cartoon setting in which Brer Rabbit, too, has an adventure while running away from home. SONG OF THE SOUTH's cartoon sequences are as fine as anything produced by the Disney animators. The live action projected into a cartoon setting transcends gimmickry, with the actors and caricatures carefully matched within the frame. Baskett's excellent performance (for which he received an honorary Academy Award) makes the technique work that much better. The film's idyllic portrayal of the Reconstruction setting was controversial, however, particularly among black Americans. The NAACP and the National Urban League, among others, protested the stereotypes in the film, though Disney officials maintained the film was "...a sincere effort to depict American folklore, to put the Uncle Remus stories into pictures." Included is the well-known song "Zip A Dee Doo Dah."

SONG TO REMEMBER, A

1945   113m   c   ★★★½
Musical/Biography   /U
Columbia

Paul Muni (*Professor Joseph Elsner*), Merle Oberon (*George Sand*), Cornel Wilde (*Frederic Chopin*), Stephen Bekassy (*Franz Liszt*), Nina Foch (*Constantia*), George Coulouris (*Louis Pleyel*), Sig Arno (*Henri Dupont*), Howard Freeman (*Kalbrenner*), George Macready (*Alfred DeMusset*), Claire DuBrey (*Mme. Mercier*)

p, Louis F. Edelman; d, Charles Vidor; w, Sidney Buchman (based on the story by Ernst Marischka); ph, Tony Gaudio, Allen Davey (Technicolor); ed, Charles Nelson; m, Miklos Rozsa; art d, Lionel Banks, Van Nest Polglase; cos, Walter Plunkett, Travis Banton

As a fictional tale of a composer who gives his all for his music, this is a fine picture; as a biography, it bears as much resemblance to the truth as NIGHT AND DAY did to the life of Cole Porter. Nonetheless, Cornell Wilde earned an Oscar nomination for his convincing performance as Frederic Chopin, whom screenwriter Sidney Buchman presents as a revolutionary Polish patriot (though, in fact, his support of Polish nationalism was never so zealous). Top-billed Paul Muni, in his only Technicolor film, portrays Chopin's mentor Prof. Joseph Elsner, while Merle Oberon essays the role of novelist George Sand, whom the infatuated Chopin meets in Paris and follows to Majorca, where he becomes consumptive (the real-life relationship between Sand and Chopin was considerably less whirlwind, lasting some 10 years), resulting in his death when he refuses to cancel a concert tour whose proceeds are earmarked for the cause.

Notwithstanding its departure from the facts and Muni's over-the-top performance, A SONG TO REMEMBER looks exquisite and received several Academy Award nominations. Miklos Rozsa won an Oscar for his adaptation of Chopin's music, Jose Iturbi performed the piano pieces, and Cornell Wilde, who studied piano for several months, looked so at home at the ivories that he was offered several concert engagements after the film came out.

SONGWRITER

1984   94m   c   ★★★
Musical   R/15
Songwriter

Willie Nelson (*Doc Jenkins*), Kris Kristofferson (*Blackie Buck*), Melinda Dillon (*Honey Carder*), Rip Torn (*Dino McLeish*), Lesley Ann Warren (*Gilda*), Mickey Raphael (*Arly and Harmonica, Gilda's Band*), Rhonda Dotson (*Corkie*), Richard C. Sarafian (*Rodeo Rocky*), Robert Gould (*Ralph*), Sage Parker (*Pattie McLeish*)

p, Sydney Pollack; d, Alan Rudolph; w, Bud Shrake; ph, Matthew F. Leonetti (Metrocolor); ed, Stephen Lovejoy, George A. Martin; m, Larry Cansler; prod d, Joel Schiller; cos, Ernest Misko, Kathleen Gore-Misko

Playing roles with which they're well familiar, Willie Nelson and Kris Kristofferson star as a pair of country & western singer-songwriters. One-time partners Doc Jenkins (Nelson) and Blackie Buck (Kristofferson) have gone their separate ways, with the former becoming the king of country music while the latter continues to rebel against record industry conventions, still an inveterate carouser. Estranged from his wife (Melinda Dillon) and daughter (Dotson), Doc takes on a talented protege (Lesley Ann Warren) who soon has her own problems, namely an over-indulgence in booze and drugs. While trying to get her on the right track and reconcile with his family, Doc also has to deal with a sleazy publisher (Richard C. Sarafian). A cut above most films that have attempted to portray the world of country & western music, SONGWRITER was directed by the immensely gifted Alan Rudolph (TROUBLE IN MIND; THE MODERNS), who came to the project after Steve Rash had begun it. The movie belongs to Nelson, who displays a natural screen charm, but Rip Torn also contributes an excellent performance as a good ol' boy concert promoter. Kristofferson's song score was nominated for an Oscar.

SONS AND LOVERS

1960   99m   bw   ★★★½
Drama   /A
FOX   (U.K.)

Trevor Howard (*Walter Morel*), Dean Stockwell (*Paul Morel*), Wendy Hiller (*Mrs. Morel*), Mary Ure (*Clara Dawes*), Heather Sears (*Miriam Lievers*), William Lucas (*William*), Conrad Phillips (*Baxter Dawes*), Donald Pleasence (*Pappleworth*), Ernest Thesiger (*Henry Hadlock*), Rosalie Crutchley (*Miriam's Mother*)

p, Jerry Wald; d, Jack Cardiff; w, Gavin Lambert, T.E.B. Clarke (based on the novel by D.H. Lawrence); ph, Freddie Francis (CinemaScope); m, Mario Nascimbene; art d, Lionel Couch; cos, Margaret Furse

They might well have titled this SON AND MOTHER, for the famous relationship between a mother and son is at the center of this respectful adaptation of Lawrence's autobiographical novel. A few characters have been altered and a sister has been dropped in the transition from print to the screen, but these changes hardly call attention to themselves. Britain's official entry at Cannes, SONS AND LOVERS won an Oscar for Francis's cinematography and nailed nominations from the Academy for Best Picture, Best Script, Best Art Direction as well as for Cardiff's direction and for Trevor Howard's and Mary Ure's performances. The only actor in the cast who was not British was former child actor Stockwell, but only Henry Higgins would have noticed any lapses in his accent. The story is set in Nottingham, where Hiller and Howard have raised three sons on Howard's miner's wages. Hiller is a forceful woman who manages men like puppets. Stockwell is the sensitive son who longs to pursue a career as an artist in London. After romancing naive local lass Sears for a while, Stockwell takes up with an older woman, Ure, who is married to Phillips. Hiller puts an end to her son's relationship with Sears, and when Ure leaves her husband for Stockwell, Hiller is livid. Stockwell listens to his mother but knows he should follow his heart; however, he appears powerless to free himself of her grasp. No matter what he does or where he goes, Stockwell feels Hiller's presence. The love that Hiller should be giving her husband is, instead, showered upon Stockwell. When one of his brothers dies in a mining accident and the other goes off to London, Stockwell is forced to abandon his dreams in order to be near his bereaved mother. Hiller eventually dies, and Stockwell leaves for London, looking forward to a life away from the claustrophobic town, but we know that the specter of his dear mother will always be with him.

Many works have been written about the domination of sons by mothers, but few have come close to the insights of Lawrence's classic, and it is much to the film's credit that a great deal of its dialogue comes straight from the novel. The film's period details are excellent, and the direction by cinematographer-turned-director Cardiff (who photographed such films as THE RED SHOES, LEAVE HER TO HEAVEN and THE AFRICAN QUEEN) is first rate. All of the actors acquit themselves well, even in the most menial roles. Crutchley is exquisite as Sears' mother and veteran Thesiger (who, at 81, was making his penultimate film in a career that begain in 1918) is equally memorable. Cardiff's assistant on the film was Peter Yates, who later directed such films as BULLITT and BREAKING AWAY.

SONS OF THE DESERT

1933 68m bw   ★★★★
Comedy   /U
MGM

Stan Laurel (Himself), Oliver Hardy (Himself), Charley Chase (Himself), Mae Busch (Mrs. Lottie Chase Hardy), Dorothy Christy (Mrs. Betty Laurel), Lucien Littlefield (Dr. Horace Meddick), John Elliott (Exalted Exhausted Ruler), Charley Young, John Merton, William Gillespie

p, Hal Roach; d, William A. Seiter; w, Frank Craven, Byron Morgan; ph, Kenneth Peach; ed, Bert Jordan; chor, David Bennett

One of Stan Laurel and Oliver Hardy's best feature-length films, SONS OF THE DESERT is a comedic send-up of lodge conventions. Based on the team's silent two-reeler WE FAW DOWN, the story involves Laurel and Hardy's trip to a convention of the Sons of the Desert. Because their wives don't want them to attend the convention, Laurel and Hardy pretend to take an ocean voyage to Honolulu, using the excuse that Hardy needs a sea cruise for health reasons. Instead, they attend their convention in grand style and are even filmed by a newsreel crew covering the festivities. Upon their return home, however, they discover that not only did the ship that they supposedly sailed on sink, but also their wives saw the newsreel they were featured in. Thus, their ruse is exposed. Songs include "Honolulu Baby" and "Sons of the Desert." SONS is faster by far than most L&H vehicles, though their childish innocence is left mercifully intact. Chase is a riot as irritatingly madcap conventioneer. And as Johhny Carson's Matinee Host used to say, "featuring the ever popular Mae Busch" (as Mrs. Hardy; that's Dorothy Christy as Mrs. Laurel—or as one of them. Stan's trips to the altar made him the Mickey Rooney of his day).

SOPHIE'S CHOICE

1982 157m c   ★★★★
Drama   R/15
ITC

Meryl Streep (Sophie Zawistowska), Kevin Kline (Nathan Landau), Peter MacNicol (Stingo), Josef Sommer (Narrator), Rita Karin (Yetta Zimmerman), Stephen D. Newman (Larry), Greta Turken (Leslie Lapidus), Josh Mostel (Morris Fink), Marcell Rosenblatt (Astrid Weinstein), Moishe Rosenfeld (Moishe Rosenblum)

p, Alan J. Pakula, Keith Barish; d, Alan J. Pakula; w, Alan J. Pakula (based on the novel by William Styron); ph, Nestor Almendros (Technicolor); ed, Evan Lottman; m, Marvin Hamlisch; prod d, George Jenkins; art d, John J. Moore; cos, Albert Wolsky

Meryl Streep's finest performance to date. William Styron's best-selling novel, supposedly based on his real experiences as a southerner living in Brooklyn in 1947, tells of Stingo (Peter MacNicol), a cornpone author who moves into a Brooklyn boarding house and meets Sophie Zawistowska (Meryl Streep) and Nathan Landau (Kevin Kline). Sophie's tales of her life in Europe have a strange and often unbelievable tint to them; she

talks for instance about her late father as a freedom-loving man, but later we learn that he was one of the most virulent anti-Semites in Poland. For most of the film one wonders what Sophie's "choice" is: is she to choose between Nathan and Stingo? But then the film flashes back to monochrome sepia for Sophie's remembrances of horrors past, and after some twists her choice is revealed.

Well directed by Pakula and featuring gorgeous cinematography by Almendros, SOPHIE'S CHOICE is gripping cinematic storytelling. Streep continues to astound audiences with the depth to which she makes characters her own. Her Oscar-winning performance here is probably the most outstanding element in what could have been an average movie. Alan Pakula's screenplay could have been at least 30 minutes shorter. The words purportedly written by Stingo are delivered as narration by Josef Sommer, not a cinematically strong device. Despite its considerable merits (and its problems), the film is nevertheless chiefly worth watching to see one of contemporary film's best actresses in action.

SORRY, WRONG NUMBER

1948 89m bw   ★★★★
Thriller   /15
Paramount

Barbara Stanwyck (Leona Stevenson), Burt Lancaster (Henry Stevenson), Ann Richards (Sally Lord Dodge), Wendell Corey (Dr. Alexander), Harold Vermilyea (Waldo Evans), Ed Begley (James Cotterell), Leif Erickson (Fred Lord), William Conrad (Morano), John Bromfield (Joe), Jimmy Hunt (Jimmy Lord)

p, Hal B. Wallis, Anatole Litvak; d, Anatole Litvak; w, Lucille Fletcher (based on her radio play); ph, Sol Polito; ed, Warren Low; m, Franz Waxman; art d, Hans Dreier, Earl Hedrick; fx, Gordon Jennings; cos, Edith Head

A gripping film version of the classic 22-minute radio play which was made famous by Agnes Moorehead in a tour-de-force performance in 1943. Because Moorehead was not a "star" in Hollywood, Barbara Stanwyck was given the role in the movie version and she made it her own. Leona Stevenson (Stanwyck) is a whining, domineering, paranoid, hypochondriac New York heiress who has developed a psychosomatic illness that has made her a bed-ridden invalid. She lives in a fancy apartment with her milquetoast husband Henry (Lancaster), her only contact with the outside world being the telephone. One evening, while trying to reach Henry at the office, she overhears two men confirming plans for a murder. She tries to contact the outside world—the police, the phone company, Henry—to warn them of the impending violence, but time is quickly running out and the hour of the murder is approaching. The film's title is also its last line of dialogue.

SORRY, WRONG NUMBER is a wonderful premise which made for a taut, fast-paced 22-minute radio play, but at 89 minutes, much of them told in flashback, the suspense ebbs somewhat. Both Lancaster and Stanwyck are excellent, the latter's incredibly intense performance earning her a fourth Best Actress nomination.

SOUND OF MUSIC, THE

1965 174m c   ★★★
Musical/Biography   G/U
FOX

Julie Andrews *(Maria)*, Christopher Plummer *(Capt. Von Trapp)*, Eleanor Parker *(The Baroness)*, Richard Haydn *(Max Detweiler)*, Peggy Wood *(Mother Abbess)*, Charmian Carr *(Liesl)*, Heather Menzies *(Louisa)*, Nicholas Hammond *(Friedrich)*, Duane Chase *(Kurt)*, Angela Cartwright *(Brigitta)*

p, Robert Wise; d, Robert Wise; w, Ernest Lehman (based on the musical play by Richard Rodgers, Oscar Hammerstein II, Howard Lindsay, Russel Crouse); ph, Ted McCord (Todd-AO, DeLuxe Color); ed, William Reynolds; m, Richard Rodgers; prod d, Boris Leven; fx, L.B. Abbott, Emil Kosa, Jr.; chor, Marc Breaux, Dee Dee Wood; cos, Dorothy Jeakins

We'd give anything to be little Von Trapp children, living our lives in the confines of this film. We'd refuse to wear clothes made from curtains. We'd sing loudly (like off-key Ethel Mermans) when we were hiding from Nazis, and never compromise our talent to sing before Papa's guests. We'd snatch Eleanor Parker's Eva Gabor wig, moon nuns, and wet Julie's bed during "My Favorite Things." What fun we'd have. And make this travesty real. For despite the political danger, we know it's leading to music swells and Andrews's million-dollar wedding gown—enough to make Grace Kelly and Princess Di and Elizabeth Taylor slap their mothers. It's so perfectly contrived and mechanical and fresh as a daisy, it's infuriating. And only the sly, insistently subversive Christopher Plummer is on our side.

Maria (Julie Andrews) is a young postulant at a nunnery who quickly realizes that the cloister is not for her. Yet she still believes in the values espoused by the church, so she goes out into the world and radiantly attempts to bring what she's learned to the lay world. Soon Maria is hired by Austrian widower Capt. Von Trapp (Christopher Plummer) as a governess for his seven singing children. Noting that the children seem cowed by their disciplinarian father, she strives to open their lives to joy. They live in one of the most beautiful sections of the Alps, but only learn to appreciate the surrounding vistas when Maria, with her fresh outlook, shows them what they have. All that is soon threatened by Nazi rule in Austria, forcing the Von Trapps to flee while en route to Salzburg for a musical festival in which they are to perform. A staple of 1960s Hollywood films, THE SOUND OF MUSIC earned an Oscar for Best Picture, delivered an unforgettable Julie Andrews performance (simulataneously damning her career; we'd have preferred the more authentic Mary Martin) and presented a most postcard view of Austria. The songs are hard to forget—"The Sound of Music," "Do Re Mi," "My Favorite Things," "Edelweiss", "Climb Every Mountain", and our pick of the litter, "The Lonely Goatherd"—but we're trying. So you expected a *serious* review?

In a nutshell: lovely to look at, scripted competently, with a few chilling moments about the lurking Nazis. But Wise can't direct Plummer to play along. And who does Eleanor Parker think she is—Anne Baxter standing in for Joan Crawford?

SOUNDER
1972 105m c   ★★★½
Drama   G/U
Radnitz/Mattel

Cicely Tyson *(Rebecca Morgan)*, Paul Winfield *(Nathan Lee Morgan)*, Kevin Hooks *(David Lee Morgan)*, Carmen Mathews *(Mrs. Boatwright)*, Taj Mahal *(Ike)*, James Best *(Sheriff Young)*, Yvonne Jarrell *(Josie Mae Morgan)*, Eric Hooks *(Earl Morgan)*, Sylvia Kuumba Williams *(Harriet)*, Janet MacLachlan *(Camille Johnson)*

p, Robert B. Radnitz; d, Martin Ritt; w, Lonne Elder, III (based on a novel by William H. Armstrong); ph, John A. Alonzo (Panavision, DeLuxe Color); ed, Sidney Levin; m, Taj Mahal; prod d, Walter Scott Herndon; cos, Nedra Watt

Heartwarming, heart-tugging, heartbreaking—all these words describe SOUNDER, a film that celebrates a family's dedication to one another through whatever travails befall them. In 1930s Louisiana, Nathan and Rebecca Morgan (Winfield and Tyson) are sharecroppers raising their three children and their dog, Sounder, as best they can in the poverty of the Depression. Nathan does the farming and hunts for game to feed his family. Rebecca takes in washing, and the trio of children take an equal part in doing the other tasks. Not much game is to be had, however, and when Nathan is arrested for stealing a ham, the family is torn apart. Rebecca and the children now begin a backbreaking schedule as they strive to work the land, make their quota, and keep body and soul together.

Adapted from a slim book that won the 1970 Newberry Award for children's literature, SOUNDER is one of the truest examples of a "family film" ever made and a triumph for all concerned. A sequel, SOUNDER, PART 2, followed in 1976, with Harold Sylvester and Ebony Wright taking over the roles played here by Winfield and Tyson. Nominated for four Academy Awards: Best Picture (losing to THE GODFATHER), Best Actor (Winfield, who lost to Brando in THE GODFATHER), Best Actress (Tyson, who lost to Liza Minnelli for CABARET) and Best Screenplay.

SOUTH PACIFIC
1958 171m c   ★★★½
Musical   /U
South Pacific/Magna

Rossano Brazzi *(Emile De Becque)*, Mitzi Gaynor *(Nellie Forbush)*, John Kerr *(Lt. Cable)*, Ray Walston *(Luther Billis)*, Juanita Hall *(Bloody Mary)*, France Nuyen *(Liat)*, Russ Brown *(Capt. Brackett)*, Jack Mullaney *(Professor)*, Ken Clark *(Stewpot)*, Floyd Simmons *(Harbison)*

p, Buddy Adler; d, Joshua Logan; w, Paul Osborn (based on the play by Oscar Hammerstein II, Richard Rodgers, Logan, from the book *Tales of the South Pacific* by James A. Michener); ph, Leon Shamroy (Todd-AO, Technicolor); ed, Robert Simpson; art d, Lyle Wheeler, John DeCuir, Walter M. Scott, Paul S. Fox; fx, L.B. Abbott; chor, LeRoy Prinz; cos, Dorothy Jeakins

SOUTH PACIFIC isn't the screen classic it should have been, but despite the fact that it pales in comparison with the long-running Rodgers and Hammerstein Broadway musical on which it is based, the film still stands up as terrific entertainment. Inspired by James Michener's book *Tales of the South Pacific*, both the stage musical and the movie were directed by Joshua Logan—not entirely a good thing, since he allows his actors to resort to stage techniques that aren't always suited to the close-up medium of film. Set on an island in (you guessed it) the South Pacific, the story concerns Nellie Forbush (Mitzi Gaynor), a midwestern nurse who falls in love with Emile De Becque (Rossano Brazzi), a widowed planter who is much older, has children, and is set in his ways (shades of THE KING AND I). At the same time, Luther Bills (John Kerr), a young Marine, falls for Liat (France Nuyen), a local native girl.

Ray Walston steals every scene in which he appears as a SeaBee conniver not unlike Sergeant Bilko, and Juanita Hall is wonderful as she repeats her stage role as Bloody Mary, though her singing is dubbed by Muriel Smith. Brazzi's voice work was provided by Giorgio Tozzi, and Bill Lee sang for Kerr, but

Gaynor handled vocal chores herself. Made for $5 million, SOUTH PACIFIC was shot on location in Hawaii with a large cast that includes such names as Tom Laughlin (BILLY JACK), Ron Ely (TV's "Tarzan"), Doug McClure, and a non-speaking cameo by Joan Fontaine. It garnered Oscar nominations for Leon Shamroy's cinematography and Alfred Newman and Ken Darby's musical direction, and it won an Oscar for Best Sound. Ultimately, though, it is the glorious Rodgers and Hammerstein songs that really distinguish the film.

SOUTHERNER, THE
1945 91m bw   ★★★★½
Drama   /A
UA

Zachary Scott (Sam Tucker), Betty Field (Nona Tucker), Beulah Bondi (Granny Tucker), Bunny Sunshine (Daisy Tucker), Jay Gilpin (Jot Tucker), Percy Kilbride (Harmie Jenkins), Blanche Yurka (Ma Tucker), Charles Kemper (Tim, the Narrator), J. Carrol Naish (Henry Devers), Norman Lloyd (Finlay Hewitt)

p, David L. Loew, Robert Hakim; d, Jean Renoir; w, Jean Renoir, Hugo Butler, William Faulkner (uncredited), Nunnally Johnson (based on the novel Hold Autumn in Your Hand by George Sessions Perry); ph, Lucien Andriot; ed, Gregg Tallas; m, Werner Janssen

A remarkably naturalistic portrayal of one family's struggle to start a farm in the South. With the coming of autumn, Scott, a man hardened by his years of working fields for other people, decides to work his own land on the advice of his dying uncle. He is given a plot of unused, out-of-the-way land and packs his wife Field, children Sunshine and Gilpin, grandmother Bondi, a dog, and all of their possessions onto a beat-up truck. What they find is a plot of unkempt, though workable, land and a dilapidated shanty that isn't fit for animals. The family gets settled in, fix the front porch, put a fire in the stove, and do their best to make the space livable. When Scott realizes the well doesn't work, he pays a visit to a neighboring farm which, after years of toiling, has become what Scott hopes his will be. The farm belongs to Naish, an embittered man who cannot appreciate the success of his hard work without thinking about how it caused the deaths of his wife and child. Naish is less than hospitable and only reluctantly agrees to let Scott use his well on the condition that Scott supply a new rope when the old one wears thin. As time passes and winter arrives, Scott and his family plow the land and ready it for a cotton crop. For days the family goes without any decent food, surviving on mash, until Scott successfully smokes a possum out of a hollow tree. Mealtime brings the family together and gives Scott reason to thank the Lord with a simple prayer. Come spring, Gilpin is stricken with pellagra, or "spring sickness," forcing Scott to plant vegetables and find milk for the boy's nourishment. The vegetables begin to grow, but Scott has no money left for milk. Out of desperation he appeals again to Naish, who, in front of Scott, proceeds to use an entire bucket of fresh milk for pig slop while refusing to spare even a drop for a sick child. Kemper, a friend of Scott's from the city who has offered the farmer a factory job, does all he can to help by buying the family a cow, thereby saving the boy's life.

In the meantime, Scott's rivalry with Naish grows stronger when Naish's livestock are found in Scott's vegetable garden. Scott goes angrily to Naish's farm and a brawl begins between them, with Naish finally being thrown into the pig pen. In retaliation, Naish grabs his rifle and heads for the river where Scott is washing up. Before Naish can fire off a shot, he sees Scott's fishing line pull taut. Both he and Scott know that the fish that has been hooked is "Lead Pencil," a legendary giant catfish with whiskers as thick as lead pencils. It's been Naish's dream to catch the fish, so rather than shoot Scott, he helps him pull in the catch. The pair strike a deal: Naish will let Scott farm his vegetable garden and use his well, and in exchange Scott will let Naish have the glory of catching "Lead Pencil." Summer comes, the cotton crop shows promise, and Scott has hopes of life improving for him and the family. While they are in town for a wedding, a terrible rainstorm rages for hours. When the family arrives back at the farm, they find their crop completely destroyed, their house battered by the storm's high winds, and the river rising high onto Scott's property. Near his wit's end, Scott must consider how his family is going to survive and what the fate of his farm will be.

THE SOUTHERNER, Renoir's most critically respected American film, is a superb depiction, in spirit if not in historical authenticity, of the plight of the farmer. The southerner of the title is not only the heroic Scott, but also the angry Naish (who, like all Renoir's "evil" characters, has his reasons for being so), the obstinate grandmother, and the unbreakable Field. As with such great pictures as OUR DAILY BREAD, THE GRAPES OF WRATH and the brilliant government documentaries of Pare Lorentz to which THE SOUTHERNER is most similar (PLOW THAT BROKE THE PLAINS and THE RIVER), this picture makes characters of the land, the cotton, the plow, and the water, granting them the same importance as the actors. In THE SOUTHERNER, man is just another element which makes up the whole of the natural world; he is not in control of the divine elements but subject to them. With the original Hugo Butler script (he later dropped out of the production, in reverence to Renoir who, Butler felt, could rewrite the script however he pleased) of the Perry novel Hold Autumn in Your Hand, Renoir and his producers, Loew and Hakim, were able to convince Hollywood to make their film.

Not surprisingly, Renoir, a native of France who had only been in the US since 1940, found it difficult to fully capture the dialogue and dialect of the southern people. Nunnally Johnson, who had scripted THE GRAPES OF WRATH, was first brought in, followed by William Faulkner (both received no screen credit), who that year also had a hand in THE MALTESE FALCON and TO HAVE AND HAVE NOT. Faulkner, who had known Renoir since the director's first American film, SWAMP WATER, and felt he was the greatest contemporary director, would later remark that working on THE SOUTHERNER had given him more pleasure than any other Hollywood production.

SPACEBALLS
1987 96m c   ★★
Comedy   PG
MGM/Brookfilms

Mel Brooks (President Skroob/Yogurt), John Candy (Barf the Mawg, Copilot), Rick Moranis (Lord Dark Helmet), Bill Pullman (Lone Starr, Space Bum), Daphne Zuniga (Princess Vespa), Dick Van Patten (King Roland, Ruler of Druidia), George Wyner (Col. Sandurz), Michael Winslow (Radar Technician), Lorene Yarnell (Dot Matrix, Droid Maid), John Hurt (Himself)

p, Mel Brooks; d, Mel Brooks; w, Mel Brooks, Thomas Meehan, Ronny Graham; ph, Nick McLean (Metrocolor); ed, Conrad Buff; m, John Morris; prod d, Terence Marsh; art d, Harold Michelson; fx, Peter Albiez, Richard Ratliff, Rick Lazzarini, Craig Boyajian, Apogee, Robert Shepherd, Percy Angress, Industrial Light & Magic; cos, Donfeld

Vaudeville pratfalls, sight gags, and ribald one-liners have always been producer-director Mel Brooks's mainstay. Here the jokes are tossed haphazardly from Brooks's gag bag and roll out ineffectively in a spoof of the "Star Wars" films. The plot, such as it is, offers pretty princess Vespa (Daphne Zuniga), daughter of kindly King Roland (Dick Van Patten), as a kidnap victim of evil Dark Helmet (Rick Moranis). Space adventurer Lone Starr (Bill Pullman) and his sidekick, Barf the Mawg (John Candy), are assigned to retrieve Vespa. Thus begins a ridiculous odyssey through space with blazing rockets, death rays, and firefights among the stars, resulting in a slaphappy ending. This is a formula film for Brooks, one that has long ago worn out its welcome with viewers. Only Brooks shines momentarily as the president of the planet Spaceball and, in a dual role, as that of his crinkled, ancient adviser, Yogurt. It's mostly forced humor all the way, a movie that rarely measures up to adequate kitsch. Aimed at younger audiences, SPACEBALLS misses its mark.

SPARTACUS
1960 196m c   ★★★★½
Historical/War   /PG
Bryna

Kirk Douglas (*Spartacus*), Laurence Olivier (*Marcus Licinius Crassus*), Tony Curtis (*Antoninus*), Jean Simmons (*Varinia*), Charles Laughton (*Gracchus*), Peter Ustinov (*Lentulus Batiatus*), John Gavin (*Julius Caesar*), Nina Foch (*Helena Glabrus*), Herbert Lom (*Tigranes*), John Ireland (*Crixus*)

p, Edward Lewis; d, Stanley Kubrick, Anthony Mann (uncredited); w, Dalton Trumbo (based on the novel by Howard Fast); ph, Russell Metty, Clifford Stine (Super Technirama-70, Technicolor); ed, Robert Lawrence, Robert Schulte, Fred Chulack; m, Alex North; prod d, Alexander Golitzen; art d, Eric Orbom; cos, Bill Thomas, Valles

Although this is the only one of Stanley Kubrick's pictures over which he did not have complete control (he was brought in by Kirk Douglas to direct when Anthony Mann was fired after the first week of shooting), SPARTACUS is still a remarkable epic—one of the greatest tales of the ancient world ever to hit the screen. It's especially strong, and more typical of Kubrick in the first half—before wiliness gives in to sentiment. But later the stars start flooding the cartoon; there's more than enough to keep you satisfied, even if the pace slackens.

It tells the true story of a slave rebellion that panicked Rome for more than two years circa 73 BC, though some historical facts have been Hollywoodized (including Spartacus' demise—he was hacked to death in battle, not crucified). Spartacus (Douglas) is a rebellious Libyan slave purchased by Lentulus Batiatus (Peter Ustinov), the proprietor of a school for gladiators. Like his fellow trainees, he is rigorously trained in fighting skills in order to be profitably peddled to Roman coliseum owners. Discovering in himself and his fellow gladiators a spark of human dignity, Spartacus helps to lead a revolt and organize an army of slaves that will descend on Rome and liberate all oppressed men from the tyrannical rule of the patricians, specifically Marcus Crassus (Laurence Olivier). Also playing parts in this battle between free will and oppression are Gracchus (Charles Laughton), a senator engaged in a political power struggle with Crassus; Varinia (Jean Simmons), the beautiful slave and wife of Spartacus whom Crassus previously arranged to purchase; and young Julius Caesar (John Gavin), a student of Gracchus who later allies himself with Crassus.

More visually restrained than usual for Kubrick (the Technirama equipment made camera movement difficult), SPARTACUS instead concentrates on the *mise-en-scene*, most notably in the preparation of the massive final battle scene, as the various Roman military units position themselves like pieces on some gigantic chessboard. SPARTACUS today remains a stirring, intelligent comment on the spirit of revolt. Olivier contributes another of his fascists—what he's best at, after all. Jean Simmons is at the peak of her beauty and spirituality; if we had never known Elizabeth Taylor's exoticism, Simmons might be one of our greatest stars. For boy-watchers, beside Douglas's lean muscle scenes, there's Curtis as Olivier's boy-toy, and Gavin, who plays Caesar as a sort of ancient Roman Kennedy star-politician. The funniest bit is when Ustinov and Laughton—both fat and splendid as ever—discuss the benefits of weightiness, which they both have down in every way. The Hearst estate, San Simeon, was used for some locations and there's fine score by Alex North.

SPELLBOUND
1945 111m bw   ★★★★
Thriller   /PG
Selznick/Vanguard

Ingrid Bergman (*Dr. Constance Peterson*), Gregory Peck (*John "J.B." Ballantine*), Jean Acker (*Matron*), Donald Curtis (*Harry*), Rhonda Fleming (*Mary Carmichael*), John Emery (*Dr. Fleurot*), Leo G. Carroll (*Dr. Murchison*), Norman Lloyd (*Garmes*), Steven Geray (*Dr. Graff*), Paul Harvey (*Dr. Hanish*)

p, David O. Selznick; d, Alfred Hitchcock; w, Ben Hecht, Angus Macphail (based on the novel *The House of Dr. Edwardes* by Francis Beeding [Hilary St. George Saunders, John Palmer]); ph, George Barnes, Rex Wimpy (uncredited); ed, William Ziegler, Hal C. Kern; m, Miklos Rozsa; prod d, James Basevi; art d, John Ewing; fx, Jack Cosgrove; cos, Howard Greer

An intriguing Hitchcock thriller which probes the dark recesses of a man's mind through psychoanalytic treatment and the love of a woman. Dr. Edwardes (Peck), a young psychiatrist, begins a new assignment as the director of a modern mental asylum. His behavior, however, is rather strange and eccentric, causing Dr. Peterson (Bergman), a brilliant but emotionally icy doctor, to grow suspicious. When she discovers that the doctor's real initials are J.B., she doubts that he is really Dr. Edwardes. She wonders not only what happened to Dr. Edwardes, but who J.B. really is, thereby involving herself professionally and emotionally as she falls in love with J.B. while digging into his past.

Generated by David O. Selznick, who purchased the rights because of his keen interest in psychoanalysis, the film often gets bogged down in psychiatric and psychoanalytic jargon, but it is counterbalanced by the love story that develops between J.B. and Dr. Peterson. Depending on the viewer's preference, the breakthrough to J.B.'s mystery can be credited to one of two things: the success of modern psychiatry or the power of love. As Hitchcock describes it, the film is "a manhunt story wrapped up in pseudo-psychoanalysis." Although heavy on dialogue, it is not without some brilliant visual touches, most obviously the heralded dream sequence created by avant-garde artist Salvador Dali. In its original conception it was far longer and more complex than the two-minute sequence that finally appeared. It was to have run 22 minutes (much of which was actually shot but edited out) and included a disturbing sequence described by Hitchcock: "He [Dali] wanted a statue to crack like a shell falling apart, with ants crawling all over it, and underneath, there would be Ingrid Bergman, covered by ants! It just wasn't possible." As it happened, Hitchcock did not even shoot the dream sequence, returning instead to London. The brilliant visual stylist Josef von Sternberg was first considered as the director of the sequence, but William Cameron Menzies (THINGS TO COME) was finally chosen, though he later expressed dissatisfaction and asked that his name be removed from the credits.

SPETTERS

1980 109m c ★★★
Drama R/18
VSE (Netherlands)

Toon Agterberg (Eve), Maarten Spanjer (Hans), Hans Van Tongeren (Reen), Marianne Boyer (Maya), Renee Soutendijk (Fientje), Jeroen Krabbe (Henkhof), Rutger Hauer (Witkamp), Peter Tuinman, Yvonne Valkenberg, Rudi Falkenhagen

p, Joop Van Den Ende; d, Paul Verhoeven; w, Gerard Soeteman; ph, Jost Vacano (Eastmancolor); ed, Ine Schenkkan; m, Ton Scherpenzeel; art d, Dick Schillemans, Peter Jasuai; cos, Yan Tax

A flashy, fast-paced drama, SPETTERS is the story of Dutch teenage motorcycle enthusiasts Eve (Toon Agterberg), Hans (Maarten Spanjer), and Reen (Hans Van Tongeren), all of whom dream of being as tough and successful as motorcycle champ Witkamp (Rutger Hauer). Their youthful rebellion ends tragically for both Reen, who is crippled in an accident, and Eve, who is raped, beaten, and killed by a gang of violent homosexuals. Providing a sexual outlet for the teenagers, and just about every other biker on the wharf, is Fientje (Renee Soutendijk), a conniving creature who runs a greasy spoon with her gay brother. SPETTERS is a violent, action-packed assault on the sensibilities of all but the most hardened filmgoers, not surprising given that it was directed by Paul Verhoeven, who would go on to score a major success in the US with his ultraviolent ROBOCOP (1987). Here he demonstrates his penchant for startling visuals, explicit sex, and graphic violence, though his intelligent direction is anything but careless or irresponsible. The beautiful blonde Soutendijk and Jeroen Krabbe would later costar again in another Verhoeven film, THE FOURTH MAN.

SPIRAL STAIRCASE, THE

1946 83m bw ★★★★★
Thriller /PG
RKO/Vanguard

Dorothy McGuire (Helen Capel), George Brent (Prof. Warren), Ethel Barrymore (Mrs. Warren), Kent Smith (Dr. Parry), Rhonda Fleming (Blanche), Gordon Oliver (Steve Warren), Elsa Lanchester (Mrs. Oates), James Bell (Constable), Charles Wagenheim (Desk Clerk), Ellen Corby (Neighbor)

p, Dore Schary; d, Robert Siodmak; w, Mel Dinelli (based on the novel Some Must Watch by Ethel Lina White); ph, Nicholas Musuraca; ed, Harry Marker, Harry Gerstad; m, Roy Webb; art d, Albert S. D'Agostino, Jack Okey; fx, Vernon L. Walker

The setting in this suspense-filled film is an old, dark Gothic mansion located in New England at the turn of the century. Young innocent Helen Capel (McGuire), long ago made mute due to a childhood trauma, is a servant for Mrs. Warren (Barrymore), a cantankerous, widowed invalid. The wealthy widow has two sons: one (Oliver), a hell-raiser, and the other (Brent), a gentle professor for whom Helen carries a secret torch. When three local girls—all physically handicapped—are murdered, everyone worries that Helen will be next. The tension builds as her suspicion of the killer's identity proves wrong and she is forced to confront the real madman.

Dorothy McGuire, one of the finest actresses of her day, gives a touching and totally convincing pantomime performance as the victimized mute in this prototype old-dark-house thriller. Not one thriller convention has been neglected in a picture that is virtually

guaranteed to suffuse audiences with gooseflesh: creaking doors, wind-gusted curtains, flickering candles, cutaways to the menacing eyes of the unseen, unknown murdering maniac, every element of terror is in place. Director Robert Siodmak, a gifted craftsman noted for his expressionistic style, had made a number of atmospheric suspense films for Universal before joining with producer Dory Schary and RKO for this one. Ethel Barrymore, Elsa Lanchester, and George Brent all turn in brilliant performances. Author White's novel was substantially modified for the film; in the book, the menaced serving girl had been a cripple rather than a mute, and the setting was contemporary England. Dismally remade in Britain in 1975 under the direction of Peter Collinson.

SPIRIT OF ST. LOUIS, THE

1957 135m c ★★★½
Biography /U
WB

James Stewart (Charles A. Lindbergh), Murray Hamilton (Bud Gurney), Patricia Smith (Mirror Girl), Bartlett Robinson (B.F. Mahoney), Robert Cornthwaite (Knight), Sheila Bond (Model/Dancer), Marc Connelly (Father Hussman), Arthur Space (Donald Hall), Harlan Warde (Boedecker), Dabbs Greer (Goldsborough)

p, Leland Hayward; d, Billy Wilder; w, Billy Wilder, Wendell Mayes, Charles Lederer (based on the book by Charles A. Lindbergh); ph, Robert Burks, Peverell Marley (CinemaScope, Warner Color); ed, Arthur Schmidt; m, Franz Waxman; art d, Art Loel; fx, H.F. Koenekamp, Louis Lichtenfield

Billy Wilder's re-creation of Charles A. Lindbergh's 1927 solo flight from New York to Paris is an intelligent piece, marked by James Stewart's strong performance as the brave pilot. The story, based on Lindbergh's autobiography, opens as Lindbergh is working as an airmail pilot. His flying goals go well beyond his mail route, however, and he begins to think about a solo voyage across the Atlantic, something no single pilot has ever accomplished. Lindbergh tries to find financial backers for his dream and, after much struggle, finds a willing group in St. Louis, Missouri. He has a special plane built for the trip, dubbing it The Spirit of St. Louis in honor of his backers. On the day he is to take off from New York, Lindbergh is forced to spend some time on the ground while waiting for the rain to stop and, in flashback, reflects on his career.

This is a well-told story, capturing the thoughts and feelings of a man alone under the most extraordinary conditions. Stewart is sincere and thoughtful in his depiction of the 1920s' greatest hero, and Wilder's direction shows the monotony of the flight while largely sidestepping the tedium which ever threatens to emerge. Perhaps the real star, though, is Waxman's marvelous score. The film gives a complete picture of Lindbergh, one that shows this dangerous journey to be the fulfillment of a devotion to and pure love of flying. The film was nominated for a Best Special Effects Oscar.

SPIRIT OF THE BEEHIVE, THE

(EL ESPIRITU DE LA COLMENA)
1976 98m c ★★★★
Drama /AA
Ellas Querejeta (Spain)

Ana Torrent *(Ana)*, Isabel Telleria *(Isabel)*, Fernando Fernan Gomez *(Fernando)*, Teresa Gimpera *(Teresa)*, Jose Villasante *(the Monster)*, Lally Soldavilla *(Milagros)*, Juan Margallo *(the Fugitive)*, Miguel Picazo *(the Doctor)*

p, Elias Querejeta; d, Victor Erice; w, Francisco J. Querejeta (based on an idea by Erice, Angel Fernandez Santos); ph, Luis Cuadrado (Eastmancolor); ed, Pablo del Amo; m, Luis de Pablo; art d, Adolfo Cofino

Praised by some as the greatest movie ever to come out of Spain, THE SPIRIT OF THE BEEHIVE is a haunting, atmospheric film that focuses on a young girl's obsession with the Frankenstein monster. Ana (the stunning Ana Torrent), a charming eight-year-old, lives in a Castillian village in 1940, just after the end of the Spanish Civil War. Although the village has been spared the destruction of battle, the after-effects of war are still felt, and the villagers buckle under Francoist repression. Ana's mother (Teresa Gimpera) shares a dream world with an imaginary lover; her father (Fernando Fernan Gomez) tends a beehive and ponders existence in an ongoing work he calls "The Spirit of the Beehive." After watching the 1931 James Whale-Boris Karloff version of FRANKENSTEIN, Ana begins to worry about the monster, and returns daily to the old house where her 10-year-old sister (Isabel Telleria) says he can be found. Eventually, an escaped convict becomes a surrogate for the monster, but though he is killed, Ana continues to cling to the idea that the monster's spirit exists, holding on to the power of imagination. Slow-moving but lyrical, Victor Erice's stunning feature-film directorial debut carefully re-creates the post-Civil War period, but much more is at work here than appears at first glance. SPIRIT OF THE BEEHIVE is a thought-provoking, highly symbolic work about the isolation engendered by Franco's stultifying reign, made by one of a generation of Spanish filmmakers forced to cloak their political messages in allegory.

SPITFIRE
1943 90m bw   ★★★½
War/Biography   /A
Misbourne/British Aviation (U.K.)

Leslie Howard *(R.J. Mitchell)*, David Niven *(Geoffrey Crisp)*, Rosamund John *(Diana Mitchell)*, Roland Culver *(Cmdr. Bride)*, Anne Firth *(Miss Harper)*, David Horne *(Higgins)*, J.H. Roberts *(Sir Robert MacLean)*, Derrick de Marney *(S.L. Jefferson)*, Rosalyn Boulter *(Mabel Livesey)*, Tonie Edgar Bruce *(Lady Houston)*

p, Leslie Howard, George King, John Stafford, Adrian Brunel; d, Leslie Howard; w, Anatole de Grunwald, Miles Malleson (based on a story by Henry C. James, Katherine Strueby); ph, Georges Perinal; ed, Douglas Myers; m, William Walton; art d, Paul Sheriff

Leslie Howard, who also produced and directed here, made his last screen appearance in this above-average biography with a strong propaganda message. Howard plays R.J. Mitchell, who designed the Spitfire fighter plane, the weapon that would foil Hitler's plans to invade England by air. The film opens as a squadron of fighter pilots sits at a base, awaiting the next wave of German planes. Squadron leader Geoffrey Crisp (David Niven) begins to tell the men about his close friend Mitchell, the designer of their craft, and the details of the origin of the Spitfire are related in a lengthy flashback that makes up most of the film's running time. This was Howard's last film before he was shot out of the sky by the Luftwaffe while returning from a semi-secret diplomatic mission in Lisbon. (There are rumors that the Germans knew Churchill was to be attending a meeting in Casablanca and that Howard's plane was used as a decoy.) Niven

was actually detached from the service to appear in SPITFIRE, and his smooth performance is probably the best in the film. Howard's direction is assured and keeps the story from getting bogged down in its message. The score, by "serious" composer William Walton, is superb.

SPLASH
1984 111m c   ★★★½
Fantasy/Comedy/Romance   PG
Touchstone

Tom Hanks *(Allen Bauer)*, Daryl Hannah *(Madison)*, Eugene Levy *(Walter Kornbluth)*, John Candy *(Freddie Bauer)*, Dody Goodman *(Mrs. Stimler)*, Shecky Greene *(Mr. Buyrite)*, Richard B. Shull *(Dr. Ross)*, Bobby Di Cicco *(Jerry)*, Howard Morris *(Dr. Zidell)*, Tony DiBenedetto *(Tim the Doorman)*

p, Brian Grazer; d, Ron Howard; w, Lowell Ganz, Babaloo Mandel, Bruce Jay Friedman (based on the story by Grazer, Friedman); ph, Don Peterman (Technicolor); ed, Daniel Hanley, Michael Hill; m, Lee Holdridge; prod d, Jack T. Collis; art d, John B. Mansbridge; fx, Mitch Suskin; cos, May Routh, Charles De Muth, Jody Berke

An "alien" picture from an alien source (Disney with a new moniker), SPLASH, for all its nudity and hip humor, is a throwback to pictures of days past such as NEPTUNE'S DAUGHTER (1914) and MR. PEABODY AND THE MERMAID (1948). Nevertheless, young viewers who never heard of the aforementioned thought that this film was wildly creative and flocked to the theaters. The premise is simple: boy meets girl, boy falls for girl, but girl is not girl at all—she's a mermaid. Mermaid Madison (Daryl Hannah) meets Allen Bauer (Tom Hanks), a bright, young man who is a wholesale fruit and vegetable dealer in New York. Allen works with his brother, Freddie (John Candy), a smarmy playboy pudge. Madison is human when on dry land but the moment she is touched by saltwater, she reverts to her half-woman, half-fish form. Walter Kornbluth (Eugene Levy), a scientist who suspects that Madison is a mermaid, tracks her and Allen until he finally pours water on Madison, transforming her in front of hundreds on a New York street. Naturally, some mean government types get interested at this point. Director Ron Howard has a good sense of the whimsical, and his film is sweet and unpretentious, though somewhat ribald when one realizes the studio from whence it sprang.

SPLENDOR IN THE GRASS
1961 124m c   ★★★
Drama   /X
NBI/Newton

Natalie Wood *(Wilma Dean Loomis)*, Warren Beatty *(Bud Stamper)*, Pat Hingle *(Ace Stamper)*, Audrey Christie *(Mrs. Loomis)*, Barbara Loden *(Ginny Stamper)*, Zohra Lampert *(Angelina)*, Fred Stewart *(Del Loomis)*, Joanna Roos *(Mrs. Stamper)*, Jan Norris *(Juanita Howard)*, Gary Lockwood *(Toots)*

p, Elia Kazan; d, Elia Kazan; w, William Inge; ph, Boris Kaufman (Technicolor); ed, Gene Milford; m, David Amram; art d, Richard Sylbert; chor, George Tapps; cos, Anna Hill Johnstone

SPLENDOR IN THE GRASS had a few firsts attached to it. It was Beatty's debut in the movies; it was Inge's first work done specifically for the screen; and it was Kazan's first picture that failed ultimately to satisfy. The title is taken from a William Wordsworth poem which reads: "There's nothing can bring back the hour / Of splendor in the grass, of glory in the flower / We will grieve not, but rather find / Strength in what remains behind." Beatty was in his early twenties and had just appeared in Inge's play "A Loss of Roses" in 1959, after having been discovered by Josh Logan and Inge while working in a small playhouse in New Jersey. Despite that play's failure, Inge was mesmerized by Beatty and wrote this screenplay for him. Later, he would adapt James Leo Herlihy's novel *All Fall Down* into a screenplay for Beatty after Beatty himself had impressed another epicene playwright, Tennessee Williams, sufficiently to get the plum role in THE ROMAN SPRING OF MRS. STONE. While making this film, Beatty began the off-screen amours that have since become legendary. Wood was married to Robert Wagner (the first time around) and she was the first of many who would fall for Beatty.

A steamy story of repressed sexuality, the film takes place in 1925, in Kansas, where Inge grew up. Beatty and Wood are high schoolers who fall in love and attempt to keep their affection on an intellectual level, for they fear it would be wrong to express their physical needs. Wood is the daughter of shrew Christie, a domineering woman who pushes her husband, Stewart, around and who continuously warns Wood against having relations with men. Beatty's father is wealthy Hingle, a blustering Midwest businessman who is stupid despite his money. Hingle discourages Beatty's love for Wood and suggests that the boy go back east, attend Yale, and if he still wants Wood after four years in New Haven, they can talk about it then. Wood and Beatty try to keep their love pristine and unsullied, and the frustration takes its toll. Since they can't get married and are having increasing difficulty denying their sexual desires, they stop seeing each other. Beatty develops pneumonia, then begins squiring Norris, who has slept with just about everyone in the county. Wood attempts to take her own life, then has a total nervous collapse and goes to an institution for mental rehabilitation. Time passes, and several calamities befall Beatty. His amoral sister, Loden, dies in an auto accident (Loden is Kazan's second wife), and when Hingle's vast fortune is obliterated by the stock market debacle in October, 1929, Hingle kills himself. Beatty quits Yale and marries Lampert, an Italian waitress from New Haven (Lampert's performance is the best acting in the movie) who is a refreshing change from the constrained types of Kansas. Wood gets out of the mental hospital and one of her pals from the sanitarium, Robinson, proposes marriage. Wood thinks about it for a while, then decides that she can't make that kind of move until she sees Beatty again.

In small bits, note Phyllis Diller as Texas Guinan, Sandy Dennis in her first film, and Gary Lockwood in his third. Youth exploitation pictures were all the rage at the time, and while this is somewhat above the others in execution and intent, it's still exactly that.

SPRINGTIME IN THE ROCKIES

1942 91m c   ★★★½
Musical   /U
FOX

Betty Grable *(Vicky)*, John Payne *(Dan)*, Carmen Miranda *(Rosita)*, Cesar Romero *(Victor)*, Charlotte Greenwood *(Phoebe Gray)*, Edward Everett Horton *(McTavish)*, Frank Orth *(Bickle)*, Harry Hayden *(Brown)*, Jackie Gleason *(Dan's Agent)*, Chick Chandler *(Stage Manager)*

p, William LeBaron; d, Irving Cummings; w, Walter Bullock, Ken Englund, Jacques Thery (based on a story by Philip Wylie); ph, Ernest Palmer (Technicolor); ed, Robert Simpson; art d, Richard Day, Joseph C. Wright; chor, Hermes Pan

Grable and Payne are a pair of Broadway performers and lovers who prove the truth of the old saying that those who love together

also fight together. The biggest problem seems to be that Payne can't keep his mind off other women, which piques Grable to no end. To get even, she hooks up with Romero as though she intends to marry him. Payne retaliates by romancing his Brazilian secretary, Miranda. Though the premise is slight, music, dance, comedy, and even some drama are combined in a very astute manner. Much of the action is played out against the backdrop of Lake Louise, Alberta, and Palmer's Technicolor cinematography fills the screen with the beauty of the Canadian Rockies. The story sets up Grable and Romero as dancing partners, and they do a little hoofing to the accompaniment of Harry James and His Music Makers. This was the first film to give Grable top billing, and it's still easy to see why she became a wartime favorite, even if the irrepressible Miranda does steal the film.

SPY WHO CAME IN FROM THE COLD, THE

1965 112m bw   ★★★★
Spy   /A
Salem (U.K.)

Richard Burton *(Alec Leamas)*, Claire Bloom *(Nan Perry)*, Oskar Werner *(Fiedler)*, Peter Van Eyck *(Hans-Dieter Mundt)*, Sam Wanamaker *(Peters)*, George Voskovec *(East German Defense Attorney)*, Rupert Davies *(Smiley)*, Cyril Cusack *(Control)*, Michael Hordern *(Ashe)*, Robert Hardy *(Carlton)*

p, Martin Ritt; d, Martin Ritt; w, Paul Dehn, Guy Trosper (based on the novel by John Le Carre); ph, Oswald Morris; ed, Anthony Harvey; m, Sol Kaplan; prod d, Hal Pereira, Tambi Larsen; art d, Edward Marshall; cos, Motley

Gripping grit, with a perfect performance from Burton, before Liz and alcohol robbed him of his center.

Spying is a grim, desperate business that is at once boring and exciting, with dirty work behind the scenes and hardly any derring-do. This superb adaptation of John Le Carre's novel artfully conveys that sense. Audiences must have preferred the more glamorous spies like James Bond because this film, which was one of the best ever made on the subject, failed to gather much interest at the box office. Produced and directed by Martin Ritt in Ireland and England, with some second-unit lensing in Europe, the film stars Richard Burton as a burnt-out case, a man who is looking forward to getting out of the spy game and retiring from British Intelligence. Just before he is to leave, Burton is called back to London and put on the carpet. It seems that several of his sub-agents have been caught by Van Eyck, who is Burton's counterpart on the East Berlin side. Van Eyck is a former Nazi who has taken over as chief of operations for the Communists, and his handiwork is putting a crimp in the British operations. Since it is well known that Burton is tired of what he's doing, Burton's boss, Cusack, gives him his final assignment. He is to masquerade as a drunk who wants to defect to the East Germans. If it works and Burton gets inside the Communist operations, he can find out if there is a "mole" in their own organization as well as get the goods on what's happening inside the East German operation. As part of his cover, Burton takes a job at a library and there meets Bloom, a member of the Communist party. He has a fling with her, then later, acting the drunken bully, he beats a shopkeeper and ends up in jail. When he is released, he is contacted by East German agents who believe he is ready to defect. He is taken to East Berlin, where he is grilled by Werner, Van Eyck's top assistant. Werner is convinced that Van Eyck is a double agent and believes Burton can provide information proving his theory. Burton genuinely believes the idea is absurd and continually insists that to Werner. Nevertheless, Werner has gathered enough evidence to have Van Eyck arrested, and a trial is begun to determine Van Eyck's fate. Burton is stunned when Bloom is brought in to testify at the trial, and he suddenly realizes his bosses have set him up—Van Eyck is indeed a double agent, and the whole plot has been constructed to discredit Werner, who is getting too close to the truth.

Burton's performance garnered him one of his five Oscar nominations (he lost that year to Lee Marvin in CAT BALLOU—an amazing example of middle-class taste). It's sad Burton never won, sad because one suspects a low self-belief at work in him. He probably drank to quell the early demons of deprivation, but could not obliterate them enough to still the pain. He had been touted as the next Olivier (we think he's *far* more interesting—and conveys heart behind the technique), before settling for celebrity as Taylor's consort. An affirmation of worth from Hollywood might have told Burton his talent not only was always apparent, but superceded his celebrity status.

There are no gimmicks, no fast cars that turn into airplanes, no weapons that fire lasers, just a tense battle of wits shot in stark black and white. The title refers to the time when an outside spy has to "come in from the cold" and take a sedentary job as another spy's control or even some menial desk assignment until the mandatory age limit forces retirement. Only Graham Greene has come close to Le Carre in detailing the emotional drudgery of the espionage world. The semidocumentary fashion in which Morris shot the film added to the believability of the story and won him the British Film Academy's award for best black-and-white cinematography.

SPY WHO LOVED ME, THE

1977 125m c   ★★
Spy   PG
Eon (U.K.)

Roger Moore *(James Bond)*, Barbara Bach *(Maj. Anya Amasova)*, Curt Jurgens *(Karl Stromberg)*, Richard Kiel *(Jaws)*, Caroline Munro *(Naomi)*, Walter Gotell *(Gen. Gogol)*, Geoffrey Keen *(Minister of Defense)*, Bernard Lee *("M")*, Shane Rimmer *(Capt. Carter)*, Bryan Marshall *(Commander Talbot)*

p, Albert R. Broccoli; d, Lewis Gilbert; w, Christopher Wood, Richard Maibaum (based on the novel by Ian Fleming); ph, Lamar Boren, Claude Renoir (Panavision, Eastmancolor); ed, John Glen; m, Marvin Hamlisch; prod d, Ken Adam; art d, Peter Lamont; fx, Derek Meddings, Alan Maley, John Evans; cos, Ronald Paterson

James Bond (Moore) teams with a beautiful Russian secret agent, Maj. Anya Amasova (Bach), to stop the Captain Nemo-esque Karl Stromberg (Jurgens) from using two stolen nuclear-armed submarines to destroy life on the Earth's surface so he can create an undersea kingdom. Stromberg dispatches 7-foot-2-inch, steel-toothed Jaws (Kiel) to take Bond out of the picture, and 007 leads the indestructible behemoth on a globe-trotting chase.

As the Bond series moved deeper into the 1970s, the emphasis moved away from the inventive scripts that made the best Sean Connery films fine examples of the spy genre and toward the kind of feats of daring and visual spectacle that abound in THE SPY WHO LOVED ME. Take for example Bond's daring jump off a 90-foot cliff, a feat that ski jumper Rick Sylvester was paid $30,000 to accomplish and which took 10 days to shoot. The largest studio set to date was also built to house the submarines and for Stromberg's menacing headquarters, and shooting was done in Egypt, Sardinia, Malta, Scotland, Okinawa, Switzerland, and Nassau; yet the film is probably best remembered for Carly Simon's hit theme song, "Nobody Does It Better" (Marvin Hamlisch, Carole Bayer Sager), which was nominated for an Oscar. Nominations also went to the art direction and score.

STAGE DOOR

1937 83m bw   ★★★★★
Comedy/Drama   /U
RKO

Katharine Hepburn *(Terry Randall)*, Ginger Rogers *(Joan Maitland)*, Adolphe Menjou *(Anthony Powell)*, Gail Patrick *(Linda Shaw)*, Constance Collier *(Catherine Luther)*, Andrea Leeds *(Kaye Hamilton)*, Samuel S. Hinds *(Henry Sims)*, Lucille Ball *(Judy Canfield)*, Pierre Watkin *(Richard Carmichael)*, Franklin Pangborn *(Harcourt)*

p, Pandro S. Berman; d, Gregory La Cava; w, Morrie Ryskind, Anthony Veiller, Gregory La Cava (based on the play by Edna Ferber, George S. Kaufman); ph, Robert de Grasse; ed, William Hamilton; art d, Van Nest Polglase, Carroll Clark; cos, Muriel King

A stellar cast, superb direction, and a screenplay that was even better than the stage play upon which it was based all add up to one of the best movies about show business or about women living together ever made. Hepburn is a wealthy debutante from an important family. She has come to New York to seek a career on the stage and, rather than take a Park Avenue apartment far removed from the mainstream, she checks into a theatrical boarding house for young, aspiring actresses. The luck of the draw puts her in a room with Rogers (in one of her finest performances), a sarcastic tough cookie who heckles everyone. The two of them are like flint and steel and are close to hair-pulling on a few occasions. All the actresses in the boarding house spend most of their time discussing work, food and potential husbands. But the ins and outs of their professional lives are central. Ball (who was appearing in her twenty-seventh movie at the age of 27) has been invited to dinner by some lumber barons from the Northwest and she asks Rogers to double date with her. Rogers has a short fuse, and there is no mistaking her likes and dislikes. Among the latter is Patrick, who is more of a mistress to Broadway producer Menjou than she is an actual working actress. Leeds hasn't worked for more than 12 months and she's trying to save some money, so she often forgoes meals. She thinks she may have a chance for the ingenue lead in a new play Menjou is planning, "Enchanted April." (The actual play shown was a rewrite of *The Lake,* a failed Hepburn vehicle that she starred in after making SPITFIRE.)

Rogers and Miller audition for Menjou with the Hal Borne-Mort Greene song "Put Your Heart Into Your Feet and Dance," and he is taken by them, especially by Rogers. He gets them a job at a nightspot in which he has a financial stake. Menjou asks Rogers for a date and she accepts—not that she finds the old lecher attractive, she just wants to make sure she and Miller get the dance job and she also wants to give the needle to Patrick. Soon Patrick is replaced by Rogers, and fumes about the turn of events. Leeds and Hepburn go together to audition for Menjou's play, but the reading is cancelled. Leeds faints from hunger in the reception area and Hepburn promptly tells Menjou off for the cavalier fashion in which he treats actors. Although he's in his office and apparently not busy, he is sending the actors away as a power play. Now attorney Watkin enters the picture, telling Menjou that a wealthy client, Hinds (who is Hepburn's father), will back Menjou's show if Hepburn is hired for the lead.

Directing his first film since MY MAN GODFREY, La Cava showed that he could handle a large group of actors as well as he could do a straight two-lead comedy. So much work was done on the script that co-author of the play George S. Kaufman suggested waggishly that it should have been called "Screen Door." Legend has it that La Cava ordered the actresses to the studio for two weeks of rehearsal and familiarization with the boarding house set. Then he had a stenographer take their dialogue down as they sat around between rehearsals, and their words were incorporated into the script. The large cast, chosen with exquisite care, included Eve Arden (in her fourth film and already taking out a patent on her particular form of comedy), Franklin Pangborn, Grady Sutton, and Jean Rouverol, who later became a well-known screenwriter with her husband, Hugo Butler. For years, impressions of Hepburn have used the line she speaks in while acting onstage: "The calla lillies are in bloom again." The best line in the film, though, is Rogers' marvelous barb to a friend over the phone when Gail Patrick enters the scene: "Hold on, gangrene just set in." The best prop, meanwhile, is the cat forever draped over Eve Arden's shoulders. A brilliant script and strong, realistic acting make this film a treat to the eyes and ears, and it affords the additional pleasure of seeing all those future stars like Ball, Miller, Arden, and Jack Carson in their early days. It's amazing how many ideas, laughs, tears, and genuine "moments" can be packed into just 83 minutes, given the talents of giants. What *is* the best way to say "Let's go up to Westchester?"

STAGE DOOR CANTEEN

1943 132m bw ★★★★
Musical/War /U
UA

Cheryl Walker *(Eileen)*, William Terry *(Ed "Dakota" Smith)*, Marjorie Riordan *(Jean Rule)*, Lon McCallister *("California")*, Margaret Early *(Ella Sue)*, Sunset Carson *("Texas")*, Dorothea Kent *(Mamie)*, Fred Brady *("Jersey" Wallace)*, Marion Shockley *(Lillian)*, Patrick O'Moore *(Australian)*

p, Sol Lesser; d, Frank Borzage; w, Delmer Daves; ph, Harry Wild; ed, Hal C. Kern; m, Freddie Rich; prod d, Harry Horner, Clem Beauchamp; art d, Hans Peters; cos, Albert Dano

In this boy-meets-canteen-girl story set in a Stage Door Canteen in Manhattan, three enlisted men on a one-day pass in New York fall in love with three young hostesses at the canteen. The story is nothing special, but the cast is: everybody who was anybody at the time, from Katharine Hepburn to Johnny Weissmuller to Gypsy Rose Lee to violinist Yehudi Menuhin, makes an appearance. The story is a trifle, but you'll want to see this movie in its full 132 minutes to revel in the sight of its 65 guest stars, playing themselves and seeming to have more fun than they had playing characters. The American Theatre Wing operated several Stage Door Canteens, with the flagship location on West 44th Street in Manhattan, and 90 percent of the movie's profits went back to the Theatre Wing to help defray expenses for the venues. In WWII, officers went to the officer's clubs, but at the Stage Door Canteen, you had to be ranked below officer status to be admitted. Jammed from start to finish with stars, music, laughs, tears, and pure entertainment, STAGE DOOR CANTEEN casts Cheryl Walker as Eileen, a young hostess at the Canteen who falls for soldier Dakota Smith (William Terry), while Jean Rule (Marjorie Riordan) hits it off with California (Lon McCallister) and Mamie (Dorothea Kent) goes ga-ga for Texas (Michael Harrison, aka Sunset Carson). The three soldiers meet the three women at the Canteen while on a one-day pass in New York; when their ship is delayed, they spend another day, and another, until love is in full bloom, despite the prohibition against hostesses seeing servicemen outside of the Canteen. When the boys finally do go off to war, they know the girls will be waiting for them upon their return. That's about it for plot, but writer Delmer Daves and director Frank Borzage insert into the story a cavalcade of musical and comedy numbers and many cameo appearances. In

the cameos, Katherine Cornell makes her only film appearance doing a snippet of "Romeo and Juliet," George Jessel reprises his famous phone call to "Mama," Harpo Marx runs around like a nut, George Raft is seen as a dishwasher, Lunt and Fontanne have an argument, and Paul Muni rehearses his new play. Fred Rich's score gained an Oscar nomination, as did Al Dubin and Jimmy Monaco for "We Mustn't Say Goodbye," sung by Lanny Ross.

STAGE FRIGHT

1950 111m bw ★★★★
Thriller /A
WB/First National (U.K.)

Jane Wyman *(Eve Gill/Doris Tinsdale)*, Marlene Dietrich *(Charlotte Inwood)*, Michael Wilding *(Wilfrid O. "Ordinary" Smith)*, Richard Todd *(Jonathan Cooper)*, Alastair Sim *(Commodore Gill)*, Kay Walsh *(Nellie Goode)*, Sybil Thorndike *(Mrs. Gill)*, Miles Malleson *(Mr. Fortesque)*, Hector MacGregor *(Freddie Williams)*, Joyce Grenfell *("Lovely Ducks")*

p, Alfred Hitchcock; d, Alfred Hitchcock; w, Whitfield Cook, Alma Reville, James Bridie, Ranald MacDougall (based on the stories "Man Running" and "Outrun the Constable" by Selwyn Jepson, uncredited); ph, Wilkie Cooper; ed, E.B. Jarvis; m, Leighton Lucas; cos, Christian Dior, Milo Anderson

The standard British murder mystery is raised to a higher plateau by Hitchcock in STAGE FRIGHT, but still falters in comparison to the best of the master's works. Over the opening credits a theatrical safety curtain rises, revealing not a stage but London street life—the actual stage for Hitchcock's mystery. Eve Gill (Wyman) is an acting student at the Royal Academy of Dramatic Art (RADA) when she runs into a former boyfriend, Jonathan Cooper (Todd), who explains how his mistress, stage and singing star Charlotte Inwood (Dietrich, in marvelous form), came to him wearing a dress bloodied when she killed her husband. Because of his involvement with the singer, Jonathan is suspected and must turn to Eve for help. The plot twists are many.

STAGE FRIGHT was far from being one of Hitchcock's most memorable or successful films, drawing criticism for both his provocative use of false flashbacks and the relative absence of any real threat of danger. Hitchcock's main interest in the film, and its most fascinating aspect today, is the concentration on acting and deception. Like MURDER in 1930 (and the same year's ALL ABOUT EVE), STAGE FRIGHT has an actress as the heroine. Here Eve gets her finest training not from RADA (where Hitchcock's daughter Patricia was enrolled, and where some of the film was photographed) but from real life. Her character's performance is not a simple one, forcing her to appear as something different to everyone—an actress, a maid, a Nancy Drew-type, and a newspaper reporter—with London serving as her stage, and death being her greatest fright. Shot at England's Elstree Studios, it was the last film Hitchcock shot in his home country until 1971 when he returned to film FRENZY. A special treat is Dietrich singing two of her standards: Cole Porter's "The Laziest Gal in Town" and Edith Piaf's "La Vie en Rose."

STAGECOACH

1939 97m bw ★★★★★
Western /U
UA

STAGECOACH

Claire Trevor (*Dallas*), John Wayne (*The Ringo Kid*), John Carradine (*Hatfield*), Thomas Mitchell (*Dr. Josiah Boone*), Andy Devine (*Buck Rickabaugh*), Donald Meek (*Mr. Samuel Peacock*), Louise Platt (*Lucy Mallory*), George Bancroft (*Sheriff Curly Wilcox*), Berton Churchill (*Henry Gatewood*), Tim Holt (*Lt. Blanchard*)

p, Walter Wanger; d, John Ford; w, Dudley Nichols (based on the short story "Stage to Lordsburg" by Ernest Haycox); ph, Bert Glennon; ed, Dorothy Spencer, Walter Reynolds; m, Richard Hageman, W. Franke Harling, Louis Gruenberg, Leo Shuken, John Leipold (adapted from 17 American folk tunes of the early 1880s); art d, Alexander Toluboff; fx, Ray Binger; cos, Walter Plunkett

The classic western, STAGECOACH is John Ford's greatest epic of the frontier. This western eclipsed all films in the genre that had gone before it, and so vastly influenced those that followed that its stamp can be found in most superior westerns made since Ford stepped into Monument Valley for the first time. Set in a landscape of endless horizons, STAGECOACH is a wonderful broad portrait of pioneer life in the untamed Great Southwest, as well as an in-depth character study of eight people, all diverse in their pursuits and all traveling to separate fates on a journey packed with danger.

High peril is present from the first scenes, which depict Geronimo on the warpath and the telegraph wires cut by raiding Apaches. Leaving the town of Tonto, New Mexico, are a bunch of social misfits accompanied by a few decent souls. Mitchell is a conniving, drunken doctor, long ago kicked out of the medical profession for malpractice. But he still carries with him his doctor's bag and is ready for any emergency, or so he says while cadging drinks at the local saloon. Leaving also on the stage is Trevor, a fallen lady whose sexual exploits have so unnerved the local women that they have banded together to oust her from their scandal-mongering society. Carradine, a shady gambler with the manners of a southern gentleman, has his own mysterious reasons for leaving Tonto, but pretends that the real reason is to offer Platt, who is pregnant and married to a cavalry officer, his "protection" as she travels to be with her husband. Churchill, a pompous and demanding banker with a shrewish wife, gets aboard the stagecoach carrying a small valise which is locked and which he will not let go of, while Meek carries a sample case which contains no mysterious contents, at least to Mitchell. Meek is a whiskey salesman, and Mitchell considers him the finest traveling companion a drunk could ever have. These six strangers make up the passenger list, and riding on top on the driver's seat is driver Devine—a garrulous type with an aversion to Indians—and tough, gruff, but fair-minded Bancroft, a lawman riding "shotgun," on the alert for a cowboy who has just broken out of the state penitentiary.

The stage moves off, heading for distant Lordsburg, but it travels only a few miles when, turning a bend, the travelers hear a rifle shot. The camera shows, in a marvelous tracking shot, Wayne, larger than life, stoically facing the stagecoach rushing at him. The camera assumes the position of the stagecoach coming to a halt before the cowboy. The tracking shot moves in fast on Wayne, losing focus for a moment, to stop in a closeup of Wayne looking up at US Marshal Bancroft, who holds a shotgun leveled at him. Wayne says that his horse came up lame and he needs to get to Lordsburg. He surrenders his rifle to Bancroft, who tells him he is under arrest as an escaped convict. Holt, the officer in charge of the cavalry escort, rides up to see that all is well and Bancroft assures him that it is. Wayne gets into the coach, and it departs. The stage rolls on through the great tracts of Monument Valley, huge, towering buttes jutting along the path of the scurrying coach. The coach comes to a way station,

and the passengers alight to have a meal. The proper Platt refuses to sit next to prostitute Trevor; only Wayne sits with her to eat, noticing that no one is sitting next to *him*. Wayne tells Trevor that he wishes he had met her earlier and that he used to be a good cowhand; he also tells her he won't go back to prison until he does a job in Lordsburg.

The passengers are called to the stagecoach for the continuing journey and all climb aboard. Some miles across the open desert the cavalry escort under Holt's command leaves the coach, going on its patrol in a different direction. Now the stage and its passengers are unprotected, racing along through the wild territory. Bancroft and Devine discuss the men who have killed Wayne's father and brother and are waiting in Lordsburg to kill him as well. Bancroft looks about him and, noticing snow on the ground, asks why Devine is taking the mountain road. The driver tells him its to avoid Indians. Inside the stagecoach, tensions rise as the passengers, except for Wayne, continue to show their contempt for Trevor. Meanwhile, Churchill complains about the cavalry escort leaving them, and Mitchell continues to vex liquor salesman Meek by drinking one sample after another from his liquor case.

The coach races onward, coming through a gap in the mountains to another rest station. The proprietor of the station, tells Bancroft and the others that the Apaches raided the station the night before and then tells Platt that her husband, a captain of the cavalry troop who had been stationed there, was wounded and taken to Lordsburg. Platt collapses and Bancroft carries her to a back room. Platt goes into labor and Mitchell, drunk from sampling Meek's wares, reluctantly goes to her aid. Later, when Trevor goes outside to get some air, Wayne follows her. He there haltingly tries asks her to join him at his ranch across the border, an invitation that stuns so much she can only decline. Bancroft appears, as if to tell Wayne he will never be far from him. The next morning, as the passengers prepare to leave, Trevor tells Wayne that if he leaves the station, heads for his ranch, and stays away from Lordsburg, she'll join him later. He makes a break for it, and Bancroft goes after him, finding him staring at the distant hills and telling him that the smoke rising from the hills are Indian war signals.

Ford had not directed a western in 13 years before making STAGECOACH, his last film in the genre being THREE BAD MEN. This film came as a shock to the movie community in that Ford was no longer thought of as a western director; now he had, out of the blue, so to speak, produced the greatest western ever seen. He would later state that "STAGECOACH blazed the trail for the 'adult' western," but this discounted too many great silent films of the genre, including his own and those of William S. Hart, who made many "adult" westerns, such as HELL'S HINGES and TUMBLEWEEDS. But STAGECOACH was the first western to portray in-depth characters with allegorical themes running just beneath the surface plot of their life and death struggles. Moreover, Ford employs a dazzling array of technical skills in presenting this film, as well as framing each breathtaking scene as if it were a painting. The landscape of the awesome Monument Valley serves both as a backdrop and a constant reminder of the freedom of the frontier and the dangers inherent in enjoying that freedom. No film had ever been made in this remote region, and its arid plains, 4,000 feet above sea level, and jutting buttes, some reaching 1,500 feet, startled audiences when it was first seen. During the 1880s, stagecoaches had actually crossed this enormous valley, and Ford made excellent use of the old coach trails which are seen running through the broad expanses like old scars.

Wanger later made claims that STAGECOACH was all his idea and even that he discovered Wayne in the B films. Ford angrily issued statements to the contrary, and Wanger backed away from his claims. The film established Wayne as a major talent and thrust Ford, as its premiere director, into the western-making limelight, where he remained to his death. The film suffered an abysmal remake in 1966, with Alex Cord and Ann-Margret in the lead roles and Bing Crosby in the role of the drunken doctor.

STAIRWAY TO HEAVEN

1946   104m   c/bw   ★★★★★
Fantasy/Romance   /A
Archers/Independent Producers   (U.K.)

David Niven (*Squadron Leader Peter D. Carter*), Kim Hunter (*June*), Roger Livesey (*Dr. Reeves*), Robert Coote (*Bob Trubshawe*), Marius Goring (*Conductor 71*), Raymond Massey (*Abraham Farlan*), Kathleen Byron (*An Angel*), Richard Attenborough (*English Pilot*), Bonar Colleano (*American Pilot*), Joan Maude (*Chief Recorder*)

p, Michael Powell, Emeric Pressburger; d, Michael Powell, Emeric Pressburger; w, Michael Powell, Emeric Pressburger; ph, Jack Cardiff (Technicolor); ed, Reginald Mills; m, Allan Gray; prod d, Alfred Junge; art d, Arthur Lawson; fx, Douglas Woolsey, Henry Harris; cos, Hein Heckroth

Superb, exquisitely photographed fantasy, mixing satire with enchanting romance. Made at the instigation of the Ministry of Information to promote goodwill between Britain and the US, Powell and Pressburger achieve what few have—walking the tightrope between fantasy and reality with deftness and impeccable taste. The fantasy sequences were shot in monochrome, the earthly ones in color. P&P seem to be saying the illusion is our "reality". Witnessing the evidence, it's hard to disagree with them.

The plot concerns an RAF pilot, Niven, who is forced to bail out of his flaming plane as it is dropping out of the sky. With all his fellow crew members either dead or having parachuted to safety and his own chute riddled with bullet holes, Niven gets on the radio and shares what he believes to be his last words with an American WAC, Hunter. Niven, a poet, has a romantic conversation with Hunter and falls hopelessly in love with her voice. When he finally jumps for his life, he lands in the ocean and is washed safely ashore. By some fateful coincidence he meets Hunter and the pair fall in love. Although Niven appears to be healthy, he actually is suffering from brain damage and must undergo an operation. Meanwhile, in heaven it is realized that a terrible mistake has been made, that Niven, who was scheduled to die, has somehow lived. This discovery is made by Heavenly Conductor Number 71, Goring, a Frenchman who was beheaded in his country's revolution. While Goring and his superiors debate Niven's fate, Niven argues that because of their mistake and because he has fallen in love with Hunter, he should be allowed to remain on Earth.

A fantastic accomplishment which shines with surrealistic cinematic bravura, STAIRWAY TO HEAVEN is a marvel, with a notable contribution from production designer Junge. Most remarkable is his monumental stairway which reaches majestically into the heavens and is peopled with a cast of history's dead. Niven and Livesey enjoy two of their finest roles here, Hunter is warm and appealing, Goring a quirky delight, and such actors as Coote, Massey and Abraham Sofaer (as God, no less) are clearly having a blast. Chosen as the first of the Royal Command Film Performances, STAIRWAY TO HEAVEN garnered some critical

acclaim in Britain but was generally attacked by stuffy detractors who felt it was anti-British (once again proving that the greatest harm inflicted on the always unstable British cinema is that imposed by British critics themselves, who prefer to cut down their finest directors, namely Powell and Pressburger, rather than build them up). In America, it was met with great enthusiasm and compared, somewhat unfairly, to the 1941 Robert Montgomery vehicle HERE COMES MR. JORDAN, which was remade in 1978 as HEAVEN CAN WAIT. An immensely enjoyable piece of escapist entertainment, though not without important underlying themes, which only improves with age.

STAKEOUT

1987   115m   c   ★★★½
Crime   R/15
Touchstone/Silver Screen Partners III/Buena Vista

Richard Dreyfuss (*Chris Leece*), Emilio Estevez (*Bill Reimers*), Madeleine Stowe (*Maria McGuire*), Aidan Quinn (*Richard "Stick" Montgomery*), Dan Lauria (*Phil Coldshank*), Forest Whitaker (*Jack Pismo*), Ian Tracey (*Caylor Reese*), Earl Billings (*Capt. Giles*), Jackson Davies (*FBI Agent Lusk*), J.J. Makaro

p, Jim Kouf, Cathleen Summers; d, John Badham; w, Jim Kouf; ph, John Seale (Deluxe Color); ed, Tom Rolf, Michael Ripps; m, Arthur B. Rubinstein; prod d, Philip Harrison; art d, Richard Hudolin, Michael Ritter

It doesn't matter that this film is a traditional cop vs. killer picture, since it is presented in very human terms and sparkles with top-flight performances from Richard Dreyfuss, Emilio Estevez, and Madeleine Stowe. Chris Leece (Dreyfuss) is a plainclothes detective on the Seattle police force, a man with a thankless job and an empty life until he and his partner, Bill Reimers (Estevez), are assigned to stake out the home of Maria McGuire (Stowe), the former girlfriend of escaped killer Stick Montgomery (Aidan Quinn). Chris meets Maria when he pretends to be a phone repairman and bugs her phones, and they are quickly attracted to each other. But fugitive Montgomery plans to retrieve not only the loot from his last job (hidden in Maria's apartment) but also his girl. STAKEOUT is a well-handled, quick-paced, and often funny film that accurately details the humdrum routine of police work. Director John Badham expertly mixes just the right amount of action with a very delightful romance. This movie is a virtuoso return for Dreyfuss, who is captivating in his role.

STALAG 17

1953   120m   bw   ★★★★½
Comedy/War   /PG
Paramount

William Holden (*Sefton*), Don Taylor (*Lt. Dunbar*), Otto Preminger (*Oberst Von Scherbach*), Robert Strauss (*"Animal" Stosh*), Harvey Lembeck (*Harry*), Richard Erdman (*Hoffy*), Peter Graves (*Price*), Neville Brand (*Duke*), Sig Rumann (*Schultz*), Michael Moore (*Manfredi*)

p, Billy Wilder; d, Billy Wilder; w, Billy Wilder, Edwin Blum (based on the play by Donald Bevan, Edmund Trzcinski); ph, Ernest Laszlo; ed, Doane Harrison, George Tomasini; m, Franz Waxman; art d, Hal Pereira, Franz Bachelin; fx, Gordon Jennings

The trenchant trenches of a German POW camp, uneven but not without its gallows humor fascination. Made just eight years after the end of WWII, writer-director Wilder's classic black comedy is too cross-pollinated by slapstick Germans, who interfere with the abrasive edge of satirical statements on free enterprise and oppressed peoples banding together to become a variation on witch-hunting fascists. But the film did amazing things for Holden. Even in SUNSET BOULEVARD he was transforming from the handsome juvenile lead of yore. His performance made him Bogie's successor to American Cynicism; without a doubt, Holden was one of the finest actors of his generation, thanks to his scrunched-face concentration which surprised you with its quick-change range. Holden won an Oscar for his portrayal of Sefton, the glib loner whose scams and scheming make life in Stalag 17 bearable for him but incurs the wrath of his fellow POWs. Still, they willingly participate in the games and attractions (like observing female Russian prisoners through a telescope) he operates for fun and profit. When two prisoners are killed while trying to escape, the Americans come to believe an informer is in their midst, and suspicion falls on Sefton. Later, after the camp's sadistic commandant, Von Scherbach (brilliantly played by director Preminger, in a take on Stroheim in LA GRANDE ILLUSION), learns how newcomer Dunbar (Don Taylor) managed to blow up a train, the POWs are certain Sefton is the rat and make life miserable for him.

Unlike previous POW films, Wilder and co-writer Edwin Blum's script, based on the play by Donald Bevan and Edmund Trzcinski, presents the prisoners not as paragons of patriotic virtue but as real, self-interested, bored soldiers trying to survive. Holden is magnificent as the heel-turned-hero, but STALAG 17 is full of wonderful, well-directed performances, including Sig Rumann as the barracks guard (the prototype for John Banner's Sgt. Schultz on "Hogan's Heroes," the long-running TV series inspired by the film); Gil Stratton, Jr., as Sefton's gopher; Harvey Lembeck and Robert Strauss as the barracks clowns; and real-life war hero Neville Brand. Peppered with Wilder's distinctive biting wit, STALAG 17 was justly a hit with the critics and at the box office.

STALKER

1982   160m   c/bw   ★★★★
Science Fiction   /PG
Mosfilm   (U.S.S.R.)

Aleksandr Kaidanovsky (Stalker), ikolai Grinko (Scientist), Anatoli Solonitsin (Writer), Alice Friendlich (Stalker's Wife), Natasha Abramova, F. Yurma, E. Kostin, R. Rendi

p, Alexandra Demidova; d, Andrei Tarkovsky; w, Boris Strugatsky, Arkady Strugatsky (based on their novel Roadside Picnic); ph, Alexander Knyazhinsky; prod d, Andrei Tarkovsky

Tarkovsky, the brilliant director of SOLARIS, continues with many of the same themes he pursued in his earlier film, most notably the search for fantasy fulfillment. Although STALKER has a sci-fi framework, its characters remain on Earth, journeying through a forbidden area called the Zone to reach its center, a room that holds many answers. But when the three explorers get to the room, they refrain from entering, preferring that the Truth remain a secret. The sets and camerawork nicely enhance an already suspenseful story.

STAMMHEIM

1986   107m   c   ★★★★
Drama
Bioskop/Thalia/Weltvertrieb   (West Germany)

Ulrich Pleitgen (Presiding Judge), Ulrich Tukur (Andreas Baader), Therese Affolter (Ulrike Meinhof), Sabine Wagner (Gudrun Ensslin), Hans Kremer (Jan-Carl Raspe), Peter Danzelsen, Hans

Christian Rudolph, Holger Mahlich, Marina Wandruszka (Defense Attorneys), Horst Mendroch

p, Eberhard Junkersdorf, Jurgen Flimm; d, Reinhard Hauff; w, Stefan Aust; ph, Frank Bruhne, Gunter Wulff; ed, Heidi Handorf; m, Marcel Wengler

The controversial winner of the 1986 Berlin Film Festival's Golden Bear Award, STAMMHEIM is based on the much-publicized Baader-Meinhof terrorist trials that shook the very foundation of Germany from 1975 to 1977. Based on the trial transcripts, the film takes place almost entirely in the Stammheim Prison in Stuttgart, West Germany, as the five defendants—Andreas Baader, Ulrike Meinhof, Gudrun Ensslin, Jan-Carl Raspe, and Holger Meins—are brought before the judge and accused of the murder of four US servicemen in a terrorist bombing attack. After a hunger strike at the trial's start, Meins dies. The next to die is Meinhof, an apparent suicide. As the trial stretches on, Baader, Ensslin, and Raspe continuously disrupt the proceedings with accusations that they are being purposely undernourished and spied upon. The trial proceeds at the most tense of levels—Baader and his defending lawyers refusing to abide by the rules of German law, while the prosecution struggles to retain a sense of order. Many months into the trial, the presiding judge is removed, defense attorneys and prosecutors come and go, witnesses appear to tell their stories, and Baader, Ensslin, and Raspe waver in their nearly unfaltering resistance. The film wraps up with a series of bizarre and violent incidents, and many unresolved questions.

Although STAMMHEIM is set almost entirely in a courtroom and based on court transcripts, it is as far from what one might expect. Rather than having the order and rigidity of a trial, the film explodes with the dynamics of the verbal battle between the defendants and the prosecutors. More than just a courtroom drama, STAMMHEIM is an examination of human nature and what happens to people when they refuse to buckle to the pressure of their oppressors. Whether or not the Baader-Meinhof group was guilty is not important to the film. What is important is to watch the accused fight against a political and judicial system that they believe is wrong.

Not surprisingly, this film split as many opinions as the trial itself did. At a press screening at the Zoo Palast Theater in Berlin, a squad of riot police was brought into the lobby because of fears that demonstrators would incite a riot. When the film was awarded the Golden Bear, festival judge Gina Lollobrigida, who was outspoken in her dislike for the film, refused to acknowledge it during the awards ceremony.

STAMMHEIM was produced without any subsidies from German television, which is usually very liberal with its financial support. Much of the funding came from the Thalia Theater ensemble, which put the film together as a labor of love—providing the money, the actors, and shooting on an extremely low-budget in a Hamburg warehouse.

STAND AND DELIVER

1988   105m   c   ★★★½
Biography   PG/15
American Playhouse

Edward James Olmos (Jaime Escalante), Lou Diamond Phillips (Angel), Rosana DeSoto (Fabiola Escalante), Andy Garcia (Ramirez), Ingrid Oliu (Lupe), Karla Montana (Claudia), Vanessa Marquez (Ana), Mark Eliot (Tito), Patrick Baca (Javier), Will Gotay (Pancho)

p, Tom Musca; d, Ramon Menendez; w, Ramon Menendez, Tom Musca; ph, Tom Richmond (Foto-Kem Color); ed, Nancy Richardson; m, Craig Safan; cos, Kathryn Morrison

STAND AND DELIVER is a powerful and enriching film about life in East Los Angeles. Based on a true story, the movie stars Edward James Olmos as Jaime Escalante, a math teacher at East LA's Garfield High. Escalante's class is filled with kids who have no desire to learn—they come late to class, can't do multiplication, talk and eat in class, and live in the fear of gang violence. Escalante is a special breed of teacher, however, who indulges in theatrics (he dresses as a chef and violently slices up apples to illustrate the concept of fractions) and refers to his class as a "show," and gradually the students respond to his style. With his school facing a loss of accreditation, Escalante makes a radical request, to teach AP Calculus and thus prepare his students for the Advanced Placement exams. Carefully scripted and exceptionally acted, STAND AND DELIVER succeeds in focusing on a large group of characters. First-time director Ramon Menendez, a Cuban UCLA graduate, takes the camera outside the classroom and into the students' own world. The film never overstates itself, concentrating instead on small, essentially non-dramatic elements to make its point. While everyone turns in a fine performance, Edward James Olmos is the standout.

STAND BY ME
1986 87m c   ★★★½
Comedy   R/15
Columbia

Wil Wheaton (Gordie Lachance), River Phoenix (Chris Chambers), Corey Feldman (Teddy Duchamp), Jerry O'Connell (Vern Tessio), Richard Dreyfuss (The Writer), Kiefer Sutherland (Ace Merrill), Casey Siemaszko (Billy Tessio), Gary Riley (Charlie Hogan), Bradley Gregg (Eyeball Chambers), Jason Oliver (Vince Desjardins)

p, Andrew Scheinman, Bruce A. Evans, Raynold Gideon; d, Rob Reiner; w, Raynold Gideon, Bruce A. Evans (based on the novella The Body by Stephen King); ph, Thomas Del Ruth (Panavision, Technicolor); ed, Robert Leighton; m, Jack Nitzsche; prod d, J. Dennis Washington; fx, Richard L. Thompson, Henry Millar; cos, Sue Moore

From the moment we hear the Ben E. King-Mike Stoller-Jerry Lieber hit "Stand By Me," we think we are in for a nostalgia trip with this film, but STAND BY ME is a lot more than that. The picture is framed by the reminiscences of a writer (Richard Dreyfuss). Hearing about a friend's death, he recalls the summer of 1959, when he and his 12-year-old friends spent their time hanging around doing what boys do. Gordie (Wil Wheaton) is the writer as a youth, and he's joined by Chris (River Phoenix), a somewhat older kid who's considered bad because of his family, Teddy (Corey Feldman), an erratic boy whose father is in a mental hospital, and pudgy Vern (Jerry O'Connell). Vern hears his older brother (Casey Siemaszko) tell a pal that his gang found the body of a missing boy while they were out for a spin in a stolen car, and when he repeats the story to his own pals, they set out to find the body.

  Directed by Rod Reiner from a semi-autobiographical Stephen King story, STAND BY ME is a lovely movie that should have been rated PG or PG-13, so that the age group it was about could have seen it. Crude language led to an R rating, but the language is honest, as is this film's remarkable re-creation of the lives of preteen boys. Reiner elicits some excellent performances from his young cast, and Kiefer Sutherland is memorable as the menacing teen hood.

STANLEY AND LIVINGSTONE
1939 101m bw   ★★★★
Biography/Adventure   /U
FOX

Spencer Tracy (Henry M. Stanley), Nancy Kelly (Eve Kingsley), Richard Greene (Gareth Tyce), Walter Brennan (Jeff Slocum), Charles Coburn (Lord Tyce), Cedric Hardwicke (Dr. David Livingstone), Henry Hull (James Gordon Bennett), Henry Travers (John Kingsley), Miles Mander (Sir John Gresham), David Torrence (Mr. Cranston)

p, Kenneth MacGowan; d, Henry King; w, Philip Dunne, Julien Josephson (based on historical research and story outline by Hal Long, Sam Hellman); ph, George Barnes, Otto Brower; ed, Barbara McLean; m, Russell Bennett, David Buttolph, Louis Silvers, R.H. Bassett, Cyril J. Mockridge, Rudy Schrager; art d, William Darling, George Dudley; cos, Royer

An intelligent, if not strictly factual, retelling of the Stanley and Livingstone legend, this hardy adventure succeeds largely because of Henry King's graceful direction and Spencer Tracy's fine, subdued performance as American journalist Henry Stanley, who searches for the missing Dr. David Livingstone (Sir Cedric Hardwicke). The film opens as Stanley returns to New York after filing reports from the West. His editor next wants the reporter to head into the African jungle and find Livingstone, a Scottish missionary who has disappeared. Stanley accepts the assignment, taking along Jeff Slocum (Walter Brennan) to accompany him on the search. The trip proves full of dangers hidden within the jungle. Stanley comes down with jungle fever, yet will not let this stop the mission. Finally he encounters the missionary in a remote jungle settlement and utters the famous line, "Dr. Livingstone, I presume?"

  Tracy gives a dignified portrait of a man who is profoundly changed as a result of his experience. The drama is well constructed, adroitly combining adventure with the humane values Livingstone espouses. The story is romanticized, with characters added to suit Hollywood conventions, and the truth about Stanley's life after his encounter with Livingstone fictionalized. Still, the final courtroom battle is a memorable one.

STAR!
1968 175m c   ★★★½
Musical/Biography   G/U
FOX

Julie Andrews (Gertrude Lawrence), Richard Crenna (Richard Aldrich), Michael Craig (Sir Anthony Spencer), Daniel Massey (Noel Coward), Robert Reed (Charles Fraser), Bruce Forsyth (Arthur Lawrence), Beryl Reid (Rose), John Collin (Jack Roper), Alan Oppenheimer (Andre Charlot), Richard Karlan (David Holtzman)

p, Saul Chaplin; d, Robert Wise; w, William Fairchild; ph, Ernest Laszlo (Todd-AO, DeLuxe Color); ed, William Reynolds; prod d, Boris Leven; fx, L.B. Abbott, Art Cruickshank, Emil Kosa, Jr.; chor, Michael Kidd; cos, Donald Brooks

Gertrude Lawrence was a huge star in England and on Broadway, but not in movies, and this cinematic biography left audiences wondering why Fox spent about $14 million to tell her story. Julie Andrews, on the other hand, was a huge marquee star after MARY POPPINS and THE SOUND OF MUSIC, and director Robert Wise and producer Saul Chaplin thought she would make a smashing Lawrence. Viewers disagreed, and the picture plummeted from its opening day. (It was re-released in a cut version, titled THOSE WERE THE HAPPY TIMES, a year later, but with no success either.) The film begins during WWII, as Lawrence, starring in the musical play *Lady in the Dark*, watches a newsreel about her own life. The film flashes back to 1915 in Clapham, England, when she leaves home to join her vaudevillian father (Bruce Forsyth), who is working in a run-down Brixton music hall. Gertrude decides to follow in her dad's footsteps and gets a job as a chorine in one of Andre Charlot's famous revues. Though Charlot (Alan Oppenheimer) is annoyed when she steals scenes and throws carefully rehearsed sketches out of whack, stage manager Jack Roper (John Collin) steps in and keeps her from getting fired. Jack and Gertrude marry but cannot agree on her role as a wife (he wants her to stay home; she wants to perform). After their daughter is born, Gertrude leaves. She becomes great friends with Noel Coward (Daniel Massey, who actually was Coward's godson), who uses his influence to get her a spot in Charlot's latest show, and she is instantly acclaimed as a new find after the opening in New York. Her career and romantic prospects soar, but her relationship with her neglected daughter (Jenny Agutter) is poor; moreover, she spends all her considerable earnings and overtaxes herself to pay her debts. After her success in Coward's *Tonight at 8:30*, she appears in *Susan and God*, showing she can play drama, then meets banker and theatrical dabbler Richard Aldrich (Richard Crenna) and appears in his staging of *Skylark*. Afterward, she moves on to *Lady in the Dark*, marries Aldrich, and is happy and fulfilled at last. There the picture ends, though in real life Lawrence lived another eight years and died at age 54. The movie lost millions, but it deserved a better fate for its enormous score, top-flight production, excellent choreography, and fine acting.

STAR 80

1983   102m   c   ★★★
Biography   R/18
Ladd/WB

Mariel Hemingway *(Dorothy Stratten)*, Eric Roberts *(Paul Snider)*, Cliff Robertson *(Hugh Hefner)*, Carroll Baker *(Dorothy's Mother)*, Roger Rees *(Aram Nicholas)*, David Clennon *(Geb)*, Josh Mostel *(Private Detective)*, Lisa Gordon *(Eileen)*, Sidney Miller *(Nightclub Owner)*, Keith Hefner *(Photographer)*

p, Wolfgang Glattes, Kenneth Utt; d, Bob Fosse; w, Bob Fosse (based on "Death of a Playmate" by Teresa Carpenter); ph, Sven Nykvist (Technicolor); ed, Alan Heim; m, Ralph Burns; art d, Jack G. Taylor, Jr., Michael Bolton; cos, Albert Wolsky

Based on the short life and gory death of *Playboy* "Playmate of the Year" Dorothy Stratten, this brutal picture might have been better had director Bob Fosse concentrated more on the young woman and less on the men who surrounded her. Played by Mariel Hemingway (who underwent breast augmentation for the role), Stratten is a sweet young thing and an easy prey for the hustling Paul Snider (Eric Roberts), the sleazy promoter who marries her and brings her to Los Angeles, where she poses for *Playboy*. Snider is portrayed as an unpredictable, insanely jealous loser, alternately gentle and violent. Stratten meets a number of sophisticated men, among them Hugh Hefner (Cliff Robertson) and Aram Nicholas (a fictionalized Peter Bogdanovich, played by Roger Rees), and begins to see Snider for the boor he is. Eventually she rejects him, and he retaliates in murderous rage. Roberts delivers a fine performance as the slippery, confused, violent Snider, bringing complexity and subtlety to his portrayal. The film degenerates into exploitation nonetheless.

STAR IS BORN, A

1937   111m   c   ★★★★½
Drama
Selznick

Janet Gaynor *(Esther Blodgett/Vicki Lester)*, Fredric March *(Norman Maine)*, Adolphe Menjou *(Oliver Niles)*, Andy Devine *(Danny McGuire)*, May Robson *(Lettie)*, Lionel Stander *(Libby)*, Owen Moore *(Casey Burke)*, Elizabeth Jenns *(Anita Regis)*, J.C. Nugent *(Theodore Smythe)*, Clara Blandick *(Aunt Mattie)*

p, David O. Selznick; d, William A. Wellman; w, Dorothy Parker, Alan Campbell, Robert Carson, David O. Selznick, William A. Wellman, Ring Lardner, Jr., Budd Schulberg, John Lee Mahin (based on the story by Wellman, Carson); ph, W. Howard Greene (Technicolor); ed, James E. Newcom; m, Max Steiner; art d, Lyle Wheeler; fx, Jack Cosgrove; cos, Omar Kiam

March is a movie superstar whose heyday has slipped by, although he is still held in high esteem by his producer and studio head, Menjou. Everyone, except March, seems to know that he is losing popularity with the public and his films are seeing less and less box-office success. At a Hollywood party where he drinks too much, as usual, March meets and is attracted to Gaynor, who is serving sandwiches and, in his cups, he proposes to make her a star. She has been longing to become an actress and has been starving while waiting for Central Casting to call her for her big break. This call never comes, which annoys her boarding house owner, Kennedy, no end. March winds up breaking the dishes Gaynor is responsible for and charming her into leaving the party with him, later painting for her a life of splendor and happiness as a movie star, encouraging her to follow his lead. March persuades a reluctant Menjou to give Gaynor a screen test. Impressed, Menjou decides to make her a star. March and Gaynor marry and, while her career accelerates, his takes a complete nosedive. Soon he's the most unemployable actor in Hollywood, shamelessly getting drunk in public and embarrassing a wife who loves him in spite of himself.

A STAR IS BORN captures wonderfully the hustle of Hollywood, especially in scenes which show Gaynor being physically (and painfully) prepared for stardom by having her perfectly acceptable face redone by cosmetic experts, facial experts, eyebrow experts, hair stylists, and makeup magicians—these scenes lack the forced "let's kid Judy" energy of the 1954 version—they're colder. It profiles the behind-the-scenes machinations of stars and producers, and it shows that, however accidentally, a person of talent, sincerity, and good-heartedness sometimes slips through the corrosive Hollywood system to become a star. The film is marvelously constructed by Wellman, who elicited superb performances from his stars.

The dialogue created for this film is tough, and most of the words Stander is given to growl portray him and the many Hollywood types similar to his character as vindictive and ruthless, people without pity, charisma, or compassion. Even after March dies of drowning, Stander can only spit out vicious quips: "First drink of water he's had in 20 years, and then he had to get it by accident. How do you wire congratulations to the Pacific Ocean?" Producer Menjou is no less cynical when evaluating the movie-going public: "Fans will write to anyone for a picture. It only takes a three-cent stamp, and that makes pictures cheaper than wallpaper." Of course, much of this acid-dripping dialogue stemmed from the black humor for which "Algonquin Round Table" member Dorothy Parker was famous.

STAR IS BORN, A
1954   176m   c   ★★★★★
Musical   PG/A
Transcona

Judy Garland *(Esther Blodgett/Vicki Lester)*, James Mason *(Norman Maine)*, Jack Carson *(Matt Libby)*, Charles Bickford *(Oliver Niles)*, Tommy Noonan *(Danny McGuire)*, Lucy Marlow *(Lola Lavery)*, Amanda Blake *(Susan Ettinger)*, Irving Bacon *(Graves)*, Hazel Shermet *(Libby's Secretary)*, James Brown *(Glenn Williams)*

p, Sidney Luft; d, George Cukor; w, Moss Hart (based on the Dorothy Parker, Alan Campbell, Robert Carson screenplay from a story by William A. Wellman, Carson, based on the film WHAT PRICE HOLLYWOOD); ph, Sam Leavitt (CinemaScope, Technicolor); ed, Folmar Blangsted, Craig Holt (reconstruction ed); m, Harold Arlen; prod d, Gene Allen; art d, Malcolm Bert; fx, H.F. Koenekamp; chor, Lize Bechtold Blyth, Eric Durst; cos, Jean Louis, Mary Ann Nyberg, Irene Sharaff

---

A thing of gut-wrenching, heartrending, lump-in-the-throat fascination with Judy Garland at her peak, pulling out all the stops, daring the gods in this dark, weighty fable of the price one pays to be at the top. *This* is the greatest one-woman performance in the history of motion pictures; a *tour de force* we are unlikely to ever see equalled, and that includes FUNNY GIRL. This version, directed by Cukor, is a fantastic orgy of emotion, lent all manner of myth by Garland teetering on the abyss before the slide. There would be other triumphs in concert, but this is the peak of her film career. Here she finally exposed her powerful dramatic range, coupled with the magnificent singing voice that she pushed further than anyone could imagine. Her genius is attached to an uncomfortable, intense plot that allows reason for the tremulous mannerisms and bottomless, dark eyes.

The plot essentially follows that of the original 1936 film (directed by William Wellman and starring Janet Gaynor and Fredric March). A young singer (Garland) saves Norman Maine (James Mason), a star actor, from making a drunken fool of himself on stage. Later, a sober Norman hears her sing and decides to help this incredible talent get started in pictures. Eventually (after she changes her name from Esther Blodgett to Vicki Lester), he manages to get her the lead in a big musical. As Vicki's star rises, however, Norman's begins to fall. The two elope, but their happiness is short-lived, and Norman's drinking increases when he is cut by his studio. Frustrated by the fickleness of his public and "friends," he drunkenly interrupts the Oscar ceremonies where Vicki has won the award for Best Actress, humbly pleading for a job and accidentally slapping his wife during the presentation ceremony. Despite all Vicki's attempts to find Norman work in Hollywood, his slide cannot be stopped by his wife's love.

Director George Cukor previously filmed the story as WHAT PRICE HOLLYWOOD? in 1932. Here he delivers a much more savage film, allowing moments and characters to speak for themselves in a way that give A STAR IS BORN that much more power. Garland is well matched by Mason, who imbues Norman's hellish descent with a deep sense of self-understanding, a dignified awareness of what is transpiring and ultimate acceptance of fate. And in the scenes of drunkenness, a threatening aura of danger that seems to give him an unhuman kind of vigor and strength. If Mason looks healthier than Garland sometimes, it works. Policing and caretaking an addict takes enormous energy; sometimes the toll is greater on the spouse than the addict themselves. Mason's work on STAR is the equal of any good performance you can name.

Garland, who had played the part on radio, asked MGM chief Louis B. Mayer if the property could be developed as a film project for her, but Mayer felt the story was too depressing and that Garland's fans would never accept her in such a screen role. Garland and new husband Sidney Luft therefore formed their own production company to bring their dream to life, and after months of maneuvers between Warner Bros. and David Selznick, the project was finally realized. Both Garland and Luft wanted Cary Grant to play Norman, but he declined, feeling his comic style might make Norman's drinking habits seem humorous rather than tragic, and Mason was hired in his stead. Harold Arlen and Ira Gershwin provided Garland with songs that would become standards in her concert repertoire, including the ten-ton torch song, "The Man That Got Away" (which earned an Oscar nomination for Best Song), rendered by Garland with incredible emotional power. Leonard Gershe's classic "Born in a Trunk" sequence is also one of Garland's finest moments, a near-autobiographical musical sequence that shows the star's rise, incorporating the songs "I'll Get By," "You Took Advantage of Me," "Black Bottom," "Peanut Vendor," "My Melancholy Baby," and "Swanee." After Garland's Oscar-nominated performance lost to Grace Kelly's amateur thesping in THE COUNTRY GIRL, many in Hollywood felt that she was being punished by her peers for her past troubles, and Groucho Marx sent a telegram to Garland saying that the loss "was the biggest robbery since Brink's." But Garland, pregnant in the hospital, was emotionally bolstered by the birth of Joey Luft, her only son and third and last child.

Warners stupidly cut A STAR IS BORN considerably after its premiere, but Cukor's version was eventually partially restored through the reinsertion of recovered soundtrack with production stills and some alternate takes that had somehow survived, giving the film a continuity that unfeeling hands had removed. Seemingly vindicated, Cukor passed away the night before he was to see his restored film, which reopened in 1983 to enthusiastic crowds. Besides that torch song, the most riveting scene: Garland's charged dressing room confession to Bickford, followed by a show-must-go-on gamine production number ("Lose That Long Face"). George Hoyningen-Huene consulted on the color, which gives the film either somber depth or hysterical, raw splashes of color—it's exactly right. If this version is more closely aligned with showbiz tradition than the 1937 version, it works, largely because it underlines the Garland legend. With Jack Carson in a definitive role as a bastard press agent, and Lucy Marlow and Joan Shawlee as putrid starlet and columnist and Tommy Noonan, surprisingly effective as Garland's jazz musician pal, in the best role of his career.

STAR IS BORN, A
1976   140m   c   ★★★
Musical   R/15
WB

Barbra Streisand *(Esther Hoffman)*, Kris Kristofferson *(John Norman Howard)*, Gary Busey *(Bobby Ritchie)*, Oliver Clark *(Gary Danziger)*, Vanetta Fields, Clydie King *(The Oreos)*, Marta Heflin *(Quentin)*, M.G. Kelly *(Bebe Jesus)*, Sally Kirkland *(Photographer)*, Joanne Linville *(Freddie)*

p, Jon Peters; d, Frank Pierson; w, John Gregory Dunne, Joan Didion, Frank Pierson (based on a story by William A. Wellman, Robert Carson); ph, Robert Surtees (Panavision, Metrocolor); ed, Peter Zinner; m, Roger Kellaway; prod d, Polly Platt; art d, William M. Hiney; fx, Chuck Gaspar; chor, David Winters; cos, Shirley Strahm, Seth Banks

---

STAR TREK: THE MOTION PICTURE

The fourth remake of this story, this is a fairly good, though overlong, film, executive-produced by Barbra Streisand and produced by her companion of the time, Jon Peters. Rock star John Norman Howard (Kris Kristofferson) takes solace in booze while his career slides. After a particularly embarrassing concert performance, the sullen star visits a nightclub where the interracial female singing trio "The Oreos" is performing. Impressed by the talents of Oreo Esther Hoffman (Streisand), John gets her an audition that leads to a recording contract. An album is released, Esther becomes a star, and she and John marry. But, as everyone watching expects, trouble looms in paradise as her career soars and his plummets. John ruins Esther's Grammy acceptance speech, staggering onstage to interrupt her triumph. Eventually he leaves her and dies in a car crash. The picture should have ended there; unfortunately, a lengthy coda follows, with Esther performing a concert dedicated to her late husband. Streisand fans will love this extra footage, but others will yawn. The songs, from several sources but mostly by Paul Williams and Kenny Ascher, range in quality from "Watch Closely Now" (a dreadful, interminable tune sung too often by Kristofferson) to the Academy Award-winning "Evergreen," cowritten by Streisand and Williams. Director Frank Pierson clashed repeatedly with Streisand and later made some much-publicized charges blasting the star for megalomania.

STAR TREK: THE MOTION PICTURE
1979   132m   c   ★★½
Science Fiction   G/U
Paramount

William Shatner (Capt. James T. Kirk), Leonard Nimoy (Mr. Spock), DeForest Kelley (Dr. Leonard "Bones" McCoy), James Doohan (Chief Engineer Montgomery "Scotty" Scott), George Takei (Sulu), Majel Barrett (Dr. Christine Chapel), Walter Koenig (Chekov), Nichelle Nichols (Uhura), Persis Khambatta (Ilia), Stephen Collins (Cmdr. Willard Decker)

p, Gene Roddenberry; d, Robert Wise; w, Harold Livingston, Gene Roddenberry (based on a story by Alan Dean Foster, from the TV program "Star Trek"); ph, Richard H. Kline (Panavision, Metrocolor); ed, Todd Ramsay; m, Jerry Goldsmith; prod d, Harold Michelson; art d, Harold Michelson, Leon Harris, Joseph Jennings, John Vallone; fx, Douglas Trumbull, John Dykstra, Dave Stewart, Don Baker, Robert Swarthe, Harry Moreau, Richard Yuricich; cos, Robert Fletcher

It finally happened. The characters loved by millions, preserved in reruns even though the TV series was canceled nearly 10 years previously, were born again. The plot of this $40-million film sometimes gets lost amid technical gadgetry, but the generation of young adults who grew up watching one of the most successful television programs ever, found it fascinating to see what has become of the crew of the starship Enterprise. Capt. James T. Kirk (William Shatner), now an admiral, is called upon one last time to take over the command of his old ship and halt a strange alien craft that is gobbling up everything in its path and is headed directly for Earth. To undertake this mission he calls upon the assistance of all the old crew members, and some new ones as well. Nominated for three Academy Awards: Best Original Score, Best Art Direction and Best Visual Effects.

STAR TREK II: THE WRATH OF KHAN
1982   113m   c   ★★★
Science Fiction   PG
Paramount

William Shatner (Adm. James T. Kirk), Leonard Nimoy (Mr. Spock), DeForest Kelley (Dr. Leonard "Bones" McCoy), James Doohan (Chief Engineer Montgomery "Scotty" Scott), Walter Koenig (Chekov), George Takei (Sulu), Nichelle Nichols (Cmdr. Uhura), Bibi Besch (Dr. Carol Marcus), Merritt Butrick (David), Paul Winfield (Capt. Terrell, Starship Reliant)

p, Robert Sallin; d, Nicholas Meyer; w, Jack B. Sowards (based on a story by Sowards and Harve Bennett and on the TV series "Star Trek"); ph, Gayne Rescher (Panavision, Movielab Color); ed, William Dornisch; m, James Horner; prod d, Joseph R. Jennings; art d, Michael Minor; fx, Bob Dawson, Ken Ralston, Jim Veillieux, Alan Howarth

Of the first three "Star Trek" films, this second entry comes closest to the spirit of the television series. Adm. James T. Kirk (William Shatner) is still in charge of a space fleet, but his desk job doesn't allow him to do the kind of work for which he was born. When cajoled by Mr. Spock (Leonard Nimoy) and "Bones" McCoy (DeForest Kelley), Kirk agrees to take command of a mission that seems simple enough, but the sudden appearance of the evil Khan (Ricardo Montalban) makes for a very sticky situation. An interesting aspect of this film, ignored in the television series, is the focus on Kirk's family life back on Earth.

STAR TREK III: THE SEARCH FOR SPOCK
1984   105m   c   ★★★
Science Fiction   PG
Paramount

William Shatner (Kirk), Leonard Nimoy (Spock), DeForest Kelley (McCoy), James Doohan (Scotty), Walter Koenig (Chekov), George Takei (Sulu), Nichelle Nichols (Uhura), Robin Curtis (Saavik), Merritt Butrick (David), Phil Morris (Trainee Foster)

p, Harve Bennett; d, Leonard Nimoy; w, Harve Bennett (based on the TV production "Star Trek" by Gene Roddenberry); ph, Charles Correll (Panavision, Movielab Color); ed, Robert F. Shugrue; m, James Horner; art d, John E. Chilberg, II; fx, Rocky Gehr; cos, Robert Fletcher

The third "Star Trek" film is not as good as the second, but it is still a very entertaining movie. Directed by Leonard Nimoy, the picture begins where STAR TREK II: THE WRATH OF KHAN left off. The crew of the Enterprise is coming home when they learn that their beloved ship is slated to be put on the shelf. Mr. Spock, who apparently died in the last feature, is now kept alive in spirit. Adm. James T. Kirk (William Shatner) must find Spock's body and bring it to the planet Vulcan, along with a crew member who is possessed by Spock's thoughts. How can Kirk complete his mission when his ship is due for the junk heap?

STAR TREK IV: THE VOYAGE HOME
1986   119m   c   ★★★★
Fantasy/Science Fiction   PG
Paramount

William Shatner (James T. Kirk), Leonard Nimoy (Mr. Spock), DeForest Kelley (Dr. Leonard "Bones" McCoy), James Doohan (Chief Engineer Montgomery "Scotty" Scott), George Takei (Sulu), Walter Koenig (Chekov), Nichelle Nichols (Comdr. Uhura), Majel Barrett (Dr. Christine Chapel), Jane Wyatt (Amanda, Spock's Mother), Catherine Hicks (Dr. Gillian Taylor) p, Harve Bennett; d, Leonard Nimoy; w, Harve Bennett, Steve Meerson, Peter Krikes, Nicholas Meyer (based on a story by Leonard Nimoy, Harve Bennett, and the TV series created by Gene Roddenberry); ph, Don Peterman (Panavision, Techniclor); ed, Peter E. Berger; m, Leonard Rosenman; prod d, Jack T. Collis; art d, Joe Aubel, Pete Smith; fx, Michael Lantieri; cos, Robert Fletcher

The fourth STAR TREK film is, to date, the best. Its silliest of all STAR TREK movie plots is all the more satisfying, allowing us to laugh along with the characters who have lived for more than two decades in America's imagination. When the crew of the *Enterprise* was last seen, Mr. Spock (Leonard Nimoy, who directed this film) had been resurrected, but his fabulous mind was wiped clean of memory. The ship had been destroyed, its crew dejected. Now they respond to an eerie sound emanating from a space probe near 23rd-century Earth. The crew identifies the sound as a duplication of a humpback whale's cry, eventually realizing that the huge probe is looking for a whale to chat with and will destroy the Earth if it doesn't find one. But centuries of hunters have killed all the whales, and to save the Earth the crew must get back to the 20th century, find a pair of the sweet-voiced mammals, and transport them to the future. They therefore drop into San Francisco, 1986, concealing their ship under a cloak of invisibility while Spock and fearless Capt. James T. Kirk (William Shatner) carry out the task. Even in the unlikely instance that you have never seen a STAR TREK movie or TV episode, you will still enjoy this film. Shatner and Nimoy's comedic byplay goes beyond Hope and Crosby and sometimes into Cheech and Chong. They've gained years and pounds, but the film makes no attempt to present them as perpetually youthful. A thoroughly enjoyable film, preceded by STAR TREK: THE MOTION PICTURE; STAR TREK II: THE WRATH OF KHAN; and STAR TREK III: THE SEARCH FOR SPOCK.

STAR TREK VI: THE UNDISCOVERED COUNTRY

1991 110m c ★★★½
Science Fiction/Action PG
Paramount

William Shatner *(Admiral James Tiberius Kirk)*, Leonard Nimoy *(Captain Spock)*, DeForest Kelley *(Doctor Leonard "Bones" McCoy)*, James Doohan *(Montgomery "Scotty" Scott)*, Walter Koenig *(Pavel Chekov)*, Nichelle Nichols *(Nytoba Uhuru)*, George Takei *(Hikaru Sulu)*, Kim Cattrall *(Lieutenant Valeris)*, Mark Lenard *(Sarek)*, Grace Lee Whitney *("Excelsior" Communications Officer)*

p, Ralph Winter, Steven-Charles Jaffe; d, Nicholas Meyer; w, Nicholas Meyer, Denny Martin Flinn (from the story by Leonard Nimoy, Lawrence Konner and Mark Rosenthal, based on the characters created by Gene Roddenberry); ph, Hiro Narita; ed, William Hoy, Ronald Roose; m, Cliff Eidelman; prod d, Herman Zimmerman; art d, Nilo Rodis-Jamero; fx, Scott Farrar; cos, Dodie Shepard

Age has crept up on the crew of the starship Enterprise. But once you stop thinking about how old everyone has gotten, and you eventually will, you'll be able to sit back and enjoy STAR TREK VI: THE UNDISCOVERED COUNTRY, the last—so they've promised—of the original Star Trek voyages. It's a worthy, witty finale.

Following an explosion on their moon, the militant Klingons face a deadly depletion of their ozone, but their economy doesn't have the resources to combat this calamity. (Or, as they tell it, "There has been an 'incident' on Praxis" and the Klingon empire has only 50 years of life left.) To survive, they have no option

left but to join the intergalactic Federation, which means an end to 70 years of hostilities.

Because of their familiarity with the Klingons, Admiral James Kirk (William Shatner) and his old crew are sent to handle the diplomacy. Slated to retire in three months, they're annoyed at being given this last mission. Frankly, they don't want to bother, and their not-too-friendly attitude runs the gamut from "Let them die" and "Bring them to their knees" to Kirk's "I never trusted Klingons. I never will." (Years before, in STAR TREK 3, they killed his son.) Sulu (George Takei)—finally commanding his own starship, the Excelsior—returns to helm the Enterprise (USS 1701-A), though it's about to be decommissioned and put back to space dock. The Klingon entourage, headed by Chancellor Gorkon (David Warner) and General Chang (Christopher Plummer), come aboard the Enterprise for preparatory peace talks, an occasion spiced with sarcasm by Kirk and his men: i.e. "Guess who's coming for dinner" and "They all look alike." Everyone's dander is up, suspicion weighs heavily over both sides, and the sparks and quotes from Shakespeare fly.

Extracts from the Bard, a recurrent motif, fall trippingly from Chang's florid Klingon tongue throughout the film, from the initial toast, "To *the undiscovered Country*, the future," to "If there is going to be a *brave new world*, our generation will have the hardest time living in it," to "Our revels now are ended"; "Once more unto the breach, dear friends"; "The Game's afoot"; and "As constant as the northern star." (There are also references to Sherlock Holmes and Peter Pan.)

The Klingons have ghastly table manners, the dinner meeting is less than satisfactory, and Chang, the Klingon ambassador, concedes they have a long way to go. Unfortunately, someone is out to sabotage the negotiations. Following the Klingons' leave-taking, Chang is poisoned by a postprandial digestif (blue Romulan ale), and two torpedoes, unquestionably emanating from the Enterprise, do deadly damage to the alien ship and personnel. (Incidentally, Klingon blood is fuschia.) Kirk and Dr. McCoy (DeForest Kelly) beam aboard the Klingon vessel to offer their help and deny responsibility for the unprovoked attack which threatens to end the peace negotiations. But despite their protestations and Gorkon's dying words to Kirk ("Don't let it end this way"), they're arrested for assassination, and, in a Kafka-esque trial, are convicted and sentenced to death.

Though several in the Klingon contingent opt for war and adamantly refuse to extradite the prisoners, Gorkon's daughter Azetbur (Rosana DeSoto) is determined the talks continue at a secret neutral site. She commutes their sentence to life at hard labor without possibility of parole at a snowy gulag in the mines of Rura Penthe, known throughout the galaxy as "The Aliens' Graveyard." While Spock (Leonard Nimoy), aboard the Enterprise, tries to piece together what happened and avoid armed conflict, Kirk and McCoy languish on the Klingon equivalent of Siberian hell. The mines are peopled with some of the most outlandishly bizarre alien creatures ever concocted by Hollywood special effects, and the pair escape with the help of another prisoner, the exotic, orange-eyed Martia (Iman). McCoy has a locator shield hidden on his back, and the trio head for the rescue party somewhere in the desolate snow-covered territory. But everything is going too smoothly. What he and Kirk discover is that Martia is not what she seems. She's really a hired assassin out to kill them and more likely a Commoloid, a species able to change shape at will. With the same fascinating degree of visual liquid wizardry found in TERMINATOR 2, she mutates into a clone of Kirk, and, as expected, is killed in a fight to the death.

When the duo return to the starship, they find that in the interim, Spock, using inimitable Vulcan logic, has uncovered evidence to exonerate Kirk and the crew. They still don't know who the guilty parties are, but deduce it's everyone who stands to lose by peace; someone who is more afraid of the future. (In this instance, it's Chang and his cohorts.) In the proverbial rush against time to get to the peace conference with the information, Spock finds the meeting's secret location through a "mind meld" (a Vulcan technique which, interestingly enough, the filmmakers felt necessary to identify; everyone knows anyway). Ultimately, the bad guys are either captured or killed, and true to form, chief villain Chang's parting words are Shakespeare's "To be, or not to be." As for the parting words from the good guys: "Once again we have saved civilization as we know it. . . ." Kirk and crew happily set the Enterprise's final course to the second star to the right and straight on till morning, a fitting ending to this complete space-Western series of high tech, high adventure and wonderful high corn.

Though much effort was given to achieve a "new look" for the production, per usual, the film has enough of the klutzy effects, silly props and costumes long familiar to and beloved by Trekkies. (The Enterprise crew's tacky uniforms still look like pajamas, and Kirk, with open collar jauntily flapping, looks like he's wearing upside-down Dr. Denton's.) It doesn't really matter. Also, in a bit of major trivia for Trekkies, after over 25 years of reruns and six feature films, Admiral James T. Kirk finally gets a middle name. It's "Tiberius." Along with their venerable captain, it's also comforting, added girth and wrinkles notwithstanding, to have the regulars back: Spock, McCoy, Scotty (James Doohan), Chekov (Walter Koenig), Uhuru (Nichelle Nichols) and Sulu. Old familiars Mark Lenard and Grace Lee Whitney also make their appearance; Michael Dorn, Worf from TV's "Star Trek: The Next Generation," briefly appears as Worf's grandfather, a Klingon defense attorney; and, in an uncredited cameo, Christian Slater pops in for mere seconds as a corpsman.

The moral of STAR TREK VI: THE UNDISCOVERED COUNTRY, with its similarity to contemporary problems caused by the sudden end of the Cold War, is that people, of whatever century, can be very frightened of change. Here, Kirk, Spock et al. All admit to those personal demons which have their very real current counterparts. In fact, this is a film with a very strong, ethical directive. Despite prejudices (Kirk was used to hating Klingons and couldn't get past the death of his son; Spock couldn't get past his Vulcan ego), the intent is clear. To quote Spock, segueing from "Has it been we have both outlived our usefulness by being too inflexible?" to "Peace is worth a great many personal risks," he rationally wraps up the issue with "Logic is the beginning of wisdom, not the end." It's advice well worth considering.

STAR TREK VI: THE UNDISCOVERED COUNTRY is dedicated to Gene Roddenberry, creator and guiding spirit of the Star Trek adventures since its inception, who, sadly, died barely a month before its opening.

STAR WARS

1977 121m c		★★★★★
Science Fiction		PG/U
FOX		

Mark Hamill *(Luke Skywalker)*, Harrison Ford *(Han Solo)*, Carrie Fisher *(Princess Leia Organa)*, Peter Cushing *(Grand Moff Tarkin)*, Alec Guinness *(Ben (Obi-Wan) Kenobi)*, Anthony Daniels *(See Threepio (C3P0))*, Kenny Baker *(Artoo-Detoo (R2D2))*, Peter Mayhew *(Chewbacca)*, David Prowse *(Lord Darth Vader)*, Phil Brown *(Uncle Owen Lars)*

p, Gary Kurtz; d, George Lucas; w, George Lucas; ph, Gilbert Taylor (Panavision, Technicolor); ed, Paul Hirsch, Marcia Lucas, Richard Chew; m, John Williams; prod d, John Barry; art d, Norman Reynolds, Leslie Dilley; fx, Rick Baker, John Dykstra; cos, John Mollo, Ron Beck; anim, Adam Beckett

"A long time ago, in a galaxy far far away," reads the opening title of STAR WARS, introducing not only this one film but, in effect, a whole new wave in Hollywood filmmaking. From this point on, American films changed—or tried to—as did audience expectations. STAR WARS left the viewers craving more; "bigger and better" spectacles became the rage for years afterwards although much that followed paled in comparison. It soon became common to hear casual fans conversing about previously arcane special effects in a critical and knowlegeable manner.

There's no denying the appeal of this historic blockbuster. George Lucas has done more than anyone except Jim Henson (and perhaps Walt Disney) to establish the gallery of characters who now populate contemporary childhood. What's fascinating from a cinematic point of view is the magnificently derivative nature of the film. It's an enormous summary of characters, styles, and plot points that surveys forty years of film history. There's probably not a frame in it that doesn't have some cinematic antecedent. This is not a criticism. STAR WARS brought back for a new generation a lot of the elements of Hollywood moviemaking that were so attractive to their parents and it did so in breathless anthology form. For young filmgoers this film acted as a doorway to the glory of the movies. For many older viewers, seeing this film made them feel young again.

STAR WARS presented us with a cast of characters who have become part of our collective film consciousness. Mark Hamill is the callow youth Luke Skywalker; Harrison Ford is the rugged roguish adventurer Han Solo; and Carrie Fisher is the lovely spunky Princess Leia. Also along for the ride are a pair of adorable 'droids, R2D2 (Kenny Baker) and C3PO (Anthony Daniels), Chewbacca (Peter Mayhew), the fierce towering bearlike Wookie navigator who's really a softie at heart and Ben "Obi-Wan" Kenobi (Alec Guinness), the wise old hermit who is actually a great Jedi Master.

Luke is an "orphan" (see THE EMPIRE STRIKES BACK) living with his aunt and uncle on their farm on a dusty remote planet called Tatooine. He yearns for a life of high adventure. He wants to go offworld to join the academy like his friends but his uncle needs his help with the coming harvest. Meanwhile the Imperial Senate has been disbanded and the galaxy has been taken over by the evil Emperor. The Empire's greatest weapon, the dreaded Death Star, is a huge globe-like craft able to disintegrate entire planets. This fearsome device is commanded by the sinister Grand Moff Tarkin (Peter Cushing) and his feared masked aide, Darth Vader (David Prowse, voiced by the uncredited James Earl Jones). Princess Lea acquires the plans for the craft and hides them in R2D2 who is jettisoned in an escape pod with the translator and protocol 'droid C3PO. R2D2 been programmed to find Obi-wan Kenobi but first he ends up on the Skywalker farm. The little 'droid wanders off one night to fulfill his mission. Luke follows and meets old Ben Kenobi who offers to teach him the mysterious ways of the Force. The rest, as they say, is movie history.

A grand battle between good and evil eventually ensues, with thundering spaceships, exploding planets, blasting blasters, and dueling light sabers. The whole glorious affair is presented at maximum warp speed with the adventure and humor settings on "stunning." Pulpy 1930s-style space opera was finally given an appropriate screen treatment in this landmark science fiction film. This is the film that *defines* "fun." Nominated for ten Academy Awards including Best Picture (it lost to ANNIE HALL), Best Supporting Actor (Guinness), Best Screenplay and Best Direction. It won Oscars for Best Visual Effects, Best Editing, Best Art Direction, Best Original Score, Best Costume Design and Best Sound.

Of the nine films planned for the STAR WARS series, only two others have been completed to date—THE EMPIRE STRIKES BACK and RETURN OF THE JEDI. Already we can look back as these three gems and ruefully say "They just don't make them like that anymore!" Let's hope that George Lucas has not lost the Force and will follow through with the projected sequels.

STARDUST MEMORIES

1980 90m bw   ★★★½
Comedy   PG/15
UA

Woody Allen *(Sandy Bates)*, Charlotte Rampling *(Dorrie)*, Jessica Harper *(Daisy)*, Marie-Christine Barrault *(Isobel)*, Tony Roberts *(Tony)*, Daniel Stern *(Actor)*, Amy Wright *(Shelley)*, Helen Hanft *(Vivian Orkin)*, John Rothman *(Jack Abel)*, Anne DeSalvo *(Sandy's Sister)*

p, Robert Greenhut; d, Woody Allen; w, Woody Allen; ph, Gordon Willis; ed, Susan E. Morse; prod d, Santo Loquasto; art d, Michael Molly

After flirting with autobiography in a few films, Woody Allen dug directly into personal experience to fashion this tale. Allen plays a prominent comedian-turned-film-director who attends a weekend film seminar where he is surrounded by hordes of adoring critics and fans who mine his every word looking for profundity and hidden meanings. The usual Allen neuroses and problems with women are given an episodic treatment, with a number of jokes along the way, but the film has an underlying angry tone that Allen fails to blend successfully with the comedy. Allen is to be commended for broadening the psychology and themes of his films, but STARDUST MEMORIES remains a disappointing outing, despite its many laughs and inside jokes. (The head of United Artists, Andy Albeck, plays a film chief who is worried that his new movie has no laughs.)

STARMAN

1984 115m c   ★★★
Science Fiction/Romance   PG
Columbia

Jeff Bridges *(Starman)*, Karen Allen *(Jenny Hayden)*, Charles Martin Smith *(Mark Shermin)*, Richard Jaeckel *(George Fox)*, Robert Phalen *(Maj. Bell)*, Tony Edwards *(Sgt. Lemon)*, John Walter Davis *(Brad Heinmuller)*, Ted White *(Deer Hunter)*, Dirk Blocker, M.C. Gainey *(Cops)*

p, Larry Franco; d, John Carpenter; w, Bruce A. Evans, Raynold Gideon; ph, Donald Morgan (Panavision, MGM Color); ed, Marion Rothman; m, Jack Nitzsche; prod d, Daniel Lomino; fx, Roy Arbogast, Bruce Nicholson, Michael McAlister; cos, Andy Hylton, Robin Bush

In this pleasant surprise from director John Carpenter, Jenny Hayden (Karen Allen) is a young Wisconsin widow still grieving over the loss of her husband. She spends her evenings looking through photo albums and watching home movies of their brief time together. One night, a bright blue light zooms from outer space and flies into Jenny's home. It hovers over the photo album and runs the home movies until it has assimilated enough char-

acteristics of Earthlings to take on the shape of one—Jenny's dead husband. She is shocked and confused when confronted with this man who looks just like her late husband (Jeff Bridges). The alien manages to explain that he has come with greetings in return for the message Earth sent into space on *Voyager II*. His people have arranged for him to be picked up in the Arizona desert in a few days, and he forces Jenny to drive him there. Meanwhile, the government, represented by a National Security Council agent (Richard Jaeckel), is out to capture the alien in order to study him. Jenny's fear is eventually overcome by her compassion for the vulnerable being who is almost childlike in his sense of wonder about Earth and its inhabitants. Slowly, hesitantly, they fall in love, knowing that he must return to his planet or die. STARMAN is a wonderful film that combines science fiction, road movies, and romance into an engaging, very entertaining whole. While the plot may have some holes and the story may be a bit hard to swallow, the film works due to the performances by Bridges and Allen. In a role that earned an Oscar nomination, Bridges manages to look as if he doesn't belong in his own body. Carpenter directs the film in a straightforward manner, and the brief forays into special effects and pyrotechnics are handled deftly without distracting from the basic story line. STARMAN is an enjoyable film filled with the kind of sensitivity, love, and humor seldom seen on today's screens.

STARS LOOK DOWN, THE

1940 104m bw   ★★★★
Drama   /A
Grand National   (U.K.)

Michael Redgrave *(David Fenwick)*, Margaret Lockwood *(Jenny Sunley)*, Emlyn Williams *(Joe Gowan)*, Nancy Price *(Martha Fenwick)*, Allan Jeayes *(Richard Barras)*, Edward Rigby *(Robert Fenwick)*, Cecil Parker *(Stanley Millington)*, Linden Travers *(Laura Millington)*, Milton Rosmer *(Harry Nugent)*, George Carney *(Slogger Gowan)*

p, Isadore Goldsmith; d, Carol Reed; w, J.B. Williams (based on the novel by A.J. Cronin); ph, Ernest Palmer (uncredited), Henry Harris (uncredited), Mutz Greenbaum; ed, Reginald Beck; m, Hans May; art d, James Carter

Made in 1939, but released in the US at around the same time as HOW GREEN WAS MY VALLEY, this superb view of the plight of British miners was unfortunately overlooked at the box office. Though related in subject, THE STARS LOOK DOWN is much grimmer than John Ford's classic.

Based on a novel by A.J. Cronin, Carol Reed's first major film is set in a bleak coal mining town in northern England, where Rigby and Price have struggled to give their son (Redgrave) an opportunity for a better life and a university education. Rigby works in the mine with his younger son (Desmond Tester) and attempts to organize his fellow miners, who are working under dangerous conditions. While away at school, Redgrave meets Lockwood. A vain young woman, Lockwood has been rejected by Williams, and now traps Redgrave into marriage. When Williams, an unctuous type, renews his affair with Lockwood, Redgrave leaves her and turns his attention to helping the miners back home, who have been forced to return to work after an aborted strike. Redgrave, who has ambitions of becoming an MP, tries to rally support for the union, but to no avail. After a cave-in at the mine in which many—including Rigby and Tester—are killed, he decides to stay in the small town and devote his life to improving the lot of the miners.

At once topical and enduring, this powerful drama influenced by the social realism of the British documentary greatly enhanced the growing reputation of Reed, then a young director. Shot partially at a colliery in Cumberland, THE STARS LOOK DOWN was also an important film for the young Michael Redgrave, who was still fresh from the British stage (and from THE LADY VANISHES). He gives a strong performance, as do Lockwood and Williams, with Rigby and Price lending fine support.

STARTING OVER

1979 106m c   ★★★½
Romance/Comedy   R/15
Paramount

Burt Reynolds (Phil Potter), Jill Clayburgh (Marilyn Homberg), Candice Bergen (Jessica Potter), Charles Durning (Michael "Mickey" Potter), Frances Sternhagen (Marva Potter), Austin Pendleton (Paul), Mary Kay Place (Marie), MacIntyre Dixon (Dan Ryan), Jay O. Sanders (Larry), Charles Kimbrough (Salesman)

p, Alan J. Pakula, James L. Brooks; d, Alan J. Pakula; w, James L. Brooks (based on the novel by Dan Wakefield); ph, Sven Nykvist (Movielab Color); ed, Marion Rothman; m, Marvin Hamlisch; prod d, George Jenkins; cos, John Boxer

In perhaps his best performance, Burt Reynolds, cast here against type, stars as a lonely man whose wife leaves him to spread her wings and try to build a career as a singer-songwriter (although she exhibits a striking lack of talent). Stunned when she announces her desire for freedom, he goes to Boston where he is consoled by Durning and Sternhagen, a duo of relatives who also happen to be psychiatrists. At first Reynolds has no idea that in addition to yearning for freedom Bergen is having an affair with her boss. Struck by this new situation, Reynolds soon meets Clayburgh, a schoolteacher who shies away from any commitment. He also joins a divorced men's group, which provides some touching and funny moments. Reynolds shaved off his moustache for the film and with it went his hirsute, macho image; he presents instead a feeling and vulnerable man. Bergen's character is gently made fun of. In a very funny sequence, she sings her dreadful autobiographical songs in a caterwauling screech. While all of the acting is top-notch, Reynolds steals the show with his underplaying and understanding of the role. He has been quoted as saying, "It was very close to the story of my life," and his grasp of the character's emotions is evident from the start. Audiences like to see their heroes in familiar roles, however, and the film was not the great success its producers hoped for, although it grossed over $20 million on initial release. Brooks, the producer-screenwriter who came from the "Mary Tyler Moore Show," later went on to make a name for himself as a director-writer-producer with TERMS OF ENDEARMENT. Shawn is the actor-playwright who was responsible for MY DINNER WITH ANDRE.

STATE FAIR

1945 100m c   ★★★★
Musical   /U
FOX

Jeanne Crain (Margy Frake), Dana Andrews (Pat Gilbert), Dick Haymes (Wayne Frake), Vivian Blaine (Emily Joyce), Charles Winninger (Abel Frake), Fay Bainter (Melissa Frake), Donald Meek (Hippenstahl), Frank McHugh (McGee), Percy Kilbride (Miller), Harry Morgan (Barker)

p, William Perlberg; d, Walter Lang; w, Oscar Hammerstein, II, Sonya Levien, Paul Green (based on the novel by Phil Stong); ph, Leon Shamroy (Technicolor); ed, J. Watson Webb; art d, Lyle Wheeler, Lewis Creber; fx, Fred Sersen

This second version of STATE FAIR improves on its predecessor of 1933. Oscar Hammerstein based his screenplay on the 1933 adaptation of Phil Stong's bucolic novel, and, with Richard Rodgers, contributed the score. The story is virtually the same, but the addition of the marvelous songs made the musical remake a smash. It's still pleasant mid-summer in Iowa, where Abel and Melissa Frake (Charles Winninger and Fay Bainter) are the parents of the teenage Margy (Jeanne Crain) and Wayne (Dick Haymes). Abel wants to enter his pig at the state fair and treats the porker like a king, lavishing more attention on the beast that his wife. Melissa is preparing her locally famous pickles and mincemeat, hoping to win a blue ribbon herself. At the fair, Wayne falls for Emily (Vivian Blaine), a dance-band singer, and Margy meets Pat (Dana Andrews), a newspaper reporter. After the obligatory romantic complications, Abel's pig hogs the show, Melissa's mincemeat is spiked with brandy and gets the judges tipsy enough to award her the prize, and the couples wind up happy. The story is as light as cotton candy, but everyone has such a good time and rural life seems so sweetly appealing that urbanites flocked to real state fairs after this movie was released. The beautiful songs include the Oscar-winning "It Might As Well Be Spring"; Alfred Newman's musical direction was also Oscar-nominated, but lost to Georgie Stoll for ANCHORS AWEIGH.

STATE OF SIEGE

(ETAT DE SIEGE)
1972 120m c   ★★★½
Political/Thriller   PG/X
Reggana/Cinema 10/Unidis/Euro Intl./Dieter Geissler
(France/U.S./Italy/West Germany)

Yves Montand (Philip Michael Santore), Renato Salvatori (Capt. Lopez), O.E. Hasse (Carlos Ducas), Jacques Weber (Hugo), Jean-Luc Bideau (Este), Evangeline Peterson (Mrs. Santore), Maurice Teynac (Minister of Internal Security), Yvette Etievant (Woman Senator), Harald Wolff (Minister of Foreign Affairs), Nemesio Antunes (President of the Republic)

p, Jacques Perrin; d, Constantin Costa-Gavras; w, Franco Solinas, Constantin Costa-Gavras; ph, Pierre-William Glenn (Eastmancolor); ed, Francoise Bonnot; m, Mikis Theodorakis; prod d, Jacques D'Ovidio; art d, Jacques d'Ovidio

Taking aim at the repressive right-wing government of a Latin American country (a thinly veiled Uruguay) and the support it received from at least one employee of the US Agency for International Development (AID), Costa-Gavras offers here another tightly knit political thriller along the lines of his Z, MISSING and THE CONFESSION. Set in the 1970s, STATE OF SEIGE chronicles the kidnaping of AID "traffic expert" Philip Santore (Yves Montand) by Tupamaro-like left-wing guerrillas who are determined to prove he is behind the introduction of sophisticated torture methods in their country and in others as well—an international criminal. As the guerrillas try to extract a confession from the wounded but cool Santore, the government's search begins to zero in on their location, with tension mounting as the demand for a prisoner exchange is rejected by the government. When Santore confesses, his captors are left with the difficult decision of whether or not to execute him. Told mostly in flashback and allegedly based on the case of real-life AID officer Daniel Mitrione, STATE OF SIEGE was banned from the American Film Institute theater in Washington upon its release, its opponents arguing that it glorified assassination and was violently anti-American. Never one to pull political punches, Costa-Gavras delivers yet another impassioned, intensely dramatic indictment of the abuse of power. As he is occasionally wont to do, the writer-director stacks the deck in favor of the Leftists, but, regardless, this is a powerful, gripping work.

STATE OF THE UNION

1948 124m bw ★★★★
Political
Liberty

Spencer Tracy (Grant Matthews), Katharine Hepburn (Mary Matthews), Van Johnson (Spike McManus), Angela Lansbury (Kay Thorndyke), Adolphe Menjou (Jim Conover), Lewis Stone (Sam Thorndyke), Howard Smith (Sam Parrish), Maidel Turner (Lulubelle Alexander), Raymond Walburn (Judge Alexander), Charles Dingle (Bill Hardy)

p, Frank Capra; d, Frank Capra; w, Anthony Veiller, Myles Connolly (based on the play by Howard Lindsay, Russel Crouse); ph, George Folsey; ed, William Hornbeck; m, Victor Young; art d, Cedric Gibbons, Urie McCleary; fx, A. Arnold Gillespie; cos, Irene

Spencer Tracy stars in this political drama as a millionaire aircraft manufacturer who is seeking the Republican presidential nomination. A party outsider, Tracy isn't given much of a chance to capture the nomination. Further, his personal life is not the kind most voters would find endearing. He has been separated from his wife, Hepburn, for some years, and is having an affair with Lansbury, a wealthy newspaper publisher. With Lansbury's newspapers supporting Tracy's candidacy, he could become a much more legitimate contender for the nomination. Still, his personal life needs to be set straight, so he asks Hepburn to return to him and pose as his loving wife during the campaign. Hepburn agrees but makes it clear that it will be on a temporary basis and that she won't stay beyond his election, if he ever gets the nomination. Tracy's campaign picks up steam and Menjou, a powerful political boss, gives Tracy his substantial support. Also joining the campaign is Johnson, a successful newspaperman who takes a leave from his job to serve as Tracy's publicist. Tracy had begun the campaign with strong convictions, but as the campaign grind continues and as the nomination becomes a very real possibility, he is soon making accommodations and compromises, most suggested to him by Lansbury and Menjou. Hepburn watches her husband alter his values to suit others, and she becomes upset by these developments. Her love for Tracy has started to return and she can't bear to see him sell out. At a dinner party, she tells him that she thinks his advisers are morally bankrupt and urges him to distance himself from them and to retain his own sense of values. Tracy is moved by Hepburn's words and then on a radio broadcast, announces to the listening audience that he is taking his name off the nominating slate because he feels he is not worthy of consideration on the voters' part. He then returns to Hepburn's open arms.

One of the joys of the Broadway hit upon which this film is based was that the authors changed the dialogue almost weekly to reflect what was happening in the news. In making the movie, the dialogue obviously was frozen, but many of the jokes and barbs were clearly aimed at events surrounding the 1948 presidential election pitting President Harry S. Truman against Republican challenger Thomas E. Dewey. The film was originally set to star Gary Cooper and Claudette Colbert, and when that casting fell through, Tracy was immediately picked for the male

lead. Despite the fact that Hepburn had turned down the same role in the play, she was anxious to do it opposite Tracy in the film and a deal was struck. There was much tension on the set between Hepburn and Menjou. During this time the government had begun to investigate the Hollywood community, searching for communists, a practice Hepburn deplored and Menjou supported. This may have helped the picture, since the characters played by Hepburn and Menjou are adversaries throughout the film. The acting is first-rate as are the script, direction, and technical credits. Though it may seem somewhat dated to younger audiences, it remains an entertaining and uplifting movie experience.

STATE OF THINGS, THE

1982 121m bw ★★★½
Drama /AA
Gray City

Isabelle Weingarten (Anna), Rebecca Pauly (Joan), Jeffrey Kime (Mark), Geoffrey Carey (Robert), Camilla Mora (Julia), Alexandra Auder (Jane), Patrick Bauchau (Friedrich), Paul Getty, III (Dennis), Viva Auder (Kate), Samuel Fuller (Joe)

p, Chris Sievernich; d, Wim Wenders; w, Wim Wenders, Robert Kramer; ph, Henri Alekan, Fred Murphy; ed, Barbara von Weitershausen; m, Jurgen Knieper; art d, Ze Branco; cos, Maria Gonzaga

THE STATE OF THINGS is the innovative and exciting saga of a filmmaker and his crew shooting a remake of the Hollywood B movie THE MOST DANGEROUS MAN ON EARTH in Spain. They are stranded with no money and, worse, no film. The adventure begins as the director searches to find an elusive American producer. The film reflects the life of director Wim Wenders. Having spent a couple of years on HAMMETT, Wenders turned to Francis Ford Coppola for funds to keep the production afloat. After a stint in filmmaking limbo, HAMMETT finally emerged, bearing little resemblance to Wenders's original conception. Wenders's debt to Hollywood movies is acknowledged in the casting of Samuel Fuller as a cameraman and Roger Corman as a lawyer. Exquisitely photographed in crisp black and white by Henri Alekan, the veteran cinematographer who would go on to shoot Wenders's WINGS OF DESIRE.

STATE'S ATTORNEY

1932 73m bw ★★★★
Drama
RKO

John Barrymore (Tom Cardigan), Helen Twelvetrees (June Perry), William "Stage" Boyd (Vanny Powers), Jill Esmond (Lillian Ulrich), Raul Roulien (Senor Alvarado), Ralph Ince (Defense Attorney), Frederick Burton (Judge), Leon Ames (Prosecutor), Lee Phelps (Bartender), Nat Pendleton (Boxer)

p, James Kevin McGuinness; d, George Archainbaud; w, Gene Fowler, Rowland Brown (based on a story by Louis Stevens); ph, Leo Tover; ed, Charles L. Kimball, William Hamilton; art d, Carroll Clark

In this entertaining though improbable courtroom drama, John Barrymore plays a young man who becomes a lawyer after leaving reform school. He becomes the attorney for William Boyd, a powerful underworld figure and a former classmate of Barrymore from reform school. Barrymore eventually turns over a new leaf, leaving Boyd and working his way up to the state's attorney's office, where he becomes an assistant DA. He is assigned to go after Boyd on gambling and murder charges, and in the course of the investigation meets Helen Twelvetrees, who is on trial through a misunderstanding of her presence at one of Boyd's gambling joints. Eventually Barrymore convicts Boyd, getting him the death penalty, but the attorney's past is exposed in the process. Barrymore graciously resigns from office but with Twelvetrees by his side the future looks bright.

In his first film at RKO, Barrymore fairly chews up the scenery then spits it out with his lively histrionics. Though the script (written especially for the actor by his good friend Gene Fowler) is pure fabrication, George Archainbaud's direction, coupled with his star's performance, weaves an interesting tale. This originally was to be directed by cowriter Rowland Brown, but he was replaced twice: first by Irving Pichel, then by Archainbaud. In 1937, this film was remade as CRIMINAL LAWYER with Lee Tracy in the Barrymore role.

STAVISKY

1974 115m c ★★★½
Political/Biography PG/A
Ariane/Cerita/Euro Intl. (France)

Jean-Paul Belmondo *(Serge Alexandre Stavisky)*, Charles Boyer *(Raoul)*, Francois Perier *(Borelli)*, Anny Duperey *(Arlette)*, Michel Lonsdale *(Mezy)*, Claude Rich *(Bonny)*, Marcel Cuvilier *(Bosseaud)*, Jacques Spiesser *(Granville)*, Gigi Balista *(Henriet)*, Roberto Bisacco *(Montalvo)*

d, Alain Resnais; w, Jorge Semprun; ph, Sacha Vierny (Eastmancolor); ed, Albert Jurgenson; m, Stephen Sondheim

A fascinating true story of the man who almost brought down the French government. Serge Stavisky committed suicide on January 3, 1934. The Russian-born promoter had been involved with the issuance of phony bonds and several other crimes, but he had evidently been protected by officials in high places (he supposedly distributed millions of francs in bribes). When one of the officials was murdered, there were accusations that this man in the public prosecutor's office was silenced to keep from spilling the beans. Factions from all of the parties began stirring up trouble and claiming that it was due to the basic corruption in the elected government. Riots began on February 6-8, and a general strike was called. The government teetered and fell, then a new coalition was formed by people who had been outside of the Stavisky influence, and France went on. That's how it ended. How it all happened is the subject of the movie by Resnais, a different kind of film from the director who helmed LAST YEAR AT MARIENBAD and HIROSHIMA, MON AMOUR. The screenplay is by the man who wrote Z, so it is literate and has more than a bit of politics attached. Belmondo plays the title role, a small-time hustler who migrates to France, becomes an embezzler, and uses his personal charm and diabolical tactics to rise quickly to a place of economic importance with a rash of bold moves. Belmondo's wife is Duperey, who goes along with his machinations, and Boyer is a poor Spanish nobleman who dreams of stirring up a civil war in Spain and taking over after the current regime has been destroyed. The picture belongs to Belmondo, who oozes confidence as he makes his way up through the whirlpools of politics and emerges as the most powerful man in the country. Then, when it seems as though he's gone too far, all of his associates desert him and he is left with only one recourse, the taking of his own life. With that, he duplicates what his father did upon hearing that his son had been clapped in jail. The picture is technically brilliant, visually stunning, and ceaselessly interesting. But the hero is a villain without much to like, and audiences want someone to root for; thus, this movie did not make a great deal at the box office. Sondheim's music is a bit too intellectual for the emotions seen on-screen.

STEALING HEAVEN

1989 110m c ★★★½
Historical/Romance /15
Amy/Jadran (U.K./Yugoslavia)

Derek De Lint *(Abelard)*, Kim Thompson *(Heloise)*, Denholm Elliott *(Fulbert)*, Bernard Hepton *(Bishop)*, Kenneth Cranham *(Suger)*, Patsy Byrne *(Agnes)*, Mark Jax *(Jourdain)*, Tim Watson *(Francois)*, Rachel Kempson *(Prioress)*, Angela Pleasence *(Sister Cecilia)*

p, Simon MacCorkindale, Andros Epaminondas; d, Clive Donner; w, Chris Bryant (based on the novel by Marion Meade); ph, Mikael Salomon; ed, Michael Ellis; m, Nick Bicat; prod d, Voytek Roman; art d, Dusko Jericevic; cos, Phyllis Dalton

Adapted by Chris Bryant from Marion Meade's historical novel of the same name, STEALING HEAVEN retells the true story of the ill-fated romance between the French religious philosopher Abelard (Derek de Lint) and Heloise (Kim Thomson), niece of a church canon, in 12th-century Paris. The finest teacher at the cathedral school of Notre Dame, Abelard is a lover of earthly delights, but his vocation requires him to practice celibacy. To protect him from the influence of his lusty students, the bishop of Paris (Bernard Hepton) orders Abelard to move into the home of the canon, Fulbert (Denholm Elliott), and it is only a matter of time before the philosopher and the bright, independent Heloise are involved in a passionate affair that enrages Fulbert. Told from Heloise's point of view, STEALING HEAVEN unfolds with the pulpy fervor of a classic bodice-ripping romance, but it's an uncommonly well-crafted one. Veteran director Clive Donner displays a sure hand with Bryant's complex script, making evocative use of Yugoslavian locations and a first-rate cast. De Lint (THE ASSAULT) is charismatic and compelling in his portrayal Abelard's interior struggle between the spirit and the flesh, and Thomson is equally effective as the provocative Heloise.

STEEL HELMET, THE

1951 84m bw ★★★★
War /A
Deputy

Gene Evans *(Sgt. Zack)*, Robert Hutton *(Pvt. "Conchie" Bronte)*, Richard Loo *(Sgt. "Buddhahead" Tanaka)*, Steve Brodie *(Lt. Driscoll)*, James Edwards *(Cpl. "Medic" Thompson)*, Sid Melton *(Joe, 2nd GI)*, Richard Monahan *(Pvt. Baldy)*, William Chun *("Short Round")*, Harold Fong *(The Red)*, Neyle Morrow *(1st GI)*

p, Samuel Fuller; d, Samuel Fuller; w, Samuel Fuller; ph, Ernest Miller; ed, Philip Cahn; m, Paul Dunlap; art d, Theobold Holsopple; fx, Ben Southland, Ray Mercer; cos, Alfred Berke

Scripted in a week, shot in 10 days, and released only six months after the start of the Korean War, Sam Fuller's THE STEEL HELMET stands as one of the best films about that war or any war. Dark, violent, and disturbing, this film does not celebrate duty, honor, and heroism; instead it shows men simply trying to survive the madness of war. The film opens as Evans, a tough veteran sergeant, crawls through a smoky battlefield littered with corpses. Wounded in the leg, his arms tied behind him, Evans slithers painfully along the ground, trying to avoid the sniper that has slaughtered his whole company. Evans is saved by Chun, a South Korean orphan whose nickname is "Short Round" (a name stolen by Steven Spielberg for his cute Oriental kid in INDIANA JONES AND THE TEMPLE OF DOOM in 1984), who cuts the soldier's binding. With scarcely a "thank you," Evans tends to his wound and packs up his belongings. Looking to settle his debt to the boy by giving him a chocolate bar, Evans discovers he has no candy, and Chun tags along. Evans soon meets up with a black medic, Edwards; he, too, is the only survivor of his unit. Evans asks the medic for a chocolate bar so that he can get rid of the kid, but the kid refuses to abandon Evans. Eventually the two soldiers and the boy meet up with a group of new recruits who have fallen into an ambush. Evans manages to extricate the soldiers from their predicament, but agrees to lead them on their mission only if one of the soldiers will give up his box of cigars. The tiny group then proceeds to an ancient Buddhist temple which is to be used as an observation post to aid the artillery. Also in the temple is a North Korean major, Fong, who is to be captured and brought back for questioning. At the temple, the cynical, somewhat racist soldiers are awestruck by the giant statue of Buddha that resides there and are moved to take their helmets off in its presence. Soon after their arrival, one of the GIs, Melton, is killed by Fong. Evans finds the Korean communist and wounds him. Once subdued, Fong makes it clear to the Americans he is not a pawn of the Russians by asserting his nationalism: "I am not a Russian! I am a North Korean communist." The defiant prisoner eventually pushes Evans too far when he ridicules Chun after the boy prays that Sergeant Zack will like him. When the boy is hit and killed by a stray bullet, Evans' repressed affection for the child surfaces and he shoots Fong for making light of the boy's prayer. After this momentary burst of emotion, Evans once agains assumes the cold, brutal attitude that has meant survival. When one of his men is killed, he tells the others not to retrieve the dog tags because ". . .a dead man is a dead man and nobody cares." When a soldier, shocked at Evans' cynicism, tries to remove the dead man's dog tags, a booby trap planted on the corpse explodes, killing the GI. Meanwhile, Fong, who is being tended to by medic Edwards, realizes he is about to die and rejects communist ideology by embracing his Buddhist roots. The dying man asks Edwards for a prayer, and the medic gently tells him, "Buddha blesses you." Soon the Americans find themselves under siege by the North Koreans. After an intense battle, the GIs manage to defeat the communists, but the film ends with the soldiers staring blankly, on the verge of madness, with many battles yet ahead.

THE STEEL HELMET is a gripping war film that does not glamorize conflict but shows soldiers trying to survive in an environment contradictory to the point of insanity. A veteran of WWII, Evans knows that if he allows himself emotion, he makes himself more vulnerable to pain. Theoretically a soldier is supposed to feel a passion for what he is fighting. In Fuller's reality, emotional attachments and deeply felt passions can mean death. This is a film made for an audience tired of war. Five short years before, the world had welcomed home its battle-weary soldiers from the violent and deadly conflict of WWII. Before Americans had time to put their lives back in order, families were again ripped apart when the men were called off to another war, one that proved not to be so clear cut. This time the public wondered whether the bloodshed was necessary. THE STEEL HELMET reflects these doubts. Those soldiers who are not confused and scared are cold and cynical. The rules of this war are different from the last. The enemy looks exactly like the people the soldiers are supposed to be defending. A confused soldier asks Evans, "How do you tell a North Korean from a South Korean?" Evans replies, "If he's running with you he's a South Korean. If he's running after you he's a North Korean." Director Fuller emphasizes this confusion visually. The film is very claustrophobic (most of the action takes place on a single set) and the

characters nearly always seem to be immersed in smoke and fog. Things are never what they seem. GI Monahan's snoring is mistaken for the whistle of incoming shells, Buddhist priests turn out to be North Korean soldiers in disguise, and Loo, the intelligent and brave South Korean soldier, isn't trusted by the American lieutenant. By the end of the film, the American soldiers who have survived are on the brink of madness. Fuller's final comment on the situation comes with the closing credit, which reads, "There is no end to this story."

STEEL MAGNOLIAS

1989 118m c   ★★★
Comedy/Drama   PG/15
Rastar

Sally Field (M'Lynn Eatenton), Dolly Parton (Truvy Jones), Shirley MacLaine (Ouiser Boudreaux), Daryl Hannah (Annelle Dupuy Desoto), Olympia Dukakis (Clairee Belcher), Julia Roberts (Shelby Eatenton Latcherie), Tom Skerritt (Drum Eatenton), Dylan McDermott (Jackson Latcherie), Kevin J. O'Connor (Sammy Desoto), Sam Shepard (Spud Jones)

p, Ray Stark; d, Herbert Ross; w, Robert Harling (based on his play); ph, John A. Alonzo; ed, Paul Hirsch; m, Georges Delerue; prod d, Gene Callahan, Edward Pisoni; art d, Hub Braden, Michael Okowita; chor, Spencer Henderson; cos, Julie Weiss

Based on screenwriter Robert Harling's award-winning off-Broadway play, STEEL MAGNOLIAS tells the story of six southern women whose lives interconnect in a beauty parlor in their small Louisiana town. M'Lynn Eatenton (Sally Field), mother of headstrong Shelby (Julia Roberts), is worried about her daughter's upcoming marriage, fearing for the children that the diabetic, seizure-prone Shelby wants to have. Their friends at the beauty parlor—Truvy (Dolly Parton), who runs the parlor; Annelle (Daryl Hannah), her assistant; Clairee (Olympia Dukakis), an aristocratic widow; and Ouiser (Shirley MacLaine), the town scold—gossip and cope with a variety of problems, among them a failing marriage for Truvy, and some chameleonlike changes for Annelle. Shelby marries and has her baby, but just when things look rosy, tragedy rears its head. STEEL MAGNOLIAS is an old-fashioned "klatsch" film, a prefeminist relic in which a group of women eschew the public world of men in favor of the community of the coffee table. Their world is inferior to men's in terms of power but superior to it in emotion and insight into the things that "really matter." Not surprisingly, the "klatscher" myth has been concocted largely by men (most notably by George Cukor). Here director Herbert Ross (TURNING POINT) gets generally strong performances from his ensemble, and an especially good one from Field in a role that really doesn't suit her. The film was shot on location in Natchitoches, Louisiana, hometown of actor-turned-writer Harling, who based his play on the experiences of his own mother and sister.

STEELYARD BLUES

1973 92m c   ★★
Crime/Comedy   PG/15
WB

Jane Fonda (Iris Caine), Donald Sutherland (Jesse Veldini), Peter Boyle (Eagle Throneberry), Garry Goodrow (Duval Jacks), Howard Hesseman (Frank Veldin), John Savage (The Kid), Richard Schaal (Zoo Official), Mel Stewart (Black Man in Jail), Morgan Upton (Police Captain), Roger Bowen (Fire Commissioner) p, Tony Bill, Michael Phillips, Julia Phillips; d, Alan Myerson; w, David S. Ward; ph, Laszlo Kovacs, Stevan Larner (Technicolor); ed, Donn Cambern, Robert Grovenor; m, Nick Gravenites, Paul Butterfield, David Shire; art d, Vincent Cresciman

STEELYARD BLUES is a terrific 1960s movie made in the 1970s. Screenwriter David S. Ward had two of his scripts filmed in 1973, both by the same producers. One was THE STING, and the other was this one. Sutherland, who was also the executive producer, is a man who loves demolition derbies, and his passion for them has caused him to steal cars. That, in turn, has sent him up the river a few times, much to the dismay of Hesseman, his ambitious brother who seeks elected office higher than the district attorney's slot he now holds. Sutherland exits the slammer for his latest offense and gets in touch with Fonda, again playing a hooker—the same thing she did with Sutherland in KLUTE. Fonda likes Sutherland and wouldn't mind reawakening the love they once had for each other, but she won't be part of his ultimate dream: the wrecking of school buses, campers, and mobile homes in a demolition derby to end all such derbies. Hesseman is acting as his brother's parole officer and gets Sutherland a job at the local zoo, cleaning out the animals' cages. In his off hours, Sutherland hangs out with Savage and Boyle, a refugee from the funny farm. Boyle dresses up in a wild array of wigs and costumes, depending on what he has to do that day. Boyle and Savage take Sutherland to meet Goodrow, who is spending all of his time attempting to rebuild a WWII plane. All agree that there must be a better world out there, a land where they don't have to worry about cops, where there are no rules. Sutherland agrees with Goodrow that the plane may be their ticket out of the conventional world. Sutherland celebrates by quitting his job at the zoo, which violates the terms of his parole. Hesseman informs the police, and the parolee gets whacked around by the men in blue. Hesseman is a regular patron of Fonda's, but, when she hears what he has done, she refuses to sleep with him and is also worked over. Goodrow announces that the plane will never get up in the air unless they can secure certain parts which are unavailable through regular sources. The only place where they can be found is in the parts department at the local naval air base. The gang dons black outfits, executes a raid and secures the goods, but Boyle somehow gets lost. They work all night on the plane, and it's ready to fly at dawn. Hesseman leads a fleet of police cars which block the runway, so the plane can't get away. Now Boyle, dressed like Marlon Brando in VIVA ZAPATA, rides in, leading a herd of horses. Sutherland sets off bombs that explode the plane. Fire and smoke cover the area, so the cops can't move in, nor can they see that Boyle has a large helicopter waiting. Fonda, Sutherland, Boyle, Savage, and Goodrow board the chopper and whirl into the air as the picture closes.

The film is a mixture of KLUTE and M*A*S*H* but without the intelligence of the former or the wit of the latter. Badly directed by first-timer Myerson, who helped found San Francisco's "The Committee," an excellent improvisational troupe, many members of which are in this film. In a small role, note Howard Storm, the former standup comic who has since become a sought-after director for sit-coms. Myerson's direction was haphazard, technically inept, failed to mine any humor in potentially hilarious situations, and showed a distinct lack of knowledge of editing or camera placement.

STELLA DALLAS
1937   104m   bw   ★★★★
Drama   /U
UA

Barbara Stanwyck (Stella Martin Dallas), John Boles (Stephen Dallas), Anne Shirley (Laurel Dallas), Barbara O'Neil (Helen Morrison), Alan Hale (Ed Munn), Marjorie Main (Mrs. Martin), Edmund Elton (Mr. Martin), George Walcott (Charlie Martin), Gertrude Short (Carrie Jenkins), Tim Holt (Richard)

p, Samuel Goldwyn; d, King Vidor; w, Sarah Y. Mason, Victor Heerman (based on the novel by Olive Higgins Prouty and the play by Harry Wagstaff Gribble, Gertrude Purcell); ph, Rudolph Mate; ed, Sherman Todd; art d, Richard Day; cos, Omar Kiam

Grand Vidor soap opera, boasting a brilliant Stanwyck performance. She's a tough cookie, a bit of a shrew and a grasping woman who snares Boles, a well-born young man whose family lost its old money when his father committed suicide. Boles has moved to a tiny New England town where he meets Stanwyck. He had been engaged to O'Neil, a woman of the same social level as himself, but when his fortune was lost he left, and she took up with another. Stanwyck is aware of his background from reading the tabloids. They have a daughter, but the difference in their classes continues to keep them distanced from one another. When Boles is offered a job in New York and asks Stanwyck to come with him, she fears being laughed at by his society friends, so he goes south and she stays in the mill town.

Stanwyck begins running around with the rough-hewn, hard-drinking friends of her youth but she remains a good mother, almost too good, as she lavishes love and affection on the child (played as an adult by Shirley). Hale would like to marry Stanwyck, but her life is devoted to her daughter. One day, while riding a train, Hale gets abusive and offends many of the townspeople, who associate him with Stanwyck and Shirley. When Shirley invites her friends to a birthday party, she and Stanwyck are snubbed in a particularly touching scene. Boles would like a divorce so he can wed O'Neil, a widow with two sons, but Stanwyck will not give her consent. Shirley and Stanwyck visit a posh resort on the strength of Boles's cash, and on this trip Stanwyck learns that her coarse behavior and garish clothing stand in the way of Shirley's happiness.

Despite unforgettable work in a slew of other films, Stanwyck was quoted as saying that this was the best acting she'd ever done and it remained her favorite role. Only 30 years old at the time of STELLA, she had to be aged considerably to look right as the mother of an adult daughter. The role demanded a vast range of emotion, and Stanwyck wrung every last smile and tear out of every speech. Even when she was simply reacting, Stanwyck emanated frustration channeled into maternal martyrdom, but without an ounce of self-pity. She is well-supported by Shirley and Hale, with John Boles his typical handsome if rather stolid self and Barbara O'Neill fine as the noble rich woman. The film was remade in 1990 as STELLA, with Bette Midler having some effective moments, with no help from anyone else.

STEPFATHER, THE
1987   90m   c   ★★★½
Horror/Thriller   R/18
ITC

Terry O'Quinn (Jerry Blake, the Stepfather/Henry Morrison/Bill Hodgkins), Jill Schoelen (Stephanie Maine), Shelley Hack (Susan Blake), Charles Lanyer (Dr. Bondurant), Stephen Shellen (Jim Ogilvie), Stephen Miller (Al Brennan), Robyn Stevan (Karen), Jeff Schultz (Paul Baker), Lindsay Bourne (Art Teacher), Anna Hagan (Mrs. Leitner) p, Jay Benson; d, Joseph Ruben; w, Donald E. Westlake (based on a story by Carolyn Lefcourt, Brian Garfield, Westlake); ph, John Lindley; ed, George Bowers; m, Patrick Moraz; prod d, James William Newport; art d, David Willson; cos, Mina Mittleman

Just when it looked like slasher movies were wholly irredeemable, director Joseph Ruben came along to prove there is some intelligent life in this otherwise bereft subgenre. Featuring a fascinating script by novelist Donald Westlake, some taut direction, and an absolutely absorbing performance by Terry O'Quinn, THE STEPFATHER is not just another slice-and-dice thriller. Loosely based on a real-life case, the film begins in a picturesque suburb, where a rugged-looking, bearded man (O'Quinn) washes blood from his hands, cuts his hair, shaves, and changes clothes to emerge a completely different person. As he walks downstairs, we see that the man's entire family has been massacred. One year later, the man resurfaces as Jerry Blake—in a new suburb, with a new job, a new wife (Shelley Hack), and a teenage stepdaughter (Jill Schoelen). Gradually the secret madness and alternate lives of Jerry Blake begin to surface. THE STEPFATHER fits in nicely among such examinations of the seedy underbelly of "perfect" family life as Alfred Hitchcock's SHADOW OF A DOUBT and David Lynch's BLUE VELVET. Although the last part of the picture disintegrates into some typical slasher-movie conventions and a plethora of clumsy Hitchcock homages, the majority of the film is *definitely* not typical. Fueled by an intense and intricate performance by O'Quinn, the movie is a fascinating examination of America's predilection for appearances over substance. Jerry Blake is the consummate actor, masking his crazed state with an air of friendliness and easy charm, whose false veneer of bliss has been spoon-fed to his diseased mind via television. He wants the perfect TV family; but when reality rears its ugly head and day-to-day problems cannot be dealt with in a matter of minutes, his repressed rage erupts.

STEPFORD WIVES, THE

1975 114m c   ★★½
Science Fiction/Comedy   PG/15
Palomar/Fadsin

Katharine Ross (*Joanna*), Paula Prentiss (*Bobby*), Peter Masterson (*Walter*), Nanette Newman (*Carol*), Patrick O'Neal (*Dale Coba*), Tina Louise (*Charmaine*), Carol Rossen (*Dr. Fancher*), William Prince (*Artist*), Paula Trueman (*Welcome Wagon Lady*), Remak Ramsay (*Atkinson*)

p, Edgar J. Scherick; d, Bryan Forbes; w, William Goldman (based on the novel by Ira Levin); ph, Owen Roizman (TVC Color); ed, Timothy Gee; m, Michael Small; prod d, Gene Callahan; fx, Dick Smith

Ira Levin is an eclectic writer who has done comedy-drama (*Sleuth*), adventure (*The Boys from Brazil*), thrillers (*Rosemary's Baby*), and science fiction such as *The Stepford Wives*. But Goldman's screenplay and Forbes's ponderous direction slow his exciting novel to a laborious pace. Goldman, an often excellent writer, scripted BUTCH CASSIDY AND THE SUNDANCE KID, and Forbes proved himself with SEANCE ON A WET AFTERNOON, as well as many other films. So what happened here? The first hour takes what feels like two, and the last 44 minutes goes like an Indy car, so the pace is alternately snail's and Lamborghini's. Ross and her husband, Masterson, leave the hectic world of Manhattan and settle in the small, tranquil town of Stepford, Connecticut (actually shot in Westport). She meets the local wives, who seem weird to her, talking about dumb things and sounding like Procter & Gamble commercials. The two women who perplex her most are Louise and Newman (Forbes's wife in real life). They are perfect—they're devoted to their husbands, to keeping their homes squeaky clean, to having every hair in place, etc. This odd contentment gnaws at Ross. Her only normal friend is also a newcomer, Prentiss. O'Neal is the important man in the town and runs a men's club that Ross and Prentiss would like to know more about. After much palaver, the truth comes out. These women are not women at all, just flawlessly executed robot replicas of the real wives who came to Stepford, and who knows what's happened to the originals? The only difference is that these women don't argue with their husbands, do everything that's asked of them, and fulfill every male chauvinist fantasy ever imagined. Ross would like to expose the truth once she learns it, but by that time it's too late. She and Prentiss are seen at the conclusion as two of a gaggle of Stepford Wives, happily exchanging recipes in the supermarket as they shop for their hubbies' favorite dishes. The film has more than a passing similarity to THE INVASION OF THE BODY SNATCHERS, although that was played totally serious and this has more than a few laughs, particularly when the wives are acting in their "whatever you want, darling" mode. With 15 minutes cut out of the opening 60, this would have been a whizzer.

STERILE CUCKOO, THE

1969 108m c   ★★★½
Romance/Comedy   PG/X
Boardwalk

Liza Minnelli (*Pookie*), Wendell Burton (*Jerry*), Tim McIntire (*Charlie Schumacher*), Elizabeth Harrower (*Landlady*), Austin Green (*Pookie's Father*), Sandra Faison (*Nancy Putnam*), Chris Bugbee (*Roe*), Jawn McKinley (*Helen Upshaw*), Fred Lerner, A. Frederick Gooseen

p, Alan J. Pakula; d, Alan J. Pakula; w, Alvin Sargent; ph, Milton Krasner (Technicolor); ed, Sam O'Steen, John W. Wheeler; m, Fred Karlin; art d, Roland Anderson; fx, Charles Spurgeon; cos, Jennifer Parsons, John A. Anderson

Pakula's directorial debut, after he had produced pictures directed by his partner, Robert Mulligan, was a smasher. Unlike many first-timers, Pakula used understatement, avoided cinematic tricks, and spent time with the actors to extract superb performances from Minnelli (who was nominated for an Oscar) and Burton, who was making his debut as well after starring on Broadway for three years in the title role of "You're a Good Man, Charlie Brown." Shot primarily at the Hamilton College campus in upstate New York, the film tells a tender story that concentrates on youth but cannot be classified as a youth picture because it transcends age. Minnelli and Burton meet on a bus going up to school. They are at different colleges—and he's glad of that, as her quirky behavior while they ride embarrasses him. Burton is a quiet young man studying etymology, and Minnelli is a motherless waif whose father has never understood her and who has sent her to a series of camps and boarding schools just to keep her away from him. It's not that her dad, Green, doesn't care about her; it's just that she is such a "weirdo" (which is what she calls everyone else). Burton disembarks from the bus and settles into his dorm room with slob McIntire, a beer-drinking boor and bore who talks endlessly of his sexual conquests. Burton is just about getting used to his new surroundings when Minnelli arrives, in a car that looks as though it should have been junked years before. She tells Burton that she intends to spend the weekend with him. He is hard-pressed to send her away after she's made a dangerous trip in that old automobile, so he puts her in a local boardinghouse. They have a marvelous time over the weekend and find something wonderful in each other—despite her prating on and on about her background. She confesses that her mother died giving birth to her. "My first victim," is how she puts it. Their schools are about 90 minutes apart, but that doesn't stop them from spending as much time with each other as they can, and the two diverse people begin to fall in love. Burton is sexually naive, and Minnelli makes sure they check into a motel to make love. While he stands there self-consciously, with his heavy coat buttoned up to his neck, she takes off all her clothes and then says, "Okay, Valentino. Hit it." It's a nervous moment for Burton, but he makes it through and a new dimension has been added to their friendship. McIntire invites Burton to come with him for the Christmas break. His parents have a cabin in the mountains, and the two boys can ski to their hearts' content. Minnelli has nowhere to go during the holidays and is hurt by Burton's decision to leave with McIntire, so she retaliates by saying that she is carrying Burton's child. He pales at this news but does the decent thing and asks her to get married, an offer she promptly declines. After returning to school, Minnelli tells Burton that she's no longer pregnant (and one wonders if she ever was). Later, he takes her to a party at his school, where she drinks too much, becomes vicious, and insults all of his pals. When she calls him later to apologize, Burton says that he won't be going home for the Easter break but will remain at school to get in some much-needed studying. She asks whether she can stay with him, as she has nowhere to go during that holiday either. At first he balks, but she prevails on him with tears and vows that she won't ever get in his way. Burton acquiesces, and she moves in for the week. Although they both try their best, it's clear that the idea was not a good one; and when the week is over and McIntire is due to return, Burton suggests they take a respite from each other. Weeks pass, and he calls her school to learn that she's left college. He locates her at the boardinghouse near his school and the film ends with a scene that will tear your heart out.

THE STERILE CUCKOO is a lovely movie that sometimes gets a bit too arch but usually remains touching and funny. Minnelli's performance is a *tour de force*; and Burton, who seemed to disappear after his next picture, FORTUNE AND MEN'S EYES, is excellent as well.

STING, THE

1973   129m   c   ★★½
Crime/Comedy   PG
Richard D. Zanuck/David Brown

Paul Newman (*Henry Gondorff/Mr. Shaw*), Robert Redford (*Johnny Hooker/Kelly*), Robert Shaw (*Doyle Lonnegan*), Charles Durning (*Lt. William Snyder*), Ray Walston (*J.J. Singleton*), Eileen Brennan (*Billie*), Harold Gould (*Kid Twist*), John Heffernan (*Eddie Niles*), Dana Elcar (*FBI Agent Polk*), Jack Kehoe ("*Erie Kid*")

p, Tony Bill, Julia Phillips, Michael Phillips; d, George Roy Hill; w, David S. Ward; ph, Robert Surtees (Technicolor); ed, William Reynolds; m, Scott Joplin, John Philip Sousa; art d, Henry Bumstead; fx, Bob Warner, Albert Whitlock; cos, Edith Head

Vastly overrated Crooks-R-Us—this time *you* wear the moustache, enhanced by fine period trappings and flavor. Ultimately empty stuff, but preferable to BUTCH CASSIDY.

By reuniting director George Roy Hill and actors Robert Redford and Paul Newman (BUTCH CASSIDY AND THE SUNDANCE KID), THE STING emerged an equally successful entertainment, outgrossing every other picture of the year. Frightening. The story begins in September, 1936, in Joliet,

Illinois. The city is run by corrupt officials, and the numbers racket runs rampant. When two-bit drifter Redford and his partner, Robert Earl Jones, the veteran bunco artist of the area, con one of the racketeers out of a $5,000 delivery, they find themselves mixed up with the big boys in Chicago and their head man, Shaw, a sleazy gangster who would gladly kill a drifter like Redford to retain control of his operation. Police lieutenant Durning shakes down Redford, who has already gambled away most of the money, threatening to kill him if he doesn't pay it back. Jones, who has decided to retire from the con game and get into a legitimate business is killed by two of Shaw's thugs. On the run from Joliet police and Shaw's goons, Redford heads for Chicago to meet a friend of Jones, a man described as "the greatest con artist of them all," Newman. Determined to avenge the murder of Jones, Redford makes plans to "sting" Shaw out of a fortune. Newman, a drunk who lives in backroom squalor in a joint run by Brennan, is wary of hooking up with the still inexperienced Redford. Newman is, however, finally convinced, and they set the gears into motion.

The gross for 1974 turned out to be a whopping $68,450,000. THE STING also ultimately won seven Oscars: Best Picture, Best Director (Hill), Best Screenplay (Ward), Best Art Direction-Set Decoration (Bumstead, Payne), Best Editing (Reynolds), Best Musical Adaptation (Hamlisch), and Best Costume Design (Head). Proving what? That it was a good year to watch television?

Much of the film's success is a result of its visual brilliance: the aged look of Surtees' photography evokes a feeling of nostalgia, and the art direction, set decoration, and costuming are equally effective. Marvin Hamlisch did a fine job of adapting Scott Joplin's classic rags, especially "The Entertainer," which was soon a radio commonplace and sparked a renewed interest in the composer. Also included from Joplin's works are "Easy Winners," "Pineapple Rag," "The Ragtime Dance," and "Gladiolus Rag." You'd be just as well off with the soundtrack.

STIR CRAZY

1980   111m   c   ★★★
Prison/Comedy   R/15
Columbia

Gene Wilder (*Skip Donahue*), Richard Pryor (*Harry Monroe*), Georg Stanford Brown (*Rory Schultebrand*), JoBeth Williams (*Meredith*), Miguel Suarez (*Jesus Ramirez*), Craig T. Nelson (*Deputy Ward Wilson*), Barry Corbin (*Warden Walter Beatty*), Charles Weldon (*Blade*), Nicolas Coster (*Warden Henry Sampson*), Joel Brooks (*Len Garber*)

p, Hannah Weinstein; d, Sidney Poitier; w, Bruce Jay Friedman; ph, Fred Schuler (Metrocolor); ed, Harry Keller; m, Tom Scott; prod d, Alfred Sweeney; chor, Scott Salmon; cos, Patricia Edwards

An essentially empty script is made palatable by Richard Pryor's ability to be funnier than his material. Pryor and Gene Wilder are two losers from New York who decide to drive to California to change their luck. Along the way they stop in a small town and take a job requiring them to wear woodpecker costumes. When two crooks don identical outfits and rob the local bank, Pryor and Wilder are arrested for the crime, convicted, and given 120-year prison terms. Wilder is his usual hyperactive self, but director Sidney Poitier gets as much as he can out of the uninspired script.

STOLEN KISSES

(BAISERS VOLES)
1968 90m c   ★★★★
Romance/Comedy   R/X
Carrosse/Artistes   (France)

Jean-Pierre Leaud *(Antoine Doinel)*, Delphine Seyrig *(Fabienne Tabard)*, Michel Lonsdale *(M. Tabard)*, Claude Jade *(Christine Darbon)*, Harry-Max *(M. Henri Tabard)*, Daniel Ceccaldi *(M. Darbon)*, Claire Duhamel *(Mme. Darbon)*, Catherine Lutz *(Mme. Catherine)*, Andre Falcon *(M. Blady)*, Paul Pavel *(Julien)*

p, Marcel Berbert; d, Francois Truffaut; w, Francois Truffaut, Bernard Revon, Claude de Givray; ph, Denys Clerval (Eastmancolor); ed, Agnes Guillemot; m, Antoine Duhamel; art d, Claude Pignot

Sadly complacent comedy of French charm, and Paris was never so beguiling. STOLEN KISSES covers the installment in the life of Antoine Doinel (Jean-Pierre Leaud), which began in THE 400 BLOWS and continued through the LOVE AT TWENTY episode entitled "Antoine and Colette." The film picks up as Doinel is discharged from the army at age 20. Unable to make Christine (Claude Jade) love him, he continues his search for the perfect woman. In the process Doinel lands a job with a detective agency, where the rookie Sherlock Holmes bungles every case he investigates. He finally gets a simple assignment in a shoe store after demonstrating his "technical proficiency" by wrapping a shoe box. Doinel is supposed to discover why the store's owner, M. Tabard (Michel Lonsdale), feels hated and whether there is a conspiracy against him; but while working late one night, he begins an affair with Tabard's wife, Fabienne (Delphine Seyrig). Dismissed, as Truffaut's work often is, as overly charming and simplistic, STOLEN KISSES was oddly enough made during a time of extremely intense political crisis in Paris, with a sidebar of artistic controversy. Dedicated to Henri Langlois and his Cinematheque Francaise, STOLEN KISSES was made while Truffaut worked with a defense committee that fought for the reinstatement of the Cinematheque director. Langlois, who in his lifetime was probably responsible for the film education of every aspiring director in France, was ordered removed by Minister of Culture Andre Malraux—a move met with opposition by the entire international film community. Truffaut stated, "If STOLEN KISSES is good, it will be thanks to Langlois." As violence erupted in the streets of Paris, Truffaut continued his filming, but, instead of making the political film one might expect to emerge from a period of revolt, the director chose to reaffirm his belief in cinema.

STONE BOY, THE

1984 93m c   ★★★½
Drama   PG/
FOX

Robert Duvall *(Joe Hillerman)*, Frederic Forrest *(Andy Jansen)*, Glenn Close *(Ruth Hillerman)*, Wilford Brimley *(George Jansen)*, Jason Presson *(Arnold Hillerman)*, Gail Youngs *(Lu Jansen)*, Cindy Fisher *(Amalie)*, Susan Blackstone *(Nora Hillerman)*, Dean Cain *(Eugene Hillerman)*, Kenneth Anderson

p, Joe Roth, Ivan Bloch; d, Christopher Cain; w, Gina Berriault (based on her short story); ph, Juan Ruiz-Anchia (DeLuxe Color); ed, Paul Rubell; m, James Horner; prod d, Joseph G. Pacelli; art d, Stephanie Wooley; cos, Gail Viola

At first glance, the story for this quiet, sensitive film would seem to bear a resemblance to ORDINARY PEOPLE. But this is *really* about ordinary people—Montana farmers who have to cope with tragedy using strength from within and without help from a professional shrink. Director Chris Cain shows enormous talent as he leads the actors through tricky territory. Arnold (Jason Presson) and Eugene Hillerman (Dean Cain, the director's son) are brothers living on a farm in Montana. They rise early to go duck hunting, but their happy plans soon turn tragic as Eugene is accidentally shot by Arnold's gun. Arnold becomes quiet, doesn't know what to do. His brother is dead and he realizes he'll have to tell everyone what happened, but he can't face the fact right away. When he finally returns home to break the terrible news to his parents (Robert Duvall and Glenn Close), he is immediately left outside of their sorrow. Since Arnold is not in tears or hysterical, his father misreads that as his not caring. His mother also can't fathom Arnold's tranquil behavior, but she is less stern. As the whirlpool swims around him, Arnold gets quieter and quieter, becoming a "stone boy" in that he cannot be part of the swirling madness of a family in chaos. A langorous movie with little of the tear jerking and often obvious sequences one might have expected, THE STONE BOY pulls no punches and makes very few statements. All it seems to do is present the story very simply and let the audience decide what's right and what's wrong.

STORMY MONDAY

1988 93m c   ★★★½
Crime/Romance   R/15
British Screen/Film Four/Moving Picture   (U.K.)

Melanie Griffith *(Kate)*, Tommy Lee Jones *(Cosmo)*, Sting *(Finney)*, Sean Bean *(Brendan)*, James Cosmo, Mark Long, Brian Lewis, Derek Hoxby, Heathcote Williams, Prunella Gee

p, Nigel Stafford-Clark; d, Mike Figgis; w, Mike Figgis; ph, Roger Deakins (Rank/Agfa Color); ed, David Martin; m, Mike Figgis; prod d, Andrew McAlpine; cos, Sandy Powell

This feature debut from British writer-director-composer Mike Figgis is a tautly constructed, deftly executed crime thriller. The action is set in Newcastle, England, an economically depressed city desperate for jobs. American business magnate-gangster, Cosmo (Tommy Lee Jones), is launching an ambitious money-laundering scheme by buying up lots of real estate. One man refuses all of Jones's lucrative offers: Finney (Sting), the owner of a successful jazz club. Caught up in the conflict are Kate (Melanie Griffith), an American who has worked for Cosmo as a call girl, and Brendan (Sean Bean), a young jazz enthusiast. When two thugs from London are hired to "persuade" Finney to sell his club, he turns the tables and sends the head assassin back to London with a broken arm. But Cosmo escalates the violence. STORMY MONDAY draws its strength from subtle shadings of character and a vivid evocation of its setting, Newcastle. The little violent action there is takes place either very quickly or offscreen. Figgis's moody realization of the screenplay is quietly effective and brimming with visual nuance and irony.

STORMY WEATHER

1943 77m bw   ★★★½
Musical   /U
FOX

Lena Horne *(Selina Rogers)*, Bill Robinson *(Corky)*, Cab Calloway and His Band, Fats Waller, The Nicholas Brothers *(Themselves)*, Ada Brown *(Ada)*, Dooley Wilson *(Gabe)*, Ned Stanfield, Johnny Horace *(The Shadracks)*, Emmett "Babe" Wallace *(Chick Bailey)*

p, William LeBaron; d, Andrew L. Stone; w, Frederick Jackson, Ted Koehler, H.S. Kraft (based on a story by Jerry Horwin, Seymour B. Robinson); ph, Leon Shamroy; ed, James B. Clark; art d, James Basevi, Joseph C. Wright; fx, Fred Sersen; chor, Clarence Robinson; cos, Helen Rose

Because it contains performances by many of the great black musical stars of its day, STORMY WEATHER will be studied for years to come. The slim story into which the acts are incorporated concerns veteran entertainer Corky (Bill Robinson), who, as he reflects on his career, flashes back to a number of scenes that are all neat musical bits in themselves. (A few were later released as short subjects in black theaters.) Corky's struggles and rise in show business, as well as his split and eventual reconciliation with his wife (Lena Horne), are thinly sketched, with a cavalcade of musical numbers in between. Cab Calloway, Fats Waller, Robinson, Horne, Mae Johnson, The Nicholas Brothers, Babe Wallace, Ada Brown, and many others are featured; about the only cast member who doesn't perform is Dooley Wilson, whose singing was so important in CASABLANCA. Horne, who had just completed CABIN IN THE SKY, was 26, making the 65-year-old Robinson old enough to be her grandfather, not her husband, but the discrepancy is overlooked. Jazz fans will recognize Zutty Singleton at the drums, Coleman Hawkins playing sax, and Taps Miller on trumpet, among several others.

STORY OF A CHEAT, THE
(LE ROMAN D'UN TRICHEUR)
1938 83m bw   ★★★★½
Drama
Cineas   (France)

Sacha Guitry (The Cheat), Jacqueline Delubac (Young Woman), Rosine Derean (The Jewel Thief), Marguerite Moreno (The Countess), Pauline Carton (Mme. Morlot), Gaston Dupray (Waiter), Serge Grave (The Cheat), Pierre Assy (The Cheat), Frehel (Singer), Henri Pfeifer (M. Charbonnier)

d, Sacha Guitry; w, Sacha Guitry (based on his novel Memoires D'un Tricheur); ph, Marcel Lucien; ed, Myriam; m, Adolphe Borchard

An exciting, funny, innovative, and brilliant effort from one of France's most prolific playwrights and filmmakers, Sacha Guitry. Considered to be Guitry's masterpiece, THE STORY OF A CHEAT is told to the audience by the cheat (Guitry, as usual, playing the role) himself, as he writes his memoirs in a Parisian cafe, while on the screen we see the events he is speaking of, acted out without dialogue. All we get to hear is Guitry's witty commentary. His life story begins with the first time he is caught being a cheat, an act which gets him sent to his room without supper. In a stroke of luck, however, his entire family eat poison mushrooms that evening and die. Thus begins a long string of events in which Guitry benefits from his cheating instead of paying for it. Not only is the film itself unique, with its cutting back and forth between past and present and its use of reverse motion and wipes, but its title sequence is also exceptional. Like Francois Truffaut's FAHRENHEIT 451, the credits are spoken by the director, but here we see the characters and filmmakers involved. Not surprisingly, his experimentation and humor have gone on to influence greatly those who've seen the picture, especially the filmmakers of the New Wave. It was chiefly the favorable criticism of filmmakers such as Truffaut, Jean-Luc Godard, and Alain Resnais (who cited THE STORY OF A CHEAT as one of the primary influences of HIROSHIMA MON

AMOUR) that have brought about the reassessment of Guitry. An outstanding contribution to cinematic and narrative technique which Guitry never quite equaled again.

STORY OF A THREE DAY PASS, THE
(LA PERMISSION)
1968 87m bw   ★★★½
Drama
OPERA   (France)

Harry Baird (Turner), Nicole Berger (Miriam), Christian Marin (Hotelman), Pierre Doris (Peasant), Hal Brav, Tria French

p, Guy Belfond; d, Melvin Van Peebles; w, Melvin Van Peebles; ph, Michel Kelber; ed, Liliane Korb; m, Mickey Baker, Melvin Van Peebles

An impressive first feature from Melvin Van Peebles has a black American soldier, Baird, stationed in France and visiting Paris on a three-day pass. He meets and falls for a French girl, Berger, and together they spend his last two days living a poetically romantic existence. Upon his return, he is demoted by his captain for having dated a white girl. The film is a moving and brutally honest achievement from Van Peebles, who moved to Paris after living in San Francisco, Mexico, and Holland. He started in Paris (without knowing the language) as an author, eventually writing in French and becoming eligible for admission to the French Cinema Center as a director. He then applied for a grant and received $70,000 after expecting no more than $10,000. With a completed film, Van Peebles went back to the US as a French filmmaker, confusing and surprising everyone when they learned he was actually a black American. Actress Berger, who also appeared in Francois Truffaut's SHOOT THE PIANO PLAYER, was killed just a short time after completing this picture.

STORY OF ADELE H., THE
(L'HISTOIRE D'ADELE H.)
1975 97m c   ★★★★
Biography   PG/A
Carrosse/Artistes   (France)

Isabelle Adjani (Adele Hugo), Bruce Robinson (Lt. Albert Pinson), Sylvia Marriott (Mrs. Saunders), Reubin Dorey (Mr. Saunders), Joseph Blatchley (Mr. Whistler), M. White (Col. White), Carl Hathwell (Lt. Pinson's Batman), Ivry Gitlis (Hypnotist), Cecil De Sausmarez (Mr. Lenoir), Raymond Falla (Judge Johnstone)

p, Marcel Berbert; d, Francois Truffaut; w, Francois Truffaut, Jean Gruault, Suzanne Schiffman, Jan Dawson (based on the book Le Journal d'Adele Hugo by Frances V. Guille); ph, Nestor Almendros (Eastmancolor); ed, Yann Dedet; m, Maurice Jaubert; art d, Jean-Pierre Kohut-Svelko; cos, Jacqueline Guyot

Truffaut's hauntingly poetic tale of obsession stars the beautiful Isabelle Adjani as Adele Hugo, daughter of France's most beloved author, Victor Hugo. The picture opens in Halifax, Nova Scotia, in 1863, after Adele has left her father's Guernsey home to seek out Albert Pinson (Bruce Robinson), a young English lieutenant who wants nothing to do with the determined young woman. Although her obsession with Pinson grows to the point that she announces to her father a pending engagement, Adele's only real contact with him is from a distance—spying on him while he makes love to another woman, or following him (or those she believes to be him) in the streets. Adele is obsessed not only with the lieutenant, but also with her own writing, paying frequent visits to a local bookstore to buy reams of paper and then retreating to her room to scrawl indecipherable coded messages in her journal.

One of Truffaut's most complex films, a love story that shows only one half of an affair, THE STORY OF ADELE H. combines the fascination with obsessive women that fills his films (Catherine from JULES AND JIM, Julie Kohler from THE BRIDE WORE BLACK, Camille Bliss from SUCH A GORGEOUS KID LIKE ME) with his love of books, diaries and the process of writing (FAHRENHEIT 451 and THE WILD CHILD). The true story of Adele Hugo is already engrossing; unable to live up to her father's expectations, she thought she could not fill the void in his heart after his favorite daughter, Leopoldine, drowned. Truffaut's disturbing film on the subject is as difficult to walk away from as it is to watch.

STORY OF ALEXANDER GRAHAM BELL, THE

1939 97m bw   ★★★½
Biography   /U
FOX

Don Ameche *(Alexander Graham Bell)*, Loretta Young *(Mrs. Bell)*, Henry Fonda *(Tom Watson)*, Charles Coburn *(Gardner Hubbard)*, Spring Byington *(Mrs. Hubbard)*, Gene Lockhart *(Thomas Sanders)*, Sally Blane *(Gertrude Hubbard)*, Polly Ann Young *(Grace Hubbard)*, Georgiana Young *(Berta Hubbard)*, Bobs Watson *(George Sanders)*

p, Kenneth MacGowan; d, Irving Cummings; w, Lamar Trotti (based on a story by Ray Harris); ph, Leon Shamroy; ed, Walter Thompson; cos, Royer

THE STORY OF ALEXANDER GRAHAM BELL is the film for which Don Ameche will be best remembered, despite his Oscar-winning performance in COCOON more than 40 years later. The film opens in 1873 with Alexander Graham Bell (Ameche) trying to earn his living by working with deaf-mutes while spending his off-hours inventing. Bell is soon enamored of a pretty young Scot (Loretta Young) whom he has been asked to teach. They fall in love, and she asks her father to unbuckle his copious money belt to back one of Bell's inventions. Bell hopes to perfect a process whereby he can use the same kind of wires Western Union uses for sending dots and dashes to transmit the sound of a human voice. After much trial and error, he succeeds and, in doing so, becomes one of the most famous inventors in history. Not even remotely factual, this Hollywood-invented story is an enjoyable feature nonetheless, especially when the boyish and earnest Ameche is onscreen.

STORY OF ESTHER COSTELLO, THE

1957 103m bw   ★★★★
Drama   /A
Romulus/Valiant (U.K.)

Joan Crawford *(Margaret Landi)*, Rossano Brazzi *(Carlo Landi)*, Heather Sears *(Esther Costello)*, Lee Patterson *(Harry Grant)*, Ron Randell *(Frank Wenzel)*, Fay Compton *(Mother Superior)*, John Loder *(Paul Marchant)*, Denis O'Dea *(Father Devlin)*, Sidney James *(Ryan)*, Bessie Love *(Matron in Art Gallery)*

p, Jack Clayton, David Miller; d, David Miller; w, Charles Kaufman (based on the novel by Nicholas Monsarrat); ph, Robert Krasker; ed, Ralph Kemplen; m, Georges Auric; art d, George Provis, Tony Masters; cos, Jean Louis

A powerful if sometimes seamy look at a problem that was later covered in William Gibson's "The Miracle Worker" when he took the true tale of Helen Keller and made it into a play, then a movie, then a sequel play, "Monday after the Miracle," which failed. Crawford is a wealthy Irish woman who arrived in the United States when she was very young, married Brazzi, and is now estranged from him due to his passion for women other than his wife. She is visiting the scenes of her childhood on the Emerald Isle when she meets Sears, a young girl who is deaf, blind, and mute as a result of an accident when she was quite small. Since she was born normal, there is no doubt that these ailments are mentally induced, not physical. Even so, they are real to Sears, and she can do nothing about them. Sears is living like an animal; no one pays any attention to her since they have no idea how to help. Since there is no medical service beyond the usual in her small town, Sears has been left to spend her life in a sightless, soundless, and wordless existence. In most Irish villages of this size, the priest is an influential figure in the community, so O'Dea, who sees that Crawford has exhibited interest in Sears, tries to get her to commit to something more than that. Crawford is having her own woes due to her failing marriage and tries hard not to care, but she is a good woman, and O'Dea's appeals touch her. So Crawford, who has no children by Brazzi, decides to take Sears into her life as a surrogate daughter. The two commence trying various sources of help, but nothing seems to work apart from Crawford's patience with Sears. Crawford learns to read Braille so she can teach it to Sears. She also learns how to communicate with "hand talk" in order to break through.

Time passes and Sears begins to respond. The press catches wind of the story, and it isn't long before it is known across the world. They are called upon to speak at many charitable dinners and fund drives and are enjoying their new status when Brazzi returns to Crawford's life. He is a slick, fast-talking promoter who knows the way back inside Crawford's heart and soon uses his Latin charm to talk her into reconciling. But Brazzi has something else in mind, a profit motive for wanting Crawford. Because Crawford and Sears are inseparable, Brazzi means to use this international story to make a lot of money for himself, with the full intent of collecting all that cash, then going off to some place like Monaco to spend it. Brazzi hires Randell to arrange a back-breaking series of tours that will fill his coffers. Since Sears is such an important story with the media, many reporters have been covering her progress; one of them is Patterson. He falls in love with the 21-year-old Sears, and she feels the same about him. Brazzi is such a satyr that he can't resist the naive loveliness of Sears, and one day, while Crawford is out of their residence on a short errand, Brazzi forces his attentions on Sears and brutally rapes the helpless girl. The shock of the act reverses the effects of the early explosion that took her faculties, and Sears miraculously regains her sight, hearing, and speech. Later, Crawford is shocked by what has happened, as well as by the cheap, conniving ideas that Brazzi has been employing to get rich. She doesn't let on that she knows, though. Now that Sears is back to normal, Crawford bids the young girl and Patterson farewell, then drives to meet Brazzi, who is coming back from a short business trip. He gets into the car unaware of what Crawford has in mind, and the finale is Joan resolving the plot in explosive fashion.

It's more melodramatic than THE MIRACLE WORKER, and the focus is as much on the people around the girl as the girl herself. Crawford showed off her acting range in familiar melodramatic territory, and the result was a Best Actress Award from the British Film Academy. A strong story, good acting, and a most literate script from Charles Kaufman, who also wrote the screenplay for FREUD.

STORY OF G.I. JOE, THE
1945 109m bw ★★★★
Biography/War
UA

Burgess Meredith (*Ernie Pyle*), Robert Mitchum (*Lt. Walker*), Freddie Steele (*Sgt. Warnicki*), Wally Cassell (*Pvt. Dondaro*), Jimmy Lloyd (*Pvt. Spencer*), Jack Reilly (*Pvt. Murphy*), William Murphy (*Pvt. Mew*), William Self (*Cookie Henderson*), Dick Rich (*Sergeant at Showers*), Billy Benedict (*Whitey*)

p, Lester Cowan; d, William A. Wellman; w, Leopold Atlas, Guy Endore, Philip Stevenson (based on the book by Ernie Pyle); ph, Russell Metty; ed, Otho Lovering, Al Joseph; m, Ann Ronell, Louis Applebaum; art d, James Sullivan, David Hall

This story of the greatest of America's WWII combat correspondents, Ernie Pyle, immortalizes the man who celebrated the common soldier in his dispatches and books (*Brave Men* and *Here Is Your War*). As the film begins, Pyle (Burgess Meredith) catches up with a tired platoon of infantrymen in Italy, observing and comforting them as they fight through town after town, enduring death, misery, boredom, and fear. Leading the platoon is Lt. Walker (Robert Mitchum), a tough but likable officer who is respected and admired by his men. The film has no real story, only the consistent wearing down of the men through combat and fatigue. Meredith is superb, conveying the humanity and caring of Pyle, but it is Mitchum, in a star-making performance, who steals the show. This great picture had the full cooperation of Pyle, who was killed in the South Pacific before seeing THE STORY OF G.I. JOE.

STORY OF LOUIS PASTEUR, THE
1936 85m bw ★★★★
Biography /A
WB

Paul Muni (*Louis Pasteur*), Josephine Hutchinson (*Mme. Pasteur*), Anita Louise (*Annette Pasteur*), Donald Woods (*Jean Martel*), Fritz Leiber (*Dr. Charbonnet*), Henry O'Neill (*Roux*), Porter Hall (*Dr. Rosignol*), Raymond Brown (*Dr. Radisse*), Akim Tamiroff (*Dr. Zaranoff*), Walter Kingsford (*Napoleon III*)

p, Henry Blanke; d, William Dieterle; w, Sheridan Gibney, Pierre Collings (based on the story by Gibney, Collings); ph, Tony Gaudio; ed, Ralph Dawson; art d, Robert Haas; cos, Milo Anderson

This film biography stars Paul Muni as Louis Pasteur, the French scientist who worked to find a cure for anthrax and hydrophobia. His colleagues at the Medical Academy are convinced his experiments are a waste of time and ridicule his research, so he and his family move to the French countryside, where he can conduct his experiments in peace. Authorities soon learn that the sheep in Pasteur's area are disease-free as a result of his efforts, a finding which causes some stir in the Medical Academy, as Pasteur is now praised for his ground-breaking work by his former critics. THE STORY OF LOUIS PASTEUR is well told, with an intelligent script, excellent performances, and careful attention to scientific accuracy. Muni's performance, which won him a Best Actor Oscar, is a fine characterization that shows the famed scientist as a man faced with extraordinary obstacles.

STORY OF ROBIN HOOD, THE
1952 84m c ★★★½
Children's/Adventure /U
RKO/Disney (U.K.)

Richard Todd (*Robin Hood*), Joan Rice (*Maid Marian*), Peter Finch (*Sheriff of Nottingham*), James Hayter (*Friar Tuck*), James Robertson Justice (*Little John*), Martita Hunt (*Queen Eleanor*), Hubert Gregg (*Prince John*), Bill Owen (*Stutely*), Reginald Tate (*Hugh Fitzooth*), Elton Haytes (*Allan-a-Dale*)

p, Perce Pearce; d, Ken Annakin; w, Lawrence E. Watkin; ph, Guy Green (Technicolor); ed, Gordon Pilkington; m, Clifton Parker; art d, Carmen Dillon, Arthur Lawson

After the success of Disney's first live-action feature, TREASURE ISLAND, the studio decided to make another, again in Britain, this time based on the legend of Robin Hood. Unfairly dismissed today as merely a Disney adventure, this version holds up nearly as well as Michael Curtiz's THE ADVENTURES OF ROBIN HOOD (1938), but doesn't offer a cast that can compare with Errol Flynn, Olivia de Havilland, Basil Rathbone, and Claude Rains. The story is a familiar one—Robin Hood and his band of merry men trying to save the poor folks of Nottingham from Prince John's greedy ways—but, given the Disney treatment, the legendary heroes and events seem even more romantic.

STORY OF VERNON AND IRENE CASTLE, THE
1939 90m bw ★★★½
Musical/Biography /U
RKO

Fred Astaire (*Vernon Castle*), Ginger Rogers (*Irene Castle*), Edna May Oliver (*Maggie Sutton*), Walter Brennan (*Walter Ash*), Lew Fields (*Himself*), Etienne Girardot (*Papa Aubel*), Janet Beecher (*Mrs. Foote*), Rolfe Sedan (*Emile Aubel*), Leonid Kinskey (*Artist*), Robert Strange (*Dr. Foote*)

p, George Haight, Pandro S. Berman; d, H.C. Potter; w, Richard Sherman, Oscar Hammerstein, II, Dorothy Yost (based on the books *My Husband* and *My Memories of Vernon Castle* by Irene Castle); ph, Robert de Grasse; ed, William Hamilton; art d, Van Nest Polglase, Perry Ferguson; fx, Vernon L. Walker, Douglas Travers; chor, Hermes Pan; cos, Walter Plunkett, Edward Stevenson, Irene Castle

This fine film biography of the title beloved dance team was Ginger Rogers and Fred Astaire's final film together for RKO. (Astaire and Rogers teamed once again a decade later, in MGM's THE BARKLEYS OF BROADWAY, but the magic of their pairing had largely fled.) After Irene Foote (Rogers), the daughter of a well-known New Rochelle physician, meets vaudeville performer Vernon Castle (Astaire), they fall in love, marry, go to Paris, and become a famous ballroom dancing duo. Soon all the world wants to be like the Castles: not only do they invent several dance steps, but her hair is duplicated in wigs; cigars are named after him, and they have their own line of cosmetics. During WWI, Vernon becomes a pilot with the Canadian Royal Flying Corps, while Irene works on the silent film PATRIA by herself. He sends for her to join him in Texas, where he has a huge romantic reunion planned, including an orchestra to play for them alone. All does not go as planned, however, and sudden tragedy strikes the Castles.

The fact that the real Vernon Castle was British didn't enter into matters; Astaire was not required to mimic an English accent because hardly anyone had ever heard the famed dancer speak. The details of the team's meteoric rise to stardom are sketchily intertwined among the many songs in the score, with Edna May Oliver providing supporting highlights as the agent who had faith in the happy couple and pushed hard to make them stars. The real Irene Castle (upon whose books the film is based) served as technical advisor, and the dancing re-creates the Castles' original steps with little in the way of alteration by Astaire and choreographer Hermes Pan. The score contains a tremendous number of songs, and it's a tribute to the talents of musical director Victor Baravalle, who died before the film was released, that they feel right and never seem crammed in for their own sake. Astaire and Rogers are both in very fine form, and if the final image of their ghosts dancing down a path comes across as exceptionally moving, it's because this film is as much a farewell to this amazing duo as it is to the characters they play onscreen.

STORY OF WOMEN

1989 110m c   ★★★
Drama
MK2/Camelia/La Sept/La Sofica Sofinergie/A2 (France)

Isabelle Huppert (Marie), Francois Cluzet (Paul), Niels Tavernier (Lucien), Marie Trintignant (Lulu/Lucie), Louis Ducreux, Michel Beaune, Dominique Blanc, Marie Bunel

p, Marin Karmitz; d, Claude Chabrol; w, Colo Tavernier O'Hagan, Claude Chabrol (based on Une Affaire de Femmes by Francis Szpiner); ph, Jean Rabier; ed, Monique Fardoulis; m, Matthieu Chabrol

In a German-occupied French village in 1941, Marie (Isabelle Huppert) struggles to eke out an existence for herself and two children, then begins supporting her family in style by performing amateur abortions. Her husband, Paul (Fracois Cluzet), whom Marie grows to despise, returns from the war a broken man, but when her affair with a young collaborator (Nils Tavernier) becomes increasingly overt, Paul turns informer, and Marie finds herself standing trial in Paris for her "crime against the state."

Loosely based on the life of Marie-Louise Giraud, an actual abortionist who was executed by the Vichy government, this absorbing account of a dark period in French history is technically impressive on every level. Chabrol's economical control of cinematic narrative, as usual, stands him in good stead, lending his depiction of the nightmare of the Occupation the kind of melodramatic tension that is his specialty. STORY OF WOMEN unfolds with inexorable logic, though it is too schematic in conception to achieve real tragic power. Huppert (who took the best actress award at the 1988 Venice Film Festival for her performance here) remains stoically in character throughout, daring viewers to sympathize with her cool demeanor, but even her fine work is not enough to overcome the problems in the script.

STRAIGHT TIME

1978 114m c   ★★★★
Crime   R/18
First Artists/Sweetwall

Dustin Hoffman (Max Dembo), Theresa Russell (Jenny Mercer), Harry Dean Stanton (Jerry Schue), Gary Busey (Willy Darin), M. Emmet Walsh (Earl Frank), Sandy Baron (Manny), Kathy Bates (Selma Darin), Edward Bunker (Mickey), Fran Ryan (Cafe Owner), Rita Taggart (Carol Schue)

p, Stanley Beck, Tim Zinnemann; d, Ulu Grosbard; w, Alvin Sargent, Edward Bunker, Jeffrey Boam (based on the novel No Beast So Fierce by Bunker); ph, Owen Roizman (Technicolor); ed, Sam O'Steen, Randy Roberts; m, David Shire; prod d, Stephen Grimes; art d, Richard Lawrence; cos, Bernie Pollack

A gripping, disturbing, and unglamorized portrait of a professional thief who thrives on the thrill and danger of his actions. Hoffman, in one of the best performances of his career, plays a thief who is released from prison after a six-year sentence for armed robbery. Unable to contact his parole officer by phone, Hoffman checks in to a cheap Los Angeles hotel and spends the night wandering the streets, relishing his freedom. The next morning he takes a bus to the parole office where he is confronted with Walsh, a slimy bureaucrat who enjoys telling racist, sexist jokes to the office help. Walsh treats Hoffman like an unruly child and warns him that he should have gone to the halfway house instead of a hotel. Hoffman tells Walsh that he tried to call and left a message with the secretary regarding his whereabouts, but Walsh says he didn't get the message. Walsh tells Hoffman he doesn't like his attitude and he'd better shape up if he wants to stay on the streets. Hoffman apologizes and reaffirms his desire to go straight. Walsh relents and says that if Hoffman can find a good place to live and a decent job in one week, he won't have to stay at the halfway house.

The next day Hoffman goes to an employment agency where he meets Russell, an attractive, young employee. Hoffman confesses he's an ex-con and tells her he is not allowed to drive a car without written permission and he can't handle money. Russell, who's intrigued by Hoffman, finds him a minimum-wage position working at a can company. Hoffman asks her if they can go out and celebrate if he gets the job, and she agrees. Meanwhile Hoffman calls Busey, his old friend and an ex-con, a lunkish and somewhat dull amateur crook who has a wife, Bates, and a young son all living on the poverty level. When Busey goes to put his son to bed, Bates asks Hoffman not to come around anymore because she doesn't want Busey to slip back into a life of crime (and besides, Hoffman is in violation of his parole just by associating with another ex-con). Hoffman understands, but Busey continues to see Hoffman on the sly. One day, while Busey visits Hoffman at his hotel, Busey pulls out his heroin paraphernalia and shoots up (he's been keeping his habit a secret from Bates). Hoffman is annoyed because associating with a drug user also violates his parole, but he lets his friend satisfy his habit. Hoffman gets the job at the can company and works hard for his meager wages. He takes Russell out on a date, and she becomes attracted to his intensity and interested in his stories about life behind bars.

One day Hoffman comes home from work to find Walsh searching his room. The parole officer finds a burned book of matches under the bed (used by Busey to heat up his heroin), and he immediately checks Hoffman's arms for track marks. Though none are evident, Walsh handcuffs Hoffman to the bed and goes to make a phone call. Hoffman soon finds himself being booked, showered, deloused, and back behind bars. Days later Walsh tells him his urine tested clean—he is free to go, but back to a halfway house. Walsh acts like he's doing Hoffman a favor and lets it slip that the results were known days ago but he was too busy to get back to Hoffman. On the ride to the halfway house Hoffman finally snaps and assaults Walsh while they drive down the freeway. He forces the car to the shoulder and drags the parole officer out of the vehicle. Hoffman handcuffs Walsh to a fence and then pulls down the man's pants leaving him hanging barebottomed for all motorists to see. Ditching the car, Hoffman quickly reverts to his former criminal lifestyle.

Based on ex-convict Edward Bunker's novel No Beast So Fierce, STRAIGHT TIME was an obsessive labor of love for its star, who had purchased the rights to the novel in 1972. Hoffman struck a deal with First Artists that would give him the right to direct the film and supervise the final cut. To research his role Hoffman had himself booked at Los Angeles County Jail and went through the procedure all inmates go through (this was later re-created for the film in documentarylike fashion). Hoffman also sneaked into San Quentin prison and mingled with the prisoners for several hours incognito to get the feel of prison life. The actor also interviewed ex-cons and visited their homes. During production, however, Hoffman found that acting and directing were too much for him, so he hired his old friend Grosbard to take over the helm. When the filming was completed, First Artists president Phil Feldman took control of the film and refused Hoffman his right to final cut (Feldman was the same man who tampered with Sam Peckinpah's THE WILD BUNCH, cutting over 20 minutes of character development behind the director's back). Hoffman sued for damages. The studio, which thought the film was a disaster, dumped the movie into release, where it received bad reviews and little box office attention. Hoffman's case was thrown out, and to this day the actor speaks little of it. But Hoffman has nothing to be ashamed of. STRAIGHT TIME is a powerful film that shows a criminal as he is. The film has no tired explanations for Hoffman's behavior, no fingers are pointed, no apologies or excuses are offered. Hoffman is a habitual criminal and that is the way he is. Though the parole system is taken to task for the "Catch 22"-type restrictions given to ex-cons, this is not presented as an excuse for Hoffman's return to crime—only a match that ignites the fuse already inside the man. The performances in STRAIGHT TIME are nothing less than superb. Walsh is perfect as the slimy parole officer who couldn't care less about his charges. Busey once again proves his versatility and is unforgettable as the pathetic addict. Russell is fine as the naive girl willing to let Hoffman drift through her life, and Stanton practically steals the film as the ex-thief yearning to escape from the boredom of his suburban lifestyle. Grosbard's direction is straightforward and professional, with the highlight being the jewelry store robbery, which keeps the viewers on the edges of their seats. STRAIGHT TIME stands as an accurate, honest portrayal of crime and criminals.

STRANGE LOVE OF MARTHA IVERS, THE

1946 116m bw   ★★★★
Crime   /A
Paramount

Barbara Stanwyck (Martha Ivers), Van Heflin (Sam Masterson), Lizabeth Scott (Toni Marachek), Kirk Douglas (Walter O'Neil), Judith Anderson (Mrs. Ivers), Roman Bohnen (Mr. O'Neil), Darryl Hickman (Sam Masterson as a Boy), Janis Wilson (Martha Ivers as a Girl), Ann Doran (Secretary), Frank Orth (Hotel Clerk)

p, Hal B. Wallis; d, Lewis Milestone; w, Robert Rossen (based on the story "Love Lies Bleeding" by John Patrick); ph, Victor Milner; ed, Archie Marshek; m, Miklos Rozsa; art d, Hans Dreier, John Meehan; fx, Farciot Edouart; cos, Edith Head

A dark and perverse melodrama which stars Stanwyck as the wicked Martha Ivers, a wealthy and powerful woman who has gained control of the small town of Iverstown, Pennsylvania, after inheriting a large family fortune. She lives with her weakling husband Walter (Douglas, in his first film), a district attorney who is preparing to make a bid for mayor. What no one in the town knows, however, is that Martha and Walter share a deep secret—as a young girl, Martha murdered her aunt while planning to elope with then-sweetheart Sam Masterson. In order to protect the family name, an innocent man was executed for the crime. After a long absence, Sam (Heflin) returns to Iverstown. The couple fear that he is preparing to blackmail them, but their paranoia only makes him more curious about Martha's childhood secret. A cruel *film noir* which, although it starts somewhat slowly, builds to a frenzied state of suspense in which the characters, all of them vile, have a perverse hold over one another. The result is an often gripping film which shows the collaborative efforts of such talents as Wallis, Milestone, Rossen, Rozsa, art director Hans Dreier, and costumer Edith Head. This film also includes among its credits four future directors: screenwriter Rossen, Kirk Douglas, assistant director Robert Aldrich, and, as a bit player, Blake Edwards.

STRANGER, THE

1946 95m bw   ★★★★
Thriller/War   /A
International Pictures

Edward G. Robinson (Wilson), Loretta Young (Mary Longstreet), Orson Welles (Prof. Charles Rankin/Franz Kindler), Philip Merivale (Judge Longstreet), Richard Long (Noah Longstreet), Byron Keith (Dr. Jeff Lawrence), Billy House (Potter), Konstantin Shayne (Konrad Meinike), Martha Wentworth (Sara), Isabel O'Madigan (Mrs. Lawrence)

p, Sam Spiegel; d, Orson Welles; w, Anthony Veiller, John Huston (uncredited), Orson Welles (based on the story by Victor Trivas, Decla Dunning); ph, Russell Metty; ed, Ernest Nims; m, Bronislau Kaper; art d, Perry Ferguson; cos, Michael Woulfe

After having made three commercial disasters in a row (THE MAGNIFICENT AMBERSONS; JOURNEY INTO FEAR; and IT'S ALL TRUE), Orson Welles was badly in need of a hit that would right him in the eyes of Hollywood. The result was THE STRANGER, the most restrained and conventional of Welles's films, but still a thrilling entertainment. Set shortly after WWII, the film casts Edward G. Robinson as Wilson, a Nazi hunter assigned the task of finding the infamous Franz Kindler, one of the architects of the genocide of the Jews. Wilson traces Kindler to the sleepy college town of Hartford, Connecticut, where he comes to suspect that Prof. Charles Rankin (Welles) is actually Kindler hiding behind a new identity. Although Rankin does a fine job of casting doubt on Wilson's suspicions, the latter's dogged pursuit of the truth wins out and Kindler is exposed. In THE STRANGER, Welles gives us one of the cinema's most realistic and chilling portrayals of a Nazi. His Franz Kindler is not a cartoon character in uniform spouting propaganda and clicking his heels, but an arrogant, cynical, amoral, and wholly self-confident creature who believes that he is superior to anyone he meets—evil incarnate. Robinson is also quite good as the hunter determined to catch his prey. Technically, as one expects with Welles, the film is superb. THE STRANGER is not as wildly creative as his other films, but all the Welles trademarks are present, including superior lighting, inventive camera angles, strong transitions, and characters silhouetted in darkness.

STRANGER, THE

(L'ETRANGER)
1967 104m c   ★★
Drama   /AA
Master Marianne Casbah/DEG   (Algeria/France/Italy)

Marcello Mastroianni (Arthur Meursault), Anna Karina (Marie Cardona), Bernard Blier (Defense Counsel), Georges Wilson (Examining Magistrate), Bruno Cremer (Priest), Pierre Bertin (Judge), Jacques Herlin (Director of Home), Marc Laurent (Emmanuel), Georges Geret (Raymond), Alfred Adam (Prosecutor)

p, Dino De Laurentiis; d, Luchino Visconti; w, Suso Cecchi D'Amico, Georges Conchon, Emmanuel Robles, Luchino Visconti (based on the novel by Albert Camus); ph, Giuseppe Rotunno (Technicolor); ed, Ruggero Mastroianni; m, Piero Piccioni; art d, Mario Garbuglia; cos, Piero Tosi

Mastroianni plays the existential Meursault, a French clerk living in Algiers who one day, for no other reason than the bright sunshine, shoots and kills a young Algerian. He is brought to trial, where he is forced to answer questions about an affair he had shortly after the death of his mother and his failure to cry at his mother's funeral. While awaiting the guillotine, Mastroianni refuses to be swayed by the prison priest's beliefs and chooses instead to think about life and existence. As is often the case when a great filmmaker brings the work of a great novelist to the screen, THE STRANGER is an utter failure, in terms of Camus. Director-writer Visconti fails to come close to Camus' style and seems unsure of his own, as if he chose to make the film in the hopes of producing a failure. All that can be said in the movie's favor lies in its stupendous technical achievements and the fine performances of Mastroianni (who somehow seems perfect as Meursault) and Karina.

STRANGER ON THE THIRD FLOOR

1940 64m bw   ★★★★
Crime   /A
RKO

Peter Lorre (Stranger), John McGuire (Michael Ward), Margaret Tallichet (Jane), Charles Waldron (District Attorney), Elisha Cook, Jr. (Joe Briggs), Charles Halton (Meng), Ethel Griffies (Mrs. Kane), Cliff Clark (Martin), Oscar O'Shea (Judge), Alec Craig (Defense Attorney)

p, Lee Marcus; d, Boris Ingster; w, Frank Partos; ph, Nicholas Musuraca; ed, Harry Marker; m, Roy Webb; art d, Van Nest Polglase; fx, Vernon L. Walker

This extremely weird B movie has been hailed as the first true *film noir*, and it certainly has all the *noir* elements, both visual and thematic. Feeling guilty because his eyewitness testimony has sent a man who could be innocent to the electric chair, reporter Michael Ward (McGuire) returns to his apartment in a state of depression. On the stairs he notices an odd-looking little man wearing a white scarf (Lorre) loitering in the building and chases him off. In his room, the reporter realizes that his nosy next door neighbor, Mr. Meng (Halton), isn't doing his usual loud snoring. Tired and upset, Michael wonders if Meng is dead and recalls the several nasty, and public, run-ins he has had with the man. Falling asleep, Michael has a nightmare where he is wrongly accused of his neighbor's murder and is sentenced to die in the electric chair. Upon awakening, Michael checks on Meng and to his horror, finds the man murdered. Arrested for the crime, Michael must rely on his fiance, Jane (Tallichet), to track down the mysterious man in the white scarf.

First-time director Boris Ingster, cinematographer Nicholas Musuraca, and art director Van Nest Polglase created a frightening, claustrophobic, and nightmarish urban environment ruled by indifference, injustice, and moral corruption. The forces of order (the police, district attorney, juries, judges, and institutions) are the true villains here as they quickly and carelessly dispense judgement on citizens. Lorre's killer is obviously mad (an escaped mental patient), but in his brief screen time he is seen to be a sympathetic victim of harsh and thoughtless treatment (he describes being held in a straight-jacket and doused with ice-water). Ingster's direction shows the heavy influence of the Germanic expressionist films of the 1920s and the film is a visual delight. He never again directed anything nearly as interesting or influential as this nearly forgotten B picture.

STRANGER THAN PARADISE

1984 95m bw   ★★★
Drama   R/15
Grokenberger/ZDF/Cinesthesia (U.S./West Germany)

John Lurie (Willie), Eszter Balint (Eva), Richard Edson (Eddie), Cecillia Stark (Aunt Lottie), Danny Rosen (Billy), Rammellzee (Man with Money), Tom Docillo (Airline Agent), Richard Boes (Factory Worker), Rockets Redglare, Harvey Perr

p, Sara Driver; d, Jim Jarmusch; w, Jim Jarmusch; ph, Tom DiCillo; ed, Jim Jarmusch, Melody London; m, John Lurie, Aaron Picht

One of the most distinctive films of the year, STRANGER THAN PARADISE offers a bleak but mordantly funny portrait of three aimless characters who discover that "paradise" isn't such an easy place to find.

Displaying a hip formalism, Jim Jarmusch's second feature (his first, 1980's PERMANENT VACATION, received scant exposure) is divided into three distinct sections; individual sequences within each section are presented in one sustained take, and are separated by blackouts. The first finds Willie (John Lurie, of Lounge Lizard renown), a Hungarian emigre and self-styled hipster, living in a stark, dreary section of New York City. Willie's day-to-day existence is interrupted when his relatives ask him to house his young female cousin, Eva (Eszter Balint), upon her arrival from the old country. Willie dutifully, but reluctantly, obliges. Eva, however, is anything but a helpless foreigner and promptly goes about her own business. Still, when she departs 10 days later, a strange affection has developed between them.

In the second section, Willie and his buddy Eddie (Richard Edson) decide to head for Cleveland in the dead of winter to visit Eva, who now lives there with her irritable Aunt Lotte (Cecilia Stark). Once again, the characters do little of import together, spending their time staring at TV and visiting Lake Erie. In the third and final section, the trio abandons the frozen north for Florida, where they check into an empty seaside motel and the boys squander most of their money at the dog races. Then Eva suddenly comes into a huge stash of loot.

Although STRANGER THAN PARADISE's premise is inarguably slight, Jarmusch compensates for it with the sheer stylishness of the film. Fortunately, he also transcends the obvious theme of alienation, fashioning instead an ironic comedy about communication and the lack thereof. The film received the Camera d'Or at the 1984 Cannes Film Festival and was cited as best picture of the year by the National Society of Film Critics.

STRANGERS KISS

1984 93m c/bw   ★★★★
Romance   R/15
Kill

Peter Coyote (Stanley, the Director), Victoria Tennant (Carol Redding/Betty), Blaine Novak (Stevie Blake/Billy), Dan Shor (Farris, the Producer), Richard Romanus (Frank Silva), Linda Kerridge (Shirley), Carlos Palomino (Estoban), Vincent Palmieri (Scandelli), Jay Rasumny (Jimmy), Jon Sloan (Mikey)

p, Douglas Dilge; d, Matthew Chapman; w, Blaine Novak, Matthew Chapman (based on a story by Novak); ph, Mikhail Suslov; ed, William Carruth; m, Gato Barbieri; art d, Virginia Randolph; cos, Tracy Tynan

A stylish, charming, honest, romantic, and obsessive look at filmmaking during the B-movie days of the 1950s that transcends its period setting and speaks to filmmakers and viewers of all times. Stanley (Peter Coyote) is a crazed, manipulative director who is driven to make his picture "Strange and Dangerous" at all costs. With his sheepish, boy-wonder producer, Farris (Dan Shor), at his side, Stanley meets with gangster Frank Silva (Richard Romanus) about funding the film. The likable but dangerous Silva agrees, with one condition—that his girl friend Carol (Victoria Tennant) get the lead role. Distressed at the lack of chemistry between Carol and her dopey, insecure costar, Stevie Blake (Blaine Novak), Stanley plots to have his stars fall in love, a scheme that will permanently sever his financial tie with Silva. Photographed in cool, vibrant color reminiscent of the 1950s and scored with a jazzy saxophone melody, STRANGERS KISS stuns with one fresh scene after another. The film shines on all levels, from technique to acting performances, from the direction to the script. What is most apparent in STRANGERS KISS is the director's and screenwriter's love for filmmaking. For anyone who is enthralled by that strange species known as "filmmakers" or for those who just love well-made entertainment reminiscent of a bygone era, STRANGERS KISS is highly recommended.

STRANGERS ON A TRAIN

1951   101m   bw   ★★★★★
Thriller   /PG
WB

Farley Granger (Guy Haines), Ruth Roman (Anne Morton), Robert Walker (Bruno Antony), Leo G. Carroll (Sen. Morton), Patricia Hitchcock (Barbara Morton), Laura Elliot (Miriam), Marion Lorne (Mrs. Antony), Jonathan Hale (Mr. Antony), Howard St. John (Capt. Turley), John Brown (Prof. Collins)

p, Alfred Hitchcock; d, Alfred Hitchcock; w, Raymond Chandler, Czenzi Ormonde, Whitfield Cook (based on the novel by Patricia Highsmith); ph, Robert Burks; ed, William Ziegler; m, Dimitri Tiomkin; art d, Ted Haworth; fx, H.F. Koenekamp; cos, Leah Rhodes

Gripping all the way, this is a Hitchcock thriller in which, through happenstance, two men, completely different, are drawn inexorably together and toward an uncommon goal—murder. Hitchcock opens this electrifying film by showing two sets of male feet, those of Guy Haines (Granger) and Bruno Antony (Walker), hurrying towards a train. Guy wears conservative-looking shoes, Bruno black and white spectator shoes, and from their very movements, the sure gait of Guy, the anxious steps of Bruno, the viewer can easily tell, once the two are shown fully on camera, their distinctive personalities. After some club car chit-chat in which both men discuss some personal problems, Bruno proposes, in theory, of course, that they each murder the person vexing the other person's life—Bruno would murder Guy's wife in exchange for Guy murdering Bruno's father. Guy is appalled at the idea, but is even more appalled when Bruno carries out his half of the deal and then expects Guy to do the same.

STRANGERS ON A TRAIN ranks at the top of Hitchcock's most accomplished works, a masterpiece that is so carefully constructed and its characters so well developed that the viewer is quickly intimate and comfortable with the story long before Bruno turns killer. After reading Patricia Highsmith's novel, Hitchcock paid $7,500 for the rights to adapt the book and then went about having a rough draft written for the screen, later bringing in Raymond Chandler to do the finished script—a collaboration which was thoroughly frustrating for both parties. At first Hitchcock insisted that he work at Chandler's side, working out every detail of the film as he, Hitchcock, envisioned it, a routine that soon had the brilliant, booze-sipping Chandler nervous and often upset. Chandler's script nevertheless was the basic one employed by Hitchcock, although the director later

asked his favorite writer, Ben Hecht, to come in and "spruce it up." Since Hecht was engaged on several other projects, he assigned Czenzi Ormonde, who worked for him, to clean up some of the dialogue and tighten some scenes before Hecht himself gave final approval. Granger is excellent as the innocent victim of the evil plot, and Walker (who would make only one more film before his death) is, like Joseph Cotten's "Uncle Charlie" in SHADOW OF A DOUBT, one of Hitchcock's most diabolical and charismatic villains—a frightening alter ego to the film's hero. Robert Burkes's extraordinary cinematography earned an Oscar nomination. Remade in 1969 as ONCE YOU KISS A STRANGER, and the basis for the 1987 comedy THROW MOMMA FROM THE TRAIN.

STRAPLESS

1989   97m   c   ★★★½
Drama   R/15
Granada/Film Four   (U.K.)

Blair Brown (Dr. Lillian Hempel), Bruno Ganz (Raymond Forbes), Bridget Fonda (Amy Hempel), Alan Howard (Mr. Cooper), Michael Gough (Douglas Brodie), Hugh Laurie (Colin), Suzanne Burden (Romaine Salmon), Camille Coduri (Mrs. Clark), Gary O'Brien (Mr. Clark), Julian Bunster (Carlos)

p, Rick McCallum; d, David Hare; w, David Hare; ph, Andrew Dunn (Technicolor); ed, Edward Marnier; m, Nick Bicat; prod d, Roger Hall

From the writer of PLENTY and writer-director of WETHERBY, British playwright David Hare, comes yet another decidedly odd but utterly irresistible study of isolation, loneliness and strength. Blair Brown stars as a cancer specialist and expatriate American, Dr. Lillian Hempel, who is unstinting in her care and support of her patients at the government-run British hospital where she works. But her emotional life is constricted and repressed. A long-term visit from her younger sister (Bridget Fonda) is turning into a comedy of horrors as Lillian's fastidiousness clashes hard and often with the free, easy and sloppy ways of her sister. As the film begins, Lillian is on vacation, visiting "every church in Europe" by herself, when she drops a handkerchief that is retrieved by Raymond Forbes. Wonderfully portrayed by Bruno Ganz, Raymond is like a character from bad romantic pulp fiction. Shady and shadowy, he is an unabashed romantic who, he tells Lillian, lives for the anticipation of love, freely given. Lillian is enchanted but cautious, accepting Raymond's invitation to tour the church and have lunch with him. But she balks at a later rendezvous at his hotel and returns to England without giving him her address. Soon Raymond abruptly shows up on Lillian's doorstep, having obtained her home address from a hotel where she stayed. He has brought with him a most unusual gift, a horse. (Lillian spoke about her love of riding during their conversation on the Continent.) Raymond begins courting Lillian in earnest, but when he proposes marriage, Lillian again balks, though she agrees to move in with him. Raymond's idea of playing house turns out to be an extended stay at a casino-hotel that ends on an ominous note when he bounces a check in attempting to cover his betting losses. Lillian makes good on Raymond's bad check and returns home. In the face of the mounting chaos in her life, Lillian suffers a minor breakdown but impulsively agrees to marry Raymond, who carries over his romantic excesses into their domestic life.

STRAPLESS is an ode to both independence and interdependence. While Lillian's repression and forced isolation lead her to be seduced by Raymond's romanticism, her independent strength allows her to take the experience on its own terms and use it to enrich her own life. That strength leads her to break out of her shell and become a participant in the lives around her. At the same time, her sister learns from Lillian the need to pull back and tend to her inner needs to make a proper environment for her new baby.

In spite of its dreamy allegorical tone and terse political overtones, STRAPLESS is anything but dour and preachy. Instead it is alive with feeling, empathy, and outright wonder for its characters and their world. Though beautifully controlled under Hare's direction, STRAPLESS is full of poignant, human moments of precise observation, gentle comedy and penetrating drama. It's also full of exquisite performances, especially from Brown, Ganz, and Fonda, who make the most of the rich roles Hare has written for them. They all help to make STRAPLESS a quietly quirky and deliciously heartwarming piece of filmmaking.

STRATEGIC AIR COMMAND
1955 114m c ★★★
Drama /U
Paramount

James Stewart *(Lt. Col. Robert "Dutch" Holland)*, June Allyson *(Sally Holland)*, Frank Lovejoy *(Gen. Ennis C. Hawkes)*, Barry Sullivan *(Lt. Col. Rocky Samford)*, Alex Nicol *(Ike Knowland)*, Bruce Bennett *(Gen. Espy)*, Jay C. Flippen *(Doyle)*, James Millican *(Gen. Castle)*, James Bell *(Rev. Thorne)*, Richard Shannon *(Aircraft Commander)*

p, Samuel J. Briskin; d, Anthony Mann; w, Valentine Davies, Beirne Lay, Jr. (based on his story); ph, William Daniels (VistaVision, Technicolor), Tom Tutwiler; ed, Eda Warren; m, Victor Young; art d, Hal Pereira, Earl Hedrick; fx, John P. Fulton; cos, Edith Head

A smash hit movie, mainly due to the sensational airplane footage. Not a war movie, not even an action picture, it's a made-up tale about a St. Louis Cardinals third baseman who is ordered back to service and put into the SAC. Stewart is the veteran hot-corner man who must leave the game of baseball when he's called into the Air Force (this actually did happen to superstar Ted Williams who was drafted to serve as a pilot during the Korean War after already having served in WWII). Like Williams, Stewart already put in his time during the battles of WWII and thinks that the authorities have singled him out because he's a star. He'd much prefer hot grounders to hot jets and makes known his feelings loud and clear. Nevertheless, he must do his country's bidding and acquiesces. He is an experienced pilot and they need men like him to handle the new B-36 and B-47 jets that have the capability of delivering the atomic bomb wherever the President orders it to be dropped. Stewart's wife is Allyson (as in THE GLENN MILLER STORY and THE STRATTON STORY) and she is expecting a child. Once in the service, Stewart settles into his job and grows to respect Lovejoy, a tough but fair commanding officer who combines a gruff manner with a soft side. There is no question that the SAC is important to the nation's security and Stewart soon comes to appreciate that, despite Allyson's whining that her husband's job is keeping him from her.

A fairly sappy story, totally contrived, with dialogue they wouldn't dare use on TV soap operas. What makes it so much fun to watch is the spectacular aerial scenes as shot by Thomas Tutwiler with Paul Mantz at the plane's controls. Mantz, who was one of the best movie pilots ever, died in a crash while making FLIGHT OF THE PHOENIX. His long-time partner was Frank Tallman (their company was TallMantz Aviation) who also died in a light-plane accident. Due to the nature of the movie, the

SAC lent support and planes to the production so if there was anything at all that might have had a negative aspect, it was never seen. This was more of a staged documentary than anything else and served to quash the complaints of the taxpayers who were carping about the billions spent on defense.

STRATTON STORY, THE
1949 106m bw ★★★½
Biography/Sports /U
MGM

James Stewart *(Monty Stratton)*, June Allyson *(Ethel Stratton)*, Frank Morgan *(Barney Wile)*, Agnes Moorehead *(Ma Stratton)*, Bill Williams *(Gene Watson)*, Bruce Cowling *(Ted Lyons)*, Eugene Bearden *(Western All-Stars Pitcher)*, Bill Dickey, Jimmy Dykes *(Themselves)*, Cliff Clark *(Higgins)*

p, Jack Cummings; d, Sam Wood; w, Douglas Morrow, Guy Trosper (based on a story by Morrow); ph, Harold Rosson; ed, Ben Lewis; art d, Cedric Gibbons, Paul Groesse; fx, A. Arnold Gillespie, Warren Newcombe; cos, Helen Rose

Directed by Sam Wood (PRIDE OF THE YANKEES), this is the true story of pitcher Monty Stratton's heroic return to professional baseball after his leg had been amputated as the result of a hunting accident. Although some liberties are taken with the story to make it play onscreen, the film doesn't stray too far from the facts. Stratton (James Stewart) is pitching in a semipro game in Texas when Barney Wile (Frank Morgan), a one-time baseball player but now a jobless hobo, recognizes his raw talent. Stratton likes the idea of hurling in the majors, and Barney offers to instruct him in the fine points that separate sandlotters from stars. The pair hitchhikes to California, where the White Sox are holding their training camp. White Sox manager Jimmy Dykes (playing himself) lets Stratton try out and the lanky right-hander is so impressive that he's given a contract. After a couple of superb years, it looks as though a great future is in store for the pitcher, until he accidentally shoots himself in the leg. With a prosthesis, Stratton learns to walk again, and then gets back into form on the pitching mound. This inspiring picture about a man who wouldn't give up (and who acted as the film's technical advisor) also features appearances by the Yankee great Bill Dickey and pitcher Gene Bearden as themselves.

STRAW DOGS
1971 118m c ★★★★
Crime R/X
ABC/Amerbroco/Talent Associates (U.K.)

Dustin Hoffman *(David Sumner)*, Susan George *(Amy Sumner)*, Peter Vaughan *(Tom Hedden)*, T.P. McKenna *(Maj. Scott)*, Del Henney *(Charlie Venner)*, Ken Hutchison *(Scutt)*, Colin Welland *(Rev. Hood)*, Jim Norton *(Cawsey)*, Sally Thomsett *(Janice)*, Donald Webster *(Riddaway)*

p, Daniel Melnick; d, Sam Peckinpah; w, David Zelag Goodman, Sam Peckinpah (based on the novel *The Siege of Trencher's Farm* by Gordon M. Williams); ph, John Coquillon (Eastmancolor); ed, Paul Davies, Roger Spottiswoode, Tony Lawson; m, Jerry Fielding; prod d, Ray Simm; art d, Ken Bridgeman; cos, Tiny Nicholls

STRAW DOGS is easily one of Sam Peckinpah's finest films. A relentless study in violence that shocks, not with simple gore tactics, but with the jolting effect it has on its characters. Even the most passive viewer may find himself cheering on the carnage at the film's climax, and in that respect, it's absolutely chilling. Hoffman is a quiet mathematician married to George. To escape urban violence, they move to her birthplace, a small

Cornish village. The pastoral setting is misleading, however, as Hoffman soon finds the town has more than its share of violence-prone louts. Four locals are hired by the couple to build a garage, and it isn't long before they start making life unpleasant for Hoffman. Lead by Henney, an ex-boyfriend of George's, the four workers blatantly ridicule Hoffman and ogle George. This abuse escalates and the couple finds George's cat strangled to death. Suspecting the workers, Hoffman vows to confront them and straighten the matter out. But he backs down and accepts an invitation from the men to accompany them on a hunting trip. Leaving the angered George alone, Hoffman goes off with the workers but is soon left in a field by himself while two of the men go back to the cottage and rape George. Hoffman returns home—infuriated at having been abandoned by the group—and George tells him nothing of the incident. Hoffman eventually fires the men and plans to finish the garage himself.

Sometime later, Hoffman and George attend a local church function, where George (haunted by memories of the rape) has a breakdown. They leave, and driving home in a dense fog, knock down the town simpleton, played by David Warner, with their car. Unknown to Hoffman and George, Warner has just strangled a young girl who taunted him. Despite George's objections, Hoffman takes the injured Warner back to their home. Trying to reach a doctor, Hoffman phones the local pub, where the dead girl's father (Vaughan)—a sadistic drunk—and a group of angered men wait for word on the whereabouts of Warner. When the group discover that Warner is at Hoffman's farm, they become a frenzied mob and march off to kill Warner. After refusing to turn Warner over to the men, Hoffman is forced to take a stand and defend his home.

When STRAW DOGS was released in 1971, it caused a great deal of controversy. Some found its violence too graphic and gratuitous, and were equally offended by the film's tone and depiction of Hoffman's character. The basic premise of the film—a pacifist having to take a stand—is simply taken to its wildest extreme. Hoffman's character is—in this vision of machismo—becoming a man: defending his honor, his home, and proving to his disbelieving wife that he is king of the castle. It's an admittedly narrow and primitive vision, but a powerful one. The film is played as a symbolic game of chess between husband and wife (Hoffman and George actually play chess on a few occasions during the film), with George pushing the boundaries of Hoffman's patience to the breaking point. George's moves include teasing the workers and disrupting Hoffman's work, while Hoffman counters by abusing the cat and accepting the hunting invitation. But Hoffman's checkmate comes when—after he's killed a few men and become shockingly abusive—he forces George to blast a hole into one of the assailants. Hoffman wins the game and in the process has lost all he has stood for. The overall effect of the film is spellbinding and disturbing, and it lingers in the mind long after it's over. Peckinpah handles it all with complete control, making an insightful examination of violence (and a blistering plunge into the heart of the male ego and macho myth), that manipulates the audience with reckless abandon. Full of wonderful images (the opening dissolve—which David Cronenberg repeats at the beginning of THE FLY—is particularly mesmerizing) and top notch production values (the photography, by John Coquillon, is beautiful, and the Oscar-nominated music, by Jerry Fielding, is appropriately eerie), STRAW DOGS is simply one of the strongest statements about violence ever put on the screen.

STRAY DOG
(NORA INU)
1949 122m bw   ★★★½
Crime
Shin Toho (Japan)

Toshiro Mifune *(Murakami)*, Takashi Shimura *(Sato)*, Ko Kimura *(Yuro)*, Keiko Awaji *(Harumi)*, Reisaburo Yamamoto *(Hondo)*, Noriko Sengoku *(Girl)*

p, Sojiro Motoki; d, Akira Kurosawa; w, Ryuzo Kikushima, Akira Kurosawa (based on a novel by Kurosawa); ph, Asakazu Nakai; ed, Yoshi Sugihara; m, Fumio Hayasaka; art d, So Matsuyama

This gripping, but somewhat flawed, Akira Kurosawa film details the efforts of young police detective Murakami (Toshiro Mifune) to recover his pistol after it is stolen from him on a crowded bus. Murakami becomes obsessed with finding the gun, taking personal responsibility for all the crimes committed with it—including murder—chasing his own criminal impulses by vicariously experiencing the killer's deeds.

Kurosawa has indicated that he considers STRAY DOG a failure in its concern with technique over character. While the analysis is debatable, technical lapses do mar the film more than the script or performances. A sloppy pace; indifferent narration; and an unbearably long montage sequence comprising nearly 10 minutes of dissolves and double-exposures, distract from the fascinating character study and threaten to cause the whole film to collapse under a ponderous weight. Despite this, STRAY DOG is a powerful film and well worth seeing.

STREAMERS
1983 118m c   ★★★½
Drama/War   R/18
UA Classics

Matthew Modine *(Billy)*, Michael Wright *(Carlyle)*, Mitchell Lichtenstein *(Richie)*, David Alan Grier *(Roger)*, Guy Boyd *(Rooney)*, George Dzundza *(Cokes)*, Albert Macklin *(Martin)*, B.J. Cleveland *(Pfc. Bush)*, Bill Allen *(Lt. Townsend)*, Paul Lazar *(MP Lieutenant)*

p, Robert Altman, Nick J. Mileti; d, Robert Altman; w, David Rabe (based on the play by Rabe); ph, Pierre Mignot (Movielab Color); ed, Norman Smith; prod d, Wolf Kroeger; art d, Steve Altman; cos, Scott Bushnell

Director Robert Altman was once heralded as being on the cutting edge of the American cinema with films like M*A*S*H, THE LONG GOODBYE and NASHVILLE. In the 1980s, however, he has seemed more interested in the stage than the screen, and the vast majority of his films have been movie versions of popular or critically acclaimed plays such as *Secret Honor*, *Come Back to the 5 and Dime, Jimmy Dean, Jimmy Dean* and *Fool for Love*. STREAMERS is no exception. Based on a play by David Rabe, it is set in an Army barracks circa 1965, where a group of young soldiers awaits assignment to Vietnam. The draftees come from a variety of backgrounds and include two blacks, a country boy and a Yale-educated homosexual. They are confronted by two brutal sergeants, veterans of the Korean War. Sexual and racial tensions build as the men await their transfer orders in the claustrophobic barracks, and eventually shocking violence erupts. Although Rabe's use of the barracks as a microcosm of the explosive emotions and issues coming to a head in America just before the Vietnam War is at times obvious, the play was an excruciatingly intense experience on stage. As filmed by Altman, however, STREAMERS becomes a distanced and rather static affair that feels more stagebound than the director's other stage-to-screen projects. While there is little of cinematic interest in the film, the performances Altman elicits from his cast—especially from Matthew Modine, Michael Wright and George Dzundza—are superb. The odd title is Army slang for a paratrooper whose chute has failed to open.

STREET SCENE

1931   80m   bw   ★★★★
Drama   /A
UA

Sylvia Sidney (Rose Maurrant), William Collier, Jr. (Sam Kaplan), Estelle Taylor (Anna Maurrant), Beulah Bondi (Emma Jones), Max Montor (Abe Kaplan), David Landau (Frank Maurrant), Matt McHugh (Vincent Jones), Russell Hopton (Steve Sankey), Greta Granstedt (Mae Jones), Tom Manning (George Jones)

p, Samuel Goldwyn; d, King Vidor; w, Elmer Rice (based on his play); ph, George Barnes; ed, Hugh Bennett; m, Alfred Newman; art d, Richard Day

Elmer Rice's Pulitzer Prize-winning play about the lives and loves of the people who live on a West Side Manhattan street proved to have national appeal under the sure hand of director King Vidor. To insure quality, eight of the original Broadway cast were hired to reprise their roles, including Beulah Bondi, who made her screen debut here and went on to have a long film career. Practically all of the shooting was done on a huge street set. It's summer and the windows are open. The neighborhood people can't bear to stay in their stifling apartments, so the action takes place outside. As the film opens, the big topic of conversation is the love affair between mature woman Estelle Taylor and Russell Hopton, a man who collects for the milk company. Taylor's husband, David Landau, suspicious of Hopton and his wife, is just waiting to catch them. As the sun rises, Taylor's daughter, Sylvia Sidney, goes off to work, while Landau mentions that he has to travel to Connecticut for the day. After Landau leaves, Sidney's beau, Max Montor, sees Hopton surreptitiously make his way to Taylor's flat. The shades come down—every other shade on the block is up to let in fresh air—and within a few seconds Landau is back in the apartment. Screams are heard, noises of a fight, then a single shot rings out. The people on the street turn their eyes to the sound, the shade comes up, and Hopton stands at the window. Then there's another shot, and Hopton disappears. An instant later, Landau, looking crazed, comes running out of the brownstone with the gun in his hand; the people on the street shrink back when he tells them to scatter. Landau turns the corner and disappears down an alley as police cars and ambulances rush into the street. A crowd gathers, eager to watch but not to help, waiting to see what will happen next.

Featuring excellent acting all around, STREET SCENE moves very quickly, with hardly a wasted word. Although somewhat dated by today's standards, it must be judged by those of the 1930s, when it was a stunning achievement. The play ran for more than two years and is still revived often. An added dimension was composer Alfred Newman's main theme (since used in many films), which ranks, to this day, among the most evocative pieces of music ever written, immediately conjuring up the crowded streets, the hustle, and the oppressive claustrophobia of the Big Apple.

STREET SMART

1987   95m   c   ★★★
Crime   R/18
Golan-Globus

Christopher Reeve (Jonathan Fisher), Morgan Freeman (Fast Black), Kathy Baker (Punchy), Mimi Rogers (Alison Parker), Jay Patterson (Leonard Pike), Andre Gregory (Ted Avery), Anna Maria Horsford (Harriet), Frederick Rolf (Joel Davis), Erik King (Reggie), Michael J. Reynolds (Art Sheffield)

p, Menahem Golan, Yoram Globus; d, Jerry Schatzberg; w, David Freeman; ph, Adam Holender (TVC Color); ed, Priscilla Nedd; m, Robert Irving, III, Miles Davis; prod d, Dan Leigh; art d, Serge Jacques; cos, Jo Ynocencio

Jonathan Fisher (Reeve) is a magazine journalist who gets an assignment to write about the lifestyle of a pimp. When he can't get any real pimps to talk to him, Fisher creates a fictional portrait that is chosen as a cover story and turns him into a celebrity with his own TV news show. Fisher then gets to know "Fast Black" (Freeman), a vicious, high-powered pimp who is being charged with murder. Meanwhile, an assistant D.A. comes to believe that Fast Black is the real-life subject of Fisher's article, and subpoenas the writer's (non-existent) notes as evidence in the trial. Fast Black exerts pressure on Fisher to create false notes that will provide him with an alibi; Fisher resists, until he realizes how far the pimp will go to get what he wants.

Thanks to a terrific performance by Freeman (it earned him an Oscar nomination as Best Supporting Actor) and slick direction by Jerry Schatzberg, this is a fast-moving, intermittently riveting crime drama. Reeve is good as the naive writer who gets in over his head, and Kathy Baker is outstanding as one of Fast Black's "girls."

STREETCAR NAMED DESIRE, A

1951   125m   bw   ★★★★★
Drama   /15
WB

Vivien Leigh (Blanche DuBois), Marlon Brando (Stanley Kowalski), Kim Hunter (Stella Kowalski), Karl Malden (Mitch), Rudy Bond (Steve Hubbell), Nick Dennis (Pablo Gonzales), Peg Hillias (Eunice Hubbell), Wright King (Young Collector), Richard Garrick (Doctor), Ann Dere (The Matron)

p, Charles K. Feldman; d, Elia Kazan; w, Tennessee Williams, Oscar Saul (adapted from the play by Williams); ph, Harry Stradling; ed, David Weisbart; m, Alex North; art d, Richard Day; cos, Lucinda Ballard

This is the classic screen version of the play which opened on Broadway in 1947 and ran for two years. Marlon Brando reprises his role from the stage and is electrifying as the brutish Stanley Kowalski. Elia Kazan directed the play in New York and made the trek west for the film, joined by Brando, Kim Hunter, Karl Malden, Rudy Bond, Nick Dennis, Peg Hillias, and Edna Thomas from the stage version. Jessica Tandy, who had been a smash as Blanche DuBois on Broadway, was the only major player to be replaced. Studio chiefs felt she wasn't well known enough for the movie, and her role went to Vivien Leigh, who had been starring in a London presentation of the play directed by her husband, Laurence Olivier.

The film opens with Leigh coming to New Orleans to visit her sister, the pregnant Hunter, and the sister's husband Brando. To get to their seedy apartment, she has to take a streetcar named Desire (named for a New Orleans street), transfer to another one named Cemetery and alight in an area of the French Quarter called Elysian Fields. The sisters are thrilled to see one another, though they couldn't be more dissimilar. Hunter is an earthy woman, happy in her marriage to the trashy but overtly sexual Brando, while Leigh is delicate, morose and deeply neurotic.

Brando immediately sees through Leigh's southern-belle facade and the two are quickly at odds.

Aware that the sisters were left a large estate (Belle Reve) by their parents, Brando starts pumping Leigh for information about the property, noting that the Napoleonic Code of Louisiana entitles him, as Hunter's husband, to half the proceeds from the sale of the estate. Leigh finally confesses that she took out a series of mortgages on the place to pay for funerals and finally lost the property. This enrages Brando and he sets out to find out all he can about his sister-in-law. In the meantime, tensions increase between the pair as they are unable to escape each other in the tiny apartment. Leigh finds Brando's behavior appalling and is equally dismayed by his friends, with the exception of the somewhat reserved Malden, a bachelor who lives with his mother. Malden is attracted to Leigh as well, and the two begin a tentative courtship, much to Brando's displeasure.

When Brando gets information about Leigh's sordid past, including the suicide of her husband and her dalliance with a high school student, he shares this information with Malden, who quickly drops Leigh, forcing her even more deeply into depression. When Hunter's labor pains commence, she is off to the hospital, leaving Brando and Leigh alone in the apartment for the first time, for a fated, horrifying confrontation.

A STREETCAR NAMED DESIRE features some of the finest ensemble acting ever offered on the screen, speaking some of the best dialogue ever written by a playwright. STREETCAR is undoubtedly Williams's masterpiece, even watered down, as it is here. Kazan's sensitive and insightful direction sometimes cannot overcome staging habits from Broadway. Leigh, in the final great triumph of her screen career, is the very picture of tattered magnificence. She's like a cracked figurine from *The Glass Menagerie* come to life; her emotional choices are tragic and horrifying at the same time. Brando's character is strictly scratch, mumble, flex and roar, but it's telegraphed through force-of-nature persona—he has no peers at locating the fear Stanley inspires. Time has proven few actors can portray Stanley. Kim Hunter is adequate in the most sketchily written role—it's hard to navigate the dichotomy in Stella's character. And Karl Malden is both touching and revolting as Mitch, exactly as it should be.

STRICTLY DISHONORABLE

1931   94m   bw   ★★★½
Comedy   /A
Universal

Paul Lukas (*Count Di Ruva*), Sidney Fox (*Isabelle Parry*), Lewis Stone (*Judge Dempsey*), George Meeker (*Henry Greene*), William Ricciardi (*Tomasso*), Sidney Toler (*Mulligan*), Samuel Bonello, Carlo Schipa (*Waiters*), Natalie Moorhead (*Lilli*), Joe Torilla (*Cook*)

p, Carl Laemmle, Jr.; d, John M. Stahl; w, Gladys Lehman (based on the play by Preston Sturges); ph, Karl Freund, Jackson Rose; ed, Arthur Tavares, Maurice Pivar

Preston Sturges's second stage play (written when he was still in his twenties) became a Broadway hit and was filmed twice: this version and the remake in 1951 that starred Janet Leigh and Ezio Pinza. Screenwriter Gladys Lehman wisely stuck close to the original, and the laughs are many. Paul Lukas portrays a rakehell opera-singer. In an illegal speakeasy one night, he meets naive southerner Sidney Fox, who is engaged to be married to boorish George Meeker. Lukas lets her know that his intentions are strictly dishonorable but it matters not to petite Fox, who is, by this time, disgusted with her aggravating suitor. The speak is owned by William Ricciardi (reprising his role in the play, as did

Meeker) and frequented by Sidney Toler, a cop who turns the other way when he sees the illegal alcohol being poured in his own glass. Lewis Stone almost steals the movie as a one-time judge who has given up the law in favor of tippling. When Fox leaves Meeker and has no place to stay, Lukas offers her the use of his apartment, making certain she knows that he is a bounder, a cad, and a ne'er-do-well. Despite his admitted degeneracy, Fox still wants to be with him, and he almost seduces her when Stone points out that she is little more than a child, and that he (Lukas) would be remiss if he allowed himself to fall prey to passion. Lukas leaves Fox in his apartment and goes up to Stone's apartment to spend the night, but the realization of love suddenly intrudes.

The writing is sharp, the characters are well drawn, and the comedy timing is on a par with the best movies of the era. And watching the patrician Stone as a drunk is great entertainment.

STRIKE UP THE BAND

1940   120m   bw   ★★★½
Musical/Comedy   /U
MGM

Mickey Rooney (*Jimmy Connors*), Judy Garland (*Mary Holden*), Paul Whiteman and His Orchestra (*Themselves*), June Preisser (*Barbara Frances Morgan*), William Tracy (*Phillip Turner*), Ann Shoemaker (*Mrs. Connors*), Larry Nunn (*Willie Brewster*), George Lessey (*Mr. Morgan*), Francis Pierlot (*Mr. Judd*), Harry McCrillis (*Booper Barton*)

p, Arthur Freed; d, Busby Berkeley; w, Herbert Fields (uncredited), Kay Van Riper (uncredited), John Monks, Jr., Fred Finklehoffe; ph, Ray June; ed, Ben Lewis; art d, Cedric Gibbons, John S. Detlie; cos, Dolly Tree, Gile Steele

Mickey Rooney and Judy Garland, two of the great young stars of their day, team up in this musical comedy as a pair of high school students. Mary (Garland) works in the library after school, and Jimmy (Rooney) spends his free time practicing the drums. He wants to smack the skins in a dance band, but his widowed mother yearns for him to become a doctor. Jimmy and a bunch of his pals form an orchestra with the intention of entering a contest sponsored by big band "King of Jazz" Paul Whiteman. The kids manage to scrape together the money for their trip to the coast, but when one of them needs an emergency operation, Jimmy decides to pay for it and sacrifice his big chance. Luckily, Paul Whiteman is in town and Jimmy and his boys get a chance to play for him anyway. Rooney and Garland deliver their usual energy-packed performances, but one unexpected scene is a standout: as Jimmy uses a bowl of fruit to illustrate an idea he has for a musical number, the fruit turns into little animated puppet models (masterminded by George Pal) that perform "Do the Conga." Also included is the big band classic "Sing, Sing, Sing."

STRIPES

1981   106m   c   ★★★½
Comedy   R/15
Columbia

Bill Murray (*John Winger*), Harold Ramis (*Russell Zitsky*), Warren Oates (*Sgt. Hulka*), P.J. Soles (*Stella*), Sean Young (*Louise*), John Candy (*Ox*), John Larroquette (*Capt. Stillman*), Judge Reinhold (*Elmo*), John Voldstad (*Aide*), John Diehl (*Cruiser*)

p, Ivan Reitman, Dan Goldberg; d, Ivan Reitman; w, Len Blum, Dan Goldberg, Harold Ramis; ph, Bill Butler (Metrocolor); ed, Eva Ruggiero, Michael Luciano, Harry Keller; m, Elmer Bernstein; prod d, James H. Spencer; chor, Ronn Forella, Arthur Goldweit; cos, Richard Bruno

Though it's occasionally tasteless and eventually crumbles, STRIPES is an often hilarious film that provided Bill Murray with a perfect opportunity in which to display his comedic skills. Murray stars as John Winger, an irresponsible goof-off who, as the film opens, has just lost his job, his girl, his apartment and his car. As he ponders his fate with his equally unsuccesful best friend, Russell Zitsky (Harold Ramis), a man who teaches English to recent immigrants, it occurs to him that enlisting in the Army seems to be a sensible career move. He persuades Howard to go along on the adventure and soon they find themselves in boot camp surrounded by a group of misfits that includes the overweight Ox (John Candy), the temperamental Psycho (Conrad Dunn), the dopey Cruiser (John Diehl), and druggie Elmo (Judge Reinhold in his film debut). Given the unenviable task of presiding over this collection of dolts is tough Army veteran Sgt. Hulka (Warren Oates), and it isn't long before Winger finds his way to the sergeant's bad side. While STRIPES was ideally suited to Murray's wise-ass, rebel-who-has-no-use-for-a-cause character, what really makes the film work is his relationship with Ramis. The two make a delightful comedy team, with the somewhat more sensible Ramis serving as the perfect foil to Murray. His expressive face and low-key manner provide a comic perspective that serves to enhance Murray's clowning. The rest of the cast is also first-rate, especially Oates who imbues his weary sergeant with an unexpected wit and intelligence. While basic training has been the subject of countless screen comedies, the subject is one which offers great comic potential, and this film exploits that potential. Unfortunately, it flags considerably once basic ends and the characters set off on their inane adventure behind enemy lines.

STUDENT PRINCE, THE

1954 107m c   ★★½
Musical   /U
MGM

Ann Blyth (Kathie), Edmund Purdom (Prince Karl), John Ericson (Count Von Asterburg), Louis Calhern (King of Karlsburg), Edmund Gwenn (Prof. Juttner), S.Z. Sakall (Joseph Ruder), Betta St. John (Princess Johanna), John Williams (Lutz), Evelyn Varden (Queen), John Hoyt (Prime Minister)

p, Joe Pasternak; d, Richard Thorpe; w, William Ludwig, Sonya Levien (based on the operetta by Dorothy Donnelly, Sigmund Romberg, and the novel and play by Wilhelm Meyer-Foerster); ph, Paul C. Vogel (CinemaScope, Ansco Color); ed, Gene Ruggiero; m, Sigmund Romberg; art d, Cedric Gibbons, Randall Duell; fx, Warren Newcombe; chor, Hermes Pan; cos, Helen Rose, Walter Plunkett

A remake of the 1927 picture based on the musical by Romberg and Donnelly and the straight play by Meyer-Foerster, this film is a pleasant trifle with some good musical numbers that were sung by Mario Lanza, but came out of the mouth of Purdom. Lanza had been scheduled to play the German prince, but his weight was always fluctuating, and when his temper began to rise and fall with the speed of his avoirdupois, the decision was made to toss him out and use Purdom. Since Lanza had already pre-recorded the tunes, that wasn't too tough, although the sound of the round tenor tones coming out of Purdom's slim chest does

seem ludicrous, for a while. After the shock of it is over, the picture has its moments. Purdom is Karl, a prince with all the accoutrements of the royal purple. His father is the king (Calhern), who feels that the prince needs to go out and see what the real world is like before he comes back to the princess (St. John) with whom a marriage has been arranged. He goes to Heidelberg, where he meets Kathie (Blyth), the daughter of a local innkeeper (Sakall). They fall in love, but when the king falls ill and dies, Karl must assume his position as king.

Unrequited love is the theme and 1954 audiences liked their love requited, so the picture didn't fare as well as the studio had hoped. The stalwart and handsome if unexciting Purdom got lots of build-up and later starred in THE EGYPTIAN, yet his career never did take off. The Romberg-Donnelly songs (with some revised lyrics by Paul Francis Webster) include "Golden Days," "Serenade," "Deep in My Heart," "To the Inn We're Marching," "Drink, Drink, Drink," and "Come Boys, Let's All Be Gay, Boys," a song that causes gales of laughter these days because the meaning of its title has changed over the years. Webster and Nicholas Brodszky added three new tunes to the score ("I'll Walk with God", "Beloved" and "Summertime in Heidelberg"), none of which was up to the original. The editing by Ruggiero was a standout and Pan's choreography properly rousing, but the time had passed for such corn by 1954.

STUNT MAN, THE

1980 129m c   ★★★★
Comedy/Drama   R/X
FOX

Peter O'Toole (Eli Cross), Steve Railsback (Cameron), Barbara Hershey (Nina Franklin), Allen Garfield (Sam), Alex Rocco (Jake), Sharon Farrell (Denise), Adam Roarke (Raymond Bailey), Philip Bruns (Ace), Chuck Bail (Chuck Barton), John Garwood (Gabe)

p, Richard Rush; d, Richard Rush; w, Larry Marcus, Richard Rush (based on the novel by Paul Brodeur); ph, Mario Tosi (Metrocolor); ed, Jack Hofstra, Caroline Ferriol; m, Dominic Frontiere; art d, James Schoppe; cos, Rosanna Norton

Peter O'Toole, a megalomaniacal film director, tyrannizes his writer and plays games with his actors, manipulating their actions in reality, just as he does in the story he is filming. Steve Railsback is on the run from the law, and he stumbles upon the movie company as they shoot a scene on the beach. After his top stuntman is killed, O'Toole, who has shielded Railsback from the law, persuades the young man to take the dead man's place. Railsback is then thrust into the not-so-glamorous world of moviemaking and gets involved with Barbara Hershey, O'Toole's beautiful star and lover. Lawrence B. Marcus's script, which pits real life against reel life, offers plenty of wit, with most of the bons mots handed to O'Toole. The script, O'Toole, and director Richard Rush were all nominated for Oscars for their contributions to this tough, funny, and enigmatic film.

SUBJECT WAS ROSES, THE

1968 107m c   ★★★★
Drama   /A
MGM

Patricia Neal (Nettie Cleary), Jack Albertson (John Cleary), Martin Sheen (Timmy Cleary), Don Saxon (Nightclub Master of Ceremonies), Elaine Williams (Woman), Grant Gordon (Man in Restaurant)

p, Edgar Lansbury; d, Ulu Grosbard; w, Frank D. Gilroy (based on his play); ph, Jack Priestley (Metrocolor); ed, Jerry Greenberg; m, Lee Pockriss; art d, George Jenkins; cos, Anna Hill Johnstone

Frank Gilroy's Pulitzer Prize-winning drama was beautifully realized in this film adaptation WWII has just ended, and Sheen returns home from the battle to live with parents Neal and Albertson. In the years since he's been away, his parents' marriage has disintegrated into rancor, disagreements and highly charged hostility. Before he left, Sheen was the apple of Neal's eye and only had a passing relationship with Albertson. Now that he's matured, however, he has a closer tie to Albertson, finding that they are two of a kind. Sheen can't bear to see his parents at such loggerheads and attempts to mediate their differences without standing in either's corner.

Neal begins a subtle campaign of sabotage against Albertson but Sheen sees through this and confronts his mother by saying that he will not side with her or Albertson in any dispute, preferring to remain completely neutral. Neal can't handle Sheen's attitude but she later discovers Sheen drunk and arguing with Albertson in much the same way he had argued with her. Sheen, despite the booze he's ingested, makes some sense. This situation will never get better as long as things remain the same. He thinks that his parents must work out their marital differences without using him as a referee, so he tells them that he is going to leave and strike out on his own.

The movie was not a hit, despite the terrific acting, sharp writing, and outstanding direction from Grosbard, who also staged the play. Never does the emotion explode into oratory, so almost every scene has an underlying tension that continues to bubble.

SUCH A GORGEOUS KID LIKE ME
(UNE BELLE FILLE COMME MOI)

1973 100m c	★★★
Comedy/Drama	R/
Carrosse (France)	

Bernadette Lafont (Camille Bliss), Claude Brasseur (Monsieur Murene), Charles Denner (Arthur), Guy Marchand (Sam Golden), Andre Dussollier (Stanislas Previne), Philippe Leotard (Clovis Bliss), Anne Kreis (Helene), Gilberte Geniat (Isobel Bliss), Daniele Girard (Florence Golden), Martine Ferriere (Prison Secretary)

p, Marcel Berbert; d, Francois Truffaut; w, Francois Truffaut, Jean-Loup Dabadie (based on the novel by Henry Farrell); ph, Pierre-William Glenn (Eastmancolor); ed, Yann Dedet; m, Georges Delerue; art d, Jean-Pierre Kohut-Svelko; cos, Monique Dury

An often ignored film by Truffaut, this black comedy is about women and their seemingly magical hold over men. Lafont, who first appeared in his 1957 short, LES MISTONS, takes up where she left off some 15 years earlier. In LES MISTONS she was tormented by a quintet of young boys who were very much in love with her. Here Lafont is able to take revenge on her tormentors.

The picture starts with a sociologist, Dussollier, preparing to write a book called *Criminal Women* (which he never gets to publish). He visits a women's prison and decides to interview convicted murderess Lafont, passing up offers to interview a woman who dismembered her victims and another who strangles them using only one hand. Dussollier discovers that Lafont is indirectly responsible for the deaths of her father and her mother-in-law, and was unsuccessful in her attempts to kill attorney Brasseur and husband Leotard with rat poison. She is eventually acquitted of her crime and rises to become a famed singer, not because of her voice (which is wretched) but because of the publicity that surrounds her case. Backstage at one of her performances, she is confronted by Leotard and Dussollier kills Leotard. But Lafont still has her own unique resources at hand.

SUCH A GORGEOUS KID LIKE ME, though it may not initially seem Truffautesque, has roots in a number of his previous films. He compares this film to THE WILD CHILD. Lafont's murderous female character is also seen in JULES AND JIM and THE BRIDE WORE BLACK (and to a lesser, non-violent extent in THE STORY OF ADELE H.). While it may not be an audience pleaser, SUCH A GORGEOUS KID LIKE ME is a definite must for those who are interested in learning about the "total" Truffaut.

SUGAR CANE ALLEY
(RUE CASES NEGRES)

1983 103m c	★★★½
Drama	PG/
Su Ma Fa/Orca/NEF Diffusion (France)	

Garry Cadenat (Jose), Darling Legitimus (M'Man Tine), Douta Seck (Medouze), Joby Bernabe (M. Saint-Louis), Francisco Charles (Le Gereur), Marie-Jo Descas (La Mere de Leopold), Marie-Ange Farot (Mme. Saint-Louis), Henri Melon (M. Roc), Eugene Mona (Douze Orteils), Joel Palcy (Carmen)

p, Michel Loulergue, Alix Regis; d, Euzhan Palcy; w, Euzhan Palcy (based on the novel La Rue Cases Negres by Joseph Zobel); ph, Dominique Chapius (Fujicolor); ed, Marie-Josephe Yoyotte; m, Groupe Malavoi; art d, Hoang Thanh At; cos, Isabelle Filleul

Set in the French colony of Martinique in the 1930s, this stark, charming film takes a look at life in "Rue Cases Negres," a wooden-shack community isolated in the middle of a sugar plantation. While the adults toil in the fields, the children romp the "alley," but for many of the youngsters this will be their last summer on the plantation. The brightest among them will find better jobs or go on to school, while the less fortunate will remain to assist their parents in the fields. Most prominently featured is Jose (Garry Cadenat), a frolicsome 11-year-old who earns a prestigious scholarship to a school in Fort-de-France. This well-acted film is an unexpected delight, showing that a ray of hope can materialize amid the despondency of a shantytown. SUGAR CANE ALLEY was a double prizewinner at the Venice Film Festival, taking a Silver Lion and Darling Legitimus garnering a Best Actress award.

SUGARBABY
(ZUCKERBABY)

1985 86m c	★★★½
Drama/Comedy	/15
Pelemele (West Germany)	

Marianne Sagebrecht (Marianne), Eisi Gulp (Huber 133), Toni Berger (Old Subway Driver), Manuela Denz (Huber's Wife), Will Spindler (Funeral Director), The Paul Wurges Combo (Dance Hall Band), Hans Stadlbauer

d, Percy Adlon; w, Percy Adlon; ph, Johanna Heer; ed, Jean-Claude Piroue; m, Dreieier; cos, Regina Batz, Silvia Risa

The first installment of Percy Adlon's delightful "Marianne" trilogy, SUGARBABY stars the utterly winning Marianne Sagebrecht in a sweetly romantic story which also bears the rare distinction of being a Teutonic comedy.

Marianne (Sagebrecht) is a hugely overweight mortuary attendant who, while commuting to work one morning on the subway, becomes infatuated with the conductor (Eisi Gulp), a handsome, blond hunk in a tight-fitting uniform. She quickly determines to win him over and, failing to locate him the following day, goes to great lengths to procure his name and route number: Huber 133. Next, under the guise of finding work for her nephew, she gets her hands on the complex work schedule for subway drivers. After an obsessive search, she finally figures out Huber's schedule. In the meantime, Marianne has been preparing herself for her future lover, buying sexy lingerie (which must be specially ordered in her size), flashy high heels and pink satin sheets. Although it seems likely that all this preparation will backfire, Huber, nicknamed "Sugarbaby" by Marianne, accepts her invitation to dinner and romance quickly blossoms.

Adlon combines the free-spirited energy of his characters with technique to match, fashioning a magnificent lighting scheme that relies heavily on color effects, a minimalist set reduced to the barest essentials and a frantic camera style that allows the camera to wander, sway, and zig-zag through the set. Rather than creating a feeling of pretension or intrusive stylization, however, Adlon's film is lighthearted and energetic. He lets no barriers stand in his way and, as a result, the entire picture is an engaging, intelligent entertainment. And in Marianne, marvelously incarnated by Sagebrecht, viewers will find a lovable heroine with whom most would gladly spend time in the real world.

SUGARLAND EXPRESS, THE

1974 109m c   ★★★
Adventure   PG
Universal

Goldie Hawn (Lou Jean Poplin), Ben Johnson (Capt. Tanner), Michael Sacks (Officer Slide), William Atherton (Clovis Poplin), Gregory Walcott (Officer Mashburn), Steve Kanaly (Jessup), Louise Latham (Mrs. Looby), Harrison Zanuck (Baby Langston), A.L. Camp (Mr. Nocker), Jessie Lee Fulton (Mrs. Nocker)

p, Richard D. Zanuck, David Brown; d, Steven Spielberg; w, Hal Barwood, Matthew Robbins (based on a story by Spielberg, Barwood, Robbins); ph, Vilmos Zsigmond (Panavision, Technicolor); ed, Edward Abroms, Verna Fields; m, John Williams; art d, Joe Alves; fx, Frank Brendel

This is Steven Spielberg's first effort at the helm in feature filmmaking (the earlier DUEL being a made-for-TV movie), and it contains much of the raw sense of adventure (though without the technical gadgetry) that would make his later films so popular and such good clean fun. After his success with THE SUGARLAND EXPRESS, he went on to direct the highly profitable, beloved, and much-imitated JAWS in 1975. Based on a true story, this film features Hawn playing a woman who helps her husband, Atherton, escape from prison. She needs him to join her in the fight against forces who want to put her child up for adoption. What ensues is one long chase across America's highways. Throughout the film, more and more police, and the media, want in on the action. Spielberg exhibits that he still had a bit to learn in the world of filmmaking. The film moves well and never loses its gripping tension, but the lighthearted tone of the beginning takes a dive into an abyss that shocks many viewers. With this role, Hawn further proves she was an actress of some talent and not just an attractive woman to be taken lightly.

SULLIVANS, THE

1944 111m bw   ★★★★
Drama/War   /U
FOX

Anne Baxter (Katherine Mary), Thomas Mitchell (Mr. Sullivan), Selena Royle (Mrs. Sullivan), Edward Ryan (Al), Trudy Marshall (Genevieve), John Campbell (Frank), James Cardwell (George), John Alvin (Matt), George Offerman, Jr. (Joe), Roy Roberts (Fr. Francis)

p, Sam Jaffe; d, Lloyd Bacon; w, Mary C. McCall, Jr. (based on a story by Edward Doherty, Jules Schermer); ph, Lucien Andriot; ed, Louis Loeffler; m, Cyril J. Mockridge; art d, James Basevi, Leland Fuller; fx, Fred Sersen

The tragic story of the Sullivans, five brothers who served together on the cruiser Juneau in WWII and who were all killed at Guadalcanal, is related in this film that reminded Americans what they were fighting for in 1944. The story begins in the small town of Waterloo, Iowa, when the Sullivans are boys. Their father, Mitchell, works for the railroad while his wife, Royle, keeps house and tries to keep an eye on their rambunctious boys, who are shown on their childhood small-town rounds, from chores to experiments with smoking. (Mitchell catches them smoking cornsilk and makes them try cigars instead—they all get sick.) Later, after the boys have grown to manhood (and are now played by Campbell, Cardwell, Alvin, Offerman, and Ryan), Ryan is the first to marry a nice girl (Baxter) and settle down. But the world invades the solitude of Waterloo in the aftermath of the Pearl Harbor bombing, and the patriotic Sullivan sons all decide to join the Navy. Even Ryan, who has a young family to think of, is urged by Baxter to join his brothers. Since they have always been a team, the Sullivans insist on serving together and are assigned duty on the Juneau. When all are killed in the same battle, the news is received at home with grief, but also with pride. Mitchell and Royle are comforted to know that their boys would have wanted to go down together. (After the Sullivans' deaths, however, the Navy prohibited the assignment of all family members on the same ship.)

THE SULLIVANS is a moving film that brings home the tragedy of loss and the cost of war. The film successfully re-creates the flavor of small-town life, with a depth that transcends the standard Hollywood Andy Hardy-style sentimentality. The casting of relative unknowns in the brothers' roles enhances the film's realism, eliminating star-power distractions; by contrast, veteran character actor Thomas Mitchell, as the film's most recognizable performer, lends an air of authority and reassurance to his role as the clan's loving patriarch. A very entertaining, warm film full of nostalgia for small-town life and values, THE SULLIVANS is also a tribute to the men who give their lives in the war, the families that suffered their loss, and the life for which they fought. The title was changed to THE FIGHTING SULLIVANS shortly after the film's release to improve its box office draw.

SULLIVAN'S TRAVELS

1941 91m bw   ★★★★★
Comedy/Drama   /A
Paramount

Joel McCrea (John L. Sullivan), Veronica Lake (The Girl), Robert Warwick (Mr. Lebrand), William Demarest (Mr. Jones), Franklin Pangborn (Mr. Casalais), Porter Hall (Mr. Hadrian), Byron Foulger (Mr. Valdelle), Margaret Hayes (Secretary), Robert Greig (Sullivan's Butler), Eric Blore (Sullivan's Valet)

p, Paul Jones; d, Preston Sturges; w, Preston Sturges; ph, John Seitz; ed, Stuart Gilmore; m, Leo Shuken, Charles Bradshaw; art d, Hans Dreier, Earl Hedrick; fx, Farciot Edouart; cos, Edith Head

A Hollywood variation on Gulliver's Travels and just as successful as satire. This brilliant, often devastating look at Hollywood and the real world behind its tinsel is Preston Sturges's greatest film. McCrea, in one of his best roles, plays a successful Hollywood film director who has made nothing but lightweight films with titles like "So Long, Sarong." When he is suddenly struck with the desire to make a searing drama about human suffering, his studio bosses (Warwick and Hall) laugh and tell him that the proposal is ridiculous, since McCrea has no personal experience of such difficulty. Accordingly, McCrea sets out to suffer. He will don hobo clothes and, with only 10 cents in his pocket, go forth into poverty and experience adversity for himself. Knowing they can't change his mind, Warwick and Hall humor the eccentric director's whim, but decide to turn McCrea's nomadic adventure into a publicity stunt that will benefit the studio. To this end they provide him with a publicity entourage and a luxury van that follows McCrea as he travels on foot, and that carries McCrea's butler, Greig, and valet, Blore, who both urge their employer to give up this mad idea, telling him that the poor insist upon their privacy and don't want him intruding upon it.

Though the plot may sound a bit contrived, everything in this wonderful film works. And it presents a spectacular array of emotions and situations that allow for Sturges's magical direction and script to quickly turn all the film's sharp corners with his characters. SULLIVAN'S TRAVELS is a wonderful comedy-drama, the type of a one-of-a-kind film for which Sturges— basically a writer with a good sense of camera use and visuals, who as a director was always trying out new techniques—was noted. Unlike many of his other films, which were made for sheer entertainment value, SULLIVAN'S TRAVELS contains a message, which Sturges himself later explained: "SULLIVAN'S TRAVELS is the result of an urge, an urge to tell some of my fellow filmwrights that they were getting a little too deep-dish and to leave the preaching to the preachers."

SUMMER
(LE RAYON VERT)
1986   98m   c   ★★★½
Drama   R/
Losange   (France)

Marie Riviere (Delphine), Lisa Heredia (Manuela), Beatrice Romand (Beatrice), Rosette (Francoise), Eric Hamm (Edouard), Vincent Gauthier (Jacques), Carita (Lena), Joel Comarlot (Joel), Amira Chemakhi, Sylvia Richez

p, Margaret Menegoz; d, Eric Rohmer; w, Eric Rohmer; ph, Sophie Maintigneux; ed, Maria-Luisa Garcia; m, Jean-Louis Valero

SUMMER is the fifth in Eric Rohmer's series of "Comedies and Proverbs" begun with THE AVIATOR'S WIFE, a film that also starred the lovely Marie Riviere. It's August in Paris, and the natives have gone on holiday, leaving the city to the throngs of tourists. Delphine (Riviere), however, has nowhere to go, having missed out on a planned trip to Greece when her girlfriend decided to go with her new lover instead. Depressed, lonely, and loveless, Delphine is determined to take a vacation before the start of her fall term at college. After accepting an invitation to stay in a friend's vacated Biarritz apartment, Delphine meets Lena (Carita), a blonde Swedish playgirl who makes every effort to pull her out of her melancholy, although ultimately Delphine must gain insight on her own.

Since his rise to prominence in the late 1950s, director-writer Rohmer has consistently delivered small but wonderful romantic episodes. Rather than filming events or spectacles, he films people—usually lovelorn Parisians on a stubborn quest. Here Delphine is the stubborn one—determined not to be stuck in Paris and to find a lover who will bring her happiness, even if her determination makes her unhappy. Riviere remarked that Rohmer "had seen some women alone on the beach on holiday and he noticed sometimes that women were looking for men in newspaper advertisements. He wanted to explore this loneliness

of young women who are not ugly, who have nothing wrong with them, but who are still alone." Filming with a typically small crew, shooting on 16mm film, and allowing his cast to improvise, Rohmer made one of his most refreshing and natural films to date in SUMMER.

SUMMER HOLIDAY
1948   92m   c   ★★★★
Musical/Comedy   /U
MGM

Mickey Rooney (Richard Miller), Gloria DeHaven (Muriel McComber), Walter Huston (Nat Miller), Frank Morgan (Uncle Sid), Jackie "Butch" Jenkins (Tommy Miller), Marilyn Maxwell (Belle), Agnes Moorehead (Cousin Lily), Selena Royle (Mrs. Miller), Michael Kirby (Arthur Miller), Shirley Johns (Mildred Miller)

p, Arthur Freed; d, Rouben Mamoulian; w, Frances Goodrich, Albert Hackett, Irving Brecher, Jean Holloway (based on the play "Ah, Wilderness!" by Eugene O'Neill); ph, Charles Schoenbaum (Technicolor); ed, Albert Akst; m, Harry Warren; art d, Cedric Gibbons, Jack Martin Smith; chor, Charles Walters; cos, Irene, Walter Plunkett

This fine musical version of Eugene O'Neill's "Ah, Wilderness!" stars Mickey Rooney as a boy struggling with the pitfalls of adolescence. In early 1900s New England we meet the Miller clan: Nat (Walter Huston), a newspaper editor and staunch upholder of Yankee tradition; his wife (Selena Royle), ever the doting mother; Richard (Rooney), their oldest son; and Tommy ("Butch" Jenkins), their youngest. Also living in their comfortable household are an old maid cousin (Agnes Moorehead) and a bachelor uncle (Frank Morgan). Richard is extraordinarily bright and has big ideas about changing the world. He adores neighbor Muriel McComber (Gloria DeHaven), but has been forbidden to see her by her conservative father. Peeved at his inability to see the girl he loves, Richard goes off on a drunk, meets a dance-hall girl, spends every cent he has, and gets kicked out of the bar. Naturally, he catches hell from his dad, but by the end he and Muriel are finally allowed to be together.

A sweet movie with good work by all the actors, SUMMER HOLIDAY benefits immeasurably from director Mamoulian's inventiveness and the handsome cinematography and production values. Even if "The Stanley Steamer" is an obvious attempt to cash in on the appeal of "The Trolley Song" from the very similar MEET ME IN ST. LOUIS, the songs are quite appealing and eminently suitable. An earlier version of the O'Neill play appeared in 1935 as AH, WILDERNESS, with Rooney playing the role of the younger brother.

SUMMER OF '42
1971   102m   c   ★★★
Drama   PG/X
WB

Jennifer O'Neill (Dorothy), Gary Grimes (Hermie), Jerry Houser (Oscy), Oliver Conant (Benjie), Katherine Allentuck (Aggie), Christopher Norris (Miriam), Lou Frizzell (Druggist), Walter Scott (Dorothy's Husband), Robert Mulligan (Narrator), Maureen Stapleton (Voice of Hermie's Mother)

p, Richard A. Roth; d, Robert Mulligan; w, Herman Raucher; ph, Robert Surtees (Technicolor); ed, Folmar Blangsted; m, Michel Legrand; prod d, Albert Brenner

People who actually recall 1942 will more greatly appreciate the waves of nostalgia that bathe this affectionate coming-of-age drama, set on a tiny island off New England. Director Mulligan (as the adult Hermie) narrates his recollections, and all of the names used in the story were the real names of the people involved (or so claimed screenwriter Raucher, who wrote the screenplay in less than two weeks). Grimes is the 15-year-old whose life we observe on the tranquil island, where the horrors of war seem a million miles away. Grimes and his friends, Houser and Conant, pal around together, get into minor scrapes, go see movies like NOW, VOYAGER, and spend a great deal of time poring over an educational sex manual. Houser reads the manual as though it were the Bible and he a seminary student; Grimes is more interested in the practical aspects of sex and yearns for O'Neill, an "older woman" in her twenties who is married to absent soldier Scott.

SUMMER STOCK

1950 109m c   ★★★½
Musical
MGM

Judy Garland (Jane Falbury), Gene Kelly (Joe D. Ross), Eddie Bracken (Orville Wingait), Gloria DeHaven (Abigail Falbury), Marjorie Main (Esme), Phil Silvers (Herb Blake), Ray Collins (Jasper G. Wingait), Carleton Carpenter (Artie), Nita Bieber (Sarah Higgins), Hans Conried (Harrison I. Keath)

p, Joe Pasternak; d, Charles Walters; w, George Wells, Sy Gomberg (based on a story by Gomberg); ph, Robert Planck (Technicolor); ed, Albert Akst; art d, Cedric Gibbons, Jack Martin Smith; chor, Nick Castle, Gene Kelly, Charles Walters; cos, Walter Plunkett, Helen Rose

A tuneful throwback to the old-fashioned "you've got the barn, I've got the instruments, let's put on a show" movie musicals, Judy Garland's last MGM film was fraught with problems resulting from the star's emotional difficulties, temperamental behavior and fluctuations in weight. Garland plays Jane Falbury, a New England farmer in financial trouble. Her sister, Abigail (Gloria DeHaven) is due to come in and help harvest the crops, but to Jane's surprise Abigail, an aspiring actress, arrives with a whole summer stock company led by Abigail's love interest, Joe D. Ross (Gene Kelly). Jane, meanwhile, is loved by Orville Wingait (Eddie Bracken), the goony son of the local general store proprietor. When Abigail suggests that they raise money by putting on a show in Jane's large barn, Jane reluctantly agrees on condition that the performers help with the harvesting and other chores to pay for their room and board—a decision which incurs the disapproval of Orville, his father, and Jane's housekeeper (Marjorie Main), none of whom think much of the acting profession. Meanwhile, Joe and Jane develop a mutual attraction, although Jane stifles her feelings out of consideration for Abigail. Soon enough, however, Abigail and Joe quarrel, sending Abigail off to New York in a huff and leaving Joe stuck for a leading lady.

Complementing the simplistic plot are several excellent songs by Harry Warren and Mack Gordon, as well as the old Ted Koehler-Harold Arlen hit "Get Happy," tacked on to the film by the studio after the rough cut was complete. Featuring a sensational performance by Garland—clad in leotard, a man's tuxedo jacket, and black fedora—the number shows the star some 15 pounds lighter than she appears in other scenes. It would be four years before Garland appeared in another film, Cukor's remake of A STAR IS BORN.

SUMMERTIME

1955 100m c   ★★★★
Romance   /PG
Lopert/London Films

Katharine Hepburn (Jane Hudson), Rossano Brazzi (Renato Di Rossi), Isa Miranda (Signora Fiorina), Darren McGavin (Eddie Jaeger), Mari Aldon (Phyl Jaeger), Jane Rose (Mrs. McIlhenny), MacDonald Parke (Mr. McIlhenny), Gaitano Audiero (Mauro), Andre Morell (Englishman), Jeremy Spenser (Vito)

p, Ilya Lopert; d, David Lean; w, David Lean, H.E. Bates (based on the play The Time of the Cuckoo by Arthur Laurents); ph, Jack Hildyard (Eastmancolor); ed, Peter Taylor; m, Alessandro Cicognini; art d, Vincent Korda

Based loosely on Arthur Laurents's play The Time Of The Cuckoo, SUMMERTIME is a romance set in Venice. Hepburn is an Ohio old maid who works as a secretary and has saved her money for a trip to Venice. She's traveling alone, and, on her first night there, she wanders around the city and sees lovers walking hand in hand. She meets Audiero, a charming child who hustles tourists, and he becomes her guide to the wonders of the city.

The next day, they go sightseeing and meet Brazzi who owns an antique shop. They fall in love, and there's a whirlwind montage as they walk, hand in hand, through the twisting streets of the main island. While waiting for Brazzi in the Piazza San Marco, she's approached by Spenser, a young man who tells her that Brazzi will be late. She soon learns that he is Brazzi's son and that her lover has a wife and family he's never mentioned. Although hurt by this revelation, Hepburn realizes that this is the most romantic interlude of her spinsterish existence; she's not about to end it now.

Touching, warm, often funny and lushly photographed. SUMMERTIME comes as close to capturing the essence of Venice as you will ever see. Lean had earlier directed BRIEF ENCOUNTER, so the story was familiar to him, although the terrain was vastly altered. There are places where the picture could have used some pruning, especially in the travelogue portions, but Hepburn and Brazzi emerge as the best middle-aged couple (short of Hepburn and Tracy) of the 1950s.

SUN ALSO RISES, THE

1957 129m c   ★★★★
Drama   /A
FOX

Tyrone Power (Jake Barnes), Ava Gardner (Lady Brett Ashley), Mel Ferrer (Robert Cohn), Errol Flynn (Mike Campbell), Eddie Albert (Bill Gorton), Gregory Ratoff (Count Mippipopolous), Juliette Greco (Georgette), Marcel Dalio (Zizi), Henry Daniell (Doctor), Bob Cunningham (Harris)

p, Darryl F. Zanuck; d, Henry King; w, Peter Viertel (based on the novel by Ernest Hemingway); ph, Leo Tover (CinemaScope, DeLuxe Color); ed, William Mace; m, Hugo Friedhofer, Alexander Courage; art d, Lyle Wheeler, Mark-Lee Kirk; cos, Charles LeMaire, Fontana Sisters

Author Hemingway's paean to the Lost Generation in the wake of WWI has been adapted to the screen more faithfully than have any of his other works. Power is the fitful postwar expatriate drifting around Europe aimlessly, seeking excitement and thrills to compensate for his war-wound-induced impotence. In the company of sultry prostitute Greco, he threads his way through the bistros of Paris, simulating enjoyment of the adventurous life despite his enforced celibacy. He falls in love with beautiful aristocrat Gardner, who once, as a volunteer, had helped him recover from his wounds during the war. She is being pursued by amorous Greek tycoon Ratoff, and also by a young would-be writer (thought to be patterned after F. Scott Fitzgerald), Ferrer, a former acquaintance. Power and Gardner—still in love with each other, despite his condition and the intervening years—make an unsuccessful attempt to be alone as the constant partying continues. One event that Power wants to experience is the famed running of the bulls at Pamplona in Spain during the San Fermin fiesta. (The bulls that will soon fight in the *corrida* are released to run in the streets, and, in a rite of passage, the brave young men of the area race before them, trying not to get gored.) Power sets off with his trusted friend, fellow expatriate Albert, arriving in Pamplona only to find that Gardner, Ferrer, and Ratoff have preceded him there. The group is joined by carefree Scottish playboy Flynn, Gardner's former fiance. Behind the hilarity and fun, tensions mount, as all the men lust after Gardner while she wants only Power. Albert and Flynn remain drunk most of the time and run with the bulls in their besotted state, miraculously avoiding injury. Gardner finds herself becoming interested in young matador Robert Evans, and the jealous Ferrer, a collegiate boxing champion, beats up the bullfighter. His actions only serve to enrage Gardner. When Evans demonstrates his courage by performing superbly in the bullring despite his injuries, Gardner elopes with him. The remaining members of the group head in different directions. Power goes to Biarritz to recuperate from the drunken festivities, knowing that he will hear from Gardner again. She telephones him from Madrid where, destitute, she has abandoned Evans. Power joins her, and the picture ends with the two hoping to find some way to fulfill what both realize to be their mutual destiny.

Producer Zanuck greatly admired Hemingway, whom he had met in Paris, introduced by screenwriter Viertel, years before. Zanuck and Hemingway both wintered in Sun Valley for a number of years and were great friends, but their friendship had been flawed by Hemingway's reaction to Zanuck's production of THE SNOWS OF KILIMANJARO. At 43, Power was old for the role. This was to be the actor's second-to-last film, and his last for Fox; he died of a heart attack the following year. This was also Flynn's penultimate picture, and his self-parody is a joy, the best thing in the film. The fourth-billed Flynn had, for the first time in years and over his weak protests, accepted less than the top spot in the credits, an honor he had been accorded ever since his success in CAPTAIN BLOOD. Power's habitually petulant facial expression is wrong for this film; a contrapuntal masculinity would have served the story better. Ferrer is fine in his part as the resentful introvert. His wife Audrey Hepburn, who joined him on location in both Pamplona and in Morelia, Mexico (which doubled for the Spain location), was the one who suggested Greco to Zanuck for the role of the sympathetic prostitute. Greco was then singing at the Waldorf-Astoria in New York City, but she had a substantial cult following in Europe, where she had appeared in movies. This was her US film debut. She and producer Zanuck had an on-location romance which was to continue long past the picture's release. Touted as a Zanuck "find," Evans had been a clothing manufacturer. He had actually been "found" by Norma Shearer, whose late husband, Irving Thalberg, he had portrayed in THE MAN WITH A THOUSAND FACES (not yet released at the time). Evans later became production chief at Paramount. Zanuck, goaded by the mischievous Flynn, actually ran with the bulls himself at Pamplona, but only after carefully timing himself to make certain he could stay ahead of them. The picture was reported to have cost $5 million, but it made money for the studio.

SUNDAY IN NEW YORK

1963 105m c   ★★★
Comedy   /X
Seven Arts

Cliff Robertson *(Adam Tyler)*, Jane Fonda *(Eileen Tyler)*, Rod Taylor *(Mike Mitchell)*, Robert Culp *(Russ Wilson)*, Jo Morrow *(Mona Harris)*, Jim Backus *(Flight Dispatcher)*, Peter Nero *(Himself)*

p, Everett Freeman; d, Peter Tewksbury; w, Norman Krasna (based on his play); ph, Leo Tover (Metrocolor); ed, Fredric Steinkamp; m, Peter Nero; art d, George W. Davis, Edward Carfagno; cos, Orry-Kelly

A fast, frantic, and sometimes funny sex comedy not unlike a thousand other sex comedies. Krasna's farce had been a fair success on Broadway and was perfect for the period. It's a lightweight piece with not much of a plot but plenty of amusing lines in the middle of familiar situations. Robertson is an airline pilot from upstate New York who lives in a well-furnished Manhattan apartment. He has the weekend off and is looking forward to having some fun with his sweetheart, Morrow. Robertson's sister is Fonda, who has just had a tiff with her fiance, Culp, a wealthy yokel. He wanted to sleep with her before they were married, but she was adamant about keeping pristine. Robertson tells her that she made the right move and that a man places a great deal of importance on his wife not having been deflowered. Robertson makes arrangements to see Morrow in another city, and she goes there to meet him. When the airline calls to say that Robertson must now fly somewhere else, he can't locate Morrow to say he won't be there. Fonda explores Robertson's apartment, and, although he preaches purity, she finds some lingerie in his closet and realizes that he has one set of rules for himself and another for her. She leaves the apartment, gets on a bus, and meets Taylor. Her attitude has changed and she thinks it's about time she stopped being a virgin, so she begins to work her wiles on Taylor. He sees how naive she really is and will not fall for her ploy, frustrating her even more. The two spend this Sunday in New York and fall in love fast (they have to; the entire movie is only 105 minutes long). Rain hits the city and they are drenched. They rush to Robertson's apartment, don bathrobes, and dry off. Then Culp shows up, thinks that Taylor is Robertson, and pleads with Fonda to come back, saying that he's now willing to wait. Robertson enters and is surprised to see the trio. Fonda introduces him as the co-pilot to her brother, who is, of course, not her brother at all, but a man she only met on a bus a few hours ago. The film ends as Culp storms out, believing that Fonda has done the deed with another. Taylor and Fonda profess their love, and Robertson decides to marry Morrow. Peter Nero did the music and shows up in a cameo. He and Carroll Coates wrote the title tune, which turned out to be a hit with Mel Torme singing. Robertson and Culp are not suited for comedy, but Taylor shows a fine flair for it.

SUNDAY IN THE COUNTRY, A

(UN DIMANCHE A LA CAMPAGNE)
1984 94m c   ★★★★½
Drama   G/18
Sara/A2   (France)

Louis Ducreux *(M. Ladmiral)*, Sabine Azema *(Irene)*, Michel Aumont *(Gonzague/(Edouard))*, Genevieve Mnich *(Marie-Therese)*, Monique Chaumette *(Mercedes)*, Claude Winter *(Mme. Ladmiral)*, Thomas Duval *(Emile)*, Quentin Ogier *(Lucien)*, Katia Wostrikoff *(Mireille)*, Valentine Suard p, Alain Sarde; d, Bertrand Tavernier; w, Bertrand Tavernier, Colo Tavernier (based on the novella *Monsieur Ladmiral Va Bientot Mourir* by Pierre Bost); ph, Bruno de Keyzer (Eastmancolor); ed, Armand Psenny; m, Gabriel Faure, Louis Ducreux, Marc Perrone; prod d, Patrice Mercier; cos, Yvonne Sassinot de Nesle

This beautiful film details a day in the life of an elderly painter, Ladmiral (Louis Ducreux), a holdover from the days of the French Impressionists. On one average Sunday in 1912, Ladmiral entertains his son (Michel Aumont) and the latter's family. They walk through the picturesque grounds of Ladmiral's country estate, prepare dinner, and tell wonderful stories about life and art. Unexpectedly, Ladmiral's daughter, Irene (Sabine Azema), pays a rare visit. Although Irene is the troubled outcast of the family, she is still her father's favorite, making this otherwise average Sunday exciting and worthwhile.

The story line may appear simple and undramatic, but the movie's beauty lies in this simplicity. The old painter's Sunday is serene. He is an old man who has lived a quiet life and enjoys reminiscing, his surroundings are bathed in a peaceful light, his canvas quietly awaits his artistic touch. The sum of these simple parts is a rich view of life. Betrand Tavernier, named Best Director at the Cannes Film Festival for this film, successfully evokes the essence of French life in the early 20th century. Tavernier and cinematographer Bruno de Keyzer have made a conscious effort to attain the appearance of French Impressionist painting. In fact, A SUNDAY IN THE COUNTRY is nothing short of a painting come to life.

SUNDAY, BLOODY SUNDAY

1971 110m c   ★★★½
Drama   R/X
Vectia (U.K.)

Glenda Jackson *(Alex Greville)*, Peter Finch *(Dr. Daniel Hirsh)*, Murray Head *(Bob Elkin)*, Peggy Ashcroft *(Mrs. Greville)*, Tony Britton *(George Harding)*, Maurice Denham *(Mr. Greville)*, Bessie Love *(Answering Service Lady)*, Vivian Pickles *(Alva Hodson)*, Frank Windsor *(Bill Hodson)*, Thomas Baptiste *(Prof. Johns)*

p, Joseph Janni; d, John Schlesinger; w, Penelope Gilliatt; ph, Billy Williams (DeLuxe Color); ed, Richard Marden; m, Ron Geesin, Wolfgang Amadeus Mozart; prod d, Luciana Arrighi; art d, Norman Dorme; cos, Jocelyn Richards

Too deliberate, but among Schlesinger's best; a strong drama about a *menage a trois* among homosexual Finch, heterosexual Jackson, and bisexual Head, who alternates between the other two. Time may decree the film a classic.

Written by *New Yorker* magazine movie critic Gilliatt, the plot presents Finch as a middle-aged bachelor doctor in London who shares his answering service with Jackson, a divorced woman who works at an employment agency. Both of them know Windsor and Pickles, a happy couple in the area, and both of them sleep with Head, a younger designer of modern sculpture. Both Jackson and Finch are aware of each other because Head is an honest sort, almost to the point of naivete. Windsor and Pickles have five children and need some time away from home, so Jackson and Head offer to stay at their home and tend the quintet while the parents go off to attend an educational seminar. On Saturday morning Head excuses himself from Jackson and only says he's "going out." She knows that he's on his way to see Finch, and the thought of it knocks her off her strict diet and into an orgy of fudge consumption. At Finch's the two men discuss an upcoming vacation to Italy, then Head returns to an annoyed Jackson, who resents having to share her lover with a man.

The characters are terribly civilized about the whole thing—too civilized, in fact, with only Jackson betraying any real emotion. The major problem with this film is that it is not easy to see what an intelligent man like Finch and an equally intelligent woman like Jackson see in Head—his character is not realized nearly so well as those of the other two. Schlesinger said that he conceived the idea of the film on the basis of some people he knew, then hired Gilliatt. She, on the other hand, claims total responsibility for the idea because she'd written a novel with a similar plot. Perhaps their differences explain the movie's unresolved undercurrent.

SUNDOWNERS, THE

1960 133m c   ★★★★½
Drama   /U
WB

Deborah Kerr *(Ida Carmody)*, Robert Mitchum *(Paddy Carmody)*, Peter Ustinov *(Venneker)*, Glynis Johns *(Mrs. Firth)*, Dina Merrill *(Jean Halstead)*, Chips Rafferty *(Quinlan)*, Michael Anderson, Jr. *(Sean)*, Lola Brooks *(Liz)*, Wylie Watson *(Herb Johnson)*, John Meillon *(Bluey)*

p, Fred Zinnemann, Gerry Blattner; d, Fred Zinnemann; w, Isobel Lennart (based on the novel by Jon Cleary); ph, Jack Hildyard (Technicolor); ed, Jack Harris; m, Dimitri Tiomkin; art d, Michael Stringer; cos, Elizabeth Haffenden

A splendid, sprawling saga of Australia. Set in the 1920s, it's the story of a single family, how they interact with the pioneers around them, how they extract a living from the land, how they live and love and cope. Lennart's adaptation of the Cleary novel is full of wit, sly philosophy and solid, motivated action. The title refers to those people who roam the land and live wherever they stop when the sun sets.

Mitchum is married to Kerr, and the two travel the land with their son, Anderson. They have no money, just a great love and a continuing hope that things will get better. Still, tiring of this nomadic existence, Kerr and Anderson yearn for a place where they can hang their hats. But instead of settling down, Mitchum takes a job leading more than a thousand sheep on a long trek to Cawndilla in western Australia. Since there are so many sheep to look after, Mitchum has to ask Ustinov, a onetime ship's captain, to help.

The journey is arduous and filled with excitement. Along the way, the four stop and visit with another group of Sundowners who have given up the road for a sedentary existence. Kerr and Anderson envy the life led by this family, but Mitchum pays it no mind. Mitchum and company continue on, finally delivering their sheep and collecting their fee. Then the four take jobs on a large station, with Kerr hoping they will be able to save enough money to buy their own spread.

Mitchum is splendid and Kerr was nominated for an Academy Award, as were Johns, Zinnemann, Lennart, and the picture itself. Kerr plays with little makeup and her natural beauty shines through all the dust. Johns is also a delight in her small but telling role, and Ustinov does his usual excellent job. Indeed, every aspect of the movie is first-rate, and even the smallest roles are wonderfully cast, including Australia's favorite actor, Chips Rafferty, as the sheep-shearing foreman. (Rafferty was in just about every Australian movie made in the 1940s, 1950s and 1960s, with his most famous appearance being in THE OVERLANDERS.) Big, funny, tender and humane all at the same time, THE SUNDOWNERS is a true "family" film, without any of the cloying connotations of that term.

SUNRISE AT CAMPOBELLO

1960 144m c   ★★★★
Biography   /U
WB

Ralph Bellamy (*Franklin D. Roosevelt*), Greer Garson (*Eleanor Roosevelt*), Hume Cronyn (*Louis Howe*), Jean Hagen (*Missy Le Hand*), Ann Shoemaker (*Sara Roosevelt*), Alan Bunce (*Al Smith*), Tim Considine (*James Roosevelt*), Zina Bethune (*Anna Roosevelt*), Pat Close (*Elliot Roosevelt*), Robin Warga (*Franklin D. Roosevelt*)

p, Dore Schary; d, Vincent J. Donehue; w, Dore Schary (based on his play); ph, Russell Harlan (Technicolor); ed, George Boemler; m, Franz Waxman; art d, Edward Carrere; cos, Marjorie Best

After a distinguished career in movies, Dore Schary decided to try his typewriter for the stage and the result was this play about FDR's first physical crisis, from 1921 through 1924. The play won the Antoinette Perry Award, after opening in January 1958, and ran for 857 performances with Bellamy in the lead. Schary wisely decided to bring Bellamy and the same director who steered his play, Donehue, along with him for the screen version. The result is a heartwarming look at the early years of the only man who was elected to the highest office in the US four times. Bellamy is superb as Roosevelt, capturing almost every nuance of a man who was the most photographed and listened-to politician of his generation. Surpassing Bellamy, though, is Garson, who doesn't *play* Eleanor Roosevelt, she *becomes* her.

It's 1921 and the Roosevelt family is vacationing on the small island of Campobello, off New Brunswick. The Roosevelts are a patrician group, with plenty of money and no worries at all. Bellamy has an eye toward public service and is the assistant secretary of the Navy, over the wishes of his mother, Shoemaker, who would prefer that he spend his time leisurely alternating between Campobello and the family's estate at Hyde Park. Returning from sailing one day, Bellamy takes to bed to recover from a "chill." When his legs suddenly become paralyzed, he's whisked to the hospital where he soon learns from doctor Ferguson that he's the victim of polio and will never again walk. Shoemaker insists that Bellamy give up his political aspirations, but Cronyn, a behind-the-scenes politico, believes his friend will be better off if he stops feeling sorry for himself and gets on with his life.

Garson excels in an atypical role; she used some prosthetic teeth to better simulate Eleanor Roosevelt's looks, but she needn't have because her acting comes from within. She's able to emulate Eleanor's unique, often quavery voice, and she submerges her own inimitable persona into that of the president's wife to such a degree that one forgets Garson ever was Mrs. Miniver. The movie was released in September 1960, just as the Kennedy-Nixon race was going strong. Kennedy's Catholicism was still an issue with many voters, and by incorporating the anti-Catholic sentiment Al Smith had faced into his screenplay, Schary helped to minimize the religious issue in the 1960 race. Since Schary was a staunch Democrat, it seems likely that the timing of the movie's release was calculated for maximum power at the polls, as well as at the box office.

SUNSET BOULEVARD

1950 110m bw   ★★★★★
Drama   /PG
Paramount

William Holden (*Joe Gillis*), Gloria Swanson (*Norma Desmond*), Erich von Stroheim (*Max von Mayerling*), Nancy Olson (*Betty Schaefer*), Fred Clark (*Sheldrake*), Lloyd Gough (*Morino*), Jack Webb (*Artie Green*), Cecil B. DeMille, Hedda Hopper, Buster Keaton

p, Charles Brackett; d, Billy Wilder; w, Billy Wilder, Charles Brackett, D.M. Marshman, Jr. (based on the story "A Can of Beans" by Brackett, Wilder); ph, John Seitz; ed, Doane Harrison, Arthur Schmidt; m, Franz Waxman, Richard Strauss; art d, Hans Dreier, John Meehan; fx, Gordon Jennings, Farciot Edouart; cos, Edith Head

No other motion picture about Hollywood comes near Billy Wilder's searing, uncompromising and utterly fascinating portrait of the film community. And beneath it all is raging vanity, madness and murder. Wilder's most important work is a haunting, unforgettable profile of an aging silent film star who lives in a dream world that turns gradually into a nightmare, and a young man half her age who is engulfed by the demented siren's illusionary past.

The movie opens with a jolt: the bullet-riddled body of a young man is seen floating face down in the pool next to a mansion. Though dead, Joe Gillis (William Holden) posthumously recounts how, six months earlier, he had been grinding out a screenplay, getting nowhere in his profession, having authored only a few B-film scripts. Desperate for money, Joe drives to Paramount Studios and tries to peddle a screenplay titled "Bases Loaded" to Sheldrake (Fred Clark), a producer. While Joe is in Sheldrake's office, Betty Shaefer (Nancy Olson, in a badly dated performance), a reader, enters and reports that Joe's script is "from hunger." When she learns that the author is present, Betty apologizes, but still calls his script trite. Sheldrake turns Joe down and, after telling him a sob story, refuses to loan him money. Later the despondent Joe, while driving aimlessly, spots two men from the finance company who are out to repossess his car; he speeds off, gets a flat, and pulls into the driveway of a run-down mansion. He's fascinated by the dilapidated old place, and then hears a woman's voice, full of authority, calling down to him, asking why he has kept her waiting so long, and ordering him into the house. Max (Erich von Stroheim), a severe-looking, bald-headed butler, waves Joe inside, where he is shown into the august presence of silent screen star Norma Desmond (Gloria Swanson). She thinks Joe is the pet mortician who is going to bury her cherished pet monkey, but he tells her that his car has broken down in her driveway, then recognizes her. After she lambasts the current state of the film industry, she offers Joe a job writing a reworking of *Salome* which she plans to use as her return to the screen. Joe takes the writing job, and Norma insists that he stay with her while working on the script. Destitute, Joe agrees and begins living in a room over the garage. Glared at by Norma from behind dark glasses and waited upon by the somber, silent Max, Joe becomes a prisoner of the actress and her strange past, virtually confined to the big house.

Gradually, Joe succumbs, allowing Norma to provide him with expensive clothes, jewelry, and pocket money. He becomes a kept man, a replacement for her pet monkey. When he goes to Norma's ornate bedroom, Joe sees her boat-shaped, gold leaf bed (once owned by silent star Gladys Desloys, borrowed for the production), and tells himself that the setting befits a silent movie queen: "Poor devil, still waving to a parade which has long since passed her by." In the meantime, Joe has learned that despite what Norma claims, no fans write to her, that the loyal Max pens and posts fan letters to keep up her spirits. Norma gives a New Year's party and has Joe wear a new tuxedo she has purchased for him. A full orchestra has been hired for the occasion and a great banquet of food and champagne waits. Norma and Joe dance across the enormous living room and he soon realizes there will be no guests, that Norma is seducing him. They quarrel; Joe flees to a noisy party, where he decides to leave Norma. But when he calls the mansion to tell Max to pack his bags, he learns that a doctor is treating Norma—the one-time star has attempted suicide, slashing both wrists over his rejection of her. Returning to the mansion to comfort her, Joe says, "You're the only person in this stinking town who's been good to me." As the orchestra downstairs plays "Auld Lang Syne," Joe sits on Norma's bed and she pulls him downward into an embrace that closes over him like a web.

In SUNSET BOULEVARD, Wilder captures the tragic, nostalgic longing for a grand Hollywood past that silent stars could never possibly reclaim. The film excels in ordinary and extraordinary passions, and Swanson's Norma provides one of many razor-sharp insights into the whole film when she says: "We didn't need dialogue. We had faces then. They don't have faces anymore, maybe one, Garbo." This was a comeback for Swanson, a return to the screen, achieving what her tragic character in SUNSET BOULEVARD could not. Yet the attention she received upon her return to Hollywood still couldn't match the adulation lavished on Swanson in the 1920s, when tens of thousands turned out to cheer her in a mammoth parade.

More than any other actress of her generation Swanson understood the glorious, fabulous, and exotic 1920s in Hollywood and the exciting, eccentric people who made it famous and infamous. There is much of Norma Desmond—the screen Norma Desmond—that *is* Swanson. Not only did she allow Wilder to exploit her hard-earned image, but she let him incorporate her silent career, including footage of her work in von Stroheim's QUEEN KELLY, into the film. Swanson, however, was never the neurotic, mentally disturbed creature that Norma is off-screen. Before Swanson was chosen, Wilder and producer-coscenarist Charles Brackett talked about the possibility of using Mary Pickford, Mae Murray, Pola Negri, or even Mae West as Norma. It is unlikely that any of them could have come close to the magnificent performance given by Swanson, whose penetrating, courageous grasp of the character astounded critics, public, and peers. In 1989, SUNSET BOULEVARD was selected by the National Film Registry of the Library of Congress as one of 25 landmark films, leading examples of American cinematic art.

SUNSHINE BOYS, THE
1975 111m c ★★★½
Comedy PG
UA

Walter Matthau *(Willy Clark)*, George Burns *(Al Lewis)*, Richard Benjamin *(Ben Clark)*, Lee Meredith *(Nurse in Sketch)*, Carol Arthur *(Doris)*, Rosetta LeNoire *(Nurse)*, F. Murray Abraham *(Mechanic)*, Howard Hesseman *(Commercial Director)*, James Cranna *(TV Director)*, Ron Rifkin *(TV Floor Manager)*

p, Ray Stark; d, Herbert Ross; w, Neil Simon

One of the best films ever made from a Neil Simon play, an engaging homage to the tradition of vaudeville in which the two halves of a once-famous double act (they now hate each other) re-team for a TV special.

The film opens in the 1970s with Matthau as a semi-retired comic scraping by doing commercials that his agent/nephew Benjamin has secured for him. He's auditioning for a silly potato chip TV spot for advertising director Hesseman when he blows his lines and decides that this isn't show business and he no longer wants to be a part of it. A nostalgic TV special is coming up, and Benjamin books Matthau on it, hoping that he will put

aside his rancor toward his former partner, Burns, and unite this last time for the benefit of all those people who never saw them together in the flesh. Burns and Matthau haven't spoken in decades, and the mere mention of Burns is enough to send Matthau's blood pressure soaring. But he buries his enmity and agrees to see his erstwhile friend. The two men meet and began rehearsing the sketch that made them household names way back when they were known as the Sunshine Boys, but battles begin immediately as they argue over the first words of the sketch.

THE SUNSHINE BOYS is a solid movie with stellar performances from all—seldom have Simon's lines been delivered with as much bite and wit as they are here. This was Burns' first film in 35 years and he was perfect, earning a Best Supporting Actor Oscar at the age of 79. Matthau earned a nomination for Best Actor (he lost to Jack Nicholson for ONE FLEW OVER THE CUCKOO'S NEST, which collected most of the statuettes in 1975), and nominations also went to the screenplay and the art direction. Simon's inspiration for the story came from real-life vaudevillians Smith and Dale. In their very advanced years, the comics teamed to do their "Dr. Kronkheit" sketch on the Ed Sullivan show, reviving a classic piece of comedy for a whole new generation of viewers.

SUPERFLY
1972 96m c ★★★★
Action/Crime R/18
WB

Ron O'Neal *(Youngblood Priest)*, Carl Lee *(Eddie)*, Sheila Frazier *(Georgia)*, Julius Harris *(Scatter)*, Charles McGregor *(Fat Freddie)*, Nate Adams *(Dealer)*, Polly Niles *(Cynthia)*, Yvonne Delaine *(Mrs. Freddie)*, Henry Shapiro *(Robbery Victim)*, K.C. *(Pimp)*

p, Sig Shore; d, Gordon Parks, Jr.; w, Phillip Fenty; ph, James Signorelli (Technicolor); ed, Bob Brady; m, Curtis Mayfield; cos, Nate Adams

This interesting feature is one of the few Hollywood films that takes an honest look at the lives of African-Americans in the ghetto. O'Neal plays a Harlem cocaine pusher whose success (via connections with corrupt police officials) has gained him the respect and envy of the neighborhood. He wants to retire from the business and enjoy the comforts this life has brought him, but first he must make one last million-dollar dope deal.

The moral ambiguity of the film may disturb some viewers, but the film smacks of realistic grit throughout. Parks, one of the few blacks to direct in Hollywood, had a real feeling for the Harlem locations and the language of its residents. The action sequences are good, and a fine score by Mayfield helps out as well. SUPERFLY was financially backed by a group of Harlem businessmen, marking one of the first times a Black-oriented film was actually financed by Blacks. It was also one of the first to use a nonwhite cast and crew. Director Parks was the son of Gordon Parks, Sr., the director of the "Shaft" movies. A sequel, SUPERFLY T.N.T., followed.

SUPERMAN
1978 143m c ★★★
Science Fiction PG
WB

Marlon Brando *(Jor-El)*, Gene Hackman *(Lex Luthor)*, Christopher Reeve *(Superman/Clark Kent)*, Ned Beatty *(Otis)*, Jackie Cooper *(Perry White)*, Glenn Ford *(Pa Kent)*, Trevor Howard *(1st Elder)*, Margot Kidder *(Lois Lane)*, Jack O'Halloran *(Non)*, Valerie Perrine *(Eve Teschmacher)*

p, Pierre Spengler; d, Richard Donner; w, Mario Puzo, David Newman, Leslie Newman, Robert Benton (based on the story by Puzo, from the comic strip created by Jerry Siegel, Joe Shuster); ph, Geoffrey Unsworth (Panavision, Technicolor); ed, Stuart Baird; m, John Williams; prod d, John Barry; fx, Colin Chilvers, Roy Field, Derek Meddings, Zoran Perisic, Denys Coop, Les Bowie; cos, Yvonne Blake

"You'll believe a man can fly," the ads said, and by SUPERMAN's end that's just about true. Christopher Reeve essays the title role and makes it his own, combining correctly chiseled features with a likable comic humanity, while the film itself nicely balances special effects with the romance of Superman and Lois Lane (Margot Kidder). The story opens on the planet Krypton, where Superman's father (Marlon Brando) sends his son off to Earth, where he grows up to be "mild-mannered reporter" Clark Kent. Flying around in tights and cape, Superman-alias-Clark saves the day—and Lois—a number of times. Eventually he rescues all mankind from the evil Lex Luthor (Gene Hackman) and his assistants (Ned Beatty and Valerie Perrine, in an excellent bit of comic caricature) as they plot to take over the world. Lois is killed in the course of events, but Superman circles the globe at such terrific speed that its rotation is reversed, bringing his beloved back to life. The film burdens itself with too many story lines and an overlong (though beautifully photographed) prologue, but things really get moving when Reeve takes the screen. A worldwide hunt was conducted to find the right man for the role, with Robert Redford, Burt Reynolds, Nick Nolte, Kris Kristofferson, Sylvester Stallone, Ryan O'Neal, Clint Eastwood, and Charles Bronson among the candidates. So excellent is Reeve, however, that it is nearly impossible to think of anyone else as the Man of Steel. Nominated for three Academy Awards: Best Sound, Best Original Score and Best Film Editing.

SUPERMAN II

1980 127m c   ★★★½
Science Fiction   PG
WB (U.S./U.K.)

Gene Hackman (Lex Luthor), Christopher Reeve (Clark Kent/Superman), Ned Beatty (Otis), Jackie Cooper (Perry White), Sarah Douglas (Ursa), Margot Kidder (Lois Lane), Jack O'Halloran (Non), Valerie Perrine (Eve Teschmacher), Susannah York (Lara), Clifton James (Sheriff)

p, Pierre Spengler; d, Richard Lester; w, Mario Puzo, David Newman, Leslie Newman (based on a story by Puzo, from characters created by Jerry Siegel, Joe Shuster); ph, Geoffrey Unsworth, Robert Paynter (Panavision, Technicolor); ed, John Victor-Smith; m, Ken Thorne; prod d, John Barry, Peter Murton; art d, Maurice Fowler; fx, Colin Chilvers, Roy Field, Zoran Perisic; cos, Yvonne Blake, Sue Yelland

Poking fun at its American mythos, but never descending into camp comedy, this sequel makes for a wonderful time. Christopher Reeve reprises his role as the bumbling reporter/Man of Steel with marvelous success. The film opens with a fury as terrorists who have taken over the Eiffel Tower threaten to blow it up with a nuclear bomb. Lois Lane (Margot Kidder), ever the inquisitive reporter, tries to interview the terrorists and finds herself in more trouble than she bargained for. Fortunately, Superman comes to save the day, rescuing Lois and flinging the bomb into outer space. But this sets off a nuclear explosion that frees some bad guys (Terence Stamp, Sarah Douglas, and Jack O'Halloran) from the cosmic prison they were sentenced to in SUPERMAN. The movie hits full stride as the villains come to

take over Earth, not knowing their fellow Kryptonian is that planet's hero. The result is an especially fun movie and a rare instance of a sequel that not only equals, but even betters, its original. The same cannot be said for SUPERMAN III or SUPERMAN IV: THE QUEST FOR PEACE, despite Reeve's continued command of the role.

SUPPORT YOUR LOCAL GUNFIGHTER

1971 92m c   ★★★
Western/Comedy   G/U
Cherokee/Brigrade

James Garner (Latigo Smith), Suzanne Pleshette (Patience Barton), Jack Elam (Jug May), Joan Blondell (Jenny), Harry Morgan (Taylor Barton), Marie Windsor (Goldie), John Dehner (Col. Ames), Henry Jones (Ez), Chuck Connors (Swifty Morgan), Dub Taylor (Doc Schultz)

p, William Finnegan; d, Burt Kennedy; w, James Edward Grant; ph, Harry Stradling, Jr. (Deluxe Color); ed, Willaim B. Gulick; m, Jack Elliott, Allyn Ferguson; art d, Phil Barber; fx, A.D. Flowers; cos, Lambert Marks, Patricia Norris

This follow-up film (though not a sequel) to SUPPORT YOUR LOCAL SHERIFF finds Garner playing a con artist running off from his madame bride-to-be, Windsor. He ends up in the small western town of Purgatory, where the citizens mistake him for a famous gunslinger. Garner decides to let them think what they want and proceeds to take Purgatory for everything he can. Elam once more is his sidekick, and Pleshette is the love interest who wants to start a Ladies Finishing School in New York State. Garner's tongue-in-cheek comic style works nicely, with some fun support in Elam's great clowning. Though not quite the film its predecessor was, this is still an enormous amount of fun, with good direction that kids around affectionately with western cliches.

SUPPORT YOUR LOCAL SHERIFF

1969 96m c   ★★★½
Western/Comedy   G/PG
Cherokee

James Garner (Jason McCullough), Joan Hackett (Prudy Perkins), Walter Brennan (Pa Danby), Harry Morgan (Mayor Olly Perkins), Jack Elam (Jake), Bruce Dern (Joe Danby), Henry Jones (Preacher Henry Jackson), Walter Burke (Fred Johnson), Dick Peabody (Luke Danby), Gene Evans (Tom Danby)

p, William Bowers; d, Burt Kennedy; w, William Bowers; ph, Harry Stradling, Jr. (Deluxe); ed, George W. Brooks; m, Jeff Alexander; art d, Leroy Coleman; fx, Marcel Vercoutere; cos, Norman Burza, Florence Hackett

This great spoof of western movie cliches features Garner as a stranger who stops off at a small town en route to Australia, a running joke that works well through the rest of the film. He's hired as the new sheriff, taking the job because he can't afford the boomtown's inflated prices. He hires Elam, the town drunk, as a deputy. After Garner arrests Dern and has the outlaw help build the new jail, Dern's father, Brennan, gets angry and summons the rest of his family to rescue the wayward son. A climactic street shootout results in a win by Garner as he holds a gang off with an apparently empty cannon. Unlike the later BLAZING SADDLES (1974), SUPPORT YOUR LOCAL SHERIFF has a good time with the western cliches but still shows respect for the formula western. Garner's performance is a marvelous study in underplaying, his expressive face saying all that needs to be said. Brennan is hilarious in a self-parody of his role in MY DARLING CLEMENTINE (1946).

SURE THING, THE

1985 94m c ★★★
Comedy PG-13/15
Monument

John Cusack *(Walter "Gib" Gibson)*, Daphne Zuniga *(Alison Bradbury)*, Anthony Edwards *(Lance)*, Boyd Gaines *(Jason)*, Lisa Jane Persky *(Mary Ann Webster)*, Viveca Lindfors *(Prof. Taub)*, Nicollette Sheridan *(The Sure Thing)*, Tim Robbins *(Gary Cooper)*, Fran Ryan *(Louise)*, George Memmoli *(Al)*

p, Roger Birnbaum, Andrew Scheinman; d, Rob Reiner; w, Steven L. Bloom, Jonathan Roberts; ph, Robert Elswit (DeLuxe Color); ed, Robert Leighton; m, Tom Scott; prod d, Lilly Kilvert; fx, John Frazier, Jeff Wischnack; cos, Durinda Wood

A charming surprise, THE SURE THING is IT HAPPENED ONE NIGHT with acne. Rob Reiner shows that he is on his way to being 10 times the director his father, Carl, is with this lovely picture. It's life in the Ivy League. Walter "Gib" Gibson (John Cusack) is a junk food junkie, a beer-swilling freshman who lives for women but strikes out more often than a pitcher. Alison Bradbury (Daphne Zuniga) is an all-American lass who has planned her life down to where she'll retire. They meet in a writing class and sparks fly, but the wrong kind of sparks. They hate each other on sight, or so it seems. Gib's pal, Lance (Anthony Edwards), invites him to spend Christmas in the West and says that he can arrange a date in California with a girl who is "a sure thing." Gib plans to drive out with a California-bound couple. At the same time, Alison arranges to go with the same couple to visit her own boy friend in California. Lots of good music, good humor, affection, and more than some passing philosophy as writers Steven L. Bloom and Jonathan Roberts poke fun at the effete East and the laidback West with equal barbs. There is no nudity and nothing sexually explicit, so this movie is a refreshing change from any of the deliberately sniggering teen-oriented films that purport to be comedies.

SURVIVORS, THE

1983 102m c ★★
Comedy R/15
Rastar

Walter Matthau *(Sonny Paluso)*, Robin Williams *(Donald Quinelle)*, Jerry Reed *(Jack Locke)*, James Wainwright *(Wes Huntley)*, Kristen Vigard *(Candice Paluso)*, Annie McEnroe *(Doreen)*, Anne Pitoniak *(Betty)*, Bernard Barrow *(TV Manager)*, Marian Hailey *(Jack's Wife)*, Joseph Carberry *(Detective Matt Burke)*

p, William Sackheim; d, Michael Ritchie; w, Michael Leeson; ph, Billy Williams (Metrocolor); ed, Richard A. Harris; m, Paul Chihara; prod d, Gene Callahan; art d, John J. Moore; cos, Ann Roth

Robin Williams plays a young executive, Donald Quinelle, who starts his business day with a visit to the boss's office, where he's informed by a large trained parrot that he's been fired. Unfortunately, this sequence is the high point of THE SURVIVORS, leaving the rest of the film an olio of undeveloped characters and unfunny jokes. Quinelle heads for the unemployment line and meets Sonny Paluso (Walter Matthau), a former gas station owner whose business was blown up. After the two witness a robbery, the culprit, Jack Locke (Jerry Reed), is determined to kill them, because they have seen his face. Meanwhile, Quinelle decides to enroll in a survivalist training school.

Considering the personnel involved, THE SURVIVORS should have been a very funny movie. But director Michael Ritchie, who had a string of successful satirical movies behind him (THE CANDIDATE, SMILE, THE BAD NEWS BEARS, and SEMI-TOUGH), doesn't seem to know what he's after here. Williams, Matthau, and Reed struggle with the material and generate some bright moments, but overall THE SURVIVORS is a bewildering, frustrating movie.

SUSAN LENOX—HER FALL AND RISE

1931 74m bw ★★★½
Romance
MGM

Greta Garbo *(Susan Lenox)*, Clark Gable *(Rodney)*, Jean Hersholt *(Ohlin)*, John Miljan *(Burlingham)*, Alan Hale *(Mondstrum)*, Hale Hamilton *(Mike Kelly)*, Hilda Vaughn *(Astrid)*, Russell Simpson *(Doctor)*, Cecil Cunningham *(Mme. Panoramia)*, Ian Keith *(Robert Lane)*

d, Robert Z. Leonard; w, Wanda Tuchock, Zelda Sears, Leon Gordon, Edith Fitzgerald (based on the novel by David Graham Phillips); ph, William Daniels; ed, Margaret Booth

The only teaming of Greta Garbo and Clark Gable ("Don't miss the one and only Garbo in the arms of Clark Gable" the ads proclaimed), SUSAN LENOX—HER FALL AND RISE was based on a rather racy novel that had caused a sensation some 15 years before. Garbo plays Susan, the illegitimate daughter of a poor, brutish farmer (Hersholt) who decides to arrange a marriage between her and a wealthier farmer (Hale). Susan detests the man, however, and runs away rather than face married life with him. During her flight she discovers a cabin inhabited by Rodney (Gable), a handsome and sophisticated engineer. The two are immediately attracted to each other and romance blooms. Unfortunately, Susan learns that her father is out searching for her, and she must flee once again. Rodney is away on a job at the time and never learns of her departure. In desperation, Susan hooks up with a carnival train and becomes the concubine of the owner (Miljan) to earn her keep. Rodney eventually resurfaces, and when he learns of her unfaithfulness, he is crushed. He dissolves their relationship and goes off to South America. Having lost the man she really loves, Susan leaves the carnival and decides to make a new life for herself, eventually becoming the mistress of a prominent politician (Hamilton). This soon ends, though, when the politician's enemies discover Susan's background and use it to ruin him. Left with no place to go, Susan travels to South America to search for Rodney, eventually making a last-ditch attempt to win his love.

Chosen solely because Garbo wanted to work with the handsome young actor, Gable was a bit miscast in SUSAN LENOX—HER FALL AND RISE. The script was weak (rumor had it that as many as 24 different screenwriters took a whack at it) and didn't really provide the proper vehicle for a Garbo-Gable sizzler. Gable's role was better suited for the less-rugged John Gilbert—the viewer has a hard time believing that the macho Gable would be destroyed and bitter over losing Garbo. Gable agreed to be in the film because it would improve his standing at the box office, and he used the opportunity to see how one of MGM's biggest stars threw her weight around. (She walked off the set six times.) Problems aside, the film is a fine, fast-paced melodrama with a strong cast that never bores. In reaction perhaps to the sensational novel it was based on, the British censors removed a few minutes of what they considered objectionable in the film and changed the title to THE RISE OF HELGA.

SUSAN SLEPT HERE

1954 98m c ★★
Comedy /A
RKO

Dick Powell *(Mark)*, Debbie Reynolds *(Susan)*, Anne Francis *(Isabella)*, Alvy Moore *(Virgil)*, Glenda Farrell *(Maude)*, Horace MacMahon *(Maizel)*, Herb Vigran *(Hanlon)*, Les Tremayne *(Harvey)*, Mara Lane *(Marilyn)*, Maidie Norman *(Georgette)*

p, Harriet Parsons; d, Frank Tashlin; w, Alex Gottlieb (based on the play "Susan" by Gottlieb, Steve Fisher); ph, Nicholas Musuraca (Technicolor); ed, Harry Marker; m, Leigh Harline; chor, Robert Sidney

Frank Tashlin before he found his form, and just *too* cutesy. This would-be comedy has Powell playing a screenwriter who is doing research for a film about juvenile delinquents. Two policeman buddies drop off an 18-year-old (Reynolds) to help him get a better handle on the subject. She proves to be more than Powell can handle and complications arise when his girlfriend (Francis) grows jealous. The premise is terrific and seemingly good material for director Tashlin. However, the film is a real mess that is more ugly than funny. There are a few humorous moments in this sex-farce, but it's a surprisingly bad outing considering all the talent involved. Powell seems tired and La Debbie is a tiny bit grating now and then. SUSAN SLEPT HERE was nominated for two Oscars: Best Sound Recording and Best Song: "Hold My Hand" (Jack Lawrence, Richard Myers).

SUSPICION

1941 99m bw ★★★½
Thriller /PG
RKO

Cary Grant *(Johnnie Aysgarth)*, Joan Fontaine *(Lina McLaidlaw)*, Cedric Hardwicke *(Gen. McLaidlaw)*, Nigel Bruce *(Beaky Thwaite)*, Dame May Whitty *(Mrs. McLaidlaw)*, Isabel Jeans *(Mrs. Newsham)*, Heather Angel *(Ethel, Maid)*, Auriol Lee *(Isobel Sedbusk)*, Reginald Sheffield *(Reggie Wetherby)*, Leo G. Carroll *(Capt. Melbeck)*

d, Alfred Hitchcock; w, Samson Raphaelson, Joan Harrison, Alma Reville (based on the novel *Before the Fact* by Frances Iles); ph, Harry Stradling; ed, William Hamilton; m, Franz Waxman; art d, Van Nest Polglase, Carroll Clark; fx, Vernon L. Walker; cos, Edward Stevenson

Johnnie Aysgarth (Cary Grant) is a cad, a rogue, a wastrel. His fiancee, Lina McLaidlaw (Joan Fontaine), is a sheltered spinster who lives in a large English manor house. They marry and, despite his spotty past, seem to be truly happy. Johnny becomes involved in an embezzlement scheme which is complicated by the death of his bumbling friend Beaky (Nigel Bruce). Putting two and two together, Lina suspects that her husband may have done Beaky in. From that moment, she begins fearing for her own life. A study in suspicion (hence the title), this Hitchcock film disappointed many because of its "trick" ending. The title change from the novel *Before the Fact* should give some clue as to the ending. Fontaine won a Best Actress Oscar for her performance, though many believed it to be a consolation for the Oscar she didn't receive for the previous year's Hitchcock film, REBECCA. The excellent Oscar-nominated score by Franz Waxman lost out to THE DEVIL AND DANIEL WEBSTER, scored by Hitchcock's future collaborator Bernard Herrmann.

SWAN LAKE, THE

1967 111m c ★★★★
Dance /U
United/Seven Arts

Rudolf Nureyev, Margot Fonteyn, The Vienna State Opera Ballet

d, Truck Branss; w, (based on the ballet by Peter Ilyich Tchaikovsky); ph, Gunther Anders (Eastmancolor); ed, Marina Runne; m, Peter Ilich Tchaikovsky; chor, Rudolf Nureyev; cos, Nicholas Georgiadis

This excellent adaption of the famous ballet differs from other ballet films in its imaginative use of cinematic technique. Rather than simply portraying the dancing, the film features numerous overhead shots and several close-ups of the dancers. Transitions are well handled, and the entire work is a visual delight, showing a group of people dancing for the sheer joy of the art. The choreography was by Nureyev. The production, said to cost over $1 million, included the participation of the Vienna Symphony Orchestra and 60 dancers from the Vienna State Opera Ballet. It was filmed on soundstages in Munich.

SWANN IN LOVE

(UN AMOUR DE SWANN)
1984 110m c ★★½
Drama R/18
Orion Classics (France/West Germany)

Jeremy Irons *(Charles Swann)*, Ornella Muti *(Odette De Crecy)*, Alain Delon *(Baron De Charlus)*, Fanny Ardant *(Duchesse de Guermantes)*, Marie-Christine Barrault *(Mme. Verdurin)*, Anne Bennent *(Chloe)*, Nathalie Juvent *(Mme. Cottard)*, Charlotte Kerr *(Sous-maitresse)*, Humbert Balsan *(Head of Protocol)*, Jean Aurenche *(M. Vinteuil)*

p, Margaret Menegoz; d, Volker Schlondorff; w, Volker Schlondorff, Peter Brook, Jean-Claude Carriere, Marie-Helene Estienne (based on the novel *Un Amour de Swann* by Marcel Proust); ph, Sven Nykvist; ed, Francoise Bonnot; m, Hans-Werner Henze, David Graham, Gerd Kuhr, Marcel Wengler; prod d, Jacques Saulnier; cos, Yvonne Sassinot de Nesle

It took four writers, several production companies, and the French Ministry of Culture to make this adaptation of the beginning of Marcel Proust's monumental *Remembrance of Things Past*. Jeremy Irons is Charles Swann, a wealthy Jewish intellectual who has overcome anti-Semitism in 19th-century Paris and managed to become part of le haute monde. The film shows his courtship and socially suicidal marriage to the courtesan Odette (Ornella Muti), condensing part of Proust's seven-volume work into a single day in the life of Swann. The couple's affair is shown in flashback as recalled by Swann, revealing that he has married this woman, his complete opposite, without benefit of really loving (much less liking) her. Paralleling this story is that of Swann's friend, the aesthete homosexual Baron de Charlus (Alain Delon), and his effort to seduce an unwilling young man. Directed by Volker Schlondorff, who made THE TIN DRUM (1979) and the Dustin Hoffman TV film of "Death of a Salesman," SWANN IN LOVE reflects a similar dedication to bringing great literature to the screen. Schlondorff's style, however, is better suited to Gunther Grass and Arthur Miller than to the unhurriedly subtle Proust. The film does lavishly re-create the period milieu and features some beautiful location settings shot by the great Sven Nykvist, as well as a top cast, but the filmmakers seem to have been too intimidated by the original material to have come up with the kind of truly satisfying, original cinematic work that would have justified the effort.

SWEET BIRD OF YOUTH

1962 120m c ★★½
Drama /X
Roxbury/MGM

Paul Newman (*Chance Wayne*), Geraldine Page (*Alexandra Del Lago*), Shirley Knight (*Heavenly Finley*), Ed Begley (*"Boss" Finley*), Rip Torn (*Thomas J. Finley*), Mildred Dunnock (*Aunt Nonnie*), Madeleine Sherwood (*Miss Lucy*), Philip Abbott (*Dr. George Scudder*), Corey Allen (*Scotty*), Barry Cahill (*Bud*)

p, Pandro S. Berman; d, Richard Brooks; w, Richard Brooks (based on the play by Tennessee Williams); ph, Milton Krasner (CinemaScope, Metrocolor); ed, Henry Berman; art d, George W. Davis, Urie McCleary; fx, Lee LeBlanc; cos, Orry-Kelly

Williams's steamy play gets the Richard Brooks whitewash—as with CAT ON A HOT TIN ROOF. Instead of Newman's hustler getting castrated, it's the original stage piece that gets emasculated here. Newman, Page, Sherwood, and Torn repeat their Broadway roles, and Hollywood replaced Sidney Blackmer, Diana Hyland, and Martine Bartlett with Begley (who won an Oscar for Best Supporting Actor), Knight, and Dunnock—all in good form. Admittedly, Brooks was under orders to make changes to the play in order to secure approval from the Production Code. But he doesn't allow the expert cast to go to the mat like they need to.

Newman is a gigolo who thinks he can make it in film; all he needs is a break. In Florida, he meets Page, a fading movie star who is at the end of her tether. Her last movie is, she is certain, a dismal flop. When she meets Newman and he gives her a ride to his home town, she begs him for more gin. Later, when they stay in a motel together, she demands an oxygen inhalator. Then she asks Newman if he can find her some hashish to smoke. In order to keep the virile Newman at her side, she tells him that she can help him get his start in Hollywood by introducing him to the right people. They travel to Newman's hometown before going back to California. Newman wants to see his one-time girlfriend, Knight, who is the apple of her father's (Begley's) eye. Begley, a corrupt politician who runs the area, hates Newman with a passion because the last time Newman came through town he left Knight pregnant and she had to get an abortion. (In the play, she was liberally infected with syphilis by her lover and had to have her ovaries removed.) Begley wants to get even with Newman for what he did to Knight, so he plots revenge with his lackey son, Torn.

All of Williams's Southern Gothic themes are intermingled here: violence, familial conflict, sexual neurosis, the mentality of the mob. Most of it comes across as overheated nonsense, but Page's egomaniacal telephone soliloquy at the film's climax is reason enough to tune in. (For devotees of camp, BIRD was filmed for TV in 1989 in an almost total misfire directed by Nicholas Roeg, with Mark Harmon more flaccid than Newman, Rip Torn moving up a generation to Begley's role, the underrated Valerie Perrine in for Sherwood, and Elizabeth Taylor playing Alexandra Del Lago like a pretty Marie Dressler.)

SWEET CHARITY

1969 157m c ★★★½
Musical/Comedy G/A
Universal

Shirley MacLaine (*Charity Hope Valentine*), Sammy Davis, Jr. (*Big Daddy*), Ricardo Montalban (*Vittorio Vitale*), John McMartin (*Oscar Lindquist*), Chita Rivera (*Nickie*), Paula Kelly (*Helene*), Stubby Kaye (*Herman*), Barbara Bouchet (*Ursula*), Alan Hewitt (*Nicholsby*), Dante D'Paulo (*Charlie*)

p, Robert Arthur; d, Bob Fosse; w, Peter Stone (based on the play by Neil Simon, Cy Coleman, Dorothy Fields, adapted from the screenplay "Notti Di Cabiria" by Federico Fellini, Tullio Ponelli, Ennio Flaiano); ph, Robert Surtees (Panavision, Technicolor); ed, Stuart Gilmore; m, Cy Coleman; art d, Alexander Golitzen, George Webb; chor, Bob Fosse; cos, Edith Head

SWEET CHARITY is a very good musical that should have been a great musical. Bob Fosse, making his film directorial debut, couldn't convey the verve he injected into the play to the movie version, which starred Shirley MacLaine as Charity, a dime-a-dance hostess in a tacky New York ballroom whose boyfriend takes all of her hard-earned savings, pushes her off a low bridge in Central Park, and absconds with the cash. Charity, however, is a die-hard optimist, down but not out. Walking along the street one evening, she comes across Italian movie star Vittorio (Ricardo Montalban) in a furious argument with his lover, Ursula (Barbara Bouchet). Vittorio takes the gamine Charity out for a night on the town in Ursula's stead—but just when sparks seem about to strike, a contrite Ursula shows up at his apartment, leaving Charity stuck hiding in a closet while Vittorio and Ursula make up. Later, Charity is trapped in a stalled elevator with Oscar (John McMartin), a mild-mannered and terribly claustrophobic insurance clerk. The two hit it off, but the romance is complicated because Oscar doesn't know Charity works in a dance hall. Eventually he does find out what she does for a living but still wants to marry her. After meeting her friends (Paula Kelly and Chita Rivera), seeing her place of employment, and discovering she wears a tattoo, however, he backs out. The film ends, as a depressed Charity is handed a flower by a band of hippies in Central Park, after which she takes new heart. Cy Coleman and Dorothy Fields wrote the fine score for the play and two new numbers for the movie, and their songs, along with Fosse's choreography and some fine supporting performances, provide the film's high points. MacLaine works very hard at not seeming to work hard but gives a somewhat studied portrayal nonetheless.

SWEET SMELL OF SUCCESS

1957 96m bw ★★★★
Drama /A
Norma/Curtleigh

Burt Lancaster (*J.J. Hunsecker*), Tony Curtis (*Sidney Falco*), Susan Harrison (*Susan Hunsecker*), Martin Milner (*Steve Dallas*), Sam Levene (*Frank D'Angelo*), Barbara Nichols (*Rita*), Jeff Donnell (*Sally*), Joseph Leon (*Robard*), Edith Atwater (*Mary*), Emile Meyer (*Harry Kello*)

p, James Hill; d, Alexander Mackendrick; w, Clifford Odets, Ernest Lehman (based on the short story "Tell Me About It Tomorrow" by Lehman); ph, James Wong Howe; ed, Alan Crosland, Jr.; m, Elmer Bernstein; art d, Edward Carrere

Curtis is a Broadway flack whose income depends on the exposure he gets for his public-relations clients in the syndicated newspaper column of the influential Lancaster, whose clout is boundless, sufficient to influence presidents. Lancaster's column of gossip, opinion, and planted publicity items is read by nearly every commuter in the country. Curtis, beholden to the powerful press pundit, panders to his every whim. Lancaster spends his evenings sipping coffee in a posh hangout for the famous and wealthy, his regular table his domain. A bachelor who, by implication, is not interested in women in any romantic way, Lancaster's demeanor is stern, his eyeglassed appearance forbidding, his manner terse. Asked to perform a favor by the ruthless columnist, Curtis—against his own judgment—must reluctantly comply. Lancaster, whose protective attitude about his sister, Harrison, seems more than merely brotherly, wants Curtis to find a way to break up her budding romance with musician Milner, whose jazz ensemble performs in the area. Unable to accomplish the task—Milner is a cleancut young man with no bad habits who might make an excellent husband for the girl—Curtis is cut off from inclusion in Lancaster's columns. Desperate, he seeks a solution. He inveigles cigarette girl Nichols into bedding down with another slimy columnist in return for a suggestion that the young musician is a pot-smoking Communist in the next day's newspaper. Fired from his gig as a result, Milner appeals to Lancaster who, evincing sympathy, uses his considerable influence to regain Milner's job for him, asking in return that Milner stop seeing Harrison. Milner, realizing the extent to which he is being manipulated, refuses. Lancaster, not wishing to alienate his sister, backs off but later extracts a promise from her that she will not see Milner again. She breaks her promise, meeting Milner at a secluded river's edge spot, where he persuades her that she is being manipulated by her possessive older brother. Harrison resumes her relationship with Milner on the sly.

When Lancaster discovers the couple's rebellious reunion, the enraged columnist contacts Curtis, promising that, if he can break up the romance, he will have a three-month entry to Lancaster's column for his clients. Unable to bring himself to resist the lucrative offer, Curtis plants marijuana in Milner's topcoat pocket, and then calls sadistic policeman Meyer, alerting the latter to the coat's contents. Meyer slowly pulls on the shot-loaded gloves he wears when he brutalizes his collars and waits for Milner to emerge from the nightclub. As Curtis celebrates, he receives a call from Harrison, who seems suicidal. He races to the apartment she shares with Lancaster, and affectionately tries to talk the half-dressed girl out of self-destruction while sitting on her bed. Lancaster arrives and assumes the worst. Everybody loses something in the end.

This remarkable, believable picture features an absolutely brilliant performance by Curtis, as the sleazy—yet sometimes compassionate—striver in thrall, through his own choosing, to a self-made slavemaster. Curtis's continual miscasting had been something of a joke to this point in his career, but here he is in his milieu, and he performed perfectly. Lancaster is wonderful as the perverse pundit, his enormous ego demanding obedience, fueled as it is by his influence over the millions who read his column. Nichols is superb as the girl who is used and humiliated by Curtis because of her affection for him. Great things occur in small compass in this picture of pallored night people, shot almost entirely indoors, a chillingly realistic realization of the misuse of power possible for the media. A stunning work by Lancaster's own production company, with British director Mackendrick demonstrating amazing skill and comprehension of Odets's superb script, and cinematographer Howe handling the lighting of Carrere's *verite* sets with his usual skill.

SWEET SWEETBACK'S BAADASSSSS SONG

1971 97m c   ★★★★
Action/Drama   X/
Cinemation Industries

Melvin Van Peebles *(Sweetback)*, Simon Chuckster *(Beetle)*, Hubert Scales *(Mu-Mu)*, John Dullaghan *(Commissioner)*, Rhetta Hughes *(Old Girl Friend)*, West Gale, Niva Rochelle, Nick Ferrari, Ed Rue, Johnny Amos

d, Melvin Van Peebles; w, Melvin Van Peebles; ph, Bob Maxwell; ed, Melvin Van Peebles; m, Melvin Van Peebles

A landmark in Black filmmaking in the U.S., this angry, extravagant, loud, belligerent movie reaches a high pitch early on and stays there. It's written, directed, photographed, scored by, and stars Melvin Van Peebles, who'd always wanted to be a filmmaker, went to France to do a conventional film (STORY OF A THREE DAY PASS), came back to try his hand in Hollywood (WATERMELON MAN), and finally wound up here, an independent in full control of his product.

The narrative is linear and relatively unimaginative. Sweetback (Van Peebles), who's working in a brothel when the film begins, is finally moved to action, stomps a couple of cops unconscious, then begins running. He runs for the rest of the film, finally escaping to Mexico.

SWEET SWEETBACK is not an easy film to admire: it's violent, even sadistic, obscene, frenzied, painful. Some critics condemned it for trading on a classic Black stereotype, the "buck." On the surface, the film has all the extreme elements of the most cynical "Blaxploitation" movies, but Van Peebles actually uses these elements in order to comment upon them. The pain with which he washes the screen is meant to be transmuted into anger by audiences, and then into political action. Obviously, this didn't happen, and probably never could. But the film succeeds as a *cri de coeur*, an announcement that Black militancy has reached your neighborhood theater and that things will never be the same.

SWEET SWEETBACK caused considerable controversy among Black commentators and critics, but it remains one of very few Black films from the 1970s to spring entirely from a Black artistic sensibility. Although this independent release didn't appear on *Variety* charts, it grossed more than $10 million, thus becoming one of the most financially rewarding independent productions of all time.

SWEETHEARTS

1938 120m c   ★★★½
Musical/Comedy   /U
MGM

Jeanette MacDonald *(Gwen Marlowe)*, Nelson Eddy *(Ernest Lane)*, Frank Morgan *(Felix Lehman)*, Ray Bolger *(Hans the Dancer)*, Florence Rice *(Kay Jordan)*, Mischa Auer *(Leo Kronk)*, Fay Holden *(Hannah the Dresser)*, Terry Kilburn *(Gwen's Brother)*, Betty Jaynes *(Una Wilson)*, Douglas McPhail *(Harvey Horton)*

p, Hunt Stromberg; d, W.S. Van Dyke, II; w, Dorothy Parker, Alan Campbell (based on the operetta by Harry B. Smith, Fred DeGresac, Robert B. Smith, Victor Herbert); ph, Oliver T. Marsh, Allen Davey (Technicolor); ed, Robert J. Kern; m, Victor Herbert, Herbert Stothart; art d, Cedric Gibbons; fx, Slavko Vorkapich; chor, Albertina Rasch; cos, Adrian

Some spice along with the sugar, and most welcome. MGM chose an old chestnut, the 1913 Victor Herbert operetta "Sweethearts," for their first three-color Technicolor movie. Audiences in 1938 were unlikely to accept the original's story about an orphan raised by a laundry operator only to find out that she was a princess by birth, however, so the studio took that plot and turned it into a show-within-the-movie, thereby retaining much of Herbert's score. MGM hired Dorothy Parker and Alan Campbell to write an entirely new backstage story, adding witty dialogue and a plot that made logical sense to the operetta's silliness. Jeanette MacDonald and Nelson Eddy play Gwen Marlowe and Ernest Lane, Broadway stars who have been both happily married and performing in the same hit show, "Sweethearts", for six years. The pair are tempted by the thought of taking a break from the arduous life of the stage and going to Hollywood, a threat to their Broadway producer, Felix Lehman (Frank Morgan), and the various other people who bank on Gwen and Ernest's talents. Lehman manipulates Gwen's jealousy to keep the show going, which eventually causes the couple to split and go on separate tours with different costars. Both come to their senses at the same time, however, and they reunite to walk into Lehman's office with movie contracts in hand, telling him they're leaving. He sobs and pleads with them to stay, whereupon Gwen and Ernest break out in smiles and sign for another six years—since what could be more fun than starring in a Broadway show with the one you love? The Parker-Campbell script is witty, wise, and gently satirical; the songs, primarily by Herbert, have new lyrics by Chet Forrest and Bob Wright. A large budget, lavish and numerous production numbers, and a great sense of fun make SWEETHEARTS a most enjoyable movie.

SWEETIE

1989 97m c   ★★★★
Comedy   /15
Arenafilm   (Australia)

Genevieve Lemon (Dawn), Karen Colston (Kay), Tom Lycos (Louis), Jon Darling (Gordon), Dorothy Barry (Flo), Michael Lake (Bob), Andre Pataczek (Clayton), Jean Hadgraft (Mrs. Schneller), Paul Livingston (Teddy Schneller), Louise Fox (Cheryl)

p, John Maynard; d, Jane Campion; w, Jane Campion, Gerard Lee (based on an idea by Jane Campion); ph, Sally Bongers; ed, Veronika Heussler; m, Martin Armiger; prod d, Peter Harris; cos, Amanda Lovejoy

To appreciate the complexity and uniqueness of SWEETIE, Jane Campion's remarkably assured first feature, try to imagine Roman Polanski's REPULSION reworked as a romantic comedy or Brian De Palma's SISTERS refashioned as a farce.

Kay (Karen Colston) is a gaunt, withdrawn young woman whose life is ruled by superstition. A control freak, she fervidly accepts a fortune teller's prediction that she'll meet a man with a question mark on his forehead and promptly steals a coworker's fiance (Tom Lycos) who fits the bill: he sports a wayward curl of hair over a beauty mark. For a while, the uptight woman relaxes, but her phobic behavior is never completely overcome. When her obese sister Dawn (Genevieve Lemon) appears on the scene, unannounced and uninvited, we begin to understand just why Kay's a paranoid bundle of repression. Manipulative and alternately petulant or hysterical, the eponymous "Sweetie" gobbles life voraciously, sampling food and men with the same relish; she's a distaff Peter Pan straitjacketed in a little girl's frilly party dress. Not surprisingly, her wildly inappropriate behavior has brought her family to the end of its rope.

In this darkly stylish debut, New Zealander Campion has fashioned a slapstick domestic tragedy. In addition to being a remarkable visual stylist (brilliantly aided by cinematographer and former classmate Sally Bongers), Campion elicits miracles of acting from her cast. In this comically heightened version of reality, the actors might all too easily have overplayed the laughs and forced the tears; instead they are effectively disquieting and colorful. Cruelly honest and pitilessly funny, SWEETIE is one of the nakedest explorations of familial love and desperation ever filmed.

SWEPT AWAY. . . BY AN UNUSUAL DESTINY IN THE BLUE SEA OF AUGUST

1974 116m c   ★★★½
Drama/Comedy   R/X
Medusa   (Italy)

Giancarlo Giannini (Gennarino), Mariangela Melato (Raffaella)

p, Romano Cardarelli; d, Lina Wertmuller; w, Lina Wertmuller; ph, Giulio Battiferri, Giuseppe Fornari, Stefano Ricciotti; m, Piero Piccioni; cos, Enrico Job

Aboard a chartered yacht a group of wealthy northern Italians discuss a variety of topics while basking in the sun. The snobbish Melato takes particular delight in taunting Giannini, a Sicilian deckhand, ridiculing his smelly shirt and communist ideology. Surely, Giannini is the last man on earth Melato would ever want to be shipwrecked with on a desert isle. SWEPT AWAY is a wild romp and certainly lives up to its elongated title. When destiny does indeed shipwreck the two, none of Melato's arrogance can keep this two-person war between the sexes and classes from taking some passionately amorous turns. Director-screenwriter Lina Wertmuller's 11th film (the fourth to gain a US release) provoked much controversy for what many perceived as a reactionary, sexist treatment of Melato's role by Wertmuller, a self-described feminist. (One beating scene goes on for a long time.) The argument has merit, although it ignores the broadness of Wertmuller's treatment here of some of her favorite themes. Gender and class politics are ever-present throughout the story, but laced with a delightfully satiric bite that provokes laughter as well as thought. Giannini and Melato are perfectly matched as the combatants/lovers, providing a chemistry that lends Wertmuller's parable some degree of naturalism and honesty. With lesser actors the story might never have worked, and it certainly wouldn't have made such a splash at the box office.

SWIMMER, THE

1988 105m c/bw   ★★★★
Biography
Gruzia   (U.S.S.R.)

Gudea Buzduli, Ruslan Mikabezidze

d, Irakli Quiricadze; w, Irakli Quiricadze; ph, Guram Tugushi; m, Temo Bakuzadze

Georgian cinema has given audiences some of the most remarkable, innovative, and beautifully photographed films ever made, from the work of Sergei Paradzhanov and Otar Iosseliani to the stunning anti-Stalinist film REPENTANCE. In THE SWIMMER, director Irakli Quiricadze, like his Georgian brothers, has rooted his work in folktales and legends. Spanning the 20th century, THE SWIMMER chronicles three generations of long-distance swimmers. It opens in the present, as a film crew is shooting a scene about Durishhan, a bearded, long-haired villager of many years ago who was quite at home in the Black Sea, with a unique gift for staying afloat for days at a time. When a famous British swimmer who has just conquered the English Channel comes to town, Durishhan declares that he can swim the distance of two Channels. The Englishman and local dignitaries laugh at Durishhan's claims, prompting the shaggy swimmer to disrobe and dive into the Black Sea. People pay no attention to him as he swims further and further away from the shore. Days later he arrives on land, having successfully swum the distance between Batumi and Poti. When he returns home, however, no one believes him, since he has failed to provide any documentation of the feat. Disgraced, Durishhan leaves town. Residing in another village, he continues to swim, but grows increasingly more dependent on alcohol, until he no longer has a swimmer's stamina. His son follows in his father's wake in the 1940s. Known around town for his willpower, he thrives on proving his ability in such feats as spending the night in a freezing meat locker (keeping warm by rearranging sides of beef nonstop). An organizer of swimming events, he finally decides to train for an upcoming long-distance competition. A rival champion, however, fearing that he will lose his title, reports the training swimmer to the authorities as an anti-Stalinist. (One event featured a group of swimmers floating Stalin's portrait out to sea, while at a family gathering the swimmer's young son sinks a bust of Stalin in the family's aquarium.) The following day the swimmer has vanished, and the reigning champion has nothing to fear. Back in the present, Durishhan's grandson, Anton, a stocky man of about 50, has arrived on the movie set where his forefathers' lives are being filmed. He meets the actors who portray them and discusses their lives with the crew's female director. Now it is Anton's turn to take to the water.

A Soviet feature from 1981, which saw a release in 1984 in a truncated version (minus its anti-Stalinism) and premiered in its full-length version in the US at the 1988 San Francisco Film Festival, THE SWIMMER is a technically inventive and often brilliant piece of filmmaking. Although much of its running time is spent in tracing the legend of Durishhan and his son, the picture is more than a piece of folklore. It is a film about man's role in documenting his own history, legends, and folktales. THE SWIMMER stresses the importance not only of the "swimmer" (literally and as a symbolic Everyman) but also of the historian, placing the storyteller on the same plane as the story. Much of the movie takes place in the present, as the director and her film crew (who, wrapped in protective plastic to ward off the elements along the Black Sea, have an almost surreal appearance) bring the legend of Durishhan to life. These filmmaking scenes, shot in color, are contrasted with the silent black-and-white and sepia footage that actually tells the story of Durishhan's life. The latter pay tribute not only to the folklore of Durishhan but to Soviet cinema's history of poetic realism.

SWINDLE, THE

(IL BIDONE)
1955 92m bw   ★★★½
Drama   /A
Titanus/SGC   (France/Italy)

Broderick Crawford (Augusto), Richard Basehart (Picasso), Franco Fabrizi (Roberto), Giulietta Masina (Iris), Lorella De Luca (Patrizia), Giacomo Gabrielli (Vargas), Sue Ellen Blake (Anna), Alberto De Amicis (Rinaldo), Irene Cefaro (Marisa), Xenia Valderi (Luciana)

p, Mario Derecchi; d, Federico Fellini; w, Federico Fellini, Ennio Flaiano, Tullio Pinelli (based on a story by Fellini, Flaiano); ph, Otello Martelli; ed, Mario Serandrei, Giuseppe Vari; m, Nino Rota

To many people the films of Fellini are an obnoxious blend of tiresome episodes filled with ugly characters and extreme symbolism. Others find these same elements to be a magical universe filled with the forces influencing an individual's fate. They appreciate the revealing caricatures, lively costumes and sets, and extenuating sounds that create a poetic vision. The latter camp will find much to entertain themselves with in THE SWINDLE, a film similar to its predecessor, LA STRADA, in its depiction of a man who goes through life almost blind to its wonders and with little pity for other humans. Crawford plays a petty thief who teams up with Basehart and Fabrizi to swindle poor people. Fabrizi is the first to back out of these schemes—not

to redeem himself but to go on to "better" things. Of the three, his character is the least sympathetic because his acts of thievery are done so casually. In a moment of enlightenment, Basehart forsakes this lifestyle to return to his wife Masina who, as in LA STRADA, looks on the events with her large round eyes. She is the direct opposite of the soulless Fabrizi. This leads Crawford to assemble another bunch to assist in his operations. In the touching final scenes, Crawford is dressed in a bishop's robes in order to execute a scheme when he is approached by an invalid, Blake, who takes him for the real thing, bending down to kiss his hand. Crawford finally feels remorse for his deeds, realizing that he has been taking advantage of people who are driven by pure faith. But by this time it's too late for him to repent. A very dark vision that isn't always pleasant to look at but is nonetheless fascinating. The film did not get a US release until 1962.

SWING SHIFT

1984 113m c   ★★
Drama/War   PG
WB

Goldie Hawn (Kay Walsh), Kurt Russell (Lucky Lockhart), Christine Lahti (Hazel Zanussi), Fred Ward (Biscuits Toohey), Ed Harris (Jack Walsh), Sudie Bond (Annie), Holly Hunter (Jeannie Sherman), Patty Maloney (Laverne), Lisa Pelikan (Violet Mulligan), Susan Peretz (Edith Castle)

p, Jerry Bick; d, Jonathan Demme; w, Nancy Dowd, Bo Goldman, Ron Nyswaner; ph, Tak Fujimoto (Technicolor); ed, Craig McKay; m, Patrick Williams; prod d, Peter Jamison; art d, Bo Welch; cos, Joe I. Tompkins

This latter-day look at "Rosie the Riveter" stars Goldie Hawn as Kay Walsh, whose husband, Jack (Ed Harris), is sent off to fight in WWII. Kay goes to work at an aircraft factory where she meets Lucky (Kurt Russell), whose heart problem has kept him out of uniform. They begin an affair, and Kay also develops a close friendship with her "loose" (i.e., emancipated) neighbor, Hazel (Christine Lahti). When Jack comes home on furlough, he discovers Kay's infidelity and goes back to war with a broken heart. In turn, Lucky, feeling rejected, sleeps with the lonely Hazel, upsetting relations among the three civilians. SWING SHIFT's view of adultery isn't very palatable—since Jack is at least as likable, if not more, than Lucky and seems to have a "good" marriage with Kay. Many castigated the film for using wartime hardships to justify Kay's affair and tarnish the patriotic image of the homefront Rosies. A fairer assessment suggests that director Jonathan Demme's characteristic generosity toward his characters and refusal to make absolute moral judgments are strong points, while the feminist subtext adds freshness to the story. The dullness of Kay and Lucky's romance, however, does damage the film, and may be the result of friction between Demme and Hawn, who reportedly had another director brought in to shoot new scenes that conventionalized the love triangle and downplayed Lahti's Hazel. Lahti nonetheless gives by far the film's best performance and was justly nominated for a Best Supporting Actress Oscar. Released at 113, 100, and 99 minutes, the movie is on videocassette at 100 minutes.

SWING TIME

1936 105m bw   ★★★★★
Musical/Romance   /U
RKO

Fred Astaire (John "Lucky" Garnett), Ginger Rogers (Penelope "Penny" Carrol), Victor Moore (Dr. Cardetti), Helen Broderick

(Mabel Anderson), Eric Blore *(Mr. Gordon)*, Betty Furness *(Margaret Watson)*, George Metaxa *(Ricardo Romero)*, Landers Stevens *(Judge Watson)*, John Harrington *(Dice Raymond)*, Pierre Watkin *(Al Simpson)*

p, Pandro S. Berman; d, George Stevens; w, Howard Lindsay, Allan Scott (based on a story by Erwin Gelsey); ph, David Abel; ed, Henry Berman; m, Jerome Kern; art d, Van Nest Polglase, Carroll Clark; fx, Vernon L. Walker; chor, Hermes Pan; cos, Bernard Newman, John Harkrider

TOP HAT may be more energetic and glossy, but SWING TIME is really the most magical of the ten films Fred Astaire and Ginger Rogers made together. Their dancing and acting rapport are at a peak and director George Stevens shows more finesse than Mark Sandrich in lending the couple's rocky romance a genuinely heartfelt quality. Somehow this film seems to be more *about* the Astaire-Rogers mystique than any of the others, so that when Fred sings that he's "Never Gonna Dance" if he can't have Ginger, we reel from the impact of his words.

The story tells of "Lucky" Garnett (Astaire), a gambler and and dancer engaged to Margaret Watson (Furness, in her pre-consumer advocacy days). When Lucky shows up late for his wedding, Margaret's father (Landers Stevens, the director's real-life father) tells him not to return until he earns $25,000 to prove that he's not just a layabout. Once Lucky meets dance teacher Penny Carrol (Rogers), however, his main problem is to *keep* from earning the 25 grand, since, of course, he falls in love with Penny. She works at an academy run by Mr. Gordon (Blore), a nefarious dance master who will do anything to sell lessons. In a very funny scene, Penny tries to teach Lucky—who is pretending to be a clod just so he can stay with her longer—some steps. Gordon watches Lucky's inept hoofing and fires Penny on the spot because she won't take money from the hopeless prospective student. Naturally, Lucky fixes things by dancing a complex and delightful routine to "Pick Yourself Up" with Penny that leaves everyone breathless. This dance is one of the greatest of all the Astaire-Rogers light courtship duets, just as their luminous turn to "Waltz in Swing Time" stands today as one of their finest romantic turns. The look they give each other after the Waltz ends perfectly sums up the incredibly erotic nature of the Astaire-Rogers dance numbers, and it's a great pleasure being "in" on the joke. Their last duet, to the aforementioned "Never Gonna Dance," really signals the end of the Astaire-Rogers golden years and both it and the scene they enact before dancing are probably their most touching five minutes together on film.

SWING TIME also features Astaire's incredible solo dance to "Bojangles of Harlem," perhaps the only blackface number on film which doesn't make one squirm today. His skin made up *as* an African-American rather than a minstrel-show caricature of one, Astaire dances an obvious tribute to the great Bill Robinson, even if the black dancer he more closely approximates is John Bubbles of PORGY AND BESS fame. The marvelous score, with music by Jerome Kern and lyrics by Dorothy Fields, consists of one classic song after another, and they are all stunningly staged. Astaire's rendition of the Oscar-winning "The Way You Look Tonight" comes while Rogers washes her hair. Her final appearance gently mocks the tender lyric, but her rubbing of Astaire's shoulder confirms the sentiment of the moment. "A Fine Romance," meanwhile, that famous sardonic love duet, appears while the couple walks around a gorgeous set of a snowy inn, the final swishing of the car's wiper blades perfectly rounding out the tune. The supporting cast, led by the acerbic Broderick, the sweetly bumbling Moore and the unctuous Blore, adds plenty of laughs, and, at the center of it all, Hollywood's ideal couple shines at their brightest. A film to cherish, and easily one of the four or five greatest musical films ever made.

SWISS FAMILY ROBINSON

1960 126m c	★★★½
Children's	G/U
Disney (U.K.)	

John Mills *(Father)*, Dorothy McGuire *(Mother)*, James MacArthur *(Fritz)*, Janet Munro *(Roberta)*, Sessue Hayakawa *(Pirate Chief)*, Tommy Kirk *(Ernst)*, Kevin Corcoran *(Francis)*, Cecil Parker *(Capt. Moreland)*, Andy Ho *(Auban)*, Milton Reid *(Big Pirate)*

p, Bill Anderson; d, Ken Annakin; w, Lowell S. Hawley (based on the novel by Johann Wyss); ph, Harry Waxman (Panavision, Technicolor); ed, Peter Boita; m, William Alwyn; prod d, John Howell; art d, John Howell; fx, Danny Lee, Walter Stones; cos, Julie Harris

Disney's version of the famous novel is a superior adventure following the exploits of the title family. Father and Mother Robinson (John Mills and Dorothy McGuire) and their three sons, Fritz, Francis, and Ernst (James MacArthur, Kevin Corcoran, and Tommy Kirk), flee Napoleon and look for someplace to live in the South Seas, but in the course of the search they are chased by pirates and their ship is pounded by an angry sea. After the ship's crew deserts the sinking vessel with only the family on board, the Robinsons crash along a rocky shore and emerge to find a tropical island Eden. Since the ship, which is only half-submerged, is filled with food and gear, they prepare to settle in. Numerous adventures follow in this exciting and humorous picture filled with classic Disney touches. It's a tongue-in-cheek movie that avoids the sappy sentiment of so many "family" films and concentrates on sheer entertainment instead. The scenery is lush and colorful; the film's success made Tobago a tourist haven for many years afterward.

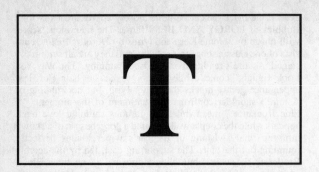

T

T-MEN

1947 91m bw ★★★★
Crime /A
Eagle-Lion

Dennis O'Keefe *(Dennis O'Brien)*, Alfred Ryder *(Tony Genaro)*, Mary Meade *(Evangeline)*, Wallace Ford *(Schemer)*, June Lockhart *(Tony's Wife)*, Charles McGraw *(Moxie)*, Jane Randolph *(Diana)*, Art Smith *(Gregg)*, Herbert Heyes *(Chief Carson)*, Jack Overman *(Brownie)*

p, Aubrey Schenck; d, Anthony Mann; w, John C. Higgins (based on a story by Virginia Kellogg); ph, John Alton; ed, Fred Allen; m, Paul Sawtell; art d, Edward C. Jewell; fx, George J. Teague; cos, Frances Ehren

One of Anthony Mann's finest forays into film noir, T-MEN was also one of the director's first financial triumphs. O'Keefe and Ryder are two treasury agents determined to crack a successful counterfeiting ring after a fellow agent is killed during the investigation. In order to obtain first-class information, the agents pose as underworld hoods and infiltrate a powerful Detroit mob family headed by Kosta. They discover that Ford, a sleazy LA-based hood with a penchant for steam baths, may hold the key to the counterfeiting ring, so O'Keefe travels west, combing every steam bath in Los Angeles to find Ford. O'Keefe manages to worm his way into the counterfeiting ring by passing off a phony bill for which he claims to have the plates (provided by the Treasury Department from their stock of confiscated counterfeit plates). He sends for Ryder, and the men bide their time by bargaining for the supposed plates while using the situation to investigate further. The agents ingratiate themselves with Ford, though they cannot uncover the secret to the operation that will enable them to crack the case. Ford is afraid he'll soon be knocked off by the boys in Detroit, and his fears are justified; they have sent McGraw to kill him. Suspecting that Ryder is a T-Man, Ford informs McGraw of his suspicions, hoping that he'll be allowed to live. McGraw accepts the news and then locks Ford in a steam bath and turns the steam on full blast. The sadistic killer stands and watches as the hysterical Ford tries to smash the glass in the tiny window to no avail. The lethal steam bath seems to take forever, but Ford finally dies. Meanwhile, Ryder finally cracks the secret of the counterfeiting operation, just as McGraw and the gang, O'Keefe among them, arrive to kill him. Ryder knows full well what is about to happen, and he manages to slip O'Keefe the essential information before he is murdered by McGraw. O'Keefe relays the information to the Treasury Department and then must work to save his own life because a member of the mob has recognized the plates to be the work of a counterfeiter he knew in prison. The climax takes place aboard a ship where McGraw closes in on O'Keefe and a tense cat and mouse game ensues.

When PRC studios and Britain's J. Arthur Rank organization merged to form Eagle-Lion, the new owners encouraged better scripts and more artistic creativity while providing bigger budgets to achieve their goals. Director Mann rose to the occasion and began a series of fascinating film noir crime dramas (T-MEN, RAW DEAL, and THE BLACK BOOK) with superb cinematographer John Alton. Presented in a documentary-like style with narration by Reed Hadley, T-MEN shifts from the bureaucratic staunchness of a voiceover to the shadowy, out-of-control world of film noir. In what would become a major theme in Mann's later work (especially in his westerns with Jimmy Stewart), the film examines the thin line between the law and the lawless, the hunters and the hunted. Though lawmen O'Keefe and Ryder plunge themselves into the criminal element with fervor, they are party to acts only sanctioned by society if one wears a badge. These themes are illustrated beautifully by Alton's visuals, which put the agents in the same shadowy light as the criminals. The film is at its most shocking during the steam bath murder and the scene is intense and horrifying enough to disturb most sensitive viewers. Mann and Alton's work for Eagle-Lion was so distinguished that MGM took note and signed both of them.

TAKE ME OUT TO THE BALL GAME

1949 93m c ★★★★
Sports/Musical /U
MGM

Frank Sinatra *(Dennis Ryan)*, Esther Williams *(K.C. Higgins)*, Gene Kelly *(Eddie O'Brien)*, Betty Garrett *(Shirley Delwyn)*, Edward Arnold *(Joe Lorgan)*, Jules Munshin *(Nat Goldberg)*, Richard Lane *(Michael Gilhuly)*, Tom Dugan *(Slappy Burke)*, Murray Alper *(Zalinka)*, Wilton Graff *(Nick Donford)*

p, Arthur Freed; d, Busby Berkeley; w, Harry Tugend, Harry Crane (uncredited), George Wells (based on a story by Gene Kelly and Stanley Donen); ph, George Folsey (Technicolor); ed, Blanche Sewell; m, Roger Edens; art d, Cedric Gibbons, Daniel B. Cathcart; fx, Warren Newcombe, Peter Ballbusch; chor, Gene Kelly, Stanley Donen; cos, Helen Rose, Valles

Dennis Ryan (Frank Sinatra) and Eddie O'Brien (Gene Kelly) are a popular song-and-dance team on the vaudeville circuit who spend their summers playing baseball in a semiprofessional league. Ready to begin a new season, the pair are surprised and delighted to find that a woman, K.C. Higgins (Esther Williams), is the new team owner as well as their manager. Both men find her attractive, but K.C. is only interested in fielding a good team. When Eddie is benched for moonlighting as a dance director for a nightclub chorus line, he falls under the spell of Joe Lorgan (Edward Arnold), a seemingly benevolent man who in reality is a big-time gambler, and trouble brews for Eddie and his team.

While there's not much baseball played here, this is an amiable film, marked by the enjoyable cast and some lively, if not memorable, music. TAKE ME OUT TO THE BALL GAME was Sinatra and Kelly's follow-up to ANCHORS AWEIGH, and the two are again well-matched partners. The film was based on an original idea of Kelly and Stanley Donen's that closely resembled a minor 1930 film, THEY LEARNED ABOUT WOMEN. After concocting the story, Kelly and Donen asked for the chance to direct, but it was decided to bring in the legendary Busby Berkeley—who had fallen on hard times—and the film turned out to be his last directorial effort. Kelly and Donen, however, were allowed to direct TAKE ME OUT TO THE BALL GAME's musical sequences and producer Arthur Freed was impressed enough to allow them to direct the next Kelly-Sinatra film, the classic ON THE TOWN, later that year. Songs include "Take Me Out to the Ball Game" (Albert von Tilzer, Jack Norworth), "The Hat My Father Wore on St. Patrick's Day" (William Jerome, Jean Schwartz), "O'Brian to Ryan to Goldberg" (Roger Edens, Betty Comden, Adolph Green), "The Right Girl for Me" (Edens, Comden, Green), "It's Fate, Baby, It's Fate" (Edens, Comden, Green), "Strictly U.S.A." (Edens, Comden, Green).

TAKE THE MONEY AND RUN

1969 85m c   ★★★½
Crime/Prison/Comedy   M/PG
Heywood/Hillary/Palomar

Woody Allen (Virgil Starkwell), Janet Margolin (Louise), Marcel Hillaire (Fritz), Jacquelyn Hyde (Miss Blaire), Lonny Chapman (Jake), Jan Merlin (Al), James Anderson (Chain Gang Warden), Howard Storm (Fred), Mark Gordon (Vince), Micil Murphy (Frank)

p, Charles H. Joffe; d, Woody Allen; w, Woody Allen, Mickey Rose; ph, Lester Shorr, Fouad Said (Eastmancolor); ed, Ralph Rosenblum, James T. Heckert, Ron Kalish, Paul Jordan; m, Marvin Hamlisch; art d, Fred Harpman; fx, A.D. Flowers

Woody Allen's first directorial achievement is a frequently hilarious, sometimes misfiring satire of crime movies. Allen plays the typical shlemiel, a put-upon wimp who becomes a compulsive criminal. Told in semidocumentary fashion, with a rambling narration by Jackson Beck (who was heard as the narrator on radio's "Superman" for years), it prefigures Allen's work years later in ZELIG. Allen begins his criminal career by robbing vending machines. His parents are seen talking about their misguided son while wearing eyeglass-nose-mustache disguises so that they won't be recognized by the neighbors when this "documentary" is released. After attempting to rob an armored car, Allen is caught and sent to a prison where the inmates are a compendium of every stock inmate character ever seen in a prison film (hilarious!). Allen tries to escape by carving a gun out of a bar of soap (a takeoff on John Dillinger's ruse). It's a bust, and two more years are added to his sentence. To get out, Allen volunteers to be a guinea pig in a dangerous medical experiment and is rewarded by being paroled. On the streets again he tries to "go straight," but the call of the criminal wild is too much for him. He plans to snatch the purse of Margolin, a lovely laundress, but changes his mind when he falls in love: "After the first 15 minutes, I knew I wanted to marry her. And after the first half hour, I totally gave up the idea of snatching her purse." Now in love and in need of money, Allen tries to rob a bank and hands his scrawled note to the tellers. An argument erupts between Allen and the bank's employees, who can't read his handwriting. Again he is thrown into jail, where Margolin makes regular visits to buoy his spirits. Through a mistake, Allen gets out of jail. He marries Margolin and moves to another state, where he takes an office job in a sincere attempt to abandon his life of crime. Hyde, one of his fellow employees at the office, discovers his true identity and tries to blackmail him. She wants his body and will stop at nothing to get it. Allen retaliates at a turkey dinner she's prepared by attempting to stab her to death with an overcooked drumstick. Margolin becomes pregnant, and Allen thinks he must try one more robbery to provide for his burgeoning family. He attempts to crack another bank and winds up in jail once more. Chained to five other convicts in a chain gang, Allen escapes and invades a farm house. (Some very funny moments here—as, for example, when one of the men wants to go to the bathroom, and all must march in close-order steps because of their "close connection"). The escapees break the

chains, after an anxious moment with some dumb cops, and go their separate ways. Allen, now topping the most-wanted list, returns to Margolin. He is soon apprehended and carted back to jail, where he reflects on his life, patiently carving up another bar of soap as the picture ends.

One-liners galore, lots of episodic scenes and some good satire, with the intercutting of actual news footage to establish the era (President Richard Nixon and Dwight Eisenhower figure prominently). A bit of homage to Claude Lelouch in the love scenes between Allen and Margolin, then into the jail sequences that can best be appreciated by those familiar with I AM A FUGITIVE FROM A CHAIN GANG, THE LAST MILE, or any of several jail movies. A spotty picture with many delicious moments, including a sequence where Allen hires an over-the-hill movie director (Hillaire) to pretend he is shooting a film about a bank robbery so that Allen and his men can use that as a cover for their actual robbery of the institution. Everything is going well until a rival gang arrives with the same intention. Several inside jokes are unfathomable to viewers from the hinterlands. By this time, Allen had written WHAT'S NEW PUSSYCAT?, helped script WHAT'S UP TIGER LILY? and had his play used as the basis for DON'T DRINK THE WATER. From this picture on, he was to become an eminent comedy writer-director-actor. Cinematographer Said was replaced on the movie and received no credit, despite a few weeks' work on it. Allen's coauthor on this and BANANAS was Rose, who decided to leave New York and try his hand at solo screenwriting in California.

TAKING OF PELHAM ONE, TWO, THREE, THE

1974 104m c   ★★★½
Crime   R/15
Palomar/Palladium

Walter Matthau (Lt. Garber), Robert Shaw (Blue), Martin Balsam (Green), Hector Elizondo (Grey), Earl Hindman (Brown), James Broderick (Denny Doyle), Dick O'Neill (Correll), Lee Wallace (The Mayor), Tom Pedi (Caz Dolowicz), Beatrice Winde (Mrs. Jenkins)

p, Gabriel Katzka, Edgar J. Scherick; d, Joseph Sargent; w, Peter Stone (based on the novel by John Godey); ph, Owen Roizman (Panavision, Technicolor); ed, Jerry Greenberg, Robert Q. Lovett; m, David Shire; art d, Gene Rudolf; cos, Anna Hill Johnstone

This exciting, suspenseful drama of a subway car held for ransom begins with Matthau, a New York transit cop, giving some visiting Japanese a guided tour of the subway control center. Matthau mocks and insults the party, not realizing that his guests speak English. Meanwhile, in the subway tunnels of New York, a train pulls out of the Pelham station at 1:23 p.m. Aboard are four men wearing identical hats, glasses, mustaches, and raincoats. The group, led by Shaw, separates one car from the train, taking the conductor (Broderick) and the passengers on board hostage. Their demands are chillingly simple: the city must pay $1 million ransom in exactly one hour or else they will begin killing hostages. A dialogue begins over the radio between Matthau and Shaw as the detective tries to negotiate a safe release for the hostages. One of the kidnappers, Balsam, is suffering from a bad cold, and Matthau blesses him with each sneeze. Shaw eventually has Broderick killed when the demands have not been met. The ransom money is finally delivered, and the gang make their plan to escape.

Though Matthau and Shaw spend most of the film communicating through a microphone, the tension between the two is well developed. The editing back and forth is sharp, accentuating the two strong performances and adding to the suspense. Shaw is excellent as the cold-blooded killer, with a steely performance that fascinates as well as frightens. The one low point is the slice-of-life group of passengers aboard the subway. Each hostage is a stereotype, ranging from a mother with two bratty children to a streetwise pimp, to Gorrin's know-it-all old man. The direction is sharp, using the small, darkened world of the subway to its fullest, and backed by Shire's exciting jazz score that complements the suspense. The film was advertised in many large cities with posters displayed in subway stations, but this ad campaign emphasizing every commuter's nightmare was dumped when subway riders across the country complained.

TAKING OFF

1971 92m c   ★★★★
Comedy/Drama   R/18
Forman/Crown/Hausman

Lynn Carlin (Lynn Tyne), Buck Henry (Larry Tyne), Linnea Heacock (Jeannie Tyne), Georgia Engel (Margot), Tony Harvey (Tony), Audra Lindley (Ann Lockston), Paul Benedict (Ben Lockston), Vincent Schiavelli (Schiavelli), David Gittler (Jamie), Ike Turner

p, Alfred W. Crown; d, Milos Forman; w, Milos Forman, John Guare, Jean-Claude Carriere, John Klein; ph, Miroslav Ondricek (Movielab Color); ed, John Carter; art d, Robert Wightman; cos, Peggy Farrell

Czech-born Forman's first US movie is a crackerjack look at the sociology of the country he had just adopted. Had it been made by an American, chances are lots of what Forman's "new eyes" had perceived would have been lost. Heacock is a runaway teenager who has settled in New York's East Village after growing up in a typical suburban home in Forest Hills, Queens, with typical parents Carlin and Henry. She's auditioning as a singer but suddenly freezes and can't perform. Back at her parents' home, Henry and Carlin are unable to find Heacock and are baring their woes to best pals Engel and Harvey. The two men leave their wives to talk and go off to report Heacock's disappearance at the police station. Before they can get to the authorities, they stop for a quick, consolatory drink at a tavern, and one leads to another. Soon they are sloshed. Back at the house, Engel is telling Carlin about her bedroom antics with her husband when Heacock walks in. Carlin is happy to see her but angry that she'd left and in a fit of pique accuses her of being a junkie. Harvey and Henry enter, and Henry hits Heacock with a drunken slap. There's a huge row between Henry and Carlin, who is angered at his drunken behavior and the fact that he's hit their daughter. Heacock reacts to the squabble by leaving again. On the following day a sober Henry travels to the seamy East Village in an attempt to find Heacock and meets Lindley, a woman in the same boat. Lindley's daughter has also run away, and Lindley thinks that the East Village is the place where most of these teens go. Lindley and her husband, Benedict, belong to an organization known as The Society for Parents of Fugitive Children (SPFC). Henry and Carlin go to a meeting of this support group, where Schiavelli (using his own name for the part) turns the whole middle-aged group on with grass. He says that they must smoke this dope in order to better understand what their children are attracted to. At first the older folks show no effects; many claim that they don't feel any response to the marijuana. Then a woman begins singing at the top of her lungs, and soon the others join in. Engel and Benedict are invited by Henry and Carlin back to their home for a nightcap. It turns out that Engel and Benedict are "swingers," and they suggest a friendly game of strip poker. Heacock has come home once more and looks down from the second story to see Henry nude on the card table singing snatches

of opera while Carlin sits topless and laughs hysterically. After Engel and Benedict depart, Henry and Carlin put their clothes on and get into a discussion with Heacock. She informs them that she is now seeing a young man. They decide that they can become closer to Heacock if they see the kind of boy she likes, so they tell her to invite the youth to their home for a family dinner. When he shows up, they are shocked to see that he's a long-haired, unshaven lad. Upon seeing him, Carlin bursts into tears. Henry attempts to be pleasant to the boy, Gittler, and wonders whether his kind of music can actually make him a living. When Gittler shyly admits that he made nearly $300,000 that year, Henry and Carlin look at the bearded boy in a new light.

The movie is more satire than farce, and satire "is what closes on Saturday nights," said George S. Kaufman. Kaufman was right, and this movie did nowhere near the business it deserved, although it did serve to introduce Forman to the US audience after his European successes with LOVES OF A BLONDE and THE FIREMAN'S BALL. Henry had done cameo appearances in THE GRADUATE and CATCH-22 and here has a full-fledged leading role. His work is exemplary, and he more than holds his own with the other, more experienced actors. Carlin first came to prominence in FACES, although her career never went as far as her talent could have taken her. Heacock was an amateur whom Forman spotted in Central Park. Forman enjoys using nonprofessionals and always seems to evoke excellent results from them. The promise of this first US movie was realized when Forman distinguished himself with ONE FLEW OVER THE CUCKOO'S NEST, AMADEUS, and the overlooked classic, RAGTIME. It's a well-made comedy that avoids the obvious at every turn. The script was written by a formidable quartet composed of Forman, playwright Guare (whose "The House of Blue Leaves" won several Tony Awards in June, 1986), French author Carriere (who co-wrote BELLE DU JOUR and THE MILKY WAY), and Klein. Lots of laughs and lots of wincing in this movie which lays bare the generation gap in a unique fashion.

TALE OF TWO CITIES, A

1935 120m bw   ★★★★★
Historical   /U
MGM

Ronald Colman (Sydney Carton), Elizabeth Allan (Lucie Manette), Edna May Oliver (Miss Pross), Blanche Yurka (Mme. DeFarge), Reginald Owen (Stryver), Basil Rathbone (Marquis St. Evremonde), Henry B. Walthall (Dr. Manette), Donald Woods (Charles Darnay), Walter Catlett (Barsad), Fritz Leiber (Gaspard)

p, David O. Selznick; d, Jack Conway; w, W.P. Lipscomb, S.N. Behrman (based on the novel by Charles Dickens); ph, Oliver T. Marsh; ed, Conrad A. Nervig; m, Herbert Stothart; art d, Cedric Gibbons, Frederic Hope; cos, Dolly Tree

Easily the best film version of Charles Dickens' classic novel (out of at least seven), A TALE OF TWO CITIES follows the turmoil and aftermath of the French Revolution. Sydney Carton (Colman) is a world-weary London barrister in love with Lucie Manette (Allan). She thinks of him only as a friend, however, and marries Charles Darnay (Woods), a descendant of a noble Frenchman who is also Carton's look-alike. Darnay's uncle, the Marquis St. Evremonde (Rathbone), is a heartless tyrant who is killed at the Revolution's onset. As the nephew of the hated Marquis, Darnay is arrested in Paris and sentenced to death. Lucie is frantic with worry over her husband, and Carton, devoted to Lucie but seeing no hope of happiness, goes to Paris, where he frees Darnay and takes his place in prison. His last words as he ascends the scaffold have become so identified with

Colman that they are almost impossible to say without slipping into his distinctive accent: "It is a far, far better thing that I do than I have ever done; it is a far, far better rest that I go to than I have ever known."

This superb, lavish production features an MGM stock company playing every small role to perfection, and Colman gives one of the best performances of his life in a role he had long wanted to play. He captures Carton's intellectualism, cynicism, self-pity and nobility in equal measure, achieving a richness of characterization that would have pleased Dickens himself. Equally memorable is Blanche Yurka as the sinister Mme. DeFarge. This is nastiness to rival Mercedes McCambridge's ripe, blistering work in JOHNNY GUITAR. And, as in that Nicholas Ray film, Yurka has her own Joan Crawford to confront: the inimitable Edna May Oliver, representing the forces of virtue. Their final struggle is one of the highlights of the film. The film, has, in fact, many great moments, among the most beautiful of which is Carton's walk through the snow as the holiday carolers go by. The finale, as Carton awaits death, is equally powerful and touching. In a small role as a seamstress also being executed, Isabel Jewell gets to pull off yet another marvelous dramatic vignette.

One of director Jack Conway's finest efforts, the film never suffers from a sense that the novel has been compressed or rushed. Moving, fresh and aware of its effects, this film stands as one of Hollywood's finest adaptations of a novel. Its huge and deserved success gave producer David O. Selznick the freedom to walk away from MGM (and his father-in-law, Louis B. Mayer) and set up Selznick International Pictures. "Tis a far, far better thing" indeed.

TALES OF MANHATTAN
1942 118m bw   ★★★½
Comedy   /A
FOX

Charles Boyer (*Paul Orman*), Henry Fonda (*George*), Rita Hayworth (*Ethel Halloway*), Charles Laughton (*Charles Smith*), Paul Robeson (*Luke*), Edward G. Robinson (*Larry Browne*), Ginger Rogers (*Diane*), Cesar Romero (*Harry Wilson*), Ethel Waters (*Esther*), J. Carrol Naish (*Costello*)

p, Boris Morros, Sam Spiegel; d, Julien Duvivier; w, Ben Hecht, Ferenc Molnar, Donald Ogden Stewart, Samuel Hoffenstein, Alan Campbell, Ladislas Fodor, Laslo Vadnay, Laszlo Gorog, Lamar Trotti, Henry Blankfort, Buster Keaton (uncredited), Edmund Beloin, William Morrow; ph, Joseph Walker; ed, Robert Bischoff; m, Sol Kaplan; art d, Richard Day, Boris Leven; cos, Irene, Dolly Tree, Bernard Newman, Gwen Wakeling, Oleg Cassini

TALES OF MANHATTAN follows the adventures of a fancy tail coat as it goes from riches to rags. A famous actor (Charles Boyer) initially buys the coat, only to be told the garment carries a curse. Later, it winds up with a man (Cesar Romero) whose fiancee (Ginger Rogers) finds a love letter in one of the pockets. He insists the coat belongs to his pal (Henry Fonda), but his strategy backfires when, impressed by the letter's passion, she runs off with the friend. The cursed jacket then passes from a composer (Charles Laughton) to an impoverished lawyer (Edward G. Robinson), who wears it to a college reunion, where three former classmates decide to help him get back on his feet. Next to own the garment is a crook (J. Carrol Naish) who wears it while he pulls off a job. Pocketing the loot, he boards a plane, but during the flight he throws the coat out the window, forgetting it's stuffed with $40,000. The money flutters to the ground and is picked up by two sharecroppers (Paul Robeson and Ethel

Waters) who take it to the local preacher, while the coat ends up on a scarecrow. TALES OF MANHATTAN unfolds with charm. Under the fine direction of Julien Duvivier (who directed the similarly episodic UN CARNET DU BAL, 1938), the episodes flow smoothly. It has, however, been criticized for its simplistic presentation of blacks in the final episode, and Robeson later denounced the film. Also unfortunate is that what might have been the best sequence, featuring W.C. Fields, didn't make the final cut.

TALES OF TERROR
1962 90m c   ★★★½
Horror   /X
Alta Vista

Vincent Price (*Locke/Fortunato/Valdemar*). MORELLA: Maggie Pierce (*Lenora*), Leona Gage (*Morella*), Edmund Cobb (*Driver*). THE BLACK CAT: Peter Lorre (*Montresor*), Joyce Jameson (*Annabel*), Lennie Weinrib, John Hackett (*Policemen*). THE CASE OF MR. VALDEMAR: Basil Rathbone (*Carmichael*), Debra Paget (*Helene*)

p, Roger Corman; d, Roger Corman; w, Richard Matheson; ph, Floyd Crosby (Panavision, Pathe Color); ed, Anthony Carras; m, Les Baxter; art d, Daniel Haller; fx, Pat Dinga

The fourth entry in Roger Corman's Edgar Allan Poe series, this film is an anthology of three short pieces based on tales by Poe, and all three—"Morella," "The Black Cat," and "The Case of Mr. Valdemar"—feature Vincent Price in the starring role. In "Morella," Price is an embittered widower who has lived alone in his gloomy mansion since the death of his wife, Gage, after giving birth some 26 years ago. His daughter, Pierce, arrives and finds that her father loathes her because he blames her for his wife's death. Prowling around the house, Pierce finds Gage's mummified body lying on a bed. Price explains he couldn't bear to have her beauty buried beneath the ground, so he had her corpse moved into the house. Pierce reveals to her father that she is dying and only has a few months left. Father and daughter are reconciled, but that night Pierce dies and her body becomes possessed by Gage, who has been waiting all these years to return and wreak her vengeance on Price—the father of the baby that killed her. In "The Black Cat," Lorre is superb as a drunken loser whose behavior forces his wife to seek comfort in the arms of wine-taster Price. To get even, Lorre captures his wife and her lover and walls them up in the cellar. Unbeknownst to him, however, the family cat is also entombed, and its wails give the scheme away. The final story, "The Case of Mr. Valdemar," features Price as a dying man who has fallen under the spell of an evil mesmerist, Rathbone. Price agrees to be the subject of an experiment wherein Rathbone will put him in a state of hypnosis at the moment of death, which will, perhaps, prevent him from dying. The trick works, but when the evil Rathbone attempts to steal Price's wife and estate, Price snaps out of the spell and attacks the mesmerist, his dead flesh melting around him. "Morella," the scariest of the tales, is an interesting precursor to THE TOMB OF LIGEIA (1965). "The Black Cat" combines the title Poe tale with Poe's "The Cask of Amontillado." It is a wonderfully funny prototype of THE RAVEN (1963), with both Lorre and Price having a grand time poking fun at the material and themselves. The final story has several memorable moments—especially when Price's disembodied voice can be heard pleading for release from his undead state—but the ending is marred by some unnecessary optical effects that obscure his melted visage (indeed, the production stills from this tale are more frightening than what appears in the movie).

TALK OF THE TOWN, THE

1942   118m   bw   ★★★★
Comedy   /U
Columbia

Cary Grant (*Leopold Dilg*), Jean Arthur (*Nora Shelley*), Ronald Colman (*Michael Lightcap*), Edgar Buchanan (*Sam Yates*), Glenda Farrell (*Regina Bush*), Charles Dingle (*Andrew Holmes*), Emma Dunn (*Mrs. Shelley*), Rex Ingram (*Tilney*), Leonid Kinskey (*Jan Pulaski*), Tom Tyler (*Clyde Bracken*)

p, George Stevens; d, George Stevens; w, Irwin Shaw, Sidney Buchman (based on a story by Sidney Harmon, adapted by Dale Van Every); ph, Ted Tetzlaff; ed, Otto Meyer; m, Frederick Hollander; art d, Lionel Banks, Rudolph Sternad; fx, Donald Starling; cos, Irene

The contrivance of plot is compensated by one of the most genial casts in history. Full of wonderful *bon mots*, TOWN is acted with comic fervor by Grant, Arthur, and Colman.

Colman plays a renowned law professor who wants to spend a quiet summer writing while he awaits an appointment to the Supreme Court. He takes lodgings in the home of Arthur, a schoolteacher, but Colman's summer proves to be anything but quiet. Grant, who has escaped from jail after being labeled as the man behind a deadly factory fire, has taken refuge in the house as well. Arthur tells the bearded professor that Grant is the gardener, taking great care to protect Grant's secret. Colman is set in his ways when it comes to legalities, but what's more, he soon learns the real reason for Grant's stay at the house. It turns out that Grant was framed by a corrupt local government. The foreman who supposedly died in the blaze is very much alive, and both Colman and Grant develop an active interest in Arthur.

Grant, Arthur, and Colman are a terrific threesome, playing well off one another in a finely constructed love triangle. Both men want Arthur, yet Colman never lets his desire for her take precedence over the justice that must be done. Stevens directs his cast well, handling the double-edged story with grace and style. He originally shot two endings, one with Colman getting Arthur, and the other having Arthur pair with Grant. Both endings were shown in preview screenings, and audience polls decided how the film would end. This was Colman's first film at Columbia since 1937's LOST HORIZON. Much to his delight, he learned that Stevens had arranged it so the actor would not have to deal with studio chief Harry Cohn during TALK OF THE TOWN's production. At the time Colman had been experiencing some popularity problems at the box office, and this hit film gave his career the desired boost.

TALK RADIO

1988   110m   c   ★★★½
Drama   R/18
Cineplex Odeon/Edward R. Pressman/Ten Four

Eric Bogosian (*Barry Champlain*), Alec Baldwin (*Dan*), Ellen Greene (*Ellen*), Leslie Hope (*Laura*), John C. McGinley (*Stu*), John Pankow (*Chuck Dietz*), Michael Wincott (*Kent*), Zach Grenier (*Sid Greenberg*), Anna Levine (*Woman at Basketball Game*), Robert Trebor (*Jeffrey Fisher*)

p, Edward R. Pressman, A. Kitman Ho; d, Oliver Stone; w, Eric Bogosian, Oliver Stone (based on the play "Talk Radio" created by Bogosian, Tad Savinar, written by Bogosian, and the book *Talked to Death: The Life and Murder of Alan Berg* by Stephen Singular); ph, Robert Richardson (DeLuxe Color); ed, David Brenner, Joe Hutshing; m, Stewart Copeland; prod d, Bruno Rubeo; cos, Ellen Mirojnick

Based on Eric Bogosian's one-act play of the same title, and set in the conservative hotbed of Dallas, Texas, TALK RADIO presents us with radio talk-show host Barry Champlain (Bogosian), a driven, self-loathing Jewish liberal who actively antagonizes his listeners. In spite of Champlain's repugnant demeanor, his show is a hit, and Champlain is shocked when he learns that a deal to go national via satellite feed has been delayed. He conducts an especially vitriolic show, victimizing his ex-wife, whom he has called to his side for moral support; fending off death threats; interviewing a sociopathic teenager; and berating his listeners for turning fear, hate, and suffering into their entertainment.

Fueled by a brilliant performance from Bogosian, TALK RADIO is an intense experience that will leave most audiences feeling drained. Director Oliver Stone confines most of the film to the radio studio, but the camera is always on the move. Less successful is the lengthy, overlit flashback sequence, which introduces some unnecessary background information: Stone and Bogosian decided to combine Bogosian's play with material from the life of the controversial talk-show host, Alan Berg, who was murdered by neofascists in 1984. Bogosian's compelling performance, however, overcomes any minor irritations in the screenplay.

TALL BLOND MAN WITH ONE BLACK SHOE, THE

(LE GRAND BLOND AVEC UNE CHAUSSURE NOIRE)
1972   90m   c   ★★½
Mystery/Comedy   PG/AA
Gueville/Madeline/Gaumont   (France)

Pierre Richard (*Francois*), Bernard Blier (*Milan*), Jean Rochefort (*Toulouse*), Mireille Darc (*Christine*), Jean Carmet (*Maurice*), Colette Castel (*Paulette*), Paul Le Person (*Perrache*), Jean Obe (*Botrel*), Robert Castel (*Georghiu*), Roger Caccia (*M. Boudart*)

p, Alain Poire, Yves Robert; d, Yves Robert; w, Yves Robert, Francis Veber; ph, Rene Mathelin (Eastmancolor); ed, Ghislaine Desjonqueres; m, Vladimir Kosma

Filled with dry humor and featuring an understated comic performance by the expressionless Pierre Richard, this French farce concentrates on the silly aspects of the espionage world. Because of infighting in the French Secret Service, chief Louis Toulouse (Jean Rochefort) sets a trap for an ambitious underling, Bernard Milan (Bernard Blier), who is after his job. As a result, the innocent Francois Perrin (Richard), a tall blond with one black shoe, is randomly chosen as a decoy to trap Milan, who immediately puts his men to work on Francois's past, his contacts, his mission, and his real identity, convinced that he is a "superagent." In the tradition of the silent comics, Francois walks through this danger zone of espionage completely oblivious to the gangs of assassins out to kill him.

What is especially funny about the film is its send-up of the genre. Milan and his top agents assume that every one of Francois' actions has a double meaning: if he goes to the dentist, they think it is to meet a contact; when he plays the violin, they think it is a secret signal. They even try to decode an innocent message inscribed on a photo from his mistress. A sequel followed in 1974 titled, appropriately enough, RETURN OF THE TALL BLOND MAN WITH ONE BLACK SHOE. The original was remade in 1985 as THE MAN WITH ONE RED SHOE, starring Tom Hanks.

TALL GUY, THE
1989 92m c   ★★
Comedy   /15
LWT/Virgin Vision/A Working Title   (U.K.)

Jeff Goldblum (Dexter King), Emma Thompson (Kate Lemon), Rowan Atkinson (Ron Anderson), Geraldine James (Carmen), Emil Wolk (Cyprus Charlie), Kim Thompson (Cheryl), Harold Innocent (Timothy), Anna Massey (Mary), Joanna Kanska (Tamara), Peter Kelly (Gavin)

p, Tim Bevan; d, Mel Smith; w, Richard Curtis; ph, Adrian Biddle (Eastmancolor); ed, Dan Rae; m, Peter Brewis; prod d, Grant Hicks; chor, Charles Augins; cos, Denise Simmons

Another British film with its roots in television, THE TALL GUY was partly financed by LWT, scripted by Richard Curtis (best known for the "Blackadder" TV series), and directed by Mel Smith—who first came to prominence in the UK as partner to Rowan Atkinson, Griff Rhys Jones, and Pamela Stephenson in the hit show "Not The Nine O'Clock News." Despite the presence of Hollywood star Jeff Goldblum, this is not A FISH CALLED WANDA. Goldblum is straight man to egotistical comedy star Atkinson in his long-running stage show, "Rubberface Revue." Depressed by the work and his miserable luck with women, Goldblum is further handicapped by violent hayfever and chronic allergies. To cure the latter he undergoes a series of injections and ends up out of work—but in love with nurse Thompson. After the usual fumbles and false starts, a date is fixed up, and soon the couple are starring in a romantic montage of the type so brilliantly parodied in THE NAKED GUN, set to the song "It Must Be Love." Goldblum's agent sends him to audition for the chorus in the Royal Shakespeare Company's new production, "Elephant!" a musical version of "The Elephant Man," and to everyone's surprise he lands the title role. The show is a big hit, but Thompson moves out on opening night, aware that Goldblum has slept with his leading lady. He is shattered and humiliated when he spots Thompson at Atkinson's side as Atkinson collects an award on television for "Rubberface Revue." In a fury, the "Elephant Man" pedals across London to take his revenge on Atkinson.

Although Curtis's screenplay and Smith's direction clearly aspire to more than a straight gag comedy, focussing on the central romance in a bid for emotional depth, THE TALL GUY never attains the authenticity nor the momentum it needs so badly. Jeff Goldblum is distinctly ill at ease in a part Curtis based on himself; the smart trading on transatlantic experience John Cleese exploited so expertly in WANDA is by-passed completely here, with only a couple of passing references to the character's nationality. Goldblum is a likable actor, but the character's insecurity, especially sexual insecurity, seems peculiarly English, and his portrayal is pitched all over the place. Likewise Thompson's prim, matter-of-fact, essentially Home Counties Nurse Lemon is an unlikely inspiration for romantic obsession, the outrageous sex scene notwithstanding.

The movie only sparkles in its second half, when it neatly satirizes the London theatrical scene: Steven Berkoff, Andrew Lloyd Webber and the RSC's crass commercial efforts. The musical "Elephant!" is an inspired and wicked swipe at the Company's dismal staging of a musical "Carrie" (and predates their forthcoming production of "A Clockwork Orange" with music by U2's the Edge). Some of these sequences are priceless (a chorus line of tap-dancing elephants; John Merrick's deathbed rising up to heaven), and finally Smith seems to get the measure of his material. Although THE TALL GUY cannot stand comparison with the likes of WANDA or WITHNAIL AND I, it does have its moments, bolstered by good support from Anna Massey as Goldblum's agent and Rowan Atkinson, very much in his element snarling lines like "If you ever do anything funny in my show again, you're out, you elongated droplet of dung!"

TALL MEN, THE
1955 122m c   ★★★½
Western   /U
FOX

Clark Gable (Ben Allison), Jane Russell (Nella Turner), Robert Ryan (Nathan Stark), Cameron Mitchell (Clint Allison), Juan Garcia (Luis), Harry Shannon (Sam), Emile Meyer (Chickasaw), Steve Darrell (Colonel), Will Wright (Gus, the Bartender), Robert Adler (Wrangler)

p, William A. Bacher, William B. Hawks; d, Raoul Walsh; w, Sydney Boehm, Frank S. Nugent (based on the novel by Clay Fisher); ph, Leo Tover (CinemaScope, DeLuxe Color); ed, Louis Loeffler; m, Victor Young; art d, Lyle Wheeler, Mark-Lee Kirk; fx, Ray Kellogg; cos, Travilla

Texas brothers Gable and Mitchell, who had ridden with Quantrill's Raiders during the Civil War, head North to Montana in search of gold. Desperate for cash, the men waylay Ryan, a wealthy businessman transporting $20,000. The fast-thinking Ryan turns the robbery to his advantage, however, by offering Gable and Mitchell a chance to be his partners in a cattle drive from Texas to Montana. They accept the offer, and Gable is made trail boss. As they head back down to Texas, Gable saves the life of Russell, a young settler whose party was attacked by Indians. She then joins the brothers in their trek. A blizzard prevents them from continuing their journey, and they are forced to seek shelter in a deserted shack. For warmth, Russell and Gable snuggle together under a large blanket, and a romance soon develops. Unfortunately, their relationship is short-lived. Gable wishes only to make enough money to buy a small ranch in Texas and settle down. Russell is more ambitious and desires the finer things in life. Gable's dreams are too small for her, so they soon break up. Once in Fort Worth, Russell meets Ryan and decides that his obsessive ambition to be one of the most powerful men in the country suits her requirements. Ryan and Russell take up together, and he insists she accompany the cattle drive back to Montana. This causes friction between Gable and Ryan, and tensions finally explode when Ryan balks upon learning that the final part of the cattle drive will take them through dangerous Indian territory. He announces his intention to abort the drive and take the loss, but Gable is determined to continue and keeps the cattle moving. Russell begins having doubts about Ryan, and their relationship cools. During the last part of the journey, Mitchell is killed, but Gable stampedes the herd through a narrow canyon and foils an Indian ambush. Once in Montana, Ryan tries to double-cross him, but Gable turns the tables on him. Gable returns to camp and discovers that Russell has finally chosen him over Ryan.

Shot in CinemaScope and color by cinematographer Leo Tover, THE TALL MEN is a beautiful film to look at and also boasts a good script, solid performances, and typically fine direction from veteran director Walsh. Though the action is supposed to take place in Texas and Montana, Walsh learned that there were not enough longhorn cattle in the area to make a decent herd for the film. The cast and crew were sent to Durango, Mexico, where large herds of longhorn roamed the countryside. Walsh was assisted by a man named Carlos, the governor's son-in-law. Carlos spoke English, was a fan of American movies, and had good connections with the local cattle ranchers. According to Walsh, in his autobiography *Each Man in His Time*, after one week of shooting, a swarthy representative of the beef-growers' association named Diaz, who wore a pistol on his hip, showed up on the set and demanded more money for the cattle. The governor's son-in-law reminded the man that they had signed a contract which stated a specific price for the cattle. According to Walsh, when this did not faze the cattleman, "… my self-appointed protector jumped in his car and raised more dust between us and the town. When he came back, he was driving a truck with 10 soldiers in it. That was the end of the holdup. The soldiers prodded Diaz into the truck after taking his gun away. 'You can roll your cameras now,' Carlos grinned, 'but I would advise you to get out of town the day you finish the picture.'" The rest of the shooting proceeded smoothly, though director Walsh and his cast enjoyed playing tricks and teasing each other. Walsh roomed with Gable, Ryan roomed with Mitchell, and Russell had a house to herself. One night the director borrowed a tame skunk that had been "deodorized" by two young Mexican boys and tossed it into Gable's bedroom. When Gable spotted the creature, he yelled for help, and Walsh calmly advised the actor to slowly get out of bed and whistle to the skunk because skunks are afraid of whistling. So Gable stood in the corner whistling "Ol' Man River" and "If I Loved You," while Walsh came over and picked up the little beast. The next day Gable told the entire company how brave Walsh was for removing the animal. Somehow, Walsh managed to keep a straight face through the entire affair.

TALL T, THE

1957 78m c ★★★★
Western /U
Columbia

Randolph Scott *(Pat Brennan)*, Richard Boone *(Usher)*, Maureen O'Sullivan *(Doretta Mims)*, Arthur Hunnicutt *(Ed Rintoon)*, Skip Homeier *(Billy Jack)*, Henry Silva *(Chink)*, John Hubbard *(Willard Mims)*, Robert Burton *(Tenvoorde)*, Robert Anderson *(Jace)*, Fred Sherman *(Hank Parker)*

p, Harry Joe Brown; d, Budd Boetticher; w, Burt Kennedy (based on the story "The Captive" by Elmore Leonard); ph, Charles Lawton, Jr. (Technicolor); ed, Al Clark; m, Heinz Roemheld; art d, George Brooks

Veteran cowboy actor Scott is on the trail again, but this is not the standard shoot-'em-up. The story has more suspense than most. Scott is captured by Boone and his thugs, who have also kidnaped newlyweds O'Sullivan and Hubbard. The film moves along at a brisk pace and includes elements of both comedy and drama. Boone and his boys want to rob a stagecoach, but the slimy Hubbard, in an attempt to save himself, tells them that O'Sullivan comes from a wealthy family, and it would be easier to get money by holding her for ransom. From there, the tension builds as Scott plans to outwit their captors.

This film has received a fair amount of critical analysis in recent years, particularly in light of the interest paid to genre films. Burt Kennedy's script and Budd Boetticher's direction have been applauded as solid in this psychological western which makes use of modern adult themes and depicts the struggle between good and evil as a complicated one—too complicated, in fact, for a black-and-white presentation. Rather, the viewer is shown how elements outside humans' control can influence the struggle and make clear-cut conclusions impossible. Scott is the strong-willed, laconic representation of the (pre-Eastwood) Western man pitted against an equally strong-minded, laconic villain. The struggle between Scott and Boone is depicted as a

delicate balance of power in which Scott, the force of good, is not necessarily stronger—or even better in all aspects of his life, he is merely more wily in the end. THE TALL T, like the Leone westerns to follow, used the American West as the perfect setting for an eternal struggle, the outcome of which is always a crap shoot.

TALVISOTA

1989 195m c ★★★★
War
National/Filmi Oy (Finland)

Taneli Makela *(Martti Hakala)*, Konsta Makela *(Paavo)*, Vesa Vierikko *(Jussi Kantola)*, Timo Torikka *(Pentti Saari)*, Heikki Paavilainen *(Vilho Errkila)*, Antti Raivio *(Erkki Somppi)*, Esko Kovero *(Juho Pernaa)*, Martti Suosalo *(Arvi Huhtala)*, Tomi Salmela *(Matti Ylinen)*, Samuli Edelman *(Maari Haapasalo)*

p, Marko Rohr; d, Pekka Parikka; w, Antii Tuurin, Pekka Parikka (based on the novel by Antii Tuurin); ph, Kari Sohlberg (Eastmancolor); ed, Keijo Virtanen; m, Juha Tikka, Jukka Haavisto; prod d, Pertti Hilkamo; cos, Tuula Hilkamo, Ilpo Nurmi

TALVISOTA, Finland's 1989 nominee for the Best Foreign Film Oscar, is a deeply moving, epic drama commemorating that country's heroic border stand against a massive Russian invading force during the Russo-Finnish War. However, one need not be a student of history to be thoroughly engrossed by TALVISOTA, which follows a single platoon into combat. These are not John Wayne-style supersoldiers charging the barricades, only farmers doing their patriotic duty with widely varying degrees of zeal.

Thrown together by chance, the platoon members are just beginning to become friends as, one by one, they die in combat. Martti (Taneli Makela) becomes the central figure by default: by film's end he's the only one of the group left standing, unable to save his own brother, though successful in helping to save his country. TALVISOTA succeeds by balancing the epic with the intimate. Rather than presenting a panoramic, detached view of history, it works through an accumulation of small details that gradually draw viewers into the drama. Pekka Parikka's direction and Kari Sohlberg's richly textured cinematography consistently keep the camera at soldier's-eye level, and TALVISOTA's battle scenes have a fearsome intensity that recalls Akira Kurosawa at his best. The cast is uniformly excellent, giving rich, understated portrayals, allowing us to become involved with history because we have become involved with its unwilling players. Even the film's 195-minute length works in its favor, since the filmmakers use the time to develop a realistic sense of day-to-day life during wartime that is as strong as any presented on the screen.

TAMPOPO

1986 114m c ★★★½
Comedy /18
Itami (Japan)

Ken Watanabe, Tsutomu Yamazaki, Nobuko Miyamoto, Koji Yakusho, Rikiya Yasuoka, Kinzo Sakura, Shuji Otaki

p, Yasushi Tamaoki, Seigo Hosogoe; d, Juzo Itami; w, Juzo Itami; ph, Masaki Tamura; ed, Akira Suzuki; m, Kunihiko Murai; art d, Takeo Kimura

A hilarious comedy from Japan concerned exclusively with food, TAMPOPO begins in a movie theater as we (the viewing audience) sit watching the audience in the film. In walks a suave yakuza attended by his girlfriend and an entourage of goons. Gangster and moll sit down in the front row, while the henchmen set up a table filled with delectable food. As the gangster eats, he suddenly notices us watching him, leans forward into the camera, and asks, "What are you eating?" He then informs us that he hates noise in movie theaters—especially people who crinkle wrappers and eat loudly. Of course, a man behind him is eating too noisily, and the gangster angrily threatens to kill the confused moviegoer if he continues. He then sits down to enjoy the show, urging us to do the same. Now TAMPOPO proper begins, a string of rollicking comic vignettes concerning food that—more or less—tell the story of a heroic truck driver and his sidekick's attempts to help a young widow improve her noodle-shop business.

The second feature by director Juzo Itami (preceded by THE FUNERAL, 1984), TAMPOPO is a wonderfully funny and creative film with a cornucopia of comical characters in absurd situations. These loony elements combine to offer some perceptive observations about human joy, fear, and passion for food. TAMPOPO also satirizes filmmaking (with references to THE SEVEN SAMURAI, American westerns, Steven Spielberg, and Japanese yakuza films), though Itami's film is itself heavily indebted to Luis Bunuel. With his first two films (his "Taxing Woman" entries, unfortunately, have less bite), Itami moved to the forefront of the irreverent young Japanese directors who have recently put a comedic spotlight on Japanese society, finding some very funny and disturbing truths about life there.

TAP

1989   110m   c   ★★★½
Dance/Drama   PG-13/PG
Tri-Star

Gregory Hines *(Max Washington)*, Suzzanne Douglas *(Amy)*, Sammy Davis, Jr. *(Little Mo)*, Savion Glover *(Louis)*, Joe Morton *(Nicky)*, Dick Anthony Williams *(Francis)*, Sandman Sims *(Sandman)*, Bunny Briggs *(Bunny)*, Steve Condos *(Steve)*, Jimmy Slyde *(Slim)*

p, Gary Adelson, Richard Vane; d, Nick Castle; w, Nick Castle; ph, David Gribble (CFI color); ed, Patrick Kennedy; m, James Newton Howard; prod d, Patricia Norris; chor, Henry Le Tang, Gregory Hines, Dorothy Wasserman; cos, Patricia Norris

TAP is the first film to attempt not only to update tap dancing from the days of Bill Robinson, Fred Astaire, and Gene Kelly, but also to consider the darker side of this truly American art form. After doing time in Sing-Sing for burglary, Max Washington (Gregory Hines), the son of a legendary hoofer, returns to his late father's seedy Harlem dance studio, where he encounters his father's best friend, the ailing Little Mo (Sammy Davis). Haunted by memories of his youth as a tap-dancing child prodigy, Max tries to rekindle his relationship with Mo's beautiful daughter, Amy (Suzzanne Douglas), and her 14-year-old son, Louis (Savion Glover), and makes attempt to return to dancing. But before he helps Mo realize his dream of combining rock and tap, Max first has to decide whether to carry out a burglary with his old partner (Joe Morton). Although too subdued in mood at times (TAP has a tendency to remain earthbound when it should soar), and despite some obvious plot contrivances, the picture still manages to be a very special one—thanks largely to the wonderful hoofing by Hines and veteran tappers Sandman Sims, Bunny Briggs, Steve Condos, Jimmy Slyde, Pat Rico, Arthur Duncan and Harold Nicholas (of the Nicholas Brothers). Musical selections include: "Forget the Girl" (Everton DeLuke McCalla, Jeffrey Calvert, performed by Tony Terry), "Can't Escape the Rhythm" (James Newton Howard, Glen Ballard, performed by Gregory Hines), "On the Sunny Side of the Street" (Dorothy Fields, Jimmy McHugh, performed by Bunny Briggs), "Stormy

Monday" (Aaron T. Walker, performed by T. Bone Walker), "Cheek to Cheek" (Irving Berlin).

TAPS

1981   119m   c   ★★★
Drama   PG
FOX

George C. Scott *(Gen. Harlan Bache)*, Timothy Hutton *(Brian Moreland)*, Ronny Cox *(Col. Kerby)*, Sean Penn *(Alex Dwyer)*, Tom Cruise *(David Shawn)*, Brendan Ward *(Charlie Auden)*, Evan Handler *(Edward West)*, John P. Navin, Jr. *(Derek Mellott)*, Billy Van Zandt *(Bug)*, Giancarlo Esposito *(J.C. Pierce)*

p, Stanley R. Jaffe, Howard B. Jaffe; d, Harold Becker; w, Darryl Ponicsan, Robert Mark Kamen, James Lineberger (based on the novel *Father Sky* by Devery Freeman); ph, Owen Roizman (DeLuxe Color); ed, Maury Winetrobe; m, Maurice Jarre; art d, Stan Jolley, Alfred Sweeney

This gripping but decidedly overwrought drama shows what happens when a military school becomes a military zone. Gen. Harlan Bache (George C. Scott, top-billed in little more than a cameo) runs the military academy, which is in danger of being closed because a greedy real estate combine wants to replace the ivy-covered, tradition-laden buildings with luxury condominiums on the valuable property. The deal is made, but when the developers try to move in and shut the place down prior to razing the structures, the students revolt. Led by Moreland (Timothy Hutton), the boys unite to demonstrate all they've learned—and taking over the armory, which is filled with weaponry and live ammunition, they keep the invaders at bay. The army is called in to quell this student revolt, but the boys continue to fight, and real bullets begin flying. Although Hutton was the hot property when the film was produced, his younger costars, Sean Penn and Tom Cruise, stole the film and became superstars in their own right. Unfortunately, director Harold Becker moves the film along at a snail's pace, giving the audience too much time to ponder holes in the plot, weakening the tension-filled climax by delaying it too long.

TARGETS

1968   90m   c   ★★★★½
Horror/Crime   /X
Saticoy

Boris Karloff *(Byron Orlok)*, Tim O'Kelly *(Bobby Thompson)*, Nancy Hsueh *(Jenny)*, James Brown *(Robert Thompson)*, Sandy Baron *(Kip Larkin)*, Arthur Peterson *(Ed Loughlin)*, Mary Jackson *(Charlotte Thompson)*, Tanya Morgan *(Ilene Thompson)*, Monty Landis *(Marshall Smith)*, Peter Bogdanovich *(Sammy Michaels)*

p, Peter Bogdanovich; d, Peter Bogdanovich; w, Peter Bogdanovich (based on a story by Polly Platt, Bogdanovich); ph, Laszlo Kovacs (Pathe Color); ed, Peter Bogdanovich; m, Charles Greene, Brian Stone; prod d, Polly Platt

On target. An unconventional horror picture that draws a comparison between the real-life horror of the 1966 Charles Whitman murder spree and the fictional horrors of movie legend Boris Karloff, TARGETS opens with a film clip (the flood scene) from Roger Corman's 1963 film, THE TERROR. The clip then ends, revealing a screening room occupied by aging horror star Byron Orlok (Karloff, extremely moving here), filmmaker Sammy Michaels (played by director Bogdanovich), and some film executives. Orlok informs them that he's had enough of horror films and plans to return to his home in England. He is aware that his films no longer frighten people and that the public is only affected by the horrors in the headlines, stating, "The world belongs to the young. Make way for them. Let them have it. I am an anachronism." Meanwhile, in a gun shop across the street, a clean-cut young man, Bobby Thompson (Tim O'Kelly), adds a high-powered rifle to the already huge arsenal of weapons stashed in his car trunk. Thompson begins a bloody rampage, first murdering his wife, then sniping at innocent drivers from a tower near a highway. TARGETS' brilliant finale, set at a drive-in premiere of the latest Orlok opus, puts both of these horrors—the movieland fiction of Orlok and the real-life danger of Thompson—up on the screen together. Down below, the audience screams in fright, not at Orlok but at Thompson, whose rifle shots are picking them off one by one. TARGETS is an insightful comment on the changing state of the horror film: Whereas Karloff's films concerned gruesome monsters with frightening physical attributes, TARGETS is about—to use Bogdanovich's phrase—"the ghouls next door," the all-American killers who are all the more frightening because the deformities exist *inside* their heads.

TARNISHED ANGELS, THE

1957 91m bw ★★★★
Drama /A
Universal

Rock Hudson (*Burke Devlin*), Robert Stack (*Roger Shumann*), Dorothy Malone (*LaVerne Shumann*), Jack Carson (*Jiggs*), Robert Middleton (*Matt Ord*), Alan Reed (*Col. Fineman*), Alexander Lockwood (*Sam Hagood*), Christopher Olsen (*Jack Shumann*), Bob Wilke (*Hank*), Troy Donahue (*Frank Burnham*)

p, Albert Zugsmith; d, Douglas Sirk; w, George Zuckerman (based on the novel *Pylon* by William Faulkner); ph, Irving Glassberg (Cinemascope); ed, Russell Schoengarth; m, Frank Skinner; art d, Alexander Golitzen, Alfred Sweeney; fx, Clifford Stine; cos, Bill Thomas

This is, perhaps, the best-ever adaptation of a Faulkner novel for the screen, directed with passion and perception by Sirk. The underrated director draws excellent portrayals from Hudson (who had come a long way as an actor by this point), Stack, Malone, and Carson in an authentic and stimulating Depression-era drama of racing pilots and daredevil exploits. Stack arrives in New Orleans in 1932 with his barnstorming troupe, his wife Malone, his son, Olsen, and his loyal-unto-death mechanic, Carson. They have arrived to participate in an air show and race, with Stack hoping to win the big prize money. His plane is a relic from WWI days, however, and he has burned it out across America. His sexy wife produces some profit for the gypsies of the air by wing-walking and then parachuting to earth, wearing a dress, of course, so that the updraft will blow her skirt skyward. Hudson, an idealistic reporter for one of the local newspapers, is assigned to write some features about the air show, so he interviews Stack and his family, intrigued by their seemingly irresponsible lifestyle. As he comes to know these people, his initial sarcastic attitude toward them changes to one of respect. Stack had been a famous ace during WWI, and he cannot bear to be on the ground, having fallen in love with airplanes as a child. During his early barnstorming days, he met and fell in love with Malone, who went off into the sky with him, staying with him ever since. Stack is full of idealism, but he forsakes his scruples to obtain the use of a new, experimental airplane when his own plane breaks down completely. Middleton, a wealthy, dirty old man who lusts after Malone, gives the plane to Stack to race in the air show, but it is understood that Stack will send his wife to him as partial payment for the plane. Malone goes to Middleton, but then

runs away from him. Stack, meanwhile, proves himself master of the air until his plane develops a problem while turning the last pylon to win the race.

The acting is first-rate here, and the script is outstanding, full of wit, black humor, and occasional fine poetic monologues, especially the lines delivered by Stack when he wistfully looks back upon WWI and those of Hudson when he returns drunk to his newspaper and describes the lives of the nomads of the air. Sirk does a marvelous job with his action scenes, all of which appear realistic. Faulkner saw this film and considered it the best picture ever made of his work. The author based much of his story on the exploits of his own brother, Dean Faulkner, who was a barnstorming pilot in the early 1930s.

TARZAN, THE APE MAN

1932 99m bw ★★★★
Adventure/Romance
MGM

Johnny Weissmuller (*Tarzan*), Neil Hamilton (*Harry Holt*), Maureen O'Sullivan (*Jane Parker*), C. Aubrey Smith (*James Parker*), Doris Lloyd (*Mrs. Cutten*), Forrester Harvey (*Beamish*), Ivory Williams (*Riano*), Cheta the Chimp

p, Irving Thalberg; d, W.S. Van Dyke, II; w, Cyril Hume, Ivor Novello (based on the characters created by Edgar Rice Burroughs); ph, Harold Rosson, Clyde De Vinna; ed, Ben Lewis, Tom Held; art d, Cedric Gibbons

The original swinger, with the original call of the wild. A legend was born when MGM cast Johnny Weissmuller, a 28-year-old Olympic swimming champion, as Tarzan in this film. The Edgar Rice Burroughs character had been popular in silent films, but this was the first sound version. Jane Parker (Maureen O'Sullivan), her father (C. Aubrey Smith), and her boyfriend (Neil Hamilton) venture into the African wilds in search of the ivory-laden Elephant's Graveyard and experience great danger in the process. Fears are heightened when Tarzan's jungle yell is heard, and before long, Jane is screaming and kicking as Tarzan carries her into the treetops. Her father and suitor threaten to shoot Tarzan, but after she is released, Jane defends the ape-man with whom she is falling in love. She is soon swinging through the trees under his arm, clowning around with the captivating chimp Cheta, and taking swims with Tarzan. Their happiness is threatened, however, when they are captured by pygmies and lowered into a pit with a giant ape.

The first of six MGM Weissmuller-O'Sullivan "Tarzan" adventures, TARZAN, THE APE MAN suffers in technological comparison with today's Steven Spielbergian jungle adventures, but still has enough thrills to put most modern films to shame. The near-nonstop excitement holds up wonderfully, making this one of Hollywood's most memorable adventure films. And the two leads, through countless casting calls, have never been beaten. Okay, Bo Derek, you can clean the cage now.

TASTE OF HONEY, A

1962 100m bw ★★★★★
Drama /18
Woodfall (U.K.)

Dora Bryan (*Helen*), Rita Tushingham (*Jo*), Robert Stephens (*Peter*), Murray Melvin (*Geoffrey*), Paul Danquah (*Jimmy*), David Boliver (*Bert*), Moira Kaye (*Doris*), Herbert Smith (*Shoe Shop Proprietor*), Valerie Scarden (*Woman in Shoe Shop*), Rosalie Scase (*Nurse*)

p, Tony Richardson; d, Tony Richardson; w, Shelagh Delaney, Tony Richardson (based on the play by Delaney); ph, Walter Lassally; ed, Anthony Gibbs; m, John Addison; art d, Ralph Brinton; cos, Sophie Harris

A taste of the British "Kitchen Sink" school at its best. Honest depiction of life in the British working class with an offbeat treatment, superb acting, realistic direction, and a complex script that sheds light on the plight of these people. What could have been a sordid story takes on a fresh glow as we are plunged into the life and times of Tushingham, a 17-year-old who lives with her promiscuous, alcoholic mother, Bryan, in various furnished rooms (which are underwritten by whomever Bryan is sleeping with at the moment). Tushingham is gawky, not terribly attractive, and desperate to be held. She gets no love whatsoever from Bryan. Bryan's current lover is Stephens, who has no use or time for the illegitimate Tushingham. While Bryan and Stephens do their thing on a short holiday in the seaside town of Blackpool, Tushingham wanders around the docks and meets Danquah, a black sailor on a brief shore leave. When she realizes that she is a thorn in the side of Bryan and Stephens, she spends the night with Danquah, who is sailing off the next morning. Tushingham arrives home and learns that Stephens and Bryan have impulsively married; she is really a fifth wheel now. Bryan moves in with Stephens, leaving Tushingham alone to take a room of her own. She secures employment in a shoe store and meets Melvin, a gentle and kind homosexual who needs a place to stay. The price of a flat is too much for Tushingham alone, so she allows him to be her platonic roommate. Melvin (repeating the role he played in the successful London production of the play) is as lonely as Tushingham, and the two find perfect company with each other. Tushingham soon realizes that she's carrying Danquah's child. Melvin is elated at the thought of the baby and plunges himself into the surrogate role that Bryan should be playing. He knits baby clothes, tidies up the residence to await the birth of the child—all of the things that a devoted husband would do—and even offers to marry Tushingham so the unborn child will have a name. Tushingham declines and becomes increasingly depressed. Melvin is worried about her condition and tells Bryan what's happening, but Bryan couldn't care less—until Stephens abandons her. With no place else to go, Bryan moves in with Melvin and Tushingham. It isn't long before the loud and vicious Bryan asserts herself, though, and problems begin anew.

The movie was shot for a pittance on location in Blackpool and on the Salford docks. Delaney was only 19 when she wrote the play, which had a long run in the West End as well as on Broadway after first trying out at Stratford-upon-Avon in May 1958. Tushingham had been a backstage worker and did a bit in Arnold Wesker's play "The Kitchen" at Liverpool Rep before she answered an ad, walked in, auditioned, and won this plum role. Bryan had spent most of her career as a comedienne in movies since she began in ODD MAN OUT. Casting her here was an inspired choice as she showed her scope. If you have a sharp ear, you may be able to recognize Johnny Dankworth's theme from SATURDAY NIGHT AND SUNDAY MORNING, which was uncredited. Richardson coproduced that film with Harry Saltzman, so it can be assumed he had permission for the tune's use. The hit song "A Taste of Honey" had nothing to do with this film. It was written by Ric Marlow and Bobby Scott and traded on the success of the movie, which won Cannes Film Festival awards for Melvin and Tushingham as well as British Film Academy Awards for Best Picture, Best Actress (Bryan), Best Screenplay (Delaney and Richardson), and Most Promising

Actress (Tushingham). Poignant, funny, moody, and never maudlin, it's a picture that haunts the memory.

TAXI BLUES
1991 110m c   ★★★½
Drama
Marin Karmitz Productions/Lenfilm Studios/Ask Eurofilm/La Sept   (France/U.S.S.R)

Pyotr Nikolajevitch Mamonov (Liocha), Piotr Zaitchenko (Schlikov), Vladimir Kachpour (Old Netchiporenko), Natalia Koliakanova (Christina), Hal Singer (Himself), Elena Saphonva (Nina—Liocha's Wife), Serguei Gazarov (Administrator), Evgueni Gortchakov (Bald Musician in the Taxi), Dimitri Prigov (Writer Typing in the Train), Igor Zolotovitsky (Petiountchik)

p, Marin Karmitz; d, Pavel Lounguine; w, Pavel Lounguine; ph, Denis Evstigneef; ed, Elizabeth Guido; m, Vladimir Chekassine; art d, Valery Yourkevitch; cos, Natalia Dianova

The precedent-shattering TAXI BLUES, helmed by screenwriter-turned-director Pavel Lounguine, is a wrenching, prolonged study in impotence and frustration.

Schlikov (Pyotr Zaitchenko) is a solidly working-class Russian taxi driver, racist and largely friendless, with the burly build of a bully. Liocha (Piotr Nikolajevitch Mamonov) is a flamboyant, self-destructive Jewish jazz musician; an emaciated, self-pitying alcoholic whose wife, Nina (Elena Saphonva), has finally thrown him out. When Liocha stiffs Schlikov for a 70-ruble fare one drunken evening, Schlikov tracks him down, beats him up and takes his saxophone. However, Schlikov is sufficiently intrigued by Liocha to offer him vodka and a bed in his flat—much to the anger of Schlikov's neighbor, the rabidly anti-Semitic Netchiporenko (Vladimir Kachpour). Liocha does little to help matters when he inadvertently floods Schlikov's apartment one morning.

To help Liocha pay off his debt, Schlikov sells off the musician's Western clothes on the black market and finds him menial work in the taxi depot. An altruistic Russian, Schlikov is really seeking to save Liocha's soul and he does, in fact, nurse the other man through an eventual breakdown. But Liocha rebels all the way, and their love-hate relationship grows ever more problematic, particularly when Schlikov's sometime girlfriend Christina (Natalia Koliakanova) starts falling for Liocha.

Shot in Moscow over a four-month period in 1989, with the flowering of *perestroika* already showing signs of blight and the crumbling of the Soviet Union soon to come, TAXI BLUES proved a rude shock to the struggling Russian film establishment. A French-Soviet co-production, the movie was financed by French coin (with the actors and technicians making double or triple their usual salaries) raised by the pan-European producer Marin Karmitz, who has produced often-controversial films for Godard, Chabrol, Resnais, Skolimowski, the Taviani brothers, Bellocchio, Loach and Scorsese.

Lounguine, who also wrote the screenplay, has described his style here as "extremist" and the story as autobiographical. The film has some of the narrative looseness of the French New Wave, as well as plenty of that movement's characteristic hand-held camerawork. Although Lounguine has termed it a comedy, Westerners will find it only occasionally amusing. To its credit, the film, styled mostly as a two-character study, never falters into an "Odd Couple"-style formula. Both characters, as superbly played by Zaitchenko and Mamonov (whom Lounguine calls "the oldest Russian rock star, mythical in Moscow for his excesses") are equally disagreeable, making audience identification nearly impossible. The excesses of both are delineated in long, boisterous, often ugly scenes (including a rape) that seem to verge on escaping directorial control.

Thankfully, there is absolutely no trace of sentimentality. The ultra-realistic tone and style (aided immensely by the importation of French sound engineers to record direct sound, as opposed to the customary Soviet and Italian practice of post-dubbing) results in a not easily forgettable catalogue of pre-dissolution Soviet social and moral ills. Lounguine shows us a Moscow beset by urban decay and bureaucratic corruption, rampant alcoholism and sexism, a virulent anti-Semitism, and a flourishing black market that trades in anything and everything.

TAXI DRIVER

1976   112m   c   ★★★★★
Drama   R/18
Bill-Phillips

Robert De Niro *(Travis Bickle)*, Cybill Shepherd *(Betsy)*, Jodie Foster *(Iris Steensman)*, Peter Boyle *(Wizard)*, Harvey Keitel *(Sport)*, Albert Brooks *(Tom)*, Leonard Harris *(Charles Palantine)*, Martin Scorsese *(Passenger)*, Diahnne Abbott *(Concession Girl)*, Frank Adu *(Angry Black Man)*

p, Michael Phillips, Julia Phillips; d, Martin Scorsese; w, Paul Schrader; ph, Michael Chapman (Panavision, Metrocolor); ed, Marcia Lucas, Tom Rolf, Melvin Shapiro; m, Bernard Herrmann; art d, Charles Rosen; fx, Dick Smith, Tony Parmalee; cos, Ruth Morley

A landmark of 70s American cinema that announced to the world the arrival of director Martin Scorsese, screenwriter Paul Schrader and star Robert De Niro. Though critics remain divided over the ultimate merits of TAXI DRIVER, it is an undeniably brilliant, nightmarish portrait of one man's personal hell—i.e. New York City.

TAXI DRIVER is an alarmingly plausible character study of Vietnam vet Travis Bickle (De Niro), an alienated insomniac who spends his nights driving a New York cab. Much of what we see of the city is viewed through his windshield. After long night shifts, he still can't sleep and spends hours in porno theatres or alone in his squalid room. He has nothing but contempt for the "scum" he sees all around him and prophesies that someday a big rain will come and clean all the filth from the streets. Travis' world brightens a little when he sees a beautiful blonde woman, Betsy (Cybill Shepherd), in the campaign offices of presidential candidate Charles Palantine (Leonard Harris). He quickly develops a crush on her, and she finds him intriguing enough to agree to go out with him. When he takes her, though, to a porn film (the only type of movie he knows) she walks out in disgust. An even more frustrated Travis then meets Iris (Jodie Foster), a 12-year-old runaway turned prostitute who is managed by a long-haired pimp known as Sport (Harvey Keitel). Travis becomes obsessed with "rescuing" Iris from her situation, turning himself into a one-man killing machine as he prepares for a bloody crusade which he believes will put the world to rights.

TAXI DRIVER is a fevered, paranoid take on the perils of contemporary urban life. Scorsese paints a picture of New York City with stark, unforgettable images—steaming sewers, rainslicked streets, glaring neon lights—that together constitute a vision of hell on earth. All this is helped immensely by Bernard Herrmann's visceral score (his last; he passed away a day after its completion), and Michael Chapman's grainy cinematography. The climactic killing sequence is a sustained, hallucinatory triumph of shot composition and editing—as stomach-churning as it is technically astonishing. (Much of the negative critical reaction to the film focused on Scorsese's moral stance toward this

bloodbath, claiming—short-sightedly—that it is portrayed as a positive, cleansing ritual that redeems Travis' character. TAXI DRIVER is far more ironic and multi-layered than such an interpretation suggests.)

De Niro's mesmerizing performance is central to the film's success. He appears in nearly every scene and we see nearly everything through his skewed vision. He commands the screen and evokes such power and authority—even during Travis's meekest moments—that we are inexorably drawn into his life. Shepherd is highly effective as the Hitchcockian icy blonde, and the young Jodie Foster effortlessly conveys both youthful innocence and a street-smart, wise-beyond-her-years quality. Her breakfast scene with De Niro is riveting. In smaller roles, Boyle is great fun as an eccentric cabbie; comedian/filmmaker Albert Brooks plays Shepherd's somewhat nerdy co-worker; and Harvey Keitel makes a memorably sleazy Sport.

TAXI DRIVER won the Golden Palm at the Cannes Film Festival, and Scorsese and De Niro were honored as Best Director and Best Actor by the New York Film Critics. The film was Oscar-nominated for Best Picture (losing to ROCKY), Best Actor (De Niro), Best Supporting Actress (Foster) and Best Musical Score.

TAXING WOMAN, A
(MARUSA NO ONNA)
1988   127m   c   ★★★½
Comedy   /18
Itami/New Century   (Japan)

Nobuko Miyamoto *(Ryoko Itakura, Tax Inspector)*, Tsutomu Yamazaki *(Hideki Gondo)*, Masahiko Tsugawa *(Assistant Chief Inspector Hanamura)*, Hideo Murota *(Ishii, Motel President)*, Shuji Otaki *(Tsuyuguchi, Tax Office Manager)*, Daisuke Yamashita *(Taro Gondo)*, Shinsuke Ashida, Keiju Kobayashi, Mariko Okada, Kiriko Shimizu

p, Yasushi Tamaoki, Seigo Hosogoe; d, Juzo Itami; w, Juzo Itami; ph, Yonezo Maeda; ed, Akira Suzuki; m, Toshiyuki Honda

Continuing his series of hilariously incisive examinations of modern Japanese culture (burial rites in THE FUNERAL, food in TAMPOPO), director Juzo Itami here turns his gaze on that most sacred of contemporary obsessions—money. Part social satire, part procedural drama, A TAXING WOMAN takes its title from spunky, dedicated tax agent Ryoko Itakura (wonderfully acted by Nobuko Miyamoto, Itami's wife), who uses her demure looks to lull tax cheats into false confidence before she lowers the boom. Most of the film details her determined attempt to get the goods on suave "adult motel" tycoon Hideki Gondo (Tsutomu Yamazaki), who launders his money through the *yakuza* (gangsters), phony corporations, real estate, and his mistress. He's sharp, but Ryoko's sharper; and by the end, not only are the interests of the Japanese Tax Office served, but love (though unrequited) makes an appearance. Although not as out-and-out loopy as TAMPOPO, Itami's portrait of money-mad Japanese society has a biting satiric edge. The boundless energy of the Japanese seems to be what really fascinates the director, who is well on his way to becoming the leading chronicler of life in modern-day Japan. His 1988 sequel to this film, A TAXING WOMAN'S RETURN, is less satisfying than the original.

TEA AND SYMPATHY
1956   122m   c   ★★★½
Drama   /X
MGM

Deborah Kerr *(Laura Reynolds)*, John Kerr *(Tom Robinson Lee)*, Leif Erickson *(Bill Reynolds)*, Edward Andrews *(Herb Lee)*, Darryl Hickman *(Al)*, Norma Crane *(Ellie Martin)*, Dean Jones *(Ollie)*, Jacqueline de Wit *(Lilly Sears)*, Tom Laughlin *(Ralph)*, Ralph Votrian *(Steve)*

p, Pandro S. Berman; d, Vincente Minnelli; w, Robert Anderson (based on the play by Anderson); ph, John Alton (CinemaScope, Metrocolor); ed, Ferris Webster; m, Adolph Deutsch; art d, William A. Horning, Edward Carfagno; cos, Helen Rose

Watered-down version of a landmark Broadway play that dealt with alleged homosexuality and an older woman's desire to prove the machismo of the suspect young man.

John Kerr is a married writer with three children who returns to his exclusive prep school in New England for a reunion. In a flashback to his troubled years at the school, we see that he is inept at every sport except tennis (which is regarded as a sissy pastime), which sets him apart from the other boys. He wears his hair long and spends his off-hours in romantic pastimes which the other students scorn. His roommate is Hickman, who is slightly embarrassed by Kerr's behavior but defends him to the others. Kerr's housemaster is big, hearty Erickson, a smiling boor who emphasizes masculine games for his charges. Erickson is in league with Andrews, Kerr's father, who shares the housemaster's belief that the boy should have his hair cut and make an attempt to get into the mainstream of the school's activities. Kerr is shunned by almost everyone at the school except Hickman and Erickson's wife, played by Deborah Kerr. She is a sensitive woman who realizes that this lad is in trouble. (He reminds her of her late first husband, a boy who volunteered for the Army during WWII in order to show everyone that he was fearless and left her widowed.) Gradually, her feelings for the boy deepen into something more than maternal concern.

The two Kerrs and Erickson all effectively reprised the roles they had played in the stage version, which opened in September, 1953, and ran for more than 700 performances. Since Anderson himself wrote the screenplay (with the censors looking over his shoulder), any bowdlerization must be attributed to him. Minnelli's direction is true to the material.

TEAHOUSE OF THE AUGUST MOON, THE

1956 123m c   ★★★★
Comedy   /U
MGM

Marlon Brando *(Sakini)*, Glenn Ford *(Capt. Fisby)*, Machiko Kyo *(Lotus Blossom)*, Eddie Albert *(Capt. McLean)*, Paul Ford *(Col. Purdy)*, Jun Negami *(Mr. Seiko)*, Nijiko Kiyokawa *(Miss Higa Jiga)*, Mitsuko Sawamura *(Little Girl)*, Harry Morgan *(Sgt. Gregovich)*, Shichizo Takeda *(Ancient Man)*

p, Jack Cummings; d, Daniel Mann; w, John Patrick (based on the novel by Vern J. Sneider and the play by Patrick); ph, John Alton (CinemaScope, Metrocolor); ed, Harold F. Kress; m, Saul Chaplin; art d, William A. Horning, Eddie Imazu; chor, Masaya Fujima

This charming adaptation of the novel and play shows that Brando has a flair for comedy. The picture opens with the same prologue seen on the Broadway stage (done there by David Wayne). Brando is the Okinawan who introduces himself and the other players and asserts with pride that Okinawa has the honor of being the most subjugated place in history. It has been overrun by the Chinese and the Japanese and, now, the Americans. The man in charge of the island is Paul Ford (who replaced Louis Calhern when the veteran actor had a fatal heart attack on location in Japan), a befuddled colonel in command of the occupation troops who have no understanding of the Okinawans. Captain Glenn Ford (no relation) arrives, and Paul Ford assigns him to bring civilization to a small village. With Brando as his official interpreter, Glenn Ford is supposed to start a women's club, build a schoolhouse, and establish democracy according to the plan sent out from Washington. Glenn Ford is a pleasant officer with a history of screwing up, so he's been exiled to Okinawa, where his superiors hope he will do no further damage. The small village doesn't care much for a school. What they desire most is a teahouse and a number of geishas to staff it. As hard as Glenn Ford tries to establish himself as a fair-but-firm officer, Brando's wily ways undo his plans. The locals bring various presents to Glenn Ford to curry favor with him. The most prominent of these gifts is Kyo. When he says he cannot accept a human being as a gift, Brando explains that to refuse would be a great loss of face for the village. If that happens, they are liable to revolt. The longer he stays, the more easily he is manipulated by Brando. Back at HQ, Paul Ford has begun to suspect something is awry because the messages coming in from the village are strangely nonspecific. After a particularly confusing phone call from Glenn Ford, the colonel orders psychiatrist Albert to the village to examine the man. Albert's hobby is growing organic foods, and, once in the village, he soon falls prey to the relaxed lifestyle and enlists the locals in doing his kind of farming. After an abortive attempt to sell local crafts as souvenirs, Glenn Ford learns that the villagers brew a very potent brandy from sweet potatoes. He jumps at the opportunity and gets the villagers working. Soon, the phone is ringing off the hook with orders for the brandy from various bases on Okinawa. The teahouse is completed, and a great celebration is about to take place. All is going well until Paul Ford arrives. No sooner does he see the teahouse than he orders Glenn Ford arrested, the teahouse razed, and the stills demolished. The colonel wonders why there is no democracy and how this poor village has been managing to have such a good lifestyle when it seems to have no industry to speak of. When he sends in his report, however, Washington is delighted that the Okinawans have shown such spunk and have embraced the recovery program. Paul Ford is beside himself, but Brando explains that the stills have only been hidden and that the teahouse was taken apart in such a manner that it can be rebuilt in no time. Once that's done, Brando tells the audience in an epilogue that the movie is over.

Paul Ford had played the role on Broadway more than 1,000 times and yet managed to bring a freshness to it for the screen. He was later to do the same kind of role on TV's "You'll Never Get Rich" when he played Sgt. Bilko's (Phil Silvers) commanding officer. Kyo spoke no English when she accepted the role. She had previously been seen in GATE OF HELL and RASHOMON. The music was mostly Okinawan and Japanese, and that lent authenticity to the affair. Although David Wayne was a marvel in the play (which won the Tony as Best Play that year), he was not a movie star, so when Brando indicated he wanted the part, he got it. Brando does one of his best roles here, submerging his own powerful personality. He spent months learning the proper way to move like an Asian. Some of the humor is labored, and Glenn Ford overplays a bit, but the ultimate result is a charming, though somewhat talky, movie that elevates whimsy to a new high.

TEMPEST

1982 140m c   ★★
Comedy/Drama   PG/15
Columbia

John Cassavetes *(Phillip)*, Gena Rowlands *(Antonia)*, Susan Sarandon *(Aretha)*, Vittorio Gassman *(Alonzo)*, Raul Julia *(Kalibanos)*, Molly Ringwald *(Miranda)*, Sam Robards *(Freddy)*, Paul Stewart *(Phillip's Father)*, Jackie Gayle *(Trinc)*, Anthony Holland *(Sebastian)*

p, Paul Mazursky; d, Paul Mazursky; w, Paul Mazursky, Leon Capetanos (based on the play "The Tempest" by William Shakespeare); ph, Don McAlpine (Metrocolor); ed, Donn Cambern; m, Stomu Yamashta; prod d, Pato Guzman; art d, Paul Eads, Gianni Quaranta; fx, Bran Ferren; chor, Gino Landi; cos, Albert Wolsky

A disappointing modernistic fantasy-drama, TEMPEST uses Shakespeare's comedy as a jumping-off point and then goes off into never-never land. Phillip (John Cassavetes), an architect married to Antonia (Gena Rowlands), an actress, takes their daughter, Miranda (Molly Ringwald in her debut), to Greece where he meets a singer, Aretha (Susan Sarandon). The three move to a bleak Greek island where they encounter a hermit, Kalibanos (Raul Julia). All the people in Phillip's life—Antonia, her producer (Paul Mazursky), casino owner Alfonso (Vittorio Gassman), his son (Sam Robards), as well as a few others—land on the island when their boat is shipwrecked.

The film roams all over the place emotionally and never settles into being much of anything. Apart from a few funny moments, the whole idea is pretentious and overloaded with intellectualism. It goes a long way around to show that having a mid-life crisis is tough. For its $13 million budget, the movie looks excellent, however. Australian cinematographer Donald McAlpine gave it better treatment than it deserved. Comedian Jackie Gayle makes an appearance and shows that he's not just another funny face. The best part of the movie is the storm sequence, but audiences could get the same effect by watching Midwestern tornadoes on the TV news.

10

1979 122m c ★★★
Comedy R/18
Orion

Dudley Moore *(George)*, Julie Andrews *(Sam)*, Bo Derek *(Jenny)*, Robert Webber *(Hugh)*, Dee Wallace Stone *(Mary Lewis)*, Sam Jones *(David)*, Brian Dennehy *(Bartender)*, Max Showalter *(Reverend)*, Rad Daly *(Josh)*, Nedra Volz *(Mrs. Kissel)*

p, Blake Edwards, Tony Adams; d, Blake Edwards; w, Blake Edwards; ph, Frank Stanley (Panavision, Metrocolor); ed, Ralph E. Winters; m, Henry Mancini; prod d, Rodger Maus; fx, Fred Cramer; cos, Patricia Edwards

A very funny if somewhat retrograde film that sent Dudley Moore's career soaring briefly, while making some telling points about the problems of middle age. Moore is a successful songwriter with four Oscars to his name. He lives in a huge southern California home, drives a Rolls, and is dissatisfied with his life. He is turning 42 and spending too much time ogling the gorgeous young women who walk the Los Angeles streets. He watches his neighbor through a telescope and sees that the man has a bevy of nude women surrounding him. The sense that life is passing him by gnaws at Moore's innards. This distresses his girlfriend, Andrews, who adores him and whose singing voice has been the reason for much of his success. Moore's partner, Webber, is having his own crisis because he is gay and, as he ages, can no longer attract the same young men he has been accustomed to cavorting with. Suffering from a combination of ennui and self-doubt, Moore sees a limousine go past in his ritzy neighborhood. In it is Derek, on her way to get married to Jones at a

Beverly Hills church. This is the woman of Moore's dreams, whom he rates "11" on a scale of one to 10. Moore goes to the church (banging up his Rolls in the process), learns Derek's identity, and finds out where she and Jones are honeymooning in Mexico. Moore flies to the resort at Las Hadas and drowns his sorrows at the bar, where a willing Dennehy keeps pouring him drinks. Without hearing Derek say a word, Moore is hopelessly in love with her, peeping at her glorious body as she romps on the beach with Jones. His fantasies run riot, and he imagines all sorts of experiences with Derek. Then he gets his chance. Jones falls asleep on a surfboard and is drifting out to sea. Moore rents a boat, goes after Jones, and saves the man's life. His deed makes him famous, newspapers herald his bravery and, most importantly, he gets to meet Derek. Jones is redder than a matador's cape and must spend some time in the local hospital to recover. Thankful for Moore's derring-do, Derek invites him to her room. She confesses that she has been watching him and thinks him very sexy "for an older man." After a dinner together, Derek takes Moore to her room again and proceeds to make a pass at him. The traditional-minded Moore can't handle her directness. He's looking for romance, soft lights, the chase. Derek just wants sex. Their encounter is a hilarious fumbling fiasco, with Ravel's "Bolero" pounding in the background. But a traditional happy ending is just waiting in the wings.

Derek enjoyed brief stardom on the basis her part in this film but has failed to achieve any further success, despite her work in several movies that might have been hits had they been handled by anyone but her indulgent director husband, John Derek. Several standout comedy bits include Moore getting drunk, being stung on the nose by a bee, and burning his feet on the hot beach sand. Moore also played the piano (which he does well) in the band that provided the background music. Mancini and Robert Wells's song "It's Easy to Say" was nominated for an Oscar. The movie made about $40 million, thus qualifying it as the "sleeper" of 1979. Since then, Moore has made one disaster after another, evidently paying more attention to the fees than to the scripts. Webber plays his role with supreme understatement. Casting Moore opposite Andrews was a mistake both because she towers above him and because there's no chemistry between them. The frank treatment of sexual themes means this is not for kids.

TEN COMMANDMENTS, THE

1956 219m c ★★★★½
Religious /U
Paramount

Charlton Heston *(Moses)*, Yul Brynner *(Rameses)*, Anne Baxter *(Nefretiri)*, Edward G. Robinson *(Dathan)*, Yvonne De Carlo *(Sephora)*, Debra Paget *(Lilia)*, John Derek *(Joshua)*, Cedric Hardwicke *(Sethi)*, Nina Foch *(Bithiah)*, Martha Scott *(Yochabel)*

p, Cecil B. DeMille; d, Cecil B. DeMille; w, Aeneas MacKenzie, Jesse Lasky, Jr., Jack Gariss, Fredric M. Frank (based on the novels *The Prince of Egypt* by Dorothy Clarke Wilson, *Pillar of Fire* by the Rev. J.H. Ingraham, and *On Eagle's Wings* by the Rev. G.E. Southon, and in accordance with the Bible, the ancient texts of Josephus, Eusebius, Philo, and The Midrash); ph, Loyal Griggs, John F. Warren, W. Wallace Kelley, Peverell Marley (VistaVision, Technicolor); ed, Anne Bauchens; m, Elmer Bernstein; art d, Hal Pereira, Walter Tyler, Albert Nozala; fx, John P. Fulton; chor, LeRoy Prinz, Ruth Godfrey; cos, Edith Head, Ralph Jester, John Jensen, Dorothy Jeakins, Arnold Friberg

A great big wallow, sublime hootchy-kootchy hokum, peppered with lightning that does automatic writing and an unsurpassed homage to the joys of jello. Director-producer Cecil B. DeMille ended his great career with this gigantic production, packed with enormous crowd scenes, lavish spectacles, and wide-screen special effects orchestrated with dazzling brilliance.

DeMille's Exodus (a tale he had also filmed in 1923) opens as the Egyptian pharaoh is told that the deliverer of the enslaved Hebrews will soon be born. He orders the slaughter of all newborn Jewish males, but one is placed on a basket in the Nile, found by the pharaoh's sister, and brought up as her own. Years pass and the now-adult Moses (Charlton Heston) has become a beloved prince, much to the chagrin of Rameses (Yul Brynner), the pharaoh's son. When Moses' lineage is revealed, he is banished into the desert, but after several peaceful years, he learns of his destiny in his encounter with the burning bush. The film then depicts his return and his confrontation with Rameses II, the mass exodus of the Hebrews, Moses' parting of the Red Sea, his receipt of the Ten Commandments, the Jews' worship of the idolatrous Golden Calf, and their 40 years of wandering as punishment. Finally, the aged Moses watches Joshua lead his people into the Promised Land.

DeMille tells the biblical story on a scale no other filmmaker ever attempted, yet the star cast cannot be overwhelmed by the epic production, even if the orgy did take three weeks to film. The exodus itself is truly moving, and Hardwicke lends a convincing old Pharaoh. Heston's stalwart prophet really does look like Michelangelo's Moses—how can he miss? Brynner and Baxter supply velvet and villainy, Robinson and Vincent Price are accomplished camps, and Paget and DeCarlo contribute beautous support. THE TEN COMMANDMENTS eventually grossed over $80 million, enjoying several re-releases, and DeMille's vision remains a powerful one, a testament to his inestimable talent as the master of epic vulgarity and self-justified righteousness.

10 RILLINGTON PLACE

1971 111m c   ★★★½
Crime   GP/15
Genesis/Filmways/Columbia   (U.K.)

Richard Attenborough (John Reginald Christie), Judy Geeson (Beryl Evans), John Hurt (Timothy John Evans), Pat Heywood (Mrs. Ethel Christie), Isobel Black (Alice), Miss Riley (Baby Geraldine), Phyllis McMahon (Muriel Eady), Ray Barron (Workman Willis), Douglas Blackwell (Workman Jones), Gabrielle Daye (Mrs. Lynch)

p, Martin Ransohoff, Leslie Linder; d, Richard Fleischer; w, Clive Exton (based on the book by Ludovic Kennedy); ph, Denys Coop (Eastmancolor); ed, Ernest Walter; m, John Dankworth; art d, Maurice Carter

Richard Attenborough portrays murderer John Reginald Christie, whose actions led to the hanging of an innocent man and the eventual abolition of capital punishment in Britain. The film picks up in 1944 as Christie coaxes a young lady into his flat, then rapes and strangles her, burying the body in his back yard. Several years later, Timothy John Evans (Hurt) and wife Beryl (Geeson), along with their baby daughter, move into the building and are charmed by Christie, who claims all sorts of medical and legal knowledge. When Beryl learns she is pregnant, the young couple allows Christie to perform an abortion. Instead of performing an abortion Christie rapes and murders Beryl, then tells Timothy his wife died during the operation and suggests he go away and leave their daughter in his care. The none-too-bright Timothy does as he is told, and that same night Christie kills his daughter. Eventually Timothy goes to the police and confesses to murdering Beryl. At his trial he relates the facts but is con-

demned by perjured testimony from Christie and hanged. Christie goes on to take the lives of several other victims, including his own wife, before justice is served.

Based on the historical Christie-Evans case, this painstakingly accurate film was shot in the building next door to the one where the actual killings took place. After filming was completed, the entire block, now renamed Ruston Close, was razed and council houses were built on the location. Attenborough is excellent as the banal, middle-class killer, and John Hurt is effective as usual as the man too dim to keep himself from being executed for a crime he didn't commit. 10 RILLINGTON STREET is somber and frightening and omits the stylistic flourishes that marred director Richard Fleischer's previous excursion into the world of true crime, THE BOSTON STRANGLER. Fleischer directed two other suspense-filled films that same year, THE LAST RUN and SEE NO EVIL.

TENANT, THE

(LE LOCATAIRE)
1976 124m c   ★★★½
Horror   R/18
Paramount   (France)

Roman Polanski (Trelkovsky), Isabelle Adjani (Stella), Shelley Winters (Concierge), Melvyn Douglas (Mr. Zy), Jo Van Fleet (Mme. Dioz), Bernard Fresson (Scope), Lila Kedrova (Mme. Gaderian), Claude Dauphin (Husband), Claude Pieplu (Neighbor), Rufus (Badar)

p, Andrew Braunsberg; d, Roman Polanski; w, Roman Polanski, Gerard Brach (based on the novel Le Locataire Chimerique by Roland Topor); ph, Sven Nykvist (Panavision, Eastmancolor); ed, Francoise Bonnot; m, Philippe Sarde; prod d, Pierre Guffroy; art d, Claude Moesching, Albert Rajau; cos, Jacques Schmidt

Roman Polanski's psychological horror film stars Polanski himself as Trelkovsky, a Polish office clerk in Paris. He rents an apartment in a quiet building whose elderly residents seem to feel malevolence toward the new tenant from the start. After he learns that the previous occupant jumped from the apartment window, he visits the dying woman—who is covered head to toe in wrappings—in the hospital, and meets her friend Stella (Isabelle Adjani). The woman suddenly lets out a bloodcurdling scream and dies, an event that forms a bond between Trelkovsky and Stella, who nearly become lovers but drift apart. Meanwhile, Trelkovsky, while experiencing increasing difficulty with his fellow tenants—they complain that he makes noise (though we don't see or hear anything) and threaten to "take steps"—grows steadily more obsessed with uncovering the mystery of the deceased woman and her fate and becomes positive his neighbors are trying to kill him. As the film progresses, however, his paranoia seems less and less justified, and his actions more and more insane.

In many ways, THE TENANT is Polanski's REPULSION (1965) with the director in the Catherine Deneuve role. In both films, a character's vision of the world clashes with "reality" to the point that no sense can be made of either, and in both the conflict leads to violence. We are never really sure that there isn't a plot against Polanski, even though logic suggests he is imagining everything, and this uneasy sense that maybe Polanski's character is right makes the film extremely, scarily effective (it is also surprisingly funny). Technically, THE TENANT is superb, with stunning camerawork by Sven Nykvist, an eerie score by Philippe Sarde, and thoroughly convincing performances from the entire cast.

TENDER MERCIES

1983 89m c ★★★½
Drama PG
EMI

Robert Duvall *(Mac Sledge)*, Tess Harper *(Rosa Lee)*, Betty Buckley *(Dixie)*, Wilford Brimley *(Harry)*, Ellen Barkin *(Sue Anne)*, Allan Hubbard *(Sonny)*, Lenny von Dohlen *(Robert)*, Paul Gleason *(Reporter)*, Michael Crabtree *(Lewis Menefee)*, Norman Bennett *(Rev. Hotchkiss)*

p, Philip S. Hobel, Mary-Ann Hobel, Horton Foote, Robert Duvall; d, Bruce Beresford; w, Horton Foote; ph, Russell Boyd (Movielab Color); ed, William Anderson; m, George Dreyfus; art d, Jeannine Oppewall; chor, Nick Felix; cos, Elizabeth McBride

This low-key drama set in Texas is one of the continuing stories of screenwriter Horton Foote's life in the hinterlands. Robert Duvall, who won an Oscar for his performance, is Mac Sledge, a down-and-out singer who has recently broken up with his wife, Dixie (Betty Buckley), also a country singer. Mac gets rip-roaring drunk and wakes up in a motel-gas-station owned by a religious widow, Rosa Lee (Tess Harper), with a young son (Allan Hubbard). Rosa offers Mac a job, so he stays on, and the two fall in love. Meanwhile, Dixie and her manager (Wilford Brimley) are lurking in the background, and Mac attempts to patch matters up with her and their daughter (Ellen Barkin). He also tries to make a comeback.

TENDER MERCIES is an episodic gem that offers little in the way of action or melodrama but gets by on fine performances (particularly from Barkin and from Duvall, who does his own singing), atmospheric cinematography, and spare, unglamorous writing. Australian director Bruce Beresford's first American assignment, the film bears interesting comparison with Englishman Michael Apted's COAL MINER'S DAUGHTER (another outsider's vision of the world of country), and with Foote's later, probably superior, THE TRIP TO BOUNTIFUL. Along with Duvall, Foote won an Academy Award for his screenplay, and the picture and Beresford's direction received nominations (both lost to TERMS OF ENDEARMENT). Austin Roberts and Bobby Hart's song "Over You" also garnered a nomination.

TENSION

1949 95m bw ★★★
Thriller /A
MGM

Richard Basehart *(Warren Quimby)*, Audrey Totter *(Claire Quimby)*, Cyd Charisse *(Mary Chanler)*, Barry Sullivan *(Lt. Collier Bonnabel)*, Lloyd Gough *(Barney Deager)*, Tom D'Andrea *(Freddie)*, William Conrad *(Lt. Edgar Gonsales)*, Tito Renaldo *(Narco)*, Philip Van Zandt *(Lt. Schiavone)*, Tommy Walker *(Man at Counter)*

p, Robert Sisk; d, John Berry; w, Allen Rivkin (based on a story by John Klorer); ph, Harry Stradling; ed, Albert Akst; m, Andre Previn; art d, Cedric Gibbons, Leonid Vasian

A tightly controlled, well-developed if slightly bland thriller of infidelity and murder, TENSION opens with a police detective speaking directly to the audience. Everybody has a breaking point, he explains, stretching a rubber band tighter and tighter, until at last it snaps. Like the rubber band, a man can only be stretched so far before he breaks. The story concerns Basehart, a modest pharmacist who is emotionally shattered when he learns that his wife (Totter) is having an affair with Gough. Basehart decides to murder his rival, devising an elaborate plan that necessitates taking a completely new identity in order for the pharmacist to have a legitimate alibi. Under this guise, Basehart

molds the perfect crime. Then he meets Charisse, falls in love with her, and decides not to carry out the killing. But Basehart goes to Gough's beach house anyway, finding himself inexplicably drawn to the place. To his horror, he finds that Gough has been murdered by someone else, and that the alter ego he created is now the prime suspect. Assigned to the case are Sullivan and Conrad, two cops who eventually expose the true killer.

This is decent, workmanlike *film noir*, creating an intriguing story of crime and passion while using the various themes and characterizations of the genre with care and precision. Basehart's essentially good man is driven to the very edge of sanity, spellbound by a cruel, manipulative woman. Totter gives an appropriately evil edge to her character and is well contrasted by Charisse, whose beauty and innocence play nicely against Totter's cold manipulations. Berry's direction from Rivkin's well-detailed script keeps a good command over the material, and the dialogue is sharp and to the point, living up to the promise of the title. The film has all the earmarks of James M. Cain's and Raymond Chandler's influence on the genre, riveting the viewer by building tension admirably.

TENTH VICTIM, THE

(LA DECIMA VITTIMA)
1965 92m c ★★★
Science Fiction /A
Champion/Concordia/Les Films (France/Italy)

Marcello Mastroianni *(Marcello Polletti)*, Ursula Andress *(Caroline Meredith)*, Elsa Martinelli *(Olga)*, Salvo Randone *(Professor)*, Massimo Serato *(Lawyer)*, Evi Rigano *(Victim)*, Milo Quesada *(Rudi)*, Luce Bonifassy *(Lidia)*, Anita Sanders *(Relaxatorium Girl)*, Mickey Knox *(Chet)*

p, Carlo Ponti; d, Elio Petri; w, Elio Petri, Ennio Flaiano, Tonino Guerra, Giorgio Salvioni (based on the on short story "The Seventh Victim" by Robert Sheckley); ph, Gianni Di Venanzo (Technicolor); ed, Ruggero Mastroianni; m, Piero Piccioni; art d, Piero Poletto; chor, Gino Landi; cos, Giulio Coltellacci

A bizarre, pop look at life in the future which stars Mastroianni and Andress as participants in a game of legalized murder known as "Man Hunt," a replacement for violence and war. Andress must kill her tenth victim to achieve the pinnacle of success, and Mastroianni happens to be the chosen one. He also is plotting to kill her, which confuses the situation, especially when they fall in love. Petri creates an eccentric and flamboyant world, with some of his wackier invention including Andress's deadly, double-barreled bra and a trendy nightery called Club Masoch.

TEOREMA

1969 93m c ★★★★
Drama /X
Aetos (Italy)

Terence Stamp *(Visitor)*, Silvana Mangano *(Mother)*, Massimo Girotti *(Father)*, Anne Wiazemsky *(Daughter)*, Laura Betti *(Maid)*, Andres Jose Cruz Soublette *(Son)*, Alfonso Gatto *(Doctor)*, Ninetto Davoli *(Messenger)*, Susanna Pasolini *(Old Peasant)*, Adele Cambria

p, Franco Rossellini, Manolo Bolognini; d, Pier Paolo Pasolini; w, Pier Paolo Pasolini (based on his novel); ph, Giuseppe Ruzzolini (Movielab); ed, Nino; m, Ennio Morricone, Wolfgang Amadeus Mozart; art d, Luciano Puccini; fx, Goffredo Rocchetti; cos, Marcella De Marchis, Roberto Capucci

A heavily symbolic and highly intellectual look at the bourgeois milieu and the effect that a mysterious visitor, Stamp, has on one specific family. Into the life of a prominent Milanese family walks Stamp, an angelic-looking stranger (although Pasolini acknowledges that he may also represent the devil), whose spiritual sexuality touches each member of the household in a different way, elevating each to a certain level of grace. He becomes involved with Mangano, the wife; Girotti, the husband; Wiazemsky, their daughter; Cruz, their son; and Betti, the house-maid. Then one day Stamp leaves as mysteriously as he arrived. The family feels the void, can no longer attain the level of spirituality that Stamp provided, and falls back into the worldli-ness of the bourgeoisie. Mangano tries to recapture that state by wandering the streets and picking up lovers at random; Wiazemsky enters a catatonic trance and completely withdraws from her society; Cruz becomes an artist whose dissatisfaction with his paintings prompts him to urinate on them; and Girotti relinquishes control of his factory to the workers and wanders naked through a vast wasteland. Only Betti, the maid, can survive without Stamp. This is because she, unlike the family that employs her, is from the peasant class and has a naive faith to sustain her—not only in Stamp's divinity but in what he has taught her faith can do. Instead of deteriorating, Betti returns to her village, performs miracles for the peasants, and even levi-tates. For her brilliant performance (the rest of the cast is equally admirable), Betti was awarded the Best Actress prize at the 1968 Venice Film Festival. The film's release, like so many of Pasolini's films, was shrouded in controversy. The left wing of the Italian Catholics gave the film an award for its "mysticism" while the Catholic right unleashed a scathing attack on the picture. According to Pasolini (whose self-analysis is usually more confusing than clarifying): "The point of the film is roughly this: a member of the bourgeoisie, whatever he does, is always wrong. . . anything done by the bourgeoisie, however sincere, profound, and noble it is, is always on the wrong side of the track." Pasolini had hoped to include Orson Welles in the cast, although he didn't make clear whether he would have had Stamp's or Girotti's role. In either case, the mind boggles.

TERMINATOR, THE

1984 108m c   ★★★★
Science Fiction/Thriller   R/18
Hemdale/Pacific Western

Arnold Schwarzenegger *(Terminator)*, Michael Biehn *(Kyle Reese)*, Linda Hamilton *(Sarah Connor)*, Paul Winfield *(Traxler)*, Lance Henriksen *(Vukovich)*, Rick Rossovich *(Matt)*, Bess Motta *(Ginger)*, Earl Boen *(Silberman)*, Dick Miller *(Pawn Shop Clerk)*, Shawn Schepps *(Nancy)*

p, Gale Anne Hurd; d, James Cameron; w, James Cameron, Gale Anne Hurd, William Wisher, Jr.; ph, Adam Greenberg (CFI Color); ed, Mark Goldblatt; m, Brad Fiedel; art d, George Costello; fx, Stan Winston, Gene Warren, Jr., Peter Kleinow; cos, Hillary Wright

Back before Arnold Schwarzenegger's ascendence to his current status as Hollywood's designated Action Hero of choice, hus-band to Kennedys, and buddy of presidents, he was still willing to play villains. As such he made an indelible impression as the titular character of THE TERMINATOR. This was the film that demonstrated to the dubious everyone that the musclebound fellow with that outrageous accent might be more than just another passing blip on our pop culture radar screens. The sleeper hit of fall 1984, THE TERMINATOR is an intelligent, smoothly crafted, and stylish low-budget science fiction action movie that astounded fans of the genre. This was an enormous career booster

for writer-director James Cameron (ALIENS, THE ABYSS, TERMINATOR 2) as well as stars Schwarzenegger and Linda Hamilton (TV's cult favorite "Beauty and the Beast" and TER-MINATOR 2).

The movie opens in the hellish Los Angeles of the year 2029. We see a world destroyed by nuclear war and run by sophisticated machines that have decided to obliterate the weak humans who created them. The action then shifts back to Los Angeles in 1984. In two separate locations, two men—the Terminator (Arnold Schwarzenegger) and Kyle Reese (Michael Biehn)—materialize out of what appear to be small electrical storms and wander off into the night. The next day, after having stolen several deadly weapons and a car, the Terminator looks up the name "Sarah Connor" in the phone book. There are three Sarah Connors listed. The stoical mystery man sets off to kill each of them. Two of the women are killed, but the third (Linda Hamilton) has gone out for the evening. Noticing she is being followed by Reese, the nervous Sarah ducks into a nightclub aptly named Tech Noir and tries to disappear into the crowd. But the Terminator has traced her to the nightclub. Fortunately for her so has Reese. From him Sarah will learn about her destiny and that of the human race.

THE TERMINATOR is an amazingly effective picture that becomes doubly impressive when one considers its small budget. Looking better than most big-budget efforts, it contains dozens of impressive visual effects, including some very good stop-mo-tion animation. For our money, this film is far superior to its mega-grossing mega-budgeted sequel. This is fresh, exciting, and surprisingly witty viewing. Like most genre films made post-STAR WARS, it alludes to many other works. However, this film went a bit further than most. The producers were success-fully sued by cult fantasy author Harlan Ellison who claimed that significant chunks of plot and imagery were lifted from two of his celebrated teleplays for "The Outer Limits," a beloved sci-ence fiction series from the early 1960s. The two episodes in question are "Soldier" and "Demon with a Glass Hand." Anyone who has seen those episodes will readily agree that THE TER-MINATOR took its homage a bit too far.

TERMINATOR 2: JUDGMENT DAY

1991 135m c   ★★★½
Science Fiction/Action   R/15
Pacific Western/Le Studio Canal Plus/Lightstorm
Entertainment/Carolco Pictures

Arnold Schwarzenegger *(The Terminator)*, Linda Hamilton *(Sarah Connor)*, Robert Patrick *(T-1000)*, Edward Furlong *(John Connor)*, Earl Boen *(Dr. Silberman)*, Joe Morton *(Miles Dyson)*, S. Epatha Merkerson *(Tarissa Dyson)*, Castulo Guerra *(Enrique Salceda)*, Danny Cooksey *(Tim)*, Jenette Goldstein *(Janelle Voight)*

p, James Cameron; d, James Cameron; w, James Cameron, William Wisher; ph, Adam Greenberg; ed, Conrad Buff, Mark Goldblatt, Richard A. Harris; m, Brad Fiedel; prod d, Joseph Nemec, III; art d, Joseph P. Lucky; fx, Stan Winston, Dennis Muren; cos, Marlene Stewart

The single *bona fide* blockbuster hit of the year, TERMINATOR 2: JUDGEMENT DAY dazzled its global audience with aston-ishing special effects and re-confirmed Arnold Schwarzenegger's status as the *uber*-star of the 90s. The trend-setting visuals compensated for a plot that lacked the imagination and edge of the 1984 original.

The film opens with a vision of a future, war-ravaged L.A., where human rebels led by an adult John Connor (Michael Edwards) do battle with silvery, skeletal robots. A voiceover informs us that two "intelligent machines" have been dispatched to the past, one to protect the young Connor, the other to kill him.

On late 20th-century Earth, the young John Connor (Edward Furlong) lives unhappily with foster parents, amusing himself by defrauding automated teller machines and spending the loot in video game arcades. Young John soon finds himself pursued by two androids. The one who would be his guardian (Arnold Schwarzenegger) is a replica of the Terminator model T-800 which dominated the original film; the other is a newer model, the T-1000 (Robert Patrick), which takes on the appearance of a young policeman—the first human it dispatches after arriving on Earth. During their first encounter, the "good" Terminator gets the drop on his rival, but a barrage of shotgun shells leaves puncture wounds that heal as we watch—the T-1000 is made of liquid metal that seems impossible to permanently damage. It is also, as we soon discover, able to assume the exact shape and appearance of anything with which it comes into contact. (Oddly, the newer model is smaller in stature than its predecessor, thus making Schwarzenegger's imposing bulk both quaintly old-fashioned and reassuringly human.)

Now convinced that androids from the future really do exist, John realizes that his mother, Sarah Connor (Linda Hamilton), is far from crazy. (Because of her ravings about killer robots and impending nuclear apocalypse, Sarah has been diagnosed as a paranoid schizophrenic and detained in Pescadero State Hospital.) Discovering that the friendly T-800 is programmed to obey his orders, he insists that it help him rescue his mother, but that it kill no more humans in the process. The T-800—which will soon start picking up John's teen slang phrases, such as "no problemo"—reluctantly agrees. After an unsuccessful attempt to lure John home by killing and impersonating his foster mother, the "bad" Terminator sets off in pursuit.

John, Sarah and the T-800 get away from the hospital and their robotic pursuer, heading south to the desert where a friend of Sarah's (Castulo Guerra) is guarding an arms cache. Sarah learns from the good Terminator that a computer scientist called Miles Dyson (Joe Morton) has been working with a microchip salvaged from the wreckage of the original T-800; if his work continues, he will design a supercomputer that will in turn orchestrate a nuclear war in 1997. She sets off to short-circuit the future by killing Dyson, but is unable to do so when she confronts him face to face, surrounded by his family.

When John and the T-800 arrive, Dyson agrees to help them destroy the lab where his work, and the original microchip, are stored. They set about blowing up the lab, but are interrupted by the arrival of the police. Dyson meets a heroic death, ensuring that all the necessary bits and pieces are destroyed, and the rest of the group make good their escape. The T-800 keeps his promise to John by immobilizing the small army of cops without causing any deaths—he aims at vehicles and kneecaps only. The T-1000 learns of the proceedings via police radio and pursues the group to a steel foundry where, after an extended struggle, he is dispatched in a vat of molten steel. The T-800 then voluntarily goes the same way, since this is the only means of ensuring that its own microchip will never fall into the wrong hands.

Though Arnold Schwarzenegger is the nominal star of TERMINATOR 2: JUDGEMENT DAY, the show is stolen from him by the film's extraordinary special effects, particularly the "morphing" or "shape-shifting" sequences in which the liquid metal T-1000 transforms itself into a multitude of organic and inorganic forms. (The process was seen earlier, in a less fully developed form, in director James Cameron's 1989 release THE ABYSS.) One scene in particular, in which the cyborg assumes the appearance of a black-and-white tiled floor, from which it

then rises up to resume the form of the young policeman, bears stunning witness to the way in which computer-generated imagery has transformed the world of special effects. Other sequences, in which the T-1000's arms become deadly steel spikes or hooks, have an uncomfortably visceral effect.

On a dramatic level, the film is less satisfactory. Like an increasing number of big-budget extravaganzas, it bears all the hallmarks of having been created by a committee, and of being self-consciously designed to appeal to a broad demographic range. Thus the inherently violent nature of the material is offset by a more user-friendly Schwarzenegger, who says things like "Hasta la vista, baby" and is forbidden to kill anyone. Meanwhile, Linda Hamilton is given a lot of New Age, motherly things to say, especially during her sojourn in the desert ("If a machine can learn the value of human life, then maybe we can, too."). Hers, nevertheless, is an enjoyably macho performance, with her muscle-bound, gun-toting persona inviting several commentators to draw parallels with other tough screen women in 1991 releases like THELMA & LOUISE, LA FEMME NIKITA, and V.I. WARSHAWSKI. Flaws aside, TERMINATOR 2 is an immensely enjoyable, often exhilarating piece of filmmaking, with a wry sense of humor to boot.

TERMS OF ENDEARMENT

1983 130m c		★★★½
Comedy/Drama		PG/15
Paramount		

Debra Winger (Emma Horton), Shirley MacLaine (Aurora Greenway), Jack Nicholson (Garrett Breedlove), Danny DeVito (Vernon Dahlart), Jeff Daniels (Flap Horton), John Lithgow (Sam Burns), Betty King (Rosie), Lisa Hart Carroll (Patsy Clark), Huckleberry Fox (Toddy), Megan Morris (Melanie)

p, James L. Brooks, Penney Finkelman, Martin Jurow; d, James L. Brooks; w, James L. Brooks (based on the novel by Larry McMurtry); ph, Andrzej Bartkowiak (Metrocolor); ed, Richard Marks, Sidney Wolinsky; m, Michael Gore; prod d, Polly Platt; art d, Harold Michelson; cos, Kristi Zea, Anthony J. Faso

Lopsided comedy turned tearjerker, saved by excellent performances. TV veteran James Brooks ("Mary Tyler Moore Show") wrote, directed, and co-produced the film which examines a 30-year period in the lives of Aurora Greenway (Shirley MacLaine) and her daughter, Emma (as a child, Jennifer Josey; as an adult, Debra Winger). Aurora is guilty of "smother" love, and, as Emma grows up, she can't wait to escape her mother's suffocating hold. In the face of her mother's anger, Emma marries Flap (Jeff Daniels), has three children, and moves away. All the while, Aurora is wooed by ex-astronaut Garrett Breedlove (Jack Nicholson), an uncouth bachelor whose persistence and unfailing good humor begin to wear her down.

Winger is absolutely winning all the way, with a deathbed scene that may not have been equalled since Bette Davis lay down in DARK VICTORY. MacLaine works like a slow-cooker. The early scenes are her usual stabs at caricature (almost every choice in a dining room scene is wrong), but she is freed by Nicholson; their scenes have a great element of play to them. About the time she demands better hospital treatment for her daughter, she begins to take chances and ventures into virtuoso territory. Nicholson, while certainly not worth the $1 million pricetag for his services, delivers an amusing variation on himself. Brooks writes some of the best dialogue around, but the film is directed in a perfunctory fashion, and many scenes go on far too long. Nonetheless, Brooks took the Oscar as Best Director, and also won for the script; MacLaine won as Best Actress,

Nicholson as Best Supporting Actor, and the movie won as Best Picture. Needless to say, it was a huge commercial success; it's one of those movies that manipulates you into thinking it touched you while it's balancing its bank account. And the box-office profited by gossip that the leading ladies despised each other—making it one of those detective watches for more hardened viewers. Something for everyone, indeed.

TESS

1979 170m c   ★★★
Drama   PG
Renn/Burrill   (France/U.K.)

Nastassja Kinski (Tess Durbeyfield), Leigh Lawson (Alec d'Urberville), Peter Firth (Angel Clare), John Collin (John Durbeyfield), David Markham (Rev. Mr. Clare), Rosemary Martin (Mrs. Durbeyfield), Richard Pearson (Vicar of Marlott), Carolyn Pickles (Marian), Pascale de Boysson (Mrs. Clare), Tony Church (Parson Tringham)

p, Claude Berri; d, Roman Polanski; w, Roman Polanski, Gerard Brach, John Brownjohn (based on the novel Tess of the d'Urbervilles by Thomas Hardy); ph, Geoffrey Unsworth, Ghislain Cloquet (Eastmancolor); ed, Alastair McIntyre, Tom Priestley; m, Philippe Sarde; prod d, Pierre Guffroy; art d, Jack Stephens; chor, Sue Lefton; cos, Anthony Powell

Roman Polanski's delicate, visually rich adaptation of Thomas Hardy's classic novel places the supremely photogenic Nastassja Kinski in the title role. Peasant girl Tess Durbeyfield is sent to the estate of the wealthy d'Urbervilles by her desperate father after he learns that the two families are distantly related. It turns out, however, that the d'Urbervilles are not the d'Urbervilles after all, but a family that bought the noble line's name. Alec d'Urberville (Leigh Lawson), the cocky young master of the household, takes Tess as his lover, but later she returns home, disillusioned and pregnant. After the death of her baby, Tess is left to work on a dairy farm, where she falls in love with Angel Clare (Peter Firth). Their romance leads to a marriage that ends abruptly on their wedding night when her outraged husband refuses to accept her past. With nowhere else to go, Tess returns to Alec, a decision that leads to a violent end.

Visually, TESS is a masterpiece, capturing in amazing detail the scenery and atmosphere of the England of yore. The film's chief drawback, however, is its lack of vitality. Instead of Hardy's passionate tale of ruin and disenchantment, TESS is cautious and reserved. It was awarded Oscars for Best Cinematography (begun by Geoffrey Unsworth, who died during the filming, and completed by Ghislain Cloquet), Best Costume Design, and Best Art Direction. Other nominations included Best Picture (won by ORDINARY PEOPLE), Best Direction, and Best Original Score. Producer Claude Berri and coscreenwriter Gerard Brach later teamed on the Berri-directed JEAN DE FLORETTE and MANON OF THE SPRING, both of which are reminiscent of TESS.

TEST PILOT

1938 118m bw   ★★★★
Drama   /A
MGM

Clark Gable (Jim Lane), Myrna Loy (Ann Barton), Spencer Tracy (Gunner Sloane), Lionel Barrymore (Howard B. Drake), Samuel S. Hinds (Gen. Ross), Arthur Aylesworth (Frank Barton), Claudia Coleman (Mrs. Barton), Gloria Holden (Mrs. Benson), Louis Jean Heydt (Benson), Ted Pearson (Joe)

p, Louis D. Lighton; d, Victor Fleming; w, Vincent Lawrence, Waldemar Young, Howard Hawks (based on a story by Frank Wead); ph, Ray June; ed, Tom Held; m, Franz Waxman; cos, Dolly Tree

One of the best Hollywood aviation dramas, TEST PILOT sparkles with a great cast and sprightly direction by Fleming, a "man's director" who had the good sense to feature a great female performer, Loy, in this action film. Gable plays a world-renowned test pilot employed by plane manufacturer Barrymore. While testing the company's new plane, The Bullet, Gable develops engine trouble and is forced to land in a Kansas cornfield. There he meets farm girl Loy, with whom he falls in love while his plane is being repaired. The two are soon married, but when Gable requests a week's vacation for his honeymoon, the cranky Barrymore refuses, telling the pilot that he wants his new plane back and in good shape. Gable quits and—accompanied not only by Loy but also by Tracy, his devoted mechanic—goes on a drinking honeymoon. Gable then goes off on his own but is tracked down by Tracy, who sobers him up and returns him to Loy, who is starting to have second thoughts about staying with her new hubby. Gable patches things up with Barrymore and settles down a bit. He and Loy begin to enjoy domestic life, though the watchful Tracy knows this calm is unlikely to last. Soon Loy becomes increasingly apprehensive about Gable's test piloting, anxiously looking on as he flies experimental planes and risks his life. It becomes obvious to her that Gable—who calls the sky "that lady all dressed in blue"—deeply enjoys putting his life on the line. Eventually Loy can no longer bear to watch the tests and begins to stay at home, where she becomes a nervous wreck. When Army general Hinds requests that Gable test the Army's new B-17 bomber (which would later become the workhorse of the Air Corps during WW II), Gable accepts the challenge. However, the mission terrifies Loy, and she is on the verge of a crackup by the time Gable and Tracy—serving as Gable's copilot—climb into the bomber. Gable pushes the plane beyond its presumed limit and keeps going, trying to reach 30,000 feet. The bomber cannot take the pressure and gives out, plummeting earthward in a screaming nosedive. Gable and Tracy frantically work the controls, but dozens of sandbags that were used for ballast break loose from the back of the plane and come crashing into the cabin, pinning the men against the controls. The two desperately throw sandbags out the window while trying to pull up the plane at the same time. Gable finally manages to yank up the controls and pull the plane level, but it's a losing struggle and the plane crashes anyway. The finale has both uplift and heartbreak.

According to some sources (though not Lynn Tornabee, author of the Gable biography Long Live the King), it was actually Tracy who, during the production of this film, gave Gable the sobriquet for which he would be forever known. Reportedly, as Tracy attempted to drive into the MGM lot one morning, his car was blocked by scores of screaming female fans who were besieging Gable, demanding that the star sign their pictures of him. Tracy beeped his horn, but the fans ignored him. Finally, the frustrated Tracy stood up in his convertible and shouted at Gable, "Long live the king! And now, for Christ's sake, let's get inside and go to work!" The prop department subsequently made Gable a cardboard crown lined with rabbit's fur, after which Ed Sullivan heard about the incident and conducted a nationwide poll to find out who the king and queen of Hollywood really were. Fans overwhelmingly elected Gable and Loy. Tracy was frequently frustrated at having to perform in support of screen idol Gable and is said to have stretched out some of his own scenes to insure that he would make a good impression. Regardless, the rapport of the three leads is the film's greatest strength. TEST PILOT was a box-office smash, with stunning aerial photography unmatched to this day. It was Oscar-nominated for Best Picture (losing to YOU CAN'T TAKE IT WITH YOU), Best Original Story, and Best Editing.

TESTAMENT OF DR. MABUSE, THE
(DAS TESTAMENT DES DR. MABUSE)
1933   122m   bw   ★★★★★
Crime   /A
Nero/Constantine/Deutsche Universal   (Germany)

Rudolf Klein-Rogge (Dr. Mabuse), Oscar Beregi, Sr. (Prof. Dr. Baum), Karl Meixner (Hofmeister), Theodor Loos (Dr. Kramm), Otto Wernicke (Commissioner Karl Lohmann), Klaus Pohl (Muller), Wera Liessem (Lilli), Gustav Diesel (Kent), Camilla Spira (Juwelen-Anna), Rudolph Schundler (Hardy)

p, Fritz Lang; d, Fritz Lang; w, Fritz Lang (based on the characters from the novel by Norbert Jacques); ph, Fritz Arno Wagner, Karl Vash; m, Hans Erdmann; prod d, Karl Vollbrecht, Emile Hasler; art d, Karl Vollbrecht, Emil Hasler

A haunting, suspenseful sequel to the great Fritz Lang's 1922 silent DR. MABUSE, THE GAMBLER picks up where the original left off—with Rudolf Klein-Rogge, reprising his role as the mad Dr. Mabuse, in a cell in an insane asylum. When Mabuse dies, Prof. Baum (Oskar Beregi), the director of the asylum, becomes possessed by the dead doctor's spirit and is compelled to carry out the madman's master plan to destroy the state through theft, violence, murder, and destruction. Although Baum engineers these chaotic acts, he manages to lead a double life, retaining his position at the asylum. Interwoven into this story is the tale of two lovers—Lilli (Wera Liessem) and Kent (Gustav Diesel), a member of Baum's gang who wants out and manages to prove the connection between Mabuse's plans and the chaos that is rocking Berlin.

Filmed in 1932 and coscripted by Lang's wife, Thea von Harbou, THE TESTAMENT OF DR. MABUSE was made during the Nazi party's rise to power, and completed just before Lang fled, without von Harbou (who would become a top Nazi screenwriter), to the US. Whether or not it was Lang's intention, there are distinct parallels between THE TESTAMENT OF DR. MABUSE and the real-life events of the day—Prof. Baum symbolizing all those whose minds had become controlled by the thought of carrying out the "master plan." It should come as no surprise, then, that this remarkable testament to Lang's artistry was banned, and nearly destroyed, by the Nazis.

TESTAMENT OF ORPHEUS, THE
(LE TESTAMENT D'ORPHEE)
1959   79m   c/bw   ★★★★★
Drama   /A
Editions Cinegraphiques   (France)

Jean Cocteau (Himself, the Poet), Edouard Dermit (Cegeste), Jean-Pierre Leaud (The Schoolboy), Henri Cremieux (The Professor), Francoise Christophe (The Nurse), Maria Casares (The Princess), Francois Perier (Heurtebise), Yul Brynner (The Court Usher), Daniel Gelin (The Intern), Nicole Courcel (The Young Mother)

p, Jean Thuillier; d, Jean Cocteau; w, Jean Cocteau; ph, Roland Pontoiseau; ed, Marie-Josephe Yoyotte; m, Georges Auric, Martial Solal, Johann Sebastian Bach, George Frederick Handel, Christophe Gluck; art d, Pierre Guffroy

Poet-filmmaker-sculptor-painter Jean Cocteau bade a fond farewell to cinema with this free-flowing, spirited collection of images and scenes that includes characters from his past films and personal friends. What there is of a story retreads the ground of Cocteau's THE BLOOD OF A POET (1930) and ORPHEUS (1949), bringing his cinematic career (which is difficult to separate from his other pursuits) full circle. For fans of Cocteau, everything in this picture will strike a familiar chord—a poet lives, must die, is resurrected, and must die again to qualify for immortality. Cocteau again employs some of the most inventive and beautiful photographic manipulations ever done in films, including the reverse motion techniques that never fail to bring a smile to his devotees. The cast reads like a cultural who's who—Pablo Picasso, Charles Aznavour, Francoise Sagan, Brigitte Bardot, Roger Vadim, Jean-Pierre Leaud, and, yes, Yul Brynner. Also making appearances are familiar faces from ORPHEUS, including Jean Marais, Maria Casares, Edouard Dermit, Francois Perier, and Henri Cremieux. Francois Truffaut, in honor of one of his masters, assisted with the production and financing of the picture. A pure, personal poem from one of the greats, THE TESTAMENT OF ORPHEUS allows Cocteau to live on forever.

TEX
1982   103m   c   ★★★
Drama   PG
Disney

Matt Dillon (Tex McCormick), Jim Metzler (Mason McCormick), Meg Tilly (Jamie Collins), Bill McKinney (Pop McCormick), Frances Lee McCain (Mrs. Johnson), Ben Johnson (Cole Collins), Emilio Estevez (Johnny Collins), Phil Brock (Lem Peters), Jack Thibeau (Coach Jackson), Zeljko Ivanek (Hitchhiker)

p, Tim Zinnemann; d, Tim Hunter; w, Tim Hunter, Charlie Haas (based on the novel by S.E. Hinton); ph, Ric Waite (Technicolor); ed, Howard Smith; m, Pino Donaggio; prod d, Jack T. Collis; art d, John B. Mansbridge

Matt Dillon takes his urban toughness to Oklahoma as Tex, a young farmboy raised by his elder brother when their mother dies and their father wanders away. The film probes the pitfalls of growing up, tackling such subjects as sex, boozing, and fighting—three areas the Disney folks have stayed clear of in the past. Dillon, though occasionally annoying, turns in a decent performance, as do Jim Metzler as his brother and Meg Tilly (THE BIG CHILL, PSYCHO II, AGNES OF GOD) as his girlfriend. The screenplay is based on a teen novel by S.E. Hinton (who also appears in the film).

TEXAS CHAINSAW MASSACRE, THE
1974   83m   c   ★★★
Horror   R/X
Vortex/Henkel/Hooper

Marilyn Burns (Sally), Allen Danziger (Jerry), Paul A. Partain (Franklin), William Vail (Kirk), Teri McMinn (Pam), Edwin Neal (Hitchhiker), Jim Siedow (Old Man), Gunnar Hansen (Leatherface), John Dugan (Grandfather), Jerry Lorenz (Pickup Driver)

p, Tobe Hooper; d, Tobe Hooper; w, Kim Henkel, Tobe Hooper; ph, Daniel Pearl (CFI Color); ed, Sallye Richardson, Larry Carroll; m, Tobe Hooper, Wayne Bell; art d, Robert Burns

Though its exploitation title would suggest that THE TEXAS CHAIN SAW MASSACRE is just another mindless gore-fest, it is in fact an intelligent, absorbing, and deeply disturbing horror film that is nearly bloodless in its depiction of violence. Using the age-old technique of suggestion, combined with a gritty, well-executed (no pun intended) visual style, the film seems much bloodier than it actually is. Disturbed by news reports that vandals have been desecrating the remote Texas cemetery where her grandfather is buried, Burns and her wheelchair-bound brother, Partain, gather some of their friends and take the family van to see if their grandfather's grave is still intact. While in the area they decide to visit the old farmhouse where Grandpa lived. Nearby is another farmhouse—one decorated with grisly items made from human and animal skin and bones—in which resides a family of unemployed slaughterhouse workers, the most frightening of whom is "Leatherface" (Hansen), who wears a mask of human flesh and has a way with a chainsaw.

Obviously based on real-life Wisconsin farmer Ed Gein (whose grotesque exploits also inspired Hitchcock's PSYCHO), THE TEXAS CHAIN SAW MASSACRE is one of the best examples of the "horror of the family" subgenre, which takes as its subject the American family—traditionally a wholesome, positive force—and examines its dark side, the side that is claustrophobic, stifling, and incestuous. Tobe Hooper's film is deeply disturbing and is meant to be. The best films in the horror genre don't exist just to "scare" people but to examine the darker impulses, fears, taboos, and repressed desires found in human beings and to purge them from our collective subconscious.

THANK YOUR LUCKY STARS
1943   127m   bw   ★★★½
Comedy/Musical   /U
WB

Eddie Cantor *(Joe Sampson/Himself)*, Joan Leslie *(Pat Dixon)*, Dennis Morgan *(Tommy Randolph)*, Dinah Shore *(Herself)*, S.Z. Sakall *(Dr. Schlenna)*, Edward Everett Horton *(Farnsworth)*, Ruth Donnelly *(Nurse Hamilton)*, Joyce Reynolds *(Girl with Book)*, Richard Lane *(Barney Jackson)*, Don Wilson *(Himself)*

p, Mark Hellinger; d, David Butler; w, Norman Panama, Melvin Frank, James V. Kern (based on a story by Everett Freeman, Arthur Schwartz); ph, Arthur Edeson; ed, Irene Morra; art d, Anton Grot, Leo K. Kuter; fx, H.F. Koenekamp; chor, LeRoy Prinz; cos, Milo Anderson

During WWII, Hollywood attempted to get behind the war effort in a big way, with every major studio—beginning with Paramount and STAR SPANGLED RHYTHM in 1942—producing a showcase musical featuring their star contract players. THANK YOUR LUCKY STARS was the Warner Bros. effort and gave audiences the opportunity to see the studio's biggest names performing in song-and-dance numbers. The flimsy story involves S.Z. Sakall and Edward Everett Horton as producers who are trying to stage a Cavalcade of Stars. They hope to line up some talent from among the guests on Eddie Cantor's radio show, like Dinah Shore (playing herself in her film debut), without involving Cantor himself, but have no such luck, as he becomes a major headache. Meanwhile, aspiring singer Tommy Randolph (Dennis Morgan), struggling songwriter Pat Dixon (Joan Leslie), and Joe Sampson (Cantor), an actor who is unable to find work because he looks too much like Cantor, come up with a kidnap scheme that provides both Tommy and Joe with their big breaks.

What the movie lacks in substance it makes up for in energy. Cantor is often quite amusing, but Leslie again proves less than ideal leading lady material. The real heart and soul of this film, though, are the musical numbers featuring such unlikely stars as Errol Flynn (performing "What You Jolly Well Get" as a Cockney sailor in a London pub), John Garfield (doing a tough-guy parody to "Blues in the Night") and Bette Davis (who contributes

a fabulous rendition of "They're Either Too Young or Too Old"), among many others.

THAT HAMILTON WOMAN
1941   128m   bw   ★★½
Biography/War   /A
UA

Vivien Leigh *(Emma Hart Hamilton)*, Laurence Olivier *(Lord Horatio Nelson)*, Alan Mowbray *(Sir William Hamilton)*, Sara Allgood *(Mrs. Cadogan-Lyon)*, Gladys Cooper *(Lady Nelson)*, Henry Wilcoxon *(Capt. Hardy)*, Heather Angel *(Street Girl)*, Halliwell Hobbes *(Rev. Nelson)*, Gilbert Emery *(Lord Spencer)*, Miles Mander *(Lord Keith)*

p, Alexander Korda; d, Alexander Korda; w, Walter Reisch, R.C. Sherriff; ph, Rudolph Mate; ed, William Hornbeck; m, Miklos Rozsa; prod d, Vincent Korda; fx, Lawrence Butler; cos, Rene Hubert

A drunken crone (played by Vivien Leigh), jailed on charges of theft and assault, begins to tell the story of her life to a cellmate, and the tale of THAT HAMILTON WOMAN unfolds in flashback. In 1786, young Emma Hart (Leigh) arrives at the court of Naples, expecting to wed the British ambassador's nephew. He proves a rascal, but Emma's *joie de vivre* soon attracts the ambassador himself, Sir William Hamilton (Alan Mowbray), and she eventually becomes his bride. Seven years later, British naval hero Lord Nelson (Laurence Olivier) arrives in Naples, seeking the king's aid in the war against Napoleon, and the rest, as they say, is history—or at least producer-director Alexander Korda's version of such. The film traces the growth in Naples of Emma and Nelson's love (to which her husband turns a blind eye, though tongues wag back home) and their return to England, where the lovers set up house, although Nelson's wife refuses to divorce him. The war goes badly, and Emma persuades Nelson to return to his command, leading to his mortal wounding in the victory at Trafalgar, which in turn begins her slide into despair. Despite the marquee pull of newlyweds Olivier and Leigh (she fresh from GONE WITH THE WIND), THAT HAMILTON WOMAN was not the hit its makers hoped it would be—though it reportedly *was* Winston Churchill's favorite movie. Korda, shooting in the US with little money, was forced to film quickly, without the lavish sets that were his specialty, and the script's "tastefulness"—which downplays Nelson's sensuality and alters facts in making Emma pay for her sins later in the classic Hollywood style—while pleasing to 1941 censors and strengthening its propaganda value for then-embattled Britain, also lowers the level of excitement. The film earned Academy Award nominations for Best Cinematography, Best Interior Decoration, and Best Special Effects. For a more accurate account, see Glenda Jackson and Peter Finch in THE NELSON AFFAIR (1973).

THAT MAN FROM RIO
(L'HOMME DE RIO)
1964   114m   c   ★★★
Comedy/Adventure   /U
Ariane/Artistes/Dear   (France/Italy)

Jean-Paul Belmondo *(Adrien Dufourquet)*, Francoise Dorleac *(Agnes)*, Jean Servais *(Prof. Catalan)*, Simone Renant *(Lola)*, Milton Ribeiro *(Tupac)*, Ubiracy de Oliveira *(Sir Winston)*, Adolfo Celi *(Senor De Castro)*, Daniel Ceccaldi, Roger Dumas, Sabu do Brasil p, Alexandre Mnouchkine, Georges Dancigers; d, Philippe de Broca; w, Jean-Paul Rappeneau, Ariane Mnouchkine, Daniel Boulanger, Philippe de Broca; ph, Edmond Sechan (Eastmancolor); ed, Laurence Mery-Clark, Francoise Javet; m, Georges Delerue; fx, Gil Delamare

A wacky adventure yarn that begins with French air force pilot Belmondo on an eight-day pass to visit girlfriend Dorleac in Paris. Unfortunately Belmondo arrives just in time to see Dorleac kidnaped by South American Indians who are trying to get a hold of a set of valuable statues that, when assembled, will point the way to an Amazon treasure. Dorleac is taken because her late father led an expedition in the area, so the Indians suspect she knows where the statues are. After a lengthy series of misadventures in the jungle, Belmondo and Dorleac eventually escape and return to Paris just in time for Belmondo to return to his unit. Belmondo, as always, is a delight. The film received an Oscar nomination for Best Screenplay.

THAT OBSCURE OBJECT OF DESIRE
(CET OBSCUR OBJECT DU DESIR)
1977 100m c   ★★★★½
Drama   R/X
Greenwich/Galaxie/Inine (France/Spain)

Fernando Rey (Mathieu), Carole Bouquet, Angela Molina (Conchita), Julien Bertheau (Judge), Milena Vukotic (Traveler), Andre Weber (Valet), Pierre Pieral (Psychologist), Maria Asquerino, Ellen Bahl, Valerie Blanco

p, Serge Silberman; d, Luis Bunuel; w, Luis Bunuel, Jean-Claude Carriere (based on the novel La Femme et la Pantin by Pierre Louys); ph, Edmond Richard (Eastmancolor); ed, Helene Plemiannikov; art d, Pierre Guffroy

The final film from the 77-year-old Luis Bunuel shows the playful director in as outrageous form as ever, casting two women—the graceful Carole Bouquet and the saucy Angela Molina—in the role of Conchita, a beautiful but elusive Spanish girl who becomes the object of obsession for Mathieu (Fernando Rey, his voice dubbed into French by Michel Piccoli), an upstanding French businessman. Widowed seven years ago, Mathieu regards love and sex moralistically, priding himself on his ability to count on one hand the number of times he had sex with a woman he didn't love. When he sees Conchita, however, his mind overflows with thoughts of her. Although Conchita professes her love to Mathieu, she leaves him and flees to Switzerland, only to return later as his maid. When Mathieu finally manages to bed her, she is dressed in such an impenetrable outfit (a chastity belt of sorts) that he is unable to satisfy his uncontrollable sexual urge.

  This straightforward tale of obsessive love is colored with the always amazing Bunuelian touches. Mathieu's story is framed by a train trip in which he speaks of Conchita to his fellow passengers: a French official, a woman and her teenage daughter, and a dwarf psychologist. Also prevalent throughout the picture is a rash of bombings by a terrorist group that calls itself the Revolutionary Army of the Infant Jesus. The most fascinating aspect of THAT OBSCURE OBJECT OF DESIRE, however, is the character of Conchita, who is exactly what the title promises—so obscure that Bunuel chose to cast two actresses in her role. LAST TANGO IN PARIS star Maria Schneider was originally cast to play Conchita by herself, but she was replaced early in the shooting. In a stroke of genius, Bunuel then cast two women in the same role—a completely logical dualism, since

Conchita seems to vary greatly in her feelings for Mathieu, loving him one day and leaving him the next.

THAT SINKING FEELING
1979 82m c   ★★★
Crime/Comedy   PG
Minor Miracle Film Cooperative (U.K.)

Robert Buchanan (Ronnie), John Hughes (Vic), Billy Greenlees (Wal), Douglas Sannachan (Simmy), Alan Love (Alec), Danny Benson (Policeman), Eddie Burt (Van Driver), Tom Mannion (Doctor), Eric Joseph (The Wee Man), Janette Rankin (Mary)

p, Bill Forsyth; d, Bill Forsyth; w, Bill Forsyth; ph, Michael Coulter (Fujicolor Negative); ed, John Gow; m, Colin Tully; prod d, Adrienne Atkinson; cos, Adrienne Atkinson

Early comedy by Scottish director Bill Forsyth (GREGORY'S GIRL, LOCAL HERO) which follows the goofy exploits of a gang of unemployed youths who steal and try to sell a shipment of stainless steel sinks. Of course the boys have a bit of trouble unloading their loot, and the film details their increasingly frustrated efforts to turn a sticky situation into a profitable one. Great performances from nonprofessionals are directed with Forsyth's usual insightful wit. Some viewers may have trouble deciphering the Scottish accents.

THAT TOUCH OF MINK
1962 99m c   ★★★
Romance/Comedy   /U
Granley/Arwin/Nob Hill

Cary Grant (Philip Shayne), Doris Day (Cathy Timberlake), Gig Young (Roger), Audrey Meadows (Connie), Alan Hewitt (Dr. Gruber), John Astin (Beasley), Richard Sargent (Young Man), Joey Faye (Short Man), John Fiedler (Mr. Smith), Willard Sage (Hodges)

p, Martin Melcher, Stanley Shapiro; d, Delbert Mann; w, Stanley Shapiro, Nate Monaster; ph, Russell Metty (Panavision, Eastmancolor); ed, Ted J. Kent; m, George Duning; art d, Alexander Golitzen, Robert Clatworthy; cos, Norman Norell, Rosemary Odell

A bouncy if rather smarmy comedy from the mind of Stanley Shapiro, who also contributed to PILLOW TALK and LOVER COME BACK. Shapiro and coauthor Monaster have come up with a thin plot but scads of funny dialogue enhanced by Grant, Day, and Young in enjoyable performances. Day is out of work in New York and about to cash her unemployment check when Grant's passing limousine splashes her with mud. Grant is a corporate raider who has spent his life gobbling up companies and neglecting his personal life. (Humphrey Bogart did the same role in SABRINA.) Day walks into the local automat. Grant sends Young, his tippling financial advisor, into the restaurant to offer Day money for her muddied dress. Meadows, Day's roommate (in a wisecracking, Eve Arden-like role), and Young tell Day to give Grant what-for if she is so indignant at him. Day marches into Grant's fabulous office, where her wrath is soon assuaged by Grant's incomparable suavity. When Grant has to make a business trip to Maryland, he invites her to join him and she agrees. Thus begins a whirlwind journey as he takes her to Philadelphia for drinks, to the UN where he gives a speech, then down to Baltimore for dinner and a game between the Yankees and the Orioles. (Seen briefly are Mickey Mantle, Roger Maris, and Yogi Berra as themselves.) This cat-and-mouse game has to end eventually, and it does when Grant asks Day if she'd like to go to Bermuda with him. The lady doth protest at first, but when Grant plies her with lavish clothing (designed by Rosemary

Odell) and a full-length mink coat, Day changes her mind. As nighttime approaches in their vacation spot, Day realizes that this is nothing out of Plato; Grant wants to take Richmond here, and there is no getting away from it. Day conveniently breaks out in a rash, leaving Grant to spend the night playing cards. The romantic trip becomes a disaster. Day feels awful about what's happened and wants another chance. Prior to their next date, Day begins to drink to relax herself and falls off a terrace. Grant feels that the whole affair has been a waste of time and won't call her anymore. Day is frustrated and wants to make Grant jealous, so she asks Young for his help. Young arranges a motel tryst with Astin, an unemployment clerk with a lecherous gleam in his eye. Then Young notifies Grant so he can rescue Day from this fate. Once Day is out of Astin's clutches, Grant realizes that she is the woman for him. Skin problems, though, once again enter the picture.

Most of the jokes are verbal rather than slapstick in this script, which, rather surprisingly, copped an Oscar nomination. It also received nominations for Best Art Direction and Best Sound. The film whips along like a Formula One car under Mann's capable direction. The main problem is that 58-year-old Grant and 38-year-old Day were getting slightly long in the tooth for this kind of "will she or won't she?" story. Astin is excellent, appearing in his second movie after WEST SIDE STORY. Right after this, he teamed with Marty Ingels in his first TV series, "I'm Dickens, He's Fenster."

THAT'LL BE THE DAY

1974   90m   c   ★★★
Drama   PG/15
Goodtimes   (U.K.)

David Essex *(Jim MacLaine)*, Ringo Starr *(Mike)*, Rosemary Leach *(Mrs. MacLaine)*, James Booth *(Mr. MacLaine)*, Billy Fury *(Stormy Tempest)*, Keith Moon *(J.D. Clover)*, Rosalind Ayres *(Jeanette)*, Robert Lindsay *(Terry)*, Beth Morris *(Jean)*, James Ottaway *(Granddad)*

p, Sandy Lieberson, David Puttnam; d, Claude Whatham; w, Ray Connolly (based on his story); ph, Peter Suschitzky (Technicolor); ed, Michael Bradsell; art d, Brian Morris

A surprisingly adept rock 'n' roll youth film set in the late 1950s starring real-life rocker David Essex (his big hit was "Rock On") as an alienated, working-class youth who goes through his rights of passage. Ex-Beatle Starr is fine as Essex's buddy. Insightful, well written and acted, THAT'LL BE THE DAY is an honest, realistic youth anthem that soon spawned a sequel, STARDUST, which is just as good.

THEATRE OF BLOOD

1973   104m   c   ★★★★
Horror   R/18
UA   (U.K.)

Vincent Price *(Edward Lionheart)*, Diana Rigg *(Edwina Lionheart)*, Ian Hendry *(Peregrine Devlin)*, Harry Andrews *(Trevor Dickman)*, Coral Browne *(Miss Chloe Moon)*, Robert Coote *(Oliver Larding)*, Jack Hawkins *(Solomon Psaltery)*, Michael Hordern *(George Maxwell)*, Arthur Lowe *(Horace Sprout)*, Robert Morley *(Meredith Merridew)*

p, John Kohn, Stanley Mann; d, Douglas Hickox; w, Anthony Greville-Bell; ph, Wolfgang Suschitzky (DeLuxe Color); ed, Malcolm Cooke; m, Michael J. Lewis; prod d, Michael Seymour; fx, John Stears; chor, Tutte Lemkow; cos, Michael Baldwin

After the horrible deaths of three of his colleagues in the prestigious London Theatre Critics Circle, Peregrine Devlin (Ian Hendry) approaches the baffled police with a bizarre theory: perhaps the murders are being committed by Edward Lionheart (Vincent Price), an aging Shakespearean actor who was outraged when the Critic's Circle award went to another actor. So incensed was Lionheart, that he pushed his way onto the stage, stole the award, and jumped into the Thames, supposedly killing himself. Since the three murders closely parallel deaths detailed in the plays of Shakespeare, the cops think that Devlin may be right. The now-insane Lionheart, aided by his lovely though equally mad daughter, Edwina (Diana Rigg), and a group of derelicts who rescued him from the Thames, is indeed killing the critics.

Clearly inspired by the success of the "Dr. Phibes" series, THEATRE OF BLOOD goes one better by allowing Price to glory in his peculiarly Gothic acting style. He is wonderful here, delighting in every grotesque killing and relishing the excerpts from Shakespeare while outfitted in a variety of outlandish costumes. While Price dominates the film with his superb performance, he is ably supported by a top-notch cast—all of whom agreed to do the film in homage to Price. Director Douglas Hickox wisely chooses a very fluid cinematic style to provide a contrast to the distinctly theatrical script. He skillfully intertwines hilarious black humor with some surprisingly intense Grand Guignol effects. Wholly entertaining and memorable, THEATRE OF BLOOD is ripe camp, an excellent film, and a lasting tribute to the career of one of the most important actors in the genre.

THELMA & LOUISE

1991   128m   c   ★★★★
Drama/Adventure/Comedy   R/15
Percy Main Productions

Geena Davis *(Thelma)*, Susan Sarandon *(Louise)*, Harvey Keitel *(Hal)*, Michael Madsen *(Jimmy)*, Christopher McDonald *(Darryl)*, Stephen Tobolowsky *(Max)*, Brad Pitt *(J.D.)*, Timothy Carhart *(Harlan)*, Lucinda Jenney *(Lena the Waitress)*, Jason Beghe *(State Trooper)*

p, Ridley Scott, Mimi Polk; d, Ridley Scott; w, Callie Khouri; ph, Adrian Biddle; ed, Thom Noble; m, Hans Zimmer; prod d, Norris Spencer; art d, Lisa Dean; cos, Elizabeth McBride

THELMA & LOUISE is a rowdy, feminist road movie in which a pair of gutsy, independent women discover the strength of sisterhood during a hell-raising, joy-riding escape from the laws of men. One of the most hotly debated films of 1991, it features two landmark performances from stars Geena Davis and Susan Sarandon.

Louise (Sarandon) is a strong-willed waitress who convinces her friend Thelma (Davis), a timid housewife, to join her on a weekend camping trip. Against the wishes of Darryl (Christopher McDonald), her possessive, sexist husband, Thelma sneaks away for the outing. Along the way the pair let loose at a country bar, drinking and dancing. A handsome but abusive man, Harlan (Timothy Carhart), attempts to rape Thelma in the parking lot and is discovered by Louise, who shoots and kills the unrepentant misogynist in anger. Louise convinces Thelma that the police are not likely to believe their version of events, so the two flee in a panic.

From Arkansas they head through Oklahoma, where they pick up J.D. (Brad Pitt), a young cowboy stud who has a one-night stand with Thelma. He also steals the money Louise had convinced Jimmy (Michael Madsen), her sometime boyfriend, to withdraw from her savings account. Again victimized by men, they turn desperado, robbing stores to finance their attempted escape to Mexico. Because Louise refuses to take the direct route through Texas (where, it turns out, she herself was once raped), their getaway turns into an extended driving tour of the Southwest. Along the way they feel oddly empowered by their ability to assert themselves against authority, and develop a penchant for improvised holdups. They even decide to teach one sleazy, lecherous truck driver a lesson by inviting him to pull over, then (to their own surprise) exploding his gasoline-filled rig.

Meanwhile, the FBI continues to close in on them. They outsmart the first Arizona state trooper to catch them, politely reducing him to a whimpering milquetoast. But the FBI's massive manhunt inevitably catches up to them. Surrounded in the middle of the desert with no way out, they agree to go out with a bang rather than surrender, speeding their convertible over the edge of the Grand Canyon.

THELMA & LOUISE does to film images of women what DANCES WITH WOLVES did to those of Native Americans: take decades of cinematic stereotypes and turn them upside down. Kevin Costner's film inverted the Hollywood Western with its sympathetic depiction of American Indians in conflict with one-dimensional white villains; Ridley Scott's free-wheeling revision of BUTCH CASSIDY AND THE SUNDANCE KID presents two funny, spirited and likable women at odds with a variety of men who are either stupid, violent, immoral, weak, disrespectful or, in the case of Thelma's husband, all of the above. Critical reaction to the film indicated that many male viewers felt threatened by these pistol-packing female outlaws, but complaints about the movie's chauvinist treatment of men are largely unjustified. Creatures like Darryl are merely comic foils for the film's wonder-women, while other male characters, such as FBI man Hal (Harvey Keitel), are fully-drawn, sympathetic figures. They, like the audience, see Thelma and Louise for what they are: exuberant women who are stifled by a male-dominated world and suffer the consequences of fighting back too strongly.

Gender warfare aside, THELMA & LOUISE is a fun, breezy roadtrip across the Western landscape. In the natural grandeur of this setting, director Scott abandons his trademark high-tech atmospherics in favor of a bright, glossy, photographic style that makes picture postcards of the Route 66 backdrop. Yet actresses Davis and Sarandon manage to upstage even Monument Valley. Their winning performances create the wind-in-the-hair, openroad sense of freedom needed to convey the film's theme of liberation. Together they forge a believable and appealing bond that carries the film through some of its improbable plot twists. Even the daring finish—a freeze-frame apotheosis of the duo's leap into the Grand Canyon—works, thanks to the vividness of Davis's and Sarandon's portrayals. It all adds up to a highly enjoyable ride.

THEM!

1954 93m bw ★★★½
Science Fiction /PG
WB

James Whitmore (Sgt. Ben Peterson), Edmund Gwenn (Dr. Harold Medford), Joan Weldon (Dr. Patricia Medford), James Arness (Robert Graham), Onslow Stevens (Brig. Gen. O'Brien), Sean McClory (Maj. Kibbee), Chris Drake (Officer Ed Blackburn), Sandy Descher (Little Girl), Mary Alan Hokanson (Mrs. Lodge), Don Shelton (Captain of Troopers)

p, David Weisbart; d, Gordon Douglas; w, Ted Sherdeman, Russell Hughes (based on a story by George Worthing Yates); ph, Sid Hickox; ed, Thomas Reilly; m, Bronislau Kaper; art d, Stanley Fleischer; fx, Ralph Ayres, William Mueller, Francis J. Scheid; cos, Edith Head

THEM! is the best of the monster movies of the 1950s which were rooted in concerns that arose due to the advent of the nuclear age. Whitmore and Drake, two New Mexico state troopers patrolling the desert, happen across a trailer home that has been peeled open like a sardine can and gutted. Hiding nearby is a little girl who is nearly catatonic from fear. All she can utter is the word "Them." As the mystery deepens, FBI man Arness, scientist Gwenn and his daughter Weldon (a scientist in her own right), are called in to help in the investigation. Eventually they learn that secret atomic testing in the area has spawned a colony of 20-foot-long ants. Realizing that if the queen is able to mate, the world may be overrun by the giant creatures, Whitmore and company hurriedly work to locate the nest and destroy it. They trace the creatures to the Los Angeles drainage system (in perhaps the best use of that overly photographed location). Armed with large flame throwers, they succeed in destroying the monstrous ants, but not without making some major sacrifices.

THEM! pulls all this off quite convincingly. The giant ants do look a bit phony, but they are never on screen long enough to become bothersome. In fact, the image of dozens of giant ants in their underground nest is unforgettable. There was no stop-motion animation used in the film. Instead, two actual-sized models were constructed by prop man Dick Smith (one entire ant, and another front section for closeups). Special effects supervisor Ayres was nominated for an Academy Award for his work on the film. The film is produced and performed with such seriousness that one becomes engrossed in the machinations of dealing with such creatures and forgets about plausibility. THEM! was Warner Brothers' highest grossing film of 1954 and inspired countless imitations, all of which were inferior to the original.

THEODORA GOES WILD

1936 94m bw ★★★½
Comedy /A
Columbia

Irene Dunne (Theodora Lynn), Melvyn Douglas (Michael Grant), Thomas Mitchell (Jed Waterbury), Thurston Hall (Arthur Stevenson), Rosalind Keith (Adelaide Perry), Spring Byington (Rebecca Perry), Elisabeth Risdon (Aunt Mary), Margaret McWade (Aunt Elsie), Nana Bryant (Ethel Stevenson), Henry Kolker (Jonathan Grant)

p, Everett Riskin; d, Richard Boleslawski; w, Sidney Buchman (based on a story by Mary E. McCarthy); ph, Joseph Walker; ed, Otto Meyer; m, M.W. Stoloff; art d, Stephen Goosson; cos, Bernard Newman

Dunne's first starring comedy role after several weepers was good enough to secure her an Oscar nomination, her second after the 1931 CIMARRON. Dunne plays the title role, a New England woman who writes a steamy best-seller about the morals of a sleepy little town located north of New York City. The book takes off and she decides to see the big city for herself. Once she arrives in Manhattan she meets the ultrasophisticated artist (Douglas) who did the illustrations for her book, and her escapades begin, arising from her situation as a fish out of water in New York. The quaint and hard-bitten Yankees from her village are examined vis-a-vis the sharp Big Apple types and the film draws the conclusion that there are nuts in both places.

The idea was to produce a screwball comedy on the style of some of Capra's Columbia pictures, but this movie had the wrong Riskin (producer Everett, rather than Capra's longtime associate and screenwriter, Robert) and it just wasn't wacky enough, despite a valiant try by Dunne to breathe life into Buchman's modest if clever script. Her efforts did earn her a Best Actress Oscar nomination, but she lost to Luise Rainer for THE GREAT ZIEGFELD.

Director Boleslawski, the Polish stage director who cut his teeth with the Moscow Arts Theatre, made a number of fine films, most notably CLIVE OF INDIA, THE PAINTED VEIL, and LES MISERABLES, which he directed in succession in 1934-35. Buchman followed this movie by writing MR. SMITH GOES TO WASHINGTON for Capra (and getting an Oscar nomination), then winning the coveted statue for his screenplay for HERE COMES MR. JORDAN. In this film, there are all the predictable situations with the foregone results. The story of a writer who exposed small-town life was done again later in SITTING PRETTY and was actually enacted by author Grace Metalious when she wrote the enormous hit PEYTON PLACE. Both films are better than this one, an enjoyable and amusing caper one wishes were a little better.

THERE'S NO BUSINESS LIKE SHOW BUSINESS
1954 117m c ★★★½
Musical /U
FOX

Ethel Merman (Molly Donahue), Donald O'Connor (Tim Donahue), Marilyn Monroe (Vicky), Dan Dailey (Terrance Donahue), Johnny Ray (Steve Donahue), Mitzi Gaynor (Katy Donahue), Richard Eastham (Lew Harris), Hugh O'Brian (Charles Gibbs), Frank McHugh (Eddie Duggan), Rhys Williams (Father Dineen)

p, Sol C. Siegel; d, Walter Lang; w, Phoebe Ephron, Henry Ephron (based on a story by Lamar Trotti); ph, Leon Shamroy (CinemaScope, DeLuxe Color); ed, Robert Simpson; m, Irving Berlin; art d, Lyle Wheeler, John De Cuir; fx, Ray Kellogg; chor, Robert Alton

Packed with tunes by the incomparable Irving Berlin, this entertaining musical concerns the plight of the Five Donahues, a vaudeville act comprised of Molly and Terrence Donahue (Ethel Merman and Dan Dailey) and their children. Steve (Johnny Ray), the oldest child, who goes off to become a priest, is the first of the brood to leave. Next brother Tim (Donald O'Connor) and sister Katy (Mitzi Gaynor) get antsy and decide to carry on the family tradition in New York. Katy's romance with songwriter Charles Gibbs (Hugh O'Brian) is no problem, but Tim's involvement with nightclub hatcheck girl and aspiring singer Vicky (Marilyn Monroe) is another story. When he believes that Vicky is cheating on him, Tim gets drunk and ends up in an automobile accident. Ultimately, though, things work out for the best, as they have a way of doing in musicals, and all of the Donahues come together for one more big number, the rousing title tune.

THERE'S NO BUSINESS LIKE SHOW BUSINESS is packed with every vaudeville cliche the movies have ever conjured up, yet it is presented in a fresh, colorful, heartwarming manner. Merman is a standout, but the lively cast never allows the singer to dominate, and Monroe, in particular, adds much-needed buoyancy to the somewhat flat story, turning up the temperature with her sexy rendition of "Heat Wave." Nominated for three Oscars: Best Score, Best Motion Picture Story and Best Costume Design.

THERESE
1986 90m c ★★★★
Biography /PG
AFC (France)

Catherine Mouchet (Therese Martin), Aurore Prieto (Celine), Sylvie Habault (Pauline), Ghislaine Mona (Marie), Clemence Massart (Prioress), Nathalie Bernart (Aimee), Beatrice DeVigan (The Singer), Noele Chantre (The Old Woman), Anna Bernelat (The Cripple), Sylvaine Massart (The Nurse)

p, Maurice Bernart; d, Alain Cavalier; w, Alain Cavalier, Camille De Casabianca; ph, Philippe Rousselot (Eclair Color); ed, Isabelle Dedieu; art d, Bernard Evein; cos, Yvette Bonnay

In 1897 Therese Martin, a young French girl, died of tuberculosis in a Carmelite convent in Lisieux. Twenty-eight years later, she was canonized and has since become known as "the Little Flower of Jesus." Her diaries, written in the convent, have been translated into numerous languages and served as the basis for this film directed by Alain Cavalier and cowritten with his daughter, Camille De Casabianca. Catherine Mouchet stars as Therese, a novice who faces the cold, hard life of the convent with great spiritual devotion, suffering in silent physical deterioration. Like all Carmelite nuns, she believes that she is the bride of Jesus Christ. Rather than viewing her "marriage" with Jesus in strictly spiritual terms, however, the schoolgirlish Therese views Him as something like a beau with whom she is infatuated. As her physical condition weakens, she is confined to bed under the care of her fellow nuns and novices—all of whom have come to love her deeply.

In respect for this young saint whose simple and pure devotion led to her canonization, Cavalier and De Casabianca have fashioned a beautiful and sensitive film. Constructed in a series of tableaux, THERESE is sparse, with very little music, limited dialogue, and, most strikingly, a set constructed in a minimal style. Rather than lose his fragile novice in an elaborate convent set, Cavalier places her against the plain grey backdrop of the sound stage, or in a simple pool of light. As Therese, Mouchet is to the film what Renee Falconetti was to Carl Dreyer's PASSION OF JOAN OF ARC: the film rests upon her face, which simply radiates with a saintly glow. Winner of the Jury Prize at the Cannes Film Festival and recipient of Cesars for Best Picture, Best Director, Best Young Female Hopeful (Mouchet), Best Script, and Best Editing (it also received nominations for cinematography, sound, and costumes).

THESE THREE
1936 93m bw ★★★★★
Drama /U
UA

Miriam Hopkins (Martha Dobie), Merle Oberon (Karen Wright), Joel McCrea (Dr. Joseph Cardin), Catharine Doucet (Mrs. Lily Mortar), Alma Kruger (Mrs. Tilford), Bonita Granville (Mary Tilford), Marcia Mae Jones (Rosalie Wells), Carmencita Johnson (Evelyn), Mary Anne Durkin (Joyce Walton), Margaret Hamilton (Agatha)

p, Samuel Goldwyn; d, William Wyler; w, Lillian Hellman (based on her play "The Children's Hour"); ph, Gregg Toland; ed, Daniel Mandell; m, Alfred Newman; art d, Richard Day; cos, Omar Kiam

One of Wyler's finest. Censors forced Lillian Hellman to eliminate the lesbian theme in the screenplay version of her play The Children's Hour, but since the essence of the play deals with the effects of a lie, it didn't really hurt this wonderful film to make the scandal a heterosexual affair instead. Bonita Granville, in an Oscar-nominated role, plays Mary Tilford, a mean, vicious girl who is censured by her teachers at a posh private school run by college friends Martha and Karen (Miriam Hopkins and Merle Oberon). Martha is an austere Yankee type, while Karen is a warm woman who is in love with local doctor Joseph Cardin (Joel McCrea). He reciprocates her passion but maintains a close friendship with Martha. Mary retaliates by telling her grandmother (Alma Kruger) that Martha and Joe had been "carrying on" in a bedroom near the student's quarters. The grandmother knows that Mary is a compulsive liar but believes her when the lie is corroborated by nine-year-old Rosalie (Marcia Mae Jones, every bit as good as Granville). Mary, it seems, is blackmailing the other girl with the knowlege that Rosalie has stolen a watch. Charges and countercharges are hurled, and though the truth eventually comes out, important changes have occurred in everyone's lives.

Lillian Hellman's *The Children's Hour* appeared on Broadway for over 600 performances. Samuel Goldwyn took advantage of the notoriety of Hellman's first stage effort by releasing the movie while the play was still running. He'd purchased the rights for $50,000, but the Production Code people insisted he remove much of what made the play such a sensation. Goldwyn hired Hellman to make the alterations. Despite the script changes, though, there are still moments when it almost seems that Hopkins's secret affections are directed more at Oberon than McCrea. However one reads it, THESE THREE is gripping, adult cinema. Oberon gives one of her best dramatic performances and McCrea is also quite fine. The two child actresses, Granville and Jones, do have the showiest parts, but perhaps the real performances to watch are those of Alma Kruger and Miriam Hopkins. Hopkins, in particular, has rarely been better, her intense, high-strung quality perfectly suited to the role of a woman unable to stop her world from falling apart around her. More than 25 years later, the movie was remade as THE CHILDREN'S HOUR with Hopkins in another role and William Wyler again directing, but that version didn't work as well as this one. In both cases, the major problem was making the audience believe in the character portrayed by Granville (Karen Balkin in the remake). This was the first of eight collaborations for Goldwyn and Wyler and the first for Wyler and the masterful Gregg Toland, who died at 44 after having photographed almost half of Goldwyn's output. Despite Granville's superb acting, she lost the Oscar for Best Supporting Actress to Gale Sondergaard for her work in ANTHONY ADVERSE. Other than MAID OF SALEM (1937) and some Nancy Drew movies, Granville never really did get another chance at bat, eventually marrying millionaire Jack Wrather and becoming a producer. Her work in THESE THREE was a revelation for audiences accustomed to seeing sweet little girls like Shirley Temple onscreen.

THEY ALL LAUGHED

1981 115m c   ★★★
Comedy   PG/
Time-Life/Moon

Audrey Hepburn (*Angela Niotes*), Ben Gazzara (*John Russo*), John Ritter (*Charles Rutledge*), Colleen Camp (*Christy Miller*), Patti Hansen (*Deborah "Sam" Wilson*), Dorothy Stratten (*Dolores Martin*), George Morfogen (*Leon Leondopolous*), Blaine Novak (*Arthur Brodsky*), Sean Ferrer (*Jose*), Linda MacEwen (*Amy Lester*)

p, George Morfogen, Blaine Novak; d, Peter Bogdanovich; w, Peter Bogdanovich; ph, Robby Muller (DeLuxe Color); ed, Scott Vickrey; m, Douglas Dilge; art d, Kert Lundell

The polished Gazzara, the bumbling Ritter, and the ultra-hip Novak work for a detective agency. Over the course of the film,

all three become romantically involved with the women they are shadowing—Hepburn, Hansen, and Stratten playing the objects of their affection. Breezy and carefree, THEY ALL LAUGHED suffers from a weak, hard-to-grasp structure. As lovable as the characters and their situations are, one is never quite sure where the film is leading. The film spent nearly a year on the shelf until director Bogdanovich bought it from Fox and distributed it himself. It is unfortunate that the movie's chief interest lies in the presence of former *Playboy* Playmate Stratten, who was murdered by her husband before the film was released. The circumstances surrounding her death were frighteningly similar to those that Bogdanovich sets up in his film. Stratten is pursued by Ritter while evading the watchful eye of her jealous husband. In real life Stratten was having an affair with Bogdanovich during the filming of THEY ALL LAUGHED and was being trailed by a detective hired by her husband, Paul Snider.

THEY DIED WITH THEIR BOOTS ON

1942 140m bw   ★★★★
Western/Biography/War   /U
WB

Errol Flynn (*George Armstrong Custer*), Olivia de Havilland (*Elizabeth Bacon Custer*), Arthur Kennedy (*Ned Sharp*), Charley Grapewin (*California Joe*), Gene Lockhart (*Samuel Bacon*), Anthony Quinn (*Crazy Horse*), Stanley Ridges (*Maj. Romolus Taipe*), John Litel (*Gen. Phil Sheridan*), Walter Hampden (*Sen. Sharp*), Sydney Greenstreet (*Gen. Winfield Scott*)

d, Raoul Walsh; w, Wally Klein, Aeneas MacKenzie; ph, Bert Glennon; ed, William Holmes; m, Max Steiner; art d, John Hughes; cos, Milo Anderson

If one can ignore the blatantly fictitious nature of this Hollywood "biography" of the still-controversial George Armstrong Custer, THEY DIED WITH THEIR BOOTS ON is a wholly entertaining movie, fueled by Raoul Walsh's direction and Errol Flynn's energetic performance. The film follows Custer (Flynn) from his youth as a West Point cadet to his service in the Civil War and finally to his days with the Seventh Cavalry, which ended with the massacre at Little Big Horn on June 25, 1876. Walsh creates a rousing film, its pace as fast as the many cavalry charges the dashing Custer leads. Unfortunately, the picture does not adhere to the facts and, in many instances, strays far afield to keep Custer's legend intact, going so far as to invest the cavalry commander with impassioned sympathy for the plight of the Indians! Though historically inaccurate, THEY DIED WITH THEIR BOOTS ON still provides sprawling, exciting epic action, with huge masses of men moved in the Civil War scenes, and particularly in the final battle against the Indians, with great skill by Walsh. Walsh used more than 1,000 extras, with mostly Filipinos doubling for the Sioux because, not surprisingly, only 16 real Sioux from the reservation at South Dakota's Fort Yates answered the casting call (the rest, presumably, refusing to insult the memories of their ancestors). Dozens of stuntmen were injured in horse falls, so many that the studio had to set up a field hospital at the location site to handle the daily injuries, with doctors and nurses—and veterinarians—attending the scores of riders and horses hobbling in for treatment after battle scenes. Indeed, three stuntmen died during the filming of this wild actioner: one from a broken neck, another from a heart attack, and, in the most bizarre and gruesome death, one impaled on his own sword—which was real at his own insistence. Despite the film's wanton distortion of history, THEY DIED WITH THEIR BOOTS ON did paint a fairly sympathetic portrait of the Indians. Director Walsh later stated: "Most westerns had depicted the

Indian as a painted, vicious savage. In THEY DIED WITH THEIR BOOTS ON I tried to show him as an individual who only turned violent when his rights as defined by treaty were violated by white men."

THEY DRIVE BY NIGHT
1940 93m bw   ★★★★½
Drama
WB

George Raft (Joe Fabrini), Ann Sheridan (Cassie Hartley), Ida Lupino (Lana Carlsen), Humphrey Bogart (Paul Fabrini), Gale Page (Pearl Fabrini), Alan Hale (Ed J. Carlsen), Roscoe Karns (Irish McGurn), John Litel (Harry McNamara), Henry O'Neill (District Attorney), George Tobias (George Rondolos)

p, Mark Hellinger; d, Raoul Walsh; w, Jerry Wald, Richard Macaulay (based on the novel The Long Haul by A.I. Bezzerides); ph, Arthur Edeson; ed, Oliver S. Garretson, Thomas Richards; m, Adolph Deutsch; art d, John Hughes; fx, Byron Haskin, H.F. Koenekamp, James Gibbons, John Holden, Edwin DuPar; cos, Milo Anderson

Amid tough competition, Ida Lupino steals it. This cult classic is one of the best road movies to emerge from a major studio in the 1940s. Raft and Bogart are truck-driving brothers who have left the large company run by Hale and bought their own truck to work as independents. The first half of the film details their rise as they drive all night, skimp on needed repairs, and struggle to keep their fledgling business afloat. Bogart is married to Page, who resents his neglect of her in favor of the business. One night, when Bogart and Raft are pulled over at a roadside diner, they meet waitress Sheridan. She has a sharp tongue and a mane of red hair, and Raft is almost instantly attracted to her. Later, the hitchhiker the two men pick up turns out to be Sheridan, who has quit her job in the face of her boss's continued advances. Raft sets her up with a room in a boardinghouse. Shyly, he makes some romantic comments, which Sheridan turns away without being discouraging. Bogart falls asleep at the wheel one night and loses his arm in the subsequent accident, forcing Raft to take a job with Hale as traffic manager. Lupino, Hale's venomous wife, sets her sights on Raft, but he refuses to fool around with the boss's wife. Lupino then decides to get rid of her husband, leaving him drunk and unconscious in the car while she closes the door and leaves the engine running. She offers to share with Raft the company she has inherited, but when he refuses, Lupino goes to the police and tells them that Raft forced her to kill her husband. In no time Raft is arrested and charged. Sheridan comes to jail and pleads with Lupino to tell the truth, but Lupino tells her that she will take Raft with her wherever she goes. Things go badly for Raft in court, with circumstantial evidence implicating him and the testimony of his friends doing nothing to clear him. But several people have yet to be heard from, and help comes from the strangest of places.

A loose remake of BORDERTOWN (in which Bette Davis asphyxiates husband Eugene Pallette in order to win Paul Muni), THEY DRIVE BY NIGHT could have been another routine film but for Lupino's incredibly forceful performance and Raft's smooth depiction of the tough trucker. Bogart—still wallowing in the lull in his career between the time THE PETRIFIED FOREST established him as a serious actor and the time HIGH SIERRA finally made him a star—is very good, especially when he is embittered by the loss of his arm. Walsh's direction is as forceful and vigorous as always and this film is among his very best.

THEY LIVE
1988 93m c   ★★★½
Science Fiction   R/18
Alive

Rowdy Roddy Piper (John Nada), Keith David (Frank), Meg Foster (Holly), George "Buck" Flower (Drifter), Peter Jason (Gilbert), Raymond St. Jacques (Street Preacher), Jason Robards, III (Family Man), John Lawrence (Bearded Man), Susan Barnes (Brown-haired Woman), Sy Richardson (Black Revolutionary)

p, Larry Franco; d, John Carpenter; w, John Carpenter (based on the short story "Eight O'Clock in the Morning" by Ray Nelson); ph, Gary B. Kibbe (Panavision, Deluxe Color); ed, Frank Jimenez, Gib Jaffe; m, John Carpenter, Alan Howarth; fx, Frank Carrisosa, Roy Arbogast; cos, Robin Bush

The most vehemently anti-Reagan Hollywood film since Alex Cox's WALKER (1987), John Carpenter's THEY LIVE is a fun-filled throwback to the science-fiction paranoia films of the 1950s. Set in Los Angeles in the near future, the movie shows a society in which the rich have gotten richer while the middle class has eroded and the ranks of the poor and homeless have swelled. A construction worker called John Nada (Roddy Piper) stumbles upon some cheap sunglasses that expose the manipulative propaganda in advertising and television and that show most of the yuppies on the street to be inhuman, with bug eyes and skull-like faces. Nada and his friend Frank (Keith David) track down a group of rebels and join in their effort to destroy Cable 54, the television station that keeps the populace from seeing things clearly. Although Carpenter tries to expose the hypnotic effect capitalism has on its citizens, THEY LIVE never rises above the intellectual level of a comic book. The movie is, however, a great deal of fun, with Carpenter's trademark action and smart, powerful visuals.

THEY LIVE BY NIGHT
1949 95m bw   ★★★★★
Crime   /A
RKO

Cathy O'Donnell (Keechie), Farley Granger (Bowie), Howard da Silva (Chickamaw), Jay C. Flippen (T-Dub), Helen Craig (Mattie), Will Wright (Mobley), Marie Bryant (Singer), Ian Wolfe (Hawkins), William Phipps (Young Farmer), Harry Harvey (Hagenheimer)

p, John Houseman; d, Nicholas Ray; w, Charles Schnee, Nicholas Ray (based on the novel Thieves Like Us by Edward Anderson); ph, George E. Diskant; ed, Sherman Todd; m, Woody Guthrie (uncredited), Leigh Harline; art d, Albert S. D'Agostino, Al Herman; fx, Russell A. Cully

Nicholas Ray's energetic first feature, THEY LIVE BY NIGHT tells the tragic story of two doomed lovers and of their short, fast life together before they are torn apart by the criminal world.

As the film opens, Granger and O'Donnell are shown kissing. A title is superimposed: "This boy and this girl were never properly introduced to the world we live in." In this manner, the young lovers' saga hits the screen. Granger, a decent enough fellow whose greatest fault is his naivete, joins a prison break engineered by da Silva and Flippen, two callous criminals who spare no sentimental thought for Granger's innocence, but simply take him along because they need a third hand for a bank job. An auto accident caused by da Silva injures Granger, who recovers in a dark hideout. He is nursed to health by O'Donnell, a young woman who quickly falls in love with Granger, sensing that he is not like his two partners. Granger returns O'Donnell's affections and the two are soon involved in passionate romance.

Soon they make it legal, marrying in the dilapidated office of a justice of the peace. When da Silva asks him to join another bank job, Granger is not strong enough to say no, but it's not long before Flippen is killed and da Silva has angrily gone off on his own. Soon da Silva, too, is killed, leaving Granger the last of the gang and still sought by the police. The young fugitive wants nothing more than a quiet home for himself and his wife, but his fate has been sealed.

More than a standard cops-and-robbers tale, THEY LIVE BY NIGHT is a Depression-era saga about lovers on the run. Entangled in a fate they cannot escape, and over which they have absolutely no control, they love to the fullest before they are inevitably, tragically separated. Though based on the novel *Thieves Like Us* by Edward Anderson (later filmed by Robert Altman under Anderson's title), THEY LIVE BY NIGHT owes an equal debt to the Bonnie and Clyde myth, which, while it bears no resemblance to this film in plot, has permeated the cinema's image of lovers on the run. (It's an image that can also be seen in 1949's GUN CRAZY and the 1937 Fritz Lang picture YOU ONLY LIVE ONCE.) Ray undertook the project enthusiastically, bringing to his film a personal style and vision evident from its beginning. After Granger and O'Donnell's kiss at the opening, a getaway car carrying the three criminals is seen traveling down a dusty road, pursued by police. Rather than shoot with a standard camera set-up, Ray demanded that the scene be photographed from a helicopter, a highly unorthodox idea that has now become a standard element of the cinematic lexicon. Not only did this sequence open the film with a burst of unharnessed energy, it also conveyed a sense of godlike fate, looking down on Granger and relentlessly pursuing him. Beautifully acted, THEY LIVE BY NIGHT stands today as one of the most poignant and unforgettable noirs ever made.

THEY SHOOT HORSES, DON'T THEY?

1969 129m c	★★★★
Drama	M/15
Palomar	

Jane Fonda *(Gloria Beatty)*, Michael Sarrazin *(Robert Syverton)*, Susannah York *(Alice)*, Gig Young *(Rocky)*, Red Buttons *(Sailor)*, Bonnie Bedelia *(Ruby)*, Bruce Dern *(James)*, Michael Conrad *(Rollo)*, Al Lewis *(Turkey)*, Robert Fields *(Joel)*

p, Irwin Winkler, Robert Chartoff, Sydney Pollack; d, Sydney Pollack; w, James Poe, Robert E. Thompson (based on the novel by Horace McCoy); ph, Philip Lathrop (Panavision, DeLuxe Color); ed, Fredric Steinkamp; m, Johnny Green; prod d, Harry Horner; fx, Blondie Anderson; chor, Tom Panko; cos, Donfeld

An allegorical, socially conscious response to the injustices of the Depression era, THEY SHOOT HORSES, DON'T THEY? has managed to survive the late 1960s, unlike so many other films of that period, without appearing the least bit dated. Preparing the audience for the inevitable, the film begins with Robert Syverton (Sarrazin) standing trial for murder, the details of which are purposely vague. The scene then switches to Chicago's famous Aragon Ballroom, where a dance marathon is about to get underway. Among the contestants is Gloria Beatty (Fonda), an independent, disagreeable loner who seems to enjoy lashing out at those around her. She replaces her original partner with Robert, a drifter with no real desire to participate. Also wearing numbers on their backs are a pregnant farm women (Bedelia), her husband (Dern), a sailor and veteran marathoner with heart trouble (Buttons), and a Jean Harlow clone (York) who hopes to be discovered while dancing in the spotlight. As the master of ceremonies, whose job it is to keep the audience content and the

dancers dancing, is the sleazy, unshaven Rocky (Young). Everyone's reason for participating is simple—three meals a day and a chance at winning the $1,500 prize, a bonanza in the days of record unemployment and bread lines. The tension builds as the emcee goads the dancers to self-destruction and the driven contestants fight among themselves. Several deaths result, and when Robert is asked why he has committed murder, responds, "They shoot horses, don't they?"

Although it is at times heavy-handed, THEY SHOOT HORSES, DON'T THEY? is a *tour de force* of acting. Fonda, best known at the time as Roger Vadim's wife and the sex toy of BARBARELLA, here got her first chance to prove herself as a serious, dramatic actress. For bringing such gritty, sweaty, hopeless self-degradation to the screen, Fonda received universal praise, as well as an Oscar nomination for Best Actress. Young, who won one of the prized statuettes for Best Supporting Actor, is superb in his role, a sharp switch from his usual *bon vivant* parts. The rest of the acting is similarly fine, even though Sarrazin, in what is admittedly one of the film's less interesting parts, doesn't really bring enough presence or imagination to his performance. Sydney Pollack does one of his best jobs of directing, even if his primary strength lies in his rapport with actors. The look of the film is just right and Pollack skillfully evokes the ratty atmosphere amid which explosive emotions come to a boil. At one point camerawork was even done on roller skates to achieve just the right effect for the bedraggled characters on the dance floor. The film uses much Depression-era music for period flavor and contains many references to the Hollywood of that era. This kind of reflexivity helps highlight the dance floor as an arena of action, a microcosm of America, and the parallels with the situation in Vietnam are pretty obvious. Based on a 1935 novel feted by French existentialists and first purchased by Charlie Chaplin, THEY SHOOT HORSES, DON'T THEY? remains a suitably glum yet cathartic film experience. It also received Oscar nominations for director, supporting actress (York), adapted screenplay, art direction and set decoration, editing, music, and costume design.

THEY WERE EXPENDABLE

1945 135m bw	★★★★★
War	/A
MGM	

Robert Montgomery *(Lt. John Brickley)*, John Wayne *(Lt. J.G. "Rusty" Ryan)*, Donna Reed *(2nd Lt. Sandy Davyss)*, Jack Holt *(Gen. Martin)*, Ward Bond *("Boots" Mulcahey)*, Marshall Thompson *(Ens. Snake Gardner)*, Paul Langton *(Ens. Andy Andrews)*, Leon Ames *(Maj. James Morton)*, Arthur Walsh *(Seaman Jones)*, Donald Curtis *(Lt. J.G. "Shorty" Long)*

p, John Ford; d, John Ford, Robert Montgomery (uncredited); w, Frank Wead (based on the book by William L. White); ph, Joseph August; ed, Frank E. Hull, Douglas Biggs; m, Herbert Stothart; art d, Cedric Gibbons, Malcolm Brown; fx, A. Arnold Gillespie

In direct contrast to the flag-waving, jingoistic propaganda films typical of Hollywood during WWII, John Ford's THEY WERE EXPENDABLE is a somber and moving account of America's defeat in the Philippines early in the war. Filming this grim failure, Ford beautifully and poetically captures the heroism and bravery of the men and women who fought there—and does so without impassioned speechifying or gushing patriotism. Instead, Ford commemorates the quiet and uncomplaining devotion to duty, the will to serve, and the nobility of sacrifice of those left in an untenable situation. Based on the exploits of Lt. John Bulkeley, commander of Motor Torpedo Boat Squadron No. 3

(the predecessor of the Navy PT boat force), the film follows the coolly professional lieutenant (Robert Montgomery, in one of his best performances), renamed "Brickley" for the film, and his hot-headed executive officer, Lt. J.G. "Rusty" Ryan (John Wayne), as they struggle to get the Navy to accept the PT boats as a valuable new tool in the war effort. The top commanders, however, see no use for the unit and relegate Brickley and crew to running messages and ferrying supplies. As Bataan and Corregidor fall to the Japanese, however, the PT unit proves itself valuable by sinking many enemy ships, although the effort proves too little too late. Japan emerges triumphant and the American brass is forced to leave their troops stranded before the enemy and to flee to Australia, where they will regroup and plan their return.

From the time Ford shot THEY WERE EXPENDABLE to the day he died, the director was ambivalent about the film, his opinion of the work alternating between disapproval and satisfaction. This may have been largely due to the fact that he was pressured into making THEY WERE EXPENDABLE soon after having seen action himself in the South Pacific as a documentary filmmaker for the Navy. Capt. Ford had lost 13 men in his unit and the making of this film no doubt stirred painful memories for the director, memories he may have preferred to ignore when asked to discuss his films later in life. Despite Ford's ambivalence, THEY WERE EXPENDABLE is one of the greatest films to come out of WWII, a lasting and poignant tribute to those who go in harm's way.

THEY WON'T FORGET

1937 95m bw ★★★★
Drama /A
WB

Claude Rains (Andrew J. Griffin), Gloria Dickson (Sybil Hale), Edward Norris (Robert Paerry Hale), Otto Kruger (Michael Gleason), Allyn Joslyn (William P. Brock), Lana Turner (Mary Clay), Linda Perry (Imogene Mayfield), Elisha Cook, Jr. (Joe Turner), Cy Kendall (Detective Laneart), Clinton Rosemond (Tump Redwine)

p, Mervyn LeRoy; d, Mervyn LeRoy; w, Robert Rossen, Aben Kandel (based on the novel Death in the Deep South by Ward Greene); ph, Arthur Edeson; ed, Thomas Richards; m, Adolph Deutsch; art d, Robert Haas

Aspiring secretary Turner takes a class in her southern hometown, learning dictation and touch-typing from young Norris, a recent arrival from the North. After class, Turner repairs to a local soda fountain (a scene that brings to mind the apocryphal tale of Turner's "discovery" in Schwab's drugstore), then heads back out into the street, where a Confederate Day parade is in progress. The camera tracks the sweatered Turner's progress, catching her figure from every angle, while a marching band plays the rebel anthem "Dixie" in the background. Returning to the deserted classroom to retrieve her misplaced vanity case—having earlier told Norris that she doesn't "feel dressed without [her] lipstick"—Turner hears the ominous sound of footsteps in the hallway. As her face, in closeup, contorts with fear, the film dissolves to a symbolic musket blast at the Confederate Day commemoration. Back at school, Rosmond, the black janitor, finds Turner's body and alerts authorities to the murder. District attorney Rains, who has long nursed political ambitions, decides to try to convict northern teacher Norris, rather than the most obvious suspect in the crime, Rosmond. "Anyone can convict a Negro in the South," says the ambitious Rains, who wants a better challenge than Rosmond might afford him.

Chiefly known now for introducing Turner to cinema audiences—she'd done bits before, but had never gotten billing—THEY WON'T FORGET (which followed close on the heels of Fritz Lang's famed lynch-mob film FURY) was touted by some critics as a true classic and cited by the National Board of Review as one of the ten best of 1937. The screenplay closely follows its source, Ward Greene's novel Death in the Deep South, which was in turn based on a true incident that occurred in Atlanta in 1915. Turner, though sixth-billed and featured only in the first few minutes of the film, nonetheless makes a vivid impression as the fresh-faced, blossoming adolescent victim. Director LeRoy's 75-foot tracking shot of Turner's sensual strut established in every viewer's mind the sex-related nature of her character's murder without in any way risking the wrath of the censors; if the character was violated, the Production Code was not.

THIEF

1981 122m c ★★★½
Crime R/X
UA

James Caan (Frank), Tuesday Weld (Jessie), Willie Nelson (Okla), James Belushi (Barry), Robert Prosky (Leo), Tom Signorelli (Attaglia), Dennis Farina (Carl), Nick Nickeas (Nick), W.R. Brown (Mitch), Norm Tobin (Guido)

p, Jerry Bruckheimer, Ronnie Caan; d, Michael Mann; w, Michael Mann (based on the book The Home Invaders by Frank Hohimer); ph, Donald Thorin (Technicolor); ed, Dov Hoenig; m, Tangerine Dream; prod d, Mel Bourne; art d, Mary Dodson

Frank (James Caan) is a professional thief, one of the best in the business, who wants to make one last big score so he can settle down with his girlfriend Jessie (Tuesday Weld). That desire gets him involved with vicious big-time mobster Leo (Robert Prosky) and the robbery of a high-security vault in Los Angeles, aided by his friend Barry (Jim Belushi). This was the first feature film for director Michael Mann (MANHUNTER, TV's "Miami Vice"), and it was a stunner. Mann demonstrates an understanding of the casting, location, costumes, music (a superior score by Tangerine Dream), and visuals. The performances by Caan, Prosky, Belushi, and Weld are nothing less than terrific. Caan has his best role since THE GODFATHER, but Prosky (TV's "Hill Street Blues") nearly steals the film by underplaying the role of the powerful mob chieftain. This film is brutally realistic in its street language and violence, so sensitive viewers should be warned.

THIEF OF BAGHDAD, THE

1940 106m c ★★★★★
Fantasy /U
London Films (U.K.)

Conrad Veidt (Jaffar), Sabu (Abu), June Duprez (Princess), John Justin (Ahmad), Rex Ingram (Djinni), Miles Malleson (Sultan), Morton Selten (King), Mary Morris (Halima), Bruce Winston (Merchant), Hay Petrie (Astrologer)

p, Alexander Korda; d, Ludwig Berger, Michael Powell, Tim Whelan, Zoltan Korda, William Cameron Menzies, Alexander Korda; w, Lajos Biro, Miles Malleson; ph, Georges Perinal, Osmond Borradaile (Technicolor); ed, William Hornbeck, Charles Crichton; m, Miklos Rozsa; prod d, Vincent Korda; fx, Lawrence Butler, Tom Howard, John Mills; cos, Oliver Messel, John Armstrong, Marcel Vertes

Perhaps the most splendid fantasy film ever made. Alexander Korda produced, Michael Powell and five others directed this breathtaking attempt to capture *The Arabian Nights* on film. An early example of outstanding Technicolor work, this became a cult favorite among young Hollywood directors of the 1970s such as Francis Coppola and George Lucas. The special effects, though quaint by today's standards, still deliver the goods. This lively collection of incidents from the Arabian Nights fables makes most modern fantasy blockbusters look anemic in comparison.

Abu (Sabu), a charming street urchin, is thrown into a Baghdad dungeon for thievery. Before long, Prince Ahmad (John Justin), the deposed ruler of the realm, joins him there. Ahmad has been overthrown by his righthand man, the evil grand vizier, Jaffar (Conrad Veidt). The unlikely duo manage to escape and flee to exotic Basra, where Ahmad is smitten by Basra's princess (June Duprez). Learning that Jaffar is about to abduct the beauty, Ahmad and Abu try to thwart the plan, but the wicked magician turns them into a blind beggar and a dog respectively. When the princess promises to wed Jaffar, he revokes his curse, and sails back to Baghdad with her. All seems lost until Abu—after a series of adventures involving a genie, an "All-Seeing Eye," and a magic carpet—finds a way to save the day.

Although six directors worked on the film, it remains surprisingly seamless as it maintains such a consistent grandeur and even pace. The marvelous set designs by Vincent Korda seem *truly* out of this world, and Miklos Rozsa has created a dynamic and memorable score. Conrad Veidt, looking cool and cruel in his dashing black outfits, is one of the screen's great villains. Sabu is simply adorable as the little thief of Baghdad. Duprez's unusual but stunning beauty is only enhanced by the rich Technicolor and the handsome Justin looks just right as the wan prince. African-American actor Rex Ingram is outstanding in the small but unforgettable role of the genie. Film fantasy just doesn't get much better than this.

THIEVES LIKE US

1974   123m   c   ★★★½
Crime   R/AA
UA

Keith Carradine *(Bowie)*, Shelley Duvall *(Keechie)*, John Schuck *(Chiçamaw)*, Bert Remsen *(T-Dub)*, Louise Fletcher *(Mattie)*, Ann Latham *(Lula)*, Tom Skerritt *(Dee Mobley)*, Al Scott *(Capt. Stammers)*, John Roper *(Jasbo)*, Mary Waits *(Noel)*

p, Jerry Bick; d, Robert Altman; w, Calder Willingham, Joan Tewkesbury, Robert Altman (based on the novel by Edward Anderson); ph, Jean Boffety; ed, Lou Lombardo

---

A well-done remake of THEY LIVE BY NIGHT that's slightly long but unusually free of Altman's customary indulgences. A 1930s crime story with humor and humanity, THIEVES LIKE US owes more than a passing nod to BONNIE AND CLYDE and BADLANDS in theme and treatment. Young killer-crook Carradine escapes from a Mississippi jail with older, hard-bitten criminals Remsen and Schuck. After a brief respite, they return to the only way they know how to make a living: robbing banks. Carradine's girlfriend is Skerritt's daughter, Duvall, and she becomes part of the team as they go on a rampage. The three men are all armed and dangerous but not very good at what they do, and that incompetency eventually catches up with them. The title is drawn from the trio's theory that everyone is a thief in one way or another and big businesses, like banks, are just as guilty of criminal activity as they are. The fact that Carradine, Schuck, and Remsen kill people as part of their daily labors never enters into their thinking. After a few thefts, Carradine intends to leave the bank robbing to move to Mexico with Duvall, where he hopes

he can find some serenity. Remsen has a fling with Latham, which proves his undoing. The robbers are celebrated in the press, feared by the towns, and chased by the cops, who begin moving closer. Remsen is erased by the law, the psychotic Schuck is nabbed, and Carradine and Duvall continue on the run until they hide out at the house of Remsen's sister-in-law, Fletcher. Carradine tries to get Schuck out of jail and succeeds, then the men quarrel and he leaves Schuck and returns to Fletcher's house where the cops are waiting. While Fletcher holds the screaming, pregnant Duvall, Carradine is mowed down by the cops. Duvall later has the baby and moves off to find a new beginning.

Unlike BONNIE AND CLYDE, there is a real love story between Carradine and Duvall that comes across. The music and background sounds were supplied by John Dunning, who is credited for "radio research." He provided radio shows like "Gangbusters," "The Heart of Gold," remote band broadcasts, and an actual "Romeo and Juliet" dramatization that is heard while Duvall and Carradine are making love. Most of the killings are referred to rather than seen, so this is a character study more than a violence film. The executive producer was George Litto, who used to be Altman's agent and was making his bow in production. Litto was later responsible for a few of De Palma's debacles. Fletcher, wife of producer Bick, makes her film debut in this picture. Remsen, who is one of Altman's stock company, has another career as one of the most respected casting directors in Hollywood. Coscreenwriter Tewkesbury makes a cameo.

THIN MAN, THE

1934   93m   bw   ★★★★½
Mystery/Comedy   /A
MGM

William Powell *(Nick Charles)*, Myrna Loy *(Nora Charles)*, Maureen O'Sullivan *(Dorothy Wynant)*, Nat Pendleton *(Lt. John Guild)*, Minna Gombell *(Mimi Wynant)*, Porter Hall *(MacCauley)*, Henry Wadsworth *(Tommy)*, William Henry *(Gilbert Wynant)*, Harold Huber *(Nunheim)*, Cesar Romero *(Chris Jorgenson)*

p, Hunt Stromberg; d, W.S. Van Dyke, II; w, Albert Hackett, Frances Goodrich (based on the novel by Dashiell Hammett); ph, James Wong Howe; ed, Robert J. Kern; m, William Axt; art d, Cedric Gibbons, David Townsend, Edwin B. Willis; cos, Dolly Tree

---

Nick Charles (Powell) is a retired detective who has married the wealthy Nora (Loy) and now intends to devote himself to looking after her money and doing some serious drinking. (You can tell this film was made just after the repeal of Prohibition.) They travel to New York for the holidays, and there meet Dorothy (O'Sullivan), who asks Nick to help her find her missing father (Ellis). He's an inventor who months before went into seclusion to work on a project but hasn't been heard from since. Nick, whose reputation precedes him, isn't anxious to end his happy retirement, but Nora, eager for thrills, prods him into it. Together with their wire-haired terrier Asta, the newlyweds solve the case.

Praise should go to the writers of the film's delightful dialogue and to the underrated Van Dyke, a director of craft who knows how to make a film move. The story, meanwhile, faithfully taken from Hammett's novel, proves eminently serviceable if not quite the stuff of genius. What really makes THE THIN MAN an enduring classic, though, is the interplay between Powell and Loy, one of the greatest *happily* married couples ever to flicker on a screen. The repartee they shoot back and forth is priceless, as in one scene the morning after a gunman has broken into their suite and superficially wounded Nick before being subdued and hauled away. As they read the morning papers about the event,

Powell says, "I'm a hero, I was shot twice in the *Tribune*." Loy: "I read you were shot five times in the tabloids." "It's not true. He didn't come anywhere near my tabloids," Powell parries. Loy has a terrific comic bit entering a scene loaded down with packages and dragged by their feisty pooch, and Powell has great fun shooting the balls off a Christmas tree with his favorite present, a gun. Loy and Powell proved so popular that they were teamed twelve more times during their careers (thirteen if you count her cameo in THE SENATOR WAS INDISCREET), six of the pairings coming in the THIN MAN series. These sleuthfests would continue with lessening success for 13 years, but at their peak (the first three films), Nick and Nora were one of the best movie buys around. Loy and Powell set a style for connubial comic banter which many performers still attempt in vain to duplicate today. Ask one of the few who caught the Broadway bomb NICK AND NORA if you don't believe us.

THING, THE

1951 87m bw   ★★★★
Science Fiction
Winchester

Kenneth Tobey *(Capt. Pat Hendry)*, James Arness *(The Thing)*, Margaret Sheridan *(Nikki Nicholson)*, Robert Cornthwaite *(Dr. Arthur Carrington)*, Douglas Spencer *(Ned "Scotty" Scott)*, James Young *(Lt. Ed Dykes)*, Dewey Martin *(Bob)*, Robert Nichols *(Lt. Ken Erickson)*, William Self *(Sgt. Barnes)*, Eduard Franz *(Dr. Stern)*

p, Howard Hawks; d, Christian Nyby, Howard Hawks (uncredited); w, Charles Lederer (based on the story "Who Goes There" by Don A. Stuart); ph, Russell Harlan; ed, Roland Gross; m, Dimitri Tiomkin; art d, Albert S. D'Agostino, John Hughes; fx, Don Steward, Linwood Dunn

Classic sci-fi chiller about a slimey alien presence (James Arness, who would later be Marshall Dillon on TV's "Gunsmoke") that invades an arctic station. THE THING is very much a film of its producer, Howard Hawks, although Christian Nyby, Hawks's editor on RED RIVER, was credited as director. Hawks's style, themes, and handling of actors, however, dominate the film.

Set in the subzero environment of the North Pole, the film follows an Air Force captain, Tobey, as he and his crew fly to Polar Expedition Six—a group of scientists led by Cornthwaite who are studying arctic conditions—to investigate reports that a flying craft of some sort has crashed into the ice. At the base camp Tobey finds an old flame, Sheridan, who is working as Cornthwaite's secretary. Sheridan is a tough woman in the Hawksian mold, and the romantic banter between her and Tobey is a joy to watch. When Tobey meets with Cornthwaite, he is shown pictures of the strange object as it streaked across the sky. A party is organized to investigate the crash site, and when they arrive they discover that the object has sunk into the ice and has been frozen. The soldiers, scientists, and Spencer, a journalist, fan out to determine the shape of the object. When they all take their places at the edge of the object, they have formed a perfect circle.

The men decide to melt the ship out of the ice by detonating thermite bombs around it, but the plan goes awry and the ship is destroyed. Gravely disappointed, the men head back for their plane only to discover something else frozen in the ice—an alien. Using axes, they cut out a block of ice encasing the extraterrestrial corpse and bring it back to the base camp. While the soldiers and scientists debate over what to do with the creature, the ice melts and the eight-foot tall thing breaks free of its prison, very much alive—and not at all friendly.

THE THING was based rather loosely on a science-fiction story by John W. Campbell, Jr. (it was first published under his pseudonym, Don A. Stuart), in which the alien had the ability to change its shape at will, causing havoc among the soldiers who begin to suspect *each other* of harboring the monster. Lederer's screenplay (rumor has it that frequent Lederer-Hawks collaborator Ben Hecht had a hand in it as well) streamlines the narrative and allows Hawks to concentrate on the human interaction in the face of crisis. Whereas the original story (and Carpenter's remake) is a study of paranoia among comrades, Hawks's film revels in the interworkings of a tough group of professionals capable of handling any crisis if they stick together. The characters operate as an ensemble with no one being given much solo screen time. Their unity is what the film is about, a familiar Hawksian theme.

In a genre often dependent upon elaborate special effects, THE THING is relatively stark and restrained. The monster is only glimpsed in shadows and darkness, thus allowing the imagination of the audience fill in the terrifying details. Harlan's cinematography and Tiomkin's eerie early electronic score (he used a theremin) provide enough chills to satisfy any horror fan. No ray-guns, strange costumes, or futuristic inventions are needed here; even the spaceship is only suggested, never seen. The fact that the alien closely resembles a man heightens the sense of personal, human struggle that is the cornerstone of all good drama.

THING, THE

1982 108m c   ★★
Science Fiction   R/18
Universal

Kurt Russell *(MacReady)*, Wilford Brimley *(Blair)*, T.K. Carter *(Nauls)*, David Clennon *(Palmer)*, Keith David *(Childs)*, Richard Dysart *(Dr. Copper)*, Charles Hallahan *(Norris)*, Peter Maloney *(Bennings)*, Richard Masur *(Clark)*, Donald Moffat *(Garry)*

p, David Foster, Lawrence Turman; d, John Carpenter; w, Bill Lancaster (based on the story "Who Goes There?" by John W. Campbell, Jr.); ph, Dean Cundey (Panavision, Technicolor); ed, Todd Ramsay; m, Ennio Morricone; prod d, John J. Lloyd; art d, Henry Larrecq; fx, Roy Arbogast, Albert Whitlock, Leroy Routly, Rob Bottin, Michael Clifford

A major disappointment. Horror director John Carpenter let the special effects run amok in this remake of the 1951 science-fiction classic THE THING, and they ooze over everything in the film. The plot is pared down to the essentials: a group of American scientists in the Antarctic find the frozen remains of an alien, which they soon thaw out. The only problem is that the alien is not dead, and it springs back to life, taking on whatever form suits its purpose (dogs, men, etc.). The cast is superb, but unfortunately the actors are not allowed to show their stuff because their characters are nothing more than fodder for the effects, and their performances are limited to standing around grimacing at the gore. Kurt Russell once again sleepwalks through his role (as he did in ESCAPE FROM NEW YORK), and the ending of the film is unsatisfying and ambiguous. The effects are absolutely fantastic, complicated, and grotesque, but this remake ultimately fails because it is more an exercise in technique than an essay in human terror.

THINGS CHANGE

1988 105m c   ★★★½
Comedy/Crime   PG
Filmhaus

Don Ameche *(Gino)*, Joe Mantegna *(Jerry)*, Robert Prosky *(Joseph Vincent)*, J.J. Johnston *(Frankie)*, Ricky Jay *(Mr. Silver)*, Mike Nussbaum *(Mr. Greene)*, Jack Wallace *(Repair Shop Owner)*, Dan Conway *(Butler)*, Willo Hausman *(Miss Bates)*, Gail Silver *(Housemaid)*

p, Michael Hausman; d, David Mamet; w, David Mamet, Shel Silverstein; ph, Juan Ruiz-Anchia; ed, Trudy Ship; m, Alaric Jans; prod d, Michael Merritt; cos, Nan Cibula

THINGS CHANGE is a surprisingly light, upbeat follow-up to David Mamet's dark directorial debut, HOUSE OF GAMES. One of the most powerful Mafia dons in the country, Mr. Greene (Mike Nussbaum), has murdered someone. An elderly Sicilian bootblack, Gino (Don Ameche), who bears more than a passing resemblance to the don, agrees to take the fall and is turned over to the custody of Jerry (Joe Mantegna), a mob goon who is "on probation." Jerry feels sorry for the old guy and impulsively decides to take him to Lake Tahoe for a final fling before jail. Because of Jerry's reticence, the staff of the mob-owned hotel treats the mysterious old man as if he were an important Mafia don. After some suspenseful moments, Jerry takes Gino back to Chicago to find things have changed in an unexpected way.

In an era in which most American comedies rely on big gags, blunt jokes, or elaborate slapstick for laughs, Mamet has taken audience expectations and played upon them brilliantly, without ever delivering the anticipated payoff. Much of the charm of THINGS CHANGE lies in the characters. Mamet's dialogue is crisp, the wit dry, and there are plenty of great lines in the film, most of which are delivered flawlessly.

THINGS TO COME

1936 113m bw   ★★★★
Science Fiction   /PG
London Films   (U.K.)

Raymond Massey *(John Cabal/Oswald Cabal)*, Edward Chapman *(Pippa Passworthy/Raymond Passworthy)*, Ralph Richardson *(The Boss)*, Margaretta Scott *(Roxana/Rowena)*, Cedric Hardwicke *(Theotocopulos)*, Maurice Braddell *(Dr. Harding)*, Sophie Stewart *(Mrs. Cabal)*, Derrick de Marney *(Richard Gordon)*, Ann Todd *(Mary Gordon)*, Pearl Argyle *(Catherine Cabal)*

p, Alexander Korda; d, William Cameron Menzies; w, H.G. Wells, Lajos Biro (based on the book *The Shape of Things to Come* by H.G. Wells); ph, Georges Perinal; ed, Charles Crichton, Francis D. Lyon; m, Arthur Bliss; prod d, Vincent Korda; fx, Ned Mann, Lawrence Butler, Edward Cohen, Harry Zech, Wally Vaevers, Ross Jacklin; cos, John Armstrong, Rene Hubert, Marchioness of Queensbury

Not since Fritz Lang's METROPOLIS had there been a science fiction film of such epic scope and vision as Alexander Korda's production of H.G. Wells's 1933 treatise on the future, *The Shape of Things to Come*. The story begins in 1940 and is set in an urban metropolis known as Everytown. It is Christmastime, but the celebration is tempered by fear of another world war. As Raymond Massey discusses the nature of war with his friends Edward Chapman and Maurice Braddell, scores of bombers are flying over the English channel to drop bombs on Everytown. Massey, a pilot, is called to duty. The war drags on for decades and the devastation is immense. By 1966 a strange disease has gripped the land, and those who have survived the destruction are succumbing to it. In 1970, the disease has run its course, having eliminated half of the world's population. The ruins of Everytown are now run by Ralph Richardson, a vagabond killer who sends his private army to do battle with other survivors who

live in the nearby hills. Richardson's dream is to repair his fleet of airplanes so that he can secure oil-rich territories. A strange looking plane lands and a much older Massey emerges wearing a jet-black spacesuit and an enormous glass helmet. He announces that he is a representative of "Wings over the World," an organization of scientists and engineers determined to end war and build a new civilization based on technology. Richardson sees Massey as a threat to his fiefdom and has him imprisoned. A fleet of planes sent by "Wings over the World" soon arrives and drops bombs containing the "gas of peace," which causes all the citizens of Everytown to temporarily lose consciousness. Richardson dies, and Massey finds this an appropriate prelude to the building of a new world. What follows is a lengthy montage sequence showing the reconstruction of Everytown. Giant digging machines plow their way under the earth where the new, entirely self-sufficent city will be constructed. Artificial sunlight is perfected, as are people-moving machines and television. By the year 2036, man turns his attention to the stars. Massey's great-grandson (whom Massey also plays), the ruler of the new Everytown, finds himself having to cope with a revolt led by Cedric Hardwicke, an artist who feels that the new society has forsaken human values for technology. The focus of Hardwicke's hatred is a giant space cannon Massey has constructed to launch a rocket to colonize the moon. Massey's daughter, Pearl Argyle, and her boyfriend, Kenneth Villiers, volunteer to be the first to travel to the moon. Hardwicke's followers revolt and charge the space cannon. Villiers and Argyle race for the spacecraft and are launched in the nick of time.

Eager to have Wells's participation in the project, producer Korda approached the great author and offered him the chance to write the screenplay. Two years and four drafts later, with considerable help from Korda, writer Lajos Biro, and director William Menzies, the script was completed. Wells was allowed to wander around the set during production influencing every detail of the film from the costumes and set design to the blocking of the actors. Everything about THINGS TO COME, its strengths and its considerable weaknesses, may be directly attributed to Wells. While the epic scope of the film and its vision of the future are impressive, the human element is sorely lacking. The dialogue is very stilted and uninteresting: there is little interaction among characters and everyone makes speeches. It is a tribute to Massey's skill as an actor that the speeches play as well as they do.

Though the film fails as a human drama, it succeeds impressively in the scenes of devastation and reconstruction—a purely visual experience. Korda's brother Vincent was in charge of the production design and he plundered every new concept in architecture, industry, and design for the Everytown of 2036. Famed Hungarian futurist Laszlo Moholy-Nagy was hired to contribute his vision, but his designs were scrapped as too impractical. Wells, of course, had final approval on everything, but eventually he grew frustrated with the filmmaking process and admitted he knew little about making movies. Menzies, one of the most influential art directors in the history of motion pictures, was the perfect choice to direct the film (though Lewis Milestone was signed on at one time). Though his skill in directing actors was negligible, Menzies possessed a true feel for design and knew how to photograph it. At Wells' insistence, Arthur Bliss was brought in before production started to compose the score based on the script and Wells' suggestions. (The author felt that the music should be incorporated into the filmmaking process from the beginning, instead of after the filming was completed.) The resulting music was thus wholly integrated with the visuals. Bliss's work on the film proved so popular with the critics and the public that his music for THINGS TO COME was the first movie score to be recorded commercially and sold in record stores. When it was all over, Korda had spent over $1.5 million on THINGS TO COME, an incredible sum for the time. The film failed to ignite the box office, but it eventually made money. The original release in Britain ran 130 minutes, but the running time was cut for the US. (There are several different versions of the film now in distribution, running the gamut from 96 min. to 130 min.) Despite its flaws, THINGS TO COME is a truly epic work which continues to fascinate.

THIRD MAN, THE

1950 104m bw   ★★★★★
Thriller   /PG
London Films   (U.K.)

Joseph Cotten (Holly Martins), Orson Welles (Harry Lime), Alida Valli (Anna Schmidt), Trevor Howard (Maj. Calloway), Paul Hoerbiger (Porter), Ernst Deutsch (Baron Kurtz), Erich Ponto (Dr. Winkel), Siegfried Breuer (Popescu), Bernard Lee (Sgt. Paine), Geoffrey Keen (British Policeman)

p, David O. Selznick, Alexander Korda, Carol Reed; d, Carol Reed; w, Graham Greene; ph, Robert Krasker; ed, Oswald Hafenrichter; m, Anton Karas; prod d, Vincent Korda, Joseph Bato, John Hawkesworth

A gripping, beautifully structured picture and a *tour de force* from British director Carol Reed. American pulp novelist Holly Martins (Cotten) arrives in bleak postwar Vienna, having been promised a job by old friend Harry Lime (Welles). Holly soon is informed that his dear friend Harry is dead, killed in an accident and, in fact, his body is about to be lowered into a grave. He attends the funeral, where he meets the beautiful Anna (Valli), Lime's one-time love. Inquiring of British officer Calloway (Howard) about Lime, Holly learns that his friend was a racketeer. Holly vows to carry out his own investigation into Lime's background and clear him of the crimes Calloway insists he committed. What results makes for a powerful examination of friendship and loyalty in the face of social obligations.

   There's so much to recommend THE THIRD MAN that one can only scratch the surface in mentioning its strengths. It gives the incredibly intoxicating feel of being a happy accident, and yet the ingredients are all there. Anton Karas's amazing zither music will haunt you for the rest of your life, and yet you will never mind. The camerawork of genius Krasker (Britain's greatest at that time) makes marvelous use of realistic city locales, darkly menacing alleys and inventively canted framings. The dozens of references to Harry Lime really prime us for his delayed appearance, and Orson Welles's enigmatic performance is so electric that one is not disappointed. (That entrance, in fact, remains one of cinema's greatest.) Cotten, meanwhile, gives a tangy yet subtle spin to the concept of the Ugly American abroad, and Howard lends both sympathy and edge to the determined police inspector. The remarkable Valli, an intense and gifted Italian star who cries out for adjectives like "Garbo", gives a wondrously poignant performance as well. Reed's direction has perhaps never been better, from the thrilling chase through the sewers to the accusations of the little boy to the quieter romantic moments. Grahame Greene's script is both adult and suspenseful, and we absolutely agree with the famous final moment (which may not please everybody, but deal with it!). It's hard to choose just one scene to sum up this somehow poetic thriller, but the legendary scene on the ferris wheel may best represent the perfect blend of great writing, acting, and directing which distinguishes

this unforgettable film. Remember: 700 years of peace equals one cuckoo clock!

THIRD MAN ON THE MOUNTAIN

1959 107m c   ★★★★
Adventure   /U
Disney

Michael Rennie (Capt. John Winter), James MacArthur (Rudi Matt), Janet Munro (Lizbeth Hempel), James Donald (Franz Lerner), Herbert Lom (Emil Saxo), Laurence Naismith (Teo Zurbriggen), Lee Patterson (Klaus Wesselhoft), Walter Fitzgerald (Herr Hempel), Nora Swinburne (Frau Mott), Ferdy Mayne (Andreas)

p, William H. Anderson; d, Ken Annakin; w, Eleanore Griffin (based on the novel Banner in the Sky by James Ramsey Ullman); ph, Harry Waxman (Technicolor); ed, Peter Boita; m, William Alwyn; prod d, John Howell; chor, Mme. Derivaz

Set against the backdrop of the Matterhorn (called the Citadel here), this exciting, beautifully photographed picture is the story of youth finding itself. MacArthur, a young boy whose father was killed while climbing the Citadel, is determined to complete the ascent himself. His youthful exuberance leads to problems when he joins the climbing party led by Rennie, then MacArthur's mother and uncle forbid the boy to climb anymore. But with the help of Munro, Naismith, and Donald, MacArthur soon masters the art of climbing. Later, MacArthur even saves Rennie during an ascent up the mountain.

   A fine film for children, THIRD MAN ON THE MOUNTAIN offers an uplifting message about courage without becoming heavy-handed. The cast is uniformly excellent, with MacArthur especially good as the film's lead. The breathtaking photography of the Alps is also well used. The cast was taught the fundamentals of mountain climbing, which MacArthur took to with great ease. He later gave the production crew and insurance company assigned to the film quite a fright when he snuck off one day to actually climb the Matterhorn by himself. MacArthur's real-life mother, Helen Hayes, makes a cameo appearance as a tourist, as does Ullman, the author of the novel that was the basis for the film. THIRD MAN ON THE MOUNTAIN was later shown on TV's "Wonderful World of Disney" under the title BANNER IN THE SKY.

1959 96m bw   ★★★
Drama
Mark VII

Jack Webb (Sam Gatlin), William Conrad (Jim Bathgate), David Nelson (Earl Collins), Whitney Blake (Peggy Gatlin), Louise Lorimer (Bernice Valentine), James Bell (Ben Quinn), Nancy Valentine (Jan Price), Joe Flynn (Hy Shapiro), Richard Bakalyan (Carl Thompson), Dick Whittinghill (Fred Kendall)

p, Jack Webb; d, Jack Webb; w, William Bowers; ph, Edward Colman; ed, Robert M. Leeds; m, Ray Heindorf; art d, Feild M. Gray, Gibson Holley

Interesting feature directed by and starring Webb as the managing editor of a newspaper working the late shift on a more or less typical Thursday night. Conrad is the crusty city editor, Lorimer, the dowager rewrite-woman who has seen it all and remained above it, and Nelson, the much put-upon copy boy. The film starts as Webb arrives in the city room late after his regular visit to the graves of his first wife and child. He is having trouble with his new wife, who wants to adopt a child, something Webb just can't bring himself to do. As the night goes on, two news items come into prominence: the first concerns a little girl who wanders into the city's storm drains and becomes lost as a storm begins to fill the sewers; the second is the story of an attempt by Air Force pilots, Lorimer's grandson among them, to set a new record flying from Hawaii to Washington, DC. The whole office holds its breath as the search for the girl continues while the waters rise, and as the planes disappear. Eventually the girl is found and the story is the headline, but the plane story is less happy, for the planes are discovered to have crashed with no survivors. Lorimer is visibly distressed and Webb tells her to go home, but she insists on writing up the story of her grandson's death before going. Webb comes to some conclusions about life and death during the evening's events and tells his wife that he no longer opposes adopting a child. Well-done newspaper story has the usual faults of Webb's films—dialogue staccato to the point of silliness and a directorial style serviceable at best, but it works here, especially in the later scenes as the staff gets down to the real work of getting the paper out. Conrad is very good as the city editor and Lorimer gives a convincing performance as a woman whose job is more important than her emotions. One of the most accurate and most memorable newspaper films ever made, this is also one of Webb's best productions.

30 IS A DANGEROUS AGE, CYNTHIA

1968 85m c ★★★½
Comedy /U
Columbia (U.K.)

Dudley Moore (*Rupert Street*), Eddie Foy, Jr. (*Oscar*), Suzy Kendall (*Louise Hammond*), John Bird (*Herbert Greenslade*), Duncan Macrae (*Jock McCue*), Patricia Routledge (*Mrs. Woolley*), Peter Bayliss (*Victor*), John Wells (*Hon. Gavin Hopton*), Harry Towb (*Mr. Woolley*), Jonathan Routh (*Capt. Gore-Taylor*)

p, Walter Shenson; d, Joseph McGrath; w, Dudley Moore, Joseph McGrath, John Wells; ph, Billy Williams; ed, Bill Blunden; m, Dudley Moore; art d, Brian Eatwell; cos, Bermans

Before suffering as a middle-aged crazy in Blake Edwards' *10*, Moore played a man depressed by the prospect of turning 30 in this comedy for which he also cowrote the script, wrote the score, and conducted his own trio playing the background music. He's a musician working in a London nightclub owned by MacRae. He wants desperately to write a smash musical and also to get married to his ideal woman, whom he hasn't found. When Kendall moves into the boarding house where he lives, he falls for her and pursues her with a vengeance, though she already has a boyfriend (Nicky Henson). When Moore comes on too strongly for Henson's taste, Henson breaks Moore's arm. Unable to play the piano, Moore heads for Dublin to work on his musical and there is inspired by a whimsical Irish storyteller (Michael MacLiammoir). He finishes his musical, but before returning to London to give the work to Bayliss, his agent, he heads for Birmingham because he heard Kendall had gone there after having a fight with Henson. Of course, he wins Kendall's heart, and his play is a smash. Yes, it's all contrived and preposterous, but there's enough humor to keep it all humming pleasantly along. Moore was married to Kendall at the time this film was made.

39 STEPS, THE

1935 85m bw ★★★★★
Spy /U
Gaumont (U.K.)

Madeleine Carroll (*Pamela*), Robert Donat (*Richard Hannay*), Lucie Mannheim (*Miss Smith/Annabella*), Godfrey Tearle (*Prof. Jordan*), Peggy Ashcroft (*Margaret*), John Laurie (*John*), Helen Haye (*Mrs. Jordan*), Wylie Watson (*Mr. Memory*), Frank Cellier (*Sheriff Watson*), Peggy Simpson (*Young Maid*)

p, Michael Balcon, Ivor Montagu; d, Alfred Hitchcock; w, Charles Bennett, Alma Reville, Ian Hay (based on the novel by John Buchan); ph, Bernard Knowles; ed, Derek Twist; m, Louis Levy; prod d, Otto Wendorff, Albert Jullion; fx, Jack Whitehead; cos, Joe Strassner

Along with THE LADY VANISHES, one of Hitchcock's best British films, and a prototype for so much of what would follow in his American career. For those who love a grand spy mystery, a wild chase, and a harrowing portrait of an innocent man struggling to prove his innocence while the world turns inexplicably against him, THE 39 STEPS is ideal. Richard Hannay (Donat) is on vacation in London when he meets a mysterious woman (Mannheim) who tells him of a spy ring which she is trying to crack. She doesn't know the identity of the masterspy, but does know that he is missing a portion of the little finger on his right hand. She also cryptically mentions something about "The 39 Steps." Later she is murdered—before Hannay can learn anything more. His own life now in danger, Hannay flees to a town in Scotland which she has circled on a map, and sets out to find the man with the disfigured finger. Along the way he meets Pamela (Carroll), who decides to assist him after the crooks handcuff her to him. An encounter with a memory expert proves to be the key to uncracking this corker.

This is simply one of the best films of its genre and it richly displays Hitchcock's complete and playful mastery of the language of filmmaking. The handcuffing sequence (which still influences films today, e.g., the remake of D.O.A.) is one of the cinema's greatest. Hitch also has great fun with the sound bridge linking a screaming woman with a train whistle, and the final assassination attempt seems nothing so much as an homage to D.W. Griffith and THE BIRTH OF A NATION. Carroll makes for an appealing heroine and Donat brings his oddly wispy quality to the man on the run. He looks curiously androgynous in this film; the oh-so-trim mustache and his lilting voice add a vulnerability to his character which distinguishes it from the run-of-the-mill hero. Tearle is splendid, as is Watson in his most famous role, but who we really like are Peggy Ashcroft and John Laurie. This gifted stage actress and this striking, reliable actor of many films lend something intense to the married couple Hannay encounters while on the run. Ashcroft is extremely moving as a woman strangled in her marriage and home life, desperately grateful for whatever the strange Hannay may bring into it. Scenes such as this linger in the memory as long as the more typically Hitchcockian setpieces, and it does credit to the master director's versatility. (It somehow seems more his style that he actually handcuffed Carroll and Donat on the set one day to get them used to their scenes together. . . he of course then vanished from the set!)

39 STEPS, THE

1960 93m c ★★
Spy /U
Rank (U.K.)

Kenneth More (*Richard Hannay*), Taina Elg (*Fisher*), Brenda de Banzie (*Nellie Lumsden*), Barry Jones (*Prof. Logan*), Reginald Beckwith (*Lumsden*), Faith Brook (*Nannie*), Michael Goodliffe

(Brown), James Hayter (Mr. Memory), Duncan Lamont (Kennedy), Jameson Clark (McDougal)

p, Betty E. Box; d, Ralph Thomas; w, Frank Harvey (based on the novel by John Buchan); ph, Ernest Steward (CinemaScope, Eastmancolor); ed, Alfred Roome; m, Clifton Parker; cos, Yvonne Caffin

"Color. That's it! Just add some color and our version will be even better than the original." That must be what the makers of this rather mundane spy thriller were thinking, forgetting that it was Hitchcock who made the original version of this John Buchan novel so brilliant. This is a remake in every sense of the term. Scene for scene, this version nearly duplicates the original. For that reason alone it can't be a bad movie, but it does remain uninspired and rather flat. More and Elg are the saving grace even though they pale in comparison to Donat and Carroll. Their coupling is engaging and fun, giving some good life to their respective roles. A third version followed in 1978.

THIRTY SECONDS OVER TOKYO

1944   138m   bw   ★★★★
War   /A
MGM

Spencer Tracy (Lt. Col. James H. Doolittle), Van Johnson (Capt. Ted W. Lawson), Robert Walker (David Thatcher), Phyllis Thaxter (Ellen Jones Lawson), Tim Murdock (Dean Davenport), Scott McKay (Davey Jones), Gordon McDonald (Bob Clever), Don De-Fore (Charles McClure), Robert Mitchum (Bob Gray), John R. Reilly (Shorty Manch)

p, Sam Zimbalist; d, Mervyn LeRoy; w, Dalton Trumbo (based on the book by Capt. Ted W. Lawson, Robert Considine); ph, Harold Rosson, Robert Surtees; ed, Frank Sullivan; m, Herbert Stothart; art d, Cedric Gibbons, Paul Groesse; fx, A. Arnold Gillespie, Warren Newcombe, Donald Jahraus

In 1942, 131 days after the Japanese bombing of Pearl Harbor, an American force retaliated, bombing the major Japanese cities of Tokyo and Yokohama. This picture, a quasi-documentary re-creation of that event, was authored by one of the survivors of the raid, Ted Lawson (played here by Van Johnson). Since land bases near the target are unavailable—and in-flight refueling techniques undeveloped—a dangerous, untried tactic must be employed for the top-secret mission: for the first time in history, twin-engine bombers are to take off from the deck of an aircraft carrier. Because the planes are too large to land on a carrier deck, after the attack they must continue on to mainland China—occupied by the Japanese—and then make their way to Allied-held territory as best they can. Weeks of preparation and training take place before the aircraft and their crews are finally loaded aboard the USS *Hornet*. Following a final shipboard briefing by mission leader Lt. Col. Jimmmy Doolittle (Spencer Tracy), the fliers man their twin-engine Mitchell bombers and are catapulted from the flight deck. The remainder of the film follows the adventures of Lawson's crew only. A well-made war film, THIRTY SECONDS OVER TOKYO was sufficiently accurate to prompt all the real-life principals to approve the use of their names in the picture. Screenwriter Dalton Trumbo wisely elected not to attempt to alter the limited perspective of Lawson's memoir by including more of the details of the famous raid. In the actual event, all 16 participating bombers made it to China, although three men died in crashes and eleven others were captured by the Japanese, who executed three of them. Although top-billed, Tracy's appearance here is basically a cameo, with Johnson the real star of the film. Popular with both critics and the public,

THIRTY SECONDS OVER TOKYO received an Oscar for Best Special Effects.

THIS ABOVE ALL

1942   110m   bw   ★★★½
War/Romance   /A
FOX

Tyrone Power (Clive Briggs), Joan Fontaine (Prudence Cathaway), Thomas Mitchell (Monty), Henry Stephenson (Gen. Cathaway), Nigel Bruce (Ramsbottom), Gladys Cooper (Iris), Philip Merivale (Dr. Roger Cathaway), Sara Allgood (Waitress in Tea Room), Alexander Knox (Rector), Queenie Leonard (Violet Worthing)

p, Darryl F. Zanuck; d, Anatole Litvak; w, R.C. Sherriff (based on the novel by Eric Knight); ph, Arthur Miller; ed, Walter Thompson; m, Alfred Newman; art d, Richard Day, Joseph C. Wright; cos, Gwen Wakeling

Prudence Cathaway (Joan Fontaine), daughter of a wealthy London surgeon of great repute, goes beneath her social station and volunteers for the WAAFs instead of entering the service as an officer, because she wants to go in at the bottom and attend training camp as a private. While in training, she gets fixed up with Clive Briggs (Tyrone Power), who is not in the service. Briggs, who was wounded at Dunkirk and placed on recuperation status, is a bitter young man from the working class who feels that the upper crust rules England and that saving their lives is hardly worth losing his. Briggs has no idea that Prudence is an aristocrat when they begin dating and, despite their vastly different backgrounds, she finds herself attracted to him. When the time for Clive to return to duty arrives, he goes AWOL and is branded a deserter, leaving Prudence to persuade him that England, despite its class conflicts, is worth fighting for. Adapted from a popular novel, THIS ABOVE ALL begins as an interesting look at heightened English class-consciousness during the war, but then disintegrates (as did the novel) into an unbelievable and treacly climax that violates the integrity of Power's character. The performances, however, are admirable, Fontaine having just received her Oscar for SUSPICION and Power finally beginning to be taken seriously as an actor. The film won an Oscar for Art/Set Decoration, and was nominated for Cinematography, Editing, and Best Sound.

THIS GUN FOR HIRE

1942   80m   bw   ★★★★½
Crime/Spy   /15
Paramount

Veronica Lake (Ellen Graham), Robert Preston (Michael Crane), Laird Cregar (Willard Gates), Alan Ladd (Philip Raven), Tully Marshall (Alvin Brewster), Mikhail Rasumny (Slukey), Marc Lawrence (Tommy), Pamela Blake (Annie), Harry Shannon (Steve Finnerty), Frank Ferguson (Albert Baker)

p, Richard Blumenthal; d, Frank Tuttle; w, Albert Maltz, W.R. Burnett (based on the novel A Gun for Sale by Graham Greene); ph, John Seitz; ed, Archie Marshek; m, David Buttolph; art d, Hans Dreier

Outstanding *film noir*, based on Graham Greene's novel *A Gun For Sale*, which presents one of the most disturbed (and disturbing) killers ever to cross the screen. Ladd is scary because he doesn't care; he is simply a killing machine hired out by whoever will pay. Only when Lake takes the time to break through the emotional fortress that he has built around himself does Ladd show any signs of humanity.

The most amazing thing about THIS GUN FOR HIRE is that it began millions of moviegoers' love affairs with Ladd—women identifying with Lake's attempt to unravel the mystery of the murderous character the actor played, and men seeing themselves as the quiet guy who tries to keep from "going soft." Although director Tuttle had originally intended to cast Preston in the lead role, he later decided to hunt for an unknown. When Tuttle was introduced to Ladd, the director was convinced that the 28-year-old blonde could make the cold-blooded killer Phillip Raven a sympathetic character. Contracted at $300 per week, Ladd underwent screen tests, and even had his hair dyed black in keeping with his character's name. Though the film was conceived as a Lake-Preston vehicle, it soon became quite apparent that the studio had something in Ladd, and the script was reworked during production to favor the actor. The film became, in more ways than one, the Alan Ladd story—with all the attention being paid to him and his role. As a result, the film's romantic angle was soon tossed away and Preston reduced to a plot device. But even though Ladd and Lake did not so much as exchange a kiss, they still became one of Hollywood's hottest and most bankable love teams, with three more pictures following—THE GLASS KEY; THE BLUE DAHLIA; and SAIGON.

THIS GUN FOR HIRE was originally to have begun with a dream in which a young Raven (played by Dickie Jones) is seen murdering his aunt and guardian (Hermine Sterler) after she attacks him and injures his wrist. This rather morbid beginning was omitted, however, and the film begins, instead, with Ladd awaking from the dream. THIS GUN FOR HIRE was remade in 1957 as the James Cagney-directed SHORT CUT TO HELL.

THIS HAPPY BREED

1944   110m   c   ★★★★
Drama   /A
Two Cities   (U.K.)

Robert Newton (Frank Gibbons), Celia Johnson (Ethel Gibbons), John Mills (Billy Mitchell), Kay Walsh (Queenie Gibbons), Stanley Holloway (Bob Mitchell), Amy Veness (Mrs. Flint), Alison Leggatt (Aunt Sylvia), Eileen Erskine (Vi), John Blythe (Reg), Guy Verney (Sam Ledbetter)

p, Noel Coward, Anthony Havelock-Allan; d, David Lean; w, David Lean, Ronald Neame, Anthony Havelock-Allan (based on the play by Noel Coward); ph, Ronald Neame (Technicolor); ed, Jack Harris; m, Noel Coward, Muir Mathieson; art d, C.P. Norman

Based on Noel Coward's hit play (in which he also starred), this cavalcade of British life between wars was one of the top moneymakers in the UK in 1944, but it took three more years to reach US screens. Laurence Olivier narrates the episodic story of a family that lives in a small row house, totally indistinguishable from all the other houses surrounding it. This average working-class family includes father Newton, mother Johnson, and their two children, Walsh (who just happened to be married to director Lean at the time) and Blythe. WWI is ending and Newton, who has served four years in the army, is coming home to take Johnson and the children away from the home they've occupied with Johnson's mother, Veness, and her sister, Leggart. The whole group moves into a larger residence in Clapham and looks forward to a happy life. But life isn't always pleasant for Leggart and Veness, who battle constantly. To get out of the house and away from Veness' sharp tongue, Leggart, a spinster, volunteers for just about every committee and charity group around. Meanwhile, the children continue to grow and become increasingly independent, watched over by Newton (in an understated performance that is a departure from his usual scene-stealing

tactics). When a general strike occurs, Blythe is right in the middle of it, coming home one evening with bruises and cuts sustained in a riot. Hoping to better her lot, Walsh takes a job in a fashionable beauty salon in London's posh West End. She's been dating Mills, the sailor son of Holloway, who lives next door, and it is just assumed that they will eventually wed. At the same time, Blythe is engaged to Betty Fleetwood. The applecart is overturned when Walsh runs off with a married man, and the family is crushed. Blythe and Fleetwood are married, but tragedy strikes when both are killed in an auto crash and the news is given to the family in one of the most memorable scenes in British cinema. Walsh walks into the parlor, tells Veness about the accident, and the grandmother exits. Walsh then walks through the French doors into Newton's garden, and the screen is empty of people for a long moment as she informs her parents of the deaths off-screen. Newton and Johnson walk silently into the room, sit down, and say nothing.

Walsh eventually marries Mills and they have a child. When Mills ships out, Walsh goes off to visit him in the Far East and entrusts her child to Newton and Johnson. The house that held so much happiness and sadness is now far too large for the couple and they opt for a small flat. Newton and Johnson take one last look around their home, he mentions that he's glad they are together, and they walk out. The camera stays inside, roves around the empty house for a last look at the rooms where people once lived. Dissolve to a high overhead shot of the row of houses, each remarkably alike, showing that No. 17 Sycamore Road is but one home and that each of these unimpressive houses has its own story to tell.

Coward and Lean codirected IN WHICH WE SERVE, and the great actor-playwright was impressed enough by Lean's work to hand the director the film rights for this film as well as for "Brief Encounter" and "Blithe Spirit." Here Lean is partnered with cinematographer Neame (who later became a producer and director) and writer Havelock-Allan. In 1944, there were almost no color cameras in England, but somehow they managed to find one of them for this film, although the color is muted and not nearly as stark as the process used in the US at the time. Still, this is an immensely charming movie, with many tears and many moments of warmth. Newton is excellent, and Johnson, who could look glamorous when the part called for it, is deliberately dressed dowdily and de-glamorized for her role here, she which performs with great aplomb.

THIS IS SPINAL TAP

1984   82m   c   ★★★½
Comedy   R/15
Spinal Tap

Rob Reiner (Marty DiBergi), Michael McKean (David St. Hubbins), Christopher Guest (Nigel Tufnel), Harry Shearer (Derek Smalls), R.J. Parnell (Mick Shrimpton), David Kaff (Viv Savage), Tony Hendra (Ian Faith), Bruno Kirby (Tommy Pischedda), Kimberly Stringer, Chazz Dominguez

p, Karen Murphy; d, Rob Reiner; w, Christopher Guest, Michael McKean, Harry Shearer, Rob Reiner; ph, Peter Smokler (CFI Color); ed, Kent Beyda, Kim Secrist, Robert Leighton; m, Christopher Guest, Michael McKean, Harry Shearer, Rob Reiner; prod d, Bryan Jones; cos, Renee Johnston

Hilarious pseudo-documentary spoof of a British rock group that was so on-target in its satire, many viewers took it for the real thing.

Spinal Tap is an aging British heavy metal band who are limping their way across the US while Marty DiBergi (Reiner)

makes a "rockumentary" film about them. (Reiner is a Yank who has been following the group since they burst onto the scene 17 years before. Now that they're fading, he decides to tell their story rather than make some commercials for Wheat Thins.) Every disaster that can befall a rock group happens to Nigel Tufnel (Guest), David St. Hubbins (McKean), and Derek Smalls (Shearer). Management woes, promotional difficulties, nonexistent hotel accommodations, phony business people, props that don't work, and an album that hasn't yet been distributed in the stores, all add up to major problems. Their new album, "Smell the Glove," is deemed to have a sexist cover, but they refuse to compromise, even after foul-mouthed promotion woman Drescher reads them the riot act at a party to launch the album's release.

Although there is a script credit, much of SPINAL TAP was improvised, with Reiner letting each scene run until he got what he wanted. Nothing was rehearsed except the tunes, which include such classics as "Hell Hole," "Tonight, I'm Gonna Rock You Tonight," "Sex Farm Woman," and "Big Bottom" ("My baby fits me like a flesh tuxedo/I love to sink her with my pink torpedo/Big bottom, drive me out my of mind/How can I leave this behind?"). Reiner and his cast perfectly capture all the hallmarks of dinosaur rock; the pomposity, the childish politics, the delusions of grandeur, the blithely unquestioned sexism. Highlights include: the band gathered at Elvis's grave, spontaneously breaking into a dismally incompetent acapella rendering of "Heartbreak Hotel"; a stage act in which the group emerge from giant pods, one of which refuses to open for the duration of the set; a member of the band playing a contemplative, solo piano piece, which he then informs us is titled "Lick My Love Pump."

The American cast make pretty convincing English rockers, and the album-of-the-film, "The Best of Spinal Tap," became a hit in Japan. In 1992, the group became the stuff of pop-culture legend, releasing a follow-up album, "Break Like the Wind," completing a national tour of the US, and even appearing in animated form on hit Fox TV show "The Simpsons."

THIS IS THE ARMY
1943 120m c   ★★★
Musical/War   /U
WB

Irving Berlin *(Himself)*, George Murphy *(Jerry Jones)*, Joan Leslie *(Eileen Dibble)*, George Tobias *(Maxie Stoloff)*, Alan Hale *(Sgt. McGee)*, Charles Butterworth *(Eddie Dibble)*, Rosemary DeCamp *(Ethel)*, Dolores Costello *(Mrs. Davidson)*, Una Merkel *(Rose Dibble)*, Stanley Ridges *(Maj. Davidson)*

p, Jack L. Warner, Hal B. Wallis; d, Michael Curtiz; w, Casey Robinson, Claude Binyon (based on the play by Irving Berlin); ph, Bert Glennon, Sol Polito (Technicolor); ed, George Amy; art d, John Keonig, John Hughes; fx, Jack Cosgrove; chor, LeRoy Prinz, Robert Sidney; cos, Orry-Kelly

This star-studded musical salute to the American soldier is filled with Irving Berlin's songs and morale-boosting patriotism. Taken from Berlin's stage play, which opened July 4, 1942, THIS IS THE ARMY also adapts portions of Berlin's earlier musical "Yip Yip Yaphank." Jerry Jones (George Murphy) is a big-time Broadway star who, at the beginning of WWI, is drafted into the service and given the job of putting on a big show. He does his bit and, when the show ends, cast and crew go off to fight in Europe. Years pass and Jerry is now a producer with a son, Johnny (Ronald Reagan, who joined Murphy in rising through California politics), who is drafted in WWII and given the same job as his father. Johnny writes a terrific show *and* marries

sweetheart Eileen Dibble (Joan Leslie). The show tours the country and at the final performance, before the boys go to war, Irving Berlin (as himself) comes onstage in Washington to sing. The plot is just barely enough to hang the musical numbers on, but it's the tunes that count. Berlin used his clout to get the Army to lend him more than 300 soldiers for the stage show, promising to donate more than a million dollars from the show's receipts to a relief fund for the families the boys left behind. The film won an Oscar for its score and earned nominations for art direction and sound.

THIS IS THE NIGHT
1932 78m bw   ★★★★
Comedy/Romance   /A
Paramount

Lily Damita *(Germaine)*, Charlie Ruggles *(Bunny West)*, Roland Young *(Gerald Grey)*, Thelma Todd *(Claire)*, Cary Grant *(Stephen)*, Irving Bacon *(Jacques)*, Claire Dodd *(Chou-Chou)*, Davison Clark *(Studio Official)*

d, Frank Tuttle; w, George Marion, Jr. (based on the play "Naughty Cinderella" by Avery Hopwood, adapted from "Pouche" by Rene Peter, Henri Falk); ph, Victor Milner; m, Ralph Rainger

This blithe comedy marked Cary Grant's film debut, a charming and engaging romp that maintains a fresh feeling from the first frame to the last. Taken from the 1925 Broadway comedy "Naughty Cinderella," the film opens with Thelma Todd in Paris making time with rich bachelor Roland Young. While escorting her to a party, Young catches Todd's long dress in a car door and the garment is torn from the woman. A cry breaks out—"Madame has lost her skirt"—and turns into a joyful song that suddenly sweeps the city, springs up from the streets, on the radio, and even from the top of the Eiffel Tower. Unperturbed, Todd merely wraps herself in her long fur coat and heads home with her lover. En route she tells Young that her husband, Grant, is back in Los Angeles competing in the Olympics as a javelin thrower. The two are naturally more than a little surprised then when they arrive at home to find Grant, javelins in tow, waiting for his wife. At that moment Young's friend Charlie Ruggles arrives at the flat, bearing two tickets to Venice meant for the lovers. Young quickly explains that he, too, is married and suggests that both couples take a holiday to Venice. Of course, this puts the previously happy bachelor in the rather awkward position of having to obtain a wife on extremely short notice. Ruggles helps out by hiring Lily Damita, a movie extra in need of some cash, to pose as Young's wife for the trip. While they're in Venice, Damita's winsome charms prove much too tantalizing for any of the men to resist. First Grant begins paying attention to her, which causes the green-eyed monster to flare up in both Todd and Damita's "husband." Ruggles is enraptured with her as well, which adds to the increasingly tangled love knot. Young confronts his friend and the two engage in an animated (and quickly inebriated) conversation. After expressing affection for one another as chums, Ruggles offers to help out Young by taking Damita off his hands. Young is outraged by this and their chat quickly degenerates into a war of words. Damita, frustrated at being the center of so much attention, decides to leave Venice altogether. But things come together amusingly by the film's close.

The comedy clearly shows the influences of Ernst Lubitsch and Rene Clair. The war between the sexes is dealt with in a sophisticated manner, the characters waltzing in and out of situations with precisely choreographed timing. The sexual tension between the principals is always held in tight rein, and the film sparkles with witty dialogue. The "Madame Has Lost Her

Skirt" number clearly takes its cue from Clair and is one of the film's most enjoyable flourishes in both style and comedy. The number becomes a running gag throughout the story, enjoyable each time without growing a bit stale. Of course, none of this could be accomplished without a skilled cast and strong direction. Frank Tuttle's helming is excellent, perhaps the best job in his varied career. Though the story is thin, he is able to move the farce along at a delightful pace, never allowing story or stylization to conflict. The ensemble could not be a finer one. Each player works well as a separate unit within the whole, creating genuine tensions of love and sex with marvelously funny results. Grant received fifth billing here but did not escape the notice of the critics, the majority of whom predicted a bright future for the handsome and witty young actor. Though it would still be a few years before he came to the forefront as a leading man, he shows here the marvelous talent that would blossom into legend.

THIS LAND IS MINE

1943   103m   bw   ★★★½
War   /A
RKO

Charles Laughton (Arthur Lory), Maureen O'Hara (Louise Martin), George Sanders (George Lambert), Walter Slezak (Maj. Erich von Keller), Kent Smith (Paul Martin), Una O'Connor (Mrs. Emma Lory), Philip Merivale (Prof. Sorel), Thurston Hall (Mayor Henry Manville), George Coulouris (Prosecuting Attorney), Nancy Gates (Julie Grant)

p, Jean Renoir, Dudley Nichols; d, Jean Renoir; w, Dudley Nichols; ph, Frank Redman; ed, Frederic Knudtson; m, Lothar Perl; prod d, Eugene Lourie; art d, Albert S. D'Agostino, Walter E. Keller; fx, Vernon L. Walker; cos, Renie

Set "somewhere in Europe" (clearly Jean Renoir's French homeland), THIS LAND IS MINE stars Charles Laughton as a cowardly schoolteacher, Arthur Lory, who whimpers during air raids and can only be comforted by his overly possessive mother (Una O'Connor). Arthur chooses to keep a low profile and go about his business unnoticed until his mentor, Prof. Sorel (Philip Merivale), lights a patriotic spark in him. Aware of his cowardice, he turns to fellow schoolteacher Louise Martin (Maureen O'Hara), who is sympathetic both to his fears and to the cause of the Resistance, of which her brother Paul (Kent Smith) is an active member who throws bombs at German officers. As much as he tries to remain neutral, Arthur finds himself increasingly sympathetic to the Resistance movement.

Although some consider THIS LAND IS MINE preachy and overly talky, it must be praised for its understanding of humanity. Instead of painting the Germans as mighty evildoers and the French as innocent victims, Renoir took a more daring and honest approach, implicating the French as being partly responsible for the Occupation, when many citizens collaborated with the Nazis to ensure that they would remain immune from punishment and that their orderly lives would not be shattered by the invaders. Renoir avoided propagandistic cliches and took into consideration human nature; human nature, however, is not what people look for in war heroes and patriotic messages. Although long considered a propaganda film, THIS LAND IS MINE is more correctly seen as anti-propagandistic. There is no black and white, no good or evil. There is only grey, and, in that grey area, an understanding of the frailty of human nature.

THIS MAN IS NEWS

1939   63m   bw   ★★★
Comedy/Mystery   /A
Pinebrook   (U.K.)

Barry K. Barnes (Simon Drake), Valerie Hobson (Pat Drake), Alastair Sim (Macgregor), John Warwick (Johnnie Clayton), Garry Marsh (Sgt. Bright), Edward Lexy (Inspector Hollis), Kenneth Buckley (Ken Marquis), Philip Leaver ("Harelip" Murphy), James Birrie (Doyle), David Keir (Brown)

p, Anthony Havelock-Allan; d, David MacDonald; w, Allan Mackinnon, Roger MacDougall, Basil Dearden (based on a story by Roger MacDougall, Allan Mackinnon); ph, Henry Harris; ed, Reginald Beck

Very spiffy indeed. One of the earlier British attempts to duplicate the success of THE THIN MAN. Barnes, a reporter, is fired by editor Sim because Barnes neglected an assignment after receiving a tip on a supposed front-page story. But soon a man connected with the phony tip is dead and Barnes finds himself looking into the London underworld. Accompanying him is his wife, Hobson, a wise-cracking, smart lady who can solve crimes herself. Though Barnes and Hobson may not quite be another William Powell and Myrna Loy, they handle the assignment with humor and great style. The film is directed with energy and the dialogue helps carry the brisk pace along. This is the first screenwriting credit for Basil Dearden, who would go on to do many stories, both serious and topical, in association with noted British producer and art director Michael Relph. A sequel, THIS MAN IN PARIS, was made in 1939.

THIS MAN MUST DIE

(QUE LA BETE MEURE)
1970   115m   c   ★★★★
Thriller   GP/A
Boetie/Rizzoli   (France/Italy)

Michel Duchaussoy (Charles Thenier), Caroline Cellier (Helene Lanson), Jean Yanne (Paul Decourt), Anouk Ferjac (Jeanne), Marc Di Napoli (Philippe Decourt), Maurice Pialat (Police Inspector), Guy Marly (Jacques Ferrand), Lorraine Rainer (Anna Ferrand), Stephane Di Napoli (Michel Thenier), Louise Chevalier (Mme. Levenes)

p, Andre Genoves; d, Claude Chabrol; w, Claude Chabrol, Paul Gegauff (based on the novel The Beast Must Die by Nicholas Blake); ph, Jean Rabier (Eastmancolor); ed, Jacques Gaillard; m, Pierre Jansen; art d, Guy Littaye

One of Chabrol's best films. When Duchaussoy's son is killed by a hit-and-run driver, the quiet author of children's books can think only of revenge. He begins a search for the killer, recording each step he takes in a diary. First, he meets a farmer who tells him that on the day of the accident he saw a damaged sports car in which TV personality Cellier was a passenger. Duchaussoy travels to Paris and meets Cellier. Soon the two are having an affair, and the writer learns that Cellier's brother-in-law (Yanne) runs an auto repair shop. Immediately, Yanne becomes Duchaussoy's prime suspect. Eventually Duchaussoy grows close to Yanne's son (Marc Di Napoli), who tells the writer that he plans to kill his father. Duchaussoy then takes Yanne out on a sailboat to drown him. However, Yanne pulls a pistol on the vengeful writer, saying that he's read Duchaussoy's diary. Duchaussoy leaves Paris with Cellier, but the plot twists don't end there. Another of the quietly handled but solidly engrossing melodramas Chabrol was making at the time, and well worth the effort.

THIS SPORTING LIFE

1963 129m bw ★★★★
Sports /15
Independent Artists (U.K.)

Richard Harris *(Frank Machin)*, Rachel Roberts *(Mrs. Hammond)*, Alan Badel *(Weaver)*, William Hartnell *(Johnson)*, Colin Blakely *(Maurice Braithwaite)*, Vanda Godsell *(Mrs. Weaver)*, Arthur Lowe *(Slomer)*, Anne Cunningham *(Judith)*, Jack Watson *(Len Miller)*, Harry Markham *(Wade)*

p, Karel Reisz; d, Lindsay Anderson; w, David Storey (based on the novel by Storey); ph, Denys Coop; ed, Peter Taylor; m, Roberto Gerhard; art d, Alan Withy; cos, Sophie Devine

From its virtuoso opening shot of a rugby scrum—from the bottom, looking up—to its final emotionally draining moments, THIS SPORTING LIFE is a captivating, visceral film experience. Not only is Lindsay Anderson's (IF; O LUCKY MAN!) first feature film one of the most poignant sports-centered movies ever made, it is also a landmark in the history of British cinema, an "Angry Young Man" classic. Adapted by David Storey (who played professional rugby at one time) from his own novel, the film follows the fortunes of Frank Machin (Richard Harris), a loutish former Yorkshire coal miner who bashes his way to local celebrity as a professional rugby player. Although pursued by a number of women, Frank starves for the love of his landlady, Mrs. Hammond (Rachel Roberts), a bitter, passionless widow, who eventually has a physical relationship with Frank but refuses to give herself to him emotionally. Meanwhile, Frank remains the darling of the rugby club's management and supporters, and as long as he performs on the field, his sullen rebelliousness is tolerated. In time, Mrs. Hammond grows tired of Frank's callousness, they fight terribly, and he moves out. Realizing how much he needs her love, Frank tries to patch things up, but tragedy awaits his attempt at reconciliation. Finally, Frank is left only with the violent world of rugby, in which he is only as good as his last game. THIS SPORTING LIFE is both a biting indictment of class-based exploitation (the club owners treat the players as mindless beasts) and a tragic story of love that founders on suppressed feelings and unconscious macho insensitivity. Nominated for an Oscar, Harris gives an extraordinary, gut-wrenching performance reminiscent of young Marlon Brando, and Roberts, who was also nominated for an Academy Award, brings considerable complexity to her exceptional portrayal of a woman whose emotional life is as dormant as Frank's is frustrated. The game action is hard-hitting and well captured, and cinematographer Denys Coop's gritty, detailed black and white is in the best tradition of British kitchen-sink realism.

THOMAS CROWN AFFAIR, THE

1968 102m c ★★★
Crime R/PG
Mirisch/Simkoe/Solar

Steve McQueen *(Thomas Crown)*, Faye Dunaway *(Vicky Anderson)*, Paul Burke *(Eddy Malone)*, Jack Weston *(Erwin Weaver)*, Biff McGuire *(Sandy)*, Yaphet Kotto *(Carl)*, Todd Martin *(Benjy)*, Sam Melville *(Dave)*, Addison Powell *(Abe)*, Sidney Armus *(Arnie)*

p, Norman Jewison; d, Norman Jewison; w, Alan R. Trustman; ph, Haskell Wexler (DeLuxe Color); ed, Hal Ashby, Ralph E. Winters, Byron Brandt; m, Michel Legrand; art d, Robert Boyle; fx, Pablo Ferro Films; cos, Ron Postal, Theadora Van Runkle, Alan Levine

A very expensive caper picture that drowns in its own artiness, using multi-images, cinematic tricks, and other pretentious film gimmicks—all of which detract from the story. Set and partially filmed in Boston, it's the tale of a self-made millionaire, McQueen, who decides that he has been a member of the Establishment long enough. With the help of aides who never actually meet him, McQueen arranges a brilliant bank robbery that nets millions. McQueen pays off his assistants (most notable is Weston) and banks the remainder, almost $3 million, in Switzerland. The bank's insurance company pays off the loss, then assigns its number one investigator, Dunaway, to the case. She is working in league with police officer Burke, and, through a totally unbelievable gut instinct, she picks McQueen as the most likely suspect (audiences groaned at this jump of logic). Dunaway moves in on McQueen, and the two recognize each other as the enemy. In an artsy sequence, Jewison sends his camera around the two (the way it was done in A MAN AND A WOMAN) as they fall in love after a chess game that parodies the eating sequence in TOM JONES. Dunaway is completely ga-ga over McQueen and thinks she can get him off without a prison sentence if he gives back the money. The chances of that are slim to none, and McQueen wants to see if she really loves him or is using her body as part of her investigation. McQueen says he's about to pull off another caper and wants her to meet him in a local cemetery after the job's done. She shows up there with Burke, and the money is in a garbage can. McQueen's Rolls-Royce arrives, and she thinks it's him. But no—further double-cross ensues.

Split-screen techniques, which were all the rage after having been seen to great advantage at the 1964 World's Fair, are used time and again. The Bergman song "The Windmills of Your Mind," written with Legrand, won an Oscar, and Legrand was nominated for his music. The supervising film editor was Hal Ashby, who also was associate producer. Walter Hill (who later became a writer-director) was one of the assistant directors and, thankfully, picked up none of Jewison's bad ideas. Trustman was a practicing attorney when he wrote the script; he has since written several more films. McQueen is charming, reads his lines well, and shows that he isn't just another short actor with an interesting face. Watching the film today, one can sense the era in which it was filmed, as many other movies of that period made the mistake of placing technique over characterization.

THOSE MAGNIFICENT MEN IN THEIR FLYING MACHINES

1965 133m c ★★★½
Comedy G/U
FOX (U.K.)

Stuart Whitman *(Orvil Newton)*, Sarah Miles *(Patricia Rawnsley)*, James Fox *(Richard Mays)*, Alberto Sordi *(Count Emilio Ponticelli)*, Robert Morley *(Lord Rawnsley)*, Gert Frobe *(Col. Manfred von Holstein)*, Jean-Pierre Cassel *(Pierre Dubois)*, Eric Sykes *(Courtney)*, Terry-Thomas *(Sir Percival Ware-Armitage)*, Irina Demick *(Brigitte/Ingrid/Marlene/Francoise/Yvette/Betty)*

p, Stan Margulies; d, Ken Annakin; w, Jack Davies, Ken Annakin; ph, Christopher Challis (Todd-AO, DeLuxe Color); ed, Gordon Stone, Anne V. Coates; m, Ron Goodwin; prod d, Tom Morahan; art d, Jim Morahan; fx, Richard Parker, Ron Ballanger; cos, Osbert Lancaster, Dinah Greet; anim, Ralph Ayres

This rip-roaring comedy takes place in 1910, when English press bigwig Lord Rawnsley (Robert Morley) sets out to prove that Great Britain is No. 1 in the air. Putting up 10,000 pounds as a prize, he invites the world's best pilots to compete in an air race from London to Paris. All sorts of dandy planes arrive, but Rawnsley roots for his daughter's (Sarah Miles's) fiance, Richard Mays (James Fox), a Royal Navy lieutenant. Other contenders include an Italian count (Alberto Sordi); a fanatical Prussian who will die before he lets anyone else win (Gert Frobe); a Frenchman (Jean-Pierre Cassel) followed by a sextet of women (all played by Irina Demick); a villainous Brit (Terry-Thomas); an inscrutable Japanese (Yujiro Ishihara); and American barnstormer Orvil Newton (Stuart Whitman), who decides that Rawnsley's daughter is the woman for him. After a series of slapstick mishaps, the competitors are winnowed until only the Italian and the two romantic rivals remain. Heroism and fair play are the order of the day in the big finish, but it's up to Rawnsley's daughter to decide which of the competitors has won her heart. Good, clean fun, with fast and furious action, good cinematography, Oscar-nominated dialogue, wonderful planes, and a host of some of the funniest people in movies in the cast.

THOUSAND CLOWNS, A

1965 117m bw   ★★★★
Comedy
UA

Jason Robards, Jr. *(Murray Burns)*, Barbara Harris *(Sandra)*, Martin Balsam *(Arnold Burns)*, Barry Gordon *(Nick)*, Gene Saks *(Leo)*, William Daniels *(Albert)*

p, Fred Coe; d, Fred Coe; w, Herb Gardner (based on his play); ph, Arthur J. Ornitz; ed, Ralph Rosenblum; m, Don Walker; cos, Ruth Morley

This warm and wonderful comedy-drama is a paen to non-conformity made just a few years before such a stance became quite widespread. Robards is an out-of-work writer who quit his last job writing a kiddie TV show known as "Chuckles the Chipmunk" when he could no longer stand the stupidity. Unemployed for five months, he needs cash to help support his nephew, Gordon, a bright 12-year-old whom his sister dropped off one afternoon seven years ago, then vanished. Gordon is illegitimate and, after living with Robards this long, more like a son than a nephew. The relationship between them is warm, loving, and respectful. Robards has never legally adopted Gordon, so a social worker, Harris, comes by to see if she can straighten out the situation. With her is Daniels, a prissy man who is a by-the-book social worker. Unless Robards can prove that he has a real job, they are going to have to take Gordon out of the ratty apartment and give him a foster home. Of course, Harris and Robards become romantically involved. Harris now has a personal stake in keeping the family together but can she and Gordon persuade Robards to return to the daily grind of a regular job? Will he willingly become one of the "thousand clowns" one sees running for the morning bus?

This was a forerunner of many movies to come because it examined independence at a time when the status quo was still very much in vogue. Touching and often hysterically funny, A THOUSAND CLOWNS offers superb performances by everyone, especially the young Gordon who read lines like a seasoned pro. Saks, who is also a well-known stage and film director, is sensational as the grotesque "Chuckles", a portrayal that is actually more memorable than Balsam's as Robard's brother, the agent, who won the Best Supporting Actor Oscar for his role. The picture, Walker's music, and Gardner's script were also Oscar nominated.

Gardner is one of the more than 40 members of the Writers Guild who attended Abraham Lincoln High in Coney Island. (He won the Tony in 1986 for his new play "I'm Not Rappaport.") Fred Coe ably directs the sterling cast. The 1962 play upon which the screenplay is based had nearly the same cast. The title song was a collaboration between saxophonist Gerry Mulligan and his wife, actress Judy Holliday, who died at 43 before the picture was released.

THOUSAND EYES OF DR. MABUSE, THE

(DIE TAUSEND AUGEN DES DR. MABUSE)
1960 103m bw   ★★★½
Crime/Science Fiction   /A
CCC/CEI Incom Criterion   (France/Italy/West Germany)

Dawn Addams *(Marion Menil)*, Peter Van Eyck *(Henry B. Travers)*, Gert Frobe *(Comm. Krauss)*, Wolfgang Preiss *(Jordan/Cornelius)*, Werner Peters *(Hieronymous P. Mistelzweig)*, Andrea Checchi *(Insp. Berg)*, Rene Kolldehoff *(The Clubfoot)*, Howard Vernon *("No. 12")*, Jean-Jacques Delbo *(Deiner the Servant)*, Christiane Maybach *(Pretty Blonde)*

p, Fritz Lang; d, Fritz Lang; w, Fritz Lang, Heinz Oskar Wuttig (based on an idea by Jan Fethke, from a character created by Norbert Jacques); ph, Karl Lob; ed, Walter Wischniewsky, Walter Wischniewsky; m, Bert Grund, Gerhard Becker; art d, Erich Kettelhut, Johannes Ott; cos, Ina Stein

Noted German director Lang returned to his native land to make his last film, a fine, low-budget sequel to his prewar films dealing with the notorious Dr. Mabuse, DR. MABUSE DER SPIELER (1922) and THE TESTAMENT OF DR. MABUSE (made in 1932, but not released in the US until 1943). Lang had fled Germany after Hitler, impressed with Lang's METROPOLIS, offered him a position as the official Nazi filmmaker. (Lang expected the offer to be a trap and feared the Nazis would learn of his mother's Jewish background.) Lang went to France, where he directed one film. In 1934, in London, he was signed by producer David O. Selznick to a one-picture deal with MGM. He sailed to the US and became a citizen in 1935. Taking his inspiration from an actual Nazi blueprint on how to bug a hotel, Lang fashioned this story about a series of strange murders in Berlin's fictional Hotel Luxor. Authorities come to believe the man behind the crimes may be someone who believes he is a reincarnation of the evil Dr. Mabuse. Van Eyck is an American millionaire who saves Addams from killing herself at the Luxor, and the two become involved in the investigation. Frobe (later of GOLDFINGER) is the police commissioner who thinks that either Preiss or Peters is the killer. Preiss is a supposedly blind clairvoyant, and Peters is an insurance salesman. Lang fills his eerie tale with a tightly controlled *mise-en-scene*, a world of hidden cameras, two-way mirrors, and mistaken impressions. This film, which was dubbed into English for American release, is pure cinema, using camera angle, shot composition, and lighting to achieve an overwhelming power that stays long after the final reel goes through the projector. Five sequels followed in the wake of this film's enormous popularity: THE RETURN OF DR. MABUSE (1961); SCOTLAND YARD HUNTS DR. MABUSE (1963); DR. MABUSE'S RAYS OF DEATH (1964); THE INVISIBLE DR. MABUSE (1965) and THE TERROR OF DR. MABUSE (1965).

THOUSANDS CHEER

1943 126m c   ★★★½
Musical   /U
MGM

Kathryn Grayson *(Kathryn Jones)*, Gene Kelly *(Eddie Marsh)*, Mary Astor *(Hyllary Jones)*, Jose Iturbi *(Himself)*, John Boles *(Col. Jones)*, Richard Simmons *(Capt. Avery)*, Ben Blue *(Chuck)*, Frank Jenks *(Sgt. Koslack)*, Frank Sully *(Alan)*, Wally Cassell *(Jack)*

p, Joe Pasternak; d, George Sidney; w, Paul Jarrico, Richard Collins (based on the story "Private Miss Jones" by Jarrico, Collins); ph, George Folsey (Technicolor); ed, George Boemler; m, Herbert Stothart; art d, Cedric Gibbons, Daniel B. Cathcart; cos, Irene

The Louis B. Mayer axiom that MGM had "more stars than there are in heaven" was proven true by this flag-waving wartime extravaganza. Promising opera singer Kathryn Jones (Kathryn Grayson) puts her career on hold to keep house for her Army colonel father (John Boles) after he and his wife (Mary Astor) separate. Kathryn's life becomes further complicated by the arrival of Pvt. Eddie Marsh (Gene Kelly), a former circus trapeze artist who doesn't much like the Army way of life but who wants to transfer to the Air Corps and realizes that by winning over Kathryn he may be able to wangle the transfer he's after from her father. Along the way, of course, he discovers that he really loves Kathryn, her parents go to great lengths to keep the two apart, and Eddie puts himself on the line to demonstrate his love for her.

Despite the rather perfunctory storyline, much of the film is taken up with the star-studded show that Kathryn organizes, featuring not only Eddie's trapeze act but a raft of MGM stars, including Eleanor Powell, Frank Morgan, Lucille Ball, Marsha Hunt, Red Skelton, Anne Sothern, and John Conte. The whole affair is emceed by Mickey Rooney, who does a very funny impression of Clark Gable (who was unable to appear in the film because he was in the service) and Lionel Barrymore from TEST PILOT. Filled with great comedy bits, boasting loud but nostalgically fun color and first-rate production values, THOUSANDS CHEER is two hours plus of solid entertainment.

THREAT, THE
1949 66m bw   ★★★★
Crime   /U
RKO

Michael O'Shea (Williams), Virginia Grey (Carol), Charles McGraw (Kluger), Julie Bishop (Ann), Frank Conroy (Mac), Robert Shayne (Murphy), Anthony Caruso (Nick), Don McGuire (Joe Turner), Frank Richards (Lefty), Michael McHale (Jensen)

p, Hugh King; d, Felix Feist; w, Hugh King, Dick Irving Hyland (based on a story by King); ph, Harry Wild; ed, Samuel E. Beetley; m, Paul Sawtell; art d, Albert S. D'Agostino, Charles F. Pyke

Despite its B-movie budget, THE THREAT is an exciting, tightly controlled film that never lets its audience down. McGraw is a vicious killer who breaks out of prison and is determined to get even with everyone responsible for putting him there. He kidnaps O'Shea, the cop who arrested him; Conroy, the district attorney who convicted him; and Grey, the nightclub singer McGraw is convinced ratted on him in the first place. Shayne is the cop who must stop McGraw and rescue the hostages. The film becomes a violent cat-and-mouse game among the principals, with tension that doesn't let up. The performances are also excellent. McGraw is the quintessential psychotic, drawing his character well and making him terrifyingly believable. The direction pays close attention to all details, from police investigations to tense confrontations. It's films like this that the writers and directors of the French New Wave rightfully recognized as true cinema.

THREE BROTHERS
1981 113m c   ★★★½
Drama   PG/A
Iter Film/Artificial Eye/Gaumont (Italy)

Philippe Noiret (Raffaele Giuranna), Charles Vanel (Donato Giuranna), Michele Placido (Nicola Giuranna), Vittorio Mezzogiorno (Rocco Giuranna/Young Donato), Andrea Ferreol (Raffaele's Wife), Maddalena Crippa (Giovanna), Sara Tafuri (Rosaria), Marta Zoffoli (Marta), Tino Schipinzi (Raffaele's Friend), Simonetta Stefanelli (Young Donato's Wife)

p, Giorgio Nocella, Antonio Macri; d, Francesco Rosi; w, Francesco Rosi (based on the story, "The Third Son," by A. Platonov); ph, Pasqualino De Santis (Technicolor); ed, Ruggero Mastroianni; m, Piero Piccioni; art d, Andrea Crisanti

Directed by Francesco Rosi, whose films have long explored Italy's complex sociopolitical milieu, THREE BROTHERS delivers a symbolic state-of-the-society message. Three brothers, each representing a significant segment of the Italian body politic, return to the village of their youth to attend their mother's funeral. Raffaele (Philippe Noiret) is a Roman judge presiding over the trial of a terrorist whose life is consequently in constant danger; Rocco (Vittorio Mezzogiorno) is a self-sacrificing teacher; and Nicola (Michele Placido) is a factory worker and organizer. None of the brothers is as happy or at peace with the world as is their father (Charles Vanel), who has lived his life simply and close to the land. Though the talk periodically becomes a little ponderous, Rosi's mise-en-scene speaks volumes about the fragmented lives of his characters and an Italy on the brink of social disintegration. THREE BROTHERS was nominated for a Best Foreign-Language Film Oscar in 1981.

THREE CABALLEROS, THE
1944 70m c   ★★★★
Animated/Musical   G/U
Disney

VOICES OF: Jose Olivera (Joe Carioca), Joaquin Garay (Panchito), Fred Shields, Sterling Holloway, Frank Graham, Aurora Miranda, Carmen Molina, Dora Luz, Nestor Amarale, Almirante

p, Norman Ferguson; d, Norman Ferguson, Clyde Geronimi, Jack Kinney, Bill Roberts, Harold Young; w, Homer Brightman, Ernest Terrazzas, Ted Sears, Bill Peet, Ralph Wright, Elmer Plummer, Roy Williams, William Cottrell, Del Connell, James Bodrero; ph, Ray Rennahan (Technicolor); ed, John Haliday; art d, Richard Irvine; chor, Billy Daniels, Aloysio Oliveira, Carmelita Maracci; anim, Ward Kimball, Eric Larson, Fred Moore, John Lounsbery, Les Clark, Milt Kahl, Hal King, Franklin Thomas, Harvey Toombs, Bob Carlson, John Sibley, Bill Justice, Oliver M. Johnston, Jr., Milt Neil, Marvin Woodward, John Patterson

A smashing follow-up to SALUDOS AMIGOS, this is one of the most dazzling achievements of the cartoon genre. Donald Duck opens presents on his birthday, the first of which is a movie projector. He puts film on the projector and we are plunged into the tale of Pablo the Penguin, who is sick and tired of the Antarctic cold and wants to live in the tropics, and a story about a little Mexican boy who finds a donkey with wings. Donald's next present is a large book. The moment he opens it, up pops Joe Carioca (from SALUDOS AMIGOS), then we're off on one of the fastest-moving cartoon sequences ever devised, as the two travel to Brazil, where Donald meets and falls in love with Aurora Miranda (in a huge production number that's as elaborate as anything Busby Berkeley ever choreographed). A breakneck trip around Mexico follows, during which Donald, Joe, and Panchito the rooster cavort with beautiful women and dance with animated plants (as well as with Carmen Molina, who does her trademark "Jesusita" number). THREE CABALLEROS also includes the famous sequence in which Donald gets into the soundtrack, represented by a moving line. So much more happens on-screen that no synopsis of this fast and funny picture will begin to do it justice. A must for all ages.

THREE CAME HOME

1950 106m bw ★★★★
War /A
FOX

Claudette Colbert (Agnes Keith), Patric Knowles (Harry Keith), Florence Desmond (Betty Sommers), Sessue Hayakawa (Col. Suga), Sylvia Andrew (Henrietta), Mark Keuning (George), Phyllis Morris (Sister Rose), Howard Chuman (Lt. Nekata), Drue Mallory, Virginia Keiley

p, Nunnally Johnson; d, Jean Negulesco; w, Nunnally Johnson (based on a book by Agnes Newton Keith); ph, Milton Krasner; ed, Dorothy Spencer; m, Hugo Friedhofer; art d, Lyle Wheeler, Leland Fuller

This is a powerful and moving picture that examines life in a Japanese POW camp from a woman's point of view. Colbert plays American writer Agnes Newton Keith, who is married to British administrator Knowles. They live in the East Indian islands and, shortly after the outbreak of WWII, are arrested along with other noncombatants, then imprisoned in a concentration camp. The prisoners are subjected to inhumane conditions. They are given paltry food rations, as well as beatings and other humiliations. Colbert refuses to lose her spirit and, at one point, crawls beneath barbed wire in order to spend a few minutes with her husband. She is later beaten by the Japanese, who will go to any lengths to draw forth a prisoner's confession. Hayakawa is the US-educated Japanese colonel who runs the camp. He is a man torn between obedience to orders and the dictates of his conscience. The prisoners, including children, manage to build some semblance of life for themselves as they struggle to maintain a daily existence, but conditions in the camp worsen and many of the inmates die. Eventually the camp is liberated but those remaining are only shadows of their former selves. Based on Keith's autobiography, this film intricately develops the relationships between characters. Colbert is stunning in the lead, delivering an honest portrait of Keith's three-year struggle. Hayakawa, a former silent-film actor, is charged with mixed emotions, creating a character of high intensity. Fighting with his own feelings towards the inmates, Hayakawa builds an unusual relationship with Colbert and handles his mixture of kindness and cruelty well. In the end, knowing that his family was obliterated by the atomic bomb, Hayakawa comes to a strange peace within himself as he reaches out to the imprisoned children under his command. A fine film in all departments.

THREE COINS IN THE FOUNTAIN

1954 101m c ★★★
Romance /U
FOX

Clifton Webb (Shadwell), Dorothy McGuire (Miss Francis), Jean Peters (Anita), Louis Jourdan (Prince Dino Di Cessi), Maggie McNamara (Maria), Rossano Brazzi (Georgio), Howard St. John (Burgoyne), Kathryn Givney (Mrs. Burgoyne), Cathleen Nesbitt (Principessa), Vincent Padula (Dr. Martinelli)

p, Sol C. Siegel; d, Jean Negulesco; w, John Patrick (based on the novel by John H. Secondari); ph, Milton Krasner (CinemaScope, DeLuxe Color); ed, William Reynolds; m, Victor Young; art d, Lyle Wheeler, John De Cuir; cos, Dorothy Jeakins

This pleasant boy-meets-girl story (times three) is more distinguished for its photography and title song than for its predictable plot. This was the first CinemaScope picture ever made on location, and Rome and Venice never looked better. Peters, McGuire, and McNamara are a trio of American women living in Rome in a posh apartment. A legend states that if you throw a coin into the Fountain of Trevi and you want to come back to the Eternal City, your wish will be granted. McNamara had come to work as a secretary and meets Italian prince Jourdan, whose mother, Nesbitt, is watching out that some gold digger doesn't snap him up. McNamara is naive but also sharp in some ways and eventually captures Jourdan as her own. McGuire is a quiet older woman who works as the secretary to Webb, an American writer who prefers living in Rome. She finally convinces Webb that she should be his life's companion and the final scene between the two, as she goes wading in the Trevi Fountain, is a lovely moment. Peters is a high-powered executive who has had it with the board rooms and now wants to find a simpler existence. She falls for Brazzi—a wolf who haunts the Via Veneto—and by the time the movie is over, he's donned sheep's clothing, for real. That's about it for the story. There are the customary romantic complications, but the conclusion is as easy to spot as an elephant at a mouse picnic. There are a few sexy (for the time) lines of dialogue but a general feeling of traditional romance sweetens the tales. The same director, Negulesco, handled another movie about a trio of women on the make, HOW TO MARRY A MILLIONAIRE. The title song, crooned unbilled by Frank Sinatra, won the Oscar for Sammy Cahn and Jule Styne. Cinematographer Krasner also took an Oscar and the movie was nominated as Best Picture (the award went to ON THE WATERFRONT). It was later remade, sort of, as THE PLEASURE SEEKERS with Negulesco again directing.

THREE COMRADES

1938 100m bw ★★★★
Drama /A
MGM

Robert Taylor (Erich Lohkamp), Margaret Sullavan (Pat Hollmann), Franchot Tone (Otto Koster), Robert Young (Gottfried Lenz), Guy Kibbee (Alfons), Lionel Atwill (Franz Breuer), Henry Hull (Dr. Heinrich Becker), George Zucco (Dr. Plauten), Charley Grapewin (Local Doctor), Monty Woolley (Dr. Jaffe)

p, Joseph L. Mankiewicz; d, Frank Borzage; w, F. Scott Fitzgerald, Edward E. Paramore (based on the novel by Erich Maria Remarque); ph, Joseph Ruttenberg; ed, Frank Sullivan; m, Franz Waxman; art d, Cedric Gibbons, Paul Groesse

Erich Maria Remarque's international best-seller was brought to the screen here with a stellar cast and a script cowritten by F. Scott Fitzgerald. The scene is post-WWI Germany, a time and place of want and astronomical inflation, where Deutschmarks are borne to the marketplace in wheelbarrows to be exchanged for a beefsteak. Three returning German soldiers—Taylor, Tone, and Young—are among the many war-weary, now homeless, hopeless young men who travel from the trenches of France to their war-ravaged homeland. Prewar friends, the three reunite and decide to try their luck in the republic-to-be's emerging automobile market, pooling their meager resources to set up a repair shop. Working with bits and pieces of salvaged wrecks, they put together a car of their own—which they affectionately dub "Heinrich"—and scramble for business in the intensely competitive field. Motoring on a highway, the three engage in an informal race with the owner of a shiny new automobile, Atwill. Victorious, they stop to eat at an inn and are joined by the vanquished Atwill. Saying, "You wiped me off the map!" Atwill admires their scrap-heap amalgam and introduces them to his driving companion, the lovely Sullavan. The travelers dine together, and Taylor persuades Sullavan to give him her telephone number. He renews the acquaintance the following day, visiting her in the elegant apartment in which Atwill has established the beauty, a child of wealth now reduced to poverty. Sullavan ultimately joins the trio of comrades, but is reluctant to marry Taylor because she suffers from tuberculosis. Eventually, she is persuaded by Taylor's two friends to live what remains of her life to the fullest, and she and Taylor wed amidst the ominous setting of an unstable, pre-Hitler Germany. Young is killed in a street riot; Sullavan, refusing further treatment for her malady, hastens her own demise. As the film ends, Tone and Taylor—joined by the spirits of their late companions (in double exposure)—face a most uncertain future.

Sullavan is superb in this bleak drama, her throaty voice and striking looks at their very best. (She was to gain an Oscar nomination for her role and was named the year's best actress by the New York Film Critics Association.) The actress was a bit difficult during filming, however. According to a long-standing superstition, she refused to work until a rainfall occurred, and she also protested that some of coscripter Fitzgerald's dialogue was unspeakable. Producer Mankiewicz agreed with his star and, with the help of other studio writers, rewrote and excised much of the script, to Fitzgerald's great disgruntlement and later vilification of Mankiewicz. In fact, Mankiewicz was himself a talented screenwriter and understood far better than the proud novelist the basic elements of a good visual presentation. (Other scenes were edited out for less obvious reasons, among them several that concerned the rise of Naziism. Objections were raised by the Breen Office—the industry's self-censorship group—and the film was also cut as a result of studio chief Louis B. Mayer's reluctance to offend the Germans and lose the export market.) Although he continued to write screenplays, and was even signed by the studio at the enormously high salary (for the time) of $1,250 weekly, this was to be Fitzgerald's only *credited* scenwriting assignment. Sullavan's leading man, Taylor, is unconvincing in his role, which he had not wanted to play. Cinemogul Mayer had to persuade the actor that the part would lend him prestige and help to erase the pretty-boy image he had developed over the course of his career. The picture is well directed by romance-drama specialist Borzage, but overlong, and only partly redeemed by Sullavan's splendid performance.

THREE CROWNS OF THE SAILOR

(LES TROIS COURONNES DU MATELOT)
1984   117m   c/bw   ★★★
Fantasy   /15
L'Institut de l'Audiovisuel/Antenne 2   (France)

Jean-Bernard Guillard *(The Sailor)*, Philippe Deplanche *(The Student)*, Jean Badin *(The Officer)*, Nadege Clair *(Maria)*, Lisa Lyon *(Mathilde)*, Claude Derepp *(The Captain)*, Frank Oger *(The Blindman)*, Raoul Guillet, Hugo Santiago *(Voices)*, Jose De Carvalho

p, Jean Lefaux, Maya Feuiette, Jose-Luis Vasconselos; d, Raul Ruiz; w, Raul Ruiz, Emilio de Solar, Francois Ede; ph, Sacha Vierny; ed, Janine Verneau, Valeria Sarmiento, Jacqueline Simoni-Adamus, Pascale Sueur; m, Jorge Arriagada

A strongly praised work of surrealism from expatriate Chilean director Ruiz—living and working in France since 1973—about a story-telling sailor, Guillard, who catches a student murdering his tutor. He proceeds to regale the lad with tales of his bizarre adventures in South American ports visiting the seedy opium dens and frequenting the brothels. It's not what happens in THREE CROWNS OF THE SAILOR but how it happens. Following the tradition of surrealism set in the 1920s, Ruiz directs this film with no basis in logic or reality—dreamy locations are filled with macabre individuals speaking mystical nonsense. As difficult as it is to pin down, THREE CROWNS OF THE SAILOR is thoroughly enjoyable just as long as you don't try to understand it.

THREE DAYS OF THE CONDOR

1975   117m   c   ★★★½
Thriller   R/AA
Wildwood/Paramount

Robert Redford *(Joe Turner)*, Faye Dunaway *(Kathy Hale)*, Cliff Robertson *(Higgins)*, Max von Sydow *(Joubert)*, John Houseman *(Mr. Wabash)*, Addison Powell *(Atwood)*, Walter McGinn *(Sam Barber)*, Tina Chen *(Janice)*, Michael Kane *(Wicks)*, Don McHenry *(Dr. Lappe)*

p, Stanley Schneider; d, Sydney Pollack; w, Lorenzo Semple, Jr., David Rayfiel (based on the novel *Six Days of the Condor* by James Grady); ph, Owen Roizman (Panavision, Technicolor); ed, Fredric Steinkamp, Don Guidice; m, Dave Grusin; prod d, Stephen Grimes; art d, Gene Rudolf; fx, Augie Lohman; cos, Joseph G. Aulisi

Redford is the bookish and bespectacled reader for the Literary Historical Society, but the organization actually serves as a CIA front located in a brownstone in Manhattan. One day he goes out to get lunch for the others (it's his turn), and while he's picking up the food, killers armed with automatic weapons enter the building and massacre everyone there. Redford returns with lunch and finds all his coworkers murdered. Fearing that he may be next, he goes to a phone booth and calls headquarters, identifying himself by his code name, "Condor." He is told to meet an agent at a nearby hotel, but when the fellow CIA man tries to kill him, Redford realizes his own organization is responsible for the slaughter. Determined to survive and to blow the whistle on the CIA, Redford kidnaps woman photographer Dunaway and forces her to help him. Based on James Grady's novel *Six Days of the Condor* (the film compresses the time frame of the novel), this taut espionage thriller gained greater plausibility during its shooting when a sudden raft of sensational post-Watergate news items began coming out of Washington regarding illegal wiretaps, surveillance, and killings motivated by political expediency. What was once merely a fanciful exploitation of antigovernment paranoia, became a thrilling pseudo-expose on the corrupt inner workings of covert organizations. The public ate it up and the film was a hit at the box office. An Oscar nomination went to film editors Steinkamp and Guidice.

THREE GODFATHERS, THE

1948   106m   c   ★★★★★
Western   /A
Argosy

John Wayne *(Robert Marmaduke Hightower)*, Pedro Armendariz *(Pedro "Pete" Roca Fuerte)*, Harry Carey, Jr. *(William Kearney, "The Abilene Kid")*, Ward Bond *(Perley "Buck" Sweet)*, Mildred Natwick *(The Mother)*, Charles Halton *(Mr. Latham)*, Jane Darwell *(Miss Florie)*, Mae Marsh *(Mrs. Perley Sweet)*, Guy Kibbee *(Judge)*, Dorothy Ford *(Ruby Latham)*

p, John Ford, Merian C. Cooper; d, John Ford; w, Laurence Stallings, Frank S. Nugent (based on the story by Peter B. Kyne); ph, Winton C. Hoch (Technicolor); ed, Jack Murray; m, Richard Hageman; art d, James Basevi

John Ford's THE THREE GODFATHERS is a wonderful western about a bad man who redeems himself. It is also a tribute to Ford's mentor and friend, actor Harry Carey, who died in 1947. The film follows a trio of outlaws—Robert Marmaduke Hightower (John Wayne), "Pete" Roca Fuerte (Pedro Armendariz), and "The Abilene Kid" (Harry Carey, Jr.)—who flee a posse after robbing the bank at Welcome. After losing their horses in a desert sandstorm, they arrive at Terrapin Tanks, where they find an abandoned woman in labor. After giving birth, the dying woman (Mildred Natwick) begs the men to save her baby, and they agree, deciding to bring it to the nearby town of New Jerusalem—a hazardous journey with a biblical analogy not lost on the outlaws. Only Hightower makes it, however, stumbling into New Jerusalem with the baby on Christmas Eve. Later, the sheriff of Welcome (Ward Bond) offers to drop the charges if the outlaw will give up custody of the baby, but Hightower's response shouldn't surprise anyone. Ford first filmed this story in 1919 as MARKED MEN with Harry Carey, who also appeared in the first version of the story, THREE GODFATHERS, in 1916. This version, Ford's first color film, begins as a silhouetted cowboy astride Carey's favorite horse rides to the top of a hill, pushing his hat back on his head as the words "Dedicated to Harry Carey, a bright star in the early western sky" appear.

THREE INTO TWO WON'T GO

1969 93m c   ★★★★
Drama   R/X
Universal (U.K.)

Rod Steiger *(Steve Howard)*, Claire Bloom *(Frances Howard)*, Judy Geeson *(Ella Patterson)*, Peggy Ashcroft *(Belle)*, Paul Rogers *(Jack Roberts)*, Lynn Farleigh *(Janet)*, Elizabeth Spriggs *(Marcia)*, Sheila Allen *(Beth)*

p, Julian Blaustein; d, Peter Hall; w, Edna O'Brien (based on a novel by Andrea Newman); ph, Walter Lassally (Technicolor); ed, Alan Osbiston; m, Francis Lai; art d, Peter Murton; cos, Ruth Myers

An intelligent drama with elements of mystery; audiences may find their perspectives shifting about the central question: who is the victim and who the victimizer? Steiger is a salesman who feels trapped in a loveless, childless marriage to Bloom, a schoolteacher. While on the road, Steiger picks up Geeson, a 19-year-old hitchhiker. The two end up at a hotel owned by Steiger's friend, Rogers. After the encounter Steiger discovers a notebook of Geeson's in which she has rated all her lovers. The experience with Steiger is detailed, and the salesman is ranked as one of her best lovers. Eventually Steiger heads home to Bloom, while Geeson remains at the hotel as an employee. On his arrival at his newly purchased suburban house, Steiger finds his wife still in the process of unpacking. The atmosphere seems stifling, so once more he leaves to seek out Geeson, and the two make love again. Then Steiger goes on a sales call. When he leaves, Geeson takes off for Steiger's home. She tells Bloom that she was forced to leave her job at the hotel because of Rogers' sexual harassment. Bloom offers Geeson the guest bedroom. Steiger returns to Rogers' hotel to find that Geeson has taken some of his money, leaving him only a farewell note. Back at his new home, he is angered to find Geeson and is further enraged when the girl announces that she may be pregnant. After she threatens to abort the unborn child, Steiger agrees to Geeson's demand that he leave Bloom. Bloom confronts her husband, offering to adopt the baby, but Steiger tells her he has decided to leave her for Geeson. Geeson herself has left by this time, however, so the depressed Steiger takes solace in drink. Once more he returns to Bloom, this time finding her with her mother (Ashcroft), whom Steiger

dislikes, and with Geeson, who now says that she is not pregnant. Steiger argues violently with his wife and mother-in-law, who respond by walking out. Geeson rejects him as well, leaving Steiger alone with his suitcase.

Much goes unsaid in this drama. The strain between the principals has the biting sting of realism. Issues, as well as villains or heroes, appear in shades of gray rather than in stark black and white. The multiple aspects of each personality are explored nonjudgmentally. Steiger's character is both a self-centered oaf and a man searching for his own identity. Bloom is a sad figure—victim of her repressive upbringing and her unfaithful husband—weak, yet in her own way the force behind Steiger's behavior. Dialogue seems authentic, including the awkward pauses and outbursts of anger that one finds in everyday conversation. The house serves as a symbol of Steiger and Bloom's marriage, a place that should hold hope for new life but seems progessively to be turning into a hollow, loveless shell that no amount of decoration can cover. Hall, an internationally acclaimed theatrical director, held this fine cast under a tight rein while making the most of the settings. He built his film on small moments, achieving a whole that is disturbing, sad, and thoroughly honest. Originally released at 93 minutes, the film had extra footage shot by the studio and edited into it for a television version. The result is not nearly as satisfying as Hall's original work.

THREE LITTLE WORDS

1950 102m c   ★★★★
Biography/Musical   /U
MGM

Fred Astaire *(Bert Kalmar)*, Red Skelton *(Harry Ruby)*, Vera-Ellen *(Jessie Brown Kalmar)*, Arlene Dahl *(Eileen Percy)*, Keenan Wynn *(Charlie Kope)*, Gale Robbins *(Terry Lordel)*, Gloria DeHaven *(Mrs. Carter DeHaven)*, Phil Regan *(Himself)*, Harry Shannon *(Clanahan)*, Debbie Reynolds *(Helen Kane)*

p, Jack Cummings; d, Richard Thorpe; w, George Wells (based on the lives and songs of Bert Kalmar and Harry Ruby); ph, Harry Jackson (Technicolor); ed, Ben Lewis; art d, Cedric Gibbons, Urie McCleary; chor, Hermes Pan

An utter delight, this musical biography portrays the lives of composers Bert Kalmar (Fred Astaire) and Harry Ruby (Red Skelton). Kalmar is a vaudeville song-and-dance man and would-be a magician who turns to writing lyrics after a knee injury puts an end to his dancing. Ruby plays the piano at a Coney Island honky-tonk and also writes lyrics, though he dreams of playing baseball. Eventually, the two meet, and a great songwriting team is born; they go on to write numerous hits for Broadway and the movies. A misunderstanding ends the partnership, but Kalmar's wife, Jessie (Vera-Ellen), and Ruby's wife, Eileen (Arlene Dahl), finally bring the two men back together for a happy, if somewhat fictionalized, conclusion. For the most part, though, this movie sticks to the facts, and it never fails to entertain. Astaire is as suave as usual and dances a couple numbers with Vera-Ellen, while Skelton gives one of the best performances of his career. The film is sparked by wonderful supporting work by Vera-Ellen and Dahl. Appearing as themselves in cameo roles are Phil Regan and Harry Mendoza. Ruby himself served as technical advisor.

THREE MUSKETEERS, THE

1948 126m c   ★★★★
Adventure/Comedy   /U
MGM

Lana Turner *(Countess Charlotte de Winter)*, Gene Kelly *(D'Artagnan)*, June Allyson *(Constance Bonacieux)*, Van Heflin *(Robert Athos)*, Angela Lansbury *(Queen Anne)*, Frank Morgan *(King Louis XIII)*, Vincent Price *(Richelieu the Prime Minister)*, Keenan Wynn *(Planchet)*, John Sutton *(George)*, Gig Young *(Porthos)*

p, Pandro S. Berman; d, George Sidney; w, Robert Ardrey (based on the novel by Alexandre Dumas); ph, Robert Planck (Technicolor); ed, Robert J. Kern, George Boemler; m, Herbert Stothart; art d, Cedric Gibbons, Malcolm Brown; fx, Warren Newcombe; cos, Walter Plunkett

THE THREE MUSKETEERS is a rollicking version of the oft-filmed Dumas classic, with Gene Kelly playing the role of D'Artagnan with great panache. The film opens as D'Artagnan leaves his country home for Paris, to join the famed Musketeers. He proves his ability in a duel with Athos (Van Heflin) and adopts the "one for all and all for one" motto, joining the Musketeers in serving King Louis XIII (Frank Morgan). Prime Minister Richelieu (Vincent Price) plots to end the king's reign, enlisting Louis's mistress, Lady de Winter (Lana Turner), in his evil scheme. The Musketeers, however, are not about to let that happen.

Kelly is a sheer delight, attacking the swashbuckling story with enormous zest. His acrobatics are a sight to behold, a marvelous extension of his much loved dancing skills. This was Kelly's favorite role in his nonmusical films, and he had hoped his performance here would convince MGM to let him do a musical version of "Cyrano de Bergerac." Alas, it didn't. The supporting cast is marvelous, especially Morgan in a wonderful portrayal of King Louis XIII. And, although Kelly is really the star of this film, La Lana steals plenty of scenes; she obviously knew damn well what she was up to.

THREE MUSKETEERS, THE

1974 105m c ★★★★
Adventure/Comedy PG/U
FOX (U.K.)

Oliver Reed *(Athos)*, Raquel Welch *(Constance)*, Richard Chamberlain *(Aramis)*, Michael York *(D'Artagnan)*, Frank Finlay *(Porthos)*, Christopher Lee *(Rochefort)*, Jean-Pierre Cassel *(Louis XIII)*, Geraldine Chaplin *(Anne of Austria)*, Simon Ward *(Duke of Buckingham)*, Faye Dunaway *(Milady)*

p, Michael Alexander, Ilya Salkind; d, Richard Lester; w, George MacDonald Fraser (based on the novel by Alexander Dumas); ph, David Watkin; ed, John Victor Smith; m, Michel Legrand; cos, Yvonne Blake, Ron Talsky

The oft-told tale by Dumas gets a terrific rendering here. York is a happy rustic youth, a bit of a bumbler, but with such high spirits that he is instantly lovable. He would like to become part of the Musketeers, the leaders of whom are Reed, Chamberlain, and Finlay, a trio more intrigued by cleavage and cash than by any sort of loyalty to their king, Cassel, who is, at best, an idiot. Cassel's wife is Chaplin, a duplicitous queen who is having a royal fling with Ward, a peer of England. Evil cardinal Charlton Heston learns of the affair and plans to use it to destroy the queen, opening the door for him to assume a more influential role with the king. He enlists the aid of the adventurous and ambitious Dunaway in his scheme. Meanwhile, the Musketeers have taken a liking to York, and he has fallen in love with Welch, Chaplin's best friend and lady-in-waiting. She is on to Heston's plot and tells York about it, and the four swordsmen set out to foil Heston's scheme. In the past, the story had been so trifled with by filmmakers that it seldom resembled what Dumas had written.

Here, writer Fraser and director Lester went back to the original and hewed closely to the source material, but adding a lot of fun. Some good slapstick combines with moments of real drama and menace to make this movie a winner. The producer, Salkind, paid the cast for one picture but shot two at the same time without telling them. In 1975, Salkind brought out a sequel, THE FOUR MUSKETEERS, and the cast banded together to sue the producer for more wages. They were awarded a considerable sum, though not nearly as much as if they'd been hired to make two movies. Despite glowing reviews, the movie did not knock audiences over at the box office, although it turned a tidy profit after all the receipts were counted.

THREE SMART GIRLS

1937 86m bw ★★★★
Musical/Comedy /A
Universal

Deanna Durbin *(Penny Craig)*, Binnie Barnes *(Donna Lyons)*, Alice Brady *(Mrs. Lyons)*, Ray Milland *(Lord Michael Stuart)*, Charles Winninger *(Judson Craig)*, Mischa Auer *(Count Arisztid)*, Nan Grey *(Joan Craig)*, Barbara Read *(Kay Craig)*, Ernest Cossart *(Binns the Butler)*, Hobart Cavanaugh *(Wilbur Lamb)*

p, Joe Pasternak; d, Henry Koster; w, Adele Comandini, Austin Parker (based on the story by Adele Comandini); ph, Joseph Valentine; ed, Ted J. Kent; art d, John Harkrider; cos, John Harkrider

In her film debut, 14-year-old singing sensation Deanna Durbin is cast as Penny Craig, one of three sisters who try to keep their father from marrying a gold digger. Penny is the devoted matchmaker who tries everything to bring about her parents' reconciliation before her father exchanges vows with his new love. By the picture's finale, Penny's efforts have been all too successful—her sisters have found prospective husbands, and her mother and father have rekindled their romance. Penny is still single, however, though thoroughly content with everyone's newfound happiness.

A highly pleasing first cousin to the screwball comedies of the day, THREE SMART GIRLS wisely centers on Durbin, a wonderful singer and a genuinely charming screen personality. The film earned Academy Award nominations for Best Picture (losing to THE GREAT ZIEGFELD), Best Original Story, and Best Sound. It spawned two sequels, THREE SMART GIRLS GROW UP, and HERS TO HOLD, both starring Durbin. There was also a remake, THREE DARING DAUGHTERS, which put Jane Powell in the Durbin role.

3:10 TO YUMA

1957 92m bw ★★★½
Western /A
Columbia

Van Heflin *(Dan Evans)*, Glenn Ford *(Ben Wade)*, Felicia Farr *(Emmy)*, Leora Dana *(Alice Evans)*, Henry Jones *(Alex Potter)*, Richard Jaeckel *(Charlie Prince)*, Robert Emhardt *(Mr. Butterfield)*, Sheridan Comerate *(Bob Moons)*, George Mitchell *(Bartender)*, Robert Ellenstein *(Ernie Collins)*

p, David Heilweil; d, Delmer Daves; w, Halsted Welles (based on the story by Elmore Leonard); ph, Charles Lawton, Jr.; ed, Al Clark; m, George Duning; art d, Frank Hotaling; cos, Jean Louis

This fine western opens with Heflin as a rancher whose family is suffering from the devastating effects of a long drought. Heflin needs $200 to build a well, then learns he can obtain the money as a reward for delivering Ford, a notorious outlaw now in the hands of the law, to the state prison in Yuma, Arizona. Though this will put Heflin in great personal danger, the peaceful man accepts the assignment, knowing what the money will mean to his family. Heflin and Ford hole up in a small hotel in another town while waiting for the train to Yuma. The outlaw begins toying with Heflin's mind, talking in a friendly manner about Heflin's job and financial situation. Playing psychological games, Ford tries to convince Heflin to take $10,000 to look the other way while he escapes. Heflin finds himself in a quandary, desperately needing the money yet being bound by his word to carry out the job. Ford's gang, led by Jaeckel, discovers where their leader is hidden and sets out to rescue him. The town officials abandon Heflin rather than put themselves in danger, leaving the troubled rancher alone to face off with the outlaws. Ford ends up assisting Heflin, helping his captor on to the 3:10 to Yuma, explaining: "I owed you that." Heflin has come through the ordeal, body and integrity intact, and, as if in answer to this baptism by fire, the skies burst forth with rain, putting an end to the drought.

Much like HIGH NOON, this film deals with a man alone after town officials have passed on their duties, leaving him to face both his adversaries and his conscience. Daves's direction is gritty, confining much of the story to the small hotel room, with a hard-hitting use of close-ups. His outdoor sequences are equally good, particularly the portrait of a land desperate for water. Heflin is superior in the role with his intense portrait of a man caught between personal needs and social duties. Ford is equally good, mixing amiable feelings with monstrous qualities. This is a landmark western, redefining what the genre was capable of doing, and is one of Daves's best works.

3 WOMEN

1977 122m c   ★★★
Drama   PG/AA
Lion's Gate

Shelley Duvall (Millie Lammoreaux), Sissy Spacek (Pinky Rose), Janice Rule (Willie Hart), Robert Fortier (Edgar Hart), Ruth Nelson (Mrs. Rose), John Cromwell (Mr. Rose), Sierra Pecheur (Mr. Bunweill), Craig Richard Nelson (Dr. Maas), Maysie Hoy (Doris), Belita Moreno (Alcira)

p, Robert Altman; d, Robert Altman; w, Robert Altman; ph, Charles Rosher, Jr.; ed, Dennis M. Hill; m, Gerald Busby; art d, James Vance; fx, Modern Film Effects

3 WOMEN is one of Robert Altman's better pictures, although it still suggests that he believes an enigma is more important than a beginning, middle and end.

Pinky Rose (Sissy Spacek), a naive young woman, arrives at a California desert community and hits it off immediately with Millie Lammoreaux (Shelly Duvall), a fellow Texan and her coworker at a nursing home that specializes in the treatment of arthritis. The fashion-conscious Millie lives in a singles apartment complex and spends her nights drinking beer at a nearby motorcycle bar. Pinky moves in with Millie and befriends Willie (Janice Rule), the silent, pregnant wife of the complex's alcoholic owner, Edgar (Robert Fortier), a former movie stuntman.

Pinky, who worships her indifferent roommate, begins borrowing Millie's clothes, using the same expressions, and generally aping Millie. Millie plans a party for some prospective suitors, but the men don't arrive and she storms out, only to return later that night with Edgar, who's roaring drunk. A distraught Pinky leaps into the swimming pool in an apparent suicide attempt. She's rescued by Willie and taken to the hospital, where

Millie remains at her side until she recovers. After recuperating, Pinky returns to the apartment, but the roles have changed.

Altman supposedly based his screenplay on a dream he had while his wife was in surgery. While the maverick director's fans will praise 3 WOMEN's narrative richness, his detractors will find it incomprehensible and tedious. Typically, however, the acting, particularly from Duvall and Spacek, is first-rate.

THREEPENNY OPERA, THE

(DIE DREIGROSCHENOPER)
1931 113m bw   ★★★
Opera
Nero/Tobis Klangfilm/WB   (U.S./Germany)

Rudolf Forster (Mackie Messer), Carola Neher (Polly), Reinhold Schunzel (Tiger Brown), Fritz Rasp (Peachum), Valeska Gert (Mrs. Peachum), Lotte Lenya (Jenny), Herman Thimig (Vicar), Ernst Busch (Street-Singer), Vladimir Sokoloff (Smith), Paul Kemp

p, Seymour Nebenzal; d, G.W. Pabst; w, Leo Lania, Bela Balasz, Ladislas Vajda, Solange Bussi, Andre Mauprey, Ninon Steinhoff (based on the play by Bertolt Brecht, adapted from The Beggar's Opera by John Gay); ph, Fritz Arno Wagner; ed, Hans Oser, Henri Rust; m, Kurt Weill; prod d, Andre Andrejew

Less revered today than the Bertolt Brecht play or the Kurt Weill songs, G.W. Pabst's film version of "The Threepenny Opera" is still a fine example of pre-Hitler German filmmaking. In the German version available on videocassette (a French version exists with a different cast, while the planned English version was never completed), Rudolf Forster plays the infamous Mackie Messer, or Mack the Knife, an underworld gangster of the 1890s whose territory is London. A dashing and respected criminal, Mackie is best of friends with the corrupt police chief, Tiger Brown (Reinhold Schunzel). After meeting Polly (Carola Neher), Mackie decides to marry her. In a dusty underground warehouse—the room lavishly prepared with goods stolen from London's top shops—the wedding is attended by a crowd of beggars and thieves, as well as Tiger Brown. Polly, however, is the daughter of Peachum (Fritz Rasp), the king of the beggars, who strongly opposes the marriage. He puts pressure on Tiger Brown to send Mackie to the gallows, threatening to organize a beggars' revolt to disrupt the queen's upcoming coronation if the police chief does not accede to his wishes.

Based on the John Gay satire of 1728, "The Beggar's Opera," Pabst's film lacks the punch that made the Brecht-Weill collaboration so potent when it hit the stage in 1928. The sting of social criticism is lessened here, with greater emphasis placed on dramatics; in fact, Brecht was so disappointed with the director's interpretation that he ended his own work on the screenplay. What the film lacks in Brechtian qualities, however, it makes up for in the aesthetics of Pabst. Having previously exposed the seedier side of London in the silent PANDORA'S BOX, Pabst once again brings it to the screen here in a unique mixture of realism and expressionism, taking great care to evoke the textures of London's underworld—populated by the lowest of low-lifes—in both his visuals and his soundtrack. Although there is a noticeable absence of some of Weill's tunes—"Ballad of Sexual Dependency," "The Ballad for the Hangman," and "The Tango Ballad"—the film does open and close with the Ernst Busch rendition of "Moritat," a song which became the 1957 pop music hit "Mack the Knife." Also prominently featured is "Pirate Jenny" (Brecht-Weill), delivered by the inimitable Lenya.

THRONE OF BLOOD
(KUMONOSUJO)
1957   110m   bw   ★★★★½
Drama/War   /PG
Brandon   (Japan)

Toshiro Mifune *(Taketoki Washizu)*, Isuzu Yamada *(Asaji)*, Takashi Shimura *(Noriyasu Odagura)*, Minoru Chiaki *(Yoshaki Miki)*, Akira Kubo *(Yoshiteru)*, Takamaru Sasaki *(Kuniharu Tsuzuki)*, Yoichi Tachikawa *(Kunimaru)*, Chieko Naniwa *(Witch)*

p, Akira Kurosawa, Sojiro Motoki; d, Akira Kurosawa; w, Hideo Oguni, Shinobu Hashimoto, Ryuzo Kikushima, Akira Kurosawa (based on the play "Macbeth" by William Shakespeare); ph, Asaichi Nakai (Tohoscope); ed, Akira Kurosawa; m, Masaru Sato; art d, Yoshiro Muraki, Kohei Ezaki

Wild. Kabuki *Macbeth*, and like nothing you've ever seen. A truly remarkable film combining beauty and terror to produce a mood of haunting power, THRONE OF BLOOD was the brilliant fulfillment of Japanese master Akira Kurosawa's longtime ambition to bring Shakespeare to Japanese audiences. Kurosawa set the story in feudal Japan, and the transposition of cultures is surprisingly successful, with all the plot elements intact. After putting down a mutinous rebellion for their lord, warriors Taketoki Washizu (Toshiro Mifune) and Yoshaki Miki (Minoru Chiaki) are called to the main castle for an audience. Riding through the dense and foggy forest that protects the warlord's castle, they encounter a mysterious old woman bathed in white light and mist. When questioned, the woman prophesies that Washizu will be given command of a castle and soon become warlord, but his reign will be brief and his throne will be occupied by his friend's son thereafter. When it appears her predictions are coming true, Washizu grows increasingly corrupted by his own ambitions. THRONE OF BLOOD is filled with unforgettable, haunting imagery. Departing from his usual (very Western) fluid camera style and fast-paced editing, Kurosawa borrowed here from the conventions of Noh theater. While the visuals are gorgeous, the compositions are static and stagy, concentrating on the emotional moment as it seems to hang in the air, unaltered by editing or camera movement. The visual and acting styles work marvelously with the material, although the film is somewhat cold and detached, containing little of the exhilarating passion found in Kurosawa's other work. Kurosawa has a lot of fun with the advance of Birnam Wood, Yamanda's Lady Macbeth is a virtuoso fright and Mifune's demise is in the most grand, outrageous Kabuki fashion. This is filmmaking with risk and greatness in its blood.

THROW MOMMA FROM THE TRAIN
1987   88m   c   ★★½
Comedy   PG-13/15
Orion

Danny DeVito *(Owen Lift)*, Billy Crystal *(Larry Donner)*, Anne Ramsey *(Momma)*, Kim Greist *(Beth)*, Kate Mulgrew *(Margaret)*, Branford Marsalis *(Lester)*, Rob Reiner *(Joel)*, Bruce Kirby, Oprah Winfrey, Joey DePinto

p, Larry Brezner; d, Danny DeVito; w, Stu Silver; ph, Barry Sonnenfeld (CFI Color); ed, Michael Jablow; m, David Newman; prod d, Ida Random; art d, William Elliott; cos, Marilyn Vance

Making a surprisingly assured directorial debut that is hampered only by a weak script, Danny DeVito stars as Owen Lift, a childlike 40-year-old bachelor whose life is totally dominated by his mean-spirited mother (Anne Ramsey). Owen meets Larry Donner (Billy Crystal) a hapless would-be writer whose ex-wife (Kate Mulgrew) ran off with his only completed manuscript, sold it as her own, and is now a millionaire. Owen gets it into his head that Larry wants to "swap" murders with him, with each committing an unmotivated crime that cannot be traced—Owen's momma for Larry's ex-wife. After beginning as a promising black comedy, THROW MOMMA FROM THE TRAIN deteriorates into a repetitive affair that betrays the brazen nastiness with which it began. DeVito does a nice job modulating his own performance, managing to evoke sympathy for his loony character. Crystal, sadly, is hampered by a script that limits him to spells of griping, whining, and full-blown hysteria. Ramsey was nominated for Best Supporting Actress, but lost the Oscar to Olympia Dukakis for MOONSTRUCK.

THUNDERBALL
1965   130m   c   ★★½
Spy   GP/PG
Eon   (U.K.)

Sean Connery *(James Bond)*, Claudine Auger *(Domino Derval)*, Adolfo Celi *(Emilio Largo)*, Luciana Paluzzi *(Fiona Volpe)*, Rik Van Nutter *(Felix Leiter)*, Bernard Lee *("M")*, Martine Beswick *(Paula Caplan)*, Guy Doleman *(Count Lippe)*, Molly Peters *(Patricia Fearing)*, Desmond Llewelyn *("Q")*

p, Kevin McClory; d, Terence Young; w, Richard Maibaum, John Hopkins (based on the characters created by Ian Fleming and the story by McClory, Jack Whittingham, Fleming); ph, Ted Moore, Lamar Boren (Panavision, Technicolor); ed, Peter Hunt; m, John Barry; prod d, Ken Adam; art d, Peter Murton; fx, John Stears; cos, Anthony Mendleson

The fourth entry in the James Bond series centers on the hijacking of a NATO bomber carrying a nuclear payload. James Bond (Connery) is dispatched to the sunny Bahamas, where the aircraft is hidden underwater. SPECTRE's No. 2 man, Largo (Celi), is behind the scheme, and Bond, well-equipped with state-of-the-art spy gadgetry, catches up with the villain and his equally well-equipped mistress, Domino (Auger), who eventually embraces both Bond and his cause. Bond locates the downed plane; calls in American aqua-paratroops, who do underwater battle with SPECTRE scuba divers; and chases Largo, who flees in his yacht-turned-hydrofoil.

It was at this point that the wildly popular Bond series started to slip, substituting gadgets and gimmicks for story and character development. The action is reasonably well-staged, and the film features a fast pace, but it can't compare to the style of the first entries. The story relating to the rights for this property is of greater interest than that offered by the script. Bond creator Ian Fleming engaged in a long legal battle over the rights to his novel, eventually losing in court to Kevin McClory. However, McClory was unable to put together a workable package to turn the novel into a movie, largely because Sean Connery was under contract to Cubby Broccoli and Harry Saltzman. Saltzman, Broccoli, and McClory struck a deal that gave McClory the producer credit and a percentage of the profits and the film was made. Despite its shortcomings, the film was the top moneymaker of 1966, grossing more than any other picture in the series. Julie Christie, Raquel Welch, and Faye Dunaway—then relatively unknown players—were all considered for the role of Domino before Claudine Auger eventually won out. Welch was actually contracted to play the part, but Broccoli reluctantly released her as a favor to 20th Century-Fox production head Richard Zanuck, who wanted her for FANTASTIC VOYAGE. Tom Jones sings the title song, written by John Barry and Don Black. THUNDERBALL won an Oscar for Best Special Visual Effects.

THUNDERBOLT AND LIGHTFOOT

1974 114m c   ★★★½
Crime   R/18
Malpaso

Clint Eastwood (John "Thunderbolt" Doherty), Jeff Bridges (Lightfoot), Geoffrey Lewis (Goody), Catherine Bach (Melody), Gary Busey (Curly), George Kennedy (Red Leary), Jack Dodson (Vault Manager), Gene Elman, Lila Teigh (Tourists), Burton Gilliam (Welder)

p, Robert Daley; d, Michael Cimino; w, Michael Cimino; ph, Frank Stanley (Panavision, DeLuxe Color); ed, Ferris Webster; m, Dee Barton; art d, Tambi Larsen; fx, Sass Bedig

Before the disastrous HEAVEN'S GATE and YEAR OF THE DRAGON, and before the success of THE DEER HUNTER, intermittently brilliant director Michael Cimino directed his marvelous first film, THUNDERBOLT AND LIGHTFOOT. Eastwood, whose production company produced the film, had become impressed with Cimino after Cimino coauthored the screenplay for another Eastwood vehicle, MAGNUM FORCE (1973). The film is a crisp, well-written cast caper movie sporting some stunning landscapes and a fine core of performances (Bridges earned an Academy Award nomination as Best Supporting Actor). Young drifter Bridges hooks up with ex-thief Eastwood, who has been on the lam from his former partners for several years because they believe he set them up and took off with the loot from a government vault they robbed in Montana. The two remaining members of his gang, Kennedy, a sadistic war buddy of Eastwood, and Lewis, a likable dimwit, are in pursuit of revenge and hot on Eastwood's tail. The thief, therefore, reluctantly strikes up a friendship with Bridges to escape. Bridges admires Eastwood and wants to prove himself worthy of his friendship, so the crazy kid takes part in the dangerous maneuvering. Eventually Kennedy and Lewis corner the pair and prepare to kill them. Eastwood convinces Kennedy he has no idea where the money is (it was hidden behind the blackboard of an old schoolhouse that no longer exists) and their lives are spared. With nothing better to do, Bridges convinces the group it should rob the same vault, the same way, all these years later because no one would suspect another attempt (they shot their way into the vault with a Howitzer cannon). After some elaborate planning, the four men successfully execute the robbery, but their getaway goes awry and Lewis is killed. Kennedy panics and becomes angry, knocks out Eastwood, severely beats Bridges (Kennedy always despised the wise-ass Bridges) and takes off with the loot. The police chase Kennedy through the streets at high speeds, and the thief ends up crashing his car into a department store and getting his throat ripped out by the store's vicious Doberman guard dogs. Meanwhile, Eastwood and Bridges manage to escape, though it is obvious that Bridges was severely wounded by Kennedy. The two friends wander down the lonely Montana roads until Eastwood spots the old schoolhouse where the original loot was stashed (the building was moved after being declared a historical monument). The two find the money and Eastwood buys Bridges his dream car, a white Cadillac convertible. As the pair drive through the beautiful Montana mountains, Bridges bravely tries to joke with Eastwood. He eventually dies, leaving Eastwood rich, but friendless.

THUNDERBOLT AND LIGHTFOOT is a multifaceted caper film told in fine detail with richly developed characters. Eastwood is nearly overshadowed by Bridges, Kennedy, and Lewis, who brings great depth to his weak-willed, somewhat stupid, character without resorting to cliches. Here, as well as in THE DEER HUNTER, Cimino's main characters—Eastwood and De Niro—seem detached from their peers and unmoved by their environment, until events beyond their control force them to realize what it was they had. It is only then that they experience a melancholy sense of loss. Cimino's first two films succeed because he allows well-drawn *characters* to affect the audience, not the *epic scale* of the production. The power of THUNDERBOLT AND LIGHTFOOT and THE DEER HUNTER stems from their eloquent, complex, honest characters.

THUNDERHEAD—SON OF FLICKA

1945 78m bw   ★★★★
Drama   /U
FOX

Roddy McDowall (Ken McLaughlin), Preston Foster (Rob McLaughlin), Rita Johnson (Nelle), James Bell (Gus), Diana Hale (Hildy), Carleton Young (Maj. Harris), Ralph Sanford (Mr. Sargent), Robert Filmer (Tim), Alan Bridge (Dr. Hicks)

p, Robert Bassler; d, Louis King; w, Dwight Cummins, Dorothy Yost (based on a novel by Mary O'Hara); ph, Charles Clarke (Technicolor); ed, Nick De Maggio; m, Cyril J. Mockridge; art d, Lyle Little, Fred J. Rode

An enjoyable and engaging tale, this follow-up to MY FRIEND FLICKA is every bit as entertaining as the original. Ken McLaughlin (Roddy McDowall, returning from the original film) is trying to break in Thunderhead, the title horse. The all-white colt is trained for racing, and Ken enters him in competition. At a county race it appears Thunderhead is going to win when the horse suddenly pulls a tendon. Ken is content to restrict his use of Thunderhead to his father's ranch, but trouble brews when the albino horse who sired Thunderhead goes wild. That horse causes trouble for all the ranchers in the valley by stealing mares, but eventually it is challenged by Thunderhead. The brave colt saves Ken, then takes on the albino. The two horses engage in a terrific fight, with Thunderhead defeating his renegade father. Ken's horse returns to his master, but shows a desire to live free on the range. Though heartbroken, Ken understands what is best for his friend and allows the horse to go free. The film is well acted, though the players are really secondary to the real stars of the film: the horses and the beautiful Utah locations. Perfect family viewing.

THX 1138

1971 88m c   ★★½
Science Fiction   PG/15
American Zoetrope

Robert Duvall (THX 1138), Donald Pleasence (SEN 5241), Don Pedro Colley (SRT), Maggie McOmie (LUH 3417), Ian Wolfe (PTO), Sid Haig (NCH), Marshall Efron (TWA), John Pearce (DWY), Johnny Weissmuller, Jr., Robert Feero (Chrome Robots)

p, Lawrence Sturhahn; d, George Lucas; w, George Lucas, Walter Murch (based on a story by Lucas); ph, David Myers, Albert Kihn (Techniscope, Technicolor); ed, George Lucas; m, Lalo Schifrin; art d, Michael Haller; cos, Donald Longhurst

This was Lucas's film debut, made after Francis Ford Coppola saw the short version that won Lucas the 1967 National Student Film Festival award while he was still a student at the University of Southern California. This picture stars a young Duvall playing a man who, along with McOmie and Pleasence, attempts to escape from a futuristic society located beneath the Earth's surface. Reminiscent of the repressive societies described in Ergenev Zamatin's *We*, George Orwell's *1984*, and Aldous Huxley's *Brave New World*, Duvall's society has outlawed love and sex, with drugs as mandatory additions to diet. McOmie plays Duvall's love interest. She awakens him to the pleasures of love after she and Duvall stop taking the repressive drugs. They are arrested, and in prison she discovers she is pregnant. While in jail, they hook up with Pleasence, who persuades the two to escape with him. Confusing and slow moving, this film shows little of the movie-making flair Lucas would later exhibit.

TIE ME UP! TIE ME DOWN!

1990 101m c   ★★★
Comedy/Romance
El Deseo (Spain)

Victoria Abril (*Marina*), Antonio Banderas (*Ricky*), Francisco Rabal (*Maximo Espejo*), Loles Leon (*Lola*), Julieta Serrano (*Alma*), Maria Barranco, Rossy De Palma

p, Agustin Almodovar; d, Pedro Almodovar; w, Pedro Almodovar; ph, Jose Luis Alcaine; ed, Jose Salcedo; m, Ennio Morricone; prod d, Esther Garcia

This outrageous title is a little deceiving, especially for a film from Spain's most controversial export, Pedro Almodovar. The director's usual campy, boisterous hilarity has been replaced in TIE ME UP! TIE ME DOWN! by anguished—albeit offbeat—romantic heterosexual yearning.

Ricky (Antonio Banderas) is released from a mental institution with one burning ambition. On a previous escape from the hospital, he met and made love to Marina (Victoria Abril), a junkie and former porn star. Obsessed by the memory of her, he determines to seek her out again and win her love. He finds her on the set of a legitimate film, working under the direction of the aged Maximo Espejo (Francisco Rabal), who is also obsessed with her. Marina has no recollection of Ricky when she sees him, but he trails her home and kidnaps her. Tying her up in her own apartment, he makes her a captive audience for his desperate romantic overtures. She is at first fiercely resistant to him, but gradually succumbs, especially when he returns to her bruised and bloodied after an attempt to score drugs for her. Eventually, Marina's sister, Lola (Loles Leon), comes to the rescue, but by that time, Marina's fate is (happily) sealed.

The shock effects of Almodovar's earlier work were considerably diluted in his Lubitschian crazy-love roundelay, WOMEN ON THE VERGE OF A NERVOUS BREAKDOWN, and TIE ME UP!, despite its bondage theme and lightly sadomasochistic overtones, makes a similar attempt to enter the mainstream. The film recalls Hitchcock's THE 39 STEPS, with its bickering handcuffed lovers, as well as the sweeping romantic intensity of Douglas Sirk's 1950s trash-fests. Ennio Morricone's ubiquitous music contributes to this attempt to explore the traditions of classic cinema, but it lacks the savvy, finger-popping verve of the more street-smart scores of other Almodovar films. The screenplay lacks the frantic multitude of characters that have typified Almodovar's work, and the non-sequiturs and comic asides we have come to expect are also kept to a minimum. Staying with TIE ME UP! demands some patience, but the director's timing never fails him, and he brings things to a close on an upbeat note.

TIGER BAY

1959 105m bw   ★★★½
Crime   /PG
Independent Artists (U.K.)

John Mills (*Supt. Graham*), Horst Buchholz (*Korchinsky*), Hayley Mills (*Gillie*), Yvonne Mitchell (*Anya*), Megs Jenkins (*Mrs. Phillips*),

Anthony Dawson (*Barclay*), George Selway (*Detective Sgt. Harvey*), Shari (*Christine*), George Pastell (*Poloma Captain*), Marne Maitland (*Dr. Das*)

p, John Hawkesworth; d, J. Lee Thompson; w, John Hawkesworth, Shelley Smith (based on the novel *Rodolphe et le Revolver* by Noel Calef); ph, Eric Cross; ed, Sidney Hayers; m, Laurie Johnson; art d, Edward Carrick

A Polish sailor on leave, Korchinsky (Horst Buchholz), heads into Tiger Bay to visit his girlfriend, Anya (Yvonne Mitchell). He finds that she is now living with another man and guns her down in a fit of anger. Their noisy argument attracts the attention of 12-year-old Gillie (Hayley Mills), a lonely tomboy who witnesses the murder through a mail slot. She gets hold of the murder weapon, convinced that having a gun will make her popular with her peers when they play cowboys and Indians. In time, the precocious youngster is confronted by a police detective (her real-life father, John Mills), but she frustrates him by reciting a convincing string of lies that get her deeper into the situation than she ever imagined. TIGER BAY operates on several levels, creating a thriller of varying intensity with the warm relationship that develops between Gillie and Korchinsky at its center. Korchinsky's interest in the girl grows from a desperate need to keep his crime a secret into genuine affection. Likewise, Gillie sees this as an adventure which will make her popular with playmates, until she develops strong feelings for the sailor. This was Hayley Mills's film debut, and she gives quite a performance for an actress of any age.

TIKI TIKI

1971 71m c   ★★★½
Animated/Comedy
Potterton/Commonwealth/United (Canada)

VOICES OF: Barrie Baldaro, Peter Cullan, Joan Stuart, Gayle Claitman, J. Shepard

d, Gerald Potterton; w, Gerald Potterton, Martin Hornstein, J. Chorodov; ph, Claude Lapierre; ed, Peter Hearn; m, Jerry Blatt, L. Burnstein

An offbeat, thoroughly enjoyable mixture of live action and animation, this Canadian feature is as much fun for adults as it is for children. It tells the story of a doctor who blasts off into space with two monkeys. They're on the run from some pirates and trying to rescue a colony of monkey children. Integrated with this adventure are some delightfully loopy animated sequences involving a Hollywood producer who is everything a hip, smarmy moviemaker should be. What makes him just a little different is that he's a monkey trying to produce the first all-people picture. The live-action sequences are culled from a Soviet children's feature, DR. ABOLIT.

TIME AFTER TIME

1979 112m c   ★★★
Science Fiction/Thriller   PG/15
Orion/WB (U.K.)

Malcolm McDowell (*Herbert G. Wells*), David Warner (*Dr. John Lesley Stevenson*), Mary Steenburgen (*Amy Robbins*), Charles Cioffi (*Lt. Mitchell*), Laurie Main (*Inspector Gregson*), Andonia Katsaros (*Mrs. Turner*), Patti D'Arbanville (*Shirley*), Keith McConnell (*Harding*), Geraldine Baron (*Carol*), James Garrett (*Edwards*) p, Herb Jaffe; d, Nicholas Meyer; w, Nicholas Meyer (based on a story by Karl Alexander and Steven Hayes); ph, Paul Lohmann (Panavision, Metrocolor); ed, Donn Cambern; m, Miklos Rozsa; prod d, Edward Carfagno; fx, Larry Fuentes, Jim Blount; cos, Sal Anthony, Yvonne Kubis

What if Jack the Ripper (David Warner) were really an old friend of H.G. Wells (Malcolm McDowell) and what if H.G. Wells actually invented a time machine and what if Jack the Ripper used it to escape to San Francisco circa 1979 and what if H.G. Wells figured out a way to follow him? What if H.G. fell in love with a kooky bank officer (Mary Steenburgen) and what if Jack tried to kill her? It's convoluted and the plot device that allows Wells to follow Jack is laughable, but this is such a conscientious undertaking you might as well take a look.

Meyer had tried this historical twist before with his screenplay for THE SEVEN-PERCENT SOLUTION, in which Sherlock Holmes meets Sigmund Freud, but TIME AFTER TIME actually works better. It's a well-crafted blend of fiction and history boosted by some excellent special effects. McDowell is marvelous as the free-thinking Victorian who is suddenly confronted with the future—a spectacle he finds both wonderful and horrifying. Steenburgen, in her first major role, does an engaging turn as the daffy bank worker, and the chemistry between the two is good. (They fell in love while making TIME AFTER TIME and were later married.) Meyer makes a fine directorial debut, pacing the film for optimal suspense despite some obvious holes in the script. For some more sophisticated treatments of time travel, see Alain Resnais' JE T'AIME, JE T'AIME, or Chris Marker's LA JETEE, a haunting parable composed almost entirely of still images.

TIME BANDITS

1981 110m c
Fantasy/Comedy ★★★★
HandMade (U.K.) PG

John Cleese (*Robin Hood*), Sean Connery (*King Agamemnon*), Shelley Duvall (*Pansy*), Katherine Helmond (*Mrs. Ogre*), Ian Holm (*Napoleon*), Michael Palin (*Vincent*), Ralph Richardson (*Supreme Being*), Peter Vaughan (*Ogre*), David Warner (*Evil Genius*), David Rappaport (*Randall*)

p, Terry Gilliam; d, Terry Gilliam; w, Michael Palin, Terry Gilliam; ph, Peter Biziou (Technicolor); ed, Julian Doyle; m, Mike Moran; prod d, Millie Burns; art d, Norman Garwood

Gilliam and Palin, from Monty Python's Flying Circus, masterminded this madcap journey through history. A curious boy, Kevin (David Warnock) is whisked out of his dreary English home by six mischievous dwarfs who possess a map stolen from the Supreme Being (Sir Ralph Richardson) that reveals gaps in the universe. Utilizing these "time holes," they travel through history encountering the likes of Robin Hood (Cleese), Greek warrior King Agamemnon (Connery), and Napoleon (Holm)— and robbing them of their treasures. God wants his map back and he keeps popping up at the most inopportune times for Kevin and the time bandits. The Evil Genius (David Warner) also wants to get his hands on this great treasure. Who will win?

This wild and sometimes woolly fantasy is delivered in the customary chaotic Python style, resulting in an onslaught of witticisms and slapstick. We can also see definite signs of the major filmmaker Gilliam (director of BRAZIL, THE ADVENTURES OF BARON MUNCHHAUSEN, THE FISHER KING) would later become. In many ways, this remains his most satisfying film. However, be warned; this film is unusually dark for

a modern children's film. At times a grimly comic fairy tale, TIME BANDITS offers little reassurance. It's a tough world out there—even in our imaginative life. Perhaps that is why we need heroes so badly.

Connery, in particular, stands out in a sterling cast. His portrayal of Agamemnon emerges as an idealized surrogate father that any boy would love to have. Cleese is priceless as a primly officious Robin Hood. Richardson as the majestic Supreme Being is initially terrifying in his displays of power a la the Wizard of Oz but ultimately a pleasant absent-minded old man. Shelley Duvall and Palin shine in multiple roles as various put upon couples throughout history. They also portray Kevin's deadened consumerist parents. The band of little people is also splendid, especially the late David Rappaport as their leader, Randall. Chances are good that this eccentric film will gain in stature in the years to come.

TIME LIMIT

1957 96m bw
Drama ★★★★
Heath /A

Richard Widmark (*Col. William Edwards*), Richard Basehart (*Maj. Harry Cargill*), Dolores Michaels (*Cpl. Jean Evans*), June Lockhart (*Mrs. Cargill*), Carl Benton Reid (*Gen. Connors*), Martin Balsam (*Sgt. Baker*), Rip Torn (*Lt. George Miller*), Alan Dexter (*Mike*), Yale Wexler (*Capt. Joe Connors*), Manning Ross (*Lt. Harvey*)

p, Richard Widmark, William Reynolds; d, Karl Malden; w, Henry Denker (based on the play by Denker and Ralph Berkey); ph, Sam Leavitt; ed, Aaron Stell; m, Fred Steiner; art d, Serge Krizman; cos, Henry West

This compelling courtroom drama features Basehart as an army major on trial for collaborating with the enemy while he was held captive in Korea. The former prisoner of war readily admits his guilt in such acts as broadcasting anti-American sentiments for his captors. Widmark, the Army colonel investigating the case, is suspicious as to why Basehart—an essentially good man— would break so readily. The truth is slowly revealed, then finally brought into the open by Torn, a young lieutenant who tells the court of Basehart's real motivation. In order to save the lives of 16 fellow POWs following the execution of an informer, Basehart had been forced to cooperate with the North Koreans, a secret the man has carried for the entire trial. This raises a moral issue that has no easy answer: is Basehart a traitor despite his good intentions? Such themes run through the film. Morality comes in varied shades of gray in the damning process, with answers coming in a process which is agonizing for both accused and the accuser. This journey into the conflict between humanism and duty is performed and directed with intensity. Basehart and Widmark are superb in their characterizations, two men in a face-off of disturbing ideas. Directed by actor Malden, the film is a tightly structured piece that forces its audience to think about the difficult issues it raises. Malden makes excellent use of his cast, wringing out emotion without bathos and adding flashbacks to Korea at crucial moments. Denker adapted the script from a play he cowrote with Ralph Berkey, constructing the story like a series of Chinese boxes, revealing information slowly until the emotional climax. TIME LIMIT is not an easy film to take, but it certainly is important in the issues it raises and the sensitive manner with which they are handled.

TIME MACHINE, THE

1960 103m c ★★★★
Science Fiction G/PG
Galaxy (U.K./U.S.)

Rod Taylor (George), Alan Young (David Filby/James Filby), Yvette Mimieux (Weena), Sebastian Cabot (Dr. Philip Hillyer), Tom Helmore (Anthony Bridewell), Whit Bissell (Walter Kemp), Doris Lloyd (Mrs. Watchell), Bob Barran (Eloi Man), Paul Frees (Voice of the History Machine)

p, George Pal; d, George Pal; w, David Duncan (based on the novel by H.G. Wells); ph, Paul C. Vogel (Metrocolor); ed, George Tomasini; m, Russell Garcia; art d, George W. Davis, William Ferrari; fx, Gene Warren, Tim Baer, Wah Chang

This smashing science-fiction adaptation of H.G. Wells's famous novel has more creativity in every frame than most latter-day rip-offs have in their entirety. Rod Taylor plays George, an inventor who confounds his contemporaries in Victorian England by unveiling his new time machine. His friends think he's lost his mind, but after they leave, George takes off in his machine, whizzing through time but not through space. Therefore, all of his adventures take place in the same general area of England but at various points in history. He makes brief stops at both World Wars, the atomic confrontations of the future (1966 according to this film), and even as far ahead as the year 802,701. In this futuristic era, he finds humanity divided into two groups—the Eloi, normal-looking humans who live above ground, and the Morlocks, horrifying mutants who live beneath the ground. The Eloi are a vapid, incredibly passive lot, and George is stunned to learn that they are nothing more than cattle for the cannibalistic Morlocks. He falls in love with Weena (Yvette Mimieux), one of the Eloi, and sets out to help her people overcome their oppressors. Producer-director George Pal had already made quite a name for himself with his "Puppetoon" stop-motion animation techniques, and here he again delivers some amazing special effects. This time he received an Oscar for his efforts.

TIME OF THE GYPSIES

1990 142m c ★★★★
Drama R/15
Forum Film/Sarajevo (Yugoslavia)

Davor Dujmovic (Perhan), Bora Todorovic (Ahmed), Ljubica Adzovic (Grandmother), Elvira Sali (Danira), Sinolicka Trpkova (Azra), Husnija Hasimovic (Merdzan)

p, Mirza Pasic; d, Emir Kusturica; w, Emir Kusturica, Gordan Mihic; ph, Vilko Filac; m, Goran Bregovic

The third film from the Yugoslavian director of the acclaimed WHEN FATHER WAS AWAY ON BUSINESS was inspired by a newspaper article on the inter-European trade in young Gypsy children. The result is an extraordinary epic that employs an elliptical, fantastic style influenced by Latin American magic realism and features nonprofessional, gypsy actors delivering most of their dialogue in Romanian (a language the director barely understands). It's a remarkable achievement.

A kindhearted Gypsy teenager, Perhan (Dujmovic, who costarred in WHEN FATHER WAS AWAY), is forced to leave his ramshackle home in the Skopje ghetto to accompany his young sister Danira (Sali) on a journey to a hospital where she is to undergo an operation on her bad leg, courtesy of Ahmed (Todorovic), the richest man in the ghetto. Danira and Perhan become separated, and he spends the rest of the film trying to find her so that he can return home and marry Azra (Trpkova),

the girl of his dreams. During his odyssey Perhan loses his innocence and learns the brutal ways of the world.

Kusturica has said that his style in this film is a mixture of Ford and Bunuel, and GYPSIES has telling echoes of both, bringing its characters vividly and vitally to life. But there are also echoes of Coppola's GODFATHER films here—in GYPSIES' operatic tone and tragic vision, as well as the parallels between both films' treatment of a criminal ethnic subculture. Kusturica also conveys a genuine sense of wonder at the Gypsies' ability to live, love, and dream amid the squalor by which they are surrounded. This is a major work that augurs well for the director's future.

TIME OF THEIR LIVES, THE

1946 82m bw ★★★½
Comedy /U
Universal

Bud Abbott (Cuthbert/Dr. Greenway), Lou Costello (Horatio Prim), Marjorie Reynolds (Melody Allen), Binnie Barnes (Mildred Prescott), John Shelton (Sheldon Gage), Jess Barker (Tom Danbury), Gale Sondergaard (Emily), Robert Barrat (Maj. Putnam), Donald MacBride (Lt. Mason), Ann Gillis (Nora)

p, Val Burton; d, Charles Barton; w, Val Burton, Walter DeLeon, Bradford Ropes, John Grant; ph, Charles Van Enger; ed, Philip Cahn; m, Milton Rosen; art d, Jack Otterson, Richard H. Reidel; fx, D.S. Hursley, Jerome Ash

A mansion serves as the setting for this funny outing in which Lou Costello plays the ghost of Horatio Prim, who was wrongfully shot as a traitor during the Revolutionary War. He is joined in this plight by a beautiful ghost named Melody (Marjorie Reynolds), both of them confined to Earth until their innocence is proven. In a dual role, Bud Abbott plays a present-day psychologist and one of the men responsible for the ghosts' long-ago deaths. For a change, Costello has a chance to get his licks in against Abbott, as Horatio uses invisibility to play numerous tricks on the psychologist. In fact, most of the film's gags are derived from the fact that ghosts Horatio and Melody cannot be seen.

TIME OF YOUR LIFE, THE

1948 109m bw ★★★½
Comedy/Drama /A
UA

James Cagney (Joe), William Bendix (Nick), Wayne Morris (Tom), Jeanne Cagney (Kitty Duval), Broderick Crawford (Policeman), Ward Bond (McCarthy), James Barton (Kit Carson), Paul Draper (Harry), Gale Page (Mary L), James Lydon (Dudley)

p, William Cagney; d, H.C. Potter; w, Nathaniel Curtis (based on the play by William Saroyan); ph, James Wong Howe; ed, Walter Hannemann, Truman K. Wood; m, Carmen Dragon, Reginald Beane; art d, Wiard Ihnen; cos, Courtney Haslam

This warm and engaging adaptation of Saroyan's superlative comedy represents a labor of love by James Cagney and his brother, producer William Cagney.

The film, set in a San Francisco waterfront saloon, is told in a helter skelter fashion, as Cagney (who remains seated through almost the entire picture) functions as the calm, controlling eye of the human hurricane that whirls on the screen. Cagney is a barroom philosopher, endlessly drinking expensive champagne as he indulges in his own peculiarities. He enjoys listening to old records as he sits, sending Morris, an earnest, mildly retarded young man, on various errands, placing bets on horses, picking up children's toys, and buying gum that this good friend loves to chew in big wads. Bendix, a member of the original Broadway cast, is the bartender, who is slightly perturbed by Cagney, though he willingly puts up with the man. He even falls for a Cagney con, hiring Draper to dance part-time at the saloon. Cagney's real-life sister Jeanne is a down-on-her-luck street-walker with a self-mocking sense of humor. By the film's end, Cagney has given her life some hope by fixing her up with Morris. Barton plays "Kit Carson," a quintessential old-timer, whom Cagney constantly prods into telling stories about the Wild West. In the end, the world inside the saloon is nearly upset by Tom Powers, but Cagney at last rises from his chair to defend his terrain and friends. He beats up Powers, and this unique world is once again in harmony.

The story's message—encouraging people to live out their dreams—is simple, and Cagney's performance is a delight. The supporting cast is marvelous, an eclectic and enjoyable bunch that keeps the film moving along at a bouncy pace. Potter's direction allows the material to flow freely, giving his cast every opportunity to excel without letting the camera call attention to itself. This was the third film Cagney did in conjunction with his brother William. The first two (JOHNNY COME LATELY and BLOOD ON THE SUN) had not done well at the box office, so the Cagney brothers were determined to find a script of quality that would also be popular with filmgoers. It wasn't: THE TIME OF YOUR LIFE lost $500,000 at the box office. It was the only Cagney picture ever to lose money, and, though the actor was proud of his artistic achievement, he remained disappointed that this never caught on with the public.

TIME TO DIE, A

(TIEMPO DE MORIR)
1985 98m c   ★★★½
Drama   /15
Focine/Icaic (Colombia/Cuba)

Gustavo Angarita (Juan Sayago), Sebastian Ospina, Jorge Emilio Salazar, Maria Eugenia Davila, Lina Botero, Enrique Almirante, Carlos Barbosa, Monica Silva, Hector Rivas, Luis Chiape

p, Gloria Zea; d, Jorge Ali Triana; w, Gabriel Garcia Marquez; ph, Mario Garcia Joya; ed, Nelson Rodriguez; m, Leo Brower, Nafer Duran

A fascinating film made from an original script by Nobel Prize laureate Gabriel Garcia Marquez. Juan Sayago (Gustavo Angarita) returns to his home village after 18 years in prison for killing a man. When he arrives, his old friends warn him to go away. The two sons of the man he killed have sworn to kill him on his release. But Juan refuses to leave and actually befriends the younger brother before the young man realizes who he is. The older brother, however, renews his vow to kill his father's killer. The rules of honor dictate that he cannot simply gun Juan down; he must provoke his father's killer into accepting a duel. A remarkably assured film for novice director Jorge Ali Triana, who cleaned up at South American film festivals with this production. The performances are all superb and understated, especially Angarita's. The pace is somewhat slow, but the film is never boring and captures the timeless feel of Marquez's fiction. The cinematography is terrific, shifting from the lush jungle that surrounds the town to the dusty heat of the main street.

TIN DRUM, THE

(DIE BLECHTROMMEL)
1979 142m c   ★★★½
Drama/War   R/X
Artemis/Hallelujah Argos (France/Yugoslavia/Poland/West Germany)

David Bennent (Oskar Matzerath), Mario Adorf (Alfred Matzerath), Angela Winkler (Agnes Matzerath), Daniel Olbrychski (Jan Bronski), Katharina Thalbach (Maria), Charles Aznavour (Sigismund Markus), Heinz Bennent (Greff), Andrea Ferreol (Lina Greff), Fritz Hakl (Bebra), Mariella Oliveri (Raswitha Raguna)

p, Franz Seitz, Anatole Dauman; d, Volker Schlondorff; w, Franz Seitz, Volker Schlondorff, Jean-Claude Carriere, Gunter Grass (based on the novel The Tin Drum by Grass); ph, Igor Luther (Eastmancolor); ed, Suzanne Baron; m, Friedrich Meyer, Maurice Jarre; prod d, Nicos Perakis; art d, Nicos Perakis; fx, Georges Jaconelli

Winner of the Academy Award for Best Foreign-Language Film and cowinner (along with APOCALYPSE NOW) of the top prize at the Cannes Film Festival, this adaptation of the Gunter Grass novel combines surreal imagery and straightforward storytelling.

Oskar (David Bennent), born to a German rural family in the 1920s, becomes disgusted with the behavior of adults and de-cides, on his third birthday, not to grow any more, preferring instead to beat his tin drum (a birthday present) and shatter glass with his shrill scream. As he "ages," little Oskar continues to observe the hypocritical behavior of adults, beating out a constant tattoo on his tin drum to control the world around him. His small stature also makes for a very peculiar relationship with a teenage girl, Maria (Katharina Thalbach), who is also mistress to a much older, and bigger, man. THE TIN DRUM is a disturbing film, rich with black humor, that takes a decidedly bitter and horrific look at the German people. Director Volker Schlondorff frames a piercing study of the origins of the German nightmare and the rise of Nazism through national complacency. Only Oskar, in his singularly demented way, is the voice of reason, proclaiming, "Once there was a credulous people who believed in Santa Claus, but Santa Claus turned out to be the gas man." The film is often difficult to watch and downright frightening, especially due to the haunting face of 12-year-old actor Bennent.

TIN MEN

1987 112m c   ★★★
Comedy   R/15
Touchstone/Silver Screen Partners II/Buena Vista

Richard Dreyfuss (Bill "BB" Babowsky), Danny DeVito (Ernest Tilley), Barbara Hershey (Nora Tilley), John Mahoney (Moe, Partner to "BB"), Jackie Gayle (Sam, Tilley's Partner), Stanley Brock (Gil), Seymour Cassel (Cheese), Bruno Kirby (Mouse), J.T. Walsh (Wing), Richard Portnow (Carly)

p, Mark Johnson; d, Barry Levinson; w, Barry Levinson; ph, Peter Sova; ed, Stu Linder; m, David Steele, Andy Cox; prod d, Peter Jamison; cos, Gloria Gresham

Director Barry Levinson (RAINMAN; GOOD MORNING, VIETNAM) returns to his hometown of Baltimore for this story of a battle between two aluminum siding salesmen in 1963. The trouble begins when Bill "BB" Babowsky (Richard Dreyfuss) backs his new Cadillac into the car owned by Ernest Tilley (Danny DeVito), who is busy arguing with his wife Nora (Barbara Hershey) at the time. Soon the two men are locked in a comical struggle for revenge. Though much of the plot action is downright silly, Dreyfuss, DeVito, and Hershey offer wonderful performances, and director Levinson keeps things moving with some nice comic touches. As he did in his first film, DINER, Levinson again effectively uses a diner setting in which his characters are allowed to engage in some rambling but very funny dialogue. Comedian Jackie Gayle provides some hilarious observations.

TIN PAN ALLEY

1940 92m bw ★★½
Musical /U
FOX

Alice Faye (Katie Blane), Betty Grable (Lily Blane), Jack Oakie (Harry Calhoun), John Payne (Skeets Harrigan), Allen Jenkins (Sgt. Casey), Esther Ralston (Nora Bayes), Harold Nicholas, Fayard Nicholas (Dance Specialty), Ben Carter (Boy), John Loder (Reggie Carstair)

p, Kenneth MacGowan; d, Walter Lang; w, Robert Ellis, Helen Logan (based on a story by Pamela Harris); ph, Leon Shamroy; ed, Walter Thompson; art d, Richard Day, Joseph C. Wright; chor, Seymour Felix; cos, Travis Banton

Harry Calhoun (Jack Oakie) and Skeets Harrigan (John Payne), a pair of struggling songsmiths, persuade the singing-and-dancing Blane sisters—Katie (Alice Faye) and Lily (Betty Grable, written into the film after her success with DOWN ARGENTINE WAY)—to perform one of their compositions. Later, Harry and Skeets have their first hit with a song they stumble on and buy from another songwriter (Elisha Cook, Jr.). When Lily lands a part in a big show, Katie decides to become part of Harry and Skeets's music publishing business; however, after they allow another, big-name singer (Esther Ralston) to perform a song that seems destined to be a hit, Katie calls it quits and joins Lily in London, where the sisters become big stars. Back in Tin Pan Alley, Skeets passes over a war song that has been submitted to the publishers, and not only does WWI break out and the song become a hit, but the brothers lose their shirts and end up in the Army. In England, on their way to the trenches, Harry and Skeets go AWOL and see the sisters, setting the stage for a happy postwar reunion. Directed at a breezy pace by Walter Lang and full of familiar old tunes (musical director Alfred Newman won a Best Score Oscar), this entertaining musical (remade in 1950 as I'LL GET BY) bubbles with energy. Payne and Faye play well off each other, Oakie and Grable provide strong support, and Ralston, once known as the "American Venus," makes her last major appearance here. The songs include: "The Sheik of Araby" (Harry B. Smith, Francis Wheeler, Ted Snyder), "You Say the Sweetest Things, Baby" (Mack Gordon, Harry Warren), "America I Love You" (Edgar Leslie, Archie Gottler), "Goodbye Broadway, Hello France" (Francis Riesner, Benny Davis, Billy Baskette), "K-K-K-Katy" (Geoffrey O'Hara), "Moonlight Bay" (Edward Madden, Percy Wenrich), "Honeysuckle Rose" (Andy Razaf, Thomas "Fats" Waller), and "Moonlight and Roses" (Ben Black, Neil Moret, Edwin H. Lemare). Significantly, "The Sheik of Araby," the movie's big production number, was edited after the Hays Office complained that an excess of female flesh was displayed in the sequence.

TITANIC

1953 98m bw ★★★½
Historical /A
FOX

Clifton Webb (Richard Sturges), Barbara Stanwyck (Julia Sturges), Robert Wagner (Giff Rogers), Audrey Dalton (Annette Sturges), Thelma Ritter (Mrs. Maude Young), Brian Aherne (Capt. E.J. Smith), Richard Basehart (George Healey), Allyn Joslyn (Earl Meeker), James Todd (Sandy Comstock), William Johnstone (John Jacob Astor)

p, Charles Brackett; d, Jean Negulesco; w, Charles Brackett, Walter Reisch, Richard Breen; ph, Joseph MacDonald; ed, Louis Loeffler; m, Sol Kaplan; art d, Lyle Wheeler, Maurice Ransford; fx, Ray Kellogg; chor, Robert Alton; cos, Dorothy Jeakins

The Titanic disaster of April 15, 1912 has been filmed several times, and this time the tragedy gets the full Hollywood melodrama treatment. Stanwyck is the mother of two children and the wife of Webb, whom she is leaving, because he is a snobbish socialite. She is taking her children back to America with her to keep them from their father's corrupting influence. Webb manages to get passage on the ship by buying the third-class tickets of a Basque family whom he has persuaded to catch another ship. He and Stanwyck have a number of confrontations on board before she drives him away once and for all by telling him that her son, Harper Carter, is not his child. Wagner is a young college student who falls in love with Dalton, Stanwyck's daughter. Basehart is a priest defrocked for alcoholism. The ship's captain, Aherne, is pushing for a record crossing-time, and is ignoring warnings of icebergs in the area. Finally the inevitable disaster strikes the "unsinkable" ship, and an underwater spur on a berg tears a long hole in the side of the ship. (When the wreck was finally located and explored in 1986, it was discovered that, in fact, rivets had popped and plates separated, rather than a hole being torn in the plate steel.) For a time, the passengers are unaware of the danger, but, before long, the ship begins to list, and the passengers start for the lifeboats, only to discover that there are entirely too few to hold all of them. Webb sees Stanwyck and his children to a boat, then goes about helping other passengers. Captain Aherne goes to the engine room to ask the chief stoker to keep the engine running as long as possible to keep power up for the lights and wireless. Back on deck, young Carter abandons his place on the lifeboat in favor of a young mother and her baby, then goes to find his father, who, of course, wants nothing to do with him anymore. One lifeboat becomes tangled in the ropes as it is lowered, and Wagner climbs down to free it. After the boat is safely in the water, though, Wagner is unable to climb back aboard and falls into the icy waters, only to be pulled by Dalton and Stanwyck into their boat (a too convenient way to get the juvenile lead to survive the disaster without looking like a coward). One woman in the boat is revealed to be a man in disguise. Webb finally accepts his son as a brave person worthy of his name, and the two hold hands as the ship goes down, the ship's orchestra playing "Nearer My God to Thee."

Despite an overly melodramatic main story line, the film is quite effective in conveying the panic and the calm of the sinking. A 20-foot-long model of the ship is featured in scenes of the sinking which are a tour de force of special effects. Even the actors were affected by the magnitude of the tragedy they were re-creating. Stanwyck later said: "The night we were filming the scene of the dying ship in the outdoor tank at Twentieth Century-Fox, it was bitter cold. I was 47 feet up in a lifeboat swinging on the davits. The water below was agitated into a heaving, rolling mass and it was thick with other lifeboats full of women and children. I looked down and thought: if one of these ropes snaps now, it's good-bye for you. Then I looked up at the faces lining the rail, those left behind to die with the ship. I thought of the men and women who had been through this thing. We were re-creating an actual tragedy and I burst into tears. I shook with great racking sobs and couldn't stop." Nominated for Best Art

TO BE OR NOT TO BE

Direction and the story and screenplay by Charles Brackett, Walter Reisch, and Richard Breen won the Oscar that year.

TO BE OR NOT TO BE

1942 99m bw ★★★★★
War/Drama/Comedy /U
UA

Carole Lombard (*Maria Tura*), Jack Benny (*Joseph Tura*), Robert Stack (*Lt. Stanislav Sobinski*), Felix Bressart (*Greenberg*), Lionel Atwill (*Rawitch*), Stanley Ridges (*Prof. Alexander Siletsky*), Sig Rumann (*Col. Ehrhardt*), Tom Dugan (*Bronski*), Charles Halton (*Dobosh*), Peter Caldwell (*Wilhelm Kunze*)

p, Ernst Lubitsch; d, Ernst Lubitsch; w, Edwin Justus Mayer (based on a story by Lubitsch, Melchior Lengyel); ph, Rudolph Mate; ed, Dorothy Spencer; m, Miklos Rozsa; prod d, Vincent Korda; fx, Lawrence Butler; cos, Irene

A masterpiece of satire and one of the more controversial films of its day, TO BE OR NOT TO BE is a brilliant example of how comedy can be as effective in raising social and political awareness as a serious propaganda film, while still providing hilarious entertainment.

The film begins in Poland, 1939, where Joseph Tura (Jack Benny), a tremendously vain Polish actor, and his wife, Maria (Carole Lombard), a conceited national institution in Warsaw, are starring in an anti-Nazi stage play that subsequently is censored and replaced with a production of "Hamlet." Maria has taken a fancy to a young Polish fighter pilot, Sobinski (Robert Stack), who is called to duty when Germany invades Poland. In England, he and his fellow pilots in the Polish squadron of the RAF bid farewell to their much-loved mentor, Prof. Siletsky (Stanley Ridges), who confides to them that he is on a secret mission to Warsaw. Sobinski, however, begins to suspect that Siletsky is a spy and flies to Warsaw to stop him from keeping an appointment with Nazi colonel Ehrhardt (Sig Rumann)—an appointment that will destroy the Warsaw underground. There, Sobinski enlists the aid and special talents of the Tura's theater group to save and protect the Resistance.

A satire built around a rather complex spy plot and directed with genius by Ernst Lubitsch, TO BE OR NOT TO BE lampoons the Nazis and paints the Poles as brave patriots fighting for their land, for whom Hamlet's question "To be or not to be" takes on national implications. Released in 1942, in the midst of America's involvement in WWII, the film drew a great deal of criticism from people who felt that Lubitsch, a German (though he left long before Hitler's rise), was somehow making fun of the Poles. TO BE OR NOT TO BE is also remembered as the last screen appearance for the dazzling Lombard, who, just after the film's completion, was killed in a plane crash while on her way to Hollywood for a war bonds spot on Benny's radio show. TO BE was a perfect and brash finale to Lombard's great comic genius, especially because of it's examination of play-acting. Was there ever as playful a spirit on a movie set as Lombard? The film came from an idea by Melchior Lengyel—as did NINOTCHKA. Mel Brooks's remake of the story was released in 1983, with Brooks and Anne Bancroft playing the leads. While not as good, it's a perfectly watchable, if unecessary, tribute to the original, with Bancroft faring better than Brooks.

TO BE OR NOT TO BE

1983 108m c ★★½
War/Comedy PG
Brooksfilms

Mel Brooks (*Frederick Bronski*), Anne Bancroft (*Anna Bronski*), Tim Matheson (*Lt. Andre Sobinski*), Charles Durning (*Col. Erhardt*), Jose Ferrer (*Prof. Siletski*), Christopher Lloyd (*Capt. Schultz*), James Haake (*Sasha*), Scamp (*Mutki*), George Gaynes (*Ravitch*), George Wyner (*Ratkowski*)

p, Mel Brooks; d, Alan Johnson; w, Thomas Meehan, Ronny Graham (based on the film written by Ernst Lubitsch and Melchior Lengyel); ph, Gerald Hirschfeld (Deluxe Color); ed, Alan Balsam; m, John Morris; prod d, Terence Marsh; art d, J. Dennis Washington; chor, Charlene Painter; cos, Albert Wolsky

Mel Brooks and his real-life wife, Anne Bancroft, starred for the first time together in the husband-and-wife roles previously played by Jack Benny and Carole Lombard in this remake of TO BE OR NOT TO BE. The plot is much the same as in the Ernst Lubitsch original, with everything played for laughs and Brooks at his funniest in impersonations of Nazis. What's missing is the relevance of the 1942 film, released while Germany occupied Poland. Charles Durning received an Oscar nomination for his supporting role.

TO CATCH A THIEF

1955 103m c ★★½
Crime/Romance/Comedy /PG
Paramount

Cary Grant (*John Robie*), Grace Kelly (*Frances Stevens*), Jessie Royce Landis (*Mrs. Jessie Stevens*), John Williams (*H.H. Hughson*), Charles Vanel (*Bertani*), Brigitte Auber (*Danielle Foussard*), Jean Martinelli (*Foussard*), Georgette Anys (*Germaine*), Roland Lessaffre (*Jean Hebey*), Rene Blancard (*Commissioner Lepic*)

p, Alfred Hitchcock; d, Alfred Hitchcock; w, John Michael Hayes (based on the novel by David Dodge); ph, Robert Burks (VistaVision, Technicolor); ed, George Tomasini; m, Lyn Murray; art d, Hal Pereira, Joseph MacMillan Johnson; fx, John P. Fulton; cos, Edith Head

Catch a thief? Throw it back. Notable as perhaps Hitchcock's worst film during perhaps his greatest decade, TO CATCH A THIEF is schoolboy naughtiness and schoolgirl slush, all decked out in chic French finery and looking mighty expensive. This doughy, stale piece of puff pastry casts Grant as a former thief whose modus operandi is being appropriated by some new crook along the French Riviera. Understandably miffed at all the suspicion blowing his way, he sets out to find out the real villain. His "girl Friday" in this one is elegant Grace Kelly, sniffing that Monaco air like she's got the crown on already. She's at her sexiest and most playful here, but the tired Grant doesn't look like he wants to tussle much. The dialogue is sexy, too, but Hitch's "wink, wink, nudge, nudge" has all the delicacy of oatmeal. If you can't figure out the real thief's identity in about twenty minutes, your Captain Crunch spy decoder ring should be taken away forever. Topping off this non-caloric sundae is a fashion extravaganza without even the camp appeal of those in THE WOMEN or the same year's LUCY GALLANT. Palms to Jesse Royce Landis, though, for giving the film's best performance. Lightweight to the point of zero gravity, this mildly enjoyable but overlong piece of K-Mart sophistication today seems a mere footnote to the career of the man in the director's chair.

TO EACH HIS OWN

1946 122m bw ★★★★
Drama /A
Paramount

Olivia de Havilland *(Miss Josephine Norris)*, John Lund *(Capt. Bart Cosgrove/Gregory Piersen)*, Mary Anderson *(Corinna Piersen)*, Roland Culver *(Lord Desham)*, Phillip Terry *(Alex Piersen)*, Bill Goodwin *(Mac Tilton)*, Virginia Welles *(Liz Lorimer)*, Victoria Horne *(Daisy Gingras)*, Griff Barnett *(Mr. Norris)*, Alma Macrorie *(Belle Ingham)*

p, Charles Brackett; d, Mitchell Leisen; w, Charles Brackett, Jacques Thery (based on a story by Brackett); ph, Daniel Fapp; ed, Alma Macrorie; m, Victor Young; art d, Hans Dreier, Roland Anderson; fx, Gordon Jennings, Farciot Edouart; cos, Edith Head

What might have been a trite soap opera is elevated to the status of superior emotional drama by a wise script, sensitive direction, and an Oscar-winning performance by de Havilland, her first and the first for an actress at Paramount. Covering 27 years in the life and times of a woman who loved neither wisely nor well, it begins during the blitz on London. Middle-aged de Havilland is an air raid warden and marches her beat with confidante Culver, a peer of the realm and another warden. Between the wars, de Havilland made a fortune in the cosmetics business and spent so much time working that there was not a moment for love in her life. When she learns that a handsome US pilot, Lund, is in town, her thoughts flash back to an earlier time in her life. As a young woman in a small town in the US, she meets a good-looking pilot (also played by Lund), spends a passionate few hours with him, and falls in love. He goes off to fight on the continent and leaves her pregnant. When he dies in the service, she gives birth in another town so as not to embarrass her druggist father, Barnett. After a struggle, she gives her son up for adoption to Anderson and Terry. She regrets having done that quickly but has no recourse, so she plunges herself into her work. When she has some money, she begins plying the young boy, Bill Ward, with toys and affection and manages to get custody of him, but he wants to go back to Anderson, whom he thinks is his real mother. She eventually allows Ward to return to Anderson, then goes to London. Years later, Lund (the son) comes to call on de Havilland because Anderson has suggested he look her up while he's in London. She asks him to stay at her posh flat and doesn't reveal their true relationship. Lund is properly deferential to this contemporary of his "mother" and shows her the greatest respect as de Havilland aches to hug him. Lund is in love with and hoping to marry Welles. Culver learns the whole story and how de Havilland wishes she could do more for Lund. Culver helps the young lovers get together and hints enough times about de Havilland for Lund to finally realize why this older woman has been so generous and doting with him. Welles and Lund are married, de Havilland is invited, and the most touching moment occurs when Lund approaches de Havilland while the wedding band is playing and says, "I believe this is our dance, Mother."

Lund, who had already established himself on Broadway, made his film debut here. An interesting sidelight is that de Havilland hadn't worked for two years. She'd been on suspension from Warner Bros. and was trying to break a contract which they claimed included all of her suspension time. She sued the studio successfully and the result was a law that limited studios to a seven-year agreement with an actor, with no clause regarding suspensions. That became known as the "de Havilland Decision," and actors have thanked her ever since. Leisen and de Havilland had worked together in HOLD BACK THE DAWN, and when she asked for him to direct, he passed on it at first, then was convinced when the studio gave him script approval as well as several other concessions. It was sentimental but never bathetic. Leisen knew that de Havilland had given a star performance and on the wrap day gifted her with a bracelet that featured a mini-Oscar. His prophecy was on the money, and she took the Oscar home at the next awards ceremony. Brackett's story was nominated for a statuette, but that was it from the Academy. Audiences loved it, and credit must be given to the studio for attempting a "soft" picture at the time. No one expected it to do as well as it did. Good editing by Macrorie and Victor Young's music kept the mood swings right on target. Miss de Havilland's winning of the Oscar was a surprise to many who had placed their bets on the formidable quartet of losers in 1946. They were Celia Johnson for BRIEF ENCOUNTER, Jane Wyman in THE YEARLING, Jennifer Jones for DUEL IN THE SUN, and Rosalind Russell as SISTER KENNY.

TO HAVE AND HAVE NOT

1944 100m bw   ★★★★
Drama   /PG
WB

Humphrey Bogart *(Harry Morgan)*, Walter Brennan *(Eddie)*, Lauren Bacall *(Marie Browning)*, Dolores Moran *(Helene De Bursac)*, Hoagy Carmichael *(Cricket)*, Walter Molnar *(Paul De Bursac)*, Sheldon Leonard *(Lt. Coyo)*, Marcel Dalio *(Gerard)*, Walter Sande *(Johnson)*, Dan Seymour *(Capt. M. Renard)*

p, Howard Hawks; d, Howard Hawks; w, Jules Furthman, William Faulkner (based on the novel by Ernest Hemingway); ph, Sid Hickox; ed, Christian Nyby; m, Franz Waxman (uncredited); art d, Charles Novi; fx, Roy Davidson; cos, Milo Anderson

The dialogue is sharp, the direction first-rate, and the acting superb, but TO HAVE AND HAVE NOT is undoubtedly best remembered for the on- and offscreen romance between Bogart and Bacall. Warner Bros. wanted another CASABLANCA, and in many ways Bogart's character here resembles his classic portrait of Rick Blaine.

It is WWII and France has just fallen to the Nazi occupation. Bogart, living on the island of Martinique, is the owner of a cabin cruiser, the *Queen Conch*, on which he takes wealthy customers on fishing trips. Working with him is Brennan, a not-too-bright alcoholic, whose amiable demeanor charms almost anybody. Sande, Bogart's current customer, loses some expensive tackle on a run and the disgusted captain brings him back to port. Claiming to have no money, Sande promises to go to the bank in the morning. Bogart is approached by Dalio, the owner of the hotel where Bogart lives. A member of the French resistance, Dalio asks Bogart to help smuggle one of the underground movement's top leaders (Molnar) into Martinique. Bogart, who cares little for politics, turns down Dalio and refuses to discuss the matter. Returning to his room at the hotel, Bogart notices a newcomer across the hall. It is, of course, Bacall, who shoots him a sultry glance, then, in a husky, and oh-so-sexy voice, asks: "Anybody got a match?" Bogart is intrigued and gives Bacall a book of matches. Later, in the hotel bar, Bogart tries to collect from Sande. Bacall steals Sande's wallet, which proves to hold enough traveler's checks to pay Bogart and then some. The Vichy police stage a raid on the hotel, and Sande is killed by a stray bullet just as he is about to sign the traveler's checks. Bogart and Bacall are brought into police headquarters for questioning, and what little money Bogart has is confiscated. The two return to the hotel and go to Bogart's room. At first Bogart is cool to Bacall's overt sexual advances; then Bacall kisses him. Finally Bogart warms up and Bacall tells him: "It's even better when you help." Bacall leaves, but later returns, asking Bogart for help in getting off the island. To help her get back to the US, Bogart agrees to make the dangerous run for Dalio.

Stylish and loaded with humor, this immensely entertaining film was the result of a argument between director Hawks and novelist Ernest Hemingway. On a fishing trip in Florida with the author, Hawks tried to convince Hemingway that he should come to Hollywood to work on a screenplay. When Hemingway indicated no interest in Hawks's proposal, the filmmaker reportedly responded by boasting that he could make a film out of Hemingway's worst book, which Hawks felt was *To Have and Have Not*. Hemingway's novel is set in Cuba and the Florida Keys in the 1930s. In it, the character Bogart plays is less heroic, a married man with children, who is forced to run booze and men on his boat when his financial situation becomes desperate. Hawks kept the title and the character, then threw out the Hemingway story. The next task for Hawks was casting. Bogart seemed perfect for the part of Harry Morgan, but who was fiery enough to play opposite him? Hawks took a chance on an unknown talent named Betty Bacall, a beautiful 18-year-old New York model who was virtually unknown in Hollywood. Hawks had become interested in Bacall after his wife spotted her on the cover of *Vogue*. The electricity between the two stars was always intended to be the heart of the film, but Bogart and Bacall's onscreen romance had a steamy verisimilitude that went way beyond anybody's expectations. As it became obvious the two were becoming involved, Hawks reportedly warned Bacall that the 45-year-old Bogart was just using his young costar to escape from a bad marriage and that when the filming was over, Bogart would forget about her. Worried that Bacall's infatuation with Bogart would cause the young actress to blow her big chance, Hawks is said to have threatened to sell her contract to Monogram. Of course, this was an empty threat, and some have even suggested that Hawks used the offscreen affair to heighten the on-screen romance. (Tellingly, in the film Bogart and Bacall refer to each other as "Steve" and "Slim," the pet names Hawks and his wife had for each another.) And as everyone knows, Bogart hardly forgot about Bacall after the filming of TO HAVE AND HAVE NOT was completed; the two were married the next year. The film was remade twice, first as THE BREAKING POINT, then as THE GUN RUNNERS.

TO KILL A MOCKINGBIRD

1962 129m bw ★★★★
Drama /PG
Universal

Gregory Peck (*Atticus Finch*), Mary Badham (*Jean Louise "Scout" Finch*), Phillip Alford (*Jem Finch*), John Megna (*Dill Harris*), Frank Overton (*Sheriff Heck Tate*), Rosemary Murphy (*Miss Maudie Atkinson*), Ruth White (*Mrs. Dubose*), Brock Peters (*Tom Robinson*), Estelle Evans (*Calpurnia*), Paul Fix (*Judge Taylor*)

p, Alan J. Pakula; d, Robert Mulligan; w, Horton Foote (based on the novel by Harper Lee); ph, Russell Harlan; ed, Aaron Stell; m, Elmer Bernstein; art d, Alexander Golitzen, Henry Bumstead; cos, Rosemary Odell, Viola Thompson

Peck's peak. Based on Harper Lee's semiautobiographical, Pulitzer Prize-winning novel of 1960, TO KILL A MOCKINGBIRD is a hauntingly nostalgic portrayal of childhood mischief set in a racially divided Alabama town in the 1930s. If the film's tone sometimes seems overly righteous, it's offset by a poetic lyricism that is difficult to resist embracing.

Gregory Peck plays incorruptible lawyer Atticus Finch, a widower with two children, 10-year-old Alford and tomboyish 6-year-old Badham. During the summer, Alford and Badham amuse themselves by rolling each other down the street in a tire or playing in a treehouse. What occupies them most, however, is

the creaky wooden house where Robert Duvall lives. According to neighborhood legend, Duvall is crazy and chained to his bed by his father, though he has never been seen, at least by the children. While the kids play, Peck agrees to represent a black man who is accused of raping a young white woman. A number of people try to pressure him into stepping down from the case, but his pursuit of justice is unwavering. As the trial proceeds, Peck, Alford, and especially Badham learn as much about each other as they do about their own fears and prejudices.

Since its release, this intelligent, atmospheric film has been warmly received by audiences responding not only to their own childhood, but also to the heroic image portrayed by Peck, a shining example of citizenship and affectionate fatherhood.

There is also a superb score by Elmer Bernstein. The language, emotions, and general subject matter of the trial scenes may be a bit rough for some children, but in Peck's solid, idealistic hands, all good things triumph. This was Robert Duvall's film debut. Both Peck and Foote's screenplay took home Oscars.

TO SIR, WITH LOVE

1967 105m c ★★★
Drama /PG
James Clavell (U.K.)

Sidney Poitier (*Mark Thackeray*), Christian Roberts (*Denham*), Judy Geeson (*Pamela Dare*), Suzy Kendall (*Gillian Blanchard*), Lulu (*Barbara Pegg*), Faith Brook (*Mrs. Evans*), Geoffrey Bayldon (*Weston*), Edward Burnham (*Florian*), Gareth Robinson (*Tich*), Grahame Charles (*Fernman*)

p, James Clavell; d, James Clavell; w, James Clavell (based on the novel by E.R. Braithwaite); ph, Paul Beeson (Technicolor); ed, Peter Thornton; m, Ron Grainer; art d, Tony Woollard

A sentimental picture starring Poitier as an engineer from British Guiana who, because he is black, cannot find work in his field. He accepts a teaching position in a slummy high school in London's East End. He quickly learns that he signed on for more than he bargained for—the students are poorly educated, viciously rebellious, and downright crude to authority figures. Rather than end up like the previous string of instructors—who gave up on the students—Poitier tries an unorthodox method. Instead of relying on textbooks, Poitier teaches from experience. His belief is that the students must be treated like adults in order for them to behave as such. They are products of an East End society that impresses upon them certain roles: the boys must be tough, the girls must be subordinate. Poitier tries to break down these societal barriers. He teaches his class how to cook, how to act respectfully as gentlemen and ladies, and how to be considerate of others. He even arranges for the class to take a field trip to a museum where, in a montage composed of still photographs (the sequence was directed by George White), they gawk at the enormous skeletons of dinosaurs. Gradually Poitier gains the students' trust and respect. They soon take to calling him "Sir," more out of affection than authority. One girl—Geeson, a dreamy blonde—develops a crush on Poitier and stands by his side in the hope that he will reciprocate. Rather than take advantage of her, Poitier gently lets her down. Others are less responsive. One cynical instructor, Bayldon, strongly disapproves of Poitier's methods and sways the school into forbidding any further field trips. Poitier's main opposition comes from Roberts, a young tough who defies all rules and tries to turn his classmates against the teacher. When a gym instructor's callousness results in an injury to a student, Roberts comes to the latter's defense and physically threatens the teacher. Poitier is called to the scene. He reprimands Roberts, but to no effect. Roberts prefers to settle the argument with a fight. Poitier straps on a pair of boxing gloves and, to everyone's surprise, delivers a healthy blow to Roberts's gut. With the school year coming to a close, the students dread the thought of losing Poitier to an engineering job. During an end-of-the-semester dance, Poitier is given a gift by the class representative, Lulu, who also sings "To Sir, with Love" for him. Poitier is driven to tears of joy by the gesture and retreats to the solitude of his classroom. The quiet is broken by a rowdy teenage couple barging into the room. They have been assigned to his class and seem to look forward to giving him a hard time. Poitier then tears up the letter informing him of the engineering job, planning instead to remain as a teacher. What makes TO SIR, WITH LOVE such an enjoyable film is the mythic nature of Poitier's character. He manages to come across as a real person, while embodying everything there is to know about morality, respect, and integrity. He is heroic yet human at the same time, and because of his care and understanding, he is able to redeem a group of children who would otherwise end up at the bottom of the social heap. As charming as TO SIR, WITH LOVE is, it does suffer from some excessive simplicity. Real-life hoodlums just aren't converted to the good life so easily, even with someone like Sir. Surprisingly (in relation to the rest of Poitier's career), the movie pays little attention to racial issues. Poitier is never considered a black man, just a teacher who happens to be black. The film's success baffled Columbia executives who just didn't know how to market it. In an attempt to learn why people liked the film so much, they even handed out questionnaires—a method that proved fruitless. One factor in the picture's popularity and its sustaining charm is the tuneful title song, which was a top hit for Lulu and is heard throughout the film. TO SIR, WITH LOVE went on to become the eighth largest grosser of the year, raking in $7.2 million.

TO SLEEP WITH ANGER

1990 95m c   ★★★★
Drama   PG/15
Edward R. Pressman/SVS

Danny Glover *(Harry Mention)*, Richard Brooks *(Babe Brother)*, Paul Butler *(Gideon)*, Mary Alice *(Suzie)*, Carl Lumbly *(Junior)*, Sheryl Lee Ralph *(Linda)*, Vonetta McGee *(Pat)*, Wonderful Smith *(Preacher)*, Ethel Ayler *(Hattie)*

p, Caldecot Chubb, Thomas S. Byrnes, Darin Scott; d, Charles Burnett; w, Charles Burnett; ph, Walt Lloyd; ed, Nancy Richardson; m, Stephen James Taylor; prod d, Penny Barrett; art d, Troy Myers; cos, Gaye Shannon-Burnett

Writer-director Charles Burnett received considerable attention as one of the current crop of new Black filmmakers in 1990 but he had already been making films for more than a decade. As an atypical look at suburban middle-class Black life, TO SLEEP WITH ANGER is notable for its honest, naturalistic presentation but this is much more than a well-intentioned exercise in positive images. By any measure, this is a superior film that boasts a rich and resonant screenplay, strong performances, and expressive direction. Human-scaled stories about day-to-day family life are rare today, regardless of the race, nationality, or religion of the characters. In this era, small-scale dramas have been consigned to television—this film itself began as a project for the Public Broadcasting System. In addition to disinterest from the all-powerful teen audience, the disappearance of this sort of production from movie theatres is also due to the industry's lack of facility of the form. Burnett demonstrates how it's done.

TO SLEEP WITH ANGER gains stature from its small and intimate scale—dictated by its small budget—to become a work as full of universal feeling as it is detailed and observant. Danny Glover, like much of the first-rank cast, agreed to appear in the film for a fraction of his usual fee and helped to raise production money as an executive producer. One can forgive any number of LETHAL WEAPON sequels if they will finance films like this. He gets a rare opportunity to show his dramatic range as actor in his portrayal of Harry Mention. Harry is a hard-bitten drifter who could be a direct descendant of Mister, the cruel husband Glover played opposite Whoopi Goldberg in THE COLOR PURPLE. Harry thoroughly disrupts the lives of a middle-class family in modern-day Los Angeles, and Burnett uses that simple plot as a pretext to examine a surprisingly wide range of human experiences and emotions.

Harry shows up one day at the suburban Los Angeles home of Gideon (Paul Butler) and his wife Suzie (Mary Alice). He is an old friend who grew up with the couple in the South. At the time, Gideon's household is filled with tension, much of it created by son Samuel (Richard Brooks), who has kept his nickname, "Babe Brother," into adulthood, largely because he's never grown up. His wife Linda (Sheryl Lee Ralph) is a successful real estate agent. Samuel harbors deep resentment against his older brother, Junior (Carl Lumbly). Junior is hard-working and successful, and Samuel feels that he has always been the favored brother. Junior, meanwhile, resents what he sees to be the way his parents dote on Samuel, despite the fact that Junior does all the heavy work around the house while supporting his pregnant wife, Pat (Vonetta McGee).

Harry's arrival initially adds some excitement to the family life as he helps his big city friends rediscover their rural roots. But Harry begins to develop an insidious edge. He starts bringing his old friends into the house. These are old acquaintances whom the family has not seen in years: blues singers, gamblers, and other shady characters who drink heavily and have vaguely violent pasts. We learn that Harry himself may have been involved with a couple of murders. Pat, who does charity work in her spare time, is treated to Harry's folksy dissertation on the values of selfishness, while Samuel's indolence is encouraged by the intruder. When Gideon is disabled by a stroke, Harry assumes control of the household with bleak results, exploiting the family's weaknesses and tensions.

While the drama focuses on the battle for Samuel's soul, there's little in the way of fiery, overwrought confrontation. There aren't even any clearcut delineations of good and evil. The family members, while basically decent, are often selfish and petty, while Harry's seedy friends aren't depicted as particularly bad people. Even Harry isn't so much diabolical—though he *does* seem to linked to the supernatural in some vague way—as he is limited by a life he never chose but tries to live as best he can. Burnett maintains a rigorously even-handed approach to his story, while bringing a wholly original lyricism to his direction. The ensemble cast is inspired, with all handling their characters with assurance. But what really sticks out in TO SLEEP WITH ANGER is its richness of imagery. The opening credits play over an image of Gideon sitting placidly in a chair as flames burn first on his feet and eventually over his entire body as the hymn "Precious Memories" plays on the soundtrack. Harry is photographed as a character who is alternately reassuring and disturbing, going from a placid shot of Harry sleeping on the floor, to a smiling Harry sitting at the kitchen table calmly cleaning his fingernails with the largest pocket knife anyone has ever seen. Other memorable scenes include shots of the kid next door struggling to play a trumpet, undercutting the stereotypes about blacks and music; Harry cutting his toenails in Gideon's favorite chair as Gideon lies stricken upstairs; and the poignant montage showing the deterioration of Gideon's beloved garden in the wake of his illness. Individually, these scenes could appear in any film, but it is their context that gives them their power here, marking Burnett as a filmmaker with a vital and important vision.

TOBACCO ROAD

1941 84m bw ★★★★
Comedy/Drama /A
FOX

Charley Grapewin (Jeeter Lester), Marjorie Rambeau (Sister Bessie), Gene Tierney (Ellie May Lester), William Tracy (Duke Lester), Elizabeth Patterson (Ada Lester), Dana Andrews (Dr. Tim), Slim Summerville (Henry Peabody), Ward Bond (Lov Bensey), Grant Mitchell (George Payne), Zeffie Tilbury (Grandma Lester)

p, Darryl F. Zanuck; d, John Ford; w, Nunnally Johnson (based on the play by Jack Kirkland and the novel by Erskine Caldwell); ph, Arthur Miller; ed, Barbara McLean; m, David Buttolph; art d, Richard Day, James Basevi

A twisted and humorous antithesis to the usual Fordian style of family bonding, TOBACCO ROAD is a beautifully photographed examination of life among the "poor white trash" of Georgia's Tobacco Road area during the Depression. One of three Nunnally Johnson-scripted Ford films—following the PRISONER OF SHARK ISLAND and THE GRAPES OF WRATH—TOBACCO ROAD takes the long-running Kirkland play, which opened in 1933 and was based on the popular Caldwell novel, and turns it into a strangely distorted story of individualism and integrity. The film opens with the apocalyptic statement, "All that they were, and all that they had, is gone with the wind and the dust," establishing a somber tone for this character study of man battered by the elements. But Ford, not to be easily pigeon-holed, plays much of the film for laughs. Diminishing the sexual tension that existed in the play between the characters of Ellie May and Lov Bensey, Ford instead concentrates on the amiability and frivolity of Jeeter Lester, played with boundless energy by Grapewin. Cast as husband and wife, Grapewin and Patterson do their best to hold their family together, while also trying to raise the necessary $100 to pay that month's bills. Regrettably, they have little luck with either undertaking. Grandmother Tilbury just gets up and leaves one day, walking into the forest, presumably to die, and is never seen again. Tracy, the rambunctious son, is more concerned with buying a car, blowing its horn, and making a wreck of it after one day than he is with helping his father in daily affairs. It is this car, however, that brings the family together in admiration of its design. This unity, however, is short-lived. Tracy taunts his parents, reveling in the idea that they cannot make ends meet and will probably be forced off their land by creditors. Meanwhile, daughter Tierney is deeply involved in making passes at neighbor Bond. The one person who has the chance to get Grapewin out of his dire financial straits is sister Rambeau, who instead carelessly spends every last cent of her money. Nearly everyone in the picture is slothful, refusing to work the land or to plant the necessary vegetables, choosing instead to steal. By the finale, the family unit is nonexistent, but Grapewin has succeeded in finding the funds to stay afloat. Amidst all the deception, carelessness, and laziness, Grapewin has somehow managed to emerge, thanks to his levity, from Tobacco Road with his dignity and individualism still in tact.

A masterful combination of Ford's pictorial skills and Johnson's character sketches (which also can be seen in the classic Jean Renoir portrait of the South, THE SOUTHERNER, to which Johnson and William Faulkner contributed), TOBACCO ROAD is an oddity in Ford's filmography, which is full of movies that celebrate family values, the love of the land, the work ethic, and honesty. In this film, however, these qualities are parodied, and the result, while unorthodox, is highly enjoyable, making TOBACCO ROAD perhaps Ford's most underrated achievement. Photographed by Arthur C. Miller, the man responsible for the breathtaking visuals of HOW GREEN WAS MY VALLEY (for which he won an Oscar), TOBACCO ROAD is, if nothing else, a marvel to look at.

TOKYO STORY

(TOKYO MONOGATARI)
1953 136m bw ★★★★★
Drama /U
Shochiku/Ofuna (Japan)

Chishu Ryu (Shukishi Hirayama), Chieko Higashiyama (Tomi Hirayama), So Yamamura (Koichi), Kuniko Miyake (Fumiko), Haruko Sugimura (Shige Kaneko), Nobuo Nakamura (Kurazo Kaneko), Kyoko Kagawa (Kyoko), Setsuko Hara (Noriko), Shiro Osaka (Keiso), Eijiro Tono (Sanpei Numata)

p, Takeshi Yamamoto; d, Yasujiro Ozu; w, Yasujiro Ozu, Kogo Noda; ph, Yushun Atsuta; ed, Yoshiyasu Hamamura; m, Takanobu Saito; prod d, Tatsuo Hamada, Itsuo Takahashi; art d, Tatsuo Hamada, Itsuo Takahashi; cos, Taizo Saito

Of Yasujiro Ozu's 53 films only a few have been released in the US, and 34 of these were silents directed before 1936, many of which have been destroyed. Even those we have seen took a long time to make it here. TOKYO STORY (made in 1953) for instance, did not make it to the US until 19 years after its initial release. It stands today, along with AN AUTUMN AFTERNOON, as one of the greatest of Ozu's films. It concerns itself with his favorite theme—the family and its discontents. An elderly couple (Ryu and Higashiyama) journey with their youngest daughter (Kagawa) to Tokyo to visit their doctor son (Yamamura) and a daughter (Sugimura) who runs a beauty salon. The children are too busy to meet with their parents, so they send them to a resort. After a sleepless night in the noisy resort the parents return to Tokyo. Before leaving, however, the mother spends a night with the widow (Hara) of another son, and the father visits some old drinking buddies. As it turns out, only this daughter-in-law gives the elderly couple the attention and love they need. The couple's own children soon have cause to regret their neglect, but their emotional ties to their parents have been all but severed by then. It comes as no surprise that they can so easily return to their own self-absorbed lives.

The film may not sound like much in a bald summary, but Ozu's cinema is remarkably powerful for those willing to give it a chance. Ryu is a familiar face in the films of many fine directors, and his marvelous low-key performance is but one of many in the film. Delicately constructed and deliberately leisurely, TOKYO STORY allows its dramatic content and thematic concerns to envelop an audience the way social mores envelop the films' characters. Ozu seems at once critical of certain aspects of Japanese tradition and reconciled to their status and use value. His trademark stylistics are equally intriguing, from his casually non-mainstream editing patterns to his limited camera movement. Most famous of all, though, are Ozu's trademark *tatami*-level shots. Using a special camera dolly to simulate the three-foot height of the average person kneeling or sitting on a *tatami* pad, Ozu creates a way of seeing the world that is specifically Japanese. Although one should resist seeing this great filmmaker as simply the most traditional of Japanese directors, his films do mirror the basics of contemporary Japan in a manner fascinating for those interested in this complex culture.

TOM BROWN'S SCHOOLDAYS
1951 93m bw ★★
Drama /U
Talisman (U.K.)

John Howard Davies (Tom Brown), Robert Newton (Dr. Arnold), Diana Wynyard (Mrs. Arnold), Hermione Baddeley (Sally Harrowell), Kathleen Byron (Mrs. Brown), James Hayter (Old Thomas), John Charlesworth (East), John Forrest (Flashman), Michael Hordern (Wilkes), Max Bygraves (Coach Guard)

p, Brian Desmond Hurst; d, Gordon Parry; w, Noel Langley (based on the novel by Thomas Hughes); ph, C. Pennington-Richards, Ray Sturgess; ed, Kenneth Heeley-Ray; m, Richard Addinsell; art d, Fred Pusey

This is a saccharine screen version of the Thomas Hughes classic, emphasizing the battles between new boy at school Davies and the brute he must contend with, Forrest. A new headmaster is also introduced, portrayed by Newton. He deals with problems in a manner the boys are not very accustomed to; that is, he treats his students as human beings instead of untrained animals. Davies is almost too likable in the lead role, while his counterpart is likewise almost too nasty, but this helps to play up the heavy dramatics. This film is a remake of TOM BROWN'S SCHOOL DAYS.

TOM HORN
1980 98m c ★★★½
Biography/Western R/15
First Artists/Solar

Steve McQueen (Tom Horn), Linda Evans (Glendolene Kimmel), Richard Farnsworth (John Coble), Billy "Green" Bush (Joe Belle), Slim Pickens (Sam Creedmore), Peter Canon (Assistant Prosecutor), Elisha Cook, Jr. (Stable Hand), Roy Jenson (Mendenhour), James Kline (Arlo Chance), Geoffrey Lewis (Walter Stoll)

p, Fred Weintraub; d, William Wiard; w, Thomas McGuane, Bud Shrake (based on Life of Tom Horn, Government Scout and Interpreter by Tom Horn); ph, John A. Alonzo (Panavision, Technicolor); ed, George Grenville; m, Ernest Gold; art d, Ron Hobbs; cos, Luster Bayless

Steve McQueen's second production for his First Artists company (following AN ENEMY OF THE PEOPLE) brings to the screen the legend of Tom Horn, the western gunman who negotiated the surrender of Geronimo, singlehandedly captured notorious outlaw Peg Leg Watson, and rode with Teddy Roosevelt's Rough Riders. As the film begins, the aging McQueen is hired by Cheyenne, Wyoming, cattle baron Richard Farnsworth to end the local range wars. Despite straying from the facts, TOM HORN is suffused in realism, the result of outstanding production design and extraordinary cinematography by John Alonzo. Like RIDE THE HIGH COUNTRY, THE SHOOTIST, and THE GREY FOX, the film is about an old cowboy's inability to adapt to the New West.

TOM JONES
1963 131m c ★★★★★
Comedy /PG
Woodfall (U.K.)

Albert Finney (Tom Jones), Susannah York (Sophie Western), Hugh Griffith (Squire Western), Edith Evans (Miss Western), Joan Greenwood (Lady Bellaston), Diane Cilento (Molly Seagrim), George Devine (Squire Allworthy), David Tomlinson (Lord Fellamar), Joyce Redman (Mrs. Waters/Jenny Jones), George A. Cooper (Fitzpatrick)

p, Tony Richardson; d, Tony Richardson; w, John Osborne (based on the novel by Henry Fielding); ph, Walter Lassally (Eastmancolor); ed, Anthony Gibbs; m, John Addison; prod d, Ralph Brinton; art d, Ted Marshall; cos, John McCorry

A rollicking comedic hack job on Fielding's sprawling novel about a lusty young man's adventures in 18th-Century England, TOM JONES was an enormous box office success that won four Oscars for Best Picture, Best Screenplay, Best Direction, and Best Score.

Featuring superb performances from Albert Finney and Susannah York and marking the film debut of Lynn Redgrave, TOM JONES is a brilliant melding of naturalistic 18th-Century backgrounds with frantic, Keystone Kops-style slapstick and silent film devices like undercranking, titles, wipes, stop-motion photography, etc. Cutting down and molding Fielding's huge 1749 episodic novel was a gargantuan task. Screenwriter Osborne, best known for social realist works like LOOK BACK IN ANGER, may have seemed an odd choice (Richardson and Osborne were both from the "Angry Young Man" school), but he succeeded beyond all expectations. (In addition to winning US Academy Awards, the filmmakers also took British Film Academy Awards for Best Film, Best British Film, and Best Screenplay.)

Several set pieces stand out in memory: the huge stag hunt at the estate of Griffith; the Georges Feydeau-style bedroom farce at the inn; but, most of all, the famous Redman-Finney scene which, while it shows nothing sexual—just two people staring into each others' eyes as they rip food apart and stuff it in their faces—remains among the most cheekily erotic few minutes in cinema. The other achievement of TOM JONES was that it put Fielding's novel back onto the best-seller lists, more than two centuries after it was published.

TOMMY
1975 111m c ★½
Musical PG/15
Columbia (U.K.)

Ann-Margret (Nora Walker Hobbs), Oliver Reed (Frank Hobbs), Roger Daltrey (Tommy Walker), Elton John (Pinball Wizard), Eric Clapton (Preacher), Jack Nicholson (Specialist), Robert Powell (Capt. Walker), Paul Nicholas (Cousin Kevin), Tina Turner (Acid Queen), Barry Winch (Young Tommy)

p, Robert Stigwood, Ken Russell; d, Ken Russell; w, Ken Russell (based on the musical drama by Pete Townshend, John Entwistle, and Keith Moon); ph, Dick Bush, Ronnie Taylor, Robin Lehman (Metrocolor); ed, Stuart Baird; m, Pete Townshend, Roger Daltrey, John Entwistle, Keith Moon; art d, John Clark; chor, Gillian Gregory; cos, Shirley Russell

Fans of the Who beware. Ken Russell applies his rococo outpourings to Pete Townshend's rock opera and botches not only the visuals but the fine score. With its beginnings as a 1969 album by the Who, one of rock music's most beloved and respected bands, TOMMY went on to become a stage smash in England. Then Russell, with his taste for the flamboyant and meaningless, added Ann-Margret and Oliver Reed, cast lead singer Roger Daltrey in the title role, and wasted a number of talents in useless cameos. The story, told entirely in song, centers on Tommy, a "deaf, dumb, and blind kid" who shuns the rest of the world after the death of his father. His mother, Ann-Margret, and stepfather, Reed, bring him to a doctor, Jack Nicholson, for treatment, but nothing seems to help—that is, until Tommy discovers pinball. "Playing by sense of smell," he beats even the Pinball Wizard (Elton John) and eventually breaks free and starts life anew. Drummer Keith Moon is a highlight as perverted Holiday Camp counsellor Uncle Ernie, Eric Clapton transfers his real-life role as rock guitar god to the screen, and Tina Turner is explosive as the Acid Queen but comes and goes with little explanation. Regrettably, Townshend's extraordinary songs are mauled by Ann-Margret, Reed, and Nicholson. Daltrey, however, proves himself an engaging screen presence and would continue to find work as an actor. Songs include "Underture," "Captain Walker Didn't Come Home," "It's a Boy," "'51 is Going to Be a Good Year," "What About the Boy?" "The Amazing Journey," "Christmas," "See Me, Feel Me," "Eyesight to the Blind," "The Acid Queen," "Do You Think It's All Right?" "Cousin Kevin," "Fiddle About," "Sparks," "Pinball Wizard," "Today It Rained Champagne," "There's a Doctor," "Go to the Mirror (The Specialist)," "Tommy Can You Hear Me?" "Smash the Mirror," "I'm Free," "Miracle Cure" (including "Extra, Extra"), "Sensation," "Sally Simpson," "Welcome," "Deceived," "Tommy's Holiday Camp," "We're Not Gonna Take It," and "Listening to You" (Peter Townshend, John Entwistle, Keith Moon). Townshend earned an Oscar nomination for Best Song Score and Ann-Margret nabbed a nomination for Best Actress (she lost to Louise Fletcher for ONE FLEW OVER THE CUCKOO'S NEST).

TONI

1934 90m bw   ★★★½
Drama
d'Aujourd'hui (France)

Charles Blavette (Antonio "Toni" Canova), Celia Montalvan (Josepha), Jenny Helia (Marie), Edouard Delmont (Fernand), Andrex (Gaby), Andre Kovachevitch (Sebastian), Max Dalban (Albert), Paul Bozzi (Jacques Bozzi the Guitarist), Jacques Mortier

p, Pierre Gault; d, Jean Renoir; w, Jean Renoir, Carl Einstein (based on material gathered by Jacques Levert); ph, Claude Renoir; ed, Marguerite Renoir, Suzanne de Troeye; m, Paul Bozzi

TONI has often been called the first "neorealist" film, preceding Luchino Visconti's OSSESSIONE by seven years; since the Italian director was one of Jean Renoir's assistants on the project, its influence on his work seems clear. Basing his film on police files dealing with an incident that occurred in the small town of Les Martigues, Renoir, seeking authenticity, brought his crew to that town and used its citizens as characters. The story centers on Toni (Charles Blavette), an Italian laborer who falls in love with his landlady (Jenny Helia) and then with a Spanish woman, Josepha (Celia Montalvan). After receiving permission from Josepha's father to marry her, Toni discovers that she has been raped by a sleazy foreman, whom Josepha ends up marrying, eventually deserts, and accidentally kills. Not surprisingly, Toni takes the blame. An insightful portrayal of male-female relationships and a skillful rendering of its near-pulp novel plot (again predating Visconti's adaptation of James M. Cain), TONI is nonetheless far from perfect, riddled with numerous technical weaknesses and some seemingly improvised direction. Still, it is clearly one of Renoir's important technical experiments.

TOOTSIE

1982 116m c   ★★½
Comedy/Romance   PG/15
Columbia

Dustin Hoffman (Michael Dorsey/Dorothy Michaels), Jessica Lange (Julie), Teri Garr (Sandy), Dabney Coleman (Ron), Charles Durning (Les), Bill Murray (Jeff), Sydney Pollack (George Fields), George Gaynes (John Van Horn), Geena Davis (April), Doris Belack (Rita)

p, Sydney Pollack, Dick Richards; d, Sydney Pollack; w, Larry Gelbart, Elaine May (uncredited), Murray Schisgal (based on a story by Don McGuire, Gelbart); ph, Owen Roizman (Technicolor); ed, Fredric Steinkamp, William Steinkamp; m, Dave Grusin; prod d, Peter Larkin; cos, Ruth Morley

A sitcom ode to the Hoffman ego. Like Hoffman in drag, it doesn't look at itself very closely; it might crack the mirror. Rather than confront what it sets up, it takes the one joke and runs—till it runs out of steam. Paging Billy Wilder.

TOOTSIE is about a man who pretends to be a woman in order to secure employment as an actor-actress. Michael Dorsey (Dustin Hoffman), a stage actor trying to make ends meet, dresses in drag and auditions for a part as a mature woman at a New York soap opera. Everyone is fooled, and he gets the part. His rise to fame as "Dorothy Michaels" is almost instant, but his personal relationships become a minefield, and the film milks the situation for all the cute yuks it will yield. His girlfriend (Teri Garr), who doesn't know he's working, wonders if he has another girl or if he's gay. The leading male actor on the soap, John Van Horn (George Gaynes), attempts to seduce him. Dorsey finds himself falling in love with the female star of the show, Julie (Jessica Lange), but Julie's father (Charles Durning) is smitten with "Dorothy."

Pollack gets something going at the first of the movie about unemployed actors' dreams vs. their realities that really moves. But after that, it's downhill. The problem is the sitcom style which doesn't really allow suspension of disbelief like SOME LIKE IT HOT. It leaves one no choice but to try and accept Hoffman at, well, face value. As Dorothy, Hoffman's Dorsey is hardly believable as a woman, much less an actress or someone playing an actress (in drag, he mumbles). He's so covered up with high collars and long sleeves, he's like a choking CHARLEY'S AUNT. Then there's the addition of the southern accent—did any southern WASP woman ever have a mug like Hoffman's Dorothy? Except for Lange (at the peak of her beauty, playing a sterotype with such effortless ease that she steals the film), the rest of the cast lacks comic energy—they're not sprightly enough. Pollack has directed them to act *around* the central idea of Hoffman's crossdressing, not in conjunction with it. Now we know what Joan Crawford's appearances on *The Secret Storm* must have been like. If that's not bad enough, Dorothy becomes a big favorite as a soap diva with female audiences. Deftly done drag by a person handsome enough to manifest some mature beauty might have raised some interesting questions about gender. As it is, this is patently an insult to women audiences, not to mention a minority whose feelings everyone seems to have neglected to consider here—professional female impersonators.

The screenplay is credited to Larry Gelbart and Murray Schisgal, but many writers contributed to it, including Elaine May; meanwhile, Hoffman's tantrums escalated set conditions to a hellish state, with Pollack, playing Hoffman's agent, and Bill Murray, Geena Davis, and Dabney Coleman around to take sides. The make-up artists worked as best they could to transform the raw material at hand—hiding Hoffman's burro ears and temporarily capping his large teeth.

The sitcom triumph shows once again that these days the lowest common denominator of audiences makes money for a film. TOOTSIE might have even made more had Hoffman also been a hired gun investigating a serial murderer on a soap opera set. Jessica Lange, up for Best Actress for her harrowing performance as Frances Farmer in FRANCES, got placated by Hollywood with a supporting one for this film.

TOP GUN

1986 110m c ★★
Drama/War PG/15
Paramount

Tom Cruise (Lt. Pete Mitchell), Anthony Edwards (Lt. Nick Bradshaw), Kelly McGillis (Charlotte Blackwood), Tom Skerritt (Cmdr. Mike Metcalf), Val Kilmer (Tom Kasanzky), Michael Ironside (Dick Wetherly), Rick Rossovich (Ron Kerner), Barry Tubb (Henry Ruth), Whip Hubley (Rick Neven), Clarence Gilyard, Jr. (Evan Gough)

p, Don Simpson, Jerry Bruckheimer; d, Tony Scott; w, Jim Cash, Jack Epps, Jr.; ph, Jeffrey L. Kimball (Metrocolor); ed, Billy Weber, Chris Lebenzon; m, Harold Faltermeyer; prod d, John De Cuir; fx, Gary Gutierrez

This paean to hotshot Navy fighter pilots and high technology attracted mass audiences despite its familiar plot and characters so vapid they vanish from memory as soon as the house lights come up. Young fighter pilot Lt. Pete Mitchell (Tom Cruise), nicknamed "Maverick" for his individualistic flying style, is sent to Miramar Naval Air Station, near San Diego, for advanced fighter training. There he trains with the best pilots from other squadrons, flying against instructors and firing electronic missiles tracked by computer. The best student from each class wins the prized "Top Gun" award, and the privilege of remaining at Miramar as an instructor. Maverick's chief competition is Tom Kasanzky (Val Kilmer), nicknamed "Ice," and eventually an international incident arises that allows the pilots to prove themselves. In an unlikely subplot, Maverick has an affair with Charlotte Blackwood (Kelly McGillis), a civilian expert on the physics of high-speed jet performance.

What TOP GUN contributes to the genre is an increased emphasis on military hardware and an almost homoerotic attraction for male bodies, mostly sweaty ones. In the final analysis, though, everything that happens on the ground is irrelevant to the real heart of the film, the flying sequences. Much praised, the airborne footage seamlessly intercuts live action shots of planes with special effects models. But for all the skill of their execution, the flying scenes are often confusing, rarely giving any idea of where the planes are in relation to one another. Jets streak by and pilots spin their heads around yelling, "Where'd he go? Where'd he go?" until the beepers aboard their planes tell them they've been shot down. The producers of TOP GUN went to the Navy with the project and received complete cooperation after certain changes were made in the plot. In fact, five different types of planes were made available to the filmmakers, in addition to a variety of other services ranging from technical advisors to air-sea rescue operations. Taxpayers, however, didn't bankroll TOP GUN; the filmmakers received a bill for $1.1 million from the Navy. The armed forces are not always so cooperative, however, as the makers of IRON EAGLE; PLATOON; and HEARTBREAK RIDGE found out when, for a variety of reasons, the Department of Defense refused to help them with those films. The Navy received yet another dividend for its trouble

when enlistment soared after the film—one of the slickest ever made—became a hit. Ultimately, TOP GUN is a facile movie in which Americans kill Russians with aplomb—proving their inherent superiority—and Tom Cruise gets the girl. The film won an Oscar for Best Song "Take My Breath Away," and was nominated for Best Film Editing, Best Sound, and Best Sound Effects Editing.

TOP HAT

1935 101m bw ★★★★★
Comedy/Musical/Romance /U
RKO

Fred Astaire (Jerry Travers), Ginger Rogers (Dale Tremont), Edward Everett Horton (Horace Hardwick), Helen Broderick (Madge Hardwick), Erik Rhodes (Alberto Beddini), Eric Blore (Bates), Lucille Ball (Flower Clerk), Leonard Mudie (Flower Salesman), Donald Meek (Curate), Florence Roberts (Curate's Wife)

p, Pandro S. Berman; d, Mark Sandrich; w, Dwight Taylor, Allan Scott (based on the musical The Gay Divorcee by Dwight Taylor, Cole Porter and the play The Girl Who Dared by Alexander Farago, Aladar Laszlo); ph, David Abel; ed, William Hamilton; art d, Van Nest Polglase, Carroll Clark; fx, Vernon L. Walker; chor, Fred Astaire, Hermes Pan; cos, Bernard Newman

The fourth pairing of Fred Astaire and Ginger Rogers and the first with a screenplay written specifically for them, TOP HAT is the quintessential Astaire-Rogers musical, complete with a silly plot, romance, dapper outfits, art deco sets, and plenty of wonderful songs and dance numbers. Set in London (though the story really unfolds in Hollywood's mythical Fred-and-Ginger-Land), TOP HAT's tale of mistaken identity concerns American song-and-dance man Jerry Travers (Astaire), who becomes as enamored of lovely Dale Tremont (Rogers) as she is of him. Problems arise, however, when Dale comes to believe that Jerry is the husband (whom she's never met) of her good friend Madge (Helen Broderick) and rebuffs his advances, finally fleeing to Venice with Madge. Jerry and Horace Hardwick (Edward Everett Horton), Madge's real husband and the producer of the show in which Jerry stars, follow them to Venice, and the confusion grows as Dale tells Madge that Horace has been unfaithful. Dale then marries her dress designer, Albert (Erik Rhodes), before Jerry gets a chance to straighten out things. Not to worry: it was actually Horace's faithful butler (Eric Blore), posing as a priest, who married Albert and Dale, which, naturally, means they aren't really married, paving the way for TOP HAT's upbeat ending. An effervescent musical that was the perfect panacea for Depression-era audiences, this wonderfully whimsical reworking of 1934's THE GAY DIVORCEE (whose leading players are reunited here) offers perhaps the most famous Astaire-Rogers duet, "Cheek to Cheek," wherein Ginger, in a gown covered with ostrich feathers, and Fred (who sneezed his way through the filming and would thereafter carefully inspect his dance partners' costumes) shift from effortless gliding to moves of dazzling exuberance. Built around Irving Berlin's hit-laden score ("Cheek to Cheek" was nominated for a Best Song Oscar), TOP HAT also boasts Astaire's brilliant solo number "Top Hat, White Tie and Tails" and excellent supporting performances from Horton and Rhodes, whose Italian caricature so offended Italian officials that TOP HAT, like THE GAY DIVORCEE (in which Rhodes played a similar character), was banned in Italy. With $3 million in receipts, TOP HAT was RKO's biggest moneymaker of the decade, and though it won no Oscars, it was nominated for Best Picture, Best Art Direction, and Best Choreography.

TOP SECRET!

1984   90m   c   ★★★
Comedy/Spy/Musical   PG/15
Paramount

Omar Sharif *(Cedric)*, Jeremy Kemp *(Gen. Streck)*, Warren Clarke *(Col. Von Horst)*, Tristram Jellinek *(Maj. Crumpler)*, Val Kilmer *(Nick Rivers)*, Billy J. Mitchell *(Martin)*, Major Wiley *(Porter)*, Gertan Klauber *(Mayor)*, Richard Mayes *(Biletnikov)*, Vyvyan Lorrayne *(Mme. Bergerone)*

p, Jon Davison, Hunt Lowry; d, Jim Abrahams, David Zucker, Jerry Zucker; w, Jim Abrahams, David Zucker, Jerry Zucker, Martyn Burke; ph, Christopher Challis (Metrocolor); ed, Bernard Gribble; m, Maurice Jarre; prod d, Peter Lamont; art d, John Fenner, Michael Lamont; fx, Nick Allder; chor, Gillian Gregory; cos, Emma Porteous

A strange mix that might have been titled "Beach Blanket Espionage," this overlooked comedy by Zucker, Abrahams, and Zucker doesn't always work, nor does it measure up to their hilarious AIRPLANE!. It is, nevertheless, very funny as it lampoons two genres: the spy movie and the teenage musical. While in East Germany to perform at big cultural festival, rock star Nick Rivers (Val Kilmer) finds himself embroiled in international intrigue involving an East German plot to take over West Germany, an imprisoned scientist (Michael Gough), and his beautiful daughter, Hillary (Lucy Gutteridge), who, naturally, becomes Nick's love interest. While helping Hillary thwart the takeover scheme, Nick, in the tradition of countless Elvis films, bursts into song on the slightest provocation. Equally without rhyme or reason is the movie's plot. In parodying pictures like THE SPY WHO CAME IN FROM THE COLD, Zucker, Abrahams, and Zucker present a narrative that is hopelessly convoluted, but that, of course, is exactly their intention as they pile joke upon joke, filling their film with inventive sight gags. Omar Sharif appears as a spy and is uproarious in what amounts to a cameo appearance, even though he gets top billing. This film hits more than it misses.

TOPAZ

1969   126m   c   ★★★½
Spy   PG/A
Universal

John Forsythe *(Michael Nordstrom)*, Frederick Stafford *(Andre Devereaux)*, Dany Robin *(Nicole Devereaux)*, John Vernon *(Rico Parra)*, Karin Dor *(Juanita de Cordoba)*, Michel Piccoli *(Jacques Granville)*, Philippe Noiret *(Henri Jarre)*, Claude Jade *(Michele Picard)*, Michel Subor *(Francois Picard)*, Roscoe Lee Browne *(Philippe Dubois)*

p, Alfred Hitchcock; d, Alfred Hitchcock; w, Samuel Taylor (based on the novel by Leon Uris); ph, Jack Hildyard (Technicolor); ed, William Ziegler; m, Maurice Jarre; prod d, Henry Bumstead; fx, Albert Whitlock; cos, Edith Head

An espionage story that takes the cameras to Copenhagen, Paris, New York City, Harlem, Virginia, and a California hacienda that doubles as Cuba. Loosely based on the true-life exploits of French spy Philippe de Vosjoli and the 1962 "Sapphire" scandals in which top French officials were uncovered as Soviet agents, the film has a sense of authenticity but fails to fire up as much suspense as most of Hitchcock's intrigues. With an international cast of semirecognizable names (Michel Piccoli, Philippe Noiret, and just one American, John Forsythe), TOPAZ gleaned most of its attention from the star status of its director. Hitchcock considered the film a disaster because it went into production without a finished script (in complete antithesis to his normal working methods of full preparedness), without full casting, and without an ending.

TOPKAPI

1964   120m   c   ★★★★
Comedy/Crime   /U
Filmways

Melina Mercouri *(Elizabeth Lipp)*, Peter Ustinov *(Arthur Simpson)*, Maximilian Schell *(William Walter)*, Robert Morley *(Cedric Page)*, Akim Tamiroff *(Geven)*, Gilles Segal *(Giulio)*, Jess Hahn *(Fischer)*, Titos Vandis *(Harback)*, Ege Ernart *(Maj. Tufan)*, Senih Orkan

p, Jules Dassin; d, Jules Dassin; w, Monja Danischewsky (based on the novel *The Light of Day* by Eric Ambler); ph, Henri Alekan (Technicolor); ed, Roger Dwyre; m, Manos Hadjidakis; art d, Max Douy; cos, Denny Vachlioti

Dassin went back to his hit RIFIFI and spoofed it with this enjoyable, fast-moving tale of a caper pulled by some of the most delightful characters ever assembled on one screen. Filmed on location in Istanbul and Greece, TOPKAPI cleverly employs every cinematic trick in the book—to an accompaniment of clever dialogue. As long as you realize TOPKAPI failed to accomplish what it set out to do—top RIFIFI—and if you don't care—this is glamorous, hambone stew.

Sexpot Mercouri (Dassin's real-life wife) and her lover want to steal a priceless dagger from the heavily secured museum in Istanbul known as Topkapi. To pull off the job, they enlist aid: Morley is an addled but brilliant British inventor and expert in electronics and burglar alarms, Segal is a mute acrobat who could climb a sheer wall with his fingernails and Hahn is a muscular, remarkably strong lout. While in Kavala, Greece, the gang hires Ustinov, a low-life con artist, to drive an expensive car across the border into Turkey. Ustinov doesn't know that the car carries weapons and gear for the robbery; when he is stopped at the border, one of the Turkish police (Ernart) thinks that some terrorists are using him as a dupe. Rather than arrest Ustinov, Ernart asks him to infiltrate the group that his hired him and to report back. Ustinov delivers the goods (some bombs, a high-powered rifle) to the gang's villa in Turkey. The daring robbery is carefully calculated. The floor of the museum is wired so that a single step will set off the alarm, so Hahn will hold a rope and lower Segal through a window. Then Segal will hang from the rope, reach down, and take the dagger without ever touching the floor. Meanwhile, at the gang's sumptuous mansion, the alcoholic cook, Tamiroff, is convinced that Mercouri and the others are Soviet agents. He passes this intelligence on to Ustinov, who still doesn't know about the robbery, and Ustinov informs Ernart. The robbery is about to take place when Tamiroff accidentally crushes Hahn's powerful hand with a door. With the strong man immobilized, Ustinov is pressed into service as the one to hold the rope, a job for which the paunchy Brit is obviously ill-equipped.

The film was based on a little-known book by Ambler and was adapted beautifully by screenwriter Danischewsky. Mercouri is the only woman of consequence in the movie, and she has a field day surrounded by the men—indeed, her touch is lighter than usual. A Supporting Oscar went to Ustinov (who keeps his numerous awards in a glass case in his bathroom. When a producer was scandalized by his placing kudos in such a room, Ustinov explained that it was the only location in his residence where he could ponder his achievements without seeming egotistical.). A great movie—with lots of laughs, a bit of the aforementioned RIFIFI, a smidgeon of BEAT THE DEVIL, and some of its own originality.

TOPPER

1937 98m bw ★★★★
Comedy /A
MGM

Constance Bennett *(Marion Kerby)*, Cary Grant *(George Kerby)*, Roland Young *(Cosmo Topper)*, Billie Burke *(Henrietta Topper)*, Alan Mowbray *(Wilkins)*, Eugene Pallette *(Casey)*, Arthur Lake *(Elevator Boy)*, Hedda Hopper *(Mrs. Stuyvesant)*, Virginia Sale *(Miss Johnson)*, Theodore von Eltz *(Hotel Manager)*

p, Hal Roach; d, Norman Z. McLeod; w, Jack Jevne, Eric Hatch, Eddie Moran (based on the novel *The Jovial Ghosts* by Thorne Smith); ph, Norbert Brodine; ed, William Terhune; m, Edward B. Powell, Hugo Friedhofer; art d, Arthur Rouce; fx, Roy Seawright; cos, Samuel Lange, Irene, Howard Schraps

Sophisticated, but a touch too mild, saved by an ebullient cast. Low-budget comedy producer Hal Roach, who had made a fortune on his Laurel and Hardy shorts, finally decided to risk a big-budget, feature-length comedy, and he came up with a winner that spawned two sequels, a television series, and a made-for-television remake.

George and Marion Kerby (Cary Grant and Constance Bennett) are a young, wealthy, happy-go-lucky married couple whose main pursuit in life is having a good time. Though they are the chief stockholders in a bank, their minds are on anything but business. One night, while driving recklessly in their big car, they hit a tree and are killed. Their spirits walk out of the wreck, but are dismayed to learn that they have not ascended to the heavens but are still on Earth, albeit in a rather astral form (they can turn invisible at will). George and Marion then decide that they will probably be trapped on Earth forever unless they make amends for their frivolous lifestyle by doing something of value.

The orignal casting for the film—Harlow for Bennett, W.C. Fields for Young—might have made for a screwier, more frenetic mix. Harlow's comedic touch had a more childlike sense of mischief. When she died a month before filming, Bennett, whose box-office was languishing due to too many formulaic weepies, landed the risk of TOPPER. She's a teasing minx, rather than a playful kitten. But audiences responded enthusiastically to her portrayal. Additional laughs result from TOPPER's special effects—the invisible duo makes objects appear to move by themselves. Avoid the the computer-colored version, which recently appeared on the market.

TORCH SONG TRILOGY

1988 120m c ★★★
Drama R/15
Howard Gottfried-Ronald K. Fierstein

Anne Bancroft *(Ma)*, Matthew Broderick *(Alan)*, Harvey Fierstein *(Arnold Beckoff)*, Brian Kerwin *(Ed)*, Karen Young *(Laurel)*, Eddie Castrodad *(David)*, Ken Page *(Murray)*, Charles Pierce *(Bertha Venation)*, Axel Vera *(Marina Del Rey)*, Benji Schulman *(Young Arnold)*

p, Howard Gottfried; d, Paul Bogart; w, Harvey Fierstein (based on his play); ph, Mikael Salomon (Metrocolor); ed, Nicholas C. Smith; m, Peter Matz; prod d, Richard Hoover; chor, Scott Salmon; cos, Colleen Atwood

When Harvey Fierstein's "Torch Song Trilogy" premiered Off-Broadway in the early 1980s, it became a word-of-mouth sensation for its caustically humorous homosexual script and performances. The film stays close to the stage production, with a story set in New York City between 1971 and 1980 that follows the roller-coaster love life of a gravel-voiced female impersonator (Fierstein). Fierstein falls for both a handsome and tender young hunk (Brian Kerwin) and a 21-year-old fashion model (Matthew Broderick), tries to act as a father to a teenage boy (Eddie Castrodad), and all the way battles his domineering mother (Anne Bancroft). Fierstein gives a strong and winning performance, and much of his story is funny and heartfelt. Kerwin and Broderick are merely perfunctory in their roles, but Bancroft nearly single-handedly destroys the picture with her scenery chewing. She's Harvey's mother because she's a star and because the script says so, not because the audience believes her.

TORRID ZONE

1940 88m bw ★★★★
Adventure/Comedy/Romance
WB

James Cagney *(Nick Butler)*, Pat O'Brien *(Steve Case)*, Ann Sheridan *(Lee Donley)*, Andy Devine *(Wally Davis)*, Helen Vinson *(Gloria Anderson)*, George Tobias *(Rosario)*, Jerome Cowan *(Bob Anderson)*, George Reeves *(Sancho)*, Victor Kilian *(Carlos)*, Frank Puglia *(Rodriguez)*

p, Mark Hellinger; d, William Keighley; w, Richard Macaulay, Jerry Wald; ph, James Wong Howe; ed, Jack Killifer; m, Adolph Deutsch; art d, Ted Smith; fx, Byron Haskin, H.F. Koenekamp; cos, Howard Shoup

In a seamy seaport nightclub in Central America, newly booked singer Sheridan—wearing a shimmering sequined gown—sexily croons a tune to local patrons and then, cheating, relieves them of their pesos at poker. Most of the patrons of the club are employed by the Baldwin Fruit Company, whose boss (O'Brien) has been observing the illicit activity from the bar. To protect his eagerly influenced employees, O'Brien orders Sheridan to leave town on the next boat back to the States, and to ensure her compliance he has her tossed in the local calaboose. Departing for the lockup, Sheridan quips to O'Brien, "The stork that brought you must have been a vulture."

In the jail cell adjacent to Sheridan's, the famed *bandido*, Tobias, awaits execution by firing squad. Befriending the clever devil, Sheridan helps him pass his few remaining hours on earth, playing cards with him through the bars. Grateful for her company, Tobias presents Sheridan with his ring as a remembrance. He also manages to cleverly evade the firing squad and make good his escape. The next day, the good-bad girl is escorted to a departing steamboat by O'Brien himself, who wants to personally witness the departure of the disruptive Sheridan. Annoyed by an amorous ship's officer aboard the vessel, Sheridan is protected by devil-may-care Cagney—wearing a *mustache*—who knocks the bounder into the briny with a single punch. Cagney, a plantation foreman for O'Brien's company, has made the mistake of messing with the boss's wife, and as a consequence is heading back to his native city, Chicago. The cocky little ladies' man makes a play for Sheridan, thinking to turn his trip into a pleasure cruise. The crafty O'Brien, however, had another motive for his dockside appearance; having shucked his faithless wife, O'Brien wants Cagney to go back to work, this time managing a troubled plantation in an area threatened by Tobias's revolutionists. Promised a substantial bonus if he succeeds in bringing in the banana crop, Cagney accepts the assignment. He finds an additional bonus at the plantation in the person of Vinson, the attractive wife of the previous plantation foreman. Their romantic idyll is interrupted by incursions of Tobias's revolutionaries, by disaffection among the workers, and—most critically—by the arrival of Sheridan, who has escaped from the ship and, pursued by police, has made her way to the plantation.

This wonderfully witty romp, laced with sexually suggestive dialogue, teams Cagney and O'Brien again in their familiar "friendly enemies" roles. But it's Sheridan, in only her second starring performance, who steals the show, proving herself the wisecracking peer of such great quipsters as Carole Lombard. Great fun.

TORTILLA FLAT
1942 105m bw   ★★★★★
Drama   /U
MGM

Spencer Tracy (Pilon), Hedy Lamarr (Dolores "Sweets" Ramirez), John Garfield (Danny), Frank Morgan (The Pirate), Akim Tamiroff (Pablo), Sheldon Leonard (Tito Ralph), John Qualen (Jose Maria Corcoran), Donald Meek (Paul D. Cummings), Connie Gilchrist (Mrs. Torrelli), Allen Jenkins (Portagee Joe)

p, Sam Zimbalist; d, Victor Fleming; w, John Lee Mahin, Benjamin Glazer (based on the novel by John Steinbeck); ph, Karl Freund; ed, James E. Newcom; m, Franz Waxman; art d, Cedric Gibbons, Paul Groesse; fx, Warren Newcombe; cos, Robert Kalloch, Gile Steele

This superlative adaptation of Steinbeck's novel features Tracy and Tamiroff as two ne'er-do-wells constantly in search of a free meal in their home of Monterey, California. Garfield is an eager young man who considers himself to be wealthy after inheriting two houses located on Tortilla Flat. Proud of his new status, Garfield allows Tracy and his friends to move into one of the homes, keeping the other for himself. Garfield then begins courting Lamarr, a beautiful young lady who works in a local cannery, but she will have nothing to do with him. Morgan, a newcomer to town, arrives with his dogs and what Tracy believes to be a good sum of money. Planning to rob Morgan, Tracy invites the newcomer to move into Garfield's home. When Morgan tells Tracy he is thinking of burying his fortune, Tracy insists this is not a safe thing to do. Morgan agrees, and much to Tracy's surprise, the amiable dog lover entrusts the would-be thief with his money, telling Tracy to keep a careful watch on the money, for he intends to use it to buy golden candlesticks in honor of St. Francis, the patron saint of animals. Morgan is convinced his prayers to the beloved saint cured one of his dogs when it was ill, and now he wants to honor his benefactor. As the story continues, Garfield's luck takes a turn for the worse: first, one of his houses burns to the ground; then he gets into a big argument with Lamarr, to whom Tracy has taken a fancy; and, eventually, Garfield gets drunk and is hurt in a fight. Blamed by Lamarr for Garfield's troubles, Tracy prays for his friend's speedy recovery and decides to help his buddy win over Lamarr. By film's end Garfield is back on his feet and married to Lamarr. Meanwhile, Tracy manages to raise enough money for Garfield to buy a fishing boat. Finally, deciding that all the trouble between friends began when Garfield became a property owner, Tracy puts a match to Garfield's remaining house when the newlyweds leave.

TORTILLA FLAT is an affectionate tale, told with sensitivity and a wonderfully offbeat sense of humor. Steinbeck's engaging characters are well treated by the talents of this ensemble and by Fleming's caring direction. Lamarr is excellent (she considered this the best of all her roles) as the level-headed, spunky woman who refuses to settle for anything she doesn't want. Her relationship with Garfield, a mixture of attraction and suspicion, is realistic and honest, a rarity for a screen romance. Garfield puts

his heart into his portrayal of the earnest Danny, contributing a memorable characterization that complements Lamarr's wonderful work. Tracy's lovable rogue and Morgan's holy roller add to the film's cast of colorful characters. Indeed, Morgan received a well-deserved Oscar nomination as Best Supporting Actor, though he lost that year to Van Heflin in JOHNNY EAGER.

Fleming captures the nuances and ambience of life in this small town, a sincere effort that guides the performers with care through the material. MGM built an entire village over three acres of land for the film that Garfield dearly wanted to do, though he had to wait some time before Warner Bros. agreed to loan him to MGM. Louis B. Mayer, MGM's head, also liked the idea of Garfield in the role, and, reportedly, the powerful mogul was not above some unorthodox pressuring to get his man. Mayer is said to have threatened to expose Warner Bros. for not making good on their pledges to certain charitable groups unless Garfield was allowed to make the film.

TORTILLA FLAT was highly praised by critics of the day—many of whom recognized it for the masterpiece it was—but the public was less receptive. The film's laid-back setting and simple characters were not what a war-minded American public wanted to see, so MGM tried spicing up the film with an ad campaign that read: "It's the gay paradise on the Pacific. . . It's as warming as the California sun. . . heady as spring wine. . . romantic as the tinkle of a guitar in the moonlight." However, the campaign didn't work, and the film failed to generate much excitement at the box office. Five years before TORTILLA FLAT was made, Paramount had considered filming the story as a musical, featuring George Raft, though that undertaking, like so many Hollywood projects, never made it to the cameras.

TOTAL RECALL
1990 109m c   ★★
Action/Science Fiction   R/18
Mario Kassar-Andrew Vajna-Carolco-Ronald Shusett

Arnold Schwarzenegger (Doug Quaid), Rachel Ticotin (Melina), Sharon Stone (Lori Quaid), Ronny Cox (Cohaagen), Michael Ironside (Richter), Marshall Bell (George/Kuato), Mel Johnson, Jr. (Benny), Michael Champion (Helm), Roy Brocksmith (Dr. Edgemar), Ray Baker (McClane)

p, Buzz Feitshans, Ronald Shusett; d, Paul Verhoeven; w, Ronald Shusett, Dan O'Bannon, Gary Goldman (based on a story by Ronald Shusett, Dan O'Bannon, Jon Povill, from the short story "We Can Remember It for You Wholesale" by Phillip K. Dick); ph, Jost Vacano (Technicolor); ed, Frank J. Urioste; m, Jerry Goldsmith; prod d, William Sandell; art d, James Tocci, Jose Rodriguez Granada; fx, Rob Bottin, Thomas L. Fisher, Eric Brevig; cos, Erica Edell Phillips; anim, Jeff Burks

Ugly, stupid, loud, offensive, and pointlessly violent—let's not mince words—this film should be called TOTAL REJECT. This is prime example of an unfortunate tendency in modern blockbuster moviemaking. Runningly mindlessly amok drunk on money and contempt, TOTAL RECALL is overloaded with inelegant special effects, bone-crunching "action," hideously cheesy make up effects, and gaping plot holes. That's entertainment? Any intelligent science fiction fan would be well advised to steer clear of this turkey and read a book instead. The late great Philip K. Dick must be retching in his grave at this "adaptation" of his short story, "We Can Remember It for You Wholesale." One would never know from watching this headache-inducing movie that Dick was one of the most cerebral writers in science fiction. Part of what makes this film so infuriating is that the premise is pure gold but the execution is insulting to the audience. Still it does have its passionate admirers. It takes all kinds. . .

Set in the year 2084, TOTAL RECALL tells the story of Doug Quaid (Schwarzenegger), a construction worker with a beautiful wife (Sharon Stone) and a nice home. This society of the future has provided a fairly good life for Quaid. Mars has become a colony of Earth but Quaid has never had time to vacation there though he dreams of it every night (and of a mysterious woman he has never met). Quaid decides to pay a visit to Rekall Inc., a "travel" service that specializes in implanting artificial memories of vacations into its customers' brains. One can recline in a high-tech chair and enjoy all the pleasures of a vacation at an accelerated rate with none of the fuss. Quaid purchases a memory of a trip to Mars. Included in the package is Rekall's special "Ego Trip" which allows the customer to take his "trip" as another person. Quaid chooses to travel as a fictional secret agent. When the doctors begin the implant, something goes terribly wrong. Even before the memory is implanted, Quaid becomes crazed, claiming that he *is* a secret agent from Mars. Is this a previous implant or is it a real memory that had been obscured? The doctors subdue and tranquilize Quaid and release him. Later, Quaid is attacked by coworkers and nearly killed by his wife. She confirms that he really is an agent posing as a construction worker. She also explains that she is not really his wife but actually another agent assigned to watch him. After fighting off would-be killers and learning more about his past (with the help of a pre-recorded message from himself), Quaid escapes to Mars to unlock the rest of the mystery.

Up to this point TOTAL RECALL is fascinating as it deals with some recurring themes from Dick's fiction such as the search for identity, the slippery nature of reality, and the effect of drugs on perception. Rumor has it that Matthew Broderick was originally slated to star. If he had been the protagonist, this would have been a radically different film, probably a much better one. Broderick would have been credible as a regular Walter Mitty-type who discovers that he may have had, unbeknownst to himself, a secret life of high adventure. In contrast, who could be less convincing as a regular guy than Schwarzenegger? The Arnold can be just fine in the right vehicle (e.g. THE TERMINATOR and PREDATOR) but here his presence, and the obligatory tone that goes with it, turns an interesting science fiction premise into just another noisy dumb shoot-em-up. Pity.

TOUCH, THE
(BE RORINGEN)
1971 112m c ★
Drama R/X
ABC/Persona/Cinematograph (U.S./Sweden)

Bibi Andersson *(Karin Vergerus)*, Elliott Gould *(David Kovac)*, Max von Sydow *(Andreas Vergerus)*, Sheila Reid *(Sara Kovac)*, Staffan Hallerstram *(Anders Vergerus)*, Maria Nolgard *(Agnes Vergerus)*, Barbro Hiort af Ornas *(Karin's Mother)*, Ake Lindstrom *(Doctor)*, Mimmi Wahlander *(Nurse)*, Elsa Ebbesen *(Hospital Matron)*

p, Ingmar Bergman; d, Ingmar Bergman; w, Ingmar Bergman; ph, Sven Nykvist; ed, Siv Kanalv; m, Jan Johansson; prod d, P.A. Lundgren; cos, Mago

If you see only one Bergman movie in your life, don't let this be it. His first film in English, THE TOUCH marks a move to a more simplistic style of drama in that it steers away from symbolic explanations of the inexplicable. The story is an uncomplicated one. Andersson and von Sydow are content in their marriage. However, when Gould, the wandering Jew, enters

Andersson's life, she begins yearning for the freedom that she no longer has. Though Andersson is attracted to Gould, she is indecisive about her situation, torn between her two worlds. The film is marred not so much by the familiarity of the story as by the embarrassing presence of Gould in a role which clearly is not suited to him. Especially disturbing is his dialogue (perhaps due to cultural unfamiliarity on Bergman's part), which seems out of place and awkward. Andersson turns in a beautiful performance.

TOUCH OF CLASS, A
1973 105m c ★★★★
Comedy/Romance PG/AA
Brut (U.K.)

George Segal *(Steve Blackburn)*, Glenda Jackson *(Vicki Allessio)*, Paul Sorvino *(Walter Menkes)*, Hildegard Neil *(Gloria Blackburn)*, Cec Linder *(Wendell Thompson)*, K. Callan *(Patty Menkes)*, Mary Barclay *(Martha Thompson)*, Michael Elwyn *(Cecil)*, Nadim Sawalha *(Night Hotel Manager)*, Ian Thompson *(Derek)*

p, Melvin Frank; d, Melvin Frank; w, Melvin Frank, Jack Rose; ph, Austin Dempster (Panavision, Technicolor); ed, Bill Butler; m, John Cameron; prod d, Terrence Marsh; art d, Alan Tomkins; cos, Ruth Myers

Joseph E. Levine (THE GRADUATE, THE LION IN WINTER, CARNAL KNOWLEDGE) picked a winner when he elected to present this very funny film about infidelity in London. It was nominated for Best Picture (it lost to THE STING), Best Song, Best Script, and Best Music, and Jackson won the Oscar as Best Actress. Segal is an American insurance executive living in London with wife Neil and children Samantha Weyson and Michael McVey. He's playing softball in the regular Sunday game near the Albert Memorial in Hyde Park one Sunday when he meets Jackson, a divorcee with two children of her own, Edward Kemp and Lisa Vanderpump. They meet again later when racing after the same cab in a London downpour. Taking this as an omen, Segal asks Jackson to have lunch. She is a fashion artist who goes to Paris, copies the latest creations, and sells them to New York garment firms who knock them off at discount prices. Segal suggests that they have a tryst in Spain and is very surprised when she agrees. Segal tells Neil that he has to take a business trip to Spain, and she wants to go along, but he manages to convince her to remain in London. When Segal and Jackson get to Heathrow Airport, he runs into Sorvino, a heavyset producer of exploitation pictures who is also taking the flight to Spain. Sorvino's presence forces Jackson to sit apart from Segal. They land at Malaga, where Segal has booked a large, comfortable car for the drive to the resort. To rid himself of Sorvino, he gives his rented car to the producer, and he and Jackson wind up with a tiny clunker. After considerable problems, they get to the resort hotel and immediately go to their room. Segal develops a back spasm and is unable to move at all. In the morning, Segal's back is finally okay, and the two make love. He is hurt when she admits that the earth didn't move for her; it was "very nice," nothing more. They have a loud argument and he exits. He runs into Sorvino and his wife, Callan, and agrees to have dinner with them that evening. Meantime, Callan has been shopping at the local marketplace, meets Jackson, and invites her to the same dinner. Jackson and Segal pretend to meet at the meal, and the scene is fraught with an underlying tension which expansive Sorvino can't quite fathom. Later, the two return to their room, and the argument erupts again, finally degenerating into a wrestling match. They laugh and make love. Sorvino learns about the affair and warns Segal against continuing it. The vacation ends, and Jackson and Segal return to London where they rent a flat to continue the affair. Segal soon finds that his family and his job are taking a toll on his relationship with Jackson. He decides to call it off and sends her a wire to that effect. Then he changes his mind and tries to stop the telegram, but it has already been sent. Jackson gets the wire at the apartment and promptly departs. Segal arrives a few moments later spots Jackson waiting for a bus. The rain is pouring down, reminiscent of their first meeting. All he has to do is call her name. But he doesn't. . . and the picture ends.

The company behind the film was Brut Productions, part of the Brut cosmetics firm headed by George Barrie. Barrie always fancied himself a composer and cowrote the film's Oscar-nominated song (lyrics by Sammy Cahn), "All That Love Went to Waste," as well as two other tunes. Shot on location in Spain and London, and interiors were done at Lee Studios in London. The picture did quite well at the box office. Segal is charming, but everyone knew he could play comedy. The big surprise was Jackson's impeccable comic timing, which some likened to that of Katharine Hepburn. The softball scene at the start of the film features many of the expatriate Americans who lived in London at the time and played regularly. Frank was not nominated for his direction, but he should have been. The film is in excellent taste and is a tribute to Frank and his cowriter, Jack Rose. Later, George Barrie would team up with Frank's former partner, Norman Panama, and produce I WILL, I WILL. . . FOR NOW with less than spectacular results.

TOUCH OF EVIL

1958 95m c ★★★★★
Crime /PG
Universal

Charlton Heston (Ramon Miguel "Mike" Vargas), Janet Leigh (Susan Vargas), Orson Welles (Hank Quinlan), Joseph Calleia (Pete Menzies), Akim Tamiroff ("Uncle Joe" Grandi), Val DeVargas (Pancho), Ray Collins (District Attorney Adair), Dennis Weaver (Motel Clerk), Joanna Moore (Marcia Linnekar), Mort Mills (Schwartz)

p, Albert Zugsmith; d, Orson Welles, Harry Keller (uncredited); w, Orson Welles (based on the novel Badge of Evil by Whit Masterson); ph, Russell Metty; ed, Virgil Vogel, Aaron Stell; m, Henry Mancini; art d, Alexander Golitzen, Robert Clatworthy; cos, Bill Thomas

Wild Welles rides again—adapting a shelved script written by Paul Manash for Albert Zugsmith, King of the Bs, from Whit Masterson's novel Badge of Evil (which Welles never bothered to read). The result? A film about love of film even more than the stinking, perverse little thriller it presents itself as. Already famous for directing perhaps the greatest film ever made, CITIZEN KANE, Welles opens TOUCH OF EVIL with what may be the greatest single shot ever put on film. It is a spectacular tracking crane shot which crosses the Mexican/US border, thereby visually foreshadowing the thematic elements to come—the differences that exist between two peoples, the Mexican and the Americans; the line Charlton Heston's character crosses from being a law-abiding husband to a vengeful madman; and the line Orson Welles's character crosses from good cop to evil cop. When a car explodes after crossing the border, both US cop Hank Quinlan (Welles) and Mexican narcotics agent Mike Vargas (Heston) begin their investigations. Almost immediately Quinlan has a suspect, Sanchez (Victor Millan), a young Mexican who is involved with the dead man's daughter Marcia (Moore). In order to secure a conviction, Quinlan plants some dynamite in Sanchez's flat, but Vargas is wise to Quinlan's game. With help

from Pete Menzies (Calleia), a long-time friend of Quinlan's, Vargas investigates Quinlan's past, all the while trying to solve the murder and protect his wife (Leigh) from a number of dangerous locals. Directing his first film in America since 1948's MACBETH, Welles was originally just supposed to act in TOUCH OF EVIL. The misunderstanding that led to this bizarre and twisted masterpiece began when Heston read a script based on the novel Badge of Evil. Hearing that Welles was involved, and assuming that his involvement meant as actor and director, Heston told producer Zugsmith that he would love to do the project. Rather than lose Heston, Zugsmith managed to get Universal to agree to let Welles direct, on the condition that he could also rewrite. Although much of the mystery element is revealed to the audience, it is Vargas who cannot unravel all the threads and make his clues add up to anything.

This nightmarish descent into dark entertainment has so much weirdness going on it's amazing. Marlene Dietrich, reprising her GOLDEN EARRINGS drag, smoking cigars and scraping pots, almost steals it. Complete with German accent and huge, light eyes at half mast, she's the most surreal excuse for a Mexican gypsy you've ever seen. When she sees Welles, big as a house with a false nose, it's the film's best line and a prophecy of Wellesian doom: "You're a mess, honey. You've been eating too much candy." Like Dietrich, Heston skips the Mexican accent as well. He looks like a muscular, surly version of an El Greco. Janet Leigh is at her most perversely innocent, and besides lots of grisly scenes (a murder by Welles the worst), there are a slew of outrageous cameos by Welles crony Joseph Cotten, Zsa Zsa Gabor (totally unaware what kind of film she's making), Dennis Weaver (unbelievably loopy), Ray Collins and the wildest, Mercedes McCambridge as a butch bitch biker. The blonde in the exploding car is Joi Lansing, the poor man's Mamie Van Doren. EVIL was filmed at Universal, with some locations at Venice Beach. It's greatly enhanced by Mancini's dangerous, Latin Rock score. Go for the rediscovered (1976) 108 minute version. Baroque, maddening, and totally inspired.

TOUT VA BIEN

1973 95m c ★★★½
Drama /X
Lido/Empire (France)

Jane Fonda (She), Yves Montand (He), Vittorio Caprioli (Factory Manager), Jean Pignol (Delegate), Pierre Ondry (Frederic), Ilizabeth Chauvin (Genevieve), Eric Chartier (Lucien), Yves Gabrielli (Leon)

p, Jean-Pierre Rassam; d, Jean-Luc Godard, Jean-Pierre Gorin; w, Jean-Luc Godard, Jean-Pierre Gorin; ph, Armand Marco; ed, Kernout Peitier

Jean-Luc Godard's most commercial film since WEEKEND and his strongest attempt to bring political thought into popular film. In order to deliver his message of class struggle Godard signed two famous actors—Jane Fonda and Yves Montand. The plot of TOUT VA BIEN exists only, as Godard says in the film, to provide "a story for those who shouldn't still need one." Fonda is an American news reporter living in Paris with her husband, Montand, a former "New Wave" film director, who has turned to directing commercials. They pay a visit to a sausage factory and find themselves in the middle of a work stoppage. The workers spout Maoist slogans and read political speeches into the cameras while taking over the factory's corporate offices. The plant manager is locked in his office and not even allowed to go to the bathroom. TOUT VA BIEN ends without neatly tying up the narrative, letting "each individual create his own history."

It is different from Godard's other political films (WIND FROM THE EAST, SEE YOU AT MAO, and VLADIMIR ET ROSA to name a few). It received a commercial release (many of his other political films were shown only to workers and students), had two "movie stars" and even received financial backing from Paramount (which opted not to distribute). It boasts stylistic camera work and set design instead of the usual hand-held graininess that is typical of his other political pictures. The most impressive visual is a multileveled cutaway of an office building which allows a view of all the offices at the same time. TOUT VA BIEN was an important step in bringing anti-bourgeois cinema to the masses.

TRADING PLACES

1983 106m c   ★★★
Comedy   R/15
Paramount

Dan Aykroyd *(Louis Winthorpe III)*, Eddie Murphy *(Billy Ray Valentine)*, Ralph Bellamy *(Randolph Duke)*, Don Ameche *(Mortimer Duke)*, Denholm Elliott *(Coleman)*, Kristin Holby *(Penelope Witherspoon)*, Paul Gleason *(Clarence Beeks)*, Jamie Lee Curtis *(Ophelia)*, Alfred Drake *(President of Exchange)*, Bo Diddley *(Pawnbroker)*

p, Aaron Russo; d, John Landis; w, Timothy Harris, Herschel Weingrod; ph, Robert Paynter (Metrocolor); ed, Malcolm Campbell; m, Elmer Bernstein; prod d, Gene Rudolf; cos, Deborah Nadoolman

The plot of this fine comedy owes more than a passing nod to Mark Twain's *The Prince and the Pauper*: street hustler Billy Ray Valentine (Eddie Murphy) and upscale yuppie Louis Winthorpe III (Dan Aykroyd) are forced to switch positions in life to resolve a bet between two rich brothers, Mortimer and Randolph Duke (Don Ameche and Ralph Bellamy), who frame Winthorpe and welcome Valentine into their business in his place. The rise of Valentine and the fall of Winthorpe are a source of great fun. The street hustler proves that his years in back alleys have stood him in good stead, providing him with all sorts of fresh business ideas. In Winthorpe's case, however, it is only when he meets and falls for hooker Ophelia (Jamie Lee Curtis) that he begins to appear in a sympathetic light. Although it tends to rely heavily on slapstick in the second half, the movie provides plenty of laughs and is one of director Landis's best efforts—despite overtones of racism that were perhaps intended ironically but have no business in the story. Elmer Bernstein's score was nominated for an Oscar.

TRAFFIC
(TRAFIC)

1972 89m c   ★★★★
Comedy   G/
Corona   (France)

Jacques Tati *(Mons. Hulot)*, Maria Kimberly *(Maria, the Public Relations Girl)*, Marcel Fravel *(Truck Driver)*, Honore Bostel *(Managing Director of ALTRA)*, Tony Kneppers *(Dutch Garage Proprietor)*, Francois Maisongrosse *(Francois)*, Franco Ressel, Mario Zanuelli

p, Robert Dorfmann; d, Jacques Tati; w, Jacques Tati, Jacques Lagrange; ph, Marcel Weiss, Edward Van Der Enden (Eastmancolor); ed, Maurice Laumain, Sophie Tatischeff, Jacques Tati; m, Charles Dumont; art d, Adrien de Rooy

Jacques Tati's fifth picture in 25 years (his fourth, PLAYTIME, was not released until 1973), TRAFFIC is a collection of sight

gags concerning the modern problem of automobile overpopulation. Tati again plays himself in this English-dubbed outing—the rain-coated, pipe-smoking eccentric—though now he has invented an ultramodern camping vehicle. With Kimberly, the public relations girl of his firm, he plans to take his new car from Paris to an Amsterdam auto show. Kimberly takes off first in her red convertible sports car, then a station wagon full of props (fake birch trees) follows, and finally Tati departs in a truck that houses his camper. The truck gets a flat tire, which Tati changes on the shoulder of the road, nearly being hit by passing traffic, and then he runs out of gas. When he doesn't show up at the car show Kimberly doubles back and looks for him. She helps him out of his mess but gets him into another by speeding through a customs check. Customs officials detain Tati and demand to know everything about his camper. He demonstrates the camper's modern devices, which include an electric shaver hidden in the steering wheel and a front grill that doubles as a cooking grill. By now Tati has missed the opening of the auto show, and adding to his misadventures is a chain of car crashes, which rivals that in Jean-Luc Godard's WEEKEND. Tati doesn't arrive at the show until everyone else has left, though a few stragglers take interest in his vehicle. He leaves with Kimberly in tow, choosing to take the train back to Paris instead of dodging traffic.

Any plot synopsis of a Tati picture proves to be fruitless since what is most important are the visual gags. So vital are the visuals that Tati rarely uses dialogUE, thereby negating the need for subtitles. One of the picture's funniest moments is Tati's attempt to climb the vines that cling to a house, pulling them down in the process. Instead of stopping there, however, he yanks them back up and winds up hanging upside down by his foot, refusing to give in and yell for help. Many of the film's brightest moments do not even include Tati (it was his wish that he would eventually be only a minor character in his films). One gag has Kimberly thinking that her dog has been crushed by the back wheel of her sports car. She is unaware that a group of mischievous passersby simply put one of their coats (which is made from the same fur as the dog) under the wheel. Other brilliant bits are created through montage. Various people are seen picking their noses while waiting for traffic to advance; or a connection is made between the car a person drives and that person's physical appearance; or a connection between the person and the movement of their windshield wipers. Tati, who's brilliant at commenting on modernization, here again provides insights into modern life that make for one of the freshest and funniest pictures to hit the screen in years.

TRAIL OF THE LONESOME PINE, THE

1936 102m c   ★★★½
Drama   /A
Paramount

Sylvia Sidney *(June Tolliver)*, Fred MacMurray *(Jack Hale)*, Henry Fonda *(Dave Tolliver)*, Fred Stone *(Judd Tolliver)*, Nigel Bruce *(Mr. Thurber)*, Beulah Bondi *(Melissa)*, Robert Barrat *(Buck Falin)*, Spanky McFarland *(Buddy)*, Fuzzy Knight *(Tater)*, Otto Fries *(Corsey)*

p, Walter Wanger; d, Henry Hathaway; w, Grover Jones, Harvey Thew, Horace McCoy (based on the novel by John Fox Jr.); ph, W. Howard Greene, Robert C. Bruce (Technicolor); ed, Robert Bischoff; art d, Hans Dreier

This was the first outdoor Technicolor three-strip film and Henry Fonda's first movie in color. Set in the backwoods of Kentucky in the early years of the 20th century, it's the story of feudin' and fussin' mountain people. Two clans have been battling for years, and, as the movie begins, Robert Barrat's family is firing at the cabin of Fred Stone's family, just as Beulah Bondi is giving birth to a daughter. Time passes and Sylvia Sidney grows up under the watchful eye of her brother, Fonda. He is almost killed in a fight with the rival clan, but Fred MacMurray, an engineer who has come to the locale with the railroad, saves his life. Fonda wants to keep his sister away from city slickers like MacMurray, believing she would be better off in love with a local boy. The advent of the railroad has brought new prosperity. MacMurray arranges for Sidney to be accepted by a school in Louisville, but Fonda is angered and lets MacMurray know it. The two men get into a fist fight, but then stop to fend off the Barrat clan, who have launched an onslaught on the railroad camp. The workers are frightened for their lives and leave the area in a shambles. Younger brother Spanky McFarland is killed in the battle, so, when Sidney returns from school in Louisville, she calls for a blood bath. MacMurray angers her when he attempts to inject a modicum of sanity into the proceedings. Fonda realizes that the feud must cease and offers to meet the rival clan leader. Barrat accepts and the time is set for the ritual handshake. In the meantime, however, Fonda is shot by one of Barrat's clan. Barrat can't believe what's happened and pays a visit to the Stone house to express his sorrow as Fonda lies moments from death. Fonda bids Stone and Barrat to shake hands, then watches as Sidney and MacMurray move close to each other.

Often poignant, filled with action, well-photographed, and even scored with four songs, this is a slice of Americana that proved successful at the box office. Cecil B. DeMille's version (1916) starred Charlotte Walker in the Sidney role, while Mary Miles Minter played the part in the 1923 version, directed by Charles Maigne. McFarland, who was only eight years old and already a veteran of several "Our Gang" shorts, shows his versatility in this film. Years later, Al Capp admitted that he'd based his famed "Li'l Abner" character on Fonda's role, and collectors of comic book lore will recognize some of Capp's early drawings as looking quite a bit like Fonda. Fuzzy Knight does a fine job acting and warbling the tunes. The song "Melody from the Sky" earned an Oscar nomination for Best Song. Other songs were: "Stack O' Lee Blues" (which may have been "Stagger Lee"), and "When It's Twilight on the Trail" (all by Sidney Mitchell and Lou Alter), plus Harry Carroll's "Trail of the Lonesome Pine."

TRAIN, THE
(LE TRAIN)
1965 140m bw   ★★★★
Thriller/War   /PG
Artistes/Ariane/Dear (France/Italy/U.S.)

Burt Lancaster (*Labiche*), Paul Scofield (*Col. von Waldheim*), Jeanne Moreau (*Christine*), Michel Simon (*Papa Boule*), Suzanne Flon (*Miss Villard*), Wolfgang Preiss (*Herren*), Richard Munch (*Von Lubitz*), Albert Remy (*Didont*), Charles Millot (*Pesquet*), Jacques Marin (*Jacques*)

p, Jules Bricken; d, John Frankenheimer; w, Franklin Coen, Frank Davis, Walter Bernstein, Albert Husson (based on the novel *Le Front de l'Art* by Rose Valland); ph, Jean Tournier, Walter Wottitz; ed, David Bretherton, Gabriel Rongier; m, Maurice Jarre; prod d, Willy Holt; fx, Lee Zavitz; cos, Jean Zay

A superior WWII film that provides plenty of edge-of-the-seat thrills, THE TRAIN also poses a rather serious philosophical question: Is the preservation of art worth a human life? Set in France in the summer of 1944, with the Germans in retreat, the film begins as a German colonel, von Waldheim (Paul Scofield), is ordered to transport the collection of the Jeu de Paume Museum—including numerous masterpieces—by train to the Fatherland. The curator of the museum gets word of the plan to the Resistance, and they persuade Labiche (Burt Lancaster), a railway inspector, to try to save the priceless works of art. THE TRAIN was originally to have been helmed by Arthur Penn, but during the first two weeks of shooting the director had some severe disagreements with Lancaster and producer Jules Bricken and left the production. Lancaster then called in John Frankenheimer, whom he had just worked with on SEVEN DAYS IN MAY (they had also collaborated on THE YOUNG SAVAGES and THE BIRDMAN OF ALCATRAZ). The film was shot entirely on location in France, and Frankenheimer employed a number of cameras shooting simultaneously so that the action with the trains would be captured from several different angles with as few takes as possible. His camera placement perfectly captures the massive trains (no models or miniatures were used) from every conceivable perspective, and their movement is directly contrasted with the chess game played by Labiche and von Waldheim. The acting in the film is superb, with Scofield taking top honors as the obsessed German colonel, though veteran French character actor Michel Simon nearly steals the film as a determined old engineer.

TRANSATLANTIC TUNNEL
1935 94m bw   ★★★
Disaster/Science Fiction   /U
Gaumont (U.K.)

Richard Dix (*McAllan*), Leslie Banks (*Robbie*), Madge Evans (*Ruth McAllan*), Helen Vinson (*Varlia*), C. Aubrey Smith (*Lloyd*), Basil Sydney (*Mostyn*), Henry Oscar (*Grellier*), Hilda Trevelyan (*Mary*), Cyril Raymond (*Harriman*), Jimmy Hanley (*Geoffrey*)

p, Michael Balcon; d, Maurice Elvey; w, Curt Siodmak, L. du Garde Peach, Clemence Dane (based on the novel by H. Kellermann); ph, Gunther Krampf; ed, Charles Frend

Set in the future, the plot deals with an undersea tunnel being constructed beneath the Atlantic Ocean which would connect England and the U.S. The special effects lend reality to the effort, showing how air locks shut down critical sections of the tunnel during a disaster and how people are trapped inside forever, as well as other troubles faced during construction. The process is shown to an attentive public via worldwide television and some scenes—such as those showing survivors of an undersea disaster and their relatives grieving at a hospital—are starkly realistic. Dix is the designer of the tunnel who gets to keep in touch with his family only through television or a telephone. Banks provides a willing shoulder for Dix's wife. A futuristic disaster movie with some very real touches.

TRAPEZE
1956 105m c   ★★★½
Drama   /U
Susan

Burt Lancaster (*Mike Ribble*), Tony Curtis (*Tino Orsini*), Gina Lollobrigida (*Lola*), Katy Jurado (*Rosa*), Thomas Gomez (*Bouglione*), Johnny Puleo (*Max the Dwarf*), Minor Watson (*John Ringling North*), Gerard Landry (*Chikki*), Jean-Pierre Kerien (*Otto*), Sidney James (*Snake Charmer*)

p, James Hill; d, Carol Reed; w, James R. Webb, Liam O'Brien (based on the novel *The Killing Frost* by Max Catto); ph, Robert Krasker (CinemaScope, DeLuxe Color); ed, Bert Bates; m, Malcolm Arnold; art d, Rino Mondellini; fx, Jack Lannan

Despite some stiff acting and a ponderous script, this was a smash at the box office, if only because audiences got to see Lancaster, himself a former circus performer, playing against the attractive Lollobrigida and the handsome Curtis. Lancaster is a lame acrobat who is famed for having done the impossible, a "triple" off the trapeze before having the accident that caused his limp. Two somersaults in mid-air are a commonplace, but a triple is the stuff of which high flyer's dreams are made. He's working as a rigger for a Parisian circus when Curtis arrives, eager to meet Lancaster and learn from him. Curtis is the son of a former circus friend of Lancaster and wants to learn to do a triple. Lancaster does everything he can to discourage Curtis, but circus-owner Gomez would love to have some enormous starring act to help business. After a while, Curtis wears Lancaster down and the older man decides that he might recapture his own glory by helping Curtis achieve the feat. The two men become very close. Lollobrigida is a scheming member of a tumbling act who would like to have the fame and fortune that trapeze artists merit. She begins using her wiles on Lancaster, but he has no interest, so she turns to the more naive Curtis. The high-wire work is very exciting and Reed's direction of the triple is breathtaking. These assets more than compensate for the shortcomings of the remainder of the movie. Seen briefly is Johnny Puleo, the little person who served for so many years as one of the Harmonica Rascals with Borah Minevitch. The ambience of circus life is quite well conveyed.

TREASURE ISLAND
1934 109m bw ★★★½
Adventure /U
MGM

Wallace Beery (Long John Silver), Jackie Cooper (Jim Hawkins), Lionel Barrymore (Billy Bones), Otto Kruger (Dr. Livesey), Lewis Stone (Capt. Alexander Smollett), Nigel Bruce (Squire Trelawney), Charles "Chic" Sale (Ben Gunn), William V. Mong (Pew), Charles McNaughton (Black Dog), Dorothy Peterson (Mrs. Hawkins)

p, Hunt Stromberg; d, Victor Fleming; w, John Lee Mahin, Leonard Praskins, John Howard Lawson (based on the novel by Robert Louis Stevenson); ph, Ray June, Harold Rosson, Clyde De Vinna; ed, Blanche Sewell; m, Herbert Stothart; art d, Cedric Gibbons, Merrill Pye, Edwin B. Willis; cos, Dwight Franklin

Robert Louis Stevenson's *Treasure Island* transfers easily from the page to the screen in this first sound version of the classic adventure tale. Wallace Beery plays the famous Long John Silver and Jackie Cooper takes the role of the doughty Jim Hawkins. The film opens at a rough-and-tumble coastal pub where young Jim meets the drunken Billy Bones (Lionel Barrymore) and learns that the old rummy has a secret map of an island in the Caribbean where a trove was left by a well-known pirate. When Billy Bones dies, Jim and two friends book passage on a ship run by Capt. Smollett (Lewis Stone). What they don't know, at first, is that practically all of the ship's men are one-time associates of the late pirate and one step from being cutthroats. What's more, all of them want their share of the booty. A beautiful production, a fine score, and a strong script all contribute to making this a respectable version of Stevenson's work.

TREASURE ISLAND
1950 96m c ★★★★
Adventure G/U
Disney (U.K.)

Bobby Driscoll (Jim Hawkins), Robert Newton (Long John Silver), Basil Sydney (Capt. Smollett), Walter Fitzgerald (Squire

Trelawney), Denis O'Dea (Dr. Livesey), Ralph Truman (George Merry), Finlay Currie (Capt. Bones), John Laurie (Pew), Francis de Wolff (Black Dog), Geoffrey Wilkinson (Ben Gunn)

p, Perce Pearce; d, Byron Haskin; w, Lawrence E. Watkin (based on the novel by Robert Louis Stevenson); ph, Freddie Young; ed, Alan Jaggs; m, Clifton Parker; prod d, Tom Morahan

This was Disney's first totally live-action movie, and it is, by far, the best film version of the familiar Stevenson story. Disney regular Bobby Driscoll takes on the coveted role of Jim Hawkins, and a number of reliable British actors round out the cast. This version has a marvelous full-bodied visual style that never appears to be studio-bound. When Disney wanted to rerelease the film in the 1970s, the MPAA rating system had arrived, and because of some rather graphic violence, the movie was given the dreaded (by Disney) "PG" rating. The offending scenes had to be snipped to acquire the desired "G" rating, depriving audiences of some excitement, but this remains an extremely satisfying film.

TREASURE OF THE SIERRA MADRE, THE
1948 126m bw ★★★★★
Adventure /PG
WB

Humphrey Bogart (Fred C. Dobbs), Walter Huston (Howard), Tim Holt (Curtin), Bruce Bennett (Cody), Barton MacLane (McCormick), Alfonso Bedoya (Gold Hat), Arturo Soto Rangel (Presidente), Manuel Donde (El Jefe), Jose Torvay (Pablo), Margarito Luna (Pancho)

p, Henry Blanke; d, John Huston; w, John Huston (based on the novel by Berwick Traven Torsvan); ph, Ted McCord; ed, Owen Marks; m, Max Steiner; art d, John Hughes; fx, William McGann, H.F. Koenekamp

Huston produced a number of major films in his long career (THE MALTESE FALCON, KEY LARGO, THE ASPHALT JUNGLE, THE AFRICAN QUEEN, PRIZZI'S HONOR) but one can make a strong case that this is the greatest of his films. This powerful tale of greed, fear, and murder in Mexico (shot on location) is one of the strongest of all American movies. There's gold in them thar hills and Humphrey Bogart, Walter Huston, and Tim Holt are hell-bent to find it. The rather preachy B. Traven novel about greed and its tragic consequences is made more lively and much more human by the father-and-son team of actor Walter Huston and director/writer John, with the invaluable assistance of Bogart. What a nice present to give your father at the end of his career. Bogart gives one of his most memorable performances as Fred C. Dobbs, an ordinary guy who gets transformed and finally consumed by greed.

On the bum in Tampico, Mexico, Bogart is reduced to panhandling. He meets and befriends another struggling American, Holt, and the two of them go to work for a shady contractor, MacLane, who takes them to a remote site where they slave away, their pay withheld until the job is done. When the work is finished and they return to Tampico, MacLane says he must go and pick up the payroll. Bogart and Holt complain that they don't have a cent, even to buy a beer, and he gives them a few dollars. They go to a cantina and drink, then check in at a flophouse where they take bunks next to a colorful, garrulous old man (Huston). Huston is regaling the other tramps about prospecting for gold, explaining that he has been at it since the Klondike days, having dug up fortunes and spent them. As Huston spins his tales, he adds that greed is usually the undoing of all prospectors. Bogart goes to sleep and the next day he and Holt look for MacLane and learn that he has a reputation for not paying his workers. They run into him on the street and have to beat him nearly senseless to get him to come up with their pay. Now that they have a little money, they decide prospecting might be a good idea, so they find Huston and ask if he wants to join them. He agrees, and says he's got a little money he can put into the venture. Just then, a young Mexican boy (Robert "Bobby" Blake, veteran of OUR GANG comedies and later famous as TV's "Baretta") who had earlier sold Bogart a lottery ticket, shows up and tells Bogart that his ticket is a winner. Bogart then adds his winnings to the stake and the three men set out to get the gear and equipment they'll need. The three start out as good buddies but wind up in a murderous tangle.

Both director John Huston and his distinguished father, Walter, won Oscars for this film, the only time father and son won the coveted gold statuettes. (In 1985, a third generation of the family won an Oscar when Anjelica Huston, John's daughter and Walter's granddaughter, was named Best Supporting Actress for her role in PRIZZI'S HONOR—also directed by John Huston.) John also won an Oscar for his screenplay, and the film was nominated for Best Picture, losing to Laurence Olivier's HAMLET.

TREE GROWS IN BROOKLYN, A

1945   128m   bw   ★★★★
Drama   /A
FOX

Dorothy McGuire *(Katie)*, Joan Blondell *(Aunt Sissy)*, James Dunn *(Johnny Nolan)*, Lloyd Nolan *(McShane)*, Peggy Ann Garner *(Francie Nolan)*, Ted Donaldson *(Neeley Nolan)*, James Gleason *(McGarrity)*, Ruth Nelson *(Miss McDonough)*, John Alexander *(Steve Edwards)*, B.S. Pully *(Christmas Tree Vendor)*

p, Louis D. Lighton; d, Elia Kazan; w, Tess Slesinger, Frank Davis (based on the novel by Betty Smith); ph, Leon Shamroy; ed, Dorothy Spencer; m, Alfred Newman; art d, Lyle Wheeler; fx, Fred Sersen; cos, Bonnie Cashin

Elia Kazan's first directorial assignment in films proved to be one of the most endearing, honest family dramas of the era and is still timeless enough to be watched and savored decades later. James Dunn won the Best Supporting Actor Oscar, Peggy Ann Garner earned a special Oscar as Best Child Actress, and the script was nominated by the Academy. Set in the Williamsburg area of Brooklyn in the first years of the 20th century, this film accurately captures the ambiance of the mighty struggle of the poor to eke out an existence against the odds as it focuses on the drama of one Irish family. McGuire is the matriarch of the family, worried about every penny because her husband, Dunn, can't ever seem to earn enough to keep her and their children, Donaldson and Garner, above the hot water they are always immersed in. McGuire is pregnant again, and although Dunn means well and truly feels that he is the best singing waiter in all of the borough, he finds success just outside his grasp and takes solace in alcohol. Dunn is not a mean drunk; there's not a scintilla of anger in his body. He is simply one of life's losers and, from the outset, we can sense that. Garner dreams of a better life, a life as a writer, somewhere away from the poverty of Brooklyn; she is the person through whom the story is told. While Donaldson is McGuire's boy, Garner is daddy's little girl. Blondell is the aunt, a woman who takes lovers and husbands with ease and who is quick to offer suggestions to everyone on how to run their lives, although she can't quite manage her own. In the tenement there is a small tree that heroically withstands the harsh winter and the humid summer, and Garner watches it as it hardily stretches its barren branches and refuses to be bent under the bludgeonings of life. She likens herself to that tree and takes strength from it as the small sapling flourishes in the midst of trouble. Dunn dies of pneumonia, and Garner fears that her link is gone, but McGuire clasps the young girl to her bosom, saying that she is going to need her to help with the birth of the new baby.

The movie is a trifle lengthy but never tedious. It's episodic, but life is often episodic, and the performances are so real, so richly detailed that one can overlook the segmented way in which the movie is unspooled. McGuire had only made one movie before, the charming CLAUDIA, and was only about 13 years older than Garner and 13 years younger than Dunn at the time of shooting. Kazan did not fall into the trap to which so many first-time directors are prey, i.e., impressing the eye with cinematic tricks. Instead, he wisely concentrated on evoking memorable performances from all concerned, and none was more rewarding than that of Dunn, who had starred in many B movies for years before getting the opportunity to show his stuff here. Dunn, for many years, had been a notorious heavy drinker, and when he was first proposed for the role of the Irish singing waiter, Fox executives said no, that he was unreliable and a drunk. But studio boss Zanuck was persuaded that that was exactly what Dunn would be playing and, against all advice, cast the easygoing tippler in the role.

TREE OF WOODEN CLOGS, THE

(L'ALBERO DEGLI ZOCCOLI)
1979   185m   c   ★★★★½
Drama   /A
G.P.C. Gruppo/Gaumont   (Italy)

Luigi Ornaghi *(Batisti)*, Francesca Moriggi *(Batistina)*, Omar Brignoli *(Minek)*, Antonio Ferrari *(Tuni)*, Teresa Brescianini *(Widow Runk)*, Giuseppe Brignoli *(Grandpa Anselmo)*, Carlo Rota *(Peppino)*, Pasqualina Brolis *(Teresina)*, Massimo Fratus *(Pierino)*, Francesca Villa *(Annetta)*

d, Ermanno Olmi; w, Ermanno Olmi; ph, Ermanno Olmi; ed, Ermanno Olmi; m, Johann Sebastian Bach

Postmodern neorealism. This naturalistic portrayal of Italian peasants neither glorifies their lives nor looks down on them. Olmi, who directed, scripted, photographed, and edited the film, concentrates on three peasant families (all finely acted by nonprofessionals) and their daily existence for the period of about one year. They live on an estate governed by a practically nonexistent landlord and work his land with the greatest of care and devotion. Interestingly, however, the least important facet of THE TREE OF WOODEN CLOGS is its plot. Instead, the focus is on the bond between people, as well as their relationship to the land. Olmi resists the urge to overly moralize the lives of these people as he considers what is beautiful as well as what is stagnant about their lives. At times he seems to suggest that here may reside a model for human existence, but he is generally content to present the film as an extended vignette. (It is interesting, though, how Olmi largely fails to consider the class relations structuring certain aspects of these people's lives.) A memorable picture which takes a sensitive, poetic look at a remarkable group of human beings without getting too romanticized about it, THE TREE OF WOODEN CLOGS was winner of the Golden Palm at the 1978 Cannes Film Festival, making it the second Italian film in a row to take top honors (the 1977 winner was the Taviani Brother's PADRE PADRONE).

TREMORS

1990   96m   c   ★★★
Comedy/Horror   PG-13/15
No Frills/Wilson-Maddock

Kevin Bacon (Valentine McKee), Fred Ward (Earl Basset), Finn Carter (Rhonda LeBeck), Michael Gross (Burt Gummer), Reba McEntire (Heather Gummer), Bobby Jacoby (Melvin Plug), Charlotte Stewart (Nancy), Tony Genaro (Miguel), Ariana Richards (Minday), Richard Marcus (Nestor)

p, Brent Maddock, S.S. Wilson; d, Ron Underwood; w, S.S. Wilson, Brent Maddock (based on a story by S.S. Wilson, Brent Maddock, and Ron Underwood); ph, Alexander Gruszynski (Deluxe Color); ed, O. Nicholas Brown; m, Ernest Troost; prod d, Ivo Cristante; art d, Donald Maskovich; fx, Gene Warren, Jr.

TREMORS fondly recalls monster movies of the 50s, but since the majority of today's moviegoers were born in the 70s, most will barely remember whence Freddy Krueger sprang, much less such films as Howard Hawks's THE THING, one of many sci-fi creature features TREMORS fondly quotes. Thus, the film draws on a genre so old that it's new. As a result, the script wisely treads a middle path between knowing sendup and cannily crafted chiller.

Trying to escape their dead-end life in the desert town of Perfection (population 14), handymen Val (Kevin Bacon) and Earl (Fred Ward) find themselves sidetracked when corpses mysteriously begin piling up around them, the causes of death ranging from the strange (an old drunk is found halfway up an electrical tower dead from dehydration) to the unknown. When the handymen have a run-in with some creepy tentacled creatures that have apparently made lunch out of a road crew, they realize they are in deep trouble and retreat to the town to spread some hysteria and prepare for Mankind's last stand against a really disgusting menace: giant, foul-smelling, flesh-eating, mutant maggots. Although these maggots are not the intellectual equals of THE THING's thinking carrot, their mental powers are still mind-boggling. Detecting a human morsel hiding in a car, the maggots dig under the vehicle, causing it to sink into the earth. When the survivors think they have outwitted the wily worms by taking refuge atop the roofs of buildings, the beasts merely destroy the buildings' foundations. The maggots are quick learners when it comes to stalking their prey, and the humans must be continually on their toes if they are to keep from becoming worm food while they try desperately to find a more permanent way to defeat the monsters.

TREMORS bends its movie cliches just enough to keep the action interesting and entertaining. One of the most fondly held conventions of 50s horror films was to withhold a straight-on view of the monsters until late in the picture; in TREMORS the beasts emerge early in the action, which, in another departure from convention, takes place almost entirely in broad daylight. The special effects are first-rate, with the maggots easily withstanding extended camera scrutiny. Another upended convention places a female scientist (Finn Carter) in the thick of the action, although she contributes little to our knowledge of the beasts and, before long, becomes irritated by the questions of the excited townsfolk. It turns out that the dumbest guys in the movie, Val and Earl, contribute the most towards eradicating the big bugs, with their prime motivation being to get the job done so they can continue their rudely interrupted journey out of Perfection.

You don't have to be a perennial late-night movie vidiot to get a kick out of TREMORS. It's fast-moving fun for kids of all ages who harbor a secret delight in movies starring gooey, smelly monsters. It's also very well cast, with Ward and Bacon proving affable and enjoyable comedy leads. Carter also has an offbeat appeal as the irritable woman of science, while Michael Gross and country star Reba McEntire, in a most unlikely film debut (she also wrote and sings the end-credit song, "Why Not Tonight?"), provide solid support as a survivalist couple who dispatch one of the creatures in a hail of bullets. It may not top anyone's 10-best list, but TREMORS is nevertheless solid entertainment.

TRIAL, THE
(LE PROCES)

1963   118m   bw   ★★★
Drama   /X
Paris Europa/Hisa   (France/Italy/West Germany)

Anthony Perkins (Josef K), Orson Welles (Hastler), Jeanne Moreau (Miss Burstner), Romy Schneider (Leni), Elsa Martinelli (Hilda), Akim Tamiroff (Bloch), Arnoldo Foa (Inspector A), William Kearns (1st Assistant Inspector), Jess Hahn (2nd Assistant Inspector), Suzanne Flon (Miss Pittl)

p, Yves Laplanche, Miguel Salkind, Alexander Salkind; d, Orson Welles; w, Orson Welles (based on the novel by Franz Kafka); ph, Edmond Richard; ed, Yvonne Martin; m, Jean Ledrut, Tomaso Albinoni; art d, Jean Mandaroux; cos, Helen Thibault

Welles applied his bravura directorial style to Kafka's landmark 1925 novel about Joseph K (Perkins), an office clerk who gets arrested without being told why.

The film opens over a series of pin-screen pictures (a technique using pins, cloth, light, and shadows created by A. Alexeieff) of a guard in front of a huge door, preventing a man from entering. For years the man awaits entrance through the door which leads to the Law, but he never gains admittance. The narrator (Welles) then explains, "It has been said that the logic of this story is the logic of a dream. Do you feel lost in a labyrinth? Do not look for a way out. You will not be able to find one. . . There is no way out."

Kafka's novel doesn't translate well into film, being too dependent on the internal thoughts and frustrations of Joseph K during his quest. Aware of this problem, Welles has chosen to concentrate on the atmosphere of K's world, accompanied by the dreamy musical leitmotif of Albinoni's "Adagio." The sets are typical Welles baroque—massive structures which engulf K in the same way Xanadu swallowed Charles Foster Kane in CITIZEN KANE. These sets alone—with their haunting shadows and claustrophobic walls and ceilings—make THE TRIAL essential viewing. Welles's enthusiasm for the film is remarkable: "Say what you like, but THE TRIAL is the best film I ever made."

The film's genesis goes back to Miguel and Alexander Salkind, the father-and-son producing team, who offered Welles a list of 15 classic novels which were in public domain. Welles was to choose one that he wanted to film and, without much enthusiasm (Welles admits he had a "lack of profound sympathy for Kafka"), he agreed to The Trial. Production began in Zagreb, Yugoslavia, but was soon shut down for lack of funds. Skipping out on bills owed there, Welles and his entourage returned to Paris to complete the film at the abandoned Gare d'Orsay train station, an overwhelming structure which seems to have been built with Welles in mind. Although the film has its admirers, its opening was less than favorable. Originally scheduled to play the 1962 Venice Film Fest, it did not open until December 21 of that year in Paris. Not only did Welles have to overcome financial and scheduling restrictions, but he had problems with the casting. He had first cast himself as a priest, but when no suitable actor could be found for the advocate, Welles took over the role, scrapping the footage he had already shot. Shot in English, THE TRIAL was dubbed for its foreign-language releases, which had a variety of running times. Two players were cut from the US release: Katina Paxinou, as a scientist, and Van Doude, who played an archivist.

The chief difference between Welles's Joseph K and Kafka's is in the extent of their guilt. While Kafka stresses ambiguity, Welles is clear in his feelings: "He is a little bureaucrat. I consider him guilty. . . He belongs to a guilty society; he collaborates with it." Welles further points to his differences with Kafka: "I do not share Kafka's point of view in *The Trial*. I believe that he is a good writer, but Kafka is not the extraordinary genius that people today see in him." Nonetheless, Kafka's story is far more successful as a novel than a film.

TRIAL OF JOAN OF ARC
(PROCES DE JEANNE D'ARC)
1965   65m   bw   ★★★
Historical
Pathe   (France)

Florence Carrez *(Jeanne D'Arc)*, Jean-Claude Fourneau *(Bishop Cauchon)*, Marc Jacquier *(Jean Lemaitre)*, Roger Honorat *(Jean Beaupere)*, Jean Gillibert *(Jean de Chatillon)*, Andre Regnier *(D'Estivet)*, Michel Herubel *(Frere Isambart de la Pierre)*, Philippe Dreux *(Frere Martin Ladvenu)*, Jean Darbaud *(Nicolas de Houppeville)*, E.R. Pratt *(Warwick)*

p, Agnes Delahaie; d, Robert Bresson; w, Robert Bresson (based on "Proces de Condamnation et de Rehabilitation de Jeanne D'Arc"); ph, L.H. Burel; ed, Germaine Artus; m, Francis Seyrig; art d, Pierre Charbonnier; cos, Lucilla Mussini

The most commonly known film rendition of the famous French legend of Joan of Arc is the 1920s version by Dreyer in which Falconetti gave a stunning performance of the girl burned as a witch. From the outset of this newer project, Bresson chose an entirely different angle from that of Dreyer, for he was concerned with creating a more objective rendition, unprejudiced by the filmmaker's camera technique and personal manipulations. His efforts were fairly successful. He based the script solely on the notes from the trial, with Carrez playing Joan in a manner that makes her appear brighter and more scheming than she has usually been represented. Joan was a French peasant girl brought to trial as an enemy of the government, and after enduring a long court case and torture she was burned as a witch. Unlike the earlier version, Bresson concentrates quite heavily on the psychological and physical torture, showing how Joan broke down during the trial and recanted her faith. The purpose of Bresson was not to destroy the myth of Joan of Arc; what he did was reveal the processes that helped to create a legend.

TRIBUTE
1980   123m   c   ★★★½
Comedy/Drama   PG/AA
FOX   (Canada)

Jack Lemmon *(Scottie Templeton)*, Robby Benson *(Jud Templeton)*, Lee Remick *(Maggie Stratton)*, Kim Cattrall *(Sally Haines)*, Colleen Dewhurst *(Gladys Petrelli)*, John Marley *(Lou Daniels)*, Gale Garnett *(Hilary)*, Teri Keane *(Evelyn)*, Rummy Bishop, John Dee

p, Joel B. Michaels, Garth H. Drabinsky; d, Bob Clark; w, Bernard Slade (based on his stage play); ph, Reginald Morris (Medallion Film Laboratories Color); ed, Richard Halsey; m, Ken Wannberg, Barry Manilow, Jack Feldman, Bruce Sussman, Jack Lemmon, Alan Jay Lerner; prod d, Trevor Williams; art d, Reuben Freed

Jack Lemmon, re-creating the role he performed onstage, is a smart-mouth Broadway press agent whose life is thrown into turmoil when he learns he has leukemia and will die if he doesn't undergo the necessary treatment. Enter Lemmon's son Robby Benson, who couldn't be more different from his father and who doesn't think much of the way Lemmon lives. Gradually they grow close, and much comedy and many deeply touching moments occur as Benson's earnestness clashes with Lemmon's irresponsibility. Strong performances by Benson and Lemmon are wonderfully supported by Lee Remick as Lemmon's ex-wife, John Marley as his partner, and Colleen Dewhurst as his doctor. Bernard Slade, who wrote SAME TIME, NEXT YEAR and ROMANTIC COMEDY, provides plenty of witty dialogue and leavens the seriousness with some inspired comedic moments.

TRIP TO BOUNTIFUL, THE
1985   105m   c   ★★★★
Drama   PG/U
Bountiful/Film Dallas

Geraldine Page *(Mrs. Watts)*, John Heard *(Ludie Watts)*, Carlin Glynn *(Jessie Mae)*, Richard Bradford *(Sheriff)*, Rebecca De Mornay *(Thelma)*, Kevin Cooney *(Roy)*, Norman Bennett, Harvey Lewis *(Bus Ticket Men)*, Kirk Sisco *(Ticket Agent)*, David Tanner *(Billy Davis)*

p, Sterling Van Wagenen, Horton Foote; d, Peter Masterson; w, Horton Foote (based on his play); ph, Fred Murphy; ed, Jay Freund; m, J.A.C. Redford; prod d, Neil Spisak; art d, Philip Lamb; cos, Gary Jones

A luminous performance by Geraldine Page won her an Oscar for this movie, one of the most touching pictures of the decade. The year is 1947; the place, Houston, Texas. Mrs. Watts (Page) is an elderly woman given to humming hymns and living the remaining years of her life with her wimp son, Ludie (John Heard), and his shrewish wife, Jessie Mae (Carlin Glynn), in a cramped apartment. Mrs. Watts's heart is weak, she has spells, and she can't get along with Jessie Mae at all. She has but one fervent desire left in her life: she wants to return to Bountiful, the small Texas town where she was born and grew up. The memories of the tranquility of Bountiful haunt her constantly as a reminder of a better time and life. When the stress gets too much for her, Mrs. Watts hides her pension check from Ludie and Jessie Mae and plans her escape. The movie is wonderfully made, and the first-time direction by stage director Peter Masterson is extraordinary. No guns, no violence, no nudity—just a caring story that will wet the driest eye and warm the coldest heart. Every single role is perfectly cast and perfectly played, and Horton Foote's script is a marvel of economy.

TRIPLE ECHO, THE
1973   90m   c   ★★
Drama   R/X
Senat   (U.K.)

Glenda Jackson *(Alice)*, Brian Deacon *(Barton)*, Oliver Reed *(Sergeant)*, Anthony May *(Subaltern)*, Gavin Richards *(Stan)*, Jenny Wright *(Christine)*, Daphne Heard *(Shopkeeper)*

p, Graham Cottle; d, Michael Apted; w, Robin Chapman (based on the novel by H.E. Bates); ph, John Coquillon (Eastmancolor); ed, Barrie Vince; m, Marc Wilkinson

In this plodding story set during WWII, Jackson is a lonely woman who stays in her country home while her husband is away in a Japanese prisoner of war camp. The drifting Deacon soon becomes her lover. A soldier, he decides not to return to the front, preferring to stay with Jackson. He dons a dress to conceal his identity, but gets over-confident. The gruff Reed, sergeant of a tank unit, passes by and uncovers Deacon's true identity when Deacon allows him to take him out dancing. Despite the love story and inescapable humor of the situation at the dance, the film's grim realism lasts to its bitter conclusion.

TRISTANA

1970 95m c ★★★★
Drama GP/A
Epoca/Talia/Selenia/Corona (Spain/Italy/France)

Catherine Deneuve (Tristana), Fernando Rey (Don Lope), Franco Nero (Horacio), Lola Gaos (Saturna), Antonio Casas (Don Cosme), Jesus Fernandez (Saturno), Vicente Soler (Don Ambrosio), Jose Calvo (Bellringer), Fernando Cebrian (Dr. Miquis), Candida Losada (Senora Burguesa)

d, Luis Bunuel; w, Luis Bunuel, Julio Alejandro (based on the novel Tristana by Benito Perez Galdos); ph, Jose F. Aguayo (Eastmancolor); ed, Pedro del Rey; art d, Enrique Alarcon; cos, Rosa Garcia

A tauting black comedy with Surrealist touches. Bunuel's reworking of Benito Perez Galdos' novel, like all the works of this prolific filmmaker, has much beneath its surface. In a role that capitalizes on her placid beauty, Deneuve is a young woman who becomes the ward of hypocritical aristocrat Rey, who makes much of the fact that he hasn't taken advantage of her beauty. The truth is—he has. Prior to receiving an inheritance from his sister, the more-or-less-impoverished Rey refuses to take a job because he believes a man of his social standing is above menial labor. Instead, he sells all his belongings. At the same time he sees himself as a leader of the common man and makes great speeches to his cronies about improving the lot of the masses. Deneuve leaves the protection of Rey's home when she falls in love with artist Nero, but she is unwilling to make a commitment to him, so she returns to Rey, who asks for her hand. After losing a leg because of a tumor, she accepts Rey's proposal and begins a passionless marriage despite her continued love for Nero.

Perhaps what makes this work so powerful is Bunuel's subtle use of key situations to represent much larger ideas. In comparison with such Bunuel masterpieces as VIRIDIANA and LOS OLVIDADOS, TRISTANA's assault on religion and politics is tame. Nevertheless, Bunuel's subtle presentation here (he uses, very little camera movement and little music), effectively conveys a world in desperate need of change.

TRIUMPH OF THE SPIRIT

1989 120m c ★★★
Biography R/15
Nova/Shimon Arama/Arnold Kopelson/Robert M. Young

Willem Dafoe (Salamo Arouch), Wendy Gazelle (Allegra), Robert Loggia (Father Arouch), Kario Salem (Jacko Levy), Kelly Wolf (Elena), Edward James Olmos (Gypsy), Costas Mandylor (Avram Arouch), Edward Zentara (Janush), Hartmut Becker (Maj. Rauscher), Burkhard Heyl (Aide to Rauscher)

p, Arnold Kopelson, Shimon Arama; d, Robert M. Young; w, Andrzej Krakowski, Laurence Heath, Robert Malcolm Young, Arthur Coburn, Millard Lampell (based on a story by Shimon Arama and Zion Haen); ph, Curtis Clark (Rank Color); ed, Arthur Coburn; m, Cliff Eidelman; art d, Krystyna Maslowska; chor, Teddy Atlas, Dimitri Papazoglou; cos, Hilary Rosenfeld

Systematically stripped of human dignity, the prisoners of Auschwitz waged a minute-to-minute struggle for mere existence. TRIUMPH OF THE SPIRIT focuses one Auschwitz internee's fight within the larger fight, telling the story of real-life Greek boxer Salamo Arouch (Willem Dafoe), who was forced to battle for his life against other inmates in boxing matches that provided off-hours diversion for the camp's SS hierarchy. The film also details Arouch's successful pre-WWII boxing career, his love affair with his future wife (Wendy Gazelle), who also survived Auschwitz, and his struggle to keep his father (Robert Loggia) alive in the camp. TRIUMPH OF THE SPIRIT was the first film of its kind to be shot on the grounds of Auschwitz, and director Robert M. Young makes judicious use of his setting—neither shrine nor stage set, it gives the film a firm grounding in history and a corresponding commitment to truth. But although interesting, well-acted, and competently made, this graphic re-creation of a singularly horrifying period offers little new insight into the evil of the Holocaust.

TROUBLE IN MIND

1985 111m c ★★
Crime/Romance R/15
Raincity

Kris Kristofferson (Hawk), Keith Carradine (Coop), Lori Singer (Georgia), Genevieve Bujold (Wanda), Joe Morton (Solo), Divine (Hilly Blue), George Kirby (Lt. Gunther), John Considine (Nate Nathanson), Dirk Blocker (Rambo), Albert Hall (Leo)

p, Carolyn Pfeiffer, David Blocker; d, Alan Rudolph; w, Alan Rudolph; ph, Toyomichi Kurita (CFI Color); ed, Sally Allen, Tom Walls; m, Mark Isham; prod d, Steven Legler; fx, Bob Burns; cos, Tracy Tynan

An ambitious but ultimately pretentious film that attempts to mix film noir, Theater of the Absurd, romance, and science fiction but falls flat on almost all counts. It's set in the near future in the mythical town of Rain City. The place is ruled by martial law but populated with 1940s gangsters and 1950s diners. Hawk (Kris Kristofferson) is an ex-cop who has just come back from jail for having killed a man in self-defense. He looks up his old flame, Wanda (Genevieve Bujold), who is now running a cafe. He would like to put his life together, mind his own business, and have a pleasant few years. Coop (Keith Carradine) and Georgia (Lori Singer) are a newlywed couple who have come to Rain City to try to find jobs. When work doesn't materialize, Coop gets involved with crook Solo (Joe Morton), soon dealing in stolen goods. When Hawk learns what's transpiring, he takes it upon himself to save Coop and protect Georgia. TROUBLE IN MIND is offbeat, unique, and interesting, and for that alone it should be noted. It is a shame that none of the elements ever come together, so this film winds up being a beautiful, atmospheric mess.

TROUBLE IN PARADISE

1932 83m bw ★★★★★
Comedy /15
Paramount

Miriam Hopkins (Lily Vautier), Kay Francis (Mariette Colet), Herbert Marshall (Gaston Monescu/La Valle), Charlie Ruggles (the Major),

Edward Everett Horton *(Francois Filiba)*, C. Aubrey Smith *(Adolph Giron)*, Robert Greig *(Jacques the Butler)*, George Humbert *(Waiter)*, Rolfe Sedan *(Purse Salesman)*, Luis Alberni *(Annoyed Opera Fan)*

p, Ernst Lubitsch; d, Ernst Lubitsch; w, Grover Jones, Samson Raphaelson (based on the play "The Honest Finder" by Laszlo Aladar); ph, Victor Milner; m, W. Franke Harling; art d, Hans Dreier; cos, Travis Banton

For six decades this film has remained unmatched in the realm of sophisticated sex farce. Films from THE AWFUL TRUTH to THE LADY EVE to SOME LIKE IT HOT are sublime on their more modest social scale and in their basic Americanness. By contrast, TROUBLE IN PARADISE has all that class and Continental elegance one came to associate with the Paramout of the 1930s. Made before the Production Code clampdown of 1934, this Ernst Lubitsch masterpiece shows his talent for sly sexual innuendo at its most witty and polished. The result is pure caviar, only tastier.

The story tells of two jewel thieves, Gaston (Marshall) and Lily (Hopkins), who together work at bilking a merry widow, Mariette Colet (Francis), out of a large sum of money. They secure jobs as her secretary and maid and all seems set. Trouble begins in paradise when Gaston starts falling for his lovely prey and when one of her many suitors (Horton), a former victim of Gaston's, begins to recognize Mme. Colet's handsome new secretary.

The many laughs in this consistently delightful souffle come not only from Raphaelson's marvelous screenplay but also from Lubitsch's supple visual wit. On one hand there's delightful repartee about a former secretary who enjoyed an antique bed a bit too much, and on the other we have the sexy silhouette of Gaston and Mariette cast over a chaise lounge. From the opening shot of an operatic gondolier who turns out to be a garbageman to a police report about theft and tonsils translated for Italian officials, this film is full of unforgettable moments of merriment.

The cast, too, is peerless. In one of his earliest Hollywood efforts, Herbert Marshall does the greatest work of his career. Too often maligned for playing stodgy consorts to dynamic star actresses such as Garbo, Davis, and Shearer, Marshall here gets to display his impeccable timing and supple grace. Frequently hilarious, his quiet approach and crushed velvet voice still let him remain suave throughout. Even Cary Grant would be hard pressed to match this portrayal. (He'd be too frantic.) Kay Francis, too, that popular sufferer of countless "women's films" with her "twoublesome" r's, gives of her very best. With her sleek, glamorous style and elegantly wry line readings, she is light, sexy, and totally captivating. Her doorway caresses and her finger-snapping seduction of Gaston are priceless. Miriam Hopkins was luckier in that she had many more chances to display her comic flair in film. Today one of the most underrated and unfairly maligned stars of the 1930s, the brittle, feisty Hopkins can rattle off witty banter at a breakneck pace or she can be deliciously languorous and coy. Her enjoyment of her own sexuality is heady even today and the thieving competition between Gaston and Lily, in which escalating crimes turn into escalating passion, remains one of the greatest scenes of foreplay ever caught on film. Ruggles and Horton prove yet again that they are two of the greatest farceurs in Hollywood, and the rest of the cast is equally choice. (One standout is Kinskey, whose role as a leftist radical only foregrounds the satiric anarchy of the entire film.) Beautifully handled from start to finish, gleamingly shot and full of Dreier's incredible Art Deco designs, TROUBLE

IN PARADISE is Lubitsch's greatest film and one of the indisputable highlights of comic cinema.

TROUBLE WITH HARRY, THE
1955 99m c ★★★½
Comedy /PG
Paramount

Edmund Gwenn *(Capt. Albert Wiles)*, John Forsythe *(Sam Marlowe, the Painter)*, Shirley MacLaine *(Jennifer Rogers, Harry's Wife)*, Mildred Natwick *(Miss Graveley)*, Mildred Dunnock *(Mrs. Wiggs)*, Jerry Mathers *(Arnie Rogers, Harry's Son)*, Royal Dano *(Calvin Wiggs)*, Parker Fennelly *(Millionaire)*, Barry Macollum *(Tramp)*, Dwight Marfield *(Dr. Greenbow)*

p, Alfred Hitchcock; d, Alfred Hitchcock; w, John Michael Hayes (based on the novel by Jack Trevor Story); ph, Robert Burks (VistaVision, Technicolor); ed, Alma Macrorie; m, Bernard Herrmann; art d, Hal Pereira, John B. Goodman; fx, John P. Fulton; cos, Edith Head

A quiet, picturesque Vermont autumn, its leaves in full color, provides the setting for this splendid Hitchcock black comedy in which Harry Worp just won't stay dead. Shirley MacLaine, in her film debut, is Jennifer Rogers, a young mother who recognizes Harry's corpse as that of her dead husband. She is certain that she accidentally killed him. Retired sea captain Albert Wiles (Gwenn), and the dotty old Miss Graveley (Natwick) also believe they are the murderers. Enter eccentric painter Sam Marlowe (Forsythe), a tongue-in-cheek nod to gumshoes Sam Spade and Philip Marlowe, who tries to get to the bottom of Harry's death. Two love stories are interspersed as Jennifer and Sam fall for each other, and the captain and Miss Graveley do the same. Jerry Mathers, of "Leave It to Beaver" fame, is MacLaine's often-hysterical young son.

TRUE BELIEVER
1989 103m c ★★★
Crime/Mystery R/
Lasker-Parkes

James Woods *(Eddie Dodd)*, Robert Downey, Jr. *(Roger Baron)*, Margaret Colin *(Kitty Greer)*, Yuji Okumoto *(Shu Kai Kim)*, Kurtwood Smith *(Robert Reynard)*, Tom Bower *(Cecil Skell)*, Miguel Fernandes *(Art Esparza)*, Charles Hallahan *(Vincent Dennehy)*, Sully Diaz *(Maraquilla Esparza)*, Misan Kim *(Mrs. Kim)*

p, Walter F. Parkes, Lawrence Lasker; d, Joseph Ruben; w, Wesley Strick; ph, John Lindley (Deluxe Color); ed, George Bowers; m, Brad Fiedel; prod d, Lawrence Miller; art d, Jim Pohl; cos, Erica Edell Phillips

Idealistic recent law school graduate Roger Baron (Robert Downey, Jr.) journeys to New York to work as a clerk for his idol, Edward Dodd (James Woods), whose inventive tactics in civil rights cases in 1960s and 70s made him one of the country's most respected attorneys. Sadly, Dodd is now a dope-smoking shyster who plies his trade in the service of sleazy drug dealers, but when Roger manages to get him to take the case of an unjustly imprisoned Korean (Yuji Okumoto), Dodd uncovers a conspiracy and redeems himself as a committed "true believer." Though its plot is thoroughly implausible, TRUE BELIEVER is still an intriguing and entertaining mystery, thanks to the performance of Woods and the direction of Joseph Ruben, who revitalizes the tired premise (crusading lawyer frees innocent man) by providing exhilarating pace and inventive action. Woods clearly relishes his chance to display a wide range of emotions within his patented maverick persona, and Downey also acquits himself well in a much less challenging role.

TRUE CONFESSIONS

1981   108m   c   ★★★★
Crime   R/15
UA

Robert De Niro (Des Spellacy), Robert Duvall (Tom Spellacy), Charles Durning (Jack Amsterdam), Ed Flanders (Dan T. Champion), Burgess Meredith (Seamus Fargo), Rose Gregorio (Brenda Samuels), Cyril Cusack (Cardinal Danaher), Kenneth McMillan (Frank Crotty), Dan Hedaya (Howard Terkel), Gwen Van Dam (Mrs. Fazenda)

p, Irwin Winkler, Robert Chartoff; d, Ulu Grosbard; w, John Gregory Dunne, Joan Didion (based on the novel by Dunne); ph, Owen Roizman (Technicolor); ed, Lynzee Klingman; m, Georges Delerue; prod d, Stephen Grimes; art d, Stewart Campbell; chor, Alfonse L. Palermo; cos, Joe I. Tompkins

Underrated at the time of release, TRUE CONFESSIONS is a fascinating film that exposes the dark underside of the Catholic Church and fixes it firmly in the seedy, corrupt world of film noir. The first on-screen teaming of De Niro and Duvall (they appeared in GODFATHER II but never in the same scene), the film is largely set in Los Angeles in the 1940s. Tom Spellacy (Duvall) is a hard-boiled homicide detective whose investigation of the grisly murder of a porno starlet leads him to believe that his brother Des (De Niro), an ambitious Catholic monsignor, is involved with corrupt local businessman Jack Amsterdam (Durning)—Spellacy's chief suspect. Adapted by the husband-and-wife team of Dunne and Didion from Dunne's fine novel, all of the characters in TRUE CONFESSIONS are corrupt to the core. The period detail is letter-perfect, the cast is uniformly excellent, and Delerue's score is haunting and evocative. TRUE CONFESSIONS is a thoughtful but deeply disturbing film, and its frank portrayal of corruption and murder makes it for adults only.

TRUE GRIT

1969   128m   c   ★★★★★
Western   G/PG
Paramount

John Wayne (Reuben J. "Rooster" Cogburn), Glen Campbell (La Boeuf), Kim Darby (Mattie Ross), Jeremy Slate (Emmett Quincy), Robert Duvall (Ned Pepper), Dennis Hopper (Moon), Alfred Ryder (Goudy), Strother Martin (Col. G. Stonehill), Jeff Corey (Tom Chaney), Ron Soble (Capt. Boots Finch)

p, Hal B. Wallis; d, Henry Hathaway; w, Marguerite Roberts (based on the novel by Charles Portis); ph, Lucien Ballard (Technicolor); ed, Warren Low; m, Elmer Bernstein; prod d, Walter Tyler; fx, Dick Johnson; cos, Dorothy Jeakins

TRUE GRIT is a rollicking western, an enormously entertaining adventure that is as much about John Wayne's image as it is about a girl seeking revenge for her father's murder. Mattie Ross (Kim Darby) is a level-headed 14-year-old who goes to Rooster Cogburn (Wayne) after her father is killed. The murderer, Tom Chaney (Jeff Corey), has since fled into Indian territory, and Mattie wants a man of "true grit" to help bring him to justice. Cogburn, a paunchy US marshal with a patch over one eye, admires Mattie's spunk and agrees to take on the job. Joining them is La Boeuf (Glen Campbell), a Texas Ranger whom Mattie despises. He, too, is searching for Chaney, hoping to collect a reward offered by the family of a murdered Texas politician.

Much of the film's entertainment comes from the obvious contrasts and subtle similarities between Cogburn and Mattie. Cogburn is fat, drunken, and not entirely honest, but he has an underlying sense of honor, that "true grit" that Mattie demands. Although Wayne's characterizations in STAGECOACH and THE SEARCHERS are more complex, TRUE GRIT provides him with some of his most memorable screen moments, and he won an Oscar for his fine work. Wayne reprised the role in ROOSTER COGBURN, costarring with Katharine Hepburn. TRUE GRIT was redone for television in 1978, with Warren Oates in the lead role, but neither project approached this film in either quality or spirit.

TRUE LOVE

1989   104m   c   ★★★
Comedy   R/15
Forward Films

Annabella Sciorra (Donna), Ron Eldard (Michael), Star Jasper (J.C.), Aida Turturro (Grace), Roger Rignack (Dom), Michael J. Wolfe (Brian), Kelly Cinnante (Yvonne), Rick Shapiro (Kevin), Suzanne Costallos (Fran), Vinny Pastore (Angelo)

p, Richard Guay, Shelley Houis; d, Nancy Savoca; w, Nancy Savoca, Richard Guay; ph, Lisa Rinzler (Duart Color); ed, John Tintori; prod d, Lester Cohen; art d, Pamela Woodbridge; cos, Deborah Anderko

The top prize-winner at the 1989 US Film festival, TRUE LOVE is a low-budget feature debut which, while no landmark, is an entertaining comedy filled with likable characters. Like fellow NYU alum Martin Scorsese, first-time director Nancy Savoca turned for inspiration to her own working-class Italian-American roots to create this story. The film centers on the strong but somewhat empty-headed Donna (Annabella Sciorra) who is determined to get her man Michael (Ron Eldard) to the altar. Michael doesn't mind getting engaged and exchanging an occasional "I love you," but who would rather pal around with his neighborhood buddies than actually exchange marriage vows. The story is as old as the movies themselves, but the uncanny resemblance its people and situations bear to real life makes TRUE LOVE enjoyable. The characters are created with care and a feeling for individuality, and each scene comes to life with humor and poignancy. Among the cast, the most pleasant surprise is Sciorra, in her first feature.

TRUE STORIES

1986   89m   c   ★★★½
Comedy   PG
True Stories Ventures

David Byrne (Narrator), John Goodman (Louis Fyne), Swoosie Kurtz (Miss Rollings), Spalding Gray (Earl Culver), Alix Elias (The Cute Woman), Annie McEnroe (Kay Culver), Roebuck "Pops" Staples (Mr. Tucker), Humberto Larriva (Ramon), John Ingle (The Preacher), Matthew Posey (The Computer Guy)

p, Gary Kurfirst; d, David Byrne; w, David Byrne, Beth Henley, Stephen Tobolowsky; ph, Ed Lachman (Technicolor); ed, Caroline Biggerstaff; m, David Byrne, The Talking Heads; prod d, Barbara Ling; chor, Meredith Monk, Dee McCandless, Gene Menger; cos, Elizabeth McBride

David Byrne, then the front man for the Talking Heads, makes his feature film directorial debut with a deliciously offbeat and affectionate look at American madness. Byrne himself plays the narrator, a friendly outsider every bit as strange as the oddball characters he observes. Wearing a large cowboy hat, he talks to the camera as he drives along in a big red convertible. Virtually plotless, the film follows Byrne as he takes us on a tour of Virgil, Texas, and its inhabitants. We meet the "Laziest Woman in the World" (Swoozie Kurtz); the "Lying Woman" (Jo Harvey Allen), who spices up her mundane workday with incredible stories; a civic leader (Spalding Gray) and his wife (Annie McEnroe), who haven't spoken directly to each other in 15 years; a paranoid preacher (John Ingle) who sees conspiracy around every corner; and the man who comes closest to being the film's main character, Louis Fyne (John Goodman), a lovable panda-bear of a man who is looking for matrimony with a capital "M." Supposedly inspired by bizarre clippings found in the slezoid tabloids that adorn grocery checkout line, TRUE STORIES attempts to provide a fond, kindly glimpse of the heartland of America. Some were offended by what they perceived to be the film's smug hipness and sense of superiority. We could not disagree more. It's a lovely loving film that also has some terrific Talking Heads tunes. The actors all do amazingly well with their rather sketchy characterizations. All in all, this is a commendable first effort from neophyte director Byrne. We hope to hear—and see—more from him.

TRULY, MADLY, DEEPLY

1991 105m c   ★★★½
Romance/Fantasy   PG
BBC Films (U.K.)

Juliet Stevenson (Nina), Alan Rickman (Jamie), Bill Paterson (Sandy), Michael Maloney (Mark), Jenny Howe (Burge), Carolyn Choa (Translator), Christopher Rozycki (Titus), Keith Bartlett (Plumber), David Ryall (George), Stella Maris (Maura)

p, Robert Cooper; d, Anthony Minghella; w, Anthony Minghella; ph, Remi Adefarasin; ed, John Stothart; m, Barrington Pheloung; prod d, Barbara Gasnold; cos, James Keast

The first feature film from writer-director Anthony Minghella, TRULY, MADLY, DEEPLY is a funny, touching story about dealing with bereavement and learning to love again.

Nina (Juliet Stevenson) is having a hard time getting over the sudden death of her lover Jamie (Alan Rickman). London is a lonely place, she finds, as she returns home from work every day to an empty flat—empty, that is, save for a recent infestation of rats. The memory of her relationship with Jamie is always on her mind, the music he played on his cello echoing her thoughts at every turn. Sandy (Bill Paterson), who runs the translation agency where she works, tries to shake Nina out of the doldrums, but without success. Titus (Christopher Rozycki), another colleague who wants to fix up her rundown flat, is smitten with her, but she good-humoredly ignores his advances. Nina admits to her bereavement therapist that she feels as though Jamie is somehow still around.

Lost in her memories, Nina begins to slip away from reality and, in the process, literally wills her dead lover back in the form of a ghost. Reunited with Jamie, she is supremely content. She notices he feels a bit cold, but that does not deter her from basking in his familiar presence and his music. Nina keeps her relationship with the returned Jamie a secret, avoiding contact with others, though she does make the acquaintance of an appealing young art-therapy teacher called Mark (Michael Maloney).

Soon, the ghostly honeymoon is over. Jamie gets into the habit of bringing several of his deceased friends back with him to the flat, where they sit around and watch classic movies on videotape, and even take to rearranging the furniture. After Nina begins a relationship with Mark, all the ghostly presences—including Jamie—disappear back from whence they came.

Labelled by many critics as a "thinking person's GHOST," TRULY, MADLY, DEEPLY is sensitively written and charmingly acted. Juliet Stevenson brings tremendous depth to a role that was created specifically for her, and Alan Rickman proves himself capable of something quite different from the bad-guy roles (DIE HARD, ROBIN HOOD: PRINCE OF THIEVES) for which he's best known. Minghella's background in TV, though (he worked with the late Jim Henson on a series of European folk tales for NBC and created the BBC drama series, "What If It's Raining") is evident in the limited scope of the piece, particularly its rather uninspired visuals. Special mention should go to Barrington Pheloung for his lilting, poignant musical score.

TRUNKS OF MR. O.F., THE

(DIE KOFFER DES HERRN O.F.)
1932 80m bw   ★★★★
Comedy
Tonbild/Syndikat AG (Germany)

Alfred Abel (The Mayor), Peter Lorre (Stix), Harald Paulsen (Stark), Hedy Lamarr (Helene), Ludwig Stossel (Hotel Owner), Margo Lion (Viola Volant), Ilse Korseck (Mayor's Wife), Liska March (Eve Lune), Aribert Mog (Stark's Assistant), Gaby Karpeles (Assistant in Salon)

p, Hans Conradi, Mark Asarow; d, Alexis Granowsky; w, Leo Lania, Alexis Granowsky (based on a story by Hans Homberg); ph, Reimar Kuntze, Heinrich Balasch; ed, Paul Falkenberg, Conrad von Molo; m, Karol Rathaus; art d, Erich Czerwonsky; cos, Edward Suhr

The citizens of a tiny German town enjoy a peaceful existence, quite separated from modern reality. However, their idyllic lives are interrupted when some expensive trunks, all marked "O.F.," arrive from Cairo, followed by a telegram asking for reservations at the town's only hotel. Since the hotel has only five rooms, the manager evicts all the tenants and proceeds to build on five more rooms. Soon the excitement spreads as everyone anticipates the arrival of Mr. O.F. Peter Lorre, wonderful in a rare comic role, is a reporter for the local paper who announces that this O.F. is actually a millionaire. Though no one knows why a millionaire would want to visit their sleepy village, the preparations continue. A movie house, casino, opera hall, cabaret, and other buildings are constructed. The town slowly grows, and still there is no O.F. The town's sudden boom is noticed by all of Europe. Why should this little burg experience such growth when the rest of the continent is suffering from a depression? An economic summit is scheduled to be held in the town, and Lorre at last decides to end it all by announcing that this millionaire (whom he made up) has been killed in an auto accident. No one really notices, though, for the O.F. momentum has built up the town beyond anyone's wildest dreams and all are anticipating the upcoming economic conference. Meanwhile, in a far-off office, the talent agent for a movie star named Ola Fallon fires his secretary for accidentally sending the actress' trunks to some obscure little town no one has ever heard of.

This is a delightful little satire, full of whimsy and marvelous performances. The story is told in an uncomplicated manner, letting the events build to a frenzied pitch and saving a great punchline for the closing moments. Sadly, this fine comedy was a victim of the new Nazi government the next year. Because Jewish performers and writers had contributed their talents, the film was severely cut to reduce their work. The resulting film was retitled BAUEN UND HEIRATEN (BUILD AND MARRY). Songs include "Hausse-Song," "Cabaretsong," "Barcarole," "Die Kleine Ansprache," and "Schluss-song" (Erich Kastner).

TRUST

1991 90m c ★★★
Romance/Comedy/Drama R/15
Zenith Productions/Last Moment Films/True Fiction Pictures

Adrienne Shelly *(Maria Coughlin)*, Martin Donovan *(Matthew Slaughter)*, Merritt Nelson *(Jean Coughlin)*, John McKay *(Jim Slaughter)*, Edie Falco *(Peg Coughlin)*, Marko Hunt *(John Coughlin)*

p, Bruce Weiss; d, Hal Hartley; w, Hal Hartley; ph, Michael Spiller; ed, Nick Gomez; m, Phil Reed; prod d, Daniel Ouellette; art d, Julie Fabian; cos, Claudia Brown

The second full-length film from director-screenwriter Hal Hartley, TRUST displays all the characteristics which made his first feature, THE UNBELIEVABLE TRUTH, a cult hit—suburban Long Island settings, deadpan dialogue mixing metaphysical ponderings with absurd *non sequiturs*, understated black humor. TRUST, though, fails to break any new ground, and lacks some of the spontaneous charm of the previous work.

The film begins with seventeen-year-old Maria Coughlin (Adrienne Shelly) confronting her father John (Marko Hunt) with the news that she's pregnant and plans to drop out of high school. He insults her, she slaps him and leaves home, he falls down dead of a heart attack. Rejected by the football-player father-to-be (Gary Sauer), Maria wanders the town and meets Rachel, a despondent housewife who confides all her woes in Maria and gives her money for food. Maria fights off a would-be-rapist shopkeeper while trying to buy beer, and emerges from the store to find that a baby has been kidnapped; she suspects Rachel of the crime. Maria hides out in an old abandoned house where she meets Matthew Slaughter (Martin Donovan), a troubled young man who carries around a hand grenade his father brought back from Korea just in case he decides to kill himself. Something of an electronics genius, Matthew has quit his job at a factory because he is unable to stomach corporate hypocrisy and incompetence.

Matthew takes Maria home, but both are driven from the house by his domineering, abusive father Jim (John MacKay). Turned down for a job at an electrical repair shop because he refuses to work on televisions, Matthew heads for a bar, where he meets Maria's sister Peg (Edie Falco), a divorced mother-of-two. Maria and Peg take Matthew home to meet their mother, Jean (Merritt Nelson), who blames Maria for her father's death and allows her to move back in only if she undertakes to do all the housework. When Maria goes to get an abortion, Matthew offers to marry her and help raise the child. She agrees, but refuses to move out of her house, as her mother needs her (i.e. needs to punish her) too much. Meanwhile, Maria begins a search for Rachel and the missing baby, based on the cryptic information the woman gave her when they met. Matthew is accepted back at the electronics factory, but the place continues to make him unhappy.

The bitter Jean tries to fix Matthew up with Peg, and thereby ruin his relationship with Maria. Neither Matthew nor Peg seem terribly interested, but Jean tricks him into getting drunk and places him in Peg's bed. Maria sees them and, disgusted, decides to have the abortion. She finds Rachel, and discovers that she and her husband have returned the kidnapped baby.

Matthew quits his job and then, informed by Maria that she has had an abortion and no longer wants to marry him, returns to the factory to set off his hand grenade. All the other workers

evacuate the building, but the grenade fails to explode. Maria finds Matthew and throws the grenade away. It blows up, he is arrested and the couple stare into each other's eyes as he is driven off by the police.

TRUST is stylishly photographed and crammed with quirky, offbeat incidents and dialogue. As in THE UNBELIEVABLE TRUTH, Adrienne Shelley gives an engaging performance as a confused, alienated suburban girl who meets up with an enigmatic, potentially violent stranger. Hartley certainly has a distinctive world-view which is both thought-and smile-provoking; those who enjoyed THE UNBELIEVABLE TRUTH, however, may feel as though they've seen it all before, and that it was better structured and more convincingly performed the first time around.

TRUTH OR DARE

1991 118m c/bw ★★★
Documentary/Musical R/18
Propaganda Films

Madonna, Donna Delory, Niki Harris, Luis Camacho, Oliver Crumes, Salim Gauwloos, Jose Guitierez, Kevin Stea, Gabriel Trupin, Carlton Wilborn *(Dancers)*

p, Tim Clawson, Jay Roewe, Steve Golin, Joni Sighvatsson; d, Alek Keshishian; ph, Robert Leacock, Doug Nichol, Christophe Lanzenberg, Marc Reshovsky, Daniel Pearl, Toby Phillips; ed, Barry Alexander Brown, John Murray; chor, Vincent Paterson

Shot during 1989's "Blond Ambition" world tour, TRUTH OR DARE is a documentary look at Madonna Louise Ciccone, arguably the most famous woman in the world today.

Director Alek Keshishian, who cut his teeth on music video, follows the pop diva from stage to hotel room to parties, press conferences, rehearsals and shopping expeditions. He photographs her talking to her family, eating, getting her hair done and horsing around with her dancers, back-up singers and other tour personnel, then intercuts the footage—shot in self-conscious B&W—with color footage of her elaborate stage show. The result is a surprisingly engaging portrait of a media phenomenon for whom the distinction between "onstage" and "offstage" is almost irrelevant.

There's an old joke about Hollywood: if you can dig through the tinsel, you'll get to the *real* tinsel. It could be a Madonna joke, and that's why the phrase "Madonna documentary" sounds like an oxymoron. Facade for facade, she just might be the deepest shallow person of all time. But TRUTH OR DARE transcends the gag and peels through layer after layer of self-conscious iconography: material girl, peep-show stripper, silver-screen goddess, spit-curled senorita, monocled *ubermadchen*, waif, whore, madonna. . . Madonna.

Keshishian is ruthless, showing Madonna as she bitches at the tech crew, strips in her dressing room, prays at her mother's grave (there's a wireless mike concealed in the dirt) and fellates a bottle during a parlor game—the "Truth or Dare" of the title. About the only thing Keshishian doesn't show is Madonna at home cleaning the toilet, but that's because she's on the road, wrapped in the cocoon of touring ritual and intense, superficial camaraderie. But you get the sense that this is her real life; when then-boyfriend Warren Beatty passes through and suggests she isn't interested in living off-camera, the remark sounds unexpectedly profound. TRUTH OR DARE isn't driven by the idea that Madonna's one thing on stage and another off; it's that she's lots of things on stage and lots of things off and, frankly, she's never really off anyway. She's just degrees of on. And the point isn't to get to the core, because there really isn't any core; it's like an onion—all in the layers.

Where TRUTH OR DARE verges on being disturbing is in its treatment of people other than Madonna. Not Beatty or Kevin Costner (Madonna makes suitable fun of him when he calls her show "neat"), but when its camera eye is turned on ordinary, life-size people, like the old friend who comes backstage to ask Madonna to be her child's godmother. As Madonna prattles in another room about their childhood sex play, the woman—pretty but ordinary, a world removed from Madonna's larger-than-life gloss—nervously denies it, then remembers she's contradicting Madonna and faults her own memory, offering a tentative apology about drugs and liquor. It's excruciating; you know how Madonna's going to live the scene down—she'll laugh, just as she laughed off butt-naked photos of herself in *Penthouse* and a raunchy underground film from her starving wannabe days—but her faded friend from the past is another story.

Madonna is a star for the voyeuristic age, an age when wars start on television and confession is only good for the soul if it's picked up by the wires. When the camera captures Madonna observing two of her male dancers kiss, she's absorbed by the same contradictory spectacle audiences experience when they look at TRUTH OR DARE: intimacy designed to be watched.

TUCKER: THE MAN AND HIS DREAM

1988   111m   c   ★★★★
Biography   PG
Lucasfilm

Jeff Bridges *(Preston Tucker)*, Joan Allen *(Vera Tucker)*, Martin Landau *(Abe Karatz)*, Frederic Forrest *(Eddie Dean)*, Mako *(Jimmy Sakuyama)*, Lloyd Bridges *(Sen. Homer Ferguson)*, Elias Koteas *(Alex Tremulis)*, Christian Slater *(Junior)*, Nina Siemaszko *(Marilyn Lee Tucker)*, Anders Johnson *(Johnny Tucker)*

p, Fred Roos, Fred Fuchs; d, Francis Ford Coppola; w, Arnold Schulman, David Seidler; ph, Vittorio Storaro (Technovision, Technicolor); ed, Priscilla Nedd; m, Joe Jackson, Carmine Coppola; prod d, Dean Tavoularis; fx, David Pier; chor, Paula Smuin; cos, Milena Canonero

A long-delayed dream project for director Francis Ford Coppola, TUCKER: THE MAN AND HIS DREAM was one of the most visually sumptuous American film of the 1980s. In a style that harkens back to the boundless optimism of 1940s American advertising art, the film tells the story of Preston Tucker—part inventor, part con man, who in the late 1940s attempted to produce his own car, which he dubbed the Tucker Torpedo, "The Car of Tomorrow—Today!" Tucker (Jeff Bridges) has worked his way up in the auto industry and starts up a company to build his dream car. Meanwhile, the big three auto manufacturers in Detroit get wind of Tucker's scheme and set out to quash the tiny interloper.

A glorious celebration of the creative process, TUCKER is Coppola's most overtly autobiographical film, even though it is about someone else's life. Coppola's treatment of the material is remarkably upbeat and joyous. Even when things get extremely dark for our hero, the film's style remains peversely buoyant. Tucker's increasingly frenzied upbeat renditions of "Hold That Tiger" begin to take on the quality of madness. As with Frank Capra heroes, there is a strong suggestion of dark undercurrents beneath the surface optimism. While a darker film would have been more honest, TUCKER: THE MAN AND HIS DREAM is a gorgeous, fluid, wonderfully exhilarating movie. Continuing and expanding upon the visual experiments he began in the notorious commercial flop ONE FROM THE HEART, Coppola fills TUCKER with some flawlessly executed scene transitions that will startle even the most jaded audience.

TUNE IN TOMORROW

1990   108m   c   ★★★
Comedy/Romance   PG-13/12
Polar

Barbara Hershey *(Aunt Julia)*, Keanu Reeves *(Martin Loader)*, Peter Falk *(Pedro Carmichael)*, Bill McCutcheon *(Puddler)*, Patricia Clarkson *(Aunt Olga)*, Jerome Dempsey *(Sam/Sid)*, Peter Gallagher *(Richard Quince)*, Dan Hedaya *(Robert Quince)*, Buck Henry *(Fr. Serafim)*, Hope Lange *(Margaret Quince)*

p, John Fiedler, Mark Tarlov; d, Jon Amiel; w, William Boyd (based on the novel *Aunt Julia and the Scriptwriter* by Mario Vargas Llosa); ph, Robert Stevens; ed, Peter Boyle; m, Wynton Marsalis; prod d, Jim Clay; chor, Quinny Sacks; cos, Betsy Heiman

TUNE IN TOMORROW, the screen adaptation of Mario Vargas Llosa's acclaimed novel *Aunt Julia and the Scriptwriter*, is an amiable comedy that overcomes its faults with the sheer charm of its performers and the talent of its director, Jon Amiel.

The film, which takes place in 1951, stars Barbara Hershey as Aunt Julia, a 36-year-old divorcee who comes to New Orleans in search of a new husband (preferably a rich old one with a heart condition), but instead begins a secret romance with her 21-year-old nephew—by marriage—Martin (Keanu Reeves), who is a newswriter at a local radio station. Another new arrival to town is eccentric scriptwriter Pedro Carmichael (Peter Falk), a self-proclaimed "artist" who likes to dress up in outlandish costumes and live out the lives of his characters. He is hired by Martin's bosses at WXBU to raise their sagging ratings by writing a new radio soap opera called "Kings of the Garden District." On their first meeting, Martin and Pedro nearly kill each other fighting over a typewriter, but soon they become friends. Pedro turns into a mentor for Martin, who has aspirations of becoming a real writer himself. Dedicated to turning Martin into a "true artist," Pedro begins manipulating Aunt Julia and Martin's relationship, as well as using their actual exchanges as dialogue for his radio show. The soap opera becomes a huge success (Amiel presents the radio show on two levels; scenes of the older, plain-looking actors reading their lines in the studio are intercut with a full and extravagantly realized unfolding of the drama, complete with a cast of well-known actors—including Buck Henry, Elizabeth McGovern, and Peter Gallagher—hamming it up riotously), but there is some backlash; Pedro has laced the show with offensive ethnic wisecracks about Albanians, causing protesters to picket the station and threaten the well-being of all those involved.

Amiel would seem to be the perfect choice to direct TUNE IN TOMORROW. The story-within-the-story construction of the film echoes the style of "The Singing Detective," the brilliant mini-series that Amiel directed for British television, and the overall sentimental tone of the script matches the feel of Amiel's terrific 1989 release QUEEN OF HEARTS. But the director fails to successfully bring these two styles together. Although extremely funny, the outrageous melodrama of the soap opera feels like an intrusion on the relationships of the real characters. The drama that unfolds between Reeves and Hershey (which remains the most interesting thing in the film) always seems to get shortchanged in favor of a cheap laugh or kooky sight-gag. The film does work, despite the wildly uneven screenplay, mainly due to the performances. Falk is absolutely hilarious (esspecially funny is the inspiring speech he gives his radio actors before they go on the air), Hershey, as usual, is wonderful and the cast of players acting out the "Kings of the Garden District" are quite amusing (with Henry, Gallagher and Dan Hedaya as the stand-outs); only Reeves seems to be struggling, and his forced southern accent is a bit distracting (much more distracting are moments in the film when he looks *exactly* like Jerry Lewis). Robert Stevens's photography is terrific, Jim Clay's production design is strikingly authentic and Wynton Marsalis's score is easily one of the best in a long while; the opening credits—which are *read* by Henry Gibson and not shown—are wonderfully original.

TUNES OF GLORY

1960 106m c   ★★★½
Drama/War   /PG
Hi Mark   (U.K.)

Alec Guinness *(Lt. Col. Jock Sinclair)*, John Mills *(Lt. Col. Basil Barrow)*, Dennis Price *(Maj. Charlie Scott)*, Susannah York *(Morag Sinclair)*, John Fraser *(Cpl. Piper Fraser)*, Allan Cuthbertson *(Capt. Eric Simpson)*, Kay Walsh *(Mary)*, John MacKenzie *(Pony Major)*, Gordon Jackson *(Capt. Jimmy Cairns)*, Duncan Macrae *(Pipe Maj. MacLean)*

p, Colin Lesslie; d, Ronald Neame; w, James Kennaway (based on his novel); ph, Arthur Ibbetson (Technicolor); ed, Anne V. Coates; m, Malcolm Arnold

A powerful and highly effective tale of military life during peacetime, TUNES OF GLORY follows two very different officers in a Scottish Highland regiment. Director Ronald Neame and the producers cast against type in giving the suave Alec Guinness the role of crude, up-from-the-ranks Lt. Col. Jock Sinclair, who had bravely led his troops to victory at El Alamein, while John Mills must convince the audience that he is Lt. Col. Basil Barrow, an Oxbridge type who is all spit, polish, and protocol. Sinclair is the interim commander of the 200-year-old unit, a man of war with little interest in commanding a peacetime unit, which suffers from a lack of discipline in the ranks. Rules are easily bent; dress rehearsals are not taken seriously. Enter military man Barrow, sent to replace Sinclair. Devoted to restoring the faded glory of the regiment, he demands respect from everyone and ruffles many feathers. However, some who served under Sinclair, appreciating his personal bravery and abilities but hating his boorish ways, flock to Barrow in the hope that he will bring back their former days of glory.

Mills and Guinness are the center of the movie and it's a tossup as to which is better, though Mills won the Best Actor Award at the 1960 Venice Film Festival. The film is all acting and character, nicely accented by the Scottish bagpipe music of Malcolm Arnold.

TURNING POINT, THE

1977 119m c   ★★★
Dance   PG
Hera

Anne Bancroft *(Emma Jacklin)*, Shirley MacLaine *(Deedee Rodgers)*, Mikhail Baryshnikov *(Kopeikine)*, Leslie Browne *(Emilia Rodgers)*, Tom Skerritt *(Wayne Rodgers)*, Martha Scott *(Adelaide)*, Antoinette Sibley *(Sevilla)*, Alexandra Danilova *(Dahkarova)*, Starr Danias *(Carolyn)*, Marshall Thompson *(Carter)*

p, Herbert Ross, Arthur Laurents; d, Herbert Ross; w, Arthur Laurents; ph, Robert Surtees (Panavision, DeLuxe Color); ed, William Reynolds; prod d, Albert Brenner; chor, John Cranko, Alvin Ailey, Marius Petipa, George Balanchine, Dennis Nahat, Alexander Minz, Jean Coralli, Jules Perrot, Harald Lander, Kenneth MacMillan, Frederick Ashton, Michel Fokine, Lev Ivanov; cos, Albert Wolsky

Only the second ballet-based picture (the first was THE RED SHOES) to ever make a dent with popular audiences, THE TURNING POINT is a well-made soap opera with a story that right out of a 1930s backstage musical.

The American Ballet Theatre is touring the US and makes a stop in Oklahoma City. The company's star is Bancroft, painfully thin, dedicated to dance, and having very little life away from her work. Living in DC is her former associate, MacLaine, who opted for love and marriage 20 years before when they were rivals for the prima ballerina role in the company. MacLaine is married to Skerritt; they have three children and a successful ballet school. MacLaine goes to the performance and is bothered by her choice in life. Had she stayed with the ABT and continued, would that prima ballerina on the stage be her and not Bancroft? MacLaine introduces 19-year-old daughter Browne to Bancroft, who recognizes herself and MacLaine in the ambitious girl. Bancroft arranges an audition for Browne, and she is accepted. As the new season approaches, Browne bids farewell to her parents and goes to New York to prepare for her work in the ABT. Bancroft has been a star for many years, and the time has come for her to hang up her tutu. The leading roles are being given to younger ballerinas, and Bancroft realizes that the moment is near when she will begin to teach more than dance. This is depressing for Bancroft, and she wonders if MacLaine didn't make the right decision by marrying Skerritt way back then. Browne is comfortably ensconced in New York by now and has been joined by MacLaine, apparently as a chaperone. But the truth is that MacLaine wants to see if she did right by leaving the ballet. Browne is the lever between the women as they both coach her in various regimens while keeping an eye on each other.

THE TURNING POINT features a few laughs, lots of maudlin moments, superior dancing from a host of real ballerinas, and an occasionally perceptive script. Executive producer Nora Kaye (wife of the director) is herself a former famed ballerina, and producer-director Ross is a one-time choreographer. Ross does his best to convince us that Bancroft can dance, but his fiddling with fast cuts and closeups won't fool anyone who knows anything about ballet.

A big winner at the box office, THE TURNING POINT received many Oscar nominations: Best Picture (losing to ANNIE HALL), Best Actress (both MacLaine and Bancroft lost to Diane Keaton for ANNIE HALL), Best Supporting Actor (Baryshnikov), Best Supporting Actress (Browne), Best Direction, Best Screenplay, Best Cinematography, Best Art Direction, Best Sound and Best Film Editing. It won none.

TURTLE DIARY

1985 97m c   ★★★½
Comedy/Drama   PG
United British Artists Britannic   (U.K.)

Glenda Jackson *(Neaera Duncan)*, Ben Kingsley *(William Snow)*, Richard Johnson *(Mr. Johnson)*, Michael Gambon *(George Fairbairn)*, Rosemary Leach *(Mrs. Inchcliff)*, Eleanor Bron *(Miss Neap)*, Harriet Walter *(Harriet)*, Jeroen Krabbe *(Sandor)*, Nigel Hawthorne *(Publisher)*, Michael Aldridge *(Mr. Meager)* p, Richard Johnson; d, John Irvin; w, Harold Pinter (based on the novel by Russell Hoban); ph, Peter Hannan (Technicolor); ed, Peter Tanner; m, Geoffrey Burgon; prod d, Leo Austin; art d, Diane Danklefsen, Judith Lang; cos, Elizabeth Waller

An intelligent, witty, offbeat, and somewhat eccentric comedy based on the novel by Russell Hoban. Neaera Duncan (Glenda Jackson) is a writer-artist who specializes in children's books. But she has come to a creative crossroads and is wondering if she has what it takes to go on. Shy Neaera lives comfortably by herself in a roomy London flat, and her only pal in the building is her enigmatic next-door neighbor Johnson (Richard Johnson). William Snow (Ben Kingsley) is a clerk in a bookshop who lives in a teeming boardinghouse populated by odd characters. William isn't happy at the job or at the rooming house, but he is doing his best to cope. Neaera and William come together at the local aquarium where both are fond of the huge turtles that swim endlessly from one end of the tank to the other. And both speculate about what would happen if these giant turtles were released into the sea. A simple tale well told. No murders, no rapes, no teenage dancing, no hardware—just good talk and lovely characters. This is a totally engaging movie, even if you don't care a whit about turtles.

12 ANGRY MEN
1957 95m bw   ★★★★
Drama   /U
Orion/Nova

Henry Fonda *(Juror No. 8)*, Lee J. Cobb *(Juror No. 3)*, Ed Begley *(Juror No. 10)*, E.G. Marshall *(Juror No. 4)*, Jack Warden *(Juror No. 7)*, Martin Balsam *(Juror No. 1)*, John Fiedler *(Juror No. 2)*, Jack Klugman *(Juror No. 5)*, Edward Binns *(Juror No. 6)*, Joseph Sweeney *(Juror No. 9)*

p, Henry Fonda, Reginald Rose; d, Sidney Lumet; w, Reginald Rose (based on his television play); ph, Boris Kaufman; ed, Carl Lerner; m, Kenyon Hopkins; art d, Robert Markell

Lumet's debut, Rose's adaptation of his television play: verbose, stage-bound, predictable and acted within an inch of its life. This classic courtroom drama begins in the final hours of a trial for murder in a hot, muggy New York City courtroom. The tired trial judge gives 12 weary jurors their instructions, exhorting them to adhere to the basic rule that weights the scales of justice: the defendant must be seen to be innocent unless proven guilty beyond a reasonable doubt. The jurors shuffle slowly to their chamber and consider the case of a teenage Puerto Rican boy accused of knifing his father to death. Expecting a rapid verdict in what appears a conclusive case, the jury foreman invites an immediate vote. When the ballots are tallied, 11 prove to be for conviction. Fonda is the lone holdout. The others breathe a nearly audible collective sigh: there's one in every crowd, their expressions attest. Grudgingly, they agree to reexamine the evidence. Afterwards, another vote is taken; this time, four are for acquittal. Once again, they deliberate, and the character of each emerges. Balsam is a man who wants no trouble, a pleasant man who will go with the majority. Fiedler, an unassuming bank clerk, is unaccustomed to framing opinions on his own. Cobb, a bullying entrepreneur who runs a transport service, insists that his is the only worthwhile opinion. Businessman Marshall enjoys deductive reasoning but seems unable to comprehend that a life is at stake in this "game" of justice. Street-wise Klugman, whose origins are too close to those of the defendant, wants only to forget them. Binns voices the prejudices and sympathies of his own class only. Warden, another small-time entrepreneur, thinks

that everything is a communist plot. Stupid Sweeney is unable to understand the evidence but becomes the pivotal juror by default. Sour-faced, dyspeptic old Begley believes that authority, as represented by police and prosecution personnel, must by its nature be infallible, as does German-American George Voskovec. Advertising executive Robert Webber views the world solely in terms of slogans. Fonda's proves to be the voice of sweet reason as he compels his 11 fellows to reevaluate the circumstantial evidence that has nearly convicted the boy.

Though the film now appears anachronistic (where are women and african americans—for starters), MEN was a landmark film in its day, one which brought a new style to cinema. The teleplay-turned-movie made use of a single static set—an actual New York City jury room—and had a total of 365 separate takes, nearly all of them from different angles. The result was cinema heresy that *worked*. Director Lumet, making his film debut (though he was accomplished in stage and television productions), was teaching lessons to the old-timers. With cameraman Kaufman (the brother of famed Soviet director Dziga Vertov), Lumet carefully plotted and sketched every visual nuance. As had been his habit with theatrical productions, he also rehearsed his cast for a full two weeks before the actual 20-day shoot. The resulting real-time drama made film history.

This was Fonda's one experience as a movie producer. He had admired the television play authored by co-producer Rose and had attempted to get Hollywood's established studios interested in it, with little success. He and Rose raised the $340,000 cost of the production themselves. Released as a conventional booking in large theaters (rather than being distributed only to small art houses, where it might have gained a major following and run for months on the strength of the uniformly favorable reviews it received), the film failed to make a profit, and Fonda never received his deferred salary. The picture continues to be screened in schools and for various organizations. Despite his financial loss, Fonda remembered it fondly as one of his three best efforts (along with THE GRAPES OF WRATH and THE OX-BOW INCIDENT). Fonda is fine in the picture, and the others in the cast (whom he hand-picked) were the leading stage and TV actors of Gotham, whose wonderful work was rewarded in many cases by eventual cinematic stardom. The film is an unsettling one in many ways, as much an indictment as an affirmation of America's jury system. One wonders what might have happened had Fonda's voice-of-reason character not been present. Eleanor Roosevelt witnessed a private screening of the movie and liked it enormously, writing about it in her widely circulated newspaper column, "My Day." Fonda received an Oscar nomination—as a coproducer, not an actor—as did Rose and Lumet. The technique of the film has been repeated since, but this is the one that set the precedent.

TWELVE CHAIRS, THE
1970 94m c   ★★★½
Comedy   GP/U
Crossbow/UMC

Ron Moody *(Ippolit Vorobyaninov)*, Frank Langella *(Ostap Bender)*, Dom DeLuise *(Father Fyodor)*, Mel Brooks *(Tikon)*, Bridget Brice *(Young Woman)*, Robert Bernal *(Curator)*, David Lander *(Engineer Bruns)*, Andreas Voutsinas *(Nikolai Sestrin)*, Vlada Petric *(Sevitsky)*, Diana Coupland *(Mme. Bruns)* p, Michael Hertzberg; d, Mel Brooks; w, Mel Brooks (based on a novel by Ilya Arnoldovich Ilf, Yevgeniy Petrov, translated by Elizabeth Hill, Doris Mudie as *Diamonds to Sit On*); ph, Djordje Nikolic (Movielab Color); ed, Alan Heim; m, John Morris; art d, Mile Nokolic; cos, Ruth Myers

One of Mel Brooks's best films, THE TWELVE CHAIRS was made before he discovered that nothing succeeds like excess. Based on a Russian novel from the 1920s that was translated into English by Doris Mudie and Elizabeth Hill and retitled *Diamonds to Sit On*, this fast-paced period piece is well-made, funny, and a pleasure to watch from start to finish. Shot on location in Yugoslavia, it begins as Moody, a onetime nobleman's son now reduced to working as a clerk for the government, is told by his dying mother that the family fortune was hidden in one of a set of a dozen chairs 10 years previously. In an attempt to claim the money, Moody returns to the family's former home and makes the mistake of telling his story to Langella, a beggar with big ideas. Now that Langella knows the secret, he is cut in as a partner when he promises to help Moody. DeLuise, a Russian Orthodox priest who heard the old woman's final confession, is now also searching for the jewels. DeLuise visits the Department of Housing, where Langella masquerades as a clerk, sending the priest on a wild goose chase to Siberia to see Lander, who supposedly has the chairs. Meanwhile, Moody and Langella find a few of the chairs reposited in a museum. They wait until the museum closes, then rip up the chairs but find nothing for their efforts. Learning that some of the remaining chairs are being used as props by a small theatrical company, Langella and Moody insinuate themselves into the acting company, slash the chairs, and are again stymied when they find zilch. As the search continues, they discover that a Russian circus performer is using one of the chairs in a highwire act. The two destroy that chair, too, but again they come up with nothing. Eleven chairs have been found and there is but one left. In a railway employees' clubroom, Moody and Langella learn that the final chair was already dismantled by the workers and that the jewels were used to provide all of the accouterments and chess games for the retired workers. The search has ended sadly, and Langella is preparing to part company with Moody, but he changes his mind when Moody goes into his "epilepsy" act and several people stop on the street to toss him some money. It becomes clear that Langella and Moody will continue their relationship as long as Moody can quiver and Langella can shout at the passers-by and gather the loose coins they toss.

Brooks plays a small role as the onetime valet of Moody's father who is now acting as the janitor in the family's old house. He does a drunk routine that is a marvel of timing and understatement (which is rare for Brooks). Unfortunately, DeLuise is out of his class opposite Moody and Langella. Moody's work proves that his brilliance in OLIVER was anything but a fluke. Langella plays it straight, which is perfect in the script by Brooks. All in all, THE TWELVE CHAIRS is a charming movie about larceny in Communist Russia, with a few moments of questionable taste that make it less than apporopriate for the kids.

TWELVE O'CLOCK HIGH

1949   132m   bw   ★★★★½
War   /U
FOX

Gregory Peck *(Gen. Frank Savage)*, Hugh Marlowe *(Lt. Col. Ben Gately)*, Gary Merrill *(Col. Keith Davenport)*, Dean Jagger *(Maj. Harvey Stovall)*, Millard Mitchell *(Gen. Pritchard)*, Robert Arthur *(Sgt. McIllhenny)*, Paul Stewart *(Capt. "Doc" Kaiser)*, John Kellogg

(Maj. Cobb), Robert Patten *(Lt. Bishop)*, Lee MacGregor *(Lt. Zimmerman)*

p, Darryl F. Zanuck; d, Henry King; w, Sy Bartlett, Beirne Lay, Jr. (based on their novel); ph, Leon Shamroy; ed, Barbara McLean; m, Alfred Newman; art d, Lyle Wheeler, Maurice Ransford

Firm film, peak Peck in this Henry King-directed drama about the physical and emotional stress that results from giving the "maximum effort" day after day. The film opens obscurely and hauntingly as a bald, bespectacled man, Harvey Stovall (Dean Jagger), wanders through postwar England, arriving at the edge of a former American air base, now overgrown with weeds. As the onetime major looks into the sky, his memory takes over: bomber squadrons return from the daylight missions in Germany. The 918th Bomber Group is under the command of Col. Keith Davenport (Gary Merrill), a likable leader who operates as a friend to his men. However, it is Col. Davenport's identification with his men—boys really—that leads to his downfall. Overly concerned with their health and well-being (after a seemingly endless succession of dangerous bombing missions, the squadron is a jumble of wounds and jangled nerves), the colonel is unable to meet the demands of his superiors, Gen. Pritchard (Millard Mitchell) and Gen. Frank Savage (Peck). Davenport is relieved of his duties and replaced by Gen. Savage, a callous martinet who tries to whip the men back into shape, immediately cutting back on three-day passes, closing the local bar, demanding that he be saluted and that everyone be properly uniformed. Most of the pilots put in for a transfer; however, one confused but heroic young pilot, Lt. Bishop (Bob Patten), rallies them. Moved by his men's show of unity, Savage becomes increasingly friendly, identifying with them even more than his predecessors had.

One of the first films to take a complex look at WWII heroism, TWELVE O'CLOCK HIGH is not afraid to show its fighting men as vulnerable. Four years after the war's end, audiences no longer needed the blatant propaganda that filled wartime screens. Instead, Savage's character (based on the real life and nervous breakdown of Air Corps Maj. Gen. Frank A. Armstrong) is entirely human—a man with real emotions, fears, and inadequacies. Peck's flawless portrayal of Gen. Savage earned an Academy Award nomination, but the film's pivotal performance is Jagger's as Maj. Stovall, and he deservedly won a Best Supporting Actor Oscar. Stovall is an introspective, older military man; friend and assistant to both Davenport and Savage, he has lived through one world war and now holds together the frayed ends of the 918th Bomber Group. In addition to the fine acting, TWELVE O'CLOCK HIGH features some gorgeous camerawork by Leon Shamroy and one of the most horrifying aerial attack sequences ever put on film. Judging from this picture alone, the subsequent devaluation of King's work is a gross injustice.

TWENTIETH CENTURY

1934   91m   bw   ★★★½
Comedy   /A
Columbia

John Barrymore *(Oscar Jaffe)*, Carole Lombard *(Mildred Plotka/Lily Garland)*, Roscoe Karns *(Owen O'Malley)*, Walter Connolly *(Oliver Webb)*, Ralph Forbes *(George Smith)*, Dale Fuller *(Sadie)*, Etienne Girardot *(Matthew J. Clark)*, Herman Bing, Lee Kohlmar *(Bearded Men)*, James Burtis *(Train Conductor)* p, Howard Hawks; d, Howard Hawks; w, Charles MacArthur, Ben Hecht (based on their play, adapted from the play "Napoleon on Broadway" by Charles Bruce Milholland); ph, Joseph August; ed, Gene Havlick

Though the film has a large cast, TWENTIETH CENTURY remains essentially a one-man show for John Barrymore, who plays one of the most preposterous and memorable characters to spring from the minds of Ben Hecht and Charles MacArthur. Directed with breakneck pace by Howard Hawks (as in his later Hecht-MacArthur adaptation, HIS GIRL FRIDAY [1940]), it's the story of a maniacal Broadway director (Barrymore) who transforms shopgirl Carole Lombard from a talented amateur to a smashing Great White Way success adored by public and press. For three years, Barrymore has been both Lombard's lover and her Svengali, shepherding her career, controlling her behavior, and directing her plays. They battle regularly, but make up passionately. Now a huge star of the New York stage, Lombard yearns for some peace and respite from the manic Barrymore. One final disagreement does the trick, and Lombard heads for the palm trees of Hollywood and a screen career. Barrymore's fortunes subsequently plummet, causing creditors to dog his heels in Chicago. To escape, he boards the Twentieth Century Limited train in the Windy City, accompanied by his manager, Walter Connolly, and press representative Roscoe Karns, heading for what they hope will be newfound success in New York. As luck would have it, Lombard and her new fiance, football player Ralph Forbes, are also on the train. Barrymore despises the ruggedly handsome Forbes and doesn't bother to hide his disdain as he moves in on Lombard (who has become as big a star on the screen as she was on the stage), trying to convince her to appear in his latest production. The remainder of the picture is a farcical series of biting verbal exchanges, opening and closing doors, hurled insults, thrown kisses, a madcap procession of several weird characters on board the train, and some of the biggest laughs Barrymore ever received. In the end, as expected, Barrymore has convinced Lombard that Broadway is the place for her, and by the time the Twentieth Century pulls into Grand Central Station, she is safely under his influence once more. Barrymore is a wonder as he does imitations of camels, tramples over his fellow actors' lines, sprinkles his dialog with foreign phrases, and generally leaves the rest of the cast looking like his stooges. The picture was not a hit when it first came out, perhaps because its satire of flamboyant theater people failed to capture the imagination of moviegoing audiences; later it became the basis for the Broadway musical "On the Twentieth Century."

20,000 LEAGUES UNDER THE SEA

1954   120m   c   ★★★★
Science Fiction   /U
Disney

Kirk Douglas (Ned Land), James Mason (Capt. Nemo), Paul Lukas (Prof. Pierre Aronnax), Peter Lorre (Conseil, His Assistant), Bob Wilke (1st Mate of "Nautilus"), Carleton Young (John Howard), Ted de Corsia (Capt. Farragut), Percy Helton (Diver), Ted Cooper (Mate of "Abraham Lincoln"), Eddie Marr (Shipping Agent)

p, Walt Disney; d, Richard Fleischer; w, Earl Felton (based on the novel Twenty Thousand Leagues under the Sea by Jules Verne); ph, Franz Planer, Ralph Hammeras, Till Gabbani (CinemaScope, Technicolor); ed, Elmo Williams; m, Paul J. Smith, Johann Sebastian Bach; art d, John Meehan; fx, John Hench, Joshua Meador; cos, Norman Martien

One of the best Disney live action films and a classic fantasy-adventure, 20,000 LEAGUES UNDER THE SEA is a fairly respectful adaptation of Jules Verne's prophetic tale (published in 1870) of submarines and atomic power. It's 1868 and San Francisco is agog over reports of a sea-roving "monster" that devours any ship that ventures near it. Many voyages are canceled and the government is forced to send a warship to investigate and clear the sea lanes. That ship is sunk by the heinous "creature" and only three people survive the ordeal: a professional harpoonist (Kirk Douglas), a professor from the Nautical Museum in Paris (Paul Lukas), and his aide (Peter Lorre). They are plucked from the sea by the dreaded "monster" which is actually the Nautilus, a fabulous submarine. The sub is commanded by Capt. Nemo (James Mason), scientist, inventor, crazed visionary, and radical peace activist. He's taken to sinking ships in a well-meaning effort to end warfare at sea. In an awesome adventure brimming over with fantastic elements, one sequence rises above the fray to become indelible: the fight with the giant squid. The marvelous sets—with their quaint blend of Victorian and futuristic elements—are worth the price of admission alone. The direction is sharp as are the special effects. All the major performances are fun but James Mason is a standout. The film won two Oscars: Best Special Effects and Best Art Direction. It was also nominated for Best Film Editing. Dare we say it? It's fun for the entire family!

20,000 YEARS IN SING SING

1933   81m   bw   ★★★★
Prison
WB/First National

Spencer Tracy (Tom Connors), Bette Davis (Fay), Lyle Talbot (Bud), A.S. Byron (Warden Long), Grant Mitchell (Dr. Ames), Warren Hymer (Hype), Louis Calhern (Joe Finn), Sheila Terry (Billie), Edward McNamara (Chief of Guards), Spencer Charters (Daniels)

p, Robert Lord; d, Michael Curtiz; w, Courtney Terrett, Robert Lord, Wilson Mizner, Brown Holmes (based on the book by Lewis E. Lawes); ph, Barney McGill; ed, George Amy; m, Bernhard Kaun; art d, Anton Grot; cos, Orry-Kelly

The praises of a prison, the famous Sing Sing, are sung in this picture authored by Sing Sing's long-term reform warden, Lewis E. Lawes. Cocksure criminal Spencer Tracy is sent to the slammer on a felony rap. There he is greeted by the kindly warden, A.S. Byron, who explains that good behavior brings certain privileges. Tough-guy Tracy rejects the offer, believing that his politically connected associates will soon win his release. The troublemaking Tracy establishes his dominance in the prison hierarchy, but when he starts a near-riot, he is consigned to solitary confinement for a 90-day period. Ruminating in his lonely cell, the convict comes to the conclusion that the only assistance he will get from his former confederates is in dividing the spoils he had amassed, including his sweetheart, Bette Davis. Tracy emerges from solitary an altered man, now believing that escape is his only remaining possibility. But the superstitious mobster believes his ill luck is attributed to the day of the week, as he was born on a Tuesday, captured on a Tuesday, sentenced on a Tuesday, and imprisoned on a Tuesday. Tracy joins some prisoners who are planning an escape attempt until he discovers that their plan calls for a try at breaching the walls on Tuesday. Beaten at last, he determines to win parole through good behavior. Meanwhile, Davis—attempting to win Tracy's parole for him by other means—seeks the assistance of powerful mob chief Harold Huber. In return for his help, Huber wants Davis's favors.

While speeding down a street in a car, Davis repels the gangster's groping and is seriously injured in the resulting automobile crash. When warden Byron hears of her condition, he offers Tracy—now a trusty—compassionate leave to visit Davis. Tracy takes a solemn oath that he will return to prison that same evening and takes a train to the big city. Arriving at Grand Central Station, Tracy is recognized by two detectives who, unaware of his pass from prison, follow him to Davis's apartment. There, Tracy finds Louis Calhern, the man responsible for his incarceration. During a fight between Tracy and Calhern, Davis shoots Calhern to protect Tracy. Hearing the shot, the waiting detectives break down the door as Tracy escapes through a window. With his dying breath, Calhern fingers Tracy as the one who shot him. Tracy redeems his promise to warden Byron by returning to Sing Sing, where he is charged with killing Calhern. At his murder trial, Tracy refuses to testify on his own behalf. Davis tries to tell the prosecutor that she was the one who pulled the trigger, but nobody will believe her. Under sentence of death, Tracy is led from the courtroom.

Tracy's role in the film seems tailored more to James Cagney's cinematic persona than to his own—indeed, Cagney, who made the mold in a number of gangster films, was Jack Warner's first choice for the part. But Tracy handled the characterization beautifully. Davis' performance is excessively histrionic; not even domineering director Michael Curtiz could hold the actress back. This was to be the only time that two-time Oscar winners Davis and Tracy worked together. At the time the picture was made, author Lawes was the warden of Sing Sing and cooperated in every possible way for the production, allowing the film crew to enter the prison to shoot and permitting real prisoners to play in the mob scenes. The film was the first of many to be based on Lawes's accounts of prison life; others include OVER THE WALL, YOU CAN'T GET AWAY WITH MURDER, INVISIBLE STRIPES, and CASTLE ON THE HUDSON, the latter a remake of 20,000 YEARS IN SING SING, starring John Garfield, Ann Sheridan, and Pat O'Brien. Despite the grimness of its subject matter, 20,000 YEARS IN SING SING is laced with humor.

TWENTY-FOUR EYES
(NIJUSHI NO HITOMI)
1954 158m c   ★★★★
Drama
Shochiku (Japan)

Hideko Takamine (Miss Oishi), Chishu Ryu, Toshiko Kobayashi, Shizue Natsukawa, Nijiko Kiyokawa, Yumeji Tsukioka, Ushio Akashi, Chieko Naniwa

p, Ryotaro Kuwata; d, Keisuke Kinoshita; w, Keisuke Kinoshita (based on the novel by Sakae Tsuboi); ph, Hiroshi Kusuda; ed, Yoshi Sugiwara; m, Chuji Kinoshita

The only film available on videotape from the masterful Keisuke Kinoshita, whose brilliance is practically unknown in the US, TWENTY-FOUR EYES chronicles 20 years in the lives of a loving teacher (Hideo Takemine, the star of 11 Kinoshita films) and 12 of her pupils in a small Inland Sea village. Concerned in many of his films with youth, purity, and innocence, the prolific Kinoshita directed some of the most visually inventive and audacious movies to come out of Japan—from his early WOMAN (a 1948 romantic thriller that has the urgency of a Hollywood B-movie) to CARMEN COMES HOME (a wild 1951 musical satire about a bubbly stripper) to THE BALLAD OF NARAYAMA (his 1958 adaptation of the popular ballad about old age that contains some of the most remarkable lighting

schemes and set designs ever put on film). Yet this is his most popular film. It centers on the teacher as she watches helplessly as her pupils are called to join the war effort, leading to much sorrow and the inevitable loss of innocence. An interesting complement to this film is Masahiro Shinoda's 1985 film MACARTHUR'S CHILDREN, a less impressive effort about the effect of the American presence on a group of schoolchildren at the close of WWII. The videocassette is in Japanese with English subtitles.

TWILIGHT'S LAST GLEAMING
1977 146m c   ★★★½
Historical/Thriller/War   R/AA
Geria/Lorimar/Bavaria   (U.S./West Germany)

Burt Lancaster (Lawrence Dell), Richard Widmark (Martin MacKenzie), Charles Durning (President Stevens), Melvyn Douglas (Zachariah Guthrie), Paul Winfield (Willis Powell), Burt Young (Augie Garvas), Joseph Cotten (Arthur Renfrew), Roscoe Lee Browne (James Forrest), Gerald S. O'Loughlin (Brig. Gen. Michael O'Rourke), Richard Jaeckel (Capt. Stanford Towne)

p, Merv Adelson; d, Robert Aldrich; w, Ronald M. Cohen, Edward Huebsch (based on the novel Viper Three by Walter Wager); ph, Robert B. Hauser (Technicolor); ed, Michael Luciano, Maury Weintrobe; m, Jerry Goldsmith; prod d, Rolf Zehetbauer; art d, Werner Achmann; fx, Henry Millar, Willy Neuner; cos, Tom Dawson

A flawed but nonetheless highly exciting political thriller, TWILIGHT'S LAST GLEAMING has some deeply disturbing things to say about the powers that be in America. The action begins in 1981 (the near future for this 1977 release) and centers on former US Air Force general Lawrence Dell (Burt Lancaster), a Vietnam veteran who served five years as a POW. Upon his return, Dell became a vocal advocate of disclosing the truth behind US involvement in Southeast Asia in the hope that a post-Watergate America would forgive its government and have renewed faith in its leaders. Because of his radical stance, however, Dell is eventually sent to prison on trumped-up manslaughter charges. Still determined, he recruits three inmates (Paul Winfield, Burt Young, and William Smith) to help him escape and take over a nearby SAC base that he helped design. Once in control of the base, Dell demands that the president (Charles Durning) reveal the truth about the Vietnam War to the American people by reading National Security Council document 9759 on national television. If these demands are not met, Dell promises to send the nine Titan missiles to their targets in the Soviet Union. TWILIGHT'S LAST GLEAMING is a stunning indictment of the arrogance of America's decision makers and the lengths to which they will go to maintain "business as usual." At the same time it also dramatizes the danger of our unthinking faith in technology. Tellingly, it comes as a deep shock to the military that their usually reliable machines and detailed procedures seem to have gone haywire on the day of the siege, leaving them powerless to stop Dell. Though a bit slow at the outset and suffering from some occasional lapses of logic, Robert Aldrich's film—shot in Germany with no cooperation from the US military—is a fascinating, tension-filled effort. Lancaster contributes a fine performance as the righteous, populist general, and Durning is superb as the president who comes to share Lancaster's high hopes. Further, Aldrich uses some remarkable split-screen techniques that add to the film's tension and speed up the complicated expository passages. Despite some flaws, TWILIGHT'S LAST GLEAMING is a gripping drama that will have you on the edge of your seat until the bitter end.

TWO ENGLISH GIRLS
(LES DEUX ANGLAISES ET LE CONTINENT)
1972 108m c   ★★★½
Drama   R/
Carosse/Simar/Cinetel (France)

Jean-Pierre Leaud *(Claude Roc)*, Kika Markham *(Anne Brown)*, Stacey Tendeter *(Muriel Brown)*, Sylvia Marriott *(Mrs. Brown)*, Marie Mansart *(Madame Roc)*, Philippe Leotard *(Diurka)*, Irene Tunc *(Ruta)*, Mark Peterson *(Mr. Flint)*, David Markham *(Palmist)*, Georges Delerue *(Claude's Business Agent)*

p, Claude Miler; d, Francois Truffaut; w, Francois Truffaut, Jean Gruault (based on the novel by Henri-Pierre Roche); ph, Nestor Almendros (Eastmancolor); ed, Yann Dedet; m, Georges Delerue; art d, Michel de Broin; cos, Gitt Magrini

Francois Truffaut's TWO ENGLISH GIRLS is a love story examining the complications of one man's romance with two women, in a reversal of JULES AND JIM (both films are based on novels by Henri-Pierre Roche). Set at the beginning of the 20th century, the film focuses on Claude (Jean-Pierre Leaud), a young art critic and aspiring author who charms his way through life. In Paris he meets Anne (Kika Markham), a liberated young woman who invites him to spend the summer at the seaside cottage she shares with her sister, Muriel (Stacey Tendeter). Though Anne shows some initial interest in Claude, she secretly intends that he fall in love with the puritanical Muriel. Her plot works, but when she herself has a tryst with Claude, the situation becomes increasingly intense. One of Truffaut's darker films, TWO ENGLISH GIRLS is compared much too often to its companion piece, JULES AND JIM. Both films shine light on the personality of Roche (Truffaut had access to his unpublished diaries), mainly through the characters of Catherine (Jeanne Moreau in JULES AND JIM) and Claude. However, TWO ENGLISH GIRLS is more interestingly viewed as a precursor to Truffaut's later film THE STORY OF ADELE H., with Muriel bearing remarkable similarities to Adele Hugo.

TWO FOR THE ROAD
1967 112m c   ★★★½
Comedy/Drama   /PG
FOX (U.K.)

Audrey Hepburn *(Joanna Wallace)*, Albert Finney *(Mark Wallace)*, Eleanor Bron *(Cathy Manchester)*, William Daniels *(Howard Manchester)*, Claude Dauphin *(Maurice Dalbret)*, Nadia Gray *(Francoise Dalbret)*, Georges Descrieres *(David)*, Gabrielle Middleton *(Ruth Manchester)*, Jacqueline Bisset *(Jackie)*, Judy Cornwell *(Pat)*

p, Stanley Donen; d, Stanley Donen; w, Frederic Raphael; ph, Christopher Challis (Panavision, DeLuxe Color); ed, Richard Marden, Madeleine Gug; m, Henry Mancini; art d, Willy Holt, Marc Frederix; fx, Gilbert Manzon; cos, Hardy Amies, Ken Scott, Michele Posier, Paco Rabanne, Mary Quant, Foale and Tuffin

Like a cheap wine, TWO FOR THE ROAD has not stood up well to the passing of time. What seemed so chic in 1967 looks like a soap opera with jumpcuts today. Still, one must measure it by the temper of the times; in 1967, it was on the money. A small cult of aficionados feels that the film remains one of the best of the genre.

Audrey Hepburn and architect Albert Finney are a married couple taking a car trip from England to the French Riviera. They are about to visit the home of Dauphin, the Frenchman who helped the successful Finney get his first break. From the nature of the biting dialogue between the two, it's obvious that this is a marriage in jeopardy. Flash back to a dozen years before when Finney and Hepburn first met. He's a backpacking student looking at European buildings, and she's one of several female music students going to a festival. Finney is attracted to Jacqueline Bisset but winds up with Hepburn as the other women all come down with chicken pox. They travel together to the edge of the sea and decide they are in love and will get married. Flash forward to their next trip on the Continent. They are newlyweds traveling with William Daniels, Eleanor Bron, and their incorrigible daughter, Gabrielle Middleton. This little girl is enough to sour any woman from having a child, but Hepburn manages to overcome her hatred for the little brat. She and Finney make a pact never again to travel with anyone else. On yet another trip along the same road, Hepburn tells Finney that she is pregnant, and they meet Dauphin, who gives Finney his chance to go from minor jobs to major homes in the south of France. The film cuts between past, present, and future, presenting Finney having a one-night stand with Karyn Balm and Hepburn submitting to the amorous advances of Georges Descrieres, a sober intellectual who turns out to be far too dour for Hepburn's lighthearted personality. The two are reunited and realize that, through it all, they love each other and no amount of petty quarreling or even major spats will ever divide them.

Finney's character remains essentially the same throughout, a slightly boorish lout. Hepburn changes visibly from a naive waif to a mature wife and mother to a bored matron. Frederic Raphael wrote the script directly for the screen; he was nominated for an Oscar but lost that year to William Rose for his orignal screenplay of GUESS WHO'S COMING TO DINNER? There were some complaints that Hepburn was too old for Finney, but she is actually just about seven years his senior. Her career had been twice the length of Finney's, and people were just used to seeing her more often. The usually fastidious Hepburn was dressed by Mary Quant, Paco Rabanne, Ken Scott, and others, and, wonder of wonders, she even wore blue jeans. Location scenes were done in Paris, Nice, St. Tropez, La Colle sur le Loup, and Beauallon. Good aerial photography by Guy Tabary and an excellent score by Henry Mancini also enhance the film. Although Bron plays an American, she is actually a British actress who scored in HELP, ALFIE, WOMEN IN LOVE, and the Dudley Moore-Peter Cook production, BEDAZZLED, also directed by Stanley Donen. Donen's direction here is a trifle trendy and frantic, with sometimes jarring results.

TWO HUNDRED MOTELS
1971 98m c   ★★★
Musical/Fantasy   R/X
UA (U.K.)

The Mothers of Invention *(Themselves)*, Theodore Bikel *(Rance Muhammitz)*, Ringo Starr *(Larry the Dwarf/Frank Zappa)*, Keith Moon *(Hot Nun)*, Jimmy Carl Black *(Lonesome Cowboy Burt)*, Martin Lickert *(Jeff)*, Janet Ferguson *(Groupies)*, Lucy Offerall *(Groupies)*, Pamela Miller *(Interviewer)*, Don Preston *(Bif Debris)*

p, Jerry Good, Herb Cohen; d, Frank Zappa, Tony Palmer; w, Frank Zappa, Tony Palmer (based on a story by Zappa); ph, Tony Palmer (Technicolor); ed, Richard Harrison, Barry Stephens; m, Frank Zappa; prod d, Calvin Schenkel; art d, Leo Austin; fx, Bert Luxford; chor, Gillian Lynne; cos, Sue Yelland; anim, Mara Kam

Always ahead of his time, avant-garde musician Zappa anticipates the rock video in what can best be described as the visual equivalent to any of his recordings in the late 1960s and early 1970s. TWO HUNDRED MOTELS is a hodgepodge of color and sound linked by ex-Beatle Starr playing Zappa, complete with curly-locked wig and the signature goatee. The film is a marvelous whirl of color and visual effects, with some fine animation and Zappa's delicious wit present throughout the entire production. This was the first color production to be transferred from videotape to film, and the technique works well. The special visual effects available at the time were used to create some amazing surreal images and optical illusions. This is certainly not for everyone, and sometimes the picture causes eyestrain, but, for the adventurous, TWO HUNDRED MOTELS is definitely a film to experience. Zappa codirected with Palmer, taking credit for "characterizations." Palmer was said to have directed the visuals and was also responsible for the shooting script from the "story" and screenplay by Zappa. Watch for Moon, the drummer of The Who, in a cameo as a nun!

TWO-LANE BLACKTOP

1971 102m c   ★★★★
Drama   R/X
Universal

James Taylor (the Driver), Warren Oates (G.T.O.), Laurie Bird (Girl), Dennis Wilson (the Mechanic), David Brake (Needles Station Attendant), Richard Ruth (Needles Station Mechanic), Rudolph Wurlitzer (Hot Rod Driver), Jaclyn Hellman (Driver's Girl), Bill Keller (Texas Hitchhiker), Harry Dean Stanton (Oklahoma Hitchhiker)

p, Michael S. Laughlin; d, Monte Hellman; w, Rudy Wurlitzer, Will Corry (based on a story by Corry); ph, Jackson Deerson (Technicolor); ed, Monte Hellman; cos, Richard Bruno

Real-life rock stars Taylor and Wilson (the latter a member of the Beach Boys) are a pair of car freaks driving down the endless roads of the American Southwest in search of a race. They drive an old 1955 Chevy, using race winnings to keep the souped-up auto in shape. The pair have little to say to each other beyond car talk. At a small Arizona diner they meet Bird, who gets in the car with them, no questions asked. After winning another race, Taylor and Bird make love; the next evening it's Wilson's turn with her. Later the three meet up with Oates, an older drifter who travels across the US in his brand new GTO. He challenges them to a cross-country race to Washington, DC, with the winner taking ownership of the loser's car. Along the way the participants' interest in the race begins to wane. Wilson suggests to Bird that they ride off together. Taylor enters a race in Memphis, and Bird, bored with the younger men, heads off to North Carolina with Oates. Later she takes off with a motorcyclist, and Oates continues his aimless driving. Eventually, Wilson and Taylor find another race to run, and the movie ends ominously as they drive away from the camera down a two-lane road and the film burns and melts in the gate, leaving only a bright white light. Certainly not an average car chase movie, TWO-LANE BLACKTOP is perhaps director Monte Hellman's finest film. Known for his small, brooding existential westerns (THE SHOOTING, RIDE IN THE WHIRLWIND), Hellman once again brings to life characters desperately searching for meaning. Oates, a close personal friend of Hellman's and lead player in nearly all his films, is magnificent in TWO-LANE BLACKTOP, bringing a perfect blend of comedy, mystery, and pathos to his role. It is a powerful and memorable screen appearance that is somewhat weakened by the amateur support from nonactors Taylor, Wilson, and Bird, whose limited abilities required delicate handling by Hellman. Expectations were high for this somber film, with the studio convinced they had another EASY RIDER on their hands. Esquire magazine ran a cover story on the film, reprinted screenwriter Wurlitzer's screenplay in its entirety, and proclaimed it "the movie of the year." The predictions fell far short; the majority of the movie-going public failed to understand the picture and found its portrayal of youthful boredom to be just that: boring. TWO-LANE BLACKTOP is very similar to the work of popular European existential filmmakers, but the fickle American "art house" crowd stayed away in droves, obviously preferring that their serious psychological dramas be imported from abroad.

TWO OF US, THE

(LE VIEIL HOMME ET L'ENFANT)
1967 86m bw   ★★★★
Drama/Comedy   /U
Valoria/PAC/Renn   (France)

Michel Simon ("Gramps"), Alain Cohen (Claude), Luce Fabiole ("Granny"), Roger Carel (Victor), Paul Preboist (Maxime), Charles Denner (Claude's Father), Zorica Lozic (Claude's Mother), Jacqueline Rouillard (Teacher), Aline Bertrand (Raymonde), Sylvine Delannoy (Suzanne)

p, Paul Cadeac; d, Claude Berri; w, Claude Berri, Michel Rivelin, Gerard Brach; ph, Jean Penzer; ed, Sophie Coussein, Denise Charvein; m, Georges Delerue; art d, Georges Levy, Maurice Petri

Life's joys and sorrows are given a fine, sensitive treatment in this autobiographical first feature from Claude Berri, who was one of many Jewish children sent by Parisian parents to live in the French countryside during the Occupation. This film, an honest portrait of one such boy, was considered by Francois Truffaut to be one of the best films ever made about the Occupation. Ten-year-old Claude (Alain Cohen, in a touching, natural performance) is sent to live with the parents of his father's Catholic friends. "Gramps" (Michel Simon), the cranky old man who looks after Claude, takes an immediate liking to the boy and begins teaching him about anti-Semitism, not realizing that his young friend is a Jew. A warm friendship grows between the two, despite their differences in age and religion. Some genuinely comic moments also arise, including Claude's accusation that the old man is a Jew (he cites Gramps's big nose as evidence). Through everything, the two remain the best of friends, bound together by the trials of everyday living, the problems incurred by the war, and the old man's aging dog. Georges Delerue delivers a moving score, and, in his comeback performance, Simon delivers one of the most memorable portrayals of his brilliant career.

TWO OR THREE THINGS I KNOW ABOUT HER

(DEUX OU TROIS CHOSES QUE JE SAIS D'ELLE)
1966 90m c   ★★★★★
Drama   /X
Anouchka/Argos/Carrosse/Parc   (France)

Marina Vlady (Juliette Janson), Anny Duperey (Marianne), Roger Montsoret (Robert Janson), Jean Narboni (Roger), Christophe Bourseiller (Christophe), Marie Bourseiller (Solange), Raoul Levy (The American), Joseph Gehrard (M. Gerard), Helena Bielicic (Girl in Bath), Robert Chevassu (Meter-Reader)

p, Raoul Levy; d, Jean-Luc Godard; w, Jean-Luc Godard (based on a letter from Catherine Vimenet that appeared in Le Nouvel Observateur); ph, Raoul Coutard (Techniscope, Eastmancolor); ed, Francoise Collin, Chantal Delattre; m, Ludwig van Beethoven; cos, Gitt Marrini

Arguably the greatest film made by arguably the most important world director to emerge since WWII. Not recognized as one of Godard's foremost achievements at the time, TWO OR THREE THINGS now seems the richest of his films, made at the perfect halfway moment between his playful iconoclasm and his later political anger. What little "plot" there is concerns a housewife (Vlady) who works part-time on the sly as a prostitute. What Godard and crew milk from this topic is extraordinary: a sociologically oriented dissection of modern middle-class life as an act of prostitution.

The film's title alone suggests the richness of what unfolds— "her" is at once our heroine Juliette, actress Vlady, Paris, consumerism, politics, structuralism and about a dozen other things. The use of disjunctive editing, saturated color schemes, endless quotation (from Marx to Wittgenstein) and deadpan performance style make this film deliberately "difficult" to engage. Godard is challenging us, asking us to consider how we watch films and how we live our lives. Unforgettable moments are numerous: the opening introduction of Vlady as Juliette ("I'm not sure which"); the little boy's dream of Vietnam, with his mother covered in the red, white and blue of her nightgown and bedding; the babysitter, paid with canned goods, attempting to comfort a squalling child; two naked women wearing airline tote bags on their heads. Perhaps greatest of all are the satiric final shot of a Paris neighborhood constructed from grocery goods and the amazing close-up wherein a cup of coffee becomes the cosmos. (As we stare in awe, the whispering voice-over of Godard himself considers the philosophical terrain underpinning contemporary French intellectual thought.) A uniquely rewarding film that requires *many* viewings, TWO OR THREE THINGS I KNOW ABOUT HER is a brilliant, powerful, overtly political film still relevant today.

TWO RODE TOGETHER

1961 108m c ★★½
Western /PG
Columbia

James Stewart (*Guthrie McCabe*), Richard Widmark (*Lt. Jim Gary*), Shirley Jones (*Marty Purcell*), Linda Cristal (*Elena de la Madriaga*), Andy Devine (*Sgt. Darius P. Posey*), John McIntire (*Maj. Frazer*), Paul Birch (*Edward Purcell*), Willis Bouchey (*Mr. Harry J. Wringle*), Henry Brandon (*Chief Quanah Parker*), Harry Carey, Jr. (*Ortho Clegg*)

p, Stan Shpetner; d, John Ford; w, Frank S. Nugent (based on the novel *Comanche Captives* by Will Cook); ph, Charles Lawton, Jr. (Eastmancolor); ed, Jack Murray; m, George Duning; art d, Robert Peterson; cos, Frank Beetson

John Ford attempts to make an adult western with this film, which seems to fall between the cracks; it's too grown-up for the children's audience and much too simplistic to be deemed a psychological film. There are attempts at comedy that barely induce a smile, and the picture winds up yawnable, one of Ford's very few bores. Gorgeous scenery and a fine acting job by Stewart in an unaccustomed semivillain role don't overcome the lackluster production overseen by TV veteran Shpetner. Stewart, a corrupt sheriff in a small town, spends most of his time seated on the verandah of the saloon run by Annelle Hayes collecting a 10 percent tithe on illicit goings-on in the village. Widmark approaches Stewart for some help. Some years before Comanche Indians kidnapped a group of whites, and Widmark wants to rescue them to bring them back to their anxious families. Stewart reckons he might help but only if Widmark arranges a bounty of $500 to be paid for each hostage recovered. The promise of the fee plus the chance to flee from the matrimonially minded Hayes

is enough to get Stewart off his duff and into the plains. They ride into the camp of Indian Brandon and secure the release of David Kent, a white boy who has been raised as an Indian, plus Cristal, a Mexican woman who had been the forced squaw of Indian warrior Woody Strode. Strode is not thrilled that they want to take away his woman and he gets into a battle with Stewart, who kills him. Widmark and Stewart bring the duo of Cristal and Kent back to the Army fort and none of the waiting families recognizes Kent. He is finally claimed by Nolan, a woman who is mentally incompetent. She thinks that the wild youth is her son and wants him. She unties Kent and he promptly kills her. The settlers capture Kent and string him up before Jones, a settler in love with Widmark, can let them know that the boy is her brother. None of the prissy women at the Army fort will have a thing to do with the tainted Cristal since, in their eyes, any woman who has lived with Indians must be a harlot. Cristal is brokenhearted and thinks that the ways of civilization are far too uncivilized. Stewart shrugs and prepares to go back to his old job as sheriff of the small town but learns that he's lost his position to his deputy, who now occupies the same spot on Hayes's verandah. Stewart takes Cristal's hand, understands that they are both outcasts, and rides off with her to find something better over the next hill as the picture goes to black. Filmed in southwest Texas, it more than resembles Ford's THE SEARCHERS in several ways but comes nowhere close to the power of the former. The picture is almost totally devoid of anything to break the despair of a mission unaccomplished. Good supporting work from a host of actors but there is a vague feeling that we've seen it before, and better.

2001: A SPACE ODYSSEY

1968 160m c ★★★★★
Science Fiction /U
Hawk/MGM (U.S./U.K.)

Keir Dullea (*David Bowman*), Gary Lockwood (*Frank Poole*), William Sylvester (*Dr. Heywood Floyd*), Daniel Richter (*Moonwatcher*), Leonard Rossiter (*Smyslov*), Margaret Tyzack (*Elena*), Robert Beatty (*Halvorsen*), Sean Sullivan (*Michaels*), Frank Miller (*Mission Controller*), Alan Gifford (*Poole's Father*)

p, Stanley Kubrick; d, Stanley Kubrick; w, Stanley Kubrick, Arthur C. Clarke (based on the short story "The Sentinel" by Clarke); ph, Geoffrey Unsworth, John Alcott (Super Panavision, Cinerama, Technicolor, Metrocolor); ed, Ray Lovejoy; prod d, Tony Masters, Harry Lange, Ernest Archer; art d, John Hoesli; fx, Stanley Kubrick, Wally Veevers, Douglas Trumbull, Con Pederson, Tom Howard, Colin J. Cantwell, Bryan Loftus, Frederick Martin, Bruce Logan, David Osborne, John Jack Malick; cos, Hardy Amies

John Lennon said of 2001: A SPACE ODYSSEY when it was first released, that the film ought to be shown in a temple 24 hours a day. He was right. It is above all else a religious experience. You have to take it on faith. People (mainly Frenchmen) have written whole books about the subject. We can't do that here. Suffice it to say that whether you see it in 70mm widescreen, or on a black-and-white TV, 2001 still has the power to mystify and thrill. It's about tools, intelligence, and lack of faith, and rebirth. It is also, among other things, definitely the most influential film of the last twenty-five years. All the special effects that make movies so successful today were first tried out by Douglas Trumbull and his crew for 2001 and of course, this is the progenitor for all the space operas that have kept George Lucas and others busy for so long.

It's got to rank with CITIZEN KANE and THE GODFATHER as an essential representative American film. Show it on a double bill with THE RIGHT STUFF to demonstrate the triumph of fiction-before-the-fact versus fiction-after-the-fact. Kubrick's "on location" photography on the moon pre-dated Neil Armstrong and company by more than a year—and had it exactly right. Only one small item seems archaic today: The HAL 9000 computer's memory bank is large enough to hold Keir Dullea as he floats graciously through, de-braining the untrusting machine. We now know HAL's memory would fit in a teacup. "Dave, my mind is going, my mind is going, I can feel it, I can feel it. . .!"

2001: A SPACE ODYSSEY is a beautiful, confounding picture that had half the audience cheering and the other half snoring. The film is based on a short story by Arthur C. Clarke. He and Kubrick wrote the screenplay, and Kubrick spent the next three years shooting it, beginning production in December 1965. Kubrick was delighted by the confusion the movie caused and maintained that he deliberately kept questions unanswered because he wanted to pique the curiosity of audiences. Made at a cost of only $10.5 million, the film began to build slowly but eventually took in almost $15 million in North America, then about half that upon rerelease in the slightly shorter version (141 minutes) in 1972. Clarke's short story was first made into a novel, then into the screenplay that MGM financed for $6 million. The budget kept rising, and the studio execs feared a disaster. They didn't reckon with Kubrick's vision. The rebirth of Dullea at the film's end has been thought to signify the next leap forward of humankind, but that is still open for discussion. No one would ever accuse Kubrick of being a sentimental humanist. The human characters are less animated than the machines. Indeed HAL is the only character allowed to be "human." The rather fey voice of HAL is that of Douglas Rain, a pleasant tone but with the slightest malevolent edge. (Martin Balsam had originally recorded the voice but was replaced.)

Understandably, the movie won the Oscar for Best Special Effects in 1968, and was nominated for Best Direction, Best Screenplay, and Best Art Direction. It also took the BFA Awards for Best Cinematography, Best Sound, and Best Art Direction. Made at Boreham Wood's British Studios in England. 2001 continues to annoy and delight audiences years later, and its real meaning cannot be explained to anyone's liking. Followed by an unfortunate sequel in 1984, 2010.

TWO WOMEN
(LA CIOCIARA)
1960   105m   bw   ★★★★
Drama/War   /X
C.C. Champion/Marceau/Cocinor/S.G.C.   (Italy/France)

Sophia Loren (Cesira), Jean-Paul Belmondo (Michele), Eleanora Brown (Rosetta), Raf Vallone (Giovanni), Renato Salvatori (Florindo), Carlo Ninchi (Michele's Father), Andrea Checchi (Fascist), Pupella Maggio, Emma Baron, Bruna Cealti

p, Carlo Ponti; d, Vittorio De Sica; w, Cesare Zavattini, Vittorio De Sica (based on the novel by Alberto Moravia); ph, Gabor Pogany, Mario Capriotti (CinemaScope); ed, Adriana Novelli; m, Armando Trovajoli; art d, Gastone Medin; cos, Elio Costanzi

Mama Mia! Loren deservedly won a Best Actress Oscar—the first to a non-American actress in a foreign-language film—for this Vittorio De Sica film, adapted by screenwriter Cesare Zavattini from an Alberto Moravia novel. It's not a great De Sica-Zavattini collaboration; much of the movie suffers from poor pacing and listlessness, but Loren is a marvel to behold.

She plays Cesira, a young widow in 1943 Italy who leaves her grocery store in San Lorenzo in the hands of her sometime lover (Raf Vallone), fleeing Allied bombing with her teenage daughter, Rosetta (Eleanora Brown), to return to her native village. There, after an arduous journey, she meets Michele (Jean-Paul Belmondo), the intellectual son of a local farmer with whom Rosetta falls in love, though he falls for her lovely mother. As the town grows increasingly besieged by bombing and shortages, Michele is forced to guide some fleeing Germans on an escape route, while Cesira and Rosetta go back to Rome for safety. Along the way, mother and daughter suffer a tragedy that changes both their lives forever, despite Cesira's best efforts to protect her child from the ravages of war. Loren also won the Best Actress Award at Cannes and the same honor from the British Film Academy; more important, she demonstrated in this film that she was a mature actress with talent to match her looks. And that deglamourized, she was still magnificent. But Eleanora Brown's role (originally meant for Loren, with Magnani to play the mother; the latter refused) is underwritten, Belmondo's character is a rehashed cliche, and Loren's affair with Vallone has had all the sex sucked out of it. It's almost as though everyone pinned their hopes on a big, international success for Loren, so they side-stepped her earth mother getting too carnal. But if the plot turns feel predictable, Loren rises to their occasions with the primal maternal force almost as old as time itself.

De Sica (who also won an Oscar for the film) and Zavattini's previous collaborations included SHOESHINE, THE BICYCLE THIEF, and UMBERTO D, while TWO WOMEN doesn't match the greatness or simplicity of those neo-realist masterworks, it remains a remarkably moving, humane vision of individual struggle in an inhumane world.

U

UFORIA

1985   100m   c   ★★★½

Science Fiction/Comedy   PG

Simon

Cindy Williams (Arlene), Harry Dean Stanton (Brother Bud), Fred Ward (Sheldon), Beverly Hope Atkinson (Naomi), Harry Carey, Jr. (George Martin), Diane Diefendorf (Delores), Robert Gray (Emile), Ted Harris (Gregory), Darrell Larson (Toby), Peggy McKay (Celia Martin)

p, Gordon Wolf, Susan Spinks; d, John Binder; w, John Binder; ph, David Myers (Deluxe Color); ed, Dennis M. Hill; m, Richard Baskin; prod d, Bill Malley; cos, Thomas Ed Sunly, Betsy Heimann

Shot independently in 1981, this funny, quirky, wholly likable little film sat on the shelf until 1985 when Universal finally decided to release it. Unfortunately, the film was given little fanfare and failed to find an audience—which is a shame, for UFORIA is a wonderfully offbeat comedy that manages to capture the eccentricities of small-town America. Set in the deserts of the Southwest, the film follows Sheldon (Fred Ward), a happy-go-lucky drifter whose wanderings bring him to a dusty desert town. In the grocery store he meets Arlene (Cindy Williams), a somewhat dippy cashier whose born-again Christianity combines faith in Jesus Christ with a strong belief that UFOs are the chariots of God. In a matter of days Sheldon has moved into Arlene's tiny trailer home. Also in town is Sheldon's seedy cousin (Harry Dean Stanton), whose latest con has put him on the evangelical bandwagon. Calling himself "Brother Bud," he has gathered a flock of the faithful who come to his tent meetings for a little preachin' and healin' in exchange for sizable donations. UFORIA is an engaging movie that has great affection for all its quirky characters. The cast is superb—with Ward, Williams, and Stanton taking top honors.

UGETSU MONOGATARI

1953   96m   bw   ★★★★★

Drama   /X

Daiei   (Japan)

Machiko Kyo (Lady Wukasa), Masayuki Mori (Genjuro), Kinuyo Tanaka (Miyagi), Sakae Ozawa (Tobei), Mitsuko Mito (Ohama), Sugisaku Aoyama (Old Priest), Ryosuke Kagawa (Village Chief), Kichijiro Tsuchida (Silk Merchant), Mitsusaburo Ramon (Captain of Tamba Soldiers), Ichisaburo Sawamura (Genichi)

p, Masaichi Nagata; d, Kenji Mizoguchi; w, Matsutaro Kawaguchi, Yoshikata Yoda (based on two classic tales by Akinari Ueda); ph, Kazuo Miyagawa; ed, Mitsuji Miyata; m, Fumio Hayasaka, Ichiro Saito; art d, Kisaku Ito; chor, Kinshichi Kodera; cos, Kusune Kainosho

Set in 16th-century Japan, this lyrical, enchanting film by Mizoguchi is one of Japanese cinema's greatest masterpieces. As civil warfare ravages the land, Genjuro and Tobei (Mori and Ozawa), peasant potters, dream of finding glory. They risk their own and their families' lives making pottery to sell at market and then head for the big city. Genjuro leaves his wife behind when he is taken in by a noblewoman (Kyo) who is not what she seems. Tobei, meanwhile, pursues his longstanding desire to become a samurai, something he achieves when, with extreme luck, he manages to kill an established warrior. What happens to the two men's wives (Tanaka and Mito), however, is another story.

Mizoguchi's background as a painter shows in the lovely and artful compositions he sets before the viewer. The image of Lady Wukasa, her servant, and Genjuro trekking through the high reeds is, among many others, unforgettable. Mizoguchi, however, does not neglect the soundtrack, and the use of offscreen sound during such moments as the opening approach of the raiders skillfully suggests the threat to village life. The aesthetic appeal of UGETSU, however, is not merely indulged for its own sake; rather, the film uses the resources of film to explore a recurrent theme in this filmmaker's work. Like a painter determined to catch one vista in canvas after canvas, Mizoguchi considers how the price of indulging men's desires is often the suffering of women. This is done in individual shots (e.g. the highway robbers in the background gorging themselves on food the victimized Miyagi was carrying) as well as in the film as a whole. On another level the film can be read as paralleling the plight of post-WWII Japan. Either way, the film's subtle mix of realism and fantasy (consider a tracking shot with a near-invisible dissolve which "impossibly" links a sensual bath with a picnic) makes for challenging viewing. Working within Japanese genre conventions which seek to validate traditional values, Mizoguchi also considers their inherent contradictions. Look carefully at the pan and tracking shot as the errant Genjuro thinks he's returning to home and hearth near the end and you will witness a great moment in the history of cinema as both art and social commentary.

ULZANA'S RAID

1972   103m   c   ★★★

Western/War   R/18

Universal

Burt Lancaster (McIntosh), Bruce Davison (Lt. Garnett DeBuin), Jorge Luke (Ke-Ni-Tay), Richard Jaeckel (Sergeant), Joaquin Martinez (Ulzana), Lloyd Bochner (Capt. Gates), Karl Swenson (Rukeyser), Douglas Watson (Maj. Cartwright), Dran Hamilton (Mrs. Riordan), John Pearce (Corporal)

p, Carter DeHaven; d, Robert Aldrich; w, Alan Sharp; ph, Joseph Biroc (Technicolor); ed, Michael Luciano; m, Frank DeVol; art d, James Vance

One of the greatest films made by often overlooked director Robert Aldrich, ULZANA'S RAID isn't a true war film, but within its traditional western format, Aldrich and screenwriter Alan Sharp transform the material into an effective and damning allegory of America's involvement in Vietnam. Set in Arizona during the late 1880s, the film centers on Lancaster, a hard-riding scout who accompanies idealistic, young lieutenant Davison in his pursuit of a group of rapacious renegade Apaches led by Martinez (playing Ulzana). On the trail it becomes apparent that Lancaster and Davison hold radically different views of Martinez's actions—the scout is cold and cynical, while Davison's Christian morality is incensed by the Apache atrocities. As the film progresses it poses a complex series of questions about the nature of heroism, racism, and American imperialism. However, as an allegorical indictment of the Vietnam War, ULZANA'S RAID avoids the preachy stance of similarly themed westerns such as SOLDIER BLUE, benefiting from Aldrich's stark, violent treatment of Sharp's well-developed script. Regrettably, this challenging film was much abused by its studio, and several different versions were circulated, including a European cut containing alternative takes and slightly altered scene construction (most noticeable in the film's opening section). This was the third time Lancaster and Aldrich had worked together, after a lapse of 18 years (their previous collaborations, APACHE and VERA CRUZ), and they would soon team again on TWILIGHT'S LAST GLEAMING.

UMBERTO D.

1952 89m bw ★★★★★
Drama
Amato/Rizzoli (Italy)

Carlo Battisti (Umberto Domenico Ferrari), Maria Pia Casilio (Maria), Lina Gennari (Landlady), Alberto Albani Barbieri (Fiance), Elena Rea (Sister), Ileana Simova (Surprised Woman), Memmo Carotenuto (Voice of Light)

p, Vittorio De Sica; d, Vittorio De Sica; w, Cesare Zavattini, Vittorio De Sica (based on a story by Zavattini); ph, Aldo Graziati; ed, Eraldo di Roma; m, Alessandro Cicognini; prod d, Virgilio Marchi

Simple on its surface but actually multi-layered and complex, this shattering portrait of an old man is an indictment of postwar Italy and its treatment of the aged. Umberto Domenico Ferrari (non-pro Carlo Battisti, a university professor) is a retired civil servant with no friends, family, or prospects, and only his dog, Flike, to keep him company. His meager pension does not provide enough for him to both eat and afford shelter, so Umberto is far behind on his rent for the room he has lived in for three decades. When he used to work during the day, his landlady (Lina Gennari) rented his room to lovers, but since his continual presence isn't adding to her income, she is planning to evict him. Umberto is one of many elderly people who voice their opposition to the way the government is treating pensionsers. Depressed by the lack of response, he determines there is no way out but suicide. He puts those thoughts aside, however, when he realizes that his dog would be at the mercy of the streets. One of the greatest films of all time and one of the handful of masterpieces to emerge from the Italian neo-realist period, UMBERTO D. is as cerebral as it is emotional, as bleak as it is warm. There is no sentimentality or pandering for sympathy in De Sica's direction. The emotions one feels watching Umberto and Flike are cathartic. This is a remarkable collaboration by De Sica, Battista, and screenwriter Cesare Zavattini.

UMBRELLAS OF CHERBOURG, THE

(LES PARAPLUIES DE CHERBOURG)
1964 90m c ★★★½
Musical
Madeleine/Parc/Beta (France/West Germany)

Catherine Deneuve (Genevieve Emery), Nino Castelnuovo (Guy), Anne Vernon (Mme. Emery), Ellen Farner (Madeleine), Marc Michel (Roland Cassard), Mireille Perrey (Aunt Elise), Jean Champion (Aubin), Harald Wolff (Dubourg), Dorothee Blank (Girl in Cafe)

p, Mag Bodard; d, Jacques Demy; w, Jacques Demy; ph, Jean Rabier (Eastmancolor); ed, Anne-Marie Cotret; m, Michel Legrand; art d, Bernard Evein; cos, Real, Jacqueline Moreau

Although inspired by the Hollywood musical, Jacques Demy's vibrant, inventive film forgoes the familiar backdrop of a Broadway show or movie premiere to revel instead in the myth and magic of everyday romance, in all its sentimental and banal glory. Not quite a musical or an operetta, THE UMBRELLAS OF CHERBOURG is, as Demy has described it, "a film in color and song." What separates it from the Hollywood musical is Demy and composer Michel Legrand's decision to deliver all the dialogue—every last meaningless word—in song form. Divided into three acts—Departure, Absence, Return—and set in Cherbourg on the coast of Normandy, the film begins with the blossoming romance of two young lovers: Genevieve (the beautiful 19-year-old Catherine Deneuve), who works in her mother's umbrella store, and Guy (Nino Castelnuovo), a service station attendant. They fall in love, have an evening of romantic bliss, and are then separated when Guy receives his draft notice. In the second act, Genevieve learns that she is pregnant and, after failing to hear from Guy, agrees to marry the accommodating Roland (Marc Michel) and move to Paris. Voila, Guy returns to Cherbourg. A feast of movement, color, and song, THE UMBRELLAS OF CHERBOURG transforms the quotidian into a celebration. By inflating the life of a common shop girl into a musical spectacle, Demy succeeds in turning a tedious existence into a fantasy, yet he and cinematographer Jean Rabier and art director Bernard Evein do so without creating a false world. Instead they discover the "poetic realism" in Genevieve's world of umbrellas, hat, chairs, and shop windows. This genuine international success was named Best Film at Cannes; it also earned an Oscar nomination in 1964 as Best Foreign-Language Film and three more in 1965 for screenplay, score, and song, "I Will Wait for You".

UNBEARABLE LIGHTNESS OF BEING, THE

1988 171m c ★★½
Romance/War R/18
Orion

Daniel Day-Lewis (Tomas), Juliette Binoche (Tereza), Lena Olin (Sabina), Derek De Lint (Franz), Erland Josephson (The Ambassador), Pavel Landovsky (Pavel), Donald Moffat (Chief Surgeon), Daniel Olbrychski (Interior Ministry Official), Stellan Skarsgard (The Engineer), Tomek Bork (Jiri)

p, Saul Zaentz; d, Philip Kaufman; w, Jean-Claude Carriere, Philip Kaufman (based on the novel by Milan Kundera); ph, Sven Nykvist (Technicolor); ed, Walter Murch; m, Mark Adler, Keith Richards, Leos Janacek; prod d, Pierre Guffroy; fx, Trielli Brothers; cos, Ann Roth

Phil Kaufman's film version of Milan Kundera's acclaimed novel opens in Prague shortly before the Soviet invasion of 1968, where Tomas (Daniel Day-Lewis), a brilliant playboy surgeon, lives a "light" existence free of commitment. Tomas falls in love with the shy, provincial Tereza (Juliette Binoche), eventually marrying her. He continues to womanize, though, especially with the similarly free and easy Sabina (Lena Olin), defending his adultery by insisting that sex and love are not the same thing. When the Soviet tanks roll into Prague, Sabina flees to Geneva, but Tomas and Tereza stay behind—she snapping pictures of the clampdown, riots, demonstrations, and violence. Eventually they, too, head for Geneva, and Tomas resumes his liaison with Sabina. When Tereza decides to return to Czechoslovakia, Tomas follows her home. There they sustain the weight of Soviet influence fairly easily, until authorities discover that Tomas once wrote an anti-Communist article. Though Tomas, typically, wrote the piece on a whim, he refuses to renounce it and suffers professionally. In the meantime, he continues to philander and Tereza continues to try to understand his philosophy of sex versus love. With its distinguished international cast and crew, volatile historical backdrop, and numerous erotic scenes, all filtered through the eye of American director Kaufman (THE RIGHT STUFF), THE UNBEARABLE LIGHTNESS OF BEING is the perfect European art film for American audiences who thirst for movies that are "intellectual" but not so much so that they can't understand them. Unfortunately, for all its credentials and the virtuoso performances of its three leads, this lengthy movie doesn't add up to much. It fails to explore its themes—love and hedonism, freedom and commitment (political and sexual)—in depth, floating haphazardly from scene to scene without emotional or intellectual development. Shot in Geneva and Lyon, France (the latter town standing in for Prague, where Kundera's work is banned), the film places greater stress on the actual events of the 1968 Soviet invasion than does its source, incorporating real black-and-white footage of the time with simulated shots featuring Binoche and Day-Lewis. Nominated by the Academy for Best Adapted Screenplay and Best Cinematography.

UNBELIEVABLE TRUTH, THE

1990 90m c   ★★½
Comedy/Drama   R/15
Action Features

Adrienne Shelly (*Audry Hugo*), Robert Burke (*Josh Hutton*), Christopher Cooke (*Vic Hugo*), Julia Mueller (*Pearl*), Mark Bailey (*Mike*), Gary Sauer (*Emmet*), Katherine Mayfield (*Liz Hugo*), David Healy (*Todd Whitbread*), Matt Malloy (*Otis*), Edie Falco (*Jane, the Waitress*)

p, Bruce Weiss, Hal Hartley; d, Hal Hartley; w, Hal Hartley; ph, Michael Spiller; ed, Hal Hartley; m, Jim Coleman, Wild Blue Yonder, The Brothers Kendall; prod d, Carla Gerona; cos, Kelly Reichardt

THE UNBELIEVABLE TRUTH is a promising feature-film debut for writer-director Hal Hartley, who shows some talent in this black comedy that manages to be original if not particularly fresh. In the vein of Jim Jarmusch's STRANGER THAN PARADISE and the work of David Lynch, THE UNBELIEVABLE TRUTH searches for the unexpected, bizarre, and magical essence of prosaic American locales. For director Hartley, Lindenhurst, Long Island, packs the allure of Lynch's Twin Peaks. Everyone has a secret or knows a secret they're dying to tell, and the hero's quirky odyssey sets the stage for self-revelation among the inhabitants and visitors of the town. Lindenhurst is the hometown of Josh Hutton (Robert Burke), a paroled convict who, as the film opens, returns to the area (where everyone remembers the details of his crime differently) because he has nowhere else to go. Haunted by a past that includes the manslaughter of his sweetheart and a prison stretch for killing her grieving father in an argument about her death, Hutton is too shell-shocked to begin his life anew until he meets Audry Hugo (Adrienne Shelly), a high-school student with an obsessive fear of nuclear attack. When Audry's father, garage owner Vic (Christopher Cooke), agrees to hire Josh for his exceptional mechanical skills, Audry and Josh can't fight off their growing attraction. Worried by his daughter's involvement with this shady character, Vic promotes Audry's fledgling modeling career, with the help of a photographer who secures her work out of town. Complicating matters is Audry's best friend, Pearl (Julia Mueller), the sister of the girl Josh killed. After a hectic climax in which everyone converges on Josh's house and clashes at cross-purposes, the unbelievable truth is revealed and sets up a happy ending for Audry and Josh, clearing Josh's name.

Hartley exhibits a born filmmaker's eye for composition and camera placement in this offbeat, dryly humorous film. His screenwriting skills are less solid, however, and the film is further damaged by the uneven quality of its cast, which weakens the already delicate balance in this black comedy. Although Burke (a combination of Christopher Walken and Michael Weller) makes the ideal loner hero providing the center for Hartley's crazy universe, Shelly is saddled with a role that's more a collection of nonconformist attitudes than a true character, and although she projects a distinct personality, she isn't resourceful enough as an actress to make Audry believable. More damaging is the casting of Cooke, whose delineation of the harried middle-class father is almost amateurish. David Healy, by contrast, does a refreshing turn as a girl-crazy photographer who uses his camera as an aphrodisiac, with poor results.

Despite these flaws, THE UNBELIEVABLE TRUTH captivates with its committedly off-center vision of suburban angst. Long Island becomes a world of identity crises, serendipitous occurrences, and genuinely surprising contrivances. It's an impressive, if not always cogent, attempt to mine humor out of tragic circumstances, and it manages to send up small-town life without being condescending—no mean feat. Unfortunately, in making his central character a passive victim of fate, Hartley condemns his film to a low energy level throughout. What seems promisingly wacky at first eventually flattens out and becomes repetitive. Instead of deepening our understanding of the characters and lifting the story toward its redemptive conclusion, the film fails to sustain its inventiveness.

Within its limits, however, THE UNBELIEVABLE TRUTH provides moments of splendid weirdness and several memorably zany characters. It is a zippy vision of everyone's hometown, relocated to a twilight zone in which all the boredom one left behind has acquired a retrospective fascination. The film challenges our perceptions and prejudices about small-town life, finding mystery in the mundane. Hartley is clearly a filmmaker to keep watching.

UNCLE BUCK

1989 100m c   ★★½
Comedy   PG/12
Universal

John Candy (*Uncle Buck Russell*), Jean Kelly (*Tia Russell*), Gaby Hoffman (*Maizy Russell*), Macaulay Culkin (*Miles Russell*), Amy Madigan (*Chanice Kobolowski*), Elaine Bromka (*Cindy Russell*), Garrett M. Brown (*Bob Russell*), Laurie Metcalf (*Marcie Dahlgren-Frost*), Jay Underwood (*Bug*), Brian Tarantina (*Rog*)

p, John Hughes, Tom Jacobson; d, John Hughes; w, John Hughes; ph, Ralf D. Bode (Deluxe Color); ed, Lou Lombardo, Tony Lombardo, Peck Prior; m, Ira Newborn; prod d, John W. Corso; chor, Miranda Garrison; cos, Marilyn Vance

John Candy stars as the eponymous Uncle Buck who becomes a most unlikely baby-sitter for eight-year-old Miles (Macaulay Culkin), six-year-old Maizy (Gaby Hoffman), and teenage Tia (Jean Kelly), when Buck's brother and sister-in-law have to leave town to visit a sick relative. Although he is supposed to be completely ill-prepared for taking care of children, Uncle Buck keeps Maizy and Miles amused and eventually wins the reluctant respect of Tia by protecting her from her creepy boyfriend. In the process, however, he nearly ruins his own eight-year relationship with Chanice (Amy Madigan). John Hughes's film is built around the notion that Uncle Buck is the last person anyone would want to have watch their children, but Candy portrays Buck as an appealing oddball in a role he was wonderfully suited to. Unfortunately, this film, like so many of Hughes efforts, is undermined by some very sloppy scripting.

UNCONQUERED

1947 146m c ★★★½
Adventure
Paramount

Gary Cooper *(Capt. Christopher Holden)*, Paulette Goddard *(Abigail Martha "Abby" Hale)*, Howard da Silva *(Martin Garth)*, Boris Karloff *(Guyasuta)*, Cecil Kellaway *(Jeremy Love)*, Ward Bond *(John Fraser)*, Katherine DeMille *(Hannah)*, Henry Wilcoxon *(Capt. Steele)*, C. Aubrey Smith *(Lord Chief Justice)*, Victor Varconi *(Capt. Simson Ecuyer)*

p, Cecil B. DeMille; d, Cecil B. DeMille; w, Charles Bennett, Fredric M. Frank, Jesse Lasky, Jr. (based on the novel *The Judas Tree* by Neil H. Swanson); ph, Ray Rennahan (Technicolor); ed, Anne Bauchens; m, Victor Young; art d, Hans Dreier, Walter Tyler; fx, Gordon Jennings, Farciot Edouart, Wallace Kelley, Paul K. Lerpae, Devereaux Jennings; chor, Jack Crosby; cos, Gwen Wakeling, Barbara Karinska

Another of Cecil B. DeMille's bloated epics about the shaping of America, UNCONQUERED stars Goddard as an indentured servant sentenced to 14 years of servitude in the American colonies. On the voyage across from England, she meets Cooper, a Virginia militia captain who takes an immediate liking to her, despite the fact that he is already engaged. Goddard also attracts the eye of da Silva, a scurrilous trader. When his attentions grow too lewd, she slaps him, prompting da Silva to try to buy her contract. He is foiled on the docks, though, when Cooper bids higher and immediately gives Goddard her freedom. However, da Silva has too many other nefarious schemes in the works to be bothered by a little setback like this. Most notably, he marries the daughter of Seneca chief Karloff and agitates the Indians to unite to drive the white men back into the sea, using muskets da Silva sells them. At Fort Pitt, Cooper's fiancee tells him that she has fallen in love with another man, a development that doesn't seem to bother Cooper much. Goddard, however, falls into da Silva's hands again when he manages to get hold of her contract and convince her that Cooper's purchase was fraudulent. He puts her to work in a saloon he owns, managed by the crude Mazurki. She scrubs the floor while the men make rude comments, but Cooper isn't long in rescuing her. Jealous of her husband's attentions toward Goddard, da Silva's Indian wife arranges with the tribe to have Goddard kidnapped. Goddard is tied to a stake and is about to be tortured when Cooper comes on the scene to rescue her yet again. They arrive back at the fort just as the Indians attack with flaming arrows. Cooper helps the settlers fight off the Indians, then manages to kill da Silva and Mazurki in a shootout in a stable. As the film ends, Cooper and Goddard are about to be married.

This huge and expensive production never really comes together. Over $5 million and 102 days were spent on the film, but it was savaged by the critics and ignored by the public. Fearing the flaming arrows that had already sent 30 extras to the hospital with burns, Goddard created problems for the director when she refused to climb the ramparts of the fort during the attack sequence. To teach her a lesson DeMille picked one lowly extra for an important part in the scene, succoring the wounded on the ramparts. Goddard was vindicated, though, when the extra joined the others at the hospital.

Karloff wasn't very good as the Indian chief, though his dedication to the part was impressive. He had originally intended to speak the role in gibberish, but DeMille insisted that he learn Seneca, which he did. In addition, the actor had recently undergone back surgery and under his bonnet, furs, and loincloth was a massive brace. Cooper is good but looks a little old to be gallivanting about the frontier, and Goddard tries too hard to be glamorous, destroying her character. Da Silva is a worthy villain and the rest of the cast is more than adequate, but the whole thing sinks under its own grand weight. DeMille simply tries too hard to get in everything, even one of his patented bathtub scenes, played here in a barrel by Goddard. The film lost a fortune at the box office.

UNDER FIRE

1983 127m c ★★★
Drama/War R/15
Lion's Gate

Nick Nolte *(Russell Price)*, Ed Harris *(Oates)*, Gene Hackman *(Alex Grazier)*, Joanna Cassidy *(Claire)*, Alma Martinez *(Isela)*, Holly Palance *(Journalist)*, Ella Laboriel *(Nightclub Singer)*, Oswaldo Doria *(Boy Photographer)*, Fernando Elizondo *(Businessman)*, Hamilton Camp *(Regis Seydor)*

p, Jonathan T. Taplin; d, Roger Spottiswoode; w, Ron Shelton, Clayton Frohman (based on a story by Frohman); ph, John Alcott (Technicolor); ed, John Bloom; m, Jerry Goldsmith; art d, Agustin Ytuarte, Toby Rafelson; fx, Laurencio Cordero, Jesus Duran; cos, Cynthia Bales

Flawed but still fascinating, UNDER FIRE looks at the Nicaraguan revolution through the eyes of Russell Price (Nick Nolte), an American photojournalist who uses his camera to distance himself from reality. In Managua, Price's noncommittal attitude is put to the test by the startling contrast between the high life enjoyed by the supporters of President Anastasio Somoza (Rene Enriquez) and the reality experienced by most Nicaraguans. The American begins to realize that the plush Hotel Continental, home of the press corps, is an obscene imperialist outpost that distances the reporters from the people they are supposed to be covering. None of this, however, is news to Claire (Joanna Cassidy), a National Public Radio reporter, and under her influence Price eventually becomes actively involved with the revolutionaries, faking a picture of a slain leader so that it will appear that he is still alive. The sensational photo brings network news anchor Alex Grazier (Gene Hackman) to Managua where he is shot and killed by one of Somoza's National Guardsmen (mirroring the horrifying true-life murder of ABC correspondent Bill Stewart by Somoza's troops in 1979—an event that was captured on videotape and shown to a shocked American audience). Price records the whole incident on film, and his pictures create worldwide outrage that helps sound the death knell for Somoza's government. Nolte gives one of his best performances as the photographer who suddenly finds himself looking past what he sees in the viewfinder in this insightful look at revolution and the world of journalism. Director Roger Spottiswoode, who edited a number of Sam Peckinpah movies, succeeds brilliantly in creating the chaotic last days of Somoza's government while at the same time incisively evaluating the moral dilemma faced by war correspondents. Where the film falters, however, is screenwriter Ron Shelton's (BULL DURHAM) overly simplistic view of both Somoza and the Sandinistas. Shown to be the white knights riding to the rescue of the oppressed masses, the Sandinistas are given almost embarrassingly reverent treatment with no hint of the ideological divisions, confusion, and suffering that would follow their takeover (problems at least hinted at in Oliver Stone's remarkable SALVADOR).

UNDER THE ROOFS OF PARIS
(SOUS LES TOITS DE PARIS)
1930   96m   bw   ★★★★
Drama   /A
Tobis   (France)

Albert Prejean (Albert), Pola Illery (Pola), Edmond T. Greville (Louis), Gaston Modot (Fred), Paul Olivier (Drunkard), Bill Bocket (Bill), Jane Pierson (Neighborhood Woman), Raymond Aimos (Thief), Thomy Bourdelle (Francois)

d, Rene Clair; w, Rene Clair; ph, Georges Perinal, Georges Raulet; ed, Rene Le Henaff; art d, Lazare Meerson

Billed upon its release as "the most beautiful film in the world," UNDER THE ROOFS OF PARIS may well have fit that description—at least at the time. In this first "100 percent French talking and singing film," Rene Clair was determined to make sound and visuals equal partners. Instead of simply employing synchronous sound techniques, he chose to use sound only when needed, refusing to toss in dialogue just for the sake of doing so.

The story itself is a simple one. Street singer Albert (Albert Prejean) and Pola (Pola Illery) are lovers, though she enjoys flirting with her best friend, Louis (Edmond Greville). When Albert finds himself in prison for a crime he didn't commit, the door is open for Pola and Edmond to act upon their mutual attraction. Upon his release from prison, Albert is enraged by Pola and Edmond's romance, but the final arrangement the three arrive at is unexpected indeed. In 1931, using practically the same set of technicians, Clair went on to make his two greatest films—LE MILLION and A NOUS LA LIBERTE, both of which continued his experiments with sound. Much of this film's visual style, however, can be attributed to the great art director Lazare Meerson, who collaborated with Clair on the director's greatest works.

UNDER THE VOLCANO
1984   112m   c   ★★★½
Drama   R/15
Ithaca/Conacine

Albert Finney (Geoffrey Firmin), Jacqueline Bisset (Yvonne Firmin), Anthony Andrews (Hugh Firmin), Ignacio Lopez Tarso (Dr. Vigil), Katy Jurado (Senora Gregoria), James Villiers (Brit), Dawson Bray (Quincey), Carlos Riquelme (Bustamante), Jim McCarthy (Gringo), Rene Ruiz (Dwarf)

p, Moritz Borman, Wieland Schulz-Keil; d, John Huston; w, Guy Gallo (based on the novel by Malcolm Lowry); ph, Gabriel Figueroa (Technicolor); ed, Roberto Silvi; m, Alex North; prod d, Gunther Gerzso; art d, Jose Rodriguez Granada; cos, Angela Dodson

A bizzare journey into the mystical Mexican underworld in 1939, UNDER THE VOLCANO is set during the morbid holiday known as the Day of the Dead—a day on which the souls of the dead spew forth from hell amid the colorful and lively festivities of the village of Cuernavaca. Geoffrey Firmin (Albert Finney), a former British consul, is there for the celebration, drinking himself to death. The spirit of celebration is alive, but Geoffrey appears lifeless, almost zombielike as he wanders the streets. His former wife, Yvonne (Jacqueline Bisset), arrives, and with the help of Geoffrey's brother, Hugh (Anthony Andrews), tries to get him away from Mexico to a farm in the US, hoping it will curb his drinking. After wandering about the village pathetically for hours on end, Geoffrey slips away and winds up in a sleazy bar-whorehouse, drinking himself into oblivion. Based on the 1947 novel by Malcom Lowry, who began the work in 1936 at the age of 27, UNDER THE VOLCANO has been a project

kicked around Hollywood since the book's publication. Lowry, a suicidal alcoholic, wrote the novel without any clear narrative line, relying instead on marvelously visual images, thereby causing many people to label the novel "unfilmable"—until it ended up in the lap of John Huston. The result is very much worth the wait, bringing to life the mysticism of Mexico with a superb script by Guy Gallo, exquisite photography, and the unparalleled performance by Finney.

UNFAITHFULLY YOURS
1948   105m   bw   ★★★★★
Comedy   /15
FOX

Rex Harrison (Sir Alfred de Carter), Linda Darnell (Daphne de Carter), Barbara Lawrence (Barbara Henshler), Rudy Vallee (August Henshler), Kurt Kreuger (Anthony), Lionel Stander (Hugo Standoff), Edgar Kennedy (Detective Sweeney), Alan Bridge (House Detective), Julius Tannen (Tailor), Torben Meyer (Dr. Schultz)

p, Preston Sturges; d, Preston Sturges; w, Preston Sturges; ph, Victor Milner; ed, Robert Fritch; m, Gioacchino Rossini, Richard Wagner, Peter Ilich Tchaikovsky; art d, Lyle Wheeler, Joseph C. Wright; fx, Fred Sersen; cos, Bonnie Cashin

The last of Sturges's Hollywood films, and one of his finest. This farce of misconceptions, infidelities, and murder is a brilliantly stylish work that imaginatively squeezes everything it can from the film medium.

Harrison, in a marvelous performance, is a famous British conductor married to Darnell. The two are much in love, but, when Harrison returns from Europe, a seed of jealousy is planted in his mind by his brother-in-law, Vallee. It seems that Vallee had a private detective, Kennedy, follow Darnell through her daily activities, and his report, which Harrison refuses to look at, suggests that Darnell indulged in some extracurricular activities with Harrison's private secretary, Kreuger, when the conductor was abroad. Harrison tears up the report and throws it out of his hotel room, but the pages are put back together and wind up back in Harrison's hands. This time Harrison burns the document, nearly setting his dressing room ablaze. However, Harrison slowly begins to think there just might be something to the report, so he goes to Kennedy's office. Kennedy, it turns out, is a big fan of Harrison (who loves how the conductor "handles Handel") and dredges up the original report from his files. Now Harrison's jealous imagination goes wild. That night, as he begins conducting Rossini's "Semiramide" overture at a concert, the camera zeros in on Harrison's eye. The scene flashes to Harrison and Darnell as they return to their hotel room. As part of an elaborate plan, Harrison has arranged for Darnell to spend a night on the town with Kreuger. Using his straight razor, Harrison murders his wife, then sets up the room so Kreuger will appear to be the culprit. Harrison's plan works to perfection, and the conductor laughs maniacally when Kreuger is found guilty of the crime. The music comes to a conclusion, and the camera pulls away from Harrison's eye, back to the concert. The entire scenario has taken place in his mind, as do the next two sequences. To the accompaniment of Wagner's "Tannhauser" overture, Harrison imagines writing a fat check for Darnell, enabling her to run off with her young lover. Finally, with Tchaikovsky's "Francesca da Rimini" wafting in the background, Harrison challenges Darnell and Kreuger to a game of Russian roulette. He ends up with a bullet in his temple as the concert comes to an end. Harrison, now convinced that Darnell and Kreuger are dallying behind his back, returns to his hotel room and tries to set up the murderous plan he imagined during the concert. His real-life plans are a disaster, and Harrison finally realizes that Kennedy's report was the result of many misconceptions.

UNFAITHFULLY YOURS is a near perfect combination of sound and image. Sturges orchestrates the fantasy sequences with care and precision, using editing and performance rhythms that are in perfect synch with the underscoring music. Harrison is a sheer delight, turning in a devilish performance brimming with wit and style. Darnell, Kreuger, Vallee, and Lawrence fill out the lead roles with elegance and wit, while consummate character player Kennedy adds a nice touch of buffoonery. Sturges had gotten the idea of music affecting the conductor's thoughts while writing the screenplay for THE POWER AND THE GLORY. "I had a scene all written and had only to put it down on paper. To my surprise, it came out quite unlike what I had planned," Sturges said later. "I sat back wondering what the hell had happened, then noticed that someone had left the radio on in the next room and realized that I had been listening to a symphony broadcast from New York and that this, added to my thoughts, had changed the total." (Quoted in James Curtis, *Between Flops*.)

Despite many critical plaudits, UNFAITHFULLY YOURS never caught on with the public—an undeserved fate for a film of such brilliance. It was remade in 1984 by Howard Zieff with Dudley Moore and Nastassja Kinski as leads.

UNFINISHED BUSINESS
1985 78m c   ★★★
Comedy/Drama
Unfinished Business (Australia)

John Clayton *(Geoff)*, Michelle Fawdon *(Maureen)*, Norman Kaye *(George)*, Bob Ellis *(Geoff's Flatmate)*, Andrew Lesnie *(Telegraph Boy)*

p, Rebel Penfold-Russell; d, Bob Ellis; w, Bob Ellis; ph, Andrew Lesnie (Eastmancolor); ed, Amanda Robson; prod d, Jane Johnston

Leaving behind a broken marriage and three children in the US, Clayton returns to his native Australia after 15 years and runs into his old flame, Fawdon. The latter is now happily married but frustrated because she and her husband have no children. To Clayton's delight, she suggests that he try to impregnate her. This proves disappointing to Clayton, who finds meeting the conditions of impregnation less alluring than he'd anticipated. Charming and witty, with good acting all around.

UNINVITED, THE
1944 98m bw   ★★★★
Horror   /A
Paramount

Ray Milland *(Roderick Fitzgerald)*, Ruth Hussey *(Pamela Fitzgerald)*, Donald Crisp *(Cmdr. Bench)*, Cornelia Otis Skinner *(Miss Holloway)*, Dorothy Stickney *(Miss Hird)*, Barbara Everest *(Lizzie Flynn)*, Alan Napier *(Dr. Scott)*, Gail Russell *(Stella Meredith)*, Jessica Newcombe *(Miss Ellis)*, John Kieran *(Foreword Narrator)*

p, Charles Brackett; d, Lewis Allen; w, Dodie Smith, Frank Partos (based on the novel by Dorothy Macardle); ph, Charles Lang; ed, Doane Harrison; m, Victor Young; art d, Hans Dreier, Ernst Fegte; fx, Farciot Edouart

An unusual and fascinating item, a ghost story that takes itself seriously. Milland and his sister, Hussey, buy a house on the Cornish cliffs and are soon bedeviled by phenomena such as cold spots in rooms, the smell of mimosas permeating the air, and the

dog refusing to go upstairs. They are often visited by a local girl, Russell, whose grandfather, Crisp, forbids her to go into the house. It's suspected that the place is haunted by the spirit of Russell's mother, who fell from the cliffs to her death. More strange things happen, such as flowers wilting immediately in a room, and eventually the phantom itself is seen at the top of the stairs (one of the most convincing and scary ghosts to appear on the screen). Russell is confined by her grandfather to an asylum, but Milland and Hussey figure out that it is not one but two ghosts that haunt their home, carrying their rivalry from life beyond the grave. They eventually solve the mystery surrounding the death of Russell's mother, and when they do the spirits depart.

This film was greatly influenced by Val Lewton's productions for RKO in which the horror is only suggested, and almost never shown—for the monster in one's mind is much more frightening than the one on the screen. Some of the film doesn't work so well; it drags in spots and much of it seems a direct cop from REBECCA (house on the cliffs, scary folks coming in and out talking about the dead woman who lived there before, etc., and the advertising for the film went out of its way to compare itself to the Hitchcock film). Milland is as good as ever, and the rest of the cast does an admirable job, particularly Crisp and Skinner. Although the film garnered favorable reviews and decent returns at the box office, it would be many years before Hollywood would get serious about the spirit world again (THE HAUNTING).

UNION PACIFIC
1939 135m bw   ★★★★
Western   /U
Paramount

Barbara Stanwyck *(Mollie Monahan)*, Joel McCrea *(Jeff Butler)*, Akim Tamiroff *(Fiesta)*, Robert Preston *(Dick Allen)*, Lynne Overman *(Leach Overmile)*, Brian Donlevy *(Sid Campeau)*, Robert Barrat *(Duke Ring)*, Anthony Quinn *(Jack Cordray)*, Stanley Ridges *(Gen. Casement)*, Henry Kolker *(Asa M. Barrows)*

p, Cecil B. DeMille; d, Cecil B. DeMille; w, Walter DeLeon, C. Gardner Sullivan, Jesse Lasky, Jr., Jack Cunningham (based on the novel *Trouble Shooters* by Ernest Haycox); ph, Victor Milner, Dewey Wrigley; ed, Anne Bauchens; m, George Antheil, Sigmund Krumgold, John Leipold; art d, Hans Dreier, Roland Anderson; fx, Gordon Jennings, Loren L. Ryder, Farciot Edouart; cos, Natalie Visart

After finishing his pirate epic THE BUCCANEER, Cecil B. DeMille was caught in a quandary regarding his next picture. Should it concern planes, ships, or trains? Deciding on trains, he faced another choice: the Union Pacific or the Sante Fe? The producer-director of spectacles reportedly flipped a coin, and UNION PACIFIC landed face up. McCrea stars in this lavishly produced western, playing the supervisor of the construction of the Union Pacific Railroad. While on the job, he meets Stanwyck, the daughter of a railroad engineer. Stanwyck, whose femininity is tempered by a tough assurance indicating she can handle herself in any situation, is the Union Pacific's postmistress. McCrea falls for her; meanwhile, Kolker, a seedy politician with a financial interest in the rival Central Pacific line, hires crooked gambler Donlevy to devise a variety of schemes to delay construction of the line. Aided by Preston, a comrade of McCrea's from the Civil War, Donlevy sets up a gambling den and begins distracting the Union Pacific workers with the prospect of gambling, liquor, and fast women. The lure of a good time causes havoc at the railroad—as does the robbery of the payroll, performed by Preston. Stanwyck, who has been seeing Preston as well as McCrea, learns that Preston is responsible for the theft and talks him into returning the money. Soon after, the train is attacked by Indians. Stanwyck holds her ground to fight alongside McCrea and Preston, and it looks as though they will all be slaughtered. The US Cavalry arrives and saves them in the nick of time, but not before the reformed Preston is murdered by Donlevy, who in turn pays for his crimes. With the villains dispatched, the Union Pacific is finally completed and the film ends in a massive celebration as the famous golden spike is driven into the last rail at Promontory Point.

UNION PACIFIC is a big, sprawling western epic produced with the usual DeMille extravagance and eye for detail. DeMille gained the cooperation of the Union Pacific Railroad, which made available heaps of old records and papers pertaining to the line's construction. In addition to the research material, the Union Pacific supplied DeMille with vintage trains and experienced crews to run them. The film was shot on locations in Utah and Oklahoma, and at the Canoga Park lot in Hollywood, where the reenactment of the golden spike ceremony was staged. Moreover, the actual golden spike (driven on May 10, 1869) that was used at that ceremony was loaned to the production by Stanford University and brought to Hollywood in great secrecy. DeMille, who assembled his usual cast of thousands for the production, was delighted by Stanwyck's professional enthusiasm as she toughed it through the action scenes with the men. The director himself was stricken with a prostate problem during the production and had to undergo an operation, which caused him to be absent for several weeks during which much of the location shooting was directed by Arthur Rosson and James Hogan. When DeMille returned to the production, he directed from a stretcher and was carried from set to set by crew members.

Even the premiere of UNION PACIFIC was a spectacle. DeMille arranged for a special Union Pacific train to carry the cast on a five-day trip from Los Angeles to Omaha, where the film was to open (and where the railway line started). There were stops along the way, of course, and special events were planned at each. In Omaha a three-day celebration with the citizenry in period costume was held, and the UNION PACIFIC cast—also in costumes—joined in. The film was a big hit at the box office, prompting Paramount Studios finally to give DeMille *carte blanche* on future productions. The film earned an Oscar nomination for Best Special Effects, the first year the Academy presented an award in that category.

UNMARRIED WOMAN, AN

1978 124m c   ★★★★
Drama/Comedy   R/18
FOX

Jill Clayburgh *(Erica)*, Alan Bates *(Saul)*, Michael Murphy *(Martin)*, Cliff Gorman *(Charlie)*, Pat Quinn *(Sue)*, Kelly Bishop *(Elaine)*, Lisa Lucas *(Patti)*, Linda G. Miller *(Jeannette)*, Andrew Duncan *(Bob)*, Daniel Seltzer *(Dr. Jacobs)*

p, Paul Mazursky, Tony Ray; d, Paul Mazursky; w, Paul Mazursky; ph, Arthur J. Ornitz (Movielab Color); ed, Stuart Pappe; m, Bill Conti; prod d, Pato Guzman; cos, Albert Wolsky

AN UNMARRIED WOMAN became a beacon of the women's movement in the 1970s, though its tentative feminism seems tame by today's standards. Jill Clayburgh, in the title role, learns to take control of her own life after her schlump of a husband (beautifully played by Michael Murphy) leaves her for a girl he met in Bloomingdale's.

Set in the New York milieus Mazursky knows so well, AN UNMARRIED WOMAN has some great insights and is su-

perbly acted by all involved. The director populates the film with his usual, very real and attractive modern characters, but you may think it cops out in the end, when Clayburgh falls into the arms of romantic SoHo painter Alan Bates. Nonetheless, Mazursky spares nobody and nothing with his comic darts. Some of the most hysterically funny scenes occur when Clayburgh and her three pals (Quinn, Bishop, and Miller) have regular luncheons in which they let down their hair and frankly talk about their sex lives. Oscar nominations were handed out to the film for Best Picture (it lost to THE DEER HUNTER), to Clayburgh as Best Actress (she lost to Jane Fonda for COMING HOME), and to Mazursky for his screenplay, which also won the New York Film Critics' Award.

UNSUITABLE JOB FOR A WOMAN, AN

1982 94m c   ★★★
Mystery   /15
Boyd's   (U.K.)

Pippa Guard *(Cordelia Gray)*, Billie Whitelaw, Paul Freeman, Dominic Guard, Elizabeth Spriggs, David Horovitch, Dawn Archibald, Bernadette Short, James Gilbey, Kelda Holmes

p, Michael Relph, Peter McKay; d, Christopher Petit; w, Elizabeth McKay, Brian Scobie, Christopher Petit (based on the novel by P.D. James); ph, Martin Schafer (Gevacolor); ed, Mick Audsley; m, Chaz Jankel; prod d, Anton Furst; art d, John Beard

Based on a novel by P.D. James, this gripping murder mystery revolves around the suicide of a tycoon's son who is found hanging in a well. Cordelia Gray (Pippa Guard), a 23-year-old female private investigator—whose unlikely career choice gives the film its title—becomes increasingly engrossed in the case, living in the dead boy's quarters, nearly hanging herself while examining the well, and even making love to the boy's father. Her snooping reveals that the boy was actually murdered and implicates the least suspect of the characters. UNSUITABLE JOB FOR A WOMAN is aptly directed by Christopher Petit (RADIO ON), whose camera never seems to be in a rush to photograph a scene—always lingering on the subject a little longer than necessary, which adds an offbeat atmosphere to the film.

UNTIL THE END OF THE WORLD

1991 178m c   ★★½
Science Fiction   R/15
Trans Pacific Films/Road Movies Film/Argos Films/
Village Roadshow   (France/Germany/Australia)

William Hurt *(Trevor McPhee/Sam Farber)*, Solveig Dommartin *(Claire Tourneur)*, Sam Neill *(Eugene Fitzpatrick)*, Max Von Sydow *(Henry Farber)*, Rudiger Vogler *(Philip Winter)*, Ernie Dingo *(Burt)*, Jeanne Moreau *(Edith Farber)*, Lois Chiles *(Elsa)*, Chick Ortega *(Chico)*, Elena Smirnowa *(Krasikova)*

p, Jonathan Taplin; d, Wim Wenders; w, Wim Wenders, Peter Carey (from the story by Wenders and Solveig Dommartin); ph, Robby Muller; ed, Peter Przygodda; m, Graeme Revell; prod d, Thierry Flamand, Sally Campbell; art d, Ian Gracie; cos, Montserrat Casanova

Wim Wenders' UNTIL THE END OF THE WORLD is really two movies, joined rather awkwardly at the hip. The first half of this three-hour marathon is an enjoyable, off-the-cuff road movie with a post-modernist, technological spin; the second is a half-baked, indulgent meditation on the nature of the recorded image.

The year is 1999, and the world is on the brink of a nuclear confrontation. Claire Tourneur (Solveig Dommartin), a disenchanted young bohemian, is involved in a lackluster relationship with novelist Eugene Fitzpatrick (Sam Neill). Driving across Europe on her way home from a decadent party, she has a car accident that involves her with two bank robbers, Chico and Raymond (Chick Ortega and Eddy Mitchell). Claire ends up agreeing to transport their heist to Paris in exchange for a cut of the proceeds. Then she meets Trevor McPhee *aka* Sam Farber (William Hurt), an enigmatic traveler who steals some of the loot from her car before going on his mysterious way. Enraged and intrigued, Claire sets off to track him down, after informing Eugene that their relationship is over. Her quest takes her around the world in a cosmopolitan blur of languages, cultures and high-tech computer images. Along the way, she has encounters with a motley group that includes an Australian bounty hunter, Burt (Ernie Dingo); a detective, Philip Winter (Rudiger Vogler); Chico the bank robber; and Eugene, who wants his former lover back.

Sam, it seems, is using a special camera to collect images from his global trek. His father (Max Von Sydow) is working on a process that will enable Sam's mother (Jeanne Moreau) to "see" these images, even though she is blind. Claire throws in her lot with him, even becoming the operator of the camera, which draws on its user's emotional response to capture an image and is also very exhausting for the operator's eyes. The detective, meanwhile, is after Sam for having stolen some expensive minerals. The caper extends through Europe via Siberia to Beijing, and from there on to Tokyo, San Francisco, and eventually the Australian outback, where Sam's father's laboratory is located under an Aboriginal settlement.

Convinced by an absence of radio signals that a nuclear holocaust has taken place, everyone devotes themselves to helping with Mr. Farber's experiments. For Mrs. Farber to be able to "see" the recorded images, Sam must "transmit" them to her, which involves recreating the emotional charge he felt during the initial act of seeing/recording. At first he is too exhausted to do this, but Claire steps into the breach and successfully transmits the images she captured. Eventually Sam is able to do the same, but the process is extremely draining for Mrs. Farber, who dies on New Year's Eve, as the others are celebrating the dawn of a new millennium.

More determined than ever, Doctor Farber, assisted by Sam and Claire, pursues his research, developing a technique for recording and playing back dream images. Those who take part in the experiments, though, become hopelessly and narcissistically addicted to the process, having no desire to do anything but continually watch playbacks of their own dreams. Eventually, Sam and Claire break free of the compulsion, and news arrives that there was no holocaust. Eugene completes a novel about his experiences, which he decides to call UNTIL THE END OF THE WORLD.

One of the most highly respected directors of the New German Cinema, Wim Wenders completed a remarkable trilogy of road movies—ALICE IN THE CITIES, WRONG MOVE and KINGS OF THE ROAD—early in his career, and made a partial return to the genre with PARIS, TEXAS. (His production company is even called Road Movies.) The themes which illuminated those earlier movies, though—the difficulty of communication, the nature of wanderlust, urban alienation—get skimpy treatment here. The first, "road movie" half of the film is a flip, if engaging romp which offers us some stylish visuals and a knowing, *fin de siecle* attitude. Once the film gets bogged down in the outback, however, things come to a literal stop. Wenders is clearly trying to say something about the emotional paucity of the recorded image as opposed to the "real thing"; but the idea has not been

through or given any dramatic form. It ends up working on an extremely banal level, exemplified by an aphorism intoned by a wise old Japanese man (Ryu Chishu): "The eye does not see the same as the heart."

Lacking both heart and brains, UNTIL THE END OF THE WORLD is a disappointing outing from one of the most interesting figures on the contemporary scene. The soundtrack includes original compositions by U2, Talking Heads, REM, Lou Reed, Robbie Robertson and others, UNTIL THE END OF THE WORLD is a disappointing outing from one of the most interesting figures on the contemporary scene.

UNTOUCHABLES, THE

1987 119m c ★★
Crime R/15
Paramount

Kevin Costner *(Eliot Ness)*, Sean Connery *(James Malone)*, Charles Martin Smith *(Oscar Wallace)*, Andy Garcia *(George Stone)*, Robert De Niro *(Al Capone)*, Richard Bradford *(Mike)*, Jack Kehoe *(Walter Payne)*, Brad Sullivan *(George)*, Billy Drago *(Frank Nitti)*, Patricia Clarkson *(Catherine Ness)*

p, Art Linson; d, Brian De Palma; w, David Mamet; ph, Stephen H. Burum (Technicolor); ed, Jerry Greenberg, Bill Pankow; m, Ennio Morricone; art d, William Elliott; cos, Marilyn Vance

THE UNTOUCHABLES pits Chicago crime kingpin Al Capone (Robert De Niro) against mild-mannered Eliot Ness (Kevin Costner), a Treasury agent assigned to smash Capone's bootleg empire. Ness recruits wily street cop James Malone (Sean Connery), who knows the ins and outs of the Chicago underworld, after which more recruits are added to form the nucleus of what will later be known as "the untouchables"—lawmen who cannot be bought or corrupted. The whole thing is sloppy, a stew brewed by writer David Mamet and served steaming hot by director Brian De Palma as true crime history, which it is not. In real life, Ness and Capone never met, and Ness had nothing to do with getting the evidence that sent Capone to prison for income tax evasion. There is something cartoonish about THE UN-TOUCHABLES, with De Niro doing an impersonation of Rod Steiger's excellent portrayal in CAPONE. Costner's interpretation is one of dreary indifference, without the forcefulness the role demands. Connery, however, is terrific as the wizened veteran cop, and he deservedly won a Best Supporting Actor Oscar for his performance. Also nominated for Best Original Score, Costume Design, and Art Direction.

UP IN ARMS

1944 106m c ★★★★
Musical/Comedy/War /U
Goldwyn

Danny Kaye *(Danny Weems)*, Constance Dowling *(Mary Morgan)*, Dinah Shore *(Virginia Merrill)*, Dana Andrews *(Joe Nelson)*, Louis Calhern *(Col. Ashley)*, George Mathews *(Blackie)*, Benny Baker *(Butterball)*, Elisha Cook, Jr. *(Info Jones)*, Lyle Talbot *(Sgt. Gelsey)*, Walter Catlett *(Maj. Brock)*

p, Don Hartman; d, Elliott Nugent; w, Don Hartman, Allen Boretz, Robert Pirosh (based on the play *The Nervous Wreck* by Owen Davis, Sr.); ph, Ray Rennahan (Technicolor); ed, Daniel Mandell, James E. Newcom; m, Ray Heindorf; art d, Perry Ferguson, Stewart Chaney, McClure Capps; fx, Clarence Slifer, Ray Binger; chor, Danny Dare

This is the lavish musical comedy that introduced 3l-year-old vaudeville and stage star Danny Kaye to the movie audience. He plays confirmed hypochondriac Danny Weems, who is so fearful of illness that he works as a medical building's elevator operator—if disease strikes, help is no more than a scream away. When Danny and his best pal, Joe (Dana Andrews), are drafted into the Army, he must tell the woman he loves, Mary (Constance Dowling), that they are going off to war. Accordingly, Mary—who really likes Joe—joins the WACs with her friend Virginia (Dinah Shore), who signs on as a nurse because, of course, she's in love with Danny. The boys are shipped out to the Far East, but fate and the screenwriters intervene when Mary and Virginia, who came to bid them goodbye, are trapped on the ship. Not being a nurse like Virginia, Mary must stow away to avoid court-martial, and is shunted around the ship to escape the eagle eye of the martinet captain (Louis Calhern). Soon enough, Mary is discovered, Danny takes the blame, and things look bleak as Danny is placed in an Army jail after the ship docks. Then the Japanese attack and take Danny prisoner, but in a series of wonderfully funny escapades our neurotic hero escapes and even manages to nab some of the enemy. Kaye's superb comic timing is already in full evidence, allowing him to dominate every scene. Excellent choreography, superb sets, fine costumes, and a host of songs (several by Harold Arlen and Ted Koehler) round out the enjoyment.

UPTOWN SATURDAY NIGHT

1974   104m   c   ★★★
Comedy   PG
First Artists

Sidney Poitier (Steve Jackson), Bill Cosby (Wardell Franklin), Harry Belafonte (Geechie Dan Beauford), Flip Wilson (The Reverend), Richard Pryor (Sharp Eye Washington), Rosalind Cash (Sarah Jackson), Roscoe Lee Browne (Congressman Lincoln), Paula Kelly (Leggy Peggy), Lee Chamberlin (Mme. Zenobia), Johnny Sekka (Geechie's Henchman)

p, Melville Tucker; d, Sidney Poitier; w, Richard Wesley; ph, Fred Koenekamp (Technicolor); ed, Pembroke J. Herring; m, Tom Scott; prod d, Alfred Sweeney; fx, Charles Spurgeon

A fine comedy starring and directed by Sidney Poitier, who plays a bored factory worker. He, along with his taxi-driving friend, Cosby, decides to live it up one night, and they venture into a seedy, illegal, underground gambling den for some fun. While they are at the club, gangsters hold up the guests, making off with jewelry, cash, and wallets. When Poitier and Cosby learn that the lottery ticket in Poitier's stolen wallet happens to be worth $50,000, the desperate friends plunge headfirst into the criminal underworld to retrieve it. Pryor turns up as an incompetent private eye, Wilson is a preacher, Browne plays a shady black congressman, and Belafonte steals the movie with a hilarious parody of Marlon Brando's "Godfather" as the mobster who owns the town. The film spawned two sequels: LET'S DO IT AGAIN and A PIECE OF THE ACTION.

URBAN COWBOY

1980   135m   c   ★★
Drama   PG/15
Paramount

John Travolta (Bud), Debra Winger (Sissy), Scott Glenn (Wes), Madolyn Smith (Pam), Barry Corbin (Uncle Bob), Brooke Alderson (Aunt Corene), Cooper Huckabee (Marshall), James Gammon

(Steve Strange), Betty Murphy (Bud's Mom), Ed Geldart (Bud's Dad)

p, Robert Evans, Irving Azoff; d, James Bridges; w, James Bridges, Aaron Latham (based on a story by Latham); ph, Reynaldo Villalobos (Panavision, Movielab Color); ed, David Rawlins; m, Ralph Burns; prod d, Stephen Grimes; art d, Stewart Campbell; chor, Patsy Swayze

If you can accept John Travolta as a Texan half of the problems of URBAN COWBOY have been surmounted. Here he plays a country boy who ventures to the big city to work at an oil refinery. Soon he is immersed in the nightlife that revolves around Gilley's, a cavernous honky-tonk, and meets sexy Debra Winger. After a brief, intense courtship the two are married, but problems soon plague the relationship. Aside from Winger's winning performance, not much else here is interesting, save for Scott Glenn's solid portrayal of a heavy. Director James Bridges fails to instill much life into this story full of vapid characters.

USED CARS

1980   113m   c   ★★★½
Comedy   R/15
Columbia

Kurt Russell (Rudy Russo), Jack Warden (Roy L. Fuchs/Luke Fuchs), Gerrit Graham (Jeff), Frank McRae (Jim, the Mechanic), Deborah Harmon (Barbara Fuchs), Joe Flaherty (Sam Slaton), David L. Lander (Freddie Paris), Michael McKean (Eddie Winslow), Michael Talbott (Mickey), Harry Northrup (Carmine)

p, Bob Gale; d, Robert Zemeckis; w, Robert Zemeckis, Bob Gale; ph, Donald Morgan (Metrocolor); ed, Michael Kahn; m, Patrick Williams; prod d, Peter Jamison

Before director-writer Bob Zemeckis found success with blockbuster hits ROMANCING THE STONE and BACK TO THE FUTURE, he directed this raunchy, hysterically funny comedy. Kurt Russell turns in a brilliant performance as Rudy Russo, the unscrupulous but likable head salesman of a dying used car lot owned by Roy L. Fuchs (Jack Warden). Roy's brother, Luke (also played by Warden), owns a successful car lot across the street and is conspiring to get Roy's property. When Roy dies Rudy and his colleague Jeff (Gerrit Graham) try to conceal the death from Roy's daughter (Deborah Harmon) and Luke. Filled with riotous plot twists and effective black humor, this is a truly inventive and memorable comedy, which was virtually ignored at the box office. Fans of television's "Hill Street Blues" may want to look for Betty Thomas as a topless dancer (a role she would no doubt like to forget) bumping and grinding in one of the R-rated commercials with which Rudy jams a Presidential address.

UTU

1984   104m   c   ★★★½
Drama   R/15
Utu/NZ Film Commission   (New Zealand)

Anzac Wallace (Te Wheke), Bruno Lawrence (Williamson), Kelly Johnson (Lt. Scott), Wi Kuki Kaa (Wiremu), Tim Elliot (Col. Elliot), Ilona Rodgers (Emily), Tania Bristowe (Kura), Martyn Sanderson (Vicar), Faenza Reuben (Henare), John Bach (Belcher)

p, Geoff Murphy, Don Blakeney; d, Geoff Murphy; w, Geoff Murphy, Keith Aberdein; ph, Graeme Cowley (Fujicolor); ed, Michael Horton, Ian John; m, John Charles; prod d, Ron Highfield; art d, Rick Kofoed; cos, Michael Kane

One of the best films yet to emerge from the budding New Zealand cinema, UTU (Maori for "retribution") deals with the

British colonial presence on the islands in the 1870s. Te Wheke (Anzac Wallace) is a Maori in the service of the British army as a scout and guide. One day, while going about his scouting duties, he comes across a village that the British have wiped out in a massacre. It is Wheke's own village, and he then deserts the British to seek revenge against them. With a small group of similarly angry renegades, he launches a campaign of terror and murder against the British. When they attack an isolated farm, murdering the woman of the house and burning it to the ground, Williamson (Bruno Lawrence) also takes up the search for revenge. Wallace, his face covered with ritual tattoos, is a superb actor, and his conversion from loyal British subject to killer is quite believable. Lawrence, the star of most of the successful films to come from New Zealand, is similarly excellent as he is driven to revenge for the same reasons. The most expensive film in New Zealand's history, UTU was a major success at home and abroad.

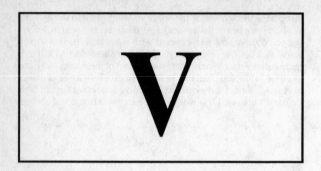

VAGABOND

(SANS TOIT NI LOI)
1985   105m   c   ★★★½
Drama   /18
Cine Tamaris/Ministere de la Culture/A2   (France)

Sandrine Bonnaire (Mona), Macha Meril (Madame Landier), Stephane Freiss (Jean-Pierre), Laurence Cortadellas (Elaine), Marthe Jarnias (Tante Lydie), Yolande Moreau (Yolande), Joel Fosse (Paulo), Patrick Lepcynski, Yahiaoui Assouna, Setti Ramdane

p, Oury Milshtein; d, Agnes Varda; w, Agnes Varda; ph, Patrick Blossier; ed, Agnes Varda, Patricia Mazuy; m, Joanna Bruzdowicz

Atmospheric, cold, and distancing, yet somehow engaging, VAGABOND combines a stylized documentary technique with the fictional vision of writer-director Agnes Varda. The picture opens in the dead of winter, as a farmhand discovers a woman's frozen corpse in a ditch—her long hair a tangle of knots, her skin hidden beneath a well-worn leather jacket and filthy blue jeans. This was Mona (Bonnaire), a fiercely independent "vagabond" whose last weeks are reconstructed in flashback and in "interviews" (both with actors and nonprofessionals Varda found during shooting) with people who met Mona. It soon becomes clear, however, that no one really knew her. Mona is not a character many will entirely like or identify with, nor is one expected to. Varda presents her story without any sentiment, and in the process she tells the stories of a number of different people whose lives were altered, perhaps permanently, by their contact with the vagabond.

After working in the shadow of the more popular French New Wave directors for years, the then 57-year-old Varda broke new ground in narrative film with her methods in VAGABOND. Her visual prowess is on ample display as well, potently rendering a rich portrait of Mona and her world. Equal credit for the movie's success, however, must go to Bonnaire, who perfectly transforms herself into the filthy, aimless, and enigmatic wanderer that the role calls for. Bonnaire justly won a French Cesar for her remarkable performance, and the film itself took the Golden Lion for Best Picture at the Venice Film Festival.

VALLEY GIRL

1983   95m   c   ★★★½
Romance   R/15
Atlantic

Nicolas Cage (Randy), Deborah Foreman (Julie Richman), Elizabeth Daily (Loryn), Michael Bowen (Tommy), Cameron Dye (Fred), Heidi Holicker (Stacey), Michelle Meyrink (Suzie), Tina Theberge (Samantha), Lee Purcell (Beth Brent), Colleen Camp (Sarah Richman)

p, Wayne Crawford, Andrew Lane; d, Martha Coolidge; w, Wayne Crawford, Andrew Lane; ph, Frederick Elmes; ed, Eva Gordos; m, Scott Wilk, Marc Levinthal; prod d, Mary Delia Javier

Insightful and genuine, VALLEY GIRL tells the unlikely tale of Julie (Deborah Foreman), a deb from the Valley, and Randy (Nicholas Cage), a punk rocker from Hollywood, falling in love. As prom time approaches, Julie bows to pressure from her friends to stop dating the "creep" from "Hollyweird." She dumps Randy for her old boyfriend, Tommy (Michael Bowen), a mindless jock. Randy tries a number of unsuccessful stunts to win her back, then reluctantly decides to go to the prom and force a confrontation. This simplified Romeo and Juliet tale was written and performed with such heart and care that it is impossible to dislike. The cast is wonderful, headed by the engaging couple of Cage and Foreman and wittily directed by Coolidge. VALLEY GIRL also boasts an eclectic pop score that features songs by Modern English, Josie Cotton, Men at Work, The Plimsouls, Sparks, Psychedelic Furs, and Eddie Grant, among others.

VAMPYR

(VAMPYR, OU L'ETRANG E AVENTURE DE DAVID GRAY)
1932   83m   bw   ★★★★★
Horror
Dreyer/Tobis/Klangfilm   (France/Germany)

Julian West (David Gray), Henriette Gerard (Marguerite Chopin), Jan Hieronimko (Doctor), Maurice Schutz (Lord of the Manor), Rena Mandel (His Daughter Gisele), Sybille Schmitz (His Daughter Leone), Albert Bras (Servant), N. Babanini (The Girl), Jane Mora (The Religious Woman)

p, Baron Nicolas de Gunzberg, Carl-Theodor Dreyer; d, Carl-Theodor Dreyer; w, Carl-Theodor Dreyer, Christen Jul (based on stories from In a Glass Darkly by Joseph Sheridan Le Fanu); ph, Rudolph Mate, Louis Nee; m, Wolfgang Zeller; art d, Hermann Warm, Hans Bittmann, Cesare Silvagni

Much to the dismay of his admirers, Danish filmmaker Dreyer followed his silent masterpiece THE PASSION OF JOAN OF ARC with a horror film. The result, his first foray into sound, was the greatest vampire film ever made and one of the few undisputed masterpieces of the horror genre. Thrillseekers, beware, though, because it's not that kind of film. VAMPYR, rather, is subtly unsettling rather than gory or shocking; it is such stuff as nightmares are made of.

Loosely based on the Le Fanu collection of stories, In a Glass Darkly, the film begins as young David Gray (West) arrives in a dark, mysterious European village and takes a room at the inn. That night a strange old man (Schutz) gives gives him a package to be opened in the event of his death. David later witnesses many strange events, among which is the murder of the old man. David meets the dead man's daughters (Schmitz and Mandel) and opens the package, which contains a copy of Strange Tales of Vampires. Realizing that the town is at the mercy of one of the undead (Gerard), David struggles to save himself and the two young women.

Such are the bare bones of the plot, but its unfolding, leisurely and fragmented, is not of tantamount importance. What really matters are features like the muffled offscreen sounds and the lack of dialogue explaining them; the misty shooting style (achieved via filters and by working at dawn); and Zeller's spare but sinister music (a highlight is his "Shadow Polka"). The sequence using this music subtly suggests the vampire's power. Angry at the villagers's revels she cannot join, she stands alone, framed in silhouette by a doorway and with large wheels around her. She shrieks for quiet and, without a cutaway, Dreyer tells us her command has been obeyed. Another sequence, in which the one-legged gamekeeper's shadow leaves his body behind to do the vampire's bidding, is also left unexplained. Throughout VAMPYR, a deep, muffling sense of terror slowly envelops both village and viewer, reinforced by Dreyer's brilliantly disjunctive construction of space. Mate's cinematography creates many memorable images, from the scythe-bearer by the water to the tainted elder sister awakening to the call of bloodlust as she eyes her innocent sibling. The marvelous Schmidt (remembered in the title role of Frank Wysbar's classic FERRYMAN MARIA), in the difficult role of the semi-vampire daughter, makes this moment one of the most horrific in the entire film. Best of all, though, are two more famous sequences. The doctor, one of the vampire's accomplices, meets his doom in a flour mill, smothered by the cascading (and purifying) white dust as the agonizingly slow workings of fate and the machinery take their toll. Earlier, David, after donating blood to help a victim, dreams of his own burial. Handled largely from David's view, with the sealing of the coffin lid, the ride to the cemetery and the icy glimpse of the elderly vampiress through the coffin window, this imitated but never duplicated sequence must rank among the greatest uses of point-of-view camera ever filmed. Sensual but remote and vague, gripping and yet somehow unsatisfying, VAMPYR is yet another of Dreyer's brilliant meditations on faith, love and salvation. For him, the vampire's curse haunts the soul foremost, and this unique film experience is likely to haunt your memory long after the film runs out.

VANISHING, THE
(SPOORLOOS)
1991   120m   c   ★★★★½
Mystery/Drama   /12
Golden Egg Films/MGS Film/Ingrid Productions
(Netherlands)

Gene Bervoets *(Rex Hofman)*, Johanna Ter Steege *(Saskia Wagter)*, Bernard-Pierre Donnadieu *(Raymond Lemorne)*, Gwen Eckhaus *(Lienexe)*, Bernadette LeSache *(Simone Lemorne)*, Tania Latarjet *(Denise)*, Lucille Glenn *(Gabrielle)*, Roger Souza *(Manager)*, Caroline Apperre *(Cashier)*, Pierre Forget *(Farmer Laurent)*

p, Anne Lordon, George Sluizer; d, George Sluizer; w, George Sluizer, Tim Krabbe (adapted from his novel *The Golden Egg*); ph, Toni Kuhn; ed, George Sluizer, Lin Friedman; m, Henry Vrienten; art d, Santiago Isidro Pin, Cor Spijk; cos, Sophie Dussaud

Through some fiendish alchemy,THE VANISHING manages to scare people out of their wits more effectively than a legion of better-known horror films. This Dutch production has a pleasantly efficient veneer to it that hides a truly awesome undercurrent.

Two young Dutch lovers are motoring through France. They are flushed with optimism and affection for each other. While arguing playfully, Saskia Wagter (Johanna Ter Steege), the young woman, tells Rex Hofman (Gene Bervoets), the young man, her recurring dream. She is trapped in a golden egg in the midst of darkness with no hope of escaping. Recently, she tells Rex, she has dreamt of another egg traveling beside her. When their car stalls in the middle of a dark tunnel, Saskia has an emotional explosion of claustrophobia and abandonment. Her lover cruelly neglects her, going off to get some gas. Returning, the two make up quickly. They stop at a nearby gas station. Saskia goes to make a purchase in the store. Rex waits for her outside. She never comes back. Three years later Rex is still searching for Saskia.

As Rex searches, the audience is introduced to Raymond Lemorne (Bernard-Pierre Donnadieu) who, through different time frames, slowly reveals Saskia's fate. It is only in the last few moments of the film that the mystery is fully revealed to us. And those moments are deeply horrific.

The choice of actors in this film is uncanny. Johanna Ter Steege's vanished Saskia is luminous in her opening scenes. Her presence continues to haunt the film after her disappearance. And Bernard-Pierre Donnadieu as Raymond Lemorne does a remarkable job. Lemorne is a sociopath and, unlike the scores of other movie villains, Donnadieu's Lemorne's humanity is not a conceit. His beneficence makes his monstrousness even more hard to take. The director, George Sluizer, lets the whole film play out in a contemporary world of freeways, efficiency lighting and sports commentary spilling over from the radio. Into this banal universe he plays out themes that haven't been so effectively conjured up since the early 60s.

THE VANISHING recalls Antonioni's L'AVVENTURA and the precise horror films of Claude Chabrol. But Sluizer's film is more deeply disturbing than any of those masters' works. It's as if, in the lapse of 30 years, cinematic existentialism has been stripped of its modishness and smugness. And Sluizer has also added a weird dose of romanticism to the existentialist bleakness, coming up with a vision of mankind's fate that is stranger than any of the old new wave masters could have imagined. In THE VANISHING we finally see with our own eyes what might have happened to the woman who disappeared in L'AVVENTURA 31 years ago.

VERA CRUZ
1954   94m   c   ★★★
Western   /A
Hecht/Hill/Lancaster

Gary Cooper *(Benjamin Trane)*, Burt Lancaster *(Joe Erin)*, Denise Darcel *(Countess Marie Duvarre)*, Cesar Romero *(Marquis de Labordere)*, Sarita Montiel *(Nina)*, George Macready *(Emperor Maximilian)*, Ernest Borgnine *(Donnegan)*, Morris Ankrum *(Gen. Aguilar)*, Henry Brandon *(Danette)*, Charles Bronson *(Pittsburgh)*

p, James Hill; d, Robert Aldrich; w, Roland Kibbee, James R. Webb (based on the story by Borden Chase); ph, Ernest Laszlo (SuperScope, Technicolor); ed, Alan Crosland, Jr.; m, Hugo Friedhofer

This broadly played, action-packed western teams Cooper and Lancaster as two American soldiers of fortune on a foray into Mexico during the revolution of 1866. Cooper, a former Confederate major, and Lancaster, a constantly grinning outlaw, leave the US in search of mercenary work. It doesn't matter to them which side they fight for, as long as it pays better than the other. In Mexico they meet a beautiful young girl, Montiel, who falls for Cooper and begs him and his partner to fight for Juarez and the revolutionaries. The American gunslingers are tugged in the opposite direction by Romero, a supporter of Maximilian, who offers them huge sums of cash. While mulling the offers over, Cooper and Lancaster encounter Darcel, a seductive and extremely rich countess who asks them to escort her while she transports a gold shipment from Mexico City to Maximilian's forces in Vera Cruz. The men agree and quickly assemble a motley crew of gunfighters and government regulars to accompany them through the rough territory. On the trail, the wily Darcel suggests that they steal the gold and split it three ways. The Americans agree to the plan, with each suspecting the other of planning double crosses. Maximilian loyalist Romero discovers the plot and takes off with the gold to make sure it gets delivered. The Americans chase Romero to the fort in Vera Cruz, and after a bloody battle, Lancaster manages to get his hands on the gold. Cooper, however, has had a change of heart due to Montiel's revolutionary fervor, and demands Lancaster hand over the gold to Juarez's forces. Lancaster doesn't buy Cooper's commitment to the revolution and refuses to release the gold. Cooper is forced to kill Lancaster in a showdown and then gives the gold to Montiel.

The film is directed with an emphasis on action by Aldrich (who had just guided Lancaster through APACHE the year before), and most of the actors in VERA CRUZ are allowed to ham it up quite a bit. For contrast there is Cooper, forever the tight-lipped, serious professional wary of those around him, especially Lancaster's grinning gunman. The film was produced by Lancaster's own company on a budget of $1.7 million and became quite a hit, grossing more than $11 million worldwide, though critical opinion at the time was extremely negative. Lancaster gladly gave top billing to Cooper, well aware of the older actor's box-office pull. As is typical with director Aldrich's work, the violence is well staged and frequent, going a bit overboard at times specifically with regard to Darcel, who is shown being slapped and knocked about by Lancaster more than once. Aldrich and Lancaster would collaborate again in the 1970s with ULZANA'S RAID and TWILIGHT'S LAST GLEAMING.

VERDICT, THE

1982 129m c ★★★★
Drama R/15
FOX

Paul Newman (Frank Galvin), Charlotte Rampling (Laura Fischer), Jack Warden (Mickey Morrissey), James Mason (Ed Concannon), Milo O'Shea (Judge Hoyle), Lindsay Crouse (Kaitlin Costello Price), Edward Binns (Bishop Brophy), Julie Bovasso (Maureen Rooney), Roxanne Hart (Sally Doneghy), James Handy (Kevin Doneghy)

p, Richard D. Zanuck, David Brown; d, Sidney Lumet; w, David Mamet (based on the novel by Barry Reed); ph, Andrzej Bartkowiak (Panavision, DeLuxe Color); ed, Peter C. Frank; m, Johnny Mandel; prod d, Edward Pisoni; art d, John Kasarda; cos, Anna Hill Johnstone

This powerful study of a man's fight to regain his dignity features a fine performance from Paul Newman as failed attorney Frank Galvin. He takes on a seemingly open-and-shut case of malpractice, in which a woman lapsed into a coma while having a baby, the apparent victim of a mistake by an anesthesiologist at a prominent Catholic hospital in Boston. At first willing to take a settlement for the victim's family, Galvin realizes after visiting the comatose woman that he should put up a fight on her behalf. Up against the powerful Catholic establishment of Boston, he works to build a case, and, with it, renewed self-respect. He is also battling his dependence on alcohol, another reason behind his downfall. Newman's portrayal of his character is a sympathetic and totally candid performance. Every wart shows, from his alcoholism to the ill-prepared opening statement he delivers in a nervous stammer to the packed courtroom. Small moments come across as something special, and the actor received a well-deserved Oscar nomination for his performance. Sidney Lumet directs effectively, keeping the tension strong, and unfolding David Mamet's intelligent screenplay slowly but with maximum impact.

VERONIKA VOSS

(DIE SEHNS UCHT DER VERONIKA VOSS)
1982 105m bw ★★★★
Drama R/AA
Rialto/Maran/Larua/Tango (West Germany)

Rosel Zech (Veronika Voss), Hilmar Thate (Robert Krohn), Cornelia Froboess (Henriette), Annemarie Duringer (Dr. Katz), Doris Schade (Josefa), Erik Schumann (Dr. Edel), Peter Berling (Fat Film Producer), Gunther Kaufmann (G.I. Dealer), Sonja Neudorfer (Saleswoman), Lilo Pempeit (Her Boss)

p, Thomas Schuhly; d, Rainer Werner Fassbinder; w, Peter Marthesheimer, Pia Frohlich, Rainer Werner Fassbinder; ph, Xaver Schwarzenberger; ed, Juliane Lorenz; m, Peer Raben; prod d, Rolf Zehetbauer

At the very end of his amazing yet tragically short career, Fassbinder still gives us his Douglas Sirk-influenced view of the world, except this time colored with Billy Wilder's SUNSET BOULEVARD and Robert Aldrich's THE LEGEND OF LYLAH CLARE for good measure. The result, in typical Fassbinder fashion, is a visually incredible portrait of German corruption as well as the UFA star system and the loneliness of once-famous screen star Veronika Voss (Zech). The fading star is drawn into an affair with sportswriter Robert Krohn (Thate), who soon discovers the actress's dependency on drugs. Her doctor (Duringer) fuels her addiction, forcing Voss to turn over all of her personal property in exchange for more morphine. Krohn and his girlfriend bring the doctor to the attention of the authorities, unaware that they, too, are involved in the doctor's scheme. On Easter Sunday, Voss is locked in her room by the doctor. Suffering from withdrawal symptoms after being refused morphine, she is given enough sleeping pills to kill herself. Zech is quite remarkable at the film's close.

One of the most stylish of Fassbinder's many films, VERONIKA VOSS features dizzying camerawork and stark black-and-white photography. Not among Fassbinder's greatest achievements, this striking film is nonetheless a worthy companion piece to his earlier two films about postwar Germany, THE MARRIAGE OF MARIA BRAUN and LOLA. The actual story is loosely based on the life of Sybille Schmitz (VAMPYR, FERRYMAN MARIA) a gifted German film star who committed suicide in the mid-1950s, unable to cope with the loss of her celebrity.

VERTIGO

1958 127m c ★★★★★
Thriller /PG
Paramount

James Stewart (John "Scottie" Ferguson), Kim Novak (Madeleine Elster/Judy Barton), Barbara Bel Geddes (Midge), Tom Helmore (Gavin Elster), Henry Jones (Coroner), Raymond Bailey (Doctor), Ellen Corby (Manageress), Konstantin Shayne (Pop Leibel), Lee Patrick (Older Mistaken Identity), Paul Bryar (Capt. Hansen)

p, Alfred Hitchcock; d, Alfred Hitchcock; w, Alec Coppel, Samuel Taylor (based on the novel D'Entre les Morts by Pierre Boileau and Thomas Narcejac); ph, Robert Burks (VistaVision, Technicolor); ed, George Tomasini; m, Bernard Herrmann; art d, Hal Pereira, Henry Bumstead; fx, John P. Fulton, Farciot Edouart, Wallace Kelly; cos, Edith Head

The most-discussed work of the master; despairingly sardonic and demanding of multiple viewings. Hitchcock's intensely personal and frighteningly self-revealing picture, VERTIGO is the story of a man Stewart as Hitch) who is possessed by the image of a former love (Novak as Vera Miles) and becomes increasingly compulsive in his attempts to make another woman (Novak as Novak) over in that image. We'll explain.

Stewart is a former San Francisco policeman who suffers from vertigo—a dizzying sensation brought on by his acrophobia. When he gets a call from a former classmate, shipping magnate Gavin Elster (Helmore), he agrees to play detective and shadow the millionaire's wife Madeleine (Novak) whom Elster fears is going to wind up dead. Elster ominously asks him "Do you believe that someone dead, someone out of the past, can take possession of a living being?" After following Madeleine for a short while Stewart becomes obsessed with her—lost deep in a labyrinthine plot from which he cannot escape.

Based on a novel by Pierre Boileau and Thomas Narcejac (who previously supplied the source material for DIABOLIQUE), VERTIGO appealed to Hitchcock for reasons which become clearer the more one knows about the director's personality. VERTIGO is, in fact, nothing less than Hitchcock revealing himself to his audience—his obsessions and desire to make over women are embodied in Stewart's character and the perfect Hitchcock woman is embodied in Madeleine. VERTIGO is also a masterpiece of filmmaking which includes one of the most important technical discoveries since the dawn of cinema— the *dolly-out, zoom-in* shot, which visually represents the dizzying sensation of vertigo. The result is a shot unique to Hitchcock, unlike any other before in film, one which will always bear his stamp.

But more than that, the behind-the-scenes preparation of VERTIGO resembles the story itself. Hitchcock had directed Vera Miles in THE WRONG MAN, and stood poised to make her a star in VERTIGO. This would be, of course, according to Hitchcock tradition: the cool blonde, whose whorish carnality is hidden beneath sleekly understated clothes and simple hair. But his plan went awry when Miles married after filming was over and soon became pregnant ("I lost interest. I couldn't get the rhythm going with her again," said Hitchcock in an interview, but later he threw her a bone in PSYCHO). He convinced Novak to take the role; her somnambulistic quality made her very effective in the role, but he and Edith Head had hell convincing her to tone down.

Yet perhaps Novak is the unsung quintessential Hitch-heroine. Hitchcock himself described Stewart's character's obsession with Novak's as a "form of necrophilia"; it's chilling when you think of the director re-creating his dreamgirl again and again. Novak's heroine is degraded by suffusing her own idenity to become what men want her to be. Did she feel degraded when Hitchcock and Head tried to bury the established Novak? Did it make her feel like a cheap pawn, forced to impersonate a lady, that is in itself an impersonation, within the confines of an acting job (an impersonation anyway)? And how much of her real self—Marilyn Novik—had fused with the manufactured Kim Novak? The latter was a star persona placed in an impossible-to-please situation in the first place. Groomed as a successor to Hayworth and a threat to Monroe, it's small wonder Novak fled the film industry to hide in Big Sur. To examine her within the context of VERTIGO is another dizzying vortex—a virtual vertigo in itself.

VICTIM

1961 100m bw   ★★★★
Crime   /15
Parkway/Allied (U.K.)

Dirk Bogarde *(Melville Farr)*, Sylvia Syms *(Laura Farr)*, Dennis Price *(Calloway)*, Anthony Nicholls *(Lord Fullbrook)*, Peter Copley *(Paul Mandrake)*, Norman Bird *(Harold Doe)*, Peter McEnery *(Jack Barrett)*, Donald Churchill *(Eddy Stone)*, Derren Nesbitt *(Sandy Youth)*, John Barrie *(Detective Inspector Harris)*

p, Michael Relph; d, Basil Dearden; w, Janet Green, John McCormick; ph, Otto Heller; ed, John D. Guthridge; m, Philip Green; art d, Alex Vetchinsky

A powerful film that deals with homosexuality in England and the fact that most of the blackmail cases in that country were aimed against men trying to stay in the closet. In 1961, any homosexual acts were illegal and, while this film was hardly an overt plea to change the laws, it did have some impact; a few years later homosexuality was no longer punishable by time in jail. Bogarde, in one of the best roles of his career to date, plays Melville Farr, a closeted lawyer aware of his own homosexual desires. He is married now to Laura (Syms), who knows about his past affairs but accepts him nonetheless. Some years before, Farr had an affair with construction worker Jack Barrett (McEnery) but denies it. Barrett is now a wanted man, having stolen money from his building company. When he's caught by the police, the truth emerges that Barrett doesn't have a brass farthing to his name. Since a great deal of money had been purloined, this sets the law to wondering where it all went. Barrett needs a lawyer and tries to contact Farr, but the eminent queen's counsel avoids him. When Barrett hangs himself rather than answer any police questions, Farr realizes that his former lover was being blackmailed and that Barrett was trying to protect Farr's good name. The blackmailers are extracting money from several people, including a barber, an actor, a used car salesman and a photographer. (The film earnestly tries to avoid stereotyping, though to some extent these "victims" do represent a variety of "types".) Although it may damage both his career and his marriage, Farr decides to go after the blackmailers and prosecute them himself.

Immensely significant in its plea for tolerance for gay men (interestingly, lesbianism is not discussed here), VICTIM works hard arguing that gays are part of the typical, healthy fabric of society. For that alone, it was highly controversial and was refused the Seal of the Motion Picture Association of America. On its own terms, the film works quite well. The drama is exciting, the writing cogent, the acting often superb and the production and direction by the team of Dearden and Relph quite fine. Every role, no matter how small, is very intelligently cast and even the blackmailers were given some depth and character contradictions. In acting terms, the film quite properly belongs to the dynamic yet sensitive Bogarde, but McEnery, as his former lover, and Price, as a blackmailed actor, also stand out. The film does, of course, shy away from certain aspects of its provocative subject matter, and a great deal of emphasis is laid on Farr's heterosexual relations with his wife. (It probably takes up more footage than is actually necessary, but this subplot broadens the role of Farr and is fairly well handled.) A liberal film on the subject of homosexuality rather than the radical film some considered it at the time, VICTIM still stands as an intelligent film attempting to address an important social issue.

VICTORIA THE GREAT

1937 110m c/bw   ★★★★
Biography/Historical   /U
Imperator (U.K.)

VICTOR/VICTORIA

Anna Neagle (*Queen Victoria*), Anton Walbrook (*Prince Albert*), Walter Rilla (*Prince Ernest*), Mary Morris (*Duchess of Kent*), H.B. Warner (*Lord Melbourne*), Grete Wegener (*Baroness Lehzen*), C.V. France (*Archbishop of Canterbury*), James Dale (*Duke of Wellington*), Charles Carson (*Sir Robert Peel*), Hubert Harben (*Lord Conyngham*)

p, Herbert Wilcox; d, Herbert Wilcox; w, Miles Malleson, Charles de Grandcourt (based on the play "Victoria Regina" by Laurence Housman); ph, Freddie Young; m, Anthony Collins

This beautiful and elaborate film gives an intimate portrait of England's long-reigning monarch, following her from the first years of her reign to the celebration of her Diamond Jubilee. Neagle is excellent as Victoria, who assumes the throne at the age of 18. The film details her courtship and marriage to Prince Albert (Walbrook), and a foiled attempt on the queen's life, thwarted when Albert risks death himself to shield Victoria from the would-be assassin. The story then concentrates on the royal couple's domestic life, with such figures as Disraeli, Wellington, and Lincoln introduced peripherally. Closing with the Jubilee, the film switches from black and white to a brilliant Technicolor.

Fictionalizing the lives of the royal family has long been a touchy issue in England, but producer-director Wilcox treats his subject respectfully, avoiding treacly sentiment. Neagle (who would later marry Wilcox) is completely believable as she takes her character from young girl to octogenarian, and is a marvel to watch as she transcends her craft and becomes the character. Released 100 years after Victoria began her reign, the film was enormously popular in England, prompting Wilcox, Neagle, and Walbrook to make a sequel, SIXTY GLORIOUS YEARS (1938), an all-color production that concentrated more on the political events of Victoria's rule. In 1942, Wilcox cut the first portion of VICTORIA THE GREAT into the latter half of SIXTY GLORIOUS YEARS to create a single feature, simply titled QUEEN VICTORIA.

Wilcox began production on VICTORIA THE GREAT after Edward VIII (who later abdicated to marry American divorcee Wallis Warfield Simpson) personally requested that the filmmaker produce a feature about the queen. It took an amazingly short five weeks to film. Attention to period detail was immaculate; Neagle's costumes were copied from Victoria's actual dresses, which were kept at the British Museum. Released in America through RKO, VICTORIA THE GREAT was popular in its initial run at Radio City Music Hall, where it turned a handsome profit, but it did not fare as well in smaller cities. Both Neagle and Wilcox toured the US to promote the film, though this too was not as successful as its backers hoped. However, Wilcox's association with RKO did result in a lucrative agreement with the studio, under which the independent producer was to turn out a number of features under the American company's banner, an arrangement that helped reduce the burden of the United Kingdom's restrictive quotas on domestic screenings of imported films. VICTORIA THE GREAT also features Paul Henreid in his first British film, appearing in a small role under his real name.

VICTOR/VICTORIA

1982 133m c   ★★★
Musical/Comedy   PG/15
MGM (U.K.)

Julie Andrews (*Victor/Victoria*), James Garner (*King*), Robert Preston (*Toddy*), Lesley Ann Warren (*Norma*), Alex Karras (*Squash*), John Rhys-Davies (*Cassell*), Graham Stark (*Waiter*), Peter Arne (*Labisse*), Sherloque Tanney (*Bovin*), Michael Robbins (*Hotel Manager*)

p, Blake Edwards, Tony Adams; d, Blake Edwards; w, Blake Edwards (based on the film VICTOR UND VIKTORIA by Rheinhold Schuenzel, Hans Hoemburg); ph, Dick Bush (Panavision, Metrocolor); ed, Ralph E. Winters; m, Henry Mancini; prod d, Rodger Maus; art d, Tim Hutchinson, William Craig Smith; chor, Paddy Stone; cos, Patricia Norris

A musical boudoir farce, captivating at times, infuriating at others. A British singer (Julie Andrews) and an aging homosexual (Robert Preston) are down-and-out nightclub performers in Paris. Hungry and broke, they're desperate for employment until Toddy (Preston) recasts his friend as the female impersonator singer-dancer Victor/Victoria—putting the chanteuse in the unusual position of being a woman who pretends to be a man who performs as a woman onstage. She is an immediate hit at a local nightclub, where King (James Garner), a gangster from Chicago traveling with his blowsy girlfriend (a Jean Harlowesque Lesley Ann Warren) and his bodyguard, Squash (Alex Karras), sees her perform. King is attracted to Victor/Victoria, but thinks, like everyone else, that she is a transvestite. The burly Squash, meanwhile, watches in amazement as his macho boss apparently loses his yen for beautiful women and becomes attracted to his own kind.

Edward's film forces audiences to examine their own ideas about gender and sexuality, and that's great. But Andrews, despite looking very Berlin Bowie in her tux, is so safe and sane, she brings no madness of her own to the farce. Everything therefore swirls around a still center—in the film's one good number, "Le Jazz Hot", she climbs a staircase like she has weights on her feet. Nor can she summon any of the impersonator's hauteur or joy to her masquerade. Robert Preston is wonderful—he plays a cliche with such malice and relish, he revitalizes it, and Garner is successful kidding his own past macho image. A platinumed Warren is also quite good, but Edwards makes her dopey sweetness go sour—he humiliates her, especially in a chorus line number that could make a feminist a raging virago. Will someone please give Warren a role worthy of her undeniable talent? The film's best moments are early on: Andrews warbling for disinterested cabaret owners, or the preparation of Victoria to become Victor. After that, this becomes increasingly coarse and overstated. Edwards directs like a grizzly bear whipping up a souffle. V/V won an Oscar for song score and adaptation. The screenplay was based on VIKTOR UND VIKTORIA, a 1933 German film, first refashioned in 1935 into a star vehicle for the ever-delightful Jessie Mathews, FIRST A GIRL.

VIDEODROME

1983 88m c   ★★★½
Horror   R/18
Filmplan (Canada)

James Woods (*Max Renn*), Sonja Smits (*Bianca O'Blivion*), Deborah Harry (*Nicki Brand*), Peter Dvorsky (*Harlan*), Les Carlson (*Barry Convex*), Jack Creley (*Prof. Brian O'Blivion*), Lynne Gorman (*Masha*), Julie Khaner (*Briley*), Reiner Schwarz (*Moses*), David Bolt (*Rafe*)

p, Claude Heroux; d, David Cronenberg; w, David Cronenberg; ph, Mark Irwin; ed, Ronald Sanders; m, Howard Shore; prod d, Carol Spier; art d, Nick Kosonic; fx, Frank Carere, Rick Baker, Michael Lennick; chor, Kirsteen Etherington; cos, Delphine White

Director David Cronenberg's most visionary and audacious film up to the time of its making, VIDEODROME is a fascinating rumination on humanity, technology, entertainment, sex, and politics that is virtually incomprehensible on first viewing and needs to be seen several times before one can even begin to unlock its mysteries. James Woods, in one of the best performances of his career, stars as Max Renn, an ambitious cable television programmer who, in his off hours, is a closet voyeur of sex and violence. Looking for something new, something "sensational" for his cable station, Renn stumbles across a show called "Videodrome" while pirating signals from satellite dishes. The show seems to depict the actual torture and murder of a different victim every night. Fascinated and excited by the program, Renn tries to find out where the show originates. During the investigation, he becomes deeply embroiled in a bizarre, intriguing, and sometimes incomprehensible fusion of television, politics, and mind-control that seems to herald some sort of "New Order" for society.

VIDEODROME very well may be the most incomprehensible mainstream film ever made. As Cronenberg's narrative veers from hallucination to reality and back again—the line between them more blurred each time—he unleashes his bizarre visual imagination, bombarding viewers with such sights as an open stomach cavity that becomes a repository for videocassettes and guns, throbbing television sets, a literal hand-gun, and humans who crack open and spew forth all manner of flesh, blood, and multicolored goo. While these images are undeniably powerful (the throbbing, living television set is amazing) and the film is compulsively watchable, it does tend to become wholly impenetrable toward the end and may leave the uninitiated frustrated or even angry. Nevertheless, this is a remarkable film that will continue to be debated and analyzed for decades to come.

VIKINGS, THE
1958 114m c   ★★★
Adventure/Historical   /A
Bryna

Kirk Douglas *(Einar)*, Tony Curtis *(Eric)*, Ernest Borgnine *(King Ragnar)*, Janet Leigh *(Princess Morgana)*, James Donald *(Lord Egbert)*, Alexander Knox *(Father Godwin)*, Frank Thring *(King Aella)*, Maxine Audley *(Enid)*, Eileen Way *(Kitala)*, Edric Connor *(Sandpiper)*

p, Jerry Bresler; d, Richard Fleischer; w, Dale Wasserman, Calder Willingham (based on the novel *The Viking* by Edison Marshall); ph, Jack Cardiff (Technirama, Technicolor); ed, Elmo Williams; m, Mario Nascimbene; prod d, Harper Goff

Viking warriors led by Borgnine raid the English coast, raping and plundering. In one small kingdom, he kills the king and rapes the queen. The child who is born as a result of that assault grows up to be Curtis, a Viking slave who knows nothing of his parentage. He and Douglas, Borgnine's legitimate son, take a dislike to each other and fight a duel, during which Curtis' falcon claws out one of Douglas' eyes. Enraged, Douglas orders the slave tossed into a pit of giant crabs. Curtis is saved when Donald, who was banished from England and is planning his return with Viking help, recognizes an amulet Curtis wears which proclaims his true identity. On another raid, the Norsemen carry off princess Leigh, and Douglas decides he wants her, although she has fallen

in love with Curtis. Leigh and Curtis escape one night, and when Douglas and Borgnine chase them, the pursuing boat crashes on the rocks in the fjord and sinks. Borgnine is pulled aboard by Curtis and taken to England as a gift for evil king Thring. Thring orders the old Viking chieftain thrown to their more civilized variation of the giant crab pit—the ravenous wolf pit. Thring laughs when Borgnine asks to die like a Viking, with a sword in his hand, but Curtis takes pity and cuts his hands free and gives him his own sword. Borgnine almost gleefully jumps into the pit with a shout and manages to take a few wolves to Valhalla with him. Thring is outraged, mostly at the loss of his precious wolves, and orders that Curtis' hand be chopped off and he be set adrift in the North Sea. The boat, of course, drifts straight back to Norway where Curtis tells Douglas the fate of his father, and the two decide to put aside their mutual hatred to seek vengeance on Thring. They sail to England and attack the castle, and Douglas then frees Leigh and proposes marriage. She tells him she loves Curtis and, when Douglas vows to kill him, she reveals that they are half-brothers. Curtis shows up and the two fight a duel on the battlements of the castle. Douglas gets the upper hand and is about to kill Curtis, but he hesitates, apparently reluctant to kill his own kin. Curtis knows nothing about any blood ties and uses Douglas' moment of indecision to drive his own blade into his foe. The film concludes as Douglas is given a Viking funeral, set adrift on a burning longship.

A rousing adventure, despite a great deal of out-and-out silliness, this film was a major ordeal to make. The projected $2.5 million budget doubled as the studio leased the rights to an entire fjord, constructed a Viking village on a rock in the middle of it, and built a fleet of longships copied from reproductions in museums. The cast and crew were housed on two ships moored in the fjord and were shuttled back and forth by a fleet of 17 old PT boats. Weather proved a problem: of the 60 shooting days in Norway, 49 were rainy and dark. Finally the camera crew improvised a way to protect the camera from the elements, and some haunting shots of Viking longships gliding through the rain and fog were captured. Douglas and Borgnine give memorably bombastic performances—Douglas leering with his milked-over eye and Borgnine shouting war cries through his bushy beard as he happily meets his death in the wolf pit. Curtis is less memorable and seems as out of place as he always does in these swashbucklers. The production values are all top drawer, and, thanks to a publicity campaign that included sending Viking dagger letter openers to reviewers, having seven Norwegians sail a longship from Oslo to New York, and lifting another longship onto the marquee of the New York theater where it debuted, the film was a big moneymaker.

VILLAGE OF THE DAMNED
1960 77m bw   ★★★
Horror/Science Fiction   /A
MGM (U.K.)

George Sanders *(Gordon Zellaby)*, Barbara Shelley *(Anthea Zellaby)*, Michael Gwynn *(Maj. Alan Bernard)*, Laurence Naismith *(Dr. Willers)*, John Phillips *(Gen. Leighton)*, Richard Vernon *(Sir Edgar Hargraves)*, Jenny Laird *(Mrs. Harrington)*, Richard Warner *(Mr. Harrington)*, Thomas Heathcote *(James Pawle)*, Alexander Archdale *(Coroner)*

p, Ronald Kinnoch; d, Wolf Rilla; w, Wolf Rilla, Stirling Silliphant, George Barclay (based on the novel *The Midwich Cuckoos* by John Wyndham); ph, Geoffrey Faithfull (Metroscope); ed, Gordon Hales; m, Ron Goodwin; art d, Ivan King; fx, Tom Howard

An incredibly frightening adaptation of the John Wyndham novel about a small English village that becomes the victim of unfriendly aliens. During a 24-hour period all the inhabitants of Midwich are put to sleep, waking to find a dozen of the women pregnant. When these babies are born, their mothers love them as if they were conceived under normal circumstances. However, all of these children look the same, with bright blond hair. The are also possessed of superior intelligence and telekinetic powers. Sanders, a physicist and the husband of Shelley, who has given birth to the leader of the children, undertakes the job of educating these youngsters and soon discovers that their mission is not a friendly one: they plan to take control of the entire planet. Sanders then sees that the children are destroyed, killing himself in the process. Sanders' role required more outward emotion than he had in his repertoire, but this casting mistake is more than compensated for by the weird atmosphere provided by the children. Made in England for less than $300,000, the picture grossed more than $1.5 million in initial release in the US and Canada alone. It spawned a host of possessed-children-as-villains films, including THE OMEN and THE BOYS FROM BRAZIL. This intriguing story also gave rise to a sequel, CHILDREN OF THE DAMNED, which proved every bit as good as the original.

VINCENT AND THEO

1990 138m c   ★★★★
Biography   R/15
Belbo/Central/La Sept/Telepool/RAI Uno/Vara/Sofica Valor
(U.K./France/U.S.)

Tim Roth *(Vincent van Gogh)*, Paul Rhys *(Theodore van Gogh)*, Jip Wijngaarden *(Sien Hoornik)*, Johanna Ter Steege *(Jo Bonger)*, Wladimir Yordanoff *(Paul Gauguin)*, Jean-Pierre Cassel *(Dr. Paul Gachet)*, Bernadette Giraud *(Marguerite Gachet)*, Adrian Brine *(Uncle Cent)*, Jean-Francois Perrier *(Leon Bouscod)*, Vincent Vallier *(Rene Valadon)*

p, Ludi Boeken; d, Robert Altman; w, Julian Mitchell; ph, Jean Lepine (Eastmancolor); ed, Francois Coispeau, Geraldine Peroni; m, Gabriel Yared; prod d, Stephen Altman; art d, Dominique Douret, Ben Van, Jan Roelfs; cos, Scott Bushnell

Altman tackles the monumental story of Vincent van Gogh and his brother Theo and, for the most part, comes up a winner. Working from a minimalist script by Julian Mitchell, the director offers us a stripped-to-the-bones drama that leaves most screen takes on the artistic life—from the Hollywood bombast of LUST FOR LIFE to the self-conscious quirkiness of Derek Jarman's CARAVAGGIO—way behind.

The film's beginning is the director's most audacious conceit. We see actual footage of the painting "Sunflowers" as it is being auctioned off at Christie's, and Altman, one of the keenest users of sound in all cinema, sustains the soundtrack of the bidding during his opening scene between Vincent and Theo. As the brothers argue over the money their rich uncle sends each month to Vincent to sustain his creative, if uncommercial, journey, the point is clearly made about the often arbitrary elusiveness of artistic success. Familiar ground is subsequently covered, including Vincent's fascination with prostitutes and Theo's syphilitic torment. The story continues through Vincent's uneasy friendship with Gauguin, his encroaching mental instability, Theo's personal financial struggles as a gallery owner, and his troubled courtship and marriage to Jo Bonger (Ter Steege). The fate of the two troubled brothers resolves the action.

As photographed by Jean Lepine, the film is visually stunning. VINCENT AND THEO is brimful of the pictorial splendors of nature and the human form, but they are captured fleetingly, in an off-the-cuff kind of way that suggests the finely attuned peripheral vision, the febrile antennae, of an artist. The early scene of Vincent observing and rapidly sketching the whore as she takes a break from posing, stretches, looks through the window at the moon, and even relieves herself, comes as close to depicting the actual creative process of painting as anything ever filmed. The creation of the sunflower paintings is aptly expressed in the silent, sketchy takes of him out in the fields, experiencing quick frustration more than anything else, with the end result a terse, panning shot of his room in Arles, filled with his finished efforts glowing from the walls.

Roth plays Vincent in the great tradition of mumbling, shambling Altman heroes such as Warren Beatty's McCabe or Elliott Gould's Philip Marlowe. His asides are often amusing and he convincingly conveys the artist's recessive nature, along with an accessible quality akin to the more raffish silent movie clowns. Rhys as Theo seems to be enjoying a real turn. If Vincent is the boho tramp of nature, then Rhys' Theo is the epitome of the over-civilized, bloodless urbanite. His performance is riddled with nervous tics, darting, piercing glances, sudden little snits, and abrupt explosions of laughter. It's an oddball performance, mostly repellant, but intermittently redeemed by its little, hard-won payoffs of humor.

VIRGIN SPRING, THE

(JUNGFRUKALLAN)
1960 88m bw   ★★★
Drama   /X
Svensk (Sweden)

Max von Sydow *(Herr Tore)*, Brigitta Pettersson *(Karin Tore)*, Birgitta Valberg *(Mareta Tore)*, Gunnel Lindblom *(Ingeri)*, Axel Duberg *(Thin Herdsman)*, Tor Isedal *(Mute Herdsman)*, Ove Porath *(Boy)*, Allan Edwall *(Beggar)*, Gudrun Brost *(Frida)*, Oscar Ljung *(Simon)*

p, Ingmar Bergman, Allan Ekelund; d, Ingmar Bergman; w, Ulla Isaksson (based on the 14th-century ballad "Tores Dotter I Vange"); ph, Sven Nykvist, Rolf Halmquist; ed, Oscar Rosander; m, Erik Nordgren; art d, P.A. Lundgren; cos, Marik Vos

The Best Foreign-Language Film Oscar awarded to THE VIRGIN SPRING was director Ingmar Bergman's first Academy Award, and the film still numbers among the director's classics. The story takes place in 13th-century Sweden, as Christianity and folklore vie for dominance in the popular belief. Karin (Birgitta Pettersson), the spoiled young virgin daughter of wealthy landowner Tore (Max von Sydow), is to go to church to light candles for the Virgin, and is allowed to wear a special gown, handmade by 15 virgins, on the occasion. Riding in the woods, Karin is raped, and then killed, by shepherds. The men take her gown, hoping to sell it, and move on, arriving at Tore's house, where they receive food and shelter. Their crime is discovered, however, moving Tore to enact bloody revenge and testing the bereaved father's faith. THE VIRGIN SPRING is based on a medieval ballad, and is full of the folk-tale oppositions (a good sister and a bad one) and motifs (the tell-tale gown, the trio of shepherds) so beloved by Bergman (the film is also true to its origins in its extreme violence). As always, those with little affinity for Bergman's preoccupations will find the film overlong and overdone. Most, however, will be rewarded by the depth of the director's moral and religious questioning, the emotional power of the story and acting, the haunting and symbolic imagery, and the excellent black-and-white photography of Sven Nykvist. Nominated by the Academy for Best Costume Design.

VIRGINIAN, THE

1929 92m bw   ★★★½
Western
Famous Players/Paramount

Gary Cooper (The Virginian), Walter Huston (Trampas), Mary Brian (Molly Stark Wood), Richard Arlen (Steve), Helen Ware ("Ma" Taylor), Chester Conklin (Uncle Hughey), Eugene Pallette ("Honey" Wiggin), Victor Potel (Nebraskey), E.H. Calvert (Judge Henry), Tex Young (Shorty)

p, Louis D. Lighton; d, Victor Fleming; w, Howard Estabrook, Edward E. Paramore, Grover Jones, Keene Thompson (based on the play by Owen Wister, Kirk La Shelle, and the novel by Owen Wister); ph, J. Roy Hunt, Edward Cronjager; ed, William Shea

Gary Cooper's first all-talkie, this film adaptation of Owen Wister's popular novel established Cooper's heroic image in the public eye. As the title character, Cooper is foreman of a Wyoming ranch. He gives a job to an old friend, Richard Arlen, with whom he is vying for the affections of schoolmarm Mary Brian. Cooper wins out and Arlen goes bad, taking up with local villain Walter Huston to rustle cattle from Cooper's herd. Cooper catches his friend changing brands and warns him, but when Arlen is later caught stealing cattle again, along with two other rustlers, Cooper oversees the lynching of all three. Plagued by guilt, Cooper swears to get Huston, whom he knows to be the leader of the gang. When Brian finds out what Cooper has done, she rejects him. Later, though, in a skirmish with Huston, Cooper is wounded and Brian takes care of him, eventually agreeing to marry him. On their wedding day, Huston brings matters to a head, and the two men square off in the street for a showdown. Cooper is faster on the draw and Huston dies in the dust. The bit for which this film is most remembered occurs during a card game, when Huston calls Cooper an insulting name. Cooper pulls his gun out, lays it on the table and says, "If you want to call me that, smile." The phrase caught on immediately and was used extensively in advertising for the film. Cooper played his role well, and his performance helped him escape the typecasting he had been saddled with. Now he could play rugged male leads instead of juvenile lovers. Huston is even better, his Trampas the essence of western villainy and the standard to be imitated for years to come. This was the third film of the novel, which had previously been done in 1921 starring Dustin Farnum, and in 1923 starring Kenneth Harlan. A major box-office success, it was remade in 1946 with Joel McCrea, and became a television series in 1962 starring James Drury in the title role.

VIRIDIANA

1961 90m bw   ★★★★★
Drama   /X
Uninci/Films 59/Gustavo Alatriste   (Mexico/Spain)

Silvia Pinal (Viridiana), Francisco Rabal (Jorge), Fernando Rey (Don Jaime), Margarita Lozano (Ramona), Victoria Zinny (Lucia), Teresa Rabal (Rita), Jose Calvo, Joaquin Roa, Luis Heredia, Jose Manuel Martin

p, Ricardo Munoz Suay; d, Luis Bunuel; w, Luis Bunuel, Julio Alejandro (based on a story by Bunuel); ed, Pedro del Rey; m, Wolfgang Amadeus Mozart, George Frederick Handel; art d, Francisco Canet

Luis Bunuel had been absent from his native land for 25 years when he was invited by the Franco government to produce a film in Spain. The result was VIRIDIANA. Ironically, it was never shown in Spanish theaters, having been banned by the Franco government immediately after its debut at the Cannes Film Festival, where it won the Golden Palm. Pinal plays the title role, a religious novitiate who visits her last remaining relative, the wealthy Don Jaime (Rey), before she takes her vows. Viridiana, firmly intent on resisting the corruption of her uncle's estate, is surprised to find him most gracious, kind, and gentle. He, however, is secretly obsessed with her resemblance to his wife, who died 30 years earlier on their wedding night. After Don Jaime attempts to ravish the nun-to-be, who has obliged the lonely man by putting on his wife's wedding gown, he feels such remorse that he commits suicide. Viridiana inherits the estate, along with Don Jaime's son Jorge (Rabal) and she intends to use her new position to benefit the local poor. Once again her virtuous intentions backfire. Oh, that final card game!

VIRIDIANA is filled with allegories concerning the general state of the world and Spain in particular, conveyed with the master surrealist's usual mix of black humor and stunning images. Foremost among them is the famous "Last Supper," in which a group of thoroughly degenerate beggars carouse drunkenly, in a visual parody of Da Vinci's painting, to the strains of Handel's "Messiah." You will never forget this moment. Viridiana, who wishes to redeem these miscreants through her idealism, is mocked in the process—as is the Catholicism that Bunuel believed had to be overthrown if Spain was to avoid becoming a decaying mess like Don Jaime's estate. Viridiana's ineffectual faith is contrasted with Jorge's more beneficial pragmatism. The changes he attempts to realize can perhaps do but minimal good, as indicated in one of Bunuel's most famous jokes: just after Jorge has rescued a dog that was being dragged mercilessly from a cart by buying it from its owner, the director shows another cur in the same predicament, attached to another cart coming from the opposite direction. Still, Jorge does represent a practical approach to achieving modest changes for the better. Immediately after the film was shot, it was shipped to Paris, where it was quickly edited in time for Cannes. Spanish authorities, who had not seen the final print before the festival screening, were shocked when it won the Golden Palm. Further scandal followed the film to Italy, where Bunuel was threatened with a prison sentence if he entered the country. Despite all this controversy, VIRIDIANA has a deceptively artless quality, stemming from the poetic formality with which Bunuel allows the picture to unfold. He steered away from complex and confusing images or camera movement, and created, along with THE EXTERMINATING ANGEL, one of the most magnificent films of his incredible career.

VITELLONI

(I VITELLONI)
1953 103m bw   ★★★★
Drama
PEG/Cite   (Italy/France)

Franco Interlenghi (Moraldo), Franco Fabrizi (Fausto), Alberto Sordi (Alberto), Leopoldo Trieste (Leopoldo), Riccardo Fellini (Riccardo), Leonora Ruffo (Sandra), Lida Baarova (Guilia), Arlette Sauvage (Woman in the Cinema), Maja Nipora (Actress), Jean Brochard (Father of Fausto)

p, Mario de Vecchi; d, Federico Fellini; w, Federico Fellini, Ennio Flaiano (based on the story by Fellini, Flaiano and Tullio Pinelli); ph, Otello Martelli, Luciano Trasatti, Carlo Carlini; ed, Rolando Benedetti; m, Nino Rota; art d, Mario Chiari

This semiautobiographical work by Federico Fellini was the first film to bring him a measure of world attention. As in AMARCORD (his film of nearly two decades later), the setting is the seaside town of Rimini, Fellini's birthplace. The plot follows the adventures of five youths who refuse to grow up and accept responsibility. Only one of the gang, Moraldo (Franco Interlenghi, the young boy from SHOESHINE) comes to understand that life in the small town is a relatively empty existence, while his friends are content to play meaningless games that lend momentary security but ultimately make them puppets to forces beyond their control. VITELLONI is filled with the cinematic excesses that were to clutter Fellini's later films, though here they seem much more insightful in describing the tribulations of adolescent rites of passage.

VIVA VILLA!

1934   115m   bw   ★★★★
Biography   /A
MGM

Wallace Beery *(Pancho Villa)*, Fay Wray *(Teresa)*, Stuart Erwin *(Johnny Sykes)*, Leo Carrillo *(Sierra)*, Donald Cook *(Don Felipe)*, George E. Stone *(Chavito)*, Joseph Schildkraut *(Gen. Pascal)*, Henry B. Walthall *(Madero)*, Katherine DeMille *(Rosita)*, David Durand *(Bugle Boy)*

p, David O. Selznick; d, Howard Hawks (uncredited), Jack Conway; w, Ben Hecht (based on the book by Edgecumb Pinchon, O.B. Stade); ph, James Wong Howe; ed, Robert J. Kern; m, Herbert Stothart; art d, Harry Oliver; cos, Dolly Tree

The life of the famous Mexican bandit and revolutionary is told in this exciting action drama. The film opens as young Pancho Villa (Phillip Cooper) watches his father whipped to death by a soldier for some minor offense. Soon afterward, the boy murders the soldier and takes to the hills where he grows into adulthood and gathers a band of followers who join him in pillaging the homes of the rich and giving part of the proceeds to the poor. On one of these raids, Villa (played as an adult by Wallace Beery) meets an American reporter (Stuart Erwin), and the two become close friends. Later he meets a wealthy landowner (Donald Cook) and his sister (Fay Wray), who are sympathetic to Beery and his goals. They introduce the bandit to the intellectual head (Henry Walthall) of the peasant revolt which is starting to gather strength. Walthall persuades Beery to add his forces to the peasant army as its fighting core. Soon a renegade general (Joseph Schildkraut) joins the rebels with his men, and the resulting body soon sweeps through Mexico to victory. The president resigns and Walthall is named in his place. Beery's army is disbanded and he is sent home to his ranch. When Beery takes up bank robbery and kills a teller in the process, Schildkraut seizes the opportunity to eliminate his closest rival and orders him executed for murder. Walthall pardons Beery on the condition that he leave the country. Schildkraut then murders Walthall and seizes power for himself. Beery returns and reactivates his army, but without the guiding intelligence of Walthall, Beery and his men run wild, robbing and killing almost at random. Cook and Wray refuse to support Beery. He attacks Wray, and when she shoots him in the arm, he orders her flogged. Later a stray bullet fired by one of Beery's men kills her. Beery's forces triumph over Schildkraut's, and, when the general is captured, Beery has him covered in honey and left out for the ants to eat. Beery takes over as president, but with his limited education the job is too much for him. He retires to his ranch once again. Some time later, he visits Mexico City and runs into his old friend Erwin. As they talk, they are spotted by Cook, who shoots the bandit to avenge his sister's death. The mortally wounded Beery feels that momentous last words are in order, so Erwin composes them for him.

Beery's performance as Villa is one of the highlights of his long and diverse career, and his portrayal of the man as equal parts child, crusader, peasant, and murderous bandito is near perfect. When finally completed, the film proved a huge success, earning stacks of money for MGM. It garnered Academy Award nominations for Best Picture (losing to IT HAPPENED ONE NIGHT), Best Screen Adaptation, and Best Sound.

VIVA ZAPATA!

1952   113m   bw   ★★★★
Biography   /PG
FOX

Marlon Brando *(Emiliano Zapata)*, Jean Peters *(Josefa Espejo)*, Anthony Quinn *(Eufemio Zapata)*, Joseph Wiseman *(Fernando Aguirre)*, Arnold Moss *(Don Nacio)*, Alan Reed *(Pancho Villa)*, Margo *(La Soldadera)*, Harold Gordon *(Don Francisco Madero)*, Lou Gilbert *(Pablo)*, Mildred Dunnock *(Senora Espejo)*

p, Darryl F. Zanuck; d, Elia Kazan; w, John Steinbeck (based on the novel *Zapata the Unconquered* by Edgcumb Pichon); ph, Joseph MacDonald; ed, Barbara McLean; m, Alex North; art d, Lyle Wheeler, Leland Fuller

Great acting exercise, Tabascoed with Brando, peppered with Quinn, but otherwise Kazan/Steinbeck refried beans.

Kazan directs this exciting biography of the peasant who rose to be a revolutionary leader and President of his country with great relish, graphically capturing a bloody era of Mexican history, and Brando gives an electrifying performance. But the adventure lags, marred by pretentious brooding as the script strains to moralize about the corruptive influence of power.

Nor can Brando's acting justify the liberties taken. The real Emiliano Zapata was a small man with large, dark eyes and delicate hands—a tenant-farmer who finally rose up against the tyrannical rule of Porfirio Diaz, as did Pancho Villa in the north, and led an army to victory over Diaz. He waged his civil wars, 1911-1919, not to conquer Mexico but to free the land for the peasants of Morelos and other southern provinces. Kazan presents a whitewashed version of the great leader; the historical Zapata was in reality barbaric and did not hesitate to execute his enemies en masse. Quinn, who won an Oscar for Best Supporting Actor, is marvelous as the hard-riding, hard-drinking brother willing to die for passion. Frank Silvera as Huerta, Roope as Diaz, and Wiseman as the intense war-mongering journalist are startling villains, not far from their real-life counterparts in posture and character. Gilbert, who acts as Brando's intellectual conscience, is a bit too dramatic and unbelievable in some scenes. Gordon as Madero gives a realistic profile, but Peters and Margo are given little to do. Though he is on camera for only a few scenes, Reed, playing Pancho Villa, captures the brooding charisma of the revolutionary leader.

VON RYAN'S EXPRESS

1965   117m   c   ★★★½
War   /PG
P-R

Frank Sinatra *(Col. Joseph L. Ryan)*, Trevor Howard *(Maj. Eric Fincham)*, Raffaella Carra *(Gabriella)*, Brad Dexter *(Sgt. Bostick)*, Sergio Fantoni *(Capt. Oriani)*, John Leyton *(Orde)*, Edward Mulhare *(Constanzo)*, Wolfgang Preiss *(Maj. von Klemment)*, James Brolin *(Pvt. Ames)*, John Van Dreelen *(Col. Gortz)* p, Saul David; d, Mark Robson; w, Wendell Mayes, Joseph Landon (based on the novel by David Westheimer); ph, William Daniels (CinemaScope, Deluxe Color); ed, Dorothy Spencer; m, Jerry Goldsmith; art d, Jack Martin Smith

Frank Sinatra stars in this implausible but relatively engaging WWII POW escape film, playing Col. Joseph Ryan, a downed US Army Air Corps pilot who leads 600 British and American prisoners in a dramatic escape through Italy aboard a commandeered train. Aided by some of their Italian jailers, who are anxious to jump sides as the 1943 Allied invasion gets under way, the POWs take over a train and, with some of their number masquerading as Germans guards, set off for neutral Switzerland. Initially called "von Ryan" by the other prisoners, who thought him too accommodating to the enemy, the American colonel proves his courage over and over again as the train makes its way to freedom, fending off attacking Messerschmitts and narrowly escaping a pursuing German troop train. Sinatra is convincing as the gutsy American officer who engineers the escape, and Trevor Howard gives a strong performance as the British major Sinatra replaces as ranking prisoner, but there isn't much else that's believable in VON RYAN'S EXPRESS. Nonetheless, Mark Robson's film is packed with action and occasionally technically impressive, especially in the duel between the train and the German planes that attack it in the mountains of northern Italy. If it's realism you're after, look elsewhere; but if you enjoy straightforward wartime thrills (or films with particularly stupid German soldiers), VON RYAN'S EXPRESS is just the ticket.

WAGES OF FEAR, THE
(LE SALAIRE DE LA PEUR)
1955   140m   bw   ★★★★½
Adventure   /A
Filmsonor/CICC/Vera/Fono Roma   (France/Italy)

Yves Montand *(Mario)*, Charles Vanel *(Jo)*, Vera Clouzot *(Linda)*, Folco Lulli *(Luigi)*, Peter Van Eyck *(Bimba)*, William Tubbs *(Bill O'Brien)*, Dario Moreno *(Hernandez)*, Jo Dest *(Smerloff)*, Antonio Centa *(Camp Chief)*, Luis de Lima *(Bernardo)*

p, Henri-Georges Clouzot; d, Henri-Georges Clouzot; w, Henri-Georges Clouzot, Jerome Geronimi (based on the novel by Georges Arnaud); ph, Armand Thirard; ed, Henri Rust, Madeleine Gug, Etiennette Muse; m, Georges Auric; prod d, Rene Renoux

Excellent, but nasty stuff. When the powerful oil company that controls the poverty-stricken Central American village of Las Piedras is faced with a well-fire disaster 300 miles away, they call for drivers to haul a load of highly volatile nitroglycerine across the dangerous terrain to the disaster site. After the driving skills of the applicants are tested, four men are chosen—Mario (Yves Montand), a French-raised Corsican; Luigi (Folco Lulli), his husky Italian roommate; Bimba (Peter Van Eyck), a cold and egotistical German; and Jo (Charles Vanel), a fifth choice who has gotten rid of the man before him. Driving two trucks at a snail's pace, they must overcome numerous obstacles to reach their destination, including a rickety wooden platform suspended over a deep ravine, a giant boulder that blocks the road and must be destroyed with a nitro charge, a swamp of oil and their greatest natural danger—fear. A superb suspense film that eats at one's nerves for its entire last half, THE WAGES OF FEAR can almost be thought of as two movies. While director Henri-Georges Clouzot, relying on visuals, devotes the latter portion of the film to the passage of the trucks, he spends the first half building characters and atmosphere—the sweaty, dusty, hellish existence in Las Piedras, which is little better than death. From the opening shot—of four frantic beetles that have been strung together by a mischievous child—it is clear that the four characters are prisoners of the place. Remade in 1977 by William Friedkin as the crummy SORCERER.

WAGONMASTER
1950   86m   bw   ★★★★
Western   /U
Argosy

Ward Bond *(Elder Wiggs)*, Ben Johnson *(Travis Blue)*, Harry Carey, Jr. *(Sandy Owens)*, Joanne Dru *(Denver)*, Charles Kemper *(Uncle Shiloh Clegg)*, Jane Darwell *(Sister Ledeyard)*, Alan Mowbray *(Dr. A. Locksley Hall)*, Ruth Clifford *(Fleuretty Phyffe)*, Russell Simpson *(Adam Perkins)*, Kathleen O'Malley *(Prudence Perkins)*

p, John Ford, Merian C. Cooper; d, John Ford; w, Frank S. Nugent, Patrick Ford (based on a story by John Ford); ph, Bert Glennon; ed, Jack Murray; m, Richard Hageman; art d, James Basevi; fx, Jack Caffee; cos, Wesley V. Jefferies, Adele Parmenter

When asked by Peter Bogdanovich to comment on WAGONMASTER during their famous interview in 1966, director Ford replied that he thought the film, "along with THE FUGITIVE and THE SUN SHINES BRIGHT. . . came closest to being what I had wanted to achieve." Written by the director's son Patrick together with Frank Nugent, and based on a story by Ford himself, WAGONMASTER is a deceptively simple tale about a Mormon wagon train headed for the promised land. Along the way the group, led by Bond, forges alliances with two young horse traders (Johnson and Carey), four members of a traveling medicine show (Mowbray, Clifford, Francis Ford, and Dru), and a tribe of nomadic Navajo Indians. Bad guys materialize in the form of a sleazy band of varmints known as the Clegg family (Kemper, Arness, Libby, Worden, and Mickey Simpson), who we have seen rob an express office and murder a clerk during the pre-credit sequence.

WAGONMASTER is a first-rate film about solidarity, sacrifice, and tolerance, with Ford displaying consummate skill in everything from the brilliant visual compositions to the casting of the bit players. The relaxed, natural feel of the film is helped by the absence of stars; by putting his supporting players in lead roles, Ford was able to develop their characters in fresh and unexpected ways. Bond, Johnson, and Dru are nothing short of brilliant, turning in performances which, together with breathtaking scenery and an engaging sense of humor, make this well worth repeated watching.

WAIT UNTIL DARK
1967   107m   c   ★★★½
Thriller   /X
WB

Audrey Hepburn *(Susy Hendrix)*, Alan Arkin *(Roat)*, Richard Crenna *(Mike Talman)*, Efrem Zimbalist, Jr. *(Sam Hendrix)*, Jack Weston *(Carlino)*, Samantha Jones *(Lisa)*, Julie Herrod *(Gloria)*, Frank O'Brien *(Shatner)*, Gary Morgan *(Boy)*, Jean Del Val *(The Old Man)*

p, Mel Ferrer; d, Terence Young; w, Robert Carrington, Jane Howard Carrington (based on the play by Frederick Knott); ph, Charles Lang (Technicolor); ed, Gene Milford; m, Henry Mancini; art d, George Jenkins

A real edge-of-your-seat thriller adapted from a Broadway stage hit written by Frederick Knott, author of DIAL M FOR MURDER. Hepburn, a blind Manhattan housewife, is terrorized by a trio of vicious killers (Crenna, Arkin, and Weston) who are after a fortune in heroin that has been hidden in a toy doll her husband, Zimbalist, gave to her. What follows is an excruciatingly suspenseful battle of wits between the blind Hepburn and her sadistic tormentors. Expertly directed by veteran British helmsman Young (Arthur Penn had directed the stage version), WAIT UNTIL DARK is an exciting, original chiller. Hepburn turns in a strong, realistic performance as the terrorized blind woman—a role she researched diligently with the help of two young blind women from the Lighthouse for the Blind school. For weeks the actress (and director Young) wore a special shade over her eyes and learned how to use a cane properly, feel the texture of different objects, and listen carefully to distinguish the quality and distance of sounds. The film was a tremendous success at the box office, and for added effect, some theater owners turned the house lights off completely during the final 15 minutes.

WAKE ISLAND

1942   78m   bw   ★★★★
War   /A
Paramount

Brian Donlevy (*Maj. Caton*), Macdonald Carey (*Lt. Cameron*), Robert Preston (*Joe Doyle*), William Bendix (*Smacksie Randall*), Albert Dekker (*Shad McClosky*), Walter Abel (*Cmdr. Roberts*), Mikhail Rasumny (*Probenzky*), Don Castle (*Pvt. Cunkel*), Rod Cameron (*Capt. Lewis*), Bill Goodwin (*Sergeant*)

p, Joseph Sistrom; d, John Farrow; w, W.R. Burnett, Frank Butler; ph, Theodor Sparkuhl; ed, LeRoy Stone; m, David Buttolph; art d, Hans Dreier, Earl Hedrick

The heroic but doomed defense of Wake Island against the Japanese in the opening days of WWII provided the basis for this slightly fictionalized, immensely popular flag-waver that garnered several Academy Award nominations. A perfect example of Hollywood's contribution to the war effort, the film demonstrated that even in defeat there was victory, and provided needed inspiration for a nation reeling from loss after loss at the hands of the Japanese. Hunkered down in foxholes and machine gun nests, the courageous Marine defenders of the island, under the command of the determined Maj. Caton (Brian Donlevy), refuse to bend to the assault of countless Japanese troops. For two weeks they hold on, but with no help coming and ammunition running low, they are doomed and know it. Still, they refuse to give up, and in the end, Maj. Caton, Joe Doyle (Robert Preston), Lt. Cameron (Macdonald Carey), Smacksie Randall (William Bendix), and the other brave Marines prove their mettle.

All the performers are good, particularly Donlevy, brilliantly evoking calm in the face of overwhelming odds, and Bendix, who earned a Best Supporting Actor Oscar nomination. The film was widely shown to soldiers at training camps all over the country, and reportedly never failed to rouse cheers. Shot on location on the shores of the Salton Sea in the California desert, the film was also nominated for Best Picture, Best Director, and Best Original Screenplay.

WALK IN THE SUN, A

1945   117m   bw   ★★★★½
War
FOX

Dana Andrews (*Sgt. Tyne*), Richard Conte (*Rivera*), John Ireland (*Windy*), George Tyne (*Friedman*), Lloyd Bridges (*Sgt. Ward*), Sterling Holloway (*McWilliams*), Herbert Rudley (*Sgt. Porter*), Norman Lloyd (*Archimbeau*), Steve Brodie (*Judson*), Huntz Hall (*Carraway*)

p, Lewis Milestone; d, Lewis Milestone; w, Robert Rossen (based on a story by Harry Brown); ph, Russell Harlan; ed, Duncan Mansfield; m, Freddie Rich; art d, Max Bertisch

One of the better films to emerge from the final days of WWII, A WALK IN THE SUN is the story of one infantry platoon, covering one morning, from the time they hit the beach at Salerno until they reach and capture their objective, a farmhouse six miles inland. Before they even get ashore things begin to go badly, and the green lieutenant in command is killed. A sergeant takes over for a time, but the stress proves too great and he cracks. The men encounter a German armored car for which they set up an ambush, raining it with grenades, then continue on their mission with natural leader Sgt. Tyne (Dana Andrews) now in command.

Eventually, the soldiers reach their objective, but the situation appears suicidal and Sgt. Tyne must devise some way to complete the mission with a minimum loss of life. Throughout the film, as it follows the men in battle, the soundtrack picks up their chatty conversations and private thoughts. They think about their place in the great scheme of the war, about their fear of being killed, and about the hard, dirty, tedious, and dangerous job of being a front-line foot soldier. A languorous sense of resignation holds sway over all: weary, hard-bitten, and somewhat cynical, they are there to do a job, and although they don't even understand what part they play in the big picture, they do it anyway, even at the cost of their lives.

Although director Lewis Milestone seemed to have put the pacifism of his earlier ALL QUIET ON THE WESTERN FRONT on hold for the duration of WWII, A WALK IN THE SUN mostly avoids the patriotic posing and outright racism (indeed, the enemy is never given a face here) of his THE PURPLE HEART from the year before and instead concentrates on the rugged day-to-day existence of the common foot soldier. While the film is consistently engaging, some of the narrative devices Milestone employs, such as the voice-over narration and the occasional off-screen singing of a somewhat sappy folk song dedicated to foot soldiers, now seem more of an intrusion on the visuals than a complement.

WALKABOUT

1971   95m   c   ★★★★½
Drama   PG/AA
FOX   (Australia/U.S.)

Jenny Agutter (*Girl*), Lucien John (*Brother*), David Gulpilil (*Aborigine*), John Meillon (*Father*), Peter Carver (*No Hoper*), John Illingsworth (*Husband*), Barry Donnelly (*Australian Scientist*), Noelene Brown (*German Scientist*), Carlo Manchini (*Italian Scientist*)

p, Si Litvinoff; d, Nicolas Roeg; w, Edward Bond (based on the novel by James Vance Marshall); ph, Nicolas Roeg (Eastmancolor); ed, Anthony Gibbs, Alan Pattillo; m, John Barry; prod d, Brian Eatwell; art d, Terry Gough

A lyrical adventure film from director Nicolas Roeg (DON'T LOOK NOW, INSIGNIFICANCE) which stars Agutter and John as a brother and sister left stranded in the Australian outback by their father, who goes insane and kills himself. Armed only with a transistor radio for survival, the children wander the wasteland with little hope of rescue. One day a young aborigine, Gumpilil, finds them and shows them how to survive in the desert. There is a sexual attraction between Gumpilil and Agutter, and the white girl even encourages the aborigine to pursue her. One night Gumpilil performs a strange ritual mating dance for Agutter, but she rejects him; the next morning she and her brother find the aborigine dead—an apparent suicide. Eventually the children make their way back to civilization, and a key revelation is made.

While the narrative is a ambiguous and laden with allegory, the visuals are stunning, and the musical score by John Barry is beautiful and haunting. A powerful film if one lets it work its magic. Songs and musical numbers include "Electronic Dance" (Billy Mitchell), "Gasoline Alley" (Rod Stewart), "Los Angeles" (Warren Marley), and excerpts from "Hymen" (Karl Heinz Stockhausen).

WALKING TALL

1973   125m   c   ★★½
Biography/Crime   R/18
BCP

Joe Don Baker *(Buford Pusser)*, Elizabeth Hartman *(Pauline Pusser)*, Gene Evans *(Sheriff Al Thurman)*, Noah Beery, Jr. *(Grandpa Carl Pusser)*, Brenda Benet *(Luan Paxton)*, John Brascia *(Prentiss Parley)*, Bruce Glover *(Grady Coker)*, Arch Johnson *(Buel Jaggers)*, Felton Perry *(Obra Eaker)*, Richard X. Slattery *(Arno Purdy)*

p, Mort Briskin; d, Phil Karlson; w, Mort Briskin; ph, Jack Marta (DeLuxe Color); ed, Harry Gerstad; m, Walter Scharf; prod d, Stan Jolley; fx, Sass Bedig; cos, Oscar Rodriguez, Phyllis Garr

Baker stars as real-life Tennessee sheriff Buford Pusser, whose one-man battle against gambling, moonshine whiskey, and prostitution in his county elevated him to folk-hero stature in three movies (WALKING TALL, PART 2 and FINAL CHAPTER—WALKING TALL followed this one) and a shortlived TV series. In this story of an angry redneck with a big stick, Baker smashes all illegal activities in his jurisdiction, much to the dismay of the criminal kingpins in Tennessee. The crooks band together in an effort to eliminate the troublesome sheriff. After several life-threatening beatings and the murder of his wife, Hartman, Baker finally gets *really mad*, grabs his stick, and cleans out the whole town, killing several people. Incredibly, the film grossed over $17 million at the box office, and the sequels were already in the works.

WALL, THE
(LE MUR)
1983   117m   c   ★★★½
Prison   /18
MK2/Guney/TF1/Ministere de la Culture   (France)

Tuncel Kurtiz, Ayse Emel Mesci, Nicolas Hossein, Isabelle Tissandier, Malik Berrichi, Ahmet Ziyrek, Ali Berktay, Selahattin Kuzuoglu, Jean-Pierre Colin, Jacques Dimanche

p, Marin Karmitz; d, Yilmaz Guney; w, Yilmaz Guney; ph, Izzet Akay (Fujicolor); ed, Sabine Mamou; m, Ozan Garip Sahin, Setrak Bakrirel, Ali Dede Altuntas, Robert Kempler

THE WALL is an unceasingly brutal film about life in a Turkish prison. Director Yilmaz Guney, who died in 1984, served three separate jail sentences (one for murder) before finally escaping in 1981. Working from this firsthand experience in France (in an abbey converted to a jail for the production), Guney brings to the screen a film that stands up defiantly and violently for the rights of the imprisoned. The prison depicted here is a re-creation of the one in Ankara, Turkey, that was the sight of an inmate rebellion in 1976. It segregates men, women, and children but has no policy of separating violent offenders from political dissidents. In an indictment of the barbaric Turkish penal system, Guney presents an overcrowded prison with no windows, heat, hot water, or decent food, and with inhumane visiting conditions. The inmates (mostly children in the film) are treated savagely: one is kicked in the eye, another is forced to swallow a louse found on his body, and yet another is savagely battered on the soles of his feet while his blood-chilling screams are transmitted through the prison's public address system. These children pray to God not to be released but simply to be sent to another prison. Although the subject has been brought to the screen before and certain elements of THE WALL have become cliches, the power of the film's message is not lessened. THE WALL is perhaps not the most artful or poetic picture (although it does contain one of the most amazingly photographed birth scenes in cinema); it is nonetheless one of the most necessary.

WALL STREET
1987   124m   c   ★★★
Drama   R/15
American Entertainment

Charlie Sheen *(Bud Fox)*, Michael Douglas *(Gordon Gekko)*, Martin Sheen *(Carl Fox)*, Terence Stamp *(Sir Larry Wildman)*, Sean Young *(Kate Gekko)*, Daryl Hannah *(Darien Taylor)*, Sylvia Miles *(Realtor)*, James Spader *(Roger Barnes)*, Hal Holbrook *(Lou Mannheim)*, Saul Rubinek *(Harold Salt)*

p, Edward R. Pressman, A. Kitman Ho; d, Oliver Stone; w, Oliver Stone, Stanley Weiser; ph, Robert Richardson (Deluxe Color); ed, Claire Simpson; m, Stewart Copeland; prod d, Stephen Hendrickson; art d, John J. Moore, Hilda Stark; cos, Ellen Mirojnick

Writer-director Oliver Stone, who shows an uncanny knack for anticipating public interest in the subjects he chooses, explores the much-publicized inside trader of the mid-1980s in WALL STREET. Set in 1985, the film follows the career of young Wall Street broker Bud Fox (Charlie Sheen) as he scrambles to make his first million. His idol is ruthless big-time corporate raider Gordon Gekko (Michael Douglas). Fox insinuates himself in Gekko's good graces by giving Gekko inside information about an airline, information he has learned from his father (Martin Sheen), an airline mechanic and local representative of his union. With the promise of big financial rewards negating his momentary apprehension about breaking the law, Fox willingly goes to work for Gekko. With WALL STREET, Stone intentionally set out to make a good old-fashioned liberal drama about the evils of unchecked capitalism. This approach results in a film with few shades of gray and lots of moralizing speeches, but Stone nearly pulls it off through his usual visual verve and keen casting instincts. Charlie Sheen is fine as the young, inexperienced kid whose soul is battled for by the forces of good and evil. Better yet is Douglas, whose Gordon Gekko is a predatory animal seducing the weak into his lair. His performance won him an Oscar for Best Actor.

WALTZ OF THE TOREADORS
1962   104m   c   ★★★½
Comedy   /15
Independent Artists   (U.K.)

Peter Sellers *(Gen. Leo Fitzjohn)*, Dany Robin *(Ghislaine)*, Margaret Leighton *(Emily Fitzjohn)*, John Fraser *(Robert)*, Cyril Cusack *(Dr. Grogan)*, Prunella Scales *(Estella)*, Denise Coffey *(Sidonia)*, Jean Anderson *(Agnes)*, Raymond Huntley *(President of the Court Martial)*, Cardew Robinson *(Midgeley)*

p, Peter de Sarigny; d, John Guillermin; w, Wolf Mankowitz (based on the play by Jean Anouilh); ph, John Wilcox (Eastmancolor); ed, Peter Taylor; m, Richard Addinsell; prod d, Wilfred Shingleton; art d, Harry Pottle; cos, Beatrice Dawson

Sellers is outstanding as a Leo Fitzjohn, a retired general looking to escape a bleak existence in this fine adaptation of Jean Anouilh's bittersweet stage comedy. The film opens just before the outbreak of WWI. Fitzjohn has retired from the army and now lives on his manor with his shrewish wife, Emily (Leighton), whom he can't stand. Tortured by loneliness, Fitzjohn pines for the days when he had a platonic affair 17 years before with Ghislaine (Robin), a beautiful young Frenchwoman. Surprisingly, Ghislaine arrives at the manor claiming fidelity to the general and demanding that they consummate the relationship. Fitzjohn jumps at the chance, but circumstances force a postponement of their rendezvous and he leaves his former love under the care of his aide, Robert (Fraser). In two days, the aide succeeds where Fitzjohn has failed, and the angry general puts the young soldier in for a court-martial. Fitzjohn learns during the trial that Robert is actually his illegitimate son, so he stops the proceedings and allows the young couple to marry. Unhinged by the reality that he is stuck with Emily for the rest of his life, Fitzjohn considers doing something desperate, but a new arrival on the scene changes his mind.

WANDA

1971 101m c   ★★★½
Crime   GP/AA
Foundation for Filmmakers

Barbara Loden (*Wanda*), Michael Higgins (*Mr. Dennis*), Charles Dosinan (*Dennis' Father*), Frank Jourdano (*Soldier*), Valerie Manches (*Girl in Roadhouse*)

p, Harry Shuster; d, Barbara Loden; w, Barbara Loden; ph, Nicholas Proferes; ed, Nick Proferes (Kodachrome)

Barbara Loden (who was married to Elia Kazan) wrote, directed, and starred in this moving and insightful film which was brought in at a budget of $115,000. It's a powerful character study of an uneducated Pennsylvania coal-country woman who allows her husband a divorce and custody of her two children because, she admits, "I'm just no good." She leaves her hometown and drifts into a series of one-night stands with traveling salesmen whom she meets in bars. One day she wanders into a tavern while it is being held up by a neurotic thief, Higgins, who kidnaps her and makes her his hostage. Loden takes a liking to the disturbed man and accompanies him on his petty criminal escapades. Eventually he grows to like her as well and allows her to assist him. He buys her a dress and even compliments her when she does particularly well on a robbery. After a while, Higgins becomes tired of his lifestyle and decides to pull one last job, a bank, and then retire. Giving Loden the job of getaway driver, Higgins enters the bank and is killed by the police. Loden gets away. Alone again, Loden wanders into another roadside dive, and the film ends with a freeze frame on her vacant face. Well worth seeing, this film won acclaim at several film festivals, including the International Critics' Prize for Best Film at the 1970 Venice Film Festival.

WANDERERS, THE

1979 113m c   ★★★★
Drama   R/18
Orion

Ken Wahl (*Richie*), John Friedrich (*Joey*), Karen Allen (*Nina*), Toni Kalem (*Despie Galasso*), Alan Rosenberg (*Turkey*), Jim Youngs (*Buddy*), Tony Ganios (*Perry*), Linda Manz (*Peewee*), William Andrews (*Emilio*), Erland Van Lidth (*Terror*)

p, Martin Ransohoff; d, Philip Kaufman; w, Rose Kaufman, Philip Kaufman (based on the novel by Richard Price); ph, Michael Chapman (Technicolor); ed, Ronald Roose, Stuart Pappe; art d, John J. Moore; cos, Robert de Mora

The best of the gang films to be released in 1979 (the list includes THE WARRIORS, WALK PROUD, and BOULEVARD NIGHTS), THE WANDERERS is a strangely compelling film directed with flair by Philip Kaufman (INVASION OF THE BODY SNATCHERS, THE RIGHT STUFF). While basically just a string of vignettes about a gang of Italian-American teenagers living in the Bronx circa 1963, the film has an air of authenticity, as if it episodes were based on adolescent recollections. The performances in the film are uniformly strong, with Wahl, the protagonist, showing a great screen promise he has

never fulfilled (FORT APACHE, THE BRONX; and THE SOLDIER being dismal wastes of his talent). Little Linda Manz (DAYS OF HEAVEN and OUT OF THE BLUE) nearly steals the film as a pint-sized tough gal who is the girlfriend of Van Lidth, the giant leader of a rival street gang known as "The Fordham Baldies." Kaufman infuses the film with a wistful sadness for an era about to end with the assassination of JFK. Many incidents will stick with the viewer, including the very funny sequence where all the members of the Fordham Baldies get drunk and join the Marines, and the haunting, almost surrealistic battle with the mysterious and violent rival gang known as "The Ducky Boys." All in all a fascinating film with an outstanding musical score consisting of jukebox hits from the period.

WAR AND PEACE

1956 208m c   ★★★★
Drama/War   /U
Ponti/DEG   (Italy/U.S.)

Audrey Hepburn (*Natasha Rostov*), Henry Fonda (*Pierre Bezukhov*), Mel Ferrer (*Prince Andrei Bolkonsky*), Vittorio Gassman (*Anatole Kuragin*), John Mills (*Platon Karatayev*), Herbert Lom (*Napoleon*), Oscar Homolka (*Gen. Mikhail Kutuzov*), Anita Ekberg (*Helene Kuragin*), Helmut Dantine (*Dolokhov*), Barry Jones (*Count Ilya Rostov*)

p, Dino De Laurentiis; d, King Vidor; w, Bridget Boland, Robert Westerby, King Vidor, Mario Camerini, Ennio De Concini, Ivo Perilli, Irwin Shaw (based on the novel by Leo Tolstoy); ph, Jack Cardiff, Aldo Tonti (VistaVision, Technicolor); ed, Stuart Gilmore, Leo Catozzo; m, Nino Rota; art d, Mario Chiari, Franz Bachelin, Gianni Polidori; cos, Maria De Matteis

King Vidor's version of Tolstoy's great novel seems insufficient at more than three hours and fared ill both with the critics and at the box office, but it does deliver the spectacular visuals expected of historical epics. As Napoleon (Herbert Lom) prepares to invade Russia, the gentle, awkward, intellectual Pierre Bezukhov (Henry Fonda) falls in undeclared love with young Natasha Rostov (Audrey Hepburn). Soon afterward, his father dies—making Pierre the wealthy new Count Bezukhov and a desirable marriage prospect—and Bezukhov marries the luscious, adulterous Helene (Anita Ekberg). Meanwhile, his dear friend Prince Andrei (Mel Ferrer), a haughty, gloomy aide to General Kutuzov (Oscar Homolka), returns home from battle after being wounded. Depressed after his wife's death in childbirth, Andrei rediscovers the joy of life when he, too, falls in love with Natasha, and she with him—the two having been introduced by Pierre, who battles his own spiritual malaise after the failure of his loveless marriage. Andrei returns to the front and is wounded critically in the disastrous Russian defeat at Borodino. Pierre observes the carnage in horror and vows to assassinate Napoleon, but he is captured and held prisoner when the French occupy Moscow. When all looks darkest, however, the Russian winter sets in, the French are routed, Pierre is reunited with Natasha, and the love that was hinted at in the opening scenes finally comes to fruition.

Lovers of Tolstoy's work are likely to be frustrated by this somewhat static film, which, inevitably, omits a great deal of Tolstoy's characterization, plots, philosophy, and historical analysis, while on the other hand plays up the Pierre-Natasha romance. The performances are similarly limited, though Hepburn charmingly captures the gamine radiance of the young Natasha and Fonda (who felt he was miscast) effectively communicates Pierre's integrity. Cinematographers Jack Cardiff and Aldo Tonti contribute the film's most stunning work, as does Mario Soldati, who directed the battle scenes.

WAR OF THE ROSES, THE

1989   116m   c   ★★★★
Comedy   R/15
Gracie

Michael Douglas (Oliver Rose), Kathleen Turner (Barbara Rose), Danny DeVito (Gavin D'Amato), Marianne Sagebrecht (Susan), Sean Astin (Josh, Age 17), Heather Fairfield (Carolyn, Age 17), G.D. Spradlin (Harry Thurmont), Trenton Teigen (Josh, Age 10), Bethany McKinney (Carolyn, Age 10), Peter Donat (Larrabee)

p, James L. Brooks, Arnon Milchan; d, Danny DeVito; w, Michael Leeson (based on the novel by Warren Adler); ph, Stephen H. Burum (Deluxe Color); ed, Lynzee Klingman, Nicholas C. Smith; m, David Newman; prod d, Ida Random; art d, Mark Mansbridge; cos, Gloria Gresham

Few things are sadder, sillier, or scarier than the break-up of a long-married pair, and in THE WAR OF THE ROSES, director Danny DeVito captures this fiasco in its full, blackly comic ingloriousness. After 17 years of wedlock, Barbara Rose (Kathleen Turner) can't stand her husband, Oliver (Michael Douglas). He still loves her—but he loves their big, beautiful, antique-filled house more, and therein lies the cautionary tale, told by Gavin D'Amato (director DeVito), a divorce lawyer who recounts the progressively crazier story to a prospective client. Stuck (for legal reasons) in the house together as they begin divorce proceedings, the Roses escalate tensions until the hostilities erupt into full-scale, no-prisoners war.

DeVito films this tale with a fiendish gusto, yet with psychological realism and meticulous attention to an inexorable logic in the plotting, even as the Roses' war moves from the outlandish to the surreal. At once horrific and hilarious, THE WAR OF THE ROSES is made with a high level of cinematic craft: Turner and Douglas (ROMANCING THE STONE, JEWEL OF THE NILE) again prove to be the quintessential antiromantic screen couple for the antiromantic 1980s, and DeVito exerts a control behind the camera that is otherwise almost nonexistent in contemporary American film comedy.

WAR OF THE WORLDS, THE

1953   85m   c   ★★★½
Science Fiction   /PG
Paramount

Gene Barry (Dr. Clayton Forrester), Ann Robinson (Sylvia Van Buren), Les Tremayne (Gen. Mann), Lewis Martin (Pastor Matthew Collins), Robert Cornthwaite (Dr. Pryor), Sandro Giglio (Dr. Bilderbeck), William Phipps (Wash Perry), Paul Birch (Alonzo Hogue), Jack Kruschen (Salvatore), Vernon Rich (Col. Heffner)

p, George Pal; d, Byron Haskin; w, Barre Lyndon (based on the novel by H.G. Wells); ph, George Barnes (Technicolor); ed, Everett Douglas; m, Leith Stevens; art d, Hal Pereira, Albert Nozaki; fx, Gordon Jennings, Paul K. Lerpae, Wallace Kelly, Ivyl Burks, Jan Domela, Irmin Roberts, Walter Hoffman, Chesley Bonestell; cos, Edith Head

A key sci-fi film of the 1950s, George Pal's THE WAR OF THE WORLDS is a vividly realized adaptation of the classic H.G. Wells novel, updated from 19th century London to 20th century California. Though it's bogged down by a stiff cast, a yawn-inspiring conventional romance, and a sappy religiosity, it remains a landmark in the history of special effects. The lumbersome triopods of the Wells novel are jettisoned in favor of cool, green,

slickly contoured flying saucers that fire death rays accompanied by one of the most fondly remembered sound effects in screen history.

Filmed on a relatively modest budget of $2 million ($1.3 million went to special effects), THE WAR OF THE WORLDS was a solid box office hit. The film was Oscar-nominated for Best Sound and Best Film Editing, and Jennings won a posthumous Oscar for special effects, having died soon after filming was completed.

WARLOCK

1959   121m   c   ★★★★
Western   /U
FOX

Richard Widmark (Johnny Gannon), Henry Fonda (Clay Blaisdell), Anthony Quinn (Tom Morgan), Dorothy Malone (Lilly Dollar), Dolores Michaels (Jessie Marlow), Wallace Ford (Judge Holloway), Tom Drake (Abe McQuown), Richard Arlen (Bacon), De Forest Kelley (Curley Burne), Regis Toomey (Skinner)

p, Edward Dmytryk; d, Edward Dmytryk; w, Robert Alan Aurthur (based on the novel by Oakley Hall); ph, Joseph MacDonald (CinemaScope, Technicolor); ed, Jack W. Holmes; m, Leigh Harline; art d, Lyle Wheeler, Herman A. Blumenthal; fx, L.B. Abbott; cos, Charles LeMaire

A unique and often overlooked adult western that goes much deeper than most movies in this genre, WARLOCK would seem on the surface to be a fairly standard story. The citizens of the small town of Warlock are a kind, God-fearing lot who live in dread because a group of brawling cowboys, led by Drake, likes to come into town from time to time and shoot up the place. Several lawmen have departed due to these rowdies, and the townspeople are livid. They hire Fonda, a well-known gunslinger, to be local marshal. It's 1881, and men of Fonda's type are either dying of old age or being shot down by younger, faster cowboys, so he's something of an anachronism. He accepts the job on the provision that he also can run the local gambling and dance parlor. His faithful companion is clubfooted Quinn, a man who worships Fonda as Tonto did the Lone Ranger. Quinn (who bleached his hair for this role) loves Fonda in an almost unspeakable manner, although this is hinted at rather than blatantly explored. Fonda soon meets Michaels, and an attraction between the two grows. Drake and his cohorts mosey back into Warlock accompanied by Widmark, who becomes disenchanted with Drake and his group so he quits the gang and decides to remain in Warlock as Fonda's deputy. Fonda manages to get Drake and the other troublemakers out of town, and for a while law and order reign. The townsfolk decide that they don't need a professional gunslinger anymore, now that Drake and the others have been cowed. Quinn agrees and suggests that he and Fonda move out of Warlock. Actually, Quinn is jealous of Fonda's relationships with both Widmark and Michaels and wants to put a stop to them. His plans are thwarted when Malone arrives in Warlock with fire in her eyes. She had once been Quinn's woman, and after their breakup Quinn murdered her fiance. Now she wants to get even. Malone and Widmark become enamored of each other and discuss the fact that Fonda is running the town his own way and must be taught a lesson. Drake and his men return for a confrontation, and Fonda wants to face them, but Quinn points a gun at him to make him stay put so that Widmark will have to face the gang by himself. The people of Warlock, every bit as cowardly as Gary Cooper's neighbors in HIGH NOON, finally decide to stand up for their rights and back up Widmark in his battle with his former compadres. This teamwork succeeds, causing Quinn to look with new eyes at Fonda—that is, his idol may no longer be the fastest gun in the West. To ensure that Fonda remains top dog, Quinn decides to kill Widmark, but Fonda tries to talk him out of it by saying that it might be better for everyone if Quinn left. Fonda means to stay in Warlock and settle in with Michaels. Quinn can't handle the rejection from the only person he ever really cared about, and during a gun battle with Fonda he dies. Widmark orders Fonda to leave the now-peaceful town, as there is no longer any room for him there. Before the conclusion, though, Fonda and Widmark have a quick-draw contest.

WARLOCK was shot partly in Utah, although not much of the glorious scenery there was utilized. The filmmakers preferred instead to concentrate on the scene within the confines of the small town and the multilayered stories going on among the principals. There's a sense of brooding and Greek tragedy here not usually presented in a cowboy movie. Yet under Dmytryk's strong direction of the Aurthur adaptation, the tone and story lines all work to great advantage. Fonda had bombed in two previous films and had to get back into mainstream movies. While this was hardly a typical western, it did reestablish him in the eyes of the movie-going public as more than the effete Easterner he had portrayed in STAGE STRUCK and 12 ANGRY MEN. Lots of action punctuates the excellent dialogue, enhanced by a strong supporting cast.

WARRIORS, THE
1979 90m c   ★★★½
Action   R/18
Paramount

Michael Beck *(Swan)*, James Remar *(Ajax)*, Thomas Waites *(Fox)*, Dorsey Wrights *(Cleon)*, Brian Taylor *(Snow)*, David Harris *(Cochise)*, Tom McKitterick *(Cowboy)*, Marcelino Sanchez *(Rembrandt)*, Terry Michos *(Vermin)*, Deborah Van Valkenburgh *(Mercy)*

p, Lawrence Gordon; d, Walter Hill; w, David Shaber, Walter Hill (based on the novel by Sol Yurick); ph, Andrew Laszlo (Panavision, Movielab Color); ed, David Holden; m, Barry DeVorzon; art d, Don Swanagan, Robert Wightman; cos, Bobbie Mannix, Mary Ellen Winston

Kinetic is the word for the films of director Walter Hill. While some of them may lack complex characterizations (particularly true of THE DRIVER and THE WARRIORS), Hill makes up for these deficiencies with stunning visual panache. THE WARRIORS advertised its subject matter in somewhat belligerent terms: "These are the Armies of the Night. They are 100,000 strong. They outnumber the cops five to one. They could run New York City," and as a result the film was widely criticized as an incitement to gang violence. While the film depicts gangs, however, it does so in a highly stylized manner, and the criticism seems therefore to reflect a naive confusion of art with life. Indeed, without moralizing, the film achieves insight into the blighted lives and emotions of the young gang members. Loosely based on Sol Yurick's 1965 novel about a reprehensible New York street gang, THE WARRIORS opens (after a marvelous credits sequence that sets the mood for the movie) at a rally held by Roger Hill, playing the ambitious leader of a gang known as the Riffs, who seeks to unite all the street gangs into one army. Each gang has sent a handful of representatives to the meeting, all of whom have agreed to come unarmed. The leader of a gang called the Rogues, however, pulls a gun, kills Hill, and frames the Warriors for the crime. The film then turns into a battle in which the Warriors try to make it home through enemy territory with every rival gang in the city out to get them. The Warriors finally straggle back to Coney Island, where the truth is revealed,

leaving Kelly and his gang in the hands of a very angry group of Riffs.

THE WARRIORS is a visual feast. Director Hill fills the frame with vibrant colors, bright lights, and nonstop motion. The uniforms of the various gangs are unique, funny, fearsome, and more than a bit theatrical. The exciting fight scenes are brilliantly choreographed, and instead of focusing on the violence, Hill concentrates on pure movement (most of the cast were actually dancers). Alongside all the glitz are a few moments of insight into the characters. In a simple but effective scene, the Warriors are sprawled exhausted in a subway car. Two teenage couples fresh from a prom enter and sit opposite gang-leader Beck and his girl, Valkenburgh. The street kids stare at the tuxedos, prom dresses, and flowers of the "wholesome" kids. The visual contrast is enough to suggest the ways in which the street kids have missed out and been denied a normal adolescence.

WATCH ON THE RHINE
1943 114m bw   ★★½
Drama/War   /U
WB

Bette Davis *(Sara Muller)*, Paul Lukas *(Kurt Muller)*, Geraldine Fitzgerald *(Marthe de Brancovis)*, Lucile Watson *(Fanny Farrelly)*, Beulah Bondi *(Anise)*, George Coulouris *(Teck de Brancovis)*, Donald Woods *(David Farrelly)*, Henry Daniell *(Phili von Ramme)*, Donald Buka *(Joshua Muller)*, Eric Roberts *(Bodo Muller)*

p, Hal B. Wallis; d, Herman Shumlin; w, Dashiell Hammett, Lillian Hellman (based on the play by Hellman); ph, Merritt Gerstad, Hal Mohr; ed, Rudi Fehr; m, Max Steiner; art d, Carl Jules Weyl; fx, Jack Holden, Edwin DuPar; cos, Orry-Kelly

Yawn. Lillian Hellman's respected play was adapted for film by Hellman and Dashiell Hammett, her longtime companion, and helmed by Herman Shumlin, who directed the stage original and cast some of its players here. The resulting drama, intermittently powerful stuff, was nominated for Best Picture, Script, and Supporting Actress (Lucile Watson) Oscars, while Paul Lukas, repeating his stage role, won as Best Actor. Kurt and Sara Muller (Lukas and Bette Davis), refugees from Nazi Germany, arrive with their children after a long absence to visit Sara's mother (Watson) in her Washington, DC, home. Already there are Teck de Brancovis (George Coulouris), a Rumanian count, and his American wife (Geraldine Fitzgerald). The Mullers plan to stay in the US only until Kurt's health improves; then he will return to his "business" abroad, the exact nature of which is unclear. When the count, who socializes at the German embassy, hears of the Gestapo's unsuccessful attempts to crack an underground resistance group, he suspects that Kurt may be one of them and offers to spy on him, then in turn tries to blackmail Kurt, who must take desperate measures to protect himself and his family.

One of the first American films to present the philosophy—rather than just the warmongering—of fascism as a danger, WATCH ON THE RHINE is rather dully helmed by stage director Shumlin, who too often fails to avoid the static pitfalls of so many play adaptations. Lukas and most of the cast (especially Coulouris) are in fine form, though, partially redeeming a film that has not worn particularly well. Davis, too, (in a fairly small role, though top-billed) tones down her usual fireworks here to fairly good effect. She's better in spitfire mode, though.

WATERLOO BRIDGE
1940 103m bw   ★★★★
Romance   /A
MGM

Vivien Leigh (Myra Lester), Robert Taylor (Capt. Roy Cronin), Lucile Watson (Lady Margaret Cronin), C. Aubrey Smith (Duke), Maria Ouspenskaya (Mme. Olga), Virginia Field (Kitty), Leo G. Carroll (Policeman), Clara Reid (Mrs. Bassett), Steffi Duna (Lydia), Leonard Mudie (Parker)

p, Sidney Franklin; d, Mervyn LeRoy; w, S.N. Behrman, Hans Rameau, George Froeschel (based on the play by Robert E. Sherwood); ph, Joseph Ruttenberg; ed, George Boemler; m, Herbert Stothart; art d, Cedric Gibbons, Urie McCleary; chor, Ernst Matray; cos, Adrian, Gile Steele

In London during WWII, a British colonel, Taylor, is caught in a blackout in his chauffeured army sedan. His passage to Waterloo Station—and, eventually, to combat in France—thus interrupted, Taylor steps from the vehicle to tread the pavement of the famed Waterloo Bridge (rebuilt following its destruction during WWI). As he paces, the middle-aged officer fondles a tiny figurine, reminiscing about days long past. In flashback, Taylor is on the old Waterloo Bridge of 1917, now a handsome young captain in the regiment commanded by his uncle, Smith. He meets Leigh, a member of a ballet troupe and goes to see her in a performance of "Swan Lake." He immediately falls hopelessly in love with her and she falls for him. They make plans to wed, but before they can do so Taylor's regiment is called into battle. Leigh abandons her performance to bid her lover farewell at Waterloo Station and is fired from the ballet company. Leigh's loyal friend and roommate, Field, quits the company in support, and the two ballerinas seek alternative employment. They descend into poverty; desperate, Field becomes a prostitute. Later, Leigh believes Taylor has been killed and, despondent and destitute, she also becomes a prostitute. She plies her trade on the Waterloo Bridge. (Historically, the bridge was a hooker haven during wartime.) On the bridge, months later, seeking a client, she meets the returning Taylor—who had spent the intervening time as a prisoner of war—and, thinking fast, conceals her profession during the shocking reunion. Their romance continues; it appears that her degradation was no more than a nightmare, best forgotten. She and Taylor travel to the country estate of his mother, Watson. Slowly, Leigh begins to realize that her indiscretions will come to light one day, besmirching the aristocratic name of her fiance and his family. Leigh recounts her recent history to Watson, imploring the latter to keep it a secret, and departs. Taylor searches for her and finds her lifeless body on Waterloo Bridge where she has been run over by a truck. The film flashes forward as the older Taylor—the blackout ended—leaves to rejoin his regiment during another world war.

Leigh is stunning in this second cinematic version of author Sherwood's hit play. (A fine first version was made in 1931 by James Whale and starred Mae Clarke and Douglass Montgomery.) WATERLOO BRIDGE was Leigh's first movie following the record-breaking David Selznick production of GONE WITH THE WIND, which had made her the most visible, most desirable actress in the world. Selznick had loaned Leigh to MGM for the picture in repayment for help that studio's head had given him for the previous picture. Leigh was in the midst of a divorce from her husband Leigh Holman at the time, her romance with Laurence Olivier—also wed at the time—a continuing scandal. She and Olivier had both invested every farthing they had in their planned theatrical production of William Shakespeare's "Romeo and Juliet," and both were desperately in need of money. Olivier accepted the male lead in PRIDE AND PREJUDICE, and the lovers were forced to separate temporarily. Leigh was irate about the parting, believing that Olivier should have gotten the role assigned to Taylor. Taylor drew kudos for his mature, restrained performance, which revitalized his then-fading career by demonstrating that he was more than just another pretty face, although critics were none too tolerant of his "Nebraska accent." Of all his seventy-plus screen performances, this was Taylor's personal favorite. The story was filmed again in 1956 as GABY, a disappointing version starring Leslie Caron and John Kerr.

WATERSHIP DOWN

1978 92m c	★★★
Animated	PG/U
Nepenthe (U.K.)	

VOICES OF: John Hurt (Hazel), Richard Briers (Fiver), Michael Graham-Cox (Bigwig), John Bennett (Capt. Holly), Simon Cadell (Blackberry), Roy Kinnear (Pipkin), Richard O'Callaghan (Dandelion), Terence Rigby (Silver), Ralph Richardson (Chief Rabbit), Denholm Elliott (Cowslip)

p, Martin Rosen; d, Martin Rosen; w, Martin Rosen (based on the novel by Richard Adams); ph, (Technicolor); ed, Terry Rawlings; m, Angela Morley, Malcolm Williamson

Expertly and realistically animated, this version of the popular novel didn't seem to have an audience. It was much too violent for kids, and wasn't the type of picture that an adult would go out and see, in part because it is animated. The spirit of the book is captured here as the rabbits, faced with problems of ecology, are forced to find a new home. Their trek is filled with surprises and adventures, as well as bloodshed. The job of personifying the rabbits is nicely achieved due to expert readings by the cast.

WAY OUT WEST

1937 65m bw	★★★★½
Comedy/Western	/U
Hal Roach	

Stan Laurel, Oliver Hardy (Themselves), James Finlayson (Mickey Finn), Sharon Lynne (Lola Marcel), Stanley Fields (Sheriff), Rosina Lawrence (Mary Roberts), James Mason (Anxious Patron), James C. Morton, Frank Mills, David Pepper (Bartenders)

p, Stan Laurel; d, James W. Horne; w, Charles Rogers, Felix Adler, James Parrott (based on a story by Jack Jevne, Charles Rogers); ph, Art Lloyd, Walter Lundin; ed, Bert Jordan; m, Marvin Hatley, LeRoy Shield, Egbert Van Alstyne, J.L. Hill, Nathaniel Shilkret, Irving Berlin, Franz von Suppe; art d, Arthur I. Royce; fx, Roy Seawright

Laurel and Hardy's only western spoof, WAY OUT WEST, ranks among the best of their films, with more exuberant laughs crammed into its scant 65 minutes than can be found in a dozen modern comedies. With their faithful mule, the boys head into Brushwood Gulch to deliver a gold mine deed to their departed partner's daughter. But they get hopelessly lost, and make the mistake of asking bartender Mickey Finn (James Finlayson) for advice. Finn's scullery maid, Mary Roberts (Rosina Lawrence), is actually the woman they seek, but he deliberately steers them toward his wife, Lola Marcel (Sharon Lynn)—a brassy blonde who is so obviously not the right person that everyone can see she cries crocodile tears upon learning of her "father's" death. Everyone, that is, except Laurel and Hardy. Included is the song "Trail of the Lonesome Pine."

WAY WE WERE, THE

1973 118m c	★★★
Romance	PG
Rastar	

Barbra Streisand *(Katie Morosky)*, Robert Redford *(Hubbell Gardiner)*, Bradford Dillman *(J.J.)*, Lois Chiles *(Carol Ann)*, Patrick O'Neal *(George Bissinger)*, Viveca Lindfors *(Paula Reisner)*, Allyn Ann McLerie *(Rhea Edwards)*, Murray Hamilton *(Brooks Carpenter)*, Herb Edelman *(Bill Verso)*, Diana Ewing *(Vicki Bissinger)*

p, Ray Stark; d, Sydney Pollack; w, Arthur Laurents, Alvin Sargent (uncredited), David Rayfiel (based on the novel by Laurents); ph, Harry Stradling, Jr. (Panavision, Eastmancolor); ed, Margaret Booth; m, Marvin Hamlisch; prod d, Stephen Grimes; chor, Grover Dale; cos, Dorothy Jeakins, Moss Mabry

Engrossing, if occasionally ludicrous, hit tearjerker with Pollack, Streisand, and Redford doing a good job of bringing Arthur Laurents' script to the screen. It's a great romance and it does tell us something about the way we were from the 30s through the 50s, but a lot of the politics of the Blacklist period are missing from the film, apparently cut just before release.

Redford is a handsome WASP college student in the late 1930s. He yearns to be a writer, spends his spare time in mindless social activities, and is politically neutral. Streisand, in her big bid for old-fashioned romantic movie star status, is a radical Jewish student who joins every political organization. She is the butt of many jokes at the college (what a surprise!), and the sharpest barbs come from Redford's pals, though he doesn't feel the same way. They meet briefly at a dance and there is an attraction, but that's put on the back burner. Years pass, and WWII begins. Streisand is on the radio talking politics, and Redford is now a member of the armed forces. They meet again, but he is drunk, so she takes him back to her apartment where he passes out in her bed. Still later, he's a published author, and she has a copy of his novel. They discuss the book, and it's evident to both that the attraction they felt in college is still there, so they begin to date. Redford's snobbish friends again try to wreck the relationship. She won't put up with their attitude, and Redford decides this might be the time to end their romance. They are reconciled, however, marry and move to California where Redford has received a screenplay assignment. She goes off to Washington to fight against the House Un-American Activities Committee. Streisand fears that Redford is selling out his talent. He begins to agree with her and is soon in trouble with the studio executives. Dillman, an old buddy of Redford's, is the wishy-washy producer assigned to the project, and he wants certain changes in the script that Redford is loath to make. While Streisand is away, Redford seeks solace in the arms of an ex-girlfriend. Pregnant, Streisand is distraught and wants to end their marriage. They will wait until after their child is born, then part amicably. Years later, though, they meet again in New York. Redford has now sold out totally and makes his living writing for TV. Streisand has remarried. They meet in Central Park, and in a rather predictable ending, bid each other farewell. She walks away handing out "Ban the Bomb" leaflets as he shakes his head and calls out after her, "You never give up, do you?"

La Strident (who lost to Glenda Jackson for A TOUCH OF CLASS), cinematographer Stradling, designer Grimes, composer Hamlisch, and lyricists Alan and Marilyn Bergman were nominated for Oscars, and the music and the song won Academy Awards.

WAYS OF LOVE
1950   119m   bw   ★★★★★
Drama
Joseph Burstyn   (Italy/France)

A DAY IN THE COUNTRY: Sylvia Bataille *(Henriette)*, Gabriel *(Mons. Doufour)*, Jeanne Marken *(Mme. Doufour)*, Georges St. Saens *(Henry)*, Bordan *(Anatole)*, Jacques Borel *(Rudolph)*, Jean Renoir *(Innkeeper)*. THE MIRACLE: Anna Magnant *(Nanni)*, Federico Fellini *(The Stranger)*. JOFROI: Vincent Scotto *(Jofroi)*

p, Pierre Braunberger; d, Jean Renoir, Roberto Rossellini, Marcel Pagnol; w, Jean Renoir, Roberto Rossellini, Tullio Pinelli (based on stories by Guy de Maupassant, Federico Fellini and Jean Giono); ph, Claude Renoir, Jean Bourgoin; ed, Marguerite Renoir; m, Joseph Kosma, Renzo Rossellini

A peculiar masterpiece since it is actually a compilation of three brilliant short films—Jean Renoir's A DAY IN THE COUNTRY (1946), Roberto Rossellini's THE MIRACLE (1948), and Marcel Pagnol's JOFROI (1933) brought together by foreign film importer Joseph Burstyn for the benefit of American audiences, who would not otherwise get a chance to see them. Renoir's film is one of his most perfect, adapting a Guy de Maupassant story about a bourgeois mother and daughter who get involved with two oarsmen. Rossellini's picture was originally released in Italy in a diptych entitled L'AMORE and was meant as a vehicle for Magnani. Besides being Fellini's only acting credit, THE MIRACLE was also the film that increased the odds for free speech in motion pictures. When New York's Cardinal Spellman saw the picture, he was morally outraged and attempted to have it banned. For once, the US Justice Department had enough good sense to let it play. The final episode, JOFROI, is a tale of a peasant who sells his land and then tries to prevent the owner from cutting down the olive trees that grow on it. All three episodes have been released as short films and are masterpieces in their own right.

WE ARE ALL MURDERERS
(NOUS SOMMES TOUS DES ASSASSINS)
1957   113m   bw   ★★★½
Drama
Union General   (France)

Marcel Mouloudji *(Rene Le Guen)*, Raymond Pellegrin *(Gino)*, Antoine Balpetre *(Dr. Albert Dutoit)*, Claude Laydu *(Philippe Arnaud, a Counsel)*, Paul Frankeur *(Leon)*, Amedeo Nazzari *(Dr. Albert Detouche)*, Georges Poujouly *(Michel Le Guen)*, Julien Verdier *(Marcel Bauchet)*, Louis Seigner *(Abbe Roussard)*, Andre Reybas *(Father Simon)*

d, Andre Cayatte; w, Andre Cayatte, Charles Spaak; ph, Jean Bourgoin; ed, Paul Cayatte; m, Raymond Legrand; art d, Jacques Colombier

A polemical picture, deliberately made by cowriter-director Cayatte to influence an audience's views about the efficacy of capital punishment as a deterrent to murder, this poses the question, "If you were the president of the Republic, would you want this man to die?" The film details, in case-history fashion, the stories of five condemned murderers. The five prisoners await the guillotine nervously, listening for the small sounds that will announce the coming of the stocking-footed guards who hope to seize the inmates unaware (a stratagem that passes for mercy) and transport them to their terminal rites. The condemned Gino (Pellegrin) is a Corsican trapped by an archaic tradition of family honor and vengeance that require him to kill a transgressor, adhering to a law older than the judicial system that condemned him. A physician (Balpetre) has been convicted on circumstantial evidence of poisoning his wife. An illiterate peasant (Verdier) murdered his infant daughter because her crying interfered with his sleep. A victim of a brain tumor (Marcel

Peres)—since surgically removed—raped and murdered a child. In the most detailed of the histories, Rene Le Guen's (Mouloudji's), the progress of this much-brutalized slum child is depicted through his adulthood and his small-arms training and recruitment into the Resistance during the occupation of WWII, a time when he found social rewards and admiration to be connected with killing.

Cayatte, himself an attorney, presents his case against judicial murder fairly; he deliberately avoids highly charged emotional scenes, preferring to undertake the method espoused by theatrical theorist Berthold Brecht, that is, giving his viewers a chance to use their own minds. This is one of four judicial films directed by Cayatte. In Britain, the film's title received a question mark, avoiding Cayatte's apparent presumption of guilt.

WE ARE NOT ALONE
1939   112m   bw   ★★★½
Drama
WB

Paul Muni (Dr. David Newcome), Jane Bryan (Leni-Krafft), Flora Robson (Jessica Newcome), Raymond Severn (Gerald Newcome), Una O'Connor (Susan), Alan Napier (Archdeacon), James Stephenson (Sir William Clintock), Montagu Love (Maj. Millman), Henry Daniell (Sir Ronald Dawson), Stanley Logan (Mr. Guy Lockhead)

p, Henry Blanke; d, Edmund Goulding; w, James Hilton, Milton Krims (based on a novel by James Hilton); ph, Tony Gaudio; ed, Warren Low; m, Max Steiner; fx, Byron Haskin, H.F. Koenekamp

This was not a hit with the war-conscious US in 1939, but star Muni felt it was one of his greatest roles. This time he's a country doctor in England with a penchant for the violin. (In the film, Muni played his own violin after studying some time to be able to play the instrument.) He and his neurotic wife, Robson, have a precocious son, Severn. The movie begins in 1914 as the physician treats an Austrian dancer, Bryan, for a broken wrist. (The part was originally cast with Dolly Haas, but when she and Muni had those old, familiar "creative differences," she was replaced with tyro Bryan after three weeks' shooting had been completed.) Bryan is sad enough over her lot to attempt suicide but Muni comes to her aid and helps her find a place to stay while she searches for work. She becomes the child's governess, and Muni hides Severn away from Robson so she can't exert her powerful influence during the day while he is out calling on patients. Bryan and Severn like each other very much, but Robson steps in and tells Muni she wants Bryan fired after learning that the sweet young thing had been a dancer and had attempted to kill herself. Robson takes the lad and sends him off to live with her pious brother, Napier, an archdeacon. It's all very British and stiff upper lip as the camera examines life in the quiet English town, but then things begin popping. Muni is irate at Robson for what she's done and continues to see Bryan, who now enters a music school. One day, Severn sneaks back to his house to find a small pocket knife Robson had confiscated earlier. In his foraging, he accidentally knocks over some pill bottles belonging to Muni. Several of the bottles are broken and, in a panic, Severn stuffs the pills into whatever bottles remain, not realizing that they are now mislabeled and the result could be fatal. WW I breaks out and the angry townspeople go wild, breaking windows and trashing shops owned by anyone with even a vaguely German sounding name. Muni, realizing that Bryan is in danger due to her Austrian heritage, gets her to another town from which she can travel back to her country. Meanwhile, Robson develops a headache and takes some tablets from Muni's medicine cabinet,

not knowing that their son has fouled matters earlier. She soon dies, the result of downing the wrong medication. Muni and Bryan are arrested on the charge of murder, tried, then convicted and finally sentenced to death. The only one who could accurately solve the crime is Severn but, at his father's insistence, the boy knows nothing. During the trial Muni comes to love Bryan, and, on the eve of the execution, the two are allowed some time together. It is here that they bare their love for each other and they go to their deaths confident that they will be together in some other time and place. Even with the downbeat conclusion, the picture has a certain dignity and conviction and is a moving experience. It was Muni's 10th and final picture for Warner Bros. and a fine bow-out to the contract that saw him appear as Louis Pasteur, Benito Juarez, and Emile Zola. The studio did well in its creation of the atmosphere of a small English village of the period, and the acting is excellent.

WE DIVE AT DAWN
1943   98m   bw   ★★★½
War   /U
Gainsborough   (U.K.)

Eric Portman (James Hobson), John Mills (Lt. Freddie Taylor), Reginald Purdell (CPO Dicky Dabbs), Niall MacGinnis (PO Mike Corrigan), Joan Hopkins (Ethel Dabbs), Josephine Wilson (Alice Hobson), Louis Bradfield (Lt. Brace), Ronald Millar (Lt. Johnson), Jack Watling (Lt. Gordon), Caven Watson (CPO Duncan)

p, Edward Black; d, Anthony Asquith; w, J.B. Williams, Val Valentine, Frank Launder (uncredited); ph, Jack Cox; ed, R.E. Dearing; art d, Walter Murton

This well-done wartime British entry, directed by Anthony Asquith, follows the crew of the submarine Sea Tiger as they proceed from a week of shore leave at home to a dangerous mission to sink the German battleship Brandenberg. The sub's commander, Lt. Taylor (John Mills), directs Sea Tiger through a mine field so it can get a shot off at the German warship, but circumstances prevent the Britons from knowing whether they have managed to sink their target (they have). After avoiding German pursuit, the submarine runs out of fuel, but a tanker is discovered in a Danish port, and the Brits and the local resistance manage to hold off the Germans long enough to complete refueling. Then it's back to England, where seaman Hobson (Eric Portman) finds his estranged wife waiting for him. This above-average submarine movie manages to avoid most of the cliches of the genre, generates more than a little tension, and offers universally strong performances.

WE LIVE AGAIN
1934   85m   bw   ★★★★
Historical   /15
UA

Anna Sten (Katusha Maslova), Fredric March (Prince Dmitri Nekhlyudov), Jane Baxter (Missy Kortchagin), C. Aubrey Smith (Prince Kortchagin), Sam Jaffe (Gregory Simonson), Ethel Griffies (Aunt Maria), Gwendolyn Logan (Aunt Sophia), Mary Forbes (Mrs. Kortchagin), Jessie Ralph (Matrona Pavlovna), Leonid Kinskey (Simon Kartinkin)

p, Samuel Goldwyn; d, Rouben Mamoulian; w, Maxwell Anderson, Leonard Praskins, Preston Sturges, Thornton Wilder (based on the novel Resurrection by Leo Tolstoy, uncredited); ph, Gregg Toland; ed, Otho Lovering; m, Alfred Newman; prod d, Sergei Sudeikin; art d, Richard Day; cos, Omar Kiam

This fine adaptation of Tolstoy's oft-filmed novel *Resurrection* begins in the countryside of Czarist Russia. Fredric March is a young prince in love with Anna Sten, a servant girl with whom he has grown up. The dashing March goes into the service and returns after two years to find Sten's affections unchanged. They attend Easter mass at a Russian Orthodox church, and afterwards he seduces her, only to slip away the next morning. He then forgets all about the girl, who, it turns out, is pregnant with his child. Sten tries to recapture his heart and at one point runs through a storm after his train as an oblivious March continues playing cards with fellow army officers. The child dies and Sten, accompanied only by another servant, buries its tiny coffin in unconsecrated ground. Seven years pass and March is engaged to Jane Baxter, the daughter of another prince, C. Aubrey Smith, who invites March to sit as a juror on a case he is trying involving a prostitute charged with murder. The accused is Sten, who is innocent of the crime. March presses for acquittal, but she is found guilty and sentenced to exile in Siberia. March tries to get her released, but she only mocks her former lover's efforts. March decides he must pay for the suffering he has caused Sten, so he gives up his land to his retainers, sells all of his possessions and joins Sten on her long journey to Siberia.

This classic story of redemption is beautifully told under Rouben Mamoulian's strong direction. March and Sten are excellent as the tragic lovers, giving their roles depth and intensity. The photography by master lensman Gregg Toland gives the film a moody, atmospheric look which further enhances the strong emotions of the story. Tolstoy's novel had been filmed three times in the silent era: first by D.W. Griffith in 1909, then in 1918 with Pauline Frederick, and again in 1927 with Dolores Del Rio and Rod LaRocque. Lupe Velez also appeared in a 1931 sound version shot in both Spanish and English. Samuel Goldwyn was furiously trying to promote Sten, an actress he considered to be "the Russian Garbo." This was her follow-up to NANA, and, though she again gave an admirable performance, Sten never caught on as Goldwyn had hoped. Maxwell Anderson and Leonard Praskins both received credit for the screenplay, though neither writer made contributions to the final script. Both had written drafts which were unacceptable by Goldwyn's standards, and though the producer was essentially distrustful of Preston Sturges, the future director was finally given the assignment at Mamoulian's urging. Condensing a 400-page novel into an 85-minute film proved to be a difficult but not insurmountable task, and Sturges turned out his script in a surprisingly short amount of time. Thornton Wilder made a small, uncredited contribution to the screenplay as well.

According to some reports, Goldwyn was highly impressed with the Russian Orthodox Easter service portrayed in the film, though the music was accidentally recorded backwards. Because of Goldwyn's enthusiasm for the scene, no one dared to tell him of the error and the sequence stayed as it was. Two more versions of Tolstoy's novel followed, a 1943 Mexican adaptation and a 1958 German-French coproduction, AUFERSTEHUNG, featuring Horst Buchholz in the March role.

WE THE LIVING

1942   174m   bw   ★★★★
Drama
Scalera/Duncan Scott   (Italy)

Alida Valli (*Kira Argounova*), Rossano Brazzi (*Leo Kovalensky*), Fosco Giachetti (*Andrei Taganov*), Giovanni Grasso (*Tishenko*), Emilio Cigoli (*Pavel Syerov*), Cesarina Gherardi (*Comrade Sonia*), Mario Pisu (*Victor Dunaev*), Guglielmo Sinaz (*Morozov*), Gero Zambuto (*Alexei Argounov*), Annibale Betrone (*Vassili Dunaev*)

p, Duncan Scott, Henry Mark Holzer, Erika Holzer; d, Goffredo Alessandrini; w, Anton Giulio Majano (based on the novel by Ayn Rand); ph, Giuseppe Caracciolo; ed, Eraldo Da Roma; m, Renzo Rossellini; art d, Andrea Beloborodoff, Giorgio Abkhasi, Amleto Bonetti; cos, Rosi Gori

They don't make films like this anymore. First shown in Italy in 1942, but banned by Mussolini's government and lost until it was rediscovered and re-edited (after an intensive search by the producers), WE THE LIVING has a syrupy score, misty photography, melodramatic confrontations, heroic renunciations, and suicides in the name of lost ideals. And it works. An adaptation of Ayn Rand's novel, the film mixes lots of anti-Communist politics with its passion, but there's still much passion in this tale set in Russia in the early 1920s. Opposed to the new Bolshevik regime are the lovers Kira Argounova (Alida Valli) and Leo Kovalensky (Rossano Brazzi). When Leo is arrested and subsequently contracts tuberculosis, Kira becomes the mistress of idealistic Party man and secret police member Andrei Taganov (Fosco Giachetti) as a means of paying for Leo's stay at a sanitarium. Unfortunately, Leo repays her sacrifice by becoming as corrupt as his erstwhile oppressors, while Andrei becomes disillusioned with the government and shoots himself after finding out that Kira doesn't care for him. The film ends as Kira, still incorruptibly anti-Red, prepares to leave Russia and Leo forever. Though filled with Rand's predictable dogma, WE THE LIVING is unforgettably romantic, and still stands up as a moving love story and as a declaration of female independence that was way ahead of its time. The lush sets, exquisite cinematography, impeccable black-and-white values, and exceptional casting lend the proceedings much splendor, even if the splendor is preposterous.

WEDDING, A

1978   125m   c   ★★½
Comedy/Drama   PG/15
Lion's Gate

Lillian Gish (*Nettie Sloan*), Ruth Nelson (*Beatrice Sloan Cory*), Ann Ryerson (*Victoria Cory*), Desi Arnaz, Jr. (*Dino Corelli*), Belita Moreno (*Daphene Corelli*), Vittorio Gassman (*Luigi Corelli*), Nina Van Pallandt (*Regina Corelli*), Virginia Vestoff (*Clarice Sloan*), Dina Merrill (*Antoinette Sloan Goddard*), Pat McCormick (*Mackenzie Goddard*)

p, Robert Altman; d, Robert Altman; w, John Considine, Patricia Resnick, Allan Nicholls, Robert Altman (based on a story by Considine and Altman); ph, Charles Rosher, Jr.; ed, Tony Lombardo; m, John Hotchkis

Altman's second most "ambitious" film is sadly one of his less successful. A WEDDING is extraordinarily self-indulgent, which is really saying something in light of this great filmmaker's astonishingly uneven career.

The setting is a wedding between the daughter of a southern parvenu family and the scion of a clan that is a combination of old money and Mafia. Altman trots more than 50 characters across the screen in what must have been an attempt to prove that he could top the feat he achieved with the 24 stars he used in NASHVILLE. In this case, though, more is less. So many people appear onscreen in so many snippets of stories that not only is it difficult to care about anyone, it's hard to remember who they are. The movie has no narrative thrust, coming across as a ragged collection of occasionally amusing scenes. This is social satire delivered with a shotgun blast.

That great gray goddess of Hollywood films, Lillian Gish, makes her 100th film appearance, but gets killed off far too early. Arnaz, the groom, is set to marry Amy Stryker, the bride with conspicuous braces. Stryker's sister Mia Farrow has already had an affair with Arnaz and is pregnant by him. Stryker's mother is Carol Burnett. She is bored with husband Paul Dooley (an Altman favorite who played Wimpy in POPEYE) and has a sexual liaison with Arnaz's uncle, McCormick. Arnaz's mother is Van Pallandt, a confirmed heroin addict. The wedding coordinator is Geraldine Chaplin, a lesbian (how amusing!), and John Cromwell is the senile priest who forgets his lines and is so myopic that he speaks to a corpse and wonders why his remarks go unanswered. Perhaps the movie's best moment goes to Howard Duff, a lech and a lush of a doctor. At one point late in the film, during a major dramatic scene, we hear him far off-screen, two floors below, very quietly reply when asked if he wants his glass refilled: "Just to the brim, please!" It's the most thrown-away of all great throwaway lines in the movies.

WEDDING IN GALILEE

(NOCE EN GALILEE)
1988 116m c ★★★★
Drama
Marisa/LPA/French Ministry of Culture/French Community Ministry/ZDF (Belgium/France)

Ali Mohammed El Akili (*Abu Adel, the Mukhtar*), Bushra Karaman (*The Mother*), Nazih Akleh (*Adel, the Groom*), Makhram Khouri (*Military General*), Anna Achdian (*Samia, the Bride*), Sonia Amar (*Sumaya, the Daughter*), Youssef Abou Warda (*Baccum*), Eyad Anis (*Hassan*), Wael Barckouti (*Ziad*), Juliano Mer Khamis

d, Michel Khleifi; w, Michel Khleifi; ph, Eddy van der Enden; ed, Marie Castro Vasquez; m, Jean-Marie Senia

WEDDING IN GALILEE is a moving and remarkable Belgian-French coproduction about Palestinian wedding customs, military and patriarchal dominance, and the quest for peace in the Middle East. Directed by the 36-year-old, Nazareth-born Michel Khleifi, who resides in Belgium, this film has not come to American shores without its share of accolades. It was awarded the 1987 Cannes Critic's Prize, named Best Film of the Year in Belgium, and took the Grand Prize at the San Sebastian Film Festival—where jury member Alain Tanner said to Khleifi, "Your film is greater than any prize we could give it."

Filmed before the escalation in Palestinian-Israeli tensions of late 1987, WEDDING IN GALILEE is set (and was photographed) in the occupied West Bank, where the village *mukhtar* (elder), played by Akili, has vowed to give his son a great wedding. The obstacle to this planned festivity is the imposed curfew that takes effect every evening at sundown. Akili appeals to the military governor, Khouri, to make an exception in this case, but to no avail. Khouri does propose that the wedding can take place on the condition that he and his Israeli aides are invited as guests of honor. Without pondering the consequences, Akili agrees and parts with the military governor on friendly terms. When he explains to his villagers that the Israelis will be in attendance, there is an immediate split, with hostilities and insults hurled about at once. Even Akili's son, groom-to-be Akleh, disagrees with his father's decision. The wedding, however, *will* take place as Akili has promised.

A rich, lyrical film of many textures, WEDDING IN GALILEE presents Western audiences with a world rarely seen onscreen, familiar only from violent television news reports. As

an anthropological film, it is educational and enlightening, presenting foreign locations and nonprofessional actors. But WEDDING IN GALILEE is much more than a film of cultural curiosity. It is a human drama, ranging in tone from comic to poignant, from tense to sensual. Director Michel Khleifi is not afraid to let his camera linger on his locations, allowing it to move through the space and stare out an open window long after the characters have left and the action has ceased. Often the haunting musical score overpowers all other sounds until it is the only thing heard.

WEE WILLIE WINKIE

1937 103m bw ★★★
Drama/Comedy
FOX

Shirley Temple (*Priscilla Williams*), Victor McLaglen (*Sgt. MacDuff*), C. Aubrey Smith (*Col. Williams*), June Lang (*Joyce Williams*), Michael Whalen (*Lt. "Coppy" Brandes*), Cesar Romero (*Khoda Khan*), Constance Collier (*Mrs. Allardyce*), Douglas Scott (*Mott*), Gavin Muir (*Capt. Bibberbeigh*), Willie Fung (*Mohammet Dihn*)

p, Gene Markey; d, John Ford; w, Ernest Pascal, Julien Josephson (based on a story by Rudyard Kipling); ph, Arthur Miller; ed, Walter Thompson; m, Louis Silvers; art d, William Darling; cos, Gwen Wakeling

Little Shirley Temple works her charms on India in this starring vehicle, which is very loosely based on a Rudyard Kipling story and directed by, of all people, John Ford, best known for his classic westerns. At the turn of the century, Priscilla (Shirley Temple) and her widowed mother (June Lang) go to live with her grandfather, Col. Williams (C. Aubrey Smith), on a British army base in India. Priscilla goes through maneuvers with the troops, donning a darling pint-sized uniform and managing to win over everyone she comes in contact with, including rebel leader Khoda Khan (Cesar Romero). The entire political situation is solved when Priscilla asks why the two factions are mad at each other, thus bringing about a peaceful resolution.

WEEDS

1987 115m c ★★★½
Drama R/18
Kingsgate

Nick Nolte (*Lee Umstetter*), Lane Smith (*Claude*), William Forsythe (*Burt the Booster*), John Toles-Bey (*Navarro*), Joe Mantegna (*Carmine*), Ernie Hudson (*Bagdad*), Mark Rolston (*Dave*), J.J. Johnson (*Lazarus*), Rita Taggart (*Lillian Bingington, Newspaper Critic*), Orville Stoeber (*Lead Guitar*)

p, Bill Badalato; d, John Hancock; w, Dorothy Tristan, John Hancock; ph, Jan Weincke (Technicolor); ed, Dennis O'Connor; m, Angelo Badalamenti; prod d, Joseph T. Garrity; art d, Pat Tagliaferro; fx, Mike Menzel, Marvin Gardner, Rick Barefoot; chor, Jerry Evans; cos, Mary Kay Stolz

WEEDS is an offbeat look at the American penal system and the criminals who pass through it. Lee Umstetter (Nick Nolte), an inmate sentenced to life with no chance of parole, tries to distract his mind from his fate by reading. Then after watching a local theater troupe perform for the prisoners, Umstetter writes his own play, basing it on the dehumanizing prison experience. He is given permission to perform the play for the inmates, and the playwright casts his work with enthusiastic prisoners. Lillian Bingington (Rita Taggart), a San Francisco drama critic, sees the play and is so impressed with both Umstetter's writing and acting that she works to get him paroled. Based loosely on the real-life saga of inmate Rick Cluchey, WEEDS is a fascinating, touching, funny, and at times brutal look at the wreckage of the American penal system. While pulling no punches when it comes to the harsh realities of the situation, the film's message is ultimately a hopeful one. The script, authored by director John Hancock and his wife, Dorothy Tristan, falters at times, but the excellent cast pulls the movie through some rough spots. Nolte is superb with a skillful, detailed performance filled with intelligence and nuance.

WEEKEND

1968   103m   c   ★★★★½
Drama   /18
Comacico/Copernic/Lira/Ascot   (France/Italy)

Mireille Darc (*Corinne*), Jean Yanne (*Roland*), Jean-Pierre Kalfon (*Leader of FLSO*), Valerie Lagrange (*His Moll*), Jean-Pierre Leaud (*Saint-Just/Man in Phone Booth*), Yves Beneyton (*Member of FLSO*), Paul Gegauff (*Pianist*), Daniel Pommereulle (*Joseph Balsamo*), Yves Alfonso (*Gros Poncet*), Blandine Jeanson (*Emily Bronte/Girl in Farmyard*)

d, Jean-Luc Godard; w, Jean-Luc Godard; ph, Raoul Coutard (Eastmancolor); ed, Agnes Guillemot; m, Antoine Duhamel, Wolfgang Amadeus Mozart (Piano Sonata K.576)

A brutally satirical film somewhat reminiscent of the works of Luis Bunuel, this was Jean-Luc Godard's most ambitious and vociferous "revolutionary" movie before he retired to the shelter of the Dziga-Vertov group. It's full of funny anti-bourgeois set pieces including one of the great sequences in all cinema: a full reel, ten-minute tracking shot that proceeds with a stately pace past a very, very long line of stalled automobiles on a French country highway lined with poplars.

This mind boggling film stacks analogy upon analogy and allegory upon allegory with hallucinatory fervor in an episodic odyssey of an unpleasant upper-class Parisian pair out for a weekend trip to visit the wife's mother. Opening with a psychiatric-session monologue by the delicate Darc, clad only in panties and perched first on a desk, then on a refrigerator as she hesitantly describes a sexual encounter involving an egg and an orifice, the movie quickly moves to the carnage of the roadways during a sunny weekend. A bumper-to-bumper carnival of cars ensues, honking, careening, crashing, overturning, and burning along with their grotesque occupants as Darc and Yanne proceed on their trip. Along the way social values regarding sex, consumerism, and family are explored in myriad surreal ways. The final result can be viewed as a darkly funny vision of Hell that culminates in one possible brave new world. One of the essential films of the 1960s.

WELCOME IN VIENNA

1988   126m   bw   ★★★★
War
Thalia/ORF/ZDF/SSR/Austrian Ministry   (Austria/
West Germany)

Gabriel Barylli (*Freddy Wolff*), Nicolas Brieger (*Sgt. Adler*), Claudia Messner (*Claudia Schutte*), Hubert Mann (*Capt. Karpeles*), Karlheinz Hackl (*Treschensky*), Liliana Nelska (*Russian Woman*), Kurt Sowinetz (*Stodola*), Joachim Kemmer (*Lt. Binder*), Heinz Trixner (*Oberst Schutte*)

d, Axel Corti; w, Axel Corti, Georg Stefan Troller; ph, Gernot Roll; ed, Ulrike Pahl, Claudia Rieneck; m, Hans Georg Koch, Franz Schubert; prod d, Matija Barl; cos, Uli Fessler

WELCOME IN VIENNA is the first and only film made on the subject of Austrian and German emigres to the US who joined the US Army and then returned to their homeland in 1944 with the American liberating forces.

Beautifully photographed in grainy black-and-white (which gives a documentary visual quality), the movie opens on Christmas Eve 1944 as the American forces are holed up in a barn in the middle of a snowy field. The two main characters are Barylli, an Austrian Jew who has longed for this return home, and Brieger, a German intellectual who fled to the States in fear of the Nazis and has now become sympathetic to the Communists. Heading their command is a tough-talking, hard-drinking German-American, Kemmer, who firmly believes in Teutonic anti-Semitism. In the battle that follows, a German deserter, Hackl, is captured who turns out to be an opportunistic Viennese and Nazi former friend of Barylli's. Time jumps ahead to May 1945 in Salzburg on the final day of the war as the liberating forces descend on the city. The first girl that Barylli lays eyes on is Messner, a pretty Austrian whose father is a colonel in the *Abwehr* (the Nazi counterintelligence). She informs US authorities that her father is willing to surrender his information, but only if the US receives him with full honors. Barylli has returned to Austria—his home—though he soon finds that things have changed. Thousands of Jews have disappeared, and as many buildings have been reduced to rubble. When he tries to locate his family's apartment, he finds it almost completely destroyed and learns that his family's possessions were sold on the street. The "home" that he hoped to find no longer exists. He works his way up in the ranks of the new government, taking a cultural job because of his smattering knowledge of theater and literature. He falls in love with Messner, who is yet another representation of that Austrian "home" that he cannot recapture. Although she loves him dearly, she uses him as a means to further her career on the stage. Brieger, in the meantime, has become disillusioned in his admiration of Stalin's Communist rule, while Hackl, still the opportunist, has moved into a position of power in the black market. As the film ends, Barylli has lost Messner to the stage and must now decide whether or not to return to America.

Funded by Austrian dollars, directed by Austrian Corti, and cowritten by Austrian expatriate Troller (now living in Paris), WELCOME IN VIENNA is the first film, according to its makers, that deals accurately with Austria's unflattering role during World War II. Echoing Jean Renoir's line of dialogue from RULES OF THE GAME that "Everybody has their reasons," Corti has presented an exceptional look at the human condition. Every element of the picture rings of a desire to tell the truth—from the newsreel quality of the film stock, to the locations and unfaltering performances.

WELCOME TO L.A.

1976   106m   c   ★★½
Drama   R/15
UA

Keith Carradine (*Carroll Barber*), Sally Kellerman (*Ann Goode*), Geraldine Chaplin (*Karen Hood*), Harvey Keitel (*Ken Hood*), Lauren Hutton (*Nona Bruce*), Viveca Lindfors (*Susan Moore*), Sissy Spacek (*Linda Murray*), Denver Pyle (*Carl Barber*), John Considine (*Jack Goode*), Richard Baskin (*Eric Wood*) p, Robert Altman; d, Alan Rudolph; w, Alan Rudolph (based on the music suite "City of the One Night Stands" by Richard Baskin); ph, David Myers (DeLuxe Color); ed, William A. Sawyer, Tom Walls; m, Richard Baskin; cos, Jules Melillo

Although heralded by some as one of the most original and innovative directorial debuts of the 1970s, Alan Rudolph's WEL-COME TO L.A., like his REMEMBER MY NAME, seems specifically designed for cult status. It takes an off-beat look at a self-important group of Los Angeles bohemians and their essentially worthless lives, which revolve mainly around sex, drinking, and driving (though not necessarily at the same time). Carradine and his fellow Altman veterans just seem to wander around a lot, and the film's success or failure depends almost entirely on how much you like them.

WEST SIDE STORY

1961   153m   c   ★★★★
Musical   /PG
Mirisch/Seven Arts/Beta

Natalie Wood (Maria), Richard Beymer (Tony), Russ Tamblyn (Riff), Rita Moreno (Anita), George Chakiris (Bernardo), Simon Oakland (Lt. Schrank), Bill Bramley (Officer Krupke), Tucker Smith (Ice), Tony Mordente (Action), Eliot Feld (Baby John)

p, Robert Wise; d, Robert Wise, Jerome Robbins; w, Ernest Lehman (based on the stage play by Arthur Laurents, based on a conception by Robbins, inspired by a play by William Shakespeare); ph, Daniel Fapp (Panavision, Technicolor); ed, Thomas Stanford; m, Leonard Bernstein; prod d, Boris Leven; chor, Jerome Robbins; cos, Irene Sharaff

When it's good, very good; when it's bad, a stinker. Winner of 10 Academy Awards, including Best Picture, WEST SIDE STORY is the filmed version of the hit Broadway musical inspired by "Romeo and Juliet." Jerome Robbins, who conceived the stage version, gets co-director credit here. He was originally slated to direct the entire film, but his perfectionism meant twice the budget. United Artists brought in Robert Wise after less than a month of rehearsals, assigning him direction of the non-musical sequences. Before long, Robbins was booted all together. The numbers he choreographed remain the most inventive, energetic sequences in the film: the lengthy opening sequence (including "The Jet Song," "America," "I Feel Pretty" and "Cool".) If Robbins had done the whole of it, we might be left with a more dynamic and explosive film. Byut there's no discounting that whenever WEST SIDE STORY proclaims the leads' love it goes predictable on us—musically, first and foremost, so no director could entirely change that. Too bad love can't be explosive too (we thought that's what WSS was about; looks like we were wrong), but as it is, Wise saddled these moments with all the usual—soft-focus camera work, stars in the sky, Rodgers and Hammerstein ballet. This is still playing to the blue-haired matinee ladies. Nor is this helped by Natalie Wood and Richard Beymer (dubbed by Marni Nixon and Jim Bryant). When they're not mouthing like fish in tanks, they're wrestling the awkward dialogue of these sequences. Lucky for us, everything— and everyone—else is first-rate; especially the three meaty supporting parts played by Moreno (alas, dubbed also, by Betty Wand— but Moreno acts with fire and can dance), gorgeous, pantherine Chakiris and winning Tamblyn.

Sticking closely to Arthur Laurents's original book, the film follows the escalating tensions between rival teenage gangs the Jets (who are white) and the Sharks (who are Puerto Rican) as they battle for turf in Manhattan's Upper West Side. The Sharks are led by Bernardo (Chakiris, who won a Best Supporting Actor Oscar), boyfriend of the tempestuous Anita (Best Supporting Actress Moreno); the Jets follow Riff (Tamblyn). Caught in the middle are Bernardo's sister, Maria (Wood), who has just arrived from Puerto Rico, and Tony (Beymer), a member of the Jets who is Riff's best friend. Tony and Maria fall in love, despite the hatred between their friends and relatives, but the romance is destined to end tragically (the musical's book was based on Romeo and Juliet).

WEST SIDE STORY became one of the most popular film musicals in history, largely on the strength of its youth appeal and the aforementioned Robbins's choreography—a spectacular combination of ballet, acrobatics, and jazz excitingly adapted for the camera. The score by Stephen Sondheim and Leonard Bernstein has become an acknowledged and much-beloved classic. Besides Moreno and Chakiris, the film's Oscar-winners were Wise and Robbins for co-direction; Daniel Fapp's cinematography; Boris Leven's art direction; Victor Gangelin's set direction; Irene Sharaff's costume design; Thomas Stanford's film editing; the musical scoring (direction and arrangement) by Johnny Green, Sid Ramin, Irwin Kostal, and Saul Chaplin; the sound; and Robbins again, who received a special honorary Oscar for "his brilliant achievements in the art of choreography on film in WEST SIDE STORY."

WESTERN UNION

1941   93m   c   ★★★★
Western   /U
FOX

Randolph Scott (Vance Shaw), Robert Young (Richard Blake), Dean Jagger (Edward Creighton), Virginia Gilmore (Sue Creighton), John Carradine (Doc Murdoch), Slim Summerville (Herman), Chill Wills (Homer), Barton MacLane (Jack Slade), Russell Hicks (Governor), Victor Kilian (Charlie)

p, Harry Joe Brown; d, Fritz Lang; w, Robert Carson (based on a story by Zane Grey); ph, Edward Cronjager, Allen Davey (Technicolor); ed, Robert Bischoff, Gene Flowler, Jr. (uncredited); m, David Buttolph; art d, Richard Day, Albert Hogsett; cos, Travis Banton

After the success of his first western, THE RETURN OF FRANK JAMES, German director Lang was assigned to do another, this one based on the construction of the Western Union telegraph line from Omaha, Nebraska, to Salt Lake City, Utah. Randolph Scott stars as an outlaw looking to reform his wicked ways.

The most epic and beautiful of Lang's westerns (it was the director's personal favorite), WESTERN UNION is an outstanding entry in the genre. Lang, who loved the American West and spent much time traveling there, researched the period thoroughly and paid painstaking attention to detail. Having studied American Indians for some time, he was delighted with the opportunity to present them in their full glory, with accurate warpaint and battle gear photographed in beautiful Technicolor. The photography by Cronjager is some of the most beautiful work of the 1940s, and the cast is filled with outstanding character actors such as Carradine, Wills, Summerville, and Kilian. There is much humor in WESTERN UNION, most of it centering around Summerville, the timid cook scared witless of the "Wild West." Lang would make only one more western, RANCHO NOTORIOUS, yet another superior entry from a German director working in a distinctly American genre.

WESTERNER, THE

1940 100m bw ★★★★★
Western /U
UA

Gary Cooper (*Cole Hardin*), Walter Brennan (*Judge Roy Bean*), Doris Davenport (*Jane-Ellen Mathews*), Fred Stone (*Caliphet Mathews*), Paul Hurst (*Chickenfoot*), Chill Wills (*Southeast*), Charles Halton (*Mort Borrow*), Forrest Tucker (*Wade Harper*), Tom Tyler (*King Evans*), Arthur Aylesworth (*Mr. Dixon*)

p, Samuel Goldwyn; d, William Wyler; w, Jo Swerling, Niven Busch (based on a story by Stuart N. Lake); ph, Gregg Toland; ed, Daniel Mandell; m, Alfred Newman (uncredited), Dimitri Tiomkin; art d, James Basevi; fx, Archie Stout, Paul Eagler; cos, Irene Saltern

A superior western that mixes fine cinematography, terrific performances, and a script of higher caliber than most to produce a film still fondly remembered today. Cooper is a drifter who runs afoul of the law when he is falsely accused of stealing a horse. He is taken in front of Brennan, who serves as a justice of the peace and *is* the "Law west of the Pecos," as a cemetery full of his victims will attest. He tries Cooper in a hasty mockery of justice and sentences him to hang, but Cooper, knowing Brennan's admiration and even love for stage star Lily Langtry (after whom Brennan has named his town), convinces the judge that he is a personal friend of Langtry and will obtain a lock of her hair for the judge if the judge lets him go. Brennan is so love-struck that he doesn't see through this obvious lie, and the two men soon become friends of a sort. That night, Cooper steals Brennan's gun and escapes, stopping at the farm of Stone and his daughter, Davenport. Brennan is conducting a campaign, through his deputies, aimed at driving the homesteaders off the range. Cooper, who has become smitten with Davenport, decides to stay in the area and be the advocate for the homesteaders with Brennan. For a time things go smoothly, and Cooper gives Brennan a lock of Davenport's hair, telling him it is from Langtry; but then Brennan's terrorizing of the farmers takes on new fervor, and Stone is murdered. Cooper sets out for a reckoning with Brennan, but learns that the judge has left Langtry to travel to Fort Davis, where he has bought every seat in the theater to see Langtry in person for the first time. The curtain rises, and it is Cooper who is standing there, guns at the ready. The two men shoot it out in the gaslit hall, and Cooper finally manages to wound Brennan mortally. Dying, Brennan is taken backstage by Cooper to meet his dream, played here by Lilian Bond, whose hand he kisses before he dies.

Cooper was initially reluctant to take the part of the drifter, thinking it too minor for an actor of his stature. Director Wyler shamed him out of that attitude, though, with a variation of the "no small parts, only small actors" bit, and he gave Cooper enough good scenes to make the actor happy. It is Brennan, however, who steals the picture, making Judge Roy Bean one of the most unforgettable characters ever seen in a western film, researching his character and adopting a neck dislocation to represent an injury the historical judge incurred when he was hanged and cut down. Cinematographer Toland's work is superb, filling his western skies with gnarled trees and amazing clouds, and underscoring the story with a strangely somber tone. The score by Tiomkin was completely scrapped at the last minute and a new one written by Alfred Newman, though he did not receive screen credit. Dana Andrews and Forrest Tucker made their debuts here. A major success, the film earned Brennan his third Oscar as Best Supporting Actor in five years. He had previously been honored for COME AND GET IT and KENTUCKY. The

film was also nominated for Best Original Story and Best Interior Decoration.

WESTWORLD

1973 91m c ★★★½
Science Fiction/Western PG/15
MGM

Yul Brynner (*Gunslinger*), Richard Benjamin (*Peter Martin*), James Brolin (*John Blane*), Norman Bartold (*Medieval Queen*), Dick Van Patten (*Banker*), Linda Scott (*Arlette*), Steve Franken (*Technician*), Michael T. Mikler (*Black Knight*), Terry Wilson (*Sheriff*), Majel Barrett (*Miss Carrie*)

p, Paul N. Lazurus III; d, Michael Crichton; w, Michael Crichton; ph, Gene Polito (Panavision, Metrocolor); ed, David Bretherton; m, Fred Karlin; art d, Herman A. Blumenthal; fx, Charles Schulthies

The title refers to a futuristic Disney-type fantasy land which features android Western figures. Benjamin and Brolin are two businessman who come to WESTWORLD to live out their fantasies, and Brynner is the robot Benjamin kills in a saloon fight. Suddenly everything goes haywire, and the machines stalk the visitors. Brynner guns down Brolin, and chases Benjamin. Brynner is very good, his austere presence and unflinching intent making him seem indestructible. The film grossed a healthy $3.4 million in the US and Canada and was the last film from MGM before it dissolved its releasing company. Ten minutes have been deleted from the original footage to allow WESTWORLD's present PG rating. The gardens of movie comedian Harold Lloyd's estate were used for some of the amusement park sequences. The film was followed by a sequel, FUTUREWORLD.

WETHERBY

1985 102m c ★★★½
Drama R/15
Greenpoint/Film Four/Zenith (U.K.)

Vanessa Redgrave (*Jean Travers*), Ian Holm (*Stanley Pilborough*), Judi Dench (*Marcia Pilborough*), Marjorie Yates (*Verity Braithwaite*), Tom Wilkinson (*Roger Braithwaite*), Tim McInnerny (*John Morgan*), Suzanna Hamilton (*Karen Creasy*), Stuart Wilson (*Mike Langdon*), Mike Kelly (*CID Policeman*), Diane Whitley

p, Simon Relph; d, David Hare; w, David Hare; ph, Stuart Harris (Technicolor); ed, Christopher Wimble; m, Nick Bicat; prod d, Hayden Griffin; art d, Jamie Leonard; cos, Jane Greenwood, Lindy Hemming

A very intelligent picture that needs to be looked at closely in order to fathom some of its subtleties. David Hare, the playwright of PLENTY, wrote and directed this film, and it's a corker. Wetherby is a small, cold town in Yorkshire. Jean Travers (Vanessa Redgrave) is a local teacher who never married. Her teenage crush was killed in Malaya in the 1950s, and she has never gotten over it. Jean is having a small dinner party in her home for two couples, Stanley (Ian Holm) and Marcia Piborough (Judi Dench), and Roger (Tom Wilkinson) and Verity Braithwaite (Marjorie Yates). When John Morgan (Tim McInnerny) shows up, Jean assumes that he is with one of the couples and they assume that he is a friend of hers. He is neither. The following day, Morgan comes by Jean's home, has a pleasant chat, then, without a bit of warning and apparently no motivation, puts a gun in his mouth and blows his brains out. It is an incredibly shocking moment. The movie flits in the present, the recent past, and sometime in the early 1950s. Hare uses an intriguing technique as he keeps going back to the seemingly ordinary dinner party in memory, and we realize that what we saw before was only the tip of the iceberg. To give away the answer to this enigma might be a disservice to anyone who likes to use his noodle. There are more questions asked than answered in this movie, but the mental gymnastics are well worth the effort. The performances are all first-rate as well, including that of Joely Richardson, Redgrave's daughter with director Tony Richardson, as the young Jean.

WHALES OF AUGUST, THE

1987 90m c   ★★★
Drama   /U
Alive/Circle/Nelson

Bette Davis (*Libby Strong*), Lillian Gish (*Sarah Webber*), Vincent Price (*Mr. Nikolai Maranov*), Ann Sothern (*Tisha Doughty*), Harry Carey, Jr. (*Joshua Brackett*), Frank Grimes (*Mr. Beckwith*), Frank Pitkin (*Old Randall*), Mike Bush (*Young Randall*), Margaret Ladd (*Young Libby*), Tisha Sterling (*Young Tisha*)

p, Carolyn Pfeiffer, Mike Kaplan; d, Lindsay Anderson; w, David Berry (based on the play by David Berry); ph, Mike Fash (CFI Color); ed, Nicolas Gaster; m, Alan Price; prod d, Jocelyn Herbert; art d, K.C. Fox, Bob Fox; cos, Rudy Dillon, Julie Weiss

It is 1954, and Libby Strong (Bette Davis) and her younger sister Sarah Webber (Lillian Gish) have returned to the small Maine island for the summer, just as they have done for the past 60 years. Libby is now blind and Sarah has cheerfully looked after her for 15 years. As girls they had stood on the cliffs and watched for whales. Now the whales come no more. Sarah still anticipates their appearance and wants to put in a new picture window, but Libby, who has grown bitter and cynical, thinks it would be frivolous and vetoes the idea. Tisha Doughty (Ann Sothern), their lifelong friend and the island's resident busybody, pays them a visit and tries to persuade Sarah to put Libby in her daughter's care and to move in with her.

With its extraordinary cast, THE WHALES OF AUGUST would have made cinema history even if its script had been taken from a cereal box. In fact, the screenplay, adapted by David Berry from his own largely autobiographical stage play, isn't one of the film's stronger elements. Suffering from heavy-handed symbolism and offering few real insights, it nonetheless provides the blueprint from which these exceptional actors are able to build their performances. THE WHALES OF AUGUST has more than a few problems, but anyone interested in the art of acting, the history of the cinema, or in seeing an unpatronizing portrait of elderly characters will find the film rewarding. Sothern was Oscar-nominated for Best Supporting Actress.

WHAT A WAY TO GO!

1964 111m c   ★½
Comedy   /15
FOX

Shirley MacLaine (*Louisa*), Paul Newman (*Larry Flint*), Robert Mitchum (*Rod Anderson*), Dean Martin (*Leonard Crawley*), Gene Kelly (*Jerry Benson*), Robert Cummings (*Dr. Stephanson*), Dick Van Dyke (*Edgar Hopper*), Reginald Gardiner (*Painter*), Margaret Dumont (*Mrs. Foster*), Roy Gordon (*Minister*)

p, Arthur P. Jacobs; d, J. Lee Thompson; w, Betty Comden, Adolph Green (based on a story by Gwen Davis); ph, Leon Shamroy (CinemaScope, DeLuxe Color); ed, Marjorie Fowler; m, Nelson Riddle; art d, Jack Martin Smith, Ted Haworth; fx, L.B. Abbott, Dick Smith, Emil Kosa, Jr.; chor, Gene Kelly, Richard Humphrey; cos, Edith Head, Moss Mabry

Former press agent Jacobs always felt that "bigger was better," so for this, his first venture into film producing, he decided to do a huge comedy, filled with stars, huge sets, and colorful costumes. It all went to prove that bigger isn't better. As the film opens, MacLaine is sharing her tale of woe with psychiatrist Cummings. Seems she's worth $200 million, but she wants to give the money to the IRS because she believes it's cursed. In flashback, the story unfolds, beginning with her refusal to marry the very wealthy Martin. Instead, she weds Van Dyke, a poor shopkeeper. Upset because Martin has told her she's made a big mistake, Van Dyke works tirelessly to amass a fortune and dies from the exertion. MacLaine, now a wealthy widow, heads for Paris, where she meets struggling Newman. MacLaine promptly falls in love with him, and they marry. Newman has invented a painting machine that is driven by sound, and when classical music is used to operate the contraption, it spews out masterpieces that take the art world by storm. Newman is soon fabulously wealthy, but he's crushed to death by his own creation. Now richer still, MacLaine returns to the US, where she meets Mitchum, an already wealthy businessman. She figures that, since he's alreay got money, he won't be affected by the curse of hers. They marry and move to the country, where they plan to live as simple farmers. Mitchum's neglected businesses prosper even more, but Mitchum soon becomes dead-husband number three when he tries to milk a bull. Despondent, MacLaine goes to a seedy night spot, where Kelly is the featured entertainer. Kelly's act is going nowhere, but he doesn't seem to mind, and MacLaine falls for him. After they marry, Kelly takes an even more relaxed approach to his act, showing up late and singing whatever appeals to him at the time. The audience loves him, his act becomes a smash, and soon he's a major star in Hollywood—until he's trampled to death by his adoring fans. That finishes MacLaine's story, and, back in Cummings's office, the IRS calls to accept MacLaine's money. She's delighted to part with it. Then, in walks Martin, now the building's janitor, having lost all of his money. He and MacLaine marry to live in dire poverty but with smiles on their faces.

The size of this production was awesome. Costumer Edith Head had half a million dollars to play with for the more than 70 MacLaine costumes, and jeweler Harry Winston lent a bauble collection of almost $4 million to the production. A musical-extravaganza number featured Kelly and MacLaine in a satire of every nautical musical ever made. Comden, Green, and Jule Styne collaborated on "Musical Extravaganza" and "I Think You and I Should Get Acquainted." Thompson employed several shooting styles. The Van Dyke episode is reminiscent of a silent movie. The Newman section is shot as a French film, right down to the English subtitles. The Mitchum section is a Doris Day-Rock Hudson Universal look-alike. And the Gene Kelly piece resembles a Busby Berkeley production. On paper this picture seemed to have everything going for it. Unfortunately, movies are made on film, and it sank. The fact was that it simply wasn't very funny. Some interesting cameos include veteran players like Dumont (in her last film after having served so long as the Marx Brothers' foil), former boxer Lou Nova, Tom Conway (in his last role; he is the former "Falcon" of the movies and brother of George Sanders), and comics Lenny Kent, Sid Gould, and Wally Vernon. A real flopperoo—which proves that excess for its own sake means little or nothing to movie audiences.

WHATEVER HAPPENED TO BABY JANE?

1962 132m bw   ★★★★
Thriller   /18
Aldrich

Bette Davis *(Jane Hudson)*, Joan Crawford *(Blanche Hudson)*, Victor Buono *(Edwin Flagg)*, Anna Lee *(Mrs. Bates)*, Maidie Norman *(Elvira Stitt)*, Marjorie Bennett *(Mrs. Della Flagg)*, Dave Willock *(Ray Hudson)*, Anne Barton *(Cora Hudson)*, Barbara D. Merrill *(Liza Bates)*, Julie Allred *(Young Jane)*

p, Robert Aldrich; d, Robert Aldrich; w, Lukas Heller (based on the novel by Henry Farrell); ph, Ernest Haller; ed, Michael Luciano; m, Frank DeVol; art d, William Glasgow; fx, Don Steward; chor, Alex Romero; cos, Norma Koch

Star wars, trenchantly served, with Davis as wharf rat and Crawford a frantic parakeet. If it sometimes looks like a posionous senior citizen show with over-the-top spoiled ham, just try to look away. Bringing the screen's queens of sadism and masochism together for this slice of Camp Hollywood gothic horror revitalized the careers of both.

The Hudson sisters—Davis and Crawford—are aging actresses who live in a rotting Los Angeles mansion. Davis had been a spoiled brat vaudeville headliner known as "Baby Jane," but as she grew older her career faded. Crawford lived in her shadow as a girl but had an enormously successful adult career as a screen glamour girl. But she was unable to help Davis gain a career in film, due to the latter's drinking and eccentric behavior. At the peak of her stardom, Crawford suffered a career-ending accident for which Davis was seemingly responsible. Ever since then the two have lived together in mutual enmity, tended to by their maid, Norman. When Davis learns that her wheelchair-bound sister is planning to sell the mansion and put her in a sanitarium, she begins terrorizing Crawford; at the same time, she enlists the service of Buono, a young pianist who she hopes will help her make a comeback. The film then suspensefully builds its way to a conclusion that puts a new spin on the relationship between the two sisters.

As in the best Hitchcock movies, suspense, rather than actual mayhem, drives the film. The screenplay, by Lukas Heller, was based on the novel by Henry Farrell (who also authored the novel HUSH, HUSH SWEET CHARLOTTE and scripted WHAT'S THE MATTER WITH HELEN?).

Aldrich had his hands full balancing the overblown but sensitive egos of the rival actresses. If full-scale battle never erupted, it is still correct to say that battle lines were constantly being drawn. The original choice to star with Davis was Tallulah Bankhead (a far more lethal combination than the eventual one) when the property began floating around Hollywood, but Crawford acquired rights to the property, and offered it to Davis while the latter was unhappily appearing on Broadway in *Night of the Iquana*. Davis commanded a larger salary, Crawford a larger percentage of the gross (Joan's years at Pepsi-Cola paid off). Davis's foot allegedly made contact with Crawford's head during a scene where Baby Jane punts her sister around the living room. Crawford supposedly retaliated by use of the old Veronica Lake trick (see I MARRIED A WITCH) by rigging weights under her robe for a scene where Davis had to drag her, and Davis hurt her back. Crawford shared a private joke on Davis by sending hairdresser Peggy Shannon to MGM to secure her old blonde wig from ICE FOLLIES OF 1939 for Davis to wear. Davis bitched to Aldrich about Crawford's drinking (both were alcoholics) and padded brassieres; Crawford insulted Davis's daughter (who appeared in the film—to put it kindly, she was not burdened by her mother's talent), and the incidents go on and on.

In a bucket of gooey make-up, Davis cried when she saw herself in rushes (the limited budget precluded re-shooting) but her excessive performance is riveting—capturing the malevolence Lynn Redgrave lacked in the 1991 TV remake. Crawford

wisely underacts—if her performance isn't as showy as Davis's, it's not any less accomplished. But Academy voters couldn't shake the outrageous nerve of Davis's histrionics: she was rewarded with a Best Actress nomination.

JANE features two girls—Julie Allred and Gina Gillespie—ideally cast as Davis and Crawford during childhood. Victor Buono won a supporting Oscar for his outrageous portrayal of Davis's obese mama's boy pianist. Beloved character actress Marjorie Bennett plays his mother and Maidie Norman gets the hammer. Frank DeVol wrote "I've Written a Letter to Daddy," the song Davis can't shake from her demented brain. For all the "career revitalization" resulting for both actresses, JANE created a downward spiral for them both—and for their peers—creating a whole genre where aging movie queens debased themselves as camp horror stooges.

WHAT'S NEW, PUSSYCAT?
(QUOI DE NEUF, PUSSYCAT?)
1965   108m   c   ★★★½
Comedy   /15
Famous Artists/Famartists   (U.S./France)

Peter Sellers *(Dr. Fritz Fassbender)*, Peter O'Toole *(Michael James)*, Romy Schneider *(Carole Werner)*, Capucine *(Renee Lefebvre)*, Paula Prentiss *(Liz)*, Woody Allen *(Victor Shakapopulis)*, Ursula Andress *(Rita)*, Eddra Gale *(Anna Fassbender)*, Katrin Schaake *(Jacqueline)*, Eleonore Hirt *(Mrs. Sylvia Werner)*

p, Charles K. Feldman; d, Clive Donner; w, Woody Allen; ph, Jean Badal (Technicolor); ed, Fergus McDonell; m, Burt Bacharach; art d, Jacques Saulnier; fx, M. MacDonald; chor, Jean Guelis; cos, Gladys de Segonzac, Mia Fonssagrives, Vicky Tiel

A most significant film to buffs in that it marks the first time Woody Allen appeared on screen in a script drawn from his own typewriter. Until this time he'd been a successful nightclub and TV variety show comic, and WHAT'S NEW PUSSYCAT? gave a wider audience to his patented neuroses. It's a good example of the "swinging sixties" style under the broad direction of Clive Donner, who had begun his career in films as an assistant director. O'Toole, fresh from his triumphs in LAWRENCE OF ARABIA and BECKET, shows that he can deliver the goods comedically as well as dramatically; here he takes the role of a lover of gorgeous women who fears nothing in this world save marriage. Sellers is a freaked-out, Beatle-wigged analyst attempting to help O'Toole deal with his problems but is so lecherous himself that he is of little value to the disturbed O'Toole. Allen is an intellectual nebbish whose life is a perpetual attempt to learn why he can't attract women. He toils as a dresser (or, rather, an "undresser") for exotic dancers at a Parisian nightspot (the famed "Crazy Horse Saloon"), and his propinquity to the femmes drives him mad. O'Toole needs a Louisville Slugger to keep the women away from him. The coterie is led by Schneider, an English teacher and pal of Allen's, the sanest in the lot of fatales who flock to O'Toole's side. She loves O'Toole and would enjoy becoming his wife, but there is no way she would ever put up with his compulsive Don Juan behavior. One of the patients at a Sellers group therapy session is the radiant Capucine, who is mad for O'Toole, much to the chagrin of her jealous husband, Paredes. Prentiss is a stripper at the club where Allen toils in frustration and she, too, chases O'Toole. She becomes suicidal over her passion for O'Toole and reaches for her overdose of sleeping pills the way other women might reach for Kleenex. Just as O'Toole has made the supreme sacrifice and decided to marry Schneider, Andress skies down from overhead in a parachute to test O'Toole's mettle. She almost succeeds in breaking O'Toole's will power, but he winds up with the comely Schneider at the conclusion when there is a raucous scene at a French country chateau and all the protagonists unite for a final madcap merry-go-round. It's in this crazy scene that we get our first indication of Allen's penchant for Marxian slapstick (Groucho, Harpo, and Chico, not Karlo) as action speaks louder than the sometimes-too-many words. All of the women in O'Toole's life are seen in Feydeau-like fashion as they race yon and hither, hide in closets, run around the countryside in go-carts, lie in wait under covers, and, in general, try to capture O'Toole, who sincerely wants to avoid them (albeit half-heartedly at times) because he knows what kind of complications would ensue if he allowed himself to be seduced by any of the bevy. O'Toole marries Schneider, but scant moments after the service, another "pussycat" (which he calls all of his women) emerges in the form of license clerk Hardy. The sight of her sends a jolt into O'Toole's just-married baby blue eyes.

WHAT'S NEW, PUSSYCAT? is a classic comedy of its time and captures the period in sight and sound. It doesn't wear as well as a true classic, though, and many of the gags would feel dated 20 years later. Sets and costumes are superb, as are the scenes at the "Crazy Horse." Burt Bacharach's music and Hal David's lyrics helped immensely, with the title tune being Oscar-nominated and reaching No. 3 in pop music polls that year. The movie was a box-office success, appealing, no doubt, to those who doubted the sexual "double standard" as well as the Teutonic psychiatrist so aptly portrayed by Sellers. Richard Burton does a cameo, as does Allen's wife at the time, Louise Lasser. By making O'Toole the editor on a Paris fashion magazine, the tale was able to move with lighting speed and also justify his coming into contact with so many gorgeous women—every man's dream, but most particularly Woody Allen's.

WHAT'S UP, DOC?

1972 94m c   ★★★
Comedy   G/U
Saticoy

Barbra Streisand (*Judy Maxwell*), Ryan O'Neal (*Prof. Howard Bannister*), Madeline Kahn (*Eunice Burns*), Kenneth Mars (*Hugh Simon*), Austin Pendleton (*Frederick Larrabe*), Sorrell Booke (*Harry*), Stefan Gierasch (*Fritz*), Mabel Albertson (*Mrs. Van Hoskins*), Michael Murphy (*Mr. Smith*), Graham Jarvis (*Bailiff*)

p, Peter Bogdanovich; d, Peter Bogdanovich; w, Buck Henry, David Newman, Robert Benton (based on a story by Bogdanovich); ph, Laszlo Kovacs (Technicolor); ed, Verna Fields; m, Artie Butler; prod d, Polly Platt; art d, Herman A. Blumenthal; fx, Robert MacDonald; cos, Nancy McArdle, Ray Phelps

Peter Bogdanovich's attempt to revive the screwball comedy genre is more imitation than homage, especially if you've seen the Howard Hawks classic BRINGING UP BABY. Still, the film has plenty of good 1930s slapstick and cartoon humor to hold your attention and to justify Bugs Bunny's famed opening line (which serves as the title) and Porky Pig's equally famed closing: "Th-th-that's all, folks!" Ryan O'Neal, a clumsy, shy professor from Iowa, hopes to win a $20,000 fellowship in musicology. He carries some ancient rocks in a plaid suitcase; the rocks demonstrate his theory on music's prehistoric origins. O'Neal arrives at a San Francisco hotel with his fiancee, Kahn (in her film debut), while other guests with identical suitcases, including the breezy Streisand, are also checking in. Naturally, the suitcases get hopelessly mixed up—a daffy coincidence leading to countless comic scenes. While WHAT'S UP, DOC? may not be as great as the classic screwball comedies of the 1930s and 40s,

director Bogdanovich has delivered a film with energy, wit, and a madcap pace that is well worth watching.

WHAT'S UP, TIGER LILY?

1966 80m c   ★★½
Comedy   PG
Toho/Benedict

Tatsuya Mihashi (*Phil Moscowitz*), Mie Hama (*Terri Yaki*), Akiko Wakabayashi (*Suki Yaki*), Tadao Nakamaru (*Shepherd Wong*), Susumu Kurobe (*Wing Fat*), Woody Allen (*Narrator/Host/Voice*), Frank Buxton, Len Maxwell, Louise Lasser, Mickey Rose

p, Woody Allen; d, Senkichi Taniguchi; w, Kazuo Yamada, Woody Allen, Frank Buxton, Len Maxwell, Louise Lasser, Mickey Rose, Bryna Wilson, Julie Bennett; ph, Kazuo Yamada (Tohoscope, Eastmancolor); ed, Richard Krown; m, Jack Lewis, The Lovin' Spoonful

Woody Allen took a low-grade Japanese spy film called KAGI NO KAGI (Key of Keys) and dubbed in new dialogue (improvised with Buxton, Maxwell, Lasser, Rose, Wilson, and Bennett) to create this wonderfully cockeyed movie. In a prologue Allen explains to an interviewer that this is the "definitive" spy picture. Allen was chosen to head the project because, he says, Hollywood knows that "death and danger are my various breads and various butters." The story describes the adventures of Phil Moscowitz, a Japanese James Bond who is searching for the world's greatest egg salad recipe. The balance of world power hangs on whether or not Moscowitz can keep this recipe—"so delicious you could *plotz*"—from falling into the wrong hands. After many plucky escapades, Moscowitz confronts Shepherd Wong, the evil mastermind trying to get the recipe for his own nefarious doings. Moscowitz defeats Wong's henchmen and then returns to his loves, Suki and Terri Yaki. They are eager for him to arrive, "bringing with him the constant promise of joy and fulfillment in its most primitive form." But alas, Moscowitz is now under the delusion that he is a Pan Am jet! WHAT'S UP, TIGER LILY?, more than any of Allen's films, is beyond the realm of synopsis. It's cleverly devised, hinging on a developed sense of the absurd. Allen and his cohorts make good use of the source movie's situations, turning its obvious cliches into some wonderful parodic gems. This is not a film that bears repeated viewing, however. The one-liners spew out like popcorn, an effect that wears a little thin towards the end. Footage of the pop group the Lovin' Spoonful edited into the story also detracts from the pell-mell pacing. Though Allen had limited control over the visual content, many of the themes and ideas he would later develop in such films as LOVE AND DEATH and HANNAH AND HER SISTERS are evident in the dialogue—themes of sexual frustration, psychiatry and neurosis, Judaism, and the influence of movies. Executive producer Saperstein paid only $66,000 for the rights to KEY OF KEYS and certainly got more than his money's worth when he turned it over to the rising comedian. Heard on the soundtrack are Lasser, Allen's second wife, and Rose, cowriter with Allen of TAKE THE MONEY AND RUN and BANANAS.

WHEELER DEALERS, THE

1963 106m c   ★★½
Comedy   /U
Filmways

James Garner (Henry Tyroon), Lee Remick (Molly Thatcher), Phil Harris (Ray Jay), Chill Wills (Jay Ray), Louis Nye (Stanislas), John Astin (Hector Vanson), Jim Backus (Bullard Bear), Elliott Reid (Leonard), Pat Crowley (Eloise), Pat Harrington, Jr. (Buddy Zack)

p, Martin Ransohoff; d, Arthur Hiller; w, George J.W. Goodman, Ira Wallach (based on the novel by Goodman); ph, Charles Lang (Panavision, Metrocolor); ed, Tom McAdoo; m, Frank DeVol; art d, George W. Davis, Addison Hehr; cos, Norman Norell

A number of outrageously zany characterizations were delivered in this spoof of Wall Street stock market ethics. Garner sets the whole thing in motion when he comes to analyst Remick to invest some of his "millions." Though Garner hardly has a penny, Remick is told by her always business-minded boss, Backus, to sell him a totally worthless stock. As it turns out, the stock is actually worth tons when oil is discovered on property belonging to the company. Garner actually turns out to be a millionaire once the deal is completed and promptly asks for the hand of Remick. Both script and direction are aimed at keeping the pace moving swiftly, much in accordance with the practices of Wall Street and greater New York in general. Garner is the only character to show any depth, though all perform with comic intention.

WHEN FATHER WAS AWAY ON BUSINESS
(OTAC NA SLUZBENOH PUTU)
1985   144m   c   ★★★½
Drama/Comedy   R/15
Centar/Forum   (Yugoslavia)

Moreno D'E Bartolli (Malik), Miki Manojlovic (Mesha), Mirjana Karanovic (Senija), Mustafa Nadarevic (Zijo), Mira Furlan (Ankica), Davor Dujmovic (Mirza), Predrag Lakovic (Franjo), Pavle Vujisic (Muzamer), Eva Ras (Zivka), Aleksandar Dorcev (Dr. Ljahaov)

d, Emir Kusturica; w, Abdulah Sidran; ph, Vilko Filac (WS Color); ed, Andrija Zafranovic; m, Zoran Simjanovic; cos, Divna Jovanovic

In only his second film, director Emir Kusturica managed to grab the prestigious Golden Palm at Cannes with this moving story. It is the early 1950s in Yugoslavia, which, under the leadership of Marshal Tito, has broken with the USSR. Nobody is sure if their next-door neighbor is shooting off his mouth or deliberately trying to bait someone else into making an antigovernment statement. If that happens, police arrive in the middle of the night and the next thing one knows, they are "away on business." Malik (Moreno D'E Bartolli) is the 6-year-old child who narrates the story of his father, Mesha (Miki Manojlovic), a former employee in the Labor Ministry and now a resident of a labor camp. The family likes everyone to think that Mesha is in jail for unspecified political actions, but just about everyone knows the truth—that he is in jail because he used his position to curry favor with women. When he left his latest lover, Ankica (Mira Furlan), she turned him in. Malik and his older brother (Davor Dujmovic) do their best to keep their mother (Mirjana Karanovic) happy while her husband is gone. But she is terribly angry because the man who arrested her husband is her very own brother, the local police commissioner, who is also sexually involved with Ankica and wanted to get his competition out of the way. The movie is charming, funny, political, tender, and poignant. There are very few films that can give you any one of those qualities, much less all of them. Though the narrator is a child himself, children should not see this film due to its explicit sexuality and excessive politics.

WHEN HARRY MET SALLY. . .
1989   96m   c   ★★★
Comedy/Romance   R/15
Castle Rock/Nelson

Billy Crystal (Harry Burns), Meg Ryan (Sally Albright), Carrie Fisher (Marie), Bruno Kirby (Jess), Steven Ford (Joe), Lisa Jane Persky (Alice), Michelle Nicastro (Amanda), Gretchen Palmer (Stewardess), Robert Alan Beuth (Man on Aisle), David Burdick (9-year-old Boy)

p, Rob Reiner, Andrew Scheinman, Jeffrey Stott, Steve Nicolaides; d, Rob Reiner; w, Nora Ephron; ph, Barry Sonnenfeld (Duart Color, CFI Color); ed, Robert Leighton; m, Marc Shaiman, Harry Connick, Jr.; prod d, Jane Musky; cos, Gloria Gresham

Harry (Billy Crystal) meets Sally (Meg Ryan) on a post-graduation drive from the University of Chicago to New York, but when she rebuffs his flip advances, instant antipathy is born. Nonetheless, over the next 10 years in Manhattan, the two bump into each other at various emotionally crucial points in their lives and eventually manage to effect a friendship. Then sex rears its insistent head once more, and, following a period of readjustment, commitment-shy Harry learns that staying an entire night—and possibly an entire life—with one's object of lust is actually possible. The plot may seem anything but fresh (and the borrowings from Woody Allen certainly are stale), but director Rob Reiner has a killer instinct for setting up jokes and punchlines, and is vastly aided by the performances and chemistry of Crystal and Ryan, as well as crisp supporting work from Carrie Fisher and Bruno Kirby. The screenplay, by Nora Ephron, was nominated for an Oscar.

WHEN THE WIND BLOWS
1988   85m   c   ★★★★
Animated   /PG
Meltdown/British Screen/Film Four/TVC London/
Penguin Books   (U.K.)

VOICES OF: Peggy Ashcroft (Hilda Bloggs), John Mills (Jim Bloggs), Robin Houston (Announcer), James Russell, Matt Irving, David Dundas

p, John Coates; d, Jimmy T. Murakami; w, Raymond Briggs (based on his book); ed, John Cary; m, Roger Waters; fx, Stephen Weston

With its striking simplicity, WHEN THE WIND BLOWS is a moving parable of nuclear holocaust. Told through animation, the story follows a retired English couple, James Bloggs (voiced by John Mills) and his wife, Hilda (voiced by Peggy Ashcroft), as they face the postnuclear winter in a small cottage in the British countryside. World tensions have been building, according to radio reports, and war is imminent. When the bomb goes off, destroying the England James and Hilda love so dearly, they are convinced the situation is merely a temporary crisis and, like WWII, one they can stick out until things get back to normal. Gradually, radiation begin taking its toll on the couple, and small but important details of their lives start to slip out of their control. These developments are handled with a gentle, sympathetic humor that subtly brings out the hopelessness of their plight. Mills and Ashcroft are perfectly cast in their cartoon roles. The variety of animation styles frequently produces captivating visual effects. WHEN THE WIND BLOWS is an eloquent vision of the ultimate tragedy.

WHERE EAGLES DARE

1968   155m   c   ★★★½
War   M/PG
Winkast   (U.K.)

Richard Burton (John Smith), Clint Eastwood (Lt. Morris Schaffer), Mary Ure (Mary Ellison), Patrick Wymark (Col. Turner), Michael Hordern (Vice Adm. Rolland), Donald Houston (Christiansen), Peter Barkworth (Berkeley), Robert Beatty (Cartwright Jones), William Squire (Thomas), Derren Nesbitt (Maj. von Hapen)

p, Elliott Kastner; d, Brian G. Hutton; w, Alistair MacLean; ph, Arthur Ibbetson (Panavision 70, Metrocolor); ed, John Jympson; m, Ron Goodwin; art d, Peter Mullins; fx, Richard Parker, Fred Hellenburgh

A high-powered, big-budget WWII espionage thriller, WHERE EAGLES DARE follows an elite group of Allied commandos, led by John Smith (Richard Burton) and assigned to rescue an American general being held captive by the Nazis in a castle high in the Bavarian Alps. Ably assisted by a young American lieutenant, Morris Schaffer (Clint Eastwood), Smith and his crew of six don German uniforms and parachute into enemy territory. One of their number is found dead after landing, and Smith begins to suspect that one of his men is a double agent. He meets up with a pair of Allied agents, Mary Ellison (Mary Ure) and Heidi (Ingrid Pitt), and they manage to infiltrate the castle, which is accessible only by a tramway. An exciting picture with much derring-do and adventure, WHERE EAGLES DARE is also a lengthy film, though there is more than enough action to keep it moving along. Of course, it's all a bit hard to credit (especially since the Germans can't seem to hit anything with their machine guns), but that's part of the fun. Burton, in a switch from the heavy dramatic roles that made him famous, is excellent as an action hero, but Eastwood is the one who makes it all worthwhile. If it's explosions, gunplay, and wartime treachery that you like, WHERE EAGLES DARE delivers.

WHERE THE BOYS ARE

1960   99m   c   ★★½
Comedy   /PG
Euterpe

Dolores Hart (Merritt Andrews), George Hamilton (Ryder Smith), Yvette Mimieux (Melanie), Jim Hutton (TV Thompson), Barbara Nichols (Lola), Paula Prentiss (Tuggle Carpenter), Connie Francis (Angie), Chill Wills (Police Captain), Frank Gorshin (Basil), Rory Harrity (Franklin)

p, Joe Pasternak; d, Henry Levin; w, George Wells (based on the novel by Glendon Swarthout); ph, Robert Bronner (CinemaScope, Metrocolor); ed, Fredric Steinkamp; m, George Stoll, Pete Rugolo; art d, George W. Davis, Preston Ames; chor, Robert Sidney; cos, Kitty Mager

It's spring break, and college kids from around the country descend en masse to Fort Lauderdale, Florida. Hart, Mimieux, Prentiss, and Francis are four friends in search of sun, parties, and boys, though not necessarily in that order. The episodic plot line follows each girl in her respective success or failure with members of the opposite gender. Prentiss (in her film debut) is a scatterbrained lass who falls for Hutton, though their relationship takes a jealous turn when Hutton is briefly infatuated with Nichols, a nightclub entertainer who performs an underwater act in a glass tank. Recording star Francis also makes her first film appearance, capitalizing more on her vocal talents than acting ability. Francis's amorous adventures propel her—where else?—into the arms of a musician, Gorshin, a myopic bass fiddler. She also sings the film's title tune, which became a hit single in 1960.

Hart is the group's sensible member. She had been reluctant to come along but, faced with expulsion from school for her in-class expounding on relationships, Hart realizes a vacation might do her some good. In Florida, she meets Ivy Leaguer Hamilton, and romance blooms. Hamilton pressures her for sex, but Hart refuses, winning both his respect and a promise of commitment in the end. Mimieux, the last girl in the quartet, is a firm believer in love at first sight. She is determined to get herself an Ivy Leaguer any way she can, mistaking sexual passion for true love. Harrity quickly catches onto the girl's idealism and uses Mimieux for sex before passing her along to his fraternity brothers. Dazed by her unpleasant experience, Mimieux wanders into traffic and is hit by a car. She winds up in the hospital, embittered by it all, then returns home to recuperate.

WHERE THE BOYS ARE is plenty moralistic, yet the film is not without a naive sense of charm. Hart, who doesn't give in so easily to Hamilton, is the pinnacle of everything good and proper, while poor Mimieux gets exactly what she deserves for responding so swiftly to Harrity's importunities—or so the film would have us believe. This sexual moralizing is a bit much, portraying women as either good or bad while the boys who chase them have just one thing in mind. Fortunately, the black-and-white ethics are balanced with the lighter involvements of the other couples. Prentiss and Hutton give their story a silly sweetness, going through predictable situations with fine comic flair. Considering the radical movements that would sweep college campuses in the 1960s, this film holds some interest as a relic of sexual attitudes in the 1950s. A 1984 remake showed just how much Hollywood had changed in portraying sexual antics on screen, though the later film has none of the original's appeal. Seen in a bit part is Sean Flynn, Errol Flynn's son by actress Lily Damita. He showed some promise as an actor but left show business for a career as a photographer. In 1970, while on assignment in a Vietnam, Flynn disappeared. Hart also gave up her screen career, surprising her Hollywood cohorts by joining a Roman Catholic convent. Francis didn't go far in the movies past this role. Though she had some appealing moments here, the singer never got another part that suited her talents. She would later appear in FOLLOW THE BOYS and WHEN THE BOYS MEET THE GIRLS, B-movies that sought to capitalize on her biggest success, WHERE THE BOYS ARE.

WHERE'S CHARLEY?

1952   97m   c   ★★★½
Musical/Comedy   /U
WB   (U.K.)

Ray Bolger (Charley Wykeham), Allyn Ann McLerie (Amy Spettigue), Robert Shackleton (Jack Chesney), Horace Cooper (Stephen Spettigue), Margaretta Scott (Dona Lucia), Howard Marion-Crawford (Sir Francis Chesney), Mary Germaine (Kitty Verdun), Henry Hewitt (Brassett), H.G. Stoker (Wilkinson), Martin Miller (Photographer)

p, Ernest Martin, Cy Feuer; d, David Butler; w, John Monks, Jr. (based on the musical play by Frank Loesser, George Abbott from the play Charley's Aunt by Brandon Thomas); ph, Erwin Hillier (Technicolor); ed, Reginald Mills; art d, David Ffolkes; chor, Michael Kidd

WHERE'S CHARLEY? is made extraordinary by its incredible star, Ray Bolger, a 48-year-old actor playing a college student at Oxford. Charley Wykeham (Bolger) and Jack Chesney (Robert Shackleton) are roommates in love with Amy Spettigue (Allyn Ann McLerie) and Kitty Verdun (Mary Germaine) and would like to have a date with them, but dating without a chaperon isn't allowed. When Charley's wealthy, widowed aunt is delayed in her arrival to chaperon them, Charley dresses up as his aunt in order to prevent an embarrassing situation. Things get awkward enough, however, when Amy's elderly uncle becomes enamored of Charley's feminine persona. Eventually, the whole tempest in a teapot is calmed, but not before we've been treated to a tour de force performance by Bolger.

WHERE'S POPPA?

1970 83m c ★★★½
Comedy R/X
UA

George Segal (Gordan Hocheiser), Ruth Gordon (Mrs. Hocheiser), Trish Van Devere (Louise Callan), Ron Leibman (Sidney Hocheiser), Rae Allen (Gladys Hocheiser), Vincent Gardenia (Coach Williams), Joe Keyes (Gang Leader), Alice Drummond (Woman in Elevator), Tom Atkins (Policeman in Apartment), Florence Tarlow (Miss Morgiani)

p, Jerry Tokofsky, Marvin Worth; d, Carl Reiner; w, Robert Klane (based on the novel by Robert Klane); ph, Jack Priestley (DeLuxe Color); ed, Bud Molin, Chic Ciccolini; m, Jack Elliott; art d, Warren Clymer; cos, Albert Wolsky

Once again, George Segal is saddled with a difficult Jewish mother, as he was in NO WAY TO TREAT A LADY and LOST AND FOUND. This time, though, she's little short of a senile psychopath. Robert Klane wrote the screenplay from his hysterical novel, and Reiner directed it, but missed many of the jokes that worked so well in the book.

A New York attorney, Segal, lives with Gordon, his aged and quite senile mother. He has never married because she has fouled up all of his relationships. She deserves to be in a home, but Segal promised his late father that he would look after her. At the beginning of the film, Segal awakens to a local radio show, showers, shaves, puts on a gorilla suit, and races into Gordon's room. We're not sure if he wants to cheer her up or cause her to have a heart attack. She responds by punching him hard in the groin and saying, "You almost scared me to death," as she laughs. Segal, doubled over in pain, mumbles, "Almost is not good enough." Gordon prepares orange slices for Segal's breakfast, then eats them herself, along with breakfast cereal smothered in Coca-Cola. Segal's brother, Leibman, is married to Allen and refuses to help in the care of Gordon, so Segal hires a succession of nurses, but none stay past noon because Gordon is impossible to deal with. Eventually Segal meets and hires Van Devere, a sweet nurse with a strange background. She's been married once, for 32 hours. After her first sexual experience with her husband, she was appalled to find that he'd defecated in bed. Van Devere is thrilled to find a man like Segal, and the two are soon in love, though Gordon does her best to scare the young woman off.

The ultimate black comedy about difficult Jewish mothers, WHERE'S POPPA? can be very funny, but suffers from the non-stop barrage of jokes. A few quieter moments would have allowed the humor more room to breathe. Reiner's son, Rob, a onetime cast member of television's "All in the Family" who would go on to be an acclaimed director in his own right (STAND BY ME, MISERY), makes a cameo appearance. Filmed on location in New York City, WHERE'S POPPA? has become a cult favorite, though it has been radically edited for television showings and must be seen in its entirety to be fully appreciated.

WHILE THE CITY SLEEPS

1956 100m bw ★★★★
Crime /PG
Thor

Dana Andrews (Edward Mobley), Rhonda Fleming (Dorothy Kyne), Sally Forrest (Nancy Liggett), Thomas Mitchell (John Day Griffith), Vincent Price (Walter Kyne), Howard Duff (Lt. Burt Kaufman), Ida Lupino (Mildred Donner), George Sanders (Mark Loving), James Craig (Harry Kritzer), John Drew Barrymore (Robert Manners)

p, Bert E. Friedlob; d, Fritz Lang; w, Casey Robinson (based on the novel The Bloody Spur by Charles Einstein); ph, Ernest Laszlo (SuperScope); ed, Gene Fowler, Jr.; m, Herschel Burke Gilbert; art d, Carroll Clark; cos, Norma

Lang's finest film since THE BIG HEAT and his last great success, WHILE THE CITY SLEEPS is a crime drama sending its lead actors on a twisted, dog-eat-dog journey into the underworld in their quest for success. The plot revolves around the aspirations of three newsmen—Mitchell, Sanders, and Craig—each in line for the job of editor-in-chief of a New York tabloid called The Sentinel. Upon the death of newspaper owner Robert Warwick, his manipulative, dilettante son Price takes charge. The city is being terrorized by a sex murderer known as "The Lipstick Killer" (played with conventional dementia by Barrymore), a mama's boy who preys on beautiful woman at night. In a perverse power game, Price offers the newspaper's top position to the man who can crack the case. Naturally, Mitchell, Sanders, and Craig become rivals. Mitchell, a leathery, hard-drinking Irishman, is clear about his motive—he needs the money that the position pays. Sanders, the head of the wire service, is a ruthless cad interested in the societal implications of being the boss. Photoeditor Craig tries to use his romantic link with Price's wife, Fleming, as his inroad to the top job, spending more time wooing her than investigating the crime. To help achieve his goal, Mitchell bribes streetwise reporter Andrews for assistance. Each character's lack of moral values is soon made evident when they all employ the services of women to find the killer—risking the ladies' lives instead of their own. Mitchell agrees to Andrews's plan to use Andrews's fiancee, Forrest, as a decoy for Barrymore. Sanders cons gutsy columnist Lupino into helping him secure information by seducing Andrews, while Craig continues working through Fleming and her influence over Price. Forrest is nearly killed when Barrymore tries to enter her apartment. A climactic chase leads Andrews, hot on the trail of the pathetic killer, to the New York subway system. A battle ensues between him and Barrymore, eventually ending up on the subway tracks. The roar of a northbound train thunders closer, while the lights of a southbound loom larger by the second. At the very last moment, Andrews is tossed past the oncoming train and lands safely, while Barrymore escapes up the stairs only to be apprehended by the police.

Although viewed rather narrow-mindedly by some as an unsuccessful thriller because Lang reveals the killer's identity too early, WHILE THE CITY SLEEPS is clearly more than a thriller. Lang's interest is not in the killer's motivation and methods, but in the journalists' ruthless, morally guilty minds. These are men who are entrusted to uphold society's morals and protect a community, yet they readily put other people in danger for their own benefit. This superbly constructed and multilayered film was Lang's second favorite film, following his 1936 US masterpiece, FURY. Produced independently, WHILE THE CITY SLEEPS was set for release by United Artists, though in the end it was distributed by RKO.

WHISPERING SMITH

1948 88m c   ★★★½
Western   /A
Paramount

Alan Ladd (Luke "Whispering" Smith), Robert Preston (Murray Sinclaire), Brenda Marshall (Marian Sinclaire), Donald Crisp (Barney Rebstock), William Demarest (Bill Dansing), Fay Holden (Emmy Dansing), Murvyn Vye (Blake Barton), Frank Faylen (Whitey DuSang), John Eldredge (George McCloud), Robert Wood (Leroy Barton)

p, Mel Epstein; d, Leslie Fenton; w, Frank Butler, Karl Kamb (based on the novel by Frank H. Spearman); ph, Ray Rennahan (Technicolor); ed, Archie Marshek; m, Adolph Deutsch; art d, Hans Dreier, Walter Tyler; fx, Gordon Jennings, Farciot Edouart; cos, Mary Kay Dodson

A big box-office success for Ladd, WHISPERING SMITH was billed by Paramount as his first western and his first picture in color. He was cast as a real-life, gun-toting railroad detective whose low voice and quiet demeanor earned him the monicker "Whispering Smith." The film opens with a spectacular credit sequence over a great western panorama—green valleys, rolling hills, snow-capped mountains, and a powerful blue sky—into which Ladd rides. A gun enters the frame, takes aim at Ladd, and shoots his horse out from under him. We then learn from a group of railroad men of the legend of "Whispering Smith," the detective in charge of investigating a recent rash of train robberies. Ladd hops a train. Before long, bandits strike. He is wounded in the battle that ensues and is knocked from the train, landing unconscious on the ground. He is found by Marshall, who brings him home to her ranch where she tends to his wounds. It turns out that she is a past love of Ladd, a secret which they both keep from her husband, Preston, a railway employee who keeps bad company. Preston offers to let Ladd stay on as ranch foreman, but Ladd declines. Instead, he begins investigating Preston, who suspiciously lives a comfortable ranch life on a meager railway salary. Before long, Preston is caught looting a wrecked railway car and is fired from his job, turning to a full-time life of crime as a member of the train-robbing Rebstock gang led by Crisp. Preston gets deeper in trouble when one of Crisp's gang, the devilish Faylen, murders a postal employee and then kills Crisp. Ladd tracks Preston back to the ranch, where they exchange gunfire. Ladd fills Preston with lead and is about to tend to the wound when the dying man pulls a concealed gun. Before he can squeeze the trigger, however, he collapses and dies, leaving Ladd to resume his past romance with Marshall.

Predating Ladd's quintessential western hero, SHANE, by five years, WHISPERING SMITH is strikingly similar with his calm but dangerous demeanor, his devotion to friends, and his gentleness with women and children. While this was Ladd's first color feature, as Paramount boasted, it was not his first western. Ladd had appeared eight years earlier as a bit player in LIGHT OF WESTERN STARS and IN OLD MISSOURI. A number of the characters in this film are based on real people. Ladd's is drawn from lawman Joe Lefors, while Preston's loosely parallels that of notorious badman Butch Cassidy, and Faylen, playing the albino, Whitey DuSang, is re-creating one of the worst killers of the Old West, Harvey Logan, who followed Cassidy in a series of spectacular train and bank holdups committed by the infamous Wild Bunch.

WHISTLE AT EATON FALLS

1951 96m bw   ★★½
Drama   /U
Columbia

Lloyd Bridges (Brad Adams), Dorothy Gish (Mrs. Doubleday), Carleton Carpenter (Eddie Talbot), Murray Hamilton (Al Webster), James Westerfield (Joe London), Lenore Lonergan (Abby), Russell Hardie (Dwight Hawkins), Helen Shields (Miss Russell), Doro Merande (Miss Pringle), Ernest Borgnine (Bill Street)

p, Louis de Rochemont; d, Robert Siodmak; w, Lemist Esler, Virginia Shaler (based on the research of J. Sterling Livingston); ph, Joseph Brun; ed, Angelo Ross; m, Louis Applebaum; art d, Herbert Andrews

This well-meaning, though not entirely successful, story of labor-management relations opens in Eaton Falls, New Hampshire, where the president of the local plastics plant has been killed in an airplane crash. Bridges, a union leader, is promoted to be president and finds he has inherited a wealth of trouble. The plant needs to be more cost-effective, and therefore faces worker layoffs. Knowing what it is like to be on the workers' side of the fence, Bridges tries to save some jobs, but the union, led by Hamilton, disagrees with his methods. They are unable to come to an understanding, and the factory closes down. Eventually, and all too easily, the dispute is settled when big orders arrive for the company's products. This, coupled with some time- and money-saving machinery, allows Bridges to bring back all the employees, settling all squabbles between union and management. The film presents some interesting problems and intelligent questions about the roles and relations between management and workers. Unfortunately, the script never delves deep enough into the issues it raises, opting for pat, simplistic solutions that just don't ring true. However, Siodmak's direction overcomes some of this with a gritty, documentary style. Filmed on location in Eaton Falls, the production used local laborers as extras in factory scenes. Gish, as the president's widow who promotes Bridges, gives an intelligent performance in her small part.

WHISTLE BLOWER, THE

1987 104m c   ★★★
Spy   PG
Portreeve   (U.K.)

Michael Caine (Frank Jones), James Fox (Lord), Nigel Havers (Robert Jones), Felicity Dean (Cynthia Goodburn), John Gielgud (Sir Adrian Chapple), Gordon Jackson (Bruce), Barry Foster (Charles Greig), Kenneth Colley (Bill Pickett), Dinah Stabb (Rose), Andrew Hawkins (Allen Goodburn)

p, Geoffrey Reeve; d, Simon Langton; w, Julian Bond (based on the novel by John Hale); ph, Fred Tammes (Technicolor); ed, Robert Morgan; m, John Scott; prod d, Morley Smith; art d, Chris Burke; cos, Raymond Hughes

Despite a superb performance from the incredibly prolific Michael Caine, THE WHISTLE BLOWER is a ponderous affair that, while intellectually interesting, fails miserably on a cinematic level. The slow, confusing, and convoluted opening introduces widower Caine, a Korean War veteran, patriot, and struggling business machine salesman who launches a one-man investigation into the mysterious death of his son (Havers), an idealistic young man who worked as a Russian translator at GCHQ (Government Communications Headquarters), British intelligence's listening center. The further he digs, the more it becomes apparent that the British government sanctioned the murder of his son because he was about to blow the whistle on the sordid operations of the agency. Because Americans are more used to cinematic portrayals of government involvement in corruption, deceit, and conspiracy, THE WHISTLE BLOWER seems strangely uninvolving. Bond's script and Langton's direction are so very proper, restrained, and subdued that the viewer has trouble maintaining much interest in revelations that should really be news to no one. Not that every spy movie needs James Bond-type action to be successful, but THE WHISTLE BLOWER is mainly dialogue with little visual nuance. As is typical of British productions, the film is brimming with fine acting.

WHISTLE DOWN THE WIND

1961 98m bw   ★★★½
Drama   /U
Beaver/Allied Film Makers   (U.K.)

Hayley Mills (Kathy Bostock), Bernard Lee (Mr. Bostock), Alan Bates (Arthur Blakey), Diane Holgate (Nan Bostock), Alan Barnes (Charles Bostock), Norman Bird (Eddie), Diane Clare (Miss Lodge), Patricia Heneghan (Salvation Army Girl), Elsie Wagstaffe (Auntie Dorothy), John Arnatt (Teesdale)

p, Richard Attenborough; d, Bryan Forbes; w, Keith Waterhouse, Willis Hall (based on the novel by Mary Hayley Bell); ph, Arthur Ibbetson; ed, Max Benedict; m, Malcolm Arnold; art d, Ray Simm

Bryan Forbes's directorial debut was a beauty. Not satisfied to cut his teeth on a proven commercial vehicle, he used the unique novel by Mary Hayley Bell as the basis for this unique film. In today's world, anyone proclaiming himself to be Jesus Christ would be whisked away by the authorities before many moments passed. And children today are a lot keener on life's realities than they were a quarter of a century ago, perhaps due to the influence of television. But on a grim Lancashire farm, a man claiming to be Christ wins the trust of three motherless children who have been strongly influenced by their strict religious training. Mills is the eldest of Lee's children. The other two are Barnes and Holgate. The trio saves some cuddly kittens from drowning and decides to hide them in the family barn, where they find a bearded man hiding. Beards are not common in that area, and when Mills asks the wild-eyed fellow who he is, he replies, "Jesus Christ," more as a mutter than an answer. Then he falls to the straw from hunger and fatigue. The truth of the matter is that the man, played superbly by Bates, is a killer on the run; but Mills had already been influenced earlier when Heneghan, a Salvation Army employee, told her that Jesus would take care of the kittens and that they would be safe from harm. So when Mills meets Bates in the barn and the kittens are nearby and still happily mewing, Mills is convinced. Word of Christ in the barn travels like wildfire, and the other children in the village bring Bates food, wine, and other gifts, eager to get on his good side. The kids keep the secret from their parents in the wondrous way kids have of doing such things. They fear that the adults will take Christ away, the way it was done 2000 years before. Bates is betrayed by accident when, at Barnes's birthday party, Holgate blurts the secret out to her aunt, Wagstaff. The cops are called at once and move in on Bates. By this time, his attitude has mellowed under the love and adoration of the children and he surrenders meekly, rather than endanger the lives of any of the youngsters. He stretches his arms out in surrender, and it almost looks as though he is to be crucified. It's done subtly, but the obvious implication is there. Two children arrive as Bates is taken away, and Mills says, "You missed him this time, but he'll come again." Mills had been a staunch believer in Bates's divinity, but 6-year-old Barnes didn't buy it when one of the kittens died and Bates didn't prevent it.

This could have been a mawkish movie if it had gone over the edge, but Forbes kept matters realistic and still managed to enfold several bits of New Testament symbolism into the picture without hammering anyone on the head. The novel's author was Mills's mother (and wife of actor John Mills), and although there is no proof that she wrote the book with her daughter in mind, the youngster was surely the right choice for the role. It was her fourth movie; she had already completed TIGER BAY, POLLYANNA, and THE PARENT TRAP before this. Bates was wonderful in his difficult role. Prior to this, he had established himself as a stage actor and had appeared in THE ENTERTAINER the year before in his debut. Holgate and Barnes are so delicious in their naivete that they almost steal the film from Mills. It's an allegory, the second film produced by actor Richard Attenborough, who later became the Oscar-winning director of GANDHI.

WHITE CHRISTMAS

1954 120m c   ★★★
Musical/Comedy   /U
Paramount

Bing Crosby (Bob Wallace), Danny Kaye (Phil Davis), Rosemary Clooney (Betty), Vera-Ellen (Judy), Dean Jagger (Gen. Waverly), Mary Wickes (Emma), John Brascia (Joe), Anne Whitfield (Susan), Richard Shannon (Adjutant), Grady Sutton (General's Guest)

p, Robert Emmett Dolan; d, Michael Curtiz; w, Norman Krasna, Norman Panama, Melvin Frank; ph, Loyal Griggs (VistaVision, Technicolor); ed, Frank Bracht; art d, Hal Pereira, Roland Anderson; chor, Robert Alton; cos, Edith Head

This eagerly awaited musical comedy had all the ingredients for success: two of its day's biggest-box office draws, a solid director, and a score by America's treasure, Irving Berlin. And though it's not as satisfying as it might have been, it still boasts great stars and catchy songs in addition to a love story, and is a perennial holiday favorite. Bob Wallace (Bing Crosby) and Phil Davis (Danny Kaye) meet during the war and team up afterward to become the hottest song-and-dance duo around. After five years of heady success, they think it's about time to take a vacation, so they travel to a New England ski resort in the company of lovely sister entertainers Betty (Rosemary Clooney) and Judy (Vera-Ellen) for some rest and recuperation. They arrive to find the place in terrible financial condition and in desperate need of an infusion of money, because there hasn't been any snow for almost a year. The man who runs the inn is their old Army topkick, Gen. Waverly (Dean Jagger). Bob and Phil decide to aid Waverly by staging a benefit show that is, of course, a smash. Included is the title song, which Irving Berlin had written for HOLIDAY INN 12 years before. With that tune as the core, the script was fashioned, and several more Berlin tunes were added, including the Oscar-nominated "Count Your Blessings Instead of Sheep."

WHITE CLIFFS OF DOVER, THE

1944 126m bw   ★★★½
War   /U
MGM

Irene Dunne (Susan Dunn Ashwood), Alan Marshal (Sir John Ashwood), Frank Morgan (Hiram Porter Dunn), Roddy McDowall (John Ashwood II as a Boy), Peter Lawford (John Ashwood II at age 24), Dame May Whitty (Nanny), C. Aubrey Smith (Colonel), Gladys Cooper (Lady Jean Ashwood), Van Johnson (Sam Bennett), John Warburton (Reggie) p, Sidney Franklin; d, Clarence Brown; w, Claudine West, Jan Lustig, George Froeschel (based on the poem "The White Cliffs of Dover" by Alice Duer Miller, with additional material by Robert Nathan); ph, George Folsey; ed, Robert J. Kern, Al Jennings; m, Herbert Stothart; art d, Cedric Gibbons, Randall Duell; fx, A. Arnold Gillespie, Warren Newcombe; cos, Irene

Alice Duer Miller's poem was the inspiration for this sentimental look at the ravages of war and at the courage of one woman who lost both her husband and son in the two world wars that dominated this century. Dunne is a Red Cross supervisor in England, awaiting casualties of WWII. At her desk, she ruminates about her past and flashes back to 1914, when she comes to England with Morgan, her father, a newspaper publisher in a medium-sized town in the US. In no time at all, Dunne meets, falls in love with, and marries wealthy and titled Marshal. They are ecstatic, but their happiness is brief; WWI breaks out, and Marshal must serve his country in France, where he is killed on the battlefield. By the time of his death, Dunne has given birth to a son, and though the war is over, she stays in England to raise the boy. Played first by McDowall, then by Lawford, the boy grows to be a credit to his father. WWII breaks out and Dunne becomes a worker for the Red Cross assigned to a hospital in London. The wounded servicemen are brought in for surgery and she is shocked to see that one of them is her son, Lawford, now 24. He is dying of his injuries and she is powerless to help. At the conclusion, Dunne looks out a window and observes a battalion of American soldiers as they march past, the first such warriors to reach the British shores.

At the advent of the war, MGM made several pro-English features, the most successful being MRS. MINIVER. The studio wanted the same type of success again, but couldn't find the right material until producer Franklin happened on Miller's poem (which was given some additional words by Robert Nathan). Dunne was busy on A GUY NAMED JOE, but that production had to go on hiatus while Van Johnson recovered from an auto accident. In the meantime, this one began, and when Johnson was able to get back before the cameras more quickly than anyone had anticipated, Dunne found herself working on two major features at the same time. Beside MRS. MINIVER, MGM had already made GOODBYE, MR. CHIPS and RANDOM HARVEST and was in danger of being classified as a strictly Anglophile studio. This movie didn't achieve the success of the aforementioned films, but still managed a respectable gross of more than $4 million. Good acting, superior production values, sensitive direction, and one of Dunne's finest performances enhance the film. In order to make the settings authentic, MGM hired Major Cyril Seys Ramsey-Hill as technical advisor; he must have done his job because Britons living in the US sobbed at the showings. The film earned an Oscar nomination for its cinematography.

WHITE DOG

1982   90m   c   ★★★½
Drama   PG/15
Edgar J. Scherick

Kristy McNichol (Julie Sawyer), Paul Winfield (Keys), Burl Ives (Carruthers), Jameson Parker (Roland Gray), Lynne Moody (Molly), Marshall Thompson (Director), Bob Minor (Joe), Vernon Weddle (Vet), Christa Lang (Nurse), Tony Brubaker (Sweeper Driver)

p, Jon Davison; d, Samuel Fuller; w, Samuel Fuller, Curtis Hanson (based on the novella by Romain Gary); ph, Bruce Surtees (Metrocolor); ed, Bernard Gribble; m, Ennio Morricone; prod d, Brian Eatwell

One of the most famous "unseen" films, WHITE DOG never got a theatrical run in the US even though it had a well-known cast, a legendary director, and a powerful subject—racism. Kristy McNichol plays Julie Sawyer, a young actress who adopts a beautiful white stray dog. When a rapist breaks into Julie's home, the dog, which has been playful and gentle up to this, attacks and nearly tears the man limb from limb before the police arrive. The beautiful dog, she learns, has been trained to kill Blacks. A Black animal-trainer, Keys (Paul Winfield), begins an attempt to recondition the dog, although Carruthers (Burl Ives), who runs the training center, maintains that it can never be completely broken of its desire to kill. In the meantime, Julie meets the person who trained the dog in the first place. The rights the award-winning novella by Romain Gary on which the film is based were bought by Paramount 10 years before production began. Once the movie was made, the studio got cold feet, fearing that the volatile subject would incite racial controversy, although Sam Fuller's film is anything but racist. When WHITE DOG finally opened in Paris and London it was hailed as a masterpiece by some critics. The film finally did show up on cable television in January of 1984, in a re-edited version from Paramount that foolishly turned the dog from a killer to one that merely bites.

WHITE HEAT

1949   114m   bw   ★★★★★
Crime   /15
WB

James Cagney (Arthur Cody Jarrett), Virginia Mayo (Verna Jarrett), Edmond O'Brien (Hank Fallon/Vic Pardo), Margaret Wycherly (Ma Jarrett), Steve Cochran (Big Ed Somers), John Archer (Phillip Evans), Wally Cassell (Giovanni Cotton Valetti), Fred Clark (Daniel Winston, the Trader), Ford Rainey (Zuckie Hommell), Fred Coby (Happy Taylor)

p, Louis F. Edelman; d, Raoul Walsh; w, Ivan Goff, Ben Roberts (based on a story by Virginia Kellogg); ph, Sid Hickox; ed, Owen Marks; m, Max Steiner; art d, Edward Carrere; fx, Roy Davidson, H.F. Koenekamp; cos, Leah Rhodes

Ten years later, a flaming farewell to the 30s gangster picture, scripted like a Greek tragedy on speed. Raoul Walsh supplies the Freudian direction, Cagney the daring acting and sizzling star power. WHITE HEAT is primal, flamboyant stuff—close your eyes and you could be watching a 30s picture. But don't close them more than momentarily; the film's visuals make it linger in the mind's eye.

Cagney plays psychopathic gangster Cody Jarrett, Margaret Wycherly the mother who drives him to crime and whose death makes him go literally berserk. Virginia Mayo is Jarrett's wife, who has a hankering for gang member Big Ed (Steve Cochran), Edmond O'Brien plays a police informant who shares a cell with Jarrett, and John Archer is the FBI agent on the madman's tail.

One of the toughest and most brilliant crime films ever made, WHITE HEAT marked a breakthrough in the explicitly psychological depiction of screen bad guys. Cagney's character was based on notorious real-life gangster Arthur "Doc" Barker, Wycherly's on the equally infamous "Ma" Barker, the alleged catalyst for his criminal exploits. Cagney graphically demonstrates Jarrett's mother fixation when the actor, following one of his epileptic-style seizures, allows her to sit him in her lap and soothe him. This startling scene, like many in this classic film noir, was Cagney's own idea. The prison mess hall sequence, where Jarrett hears of his mother's murder, is the most charged moment in Cagney's outstanding career. The final image, shot atop an actual oil refinery in Torrance, CA, in which Jarrett calls out his warped triumph to his dead mother before blowing himself skyward, is one of the best-known scenes in film history.

WHITE HUNTER, BLACK HEART

1990 112m c   ★★½
Adventure/Drama   PG
Malpaso/Rastar

Clint Eastwood (John Wilson), Jeff Fahey (Pete Verrill), Charlotte Cornwell (Miss Wilding), Norman Lumsden (Butler George), George Dzundza (Paul Landers), Edward Tudor Pole (Reissar), Roddy Maude-Roxby (Thompson), Richard Warwick (Basil Fields), John Rapley (Gun Shop Salesman), Catherine Neilson (Irene Saunders)

p, Clint Eastwood; d, Clint Eastwood; w, Peter Viertel, James Bridges, Burt Kennedy (based on the novel Roman a Clef by Peter Viertel); ph, Jack N. Green (Technicolor); ed, Joel Cox; m, Lennie Niehaus; prod d, John Graysmark; art d, Tony Reading; fx, John Evans, Roy Field; chor, Arlene Phillips; cos, John Mollo

Based on Peter Viertel's *roman a clef*, WHITE HUNTER, BLACK HEART uses the making of a classic film, THE AFRICAN QUEEN, as the setting for an investigation into the creative process. It's also the story of one enigmatic film director as told by another. Star-director Clint Eastwood plays a thinly disguised John Huston, here called John Wilson.

Set in 1951, the film begins as Wilson has summoned an old friend, writer Pete Verrill (Jeff Fahey), to his Irish estate to recruit him for his latest project—the title of which he never can remember—about a salty, hard-drinking boat captain and a prissy schoolmarm who take on the German navy in Africa during WWII. All Wilson really cares about is that the film will give him a fast infusion of cash to put a dent in personal debts totalling a quarter of a million dollars. Even more important, it will provide him with an all-expenses-paid opportunity to fulfill his longtime dream of going big-game hunting. Meetings with producer Paul Landers (George Dzundza, playing a role modeled on real-life producer Sam Spiegel) and potential backers put the production on track, and Wilson and Verrill begin work on the script. But a major dispute arises over the fate of the leading characters, who, in Wilson's version, are killed, while Verrill insists they should live as the fair reward for their extraordinary heroism. Even after Wilson and Verrill's arrival in Africa, the film continues to take a back seat to the director's planned safari to kill an elephant.

WHITE HUNTER is an ambitious and intriguing project that never amounts to anything more than the sum of its parts—a trait shared by many of Eastwood's other major project as an independent filmmaker, BIRD. The personification of the post-Hemingway action hero, Eastwood looks and sounds uncomfortable filling Huston's decidedly Hemingwayesque shoes. As the action shifts to Africa, he seems inordinately laid-back as his character's obsession grows. He can't quite get a hold on the first predominantly unsympathetic character he's played since TIGHTROPE. And as a director, Eastwood has yet to pose much of a threat to Huston. WHITE HUNTER, like other Eastwood-directed films, lacks precisely the clear, lean narrative approach that characterizes Huston's best work (including THE AFRICAN QUEEN) or even that of Eastwood's mentor, director Don Siegel (DIRTY HARRY, ESCAPE FROM ALCATRAZ).

WHITE SHEIK, THE

(LO SCEICCO BIANCO)
1952 86m bw   ★★½
Comedy   /PG
Producers Distributors/OFI   (France/Italy)

Alberto Sordi (Fernando Rivoli), Brunella Bovo (Wanda Cavalli), Leopoldo Trieste (Ivan Cavalli), Giulietta Masina (Cabiria), Lilia Landi (Felga), Ernesto Almirante (Director of "White Sheik" Strip), Fanny Marchio (Marilena Vellardi), Gina Mascetti (White Sheik's Wife), Enzo Maggio (Hotel Concierge), Ettore Margadonna (Ivan's Uncle)

p, Luigi Rovere; d, Federico Fellini; w, Federico Fellini, Tullio Pinelli, Ennio Flaiano (based on a story by Federico Fellini and Tullio Pinelli from an idea by Michelangelo Antonioni); ph, Arturo Galea; ed, Rolando Bebedetti; m, Nino Rota; art d, Raffaello Tolfo

Federico Fellini's first solo directorial effort (he codirected VARIETY LIGHTS with Alberto Lattuada in 1951) is an enjoyable romp that shows the director's early promise. Newlyweds Wanda (Brunella Bovo) and Ivan Cavalli (Leopoldo Trieste) are honeymooning in Rome. The couple is mismatched: Ivan is conservative in nature, while his bride is full of spontaneity and eager to pursue her dreams. When Wanda learns that the popular photographic comic book "The White Sheik" is being shot nearby, she heads off to ogle the sheik (Alberto Sordi), sending Ivan on a frantic search for her all over Rome and jeopardizing their planned papal audience. When Wanda actually meets her idol, however, the sheik proves to be less than dashing. Already displaying his fascination with the romantic dreams of everyday people, Fellini orchestrates fantasy and reality deftly here as the newlyweds' perceptions of life and of each other change under the pressure of their unusual circumstances. The film falters in its pacing, however, which is somewhat too slow. Originally proposed as a project for Michelangelo Antonioni, THE WHITE SHEIK is not one of Fellini's masterworks (and uncharacteristically farcical), but it is a must-see for those interested in the director's oeuvre and an entertaining piece on its own.

WHO FRAMED ROGER RABBIT?

1988 103m c   ★★★
Animated/Comedy/Mystery   PG
Touchstone/Amblin/Silver Screen Partners III

Bob Hoskins (Eddie Valiant), Christopher Lloyd (Judge Doom), Joanna Cassidy (Dolores), Stubby Kaye (Marvin Acme), Alan Tilvern (R.K. Maroon), Richard Le Parmentier (Lt. Santino), Joel Silver (Raoul Raoul, Director), Paul Springer (Augie), Richard Ridings (Angelo), Edwin Craig (Arthritic Cowboy)

p, Robert Watts, Frank Marshall; d, Robert Zemeckis; w, Jeffrey Price, Peter Seaman (based on the book Who Censored Roger Rabbit? by Gary K. Wolf); ph, Dean Cundey (Rank Color); ed, Arthur Schmidt; m, Alan Silvestri; prod d, Elliot Scott, Roger Cain; fx, Peter Biggs, Brian Morrison, Roger Nichols, David Watkins, Brian Lince, Tony Dunsterville, Brian Warner; chor, Quinny Sacks, David Toguri; cos, Joanna Johnston; anim, Richard Williams

A startling combination of live action and animation, WHO FRAMED ROGER RABBIT? was instantly catapulted into the ranks of cinema classics. While flawlessly delivered, it's overkill—so loud and excessive, it makes our head swim. And its peak comes early on, when Jessica Rabbit sings, "Why Don't You Do Right?". Adult viewers are generally used to only Disney—104 minutes of the racous rukus of Warners style cartoons is well, too much of a dumb thing. This film could only

WHO IS KILLING THE GREAT CHEFS OF EUROPE?

have been made during the decade when Miss Piggy became a star.

Set in Los Angeles circa 1947, the film takes place in a universe where cartoon characters really exist and work alongside human beings. Disdainfully referred to as "Toons" by humans, the cartoon characters are underpaid by human standards and are forced to live in a segregated ghetto known as Toontown. When Maroon Cartoons studio chief R.K. Maroon (Alan Tilvern) is found murdered, it appears that the studio's biggest star, Roger Rabbit, is the culprit. Desperate to clear his name, Roger hires down-on-his-luck private detective Eddie Valiant (Bob Hoskins) to crack the case. A human, Eddie is reluctant to take the case, for he hates Toons because his brother was killed by one. As the plot thickens, however, Roger begins to grow on Eddie and the pair team up to solve the mystery of Toontown, battling the sinister Judge Doom (Christopher Lloyd) in the process.

We salute the technical brilliance of this movie. A small army of animators led by Richard Williams and assisted by Industrial Light and Magic performed the meticulous task of matching animation with camera movement and film noir lighting to give the cartoon characters a 3-D effect. And admittedly Hoskins had a tough job—interacting with thin air and floating props (the Toons handle real objects) because the animation was added to the frame months after principal photography had been completed. Director Bob Zemeckis deserves a Purple Heart for taking on the monumental technical headaches involved in the production and somehow managing to deliver a film that works. A must-see for all ages, but not a work that lingers in the imagination. It's like a sumptuous banquet composed entirely of fast food; fills you up but entirely forgettable.

WHO IS KILLING THE GREAT CHEFS OF EUROPE?

1978 112m c   ★★★
Comedy/Mystery   PG/A
Lorimar/Aldrich/Geria/Bavaria   (U.S./West Germany)

George Segal (Robby), Jacqueline Bisset (Natasha), Robert Morley (Max), Jean-Pierre Cassel (Kohner), Philippe Noiret (Moulineau), Jean Rochefort (Grandvilliers), Luigi Proietti (Ravello), Stefano Satta Flores (Fausto Zoppi), Madge Ryan (Beecham), Frank Windsor (Blodgett)

p, William Aldrich, Merv Adelson; d, Ted Kotcheff; w, Peter Stone (based on the novel Someone is Killing the Great Chefs of Europe by Nan Lyons and Ivan Lyons); ph, John Alcott (Metrocolor); ed, Thom Noble; m, Henry Mancini; art d, Werner Achmann; cos, Judy Moorcroft

The title of this movie tells it all. Morley is a gourmand whose doctor orders him to lose 140 pounds, lest his overworked heart give out. But how can he lose all this excess weight when his favorite chefs are still cooking up delectable dishes? Suddenly the finest of Europe's chefs mysteriously are done in with the most bizarre style of murder one might imagine. Each chef is killed in accordance with his specialty. A duck press crushes the head of one chef; another is baked in his own oven. What's in store for Bisset, a world-renowned dessert specialist and ex-wife of fast-food entrepreneur Segal? The string of murders takes the viewer on a rollicking trans-European chase with all the clues pointing to Morley. But is he the killer? This unusual comedy has some wonderful moments of black humor. The direction moves at a slick pace but keeps the tone light, with some witty results. Morley steals the entire film.

WHOLE TOWN'S TALKING, THE

1935 95m bw
Comedy/Crime
Columbia

Edward G. Robinson (Arthur Ferguson Jones/Killer Mannion), Jean Arthur (Wilhelmina "Bill" Clark), Arthur Hohl (Detective Sgt. Mike Boyle), Wallace Ford (Healy), A.S. Byron (District Atty. Spencer), Donald Meek (Hoyt), Paul Harvey (J.G. Carpenter), Edward Brophy (Bugs Martin), Etienne Girardot (Seaver), James Donlan (Detective Sgt. Pat Howe)

p, Lester Cowan; d, John Ford; w, Jo Swerling, Robert Riskin (based on the novel by W.R. Burnett); ph, Joseph August; ed, Viola Lawrence

One of the most underrated of John Ford's early films, THE WHOLE TOWN'S TALKING is a marvelous gangster film told in a comic vein and sporting a superb performance from Edward G. Robinson, playing a timid clerk working for a hardware company. He has a superlative work record and has been on time every morning for eight years. He is in love with one of his coworkers (Jean Arthur) from afar. While he is having lunch with her one day, the police arrive and arrest him, having mistaken him for Public Enemy No. 1, Killer Mannion, recently escaped from prison and the hardware clerk's exact double. After much confusion over his identity, the district attorney is satisfied that Robinson isn't the gangster they are looking for and issues the clerk an identity card he can show police to avoid being arrested by mistake again. Unfortunately, the news about Robinson's misadventure hits all the newspapers—partly because Robinson's boss urges his employee to write about Mannion for the papers—and the real Killer Mannion (also played by Robinson) reads the story. The gangster shows up at the clerk's house and demands that the identity card be turned over to him every evening so that he can move about more freely. The gangster also begins dictating the details of his sordid life to the clerk, to be included in the newspaper column. To ensure the clerk's cooperation, the gangster kidnaps Arthur and the clerk's aunt (Effie Ellsler). Posing as the clerk, the gangster and his thugs commit several robberies in the area and the police put the innocent Robinson in jail for his own protection. To kill two birds with one stone, the gangster decides to pose as the clerk, get into jail, kill a stoolie that once double-crossed him, and then send the clerk out on a bank job where he is sure to be killed—thus "Killer Mannion" would be dead and "Arthur Ferguson" could be released. The clerk heads for the bank, but when he realizes that he's forgotten his gun, he goes back to the gang's hideout. Before entering, he overhears the gangsters joking about the setup. The clerk then decides to act like the gangster, and when the real gangster enters the room, the clerk orders the men to kill him, which they do, thinking the clerk is their boss. The clerk then gets the drop on the gang with a Tommy gun, rescues Arthur and his aunt, and delivers the gang to the police. The newly confident Robinson finally asks Arthur to marry him.

Adapted by screenwriters Jo Swerling and Robert Riskin from a story by W.R. Burnett (who wrote the novel Little Caesar), THE WHOLE TOWN'S TALKING is a masterful balance of comedy and drama with a very dark subtext. Robinson the clerk and Robinson the gangster are two sides of the same coin. The clerk is a milquetoast who can't bring himself to tell the woman he loves how he feels about her, but once he dons the identity of the gangster and orders a man to be killed, he is suddenly infused with self-confidence and power which finally enable him to speak his mind and take action. Though the film is essentially a comedy and Robinson the clerk's actions are well enough motivated for his character to remain sympathetic, it is an undeniably chilling and ambiguous moment. Robinson handles the role beautifully, bringing several shadings and subtleties to a double role that could easily have disintegrated into gimmicky silliness. Because of the ambiguity and subtle handling of the darker aspects of the story, director Ford and actor Robinson turned what could have been dismissed as just another light, frivolous entertainment into an evocative work of art.

WHO'LL STOP THE RAIN?

1978 125m c   ★★★½
Crime/War   R/18
UA

Nick Nolte *(Ray Hicks)*, Tuesday Weld *(Marge Converse)*, Michael Moriarty *(John Converse)*, Anthony Zerbe *(Antheil)*, Richard Masur *(Danskin)*, Ray Sharkey *(Smitty)*, Gail Strickland *(Chairman)*, Charles Haid *(Eddy)*, David Opatoshu *(Bender)*

p, Herb Jaffe, Gabriel Katzka; d, Karel Reisz; w, Judith Rascoe, Robert Stone (based on the novel *Dog Soldiers* by Stone); ph, Richard H. Kline; ed, John Bloom; m, Laurence Rosenthal

An effective film adaptation of Robert Stone's excellent novel *Dog Soldiers*, WHO'LL STOP THE RAIN? begins in Vietnam and follows jaded, cynical, and bitter photojournalist John Converse (Michael Moriarty) as he arranges to smuggle a large shipment of Asian heroin into the US. To assist him, Converse enlists Vietnam vet Ray Hicks (Nick Nolte). Once a Marine, now working for the Merchant Marine, Hicks can easily smuggle the heroin out of Vietnam and into the docks at Oakland, California, where he is to hook up with Converse's wife, Marge (Tuesday Weld), and await Converse's return to the US. Unfortunately, Antheil (Anthony Zerbe), a corrupt federal drug enforcement agent, has gotten wind of the shipment and has sent two of his men (Richard Masur and Ray Sharkey) to kill Marge and Hicks and confiscate the heroin for his own purposes. Fueled by excellent performances from the entire cast—with Nolte a definite standout—WHO'LL STOP THE RAIN? is a gripping action film that also illustrates the bitter disillusionment of Americans who witnessed the corruption, confusion, and moral chaos of the country's leadership during the Vietnam era. Smartly directed by Karel Reisz (a Czech-born Englishman), whose previous feature was the memorable THE GAMBLER with James Caan, the film boasts fine photography by Richard H. Kline and an unforgettable climax in the surreal ruins of an abandoned hippie commune.

WHOOPEE

1930 94m c   ★★★½
Musical/Comedy
UA

Eddie Cantor *(Henry Williams)*, Eleanor Hunt *(Sally Morgan)*, Paul Gregory *(Wanenis)*, Jack Rutherford *(Sheriff Bob Wells)*, Ethel Shutta *(Mary Custer)*, Spencer Charters *(Jerome Underwood)*, Chief Caupolican *(Black Eagle)*, Albert Hackett *(Chester Underwood)*, William H. Philbrick *(Andy McNabb)*, Walter Law *(Judd Morgan)*

p, Samuel Goldwyn, Florenz Ziegfeld; d, Thornton Freeland; w, William Conselman (based on the Ziegfeld musical "Whoopee" by William Anthony McGuire, Walter Donaldson, Gus Kahn, the comedy "The Nervous Wreck" by Owen Davis, Sr., and the story "The Wreck" by E.J. Rath); ph, Lee Garmes, Ray Rennahan, Gregg Toland; ed, Stuart Heisler; art d, Richard Day; chor, Busby Berkeley; cos, John Harkrider

After the smash hit Broadway show in 1928-29 finished its long run, Sam Goldwyn joined forces with Flo Ziegfeld to re-create "Whoopee" for one of the first Technicolor films, making Eddie Cantor a Goldwyn star and the song "Making Whoopee" a standard. Cantor plays Henry Williams, a hypochondriac whose supposedly poor health causes him to travel West with his nurse-companion Mary Custer (Ethel Shutt). They wind up in Arizona, where busybody Henry pokes his nose into the affairs of Sally Morgan (Eleanor Hunt). Sally is engaged to local sheriff Bob Wells (John Rutherford), but really loves Indian brave Wanenis (Paul Gregory). Henry manages to extricate Sally from Bob's arms into those of Wanenis, who, it later turns out, is really a paleface who had been abandoned and raised by local Native Americans. Several splendid Busby Berkeley production numbers, a bevy of "Goldwyn Girls" (among them a very young Betty Grable), and Oscar-nominated art direction by Capt. Richard Day enliven the silly plot—but the real drawing card is Cantor (just as it was Danny Kaye, when Goldwyn remade this movie as 1944's UP IN ARMS). Neither Goldwyn nor Ziegfeld enjoyed working with a partner, and the two split when Ziegfeld wanted his name first in the billing of the company. Goldwyn released the film in the nadir of the Depression and charged $5 per ticket, the equivalent of a day's pay back then.

WHOOPING COUGH

(SZAMARKOHOGES)
1987 90m c   ★★★★
War
Mafilm/Hunnia   (Hungary)

Marcell Toth *(Tomi)*, Eszter Karasz *(Annamari)*, Dezso Garas *(Father)*, Judit Hernadi *(Mother)*, Mari Torocsik *(Grandmother)*, Anna Feher *(The Maid)*, Karoly Eperjes *(Akos)*

d, Peter Gardos; w, Andras Osvat, Peter Gardos; ph, Tibor Mathe (Eastmancolor); ed, Maria Rigo; m, Janos Novak; prod d, Jozsef Romvari; cos, Agnes Gyarmathy

On May 1, 1956, Torocsik is the custodian of a rooftop air raid siren. She tells her 10-year-old grandson, Toth, they must remain vigilant in case they come under attack from the imperialist troops. In October 1956 the calm has been shattered, and Budapest is in the midst of a bloody uprising. A curfew is imposed as gunfire resounds throughout the city, and families seal themselves behind closed doors. Torocsik is now engrossed in reading and rarely ventures out of doors. Her grandson is ecstatic about the state of insurrection because his school has been shut down until the curfew is lifted. He is confined to his home with the remainder of his family, which includes his father, Garas, who has lost his management job because he struck an employee, and his mother, Hernadi, who has secretly begun an affair. His eight-year-old sister, Karasz, perpetually bewilders the family with her obscene and slanderous remarks. At one point, Toth decides to break into the school building to retrieve his grandmother's typewriter, which he earlier smuggled out of his home. He is apprehended by the brutal custodian and beaten for stealing what appears to be school property. Back home, Karasz's sudden coughing fit leads to fears of whooping cough, and a doctor is summoned. The doctor, a young and attractive female, examines Karasz and finds her free of the disease. She then examines Toth, an experience that leads to the boy's sexual awakening. The children then take advantage of a rare opportunity to enjoy the outdoors by undertaking a rail journey with a group of their school friends on a borrowed flat car. They glide along through the forest until a group of soldiers opens fire on them, killing one of their classmates. Meanwhile, Garas longs for his wife, who has left him to spend the night with her lover. His mother-in-law surprisingly treats him with a rare display of affection, thus enabling him to endure the loneliness until his repentant wife returns the following morning. After the insurrection has been quelled, Torocsik is unjustly jailed for allegedly printing subversive material with her typewriter. When she is released, she marches directly to the roof of her building and pulls the alarm, setting off a violent and deafening wail.

"Most people wanted to survive the shooting outside the house. They wanted to survive history and go beyond it," explains director Peter Gardos about the focus of his second feature film. This is a charmingly astute portrait of a small world turned upside down by the cataclysmic events of 1956. The story follows the exploits of an ordinary family, one of the multitude of fearful ones during the uprising, who shut their doors and windows to the terror of the outside world. In his earlier film, THE PHILADELPHIA ATTRACTION (1985), Gardos explored the obsessive yearnings and the accompanying solitariness of the artist; in WHOOPING COUGH, he focuses on the frustrated artistic inclinations of a common man who rarely explores either of these leanings. The bond of Garas's family loosens as its individual members compromise their commitment to the unit. The delight he feels over his artistic intents forces him to experience the pain of vulnerability when he's greeted with criticism from his judgmental family. Eventually his children arrive at the painful realization that he and the members of the family are just ordinary people and that their attempts at displaying creativity produce little more than hollow failures. Yet, unbeknownst to any of them, it is their ordinary actions that produce the real artistic creativity. Winner of the top prize at the 1987 Chicago International Film Festival.

WHO'S AFRAID OF VIRGINIA WOOLF?

1966   131m   bw   ★★★★
Drama   /15
WB

Elizabeth Taylor *(Martha)*, Richard Burton *(George)*, George Segal *(Nick)*, Sandy Dennis *(Honey)*

p, Ernest Lehman; d, Mike Nichols; w, Ernest Lehman (based on the play by Edward Albee); ph, Haskell Wexler; ed, Sam O'Steen; m, Alex North; prod d, Richard Sylbert; cos, Irene Sharaff

The Liz and Dick Show. A vitriol Valentine to that most public of famous marriages, The Battling Burtons, in their finest work (together). Our tabloid awareness of their union informs us they were living out their real-life roles, so a side of the viewer champions the authenticity, even when it sometimes looks actorly. Albee's play opened in October, 1962, and shocked even blase New Yorkers with its language and dark subject matter (Uta Hagen and Arthur Hiller created the Broadway roles). The attendent publicity when the film was cast guaranteed an audience no matter what. And many big names had wanted the roles. (Bette Davis wanted to play it opposite Jimmy Stewart, supposedly. Can you imagine Davis doing a parody of herself saying, "What a dump!"? We ideally would have cast Susan Hayward and Henry Fonda.) If Taylor's early scenes sometimes seem more like showing off, she ultimately ropes you in—it's a pity so few films have taken advantage of her bawdy penchant for black comedy. Burton's only disadvantage is his accent; his portrayal seems a trifle more fully realized than hers.

It's two in the morning in New England. Burton is a defeated history professor married to Taylor, a harridan whose father is the president of the college where Burton lectures. After two decades their union is alternately loving and vicious. Taylor likes to compare her weakling husband with her strong father (who is never seen) because she knows it rankles Burton. They have invented a son and talk about him as though he actually exists. Earlier that night, they attended a faculty party where they met Segal and Dennis, a self-proclaimed ladies' man and a sniveling mouse of a woman. The older couple have invited the younger to their comfortable home for a nightcap. Enter Segal and Dennis. She is already tipsy but has more to drink, which makes her worse. Taylor, behaving boorishly, makes advances at Segal which Burton does nothing to stop. Dennis begins to feel sick and Segal gets increasingly drunk. Segal confides to Burton that Dennis trapped him into marriage by pretending to be pregnant. As the late evening drags into early morning, Taylor takes Segal up to her bedroom. Burton stands in the yard below and watches their shadows in the window. Later, Segal mentions Burton's and Taylor's "son," and Burton explodes, vowing to destroy Taylor, who matches his threat.

Producer Lehman's screenplay left most of Albee's play intact, which shocked movie audiences not accustomed to hearing four-letter words cannonading off the screen. At first, the Production Code seal was denied to the movie, but Jack Warner used his personal clout and secured the seal. The play was bought by Warners for half a million dollars; an additional million each went to the Burtons—out of a total budget of $5 million. The movie grossed large numbers at the box office, nearly $15 million the first time around, due, in part, to the draw of the stars.

The film received 13 Oscar nominations and ended up winning five awards. Taylor took Best Actress and Dennis won for Best Supporting Actress (in her second role after a small part in SPLENDOR IN THE GRASS—and she was absolutely right in a part that became the definitive Dennis role. The same cannot be said for Segal, who lacks the bulk and WASP look for Nick—where was Robert Redford when Nichols needed him?). Richard Sylbert and George James Hopkins also won for black-and-white art direction and set decoration; Irene Sharaff for black-and-white costumes; and Wexler for black-and-white cinematography. Both Burton and Taylor both took British Oscars for their work. Hiring Nichols (comedy partner of Elaine May) in his directorial debut was a risk because the former nightclub comic had done only lighter work. But the script is fueled by acid, sarcastic dialogue which his direction paces flawlessly, his sense of comic timing serving him well. The film was rehearsed like a play for three weeks before a camera ever turned. This also marked Lehman's debut as a producer. Strong stuff, intensely watchable, but definitely not for children.

WICKER MAN, THE

1974   102m   c   ★★★½
Horror/Mystery   R/18
British Lion   (U.K.)

Edward Woodward *(Sgt. Neil Howie)*, Christopher Lee *(Lord Summerisle)*, Diane Cilento *(Miss Rose)*, Britt Ekland *(Willow MacGregor)*, Ingrid Pitt *(Librarian-Clerk)*, Lindsay Kemp *(Alder MacGregor)*, Russell Waters *(Harbormaster)*, Aubrey Morris *(Old Gardener-Gravedigger)*, Irene Sunters *(May Morrison)*, Walter Carr *(Schoolmaster)*

p, Peter Snell; d, Robin Hardy; w, Anthony Shaffer; ph, Harry Waxman; ed, Eric Boyd-Perkins; m, Paul Giovanni; art d, Seamus Flannery; chor, Stewart Hopps; cos, Sue Yelland

Sgt. Neil Howie (Woodward) is a devoutly Christian policeman and lay minister, still an unmarried virgin though middle-aged. After receiving an anonymous lead pertaining to the whereabouts of a missing girl, Neil heads out to Summerisle, a Scottish island community within his jurisdiction, in search of clues. What he finds on the island is a pagan cult led by Lord Summerisle (Lee), which offers a human sacrifice every year. Here we have the unusual case of a film about a pagan cult that has developed a cult of its very own. Drastically cut by its original distributors (from 102 minutes to 87 minutes), poorly marketed, and subsequently little seen, THE WICKER MAN developed a reputation as a lost masterpiece of mystery and the macabre. Fueled by actor Christopher Lee's comments that the film contained his best performance, a rabid group of fans went about extolling the movie's virtues. When director Robin Hardy's reconstructed original cut of the film was finally released on videocassette (seven minutes are still missing), opinion over the much-anticipated film was split: people either loved it or hated it. While no masterpiece, the film is a fascinating examination of the conflict between fundamental Christianity and paganism. The performances are uniformly excellent, and Hardy's direction is quite evocative, bizarre, witty, erotic, and downright chilling.

WILD AT HEART

1990 126m c   ★★½
Comedy/Drama/Romance   R/18
Polygram-Propaganda

Nicolas Cage (Sailor Ripley), Laura Dern (Lula Pace Fortune), Diane Ladd (Marietta Pace), Willem Dafoe (Bobby Peru), Isabella Rossellini (Perdita Durango), Harry Dean Stanton (Johnnie Farragut), Crispin Glover (Dell), Grace Zabriskie (Juana), J.E. Freeman (Marcello Santos), W. Morgan Sheppard (Mr. Reindeer)

p, Monty Montgomery, Steve Golin, Joni Sighvatsson; d, David Lynch; w, David Lynch (based on the novel by Barry Gifford); ph, Frederick Elmes; ed, Duwayne Dunham; m, Angelo Badalamenti; prod d, Patricia Norris; fx, David B. Miller, Louis Lazara, David Domeyer; cos, Patricia Norris

Based on the novel by Barry Gifford, this winner of the Cannes Film Festival's Palme d'Or is a wacky, occasionally inventive road movie that fails to display the vision or the dark intensity of director Lynch's earlier work.

Sailor Ripley (Nicolas Cage) is a rebellious, 23-year-old Elvis acolyte who has just served 22 months and 18 days in the Pee Dee correctional facility for manslaughter. Waiting for him on the outside is Lula Fortune (Laura Dern), a 20-year-old, gum-popping, sex-loving cyclone of a gal who picks him up from prison the day of his release. They are in love and spend most of their time smoking (their philosophical conversations about cigarettes echo the similar conversations about beer in BLUE VELVET), dancing, and having sex. Embarking on a journey that takes them from the Carolinas to Texas, they encounter nightmarish accidents and outrageously evil characters, all the while trying to keep one step ahead of Lula's murderous, witchlike mother, Marietta (Diane Ladd, Dern's real-life mother). Sailor's arrest and imprisonment were actually Marietta's doing. After failing to seduce him in a bathroom stall at a ballroom dance, Marietta paid a man to attack Sailor (who, in addition to spurning Marietta's advances, may also know a little too much about the mysterious death of her husband). When Sailor beat his assailant to death, he was thrown in prison. Even now, after Sailor's release, Marietta harbors a bizarre hatred for the young man, and hires her private-detective boyfriend, Johnnie Farragut (Harry Dean Stanton), to find her daughter and get her away from the rebellious Sailor. Marietta is so determined to separate Sailor and Lula that she also asks ex-lover Marcello Santos (J.E. Freeman), a mobster, to find Sailor and kill him. Meanwhile, Lula and Sailor continue to drive, smoke, dance, and have lots of sex. Interwoven

into their cross-country odyssey are numerous references to THE WIZARD OF OZ.

Besides Crispin Glover as a cousin of Lula's who likes to put cockroaches in his underwear, and Willem Dafoe as a psychotic, rotten-toothed ex-marine called Bobby Peru, Lynch's Rogues Gallery includes W. Morgan Sheppard as Mr. Reindeer, a mysterious crime lord who is constantly surrounded by topless hookers; Freddie Jones as a bar patron with a mangled voice; Isabella Rossellini as Perdita, Peru's bleached-blonde girlfriend; Jack Nance, John Lurie, and Scott Coffey as three of the many eccentrics that populate Big Tuna, Texas; and David Patrick Kelly, Calvin Lockhart, and Grace Zabriskie as a trio of psycho killers. At the center of this wild hodge-podge, Cage and Dern turn in undeniably effective performances. Dern is particularly impressive, creating a character far different from anything she has done before (miles from the innocent Sandy of BLUE VELVET). Cage is, as always, goofily engaging, and even turns in affecting renditions of Elvis' "Love Me" and "Love Me Tender."

There are many powerful moments in WILD AT HEART—particularly one sequence in which Sailor and Lula come upon the scene of a nighttime accident, and find Sherilyn Fenn (best known for Lynch's TV show "Twin Peaks") wandering in a bloody daze by the side of the road. But these moments never add up to very much; the film plays as a series of vignettes, each with its own visual or aural or psychological raison d'etre, but never really tying into anything else that's going on.

Alternating between jolting violence and manic comedy, WILD AT HEART proudly displays all of Lynch's directorial trademarks—exotically dangerous characters, painterly visuals, surrealistic sound design, and a healthy dose of sex and violence. But unlike BLUE VELVET, where all these elements seemed fused for the purpose of creating a particular world vision, much of WILD AT HEART seems gratuitous, as though the director is re-hashing his earlier triumph to satisfy the now-formulaic demands of his audience.

WILD BOYS OF THE ROAD

1933 77m bw   ★★★★★
Drama
WB/First National

Frankie Darro (Eddie Smith), Dorothy Coonan (Sally), Edwin Phillips (Tommy), Rochelle Hudson (Grace), Ann Hovey (Lola), Arthur Hohl (Dr. Heckel), Grant Mitchell (Mr. Smith), Claire McDowell (Mrs. Smith), Sterling Holloway (Ollie), Charley Grapewin (Mr. Cadmust)

p, Robert Presnell; d, William A. Wellman; w, Earl Baldwin (based on the story "Desperate Youth" by Daniel Ahearn); ph, Arthur Todd; ed, Thomas Pratt; art d, Esdras Hartley

WILD BOYS OF THE ROAD is a marvelous piece of Americana, a look at the social confusion of the Depression era. The film's two chief characters, Frankie Darro and Edwin Phillips, are California youths enjoying a comfortable lifestyle with their parents. When the Depression hits and their fathers lose their jobs, the boys hop an eastbound freight train to find work. They soon learn that there are thousands just like themselves, all looking for work, all trying to fight the economic depression that is destroying the country. Darro and Phillips find not only a number of other "wild boys" but also Dorothy Coonan and Rochelle Hudson, tough girls who take to the rails with them. Along the way, this mobile group of naive vagrants become a pack of outlaws when they kill a brakeman who has raped Hudson. The kids are finally forced off the tracks in Ohio, where they assemble their own "sewer city" from sewer pipes and supplies—a city founded on new ideals and a commitment to equality. Their city, however, breeds theft in the nearby community, prompting the police and fire department to wash away the vagrants with fire hoses. The gang moves on, suffering from lack of food and money, as well as a disastrous accident in which one member loses a leg under the wheels of a train. By time they arrive in New York, the remaining three, Darro, Phillips, and Coonan, have been almost completely broken in spirit, no longer looking for the sort of comfortable living they had in California but merely trying to stay alive. After getting involved in a theft ring, they're arrested and hauled off to court. Coming before the judge, who sits proudly under the blue eagle of the National Recovery Administration, the young thieves are given the customary lecture. This one, however, smacks of Franklin Roosevelt's New Deal ideology as the judge confidently tells the youngsters that things are going to get better.

Blasted by countless critics for its political stance, WILD BOYS OF THE ROAD, if sometimes naive politically, is still superb entertainment. Director William A. Wellman tackled a straightforward "road movie" structure and applied the simplest of New Deal ideas to it. WILD BOYS OF THE ROAD shows with amazing accuracy the feeling of emptiness and apparent hopelessness that ran rampant in the country. The chief problem with the film is its refusal to lay the blame for the Depression at anyone's feet. The film's finish, though technically a happy ending, is rather mindless, leaving the audience with a "don't worry, everything will be fine" promise. Despite these faults, WILD BOYS OF THE ROAD is one of the finest films about youthful idealism to hit the screen. Costing $203,000 to produce, the film had only minimal success at the box office. Besides the superb Coonan (Wellman's fourth wife), the film is peopled with numerous teens, most of whom were, before and after the film, unknowns, adding to the authenticity of the film's atmosphere. The standout among the cast, however, is the appealing, pint-sized Darro, who became one of the foremost Depression era tough kids of the screen.

WILD BUNCH, THE

1969   143m   c   ★★★★★
Western   R/18
WB

William Holden (Pike Bishop), Ernest Borgnine (Dutch Engstrom), Robert Ryan (Deke Thornton), Edmond O'Brien (Sykes), Warren Oates (Lyle Gorch), Jaime Sanchez (Angel), Ben Johnson (Tector Gorch), Emilio Fernandez (Mapache), Strother Martin (Coffer), L.Q. Jones (T.C.).

p, Phil Feldman; d, Sam Peckinpah; w, Walon Green, Sam Peckinpah (based on a story by Green, Roy N. Sickner); ph, Lucien Ballard (Panavision, Technicolor); ed, Lou Lombardo; m, Jerry Fielding; art d, Edward Carrere; fx, Bud Hulburd

An extraordinarily well-made film about out-of-date outlaws in the early 20th century, Sam Peckinpah's THE WILD BUNCH feels like it should have been the final western. This harsh yet elegaic story proved controversial upon its release not only because, like BONNIE AND CLYDE two years before, it upped the ante on American screen violence but also, in industry circles, because of the war it started between the producer, Feldman, and the director.

As with the majority of Peckinpah's work, the studios and producers mutilated the film to suit their needs (to cut its length, to eliminate controversy, to prove their power over the ever-difficult Peckinpah) and distributed a movie vastly different from the one the director had originally envisioned. The cutting occurred while Peckinpah was vacationing in Hawaii, *after* his film had been shown uncut to reviewers on the East Coast. (*New York Times* critic Vincent Canby expressed dismay when he went to see the film again and discovered scenes missing.) Certainly it was not adverse preview reaction that spurred Feldman to make the cuts (the trimmed scenes contained important motivational information vital to the portrayals of the main characters—none of the deletions was a particularly violent scene). These revisions were simply made to bring the film's running time down to two hours, to enable theater owners to turn more of a profit from the feature. With the director's uncut version now readily available on video and laserdisc, there is no reason for anyone to subject themselves to the butchered version.

WILD CHILD, THE

(L'ENFANT SAUVAGE)
1970   90m   bw   ★★★★½
Drama   G/
Carrosse/Artistes   (France)

Jean-Pierre Cargol (Victor the Boy), Francois Truffaut (Dr. Jean Itard), Jean Daste (Prof. Philippe Pinel), Francoise Seigner (Mme. Guerin), Paul Ville (Remy), Claude Miler (M. Lemeri), Annie Miler (Mme. Lemeri), Pierre Fabre (Orderly at Institute), Rene Levert (Police Offical), Jean Mandaroux (Itard's Doctor)

p, Marcel Berbert; d, Francois Truffaut; w, Francois Truffaut, Jean Gruault (based on Memoire et Rapport sur Victor de L'Aveyron by Jean-Marc Gaspard Itard); ph, Nestor Almendros; ed, Agnes Guillemot; m, Antonio Vivaldi; art d, Jean Mandaroux; cos, Gitt Magrini

As in Francois Truffaut's THE 400 BLOWS and SMALL CHANGE, THE WILD CHILD is devoted to the perceptual honesty and education of children. In this case, director and star Truffaut has made a deceptively clear and simple picture on the classic subject (Romulus and Remus, Tarzan) of the socialization of a boy discovered in the forest. Based on an actual case study published in 1806, THE WILD CHILD stars Jean-Pierre Cargol as Victor, a long-haired nature boy who, apparently abandoned in the woods by his parents years earlier, is found and placed in the Institute for the Deaf and Dumb in Paris. The boy is treated as a perverse outcast and freak, but Jean Itard (Truffaut), a patient and enlightened doctor, intervenes and cares for the child in his country home rather than allow him to be sent to an asylum. Raised in an orphanage himself, Truffaut had an affinity for children that was expressed in nearly all his pictures. Probably the director's most ambitious film, THE WILD CHILD spins a modern myth with resonances for parents and children, teachers and students, and even filmmakers, actors and audiences. Its concern with language and images mirrors the longstanding French philosophical interest in linguistics, and through it all Truffaut examines the many issues at hand with warmth, concern and wisdom.

WILD IN THE COUNTRY

1961   112m   c   ★★½
Drama
FOX

Elvis Presley (Glenn Tyler), Hope Lange (Irene Sperry), Tuesday Weld (Noreen), Millie Perkins (Betty Lee Parsons), Rafer Johnson (Davis), John Ireland (Phil Macy), Gary Lockwood (Cliff Macy), William Mims (Uncle Rolfe), Raymond Greenleaf (Dr. Underwood), Christina Crawford (Monica George)

p, Jerry Wald; d, Philip Dunne; w, Clifford Odets (based on the novel *The Lost Country* by J.R. Salamanca); ph, William Mellor (CinemaScope, DeLuxe Color); ed, Dorothy Spencer; m, Kenyon Hopkins; art d, Jack Martin Smith, Preston Ames; cos, Don Feld

Presley is a backwoods delinquent youngster who, after a fight, is paroled into the care of his crooked uncle, a tonic manufacturer. He also must pay weekly visits to psychiatrist Lange, a widow, who discovers a talent for writing in the young man and nurses it along, finally becoming attracted to him. In the meantime, Presley is carrying on with the pushy Weld and the more reserved Perkins. Instead of concerning himself with romance, he concentrates on his education and leaves for college, presumably to become a literary giant. The well-versed fellow also manages a few tunes: "In My Way," "I Slipped, I Stumbled, I Fell" (Fred Weiss, Ben Weidman), "Lonely Man" (Bennie Benjamin, Sol Marcus), "Wild in the Country" (Hugo Peretti, Luigi Creatore, George David Weiss). Presley's character may be tough to swallow, but he makes the attempt in an enjoyable dramatic role that was a change from the typical swooning and singing pictures he churned out. One of the less-than-memorable efforts of screenwriter Odets, the once proletarian dramatist ("Golden Boy," "Awake and Sing") who turned to Hollywood in the middle 1940s after several successes on Broadway. Most of the critics of WILD IN THE COUNTRY called the premise—a country boy from the Shenandoah Valley in Virginia being groomed for a career in literature—unconvincing and romantic, without realizing that the author, J.R. Salamanca, may have based part of his story on the poet and novelist Jesse Stuart (*Taps for Private Tussy*), who came out of the hills of Kentucky to become the toast of New York literary circles in the 1930s and 1940s.

WILD ONE, THE

1953 79m bw   ★★★½
Drama   /PG
Columbia

Marlon Brando (*Johnny*), Mary Murphy (*Kathie*), Robert Keith (*Harry Bleeker*), Lee Marvin (*Chino*), Jay C. Flippen (*Sheriff Singer*), Peggy Maley (*Mildred*), Hugh Sanders (*Charlie Thomas*), Ray Teal (*Frank Bleeker*), John Brown (*Bill Hannegan*), Will Wright (*Art Kleiner*)

p, Stanley Kramer; d, Laslo Benedek; w, John Paxton (based on a story by Frank Rooney); ph, Hal Mohr; ed, Al Clark; m, Leith Stevens; prod d, Rudolph Sternad; art d, Walter Holscher

The first and best biker movie begins as a group of 40 leather-jacketed motorcyclists roar down a lonely country road straight at the camera. The bikers, who call themselves the Black Rebels, invade a legitimate motorcycle race and try to join the competition, but they are soon thrown out by the mass of motorcycle enthusiasts. Before leaving, a gang member manages to snatch the first-prize trophy and presents it to their leader, Brando. With the trophy strapped to his handlebars, Brando leads his pack of rowdies into the small town of Wrightsville where they drag up and down the street, forcing an old man to drive his car into a light pole. Many of the bikers pile into the local bar, Bleeker's Cafe, which is owned and operated by the sheriff, Keith. Keith is overwhelmed by the disturbance and does little to calm things down as the bikers drink themselves into oblivion. Brando's minions amuse themselves by terrorizing the town, while Brando spots a good-looking girl, Murphy, and follows her into the bar. To his surprise he learns that she is Keith's daughter, and he tries to impress her by giving her the stolen trophy. Though she is intrigued by this strange, somewhat withdrawn, brutish young

man, she refuses the gift. More trouble soon thunders into town in the guise of Marvin, a former member of Brando's gang who has left and formed his own pack.

THE WILD ONE was inspired by an incident in 1947 in which a gang of 4,000 motorcyclists took over the small town of Hollister, California, for the Fourth of July weekend and destroyed it. Producer Kramer put together a film that he hoped would illustrate the frustration and alienation felt by a younger generation, and the result became an anthem for disaffected American youth. Brando's performance enthralled audiences, who became fascinated with his contradictory character. He seemed powerful and brutal, but also demonstrated a caring, vulnerable side that he tried hard to repress—laying the groundwork for a whole school of moody antiheroes that would include James Dean in REBEL WITHOUT A CAUSE. Even without these virtues, the film would be immortal merely for the legendary exchange in which Murphy asks Brando, "What are you rebelling against?" and he replies, "What have you got?"

WILD PARTY, THE

1929 77m bw   ★★★
Comedy/Romance
Paramount

Clara Bow (*Stella Ames*), Fredric March (*Gil Gilmore*), Shirley O'Hara (*Helen Owens*), Marceline Day (*Faith Morgan*), Joyce Compton (*Eva Tutt*), Adrienne Dore (*Babs*), Virginia Thomas (*Tess*), Kay Bryant (*Thelma*), Alice Adair (*Mazie*), Jean Lorraine (*Ann*)

p, E. Lloyd Sheldon; d, Dorothy Arzner; w, E. Lloyd Sheldon, John V.A. Weaver, George Marion, Jr. (based on a story by Warner Fabian); ph, Victor Milner; ed, Otho Lovering; cos, Travis Banton

Though the plot practically grows mold before the viewer's eyes, and some of the production qualities are laughable, THE WILD PARTY remains fascinating to watch from first reel to last. One of the popular happy-go-lucky college-based films of the era, this has an added benefit in featuring Bow in her talkie debut. She is, naturally, a wild party girl who's enrolled in college for the good times rather than to advance her education. Bow and her girlfriends decide to take a class taught by March, not for his stunning classroom abilities, but because he's cute! March is a no-nonsense type and the course proves to be much more difficult than Bow and company had anticipated. To relieve this academic pressure, the coeds pull a few classroom pranks. Bow attends a ball but is kicked out for wearing a low-cut dress. She later goes to a roadhouse, where an inebriated Ben Hendricks tries to have his way with her. March, who inexplicably is also at the roadhouse, puts a stop to this, then gives Bow a lift. Compton, a fellow classmate of Bow's, sees the campus flirt leaving March's car, and her nimble mind immediately assumes there's funny business involved. Gossip spreads thick, so March chews out Bow in front of other students to prove they aren't an item. Bow angrily walks out of the classroom. She and roommate O'Hara go to a party (no one ever studies at this school), where O'Hara falls for Jack Luden. Hendricks, still angry with March for the earlier altercation, finds the professor and shoots him. Bow tells the wounded March of her love for him, giving Compton more fuel for her gossip mill. A letter from O'Hara to Luden turns up, and its spicy contents create a scandal.

It's silly, but so what? Arzner's direction is good and Bow gives an energetic performance, her Brooklyn accent serving the "It" girl's well-known personality with absolute perfection. The advertising campaign played up on this with glee, claiming: "You've had an eyeful of *IT*. . . now get an earful!" March, in only his second film, takes his part seriously, which adds to the picture's inherent campiness. Bow was terrified of making a talkie, but she handled herself well in the funfest. Reportedly, her voice was so loud it blew meters on the sound equipment when she spoke her first line. At times her voice is muddled on the soundtrack, partly the fault of the new technology and partly due to her accent. In England, THE WILD PARTY was released as a silent film. Within a few years Bow would be gone from the screen forever, while March would become one of filmdom's most respected thespians.

WILD RIVER

1960 115m c   ★★★★
Drama   /A
FOX

Montgomery Clift (Chuck Glover), Lee Remick (Carol Baldwin), Jo Van Fleet (Ella Garth), Albert Salmi (F.J. Bailey), Jay C. Flippen (Hamilton Garth), James Westerfield (Cal Garth), Big Jeff Bess (Joe John Garth), Robert Earl Jones (Ben), Frank Overton (Walter Clark), Barbara Loden (Betty Jackson)

p, Elia Kazan; d, Elia Kazan; w, Paul Osborn (based on the novels Mud on the Stars by William Bradford Huie and Dunbar's Cove by Borden Deal); ph, Ellsworth Fredricks (CinemaScope, DeLuxe Color); ed, William Reynolds; m, Kenyon Hopkins; art d, Lyle Wheeler, Herman A. Blumenthal; cos, Anna Hill Johnstone

Although it was not a great success at the box office (issue-oriented films were not what the public seemed to want in 1960), this dramatic tug-of-war between progress and tradition remains a memorable example of director Kazan at his best. Set in the 1930s, the story focuses on Clift, an agent for the Tennessee Valley Authority (TVA), which is in the process of clearing land to build much-needed dams. This project cannot be accomplished without the demolition of many homes and the relocation of their inhabitants. One of Clift's most unpleasant tasks is the removal of Van Fleet, an 80-year-old widow, from her home. Van Fleet, who has lived on her land for more than 50 years, refuses to leave. As if Clift's plight isn't bad enough, the locals look upon him as an interloper and make his life miserable. Local whites grow particularly hostile when Clift treats the area's blacks fairly, and it isn't long before some of the more racist townsfolk try to beat some sense into the TVA man. Nevertheless, Van Fleet's young widowed granddaughter, Remick, falls in love with Clift and they eventually marry. In time, Van Fleet finally gives up her battle, the land is flooded, and the proud old woman dies shortly after moving into her new home.

An emotionally charged movie that offers little respite for the viewer, WILD RIVER was skillfully scripted by Osborn, masterfully directed by Kazan, and features excellent acting and strong production values. Shot on location in Tennessee at Lake Chickamauga, the Hiwassee River, and in the towns of Cleveland and Charleston, this film was the end of a 25-year dream for Kazan. He had been to the area in the mid-1930s and always wanted to do a movie about the TVA, but it took more than two decades to find a studio and the right script to fulfill his desire. Many nonprofessional Tennesseans appear in the film, lending it a realism seldom seen when Hollywood extras are employed. Kazan's wife, Barbara Loden, plays a small role, and if you keep an eye out you'll see a very young Bruce Dern appearing in his first movie. However, Van Fleet's performance is the film's standout; though she was only 41 at the time the film was made, the actress is completely convincing as an 80-year-old, thanks in no small part to Ben Nye's wonderful makeup work. Clift also gives a fine performance. He was never easy to work with, as he

had several personal problems, not the least of which was his drinking and his difficulty in coming to grips with his homosexuality. Reportedly, he'd promised to stay off the sauce for the picture and kept his word until the final week when he went on a bender that almost submarined the movie.

WILD STRAWBERRIES
(SMULTRONSTALLET)
1957 90m bw   ★★★★★
Drama   /15
Svensk (Sweden)

Victor Seastrom (Prof. Isak Borg), Bibi Andersson (Sara), Ingrid Thulin (Marianne Borg), Gunnar Bjornstrand (Evald Borg), Jullan Kindahl (Agda), Folke Sundquist (Anders), Bjorn Bjelvenstam (Viktor), Naima Wifstrand (Isak's Mother), Gunnel Brostrom (Mrs. Berit Almann), Gertrud Fridh (Isak's Wife)

p, Allan Ekelund; d, Ingmar Bergman; w, Ingmar Bergman; ph, Gunnar Fischer, Bjorn Thermenius; ed, Oscar Rosander; m, Erik Nordgren; art d, Gittan Gustafsson; cos, Millie Strom

Possibly Ingmar Bergman's finest film and a staple in film history, WILD STRAWBERRIES not only exemplifies one of Sweden's greatest directors' greatest works, but the importance of a superb performance as well. Victor Sjostrom stars as Isak Borg, a medical professor on his way to accept an honorary degree on the 50th anniversary of his graduation from the University at Lund. He rides with his daughter-in-law, Marianne (Ingrid Thulin), who has decided to leave her husband. Animosity exists between the opinionated Isak (as she sees him) and Marianne, mainly because the old man reminds her so much of her husband. En route, they stop at Isak's childhood house, where he recalls his family in the days of his youth (although he is unseen by the characters and not present in the flashback). He sees his sweetheart, Sara (Bibi Andersson), picking wild strawberries and carrying on semi-innocently with his brother. Later he is awakened (in the present) by a teenage girl named Sara (again played by Andersson). She asks the old man for a ride, bringing along two male friends. This foray proves less than ideal, hampered by a car crash and Isak's disturbing nightmares.

A fascinating, compelling picture, WILD STRAWBERRIES is viewed by many as Bergman's greatest achievement. Its most striking segment, which perhaps best illustrates Bergman's talents, is a dream sequence in which Isak walks through a desolate city, is approached by a faceless man, sees a clock without hands, and watches a funeral wagon crash and leave a coffin in the middle of the street. As he nears the coffin, it opens, and the corpse—again Isak—emerges and attempts to pull him into the afterlife. The visual and aural symbolism is chilling, and the entire scene is perfectly integrated into the "reality" of the rest of the picture. Sjostrom, in his final film, delivers the finest performance in any Bergman film—a major accomplishment considering the virtuosity that Bergman's actors consistently display.

WILDROSE
1985 95m c   ★★★½
Drama
New Front/Ely Lake

Lisa Eichhorn (June Lorich), Tom Bower (Rick Ogaard), Jim Cada (Pavich), Cinda Jackson (Karen), Dan Nemanick (Ricotti), Lydia Olsen (Katri Sippola), Bill Schoppert (Timo Maki), James Stowell (Doobie), Stephen Yokam (Billy), Vienna Maki (Vienna Lorich)

p, Sandra Schulberg; d, John Hanson; w, John Hanson, Eugene Corr (based on a story by Sandra Schulberg, John Hanson); ph, Peter Stein; ed, Arthur Coburn; m, Bernard Krause, Gary S. Remal, Cris Williamson

Though WILDROSE tells its story in the classic Hollywood format, this is an intelligent and often moving story of one woman's struggle to achieve independence. June Lorich (Lisa Eichhorn) works as a laborer and heavy-machine operator at an iron mine in Minnesota. Having recently divorced a drunken wife-beater, June is eager to find her own place in the world. Though she is not the only woman working the strip mines, she is confronted by sexist attitudes when she is transferred to an otherwise all-male crew. Only Rick Ogaard (Tom Bower), a fellow crew member, refuses to harass her. They begin a friendship that develops into an unexpected love affair, while June grapples with the problems that come with independence. WILDROSE develops with a quiet understanding for Eichhorn's predicaments and desires, making effective use of small, everyday moments under John Hanson's semidocumentary directorial style. Eichhorn gives the story a firm center, with a natural and emotionally sincere performance.

WILL SUCCESS SPOIL ROCK HUNTER?
1957 94m c
Comedy
FOX
★★★★

Jayne Mansfield (Rita Marlowe), Tony Randall (Rock Hunter), Betsy Drake (Jenny), Joan Blondell (Violet), John Williams (Le Salle), Henry Jones (Rufus), Lili Gentle (April), Mickey Hargitay (Bobo), Georgia Carr (Calypso Number), Groucho Marx (Surprise Guest)

p, Frank Tashlin; d, Frank Tashlin; w, Frank Tashlin (based on the play by George Axelrod); ph, Joseph MacDonald (CinemaScope, DeLuxe Color); ed, Hugh S. Fowler; m, Cyril J. Mockridge; art d, Lyle Wheeler, Leland Fuller; fx, L.B. Abbott; cos, Charles LeMaire

A panic. Jayne's twin peaks triumph, for which she received a Tony, gets transferred from Hollywood lampoon to advertising satire. Tashlin produced, directed and wrote the screenplay, and in true Tashlin form, it feels like a like an outrageous, gaudy cartoon. The frantic Randall performance, Blondell's usual canny job and Hargitay, Mansfield's real life muscleman husband doing a turn as a TV Tarzan, all score. But it's Jayne's last word on Hollywood Blondes that will have you howling. Her best takes: Seclusion and Catherine the Great. And wait until you see who she really carries a torch for. Jayne's broad comedic talent was only properly utilized twice by Fox. Instead of basing her persona on Marilyn Monroe, her studio should have built her along the lines of a combo of Mae West and Jane Russell, and taken advantage of her unique brand of sexual anarchy. French critics enjoyed this picture immensely, and Jean-Luc Godard had it on his 10-best list. In a small role as one of the scrubwomen appears Minta Durfee, former silent-screen comedienne who worked with Charlie Chaplin, among others, and married Roscoe "Fatty" Arbuckle.

WILLIE AND PHIL
1980 116m c
Drama
FOX
★★½
R/18

Michael Ontkean (Willie Kaufman), Margot Kidder (Jeannette Sutherland), Ray Sharkey (Phil D'Amico), Jan Miner (Mrs. Kaufman), Tom Brennan (Mr. Kaufman), Julie Bovasso (Mrs. D'Amico), Louis Guss (Mr. D'Amico), Kathleen Maguire (Mrs. Sutherland), Kaki Hunter (Patti Sutherland), Kristine DeBell (Rena)

p, Paul Mazursky, Tony Ray; d, Paul Mazursky; w, Paul Mazursky; ph, Sven Nykvist (Movielab Color); ed, Donn Cambern; m, Claude Bolling, Georges Delerue; prod d, Pato Guzman; cos, Albert Wolsky

Director-writer Paul Mazursky creates a light, pleasant situation but never really gets at what makes his characters tick. Michael Ontkean and Ray Sharkey become incredibly close friends, not even allowing their mutual attraction to Margot Kidder to interfere with their friendship. Though Kidder is fond of both men, and they feel the same about her, she marries Ontkean. Then the setting switches from New York to California, the marriage fails, and Kidder takes up with Sharkey. WILLIE AND PHIL looks like a glossy remake of JULES ET JIM (one scene even uses a portion of George Delerue's score from that movie), though it lacks all the cinematic subtleties and human insights that fill Francois Truffaut's film. It is almost impossible not to like the characters, which makes it all the more irritating to watch them make fools of themselves.

WILSON
1944 154m c
Biography
FOX
★★★
/U

Alexander Knox (Woodrow Wilson), Charles Coburn (Prof. Henry Holmes), Geraldine Fitzgerald (Edith Wilson), Thomas Mitchell (Joseph Tumulty), Ruth Nelson (Ellen Wilson), Cedric Hardwicke (Henry Cabot Lodge), Vincent Price (William G. McAdoo), William Eythe (George Felton), Mary Anderson (Eleanor Wilson), Sidney Blackmer (Josephus Daniels)

p, Darryl F. Zanuck; d, Henry King; w, Lamar Trotti; ph, Leon Shamroy (Technicolor); ed, Barbara McLean; m, Alfred Newman; art d, Wiard Ihnen, James Basevi; fx, Fred Sersen; cos, Rene Hubert

A lavish biography of Woodrow Wilson, this film was Darryl F. Zanuck's first production after he returned from WWII service in North Africa. Knox plays the president, first as the head of Princeton University and the author of books on political theory. He is chosen to run for governor of New Jersey and is such a success that he is soon running for president. He wins and during his first term WWI erupts in Europe. He is steadfast in his determination to keep the US out of the war, keeping with the largely isolationist sentiment of the country. Eventually, though, German attacks on US merchant ships lead Wilson to declare war. After the war is won, thanks to the massive infusion of fresh American boys into the exhausted and depleted Allied armies, Wilson goes to Versailles to help form the peace treaty. He conceives the idea of the League of Nations and convinces most of the former combatants to join, but back in the US he is unable to drum up support; isolationism is still running strong. He goes on a cross-country campaign to bring his idea to the masses, but the trip only ruins his own health and the US votes to stay out of the League.

More than $3 million was spent on the production, and the lavish sets included a nearly perfect re-creation of the White House. Henry Fonda and Gary Cooper were considered for the lead, but eventually a supporting contract player, Knox, was tagged for the role. Zanuck and Lamar Trotti wrote most of the script. Zanuck also oversaw the cutting, seeing that the film moved quickly depite its length. When the film was finally ready, Zanuck reportedly predicted that it would win an Oscar. (It didn't, but when Zanuck did recieve one for GENTLEMAN'S AGREEMENT in 1947 he told the Academy in his acceptance speech, "I should have got this for WILSON.") The film won Oscars for its screenplay, cinematography, art direction, and sound, and was nominated for Best Picture, Best Actor, Best Director (losing on all three counts to GOING MY WAY), Best Score, and Best Special Effects. Not quite as good as all those nominations might suggest (but then since when do Oscars *mean* anything?), but a solid film just the same, with Knox doing a good job in the title role.

WINCHESTER '73

1950 92m bw ★★★★
Western /U
Universal

James Stewart (*Lin McAdam*), Shelley Winters (*Lola Manners*), Dan Duryea (*Waco Johnny Dean, the Kansas Kid*), Stephen McNally (*Dutch Henry Brown*), Millard Mitchell (*Johnny "High Spade" Williams*), Charles Drake (*Steve Miller*), John McIntire (*Joe Lamont*), Will Geer (*Wyatt Earp*), Jay C. Flippen (*Sgt. Wilkes*), Rock Hudson (*Young Bull*)

p, Aaron Rosenberg; d, Anthony Mann; w, Robert L. Richards, Borden Chase (based on the story by Stuart N. Lake); ph, William Daniels; ed, Edward Curtiss; m, Joseph Gershenson (assisted by Jesse Hibbs); art d, Bernard Herzbrun, Nathan Juran, Russell A. Gausman, A. Roland Fields; cos, Yvonne Wood

The first collaboration between director Mann and actor Stewart, a team that would create a series of superior westerns that added a new, psychological dimension to the genre.

WINCHESTER '73 begins as Stewart, who is pursuing his father's killer, rides into Dodge City with his friend, Mitchell. The whole town is celebrating the Fourth of July under the watchful eye of the fatherly Wyatt Earp (Geer), who collects pistols from gun-toting strangers and keeps them in his office until they leave. Stewart enters the local saloon and orders a drink. Out of the corner of his eye he sees McNally, and both men spastically grope for their sidearms, only to find empty holsters. Stewart's nerves are frazzled by the event, and he leaves the saloon shaking. The two men square off again, this time in a shooting contest with a brand new "one-of-1,000" Winchester '73 rifle as the first prize. The contestants are evenly matched in an intense fight, but Stewart manages to best McNally and wins the coveted rifle. Before Stewart can leave town with his prize, however, McNally attacks him and steals the rifle. Stewart then sets off on a maniacal pursuit of McNally and his rifle which culminates in a memorable shoot-out with decidedly Oedipal overtones.

WINCHESTER '73 was the first of the so-called "psychological" westerns that became the benchmark of the genre in the 1950s. Mann and Stewart present a basically decent hero driven to the brink of madness by dark forces from his past. Played out against breathtaking landscapes that reflect the emotional turmoil of the main characters, Mann's film gives us one of Stewart's greatest performances, his manic intensity evoking both terror and pathos. The supporting cast is fine, with both Tony Curtis and Rock Hudson appearing in small roles.

WINCHESTER '73 was once a project for Fritz Lang, who worked on the script with Silvia Richards in 1948. Lang eventually walked away from the film, and Mann took over at Stewart's suggestion. Beginning a collaboration that would last through two more westerns (BEND OF THE RIVER, 1952, and THE FAR COUNTRY, 1955), Mann rewrote the script with Borden Chase. WINCHESTER '73 was a great success at the box office

and reestablished Stewart (who was suffering a decline in popularity) as one of Hollywood's top actors. In addition to providing both star and director with a career boost, the film launched a whole new series of adult westerns directed by such notables as Mann, Budd Boetticher, Don Siegel, Sam Fuller, and Nicholas Ray.

WIND, THE

1987 93m c ★★★½
Thriller
Omega

Meg Foster (*Sian Anderson*), Wings Hauser (*Phil*), David McCallum (*John*), Robert Morley (*Elias Appleby*), Steve Railsback (*Kesner*), Michael Yannatos (*Policeman*), Summer Thomas (*Sian's Friend*), John Michaels, Tracy Young (*Newlyweds*), Dina Yannou (*Elias' Wife*)

p, Nico Mastorakis; d, Nico Mastorakis; w, Nico Mastorakis, Fred C. Perry (based on a story by Mastorakis); ph, Andrew Bellis (Technicolor); ed, Nico Mastorakis, Bruce Cannon; m, Stanley Myers, Hans Zimmer; prod d, Lester Gallagher; art d, Dotty Engfeld, G. Koliopandos, Lenny Schultz; fx, L. Ludovik, A. Bellek, Yannis Samiotis; cos, Richard Abramson

Sian Anderson (Meg Foster) is a writer of trashy novels who decides to take a break and rents a villa on a remote Greek island for the winter. The eccentric Englishman renting her place is Elias Appleby (Robert Morley), who warns her about the fierce winds that blow at night, sometimes with fatal results. She settles down and tries to begin working on her next book. Later Appleby fires the caretaker, Phil (Wings Hauser), a former seaman and mercenary at the end of his tether. Then Sian sees Phil kill Appleby and bury him in the yard. Speaking no Greek, she is only able to call her boyfriend (David McCallum) in Los Angeles and have him call back for help. Meanwhile, Phil knows what Sian has seen.

An entertaining, suspenseful drama, THE WIND benefits most from excellent performances by Foster and Hauser. The other cast members have little to do but die or move the plot along, though Morley is as delightful as ever. Shot on the island of Monemvassia off the coast of Greece, the movie is full of spectacular scenery. With THE WIND, producer-writer-director Nico Mastorakis proves he can make as good a film as anyone, and better than most.

WIND AND THE LION, THE

1975 119m c ★★★½
Adventure/Historical/War PG/A
MGM

Sean Connery (*Mulay el Raisuli*), Candice Bergen (*Eden Pedecaris*), Brian Keith (*Theodore Roosevelt*), John Huston (*John Hay*), Geoffrey Lewis (*Gummere*), Steve Kanaly (*Capt. Jerome*), Vladek Sheybal (*The Bashaw*), Nadim Sawalha (*Sherif of Wazan*), Roy Jenson (*Adm. Chadwick*), Deborah Baxter (*Alice Roosevelt*)

p, Herb Jaffe; d, John Milius; w, John Milius; ph, Billy Williams (Panavision, Metrocolor); ed, Robert Wolfe; m, Jerry Goldsmith; prod d, Gil Parando; art d, Antonio Paton; cos, Richard LaMotte

A stirring, if grossly inaccurate, look at the dawn of US interventionism, THE WIND AND THE LION features Brian Keith as a Teddy Roosevelt determined to establish his Presidential identity, having come to office after the death of William McKinley. When a rebellious Arab chieftain, Mulay el Raisuli (Sean Connery), seizes American woman Eden Pedecaris (Candice Bergen) and her children, Roosevelt prepares to send in the Marines. At the same time the Germans land in North Africa in force, looking for a way to turn the situation to their advantage. The chieftain and Eden talk a great deal of philosophy, and the Arab ruler begins to take on heroic stature in the eyes of her son. Eventually, under pressure from Roosevelt, Raisuli releases his hostages to the Marines and is immediately arrested and imprisoned by the Germans. The Marines are none too happy about this development—since Roosevelt had promised Raisuli his freedom if he released his prisoners—so they march into the town (in a scene almost directly stolen from THE WILD BUNCH) and shoot it out with the Germans.

THE WIND AND THE LION is certainly jingoistic to a fault, and its portrayal of the various factions is little above the cartoon level, but thanks to marvelous performances by Keith and Connery, the film works as a maker of myths. The real facts of the incident were not so grand: Raisuli, a brigand chief, kidnapped a balding, overweight businessman who bore no resemblance to the lovely Bergen, to embarrass the Sultan of Morocco, who was already having troubles with the US. The man was freed after only a couple of days, but before his release was made public, the Republican Party, looking for a rallying issue, announced that a telegram had been sent to the kidnapper demanding the man be freed or Raisuli would be pay with his life. No troops landed No one was killed. But historical truth isn't what's important here; heroes and myth are the currency of this film, and it delivers two heroes in admirable fashion. Nominated for two Academy Awards: Best Sound and Best Score.

WINDOW, THE
1949 73m bw   ★★★★★
Thriller   /A
RKO

Barbara Hale *(Mrs. Woodry)*, Bobby Driscoll *(Tommy Woodry)*, Arthur Kennedy *(Mr. Woodry)*, Paul Stewart *(Mr. Kellerton)*, Ruth Roman *(Mrs. Kellerton)*, Anthony Ross *(Ross)*, Richard Benedict *(Drunken Seaman)*, Jim Nolan *(Stranger on Street)*, Ken Terrell *(Man)*, Lee Phelps

p, Frederic Ullman, Jr.; d, Ted Tetzlaff; w, Mel Dinelli (based on the novelette *The Boy Cried Murder* by Cornell Woolrich); ph, William Steiner; ed, Frederic Knudtson; m, Roy Webb; art d, Walter E. Keller, Sam Corso; fx, Russell A. Cully

Set in the tenement section of New York's Lower East Side, this incredibly tense nail-biter stars Driscoll as a young boy who has a habit of crying wolf. One night, while trying to beat the heat by making his bed on the fire escape, he climbs up to the next floor and sees Stewart and Roman murder a drunken seaman, Benedict. Of course, no one, not even the boy's parents (Kennedy and Hale), believes Driscoll when he tells what he has seen, since they all assume that this is just another of the boy's tales. Danger lurks.

Based on a story by Cornell Woolrich (whose writing was also the basis for Hitchcock's similar REAR WINDOW), THE WINDOW presents a frightening vision of helplessness, vividly conveying childish frustration at being dismissed or ignored by one's parents. Director and onetime cameraman Tetzlaff adroitly injects a maximum of suspense into the film, enabling the audience to identify with Driscoll's predicament and, interestingly, to view his parents as evil, almost as evil as the murderers themselves. Having photographed Hitchcock's NOTORIOUS just three years before, Tetzlaff had, without a shadow of a doubt, learned something of his suspense-building craft from the master of that art (as did just about every working director). By casting the 12-year-old Driscoll, star of such heart-warming Disney pictures

as SONG OF THE SOUTH and SO DEAR TO MY HEART, Tetzlaff was able to twist the idyllic Disney image of childhood into a nightmare world of death and violence, in which parents and neighbors are the child's worst fears come true. Adding to the film's effect is the on-location photography and the dark ambience of the tenements, where evil and death seem to lurk in every shadow, where the seaman's corpse is found, and where the pursued boy is nearly killed. (In a perverse twist of fate, it was in an abandoned, crumbling New York City tenement that actor Driscoll was found dead some 20 years later, the victim of an apparent drug overdose.) THE WINDOW, which cost only $210,000 to produce and made many times that at the box office, was voted the best mystery film of the year by the Mystery Writers of America. Editor Knudtson was nominated for an Academy Award, while Driscoll was named Outstanding Juvenile Actor and given a miniature statuette. An exceptional film.

WINGED VICTORY
1944 130m bw   ★★★½
War   /U
FOX

Lon McCallister *(Frankie Davis)*, Jeanne Crain *(Helen)*, Edmond O'Brien *(Irving Miller)*, Jane Ball *(Jane Preston)*, Mark Daniels *(Alan Ross)*, Jo-Carroll Dennison *(Dorothy Ross)*, Don Taylor *(Danny "Pinky" Scariano)*, Lee J. Cobb *(Doctor)*, Judy Holliday *(Ruth Miller)*, Peter Lind Hayes *(O'Brian)*

p, Darryl F. Zanuck; d, George Cukor; w, Moss Hart (based on the play by Moss Hart); ph, Glen MacWilliams; ed, Barbara McLean; m, David Rose; art d, Lyle Wheeler, Lewis Creber; fx, Fred Sersen

Decent if not terrific. A paean to the Army Air Force training program, this film was adapted from the smash hit Broadway play by Moss Hart. Much of the same cast, most of them actual members of the AAF, is also carried over from the play. The plot, what there is of it, follows McCallister through his flight training, along with his friends and comrades from all over the country, O'Brien, Daniels, Taylor, and others. Their trials and tests on the way to getting their wings is contrasted with the worries of their wives, mothers, and girlfriends, including Holliday, Crain, Dennison, and Ball.

This film marked the first meeting of director George Cukor and Judy Holliday, who would later become one of his favorite actresses, appearing in such films as ADAM'S RIB (1949), THE MARRYING KIND (1952), and IT SHOULD HAPPEN TO YOU (1953) for the director. Her performance here is excellent, making the other women look stiff and artificial by comparison. The profits from this film, like those of the stage production, went to assorted Army charities, and the film made a lot of money for those coffers.

WINGS OF DESIRE
(DER HIMMEL UBER BERLIN)
1987 130m c/bw   ★★★★½
Fantasy   PG-13/15
Road Movies/Argos/WDR   (France/West Germany)

Bruno Ganz *(Damiel)*, Solveig Dommartin *(Marion)*, Otto Sander *(Cassiel)*, Curt Bois *(Homer)*, Peter Falk *(Himself)*

p, Wim Wenders, Anatole Dauman; d, Wim Wenders; w, Wim Wenders, Peter Handke; ph, Henri Alekan; ed, Peter Przygodda; m, Jurgen Knieper; prod d, Heidi Ludi; cos, Monika Jacobs

A rich, mystical near-masterpiece. With WINGS OF DESIRE, Wim Wenders creates a visual poem about the walls that exist in our world—those that separate fiction from reality, Heaven from

Earth, history from the present, those who observe from those who feel. Bruno Ganz and Otto Sander play two angels who circulate in a black-and-white Berlin, where they "observe, collect, testify to, and preserve" the world around them, unseen by all but innocent children. The angels focus their attentions on three individuals—an octogenarian poet (Curt Bois); an American film and TV star (Peter Falk, playing himself); and a French trapeze artist (Solveig Dommartin). But, while helping these mortals, Ganz also struggles with his own desires to be able to feel, not just emotionally but physically as well. Although WINGS OF DESIRE draws on many sources, from Cocteau's filmic depiction of angels to the writings of Rainer Maria Rilke, the film's roots are perhaps closest to Walter Ruttmann's classic 1927 silent documentary, BERLIN: SYMPHONY OF A CITY. WINGS OF DESIRE, too, is a symphony on Berlin, though under Wenders's direction the city limits (which have been bisected by the Wall) become fantastic, extending far above to include those angels who keep a watchful eye on the world below. WINGS OF DESIRE enjoyed an overwhelmingly positive reception both at the box office—where it exceeded the success normally enjoyed by art-house offerings—and at the hands of the critics. The jury of the 1987 Cannes Film Festival named Wenders Best Director.

WINNER TAKE ALL

1932 68m bw   ★★★½
Sports   /U
WB

James Cagney (Jim Kane), Marian Nixon (Peggy Harmon), Virginia Bruce (Joan Gibson), Guy Kibbee (Pop Slavin), Clarence Muse (Rosebud, the Trainer), Dickie Moore (Dickie Harmon), Allan Lane (Monty), John Roche (Roger Elliott), Ralf Harolde (Legs Davis), Alan Mowbray (Forbes)

d, Roy Del Ruth; w, Wilson Mizner, Robert Lord (based on the story "133 at 3" by Gerald Beaumont); ph, Robert Kurrle; ed, Thomas Pratt; m, W. Franke Harling; art d, Robert Haas; cos, Orry-Kelly

For his first boxing picture, James Cagney plays Jim Kane, a fighter on the mend in a New Mexico health resort. He's been sent there courtesy of fans' donations, having spent most of his own money on alcohol and women. At the resort, he meets Peggy (Marian Nixon) and her small son, Dickie (Dickie Moore), who are about to be kicked out because she can't pay her bill. Jim agrees to help out by entering the ring once more, and wins the prize money, but gets his nose smashed for his efforts. Returning to New York City determined to take the town by storm, Jim meets socialite Joan (Virginia Bruce) and falls for her. He gets his nose fixed to impress her, and takes care to protect his new snooter in the ring, but his skills as a fighter suffer as a result. The fans turn on him, Joan begins to grow bored, and the pug begins to realize that his life has taken a wrong turn. Though the story is simplistic, this is a strong drama, delivered with gusto by the cast. Cagney is at his best, creating a realistic portrait of a fighter who lets his ego balloon out of proportion. Roy Del Ruth's direction wisely concentrates on the characters, allowing the fine ensemble to give the drama its power. Cagney, who approached his role with the utmost seriousness and was determined to make his characterization realistic, trained with Harvey Perry, an ex-welterweight who also has a bit part in the film. The sparring sessions paid off, for Cagney's moves look like the real thing and it's obvious he's in the thick of the fray in both closeups and long shots. Cagney's skills in the film were so impressive that the rumor circulated for some time that the actor was a former prizefighter.

WINNING TEAM, THE

1952 98m bw   ★★★
Biography/Sports   /U
WB

Doris Day (Aimee Alexander), Ronald Reagan (Grover Cleveland Alexander), Frank Lovejoy (Rogers Hornsby), Eve Miller (Margaret), James Millican (Bill Killefer), Russ Tamblyn (Willie Alexander), Gordon Jones (Glasheen), Hugh Sanders (McCarthy), Frank Ferguson (Sam Arrants), Walter Baldwin (Pa Alexander)

p, Bryan Foy; d, Lewis Seiler; w, Ted Sherdeman, Seeleg Lester, Merwin Gerard (based on the story by Lester, Gerard); ph, Sid Hickox; ed, Alan Crosland, Jr.; m, David Buttolph; art d, Douglas Bacon; fx, H.F. Koenekamp; cos, Leah Rhodes

After portraying the immortal George Gipp in KNUTE ROCKNE—ALL AMERICAN, Ronald Reagan took on the role of another sporting great in this well-made but sanitized screen biography of legendary pitcher Grover Cleveland Alexander. The film follows Alexander from his early days as a telephone lineman and barnstorming pro through his major-league pitching success with the Phillies and Cubs, and on to his strong-willed comeback after succumbing to the bottle. Plagued by double vision and dizzy spells—the result of a head injury that temporarily ended his career even before he reached the majors—Alexander begins drinking when his curse returns, driving away his loving wife, Aimee (Doris Day). Leaving the game again, Alexander hits bottom, supporting himself by working for a two-bit circus. When Aimee persuades St. Louis Cardinal manager Rogers Hornsby (Frank Lovejoy) to give Alexander another shot, the great pitcher rises to the challenge, leading the Cards to a victory in the 1926 World Series.

Reportedly, this was one of Reagan's favorite roles, and he gives a credible if not particularly imaginative performance, portraying Alexander as a remarkable talent beset by all-too-human problems. To prepare for his role, Reagan trained with Arnold "Jigger" Statz, a contemporary of Alexander's, and Jerry Priddy, second baseman for the Detroit Tigers, spending two hours a day for three weeks working on his pitching.

WINSLOW BOY, THE

1950 97m bw   ★★★½
Drama   /U
Anatole de Grunwald/London Films/Eagle-Lion   (U.K.)

Robert Donat (Sir Robert Morton), Margaret Leighton (Catherine Winslow), Cedric Hardwicke (Arthur Winslow), Basil Radford (Esmond Curry), Kathleen Harrison (Violet), Francis L. Sullivan (Attorney General), Marie Lohr (Grace Winslow), Jack Watling (Dickie Winslow), Frank Lawton (John Watherstone), Neil North (Ronnie Winslow)

p, Anatole de Grunwald; d, Anthony Asquith; w, Terence Rattigan, Anthony Asquith, Anatole de Grunwald (based on the play by Rattigan); ph, Freddie Young, Osmond Borradaile; ed, Gerald Turney-Smith; m, William Alwyn; prod d, Andre Andrejew; cos, William Chappell

In 1912 in London, Hardwicke is a retired bank official whose 14-year-old son, North, is expelled from naval college when he is accused of stealing a five-shilling postal order from another cadet. Hardwicke is convinced of his son's innocence but he is prevented by British law and unconcerned bureaucrats from fighting for his son's honor. Stymied at every turn, he hires the most famous attorney in Britain, Donat. Donat makes an impassioned speech in the House of Commons that results in a Petition of Right that allows Hardwicke to sue the Admiralty and make them prove in the courts that his son stole the postal order. The case is making headlines now and Hardwicke's family is facing the consequences: Hardwicke's daughter, suffragette Leighton, is left by her fiance; son Watling is forced to leave Oxford; and various legal fees are bringing Hardwicke almost to bankruptcy. In a courtroom trial, Donat finally gets North to admit the truth about what he was doing when the postal order was stolen: sneaking a cigarette in the locker room. The court finds in favor of North and Donat makes clear that he intends to see a great deal more of Leighton.

The story may seem rather dry, but the performances of Hardwicke, as the father prepared to face ruin to restore his son's honor, and of Donat, as the brilliant lawyer who finally breaks through the boy's own personal code of honor to exonerate him, keep the movie an engrossing experience. Based on the true Archer-Shee case of 1912.

WINTER KILLS

1979 97m c   ★★★★
Comedy/Mystery/Political   R/18
Avco Embassy

Jeff Bridges (*Nick Kegan*), John Huston (*Pa Kegan*), Anthony Perkins (*John Ceruti*), Sterling Hayden (*Z.K. Dawson*), Eli Wallach (*Joe Diamond*), Dorothy Malone (*Emma Kegan*), Tomas Milian (*Frank Mayo*), Belinda Bauer (*Yvette Malone*), Ralph Meeker (*Gameboy Baker*), Toshiro Mifune (*Keith*)

p, Fred Caruso; d, William Richert; w, William Richert (based on the novel by Richard Condon); ph, Vilmos Zsigmond; ed, David Bretherton; m, Maurice Jarre; prod d, Robert Boyle; art d, Norman Newberry

Bridges stars as Nick Kegan, the youngest son of a Kennedy-esque family presided over by an eccentric tycoon (Huston). Not wanting to follow in the footsteps of his older brother, who became president and was then assassinated, Nick has drifted through life trying to avoid the influence of his father. But when a dying man claims to have been the "second rifle" at the president's assassination 19 years before, the revelation sets into motion a bizarre series of events which sees Nick dig deeper and deeper into the past to find out who is truly responsible for his brother's assassination. Director William Richert has turned Richard Condon's novel about the insanity of the American power structure into a wickedly funny black comedy spiced up by some deliciously off-the-wall performances. The fact that Richert got the project off the ground at all is a miracle. To be taken seriously by the studio, this first-time director went out and got written commitments from such acting notables as Huston, Bridges, Perkins, and Elizabeth Taylor. Filling out his cast with Mifune, Malone, Hayden, Wallach, and Richard Boone, he began production and acquired Alfred Hitchcock's favorite production designer, Robert Boyle (who also makes a humorous cameo as a hotel desk clerk) to execute the lush, detailed look of the film. About a week before the $6.5 million production was completed, the studio inexplicably pulled the financial plug. Richert finished the project on his own and struck complicated financial deals with Avco Embassy in an effort to complete and distribute it. Though it garnered little attention in theaters, it has become a cult favorite on video.

WISE BLOOD

1979 108m c   ★★★½
Drama   PG/15
Ithaca/Anthea   (U.S./West Germany)

Brad Dourif (*Hazel Motes*), Ned Beatty (*Hoover Shoates*), Harry Dean Stanton (*Asa Hawks*), Dan Shor (*Enoch Emery*), Amy Wright (*Sabbath Lilly*), Mary Nell Santacroce (*Landlady*), John Huston (*Grandfather*)

p, Michael Fitzgerald, Kathy Fitzgerald; d, John Huston; w, Benedict Fitzgerald (based on the novel by Flannery O'Connor); ph, Gerry Fisher; ed, Roberto Silvi; m, Alex North; cos, Sally Fitzgerald

A rich slice of Southern Gothic, adapted from the novel by Flannery O'Connor and directed by John Huston, who also makes an appearance as a preacher. Hazel Motes (Brad Dourif) is a fanatical young evangelist who, through his one-man "Church of Truth Without Jesus Christ," wages a private war against the crass commercialization of religion—the "Jesus trade." He is "helped" by various unsavory types including Harry Dean Stanton, as a preacher who feigns blindness and persuades Motes to put out his own eyes, and Ned Beatty, as a guitar-strumming hustler. By turns disturbing and hilarious, this is as dark a take on Southern small-town life as you will find.

WITCHES, THE

1990 91m c   ★★★½
Fantasy   PG
Jim Henson/Lorimar   (U.K./U.S.)

Anjelica Huston (*Mrs. Ernst/Grand High Witch*), Mai Zetterling (*Helga*), Jasen Fisher (*Luke*), Rowan Atkinson (*Mr. Stringer*), Bill Paterson (*Mr. Jenkins*), Brenda Blethyn (*Mrs. Jenkins*), Charlie Potter (*Bruno Jenkins*), Anna Lambton (*Woman in Black*), Jane Horrocks (*Miss Irvine*), Sukie Smith (*Marlene*)

p, Mark Shivas; d, Nicolas Roeg; w, Allan Scott (based on the book by Roald Dahl); ph, Harvey Harrison (Eastman Color); ed, Tony Lawson; m, Stanley Myers; prod d, Andrew Sanders; art d, Norman Dorme; fx, Jim Henson's Creature Shop, Steve Norrington, Nigel Booth, John Stephenson; cos, Marit Allen

Never known for the accessibility of his films, director Nicolas Roeg (DON'T LOOK NOW, THE MAN WHO FELL TO EARTH, INSIGNIFICANCE) here has created a wildly entertaining fairy tale.

The film begins in Germany, where a little boy named Luke (Jasen Fisher) listens to bedtime stories read by his grandmother Helga (Mai Zetterling). Helga tells Luke that she has had experience with witchcraft, adding that it cost her a finger on her left hand. She wants to prepare the boy to protect himself against the witches in the world, who are constantly plotting to kill children. She gives him tips on how to spot a witch, noting that they have a purple tinge to their eyes, wear squared shoes because they have no toes, and always wear gloves to hide their hideous hands. They also have a keen sense of smell which enables them to locate children. Helga relates the story of a girl who was captured by witches and thought to be gone forever until she suddenly appeared as an image in a painting owned by her parents. Over the years, the image aged from that of a little girl to that of an old lady, until finally the image disappeared. After the story-telling session, Luke's parents are killed in a car accident, leaving the boy and his grandmother alone. They travel to England where Helga buys a pair of mice as pets for Luke. When she is stricken with a mild attack of diabetes, they head for a seaside resort while Helga recovers. Coincidentally, all the witches in England arrive at the resort, summoned there by Mrs. Ernst (Anjelica Huston) for seminars on how to capture British children. The witches pose as conventioneers who are members of the fictional Royal Commission for the Prevention of Cruelty to Children. While exploring the hotel, Luke stumbles upon a meeting of the witches. He watches from a hiding place and is stunned to see Mrs. Ernst, as she removes her disguise, transform herself into the frightening Grand High Witch. The head witch says she is disappointed in efforts to wipe out the children of England, and has developed a magic potion that turns children into mice. When the witches' smelling abilities lead them to discover Luke, he is forced to drink some of the potion and is quickly turned into a mouse. It's now up to Luke to thwart the heinous plan concocted by Mrs. Ernst, a difficult task for a mouse, and one which requires the assistance of the wily Helga.

Based on a story by Roald Dahl (source author of WILLY WONKA AND THE CHOCOLATE FACTORY, and screenwriter for CHITTY CHITTY BANG BANG), THE WITCHES weaves many classic childhood fears into its entertaining—and genuinely eerie—action. Roeg directs with his usual visual flair, notably excelling during the wondrous mouse point-of-view scenes. (These sequences feature mouse puppets designed by the late Jim Henson, who served as the film's executive producer, the last film in which he was involved before his death in 1990.) In addition to the lively visuals, THE WITCHES features sharp art direction and beautiful locations. The actors seem to be having a good time, particularly Huston, who gives a wonderfully over-the-top performance as the Grand High Witch. Zetterling, making her first appearance in a US release since THE MAN WHO FINALLY DIED in 1967, is impressive, turning in a performance that is both rich and comic, and giving the film its emotional center.

WITCHES OF EASTWICK, THE

1987 118m c   ★★
Horror/Comedy   R/18
WB

Jack Nicholson (Daryl Van Horne), Cher (Alexandra Medford), Susan Sarandon (Jane Spofford), Michelle Pfeiffer (Sukie Ridgemont), Veronica Cartwright (Felicia Alden), Richard Jenkins (Clyde Alden), Keith Jochim (Walter Neff), Carel Struycken (Fidel), Helen Lloyd Breed (Mrs. Biddle), Caroline Struzik (Carol Medford)

p, Neil Canton, Peter Guber, Jon Peters; d, George Miller; w, Michael Cristofer (based on the novel by John Updike); ph, Vilmos Zsigmond (Panavision, Technicolor); ed, Richard Francis-Bruce, Hubert C. de La Bouillerie; m, John Williams; prod d, Polly Platt; art d, Mark Mansbridge, Dave Howard Stein; fx, Mike Lanteri, Rob Bottin; cos, Aggie Guerard Rodgers; anim, Ellen Lichtwardt, John Armstrong, Chris Green

A haphazard and slickly dumb adaptation of John Updike's best-selling novel, THE WITCHES OF EASTWICK is a star-studded special-effects extravaganza about the battle of the sexes. A trio of bored, sexually repressed New England women—Alex (Cher), Jane (Susan Sarandon), and Sukie (Michelle Pfeiffer), each of them left to live without their respective husbands—innocently conjures up a mysterious stranger who, they are convinced, will relieve their frustrations. This mystery man is Daryl Van Horne (Jack Nicholson), the filthy rich, wild-eyed Devil incarnate, who buys a local mansion. Within days, Alex, Jane, and Sukie have all been to bed with the Devil and discovered in themselves the almighty power of the female form. By the finale, the female trinity is pitted against the Devil, a mildly sympathetic misogynist who only wants to be loved and have someone to iron his shirts. While the underlying message of THE WITCHES OF EASTWICK may be of interest, the execution by George (MAD MAX) Miller is downright pathetic. The film plays like a TV sitcom, with an overdose of raunch added to the proceedings; when the Devil spews forth his pro-

fanities, one almost expects to hear a diabolical laugh track. Nominated by the Academy for Best Original Score and Best Sound.

WITH A SONG IN MY HEART

1952 116m c   ★★★½
Musical/Biography   /U
FOX

Susan Hayward (Jane Froman), Rory Calhoun (John Burns), David Wayne (Don Ross), Thelma Ritter (Clancy), Robert Wagner (GI Paratrooper), Helen Westcott (Jennifer March), Una Merkel (Sister Marie), Richard Allan (Dancer), Max Showalter (Guild), Lyle Talbot (Radio Director)

p, Lamar Trotti; d, Walter Lang; w, Lamar Trotti; ph, Leon Shamroy (Technicolor); ed, J. Watson Webb; art d, Lyle Wheeler, Joseph C. Wright, Earle Hagen; fx, Fred Sersen, Ray Kellogg; chor, Billy Daniel; cos, Charles LeMaire

This fairly accurate film biography stars Susan Hayward as singer Jane Froman, whose story is told in flashback. In 1936 she gets her first break on a Cincinnati radio station, and from there it's on to personal appearances at Radio City Music Hall and across the country. Although she's somewhat ambivalent about the match, Jane eventually marries her mentor, Don Ross (David Wayne). Problems arise, however, as Don becomes jealous of his wife's success. When Jane goes off to entertain the troops during WWII, her plane crashes off the Portuguese coast. Rescued by pilot John Burn (Rory Calhoun), the badly injured singer undergoes a difficult recuperation in a Lisbon hospital, becoming fast friends with her nurse, Clancy (Thelma Ritter, whose character is fictional). John, meanwhile, falls in love with Jane, who stifles her own feelings because she is married. She returns to the US, undergoes a series of painful operations (with faithful Clancy by her side), and works with Don's help to get her career back on track. There are setbacks along the way, including a serious argument with Don, but eventually Jane makes a triumphant comeback and Don frees her to marry John.

Hayward and Ritter were nominated for Oscars; Alfred Newman won the award for his musical direction. Froman provides Hayward's singing voice, to glorious effect, in a host of standards from various writers (with uncredited background vocals provided by the Skylarks, Modernaires, Melody Men, King's Men, Starlighters, and Four Girlfriends). Five-time Oscar nominee Hayward, as always, gives her best, making WITH A SONG IN MY HEART a satisfying film on all levels.

WITHNAIL & I

1987 108m c   ★★★½
Drama   R/15
HandMade (U.K.)

Richard E. Grant (Withnail), Paul McGann (Marwood), Richard Griffiths (Monty), Ralph Brown (Danny), Michael Elphick (Jake), Daragh O'Malley (Irishman), Michael Wardle (Issac Parkin), Una Brandon-Jones (Mrs. Parkin), Noel Johnson (General), Irene Sutcliffe (Waitress)

p, Paul M. Heller; d, Bruce Robinson; w, Bruce Robinson (based on his novel); ph, Peter Hannan; ed, Alan Strachan; m, David Dundas; prod d, Michael Pickwoad; art d, Henry Harris; cos, Andrea Galer

A hilarious black comedy and already something of a cult favorite, WITHNAIL & I opens in a cluttered, refuse-ridden flat in North London. This confused mess is home for two out-of-work actors: gaunt, sarcastic, vaguely aristocratic, and dissipated

Withnail (Richard E. Grant); and handsome, bespectacled Marwood (Paul McGann), whose journal notations, heard in voice-over, serve as the film's narration. It is 1969, and the pair visit Withnail's wealthy eccentric uncle Monty (Richard Griffiths) in hopes of getting the use of his country cottage for a weekend away to "rejuvenate." Uncle is agreeable, and the two drive off to the cottage only to find it a rustic version of their own flat—ice cold, damp, totally without provisions. As usual, Withnail leaves the practical matters to Marwood to solve. WITHNAIL & I is a wry portrait of 60s low-life bohemia which gets plenty of comic mileage from the rapid-fire repartee, colorfully drawn characters, and occasionally Monty Pythonesque moments of director-writer Bruce Robinson's script.

WITHOUT APPARENT MOTIVE
(SANS MOBILE APPARENT)
1972 102m c   ★★★
Mystery   PG/
President/Cineteleuro   (France)

Jean-Louis Trintignant *(Stephane Carella)*, Dominique Sanda *(Sandra Forest)*, Sacha Distel *(Julien Sabirnou)*, Carla Gravina *(Jocelyne Rocca)*, Paul Crauchet *(Francis Palombo)*, Laura Antonelli *(Juliette Vaudreuil)*, Jean-Pierre Marielle *(Perry Rupert-Foote)*, Stephane Audran *(Helene Vallee)*, Pierre Dominique *(Di Bozzo)*, Erich Segal *(Hans Kleinberg)*

p, Jacques Strauss; d, Philippe Labro; w, Philippe Labro, Jacques Lanzmann (based on the novel *Ten Plus One* by Ed McBain); ph, Jean Penzer (Eastmancolor); ed, Claude Barrois, Nicole Saunier; m, Ennio Morricone; prod d, Andre Hoss

A deft thriller in the hardboiled tradition of Raymond Chandler and Dashiell Hammett, this story of murderous revenge opens with Michel Bardinet, playing a wealthy Frenchman, being gunned down in broad daylight. Trintignant, the detective assigned to the case, can find no motive behind the slaying. Soon two others are killed in the same mysterious way. Trintignant is convinced a link exists between the three deaths, yet he has nothing to go on. A slim thread of hope comes when Sanda, Bardinet's stepdaughter, gives the detective a pocket diary that had belonged to the dead man. The diary contains, among other things, a list of Bardinet's lovers. One woman on this roll call is Gravina, a former passion of Trintignant's as well. Gravina meets the detective at his flat, hoping to rekindle their affair. After it's revealed that she had known all three of the murdered men, Gravina leaves, disappointed this liaison was for business reasons rather than sex. Before Trintignant can catch up with her, a shot rings out, adding Gravina to the list of mysterious sniper killings. Trintignant goes with Sanda to a local university, acting on a tip from her boyfriend, television personality Distel. There they recover a theater program from a play performed some eight years earlier. The first four names on the cast list have all been victims of the mysterious sniper. Distel is the next name in the cast. Trintignant rushes to an outdoor location where Distel is shooting his television program and manages to save the man just as the sniper's gun goes off. Audran, another member of the play's cast, goes to the police. She tells of a long-ago cast party that had turned into an all-out orgy. The male cast members at the party gang-raped Antonelli, a shy actress also appearing in the play. Trintignant goes to Antonelli's apartment but is met by her husband, Marielle, who shoots at the detective with a high-powered rifle. Trintignant fires back, killing the man. Antonelli is taken away by authorities, and her secret is exposed. As a result of the gang rape Antonelli had gone mad and her husband decided to assassinate those responsible in his quest for revenge. Trintign-

ant, beaten down by the horrors he has experienced in this case, decides the time has come for him to leave police work.

Though the plot, adapted from a pulp novel by Ed McBain, clearly takes its cue from *film noir*, director Labro takes some interesting chances with his adaptation. Rather than use the classic darkened settings of a 1940s crime film, Labro shoots in the sun-drenched streets of the French Riviera city of Nice. Despite the antithetical settings, the mood is just as dark here as in a good Humphrey Bogart crime story. Labro slowly builds up a feeling of impending doom, holding the mystery's solution until the very end and maintaining a consistent mood. The background music, a pulsating rhythm, enhances the atmosphere. Labro also understands the essentials of creating a thriller, building suspense before letting out the short bursts of violence. As the lone detective, Trintignant also owes a great deal to Bogart. His performance, filled with suppressed emotion, shows the influence of his cinematic forerunner but wisely avoids parodying him. A real surprise in the cast is Erich Segal, better known for his novel *Love Story*. In his cameo role the author shows a genuine flair for acting and handles his French dialogue with ease.

WITNESS
1985 112m c   ★★★★½
Crime   R/15
Paramount

Harrison Ford *(John Book)*, Kelly McGillis *(Rachel)*, Josef Sommer *(Schaeffer)*, Lukas Haas *(Samuel)*, Jan Rubes *(Eli Lapp)*, Alexander Godunov *(Daniel Hochleitner)*, Patti LuPone *(Elaine)*, Danny Glover *(McFee)*, Brent Jennings *(Carter)*, Angus MacInnes *(Fergie)*

p, Edward S. Feldman; d, Peter Weir; w, Earl W. Wallace, William Kelley (based on a story by Kelley, Wallace, Pamela Wallace); ph, John Seale (Technicolor); ed, Thom Noble; m, Maurice Jarre; prod d, Stan Jolley; fx, John R. Elliott; cos, Shari Feldman, Dallas Dornan

Sure-footed thriller, beautifully photographed, with Ford's best performance thus far. Australian director Peter Weir's first American film proved to be a success both critically and commercially, garnering rave reviews and receiving eight Oscar nominations. The story begins as Rachel (Kelly McGillis), a young Amish widow, is traveling into the city with her young son, Samuel (Lukas Haas). While they're waiting for their train in the crowded Philadelphia station, Samuel wanders into the men's room where, undetected, he witnesses a man getting his throat slit. John Book (Harrison Ford), the investigator who questions the boy, manages to win the confidence of both Samuel and Rachel, who are out of their element in the big city, living simple, peaceful, religious lives in the isolation of their farm home and Amish community. Book is quite the opposite—a tough, gun-toting city cop surrounded by hate and brutality. Later, during questioning at the police station, Samuel identifies the photograph of a narcotics officer (Danny Glover) as the killer. Suspecting the worst and fearing for the safety of his young witness, Book tries to get Samuel and Rachel back to the safe obscurity of Lancaster County. But trouble follows, even as Rachel and Book become attracted to each other.

WITNESS, budgeted at $11.5 million, more than returned its investment when it went on to win Oscars for Best Original Screenplay and Best Editing.

WITNESS FOR THE PROSECUTION

1957   114m   bw   ★★★★½
Mystery   /U
Theme

Tyrone Power *(Leonard Stephen Vole)*, Marlene Dietrich *(Christine Helm/Vole)*, Charles Laughton *(Sir Wilfrid Robarts)*, Elsa Lanchester *(Miss Plimsoll)*, John Williams *(Brogan Moore)*, Henry Daniell *(Mayhew)*, Ian Wolfe *(Carter)*, Una O'Connor *(Janet MacKenzie)*, Torin Thatcher *(Mr. Meyers)*, Francis Compton *(Judge)*

p, Arthur Hornblow, Jr.; d, Billy Wilder; w, Billy Wilder, Harry Kurnitz, Larry Marcus (based on the novel and the play by Agatha Christie); ph, Russell Harlan; ed, Daniel Mandell; m, Matty Malneck; art d, Alexander Trauner; cos, Edith Head, Joe King

Dietrich steals it. WITNESS FOR THE PROSECUTION is a witty, terse adaptation of the Agatha Christie hit play brought to the screen with ingenuity and vitality by Billy Wilder. Sir Wilfrid Robarts (Laughton) is a sickly barrister who is told by his doctors and forced by his pesty nurse Miss Plimsoll (Lanchester, Laughton's real-life wife), to retire from criminal cases. When his solicitor Mayhew (Daniell) arrives at his home with murder suspect Leonard Vole (Power), Robarts cannot resist. Hearing Vole's story, Robarts becomes convinced of the man's innocence, but because his only alibi is his wife Christine (Dietrich), prospects for an acquittal look dim. Before their meeting ends, word is received that Vole has inherited a fortune from the deceased's estate. Because of the apparent clarity of Vole's motive, Scotland Yard places him under arrest. Robarts, however, is not completely convinced and continues examining the clues, uncovering more than even he imagined.

Improving on Christie's play, Wilder has rid WITNESS FOR THE PROSECUTION of much of the usual static courtroom scenes and filled the film with an active, visual excitement. Whether it be the fluidity of the camera, the use of an occasional flashback, or the diversion of Robarts's constant medical attention, Wilder succeeds in finding a way to relieve the boredom that typically accompanies the courtroom. Wilder even introduces the Miss Plimsoll character into Christie's scenario to add some life and a comic angle. At the film's halfway point Wilder flashes back to wartime Germany for the standard Dietrich-as-cabaret-singer scene, giving her a chance to show off one of her attractive legs, play the accordion, and deliver "I Never Go There Anymore" (Ralph Arthur Roberts, Jack Brooks). The part, one of her finest, was pure Dietrich, casting her as a woman who throws away everything—her homeland, her reputation, and her life—for the man she loves. In addition to receiving an Academy Award nomination for Best Picture (it lost to THE BRIDGE ON THE RIVER KWAI), WITNESS FOR THE PROSECUTION justly garnered nominations for the hilarious husband-and-wife team of Laughton and Lanchester for Best Actor (Laughton lost to Alec Guinness for RIVER KWAI) and Best Supporting Actress (Lanchester lost to Miyoshi Umeki for SAYONARA). Tyrone Power, in his final role before his fatal heart attack the following year, turned in a superb performance but was unfairly overlooked by the Academy. Other Oscar nominations were handed out for Best Director, Best Sound, and Best Editing.

WIZARD OF OZ, THE

1939   101m   c/bw   ★★★★★
Fantasy/Musical   /U
MGM

Judy Garland *(Dorothy)*, Ray Bolger *(Hunk/The Scarecrow)*, Bert Lahr *(Zeke/The Cowardly Lion)*, Jack Haley *(Hickory/The Tin Woodsman)*, Billie Burke *(Glinda)*, Margaret Hamilton *(Miss Gulch/The Wicked Witch)*, Charley Grapewin *(Uncle Henry)*, Clara Blandick *(Auntie Em)*, Pat Walsh *(Nikko)*, Frank Morgan *(Prof. Marvel/The Wizard/Guard/Coachman)*

p, Mervyn LeRoy; d, Victor Fleming, King Vidor (uncredited); w, Noel Langley, Florence Ryerson, Edgar Allan Woolf (based on the novel by L. Frank Baum); ph, Harold Rosson (Technicolor); ed, Blanche Sewell; m, Herbert Stothart; art d, Cedric Gibbons; fx, A. Arnold Gillespie; chor, Bobby Connolly; cos, Adrian

There's no place like home, and there will never be another movie like THE WIZARD OF OZ. Forget that it's over 50 years old, that here and there it creaks a tiny bit: it stirs in all of us the feeling of wanting to belong, of having security, but wanting enchantment at the same time. OZ gives us enchantment unparalleled for a hundred different reasons, foremost among which is the ageless appeal of young Judy Garland, perhaps the most beloved of all film actresses. Watching her now, we're aware of all the sadness Garland's life would encompasses (the consummate showbiz pro, she was quick to milk her suffering), but Dorothy captures her poised on the brink of legend, before the ravages of unhappiness set in. And chances are, for most of us, we first saw her in OZ before life took any serious tolls upon us, before broken hearts, or deaths, or money troubles or career disappointments. Sometimes you watch Garland longingly sing "Over the Rainbow" and it sweeps you away to somewhere you can't even explain. THE WIZARD OF OZ is a dazzling fantasy musical, so beautifully directed and acted that it deserves its classic status.

Dorothy (Garland) is a schoolgirl living in Kansas with family and her little dog, Toto. One afternoon, a twister sucks up Dorothy's house and she and Toto are dropped beyond the rainbow into Munchkinland. With a pair of magical red slippers and some advice from Glinda the Good Witch (Billie Burke), Dorothy, Toto and three new friends—the Scarecrow (Ray Bolger), Tin Man (Jack Haley), and Cowardly Lion (Bert Lahr)—follow the yellow brick road to the Emerald City, where they must ask the all-powerful Wizard of Oz (Frank Morgan) to get Dorothy and Toto back home. The Wicked Witch (Margaret Hamilton), however, is determined to get her hands on the slippers, and sends out her flying monkeys to capture the group—as if you needed to know any of this.

Curiously, Garland, forever to be identified with the wide-eyed Dorothy, was not the first choice for the part; both Shirley Temple and Deanna Durbin were considered for the role. Had Jean Harlow not died, ending the loan-out deal to exchange her for IN OLD CHICAGO with Temple for OZ, we'd be watching Temple's forthright moppet, instead of Garland's tender waif. The mind boggles. We could regale you for hours on end with behind the scenes trivia on OZ. Books have been written on nothing but, and they're not hard to find. But we'll toss you a few: Frank Morgan spent half his time on set drunk. Clara Blandick (Auntie Em) was just as unhappy as she appears; she ended up a recluse who eventually took her own life. Harlow's third and last husband, Harold Rosson, did OZ's cinematography and King Vidor did some uncredited directorial work. L.B. Mayer's nickname for Garland was his "little humpback." The original Wizard was to have been W.C. Fields, the original Tin Man Buddy Ebsen (who fell ill from all the makeup preparation) and the original Wicked Witch was to have been played as an evil siren by Gale Sondergaard. Bolger, Haley, Lahr, and Morgan were not the kindly uncles you might think. All were grizzled showbiz vets not about to give Garland an inch of scene-stealing capacity onscreen; when she takes a scene, it's not because anyone let her. See if you can hear the female Munchkin who runs forward to Garland and shouts "Judy" instead of "Dorothy" after Hamilton's first exit. And watch for inconsistencies in Garland's hairstyles during the time she is beautified in OZ.

Some of Hollywood's most beloved songs are included, namely "Somewhere over the Rainbow," "Ding Dong, the Witch Is Dead," "If I Only Had a Brain/a Heart/the Nerve," "Follow the Yellow Brick Road," and "We're Off to See the Wizard." Variations on this classic include the animated JOURNEY BACK TO OZ (with Liza Minnelli's voice in for Garland, and Hamilton reprising her character), the silent 1925 WIZARD OF OZ, the overblown 1978 musical THE WIZ starring Diana Ross, and the intriguingly dismal RETURN TO OZ. They can't make 'em like this anymore.

WOLF MAN, THE
1941 71m bw   ★★★★
Horror   /PG
Universal

Claude Rains (Sir John Talbot), Lon Chaney, Jr. (Larry Talbot), Evelyn Ankers (Gwen Conliffe), Ralph Bellamy (Capt. Paul Montford), Warren William (Dr. Lloyd), Patric Knowles (Frank Andrews), Maria Ouspenskaya (Maleva), Bela Lugosi (Bela), Fay Helm (Jenny Williams), Leyland Hodgson (Kendall)

p, George Waggner; d, George Waggner; w, Curt Siodmak; ph, Joseph Valentine; ed, Ted J. Kent; art d, Jack Otterson

A feast of horror, for animals of all kinds. Bearing no resemblance to Universal's 1935 film THE WEREWOLF OF LONDON, THE WOLF MAN was given a whole new look and treatment by the studio. Lon Chaney, Jr., stars as Larry Talbot, a young British heir who returns to the mansion of his father (Claude Rains) after getting a college education in America. Learning about the legend of the werewolf from antique store employee Gwen (Evelyn Ankers), gypsy fortune teller Maleva (Maria Ouspenskaya), and Maleva's son, Bela (Bela Lugosi), Larry laughs it off as superstition. When the young man hears a bone-chilling wolf's howl and a blood-curdling scream emanating from the foggy moors, however, he rushes to the source of the hideous noises and is attacked and bitten by a vicious, hairy beast. Later, Maleva tells Larry that he will transform into a savage, murderous wolf when the moon is full and that he can only be killed by silver—be it a silver bullet, knife, or cane. Larry tries to deny her superstitious forecast, but when the next full moon arises, his nose becomes a wet snout, his hands and feet turn to paws, and his body is covered with thick fur. An animal trapped in a bedroom, the wolf man crashes through the window and runs off into the night in search of his prey.

Fearing comparison with his famous father, Lon Jr. avoided appearing in horror films, but as he gained confidence in his abilities he agreed to try the genre and created the character with whom he would always be identified—the wolf man. Through the genius of Universal makeup artist Jack Pierce, Chaney underwent a complete transformation nearly as complete as his character's—gaining a rubber snout, fangs, claws, and lots of yak hair. Screenwriter Curt Siodmak patched together the legend of the werewolf by combining elements from lycanthropic folklore, witchcraft, and Bram Stoker's *Dracula*, creating a new monster for the screen. All elements combined to make a thrilling, scary, and ultimately tragic horror classic. Chaney essayed the role of the werewolf five more times, in FRANKENSTEIN MEETS THE WOLFMAN, HOUSE OF FRANKENSTEIN, HOUSE OF DRACULA, and ABBOTT AND COSTELLO MEET FRANKENSTEIN, as well as a guest appearance on the television show "Route 66."

WOLFEN
1981 115m c   ★★★½
Horror   R/18
Orion

Albert Finney (Dewey Wilson), Diane Venora (Rebecca Neff), Edward James Olmos (Eddie Holt), Gregory Hines (Whittington), Tom Noonan (Ferguson), Dick O'Neill (Warren), Dehl Berti (Old Indian), Peter Michael Goetz (Ross), Sam Gray (Mayor), Ralph Bell (Commissioner)

p, Rupert Hitzig; d, Michael Wadleigh; w, David Eyre, Michael Wadleigh (based on the novel by Whitley Strieber); ph, Gerry Fisher (Panavision, Technicolor); ed, Chris Lebenzon, Dennis Dolan, Martin Bram, Marshall M. Borden; m, James Horner; prod d, Paul Sylbert; art d, David Chapman; fx, Carl Fullerton, Robert Blalack, Betz Bromberg; cos, John Boxer

This straightforward, intelligent film puts a new spin on the werewolf legend, presenting the creatures as a superior species living in the slums of New York City. Police detective Dewey Wilson (Albert Finney) is assigned to investigate the savage murder of a rich industrialist. When the city coroner (Gregory Hines, in his film debut) suggests that the dead man was mutilated by a wild animal, Wilson and criminal psychologist Rebecca Neff (Diane Venora) connect the killing with several murders that have occurred in which the bodies of winos, drug addicts, and bums have been found with their throats ripped out. Further investigation by Wilson and Neff leads to a group of Native American construction workers and to a strange tale of the "Wolfen" that once roamed the land that is now New York City. Directed by Michael Wadleigh, whose only other feature is the 1970 rock documentary WOODSTOCK, WOLFEN is an intelligent, insightful, and visually creative twist on the werewolf legend. Although occasionally preachy, it is a fascinating horror tale that is as engrossing as it is horrifying. The visual effects are sensational, introducing to the screen a previously unseen "Wolfen vision" that, through a variety of optical printing techniques, conveys the wolves' heightened awareness of heat, smell, movement, and texture. The gore effects by Carl Fullerton are effective, if somewhat gratuitous.

WOLFPEN PRINCIPLE, THE
1974 96m c   ★★★½
Comedy/Drama
Image Flow   (Canada)

Vladimir Valenta (Henry Manufort), Doris Chillcot (His Wife), Alicia Ammon (Her Mother), Tom Snelgrove (Her Father), Lawrence Brown (Indian Smith), Janet Wright (Miss Mervin), Lee Taylor (Sailor), Ivor Harries (Watchman), Bullus Hutton (Clergyman)

p, Werner Aellen; d, Jack Darcus; w, Jack Darcus; ph, Hans Klardie; ed, Raymond Hall; m, Don Druick; art d, Hagen Beggs

Henry Manufort (Vladimir Valenta) is a middle-aged man looking for something to do with his life who begins spending his evenings at the local zoo, endlessly watching the wolves. He meets Indian Smith (Lawrence Brown), a Northern Indian who shares his fascination with the animals. Together they concoct a plan to free the wolf pack, but they ultimately are defeated by the animals themselves, who don't care to leave the security of their cage. The film delivers its message with grace and subtlety, and the story is told with genuine feeling for its characters (including the wolf pack) while adding a nice comic touch. Another fine example of what an imaginative low-budget filmmaker can do.

WOMAN IN THE DUNES
(SUNA NO ONNA)

1964 123m bw   ★★★★★

Drama   /18

Teshigahara (Japan)

Eiji Okada *(Niki Jumpei)*, Kyoko Kishida *(Woman)*, Koji Mitsui, Hiroko Ito, Sen Yano, Ginzo Sekigushi, Kiyohiko Ichiha, Tamutsu Tamura, Hiroyuki Nishimo

p, Kiichi Ichikawa, Tadashi Ohono; d, Hiroshi Teshigahara; w, Kobo Abe (based on the novel *Suna no Onna* by Abe); ph, Hiroshi Segawa; ed, F. Susui; m, Toru Takemitsu

A profoundly moving parable of man's search for meaning in life and love, told with beautiful simplicity, WOMAN IN THE DUNES begins as Niki Jumpei (Eiji Okada), a reserved entomologist, collects specimens along a Japanese beach. He is met by some villagers, who offer him both a place to sleep and a woman, and is led to a shack located at the bottom of a sand pit, where he climbs down a rope ladder to the woman, Kyoko (Kyoko Kishida). The next morning, he notices that the ladder has been removed. A panicky urge to climb out of the pit is followed by a futile attempt to scale the sand walls, which cascade beneath his feet. Helpless, he watches as Kyoko endlessly shovels the sand into buckets, which are then hoisted by the villagers above. In return, food and water are sent down—no shoveling, no food. Niki soon realizes the necessity of the woman's work. He becomes accustomed to his new lifestyle and takes the woman as his lover. She becomes pregnant, and he must wrestle with his urge to escape and his growing devotion to Kyoko and his new life.

Beautifully photographed and confined almost exclusively to a single set, WOMAN IN THE DUNES is a poetic affirmation of life. As frustrating and claustrophobic as the man's situation may first appear, the film becomes increasingly seductive as it lulls the audience into the woman's sandpit existence. Based on a novel by Kobo Abe, Hiroshi Teshigahara's emotionally draining picture was nominated for Best Foreign Film at the 1964 Academy Awards and the following year earned him a nomination for Best Director.

WOMAN IN THE WINDOW, THE

1945 99m bw   ★★★★

Thriller   /A

Christie/International Pictures

Edward G. Robinson *(Prof. Richard Wanley)*, Joan Bennett *(Alice Reed)*, Raymond Massey *(Frank Lalor)*, Edmund Breon *(Dr. Michael Barkstone)*, Dan Duryea *(Heidt/Doorman)*, Thomas Jackson *(Inspector Jackson)*, Arthur Loft *(Claude Mazard/Frank Howard)*, Dorothy Peterson *(Mrs. Wanley)*, Frank Dawson *(Collins, the Steward)*, Carol Cameron *(Elsie Wanley)*

p, Nunnally Johnson; d, Fritz Lang; w, Nunnally Johnson (based on the novel *Once Off Guard* by J.H. Wallis); ph, Milton Krasner; ed, Marjorie Johnson, Gene Fowler, Jr.; m, Arthur Lange; art d, Duncan Cramer; fx, Vernon L. Walker; cos, Muriel King

A gripping psychological thriller which stars Robinson as a fortyish, intellectual college professor who, with his friends, discusses the dangers of becoming too adventurous at their age. Robinson has a wife and children (who are away on vacation) and sees no reason to wander from his staid, secure path. However, while admiring a portrait of a beautiful model in a gallery window, he notices the model, Bennett, standing beside him. Bennett asks if Robinson would like to come up to her apartment under honest pretenses: "I'm not married. I have no designs on

you," she assures him. Once in her apartment, this fantasy girl of Robinson's brings about his downfall, though unintentionally. Her boyfriend, wealthy financier Loft, arrives unexpectedly and, thinking that the two are having an affair, begins to slap his mistress around. He then lunges at Robinson, who grabs a nearby scissors and, in self-defense, stabs his attacker in the back. Frightened both of the police and of the disgrace he will cause his family, Robinson plots, with Bennett, to dispose of the body. Battling countless obstacles and nearly getting caught a number of times, they take the corpse, sitting up in the back seat of a car with open, glazed eyes, to a secluded woody area. They manage to carry out their plan without getting caught. Robinson, however, is still subject to mental torture, especially by his friend, Massey, a district attorney who continually talks about the case, unaware that Robinson is the man he's after. Through Massey, Robinson learns all the most intricate details of the investigation and is able to follow the progress of the police. He also learns his mistakes, which mount by the day. Making matters worse is a blackmail scheme engineered by Loft's bodyguard, Duryea, who has discovered Robinson's guilt.

With its terse pacing and elegant camerawork, THE WOMAN IN THE WINDOW was a great box-office success and one of the most praised *films noir* of its time. Robinson, in a role different from his standard gangster part, shines and holds the film's credibility together by turning in a convincing portrayal of a good man who is caught off guard just once (to paraphrase the title of the novel, *Once Off Guard*, on which the film is based). Bennett, in her second Lang film after 1941's MAN HUNT, is dazzlingly alluring as the fantasy girl who comes to life for Robinson. The collaboration between Bennett and Lang was so amiable that they would work together two more times, in SCARLET STREET with Robinson again as costar, and in SECRET BEYOND THE DOOR, both produced by her and husband Walter Wanger's own Diana Productions. Although many people feel cheated by the film's ending, Lang always felt (in later interviews) that his decision was justified. Either way, it's still a fine film.

WOMAN IS A WOMAN, A
(UNE FEMME EST UNE FEMME)

1961 80m c   ★★★★

Drama   /X

Rome/Paris Pathe (France/Italy)

Anna Karina *(Angela)*, Jean-Claude Brialy *(Emile Recamier)*, Jean-Paul Belmondo *(Alfred Lubitsch)*, Nicole Paquin *(Suzanne)*, Marie Dubois *(1st Prostitute)*, Marion Sarraut *(2nd Prostitute)*, Jeanne Moreau *(Woman in Bar)*, Catherine Demongeot

p, Carlo Ponti, Georges de Beauregard; d, Jean-Luc Godard; w, Jean-Luc Godard (based on an idea by Genevieve Cluny); ph, Raoul Coutard (FranScope, Eastmancolor); ed, Agnes Guillemot, Lila Herman; m, Michel Legrand; art d, Bernard Evein; cos, Bernard Evein

Godard's third feature film and his first in color, A WOMAN IS A WOMAN is one of the most enjoyable of all the master's works. Taking an extremely lighthearted approach, it bursts with a passion for the medium of film expressed in every shot. The plot is very simple and could almost be taken for homage to Hollywood musical comedy, but homage seems much too tacky a term to express the fascination Godard had and the playful manner in which he approached this film. Karina (Godard's wife at the time) plays a stripper living with her boyfriend (Brialy), who refuses to marry her in spite of her expressed desire to have a child. Using an old feminine ploy, she starts to turn her attentions toward another man (Belmondo), easily making him fall in love with her. Sure enough, it works, with the boyfriend breaking down when faced with the prospect of losing the girl he loves.

Every moment of this picture is filled with charm, from Brialy riding a bicycle around their apartment in a strange mating dance to the buffoonish manner in which Belmondo tries to declare his love for Karina. The loose style almost seems to suggest that Godard just placed the camera down and then told his three stars to play; they look like children who have not yet outgrown the play lot and are unwilling to accept responsibility. The way Karina announces that she wants to have a baby is totally whimsical, a thing to do because that is what couples do when they are in love. Next to Godard's nonstylish stylishness, the most outstanding feature is the mere presence of Karina; her subtle glance and loftiness coincide with little mistakes in technical performance that most directors would not tolerate, but which actually serve to make her that much more human and irresistible. In fact, the picture appears almost to be a private photograph album showcasing the charming Karina in many moods. This is the first of Godard's films to be shot largely in a studio under tightly controlled conditions. The director insisted on using sets with ceilings in the interest of naturalism. This was also Godard's first experience with direct synchronous sound; his previous films had been dubbed. Elements of some of the director's earlier short subjects—most notably the 10-minute UNE FEMME COQUETTE—can be seen in the plot and the characterizations.

WOMAN NEXT DOOR, THE
(LA FEMME D'A COTE)
1981   106m   c   ★★★
Drama   R/AA
Carrosse/TF-1   (France)

Gerard Depardieu *(Bernard Coudray)*, Fanny Ardant *(Mathilde Bauchard)*, Henri Garcin *(Philippe Bauchard)*, Michele Baumgartner *(Arlette Coudray)*, Veronique Silver *(Mme. Jouve)*, Philippe Morier-Genoud *(Doctor)*, Roger Van Hool *(Roland Duguet)*, Olivier Becquaert, Nicole Vauthier, Muriel Combe

d, Francois Truffaut; w, Francois Truffaut, Suzanne Schiffman, Jean Aurel; ph, William Lubtchansky (Fujicolor); ed, Martine Barraque; m, Georges Delerue; art d, Jean-Pierre Kohut-Svelko; cos, Michele Cerf

This dark entry from Truffaut pairs French superstar Depardieu with newcomer Ardant as former flames who have married other people and now live next door to each other. Depardieu, who has been living a comfortable though joyless bourgeois existence with his wife and young son, tries to avoid Ardant at every turn. A chance meeting at the supermarket, however, opens a floodgate of buried emotions, and the romance is resumed. Gradually, Depardieu and Ardant's mutual obsession builds to a dangerous level that neither can control. As he did in JULES AND JIM and THE STORY OF ADELE H., Truffaut once again displays his interest in obsessive love and the pain and destruction it can cause. Here as in THE SOFT SKIN and THE BRIDE WORE BLACK, the shadow of Hitchcock looms large, resulting in a taut, psychological narrative that stifles the director's poetic impulse. Stage actress Ardant, who makes a stunning starring debut here as the woman obsessed, also appears in Truffaut's final film, CONFIDENTIALLY YOURS.

WOMAN OF THE YEAR
1942   112m   bw   ★★★★
Comedy/Drama   /A
MGM

Spencer Tracy *(Sam Craig)*, Katharine Hepburn *(Tess Harding)*, Fay Bainter *(Ellen Whitcomb)*, Reginald Owen *(Clayton)*, Minor Watson *(William Harding)*, William Bendix *(Pinkie Peters)*, Gladys Blake *(Flo Peters)*, Dan Tobin *(Gerald)*, Roscoe Karns *(Phil Whittaker)*, William Tannen *(Ellis)*

p, Joseph L. Mankiewicz; d, George Stevens; w, Ring Lardner, Jr., Michael Kanin; ph, Joseph Ruttenberg; ed, Frank Sullivan; m, Franz Waxman; art d, Cedric Gibbons, Randall Duell; cos, Adrian

The first onscreen pairing of Tracy and Hepburn, a team that would last 25 years until Tracy's death in 1967. He plays a sportswriter for a New York newpaper who becomes angry after hearing Hepburn on a radio broadcast boldly state that baseball should be eliminated until WWII comes to an end. Hepburn, the daughter of diplomat Watson and an international affairs writer, works on the same paper as Tracy, and her remarks begin a battle waged in their respective columns. Once they meet in person, they are attracted to each other, much to the surprise of their friends and colleagues. Eventually Tracy and Hepburn wed, but their marriage rests on shaky ground. Hepburn's attempts at homemaking are an outright disaster, as she feels her job must come before anything else. Tracy is angered by her lack of commitment to the marriage and ends up getting too drunk to write his column. Hepburn, whose knowledge of sports isn't much better than her abilities as a housewife, pens Tracy's column and the results are catastrophic. Hepburn is voted "Woman of the Year," ironically hearing the news while she is contemplating whether to remain with Tracy. When her father remarries, Hepburn listens closely as marriage vows are read. The words move her and she decides to go back to Tracy with renewed zeal for married life.

WOMAN OF THE YEAR is a marvelous comedy-drama, brimming with wit, style, and sophistication. Hepburn is strong and assured, a woman fueled by intense pride along with a good-sized ego. (Maybe that's why the final breakfast scene, amusing as it is, leaves a bad taste in the mouth, as it milks rather obvious laughs from Hepburn's lack of traditonally "feminine" skills.) Tracy is her male opposite, just as opinionated and just as stubborn. Their chemistry is engaging, a solid teaming that enhances the accomplished script.

Garson Kanin's idea for the film was inspired by renowned columnist Dorothy Thompson. Because of Kanin's other commitments, he was unable to develop the story further, instead giving the project to his brother Michael and Ring Lardner, Jr. The writers concocted a 30,000-word treatment, and Hepburn immediately fell in love with the property. It was decided that Hepburn would talk MGM into buying the script. Hepburn, at 5 feet 7 inches, was already considered to be tall among the actresses on the MGM lot. For her meeting with studio head Louis B. Mayer, Hepburn donned four-inch heels, thus increasing her height to an even more imposing stature. Mayer, who was not a tall man, listened to her every demand. Though Hepburn was convinced she had not succeeded, the strong-minded actress was shocked when she learned Mayer had given her everything she wanted on WOMAN OF THE YEAR. In addition to her own salary of $100,000, Hepburn received a $11,000 commission as a script agent, plus her choice of director and costar. Kanin and Lardner each received $50,000 for their efforts, far beyond the $200 to $300 a week they normally got.

WOMAN TIMES SEVEN

For her leading man, Hepburn had only one choice. She wanted Tracy, but at the time he was on location in Florida, working on MGM's production of THE YEARLING. However, various problems on the set caused that project to be halted (Gregory Peck would eventually play Tracy's role), leaving Tracy free for WOMAN OF THE YEAR. The two were introduced in the studio commissary by producer Mankiewicz. Hepburn, decked out in her four-inch heels, said to her costar, "I'm afraid I'm a little tall for you, Mr. Tracy." "Don't worry, Miss Hepburn," Tracy shot back, "I'll cut you down to my size." (In years to follow, Mankiewicz took credit for the clever retort whenever he told the story.)

An instant success popular with both the public and critics, WOMAN OF THE YEAR received Academy Award nominations for Best Actress and Best Original Screenplay. Though Hepburn lost that year to Greer Garson for MRS. MINIVER, Kanin and Lardner won Oscars for their wonderful script.

WOMAN TIMES SEVEN

(SEPT FOIS FEMME)

1967 99m c ★★★

Comedy/Drama /15

FOX/Cormoran (U.S./France/Italy)

Shirley MacLaine (Paulette/Maria Terese/Linda/Edith/Eve Minou/Marie/Jeanne). FUNERAL PROCESSION: Elspeth March (Annette). AMATEUR NIGHT: Rossano Brazzi (Giorgio), Catherine Samie (Jeannine), Judith Magre (2nd Prostitute). TWO AGAINST ONE: Vittorio Gassman (Cenci), Clinton Greyn (MacCormick), Lex Barker (Rik). THE SUPER-SIMONE: Elsa Martinelli (Woman in Market), Robert Morley (Dr. Xavier)

p, Arthur Cohn; d, Vittorio De Sica; w, Cesare Zavattini; ph, Christian Matras (Pathe Color); ed, Teddy Darvas, Victoria Mercanton; m, Riz Ortolani; art d, Bernard Evein; cos, Marcel Escoffier

It's difficult enough doing one role well, but playing several parts in the same movie is a nearly impossible feat requiring the talents of an Alec Guinness or a Peter Sellers. MacLaine had not yet achieved the maturity or the acting ability to bring this off, and the result is just ol' Shirl' in a host of different costumes, hairstyles, and makeup. Gallic. Shot on location in Paris with interiors at the Boulogne Studios, this set out to be a *tour de force* but ends up only a *tour de France*.

In the first segment, she's a widow accompanying the coffin of her late husband to the cemetery. Her close pal, Sellers, offers her balm and solace. As they move slowly along the road, Sellers admits that he loves her and always has. She is delighted by his confession, and her tears dry as the couple begins to talk about the good times they are going to have. They approach a crossroad and are so enraptured by their conversation that they miss the turn. The hearse goes right and they go left. Black humor, but not very funny except for Sellers' amorous ogling.

The second segment has MacLaine returning to her home to find her husband, Brazzi, cavorting in the sack with another woman. MacLaine is incensed, exits, and swears that she will exact revenge by making love to the very first man who talks to her. She meets a group of hookers lead by Samie and Magre. They teach her some things about walking the streets, but when push comes to shove, MacLaine can't come across. A local pimp gives her a lift home. They arrive, and Brazzi showers them both with invective. The pimp decks Brazzi then turns, expecting MacLaine to come with him. Instead, she berates him and races to kneel by the semiconscious Brazzi. Little more than an extended joke.

The third section gets a little racy as MacLaine is seen as a hippy interpreter working at a convention of cybernetics experts. She has an off-stage lover but complains that he's boring to Gassman, an Italian, and Greyn, a Scot. Both men find her attractive, if a bit dippy. She takes them to her apartment where she doffs her clothes and begins to read the collected works of T.S. Eliot. The sight of the nude woman fans the passions of the men. When they make an advance, MacLaine responds by saying that they are animals, little better than cavemen. She reads them the riot act, and the two men begin to hit each other to prove that they have been properly chastised. MacLaine watches this new behavior with delight and responds by throwing her lover's photo away and promptly engaging with Gassman and Greyn in a *menage a trois*.

The fourth segment is a good one, with MacLaine as a grumpy housewife married to Barker, a successful author of trashy novels that feature a heroine named "Simone." The creation is the type of hoyden who drives men mad with her passionate ways and wild ideas. MacLaine begins to act strangely in an attempt to compete with her husband's fantasies, but Barker brings in Morley, a psychiatrist, to see what's brought on this "insane" behavior. After a while, MacLaine understands that they think she's bananas and must rectify the situation before she is committed. She runs onto the roof of their apartment building and shouts that she's not crazy, she's simply in love with her own husband. Morley does his usual delicious work in this one, and Barker shows that he's not just a handsome face.

The fifth episode has MacLaine as a rich Parisian matron married to Patrick Wymark. The opera season is about to open, and MacLaine intends to wear a spectacular new gown. She is disgruntled to discover that her chief social competitor, Adrienne Corri, will be wearing the same dress to the festivities. Determined to be the belle of the ball, MacLaine prevails upon Wymark to sabotage Corri by having three of his assistants plant an explosive in Corri's limo. When MacLaine gets to the opera first, she is chagrined to learn that yet a third woman—older and rotund—has arrived wearing the same dress. As MacLaine runs angrily from the theater, she sees Corri, now in tatters and with a blackened face from the explosion, walking into the opera undaunted, about to make her grand appearance. MacLaine laughs when she sees Corri and wonders how the woman will respond to seeing the fat lady in the same gown. Silly and mean-spirited.

In No. 6, MacLaine and Alan Arkin are lovers married to other people. They are depressed that their love will never be permanent, and since they can't be united in life, they plan to be wed in death. They don bride and groom costumes and conspire to take their own lives in a seedy hotel room. Their calm determination begins to rock when they can't agree on the means to their deaths, and an argument breaks out. MacLaine takes refuge in the tacky bathroom, while Arkin sits by himself, begins to pace, then thinks that maybe life is better than death after all. He makes a move toward the door and begins to open it quietly when he hears the window break in the bathroom. He looks outside and sees MacLaine scampering down the fire escape.

The final section of the film has MacLaine out shopping with her best pal, Anita Ekberg. MacLaine is deeply in love with her husband, Philippe Noiret, but when the two women spot Michael Caine watching them, they are thrilled that such a good-looking man would find them attractive. Ekberg departs, and Caine continues to follow MacLaine. She arrives home, is met by Noiret, then looks out the window and sees Caine is still there. She smiles happily with the belief that she is appealing to other men, never dreaming that Caine has been hired to keep an eye on her by her jealous husband.

All of the segments, save the first, run between 14 and 16 minutes. The funeral episode goes about eight minutes, which is all it's worth. Ortolani's music is second-rate, but the rest of the technical credits are all excellent. Special note should be taken of Alex Archambault's hairstyles and the makeup work done by Alberto De Rossi and Georges Bouban. Although Marcel Escoffier gets credit for the well-planned costumes, it was Pierre Cardin who designed MacLaine's gowns.

WOMAN UNDER THE INFLUENCE, A

1974　155m　c	★★★½
Drama	R/15
Faces	

Peter Falk (Nick Longhetti), Gena Rowlands (Mabel Longhetti), Matthew Cassel (Tony Longhetti), Matthew Laborteaux (Angelo Longhetti), Christina Grisanti (Maria Longhetti), Katherine Cassavetes (Mama Longhetti), Lady Rowlands (Martha Mortensen), Fred Draper (George Mortensen), O.G. Dunn (Garson Cross), Mario Gallo (Harold Jensen)

p, Sam Shaw; d, John Cassavetes; w, John Cassavetes; ph, Mitch Breif (MGM Color); ed, David Armstrong, Elizabeth Bergeron, Sheila Viseltear, Tom Cornwell; m, Bo Harwood; art d, Phedon Papamichael

Rambling, overlong study of a working-class housewife's mental breakdown, redeemed by superb performances from Rowlands, in the title role, and Falk as her husband. Laborteaux, Grisanti, and Cassel play the children. A kind of tragic duet between the two leads, A WOMAN remains an insightful essay on sexual politics. As Rowlands delicately crosses the line of sanity, it becomes apparent that imposed social roles are the cause.

Both Rowlands (who lost to Ellen Burstyn for ALICE DOESN'T LIVE HERE ANYMORE) and Cassavetes (for direction) were nominated for Oscars for this unexpected minor hit, which grossed well over $6 million the first time around. It began as a theatrical piece for Rowlands, but she balked at having to play such a demanding role nightly and the suggestion was made to transform it into a movie. Cassavetes took out a mortgage on his home, contacted friends and relatives for financing, and then began a two-year shooting schedule dictated by his own personal finances. Cassavetes's work is often mistaken as improvisational, or even as *cinema verite*. In fact, his films are thoughtful celebrations of the art of acting and, in most cases, are shot from precise scripts (even if those scripts are themselves based on extensive improvisational exercises).

WOMEN, THE

1939　132m　c/bw	★★★★
Comedy	/A
MGM	

Norma Shearer (Mary Haines), Joan Crawford (Chrystal Allen), Rosalind Russell (Sylvia Fowler), Mary Boland (Countess DeLave), Paulette Goddard (Miriam Aarons), Joan Fontaine (Peggy Day), Lucile Watson (Mrs. Moorehead), Phyllis Povah (Edith Potter), Florence Nash (Nancy Blake), Virginia Weidler (Little Mary)

p, Hunt Stromberg; d, George Cukor; w, Anita Loos, Jane Murfin (based on the play by Clare Boothe Luce); ph, Oliver T. Marsh, Joseph Ruttenberg (Part Technicolor); ed, Robert J. Kern; m, Edward Ward, David Snell; art d, Cedric Gibbons, Wade B. Rubottom; cos, Adrian

Every feminist's nightmare? In some ways, yes; in others no. Adapted from the hit Broadway play by Clare Boothe (who was also Mrs. Luce, by dint of marriage to the founder of *Time* magazine), THE WOMEN does portray its subjects as inordinately fond of catty gossip, but also has some interesting points to make about female bonding and societal pressures.

Heading a cast of 130 women and no men, Norma Shearer plays Mary Haines, a wealthy and loving woman married to an adoring husband and the mother of sweet Little Mary (Weidler, admirably pulling off a difficult part). Contented Mary, though, has no idea that her husband is having an affair with predatory perfume seller Crystal Allen (Joan Crawford). Mary's girlfriends know, and the bitchiest of the lot, Sylvia Fowler (Rosalind Russell), arranges for Mary to get the news herself from the gossipy manicurist (Dennie Moore) who first started circulating the story. Mary's mother, Mrs. Morehead (Lucile Watson), though, advises her to say nothing and simply let the affair play itself out. Unfortunately, Mary encounters Crystal at a fancy clothing salon and, in a blistering scene, the two women exchange words. Mary leaves New York to race to Reno for a six-week divorce and meets the Countess de Lave (Boland), an aging former showgirl who has been married several times. She also encounters younger chorine Miriam Aarons (Goddard), who is having an affair with Sylvia's husband. Mary and the others check in to a ranch owned by Lucy (Main, along with Phyllis Povah, the only holdover from the original Broadway cast), a funny and voluble woman. Sylvia arrives, and when she realizes that it was Miriam who stole her husband, a battle ensues between the two women. Mary's surprise, though, is soon tempered as she learns that her former mate, rather than calling her to stop the divorce at the 11th hour, has married Crystal.

Later, when she gets home to New York, Mary discovers that her ex is unhappy in his new marriage, and that Crystal has taken to both spending money with a passion and having an affair with a radio singing cowboy married to the former Countess. Finally showing her mother that, she, too, has had her nails done in "Jungle Red", Mary embraces the predatory principles of her friends and artfully tries to win her husband back.

Filled with witty repartee and vicious gossip, THE WOMEN portrays a world where women seem to do nothing but obsess over men. Playwright Clare Boothe always defended her work, claiming that only empty-headed, spoilt rich women were being satirized here. Inspection of her play, however, shows that all women are, to some extent, under scrutiny, and the portrait which emerges is undoubtedly harsh. (Her one undeniable talent as a writer, rather, is her remarkable talent for hilarious, nasty wisecracking.) Close examination of the film script, though, reveals considerable insight into female bonding. The several mother-daughter relationships are interestingly portrayed, and even the fights over men, as dramatized in this vast improvement on Boothe's original, are not without their lessons about the roles imposed on women by society.

The famous opening credit sequence has the leading actresses' faces shown before each one dissolves to a shot of an animal which categorizes her "type." Russell is shown as a black cat, Main a donkey, Weidler a doe, Povah a cow, Goddard a fox, Fontaine a lamb, Boland a chimpanzee, Watson an owl, Crawford a leopard, and Shearer, who was top-billed, a fawn.

Many of the performances are joys. Shearer has never been more restrained, and but for two moments (dropping to her knees to cry at her mother's feet, and the final reconciliation), her performance never falters. Her crying jag in Reno is one of the most convincing of its kind; even technically better actresses like Davis and Hepburn couldn't always pull tears off this well.

WOMEN IN LOVE

Another moment to look for is the way Shearer hits the flowers her errant husband sends her. Crawford, meanwhile, brilliantly revitalized her career with one of her finest acting achievement, a funny, spot-on portrait of the scheming, sexy Crystal. Hard as nails throughout, she uses her velvet voice to great effect, and her parting salvo at the end is a killer ("There's a word for you ladies, but it is seldom used in high society, outside of a kennel"). Cukor's direction is rich and confident, and the whole production fairly shimmers.

WOMEN IN LOVE
1969 130m c   ★★★½
Drama   R/18
Brandywine   (U.K.)

Alan Bates *(Rupert Birkin)*, Oliver Reed *(Gerald Crich)*, Glenda Jackson *(Gudrun Brangwen)*, Jennie Linden *(Ursula Brangwen)*, Eleanor Bron *(Hermione Roddice)*, Alan Webb *(Thomas Crich)*, Vladek Sheybal *(Loerke)*, Catherine Willmer *(Mrs. Crich)*, Sarah Nicholls *(Winifred Crich)*, Sharon Gurney *(Laura Crich)*

p, Larry Kramer; d, Ken Russell; w, Larry Kramer (based on the novel by D.H. Lawrence); ph, Billy Williams (DeLuxe Color); ed, Michael Bradsell; m, Georges Delerue, Peter Ilich Tchaikovsky; art d, Ken Jones; chor, Terry Gilbert; cos, Shirley Russell

Fine adaptation of D.H. Lawrence's classic novel with some interesting visual sequences typical of director Russell's style.

It is 1920s England. Jackson is a free-thinking artist who, along with her schoolteacher sister, Linden, watches from a graveyard as Gurney and Christopher Gable are married. Later, at an outdoor luncheon given for the couple, the two women meet Reed and Bates. Bates, a school inspector, constantly ruminates on the topic of love and begins a fledgling relationship with Linden. At a picnic at the plush home of Gurney's wealthy family, the newlyweds are lost beneath the dark waters of the estate's lake. When the water is drained from the lake, the two drowned bodies are discovered entwined together in the muddy lake bed. That night Bates and Reed, in a discussion on friendship, strip before a fireplace and engage in a nude wrestling match. After Bates and Linden marry, they go with Reed and Jackson for a honeymoon in Switzerland. Jackson meets Sheybal, a sculptor like herself, and engages in an affair with the bisexual man, when her sister and brother-in-law leave Switzerland. Reed, enraged at Sheybal's intrusion, attacks the man and tries to choke Jackson. Then Reed flees into the snow and wanders until he dies. Bates, stunned by the death, still questions the mystery of relations between men and women.

There are moments of great beauty here, such as the view of Bates and Linden running naked into each other's arms in a wheatfield. The camera is turned horizontally, and the bodies seem to defy gravity, moving up and down within the frame through the golden vegetation. In another, much-heralded piece of editing, Russell cuts from the intertwined bodies of Bates and Linden after a lovemaking session to the cold, stiff corpses of Gurney and Gable on the bottom of the emptied lake. Russell did some of his own camerawork (although Williams received credit as cinematographer) and showed an excellent eye for shot composition and editing rhythms. His ability as a storyteller is less in evidence, however. Despite the passion of the topic and the beauty of the images, the narrative tends toward the static, particularly in the later stages. Russell incorporated many dance images into WOMEN IN LOVE, expanding on what he considered to be a central theme of the novel. He later stated that he "should have turned the whole thing into a musical; it wasn't far off in some ways." He received an Oscar nomination for Best

Director, with nominations also going to Kramer for his script, and Williams for his lovely cinematography. Jackson, in a restrained, elegant performance, won the Oscar for Best Actress.

WOMEN ON THE VERGE OF A NERVOUS BREAKDOWN
1988 98m c   ★★★★
Drama   /15
Lauren Films/El Desea   (Spain)

Carmen Maura *(Pepa)*, Antonio Banderas *(Carlos)*, Fernando Guillen *(Ivan)*, Julieta Serrano *(Lucia)*, Maria Barranco *(Candela)*, Rossy de Palma *(Marisa)*, Kiti Manver *(Paulina)*, Chus Lampreave, Yayo Calvo, Lotes Leon

d, Pedro Almodovar; w, Pedro Almodovar; ph, Jose Luis Alcaine (Eastmancolor); ed, Jose Salcedo; m, Bernardo Bonezzi; cos, Jose Maria de Cossio

In WOMEN ON THE VERGE OF A NERVOUS BREAKDOWN, Pedro Almodovar has written and directed an incisive, fast-paced romp with the serious theme of obsessive love. The film's cascade of missed connections and riotous coincidences is triggered when Ivan (Fernando Guillen) abruptly abandons his longtime lover, Pepa (Carmen Maura). Finding herself pregnant, Pepa frantically tries to track down the elusive Ivan. In the course of her search she discovers some of his secrets, including Lucia (Julieta Serrano), by whom he has fathered a now-grown son. Pepa, distraught and contemplating suicide, prepares a batch of gazpacho laced with enough barbiturates to put a small town into coma and puts her apartment up for rent—after which people start showing up in waves. The pitcher of gazpacho becomes the key to some strange and unexpected events, culminating in a loopy car chase. Almodovar, who was an obscure telephone company employee just six years earlier, consolidates his reputation as a cult moviemaker with this one. He is great at inventing simple but stunning visual jokes and staging running gags. Further, he brings the best out of his uniformly skillful cast, in particular Carmen Maura. An Almodovar regular and consummate farceur, Maura can also play the pathos of the role with moving veracity. The film is flushed with bright light and cartoon hues, nicely accenting the fast-paced stew of incidents.

WONDER MAN
1945 98m c   ★★★★
Comedy/Musical   /U
Goldwyn

Danny Kaye *(Buzzy Bellew/Edwin Dingle)*, Virginia Mayo *(Ellen Shanley)*, Vera-Ellen *(Midge Mallon)*, Donald Woods *(Monte Rossen)*, S.Z. Sakall *(Schmidt)*, Allen Jenkins *(Chimp)*, Edward Brophy *(Torso)*, Steve Cochran *(Ten-Grand Jackson)*, Otto Kruger *(District Attorney R.J. O'Brien)*, Richard Land *(Assistant District Attorney Grosset)*

p, Samuel Goldwyn; d, H. Bruce Humberstone; w, Don Hartman, Melville Shavelson, Philip Rapp, Jack Jevne, Eddie Moran (based on a story by Arthur Sheekman); ph, Victor Milner, William Snyder (Technicolor); ed, Daniel Mandell; m, Ray Heindorf; art d, Ernst Fegte, McClure Capps; fx, John P. Fulton; chor, John Wray

In one of his most likable films, Danny Kaye takes on a dual role, playing two brothers—one an entertainer about to marry who is killed when he witnesses a mob hit, and the other an intellectual in love with a librarian. The dead brother's spirit approaches the living brother and asks that he help bring the murderous mobsters to justice. Since the egghead is afraid to get involved, the spirit of the dead brother enters the body of the living one. Not surprisingly, this causes a great deal of confusion, especially for the two women who are now in love with him, the librarian and the dead brother's fiancee. Filled with lots of laughs, WONDER MAN features a splendid performance by Kaye that is spiced with verve and zeal. There are, a number of fine, funny musical numbers and the special effects are well deserving of the Oscar they earned.

WOODEN HORSE, THE
1951   101m   bw   ★★★½
War/Prison   /U
Wessex   (U.K.)

Leo Genn *(Peter)*, David Tomlinson *(Phil)*, Anthony Steel *(John)*, David Greene *(Bennett)*, Peter Burton *(Nigel)*, Patrick Waddington *(Senior British Officer)*, Michael Goodliffe *(Robbie)*, Anthony Dawson *(Pomfret)*, Bryan Forbes *(Paul)*, Franz Schaftheitlin *(Commandant)*

p, Ian Dalrymple; d, Jack Lee; w, Eric Williams (based on the book by Williams); ph, C. Pennington-Richards; ed, John Seabourne, Peter Seabourne; m, Clifton Parker; prod d, William Kellner

One of the cleverest escapes of WWII was pulled off by British prisoners in 1943, and this film tells their story. Pondering a method of escaping their camp, POWs Peter (Leo Genn), John (Anthony Steel), and Phil (David Tomlinson) hit upon a brilliant scheme. They construct a boxlike vaulting horse, which is brought out to the yard daily for a few hours of exercise by their fellow internees. Inside the horse, however, are one and sometimes two men who start a tunnel from underneath the horse, then cover it up at the end of each day's vaulting. After months of digging and close calls, the tunnel is ready. Three men remain inside it until after dark, then break through the last few feet of ground to the surface beyond the fence. Peter and John travel together and are eventually spirited by the Danish underground to Sweden, where they rejoin Phil. This was the first of the British POW films and set the subgenre's style, in which Stalag life takes on the character of a British public school, a rigorous discipline and hierarchy in which the Germans function as "rather nasty prefects, who exist simply to be tricked and humiliated," as one critic put it. THE WOODEN HORSE subscribes to this trivialization of what was really a horrible, degrading experience, but as an adventure the film is very successful—suspenseful and fast-paced, with all the leads well done in suitably stiff-upper-lip style.

WORKING GIRL
1988   113m   c   ★★★½
Romance   R/15
FOX

Harrison Ford *(Jack Trainer)*, Sigourney Weaver *(Katharine Parker)*, Melanie Griffith *(Tess McGill)*, Alec Baldwin *(Mick Dugan)*, Joan Cusack *(Cyn)*, Philip Bosco *(Oren Trask)*, Nora Dunn *(Ginny)*, Oliver Platt *(Lutz)*, James Lally *(Turkel)*, Kevin Spacey *(Bob Speck)*

p, Douglas Wick; d, Mike Nichols; w, Kevin Wade; ph, Michael Ballhaus (Deluxe Color); ed, Sam O'Steen; m, Carly Simon; prod d, Patrizia von Brandenstein; cos, Ann Roth

Melanie Griffith, excellent in another strong 1988 film, STORMY MONDAY, gives an even more dazzling performance here as Tess McGill, an industrious secretary at a brokerage firm who longs to break out of the secretarial mold. After a run-in with her boss, she finds herself in a last-chance opportunity as the secretary to Katharine Parker (Sigourney Weaver). The astute secretary has an idea for putting together a deal for a client (Philip

Bosco). Later, while Katharine recovers from a skiing accident, Tess learns that her boss has been moving ahead on the idea with no apparent intention of giving Tess any credit. Tess decides to engineer the big deal herself, with the help of Jack Trainer (Harrison Ford), an outside deal-maker who also happens to be Katharine's lover. Director Mike Nichols (THE GRADUATE; CATCH-22; BILOXI BLUES) demonstrates again his assured command of the film medium—coaxing outstanding performances from lead and supporting players alike, using the camera to brilliant effect, and infusing the story with tension, romance, and humor. Funny, touching, and ultimately tremendously buoyant, WORKING GIRL is a "feel good" movie with intelligence.

WORKING GIRLS
1986   90m   c   ★★★★
Drama   /18
Lizzie Borden/Alternate Current

Louise Smith *(Molly)*, Ellen McElduff *(Lucy)*, Amanda Goodwin *(Dawn)*, Marusia Zach *(Gina)*, Janne Peters *(April)*, Helen Nicholas *(Mary)*

p, Lizzie Borden, Andi Gladstone; d, Lizzie Borden; w, Lizzie Borden, Sandra Kay; ph, Judy Irola (Eastmancolor); ed, Lizzie Borden; m, David van Tieghem; prod d, Kurt Ossenfort

WORKING GIRLS concentrates on the daily routine of a modern-day Manhattan prostitute in a detached, clinical manner, breaking away from old myths to create an insightful and, in many ways, disturbing interpretation of what has been called the "world's oldest profession." Molly (Louise Smith) is a Yale graduate, nearing 30, who temporarily works in a Manhattan brothel to help make ends meet. The Manhattan brothel she works in appears as a normal office. The girls dress like secretaries, and harmlessly chat about their personal lives, the job, and their general disdain for their boss, as they patiently wait for the day to end so they can go home.

Director Lizzie Borden's usually sharp eye for detail pervades WORKING GIRLS, and here maintains a high level of interest throughout. The down-to-earth portrayals possess none of the stereotypes popular in media representations of prostitutes, and, as a result, are frighteningly realistic. A film with an interesting and provocative feminist edge.

WORLD ACCORDING TO GARP, THE
1982   136m   c   ★★½
Comedy/Drama   R/15
Pan Arts

Robin Williams *(T.S. Garp)*, Mary Beth Hurt *(Helen Holm)*, Glenn Close *(Jenny Fields)*, John Lithgow *(Roberta Muldoon)*, Hume Cronyn *(Mr. Fields)*, Jessica Tandy *(Mrs. Fields)*, Swoosie Kurtz *(Hooker)*, James McCall *(Young Garp)*, Peter Michael Goetz *(John Wolfe)*, George Ede *(Dean Bodger)*

p, George Roy Hill, Robert L. Crawford; d, George Roy Hill; w, Steve Tesich (based on the novel by John Irving); ph, Miroslav Ondricek (Technicolor); ed, Ronald Roose, Stephen A. Rotter; prod d, Henry Bumstead; art d, Woods Mackintosh; cos, Ann Roth; anim, John Canemaker

Empty shortening of Irving's book reaches for profundity, and comes up courageous but brainless. It's actually a bittersweet string of sketches, attempting to explain a man's growth from birth to adulthood and how he deals with the vices of lust and fanaticism that whirl around him.

Garp is born to a formidable unmarried mother, Jenny Fields, played by Glenn Close. (The various stages of Garp's childhood are played by Thomas Peter Daikos, Brendon Roth, and James McCall before Robin Williams takes over as Garp reaches young adulthood.) The story follows him through childhood at a boys' prep school, where Jenny is the school nurse, through his high school passions—wrestling, writing, and sex—to marriage with his high school sweetheart, children, marital disaffection, and a career as a writer. Jenny meanwhile has become a famous feminist, espousing an eccentric cause. The plot details an abundance of comic and tragicomic episodes, outlandish physical, emotional, and sexual adventures. Williams gives another puppy-dog performance—he has yet to land a script that takes advantage of his wildness and anarchy. Although these qualities are undoubtedly couched in the cuteness of Williams's persona, they come from anywhere but. He's like a wild bird with clipped wings. GARP is stolen by Lithgow, who imparts dignity and depth to his role of a king-sized transsexual, and Close's feminist mom. The movie was not a success—even at 136 minutes, GARP still feels like its dialogue and its action are going in opposite directions. Audiences were confused; we're not—we can't work up that much of a lather.

WORLD APART, A

1988   113m   c   ★★★★
Biography   PG
Working Title/British Screen   (U.K.)

Barbara Hershey (Diana Roth), Jodhi May (Molly Roth), Jeroen Krabbe (Gus Roth), Carolyn Clayton-Cragg (Miriam Roth), Merav Gruer (Jude Roth), Yvonne Bryceland (Bertha), Albee Lesotho (Solomon), Linda Mvusi (Elsie), Rosalie Crutchley (Mrs. Harris), Mackay Tickey (Milius)

p, Sarah Radclyffe; d, Chris Menges; w, Shawn Slovo; ph, Peter Biziou (Eastmancolor); ed, Nicolas Gaster; m, Hans Zimmer; prod d, Brian Morris; cos, Nic Ede

Set in Johannesburg in 1963, A WORLD APART is an utterly convincing, impeccably constructed indictment of apartheid, based on a semiautobiographical screenplay by Shawn Slovo. (Slovo is the daughter of Joe Slovo, head of the South African Communist Party and one of two white members of the ANC executive council, and Ruth First, who was assassinated by a parcel bomb in Mozambique in 1982.) Jodhi May plays Slovo as a 13-year-old whose world revolves around Spanish dancing lessons, hula-hooping, and swimming in the pool of her equally privileged best friend (Nadine Chalmers). Her world is turned upside down when her father (Jeroen Krabbe), an ANC official, departs in the middle of the night not to return, leaving her journalist mother (Barbara Hershey) both to take care of May and her two younger sisters and to continue the political struggle. Much to May's confusion, Hershey's involvement with the movement makes her, not a bad mother, but a distracted, inattentive one—distant because she fears she cannot trust her daughter with life-and-death secrets. The film is driven by the tension between May's resentment at what she perceives as her mother's neglect of the family, and her gradual acknowledgment of the importance of the political imperatives by which her mother is compelled.

The feature-film directorial debut of Academy Award-winning cinematographer Chris Menges (THE KILLING FIELDS; THE MISSION), A WORLD APART was the second major film in two years to deal with South African issues, coming soon after Richard Attenborough's 1987 effort, CRY FREEDOM. In A WORLD APART, Menges has chosen to explore apartheid primarily through the eyes of whites, though his black characters—particularly Elsie (Linda Mvusi), the family's live-in maid, and

her brother Solomon (Albee Lesotho), a political activist—are considerably more developed than those in Attenborough's film.

The performances in A WORLD APART are uniformly excellent, and the extraordinarily moving work of Barbara Hershey, Jodhi May, and Linda Mvusi garnered a shared Best Actress award at the Cannes Film Festival. Director Menges took a special interest in the story because in 1963, the year of Ruth First's arrest, he was in South Africa at age 22, filming a documentary on the 90-Day Detention Act for BBC-TV's "World in Action." Obviously, though, no one is closer to the story than its author, Shawn Slovo, who wrote the screenplay as a response to her mother's murder in her office at the University of Mozambique on August 17, 1982. Using her own experiences, her father's recollections, and her mother's book *One Hundred and Seventeen Days* as the basis, Slovo wrote the screenplay while a student at Britain's National Film School. After receiving a cool reception from American film producers, she took it to Britain's Working Title, the risk-taking production company responsible for MY BEAUTIFUL LAUNDRETTE. The $5 million production was shot in 19 weeks in Bulawayo, Zimbabwe, which substitutes for suburban Johannesburg. Slovo was on hand for the shooting, but she was forced to travel under a false name with her hair dyed.

WORLD IN HIS ARMS, THE

1952   104m   c   ★★★
Adventure   /U
Universal

Gregory Peck (Jonathan Clark), Ann Blyth (Countess Marina Selanova), Anthony Quinn (Portugee), John McIntire (Deacon Greathouse), Andrea King (Mamie), Carl Esmond (Prince Semyon), Eugenie Leontovich (Anna Selanova), Sig Rumann (Gen. Ivan Vorashilov), Hans Conried (Eustace), Bryan Forbes (William Cleggett)

p, Aaron Rosenberg; d, Raoul Walsh; w, Borden Chase, Horace McCoy (based on the novel by Rex Beach); ph, Russell Metty (Technicolor); ed, Frank Gross; m, Frank Skinner; art d, Bernard Herzbrun, Alexander Golitzen; chor, Hal Belfaer; cos, Bill Thomas

Strong period adventure film set in Alaska that marked the first of three joint projects for Peck and Quinn.

Peck is captain of a vessel that illegally hunts seals. He returns to San Francisco's Barbary Coast after a good voyage and checks into a hotel with his crew. Blyth, a Russian countess, is also a guest there with her coterie of servants. She is fleeing an arranged marriage with Esmond, a Czarist peer, and thinks she can find safety in Sitka, Alaska, under the aegis of her uncle, Rumann, who is the governor general of the area. She approaches Quinn, a Portuguese seal hunter and Peck's rival, and says she'll pay well to be taken north, but Quinn can't raise a crew to make the voyage. When Blyth discovers that Peck has a ship and a crew, she asks him to take her to Alaska. Peck finds her most attractive and doesn't know that royal blood pumps in her veins when he takes her around the city for a nighttime tour of Baghdad by the Bay. By dawn the two become close and decide to get married. They are about to be wed when Esmond, at the helm of a Russian boat, comes into San Francisco harbor, steals Blyth and her entourage, and sets sail for Alaska, promising to kill Rumann if Blyth doesn't fulfill her previous marriage obligation. Peck finds that Blyth is gone, drinks himself into a stupor, has a huge fist fight with Quinn, and winds up broke. To raise money, Peck proposes a bet with Quinn. The two will race to Sitka, and the winner will get the other captain's seal catch as well as his boat. Quinn agrees and the race begins. Peck's boat arrives slightly ahead of Quinn's, but then the Russians capture both ships and impound them along with their catches and crews. Peck and Quinn are arrested as seal poachers and tossed into jail. Blyth saves them by agreeing to marry Esmond if he will order their release. This he does, and Quinn and Peck are taken back to their ships under guard. Later, they stealthily make their way to Rumann's residence, where the wedding is about to commence, and join forces to snatch Blyth away from the cunning Esmond. Then, to ensure their safe arrival back in the US, Quinn oversees the wrecking of the Russian gunboat. Peck and Blyth sail south, happily planning the rest of their lives together.

Superb sea footage, lots of action, and a robust relationship between Peck and Quinn combine to make this highly enjoyable, despite occasional overtones of anticommunism (this was the time of the Hollywood "witch hunts"). It would be hard to present a seal-hunter as a modern-day hero, but producer Rosenberg and director Walsh admittedly keep the hunting scenes to a minimum. Appearing in his first US film (he'd done two in the UK) is Bryan Forbes, who later abandoned acting for writing, producing, and directing.

WORLD OF APU, THE

(APUR SANSAR)
1959 103m bw   ★★★★
Drama   /U
Satyajit Ray   (India)

Soumitra Chatterjee *(Apurba Kumar Roy)*, Sharmila Tagore *(Aparna)*, Shapan Mukerji *(Pulu)*, S. Alke Chakravarty *(Kajal)*

p, Satyajit Ray; d, Satyajit Ray; w, Satyajit Ray (based on the novel *Aparajito* by Bibhutibhusan Bandopadhaya); ph, Subrata Mitra; ed, Dulal Dutta; m, Ravi Shankar; art d, Banshi Chandra Gupta

THE WORLD OF APU is the third and final installment of Satyajit Ray's "Apu Trilogy," the most famous group of films to come out of India. After following the young character of Apu from his early years (PATHER PANCHALI) to his schooldays (APARAJITO), the trilogy picks up with Soumitra Chatterjee in the role of Apu as a young man. His desire is to become a writer, but a lack of finances has forced him to abandon his university studies. His life changes, however, when he again meets his old friend Pulu (Shapan Mukerji). Together, the two travel to the wedding of Pulu's cousin, Aparna (Sharmila Tagore). When the bridegroom turns out to be insane and the wedding is canceled, Apu agrees to marry Aparna to save her from ridicule. They return to his Calcutta apartment to start a new life, but destiny does not look kindly upon the newlyweds. In this final entry, Ray rounds out the life of Apu, charting his loss of innocence and painting a detailed and textured portrait of Indian life in the process. In Apu, Ray has brought to the screen a character who lives out his story, though he is never able to finally put it on paper. A rich and insightful picture, THE WORLD OF APU, despite being rooted deep in Indian culture, strikes a universal humanistic chord.

WORLD OF HENRY ORIENT, THE

1964 115m c   ★★★
Comedy   /U
UA

Peter Sellers *(Henry Orient)*, Paula Prentiss *(Stella)*, Tippy Walker *(Valerie Boyd)*, Merrie Spaeth *(Marian "Gil" Gilbert)*, Angela Lansbury *(Isabel Boyd)*, Tom Bosley *(Frank Boyd)*, Phyllis Thaxter *(Mrs. Gilbert)*, Bibi Osterwald *(Boothy)*, Peter Duchin *(Joe Byrd)*, John Fiedler *(Sidney)*

p, Jerome Hellman; d, George Roy Hill; w, Nora Johnson, Nunnally Johnson (based on the novel by Nora Johnson); ph, Boris Kaufman, Arthur J. Ornitz (Panavision, DeLuxe Color); ed, Stuart Gilmore; m, Elmer Bernstein, Ken Lauber; prod d, James Sullivan; art d, Jan Scott; fx, Dick Smith; cos, Ann Roth

THE WORLD OF HENRY ORIENT is a charming comedy about the agony of adolescent infatuation. Walker and Spaeth are boarding school chums who keep busy pursuing egotistical concert pianist Sellers. The girls, just 14 or so, believe that they are in love with Sellers, a Casanova whose latest conquest is the married Prentiss. Prentiss is convinced that the girls have been hired by her husband to trail her, and after that the groupies' idolatry creates a number of ridiculous situations. This is one of the rare films in which someone steals scenes from Sellers. Walker and Spaeth are a joy—with none of the professional, cloying sweetness so often seen in younger performers—and the best part of the movie is the depiction of the girls, which never strays from truth, even when the teens are on wild flights of fancy. Director George Roy Hill made another, equally charming, tale of young love 15 years later: A LITTLE ROMANCE.

WRITTEN ON THE WIND

1956 99m c   ★★★★½
Drama   /A
Universal

Rock Hudson *(Mitch Wayne)*, Lauren Bacall *(Lucy Moore Hadley)*, Robert Stack *(Kyle Hadley)*, Dorothy Malone *(Marylee Hadley)*, Robert Keith *(Jasper Hadley)*, Grant Williams *(Biff Miley)*, Bob Wilke *(Dan Willis)*, Edward Platt *(Dr. Paul Cochrane)*, Harry Shannon *(Hoak Wayne)*, John Larch *(Roy Carter)*

p, Albert Zugsmith; d, Douglas Sirk; w, George Zuckerman (based on the novel by Robert Wilder); ph, Russell Metty (Technicolor); ed, Russell Schoengarth; m, Frank Skinner; art d, Alexander Golitzen, Robert Clatworthy; fx, Clifford Stine; cos, Bill Thomas, Jay A. Morley, Jr.

The ultimate in lush melodrama, WRITTEN ON THE WIND is, along with IMITATION OF LIFE, Douglas Sirk's finest directorial effort, and one of the most notable critiques of the American family ever made.

A Texas oil baron (Stack) has a whirlwind romance with a secretary (Bacall) and then marries her, but later has doubts as to whether the child she is expecting is really his. Stacks's nymphomaniac sister (Malone) stokes up his suspicions that his best friend, geologist Rock Hudson, is really the father, and sets off a series of larger-than-life confrontations and crises from which no-one escapes lightly.

WRITTEN ON THE WIND successfully combines all the elements of the genre that has has become synonymous with Sirk's name. Sirk's melodrama, though, diverges from what is usually understood by that term to encompass a highly developed sense of ironic social critique. Some critics have seen his sumptuous visual style, full of parody and cliche, as a kind of Brechtian distancing that draws attention to the artificiality of the film medium, in turn commenting on the hollowness of middle-class American life. The lake in WRITTEN ON THE WIND, for example, is presented as a patently artificial studio interior, ironically pointing up the romantic self-delusion with which Malone sees her world.

Malone picked up an Academy Award for her supporting performance, and the film was nominated for Best Supporting Actor (Stack) and Best Song ("Written on the Wind" by Victor Young and Sammy Cahn).

WRONG BOX, THE

1966 107m c   ★★★
Comedy   /U
Salamander (U.K.)

John Mills *(Masterman Finsbury)*, Ralph Richardson *(Joseph Finsbury)*, Michael Caine *(Michael Finsbury)*, Peter Cook *(Morris Finsbury)*, Dudley Moore *(John Finsbury)*, Nanette Newman *(Julia Finsbury)*, Tony Hancock *(Detective)*, Peter Sellers *(Dr. Pratt)*, Cicely Courtneidge *(Maj. Martha)*, Wilfrid Lawson *(Peacock)*

p, Bryan Forbes; d, Bryan Forbes; w, Larry Gelbart, Burt Shevelove (based on the novel by Robert Louis Stevenson, Lloyd Osbourne); ph, Gerry Turpin (Eastmancolor); ed, Alan Osbiston; m, John Barry; art d, Ray Simm; cos, Julie Harris

This funny period comedy is based on a story coauthored by Robert Louis Stevenson and Lloyd Osbourne in the last century. Americans Gelbart and Shevelove expanded on the tale, adding a great deal of comedy and writing the script for this gag-filled farce.

Mills and Richardson are brothers in Victorian London. They haven't seen each other for four decades, and for good reason. When they were young lads, they were part of a multi-youth "tontine" and they are the last survivors of the odd pact. Years before, several parents had tossed about $2,800 each into a pool. As the calendar pages were ripped off, the money began to mount through good investments, until it is now quite a bundle. In an extended series of gags, we see how the other members of the strange lottery have gone to their final destinies. Meanwhile, the brothers are each awaiting the news that the other has died, so the remaining one can have all the money.

Sellers is on screen only a few minutes but registers quite well, as does Lawson as the butler. The picture is shot like a British version of a Mack Sennett film, replete with subtitles. All of the smaller roles are deliciously cast, with several of the best comic actors England had to offer in that decade, a heyday of British humor. The picture gets flabby from time to time but comes alive when the old masters, Mills and Richardson, are on screen. The plot works, but there are so many sight gags that fall flat, it begins to pall occasionally. The score is by John Barry and The Temperance Seven perform funeral and military airs.

WRONG MAN, THE

1956 105m bw   ★★★★★
Crime   /PG
WB

Henry Fonda *(Christopher Emmanuel "Manny" Balestrero)*, Vera Miles *(Rose Balestrero)*, Anthony Quayle *(Frank O'Connor)*, Harold J. Stone *(Lt. Bowers)*, Esther Minciotti *(Mrs. Balestrero)*, Charles Cooper *(Detective Matthews)*, Nehemiah Persoff *(Gene Conforti)*, Laurinda Barrett *(Constance Willis)*, Norma Connolly *(Betty Todd)*, Doreen Lang *(Ann James)*

p, Alfred Hitchcock; d, Alfred Hitchcock; w, Maxwell Anderson, Angus Macphail (based on "The True Story of Christopher Emmanuel Balestrero" by Anderson); ph, Robert Burks; ed, George Tomasini; m, Bernard Herrmann; art d, Paul Sylbert, William L. Kuehl

The bleakest of Hitchcock's films, this stark, deliberate probing of a man wrongfully accused is almost wholly based on fact, creating its drama from a celebrated New York City case. Fonda plays Manny Balestrero, a family man who plays stand-up bass at a Queens nightspot called the Stork Club. Although he doesn't have much money, he manages to keep his life together with the help of his devoted wife, Rose (Miles). When she complains of

dental pains, Manny decides to borrow on her life insurance policy (the last place they can borrow money since their debts have already piled too high) to pay for medical attention. Although he makes a practice of picking horses in the race section of the newspaper, he never dares to actually bet on them even though a win could get him out of debt. The following morning, Manny goes to the insurance office where he is identified by the office girls as the man who had robbed them previously. Later that night, he is arrested at the Stork Club. After being identified by a number of witnesses, Manny is interrogated at the police station. When he makes a nervous mistake in a handwriting test (misspelling the word "drawer" as "draw"—the same mistake made on the robber's ransom note), he is fingerprinted, photographed, and imprisoned. Finally released on bail, Manny is joyfully reunited with Rose and hires defense attorney (Quayle). When Manny cannot find any witnesses to provide his alibi, the prospect of an acquittal looks dim. Meanwhile, Rose begins to crack under the pressure and is no longer able to deal with her husband's trial and defense. Although legal justice is ultimately served, Manny's family must nonetheless pay a considerable price for his freedom.

Having become accustomed to the lighter, more commercial tone of such films as TO CATCH A THIEF; THE TROUBLE WITH HARRY; and THE MAN WHO KNEW TOO MUCH, the public was taken aback when they viewed the unexpectedly bleak, hopeless, Kafka-esque style (more frightening than Orson Welles's THE TRIAL) of THE WRONG MAN. Basing the film on incidents occurring to a real-life Queens bass player that began with his arrest on January 13, 1953 (Hitchcock learned of the case through a *Life* magazine article), Hitchcock takes us to the actual locations—the Stork Club, a Long Island Prudential insurance office, Balestrero's 74th Street Queens home, the asylum where his wife was committed, the actual police station, and Balestrero's prison cell—with the intent of representing the case in all its authenticity. Hitchcock spares us nothing in procedural terms. The questioning of the suspect, for example, is done in necessary tedium, wearing down the audience as much as Fonda's character. We see him fingerprinted—the ink being applied to his fingertips, the printing, the paper he is given to clean his hands. We are forced to sit through the entirety of his handwriting analysis as well. In THE WRONG MAN Hitchcock has succeeded in filming a true story that is indeed Hitchcockian—the idea of the wrong man accused—as if to present evidence to any critics or viewers who thought the director's films were not credible. To add legitimacy to the story's events, Hitchcock even tacked on a prologue in which he introduced himself and then verified that the story about to be shown was based on fact. While the film centers chiefly on Manny's trauma, Hitchcock doesn't ignore the mental torture Rose is put through, temporarily departing from the story of Fonda's conviction to delve further into her problems. It was Miles's first of two appearances in a Hitchcock film (PSYCHO was the second), although she did act in the first episode of the director's television series "Alfred Hitchcock Presents. . ." (one of the handful to be directed by Hitchcock himself). Hitchcock planned to cast her in VERTIGO but had to cast Kim Novak instead when the newly wed actress became pregnant. Don't look for Hitchcock's trademark cameo in this picture; he had originally intended to be seen as a customer walking into the Stork Club but edited himself out of the final print. There are a few other interesting appearances, however—Harry Dean Stanton in one of his countless minor roles, and two giggling girls who later found fame, Bonnie Franklin and Tuesday Weld.

WUTHERING HEIGHTS
1939   103m   bw   ★★★★½
Romance   /U
Goldwyn

Merle Oberon *(Cathy Linton)*, Laurence Olivier *(Heathcliff)*, David Niven *(Edgar Linton)*, Donald Crisp *(Dr. Kenneth)*, Flora Robson *(Ellen Dean)*, Hugh Williams *(Hindley Earnshaw)*, Geraldine Fitzgerald *(Isabella Linton)*, Leo G. Carroll *(Joseph)*, Cecil Humphreys *(Judge Linton)*, Miles Mander *(Lockwood)*

p, Samuel Goldwyn; d, William Wyler; w, Ben Hecht, Charles MacArthur (based on the novel by Emily Bronte); ph, Gregg Toland; ed, Daniel Mandell; art d, James Vasevi; cos, Omar Kiam

Haunting, beautiful film version of Emily Bronte's tragic novel, with Olivier at his romance period peak, but marred slightly by Oberon's relative lack of passion.

WUTHERING HEIGHTS is a beautifully told story, displaying impeccable talent both in front of and behind the camera. Wyler had been interested in Bronte's story as a vehicle for Charles Boyer and Sylvia Sidney, who had starred in his 1937 film DEAD END. Hecht and MacArthur were assigned to write the film, and they headed for the island home of drama critic Alexander Woolcott. Here they labored to create a script faithful to the novel, though Woolcott was convinced the two writers would destroy Bronte's passionate and poetic story. Wyler eventually got Goldwyn to back the script, though Boyer was no longer being considered for the lead. The next choice was Olivier, a relative unknown to American audiences at the time. Hecht, who was an uncredited writer on QUEEN CHRISTINA, remembered Olivier from that film. The Briton had originally been hired to play opposite Garbo in that film, but was removed from the production in favor of John Gilbert. Olivier was furious, and had harbored ill feelings towards Hollywood ever since. He was interested in the part of Heathcliff however, and agreed to portray the doomed lover only if his wife, Vivien Leigh, could be his Cathy. But Oberon had already been signed for the role, and Goldwyn would not consider firing her. Leigh was offered the role of Olivier's unloved wife instead, but she turned this down, saying she felt more akin to the tragic lead character. Besides, Leigh had already been featured as the lead in several British films and was simply unwilling to step down for Hollywood. Eventually Olivier agreed to take the role, and Leigh ended up playing Scarlett O'Hara in GONE WITH THE WIND that year. Olivier and Oberon had previously appeared together in THE DIVORCE OF LADY X, a 1938 British film; many believe they made an unforgettable romantic duo.

Though the film understandably condenses Bronte's lengthy novel, Goldwyn spared no expense in creating the right atmosphere for the picture. A tract of 450 acres of land in California's Conejo Hills was transformed into authentic-looking English moors. One thousand heather plants were transplanted, and Goldwyn completed his re-creation by building a period manor on the site. However, he switched the novel's period from the original Regency to the Georgian era. His reasoning was simple: the Georgian period was marked by fancier dresses for women, and he was eager to show off Oberon in beautiful costumes. Gregg Toland won an Academy Award for his brilliant photography, a moody black-and-white perfectly suited to the material.

WUTHERING HEIGHTS
(ABISMOS DE PASION)
1953   90m   bw   ★★★★
Romance
Tepeyac   (Mexico)

Irasema Dilian *(Catalina)*, Jorge Mistral *(Alejandro)*, Lilia Prado, Ernesto Alonso, Luis Aceves Castaneda, Francisco Reiguera, Hortensia Santovena, Jaime Gonzalez

p, Oscar Dancigers; d, Luis Bunuel; w, Luis Bunuel, Julio Alejandro, Dino Maiuri (based on the novel by Emily Bronte); ph, Agustin Jiminez; ed, Carlos Savage; m, Raul Lavista, Richard Wagner

Luis Bunuel's long-planned version of Emily Bronte's novel (the screenplay was written some 20 years before the film was made, but no backer could be found), a favorite work of the Surrealists, shifts the setting from the English moors to a small Mexican estate and turns Heathcliff into Alejandro (Jorge Mistral) and Cathy into Catalina (Irasema Dilian). As the Spanish title implies, the lovers fall into an "abyss of passion"—a place where love exists above and beyond all else. Unlike Hollywood's sanitized backlot version of Bronte, Bunuel's reworking is rooted in the darker aspects of love. The film opens with a slow-motion image of crows as they scatter from a twisted, leafless tree, frightened by an off-screen gunshot. This image of death and decay hangs over the film. The film is flawed (the acting is flatter than usual, the emphasis is overly literary), but it is one of the most passionate and expressionistic works of Bunuel's Mexican period, featuring an ending as brilliant as anything ever accomplished by a surrealist artist.

YZ

YAABA

1989 90m c ★★★★
Drama /PG
Arcadia/L'Avenir/Thelma/Suisse Romande TV/ZDF/La
Sept/Centre de la Cinemagraphic/Department des Affaires
Etrangeres/Coe (Burkina Faso)

Fatimata Sanga (Yaaba), Noufou Ouedraogo (Bila), Roukietou
Barry (Nopoko), Adama Ouedraogo (Kougri), Amade Toure (Tibo),
Sibidou Ouedraogo (Poko), Adama Sidibe (Razougou), Rasmane
Ouedraogo (Noaga), Kinda Moumouni (Finse), Assita Ouedraogo
(Koudi)

p, Freddy Denaes, Michel David, Pierre-Alain Meier, Idressa
Ouedraogo; d, Idressa Ouedraogo; w, Idressa Ouedraogo; ph,
Matthias Kalin; ed, Loredana Cristelli; m, Francis Bebey

Set in a village in Burkina Faso, YAABA concerns two young
cousins, Bila (Noufou Ouedraogo) and Nopoko (Roukietou
Barry), whose lives are forever changed by their association with
the mysterious Sana (Fatimata Sanga), an old woman who has
been branded a witch and ostracized by the adults in their village.
While carefully depicting the social codes of the village's quar-
relsome extended family, director Idrissa Ouedraogo pits the
innocence of Bila and Nopoko against the intrigue and superstition among the elders. The curious and sensitive Bila becomes
something of a "problem child" when he develops a relationship
with the outcast Sana—who, far from being a witch, is a contemplative sort given to dispensing small nuggets of wisdom. Bila
savors these nuggets and respectfully calls her "Yaaba" (Grandmother). When Nopoko suffers an injury that leads to an infection
that is misdiagnosed as malaria, Sana journeys to get a healer to
help her. However, the villagers continue to persecute Sana right
up to the film's touching closing.

The winner of the International Critics Prize at the 1989
Cannes Film Festival, YAABA is a visually striking, poignant
film that communicates much through refreshingly economical
means. Director Ouedraogo (YAM DAABO) filmed this elegant
work in his own village, using a nonprofessional cast that renders
uniformly convincing and natural performances. Relying on deft
mise-en-scene, Ouedraogo captures the village's unique rhythms
with precision and wrests great emotional power from the simple
story.

YAKUZA, THE

1975 112m c ★★★½
Crime R/AA
WB/Toei (U.S./Japan)

Robert Mitchum (Harry Kilmer), Ken Takakura (Tanaka Ken), Brian
Keith (George Tanner), Herb Edelman (Oliver Wheat), Richard
Jordan (Dusty), Kishi Keiko (Tanaka Eiko), Okada Eiji (Tono

Toshiro), James Shigeta (Goro), Kyosuke Mashida (Kato Jiro),
Christina Kokubo (Hanako)

p, Sydney Pollack; d, Sydney Pollack; w, Paul Schrader, Robert
Towne (based on a story by Leonard Schrader); ph, Okazaki Kozo,
Duke Callaghan (Panavision, Technicolor); ed, Fredric Steinkamp,
Thomas Stanford, Don Guidice; m, Dave Grusin; prod d, Stephen
Grimes; art d, Ishida Yoshiyuki; fx, Richard Parker, Kasai Tomoo;
cos, Dorothy Jeakins

Interesting and well-acted, if clumsy, American take on the
Japanese gangster genre. Robert Mitchum stars as a private
detective who goes to Japan to rescue an American girl who has
been kidnapped by a yakuza, with Japanese screen idol Ken
Takakura as a former gangster who helps him in his quest. Kishi
Keiko plays a woman with whom Mitchum had had a love affair
while stationed in Japan at the end of WWII, and whom he now
re-encounters.

Written by Paul Schrader from a story by his brother Leonard
(the screenplay was then rewritten by famed script doctor Robert
Towne), THE YAKUZA was a commendable attempt to expose
American audiences to some of the conventions of Japanese
genre films. By making the Ken character an anachronistic
yakuza who still lives by the codes of the past (he's described as
a "lone wolf" by his brother) while trying to exist in present-day
capitalist Japan, the filmmakers were able to interestingly compare ancient rituals and values with more contemporary practices. Director Pollack does a workmanlike job, neither giving
added resonance to the material, nor ruining a good idea with
overbearing direction. His camera is just there to record the
performances and really does little else. This film belongs to the
actors, and they succeed in making it fascinating viewing. Co-
screenwriter Paul Schrader is a student of Japanese culture and
cinema, and his obsession with their notion of honor and sacrifice
climaxed in 1985 with MISHIMA.

YANKEE DOODLE DANDY

1942 126m bw ★★★★★
Musical /U
WB

James Cagney (George M. Cohan), Joan Leslie (Mary), Walter
Huston (Jerry Cohan), Richard Whorf (Sam Harris), George Tobias
(Dietz), Irene Manning (Fay Templeton), Rosemary DeCamp (Nel-
lie Cohan), Jeanne Cagney (Josie Cohan), S.Z. Sakall (Schwab),
George Barbier (Erlanger)

p, William Cagney; d, Michael Curtiz; w, Robert Buckner, Edmund
Joseph (based on a story by Robert Buckner); ph, James Wong
Howe; ed, George Amy; art d, Carl Jules Weyl; chor, LeRoy Prinz,
Seymour Felix, John Boyle; cos, Milo Anderson

The real George M. Cohan had just had a serious operation and
was recuperating at his upstate New York home when he was
shown, in a private screening, this film of his life starring the
indefatigable James Cagney. The great showman watched the
movie without a word. When it was finished he was asked how
he liked it. Cohan grinned, shook his head, and paid the great
Cagney his highest compliment: "My God, what an act to follow!" This beguiling film, which deservedly won Cagney a Best
Actor Oscar, presents an irresistible portrait of song-and-dance
man Cohan and of early 20th-century America. It's heartfelt
entertainment and anyone who ever whistled a tune, tapped a toe
or hummed a bar of music will love it. This was Cagney's favorite
film and his favorite number was, in his own words, "when I did
the 'wings' coming down the stairs at the White House. Didn't

think of it until five minutes before I went on. I didn't consult with the director or anything, I just did it."

YANKS
1979   141m   c   ★★½
War/Romance   R/15
Universal   (U.K.)

Richard Gere *(Matt)*, Lisa Eichhorn *(Jean Moreton)*, Vanessa Redgrave *(Helen)*, William Devane *(John)*, Chick Vennera *(Danny)*, Wendy Morgan *(Mollie)*, Rachel Roberts *(Mrs. Moreton)*, Tony Melody *(Mr. Moreton)*, Martin Smith *(Geoff)*, Philip Whileman *(Billy)*

p, Joseph Janni, Lester Persky; d, John Schlesinger; w, Colin Welland, Walter Bernstein (based on a story by Welland); ph, Dick Bush (Technicolor); ed, Jim Clark; m, Richard Rodney Bennett; prod d, Brian Morris; art d, Milly Burns; chor, Eleanor Fazan; cos, Shirley Russell

This well-made but often-boring movie examines, soap-opera style, a trio of couples. A small English village is thrown for a loop when a bunch of Americans show up, tossing money around and wooing the local women. The first two relationships are creakingly predictable. Gere is a hotshot who falls in love with Eichhorn, the prim daughter of Roberts and Melody. As much as she likes Gere, her heart belongs to her absent boyfriend, Derek Thompson. Devane and Redgrave are both married—to absent spouses. His wife is in the US, and her husband is off fighting. They have a brief affair but realize it's not in the cards. The relationship between Vennera and Morgan escapes the kind of obvious plotting that mars the other two; Vennera is a breath of fresh air, rushing Morgan into bed, and their story is the most passionate and enjoyable of the lot. Several less idyllic moments counterpoint the three love stories: a racist fight at a dance, a snippet of some of the training the soldiers must go through, and a boxing match at a local site. Those scenes stand out only because the rest of the movie is ho-hum. The film pays close attention to detail and the re-creation of the era, however, and the costumes by Shirley Russell won a British Academy Award. In a small role as a Red Cross employee, look for Annie Ross, who teamed with Dave Lambert and Jon Hendricks in the 1960s to form one of the hottest jazz singing group of the era. Bennett's music is properly evocative, with excerpts from swing pieces of the era including "Two O'Clock Jump."

YEAR OF LIVING DANGEROUSLY, THE
1982   115m   c   ★★★★
Adventure/Romance   PG
MGM   (Australia)

Mel Gibson *(Guy Hamilton)*, Sigourney Weaver *(Jill Bryant)*, Linda Hunt *(Billy Kwan)*, Michael Murphy *(Pete Curtis)*, Bembol Roco *(Kumar)*, Domingo Landicho *(Hortono)*, Hermono De Guzman *(Immigration Officer)*, Noel Ferrier *(Wally O'Sullivan)*, Paul Sonkkila *(Kevin Condon)*, Ali Nur *(Ali)*

p, James McElroy; d, Peter Weir; w, David Williamson, Peter Weir, C.J. Koch (based on the novel by Koch); ph, Russell Boyd (Panavision, Metrocolor); ed, Bill Anderson; m, Maurice Jarre; art d, Herbert Pinter; cos, Terry Ryan

Ambitious, gripping, and stylish, THE YEAR OF LIVING DANGEROUSLY falters slightly in its attempts to be thriller, romance, and political tract, and to encompass director Peter Weir's penchant for mysticism all at the same time. Still, it's an excellent film, set in 1965 as Australian reporter Guy Hamilton (Gibson) arrives in Jakarta, Indonesia. His photographer, Billy

Kwan (Hunt), a Chinese-Australian, shows him the ropes, introducing him to the city's poverty and corruption and to various contacts, including Jill Bryant (Weaver), an embassy attache with whom Guy begins a romance. When Jill secures information on the planned Communist coup against President Sukarno and urges Guy to leave, he betrays her confidence and files a major story—for which she is the obvious source. Billy, previously a fence-sitter, now comes out against Sukarno, feeling that he has betrayed Indonesia in much the same way as Guy betrayed Jill (whom Billy also loves). Revolt and reaction explode on all sides.

Weir is only partly successful in attempting to link his various themes symbolically with images of Indonesian shadow puppetry and Billy's advice to "look at the shadows, not at the puppets," but the director indisputably made the right move in his risky casting of the tiny, gravel-voiced Hunt to play Billy Kwan. She eventually (and deservedly) won a Best Supporting Actress Oscar and a New York Film Critics Award for her compelling performance. Physically convincing in the role, Hunt's achievement is not merely cosmetic; her Billy negotiates among a compelling range of motivations and emotions. Gibson and Weaver, too, enjoy two of their few interesting roles to date, and respond to the challenges put them with intensity and intelligence. The film's hot, humid, seedy ambience is nearly palpable, enhancing this fascinating story of Sukarno's downfall. Whatever its shortcomings, THE YEAR OF LIVING DANGEROUSLY is one of those rare contemporary films to embrace a political issue and to aim itself at an audience older than the average shoe size.

YEAR ONE
(ANNO UNO)
1974   123m   c   ★
Biography/Political
Rusconi Film   (Italy)

Luigi Vannucchi *(Alcide De Gasperi)*, Dominique Darel *(Romanoa De Gasperi)*, Rita Calderoni *(Giornalista)*, Valeria Sabel *(Francesca De Gasperi)*, Ennio Balbo *(Ninni)*

d, Roberto Rossellini; w, Roberto Rossellini, Luciano Scaffa, Marcello Mariani; ph, Mario Montuori (Eastmancolor); ed, Jolanda Benvenuti; m, Mario Nascimbene

In the midst of a string of historical pictures made for Italian television, Rossellini directed this biography of political leader De Gasperi for the cinema. Vannucchi coldly portrays the leader who in the postwar years headed the Christian Democratic Party. Dialogue is held to a bare minimum, Rossellini relying on historical documents rather than invention. Gregory Peck was rumored to have been considered for the lead, which at the very least would have made the picture more appealing to American viewers.

YEARLING, THE
1946   134m   c   ★★★★
Drama   /U
MGM

Gregory Peck *(Pa Baxter)*, Jane Wyman *(Ma Baxter)*, Claude Jarman, Jr. *(Jody Baxter)*, Chill Wills *(Buck Forrester)*, Clem Bevans *(Pa Forrester)*, Margaret Wycherly *(Ma Forrester)*, Henry Travers *(Mr. Boyles)*, Forrest Tucker *(Lem Forrester)*, Donn Gift *(Fodderwing)*, Dan White *(Millwheel)* p, Sidney Franklin; d, Clarence Brown; w, Paul Osborn (based on the novel by Marjorie Kinnan Rawlings); ph, Charles Rosher, Leonard Smith, Arthur E. Arling (Technicolor); ed, Harold F. Kress; m, Herbert Stothart; art d, Cedric Gibbons, Paul Groesse; fx, Warren Newcombe, Chester M. Franklin

THE YEARLING is a splendid family film set just after the Civil War in the wilds of southern Florida, where the Baxters—Ma, Pa, and their one surviving child, Jody (Gregory Peck, Jane Wyman, and Claude Jarman)—are having a tough time eking out a living on their small farm. Pa's ambition is to earn enough from his next crop to be able to sink a well nearer the house, so that Ma won't have to tote water. As an only child in the wilderness, Jody needs some company and asks his parents if he might have a pet. When Pa is bitten by a rattlesnake and in danger of dying, Ma and Jody must kill a deer and make an elixir out of its innards. The doe has a fawn, and when Jody begs his parents to allow him to raise the baby, they do. Time passes and the bond between boy and animal deepens, but as the deer grows it begins eating some of the crops so vital to the family's existence. Pa is left with no choice but to tell Jody that the youth must kill his beloved companion. Similar to OLD YELLER in its lessons, THE YEARLING was a huge success and one of MGM's top moneymakers, earning Oscar nominations for Best Film, Best Actor (Peck), and Best Actress (Wyman). Jarman, however, was the only cast member to take home a statuette—as Outstanding Child Actor of 1946. A remarkable film that is truly for the entire family.

YELLOW EARTH

1986 89m c   ★★★½
Drama   /U
World Entertainment Release (China)

Xue Bai (Ciu Qiao), Wang Xueqi (Gu Qing), Tan Tuo (The Father), Liu Qiang (Hanhan)

d, Chen Kaige; w, Zhang Ziliang (based on the essay "Sanwen" by Ke Lan); ph, Zhang Yimou

One of a handful of films by the group of young Chinese directors labeled "the Fifth Generation," YELLOW EARTH is set during the skirmishes between China and Japan prior to WWII. Xueqi plays a communist soldier studying the local folk songs of the Shaanxi province. He settles in the house of Tuo, a farmer who continues to plough his barren land in the hope the gods will reward him with a good crop. Along with Tuo are his 10-year-old son, and 14-year-old daughter, Bai, rumored to have the most beautiful voice in the province. The taciturn family slowly begins to open up to Xueqi as he helps them with their daily work, but the tension between his "progressive" ideals and the time-honored protocols of village life leads to tragedy.

YELLOW EARTH was one of the first "Fifth Generation" films to reach Western eyes and was justifiably celebrated for its daring, colorful visuals and innovative, eye-opening rhythms.

YELLOW SKY

1948 98m bw   ★★★★★
Western   /A
FOX

Gregory Peck (Stretch), Anne Baxter (Mike), Richard Widmark (Dude), Robert Arthur (Bull Run), John Russell (Lengthy), Harry Morgan (Half Pint), James Barton (Grandpa), Charles Kemper (Walrus), Robert Adler (Jed), Victor Kilian (Bartender)

p, Lamar Trotti; d, William A. Wellman; w, Lamar Trotti (based on the novel by W.R. Burnett); ph, Joseph MacDonald; ed, Harmon Jones; m, Alfred Newman; art d, Lyle Wheeler, Albert Hogsett; fx, Fred Sersen

Set in the post-Civil War Old West, the film begins as Peck leads a band of seven masked desperadoes in a bank robbery. Loading the bullion into their saddlebags, the robbers gallop off, the US Cavalry in hot pursuit. An enormous salt flat is the outlaws' only conceivable avenue of escape, so Peck leads his men into the arid, sun-blistered area. Reining their horses, the pursuing troopers abort the chase, believing the gang to be as good as dead. The bandits' transit through the waterless sea is a painful, difficult one. They walk their parched, weary steeds; Peck pours a little precious water from his nearly empty canteen onto his neckerchief and wipes the saline rime from his mount's mouth. Their water gone, the dehydrated desperadoes chance upon a ghost town, heralded by a sign that reads "Yellow Sky—fastest growing town in the territory." The town is completely deserted, save for dotty old prospector Barton and his tomboy granddaughter Baxter. Greed for both the gold and the girl causes dissension among the men, a situation further exacerbated when Barton hides the outlaws' loot. Villain Widmark makes a try at wresting the role of leader from Peck and poses a threat to both beautiful Baxter and her grandfather. In a showdown, Widmark and one of his partisans are gunned down by the quick-drawing Peck. Driven by a desire to reform through his association with the small family, Peck returns to the bank to return the gold he and his band had stolen.

The unlikely ending doesn't injure this brilliantly filmed and directed Western, which qualifies as one of the best of the genre. The high-contrast black-and-white photography by MacDonald is stunning; the salt-flat scenes made audiences run to the theater lobby water fountain. Dialogue is all the more telling for being sparse; the story is carried visually. As actor Peck said of director Wellman, who had started his career with silent films, he was "another master of the art of telling a story with pictures. Words are. . . of secondary importance to these pioneer directors." Wellman's fine cast tells the tale in delicate nuances. The music by Newman is fine, beginning the action of each scene, then fading as stark realism takes hold and only natural sounds are heard. Peck is thoroughly believable in a part which contrasts so greatly with many of his others. Tanned and lined, etched with fatigue and thirst, his usually pallid countenance completely altered by makeup artist Nye's fine simulation of the ravages of weather, the leadership qualities of Peck's strong, short-of-speech badman are never in doubt. Basically a formula Western, the film was transmuted into a movie of major impact by the talents of its production staff and its cast. Baxter (an Oscar winner two years previously for her Best Supporting role in THE RAZOR'S EDGE) had begun her screen career at the age of 17 in a 1940 western, TWENTY MULE TEAM. Her naively hoydenish characterization here is wonderful. In his first film in this genre, Widmark plays the sort of smiling psychopath that brought him fame in his screen debut, KISS OF DEATH. The supporting cast members all do a fine job. Screenwriter Trotti and author Burnett received an award from the Writers Guild of America for Best Written American Western of the year. The versatile Wellman, director of such cinematic masterpieces as PUBLIC ENEMY and A STAR IS BORN—which he also wrote—demonstrates motion picture alchemy here as he takes basic western dross and turns it into gold. A less-than-successful remake with a South African setting, THE JACKALS, starring Vincent Price and Dana Ivarson, was made in 1967.

YELLOW SUBMARINE
1968   85m   c   ★★★½
Animated/Musical   G/U
King Features/Subafilms   (U.K.)

Paul McCartney, John Lennon, Ringo Starr, George Harrison *(The Beatles)*. VOICES OF: John Clive *(John)*, Geoffrey Hughes *(Paul)*, Peter Batten *(George)*, Paul Angelis *(Ringo/Chief Blue Meanie)*, Dick Emery *(Lord Mayor/Nowhere Man/Max)*, Lance Percival *(Old Fred)*

p, Al Brodax; d, George Dunning; w, Lee Minoff, Al Brodax, Erich Segal, Jack Mendelsohn (based on a story by Minoff, from the song by John Lennon and Paul McCartney); ph, John Williams (DeLuxe Color); ed, Brian J. Bishop; art d, Heinz Edelmann; fx, Charles Jenkins; anim, Jack Stokes, Robert Balser

A zesty, satisfying celebration of animation, fantasy, love, and the Beatles that pleases the eyes as much as the ears. YELLOW SUBMARINE tells the glorious tale of a make-believe world inhabited by Blue Meanies, a wicked little bunch who suck the color out of people and bop them on the heads with apples. The Beatles and Old Fred are called in to stop the Blue Meanies' rage. The singing heroes hop in their yellow submarine and sail the seas—of green, of science, of time, of monsters, and, best of all, of holes—until they finally reach Pepperland and straighten out the villains by overpowering them with love, love, love. The animation is superb, filled with exciting and unexpected transformations that are thoughtfully complemented by the music. The Fab Four themselves appear in the live-action coda. This was the first animated feature made in Britain in 14 years; no wonder everyone got a hand in it. Director Dunning contributed the memorable "Lucy" section himself. Erich Segal, who wrote the fast-food romance *Love Story*, had a hand in the script.

YENTL
1983   134m   c   ★★★
Musical   PG
Ladbroke/Barwood

Barbra Streisand *(Yentl)*, Mandy Patinkin *(Avigdor)*, Amy Irving *(Hadass)*, Nehemiah Persoff *(Papa)*, Steven Hill *(Reb Alter Vishkower)*, Allan Corduner *(Shimmele)*, Ruth Goring *(Esther Rachel)*, David De Keyser *(Rabbi Zalman)*, Bernard Spear *(Tailor)*, Doreen Mantle *(Mrs. Shaemen)*

p, Barbra Streisand, Rusty Lemorande; d, Barbra Streisand; w, Barbra Streisand, Jack Rosenthal (based on the short story "Yentl, the Yeshiva Boy" by Isaac Bashevis Singer); ph, David Watkin (Technicolor); ed, Terry Rawlings; m, Michel Legrand; prod d, Roy Walker; art d, Leslie Tomkins; fx, Alan Whibley; chor, Gillian Lynne; cos, Judy Moorcroft

Isaac Bashevis Singer's beautiful short story "Yentl, the Yeshiva Boy" is turned into a musical ego trip in Barbra Streisand's directorial debut. Set in Eastern Europe in 1904, the story concerns the fortunes of Yentl (Streisand), a girl who wants to study the Torah. Strict Jewish law prohibits such knowledge for women, but Yentl won't give in to community pressure, so, after the death of her father, she disguises herself as a young man and leaves home, hoping to be accepted into a yeshiva. In this guise, she falls in love with fellow student Avigdor (Mandy Patinkin), who takes a liking to young Yentl, but never realizes that his friend is really a woman. When Avigdor's engagement to Hadass (Amy Irving) breaks off because her parents disapprove of him, Avigdor asks Yentl to marry Hadass in his stead. Yentl does so, stalling consummation of the union and attempting to teach Hadass the Torah, but finds her bride's increasing desires more

than she can bear. Eventually, she reveals her secret to an angry Avigdor, who returns to Hadass and, in time, accepts Yentl for who she really is. Yentl leaves for America, hoping to continue her studies in the New World.

Streisand has undertaken an extremely ambitious project to mark her directorial debut and, while far from perfect, the superstar performer shows undeniable promise. The production values are topflight but Streisand lacks visual skill and relies on the musical numbers to link episodes and detail character motivation. In the opening sequences these songs, all sung by Streisand and structured as musical soliloquies, work quite well but they later become repetitious and intrusive—important characters are tossed aside to make room for her to belt out another tune. In all fairness, however, Streisand is actually quite credible in her role and she elicits beautifully shaded performances from a large cast, particularly Patinkin and Irving. Streisand owned the movie rights to Singer's story for 14 years and finally acquired the clout to bring the project to life after many years of trying. Singer was appalled by the end result, a fate that has befallen many an author adapted by Hollywood.

YESTERDAY, TODAY, AND TOMORROW
(IERI, OGGI E DOMANI)
1963   119m   c   ★★★
Comedy/Drama   /X
C.C. Champion/Concordia   (Italy/France)

Sophia Loren *(Adelina/Anna/Mara)*, Marcello Mastroianni *(Carmine/Renzo/Augusto Rusconi)*, Aldo Giuffre *(Pasquale Nardella)*, Agostino Salvietti *(Lawyer Verace)*, Lino Mattera *(Amadeo Scapece)*, Tecla Scarano *(Bianchina Verace)*, Silvia Monelli *(Elvira Nardella)*, Carlo Croccolo *(Auctioneer)*, Pasquale Cennamo *(Police Captian)*, Armando Trovajoli *(Other Man)*

p, Carlo Ponti; d, Vittorio De Sica; w, Eduardo De Filippo, Isabella Quarantotti, Cesare Zavattini, Billa Billa Zanuso (based on the story "Troppo Ricca" by Alberto Moravia); ph, Giuseppe Rotunno (Techniscope, Technicolor); ed, Adriana Novelli; m, Armando Trovajoli; art d, Ezio Frigerio; chor, Jacques Ruet; cos, Piero Tosi, Christian Dior, Annamode, Jean Barthet

This Italian sex trilogy teams up two of that country's biggest stars, Sophia Loren and Marcello Mastroianni, with director Vittorio De Sica. The first and most interesting episode, "Adelina," features Loren as the title Neopolitan who is in trouble with the law and Mastroianni as her husband who discovers a legal loophole: pregnant women cannot be jailed until six months after the child's birth. Adelina duly gets pregnant, and pregnant again, and so on until her mate can no longer take it. "Anna" casts Loren as the Milanese wife of an industrialist who drops her lover (Mastroianni) after he nearly wrecks her beloved sports car. Lastly, in "Mara," the eponymous Roman prostitute (Loren) resists the temptation to seduce a young seminarian (Giovanni Ridolfi) who has fallen in love with her and even takes a one-week vow of chastity herself, much to the frustration of her most devoted client (Mastroianni). Although YESTERDAY, TODAY AND TOMORROW won a Best Foreign-Language Film Academy Award, it's hardly representative of the best work of its stars, director (UMBERTO D, THE BICYCLE THIEF, SHOESHINE), or screenwriters (Cesare Zavattini, De Sica's frequent collaborator, contributes "Anna" and "Mara"). It is, however, an enjoyable romp, buoyed by the professionalism of all concerned.

YESTERDAY'S ENEMY

1959 95m bw ★★★★
War /A
Hammer (U.K.)

Stanley Baker (Capt. Langford), Guy Rolfe (Padre), Leo McKern (Max), Gordon Jackson (Sgt. MacKenzie), David Oxley (Doctor), Richard Pasco (2nd Lt. Hastings), Russell Waters (Brigadier), Philip Ahn (Yamazaki), Bryan Forbes (Dawson), Wolfe Morris (Informer)

p, Michael Carreras; d, Val Guest; w, Peter R. Newman (based on his television play); ph, Arthur Grant (MegaScope); ed, James Needs, Alfred Cox; art d, Bernard Robinson, Don Mingaye

This disturbing WWII film focuses on the survivors of a battle-decimated brigade as they try to make their way through the Burmese jungle to rejoin the main British force. Led by Baker, the survivors come upon a village where they surprise a small Japanese detachment. Found on a dead Japanese colonel is a coded map that details future Japanese battle strategy. Baker interrogates a captured Burmese agent, demanding an explanation of the code. The prisoner refuses to talk, so Baker carries through a threat to shoot two innocent villagers. In the wake of these executions, the prisoner confesses all. Rolfe and McKern, a priest and reporter, respectively, are appalled by Baker's sadistic actions. Baker tries to get the information to divisional headquarters, but he and his men are captured by Japanese troops. Now Baker is on the receiving end of similar torture. When Baker refuses to talk, the Japanese kill him and his men.

YESTERDAY'S ENEMY takes an unflinching look at the effects of war on the human psyche. Applying their own standards to a situation unlike any either of them has experienced, Rolfe and McKern are unable to fathom Baker's actions. Yet there is no right and wrong in Baker's act. Instead, his brutality is depicted as an evil that has become necessary at a specific moment. The perverse irony of war then reverses the entire situation. Guest's direction is excellent—particularly his skillful building of tension—and the ensemble performances are riveting. Though shot in the studio, the film is highly realistic, putting the viewer in the midst of the Burmese jungle.

YOJIMBO

1961 110m bw ★★★½
Action /A
Toho/Kurosawa (Japan)

Toshiro Mifune (Sanjuro Kuwabatake), Eijiro Tono (Gonji the Sake Seller), Seizaburo Kawazu (Seibei), Isuzu Yamada (Orin), Hiroshi Tachikawa (Yoichiro), Kyu Sazanka (Ushitora), Daisuke Kato (Inokichi), Tatsuya Nakadai (Unosuke), Kamatari Fujiwara (Tazaemon), Takashi Shimura (Tokuemon)

d, Akira Kurosawa; w, Akira Kurosawa, Ryuzo Kikushima, Hideo Oguni; ph, Kazuo Miyagawa (Tohoscope); m, Masaru Sato; art d, Yoshiro Muraki; cos, Yoshiro Muraki

Directed by Japanese master Akira Kurosawa, YOJIMBO is the spirited, strangely moralistic tale of Sanjuro Kuwabatake (Toshiro Mifune), a samurai who wanders into a town divided by a civil war. On one side stands silk merchant Tazaemon (Kamatari Fujiwara), on the other sake merchant Tokuemon (Takashi Shimura)—both equally evil. Sanjuro views their conflict as an opportunity to make some money and secure food and lodging. Hired by Tazaemon as a yojimbo (bodyguard), Sanjro puts a devious plan of his own into effect, pretending to enter the employ of Tokuemon, then secretly killing some of his men. Sanjuro is caught, however, brutally beaten, and tossed in prison.

He escapes, in time to witness the momentous battle between the two factions that ultimately brings peace to the war-ravaged village. Kurosawa's entertaining direction, Kazuo Miyagawa's beautiful widescreen photography, and Mifune's eccentric acting combined to make YOJIMBO such a box-office success that Toho Studios asked the director to make another film along similar lines. The result was SANJURO, which again starred Mifune as an unorthodox samurai.

YOL

1981 111m c ★★★½
Drama PG/15
Guney/Cactus (Turkey)

Tarik Akan (Seyit Ali), Halil Ergun (Mehmet Salih), Necmettin Cobanoglu (Omer), Serif Sezer (Zine), Meral Orhousoy (Emine), Semra Ucar (Gulbahar), Hikmet Celik (Mevlut)

p, Edi Hubschmid, K.L. Puldi; d, Serif Goren; w, Yilmaz Guney; ph, Erdogan Engin (Fujicolor); ed, Yilmaz Guney, Elisabeth Waelchli; m, Sebastian Argol, Kendal

Five Turkish convicts are given a week's leave from prison to visit their loved ones in this extraordinarily painful drama. What has promised to be an emotionally uplifting period of freedom takes a disastrous and tragic turn for each of the prisoners, one of whom comes home to find that his brother has been murdered by police, while another learns of his wife's infidelity. A visually intense examination of Turkish mores and customs (the scene of the prisoner dragging his unfaithful wife into a snowy wasteland is both powerful and alien for Western audiences), YOL was written by actor-turned-director Yilmaz Guney while he was behind bars and directed by one of Guney's former assistants under his supervision. Guney escaped from prison in 1981, and died three years later, after completing his final picture, THE WALL. YOL shared the top prize at Cannes with Costa-Gavras's MISSING, another grim tale of political oppression.

YOU CAN'T CHEAT AN HONEST MAN

1939 76m bw ★★★½
Comedy /U
Universal

W.C. Fields (Larson E. Whipsnade), Edgar Bergen, Charlie McCarthy, Mortimer Snerd, Pietro Blacaman, Princess Baba (Themselves), Constance Moore (Vicky Whipsnade), Mary Forbes (Mrs. Bel-Goodie), Thurston Hall (Archibald Bel-Goodie), John Arledge (Phineas Whipsnade)

p, Lester Cowan; d, George Marshall, Edward F. Cline (uncredited); w, George Marion, Jr., Richard Mack, Everett Freeman (based on a story by W.C. Fields); ph, Milton Krasner; ed, Otto Ludwig; art d, Jack Otterson; cos, Vera West

Universal Studios waved big money under comedian Fields's legendary proboscis and wooed him away from Paramount. In his first film for his new studio, Fields returned to the kind of character he loved best—a terminally broke and nomadic huckster who must live by his wits to stay one step ahead of the law. Owner of "Larson E. Whipsnade's Circus Giganticus," Fields is first seen hustling his caravan of wagons over the county line to escape the police he had angered at his previous stop. While setting up tents in a new town, Fields is confronted by ventriloquist Bergen and his smart-aleck dummy Charlie McCarthy. The two are the bane of Fields's existence, but he cannot fire them because of a strange clause in their contract. Luckily for Fields, Bergen has decided to quit because he hasn't been paid in months.

The ventriloquist quickly changes his mind, however, when he meets Fields's beautiful daughter, Moore.

Like most Fields vehicles, YOU CAN'T CHEAT AN HONEST MAN is a virtually plotless array of hilarious verbal and visual gags designed to make the most of the comedian's prodigious talents. The script was actually a reworking of two previous projects, a rejected screenplay titled "Grease Paint," written by H.M. Walker in 1933, with added plot lines from Fields' silent movie TWO FLAMING YOUTHS. Once again Fields wrote the story under the pseudonym of "Charles Bogle," but Universal and director Marshall removed several important scenes that Fields felt were essential to his character development. In the film, Fields seems to be an entirely unlikable character with little or no compassion for his workers or family. In the script, Fields began the film with a tender scene where his wife, a trapeze artist who has suffered a fall, dies in his arms. Despite—or perhaps because of—trimmings of this nature, YOU CAN'T CHEAT is one of Fields's most sustained comic triumphs, containing several classic moments.

YOU CAN'T TAKE IT WITH YOU
1938 126m bw   ★★★½
Comedy   /U
Columbia

Jean Arthur (Alice Sycamore), Lionel Barrymore (Martin Vanderhof), James Stewart (Tony Kirby), Edward Arnold (Anthony P. Kirby), Mischa Auer (Kolenkhov), Ann Miller (Essie Carmichael), Spring Byington (Penny Sycamore), Samuel S. Hinds (Paul Sycamore), Donald Meek (Poppins), H.B. Warner (Ramsey)

p, Frank Capra; d, Frank Capra; w, Robert Riskin (based on the play by George S. Kaufman and Moss Hart); ph, Joseph Walker; ed, Gene Havlick; m, Dimitri Tiomkin; art d, Stephen Goosson; cos, Bernard Newman, Irene

Frank Capra took the phenomenally successful (if somewhat overrated) Kaufman-Hart stage play "You Can't Take It with You" and turned it into this well-received (if somewhat overrated) film. Amazingly, it garnered Capra his third Oscar for Best Director, as well as winning the Best Picture Oscar (it was also nominated for Best Supporting Actress [Byington], screenplay, cinematography, editing, and sound recording).

Barrymore is the eccentric patriarch of a clan of frustrated artists who decided 30 years earlier to retire from the rat-race and use his fortune to encourage friends and family to pursue vocations that really interest them. He has taken up painting, which he does badly, but at least he enjoys himself. His daughter, Byington, has taken up writing mystery novels, which she was inspired to do when a typewriter was left on the doorstep one day. Byington's husband, Hinds, tinkers with explosives in the basement, working towards perfecting the Roman Candle and the rocket. Their daughter Miller desires to be a ballet dancer, and her cynical Russian teacher, Auer, follows her around barking instructions. Miller's husband, Dub Taylor, practices playing the xylophone, while Barrymore's friend Meek invents new toys and party masks. The huge house is a frenzy of bizarre activities and in the center of it all is Barrymore's other granddaughter, Arthur, who is pursuing a relatively normal life by working as a receptionist in the offices of Arnold, a powerful, very dour businessman who has been known to make shady deals and wants to have Barrymore's mansion torn down so he can build on the property. Arthur is in love with Arnold's son Stewart, and while Stewart is amused at her family's eccentricities, he fears that his father will never approve of a girl from such a family. The couple decides to arrange a dinner for the families to be held at Arthur's

house, and Barrymore commands the clan to tone down their normal antics in order to make a good impression on Arnold and his stuffy wife, Mary Forbes. Unfortunately, there is confusion over the date of the dinner, and Stewart shows up with his parents a day early. As Arthur and her family rush around to prepare a decent dinner for their guests, Arnold and Forbes become mortified at the strange goings-on. Before the guests can leave, Hinds accidentally sets off a flurry of fireworks in the basement and the whole neighborhood is treated to the show. The police arrive and cart everyone off to jail, including an outraged Arnold and Forbes. Luckily, everyone is eventually released by a bemused judge, but Stewart's parents force him to break up with Arthur. Worried that she will never have a normal life if she stays in the house, Arthur decides to leave, but she is dissuaded by Barrymore, who tells her he's decided to sell the mansion to Arnold and move the clan to the country. Meanwhile Stewart, angry with his father because of the situation with Arthur and the fact that he has discovered his father's shady business dealings, lets loose with a tirade of insults at Arnold and concludes that his father has become a heartless monster. A heartfelt talk from Barrymore, though, is all that is needed to save the day for all concerned.

YOU CAN'T TAKE IT WITH YOU is an entertaining, if saccharine film, packed with enough loony activity to keep the laughs coming from start to finish. Capra assembled a superb cast of players, and all score solidly in their roles, even if their behavior doesn't today seem as anarchic as it must have then. Capra himself, however, doesn't do as well, turning out a stagey product that represents one of his lesser directorial efforts. Perhaps the most amusing character in the film is Meek, a milquetoast of a man who enjoys sneaking up on family members and scaring them with his latest Halloween mask. YOU CAN'T TAKE IT WITH YOU was the first film for veteran actor Barrymore in which the crippling arthritis which would soon put him in a wheelchair became evident. To remedy the situation, Capra had a fake leg cast put on the actor and explained it by having him state that he broke his leg while sliding down a bannister—just the kind of reckless, carefree act one would expect from his character. Character actor Dub Taylor, who has appeared in hundreds of films and television shows, made his acting debut in this film.

YOU ONLY LIVE ONCE
1937 86m bw   ★★★★
Crime   /A
UA

Sylvia Sidney (Joan Graham), Henry Fonda (Eddie Taylor), Barton MacLane (Stephen Whitney), Jean Dixon (Bonnie Graham), William Gargan (Father Dolan), Warren Hymer (Muggsy), Charles "Chic" Sale (Ethan), Margaret Hamilton (Hester), Guinn "Big Boy" Williams (Rogers), Jerome Cowan (Dr. Hill)

p, Walter Wanger; d, Fritz Lang; w, Gene Towne, Graham Baker (based on a story by Towne); ph, Leon Shamroy; ed, Daniel Mandell; m, Alfred Newman; art d, Alexander Toluboff

This brooding and powerful tale, which suggests the story of Bonnie and Clyde, is one of Lang's best efforts in Hollywood. Fonda and Sidney are excellent as the average Depression-era couple made into criminals through circumstances and just plain bad luck. Fonda is not the average law-abiding citizen, however; he has committed many robberies in the past and has served three prison terms. He vows, however, that he is going straight. He gets a job and marries his patient, long-time sweetheart, Sidney. But his past catches up with him when his landlord turns him and his wife out of their room after finding out he has a record. Soon after, his employer at the trucking firm fires him. Then Fonda's hat is found at the scene of a bank holdup where a guard has been killed. He is quickly tried and sentenced to death. Once in prison, Fonda resolves to fight back against a system that offers him no way of surviving. He pretends to be ill and is sent to the prison hospital. There he obtains a gun and uses the prison doctor as a shield to get to the prison yard. The prison chaplain runs to him to say that he has been pardoned but by then Fonda will believe nothing any authority figure tells him. He thinks the chaplain is trying to hoodwink him into surrendering and, when the priest makes the wrong move, Fonda fires, killing the chaplain. He manages to escape the prison and rejoin wife Sidney. Together they drive toward the Canadian border, trying to get out of a country that has persecuted and hounded them. They do manage to reach the border but their joy is only momentary. A sharpshooting member of the New York State Police raises his rifle and spots the fugitives through his telescopic sights. He fires several rounds which mortally wound both Fonda and Sidney. Sidney is first hit and Fonda takes her in his arms, carrying her the last few steps into Canada, freedom, and death for both of them. This tragedy is distinguished by Lang's meticulous direction and carefully constructed scenes. Fonda gives a terrific performance as the social pariah fighting for his very existence. Sidney's performance is poignant and beautiful. It was once stated that this superb actress had the face of the Great Depression, and this film is undoubtedly the reason for the sobriquet. There is little mirth in this film loaded with permanent steel-gray skies, and the director's murky, diffused shots suggest a kind of unbearable futility to life. His figures, especially in the prison escape scenes, are hazy, almost transparent, as mist covers the yard and searchlights reach out for Fonda who moves like a ghost before them. Fonda held Lang in high regard as a director but felt that Lang pushed his actors too hard in his quest to attain perfection, causing, in the 46-day shooting schedule of this film, his cast and crew to go without sleep and to physically exhaust themselves to achieve the effect he desired. There is a grimness to this film that is often overwhelming, and though it is technically flawless, it offers little hope to the viewer for satisfaction. Justice is not served here, only irony.

YOU WERE NEVER LOVELIER

1942 97m bw   ★★★½
Musical   /U
Columbia

Fred Astaire (*Robert Davis*), Rita Hayworth (*Maria Acuna*), Adolphe Menjou (*Edwardo Acuna*), Leslie Brooks (*Cecy Acuna*), Adele Mara (*Lita Acuna*), Isobel Elsom (*Mrs. Maria Castro*), Gus Schilling (*Fernando*), Barbara Brown (*Mrs. Delfina Acuna*), Douglas Leavitt (*Juan Castro*), Catherine Craig (*Julia Acuna*)

p, Louis F. Edelman; d, William A. Seiter; w, Michael Fessier, Ernest Pagano, Delmer Daves (based on the story and screenplay "The Gay Senorita" by Carlos Olivari, Sixto Pondal Rios); ph, Ted Tetzlaff; ed, William Lyon; m, Jerome Kern; art d, Lionel Banks, Rudolph Sternad; chor, Val Raset; cos, Irene

The second and last screen pairing of Fred Astaire and Rita Hayworth features the former as Robert Davis, an American dancer stranded in Buenos Aires. Desperate for funds (he lost his money gambling), he seeks work at the hotel owned by Edwardo Acuna (Adolphe Menjou), where Xavier Cugat and His Orchestra are currently playing. Edwardo, however, has more pressing matters to deal with: his eldest daughter is about to wed and his two youngest want to, but his second child, Maria (Hayworth), is ruining everyone's plans. Edwardo has a strict rule for his

children: they must marry in order of their age, and Maria's romantic ideals are so lofty no man can measure up to them. Edwardo has been secretly sending her flowers and love notes, hoping to put a dent in her fantasies. Robert is mistaken for a messenger and sent to deliver the latest bouquet, and Maria thinks he's her mystery man. Edwardo now hires Robert to play Maria's secret admirer, but idealistic Maria has a counter to every argument for marriage. More complications arise when Mrs. Acuna starts wondering who her spouse has been sending *billets-doux*, but all works out happily in the end, of course. Hayworth is a wonderful complement to Astaire in the dance numbers, gliding about the floor with natural ease and looking ravishing. Her singing is dubbed for the film by Nan Wynn. The film gained Oscar nominations for the sound, the Jerome Kern score, and the musical direction by Leigh Harline.

YOUNG AND INNOCENT

1938 84m bw   ★★★½
Crime   /U
G.B./Gaumont (U.K.)

Nova Pilbeam (*Erica Burgoyne*), Derrick de Marney (*Robert Tisdall*), Percy Marmont (*Col. Burgoyne*), Edward Rigby (*Old Will*), Mary Clare (*Aunt Margaret*), John Longden (*Inspector Kent*), George Curzon (*Guy*), Basil Radford (*Uncle Basil*), Pamela Carme (*Christine Clay*), George Merritt (*Sgt. Miller*)

p, Edward Black; d, Alfred Hitchcock; w, Charles Bennett, Alma Reville, Anthony Armstrong, Edwin Greenwood, Gerald Savory (based on the novel *A Schilling for Candles* by Josephine Tey); ph, Bernard Knowles; ed, Charles Frend; m, Louis Levy; art d, Alfred Junge

One of Hitchcock's more charming efforts, this thriller stars the endearing 18-year-old Pilbeam as Erica Burgoyne, the daughter of police constable Col. Burgoyne (Marmount), who is heading an investigation into the strangulation death of an actress whose body has washed ashore, along with the murder weapon—the belt of a raincoat. The prime, and in fact only, suspect is Robert Tisdall (de Marney) who maintains his innocence, despite the fact that everything is against him—he was friendly with the dead woman, he was included in her will, and his raincoat is missing. After giving the suspect a ride to a desolate farmhouse, Erica is faced with the choice of helping Tisdall prove his innocence, despite her fear of the repercussions of her father and his office. Naturally she finds herself falling in love with him, and he with her, and together the young and innocent fugitives must steer clear of the authorities and find the real murderer. While not generally considered one of Hitchcock's finer films, YOUNG AND INNOCENT, because of its simplicity (or innocence, in keeping with the title), is often overlooked, especially in light of the director's other British successes, THE MAN WHO KNEW TOO MUCH, THE 39 STEPS, and THE LADY VANISHES. Although its plot is simply a reworking of THE 39 STEPS without the spy angle, YOUNG AND INNOCENT has a certain delightful charm to it, due entirely to the young Pilbeam, with her glowing Sylvia Sidney-type face. The film also boasts some of Hitchcock's most memorable visual effects, namely a remarkable crane and dolly shot which travels across a grand ballroom and into the face of the murderer with his twitching eye.

YOUNG AT HEART

1955 117m c   ★★★
Musical   /U
Arwin

Doris Day *(Laurie Tuttle)*, Frank Sinatra *(Barney Sloan)*, Gig Young *(Alex Burke)*, Ethel Barrymore *(Aunt Jessie)*, Dorothy Malone *(Fran Tuttle)*, Robert Keith *(Gregory Tuttle)*, Elisabeth Fraser *(Amy Tuttle)*, Alan Hale, Jr. *(Robert Neary)*, Lonny Chapman *(Ernest Nichols)*, Frank Ferguson *(Bartell)*

p, Henry Blanke; d, Gordon Douglas; w, Liam O'Brien (based on the screenplay for the film FOUR DAUGHTERS by Julius J. Epstein, Lenore Coffee, from the story "Sister Act" by Fanny Hurst); ph, Ted McCord (Warner Color); ed, William Ziegler; art d, John Beckman; fx, H.F. Koenekamp; cos, Howard Shoup

This is a smooth but empty musical remake of 1938's FOUR DAUGHTERS, sans one daughter. Laurie Tuttle (Doris Day) and sisters Fran and Amy (Dorothy Malone and Elizabeth Fraser) live with their father (Robert Keith) and Aunt Jessie (Ethel Barrymore). When Alex Burke (Gig Young), a composer working on a musical comedy, arrives on the scene, both Laurie and Fran fall in love with him. Alex calls in a friend, the embittered pianist and composer Barney Sloan (Frank Sinatra), to help him arrange the musical's score, and Barney promptly falls for Laurie, who has gotten engaged to Alex. On the eve of her wedding to Alex, however, Laurie finds out about Fran's feelings for Alex; Laurie then nobly backs out of the wedding and heads for the city with Barney. They get married, and in time she comes to love him truly, though he is unconvinced of the sincerity of her emotion. Bad luck strikes again and again, until Barney finally comes to have faith in Laurie's love and they embark on married life anew. Despite all the talent involved, this soap opera fails to generate much interest, especially since Day and Sinatra generate few sparks.

YOUNG CASSIDY
1965 108m c   ★★★
Biography   /A
Sextant (U.S./U.K.)

Rod Taylor *(John Cassidy)*, Flora Robson *(Mrs. Cassidy)*, Jack MacGowran *(Archie)*, Sian Phillips *(Ella)*, T.P. McKenna *(Tom)*, Julie Ross *(Sara)*, Robin Sumner *(Michael)*, Philip O'Flynn *(Mick Mullen)*, Maggie Smith *(Nora)*, Julie Christie *(Daisy Battles)*

p, Robert D. Graff, Robert Emmett Ginna; d, Jack Cardiff, John Ford; w, John Whiting (based on the autobiography *Mirror in My House* by Sean O'Casey); ph, Ted Scaife (Metrocolor); ed, Anne V. Coates; m, Sean O'Riada; art d, Michael Stringer; cos, Margaret Furse

The massive 13-volume autobiography of Irish playwright and rebel Sean O'Casey serves as the source material for this film. Taylor is a young Irishman from a poor family. He spends his days digging ditches and his nights at political meetings and reading books. He eventually turns his attention away from fighting the British to writing pamphlets against them. When a riot, sparked by a Taylor pamphlet, breaks out, Taylor meets Christie, a music hall dancer, and they enter into an affair. After a time he leaves her and takes up with Smith, the owner of a small bookshop Taylor frequents. His plays are produced at the Abbey Theatre, and he comes to the attention of the literary world. Yet he constantly struggles against his own background in poverty and tries to keep from being co-opted by the literary establishment. When his play "The Plough and the Stars" is produced, the audience riots, but later it is hailed as a work of brilliance. As the film ends, Taylor is leaving his home for England and international acclaim. Although the film carries a title at the beginning claiming this as "A John Ford Film," the great director's contributions are small, totaling less than 10 minutes of screen time.

Although he was not in great health and was thoroughly occupied with making CHEYENNE AUTUMN, Ford jumped at the chance to direct this film, offering to forego his usual fee for a mere $50,000. When the shooting of CHEYENNE AUTUMN was complete, Ford went to Ireland to look over locations. He drank steadily on the flight to Dublin, and when he got off the airplane, the producers of the film, Robert Ginna and Robert Graff, whom Ford came to call "the Bobs," had trouble believing that the drunken, unshaven man who stumbled off the airplane was really Ford. Ford had only a week to spend in Dublin before returning to California for the premiere of CHEYENNE AUTUMN. When the Bobs expressed their dismay over the little time Ford could give them, the crusty director replied, "What do you expect for a lousy 50 grand?" When he returned to Ireland after the disastrous reception of CHEYENNE AUTUMN, he worked only 13 days on the film before falling ill. The Bobs, who had never had much faith in Ford after that initial meeting, were just as happy when they replaced him with Jack Cardiff. The film is unsuccessful on a number of counts, but mainly in that it lacks a focal point. The performances are good, though, especially those of Taylor and Christie.

YOUNG DR. KILDARE
1938 81m bw   ★★★½
Drama   /A
MGM

Lew Ayres *(Dr. James Kildare)*, Lionel Barrymore *(Dr. Leonard Gillespie)*, Lynne Carver *(Alice Raymond)*, Nat Pendleton *(Joe Wayman)*, Jo Ann Sayers *(Barbara Chanler)*, Samuel S. Hinds *(Dr. Stephen Kildare)*, Emma Dunn *(Mrs. Martha Kildare)*, Walter Kingsford *(Dr. Walter Carew)*, Nella Walker *(Mrs. Chanler)*, Pierre Watkin *(Mr. Chanler)*

p, Lou Ostrow; d, Harold S. Bucquet; w, Harry Ruskin, Willis Goldbeck (based on characters created by Max Brand); ph, John Seitz; ed, Elmo Veron; m, David Snell; art d, Cedric Gibbons, Malcolm Brown

Newly graduated from medical school, Ayres returns to his home town and the prospect of joining his father's medical practice. To the disappointment of his parents and his sweetheart, Carver, Ayres elects to accept a proffered internship in a large New York City hospital. There he incurs adverse publicity in the newspapers when a powerful politician dies while under his care. He is exonerated of blame when it is discovered that an ambulance attendant failed to follow Ayres's orders to administer oxygen to the alcoholic politician. Crusty old wheelchair-bound diagnostician Barrymore takes the young man under his abrasive wing, to Ayres's discomfort. (Ayres has yet to learn that Barrymore's bark is directed mostly at those in whom he sees some potential.) One of Ayres's patients is Sayers, daughter of wealthy Watkin and Walker. Sayers has attempted suicide, and eminent psychiatrist Monty Woolley has adjudged her mentally unbalanced, decreeing that she be institutionalized. Ayres disagrees with the opinion and countermands the decision on his own authority. As the youthful physician is about to be discharged for insubordination, the ever-irascible Barrymore—who agrees with his diagnosis—appoints Ayres as his new assistant.

The first of MGM's "Dr. Kildare" series, this was not the first filmed adaptation of author Brand's characters. That honor belongs to INTERNES CAN'T TAKE MONEY, starring Joel McCrea and Barbara Stanwyck. MGM had recently started its "Hardy Family" series to considerable acclaim, and Louis B. Mayer wanted another profitable series vehicle. He assigned the HARDY staff to search for something suitable and settled on a hospital theme partly because of the nearly infinite plot variations it appeared to afford and partly because it offered a continuing role for his favorite actor, Barrymore (who had only recently suffered the crippling hip injury that required him to use a wheelchair). Ayres, with his gentle manner, was a fortuitous selection as Kildare, though he was none too pleased with the series at the outset (he's been quoted as saying of this initial entry, "Frankly, I thought it was terrible"). Ayres and Barrymore were to work together in eight more films in the series (Barrymore continued beyond these eight, with other actors assuming the young doctor characterization). Players Pendleton, Hinds, Dunn, and Kingsford were to become regulars on the series. Actress Laraine Day joined the group in the next picture in the series, CALLING DR. KILDARE. The studio's feature-release series ended in 1947 with DARK DELUSION, but the young doctor and his mentor were to be rejuvenated on television.

YOUNG FRANKENSTEIN

1974 108m bw ★★★★½
Comedy/Horror PG/15
FOX

Gene Wilder (Dr. Frederick Frankenstein), Peter Boyle (Monster), Marty Feldman (Igor), Madeline Kahn (Elizabeth), Cloris Leachman (Frau Blucher), Teri Garr (Inga), Kenneth Mars (Inspector Kemp), Gene Hackman (Blind Hermit), Richard Haydn (Herr Falkstein), Liam Dunn (Mr. Hilltop)

p, Michael Gruskoff; d, Mel Brooks; w, Gene Wilder, Mel Brooks (based on the characters from the novel Frankenstein by Mary Wollstonecraft Shelley); ph, Gerald Hirschfeld; ed, John C. Howard; m, John Morris; art d, Dale Hennesy; fx, Hal Millar, Henry Miller, Jr.; cos, Dorothy Jeakins

Mel Brooks's follow-up to his enormously successful western spoof, BLAZING SADDLES, tackles the horror genre—specifically, FRANKENSTEIN and THE BRIDE OF FRANKENSTEIN. This time Brooks tones down his broad humor a bit to create a work that is both an affectionate parody and a knowlegeable homage to its cinematic forebears. Gene Wilder plays Dr. Frederick Frankenstein (now defiantly pronounced "FRONK-ensteen"), a med school lecturer who thinks his infamous grandfather's work is "doo-doo." The younger Frankenstein must finally face his destiny when he inherits his grandfather's Transylvanian estate. Once there, he meets Igor (pronounced "eye-gore" and played by the eye-popping Marty Feldman), whose hunchback inexplicably changes from the left side to the right throughout the movie; Inga (Teri Garr), a young woman who will assist the doctor; and Frau Blucher (Cloris Leachman), a hideous old woman who causes horses to whinny in fright at the mere mention of her name. Eventually, Frederick finds his grandfather's private library and a copy of his book, How I Did It. Of course, Frederick cannot keep himself from righting his grandfather's wrongs and creating a new monster (Peter Boyle), a big, dumb corpse with a zipper round his neck and an abnormal brain in his head. The laughs come along at a fast and furious rate. One of the film's highlights is the "Puttin' on the Ritz" duet performed by Frederick and the Monster.

YOUNG FRANKENSTEIN is Brooks's most accomplished work, combining his well-known brand of comedy with stylish direction and a uniformly excellent cast. The handsome black-and-white cinematography really captures the look of an early 1930s film. The direction achieves a seemingly impossible task, balancing Brooks's off-the-wall humor within the framework of the style of a classic Universal Frankenstein film. The Frankenstein castle, with its cobwebs, dust, skulls, original lab equipment,

and strange goings-on, could easily have been inhabited by Boris Karloff or Bela Lugosi. Wilder, wildly funny here, later attempted his own genre spoof, HAUNTED HONEYMOON, which came nowhere near YOUNG FRANKENSTEIN. Nominated for two Oscars: Best Adapted Screenplay and Best Sound.

YOUNG LIONS, THE

1958 167m bw ★★★★
War /PG
FOX

Marlon Brando (Christian Diestl), Montgomery Clift (Noah Ackerman), Dean Martin (Michael Whiteacre), Hope Lange (Hope Plowman), Barbara Rush (Margaret Freemantle), May Britt (Gretchen Hardenberg), Maximilian Schell (Capt. Hardenberg), Dora Doll (Simone), Lee Van Cleef (Sgt. Rickett), Liliane Montevecchi (Francoise)

p, Al Lichtman; d, Edward Dmytryk; w, Edward Anhalt (based on the novel by Irwin Shaw); ph, Joseph MacDonald (CinemaScope); ed, Dorothy Spencer; m, Hugo Friedhofer; art d, Lyle Wheeler, Addison Hehr; fx, L.B. Abbott; cos, Adele Balkan, Charles LeMaire

A somewhat bloated adaptation of Irwin Shaw's sprawling WWII novel, THE YOUNG LIONS follows three soldiers—one German, two American—from the time of their enlistment until the end of the war. Christian Diestl (Marlon Brando) is an idealistic young German who believes in Hitler and becomes a lieutenant in the Wehrmacht. As he makes his way from the occupation of Paris to duty in Rommel's Afrika Korps and then back into Europe, Diestl becomes disillusioned and embittered over Nazi brutality and comes to hate his uniform and everything it represents. Meanwhile, in the US, a young Jew, Noah Ackerman (Montgomery Clift), and a popular singer, Michael Whiteacre (Dean Martin), meet as draftees and become fast friends. Although patriotic and dedicated, Ackerman becomes the victim of the Army's anti-Semitism, and is forced to fight his fellow Americans before ever facing the Germans. As the years go by, the fates of Ackerman, Whiteacre, and Diestl grow closer, until they eventually intersect outside a concentration camp. Great departures were made in the script from Shaw's original story, mostly in the character of the German, Diestl. In the book, he is an unredeemed Nazi to the last, and in the final confrontation kills the Jewish soldier, then is killed by the other American. It was largely Brando who made the German a sympathetic character, arguing that Shaw had written his book in the immediate, angry aftermath of the war, although Shaw later told the actor that he wouldn't have changed his opinions even if he had written the book 10 years later. Although Edward Dmytryk's direction was never more than workmanlike and the film is bit overlong and draggy at times, it does contain a pair of worthwhile performances from Brando and Clift.

YOUNG MAN WITH A HORN

1950 111m bw ★★★★
Musical /PG
WB

Kirk Douglas (Rick Martin), Lauren Bacall (Amy North), Doris Day (Jo Jordan), Hoagy Carmichael (Smoke Willoughby), Juano Hernandez (Art Hazzard), Jerome Cowan (Phil Morrison), Mary Beth Hughes (Margo Martin), Nestor Paiva (Louis Galba), Orley Lindgren (Rick as a Boy), Walter Reed (Jack Chandler)

p, Jerry Wald; d, Michael Curtiz; w, Carl Foreman, Edmund H. North (based on the novel by Dorothy Baker); ph, Ted McCord; ed, Alan Crosland, Jr.; art d, Edward Carrere; cos, Milo Anderson

Inspired by the tragic life of jazz cornet player Bix Beiderbecke, who died at age 28 in 1931 after a long battle with alcoholism, YOUNG MAN WITH A HORN stars Kirk Douglas as the great musician's fictional counterpart, Rick Martin. While pianist Smoke Willoughby (Hoagy Carmichael) reminisces about the talented trumpeter, Rick's life is shown in flashback, beginning with his youthful fascination with music and Art Hazzard (Juano Hernandez), a black jazz musician. Rick saves up to buy a trumpet and learns to play under Art's tutelage, and by age 20 Rick is performing with a dance band that includes Smoke and torch singer Jo Jordon (Doris Day). He's quickly frustrated by the band's dull sound, however, and gets himself and Smoke fired. The two continue to play in cheap dives, broke but having fun, after which Rick ends up in New York City, where he finds Jo singing with a new band. Rick's brilliant playing soon makes him a sensation, but stardom brings trouble in the form of a rich, neurotic, beautiful, and controlling Amy North (Lauren Bacall), who both marries Rick and ruins him—although the film's ending suggest that he may be on his way back, with the help of the loyal Smoke and Jo. YOUNG MAN WITH A HORN suffers from excessive melodrama, but boasts several fine performances and plenty of enjoyable jazz. Douglas studied under trumpeter Larry Sullivan and learned how to "play" convincingly, although all his trumpeting is dubbed by Harry James, the film's musical adviser (some of Carmichael's piano was dubbed by Buddy Cole, and Jimmy Zito handled Hernandez's playing).

YOUNG MR. LINCOLN
1939 100m bw   ★★★★
Biography/Political   /A
FOX

Henry Fonda (Abraham Lincoln), Alice Brady (Abigail Clay), Marjorie Weaver (Mary Todd), Arleen Whelan (Hannah Clay), Eddie Collins (Efe Turner), Pauline Moore (Ann Rutledge), Richard Cromwell (Matt Clay), Ward Bond (John Palmer Cass), Donald Meek (John Felder), Spencer Charters (Judge Herbert A. Bell)

p, Kenneth MacGowan; d, John Ford; w, Lamar Trotti; ph, Bert Glennon, Arthur Miller; ed, Walter Thompson; m, Alfred Newman; art d, Richard Day, Mark-Lee Kirk; cos, Royer

The early days of Abraham Lincoln get the full treatment in this film by Ford, who simultaneously makes Lincoln both a man and a myth. The film opens with a poem familiar to most: "If Nancy Hanks/came back as a ghost/seeking news/of what she loved most/She'd ask first/'Where's my son?/What's happened to Abe?/What's he done?'" This sets the tone for the rest of the film, in which these questions are answered, but only in the context of what Lincoln (played by Fonda) had done by 1837. The film's first scene has Fonda making a speech to a convention of the Whig party in 1832, in which the first words from his mouth are "You all know me." In that same year he talks with his girlfriend, Moore, by a riverside, which dissolves to the same riverside five years later, covered with ice. Moore is dead, and her grave is on the same spot where they had spoken. Fonda speaks to it and asks her to help him decide his future. He stands a stick up on the grave, holding it with his finger at the top, and tells her that if it falls on her grave, he'll go into the legal profession. It falls for the law, and soon we see Fonda practicing his first case, a dispute between two men. Fonda listens to both of them, then proposes a compromise. They both refuse that solution, so he threatens them: "Did you fellas ever hear 'bout the time I butted two heads together?" They acquiesce, and it is with great satisfaction that Fonda collects his fee. Following a fair in which Fonda serves as the pie judge, there is a murder during a fight involving the two

sons of an old friend, Brady, and two local roughnecks, of whom the survivor is Bond. Fonda takes on the boys' defense, first by stopping a lynch mob from killing the pair on the spot. He tries to learn from Brady which of her sons killed the victim, but she can't say. Bond indicates that it was the bigger of the two, though neither is especially larger than the other. The judge tries to convince Fonda that he is too inexperienced for a case of this importance and suggests that he let an established lawyer take on the defense, namely Milburn Stone, a noted trial lawyer and Fonda's rival for the hand of socialite Weaver. Fonda refuses, and in court he manages to uses the Farmer's Almanac to trap Bond into confessing to the crime himself. Fonda is triumphant, and Stone comes up to him and says he'll never underestimate him again. Fonda walks away in a rainstorm that just happened to come up that day of shooting, and as he is lost in the rain, the film dissolves to a picture of the statue in the Lincoln Memorial.

Ford was originally reluctant to take on the film. He had just made STAGECOACH and was in a position to pick and choose his work. Two plays had recently been on Broadway on the subject of Lincoln's early years, and Ford felt that the subject had been "worked to death." But when he read the Lamar Trotti script he changed his mind. Executive Producer Darryl F. Zanuck wanted rising actor Fonda to take on the title role, but Fonda was too much in awe of the character and he turned it down at first. But after talking to Ford, Fonda changed his mind and took the part, turning in a marvelous performance that simultaneously captures both the awkwardness of the young man and his promise. Unlike most of Ford's films after STAGECOACH, this was very much a studio project, and Ford knew he was going to move on to his next film almost immediately after finishing work on this, leaving control of the editing to others. Since Ford had already argued with Zanuck over the slow, elegiac pace Ford was taking with the material, the director ensured that the film would be cut the way he wanted by editing in the camera, setting up slow dissolves, and destroying the negatives of all the takes except the ones he wanted. Throughout the film Zanuck gave Ford a lot of input about how he thought the film should go, mostly suggesting it move faster. The story of the murder in the film was taken from Trotti's own experiences as a reporter in the South. There he had reported on a murder case in which one of two brothers was accused of killing a man. Their mother refused to tell which of them did it, so both were hanged. Trotti earned an Oscar nomination for Best Original Story, but lost to Lewis Foster for MR. SMITH GOES TO WASHINGTON. A superb motion picture, and one in which Ford's obsession with Americana and the forces and emotions that made this country what it is are plainly in view.

YOUNG WINSTON
1972 145m c   ★★★
Biography/Adventure/Political   PG
Highroad/Hugh French (U.K.)

Simon Ward (Winston Churchill/Sir Winston Churchill's Voice), Peter Cellier (Captain 35th Sikhs), Ronald Hines (Adjutant 35th Sikhs), Dino Shafeek (Sikh Soldier), John Mills (Gen. Herbert Kitchener), Anne Bancroft (Lady Jennie Churchill), Russell Lewis (Winston, Age 7), Pat Heywood (Mrs. Everest), Robert Shaw (Lord Randolph Churchill), Laurence Naismith (Lord Salisbury) p, Carl Foreman; d, Richard Attenborough; w, Carl Foreman (based on *My Early Life: A Roving Commission* by Sir Winston Churchill); ph, Gerry Turpin (Panavision, Eastmancolor); ed, Kevin Connor; m, Alfred Ralston, Sir Edward Elgar; prod d, Geoffrey Drake, Don Ashton; art d, John Graysmark, William Hutchinson; fx, Cliff Richardson, Tom Howard, Charles Staffel; cos, Anthony Mendleson

After viewing Carl Foreman's production of THE GUNS OF NAVARONE, Churchill himself decided that Foreman was just the man to adapt and produce Churchill's memoirs of his adventures as a young man, *My Early Life: A Roving Commission*, as a motion picture. (No comment as to what that tells you about Churchill.) As it happened, Foreman was busy and Churchill died in 1965 before the film could be shot. Finally, in 1972 the film was completed with a script by Foreman and direction by the current master (or at least the most frequent practitioner) of the historical epic, Richard Attenborough.

The film opens with Churchill (Ward) a junior officer in India out to make a name for himself. One of his superiors suggests that becoming a war correspondent is a good way to get his name into the newspapers. As luck would have it, a native uprising occurs and Churchill helps suppress it, providing the material for his first dispatches from the field and eventually a book that angers many of the top brass with its outspoken opinions. Back in England, Churchill's father (Shaw) resigns his post as Chancellor of the Exchequer over his disagreement with the ruling party concerning new arms expenditures. The elder Churchill's career goes downhill quickly after that, particularly when he contracts syphilis. Winston and his mother (Bancroft) can only watch horror-stricken from the gallery as Randolph babbles incoherently while trying to make a speech before the House of Commons. After his father's death Churchill returns to the army and goes to the Sudan to put down the Dervish uprising. The Arabs fight furiously, but the British machine guns destroy the Dervish army at Omdurman. On the strength of his record in that war Churchill returns to England and runs for Parliament but loses. He goes off to the Boer War as a correspondent and has a number of adventures not quite in keeping with his status as a noncombatant. After helping to foil a Boer ambush of an armored train Churchill is captured and put into a Boer concentration camp (the term originates from this war). Along with Haldane (Edward Woodward), he escapes and makes his way back to the British lines. (Woodward would later return to the Boer War in the film that made him something of an international star, BREAKER MORANT). His adventures have made him a household name and he easily wins election to Parliament at age 26. In his first speech before the House of Commons, Churchill drives home his father's beliefs as his mother proudly sits watching from the gallery. (A scene cut from most prints ends the film with Churchill [Sanders Watney], now an old man, sleeping in front of one of his unfinished landscapes, dreaming of his father coming to him and telling him he doesn't understand the son's actions.)

YOUNG WINSTON works as an action-packed adventure, with lots of rousing battle scenes and hairsbreadth escapes, but its attempt to penetrate the motivations of its hero is about as profound as a high school psychology text. Ward is convincing as Churchill, and the other performances, particularly that of Shaw, are of a high order. Attenborough's direction, in his debut feature, is fairly accomplished and even innovative—he experimented with "flashing" techniques here, exposing the film before shooting to get subtle color tints. Well-paced, but still very long at almost two and a half hours.

YOU'RE A BIG BOY NOW

1966 96m c ★★★
Comedy/Drama /X
Seven Arts

Elizabeth Hartman *(Barbara Darling)*, Geraldine Page *(Margery Chanticleer)*, Julie Harris *(Miss Thing)*, Peter Kastner *(Bernard Chanticleer)*, Rip Torn *(I.H. Chanticleer)*, Michael Dunn *(Richard Mudd)*, Tony Bill *(Raef)*, Karen Black *(Amy)*, Dolph Sweet *(Policeman Francis Graf)*, Michael O'Sullivan *(Kurt Doughty)*

p, Phil Feldman; d, Francis Ford Coppola; w, Francis Ford Coppola (based on the novel by David Benedictius); ph, Andrew Laszlo (Pathe Color); ed, Aram Avakian; m, Robert Prince; art d, Vassele Fotopoulos; chor, Robert Tucker; cos, Theoni V. Aldredge

YOU'RE A BIG BOY NOW is significant as an early example of the developing talent of one of the most important (if not the most important) American directors of the 1970s. Coppola scripted and directed this whimsical look at coming of age in the 1960s as part of his graduate thesis at UCLA. Though not his first film, it revealed a willingness to experiment with technique and themes that would continue throughout his career. As in both RUMBLE FISH and THE OUTSIDERS, made by Coppola nearly two decades later, his subject here is a teenager's passage into manhood. The tone in this film is much less serious, though, more appropriate for the 1960s, when a laid-back attitude toward drama in general was prevalent, and deep messages lurked beneath surfaces. But unlike the work of either Jean-Luc Godard or Richard Lester (both obvious influences on Coppola at this point in his career), YOU'RE A BIG BOY NOW fails to have much impact beyond its lightheartedness. It is as if Coppola were too concerned with creating a style to put much effort into the implications of his material. Kastner plays a young Long Islander given his first taste of what it's like to be on his own. His move to New York City has come at the behest of Torn, his father, who wants to get the boy away from his security-blanket existence with doting mother Page. Kastner moves into a boarding house run by Harris and discovers sex and drugs under the guidance of older and wiser Bill, with whom he works at the New York Public Library. Kastner is obsessed with discotheque dancer and actress Hartman in a big way, but his pursuit of her leaves him with an extremely bitter taste of romance. He eventually does discover something about love through his relationship with Black, the woman who has been waiting on the sidelines all along, acting as his friend while harboring a gigantic crush. Though YOU'RE A BIG BOY NOW has been criticized for being too whimsical, it offers a wide range of fascinating characters and situations that make for great entertainment. The soundtrack by the Lovin' Spoonful is also a delight. Like much of Coppola's early work, however, it presents his themes in a cliched manner, almost as if he has learned about human experience and emotions through the cinema instead of real life. That Coppola, an unknown just embarking on his career, was able to persuade so many established performers to appear in the film, is indicative of the organization skills and the ability to gain people's trust and respect that have made him such an outstanding director. Page received an Oscar nomination for Best Supporting Actress.

YOU'RE TELLING ME

1934 67m bw ★★★★
Comedy /U
Paramount

W.C. Fields *(Sam Bisbee)*, Joan Marsh *(Pauline Bisbee)*, Buster Crabbe *(Bob Murchison)*, Adrienne Ames *(H.R.H. Princess Lescaboura)*, Louise Carter *(Mrs. Bessie Bisbee)*, Kathleen Howard *(Mrs. Murchison)*, James B. "Pop" Kenton *(Doc Beebe)*, Bob McKenzie *(Charlie Bogle)*, George Irving *(President of the Tire Company)*, Jerry Stewart *(Frobisher)*

p, William Le Baron; d, Erle C. Kenton; w, J.P. McEvoy, Walter DeLeon, Paul M. Jones (based on the short story "Mr. Bisbee's Princess" by Julian Street); ph, Alfred Gilks; ed, Otho Lovering; m, Arthur Johnston; art d, Hans Dreier, Robert Odell

Sam Bisbee (W.C. Fields) is a struggling inventor having trouble scraping up enough money to support his family. He devises a puncture-proof tire, but a demonstration for auto company executives goes awry. Eventually, Bisbee's efforts are rewarded with a check for $1 million. While most of Fields's films were virtually plotless, YOU'RE TELLING ME has a complex, linear story line that gives him lots of room for comedy and a surprising number of opportunities to show off his talents as a serious actor. Fields demonstrates heretofore untapped sensitivity in several scenes—especially when he delivers an antisuicide speech. This is also a superior Fields vehicle in that the comedian is on screen throughout—unlike many of his other films, in which his appearances are infrequent and sometimes almost incidental to other plot lines, romances, or musical numbers. Held to a taut 67 minutes, the film concentrates wholly on Fields and allows him to develop a full, emotionally complex, fascinating character. The stronger the characterization, the better the film, and YOU'RE TELLING ME is a great testament to Fields's skills as comedian and actor. One of its finest moments is Fields's famed golf routine, which is also seen in SO'S YOUR OLD MAN and in the sound short THE GOLF SPECIALIST.

Z

1969   127m   c   ★★★★
Political   M/A
Reggane   (France/Algeria)

Yves Montand *(The Deputy)*, Jean-Louis Trintignant *(The Examining Magistrate)*, Irene Papas *(Helene, the Deputy's Wife)*, Jacques Perrin *(Photojournalist)*, Charles Denner *(Manuel)*, Francois Perier *(Public Prosecutor)*, Pierre Dux *(The General)*, Julien Guiomar *(The Colonel)*, Bernard Fresson *(Matt)*, Renato Salvatori *(Yago)*

p, Jacques Perrin, Hamed Rachedi; d, Constantin Costa-Gavras; w, Constantin Costa-Gavras, Jorge Semprun (based on the novel by Vassili Vassilikos); ph, Raoul Coutard (Technicolor); ed, Francoise Bonnot; m, Mikis Theodorakis; art d, Jacques d'Ovidio

A chilling, manipulative rollercoaster ride. Originally subtitled "The Anatomy of a Political Assassination," this intense political thriller is based on the real-life 1963 killing of Gregorios Lambrakis, a Greek liberal whose extreme popularity and advocacy of peace shook the stability of the government in power. Starring is Yves Montand, who, although referred to only as "the Deputy," is clearly Lambrakis. After his liberal organization, the Friends of Peace, loses a large meeting hall at the last moment, the Deputy is forced to find another venue. He appeals and is given a permit to hold the meeting in a small, 200-seat auditorium, although it is expected to draw over 4,000. During the meeting, the Deputy's supporters are taunted by a violent right-wing faction, while the police "protection" stands by passively. Later, the police do little to protect the Deputy from a truck that speeds by, from which one of the passengers ferociously clubs the Deputy in the head, killing him. In order to give the appearance of an investigation, the general in charge appoints an

Examining Magistrate (Jean-Louis Trintignant), who is believed to be a pawn of the government, but soon surprises all by probing deep into a government conspiracy and cover-up.

Rather than appealing only to a politically minded audience, Z found a great deal of enthusiastic support from almost everyone who saw it. At the Cannes Film Festival it received a unanimous vote for the Jury Prize, with Trintignant receiving Best Actor honors. The Academy Awards also responded, with Oscars for Best Foreign Film and Best Editing (it was nominated for Best Picture as well). Z succeeds where so many political pictures have failed because of its concentration on the thriller aspects of the story. Borrowing heavily from American gangster/prison/anti-Facist melodrama conventions, Costa-Gavras' film contains many breathtaking, pressure-filled scenes that help pummel home the sometimes confusing politics. Rather than worrying about which right-wing general did what, the audience becomes wrapped up in whether or not a character will survive a beating, or be run down by a speeding car. Detractors complained that the film commercialized and simplified the Lambrakis incident and politics in general. Costa-Gavras responded: "That's the way it is in Greece. Black and White. No nuances." The glorious Irene Papas plays Montand's wife—she's an actress whose eyes speak volumes even when she's standing stock-still. The score is by Mikis Theodorakis—who was under arrest in Greece at the time. Z was filmed in Algeria, in French.

ZABRISKIE POINT

1970   112m   c   ★★
Drama   R/15
MGM/Trianon

Mark Frechette *(Mark)*, Daria Halprin *(Daria)*, Rod Taylor *(Lee Allen)*, Paul Fix *(Cafe Owner)*, G.D. Spradlin *(Lee's Associate)*, Bill Garaway *(Morty)*, Kathleen Cleaver *(Kathleen)*

p, Carlo Ponti; d, Michelangelo Antonioni; w, Michelangelo Antonioni, Fred Gardner, Sam Shepard, Tonino Guerra, Clare Peploe (based on a story by Michelangelo Antonioni); ph, Alfio Contini (Panavision, Metrocolor); ed, Franco Arcalli; prod d, Dean Tavoularis; fx, Earl McCoy; cos, Ray Summers

In his super-successful BLOW-UP, Antonioni made an attempt to understand the English youth movement of the 1960s. Here, in his first American film, Antonioni took his search for answers to the States. Unfortunately, with this picture the director falls into two traps: employing endless "anti-Establishment" cliches and saddling himself with the underwhelming talents of Mark Frechette. The picture opens in documentary style, with a meeting of college radicals discussing the meaning of revolution. Mark (Frechette), disgusted with the students' stagnant ideals, declares that he is ready to die—but not of boredom—and walks out. Identified as a cop killer during a campus riot, Mark flees to a nearby airfield, steals a small private plane, flies through Death Valley, and meets Daria (Daria Halprin), a pretty, pot-smoking, meditative secretary. It's not long before they are holding hands at Zabriskie Point, a tourist spot marked by a small plaque explaining that a man named Zabriskie discovered mineral matter there. The psychedelic happenings plod along until the explosive, apocalyptic finale. On the basis of Antonioni's "art-house" following in the US, MGM decided to jump on the bandwagon and give the director carte blanche for this film. The result is a critical but relatively accurate portrait of America in the late 1960s, which, however, now seems horribly dated. Antonioni concentrates chiefly on the gaps between student radicals and the establishment, naturalism and plasticity, free-spirited individualism and the restraints of modern life. While Antonioni's visual

1095

sense is once again in top form, his "mind-expanding" hippie dialogue, as delivered by his amateur leads, is painful to experience. MGM hoped that a combination of art-house and hippie audiences would help return their $7 million investment. Instead the film was a box-office and critical bomb, surviving today as a nugget of the hippie culture.

ZANDY'S BRIDE

1974 116m c   ★★½
Western   PG/AA
WB

Gene Hackman (Zandy Allan), Liv Ullmann (Hannah Lund), Eileen Heckart (Ma Allan), Harry Dean Stanton (Songer), Joe Santos (Frank Gallo), Frank Cady (Pa Allan), Sam Bottoms (Mel Allan), Susan Tyrrell (Maria Cordova), Bob Simpson (Bill Pincus), Fabian Gregory Cordova (Paco)

p, Harvey Matofsky; d, Jan Troell; w, Marc Norman (based on the novel The Stranger by Lillian Bos Ross); ph, Jordan Cronenweth (Panavision, Technicolor); ed, Gordon Scott; m, Michael Franks; prod d, Albert Brenner; cos, Patricia Norris

A beautifully photographed, intimate little western shot in the Big Sur area of California that boasts some fine acting but really nothing more. Hackman stars as an ill-tempered rancher who decides to end his loneliness by sending off for a mail-order bride (Ullmann). When the woman arrives, she is shocked by Hackman's apparent cruelty and heartlessness toward her as he treats her like a slave. She decides to fight back against his tyranny, and the shock of someone standing up to him begins to arouse long-repressed feelings of tenderness and compassion in Hackman. By the end of the film, Hackman accepts Ullmann as an equal and demonstrates his ability to be a loving father when she bears his child. Despite the gorgeous scenery and strong performances, ZANDY'S BRIDE is a rather hollow film that suffers from lackadaisical scripting. There is not much plot here (and there is nothing wrong with that if the characters are interesting), and the people and their actions are cliched and predictable. There is no spontaneity; it all seems very cold and mannered. Hackman and Ullmann (with able support from Heckart, Stanton, and Bottoms) struggle to wring some life and meaning out of the material, and it is through their efforts that ZANDY'S BRIDE works at all. Directed by celebrated Swedish director Troell, whose films THE EMIGRANTS and THE NEW LAND were magnificent period pieces about Swedes settling in America during the 19th century, ZANDY'S BRIDE suffered because of his inability to adjust to American production methods. In Sweden, Troell worked with a close-knit crew of 15 and had complete access to the camera—even shooting scenes himself if he chose to. Warner Bros. gave the director a union crew of 100. The sheer number of these strangers intimidated the director and made him extremely nervous and self-conscious. He was also not allowed anywhere near the camera—union rules. In her book Changing, Ullmann relates how Troell and his actors sneaked a camera into the cabin and "rehearsed" while the director photographed the whole scene hand-holding the camera—finally able to feel as if he controlled the set. Problems aside, ZANDY'S BRIDE is beautiful to watch and at times an interesting look into frontier life.

ZAZIE

(ZAZIE DANS LE METRO)
1961 86m c   ★★★½
Comedy   /X
Nouvelle Editions de Films   (France)

Catherine Demongeot (Zazie), Philippe Noiret (Uncle Gabriel), Hubert Deschamps (Turnadot), Antoine Roblot (Charles), Annie Fratellini (Mado), Carla Marlier (Albertine), Vittorio Caprioli (Trouscaillon), Yvonne Clech (Mme. Mouaque), Nicolas Bataille (Fedor), Jacques Dufilho (Gridoux)

p, Louis Malle; d, Louis Malle; w, Louis Malle, Jean-Paul Rappeneau (based on the book Zazie dans le Metro by Raymond Queneau); ph, Henri Raichi (Eastmancolor); ed, Kenout Peltier; m, Andre Pontin, Fiorenzo Carpi; art d, Bernard Evein; fx, Locafilms; cos, Marc Doelnitz

Demongeot is an 11-year-old nuisance who must spend a few days with her uncle, Noiret, in Paris when her mother goes off with a new lover. She wants nothing more than to ride the subway, but a strike by the Paris Metro workers prevents this. The foul-mouthed girl blames it on grownups but decides to have fun in spite of this setback. She takes Noiret on a mad chase through the town, and at one point he's forced to leap from the Eiffel Tower using a balloon as a parachute. Finally she is granted her wish when the strike ends, but Demongeot is tuckered out from all the loony goings on and ends up falling asleep on the way home. This is a great romp with some wonderfully wild moments. A fine early effort from the director of ATLANTIC CITY and MURMUR OF THE HEART.

ZELIG

1983 80m c/bw   ★★½
Comedy   PG
Orion

Woody Allen (Leonard Zelig), Mia Farrow (Dr. Eudora Fletcher), John Buckwalter (Dr. Sindell), Marvin Chatinover (Glandular Diagnosis Doctor), Stanley Swerdlow (Mexican Food Doctor), Paul Nevens (Dr. Birsky), Howard Erskine (Hypodermic Doctor), George Hamlin (Experimental Drugs Doctor), Ralph Bell, Richard Whiting

p, Robert Greenhut; d, Woody Allen; w, Woody Allen; ph, Gordon Willis; ed, Susan E. Morse; m, Dick Hyman; prod d, Mel Bourne; art d, Speed Hopkins; fx, John Caglione, Jr., Joel Hynick, Stuart Robinson, Richard Greenberg; chor, Danny Daniels; cos, Santo Loquasto; anim, Steven Plastrik

ZELIG relies on gimmick filmmaking to deliver a simple, heavy-handed message. Leonard Zelig (Woody Allen) is a minor celebrity of the Depression era whose abilities as a "human chameleon" astounded the world. He is desperate to be accepted by others and goes to extraordinary lengths to become one of the crowd. In "documentary footage," Zelig is seen waiting in the on-deck circle as Babe Ruth is batting, among a crowd of Nazis cheering Hitler, and growing a beard to become a Hassidic rabbi. His case captures the imagination of America, as well as the attentions of a psychiatrist (Mia Farrow) who falls in love with him. While the footage showing Zelig in a variety of historical situations is very well done and fun to watch, the trick soon gets old. Nominated by the Academy for Best Cinematography and Best Costume Design.

ZELLY AND ME

1988 87m c   ★★★½
Drama   PG/15
Cypress

Alexandra Johnes *(Phoebe)*, Isabella Rossellini *(Joan, "Zelly")*, Glynis Johns *(Co-Co)*, Kaiulani Lee *(Nora)*, David Lynch *(Willie)*, Joe Morton *(Earl)*, Courtney Vickery *(Dora)*, Lindsay Dickon *(Kitty)*, Jason McCall *(Alexander)*, Aaron Boone *(David)*

p, Sue Jett, Tony Mark; d, Tina Rathborne; w, Tina Rathborne; ph, Mikael Salomon (Technicolor); ed, Cindy Kaplan Rooney; m, Pino Donaggio, Jeremiah Clarke; prod d, David Morong; cos, Kathleen Detoro

In this deceptively cuddly picture about the psychological violence inflicted by a grandmother on her granddaughter, Alexandra Johnes plays Phoebe, an orphaned eight-year-old who lives with her grandmother (Glynis Johns) on an immaculate Virginia estate. Phoebe is deeply attached to her French nanny, Joan, called "Zelly" (a childish version of "Mademoiselle"), played by Isabella Rossellini. Phoebe's favorite pastime is learning about St. Joan of Arc. The grandmother, a lonely, bereaved woman, tries to bind Phoebe to her by separating the youngster from anyone who might come between them. She gradually banishes the gardener for giving Phoebe a gift, Zelly for an imagined violation of trust, and the child's stuffed animals because they are close to Phoebe's heart. A gentle and spiritual film, ZELLY AND ME is directed with great grace. It is also a film of unrelenting psychological and spiritual cruelty. In addition to Tina Rathborne's fine direction and some excellent technical credits, ZELLY AND ME offers impeccable performances from Alexandra Johnes and Glynis Johns, and a superlative one from Isabella Rossellini.

ZERO FOR CONDUCT
(ZERO DE CONDUITE)
1933   44m   bw   ★★★★★
Drama
Gaumont/Franco Film/Aubert   (France)

Jean Daste, le nain Delfin, Robert Le Flem, Louis de Gonzague-Frick, Louis Lefevre, Gilbert Pluchon, Gerard de Bedarieux, Constantin Goldstein-Kehler

p, Jean Vigo; d, Jean Vigo; w, Jean Vigo; ph, Boris Kaufman; ed, Jean Vigo; m, Maurice Jaubert

One of the greatest films about children ever made and a haunting celebration of anarchic rebellion. The first fictional work from writer/director/scenarist/editor Jean Vigo, ZERO FOR CONDUCT was closely based on his own miserable experiences as a boarding-school pupil and influenced other screen classics of disaffected youth including Truffaut's THE 400 BLOWS and Lindsay Anderson's IF. . .

The plot follows the misadventures of a group of young students as they endure the absurdities and deprivations forced upon them by their petty, authoritarian teachers. After a confrontation in which one of the students repeats before the entire assembled faculty the phrase with which he has rebuffed the sexual advances of one of his teachers (literally, "shit on you"), matters escalate into a full-scale dormitory rebellion. Beds are overturned and pillows ripped open, resulting in a rain of feathers which falls over everything—one of the most beautiful images in this, or any, film. Finally, locked in an attic for the duration of the school fete, the young rebels escape onto the roof and rain down a barrage of books, stones, and shoes onto a group of visiting dignitaries, inspiring the rest of the boys to revolt and take over the school.

Vigo, whose extraordinarily promising career was cut short by his death from septicemia at the age of 29, demonstrates a complete mastery of his art in ZERO, only the third film he had

made. Despite occasionally poor acting (the cast was largely nonprofessional), several sequences stand out as near-perfect fusions of shot composition, editing, lighting, and dialogue. The "rain of feathers" sequence is justly celebrated; so is the scene in which three of the boys, after being ordered to stand still for two hours at the bedside of a supervisor, plead with him to allow one of them, who has developed a stomach ache, to visit the bathroom. Their repeated pleas become a kind of incantation which takes on a haunting, other-worldly quality.

ZERO was made for a mere 200,000 francs, and shot by Vigo's friend Boris Kaufman, younger brother of Soviet "Kino-Eye" pioneer Dziga Vertov. It received a mixed reception on its initial 1933 release and was soon banned for fear it would instigate civil unrest. Rereleased in 1945, it has since been accepted as a landmark of world cinema.

ZIEGFELD FOLLIES
1945   110m   c   ★★★★
Musical   /U
MGM

William Powell *(The Great Ziegfeld)*, Fred Astaire, Lucille Ball, Judy Garland, Lena Horne, Esther Williams, Red Skelton, Gene Kelly, Fanny Brice, Edward Arnold

p, Arthur Freed; d, Vincente Minnelli, George Sidney, Charles Walters, Roy Del Ruth, Lemuel Ayers; w, E.Y. Harburg, Jack McGowan, Guy Bolton, Frank Sullivan, John Murray Anderson, Lemuel Ayers, Don Loper, Kay Thompson, Roger Edens, Hugh Martin, Ralph Blane, William Noble, Wilkie Mahoney, Cal Howard, Erik Charell, Max Liebman, Bill Schorr, Harry Crane, Lou Holtz, Eddie Cantor, Allen Boretz, Edgar Allan Woolf, Philip Rapp, Al Lewis, Joseph Schrank, Robert Alton, Eugene Loring, Robert Lewis, Charles Walters, James O'Hanlon, David Freedman, Joseph Erons, Irving Brecher, Samson Raphaelson, Everett Freeman, Devery Freeman; ph, George Folsey, Charles Rosher, William Ferrari (Technicolor); ed, Albert Akst; art d, Cedric Gibbons, Jack Martin Smith, Merrill Pye, Lemuel Ayers; chor, Robert Alton; cos, Florence Bunin, Irene, Helen Rose

On his deathbed, a delirious Florenz Ziegfeld reportedly cried out stage directions ("Ready for the last finale! Great! The show looks good! The show looks good!") continually. ZIEGFELD FOLLIES takes its cue from there, and the film opens up with Ziegfeld (William Powell, reprising his role in THE GREAT ZIEGFELD) up in heaven, dreaming about a new show. A group of puppets (caricatures of some of his original Follies stars) entertain him, followed by Fred Astaire, Lucille Ball, and Cyd Charisse in the first of a whopping 13 musical and comic sequences featuring MGM's top stars (Astaire and Gene Kelly among them, dancing together for the first time in "The Babbitt and the Bromide"). The film was shot by several directors, starting with George Sidney, who was replaced by Vincente Minnelli, while Robert Lewis, Norman Taurog, Charles Walters, Roy Del Ruth, Merrill Pye, and Lemuel Ayres also lent uncredited hands. With so many big names in the cast, it had to be shot bit by bit, with the actors called off other productions and many writers paged from other projects. The film premiered with 19 sequences, clocking in at 273 minutes, too long for any sensible release, so several segments were cut, including a duet between Mickey Rooney and Judy Garland (who parodies Greer Garson in "A Great Lady Has an Interview") and some comic bits. The film eventually made over $5 million in theaters—deservedly, since ZIEGFELD FOLLIES is a marvel of music and dance as only MGM could do it.

ZIEGFELD GIRL
1941   131m   bw   ★★★½
Musical   /A
MGM

James Stewart *(Gilbert Young)*, Judy Garland *(Susan Gallagher)*, Hedy Lamarr *(Sandra Kolter)*, Lana Turner *(Sheila Regan)*, Tony Martin *(Frank Merton)*, Jackie Cooper *(Jerry Regan)*, Ian Hunter *(Geoffrey Collis)*, Charles Winninger *(Pop Gallagher)*, Edward Everett Horton *(Noble Sage)*, Paul Kelly *(John Slayton)*

p, Pandro S. Berman; d, Robert Z. Leonard; w, Marguerite Roberts, Sonya Levien (based on a story by William Anthony McGuire); ph, Ray June; ed, Blanche Sewell; m, Herbert Stothart; art d, Cedric Gibbons, Daniel B. Cathcart; chor, Busby Berkeley; cos, Adrian

This MGM extravaganza details the fortunes of Ziegfeld girls Susan Gallagher (Judy Garland), Sandra Kolter (Hedy Lamarr), and Sheila Regan (Lana Turner). Show business trouper Susan quits the vaudeville act run by her father (Charles Winninger) to further her Follies career, and soon falls in love with the brother (Jackie Cooper) of former elevator operator Sheila, another new Ziegfeld girl. Meanwhile, Sheila's head is turned by the glamor of it all, and she begins to hobnob with high society, especially Park Avenue socialite Geoffrey Collis (Ian Hunter). Left behind is truck driver Gilbert Young (James Stewart), who, in the hopes of winning back his wayward love, tries to make extra money as a bootlegger and winds up in prison. Sandra, the third Ziegfeld girl, finds life on the stage more eventful than life with her penniless violinist husband (Philip Dorn)—until she finally comes to her senses and realizes that love means more to her than show business. Eventually, Susan uses her success to renew interest in her father's career, while Sheila botches her life and career, becoming an alcoholic. For all the melodramatic goings on among the principals, the true stars of this entertaining film are, quite fittingly, the lavish, spectacular dance numbers, employing hundreds of Ziegfeld girls in glittering costumes in the best style of both Florenz Ziegfeld and Busby Berkeley.

ZOOT SUIT
1981   103m   c   ★★
Drama   R/
Universal

Daniel Valdez *(Henry Reyna)*, Edward James Olmos *(El Pachuco)*, Charles Aidman *(George)*, Tyne Daly *(Alice)*, John Anderson *(Judge)*, Abel Franco *(Enrique)*, Mike Gomez *(Joey)*, Alma Martinez *(Lupe)*, Frank McCarthy *(Press)*, Lupe Ontiveros *(Dolores)*

p, Peter Burrell, Kenneth Brecher, William P. Wingate; d, Luis Valdez; w, Luis Valdez (based on his play); ph, David Myers (Technicolor); ed, Jacqueline Cambas; m, Daniel Valdez, Shorty Rogers; prod d, Tom H. John; chor, Patricia Birch; cos, Yvonne Wood

This is the film adaptation of the play "Zoot Suit," based on the real-life Sleepy Lagoon case in Los Angeles, in which several Hispanics were sent to jail in 1942 on trumped-up murder charges. Attempts were made to free the group but to no avail. Valdez, who adapted his play for the screen, keeps the story and the camera moving nicely. Shot in 11 days on a tiny budget of $2.5 million, the film showcases the talents of several Hispanic-American actors, including future "Miami Vice" star Olmos.

ZORBA THE GREEK
(ZORBA)
1964   142m   bw   ★★★½
Drama   /PG
FOX/Cacoyannis-Rochley   (U.S./Greece)

Anthony Quinn *(Alexis Zorba)*, Alan Bates *(Basil)*, Irene Papas *(The Widow)*, Lila Kedrova *(Mme. Hortense)*, George Foundas *(Mavrandoni)*, Eleni Anousaki *(Lola)*, Sotiris Moustakas *(Mimithos)*, Takis Emmanuel *(Manolakas)*, Yorgo Voyagis *(Pavlo)*, Anna Kyriakou *(Soul)*

p, Michael Cacoyannis; d, Michael Cacoyannis; w, Michael Cacoyannis (based on the novel by Nikos Kazantzakis); ph, Walter Lassally; ed, Michael Cacoyannis; m, Mikis Theodorakis; art d, Vassele Fotopoulos; cos, Anna Stavropoulou

As spritely and exuberant as a tank, but worth a watch. Although Quinn has often played earthy, force-of-nature characters, his title role in ZORBA THE GREEK was a career performance loved by both critics and audiences—so much, in fact, that he's been doing it ever since.

The film opens with Bates, a young English writer, arriving in Greece to collect his thoughts and discover his own identity. When he goes to Crete to work at a lignite mine, an inheritance from his native-Greek father, he is joined by Quinn, a lusty Greek peasant who also wants to work at the mine. The unusual duo move into a hotel run by Kedrova, a tattered French prostitute, former lover to four different admirals, and ex-cabaret dancer. Quinn begins wooing her and encourages Bates to show some attention to Papas, a beautiful widow much desired by the local male population. The mine is in need of some repairs, so the irrepressible Quinn cons a group of monks into letting him remove some lumber from a forest on a nearby mountain. Quinn devises a scheme to transport the lumber to the mine but must first obtain the necessary equipment. When Quinn ventures into the city, Kedrova helps Bates overcome his bashfulness, and the Englishman gathers up the courage to visit Papas. They make love, and rumors begin spreading about the island after Bates is seen leaving the house.

Through several upheavals, ZORBA boils down to the joyful dance that expresses Quinn's surpassingly positive philosophy—life may be painful, but it is beautiful nonetheless.

Quinn brings all his larger-than-life magic to his part—that of a character who is happy, devil-may-care, and zestfully mad. (When ZORBA THE GREEK was adapted into a spirited Broadway musical, "Zorba," for the 1968-1969 season, Quinn was chosen for the title role.) Bates, as the inhibited Englishman, is a fine contrast, never overshadowed by the enormity of Quinn's character as he learns about the forces of life. And both Kedrova and Papas are wonderful.

Despite its loose structure and excessive length, ZORBA THE GREEK has some marvelous moments. The film itself was somewhat revolutionary in its language and irreverent sense of humor, although these elements, controversial in 1964, have since become commonplace. Kedrova won a supporting Oscar; the film also won Oscars for art direction and cinematography (in the now-defunct black-and-white category).

ZULU
1964   135m   c   ★★★★★
Historical/War   /PG
Diamond   (U.K.)

Stanley Baker *(Lt. John Chard)*, Jack Hawkins *(Rev. Otto Witt)*, Ulla Jacobsson *(Margareta Witt)*, James Booth *(Pvt. Henry Hook)*, Michael Caine *(Lt. Gonville Bromhead)*, Nigel Green *(Color Sgt. Bourne)*, Ivor Emmanuel *(Pvt. Owen)*, Paul Daneman *(Sgt. Max-field)*, Glynn Edwards *(Cpl. Allen)*, Neil McCarthy *(Pvt. Thomas)*

p, Stanley Baker; d, Cy Endfield; w, John Prebble, Cy Endfield (based on a story by Prebble); ph, Stephen Dade (Technirama, Technicolor); ed, John Jympson; m, John Barry; art d, Ernest Archer; cos, Arthur Newman

Set in 1879 in Natal, this magnificently staged, brilliantly acted film tells the story of the heroic defense by overwhelmingly outnumbered British troops of the tiny outpost Rorke's Drift. Having been warned by a pacifist missionary (Jack Hawkins) that a British army contingent has been massacred by Zulu warriors, Lt. John Chard (Stanley Baker, the film's producer) orders his troops to dig in, despite the pleas of Lt. Gonville Bromhead (Michael Caine), the blueblood second-in-command who wants to abandon the post and who feels that he, rather than Chard (an engineer), should be in charge. Rather than fleeing, however, the courageous Brits withstand attack after attack, night and day, from 4,000 Zulus, and eventually triumph through a combination of ingenuity, determination, and luck. This amazing film is devastatingly accurate in its depiction of the Rorke's Drift action, and is superbly directed by Cy Endfield, whose battle scenes are some of the most terrifying ever committed to film. Producer Baker, however, had a difficult time getting his Zulu extras to cooperate on the location shoot in Natal. None had ever seen a motion picture, and he couldn't make the chiefs understand what he wanted to do. Finally, Baker had an old western starring Gene Autry flown in and showed it to the Zulus, who, grasping the fictional game at hand, later cooperated and lent the battle scenes tremendous power. ZULU is dramatically narrated by Richard Burton, who points out that of the 1,344 Victoria Crosses awarded since 1856, 11 were given to the defenders at Rorke's Drift, an all-time record for one engagement.

ZULU DAWN
1980 117m c   ★★★
Historical/War   PG/A
Samarkand/Lamitas   (U.K.)

Burt Lancaster *(Col. Durnford)*, Peter O'Toole *(Lord Chelmsford)*, Simon Ward *(William Vereker)*, John Mills *(Sir Bartle Frere)*, Nigel Davenport *(Col. Hamilton-Brown)*, Michael Jayston *(Col. Crealock)*, Ronald Lacey *(Norris Newman)*, Denholm Elliott *(Lt. Col. Pulleine)*, Freddie Jones *(Bishop Colenso)*, Christopher Cazenove *(Lt. Coghill)*

p, Nate Kohn; d, Douglas Hickox; w, Cy Endfield, Anthony Storey (based on a story by Endfield); ph, Ousama Rawi (Panavision, Technicolor); ed, Malcolm Cooke; m, Elmer Bernstein; prod d, John Rosewarne; art d, Peter Williams

Fifteen years after the release of ZULU, the British film industry offered this prequel. ZULU was Cy Endfield's masterful re-creation of the 1879 battle of Rorke's Drift in which Stanley Baker and Michael Caine lead the heroic stand by a vastly outnumbered contingent of British soldiers against thousands of Zulu warriors. ZULU DAWN documents the circumstances leading up to that confrontation, focusing on the increasing tensions between British colonial officials and the Zulus, and culminates with the extermination of 1,500 British soldiers at the battle of Isandhlwana. This battle occurred only hours before the events depicted in ZULU. Peter O'Toole commands the British forces in Natal, and Burt Lancaster is the one-armed hero who leads his men to their deaths when their column is attacked and annihilated by Zulu forces that outnumber them sixteen to one. That attack, as well as the scenes of the Zulus preparing to descend upon the marching British, are impressively staged and shot. While ZULU DAWN succeeds in painting these events on a broad canvas, it lacks the interpersonal conflicts that made ZULU so fascinating, and ultimately this film, penned by Endfield but directed by Douglas Hickox, is a far cry from that classic war film.

ZYDECKO MULATTO
1983 187m c   ★★★★
Documentary
Wild Entrepreneurs, Inc.

Janet Fille *(Singer)*, Jacques Pallette *(Composer)*, S. Cohn *(Narrator)*, Antoine Boitano *(Chef Tony)*, The People of Fil-au-fond, LA

p, Radha Homay; d, Jacob Munch

This charming if obscure documentary limning the struggles of a small group of aspiring musicians from a village in the bayou garnered little attention at the time of its release in the early 80s. It was only with the increasing interest in Zydeco music in the late 80s that bootleg videocassettes began circulating in the entertainment community. Music/Food/Film critic Michael Goodwin, who did so much for various facets of Acadian culture in the 70s, championed Munch's work for years before turning his attention elsewhere. The film is still little known outside the professional community, where it has since become a well-established underground classic, as much for the story of its production as for its music. Munch, the Swiss critic and erstwhile filmmaker, struggled for years to raise the funding for the enterprise, relying on a dedicated crew who often worked without pay.

The result is a colorful canvas replete with meticulous detail, with all sorts of enjoyable nuances buried deep within the soundtrack or delicately sketched in the background, on the edges of the frame. Coming through strongly is the courage and humor of the small group of musicians, set against the multiethnic canvas of the community, who almost—but not quite—make it to the big time at the end of the lengthy film. It's as if Robert Altman and Richard Lester collaborated with Les Blank. Although the subject of the film is clearly the music, Munch often gets carried away with portraits of minor characters (often children), meticulous financial details of the Zydeco business, and food and gardening tips. (In the cassette version we saw, several recipes are included in the credits.) This fullness and variety are in large part responsible for the charm of the film, which was just slightly ahead of its time.

Welcome to Perigee's television and film library, with fabulous books written by some of the industry's greatest authorities.

The Encyclopedia of Film
by James Monaco and the editors of BASELINE
A comprehensive guide to Hollywood's major players: stars, producers, directors, writers, and more.

The Movie Guide
by James Monaco and the editors of BASELINE
The inside word on 3,5000 of the best pictures ever made.

The TV Encyclopedia
David Inman
More than 10,000 entries on the performers and behind-the scenes players who have worked in television since its inception.

Abbott and Costello in Hollywood
Bob Furmanek and Ron Palumbo
This one-of-a-kind, illustrated volume provides in-depth coverage of each of Bud and Lou's thirty-six films.

These books are available at your bookstores or whenever books are sold, or for your convenience, we'll send them directly to you. Just call 1-800-631-8571 (press 1 for inquiries and orders), or fill out the coupon below and send it to:

The Putnam Publishing Group
390 Murray Hill Parkway, Dept. B — East Rutherford, NJ 07073

			Price	
			U.S.	Canada
_____	The Encyclopedia of Film	399-51606-9	$18.95	$24.95
_____	The Movie Guide	399-51780-4	24.95	32.50
_____	The TV Encyclopedia	399-51704-9	18.95	24.95
_____	Abbott and Costello in Hollywood	399-51605-0	16.95	22.50

Subtotal $ _____

Postage & handling* $ _____

Sales tax (CA, NJ, NY, PA) $ _____

Total amount due $ _____

Payable in U.S. (no cash orders accepted). $15.00 minimum on credit card orders.
*Postage & handling: $2.50 for 1 book, 75¢ for each additional book up to a maximum of $6.25.

Enclosed is my ☐ Check ☐ Money Order

Please charge my ☐ Visa ☐ MasterCard ☐ American Express

Card # _____ Expiration date_____

Signature as on charge card_____

Name _____

Address_____

City _____ State _____ Zip_____

Please allow six weeks for delivery. Prices subject to change without notice.   Source Key #45